Circulating Issues • 1901-Present • 12th Edition

Colin R. Bruce II
Senior Editor

Thomas Michael
Market Analyst

George Cuhaj
Editor

Randy Thern
Numismatic Cataloging Supervisor

Merna Dudley
Coordinating Editor

Deb McCue
Database Coordinator

Bullion Value (BV) Market Valuations

Valuations for all platinum, gold, palladium and silver coins of the more common, basically bullion types, or those possessing only modest numismatic premiums are presented in this edition based on the market levels of:

$1,450-2000 per ounce for **platinum**
$800-950 per ounce for **gold**
$350-470 per ounce for **palladium**
$14.50-18.50 per ounce for **silver**

Published by

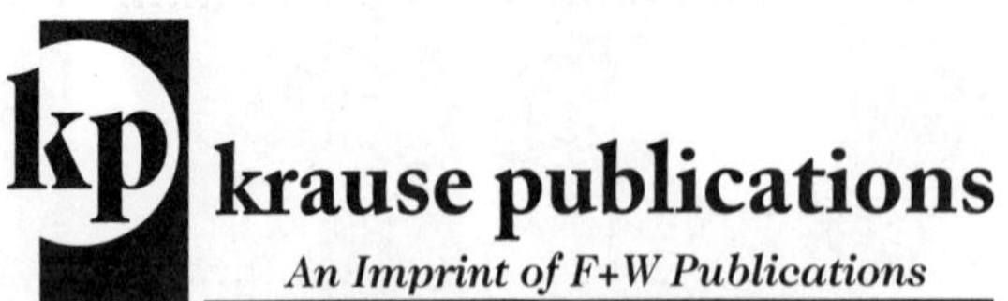

700 East State Street • Iola, WI 54990-0001
715-445-2214 • 888-457-2873
www.krausebooks.com

Library of Congress Catalog Number: ISSN 1532-8104

ISBN 13-digit: 978-0-89689-713-7

ISBN 10-digit: 0-89689-713-3

Edited by: Randy Thern

Designed by: Wendy Wendt

Printed in the United States of America

TABLE OF CONTENTS

INTRODUCTION

Collecting World Coins is designed to offer a focused approach to world coin collecting, catering to the needs of the beginner, novice or casual collector; or the experienced collector interested only in coinage minted for circulation. No commemoratives, sets, or special issues are included in this catalog. This reference is not intended as an enhancement to our other numismatic catalogs – rather a response to a specific need.

The scope of this volume embraces issues since 1901 circulated by nations around the globe. The coverage of silver and non-precious metal coinages is broad based, generally speaking, while the coverage of gold coinages is limited to those which enjoyed currency status at the time of issue, or have been popularly traded in later years as bullion issues.

The presentation of listings is detailed and comprehensive. The catalog presents listings of all issues which were struck for circulation, including dates and mints of issue, along with mintage figures where available and valuations in up to five grades of preservation.

This book provides thorough, but not absolute coverage of its broad sweeping range. What you will not find listed are those coin issues expressly created for non-monetary purposes, including limited issue commemorative coinages. You will find a few gold issues, as prior to World War II many were produced to serve circulating monetary needs.

The objective of this volume, then, is to provide users with accurate, reliable and instructive information on 20th and 21st century monetary issue coins – coins of great historical value, which attribute is drawn from the people, events and symbols emblazoned on them.

This book is keyed to enabling all to easily and quickly identify coins which require attribution to country or valuation. Two key features facilitate this purpose; an Instant Identifier guide that focuses on dominant design characteristics, including monograms, which when coupled with a comprehensive Country Index documenting the variable forms of country names that appear on subject coins, enables the user to quickly attribute any monetary world coin issue to its' country of origin.

The key feature of the country listings is the integration of actual size coin illustrations, which allows quick identification, by type, of all denominations and design changes. Listings are accompanied by complete documentation of dates of issue and mintages as well as metals of issue, with the addition of Actual Silver Weight (ASW) and Actual Gold Weight (AGW) figures for all listed coins struck of silver or gold alloys.

From Afghanistan to Zimbabwe, the listings are catalogued, in most cases, according to the name found on the coins. Thus the coins of the old Belgian Congo are listed under B, and not under their current geographic country of Zaire. Coins of the German States are listed alphabetically under the group heading of German States. If you have a concern, please check the country index.

The country listings are arranged, generally, in ascending denomination and date of issue cataloging style popularly employed in American coin catalogs. In a few cases, many of the countries in the Islamic world, coins are listed by ruler and then in ascending denomination order. Furthermore, divisions are made for monetary reforms, thus the coins of France are separated by pre-war and post–war monetary reforms, as well as the new euro coinage. Catalog numbers accompany each coin cataloged. Prefixes are those that prevail in the marketplace; principally they are the KM# carried in the *Standard Catalog of World Coins* authored by Chester L. Krause and Clifford Mishler.

Users of this catalog seeking to advance their collecting pursuit are referred to the complete listings offered in the comprehensive *Standard Catalog of World Coins*, 20th Century edition, an annual volume providing coverage of all countries from 1901 to 2000. Companion 17th, 18th, 19th and 21st century editions present in five volumes total, world coin issues from 1601 to the present.

Collectors seriously interested in expanding their pursuit of world coins should consider subscribing to *World Coin News*, another Krause Publications product, the only monthly hobby newspaper devoted exclusively to world numismatic subjects. In addition to presenting a wide range of news reports covering various aspects of the world coin collecting realm, each issue also features *World Coin Roundup*, a detailed presentation of timely information on newly released issues from around the globe, plus newly discovered varieties unearthed by scholars form many countries. More information on these products can be found at www.krause.com.

The Editorial Staff

A GUIDE TO INTERNATIONAL NUMERICS

	ENGLISH	CZECH	DANISH	DUTCH	ESPERANTO	FRENCH
1/4	one-quarter	jeden-ctvrt	én kvart	een-kwart	unu-kvar'ono	un-quart
1/2	one-half	jeden-polovieni or pul	én halv	een-half	unu-du'one	un-demi
1	one	jeden	én	een	unu	un
2	two	dve	to	twee	du	deux
3	three	tri	tre	drie	tri	trois
4	four	ctyri	fire	vier	kvar	quatre
5	five	pet	fem	vijf	kvin	cinq
6	six	sest	seks	zes	ses	six
7	seven	sedm	syv	zeven	sep	sept
8	eight	osm	otte	acht	ok	huit
9	nine	devet	ni	negen	nau	neuf
10	ten	deset	ti	tien	dek	dix
12	twelve	dvanáct	tolv	twaalf	dek du	douze
15	fifteen	patnáct	femten	vijftien	dek kvin	quinze
20	twenty	dvacet	tyve	twintig	du'dek	vingt
24	twenty-four	dvacet-ctyri	fire og tyve	twintig-vier	du'dek kvar	vingt-quatre
25	twenty-five	dvacet-pet	fem og tyve	twintig-vijf	du'dek kvin	vingt-cinq
30	thirty	tricet	tredive	dertig	tri'dek	trente
40	forty	ctyricet	fyrre	veertig	kvar'dek	quarante
50	fifty	padesát	halvtreds	vijftig	kvin'dek	cinquante
60	sixty	sedesát	tres	zestig	ses'dek	soixante
70	seventy	sedmdesát	halvfjerds	zeventig	sep'dek	soixante dix
80	eighty	osemdesát	firs	tachtig	ok'dek	quatre-vingt
90	ninety	devadesát	halvfems	negentig	nau'dek	quatre-vingt-dix
100	one hundred	jedno sto	et hundrede	een-honderd	unu-cento	un-cent
1000	thousand	tisíc	tusind	duizend	mil	mille

	GERMAN	HUNGARIAN	INDONESIAN	ITALIAN	NORWEGIAN	POLISH
1/4	ein viertel	egy-negyed	satu-suku	uno-guarto	en-fjeerdedel	jeden-c weirc
1/2	einhalb	egy-fél	satu-setengah	un-mezzo	en-halv	jeden-polowa
1	ein	egy	satu	uno	en	jeden
2	zwei	kettö	dud	due	to	dwa
3	drei	három	tiga	tre	tre	trzy
4	vier	négy	empot	quattro	fire	cztery
5	fünf	öt	lima	cinque	fem	piec'
6	sechs	hat	enam	sei	seks	szes'c'
7	sieben	hét	tudjuh	sette	sju	siedem
8	acht	nyolc	delapan	otto	atte	osiem
9	neun	kilenc	sembilan	nove	ni	dziewiec'
10	zehn	tí z	sepuluh	dieci	ti	dziesiec'
12	zwölf	tizenketto	duabelas	dodici	tolv	dwanas' cie
15	fünfzehn	tizenöt	lima belas	quindici	femten	pietnas'cie
20	zwanzig	húsz	dua pulah	venti	tjue or tyve	dwadzies'cia
24	vierundzwanzig	húsz-négy	dua pulah-empot	venti-quattro	tjue-fire or tyve-fire	dwadzies'cia-cztery
25	fünfundzwanzig	húsz-öt	dua-pulah-lima	venti-cinque	tjue-fem or tyve-fem	dwadzies'cia-piec
30	dreissig	harminc	tigapulah	trenta	tredve	trydzies'ci
40	vierzig	negyven	empat pulah	quaranta	forti	czterdries'ci
50	fünfzig	otven	lima pulah	cinquanta	femti	piec'dziesiat
60	sechzig	hatvan	enam pulah	sessanta	seksti	szes'c'dziesiat
70	siebzig	hetven	tudjuh pulu	settanta	sytti	siedemdziesiat
80	achtzig	nyolvan	delapan puluh	ottonta	atti	osiemdziesiat
90	neunzig	kilencven	sembilan puluh	novanta	nitty	dziewiec'dziesiat
100	ein hundert	egy-száz	satu-seratus	uno-cento	en-hundre	jeden-sto
1000	tausend	ezer	seribu	mille	tusen	tysiac

	PORTUGUESE	ROMANIAN	SERBO-CROATIAN	SPANISH	SWEDISH	TURKISH
1/4	um-quarto	un-sfert	jedan-ceturtina	un-cuarto	en-fjärdedel	bir-ceyrek
1/2	un-meio	o-jumatate	jedan-polovina	un-medio	en-hälft	bir-yarim
1	um	un	jedan	uno	en	bir
2	dois	doi	dva	dos	tva	iki
3	trés	trei	tri	tres	tre	üc
4	quatro	patru	cetiri	cuatro	fyra	dört
5	cinco	cinci	pet	cinco	fem	bes
6	seis	sase	sest	seis	sex	alti
7	sete	sapte	sedam	siete	sju	yedi
8	oito	opt	osam	ocho	atta	sekiz
9	nove	noua	devet	nueve	io	dokuz
10	dez	zece	deset	diez	tio	on
12	doze	doisprezece	dvanaest	doce	tolv	on iki
15	quinze	cincisprezece	petnaest	quince	femton	on bes
20	vinte	douazeci	dvadset	veinte	tjugu	yirmi
24	vinte-quatro	douazeci-patru	dvadesel-citiri	veinticuatro	tjugu-fyra	yirmi-dört
25	vinte-cinco	douazeci-cinci	dvadeset-pet	veinticinco	tjugu-fem	yirmi-bes
30	trinta	treizeci	trideset	treinta	trettio	otuz
40	quarenta	patruzeci	cetrdeset	cuarenta	fyrtio	kirk
50	cinqüenta	cincizeci	padeset	cincuenta	femtio	elli
60	sessenta	saizeci	sezdeset	sesenta	sextio	altmis
70	setenta	saptezeci	sedamdeset	setenta	sjuttio	yetmis
80	oitenta	optzeci	osamdeset	ochenta	attio	seksen
90	noventa	novazeci	devedeset	noventa	nittio	doksan
100	un-cem	o-suta	jedan-sto	cien	en-hundra	bir-yüz
1000	mil	mie	hiljada	mil	tusen	bin

COUNTRY INDEX

A

B

C

D

E

F

G

H

I

J

K

L

HOW TO USE THIS CATALOG

This catalog series is designed to serve the needs of both the novice and advanced collectors. It provides a comprehensive guide to over 100 years of world coinage. It is generally arranged so that persons with no more than a basic knowledge of world history and a casual acquaintance with coin collecting can consult it with confidence and ease. The following explanations summarize the general practices used in preparing this catalog's listings. However, because of specialized requirements, which may vary by country and era, these must not be considered ironclad. Where these standards have been set aside, appropriate notations of the variations are incorporated in that particular listing.

ARRANGEMENT

Countries are arranged alphabetically. Political changes within a country are arranged chronologically. In countries where Rulers are the single most significant political entity a chronological arrangement by Ruler has been employed. Distinctive sub-geographic regions are listed alphabetically following the countries main listings. A few exceptions to these rules may exist. Refer to the Country Index.

Diverse coinage types relating to fabrication methods, revaluations, denomination systems, non-circulating categories and such have been identified, separated and arranged in logical fashion. Chronological arrangement is employed for most circulating coinage, i.e., Hammered coinage will normally precede Milled coinage, monetary reforms will flow in order of their institution.

Within a coinage type coins will be listed by denomination, from smallest to largest. Numbered types within a denomination will be ordered by their first date of issue.

IDENTIFICATION

The most important step in the identification of a coin is the determination of the nation of origin. This is generally easily accomplished where English-speaking lands are concerned, however, use of the country index is sometimes required. The coins of Great Britain provide an interesting challenge. For hundreds of years the only indication of the country of origin was in the abbreviated Latin legends. In recent times there have been occasions when there has been no indication of origin. Only through the familiarity of the monarchical portraits, symbols and legends or indication of currency system are they identifiable.

The coins of many countries beyond the English-language realm, such as those of French, Italian or Spanish heritage, are also quite easy to identify through reference to their legends, which appear in the national languages based on Western alphabets. In many instances the name is spelled exactly the same in English as in the national language, such as France; while in other cases it varies only slightly, like Italia for Italy, Belgique or Belgie for Belgium, Brasil for Brazil and Danmark for Denmark.

This is not always the case, however, as in Norge for Norway, Espana for Spain, Sverige for Sweden and Helvetia for Switzerland. Some other examples include:

DEUTSCHES REICH - Germany 1873-1945

BUNDESREPUBLIC DEUTSCHLAND - Federal Republic of Germany.

DEUTSCHE DEMOKRATISCHE REPUBLIK - German Democratic Republic.

EMPIRE CHERIFIEN MAROC - Morocco.

ESTADOS UNIDOS MEXICANOS - United Mexican States (Mexico).

ETAT DU GRAND LIBAN - State of Great Lebanon (Lebanon).

Thus it can be seen there are instances in which a little schooling in the rudiments of foreign languages can be most helpful. In general, colonial possessions of countries using the Western alphabet are similarly identifiable as they often carry portraits of their current rulers, the familiar lettering, sometimes in combination with a companion designation in the local language.

Collectors have the greatest difficulty with coins that do not bear legends or dates in the Western systems. These include coins bearing Cyrillic lettering, attributable to Bulgaria, Russia, the Slavic states and Mongolia, the Greek script peculiar to Greece, Crete and the Ionian Islands; The Amharic characters of Ethiopia, or Hebrew in the case of Israel. Dragons and sunbursts along with the distinctive word characters attribute a coin to the Oriental countries of China, Japan, Korea, Tibet, Viet Nam and their component parts.

The most difficult coins to identify are those bearing only Persian or Arabic script and its derivatives, found on the issues of nations stretching in a wide swath across North Africa and East Asia, from Morocco to Indonesia, and the Indian subcontinent coinages which surely are more confusing in their vast array of Nagari, Sanskrit, Ahom, Assamese and other local dialects found on the local issues of the Indian Princely States. Although the task of identification on the more modern issues of these lands is often eased by the added presence of Western alphabet legends, a feature sometimes adopted as early as the late 19th Century, for the earlier pieces it is often necessary for the uninitiated to laboriously seek and find.

Except for the cruder issues, however, it will be found that certain characteristics and symbols featured in addition to the predominant legends are typical on coins from a given country or group of countries. The toughra monogram, for instance, occurs on some of the coins of Afghanistan, Egypt, the Sudan, Pakistan, Turkey and other areas of the late Ottoman Empire. A predominant design feature on the coins of Nepal is the trident; while neighboring Tibet features a lotus blossom or lion on many of their issues.

To assist in identification of the more difficult coins, we have assembled the Instant Identifier and Monogram sections presented on the following pages. They are designed to provide a point of beginning for collectors by allowing them to compare unidentified coins with photographic details from typical issues.

We also suggest reference to the Index of Coin Denominations presented here and also the comprehensive Country Index, where the inscription will be found listed just as it appears on the coin for nations using the Western alphabet.

DATING

Coin dating is the final basic attribution consideration. Here, the problem can be more difficult because the reading of a coin date is subject not only to the vagaries of numeric styling, but to calendar variations caused by the observance of various religious eras or regal periods from country to country, or even within a country. Here again with the exception of the sphere from North Africa through the Orient, it will be found that most countries rely on Western date numerals and Christian (AD) era reckoning, although in a few instances, coin dating has been tied to the year of a reign or government. The Vatican, for example dates its coinage according to the year of reign of the current pope, in addition to the Christian-era date.

Countries in the Arabic sphere generally date their coins to the Muslim era (AH), which commenced on July 16, 622 AD (Julian calendar), when the prophet Mohammed fled from Mecca to Medina. As their calendar is reckoned by the lunar year of 354 days, which is about three percent (precisely 2.98%) shorter than the Christian year, a formula is required to convert AH dating to its Western equivalent. To convert an AH date to the approximate AD date, subtract three percent of the AH date (round to the closest whole number) from the AH date and add 622. A chart converting all AH years from 1010 (July 2, 1601) to 1421 (May 25, 2028) is presented as the Heijra Chart on page 35.

The Muslim calendar is not always based on the lunar year (AH), however, causing some confusion, particularly in Afghanistan and Iran, where a calendar based on the solar year (SH) was introduced around 1920. These dates can be converted to AD by simply adding 621. In 1976 the government of Iran implemented a new solar calendar based on the foundation of the Iranian monarchy in 559 BC. The first year observed on the new calendar was 2535 (MS), which commenced March 20, 1976. A reversion to the traditional SH dating standard occurred a few years later.

Several different eras of reckoning, including Christian and Muslim (AH), have been used to date coins of the Indian subcontinent. The two basic systems are the Vikrama Samvat (VS), which dates from Oct. 18, 58 BC, and the Saka era, the origin of which is reckoned from March 3, 78 AD. Dating according to both eras appears on various coins of the area.

Coins of Thailand (Siam) are found dated by three different eras. The most predominant is the Buddhist era (BE), which originated in 543 BC. Next is the Bangkok or Ratanakosindsok (RS) era, dating from 1781 AD; followed by the Chula-Sakarat (CS) era, dating from 638 AD. The latter era originated in Burma and is used on that country's coins.

Other calendars include that of the Ethiopian era (EE), which commenced seven years, eight months after AD dating; and that of the Jewish people, which commenced on Oct. 7, 3761 BC. Korea claims a legendary dating from 2333 BC, which is acknowledged in some of its coin dating. Some coin issues of the Indonesian area carry dates determined by the Javanese Aji Saka era (AS), a calendar of 354 days (100 Javanese years equal 97 Christian or Gregorian calendar years), which can be matched to AD dating by comparing it to AH dating.

The following table indicates the year dating for the various eras, which correspond to 2006 in Christian calendar reckoning, but it must be remembered that there are overlaps between the eras in some instances.

Christian era (AD)	-2008
Muslim era (AH)	-AH1429
Solar year (SH)	-SH1386
Monarchic Solar era (MS)	-MS2567
Vikrama Samvat (VS)	-VS20605
Saka era (SE)	-SE1930
Buddhist era (BE)	-BE2549
Bangkok era (RS)	-RS227
Chula-Sakarat era (CS)	-CS1370
Ethiopian era (EE)	-EE2002
Jewish era	-5768
Korean era	-4341
Javanese Aji Saka era (AS)	-AS1941
Fasli era (FE)	-FE1418

Coins of Asian origin - principally Japan, Korea, China, Turkestan and Tibet and some modern gold issues of Turkey - are generally dated to the year of the government, dynasty, reign or cyclic eras, with the dates indicated in Asian characters which usually read from right to left. In recent years, however, some dating has been according to the Christian calendar and in Western numerals. In Japan, Asian character dating was reversed to read from left to right in Showa year 23 (1948 AD).

More detailed guides to less prevalent coin dating systems, which are strictly local in nature, are presented with the appropriate listings.

Some coins carry dates according to both locally observed and Christian eras. This is particularly true in the Arabic world, where the Hejira date may be indicated in Arabic numerals and the Christian date in Western numerals, or both dates in either form.

The date actually carried on a given coin is generally cataloged here in the first column (Date) to the right of the catalog number. If this date is by a non-Christian dating system, such as 'AH'(Muslim), the Christian equivalent date will appear in parentheses(), for example AH1336(1917). Dates listed alone in the date column which do not actually appear on a given coin, or dates which are known, but do not appear on the coin, are generally enclosed by parentheses with 'ND' at the left, for example ND(1926).

Timing differentials between some era of reckoning, particularly the 354-day Mohammedan and 365-day Christian years, cause situations whereby coins which carry dates for both eras exist bearing two year dates from one calendar combined with a single date from another.

Countermarked Coinage is presented with both 'Countermark Date' and 'Host Coin' date for each type. Actual date representation follows the rules outlined above.

NUMBERING SYSTEM

Some catalog numbers assigned in this volume are based on established references. This practice has been observed for two reasons: First, when world coins are listed chronologically they are basically self-cataloging; second, there was no need to confuse collectors with totally new numeric designations where appropriate systems already existed. As time progressed we found many of these established systems incomplete and inadequate and have now replaced many with new KM numbers. When numbers change appropriate cross-referencing has been provided.

Some of the coins listed in this catalog are identified or cross-referenced by numbers assigned by R.S. Yeoman (Y#), or slight adaptations thereof, in his *Modern World Coins*, and *Current Coins of the World*. For the pre-Yeoman dated issues, the numbers assigned by William D. Craig (C#) in his *Coins of the World* (1750-1850 period), 3rd edition, have generally been applied.

In some countries, listings are cross-referenced to Robert Friedberg's (FR#) *Gold Coins of the World* or *Coins of the British World*. Major Fred Pridmore's (P#) studies of British colonial coinage are also referenced, as are W.H. Valentine's (V#) references on the *Modern Copper Coins of the Muhammadan States*. Coins issued under the Chinese sphere of influence are assigned numbers from E. Kann's (K#) *Illustrated Catalog of Chinese Coins* and T.K. Hsu's (Su) work of similar title. In most cases, these cross-reference numbers are presented in the descriptive text for each type.

DENOMINATIONS

The second basic consideration to be met in the attribution of a coin is the determination of denomination. Since denominations are usually expressed in numeric, rather than word form on a coin, this is usually quite easily accomplished on coins from nations, which use Western numerals, except in those instances where issues are devoid of any mention of face value, and denomination must be attributed by size, metallic composition or weight. Coins listed in this volume are generally illustrated in actual size. Where size is critical to proper attribution, the coin's millimeter size is indicated.

The sphere of countries stretching from North Africa through the Orient, on which numeric symbols generally unfamiliar to Westerners are employed, often provide the collector with a much greater challenge. This is particularly true on nearly all pre-20th Century issues. On some of the more modern issues and increasingly so as the years progress, Western-style numerals usually presented in combination with the local numeric system are becoming more commonplace on these coins.

Determination of a coin's currency system can also be valuable in attributing the issue to its country of origin. A comprehensive alphabetical index of currency names, applicable to the countries as cataloged in this volume, with all individual nations of use for each, is presented in this section.

The included table of Standard International Numeral Systems presents charts of the basic numeric designations found on coins of non-Western origin. Although denomination numerals are generally prominently displayed on coins, it must be remembered that these are general representations of characters, which individual coin engravers may have rendered in widely varying styles. Where numeric or script denominations designation forms peculiar to a given coin or country apply, such as the script used on some Persian (Iranian) issues. They are so indicated or illustrated in conjunction with the appropriate listings.

MINTAGES

Quantities minted of each date are indicated where that information is available, generally stated in millions, and usually rounded off to the nearest 10,000 pieces. On quantities of a few thousand or less, actual mintages are generally indicated. For combined mintage figures the abbreviation "Inc. Above" means Included Above, while "Inc. Below" means Included

Below. "Est." beside a mintage figure indicates the number given is an estimate or mintage limit.

MINT AND PRIVY MARKS

The presence of distinctive, but frequently inconspicuously placed, mintmarks indicates the mint of issue for many of the coins listed in this catalog. An appropriate designation in the date listings notes the presence, if any, of a mint mark on a particular coin type by incorporating the letter or letters of the mint mark adjoining the date, i.e., 1950D or 1927R.

The presence of mint and/or mintmaster's privy marks on a coin in non-letter form is indicated by incorporating the mint letter in lower case within parentheses adjoining the date; i.e. 1927(a). The corresponding mark is illustrated or identified in the introduction of the country.

In countries such as France and Mexico, where many mints may be producing like coinage in the same denomination during the same time period, divisions by mint have been employed. In these cases the mint mark may appear next to the individual date listings and/or the mint name or mint mark may be listed in the Note field of the type description.

Where listings incorporate mintmaster initials, they are always presented in capital letters separated from the date by one character space; i.e., 1850 MF. The different mintmark and mintmaster letters found on the coins of any country, state or city of issue are always shown at the beginning of listings.

METALS

Each numbered type listing will contain a description of the coins metallic content. The traditional coinage metals and their symbolic chemical abbreviations sometimes used in this catalog are:

Platinum - (PT)	Copper - (Cu)
Gold - (Au)	Brass -
Silver - (Ag)	Copper-nickel - (CN)
Billion -	Lead - (Pb)
Nickel - (Ni)	Steel -
Zinc - (Zn)	Tin - (Sn)
Bronze - (Ae)	Aluminum - (Al)

During the 18th and 19th centuries, most of the world's coins were struck of copper or bronze, silver and gold. Commencing in the early years of the 20th century, however, numerous new coinage metals, primarily non-precious metal alloys, were introduced. Gold has not been widely used for circulation coinages since World War I, although silver remained a popular coinage metal in most parts of the world until after World War II. With the disappearance of silver for circulation coinage, numerous additional compositions were introduced to coinage applications.

Most recent is the development of clad or plated planchets in order to maintain circulation life and extend the life of a set of production dies as used in the production of the copper-nickel clad copper 50 centesimos of Panama or in the latter case to reduce production costs of the planchets and yet provide a coin quite similar in appearance to its predecessor as in the case of the copper plated zinc core United States 1983 cent.

Modern commemorative coins have employed still more unusual methods such as bimetallic coins, color applications and precious metal or gem inlays.

OFF-METAL STRIKES

Off-metal strikes previously designated by "(OMS)" which also included the wide range of error coinage struck in other than their officially authorized compositions have been incorporated into Pattern listings along with special issues, which were struck for presentation or other reasons.

Collectors of Germanic coinage may be familiar with the term "Abschlag" which quickly identifies similar types of coinage.

PRECIOUS METAL WEIGHTS

Listings of weight, fineness and actual silver (ASW), gold (AGW), platinum or palladium (APW) content of most machine-struck silver, gold, platinum and palladium coins are provided in this edition. This information will be found incorporated in each separate type listing, along with other data related to the coin.

The ASW, AGW and APW figures were determined by multiplying the gross weight of a given coin by its known or tested fineness and converting the resulting gram or grain weight to troy ounces, rounded to the nearest ten-thousandth of an ounce. A silver coin with a 24.25-gram weight and .875 fineness for example, would have a fine weight of approximately 21.2188 grams, or a .6822 ASW, a factor that can be used to accurately determine the intrinsic value for multiple examples.

The ASW, AGW or APW figure can be multiplied by the spot price of each precious metal to determine the current intrinsic value of any coin accompanied by these designations.

Coin weights are indicated in grams (abbreviated "g") along with fineness where the information is of value in differentiating between types. These weights are based on 31.103 grams per troy (scientific) ounce, as opposed to the avoirdupois (commercial) standard of 28.35 grams. Actual coin weights are generally shown in hundredths or thousands of a gram; i.e., 0.500 SILVER 2.9200g.

WEIGHTS AND FINENESSES

As the silver and gold bullion markets have advanced and declined sharply in recent years, the fineness and total precious metal content of coins has become especially significant where bullion coins - issues which trade on the basis of their intrinsic metallic content rather than numismatic value - are concerned. In many instances, such issues have become worth more in bullion form than their nominal collector values or denominations indicate.

Establishing the weight of a coin can also be valuable for determining its denomination. Actual weight is also necessary to ascertain the specific gravity of the coin's metallic content, an important factor in determining authenticity.

TROY WEIGHT STANDARDS

24 Grains = 1 Pennyweight
480 Grains = 1 Ounce
31.103 Grams = 1 Ounce

UNIFORM WEIGHTS

15.432 Grains = 1 Gram
0.0648 Gram = 1 Grain

AVOIRDUPOIS STANDARDS

27-11/32 Grains = 11 Dram
437-1/2 Grains = 1 Ounce
28.350 Grams = 1 Ounce

BULLION VALUE CHARTS

The simplest method for determining the bullion value of a precious metal coin is to multiply the actual precious metal weight by the current spot price for that metal. Using the example above, a silver coin with a .6822 actual silver weight (ASW) would have an intrinsic value of $6.65 when the spot price of silver is $9.75. If the spot price of silver rose to $11.00 that same coins intrinsic value would rise to $7.50.

Valuations for most of the silver, gold, platinum and palladium coins listed in this edition are based on assumed market values of **$14.50-18.50** per troy ounce for silver, **$800-950** for gold, **$1450-2,000** for platinum, and **$350-470** for palladium. To arrive at accurate current market indications for these issues, increase or decrease the valuations appropriately based on any variations in these indicated levels.

The silver bullion chart provides silver values in thousandths from .001 to .009 troy ounce, and in hundredths from .01 to 1.00 in 50¢ value increments from $3.00 to $10.50. If the market value of silver exceeds $10.50, doubling the increments presented will provide valuations in $1 steps from $6.00 to $21.00.

The gold bullion chart is similarly arranged in $10 increments from $350 to $1000.

Valuations for most of the silver, gold, platinum and palladium coins listed in this edition are based on assumed market values of $14.50-18.50 per troy ounce for silver, $800-950 for gold, $1450-2000 for platinum, and $350-470 for palladium. To arrive at accurate current market indications for these issues, increase or decrease the valuations appropriately based on any variations in these indicated levels.

HOMELAND TYPES

Homeland types are coins which colonial powers used in a colony, but do not bear that location's name. In some cases they were legal tender in the

Coin Alignment

Medal Alignment

COIN vs MEDAL ALIGNMENT

Some coins are struck with obverse and reverse aligned at a rotation of 180 degrees from each other. When a coin is held for vertical viewing with the obverse design aligned upright and the index finger and thumb at the top and bottom, upon rotation from left to right for viewing the reverse, the latter will be upside down. Such alignment is called "coin rotation." Other coins are struck with the obverse and reverse designs mated on an alignment of zero or 360 degrees. If such an example is held and rotated as described, the reverse will appear upright. This is the alignment, which is generally observed in the striking of medals, and for that reason coins produced in this manner are considered struck in "medal rotation". In some instances, often through error, certain coin issues have been struck to both alignment standards, creating interesting collectible varieties, which will be found noted in some listings. In addition, some countries are now producing coins with other designated overse to reverse alignments which are considered standard for this type.

homeland, in others not. They are listed under the homeland and cross-referenced at the colony listing.

COUNTERMARKS/COUNTERSTAMPS

There is some confusion among collectors over the terms "countermark" and "counterstamp" when applied to a coin bearing an additional mark or change of design and/or denomination.

To clarify, a countermark might be considered similar to the "hall mark" applied to a piece of silverware, by which a silversmith assured the quality of the piece. In the same way, a countermark assures the quality of the coin on which it is placed, as, for example, when the royal crown of England was countermarked (punched into) on segmented Spanish reales, allowing them to circulate in commerce in the British West Indies. An additional countermark indicating the new denomination may also be encountered on these coins.

Countermarks are generally applied singularly and in most cases indiscriminately on either side of the "host" coin.

Counterstamped coins are more extensively altered. The counterstamping is done with a set of dies, rather than a hand punch. The coin being counterstamped is placed between the new dies and struck as if it were a blank planchet as found with the Manila 8 reales issue of the Philippines. A more unusual application where the counterstamp dies were smaller than the host coin in the revalidated 50 centimos and 1 colon of Costa Rica issued in 1923.

PHOTOGRAPHS

To assist the reader in coin identification, every effort has been made to present actual size photographs of every coinage type listed. Obverse and reverse are illustrated, except when a change in design is restricted to one side, and the coin has a diameter of 39mm or larger, in which case only the side required for identification of the type is generally illustrated. All coins up to 60mm are illustrated actual size, to the nearest 1/2mm up to 25mm, and to the nearest 1mm thereafter. Coins larger than 60mm diameter are illustrated in reduced size, with the actual size noted in the descriptive text block. Where slight change in size is important to coin type identification, actual millimeter measurements are stated.

TRADE COINS

From approximately 1750-1940, a number of nations, particularly European colonial powers and commercial traders, minted trade coins to facilitate commerce with the local populace of Africa, the Arab countries, the Indian subcontinental, Southeast Asia and the Far East. Such coins generally circulated at a value based on the weight and fineness of their silver or gold content, rather than their stated denomination. Examples include the sovereigns of Great Britain and the gold ducat issues of Austria, Hungary and the Netherlands. Trade coinage will sometimes be found listed at the end of the domestic issues.

VALUATIONS

Values quoted in this catalog represent the current market and are compiled from recommendations provided and verified through various source documents and specialized consultants. It should be stressed, however, that this book is intended to serve only as an aid for evaluating coins, actual market conditions are constantly changing and additional influences, such as particularly strong local demand for certain coin series, fluctuation of international exchange rates and worldwide collection patterns must also be considered. Publication of this catalog is not intended as a solicitation by the publisher, editors or contributors to buy or sell the coins listed at the prices indicated.

All valuations are stated in U.S. dollars, based on careful assessment of the varied international collector market. Valuations for coins priced below $100.00 are generally stated in full amounts - i.e. 37.50 or 95.00 - while valuations at or above that figure are rounded off in even dollars - i.e. $125.00 is expressed 125. A comma is added to indicate thousands of dollars in value.

For the convenience of overseas collectors and for U.S. collectors doing business with overseas dealers, the base exchange rate for the national currencies of approximately 180 countries are presented in the Foreign Exchange Table.

It should be noted that when particularly select uncirculated or proof-like examples of uncirculated coins become available they can be expected to command proportionately high premiums. Such examples in reference to choice Germanic Thalers are referred to as "erst schlage" or first strikes.

RESTRIKES, COUNTERFEITS

Deceptive restrike and counterfeit (both contemporary and modern) examples exist of some coin issues. Where possible, the existence of restrikes is noted. Warnings are also incorporated in instances where particularly deceptive counterfeits are known to exist. Collectors who are uncertain about the authenticity of a coin held in their collection, or being offered for sale, should take the precaution of having it authenticated by the American Numismatic Association Authentication Bureau, 818 N. Cascade, Colorado Springs, CO 80903. Their reasonably priced certification tests are widely accepted by collectors and dealers alike.

EDGE VARIETIES

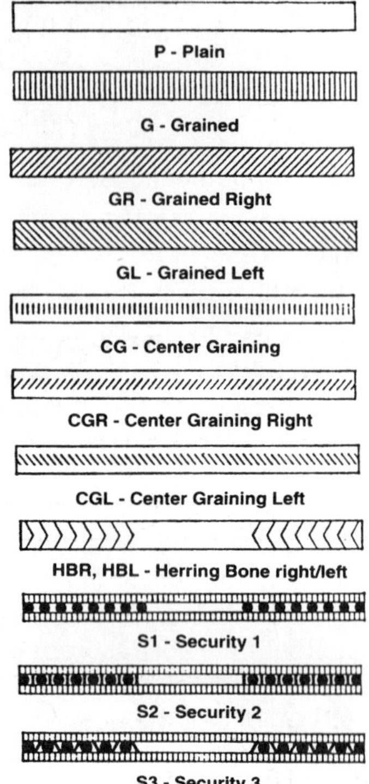

NEW ISSUES

All newly released coins that have been physically observed by our staff and those that have been confirmed by press time have been incorporated in this edition. Exceptions exist in some countries where current date coin production lags far behind and other countries whose fiscal year actually begins in the latter half of the current year.

Collectors and dealers alike are kept up to date with worldwide new issues having newly assigned catalog reference numbers in the monthly feature "World Coin Roundup" in World Coin News. A free sample copy will be sent upon request. Overseas requests should include 1 international postal reply coupon for surface mail or 2 international postal reply coupons for air mail dispatch: Write to World Coin News, 700 East State St., Iola, WI 54990 USA.

CONDITIONS/GRADING

Wherever possible, coin valuations are given in four or five grades of preservation. For modern commemoratives, which do not circulate, only uncirculated values are usually sufficient. Proof issues are indicated by the word "Proof" next to the date, with valuation proceeded by the word "value" following the mintage. For very recent circulating coins and coins of limited value, one, two or three grade values are presented.

There are almost no grading guides for world coins. What follows is an attempt to help bridge that gap until a detailed, illustrated guide becomes available.

In grading world coins, there are two elements to look for: 1) Overall wear, and 2) loss of design details, such as strands of hair, feathers on eagles, designs on coats of arms, etc.

The age, rarity or type of a coin should not be a consideration in grading.

Grade each coin by the weaker of the two sides. This method appears to give results most nearly consistent with conservative American Numismatic Association standards for U.S. coins. Split grades, i.e., F/VF for obverse and reverse, respectively, are normally no more than one grade apart. If the two sides are more than one grade apart, the series of coins probably wears differently on each side and should then be graded by the weaker side alone.

Grade by the amount of overall wear and loss of design detail evident on each side of the coin. On coins with a moderately small design element, which is prone to early wear, grade by that design alone. For example, the 5-ore (KM#554) of Sweden has a crown above the monogram on which the beads on the arches show wear most clearly. So, grade by the crown alone.

For **Brilliant Uncirculated** (BU) grades there will be no visible signs of wear or handling, even under a 30-power microscope. Full mint luster will be present. Ideally no bags marks will be evident.

For **Uncirculated** (Unc.) grades there will be no visible signs of wear or handling, even under a 30-power microscope. Bag marks may be present.

For **Almost Uncirculated** (AU), all detail will be visible. There will be wear only on the highest point of the coin. There will often be half or more of the original mint luster present.

On the **Extremely Fine** (XF or EF) coin, there will be about 95% of the original detail visible. Or, on a coin with a design with no inner detail to wear down, there will be a light wear over nearly all the coin. If a small design is used as the grading area, about 90% of the original detail will be visible. This latter rule stems from the logic that a smaller amount of detail needs to be present because a small area is being used to grade the whole coin.

The **Very Fine** (VF) coin will have about 75% of the original detail visible. Or, on a coin with no inner detail, there will be moderate wear over the entire coin. Corners of letters and numbers may be weak. A small grading area will have about 66% of the original detail.

For **Fine** (F), there will be about 50% of the original detail visible. Or, on a coin with no inner detail, there will be fairly heavy wear over all of the coin. Sides of letters will be weak. A typically uncleaned coin will often appear as dirty or dull. A small grading area will have just under 50% of the original detail.

On the **Very Good** (VG) coin, there will be about 25% of the original detail visible. There will be heavy wear on all of the coin.

The **Good** (G) coin's design will be clearly outlined but with substantial wear. Some of the larger detail may be visible. The rim may have a few weak spots of wear.

On the **About Good** (AG) coin, there will typically be only a silhouette of a large design. The rim will be worn down into the letters if any.

Strong or weak strikes, partially weak strikes, damage, corrosion, attractive or unattractive toning, dipping or cleaning should be described along with the above grades. These factors affect the quality of the coin just as do wear and loss of detail, but are easier to describe.

In the case of countermarked/counterstamped coins, the condition of the host coin will have a bearing on the end valuation. The important factor in determining the grade is the condition, clarity and completeness of the countermark itself. This is in reference to countermarks/counterstamps having raised design while being struck in a depression.

Incuse countermarks cannot be graded for wear. They are graded by the clarity and completeness including the condition of the host coin which will also have more bearing on the final grade/valuation determined.

STANDARD INTERNATIONAL GRADING TERMINOLOGY AND ABBREVIATIONS

	PROOF	UNCIRCULATED	EXTREMELY FINE	VERY FINE	FINE	VERY GOOD	GOOD	POOR
U.S. and ENGLISH SPEAKING LANDS	PRF	UNC	EF or XF	VF	F	VG	G	PR
BRAZIL	—	(1)FDC or FC	(3) S	(5) MBC	(7) BC	(8) BC/R	(9) R	UT GeG
DENMARK	M	0	01	1+	1	1÷	2	3
FINLAND	00	0	01	1+	1	1?	2	3
FRANCE	FB Flan Bruni	FDC Fleur de Coin	SUP Superbe	TTB Très très beau	TB Très beau	B Beau	TBC Très Bien Conservée	BC Bien Conservée
GERMANY	PP Polierte Platte	STG Stempelglanz	VZ Vorzüglich	SS Sehr schön	S Schön	S.G.E. Sehr gut erhalten	G.E. Gut erhalten	Gering erhalten
ITALY	FS Fondo Specchio	FDC Fior di Conio	SPL Splendido	BB Bellissimo	MB Molto Bello	B Bello	M	—
JAPAN	—	未使用	極美品	美品	並品	—	—	—
NETHERLANDS	— Proef	FDC Fleur de Coin	Pr. Prachtig	Z.f. Zeer fraai	Fr. Fraai	Z.g. Zeer goed	G	—
NORWAY	M	0	01	1+	1	1÷	2	3
PORTUGAL	—	Soberba	Bela	MBC	BC	MREG	REG	MC
SPAIN	Prueba	SC	EBC	MBC	BC+	BC	RC	MC
SWEDEN	Polerad	0	01	1+	1	1?	2	—

Sending Scanned Images by Email

Over the past 5 years or so, we have been receiving an ever-increasing flow of scanned images from sources worldwide. Unfortunately, many of these scans could not be used due to the type of scan, or simple incompatability with our systems. We appreciate the effort it takes to produce these images and accuracy they add to the catalog listings.

Here are a few simple instructions to follow when producing these scans. We encourage you to continue sending new images or upgrades to those currently illustrated and please do not hesitate to ask questions about this process.

- **Scan all images within a resolution of 300 dpi**
- **Size setting should be at 100%**
- **Scan in true 4-color**
- **Save images as 'jpeg' or 'tiff' and name in such a way, which clearly identifies the country of origin of the coin**
- **Please email with a request to confirm receipt of the attachment**
- **Please send images to randy.thern@fwpubs.com**

COIN DENOMINATION INDEX

- **ABBASI** - Afghanistan
  - Iran
- **AFGHANI** - Afghanistan
- **AGORA** - Israel
- **AGOROT** - Israel
- **AMANI** - Afghanistan
- **ANNA** - India-British
  - India-Republic
  - Pakistan
- **ARI** - Albania
- **ARIARY** - Madagascar
- **ASARFI** - Nepal
- **ASARPHI** - Nepal
- **ASHRAPHI** - Nepal
- **ATT** - Lao
  - Thailand
- **AURAR** - Iceland
- **AUSTRAL** - Argentina
- **AVOS** - Macao
  - Timor
- **BAHT** - Thailand
- **BAISA** - Muscat & Oman
  - Oman
- **BALBOA** - Panama
- **BAN** - Moldova
  - Romania
- **BANI** - Moldova
  - Romania
- **BESA** - Italian Somaliland
- **BESE** - Italian Somaliland
- **BIPKWELE** - Equatorial Guinea
- **BIRR** - Ethiopia
- **BOLIVAR** - Venezuela
- **BOLIVIANO** - Bolivia
- **BUQSHA** - Yemen Arab Republic
- **BUTUT** - Gambia, The
- **CASH** - China
  - China, Republic Of
- **CAURIS** - Guinea
- **CEDI** - Ghana
- **CEDIS** - Ghana
- **CENT** - Aruba
  - Australia
  - Bahamas
  - Barbados
  - Belize
  - Bermuda
  - British Honduras
  - British North Borneo
  - British Virgin Islands
  - Canada
  - Cayman Islands
  - Ceylon
  - China
  - China, People'S Republic
  - China, Republic Of
  - Cook Islands
  - Curacao
  - Cyprus
  - Danish West Indies
  - East Africa
  - East Caribbean States
  - Eritrea
  - Ethiopia
  - Fiji
  - French Indo-China
  - Guyana
  - Hong Kong
  - Jamaica
  - Kenya
  - Kiau Chau
  - Kiribati
  - Lao
  - Liberia
  - Malay Peninsula
  - Malaya
  - Malaya & British Borneo
  - Malta
  - Mauritius
  - Namibia
  - Netherlands
  - Netherlands Antilles
  - Netherlands East Indies
  - New Zealand
  - Newfoundland
  - Nova Scotia
  - Rhodesia
  - Sarawak
  - Seychelles
  - Sierra Leone
  - Singapore
  - Solomon Islands
  - South Africa
  - Sri Lanka
  - Straits Settlements
  - Suriname
  - Swaziland
  - Trinidad & Tobago
  - Tuvalu
  - Uganda
  - United States
  - Zanzibar
  - Zimbabwe
- **CENTAI** - Lithuania
- **CENTAS** - Lithuania
- **CENTAVO** - Angola
  - Argentina
  - Bolivia
  - Brazil
  - Cape Verde
  - Chile
  - Colombia
  - Costa Rica
  - Cuba
  - Dominican Republic
  - East Timor
  - Ecuador
  - El Salvador
  - Guatemala
  - Guinea-Bissau
  - Honduras
  - India-Portuguese
  - Mexico
  - Mozambique
  - Nicaragua
  - Paraguay
  - Peru
  - Philippines
  - Portugal
  - Saint Thomas & Prince Island
  - Timor
- **CENTESIMI** - Italy
  - San Marino
  - Somalia
  - Vatican City
- **CENTESIMO** - Chile
  - Italy
  - Panama
  - Somalia
  - Uruguay
- **CENTIM** - Andorra
- **CENTIME** - Algeria
  - Belgian Congo
  - Belgium
  - Cambodia
  - Cameroon
  - Congo Free State
  - Congo, Democratic Republic
  - France
  - French Equatorial Africa
  - French Oceania
  - French Polynesia
  - French West Africa
  - Guadeloupe
  - Haiti
  - Luxembourg
  - Madagascar
  - Martinique
  - Monaco
  - Morocco
  - New Caledonia
  - Togo
  - Tunisia
- **CENTIMO** - Angola
  - Costa Rica
  - Mozambique
  - Paraguay
  - Peru
  - Philippines
  - Saint Thomas & Prince Island
  - Spain
  - Venezuela
- **CENTIMS** - Andorra
- **CENTU** - Lithuania
- **CFA** - Congo Republic
- **CHERVONETZ** - Russia
- **CHETRUM** - Bhutan
- **CHHERTUM** - Bhutan
- **CHIAO** - China, Japanese Puppet States
  - China, Republic Of
- **CHON** - Korea
  - Korea-North
- **COLON** - Costa Rica
  - El Salvador
- **CONDOR** - Ecuador
- **CORDOBA** - Nicaragua
- **CORONA** - Austria
- **CROWN** - Australia
  - Bermuda
  - Gibraltar
  - Great Britain
  - Ireland Republic
  - Malawi
  - New Zealand
  - Rhodesia And Nyasaland
  - Southern Rhodesia
  - Tibet
- **CRUZADO** - Brazil
- **CRUZEIRO** - Brazil
- **CRUZEIROS** - Brazil
- **CRUZEIROS REAIS** - Brazil
- **DALASI** - Gambia, The
- **DALER** - Danish West Indies
- **DAM** - Nepal
- **DECIME** - Monaco
- **DECIMO** - Ecuador
- **DENAR** - Macedonia
- **DENARI** - Macedonia
- **DENI** - Macedonia
- **DENOMINATION** - United States
- **DINAR** - Algeria
  - Hejaz
  - Iran
  - Iraq
  - Jordan
  - Libya
  - Serbia
  - Sudan
  - Tunisia
  - Yugoslavia
- **DINARA** - Serbia
  - Yugoslavia
- **DINER** - Andorra
- **DINERO** - Peru
- **DIRHAM** - Libya
  - Morocco
  - Qatar
  - United Arab Emirates
- **DIRHEM** - Qatar & Dubai
- **DOBRA** - Saint Thomas & Prince Island
- **DOLLAR** - Australia
  - Bahamas
  - Barbados
  - Belize
  - Bermuda
  - British Virgin Islands
  - Brunei
  - Canada
  - China
  - China, People'S Republic
  - China, Republic Of
  - Conch Republic
  - Cook Islands
  - East Caribbean States
  - Fiji
  - Great Britain
  - Grenada
  - Guyana
  - Hong Kong
  - Jamaica
  - Kiribati
  - Liberia
  - Namibia
  - New Zealand
  - Singapore
  - Solomon Islands
  - Straits Settlements
  - Trinidad & Tobago
  - Tuvalu
  - United States
  - Zimbabwe
- **DONG** - Viet Nam
- **DOUBLE** - Guernsey
- **DRACHMA** - Crete
  - Greece
- **DRACHMAI** - Crete
  - Greece
- **DRACHMES** - Greece
- **DRAM** - Armenia
  - Nagorno-Karabakh
  - Tajikistan
- **DUCAT** - Austria
  - German States
  - Netherlands
- **DUKAT** - Czechoslovakia
  - Yugoslavia
- **DUKATA** - Yugoslavia
- **DUKATU** - Czechoslovakia
- **DUKATY** - Czechoslovakia
- **EKUELE** - Equatorial Guinea
- **EMALANGENI** - Swaziland
- **ESCUDO** - Angola
  - Azores
  - Cape Verde
  - Chile
  - Guinea-Bissau
  - India-Portuguese
  - Madeira Islands
  - Mozambique
  - Portugal
  - Saint Thomas & Prince Island
  - Timor
- **EURO** - Austria
  - Belgium
  - Cyprus
  - Finland
  - France
  - Germany - Federal Republic
  - Greece
  - Ireland Republic
  - Italy
  - Luxembourg
  - Malta
  - Monaco
  - Netherlands
  - Portugal
  - San Marino
  - Slovenia
  - Spain
  - Vatican City
- **EYRIR** - Iceland
- **FARTHING** - Great Britain
  - Ireland Republic
  - Jamaica
- **FEN** - China, Japanese Puppet States
  - China, People'S Republic
  - China, Republic Of
- **FENIG** - Poland
- **FENIGOW** - Poland
- **FENINGA** - Bosnia-Herzegovina
- **FIL** - Bahrain
  - Iraq
  - Jordan
  - Kuwait
  - South Arabia
  - United Arab Emirates
  - Yemen Arab Republic
  - Yemen, Democratic Republic Of
- **FILLER** - Hungary
- **FLORIN** - Aruba
  - Australia
  - East Africa
  - Fiji
  - Great Britain
  - Ireland Republic
  - Malawi
  - New Zealand
  - South Africa
- **FORINT** - Hungary
- **FRANC** - Algeria
  - Belgian Congo
  - Belgium
  - Burundi
  - Cameroon
  - Central African Republic
  - Central African States
  - Chad
  - Comoros
  - Congo Republic
  - Congo, Democratic Republic
  - Djibouti
  - Equatorial African States
  - France
  - French Afars & Issas
  - French Equatorial Africa
  - French Oceania
  - French Polynesia
  - French Somaliland
  - French West Africa
  - Gabon
  - Guadeloupe
  - Guinea
  - Katanga
  - Luxembourg
  - Madagascar
  - Mali
  - Martinique
  - Monaco
  - Morocco
  - New Caledonia
  - New Hebrides
  - Reunion
  - Rwanda
  - Rwanda & Burundi
  - Saint Pierre & Miquelon
  - Switzerland
  - Togo
  - Tunisia
  - West African States
- **FRANCO** - Equatorial Guinea
- **FRANG AR** - Albania
- **FRANK** - Liechtenstein
- **FRANKEN** - Liechtenstein
  - Saarland
- **FUANG** - Thailand
- **FULUS** - Central Asia
- **FUN** - Korea
- **GERSH** - Ethiopia
- **GHIRSH** - Saudi Arabia
  - Sudan
- **GOURDE** - Haiti
- **GRAM** - Venezuela
- **GRAMS** - Afghanistan
- **GROSCHEN** - Austria
- **GROSZ** - Poland
- **GROSZE** - Poland
- **GROSZY** - Poland
- **GUARANI** - Paraguay
- **GUINEA** - Saudi Arabia
- **GULDEN** - Curacao
  - Danzig
  - Netherlands
  - Netherlands Antilles
  - Netherlands East Indies
  - Suriname
- **HABIBI** - Afghanistan
- **HALALA** - Saudi Arabia
  - Yemen
- **HALER** - Czechoslovakia
- **HALERE** - Czechoslovakia
- **HALERU** - Bohemia & Moravia
  - Czech Republic
  - Czechoslovakia
- **HALIEROV** - Slovakia
- **HAO** - Viet Nam
- **HARF** - Yemen
- **HELLER** - Austria
  - German East Africa

HRYVEN - Ukraine
HRYVNIA - Ukraine
HWAN - Korea-South
IMADI RIYAL - Yemen
INTI - Peru
JIAO - China, People'S Republic
KABIR - Yemen
KEPING - Malay Peninsula
KHUMSI - Yemen Eastern Aden Protectorate
KINA - Papua New Guinea
KIP - Lao
KOBO - Nigeria
KOPEEK - Transnistria
KOPEJEK - Tannu Tuva
KOPEK - Russia
KOPIYKA - Ukraine
KOPIYKY - Ukraine
KOPIYOK - Ukraine
KORONA - Hungary
KORUN - Czech Republic
Czechoslovakia
Slovakia
KORUNA - Bohemia & Moravia
Czech Republic
Czechoslovakia
Slovakia
KRAN - Iran
KRONA - Iceland
Sweden
KRONE - Denmark
Greenland
Liechtenstein
Norway
KRONEN - Austria
Liechtenstein
KRONER - Denmark
Greenland
Norway
KRONOR - Sweden
KRONUR - Iceland
KROONI - Estonia
KUNA - Croatia
KURUS - Turkey
KURUSH - Turkey
KWACHA - Malawi
Zambia
KWANZA - Angola
KYAT - Myanmar
KYATS - Myanmar
LAARI - Maldive Islands
LARI - Georgia
LARIAT - Maldive Islands
LARIN - Maldive Islands
LATI - Latvia
LATS - Latvia
LEI - Moldova
Romania
LEK - Albania
LEKE - Albania
LEKU - Albania
LEMPIRA - Honduras
LEONE - Sierra Leone
LEPTA - Crete
Greece
LEPTON - Crete
LEU - Moldova
Romania
LEV - Bulgaria
LEVA - Bulgaria
LI - China, Japanese Puppet States
LIBRA - Peru
LICENTE - Lesotho
LIKUTA - Congo, Democratic Republic
LILANGENI - Swaziland
LIPA - Croatia
LIPE - Croatia
LIRA - Israel
Italy
Malta
San Marino
Syria
Turkey
Vatican City
LIRE - Italian Somaliland
Italy
San Marino
Vatican City
LIROT - Israel
LISENTE - Lesotho
LITAI - Lithuania
LITAS - Lithuania
LITU - Lithuania
LIVRE - Lebanon
LIVRES - Lebanon
LOTI - Lesotho
LUMA - Armenia
Nagorno-Karabakh
LWEI - Angola
MAKUTA - Congo, Democratic Republic
Zaire
MALOTI - Lesotho
MANAT - Turkmenistan
MARK - Estonia
German States
German-Democratic Republic
Germany - Federal Republic
Germany, Empire
Germany, Weimar Republic
MARKA - Bosnia-Herzegovina
Estonia
MARKKA - Finland
MARKKAA - Finland
MATONA - Ethiopia
MATONAS - Ethiopia
MAZUNAS - Morocco
METICA - Mozambique
METICAIS - Mozambique
METICAL - Mozambique
MIL - Cyprus
Israel
Malta
Palestine
MILLIEME - Egypt
Libya
MILLIM - Sudan
Tunisia
MOHAR - Nepal
MONGO - Mongolia
MUZUNA - Morocco
NAIRA - Nigeria
NGULTRUM - Bhutan
NGWEE - Zambia
NUMISMAS - Kamberra Island
ORE - Denmark
Faeroe Islands
Greenland
Norway
Sweden
OUGUIYA - Mauritania
OUNCE - Burkina Faso
PA'ANGA - Tonga
PAHLAVI - Iran
PAISA - Afghanistan
Bhutan
India-Republic
Nepal
Pakistan
PAISE - Afghanistan
India-Republic
PARA - Hejaz
Montenegro
Serbia
Turkey
Yugoslavia
PARE - Montenegro
Serbia
PATACA - Macao
PE - Myanmar
PENCE - Australia
Biafra
British West Africa
Falkland Islands
Fiji
Gambia, The
Ghana
Gibraltar
Great Britain
Guernsey
Guyana
Ireland Republic
Isle Of Man
Jersey
Malawi
New Guinea
New Zealand
Nigeria
Rhodesia
Rhodesia And Nyasaland
Saint Helena & Ascension
South Africa
Southern Rhodesia
Zambia
PENGO - Hungary
PENNIA - Finland
PENNY - Australia
British West Africa
Falkland Islands
Fiji
Gambia, The
Ghana
Gibraltar
Great Britain
Guernsey
Ireland Republic
Isle Of Man
Jamaica
Jersey
Malawi
New Guinea
New Zealand
Nigeria
Rhodesia And Nyasaland
Saint Helena & Ascension
South Africa
Southern Rhodesia
Zambia
PERPER - Montenegro
PERPERA - Montenegro
PESETA - Equatorial Guinea
Spain
PESEWA - Ghana
PESO - Argentina
Bolivia
Chile
Colombia
Cuba
Dominican Republic
El Salvador
Guatemala
Guinea-Bissau
Honduras
Mexico
Paraguay
Philippines
Uruguay
PESOS - Uruguay
PFENNIG - Danzig
German-Democratic Republic
Germany - Federal Republic
Germany, Empire
Germany, Weimar Republic
PHAN - Viet Nam
PIASTRE - Cyprus
Egypt
French Indo-China
Hejaz
Jordan
Lebanon
Libya
Nejd
Sudan
Syria
Tonkin
PICE - Bhutan
India-British
India-Republic
Pakistan
PIE - Pakistan
PISO - Philippines
PITIS - Malay Peninsula
POISHA - Bangladesh
POLUSHKA - Russia
POND - South Africa
POUND - Cyprus
Egypt
Falkland Islands
Gibraltar
Great Britain
Guernsey
Isle Of Man
Jersey
Malta
Saint Helena & Ascension
Sudan
Syria
PRUTA - Israel
PRUTOT - Israel
PUL - Afghanistan
Central Asia
PULA - Botswana
PUNT - Ireland Republic
PYA - Myanmar
QAPIK - Azerbaijan
QINDAR AR - Albania
QINDARKA - Albania
QIRSH - Egypt
Jordan
QUETZAL - Guatemala
RAND - South Africa
RAPPEN - Switzerland
REAL - Brazil
El Salvador
Guatemala
REICHSMARK - Germany, Third Reich
Germany, Weimar Republic
REICHSPFENNIG - Germany, Third Reich
Germany, Weimar Republic
REIS - Azores
Brazil
Portugal
RENTENPFENNIG - Germany, Weimar Republic
RIAL - Iran
Morocco
Muscat & Oman
Oman
Yemen Republic
RIEL - Cambodia
RIN - Japan
RINGGIT - Malaysia
RIYAL - Iraq
Saudi Arabia
Yemen
Yemen Arab Republic
Yemen Republic
ROUBLE - Central Asia
Russia
RUFIYAA - Maldive Islands
RUPEE - Afghanistan
Bhutan
Ceylon
India-British
India-Republic
Mauritius
Nepal
Pakistan
Seychelles
Sri Lanka
Tibet
RUPIA - India-Portuguese
Indonesia
Italian Somaliland
RUPIAH - Indonesia
RUPIE - German East Africa
SALUNG - Thailand
SANAR - Afghanistan
SANTIM - Morocco
SANTIMAT - Morocco
SANTIMI - Latvia
SANTIMS - Latvia
SANTIMU - Latvia
SAPEQUE - French Indo-China
SATANG - Thailand
SCHILLING - Austria
SEN - Brunei
Cambodia
Indonesia
Japan
Malaysia
SENE - Samoa
SENGI - Congo, Democratic Republic
SENITI - Tonga
SENT - Estonia
SENTE - Lesotho
SENTI - Estonia
Somalia
Tanzania
SENTIMO - Philippines
SHAHI - Afghanistan
Iran
SHEQALIM - Israel
SHEQEL - Israel
SHILINGI - Tanzania
SHILLING - Australia
Biafra
British West Africa
Cyprus
East Africa
Fiji
Gambia, The
Ghana
Great Britain
Guernsey
Ireland Republic
Jersey
Kenya
Malawi
New Guinea
New Zealand
Nigeria
Rhodesia
Rhodesia And Nyasaland
Somalia
Somaliland
South Africa
Southern Rhodesia
Uganda
Zambia
SHILLINGS - Kenya
Somalia
SHO - Tibet
SKAR - Tibet
SOL - Peru
SOLDI - Montecristo
SOLDO - Montecristo
SOLE - Peru
SOM - Kyrgyzstan
Uzbekistan
SOMALO - Somalia
SOMONI - Tajikistan
SOVEREIGN - Australia
Canada
Great Britain
India-British
Isle Of Man
South Africa
SRANG - Tibet
STOTINKA - Bulgaria
STOTINKI - Bulgaria
STOTINOV - Slovenia
SU - Viet Nam
SUCRE - Ecuador
SYLI - Guinea
SYLIS - Guinea
TAKA - Bangladesh
TALA - Samoa
TALLERO - Eritrea
TAMBALA - Malawi
TANGA - India-Portuguese
TANGKA - Tibet
TENE - Cook Islands
TENGA - Central Asia
TENGE - Kazakhstan
Turkmenistan
THEBE - Botswana
THETRI - Georgia
TILLA - Afghanistan
Central Asia
TIYIN - Kyrgyzstan
Uzbekistan
TOEA - Papua New Guinea
TOLA - Nepal
TOLAR - Slovenia
TOLARJA - Slovenia
TOLARJEV - Slovenia
TOMAN - Iran
TUGRIK - Mongolia
TYIN - Kazakhstan
VAN - Viet Nam
VATU - Vanuatu
WERK - Ethiopia
WON - Korea
Korea-North
Korea-South
XU - Viet Nam
YANG - Korea
YEN - Japan
YUAN - China, People'S Republic
China, Republic Of
ZAIRE - Zaire
ZALAT - Yemen
ZLOTE - Poland
ZLOTY - Poland
ZLOTYCH - Poland

INSTANT IDENTIFIER

Aachen (German States)

Albania

Austria

Baden (German States)

Brandenburg Ansbach (German States)

Finland

Jever (German States)

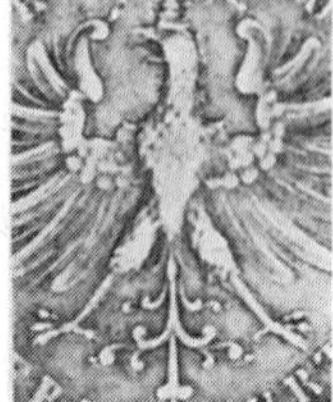

Frankfurt (German States)

Furstenberg (German States)

Geneva (Swiss Cantons)

German Empire

Montenegro (Yugoslavia)

Nürnberg (German States)

Milan (Italian States)

Prussia (German States)

Russia (Czarist) Russian Poland

Schwarzburg-Rudolstadt (German States)

Schwarzburg-Sondershausen (German States)

Serbia (Yugoslavia)

Teutonic Order (German States)

Genoa (Italian States)

Syrian Arab Republic

United Arab Republic (Egypt, Syria)

Arab Republic of Egypt Libya

Yemen Arab Republic

Bulgaria

Burma (Myanmar)

Ethiopia

Finland

Norway

Gorizia (Italian States)

Hannover (German States)

Hesse-Darmstadt (German States)

Hohenlohe-Neuenstein-Oehringen (German States)

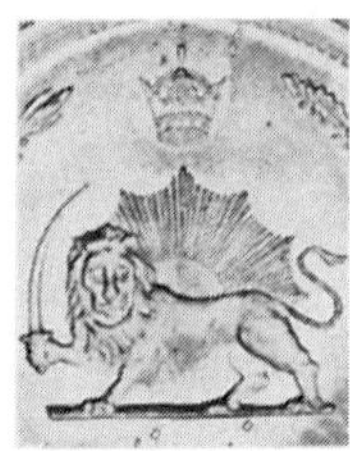

Iran (Persia)

Morocco

Siberia

Tibet (China)

Nepal

Morocco (AH1371-1951AD)

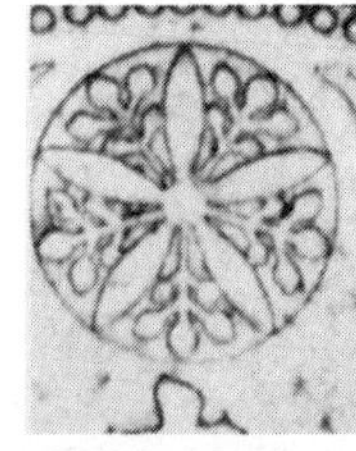

Manchoukuo (Puppet State-China)

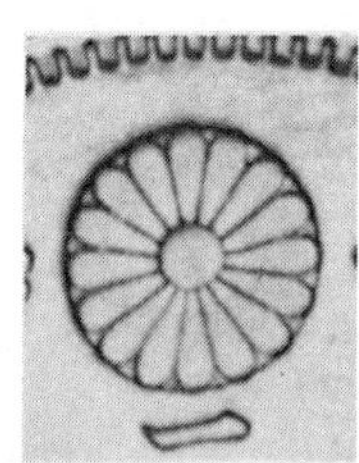

Japan

INSTANT IDENTIFIER

Hanau-Munzenberg (German States)

Nassau (German States)

Hesse-Cassel (German States)

Sri Lanka (Ceylon)

Tibet (China)

Utrecht (Netherlands)

Venice (Italian States)

Neuchatel (Swiss Cantons)

China (Empire-Provincial)

China (Empire-Provincial)

Japan

Japan

African States

Bretzenheim (German States)

Hall in Swabia (German States)

Greenland

German New Guinea (Papua New Guinea)

Lithuania

Mongolia

Sudan

Algeria

Lowenstein-Wertheim (German States)

Maldive Islands

Afghanistan

Ireland

Israel

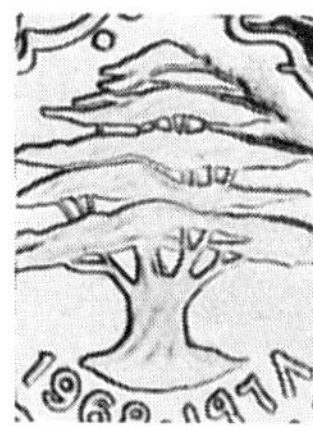
Lebanon

Papal States (Italian States)

Regensburg (German States)

Sweden

North Korea

CCCP-Russia

CCCP-Russia

Yugoslavia

Taiwan (Rep. of China)

Mainz (German States)

Solms-Laubach (German States)

Ticino (Swiss Cantons)

Fugger (German States)

Naples & Sicily (Italian States)

Saxe-Saalfeld (German States)

Stolberg-Stolberg (German States)

INSTANT IDENTIFIER

French Colonial

French Colonial

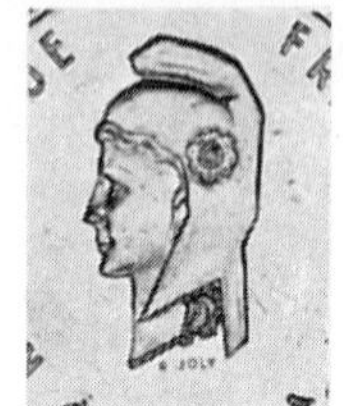
French Colonial

Bangladesh

Isle of Man
Sicily

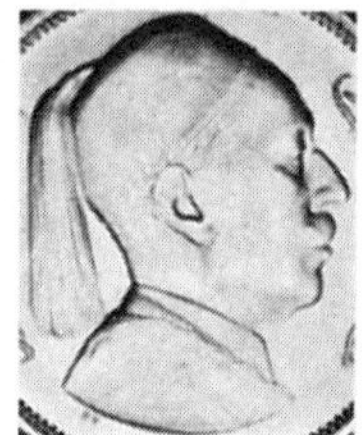
Libya

Anhalt-Bernburg
(German States)

Aargau
(Swiss Cantons)

Augsburg
(German States)

Basel
(Swiss Cantons)

Bavaria
(German States)

Brazil

Bremen
(German States)

Luzern
(Swiss Cantons)

Chur Pfalz
(German States)

Fulda
(German States)

Glarus
(Swiss Cantons)

Grand Duchy
of Warsaw
(Poland)

Graubunden
(Swiss Cantons)

Hamburg
(German States)

Lucca
(Italian States)

Hesse-Cassel
(German States)

Hesse-Homburg
(German States)

Hildesheim
(German States)

Hohenzollern-
Hechingen
(German States)

Hungary

Julich-Berg
(German States)

Gelderland
(Netherlands)

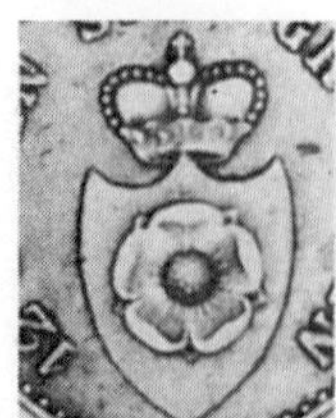
Lippe-Detmold
(German States)

Lübeck
(German States)

Mecklenburg-
Strelitz
(German States)

Oldenburg
(German States)

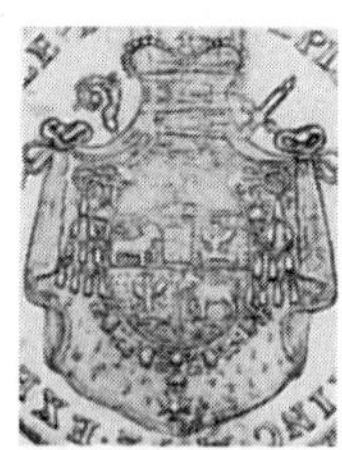
Passau
(German States)

Portugal

Vaud
(Swiss Cantons)

Anhalt
(Joint Coinage)
(German States)

Oldenburg
(German States)

Schwarzenberg
(German States)

Schaffhausen
(Swiss Cantons)

Paderborn
(German States)

Thurgau
(Swiss Cantons)

Westfrisia
(Netherlands)

INSTANT IDENTIFIER

Arenberg (German States)

Rhenish Confederation (German States)

Reuss-Greiz (German States)

Sardinia (Italian States)

Saxony (German States)

Schaumburg-Lippe (German States)

Schleswig-Holstein (German States)

St. Gall (Swiss Cantons)

Slovakia

Solothurn (Swiss Cantons)

Unterwalden (Nidwalden) (Swiss Cantons)

Württemberg (German States)

Würzburg (German States)

Zurich (Swiss Cantons)

Waldeck-Pyrmont (German States)

Iraq

Pakistan

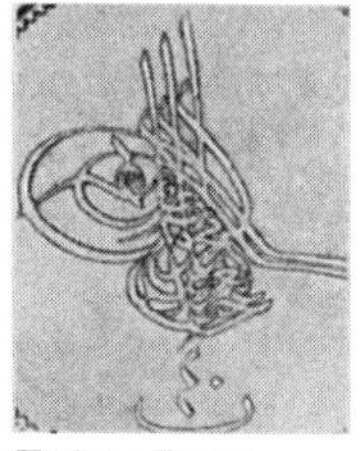
Turkey-Egypt Sudan, Algeria (Ottoman Empire)

Muscat & Oman, Oman

Saudi Arabia

Tunisia

Wismar (German States)

Order of Malta

Bamberg (German States)

Brunswick-Wolfenbüttel (German States)

Brunswick-Lüneburg (German States

Erfurt Mainz (German States)

Hannover (German States)

Eichstätt (German States)

Greece

Serbia

Switzerland

Thailand (Siam)

Japan (Dai Nippon)

South Korea

Sitten (Swiss Cantons)

Rostock (German States)

Saint Alban (German States)

English East India Co. (Sumatra)

China, Japan, Annam, Korea
(All Holed 'cash' coins look quite similar.)

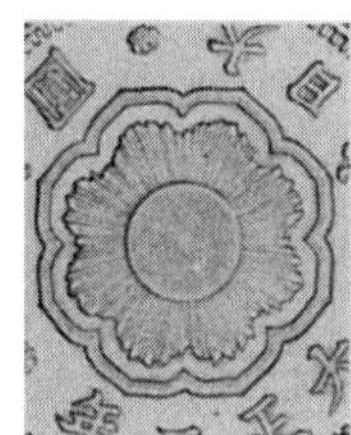
Japan

Korea

MONOGRAMS

MJ
Maximilian IV
Joseph Berg

CC99
Christian IX
Danish West Indies

VOC
Dutch East India
Co. (Indonesia)

CVII
Christian VII
Danish West Indies

CCX
Christian X
Danish West Indies

G
Georg Mexklenburg-
Strelitz

CWF Carl Welhelm
Ferdinand Brunswick-
Wolfenbuttel

H7
Haakon VII
Norway

A
Albert I
Belgium

GRI Georgius Rex
Imperator
New Guinea

L
Leopold II
Belgium

EAR
Ernest August Rex
Hannover

FRVI
Frederick VI Rex
Denmark

CX
Christian X
Denmark

H7
Haakon VII
Norway

A
Albert I
Belgium

GRI Georgius Rex
Imperator
New Guinea

L
Leopold II
Belgium

EAR
Ernest August Rex
Hannover

FRVI
Frederick VI Rex
Denmark

CX
Christian X
Denmark

C7
Christian VII
Tranquebar

C7
Christian VII
Denmark

CIX
Christian IX
Denmark

CCX
Christian X
Denmark

CCXIII
Charles XIII
Sweden

CLXIV
Carl XIV Johann
Norway

CXIV
Carl XIV Johann
Sweden

EP
Elizabeth-Philip
Great Britain

ERI Edward Rex
Imperator
New Guinea

EIIR
Elizabeth II Regina
Cook Island

FA
Friedrich August
Lubeck Bishopric

FF
Friedrich Franz
Mecklenburg-Schwerin

FJI
Franz Joseph I
Austria

O
Oscar I
Sweden

AFC
Alexius Friedrich
Great Britain
Anhalt-Bernburg

NII
Nicholas II
Russia

FRVII
Frederik VII Rex
Danish West Indies
Denmark

FC
Friedrich Christian
Brandenburg-
Bayreuth

AIII
Alexander III
Russia

W
William I
Netherlands

LLX
Ludwig X
Hesse-Darmstadt

MONOGRAMS

MJ
Maximilian IV Joseph
Berg

FI
Frederick IX & Ingrid
Denmark

F VI R
Fred. VI Denmark
Tranquebar

FVII
Frederick VII
Denmark

FF8
Frederick VIII
Denmark

F IX R
Frederick IX
Denmark

FVII
Ferdinand VII
Mexico

PI
Paul I
Russia

FVII
Ferdinand VII
Mexico

FW
Fredrich Wilhelm III
Prussia

GA IV
Gustav Adolf IV
Sweden

HI
Nicholas I
Russia

HC
Henri Christophe
Haiti

HVII
Haakon VII
Norway

HN Hieronymus
Napoleon
Westphalia

J
Joachim (Murat)
Berg

E(K)I II
Katherine II
Russia

L
Ludwig
Hesse-Darmstadt

L
Leopold
Belgium

LL III
Leopold III
Belgium

LL
Louis XVIII
Antwerp

C XIVJ
Carl XIV Johann
Norway

M Morelos
Revolutionary
Mexico

M 2 R
Margrethe II Regina
Denmark

NII
Nicholas II
Russia

NI
Nicholas I
Russia

NFP
Nicholas Friedrich
Peter Oldenburg

OII
Oscar II
Norway

E
Ernest I
Saxe-Coburg-Gotha

O V
Olav V
Norway

P I
Paul I
Russia

P III
Peter III
Russia

R
Rainier III
Monaco

WL
Wilhelm Landgraf
Hesse-Cassel

WR
William Rex
Hannover

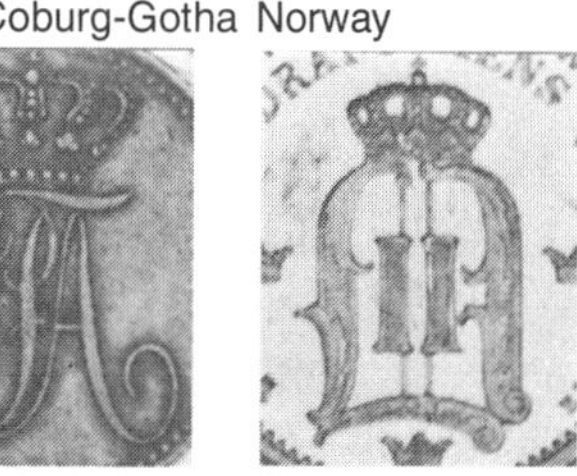
PFA
Peter Friedrich
August Oldenburg

OII
Oscar II
Sweden

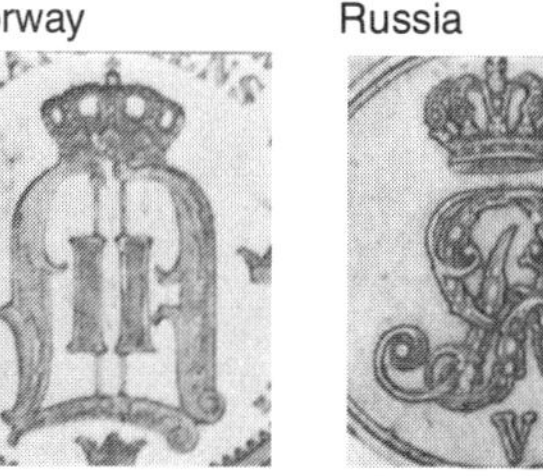
GR
Georgius Rex
Hannover

FRVI
Frederik VI Rex
Tranquebar

PF
Paul Friedrich
Mecklenburg-Schwerin

FII
Friedrich II
Wurttemberg

FER VII
Ferdinand VII
(Spain) Gerona

ILLUSTRATED GUIDE TO EASTERN MINT NAMES

Compiled by Dr. N. Douglas Nicol, 2006

Abarquh (Iran) ابرقوه

'Abdullahnagar (Pihani) عبدالله نگر

Abivard ابي ورد ابيورد باورد

Abu Arish (the Yemen) ابو عريش

Abushahr (Bushire - Iran) ابو سهر

'Adan (Aden-the Yemen) عدن

Adoni (Imtiyazgarh-Mughal) ادوني

Adrana (see Edirne)

Advani (Adoni - Mughal) ادواني

Afghanistan افغانستان

Agra (Mughal) اگره

Ahmadabad (Gujarat Sultanate, Mughal, Maratha, Bombay Presidency, Baroda) احمداباد

Ahmadnagar (Ahmadnagar Sultanate, Mughal) احمدنگر

Ahmadnagar Farrukhabad (state, Afghanistan) احمدنگر فرخ اباد

Ahmadpur (Bahawalpur, Afghanistan) احمدپور

Ahmadshahi (Qandahar-Afghanistan) احمدشاهي

Ahsanabad (Kulbarga - Mughal) احسن اباد

Ajman (United Arab Emirates) عجمان

Ajmer (Salimabad - Mughal, Maratha, Gwalior, Jodhpur) اجمير

Ajmer Salimabad (Mughal) اجمير سليم اباد

Akalpurakh (Kashmir, Sikh) اكال پورخ

Akbarabad (Agra - Mughal, Maratha, Bharatpur) اكبراباد

Akbarnagar (Rajmahal - Mughal) اكبرنگر

Akbarpur (Tanda - Mughal) اكبرپور

Akbarpur Tanda (Mughal) اكبرپور تانده

Akhshi, Akhshikath (Central Asia) اخشي اخشيكاث

Akhtarnagar (Awadh - Mughal) اخترنگر

'Akka (Ottoman Turkey) عكّا عكّة

Aksu (China - Sinkiang) اقسو اقصو

al-Aliya العالية

'Alamgirnagar (Mughal, Koch Bihar) عالمگيرنگر

'Alamgirpur (Bhilsa, Vidisha-Mughal, Gwalior) عالم گيرپور

Amul (Iran) آمل

al-'Arabiya as-Sa'udiya (Saudi Arabia) العربية السعودية

al-'Ara'ish (Larache - Morocco) العرائش

Algeria (al-Jaza'ir) الجزائر

'Alinagar (Calcutta - Mughal) علي نگر

'Alinagar Kalkatah (Calcutta - Bengal Pres.) علي نگر كلكته

Allahabad (Mughal, Awadh) الله اباد

Almora (Gurkha)

Alwar (Mughal) الوار

Amaravati (Hyderabad) امراوتي

Amasya (Amasia - Turkey) اماسية

Amid (Turkey) آمد

Amritsar (Ambratsar - Sikh) امبرت سر امرت سر

Amirkot (Umarkot - Mughal) اميركوت

Anandgharh (Anandpur - Mughal) انندگهره

Andijan (Andigan - Central Asia) اندجان اندگان

Anhirwala Pattan (Mughal) انحيروالا پتن

Ankaland (Bi-Ankaland - in England, Birmingham and London mints for Morocco) انكلند بانكلند

Ankara (Anguriya, Engüriye - Turkey) انگورية انقرية انقرة

Anupnagar Shahabad (Mughal) انوپنگر شاه باد

Anwala (Anola - Mughal, Rohilkhand, Afghanistan) انوله

Aqsara (Aqsaray, Aksara - the Yemen) اقصرا اقصراي اكصرا

Ardabil (Iran) اردبيل

Ardanuç (Turkey) اردنوچ اردانيچ

Ardanush (Iran) اردنوش

Arjish (Iran) ارجيش

Arkat (Arcot - Mughal, French India, Madras Presidency) اركات

Asafabad (Bareli - Mughal, Awadh) اصف اباد

Asafabad Bareli (Mughal, Awadh) اصفاباد

Asafnagar (Aklooj - Mughal, Rohilkhand, Awadh) اصف نگر اصفنگر

Asfarayin (Central Asia, Iran) اسفراين

Asfi (Safi - Morocco) اسفي

Asir (Asirgarh - Mughal) اسير

Astarabad (Central Asia, Iran) استراباد

Atak (Attock - Mughal, Afghanistan) اتك

Atak Banaras (Mughal) اتك بنارس

Atcheh (Sultanate, Netherlands East Indies) اچه

Athani (Maratha) اثاني

Aurangabad (Khujista Bunyad - Mughal, Hyderabad) اورنگ اباد

Aurangnagar (Mughal, Maratha) اورنگ نگر

Ausa (Mughal) اوسا

Awadh (Oudh, Khitta - Awadh state) اوده

Awbah (Central Asia) اوبه

Ayasluk (Ayasoluq, Ephesus - Turkey) اياسلق اياثلق

Aydaj (Iran) ايدج

Azak (Azow - Turkey) آزاق آزق

A'zamnagar (Gokak - Mughal) اعظم نگر

A'zamnagar Bankapur (Mughal) اعظم نگر بنكاپور

A'zamnagar Gokak (Belgaum - Mughal, Kolhapur) اعظم نگر گوكاك

'Azimabad (Patna - Mughal, Bengal Presidency) عظيم اباد

Badakhshan (Mughal, Central Asia, Afghanistan) بدخشان

Bagalkot (Maratha) بگلكوت

Bagchih Serai (Krim) باغچه سراي

Baghdad (Bagdad - Iraq) بغداد

Bahadurgarh (Mughal) بهادرگره

Bahawalpur (Bahawalpur state, Afghanistan) بهاولپور

Bahraich (Mughal) بهرايچ بهريچ

Bahrain (al-Bahrayn) البحرين

Bairata (Mughal) بيراتة

Bakhar (Bakkar, Bakhar, Bhakhar, Bhakkar - Mughal, Sind, Afghanistan) بهكّر بهكهر

Baku (Bakuya - Iran) باكو باكويه

Balanagor Gadha (Mandla - Maratha) بالانگر گدها

Balapur (two places - one in Kandesh, one in Sira - Mughal) بالاپور

Balhari (Bellary - Mysore) بلهاري

Balikesir (Turkey) بالكسير

Balkh (Mughal, Central Asia, Afghanistan) بلخ

Balwantnagar (Jhansi - Mughal, Maratha, Gwalior) بلونت نگر

Banaras (Benares, Varanasi - Mughal, Bengal Presidency, Awadh) بنارس

Banda Malwari (Maratha) بنده ملواري

Bandar (Iran) بندر

Bandar Abbas (Iran) بندر عباس

Bandar Abu Shahr (Iran) بندر ابو شهر

Bandar Shahi (Mughal) بندرشاهي

Bandhu (Qila - Mughal) بندهو

Bangala (Mughal) بنگالة

Banjarmasin (Netherlands East Indies) بنجرمسن

Bankapur (Mughal) بنكپ بنكاپور

Baramati (Sultanate, Mughal) بنده ملواري

Bareli (Bareilly - Mughal, Rohilkhand, Awadh, Afghanistan) بريلي

Bariz (Paris, in Paris - Morocco) باريز بباريز

Baroda (Vadodara - Baroda state) بروده

Basoda (Gwalior) بسوده

al-Basra (Basra - Iraq) البصرة

Batan (Baltistan? - Ladakh) بتان

Bela (Las Bela state) بيله

Belgrad (Turkey) بنگالور

Bengalur (Bangalor - Mysore) بنگالور

Berar (Mughal) برار

Berlin (for Morocco) برلين

Bhakkar, Bhakhar (See Bakkar)

Bharatpur (Braj Indrapur) بهرت پور

Bhaunagar (Mughal) بهاونگر

Bhelah (See Bela) بهله

Bhilsa (Alamgirpur - Mughal) بهيلسة

Bhilwara (Mewar) بهيلوارا

Bhopal (Bhopal state) بهوپال

Bhuj (Kutch) بهوج

Bhujnagar (Bhuj - Kutch) بهوج نگر

Bidlis (Bitlis - Turkey) بدليس بتليس

Bidrur (Mughal) بدرور

Bihbihan (Behbehan - Iran) بهبهان

Bijapur (Bijapur Sultanate, Mughal) بيجاپور

Bikanir (Mughal, Bikanir state) بيكانير

Bindraban (Vrindavan - Mughal, Bindraban state) بندربن

Bisauli (Rohilkhand) بسولے بسولي

Bistam (Central Asia) بسطام

Biyar (Iran) بيار

Borujerd (Iran) بروجرد

Bosna (Sarajevo - Turkey) بوسنه

Bosna Saray (Sarajevo - Turkey) بوسنة سراي

Braj Indrapur (Bharatpur) برج اندرپور

Broach (Baroch, Bharoch - Mughal, Broach state, Gwalior) بروني

Brunei (Malaya) بروني

Bukhara (Central Asia) بخارا

Bukhara-yi Sharif (Central Asia) بخاراي شريف

Bundi (Bundi state) بوندي

Burhanabad (Mughal) برهان اباد

Burhanpur (Mughal, Maratha, Gwalior) برهانپور

Bursa (Brusa - Turkey) برسه بروسه

Bushanj (Iran) بوشنج

Bushire (see Abushahr)

Çaniçe (Chanicha - Turkey) چانيچه چاينيچه

Chakan (Maratha) چاكن

Champanir (Gujarat Sultanate) چانپانير

Chanda (Maratha) چانده

Chanderi (Gwalior) چنديري

Chandor (Maratha, Indore) چاندور

Chhachrauli (Kalsia) چهچرولي

Chhatarpur (Chhatarpur state) چترپور

Chikodi (Maratha) چكودي

Chinapattan (Madras - Mughal) چيناپتن

Chinchwar (Maratha) چنچور

Chitor (Akbarpur - Mughal) چيتور

Chunar (Mughal) چنار

Cuttack (see Katak)

Dadiyan (Iran) داديان

Dalipnagar (Datia) دليپ نگر

Damarvar (Mysore) دماروار

Damghan (Central Asia) دامغان

al-Damigh (the Yemen) الدامغ

Damla (Mughal) داملا

Darband (Derbent - Azerbaijan, Iran) دربند

Darfur (see al-Fashir)

Darur (Mughal) درور دارر

Daulatabad (Deogir - Mughal, Hyderabad) دولت اباد دولتاباد

Daulat Anjazanchiya (see Comoros) دولة انجزنچية

Daulatgarh (Rahatgarh - Bharatpur, Gwalior) دولت گره

Daulat Qatar (State of Qatar - Qatar) دولة قطر

Dawar (Iran) داور

al-Dawla al-Mughribiya (Empire of Morocco) الدولة المغربية

Dawlatabad (Iran) دولتاباد

Dawraq (Iran) دورق

Dehdasht (Iran) دهدشت

Dehli (Shahjahanabad - Mughal, Afghanistan) دهلي

Deli (Netherlands East Indies) دلي

Deogarh (Partabgarh) ديوگره

Deogir (Daulatabad - Mughal) ديوگير

Dera (Derah - Mughal, Sikh, Afghanistan) ديره

Derajat (Mughal, Sikh, Afghanistan) ديره جات

Dewal Bandar (Mughal) ديول بندر

Dezful (Iran) دزفول

Dhamar (the Yemen) ذمار ذمر

Dharwar (Mysore) دہاروار

Dholapur (Dholapur state) دهولپور دہولپور

Dicholi (Mughal, Maratha) ديچولي

Dilshadabad (Mughal, Narayanpett) دلشاداباد

Dimashq (Damascus - Syria) دمشق

Diyar Bakr (Turkey) جيبوتي

Djibouti (Jaibuti - French Somaliland) جيبوتي

Dogam (Dogaon - Mughal) دوگام

Dogaon (Mughal) دوگاون

Edirne (Adrianople - Turkey) ادرنه

Elichpur (Mughal, Hyderabad) ايلچپور

Erzurum (Theodosiopolis - Turkey) ارزروم

Faiz Hisar (Gooty - Mysore) فعز حصار

Farahabad (Iran) فرح اباد

Farkhanda Bunyad (Hyderabad - Mughal) فرخنده بنياد

Farrukhabad (Ahmadnagar - Mughal, Bengal Presidency) فرخ اباد

Farrukhi (Feroke - Mysore) فرخي

Farrukhnagar (Mughal) فرخ نگر

Farrukhyab Hisar (Chitradurga - Mysore) فرخياب حصار

Fas (Fez - Morocco) فاس

Fas al-Jadid (see al-Madina al-Bayda' - Morocco) فاش الجديد

al-Fashir (Darfur, Sudan) الفشير

Fathabad Dharur (Mughal) فبح اباد دهرور

Fathnagar (Aurangabad - فتحنگر

Fathpur (Nusratabad, Sikri - Mughal) فتحپور

Fedala (Fadalat al-Muhammadiya - Morocco) فضالة

Fergana (Central Asia) فرغانة

Filastin (Palestine) فاسطين

Filibe (Philipopolis, Plovdiv - Turkey) فيليپ فلبه

Firozgarh (Yadgir - Mughal) فيروزگره

Firoznagar (Mughal, Hyderabad) فيروزنگر

al-Fujaira (United Arab Emir- الفجيرة

Fuman (Iran) فومان

Gadraula (Mughal) گدرولة

Gadwal (Hyderabad) گدوال

Gajjikota (Mughal) گجيكوتا

Ganja (Ganjah, Genje - Elizabethpol, Kirovabad in Azerbaijan, Iran, Turkey) گنجه

Ganjikot (Genjikot - Mughal) گنجيكوت

Gargaon (Assam) گرگاو

Garha (Mughal) گارحة

Gelibolu (Gallipoli - Turkey) گليبولى

Ghazni (Afghanistan) غزني

al-Ghurfa (Hadhramaut) الغرفة

Gilan (Iran) گنلان

Gobindpur (Mughal) گوبندپور

Gohad (Mughal, Dholapur) گوهد

Gokak (Belgaum, 'Azamnagar - Mughal) گوكاك

Gokul (Bindraban) گوكل

Gokulgarh (Mughal) گوكل گره

Gorakpur (Muazzamabad - Mughal) گوركپور

Gözlü (see Shahr-Gözlü - Krim) گوزلو

Gulbarga (Kulbarga, Ahsanabad - Mughal) گلبرگة

Gulkanda (Golkona - Sultanate, Mughal) گلكندة

Gulshanabad (Nasik - Mughal, Maratha) گلشن اباد

Gümüsh-hane (Turkey) گمشخانه

Guti (Gooty - Mughal, Mysore) گوتي

Guzelhisar (Turkey) گوزلحصر

Gwaliar (Mughal, Gwalior state, گواليار

Hafizabad (Mughal) هافظاباد

Haidarabad (Hyderabad, Haidrabad, Farkhanda Bunyad - Golkanda Sultanate, Mughal, Hyderabad state, Sind, Afghanistan) حيدراباد

Haidarnagar (Bednur, Nagar - Mysore) حيدرنگر

Hajipur (Mughal) حجيپور

Halab (Aleppo - Syria) بلب

Hamadan (Iran) همدان

Hansi (Qanauj - Mughal, Awadh) هانسي

al-Haramayn ash-Sharifayn (Mecca and Medina in Arabia - Ottoman Turkey) الشريفين الحرمين

al-Harar (Ethiopia) الهرر

Hardwar (Haridwar, Tirath - Mughal, Saharanpur) هاردوار

Harput, Harburt (see Khartapirt)

Harran (Turkey) حران

Hasanabad (Mughal) حسن اباد

Hathras (Mughal, Awadh) هاتهرس

Hathrasa (Hathras) هاتهرسا

Hawran (Horan - Syria) حوران

Hawta (the Yemen) حوطة

Hawz (Morocco) حوز

al-Hejaz (Saudi Arabia) الحجاز

Herat (Afghanistan, Central Asia, Iran) — هراة هرات

al-Hilla (Hille - Iraq) — الحلة

Hinganhat (Maratha) — حنگنهات

Hisar (Central Asia) — حصر حصار

Hisar Firoza (Mughal) — حصار فيروزة

al-Hisn (el-Hisin - Turkey) — الحصن

Hizan (Khizan - Turkey) — هزان خيزان

Hukeri (Mughal, Maratha) — هوكري

Husaingarh (Mughal) — حسين گره

Huwayza (Iran) — حويزة

Ibb (the Yemen) — ايب

Ilahabad (Allahabad) — اله اباد

Ilahabas (Mughal) — اله اباس

Ili (China - Sinkiang) — الي

al-Imarat al-'Arabiya al-Muttahida (United Arab Emirates) — امتيازگره

Imtiyazgarh (Adoni - Mughal) — امتيازگره

Indore (Indore state) — اندور

Inebolu (Turkey) — اينه بولى

Inegöl (Turkey) — اينه كول

Iran — ايران

al-Iraq

Iravan (Eravan, Erewan, Revan – Iran, Yeravan – Armenia) — ايروان

'Isagarh (Gwalior) — عيسى گره

Isfahan (Iran) — اصفهان

Islamabad (Mathura – Mughal, Bindraban — اسلام اباد

Islam Bandar (Rajapur – Mughal) — اسلام بندر

Islambul (Istanbul – Turkey) — اسلامبول

Islamnagar (Navanagar – Mughal) — اسلام نگر

Ismailgarh (Mughal) — اسمعيل گره

Italian Somaliland (Somalia) — الصومال الايطاليانية

Itawa (Mughal, Maratha, Rohilkhand, Awadh — اتاوه اتاوا

Izmir (Turkey) — ازمير ازمر

Jabbalpur (Mughal) — جَبالپور

Ja'farabad urf Chandor (Indore) — جعفراباد عرف چاندور

Jahangirnagar (Dacca - Mughal, Bengal Presidency) — جهانگيرنگر

Jaipur (Sawai - Mughal) — جي پور

Jaisalmir (Jaisalmir state) — جيسلمير

Jalalnagar (Mughal) — جلال نگر

Jalalpur (Mughal) — جلالپور

Jalaun (Jalon - Maratha) — جلون

Jalesar (Mughal) — جليسار

Jallandar (Jullundur - Mughal) — جالندر جلّندر

Jalnapur (Jalna - Mughal) — جالنة پور

Jambusar (Baroda) — جمبوسر

Jammu (Jamun - Kashmir) — جمون

Jaora (Jaora state) — جاوره

Jaunpur (Mughal) — جونپور

Java (Netherlands East Indies) — جاو جاوا

Jaytapur (Jaiyatpur - Mughal) — جيت پور

Jaza'ir (Algiers) — جزائر

Jaza'ir Gharb (Algiers) — جزائر غرب

al-Jaza'ir-i Gharb (Algiers) — الجزائر غرب

Jelu (Jelou - Iran) — جلو

Jerba (Cerbe, Gabes - — جربة

Jering (Jaring, Jerin - Thai- — جريج جرين

Jhalawar (Jhalawar state) — جهالاوار

Jinji (Nusratgarh - — جنجي

Jind (Jind state) — جيند

Jodhpur (Mughal, Jodhpur state) — جودهپور

Jordan (al-Urdunn) — الاردن

al-Jumhuriya al-'Arabiya al-Muttahida (The United Arab Republic - Egypt, Syria and the Yemen) — الجمهورية العربية المتحدة

al-Jumhuriya al-'Arabiya al-Suriya (The Arab Republic of Syria) — الجمهورية العربية السورية

al-Jumhuriya al-'Arabiya al-Yamaniya (The Arab Republic of the Yemen) — الجمهورية العربية اليمنية

al-Jumhuriya al-'Iraqiya (The Republic of Iraq) — الجمهورية العراقية

al-Jumhuriya al-Libiya (The Republic of Libya) — الجمهورية الليبية

al-Jumhuriya al-Lubnaniya (The Republic of Leba- — الجمهورية اللبنانية

al-Jumhuriya as-Somal (The Republic of Somalia) — الجمهورية الصومال

al-Jumhuriya as-Sudan (The Republic of the Sudan) — الجمهورية السودان

al-Jumhuriya as-Sudan al-Dimuqratiya (The Democratic Republic of the Sudan) — الجمهورية السودان الديمقراطية

al-Jumhuriya as-Suriiya (The Republic of Syria) — الجمهورية السورية

al-Jumhuriya at-Tunisiya (The Republic of Tunisia) — الجمهورية العراقية

al-Jumhuriya al-Yaman al-Dimuqratia al-Shu'ubiya (The Peoples' Democratic Republic of the Yemen) — الجمهورية اليمن الديمقراطية الشعبية

Jumhuriyeti Turkiye (The Republic of Turkey) — جمهوريتى توركيه

Junagarh (Junagadh - Mughal) — جونة گره

al-Junub al-Arabi (South Arabia) — الجنوب العربي

Kabul (Mughal, Afghanistan) — كابل

Kaffa (Krim) — كفّة

Kalanur (Mughal) — كالانور

Kalat (Kalat state) — قلات كلات

Kalian (Kalayani - Hydera- — كليان

Kalikut (Calicut, Kozhikode - Mysore) — كليكوت

Kalkatah (Calcutta, Alinagar - Mughal, Bengal Presidency) — كلكته

Kalpi (Mughal, Maratha) — كلپي

Kanauj (Qanauj - Mughal, Awadh) — قنوج

Kanauj urf Shahgarh (Qanauj - Mughal, Awadh) — قنوج عرف شاه گره

Kanbayat (Kambayat, Kanbat, Khambayat - Mughal, Cambay state) — كمبايت كهنبايت كنبات كنبايت

Kandahar (see Qandahar)

Kangun (Hosakote - Mughal) — كنگون

Kanji (Conjeeveram - Mughal) — كنجي

Kankurti (Mughal, Maratha) — كانكرتي

Kara Amid (Turkey) — قره آمد

Karahisar (Qara-Hisar - Turkey) — قراحصار قره حسار

Kararabad (Karad - Mughal) — كراراباد

Karatova (Kratova - Turkey) — قراطوه قراطوه

Karauli (Karauli state) — كرولي

Karimabad (Mughal)	كريم اباد
Karmin (Central Asia)	كرمين
Karnatak (Carnatic - Mughal)	كرناتك
Karpa (Kurpa - Mughal)	كرپا
Kars (Qars - Turkey)	قارص قارس
Kashan (Iran)	كاشان
Kashgar (China - Sinkiang)	كاشغر كشقر
Kashmir (Srinagar - Kashmir Sultanate, Mughal, Sikh, Afghanistan)	كشمير
Kastamonu (Turkey)	قسطمونى
Katak (Cuttack - Mughal, Maratha)	كتك
Katak Banaras (Mughal)	كتك بنارس
Kawkaban (the Yemen)	كوكبان
Kayeri (Turkey)	قيصري قيسري
Kedah (Straits Settlements, Malaya)	كداه
Kelantan (Straits Settlements, Malaya)	كلنتن
Kemasin (Straits Settlements, Malaya)	كماسن
Khairabad (Mughal)	خيراباد
Khairnagar (Mughal)	خيرنگر
Khairpur (Mughal, Sind)	خيرپور
Khaliqabad (Dindigal - Mysore)	خالق اباد
Khambayat (Kanbayat - Mughal)	كمنبايت
Khanabad (Afghanistan)	خان اباد
Khanja (Canca, Hanca - Turkey)	خانجة خانجا
Khanpur (Bahawalpur)	خانپور
Khartapirt (Harput, Harburt - Turkey)	خرتبرت خربت خربرت
Khizan (Turkey)	خيزان
Khoqand (Central Asia)	خوقند
Khotan (Khutan, China - Sinkiang)	خوتن ختن
Khoy (Khoi, Khui - Iran)	خوي
Khujista Bunyad (Aurangabad - Mughal, Hyderabad)	خجسته بنياد
al-Khurfa (the Yemen)	الخرفاة
Khurshid Sawad (Mysore)	خورشيد سواد
Khwarizm (Central Asia)	خوارزم
Kighi (Turkey)	كيغي
Kirman (Kerman - Iran)	كرمان
Kirmanshahan (Kermanshah - Iran)	كرمانساهان
Kish (Central Asia)	كش
Kishangar (Kishangar state)	كشنگره
Kishtwar (Mughal)	كشتوار
Koçaniye (Kochana - Turkey)	قوچانية
Koilkunda (Mughal)	كويلكونده
Kolapur (Mughal, Kolhapur)	كولاپور كلاپور
Konya (Turkey)	قونية
Kora (Mughal, Maratha, Awadh)	كورا
Kosantina (see Qusantinia)	
Kosova (Kosovo - Turkey)	قوصوه قوسوه
Kostantaniye (see Qustantaniya)	
Kotah (Kotah state)	كوته
Kotah urf Nandgaon	كوته عرف نندگانو
Kubrus (Cyprus - Turkey)	قبرص
Kuch Hijri (Kunch)	كوچ حجري
Kuchaman (Mughal)	كچامن
Kuche (China - Sinkiang)	كوچا
Kufan (Kufin - Central Asia)	كوفن كوفين
Kulbarga (see Gulbarga)	
Kumber (Kumbar - see Maha Indrapur)	
Kunar (Maratha)	كنار
Kunch (Maratha)	كونچ
Kurdasht (Azerbaijan)	كرداشت كردشت
Kuwait (al-Kuwayt)	الكويت
Ladakh (Ladakah - Kashmir, Afghanistan)	لداكه لداخ
Lahej (the Yemen)	لحج
Lahijan (Iran)	لاهيجان
Lahore (Lahur - Mughal, Sikh, Afghanistan)	لاهور
Lahri Bandar (Mughal)	لهري بندر
Langar (Central Asia)	لنگر
Lar (Iran)	لار
Larenda (Turkey)	لارندة
Lashkar (Gwalior)	لاشكار
Lebanon (Lubnan)	لبنان
Legeh (Thailand)	لغكه
Libya	ليبيا
Lucknow (Lakhnau - Mughal, Awadh)	لكهنو
Machhli Bandar (Masulipatam)	مچهلي بندر
Machhlipatan (Masulipatam - Mughal, French India, Madras Pres.)	مچهلي پتن
Madankot (Mughal)	مدنكوت
al-Madina al-Bayda' (see Fas al-Jadid - Morocco)	المدينة البيضاء
Madrid (for Morocco)	مدريد
al-Maghrib (Morocco)	المغرب
Maha Indrapur (Dig, Kumbar - Mughal, Bharatpur)	مهه اندرپور
Mahle (Male - Maldive Islands)	محلي
Mahmud Bandar (Porto Novo - Mughal)	محمودبندر
Mahoba (Maratha)	مهوبة
Mailapur (Madras - Mughal)	ميلاپور
Makhsusabad (Murshidabad - Mughal)	مخصوص اباد
Malharnagar (Indore, also for Maheshwar)	ملهارنگر
Malher (Malhar, Mulher - Mughal)	ملهر
Maliknagar (Mughal)	ملك نگر
Malnapur (Mughal)	مالناپور
Malpur (Mughal)	مالپور
Maluka (Netherlands East Indies)	ملوكة
al-Mamlaka al-'Arabiya as-Sa'udiya (The Kingdom of Saudi Arabia)	المملكة العربية السعودية
al-Mamlaka al-Libiya (The Kingdom of Libya)	المملكة الليبية
al-Mamlaka al-Maghribiya (The Kingdom of Morocco)	المملكة المغربية
al-Mamlaka al-Misriya (The Kingdom of Egypt)	المملكة المصرية
al-Mamlaka al-Mutawakkiliya al-Yamaniya (The Mutawakkilite Kingdom of the Yemen)	المملكة المتوكلية اليمنية

al-Mamlaka al-Tunisiya (The Kingdom of Tunisia)	المملكة التونسية
al-Mamlaka al-Urdunniya al-Hashimiya (The Hashimite Kingdom of Jordan)	الاردنية الهاسمية
Manastir (Turkey)	مناستر
Mandasor (Gwalior)	منديسور
Mandla (Maratha)	مندلا
Mandu (Mughal)	مندو
Mangarh (Mughal)	مانگره
Manghir (Monghyr - Bihar)	مانگهير
Manikpur (Mughal)	مانكپور
Maragha (Azerbaijan, Iran)	مراغة
Marakesh (Marrakech - Morocco)	مراكش
Mar'ash (Turkey)	مرعش
Mardin (Turkey)	ماردين
Marv (Central Asia, Iran)	ماروار
Marwar (Jodhpur, Nagor, Pali, Sojat)	ماروار
al-Mu'askar (Mascara - Algeria)	المعسكر
Mashhad (Iran)	مشهد
Mashhad Imam Rida (Iran)	مشهد امام رضى
Mathura (Islamabad - Mughal, Bindraban)	متهره
Mazandaran (Iran)	مازندران
Mecca (Makkah - al-Hejaz)	مكّة
Medea (Algeria)	مدية
Meknes (Miknas - Morocco)	مكناس
Menangkabau (Netherlands East Indies)	منقكابو
Merta (Mirath - Mughal, Jodhpur)	ميرتا ميرتة
Misr (Egypt, Turkey)	مصر
Modava (Moldava - Turkey)	موداوه مداوه
Mombasa (Kenya)	ممباسة
Mosul (al-Mawsil - Iraq)	موصل الموصل
Muazzamabad (Gorakpur - Mughal, Awadh)	معظم اباد
Muhammadabad (Udaipur - Mughal)	محمداباد
Muhammadabad Banaras (Mughal, Awadh, Bengal Presidency, fictitious for Lucknow)	محمداباد بنارس
Muhammadabad urf Kalpi (Kalpi)	محمداباد عرف كلپي
al-Muhammadiya (al-Masila - Morocco)	المحمدية
al-Muhammadiya ash-Sharifa (Morocco)	المحمدية الشريفة
Muhammadnagar Tandah (Awadh)	محمدنگر تانده
Muhiabad Poona (Maratha)	محيى اباد پونه
Mujahidabad (Mughal)	مجاحداباد
Mujibalanagar (Rohilkhand)	مجى بالانگر
al-Mukala (the Yemen)	المكلا
Mukha (Mocca - the Yemen)	مخا
Mukhtara (the Yemen)	مختارة
Müküs (Turkey)	مكس
Multan (Mughal, Sikh, Afghanistan)	ملتان
Muminabad (Bindraban)	مؤمن اباد
Munbai (Mumbai, Bombay - Mughal, Bombay Presidency)	منبي
Mungir (Mughal)	مهنگير
Muradabad (Mughal, Rohilkhand, Awadh, Afghanistan)	مراداباد
Murshidabad (Makhsusabad - Mughal, French India, Bengal Pres.)	مرشداباد
Murtazabad (Mughal)	مرتضاباد
Muscat (Oman)	مسقط
Mustafabad (Rampur - Rohilkhand)	مصطفاباد
Muzaffargarh (Jhajjar - Mughal)	مظفرگره
Mysore (Mahisur - Mysore state)	مهيسور مهي سور
Nabha (Sirkar - Nabha state)	سركار نابهه
Nagar (Ahmadnagar, Bednur - Maratha, Mysore)	نگر
Nagar Ijri (Srinagar in Bundelkand)	نگر يجري
Nagor (Mughal, Jodhpur)	ناگور
Nagpur (Maratha)	ناگپور
Nahan (Sirmur)	ناهن
Nahtarnagar (Trichinopoly - Arcot)	نهتر نگر
Najafgarh (Mughal, Rohilkhand)	نجف گره
Najibabad (Mughal, Sikh, Rohilkhand, Awadh, Afghanistan)	نجيب اباد نجيباباد
Nakhjuvan (Iran, Azerbaijan)	نخجوان
Nandgaon (Nandgano - Kotah)	نندگانو
Nandgaon urf Kotah	نندگانو عرف كوته
Narnol (Mughal)	نارنول
Narwar (Sipri - Mughal, Gwalior, Narwar state)	نرور
Nasaf (Central Asia)	نسف
Nasirabad (Sagar, Wanparti - Hyderabad)	نصر اباد
Nasirabad (Dharwar - Mughal)	نصيراباد
Nasiri (Iran)	ناصري
Nasrullahnagar (Rohilkhand)	نصرالله نگر
Nazarbar (Mysore)	نظربار
Nejd (Saudi Arabia)	نجد
Nigbolu (Turkey)	نگبولو
Nihavand (Iran)	نهاوند
Nimak (Sikh)	نمك
Nimruz (Central Asia, Iran)	نمرز نيمروز
Nipani (Maratha)	نپني
Nisa (Iran)	نسا
Nishapur (Naysabur - Iran)	نيشاپور
Novabirda (Novoberda - Turkey)	نوابرده
Novar (Turkey)	نوار
Nukhwi (Iran, Azerbaijan)	نخوي
Nusratabad (Dharwar, Nasratabad, Fathpur - Mughal)	نصرت اباد
Nusratgarh (Jinji - Mughal)	نصرت گره
Ohri (Okhri, Ochrida - Turkey)	اوخرى
Oman ('Uman)	عمان
Omdurman (Umm Durman - the Sudan)	ام درمان
Orchha (Orchha state)	اورچحه
Ordu-Bagh (Iran)	اوردوباغ
Ordu-yi Humayun (Turkey)	اردو همايون
Orissa (Mughal)	اوريسة
Pahang (Straits Settlements)	فاحغ
Pakistan	پاكستان

Palembang (Netherlands East Indies) فلمبغ

Palestine (see Filastin)

Pali (Jodhpur) پالي

Panahabad (Iran, Karabagh) پناه اباد

Panipat (Mughal) پاني پت

Parenda (Purenda - Mughal) پرينده پرنده

Parnala (Qila) (Mughal) پرنالا (قلع)

Patan (Seringapatan - Mysore) پتن

al-Patani (Patani - Thailand) الفطاني

Pathankot پثنكوت

Patna (Azimabad - Mughal, Bengal Presidency) پتنة

Pattan (Anhirwala - Mughal) پتن

Pattan Deo (Somnath – Mughal) پتن ديو

Perak (Straits Settlements, Malaya) فيرق

Peshawar (Mughal, Sikh, Afghanistan, Iran) پشاور

Petlad (Baroda) پتلاد

Phonda (Mughal) پهونده

Pondichery (Pholcheri - French India) پهلچري

Pondichery (Porcheri - French India) پرچري

Poona (Punah, Pune, Muhiabad - Mughal, Maratha) پونه

Pulu Malayu (IslandoftheMalays-Sumatra, Netherlands East Indies) فولو ملايو

Pulu Penang (Penang, Prince of Wales Island - Straits Settlements, Malaya) فولو فنيغ

Pulu Percha (Island of Sumatra - Netherlands East Indies) فولو فرج

Punamali (Mughal) پونامالي

Punch (Mughal) پونچ

Purbandar (Porbandar - Mughal) پوربندر

Qafsa (Capsa - Tunis, Tunisia) قفصة

al-Qahira (Cairo - Egypt) القاهرة

Qaiti (the Yemen) القعياطي

Qamarnagar (Karnul - Mughal) قمرنگر

Qanauj (see Kanauj)

Qandahar (Ahmadshahi - Mughal, Afghanistan, Iran) قندهار

Qarshi (Central Asia) قرشي

Qasbah Panipat (Rohilkhand) قصبة پاني پت

Qatar wa Dubai (Qatar and Dubai - Qatar) قطر و دبي

Qayin (Central Asia) قاين

Qazvin (Iran) قزوين

Qubba (Azerbaijan) قبة

Qumm (Qomm - Iran) قم

Qunduz (Central Asia) قندوز

Qusantinia (Qustantina, Qusantina - Constantine, Algiers) قسنطينية قسطنطينة قسنطينة

Qustantaniya (Constantinople - Turkey) قسطنطنية

Rabat (Morocco) رباط

Rabat al-Fath (Rabat - Morocco) رباط الفتح

Rada' (the Yemen) راداء

Radhanpur (Radhanpur state) رادهنپور

Rajapur (Islam Bandar - Mughal) راجاپور

Rajgarh (Alwar) راج گره

Ramhurmuz (Iran) رامهرمز

Ra'nash (Ramhurmuz - Iran) رعنش

Rangpur (Assam) رنگپور

Ranthor (Ranthambhor - Mughal) رنتهور

Ras al-Khaima (United Arab Emirates) رأس الخيمة

Rasht (Resht - Iran) رشت

Ratlam (Ratlam state) رتلام

Ravishnagar Sagar (Garhakota - Maratha - Gwalior) روش نگر ساگر

Rehman (Reman - Thailand) رحمن

Revan (Iravan - Armenia) روان

Rewan (Rewa) ريوان

Reza'iyeh (Urumi - Iran) رضائية

Rikab (Rekab - Afghanistan, Iran) ركاب

Rohtas (Rohtak - Mughal) رحتاس رهتاس

Rudana (Taroudant - Morocco) ردانة

Ruha (al-Ruha - Turkey) الرها رها رهى

Sa'adnagar (Aklaj - Mughal) سعدنگر

Sabzavar (Iran) سبزوار

Sa'da (the Yemen) صعدة

Sagar (Maratha, Bengal Pres.) ساگر

Saharanpur (Mughal) سهارنپور

Sahibabad Hansi (Hansi state) صاحب اباد هنسي

Sahrind (Sarhind - Mughal, Cis-Sutlej Patiala, Afghanistan) سرهند سهرند

Sailana (Sailana state) سيلانه

Saimur (Mughal) سيمور

al-Saiwi (Sai, Saiburi, Teluban - Thailand) السيوي

Sakiz (Saqyz, Scio - Turkey) سكيز ساقز

Sakkhar (Mughal) سكهر

Sala (Sale - Morocco) سلا

Salamabad (Satyamangalam - Mysore) سلام اباد

Salimabad (Ajmer - Mughal) سليم اباد

Samandra (Turkey) سمندره

Samarqand (Central Asia) سمرقند

San'a (the Yemen) صنعاء

Sanbal (Sambhal - Mughal) سنبل

Sanbhar (Sambhar - Mughal) سانبهر

Sangamner (Mughal) سنگمنر

Sangli (Maratha) سنگلي

al-Saniya (Turkey) السنية

Sarakhs (Iran) سرخس

Sarangpur (Mughal) سارنگپور

Saray (Turkey) سراي

Sari (Iran) ساري

Sari Pol (Afghanistan) سر پل

Sarhind (see Sahrind)

Sashti (in Devanagari) (Maratha)

Satara (Mughal) ستارا

Saudi Arabia (see al-Hejaz, Nejd) — العربية السعودية

Sawai Jaipur (Jaipur, fictitious for Karauli) — سواي جيپور

Sawai Madhopur (Jaipur, fictitious for Sikar) — سواي مادهوپور

Sawuj Balaq (Iran) — ساوج بلاق

Selam (Selam state) — سيلم

Selanghur (Selangor - Straits Settlements, Malaya) — سلاغور

Selanik (Salonika - Turkey) — سلانيك

Selefke (Turkey) — سلفكه

Semnan (Simnan - Iran) — سمنان

Serbernik (Turkey) — سربرنيك

Serez (see Siroz - Turkey) — سرز سريز

Seringapatan (Mysore)

Shadiabad Urf Mandu (Mughal) — شادياباد ارف مندو

Shadman (Central Asia) — شادمان

Shadora (Gwalior) — شادهوره

Shahabad (Awadh) — شاه اباد قنوج شاهاباد

Shahabad Qanauj (Mughal, Rohilkhand, Awadh) — شاه اباد قنوج

Shahgarh Qanauj (Mughal) — شاه گره قنوج

Shahjahanabad (Dehli - Mughal, Bhilwara, Bindraban, Chitor, Mathura, Shapura, Udaipur, also fictitious for Bagalkot, Jaisalmir, Satara-EIC) — شاه جهان اباد

Shahr-Gözlü (see Gözlü - Krim) — شهرگوزلو

Shakola (Mughal) — شكولا

Shamakhi (Shamakha, Shemakhi - Iran, Azerbaijan) — شماخي شماخه

Sharakat Almaniya (German East Africa Co.) — شراكة المانيا

ash-Sharja (Sharja - United Arab Emirates) — الشارجة

Shekki (Iran) — شكّي

Sheopur (Gwalior) — شيوپور

Shergarh (Shirgarh - Mughal) — شيرگره

Sherkot (Mughal) — شيركوت

Sherpur (Shirpur - Mughal) — شيرپور

Shikarpur (Sind) — شكارپور

Shiraz (Iran) — شيراز

Shirvan (Azerbaijan, Iran, Turkey) — شيروان شروان

Sholapur (Mughal) — شولاپور

Shustar (Iran) — شوستر

Siak (Netherlands East Indies) — سيك

Sidrekipsi (Turkey) — بسدره قپسى

Siirt (Sa'irt - Turkey) — سعرت

Sijilmasa (Sizilmassa - Morocco) — سجلماسة

Sikakul (Chicacole - Mughal) — سيكاكل

Sikandarah (Sikandra – Mughal) — سكندره

Sind (Mughal, Sind state, Afghanistan, Iran) — سند

Singgora (Thailand) — سڠگورا

Sira (Mughal) — سيرة

Sironj (Mughal, Indore, Tonk) — سرونج

Siroz (see Serez - Turkey) — سيروز

Sistan (Iran) — سيستان

Sitamau (Sitamo) — سيتامو

Sitapur (Mughal) — سيتاپور

Sitpur (Sidhpur in Gujarat? - Mughal) — سيتپور

Sivas (Siwas - Turkey) — سيواس

Sofia (Turkey) — صوفية

Sojat (Jodhpur) — سوجت

al-Somal al-Italyaniya (Italian Somaliland, Somalia) — الصومال الايطاليانية

Srebrenice (Serbernichna - Turkey) — سربرنيچه

Sri (Amritsar) — سري

Sri Akalpur (Malkarian) — سري اكلپور

Srinagar (Mughal, Garhwal, Kashmir) — سرينگر

Srinagar (in Bundelkhand - Maratha) — سرينگر

Sultanabad (Iran) — سلطاناباد

Sultanpur (Mughal) — سلطانپور

Sumenep (Netherlands East Indies) — سمنف

Surat (Mughal, French India, Bombay Presidency, fictitious for Chand) — سورت

Suriya (Syria) — سورية

al-Suwair/al-Suwaira (Essaouir, Essaouira - Mogador, Morocco) — السوير الصويرة

Tabaristan (Iran) — طبرستان

Tabriz (Iran, Turkey) — تبريز

Tadpatri (Mughal) — تدپتري

Ta'izz (the Yemen) — تعز

Tanah Malayu (Land of the Malays - Sumatra, Malacca, Straits Settlements) — تانة ملايو

Tana Ugi (Land of the Bugis - Netherlands East Indies) — تانة اغيسى

Tanda (Akbarpur - Bengal Sultanate, Mughal, Awadh) — تانده

Tanja (Tangier - Morocco) — طنجة

Tappal (Mughal) — ابرقوه

Taqidemt (Algiers) — تاقدمت

Tarablus (Tripoli in Lebanon) — طرابلس

Tarablus Gharb (Tripoli West - in Libya) — طرابلس غرب

Tarapatri (Mughal) — تراپتري

Tarim (the Yemen) — تريم

Tashkand (Tashkent - Central Asia) — تشكند

Tashqurghan (Afghanistan) — تاشقورغان

Tatta (Tattah - Mughal, Sind, Afghanistan) — تته

Tehran (Iran) — طهران

Tellicherry (French India, Bombay Presidency) — تلچري تالچري تلجري

Termez (Central Asia) — ترمذ

Tetuan (Tetouan, Titwan - Morocco) — تطوان

Tibet (Mughal, Ladakh) — تبت

Tiflis (Georgia, Iran) — تفليس

Tilimsan (Tlemcen, Aghadir - Algiers) — تلمسان

Tirat Hardwar (Hardwar) — تيرتهردوار

Tire (Turkey) — تيره

Tokat (Tuqat - Turkey) — توقاط توقات دوقات طوقات

Tonk (Tonk state) — تونك

Toragal (Mughal, Maratha) — تورگل توراگال

Trabzon (Trebizond - Turkey) — طرابزون طرابزن

Trengganu (Straits Settlements, Malaya) — ترغگانو

Tun (Central Asia) تون

Tunis (Tunisia) تونس

Turbat (Central Asia) تربت

Tuyserkan (Iran) توي سركان

Udaipur (Muhammadabad - Mughal) اوديپور اديپور

Udgir (Mughal) اجين

Ujjain (Mughal, Gwalior) اجين

Ujjain Dar al-Fath (Gwalior) اجين دارالفتح

Ujjainpur (Mughal) اجين پور

Umarkot (Mughal) امركوت

Umm al-Qaiwain (United Arab Emirates) ام القيوين

United Arab Emirates (see al-Imarat al-'Arabiya al-Muttahida)

Urdu (Camp mint - Mughal, Central Asia, Iran) اردو

Urdu Dar Rahi-i-Dakkin (Mughal) اردو دار راه دكين

Urdu Zafar Qirin (Mughal) اردو ظفر قرين

al-Urdunn (Jordan) الاردن

Urumchi (China - Sinkiang) ارومچي

Urumi (Urumia, Urmia, Reza'iya - Iran) ارومي ارومية ارمية

Ushi (China - Sinkiang) اوش

Usküp (Uskub, Skopje, Kosovo - Turkey) اسكوپ

Van (Wan - Turkey, Armenia) وان

Varne (Turkey) ورنه

al-Yaman (the Yemen) اليمن

Yarkand (China - Sinkiang) يارقند

Yarkhissarmaran (China - Sinkiang) ياركسارمرن

Yazd (Iran) يزد

Yazur (Cemtral Asia) يازر

Yenishehr (Larissa - Turkey) ينكى شهر

Za (Taorirt - Morocco) صا

Zabid (the Yemen) زبيد

Zafarabad (Bidar - Mughal, Gurramkonda - Mysore) ظفراباد

Zafarnagar (Fathabad - Mughal) ظفرنگر

Zafarpur (Mughal) ظفرپور

Zain-ul-Bilad (Ahmadabad) زين البلاد

Zanjibar (Zanjibara - Zanzibar) زنجبار زنجبارا

Zebabad (Mughal, Sardhanah) زيب اباد

Zegam (Zigam - Iran) زگام

Zinjan (Zanjan - Iran) زنجان

al-Zuhra (the Yemen) الزهرة

MINT EPITHETS

Geographical Terms:

Baldat (City - Agra, Allahabad, Burhanpur, Bikanir, Patna, Sarhind, Ujjain) بلدات

Bandar (Port - Dewal, Hari, Surat, Machhlipatan) بندر

Dakhil (Breach, Entrance - Chitor) داخل

Dawla/Daula (State, State of) دولة

Hazrat (Royal Residence - Fas, Marakesh, Dehli) حضرة

Khitta (District - Awadh, Kalpi, Kashmir, Lakhnau) خطة

Negri (State of - Straits Settlements, Malaya, Netherlands East Indies, Thailand) نكري

Qasba (Town - Panipat, Sherkot) قصبة

Qila (Fort - Agra, Alwar, Bandhu, Gwalior, Punch) قلع قلعة

Qila Muqam (Fort Residence - Gwalior) قلعة مقام

Qita (District - Bareli) قطة

Sarkar (County - Lakhnau, Torgal) سركار

Shahr (City - Anhirwala Pattan) شهر

Suba (Province - Awadh) سوبة

Tirtha (Shrine - Hardwar) ترتة

Poetic Allusion:

Ashraf al-Bilad (Most Noble of Cities - Qandahar/Ahmadshahi) اشراف البلاد

Baldat-i-Fakhira (Splendid City - Burhanpur) بلدات فخيرة

Bandar-i-Mubarak (Blessed Port - Surat) بندر مبارك

Dar-ul-Aman (Abode of Security - Agra, Jammu, Multan, Sarhind) دار الامان

Dar-ul-Barakat (Abode of Blessings - Jodhpur, Nagor) دار البركات

Dar-ul-Fath (Seat of Conquest - Ujjain) دار الفتح

Dar-ul-Islam (Abode of Islam - Bahawalpur, Dogaon, Mandisor) دار الاسلام

Dar-ul-Jihad (Seat of Holy War - Hyderabad) دار الجهاد

Dar-ul-Khair (Abode of Beneficence - Ajmer) دار الخير

Dar-ul-Khilafa (Abode of the Caliphate - Agra, Ahmadabad, Akbarabad, Akbarpur Tanda, Awadh, Bahraich, Daulatabad, Dogaon, Gorakpur, Gwalior, Jaunpur, Kanauj, Lahore, Lakhnau, Malpur, Shahgarh, Shahjahanabad, Tehran, the Yemen) دار الخلافة

Dar-ul-Mansur (Abode of the Victorious - Ajmer, Jodhpur) دار المنصور

Dar-ul-Mulk (Seat of Kingship - Dehli, Fathpur, Kabul) دار الملك

Dar an-Nusrat (Abode of Succor - Herat) دار النصرات

Dar-ur-Riyasa (Seat of the Chief of State - Jaisalmir) دار الرياسة

Dar-us-Salam (Abode of Peace - Dogaon, Mandisor, Legeh) دار السلام

Dar-us-Saltana (Seat of the Sultanate - Ahmadabad, Burhanpur, Fathpur, Herat, Kabul, Kora, Lahore) دار السلطنة

Dar-ul-Surur (Abode of Happiness - Bahawalpur, Burhanpur, Saharanpur) دار السرور

Dar-uz-Zafar (Seat of Victory - Advani, Bijapur) دار الظفر

Dar-uz-Zarb (Seat of the Mint - Jaunpur, Kalpi, Patna) دار الضرب

Farkhanda Bunyad (Of Auspicious Foundation - Hyderabad) فرخنده بنياد

Hazrat (Venerable - Dehli) حضرت

Khujista Bunyad (Of Fortunate Foundation - Aurangabad) خجستة بنياد

Mustaqarr-ul-Khilafa (Residence of the Caliphate - Akbarabad, Ajmer) مستقر الخلافة

Mustaqarr-ul-Mulk (Abode of Kingship - Akbarabad, Azimabad) مستقر الملك

Sawai (One-fourth, i.e. "a notch better" - Jaipur) سواي

Umm al-Bilad (Mother of Cities - Balkh) ام البلاد

Zain-ul-Bilad (The Most-Beautiful of Cities – Ahmadabad) زين البلاد

HEJIRA DATE CONVERSION CHART

JEHIRA DATE CHART

HEJIRA (Hijira, Hegira), the name of the Muslim era (A.H. = Anno Hegirae) dates back to the Christian year 622 when Mohammed "fled" from Mecca, escaping to Medina to avoid persecution from the Koreish tribemen. Based on a lunar year the Muslim year is 11 days shorter.

*=Leap Year (Christian Calendar)

AH Hejira	AD Christian Date
1010	1601, July 2
1011	1602, June 21
1012	1603, June 11
1013	1604, May 30
1014	1605, May 19
1015	1606, May 19
1016	1607, May 9
1017	1608, April 28
1018	1609, April 6
1017	1608, April 28
1018	1609, April 6
1019	1610, March 26
1020	1611, March 16
1021	1612, March 4
1022	1613, February 21
1023	1614, February 11
1024	1615, January 31
1025	1616, January 20
1026	1617, January 9
1027	1617, December 29
1028	1618, December 19
1029	1619, December 8
1030	1620, November 26
1031	1621, November 16
1032	1622, November 5
1033	1623, October 25
1034	1624, October 14
1035	1625, October 3
1036	1626, September 22
1037	1627, Septembe 12
1038	1628, August 31
1039	1629, August 21
1040	1630, July 10
1041	1631, July 30
1042	1632, July 19
1043	1633, July 8
1044	1634, June 27
1045	1635, June 17
1046	1636, June 5
1047	1637, May 26
1048	1638, May 15
1049	1639, May 4
1050	1640, April 23
1051	1641, April 12
1052	1642, April 1
1053	1643, March 22
1054	1644, March 10
1055	1645, February 27
1056	1646, February 17
1057	1647, February 6
1058	1648, January 27
1059	1649, January 15
1060	1650, January 4
1061	1650, December 25
1062	1651, December 14
1063	1652, December 2
1064	1653, November 22
1065	1654, November 11
1066	1655, October 31
1067	1656, October 20
1068	1657, October 9
1069	1658, September 29
1070	1659, September 18
1071	1660, September 6
1072	1661, August 27
1073	1662, August 16
1074	1663, August 5
1075	1664, July 25
1076	1665, July 14
1077	1666, July 4
1078	1667, June 23
1079	1668, June 11
1080	1669, June 1
1081	1670, May 21
1082	1671, may 10
1083	1672, April 29
1084	1673, April 18
1085	1674, April 7

AH Hejira	AD Christian Date
1086	1675, March 28
1087	1676, March 16*
1088	1677, March 6
1089	1678, February 23
1090	1679, February 12
1091	1680, February 2*
1092	1681, January 21
1093	1682, January 10
1094	1682, December 31
1095	1683, December 20
1096	1684, December 8*
1097	1685, November 28
1098	1686, November 17
1099	1687, November 7
1100	1688, October 26*
1101	1689, October 15
1102	1690, October 5
1103	1691, September 24
1104	1692, September 12*
1105	1693, September 2
1106	1694, August 22
1107	1695, August 12
1108	1696, July 31*
1109	1697, July 20
1110	1698, July 10
1111	1699, June 29
1112	1700, June 18
1113	1701, June 8
1114	1702, May 28
1115	1703, May 17
1116	1704, May 6*
1117	1705, April 25
1118	1706, April 15
1119	1707, April 4
1120	1708, March 23*
1121	1709, March 13
1122	1710, March 2
1123	1711, February 19
1124	1712, Feburary 9*
1125	1713, January 28
1126	1714, January 17
1127	1715, January 7
1128	1715, December 27
1129	1716, December 16*
1130	1717, December 5
1131	1718, November 24
1132	1719, November 14
1133	1720, November 2*
1134	1721, October 22
1135	1722, October 12
1136	1723, October 1
1137	1724, September 19
1138	1725, September 9
1139	1726, August 29
1140	1727, August 19
1141	1728, August 7*
1142	1729, July 27
1143	1730, July 17
1144	1731, July 6
1145	1732, June 24*
1146	1733, June 14
1147	1734, June 3
1148	1735, May 24
1149	1736, May 12*
1150	1737, May 1
1151	1738, April 21
1152	1739, April 10
1153	1740, March 29*
1154	1741, March 19
1155	1742, March 8
1156	1743, Febuary 25
1157	1744, February 15*
1158	1745, February 3
1159	1746, January 24
1160	1747, January 13
1161	1748, January 2
1162	1748, December 22*
1163	1749, December 11
1164	1750, November 30
1165	1751, November 20
1166	1752, November 8*
1167	1753, October 29
1168	1754, October 18
1169	1755, October 7
1170	1756, September 26*
1171	1757, September 15
1172	1758, September 4
1173	1759, August 25
1174	1760, August 13*
1175	1761, August 2
1176	1762, July 23

AH Hejira	AD Christian Date
1177	1763, July 12
1178	1764, July 1*
1179	1765, June 20
1180	1766, June 9
1181	1767, May 30
1182	1768, May 18*
1183	1769, May 7
1184	1770, April 27
1185	1771, April 16
1186	1772, April 4*
1187	1773, March 25
1188	1774, March 14
1189	1775, March 4
1190	1776, February 21*
1191	1777, February 91
1192	1778, January 30
1193	1779, January 19
1194	1780, January 8*
1195	1780, December 28*
1196	1781, December 17
1197	1782, December 7
1198	1783, November 26
1199	1784, November 14*
1200	1785, November 4
1201	1786, October 24
1202	1787, October 13
1203	1788, October 2*
1204	1789, September 21
1205	1790, September 10
1206	1791, August 31
1207	1792, August 19*
1208	1793, August 9
1209	1794, July 29
1210	1795, July 18
1211	1796, July 7*
1212	1797, June 26
1213	1798, June 15
1214	1799, June 5
1215	1800, May 25
1216	1801, May 14
1217	1802, May 4
1218	1803, April 23
1219	1804, April 12*
1220	1805, April 1
1221	1806, March 21
1222	1807, March 11
1223	1808, February 28*
1224	1809, February 16
1225	1810, Febauary 6
1226	1811, January 26
1227	1812, January 16*
1228	1813, Janaury 26
1229	1813, December 24
1230	1814, December 14
1231	1815, December 3
1232	1816, November 21*
1233	1817, November 11
1234	1818, October 31
1235	1819, October 20
1236	1820, October 9*
1237	1821, September 28
1238	1822, September 18
1239	1823, September 18
1240	1824, August 26*
1241	1825, August 16
1242	1826, August 5
1243	1827, July 25
1244	1828, July 14*
1245	1829, July 3
1246	1830, June 22
1247	1831, June 12
1248	1832, May 31*
1249	1833, May 21
1250	1834, May 10
1251	1835, April 29
1252	1836, April 18*
1253	1837, April 7
1254	1838, March 27
1255	1839, March 17
1256	1840, March 5*
1257	1841, February 23
1258	1842, February 12
1259	1843, February 1
1260	1844, January 22*
1261	1845, January 10
1262	1845, December 30
1263	1846, December 20
1264	1847, December 9
1265	1848, November 27*
1266	1849, November 17
1267	1850, November 6

AH Hejira	AD Christian Date
1268	1851, October 27
1269	1852, October 15*
1270	1853, October 4
1271	1854, September 24
1272	1855, September 13
1273	1856, September 1*
1274	1857, August 22
1275	1858, August 11
1276	1859, July 31
1277	1860, July 20*
1278	1861, July 9
1279	1862, June 29
1280	1863, June 18
1281	1864, June 6*
1282	1865, May 27
1283	1866, May 16
1284	1867, May 5
1285	1868, April 24*
1286	1869, April 13
1287	1870, April 3
1288	1871, March 23
1289	1872, March 11*
1290	1873, March 1
1291	1874, February 18
1292	1875, Febuary 7
1293	1876, January 28*
1294	1877, January 16
1295	1878, January 5
1296	1878, December 26
1297	1879, December 15
1298	1880, December 4*
1299	1881, November 23
1300	1882, November 12
1301	1883, November 2
1302	1884, October 21*
1303	1885, October 10
1304	1886, September 30
1305	1887, September 19
1306	1888, September 7*
1307	1889, August 28
1308	1890, August 17
1309	1891, August 7
1310	1892, July 26*
1311	1893, July 15
1312	1894, July 5
1313	1895, June 24
1314	1896, June 12*
1315	1897, June 2
1316	1898, May 22
1317	1899, May 12
1318	1900, May 1
1319	1901, April 20
1320	1902, april 10
1321	1903, March 30
1322	1904, March 18*
1323	1905, March 8
1324	1906, February 25
1325	1907, February 14
1326	1908, February 4*
1327	1909, January 23
1328	1910, January 13
1329	1911, January 2
1330	1911, December 22
1332	1913, November 30
1333	1914, November 19
1334	1915, November 9
1335	1916, October 28*
1336	1917, October 17
1337	1918, October 7
1338	1919, September 26
1339	1920, September 15*
1340	1921, September 4
1341	1922, August 24
1342	1923, August 14
1343	1924, August 2*
1344	1925, July 22
1345	1926, July 12
1346	1927, July 1
1347	1928, June 20*
1348	1929, June 9
1349	1930, May 29
1350	1931, May 19
1351	1932, May 7*
1352	1933, April 26
1353	1934, April 16
1354	1935, April 5
1355	1936, March 24*
1356	1937, March 14
1357	1938, March 3
1358	1939, February 21
1359	1940, February 10*

AH Hejira	AD Christian Date
1360	1941, January 29
1361	1942, January 19
1362	1943, January 8
1363	1943, December 28
1364	1944, December 17*
1365	1945, December 6
1366	1946, November 25
1367	1947, November 15
1368	1948, November 3*
1369	1949, October 24
1370	1950, October 13
1371	1951, October 2
1372	1952, September 21*
1373	1953, September 10
1374	1954, August 30
1375	1955, August 20
1376	1956, August 8*
1377	1957, July 29
1378	1958, July 18
1379	1959, July 7
1380	1960, June 25*
1381	1961, June 14
1382	1962, June 4
1383	1963, May 25
1384	1964, May 13*
1385	1965, May 2
1386	1966, April 22
1387	1967, April 11
1388	1968, March 31*
1389	1969, march 20
1390	1970, March 9
1391	1971, February 27
1392	1972, February 16*
1393	1973, February 4
1394	1974, January 25
1395	1975, January 14
1396	1976, January 3*
1397	1976, December 23*
1398	1977, December 12
1399	1978, December 2
1400	1979, November 21
1401	1980, November 9*
1402	1981, October 30
1403	1982, October 19
1404	1984, October 8
1405	1984, September 27*
1406	1985, September 16
1407	1986, September 6
1409	1987, August 26
1409	1988, August 14*
1410	1989, August 3
1411	1990, July 24
1412	1991, July 13
1413	1992, July 2*
1414	1993, June 21
1415	1994, June 10
1416	1995, May 31
1417	1996, May 19*
1418	1997, May 9
1419	1998, April 28
1420	1999, April 17
1421	2000, April 6*
1422	2001, March 26
1423	2002, March 15
1424	2003, March 5
1425	2004, February 22*
1426	2005, February 10
1427	2006, January 31
1428	2007, January 20
1429	2008, January 10*
1430	2008, December 29
1431	2009, December 18
1432	2010, December 8
1433	2011, November 27*
1434	2012, November 15
1435	2013, November 5
1436	2014, October 25
1437	2015, October 15*
1438	2016, October 3
1439	2017, September 22
1440	2018, September 12
1441	2019, September 11*
1442	2020, August 20
1443	2021, August 10
1444	2022, July 30
1445	2023, July 19*
1446	2024, July 8
1447	2025, June 27
1448	2026, June 17
1449	2027, June 6*
1450	2028, May25

GOLD BULLION VALUE CHART

Oz.	800.00	810.00	820.00	830.00	840.00	850.00	860.00	870.00	880.00	890.00	900.00	910.00	920.00	930.00	940.00	950.00
0.001	0.80	0.81	0.82	0.83	0.84	0.85	0.86	0.87	0.88	0.89	0.90	0.91	0.92	0.93	0.94	0.95
0.002	1.60	1.62	1.64	1.66	1.68	1.70	1.72	1.74	1.76	1.78	1.80	1.82	1.84	1.86	1.88	1.90
0.003	2.40	2.43	2.46	2.49	2.52	2.55	2.58	2.61	2.64	2.67	2.70	2.73	2.76	2.79	2.82	2.85
0.004	3.20	3.24	3.28	3.32	3.36	3.40	3.44	3.48	3.52	3.56	3.60	3.64	3.68	3.72	3.76	3.80
0.005	4.00	4.05	4.10	4.15	4.20	4.25	4.30	4.35	4.40	4.45	4.50	4.55	4.60	4.65	4.70	4.75
0.006	4.80	4.86	4.92	4.98	5.04	5.10	5.16	5.22	5.28	5.34	5.40	5.46	5.52	5.58	5.64	5.70
0.007	5.60	5.67	5.74	5.81	5.88	5.95	6.02	6.09	6.16	6.23	6.30	6.37	6.44	6.51	6.58	6.65
0.008	6.40	6.48	6.56	6.64	6.72	6.80	6.88	6.96	7.04	7.12	7.20	7.28	7.36	7.44	7.52	7.60
0.009	7.20	7.29	7.38	7.47	7.56	7.65	7.74	7.83	7.92	8.01	8.10	8.19	8.28	8.37	8.46	8.55
0.010	8.00	8.10	8.20	8.30	8.40	8.50	8.60	8.70	8.80	8.90	9.00	9.10	9.20	9.30	9.40	9.50
0.020	16.00	16.20	16.40	16.60	16.80	17.00	17.20	17.40	17.60	17.80	18.00	18.20	18.40	18.60	18.80	19.00
0.030	24.00	24.30	24.60	24.90	25.20	25.50	25.80	26.10	26.40	26.70	27.00	27.30	27.60	27.90	28.20	28.50
0.040	32.00	32.40	32.80	33.20	33.60	34.00	34.40	34.80	35.20	35.60	36.00	36.40	36.80	37.20	37.60	38.00
0.050	40.00	40.50	41.00	41.50	42.00	42.50	43.00	43.50	44.00	44.50	45.00	45.50	46.00	46.50	47.00	47.50
0.060	48.00	48.60	49.20	49.80	50.40	51.00	51.60	52.20	52.80	53.40	54.00	54.60	55.20	55.80	56.40	57.00
0.070	56.00	56.70	57.40	58.10	58.80	59.50	60.20	60.90	61.60	62.30	63.00	63.70	64.40	65.10	65.80	66.50
0.080	64.00	64.80	65.60	66.40	67.20	68.00	68.80	69.60	70.40	71.20	72.00	72.80	73.60	74.40	75.20	76.00
0.090	72.00	72.90	73.80	74.70	75.60	76.50	77.40	78.30	79.20	80.10	81.00	81.90	82.80	83.70	84.60	85.50
0.100	80.00	81.00	82.00	83.00	84.00	85.00	86.00	87.00	88.00	89.00	90.00	91.00	92.00	93.00	94.00	95.00
0.110	88.00	89.10	90.20	91.30	92.40	93.50	94.60	95.70	96.80	97.90	99.00	100.10	101.20	102.30	103.40	104.50
0.120	96.00	97.20	98.40	99.60	100.80	102.00	103.20	104.40	105.60	106.80	108.00	109.20	110.40	111.60	112.80	114.00
0.130	104.00	105.30	106.60	107.90	109.20	110.50	111.80	113.10	114.40	115.70	117.00	118.30	119.60	120.90	122.20	123.50
0.140	112.00	113.40	114.80	116.20	117.60	119.00	120.40	121.80	123.20	124.60	126.00	127.40	128.80	130.20	131.60	133.00
0.150	120.00	121.50	123.00	124.50	126.00	127.50	129.00	130.50	132.00	133.50	135.00	136.50	138.00	139.50	141.00	142.50
0.160	128.00	129.60	131.20	132.80	134.40	136.00	137.60	139.20	140.80	142.40	144.00	145.60	147.20	148.80	150.40	152.00
0.170	136.00	137.70	139.40	141.10	142.80	144.50	146.20	147.90	149.60	151.30	153.00	154.70	156.40	158.10	159.80	161.50
0.180	144.00	145.80	147.60	149.40	151.20	153.00	154.80	156.60	158.40	160.20	162.00	163.80	165.60	167.40	169.20	171.00
0.190	152.00	153.90	155.80	157.70	159.60	161.50	163.40	165.30	167.20	169.10	171.00	172.90	174.80	176.70	178.60	180.50
0.200	160.00	162.00	164.00	166.00	168.00	170.00	172.00	174.00	176.00	178.00	180.00	182.00	184.00	186.00	188.00	190.00
0.210	168.00	170.10	172.20	174.30	176.40	178.50	180.60	182.70	184.80	186.90	189.00	191.10	193.20	195.30	197.40	199.50
0.220	176.00	178.20	180.40	182.60	184.80	187.00	189.20	191.40	193.60	195.80	198.00	200.20	202.40	204.60	206.80	209.00
0.230	184.00	186.30	188.60	190.90	193.20	195.50	197.80	200.10	202.40	204.70	207.00	209.30	211.60	213.90	216.20	218.50
0.240	192.00	194.40	196.80	199.20	201.60	204.00	206.40	208.80	211.20	213.60	216.00	218.40	220.80	223.20	225.60	228.00
0.250	200.00	202.50	205.00	207.50	210.00	212.50	215.00	217.50	220.00	222.50	225.00	227.50	230.00	232.50	235.00	237.50
0.260	208.00	210.60	213.20	215.80	218.40	221.00	223.60	226.20	228.80	231.40	234.00	236.60	239.20	241.80	244.40	247.00
0.270	216.00	218.70	221.40	224.10	226.80	229.50	232.20	234.90	237.60	240.30	243.00	245.70	248.40	251.10	253.80	256.50
0.280	224.00	226.80	229.60	232.40	235.20	238.00	240.80	243.60	246.40	249.20	252.00	254.80	257.60	260.40	263.20	266.00
0.290	232.00	234.90	237.80	240.70	243.60	246.50	249.40	252.30	255.20	258.10	261.00	263.90	266.80	269.70	272.60	275.50
0.300	240.00	243.00	246.00	249.00	252.00	255.00	258.00	261.00	264.00	267.00	270.00	273.00	276.00	279.00	282.00	285.00
0.310	248.00	251.10	254.20	257.30	260.40	263.50	266.60	269.70	272.80	275.90	279.00	282.10	285.20	288.30	291.40	294.50
0.320	256.00	259.20	262.40	265.60	268.80	272.00	275.20	278.40	281.60	284.80	288.00	291.20	294.40	297.60	300.80	304.00
0.330	264.00	267.30	270.60	273.90	277.20	280.50	283.80	287.10	290.40	293.70	297.00	300.30	303.60	306.90	310.20	313.50
0.340	272.00	275.40	278.80	282.20	285.60	289.00	292.40	295.80	299.20	302.60	306.00	309.40	312.80	316.20	319.60	323.00
0.350	280.00	283.50	287.00	290.50	294.00	297.50	301.00	304.50	308.00	311.50	315.00	318.50	322.00	325.50	329.00	332.50
0.360	288.00	291.60	295.20	298.80	302.40	306.00	309.60	313.20	316.80	320.40	324.00	327.60	331.20	334.80	338.40	342.00
0.370	296.00	299.70	303.40	307.10	310.80	314.50	318.20	321.90	325.60	329.30	333.00	336.70	340.40	344.10	347.80	351.50
0.380	304.00	307.80	311.60	315.40	319.20	323.00	326.80	330.60	334.40	338.20	342.00	345.80	349.60	353.40	357.20	361.00
0.390	312.00	315.90	319.80	323.70	327.60	331.50	335.40	339.30	343.20	347.10	351.00	354.90	358.80	362.70	366.60	370.50
0.400	320.00	324.00	328.00	332.00	336.00	340.00	344.00	348.00	352.00	356.00	360.00	364.00	368.00	372.00	376.00	380.00
0.410	328.00	332.10	336.20	340.30	344.40	348.50	352.60	356.70	360.80	364.90	369.00	373.10	377.20	381.30	385.40	389.50
0.420	336.00	340.20	344.40	348.60	352.80	357.00	361.20	365.40	369.60	373.80	378.00	382.20	386.40	390.60	394.80	399.00
0.430	344.00	348.30	352.60	356.90	361.20	365.50	369.80	374.10	378.40	382.70	387.00	391.30	395.60	399.90	404.20	408.50
0.440	352.00	356.40	360.80	365.20	369.60	374.00	378.40	382.80	387.20	391.60	396.00	400.40	404.80	409.20	413.60	418.00
0.450	360.00	364.50	369.00	373.50	378.00	382.50	387.00	391.50	396.00	400.50	405.00	409.50	414.00	418.50	423.00	427.50
0.460	368.00	372.60	377.20	381.80	386.40	391.00	395.60	400.20	404.80	409.40	414.00	418.60	423.20	427.80	432.40	437.00
0.470	376.00	380.70	385.40	390.10	394.80	399.50	404.20	408.90	413.60	418.30	423.00	427.70	432.40	437.10	441.80	446.50
0.480	384.00	388.80	393.60	398.40	403.20	408.00	412.80	417.60	422.40	427.20	432.00	436.80	441.60	446.40	451.20	456.00
0.490	392.00	396.90	401.80	406.70	411.60	416.50	421.40	426.30	431.20	436.10	441.00	445.90	450.80	455.70	460.60	465.50
0.500	400.00	405.00	410.00	415.00	420.00	425.00	430.00	435.00	440.00	445.00	450.00	455.00	460.00	465.00	470.00	475.00
0.510	408.00	413.10	418.20	423.30	428.40	433.50	438.60	443.70	448.80	453.90	459.00	464.10	469.20	474.30	479.40	484.50
0.520	416.00	421.20	426.40	431.60	436.80	442.00	447.20	452.40	457.60	462.80	468.00	473.20	478.40	483.60	488.80	494.00
0.530	424.00	429.30	434.60	439.90	445.20	450.50	455.80	461.10	466.40	471.70	477.00	482.30	487.60	492.90	498.20	503.50
0.540	432.00	437.40	442.80	448.20	453.60	459.00	464.40	469.80	475.20	480.60	486.00	491.40	496.80	502.20	507.60	513.00

GOLD BULLION VALUE CHART

Oz.	800.00	810.00	820.00	830.00	840.00	850.00	860.00	870.00	880.00	890.00	900.00	910.00	920.00	930.00	940.00	950.00
0.550	440.00	445.50	451.00	456.50	462.00	467.50	473.00	478.50	484.00	489.50	495.00	500.50	506.00	511.50	517.00	522.50
0.560	448.00	453.60	459.20	464.80	470.40	476.00	481.60	487.20	492.80	498.40	504.00	509.60	515.20	520.80	526.40	532.00
0.570	456.00	461.70	467.40	473.10	478.80	484.50	490.20	495.90	501.60	507.30	513.00	518.70	524.40	530.10	535.80	541.50
0.580	464.00	469.80	475.60	481.40	487.20	493.00	498.80	504.60	510.40	516.20	522.00	527.80	533.60	539.40	545.20	551.00
0.590	472.00	477.90	483.80	489.70	495.60	501.50	507.40	513.30	519.20	525.10	531.00	536.90	542.80	548.70	554.60	560.50
0.600	480.00	486.00	492.00	498.00	504.00	510.00	516.00	522.00	528.00	534.00	540.00	546.00	552.00	558.00	564.00	570.00
0.610	488.00	494.10	500.20	506.30	512.40	518.50	524.60	530.70	536.80	542.90	549.00	555.10	561.20	567.30	573.40	579.50
0.620	496.00	502.20	508.40	514.60	520.80	527.00	533.20	539.40	545.60	551.80	558.00	564.20	570.40	576.60	582.80	589.00
0.630	504.00	510.30	516.60	522.90	529.20	535.50	541.80	548.10	554.40	560.70	567.00	573.30	579.60	585.90	592.20	598.50
0.640	512.00	518.40	524.80	531.20	537.60	544.00	550.40	556.80	563.20	569.60	576.00	582.40	588.80	595.20	601.60	608.00
0.650	520.00	526.50	533.00	539.50	546.00	552.50	559.00	565.50	572.00	578.50	585.00	591.50	598.00	604.50	611.00	617.50
0.660	528.00	534.60	541.20	547.80	554.40	561.00	567.60	574.20	580.80	587.40	594.00	600.60	607.20	613.80	620.40	627.00
0.670	536.00	542.70	549.40	556.10	562.80	569.50	576.20	582.90	589.60	596.30	603.00	609.70	616.40	623.10	629.80	636.50
0.680	544.00	550.80	557.60	564.40	571.20	578.00	584.80	591.60	598.40	605.20	612.00	618.80	625.60	632.40	639.20	646.00
0.690	552.00	558.90	565.80	572.70	579.60	586.50	593.40	600.30	607.20	614.10	621.00	627.90	634.80	641.70	648.60	655.50
0.700	560.00	567.00	574.00	581.00	588.00	595.00	602.00	609.00	616.00	623.00	630.00	637.00	644.00	651.00	658.00	665.00
0.710	568.00	575.10	582.20	589.30	596.40	603.50	610.60	617.70	624.80	631.90	639.00	646.10	653.20	660.30	667.40	674.50
0.720	576.00	583.20	590.40	597.60	604.80	612.00	619.20	626.40	633.60	640.80	648.00	655.20	662.40	669.60	676.80	684.00
0.730	584.00	591.30	598.60	605.90	613.20	620.50	627.80	635.10	642.40	649.70	657.00	664.30	671.60	678.90	686.20	693.50
0.740	592.00	599.40	606.80	614.20	621.60	629.00	636.40	643.80	651.20	658.60	666.00	673.40	680.80	688.20	695.60	703.00
0.750	600.00	607.50	615.00	622.50	630.00	637.50	645.00	652.50	660.00	667.50	675.00	682.50	690.00	697.50	705.00	712.50
0.760	608.00	615.60	623.20	630.80	638.40	646.00	653.60	661.20	668.80	676.40	684.00	691.60	699.20	706.80	714.40	722.00
0.770	616.00	623.70	631.40	639.10	646.80	654.50	662.20	669.90	677.60	685.30	693.00	700.70	708.40	716.10	723.80	731.50
0.780	624.00	631.80	639.60	647.40	655.20	663.00	670.80	678.60	686.40	694.20	702.00	709.80	717.60	725.40	733.20	741.00
0.790	632.00	639.90	647.80	655.70	663.60	671.50	679.40	687.30	695.20	703.10	711.00	718.90	726.80	734.70	742.60	750.50
0.800	640.00	648.00	656.00	664.00	672.00	680.00	688.00	696.00	704.00	712.00	720.00	728.00	736.00	744.00	752.00	760.00
0.810	648.00	656.10	664.20	672.30	680.40	688.50	696.60	704.70	712.80	720.90	729.00	737.10	745.20	753.30	761.40	769.50
0.820	656.00	664.20	672.40	680.60	688.80	697.00	705.20	713.40	721.60	729.80	738.00	746.20	754.40	762.60	770.80	779.00
0.830	664.00	672.30	680.60	688.90	697.20	705.50	713.80	722.10	730.40	738.70	747.00	755.30	763.60	771.90	780.20	788.50
0.840	672.00	680.40	688.80	697.20	705.60	714.00	722.40	730.80	739.20	747.60	756.00	764.40	772.80	781.20	789.60	798.00
0.850	680.00	688.50	697.00	705.50	714.00	722.50	731.00	739.50	748.00	756.50	765.00	773.50	782.00	790.50	799.00	807.50
0.860	688.00	696.60	705.20	713.80	722.40	731.00	739.60	748.20	756.80	765.40	774.00	782.60	791.20	799.80	808.40	817.00
0.870	696.00	704.70	713.40	722.10	730.80	739.50	748.20	756.90	765.60	774.30	783.00	791.70	800.40	809.10	817.80	826.50
0.880	704.00	712.80	721.60	730.40	739.20	748.00	756.80	765.60	774.40	783.20	792.00	800.80	809.60	818.40	827.20	836.00
0.890	712.00	720.90	729.80	738.70	747.60	756.50	765.40	774.30	783.20	792.10	801.00	809.90	818.80	827.70	836.60	845.50
0.900	720.00	729.00	738.00	747.00	756.00	765.00	774.00	783.00	792.00	801.00	810.00	819.00	828.00	837.00	846.00	855.00
0.910	728.00	737.10	746.20	755.30	764.40	773.50	782.60	791.70	800.80	809.90	819.00	828.10	837.20	846.30	855.40	864.50
0.920	736.00	745.20	754.40	763.60	772.80	782.00	791.20	800.40	809.60	818.80	828.00	837.20	846.40	855.60	864.80	874.00
0.930	744.00	753.30	762.60	771.90	781.20	790.50	799.80	809.10	818.40	827.70	837.00	846.30	855.60	864.90	874.20	883.50
0.940	752.00	761.40	770.80	780.20	789.60	799.00	808.40	817.80	827.20	836.60	846.00	855.40	864.80	874.20	883.60	893.00
0.950	760.00	769.50	779.00	788.50	798.00	807.50	817.00	826.50	836.00	845.50	855.00	864.50	874.00	883.50	893.00	902.50
0.960	768.00	777.60	787.20	796.80	806.40	816.00	825.60	835.20	844.80	854.40	864.00	873.60	883.20	892.80	902.40	912.00
0.970	776.00	785.70	795.40	805.10	814.80	824.50	834.20	843.90	853.60	863.30	873.00	882.70	892.40	902.10	911.80	921.50
0.980	784.00	793.80	803.60	813.40	823.20	833.00	842.80	852.60	862.40	872.20	882.00	891.80	901.60	911.40	921.20	931.00
0.990	792.00	801.90	811.80	821.70	831.60	841.50	851.40	861.30	871.20	881.10	891.00	900.90	910.80	920.70	930.60	940.50
1.000	800.00	810.00	820.00	830.00	840.00	850.00	860.00	870.00	880.00	890.00	900.00	910.00	920.00	930.00	940.00	950.00

SILVER VALUE CHART

Oz.	15.00	15.50	16.00	16.50	17.00	17.50	18.00	18.50	19.00	19.50	20.00
0.001	0.015	0.016	0.016	0.017	0.017	0.018	0.018	0.019	0.019	0.020	0.020
0.002	0.030	0.031	0.032	0.033	0.034	0.035	0.036	0.037	0.038	0.039	0.040
0.003	0.045	0.047	0.048	0.050	0.051	0.053	0.054	0.056	0.057	0.059	0.060
0.004	0.060	0.062	0.064	0.066	0.068	0.070	0.072	0.074	0.076	0.078	0.080
0.005	0.075	0.078	0.080	0.083	0.085	0.088	0.090	0.093	0.095	0.098	0.100
0.006	0.090	0.093	0.096	0.099	0.102	0.105	0.108	0.111	0.114	0.117	0.120
0.007	0.105	0.109	0.112	0.116	0.119	0.123	0.126	0.130	0.133	0.137	0.140
0.008	0.120	0.124	0.128	0.132	0.136	0.140	0.144	0.148	0.152	0.156	0.160
0.009	0.135	0.140	0.144	0.149	0.153	0.158	0.162	0.167	0.171	0.176	0.180
0.010	0.150	0.155	0.160	0.165	0.170	0.175	0.180	0.185	0.190	0.195	0.200
0.020	0.300	0.310	0.320	0.330	0.340	0.350	0.360	0.370	0.380	0.390	0.400
0.030	0.450	0.465	0.480	0.495	0.510	0.525	0.540	0.555	0.570	0.585	0.600
0.040	0.600	0.620	0.640	0.660	0.680	0.700	0.720	0.740	0.760	0.780	0.800
0.050	0.750	0.775	0.800	0.825	0.850	0.875	0.900	0.925	0.950	0.975	1.000
0.060	0.900	0.930	0.960	0.990	1.020	1.050	1.080	1.110	1.140	1.170	1.200
0.070	1.050	1.085	1.120	1.155	1.190	1.225	1.260	1.295	1.330	1.365	1.400
0.080	1.200	1.240	1.280	1.320	1.360	1.400	1.440	1.480	1.520	1.560	1.600
0.090	1.350	1.395	1.440	1.485	1.530	1.575	1.620	1.665	1.710	1.755	1.800
0.100	1.500	1.550	1.600	1.650	1.700	1.750	1.800	1.850	1.900	1.950	2.000
0.110	1.650	1.705	1.760	1.815	1.870	1.925	1.980	2.035	2.090	2.145	2.200
0.120	1.800	1.860	1.920	1.980	2.040	2.100	2.160	2.220	2.280	2.340	2.400
0.130	1.950	2.015	2.080	2.145	2.210	2.275	2.340	2.405	2.470	2.535	2.600
0.140	2.100	2.170	2.240	2.310	2.380	2.450	2.520	2.590	2.660	2.730	2.800
0.150	2.250	2.325	2.400	2.475	2.550	2.625	2.700	2.775	2.850	2.925	3.000
0.160	2.400	2.480	2.560	2.640	2.720	2.800	2.880	2.960	3.040	3.120	3.200
0.170	2.550	2.635	2.720	2.805	2.890	2.975	3.060	3.145	3.230	3.315	3.400
0.180	2.700	2.790	2.880	2.970	3.060	3.150	3.240	3.330	3.420	3.510	3.600
0.190	2.850	2.945	3.040	3.135	3.230	3.325	3.420	3.515	3.610	3.705	3.800
0.200	3.000	3.100	3.200	3.300	3.400	3.500	3.600	3.700	3.800	3.900	4.000
0.210	3.150	3.255	3.360	3.465	3.570	3.675	3.780	3.885	3.990	4.095	4.200
0.220	3.300	3.410	3.520	3.630	3.740	3.850	3.960	4.070	4.180	4.290	4.400
0.230	3.450	3.565	3.680	3.795	3.910	4.025	4.140	4.255	4.370	4.485	4.600
0.240	3.600	3.720	3.840	3.960	4.080	4.200	4.320	4.440	4.560	4.680	4.800
0.250	3.750	3.875	4.000	4.125	4.250	4.375	4.500	4.625	4.750	4.875	5.000
0.260	3.900	4.030	4.160	4.290	4.420	4.550	4.680	4.810	4.940	5.070	5.200
0.270	4.050	4.185	4.320	4.455	4.590	4.725	4.860	4.995	5.130	5.265	5.400
0.280	4.200	4.340	4.480	4.620	4.760	4.900	5.040	5.180	5.320	5.460	5.600
0.290	4.350	4.495	4.640	4.785	4.930	5.075	5.220	5.365	5.510	5.655	5.800
0.300	4.500	4.650	4.800	4.950	5.100	5.250	5.400	5.550	5.700	5.850	6.000
0.310	4.650	4.805	4.960	5.115	5.270	5.425	5.580	5.735	5.890	6.045	6.200
0.320	4.800	4.960	5.120	5.280	5.440	5.600	5.760	5.920	6.080	6.240	6.400
0.330	4.950	5.115	5.280	5.445	5.610	5.775	5.940	6.105	6.270	6.435	6.600
0.340	5.100	5.270	5.440	5.610	5.780	5.950	6.120	6.290	6.460	6.630	6.800
0.350	5.250	5.425	5.600	5.775	5.950	6.125	6.300	6.475	6.650	6.825	7.000
0.360	5.400	5.580	5.760	5.940	6.120	6.300	6.480	6.660	6.840	7.020	7.200
0.370	5.550	5.735	5.920	6.105	6.290	6.475	6.660	6.845	7.030	7.215	7.400
0.380	5.700	5.890	6.080	6.270	6.460	6.650	6.840	7.030	7.220	7.410	7.600
0.390	5.850	6.045	6.240	6.435	6.630	6.825	7.020	7.215	7.410	7.605	7.800
0.400	6.000	6.200	6.400	6.600	6.800	7.000	7.200	7.400	7.600	7.800	8.000
0.410	6.150	6.355	6.560	6.765	6.970	7.175	7.380	7.585	7.790	7.995	8.200
0.420	6.300	6.510	6.720	6.930	7.140	7.350	7.560	7.770	7.980	8.190	8.400
0.430	6.450	6.665	6.880	7.095	7.310	7.525	7.740	7.955	8.170	8.385	8.600
0.440	6.600	6.820	7.040	7.260	7.480	7.700	7.920	8.140	8.360	8.580	8.800
0.450	6.750	6.975	7.200	7.425	7.650	7.875	8.100	8.325	8.550	8.775	9.000
0.460	6.900	7.130	7.360	7.590	7.820	8.050	8.280	8.510	8.740	8.970	9.200
0.470	7.050	7.285	7.520	7.755	7.990	8.225	8.460	8.695	8.930	9.165	9.400
0.480	7.200	7.440	7.680	7.920	8.160	8.400	8.640	8.880	9.120	9.360	9.600
0.490	7.350	7.595	7.840	8.085	8.330	8.575	8.820	9.065	9.310	9.555	9.800
0.500	7.500	7.750	8.000	8.250	8.500	8.750	9.000	9.250	9.500	9.750	10.000
0.510	7.650	7.905	8.160	8.415	8.670	8.925	9.180	9.435	9.690	9.945	10.200
0.520	7.800	8.060	8.320	8.580	8.840	9.100	9.360	9.620	9.880	10.140	10.400
0.530	7.950	8.215	8.480	8.745	9.010	9.275	9.540	9.805	10.070	10.335	10.600
0.540	8.100	8.370	8.640	8.910	9.180	9.450	9.720	9.990	10.260	10.530	10.800
0.550	8.250	8.525	8.800	9.075	9.350	9.625	9.900	10.175	10.450	10.725	11.000
0.560	8.400	8.680	8.960	9.240	9.520	9.800	10.080	10.360	10.640	10.920	11.200
0.570	8.550	8.835	9.120	9.405	9.690	9.975	10.260	10.545	10.830	11.115	11.400
0.580	8.700	8.990	9.280	9.570	9.860	10.150	10.440	10.730	11.020	11.310	11.600
0.590	8.850	9.145	9.440	9.735	10.030	10.325	10.620	10.915	11.210	11.505	11.800
0.600	9.000	9.300	9.600	9.900	10.200	10.500	10.800	11.100	11.400	11.700	12.000
0.610	9.150	9.455	9.760	10.065	10.370	10.675	10.980	11.285	11.590	11.895	12.200
0.620	9.300	9.610	9.920	10.230	10.540	10.850	11.160	11.470	11.780	12.090	12.400
0.630	9.450	9.765	10.080	10.395	10.710	11.025	11.340	11.655	11.970	12.285	12.600
0.640	9.600	9.920	10.240	10.560	10.880	11.200	11.520	11.840	12.160	12.480	12.800
0.650	9.750	10.075	10.400	10.725	11.050	11.375	11.700	12.025	12.350	12.675	13.000
0.660	9.900	10.230	10.560	10.890	11.220	11.550	11.880	12.210	12.540	12.870	13.200
0.670	10.050	10.385	10.720	11.055	11.390	11.725	12.060	12.395	12.730	13.065	13.400

SILVER VALUE CHART

Oz.	15.00	15.50	16.00	16.50	17.00	17.50	18.00	18.50	19.00	19.50	20.00
0.680	10.200	10.540	10.880	11.220	11.560	11.900	12.240	12.580	12.920	13.260	13.600
0.690	10.350	10.695	11.040	11.385	11.730	12.075	12.420	12.765	13.110	13.455	13.800
0.700	10.500	10.850	11.200	11.550	11.900	12.250	12.600	12.950	13.300	13.650	14.000
0.710	10.650	11.005	11.360	11.715	12.070	12.425	12.780	13.135	13.490	13.845	14.200
0.720	10.800	11.160	11.520	11.880	12.240	12.600	12.960	13.320	13.680	14.040	14.400
0.730	10.950	11.315	11.680	12.045	12.410	12.775	13.140	13.505	13.870	14.235	14.600
0.740	11.100	11.470	11.840	12.210	12.580	12.950	13.320	13.690	14.060	14.430	14.800
0.750	11.250	11.625	12.000	12.375	12.750	13.125	13.500	13.875	14.250	14.625	15.000
0.760	11.400	11.780	12.160	12.540	12.920	13.300	13.680	14.060	14.440	14.820	15.200
0.770	11.550	11.935	12.320	12.705	13.090	13.475	13.860	14.245	14.630	15.015	15.400
0.780	11.700	12.090	12.480	12.870	13.260	13.650	14.040	14.430	14.820	15.210	15.600
0.790	11.850	12.245	12.640	13.035	13.430	13.825	14.220	14.615	15.010	15.405	15.800
0.800	12.000	12.400	12.800	13.200	13.600	14.000	14.400	14.800	15.200	15.600	16.000
0.810	12.150	12.555	12.960	13.365	13.770	14.175	14.580	14.985	15.390	15.795	16.200
0.820	12.300	12.710	13.120	13.530	13.940	14.350	14.760	15.170	15.580	15.990	16.400
0.830	12.450	12.865	13.280	13.695	14.110	14.525	14.940	15.355	15.770	16.185	16.600
0.840	12.600	13.020	13.440	13.860	14.280	14.700	15.120	15.540	15.960	16.380	16.800
0.850	12.750	13.175	13.600	14.025	14.450	14.875	15.300	15.725	16.150	16.575	17.000
0.860	12.900	13.330	13.760	14.190	14.620	15.050	15.480	15.910	16.340	16.770	17.200
0.870	13.050	13.485	13.920	14.355	14.790	15.225	15.660	16.095	16.530	16.965	17.400
0.880	13.200	13.640	14.080	14.520	14.960	15.400	15.840	16.280	16.720	17.160	17.600
0.890	13.350	13.795	14.240	14.685	15.130	15.575	16.020	16.465	16.910	17.355	17.800
0.900	13.500	13.950	14.400	14.850	15.300	15.750	16.200	16.650	17.100	17.550	18.000
0.910	13.650	14.105	14.560	15.015	15.470	15.925	16.380	16.835	17.290	17.745	18.200
0.920	13.800	14.260	14.720	15.180	15.640	16.100	16.560	17.020	17.480	17.940	18.400
0.930	13.950	14.415	14.880	15.345	15.810	16.275	16.740	17.205	17.670	18.135	18.600
0.940	14.100	14.570	15.040	15.510	15.980	16.450	16.920	17.390	17.860	18.330	18.800
0.950	14.250	14.725	15.200	15.675	16.150	16.625	17.100	17.575	18.050	18.525	19.000
0.960	14.400	14.880	15.360	15.840	16.320	16.800	17.280	17.760	18.240	18.720	19.200
0.970	14.550	15.035	15.520	16.005	16.490	16.975	17.460	17.945	18.430	18.915	19.400
0.980	14.700	15.190	15.680	16.170	16.660	17.150	17.640	18.130	18.620	19.110	19.600
0.990	14.850	15.345	15.840	16.335	16.830	17.325	17.820	18.315	18.810	19.305	19.800
1.000	15.000	15.500	16.000	16.500	17.000	17.500	18.000	18.500	19.000	19.500	20.000

FOREIGN EXCHANGE TABLE

The latest foreign exchange rates below apply to trade with banks in the country of origin. The left column shows the number of units per U.S. dollar at the official rate. The right column shows the number of units per dollar at the free market rate.

Country	Official #/$	Market #/$
Afghanistan (New Afghani)	49.5	–
Albania (Lek)	80	–
Algeria (Dinar)	67	–
Andorra uses Euro	.65	–
Angola (Readjust K wanza)	75	–
Anguilla uses E.C. Dollar	2.7	–
Antigua uses E.C. Dollar	2.7	–
Argentina (Peso)	3.16	–
Armenia (Dram)	300	–
Aruba (Florin)	1.79	–
Australia (Dollar)	1.09	–
Austria (Euro)	.65	–
Azerbaijan (New Manat)	.85	–
Bahamas (Dollar)	1.0	–
Bahrain Is. (Dinar)	.377	–
Bangladesh (Taka)	68.6	–
Barbados (Dollar)	2.0	–
Belarus (Ruble)	2,150	–
Belgium (Euro)	.65	–
Belize (Dollar)	1.97	–
Benin uses CFA Franc West	425	–
Bermuda (Dollar)	1.0	–
Bhutan (Ngultrum)	40	–
Bolivia (Boliviano)	7.5	–
Bosnia-Herzegovina (Conv. marka)	1.27	–
Botswana (Pula)	6.5	–
British Virgin Islands uses U.S. Dollar	1.00	–
Brazil (Real)	1.70	–
Brunei (Dollar)	1.39	–
Bulgaria (Lev)	1.27	–
Burkina Faso uses CFA Fr.West	425	–
Burma (Kyat)	6.42	1,250
Burundi (Franc)	1,175	–
Cambodia (Riel)	4,000	–
Cameroon uses CFA Franc Central	425	–
Canada (Dollar)	.995	–
Cape Verde (Escudo)	75	–
Cayman Is.(Dollar)	0.82	–
Central African Rep.	425	–
CFA Franc Central	425	–
CFA Franc West	425	–
CFP Franc	78	–
Chad uses CFA Franc Central	425	–
Chile (Peso)	440	–
China, P.R. (Renminbi Yuan)	7.11	–
Colombia (Peso)	1,875	–
Comoros (Franc)	320	–
Congo uses CFA Franc Central	425	–
Congo-Dem.Rep. (Congolese Franc)	550	–
Cook Islands (Dollar)	1.73	–
Costa Rica (Colon)	495	–
Croatia (Kuna)	4.74	–
Cuba (Peso)	1.00	27.00
Cyprus (Pound)	.38	–
Czech Republic (Koruna)	16.3	–
Denmark (Danish Krone)	4.9	–
Djibouti (Franc)	178	–
Dominica uses E.C. Dollar	2.7	–
Dominican Republic (Peso)	34	–
East Caribbean (Dollar)	2.7	–
Ecuador (U.S. Dollar)	1.00	–
Egypt (Pound)	5.5	–
El Salvador (U.S. Dollar)	1.00	–
England (Sterling Pound)	.497	–
Equatorial Guinea uses CFA Franc Central	425	–
Eritrea (Nafka)	15	–
Estonia (Kroon)	10.2	–
Ethiopia (Birr)	9.4	–
Euro	.65	–
Falkland Is. (Pound)	.497	–
Faroe Islands (Krona)	4.9	–
Fiji Islands (Dollar)	1.49	–
Finland (Euro)	.65	–
France (Euro)	.65	–
French Polynesia uses CFP Franc	78	–
Gabon (CFA Franc)	425	–
Gambia (Dalasi)	22	–
Georgia (Lari)	1.5	–
Germany (Euro)	.65	–
Ghana (New Cedi)	.972	–
Gibraltar (Pound)	.497	–
Greece (Euro)	.65	–
Greenland uses Danish Krone	4.9	–
Grenada uses E.C. Dollar	2.7	–
Guatemala (Quetzal)	7.7	–
Guernsey uses Sterling Pound	.497	–
Guinea Bissau (CFA Franc)	425	–
Guinea Conakry (Franc)	4,375	–
Guyana (Dollar)	205	–
Haiti (Gourde)	38	–
Honduras (Lempira)	18.9	–
Hong Kong (Dollar)	7.789	–
Hungary (Forint)	170	–
Iceland (Krona)	68	–
India (Rupee)	40.5	–
Indonesia (Rupiah)	9,175	–
Iran (Rial)	9,200	–
Iraq (Dinar)	1,210	–
Ireland (Euro)	.65	–
Isle of Man uses Sterling Pound	.497	–
Israel (New Sheqalim)	3.6	–
Italy (Euro)	.65	–
Ivory Coast uses CFA Franc West	425	–
Jamaica (Dollar)	71	–
Japan (Yen)	102.2	–
Jersey uses Sterling Pound	.497	–
Jordan (Dinar)	.71	–
Kazakhstan (Tenge)	120	–
Kenya (Shilling)	65	–
Kiribati uses Australian Dollar	1.09	–
Korea-PDR (Won)	2.2	425
Korea-Rep. (Won)	965	–
Kuwait (Dinar)	.272	–
Kyrgyzstan (Som)	36	–
Laos (Kip)	8,825	–
Latvia (Lats)	.45	–
Lebanon (Pound)	1,510	–
Lesotho (Maloti)	8	–
Liberia (Dollar)	63	–
Libya (Dinar)	1.2	–
Liechtenstein uses Swiss Franc	1.02	–
Lithuania (Litas)	2.25	–
Luxembourg (Euro)	.65	–
Macao (Pataca)	8	–
Macedonia (New Denar)	40	–
Madagascar (Franc)	1,750	–
Malawi (Kwacha)	140	–
Malaysia (Ringgit)	3.2	–
Maldives (Rufiya)	12.8	–
Mali uses CFA Franc West	425	–
Malta (Lira)	.28	–
Marshall Islands uses U.S.Dollar	1.00	–
Mauritania (Ouguiya)	250	–
Mauritius (Rupee)	27	–
Mexico (Peso)	10.84	–
Moldova (Leu)	10.8	–
Monaco uses Euro	.65	–
Mongolia (Tugrik)	1,170	–
Montenegro uses Euro	.65	–
Montserrat uses E.C. Dollar	2.7	–
Morocco (Dirham)	7.5	–
Mozambique (New Metical)	24.4	–
Myanmar (Burma) (Kyat)	6.42	1,250
Namibia (Rand)	8	–
Nauru uses Australian Dollar	1.09	–
Nepal (Rupee)	65	–
Netherlands (Euro)	.65	–
Netherlands Antilles (Gulden)	1.79	–
New Caledonia uses CFP Franc	78	–
New Zealand (Dollar)	1.27	–
Nicaragua (Cordoba Oro)	19	–
Niger uses CFA Franc West	425	–
Nigeria (Naira)	117	–
Northern Ireland uses Sterling Pound	.497	–
Norway (Krone)	5.14	–
Oman (Rial)	.385	–
Pakistan (Rupee)	63	–
Palau uses U.S.Dollar	1.00	–
Panama (Balboa) uses U.S.Dollar	1.00	–
Papua New Guinea (Kina)	2.81	–
Paraguay (Guarani)	4,600	–
Peru (Nuevo Sol)	2.8	–
Philippines (Peso)	41	–
Poland (Zloty)	2.32	–
Portugal (Euro)	.65	–
Qatar (Riyal)	3.64	–
Romania (New Leu)	2.42	–
Russia (Ruble)	23.9	–
Rwanda (Franc)	545	–
St. Helena (Pound)	.497	–
St. Kitts uses E.C. Dollar	2.7	–
St. Lucia uses E.C. Dollar	2.7	–
St. Vincent uses E.C. Dollar	2.7	–
San Marino uses Euro	.65	–
Sao Tome e Principe (Dobra)	14,525	–
Saudi Arabia (Riyal)	3.75	–
Scotland uses Sterling Pound	.497	–
Senegal uses CFA Franc West	425	–
Serbia (Dinar)	54	–
Seychelles (Rupee)	8	–
Sierra Leone (Leone)	3,000	–
Singapore (Dollar)	1.39	–
Slovakia (Sk. Koruna)	21.1	–
Slovenia (Tolar)	155	–
Solomon Is. (Dollar)	7.4	–
Somalia (Shilling)	1,400	–
Somaliland (Somali Shilling)	1,800	4,000
South Africa (Rand)	8	–
Spain (Euro)	.65	–
Sri Lanka (Rupee)	107	–
Sudan (Pound)	2.01	–
Surinam (Dollar)	2.75	–
Swaziland (Lilangeni)	8	–
Sweden (Krona)	6.1	–
Switzerland (Franc)	1.02	–
Syria (Pound)	51	–
Taiwan (NT Dollar)	30.5	–
Tajikistan (Somoni)	3.5	–
Tanzania (Shilling)	1,170	–
Thailand (Baht)	31.5	–
Togo uses CFA Franc West	425	–
Tonga (Pa'anga)	1.8	–
Transdniestria (Ruble)	–	–
Trinidad & Tobago (Dollar)	6.3	–
Tunisia (Dinar)	1.18	–
Turkey (New Lira)	1.25	–
Turkmenistan (Manat)	6,250	–
Turks & Caicos uses U.S. Dollar	1.00	–
Tuvalu uses Australian Dollar	1.09	–
Uganda (Shilling)	1,675	–
Ukraine (Hryvnia)	5.05	–
United Arab Emirates (Dirham)	3.673	–
Uruguay (Peso Uruguayo)	20.5	–
Uzbekistan (Sum)	1,300	–
Vanuatu (Vatu)	97	–
Vatican City uses Euro	.65	–
Venezuela (New Bolivar)	2.15	5.7
Vietnam (Dong)	15,900	–
Western Samoa (Tala)	2.49	–
Yemen (Rial)	200	–
Zambia (Kwacha)	3,700	–
Zimbabwe (revalued Dollar)	30,000	–

HOW TO USE THE DVD

This DVD is PC and Macintosh® compatible when used with Adobe Acrobat Reader® version 6.0 or later. A step-by-step free download of Adobe Acrobat Reader® 8 is available at www.adobe.com. Adobe Reader® 8 was used in creating the instructions that follow.

To help you successfully navigate through the PDF document, several types of searches are available.

USING BOOKMARKS

Click on the Bookmarks icon to open the Bookmarks window. Use these links to go to specific points of interest. To scroll through pages in each section, use the arrows at the top of the screen (see next page for instructions to find page navigators).

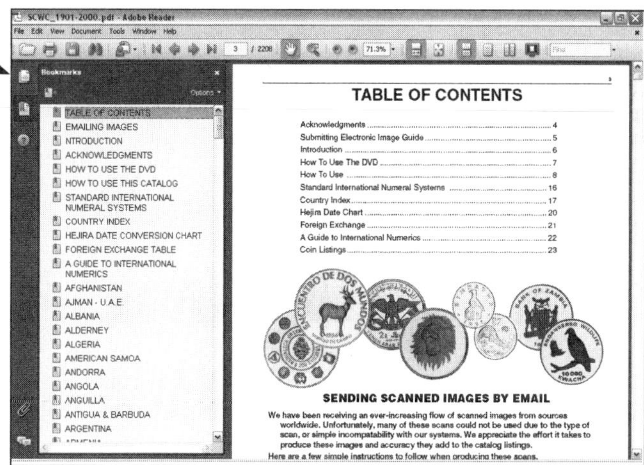

USING THE FIND BOX

Locate the find box in the tool bar and enter the word(s) you are searching for.

To navigate through the results of your search, use the Find Next icon.

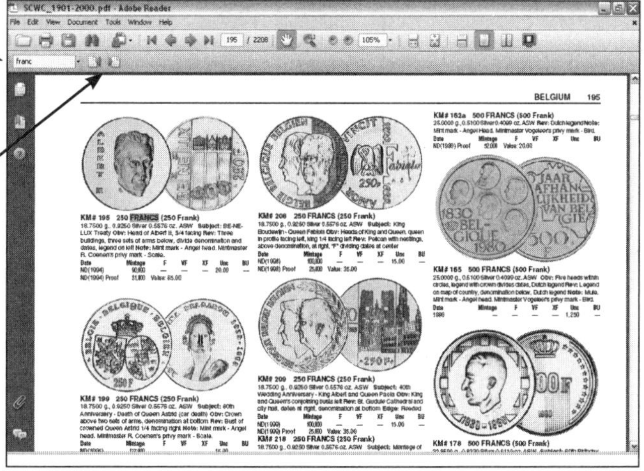

USING THE SEARCH OPTION

Locate the Search button by choosing Customize Toolbars in the Tools pull-down menu. Check Search (binocular icon) to have the Search option available in the toolbar.

Click on the Search icon to open the Search dialog box.

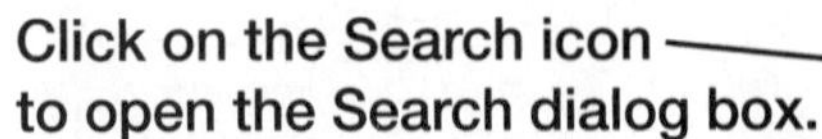

In the Search dialog box, enter the word(s) you are searching for and click on the Search button.

The list of results will appear in the dialog box. Click on the listings to view each page that contains your searched word(s).

To begin a new word search, click on the New Search button.

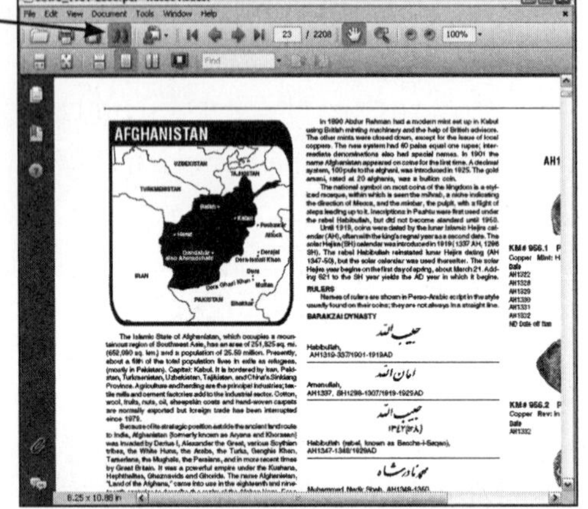

USING PAGE NAVIGATORS

Activate the Page Navigator Toolbar by choosing Customize Toolbars in the Tools pull-down menu. Check each tool as shown at right. You are now able to page through the PDF document by using the arrows at the top of the screen or by entering a page number you wish to view.

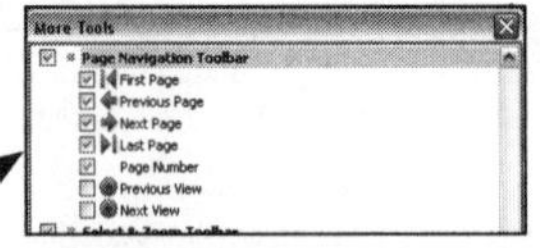

The Table of Contents is on page 3 and the Country Index starts on page 17.

You may also enlarge the images of the coins up to 400% for easy viewing

The Islamic State of Afghanistan, which occupies a mountainous region of Southwest Asia, has an area of 251,825 sq. mi. (652,090 sq. km.) and a population of 25.59 million. Presently, about a fifth of the total population lives in exile as refugees, (mostly in Pakistan). Capital: Kabul. It is bordered by Iran, Pakistan, Turkmenistan, Uzbekistan, Tajikistan, and China's Sinkiang Province. Agriculture and herding are the principal industries; textile mills and cement factories add to the industrial sector. Cotton, wool, fruits, nuts, oil, sheepskin coats and hand-woven carpets are normally exported but foreign trade has been interrupted since 1979.

Because of its strategic position astride the ancient land route to India, Afghanistan (formerly known as Aryana and Khorasan) was invaded by Darius I, Alexander the Great, various Scythian tribes, the White Huns, the Arabs, the Turks, Genghis Khan, Tamerlane, the Mughals, the Persians, and in more recent times by Great Britain. It was a powerful empire under the Kushans, Hephthalites, Ghaznavids and Ghorids. The name Afghanistan, "Land of the Afghans," came into use in the eighteenth and nineteenth centuries to describe the realm of the Afghan kings. For a short period, this mountainous region was the easternmost frontier of the Iranian world, with strong cultural influences from the Turks and Mongols to the north and India to the south.

Previous to 1747, Afghan Kings ruled not only in Afghanistan, but also in India, of which Sher Shah Suri was one. Ahmad Shah Abdali, founder of the Durrani dynasty, established his rule at Qandahar in 1747. His clan was known as Saddozai. He conquered large territories in India and eastern Iran, which were lost by his grandson Shah Zaman. A new family, the Barakzai, drove the Durrani king out of Kabul, the capital, in 1819, but the Durranis were not eliminated completely until 1858. Further conflicts among the Barakzai prevented full unity until the reign of Abdur Rahman in 1880. In 1929, King Amanullah, grandson of Abdul Rahman, was driven out of the country by a commoner known as Baccha-i-Saqao, "Son of the Water-Carrier", who ruled as Habibullah for less than a year before he was defeated by Muhammad Nadir Shah, a relative of the Barakzai. The last king, Muhammad Zahir Shah, became a constitutional though still autocratic monarch in 1964. In 1973 a coup d'etat displaced him and created the Republic of Afghanistan. A subsequent military coup established the pro-Soviet Democratic Republic of Afghanistan in 1978. Mounting resistance in the countryside and violence within the government led to the Soviet invasion of late 1979 and the installation of Babrak Karmal as prime minister. A brutal civil war ensued, which continues to the present, even after Soviet forces withdrew in 1989 and Karmal's government was defeated. An unstable coalition of former *Mujahideen* (Freedom Fighters) factions attempted to govern for several years but have been gradually overcome by the Taliban, a Muslim fundamentalist force supported from Pakistan.

On September 11, 2001, a terrorist attack on the United States, supported by the Taliban, led to retaliatory strikes by the U.S. Military and subsequent dismantling of the Taliban regime. During a UN-sponsored conference on Afghanistan that was held in Bonn, Germany, in early November 2001, an agreement was reached for an Interim Authority, under the leadership of Hamid Karzai, to be instated in Afghanistan on December 22, 2001 and to hold power for the following four to six months. During that time a "loya jirga" (Grand Council) is scheduled to decide on the follow-on Transitional Authority.

Afghanistan's traditional coinage was much like that of its neighbors Iran and India. There were four major mints: Kabul, Qandahar, Balkh and Herat. The early Durranis also controlled mints in Iran and India. On gold and silver coins, the inscriptions in Persian (called *Dari* in Afghanistan) included the name of the mint city and, normally, of the ruler recognized there, but some issues are anonymous. The arrangement of the inscriptions, and frequently the name of the ruler, was different at each mint. Copper coins were controlled locally and usually did not name any ruler. For these reasons the coinage of each mint is treated separately. The relative values of gold, silver, and copper coins were not fixed but were determined in the marketplace.

In 1890 Abdur Rahman had a modern mint set up in Kabul using British minting machinery and the help of British advisors. The other mints were closed down, except for the issue of local coppers. The new system had 60 paisa equal one rupee; intermediate denominations also had special names. In 1901 the name Afghanistan appeared on coins for the first time. A decimal system, 100 puls to the afghani, was introduced in 1925. The gold amani, rated at 20 afghanis, was a bullion coin.

The national symbol on most coins of the kingdom is a stylized mosque, within which is seen the *mihrab*, a niche indicating the direction of Mecca, and the *minbar*, the pulpit, with a flight of steps leading up to it. Inscriptions in Pashtu were first used under the rebel Habibullah, but did not become standard until 1950.

Until 1919, coins were dated by the lunar Islamic Hejira calendar (AH), often with the king's regnal year as a second date. The solar Hejira (SH) calendar was introduced in 1919 (1337 AH, 1298 SH). The rebel Habibullah reinstated lunar Hejira dating (AH 1347-50), but the solar calendar was used thereafter. The solar Hejira year begins on the first day of spring, about March 21. Adding 621 to the SH year yields the AD year in which it begins.

RULERS

Names of rulers are shown in Perso-Arabic script in the style usually found on their coins; they are not always in a straight line.

BARAKZAI DYNASTY

امان الله

Habibullah,
AH1319-337/1901-1919AD

حبیب الله
۱۳۴۷(۵۳۸)

Amanullah,
AH1337, SH1298-1307/1919-1929AD

حبیب الله

Habibullah (rebel, known as Baccha-i-Saqao),
AH1347-1348/1929AD

محمد نادر شاه

Muhammed Nadir Shah, AH1348-1350,
SH1310-1312/1929-1933AD

محمد ظاهر شاه

Muhammad Zahir Shah,
SH1312-1352/1933-1973AD

Republic, SH1352-1358/1973-1979AD
Democratic Republic, SH1358-1373/1979-1994 AD
Islamic Republic, SH1373-1381/1994-2002AD

MINT NAMES

Coins were struck at numerous mints in Afghanistan and adjacent lands. These are listed below, together with their honorific titles, and shown in the style ordinarily found on the coins.

افغانستان

Afghanistan

غزني

Ghazni

هرات

Herat

كابل

Kabul

"Dar al-Nusrat"

دار الملك

Qandahar

MINT EPITHET

قندهار

"Dar al-Mulk"
Abode of the King

MINT MARKS

(k) - key Havana, Cuba

KINGDOM

Habibullah

AH1319-1337 / 1901-1919AD

LOCAL COINAGE

KM# 957 PAISA

Copper **Note:** Counterstruck over Iran, 50 Dinars, Y#4.

Date	Mintage	Good	VG	F	VF	XF
AH1322	—	4.00	6.50	12.50	18.00	—
AH1328	—	3.00	5.00	10.00	16.00	—

KM# 956.1 PAISA

Copper **Note:** Round or irregular flan.

Date	Mintage	Good	VG	F	VF	XF
AH1322	—	2.50	4.00	7.50	12.50	—
AH1328	—	2.50	4.00	7.50	12.50	—
AH1329	—	2.50	4.00	7.50	12.50	—
AH1330	—	2.50	4.00	7.50	12.50	—
AH1331	—	2.50	4.00	7.50	12.50	—
AH1332	—	2.50	4.00	7.50	12.50	—
ND Date off flan	—	1.50	2.50	5.00	8.00	—

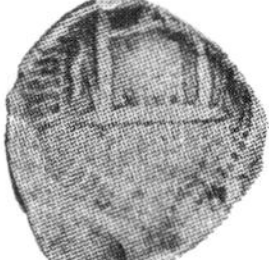

KM# 956.2 PAISA

Copper **Rev:** In a rayed circle

Date	Mintage	Good	VG	F	VF	XF
AH1332	—	3.00	5.00	8.50	15.00	—

KM# 956.3 PAISA

Copper **Obv:** Scroll symbol

Date	Mintage	Good	VG	F	VF	XF
AH1325	—	3.00	5.00	8.50	15.00	—

KM# 960.1 PAISA

Copper **Rev:** Mosque **Note:** Dump.

Date	Mintage	Good	VG	F	VF	XF
AH1322	—	4.50	7.50	12.50	17.50	—

KM# 960.2 PAISA

Copper **Rev:** Mosque **Note:** Counterstruck on Iran 50 dinars, Y#4.

Date	Mintage	Good	VG	F	VF	XF
AH1321	—	3.00	5.00	8.00	15.00	—
AH1322	—	3.00	5.00	8.00	15.00	—

KM# 960.3 PAISA

Copper **Rev:** Mosque **Note:** Counterstruck on Muscat and Oman, 1/4 Anna, KM#4.

Date	Mintage	Good	VG	F	VF	XF
AH1322	—	3.75	6.50	10.00	16.00	—

KM# 960.5 PAISA

Copper **Rev:** Mosque **Note:** Overstruck on Oman, 1/4 Anna, KM#3.1.

Date	Mintage	Good	VG	F	VF	XF
AH1322	—	3.75	6.50	10.00	16.00	—

KM# 963 PAISA

Copper **Obv:** Text **Rev:** Star with five points within wreath **Note:** Struck over British East India Co., 1/4 Anna.

Date	Mintage	Good	VG	F	VF	XF
AH1322	—	10.00	20.00	35.00	75.00	—

KM# 958.2 PAISA

Copper **Rev:** Date below mosque

Date	Mintage	Good	VG	F	VF	XF
AH1331	—	3.50	5.00	8.50	15.00	—

KM# 964 PAISA

Copper **Obv:** Text **Rev:** Mosque

Date	Mintage	Good	VG	F	VF	XF
AH1333	—	2.00	3.50	6.00	10.00	—
AH1334	—	2.00	3.50	6.00	10.00	—

KM# 973 PAISA

Copper

Date	Mintage	Good	VG	F	VF	XF
ND	—	—	—	—	—	—

KM# 959 2 PAISE

Copper **Note:** Similar to Paisa, KM#965 but inscribed "Do Paisa" below mosque.

Date	Mintage	Good	VG	F	VF	XF
AH1329	—	3.00	5.00	8.50	15.00	—

MILLED COINAGE

10 Dinar = 1 Paisa; 5 Paise = 1 Shahi; 2 Shahi = 1 Sanar; 2 Sanar = 1 Abbasi; 1-1/2 Abbasi = 1 Qiran; 2 Qiran = 1 Kabuli Rupee; 1 Tilla = 10 Rupees

KM# 848 PAISA

Bronze Or Brass **Obv:** Text within beaded circle **Rev:** Mosque

Date	Mintage	VG	F	VF	XF	Unc
AH1329	—	6.00	12.00	25.00	45.00	—
AH1329/17	—	8.00	16.00	35.00	60.00	—

Note: On KM#828 obverse die

KM# 849 PAISA

Brass, 21 mm. **Obv:** Text **Rev:** Mosque within 8-pointed star

Date	Mintage	VG	F	VF	XF	Unc
AH1329	—	2.00	4.00	7.50	15.00	—
AH1331	—	2.00	4.00	7.50	15.00	—

KM# 849a PAISA

Bronze, 21 mm. **Obv:** Text **Rev:** Mosque within 8-pointed star

Date	Mintage	VG	F	VF	XF	Unc
AH1334	—	3.00	6.00	11.50	20.00	—

KM# 854 PAISA

Bronze Or Brass, 19 mm. **Obv:** Text within circle **Rev:** Mosque within 8-pointed star, circle surrounds **Note:** Thick flan, reduced size.

Date	Mintage	VG	F	VF	XF	Unc
AH1336	—	3.00	6.00	12.00	25.00	—

KM# 855 PAISA

Bronze Or Brass **Note:** Thin flan.

Date	Mintage	VG	F	VF	XF	Unc
AH1336	—	6.50	10.00	20.00	35.00	—
AH1337	—	2.00	4.00	8.00	16.00	—

KM# 857 PAISA

Bronze Or Brass, 20 mm. **Obv:** Text within wreath **Rev:** Mosque within 8-pointed star **Note:** Thin flan.

Date	Mintage	VG	F	VF	XF	Unc
AH1337	—	6.50	10.00	20.00	35.00	—

KM# 858 PAISA

Bronze Or Brass, 19-20 mm. **Note:** Thin flan. Size varies.

Date	Mintage	VG	F	VF	XF	Unc
AH1337 (1918)	—	3.00	6.00	10.00	20.00	—
Note: Three varieties are known dated AH1337						
SH1298 (1919)	—	4.50	8.00	15.00	32.50	—

KM# 846 SANAR (10 Paisa)

1.5500 g., 0.5000 Silver 0.0249 oz. ASW, 13 mm. **Rev:** Mosque above crossed cannons and swords, wreath surrounds

Date	Mintage	VG	F	VF	XF	Unc
AH1325	—	10.00	20.00	35.00	60.00	—
AH1326	—	5.00	7.50	12.50	22.50	—
AH1328	—	5.00	7.50	12.50	22.50	—
AH1329	—	5.75	8.50	14.00	25.00	—

KM# 850 SANAR (10 Paisa)

1.5500 g., 0.5000 Silver 0.0249 oz. ASW, 13 mm. **Obv:** Text and date **Rev:** Mosque within 7-pointed star **Note:** Coins dated AH1333 and 1337 are known in two varieties.

Date	Mintage	VG	F	VF	XF	Unc
AH1329	—	4.00	7.00	12.00	22.00	—
AH1330	—	3.00	6.00	10.00	20.00	—
AH1331	—	3.00	6.00	10.00	20.00	—
AH1332	—	3.00	6.00	10.00	20.00	—
AH1333	—	3.00	5.00	9.00	16.00	—
AH1335	—	3.00	5.00	9.00	16.00	—
AH1337	—	3.00	6.00	10.00	20.00	—

KM# 863 3 SHAHI (15 Paisa)

Copper, 32-33 mm. **Obv:** Without "Al-Ghazi" **Rev:** Mosque within 8-pointed star inside circle, stars surround **Note:** Size varies.

Date	Mintage	VG	F	VF	XF	Unc
AH1337 (1918)	—	5.00	12.00	22.00	40.00	—

Note: Three varieties are known

KM# 869 3 SHAHI (15 Paisa)

Copper **Obv:** "Shamsi" left and below date **Rev:** Mosque within 8-pointed star within circle, stars surround

Date	Mintage	VG	F	VF	XF	Unc
SH1298 (1919)	—	2.00	4.00	10.00	20.00	—

Note: Shamsi (Solar) is an additional word written on some of the coins dated SH1298, to show the change from a lunar to solar calendar

KM# 837 ABBASI (20 Paisa)

3.1100 g., 0.5000 Silver 0.0500 oz. ASW, 16 mm. **Obv:** Tughra within wreath **Rev:** Mosque above crossed cannons and swords, wreath surrounds

Date	Mintage	VG	F	VF	XF	Unc
AH1320	—	30.00	60.00	100	225	—

KM# 845 ABBASI (20 Paisa)

3.1100 g., 0.5000 Silver 0.0500 oz. ASW, 17 mm. **Obv:** Tughra within wreath **Rev:** Mosque above crossed cannons and swords, wreath surrounds

Date	Mintage	VG	F	VF	XF	Unc
AH1324	—	35.00	70.00	125	250	—
AH1328	—	35.00	70.00	125	250	—
AH1329	—	50.00	100	175	300	—

KM# 851 ABBASI (20 Paisa)

3.1100 g., 0.5000 Silver 0.0500 oz. ASW, 17 mm. **Obv:** Tughra within wreath **Rev:** Mosque above crossed cannons and swords, wreath surrounds

Date	Mintage	VG	F	VF	XF	Unc
AH1329	—	6.00	11.00	16.00	24.00	—
AH1330	—	6.00	11.00	16.00	24.00	—
AH1333	—	5.00	10.00	15.00	22.50	—
AH1334	—	5.00	10.00	15.00	22.50	—
AH1335	—	5.00	10.00	15.00	22.50	—
AH1337	—	5.00	10.00	15.00	22.50	—

KM# 831 1/2 RUPEE (Qiran)

4.6500 g., 0.5000 Silver 0.0747 oz. ASW **Obv:** Toughra **Rev:** Crossed cannons below mosque, wreath surrounds

Date	Mintage	VG	F	VF	XF	Unc
AH1319	—	20.00	40.00	75.00	125	—

KM# 838 1/2 RUPEE (Qiran)

4.6500 g., 0.5000 Silver 0.0747 oz. ASW, 19 mm. **Obv:** Toughra divides date **Rev:** Mosque above crossed cannons and swords, wreath surrounds

Date	Mintage	VG	F	VF	XF	Unc
AH1320	—	25.00	45.00	85.00	140	—
AH1325	—	20.00	40.00	75.00	125	—

KM# 841 1/2 RUPEE (Qiran)

4.6500 g., 0.5000 Silver 0.0747 oz. ASW, 19 mm. **Obv:** Date at upper right of toughra **Rev:** Mosque above crossed cannons and swords, wreath surrounds, dated AH1320

Date	Mintage	VG	F	VF	XF	Unc
AH1321	—	25.00	45.00	85.00	140	—
AH1323	—	30.00	55.00	100	170	—

KM# 844.1 1/2 RUPEE (Qiran)

4.6500 g., 0.5000 Silver 0.0747 oz. ASW, 19 mm. **Obv:** Inscription and date within wreath **Rev:** Frozen date AH1320 split above mosque, crossed cannons and swords below, wreath surrounds

Date	Mintage	VG	F	VF	XF	Unc
AH1323	—	6.00	9.00	16.00	28.00	—
AH1324	—	6.00	9.00	15.00	25.00	—
AH1326	—	6.00	9.00	15.00	25.00	—
AH1327/6	—	6.00	9.00	15.00	25.00	—
AH1327	—	6.00	9.00	15.00	25.00	—

KM# 844.2 1/2 RUPEE (Qiran)

4.6500 g., 0.5000 Silver 0.0747 oz. ASW, 19 mm. **Obv:** Inscription and date within wreath **Rev:** Mosque above crossed cannons and swords, wreath surrounds, actual date at top

Date	Mintage	VG	F	VF	XF	Unc
AH1326/3	—	25.00	45.00	75.00	135	—
Note: AH1326/0 for actual date on reverse						
AH1328	—	25.00	45.00	75.00	135	—
AH1329	—	25.00	45.00	75.00	135	—

KM# 852 1/2 RUPEE (Qiran)

4.6000 g., 0.5000 Silver 0.0739 oz. ASW, 20 mm. **Obv:** Text within wreath **Rev:** Mosque within 8-pointed star, wreath surrounds

Date	Mintage	VG	F	VF	XF	Unc
AH1329	—	3.50	5.50	8.50	16.00	—
AH1333	—	3.50	5.50	8.50	16.00	—
AH1334	—	4.50	7.50	12.50	22.50	—
AH1335	—	4.50	7.50	12.50	22.50	—
AH1337	—	3.50	5.50	8.50	16.00	—

KM# 864 1/2 RUPEE (Qiran)

5.0000 g., Silver **Obv. Legend:** "Habibullah" **Rev:** Star of Solomon

Date	Mintage	VG	F	VF	XF	Unc
AH1335	—	—	300	500	—	—

KM# 865 1/2 RUPEE (Qiran)

Silver **Obv:** Uncircled inscription **Rev:** Mosque within 8-pointed star, wreath surrounds

Date	Mintage	VG	F	VF	XF	Unc
AH1337 (1918)	—	4.00	9.00	15.00	25.00	—
Note: Five varieties are known						

KM# 832 RUPEE

9.2000 g., 0.5000 Silver 0.1479 oz. ASW, 25 mm. **Obv:** Toughra of Habibullah in wreath, star above **Rev:** Mosque above crossed swords and cannons, wreath surrounds

Date	Mintage	VG	F	VF	XF	Unc
AH1319	—	8.00	12.00	25.00	70.00	—
Note: Two varieties are known						

KM# 833.1 RUPEE

9.2000 g., 0.5000 Silver 0.1479 oz. ASW, 25 mm. **Obv:** "Afghanistan" above small toughra, star at right **Rev:** Mosque above crossed swords and cannons, large inverted pyramid dome

Date	Mintage	VG	F	VF	XF	Unc
AH1319	—	4.00	5.50	10.00	25.00	—
AH1320	—	4.00	5.50	8.50	20.00	—
AH1325	—	7.00	15.00	25.00	50.00	—

KM# 833.2 RUPEE

9.2000 g., 0.5000 Silver 0.1479 oz. ASW, 25 mm. **Obv:** Tughra within wreath, without star **Rev:** Swords and cannons crossed below mosque, wreath surrounds

Date	Mintage	VG	F	VF	XF	Unc
AH1319	—	4.00	5.50	10.00	25.00	—
AH1325	—	7.00	15.00	25.00	50.00	—

KM# 839 RUPEE

9.2000 g., 0.5000 Silver 0.1479 oz. ASW, 25 mm. **Obv:** "Afghanistan" divided by a star above large toughra **Rev:** Swords and cannons below mosque, wreath surrounds

Date	Mintage	VG	F	VF	XF	Unc
AH1320	—	4.00	6.00	10.00	20.00	—

KM# 840.1 RUPEE

9.2000 g., 0.5000 Silver 0.1479 oz. ASW, 25 mm. **Obv:** Tughra within wreath **Rev:** Small dome mosque above weapons within wreath

Date	Mintage	VG	F	VF	XF	Unc
AH1320	—	5.00	8.00	15.00	35.00	—

KM# 840.2 RUPEE

9.2000 g., 0.5000 Silver 0.1479 oz. ASW, 25 mm. **Obv:** Date in loop of toughra, wreath surrounds **Rev:** Mosque above weapons within wreath

Date	Mintage	VG	F	VF	XF	Unc
AH1321	—	10.00	15.00	25.00	50.00	—

KM# 842.1 RUPEE

9.2000 g., 0.5000 Silver 0.1479 oz. ASW, 25 mm. **Obv:** Text within wreath **Rev:** "Afghanistan" above mosque, crossed swords and cannons below, wreath surrounds

Date	Mintage	VG	F	VF	XF	Unc
AH1321	—	4.00	7.00	11.00	22.50	—
Note: Two varieties exist for AH1321 date						
AH1322	—	4.00	7.00	11.00	22.50	—

KM# 842.2 RUPEE

9.2000 g., 0.5000 Silver 0.1479 oz. ASW, 25 mm. **Obv:** Text within wreath **Rev:** Mosque above crossed cannons, wreath surrounds

Date	Mintage	VG	F	VF	XF	Unc
AH1322	—	4.00	5.00	9.00	20.00	—
AH1324	—	4.00	5.00	9.00	20.00	—
AH1325	—	5.00	8.00	12.00	25.00	—
AH1326	—	4.00	6.00	10.00	20.00	—
AH1327/6	—	6.00	8.00	15.00	30.00	—
AH1327	—	4.00	6.00	10.00	20.00	—
AH1328	—	6.00	8.00	15.00	30.00	—
Note: Two varieties exist for AH1328 date.						
AH1329	—	6.00	8.00	15.00	30.00	—

KM# 847.1 RUPEE

9.2000 g., 0.5000 Silver 0.1479 oz. ASW, 25 mm. **Obv:** Date divided 13 Arabic "j" 28 **Rev:** Large dome mosque without "Afghanistan"

Date	Mintage	VG	F	VF	XF	Unc
AH1328	—	7.00	15.00	25.00	50.00	—

KM# 847.2 RUPEE

9.2000 g., 0.5000 Silver 0.1479 oz. ASW, 25 mm. **Obv:** Date divided 132 Arabic "j" 8 **Rev:** Mosque above weapons, wreath surrounds

Date	Mintage	VG	F	VF	XF	Unc
AH1328	—	10.00	20.00	30.00	60.00	—

KM# 853 RUPEE

9.2000 g., 0.5000 Silver 0.1479 oz. ASW, 25-26 mm. **Obv:** Name and titles of Habibullah within wreath **Rev:** Mosque within 8-pointed star, wreath surrounds **Note:** Size varies. Two varieties exist for AH1330, 1331, and 1337 and three varieties exist for AH1333; thickness of obverse inscription and size of mosque dome on reverse vary.

Date	Mintage	VG	F	VF	XF	Unc
AH1329	—	4.00	6.00	10.00	20.00	—
AH1330	—	4.00	6.00	9.00	18.50	—
AH1331/0	—	4.00	6.00	9.00	18.50	—
AH1331	—	4.00	6.00	9.00	18.50	—
AH1332	—	4.00	6.00	9.00	18.50	—
AH1333	—	4.00	6.00	9.00	18.50	—

Date	Mintage	VG	F	VF	XF	Unc
AH1334	—	4.00	6.00	9.00	18.50	—
AH1335	—	4.00	6.00	9.00	18.50	—
AH1337	—	4.00	6.00	10.00	20.00	—

KM# 835 TILLA (10 Rupees)
4.6000 g., 0.9000 Gold 0.1331 oz. AGW, 21 mm. **Obv:** Star above toughra within wreath **Rev:** Flags flank mosque above weapons, wreath surrounds

Date	Mintage	VG	F	VF	XF	Unc
AH1319	—	125	140	175	240	—

KM# 836.1 TILLA (10 Rupees)
4.6000 g., 0.9000 Gold 0.1331 oz. AGW, 21 mm. **Obv:** Legend divided by star above toughra, wreath surrounds **Obv. Legend:** "Afghanistan" **Rev:** Flags flank mosque above weapons, wreath surrounds

Date	Mintage	VG	F	VF	XF	Unc
AH1319	—	130	145	185	250	—

KM# 836.2 TILLA (10 Rupees)
4.6000 g., 0.9000 Gold 0.1331 oz. AGW, 21 mm. **Obv:** Legend above toughra with star to right, wreath surrounds **Obv. Legend:** "Afghanistan" **Rev:** Flags flank mosque above weapons, wreath surrounds

Date	Mintage	VG	F	VF	XF	Unc
AH1320	—	130	145	185	250	—

KM# A856 TILLA (10 Rupees)
4.6000 g., 0.9000 Gold 0.1331 oz. AGW **Obv:** Date divided

Date	Mintage	VG	F	VF	XF	Unc
AH1325	—	—	450	650	900	—

KM# 856 TILLA (10 Rupees)
4.6000 g., 0.9000 Gold 0.1331 oz. AGW, 21 mm. **Obv. Legend:** Habibullah...

Date	Mintage	VG	F	VF	XF	Unc
AH1335	—	170	200	260	330	—
AH1336	—	125	140	175	240	—
AH1337	—	130	145	180	245	—

KM# 879 2 TILLAS (20 Rupees)
9.2000 g., 0.9000 Gold 0.2662 oz. AGW, 22 mm. **Obv:** Text above date, wreath surrounds **Rev:** Mosque within 8-pointed star, denomination above, wreath surrounds

Date	Mintage	F	VF	XF	Unc
SH1298 (1919)	—	—	BV	275	400

KM# 903 4 TILLAS (40 Rupees)
18.5300 g., 0.9000 Gold 0.5362 oz. AGW **Obv:** Text within wreath **Rev:** Mosque within 8-pointed star, spray below

Date	Mintage	VG	F	VF	XF	Unc
AH1337 Rare	—	—	—	—	—	—

KM# 889 5 AMANI (50 Rupees)
23.0000 g., 0.9000 Gold 0.6655 oz. AGW, 34 mm. **Obv:** Tughra within wreath, Persian "5" above toughra; "Al Ghazi" at right **Rev:** Legend above mosque within 7-pointed star, wreath surrounds **Rev. Legend:** "Amaniya"

Date	Mintage	VG	F	VF	XF	Unc
SH1299 (1920)	—	BV	650	750	1,500	—

KM# 890 5 AMANI (50 Rupees)
23.0000 g., 0.9000 Gold 0.6655 oz. AGW, 34 mm. **Obv:** Star above toughra within wreath **Rev:** Mosque within 7-pointed star, wreath surrounds, persian "5" above mosque

Date	Mintage	VG	F	VF	XF	Unc
SH1299	—	BV	600	750	1,500	—

Amanullah
AH1337-1348 / 1919-1929AD

LOCAL COINAGE

KM# 965 PAISA
Copper, 20 mm. **Obv:** Denomination "Yek Paisa" **Note:** Crudely struck. Believed to be struck at Kabul.

Date	Mintage	Good	VG	F	VF	XF
SH1298 (1919)	—	4.50	7.50	12.50	22.00	—
SH1299 (1920)	—	4.50	7.50	12.50	22.00	—

KM# 966 PAISA
Copper **Note:** Crudely struck; without mint name, believed to be struck at Kabul.

Date	Mintage	Good	VG	F	VF	XF
SH1299 (1920)	—	6.00	10.00	16.50	27.50	—

KM# 967 SHAHI (5 Paise)
Copper **Rev:** Both denominations **Note:** Crudely struck; without mint name, believed to be struck at Kabul.

Date	Mintage	Good	VG	F	VF	XF
AH1338 - SH1298 (1919)	—	6.00	10.00	16.50	27.50	—
AH1338 - SH1299 (1920)	—	7.50	12.50	20.00	35.00	—
AH1339 - SH1299 (1920)	—	6.00	10.00	16.50	27.50	—

KM# A846 10 PAISE
Copper **Note:** Crudely struck; believed to be struck at Kabul.

Date	Mintage	Good	VG	F	VF	XF
SH1299 (1920)	—	7.50	12.50	20.00	35.00	—

MILLED COINAGE

10 Dinar = 1 Paisa; 5 Paise = 1 Shahi; 2 Shahi = 1 Sanar; 2 Sanar = 1 Abbasi; 1-1/2 Abbasi = 1 Qiran; 2 Qiran = 1 Kabuli Rupee; 1 Tilla = 10 Rupees

KM# 880 PAISA
Bronze Or Brass

Date	Mintage	VG	F	VF	XF	Unc
SH1299 (1920)	—	2.50	5.50	12.00	22.50	—
SH1300 (1921)	—	3.50	7.00	15.00	25.00	—
SH1301 (1922)	—	3.50	7.00	15.00	25.00	—

Note: Two varieties are known dated SH1301

Date	Mintage	VG	F	VF	XF	Unc
SH1302 (1923)	—	2.50	5.50	12.00	22.50	—
SH1303 (1924)	—	2.50	5.50	12.00	22.50	—

KM# 859 SHAHI (5 Paise)
Copper Or Brass, 25 mm. **Note:** Thick flan.

Date	Mintage	VG	F	VF	XF	Unc
AH1337	—	12.00	22.00	40.00	70.00	—

KM# 860 SHAHI (5 Paise)
Copper Or Brass, 25 mm. **Note:** Thin flan.

Date	Mintage	VG	F	VF	XF	Unc
AH1337	—	10.00	20.00	35.00	55.00	—

KM# 861 SANAR (10 Paisa)
Copper Or Brass, 29-30 mm. **Obv:** Text within inner circle, stars surround **Rev:** Mosque within 8-pointed star, within circle, stars surrounds **Note:** Thick flan. Size varies.

Date	Mintage	VG	F	VF	XF	Unc
AH1337	—	10.00	17.50	30.00	55.00	—

KM# 862 SANAR (10 Paisa)
Copper Or Brass, 29-30 mm. **Note:** Thin flan. Size varies.

Date	Mintage	VG	F	VF	XF	Unc
AH1337	—	9.00	14.00	20.00	35.00	—

KM# 881 3 SHAHI (15 Paisa)
Copper, 33 mm. **Obv:** Stars surround inner circle, without "Shamsi" **Rev:** Mosque within 7-pointed star, within circle, stars surrounds **Note:** Four varieties for date SH1299 and three varieties for date SH1300 are known.

Date	Mintage	VG	F	VF	XF	Unc
SH1298 (1919)	—	4.00	15.00	22.00	40.00	—
AH1299 (1920)	—	1.50	3.50	8.00	17.00	—
AH1300 (1921)	—	1.50	3.50	8.00	17.00	—

KM# 881a 3 SHAHI (15 Paisa)
Brass, 33 mm. **Obv:** Stars surround inner circle, without "Shamsi" **Rev:** Mosque within 7-pointed star, within circle, stars surrounds **Note:** Prev. KM#892.

Date	Mintage	VG	F	VF	XF	Unc
SH1300 (1921)	—	4.00	8.00	15.00	30.00	—

KM# 870 3 SHAHI (15 Paisa)
Copper, 32-33 mm. **Obv:** "Al-Ghazi", without "Shamsi" by date **Rev:** Mosque within 8-pointed star, within circle, stars surrounds **Note:** Size varies.

Date	Mintage	VG	F	VF	XF	Unc
SH1298 (1919)	—	3.00	5.00	10.00	20.00	—
SH1299 (1920)	—	3.00	5.00	10.00	20.00	—

Note: 2 varieties of SH1299 exist

KM# 871.1 3 SHAHI (15 Paisa)
11.5000 g., Copper, 33 mm. **Obv:** "Al-Ghazi, Shamsi" **Rev:** Mosque within 8-pointed star, within circle, stars surrounds **Note:** Thick flan.

Date	Mintage	VG	F	VF	XF	Unc
SH1298 (1919)	—	10.00	15.00	22.00	40.00	—

KM# 871.2 3 SHAHI (15 Paisa)
9.0000 g., Copper, 33 mm. **Obv:** "Al-Ghazi, Shamsi" **Rev:** Mosque within 8-pointed star, within circle, stars surrounds **Note:** Thin flan.

Date	Mintage	VG	F	VF	XF	Unc
SH1298 (1919)	—	2.00	4.00	9.00	18.00	—

Note: Two reverse varieties with 10 or 11 circular stars exist

KM# 872 3 SHAHI (15 Paisa)
Copper, 33 mm. **Obv:** "Shamsi" **Rev:** Mosque in seven-pointed star

Date	Mintage	VG	F	VF	XF	Unc
SH1298 (1919)	—	2.00	4.00	9.00	18.00	—

KM# 891 3 SHAHI (15 Paisa)

Brass **Obv:** Eight stars around perimeter **Rev:** Eight stars around perimeter

Date	Mintage	VG	F	VF	XF	Unc
SH1300 (1921)	—	—	—	—	—	—

KM# 893 3 SHAHI (15 Paisa)

Copper, 33 mm. **Obv:** Tughra, stars surround **Rev:** Mosque within 7-pointed star, within circle, stars surrounds

Date	Mintage	VG	F	VF	XF	Unc
SH1300 (1921)	—	1.50	3.50	8.00	17.00	—
SH1301 (1922)	—	1.50	3.50	8.00	17.00	—
Note: 2 varieties of SH1301 exist						
SH130x (1923) (error)	—	—	—	—	—	—
SH1303 (1924)	—	1.50	3.50	8.00	17.00	—

KM# 874 ABBASI (20 Paisa)

Copper Or Billon, 20 mm. **Obv:** Text within circle, stars surround **Rev:** Mosque within 8-pointed star, within circle, stars surrounds

Date	Mintage	VG	F	VF	XF	Unc
SH1298 (1919)	—	50.00	75.00	90.00	150	—

KM# 882 ABBASI (20 Paisa)

Copper Or Billon, 25 mm.

Date	Mintage	VG	F	VF	XF	Unc
SH1299 (1920)	—	15.00	30.00	50.00	75.00	—

KM# 883 ABBASI (20 Paisa)

Copper Or Billon, 25 mm. **Obv:** Tughra, stars surround **Rev:** Mosque within 7-pointed star, stars surrounds

Date	Mintage	VG	F	VF	XF	Unc
SH1299 (1920)	—	2.00	6.00	15.00	30.00	—
SH1300 (1921)	—	2.00	6.00	15.00	30.00	—
SH1301 (1922)	—	2.00	6.00	15.00	30.00	—
Note: Two varieties for date SH1301 exist						
SH1302 (1923)	—	2.00	6.00	15.00	30.00	—
SH2031 (1923) Error	—	7.00	15.00	30.00	50.00	—
SH1303 (1924)	—	2.00	6.00	15.00	30.00	—

KM# 866 1/2 RUPEE (Qiran)

Silver **Obv:** Legend within circle and wreath **Rev:** Mosque within 8-pointed star, wreath surrounds

Date	Mintage	VG	F	VF	XF	Unc
AH1337 (1918)	—	150	300	500	725	—

KM# 875 1/2 RUPEE (Qiran)

4.7500 g., 0.5000 Silver 0.0764 oz. ASW, 20 mm. **Obv:** Star above inscription, "Shamsi" **Rev:** Mosque within 8-pointed star, wreath surrounds

Date	Mintage	VG	F	VF	XF	Unc
SH1298 (1919)	—	3.00	6.00	10.00	20.00	—
Note: Two varieties are known						

KM# 876 1/2 RUPEE (Qiran)

4.7500 g., 0.5000 Silver 0.0764 oz. ASW, 20 mm. **Obv:** "Al-Ghazi" above inscription, "Shamsi" **Rev:** Mosque within 8-pointed star, wreath surrounds

Date	Mintage	VG	F	VF	XF	Unc
SH1298 (1919)	—	15.00	30.00	50.00	75.00	—

KM# 884 1/2 RUPEE (Qiran)

4.7500 g., 0.5000 Silver 0.0764 oz. ASW, 20 mm. **Obv:** Without "Shamsi"

Date	Mintage	VG	F	VF	XF	Unc
SH1299 (1920)	—	3.00	4.00	7.00	15.00	—
Note: Two varieties are known dated 1299						
SH1300 (1921)	—	3.00	4.00	7.00	15.00	—

KM# 894 1/2 RUPEE (Qiran)

4.7500 g., 0.5000 Silver 0.0764 oz. ASW, 20 mm. **Obv:** Tughra within wreath **Rev:** Mosque within 7-pointed star, wreath surrounds

Date	Mintage	VG	F	VF	XF	Unc
SH1300 (1921)	—	2.00	4.00	7.00	12.00	—
SH1301 (1922)	—	2.00	4.00	7.00	12.00	—
SH1302 (1923)	—	2.00	4.00	7.00	12.00	—
SH1303 (1924)	—	2.00	4.00	7.00	12.00	—

KM# 867 RUPEE

9.2000 g., 0.5000 Silver 0.1479 oz. ASW, 25 mm. **Obv:** Name and titles of Amanullah, star above inscription **Rev:** Mosque within 8-pointed star, wreath surrounds

Date	Mintage	VG	F	VF	XF	Unc
AH1337 (1918)	—	6.00	10.00	18.00	30.00	—
Note: Seven varieties are known						

KM# 877 RUPEE

9.0000 g., 0.9000 Silver 0.2604 oz. ASW, 25 mm. **Obv:** "Al-Ghazi" above inscription **Rev:** Mosque within 8-pointed star, wreath surrounds

Date	Mintage	VG	F	VF	XF	Unc
SH1298 (1919)	—	5.00	6.50	10.00	18.50	—
Note: Four varieties are known for date SH1298						
SH1299 (1920)	—	5.00	6.50	10.00	18.50	—
Note: Two varieties are known for date SH1299						

KM# 885 RUPEE

9.2500 g., 0.9000 Silver 0.2676 oz. ASW, 27 mm. **Obv:** Toughra of Amanullah **Rev:** Mosque within 7-pointed star, wreath surrounds

Date	Mintage	VG	F	VF	XF	Unc
SH1299 (1920)	—	5.25	6.50	8.00	16.50	—
SH1300 (1921)	—	5.25	6.50	8.00	16.50	—
SH1301 (1922)	—	5.25	6.50	8.00	16.50	—
SH1302/1 (1923)	—	5.25	6.50	8.00	16.50	—
SH1302 (1923)	—	5.25	6.50	8.00	16.50	—
SH1303 (1924)	—	5.25	6.50	8.00	16.50	—

KM# 878 2-1/2 RUPEES

22.9200 g., 0.9000 Silver 0.6632 oz. ASW, 34 mm. **Obv:** Tughra above date within wreath **Rev:** Mosque within 7-pointed star, wreath surrounds **Note:** Two varieties each are known for dates SH1298-1300.

Date	Mintage	VG	F	VF	XF	Unc
SH1298 (1919)	—	12.50	16.50	20.00	45.00	—
SH1299 (1920)	—	9.50	12.50	17.50	40.00	—
SH1300 (1921)	—	9.50	12.50	17.50	40.00	—
SH1301 (1922)	—	9.50	12.50	15.00	35.00	—
SH1302 (1923)	—	9.50	12.50	15.00	35.00	—
SH1303 (1924)	—	9.50	12.50	15.00	35.00	—

KM# 834.1 5 RUPEES

45.6000 g., 0.9000 Silver 1.3194 oz. ASW, 46 mm. **Obv:** Tughra divides date, wreath surrounds **Rev:** Similar to KM#826

Date	Mintage	VG	F	VF	XF	Unc
AH1319	—	28.00	45.00	90.00	175	—

KM# 834.2 5 RUPEES

45.6000 g., 0.9000 Silver 1.3194 oz. ASW, 46 mm. **Obv:** Date at left of tughra, wreath surrounds

Date	Mintage	VG	F	VF	XF	Unc
AH1319	—	28.00	45.00	90.00	175	—

KM# 843 5 RUPEES

45.6000 g., 0.9000 Silver 1.3194 oz. ASW, 45 mm. **Obv:** Wreath surrounds text **Rev:** Mosque within beaded circle, wreath surrounds **Note:** Most dates are recut dies. Two varieties are known for each date, AH1324 and 1327.

Date	Mintage	VG	F	VF	XF	Unc
AH1322	—	27.50	32.50	50.00	100	—
AH1324	—	27.50	30.00	45.00	90.00	—
AH1326	—	27.50	30.00	45.00	90.00	—
AH1327/6	—	27.50	30.00	45.00	90.00	—
AH1328	—	30.00	35.00	55.00	120	—
AH1329	—	27.50	40.00	70.00	145	—

KM# 886 1/2 AMANI (5 Rupees)
2.3000 g., 0.9000 Gold 0.0665 oz. AGW, 16 mm. **Obv:** Tughra within wreath **Rev:** Mosque within 7-pointed star, wreath surrounds

Date	Mintage	VG	F	VF	XF	Unc
SH1299 (1920)	—	65.00	75.00	95.00	135	—

KM# 868.1 TILLA (10 Rupees)
4.6000 g., 0.9000 Gold 0.1331 oz. AGW, 21 mm. **Obv:** Text within wreath **Obv. Legend:** "Amanullah..." **Rev:** Mosque within 8-pointed star, crossed swords below mosque, wreath surrounds

Date	Mintage	VG	F	VF	XF	Unc
AH1337 (1918)	—	125	140	165	225	—

KM# 868.2 TILLA (10 Rupees)
4.6000 g., 0.9000 Gold 0.1331 oz. AGW, 21 mm. **Obv:** Text within wreath **Rev:** Mosque within 8-pointed star, 6-pointed star below mosque, wreath surrounds

Date	Mintage	VG	F	VF	XF	Unc
AH1337 (1918)	—	125	150	175	250	—

KM# 887 AMANI (10 Rupees)
4.6000 g., 0.9000 Gold 0.1331 oz. AGW, 22 mm. **Obv:** Tughra above date within wreath **Rev:** Mosque within 7-pointed star, wreath surrounds

Date	Mintage	VG	F	VF	XF	Unc
SH1299 (1920)	—	—	BV	135	175	—

KM# 888 2 AMANI (20 Rupees)
9.2000 g., 0.9000 Gold 0.2662 oz. AGW, 24 mm. **Obv:** Tughra above date within wreath **Rev:** Mosque within 7-pointed star, wreath surrounds

Date	Mintage	VG	F	VF	XF	Unc
SH1299 (1920)	—	—	BV	260	285	320
SH1300 (1921)	—	—	BV	260	285	320
SH1301 (1922)	—	—	BV	260	285	320
SH1302 (1923)	—	—	BV	260	285	320
SH1303 (1924)	—	—	BV	260	285	320

KM# 900 HABIBI (30 Rupees)
4.6000 g., 0.9000 Gold 0.1331 oz. AGW **Obv:** Small star replaces "30 Rupees" in legend **Rev:** Value stated as "Habibi"

Date	Mintage	VG	F	VF	XF	Unc
AH1347	—	BV	135	200	325	—

DECIMAL COINAGE

100 Pul = 1 Afghani; 20 Afghani = 1 Amani

KM# 905 2 PUL
2.0000 g., Bronze Or Brass, 18 mm. **Obv:** Tughra within inner circle, spray below **Rev:** Denomination within inner circle, spray below

Date	Mintage	F	VF	XF	Unc
SH1304 (1925)	—	3.00	5.00	9.00	15.00
SH1305 (1926)	—	3.00	5.00	9.00	15.00

KM# 906 5 PUL
3.0000 g., Bronze Or Brass, 22 mm. **Obv:** Tughra within inner circle, spray below **Rev:** Denomination within inner circle, spray below

Date	Mintage	F	VF	XF	Unc
SH1304 (1925)	—	1.75	3.50	6.00	14.00
SH1305 (1926)	—	1.50	3.00	5.50	14.00

KM# 907 10 PUL
6.0000 g., Copper, 24 mm. **Obv:** Tughra within inner circle, spray below **Rev:** Denomination within inner circle, spray below

Date	Mintage	F	VF	XF	Unc
SH1304 (1925)	—	2.00	4.00	6.00	15.00
SH1305 (1926)	—	2.50	4.50	7.00	20.00
SH1306 (1927)	—	2.50	4.50	7.00	20.00

KM# 908 20 PUL
2.0000 g., Billon, 19 mm. **Obv:** Tughra within inner circle, spray below **Rev:** Denomination within inner circle, spray below **Note:** Varieties exist.

Date	Mintage	F	VF	XF	Unc
SH1304 (1925)	—	50.00	75.00	100	170
SH134 (1925) Error	—	—	—	—	—
ND(ca.1926)	—	35.00	60.00	90.00	160

KM# 909 1/2 AFGHANI (50 Pul)
5.0000 g., 0.5000 Silver 0.0804 oz. ASW, 25 mm. **Obv:** Tughra, date and spray below **Rev:** Mosque with flags flanking within wreath

Date	Mintage	F	VF	XF	Unc
SH1304/7 (1925)	—	2.00	3.50	6.50	18.50
Note: Two varieties are known dated SH1304					
SH1305/8 (1926)	—	2.00	3.50	6.50	18.50
SH1306/9 (1927)	—	2.00	3.50	6.50	18.50

KM# 915 1/2 AFGHANI (50 Pul)
5.0000 g., 0.5000 Silver 0.0804 oz. ASW, 25 mm. **Obv:** Date below mosque

Date	Mintage	F	VF	XF	Unc
SH1307/10 (1928)	—	3.00	6.00	12.00	35.00

KM# 910 AFGHANI (100 Pul)
10.0000 g., 0.9000 Silver 0.2893 oz. ASW, 29 mm. **Obv:** Date below toughra **Note:** Two varieties each are known for dates SH1305-06.

Date	Mintage	F	VF	XF	Unc
SH1304/7 (1925)	—	6.00	7.00	12.50	28.00
Note: Three varieties are known for date SH1304					
SH1305/8 (1926)	—	6.00	7.00	12.50	28.00
SH1305/9 (1926)	—	6.00	7.00	12.50	28.00
SH1306/9 (1927)	—	6.00	7.00	12.50	28.00

KM# 913 2-1/2 AFGHANIS
25.0000 g., 0.9000 Silver 0.7234 oz. ASW, 38 mm. **Obv:** Tughra within wreath **Rev:** Mosque within wreath **Note:** Two varieties are known for each date.

Date	Mintage	F	VF	XF	Unc
SH1305/8 (1926)	—	15.00	25.00	50.00	125
SH1306/9 (1927)	—	15.00	20.00	40.00	90.00

KM# 911 1/2 AMANI (5 Rupees)
3.0000 g., 0.9000 Gold 0.0868 oz. AGW, 18 mm.

Date	Mintage	VG	F	VF	XF	Unc
SH1304/7 (1925)	—	—	BV	95.00	120	165
SH1305/8 (1926)	—	—	BV	95.00	120	165
SH1306/9 (1927)	—	—	BV	95.00	120	165

KM# 912 AMANI
6.0000 g., 0.9000 Gold 0.1736 oz. AGW, 23 mm.

Date	Mintage	F	VF	XF	Unc
SH1304/7 (1925)	—	—	BV	170	185
SH1305/8 (1926)	—	—	BV	170	220
SH1306/9 (1927)	—	—	BV	170	185

KM# 914 2-1/2 AMANI
15.0000 g., 0.9000 Gold 0.4340 oz. AGW, 29 mm. **Obv:** Tughra above date within wreath **Rev:** Mosque within wreath

Date	Mintage	F	VF	XF	Unc
SH1306/9 (1927)	—	—	—	5,000	7,000

Habibullah Ghazi

Rebel ; AH1347-1348 / 1929AD; Struck in the name of Baccha-i-Saqao

LOCAL COINAGE

KM# 969 5 PAISE
Brass

Date	Mintage	Good	VG	F	VF	XF
AH1347	—	5.00	8.50	15.00	25.00	—

KM# 970.1 10 PAISE
Brass **Rev:** Denomination "Dah" written above "Paisa"

Date	Mintage	Good	VG	F	VF	XF
AH1347	—	6.00	10.00	16.50	27.50	—

KM# 970.2 10 PAISE
Brass **Rev:** Denomination "Dah" written at right of "Paisa"

Date	Mintage	Good	VG	F	VF	XF
AH1347	—	7.50	12.50	20.00	35.00	—

KM# 972 20 PAISE
Brass

Date	Mintage	Good	VG	F	VF	XF
AH1347	—	7.50	12.50	20.00	35.00	—
AH1348	—	10.00	15.00	25.00	40.00	—

Muhammed Nadir Shah

AH1348-1350 / 1929-1933AD

MILLED COINAGE

10 Dinar = 1 Paisa; 5 Paise = 1 Shahi; 2 Shahi = 1 Sanar; 2 Sanar = 1 Abbasi; 1-1/2 Abbasi = 1 Qiran; 2 Qiran = 1 Kabuli Rupee; 1 Tilla = 10 Rupees

KM# 901 10 PAISE
4.1000 g., Copper, 22 mm. **Obv:** Text above spray **Rev:** Mosque within 8-pointed star, spray below

Date	Mintage	VG	F	VF	XF	Unc
AH1348	—	6.00	12.00	20.00	40.00	—

KM# 895 20 PAISE
5.7000 g., Bronze Or Brass, 25 mm. **Obv:** Text within wreath **Rev:** Mosque within 8-pointed star, wreath surrounds

Date	Mintage	VG	F	VF	XF	Unc
AH1347	—	3.00	5.00	7.50	18.00	—

KM# 896 1/2 RUPEE (Qiran)
4.7000 g., 0.5000 Silver 0.0756 oz. ASW, 21 mm. **Obv:** Text within wreath **Rev:** Value (Qiran) above mosque within 8-pointed star, wreath surrounds

Date	Mintage	VG	F	VF	XF	Unc
AH1347	—	4.00	7.00	12.00	20.00	—

KM# 902 1/2 RUPEE (Qiran)
4.7000 g., 0.5000 Silver 0.0756 oz. ASW, 21 mm. **Obv:** Text within wreath **Rev:** Value (Qiran) above mosque within 8-pointed star, wreath surrounds

Date	Mintage	VG	F	VF	XF	Unc
AH1348	—	12.00	20.00	32.00	50.00	—

KM# 897 RUPEE
9.1000 g., 0.9000 Silver 0.2633 oz. ASW, 25 mm. **Obv:** Name and titles of Amir Habibullah (The Usurper) **Rev:** Mosque within 8-pointed star, wreath surrounds

Date	Mintage	VG	F	VF	XF	Unc
AH1347	—	5.00	9.00	15.00	25.00	—

KM# 898 RUPEE
9.1000 g., 0.9000 Silver 0.2633 oz. ASW **Obv:** Title in circle **Rev:** Mosque within 8-pointed star, wreath surrounds

Date	Mintage	VG	F	VF	XF	Unc
AH1347	—	25.00	35.00	55.00	90.00	—

KM# 899 HABIBI (30 Rupees)
4.6000 g., 0.9000 Gold 0.1331 oz. AGW, 21 mm. **Obv:** Value text within wreath **Rev:** Mosque within 8-pointed star, wreath surrounds, value stated as Habibi (2 values on coin)

Date	Mintage	VG	F	VF	XF	Unc
AH1347	—	BV	140	200	325	—

DECIMAL COINAGE

100 Pul = 1 Afghani; 20 Afghani = 1 Amani

KM# A922 PUL
1.0000 g., Bronze Or Brass, 15 mm. **Obv:** Text, stars surround **Rev:** Denomination within inner circle, stars surround

Date	Mintage	F	VF	XF	Unc
AH1349 (1930)	—	0.75	1.25	1.75	2.50

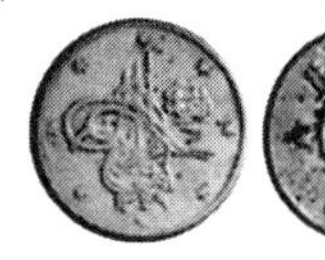

KM# 922 PUL
Bronze Or Brass, 15 mm. **Obv:** Toughra **Rev:** Denomination within inner circle

Date	Mintage	F	VF	XF	Unc
AH1349 (1930)	—	100	250	300	400

KM# 917 2 PUL
2.0000 g., Bronze Or Brass, 18 mm. **Obv:** Tughra within inner circle **Rev:** Denomination within inner circle, spray below

Date	Mintage	F	VF	XF	Unc
AH1348 (1929)	—	1.25	2.50	3.50	8.00
AH1349/8 (1930)	—	1.25	2.50	3.50	8.00

KM# 923 5 PUL
3.0000 g., Bronze Or Brass, 22 mm. **Obv:** Tughra within inner circle, wreath surrounds **Rev:** Denomination within inner circle, spray below

Date	Mintage	F	VF	XF	Unc
AH1349 (1930)	—	1.75	2.75	4.50	12.50
AH1350 (1931)	—	1.25	2.25	3.50	12.50

Note: Two varieties are known dated AH1350

KM# 929 5 PUL
3.0000 g., Bronze Or Brass, 21 mm. **Obv:** Text within beaded circle, wreath surrounds **Rev:** Denomination within beaded circle, spray below

Date	Mintage	F	VF	XF	Unc
SH1311 (1932)	—	2.50	5.50	9.00	20.00
SH1312 (1933)	—	2.50	5.50	9.00	20.00
SH1313 (1934)	—	2.50	5.50	9.00	20.00
SH1314 (1935)	—	2.50	5.50	9.00	20.00

KM# 918 10 PUL
5.8000 g., Copper Or Brass, 25 mm. **Obv:** Tughra within circle **Rev:** Denomination within circle **Note:** Illustration shows an example struck off-center; prices are for properly struck specimens.

Date	Mintage	F	VF	XF	Unc
AH1348 (1929)	—	2.00	3.50	5.00	15.00
AH1349 (1930)	—	2.25	4.00	5.50	15.00

Note: Small or large letters, weight varies: 5.8 or 5.3

KM# 930 10 PUL
Bronze Or Brass, 23 mm. **Obv:** Text within beaded circle, spray below **Rev:** Denomination within small beaded circle, spray below

Date	Mintage	F	VF	XF	Unc
SH1311 (1932)	—	1.50	2.50	4.00	15.00
SH1312 (1933)	—	1.50	2.50	4.00	15.00
SH1313 (1934)	—	1.50	2.50	4.00	15.00
SH1314 (1935)	—	1.50	2.50	4.00	15.00

KM# 919 20 PUL
5.5589 g., Copper Or Brass, 25 mm. **Obv:** Tughra within inner circle, wreath surrounds **Rev:** Denomination within circle, wreath surrounds

Date	Mintage	F	VF	XF	Unc
AH1348 (1929)	—	2.00	4.00	10.00	22.00
AH1349 (1930)	—	3.00	5.00	12.00	25.00

KM# 924 25 PUL

6.0000 g., Copper Or Brass, 25 mm. **Obv:** Tughra within circle, wreath surrounds **Rev:** Denomination within circle, wreath surrounds **Note:** 2 varieties of letters

Date	Mintage	F	VF	XF	Unc
AH1349	—	2.50	5.00	10.00	20.00
Note: Two varieties are known dated AH1349.					
134x	—	2.50	5.00	10.00	20.00

KM# 920 1/2 AFGHANI (50 Pul)

5.0000 g., 0.5000 Silver 0.0804 oz. ASW, 24 mm. **Obv:** Mosque above date within wreath **Note:** Prev. KM#919.

Date	Mintage	F	VF	XF	Unc
AH1348/1 (1929)	—	1.75	2.50	5.00	14.00
AH1349/2 (1930)	—	1.75	2.50	5.00	14.00
AH1350/3 (1931)	—	1.75	2.50	5.00	14.00

KM# 926 1/2 AFGHANI (50 Pul)

1.8000 g., 0.5000 Silver 0.0289 oz. ASW, 24 mm. **Obv:** Text within beaded circle, wreath surrounds **Rev:** Mosque within wreath

Date	Mintage	F	VF	XF	Unc
SH1310 (1931)	—	2.00	3.00	5.50	15.00
SH1311 (1932)	—	1.75	2.25	4.50	12.50
Note: Two die varieties exist					
SH1312 (1933)	—	2.00	3.00	5.50	15.00
Note: With and without diamond-shaped dot beneath the wreath on the obverse					

KM# 921 AFGHANI (100 Pul)

9.9500 g., 0.9000 Silver 0.2879 oz. ASW, 30 mm. **Obv:** Tughra within wreath **Rev:** Mosque within wreath

Date	Mintage	F	VF	XF	Unc
AH1348 (1929)	—	6.00	7.00	9.00	16.50
AH1349 (1930)	—	6.00	7.00	9.00	16.50
AH1350 (1931)	—	6.00	7.00	9.00	16.50

KM# 927.1 AFGHANI (100 Pul)

10.0000 g., 0.9000 Silver 0.2893 oz. ASW, 27 mm. **Obv:** Text within beaded circle, wreath surrounds **Rev:** Mosque within wreath

Date	Mintage	F	VF	XF	Unc
SH1310 (1931) Rare	—	—	—	—	—
SH1311 (1932)	—	110	160	180	260

KM# 927.2 AFGHANI (100 Pul)

10.0000 g., 0.9000 Silver 0.2893 oz. ASW, 27 mm. **Obv:** Text within beaded circle, wreath surrounds **Rev:** Mosque within wreath **Note:** Thick flan.

Date	Mintage	F	VF	XF	Unc
SH1310 (1931) Rare	—	—	—	—	—

KM# 925 20 AFGHANIS

6.0000 g., 0.9000 Gold 0.1736 oz. AGW, 22 mm.

Date	Mintage	F	VF	XF	Unc
AH1348	—	BV	175	200	300
AH1349	—	—	BV	170	240
AH1350	—	—	BV	170	240

Muhammed Zahir Shah

SH1312-1352 / 1933-1973AD

DECIMAL COINAGE

100 Pul = 1 Afghani; 20 Afghani = 1 Amani

KM# 928 2 PUL

2.0000 g., Bronze Or Brass, 18 mm. **Obv:** Text within beaded circle, wreath surrounds **Rev:** Denomination within beaded circle, wreath surrounds

Date	Mintage	F	VF	XF	Unc
SH1311 (1932)	—	2.00	3.00	4.00	12.00
SH1312 (1933)	—	1.50	2.25	3.00	10.00
SH1313 (1934)	—	1.75	2.75	3.75	10.00
SH1314 (1935)	—	2.00	3.00	4.00	12.00

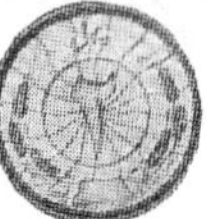

KM# 936 2 PUL

2.0000 g., Bronze, 15 mm. **Obv:** Arms within wreath, radiant background **Rev:** Denomination within inner circle, wreath surrounds, radiant background

Date	Mintage	F	VF	XF	Unc
SH1316 (1937)	—	0.15	0.20	0.35	1.00

KM# 937 3 PUL

2.5000 g., Bronze, 16 mm. **Obv:** Arms within wreath, radiant background **Rev:** Denomination within inner circle, radiant background

Date	Mintage	F	VF	XF	Unc
SH1316 (1937)	—	0.35	0.50	0.75	2.00

KM# 938 5 PUL

3.0300 g., Bronze, 17.1 mm. **Obv:** Arms within wreath, radiant background **Rev:** Denomination within inner circle, radiant background

Date	Mintage	F	VF	XF	Unc
SH1316 (1937)	—	0.35	0.50	0.75	2.00

KM# 939 10 PUL

2.5000 g., Copper-Nickel, 18 mm. **Obv:** Arms within wreath, radiant background **Rev:** Denomination within inner circle, radiant background

Date	Mintage	F	VF	XF	Unc
SH1316 (1937)	—	0.40	0.65	1.00	3.00

KM# 931 25 PUL

7.0000 g., Bronze Or Brass, 24-25 mm. **Obv:** Text within beaded circle, wreath surrounds **Rev:** Denomination within inner circle, wreath surrounds **Note:** Size varies.

Date	Mintage	F	VF	XF	Unc
SH1312 (1933)	—	2.00	4.00	12.00	25.00
SH1313 (1934)	—	2.00	4.00	12.00	25.00
SH1314 (1935)	—	2.00	4.50	14.00	28.00
SH1316 (1937)	—	2.00	4.50	14.00	28.00

KM# 940 25 PUL

2.9000 g., Copper-Nickel, 20 mm. **Obv:** Text within inner circle, text surrounds **Rev:** Arms within wreath

Date	Mintage	F	VF	XF	Unc
SH1316 (1937)	—	0.60	0.75	1.50	3.50

KM# 941 25 PUL

3.0000 g., Bronze, 20 mm. **Obv:** Text within inner circle, text surrounds **Rev:** Arms within wreath

Date	Mintage	F	VF	XF	Unc
SH1330 (1951)	—	0.30	0.50	0.75	2.50
SH1331 (1952)	—	0.30	0.50	0.75	2.50
SH1332 (1953)	—	0.30	0.50	0.75	2.50
SH1333 (1954)	—	1.00	2.00	3.50	6.00

KM# 943 25 PUL

3.0000 g., Nickel Clad Steel **Edge:** Reeded

Date	Mintage	F	VF	XF	Unc
SH1331 (1952)	—	1.00	2.00	3.50	7.00
SH1332 (1953)	—	1.50	3.00	5.00	9.00

KM# 944 25 PUL

3.0000 g., Nickel Clad Steel **Edge:** Plain

Date	Mintage	F	VF	XF	Unc
SH1331 (1952)	—	0.35	0.65	1.00	3.00
SH1332 (1953)	—	0.35	0.65	1.00	3.00
SH1333 (1954)	—	0.35	0.65	1.00	3.00
SH1334/2 (1955)	—	1.50	3.00	5.00	9.00
SH1334 (1955)	—	0.35	0.65	1.00	3.00

KM# 945 25 PUL

Aluminum, 24 mm. **Obv:** Text within inner circle, text surrounds **Rev:** Arms within wreath **Note:** Struck on oversize 2 Afghani KM#949 planchets in 1970.

Date	Mintage	F	VF	XF	Unc
SH1331 (1952)	—	0.50	1.00	3.00	10.00

KM# 932.1 1/2 AFGHANI (50 Pul)

4.7500 g., 0.5000 Silver 0.0764 oz. ASW, 24 mm. **Obv:** Smaller dotted circle within wreath **Rev:** Arms within wreath

Date	Mintage	F	VF	XF	Unc
SH1312 (1933)	—	1.75	3.00	6.00	16.00

KM# 932.2 1/2 AFGHANI (50 Pul)

4.7500 g., 0.5000 Silver 0.0764 oz. ASW, 24 mm. **Obv:** Large dotted field in circle within wreath **Rev:** Arms within wreath

Date	Mintage	F	VF	XF	Unc
SH1313 (1934)	—	1.75	3.00	6.00	16.00
Note: 60 dots in circle					
SH1314 (1935)	—	1.75	3.00	6.00	16.00
Note: 60 dots in circle					
SH1315 (1936)	—	1.50	2.50	5.50	15.00
Note: 40 dots in circle					
SH1316 (1937)	—	1.50	2.50	5.50	15.00
Note: 40 dots in circle					

KM# 947 1/2 AFGHANI (50 Pul)
5.0000 g., Nickel Clad Steel, 22.3 mm. **Obv:** Value on coin is "50 Pul" in Pashto. **Rev:** Arms within wreath

Date	Mintage	F	VF	XF	Unc
SH1331 (1952)	—	0.50	1.00	2.00	4.00
SH133x (1953)	—	5.00	7.50	12.50	20.00

KM# 942.1 50 PUL
4.8000 g., Bronze, 22.5 mm. **Obv:** Denomination in numerals **Rev:** Arms within wreath

Date	Mintage	F	VF	XF	Unc
SH1330 (1951)	—	0.50	1.00	2.00	4.00
SH133x (1951)	—	1.50	3.00	5.00	9.00

KM# 942.2 50 PUL
Bronze, 24 mm. **Obv:** Denomination in numerals **Rev:** Arms within wreath

Date	Mintage	F	VF	XF	Unc
SH1330 (1951)	—	20.00	30.00	40.00	50.00

KM# 946 50 PUL
5.0000 g., Nickel Clad Steel, 22.3 mm. **Obv:** Denomination within inner circle **Rev:** Arms within wreath

Date	Mintage	F	VF	XF	Unc
SH1331 (1952)	—	0.20	0.35	0.65	2.00
SH1332 (1953)	—	0.20	0.35	0.65	2.00
SH1333 (1954)	—	1.00	2.00	3.50	6.00
SH1334/2 (1955)	—	0.40	0.65	1.00	2.50
SH1334 (1955)	—	0.20	0.35	0.65	2.00

KM# 953 AFGHANI (100 Pul)
4.0000 g., Nickel Clad Steel, 23 mm. **Obv:** Three wheat sprigs **Rev:** Denomination and stars **Edge:** Reeded

Date	Mintage	F	VF	XF	Unc
SH1340 (1961)	—	0.20	0.35	0.60	1.25

KM# 949 2 AFGHANIS
2.5000 g., Aluminum **Obv:** Arms within wreath, circle surrounds **Rev:** Denomination within inner circle **Note:** This issue was withdrawn and demonetized due to extensive counterfeiting.

Date	Mintage	F	VF	XF	Unc
SH1337 (1958)	—	0.60	1.00	1.50	2.50

KM# 954.1 2 AFGHANIS
5.3000 g., Nickel Clad Steel, 25.1 mm. **Obv:** Radiant eagle statue, with wings spread **Rev:** Wheat sprig left of denomination **Edge:** Plain **Note:** Coin turn.

Date	Mintage	F	VF	XF	Unc
SH1340 (1961)	—	0.25	0.45	0.85	2.00

KM# 954.2 2 AFGHANIS
5.3000 g., Nickel Clad Steel, 25.1 mm. **Obv:** Radiant eagle statue, with wings spread **Rev:** Wheat sprig left of denomination **Note:** Medallic die orientation.

Date	Mintage	F	VF	XF	Unc
SH1340 (1961)	—	0.75	1.25	2.25	5.00

Note: Some evidence indicates that this variety was the first Republican issue struck in 1973

KM# 950 5 AFGHANIS
3.0000 g., Aluminum **Obv:** Tughra within beaded circle **Rev:** Arms within beaded circle, denomination below **Note:** This issue was withdrawn and demonetized due to extensive counterfeiting.

Date	Mintage	F	VF	XF	Unc
SH1337 (1958)	—	1.00	2.00	3.50	5.00

KM# 955 5 AFGHANIS
8.0400 g., Nickel Clad Steel, 29.2 mm. **Obv:** Bust 3/4 right divides dates **Rev:** Wheat sprigs flank denomination **Edge:** Reeded

Date	Mintage	F	VF	XF	Unc
SH1340 (1961)	—	0.35	0.75	1.50	3.00

KM# 948 10 AFGHANIS
Aluminum **Obv:** Tughra within beaded circle, denomination below **Rev:** Arms within wreath, date below, stars flank

Date	Mintage	F	VF	XF	Unc
SH1336 (1957)	—	—	—	—	900

KM# 935 4 GRAMS
4.0000 g., 0.9000 Gold 0.1157 oz. AGW, 19 mm.

Date	Mintage	F	VF	XF	Unc
SH1315 (1936)	—	—	BV	125	175
SH1317 (1938)	—	—	BV	125	175

KM# 933 TILLA
6.0000 g., 0.9000 Gold 0.1736 oz. AGW, 22 mm.

Date	Mintage	F	VF	XF	Unc
SH1313 (1934)	—	BV	165	185	275

KM# 934 8 GRAMS
8.0000 g., 0.9000 Gold 0.2315 oz. AGW, 22 mm.

Date	Mintage	F	VF	XF	Unc
SH1314 (1935)	—	—	BV	225	275
SH1315 (1936)	—	—	BV	225	275
SH1317 (1938)	—	—	BV	225	275

KM# 952 8 GRAMS
8.0000 g., 0.9000 Gold 0.2315 oz. AGW, 22 mm. **Obv:** Tughra **Rev:** Eagles divide date and flank figure above horse within cornucopias

Date	Mintage	F	VF	XF	Unc
SH1339-AH1380 (1960)	200	—	—	375	800

Note: Struck for royal presentation purposes. Specimens struck with the same dies (including the "8 grams", the "8" having been effaced after striking), but on thin planchets weighing 3.9-4.0 grams, exist, they are regarded as "mint sports". Market value $275.00 in Unc

REPUBLIC
SH1352-1357 / 1973-1978AD

STANDARD COINAGE

KM# 975 25 PUL
2.5200 g., Brass Clad Steel **Obv:** National arms **Rev:** Denomination, six stars

Date	Mintage	F	VF	XF	Unc
SH1352(1973)	45,950,000	0.25	0.50	1.00	2.00

KM# 976 50 PUL
Copper Clad Steel, 21 mm. **Obv:** National arms **Rev:** Denomination, six stars **Edge:** Plain

Date	Mintage	F	VF	XF	Unc
SH1352(1973)	24,750,000	0.50	1.00	2.00	4.00

KM# 977 5 AFGHANIS
Copper-Nickel Clad Steel **Obv:** National arms **Rev:** Denomination within stylized grain sprig wreath

Date	Mintage	F	VF	XF	Unc
SH1352(1973)	34,750,000	1.75	3.50	5.00	10.00

DEMOCRATIC REPUBLIC
SH1358-1371 / 1979-1992AD

STANDARD COINAGE

KM# 990 25 PUL
Aluminum-Bronze **Obv:** National arms **Rev:** Value at center

Date	Mintage	F	VF	XF	Unc
SH1357 (1978)	—	0.25	0.50	1.00	2.00

KM# 996 25 PUL
2.3000 g., Aluminum-Bronze, 19 mm. **Obv:** National arms **Rev:** Value at center

Date	Mintage	F	VF	XF	Unc
SH1359 (1980)	—	0.20	0.35	0.70	1.50

KM# 992 50 PUL
3.1000 g., Aluminum-Bronze, 20.9 mm. **Obv:** National arms **Rev:** Value at center

Date	Mintage	F	VF	XF	Unc
SH1357 (1978)	—	0.50	0.80	1.50	2.50

KM# 997 50 PUL
3.1600 g., Aluminum-Bronze, 21 mm. **Obv:** National arms **Rev:** Value at center

Date	Mintage	F	VF	XF	Unc
SH1359 (1980)	—	0.25	0.50	1.00	2.00

KM# 993 AFGHANI
4.6000 g., Copper-Nickel, 23 mm. **Obv:** National arms **Rev:** Value at center

Date	Mintage	F	VF	XF	Unc
SH1357 (1978)	—	0.60	1.00	2.00	4.00

KM# 998 AFGHANI
6.1800 g., Copper-Nickel **Obv:** National arms **Rev:** Value at center

Date	Mintage	F	VF	XF	Unc
SH1359 (1980)	—	0.50	0.80	1.50	2.50

KM# 994 2 AFGHANIS
6.0000 g., Copper-Nickel, 25 mm. **Obv:** National arms **Rev:** Value at center

Date	Mintage	F	VF	XF	Unc
SH1357 (1978)	—	1.00	1.50	2.00	4.00
SH1358 (1979)	—	1.00	1.50	2.00	4.00

KM# 999 2 AFGHANIS
6.2100 g., Copper-Nickel **Obv:** Similar to 1 Afghani, KM#998

Date	Mintage	F	VF	XF	Unc
SH1359 (1980)	—	0.60	1.00	1.50	3.00

KM# 995 5 AFGHANIS
7.4000 g., Copper-Nickel **Obv:** National arms **Rev:** Value at center

Date	Mintage	F	VF	XF	Unc
SH1357 (1978)	—	1.00	2.00	4.00	6.50

KM# 1000 5 AFGHANIS
7.4000 g., Copper-Nickel

Date	Mintage	VG	F	VF	XF	Unc
SH1359	—	—	1.00	1.50	2.00	4.00

KM# 1001 5 AFGHANIS
Brass **Series:** F.A.O. **Subject:** World Food Day **Obv:** National arms **Rev:** FAO logo

Date	Mintage	F	VF	XF	Unc
SH1360 (1981)	—	0.25	0.50	1.00	1.75

KM# 1015 10 AFGHANIS
Brass **Subject:** 70th Anniversary of Independence **Obv:** Arch **Rev:** Bank logo

Date	Mintage	F	VF	XF	Unc
1989	—	—	—	—	3.50

REPUBLIC

SH1381- / 2002- AD

DECIMAL COINAGE

100 Pul = 1 Afghani; 20 Afghani = 1 Amani

KM# 1044 AFGHANI
3.2500 g., Copper-Plated-Steel, 19.5 mm. **Obv:** Value, legend above, legend and date below **Rev:** Mosque with flags in wreath

Date	Mintage	F	VF	XF	Unc
SH1383(2004)	—	—	—	—	1.50
SH1384(2005)	—	—	—	—	—

KM# 1045 2 AFGHANIS
4.2500 g., Stainless Steel, 21 mm. **Obv:** Value, legend above, legend and date below **Rev:** Mosque with flags in wreath

Date	Mintage	F	VF	XF	Unc
SH1383(2004)	—	—	—	—	2.00
SH1384(2005)	—	—	—	—	—

KM# 1046 5 AFGHANIS
5.2600 g., Brass, 23.5 mm. **Obv:** Value, legend above, legend and date below **Rev:** Mosque with flags in wreath

Date	Mintage	F	VF	XF	Unc
SH1383(2004)	—	—	—	—	2.50
SE1384(2005)	—	—	—	—	—

ALBANIA

The Republic of Albania, a Balkan republic bounded by Macedonia, Greece, Montenegro, and the Adriatic Sea, has an area of 11,100 sq. mi. (28,748 sq. km.) and a population of 3.49 million. Capital: Tirane. The country is predominantly agricultural, although recent progress has been made in the manufacturing and mining sectors. Petroleum, chrome, iron, copper, cotton textiles, tobacco and wood products are exported.

Independence was re-established by revolt in 1912, and the present borders established in 1913 by a conference of European powers, which, in 1914, placed Prince William of Wied on the throne; popular discontent forced his abdication within months. In 1920, following World War I occupancy by several nations, a republic was set up. Ahmed Zogu seized the presidency in 1925, and in 1928 he proclaimed himself king with the title of Zog I. King Zog fled when Italy occupied Albania in 1939 and enthroned King Victor Emanuel of Italy. Upon the surrender of Italy to the Allies in 1943, German troops occupied the country. They withdrew in 1944, and communist partisans seized power, naming Gen. Enver Hoxha provisional president. In 1946, following a victory by the communist front in the 1945 elections, a new constitution modeled on that of the USSR was adopted. In accordance with the constitution of Dec. 28, 1976, the official name of Albania was changed from the Peoples Republic of Albania to the Peoples Socialist Republic of Albania.

Albania's former communists were routed in elections. March 1992, amid economic collapse and social unrest, Sali Berisha was elected as the first non-communist president since World War II. Rexhep Mejdani, elected president in 1997, succeeds him.

RULERS
Ahmed Bey Zogu - King Zog I, 1928-1939
Vittorio Emanuele III, 1939-1943

MINT MARKS
L – London
R - Rome
V – Vienna

MONETARY SYSTEM
100 Qindar Leku = 1 Lek
100 Qindar Ari = 1 Frang Ar = 5 Lek

KINGDOM

STANDARD COINAGE

KM# 1 5 QINDAR LEKU
Bronze **Ruler:** Ahmed Bey Zogu - King Zog I **Obv:** Lion head left **Rev:** Value above oak branch **Designer:** Giuseppe Romagnoli

Date	Mintage	F	VF	XF	Unc	BU
1926R	512,000	22.00	60.00	95.00	210	—

KM# 2 10 QINDAR LEKU
Bronze **Obv:** Eagle's head right **Rev:** Value between olive branches **Designer:** Giuseppe Romagnoli

Date	Mintage	F	VF	XF	Unc	BU
1926R	511,000	16.00	50.00	85.00	165	—

KM# 14 QINDAR AR
Bronze **Ruler:** Ahmed Bey Zogu - King Zog I **Obv:** Two headed Eagle **Rev:** Value above oak leaves and acorn

Date	Mintage	F	VF	XF	Unc	BU
1935R	2,000,000	2.50	6.00	14.00	34.00	—

KM# 15 2 QINDAR ARI

Bronze **Ruler:** Ahmed Bey Zogu - King Zog I **Obv:** Two headed Eagle **Rev:** Value above oak leaves

Date	Mintage	F	VF	XF	Unc	BU
1935R	1,500,000	3.50	10.00	18.00	40.00	—

KM# 3 1/4 LEKU

Nickel **Obv:** Lion advancing left **Rev:** Oak branch above value **Designer:** Giuseppe Romagnoli

Date	Mintage	F	VF	XF	Unc	BU
1926R	506,000	3.50	8.00	24.00	50.00	55.00
1927R	756,000	3.50	8.00	16.00	38.00	50.00

KM# 4 1/2 LEK

6.0700 g., Nickel, 23.96 mm. **Obv:** Two headed Eagle **Rev:** Hercules wrestling Nemean lion **Designer:** Giuseppe Romagnoli

Date	Mintage	F	VF	XF	Unc	BU
1926R	1,002,000	3.00	6.00	14.00	30.00	—

KM# 13 1/2 LEK

Nickel **Ruler:** Ahmed Bey Zogu - King Zog I **Obv:** Kings arms **Rev:** Hercules wrestling Nemean lion **Designer:** Giuseppe Romagnoli

Date	Mintage	F	VF	XF	Unc	BU
1930V	500,000	3.00	5.50	12.00	28.00	—
1931L	500,000	3.00	5.50	12.00	28.00	—
1931L Proof	—	Value: 200				

KM# 5 LEK

8.0000 g., Nickel, 26.7 mm. **Obv:** Head right **Rev:** Caped man on horse right **Designer:** Giuseppe Romagnoli

Date	Mintage	F	VF	XF	Unc	BU
1926R	1,004,000	2.00	4.00	10.00	25.00	—
1927R	506,000	3.00	7.00	18.00	38.00	—
1930V	1,250,000	1.50	3.00	7.00	22.00	—
1931L	1,000,000	2.00	4.00	10.00	25.00	—
1931L Proof	—	Value: 220				

KM# 6 FRANG AR

5.0000 g., 0.8350 Silver 0.1342 oz. ASW, 23 mm. **Obv:** Helmeted head right **Rev:** Prow of ancient ship **Designer:** Giuseppe Romagnoli

Date	Mintage	F	VF	XF	Unc	BU
1927R	100,000	70.00	130	200	385	—
1928R	60,000	70.00	140	220	410	—

KM# 16 FRANG AR

5.0000 g., 0.8350 Silver 0.1342 oz. ASW, 23.20 mm. **Ruler:** Ahmed Bey Zogu - King Zog I **Obv:** Head right, date below **Rev:** Kings Arms

Date	Mintage	F	VF	XF	Unc	BU
1935R	700,000	5.00	10.00	24.00	65.00	—
1937R	600,000	5.00	12.00	30.00	75.00	—

KM# 18 FRANG AR

5.0000 g., 0.8350 Silver 0.1342 oz. ASW, 23 mm. **Ruler:** Ahmed Bey Zogu - King Zog I **Subject:** 25th Anniversary of Independence **Obv:** Head right, date below **Rev:** Kings Arms **Designer:** Romagnoli

Date	Mintage	F	VF	XF	Unc	BU
1937R	50,000	8.00	16.00	36.00	95.00	—

KM# 7 2 FRANGA ARI

10.0000 g., 0.8350 Silver 0.2684 oz. ASW, 28 mm. **Obv:** Standing eagle with wings spread divides denomination **Rev:** Seed sower **Designer:** Romagnoli

Date	Mintage	F	VF	XF	Unc	BU
1926R	50,000	60.00	130	250	420	—
1927R	50,000	70.00	150	270	420	—
1928R	60,000	60.00	130	250	410	—

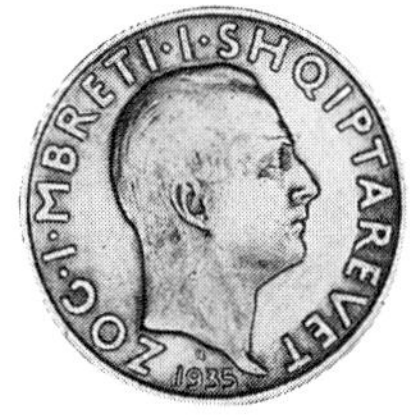

KM# 17 2 FRANGA ARI

10.0000 g., 0.8350 Silver 0.2684 oz. ASW **Ruler:** Ahmed Bey Zogu - King Zog I **Obv:** Head right, date below **Rev:** Kings Arms

Date	Mintage	F	VF	XF	Unc	BU
1935R	150,000	10.00	30.00	75.00	135	—

KM# 19 2 FRANGA ARI

10.0000 g., 0.8350 Silver 0.2684 oz. ASW **Ruler:** Ahmed Bey Zogu - King Zog I **Subject:** 25th Anniversary of Independence **Obv:** Head right, date below **Rev:** Kings arms

Date	Mintage	F	VF	XF	Unc	BU
1937R	25,000	15.00	30.00	80.00	160	—

KM# 8.1 5 FRANGA ARI

25.0000 g., 0.9000 Silver 0.7234 oz. ASW **Ruler:** Ahmed Bey Zogu - King Zog I **Obv:** Head right **Rev:** Man with plow left, value below **Designer:** Giuseppe Romagnoli

Date	Mintage	F	VF	XF	Unc	BU
1926R	60,000	100	220	450	750	—
1927V	Est. 40,000	—	—	—	—	—

Note: Only exist as provas

KM# 8.2 5 FRANGA ARI

25.0000 g., 0.9000 Silver 0.7234 oz. ASW **Ruler:** Ahmed Bey Zogu - King Zog I **Obv:** Hed right, star below head **Rev:** Man with plow left, value below **Designer:** Giuseppe Romagnoli

Date	Mintage	F	VF	XF	Unc	BU
1926R	Inc. above	130	300	490	800	—

KM# 9 10 FRANGA ARI

3.2258 g., 0.9000 Gold 0.0933 oz. AGW **Ruler:** Ahmed Bey Zogu - King Zog I **Obv:** Head left **Rev:** Double imperial eagle divides denomination below **Designer:** Romagnoli

Date	Mintage	F	VF	XF	Unc	BU
1927R	6,000	160	175	275	385	—

KM# 10 20 FRANGA ARI

6.4516 g., 0.9000 Gold 0.1867 oz. AGW, 21 mm. **Ruler:** Ahmed Bey Zogu - King Zog I **Obv:** Head left **Rev:** Double imperial eagle divides denomination below **Designer:** Romagnoli

Date	Mintage	F	VF	XF	Unc	BU
1926R	—	BV	190	270	365	—
1927R	6,000	BV	185	260	375	—

KM# 12 20 FRANGA ARI

6.4516 g., 0.9000 Gold 0.1867 oz. AGW, 21 mm. **Subject:** George Kastrioti "Skanderbeg" **Obv:** Lion of St. Mark right divides denomination, date below **Rev:** Bust right **Designer:** Romagnoli

Date	Mintage	F	VF	XF	Unc	BU
1926R	5,900	BV	200	330	450	—
1926 Fasces	100	—	—	4,200	6,600	—

Note: 90 pieces were reported melted

Date	Mintage	F	VF	XF	Unc	BU
1927V	5,053	BV	180	290	400	—

KM# 20 20 FRANGA ARI

6.4516 g., 0.9000 Gold 0.1867 oz. AGW, 21 mm. **Ruler:** Ahmed Bey Zogu - King Zog I **Subject:** 25th Anniversary of Independence **Obv:** Head right, date below **Rev:** Kings arms, denomination below

Date	Mintage	F	VF	XF	Unc	BU
1937R	2,500	—	225	350	500	—

KM# 22 20 FRANGA ARI

6.4516 g., 0.9000 Gold 0.1867 oz. AGW, 21 mm. **Ruler:** Ahmed Bey Zogu - King Zog I **Subject:** Marriage of King Zog to Countess Geraldine Apponyi, April 27, 1938 **Obv:** Head right, date below **Rev:** Kings arms, denomination below

Date	Mintage	F	VF	XF	Unc	BU
1938R	2,500	—	225	350	500	—

KM# 24 20 FRANGA ARI

6.4516 g., 0.9000 Gold 0.1867 oz. AGW, 21 mm. **Ruler:** Ahmed Bey Zogu - King Zog I **Subject:** 10th Anniversary - Reign of King

Zog **Obv:** Head right, date below **Rev:** Kings arms, denomination below

Date	Mintage	F	VF	XF	Unc	BU
1938R	1,000	—	250	400	600	—

Note: Pieces struck in 1969 from new dies

KM# 25 50 FRANGA ARI

16.1290 g., 0.9000 Gold 0.4667 oz. AGW **Ruler:** Ahmed Bey Zogu - King Zog I **Subject:** 10th Anniversary - Reign of King Zog **Obv:** Head right, date below **Rev:** Kings Arms, denomination below

Date	Mintage	F	VF	XF	Unc	BU
1938R	600	—	600	900	1,650	—

Note: Pieces struck in 1969 from new dies

KM# 11.1 100 FRANGA ARI

32.2580 g., 0.9000 Gold 0.9334 oz. AGW, 35 mm. **Ruler:** Ahmed Bey Zogu - King Zog I **Obv:** Head left **Rev:** Biga right, denomination below **Designer:** Giuseppe Romagnoli

Date	Mintage	F	VF	XF	Unc	BU
1926R	6,614	—	900	1,100	1,650	—

Note: Mintage figures includes provas, Pr7-9

KM# 11.2 100 FRANGA ARI

32.2580 g., 0.9000 Gold 0.9334 oz. AGW, 35 mm. **Ruler:** Ahmed Bey Zogu - King Zog I **Obv:** Head left, star below **Rev:** Biga right, denomination below **Designer:** Giuseppe Romagnoli

Date	Mintage	F	VF	XF	Unc	BU
1926R	Inc. above	—	925	1,150	1,750	—

KM# 11.3 100 FRANGA ARI

32.2580 g., 0.9000 Gold 0.9334 oz. AGW, 35 mm. **Ruler:** Ahmed Bey Zogu - King Zog I **Obv:** Head left, two stars below **Rev:** Biga right, denomination below **Designer:** Romagnoli

Date	Mintage	F	VF	XF	Unc	BU
1926R	Inc. above	—	925	1,150	1,750	—

KM# 11a.1 100 FRANGA ARI

32.2580 g., 0.9000 Gold 0.9334 oz. AGW, 35 mm. **Ruler:** Ahmed Bey Zogu - King Zog I **Obv:** Head left **Rev:** Biga right, denomination below **Designer:** Romagnoli

Date	Mintage	F	VF	XF	Unc	BU
1927R	5,000	—	900	1,000	1,450	—

Note: Mintage figure includes provas, Pr17-19

KM# 11a.2 100 FRANGA ARI

32.2580 g., 0.9000 Gold 0.9334 oz. AGW **Ruler:** Ahmed Bey Zogu - King Zog I **Obv:** Head left, star below **Rev:** Biga right, denomination below

Date	Mintage	F	VF	XF	Unc	BU
1927R	Inc. above	—	950	1,150	2,000	—

KM# 11a.3 100 FRANGA ARI

32.2580 g., 0.9000 Gold 0.9334 oz. AGW **Ruler:** Ahmed Bey Zogu - King Zog I **Obv:** Head left, two stars below **Rev:** Biga right, denomination below

Date	Mintage	F	VF	XF	Unc	BU
1927R	Inc. above	—	950	1,150	2,000	—

KM# 21 100 FRANGA ARI

32.2580 g., 0.9000 Gold 0.9334 oz. AGW, 35 mm. **Ruler:** Ahmed Bey Zogu - King Zog I **Subject:** 25th Anniversary of Independence **Obv:** Head right, date below **Rev:** Kings arms divide denomination below

Date	Mintage	F	VF	XF	Unc	BU
1937R	500	—	1,000	1,600	2,350	—

KM# 23 100 FRANGA ARI

32.2580 g., 0.9000 Gold 0.9334 oz. AGW, 35 mm. **Ruler:** Ahmed Bey Zogu - King Zog I **Subject:** Marriage of King Zog to Countess Geraldine Apponyi, April 27, 1938 **Obv:** Head right, date below **Rev:** Kings Arms divide denomination below

Date	Mintage	F	VF	XF	Unc	BU
1938R	500	—	1,000	1,600	2,350	—

KM# 26 100 FRANGA ARI

32.2580 g., 0.9000 Gold 0.9334 oz. AGW, 35 mm. **Ruler:** Ahmed Bey Zogu - King Zog I **Subject:** 10th Anniversary - Reign of King Zog **Obv:** Head right, date below **Rev:** Kings Arms divide denomination below

Date	Mintage	F	VF	XF	Unc	BU
1938R	500	—	1,000	1,600	2,350	—

Note: Pieces restruck in 1969 from new dies

ITALIAN OCCUPATION WWII

STANDARD COINAGE

KM# 27 0.05 LEK

Aluminum-Bronze **Ruler:** Vittorio Emanuele III **Obv:** Head right **Rev:** Value below oak branch **Designer:** Romagnoli

Date	Mintage	F	VF	XF	Unc	BU
1940R	1,400,000	3.00	6.00	16.00	32.00	—
1941R Rare	200,000	100	150	330	570	—

KM# 28 0.10 LEK

Aluminum-Bronze **Ruler:** Vittorio Emanuele III **Obv:** Head left **Rev:** Value below olive branch **Designer:** Romagnoli

Date	Mintage	F	VF	XF	Unc	BU
1940R	550,000	4.00	8.00	20.00	35.00	—
1941R	250,000	18.00	50.00	100	170	—

KM# 29 0.20 LEK

4.0000 g., Stainless Steel, 21.7 mm. **Ruler:** Vittorio Emanuele III **Obv:** Helmeted head right **Rev:** Double eagle between columns, value below **Designer:** Romagnoli

Date	Mintage	F	VF	XF	Unc	BU
1939R	900,000	1.00	4.00	8.00	14.00	—

Note: 1939 dated coins exist in 2 varieties, magnetic and non-magnetic

Date	Mintage	F	VF	XF	Unc	BU
1940R	700,000	1.00	2.00	6.00	16.00	—
1941R	1,400,000	1.00	2.00	4.00	12.00	—

KM# 30 0.50 LEK

Stainless Steel **Ruler:** Vittorio Emanuele III **Obv:** Helmeted head left **Rev:** Double eagle between columns, value below **Designer:** Romagnoli

Date	Mintage	F	VF	XF	Unc	BU
1939R	100,000	1.50	4.00	10.00	28.00	—

Note: 1939 dated coins exist in two varieties, magnetic and non-magnetic

Date	Mintage	F	VF	XF	Unc	BU
1940R	500,000	1.50	3.00	6.00	16.00	—
1941R	—	1.50	3.00	7.00	18.00	—

KM# 31 LEK

Stainless Steel **Ruler:** Vittorio Emanuele III **Obv:** Helmeted head right **Rev:** Double eagle between columns, value below **Designer:** Romagnoli **Note:** Coins dated after 1939 were not struck for circulation.

Date	Mintage	F	VF	XF	Unc	BU
1939R	2,100,000	1.50	2.50	5.00	15.00	—

Note: 1939 dated coins exist in two varieties, magnetic and non-magnetic

Date	Mintage	F	VF	XF	Unc	BU
1940R Rare	1,500,000	—	—	—	—	—

Note: The official mintage figure is large, but few examples are known

Date	Mintage	F	VF	XF	Unc	BU
1941R Rare	1,000,000	—	—	—	—	—

Note: The official mintage figure is large, but few examples are known

KM# 32 2 LEK

Stainless Steel **Ruler:** Vittorio Emanuele III **Obv:** Helmeted head left **Rev:** Double eagle between columns,value below **Designer:** Romagnoli **Note:** Coins dated after 1939 were not struck for circulation.

Date	Mintage	F	VF	XF	Unc	BU
1939R	1,300,000	2.00	4.00	9.00	20.00	—

Note: 1939 dated coins exist in 2 varieties, magnetic and non-magnetic

Date	Mintage	F	VF	XF	Unc	BU
1940R Rare	—	—	—	—	—	—
1941R Rare	—	—	—	—	—	—

KM# 33 5 LEK
5.0000 g., 0.8350 Silver 0.1342 oz. ASW **Ruler:** Vittorio Emanuele III **Obv:** Head left **Rev:** Double eagle between columns, value

Date	Mintage	F	VF	XF	Unc	BU
1939R	1,350,000	6.00	12.00	35.00	75.00	—

KM# 34 10 LEK
10.0000 g., 0.8350 Silver 0.2684 oz. ASW **Ruler:** Vittorio Emanuele III **Obv:** Head right **Rev:** Double eagle between columns, value

Date	Mintage	F	VF	XF	Unc	BU
1939R	175,000	40.00	70.00	120	220	—

PEOPLE'S SOCIALIST REPUBLIC
1945 - 1990

STANDARD COINAGE

KM# 39 5 QINDARKA
0.7500 g., Aluminum, 18 mm. **Obv:** National Arms, date below **Rev:** Five stars across top, value in center of wheat

Date	Mintage	F	VF	XF	Unc	BU
1964	—	0.10	0.25	0.50	1.25	1.50

KM# 44 5 QINDARKA
0.8000 g., Aluminum, 18 mm. **Subject:** 25th Anniversary of Liberation **Obv:** National Arms, two dates below **Rev:** Five stars across top, value in center of wheat

Date	Mintage	F	VF	XF	Unc	BU
ND (1969)	—	0.10	0.20	0.30	0.85	1.25

KM# 71 5 QINDARKA
Aluminum **Obv:** National Arms, date below **Rev:** Value between wheat **Edge:** Plain

Date	Mintage	F	VF	XF	Unc	BU
1988	—	—	—	0.20	0.65	1.00

KM# 40 10 QINDARKA
1.0900 g., Aluminum, 17.95 mm. **Obv:** National Arms, date below **Rev:** Five stars across top, value at center between wheat

Date	Mintage	F	VF	XF	Unc	BU
1964	—	0.15	0.30	0.60	1.50	1.75

KM# 45 10 QINDARKA
1.2000 g., Aluminum, 20 mm. **Subject:** 25th Anniversary of Liberation **Obv:** National Arms, two dates **Rev:** Five stars across top, value at center between wheat

Date	Mintage	F	VF	XF	Unc	BU
ND (1969)	—	0.10	0.20	0.35	1.00	1.25

KM# 60 10 QINDARKA
Aluminum, 20 mm. **Obv:** National Arms, date below **Rev:** Value at center between wheat **Edge:** Plain

Date	Mintage	F	VF	XF	Unc	BU
1988	—	—	—	0.30	0.80	1.25

KM# 41 20 QINDARKA
1.5000 g., Aluminum, 22 mm. **Obv:** National Arms, date below **Rev:** Five stars across top, value at center between wheat

Date	Mintage	F	VF	XF	Unc	BU
1964	—	0.20	0.40	0.60	1.75	2.00

KM# 46 20 QINDARKA
1.6000 g., Aluminum, 22 mm. **Subject:** 25th Anniversary of Liberation **Obv:** National Arms, two dates **Rev:** Five stars across top, value at center between wheat

Date	Mintage	F	VF	XF	Unc	BU
ND (1969)	—	0.15	0.30	0.50	1.25	1.50

KM# 65 20 QINDARKA
Aluminum **Obv:** National Arms, date below **Rev:** Value at center between wheat

Date	Mintage	F	VF	XF	Unc	BU
1988	—	—	—	0.20	0.80	1.25

KM# 42 50 QINDARKA
2.0000 g., Aluminum, 24.49 mm. **Obv:** National Arms, date below **Rev:** Five stars across top, value at center between wheat

Date	Mintage	F	VF	XF	Unc	BU
1964	—	0.50	0.75	2.00	4.00	6.00

KM# 47 50 QINDARKA
2.0000 g., Aluminum, 24.4 mm. **Subject:** 25th Anniversary of Liberation **Rev:** Two half-length figures holding torch aloft, value below

Date	Mintage	F	VF	XF	Unc	BU
ND (1969)	—	0.30	0.50	1.00	2.00	3.00

KM# 72 50 QINDARKA
2.0000 g., Aluminum, 24.1 mm. **Obv:** National Arms, date below **Rev:** Value at center between wheat, inside beaded circle **Edge:** Plain

Date	Mintage	F	VF	XF	Unc	BU
1988	—	—	—	0.50	1.40	2.25

KM# 35 1/2 LEKU
Zinc **Obv:** National Arms inside 3/4 circle of stars **Rev:** Value inside circle of stars, date at bottom

Date	Mintage	F	VF	XF	Unc	BU
1947	—	0.40	0.80	2.00	5.00	7.00
1957	—	0.25	0.50	1.00	2.00	3.00

KM# 36 LEK
Zinc **Obv:** National Arms inside 3/4 circle of stars **Rev:** Value inside circle of stars, date at bottom

Date	Mintage	F	VF	XF	Unc	BU
1947	—	0.60	1.00	3.00	6.00	8.00
1957	—	0.35	0.75	1.50	3.00	4.00

KM# 43 LEK
2.3000 g., Aluminum, 26.5 mm. **Obv:** National Arms between stars, date at bottom **Rev:** Five stars across top, value at center of wheat

Date	Mintage	F	VF	XF	Unc	BU
1964	—	0.50	1.00	2.00	4.00	5.50

KM# 48 LEK
2.3000 g., Aluminum, 26.5 mm. **Subject:** 25th Anniversary of Liberation **Obv:** National Arms between stars, two dates at bottom **Rev:** Armed man with knee on man on ground, value below

Date	Mintage	F	VF	XF	Unc	BU
ND (1969)	—	0.35	0.75	1.25	3.00	4.50

KM# 66 LEK
Aluminum-Bronze **Obv:** National Arms inside legend, date below **Rev:** Large value above wheat inside beaded circle

Date	Mintage	F	VF	XF	Unc	BU
1988	—	—	—	0.50	1.80	2.25

KM# 74 LEK
2.0000 g., Aluminum, 24.2 mm. **Obv:** National Arms, date below **Rev:** Large value above wheat inside beaded circle

Date	Mintage	F	VF	XF	Unc	BU
1988	—	—	—	0.40	1.60	2.00

KM# 37 2 LEKE
Zinc **Obv:** National Arms within 3/4 circle of stars, beaded edge **Rev:** Large value at center of circle stars, date below, beaded edge

Date	Mintage	F	VF	XF	Unc	BU
1947	—	0.50	1.25	3.00	6.00	8.00
1957	—	0.35	0.75	1.50	3.00	4.00

KM# 67 2 LEKE
7.6000 g., Copper-Nickel, 26 mm. **Subject:** 45th Anniversary - WWII **Obv:** National Arms, date below **Rev:** Armed man standing inside star, right arm raised, value to right

Date	Mintage	F	VF	XF	Unc	BU
1989	—	—	—	1.00	3.75	5.50

KM# 73 2 LEKE
Copper-Nickel **Obv:** National Arms, date below **Rev:** Large value above wheat within beaded circle **Edge:** Plain

Date	Mintage	F	VF	XF	Unc	BU
1989	—	—	—	1.20	4.00	5.50

KM# 38 5 LEKE
Zinc **Obv:** National Arms within 3/4 circle of stars **Rev:** Large value within circle of stars, date below

Date	Mintage	F	VF	XF	Unc	BU
1947	—	1.00	1.75	4.50	8.00	10.00
1957	—	0.50	1.00	2.00	3.50	5.00

REPUBLIC

STANDARD COINAGE

KM# 75 LEK
3.0000 g., Bronze, 18.1 mm. **Obv:** Pelican **Rev:** Denomination **Edge:** Plain

Date	Mintage	F	VF	XF	Unc	BU
1996	—	—	—	0.40	1.50	2.00

KM# 76 5 LEKE
3.1000 g., Steel, 20 mm. **Obv:** Imperial eagle **Rev:** Olive branch, denomination

Date	Mintage	F	VF	XF	Unc	BU
1995	—	—	—	—	1.00	1.25
2000	—	—	—	—	1.00	1.25

KM# 77 10 LEKE
3.6000 g., Brass, 21.1 mm. **Obv:** Fortress **Rev:** Denomination above sprig with berries

Date	Mintage	F	VF	XF	Unc	BU
1996	—	—	—	—	1.25	1.50
2000	—	—	—	—	1.25	1.50

KM# 93 10 LEKE
3.5400 g., Aluminum-Nickel-Bronze, 21.34 mm. **Subject:** 85th Anniversary Tirana as capital **Obv:** Archaic tomb **Obv. Legend:** SHQIPERI • ALBANIA **Rev:** Outlined bird above value **Edge:** Reeded

Date	Mintage	F	VF	XF	Unc	BU
2005	—	—	—	—	2.00	3.00

KM# 94 10 LEKE
3.6600 g., Aluminum-Nickel-Bronze, 21.40 mm. **Subject:** Culture **Obv:** Ornate vest **Obv. Legend:** SHQIPERI • ALBANIA **Rev:** Ornate value **Rev. Legend:** OBJEKTE TE TRASHEGIMISE KULTURORE **Edge:** Reeded

Date	Mintage	F	VF	XF	Unc	BU
2005	—	—	—	—	2.00	3.00

KM# 78 20 LEKE
4.9000 g., Brass, 23.5 mm. **Obv:** Ancient sailing vessel **Rev:** Denomination

Date	Mintage	F	VF	XF	Unc	BU
1996	—	—	—	—	1.60	2.00
2000	—	—	—	—	1.60	2.00

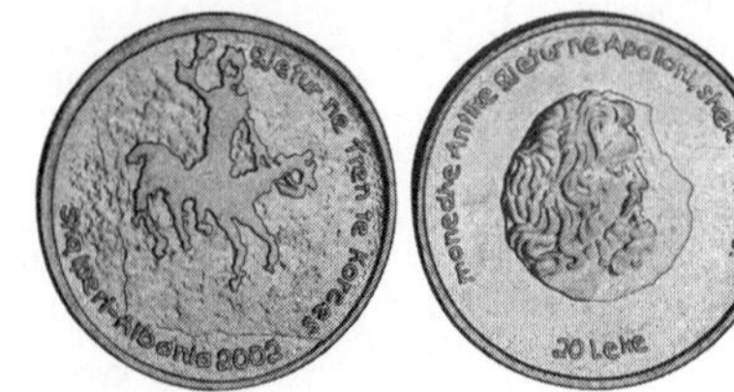

KM# 87 20 LEKE
8.5400 g., Brass, 26.1 mm. **Subject:** Prehistoric art **Obv:** Horseman **Rev:** Ancient coin design with Apollo portrait **Edge:** Reeded

Date	Mintage	F	VF	XF	Unc	BU
2002	—	—	—	—	3.00	4.00

KM# 79 50 LEKE
5.5000 g., Copper-Nickel, 24.5 mm. **Obv:** Ancient equestrian **Rev:** Denomination, tied oak sprigs

Date	Mintage	F	VF	XF	Unc	BU
1996	—	—	—	—	2.00	3.00
2000	—	—	—	—	2.00	3.00

KM# 88 50 LEKE
11.9200 g., Brass, 28.1 mm. **Obv:** Value within circle **Rev:** Bust facing, dates below **Edge:** Reeded

Date	Mintage	F	VF	XF	Unc	BU
2002	—	—	—	—	3.00	4.00

KM# 89 50 LEKE
11.8400 g., Brass, 28 mm. **Obv:** Bust 3/4 facing, dates below, circle surrounds **Rev:** Value within box within circle **Edge:** Plain

Date	Mintage	F	VF	XF	Unc	BU
2003	—	—	—	—	3.00	4.00

KM# 86 50 LEKE
5.4600 g., Copper-Nickel, 24.2 mm. **Obv:** Value and legend **Rev:** Ancient Illyrian helmet **Edge:** Reeded

Date	Mintage	F	VF	XF	Unc	BU
2003 (2004)	200,000	—	—	—	6.00	7.50

KM# 90 50 LEKE
5.5000 g., Copper-Nickel, 24.2 mm. **Obv:** Wheel design **Rev:** Ancient bust above value within circle **Edge:** Reeded

Date	Mintage	F	VF	XF	Unc	BU
2004	—	—	—	—	3.00	4.00

KM# 91 50 LEKE
5.5000 g., Copper-Nickel, 24.2 mm. **Obv:** Soldier within circle **Rev:** Value within circle **Edge:** Reeded

Date	Mintage	F	VF	XF	Unc	BU
2004	—	—	—	—	3.00	4.00

KM# 80 100 LEKE

6.7000 g., Bi-Metallic Aluminum-Bronze center in Copper-Nickel ring, 24.7 mm. **Obv:** Teuta, Illyrian queen, stateswoman, reigned 231 BC **Rev:** Denomination in wreath. **Edge:** Reeded

Date	Mintage	F	VF	XF	Unc	BU
2000	—	—	—	—	4.00	5.00

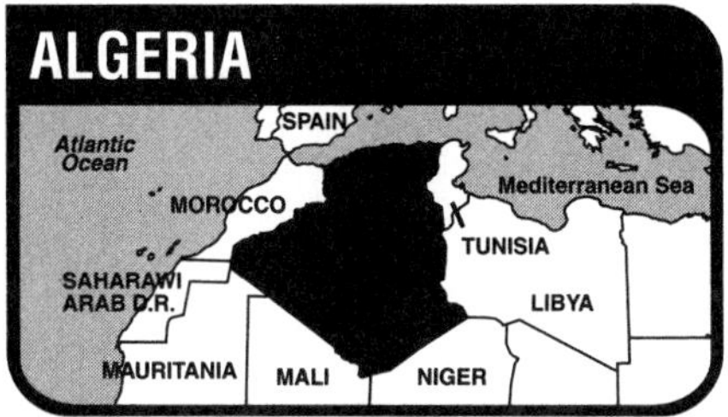

The Democratic and Popular Republic of Algeria, a North African country fronting on the Mediterranean Sea between Tunisia and Morocco, has an area of 919,595 sq. mi. (2,381,740 sq. km.) and a population of 31.6 million. Capital: Algiers (Alger). Most of the country's working population is engaged in agriculture although a recent industrial diversification, financed by oil revenues, is making steady progress. Wines, fruits, iron and zinc ores, phosphates, tobacco products, liquified natural gas, and petroleum are exported.

Following the armistice signed by France and Nazi Germany on June 22, 1940, Algeria fell under Vichy Government control until liberated by the Allied invasion forces under the command of Gen. D. D. Eisenhower on Nov. 8, 1942. The inability to obtain equal rights with Frenchmen led to an organized revolt which began on Nov. 1, 1954 and lasted until a ceasefire was signed on July l, 1962. Independence was proclaimed on July 5, 1962, following a self-determination referendum, and the Republic was declared on September 25, 1962.

MINT MARK

(a) – Paris, privy marks only

MONETARY SYSTEM

100 Centimes = 1 Franc

FRENCH OCCUPATION

COLONIAL COINAGE

KM# 91 20 FRANCS

Copper-Nickel **Obv:** Head with laureled hood, right **Rev:** Value between columns of wheat, date at center **Designer:** P. Turin

Date	Mintage	F	VF	XF	Unc	BU
1949(a)	25,556,000	1.00	2.00	5.00	10.00	—
1956(a)	7,500,000	1.00	2.50	6.00	12.50	—

KM# 92 50 FRANCS

Copper-Nickel **Obv:** Man with laureled hood, right **Rev:** Value between columns of wheat, date below **Designer:** P. Turin

Date	Mintage	F	VF	XF	Unc	BU
1949(a)	18,000,000	1.50	3.00	9.00	18.00	—

KM# 93 100 FRANCS

Copper-Nickel, 29.8 mm. **Obv:** Man with laureled hood. right **Rev:** Value between wheat columns, date below **Edge:** Reeded **Designer:** P. Turin **Note:** During World War II homeland coins were struck at the Paris Mint and the French 2 Francs, Y#89 were struck at the Philadelphia Mint for use in French African Territories.

Date	Mintage	F	VF	XF	Unc	BU
1950(a)	22,189,000	1.50	3.00	10.00	20.00	—
1952(a)	12,000,000	2.00	4.00	12.00	25.00	—

REPUBLIC

MONETARY SYSTEM

100 Centimes = 1 Dinar

STANDARD COINAGE

KM# 94 CENTIME

Aluminum, 11.5 mm. **Obv:** Small arms within wreath **Rev:** Value at center of scalloped circle **Edge:** Plain

Date	Mintage	F	VF	XF	Unc	BU
AH1383-1964	35,000,000	—	0.20	0.40	1.00	2.00

KM# 95 2 CENTIMES

0.6000 g., Aluminum, 18.3 mm. **Obv:** Arms within wreath **Rev:** Value at center of scalloped circle **Edge:** Plain

Date	Mintage	F	VF	XF	Unc	BU
AH1383-1964	50,000,000	—	0.20	0.40	1.00	2.00

KM# 96 5 CENTIMES

0.8500 g., Aluminum, 21.1 mm. **Obv:** Arms within wreath **Rev:** Value at center of scalloped circle

Date	Mintage	F	VF	XF	Unc	BU
AH1383-1964	40,000,000	—	0.25	0.45	1.25	2.50

KM# 101 5 CENTIMES

Aluminum **Series:** F.A.O. **Subject:** 1st Four Year Plan **Obv:** Value at center **Rev:** Two dates center of circle, circle consists of gear teeth on left, sprays of grain on right **Note:** Varieties exist.

Date	Mintage	F	VF	XF	Unc	BU
ND(1970)	50,000,000	—	0.15	0.30	0.75	—

KM# 106 5 CENTIMES

Aluminum **Series:** F.A.O. **Subject:** 2nd Four Year Plan **Obv:** Large value at center **Rev:** Two dates at center of circle, circle consists of gear teeth on left, sprays of grain on right

Date	Mintage	F	VF	XF	Unc	BU
ND(1974)	10,000,000	—	0.15	0.30	0.75	1.50

KM# 113 5 CENTIMES

Aluminum **Series:** F.A.O. **Subject:** 1st Five Year Plan **Obv:** Large value at center **Rev:** Inscription within circle of gear teeth on left, grain spray on right

Date	Mintage	F	VF	XF	Unc	BU
ND(1980)	—	2.00	5.00	12.00	25.00	—

KM# 116 5 CENTIMES

Aluminum **Series:** F.A.O. **Subject:** 2nd Five Year Plan **Obv:** Large value at center **Rev:** Two dates center of circle, circle consists of geared teeth on right, sprays of grain on left **Note:** Varieties exist in planchet thickness.

Date	Mintage	F	VF	XF	Unc	BU
ND(1985)	—	—	0.10	0.25	0.70	1.50

KM# 97 10 CENTIMES

Aluminum-Bronze **Obv:** Small arms within wreath **Rev:** Value in circle

Date	Mintage	F	VF	XF	Unc	BU
AH1383-1964	—	—	0.25	0.75	2.00	3.00

KM# 115 10 CENTIMES

Aluminum **Obv:** Large value in circle **Rev:** Palm tree flanked by rosettes, date below tree **Note:** Varieties exist.

Date	Mintage	F	VF	XF	Unc	BU
1984	—	0.15	0.25	0.75	3.00	4.00

KM# 98 20 CENTIMES

Aluminum-Bronze **Obv:** Arms within wreath **Rev:** Value in circle

Date	Mintage	F	VF	XF	Unc	BU
AH1383-1964	—	—	0.25	0.75	2.00	3.00

KM# 103 20 CENTIMES

Brass **Series:** F.A.O. **Subject:** Agricultural Revolution **Obv:** Value in circle **Rev:** Cornucopeia, date above **Designer:** Mohamed Temmam

Date	Mintage	F	VF	XF	Unc	BU
1972	20,000,000	—	0.10	0.25	0.75	1.25

KM# 107.1 20 CENTIMES
Aluminum-Bronze **Series:** F.A.O. **Obv:** Value at center of circle **Rev:** Rams head left, date below

Date	Mintage	F	VF	XF	Unc	BU
1975	50,000,000	—	0.20	0.45	1.75	2.00

KM# 107.2 20 CENTIMES
Aluminum-Bronze **Series:** F.A.O. **Obv:** Small flower above 20 **Rev:** Rams head left, date below

Date	Mintage	F	VF	XF	Unc	BU
1975	Inc. above	—	0.15	0.30	1.50	2.00

KM# 118 20 CENTIMES
Aluminum-Bronze **Series:** F.A.O. **Obv:** Value in circle **Rev:** Rams head left, date below

Date	Mintage	F	VF	XF	Unc	BU
1987	60,000,000	0.50	1.00	2.00	8.00	12.00

KM# 99 50 CENTIMES
Aluminum-Bronze **Obv:** Arms within wreath **Rev:** Value in circle

Date	Mintage	F	VF	XF	Unc	BU
AH1383-1964	—	—	0.25	0.75	2.00	3.50

KM# 102 50 CENTIMES
Copper-Nickel-Zinc **Obv:** Book, divider on top, bottle at bottom **Rev:** Value in circle **Edge:** Reeded

Date	Mintage	F	VF	XF	Unc	BU
AH1391-1971(a)	10,000,000	0.25	0.50	1.50	6.00	—
AH1393-1973	10,000,000	0.25	0.50	1.50	6.00	—

KM# 109 50 CENTIMES
5.0000 g., Brass, 24 mm. **Subject:** 30th Anniversary French-Algerian Clash **Obv:** Value in circle **Rev:** Inscription

Date	Mintage	F	VF	XF	Unc	BU
ND(1975)	18,000,000	—	0.20	0.50	2.00	—

KM# 111 50 CENTIMES
Aluminum-Bronze **Subject:** 1400th Anniversary of Mohammad's Flight **Obv:** Value in circle **Rev:** Value, outline of Mosque

Date	Mintage	F	VF	XF	Unc	BU
AH1400-1980	—	0.15	0.25	0.50	2.50	4.50

KM# 119 50 CENTIMES
Aluminum-Bronze **Subject:** 25th Anniversary of Constitution **Obv:** Value in circle **Rev:** Stylized design

Date	Mintage	F	VF	XF	Unc	BU
1988	40,000,000	0.15	0.25	0.75	3.00	6.00

KM# 127 1/4 DINAR
1.1500 g., Aluminum **Subject:** Fennec Fox **Obv:** Value in small circle **Rev:** Head facing

Date	Mintage	F	VF	XF	Unc	BU
1992-AH1413	—	—	0.65	1.25	2.50	3.00
1992-AH1413 Proof	—	Value: 12.00				
1998-AH1418	—	—	0.65	1.25	2.50	3.00
2003-AH1423	—	—	1.50	3.00	4.50	5.50

KM# 128 1/2 DINAR
Steel **Subject:** Barbary Horse **Obv:** Value in small circle **Rev:** Encirled Barbary horse head dividing date at top, facing 3/4 left

Date	Mintage	F	VF	XF	Unc	BU
AH1413-1992	—	—	0.65	1.25	3.00	3.50
AH1413-1992 Proof	—	Value: 12.00				

KM# 100 DINAR
Copper-Nickel **Obv:** Large arms within wreath **Rev:** Large value in circle

Date	Mintage	F	VF	XF	Unc	BU
AH1383-1964	15,000,000	0.25	0.50	1.00	4.00	—
AH1383-1964 Proof	—	Value: 40.00				

KM# 104.1 DINAR
Copper-Nickel **Series:** F.A.O. **Obv:** Large value in circle **Rev:** Hands grasped at top, man on tractor facing flanked by sprigs, date below **Designer:** Mohamed Temmam

Date	Mintage	F	VF	XF	Unc	BU
1972	20,000,000	0.25	0.50	1.00	2.50	3.50

KM# 104.2 DINAR
Copper-Nickel **Obv:** Legend touches inner circle **Designer:** Mohamed Temmam

Date	Mintage	F	VF	XF	Unc	BU
1972	Inc. above	0.20	0.45	0.85	2.00	3.00

KM# 112 DINAR
Copper-Nickel **Subject:** 20th Anniversary of Independence **Obv:** Large value in circle **Rev:** Circle of hands

Date	Mintage	F	VF	XF	Unc	BU
ND(1983)	—	0.35	0.75	1.50	4.50	6.50

KM# 117 DINAR
Copper-Nickel **Subject:** 25th Anniversary of Independence - Monument **Obv:** Large value in circle **Rev:** Monument within grain wreath

Date	Mintage	F	VF	XF	Unc	BU
1987	—	0.35	0.75	1.50	4.00	6.00

KM# 129 DINAR
4.2400 g., Steel **Subject:** Buffalo **Obv:** Value on silhouette of country, within circle **Rev:** Prehistoric head 3/4 facing, ancient drawings back of horns

Date	Mintage	F	VF	XF	Unc	BU
AH1413-1992	—	—	1.00	2.00	4.00	6.00
AH1413-1992 Proof	—	Value: 15.00				
AH1417-1997	—	—	—	2.00	4.00	6.00
AH1419-1999	—	—	1.00	2.00	4.00	6.00
AH1420-2000	—	—	1.00	2.00	4.00	6.00
AH1421 -2000	—	—	1.00	2.00	3.50	5.50
AH1422-2002	—	—	1.00	2.00	3.50	5.50
AH1423-2003	—	—	1.00	2.00	3.50	5.50
AH1424-2004	—	—	1.00	2.00	3.50	5.50
AH1426-2005	—	—	1.00	2.00	3.50	5.50
AH1427-2006	—	—	1.00	2.00	3.50	5.50
AH1428-2007	—	—	1.00	2.00	3.50	5.50

KM# 130 2 DINARS
5.1300 g., Steel, 22.5 mm. **Subject:** Camel **Obv:** Value on silhouette of country **Rev:** Head right

Date	Mintage	F	VF	XF	Unc	BU
AH1413-1992	—	—	1.00	2.50	5.00	6.50
AH1413-1992 Proof	—	Value: 18.00				
AH1414-1993	—	—	1.00	2.50	5.00	6.50
AH1417-1996	—	—	—	—	—	—
AH1417-1997	—	—	1.00	2.50	5.00	6.50
AH1419-1999	—	—	1.00	2.50	5.00	6.50
AH1422-2002	—	—	1.00	2.00	4.00	6.00
AH1423-2002	—	—	1.00	2.00	4.00	6.00
AH1424-2003	—	—	1.00	2.00	4.00	6.00
AH1424-2004	—	—	1.00	2.00	4.00	6.00
AH1426-2005	—	—	1.00	2.00	4.00	6.00
AH1427-2006	—	—	1.00	2.00	4.00	6.00
AH1428-2007	—	—	1.00	2.00	4.00	6.00

KM# 105 5 DINARS

12.0000 g., 0.7500 Silver 0.2893 oz. ASW, 31 mm. **Series:** F.A.O. **Subject:** 10th Anniversary **Obv:** Large value flanked by small flowers within circle **Rev:** Tower with grain head at base dividing dates at bottom, Five stars flanking **Note:** Privy mark: owl.

Date	Mintage	F	VF	XF	Unc	BU
ND(1972)(a)	5,000,000	—	6.00	10.00	16.50	—

KM# 105a.1 5 DINARS

Nickel, 31 mm. **Edge:** Reeded

Date	Mintage	F	VF	XF	Unc	BU
ND(1972)(a)	10,000,000	—	4.00	8.00	14.50	—

KM# 105a.2 5 DINARS

Nickel, 31 mm. **Note:** Privy mark: dolphin.

Date	Mintage	F	VF	XF	Unc	BU
ND(1972)(a)	10,000,000	—	4.00	8.00	14.50	—

KM# 108 5 DINARS

Nickel, 31 mm. **Subject:** 20th Anniversary of Revolution **Obv:** Large value in circle flanked by rosettes **Rev:** Armed revolutionary man leaning, right, two dates lower right

Date	Mintage	F	VF	XF	Unc	BU
ND(1974)(a)	—	—	3.50	7.00	12.50	—

KM# 114 5 DINARS

Nickel **Subject:** 30th Anniversary of Revolution **Obv:** Value flanked by small rosettes in circle **Rev:** Hands holding symbol, flanked by dates divided by stars

Date	Mintage	F	VF	XF	Unc	BU
ND(1984)	—	—	2.50	5.00	10.00	—

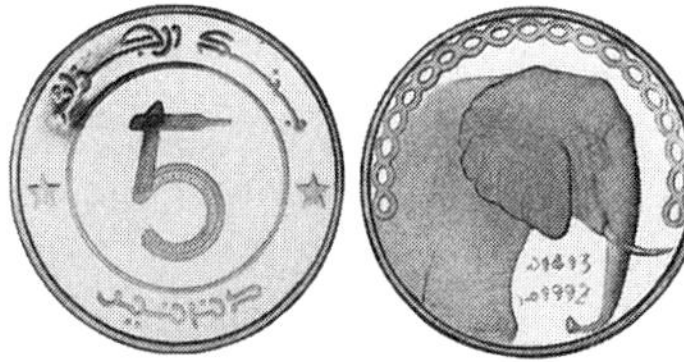

KM# 123 5 DINARS

6.2000 g., Steel **Subject:** Elephant **Obv:** Denomination within circle **Rev:** Head right

Date	Mintage	F	VF	XF	Unc	BU
AH1413-1992	—	—	1.50	3.50	7.00	10.00
AH1413-1992 Proof	—	Value: 20.00				
AH1414-1993	—	—	1.50	3.50	7.00	10.00
AH1418-1997	—	—	1.50	3.50	7.00	10.00
AH1417-1997	—	—	1.50	3.50	7.00	10.00
AH1418-1998	—	—	1.50	3.50	7.00	10.00
AH1419-1998	—	—	1.50	3.50	7.00	10.00
AH1420-1999	—	—	1.50	3.50	7.00	10.00
AH1420-2000	—	—	1.50	3.50	7.00	10.00
AH1422-2003	—	—	1.50	3.50	6.50	9.50
AH1423-2003	—	—	1.50	3.50	6.50	9.50
AH1424-2004	—	—	1.50	3.50	6.50	9.50
AH1426-2005	—	—	1.00	3.00	5.50	8.00
AH1426-2006	—	—	1.00	3.50	6.50	9.50
AH1427-2006	—	—	1.00	3.00	5.50	8.00
AH1428-2007	—	—	1.00	3.00	5.50	8.00

KM# 110 10 DINARS

11.3700 g., Aluminum-Bronze **Obv:** Inscription within circle, wreath surrounds **Rev:** Large value within circle, date above **Shape:** 10-sided

Date	Mintage	F	VF	XF	Unc	BU
1979	25,001,000	—	2.00	4.00	8.00	—
1981(a)	40,000,000	—	2.00	4.00	8.00	—

KM# 124 10 DINARS

4.9500 g., Bi-Metallic Aluminum center in Steel ring, 26.5 mm. **Subject:** Falcon **Obv:** Denomination **Rev:** Head right

Date	Mintage	F	VF	XF	Unc	BU
AH1413-1992	—	—	2.00	4.50	10.00	—
AH1413-1992 Proof	—	—	—	—	—	—
AH1414-1993	—	—	2.00	4.50	10.00	—
AH1418-1997	—	—	2.00	4.50	10.00	—
AH1423-2002	—	—	1.75	4.00	9.00	—
AH1425-2004	—	—	1.75	4.00	9.00	—
AH1427-2006	—	—	—	4.00	9.00	—

KM# 125 20 DINARS

8.6200 g., Bi-Metallic Brass center in Steel ring, 27.5 mm. **Subject:** Lion **Obv:** Denomination **Rev:** Head left

Date	Mintage	F	VF	XF	Unc	BU
AH1413-1992	—	—	3.00	6.00	12.50	—
AH1413-1992 Proof	—	—	—	—	—	—
AH1414-1993	—	—	3.00	6.00	12.50	—
AH1416-1996	—	—	3.00	6.00	12.50	—
AH1417-1996	—	—	3.00	6.00	12.50	—
AH1417-1997	—	—	3.00	6.00	12.50	—
AH1418-1997	—	—	3.00	6.00	12.50	—
AH1420-1999	—	—	3.00	6.00	12.50	—
AH1421-2000	—	—	3.00	6.00	12.50	—
AH1424-2004	—	—	3.00	6.00	12.00	—
AH1426-2005	—	—	—	6.00	12.00	—
AH1428-2007	—	—	—	6.00	12.00	—

KM# 126 50 DINARS

9.2700 g., Bi-Metallic Steel center in Brass ring, 28.5 mm. **Subject:** Gazelle **Obv:** Denomination **Rev:** Head left

Date	Mintage	F	VF	XF	Unc	BU
AH1413-1992	—	—	4.00	8.00	15.00	—
AH1413-1992 Proof	—	Value: 35.00				
AH1414-1993	—	—	4.00	8.00	15.00	—
AH1416-1996	—	—	4.00	8.00	15.00	—
AH1417-1996	—	—	4.00	8.00	15.00	—
AH1414-1996	—	—	4.00	8.00	15.00	—
AH1418-1998	—	—	4.00	8.00	15.00	—
AH1419-1999	—	—	4.00	8.00	15.00	—
AH1420-1999	—	—	4.00	8.00	15.00	—
AH1424-2003	—	—	4.00	8.00	16.50	—
AH1425-2004	—	—	4.00	8.00	16.50	—

KM# 131 50 DINARS

9.2600 g., Bi-Metallic Steel center in Brass ring, 28.5 mm. **Subject:** 40th Anniversary - Start of the Revolution **Obv:** Large value in circle **Rev:** Star dividing dates at right in circle

Date	Mintage	F	VF	XF	Unc	BU
ND(1994)	—	—	6.00	10.00	17.50	—
ND(1994) Proof	—	Value: 37.50				

KM# 138 50 DINARS

Bi-Metallic **Rev:** Two men with guns

Date	Mintage	F	VF	XF	Unc	BU
AH1425-2004	—	—	—	—	12.50	15.00

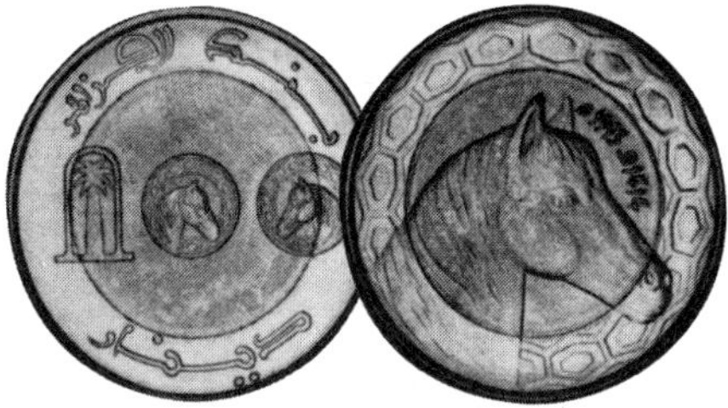

KM# 132 100 DINARS

11.0000 g., Bi-Metallic Aluminum-Bronze center in Stainless Steel ring, 29.5 mm. **Obv:** Denomination stylized with reverse design **Rev:** Horse head right

Date	Mintage	F	VF	XF	Unc	BU
AH1413-1992	—	—	6.00	12.00	20.00	24.00
AH1414-1993	—	—	6.00	12.00	20.00	24.00
AH1415-1994	—	—	6.00	12.00	20.00	24.00
AH1417-1997	—	—	6.00	12.00	20.00	24.00
AH1418-1998	—	—	6.00	12.00	20.00	24.00
AH1421-2000	—	—	6.00	12.00	20.00	24.00
AH1422-2002	—	—	6.00	12.00	20.00	24.00
AH1423-2002	—	—	6.00	12.00	20.00	24.00
AH1425-2004	—	—	6.00	12.00	20.00	24.00

KM# 137 100 DINARS

11.0000 g., Bi-Metallic Brass center in Stainless Steel ring, 29.5 mm. **Subject:** 40th Anniversary of Independence **Obv:** Stylized value **Rev:** Number 40 and stylized face **Edge:** Reeded

Date	Mintage	F	VF	XF	Unc	BU
AH1422-2002	—	—	—	—	25.00	27.50

ANGOLA

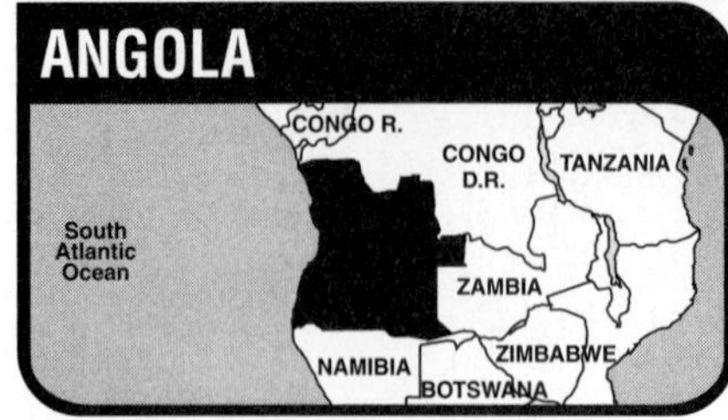

The Republic of Angola, a country on the west coast of southern Africa bounded by Congo Democratic Republic, Zambia, and Namibia (Southwest Africa), has an area of 481,351 sq. mi. (1,246,700 sq. km.) and a population of 12.78 million, predominantly Bantu in origin. Capital: Luanda. Most of the people are engaged in subsistence agriculture. However, important oil and mineral deposits make Angola potentially one of the richest countries in Africa. Iron and diamonds are exported.

The Portuguese navigator, Diogo Cao, discovered Angola in 1482 Angola. Portuguese settlers arrived in 1491, and established Angola as a major slaving center, which sent about 3 million slaves to the New World.

A revolt, characterized by guerrilla warfare, against Portuguese rule began in 1961 and continued until 1974, when a new regime in Portugal offered independence. The independence movement was actively supported by three groups; the National Front, based in Zaire, the Soviet-backed Popular Movement, and the moderate National Union. Independence was proclaimed on Nov. 11, 1975, and the Portuguese departed, leaving the Angolan people to work out their own political destiny. Within hours, each of the independence groups proclaimed itself Angola's sole ruler. A bloody intertribal civil war erupted in which the Communist Popular Movement, assisted by Soviet arms and Cuban mercenaries, was the eventual victor.

RULER
Portuguese until 1975

MINT MARK
KN - King's Norton

PORTUGUESE COLONY

DECIMAL COINAGE

Commencing 1910

100 Centavos = 20 Macutas = 1 Escudo

100 Centavos = 1 Escudo

KM# 60 CENTAVO

Bronze **Obv:** Value **Rev:** Arms, date below

Date	Mintage	F	VF	XF	Unc	BU
1921	1,360,000	7.50	20.00	60.00	125	170

KM# 61 2 CENTAVOS

Bronze **Obv:** Value **Rev:** Arms, date below

Date	Mintage	F	VF	XF	Unc	BU
1921	530,000	10.00	15.00	60.00	135	—

KM# 62 5 CENTAVOS

Bronze **Obv:** Value **Rev:** Arms, date below

Date	Mintage	F	VF	XF	Unc	BU
1921	720,000	5.00	18.00	45.00	80.00	—
1922	5,680,000	4.00	14.00	30.00	55.00	90.00
1923	5,840,000	4.00	14.00	30.00	55.00	90.00
1924	—	12.00	35.00	70.00	140	—

KM# 66 5 CENTAVOS (1 Macuta)

Nickel-Bronze **Obv:** Head left **Rev:** Arms, value below

Date	Mintage	F	VF	XF	Unc	BU
1927	2,001,999	2.50	6.00	15.00	27.50	—

KM# 63 10 CENTAVOS

Copper-Nickel **Obv:** Value **Rev:** Head, left

Date	Mintage	F	VF	XF	Unc	BU
1921	160,000	10.00	30.00	65.00	120	—
1922	340,000	7.50	15.00	45.00	85.00	175
1923	2,960,000	3.50	8.00	20.00	45.00	115

KM# 70 10 CENTAVOS

Bronze, 17.8 mm. **Subject:** 300th Anniversary - Revolution of 1648 **Obv:** Value **Rev:** Five crowns above arms, date below **Edge:** Plain

Date	Mintage	F	VF	XF	Unc	BU
1948	10,000,000	0.50	1.00	3.50	7.50	10.00
1949	10,000,000	0.35	0.75	3.00	6.50	9.00

KM# 82 10 CENTAVOS

Aluminum **Obv:** Value **Rev:** Five crowns above arms, date below

Date	Mintage	F	VF	XF	Unc	BU
1974	4,000,000	—	—	—	17.50	22.00

Note: Not released for circulation, but relatively available

KM# 67 10 CENTAVOS (2 Macutas)

Copper-Nickel **Obv:** Head, left **Rev:** Arms, value below

Date	Mintage	F	VF	XF	Unc	BU
1927	2,003,000	2.00	4.00	16.00	32.00	—
1928	1,000,000	2.00	4.00	16.00	32.00	45.00

KM# 64 20 CENTAVOS

Copper-Nickel **Obv:** Value **Rev:** Head left

Date	Mintage	F	VF	XF	Unc	BU
1921	2,115,000	4.00	9.00	22.00	40.00	100
1922	1,730,000	6.50	14.50	35.00	65.00	—

KM# 71 20 CENTAVOS

2.8400 g., Bronze, 20.5 mm. **Subject:** 300th Anniversary - Revolution of 1648 **Obv:** Value **Rev:** Five crowns above arms, date below **Edge:** Plain

Date	Mintage	F	VF	XF	Unc	BU
1948	7,850,000	0.50	1.00	2.00	4.50	25.00
1949	2,150,000	10.00	30.00	60.00	100	140

KM# 78 20 CENTAVOS

Bronze, 18.2 mm. **Obv:** Value **Rev:** Five crowns above arms, date below **Edge:** Plain

Date	Mintage	F	VF	XF	Unc	BU
1962	3,000,000	—	0.25	0.65	1.75	—

KM# 68 20 CENTAVOS (4 Macutas)

Copper-Nickel **Obv:** Laureled head, left **Rev:** Arms, value below

Date	Mintage	F	VF	XF	Unc	BU
1927	2,001,000	2.50	4.00	12.00	25.00	—
1928	500,000	3.50	6.00	20.00	35.00	50.00

KM# 65 50 CENTAVOS

Nickel **Obv:** Head left, date below **Rev:** Arms, value in legend

Date	Mintage	F	VF	XF	Unc	BU
1922	6,000,000	3.00	10.00	25.00	40.00	—
1923	6,000,000	3.00	10.00	25.00	40.00	—
1923 KN	Inc. above	—	—	225	375	—

Note: Not released for circulation

KM# 69 50 CENTAVOS

Nickel-Bronze **Obv:** Laureled, hooded bust with long hair, left **Rev:** Arms, value below

Date	Mintage	F	VF	XF	Unc	BU
1927	1,608,000	5.00	18.00	35.00	70.00	—
1928/7	1,600,000	5.00	18.00	40.00	75.00	—
1928	Inc. above	3.50	12.50	30.00	65.00	—

KM# 72 50 CENTAVOS

Nickel-Bronze **Subject:** 300th Anniversary - Revolution of 1648 **Obv:** Value **Rev:** Five crowns above arms, date below

Date	Mintage	F	VF	XF	Unc	BU
1948	4,000,000	0.50	1.00	5.00	12.00	27.50
1950	4,000,000	0.50	1.00	5.00	12.00	27.50

KM# 75 50 CENTAVOS

4.0700 g., Bronze, 20 mm. **Obv:** Value **Rev:** Five crowns above arms, date below **Edge:** Plain

Date	Mintage	F	VF	XF	Unc	BU
1953	5,000,000	—	0.25	0.65	2.50	6.00
1954	11,731,000	—	0.20	0.40	1.75	4.50

Date	Mintage	F	VF	XF	Unc	BU
1955 Rare	1,126,000	—	3.00	10.00	40.00	85.00
1957	8,873,000	—	0.20	0.45	2.00	4.50
1958	17,520,000	—	0.15	0.35	1.50	4.00
1961	8,750,000	—	0.20	0.45	2.00	4.50

KM# 76 ESCUDO

8.0200 g., Bronze, 26 mm. **Obv:** Value **Rev:** Five crowns above arms, date below

Date	Mintage	F	VF	XF	Unc	BU
1953	2,001,000	—	1.50	6.00	15.00	—
1956	2,989,000	—	1.00	4.00	10.00	—
1963	5,000,000	—	1.00	2.00	7.00	18.00
1965	5,000,000	—	1.00	2.00	7.00	18.00
1972	10,000,000	—	0.75	1.50	4.50	10.00
1974	6,214,000	—	0.75	1.50	4.50	15.00

KM# 76a ESCUDO

Copper-Nickel **Note:** Not released for circulation.

Date	Mintage	F	VF	XF	Unc	BU
1972 Rare	—	—	—	—	—	—
1974 Rare	—	—	—	—	—	—

KM# 77 2-1/2 ESCUDOS

3.5300 g., Copper-Nickel, 20 mm. **Obv:** Arms, date below **Rev:** Five crowns above arms, value below **Edge:** Reeded

Date	Mintage	F	VF	XF	Unc	BU
1953	6,008,000	—	1.00	7.00	15.00	27.50
1956	9,992,000	—	0.35	2.00	4.00	9.50
1967	6,000,000	—	0.35	2.00	4.00	9.50
1968	5,000,000	—	0.35	2.00	4.00	9.50
1969	5,000,000	—	0.35	2.00	4.00	9.50
1974	19,999,000	—	0.25	1.00	3.00	9.00

KM# 81 5 ESCUDOS

Copper-Nickel **Obv:** Arms, date below **Rev:** Five crowns above arms, value below

Date	Mintage	F	VF	XF	Unc	BU
1972	8,000,000	—	10.00	20.00	45.00	80.00
1974	Est. 3,343,000	—	—	250	450	—

Note: Not released for circulation

KM# 73 10 ESCUDOS

5.0000 g., 0.7200 Silver 0.1157 oz. ASW, 24.0 mm. **Obv:** Arms, date below **Rev:** Five crowns above arms, value below

Date	Mintage	F	VF	XF	Unc	BU
1952	2,023,000	—	2.50	5.00	10.00	20.00
1955	1,977,000	—	2.50	5.00	10.00	20.00

KM# 79 10 ESCUDOS

Copper-Nickel **Obv:** Arms, date below **Rev:** Five crowns above arms, value below

Date	Mintage	F	VF	XF	Unc	BU
1969	3,022,000	—	1.50	3.00	6.00	14.50
1970	978,000	—	2.00	4.00	7.00	18.00

KM# 74 20 ESCUDOS

10.0000 g., 0.7200 Silver 0.2315 oz. ASW **Obv:** Arms, date below **Rev:** Five crowns above arms, value below

Date	Mintage	F	VF	XF	Unc	BU
1952	1,002,999	—	4.75	7.00	14.00	32.50
1955	997,000	—	4.75	6.00	12.00	28.00

KM# 80 20 ESCUDOS

12.0600 g., Nickel **Obv:** Arms on ornate shield, date below **Rev:** Arms, value below

Date	Mintage	F	VF	XF	Unc	BU
1971	1,572,000	—	0.75	2.00	4.00	7.50
1972	428,000	—	2.50	5.00	10.00	30.00

PEOPLES REPUBLIC

DECIMAL COINAGE

1975 - 1998

100 Lwei = 1 Kwanza

KM# 90 50 LWEI

Copper-Nickel **Obv:** National arms **Rev:** Large value, dots near rim

Date	Mintage	F	VF	XF	Unc	BU
ND(1977)	—	—	0.15	0.35	1.25	2.50
1979	—	—	0.10	0.30	1.00	1.50

KM# 83 KWANZA

3.9100 g., Copper-Nickel, 20.9 mm. **Obv:** National arms **Rev:** Large value, dots near rim

Date	Mintage	F	VF	XF	Unc	BU
ND(1977)	—	—	0.30	0.50	1.50	—
1978	—	—	0.25	0.40	1.50	—
1979	—	—	0.25	0.40	1.50	—

KM# 84 2 KWANZAS

5.0000 g., Copper-Nickel, 23.2 mm. **Obv:** National arms **Rev:** Large value, dots near rim

Date	Mintage	F	VF	XF	Unc	BU
ND(1977)	—	—	0.40	0.60	1.75	—

KM# 85 5 KWANZAS

6.9000 g., Copper-Nickel, 25.5 mm. **Obv:** National arms **Rev:** Large value, dots near rim

Date	Mintage	F	VF	XF	Unc	BU
ND(1977)	—	—	0.65	1.25	3.00	—

KM# 86.1 10 KWANZAS

Copper-Nickel **Obv:** National arms **Rev:** Small date, dots near rim, Large value

Date	Mintage	F	VF	XF	Unc	BU
ND(1977)	—	—	1.25	2.00	3.50	—
1978	—	—	1.50	2.50	4.50	—

KM# 86.2 10 KWANZAS

Copper-Nickel **Rev:** Large date, dots away from rim

Date	Mintage	F	VF	XF	Unc	BU
1978	—	—	1.50	2.50	4.50	—

KM# 87 20 KWANZAS

10.0000 g., Copper-Nickel **Obv:** National arms **Rev:** Large value, dots near rim

Date	Mintage	F	VF	XF	Unc	BU
1978	—	—	2.00	3.00	6.00	—

KM# 91 50 KWANZAS

Copper **Obv:** National arms **Rev:** Large value, dots near rim

Date	Mintage	F	VF	XF	Unc	BU
ND(1978)	—	—	2.50	4.50	9.00	—
ND(1991)	—	—	2.50	4.50	9.00	—

KM# 101 50 KWANZAS

Copper Clad Steel, 23.3 mm. **Subject:** 15th Anniversary of the Angolan Kwanza Currency **Obv:** National arms within legend **Rev:** Value above anniversary date "8 Jan. 92" **Edge:** Reeded

Date	Mintage	F	VF	XF	Unc	BU
ND(1992)	—	—	55.00	90.00	—	—

KM# 92 100 KWANZAS

Copper **Obv:** National arms **Rev:** Large value, dots near rim

Date	Mintage	F	VF	XF	Unc	BU
ND(1991)	—	—	3.50	6.50	14.00	—

REFORM COINAGE

1999 -

KM# 95 10 CENTIMOS

1.5000 g., Copper Plated Steel, 15 mm. **Obv:** National arms, country name and date **Rev:** Denomination **Edge:** Plain

Date	Mintage	F	VF	XF	Unc	BU
1999	—	—	—	—	0.50	—

KM# 96 50 CENTIMOS

3.0000 g., Copper Plated Steel, 18 mm. **Obv:** National arms, country name and date **Rev:** Denomination **Edge:** Plain

Date	Mintage	F	VF	XF	Unc	BU
1999	—	—	—	—	1.00	—

KM# 97 KWANZA

4.5000 g., Nickel Plated Steel, 21 mm. **Obv:** National arms, country name and date **Rev:** Denomination **Edge:** Reeded

Date	Mintage	F	VF	XF	Unc	BU
1999	—	—	—	—	1.50	—

KM# 98 2 KWANZAS

5.0000 g., Nickel Plated Steel, 22 mm. **Obv:** National arms, country name and date **Rev:** Denomination **Edge:** Reeded

Date	Mintage	F	VF	XF	Unc	BU
1999	—	—	—	—	2.00	—

KM# 99 5 KWANZAS

7.0000 g., Nickel Plated Steel, 26 mm. **Obv:** National arms, country name and date **Rev:** Denomination **Edge:** Reeded

Date	Mintage	F	VF	XF	Unc	BU
1999	—	—	—	—	3.50	—

ARGENTINA

The Argentine Republic, located in southern South America, has an area of 1,073,518 sq. mi. (3,761,274 sq. km.) and an estimated population of 37.03 million. Capital: Buenos Aires. Its varied topography ranges from the subtropical lowlands of the north to the towering Andean Mountains in the west and the wind-swept Patagonian steppe in the south. The rolling, fertile pampas of central Argentina are ideal for agriculture and grazing, and support most of the republic's population. Meatpacking, flour milling, textiles, sugar refining and dairy products are the principal industries. Oil is found in Patagonia, but most mineral requirements must be imported.

Argentina was discovered in 1516 by the Spanish navigator Juan de Solis. A permanent Spanish colony was established at Buenos Aires in 1580, but the colony developed slowly. When Napoleon conquered Spain, the Argentines set up their own government on May 25, 1810. Independence was formally declared on July 9, 1816. A strong tendency toward local autonomy, fostered by difficult transportation, resulted in a federalized union with much authority left to the states or provinces, which resulted in the coinage of 1817-1867.

Internal conflict through the first half century of Argentine independence resulted in a provisional national coinage, chiefly of crown-sized silver. Provincial issues mainly of minor denominations supplemented this.

MINT MARKS

A = Korea
B = Great Britain
BA = Buenos Aires
CORDOBA, CORDOVA
C = France
PTS = Potosi monogram (Bolivia)
R, RA, RIOJA, RIOXA
SE = Santiago del Estero
T, TM = Tucuman
TIERRA DEL FUEGO

MONETARY SYSTEM

8 Reales = 8 Soles = 1/2 Escudo
16 Reales or Soles = 1 Escudo
10 Decimos = 1 Real
100 Centavos = 1 Peso
10 Pesos = 1 Argentino
(Commencing 1970)
100 Old Pesos = 1 New Peso
(Commencing June 1983)
10,000 New Pesos = 1 Peso Argentino
1,000 Pesos Argentino = 1 Austral
(Commencing 1985)
1,000 Pesos Argentinos = 1 Austral
100 Centavos = 1 Austral
(Commencing 1992)
100 Centavos = 1 Peso

REPUBLIC

DECIMAL COINAGE

KM# 37 CENTAVO

2.0200 g., Bronze **Obv:** Argentine arms **Rev:** Value within wreath **Note:** Prev. KM#12.

Date	Mintage	F	VF	XF	Unc	BU
1939	3,488,000	0.25	0.50	1.50	4.00	—
1940	3,140,000	0.15	0.35	1.00	2.00	—
1941	4,572,000	0.15	0.35	1.00	2.00	—
1942	495,000	0.30	0.75	1.50	7.50	—
1943	1,293,500	0.10	0.25	0.55	1.50	—
1944	3,102,743	0.20	0.50	1.00	2.75	—

KM# 37a CENTAVO

Copper **Obv:** Argentine arms **Rev:** Value within wreath **Note:** Cruder diework. Prev. KM#12a.

Date	Mintage	F	VF	XF	Unc	BU
1945	420,000	0.20	0.50	1.00	4.00	—
1946/6	4,450,000	0.15	0.35	0.50	2.00	3.00
1947	5,630,000	0.15	0.35	0.50	2.00	3.00
1948	4,419,545	0.15	0.35	0.50	2.00	3.00

KM# 38 2 CENTAVOS

3.4400 g., Bronze **Obv:** Argentine arms **Rev:** Value within wreath **Note:** Prev. KM#13.

Date	Mintage	F	VF	XF	Unc	BU
1939	5,490,000	0.15	0.35	1.00	4.50	—
1940	4,625,000	0.15	0.35	1.00	5.00	—
1941	4,566,805	0.15	0.35	1.00	5.00	—
1942	2,082,492	0.15	0.35	1.00	5.50	—
1944	387,072	0.25	0.50	1.25	7.50	—
1945	4,585,000	0.15	0.35	1.00	5.00	—
1946/1946	3,395,000	0.15	0.35	1.00	5.00	—
1947	4,395,000	0.15	0.35	1.00	5.00	—

KM# 38a 2 CENTAVOS

Copper **Obv:** Argentine arms **Rev:** Value within wreath **Note:** Cruder diework. Prev. KM#13a.

Date	Mintage	F	VF	XF	Unc	BU
1947	Inc. above	0.15	0.35	1.00	5.50	—
1948	3,645,000	0.15	0.35	1.00	5.50	—
1949/9	7,290,000	0.15	0.35	1.00	3.50	5.00
1950	903,070	0.25	0.65	1.25	6.50	—

KM# 34 5 CENTAVOS

2.0000 g., Copper-Nickel, 17.3 mm. **Obv:** Capped liberty head left **Rev:** Denomination within wreath **Note:** Prev. KM#9.

Date	Mintage	F	VF	XF	Unc	BU
1896	1,499,000	1.50	4.00	8.00	30.00	—
1897	3,981,000	0.50	1.00	4.00	22.00	—
1898	2,661,000	0.50	1.00	4.00	22.00	—
1899	2,835,000	0.25	0.50	3.00	18.00	—
1903	2,502,000	0.25	0.50	3.00	18.00	—
1904	2,518,000	0.25	0.50	3.00	18.00	—
1905	4,359,000	0.25	0.50	3.00	18.00	—
1906	3,939,000	0.25	0.50	3.00	18.00	—
1907	1,682,000	0.50	1.00	5.00	20.00	—
1908	1,693,000	0.50	1.00	5.00	20.00	—
1909	4,650,000	0.25	0.50	3.50	20.00	—
1910	1,469,000	0.75	2.00	6.00	24.00	—
1911	1,431,000	0.25	0.75	4.00	20.00	—
1912	2,377,000	0.25	0.75	4.00	20.00	—
1913	1,477,000	0.25	0.75	4.00	20.00	—
1914	1,097,000	0.50	1.00	5.00	22.00	—
1915	1,310,000	0.30	0.75	3.50	20.00	—
1916	1,310,000	0.30	0.75	3.50	18.00	—
1917	1,009,000	0.75	1.50	4.00	20.00	—
1918	2,287,000	0.25	0.50	3.00	15.00	—
1919	2,476,000	0.25	0.50	3.00	10.00	—
1920	5,235,000	0.25	0.50	3.00	10.00	—
1921	7,040,000	0.20	0.35	2.00	8.00	—
1922	9,427,000	0.20	0.35	2.00	10.00	—
1923	6,256,000	0.20	0.35	2.00	10.00	—
1924	6,355,000	0.20	0.35	2.00	10.00	—
1925	3,955,000	0.20	0.35	2.00	10.00	—
1926	3,560,000	0.20	0.35	2.00	10.00	—
1927	5,650,000	0.20	0.35	2.00	10.00	—
1928	6,380,000	0.20	0.35	2.00	10.00	—
1929	11,831,000	0.20	0.35	2.00	10.00	—
1930 round top 3	7,110,000	0.20	0.35	2.00	10.00	—
1931 flat top 3	506,000	2.00	4.00	9.00	25.00	—
1933 round top 3	5,537,000	0.10	0.25	1.00	4.00	—
1934 round top 3	1,288,000	0.25	0.50	3.00	8.00	—
1935	3,052,000	0.10	0.25	1.00	4.00	—
1936	7,175,000	0.10	0.25	1.00	4.00	—
1937	7,063,000	0.10	0.25	1.00	4.00	—
1938	10,252,000	0.10	0.25	1.00	3.50	—
1939	7,171,000	0.10	0.25	1.00	4.00	—
1940	10,191,000	0.10	0.25	1.00	3.50	—
1941	951,000	0.50	1.00	3.00	12.00	—
1942	8,692,000	0.10	0.25	1.00	3.50	—

KM# 40 5 CENTAVOS

2.0600 g., Aluminum-Bronze **Obv:** Value at center, grain spray on left, head of cow on right **Rev:** Grain sprig behind capped head, right **Note:** Prev. KM#15.

Date	Mintage	F	VF	XF	Unc	BU
1942	2,130,000	0.25	0.50	1.50	5.00	—
1943 round top 3	15,778,000	0.10	0.25	0.75	3.00	4.00
1944	21,081,000	0.10	0.25	0.75	3.00	4.00
1945	21,600,000	0.10	0.25	0.75	3.00	4.00
1946	20,460,000	0.10	0.25	0.75	3.00	4.00
1947	22,520,000	0.10	0.25	0.75	3.00	4.00
1948	42,790,000	0.10	0.25	0.50	2.00	3.00
1949	35,470,000	0.10	0.25	0.75	3.00	4.00
1950	13,500,000	0.10	0.25	0.75	3.00	4.00

KM# 43 5 CENTAVOS

Copper-Nickel, 17 mm. **Obv:** Value **Rev:** Jose de San Martin bust facing right **Edge:** Reeded **Designer:** Mario Baiardi **Note:** Prev. KM#18.

Date	Mintage	F	VF	XF	Unc	BU
1950	3,460,000	0.20	0.40	0.60	2.00	3.00

KM# 46 5 CENTAVOS

1.9500 g., Copper-Nickel, 17 mm. **Obv:** Value **Rev:** Jose de San Martin bust facing right **Edge:** Reeded **Designer:** Mario Baiardi **Note:** Prev. KM#21.

Date	Mintage	F	VF	XF	Unc	BU
1951	34,994,000	—	0.20	0.30	0.50	0.75
1952	33,110,000	—	0.20	0.30	0.50	0.75
1953	20,129,000	—	0.20	0.30	0.50	0.75

KM# 46a 5 CENTAVOS

Copper-Nickel Clad Steel, 17 mm. **Rev:** Jose de San Martin bust facing right **Edge:** Plain **Designer:** Mario Baiardi **Note:** Prev. KM#21a.

Date	Mintage	F	VF	XF	Unc	BU
1953	36,300,000	—	0.15	0.20	0.35	0.50

KM# 50 5 CENTAVOS

Copper-Nickel Clad Steel, 17.2 mm. **Obv:** Value **Rev:** Jose de

San Martin bust facing right **Edge:** Plain **Designer:** Mario Baiardi **Note:** Prev. KM#25.

Date	Mintage	F	VF	XF	Unc	BU
1954	50,640,000	—	0.15	0.20	0.35	0.50
1955	42,200,000	—	0.15	0.20	0.35	0.50
1956	36,870,000	—	0.15	0.20	0.35	0.50

KM# 53 5 CENTAVOS

Copper-Nickel Clad Steel **Obv:** Capped liberty head, left **Rev:** Value within wreath **Edge:** Plain **Note:** Prev. KM#28.

Date	Mintage	F	VF	XF	Unc	BU
1957	26,930,000	—	0.15	0.20	0.35	0.50
1958	13,108,000	—	0.15	0.20	0.35	0.50
1959	14,971,000	—	0.15	0.20	0.35	0.50

KM# 35 10 CENTAVOS

3.0000 g., Copper-Nickel **Obv:** Capped liberty head **Rev:** Denomination **Edge:** Reeded **Note:** Prev. KM#10.

Date	Mintage	F	VF	XF	Unc	BU
1896	1,877,000	2.00	7.50	20.00	45.00	—
1897	8,582,000	0.50	1.50	6.50	26.00	—
1898	8,534,000	0.50	1.50	6.50	26.00	—
1899	8,889,000	0.50	1.50	6.50	26.00	—
1905	3,785,000	0.50	1.00	3.50	20.00	—
1906	3,854,000	0.50	1.00	3.50	20.00	—
1907	2,355,000	0.50	1.00	4.50	22.00	—
1908	2,280,000	0.50	1.00	4.50	22.00	—
1909	3,738,000	0.50	1.00	3.50	20.00	—
1910	3,026,000	0.50	1.00	3.50	20.00	—
1911	2,142,000	0.75	2.00	5.00	24.00	—
1912	2,993,000	0.75	2.00	5.00	24.00	—
1913 round top 3	1,828,000	1.00	2.50	5.50	25.00	—
1914	751,000	1.00	2.50	5.50	25.00	—
1915	2,607,000	0.50	1.00	3.50	20.00	—
1916	835,000	1.00	2.50	5.50	25.00	—
1918	3,897,000	0.50	1.00	3.50	20.00	—
1919	2,517,000	0.50	1.00	3.50	25.00	—
1920	7,509,000	0.25	0.75	2.50	20.00	—
1921	11,564,000	0.25	0.60	2.00	15.00	—
1922	6,542,000	0.20	0.50	2.00	20.00	—
1923	5,301,000	0.20	0.50	2.00	15.00	—
1924	3,489,000	0.20	0.50	1.75	10.00	—
1925	5,415,000	0.20	0.50	1.75	10.00	—
1926	5,055,000	0.15	0.35	1.50	9.00	—
1927	5,205,000	0.15	0.35	1.50	9.00	—
1928	8,255,000	0.15	0.35	1.50	9.00	—
1929	2,501,000	0.15	0.35	1.50	9.00	—
1930 round top 3	14,586,000	0.15	0.35	1.00	6.00	—
1931 flat top 3	893,000	0.50	1.00	2.50	20.00	—
1933	5,394,000	0.15	0.35	1.50	8.00	—
1934	3,319,000	0.15	0.35	1.50	8.00	—
1935	1,018,000	0.30	0.75	2.00	15.00	—
1936	3,000,000	0.15	0.35	1.50	12.00	—
1937	11,766,000	0.15	0.35	1.00	4.00	—
1938	10,494,000	0.15	0.35	1.00	4.00	—
1939	5,585,000	0.15	0.35	1.00	5.00	—
1940	3,955,000	0.15	0.35	1.00	5.00	—
1941	4,101,000	0.15	0.35	1.00	5.00	—
1942	2,962,000	0.15	0.25	1.00	5.00	—

KM# 41 10 CENTAVOS

Aluminum-Bronze **Obv:** Value center, grain sprig on left, head of cow on right **Rev:** Grain sprig behind capped head facing right **Note:** Prev. KM#16.

Date	Mintage	F	VF	XF	Unc	BU
1942	15,541,000	0.15	0.25	1.00	4.00	—
1943	13,916,000	0.15	0.35	1.25	6.00	—
1944	16,411,000	0.15	0.25	1.00	4.00	—
1945	12,500,000	0.25	0.50	2.00	7.00	—
1946	15,790,000	0.15	0.25	1.00	4.00	—
1947	36,430,000	0.15	0.25	1.00	2.50	3.50
1948	54,685,000	0.15	0.25	1.00	2.50	3.50
1949	57,740,000	0.15	0.25	1.00	2.50	3.50
1950	42,825,000	0.15	0.25	1.00	2.50	3.50

KM# 44 10 CENTAVOS

Copper-Nickel, 19 mm. **Obv:** Value **Rev:** Jose de San Martin bust facing right **Edge:** Reeded **Designer:** Mario Baiardi **Note:** Prev. KM#19.

Date	Mintage	F	VF	XF	Unc	BU
1950	17,505,000	0.20	0.40	0.60	1.75	2.50

KM# 47 10 CENTAVOS

Copper-Nickel, 19 mm. **Obv:** Value **Rev:** Jose de San Martín bust right **Edge:** Reeded **Designer:** Mario Baiardi **Note:** Prev. KM#22.

Date	Mintage	F	VF	XF	Unc	BU
1951	98,521,000	—	0.20	0.30	0.50	0.75
1952	67,328,000	—	0.20	0.30	0.50	0.75

KM# 47a 10 CENTAVOS

Nickel Clad Steel, 19 mm. **Edge:** Plain **Designer:** Mario Baiardi **Note:** Prev. KM#22a.

Date	Mintage	F	VF	XF	Unc	BU
1952	33,240,000	—	0.10	0.15	0.25	0.50
1953	106,685,000	—	0.10	0.15	0.25	0.50

KM# 51 10 CENTAVOS

3.0500 g., Nickel Clad Steel, 19 mm. **Obv:** Value **Rev:** Jose de San Martin facing right **Edge:** Plain **Designer:** Mario Baiardi **Note:** Prev. KM#26.

Date	Mintage	F	VF	XF	Unc	BU
1954	117,200,000	—	0.10	0.15	0.25	0.50
1955	97,045,000	—	0.10	0.15	0.25	0.50
1956	122,630,000	—	0.10	0.15	0.25	0.50

KM# 54 10 CENTAVOS

2.9500 g., Nickel Clad Steel, 19.24 mm. **Obv:** Capped liberty head facing left **Rev:** Value within wreath **Edge:** Plain **Note:** Prev. KM#29.

Date	Mintage	F	VF	XF	Unc	BU
1957	52,810,000	—	0.10	0.15	0.25	0.50
1958	41,916,000	—	0.10	0.15	0.25	0.50
1959	29,183,000	—	0.10	0.15	0.25	0.50

KM# 36 20 CENTAVOS

4.0000 g., Copper-Nickel **Obv:** Capped liberty head left **Rev:** Denomination within wreath **Note:** Prev. KM#11.

Date	Mintage	F	VF	XF	Unc	BU
1896	2,030,000	2.00	8.00	20.00	60.00	90.00
1897	5,263,000	1.50	6.00	12.00	50.00	—
1898	1,264,000	2.00	8.00	20.00	60.00	—
1899	840,000	20.00	55.00	100	200	—
1905	4,455,000	0.75	2.00	5.00	38.00	—
1906	4,331,000	0.75	2.00	5.00	38.00	—
1907	3,730,000	1.00	3.00	7.00	40.00	—
1908	719,000	2.25	5.00	10.00	45.00	—
1909	1,329,000	0.50	1.50	4.00	35.00	—
1910	1,845,000	0.50	1.50	4.00	35.00	—
1911	1,110,000	0.50	1.50	4.00	35.00	—
1912	2,402,000	0.50	1.50	4.00	35.00	—
1913	1,579,000	0.50	1.00	3.00	30.00	—
1914	527,000	2.25	5.00	12.00	50.00	—
1915	1,921,000	0.50	1.00	3.00	30.00	—
1916	985,000	0.50	1.25	4.00	35.00	—
1918	1,638,000	0.40	0.75	3.00	30.00	—
1919	2,280,000	0.40	0.75	3.00	30.00	—
1920	7,572,000	0.40	0.75	2.50	20.00	—
1921	5,286,000	0.25	0.60	2.50	30.00	—
1922	2,324,000	0.25	0.60	2.50	30.00	—
1923	4,416,000	0.25	0.60	2.50	30.00	—
1924	3,676,000	0.25	0.60	2.00	30.00	—
1925	3,799,000	0.25	0.60	2.00	30.00	—
1926	3,250,000	0.25	0.50	2.00	25.00	—
1927	2,880,000	0.25	0.50	2.00	25.00	—
1928	2,886,000	0.25	0.50	2.00	25.00	—
1929	8,361,000	0.25	0.50	1.25	12.00	—
1930	8,281,000	0.25	0.50	1.25	12.00	—
1931	315,000	2.25	5.00	10.00	35.00	—
1935	1,127,000	0.25	0.60	1.75	12.50	—
1936	855,000	0.50	1.25	2.50	15.00	—
1937	3,314,000	0.25	0.50	1.50	9.00	—
1938	6,449,000	0.25	0.50	1.25	9.00	—
1939	3,555,000	0.25	0.50	1.25	9.00	—
1940	4,465,000	0.25	0.50	1.25	9.00	—
1941	600,000	0.50	1.00	2.00	12.50	—
1942	4,844,000	0.25	0.50	1.25	9.00	—

KM# 42 20 CENTAVOS

4.2000 g., Aluminum-Bronze, 21.2 mm. **Obv:** Value at center, grain sprig to left, head of cow to right **Rev:** Grain sprig behind capped head right **Note:** Prev. KM#17.

Date	Mintage	F	VF	XF	Unc	BU
1942	10,255,000	0.25	0.50	2.00	10.00	—
1943	13,775,000	0.15	0.35	1.50	7.00	—
1944	12,225,000	0.15	0.35	1.75	8.00	—
1945	13,340,000	0.15	0.35	1.50	7.00	—
1946	14,625,000	0.15	0.35	1.50	7.00	—
1947	23,165,000	0.15	0.25	1.25	6.00	7.50
1948	32,245,000	0.15	0.25	1.25	6.00	7.50
1949	67,115,000	0.15	0.25	1.25	6.00	7.50
1950	40,071,000	0.15	0.25	1.25	6.00	7.50

KM# 45 20 CENTAVOS

4.0200 g., Copper-Nickel, 21 mm. **Obv:** Value **Rev:** Jose de San Martín portrait right **Edge:** Reeded **Designer:** Mario Baiardi **Note:** Prev. KM#20.

Date	Mintage	F	VF	XF	Unc	BU
1950	86,770,000	0.15	0.25	0.60	1.50	2.00

KM# 48 20 CENTAVOS

Copper-Nickel, 21 mm. **Obv:** Value **Rev:** Jose de San Martín bust right **Edge:** Reeded **Designer:** Mario Baiardi **Note:** Prev. KM#23.

Date	Mintage	F	VF	XF	Unc	BU
1951	85,782,000	0.10	0.20	0.30	0.50	0.75
1952	69,796,000	0.10	0.20	0.30	0.50	0.75

KM# 48a 20 CENTAVOS

4.0000 g., Nickel Clad Steel, 21 mm. **Rev:** Jose de San Martín portrait right **Edge:** Plain **Designer:** Mario Baiardi **Note:** Prev. KM#23a.

Date	Mintage	F	VF	XF	Unc	BU
1952	12,863,000	—	0.15	0.25	0.50	0.75
1953	36,893,000	—	0.15	0.40	1.00	1.50

KM# 52 20 CENTAVOS

3.9100 g., Nickel Clad Steel, 21 mm. **Obv:** Value **Rev:** Jose de San Martin bust facing right **Designer:** Mario Baiardi **Note:** Head size reduced slightly. Prev. KM#27.

Date	Mintage	F	VF	XF	Unc	BU
1954	52,563,000	—	0.15	0.20	0.25	0.50
1955	46,952,000	—	0.15	0.20	0.25	0.50
1956	35,995,000	—	0.15	0.20	0.25	0.50

KM# 55 20 CENTAVOS

4.0000 g., Nickel Clad Steel, 19.59 mm. **Obv:** Capped liberty head left **Rev:** Value within wreath **Edge:** Plain **Note:** Prev. KM#30.

Date	Mintage	F	VF	XF	Unc	BU
1957	89,365,000	—	0.15	0.20	0.25	0.50
1958	52,710,000	—	0.15	0.20	0.25	0.50
1959	56,585,000	—	0.15	0.20	0.25	0.50
1960	21,254,000	—	0.15	0.20	0.25	0.50
1961	2,083,000	—	0.25	0.50	1.50	2.00

KM# 39 50 CENTAVOS

6.0000 g., Nickel, 24.50 mm. **Obv:** Capped liberty head, left **Rev:** Value within wreath **Edge:** Reeded **Note:** Prev. KM#14.

Date	Mintage	F	VF	XF	Unc	BU
1941	1,000,000	0.40	1.00	2.00	6.00	—

KM# 49 50 CENTAVOS

Nickel Clad Steel **Obv:** Value **Rev:** Jose de San Martín bust right **Edge:** Plain **Designer:** Mario Baiardi **Note:** Prev. KM#24.

Date	Mintage	F	VF	XF	Unc	BU
1952	29,736,000	0.10	0.20	0.35	1.25	2.00
1953	62,814,000	0.10	0.20	0.35	1.25	2.00
1954	132,224,000	0.10	0.20	0.35	1.00	1.50
1955	75,490,000	0.10	0.20	0.35	1.25	2.00
1956	19,120,000	0.10	0.20	0.50	2.00	3.00

KM# 56 50 CENTAVOS

5.0500 g., Nickel Clad Steel, 23.2 mm. **Obv:** Capped liberty head left **Rev:** Value within wreath **Edge:** Plain **Note:** Prev. KM#31.

Date	Mintage	F	VF	XF	Unc	BU
1957	18,139,000	0.10	0.20	0.45	1.25	2.00
1958	51,750,000	0.10	0.20	0.35	1.00	1.50
1959	13,997,000	0.10	0.20	0.45	1.25	2.00
1960	26,038,000	0.10	0.20	0.35	1.00	1.50
1961	11,106,000	0.10	0.20	0.45	1.25	2.00

KM# 57 PESO

6.4100 g., Nickel Clad Steel **Obv:** Capped liberty head left **Rev:** Value within wreath **Note:** Prev. KM#32.

Date	Mintage	F	VF	XF	Unc	BU
1957	118,118,000	0.10	0.20	0.40	2.00	3.00
1958	118,151,000	0.10	0.20	0.40	2.00	3.00
1959	237,733,000	0.10	0.20	0.30	1.50	2.50
1960	75,048,000	0.10	0.30	0.50	2.50	3.50
1961	76,897,000	0.10	0.30	0.50	2.50	3.50
1962	30,006,000	0.10	0.30	0.50	3.00	4.00

KM# 58 PESO

6.6200 g., Nickel Clad Steel, 25.5 mm. **Subject:** 150th Anniversary - Removal of Spanish Viceroy **Obv:** Argentine arms, value at bottom **Rev:** Building, two dates below **Edge:** Reeded **Note:** Prev. KM#33.

Date	Mintage	F	VF	XF	Unc	BU
ND(1960)	98,751,000	0.20	0.50	0.75	2.00	3.00

KM# 59 5 PESOS

4.0000 g., Nickel Clad Steel, 21.5 mm. **Obv:** Sailing ship-Fragata Sarmiento **Rev:** Value above date flanked by sprays **Edge:** Plain **Note:** Prev. KM#34.

Date	Mintage	F	VF	XF	Unc	BU
1961	37,423,000	0.15	0.25	0.50	3.00	3.50
1962	42,362,000	0.15	0.25	0.50	3.00	3.50
1963	71,769,000	0.15	0.25	0.40	2.00	2.50
1964	12,302,000	0.20	0.35	0.60	3.50	4.00
1965	19,450,000	0.15	0.25	0.50	3.00	3.50
1966	17,259,000	0.15	0.25	0.50	3.00	3.50
1967	17,806,000	0.15	0.25	0.50	3.00	3.50
1968	12,634,000	0.20	0.35	0.60	3.50	4.00

KM# 60 10 PESOS

Nickel Clad Steel, 23.6 mm. **Obv:** Gaucho **Edge:** Plain **Note:** Prev. KM#35.

Date	Mintage	F	VF	XF	Unc	BU
1962	57,401,000	0.15	0.25	0.50	3.00	3.50
1963	136,792,000	0.15	0.20	0.35	2.00	2.50
1964	46,576,000	0.15	0.25	0.50	3.00	3.50
1965	40,640,000	0.15	0.25	0.50	3.00	3.50
1966	50,733,000	0.15	0.20	0.40	2.50	3.00
1967	43,050,000	0.15	0.25	0.50	3.00	3.50
1968	36,588,000	0.15	0.25	0.50	3.00	3.50

KM# 62 10 PESOS

Nickel Clad Steel **Subject:** 150th Anniversary - Declaration of Independence. **Rev:** Building facing right, two dates below **Note:** Prev. KM#37.

Date	Mintage	F	VF	XF	Unc	BU
ND(1966)	29,336,000	0.15	0.25	0.50	3.00	3.50

KM# 61 25 PESOS

6.4500 g., Nickel Clad Steel, 26 mm. **Subject:** 1st issue of National Coinage in 1813. **Obv:** Radiant sunface within circle **Rev:** Argentine arms within circle **Edge:** Plain **Note:** Prev. KM#36.

Date	Mintage	F	VF	XF	Unc	BU
1964	20,485,000	0.15	0.25	0.50	3.00	3.75
1965	14,884,000	0.15	0.25	0.50	3.00	3.75
1966	16,426,000	0.15	0.25	0.50	3.00	3.75
1967	15,734,000	0.15	0.25	0.50	3.00	3.75
1968	4,446,000	0.15	0.25	0.75	3.50	4.50

KM# 63 25 PESOS

Nickel Clad Steel, 26 mm. **Subject:** 80th Anniversary - Death of D. Faustino Sarmiento **Rev:** Head of Domingo Faustino Samiento, left, date below **Note:** Prev. KM#38.

Date	Mintage	F	VF	XF	Unc	BU
1968	15,804,000	0.25	0.60	0.85	1.65	2.00

REFORM COINAGE

1970-1983; 100 Old Pesos = 1 New Peso

KM# 64 CENTAVO

0.6200 g., Aluminum, 15.62 mm. **Obv:** Capped Liberty head, left **Rev:** Value to left of grain sprig, date below **Edge:** Plain **Note:** Prev. KM#39.

Date	Mintage	F	VF	XF	Unc	BU
1970	54,568,115	—	—	0.10	0.30	0.50
1971	44,644,000	—	—	0.10	0.30	0.50
1972	92,430,000	—	—	0.10	0.30	0.50
1973	29,515,000	—	—	0.10	0.30	0.50
1974	5,162,000	—	—	0.15	0.35	0.60
1975	3,840,000	—	0.10	0.20	0.50	0.75

KM# 65 5 CENTAVOS

0.9800 g., Aluminum, 16.63 mm. **Obv:** Capped liberty head left **Rev:** Value with grain sprig to left **Edge:** Plain **Note:** Prev. KM#40.

Date	Mintage	F	VF	XF	Unc	BU
1970	56,174,000	—	0.10	0.15	0.40	0.60
1971	3,798,000	0.10	0.20	0.35	0.65	0.90
1972	84,250,000	—	0.10	0.15	0.40	0.60
1973	113,912,000	—	0.10	0.15	0.40	0.60
1974	18,150,000	—	0.10	0.15	0.40	0.60
1975	6,940,000	0.10	0.20	0.35	0.65	0.90

KM# 66 10 CENTAVOS

Brass **Obv:** Capped liberty head, left **Rev:** Value with grain sprig to left **Note:** Prev. KM#41.

Date	Mintage	F	VF	XF	Unc	BU
1970	64,585,300	—	0.10	0.15	0.35	0.55
1971	135,623,000	—	0.10	0.15	0.35	0.55
1973	19,930,000	—	0.10	0.15	0.35	0.55
1974	79,156,000	—	0.10	0.15	0.35	0.55
1975	31,270,000	—	0.10	0.15	0.35	0.55
1976	730,000	0.10	0.20	0.35	1.00	1.75

KM# 67 20 CENTAVOS

3.0700 g., Brass, 18.75 mm. **Obv:** Capped liberty head, left **Rev:** Value with grain sprig to left **Edge:** Reeded **Note:** Prev. KM#42.

Date	Mintage	F	VF	XF	Unc	BU
1970	27,029,000	—	0.10	0.15	0.35	0.55
1971	33,211,000	—	0.10	0.15	0.35	0.55
1972	220,000	1.00	2.00	4.00	8.00	10.00
1973	9,676,000	—	0.10	0.15	0.35	0.55
1974	41,024,000	—	0.10	0.15	0.35	0.55
1975	26,540,000	—	0.10	0.15	0.35	0.55
1976	960,000	—	0.10	0.15	0.35	0.55

KM# 68 50 CENTAVOS

4.3500 g., Brass **Obv:** Capped liberty head left **Rev:** Value with grain sprig to left **Note:** Prev. KM#43.

Date	Mintage	F	VF	XF	Unc	BU
1970	56,103,729	0.10	0.15	0.30	0.60	0.80
1971	34,947,000	0.10	0.15	0.30	0.60	0.80
1972	40,960,000	0.10	0.15	0.30	0.60	0.80
1973	59,472,124	0.10	0.15	0.30	0.60	0.80
1974	64,063,000	0.10	0.15	0.30	0.60	0.80
1975	64,859,000	0.10	0.15	0.30	0.60	0.80
1976	9,768,000	0.10	0.15	0.30	0.60	0.80

KM# 69 PESO

5.0000 g., Aluminum-Brass, 22 mm. **Obv:** Radiant sunface, grain sprays below **Rev:** Value with grain sprig to left **Edge:** Reeded **Note:** Wide and narrow rim varieties exist. Prev. KM#44.

Date	Mintage	F	VF	XF	Unc	BU
1974	77,292,000	—	0.10	0.25	0.75	1.00
1975	423,000,000	—	0.10	0.20	0.50	0.75
1976	100,075,000	—	0.10	0.20	0.50	0.75

KM# 71 5 PESOS

Aluminum-Bronze **Obv:** Radiant sunface, grain sprays below **Rev:** Value with grain sprig to left **Note:** Prev. KM#46.

Date	Mintage	F	VF	XF	Unc	BU
1976	118,353,000	—	0.10	0.20	0.65	1.00
1977	66,765,684	—	0.10	0.20	0.65	1.00

KM# 73 5 PESOS

Aluminum-Bronze **Subject:** Admiral G. Brown Bicentennial **Note:** Prev. KM#48.

Date	Mintage	F	VF	XF	Unc	BU
1977	11,297,808	0.10	0.15	0.30	0.75	1.00

KM# 72 10 PESOS

Aluminum-Bronze **Obv:** Radiant sunface, grain sprays below **Rev:** Value with grain sprig to left **Note:** Prev. KM#47.

Date	Mintage	F	VF	XF	Unc	BU
1976	130,216,724	0.10	0.15	0.35	1.00	1.50
1977	191,520,382	0.10	0.15	0.35	1.00	1.50
1978	259,424,310	0.10	0.15	0.35	1.00	1.50

KM# 74 10 PESOS

Aluminum-Bronze **Subject:** Admiral G. Brown Bicentennial **Obv:** Armored bust of Admiral G. Brown right dividing dates **Rev:** Value with grain sprigs to left, date below **Note:** Prev. KM#49.

Date	Mintage	F	VF	XF	Unc	BU
1977	60,008,179	0.10	0.20	0.50	1.25	1.50

KM# 75 20 PESOS

Aluminum-Bronze **Subject:** 1978 World Soccer Championship **Obv:** Two soccer players, country above with two numbered year below country to right **Rev:** Soccer ball within symbol, top right, small mark to left, value below, date at bottom **Note:** Prev. KM#50.

Date	Mintage	F	VF	XF	Unc	BU
1977	1,506,000	0.10	0.20	0.40	1.00	1.25
1978	2,000,000	0.10	0.20	0.40	1.00	1.25

KM# 76 50 PESOS

Aluminum-Bronze **Subject:** 1978 World Soccer Championship **Obv:** Soccer player on lined globe, country name above with two numbered year below at right **Rev:** Soccer ball within symbol, top right, value below, date at bottom, small mark to left of symbol **Note:** Prev. KM#51.

Date	Mintage	F	VF	XF	Unc	BU
1977	1,506,000	0.10	0.20	0.40	1.00	1.25
1978	2,000,000	0.10	0.20	0.40	1.00	1.25

KM# 81 50 PESOS

Aluminum-Bronze **Subject:** 200th Anniversary - Birth of Jose de San Martín **Obv:** Value, date below flanked by stars **Rev:** Armored bust of Jose de San Martin left, two dates at right **Note:** Prev. KM#56.

Date	Mintage	F	VF	XF	Unc	BU
1978	40,601,000	0.20	0.50	1.00	2.00	2.50

KM# 83 50 PESOS

Aluminum-Bronze **Obv:** Value, date below **Rev:** Bust of Jose de San Martin left **Note:** Prev. KM#58.

Date	Mintage	F	VF	XF	Unc	BU
1979	21,728,900	0.10	0.25	0.65	1.50	2.00
1980	—	0.10	0.25	0.65	1.50	2.00

Note: Mintage included with 1980 date of KM#83a

KM# 83a 50 PESOS

7.3900 g., Brass Clad Steel, 26.14 mm. **Rev:** Jose de San Martín portrait right **Edge:** Reeded **Note:** Prev. KM#58a.

Date	Mintage	F	VF	XF	Unc	BU
1980	94,730,000	0.10	0.25	0.65	1.25	1.50
1981	26,507,500	0.10	0.25	0.65	1.25	1.50

KM# 84 50 PESOS

Aluminum-Bronze **Subject:** Conquest of Patagonia Centennial **Obv:** Value, date below **Rev:** Man on horse, lance in right hand, facing left **Note:** Prev. KM#59.

Date	Mintage	F	VF	XF	Unc	BU
1979	34,761,829	0.10	0.25	0.65	2.50	3.50

KM# 77 100 PESOS

Aluminum-Bronze **Subject:** 1978 World Soccer Championship **Obv:** Stadium on lined globe, country name above with two numbered year below at right **Rev:** Soccer ball within symbol, top right, value below, date at bottom, small mark at left of symbol **Note:** Prev. KM#52.

Date	Mintage	F	VF	XF	Unc	BU
1977	1,506,000	0.15	0.30	0.75	1.50	2.00
1978	2,000,000	0.15	0.30	0.75	1.50	2.00

KM# 82 100 PESOS

Aluminum-Bronze **Subject:** 200th Anniversary - Birth of Jose de San Martín **Obv:** Value at center, small mark at top, date at bottom **Rev:** Armored bust of Jose de San Martin, left **Note:** Prev. KM#57.

Date	Mintage	F	VF	XF	Unc	BU
1978	113,826,000	—	0.50	1.00	2.00	2.50
1979	—	—	—	—	—	800

KM# 85 100 PESOS

Aluminum-Bronze, 27.4 mm. **Obv:** Value at center, small mark at top, date at bottom **Rev:** Jose de San Martín portrait left **Note:** Prev. KM#60.

Date	Mintage	F	VF	XF	Unc	BU
1978	—	—	—	—	—	300
1979	43,389,383	0.15	0.30	0.75	1.25	1.50
1980	154,260,000	0.15	0.30	0.75	1.25	1.50

KM# 85a 100 PESOS

7.9100 g., Brass Clad Steel **Rev:** Jose de San Martín portrait left **Note:** Prev. KM#60a.

Date	Mintage	F	VF	XF	Unc	BU
1980	Inc. above	0.15	0.30	0.75	1.50	1.75
1981	99,512,000	0.15	0.30	0.75	1.25	1.50

KM# 86 100 PESOS

Aluminum-Bronze **Subject:** Conquest of Patagonia Centennial **Obv:** Value center, small mark at top, date below **Rev:** Man on horse holding lance in right, facing left **Note:** Prev. KM#61.

Date	Mintage	F	VF	XF	Unc	BU
1979	34,132,135	0.15	0.30	0.75	2.50	3.50

REFORM COINAGE

1983-1985; 10,000 Pesos = 1 Peso Argentino;
100 Centavos = 1 Peso Argentino

KM# 87 CENTAVO

Aluminum **Obv:** Capped liberty head, left **Rev:** Value, date below **Note:** Prev. KM#62.

Date	Mintage	F	VF	XF	Unc	BU
1983	19,959,000	—	—	—	0.20	0.35

KM# 88 5 CENTAVOS

1.2400 g., Aluminum **Obv:** Capped liberty head left **Rev:** Value, date below **Note:** Prev. KM#63.

Date	Mintage	F	VF	XF	Unc	BU
1983	59,870,000	—	—	—	0.25	0.40

KM# 89 10 CENTAVOS

1.5500 g., Aluminum, 20.08 mm. **Obv:** Capped liberty head, left **Rev:** Value, date below **Edge:** Plain **Note:** Prev. KM#64. Struck at the British Royal Mint.

Date	Mintage	F	VF	XF	Unc	BU
1983	307,513,000	—	—	—	0.25	0.40

KM# 90 50 CENTAVOS

Aluminum **Obv:** Capped liberty head, left **Rev:** Value, date below **Note:** Prev. KM#65.

Date	Mintage	F	VF	XF	Unc	BU
1983	243,909,000	—	—	—	0.45	0.60

KM# 91 PESO

Aluminum **Obv:** Capitol building **Rev:** Value, date below **Note:** National Congress. Prev. KM#66.

Date	Mintage	F	VF	XF	Unc	BU
1984	184,691,379	—	—	—	0.50	0.65

KM# 92 5 PESOS

Brass **Obv:** Buenos Aires City Hall **Rev:** Value, date at bottom **Note:** Prev. KM#67.

Date	Mintage	F	VF	XF	Unc	BU
1984	11,206,000	—	—	—	0.65	0.80
1985	14,168,000	—	—	—	0.65	0.80

KM# 93 10 PESOS

Brass **Obv:** Independence Hall at Tucuman **Rev:** Value, date at bottom **Note:** Prev. KM#68.

Date	Mintage	F	VF	XF	Unc	BU
1984	16,528,000	—	—	—	0.85	1.00
1985	9,898,717	—	—	—	0.85	1.00

KM# 94 50 PESOS

4.8300 g., Aluminum-Bronze **Subject:** 50th Anniversary of Central Bank **Obv:** Value, date at bottom **Rev:** Small capped liberty head within wreath, circle surrounding **Note:** Prev. KM#69.

Date	Mintage	F	VF	XF	Unc	BU
1985	3,300,000	—	—	—	1.25	1.50

REFORM COINAGE

1985-1992; 1,000 Pesos Argentinos = 1 Austral; 100 Centavos = 1 Austral

KM# 95 1/2 CENTAVO

Brass **Obv:** Rufous Hornero Bird **Rev:** Value, date below **Note:** Prev. KM#70.

Date	Mintage	F	VF	XF	Unc	BU
1985	7,490,000	—	—	—	0.45	1.00

KM# 96.1 CENTAVO

Brass, 20 mm. **Obv:** Common Rhea **Rev:** Value, date below **Note:** Thick flan. Prev. KM#71.1.

Date	Mintage	F	VF	XF	Unc	BU
1985	76,082,000	—	—	—	0.75	1.25

KM# 96.2 CENTAVO

3.1900 g., Brass, 20.56 mm. **Obv:** Common Rhea **Edge:** Plain **Note:** Thin flan. Prev. KM#71.2.

Date	Mintage	F	VF	XF	Unc	BU
1986	118,934,000	—	—	—	0.75	1.25
1987	87,315,000	—	—	—	0.75	1.25

KM# 97.1 5 CENTAVOS

Brass, 23 mm. **Obv:** Pampas Cat **Rev:** Value, date below **Edge:** Plain **Note:** Thick flan. Prev. KM#72.1.

Date	Mintage	F	VF	XF	Unc	BU
1985	36,924,000	—	—	—	1.60	3.00

KM# 97.2 5 CENTAVOS

4.9000 g., Brass, 23 mm. **Obv:** Pampas Cat **Edge:** Plain **Note:** Thin flan. Prev. KM#72.2.

Date	Mintage	F	VF	XF	Unc	BU
1986	66,414,000	—	—	—	1.50	3.00
1987	56,181,000	—	—	—	1.50	3.00
1988	23,895,000	—	—	—	1.50	3.00

KM# 98 10 CENTAVOS

4.4500 g., Brass, 21.5 mm. **Obv:** Argentine arms **Rev:** Value, date below **Note:** Prev. KM#73.

Date	Mintage	F	VF	XF	Unc	BU
1985	23,268,000	—	—	—	0.65	0.85
1986	158,427,000	—	—	—	0.65	0.85
1987	184,330,000	—	—	—	0.65	0.85
1988	174,003,000	—	—	—	0.65	0.85

KM# 99 50 CENTAVOS

5.4000 g., Brass, 24.5 mm. **Obv:** Capped liberty head, left **Rev:** Value, date below **Note:** Varieties exist. Previous KM#74.

Date	Mintage	F	VF	XF	Unc	BU
1985	13,884,000	—	—	—	1.50	2.00
1986	59,074,000	—	—	—	1.45	1.85
1987	64,525,000	—	—	—	1.45	1.85
1988	62,388,000	—	—	—	1.45	1.85

KM# 100 AUSTRAL

1.5500 g., Aluminum, 20.11 mm. **Obv:** Buenos Aires City Hall **Rev:** Large value in box at right, double lined "A" at top left, date below "A" **Edge:** Plain **Note:** Prev. KM#75.

Date	Mintage	F	VF	XF	Unc	BU
1989	57,400,000	—	—	—	0.15	0.30

KM# 101 5 AUSTRALES

Aluminum, 21.6 mm. **Obv:** Independence Hall at Tucuman **Rev:** Large value in box at right, double lined "A" at left top, date below "A" **Edge:** Plain **Note:** Prev. KM#76.

Date	Mintage	F	VF	XF	Unc	BU
1989	46,894,977	—	—	—	0.25	0.40

KM# 102 10 AUSTRALES

2.0000 g., Aluminum, 23.2 mm. **Obv:** Casa del Acuerdo **Rev:** Large value in box at right, double lined "A" at top left, date below "A" **Edge:** Plain **Note:** Prev. KM#77.

Date	Mintage	F	VF	XF	Unc	BU
1989	99,600,000	—	—	—	0.35	0.50

KM# 103 100 AUSTRALES

1.5000 g., Aluminum, 19.52 mm. **Obv:** Argentine arms **Rev:** Large value in box, small double lined "A" at top, date below box **Edge:** Plain **Note:** Prev. KM#78.

Date	Mintage	F	VF	XF	Unc	BU
1990	18,003,500	—	—	—	0.25	0.40
1991	31,996,500	—	—	—	0.25	0.40

KM# 104 500 AUSTRALES

Aluminum **Obv:** Argentine arms **Rev:** Large value in box, small double lined "A" at top, date below box **Note:** Prev. KM#79.

Date	Mintage	F	VF	XF	Unc	BU
1990	29,312,000	—	—	—	0.35	0.50
1991	50,087,100	—	—	—	0.35	0.50

KM# 105 1000 AUSTRALES
Aluminum, 24.5 mm. **Obv:** Argentine arms **Rev:** Large value in box, small double lined "A" at top, date below box **Edge:** Plain **Note:** Prev. KM#80.

Date	Mintage	F	VF	XF	Unc	BU
1990	8,282,000	—	—	—	0.60	0.75
1991	41,618,000	—	—	—	0.60	0.75

REFORM COINAGE

1992; 100 Centavos = 1 Peso

KM# 108 CENTAVO
Brass **Obv:** Five line inscription within wreath **Rev:** Large value, date below **Edge:** Plain **Shape:** Octagonal **Note:** Prev. KM#83.

Date	Mintage	F	VF	XF	Unc	BU
1992	30,000,000	—	—	—	0.25	0.40

KM# 113 CENTAVO
Brass **Edge:** Reeded **Shape:** Round **Note:** Prev. KM#88.

Date	Mintage	F	VF	XF	Unc	BU
1992	30,000,000	—	—	—	0.25	0.40
1993	79,000,000	—	—	—	0.25	0.40

KM# 113a CENTAVO
2.0200 g., Bronze, 16.2 mm. **Edge:** Reeded **Shape:** Round **Note:** Prev. KM#88a.

Date	Mintage	F	VF	XF	Unc	BU
1993	48,000,000	—	—	—	0.25	0.40
1997	50,000,000	—	—	—	0.25	0.40
1998	50,000,000	—	—	—	0.25	0.40
1999	70,000,000	—	—	—	0.25	0.40
2000	37,000,000	—	—	—	0.25	0.40

KM# 109 5 CENTAVOS
Brass **Obv:** Radiant sunface **Rev:** Large value, date below **Note:** Prev. KM#84.

Date	Mintage	F	VF	XF	Unc	BU
1992	230,000,000	—	—	—	0.45	0.60
1993	20,000,000	—	—	—	0.45	0.60
2005	—	—	—	—	0.45	0.60

KM# 109a.1 5 CENTAVOS
Copper-Nickel **Obv:** Radiant sunface, Fine lettering **Rev:** Value, date below **Note:** Prev. KM#84a.1.

Date	Mintage	F	VF	XF	Unc	BU
1993	245,500,000	—	—	—	0.45	0.65

KM# 109a.2 5 CENTAVOS
Copper-Nickel **Obv:** Radiant sunface. Bold lettering **Note:** Prev. KM#84a.2.

Date	Mintage	F	VF	XF	Unc	BU
1994	5,000,000	—	—	—	0.45	0.65
1995	25,000,000	—	—	—	0.45	0.60
2004	30,000,000	—	—	—	0.45	0.60
2005	76,000,000	—	—	—	0.45	0.60

KM# 107 10 CENTAVOS
Aluminum-Bronze **Obv:** Argentine arms **Rev:** Value, date below **Edge:** Reeded **Note:** Prev. KM#82.

Date	Mintage	F	VF	XF	Unc	BU
1992	805,000,000	—	—	—	0.65	0.85
1993	500,000,000	—	—	—	0.65	0.85
1994	80,000,000	—	—	—	0.65	0.85
2004	190,000,000	—	—	—	0.65	0.85
2005	114,400,000	—	—	—	0.65	0.85
2006	99,600,000	—	—	—	0.65	0.85

KM# 110.1 25 CENTAVOS
Brass **Obv:** Towered building, fine lettering **Rev:** Large value, date below **Note:** Prev. KM#85.1.

Date	Mintage	F	VF	XF	Unc	BU
1992	150,000,000	—	—	—	1.25	1.50

KM# 110.2 25 CENTAVOS
Brass **Obv:** Towered building, bold lettering **Note:** Prev. KM#85.2.

Date	Mintage	F	VF	XF	Unc	BU
1993	80,000,000	—	—	—	1.25	1.50

KM# 110a 25 CENTAVOS
Copper-Nickel **Obv:** Towered building, bold lettering **Note:** Prev. KM#85a.

Date	Mintage	F	VF	XF	Unc	BU
1993	390,000,000	—	—	—	1.25	1.50
1994	200,000,000	—	—	—	1.25	1.50
1996	96,000,000	—	—	—	1.25	1.50

KM# 111.1 50 CENTAVOS
Brass **Obv:** Tucuman Province Capital Building; fine lettering **Rev:** Large value, date below **Note:** Prev. KM#86.1.

Date	Mintage	F	VF	XF	Unc	BU
1992	290,000,000	—	—	—	1.75	2.00
1993	—	—	—	—	1.75	2.00
1994	—	—	—	—	1.75	2.00

KM# 111.2 50 CENTAVOS
Copper-Nickel **Obv:** Tucuman Province Capital Building; bold lettering. **Note:** Prev. KM#86.2.

Date	Mintage	F	VF	XF	Unc	BU
1993	120,000,000	—	—	—	1.75	2.00
1994	304,000,000	—	—	—	1.75	2.00

KM# 119 50 CENTAVOS
Copper-Aluminum **Subject:** 50th Anniversary - UNICEF **Obv:** Girl with rag doll **Rev:** UNICEF logo above denomination **Note:** Prev. KM#94.

Date	Mintage	F	VF	XF	Unc	BU
1996	1,000,000	—	—	—	2.00	2.25

KM# 121 50 CENTAVOS
Copper-Aluminum **Subject:** 50th Anniversary - Women's Right to Vote **Obv:** Bust of Eva Peron right **Rev:** Value with two dates above in circle, legend across top, date at bottom divides wreath **Designer:** Mario Baiardi **Note:** Prev. KM#96.

Date	Mintage	F	VF	XF	Unc	BU
1997	2,000,000	—	—	—	2.25	2.50

KM# 124 50 CENTAVOS
Copper-Aluminum **Subject:** Mercosur **Obv:** Southern Cross constellation **Rev:** Value in circle, date below circle **Note:** Prev. KM#99.

Date	Mintage	F	VF	XF	Unc	BU
1998	1,000,000	—	—	—	2.25	2.50

KM# 129.1 50 CENTAVOS
5.9200 g., Brass, 25.1 mm. **Subject:** General Guemes **Obv:** Bearded portrait, right **Rev:** Value in circle **Edge:** Plain **Note:** Prev. KM#129

Date	Mintage	F	VF	XF	Unc	BU
2000	1,695,000	—	—	—	2.25	2.50

KM# 129.2 50 CENTAVOS
5.9200 g., Brass, 25.1 mm. **Subject:** General Guemes **Obv:** Bearded portrait **Rev:** Denomination **Edge:** Reeded

Date	Mintage	F	VF	XF	Unc	BU
2000	5,000	—	—	—	4.50	6.00

KM# 130.1 50 CENTAVOS
5.9200 g., Brass, 25.1 mm. **Subject:** General San Martin **Obv:** Stylized portrait, facing **Rev:** Value to right of building **Edge:** Reeded **Note:** Previous KM#130

Date	Mintage	F	VF	XF	Unc	BU
2000	995,000	—	—	—	2.25	2.50

KM# 130.2 50 CENTAVOS
5.9200 g., Brass, 25.1 mm. **Subject:** General San Martin **Obv:** Stylized portrait **Rev:** Denomination and building **Edge:** Plain

Date	Mintage	F	VF	XF	Unc	BU
2000	5,000	—	—	—	4.50	6.00

KM# 112.1 PESO
Bi-Metallic Brass center in Copper-Nickel ring **Obv:** Argentine arms in outer ring, design of first Argetine coin in center **Note:** Prev. KM#87.1.

Date	Mintage	F	VF	XF	Unc	BU
1994A	75,000,000	—	—	—	4.50	5.00
Note: Medal rotation						
1995A	185,000,000	—	—	—	4.50	5.00
Note: Medal rotation						
1995B	14,000,000	—	—	—	4.50	5.00
1996A	30,000,000	—	—	—	4.50	5.00
2006	—	—	—	—	—	—
2007	—	—	—	—	—	—

KM# 112.2 PESO
Bi-Metallic Brass center in Copper-Nickel ring **Obv:** Smaller Argentine arms in outer ring, design of first Argetine coin in center **Note:** Prev. KM#87.2.

Date	Mintage	F	VF	XF	Unc	BU
1995C	90,000,000	—	—	—	4.50	5.00

KM# 112.3 PESO
Bi-Metallic Brass center in Copper-Nickel ring **Obv:** Argentine arms in outer ring, design of first Argetine coin in center **Rev:** Error, PROVINGIAS, radiant sun, legend in circle, value at top, date at bottom **Note:** Prev. KM#87.3.

Date	Mintage	F	VF	XF	Unc	BU
1995B	56,000,000	—	—	—	7.50	8.00

KM# 120 PESO

Bi-Metallic Brass center in Copper-Nickel ring, 23 mm. **Subject:** 50th Anniversary - UNICEF **Obv:** Girl with rag doll **Rev:** UNICEF logo above denomination **Note:** Prev. KM#95. Medal rotation.

Date	Mintage	F	VF	XF	Unc	BU
1996	1,000,000	—	—	—	4.50	5.00

KM# 122 PESO

Bi-Metallic Brass center in Copper-Nickel ring, 23 mm. **Subject:** 50th Anniversary - Women's Suffrage Law **Obv:** Bust of Eva Duarte de Peron right (social reformer) **Rev:** Denomination **Edge:** Reeded **Designer:** Mario Baiardi **Note:** Prev. KM#97. Medal rotation.

Date	Mintage	F	VF	XF	Unc	BU
1997	1,000,000	—	—	—	5.00	5.50

KM# 125 PESO

Bi-Metallic Brass center in Copper-Nickel ring, 23 mm. **Subject:** Mercosur **Obv:** Southern Cross constellation **Rev:** Denomination **Note:** Prev. KM#100. Medal rotation.

Date	Mintage	F	VF	XF	Unc	BU
1998	496,715	—	—	—	4.00	5.00

KM# 132.1 PESO

6.3500 g., Bi-Metallic Brass center in Copper-Nickel ring, 23 mm. **Subject:** General Urquiza **Obv:** Stylized portrait facing **Rev:** Church tower and denomination **Edge:** Reeded

Date	Mintage	F	VF	XF	Unc	BU
2001	995,000	—	—	—	3.75	4.50

KM# 132.2 PESO

6.3500 g., Bi-Metallic Copper-Aluminum-Nickel center in Copper-Nickel ring, 23 mm. **Subject:** General Urquiza **Obv:** Stylized portrait facing **Rev:** Church tower and denomination **Edge:** Plain

Date	Mintage	F	VF	XF	Unc	BU
2001	5,000	—	—	—	7.50	8.00

KM# 112.4 PESO

Bi-Metallic Brass center in Copper-Nickel ring **Obv:** Argentine arms in outer ring, design of first Argetine coin in center **Rev:** Radiant sun, legend in circle, value at top, date at bottom

Date	Mintage	F	VF	XF	Unc	BU
2006	30,000,000	—	—	—	4.50	5.00

KM# 135 2 PESOS

10.4400 g., Copper-Nickel, 30.2 mm. **Subject:** Eva Peron **Obv:** Head left **Rev:** Stylized crowd scene and value **Edge:** Reeded

Date	Mintage	F	VF	XF	Unc	BU
2002	—	—	—	—	7.50	9.00

KM# 145 2 PESOS

Copper Nickel, 30.35 mm. **Subject:** !00th Anniversary First Oil Well **Obv:** First oil well **Obv. Legend:** REPÚBLICA ARGENTINA - DESCUBRIMIENTO DEL PETRÓLEO **Rev:** Modern pump **Rev. Inscription:** CHUBUT **Edge:** Reeded

Date	Mintage	F	VF	XF	Unc	BU
2007	—	—	—	—	—	—

ARMENIA

The Republic of Armenia, formerly Armenian S.S.R., is bordered to the north by Georgia, the east by Azerbaijan and the south and west by Turkey and Iran. It has an area of 11,506 sq. mi. (29,800 sq. km) and an estimated population of 3.66 million. Capital: Yerevan. Agriculture including cotton, vineyards and orchards, hydroelectricity, chemicals - primarily synthetic rubber and fertilizers, vast mineral deposits of copper, zinc and aluminum, and production of steel and paper are major industries.

Russia occupied Armenia in 1801 until the Russo-Turkish war of 1878. British intervention excluded either side from remaining although the Armenians remained more loyal to the Ottoman Turks, but in 1894 the Ottoman Turks sent in an expeditionary force of Kurds fearing a revolutionary movement. Large massacres were followed by retaliations, then amnesty was proclaimed which led right into WW I and once again occupation by Russian forces in 1916. After the Russian revolution the Georgians, Armenians and Azerbaijanis formed the short-lived Transcaucasian Federal Republic on Sept. 20, 1917, which broke up into three independent republics on May 26, 1918. Communism developed and in Sept. 1920 the Turks attacked the Armenian Republic; the Russians soon followed suit from Azerbaijan routing the Turks. On Nov. 29, 1920 Armenia was proclaimed a Soviet Socialist Republic. On March 12, 1922, Armenia, Georgia and Azerbaijan were combined to form the Transcaucasian Soviet Federated Socialist Republic, which on Dec. 30, 1922, became a part of U.S.S.R. On Dec. 5, 1936, the Transcaucasian federation was dissolved and Armenia became a constituent Republic of the U.S.S.R. A new constitution was adopted in April 1978. Elections took place on May 20, 1990. The Supreme Soviet adopted a declaration of sovereignty in Aug. 1991, voting to unite Armenia with Nagorno - Karabakh. This newly constituted "Republic of Armenia" became fully independent by popular vote in Sept. 1991. It became a member of the CIS in Dec. 1991.

Fighting between Christians in Armenia and Muslim forces of Azerbaijan escalated in 1992 and continued through early 1994. Each country claimed the Nagorno-Karabakh, an Armenian ethnic enclave, in Azerbaijan. A temporary cease-fire was announced in May 1994.

MONETARY SYSTEM

100 Luma = 1 Dram

MINT NAME

Revan, (Erevan, now Yerevan)

REPUBLIC

STANDARD COINAGE

KM# 51 10 LUMA

0.6000 g., Aluminum, 16 mm. **Obv:** National arms **Rev:** Value over date **Edge:** Plain

Date	Mintage	F	VF	XF	Unc	BU
1994	—	—	—	—	0.40	0.50

KM# 52 20 LUMA

0.7500 g., Aluminum, 18 mm. **Obv:** National arms **Rev:** Value over date **Edge:** Plain

Date	Mintage	F	VF	XF	Unc	BU
1994	—	—	—	—	0.50	0.65

KM# 53 50 LUMA

0.9500 g., Aluminum, 20 mm. **Obv:** National arms **Rev:** Value over date **Edge:** Plain

Date	Mintage	F	VF	XF	Unc	BU
1994	—	—	—	—	0.60	0.75

KM# 54 DRAM

1.4000 g., Aluminum, 20.29 mm. **Obv:** National arms **Rev:** Value over date in sprays **Edge:** Reeded

Date	Mintage	F	VF	XF	Unc	BU
1994	—	—	—	—	0.75	1.00

KM# 55 3 DRAM

1.6500 g., Aluminum, 24 mm. **Obv:** National arms **Rev:** Value over date within sprays **Edge:** Reeded

Date	Mintage	F	VF	XF	Unc	BU
1994	—	—	—	—	1.00	1.25

KM# 56 5 DRAM

2.0000 g., Aluminum, 26 mm. **Obv:** National arms **Rev:** Value over date within sprays **Edge:** Plain

Date	Mintage	F	VF	XF	Unc	BU
1994	—	—	—	—	1.50	1.75

KM# 58 10 DRAM

2.3000 g., Aluminum, 26.3 mm. **Obv:** National arms **Rev:** Value over date within sprays **Edge:** Plain

Date	Mintage	F	VF	XF	Unc	BU
1994	—	—	—	—	2.00	2.50

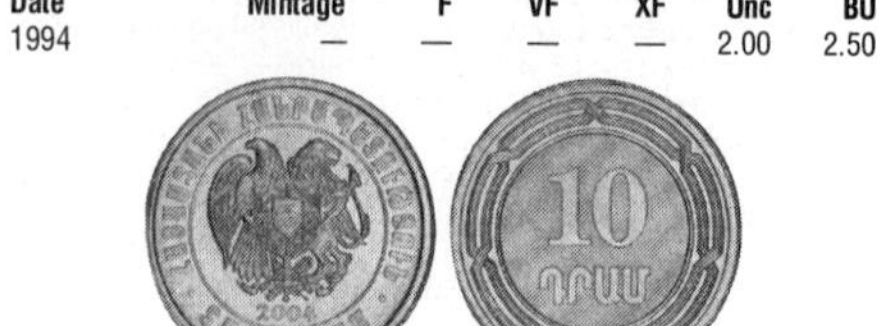

KM# 112 10 DRAM

1.3000 g., Aluminum, 20 mm. **Obv:** National arms **Rev:** Value **Edge:** Reeded

Date	Mintage	F	VF	XF	Unc	BU
2004	—	—	—	—	1.00	1.50

KM# 93 20 DRAM

2.8000 g., Copper Plated Steel, 20.5 mm. **Obv:** National arms **Rev:** Denomination **Edge:** Plain

Date	Mintage	F	VF	XF	Unc	BU
2003	—	—	—	—	1.00	1.50

KM# 94 50 DRAM

3.4500 g., Brass Plated Steel, 21.5 mm. **Obv:** National arms **Rev:** Value **Edge:** Reeded

Date	Mintage	F	VF	XF	Unc	BU
2003	—	—	—	—	1.25	1.50

KM# 95 100 DRAM

4.0000 g., Nickel Plated Steel, 22.5 mm. **Obv:** National arms **Rev:** Value **Edge:** Reeded

Date	Mintage	F	VF	XF	Unc	BU
2003	—	—	—	—	1.50	2.00

KM# 96 200 DRAM

4.5000 g., Brass, 24 mm. **Obv:** National arms **Rev:** Value **Edge:** Reeded

Date	Mintage	F	VF	XF	Unc	BU
2003	—	—	—	—	3.00	4.00

KM# 97 500 DRAM

5.0000 g., Bi-Metallic Copper-Nickel center in a Brass ring, 22 mm. **Obv:** National arms **Rev:** Value **Edge:** Segmented reeding

Date	Mintage	F	VF	XF	Unc	BU
2003	—	—	—	—	6.00	8.00

ARUBA

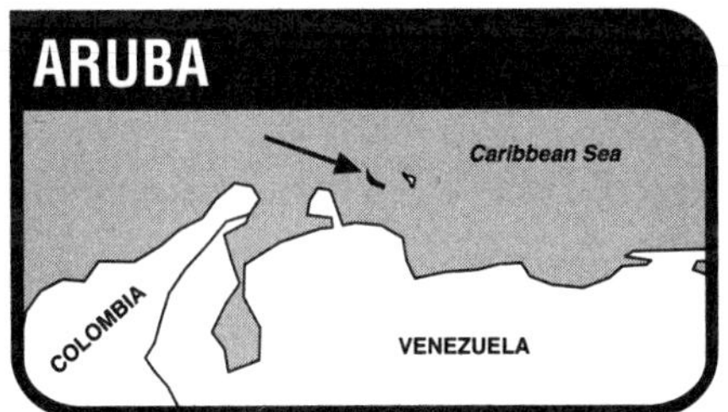

Aruba, formerly a part of the Netherlands Antilles, achieved on Jan. 1, 1986 a special status, "status aparte" as the third state under the Dutch crown, together with the Netherlands and the remaining five islands of the Netherlands Antilles. On Dec. 15, 1954 the Netherlands Antilles were given complete domestic autonomy and granted equality within the Kingdom of the Netherlands. The separate constitution put in place for Aruba in 1986 established it as an autonomous government within the Kingdom of the Netherlands. In 1990 Aruba opted to remain a part of the Kingdom without the promise of future independence.

The second largest island of the Netherlands Antilles, Aruba is situated near the Venezuelan coast. The island has an area of 74-1/2 sq. mi. (193 sq. km.) and a population of 65,974. Capital: Oranjestad, named after the Dutch royal family. Aruba was important in the processing and transportation of petroleum products in the first part of the twentieth century, but today the chief industry is tourism.

For earlier issues see Curacao and the Netherlands Antilles.

RULER

Dutch

MINT MARKS

(u) Utrecht - Privy marks only
- Anvil, 1986-1988
- Bow and Arrow, 1989-1999
- Bow and Arrow w/star, 2000-

MONETARY SYSTEM

100 Cents = 1 Florin

DUTCH STATE

"Status Aparte"

REGULAR COINAGE

KM# 1 5 CENTS

2.0000 g., Nickel Bonded Steel, 16 mm. **Ruler:** Beatrix 1980- **Obv:** National arms **Rev:** Geometric design with value **Edge:** Plain

Date	Mintage	F	VF	XF	Unc	BU
1986(u)	776,000	—	0.10	0.15	0.30	0.50
1987(u)	461,651	—	0.10	0.15	0.30	0.50
1988(u)	656,500	—	—	0.20	0.40	0.60
1989(u)	770,000	—	—	0.20	0.40	0.60
1990(u)	612,000	—	—	0.20	0.40	0.60
1991(u)	412,000	—	—	0.20	0.50	1.00
1992(u)	810,500	—	—	—	0.20	0.50
1993(u)	709,100	—	—	—	0.20	0.50
1994(u)	709,100	—	—	—	0.20	0.50
1995(u)	808,500	—	—	—	0.20	0.50
1996(u)	587,500	—	—	—	0.20	0.50
1997(u)	535,500	—	—	—	0.20	0.50
1998(u)	920,000	—	—	—	0.20	0.50
1999(u)	823,000	—	—	—	0.20	0.50
2000(u)	886,500	—	—	—	0.20	0.50
2001(u)	946,900	—	—	—	0.30	0.60
2002(u)	1,006,000	—	—	—	0.20	0.50
2003(u)	1,104,100	—	—	—	0.20	0.50
2004(u)	502,500	—	—	0.20	0.50	1.00
2005(u)	602,500	—	—	—	0.20	0.50
2006(u)	602,000	—	—	—	0.20	0.50
2007(u)	1,152,000	—	—	—	0.20	0.50
2008(u)	—	—	—	—	0.20	0.50

KM# 2 10 CENTS

3.0000 g., Nickel Bonded Steel, 18 mm. **Ruler:** Beatrix 1980- **Obv:** National arms **Rev:** Geometric design with value **Edge:** Reeded

Date	Mintage	F	VF	XF	Unc	BU
1986(u)	856,200	—	0.20	0.35	0.60	0.75
1987(u)	371,651	—	0.20	0.35	0.60	0.75
1988(u)	986,500	—	—	0.15	0.35	0.50
1989(u)	610,000	—	—	0.15	0.35	0.50
1990(u)	762,000	—	0.20	0.35	0.60	0.75
1991(u)	512,000	—	0.20	0.35	0.60	0.75
1992(u)	610,500	—	0.20	0.35	0.60	0.75
1993(u)	1,009,100	—	—	—	0.30	0.50
1994(u)	409,100	—	0.20	0.35	0.60	0.75
1995(u)	918,500	—	—	—	0.30	0.50
1996(u)	457,500	—	0.20	0.35	0.60	0.75
1997(u)	423,500	—	0.20	0.35	0.60	0.75
1998(u)	954,000	—	—	—	0.30	0.50
1999(u)	1,004,000	—	—	—	0.30	0.50
2000(u)	759,500	—	—	—	0.30	0.50
2001(u)	1,006,900	—	—	—	0.30	0.50
2002(u)	1,006,000	—	—	—	0.30	0.50
2003(u)	1,004,000	—	—	—	0.30	0.50
2004(u)	402,500	—	0.20	0.35	0.60	0.75
2005(u)	602,500	—	—	—	0.30	0.50
2006(u)	602,000	—	—	—	0.30	0.50
2007(u)	1,152,000	—	—	—	0.30	0.50
2008(u)	—	—	—	—	0.30	0.50

KM# 3 25 CENTS

3.5000 g., Nickel Bonded Steel, 20 mm. **Ruler:** Beatrix 1980- **Obv:** National arms **Rev:** Geometric design with value **Edge:** Plain

Date	Mintage	F	VF	XF	Unc	BU
1986(u)	856,200	—	0.20	0.40	0.75	1.50
1987(u)	331,651	—	0.20	0.40	0.75	1.50
1988(u)	116,500	—	0.20	0.40	0.75	1.50
1989(u)	360,000	—	0.20	0.40	0.75	1.50
1990(u)	512,000	—	—	—	0.45	0.80
1991(u)	612,000	—	—	—	0.45	0.80
1992(u)	460,500	—	—	—	0.45	0.80
1993(u)	609,100	—	—	—	0.45	0.80
1994(u)	109,100	—	0.20	0.40	0.75	1.50
1995(u)	608,500	—	—	—	0.35	0.80
1996(u)	287,500	—	—	—	0.60	1.00
1997(u)	467,500	—	—	—	0.50	0.90
1998(u)	641,000	—	—	—	0.35	0.80
1999(u)	332,000	—	—	—	0.40	0.80
2000(u)	330,500	—	—	—	0.40	0.80
2001(u)	716,900	—	—	—	0.35	0.80
2002(u)	806,000	—	—	—	0.35	0.80
2003(u)	804,000	—	—	—	0.35	0.80
2004(u)	362,500	—	—	—	0.40	0.80
2005(u)	302,500	—	—	—	0.40	0.80
2006(u)	302,000	—	—	—	0.40	0.80
2007(u)	202,000	—	—	—	0.50	1.00
2008(u)	—	—	—	—	0.50	1.00

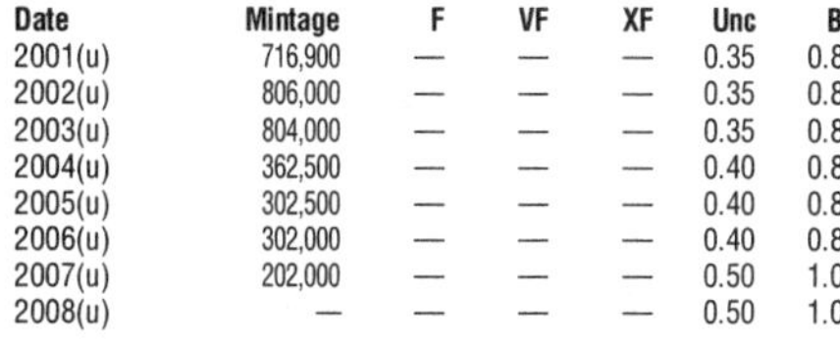

KM# 4 50 CENTS

5.0000 g., Nickel Bonded Steel, 20 mm. **Ruler:** Beatrix 1980- **Obv:** National arms **Rev:** Geometric design with value **Edge:** Plain **Shape:** 4-sided

Date	Mintage	F	VF	XF	Unc	BU
1986(u)	486,200	—	0.30	0.50	1.00	1.50
1987(u)	121,651	—	0.30	0.50	1.00	1.50
1988(u)	216,500	—	0.25	0.45	1.00	1.50
1989(u)	110,000	—	0.30	0.50	1.25	2.25
1990(u)	262,000	—	0.25	0.45	1.00	1.50
1991(u)	312,000	—	—	0.40	0.90	1.10
1992(u)	310,500	—	—	0.40	0.90	1.10
1993(u)	459,100	—	—	0.35	0.65	0.80
1994(u)	309,100	—	—	0.35	0.65	0.80
1995(u)	258,500	—	—	0.40	0.90	1.10
1996(u)	392,500	—	—	0.35	0.65	0.80
1997(u)	27,500	—	—	1.00	2.00	3.00
1998(u)	197,000	—	—	0.35	0.65	0.80
1999(u)	445,000	—	—	0.35	0.65	0.80
2000(u)	54,500	—	—	0.50	1.00	1.20
2001(u)	506,900	—	—	0.30	0.65	0.80
2002(u)	306,000	—	—	0.30	0.65	0.80
2003(u)	279,000	—	—	0.40	0.80	1.00
2004(u)	402,500	—	—	0.50	0.85	1.10
2005(u)	102,500	—	—	0.35	0.65	0.85
2006(u)	102,000	—	—	0.35	0.65	0.85
2007(u)	32,000	—	—	0.60	1.20	1.50

KM# 5 FLORIN

8.5000 g., Nickel Bonded Steel, 26 mm. **Ruler:** Beatrix 1980- **Obv:** Head left **Rev:** National arms **Edge:** Lettered **Edge Lettering:** GOD * ZiJ * MET * ONS

Date	Mintage	F	VF	XF	Unc	BU
1986(u)	586,200	—	0.60	1.00	2.00	3.00
1987(u)	271,651	—	0.60	1.00	2.00	3.00
1988(u)	566,500	—	—	0.65	1.25	2.25
1989(u)	410,000	—	—	0.65	1.25	2.25
1990(u)	412,000	—	—	0.65	1.25	2.25
1991(u)	162,000	—	—	0.75	1.75	3.00
1992(u)	510,500	—	—	0.65	1.25	2.25
1993(u)	409,100	—	—	0.65	1.25	2.25
1994(u)	109,100	—	—	0.65	1.25	2.25
1995(u)	208,500	—	—	0.65	1.25	2.25
1996(u)	132,500	—	—	0.75	1.75	3.00
1997(u)	415,500	—	—	0.65	1.25	2.25
1998(u)	300,000	—	—	0.65	1.25	2.25
1999(u)	430,000	—	—	0.65	1.25	2.25
2000(u)	295,500	—	—	0.65	1.25	2.25
2001(u)	406,900	—	—	0.65	1.25	2.25
2002(u)	206,000	—	—	0.75	1.30	2.50
2003(u)	179,000	—	—	0.80	1.50	3.00
2004(u)	410,000	—	—	0.70	1.35	2.35
2005(u)	352,500	—	—	0.70	1.35	2.35
2006(u)	402,000	—	—	0.70	1.35	2.35
2007(u)	502,000	—	—	0.70	1.35	2.35
2008(u)	—	—	—	0.70	1.35	2.35

KM# 6 2-1/2 FLORIN
10.3000 g., Nickel Bonded Steel, 30 mm. **Ruler:** Beatrix 1980- **Obv:** Head left **Rev:** National arms **Edge:** Lettered **Edge Lettering:** GOD * ZiJ * MET * ONS

Date	Mintage	F	VF	XF	Unc	BU
1986(u)	106,200	—	—	1.75	2.50	3.75
1987(u)	31,651	—	—	2.00	2.75	4.00
1988(u)	26,500	—	—	2.00	2.75	4.00
1989(u)	15,000	—	—	2.00	3.00	4.50
1990(u)	17,000	—	—	2.00	3.00	4.50
1991(u)	17,000	—	—	2.00	3.00	4.50
1992(u)	12,500	—	—	2.00	3.00	4.75
1993(u)	11,100	—	—	2.00	3.00	4.75
1994(u)	11,100	—	—	2.00	3.00	4.75
1995(u)	10,500	—	—	2.00	3.00	4.75
1996(u)	7,500	—	—	2.00	3.50	5.00
Note: In sets only						
1997(u)	7,500	—	—	1.75	3.50	5.00
Note: In sets only						
1998(u)	8,000	—	—	1.75	3.50	5.00
Note: In sets only						
1999(u)	7,500	—	—	1.75	3.50	5.00
Note: In sets only						
2000(u)	7,500	—	—	1.75	3.50	5.00
Note: In sets only						
2001(u)	6,900	—	—	—	3.50	5.00
Note: In sets only						
2002(u)	6,000	—	—	—	3.50	5.00
Note: In sets only						
2003(u)	4,000	—	—	—	3.50	5.00
Note: In sets only						
2004(u)	2,500	—	—	—	3.50	5.00
Note: In sets only						
2005(u)	2,500	—	—	—	3.50	5.00
Note: In sets only						
2006(u)	2,000	—	—	—	3.50	5.00
Note: In sets only						
2007(u)	2,000	—	—	—	3.50	5.00
2008(u)	—	—	—	—	3.50	5.00

KM# 12 5 FLORIN
8.6400 g., Nickel Bonded Steel, 26 mm. **Ruler:** Beatrix 1980- **Obv:** Head left **Rev:** National arms **Edge:** Plain **Shape:** Square

Date	Mintage	F	VF	XF	Unc	BU
1995(u)	200,500	—	—	2.00	4.50	6.00
1996(u)	357,500	—	—	2.00	4.50	6.00
1997(u)	27,500	—	—	2.25	5.50	7.00
1998(u)	162,000	—	—	2.00	4.50	6.00
1999(u)	86,200	—	—	2.25	5.50	7.00
2000(u)	7,500	—	—	3.00	6.00	7.50
Note: In sets only						
2001(u)	6,900	—	—	—	6.00	7.50
Note: In sets only						
2002(u)	6,000	—	—	—	6.00	7.50
Note: In sets only						
2003(u)	4,000	—	—	—	6.00	7.50
Note: In sets only						
2004(u)	2,500	—	—	—	7.00	8.50
Note: In sets only						
2005(u)	2,500	—	—	—	7.00	8.50
Note: In sets only						

KM# 38 5 FLORIN
8.4000 g., Nickel Bonded Steel, 22.5 mm. **Ruler:** Beatrix 1980- **Obv:** Queen **Rev:** Value and arms **Edge:** Reeded and lettered **Edge Lettering:** GOD Z'J MET ONS **Shape:** Round

Date	Mintage	F	VF	XF	Unc	BU
2005(u)	827,500	—	—	—	5.50	7.00
2006(u)	102,000	—	—	—	5.50	8.00
2007(u)	52,000	—	—	—	5.50	8.00
2008(u)	—	—	—	—	5.50	7.00

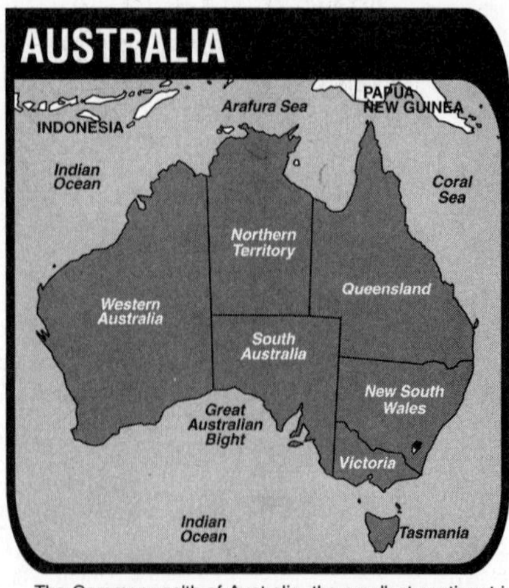

The Commonwealth of Australia, the smallest continent in the world, is located south of Indonesia between the Indian and Pacific oceans. It has an area of 2,967,893 sq. mi. (7,686,850 sq. km.) and an estimated population of 18.84 million. Capital: Canberra. Due to its early and sustained isolation, Australia is the habitat of such curious and unique fauna as the kangaroo, koala, platypus, wombat, echidna and frilled-necked lizard. The continent possesses extensive mineral deposits, the most important of which are iron ore, coal, gold, silver, nickel, uranium, lead and zinc. Raising livestock, mining and manufacturing are the principal industries. Chief exports are wool, meat, wheat, iron ore, coal and nonferrous metals.

The first Caucasians to see Australia probably were Portuguese and Spanish navigators of the late 16th century. In 1770, Captain James Cook explored the east coast and annexed it for Great Britain. New South Wales was founded as a penal colony, following the loss of British North America, by Captain Arthur Phillip on January 26, 1788, a date now celebrated as Australia Day. Dates of creation of the six colonies that now comprise the states of the Australian Commonwealth are: New South Wales, 1823; Tasmania, 1825; Western Australia, 1838; South Australia, 1842; Victoria, 1851; Queensland, 1859. The British Parliament approved a constitution providing for the federation of the colonies in 1900. The Commonwealth of Australia came into being in 1901. Australia passed the Statute of Westminster Adoption Act on October 9, 1942, which officially established Australia's complete autonomy in external and internal affairs, thereby formalizing a situation that had existed for years. Australia is a member of the Commonwealth of Nations. Elizabeth II is Head of State as Queen of Australia.

Australia's currency system was changed from Pounds-Shillings-Pence to a decimal system of Dollars and Cents on Feb. 14, 1966.

RULER
British until 1942

MINT MARKS

Abbr.	Mint	Mint Marks
A	Adelaide	-
(b)	Bombay	I below bust; dots before and after HALF PENNY, 1942-43
(b)	Bombay	I below bust dots before and after PENNY, 1942-43
B	Brisbane	-
(c)	Calcutta	I above date, 1916-18
(c)	Canberra	None, 1966 to date
C	Canberra	-
D	Denver	D above date 1/-& 2/-, below date on 3d
D	Denver	D below date on 6d
H	Heaton	H below date on silvere coins, 1914-15
H	Heaton	H above date on bronze coins
(L)	London	1910-1915 (no marks), 1966
M	Melbourne	M below date on silver coins, 1916-20
M	Melbourne	M above date on the ground on gold coins w/St. George
M	Melbourne	-
(m)	Melbourne	Dot below scroll on penny, 1919-20
(m)	Melbourne	Two dots; below lower scroll and above upper, 1919-20
(m)	Melbourne	None, 1921-1964, 1966
P	Perth	P above date on the ground on gold coins w/St. George
(p)	Perth	Dot between KG (designer's initials), 1940-41
(p)	Perth	Dot after PENNY, 1941-51, 1954-64
(p)	Perth	Dot after AUSTRALIA, 1952-53
(p)	Perth	Dot before SHILLING, 1946
(p)	Perth	None, 1922 penny, 1966
P	Perth	Nuggets, 1986
PL	London	PL after PENNY in 1951
PL	London	PL on bottom folds of ribbon, 1951 threepence
PL	London	PL above date on sixpence
PL		1951
S	San Francisco	S above or below date, 1942-44, mm exists w/ and w/o bulbous serifs
S	Sydney	S above date on the ground on gold coins w/St. George
S	Sydney	-
(sy)	Sydney	Dot above bottom scroll on penny 1920
(sy)	Sydney	None, 1919-1926

Mint designations are shown in ( ). Ex. 1978(m).
Mint marks are shown after date. Ex. 1978M.

PRIVY MARKS

(ae) - American Eagle

(aa) - Adelaide Assay

(ba) - Basler Stab

(bg) - Brandenburg Gate

(d) – Ducat

(dp) – Dump

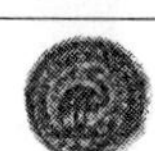

(e) – Emu

(ev) - Edward V

(f) – Fok

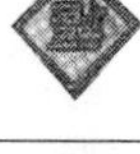

(f1) - Rev. 1 Florin, KM#31

(f3) - Rev. 1 Florin, KM#33

(f7) - Rev. 1 Florin, KM#47

(ge) - Golden Eagle

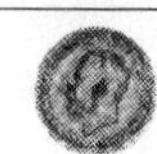

(gv) - George V, small head

(gV) - George V, large head

(h) – Hague

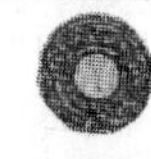

(hd) - Holey Dollar

(j) – Johanna

(jw) - Japanese Royal Wedding

(l) – Luk

(lh) - Liberty Head

(p) – Prospector

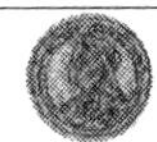

(qv) - Queen Victoria

(rv) - Royal Visit Florin, Rev. 1 Florin, KM#55

(s) – Shu

(sg) - Spade Guinea

(sm) - Sydney Mint Sovereign

(so) - Sydney Opera House

(sp) - Star Pagoda

(sq) – State Quarter

(sr) - Swan River/Rottnest Island Tercentenary

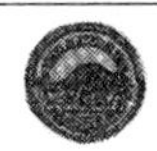

(ta) - Team Australia (Commonwealth Games)

(hd) - Holey Dollar

(w) – Whales

(ww) - 50 Years Beyond WWII

MONETARY SYSTEM

Sterling Coinage (Until 1966)
12 Pence = 1 Shilling
2 Shillings = 1 Florin
5 Shillings = 1 Crown
20 Shillings = 1 Pound
1 Sovereign = 1 Pound

Decimal Coinage (Commencing 1966)
100 Cents = 1 Dollar

COMMONWEALTH OF AUSTRALIA

MINT MARKS
M – Melbourne
P – Perth
S – Sydney
(sy) - Sydney

STERLING COINAGE

KM# 22 1/2 PENNY

Bronze **Ruler:** George V **Obv:** Crowned bust left **Obv. Designer:** E. B. MacKennal **Rev:** Denomination within circle **Edge:** Plain

Date	Mintage	F	VF	XF	Unc	BU
1911(L)	2,832,000	1.00	4.00	17.50	225	350
1911(L) Proof	—	Value: 15,000				
1912H	2,400,000	1.50	5.00	21.00	320	500
1912H Proof	—	Value: 15,000				
1913(L) Wide date	2,160,000	2.00	5.50	38.00	625	900
1913(L) Narrow date	Inc. above	1.50	5.00	36.00	600	875
1914(L)	1,440,000	3.00	15.00	70.00	925	1,500
1914H	1,200,000	3.50	15.00	65.00	800	1,200
1915H	720,000	25.00	75.00	350	3,250	—
1916(c) I	3,600,000	0.50	1.50	17.50	230	350
1916(c) I Proof	—	Value: 15,000				
1917(c) I	5,760,000	0.50	1.50	17.00	230	330
1918(c) I	1,440,000	6.00	22.00	185	2,350	—
1919(sy)	3,326,000	0.25	1.00	15.00	230	325
1919(sy) Proof	—	Value: 17,000				
1920(sy)	4,114,000	1.00	5.00	30.00	350	520
1920(m) Proof	—	Value: 21,000				
1921(sy)	5,280,000	0.25	1.00	16.00	230	320
1922(sy)	6,924,000	0.25	1.00	17.00	235	350
1923(sy)	Est. 1,113,000	1,300	3,500	14,000	50,000	—

Note: Dies dated 1922 were used for the majority of the calendar year 1923, leaving only a small portion of this mintage figure as 1923 dated coins.

Date	Mintage	F	VF	XF	Unc	BU
1923(sy) Proof; Rare	—	Value: 100,000				

Note: Noble Numismatics sale No. 62, 11-99, nearly FDC proof realized $56,745.

Date	Mintage	F	VF	XF	Unc	BU
1924(m)	682,000	3.50	12.50	70.00	1,000	1,500
1924(m) Proof	—	Value: 20,000				
1925(m)	1,147,000	1.00	5.00	30.00	825	—
1925(m) Proof	—	Value: 32,000				
1926(m & sy)	4,139,000	0.25	1.00	17.00	400	800
1926(m) Proof	—	Value: 15,000				
1927(m)	3,072,000	0.25	1.00	15.00	250	400
1927(m) Proof	50	Value: 15,500				
1928(m)	2,318,000	1.00	5.00	25.00	625	1,000
1928(m) Proof	—	Value: 15,500				
1929(m)	2,635,000	0.25	1.00	15.00	275	450
1929(m) Proof	—	Value: 15,000				
1930(m)	638,000	1.50	6.00	35.00	900	1,250
1930(m) Proof	—	Value: 40,000				
1931(m)	370,000	1.50	6.00	35.00	900	1,250
1931(m) Proof	—	Value: 16,000				
1932(m)	2,554,000	0.25	1.00	10.00	175	285
1932(m) Proof	—	Value: 16,000				
1933(m)	4,608,000	0.20	0.50	9.00	125	200
1933(m) Proof	—	Value: 15,500				
1934(m)	3,816,000	0.20	0.50	9.00	125	200
1934(m) Proof	100	Value: 11,500				
1935(m)	2,916,000	0.20	0.50	9.00	125	200
1935(m) Proof	100	Value: 11,000				
1936(m)	2,562,000	0.20	0.40	5.00	75.00	125
1936(m) Proof	—	Value: 15,000				

KM# 30 1/2 PENNY

Bronze **Ruler:** George V **Obv:** India 1/4 Anna, KM#511 **Rev:** Value in inner circle **Note:** Mule.

Date	Mintage	F	VF	XF	Unc	BU
1916(c) I	Est. 10	55,000	85,000	—	—	—

KM# 35 1/2 PENNY

Bronze **Ruler:** George VI **Obv:** Head left **Obv. Designer:** T.H. Paget **Rev:** Value in inner circle **Edge:** Plain

Date	Mintage	F	VF	XF	Unc	BU
1938(m)	3,014,000	0.20	0.40	3.00	35.00	60.00
1938(m) Proof	250	Value: 6,500				
1939(m)	4,382,000	0.20	0.40	3.50	60.00	100
1939(m) Proof	—	Value: 14,000				

KM# 41 1/2 PENNY

5.7000 g., Bronze **Ruler:** George VI **Obv:** Head left **Obv. Designer:** T. H. Paget **Rev:** Kangaroo leaping right above value **Rev. Designer:** George Kruger Gray

Date	Mintage	F	VF	XF	Unc	BU
1939(m)	504,000	9.50	15.00	60.00	650	1,100
1939(m) Proof	100	Value: 11,000				
1940(m)	2,294,000	0.25	1.00	6.50	125	170
1940(m) Proof	—	Value: 15,500				
1941(m)	5,011,000	0.20	0.75	4.00	70.00	100
1941(m) Proof	—	Value: 15,500				
1942(m)	720,000	1.00	3.75	20.00	175	300
1942(m) Proof	—	Value: 11,000				
1942(p)	4,334,000	0.20	0.50	6.00	90.00	120
1942(p) Proof	—	Value: 10,500				
1942(b) I Wide date	6,000,000	0.20	0.50	3.00	40.00	60.00
1942(b) I Narrow date	Inc. above	0.20	0.50	3.00	40.00	60.00
1942(b) I Proof	—	Value: 10,500				
1943(m)	33,989,000	0.10	0.25	2.00	17.50	28.00
1943(p) Proof	—	Value: 12,000				
1943(b) I	6,000,000	0.10	0.30	2.75	30.00	42.00
1943(b) I Proof	—	Value: 10,500				
1944(m)	720,000	1.00	3.75	27.50	185	375
1945(p)	3,033,000	0.75	2.00	13.50	85.00	150
1945(p) Proof	—	Value: 11,500				
1945(p) Without dot	Inc. above	1.00	2.25	13.50	85.00	150
1946(p)	13,747,000	0.10	0.25	2.00	20.00	30.00
1946(p) Proof	—	Value: 11,500				
1947(p)	9,293,000	0.10	0.25	2.50	25.00	37.50
1947(p) Proof	—	Value: 12,000				
1948(m)	4,608,000	0.25	0.50	3.50	32.50	42.00
1948(m) Proof	—	Value: 12,000				
1948(p)	25,553,000	0.10	0.25	2.00	21.50	30.00
1948(p) Proof	—	Value: 11,500				

KM# 42 1/2 PENNY

5.6000 g., Bronze **Ruler:** George VI **Obv:** Head left **Obv. Legend:** IND: IMP: dropped **Obv. Designer:** T.H. Paget **Rev:** Kangaroo leaping right **Rev. Designer:** George Kruger Gray

Date	Mintage	F	VF	XF	Unc	BU
1949(m) Proof	—	Value: 13,500				

Note: Some consider this a pattern

Date	Mintage	F	VF	XF	Unc	BU
1949(p)	22,310,000	0.10	0.25	2.00	21.50	27.50
1949(p) Proof	—	Value: 11,500				
1950(p)	12,014,000	0.10	0.25	2.00	32.50	40.00
1950(p) Proof	—	Value: 11,500				
1951(p) With dot	—	0.10	0.25	2.00	21.50	27.50
1951(p) With dot, Proof	—	Value: 12,000				
1951(p) Without dot	29,422,000	0.10	0.50	3.50	23.50	32.50
1951(p) Without dot; Proof	—	Value: 12,000				
1951PL	17,040,000	0.10	0.15	0.75	6.25	10.00

Note: 5,040,000 struck at the Birmingham Mint.

Date	Mintage	F	VF	XF	Unc	BU
1951PL Proof	—	Value: 7,250				
1952(p)	1,832,000	0.50	1.50	4.00	55.00	85.00
1952(p) Proof	—	Value: 7,500				

KM# 49 1/2 PENNY

5.6700 g., Bronze **Ruler:** Elizabeth II **Obv:** Laureate bust right **Obv. Legend:** DEI • GRATIA • REGINA + ELIZABETH • II • **Obv. Designer:** Mary Gillick **Rev:** Kangaroo leaping right **Rev. Designer:** George Kruger Gray

Date	Mintage	F	VF	XF	Unc	BU
1953(p)	23,967,000	0.10	0.15	0.50	10.00	15.00
1953(p) Proof	16	Value: 7,500				
1954(p)	21,963,000	0.10	0.15	0.50	10.00	15.00
1954(p) Proof	—	Value: 7,500				
1955(p) Without dot	9,343,000	0.10	0.15	0.50	10.00	14.00
1955(p) Without dot; Proof	301	Value: 4,500				

KM# 61 1/2 PENNY

5.9000 g., Bronze **Ruler:** Elizabeth II **Obv:** Laureate bust right **Obv. Legend:** DEI • GRATIA • REGINA • F:D: + ELIZABETH • II • **Obv. Designer:** Mary Gillick **Rev:** Kangaroo leaping right **Rev. Designer:** George Kruger Gray

Date	Mintage	F	VF	XF	Unc	BU
1959(m)	10,166,000	0.10	0.15	0.25	1.50	3.00
1959(m) Proof	1,506	Value: 350				
1960(p)	17,812,000	0.10	0.15	0.25	1.00	1.50
1960(p) Proof	1,030	Value: 300				
1961(p)	20,183,000	0.10	0.15	0.25	1.00	1.50
1961(p) Proof	1,040	Value: 300				
1962(p)	10,259,000	0.10	0.15	0.25	1.00	1.50
1962(p) Proof	1,064	Value: 300				
1963(p)	16,410,000	0.10	0.15	0.25	0.75	1.00
1963(p) Proof	1,060	Value: 300				
1964(p)	18,230,000	0.10	0.15	0.25	0.75	1.00
1964(p) Proof; 1 known	—	Value: 16,500				

KM# 23 PENNY

9.4000 g., Bronze, 30.5 mm. **Ruler:** George V **Obv:** Crowned bust left **Obv. Legend:** GEORGIVS V D.G. BRITT: OMN: REX F.D: IND: IMP **Obv. Designer:** E.B. MacKennal **Rev:** Value in inner circle **Edge:** Plain

Date	Mintage	F	VF	XF	Unc	BU
1911(L)	3,768,000	1.00	4.00	22.50	200	400
1911(L) Proof	—	Value: 21,000				
1912H	3,600,000	1.25	4.50	27.50	350	775
1912H Proof	—	Value: 21,000				
1913(L) Narrow date	2,520,000	1.25	5.00	32.50	650	1,100
1913(L) Wide date	Inc. above	1.25	5.00	32.50	675	1,125
1914(L)	720,000	3.00	12.50	200	1,500	2,500
1915(L)	960,000	2.00	10.00	220	1,750	2,650
1915H	1,320,000	1.75	8.50	160	1,400	2,000
1916(c) I	3,324,000	0.50	1.50	20.00	250	650
1916(c) I Proof	—	Value: 36,500				
1917(c) I	6,240,000	0.50	1.50	20.00	200	650
1918(c) I	1,200,000	1.75	10.00	220	1,850	2,300
1919(m)	5,810,000	0.50	1.50	25.00	250	650
Note: Without dots						
1919(m)	Inc. above	0.50	1.50	25.00	250	650
Note: Dot below bottom scroll						
1919(m)	—	40.00	125	800	2,750	4,000
Note: Dots below bottom scroll and above upper						
1919(m) Proof	—	Value: 37,500				
1920(m & sy)	9,041,000	20.00	150	850	7,500	12,500
Note: Without dots						
1920(m)	Inc. above	1.75	10.00	145	1,350	1,750
Note: Dot below bottom scroll						
1920(m) Proof	—	Value: 35,000				
1920(sy)	Inc. above	1.75	10.00	145	1,350	1,750
Note: Dot above bottom scroll						
1920	Inc. above	20.00	125	725	5,000	—
Note: Dots below bottom scroll and above upper						
1921(m & sy)	7,438,000	0.50	6.00	35.00	600	1,050
1922(m & p)	12,697,000	0.50	6.00	40.00	650	1,100
1923(m)	5,654,000	0.50	6.00	35.00	575	1,000
1923(m) Proof	—	Value: 30,000				
1924(m & sy)	4,656,000	0.50	5.00	35.00	550	900
1924(m) Proof	—	Value: 19,500				
1925(m)	1,639,000	85.00	210	1,100	9,000	13,500
1925(m) Proof	—	Value: 95,000				
1926(m & sy)	1,859,000	1.50	8.00	160	1,250	2,000
1926(m) Proof	—	Value: 19,000				
1927(m)	4,922,000	0.50	2.25	35.00	275	450
1927(m) Proof	50	Value: 21,500				
1928(m)	3,038,000	0.50	3.00	50.00	950	1,500
1928(m) Proof	—	Value: 18,500				
1929(m)	2,599,000	0.50	3.00	55.00	1,100	1,900
1929(m) Proof	—	Value: 18,500				
1930(m)	Est. 3,000	8,500	13,000	33,000	65,000	100,000
1930(m) Proof; Rare	Est. 6	Value: 300,000				
Note: Noble Numismatics sale No. 52, 7-97, nearly FDC proof realized $126,500. Noble Numismatics sale No. 62, 11-99, FDC proof realized $162,665.						
1931(m) Normal date alignment	494,000	2.00	7.50	100	1,200	2,000
1931(m) Fallen 1 in date	Inc. above	2.00	7.50	100	1,200	2,000
1931(m) Proof	—	Value: 35,000				
1932(m)	2,117,000	0.50	3.00	50.00	275	500
1933/2(m)	5,818,000	15.00	30.00	150	1,100	1,800
1933(m)	Inc. above	0.25	1.50	20.00	125	200
1933(m) Proof	—	Value: 21,500				
1934(m)	5,808,000	0.25	1.50	20.00	125	200
1934(m) Proof	100	Value: 12,000				
1935(m)	3,725,000	0.25	1.50	20.00	120	200
1935(m) Proof	100	Value: 8,500				
1936(m)	9,890,000	0.25	0.75	10.00	80.00	140
1936(m) Proof	—	Value: 19,500				

KM# 36 PENNY

9.4100 g., Bronze, 30.5 mm. **Ruler:** George VI **Obv:** Head left **Obv. Legend:** GEORGIVS VI D:G:BR: OMN: REX F.D: IND: IMP **Obv. Designer:** T. H. Paget **Rev:** Kangaroo leaping left **Rev. Designer:** George Kruger Gray **Edge:** Plain

Date	Mintage	F	VF	XF	Unc	BU
1938(m)	5,552,000	0.25	0.75	8.00	45.00	80.00
1938(m) Proof	250	Value: 8,500				
1939(m)	6,240,000	0.25	0.75	8.00	50.00	85.00
1939(m) Proof	—	Value: 15,000				
1940(m)	4,075,000	0.50	1.50	20.00	100	180
1940(p) K.G.	1,114,000	1.50	5.00	50.00	500	1,000
1941(m)	1,588,000	0.25	1.50	12.00	80.00	150
1941(p) K.G.	12,794,000	1.00	2.00	30.00	180	275
1941(p) Proof	—	Value: 15,000				
1941(p)	Inc. above	0.25	0.75	12.00	75.00	140
1941(p) K.G. high dot after Y	Inc. above	2.00	7.50	100	1,000	—
1942(p)	12,245,000	0.15	0.50	7.00	35.00	80.00
1942(b) I	9,000,000	0.15	0.50	5.00	22.50	60.00
1942(b) Without I	Inc. above	2.00	5.00	40.00	275	—
1942(b) Proof	—	Value: 9,500				
1943(m)	11,112,000	0.20	0.50	10.00	35.00	60.00
1943(p)	33,086,000	0.15	0.50	9.00	35.00	60.00
1943(p) Proof	—	Value: 12,500				
1943(b) I	9,000,000	0.15	0.50	8.00	35.00	60.00
Note: Small and large denticle varieties exist.						
1943(b) I Without I	Inc. above	2.00	4.00	25.00	125	—
1943(b) Proof	—	Value: 11,500				
1944(m)	2,112,000	0.50	3.00	25.00	145	260
1944(p)	27,830,000	0.15	0.50	7.00	35.00	50.00
1944(p) Proof	—	Value: 12,500				
1945(p)	15,173,000	0.20	0.75	9.00	60.00	100
Note: With and without a large dot after the KG.						
1945(p) Proof	—	Value: 12,500				
1945(b) I Rare	6	—	—	—	—	—
1945(m) Rare	—	Value: 100,000				
Note: Considered by many to be a pattern						
1946(m)	240,000	42.50	75.00	275	1,650	2,500
1947(m)	6,864,000	0.15	0.40	4.50	25.00	40.00
1947(p)	4,490,000	0.50	2.00	35.00	275	550
1947(p) Proof	—	Value: 12,500				
1948(m)	26,616,000	0.15	0.40	3.50	20.00	30.00
1948(p)	1,534,000	0.75	4.00	60.00	400	900
1948(p) Proof	—	Value: 15,000				

KM# 43 PENNY

Bronze, 30.5 mm. **Ruler:** George VI **Obv:** Head left **Obv. Legend:** IND: IMP. dropped **Obv. Designer:** T. H. Paget **Rev:** Kangaroo leaping left **Rev. Designer:** George Kruger Gray **Edge:** Plain

Date	Mintage	F	VF	XF	Unc	BU
1949(m)	27,065,000	0.15	0.25	2.50	16.00	28.00
1949(m) Proof	—	Value: 16,000				
1950(m)	36,359,000	0.15	0.25	2.50	18.00	28.00
1950(m) Proof	—	Value: 16,000				
1950(p)	21,488,000	0.20	0.75	12.50	60.00	100
1950(p) Proof	—	Value: 16,000				
1951(m)	21,240,000	0.15	0.20	1.00	15.00	25.00
1951(p)	12,888,000	0.20	0.75	10.00	50.00	85.00
1951(p) Proof	—	Value: 15,000				
1951PL	18,000,000	0.15	0.25	0.85	10.00	15.00
1951PL Proof	—	Value: 14,500				
1952(m)	12,408,000	0.15	0.30	1.00	12.00	17.50
1952(m) Proof	—	Value: 12,000				
1952(p)	45,514,000	0.15	0.25	0.85	9.00	15.00
Note: Two varieties of the 2 in the date.						
1952(p) Proof	—	Value: 12,000				

KM# 50 PENNY

Bronze, 30.5 mm. **Ruler:** Elizabeth II **Obv:** Laureate bust, right **Obv. Legend:** DEI • GRATIA • REGINA + ELIZABETH • II • **Obv. Designer:** Mary Gillick **Rev:** Kangaroo leaping left **Rev. Designer:** George Kruger Gray **Edge:** Plain

Date	Mintage	F	VF	XF	Unc	BU
1953(m)	6,936,000	0.20	0.50	2.00	20.00	35.00
Note: Two varieties to the numeral 5.						
1953(m) Proof	—	Value: 10,500				
1953(p)	6,203,000	0.20	0.65	2.50	20.00	35.00
1953(p) Proof	16	Value: 10,500				

KM# 56 PENNY

9.4500 g., Bronze, 30.5 mm. **Ruler:** Elizabeth II **Obv:** Laureate bust right **Obv. Legend:** F:D: added **Obv. Designer:** Mary Gillick **Rev:** Kangaroo leaping left **Rev. Designer:** George Kruger Gray **Edge:** Plain

Date	Mintage	F	VF	XF	Unc	BU
1955(m)	6,336,000	0.20	0.50	2.00	12.00	20.00
1955(m) Proof	1,200	Value: 400				
1955(p)	11,110,000	0.25	0.75	2.00	15.00	27.50
1955(p) Proof	301	Value: 3,150				
1956(m)	13,872,000	0.10	0.20	0.50	8.00	17.50
1956(m) Proof	1,500	Value: 400				
1956(p)	12,121,000	0.10	0.20	0.50	8.00	18.50
1956(p) Proof	417	Value: 2,900				
1957(p)	15,978,000	0.10	0.20	0.50	5.00	9.00
1957(p) Proof	1,112	Value: 550				
1958(m)	10,012,000	0.10	0.20	0.50	5.00	9.00
1958(m) Proof	1,506	Value: 400				
1958(p)	14,428,000	0.10	0.20	0.50	6.00	9.00
1958(p) Proof	1,028	Value: 500				
1959(m)	1,617,000	0.50	1.25	8.00	50.00	90.00
1959(m) Proof	1,506	Value: 500				
1959(p)	14,428,000	0.10	0.20	0.50	3.00	6.00
1959(p) Proof	1,030	Value: 500				
1960(p)	20,515,000	0.10	0.20	0.50	1.50	2.00
1960(p) Proof	1,030	Value: 475				
1961(p)	30,607,000	0.10	0.20	0.40	1.00	1.75
1961(p) Proof	1,040	Value: 475				
1962(p)	34,851,000	0.10	0.20	0.30	0.75	1.25
1962(p) Proof	1,064	Value: 475				
1963(p)	10,258,000	0.10	0.20	0.30	0.75	1.25
1963(p) Proof	1,100	Value: 475				
1964(m)	49,130,000	0.10	0.15	0.20	0.75	1.00
1964(p)	54,590,000	0.10	0.15	0.30	0.75	1.00
1964(p) Proof; 1 known	—	Value: 12,500				

KM# 18 THREEPENCE

1.4100 g., 0.9250 Silver 0.0419 oz. ASW, 16 mm. **Ruler:** Edward VII **Obv:** Bust right **Obv. Designer:** G. W. de Saulles **Rev:** Arms **Rev. Designer:** W. H. J. Blakemore **Edge:** Plain

Date	Mintage	F	VF	XF	Unc	BU
1910(L)	4,000,000	1.75	7.00	20.00	65.00	100
1910(L) Proof	—	Value: 7,500				

KM# 24 THREEPENCE

1.4100 g., 0.9250 Silver 0.0419 oz. ASW, 16 mm. **Ruler:** George V **Obv:** Crowned bust left **Obv. Designer:** E. B. MacKennal **Rev:** Arms **Rev. Designer:** W. H. J. Blakemore **Edge:** Plain

Date	Mintage	F	VF	XF	Unc	BU
1911(L)	2,000,000	5.00	17.50	80.00	325	600
1911(L) Proof	—	Value: 14,500				
1911(L) Proof	—	Value: 45,000				
Note: Reeded edge						
1912(L)	2,400,000	10.00	50.00	200	1,250	2,250
1914(L)	1,600,000	11.00	40.00	190	800	1,600
1915(L)	800,000	25.00	90.00	325	1,650	2,750
1916M	1,913,000	5.00	17.50	110	600	1,000
1916M Proof	25	Value: 8,000				
1917M	3,808,000	1.75	7.00	35.00	200	375
1918M	3,119,000	1.75	7.00	35.00	200	375
1918M Proof	—	Value: 35,000				
1919M	3,201,000	1.75	7.00	40.00	220	395
1919M Proof	—	Value: 13,500				
1920M	4,196,000	5.00	25.00	100	675	1,100
1920M Proof	—	Value: 14,000				
1921M	7,378,000	1.25	3.50	35.00	145	250
1921(m)	Inc. above	5.00	35.00	175	725	1,150
1921M Proof	—	Value: 14,000				
1922/1(m)	900	8,500	22,500	42,000	—	—
1922(m)	5,531,000	1.75	7.00	50.00	260	500
1922(m) Proof	—	Value: 14,000				
1923(m)	815,000	14.00	60.00	215	1,300	2,250
1924(m & sy)	2,013,999	5.00	17.50	90.00	575	475
1924(m) Proof	—	Value: 11,000				
1925(m & sy) Proof	4,347,000	1.00	4.00	45.00	200	375
1925(m) Proof	—	Value: 12,500				
1926(m & sy)	6,158,000	1.00	3.00	27.50	150	250
1926(m) Proof	—	Value: 11,500				
1927(m)	6,720,000	0.85	2.25	27.00	145	245
1927(m) Proof	50	Value: 11,500				
1928(m)	5,000,000	0.85	3.00	30.00	170	300
1928(m) Proof	—	Value: 11,500				
1934/3(m)	1,616,000	25.00	90.00	300	1,250	2,250
1934(m)	Inc. above	0.85	2.25	27.00	140	240
1934(m) Proof	100	Value: 6,000				
1935(m)	2,800,000	0.85	2.25	21.50	140	240
1935(m) Proof	—	Value: 6,000				
1936(m)	3,600,000	BV	1.00	12.50	75.00	135
1936(m) Proof	—	Value: 6,000				

KM# 37 THREEPENCE

1.4100 g., 0.9250 Silver 0.0419 oz. ASW, 16 mm. **Ruler:** George VI **Obv:** Head left **Obv. Designer:** T. H. Paget **Rev:** Three wheat stalks divide date **Rev. Designer:** George Kruger Gray

Date	Mintage	F	VF	XF	Unc	BU
1938(m)	4,560,000	BV	1.00	6.50	27.50	45.00
1938(m) Proof	250	Value: 5,000				
1939(m)	3,856,000	BV	1.00	10.00	50.00	100
1939(m) Proof	—	—	—	—	—	—
1940(m)	3,840,000	BV	1.00	10.00	55.00	110
1941(m)	7,584,000	BV	0.75	6.50	30.00	55.00
1942(m)	528,000	12.50	35.00	250	1,300	2,400
1942D	16,000,000	—	BV	1.00	11.50	18.50
1942S	8,000,000	—	BV	1.00	11.50	18.50
1943(m)	24,912,000	—	BV	1.00	11.50	18.50
1943D	16,000,000	—	BV	1.00	11.50	18.50
1943S	8,000,000	—	BV	1.00	12.00	18.50
1944S	32,000,000	—	BV	0.85	5.00	9.50
Note: Two varieties to the "S" mintmark.						

KM# 37a THREEPENCE

1.4100 g., 0.5000 Silver 0.0227 oz. ASW, 16 mm. **Ruler:** George VI **Obv:** Head left **Obv. Designer:** T. H. Paget **Rev:** 3 wheat stalks divide date **Rev. Designer:** George Kruger Gray

Date	Mintage	F	VF	XF	Unc	BU
1947(m)	4,176,000	0.85	1.50	10.00	55.00	110
1948(m)	26,208,000	—	BV	0.85	7.00	14.00

KM# 44 THREEPENCE

1.4100 g., 0.5000 Silver 0.0227 oz. ASW, 16 mm. **Ruler:** George VI **Obv:** Head left **Obv. Legend:** IND: IMP. dropped **Obv. Designer:** T. H. Paget **Rev:** Three wheat stalks divide date **Rev. Designer:** George Kruger Gray

Date	Mintage	F	VF	XF	Unc	BU
1949(m)	26,400,000	—	BV	0.85	6.50	16.00
1949(m) Proof	—	—	—	—	—	—
1950(m)	35,456,000	—	BV	0.85	6.50	14.00
1951(m)	15,856,000	—	0.50	1.00	11.50	23.50
1951PL	40,000,000	—	BV	0.50	4.00	7.00
1951PL Proof	—	Value: 7,500				
1952(m)	21,560,000	—	BV	1.00	8.00	15.00

KM# 51 THREEPENCE

1.4100 g., 0.5000 Silver 0.0227 oz. ASW, 16 mm. **Ruler:** Elizabeth II **Obv:** Laureate bust, right **Obv. Designer:** Mary Gillick **Rev:** Three wheat stalks divide date **Rev. Designer:** George Kruger Gray **Edge:** Plain

Date	Mintage	F	VF	XF	Unc	BU
1953(m)	7,664,000	BV	1.50	4.00	20.00	40.00
1953(m) Proof	—	Value: 7,500				
1954(m)	2,672,000	0.85	2.50	5.00	32.50	55.00
1954(m) Proof	—	Value: 7,500				

KM# 57 THREEPENCE

1.4100 g., 0.5000 Silver 0.0227 oz. ASW, 16 mm. **Ruler:** Elizabeth II **Obv:** Laureate bust right **Obv. Legend:** F:D: added **Obv. Designer:** Mary Gillick **Rev:** Three wheat stalks divide date **Rev. Designer:** George Kruger Gray **Edge:** Plain

Date	Mintage	F	VF	XF	Unc	BU
1955(m)	27,088,000	—	BV	1.00	6.00	11.50
1955(m) Proof	1,040	Value: 250				
1956(m)	14,088,000	—	BV	1.00	6.00	11.50
1956(m) Proof	1,500	Value: 70.00				
1957(m)	26,704,000	—	BV	0.75	4.00	7.50
1957(m) Proof	1,256	Value: 70.00				
1958(m)	11,248,000	—	BV	0.75	6.00	11.50
1958(m) Proof	1,506	Value: 70.00				
1959(m)	19,888,000	—	BV	0.75	4.00	7.50
1959(m) Proof	1,506	Value: 70.00				
1960(m)	19,600,000	—	BV	0.50	1.50	3.00
1960(m) Proof	1,509	Value: 70.00				
1961(m)	33,840,000	—	BV	0.50	1.50	3.00
1961(m) Proof	1,506	Value: 70.00				
1962(m)	15,968,000	—	BV	0.50	1.50	3.00
1962(m) Proof	2,016	Value: 65.00				
1963(m)	44,016,000	—	BV	0.50	1.50	3.00
1963(m) Proof	5,042	Value: 55.00				
1964(m)	20,320,000	—	BV	0.50	1.00	2.00

KM# 19 SIXPENCE

2.8200 g., 0.9250 Silver 0.0839 oz. ASW, 19.5 mm. **Ruler:** Edward VII **Obv:** Crowned bust right **Obv. Designer:** G. W. de Salles **Rev:** Arms **Rev. Designer:** W. H. J. Blakemore **Edge:** Reeded

Date	Mintage	F	VF	XF	Unc	BU
1910(L)	3,046,000	6.00	17.00	60.00	200	325
1910(L) Proof	—	Value: 10,500				

KM# 25 SIXPENCE

2.8200 g., 0.9250 Silver 0.0839 oz. ASW, 19.5 mm. **Ruler:** George V **Obv:** Crowned bust left **Obv. Designer:** E. B. MacKennal **Rev:** Arms **Rev. Designer:** W. H. J. Blakemore **Edge:** Reeded

Date	Mintage	F	VF	XF	Unc	BU
1911(L)	1,000,000	9.00	30.00	145	950	2,250
1911(L) Proof	—	Value: 20,000				
1912(L)	1,600,000	30.00	85.00	400	1,500	3,250
1914(L)	1,800,000	9.00	25.00	140	875	1,800
1916M	1,769,000	22.00	75.00	275	1,250	2,500
1916M Proof	25	Value: 12,500				
1917M	1,632,000	20.00	60.00	220	950	1,900
1917M Proof	—	Value: 20,000				
1918M	915,000	50.00	170	700	2,700	5,500
1918M Proof	—	Value: 60,000				
1919M	1,521,000	10.00	30.00	140	875	1,500
1919M Proof	—	Value: 20,000				
1920M	1,476,000	15.00	60.00	220	1,050	2,600
1920M Proof	—	Value: 20,000				
1921(m) Proof	—	Value: 20,000				
1921(m & sy)	3,795,000	5.00	16.50	75.00	400	700
1922(sy)	1,488,000	20.00	100	450	1,900	2,850
1922(sy) Proof	—	Value: 30,000				
1923(m & sy)	1,458,000	10.00	35.00	220	1,000	1,850
1924(m) Proof	—	Value: 16,500				
1924(m & sy)	1,038,000	15.00	60.00	275	1,500	2,600
1925(m) Proof	—	Value: 15,000				
1925(m & sy)	3,266,000	5.00	20.00	90.00	425	1,000
1926(m) Proof	—	Value: 15,000				
1926(m & sy)	3,609,000	2.50	9.00	30.00	190	350
1927(m)	3,592,000	2.50	8.00	25.00	180	350
1927(m) Proof	50	Value: 15,000				
1928(m)	2,721,000	2.50	8.00	25.00	185	400
1928(m) Proof	—	Value: 15,000				
1934(m)	1,024,000	2.50	9.00	55.00	400	1,000
1934(m) Proof	100	Value: 6,500				
1935(m)	392,000	5.00	18.00	100	675	1,300
1935(m) Proof	—	Value: 15,000				
1936(m)	1,800,000	1.50	3.00	10.00	130	295
1936(m) Proof	—	Value: 15,000				

KM# 38 SIXPENCE

2.8200 g., 0.9250 Silver 0.0839 oz. ASW, 19.5 mm. **Ruler:** George VI **Obv:** Head left **Obv. Designer:** T. H. Paget **Rev:** Arms **Rev. Designer:** W. H. J. Blakemore **Edge:** Reeded

Date	Mintage	F	VF	XF	Unc	BU
1938(m)	2,864,000	BV	2.25	6.00	40.00	70.00
1938(m) Proof	250	Value: 5,000				
1939(m)	1,600,000	BV	2.50	15.00	160	500
1940(m)	1,600,000	BV	2.25	10.00	80.00	150
1941(m)	2,912,000	BV	2.25	6.50	45.00	75.00
1942(m)	8,968,000	BV	1.75	3.00	30.00	50.00
1942D	12,000,000	BV	1.75	2.25	16.00	25.00
1942S	4,000,000	BV	1.75	2.25	20.00	30.00
1943D	8,000,000	BV	1.75	2.25	16.00	25.00
1943S	4,000,000	BV	1.75	2.25	20.00	30.00
1944S	4,000,000	BV	1.75	2.25	16.00	25.00
1945(m)	10,096,000	BV	1.75	2.50	20.00	30.00

KM# 38a SIXPENCE

2.8200 g., 0.5000 Silver 0.0453 oz. ASW **Ruler:** George VI **Obv:** Head left **Obv. Designer:** T. H. Paget **Rev:** Arms **Rev. Designer:** W. H. J. Blakemore **Edge:** Reeded

Date	Mintage	F	VF	XF	Unc	BU
1946(m)	10,024,000	—	BV	3.00	30.00	50.00
1946(m) Proof	—	Value: 10,000				
1948(m)	1,584,000	—	BV	3.00	37.50	60.00

KM# 45 SIXPENCE

2.8200 g., 0.5000 Silver 0.0453 oz. ASW, 19.5 mm. **Ruler:** George VI **Obv:** Head left **Obv. Legend:** IND: IMP. dropped **Obv. Designer:** T. H. Paget **Rev:** Arms **Rev. Designer:** W. H. J. Blakemore **Edge:** Plain

Date	Mintage	F	VF	XF	Unc	BU
1950(m)	10,272,000	BV	BV	3.00	37.50	55.00
1951(m)	13,760,000	BV	BV	2.50	25.00	47.50
1951PL	20,024,000	—	BV	2.00	7.50	12.50
1951PL Proof	—	Value: 9,000				
1952(m)	2,112,000	1.25	5.00	35.00	210	400

KM# 52 SIXPENCE

2.8200 g., 0.5000 Silver 0.0453 oz. ASW, 19.5 mm. **Ruler:** Elizabeth II **Obv:** Laureate bust right **Obv. Designer:** Mary Gillick **Rev:** Arms **Rev. Designer:** W. H. J. Blakemore **Edge:** Reeded

Date	Mintage	F	VF	XF	Unc	BU
1953(m)	1,152,000	1.25	4.00	25.00	150	295
1953(m) Proof	—	Value: 7,500				
1954(m)	7,672,000	—	BV	1.75	5.00	8.00
1954(m) Proof	—	Value: 8,000				

KM# 58 SIXPENCE

2.8200 g., 0.5000 Silver 0.0453 oz. ASW, 19.5 mm. **Ruler:** Elizabeth II **Obv:** Laureate bust right **Obv. Legend:** F:D: added **Obv. Designer:** Mary Gillick **Rev:** Arms **Rev. Designer:** W. H. J. Blakemore **Edge:** Reeded

Date	Mintage	F	VF	XF	Unc	BU
1955(m)	14,248,000	—	BV	2.00	12.50	20.00
1955(m) Proof	1,200	Value: 150				
1956(m)	7,904,000	—	2.00	5.00	30.00	60.00
1956(m) Proof	1,500	Value: 90.00				
1957(m)	13,752,000	—	BV	1.25	4.00	6.50
1957(m) Proof	1,256	Value: 100				
1958(m)	17,944,000	—	BV	1.25	4.00	6.50
1958(m) Proof	1,506	Value: 95.00				
1959(m)	11,728,000	—	BV	1.25	6.00	9.00
1959(m) Proof	1,506	Value: 85.00				
1960(m)	18,592,000	—	BV	1.25	7.00	11.00
1960(m) Proof	1,509	Value: 85.00				
1961(m)	9,152,000	—	BV	1.25	3.00	5.00
1961(m) Proof	1,506	Value: 85.00				
1962(m)	44,816,000	—	BV	BV	1.50	3.00
1962(m) Proof	2,016	Value: 75.00				
1963(m)	25,056,000	—	BV	BV	1.50	3.00
1963(m) Proof	5,042	Value: 65.00				

KM# 20 SHILLING

5.6500 g., 0.9250 Silver 0.1680 oz. ASW, 23.5 mm. **Ruler:** Edward VII **Obv:** Crowned bust right **Obv. Designer:** G. W. de Saulles **Rev:** Arms **Rev. Designer:** W. H. J. Blakemore **Edge:** Reeded

Date	Mintage	F	VF	XF	Unc	BU
1910(L)	2,536,000	5.00	20.00	70.00	175	325
1910(L) Proof	—	Value: 21,000				

KM# 26 SHILLING

5.6500 g., 0.9250 Silver 0.1680 oz. ASW, 23.5 mm. **Ruler:** George V **Obv:** Crowned bust left **Obv. Designer:** E. B. MacKennal **Rev:** Arms **Rev. Designer:** W. H. J. Blakemore **Edge:** Reeded

Date	Mintage	F	VF	XF	Unc	BU
1911(L)	1,700,000	10.00	35.00	180	1,000	1,850
1911(L) Proof	—	Value: 36,000				
1912(L)	1,000,000	20.00	65.00	300	3,000	5,250
1913(L)	1,200,000	16.00	50.00	250	2,750	4,850
1914(L)	3,300,000	6.50	20.00	90.00	600	1,400
1915(L)	800,000	40.00	125	600	4,000	7,000
1915H	500,000	60.00	175	900	7,000	12,500
1915H Proof	—	Value: 55,000				
1916M	5,141,000	3.50	10.00	35.00	200	350
1916M Proof	25	Value: 13,000				
1917M	5,274,000	3.50	9.00	30.00	175	325
1918M	3,761,000	4.00	17.50	65.00	325	600
1919M	—	Value: 100,000				
Note: Some consider this a pattern.						
1920M	520,000	7.00	35.00	225	1,700	3,000
1920M	—	Value: 60,000				
Note: Some consider this to be a pattern						
1921(sy) Star	1,641,000	25.00	80.00	500	3,500	6,500
1921(m) Star; Proof	—	Value: 40,000				
1922(m)	2,040,000	7.50	22.50	150	700	1,850
1922(m) Proof	—	Value: 22,000				
1924(m & sy)	674,000	10.00	45.00	250	2,000	3,750
1924(m) Proof	—	Value: 27,000				
1925/3(m & sy)	1,448,000	3.50	10.00	60.00	325	600
1925(m) Proof	—	Value: 22,000				
1926(m & sy)	2,352,000	3.50	10.00	70.00	350	700
1926(m) Proof	—	Value: 22,000				
1927(m)	1,146,000	3.50	50.00	300	550	—
1927(m) Proof	50	Value: 16,000				
1928(m)	664,000	12.00	35.00	235	1,700	2,800
1928(m) Proof	—	Value: 24,000				
1931(m)	1,000,000	3.50	7.50	50.00	300	550
1931(m) Proof	—	Value: 19,000				
1933(m)	220,000	65.00	190	900	4,500	7,500
1933(m) Proof	—	Value: 50,000				
1934(m)	480,000	7.50	22.50	110	500	900
1934(m) Proof	100	Value: 7,250				
1935(m)	500,000	3.50	9.00	45.00	325	600
1935(m) Proof	—	Value: 9,000				
1936(m)	2,000,000	BV	5.00	27.50	250	450
1936(m) Proof	—	Value: 15,000				

KM# 39 SHILLING

5.6500 g., 0.9250 Silver 0.1680 oz. ASW, 23.5 mm. **Ruler:** George VI **Obv:** Head left **Obv. Designer:** T. H. Paget **Rev:** Rams head left above value and date **Rev. Designer:** George Kruger Gray **Edge:** Reeded

Date	Mintage	F	VF	XF	Unc	BU
1938(m)	1,484,000	2.00	4.00	11.00	60.00	100
1938(m) Proof	250	Value: 5,100				
1939(m)	1,520,000	2.00	5.00	25.00	130	210
1939(m) Proof	—	Value: 19,000				
1940(m)	760,000	4.00	11.50	40.00	275	500
1941(m)	3,040,000	BV	3.00	7.00	50.00	90.00
1942(m)	1,380,000	BV	3.00	6.00	40.00	70.00
1942S	4,000,000	BV	2.00	3.50	25.00	40.00
1943(m)	2,720,000	2.50	5.00	20.00	100	180
1943S	16,000,000	BV	2.00	3.00	15.00	25.00
1944(m)	14,576,000	BV	2.75	8.00	52.50	95.00
1944S	8,000,000	BV	2.00	3.00	15.00	25.00

KM# 39a SHILLING

5.6500 g., 0.5000 Silver 0.0908 oz. ASW, 23.5 mm. **Ruler:** George VI **Obv:** Head left **Obv. Designer:** T. H. Paget **Rev:** Ram's head left above value **Rev. Designer:** George Kruger-Grey **Edge:** Reeded

Date	Mintage	F	VF	XF	Unc	BU
1946(m)	10,072,000	BV	2.00	4.00	25.00	40.00
1946(p)	1,316,000	3.00	10.00	30.00	160	240
1948(m)	4,131,999	BV	2.00	5.00	28.00	45.00

KM# 46 SHILLING

5.6500 g., 0.5000 Silver 0.0908 oz. ASW, 23.5 mm. **Ruler:** George VI **Obv:** Head left **Obv. Legend:** IND: IMP. dropped **Obv. Designer:** T. H. Paget **Rev:** Ram's head left above value, date **Rev. Designer:** George Kruger Gray **Edge:** Reeded

Date	Mintage	F	VF	XF	Unc	BU
1950(m)	7,188,000	BV	2.00	4.00	22.50	40.00
1952(m)	19,644,000	BV	2.00	3.50	15.00	25.00

KM# 53 SHILLING

5.5600 g., 0.5000 Silver 0.0894 oz. ASW, 23.5 mm. **Ruler:** Elizabeth II **Obv:** Laureate bust right **Obv. Designer:** Mary Gillick **Rev:** Ram's head left above value, date **Rev. Designer:** George Kruger Gray **Edge:** Reeded

Date	Mintage	F	VF	XF	Unc	BU
1953(m)	12,204,000	BV	2.00	3.00	13.00	20.00
1953(m) Proof	—	Value: 7,500				
1954(m)	16,187,999	BV	2.00	3.00	13.00	20.00
1954(m) Proof	—	Value: 8,000				

KM# 59 SHILLING

5.5600 g., 0.5000 Silver 0.0894 oz. ASW, 23.5 mm. **Ruler:** Elizabeth II **Obv:** Laureate bust right **Obv. Legend:** F:D: added **Obv. Designer:** Mary Gillick **Rev:** Ram's head left above value, date **Rev. Designer:** George Kruger Gray **Edge:** Reeded

Date	Mintage	F	VF	XF	Unc	BU
1955(m)	7,492,000	BV	BV	3.50	22.50	37.50
1955(m) Proof	1,200	Value: 150				
1956(m)	6,064,000	BV	2.00	4.50	40.00	75.00
1956(m) Proof	1,500	Value: 110				
1957(m)	12,668,000	—	BV	2.00	6.00	10.00
1957(m) Proof	1,256	Value: 130				
1958(m)	7,412,000	—	BV	2.00	6.00	10.00
1958(m) Proof	1,506	Value: 110				
1959(m)	10,876,000	—	BV	2.00	5.00	8.50
1959(m) Proof	1,506	Value: 95.00				
1960(m)	14,512,000	—	—	BV	4.50	8.00
1960(m) Proof	1,509	Value: 95.00				
1961(m)	31,864,000	—	—	BV	2.00	3.00
1961(m) Proof	1,506	Value: 95.00				
1962(m)	6,592,000	—	—	BV	2.00	3.00
1962(m) Proof	2,016	Value: 90.00				
1963(m)	10,072,000	—	—	BV	2.00	3.00
1963(m) Proof	5,042	Value: 80.00				

KM# 21 FLORIN

11.3100 g., 0.9250 Silver 0.3363 oz. ASW, 28.5 mm. **Ruler:** Edward VII **Obv:** Crowned bust right **Obv. Designer:** G. W. de Saulles **Rev:** Arms **Rev. Designer:** W. H. J. Blakemore **Edge:** Reeded

Date	Mintage	F	VF	XF	Unc	BU
1910(L)	1,259,000	27.00	150	375	1,400	2,500
1910(L) Proof	—	Value: 32,500				

KM# 27 FLORIN

11.3100 g., 0.9250 Silver 0.3363 oz. ASW, 28.5 mm. **Ruler:** George V **Obv:** Crowned bust left **Obv. Designer:** E. B. MacKennal **Rev:** Arms **Rev. Designer:** W. H. J. Blakemore **Edge:** Reeded

Date	Mintage	F	VF	XF	Unc	BU
1911(L)	950,000	27.00	200	800	4,200	8,000
1911(L) Proof	—	Value: 45,000				
1912(L)	1,000,000	25.00	225	1,050	6,000	12,000
1913(L)	1,200,000	22.50	200	1,050	5,750	11,500
1913(L) Proof	—	Value: 45,000				
1914(L)	2,300,000	8.00	40.00	350	1,450	2,800
1914H	500,000	45.00	300	1,200	6,800	12,500
1914H Proof	—	Value: 60,000				
1915(L)	500,000	50.00	310	1,300	7,500	13,500
1915H	750,000	27.00	210	700	3,250	5,900
1915H Proof	—	Value: 50,000				
1916M	2,752,000	7.50	30.00	275	1,000	1,800
1916M Proof	25	Value: 15,000				
1917M	4,305,000	7.50	28.00	275	900	1,600
1917M Proof	—	Value: 37,500				
1918M	2,095,000	10.00	30.00	300	1,050	2,000
1918M Proof	—	Value: 37,500				
1919M	1,677,000	20.00	200	700	2,500	4,500
1919M Proof	—	Value: 40,000				
1920M Star; Proof	—	Value: 100,000				
1921(m)	1,247,000	17.50	175	700	3,000	6,000
1921(m) Proof	—	Value: 40,000				
1922(m)	2,057,999	17.50	125	550	2,250	4,200
1922(m) Proof	—	Value: 40,000				
1923(m)	1,038,000	15.00	125	350	1,800	3,400
1923(m) Proof	—	Value: 37,500				
1924(m & sy)	1,582,000	10.00	60.00	315	1,250	2,200
1925(m & sy)	2,960,000	7.00	25.00	250	1,050	1,750
1925(m) Proof	—	Value: 30,000				
1926(m & sy)	2,487,000	7.00	25.00	300	1,200	2,500
1926(m) Proof	—	Value: 30,000				
1927(m)	3,420,000	7.00	15.00	70.00	425	800
1927(m) Proof	50	Value: 26,000				
1928(m)	1,962,000	7.00	15.00	75.00	550	850
1928(m) Proof	—	Value: 30,000				
1931(m)	3,129,000	7.00	9.00	27.50	160	295
1931(m) Proof	—	Value: 26,000				
1932(m)	188,000	100	425	1,500	6,600	12,000
1933(m)	488,000	22.50	200	750	6,000	11,750
1934(m)	1,674,000	7.00	12.50	55.00	350	600
1934(m) Proof	100	Value: 10,000				
1935(m)	915,000	7.00	12.50	65.00	425	800
1935(m) Proof	—	Value: 30,000				
1936(m)	2,382,000	BV	7.00	20.00	180	310
1936(m) Proof	—	Value: 23,500				

KM# 31 FLORIN

11.3100 g., 0.9250 Silver 0.3363 oz. ASW, 28.5 mm. **Ruler:** George V **Subject:** Opening of Parliament House, Canberra **Obv:** Crowned head left **Rev. Designer:** George Kruger Gray **Edge:** Reeded

Date	Mintage	F	VF	XF	Unc	BU
1927(m)	2,000,000	BV	7.00	15.00	85.00	150
1927(m) Proof	400	Value: 15,000				

KM# 33 FLORIN

11.3100 g., 0.9250 Silver 0.3363 oz. ASW, 28.5 mm. **Ruler:** George V **Subject:** Centennial of Victoria and Melbourne **Obv:** Crowned bust left **Rev:** Horse prancing left with rider holding torch **Rev. Designer:** George Kruger Gray

Date	Mintage	F	VF	XF	Unc	BU
ND(1934)	Est. 54,000	100	130	175	300	550
Note: 21,000 pieces were melted						
ND(1934) Proof	—	Value: 16,500				

KM# 40 FLORIN

11.3100 g., 0.9250 Silver 0.3363 oz. ASW, 28.5 mm. **Ruler:** George VI **Obv:** Head left **Obv. Designer:** T. H. Paget **Rev:** Arms **Rev. Designer:** George Kruger Gray **Edge:** Reeded

Date	Mintage	F	VF	XF	Unc	BU
1938(m)	2,990,000	BV	4.50	15.00	45.00	80.00
1938(m) Proof	—	Value: 6,000				
1939(m)	630,000	10.00	30.00	250	1,000	1,700
1940(m)	8,410,000	—	BV	8.50	35.00	50.00
1941(m)	7,614,000	—	BV	7.50	30.00	40.00
1942(m)	17,986,000	—	BV	7.00	25.00	35.00
1942S	6,000,000	—	BV	7.00	20.00	30.00
1943(m)	12,762,000	—	BV	7.00	18.00	27.00
1943S	11,000,000	—	BV	7.00	18.00	27.00
1944(m)	22,440,000	—	BV	7.00	18.00	27.00
1944S	11,000,000	—	BV	7.00	18.00	25.00
1945(m)	11,970,000	—	BV	15.00	50.00	80.00

KM# 40a FLORIN

11.3100 g., 0.5000 Silver 0.1818 oz. ASW, 28.5 mm. **Ruler:** George VI **Obv:** Head left **Obv. Designer:** T. H. Paget **Rev:** Arms **Rev. Designer:** George Kruger-Grey

Date	Mintage	F	VF	XF	Unc	BU
1946(m)	22,154,000	—	BV	4.00	16.50	23.00
1946(m) Proof	—	Value: 13,000				
1947(m)	39,292,000	—	BV	4.00	16.50	23.00
1947(m) Proof	—	Value: 13,000				

KM# 47 FLORIN

11.3100 g., 0.5000 Silver 0.1818 oz. ASW, 28.5 mm. **Ruler:** George VI **Subject:** 50th Year Jubilee **Obv:** Head left **Obv. Designer:** T. H. Paget **Rev:** Crowned crossed scepter and sword divide Jubilee dates **Rev. Designer:** Leslie Bowles **Edge:** Reeded

Date	Mintage	F	VF	XF	Unc	BU
1951(m)	2,000,000	—	BV	4.00	15.00	21.00

KM# 47a FLORIN

Copper-Nickel, 28.5 mm. **Ruler:** George VI **Subject:** 50th Year - Jubilee **Obv:** Head left **Obv. Designer:** T. H. Paget **Rev:** Crowned crossed scepter and sword divide Jubilee dates **Rev. Designer:** Leslie Bowles **Edge:** Reeded

Date	Mintage	F	VF	XF	Unc	BU
1951(L) Proof	—	Value: 17,500				
Note: Thought by many to be a trial strike or pattern						

KM# 48 FLORIN

11.3100 g., 0.5000 Silver 0.1818 oz. ASW, 28.5 mm. **Ruler:** George VI **Obv:** Head left **Obv. Legend:** IND: IMP. dropped **Obv. Designer:** T. H. Paget **Rev:** Arms **Rev. Designer:** George Kruger Gray **Edge:** Reeded

Date	Mintage	F	VF	XF	Unc	BU
1951(m)	10,068,000	BV	BV	10.00	45.00	90.00
1952(m)	10,044,000	BV	BV	10.00	45.00	90.00

KM# 54 FLORIN

11.3100 g., 0.5000 Silver 0.1818 oz. ASW, 28.5 mm. **Ruler:** Elizabeth II **Obv:** Laureate bust right **Obv. Designer:** Mary Gillick **Rev:** Arms **Rev. Designer:** George Kruger Gray **Edge:** Reeded

Date	Mintage	F	VF	XF	Unc	BU
1953(m)	12,658,000	—	BV	4.00	16.50	25.00
Note: Normal and large beads on the reverse.						
1953(m) Proof	—	Value: 8,000				
1954(m)	15,366,000	—	BV	5.00	25.00	50.00
1954(m) Proof	—	Value: 27,500				

KM# 55 FLORIN

11.3100 g., 0.5000 Silver 0.1818 oz. ASW, 28.5 mm. **Ruler:** Elizabeth II **Subject:** Royal Visit **Obv:** Laureate bust right **Obv. Designer:** Mary Gillick **Rev:** Lion and kangaroo facing right **Rev. Designer:** Leslie Bowles

Date	Mintage	F	VF	XF	Unc	BU
1954(m)	4,000,000	BV	BV	4.00	15.00	20.00
1954(m) Proof	—	Value: 15,000				

KM# 60 FLORIN

11.3100 g., 0.5000 Silver 0.1818 oz. ASW, 28.5 mm. **Ruler:** Elizabeth II **Obv:** Laureate bust right **Obv. Legend:** F:D: added **Obv. Designer:** Mary Gillick **Rev:** Arms **Rev. Designer:** George Kruger Gray **Edge:** Reeded

Date	Mintage	F	VF	XF	Unc	BU
1956(m)	8,090,000	BV	4.00	8.00	55.00	110
1956(m) Proof	1,500	Value: 140				
1957(m)	9,278,000	—	BV	3.75	8.00	13.00
1957(m) Proof	1,256	Value: 150				
1958(m)	8,972,000	—	BV	3.75	7.00	12.00
1958(m) Proof	1,506	Value: 140				
1959(m)	3,500,000	—	BV	3.75	6.00	11.00
1959(m) Proof	1,506	Value: 150				
1960(m)	15,760,000	—	BV	3.75	5.00	10.00
1960(m) Proof	1,509	Value: 140				
1961(m)	9,452,000	—	BV	3.75	5.00	10.00
1961(m) Proof	1,506	Value: 140				
1962(m)	13,748,000	—	BV	3.75	5.00	9.00
1962(m) Proof	2,016	Value: 110				
1963(m)	12,002,000	—	BV	3.75	5.00	9.00
1963(m) Proof	5,042	Value: 100				

KM# 34 CROWN

28.2800 g., 0.9250 Silver 0.8410 oz. ASW, 38 mm. **Ruler:** George VI **Obv:** Head left **Obv. Designer:** T. H. Paget **Rev:** Crown above date and value **Rev. Designer:** George Kruger Gray **Edge:** Reeded

Date	Mintage	F	VF	XF	Unc	BU
1937(m)	1,008,000	BV	17.50	22.50	75.00	150
1937(m) Proof	100	Value: 15,000				
1938(m)	102,000	40.00	60.00	90.00	375	800
1938(m) Proof	250	Value: 35,000				

TRADE COINAGE

KM# 14 1/2 SOVEREIGN

3.9940 g., 0.9170 Gold 0.1177 oz. AGW **Ruler:** Edward VII **Obv:** Head right **Obv. Designer:** G.W. DeSaulles **Rev:** St. George slaying dragon

Date	Mintage	F	VF	XF	Unc	BU
1902S	84,000	BV	115	125	550	750
1902S Proof	—	Value: 50,000				
1902S Frosted, Proof	—	Value: 50,000				
1903S	231,000	BV	115	125	700	1,500
1904P	60,000	115	230	1,300	5,000	—
1906S	308,000	BV	115	125	550	750
1906M	82,000	115	150	900	3,000	5,000
1907M	400,000	BV	115	125	950	1,550
1908S	538,000	BV	110	125	450	600
1908M	—	BV	115	125	750	1,200
1908P	25,000	120	250	1,500	5,000	—
1909M	186,000	BV	115	125	1,000	1,500
1909P	44,000	115	175	600	3,000	5,000
1910S	474,000	BV	115	125	400	600

KM# 28 1/2 SOVEREIGN

3.9940 g., 0.9170 Gold 0.1177 oz. AGW **Ruler:** George V **Obv:** Head left **Rev:** St. George slaying dragon

Date	Mintage	F	VF	XF	Unc	BU
1911S	252,000	BV	115	125	150	175
1911S Matte Proof	—	Value: 50,000				
1911P	130,000	BV	120	150	275	325
1912S	278,000	BV	115	125	125	150
1914S	322,000	BV	115	125	130	145
1915P	138,000	BV	115	140	255	300
1915S	892,000	—	BV	110	120	145
1915M	125,000	BV	115	125	150	175
1916S	448,000	—	BV	110	120	145
1918P	—	275	500	1,900	3,100	4,000
Note: Estimated 200-250 pieces minted						

KM# 15 SOVEREIGN

7.9881 g., 0.9170 Gold 0.2355 oz. AGW **Ruler:** Edward VII **Obv:** Head right **Obv. Designer:** G.W. DeSaulles **Rev:** St. George on horseback with sword slaying the dragon

Date	Mintage	F	VF	XF	Unc	BU
1902S	2,813,000	—	—	BV	235	350
1902S Proof	—	Value: 55,000				
1902S Frosted proof	—	Value: 55,000				
1902M	4,267,000	—	—	BV	235	350
1902P	4,289,000	—	—	BV	235	400
1903S	2,806,000	—	—	BV	235	400
1903M	3,521,000	—	—	BV	235	325
1903P	4,674,000	—	—	BV	235	300
1904S	2,986,000	—	—	BV	235	300
1904M	3,743,000	—	—	BV	235	350
1904M Proof	—	Value: 50,000				
1904P	4,506,000	—	—	BV	235	400
1905S	2,778,000	—	—	BV	235	325
1905M	3,633,000	—	—	BV	235	325
1905P	4,876,000	—	—	BV	235	325
1906S	2,792,000	—	—	BV	235	300
1906M	3,657,000	—	—	BV	235	300
1906P	4,829,000	—	—	BV	235	400
1907S	2,539,000	—	—	BV	235	265
1907M	3,332,000	—	—	BV	235	265
1907P	4,972,000	—	—	BV	235	325
1908S	2,017,000	—	—	BV	235	265
1908M	3,080,000	—	—	BV	235	265
1908P	4,875,000	—	—	BV	235	265
1909S	2,057,000	—	—	BV	235	265
1909M	3,029,000	—	—	BV	235	265
1909P	4,524,000	—	—	BV	235	265
1910S	2,135,000	—	—	BV	235	265
1910M	3,054,000	—	—	BV	235	265
1910M Proof	—	Value: 45,000				
1910P	4,690,000	—	—	BV	235	265

KM# 29 SOVEREIGN

7.9881 g., 0.9170 Gold 0.2355 oz. AGW **Ruler:** George V **Obv:** Head left **Rev:** St. George on horseback with sword slaying the dragon

Date	Mintage	F	VF	XF	Unc	BU
1911S	2,519,000	—	—	BV	235	250
1911S Proof	—	Value: 50,000				
1911M	2,851,000	—	—	BV	235	250
1911M Proof	—	Value: 50,000				
1911P	4,373,000	—	—	BV	235	250
1912S	2,227,000	—	—	BV	235	250
1912M	2,467,000	—	—	BV	235	250
1912P	4,278,000	—	—	BV	235	250
1913S	2,249,000	—	—	BV	235	250
1913M	2,323,000	—	—	BV	235	250
1913P	4,635,000	—	—	BV	235	250
1914S	1,774,000	—	—	BV	235	250
1914S Proof	—	Value: 50,000				
1914M	2,012,000	—	—	BV	235	250
1914P	4,815,000	—	—	BV	235	250
1915S	1,346,000	—	—	BV	235	250
1915M	1,637,000	—	—	BV	235	250
1915P	4,373,000	—	—	BV	235	250
1916S	1,242,000	—	—	BV	235	250
1916M	1,277,000	—	—	BV	235	250
1916P	4,906,000	—	—	BV	235	250
1917S	1,666,000	—	—	BV	235	250
1917M	934,000	—	—	BV	235	250
1917P	4,110,000	—	—	BV	235	250
1918S	3,716,000	—	—	BV	235	250
1918M	4,969,000	—	—	BV	235	250
1918P	3,812,000	—	—	BV	235	250
1919S	1,835,000	—	—	BV	235	250
1919M	514,000	—	—	BV	235	300
1919P	2,995,000	—	—	BV	235	250
1920S	360,000	40,000	75,000	150,000	275,000	—
1920M	530,000	1,200	2,700	3,900	5,000	6,000
1920P	2,421,000	—	—	BV	235	250
1921S	839,000	500	750	1,200	1,700	2,200
1921M	240,000	4,500	8,000	12,000	16,000	18,000
1921P	2,314,000	—	—	BV	235	250
1922S	578,000	5,000	8,500	12,500	17,000	19,000
1922S Proof	—	Value: 50,000				
1922M	608,000	3,000	5,000	7,500	10,000	12,500
1922P	2,298,000	—	—	BV	235	250
1923S	416,000	3,000	5,200	8,000	12,500	14,000
1923S Proof	—	Value: 50,000				
1923M	510,000	Value: 300				
1923P	2,124,000	—	—	BV	235	250
1924S	394,000	500	750	1,200	1,700	2,200
1924M	278,000	—	—	BV	235	300
1924P	1,464,000	—	BV	235	250	350
1925S	5,632,000	—	—	BV	235	250
1925M	3,311,000	—	—	BV	235	250
1925P	1,837,000	—	—	BV	250	350
1926S	1,030,999	5,250	10,000	15,000	20,000	22,500
1926S Proof	—	Value: 60,000				
1926M	211,000	—	—	BV	235	300
1926P	1,131,000	500	750	1,250	2,500	2,800
1927M	310,000	—	—	—	—	—
Note: None known.						
1927P	1,383,000	—	BV	235	350	500
1928M	413,000	900	1,400	2,750	3,150	—
1928P	1,333,000	—	BV	235	245	265

KM# 32 SOVEREIGN

7.9881 g., 0.9170 Gold 0.2355 oz. AGW **Ruler:** George V **Obv:** Head left **Rev:** St. George on horseback with sword slaying the dragon

Date	Mintage	F	VF	XF	Unc	BU
1929M	436,000	600	1,000	1,750	2,500	3,000
1929M Proof	—	Value: 50,000				
1929P	1,606,000	—	—	BV	235	250
1930M	77,000	BV	235	250	275	300
1930M Proof	—	Value: 50,000				
1930P	1,915,000	—	—	BV	235	250
1931M	57,000	235	260	350	550	700
1931M Proof	—	Value: 50,000				
1931P	1,173,000	—	—	BV	235	250

DECIMAL COINAGE

KM# 62 CENT

2.6000 g., Bronze, 17.51 mm. **Ruler:** Elizabeth II **Obv:** Young bust right **Obv. Designer:** Arnold Machin **Rev:** Feather-tailed Glider **Rev. Designer:** Stuart Devlin **Edge:** Plain

Date	Mintage	F	VF	XF	Unc	BU
1966(c)	146,457,000	—	—	—	0.65	1.00
1966(c) Proof	18,000	Value: 5.00				
1966(m)	238,990,000	—	—	—	1.00	2.50
Note: Blunted whisker on right						
1966(p)	26,620,000	—	—	1.25	5.00	10.00
Note: Blunted 2nd whisker from right						
1967	110,055,000	—	—	—	1.50	3.00
1968	19,930,000	0.15	0.30	1.25	9.00	18.00
1969	87,680,000	—	—	—	0.65	1.50
1969 Proof	13,000	Value: 3.00				
1970	72,560,000	—	—	—	0.50	0.85
1970 Proof	15,000	Value: 2.50				
1971	102,455,000	—	—	—	0.50	0.85
1971 Proof	10,000	Value: 2.50				
1972	82,400,000	—	—	—	0.50	0.85
1972 Proof	10,000	Value: 2.50				
1973	140,710,000	—	—	—	0.50	0.85
1973 Proof	10,000	Value: 2.50				
1974	131,720,000	—	—	—	0.40	0.60
1974 Proof	11,000	Value: 2.50				
1975	134,775,000	—	—	—	0.20	0.40
1975 Proof	23,000	Value: 1.00				
1976	172,935,000	—	—	—	0.20	0.40
1976 Proof	21,000	Value: 1.25				
1977	153,430,000	—	—	—	0.20	0.40
1977 Proof	55,000	Value: 1.00				
1978	97,253,000	—	—	—	0.20	0.40
1978 Proof	39,000	Value: 1.00				
1979	130,339,000	—	—	—	0.20	0.40
1979 Proof	36,000	Value: 1.00				
1980	137,892,000	—	—	—	0.20	0.40
1980 Proof	68,000	Value: 1.00				
1981	223,900,000	—	—	—	—	0.40
1981 Proof	86,000	Value: 1.00				
1982	134,290,000	—	—	—	0.20	0.40
1982 Proof	100,000	Value: 1.00				
1983	205,625,000	—	—	—	0.20	0.40
1983 Proof	80,000	Value: 1.00				
1984	74,735,000	—	—	—	0.20	0.40
1984 Proof	61,000	Value: 1.00				

KM# 78 CENT

2.6000 g., Bronze, 17.51 mm. **Ruler:** Elizabeth II **Obv:** Crowned head right **Obv. Designer:** Raphael Maklouf **Rev:** Feather-tailed Glider **Rev. Designer:** Stuart Devlin

Date	Mintage	F	VF	XF	Unc	BU
1985	38,300,000	—	—	—	0.20	0.40
1985 Proof	75,000	Value: 1.00				
1986 In sets only	180,000	—	—	—	2.25	3.00
1986 Proof	67,000	Value: 3.00				
1987	127,000,000	—	—	—	0.20	0.40
1987 Proof	70,000	Value: 1.00				
1988	105,900,000	—	—	—	0.20	0.40
1988 Proof	106,000	Value: 1.00				
1989	150,000,000	—	—	—	0.20	0.40
1989 Proof	67,000	Value: 1.00				
1990	51,900,000	—	—	—	0.20	0.40
1990 Proof	53,000	Value: 2.00				
1991 In sets only	148,000	—	—	—	2.25	3.00
1991 Proof	41,000	Value: 3.00				

KM# 767 CENT

2.5900 g., Bronze, 17.53 mm. **Ruler:** Elizabeth II **Obv:** Head with tiara right **Obv. Designer:** Ian Rank-Broadley **Rev:** Feather-tailed glider **Rev. Designer:** Stuart Devlin **Edge:** Plain

Date	Mintage	F	VF	XF	Unc	BU
2006	—	—	—	—	2.25	3.00
Note: In sets only						
2006 Proof	—	Value: 5.00				

KM# 63 2 CENTS

5.2000 g., Bronze, 21.6 mm. **Ruler:** Elizabeth II **Obv:** Young bust right **Obv. Designer:** Arnold Machin **Rev:** Frilled Lizard **Rev. Designer:** Stuart Devlin

Date	Mintage	F	VF	XF	Unc	BU
1966(c)	145,226,000	—	—	—	0.65	1.00
1966(c) Proof	18,000	Value: 6.00				
1966(m)	66,575,000	—	—	—	2.25	4.00
Note: Blunted 3rd left claw						
1966(p)	217,735,000	—	—	—	1.25	2.00
Note: Blunted 1st right claw						
1967	73,250,000	—	—	—	3.50	6.00
1967	Inc. above	—	—	—	50.00	60.00
Note: Without designer's initials on reverse						
1968	17,000,000	—	0.25	0.85	10.00	20.00
1969	12,940,000	—	—	—	2.25	4.00
1969 Proof	13,000	Value: 4.75				
1970	39,872,000	—	—	—	0.60	0.75
1970 Proof	15,000	Value: 4.00				
1971	60,735,000	—	—	—	0.60	0.75
1971 Proof	10,000	Value: 4.00				
1972	77,570,000	—	—	—	0.60	0.75
1972 Proof	10,000	Value: 4.00				
1973	94,058,000	—	—	—	0.60	0.75
1973 Proof	10,000	Value: 4.00				
1974	177,723,000	—	—	—	0.50	0.75
1974 Proof	11,000	Value: 3.00				
1975	100,045,000	—	—	—	0.50	0.75
1975 Proof	23,000	Value: 1.25				
1976	121,882,000	—	—	—	0.35	0.50
1976 Proof	21,000	Value: 2.00				
1977	102,000,000	—	—	—	0.35	0.50
1977 Proof	55,000	Value: 1.25				
1978	128,700,000	—	—	—	0.35	0.50
1978 Proof	39,000	Value: 1.25				
1979	69,705,000	—	—	—	0.35	0.50
1979 Proof	36,000	Value: 1.25				
1980	145,603,000	—	—	—	0.35	0.50
1980 Proof	68,000	Value: 1.25				
1981	247,300,000	—	—	—	0.35	0.50
1981 Proof	86,000	Value: 1.25				
1982	121,770,000	—	—	—	0.35	0.50
1982 Proof	100,000	Value: 1.25				
1983	177,227,000	—	—	—	0.35	0.50
1983 Proof	80,000	Value: 1.25				
1984	57,963,000	—	—	—	0.35	0.50
1984 Proof	61,000	Value: 1.25				

KM# 79 2 CENTS

5.2000 g., Bronze, 21.6 mm. **Ruler:** Elizabeth II **Obv:** Crowned head right **Obv. Designer:** Raphael Maklouf **Rev:** Frilled Lizard **Rev. Designer:** Stuart Devlin **Edge:** Plain

Date	Mintage	F	VF	XF	Unc	BU
1985	34,700,000	—	—	—	0.35	0.50
1985 Proof	75,000	Value: 1.25				
1986 In sets only	180,000	—	—	—	2.50	3.50
1986 Proof	67,000	Value: 3.50				
1987 In sets only	200,000	—	—	—	2.50	3.50
1987 Proof	70,000	Value: 3.50				
1988	28,905,000	—	—	—	0.35	0.50
1988 Proof	106,000	Value: 1.25				
1989	110,000,000	—	—	—	0.35	0.50
1989 Proof	67,000	Value: 2.00				
1990 In sets only	103,000	—	—	—	25.00	30.00
1990 Proof	53,000	Value: 25.00				
1991 In sets only	148,000	—	—	—	5.00	7.00
1991 Proof	41,000	Value: 5.00				

KM# 768 2 CENTS

5.1800 g., Bronze, 21.59 mm. **Ruler:** Elizabeth II **Obv:** Head with tiara right **Obv. Designer:** Ian Rank-Broadley **Rev:** Frilled-necked lizard

Date	Mintage	F	VF	XF	Unc	BU
2006	—	—	—	—	2.25	3.00
2006 Proof	—	Value: 5.00				

KM# 64 5 CENTS

2.8000 g., Copper-Nickel, 19.4 mm. **Ruler:** Elizabeth II **Obv:** Young bust right **Obv. Designer:** Arnold Machin **Rev:** Short-beaked Spiny Anteater **Rev. Designer:** Stuart Devlin **Note:** For 1966 dated examples, the length of the whisker on top of the forward-most claw at left will indicate the mint: Canberra (less than .5mm) or London (greater than .6mm).

Date	Mintage	F	VF	XF	Unc	BU
1966(c)	45,427,000	—	—	—	0.85	1.50
1966(c) Proof	18,000	Value: 7.50				
1966(L)	30,000,000	—	—	—	1.00	1.75
1967	62,144,000	—	—	—	0.85	1.50
1968	67,336,000	—	—	—	0.85	1.50
1969	38,170,000	—	—	—	0.85	1.50
1969 Proof	13,000	Value: 7.50				
1970	46,058,000	—	—	—	0.60	0.80
1970 Proof	15,000	Value: 5.00				
1971	39,516,000	—	—	—	0.60	0.80
1971 Proof	10,000	Value: 5.00				
1972	8,256,000	0.15	0.30	1.50	12.50	20.00
1972 Proof	10,000	Value: 5.00				
1973	48,816,000	—	—	—	0.60	0.80
1973 Proof	10,000	Value: 5.00				
1974	64,248,000	—	—	—	0.60	0.80
1974 Proof	11,000	Value: 5.00				
1975	44,256,000	—	—	—	0.50	0.60
1975 Proof	23,000	Value: 2.00				
1976	113,180,000	—	—	—	0.50	0.60
1976 Proof	21,000	Value: 3.00				
1977	108,800,000	—	—	—	0.50	0.60
1977 Proof	55,000	Value: 2.00				
1978	25,210,000	—	—	—	0.50	0.60
1978 Proof	39,000	Value: 2.00				
1979	44,533,000	—	—	—	0.50	0.60
1979 Proof	36,000	Value: 2.00				
1980	115,042,000	—	—	—	0.50	0.60
1980 Proof	68,000	Value: 2.00				
1981	162,264,000	—	—	—	0.50	0.60
1981 Proof	86,000	Value: 2.00				
1982	139,468,000	—	—	—	0.50	0.60
1982 Proof	100,000	Value: 2.00				
1983	131,568,000	—	—	—	0.50	0.60
1983 Proof	80,000	Value: 2.00				
1984	35,436,000	—	—	—	0.50	0.60
1984 Proof	61,000	Value: 2.00				

KM# 80 5 CENTS

2.8000 g., Copper-Nickel, 19.25 mm. **Ruler:** Elizabeth II **Obv:** Crowned head right **Obv. Designer:** Raphael Maklouf **Rev:** Short-beaked Spiny Anteater **Rev. Designer:** Stuart Devlin **Edge:** Reeded

Date	Mintage	F	VF	XF	Unc	BU
1985	170,000	—	—	—	10.00	15.00
Note: In Mint sets only						
1985 Proof	75,000	Value: 15.00				
1986	180,000	—	—	—	2.50	3.50
Note: In Mint sets only						
1986 Proof	67,000	Value: 3.50				
1987	73,500,000	—	—	—	0.50	0.60
1987 Proof	70,000	Value: 2.00				
1988	106,100,000	—	—	—	0.50	0.60
1988 Proof	106,000	Value: 2.00				
1989	75,000,000	—	—	—	0.50	0.60
1989 Proof	67,000	Value: 2.00				
1990	33,200,000	—	—	—	0.50	0.60
1990 Proof	53,000	Value: 2.00				
1991	18,400,000	—	—	—	0.50	0.60
1991 Proof	41,000	Value: 2.00				
1992	36,200,000	—	—	—	0.50	0.60
1992 Proof	56,000	Value: 2.00				
1993	93,840,000	—	—	—	0.50	0.60
1993 Proof	46,000	Value: 2.00				
1994	146,669,000	—	—	—	0.50	0.60
1994 Proof	39,000	Value: 2.00				
1995	84,987,000	—	—	—	0.50	0.60
1995 Proof	48,000	Value: 2.00				
1996	79,210,000	—	—	—	0.50	0.60
1996 Proof	41,000	Value: 2.00				
1997	100,680,000	—	—	—	0.50	0.60
1997 Proof	32,000	Value: 3.00				
1998	88,532,000	—	—	—	0.40	0.50
1998 Proof	32,000	Value: 3.00				

KM# 401 5 CENTS

2.8300 g., Copper-Nickel, 19.4 mm. **Ruler:** Elizabeth II **Obv:** Head with tiara right **Obv. Designer:** Ian Rank-Broadley **Rev:** Short-beaked Spiny Anteater **Rev. Designer:** Stuart Devlin **Edge:** Reeded

Date	Mintage	F	VF	XF	Unc	BU
1999	179,016,000	—	—	—	—	0.20
1999 Proof	28,000	Value: 3.00				
2000	97,422,000	—	—	—	—	0.20
2000 Proof	64,000	Value: 4.00				
2001	174,579,000	—	—	—	—	0.20
Note: Large obverse head, IRB spaced						
2001	Inc. above	—	—	—	—	0.20
Note: Smaller obverse head, RB joined						
2001 Proof	59,569	Value: 3.00				
2002	148,812,000	—	—	—	—	0.20
2002 Proof	39,514	Value: 2.50				
2003	113,470,000	—	—	—	—	0.20
2003 Proof	39,090	Value: 2.00				
2004	147,658,000	—	—	—	—	0.20
Note: Normal sized SD						
2004	Inc. above	—	—	—	—	0.20
Note: Smaller SD						
2004 Proof	50,000	Value: 2.50				
2005	194,300,000	—	—	—	—	0.20
Note: Normal sized SD						
2005	Inc. above	—	—	—	—	0.20
Note: Smaller SD						
2005 Proof	33,520	Value: 2.50				
2006	—	—	—	—	—	0.20
2006 Proof	—	Value: 2.50				
2007	—	—	—	—	—	0.20
2007 Proof	—	Value: 2.00				

KM# 65 10 CENTS

5.6500 g., Copper-Nickel, 23.6 mm. **Ruler:** Elizabeth II **Obv:** Young bust right **Obv. Designer:** Arnold Machin **Rev:** Superb Lyre-bird **Rev. Designer:** Stuart Devlin **Note:** For 1966 dated examples, 11 spikes on the left Lyre-bird indicates a strike from Canberra, 12 spikes indicate a London strike.

Date	Mintage	F	VF	XF	Unc	BU
1966(c)	10,984,000	—	—	—	2.00	3.00
1966(c) Proof	18,000	Value: 8.00				
1966(L)	30,000,000	—	—	—	2.00	3.00
1967	51,032,000	—	—	—	4.00	6.00
1968	57,194,000	—	—	—	4.50	6.50
1969	22,146,000	—	—	—	2.75	3.50
1969 Proof	13,000	Value: 8.50				
1970	22,306,000	—	—	—	2.00	3.00
1970 Proof	15,000	Value: 6.50				
1971	20,726,000	—	—	—	5.00	7.50
1971 Proof	10,000	Value: 6.50				
1972	12,502,000	—	—	—	8.00	11.00
1972 Proof	10,000	Value: 6.50				
1973	27,320,000	—	—	—	2.00	3.00
1973 Proof	10,000	Value: 6.50				
1974	46,550,000	—	—	—	2.00	3.00
1974 Proof	11,000	Value: 6.50				
1975	50,900,000	—	—	—	0.75	1.00
1975 Proof	23,000	Value: 2.00				
1976	57,060,000	—	—	—	0.75	1.00
1976 Proof	21,000	Value: 3.75				
1977	10,940,000	—	—	—	0.75	1.00
1977 Proof	55,000	Value: 2.00				
1978	48,400,000	—	—	—	0.50	0.75
1978 Proof	39,000	Value: 2.00				
1979	36,950,000	—	—	—	0.50	0.75
1979 Proof	36,000	Value: 2.00				
1980	55,084,000	—	—	—	0.50	0.75
1980 Proof	68,000	Value: 2.00				
1981	116,060,000	—	—	—	0.50	0.75
Note: One 1981 coin was struck on a Sri Lanka 50 cents planchet, KM#135.1. It carries an approximate value of $600						
1981 Proof	86,000	Value: 2.00				
1982	61,492,000	—	—	—	0.50	0.75
1982 Proof	100,000	Value: 2.00				
1983	82,318,000	—	—	—	0.50	0.75
1983 Proof	80,000	Value: 2.00				
1984	25,728,000	—	—	—	0.50	0.75
1984 Proof	61,000	Value: 2.00				

KM# 81 10 CENTS

5.6500 g., Copper-Nickel, 23.6 mm. **Ruler:** Elizabeth II **Obv:** Crowned head right **Obv. Designer:** Raphael Maklouf **Rev:** Superb Lyre-bird **Rev. Designer:** Stuart Devlin

Date	Mintage	F	VF	XF	Unc	BU
1985	2,100,000	—	—	—	0.50	0.75
1985 Proof	75,000	Value: 3.00				
1986	180,000	—	—	—	2.50	3.50
Note: In mint sets only						
1986 Proof	67,000	Value: 3.50				
1987	200,000	—	—	—	2.50	3.50
Note: In mint sets only						
1987 Proof	70,000	Value: 3.50				
1988	46,900,000	—	—	—	0.50	0.75
1988 Proof	106,000	Value: 2.50				
1989	45,000,000	—	—	—	0.50	0.75
1989 Proof	67,000	Value: 2.50				
1990	17,000,000	—	—	—	0.50	0.75
1990 Proof	53,000	Value: 2.50				
1991	3,174,000	—	—	—	0.50	0.75
1991 Proof	41,000	Value: 2.50				
1992	29,800,000	—	—	—	0.50	0.75
1992 Proof	56,000	Value: 2.50				
1993	23,100,000	—	—	—	0.50	0.75
1993 Proof	46,000	Value: 2.50				
1994	43,726,000	—	—	—	0.50	0.75
1994 Proof	39,000	Value: 2.50				
1995 Mint sets only	96,000	—	—	—	10.00	15.00
1995 Proof	41,000	Value: 15.00				
1996	108,000	—	—	—	10.00	15.00
1996 Proof	41,000	Value: 15.00				
1997	5,700,000	—	—	—	20.00	30.00
1997 Proof	32,000	Value: 30.00				
1998	47,989,000	—	—	—	0.50	0.75
1998 Proof	32,000	Value: 3.50				

KM# 402 10 CENTS

5.6600 g., Copper-Nickel, 23.6 mm. **Ruler:** Elizabeth II **Obv:** Head with tiara right **Obv. Designer:** Ian Rank-Broadley **Rev:** Superb Lyre-bird **Rev. Designer:** Stuart Devlin **Edge:** Reeded

Date	Mintage	F	VF	XF	Unc	BU
1999	94,889,000	—	—	—	—	0.50
1999 Proof	28,000	Value: 3.00				
2000	51,117,000	—	—	—	—	0.50
2000 Proof	64,000	Value: 4.00				
2001	109,357,000	—	—	—	—	0.50
Note: Large obverse head, IRB spaced						
2001	Inc. above	—	—	—	—	0.50
Note: Smaller obverse head, RB joined						
2001 Proof	59,569	Value: 3.00				
2002	70,329,000	—	—	—	—	0.50
2002 Proof	39,514	Value: 3.00				
2003	53,635,000	—	—	—	—	0.50
2003 Proof	39,090	Value: 3.00				
2004	147,658,000	—	—	—	—	0.50
2004 Proof	50,000	Value: 3.00				
2005	—	—	—	—	—	0.50
2005 Proof	33,520	Value: 3.00				
2006	—	—	—	—	—	0.50
2006 Proof	—	Value: 3.00				
2007	—	—	—	—	—	0.50
2007 Proof	—	Value: 3.00				

KM# 66 20 CENTS

11.3000 g., Copper-Nickel, 28.5 mm. **Ruler:** Elizabeth II **Obv:** Young bust right **Obv. Designer:** Arnold Machin **Rev:** Duckbill Platypus **Rev. Designer:** Stuart Devlin **Note:** For 1966 dated examples, strikes from Canberra show a gap between sea line and right face of platypus

Date	Mintage	F	VF	XF	Unc	BU
1966(c)	28,223,000	—	—	—	10.00	16.00
1966(c) Proof	18,000	Value: 12.00				
1966(L)	—	—	—	—	500	850
Note: Wave on base of 2						
1966(L) Proof	—	Value: 12.50				
1967	83,848,000	—	—	1.00	15.00	22.00
1968	40,537,000	—	1.00	5.00	30.00	40.00
1969	16,501,999	—	—	—	15.00	22.00
1969 Proof	13,000	Value: 13.50				
1970	23,271,000	—	—	—	7.00	10.00
1970 Proof	15,000	Value: 11.50				
1971	8,947,000	—	—	5.00	25.00	32.00
1971 Proof	10,000	Value: 11.50				
1972	16,643,000	—	—	—	8.00	11.00
1972 Proof	10,000	Value: 10.00				
1973	23,356,000	—	—	—	8.00	11.00
1973 Proof	10,000	Value: 10.00				
1974	33,548,000	—	—	—	8.00	11.00
1974 Proof	11,000	Value: 10.00				
1975	53,300,000	—	—	—	1.75	2.50
1975 Proof	23,000	Value: 2.25				
1976	59,774,000	—	—	—	1.00	1.50
1976 Proof	21,000	Value: 3.75				
1977	41,272,000	—	—	—	1.00	1.50
1977 Proof	55,000	Value: 2.25				
1978	37,400,000	—	—	—	1.00	1.50
1978 Proof	39,000	Value: 2.25				
1979	22,300,000	—	—	—	1.00	1.50
1979 Proof	36,000	Value: 2.25				
1980	84,400,000	—	—	—	0.70	1.00
1980 Proof	68,000	Value: 2.25				
1981	165,500,000	—	—	—	0.60	0.80
Note: Some 1981 dated coins were struck on a Hong Kong 2 Dollar planchet, KM#37. 6 pieces are reported. Each carries an approximate value of $800						
1981 Proof	86,000	Value: 2.25				
1982	76,600,000	—	—	—	0.60	0.80
1982 Proof	100,000	Value: 2.25				
1983	55,113,000	—	—	—	10.00	15.00
1983 Proof	80,000	Value: 10.00				
1984	27,820,000	—	—	—	12.00	17.00
1984 Proof	61,000	Value: 10.00				

KM# 82 20 CENTS

11.3000 g., Copper-Nickel, 28.5 mm. **Ruler:** Elizabeth II **Obv:** Crowned head right **Obv. Designer:** Raphael Maklouf **Rev:** Duckbill Platypus **Rev. Designer:** Stuart Devlin

Date	Mintage	F	VF	XF	Unc	BU
1985	2,700,000	—	—	—	6.00	10.00
1985 Proof	75,000	Value: 10.00				
1986	180,000	—	—	—	6.00	10.00
Note: In mint sets only						
1986 Proof	67,000	Value: 10.00				
1987	200,000	—	—	—	6.00	10.00
Note: In mint sets only						
1987 Proof	70,000	Value: 10.00				
1988	240,000	—	—	—	6.00	10.00
Note: In mint sets only						
1988 Proof	106,000	Value: 10.00				
1989	150,000	—	—	—	6.00	10.00
1989 Proof	67,000	Value: 10.00				
1990	103,000	—	—	—	6.00	10.00
1990 Proof	53,000	Value: 10.00				
1991	148,000	—	—	—	6.00	10.00
1991 Proof	41,000	Value: 10.00				
1992	118,000	—	—	—	6.00	10.00
1992 Proof	56,000	Value: 10.00				
1993	84,000	—	—	—	6.00	10.00
1993 Proof	46,000	Value: 10.00				
1994	14,330,000	—	—	—	1.00	2.00
1994 Proof	39,000	Value: 3.50				
1995	4,840,000	—	—	—	15.00	25.00
1995 Proof	41,000	Value: 25.00				
1996	20,596,000	—	—	—	1.00	2.00
1996 Proof	41,000	Value: 10.00				
1997	16,730,000	—	—	—	1.00	2.00
1997 Proof	32,000	Value: 15.00				
1998	28,830,000	—	—	—	1.00	2.00
1998 Proof	32,000	Value: 10.00				

KM# 403 20 CENTS

11.3000 g., Copper-Nickel, 26.87 mm. **Ruler:** Elizabeth II **Obv:** Head with tiara right **Obv. Designer:** Ian Rank-Broadley **Rev:** Duckbill Platypus **Rev. Designer:** Stuart Devlin **Edge:** Reeded

Date	Mintage	F	VF	XF	Unc	BU
1999	64,181,000	—	—	—	—	0.80
1999 Proof	28,000	Value: 10.00				
2000	35,584,000	—	—	—	—	0.80
2000 Proof	64,000	Value: 15.00				
2001	81,967,000	—	—	—	—	0.80
Note: IRB spaced						
2001	Inc. above	—	—	—	—	0.80
Note: RB joined						
2001	Inc. above	—	—	—	—	0.80
Note: IRB joined						
2001 Proof	59,569	Value: 10.00				
2002	27,244,000	—	—	—	—	0.80
2002 Proof	39,514	Value: 6.00				
2004	74,609,000	—	—	—	—	0.80
Note: Small obverse head, flat top A						
2004	Est. 400,000	—	—	—	4.00	7.00
Note: Large obverse head, pointed A						
2004 Proof	50,000	Value: 6.00				
2005	1,600,000	—	—	—	5.00	7.50
2006	—	—	—	—	—	0.80
2006 Proof	—	Value: 6.00				
2007	—	—	—	—	—	0.80
2007 Proof	—	Value: 6.00				

KM# 589 20 CENTS

11.3000 g., Copper-Nickel, 28.5 mm. **Ruler:** Elizabeth II **Subject:** Sir Donald Bradman **Obv:** Head with tiara right **Obv. Designer:** Ian Rank-Broadley **Rev:** Cricket batsman **Edge:** Reeded

Date	Mintage	F	VF	XF	Unc	BU
2001	10,000,000	—	—	—	1.50	3.00

KM# 688 20 CENTS

11.3000 g., Copper-Nickel, 28.52 mm. **Ruler:** Elizabeth II **Obv:** Head with tiara right **Obv. Designer:** Ian Rank-Broadley **Rev:** Group of Australian Volunteers **Edge:** Reeded

Date	Mintage	F	VF	XF	Unc	BU
2003	7,600,000	—	—	—	1.50	2.50

KM# 745 20 CENTS

11.3000 g., Copper-Nickel, 28.52 mm. **Ruler:** Elizabeth II **Obv:** Head right **Rev:** Soldier with wife and child **Edge:** Reeded

Date	Mintage	F	VF	XF	Unc	BU
2005	33,500,000	—	—	—	1.50	2.00
2005 Proof	—	Value: 6.00				

KM# 67 50 CENTS

13.2800 g., 0.8000 Silver 0.3416 oz. ASW, 31.5 mm. **Ruler:** Elizabeth II **Obv:** Young bust right **Obv. Designer:** Arnold Machin **Rev:** Coat of arms with kangaroo and emu supporters **Rev. Designer:** Stuart Devlin

Date	Mintage	F	VF	XF	Unc	BU
1966	36,454,000	—	—	BV	5.50	8.00
Note: On reverse, two parallel horizontal bars behind Emu's head.						
1966 Proof	18,000	Value: 75.00				

KM# 68 50 CENTS

15.5500 g., Copper-Nickel, 31.5 mm. **Ruler:** Elizabeth II **Obv:** Young bust right **Obv. Designer:** Arnold Machin **Rev:** Coat of arms with kangaroo and emu supporters **Rev. Designer:** Stuart Devlin **Edge:** 12-sided

Date	Mintage	F	VF	XF	Unc	BU
1969	14,015,000	—	—	—	10.00	16.50
1969 Proof	13,000	Value: 55.00				
1971	21,056,000	—	—	—	13.50	16.50
1971 Proof	10,000	Value: 35.00				
1972	5,586,000	—	—	2.50	20.00	30.00
1972 Proof	10,000	Value: 35.00				
1973	4,009,000	—	—	3.00	25.00	35.00
1973 Proof	10,000	Value: 35.00				
1974	8,962,000	—	—	—	15.00	20.00
1974 Proof	11,000	Value: 30.00				
1975	19,025,000	—	—	—	3.00	5.00
1975 Proof	23,000	Value: 10.00				
1976	27,280,000	—	—	—	3.00	5.00
1976 Proof	21,000	Value: 15.00				

Date	Mintage	F	VF	XF	Unc	BU
1978	25,765,000	—	—	—	2.00	3.00
1978 Proof	39,000	Value: 4.00				
1979	24,886,000	—	—	—	2.00	3.00
1979 Proof	36,000	Value: 4.00				
1979	Inc. above	—	—	—	6.00	8.50

Note: On reverse, two parallel horizontal bars behind Emu's head.

Date	Mintage	F	VF	XF	Unc	BU
1980	38,681,000	—	—	—	2.00	3.00
1980	Inc. above	—	—	—	5.00	7.00

Note: On reverse, two parallel horizontal bars behind Emu's head.

Date	Mintage	F	VF	XF	Unc	BU
1980 Proof	68,000	Value: 3.50				
1981	24,168,000	—	—	—	1.00	1.50
1981 Proof	86,000	Value: 3.50				
1983	48,923,000	—	—	—	1.00	1.50
1983 Proof	80,000	Value: 3.75				
1984	26,281,000	—	—	—	1.00	1.50
1984 Proof	61,000	Value: 4.00				

KM# 69 50 CENTS

15.5500 g., Copper-Nickel, 31.5 mm. **Ruler:** Elizabeth II **Subject:** 200th Anniversary - Cook's Australian Voyage **Obv:** Young bust right **Obv. Designer:** Arnold Machin **Rev:** Bust of Captain Cook at left, map of Australia at right **Rev. Designer:** Stuart Devlin **Shape:** 12-sided

Date	Mintage	F	VF	XF	Unc	BU
1970	16,540,000	—	—	0.50	2.00	3.50
1970 Proof	15,000	Value: 40.00				

KM# 70 50 CENTS

15.5500 g., Copper-Nickel, 31.5 mm. **Ruler:** Elizabeth II **Subject:** Queen's Silver Jubilee **Obv:** Young bust right **Obv. Designer:** Arnold Machin **Rev:** Circular geometric design **Shape:** 12-sided

Date	Mintage	F	VF	XF	Unc	BU
1977	25,076,000	—	—	—	1.00	1.75
1977 Proof	55,000	Value: 4.00				

KM# 72 50 CENTS

15.5500 g., Copper-Nickel, 31.5 mm. **Ruler:** Elizabeth II **Subject:** Wedding of Prince Charles and Lady Diana **Obv. Designer:** Arnold Machin **Rev:** Conjoined heads of Prince Charles and Lady Diana, left **Rev. Designer:** Stuart Devlin

Date	Mintage	F	VF	XF	Unc	BU
1981	44,100,000	—	0.40	0.50	1.00	1.50

KM# 74 50 CENTS

15.5500 g., Copper-Nickel, 31.5 mm. **Ruler:** Elizabeth II **Subject:** XII Commonwealth Games - Brisbane **Obv:** Young bust right **Obv. Designer:** Arnold Machin **Rev:** Circle of images representing different sporting events **Rev. Designer:** Stuart Devlin **Shape:** 12-sided

Date	Mintage	F	VF	XF	Unc	BU
1982	49,500,000	—	—	—	1.00	1.25
1982 Proof	100,000	Value: 4.00				

KM# 83 50 CENTS

15.5500 g., Copper-Nickel, 31.5 mm. **Ruler:** Elizabeth II **Obv:** Young bust with tiara right **Obv. Designer:** Raphael Maklouf **Rev:** Coat of arms with kangaroo and emu supporters **Rev. Designer:** Stuart Devlin **Shape:** 12-sided

Date	Mintage	F	VF	XF	Unc	BU
1985	1,000,000	—	—	2.00	6.00	10.00
1985 Proof	75,000	Value: 10.00				
1986 In sets only	180,000	—	—	—	6.00	10.00
1986 Proof	67,000	Value: 10.00				
1987 In sets only	200,000	—	—	—	6.00	10.00
1987 Proof	70,000	Value: 10.00				
1989 In sets only	—	—	—	—	6.00	10.00
1989 Proof	—	Value: 10.00				
1990 In sets only	—	—	—	—	6.00	10.00
1990 Proof	—	Value: 10.00				
1992 In sets only	—	—	—	—	6.00	10.00
1992 Proof	47,000	Value: 10.00				
1993	980,000	—	—	—	6.00	10.00
1993 Proof	—	Value: 10.00				
1996	19,297,000	—	—	—	1.50	2.25
1996 Proof	—	Value: 6.00				
1997	4,340,000	—	—	—	6.00	10.00
1997 Proof	—	Value: 16.00				

KM# 99 50 CENTS

15.5500 g., Copper-Nickel, 31.5 mm. **Ruler:** Elizabeth II **Subject:** Australian Bicentennial **Obv:** Crowned head right **Obv. Designer:** Raphael Maklouf **Rev:** Captain Cook's ship sailing towards gridmarked map of Australia, compass at upper center **Rev. Legend:** AUSTRALIA - 1788-1988 **Rev. Designer:** Michael Tracey **Shape:** 12-sided

Date	Mintage	F	VF	XF	Unc	BU
1988	8,100,000	—	—	—	2.25	3.00
1988 Proof	106,000	Value: 4.00				

KM# 139 50 CENTS

15.5500 g., Copper-Nickel, 31.5 mm. **Ruler:** Elizabeth II **Subject:** 25th Anniversary of Decimal Currency **Obv:** Crowned head right **Obv. Designer:** Raphael Maklouf **Rev:** Head of Merino ram **Rev. Designer:** George Kruger-Grey

Date	Mintage	F	VF	XF	Unc	BU
1991	4,364,000	—	—	1.00	5.00	10.00
1991 Proof	—	Value: 12.50				

KM# 257 50 CENTS

15.5000 g., Copper-Nickel, 31.5 mm. **Ruler:** Elizabeth II **Subject:** International Year of the Family **Obv:** Crowned head right **Obv. Designer:** Raphael Maklouf **Rev:** Crude drawings depicting a family **Rev. Designer:** Carolyn Rossier

Date	Mintage	F	VF	XF	Unc	BU
1994	21,200,000	—	—	1.00	3.00	5.00
1994 Proof	39,000	Value: 11.50				

KM# 294 50 CENTS

15.5000 g., Copper-Nickel, 31.5 mm. **Ruler:** Elizabeth II **Subject:** Weary Dunlop **Obv:** Crowned head right **Obv. Designer:** Raphael Maklouf **Rev:** Bust of Dunlop at center, value below **Rev. Designer:** Louis Laumen & Horst Hahne

Date	Mintage	F	VF	XF	Unc	BU
1995	15,860,000	—	—	—	1.50	2.50
1995 Proof	48,000	Value: 11.50				

KM# 364 50 CENTS

15.5500 g., Copper-Nickel, 31.5 mm. **Ruler:** Elizabeth II **Subject:** Discovery of Bass Strait **Obv:** Crowned head right **Obv. Designer:** Raphael Maklouf **Rev:** Busts of Bass and Flinders, map of Australia at lower left

Date	Mintage	F	VF	XF	Unc	BU
1998	22,390,000	—	—	—	1.50	2.50
1998 Proof	32,000	Value: 11.50				

KM# 404 50 CENTS

15.5500 g., Copper-Nickel, 31.51 mm. **Ruler:** Elizabeth II **Obv:** Head with tiara right **Obv. Designer:** Ian Rank-Broadley **Rev:** Australian coat of arms with kangaroo and emu supporters **Rev. Designer:** Stuart Devlin **Edge:** Plain **Shape:** 12-sided

Date	Mintage	F	VF	XF	Unc	BU
1999	20,318,000	—	—	—	1.50	2.50
1999 Proof	28,000	Value: 12.50				
2004	17,918,000	—	—	—	2.00	3.00
2004 Proof	—	Value: 10.00				
2005	30,000	—	—	—	25.00	40.00

Note: Issued as part of a PNC only

Date	Mintage	F	VF	XF	Unc	BU
2006	—	—	—	—	1.00	1.50
2007	—	—	—	—	1.00	1.50

KM# 533 50 CENTS

15.6000 g., Copper-Nickel, 31.51 mm. **Ruler:** Elizabeth II **Subject:** Centennial - Norfolk Island Federation **Obv:** Head with tiara right **Obv. Designer:** Ian Rank-Broadley **Rev:** Norfolk Island coat of arms **Edge:** Plain **Shape:** 12-sided

Date	Mintage	F	VF	XF	Unc	BU
2001	2,000,000	—	—	—	3.50	5.00
2001 Proof	—	Value: 12.50				

KM# 551 50 CENTS
15.5500 g., Copper-Nickel, 31.5 mm. **Ruler:** Elizabeth II **Series:** Centenary of Federation - New South Wales **Obv:** Head with tiara right **Rev:** New South Wales state arms **Edge:** Plain **Shape:** 12-sided

Date	Mintage	F	VF	XF	Unc	BU
2001	3,000,000	—	—	—	3.50	5.00
2001 Proof	—	Value: 12.50				

KM# 553 50 CENTS
15.5500 g., Copper-Nickel, 31.5 mm. **Ruler:** Elizabeth II **Series:** Centenary of Federation - Australian Capital Territory **Obv:** Head right **Rev:** Austrian Capital Territory arms **Edge:** Plain **Shape:** 12-sided

Date	Mintage	F	VF	XF	Unc	BU
2001	2,000,000	—	—	—	3.50	5.00
2001 Proof	—	Value: 12.50				

KM# 555 50 CENTS
15.5500 g., Copper-Nickel, 31.5 mm. **Ruler:** Elizabeth II **Series:** Centenary of Federation - Queensland **Obv:** Head with tiara right **Rev:** Queensland state arms **Edge:** Plain **Shape:** 12-sided

Date	Mintage	F	VF	XF	Unc	BU
2001	2,300,000	—	—	—	3.50	5.00
2001 Proof	—	Value: 12.50				

KM# 557 50 CENTS
15.5500 g., Copper-Nickel, 31.5 mm. **Ruler:** Elizabeth II **Series:** Centenary of Federation - Victoria **Obv:** Head with tiara right **Rev:** Victoria state arms **Edge:** Plain **Shape:** 12-sided

Date	Mintage	F	VF	XF	Unc	BU
2001	2,800,000	—	—	—	3.50	5.00
2001 Proof	—	Value: 12.50				

KM# 559 50 CENTS
15.5500 g., Copper-Nickel, 31.5 mm. **Ruler:** Elizabeth II **Series:** Centenary of Federation - Northern Territory **Obv:** Head with tiara right **Rev:** Northern Territory state arms **Edge:** Plain **Shape:** 12-sided

Date	Mintage	F	VF	XF	Unc	BU
2001	2,100,000	—	—	—	3.50	5.00
2001 Proof	—	Value: 12.50				

KM# 561 50 CENTS
15.5500 g., Copper-Nickel, 31.5 mm. **Ruler:** Elizabeth II **Series:** Centenary of Federation - South Australia **Obv:** Head with tiara right **Rev:** South Australia state arms **Edge:** Plain **Shape:** 12-sided

Date	Mintage	F	VF	XF	Unc	BU
2001	2,400,000	—	—	—	3.50	5.00
2001 Proof	—	Value: 12.50				

KM# 563 50 CENTS
15.5500 g., Copper-Nickel, 31.5 mm. **Ruler:** Elizabeth II **Series:** Centenary of Federation - Western Australia **Obv:** Head with tiara right **Rev:** Western Australia state arms **Edge:** Plain **Shape:** 12-sided

Date	Mintage	F	VF	XF	Unc	BU
2001	2,400,000	—	—	—	3.50	5.00
2001 Proof	—	Value: 12.50				

KM# 565 50 CENTS
15.5500 g., Copper-Nickel, 31.5 mm. **Ruler:** Elizabeth II **Series:** Centenary of Federation - Tasmania **Obv:** Head with tiara right **Rev:** Tasmania state arms **Edge:** Plain **Shape:** 12-sided

Date	Mintage	F	VF	XF	Unc	BU
2001	2,200,000	—	—	—	3.50	5.00
2001 Proof	—	Value: 12.50				

KM# 491.1 50 CENTS
Copper-Nickel, 31.5 mm. **Ruler:** Elizabeth II **Subject:** Centenary of Federation, 1901-2001 **Obv:** Head with tiara right **Rev:** Commonwealth coat of arms **Edge:** Plain **Shape:** 12-sided **Note:** Prev. KM#491.

Date	Mintage	F	VF	XF	Unc	BU
2001	43,149,600	—	—	—	2.00	3.00

KM# 491.2 50 CENTS
15.5500 g., Copper-Nickel, 31.51 mm. **Ruler:** Elizabeth II **Subject:** Federation Centennial **Obv:** Elizabeth II right **Rev:** Multicolor arms above value **Edge:** Plain **Shape:** 12-sided

Date	Mintage	F	VF	XF	Unc	BU
2001 Proof	60,000	Value: 20.00				

KM# 602 50 CENTS
15.5500 g., Copper-Nickel, 31.5 mm. **Ruler:** Elizabeth II **Subject:** The Outback Region **Obv:** Head right **Rev:** Windmill **Rev. Designer:** Wojciech Pietronik **Edge:** Plain **Shape:** 12-sided

Date	Mintage	F	VF	XF	Unc	BU
2002	11,507,000	—	—	—	3.00	4.50
2002 Proof	39,000	Value: 10.00				

KM# 689 50 CENTS
15.5500 g., Copper-Nickel, 31.5 mm. **Ruler:** Elizabeth II **Obv:** Head right **Rev:** Value within circle of volunteer activities **Rev. Designer:** Wojciech Pietronik **Edge:** Plain **Shape:** 12-sided

Date	Mintage	F	VF	XF	Unc	BU
2003	13,927,000	—	—	—	3.00	4.50

KM# 799 50 CENTS
14.0900 g., Aluminum-Bronze, 31.51 mm. **Ruler:** Elizabeth II **Subject:** 50th Anniversary of the Coronation of Elizabeth II **Obv:** Head with tiara right **Obv. Designer:** Ian Rank-Broadley **Rev:** Crown, Federation star, dates **Rev. Designer:** Peter Soobik **Edge:** Plain **Shape:** 12-sided

Date	Mintage	F	VF	XF	Unc	BU
2006	65,003	—	—	—	15.00	17.50

KM# 694 50 CENTS
15.5500 g., Copper-Nickel, 31.5 mm. **Ruler:** Elizabeth II **Obv:** Head with tiara right **Obv. Designer:** Ian Rank-Broadley **Rev:** Koala, Lorikeet (bird) and a Wombat **Rev. Designer:** John Serrano **Edge:** Plain **Shape:** 12-sided

Date	Mintage	F	VF	XF	Unc	BU
2004	10,577,000	—	—	—	3.00	5.00

KM# 746 50 CENTS
15.5500 g., Copper-Nickel, 31.51 mm. **Ruler:** Elizabeth II **Obv:** Head with tiara right **Rev:** Military cemetery scene **Edge:** Plain **Shape:** 12-sided

Date	Mintage	F	VF	XF	Unc	BU
2005	11,033,000	—	—	—	2.50	3.50
2005 Proof	—	Value: 10.00				

KM# 769 50 CENTS
Copper-Nickel **Ruler:** Elizabeth II **Subject:** Commonweath Games, Secondary School Design Competition **Obv:** Head with tiara right **Rev:** Athletes **Rev. Designer:** Kelly Jost

Date	Mintage	F	VF	XF	Unc	BU
2005	20,500,000	—	—	—	2.50	3.50
2005 Proof	5,402	Value: 35.00				

KM# 801 50 CENTS
15.5500 g., Copper-Nickel, 31.51 mm. **Ruler:** Elizabeth II **Subject:** 80th Birthday of Queen Elizabeth II **Obv:** Head with tiara right **Obv. Designer:** Ian Rank-Broadley **Rev:** Royal Cipher **Rev. Designer:** Stuart Devlin **Edge:** Plain **Shape:** 12-sided

Date	Mintage	F	VF	XF	Unc	BU
2006	—	—	—	—	5.00	8.50

KM# 802 50 CENTS

15.5500 g., Copper-Nickel, 31.51 mm. **Ruler:** Elizabeth II **Subject:** Visit of Queen Elizabeth II **Obv:** Head with tiara right **Obv. Designer:** Ian Rank-Broadley **Rev:** Australian map and world globe **Rev. Designer:** Stuart Devlin **Edge:** Plain **Shape:** 12-sided

Date	Mintage	F	VF	XF	Unc	BU
2006	—	—	—	—	5.00	8.50

KM# 1001 50 CENTS

15.5500 g., Copper Nickel, 31.50 mm. **Ruler:** Elizabeth II **Subject:** Squash **Obv:** Head with tiarra right **Obv. Legend:** ELIZABETH II - AUSTRALIA **Obv. Designer:** Ian Rank-Broadley **Rev:** Player, Melbourne 2006 logo **Rev. Legend:** XVIII COMMONWEALTH GAMES **Rev. Designer:** Wojciech Pietranik **Edge:** Plain **Shape:** 12-sided

Date	Mintage	F	VF	XF	Unc	BU
2006	—	—	—	—	2.50	4.50

KM# 1002 50 CENTS

15.5500 g., Copper Nickel, 31.50 mm. **Ruler:** Elizabeth II **Subject:** Lawn bowling **Obv:** Head with tiarre right **Obv. Legend:** ELIZABETH II - AUSTRALIA **Obv. Designer:** Ian Rank-Broadlet **Rev:** Bowler, Melbourne 2006 **Rev. Legend:** XVIII COMMONWEALTH GAMES **Rev. Designer:** Wojciech Pietranik **Edge:** Plain **Shape:** 12-sided

Date	Mintage	F	VF	XF	Unc	BU
2006	—	—	—	—	2.50	4.50

KM# 1003 50 CENTS

15.5500 g., Copper Nickel, 31.50 mm. **Ruler:** Elizabeth II **Subject:** Boxing **Obv:** Head with tiarra right **Obv. Legend:** ELIZABETH II - AUSTRALIA **Obv. Designer:** Ian Rank-Broadley **Rev:** Boxer, Melbourne 2006 logo **Rev. Legend:** XVIII COMMONWEALTH GAMES **Rev. Designer:** Wojciech Pietranik **Edge:** Plain **Shape:** 12-sided

Date	Mintage	F	VF	XF	Unc	BU
2006	—	—	—	—	2.50	4.50

KM# 1004 50 CENTS

Aluminum-Bronze, 30.00 mm. **Ruler:** Elizabeth II **Obv:** Head with tiara right **Obv. Legend:** ELIZABETH II - AUSTRALIA **Obv. Designer:** Ian Rank-Broadley **Rev:** Everage head facing, multicolor **Rev. Legend:** DAME EDNA EVERAGE - 50TH ANNIVERSARY

Date	Mintage	F	VF	XF	Unc	BU
ND(2006)P	—	—	—	—	2.50	4.50

KM# 77 DOLLAR

9.0000 g., Nickel-Aluminum-Copper, 25 mm. **Ruler:** Elizabeth II **Obv:** Young bust right **Obv. Designer:** Arnold Machin **Rev:** 5 kangaroos, denomination **Rev. Designer:** Stuart Devlin **Edge:** Smooth, reeded alternating edge

Date	Mintage	F	VF	XF	Unc	BU
1984	185,985,000	—	—	1.00	2.00	5.00
1984 Proof	159,000	Value: 9.00				

KM# 84 DOLLAR

9.0000 g., Nickel-Aluminum-Copper, 25 mm. **Ruler:** Elizabeth II **Obv:** Crowned head right **Obv. Designer:** Raphael Maklouf **Rev:** 5 kangaroos, value **Rev. Designer:** Stuart Devlin **Edge:** Smooth, reeded alternating edge

Date	Mintage	F	VF	XF	Unc	BU
1985	91,400,000	—	—	1.00	4.00	5.00
1985 Proof	75,000	Value: 9.00				
1987 In sets only	200,000	—	—	—	5.00	6.00
1987 Proof	70,000	Value: 9.00				
1989	—	—	—	1.00	4.00	5.00
1989 Proof	—	Value: 9.00				
1990	—	—	—	1.00	9.00	11.00
1990 Proof	—	Value: 9.00				
1991	—	—	—	1.00	4.00	5.00
1991 Proof	—	Value: 9.00				
1994	47,639,000	—	—	1.00	6.00	9.00
1994 Proof	—	Value: 9.00				
1995	21,412,000	—	—	1.00	4.00	6.00
1995 Proof	—	Value: 9.00				
1998	16,248,000	—	—	1.00	4.00	6.00
1998 Proof	—	Value: 9.00				

KM# 87 DOLLAR

9.0000 g., Nickel-Aluminum-Copper, 25 mm. **Ruler:** Elizabeth II **Subject:** International Year of Peace **Obv:** Crowned head right **Obv. Designer:** Raphael Maklouf **Rev:** Dove above hands within wreath, value and legend below **Rev. Legend:** INTERNATIONAL YEAR OF PEACE **Rev. Designer:** Horst Hahne **Edge:** Smooth, reeded alternating edge

Date	Mintage	F	VF	XF	Unc	BU
1986	25,100,000	—	—	—	4.00	6.00
1986 Proof	67,000	Value: 20.00				

KM# 100 DOLLAR

9.0000 g., Aluminum-Bronze, 25 mm. **Ruler:** Elizabeth II **Subject:** Aboriginal Art **Obv:** Crowned head right **Obv. Designer:** Raphael Maklouf **Rev:** Kangaroo on artistic patterned background, denomination below **Rev. Designer:** Stuart Devlin **Edge:** Reeded, smooth alternating edge

Date	Mintage	F	VF	XF	Unc	BU
1988	20,294,000	—	—	—	4.00	6.00
1988 Proof	106,000	Value: 20.00				

KM# 175 DOLLAR

9.0000 g., Nickel-Aluminum-Copper, 25.12 mm. **Ruler:** Elizabeth II **Subject:** Barcelona - 25th Olympics **Obv:** Crowned head right **Obv. Designer:** Raphael Maklouf **Rev:** Female javelin thrower **Rev. Designer:** Margaret Priest **Edge:** Alternating reeded and plain sections

Date	Mintage	F	VF	XF	Unc	BU
1992	13,996	—	—	—	65.00	—
Note: RAM wallet						
1992	Inc. above	—	—	—	55.00	—
Note: Olympic wallet						
1992 Proof	2,940	Value: 165				
1992	23,500	—	—	—	70.00	—
Note: Olympic card						

KM# 208 DOLLAR

9.0000 g., Nickel-Aluminum-Copper, 25 mm. **Ruler:** Elizabeth II **Obv:** Crowned head right **Obv. Designer:** Raphael Maklouf **Rev:** Stylized tree above value, 2 hands above Landcare Australia **Rev. Designer:** Vladimir Gottwald **Edge:** Reeded, smooth alternating edge **Note:** Visitors at mints and coin shows were allowed to strike a coin for a fee at the following C - Canberra, M - Hall of Manufacturers Pavilion Coin Show, Melbourne and S - Sydney International Coin Fair.

Date	Mintage	F	VF	XF	Unc	BU
1993	17,917,000	—	—	—	3.00	4.50
1993 Proof	—	Value: 16.50				
1993C	91,993	—	—	—	6.00	8.00
1993M	60,104	—	—	—	7.50	10.00
1993S	87,939	—	—	—	6.00	8.00

KM# 258 DOLLAR

9.0000 g., Nickel-Aluminum-Copper, 25 mm. **Ruler:** Elizabeth II **Subject:** 10th Anniversary - Introduction of Dollar Coin **Obv. Designer:** Raphael Maklouf **Rev:** Paper money with coin design at left divides dates **Rev. Designer:** Vladimir Gottwald **Edge:** Reeded, smooth alternating edge

Date	Mintage	F	VF	XF	Unc	BU
1994C	123,318	—	—	—	15.00	17.50
1994M	65,440	—	—	—	17.50	20.00
1994S	74,426	—	—	—	17.50	20.00

KM# 269 DOLLAR

9.0000 g., Nickel-Aluminum-Copper, 25 mm. **Ruler:** Elizabeth II **Subject:** A.B. Banjo Paterson - Waltzing Matilda **Obv:** Crowned head right **Obv. Designer:** Raphael Maklouf **Rev:** 3/4-length figure of Banjo Paterson on a walkabout with walking stick **Rev. Designer:** Vladimir Gottwald **Edge:** Reeded, smooth alternating edge

Date	Mintage	F	VF	XF	Unc	BU
1995B	74,353	—	—	—	35.00	45.00
1995C	156,453	—	—	—	28.00	30.00
1995M	74,255	—	—	—	35.00	40.00
1995S	82,810	—	—	—	30.00	35.00

KM# 310 DOLLAR

9.0000 g., Nickel-Aluminum-Copper, 25 mm. **Ruler:** Elizabeth II **Subject:** Sir Henry Parkes **Obv:** Crowned head right **Obv. Designer:** Raphael Maklouf **Rev:** Large head of Sir Henry Parkes half facing right, legend around **Rev. Legend:** SIR HENRY PARKES 1815-1896, FATHER OF FEDERATION **Edge:** Reeded, smooth alternating edge

Date	Mintage	F	VF	XF	Unc	BU
1996	26,200,000	—	—	—	5.00	6.00
1996 Proof	—	—	—	—	—	—
1996A	29,127	—	—	—	11.50	13.50
1996B	41,128	—	—	—	7.50	10.00
1996C	272,980	—	—	—	6.00	8.00
1996M	38,030	—	—	—	11.50	13.50
1996S	72,186	—	—	—	7.50	10.00

KM# 327 DOLLAR

9.0000 g., Nickel-Aluminum-Copper, 25 mm. **Ruler:** Elizabeth II **Subject:** Sir Charles Kingsford Smith **Obv:** Crowned head right **Obv. Designer:** Raphael Maklouf **Rev:** Pilot above airplane, dates

Date	Mintage	F	VF	XF	Unc	BU
1997	24,381,000	—	—	—	20.00	22.50

KM# 355 DOLLAR

9.0000 g., Nickel-Aluminum-Copper, 25 mm. **Ruler:** Elizabeth II **Subject:** Sir Charles Kingsford Smith **Obv:** Crowned head right **Obv. Designer:** Raphael Maklouf **Rev:** Head of Sir Smith over airplane over world map

Date	Mintage	F	VF	XF	Unc	BU
1997A	33,060	—	—	—	22.50	25.00
1997B	40,800	—	—	—	22.50	25.00
1997C	244,450	—	—	—	18.50	20.00
1997M	48,120	—	—	—	22.50	25.00
1997S	89,800	—	—	—	20.00	22.50

KM# 366 DOLLAR

9.0000 g., Nickel-Aluminum-Copper, 25 mm. **Ruler:** Elizabeth II **Obv:** Crowned head right **Obv. Designer:** Raphael Maklouf **Rev:** Bust of Howard Florey facing **Rev. Designer:** Horst Hahne

Date	Mintage	F	VF	XF	Unc	BU
1998A	21,120	—	—	—	11.50	13.50
1998B	29,914	—	—	—	11.50	13.50
1998C	82,035	—	—	—	9.00	11.50
1998M	21,309	—	—	—	11.50	13.50
1998S	58,514	—	—	—	9.00	11.50

KM# 400 DOLLAR

9.0000 g., Nickel-Aluminum-Copper, 25 mm. **Ruler:** Elizabeth II **Obv:** Rank-Broadley head with tiara right **Obv. Designer:** Ian Rank-Broadley **Rev:** Anzac soldier wearing bush hat, 3/4 left **Rev. Designer:** Wojciech Pietranik

Date	Mintage	F	VF	XF	Unc	BU
1999A	28,681	—	—	—	25.00	28.00
1999C	126,161	—	—	—	22.50	25.00
1999M	49,841	—	—	—	22.50	25.00
1999S	53,286	—	—	—	22.50	25.00
1999B	33,634	—	—	—	25.00	28.00
2000	47,830	—	—	—	85.00	95.00

KM# 405 DOLLAR

9.0000 g., Nickel-Aluminum-Copper, 25 mm. **Ruler:** Elizabeth II **Subject:** International Year of Older People **Obv:** Crowned head right **Obv. Designer:** Ian Rank-Broadley **Rev:** IYOP logo **Rev. Legend:** TOWARDS A SOCIETY FOR ALL AGES - INTERNATIONAL YEAR OF OLDER PERSONS

Date	Mintage	F	VF	XF	Unc	BU
1999	29,218,000	—	—	—	4.50	5.50
1999 Proof	—	Value: 18.50				

KM# 489 DOLLAR

9.0000 g., Aluminum-Bronze, 25 mm. **Ruler:** Elizabeth II **Subject:** Kangaroos **Obv:** Head with tiara right **Obv. Designer:** Ian Rank-Broadley **Rev:** Circle of 5 kangaroos **Rev. Designer:** Stuart Devlin **Edge:** Reeded and plain sections

Date	Mintage	F	VF	XF	Unc	BU
2000	7,592,000	—	—	—	18.00	20.00
2001 Proof	1,001,000	Value: 45.00				
2004	9,565,000	—	—	—	3.50	5.00
2004 Proof	50,000	Value: 65.00				
2005	5,792,000	—	—	—	3.50	5.00
2005 Proof	33,520	Value: 75.00				
2006	—	—	—	—	—	5.00
2007	—	—	—	—	—	5.00

KM# 422 DOLLAR

9.0000 g., Nickel-Aluminum-Copper, 25 mm. **Ruler:** Elizabeth II **Subject:** HMAS Sydney II **Obv:** Head with tiara right **Obv. Designer:** Ian Rank-Broadley **Rev:** Ship above denomination **Rev. Designer:** Vladimir Gottwald **Edge:** Reeded

Date	Mintage	F	VF	XF	Unc	BU
2000C	71,367	—	—	—	18.00	20.00
2000S	34,277	—	—	—	18.00	20.00

KM# 493 DOLLAR

9.0000 g., Nickel-Aluminum-Copper, 24.9 mm. **Ruler:** Elizabeth II **Subject:** Victoria Cross **Obv:** Head with tiara right **Obv. Designer:** Ian Rank-Broadley **Rev:** The Victoria Cross **Edge:** Reeded and plain sections

Date	Mintage	F	VF	XF	Unc	BU
2000	49,877	—	—	—	165	175

KM# 529.1 DOLLAR

9.0000 g., Nickel-Aluminum-Copper, 24.9 mm. **Ruler:** Elizabeth II **Subject:** Olymphilex Exhibition **Obv:** Head with tiara right **Obv. Designer:** Ian Rank-Broadley **Rev:** Denomination and Olympic logo **Edge:** Plain **Edge Lettering:** Incuse SYDNEY

Date	Mintage	F	VF	XF	Unc	BU
2000	98,567	—	—	—	15.00	17.50

KM# 529.2 DOLLAR

9.0000 g., Nickel-Aluminum-Copper, 24.9 mm. **Ruler:** Elizabeth II **Obv:** Head with tiara right **Obv. Designer:** Ian Rank-Broadley **Rev:** Denomination and Olympic logo **Edge:** Plain **Edge Lettering:** Incuse CANBERRA

Date	Mintage	F	VF	XF	Unc	BU
2000	72,573	—	—	—	15.00	17.50

KM# 530 DOLLAR

9.0000 g., Aluminum-Bronze, 25 mm. **Ruler:** Elizabeth II **Subject:** Army Centennial **Obv:** Head with tiara right **Obv. Designer:** Ian Rank-Broadley **Rev:** Army crest **Rev. Designer:** Vladimir Gottwald **Edge:** Reeded and plain sections

Date	Mintage	F	VF	XF	Unc	BU
2001C	125,186	—	—	—	6.00	10.00
Note: IRB spaced						
2001C	Inc. above	—	—	—	6.00	10.00
Note: IRB joined						
2001S	38,095	—	—	—	10.00	15.00
Note: IRB joined only						

KM# 531 DOLLAR

9.0000 g., Aluminum-Bronze, 25 mm. **Ruler:** Elizabeth II **Subject:** 80th Anniversary Royal Australian Air Force **Obv:** Head with tiara right **Obv. Designer:** Ian Rank-Broadley **Rev:** Air Force crest **Rev. Designer:** Vladimir Gottwald **Edge:** Reeded and plain sections

Date	Mintage	F	VF	XF	Unc	BU
2001	99,281	—	—	—	6.00	10.00
Note: IRB spaced						
2001	Inc. above	—	—	—	6.00	10.00
Note: IRB joined						

KM# 534.1 DOLLAR

9.0000 g., Aluminum-Bronze, 25 mm. **Ruler:** Elizabeth II **Subject:** Centenary - Norfolk Island Federation **Obv:** Head with tiara right **Obv. Designer:** Ian Rank-Broadley **Rev:** Stylized ribbon map of Australia with star **Rev. Designer:** Wojciech Pietranik **Edge:** Plain and reeded sections **Note:** Reverse design raised above field. Prev. KM#534.

Date	Mintage	F	VF	XF	Unc	BU
2001	6,781,200	—	—	—	2.50	3.50
Note: IRB joined						
2001	Inc. above	—	—	—	5.00	10.00
Note: IRB spaced						

KM# 588 DOLLAR

9.0000 g., Aluminum-Bronze, 25 mm. **Ruler:** Elizabeth II **Subject:** 90th Anniversary Royal Australian Navy **Obv:** Head with tiara right **Obv. Designer:** Ian Rank-Broadley **Rev:** Navy crest **Rev. Designer:** Vladimir Gottwald **Edge:** Reeded and plain sections

Date	Mintage	F	VF	XF	Unc	BU
2001	62,429	—	—	—	15.00	20.00

KM# 682 DOLLAR

9.0000 g., Aluminum-Nickel-Bronze, 25 mm. **Ruler:** Elizabeth II **Subject:** International Year of Volunteers **Rev:** Volunteers in wreath **Designer:** Wojciech Pietranik

Date	Mintage	F	VF	XF	Unc	BU
2001	6,000,000	—	—	—	3.00	4.50

KM# 600.1 DOLLAR

9.0000 g., Aluminum-Bronze, 25 mm. **Ruler:** Elizabeth II **Subject:** Year of the Outback **Obv:** Head with tiara right **Obv. Designer:** Ian Rank-Broadley **Rev:** Stylized Australian map **Rev. Designer:** Wojciech Pietranik **Edge:** Reeded and plain sections **Note:** Prev. KM#600.

Date	Mintage	F	VF	XF	Unc	BU
2002	34,074,000	—	—	—	2.50	3.50
2002 Proof	—	Value: 4.00				
2002B	32,698	—	—	—	4.50	6.50
2002C	68,447	—	—	—	3.50	5.00
2002M	—	—	—	—	2.50	3.00
2002S	36,931	—	—	—	4.00	6.00

KM# 803 DOLLAR

Aluminum-Bronze, 25 mm. **Ruler:** Elizabeth II **Subject:** Vietnam War 1962-1997 **Obv:** Head with tiara right

Date	Mintage	F	VF	XF	Unc	BU
2003	—	—	—	—	3.50	5.00

KM# 663 DOLLAR

9.0000 g., Aluminum-Bronze, 25 mm. **Ruler:** Elizabeth II **Subject:** 50th Anniversary of the end of Korean War **Obv:** Head with tiara right **Obv. Designer:** Ian Rank-Broadley **Rev:** Dove of Peace **Rev. Designer:** Vladimir Gottwald **Edge:** Segmented reeding

Date	Mintage	F	VF	XF	Unc	BU
2003C	93,572	—	—	—	2.50	3.50
2003B	34,949	—	—	—	3.50	5.00
2003M	36,142	—	—	—	3.50	5.00
2003S	36,091	—	—	—	3.50	5.00

KM# 690 DOLLAR

9.0000 g., Aluminum-Bronze, 25 mm. **Ruler:** Elizabeth II **Obv:** Queens head right **Rev:** Australia Volunteers logo **Edge:** Segmented reeding

Date	Mintage	F	VF	XF	Unc	BU
2003	4,149,000	—	—	—	3.50	4.50

KM# 754 DOLLAR

9.0000 g., Aluminum-Bronze, 25 mm. **Ruler:** Elizabeth II **Subject:** Womens Suffrage **Obv:** Queens head right **Rev:** Suffragette talking to Britannia **Edge:** Segmented reeding

Date	Mintage	F	VF	XF	Unc	BU
2003	10,007,000	—	—	—	3.00	4.00

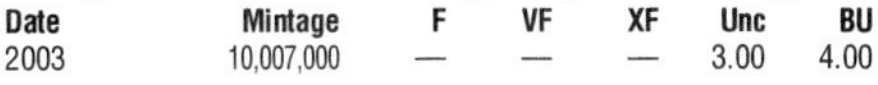

KM# 726 DOLLAR

9.0000 g., Aluminum-Bronze, 25 mm. **Ruler:** Elizabeth II **Subject:** Eureka Stockade 1854-2004 **Obv:** Head with tiara right **Obv. Designer:** Ian Rank-Broadley **Rev:** Stockade and stylized soldiers **Rev. Designer:** Wojciech Pietranik **Edge:** Reeded and plain sections

Date	Mintage	F	VF	XF	Unc	BU
2004	—	—	—	—	20.00	50.00
Note: no mintmark						
2004 B	32,142	—	—	—	3.50	5.00
2004 C	70,913	—	—	—	2.50	3.50
2004 E	89,276	—	—	—	2.50	3.50
2004 S	35,483	—	—	—	3.50	5.00
2004 M	37,526	—	—	—	3.50	5.00

KM# 733.1 DOLLAR

9.0000 g., Aluminum-Bronze, 25 mm. **Ruler:** Elizabeth II **Obv:** Elizabeth II **Rev:** Five kangaroos, not colored or holographic **Edge:** Segmented reeding

Date	Mintage	F	VF	XF	Unc	BU
2004	—	—	—	—	—	4.50

KM# 748 DOLLAR

9.0000 g., Aluminum-Bronze, 38.74 mm. **Ruler:** Elizabeth II **Subject:** 90th Anniversary Gallipoli Landing 1915-2005 **Obv:** Head with tiara right **Obv. Designer:** Ian Rank-Broadley **Rev:** Bugler silhouette **Rev. Designer:** Vladimir Gottwald **Edge:** Segmented reeding

Date	Mintage	F	VF	XF	Unc	BU
2005	15,000	—	—	—	25.00	30.00
2005B	36,108	—	—	—	3.50	5.00
2005C	76,173	—	—	—	2.50	3.50
2005G	35,452	—	—	—	20.00	30.00
2005M	—	—	—	—	2.50	3.50
2005S	39,569	—	—	—	3.50	5.00

KM# 747 DOLLAR

9.0000 g., Aluminum-Bronze, 25 mm. **Ruler:** Elizabeth II **Subject:** 60th Anniversary World War II **Obv:** Head with tiara right **Obv. Designer:** Ian Rank-Broadley **Rev:** Rejoicing serviceman **Rev. Designer:** Wojciech Pietranik **Edge:** Segmented reeding

Date	Mintage	F	VF	XF	Unc	BU
2005	10,607,000	—	—	—	2.00	3.00
2005 Proof	—	Value: 35.00				

KM# 805 DOLLAR

9.0000 g., Aluminum-Bronze, 25 mm. **Ruler:** Elizabeth II **Subject:** 50 Years of Television **Obv:** Head with tiara right **Obv. Designer:** Ian Rank-Broadley **Rev:** TV mast and camera **Rev. Designer:** Vladimir Gottwald **Edge:** Segmented reeding

Date	Mintage	F	VF	XF	Unc	BU
2006C	—	—	—	—	2.50	3.50
2006 TV	—	—	—	—	7.50	10.00
2006S	—	—	—	—	2.50	3.50
2006B	—	—	—	—	3.50	5.50
2006M	—	—	—	—	3.50	5.50

KM# 807 DOLLAR

9.0000 g., Aluminum-Bronze, 25 mm. **Ruler:** Elizabeth II **Subject:** Colored Oceans **Obv:** Head with tiara right **Obv. Designer:** Ian Rank-Broadley **Rev:** Multicolor clown fish **Rev. Designer:** Vladimir Gottwald **Edge:** Segmented reeding

Date	Mintage	F	VF	XF	Unc	BU
2006	—	—	—	—	3.00	4.00

KM# 806 DOLLAR

9.0000 g., Aluminum-Bronze, 25 mm. **Ruler:** Elizabeth II **Subject:** Colored Oceans **Obv:** Head with tiara right **Obv. Designer:** Ian Rank-Broadley **Rev:** Multicolor jumping dolphins **Rev. Designer:** Vladimir Gottwald **Edge:** Segmented reeding

Date	Mintage	F	VF	XF	Unc	BU
2006	—	—	—	—	3.00	4.00

KM# 804 DOLLAR

Aluminum-Bronze, 25 mm. **Ruler:** Elizabeth II **Subject:** XXIII Commonwealth Games **Obv:** Head with tiara right

Date	Mintage	F	VF	XF	Unc	BU
2006	—	—	—	—	3.50	5.00

KM# 809 DOLLAR

9.0000 g., Aluminum-Bronze, 25 mm. **Ruler:** Elizabeth II **Subject:** Year of the Pig **Obv:** Head with tiara right **Obv. Designer:** Ian Rank-Broadley **Rev:** Pig **Rev. Designer:** Vladimir Gottwald **Edge:** Segmented reeding

Date	Mintage	F	VF	XF	Unc	BU
2007	—	—	—	—	3.00	4.00

KM# 808 DOLLAR

9.0000 g., Aluminum-Bronze, 25 mm. **Ruler:** Elizabeth II **Subject:** Ashes Cricket Series 1882-2007 **Obv:** Head with tiara right **Obv. Designer:** Ian Rank-Broadley **Rev:** Urn with supporters **Rev. Designer:** Vladimir Gottwald **Edge:** Segmented reeding

Date	Mintage	F	VF	XF	Unc	BU
2007	—	—	—	—	3.00	4.00

KM# 101 2 DOLLARS

6.6000 g., Aluminum-Bronze, 20.62 mm. **Ruler:** Elizabeth II **Subject:** Aboriginal Man **Obv:** Crowned head right **Obv. Designer:** Raphael Maklouf **Rev:** 1/2-length figure of Aboriginal man at left, 5 stars above value **Rev. Designer:** Horst Hahne **Edge:** Reeded, smooth alternating edge

Date	Mintage	F	VF	XF	Unc	BU
1988	160,700,000	—	—	—	4.25	5.00
1988 Proof	106,000	Value: 7.50				
1989	30,000,000	—	—	—	4.25	5.00
1989 Proof	—	Value: 7.50				
1990	8,700,000	—	—	—	4.25	5.00
1990 Proof	—	Value: 7.50				
1991	—	—	—	—	4.25	5.00
1991 Proof	—	Value: 7.50				
1992	11,500,000	—	—	—	4.25	5.00
1992 Proof	47,000	Value: 7.50				
1993	4,870,000	—	—	—	6.00	9.00
1993 Proof	—	Value: 7.50				
1994	22,143,000	—	—	—	4.50	6.00
1994 Proof	—	Value: 10.00				
1995	13,929,000	—	—	—	4.25	5.00
1995 Proof	—	Value: 10.00				
1996	13,909,000	—	—	—	4.25	5.00
1996 Proof	—	Value: 10.00				
1997	19,039,000	—	—	—	4.50	6.00
1997 Proof	—	Value: 10.00				
1998	8,719,000	—	—	—	4.25	5.00
1998 Proof	—	Value: 10.00				

KM# 406 2 DOLLARS

6.6000 g., Aluminum-Bronze, 20.62 mm. **Ruler:** Elizabeth II **Obv:** Head right **Obv. Designer:** Ian Rank-Broadley **Rev:** Aboriginal man at left, stars above at right **Rev. Designer:** Horst Hahn **Edge:** Reeded, smooth alternating edge

Date	Mintage	F	VF	XF	Unc	BU
1999	10,494,000	—	—	—	6.00	10.00
1999 Proof	—	Value: 11.50				
2000	5,706,000	—	—	—	7.50	12.50
2000 Proof	—	Value: 20.00				
2001	3,565,000	—	—	—	4.00	6.00
Note: Large obverse head, IRB spaced						
2001	Inc. above	—	—	—	—	—
Note: Smaller obverse head, IRB joined						
2001 Proof	59,569	Value: 8.00				
2002	29,689,000	—	—	—	4.00	6.00
2002 Proof	39,514	Value: 8.00				
2003	13,656,000	—	—	—	4.00	6.00
2003 Proof	39,090	Value: 8.00				
2004	20,084,000	—	—	—	3.50	5.00
2004 Proof	50,000	Value: 7.00				
2005	—	—	—	—	3.50	5.00
2005 Proof	33,520	Value: 7.00				
2006	—	—	—	—	3.50	5.00
2006 Proof	—	Value: 7.00				
2007	—	—	—	—	3.00	4.50
2007 Proof	—	Value: 6.00				

The Republic of Austria, a parliamentary democracy located in mountainous central Europe, has an area of 32,374 sq. mi. (83,850 sq. km.) and a population of 8.08 million. Capital: Wien (Vienna). Austria is primarily an industrial country. Machinery, iron, steel, textiles, yarns and timber are exported.

The territories later to be known as Austria were overrun in pre-Roman times by various tribes, including the Celts. Upon the fall of the Roman Empire, the country became a margravate of Charlemagne's Empire. Premysl II of Otakar, King of Bohemia, gained possession in 1252, only to lose the territory to Rudolf of Habsburg in 1276. Thereafter, until World War I, the story of Austria was conducted by the ruling Habsburgs.

During the 17th century, Austrian coinage reflected the geopolitical strife of three wars. From 1618-1648, the Thirty Years' War between northern Protestants and southern Catholics produced low quality, "kipperwhipper" strikes of 12, 24, 30, 60, 75 and 150 Kreuzer. Later, during the Austrian-Turkish War, 1660-1664, coinages used to maintain soldier's salaries also reported the steady division of Hungarian territories. Finally, between 1683 and 1699, during the second Austrian-Turkish conflict, new issues of 3, 6 and 15 Kreuzers were struck, being necessary to help defray mounting expenses of the war effort.

During World War I, the Austro-Hungarian Empire was one of the Central Powers with Germany, Bulgaria and Turkey. At the end of the war, the Empire was dismembered and Austria established as an independent republic. In March 1938, Austria was incorporated into Hitler's short-lived Greater German Reich. Allied forces of both East and West occupied Austria in April 1945, and subsequently divided it into 4 zones of military occupation. On May 15, 1955, the 4 powers formally recognized Austria as a sovereign independent democratic state.

NOTE: During the **GERMAN OCCUPATION** (1938-1945), the German Reichsmark coins and banknotes were circulated.

MONETARY SYSTEM

150 Schillings = 100 Reichsmark

RULERS

Franz Joseph I, 1848-1916
Karl I, 1916-1918

EMPIRE

REFORM COINAGE

100 Heller = 1 Corona

KM# 2800 HELLER

1.6700 g., Bronze **Ruler:** Franz Joseph I

Date	Mintage	F	VF	XF	Unc	BU
1892	—	35.00	75.00	150	350	—
1893	29,000,000	0.20	0.35	0.50	4.00	—
1894	30,100,000	0.20	0.35	0.50	4.00	—
1895	49,500,000	0.20	0.35	0.50	3.00	—
1896	15,600,000	0.35	1.50	3.00	8.00	—
1897	12,400,000	0.35	2.00	4.00	10.00	—
1898	6,780,000	5.00	10.00	20.00	35.00	—
1899	1,901,000	3.00	12.00	25.00	60.00	—
1900	26,981,000	0.20	0.50	1.50	4.00	—
1901	52,096,000	0.20	0.35	1.00	3.00	—
1902	20,553,000	0.20	0.50	1.25	3.00	—
1903	13,779,000	0.20	0.35	0.50	2.50	—
1909	12,668,000	0.20	0.35	0.50	2.50	—
1910	21,941,000	0.20	0.35	0.50	2.50	—
1911	18,387,000	0.20	0.35	0.50	2.50	—
1912	27,053,000	0.20	0.35	0.50	2.50	—
1913	8,782,000	0.20	0.35	0.50	2.50	—
1914	9,906,000	0.20	0.35	0.50	2.50	—
1915	5,673,000	0.20	0.35	0.75	2.50	—
1916	12,484,000	0.35	0.75	1.50	4.00	—

KM# 2823 HELLER

Bronze, 17 mm. **Ruler:** Franz Joseph I **Obv:** Austrian shield on crowned double eagle's breast **Rev:** Value above sprays, date below, within shield

Date	Mintage	F	VF	XF	Unc	BU
1916	Inc. above	4.00	6.00	14.00	20.00	—

KM# 2801 2 HELLER

3.3500 g., Bronze, 19 mm. **Ruler:** Franz Joseph I **Obv:** Crowned imperial double eagle **Rev:** Value above sprays, date below within shield **Edge:** Smooth

Date	Mintage	F	VF	XF	Unc	BU
1892	260,000	50.00	100	200	450	—
1893	41,507,000	0.20	0.50	1.75	5.00	—
1894	78,036,000	0.15	0.25	0.75	3.00	—
1895	25,610,000	0.20	0.50	2.25	6.25	—
1896	43,080,000	0.15	0.25	0.75	3.50	—
1897	98,000,000	0.15	0.25	0.75	3.00	—
1898	10,720,000	0.75	1.50	4.00	12.00	—
1899	42,734,000	0.15	0.25	1.00	4.00	—
1900	7,942,000	0.50	1.00	3.00	9.00	—
1901	12,157,000	2.50	5.00	15.00	35.00	—
1902	18,760,000	0.15	0.50	1.50	3.00	—
1903	26,983,000	0.50	1.50	3.00	8.00	—
1904	12,863,000	0.15	0.50	4.00	14.00	—
1905	6,679,000	0.75	2.75	5.50	15.00	—
1906	20,104,000	0.50	1.50	3.00	8.00	—
1907	23,804,000	0.15	0.25	0.75	3.00	—
1908	21,984,000	0.15	0.25	0.75	3.00	—
1909	25,975,000	0.15	0.25	0.75	3.00	—
1910	28,406,000	0.50	1.50	3.00	8.00	—
1911	50,007,058	0.15	0.25	0.50	2.00	—
1912	74,234,000	0.15	0.20	0.35	2.00	—
1913	27,432,000	0.35	0.75	2.25	6.00	—
1914	60,674,000	0.15	0.20	0.35	2.00	—
1915	7,871,000	0.15	0.20	0.35	2.00	—

KM# 2824 2 HELLER

Iron **Ruler:** Karl I **Obv:** Austrian shield on crowned double eagle's breast **Rev:** Value above date, within wreath

Date	Mintage	F	VF	XF	Unc	BU
1916	61,909,000	0.50	1.00	2.00	7.50	—
1917	81,186,000	0.25	0.50	1.00	5.00	—
1918	66,352,999	0.25	0.50	1.00	4.00	—

KM# 2802 10 HELLER

Nickel **Ruler:** Franz Joseph I **Obv:** Crowned imperial double eagle **Rev:** Value above date at center of ornate shield

Date	Mintage	F	VF	XF	Unc	BU
1892	—	125	250	450	1,150	—
1892 Proof	—	Value: 1,500				
1893	43,524,000	0.25	0.50	1.50	4.00	—
1894	45,558,000	0.25	0.50	1.25	4.00	—
1895	79,918,000	0.25	0.50	1.00	3.50	—
1907	8,662,000	0.25	0.50	1.00	4.00	—
1908	7,772,000	0.75	1.50	2.50	6.00	—
1909	20,462,000	0.15	0.25	0.75	2.50	—
1910	10,164,000	0.15	0.25	0.75	2.50	—
1911	3,634,000	1.00	2.00	3.50	8.00	—

KM# 2822 10 HELLER

Copper-Nickel-Zinc **Ruler:** Franz Joseph I **Obv:** Shield on crowned double eagle's breast **Rev:** Value within wreath, date below

Date	Mintage	F	VF	XF	Unc	BU
1915	18,366,000	0.15	0.25	0.50	2.00	—
1916	27,487,000	0.15	0.25	0.50	2.00	—

KM# 2825 10 HELLER

Copper-Nickel-Zinc **Ruler:** Franz Joseph I **Obv:** Austrian shield on crowned double eagle's breast **Rev:** Value within wreath, date below

Date	Mintage	F	VF	XF	Unc	BU
1916	14,804,000	0.75	1.50	3.00	5.00	—

KM# 2803 20 HELLER

Nickel, 21 mm. **Ruler:** Franz Joseph I **Obv:** Crowned imperial double eagle **Rev:** Value above date at center of ornate shield

Date	Mintage	F	VF	XF	Unc	BU
1892	1,500,000	7.50	15.00	35.00	75.00	—
1892 Proof	—	Value: 250				
1893	41,457,000	0.25	0.65	1.50	7.00	—
1894	50,116,000	0.25	0.65	1.50	7.00	—
1895	32,927,000	0.25	0.65	1.50	7.00	—
1907	7,650,000	0.75	1.50	3.00	12.00	—
1908	7,469,000	0.75	1.25	2.50	9.00	—
1909	7,592,000	3.00	6.00	12.00	20.00	—
1911	19,560,000	0.25	0.35	1.00	5.00	—
1914	2,342,000	5.00	10.00	15.00	25.00	—

KM# 2826 20 HELLER

Iron **Ruler:** Karl I **Obv:** Austrian shield on crowned double eagle's breast **Rev:** Value within wreath, date below

Date	Mintage	F	VF	XF	Unc	BU
1916	130,770,000	0.50	1.25	2.00	6.50	—
1917	127,420,000	0.50	1.25	2.00	5.50	—
1918	48,985,000	0.25	0.65	1.25	4.50	—

KM# 2804 CORONA

5.0000 g., 0.8350 Silver 0.1342 oz. ASW **Ruler:** Franz Joseph I **Obv:** Laureate head

Date	Mintage	F	VF	XF	Unc	BU
1892	235,000	80.00	160	275	700	—
1893	50,124,000	2.00	3.00	5.00	10.00	—
1894	28,003,000	2.00	3.00	5.00	12.00	—
1895	15,115,000	3.75	6.00	15.00	35.00	—
1896	3,068,000	7.50	15.00	25.00	55.00	—
1897	2,142,000	20.00	30.00	60.00	150	—
1898	5,855,000	2.50	5.00	8.00	25.00	—
1899	11,820,000	2.00	3.00	5.00	10.00	—
1900	3,745,000	2.50	5.00	8.00	14.00	—
1901	10,387,000	2.00	3.00	5.00	10.00	—
1902	2,947,000	2.00	4.25	7.50	15.00	—
1903	2,198,000	2.00	4.25	8.00	29.00	—
1904	993,000	4.00	8.50	17.50	50.00	—
1905	505,000	10.00	25.00	45.00	70.00	—
1906	164,500	80.00	125	200	450	—
1907	244,000	30.00	60.00	100	300	—

KM# 2808 CORONA

5.0000 g., 0.8350 Silver 0.1342 oz. ASW **Ruler:** Franz Joseph I **Subject:** 60th Anniversary of Reign **Obv:** Head right **Rev:** Crown at top divides dates, FII on spray at center, value at bottom **Designer:** R. Marshall & R. Neuberger

Date	Mintage	F	VF	XF	Unc	BU
ND(1908)	4,784,992	2.50	3.50	6.00	12.00	—

KM# 2820 CORONA

5.0000 g., 0.8350 Silver 0.1342 oz. ASW **Ruler:** Franz Joseph I **Obv:** Head right **Rev:** Crown above value, date at bottom, sprays flanking

Date	Mintage	F	VF	XF	Unc	BU
1912	8,457,000	BV	2.25	3.50	8.00	—
1913	9,345,000	BV	2.25	3.50	7.00	—
1914	37,897,000	BV	2.25	3.00	6.00	—
1915	23,000,134	BV	2.25	3.00	6.00	—
1916	12,415,404	BV	2.25	3.00	6.00	—

KM# 2821 2 CORONA

10.0000 g., 0.8350 Silver 0.2684 oz. ASW **Ruler:** Franz Joseph I **Obv:** Head right **Rev:** Crowned double eagle above date

Date	Mintage	F	VF	XF	Unc	BU
1912	10,244,500	BV	5.00	7.00	10.00	—
1913	7,256,002	BV	5.00	7.00	10.00	—

KM# 2807 5 CORONA

24.0000 g., 0.9000 Silver 0.6944 oz. ASW **Ruler:** Franz Joseph I **Obv:** Laureate, bearded head right **Rev:** Crowned imperial double eagle within circle surrounded by wreath of circled crowns and leaves

Date	Mintage	F	VF	XF	Unc	BU
1900	8,525,000	10.00	13.50	30.00	110	—
1907	1,539,000	16.00	20.00	45.00	145	—
1907 Proof	—	Value: 650				

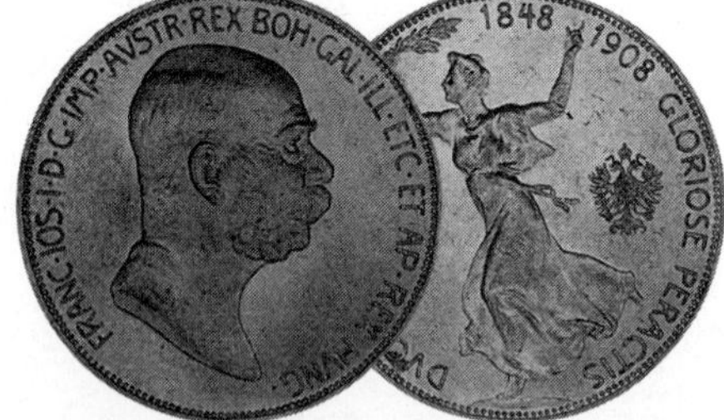

KM# 2809 5 CORONA

24.0000 g., 0.9000 Silver 0.6944 oz. ASW, 35 mm. **Ruler:** Franz Joseph I **Subject:** 60th Anniversary of Reign **Obv:** Head right **Rev:** Running figure of Fame **Designer:** R. Marshall & R. Neuberger

Date	Mintage	F	VF	XF	Unc	BU
ND(1908)	5,089,700	14.00	16.00	28.00	65.00	—
ND(1908) Proof	—	Value: 650				

KM# 2813 5 CORONA
24.0000 g., 0.9000 Silver 0.6944 oz. ASW **Ruler:** Franz Joseph I **Obv:** Large head, right, continuous legend **Rev:** Crowned double eagle with shield on breast within circle, five crowns in circles and leaf sprays surrounding, date divides value at bottom

Date	Mintage	F	VF	XF	Unc	BU
1909	1,708,800	15.00	18.00	40.00	125	—

KM# 2814 5 CORONA
24.0000 g., 0.9000 Silver 0.6944 oz. ASW **Ruler:** Franz Joseph I **Obv:** Head right **Rev:** National arms, date below divides denomination

Date	Mintage	F	VF	XF	Unc	BU
1909	1,775,787	15.00	17.00	35.00	90.00	—

KM# 2805 10 CORONA
3.3875 g., 0.9000 Gold 0.0980 oz. AGW, 19 mm. **Ruler:** Franz Joseph I **Obv:** Laureate, bearded head right **Rev:** Crowned imperial double eagle

Date	Mintage	F	VF	XF	Unc	BU
1892 - MDCCCXCII	—	1,000	1,500	2,500	3,500	—
1893 - MDCCCXCIII Rare	—	—	—	—	—	—
1896 - MDCCCXCVI	211,000	—	BV	100	120	—
1897 - MDCCCXCVII	1,803,000	—	BV	100	120	—
1905 - MDCCCCV	1,933,230	—	BV	100	120	—
1906 - MDCCCCVI	1,081,161	—	BV	100	120	—

KM# 2810 10 CORONA
3.3875 g., 0.9000 Gold 0.0980 oz. AGW, 19 mm. **Ruler:** Franz J oseph I **Subject:** 60th Anniversary of Reign **Obv:** Small plain head right **Rev:** Crowned double eagle, tail divides two dates, value at bottom **Designer:** R. Marshall & R. Neuberger

Date	Mintage	F	VF	XF	Unc	BU
ND(1908)	654,022	—	BV	85.00	100	110

KM# 2815 10 CORONA
3.3875 g., 0.9000 Gold 0.0980 oz. AGW, 19 mm. **Ruler:** Franz Joseph I **Obv:** Head right **Rev:** Crowned double eagle, date and value at bottom

Date	Mintage	F	VF	XF	Unc	BU
1909 - MDCCCCIX	2,319,872	—	BV	85.00	100	110

KM# 2816 10 CORONA
3.3875 g., 0.9000 Gold 0.0980 oz. AGW, 19 mm. **Ruler:** Franz Joseph I **Obv:** Large right **Rev:** Crowned double eagle, date and value at bottom

Date	Mintage	F	VF	XF	Unc	BU
1909 - MDCCCCIX	192,135	—	BV	90.00	110	120
1910 - MDCCCCX	1,055,387	—	BV	85.00	100	110
1911 - MDCCCCXI	1,285,667	—	BV	85.00	100	110
1912 - MDCCCCXII Restrike	—	—	—	—	BV+ 10%	—

KM# 2806 20 CORONA
6.7751 g., 0.9000 Gold 0.1960 oz. AGW, 21 mm. **Ruler:** Franz Joseph I **Obv:** Laureate, bearded head right **Rev:** Crowned imperial double eagle

Date	Mintage	F	VF	XF	Unc	BU
1892 - MDCCCXCII	653,000	—	BV	175	185	195
1893 - MDCCCXCIII	7,872,000	—	—	BV	175	185
1894 - MDCCCXCIV	6,714,000	—	—	BV	175	185
1895 - MDCCCXCV	2,266,000	—	—	BV	175	185
1896 - MDCCCXCVI	6,868,000	—	—	BV	175	185
1897 - MDCCCXCVII	5,133,000	—	—	BV	175	185
1898 - MDCCCXCVIII	1,874,000	—	—	BV	175	185
1899 - MDCCCXCIX	98,000	—	BV	175	185	195
1900 - MDCCCC	27,000	200	400	600	800	950
1901 - MDCCCCI	48,677	200	400	600	800	950
1902 - MDCCCCII	440,751	—	BV	185	195	200
1903 - MDCCCCIII	322,679	—	BV	185	195	200
1904 - MDCCCCIV	494,356	—	BV	185	195	200
1905 - MDCCCCV	146,097	—	BV	185	195	210

KM# 2811 20 CORONA
6.7751 g., 0.9000 Gold 0.1960 oz. AGW, 21 mm. **Ruler:** Franz Joseph I **Subject:** 60th Anniversary of Reign **Obv:** Head right **Rev:** Crowned double eagle, crown divides two dates, value at bottom **Designer:** R. Marshall & R. Neuberger

Date	Mintage	F	VF	XF	Unc	BU
1908	188,000	BV	195	285	380	425

KM# 2817 20 CORONA
6.7751 g., 0.9000 Gold 0.1960 oz. AGW, 21 mm. **Ruler:** Franz Joseph I **Rev:** Crowned double eagle, value and date at bottom **Designer:** Rudolf Marschall

Date	Mintage	F	VF	XF	Unc	BU
1909 - MDCCCCIX	227,754	450	750	1,400	1,800	2,100

KM# 2818 20 CORONA
6.7751 g., 0.9000 Gold 0.1960 oz. AGW, 21 mm. **Ruler:** Franz Joseph I **Obv:** Head of Franz Joseph I, right

Date	Mintage	F	VF	XF	Unc	BU
MDCCCCIX (1909)	102,404	575	1,150	2,000	2,800	—
MDCCCCX (1910)	386,031	BV	195	250	350	—
MDCCCCXI (1911)	59,313	185	550	800	975	—
MDCCCCXII (1912)	4,460	250	550	1,350	2,000	—
MDCCCCXIII (1913)	28,058	350	900	1,800	3,000	—
MDCCCCXIV (1914)	82,104	185	550	800	1,000	—
MDCCCCXV (1915) Restrike	—	—	—	—	BV+ 5%	—
MDCCCCXVI (1916)	71,763	2,500	3,500	5,500	7,500	—

KM# 2827 20 CORONA
6.7751 g., 0.9000 Gold 0.1960 oz. AGW, 21 mm. **Ruler:** Franz Joseph I **Obv:** Head right **Rev:** Austrian shield on crowned double eagle, value and date at bottom

Date	Mintage	F	VF	XF	Unc	BU
1916 - MDCCCCXVI	Inc. above	450	750	900	1,200	—

KM# 2812 100 CORONA
33.8753 g., 0.9000 Gold 0.9802 oz. AGW, 37 mm. **Ruler:** Franz Joseph I **Subject:** 60th Anniversary of Reign **Obv:** Head right **Rev:** Resting figure of Fame **Designer:** Rudolf Marschall

Date	Mintage	F	VF	XF	Unc	BU
ND(1908)	16,000	BV	1,000	1,200	1,700	—
ND(1908) Proof	—	Value: 1,850				

KM# 2819 100 CORONA
33.8753 g., 0.9000 Gold 0.9802 oz. AGW, 37 mm. **Ruler:** Franz Joseph I **Obv:** Head right **Obv. Designer:** Stefan Schwartz **Rev:** Crowned double eagle, tail dividing value, date at bottom

Date	Mintage	F	VF	XF	Unc	BU
1909	3,203	BV	950	1,000	1,500	—
1910	3,074	BV	950	1,000	1,500	—
1911	11,165	BV	950	1,000	1,500	—
1912	3,591	950	1,000	1,150	2,000	—
1913	2,696	BV	1,000	1,200	1,700	—
1914	1,195	BV	950	1,000	1,600	—
1915 Restrike	—	—	—	—	BV+ 2%	—
1915 Restrike, Proof	—	—	—	—	—	—

TRADE COINAGE

KM# 2267 DUCAT
3.4909 g., 0.9860 Gold 0.1107 oz. AGW **Ruler:** Franz Joseph I **Obv:** Laureate head right, heavy whiskers **Rev:** Crowned imperial double eagle **Note:** 996,721 pieces were struck from 1920-1936.

Date	Mintage	F	VF	XF	Unc	BU
1872	460,000	BV	100	125	175	185
1873	516,000	BV	100	125	175	185
1874	353,000	BV	100	125	175	185
1875	184,000	BV	100	125	175	185
1876	680,000	BV	95.00	125	150	175
1877	823,000	BV	95.00	125	175	185
1878	281,000	BV	95.00	125	175	185
1879	362,000	BV	95.00	125	175	185
1880	341,000	BV	100	150	225	245
1881	477,000	BV	95.00	125	175	185

Date	Mintage	F	VF	XF	Unc	BU
1882	390,000	BV	100	125	175	185
1883	409,000	BV	100	125	175	185
1884	238,000	BV	95.00	125	175	185
1885	257,000	BV	95.00	125	150	160
1886	291,000	BV	95.00	125	150	160
1887	223,000	BV	95.00	105	150	160
1888	309,000	BV	95.00	105	150	160
1889	335,000	BV	95.00	105	150	160
1890	374,000	BV	95.00	105	150	160
1891	325,000	BV	95.00	105	150	160
1901	348,621	BV	115	125	175	185
1902	311,471	BV	115	125	175	185
1903	380,014	BV	115	125	175	185
1904	517,118	BV	115	125	175	185
1905	391,534	BV	125	150	200	210
1906	491,574	BV	125	150	200	210
1907	554,205	BV	110	175	250	260
1908	408,832	BV	110	125	175	187
1909	366,318	BV	110	105	150	160
1910	440,424	BV	110	105	150	160
1911	590,826	BV	110	105	125	135
1912	494,991	BV	110	105	125	135
1913	319,926	BV	110	105	125	135
1914	378,241	BV	110	105	125	135
1915 Restrike	—	—	—	—	—	BV+10%
1915 Restrike, Proof	—	BV+5%				
1951 Error for 1915	—	BV	125	150	225	235

KM# 2276 4 DUCAT

13.9636 g., 0.9860 Gold 0.4426 oz. AGW **Ruler:** Franz Joseph I **Obv:** Laureate, armored bust right **Rev:** Crowned imperial double eagle **Note:** without mint

Date	Mintage	F	VF	XF	Unc	BU
1872	Est. 12,000	380	625	975	1,650	—
1873	24,000	380	475	875	1,400	—
1874	15,000	380	475	875	1,400	—
1875	12,000	380	450	875	1,400	—
1876	5,243	380	550	1,000	1,750	—
1877	5,970	380	550	1,000	1,750	—
1878	23,000	380	460	850	1,200	—
1879	29,000	380	460	850	1,200	—
1880	23,000	380	460	850	1,200	—
1881	35,000	380	460	850	1,200	—
1882	29,000	380	460	850	1,200	—
1883	37,000	380	460	850	1,200	—
1884	35,000	380	460	850	1,200	—
1885	28,000	380	460	850	1,200	—
1886	18,000	380	450	825	1,200	—
1887	27,000	380	450	825	1,200	—
1888	36,000	380	450	825	1,200	—
1889	31,000	380	450	825	1,200	—
1890	47,000	380	450	825	1,200	—
1891	54,000	380	450	825	1,200	—
1892	58,000	380	450	825	1,200	—
1893	54,000	380	450	800	1,150	—
1894	35,000	380	450	800	1,150	—
1895	40,000	380	450	800	1,150	—
1896	49,000	380	450	800	1,150	—
1897	35,000	380	450	800	1,150	—
1898	54,000	380	450	800	1,150	—
1899	54,000	380	450	800	1,100	1,200
1900	47,000	380	450	800	1,100	1,200
1901	51,597	BV	450	800	1,100	1,200
1902	69,380	BV	450	800	1,100	1,200
1903	72,658	BV	450	800	1,100	1,200
1904	80,086	BV	450	800	1,100	1,200
1905	90,906	BV	450	800	1,100	1,200
1906	123,443	BV	425	500	800	850
1907	104,295	BV	425	500	800	850
1908	80,428	BV	425	550	870	900
1909	83,852	BV	400	450	680	710
1910	101,000	BV	400	425	580	600
1911	141,857	BV	400	425	450	500
1912	150,691	BV	400	425	450	500
1913	119,133	BV	400	425	450	500
1914	102,712	BV	400	425	450	500
1915 (- 1936) Restrike	—	—	—	—	BV+ 8%	—

Note: 496,501 pieces were struck from 1920-1936

REPUBLIC

REFORM COINAGE

10,000 Kronen = 1 Schilling

KM# 2830 20 KRONEN

6.7751 g., 0.9000 Gold 0.1960 oz. AGW **Obv:** Imperial Eagle, date below **Rev:** Value within wreath **Designer:** Richard Placht

Date	Mintage	F	VF	XF	Unc	BU
1923	6,988	650	1,400	1,850	2,500	—
1924	10,337	650	1,400	1,850	2,500	—

KM# 2831 100 KRONEN

33.8753 g., 0.9000 Gold 0.9802 oz. AGW **Obv:** Imperial Eagle, date below **Rev:** Value within wreath **Designer:** Richard Placht

Date	Mintage	F	VF	XF	Unc	BU
1923	617	950	1,550	2,250	3,500	—
1923 Proof	—	Value: 4,000				
1924	2,851	950	1,550	2,250	3,500	—

KM# 2832 100 KRONEN

Bronze **Obv:** Eagle's head, right **Rev:** Value to right of leaf, date below **Designer:** Heinrich Zita

Date	Mintage	F	VF	XF	Unc	BU
1923	6,403,680	4.00	8.00	15.00	30.00	—
1924	43,013,920	0.25	0.50	1.50	4.50	—

KM# 2833 200 KRONEN

Bronze **Obv:** Thick cross, date below **Rev:** Large value **Designer:** Filip Häuslerr

Date	Mintage	F	VF	XF	Unc	BU
1924	57,160,000	0.50	1.00	2.00	6.50	—

KM# 2834 1000 KRONEN

Copper-Nickel **Obv:** Woman of Tyrol, right **Rev:** Value within wreath **Designer:** Heinrich Zita

Date	Mintage	F	VF	XF	Unc	BU
1924	72,353,000	0.75	1.50	3.00	8.00	—

PRE WWII DECIMAL COINAGE

100 Groschen - 1 Schilling

KM# 2836 GROSCHEN

Bronze **Obv:** Eagle's head, right **Rev:** Large value, date below **Designer:** Heinrich Zita

Date	Mintage	F	VF	XF	Unc	BU
1925	30,465,000	0.10	0.20	0.50	2.00	—
1926	15,487,000	0.10	0.30	0.75	2.00	—
1927	9,318,000	0.10	0.30	0.75	2.50	—
1928	17,189,000	0.10	0.30	0.75	2.50	—
1929	11,400,000	0.10	0.30	0.75	2.50	—
1930	8,893,000	0.10	0.30	0.75	2.50	—
1931	971,000	10.00	20.00	30.00	60.00	—
1932	3,040,000	1.00	2.50	5.00	7.50	—
1933	3,940,000	0.50	1.00	2.00	6.00	—
1934	4,232,000	0.15	0.50	1.00	4.00	—
1935	3,740,000	0.15	0.50	1.00	4.00	—
1936	6,020,000	0.50	1.00	3.00	9.00	—
1937	5,830,000	0.50	1.00	2.00	7.50	—
1938	1,650,000	2.00	3.00	6.00	15.00	—

KM# 2837 2 GROSCHEN

Bronze **Obv:** Thick cross, date below **Rev:** Large value

Date	Mintage	F	VF	XF	Unc	BU
1925	29,892,000	0.10	0.25	0.50	1.50	—
1926	17,700,000	0.10	0.30	0.75	2.00	—
1927	7,757,000	0.20	0.75	2.00	5.00	—
1928	19,478,000	0.10	0.30	0.75	2.00	—
1929	16,184,000	0.10	0.30	0.75	2.00	—
1930	5,709,000	0.20	0.60	1.50	4.00	—
1934	812,000	7.00	12.00	15.00	25.00	—
1935	3,148,000	0.20	0.60	1.50	4.00	—
1936	4,410,000	0.15	0.30	1.00	3.00	—
1937	3,790,000	0.20	0.40	1.25	3.50	—
1938	860,000	2.50	4.00	6.50	12.50	—

KM# 2846 5 GROSCHEN

Copper-Nickel **Obv:** Thick cross, date below **Obv. Designer:** Adolf Hofmann **Rev:** Large value **Rev. Designer:** Philipp Häusler

Date	Mintage	F	VF	XF	Unc	BU
1931	16,631,000	0.15	0.40	0.80	2.00	—
1932	4,700,000	0.25	1.00	2.00	5.00	—
1934	3,210,000	0.30	1.00	2.50	6.00	—
1936	1,240,000	2.00	4.00	7.50	15.00	—
1937	1,540,000	20.00	30.00	45.00	80.00	—
1938	870,000	125	175	250	425	—

KM# 2838 10 GROSCHEN

Copper-Nickel, 22 mm. **Obv:** Woman of Tyrol, right **Rev:** Value above date within wreath **Designer:** Heinrich Zita

Date	Mintage	F	VF	XF	Unc	BU
1925	66,199,000	0.10	0.25	0.50	3.00	—
1928	11,468,000	0.50	1.00	4.00	12.00	—
1929	12,000,000	0.40	0.75	1.50	4.50	—

KM# 2850 50 GROSCHEN

Copper-Nickel **Obv:** Numeric value in box within circle, value at bottom **Obv. Designer:** G. Baudisch **Rev:** Austrian shield on haloed double eagle's breast, tail dividing date **Rev. Designer:** Michael Powolny

Date	Mintage	F	VF	XF	Unc	BU
1934	8,224,822	20.00	35.00	50.00	90.00	—
1934 Proof	Inc. above	Value: 125				

KM# 2854 50 GROSCHEN

5.5100 g., Copper-Nickel **Obv:** Austrian shield on haloed double eagle's breast, value at bottom **Rev:** Large value above date

Date	Mintage	F	VF	XF	Unc	BU
1935	11,435,000	0.75	1.25	2.50	5.00	—
1935 Proof	Inc. above	Value: 80.00				
1936	1,000,000	30.00	40.00	60.00	115	—
1936 Proof	Inc. above	Value: 140				

KM# 2839 1/2 SCHILLING

3.0000 g., 0.6400 Silver 0.0617 oz. ASW **Obv:** Austrian shield at center **Rev:** Numeric value in diamond at center **Designer:** Philipp Häusler

Date	Mintage	F	VF	XF	Unc	BU
1925	18,370,000	1.25	2.50	4.00	8.00	—
1926	12,943,000	2.00	4.00	7.00	12.50	—

KM# 2835 SCHILLING

7.0000 g., 0.8000 Silver 0.1800 oz. ASW **Obv:** Parliament building in Vienna, date below **Rev:** Coat of arms on spray of edelweiss, value

Date	Mintage	F	VF	XF	Unc	BU
1924	11,086,000	BV	3.50	6.00	10.00	—

KM# 2840 SCHILLING

6.0000 g., 0.6400 Silver 0.1235 oz. ASW **Obv:** Parliament building in Vienna, date below **Rev:** Coat of arms on spray of edelweiss, value

Date	Mintage	F	VF	XF	Unc	BU
1925	38,209,000	BV	2.25	3.50	7.00	—
1926	20,157,000	BV	2.50	4.00	8.00	—
1932	700,000	30.00	65.00	90.00	150	—

KM# 2851 SCHILLING

Copper-Nickel **Obv:** Two sprigs of grain in center with large numeric value on top **Rev:** Austrian shield on haloed double eagles breast, tail dividing date

Date	Mintage	F	VF	XF	Unc	BU
1934	30,641,000	1.00	2.00	3.50	7.50	—
1934 Proof	—	Value: 150				
1935	11,987,000	3.00	6.00	12.50	30.00	—

KM# 2843 2 SCHILLING

12.0000 g., 0.6400 Silver 0.2469 oz. ASW **Subject:** Centennial - Death of Franz Schubert **Obv:** Value within circle of shields **Rev:** Head of Franz Schubert, left, date at bottom left **Rev. Designer:** Edwin Grienauer

Date	Mintage	F	VF	XF	Unc	BU
1928	6,900,000	BV	5.00	8.00	16.00	—

KM# 2844 2 SCHILLING

12.0000 g., 0.6400 Silver 0.2469 oz. ASW **Subject:** 100th Anniversary - Birth of Dr. Theodor Billroth, Surgeon **Obv:** Value within circle of shields **Rev:** Head of Dr. Theodor Billroth, left, date below **Rev. Designer:** Edwin Grienauer

Date	Mintage	F	VF	XF	Unc	BU
1929	2,000,000	6.00	9.00	18.00	32.50	—

KM# 2845 2 SCHILLING

12.0000 g., 0.6400 Silver 0.2469 oz. ASW **Subject:** 7th Centennial - Death of Walther von der Vogelweide, Minstrel **Obv:** Value within circle of shields **Rev:** Figure of Walther von der Vogelweide sitting, left, with doves, harp on lower left. date at bottom **Rev. Designer:** Edwin Grienauer

Date	Mintage	F	VF	XF	Unc	BU
1930	500,000	5.00	6.00	9.00	18.00	—
1930 Proof	Inc. above	Value: 125				

KM# 2847 2 SCHILLING

12.0000 g., 0.6400 Silver 0.2469 oz. ASW **Subject:** 175th Anniversary - Birth of Wolfgang Mozart, Composer **Obv:** Value within circle of shields **Rev:** Head of Wolfgang Mozart, right, two dates at bottom **Rev. Designer:** Edwin Grienauer

Date	Mintage	F	VF	XF	Unc	BU
1931	500,000	9.00	18.00	28.00	50.00	—
1931 Proof	Inc. above	Value: 300				

KM# 2848 2 SCHILLING

12.0000 g., 0.6400 Silver 0.2469 oz. ASW **Subject:** 200th Anniversary - Birth of Joseph Haydn, Composer **Obv:** Value within circle of shields **Rev:** Head of Joseph Haydn, left, date below **Rev. Designer:** Edwin Grienauer

Date	Mintage	F	VF	XF	Unc	BU
1932	300,000	25.00	50.00	100	175	—
1932 Proof	Inc. above	Value: 550				

KM# 2849 2 SCHILLING

12.0000 g., 0.6400 Silver 0.2469 oz. ASW **Subject:** Death of Dr. Ignaz Seipel, Chancellor **Obv:** Value within circle of shields **Rev:** Head of Dr. Ignaz Seipel, right, two dates at bottom **Rev. Designer:** Hanisch and Concée

Date	Mintage	F	VF	XF	Unc	BU
ND(1933)	400,000	10.00	20.00	35.00	60.00	—
ND(1933) Proof	Inc. above	Value: 400				

KM# 2852 2 SCHILLING

12.0000 g., 0.6400 Silver 0.2469 oz. ASW **Subject:** Death of Dr. Engelbert Dollfuss, Chancellor **Obv:** Value within circle of shields **Rev:** Head of Dr. Engelbert Dollfuss, right, two dates at bottom **Rev. Designer:** Edwin Grienauer

Date	Mintage	F	VF	XF	Unc	BU
1934	1,500,000	7.00	12.00	20.00	32.50	—
1934 Proof	Inc. above	Value: 275				

KM# 2855 2 SCHILLING

12.0000 g., 0.6400 Silver 0.2469 oz. ASW **Subject:** 25th Anniversary - Death of Dr. Karl Lueger, Politician, Social reformer **Obv:** Haloed double eagle with Austrian shield, date divides value at bottom **Rev:** Head of Dr. Karl Lueger, right **Rev. Designer:** Rudolf Marschall

Date	Mintage	F	VF	XF	Unc	BU
1935	500,000	8.00	16.00	25.00	45.00	—
1935 Proof	Inc. above	Value: 285				

KM# 2858 2 SCHILLING

12.0000 g., 0.6400 Silver 0.2469 oz. ASW **Subject:** Bicentennial - Death of Prince Eugen of Savoy, Imperial Austrian Field Marshal **Obv:** Haloed double eagle with Austrian shield, date divides value below **Rev:** Head of Prince Eugen of Savoy, left **Rev. Designer:** Edwin Grienauer

Date	Mintage	F	VF	XF	Unc	BU
1936	500,000	6.00	9.00	18.00	30.00	—
1936 Proof	Inc. above	Value: 225				

KM# 2859 2 SCHILLING

12.0000 g., 0.6400 Silver 0.2469 oz. ASW **Subject:** Bicentennial - Completion of St. Charles Church 1737 **Obv:** Haloed double eagle with Austrian shield, date divides value below **Rev:** St. Charles Church, date at bottom **Rev. Designer:** Edwin Grienauer

Date	Mintage	F	VF	XF	Unc	BU
1937	500,000	6.00	9.00	18.00	30.00	—
1937 Proof	Inc. above	Value: 185				

KM# 2853 5 SCHILLING

15.0000 g., 0.8350 Silver 0.4027 oz. ASW **Obv:** Haloed double eagle with Austrian shield, value **Rev:** Standing figure of Madonna of Mariazell, date below

Date	Mintage	F	VF	XF	Unc	BU
1934	3,066,000	11.50	17.50	32.50	60.00	—
1934 Proof	—	Value: 220				
1935	5,377,000	11.50	17.50	32.50	60.00	—
1936	1,557,000	45.00	85.00	125	185	—

KM# 2841 25 SCHILLING

5.8810 g., 0.9000 Gold 0.1702 oz. AGW **Obv:** Imperial Eagle with Austrian shield on breast, holding hammer and sickle, **Rev:** Value at top flanked by edelweiss sprays, date divided by sprigs at bottom **Designer:** Arnold Hartig

Date	Mintage	F	VF	XF	Unc	BU
1926 Prooflike	276,705	—	—	—	175	—
1927 Prooflike	72,672	—	—	—	185	—
1928 Prooflike	134,041	—	—	—	175	—
1929 Prooflike	243,269	—	—	—	175	—
1930 Prooflike	129,535	—	—	—	185	—
1931 Prooflike	169,002	—	—	—	175	—
1933 Prooflike	4,944	—	—	—	1,850	—
1934 Prooflike	11,000	—	—	—	600	—

KM# 2856 25 SCHILLING

5.8810 g., 0.9000 Gold 0.1702 oz. AGW **Obv:** Haloed double eagle with Austrian shield on breast, value below **Obv. Designer:** Joseph Prinz **Rev:** Half figure of St. Leopold, facing 3/4 forward, date at bottom **Rev. Designer:** Edwin Grienauer

Date	Mintage	F	VF	XF	Unc	BU
1935 Prooflike	2,880	—	—	—	1,000	—
1936 Prooflike	7,260	—	—	—	850	—
1937 Prooflike	7,660	—	—	—	850	—
1938 Prooflike	1,360	—	—	—	25,000	—

KM# 2842 100 SCHILLING

23.5245 g., 0.9000 Gold 0.6807 oz. AGW **Obv:** Imperial Eagle with Austrian shield on breast holding hammer and sickle **Rev:** Value at top flanked by edelweiss sprays, date below, one star on either side **Designer:** Arnold Hartig

Date	Mintage	F	VF	XF	Unc	BU
1926 Prooflike	63,795	—	—	—	675	—
1927 Prooflike	68,746	—	—	—	675	—
1928 Prooflike	40,188	—	—	—	750	—
1929 Prooflike	74,849	—	—	—	675	—
1930 Prooflike	24,849	—	—	—	675	—
1931 Prooflike	101,935	—	—	—	675	—
1933 Prooflike	4,727	—	—	—	1,550	—
1934 Prooflike	9,383	—	—	—	800	—

KM# 2857 100 SCHILLING

23.5245 g., 0.9000 Gold 0.6807 oz. AGW **Obv:** Haloed eagle with Austrian shield on breast, value below **Rev:** Standing figure of Madonna of Mariazell, facing, date below

Date	Mintage	F	VF	XF	Unc	BU
1935 Prooflike	951	—	—	—	5,500	—
1936 Prooflike	12,000	—	—	—	1,650	—
1937 Prooflike	2,900	—	—	—	2,250	—
1938 Prooflike	1,400	—	—	—	25,000	—

POST WWII DECIMAL COINAGE

100 Groschen - 1 Schilling

KM# 2873 GROSCHEN

Zinc **Obv:** Imperial Eagle with Austrian shield on breast **Rev:** Large value above date, spray of leaves below

Date	Mintage	F	VF	XF	Unc	BU
1947	23,758,000	0.15	0.25	0.75	2.50	—

KM# 2876 2 GROSCHEN

0.9000 g., Aluminum, 18 mm. **Obv:** Imperial Eagle with Austrian shield on breast, holding hammer and sickle **Obv. Designer:** Michael Powolny **Rev:** Large value in circle, date below circle **Rev. Designer:** Benno Rost **Edge:** Plain

Date	Mintage	F	VF	XF	Unc	BU
1950	21,652,000	—	0.15	0.60	4.00	—
1950 Proof	—	Value: 28.00				
1951	7,377,000	—	0.25	1.00	4.50	—
1951 Proof	—	Value: 300				
1952	37,851,000	—	0.15	0.50	2.50	—
1952 Proof	—	Value: 25.00				
1954	46,167,000	—	0.15	0.50	2.50	—
1954 Proof	—	Value: 50.00				
1957	26,923,000	—	0.15	0.50	3.00	—
1957 Proof	—	Value: 45.00				
1962	6,692,000	—	0.15	0.50	2.50	—
1962 Proof	—	Value: 28.00				
1964 Proof	173,000	Value: 6.50				
1965	14,475,000	—	0.10	0.30	1.50	—
1965 Proof	—	Value: 2.50				
1966	7,454,000	—	0.10	0.30	1.50	—
1966 Proof	—	Value: 7.50				
1967 Proof	13,000	Value: 100				
1968	1,803,400	—	0.10	0.30	1.50	—
1968 Proof	21,600	Value: 10.00				
1969 Proof	57,000	Value: 6.00				
1970 Proof	260,000	Value: 2.50				

Date	Mintage	F	VF	XF	Unc	BU
1971 Proof	145,000	Value: 2.50				
1972	2,763,000	—	—	0.20	0.50	—
1972 Proof	132,000	Value: 1.00				
1973	5,883,000	—	—	0.20	0.50	—
1973 Proof	149,000	Value: 1.00				
1974	1,387,000	—	—	0.20	0.50	—
1974 Proof	93,000	Value: 1.00				
1975	1,096,000	—	—	0.20	0.50	—
1975 Proof	52,000	Value: 1.00				
1976	2,755,000	—	—	0.20	0.50	—
1976 Proof	45,000	Value: 1.00				
1977	1,837,000	—	—	0.20	0.50	—
1977 Proof	47,000	Value: 1.00				
1978	1,527,000	—	—	0.20	0.50	—
1978 Proof	44,000	Value: 1.00				
1979	2,434,000	—	—	0.20	0.50	—
1979 Proof	44,000	Value: 1.00				
1980	1,893,000	—	—	0.20	0.50	—
1980 Proof	48,000	Value: 10.00				
1981	950,000	—	—	0.20	0.50	—
1981 Proof	49,000	Value: 10.00				
1982	3,950,000	—	—	0.20	0.50	—
1982 Proof	50,000	Value: 3.00				
1983	2,665,000	—	—	0.20	0.50	—
1983 Proof	65,000	Value: 2.00				
1984	500,000	—	—	0.20	0.50	—
1984 Proof	65,000	Value: 2.00				
1985	1,060,000	—	—	0.20	0.50	—
1985 Proof	45,000	Value: 5.00				
1986	1,798,000	—	—	0.20	0.50	—
1986 Proof	42,000	Value: 10.00				
1987	958,000	—	—	0.20	0.50	—
1987 Proof	42,000	Value: 6.00				
1988	1,061,000	—	—	0.20	0.50	—
1988 Proof	39,000	Value: 2.00				
1989	950,000	—	—	0.20	0.50	—
1989 Proof	38,000	Value: 2.00				
1990 Proof	35,000	Value: 22.00				
1991	2,600,000	—	—	0.20	0.50	—
1991 Proof	27,000	Value: 5.00				
1992	25,000	—	—	—	20.00	—
Note: In sets only						
1992 Proof	25,000	Value: 15.00				
1993	35,000	—	—	—	20.00	—
Note: In sets only						
1993 Proof	28,000	Value: 7.00				
1994	25,000	—	—	—	25.00	—
Note: In sets only						
1994 Proof	25,000	Value: 30.00				

KM# 2875 5 GROSCHEN

2.5000 g., Zinc, 18.86 mm. **Obv:** Imperial Eagle with Austrian shield on breast, holding hammer and sickle **Obv. Designer:** Michael Powolny **Rev. Designer:** Adolf Hofmann **Edge:** Reeded

Date	Mintage	F	VF	XF	Unc	BU
1948	17,269,000	—	0.20	0.75	12.00	—
1950	19,426,431	—	0.20	0.75	8.00	—
1950 Proof	—	Value: 200				
1951	12,454,569	—	0.20	0.75	12.00	—
1951 Proof	—	Value: 35.00				
1953	14,931,000	—	0.15	0.75	8.00	—
1955	12,288,000	—	0.15	0.75	12.00	—
1957	26,809,000	—	0.15	0.75	6.00	—
1957 Proof	—	Value: 50.00				
1961	3,429,000	—	0.20	0.75	8.00	—
1961 Proof	—	Value: 25.00				
1962	5,999,000	—	0.20	0.75	8.00	—
1963	13,293,000	—	0.15	0.75	8.00	—
1963 Proof	—	Value: 40.00				
1964	4,659,000	—	0.15	0.75	4.00	—
1964 Proof	—	Value: 2.50				
1965	13,704,000	—	0.10	0.50	3.00	—
1965 Proof	—	Value: 2.50				
1966	9,348,000	—	0.10	0.50	3.00	—
1966 Proof	—	Value: 8.00				
1967	4,404,000	—	0.10	0.50	3.00	—
1967 Proof	—	Value: 10.00				
1968	31,418,400	—	0.10	0.50	3.00	—
1968 Proof	15,600	Value: 8.00				
1969 Proof	44,000	Value: 10.00				
1970 Proof	144,000	Value: 2.50				
1971 Proof	125,000	Value: 2.50				
1972	10,979,000	—	—	0.20	0.75	—
1972 Proof	116,000	Value: 1.00				
1973	10,336,000	—	—	0.20	0.75	—
1973 Proof	120,000	Value: 1.00				
1974	2,911,000	—	—	0.20	0.75	—
1974 Proof	87,000	Value: 1.00				
1975	7,102,000	—	—	0.20	0.75	—
1975 Proof	51,000	Value: 1.00				
1976	8,079,000	—	—	0.20	0.75	—
1976 Proof	45,000	Value: 1.00				
1977	1,600,000	—	—	0.20	0.75	—
1977 Proof	45,000	Value: 1.00				

Date	Mintage	F	VF	XF	Unc	BU
1978	2,657,000	—	—	0.20	0.75	—
1978 Proof	44,000	Value: 1.00				
1979	4,927,000	—	—	0.20	0.75	—
1979 Proof	44,000	Value: 1.00				
1980	3,100,000	—	—	0.20	0.75	—
1980 Proof	48,000	Value: 8.00				
1981	450,000	—	—	0.20	0.75	—
1981 Proof	49,000	Value: 8.00				
1982	3,950,000	—	—	0.20	0.75	—
1982 Proof	50,000	Value: 2.50				
1983	501,000	—	—	0.20	0.75	—
1983 Proof	65,000	Value: 2.50				
1984	988,000	—	—	0.20	0.75	—
1984 Proof	65,000	Value: 2.50				
1985	1,914,000	—	—	0.20	0.75	—
1985 Proof	45,000	Value: 4.00				
1986	1,008,000	—	—	0.20	0.75	—
1986 Proof	42,000	Value: 7.00				
1987	1,458,000	—	—	0.20	0.75	—
1987 Proof	42,000	Value: 4.00				
1988	1,261,000	—	—	0.20	0.75	—
1988 Proof	39,000	Value: 3.00				
1989	2,604,000	—	—	0.20	0.75	—
1989 Proof	38,000	Value: 2.00				
1990	2,608,000	—	—	0.20	0.75	—
1990 Proof	35,000	Value: 6.00				
1991	2,400,000	—	—	0.20	0.75	—
1991 Proof	27,000	Value: 6.00				
1992	671,000	—	—	0.20	0.75	—
1992 Proof	25,000	Value: 10.00				
1993	35,000	—	—	—	12.00	—
Note: In sets only						
1993 Proof	28,000	Value: 7.00				
1994	25,000	—	—	—	15.00	—
Note: In sets only						
1994 Proof	25,000	Value: 20.00				

KM# 2874 10 GROSCHEN

3.5000 g., Zinc, 21 mm. **Obv:** Imperial Eagle with Austrian shield on breast, holding hammer and sickle **Rev:** Large value above date, trumpet flower spray below **Edge:** Plain

Date	Mintage	F	VF	XF	Unc	BU
1947	6,845,000	0.75	2.00	4.00	22.00	—
1947 Proof	—	Value: 55.00				
1948	66,205,000	0.20	0.50	1.00	3.50	—
1948 Proof	—	Value: 65.00				
1949	51,202,000	0.20	0.50	1.00	3.50	—
1949 Proof	—	Value: 75.00				

KM# 2878 10 GROSCHEN

1.1000 g., Aluminum, 20 mm. **Obv:** Small Imperial Eagle with Austrian shield on breast, at top between numbers, scalloped rim, stylized inscription below **Rev:** Large value above date, scalloped rim **Edge:** Plain **Designer:** Hans Köttenstorfer

Date	Mintage	F	VF	XF	Unc	BU
1951	9,573,000	—	0.20	0.75	8.00	—
1951 Proof	—	Value: 85.00				
1952	45,911,400	—	0.10	0.50	4.00	—
1952 Proof	—	Value: 50.00				
1953	22,577,600	—	0.10	0.50	4.00	—
1953 Proof	—	Value: 175				
1955	51,707,000	—	0.10	0.50	4.00	—
1955 Proof	—	Value: 28.00				
1957	33,509,000	—	0.10	0.50	4.00	—
1957 Proof	—	Value: 150				
1959	80,719,000	—	0.10	0.35	3.50	—
1959 Proof	—	Value: 45.00				
1961	11,283,000	—	0.20	0.75	8.00	—
1961 Proof	—	—	—	—	—	—
1962	24,635,000	—	0.10	0.35	3.50	—
1962 Proof	—	Value: 40.00				
1963	38,062,000	—	0.10	0.35	3.50	—
1963 Proof	—	Value: 45.00				
1964	34,928,000	—	0.10	0.20	2.00	—
1964 Proof	—	Value: 1.50				
1965	40,615,000	—	0.10	0.20	2.00	—
1965 Proof	—	Value: 1.50				
1966	24,991,000	—	0.10	0.20	2.00	—
1966 Proof	—	Value: 6.00				
1967	32,552,999	—	0.10	0.20	2.00	—
1967 Proof	—	Value: 12.00				
1968	42,395,800	—	0.10	0.20	2.00	—
1968 Proof	16,000	Value: 8.00				
1969	19,953,000	—	0.10	0.20	2.00	—
1969 Proof	27,000	Value: 5.00				
1970	36,997,500	—	—	0.10	0.45	—
1970 Proof	102,000	Value: 1.00				
1971	57,450,000	—	—	0.10	0.45	—
1971 Proof	82,000	Value: 1.00				
1972	75,661,000	—	—	0.10	0.45	—
1972 Proof	81,000	Value: 1.00				
1973	60,244,000	—	—	0.10	0.45	—
1973 Proof	97,000	Value: 0.75				
1974	55,924,000	—	—	0.10	0.45	—
1974 Proof	78,000	Value: 0.75				
1975	60,576,000	—	—	0.10	0.45	—
1975 Proof	49,000	Value: 0.75				
1976	39,357,000	—	—	0.10	0.45	—
1976 Proof	44,000	Value: 0.75				
1977	53,610,000	—	—	0.10	0.45	—
1977 Proof	44,000	Value: 0.75				
1978	57,857,000	—	—	0.10	0.45	—
1978 Proof	43,000	Value: 0.75				
1979	103,686,000	—	—	—	0.45	—
1979 Proof	44,000	Value: 0.75				
1980	79,848,000	—	—	—	0.45	—
1980 Proof	48,000	Value: 2.00				
1981	92,268,000	—	—	—	0.45	—
1981 Proof	49,000	Value: 2.00				
1982	99,950,000	—	—	—	0.45	—
1982 Proof	50,000	Value: 0.75				
1983	93,768,000	—	—	—	0.45	—
1983 Proof	65,000	Value: 0.75				
1984	86,603,000	—	—	—	0.45	—
1984 Proof	65,000	Value: 0.75				
1985	86,304,000	—	—	—	0.45	—
1985 Proof	45,000	Value: 0.75				
1986	108,912,000	—	—	—	0.45	—
1986 Proof	42,000	Value: 1.50				
1987	114,058,000	—	—	—	0.45	—
1987 Proof	42,000	Value: 0.75				
1988	114,461,000	—	—	—	0.45	—
1988 Proof	39,000	Value: 0.75				
1989	127,784,000	—	—	—	0.45	—
1989 Proof	38,000	Value: 0.75				
1990	182,050,000	—	—	—	0.45	—
1990 Proof	35,000	Value: 1.50				
1991	145,000,000	—	—	—	0.45	—
1991 Proof	27,000	Value: 1.50				
1992	125,000,000	—	—	—	0.45	—
1992 Proof	25,000	Value: 1.50				
1993	120,000,000	—	—	—	0.45	—
1993 Proof	28,000	Value: 1.50				
1994	110,000,000	—	—	—	0.45	—
1994 Proof	25,000	Value: 2.00				
1995	80,000,000	—	—	—	0.45	—
1995 Proof	27,000	Value: 1.50				
1996	100,000,000	—	—	—	0.45	—
1996 Proof	25,000	Value: 2.50				
1997	—	—	—	—	0.45	—
1997 Proof	25,000	Value: 2.50				
1998	32,000,000	—	—	—	0.45	—
1998 Proof	25,000	Value: 3.00				
1999	—	—	—	—	0.45	—
1999 Proof	50,000	Value: 1.50				
2000	—	—	—	—	0.45	—
2000 Proof	75,000	Value: 1.50				
2001	—	—	—	—	0.45	—
2001 Proof	75,000	Value: 1.50				

KM# 2877 20 GROSCHEN

Aluminum-Bronze **Obv:** Imperial Eagle with Austrian shield on breast, holding hammer and sickle **Rev:** Value at center above date

Date	Mintage	F	VF	XF	Unc	BU
1950	1,610,000	0.20	0.50	2.00	13.50	—
1950 Proof	—	Value: 40.00				
1951	7,781,000	0.10	0.25	0.75	2.75	—
1951 Proof	—	Value: 25.00				
1954	5,343,000	0.10	0.25	0.75	2.75	—
1954 Proof	—	Value: 275				

KM# 2870 50 GROSCHEN

1.3400 g., Aluminum, 21.9 mm. **Obv:** Imperial Eagle with Austrian shield on breast holding hammer and sickle **Rev:** Numeric value on Austrian shield at center, date divided below shield

Date	Mintage	F	VF	XF	Unc	BU
1946	13,058,000	0.20	0.50	1.75	10.00	—
1946 Proof	—	Value: 75.00				
1947	26,990,000	0.15	0.35	1.25	6.50	—
1947 Proof	—	Value: 35.00				
1952	7,455,000	0.40	1.00	2.50	8.50	—
1952 Proof	—	Value: 55.00				
1955	16,919,000	0.20	0.40	1.25	4.50	—
1955 Proof	—	Value: 55.00				

KM# 2885 50 GROSCHEN

2.9700 g., Aluminum-Bronze, 19.44 mm. **Obv:** Austrian shield **Obv. Designer:** Hans Köttenstorfer **Rev:** Large value above date **Rev. Designer:** Ferdinand Welz **Edge:** Reeded

Date	Mintage	F	VF	XF	Unc	BU
1959	14,122,000	—	0.50	2.00	15.00	—
1959 Proof	—	Value: 25.00				
1960	22,404,000	—	0.20	1.50	12.00	—
1960 Proof	—	Value: 100				
1961	19,891,000	—	0.50	2.00	15.00	—
1961 Proof	—	Value: 75.00				
1962	10,008,000	—	0.40	1.75	15.00	—
1962 Proof	—	Value: 40.00				
1963	9,483,000	—	0.50	2.00	18.00	—
1963 Proof	—	Value: 40.00				
1964	5,331,000	—	0.15	0.75	3.00	—
1964 Proof	—	Value: 1.50				
1965	1,500,700	—	0.15	0.75	3.00	—
1965 Proof	—	Value: 1.50				
1966	7,322,000	—	0.15	0.75	3.00	—
1966 Proof	—	Value: 10.00				
1967	8,237,000	—	0.15	0.75	3.00	—
1967 Proof	—	Value: 15.00				
1968	7,741,600	—	0.15	0.75	3.00	—
1968 Proof	15,400	Value: 10.00				
1969	7,070,000	—	0.15	0.75	3.00	—
1969 Proof	26,000	Value: 5.00				
1970	29,941,000	—	0.10	0.50	2.00	—
1970 Proof	128,000	Value: 3.00				
1971	14,217,000	—	—	0.25	1.50	—
1971 Proof	84,000	Value: 2.50				
1972	17,367,000	—	—	0.25	1.50	—
1972 Proof	80,000	Value: 2.00				
1973	17,902,000	—	—	0.25	1.50	—
1973 Proof	90,000	Value: 2.00				
1974	15,852,000	—	—	0.25	1.50	—
1974 Proof	76,000	Value: 2.00				
1975	7,726,000	—	—	0.15	1.00	—
1975 Proof	49,000	Value: 1.50				
1976	11,150,000	—	—	0.15	1.00	—
1976 Proof	44,000	Value: 1.50				
1977	7,258,000	—	—	0.15	1.00	—
1977 Proof	44,000	Value: 1.50				
1978	12,407,000	—	—	0.15	1.00	—
1978 Proof	43,000	Value: 1.50				
1979	16,351,000	—	—	0.15	1.00	—
1979 Proof	44,000	Value: 1.50				
1980	29,884,000	—	—	0.15	1.25	—
1980 Proof	48,000	Value: 3.50				
1981	12,993,000	—	—	0.15	1.25	—
1981 Proof	49,000	Value: 3.50				
1982	9,950,000	—	—	0.15	1.00	—
1982 Proof	50,000	Value: 1.50				
1983	15,182,000	—	—	0.15	1.00	—
1983 Proof	65,000	Value: 1.50				
1984	20,742,000	—	—	0.15	1.00	—
1984 Proof	65,000	Value: 2.00				
1985	15,654,000	—	—	0.15	1.00	—
1985 Proof	45,000	Value: 2.00				
1986	17,016,000	—	—	0.15	0.75	—
1986 Proof	42,000	Value: 2.00				
1987	7,258,000	—	—	0.15	0.75	—
1987 Proof	42,000	Value: 2.00				
1988	16,267,000	—	—	0.15	0.75	—
1988 Proof	39,000	Value: 2.00				
1989	17,353,000	—	—	0.15	0.75	—
1989 Proof	38,000	Value: 2.00				
1990	29,653,000	—	—	0.15	0.75	—
1990 Proof	35,000	Value: 2.00				
1991	44,990,000	—	—	0.15	0.75	—
1991 Proof	27,000	Value: 2.00				
1992	20,000,000	—	—	—	0.45	—
1992 Proof	25,000	Value: 2.00				
1993	15,000,000	—	—	—	0.45	—
1993 Proof	28,000	Value: 2.00				
1994	10,000,000	—	—	—	0.45	—
1994 Proof	25,000	Value: 2.50				
1995	20,000,000	—	—	—	0.45	—
1995 Proof	27,000	Value: 2.00				
1996	15,000,000	—	—	—	0.45	—
1996 Proof	25,000	Value: 2.50				
1997	10,000,000	—	—	—	0.45	—
1997 Proof	25,000	Value: 2.50				
1998	—	—	—	—	0.45	—
1998 Proof	25,000	Value: 3.00				
Note: In sets only						
1999	—	—	—	—	0.45	—

Date	Mintage	F	VF	XF	Unc	BU
1999 Proof	50,000	Value: 2.00				
Note: In sets only						
2000	4,300,000	—	—	—	0.45	—
2000 Proof	75,000	Value: 2.00				
Note: In sets only						
2001	—	—	—	—	0.45	—
2001 Proof	75,000	Value: 2.00				
Note: In sets only						

KM# 2871 SCHILLING

Aluminum **Obv:** Full figure with seedbag on left hip, dropping seed from right hand, divides value **Rev:** Imperial Eagle with Austrian shield, tail dividing date

Date	Mintage	F	VF	XF	Unc	BU
1946	27,336,000	0.30	1.00	2.50	20.00	—
1946 Proof	—	Value: 500				
1947	35,838,000	0.20	0.50	1.50	6.00	—
1947 Proof	—	Value: 35.00				
1952	23,231,000	0.25	0.75	1.65	7.00	—
1952 Proof	—	Value: 50.00				
1957	28,649,000	0.25	0.75	1.65	7.00	—
1957 Proof	—	Value: 145				

KM# 2886 SCHILLING

4.2000 g., Aluminum-Bronze, 22.5 mm. **Obv:** Large value above date **Obv. Designer:** Edwin Grienauer **Rev:** Edelweiss flower **Rev. Designer:** Ferdinand Welz **Edge:** Plain

Date	Mintage	F	VF	XF	Unc	BU
1959	46,726,000	—	0.25	0.75	12.00	—
1959 Proof	—	Value: 15.00				
1960	46,111,000	—	0.25	1.50	20.00	—
1960 Proof	—	Value: 200				
1961	51,115,000	—	0.25	1.50	15.00	—
1961 Proof	—	Value: 400				
1962	9,303,000	—	0.25	1.50	15.00	—
1962 Proof	—	Value: 65.00				
1963	24,845,000	—	0.25	1.50	20.00	—
1963 Proof	—	Value: 45.00				
1964	11,709,000	—	0.25	1.25	3.50	—
1964 Proof	—	Value: 2.00				
1965	9,155,100	—	0.25	0.75	3.50	—
1965 Proof	27,900	Value: 8.00				
1966	18,688,000	—	0.25	0.75	3.50	—
1966 Proof	—	Value: 8.00				
1967	22,214,000	—	0.25	0.75	3.50	—
1967 Proof	—	Value: 12.00				
1968	30,860,000	—	0.25	0.75	3.50	—
1968 Proof	17,000	Value: 8.00				
1969	10,285,000	—	0.25	0.75	3.50	—
1969 Proof	28,000	Value: 4.00				
1970	10,678,600	—	0.20	0.50	2.50	—
1970 Proof	100,400	Value: 1.75				
1971	27,974,000	—	0.20	0.50	2.50	—
1971 Proof	82,000	Value: 1.75				
1972	54,577,000	—	0.15	0.30	1.50	—
1972 Proof	78,000	Value: 1.25				
1973	41,332,000	—	0.15	0.30	1.50	—
1973 Proof	90,000	Value: 1.25				
1974	43,712,000	—	0.15	0.30	1.50	—
1974 Proof	77,000	Value: 1.25				
1975	13,989,000	—	0.15	0.30	1.50	—
1975 Proof	49,000	Value: 1.25				
1976	28,748,000	—	0.15	0.30	1.50	—
1976 Proof	44,000	Value: 1.25				
1977	19,584,000	—	0.15	0.30	1.50	—
1977 Proof	44,000	Value: 1.25				
1978	35,632,000	—	0.15	0.30	1.50	—
1978 Proof	43,000	Value: 1.25				
1979	64,802,000	—	0.15	0.30	1.50	—
1979 Proof	44,000	Value: 1.25				
1980	49,855,000	—	—	0.15	0.75	—
1980 Proof	48,000	Value: 2.50				
1981	37,502,000	—	—	0.15	0.75	—
1981 Proof	49,000	Value: 2.50				
1982	29,950,000	—	—	0.15	0.75	—
1982 Proof	50,000	Value: 1.50				
1983	38,186,000	—	—	0.15	0.75	—
1983 Proof	65,000	Value: 1.50				
1984	31,891,000	—	—	0.15	0.75	—
1984 Proof	65,000	Value: 1.50				
1985	49,154,000	—	—	0.15	0.75	—
1985 Proof	45,000	Value: 1.50				

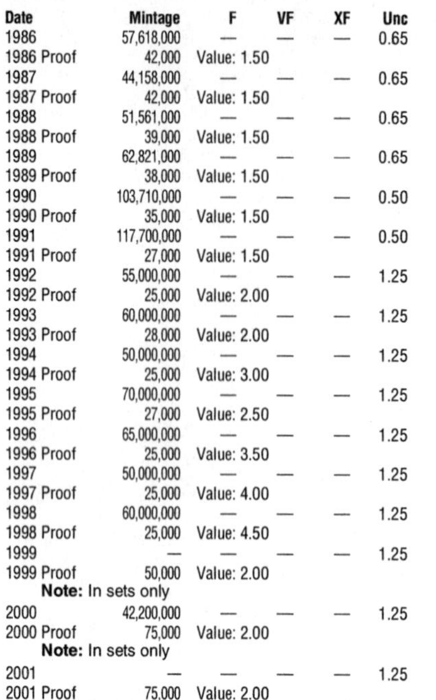

Date	Mintage	F	VF	XF	Unc	BU
1986	57,618,000	—	—	—	0.65	—
1986 Proof	42,000	Value: 1.50				
1987	44,158,000	—	—	—	0.65	—
1987 Proof	42,000	Value: 1.50				
1988	51,561,000	—	—	—	0.65	—
1988 Proof	39,000	Value: 1.50				
1989	62,821,000	—	—	—	0.65	—
1989 Proof	38,000	Value: 1.50				
1990	103,710,000	—	—	—	0.50	—
1990 Proof	35,000	Value: 1.50				
1991	117,700,000	—	—	—	0.50	—
1991 Proof	27,000	Value: 1.50				
1992	55,000,000	—	—	—	1.25	—
1992 Proof	25,000	Value: 2.00				
1993	60,000,000	—	—	—	1.25	—
1993 Proof	28,000	Value: 2.00				
1994	50,000,000	—	—	—	1.25	—
1994 Proof	25,000	Value: 3.00				
1995	70,000,000	—	—	—	1.25	—
1995 Proof	27,000	Value: 2.50				
1996	65,000,000	—	—	—	1.25	—
1996 Proof	25,000	Value: 3.50				
1997	50,000,000	—	—	—	1.25	—
1997 Proof	25,000	Value: 4.00				
1998	60,000,000	—	—	—	1.25	—
1998 Proof	25,000	Value: 4.50				
1999	—	—	—	—	1.25	—
1999 Proof	50,000	Value: 2.00				
Note: In sets only						
2000	42,200,000	—	—	—	1.25	—
2000 Proof	75,000	Value: 2.00				
Note: In sets only						
2001	—	—	—	—	1.25	—
2001 Proof	75,000	Value: 2.00				
Note: In sets only						

KM# 2872 2 SCHILLING

Aluminum **Obv:** Imperial Eagle with Austrian shield on breast, holding hammer and sickle **Rev:** Thick value above spray of leaves and berries, grain sprigs at top

Date	Mintage	F	VF	XF	Unc	BU
1946	10,082,000	0.45	1.25	2.75	25.00	—
1946 Proof	—	Value: 700				
1947	20,140,000	0.45	1.25	2.50	20.00	—
1947 Proof	—	Value: 40.00				
1952	149,000	55.00	100	200	350	—
1952 Proof	—	Value: 900				

KM# 2879 5 SCHILLING

4.0000 g., Aluminum, 30.94 mm. **Obv:** Large value at center, geared rim **Rev:** Imperial Eagle with Austrian shield on breast, holding hammer and sickle

Date	Mintage	F	VF	XF	Unc	BU
1952	29,873,000	1.00	2.00	5.00	12.50	—
1952 Proof	—	Value: 45.00				
1957	240,000	100	380	540	900	—
1957 Proof	—	Value: 700				

KM# 2889 5 SCHILLING

5.2000 g., 0.6400 Silver 0.1070 oz. ASW, 23.5 mm. **Obv:** Lippizaner stallion with rider, rearing, left **Obv. Designer:** Hans Köttenstorfer **Rev:** Austrian shield divides date, value above, sprays below **Rev. Designer:** Josef Köblinger **Edge:** Reeded

Date	Mintage	F	VF	XF	Unc	BU
1960	12,618,000	—	BV	2.50	5.50	—
1960 Proof	1,000	Value: 65.00				
1961	17,902,000	—	BV	2.50	4.50	—
1961 Proof	—	Value: 25.00				
1962	6,771,000	—	BV	2.50	4.50	—
1962 Proof	—	Value: 50.00				
1963	1,811,000	BV	2.00	4.00	14.50	—
1963 Proof	—	Value: 120				
1964	4,030,000	—	BV	2.00	3.50	—
1964 Proof	—	Value: 3.50				
1965	4,759,000	—	BV	2.00	3.50	—
1965 Proof	—	Value: 3.50				
1966	4,481,000	—	BV	2.00	3.50	—
1966 Proof	—	Value: 8.00				
1967	1,900,000	BV	2.00	4.00	6.00	—
1967 Proof	—	Value: 15.00				
1968	4,792,300	—	BV	2.00	3.50	—
1968 Proof	19,700	Value: 8.00				

KM# 2889a 5 SCHILLING

4.8000 g., Copper-Nickel, 23.5 mm. **Obv:** Lippizaner stallion with rider, rearing left **Obv. Designer:** Hans Köttenstorfer **Rev:** Austrian shield divides date, value above, sprays below **Rev. Designer:** Josef Köblinger **Edge:** Plain

Date	Mintage	F	VF	XF	Unc	BU
1968	2,075,000	—	1.00	2.50	5.00	—
1969	41,222,000	—	0.75	1.50	4.00	—
1969 Proof	21,000	Value: 6.00				
1970	15,770,700	—	—	1.00	4.00	—
1970 Proof	92,300	Value: 2.50				
1971	21,422,000	—	—	1.00	4.00	—
1971 Proof	84,000	Value: 2.50				
1972	5,430,000	—	—	1.00	4.00	—
1972 Proof	75,000	Value: 2.50				
1973	8,259,000	—	—	1.00	4.00	—
1973 Proof	87,000	Value: 2.50				
1974	17,956,000	—	—	1.00	4.00	—
1974 Proof	76,000	Value: 2.50				
1975	6,849,000	—	—	0.75	4.00	—
1975 Proof	49,000	Value: 2.50				
1976	1,458,000	—	—	1.00	5.00	—
1976 Proof	44,000	Value: 4.00				
1977	6,423,000	—	—	0.65	2.50	—
1977 Proof	44,000	Value: 2.75				
1978	9,907,000	—	—	0.65	2.50	—
1978 Proof	43,000	Value: 2.75				
1979	11,607,000	—	—	0.65	2.50	—
1979 Proof	44,000	Value: 2.75				
1980	14,898,000	—	—	0.65	2.50	—
1980 Proof	48,000	Value: 3.50				
1981	13,837,000	—	—	0.65	2.50	—
1981 Proof	49,000	Value: 3.50				
1982	4,950,000	—	—	0.65	2.00	—
1982 Proof	50,000	Value: 2.50				
1983	9,268,000	—	—	0.65	2.00	—
1983 Proof	65,000	Value: 2.50				
1984	13,763,000	—	—	0.65	2.00	—
1984 Proof	65,000	Value: 2.50				
1985	12,754,000	—	—	0.60	2.00	—
1985 Proof	45,000	Value: 3.00				
1986	16,558,000	—	—	0.60	2.00	—
1986 Proof	42,000	Value: 3.00				
1987	9,758,000	—	—	0.60	2.00	—
1987 Proof	42,000	Value: 3.00				
1988	10,161,000	—	—	0.60	2.00	—
1988 Proof	39,000	Value: 3.00				
1989	24,043,000	—	—	0.60	2.00	—
1989 Proof	38,000	Value: 3.00				
1990	36,512,000	—	—	0.60	2.00	—
1990 Proof	35,000	Value: 2.50				
1991	24,000,000	—	—	0.60	2.00	—
1991 Proof	27,000	Value: 2.50				
1992	20,000,000	—	—	—	2.00	—
1992 Proof	25,000	Value: 2.50				
1993	20,000,000	—	—	—	2.00	—
1993 Proof	28,000	Value: 2.50				
1994	10,000,000	—	—	—	2.00	—
1994 Proof	25,000	Value: 3.50				
1995	20,000,000	—	—	—	2.00	—
1995 Proof	27,000	Value: 2.50				
1996	10,000,000	—	—	—	2.00	—
1996 Proof	25,000	Value: 3.50				
1997	10,000,000	—	—	—	2.00	—
1997 Proof	25,000	Value: 4.00				
1998	10,000,000	—	—	—	2.00	—
1998 Proof	25,000	Value: 4.50				
1999	—	—	—	—	2.00	—
1999 Proof	50,000	Value: 2.50				
Note: In sets only						
2000	1,500,000	—	—	—	2.00	—
2000 Proof	75,000	Value: 2.50				
Note: In sets only						
2001	—	—	—	—	2.00	—
2001 Proof	75,000	Value: 2.50				
Note: In sets only						

KM# 2882 10 SCHILLING

7.5000 g., 0.6400 Silver 0.1543 oz. ASW **Obv:** Austrian shield **Obv. Designer:** Kurt Bodlak **Rev:** Woman of Wachau, left, value at lower right, date to right of hat **Rev. Designer:** Ferdinand Welz

Date	Mintage	F	VF	XF	Unc	BU
1957	15,635,500	BV	2.25	3.00	7.50	—
1957 Proof	—	Value: 80.00				
1958	27,280,000	BV	2.25	3.00	7.50	—
1958 Proof	—	Value: 700				
1959	4,739,500	BV	2.25	3.50	11.50	—
1959 Proof	—	Value: 40.00				
1964	187,000	7.00	10.00	25.00	45.00	—
1964 Proof	27,000	Value: 15.00				
1965	1,721,000	BV	2.25	3.50	11.50	—
1965 Proof	—	Value: 8.00				
1966	3,430,500	BV	2.25	3.50	9.00	—
1966 Proof	—	Value: 12.00				
1967	1,393,500	BV	2.25	3.50	11.50	—
1967 Proof	—	Value: 15.00				
1968	1,525,000	BV	2.25	3.50	10.00	—
1968 Proof	15,000	Value: 9.00				
1969	1,317,500	BV	2.25	3.50	11.50	—
1969 Proof	20,000	Value: 12.00				
1970	4,493,900	—	BV	2.75	6.50	—
1970 Proof	89,100	Value: 5.00				
1971	7,320,500	—	BV	2.75	5.50	—
1971 Proof	80,000	Value: 5.00				
1972	14,210,500	—	BV	2.75	4.50	—
1972 Proof	75,000	Value: 5.00				
1973	14,559,000	—	BV	2.75	4.50	—
1973 Proof	80,000	Value: 5.00				

KM# 2918 10 SCHILLING

6.2000 g., Copper-Nickel Plated Nickel, 26 mm. **Obv:** Imperial Eagle with Austrian shield on breast, holding hammer and sickle **Obv. Designer:** Kurt Bodlak **Rev:** Woman of Wachau left, value and date right of hat **Rev. Designer:** Ferdinand Welz

Date	Mintage	F	VF	XF	Unc	BU
1974	59,877,000	—	—	2.00	6.00	—
1974 Proof	75,500	Value: 4.00				
1975	16,869,500	—	—	2.00	6.00	—
1975 Proof	49,000	Value: 3.00				
1976	13,459,500	—	—	2.00	6.00	—
1976 Proof	44,000	Value: 3.00				
1977	3,804,000	—	—	2.00	6.00	—
1977 Proof	44,000	Value: 3.00				
1978	6,813,000	—	—	2.00	6.00	—
1978 Proof	43,000	Value: 3.00				
1979	11,702,000	—	—	2.00	6.00	—
1979 Proof	44,000	Value: 2.50				
1980	10,884,000	—	—	2.00	6.00	—
1980 Proof	48,000	Value: 6.50				
1981	9,470,000	—	—	2.00	6.00	—
1981 Proof	49,000	Value: 6.50				
1982	4,950,000	—	—	2.00	5.00	—
1982 Proof	50,000	Value: 2.50				
1983	8,993,000	—	—	1.50	4.00	—
1983 Proof	65,000	Value: 2.50				
1984	7,936,000	—	—	1.50	4.00	—
1984 Proof	65,000	Value: 2.50				
1985	9,009,000	—	—	1.50	4.00	—
1985 Proof	45,000	Value: 2.50				
1986	8,189,000	—	—	1.50	4.00	—
1986 Proof	42,000	Value: 2.50				
1987	9,258,000	—	—	1.50	4.00	—
1987 Proof	42,000	Value: 2.50				
1988	9,011,000	—	—	1.50	4.00	—
1988 Proof	39,000	Value: 4.50				
1989	16,233,000	—	—	1.25	3.00	—
1989 Proof	38,000	Value: 2.50				
1990	27,150,000	—	—	1.25	3.00	—
1990 Proof	35,000	Value: 2.50				
1991	18,000,000	—	—	1.25	3.00	—
1991 Proof	27,000	Value: 2.50				
1992	10,952,000	—	—	—	2.00	—
1992 Proof	25,000	Value: 2.50				
1993	12,500,000	—	—	—	2.00	—
1993 Proof	28,000	Value: 2.50				
1994	15,000,000	—	—	—	2.00	—
1994 Proof	25,000	Value: 3.50				
1995	12,500,000	—	—	—	2.00	—
1995 Proof	27,000	Value: 2.50				
1996	12,500,000	—	—	—	2.00	—
1996 Proof	25,000	Value: 4.00				
1997	11,000,000	—	—	—	2.00	—
1997 Proof	25,000	Value: 4.50				
1998	5,000,000	—	—	—	2.00	—
1998 Proof	25,000	Value: 5.00				
1999	—	—	—	—	2.00	—
1999 Proof	50,000	Value: 2.50				
Note: In sets only						
2000	1,175,000	—	—	—	2.00	—
2000 Proof	75,000	Value: 2.50				
Note: In sets only						
2001	—	—	—	—	2.00	—
2001 Proof	75,000	Value: 2.50				
Note: In sets only						

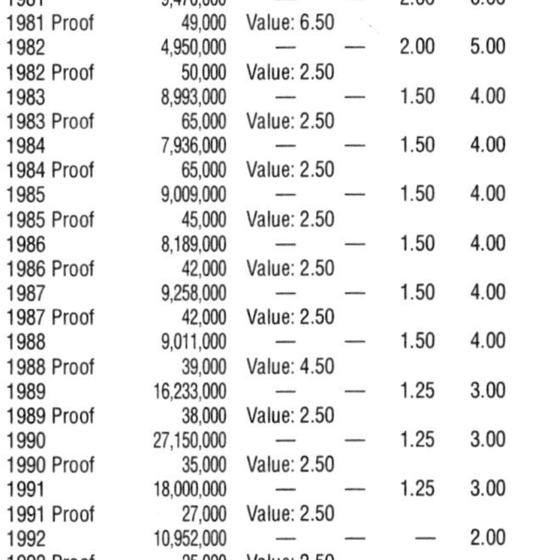

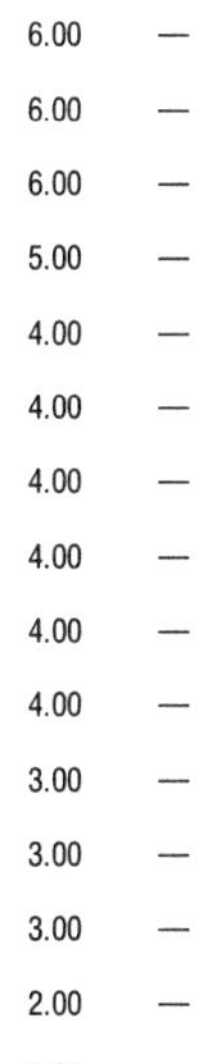

KM# 2946.1 20 SCHILLING

8.0000 g., Copper-Aluminum-Nickel, 27.8 mm. **Obv:** Nine people standing (representing the nine Austrian provinces), center figure holding Austrian shield aloft **Rev:** Numeric value within shaded box within circle, date below box **Edge:** Edge with incuse dots **Designer:** Helmut Zobol

Date	Mintage	F	VF	XF	Unc	BU
1980	9,851,500	—	—	2.50	3.50	—
1980 Proof	48,000	Value: 20.00				
1981	450,500	—	—	4.50	7.50	—
1981 Proof	49,000	Value: 22.50				
1991	140,000	—	—	2.25	5.00	—

KM# 2955.1 20 SCHILLING

8.0000 g., Copper-Aluminum-Nickel, 27.8 mm. **Subject:** 250th Anniversary - Birth of Joseph Haydn **Obv:** Value within box, small Austrian shield divides date below **Obv. Designer:** Kurt Bodlak **Rev:** Bust of Joseph Haydn, 3/4 right, two dates to his left, his name to his right **Rev. Designer:** Thomas Pesendorfer **Edge:** With incuse dots

Date	Mintage	F	VF	XF	Unc	BU
1982	3,100,000	—	—	2.25	3.50	—
1982 Proof	50,000	Value: 9.00				
1991	140,000	—	—	2.25	5.00	—

KM# 2955.2 20 SCHILLING

8.0000 g., Copper-Aluminum-Nickel, 27.8 mm. **Edge:** Plain

Date	Mintage	F	VF	XF	Unc	BU
1992	100,000	—	—	2.25	6.00	—
1993	180,000	—	—	2.25	5.00	—

KM# 2960.1 20 SCHILLING

8.0000 g., Copper-Aluminum-Nickel, 27.8 mm. **Obv:** Value within box, Austrian shield divides date below **Rev:** Hochosterwitz Castle **Edge:** With incuse dots **Designer:** Kurt Bodlak

Date	Mintage	F	VF	XF	Unc	BU
1983	1,002,000	—	—	2.25	3.50	—
1983 Proof	65,000	Value: 7.50				
1991	140,000	—	—	2.25	4.50	—

KM# 2965.1 20 SCHILLING

8.0000 g., Copper-Aluminum-Nickel, 27.8 mm. **Obv:** Value within box, Austrian shield divides date below **Obv. Designer:** Kurt Bodlak **Rev:** Grafenegg Palace, date at upper left **Rev. Designer:** Josef Kaiser **Edge:** With incuse dots

Date	Mintage	F	VF	XF	Unc	BU
1984	1,203,000	—	—	2.25	3.50	—
1984 Proof	65,000	Value: 7.50				
1991	140,000	—	—	2.25	4.50	—

KM# 2970.1 20 SCHILLING

8.0000 g., Copper-Aluminum-Nickel, 27.8 mm. **Subject:** 200th Anniversary - Diocese of Linz **Obv:** Value within box, Austrian shield divides date below **Obv. Designer:** Kurt Bodlak **Rev:** Two shields on decorative background within circle, two dates below circle **Rev. Designer:** Josef Fösleiter **Edge:** With incuse dots

Date	Mintage	F	VF	XF	Unc	BU
1985	814,000	—	—	2.25	4.50	—
1985 Proof	45,000	Value: 11.50				
1991	140,000	—	—	2.25	4.50	—

KM# 2975.1 20 SCHILLING

8.0000 g., Copper-Aluminum-Nickel, 27.8 mm. **Subject:** 800th Anniversary - Georgenberger Treaty **Obv:** Value within box, Austrian shield divides date below **Obv. Designer:** Kurt Bodlak **Rev:** Ottakar IV of Steyr and Leopold V of Austria holding the secret treaty **Rev. Designer:** Thomas Pesendorfer **Edge:** With incuse dots

Date	Mintage	F	VF	XF	Unc	BU
1986	801,000	—	—	2.25	4.50	—
1986 Proof	42,000	Value: 16.50				
1991	140,000	—	—	2.25	4.50	—

KM# 2975.2 20 SCHILLING

8.0000 g., Copper-Aluminum-Nickel, 27.8 mm. **Edge:** Plain

Date	Mintage	F	VF	XF	Unc	BU
1992	100,000	—	—	2.25	5.00	—
1993	180,000	—	—	2.25	4.50	—

KM# 2980.1 20 SCHILLING

8.0000 g., Copper-Aluminum-Nickel, 27.8 mm. **Subject:** 300th Anniversary - Birth of Salzburg's Archbishop Thun **Obv:** Value within box, Austrian shield divides date below **Obv. Designer:** Kurt Bodlak **Rev:** Bishop's hat above supported arms, dates below supporters, subject name at bottom with date below **Rev. Designer:** Josef Kaiser **Edge:** With incuse dots

Date	Mintage	F	VF	XF	Unc	BU
1987	508,000	—	—	2.25	4.50	—
1987 Proof	42,000	Value: 11.50				
1991	140,000	—	—	2.25	4.50	—

KM# 2980.2 20 SCHILLING

8.0000 g., Copper-Aluminum-Nickel, 27.8 mm. **Edge:** Plain

Date	Mintage	F	VF	XF	Unc	BU
1992	100,000	—	—	2.25	5.00	—
1993	180,000	—	—	2.25	4.50	—

KM# 2988.1 20 SCHILLING

8.0000 g., Copper-Aluminum-Nickel, 27.8 mm. **Obv:** Value within box, Austrian shield divides date below **Obv. Designer:** Kurt Bodlak **Rev:** Crowned eagle - Tyrol **Rev. Designer:** Thomas Pesendorfer **Edge:** With incuse dots

Date	Mintage	F	VF	XF	Unc	BU
1989	252,000	—	—	2.25	4.50	—
1989 Proof	38,000	Value: 8.00				
1991	140,000	—	—	2.25	4.50	—

KM# 2988.2 20 SCHILLING

8.0000 g., Copper-Aluminum-Nickel, 27.8 mm. **Edge:** Plain

Date	Mintage	F	VF	XF	Unc	BU
1992	100,000	—	—	2.25	5.00	—
1993	180,000	—	—	2.25	4.50	—

KM# 2993.1 20 SCHILLING

8.0000 g., Copper-Aluminum-Nickel, 27.8 mm. **Obv:** Value within box, Austrian shield divides date below **Obv. Designer:** Kurt Bodlak **Rev:** Martinsturm in Bregenz, small shield at upper left **Rev. Designer:** Herbert Wähner **Edge:** With incuse dots

Date	Mintage	F	VF	XF	Unc	BU
1990	250,000	—	—	2.25	4.50	—
1990 Proof	35,000	Value: 10.00				
1991	—	—	—	—	—	—
1991	140,000	—	—	2.25	4.50	—

KM# 2993.2 20 SCHILLING

8.0000 g., Copper-Aluminum-Nickel, 27.8 mm. **Edge:** Plain

Date	Mintage	F	VF	XF	Unc	BU
1992	100,000	—	—	2.25	5.00	—
1993	180,000	—	—	2.25	4.50	—

KM# 2995.1 20 SCHILLING

8.0000 g., Copper-Aluminum-Nickel, 27.8 mm. **Subject:** 200th Anniversary - Birth of Franz Grillparzer **Obv:** Value within shield, Austrian shield divides date below **Obv. Designer:** Kurt Bodlak **Rev:** Bust of Franz Grillparzer on left, looking right, theater building on the right **Rev. Designer:** Alfred Zierler **Edge:** With incuse dots

Date	Mintage	F	VF	XF	Unc	BU
1991	1,860,000	—	—	2.25	4.50	—
1991 Proof	27,000	Value: 10.00				

KM# 2995.2 20 SCHILLING

8.0000 g., Copper-Aluminum-Nickel, 27.8 mm. **Edge:** Plain

Date	Mintage	F	VF	XF	Unc	BU
1992	1,000,000	—	—	2.25	5.00	—
1992 Proof	25,000	Value: 12.50				
1993	1,800,000	—	—	2.25	4.50	—
1993 Proof	28,000	Value: 10.00				

KM# 2965.2 20 SCHILLING

8.0000 g., Copper-Aluminum-Nickel, 27.8 mm. **Edge:** Plain

Date	Mintage	F	VF	XF	Unc	BU
1992	100,000	—	—	2.25	5.00	—
1993	180,000	—	—	2.25	4.50	—

KM# 2960.2 20 SCHILLING

8.0000 g., Copper-Aluminum-Nickel, 27.8 mm. **Edge:** Plain

Date	Mintage	F	VF	XF	Unc	BU
1992	100,000	—	—	2.25	5.00	—
1993	180,000	—	—	2.25	4.50	—

KM# 2946.2 20 SCHILLING

8.0000 g., Copper-Aluminum-Nickel, 27.8 mm. **Edge:** Plain

Date	Mintage	F	VF	XF	Unc	BU
1992	100,000	—	—	2.25	6.00	—
1992 Proof	25,000	Value: 10.00				
1993	180,000	—	—	2.25	5.00	—
1993 Proof	28,000	Value: 10.00				

KM# 2970.2 20 SCHILLING

8.0000 g., Copper-Aluminum-Nickel, 27.8 mm. **Edge:** Plain

Date	Mintage	F	VF	XF	Unc	BU
1992	100,000	—	—	2.25	5.00	—
1993	180,000	—	—	2.25	4.50	—

KM# 3016 20 SCHILLING

8.0000 g., Copper-Aluminum-Nickel, 27.8 mm. **Subject:** 800th Anniversary - Vienna Mint **Obv:** Value within box, Austrian shield divides date below **Obv. Designer:** Kurt Bodlak **Rev:** Vienna Mint, two dates below **Rev. Designer:** Thomas Pesendorfer

Date	Mintage	F	VF	XF	Unc	BU
1994	2,000,000	—	—	—	4.50	—
1994 Proof	25,000	Value: 12.50				

KM# 3022 20 SCHILLING

8.0000 g., Copper-Aluminum-Nickel, 27.8 mm. **Subject:** 1000th Anniversary - Krems **Obv:** Value within box, Austrian shield below **Obv. Designer:** Kurt Bodlak **Rev:** Krems within box, dates flanking, legend at top **Rev. Designer:** Thomas Pesendorfer and Christa Reiter

Date	Mintage	F	VF	XF	Unc	BU
1995	2,000,000	—	—	—	4.50	—
1995 Proof	27,000	Value: 10.00				

KM# 3033 20 SCHILLING

8.0000 g., Copper-Aluminum-Nickel, 27.8 mm. **Obv:** Value within box, Austrian shield divides date at bottom **Obv. Designer:** Kurt Bodlak **Rev:** Bust of Anton Bruckner, 3/4 facing, two dates below, name on the left, building on the right **Rev. Designer:** Christa Reiter

Date	Mintage	F	VF	XF	Unc	BU
1996	—	—	—	—	4.50	—
1996 Proof	25,000	Value: 15.00				

KM# 3041 20 SCHILLING

8.0000 g., Copper-Aluminum-Nickel, 27.8 mm. **Subject:** 850th Anniversary of St. Stephen's Cathedral **Obv:** Value within box, Austrian shield divides date below **Obv. Designer:** Kurt Bodlak **Rev:** St. Stephen's Cathedral, two dates above **Rev. Designer:** Thomas Pesendorfer

Date	Mintage	F	VF	XF	Unc	BU
1997	700,000	—	—	—	4.50	—
1997 Proof	25,000	Value: 16.50				

KM# 3048 20 SCHILLING

8.0000 g., Copper-Aluminum-Nickel, 27.8 mm. **Subject:** 500th Anniversary of Michael Pacher's Death **Obv:** Value within box, Austrian shield divides date below **Rev:** Pacher's altar at St. Wolfgang **Designer:** Herbert Wähner

Date	Mintage	F	VF	XF	Unc	BU
1998	200,000	—	—	—	5.00	—
1998 Proof	25,000	Value: 17.50				

KM# 3056 20 SCHILLING

8.0000 g., Copper-Aluminum-Nickel, 27.8 mm. **Obv:** Value within box, Austrian shield divides date below **Rev:** Hugo Von Hofmannsthal **Designer:** Herbert Wähner

Date	Mintage	F	VF	XF	Unc	BU
1999	400,000	—	—	—	4.50	—
1999 Proof	50,000	Value: 12.50				

KM# 3064 20 SCHILLING

8.0000 g., Brass, 27.8 mm. **Subject:** 150th Anniversary - First Austrian Postage Stamp **Obv:** Value within box, Austrian shield divides date below **Rev:** Canceled stamp design **Edge:** Plain **Designer:** Andreas Zanaschka

Date	Mintage	F	VF	XF	Unc	BU
2000	400,000	—	—	—	4.50	—
2000 Proof	75,000	Value: 12.50				

KM# 3075 20 SCHILLING

8.1300 g., Brass, 27.8 mm. **Subject:** Johann Nepomuk Nestroy **Obv:** Denomination within square **Rev:** Bust half left **Edge:** Plain **Designer:** Herbert Wähner

Date	Mintage	F	VF	XF	Unc	BU
2001	300,000	—	—	—	4.50	—
2001 Proof	75,000	Value: 10.00				

KM# 3053 50 SCHILLING

Bi-Metallic Copper-Nickel Clad Nickel center in Aluminum-Bronze ring, 26.5 mm. **Obv:** Value within circle of provincial arms **Obv. Designer:** Herbert Wähner **Rev:** Head of Konrad Lorenz, looking right, with three Greylag geese on the right, within circle, two dates below circle **Rev. Designer:** Thomas Pesendorfer

Date	Mintage	F	VF	XF	Unc	BU
1998	1,200,000	—	—	—	7.00	—
1998 Special Unc	100,000	—	—	—	9.00	—

KM# 3057 50 SCHILLING

Bi-Metallic Copper-Nickel Clad Nickel center in Aluminum-Bronze ring, 26.5 mm. **Subject:** Euro Currency **Obv:** Value within circle of provincial arms **Obv. Designer:** Herbert Wähner **Rev:** Euro currency designs within circle, date below **Rev. Designer:** Thomas Pesendorfer

Date	Mintage	F	VF	XF	Unc	BU
1999	1,200,000	—	—	—	7.00	—
1999 Special Unc	100,000	—	—	—	9.00	—

KM# 3061 50 SCHILLING

Bi-Metallic Copper-Nickel clad Nickel center in Aluminum-Bronze ring, 26.5 mm. **Subject:** Centenary - Death of Johann Strauss **Obv:** Value within circle of provincial arms **Obv. Designer:** Herbert Wähner **Rev:** Bust of Johann Strauss, facing right, two dates to his right, two figures to his left, all within circle, music notes below circle **Rev. Designer:** Helmut Andexlinger

Date	Mintage	F	VF	XF	Unc	BU
ND(1999)	600,000	—	—	—	7.00	—
ND(1999) Special Unc	100,000	—	—	—	9.00	—

KM# 3066 50 SCHILLING

Bi-Metallic Copper-Nickel clad Nickel center in Aluminum-Bronze ring, 26.5 mm. **Obv:** Value within circle of provincial arms **Obv. Designer:** Herbert Wähner **Rev:** Bust of Sigmund Freud facing 1/4 left, two dates at upper right, all within circle **Rev. Designer:** Thomas Pesendorfer and Gustav Klimt **Edge:** Plain

Date	Mintage	F	VF	XF	Unc	BU
ND(2000)	600,000	—	—	—	7.00	—
ND(2000) Special Unc	90,000	—	—	—	9.00	—

KM# 3076 50 SCHILLING

8.1100 g., Bi-Metallic Copper-Nickel clad Nickel center in Aluminumn-Bronze ring, 26.5 mm. **Subject:** The Schilling Era **Obv:** Denomination and shields **Rev:** Four old coin designs **Edge:** Plain

Date	Mintage	F	VF	XF	Unc	BU
2001	600,000	—	—	—	7.50	—
2001 Special Unc.	100,000	—	—	—	9.50	—

EURO COINAGE

European Union Issues

KM# 3082 EURO CENT

2.3500 g., Copper Plated Steel, 16.18 mm. **Obv:** Gentian flower **Obv. Legend:** EIN EURO CENT **Obv. Designer:** Josef Kaiser **Rev:** Denomination and globe **Rev. Designer:** Luc Luycx **Edge:** Plain

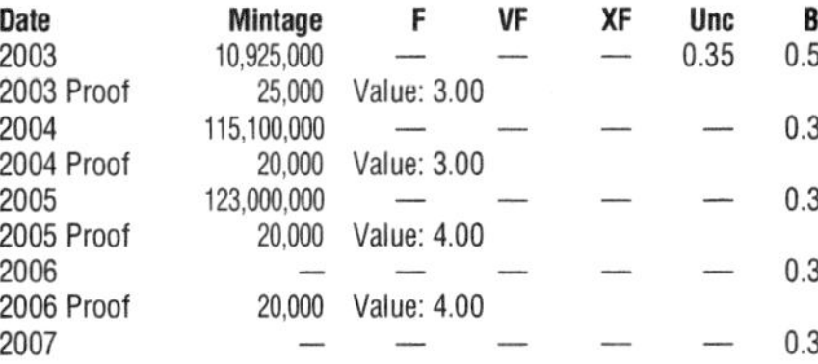

Date	Mintage	F	VF	XF	Unc	BU
2002	378,500,000	—	—	—	0.35	0.50
2002 Proof	10,000	Value: 15.00				
2003	10,925,000	—	—	—	0.35	0.50
2003 Proof	25,000	Value: 3.00				
2004	115,100,000	—	—	—	—	0.35
2004 Proof	20,000	Value: 3.00				
2005	123,000,000	—	—	—	—	0.35
2005 Proof	20,000	Value: 4.00				
2006	—	—	—	—	—	0.35
2006 Proof	20,000	Value: 4.00				
2007	—	—	—	—	—	0.35

KM# 3083 2 EURO CENT

3.0700 g., Copper Plated Steel, 18.69 mm. **Obv:** Edelweiss flower in inner circle, stars in outer circle **Obv. Legend:** ZWEI EURO CENT **Obv. Designer:** Josef Kaiser **Rev:** Denomination and globe **Rev. Designer:** Luc Luycx **Edge:** Plain

Date	Mintage	F	VF	XF	Unc	BU
2002	326,500,000	—	—	—	0.50	0.65
2002 Proof	10,000	Value: 20.00				
2003	118,625,000	—	—	—	0.50	0.65
2003 Proof	25,000	Value: 5.00				
2004	156,500,000	—	—	—	—	0.50
2004 Proof	20,000	Value: 5.00				
2005	113,000,000	—	—	—	—	0.50
2005 Proof	20,000	Value: 6.00				
2006	—	—	—	—	—	0.50
2006 Proof	20,000	Value: 6.00				
2007	—	—	—	—	—	0.35

KM# 3084 5 EURO CENT

3.8600 g., Copper Plated Steel, 21.25 mm. **Obv:** Alpine prim rose flower in inner ring, stars in outer ring **Obv. Legend:** FUNF EURO CENT **Obv. Designer:** Josef Kaiser **Rev:** Denomination and globe **Rev. Designer:** Luc Luycx **Edge:** Plain

Date	Mintage	F	VF	XF	Unc	BU
2002	217,100,000	—	—	—	0.75	1.00
2002 Proof	10,000	Value: 30.00				
2003	108,625,000	—	—	—	0.75	1.00
2003 Proof	25,000	Value: 8.50				
2004	89,400,000	—	—	—	—	0.75
2004 Proof	20,000	Value: 9.00				
2005	66,300,000	—	—	—	—	0.75
2005 Proof	20,000	Value: 10.00				
2006	—	—	—	—	—	0.75
2006 Proof	20,000	Value: 10.00				
2007	—	—	—	—	—	0.75

KM# 3085 10 EURO CENT

4.0700 g., Brass, 19.75 mm. **Obv:** St. Stephen's Cathedral spires **Obv. Designer:** Josef Kaiser **Rev:** Relief map of European Union at left, denomination at center right **Rev. Designer:** Luc Luycx **Edge:** Reeded

Date	Mintage	F	VF	XF	Unc	BU
2002	441,700,000	—	—	—	0.75	1.00
2002 Proof	10,000	Value: 45.00				
2003	125,000	—	—	—	0.75	1.00
2003 Proof	25,000	Value: 8.50				
2004	5,300,000	—	—	—	—	0.75
2004 Proof	20,000	Value: 9.00				
2005	5,300,000	—	—	—	—	0.75
2005 Proof	20,000	Value: 10.00				
2006	—	—	—	—	—	0.75
2006 Proof	20,000	Value: 10.00				
2007	—	—	—	—	—	0.75

KM# 3139 10 EURO CENT

4.0700 g., Brass, 19.7 mm. **Obv:** St. Stephen's Cathedral spires **Obv. Designer:** Josef Kaiser **Rev:** Relief Map of Western Europe, stars, lines and value **Rev. Designer:** Luc Luycx **Edge:** Reeded

Date	Mintage	F	VF	XF	Unc	BU
2008	—	—	—	—	—	0.75
2008 Proof	—	Value: 10.00				

KM# 3086 20 EURO CENT

5.7300 g., Brass, 22.25 mm. **Obv:** Belvedere Palace gate **Obv. Designer:** Josef Kaiser **Rev:** Relief map of European Union at left, denomination at center right **Rev. Designer:** Luc Luycx **Edge:** Notched

Date	Mintage	F	VF	XF	Unc	BU
2002	203,500,000	—	—	—	1.00	1.25
2002 Proof	10,000	Value: 60.00				
2003	51,038,200	—	—	—	1.00	1.25
2003 Proof	25,000	Value: 10.00				
2004	54,900,000	—	—	—	—	1.00
2004 Proof	20,000	Value: 11.50				
2005	4,200,000	—	—	—	—	1.00
2005 Proof	20,000	Value: 12.50				
2006	—	—	—	—	—	1.00
2006 Proof	20,000	Value: 12.50				
2007	—	—	—	—	—	1.00

KM# 3087 50 EURO CENT

7.8100 g., Brass, 24.25 mm. **Obv:** Secession building in Vienna **Obv. Designer:** Josef Kaiser **Rev:** Relief map of European Union at left, denomination at center right **Rev. Designer:** Luc Luycx **Edge:** Reeded

Date	Mintage	F	VF	XF	Unc	BU
2002	169,200,000	—	—	—	1.25	1.50
2002 Proof	10,000	Value: 75.00				
2003	9,199,000	—	—	—	1.25	1.50
2003 Proof	25,000	Value: 12.50				
2004	3,200,000	—	—	—	—	1.25
2004 Proof	20,000	Value: 13.50				
2005	3,200,000	—	—	—	—	1.25
2005 Proof	20,000	Value: 15.00				
2006	—	—	—	—	—	1.25
2006 Proof	20,000	Value: 15.00				
2007	—	—	—	—	—	1.25

KM# 3088 EURO

7.5000 g., Bi-Metallic Copper-Nickel center in Brass ring, 23.25 mm. **Obv:** Bust of Mozart right within inner circle, stars in outer circle **Obv. Designer:** Josef Kaiser **Rev:** Value at left, relief map of European Union at right **Rev. Designer:** Luc Luycx **Edge:** Reeded and plain sections

Date	Mintage	F	VF	XF	Unc	BU
2002	223,600,000	—	—	—	2.50	2.75
2002 Proof	10,000	Value: 100				
2003	125,000	—	—	—	2.50	2.75
2003 Proof	25,000	Value: 16.50				
2004	2,700,000	—	—	—	—	2.50
2004 Proof	20,000	Value: 17.50				
2005	2,700,000	—	—	—	—	2.50
2005 Proof	20,000	Value: 18.50				
2006	—	—	—	—	—	2.50
2006 Proof	20,000	Value: 18.50				
2007	—	—	—	—	—	2.50

KM# 3089 2 EURO

8.5200 g., Bi-Metallic Brass center in Copper-Nickel ring, 25.75 mm. **Obv:** Bust of Bertha von Suttner, Novelist and winner of 1905 Peace Prize, facing left within inner circle, stars in outer circle **Obv. Designer:** Joaef Kaiser **Rev:** Value at left, relief map of European Union at right **Rev. Designer:** Luc Luycx **Edge:** Reeded and lettered: 2 EURO (star) (star) (star) (star)

Date	Mintage	F	VF	XF	Unc	BU
2002	196,500,000	—	—	—	3.75	4.00
2002 Proof	10,000	Value: 125				
2003	4,804,500	—	—	—	3.75	4.00
2003 Proof	25,000	Value: 25.00				
2004	2,600,000	—	—	—	—	3.75
2004 Proof	20,000	Value: 27.50				
2006	—	—	—	—	—	3.75
2006 Proof	20,000	Value: 27.50				

KM# 3124 2 EURO

8.5200 g., Bi-Metallic Brass center in Copper-Nickel ring, 25.7 mm. **Subject:** 50th Anniversary of the State Treaty **Obv:** Treaty seals and signatures **Rev:** Denomination and map **Edge:** Reeding over lettering **Edge Lettering:** "2 EURO" and 3 stars repeated four times **Note:** No country name on this coin!

Date	Mintage	F	VF	XF	Unc	BU
2005	6,880,000	—	—	—	5.00	6.00
2005 Proof	20,000	Value: 27.50				

KM# 3150 2 EURO

Center Composition: Bi-Metallic Brass center in Copper-Nickel Ring **Subject:** 50th Anniversary - Treaty of Rome

Date	Mintage	F	VF	XF	Unc	BU
2007	8,900,000	—	—	—	4.00	5.00
2007 Proof	20,000	Value: 27.50				

KM# 3152 2 EURO

8.5200 g., Bi-Metallic **Ring Composition:** Copper-Nickel **Center Composition:** Brass, 25.75 mm. **Subject:** 50th Anniversary Treaty of Rome **Obv:** Open Treaty book on Michelangelo's star or rose shaped background **Rev:** Value at left, expanded relief map of European Union at right **Rev. Designer:** Luc Luycx **Edge:** Reeded and lettered: 2 EURO (star) (star) (star) (star)

Date	Mintage	F	VF	XF	Unc	BU
2007	—	—	—	—	4.00	5.00

KM# 3143 2 EURO

8.5200 g., Bi-Metallic Brass center in Copper-Nickel ring, 25.75 mm. **Obv:** Bust of Bertha von Suttner, Novelist and winner of 1905 Peace Prize, at right facing left in inner circle, stars in outer circle **Obv. Designer:** Josef Kaiser **Rev:** Value at left, expanded relief map of European Union at right **Rev. Designer:** Luc Luycx **Edge:** Reeded and lettered: 2 EURO ★ ★ ★

Date	Mintage	F	VF	XF	Unc	BU
2008	—	—	—	—	5.00	6.00

AZERBAIJAN

The Republic of Azerbaijan (formerly Azerbaijan S.S.R.) includes the Nakhichevan Autonomous Republic. Situated in the eastern area of Transcaucasia, it is bordered in the west by Armenia, in the north by Georgia and Dagestan, to the east by the Caspian Sea and to the south by Iran. It has an area of 33,430 sq. mi. (86,600 sq. km.) and a population of 7.8 million. Capital: Baku. The area is rich in mineral deposits of aluminum, copper, iron, lead, salt and zinc, with oil as its leading industry. Agriculture and livestock follow in importance.

Until the Russian Revolution of 1905, there was no political life in Azerbaijan. A Mussavat (Equality) party was formed in 1911 by Mohammed Emin Rasulzade, a former Social Democrat. After the Russian Revolution of March 1917, the party started a campaign for independence. Baku, however, the capital with its mixed population, constituted an alien enclave in the country. While a national Azerbaijani government was established at Gandzha (Elizavetpol), a Communist controlled council assumed power at Baku with Stepan Shaumian, an Armenian, at its head. The Gandzha government joined first, on Sept. 20, 1917, a Transcaucasian federal republic, but on May 28, 1918, proclaimed the independence of Azerbaijan. On June 4, 1918, at Batum, a peace treaty was signed with Turkey. Turko-Azerbaijani forces started an offensive against Baku, occupied since Aug. 17, 1918 by 1,400 British troops coming by sea from Anzali, Persia. On Sept. 14 the British evacuated Baku, returning to Anzali, and three days later the Azerbaijan government, headed by Fath Khoysky, established itself at Baku.

After the collapse of the Ottoman Empire, the British returned to Baku, at first ignoring the Azerbaijan government. A general election with universal suffrage for the Azerbaijan constituent assembly took place on Dec. 7, 1918 and out of 120 members there were 84 Mussavat supporters. On Jan. 15, 1920, the Allied powers recognized Azerbaijan de facto, but on April 27 of the same year the Red army invaded the country, and a Soviet republic of Azerbaijan was proclaimed the next day. Later it became a member of the Transcaucasian Federation joining the U.S.S.R. on Dec. 30, 1922, it became a self-constituent republic in 1936.

The Azerbaijan Communist party held its first congress at Baku in Feb. 1920. From 1921 to 1925 its first secretary was a Russian, S.M. Kirov, who directed a mass deportation to Siberia of about 120,000 Azerbaijani "nationalist deviationists," among them the country's first two premiers.

In 1990 it adopted a declaration of republican sovereignty and in Aug. 1991 declared itself formally independent. This action was approved by a vote of referendum in Jan. 1992. It announced its intention of joining the CIS in Dec. 1991, but a parliamentary resolution of Oct. 1992 declined to confirm its involvement. On Sept. 20, 1993, Azerbaijan became a member of the CIS. Communist President Mutaibov was relieved of his office in May 1992. On June 7, in the first democratic election in the country's history, a National Council replaced Mutaibov with Abulfez Elchibey. Surat Huseynov led a military coup against Elchibey and seized power on June 30, 1993. Huseynov became prime minister with former communist Geidar Aliyev, president.

Fighting commenced between Muslim forces of Azerbaijan and Christian forces of Armenia in 1992 and continued through early 1994. Each faction claimed the Nagorno-Karabakh, an Armenian ethnic enclave, in Azerbaijan. A cease-fire was declared in May 1994.

MONETARY SYSTEM

100 Qapik = 1 Manat

REPUBLIC

DECIMAL COINAGE

KM# 39 QAPIK

2.7300 g., Copper Plated Steel, 16.2 mm. **Obv:** Map above value **Rev:** Value and musical instruments **Edge:** Plain

Date	Mintage	F	VF	XF	Unc	BU
ND (2006)	—	—	—	—	—	2.00

KM# 40 3 QAPIK

3.3600 g., Copper-Plated-Steel, 17.9 mm. **Obv:** Map above value **Rev:** Value above books **Edge:** Grooved

Date	Mintage	F	VF	XF	Unc	BU
ND (2006)	—	—	—	—	—	2.50

KM# 1 5 QAPIK

Brass **Obv:** Value **Rev:** Three symbols above date at center of sun

Date	Mintage	F	VF	XF	Unc	BU
1992	—	—	—	2.00	4.00	5.00

KM# 1a 5 QAPIK

0.8500 g., Aluminum, 17.1 mm. **Obv:** Value **Rev:** Three symbols above date at center of sun **Edge:** Plain

Date	Mintage	F	VF	XF	Unc	BU
1993	—	—	—	—	1.00	1.50

KM# 41 5 QAPIK

4.7200 g., Copper-Plated-Steel, 29.75 mm. **Obv:** Map above value **Rev:** Building above value **Edge:** Reeded

Date	Mintage	F	VF	XF	Unc	BU
ND (2006)	—	—	—	—	—	2.75

KM# 2 10 QAPIK

1.0500 g., Aluminum, 18.6 mm. **Obv:** Denomination **Rev:** Star with date **Edge:** Plain

Date	Mintage	F	VF	XF	Unc	BU
1992	—	—	—	1.00	2.00	2.50

KM# 42 10 QAPIK

5.1000 g., Brass-Plated Steel, 22.2 mm. **Obv:** Map above value **Rev:** Dome shaped object to right of value **Edge:** Notched

Date	Mintage	F	VF	XF	Unc	BU
ND (2006)	—	—	—	—	—	3.00

KM# 3 20 QAPIK

Brass **Obv:** Moon and star at center **Rev:** Value above date within star **Edge:** Plain

Date	Mintage	F	VF	XF	Unc	BU
1992	—	—	—	1.00	2.00	2.50

KM# 3a 20 QAPIK

1.1500 g., Aluminum, 20.1 mm. **Edge:** Plain **Note:** Varieties in spelling of Respublikas exist.

Date	Mintage	F	VF	XF	Unc	BU
1993	—	—	—	—	0.75	1.00

Note: Two die varieties exist

KM# 43 20 QAPIK

6.3500 g., Brass Plated Steel, 24.2 mm. **Obv:** Map above value **Rev:** Value and spiral staircase **Edge:** Segmented reeding

Date	Mintage	F	VF	XF	Unc	BU
ND (2006)	—	—	—	—	—	4.00

KM# 4 50 QAPIK

Copper-Nickel **Obv:** Maiden tower ruins **Rev:** Value above date within ornate circle **Edge:** Plain

Date	Mintage	F	VF	XF	Unc	BU
1992	—	—	—	1.50	3.50	4.50
1994	—	—	—	1.50	3.50	4.50

KM# 4a 50 QAPIK

1.4500 g., Aluminum, 23 mm. **Edge:** Plain

Date	Mintage	F	VF	XF	Unc	BU
1992	—	—	—	—	1.25	1.50
1993	—	—	—	—	0.75	1.00

KM# 44 50 QAPIK

7.4200 g., Bi-Metallic Brass plated Steel center in Stainless Steel ring, 25.4 mm. **Obv:** Map above value **Rev:** Two oil wells **Edge:** Reeding over lettering

Date	Mintage	F	VF	XF	Unc	BU
ND (2006)	—	—	—	—	—	5.00

AZORES

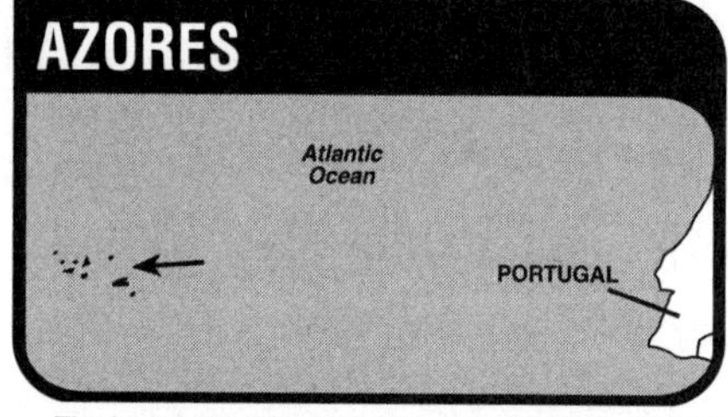

The Azores, an archipelago of nine islands of volcanic origin, are located in the Atlantic Ocean 740 miles (1,190 km.) west of Cape de Roca, Portugal. They are the westernmost region of Europe under the administration of Portugal and have an area of 902 sq. mi. (2,305 sq. km.) and a population of 236,000. Principal city: Ponta Delgada. The natives are mainly of Portuguese descent and earn their livelihood by fishing, wine making, basket weaving and the growing of fruit, grains and sugar cane. Pineapples are the chief item of export. The climate is particularly temperate, making the islands a favorite winter resort.

The Azores were discovered about 1427 by the Portuguese navigator Diogo de Sevill. Portugal secured the islands in the 15th century and established the first settlement on Santa Maria about 1439. From 1580 to 1640 the Azores were subject to Spain.

The Azores' first provincial coinage was ordered by law of August 19, 1750. Copper coins were struck for circulation in both the Azores and Madeira Islands, keeping the same technical specifications but with different designs. In 1795 a second provincial coinage was introduced but the weight was reduced by 50 percent.

Angra on Terceira Island became the capital of the captaincy-general of the Azores in 1766 and it was here in 1826 that the constitutionalists set up a pro-Pedro government in opposition to King Miguel in Lisbon. The whole Portuguese fleet attacked Terceira and was repelled at Praia, after which Azoreans, Brazilians and British mercenaries defeated Miguel in Portugal. Maria de Gloria, Pedro's daughter, was proclaimed queen of Portugal on Terceira in 1828.

A U.S. naval base was established at Ponta Delgada in 1917.

After World War II, the islands acquired a renewed importance as a refueling stop for transatlantic air transport. The United States maintains defense bases in the Azores as part of the collective security program of NATO.

In 1976 the archipelago became the Autonomous Region of Azores.

Note: Portuguese 50 Centavos and 1 Escudo pieces dated 1935 were issued for circulation in Azores. These are found under the appropriate listing in Portugal.

RULER
Portuguese

MONETARY SYSTEM
1000 Reis (Insulanos) = 1 Milreis

PORTUGUESE ADMINISTRATION

PROVINCIAL COINAGE

KM# 16 5 REIS
Copper **Subject:** Carlos I **Obv:** Crowned arms **Rev:** Value within wreath, date below

Date	Mintage	F	VF	XF	Unc	BU
1901	800,000	1.75	3.50	9.00	25.00	—

KM# 17 10 REIS
Copper **Subject:** Carlos I **Obv:** Crowned arms **Rev:** Value within wreath, date below

Date	Mintage	F	VF	XF	Unc	BU
1901	600,000	2.00	4.00	10.00	28.00	—

REPUBLIC

DECIMAL COINAGE

KM# 43 25 ESCUDOS
11.0500 g., Copper-Nickel, 28.5 mm. **Subject:** Regional Autonomy **Obv:** Shields above denomination, stars below **Rev:** Supported arms **Edge:** Reeded

Date	Mintage	F	VF	XF	Unc	BU
1980	770,000	—	—	2.50	5.00	7.50

KM# 44 100 ESCUDOS
Copper-Nickel **Subject:** Regional Autonomy **Obv:** Shields above denomination, stars below **Rev:** Supported arms

Date	Mintage	F	VF	XF	Unc	BU
1980	270,000	—	—	4.50	10.00	12.50

KM# 45 100 ESCUDOS
16.5000 g., Copper-Nickel **Subject:** 10th Anniversary of Regional Autonomy **Obv:** Supported arms, value below **Rev:** Hydrangea plant, date below **Designer:** Isabel and F. Branca

Date	Mintage	F	VF	XF	Unc	BU
1986	750,000	—	—	—	6.50	8.50

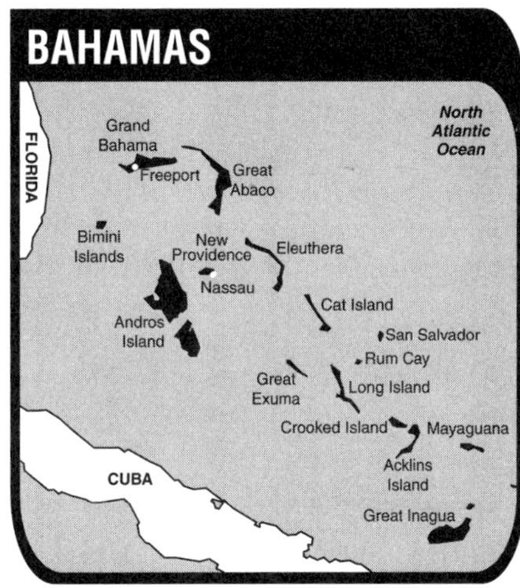

The Commonwealth of the Bahamas is an archipelago of about 3,000 islands, cays and rocks located in the Atlantic Ocean east of Florida and north of Cuba. The total land area of the 800 mile (1,287 km.) long chain of islands is 5,382 sq. mi. (13,935 sq. km.). They have a population of 302,000. Capital: Nassau. The Bahamas import most of their food and manufactured products and export cement, refined oil, pulpwood and lobsters. Tourism is the principal industry.

The Bahamas were discovered by Columbus October, 1492, upon his sighting of the island of San Salvador, but Spain made no attempt to settle them. British influence began in 1626 when Charles I granted them to the lord proprietors of Carolina, with settlements in 1629 at New Providence by colonists from the northern territory. Although the Bahamas were temporarily under Spanish control in 1641 and 1703, they continued under British proprietors until 1717, when, as the result of political and economic mismanagement, the civil and military governments were surrendered to the King and the islands designated a British Crown Colony. Full international agreement on British possession of the islands resulted from the Treaty of Versailles in 1783. The Bahamas obtained complete internal self-government under the constitution of Jan. 7, 1964. Full independence was achieved on July 10, 1973. The Bahamas is a member of the Commonwealth of Nations. Elizabeth II is Head of State as Queen of The Bahamas.

The coinage of Great Britain was legal tender in the Bahamas from 1825 to the issuing of a definitive coinage in 1966.

RULER
British

MINT MARKS
Through 1969 all decimal coinage of the Bahamas was executed at the Royal Mint in England. Since that time issues have been struck at both the Royal Mint and at the Franklin Mint (FM) in the U.S.A. While the mint mark of the latter appears on coins dated 1971 and subsequently, it is missing from the 1970 issues.
JP – John Pinches, London
None - Royal Mint
(t) - Tower of London
FM - Franklin Mint, U.S.A.

***NOTE**: From 1975-1985 the Franklin Mint produced coinage in up to 3 different qualities. Qualities of issue are designated in ( ) after each date and are defined as follows:

(M) MATTE - Normal circulation strike or a dull finish produced by sandblasting special uncirculated (polish finish) or proof quality dies.

(U) SPECIAL UNCIRCULATED - Polished or proof-like in appearance without any frosted features.

(P) PROOF - The highest quality obtainable having mirror-like fields and frosted features.

MONETARY SYSTEM
12 Pence = 1 Shilling

COMMONWEALTH

DECIMAL COINAGE

100 Cents = 1 Dollar

KM# 2 CENT
4.1600 g., Nickel-Brass, 23 mm. **Ruler:** Elizabeth II **Obv:** Queen Elizabeth II right **Rev:** Starfish above date, value at top **Edge:** Smooth **Designer:** Arnold Machin

Date	Mintage	F	VF	XF	Unc	BU
1966	7,312,000	—	—	0.10	0.50	2.00
1968	800,000	—	—	0.25	0.75	2.25
1969	4,036,000	—	—	0.10	0.50	2.00
1969 Proof	10,000	Value: 1.50				

KM# 15 CENT
Bronze, 19 mm. **Ruler:** Elizabeth II **Obv:** Bust of Queen Elizabeth II right with tiara **Rev:** Starfish above date, value at top **Edge:** Smooth **Designer:** Arnold Machin **Note:** Proof specimens of this date are struck in "special brass" which looks like a pale bronze.

Date	Mintage	F	VF	XF	Unc	BU
1970	125,000	—	0.10	0.25	0.50	1.50
1970 Proof	23,000	Value: 1.00				

KM# 16 CENT
3.1300 g., Brass **Ruler:** Elizabeth II **Obv:** Bust of Queen Elizabeth II right with tiara **Rev:** Starfish above date, value at top **Edge:** Smooth **Designer:** Arnold Machin

Date	Mintage	F	VF	XF	Unc	BU
1971FM	1,007,000	—	—	0.10	0.50	2.00
1971FM (P)	31,000	Value: 1.50				
1972FM	1,037,000	—	—	0.10	0.50	2.00
1972FM (P)	35,000	Value: 1.50				
1973	7,000,000	—	—	0.20	0.50	2.00
1973FM	1,040,000	—	—	0.10	0.50	2.00
1973FM (P)	35,000	Value: 1.50				

KM# 59 CENT
3.1600 g., Brass, 19 mm. **Ruler:** Elizabeth II **Obv:** National arms above date **Rev:** Starfish, value at top **Rev. Designer:** Arnold Machin **Edge:** Smooth

Date	Mintage	F	VF	XF	Unc	BU
1974	11,000	—	—	0.20	0.50	1.50
1974FM	71,000	—	—	0.10	0.25	1.00
1974FM (P)	94,000	Value: 1.50				
1975FM (M)	60,000	—	—	0.10	0.25	1.00
1975FM (U)	3,845	—	—	0.10	0.50	1.50
1975FM (P)	29,000	Value: 1.50				
1976FM (M)	60,000	—	—	0.10	0.25	1.00
1976FM (U)	1,453	—	—	0.10	0.50	1.50
1976FM (P)	23,000	Value: 1.50				
1977	3,000,000	—	—	0.10	0.25	1.00
1977FM (M)	60,000	—	—	0.10	0.25	1.00
1977FM (U)	713	—	—	0.50	1.50	4.50
1977FM (P)	11,000	Value: 1.50				
1978FM (M)	60,000	—	—	0.10	0.25	1.00
1978FM (U)	767	—	—	0.50	1.50	4.50
1978FM (P)	6,931	Value: 1.50				
1979	—	—	—	0.10	0.25	1.00
1979FM (P)	2,053	Value: 2.00				
1980	4,000,000	—	—	0.10	0.25	1.00
1980FM (P)	2,084	Value: 2.00				
1981	5,000,000	—	—	0.10	0.25	1.00
1981FM (M)	—	—	—	0.10	0.25	1.00
1981FM (P)	1,980	Value: 2.00				
1982	5,000,000	—	—	0.10	0.25	1.00
1982FM (M)	—	—	—	0.10	0.25	1.00
1982FM (P)	1,217	Value: 2.00				
1983	8,000,000	—	—	0.10	0.25	1.00
1983FM (P)	1,020	Value: 2.00				

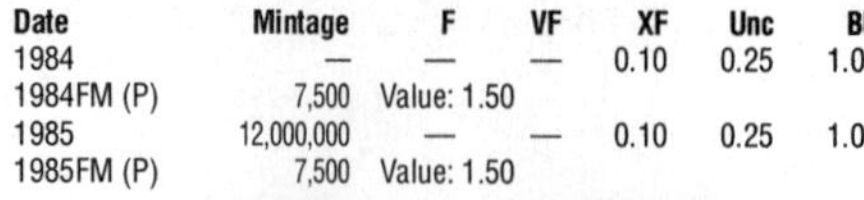

Date	Mintage	F	VF	XF	Unc	BU
1984	—	—	—	0.10	0.25	1.00
1984FM (P)	7,500	Value: 1.50				
1985	12,000,000	—	—	0.10	0.25	1.00
1985FM (P)	7,500	Value: 1.50				

KM# 59a CENT

2.5800 g., Copper Plated Zinc, 19.02 mm. **Ruler:** Elizabeth II **Obv:** National arms above date **Obv. Legend:** COMMONWEALTH OF THE BAHAMAS **Rev:** Starfish, value at top **Edge:** Plain

Date	Mintage	F	VF	XF	Unc	BU
1985	—	—	—	0.10	0.25	0.75
1987	12,000,000	—	—	0.10	0.25	0.75
1989	12,000,000	—	—	0.10	0.25	0.75
1989 Proof	—	Value: 2.00				
1990	—	—	—	0.10	0.25	0.75
1991	—	—	—	0.10	0.25	0.75
1992	—	—	—	0.10	0.25	0.75
1995	—	—	—	0.10	0.25	0.75
1997	—	—	—	0.10	0.25	0.75
1998	—	—	—	0.10	0.25	0.75
1999	—	—	—	0.10	0.25	0.75
2000	—	—	—	0.10	0.25	0.75
2001	—	—	—	0.10	0.25	0.75
2006	—	—	—	0.10	0.25	0.75
2007	—	—	—	0.10	0.25	0.75

KM# 208 CENT

2.5800 g., Copper Plated Zinc **Ruler:** Elizabeth II **Obv:** National arms above date **Rev:** Multiple starfish

Date	Mintage	F	VF	XF	Unc	BU
2006	—	—	—	0.10	0.25	0.75

KM# 3 5 CENTS

3.8700 g., Copper-Nickel, 21 mm. **Ruler:** Elizabeth II **Obv:** Bust of Queen Elizabeth II right with tiara **Rev:** Pineapple above garland divides date and value **Edge:** Smooth **Designer:** Arnold Machin **Note:** The obverse of this coin also comes muled with the reverse of a New Zealand 2-cent piece, KM#32. The undated 1967 error is listed as New Zealand KM#33.

Date	Mintage	F	VF	XF	Unc	BU
1966	2,571,000	—	—	0.10	0.25	0.75
1968	600,000	—	—	0.30	1.25	3.00
1969	2,026,000	—	—	0.10	0.25	0.75
1969 Proof	75,000	Value: 1.00				
1970	26,000	—	—	0.30	0.60	1.80
1970 Proof	23,000	Value: 1.50				

KM# 17 5 CENTS

Copper-Nickel, 21 mm. **Ruler:** Elizabeth II **Obv:** Bust of Queen Elizabeth II right with tiara **Rev:** Pineapple above garland divides date and value **Edge:** Smooth **Designer:** Arnold Machin

Date	Mintage	F	VF	XF	Unc	BU
1971FM	13,000	—	—	0.15	0.40	1.20
1971FM (P)	31,000	Value: 1.00				
1972FM	11,000	—	—	0.15	0.40	1.20
1972FM (P)	35,000	Value: 1.00				
1973FM	21,000	—	—	0.15	0.40	1.20
1973FM (P)	35,000	Value: 1.00				

KM# 38 5 CENTS

3.9000 g., Copper-Nickel, 21 mm. **Ruler:** Elizabeth II **Obv. Legend:** THE COMMONWEALTH OF THE BAHAMAS **Edge:** Smooth **Designer:** Arnold Machin

Date	Mintage	F	VF	XF	Unc	BU
1973	1,000,000	—	—	0.10	0.65	1.75

KM# 60 5 CENTS

3.9400 g., Copper-Nickel, 21 mm. **Ruler:** Elizabeth II **Obv:** National arms above date **Obv. Legend:** COMMONWEALTH OF THE BAHAMAS **Rev:** Pineapple above garland divides value at top **Rev. Designer:** Arnold Machin **Edge:** Smooth

Date	Mintage	F	VF	XF	Unc	BU
1974FM	23,000	—	—	0.10	0.50	1.50
1974FM (P)	94,000	Value: 1.00				
1975	—	—	—	0.10	0.30	0.90
1975FM (M)	12,000	—	—	0.10	0.50	1.50
1975FM (U)	3,845	—	—	0.15	0.75	2.25
1975FM (P)	29,000	Value: 1.00				
1976FM (M)	12,000	—	—	0.10	0.25	0.75
1976FM (U)	1,453	—	—	0.50	1.00	3.00
1976FM (P)	23,000	Value: 1.00				
1977FM (M)	12,000	—	—	0.10	0.35	1.00
1977FM (U)	713	—	—	0.50	1.50	4.50
1977FM (P)	11,000	Value: 1.00				
1978FM (M)	12,000	—	—	0.10	0.35	1.00
1978FM (U)	767	—	—	0.50	1.50	4.50
1978FM (P)	6,931	Value: 1.00				
1979FM (P)	2,053	Value: 1.50				
1980FM (P)	2,084	Value: 1.50				
1981	—	—	—	0.10	0.25	0.75
1981FM (P)	1,980	Value: 1.50				
1982FM (P)	1,217	Value: 1.50				
1983	2,000,000	—	—	0.10	0.25	0.75
1983FM (P)	1,020	Value: 1.50				
1984	—	—	—	0.10	0.25	0.75
1984FM (P)	1,036	Value: 1.50				
1985FM (P)	7,500	Value: 1.50				
1987	4,000,000	—	—	0.10	0.25	0.75
1989	—	—	—	0.10	0.25	0.75
1989 (P)	—	Value: 1.50				
1991	—	—	—	0.10	0.25	0.75
1992	—	—	—	0.10	0.25	0.75
1998	—	—	—	0.10	0.25	0.75
1999	—	—	—	0.10	0.25	0.75
2000	—	—	—	0.10	0.25	0.75
2004	—	—	—	0.10	0.25	0.75

KM# 4 10 CENTS

6.5500 g., Copper-Nickel, 23.5 mm. **Ruler:** Elizabeth II **Obv:** Bust of Queen Elizabeth II right with tiara, within beaded circle **Rev:** Bone Fish, value below, date above **Edge:** Smooth **Designer:** Arnold Machin

Date	Mintage	F	VF	XF	Unc	BU
1966	2,198,000	—	—	0.10	0.50	1.50
1968	550,000	—	—	2.00	4.00	8.00
1969	2,026,000	—	—	0.10	0.50	1.50
1969 Proof	10,000	Value: 1.00				
1970	27,000	—	—	0.15	0.60	1.80
1970 Proof	23,000	Value: 1.00				

KM# 18 10 CENTS

Copper-Nickel, 23.5 mm. **Ruler:** Elizabeth II **Obv:** Bust of Queen Elizabeth II right with tiara, within beaded circle **Rev:** Bone Fish, value below, date above **Edge:** Smooth **Designer:** Arnold Machin

Date	Mintage	F	VF	XF	Unc	BU
1971FM	13,000	—	—	0.15	0.50	1.50
1971FM (P)	31,000	Value: 1.00				
1972FM	11,000	—	—	0.15	0.50	1.50
1972FM (P)	35,000	Value: 1.00				
1973FM	15,000	—	—	0.15	0.50	1.50
1973FM (P)	35,000	Value: 1.00				

KM# 39 10 CENTS

Copper-Nickel, 23.5 mm. **Ruler:** Elizabeth II **Obv. Legend:** THE COMMONWEALTH OF THE BAHAMAS **Edge:** Smooth **Designer:** Arnold Machin

Date	Mintage	F	VF	XF	Unc	BU
1973	1,000,000	—	—	0.15	1.00	2.00

KM# 61 10 CENTS

5.5400 g., Copper-Nickel, 23.5 mm. **Ruler:** Elizabeth II **Obv:** National arms, date below, within beaded circle **Rev:** Arnold Machin **Edge:** Smooth

Date	Mintage	F	VF	XF	Unc	BU
1974FM	17,000	—	—	0.10	0.50	1.50
1974FM (P)	94,000	Value: 1.50				
1975	3,000,000	—	—	0.10	0.50	1.50
1975FM (M)	6,000	—	—	0.15	0.50	1.50
1975FM (U)	3,845	—	—	0.15	0.50	1.50
1975FM (P)	29,000	Value: 1.50				
1976FM (M)	6,000	—	—	0.15	0.50	1.50
1976FM (U)	1,453	—	—	0.25	1.00	3.00
1976FM (P)	23,000	Value: 1.50				
1977FM (M)	6,000	—	—	0.15	0.50	1.50
1977FM (U)	713	—	—	0.50	1.50	3.00
1977FM (P)	11,000	Value: 1.50				
1978FM (M)	6,000	—	—	0.15	0.50	1.50
1978FM (U)	767	—	—	0.50	1.50	3.00
1978FM (P)	6,931	Value: 2.00				
1979FM (P)	2,053	Value: 2.50				
1980	2,500,000	—	—	0.10	0.50	1.50
1980FM (P)	2,084	Value: 2.50				
1981FM (P)	1,980	Value: 2.50				
1982	2,000,000	—	—	0.10	0.50	1.50
1982FM (P)	1,217	Value: 2.50				
1983FM (P)	1,020	Value: 2.50				
1984FM (P)	1,036	Value: 2.50				
1985	2,000,000	—	—	0.10	0.50	1.50
1985FM (M)	—	—	—	0.15	0.50	1.50
1985FM (P)	7,500	Value: 2.00				
1987	3,000,000	—	—	0.15	0.50	1.50
1989	—	—	—	0.15	0.50	1.50
1989	—	Value: 2.00				
1991	—	—	—	0.15	0.50	1.50
1992	—	—	—	0.15	0.50	1.50
1998	—	—	—	0.15	0.50	1.50
2000	—	—	—	0.15	0.50	1.00

KM# 5 15 CENTS

Copper-Nickel, 25 mm. **Ruler:** Elizabeth II **Obv:** Bust of Queen Elizabeth II right with tiara **Rev:** Hibiscus, date divides value at bottom **Edge:** Smooth **Shape:** 4-sided **Designer:** Arnold Machin

Date	Mintage	F	VF	XF	Unc	BU
1966	930,000	—	—	1.00	2.00	3.00
1969	1,026,000	—	—	0.20	0.75	2.25
1969 Proof	10,000	Value: 2.00				
1970	28,000	—	—	0.25	0.75	2.25
1970 Proof	23,000	Value: 1.50				

KM# 19 15 CENTS

Copper-Nickel, 25 mm. **Ruler:** Elizabeth II **Obv:** Bust of Queen Elizabeth II right with tiara **Rev:** Hibiscus, date divides value below **Edge:** Smooth **Shape:** 4-sided **Designer:** Arnold Machin

Date	Mintage	F	VF	XF	Unc	BU
1971FM	13,000	—	—	0.20	0.50	1.50
1971FM Proof	31,000	Value: 1.50				
1972FM	11,000	—	—	0.20	0.50	1.50
1972FM Proof	35,000	Value: 1.50				
1973FM	14,000	—	—	0.20	0.50	1.50
1973FM Proof	35,000	Value: 1.50				

KM# 62 15 CENTS

Copper-Nickel, 25 mm. **Ruler:** Elizabeth II **Obv:** National arms above date **Rev:** Hibiscus, value divided at bottom **Rev. Designer:** Arnold Machin **Edge:** Smooth **Shape:** 4-sided

Date	Mintage	F	VF	XF	Unc	BU
1974FM	15,000	—	—	0.20	0.50	1.50
1974FM (P)	94,000	Value: 1.50				
1975FM (M)	3,500	—	—	0.25	1.00	3.00
1975FM (U)	3,845	—	—	0.25	1.00	3.00
1975FM (P)	29,000	Value: 1.50				
1976FM (M)	3,500	—	—	0.25	1.00	3.00
1976FM (U)	1,453	—	—	0.30	1.50	4.50
1976FM (P)	23,000	Value: 1.50				
1977FM (M)	3,500	—	—	0.25	1.00	3.00
1977FM (U)	713	—	—	0.50	2.00	6.00
1977FM (P)	11,000	Value: 1.00				
1978FM (M)	3,500	—	—	0.25	1.00	3.00
1978FM (U)	767	—	—	0.50	2.00	6.00
1978FM (P)	6,931	Value: 1.50				
1979FM (P)	2,053	Value: 2.00				
1980FM (P)	2,084	Value: 2.00				
1981FM (P)	1,980	Value: 2.00				
1982FM (P)	1,217	Value: 2.50				
1983FM (P)	1,020	Value: 3.00				
1984FM (P)	1,036	Value: 3.00				
1985FM (P)	7,500	Value: 2.25				
1989	—	—	—	0.20	0.50	1.50
1989 (P)	—	Value: 3.00				
1991	—	—	—	0.20	0.50	1.50
1992	—	—	—	0.20	0.50	1.50

KM# 6 25 CENTS

Nickel, 24 mm. **Ruler:** Elizabeth II **Obv:** Bust of Queen Elizabeth II right with tiara **Rev:** Bahaminian sloop, value, date **Edge:** Reeded **Designer:** Arnold Machin

Date	Mintage	F	VF	XF	Unc	BU
1966	3,685,000	—	—	0.30	0.50	1.50
1969	1,026,000	—	—	0.30	0.50	1.50
1969	10,000	Value: 1.50				
1970	26,000	—	—	0.35	0.75	2.25
1970FM (P)	23,000	Value: 2.00				
1970FM (M)	—	—	—	—	—	—

KM# 20 25 CENTS

Nickel, 24 mm. **Ruler:** Elizabeth II **Obv:** Bust of Queen Elizabeth II right with tiara **Rev:** Bahaminian Sloop, value, date **Edge:** Reeded **Designer:** Arnold Machin

Date	Mintage	F	VF	XF	Unc	BU
1971FM	13,000	—	—	0.30	0.50	1.50
1971FM (P)	31,000	Value: 1.50				
1972FM	11,000	—	—	0.30	0.50	1.50
1972FM (M)	—	—	—	0.30	0.50	1.50
1972FM (P)	35,000	Value: 1.50				
1973FM	12,000	—	—	0.30	0.50	1.50
1973FM (P)	35,000	Value: 1.50				

KM# 63.1 25 CENTS

6.9000 g., Nickel, 24 mm. **Ruler:** Elizabeth II **Obv:** National arms above date, beaded rim **Rev:** Bahaminian Sloop, value above **Rev. Designer:** Arnold Machin **Edge:** Reeded

Date	Mintage	F	VF	XF	Unc	BU
1974FM	13,000	—	—	0.30	0.50	1.50
1974FM (P)	94,000	Value: 1.50				
1975FM (M)	2,400	—	—	0.35	1.00	3.00
1975FM (U)	3,845	—	—	0.35	1.00	3.00
1975FM (P)	29,000	Value: 1.50				
1976FM (M)	2,400	—	—	0.35	1.00	3.00
1976FM (U)	1,453	—	—	0.35	1.25	3.75
1976FM (P)	23,000	Value: 1.50				
1977	—	—	—	0.30	0.50	1.50
1977FM (M)	2,400	—	—	0.35	1.00	3.00
1977FM (U)	713	—	—	0.50	3.00	9.00
1977FM (P)	11,000	Value: 1.50				
1978FM	2,400	—	—	0.35	1.00	3.00
1978FM (U)	767	—	—	0.50	3.00	9.00
1978FM (P)	6,931	Value: 2.00				
1979	—	—	—	0.30	0.50	1.50
1979FM (P)	2,053	Value: 3.00				
1980FM (P)	2,084	Value: 3.00				
1981	1,600,000	—	—	0.30	0.50	1.50
1981FM (P)	1,980	Value: 3.00				
1982FM (P)	1,217	Value: 4.00				
1983FM (P)	1,020	Value: 4.00				
1984FM (P)	1,036	Value: 4.00				
1985	2,000,000	—	—	0.30	0.50	1.50
1985FM (P)	7,500	Value: 2.00				
1987	—	—	—	0.30	0.50	1.50
1989	—	—	—	0.30	0.50	1.50
1989 (P)	—	Value: 3.00				

KM# 63.2 25 CENTS

5.7000 g., Copper-Nickel, 24 mm. **Ruler:** Elizabeth II **Edge:** Reeded

Date	Mintage	F	VF	XF	Unc	BU
1991	—	—	—	0.30	0.50	1.50
1992	—	—	—	0.30	0.50	1.50
1998	—	—	—	0.30	0.50	1.50
2000	—	—	—	0.30	0.50	1.50

KM# 7 50 CENTS

10.3700 g., 0.8000 Silver 0.2667 oz. ASW, 29 mm. **Ruler:** Elizabeth II **Obv:** Bust of Queen Elizabeth II right with tiara **Rev:** Blue Marlin, value and date at right **Designer:** Arnold Machin

Date	Mintage	F	VF	XF	Unc	BU
1966	701,000	—	—	BV	4.25	5.50
1969	26,000	—	—	BV	4.25	5.50
1969 Proof	10,000	Value: 6.00				
1970	25,000	—	—	BV	4.25	5.50
1970 Proof	23,000	Value: 6.00				

KM# 21 50 CENTS

10.3700 g., 0.8000 Silver 0.2667 oz. ASW, 29 mm. **Ruler:** Elizabeth II **Obv:** Bust of Queen Elizabeth II right with tiara **Rev:** Blue Marlin, value and date at right **Designer:** Arnold Machin

Date	Mintage	F	VF	XF	Unc	BU
1971FM	14,000	—	—	BV	4.25	5.50
1971FM (P)	31,000	Value: 6.00				
1972FM	12,000	—	—	BV	4.25	5.50
1972FM (P)	35,000	Value: 6.00				
1973FM	11,000	—	—	BV	4.25	5.50
1973FM (P)	35,000	Value: 6.00				

KM# 64 50 CENTS

Copper-Nickel, 29 mm. **Ruler:** Elizabeth II **Obv:** National arms, date below **Rev:** Blue Marlin, value at right **Rev. Designer:** Arnold Machin

Date	Mintage	F	VF	XF	Unc	BU
1974FM	12,000	—	—	0.60	2.00	4.00
1975FM (M)	1,200	—	—	1.00	6.00	12.00
1975FM (U)	3,828	—	—	0.65	4.00	8.00
1976FM (M)	1,200	—	—	0.75	5.00	10.00
1976FM (U)	1,453	—	—	0.65	4.00	8.00
1977FM (M)	1,200	—	—	0.75	5.00	10.00
1977FM (U)	713	—	—	1.25	10.00	15.00
1978FM (M)	1,200	—	—	1.00	8.00	12.00
1978FM (U)	767	—	—	1.25	10.00	15.00
1981FM (P)	1,980	Value: 6.00				
1982FM (P)	1,217	Value: 7.00				
1983FM (P)	1,020	Value: 7.00				
1984FM (P)	1,036	Value: 7.00				
1985FM (P)	7,500	Value: 5.00				
1989	—	—	—	0.75	2.25	3.00
1989 Proof	—	Value: 5.00				
1991	—	—	—	0.75	2.25	3.00
1992	—	—	—	0.75	2.25	3.00

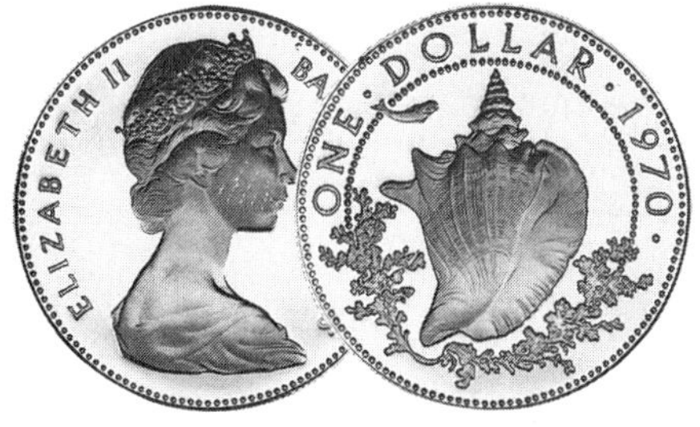

KM# 8 DOLLAR

18.1400 g., 0.8000 Silver 0.4666 oz. ASW, 34 mm. **Ruler:** Elizabeth II **Obv:** Bust of Queen Elizabeth II right with tiara **Rev:** Conch shell above garland, within 3/4 beaded circle, value and date above circle **Designer:** Arnold Machin

Date	Mintage	F	VF	XF	Unc	BU
1966	406,000	—	—	BV	7.50	11.00
1969	26,000	—	—	BV	7.50	11.00
1969 Proof	10,000	Value: 8.00				
1970	27,000	—	—	BV	7.50	11.00
1970 Proof	23,000	Value: 8.00				

KM# 22 DOLLAR

18.1400 g., 0.8000 Silver 0.4666 oz. ASW, 34 mm. **Ruler:** Elizabeth II **Obv:** Bust of Queen Elizabeth II right with tiara **Rev:** Conch shell above garland within 3/4 beaded circle, value and date above **Designer:** Arnold Machin

Date	Mintage	F	VF	XF	Unc	BU
1971FM	15,000	—	—	BV	7.50	11.00
1971FM (P)	31,000	Value: 8.00				
1972FM	18,000	—	—	BV	7.50	11.00
1972FM (P)	35,000	Value: 8.00				
1973FM	10,000	—	—	BV	7.50	11.00
1973FM (P)	35,000	Value: 8.00				

KM# 65 DOLLAR

Copper-Nickel, 34 mm. **Ruler:** Elizabeth II **Obv:** National arms above daate **Rev:** Conch shell above garland within 3/4 beaded circle, value at top **Rev. Designer:** Arnold Machin

Date	Mintage	F	VF	XF	Unc	BU
1974FM	12,000	—	—	1.25	4.00	6.00
1975FM (M)	600	—	—	7.50	25.00	—
1975FM (U)	3,845	—	—	1.50	9.00	12.00
1976FM (M)	600	—	—	7.50	25.00	—
1976FM (U)	1,453	—	—	1.75	10.00	13.50
1977FM (M)	600	—	—	7.50	25.00	—
1977FM (U)	713	—	—	5.00	25.00	—
1978FM (U)	1,367	—	—	2.00	10.00	13.50

KM# 65b DOLLAR

Copper-Nickel, 32 mm. **Ruler:** Elizabeth II

Date	Mintage	F	VF	XF	Unc	BU
1981FM (P)	1,980	Value: 17.00				
1989	—	—	—	1.50	4.00	6.00
1989 (P)	Est. 2,000	Value: 17.00				

Date	Mintage	F	VF	XF	Unc	BU
1991	—	—	—	1.50	4.00	6.00
1992	—	—	—	1.50	4.00	6.00

KM# 9 2 DOLLARS

29.8000 g., 0.9250 Silver 0.8862 oz. ASW, 40 mm. **Ruler:** Elizabeth II **Obv:** Bust of Queen Elizabeth II right with tiara **Rev:** National bird - two flamingos, value and date at top **Designer:** Arnold Machin

Date	Mintage	F	VF	XF	Unc	BU
1966	104,000	—	—	BV	13.50	15.00
1969	26,000	—	—	BV	13.50	15.00
1969 Proof	10,000	Value: 12.00				
1970	32,000	—	—	BV	13.50	15.00
1970 Proof	23,000	Value: 12.00				

KM# 23 2 DOLLARS

29.8000 g., 0.9250 Silver 0.8862 oz. ASW, 40 mm. **Ruler:** Elizabeth II **Obv:** Bust of Queen Elizabeth II right with tiara **Rev:** National bird-two flamingos, value and date at top **Designer:** Arnold Machin

Date	Mintage	F	VF	XF	Unc	BU
1971FM	88,000	—	—	BV	13.50	15.00
1971FM (P)	60,000	Value: 12.00				
1972FM	65,000	—	—	BV	13.50	15.00
1972FM (P)	59,000	Value: 12.00				
1973FM	43,000	—	—	BV	13.50	15.00
1973FM (P)	50,000	Value: 13.00				

KM# 66 2 DOLLARS

Copper-Nickel, 40 mm. **Ruler:** Elizabeth II **Obv:** National arms, date below **Rev:** National bird-two flamingos, value above **Edge:** Reeded

Date	Mintage	F	VF	XF	Unc	BU
1974FM	37,000	—	—	2.25	6.00	8.00
1975FM (M)	300	—	—	9.00	25.00	—
1975FM (U)	8,810	—	—	2.25	7.00	9.00

Date	Mintage	F	VF	XF	Unc	BU
1976FM (M)	300	—	—	9.00	25.00	—
1976FM (U)	4,381	—	—	2.50	10.00	12.00
1977FM (M)	300	—	—	9.00	25.00	—
1977FM (U)	946	—	—	3.00	20.00	—
1978FM (U)	1,067	—	—	3.00	15.00	—
1979FM (U)	300	—	—	7.50	25.00	—
1980FM (U)	—	—	—	—	75.00	—

BAHRAIN

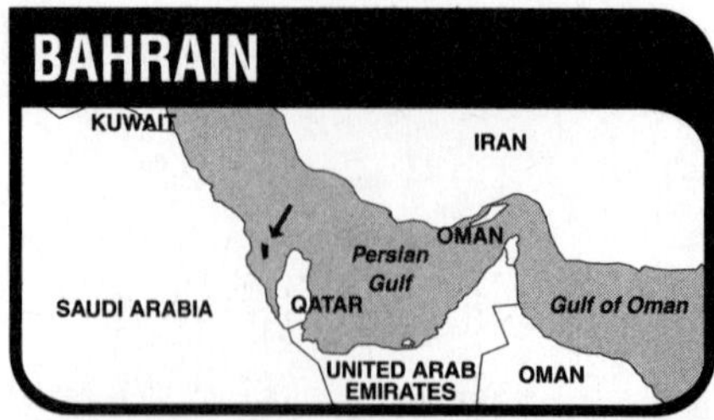

The State of Bahrain, a group of islands in the Persian Gulf off Saudi Arabia, has an area of 268 sq. mi. (622 sq. km.) and a population of 618,000. Capital: Manama. Prior to the depression of the 1930's, the economy was based on pearl fishing. Petroleum and aluminum industries and transit trade are the vital factors in the economy today.

The Portuguese occupied the islands in 1507 but were driven out in 1602 by Arab subjects of Persia. They in turn were ejected by Arabs of the Ataiba tribe from the Arabian mainland who have maintained possession up to the present time. The ruling sheikh of Bahrain entered into relations with Great Britain in 1805 and concluded a binding treaty of protection in 1861. In 1968 Great Britain decided to terminate treaty relations with the Persian Gulf sheikhdoms. Unable to agree on terms of union with the other sheikhdoms, Bahrain decided to seek independence as a separate entity and became fully independent on August 14, 1971.

Bahrain took part in the Arab oil embargo against the U.S. and other nations. The government bought controlling interest in the oil industry in 1975.

The coinage of the State of Bahrain was struck at the Royal Mint, London, England.

RULERS

Al Khalifa Dynasty

Isa Bin Ali, 1869-1932
Hamad Bin Isa, 1932-1942
Salman Bin Hamad, 1942-1961
Isa Bin Salman, 1961-1999
Hamed Bin Isa, 1999-

MINT MARKS

بحرين

Bahrain

البحرين

al-Bahrain = of the two seas

MONETARY SYSTEM

Falus, Fulus **Fals, Fils** **Falsan**

1000 Fils = 1 Dinar

KINGDOM

STANDARD COINAGE

KM# 1 FILS

Bronze, 1.5 mm. **Obv:** Palm tree within inner circle **Rev:** Denomination

Date	Mintage	F	VF	XF	Unc	BU
AH1385-1965	1,500,000	—	0.10	0.20	0.40	0.60
AH1385-1965 Proof	12,000	Value: 1.00				
AH1386-1966	1,500,000	—	0.10	0.20	0.40	0.60
AH1386-1966 Proof	—	Value: 2.00				

KM# 2 5 FILS

2.0000 g., Bronze, 18.5 mm. **Obv:** Palm tree within inner circle **Rev:** Denomination

Date	Mintage	F	VF	XF	Unc	BU
AH1385-1965	8,000,000	—	0.10	0.20	0.40	0.60
AH1385-1965 Proof	12,000	Value: 1.00				

KM# 16 5 FILS

2.5000 g., Brass, 18.98 mm. **Obv:** Palm tree within inner circle **Obv. Legend:** KINGDOM OF BAHRAIN **Rev:** Numeric denomination back of boxed denomination within circle, chain surrounds

Date	Mintage	F	VF	XF	Unc	BU
AH1412-1991	—	—	—	—	0.50	0.75
AH1412-1992	—	—	—	—	0.50	0.75
AH1426-2005	—	—	—	—	0.50	0.75

KM# 3 10 FILS

4.7500 g., Bronze, 23.5 mm. **Obv:** Palm tree within inner circle **Rev:** Denomination

Date	Mintage	F	VF	XF	Unc	BU
AH1385-1965	8,500,000	—	0.10	0.25	0.50	0.75
AH1385-1965 Proof	12,000	Value: 1.50				

KM# 17 10 FILS

3.4500 g., Brass, 19.22 mm. **Obv:** Palm tree within inner circle **Rev:** Numeric denomination back of boxed denomination within circle, chain surrounds **Edge:** Plain

Date	Mintage	F	VF	XF	Unc	BU
AH1412-1991	—	—	—	—	0.75	1.00
AH1412-1992	—	—	—	—	0.75	1.00
AH1420-2000	—	—	—	—	0.75	1.00

KM# 28 10 FILS

3.3500 g., Brass, 21 mm. **Ruler:** Hamed Bin Isa **Obv:** Palm Tree, "Kingdom Of Bahrain" **Rev:** Value **Edge:** Plain

Date	Mintage	F	VF	XF	Unc	BU
AH 1423- 2002	—	—	—	—	0.75	1.00
AH1424-2004	—	—	—	—	0.75	1.00

KM# 4 25 FILS

1.7500 g., Copper-Nickel, 16.5 mm. **Obv:** Palm tree within inner circle **Rev:** Denomination **Edge:** Reeded

Date	Mintage	F	VF	XF	Unc	BU
AH1385-1965	11,250,000	—	0.20	0.35	0.75	1.25
AH1385-1965 Proof	12,000	Value: 2.00				

KM# 18 25 FILS

Copper-Nickel **Obv:** Ancient painting within circle **Rev:** Numeric denomination back of boxed denomination within circle, chain surrounds

Date	Mintage	F	VF	XF	Unc	BU
AH1412-1992	—	—	—	—	1.25	1.50
AH1420-2000	—	—	—	—	1.25	1.50

KM# 24 25 FILS
3.5300 g., Copper-Nickel, 19.8 mm. **Obv:** Ancient painting within circle, dates at either side **Obv. Legend:** KINGDOM OF BAHRAIN **Rev:** Numeric denomination back of boxed denomination within circle, chain surrounds **Edge:** Reeded

Date	Mintage	F	VF	XF	Unc	BU
AH1423-2002	—	—	—	—	1.25	1.50

KM# 5 50 FILS
3.1000 g., Copper-Nickel, 20 mm. **Obv:** Palm tree within inner circle **Rev:** Denomination

Date	Mintage	F	VF	XF	Unc	BU
AH1385-1965	6,909,000	—	0.25	0.55	1.25	1.65
AH1385-1965 Proof	12,000	Value: 2.50				

KM# 19 50 FILS
4.4600 g., Copper-Nickel **Obv:** Stylized sailboat **Rev:** Numeric denomination back of boxed denomination within circle, chain surrounds

Date	Mintage	F	VF	XF	Unc	BU
AH1412-1992	—	—	—	—	1.50	1.75
AH1420-2000	—	—	—	—	1.50	1.75

KM# 25 50 FILS
4.4700 g., Copper-Nickel, 21.8 mm. **Subject:** Kingdom **Obv:** Stylized sailboats within circle, dates at either side **Obv. Legend:** KINGDOM OF BAHRAIN **Rev:** Numeric denomination back of boxed denomination within circle, chain surrounds **Edge:** Reeded

Date	Mintage	F	VF	XF	Unc	BU
AH1423-2002	—	—	—	—	1.50	1.75

KM# 6 100 FILS
6.5000 g., Copper-Nickel, 25 mm. **Obv:** Palm tree within inner circle **Rev:** Denomination **Edge:** Reeded

Date	Mintage	F	VF	XF	Unc	BU
AH1385-1965	8,300,000	—	0.35	0.75	1.50	2.00
AH1385-1965 Proof	12,000	Value: 3.50				

KM# 20 100 FILS
5.9600 g., Bi-Metallic Copper-Nickel center in Brass ring, 24 mm. **Obv:** Coat of arms within circle, dates at either side **Obv. Legend:** STATE OF BAHRAIN **Rev:** Numeric denomination back of boxed denomination within circle, chain surrounds **Edge:** Reeded

Date	Mintage	F	VF	XF	Unc	BU
AH1412-1991	—	—	—	—	3.50	4.00
AH1412-1992	—	—	—	—	3.50	4.00
AH1415-1994	—	—	—	—	3.50	4.00
AH1416-1995	—	—	—	—	3.50	4.00
AH1417-1997	—	—	—	—	3.50	4.00
AH1420-2000	—	—	—	—	3.50	4.00
AH1420-2001	—	—	—	—	3.50	4.00
AH1422-2001	—	—	—	—	3.50	4.00

KM# 26 100 FILS
5.9500 g., Bi-Metallic Copper-Nickel center in Brass ring, 23.9 mm. **Subject:** Kingdom **Obv:** Coat of arms within circle, dates at either side **Obv. Legend:** KINGDOM OF BAHRAIN **Rev:** Numeric denomination back of boxed denomination within circle, chain surrounds **Edge:** Reeded

Date	Mintage	F	VF	XF	Unc	BU
AH1423-2002	—	—	—	—	3.50	5.00
AH1426-2005	—	—	—	—	3.50	5.00
AH1427-2006	—	—	—	—	3.50	5.00
AH1428-2007	—	—	—	—	3.50	5.00

KM# 29 100 FILS
5.9500 g., Bi-Metallic Copper-Nickel center in Brass ring, 23.9 mm. **Subject:** 1st Bahrain Grand Prix **Obv:** Maze design within circle **Rev:** Numeric denomination back of boxed denomination within circle, chain surrounds **Edge:** Reeded

Date	Mintage	F	VF	XF	Unc	BU
AH1425-2004	30,000	—	—	—	12.50	15.00

KM# 7 250 FILS
Copper-Nickel **Series:** F.A.O. **Obv:** Sailboat, palm tree at right **Rev:** F.A.O. logo divided by grain sprig

Date	Mintage	F	VF	XF	Unc	BU
AH1389-1969	50,000	—	1.50	2.50	5.00	6.50
AH1389-1969 Proof	—	Value: 8.00				
AH1403-1983	3,000	—	1.75	3.50	10.00	12.50

KM# 8 500 FILS
18.3000 g., 0.8000 Silver 0.4707 oz. ASW **Ruler:** Isa Bin Salman **Obv:** Bust left **Rev:** Opening of Isa Town, crowned arms at center of octagon, dates appear in western and arabic script: 1368-1968

Date	Mintage	F	VF	XF	Unc	BU
ND	50,000	—	8.00	10.00	15.00	18.00
ND Proof	—	Value: 20.00				

KM# 22 500 FILS
Bi-Metallic Brass center in Copper-Nickel ring, 27 mm. **Ruler:** Hamed Bin Isa **Obv:** Monument and inscription **Obv. Inscription:** STATE OF BAHRAIN **Rev:** Denomination **Edge:** Reeded **Note:** Total weight: 9.05 grams.

Date	Mintage	F	VF	XF	Unc	BU
2000	—	—	—	—	6.00	7.50
2001	—	—	—	—	6.00	7.50

KM# 27 500 FILS
9.0500 g., Bi-Metallic Brass center Copper-Nickel ring, 27 mm. **Subject:** Kingdom **Obv:** Monument and inscription **Obv. Legend:** KINGDOM OF BAHRAIN **Rev:** Denomination **Edge:** Reeded

Date	Mintage	F	VF	XF	Unc	BU
2002	—	—	—	—	6.50	8.00

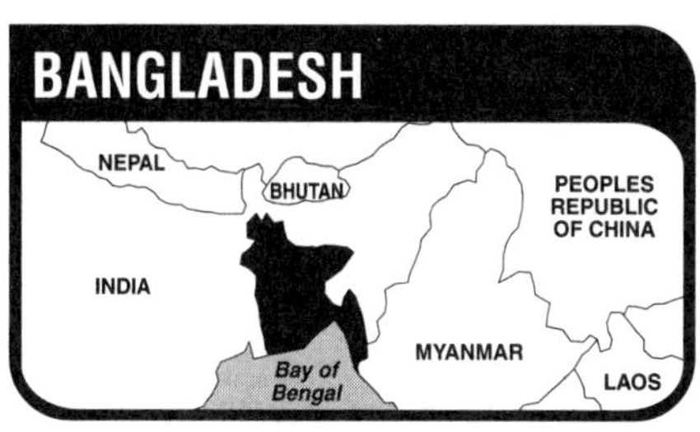

The Peoples Republic of Bangladesh (formerly East Pakistan), a parliamentary democracy located on the Bay of Bengal bordered by India and Burma, has an area of 55,598 sq. mi. (143,998 sq. km.) and a population of 128.1 million. Capital: Dhaka. The economy is predominantly agricultural. Jute products, jute and tea are exported.

British rule over the vast Indian sub-continent ended in 1947 when British India attained independence and was partitioned into the two successor states of India and Pakistan. Pakistan consisted of East and West Pakistan, two areas united by the Moslem religion but separated by culture and 1,000 miles of Indian territory. Restive under the de facto rule of the militant but fewer West Pakistanis, the East Pakistanis unsuccessfully demanded greater economic benefits and political reforms. The inability of the leaders of East and West Pakistan to resolve a political breakdown occasioned by the East Pakistan success in the general elections of 1970 precipitated massive civil disobedience in East Pakistan which West Pakistan sought to suppress militarily. East Pakistan seceded from Pakistan, March 26, 1971, and with the support of India declared an independent Peoples Republic of Bangladesh.

Bangladesh is a member of the Commonwealth of Nations. The president is the Head of State and the Government.

MONETARY SYSTEM
100 Poisha = 1 Taka

DATING
Christian era using Bengali numerals.

PEOPLES REPUBLIC

STANDARD COINAGE

KM# 5 POISHA
0.5300 g., Aluminum, 15.91 mm. **Obv:** National emblem, Shapla (water lily) **Rev:** Value within decorative circle **Edge:** Plain

Date	Mintage	F	VF	XF	Unc	BU
1974	300,000,000	—	—	0.10	0.15	—

KM# 1 5 POISHA
Aluminum **Obv:** National emblem, Shapla (water lily) **Rev:** Value and symbol within dentiled circle **Shape:** 4-sided

Date	Mintage	F	VF	XF	Unc	BU
1973	Est. 47,088,000	—	—	0.10	0.20	—
1974	—	—	—	0.10	0.20	—

KM# 6 5 POISHA
1.4000 g., Aluminum **Series:** F.A.O. **Obv:** National emblem, Shapla (water lily) **Rev:** Value and sumbol within dentiled circle **Shape:** 4-sided

Date	Mintage	F	VF	XF	Unc	BU
1974	5,000,000	—	—	0.10	0.20	—
1975	3,000,000	—	—	0.10	0.20	—
1976	3,000,000	—	—	0.10	0.20	—
1977	—	—	—	0.10	0.20	—

KM# 10 5 POISHA
1.4300 g., Aluminum **Series:** F.A.O. **Obv:** National emblem, Shapla (water lily) **Rev:** Value at right, 2/3 dentiled circle at left, symbol wihin **Edge:** Plain **Shape:** 4-sided square

Date	Mintage	F	VF	XF	Unc	BU
1977	90,000,000	—	—	0.10	0.15	—
1978	52,432,000	—	—	0.10	0.25	—
1979	120,096,000	—	—	0.10	0.15	—
1980	127,008,000	—	—	0.10	0.15	—
1981	72,992,000	—	—	0.10	0.15	—
1994	—	—	—	0.10	0.15	—

KM# 2 10 POISHA
1.9600 g., Aluminum, 24 mm. **Obv:** National emblem, Shapla (water lily) **Rev:** Large leaf at center, stem divides value **Shape:** Scalloped

Date	Mintage	F	VF	XF	Unc	BU
1973	Est. 21,500,000	—	—	0.10	0.35	—
1974	—	—	—	0.10	0.35	—

KM# 7 10 POISHA
2.0000 g., Aluminum, 24 mm. **Series:** F.A.O. **Obv:** National emblem, Shapla (water lily) **Rev:** Value at bottom, vehicle and plant at center **Shape:** Scalloped

Date	Mintage	F	VF	XF	Unc	BU
1974	5,000,000	—	—	0.15	0.35	—
1975	4,000,000	—	—	0.15	0.35	—
1976	4,000,000	—	—	0.15	0.35	—
1977	4,000,000	—	—	0.15	0.35	—
1978	141,744,000	—	—	0.15	0.30	—
1979	—	—	—	0.15	0.40	—

KM# 11.1 10 POISHA
1.9800 g., Aluminum, 24 mm. **Series:** F.A.O. **Obv:** National emblem, Shapla (water lily) **Rev:** Family above value **Shape:** Scalloped

Date	Mintage	F	VF	XF	Unc	BU
1977	48,000,000	—	—	0.15	0.30	—
1978	77,518,000	—	—	0.15	0.30	—
1979	170,112,000	—	—	0.15	0.30	—
1980	200,000,000	—	—	0.15	0.30	—

KM# 11.2 10 POISHA
1.3900 g., Aluminum, 22 mm. **Series:** F.A.O. **Obv:** National emblem, Shapla (water lily) within wreath above water **Rev:** Family, value below **Shape:** Scalloped **Note:** Reduced size.

Date	Mintage	F	VF	XF	Unc	BU
1981	—	—	—	0.25	0.50	—
1983	142,848,000	—	—	0.15	0.30	—
1984	57,152,000	—	—	0.15	0.30	—
1994	—	—	—	0.15	0.30	—

KM# 3 25 POISHA
2.6800 g., Steel, 19 mm. **Obv:** National emblem, Shapla (water lily) **Rev:** Rohu, right, value below

Date	Mintage	F	VF	XF	Unc	BU
1973	Est. 25,072,000	—	—	0.25	0.75	1.00

KM# 8 25 POISHA
2.6600 g., Steel, 19 mm. **Series:** F.A.O. **Obv:** National emblem, Shapla (water lily) **Rev:** Carp, egg, banana, squash, value at bottom

Date	Mintage	F	VF	XF	Unc	BU
1974	5,000,000	—	—	0.20	0.50	—
1975	6,000,000	—	—	0.20	0.50	—
1976	6,000,000	—	—	0.20	0.50	—
1977	51,300,000	—	—	0.15	0.50	—
1978	66,750,000	—	—	0.15	0.50	—
1979	—	—	—	0.15	0.50	—

KM# 12 25 POISHA
2.6400 g., Steel, 19 mm. **Obv:** National emblem, Shapla (water lily) **Rev:** Tiger head left within inner circle **Edge:** Reeded

Date	Mintage	F	VF	XF	Unc	BU
1977	45,300,000	—	—	0.20	0.75	—
1978	66,750,000	—	—	0.20	0.75	—
1979	56,704,000	—	—	0.20	0.75	—
1980	228,992,000	—	—	0.20	0.75	—
1981	45,072,000	—	—	0.20	0.75	—
1983	96,128,000	—	—	0.20	0.75	—
1984	203,872,000	—	—	0.20	0.75	—
1991	50,002,000	—	—	0.20	0.75	—
1994	—	—	—	0.20	0.75	—

KM# 4 50 POISHA
Steel **Obv:** National emblem, Shapla (water lily) **Rev:** Bird left, value below

Date	Mintage	F	VF	XF	Unc	BU
1973	18,000,000	—	0.25	0.75	2.50	3.50

KM# 13 50 POISHA
1.4500 g., Steel, 20.33 mm. **Series:** F.A.O. **Obv:** National emblem, Shapla (water lily) **Rev:** Symbols within inner ring, value at bottom **Edge:** Plain **Shape:** Scalloped

Date	Mintage	F	VF	XF	Unc	BU
1977	12,700,000	—	—	0.20	0.75	—
1978	37,300,000	—	—	0.20	0.75	—
1979	2,208,000	—	—	0.20	0.75	—
1980	124,512,000	—	—	0.20	0.50	—
1981	36,680,000	—	—	0.20	0.75	—
1983	31,392,000	—	—	0.20	0.75	—
1984	168,608,000	—	—	0.20	0.50	—
1994	—	—	—	0.20	0.50	—

KM# 24 50 POISHA
2.6000 g., Stainless Steel, 19.3 mm. **Obv:** National emblem, Shapla (water lily) within wreath above water **Rev:** Fish, chicken and produce within inner circle **Edge:** Plain **Shape:** Octagonal

Date	Mintage	F	VF	XF	Unc	BU
2001	—	—	—	—	1.50	—

KM# 9.1 TAKA
Copper-Nickel **Series:** F.A.O. **Obv:** National emblem, Shapla (water lily) **Rev:** Stylized family, value at right

Date	Mintage	F	VF	XF	Unc	BU
1975	4,000,000	—	0.15	0.45	1.00	—
1976	—	—	0.15	0.45	1.00	—
1977	—	—	0.15	0.45	1.00	—

KM# 9.3 TAKA
3.9800 g., Brass **Obv:** National emblem, Shapla (water lily) **Rev:** Stylized family, value at right **Edge:** Reeded

Date	Mintage	F	VF	XF	Unc	BU
1996	—	—	0.20	0.65	1.85	—
1997	—	—	0.20	0.65	1.85	—
1999	—	—	0.20	0.65	1.85	—
2003	—	—	0.20	0.65	1.85	—

KM# 9.4 TAKA
Brass **Obv:** National emblem, Shapla (water lily) **Rev:** Stylized family, value at right

Date	Mintage	F	VF	XF	Unc	BU
1998	—	—	—	0.50	1.25	—
1999	—	—	—	0.50	1.25	—

KM# 9.5 TAKA
4.2500 g., Stainless Steel, 24.91 mm. **Obv:** National emblem, Shapla (water lily) within wreath above water in octagonal frame **Rev:** Stylized family, value at right within octagonal frame

Date	Mintage	F	VF	XF	Unc	BU
2002	—	—	0.20	0.65	1.75	—
2007	—	—	0.20	0.65	1.75	—

KM# 25 2 TAKA
7.0000 g., Stainless Steel, 26 mm. **Obv:** State emblem and "TWO 2 TAKA" within beaded border **Rev:** Two children reading and legend within beaded border **Edge:** Plain

Date	Mintage	F	VF	XF	Unc	BU
2004	—	—	—	—	3.00	5.00

KM# 18.1 5 TAKA
7.8700 g., Steel **Obv:** Shapla flower on waves within wreath **Rev:** Bridge, value below **Shape:** 12-sided

Date	Mintage	F	VF	XF	Unc	BU
1994	—	—	—	—	1.75	2.50
1996	—	—	—	—	1.75	2.50

KM# 18.2 5 TAKA
8.1700 g., Steel, 26.68 mm. **Obv:** Shapla flower on waves within wreath, thicker design **Rev:** Bridge, value, denomination at bottom **Shape:** 12-sided

Date	Mintage	F	VF	XF	Unc	BU
1996	—	—	—	—	1.50	3.00
1998	—	—	—	—	1.50	—

KM# 18.3 5 TAKA
8.1700 g., Steel **Obv:** National emblem, Shapla (water lily) within wreath above water **Rev:** Bridge, date and denomination below

Date	Mintage	F	VF	XF	Unc	BU
2006	—	—	—	—	2.50	3.50

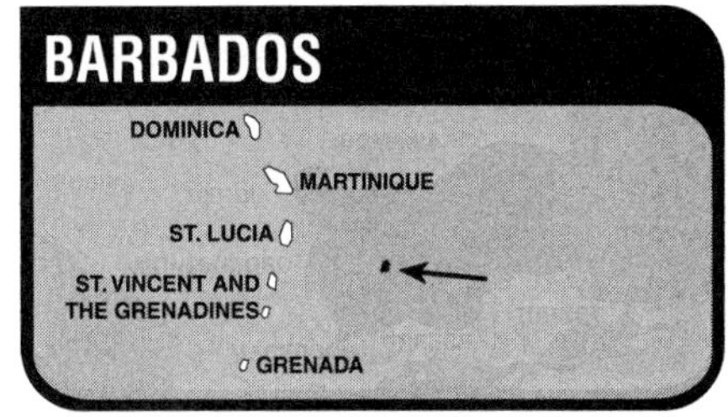

Barbados, a Constitutional Monarchy within the Commonwealth of Nations, is located in the Windward Islands of the West Indies east of St. Vincent. The coral island has an area of 166 sq. mi. (430 sq. km.) and a population of 269,000. Capital: Bridgetown. The economy is based on sugar and tourism. Sugar, petroleum products, molasses, and rum are exported.

Barbados was named by the Portuguese who achieved the first landing on the island in 1563. British sailors landed at the site of present-day Holetown in 1624. Barbados was under uninterrupted British control from the time of the first British settlement in 1627 until it obtained independence on Nov. 30, 1966. It is a member of the Commonwealth of Nations. Elizabeth II is Head of State as Queen of Barbados.

Unmarked side cut pieces of Spanish and Spanish Colonial 1, 2 and 8 reales were the principal coinage medium of 18th-century Barbados. The "Neptune" tokens issued by Sir Phillip Gibbs, a local plantation owner, circulated freely but were never established as legal coinage. The coinage and banknotes of the British Caribbean Territories (Eastern Group) were employed prior to 1973 when Barbados issued a decimal coinage.

RULER

British, until 1966

MINT MARKS

FM - Franklin Mint, U.S.A.*

None - Royal Mint

***NOTE**: From 1973-1985 the Franklin Mint produced coinage in up to 3 different qualities. Qualities of issue are designated in ( ) after each date and are defined as follows:

(M) MATTE - Normal circulation strike or a dull finish produced by sandblasting special uncirculated (polish finish) or proof quality dies.

(U) SPECIAL UNCIRCULATED - Polished or proof-like in appearance without any frosted features.

(P) PROOF - The highest quality obtainable having mirror-like fields and frosted features.

MONETARY SYSTEM

100 Cents = 1 Dollar

COMMONWEALTH

DECIMAL COINAGE

KM# 10 CENT

3.1400 g., Bronze, 19 mm. **Obv:** National arms **Rev:** Trident above value **Edge:** Plain **Designer:** Philip Nathan

Date	Mintage	F	VF	XF	Unc	BU
1973	5,000,000	—	—	0.10	0.25	0.75
1973FM (M)	7,500	—	—	0.50	1.00	3.00
1973FM (P)	97,000	Value: 1.00				
1974FM (M)	8,708	—	—	0.50	1.00	3.00
1974FM (P)	36,000	Value: 1.00				
1975FM (M)	5,000	—	—	0.35	0.75	2.25
1975FM (U)	1,360	—	—	0.50	1.00	3.00
1975FM (P)	20,000	Value: 1.00				
1977FM (M)	2,102	—	—	—	0.75	1.50
1977FM (U)	468	—	—	1.50	3.00	6.00
1977FM (P)	5,014	Value: 1.00				
1978	4,807,000	—	—	0.10	0.25	0.75
1978FM (M)	2,000	—	—	0.50	1.00	3.00
1978FM (U)	2,517	—	—	1.50	3.00	6.00
1978FM (P)	4,436	Value: 1.50				
1979	5,606,000	—	—	0.10	0.25	0.75
1979FM (M)	1,500	—	—	—	1.00	3.00
1979FM (U)	523	—	—	1.50	3.00	6.00
1979FM (P)	4,126	Value: 1.50				
1980	14,400,000	—	—	0.10	0.25	0.75
1980FM (M)	1,500	—	—	0.50	1.00	3.00
1980FM (U)	649	—	—	1.50	3.00	6.00
1980FM (P)	2,111	Value: 3.00				
1981	10,160,000	—	—	0.10	0.25	0.75
1981FM (M)	1,500	—	—	—	1.00	3.00
1981FM (U)	327	—	—	1.50	3.00	6.00
1981FM (P)	943	Value: 4.50				
1982	5,040,000	—	—	0.10	0.25	0.75
1982FM (U)	1,500	—	—	—	1.25	3.75
1982FM (P)	843	Value: 4.50				
1983FM (M)	1,500	—	—	—	1.00	4.50
1983FM (U)	—	—	—	—	1.25	3.75
1983FM (P)	459	Value: 4.50				
1984	5,008,000	—	—	0.10	0.25	0.75
1984FM (M)	868	—	—	—	1.25	4.50
1984FM (P)	—	Value: 3.00				
1985	—	—	—	0.10	0.25	0.75
1986	—	—	—	0.10	0.25	0.75
1987	10,000,000	—	—	0.10	0.25	0.75
1988	12,136,000	—	—	0.10	0.25	0.75
1989	—	—	—	0.10	0.25	0.75
1990	—	—	—	0.10	0.25	0.75
1991	—	—	—	0.10	0.25	0.75

KM# 10a CENT

2.5000 g., Copper Plated Zinc, 19 mm. **Obv:** National arms **Rev:** Broken trident above value **Rev. Designer:** Philip Nathan **Edge:** Plain

Date	Mintage	F	VF	XF	Unc	BU
1992	—	—	—	0.10	0.25	0.75
1993	—	—	—	0.10	0.25	0.75
1995	—	—	—	0.10	0.25	0.75
1996	—	—	—	0.10	0.25	0.75
1997	—	—	—	0.10	0.25	0.75
1998	—	—	—	0.10	0.25	0.75
1999	—	—	—	0.10	0.25	0.75
2000	—	—	—	0.10	0.25	0.75
2001	—	—	—	0.10	0.25	0.75
2004	—	—	—	0.10	0.25	0.75

KM# 11 5 CENTS

3.8100 g., Brass, 19.21 mm. **Obv:** National arms **Rev:** South Point Lighthouse **Rev. Designer:** Philip Nathan **Edge:** Plain

Date	Mintage	F	VF	XF	Unc	BU
1973FM (M)	7,500	—	—	—	1.25	3.75
1973	3,000,000	—	0.10	0.15	0.35	1.00
1973FM (P)	97,000	Value: 1.50				
1974FM (M)	8,708	—	—	—	1.25	3.75
1974FM (P)	36,000	Value: 1.50				
1975FM (M)	5,000	—	—	—	1.00	3.00
1975FM (U)	1,360	—	—	—	1.25	3.75
1975FM (P)	20,000	Value: 1.50				
1977FM (M)	2,100	—	—	1.00	2.00	5.00
1977FM (U)	468	—	—	1.50	3.00	6.00
1977FM (P)	5,014	Value: 1.50				
1978FM (M)	2,000	—	—	—	0.75	1.25
1978FM (U)	2,517	—	—	1.25	2.75	5.00
1978FM (P)	4,436	Value: 3.75				
1979	4,800,000	—	0.10	0.15	0.35	1.00
1979FM (M)	1,500	—	—	—	0.75	1.50
1979FM (U)	523	—	—	—	2.75	5.00
1979FM (P)	4,126	Value: 3.75				
1980FM (M)	1,500	—	—	—	1.00	3.00
1980FM (U)	649	—	—	1.00	2.25	6.75
1980FM (P)	2,111	Value: 4.25				
1981FM (M)	1,500	—	—	—	1.00	3.00
1981FM (U)	327	—	—	1.00	2.25	6.75
1981FM (P)	943	Value: 4.25				
1982	2,100,000	—	0.10	0.15	0.35	1.00
1982FM (U)	1,500	—	—	0.75	1.50	4.50
1982FM (P)	843	Value: 4.25				
1983FM (M)	1,500	—	—	0.75	1.50	4.50
1983FM (U)	—	—	—	0.75	1.50	4.50
1983FM (P)	459	Value: 4.25				
1984FM	1,737	—	—	0.75	1.50	4.50
1984FM (P)	—	Value: 4.25				
1985	—	—	—	0.10	0.25	0.75
1986	—	—	—	0.10	0.25	0.75
1988	4,200,000	—	—	0.10	0.25	0.75
1989	—	—	—	0.10	0.25	0.75
1991	—	—	—	0.10	0.25	0.75
1994	—	—	—	0.10	0.25	0.75
1995	—	—	—	0.10	0.25	0.75
1996	—	—	—	0.10	0.25	0.75
1997	—	—	—	0.10	0.25	0.75
1998	—	—	—	0.10	0.25	0.75
1999	—	—	—	0.10	0.25	0.75
2000	—	—	—	0.10	0.25	0.75
2001	—	—	—	0.10	0.25	0.75

KM# 12 10 CENTS

2.2900 g., Copper-Nickel, 17.5 mm. **Obv:** National arms **Rev:** Laughing Gull left **Rev. Designer:** Philip Nathan **Edge:** Reeded

Date	Mintage	F	VF	XF	Unc	BU
1973	4,000,000	—	0.10	0.15	0.50	1.50
1973FM (M)	5,000	—	—	—	1.50	3.00
1973FM (P)	97,000	Value: 2.00				
1974FM (M)	6,208	—	—	—	1.50	3.00
1974FM (P)	36,000	Value: 2.00				
1975FM (M)	2,500	—	—	—	1.00	3.00
1975FM (U)	1,360	—	—	—	1.50	3.00
1975FM (P)	20,000	Value: 2.00				
1977FM (M)	2,100	—	—	—	1.00	3.00
1977FM (U)	468	—	—	2.50	4.00	8.00
1977FM (P)	5,014	Value: 2.00				
1978FM (M)	2,000	—	—	—	1.00	3.00
1978FM (U)	2,517	—	—	—	3.00	6.00
1978FM (P)	4,436	Value: 3.00				
1979	2,500,000	—	0.10	0.20	0.60	1.25
1979FM (M)	1,500	—	—	1.00	2.50	5.00
1979FM (U)	523	—	—	1.50	3.00	8.00
1979FM (P)	4,126	Value: 3.00				
1980	3,500,000	—	0.10	0.15	0.50	1.25
1980FM (M)	1,500	—	—	—	1.00	3.00
1980FM (U)	649	—	—	1.00	2.50	7.00
1980FM (P)	2,111	Value: 4.00				
1981FM (M)	1,500	—	—	—	1.00	3.00
1981FM (U)	327	—	—	—	2.50	7.00
1981FM (P)	943	Value: 4.00				
1982FM (M)	—	—	—	—	1.00	3.00
1982FM (U)	1,500	—	—	—	1.75	4.25
1982FM (P)	843	Value: 4.00				
1983FM (M)	1,500	—	—	—	1.75	4.25
1983FM (U)	—	—	—	—	1.75	4.25
1983FM (P)	459	Value: 4.00				
1984	3,400,000	—	0.10	0.15	0.50	1.50
1984FM (P)	—	Value: 4.50				
1985	—	—	0.10	0.15	0.50	1.50
1986	—	—	0.10	0.15	0.50	1.50
1987	3,500,000	—	0.10	0.15	0.50	1.50
1988	—	—	0.10	0.15	0.50	1.50
1989	—	—	0.10	0.15	0.50	1.50
1990	—	—	0.10	0.15	0.50	1.50
1992	—	—	0.10	0.15	0.50	1.50
1995	—	—	0.10	0.15	0.50	1.50
1996	—	—	0.10	0.15	0.50	1.50
1998	—	—	0.10	0.15	0.50	1.50
2000	—	—	0.10	0.15	0.50	1.50
2001	—	—	0.10	0.15	0.50	1.50

KM# 13 25 CENTS

5.6700 g., Copper-Nickel, 23.6 mm. **Obv:** National arms **Rev:** Morgan Lewis Sugar Mill **Edge:** Reeded **Designer:** Philip Nathan

Date	Mintage	F	VF	XF	Unc	BU
1973	6,000,000	—	0.15	0.30	0.60	1.20
1973FM (M)	4,300	—	—	—	1.75	3.50
1973FM (P)	97,000	Value: 2.50				
1974FM (M)	5,508	—	—	—	1.75	3.50
1974FM (P)	36,000	Value: 2.50				
1975FM (M)	1,800	—	—	—	1.25	3.00
1975FM (U)	1,360	—	—	—	1.75	3.50
1975FM (P)	20,000	Value: 2.50				
1977FM (M)	2,100	—	—	—	1.00	3.00
1977FM (U)	468	—	—	—	4.25	10.00
1977FM (P)	5,014	Value: 2.50				
1978	2,407,000	—	0.20	0.40	0.80	1.60
1978FM (M)	2,000	—	—	—	1.00	3.00
1978FM (U)	2,517	—	—	—	3.25	9.00
1978FM (P)	4,436	Value: 3.50				
1979	1,200,000	—	0.20	0.40	0.80	1.60
1979FM (M)	1,500	—	—	—	1.00	3.00
1979FM (U)	523	—	—	—	3.00	9.00
1979FM (P)	4,126,000	Value: 3.50				
1980	2,700,000	—	0.15	0.30	0.60	1.60
1980FM (M)	1,500	—	—	0.75	3.00	8.00
1980FM (U)	649	—	—	—	2.75	10.00
1980FM (P)	2,111	Value: 3.50				
1981	4,365,000	—	0.15	0.30	0.60	1.60
1981FM (M)	1,500	—	—	0.75	3.00	8.00
1981FM (U)	327	—	—	—	2.75	10.00
1981FM (P)	943	Value: 4.50				
1982FM (U)	1,500	—	—	—	2.00	4.50
1982FM (P)	843	Value: 4.50				
1983FM (M)	1,500	—	—	—	2.00	4.50
1983FM (U)	—	—	—	—	2.00	4.50
1983FM (P)	459	Value: 4.50				
1984FM	868	—	—	—	2.00	4.50
1984FM (P)	—	Value: 5.00				
1985	—	—	0.15	0.30	0.60	1.60
1986	—	—	0.15	0.30	0.60	1.60
1987	3,150,000	—	—	—	2.00	3.00
1988	—	—	0.15	0.30	0.60	1.60
1989	—	—	0.15	0.30	0.60	1.60
1990	—	—	0.15	0.30	0.60	1.60
1994	—	—	0.15	0.30	0.60	1.60
1996	—	—	0.15	0.30	0.60	1.60
1998	—	—	0.15	0.30	0.60	1.60
2000	—	—	0.15	0.30	0.60	1.60

KM# 14.1 DOLLAR

9.9000 g., Copper-Nickel, 28 mm. **Obv:** National arms **Rev:** Flying fish left **Edge:** Plain **Shape:** Seven sided coin **Designer:** Philip Nathan

Date	Mintage	F	VF	XF	Unc	BU
1973	3,955,000	—	0.60	0.75	1.50	3.00
1973FM (M)	3,000	—	—	—	2.00	6.00
1973FM (P)	97,000	Value: 2.00				
1974FM (M)	4,208	—	—	—	2.00	6.00
1974FM (P)	36,000	Value: 3.00				
1975FM (M)	500	—	—	1.25	3.50	9.00
1975FM (U)	1,360	—	—	—	2.00	6.00
1975FM (P)	20,000	Value: 3.00				
1977FM (M)	600	—	—	1.75	5.00	9.00
1977FM (U)	468	—	—	1.50	4.50	10.00
1977FM (P)	5,014	Value: 6.00				
1978FM (M)	—	—	—	—	—	—
Note: Reported, not confirmed						
1978FM (U)	1,017	—	—	1.25	3.50	6.00
1978FM (P)	4,436	Value: 6.00				
1979	2,000,000	—	0.75	1.25	1.75	2.50
1979FM (M)	600	—	—	1.50	3.00	9.00
1979FM (U)	523	—	—	1.25	3.50	9.00
1979FM (P)	4,126	Value: 6.00				
1980FM (M)	600	—	—	1.50	3.50	9.00
1980FM (U)	649	—	—	1.50	3.50	9.00
1980FM (P)	2,111	Value: 6.00				
1981FM (M)	600	—	—	1.25	3.00	9.00
1981FM (U)	327	—	—	1.50	3.50	9.00
1981FM (P)	943	Value: 6.00				
1982FM (U)	600	—	—	1.25	3.00	9.00
1982FM (P)	843	Value: 6.00				
1983FM (M)	600	—	—	1.25	3.00	9.00
1983FM (U)	—	—	—	1.25	3.00	9.00
1983FM (P)	459	Value: 7.50				
1984FM	469	—	—	—	3.50	9.00
1984FM (P)	—	Value: 4.50				
1985	—	—	—	—	1.50	3.00
1986	—	—	—	—	1.50	3.00

KM# 15 2 DOLLARS

Copper-Nickel, 37 mm. **Obv:** National arms **Rev:** Staghorn coral **Edge:** Reeded **Designer:** Philip Nathan

Date	Mintage	F	VF	XF	Unc	BU
1973FM (M)	3,000	—	—	1.25	5.00	9.00
1973FM (P)	97,000	Value: 6.00				
1974FM (M)	4,208	—	—	1.25	5.00	9.00
1974FM (P)	36,000	Value: 6.00				
1975FM (M)	500	—	—	1.25	5.00	9.00
1975FM (U)	1,360	—	—	1.25	5.00	9.00
1975FM (P)	20,000	Value: 6.00				
1977FM (M)	600	—	—	1.25	5.00	9.00
1977FM (U)	468	—	—	1.50	5.50	10.00
1977FM (P)	5,014	Value: 9.00				
1978FM (M)	—	—	—	—	—	—
Note: Reported, not confirmed						
1978FM (U)	1,017	—	—	1.25	5.00	9.00
1978FM (P)	4,436	Value: 9.00				
1979FM (M)	600	—	—	1.25	5.00	10.00
1979FM (U)	523	—	—	1.25	5.00	10.00
1979FM (P)	4,126	Value: 9.00				
1980FM (M)	600	—	—	1.25	5.00	10.00
1980FM (U)	649	—	—	1.25	5.00	10.00
1980FM (P)	2,111	Value: 9.00				
1981FM (M)	600	—	—	1.25	5.00	10.00
1981FM (U)	327	—	—	1.25	5.00	10.00
1981FM (P)	943	Value: 9.00				
1982FM (U)	600	—	—	1.25	5.00	10.00
1982FM (P)	843	Value: 9.00				
1983FM (U)	—	—	—	1.25	5.00	10.00
1983FM (P)	459	Value: 9.00				
1984FM (U)	473	—	—	1.25	5.00	10.00
1984FM (P)	—	Value: 9.00				

KM# A9 4 DOLLARS

Copper-Nickel, 38.5 mm. **Series:** F.A.O. **Obv:** National arms **Rev:** Sugarcane and banana tree branch **Edge:** Reeded

Date	Mintage	F	VF	XF	Unc	BU
1970	30,000	—	4.00	7.00	15.00	20.00
1970 Proof	2,000	Value: 25.00				

BELGIAN CONGO

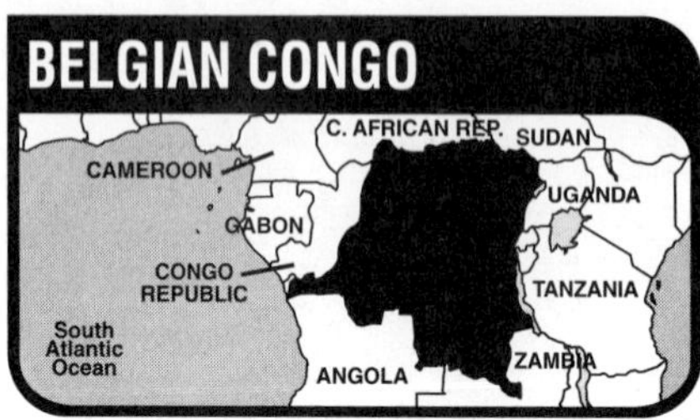

The Belgian Congo and Ruanda-Urundi were united administratively from 1925 to 1960. Ruanda-Urundi was made a U.N. Trust territory in 1946. Coins for these 2 areas were made jointly between 1952 and 1960. Ruanda-Urundi became the Republic of Rwanda on June 1, 1962.

MONETARY SYSTEM

100 Centimes = 1 Franc

RULER

Belgium

COLONY

DECIMAL COINAGE

KM# 15 CENTIME

Copper **Obv:** Hole at center of crowned "A"s, circle surrounds **Rev:** Center hole within star, date below star, value above

Date	Mintage	F	VF	XF	Unc	BU
1910	2,000,000	1.00	2.00	3.00	10.00	25.00
1919	500,000	1.00	2.00	3.00	15.00	40.00

KM# 16 2 CENTIMES

Copper **Obv:** Hole at center of crowned "A"s, circle surrounds **Rev:** Hole at center of star, date below star, value above

Date	Mintage	F	VF	XF	Unc	BU
1910	1,500,000	1.00	3.00	7.00	30.00	60.00
1919	500,000	1.50	3.50	10.00	35.00	75.00

KM# 12 5 CENTIMES

Copper-Nickel **Obv:** Hole at cente of crowned"JL", circle surrounds **Rev:** Hole at center of star, date below star, value above

Date	Mintage	F	VF	XF	Unc	BU
1909	1,800,000	5.00	12.50	40.00	125	210

KM# 17 5 CENTIMES

2.3900 g., Copper-Nickel, 19 mm. **Obv:** Hole at center of crowned "A"s, within circle **Rev:** Hole at center of star, date below star, value above

Date	Mintage	F	VF	XF	Unc	BU
1910(H)	6,000,000	0.75	1.50	3.50	16.00	60.00
1911(H)	5,000,000	0.75	1.50	3.50	16.00	50.00
1917(H)	1,000,000	3.00	7.00	18.00	55.00	100
1917(H) Proof	—	Value: 175				
1919(H)	3,000,000	1.50	3.00	7.00	25.00	—
1919	6,850,000	0.50	1.00	2.50	16.00	—
1920	2,740,000	0.50	1.00	3.50	18.00	—
1920/10(H)	—	—	—	—	—	—
1921	17,260,000	0.25	0.75	1.50	10.00	—
1921(H)	3,000,000	1.00	2.00	6.00	20.00	—
1925	11,000,000	0.25	0.75	2.00	10.00	—
1926/5	5,770,000	2.25	4.50	—	—	—
1926	Inc. above	0.25	1.00	2.00	9.00	—
1927	2,000,000	0.50	1.00	2.50	10.00	—
1928/6	1,500,000	2.00	4.00	8.00	20.00	—
1928	Inc. above	0.75	1.25	3.00	10.00	—

KM# 13 10 CENTIMES

Copper-Nickel **Obv:** Hole at center of crowned "L"s, backs touching, within circle **Rev:** Hole at center of star, date below star, value above

Date	Mintage	F	VF	XF	Unc	BU
1909	1,500,000	8.00	20.00	70.00	200	300

KM# 18 10 CENTIMES

Copper-Nickel **Obv:** Hole at center of crowned "A"s, within circle **Rev:** Hole at center of star, date below star, value above

Date	Mintage	F	VF	XF	Unc	BU
1910	5,000,000	0.50	1.00	3.00	15.00	50.00
1911	5,000,000	0.50	1.00	3.00	15.00	50.00
1917(H)	500,000	5.00	10.00	25.00	75.00	—
1919	3,430,000	0.50	1.00	3.50	16.50	—
1919(H)	1,500,000	0.75	1.25	4.00	18.00	—
1920	1,510,000	0.75	1.25	4.00	18.00	—
1921	13,540,000	0.25	0.75	2.00	10.00	—
1921(H)	3,000,000	0.75	1.50	3.50	16.50	—
1922	14,950,000	0.25	1.00	2.50	10.00	—
1924	3,600,000	0.50	1.50	3.00	15.00	—
1925/4	4,800,000	2.00	4.00	8.00	50.00	—
1925	Inc. above	0.25	1.00	3.00	15.00	—
1927	2,020,000	0.25	1.00	3.00	12.00	—
1928/7	5,600,000	1.00	3.00	8.00	40.00	—
1928	Inc. above	0.25	1.00	3.00	12.00	—
1928/3	—	—	—	—	—	—
1928/5	—	—	—	—	—	—

KM# 14 20 CENTIMES

Copper-Nickel **Obv:** Hole at center of crowned "L"s, backs touching, within circle **Rev:** Hole at center of star, date below star, value above

Date	Mintage	F	VF	XF	Unc	BU
1909	300,000	10.00	25.00	65.00	180	—

KM# 19 20 CENTIMES
5.9200 g., Copper-Nickel, 25.1 mm. **Obv:** Hole at center of crowned "A"s, within circle **Rev:** Hole at center of star, date below star, value above

Date	Mintage	F	VF	XF	Unc	BU
1910	1,000,000	2.00	5.00	12.00	40.00	120
1911	1,250,000	1.50	4.00	10.00	35.00	120

KM# 22 50 CENTIMES
6.4300 g., Copper-Nickel, 24.2 mm. **Obv:** Laureate head left, French legend **Rev:** Oil palm divides denomination and date **Rev. Legend:** CONGO BELGE **Edge:** Reeded

Date	Mintage	F	VF	XF	Unc	BU
1921	4,000,000	0.60	2.00	8.00	35.00	80.00
1922	6,000,000	0.60	2.00	8.00	30.00	80.00
1923	7,200,000	0.60	2.00	8.00	30.00	80.00
1924	1,096,000	0.75	3.00	10.00	45.00	—
1925	16,104,000	0.60	2.00	7.00	30.00	80.00
1926/5	16,000,000	1.00	4.00	12.00	50.00	—
1926	Inc. above	0.60	2.00	8.00	30.00	80.00
1927	10,000,000	0.60	2.00	8.00	30.00	80.00
1929/7	7,504,000	0.60	2.00	9.00	50.00	—
1929/8	Inc. above	1.00	4.00	15.00	90.00	—
1929	Inc. above	0.60	2.00	7.00	30.00	80.00

KM# 23 50 CENTIMES
6.5100 g., Copper-Nickel **Obv:** Laureate head left **Rev:** Oil palm divides denomination and date, Flemish legend **Rev. Legend:** BELGISCH CONGO

Date	Mintage	F	VF	XF	Unc	BU
1921	4,000,000	0.60	2.00	8.00	32.00	—
1922	5,592,000	0.60	2.00	7.00	30.00	—
1923	7,208,000	0.60	2.00	7.00	30.00	—
1924	7,000,000	0.60	2.00	8.00	32.00	—
1925/4	10,600,000	1.50	7.00	20.00	90.00	—
1925	Inc. above	0.60	2.00	7.00	30.00	—
1926	25,200,000	0.60	2.00	7.00	27.50	—
1927	4,800,000	0.60	2.00	8.00	30.00	—
1928	7,484,000	0.60	2.00	7.00	30.00	—
1929/8	116,000	25.00	50.00	75.00	120	—
1929	Inc. above	20.00	40.00	70.00	100	—
1923/1	—	—	—	—	—	—

KM# 20 FRANC
10.0000 g., Copper-Nickel **Obv:** Laureate head left **Rev:** Oil palm divides denomination and date, French legend **Rev. Legend:** CONGO BELGE

Date	Mintage	F	VF	XF	Unc	BU
1920	4,000,000	0.85	2.75	10.00	37.50	—
1922	5,000,000	0.85	2.75	9.00	32.00	—
1923/2	5,000,000	2.00	7.00	16.00	45.00	—
1923	Inc. above	0.85	2.75	9.00	32.00	—
1924	6,030,000	0.85	2.75	9.00	35.00	—
1925	10,470,000	0.85	2.75	9.00	32.00	—
1926/5	12,500,000	2.00	7.00	16.50	50.00	—
1926	Inc. above	0.85	2.75	8.00	30.00	—
1927	15,250,000	0.85	2.75	8.00	30.00	—
1929	5,763,000	0.85	2.75	9.00	32.00	—
1930	5,000,000	0.85	2.75	10.00	40.00	—

KM# 21 FRANC
10.1500 g., Copper-Nickel, 29 mm. **Obv:** Laureate head left **Rev:** Oil palm divides denomination and date, Flemish legend **Rev. Legend:** BELGISCH CONGO

Date	Mintage	F	VF	XF	Unc	BU
1920	475,000	2.00	5.00	16.50	50.00	—
1921	3,525,000	0.85	3.00	9.00	37.50	—
1922	5,000,000	0.85	3.00	9.00	37.50	—
1923/2	7,362,000	2.00	5.00	17.00	55.00	—
1923	Inc. above	0.85	2.75	9.00	32.00	—
1924	4,608,000	0.85	3.00	10.00	37.50	—
1925	9,530,000	0.85	2.75	9.00	32.00	—
1925/3	—	—	—	—	—	—
1926/5	17,000,000	2.00	5.00	17.00	55.00	—
1926	Inc. above	0.85	2.75	9.00	32.00	—
1928	9,250,000	0.85	2.75	9.00	32.00	—
1929	4,250,000	0.85	3.00	10.00	37.50	—

KM# 26 FRANC
2.4800 g., Brass, 19.20 mm. **Obv:** Denomination, legend at top and bottom **Rev:** African elephant, date below

Date	Mintage	F	VF	XF	Unc	BU
1944	25,000,000	0.50	1.00	3.00	10.00	12.50
1946	15,000,000	0.75	1.50	3.50	11.00	13.50
1949	15,000,000	0.75	1.50	3.00	11.00	13.50

KM# 25 2 FRANCS
5.8900 g., Brass **Obv:** Denomination, stars flanking **Rev:** African elephant left, date below **Shape:** 6-sided

Date	Mintage	F	VF	XF	Unc	BU
1943	25,000,000	2.50	6.00	15.00	50.00	75.00

KM# 28 2 FRANCS
Brass **Obv:** Denomination, stars flanking, legend at top and bottom **Rev:** African elephant left, date below

Date	Mintage	F	VF	XF	Unc	BU
1946	13,000,000	1.00	2.00	3.50	22.00	—
1947	12,000,000	1.00	2.00	4.00	25.00	—

KM# 24 5 FRANCS
Nickel-Bronze **Obv:** Head of Leopold III, left **Rev:** Lion above denomination, star at left of denomination, legend surrounds

Date	Mintage	F	VF	XF	Unc	BU
1936	2,600,000	5.00	10.00	30.00	125	150
1937	11,400,000	4.00	12.00	35.00	140	170

KM# 29 5 FRANCS
Brass **Obv:** Denomination at center, stars flanking, legend at top and bottom **Rev:** Africian elephant left, date below

Date	Mintage	F	VF	XF	Unc	BU
1947	10,000,000	3.00	7.00	15.00	50.00	90.00

KM# 27 50 FRANCS
17.5000 g., 0.5000 Silver 0.2813 oz. ASW **Obv:** Denomination at center, stars flanking, legend at top and bottom **Rev:** Africian elephant left, date below

Date	Mintage	F	VF	XF	Unc	BU
1944	1,000,000	20.00	50.00	90.00	175	425

RUANDA-URUNDI

PROVINCE

DECIMAL COINAGE

KM# 2 50 CENTIMES
0.6700 g., Aluminum **Obv:** Crowned arms divide date **Rev:** Oil palm divides denomination

Date	Mintage	F	VF	XF	Unc	BU
1954 DB	4,700,000	—	0.35	0.75	2.00	3.00
1955 DB	20,300,000	—	0.15	0.60	1.50	2.50

KM# 4 FRANC
1.4000 g., Aluminum **Obv:** Crowned arms divide date **Rev:** Oil palm divides denomination

Date	Mintage	F	VF	XF	Unc	BU
1957	10,000,000	—	0.50	1.00	2.00	3.50
1958	20,000,000	—	0.50	1.00	2.00	3.00
1959	20,000,000	—	0.50	1.00	2.00	3.00
1960	20,000,000	—	0.50	1.00	2.00	3.00

KM# 1 5 FRANCS
7.3000 g., Brass

Date	Mintage	F	VF	XF	Unc	BU
1952	10,000,000	—	2.50	5.00	10.00	15.00

KM# 3 5 FRANCS

2.2000 g., Aluminum, 31 mm. **Obv:** Crowned arms divide date **Rev:** Oil palm divides denomination **Edge:** Reeded

Date	Mintage	F	VF	XF	Unc	BU
1956 DB	10,000,000	—	1.00	2.00	4.00	6.00
1958 DB	26,110,000	—	0.75	1.75	3.50	5.00
1959 DB	3,890,000	—	1.00	2.50	5.00	7.00

BELGIUM

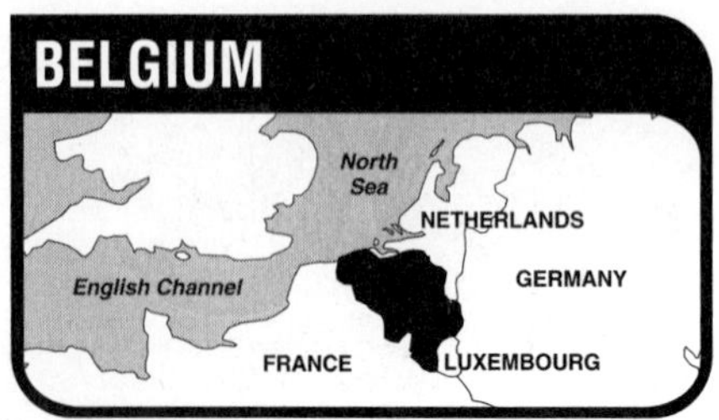

The Kingdom of Belgium, a constitutional monarchy in northwest Europe, has an area of 11,780 sq. mi. (30,519 sq. km.) and a population of 10.1 million, chiefly Dutch-speaking Flemish and French-speaking Walloons. Capital: Brussels. Agriculture, dairy farming, and the processing of raw materials for re-export are the principal industries. Beurs voor Diamant in Antwerp is the world's largest diamond trading center. Iron and steel, machinery motor vehicles, chemicals, textile yarns and fabrics comprise the principal exports.

At the Congress of Vienna in 1815 the area was reunited with the Netherlands, but in 1830 independence was gained and the constitutional monarchy of Belgium was established. A large part of the Duchy of Luxembourg was incorporated into Belgium and the first king was Leopold I of Saxe-Coburg-Gotha. It was invaded by the German Army in August, 1914 and the German forces carried on a devastating occupation of most of the territory until the Armistice. Belgium joined the League of Nations. On May 10, 1940 it was invaded again by the German army. The Belgian and Allied forces were quickly overwhelmed and were evacuated through Dunkirk. Allied troops reached Belgium again in Sept. 1944. Prince Charles, Count of Flanders, assumed King Leopold's responsibilities until liberation by the U.S. Army in Austria on May 8, 1945. As of January 1, 1989, Belgium became a federal kingdom.

RULERS

Leopold II, 1865-1909
Albert I, 1909-1934
Leopold III, 1934-1950
Baudouin I, 1951-1993
Albert II, 1993-

MINT MARK

Angel head - Brussels

MINTMASTERS' INITIALS & PRIVY MARKS

(b) - bird - Vogelier
Lamb head – Lambret

NOTE: Beginning in 1987, the letters "qp" appear on the coins - (quality proof)

MONETARY SYSTEM

100 Centimes = 1 Franc
1 Euro = 100 Cents

LEGENDS

Belgian coins are usually inscribed either in Dutch, French or both. However some modern coins are being inscribed in Latin or German. The language used is best told by noting the spelling of the name of the country.

(Fr) French: BELGIQUE or BELGES
(Du) Dutch: BELGIE or BELGEN
(La) Latin: BELGICA
(Ge) German: BELGIEN

Many Belgian coins are collected by what is known as Position A and Position B edges. Some dates command a premium depending on the position which are as follows:

Position A: Coins with portrait side down having upright edge lettering.

Position B: Coins with portrait side up having upright edge lettering.

KINGDOM

DECIMAL COINAGE

KM# 33.1 CENTIME

2.0000 g., Copper, 18 mm. **Ruler:** Leopold II **Obv:** Crowned monogram, legend in French **Obv. Legend:** DES BELGES **Rev:** Seated lion with tablet **Rev. Legend:** L'UNION FAIT LA FORCE

Date	Mintage	F	VF	XF	Unc	BU
1869	5,064,000	1.00	7.00	20.00	45.00	—
1870	3,930,000	1.00	7.00	20.00	45.00	—
1873	2,036,000	1.00	7.00	20.00	45.00	—
1874	3,907,000	1.00	7.00	20.00	45.00	—
1875	2,970,000	1.00	7.00	20.00	45.00	—
1876	2,966,000	1.00	7.00	20.00	45.00	—
1882	5,000,000	0.50	2.50	6.00	15.00	—
1883	—	60.00	125	450	1,000	—
1899	2,500,000	0.50	3.00	6.00	12.00	—
1901/801 Near 1	3,743,000	0.50	2.50	5.00	18.00	—
1901/801 Far 1	Inc. above	0.50	2.50	5.00	18.00	—
1901	Inc. above	0.25	0.50	1.50	5.00	—
1902/802 Near 2	2,847,000	1.00	2.00	4.00	10.00	—
1902/802 Far 2	Inc. above	1.00	2.00	4.00	10.00	—
1902/801	Inc. above	1.00	2.00	4.00	10.00	—
1902/1	Inc. above	1.00	2.00	4.00	10.00	—
1902	Inc. above	0.20	0.50	1.50	5.00	—
1907	3,967,000	0.20	0.50	1.50	4.00	—

KM# 34.1 CENTIME

Copper **Ruler:** Leopold II **Obv:** Crowned monogram, legend in Dutch **Obv. Legend:** DER BELGEN **Rev:** Seated lion with tablet **Rev. Legend:** L'UNION FAIT LA FORCE

Date	Mintage	F	VF	XF	Unc	BU
1882	Inc. above	50.00	150	325	550	—
1887	5,000,000	0.50	2.50	6.00	15.00	—
1892	—	30.00	100	400	900	—
1894	5,000,000	0.50	2.00	5.00	12.00	—
1899	2,500,000	0.50	2.00	5.00	12.00	—
1901/899	Inc. above	0.75	2.25	4.50	18.00	—
1901	Inc. above	0.25	0.50	1.50	5.00	—
1902/1	2,482,000	1.25	3.50	9.00	10.00	—
1902	Inc. above	0.25	0.50	1.50	5.00	—
1907	3,966,000	0.25	0.50	1.50	4.00	—

KM# 33.2 CENTIME

Copper **Ruler:** Leopold II **Obv:** Crowned monogram **Rev:** Lion with tablet **Note:** Thin flan.

Date	Mintage	F	VF	XF	Unc	BU
1882	Inc. above	0.50	1.50	6.00	15.00	—
1901	Inc. above	1.00	1.50	4.00	12.50	—
1902	Inc. above	1.00	1.50	6.00	15.00	—

KM# 34.2 CENTIME

Copper **Ruler:** Leopold II **Obv:** Crowned monogram **Rev:** Lion with tablet **Note:** Thin flan.

Date	Mintage	F	VF	XF	Unc	BU
1887	Inc. above	3.00	4.50	12.00	35.00	—
1901	Inc. above	1.00	1.50	8.00	25.00	—
1902	Inc. above	1.00	1.50	8.00	25.00	—

KM# 33.3 CENTIME

Copper **Rev:** Additional stop in signature... BRAEMT.F.

Date	Mintage	F	VF	XF	Unc	BU
1902	Inc. above	1.00	2.00	10.00	30.00	—

KM# 76 CENTIME

Copper, 11 mm. **Obv:** Crowned letter "A", date below, legend in French **Obv. Legend:** DES BELGES **Rev:** Tablet at left of seated lion looking right, denomination below **Edge:** Reeded

Date	Mintage	F	VF	XF	Unc	BU
1912	2,540,000	0.20	0.50	2.50	7.00	—
1914	870,000	0.25	0.75	3.50	10.00	—

KM# 77 CENTIME

2.0000 g., Copper, 11 mm. **Obv:** Crowned letter "A", date below, legend in Dutch **Obv. Legend:** DER BELGEN **Rev:** Tablet to left of seated lion looking right, denomination below **Edge:** Reeded

Date	Mintage	F	VF	XF	Unc	BU
1912	2,542,000	0.20	0.50	1.50	4.00	—

KM# 35.1 2 CENTIMES

Copper **Ruler:** Leopold II **Obv:** Legend in French **Obv. Legend:** DES BELGES

Date	Mintage	F	VF	XF	Unc	BU
1869	2,972,000	10.00	60.00	125	200	—
1869 Plain edge; restrike	—	—	—	—	—	—
1870	5,654,000	0.25	1.00	7.00	12.00	—
1870/1	Inc. above	1.25	2.00	12.50	30.00	—
1871 Inc.1870	—	0.25	5.00	20.00	70.00	—
1873	7,491,000	0.25	1.00	5.00	12.00	—
1874 Small wide date	7,876,000	0.25	1.00	5.00	12.00	—
1874 Large narrow date	Inc. above	0.25	1.00	5.00	12.00	—
1875	7,932,000	0.25	1.00	5.00	12.00	—
1876	10,472,000	0.25	1.00	3.00	10.00	—
1902	2,490,000	0.15	0.50	4.00	15.00	—
1905	4,981,000	0.15	0.50	4.00	10.00	—
1909/5	4,983,000	0.75	3.00	15.00	50.00	—
1909	Inc. above	0.15	0.50	4.00	10.00	—
1909/1809	Inc. above	1.00	5.00	30.00	85.00	—

KM# 36 2 CENTIMES

4.0000 g., Copper, 21.6 mm. **Obv:** Crowned design, date below, legend in Dutch **Obv. Legend:** DER BELGEN **Rev:** Tablet to left of seated lion looking right, denomination below

Date	Mintage	F	VF	XF	Unc	BU
1902	2,488,000	0.15	1.50	4.00	15.00	—
1905/2	4,986,000	1.50	3.00	15.00	50.00	—
1905	Inc. above	0.15	1.00	4.00	10.00	—
1909	565,000	0.50	2.00	12.00	50.00	—

KM# 35.2 2 CENTIMES

Copper **Note:** Thin flan.

Date	Mintage	F	VF	XF	Unc	BU
1902	Inc. above	3.00	5.00	35.00	75.00	125

KM# 65 2 CENTIMES

3.9700 g., Copper, 21.64 mm. **Obv:** Crowned letter "A", date below, legend in Dutch **Obv. Legend:** DER BELGEN **Rev:** Tablet to left of seated lion looking right, denomination below

Date	Mintage	F	VF	XF	Unc	BU
1910	1,248,000	0.25	0.50	3.00	10.00	—
1911 Large date	6,441,000	0.15	0.35	1.50	5.00	—
1911 Small date	Inc. above	0.15	0.35	1.50	5.00	—
1912	1,602,000	0.35	1.00	3.00	8.00	—
1919	4,998,000	0.15	0.35	0.75	3.00	—

KM# 64 2 CENTIMES

Copper **Obv:** Crowned letter "A", date below, legend in French **Obv. Legend:** DES BELGES **Rev:** Tablet to left of seated lion looking right, denomination below

Date	Mintage	F	VF	XF	Unc	BU
1911	645,000	1.50	3.00	14.00	40.00	—
1912/1	4,928,000	1.00	3.00	10.00	25.00	—
1912	Inc. above	0.15	0.50	2.00	5.00	—
1914	491,000	1.00	2.50	12.00	30.00	—
1919/4	5,000,000	0.75	1.00	3.00	7.00	—
1919	Inc. above	0.15	0.25	1.00	3.00	—

KM# 40 5 CENTIMES

Copper-Nickel **Ruler:** Leopold II **Obv:** Legend in French **Obv. Legend:** DES BELGES

Date	Mintage	F	VF	XF	Unc	BU
1894	3,111,000	1.00	4.00	9.00	20.00	—
1895	3,693,000	1.00	4.00	9.00	20.00	—
1898	1,004,000	8.00	40.00	70.00	120	—
1900/891	1,666,000	7.00	12.00	55.00	125	—
1900	Inc. above	5.00	30.00	65.00	90.00	—
1901	—	10.00	30.00	65.00	140	—

KM# 44 5 CENTIMES

Copper-Nickel **Obv:** Denomination above star, circle surrounds **Rev:** Rampant lion left within circle, date below

Date	Mintage	F	VF	XF	Unc	BU
1901	2,494,000	3.00	20.00	35.00	70.00	—

KM# 45 5 CENTIMES

Copper-Nickel **Obv:** Denomination above star, circle surrounds, legend in Dutch **Obv. Legend:** DER BELGEN **Rev:** Rampant lion left within circle, date below

Date	Mintage	F	VF	XF	Unc	BU
1901	2,491,000	3.00	20.00	35.00	70.00	—

KM# 46 5 CENTIMES

2.3900 g., Copper-Nickel **Obv:** Hole at center of crowned monogram, small date below, legend in French **Obv. Legend:** BELGIQUE **Rev:** Spray of leaves to left of center hole, denomination at right **Designer:** A. Michaux

Date	Mintage	F	VF	XF	Unc	BU
1901	202,000	15.00	50.00	90.00	175	—
1902/1	1,416,000	0.50	8.00	15.00	45.00	—
1902	Inc. above	0.25	3.00	7.00	22.00	—
1903	864,000	1.00	8.00	15.00	45.00	—

KM# 47 5 CENTIMES

Copper-Nickel **Obv:** Center hole within crowned monogram, small date below, legend in Dutch **Obv. Legend:** BELGIE **Rev:** Spray of leaves to left of center hole, denomination to right **Designer:** A. Michaux

Date	Mintage	F	VF	XF	Unc	BU
1902/1	1,485,000	1.75	5.50	22.50	45.00	—
1902	Inc. above	0.15	3.00	7.00	22.00	—
1903	1,002,000	1.00	8.00	25.00	50.00	—

KM# 54 5 CENTIMES

Copper-Nickel **Obv:** Center hole within crowned monogram, large date below, legend in French **Obv. Legend:** BELGIQUE **Rev:** Spray of leaves to left of center hole, denomination to right **Designer:** A. Michaux

Date	Mintage	F	VF	XF	Unc	BU
1904	5,814,000	0.15	0.35	2.00	7.00	—
1905/4	9,575,000	0.30	1.00	3.00	15.00	—
1905	Inc. above	0.15	0.35	2.00	7.00	—
1905 WICHAUX (error)	Inc. above	2.00	15.00	25.00	60.00	—
1905 A. MICHAUX	Inc. above	1.00	3.50	15.00	40.00	—
1906/5	8,463,000	0.30	1.50	3.00	12.00	—
1906	Inc. above	0.15	0.35	2.00	6.00	—
1907	993,000	1.00	6.00	12.00	30.00	—

KM# 55 5 CENTIMES

Copper-Nickel **Obv:** Center hole within crowned monogram, large date below, legend in Dutch **Obv. Legend:** BELGIE **Rev:** Spray of leaves to left of center hole, denomination to right **Designer:** A. Michaux

Date	Mintage	F	VF	XF	Unc	BU
1904	5,812,000	0.15	0.35	2.00	7.00	—
1905/3	7,002,000	0.35	2.50	15.00	30.00	—
1905/4	Inc. above	0.30	1.50	4.00	15.00	—
1905	Inc. above	0.15	0.35	2.00	7.00	—
1905 Without cross	Inc. above	—	1.50	6.00	20.00	—
1906	11,016,000	0.15	0.35	2.00	7.00	—
1906 Without cross	Inc. above	0.30	1.50	4.00	15.00	—
1907	998,000	1.00	3.00	15.00	30.00	—

KM# 66 5 CENTIMES

Copper-Nickel **Obv:** Center hole within crowned monogram, date below,legend in French **Obv. Legend:** BELGIQUE **Rev:** Spray of leaves to left of center hole, denomination to right **Designer:** A. Michaux

Date	Mintage	F	VF	XF	Unc	BU
1910	8,011,000	0.10	0.35	1.25	4.00	—
1913/0	5,005,000	0.20	0.75	2.25	10.00	—
1913	Inc. above	0.10	0.40	1.50	7.00	—
1914	1,004,000	1.00	3.00	8.00	25.00	—
1920/10	10,040,000	0.10	1.00	3.00	7.00	—
1920	Inc. above	0.10	0.35	1.25	4.00	—
1922/0	12,640,000	0.10	1.50	4.00	9.00	—
1922/1	Inc. above	0.10	1.50	3.50	9.00	—
1922	Inc. above	0.10	0.35	1.25	4.00	—
1923/13	9,000,000	0.10	0.75	2.50	8.00	—
1923	Inc. above	0.10	0.35	1.25	4.00	—
1925/13	15,860,000	0.10	0.50	2.00	8.00	—
1925/23	Inc. above	0.10	0.50	2.00	8.00	—
1925	Inc. above	0.10	0.35	1.25	4.00	—
1926/5	7,000,000	0.10	1.00	2.50	8.00	—
1926	Inc. above	0.10	0.35	1.25	4.00	—
1927	2,000,000	0.10	1.00	2.50	9.00	—
1927 5 Cen	—	10.00	20.00	50.00	100	—
Note: Obverse of KM#66 in French paired with the reverse of KM#67 in Flemish						
1928	12,507,000	0.10	0.35	1.25	4.00	—

KM# 67 5 CENTIMES

Copper-Nickel **Obv:** Center hole within crowned monogram, date below, legend in Dutch **Obv. Legend:** BELGIE **Rev:** Spray of leaves to left of center hole, denomination to right, plain field above 5 **Designer:** A. Michaux

Date	Mintage	F	VF	XF	Unc	BU
1910	8,033,000	0.10	0.35	1.25	4.00	—
1914	6,040,000	0.10	0.35	1.25	4.00	—
1920/10	10,030,000	0.10	0.35	1.25	6.00	—
1920	Inc. above	0.10	0.50	3.00	12.00	—
1921/11	4,200,000	0.10	1.00	2.50	12.00	—
1921	Inc. above	0.10	1.00	2.00	9.00	—
1922/12	13,180,000	0.10	1.00	2.50	8.00	—
1922/0	Inc. above	0.10	1.00	3.00	9.00	—
1922	Inc. above	0.10	0.35	1.25	4.00	—
1923/13	3,530,000	0.10	1.00	3.00	10.00	—
1923	Inc. above	0.10	0.75	2.00	9.00	—
1924/11	5,260,000	0.10	1.00	2.50	9.00	—
1924/14	Inc. above	0.10	0.50	1.75	9.00	—
1924	Inc. above	0.10	0.35	1.25	4.00	—
1925/13	13,000,000	0.10	1.00	2.50	8.00	—
1925/15 High 2	Inc. above	0.10	1.00	2.00	9.00	—
1925/15 Level 2	Inc. above	0.10	1.00	2.00	9.00	—
1925/3	Inc. above	0.10	0.60	2.00	9.00	—
1925	Inc. above	0.10	0.35	1.25	4.00	—
1927	6,938,000	0.10	0.35	1.25	4.00	—
1928/3	6,252,000	0.10	0.75	2.50	9.00	—
1928	Inc. above	0.10	0.35	1.25	4.00	—

KM# 80 5 CENTIMES

Zinc **Obv:** Denomination within circle, date below circle, legend in French **Obv. Legend:** BELGIQUE-BELGIE **Rev:** Rampant lion, left, within circle **Note:** German Occupation WW I

Date	Mintage	F	VF	XF	Unc	BU
1915	10,199,000	0.15	2.00	4.00	15.00	30.00
1916	45,464,000	0.10	0.60	2.00	7.00	15.00

KM# 94 5 CENTIMES

Nickel-Brass **Obv:** Center hole within crowned monogram, date below, legend in Dutch **Obv. Legend:** BELGIE **Rev:** Spray of leaves to left of center hole, denomination at right, star added above 5

Date	Mintage	F	VF	XF	Unc	BU
1930	3,000,000	0.10	0.20	0.35	3.00	—
1931	7,430,000	0.10	0.20	0.35	3.00	—

KM# 93 5 CENTIMES

Nickel-Brass **Obv:** Legend in French **Obv. Legend:** BELGIQUE **Rev:** Star added above 5

Date	Mintage	F	VF	XF	Unc	BU
1932	5,520,000	0.10	0.20	0.35	3.00	—

KM# 110.1 5 CENTIMES

Nickel-Brass **Obv:** Three shields above denomination, legend in French, hole at center **Obv. Legend:** BELGIQUE-BELGIE **Rev:** Hole at center of crowned design, date below

Date	Mintage	F	VF	XF	Unc	BU
1938	4,970,000	0.10	0.20	0.75	2.00	—
1939	—	—	—	—	—	—
Note: Struck at a later date						

KM# 110.2 5 CENTIMES

Nickel-Brass **Note:** Medal alignment.

Date	Mintage	F	VF	XF	Unc	BU
1938	Inc. above	7.00	12.00	20.00	40.00	—

KM# 111 5 CENTIMES

Nickel-Brass **Obv:** Three shields above denomination, hole at center, legend in Dutch **Obv. Legend:** BELGIE-BELGIQUE **Rev:** Crowned design above date, hole at center

Date	Mintage	F	VF	XF	Unc	BU
1939	3,000,000	0.10	0.20	0.75	3.00	—
1940	1,970,000	0.20	0.50	1.50	5.00	—

KM# 124 5 CENTIMES

Zinc **Obv:** Legend in Dutch **Obv. Legend:** BELGIE-BELGIQUE

Date	Mintage	F	VF	XF	Unc	BU
1941	4,000,000	0.15	0.75	2.50	15.00	—
1942	18,430,000	0.10	0.20	1.00	4.00	—

KM# 123 5 CENTIMES

Zinc **Obv:** Three shields above denomination, dots flank denomination, hole at center, legend in French **Obv. Legend:** BELGIQUE-BELGIE **Rev:** Crowned design above date, hole at center **Note:** German Occupation WW II

Date	Mintage	F	VF	XF	Unc	BU
1941	10,000,000	0.10	0.20	1.00	4.00	—
1943	7,606,000	0.10	0.20	1.50	6.00	—

KM# 42 10 CENTIMES

Copper-Nickel **Ruler:** Leopold II **Obv:** Denomination and star within shaded circle **Obv. Legend:** LEOPOLD II ROI DES BELGES **Rev:** Rampant lion left within circle **Rev. Legend:** L'UNION FAIT LA FORCE

Date	Mintage	F	VF	XF	Unc	BU
1894	11,886,000	0.75	3.00	7.00	15.00	20.00
1895/4	736,000	30.00	80.00	140	250	—
1895	Inc. above	15.00	80.00	140	250	—
1898	3,499,000	3.00	9.00	20.00	45.00	—
1901	551,000	30.00	140	200	325	375

KM# 43 10 CENTIMES

Copper-Nickel **Ruler:** Leopold II **Obv:** Denomination above star, within circle, legend in Dutch **Obv. Legend:** LEOPOLD II KONING DER BELGEN **Rev:** Rampant lion left within circle **Rev. Legend:** EENDRACHT MAAKT MACHT

Date	Mintage	F	VF	XF	Unc	BU
1894	9,209,000	0.75	3.00	9.00	20.00	25.00
1895/4	3,529,000	9.00	50.00	100	150	—
1895	Inc. above	1.00	9.00	20.00	35.00	—
1898	3,500,000	3.00	9.00	20.00	45.00	—
1901	556,000	30.00	175	225	350	450

KM# 48 10 CENTIMES

Copper-Nickel, 22 mm. **Obv:** Center hole within crowned monogram, small date below, legend in French **Obv. Legend:** BELGIQUE **Rev:** Spray of leaves to left of center hole, denomination to right **Designer:** A. Michaux

Date	Mintage	F	VF	XF	Unc	BU
1901	582,000	6.00	15.00	40.00	130	—
1902/1	5,866,000	0.50	3.00	15.00	30.00	—
1902	Inc. above	0.15	1.00	3.00	7.00	—
1903	763,000	1.00	4.00	15.00	35.00	—

KM# 49 10 CENTIMES

Copper-Nickel, 22 mm. **Obv:** Center hole within crowned monogram, date below, legend in Dutch, **Obv. Legend:** BELGIE **Rev:** Spray of leaves to left of center hole, denomination to right **Designer:** A. Michaux

Date	Mintage	F	VF	XF	Unc	BU
1902	1,560,000	0.20	2.00	8.00	15.00	—
1903/2	—	0.50	1.25	7.00	20.00	—
1903	5,658,000	0.20	1.00	2.50	7.00	—

KM# 52 10 CENTIMES

3.9000 g., Copper-Nickel, 22.6 mm. **Obv:** Center hole within crowned monogram, large date below, legend in French **Obv. Legend:** BELGIQUE **Rev:** Spray of leaves to left center hole, denomination to right **Designer:** A. Michaux

Date	Mintage	F	VF	XF	Unc	BU
1903	Inc. above	2.00	15.00	30.00	55.00	—
1904	16,354,000	0.15	1.00	3.00	7.00	—
1905/4	14,392,000	0.25	1.00	5.00	15.00	—
1905	Inc. above	0.15	0.60	2.00	7.00	—
1906/5	1,483,000	0.50	1.50	5.00	18.00	—
1906	Inc. above	0.25	0.75	5.00	15.00	—

KM# 53 10 CENTIMES

Copper-Nickel, 22 mm. **Obv:** Center hole within crowned monogram, large date below, legend in Dutch **Obv. Legend:** BELGIE **Rev:** Spray of leaves to left of center hole, denomination to right **Designer:** A. Michaux

Date	Mintage	F	VF	XF	Unc	BU
1903	Inc. above	1.00	4.00	15.00	35.00	—
1904	16,834,000	0.20	0.50	2.00	7.00	—
1905/3	13,758,000	0.35	1.00	3.00	15.00	—
1905/4	Inc. above	0.30	1.00	3.00	15.00	—
1905	Inc. above	0.20	0.50	2.00	7.00	—
1906/5	2,017,000	0.50	1.25	4.00	15.00	—
Note: Point above center of 6						
1906/5	Inc. above	0.50	1.25	4.00	15.00	—
Note: Point above right side of 6						
1906	Inc. above	0.10	0.75	5.00	18.00	—

KM# 81 10 CENTIMES

3.9500 g., Zinc **Obv:** Denomination within circle, date below, legend in French **Obv. Legend:** BELGIQUE-BELGIE **Rev:** Rampant lion, left, within circle **Note:** German Occupation. All of KM#81 have dots after the date. The 1916 is distinguished by a period after the date.

Date	Mintage	F	VF	XF	Unc	BU
1915	9,681,000	0.25	1.50	4.00	15.00	30.00
1916/15	37,382,000	20.00	30.00	100	175	225
.1916.	Inc. above	0.15	0.75	3.00	10.00	20.00
Note: With dots before and after date						
.1916	Inc. above	7.00	15.00	50.00	100	—
Note: With dot before date only						
1916.	Inc. above	10.00	25.00	100	200	—
Note: With dot after date only						
1917	1,447,000	17.50	25.00	85.00	200	—

KM# 85.1 10 CENTIMES

Copper-Nickel, 22 mm. **Obv:** Center hole within crowned monogram, date below, legend in French **Obv. Legend:** BELGIQUE **Rev:** Spray of leaves to left of center hole, denomination to right **Designer:** A. Michaux

Date	Mintage	F	VF	XF	Unc	BU
1911	—	—	—	—	—	—
Note: Struck at a later date						
1920	6,520,000	0.15	0.40	1.50	4.50	—
1921	7,215,000	0.15	0.20	1.00	4.00	—
1923	20,625,000	0.10	0.20	1.00	4.00	—
1926/3	6,916,000	0.20	0.75	3.00	12.00	—
1926/5	Inc. above	0.20	0.75	3.00	12.00	—
1926	Inc. above	0.15	0.20	1.00	4.00	—
1927	8,125,000	0.15	0.20	1.00	4.00	—
1928/3	6,895,000	0.20	1.00	4.00	10.00	—
1928/5	Inc. above	0.20	1.00	4.00	10.00	—
1928	Inc. above	0.15	0.20	1.00	4.00	—
1929	12,260,000	0.15	0.20	1.00	4.00	—

KM# 85.2 10 CENTIMES

Copper-Nickel, 22 mm. **Rev:** Single line below ES of CES **Designer:** A. Michaux

Date	Mintage	F	VF	XF	Unc	BU
1920	Inc. above	0.50	3.00	10.00	20.00	—
1921	Inc. above	1.50	10.00	18.00	45.00	—

KM# 86 10 CENTIMES

Copper-Nickel, 22 mm. **Obv:** Center hole within crowned monogram, date below, legend in Dutch **Obv. Legend:** BELGIE **Rev:** Spray of leaves to left of center hole, denomination to right, plain field above 10 **Edge:** Plain **Designer:** A. Michaux

Date	Mintage	F	VF	XF	Unc	BU
1920	5,050,000	0.15	0.20	1.00	5.00	—
1921	7,580,000	0.15	0.20	1.00	4.00	—
1922	6,250,000	0.15	0.20	1.00	4.00	—
1924	5,825,000	0.15	0.20	1.00	6.00	—
1925/4	8,160,000	0.20	0.40	2.00	10.00	—
1925/3	Inc. above	0.20	0.40	2.00	10.00	—
1925	Inc. above	0.10	0.20	1.00	4.00	—
1926/5	6,250,000	0.20	0.40	2.00	10.00	—
1926/3	Inc. above	0.20	0.40	2.00	10.00	—
1926	Inc. above	0.15	0.20	1.00	4.00	—
1927	10,625,000	0.15	0.20	1.00	4.00	—
1928/5	6,750,000	0.20	0.40	2.00	10.00	—
1928/3	Inc. above	0.20	0.40	2.00	10.00	—
1928	Inc. above	0.15	0.20	1.00	4.00	—
1929	4,668,000	0.15	0.20	1.00	4.00	—
1930	—	15.00	30.00	100	250	—

KM# 95.1 10 CENTIMES

Nickel-Brass, 22 mm. **Obv:** Legend in French **Obv. Legend:** BELGIQUE **Rev:** Star added above 10

Date	Mintage	F	VF	XF	Unc	BU
1930/20	2,000,000	50.00	120	275	450	—
1930	Inc. above	20.00	100	250	400	—
1931	6,270,000	5.00	10.00	20.00	50.00	—
1932	1,270,000	35.00	200	300	450	—
1932	Inc. above	50.00	220	350	500	—
Note: A instead of signature						

KM# 95.2 10 CENTIMES

Nickel-Brass, 22 mm. **Rev:** Single line below ES of CES

Date	Mintage	F	VF	XF	Unc	BU
1931	Inc. above	2.00	8.00	20.00	50.00	—
1932	Inc. above	45.00	200	350	500	—

KM# 96 10 CENTIMES

Nickel-Brass, 22 mm. **Obv:** Center hole within crowned monogram, date below, legend in Dutch **Obv. Legend:** BELGIE **Rev:** Spray of leaves to left of center hole, denomination to right, star added above 10 **Designer:** A. Michaux

Date	Mintage	F	VF	XF	Unc	BU
1930	1,581,000	0.30	0.75	3.00	10.00	—
1931	5,000,000	25.00	100	200	350	—

KM# 112 10 CENTIMES

Nickel-Brass, 22 mm. **Obv:** Three shields above denomination, hole at center, legend in French **Obv. Legend:** BELGIQUE-BELGIE **Rev:** Crowned design above date, hole at center

Date	Mintage	F	VF	XF	Unc	BU
1938	6,000,000	0.10	0.25	0.50	1.50	—
1939	7,000,000	0.50	1.00	3.00	15.00	—

KM# 113.1 10 CENTIMES

Nickel-Brass, 22 mm. **Obv:** Three shields above denomination, hole at center, legend in Dutch **Obv. Legend:** BELGIE-BELGIQUE **Rev:** Crowned design above date, hole at center

Date	Mintage	F	VF	XF	Unc	BU
1939	8,425,000	0.10	0.25	0.50	1.50	—

KM# 113.2 10 CENTIMES

Nickel-Brass, 22 mm. **Note:** Thin flan.

Date	Mintage	F	VF	XF	Unc	BU
1939	Inc. above	1.25	3.00	10.00	35.00	—

KM# 126 10 CENTIMES

Zinc, 22 mm. **Obv:** Three shields above denomination, hole at center, legend in Dutch **Obv. Legend:** BELGIE-BELGIQUE **Rev:** Crowned design above date, hole at center **Edge:** Plain

Date	Mintage	F	VF	XF	Unc	BU
1941	7,000,000	0.15	2.00	5.00	10.00	—
1942	21,000,000	0.15	0.25	1.50	4.00	—
1943	22,000,000	0.15	0.25	1.50	4.00	—
1944	28,140,000	0.15	0.25	1.50	4.00	—
1945	8,000,000	0.15	2.00	5.00	10.00	—
1946	5,370,000	0.15	1.00	2.00	8.00	—

KM# 125 10 CENTIMES

Zinc, 22 mm. **Obv:** Three shields above denomination, hole at center, legend in French **Obv. Legend:** BELGIQUE-BELGIE **Rev:** Crowned design above date, hole at center **Edge:** Plain **Note:** German Occupation WW II.

Date	Mintage	F	VF	XF	Unc	BU
1941	10,000,000	0.15	0.25	1.50	4.00	—
1942	17,000,000	0.15	0.25	1.50	4.00	—

Date	Mintage	F	VF	XF	Unc	BU
1943	22,500,000	0.15	0.25	1.50	4.00	—
1945	—	—	—	—	—	—
Note: Struck at a later date						
1946	Est. 10,370,000	—	—	—	—	—
Note: Not released for circulation						

KM# 146 20 CENTIMES

Bronze, 17 mm. **Obv:** Crowned denomination divides date, legend in French **Obv. Legend:** BELGIQUE **Rev:** Helmeted head, left, small miner's lamp at right **Edge:** Plain

Date	Mintage	F	VF	XF	Unc	BU
1953	14,150,000	—	0.10	0.20	0.50	—
1953	—	—	0.10	0.75	2.50	—
Note: CENTIMES not touching rim						
1954	—	—	600	800	1,000	—
Note: Considered by some to be an Essai						
1957	13,300,000	—	—	0.10	0.50	—
1958	8,700,000	—	—	0.10	0.50	—
1959	19,670,000	—	—	0.10	0.50	—
1962	410,000	—	6.00	10.00	18.00	—
1963	2,550,000	0.10	0.20	0.50	1.00	—

KM# 147.1 20 CENTIMES

Bronze, 17 mm. **Obv:** Crowned denomination divides date, legend in Dutch **Obv. Legend:** BELGIE **Rev:** Helmeted head, left, small miner's lamp at right **Edge:** Plain

Date	Mintage	F	VF	XF	Unc	BU
1954	50,130,000	—	—	0.10	0.50	—
1960	7,530,000	—	—	0.10	0.50	—

KM# 147.2 20 CENTIMES

Bronze, 17 mm. **Obv:** CENTIMES touching rim **Edge:** Plain

Date	Mintage	F	VF	XF	Unc	BU
1954	Inc. above	—	0.15	0.75	2.50	—
1960	Inc. above	—	0.15	0.75	2.50	—

KM# 62 25 CENTIMES

Copper-Nickel **Obv:** Center hole within crowned monogram, date below, legend in French **Obv. Legend:** BELGIQUE **Rev:** Spray of leaves to left of center hole, denomination to right **Designer:** A. Michaux

Date	Mintage	F	VF	XF	Unc	BU
1908	4,007,000	0.50	4.00	20.00	50.00	—
1909/8	1,998,000	4.00	40.00	150	275	—
1909	Inc. above	1.00	8.00	30.00	70.00	—

KM# 63 25 CENTIMES

Copper-Nickel **Obv:** Center hole within crowned monogram, date below, legend in Dutch **Obv. Legend:** BELGIE **Rev:** Spray of leaves to left of center hole, denomination to right **Designer:** A. Michaux

Date	Mintage	F	VF	XF	Unc	BU
1908	4,011,000	0.50	4.00	20.00	50.00	—

KM# 69 25 CENTIMES

6.4500 g., Copper-Nickel, 25.8 mm. **Obv:** Center hole within crowned monogram, date below, legend in Dutch **Obv. Legend:** BELGIE **Rev:** Sprays to left of center hole, denomination to right **Designer:** A. Michaux

Date	Mintage	F	VF	XF	Unc	BU
1910	2,006,000	0.15	1.00	8.00	20.00	—
1911	—	—	—	—	—	—
Note: Struck at a later date						
1913	2,010,000	0.15	3.00	8.00	20.00	—
1921	11,173,000	0.15	0.25	2.00	6.00	—
1922/1	14,200,000	1.00	10.00	20.00	45.00	—
1922	Inc. above	0.15	0.25	2.00	6.00	—
1926/3	6,400,000	0.35	6.00	12.00	25.00	—
1926	Inc. above	0.10	0.40	2.00	6.00	—
1927/3	3,799,000	0.35	5.00	10.00	25.00	—
1927	Inc. above	0.10	0.25	2.00	8.00	—
1928	9,200,000	0.10	0.25	2.00	6.00	—
1929	8,980,000	0.10	0.25	2.00	6.00	—

KM# 68.1 25 CENTIMES

Copper-Nickel **Obv:** Center hole within crowned monogram, date below, legend in French **Obv. Legend:** BELGIQUE **Rev:** Spray of leaves to left of center hole, denomination to right **Designer:** A. Michaux

Date	Mintage	F	VF	XF	Unc	BU
1913	2,011,000	0.15	3.00	8.00	20.00	—
1920	2,844,000	0.15	2.00	7.00	18.00	—
1921	7,464,000	0.10	0.25	2.00	6.00	—
1922	7,600,000	0.10	0.25	2.00	6.00	—
1923	11,356,000	0.15	0.25	2.00	6.00	—
1926/3	1,300,000	1.00	5.00	12.00	30.00	—
1926	Inc. above	0.50	5.00	12.00	30.00	—
1927/3	8,800,000	1.00	10.00	20.00	45.00	—
1927	Inc. above	0.10	0.25	2.00	6.00	—
1928	4,351,000	0.10	1.00	2.00	8.00	—
1929	9,600,000	0.10	0.25	2.00	6.00	—

KM# 68.2 25 CENTIMES

Copper-Nickel **Rev:** Single line below ES of CES

Date	Mintage	F	VF	XF	Unc	BU
1920	Inc. above	0.50	2.00	8.00	25.00	—
1921	Inc. above	0.35	1.50	6.00	15.00	—

KM# 82 25 CENTIMES

6.4200 g., Zinc, 25.7 mm. **Obv:** Denomination within beaded circle, stars flank date below, legend in French **Obv. Legend:** BELGIQUE-BELGIE **Rev:** Rampant lion left within beaded circle **Note:** German Occupation WW I

Date	Mintage	F	VF	XF	Unc	BU
1915	8,080,000	0.50	4.00	9.00	22.00	—
1916	10,671,000	0.50	3.00	7.00	15.00	—
1917	3,555,000	2.00	10.00	18.00	40.00	—
1918	5,489,000	1.00	8.00	12.00	30.00	—

KM# 114.1 25 CENTIMES

Nickel-Brass **Obv:** Three shields above denomination, hole in center, legend in French **Obv. Legend:** BELGIQUE-BELGIE **Rev:** Crowned design above date, hole in center

Date	Mintage	F	VF	XF	Unc	BU
1938	7,200,000	—	0.25	1.00	4.00	—
1939	7,732,000	—	0.25	1.00	4.00	—

KM# 114.2 25 CENTIMES

Nickel-Brass **Note:** Medal alignment.

Date	Mintage	F	VF	XF	Unc	BU
1939	Inc. above	5.00	10.00	20.00	35.00	—

KM# 115.1 25 CENTIMES

Nickel-Brass **Obv:** Three shields above denomination, hole at center, legend in Dutch **Obv. Legend:** BELGIE-BELGIQUE **Rev:** Crowned design above date, hole at center

Date	Mintage	F	VF	XF	Unc	BU
1938	14,932,000	—	0.25	1.00	3.00	—

KM# 115.2 25 CENTIMES

Nickel-Brass **Note:** Medal alignment.

Date	Mintage	F	VF	XF	Unc	BU
1938	Inc. above	5.00	10.00	20.00	30.00	—

KM# 131 25 CENTIMES

Zinc **Obv:** Three shields above denomination, hole at center, legend in French **Obv. Legend:** BELGIQUE-BELGIE **Rev:** Crowned design above date, hole at center **Note:** German Occupation WW II.

Date	Mintage	F	VF	XF	Unc	BU
1941 Rare	—	—	—	—	—	—
1942	14,400,000	—	0.20	0.75	3.00	10.00
1943	21,600,000	—	0.20	0.75	3.00	10.00
1945	—	—	—	—	—	—
Note: Struck at a later date						
1946	21,428,000	—	0.20	0.75	3.00	10.00
1947	Est. 300,000	—	—	—	—	—
Note: Not released for circulation						

KM# 132 25 CENTIMES

Zinc **Obv:** Three shields above denomination, hole at center, legend in Dutch **Obv. Legend:** BELGIE-BELGIQUE **Rev:** Crowned design above date, hole at center

Date	Mintage	F	VF	XF	Unc	BU
1942	14,400,000	—	1.00	2.00	6.00	18.00
1943	21,600,000	—	0.20	0.75	3.00	10.00
1944	25,960,000	—	0.20	0.75	3.00	10.00
1945	8,200,000	—	0.50	2.50	8.00	22.00
1946	11,652,000	—	0.50	2.50	10.00	30.00
1947	Est. 316,000	—	—	—	—	—
Note: Not released for circulation						

KM# 153.1 25 CENTIMES

Copper-Nickel, 16 mm. **Obv:** Large denomination between mint marks, legend in French **Obv. Legend:** BELGIQUE **Rev:** Crowned "B" divides date **Note:** Mint mark - Angel Head. Mintmaster Vogeleer's privy mark - Bird.

Date	Mintage	F	VF	XF	Unc	BU
1964	21,770,000	—	—	0.10	0.15	—
1965	11,440,000	—	—	0.10	0.15	—
1966	19,990,000	—	—	0.10	0.15	—
1967	6,820,000	—	—	0.10	0.50	—
1968	25,250,000	—	—	0.10	0.15	—
1969	7,670,000	—	—	0.10	0.30	—
1970	27,000,000	—	—	0.10	0.15	—
1971	16,000,000	—	—	0.10	0.15	—
1972	20,000,000	—	—	0.10	0.15	—
1973	12,500,000	—	—	0.10	0.15	—
1974	20,000,000	—	—	0.10	0.15	—
1975	12,000,000	—	—	0.10	0.15	—

KM# 153.2 25 CENTIMES

Copper-Nickel, 16 mm. **Note:** Medal alignment. Mint mark - Angel Head. Mintmaster Vogeleer's privy mark - Bird.

Date	Mintage	F	VF	XF	Unc	BU
1964	Inc. above	—	—	5.00	12.00	—
1965	Inc. above	—	—	10.00	25.00	—
1967	Inc. above	—	—	10.00	25.00	—

Date	Mintage	F	VF	XF	Unc	BU
1970	Inc. above	—	—	5.00	12.00	—
1971	Inc. above	—	—	5.00	12.00	—
1974	Inc. above	—	—	10.00	25.00	—

KM# 154.1 25 CENTIMES

Copper-Nickel, 16 mm. **Obv:** Large denomination between mint marks, legend in Dutch **Obv. Legend:** BELGIE **Rev:** Crowned "B" divides date **Edge:** Plain **Note:** Mint mark - Angel Head. Mintmaster Vogeleer's privy mark - Bird.

Date	Mintage	F	VF	XF	Unc	BU
1964	21,300,000	—	—	0.10	0.15	—
1965	7,900,000	—	—	0.10	0.30	—
1966	23,420,000	—	—	0.10	0.15	—
1967	7,720,000	—	—	0.10	0.30	—
1968	22,750,000	—	—	0.10	0.15	—
1969	25,190,000	—	—	0.10	0.15	—
1970	12,000,000	—	—	0.10	0.15	—
1971	16,000,000	—	—	0.10	0.15	—
1972	20,000,000	—	—	0.10	0.15	—
1973	12,500,000	—	—	0.10	0.15	—
1974	20,000,000	—	—	0.10	0.15	—
1975	12,000,000	—	—	0.10	0.15	—

KM# 154.2 25 CENTIMES

Copper-Nickel, 16 mm. **Edge:** Plain **Note:** Medal alignment. Mint mark - Angel Head. Mintmaster Vogeleer's privy mark - Bird.

Date	Mintage	F	VF	XF	Unc	BU
1964	Inc. above	—	—	5.00	12.00	—
1965	Inc. above	—	—	5.00	15.00	—
1966	Inc. above	—	—	5.00	12.00	—
1967	Inc. above	—	—	6.00	15.00	—
1969	Inc. above	—	—	5.00	12.00	—
1971	Inc. above	—	—	6.00	15.00	—
1972	Inc. above	—	—	5.00	12.00	—

KM# 50 50 CENTIMES

2.5000 g., 0.8350 Silver 0.0671 oz. ASW **Obv:** Bearded head of Leopold II, left, legend in French **Obv. Legend:** DES BELGES **Rev:** Tablet to right of seated lion, looking left, denomination below, date to left of lion

Date	Mintage	F	VF	XF	Unc	BU
1901	3,000,000	2.00	8.00	30.00	75.00	160

KM# 51 50 CENTIMES

2.5000 g., 0.8350 Silver 0.0671 oz. ASW **Obv:** Legend in Dutch **Obv. Legend:** DER BELGEN

Date	Mintage	F	VF	XF	Unc	BU
1901	3,000,000	2.00	8.00	30.00	75.00	150

KM# 60.1 50 CENTIMES

2.5000 g., 0.8350 Silver 0.0671 oz. ASW **Obv:** Bearded head of Leopold II, left, legend in French **Obv. Legend:** DES BELGES **Rev:** Denomination above date within wreath

Date	Mintage	F	VF	XF	Unc	BU
1907	545,000	3.00	8.00	18.00	70.00	140
1909	2,503,000	1.00	4.00	12.00	35.00	—

KM# 60.2 50 CENTIMES

2.5000 g., 0.8350 Silver 0.0671 oz. ASW **Obv:** Without period in signature

Date	Mintage	F	VF	XF	Unc	BU
1907	Inc. above	4.00	10.00	25.00	100	140
1909	Inc. above	2.00	5.00	12.00	35.00	—

KM# 61.1 50 CENTIMES

2.5000 g., 0.8350 Silver 0.0671 oz. ASW **Obv:** Bearded head of Leopold II, left, legend in Dutch **Obv. Legend:** DER BELGEN **Rev:** Denomination above date within wreath

Date	Mintage	F	VF	XF	Unc	BU
1907	545,000	3.00	10.00	25.00	70.00	140
1909	2,510,000	1.00	5.00	12.00	35.00	—

KM# 61.2 50 CENTIMES

2.5000 g., 0.8350 Silver 0.0671 oz. ASW **Obv:** Bearded head of Leopold II, left, legend in Dutch **Obv. Legend:** DER BELGEN **Note:** Medal alignment

Date	Mintage	F	VF	XF	Unc	BU
1909	Inc. above	12.50	15.00	45.00	135	180

KM# 70 50 CENTIMES

2.5000 g., 0.8350 Silver 0.0671 oz. ASW **Obv:** Head of Albert, left, legend in French **Obv. Legend:** DES BELGES **Rev:** Denomination above date within wreath

Date	Mintage	F	VF	XF	Unc	BU
1910	1,900,000	1.00	5.00	12.00	30.00	—
1911	2,063,000	3.00	10.00	15.00	60.00	—
1912	1,000,000	0.85	1.25	2.00	6.00	—
1914	240,000	2.50	9.00	15.00	40.00	—

KM# 71 50 CENTIMES

2.5000 g., 0.8350 Silver 0.0671 oz. ASW **Obv:** Head of Albert, left, legend in Dutch **Obv. Legend:** DER BELGEN **Rev:** Denomination above date within wreath

Date	Mintage	F	VF	XF	Unc	BU
1910	1,900,000	3.00	10.00	15.00	60.00	—
1911	2,063,000	0.85	1.25	2.00	6.00	—
1912	1,000,000	0.85	1.25	2.00	6.00	—

KM# 83 50 CENTIMES

Zinc **Obv:** Hole at center of star, tiny stars flank date below, legend in Dutch **Obv. Legend:** BELGIE-BELGIQUE **Rev:** Spray of leaves to left of center hole, denomination to right, small shield with rampant lion on spray **Note:** German Occupation WW I

Date	Mintage	F	VF	XF	Unc	BU
1918	7,394,000	0.50	6.00	10.00	25.00	50.00

KM# 87 50 CENTIMES

Nickel **Obv:** Allegorically female figure of Belgium kneeling, wounded but recovering **Obv. Legend:** BELGIQUE **Rev:** Caduceus divides denomination and dates **Designer:** Bonnitain

Date	Mintage	F	VF	XF	Unc	BU
1922	6,180,000	0.15	0.25	0.50	3.00	—
1923	8,820,000	0.15	0.25	0.50	3.00	—
1927	1,750,000	0.15	0.30	0.50	3.00	—
1928	3,000,000	0.15	0.35	1.00	4.00	—
1929	1,000,000	0.25	0.50	3.00	12.00	—
1930	1,000,000	0.25	0.50	3.00	10.00	—
1932/23	2,530,000	1.00	3.00	10.00	25.00	—
1932	Inc. above	0.15	0.50	1.00	4.00	—
1933	2,861,000	0.15	0.25	0.75	4.00	—

KM# 88 50 CENTIMES

Nickel **Obv:** Allegorically female figure of Belgium kneeling, wounded but recovering **Obv. Legend:** BELGIE **Rev:** Caduceus divides denomination and date **Designer:** Bonnitain

Date	Mintage	F	VF	XF	Unc	BU
1922	—	—	—	—	—	—
Note: Struck at a later date						
1923	15,000,000	0.20	0.25	0.50	3.00	—
1928/3	10,000,000	0.25	0.50	3.00	10.00	—
1928	Inc. above	0.20	0.25	0.50	3.00	—
1930/20	2,252,000	0.50	2.00	3.50	16.00	—
1930	Inc. above	0.20	0.75	2.50	6.00	—
1932/22	—	0.25	3.00	3.00	15.00	—
1932	2,000,000	0.20	0.50	1.00	4.00	—
1933	1,189,000	1.00	5.00	9.00	16.50	—
1934	935,000	75.00	175	225	300	—

KM# 118 50 CENTIMES

Nickel **Obv:** Legend in French **Obv. Legend:** BELGIQUE-BELGIE **Note:** Striking interrupted by the war. Very few coins have been officially released into circulation.

Date	Mintage	F	VF	XF	Unc	BU
1939	15,500,000	200	400	800	1,300	—

KM# 144 50 CENTIMES

2.7500 g., Bronze, 19 mm. **Obv:** Crowned denomination divides date, legend in French **Obv. Legend:** BELGIQUE **Rev:** Helmeted mine worker, left, miner's lamp at r. Large head, tip of neck 1/2 mm from rim **Edge:** Plain **Designer:** Rau

Date	Mintage	F	VF	XF	Unc	BU
1952	3,520,000	—	0.10	0.50	2.50	—
1953	22,620,000	—	—	0.10	0.35	—
1955	29,160,000	—	—	0.10	0.35	—

KM# 145 50 CENTIMES

2.7500 g., Bronze, 19 mm. **Obv:** Crowned denomination divides date, legend in Dutch **Obv. Legend:** BELGIE **Rev:** Helmeted mine worker left, miner's lamp at right, large head **Edge:** Plain **Designer:** Rau

Date	Mintage	F	VF	XF	Unc	BU
1952	5,830,000	—	0.10	0.50	2.00	—
1953	22,930,000	—	—	0.10	0.35	—
1954	15,730,000	—	—	0.10	0.35	—

KM# 148.1 50 CENTIMES

2.7500 g., Bronze, 19 mm. **Ruler:** Baudouin I **Obv:** Crowned denomination divides date, legend in French **Obv. Legend:** BELGIQUE **Rev:** Helmeted miner left, miners lamp at right, smaller head, tip of neck 1mm from rim **Edge:** Plain **Designer:** Rau

Date	Mintage	F	VF	XF	Unc	BU
1958	9,750,000	—	—	0.10	0.25	—
1959	17,350,000	—	—	0.10	0.20	—
1962	6,160,000	—	—	0.10	2.00	—
1964	5,860,000	—	—	0.10	2.00	—
1965	10,320,000	—	—	0.10	0.15	—
1966	11,040,000	—	—	0.10	0.15	—
1967	7,200,000	—	—	0.10	0.15	—
1968	2,000,000	—	—	0.10	2.00	—
1969	10,000,000	—	—	0.10	0.15	—
1970	16,000,000	—	—	0.10	0.15	—
1971	1,250,000	—	—	0.10	2.00	—
1972	3,000,000	—	—	0.10	0.15	—
1973	3,000,000	—	—	0.10	0.15	—
1974	5,000,000	—	—	0.10	0.15	—
1974 Wide rim	Inc. above	—	—	0.10	0.15	—
1975	7,000,000	—	—	0.10	0.15	—
1976	8,000,000	—	—	0.10	0.15	—
1977	13,000,000	—	—	0.10	0.15	—
1978	2,500,000	—	—	0.10	1.00	—
1979	20,000,000	—	—	0.10	0.15	—
1980	20,000,000	—	—	0.10	0.15	—
1981	2,000,000	—	—	0.10	1.00	—
1982	7,000,000	—	—	0.10	0.15	—
1983	14,100,000	—	—	0.10	0.15	—
1985	6,000,000	—	—	0.10	0.15	—
1987	9,000,000	—	—	0.10	0.15	—
1988	4,500,000	—	—	0.10	0.15	—
1989	60,000	—	—	—	3.00	—
Note: In sets only						
1990	60,000	—	—	—	3.00	—
Note: In sets only						
1991	6,000,000	—	—	—	0.10	—
1992	7,060,000	—	—	0.10	0.15	—
1993	10,000,000	—	—	0.10	0.15	—
1994	10,000,000	—	—	0.10	0.15	—
1995	60,000	—	—	—	2.00	—
Note: In sets only						
1996	11,000,000	—	—	0.10	0.15	—
1997	60,000	—	—	—	2.00	—
Note: In sets only						
1998	30,000,000	—	—	—	0.10	—
1999	60,000	—	—	—	2.00	—

Date	Mintage	F	VF	XF	Unc	BU
Note: In sets only						
2000	60,000	—	—	—	2.00	—
Note: In sets only						
2001	60,000	—	—	—	2.00	—
Note: In sets only						
2001 Proof	5,000	Value: 25.00				
Note: Medal alignment						

KM# 148.2 50 CENTIMES

2.7500 g., Bronze, 19 mm. **Edge:** Plain **Note:** Medal alignment.

Date	Mintage	F	VF	XF	Unc	BU
1953	Inc. above	—	—	15.00	30.00	—
1959	Inc. above	—	—	15.00	30.00	—
1965	Inc. above	—	—	15.00	30.00	—
1966	Inc. above	—	—	15.00	30.00	—
1969	Inc. above	—	—	15.00	30.00	—
1974	Inc. above	—	—	15.00	30.00	—
1976	Inc. above	—	—	15.00	30.00	—
1999 Proof	—	Value: 30.00				
Note: In sets only						
2000 Proof	—	Value: 30.00				
Note: In sets only						
2001 Proof	—	Value: 30.00				
Note: In sets only						

KM# 149.1 50 CENTIMES

2.7500 g., Bronze, 19 mm. **Ruler:** Baudouin I **Obv:** Crowned denomination divides date **Obv. Legend:** BELGIE **Rev:** Helmeted miner left, miners lamp at right, smaller head, legend in Dutch **Edge:** Plain **Designer:** Rau

Date	Mintage	F	VF	XF	Unc	BU
1956	5,640,000	—	—	0.10	0.75	—
1957	13,800,000	—	—	0.10	0.25	—
1958	19,480,000	—	—	0.10	0.20	—
1962	4,150,000	—	—	0.10	2.00	—
1963	1,110,000	—	—	0.10	3.00	—
1964	10,340,000	—	—	0.10	0.15	—
1965	9,590,000	—	—	0.10	0.15	—
1966	6,930,000	—	—	0.10	0.15	—
1967	6,970,000	—	—	0.10	0.15	—
1968	2,000,000	—	—	0.10	1.00	—
1969	10,000,000	—	—	0.10	0.15	—
1970	12,000,000	—	—	0.10	0.15	—
1971	1,250,000	—	—	0.10	1.00	—
1972	7,000,000	—	—	0.10	0.15	—
1973	3,000,000	—	—	0.10	0.15	—
1974	5,000,000	—	—	0.10	0.15	—
1975	7,000,000	—	—	0.10	0.15	—
1976	8,000,000	—	—	0.10	0.15	—
1977	13,000,000	—	—	0.10	0.15	—
1978	2,500,000	—	—	0.10	1.00	—
1979	40,000,000	—	—	0.10	0.15	—
1980	20,000,000	—	—	0.10	0.15	—
1981	2,000,000	—	—	0.10	1.00	—
1982	7,000,000	—	—	0.10	0.15	—
1983	14,100,000	—	—	0.10	0.15	—
1985	6,000,000	—	—	0.10	0.15	—
1987	9,000,000	—	—	0.10	0.15	—
1988	9,000,000	—	—	0.10	0.15	—
1989	60,000	—	—	—	3.00	—
Note: In sets only						
1990	60,000	—	—	—	3.00	—
Note: In sets only						
1991	6,000,000	—	—	—	0.50	—
1992	7,060,000	—	—	0.10	0.15	—
1993	10,000,000	—	—	0.10	0.15	—
1994	10,000,000	—	—	0.10	0.15	—
1995	60,000	—	—	—	2.00	—
Note: In sets only						
1996	11,000,000	—	—	—	0.50	—
1997	60,000	—	—	—	2.00	—
Note: In sets only						
1998	30,000,000	—	—	—	0.10	—
1999	60,000	—	—	—	2.00	—
Note: In sets only						
2000	60,000	—	—	—	2.00	—
Note: In sets only						
2001	60,000	—	—	—	3.00	—
Note: In sets only						
2001 Proof	5,000	Value: 25.00				
Note: Medal alignment						
2007	60,000	—	—	—	2.00	—
Note: In sets only						

KM# 149.2 50 CENTIMES

2.7500 g., Bronze, 19 mm. **Edge:** Plain **Note:** Medal alignment.

Date	Mintage	F	VF	XF	Unc	BU
1953	Inc. above	—	—	15.00	30.00	—
1967	Inc. above	—	—	15.00	30.00	—
1969	Inc. above	—	—	15.00	30.00	—
1979	Inc. above	—	—	15.00	30.00	—
1988	Inc. above	—	—	15.00	30.00	—
1999 Proof	—	Value: 30.00				
Note: In sets only						

Date	Mintage	F	VF	XF	Unc	BU
2000 Proof	—	Value: 30.00				
Note: In sets only						
2001 Proof	—	Value: 30.00				
Note: In sets only						

KM# 56.1 FRANC

5.0000 g., 0.8350 Silver 0.1342 oz. ASW **Obv:** Legend in French **Obv. Legend:** DES BELGES

Date	Mintage	F	VF	XF	Unc	BU
1904	803,000	3.00	14.00	40.00	75.00	160
1909	2,250,000	1.50	10.00	30.00	45.00	—

KM# 56.2 FRANC

5.0000 g., 0.8350 Silver 0.1342 oz. ASW **Obv:** Without period in signature

Date	Mintage	F	VF	XF	Unc	BU
1904	Inc. above	5.00	35.00	60.00	140	325
1909	Inc. above	1.50	10.00	30.00	45.00	—

KM# 57.1 FRANC

5.0000 g., 0.8350 Silver 0.1342 oz. ASW **Obv:** Bearded head of Leopold II, left, legend in Dutch **Obv. Legend:** DER BELGEN **Rev:** Denomination above date within wreath

Date	Mintage	F	VF	XF	Unc	BU
1904	803,000	3.00	14.00	40.00	75.00	—
1909	2,250,000	2.50	10.00	30.00	50.00	—

KM# 57.2 FRANC

5.0000 g., 0.8350 Silver 0.1342 oz. ASW **Obv:** Without period in signature

Date	Mintage	F	VF	XF	Unc	BU
1909	Inc. above	1.50	8.00	30.00	45.00	—

KM# 73.1 FRANC

5.0000 g., 0.8350 Silver 0.1342 oz. ASW, 23 mm. **Obv:** Head of Albert, left, legend in Dutch **Obv. Legend:** DER BELGEN **Rev:** Denomination above date within wreath

Date	Mintage	F	VF	XF	Unc	BU
1910	2,750,000	2.00	15.00	35.00	65.00	145
1911	2,250,000	BV	2.00	5.00	12.00	—
1912	3,250,000	BV	1.50	2.50	5.00	—
1913	3,000,000	BV	1.50	2.50	5.00	—
1914	10,222,000	BV	1.50	2.50	5.00	—
1918	—	300	600	1,400	2,000	—

KM# 73.2 FRANC

5.0000 g., 0.8350 Silver 0.1342 oz. ASW **Note:** Medal alignment.

Date	Mintage	F	VF	XF	Unc	BU
1914	Inc. above	4.50	12.50	50.00	125	275

KM# 72 FRANC

5.0000 g., 0.8350 Silver 0.1342 oz. ASW **Obv:** Legend in French **Obv. Legend:** DES BELGES **Note:** Prev. KM#72.1.

Date	Mintage	F	VF	XF	Unc	BU
1910	2,190,000	1.75	5.00	18.00	35.00	—
1911	2,810,000	BV	2.00	5.00	12.00	—
1912	3,250,000	BV	1.50	2.50	5.00	—
1913	3,000,000	BV	1.50	2.50	5.00	—
1914	10,563,000	BV	1.50	2.50	5.00	—
1917	8,540,000	350	700	1,500	2,000	—
1918	1,469,000	300	600	1,400	2,000	—

KM# 89 FRANC

4.8900 g., Nickel, 22.5 mm. **Obv:** Kneeling figure, legend in French **Obv. Legend:** BELGIQUE **Rev:** Caduceus divides denomination and date **Edge:** Reeded **Designer:** Bonnitain

Date	Mintage	F	VF	XF	Unc	BU
1922	14,000,000	0.15	0.25	1.00	3.00	—
1923	22,500,000	0.15	0.25	1.00	3.00	—
1928/3	5,000,000	0.25	1.50	5.00	12.00	—
1928/7	Inc. above	0.25	1.50	5.00	12.00	—
1928	Inc. above	0.15	0.25	1.00	4.00	—
1929	7,415,000	0.15	0.25	1.00	3.50	—
1930	5,365,000	0.15	0.25	1.00	5.00	—
1931	—	250	700	1,000	1,800	—
1933	1,998,000	0.25	1.50	5.00	15.00	—
1934/24	10,263,000	0.25	1.50	6.00	12.00	—
1934	Inc. above	0.15	0.25	1.00	3.00	—

KM# 90 FRANC

Nickel, 22.5 mm. **Obv:** Kneeling figure, legend in Dutch **Obv. Legend:** BELGIE **Rev:** Caduceus divides denomination and date **Edge:** Reeded **Designer:** Bonnitain

Date	Mintage	F	VF	XF	Unc	BU
1922	19,000,000	0.15	0.25	1.00	3.00	—
1923/2	17,500,000	0.20	1.50	4.00	12.00	—
1923	Inc. above	0.15	0.25	1.00	3.00	—
1928/3	4,975,000	0.20	2.00	5.00	12.00	—
1928/7	Inc. above	0.20	2.00	5.00	12.00	—
1928	Inc. above	0.15	0.50	2.00	6.00	—
1929	10,365,000	0.15	0.25	1.00	3.00	—
1933	786,000	200	900	1,200	2,000	—
1934/24	8,025,000	0.35	2.50	7.00	15.00	—
1934	Inc. above	0.15	0.50	1.00	3.00	—
1935/23	2,238,000	1.50	4.00	12.00	35.00	—
1935	Inc. above	0.25	0.75	2.00	6.00	—

KM# 119 FRANC

Nickel, 21.5 mm. **Obv:** Three shields, legend in French **Obv. Legend:** BELGIQUE-BELGIE **Rev:** Seated lion, right, facing left above date, denomination to right

Date	Mintage	F	VF	XF	Unc	BU
1939	46,865,000	0.15	0.25	0.50	1.50	—

KM# 120 FRANC

Nickel, 21.5 mm. **Obv:** Three shields, legend in Dutch **Obv. Legend:** BELGIE-BELGIQUE **Rev:** Seated lion, right, facing left above date, denomination at right

Date	Mintage	F	VF	XF	Unc	BU
1939	36,000,000	0.15	0.25	0.50	1.50	—
1940	10,865,000	0.20	0.40	0.75	2.50	—

KM# 127 FRANC

Zinc, 21.5 mm. **Obv:** Rampant lion, left on shield, legend in French **Obv. Legend:** BELGIQUE-BELGIE **Rev:** Crowned letter "L"s, backs touching, divide denomination, date below **Edge:** Reeded **Note:** German Occupation WW II.

Date	Mintage	F	VF	XF	Unc	BU
1941	16,000,000	0.20	0.75	1.50	12.00	25.00
1942	25,000,000	0.20	0.75	1.50	5.00	10.00
1943	28,000,000	0.20	0.75	1.50	5.00	10.00
1947	3,175,000	60.00	125	400	700	1,000

KM# 128 FRANC

Zinc, 21.5 mm. **Obv:** Rampant lion, left, on shield, legend in Dutch **Obv. Legend:** BELGIE-BELGIQUE **Rev:** Crowned "L"s, backs touching, divide denomination, date below **Edge:** Reeded

Date	Mintage	F	VF	XF	Unc	BU
1942	42,000,000	0.20	0.75	1.50	5.00	10.00
1943	28,000,000	0.20	0.75	1.50	5.00	10.00
1944	24,190,000	0.20	0.75	1.50	5.00	10.00
1945	15,930,000	0.20	1.00	4.00	12.00	25.00

Date	Mintage	F	VF	XF	Unc	BU
1946	36,000,000	0.20	0.75	1.50	6.00	18.00
1947	3,000,000	25.00	40.00	100	200	350

KM# 142.1 FRANC

4.0000 g., Copper-Nickel, 21 mm. **Obv:** Plant divides denomination , crown at top, legend in French **Obv. Legend:** BELGIQUE **Rev:** Laureate bust, left, small symbol at right, date at left **Rev. Designer:** Rau **Edge:** Reeded

Date	Mintage	F	VF	XF	Unc	BU
1950	13,630,000	—	—	0.10	8.00	—
1951	51,025,000	—	—	0.10	3.00	—
1952	53,205,000	—	—	0.10	5.00	—
1954	4,980,000	—	0.10	0.25	4.00	—
1955	3,960,000	—	0.10	0.25	3.00	—
1956	10,000,000	—	—	0.10	1.00	—
1958	31,750,000	—	—	0.10	1.00	—
1959	9,000,000	—	—	0.10	1.00	—
1960	10,000,000	—	—	0.10	1.00	—
1961	5,030,000	—	—	0.10	2.00	—
1962	12,250,000	—	—	0.10	0.50	—
1963	18,700,000	—	—	0.10	0.50	—
1964	10,110,000	—	—	0.10	0.50	—
1965	10,185,000	—	—	0.10	0.50	—
1966	16,430,000	—	—	0.10	0.50	—
1967	32,945,000	—	—	0.10	0.50	—
1968	8,000,000	—	—	0.10	0.50	—
1969	21,950,000	—	—	0.10	0.50	—
1970	35,500,000	—	—	0.10	0.50	—
1971	10,000,000	—	—	0.10	0.30	—
1972	35,000,000	—	—	0.10	0.30	—
1973	42,500,000	—	—	0.10	0.30	—
1974	30,000,000	—	—	0.10	0.30	—
1975	80,000,000	—	—	0.10	0.30	—
1976	18,000,000	—	—	0.10	0.30	—
1977	68,500,000	—	—	0.10	0.30	—
1978	47,500,000	—	—	0.10	0.30	—
1979	25,000,000	—	—	0.10	0.30	—
1980	66,500,000	—	—	0.10	0.30	—
1981	2,000,000	0.10	0.20	0.50	3.00	—
1988	17,500,000	—	—	0.10	0.30	—

KM# 143.1 FRANC

4.0000 g., Copper-Nickel, 21 mm. **Obv:** Plant divides denomination, crown at top, legend in Dutch **Obv. Legend:** BELGIE **Rev:** Laureate bust, left, date at left, small symbol at right **Rev. Designer:** Rau **Edge:** Reeded

Date	Mintage	F	VF	XF	Unc	BU
1950	10,000,000	—	—	0.10	8.00	—
1951	53,750,000	—	—	0.10	3.00	—
1952	49,145,000	—	—	0.10	5.00	—
1953	9,915,000	—	—	0.10	3.00	—
1954	4,940,000	—	0.10	0.25	4.00	—
1955	3,960,000	—	0.10	0.25	4.00	—
1956	10,040,000	—	—	0.10	1.00	—
1957	18,315,000	—	—	0.10	1.00	—
1958	17,365,000	—	—	0.10	1.00	—
1959	5,830,000	—	—	0.10	2.00	—
1960	5,555,000	—	—	0.10	2.00	—
1961	9,350,000	—	—	0.10	1.00	—
1962	10,720,000	—	—	0.10	0.50	—
1963	23,460,000	—	—	0.10	0.50	—
1964	7,430,000	—	—	0.10	0.50	—
1965	11,190,000	—	—	0.10	0.50	—
1966	20,990,000	—	—	0.10	0.50	—
1967	27,470,000	—	—	0.10	0.50	—
1968	8,170,000	—	—	0.10	0.30	—
1969	21,730,000	—	—	0.10	0.30	—
1970	35,730,000	—	—	0.10	0.30	—
1971	10,000,000	—	—	0.10	0.30	—
1972	35,000,000	—	—	0.10	0.30	—
1973	42,500,000	—	—	0.10	0.30	—
1974	30,000,000	—	—	0.10	0.30	—
1975	80,000,000	—	—	0.10	0.30	—
1976	18,000,000	—	—	0.10	0.30	—
1977	68,500,000	—	—	0.10	0.30	—
1978	47,500,000	—	—	0.10	0.30	—
1979	50,000,000	—	—	0.10	0.30	—
1980	66,500,000	—	—	0.10	0.30	—
1981	2,000,000	—	—	0.10	3.00	—
1988	17,500,000	—	—	0.10	0.30	—

KM# 143.2 FRANC

4.0000 g., Copper-Nickel, 21 mm. **Edge:** Reeded **Note:** Medal alignment.

Date	Mintage	F	VF	XF	Unc	BU
1952	Inc. above	—	10.00	30.00	60.00	—
1958	Inc. above	—	10.00	30.00	60.00	—
1970	Inc. above	—	10.00	30.00	60.00	—
1971	Inc. above	—	10.00	30.00	60.00	—
1973	Inc. above	—	10.00	30.00	60.00	—
1979	Inc. above	—	10.00	30.00	60.00	—

KM# 142.2 FRANC

4.0000 g., Copper-Nickel, 21 mm. **Edge:** Reeded **Note:** Medal alignment.

Date	Mintage	F	VF	XF	Unc	BU
1952	Inc. above	—	10.00	30.00	60.00	—
1959	Inc. above	—	10.00	30.00	60.00	—
1963	Inc. above	—	10.00	30.00	60.00	—
1965	Inc. above	—	10.00	30.00	60.00	—
1970	Inc. above	—	10.00	30.00	60.00	—
1974	Inc. above	—	10.00	30.00	60.00	—
1977	Inc. above	—	10.00	30.00	60.00	—
1978	Inc. above	—	10.00	30.00	60.00	—
1979	Inc. above	—	10.00	30.00	60.00	—

KM# 171 FRANC

Nickel Plated Iron, 18 mm. **Obv:** Head, left, small mark lower right, dutch legend **Obv. Legend:** BOUDEWIJN I **Rev:** Center symbol divides Crown at left from denomination at right and dates, legend in Dutch **Rev. Legend:** BELGIE

Date	Mintage	F	VF	XF	Unc	BU
1989	200,060,000	—	—	—	0.35	—
1989 medal alignment	—	—	10.00	30.00	60.00	—
1990	200,060,000	—	—	—	0.35	—
1990 medal alignment	—	—	10.00	30.00	60.00	—
1991	200,060,000	—	—	—	0.35	—
1991 medal alignment	—	—	10.00	30.00	60.00	—
1992 In sets only	60,000	—	—	—	18.00	—
1993	15,060,000	—	—	—	0.35	—

KM# 170 FRANC

Nickel Plated Iron, 18 mm. **Obv:** Head left, French legend **Obv. Legend:** BAUDOUIN I **Rev:** Center symbol divides Crown on left from denomination on right and dates, legend in French **Rev. Legend:** BELGIQUE

Date	Mintage	F	VF	XF	Unc	BU
1989	200,060,000	—	—	—	0.35	—
1989 medal alignment	—	—	10.00	30.00	60.00	—
1990	200,060,000	—	—	—	0.35	—
1991	200,060,000	—	—	—	0.35	—
1991 medal alignment	—	—	10.00	30.00	60.00	—
1992 In sets only	60,000	—	—	—	18.00	—
1993	15,060,000	—	—	—	0.35	—

KM# 188 FRANC

2.7700 g., Nickel Plated Iron, 18 mm. **Ruler:** Albert II **Obv:** Head left, outline around back of head **Rev:** Vertical line divides date and large denomination, legend in Dutch **Rev. Legend:** BELGIE **Edge:** Plain

Date	Mintage	F	VF	XF	Unc	BU
1994	75,060,000	—	—	—	0.30	—
1995	75,060,000	—	—	—	0.30	—
1996	95,060,000	—	—	—	0.30	—
1997	95,060,000	—	—	—	0.30	—
1998	75,060,000	—	—	—	0.30	—
1999	60,000	—	—	—	3.00	—
Note: In sets only						
1999 Proof	5,000	Value: 25.00				
Note: Medal alignment; in sets only						
2000	60,000	—	—	—	3.00	—
Note: In sets only						
2000 Proof	5,000	Value: 25.00				
Note: Medal alignment; in sets only						
2001	60,000	—	—	—	3.00	—
Note: In sets only						
2001 Proof	5,000	Value: 25.00				
Note: Medal alignment; in sets only						

KM# 187 FRANC

Nickel Plated Iron, 18 mm. **Ruler:** Albert II **Obv:** Head left, outline around back of head **Rev:** Vertical line divides date and large denomination, legend in French **Rev. Legend:** BELGIQUE **Note:** Mint mark - Angel Head. Unknown mintmaster's privy mark - scales.

Date	Mintage	F	VF	XF	Unc	BU
1994	75,060,000	—	—	—	0.30	—
1995	75,060,000	—	—	—	0.30	—
1996	75,060,000	—	—	—	0.30	—
1997	95,060,000	—	—	—	0.30	—
1998	75,060,000	—	—	—	0.30	—
1999	60,000	—	—	—	3.00	—
Note: In sets only						
1999 Proof	5,000	Value: 25.00				
Note: Medal alignment; in sets only						
2000	60,000	—	—	—	3.00	—
Note: In sets only						
2000 Proof	5,000	Value: 25.00				
Note: Medal alignment; in sets only						
2001	60,000	—	—	—	3.00	—
Note: In sets only						
2001 Proof	5,000	Value: 25.00				
Note: Medal alignment; in sets only						

KM# 58.1 2 FRANCS (2 Frank)

10.0000 g., 0.8350 Silver 0.2684 oz. ASW **Obv:** Legend in French **Obv. Legend:** DES BELGES

Date	Mintage	F	VF	XF	Unc	BU
1904	400,000	6.00	20.00	55.00	100	250
1909	1,088,000	3.50	10.00	30.00	50.00	—

KM# 58.2 2 FRANCS (2 Frank)

10.0000 g., 0.8350 Silver 0.2684 oz. ASW **Obv:** Without period in signature

Date	Mintage	F	VF	XF	Unc	BU
1904	Inc. above	9.00	50.00	120	225	500

KM# 59 2 FRANCS (2 Frank)

10.0000 g., 0.8350 Silver 0.2684 oz. ASW **Obv:** Bearded head of Leopold II, left, legend in Dutch **Obv. Legend:** DER BELGEN **Rev:** Denomination above date within wreath

Date	Mintage	F	VF	XF	Unc	BU
1904	400,000	6.00	20.00	55.00	100	—
1909	1,088,000	3.50	10.00	30.00	50.00	—

KM# 74 2 FRANCS (2 Frank)

10.0000 g., 0.8350 Silver 0.2684 oz. ASW **Obv:** Head of Albert, left, legend in French **Obv. Legend:** DES BELGES **Rev:** Denomination above date within wreath

Date	Mintage	F	VF	XF	Unc	BU
1910	800,000	BV	10.00	25.00	50.00	—
1911	1,000,000	BV	7.00	15.00	30.00	—
1912	375,000	3.50	15.00	30.00	55.00	—

KM# 75 2 FRANCS (2 Frank)

10.0000 g., 0.8350 Silver 0.2684 oz. ASW **Obv:** Head of Albert, left, legend in Dutch **Obv. Legend:** DER BELGEN **Rev:** Denomination above date within wreath

Date	Mintage	F	VF	XF	Unc	BU
1911	1,775,000	BV	4.00	10.00	25.00	—
1912	375,000	BV	10.00	20.00	50.00	—

KM# 91.1 2 FRANCS (2 Frank)
Nickel **Obv:** Kneeling figure, legend in French **Obv. Legend:** BELGIQUE **Rev:** Caduceus divides denomination and date

Date	Mintage	F	VF	XF	Unc	BU
1923	7,500,000	0.50	2.00	8.00	20.00	—
1930/20	1,250,000	12.00	60.00	140	250	—
1930	Inc. above	10.00	50.00	100	200	—

KM# 92 2 FRANCS (2 Frank)
Nickel **Obv:** Kneeling figure, legend in Dutch **Obv. Legend:** BELGIE **Rev:** Caduceus divides denomination and date

Date	Mintage	F	VF	XF	Unc	BU
1923	6,500,000	0.25	3.00	10.00	25.00	—
1924	1,000,000	5.00	20.00	45.00	100	—
1930/20	1,252,000	15.00	55.00	125	250	—
1930	Inc. above	8.00	45.00	100	200	—

KM# 91.2 2 FRANCS (2 Frank)
Nickel **Note:** Medal alignment

Date	Mintage	F	VF	XF	Unc	BU
1923	Inc. above	5.00	8.00	45.00	110	—

KM# 133 2 FRANCS (2 Frank)
2.6800 g., Zinc Coated Steel, 19 mm. **Obv:** Sprays below legend, small star at top, legend in French **Obv. Legend:** BELGIQUE-BELGIE **Rev:** Denomination flanked by sprays, date below **Edge:** Plain **Note:** Allied Occupation issue. Made in U.S.A. on blanks for 1943 cents.

Date	Mintage	F	VF	XF	Unc	BU
1944	25,000,000	0.25	0.50	1.50	5.00	10.00

KM# 133a 2 FRANCS (2 Frank)
Silver **Note:** Made in error in U.S.A. on blanks for Netherlands 25 cents.

Date	Mintage	F	VF	XF	Unc	BU
1944	—	200	300	325	450	700

KM# 97.1 5 FRANCS (5 Frank)
13.8900 g., Nickel, 31 mm. **Obv:** Head of Albert, left **Obv. Legend:** DES BELGES **Rev:** Wreath surrounds denomination and date, crown at top, value: UN BELGA **Note:** All dates exist in position A and B, values are the same.

Date	Mintage	F	VF	XF	Unc	BU
1930	1,600,000	1.50	6.00	12.00	25.00	—
1931	9,032,000	1.00	4.00	10.00	20.00	—
1932	3,600,000	1.50	7.00	14.00	30.00	—
1933	1,387,000	6.00	15.00	35.00	80.00	—
1934	1,000,000	30.00	75.00	160	350	—

KM# 98 5 FRANCS (5 Frank)
Nickel **Obv:** Head of Albert, legend in Dutch **Obv. Legend:** DER BELGEN **Rev:** Denomination and date within wreath, Crown at top, value: EEN BELGA **Note:** All dates exist in position A and B, values are the same.

Date	Mintage	F	VF	XF	Unc	BU
1930	5,086,000	2.00	8.00	16.00	40.00	—
1931	5,336,000	1.50	6.00	12.00	25.00	—
1932	3,683,000	1.50	7.00	14.00	30.00	—
1933	2,514,000	8.00	20.00	40.00	80.00	—

KM# 97.2 5 FRANCS (5 Frank)
Nickel **Note:** Medal alignment. Edge varieties exist.

Date	Mintage	F	VF	XF	Unc	BU
1930	Inc. above	17.50	50.00	150	350	—

KM# 108 5 FRANCS (5 Frank)
Nickel, 31 mm. **Obv. Designer:** Rau **Rev:** Crown above denomination, sprays below **Rev. Legend:** BELGIQUE **Note:** Both dates exist in position A and B, values are the same. Prev. KM#108.1.

Date	Mintage	F	VF	XF	Unc	BU
1936	650,000	6.00	25.00	50.00	85.00	—
1937	1,848,000	6.00	20.00	40.00	70.00	—

KM# 109.1 5 FRANCS (5 Frank)
Nickel, 31 mm. **Obv:** Head of Leopold III, left, small date, lower right **Obv. Designer:** Rau **Rev:** Crown above denomination, sprays below, legend in Dutch **Rev. Legend:** BELGIE **Note:** Both dates exist in position A and B, values are the same.

Date	Mintage	F	VF	XF	Unc	BU
1936	2,498,000	4.00	15.00	35.00	50.00	—

KM# 109.2 5 FRANCS (5 Frank)
Nickel **Note:** Medal alignment. Edge varieties exist.

Date	Mintage	F	VF	XF	Unc	BU
1936	Inc. above	15.00	50.00	150	325	—

KM# 117.1 5 FRANCS (5 Frank)
Nickel **Obv:** Three shields, legend in Dutch **Obv. Legend:** BELGIE-BELGIQUE **Rev:** Seated lion, right, looking left, date below, denomination at right **Note:** Milled edge, lettering with crown.

Date	Mintage	F	VF	XF	Unc	BU
1938 Position A	3,200,000	20.00	50.00	80.00	125	—
1938 Position B	Inc. above	20.00	50.00	80.00	125	—
1939 Position A	8,219,000	20.00	50.00	80.00	125	—
1939 Position B	Inc. above	20.00	50.00	80.00	125	—

KM# 117.2 5 FRANCS (5 Frank)
9.0400 g., Nickel **Note:** Milled edge, lettering with star.

Date	Mintage	F	VF	XF	Unc	BU
1938 Position B	Inc. above	25.00	60.00	90.00	160	—
1938 Position A	Inc. above	25.00	60.00	90.00	160	—
1939 Position A	Inc. above	0.15	2.00	3.00	5.00	—
1939 Position B	Inc. above	0.15	2.00	3.00	5.00	—

KM# 117.3 5 FRANCS (5 Frank)
Nickel **Note:** Milled edge, without lettering (error).

Date	Mintage	F	VF	XF	Unc	BU
1939	Inc. above	30.00	60.00	175	350	—

KM# 116.1 5 FRANCS (5 Frank)
Nickel **Obv:** Three shields, legend in French **Obv. Legend:** BELGIQUE-BELGIE **Rev:** Seated lion, right, looking left, denomination at right, date below **Note:** Milled edge lettering with crown.

Date	Mintage	F	VF	XF	Unc	BU
1938 Position A	11,419,000	0.20	4.00	7.00	10.00	—
1938 Position B	Inc. above	0.30	4.00	7.00	10.00	—

KM# 116.2 5 FRANCS (5 Frank)
Nickel **Note:** Milled edge, lettering with star.

Date	Mintage	F	VF	XF	Unc	BU
1939 Position A	Inc. above	500	1,200	2,000	3,000	—
1939 Position B	Inc. above	500	1,200	2,000	3,000	—

KM# 116.3 5 FRANCS (5 Frank)
Nickel **Note:** Milled edge, without lettering (error).

Date	Mintage	F	VF	XF	Unc	BU
1938	Inc. above	40.00	70.00	135	300	—

KM# 129.1 5 FRANCS (5 Frank)
Zinc, 24.8 mm. **Obv:** Head of Leopold III, right, legend in French **Obv. Legend:** DES BELGES **Obv. Designer:** Rau **Rev:** Crown above large decorated denomination, flanked by symbols, date at bottom **Edge:** Reeded **Note:** German Occupation WW II.

Date	Mintage	F	VF	XF	Unc	BU
1941	15,200,000	1.00	2.50	5.00	12.00	—
1943	16,236,000	1.00	2.50	5.00	12.00	—
1944	1,868,000	6.00	17.00	35.00	65.00	—
1945	3,200,000	2.00	5.00	10.00	25.00	—
1946	4,452,000	5.00	12.00	20.00	35.00	—
1947	3,100,000	30.00	80.00	150	240	—

KM# 129.2 5 FRANCS (5 Frank)
Zinc, 24.8 mm. **Note:** Medal alignment.

Date	Mintage	F	VF	XF	Unc	BU
1943	Inc. above	5.00	15.00	50.00	130	—

KM# 130 5 FRANCS (5 Frank)
Zinc, 24.8 mm. **Obv:** Head of Leopold III, right, legend in Dutch **Obv. Legend:** DER BELGEN **Obv. Designer:** Rau **Rev:** Crown above large decorated denomination flanked by symbols, date at bottom

Date	Mintage	F	VF	XF	Unc	BU
1941	27,544,000	0.75	2.00	4.00	10.00	—
1945	3,200,000	30.00	80.00	125	200	—
1946 Rare	4,000,000	—	—	—	—	—
1947	36,000	175	650	900	1,500	—

KM# 134.1 5 FRANCS (5 Frank)
6.0000 g., Copper-Nickel, 24 mm. **Obv:** Plant divides denomination, Crown at top, legend in French **Obv. Legend:** BELGIQUE **Obv. Designer:** Rau **Rev:** Laureate head, left, small diamonds flank date at left, symbol at right **Edge:** Reeded

Date	Mintage	F	VF	XF	Unc	BU
1948	5,304,000	—	4.00	10.00	25.00	—
1949	38,752,000	—	—	1.00	6.00	—
1950	23,948,000	—	—	1.00	6.00	—
1958	9,088,000	—	—	1.00	3.00	—
1961	6,000,000	—	—	1.00	3.00	—
1962	6,576,000	—	—	1.00	3.00	—
1963	11,144,000	—	—	1.00	3.00	—
1964	3,520,000	—	1.00	2.00	5.00	—
1965	11,988,000	—	—	1.00	3.00	—
1966	6,772,000	—	—	1.00	3.00	—
1967	13,268,000	—	—	1.00	3.00	—
1968	5,192,000	—	1.00	2.00	4.00	—
1969	22,235,000	—	—	1.00	3.00	—
1969	Inc. above	3.00	5.00	10.00	20.00	—
Note: Without engraver's name						
1970	2,000,000	—	1.00	2.00	5.00	—
1971	15,000,000	—	—	0.20	0.50	—
1972	17,500,000	—	—	0.20	0.50	—
1973	10,000,000	—	—	0.20	0.50	—
1974	25,000,000	—	—	0.20	0.50	—
1975	34,000,000	—	—	0.20	0.50	—
1975	—	1.00	5.00	8.00	15.00	—
Note: Without engraver's name						
1976	7,500,000	—	—	0.20	0.75	—
1977	22,500,000	—	—	0.20	0.50	—
1978	27,500,000	—	—	0.20	0.50	—
1979	5,000,000	—	—	0.50	1.00	—
1980	11,000,000	—	—	0.20	0.35	—
1981	2,000,000	—	—	1.00	2.00	—

KM# 134.2 5 FRANCS (5 Frank)
6.0000 g., Copper-Nickel, 24 mm. **Note:** Medal alignment.

Date	Mintage	F	VF	XF	Unc	BU
1949	Inc. above	—	4.00	10.00	30.00	—
1950	Inc. above	—	4.00	10.00	30.00	—

Date	Mintage	F	VF	XF	Unc	BU
1963	Inc. above	—	4.00	10.00	30.00	—
1966	Inc. above	—	4.00	10.00	30.00	—
1969	Inc. above	—	4.00	10.00	30.00	—
1975	Inc. above	—	4.00	10.00	30.00	—

KM# 135.1 5 FRANCS (5 Frank)

6.0000 g., Copper-Nickel, 24 mm. **Obv:** Plant divides denomination, Crown at top, legend in Dutch **Obv. Legend:** BELGIE **Obv. Designer:** Rau **Rev:** Laureate head, left, small diamonds flank date at left, symbol at right **Edge:** Reeded

Date	Mintage	F	VF	XF	Unc	BU
1948	4,800,000	—	4.00	10.00	25.00	—
1948	—	—	3.00	15.00	40.00	—
Note: Without engraver's name						
1949	31,500,000	—	—	1.00	6.00	—
1950	34,728,000	—	—	1.00	6.00	—
1958	2,672,000	—	1.00	2.00	6.00	—
1960	5,896,000	—	—	1.00	3.00	—
1961	4,120,000	—	1.00	2.00	5.00	—
1962	7,624,000	—	—	1.00	3.00	—
1963	6,136,000	—	—	1.00	3.00	—
1964	8,128,000	—	—	1.00	3.00	—
1965	9,956,000	—	—	1.00	3.00	—
1966	7,136,000	—	—	1.00	3.00	—
1966	—	3.00	5.00	10.00	20.00	—
Note: Without engraver's name						
1967	16,132,000	—	—	1.00	3.00	—
1968	3,200,000	—	1.00	2.00	5.00	—
1969	21,500,000	—	—	1.00	3.00	—
1970	2,000,000	—	1.00	2.00	5.00	—
1971	15,000,000	—	—	0.20	0.50	—
1972	17,500,000	—	—	0.20	0.50	—
1972	Inc. above	1.00	5.00	8.00	15.00	—
Note: Without engraver's name						
1973	10,000,000	—	—	0.20	0.50	—
1974	25,000,000	—	—	0.20	0.50	—
1974	—	1.00	5.00	8.00	15.00	—
Note: Without engraver's name						
1975	34,000,000	—	—	0.20	0.50	—
1976	7,500,000	—	—	0.20	0.75	—
1977	22,500,000	—	—	0.20	0.50	—
1978	27,500,000	—	—	0.20	0.50	—
1979	10,000,000	—	—	0.50	1.00	—
1980	11,000,000	—	—	0.20	0.50	—
1981	2,000,000	—	—	1.00	2.00	—

KM# 135.2 5 FRANCS (5 Frank)

6.0000 g., Copper-Nickel, 24 mm. **Note:** Medal alignment.

Date	Mintage	F	VF	XF	Unc	BU
1950	Inc. above	—	4.00	10.00	30.00	—
1962	Inc. above	—	4.00	10.00	30.00	—
1965	Inc. above	—	4.00	10.00	30.00	—
1974	Inc. above	—	4.00	10.00	30.00	—

KM# 163 5 FRANCS (5 Frank)

Brass Or Aluminum-Bronze, 24 mm. **Obv:** Face, left, on divided coin **Rev:** Stylized denomination, date at bottom, legend in French **Rev. Legend:** BELGIQUE

Date	Mintage	F	VF	XF	Unc	BU
1986	208,400,000	—	—	0.35	0.65	—
1987	22,500,000	—	—	0.35	1.00	—
1988	26,500,000	—	—	0.35	1.00	—
1989	60,000	—	—	—	4.00	—
Note: In sets only						
1990	60,000	—	—	—	4.00	—
Note: In sets only						
1991	60,000	—	—	—	4.00	—
Note: In sets only						
1992	5,060,000	—	—	0.35	2.00	—
1993	15,060,000	—	—	0.35	1.00	—

KM# 164 5 FRANCS (5 Frank)

Brass Or Aluminum-Bronze, 24 mm. **Obv:** Face, left, on divided coin **Rev:** Stylized denomination, date at bottom, legend in Dutch **Rev. Legend:** BELGIE

Date	Mintage	F	VF	XF	Unc	BU
1986	208,400,000	—	—	0.35	0.65	—
1987	22,500,000	—	—	0.35	1.00	—
1988	26,500,000	—	—	0.35	1.00	—
1989	60,000	—	—	—	4.00	—
Note: In sets only						
1990	60,000	—	—	—	4.00	—
Note: In sets only						
1991	60,000	—	—	—	4.00	—
Note: In sets only						
1992	5,060,000	—	—	0.35	2.00	—
1993	15,060,000	—	—	0.35	1.00	—

KM# 189 5 FRANCS (5 Frank)

5.5000 g., Aluminum-Bronze, 24 mm. **Ruler:** Albert II **Obv:** Head left, outline around back of head **Rev:** Vertical line divides date and denomination, legend in French **Rev. Legend:** BELGIQUE **Note:** Mint mark - Angel head. Mintmaster R. Coenen's privy mark - Scale.

Date	Mintage	F	VF	XF	Unc	BU
1994	15,060,000	—	—	—	0.50	—
1995	60,000	—	—	—	4.00	—
Note: In sets only						
1996	6,860,000	—	—	—	1.00	—
1997	60,000	—	—	—	5.00	—
Note: In sets only						
1998	32,560,000	—	—	—	0.50	—
1999	60,000	—	—	—	4.00	—
Note: In sets only						
1999 Proof	5,000	Value: 25.00				
Note: Medal alignment; in sets only						
2000	60,000	—	—	—	4.00	—
Note: In sets only						
2000 Proof	5,000	Value: 25.00				
Note: Medal alignment; in sets only						
2001	60,000	—	—	—	4.00	—
Note: In sets only						
2001 Proof	5,000	Value: 25.00				
Note: Medal alignment; in sets only						

KM# 190 5 FRANCS (5 Frank)

Aluminum-Bronze, 24 mm. **Ruler:** Albert II **Obv:** Head left, outline around back of head **Rev:** Vertical line divides date and large denomination, legend in Dutch **Rev. Legend:** BELGIE **Note:** Mint mark - Angel head. Mintmaster R. Coenen's privy mark - Scale.

Date	Mintage	F	VF	XF	Unc	BU
1994	30,060,000	—	—	—	0.50	—
1995	60,000	—	—	—	2.00	—
Note: In sets only						
1996	3,133,000	—	—	—	1.00	—
1997	60,000	—	—	—	5.00	—
Note: In sets only						
1998	6,500,000	—	—	—	0.50	—
1999	60,000	—	—	—	4.00	—
Note: In sets only						
1999	5,000	—	—	—	20.00	—
Note: Medal alignment						
2000	60,000	—	—	—	4.00	—
Note: In sets only						
2000 Proof	5,000	Value: 25.00				
Note: Medal alignment; in sets only						
2001	60,000	—	—	—	4.00	—
Note: In sets only						
2001 Proof	5,000	Value: 25.00				
Note: Medal alignment, in sets only						

KM# 99 10 FRANCS-10 FRANK (Deux / Twee Belgas)

Nickel **Subject:** Independence Centennial **Rev:** Legend in French **Rev. Legend:** BELGIQUE **Note:** Exists in position A or B, values are the same.

Date	Mintage	F	VF	XF	Unc	BU
1930	2,699,000	25.00	70.00	130	200	—

KM# 100 10 FRANCS-10 FRANK (Deux / Twee Belgas)

Nickel **Obv:** Conjoined heads of Leopold I, Leopold II and Albert I, left, two dates at bottom **Rev:** Denomination flanked by sprays, legend in Dutch **Rev. Legend:** BELGIE **Note:** Exists in position A or B, values are the same.

Date	Mintage	F	VF	XF	Unc	BU
1930	3,000,000	30.00	75.00	140	250	500

KM# 155.1 10 FRANCS (10 Frank)

8.0000 g., Nickel, 27 mm. **Obv:** Head, left **Obv. Designer:** Harry Elstrom **Rev:** Crowned arms divide denomination, date at bottom, legend in French **Rev. Legend:** BELGIQUE **Rev. Designer:** J. DeBast **Edge:** Plain **Note:** Mint mark - Angel head. Mintmaster Vogeleer's privy mark - Bird.

Date	Mintage	F	VF	XF	Unc	BU
1969	22,235,000	—	—	0.40	0.70	—
1970	9,500,000	—	—	0.40	0.70	—
1971	15,000,000	—	—	0.40	0.70	—
1972	10,000,000	—	—	0.40	0.70	—
1973	10,000,000	—	—	0.40	0.70	—
1974	5,000,000	—	—	0.50	1.00	—
1975	5,000,000	—	—	0.50	1.00	—
1976	7,500,000	—	—	0.50	1.00	—
1977	7,000,000	—	—	0.50	1.00	—
1978	2,500,000	—	—	1.00	2.50	—
1979	5,000,000	—	—	0.60	1.50	—

KM# 155.2 10 FRANCS (10 Frank)

8.0000 g., Nickel, 27 mm. **Note:** Medal alignment. Mint mark - Angel head. Mintmaster Vogeleer's privy mark - Bird.

Date	Mintage	F	VF	XF	Unc	BU
1969	Inc. above	—	6.00	12.00	35.00	—
1974	Inc. above	—	6.00	12.00	35.00	—

KM# 156.1 10 FRANCS (10 Frank)

8.0000 g., Nickel, 27 mm. **Obv:** Head, left **Obv. Designer:** Harry Elstrom **Rev:** Crowned arms divide denomination, date at bottom, legend in Dutch **Rev. Legend:** BELGIE **Rev. Designer:** J. DeBast **Edge:** Plain **Note:** Mint mark - Angel head. Mintmaster Vogeleer's privy mark - Bird.

Date	Mintage	F	VF	XF	Unc	BU
1969	21,500,000	—	—	0.40	0.70	—
1970	10,000,000	—	—	0.40	0.70	—
1971	15,000,000	—	—	0.40	0.70	—
1972	10,000,000	—	—	0.40	0.70	—
1973	10,000,000	—	—	0.40	0.70	—
1974	5,000,000	—	—	0.50	1.00	—
1975	5,000,000	—	—	0.50	1.00	—
1976	7,500,000	—	—	0.50	1.00	—
1977	7,000,000	—	—	0.50	1.00	—
1978	2,500,000	—	—	1.00	2.50	—
1979	10,000,000	—	—	0.60	1.50	—

KM# 156.2 10 FRANCS (10 Frank)

8.0000 g., Nickel, 27 mm. **Note:** Medal alignment. Struck at Brussels Mint. Mint mark - Angel head. Mintmaster Vogeleer's privy mark - Bird.

Date	Mintage	F	VF	XF	Unc	BU
1971	Inc. above	—	6.00	12.00	35.00	—
1976	Inc. above	—	6.00	12.00	35.00	—
1978	Inc. above	—	6.00	12.00	35.00	—

KM# 78 20 FRANCS (20 Frank)
6.4516 g., 0.9000 Gold 0.1867 oz. AGW **Obv:** Armored bust of Albert, left, legend in French **Obv. Legend:** DES BELGES **Rev:** Crowned arms divide denomination and date

Date	Mintage	F	VF	XF	Unc	BU
1914 Position A	125,000	—	—	BV	165	250
1914 Position B	Inc. above	300	600	800	1,200	—

KM# 79 20 FRANCS (20 Frank)
6.4516 g., 0.9000 Gold 0.1867 oz. AGW **Obv:** Armored bust of Albert, left, legend in Dutch **Obv. Legend:** DER BELGEN **Rev:** Crowned arms divide denomination and date

Date	Mintage	F	VF	XF	Unc	BU
1914 Position A	125,000	—	—	BV	160	175
1914 Position B	Inc. above	—	BV	160	170	200

KM# 103.1 20 FRANCS (20 Frank)
11.0000 g., 0.6800 Silver 0.2405 oz. ASW **Obv:** Head of Albert, left, legend in French **Obv. Legend:** DES BELGES **Rev:** Crowned arms divide denomination and date

Date	Mintage	F	VF	XF	Unc	BU
1933 Position A	200,000	20.00	60.00	100	150	—
1933 Position B	Inc. above	25.00	75.00	120	175	—
1934 Position A	12,300,000	—	4.00	8.00	12.00	—
1934 Position B	Inc. above	—	4.00	8.00	12.00	—

KM# 103.2 20 FRANCS (20 Frank)
11.0000 g., 0.6800 Silver 0.2405 oz. ASW **Note:** Medal alignment.

Date	Mintage	F	VF	XF	Unc	BU
1934	Inc. above	35.00	80.00	190	400	—

KM# 104.1 20 FRANCS (20 Frank)
11.0000 g., 0.6800 Silver 0.2405 oz. ASW **Obv:** Head of Albert, left, legend in Dutch **Obv. Legend:** DER BELGEN **Rev:** Crowned arms divide denomination and date

Date	Mintage	F	VF	XF	Unc	BU
1933 Position B	Inc. above	16.00	40.00	65.00	125	—
1933 Position A	200,000	14.00	30.00	60.00	110	—
1934 Position A	12,300,000	—	2.00	4.00	7.00	—
1934 Position B	Inc. above	—	2.00	4.00	7.00	—

KM# 104.2 20 FRANCS (20 Frank)
11.0000 g., 0.6800 Silver 0.2405 oz. ASW **Note:** Medal alignment.

Date	Mintage	F	VF	XF	Unc	BU
1934	Inc. above	30.00	70.00	170	350	—

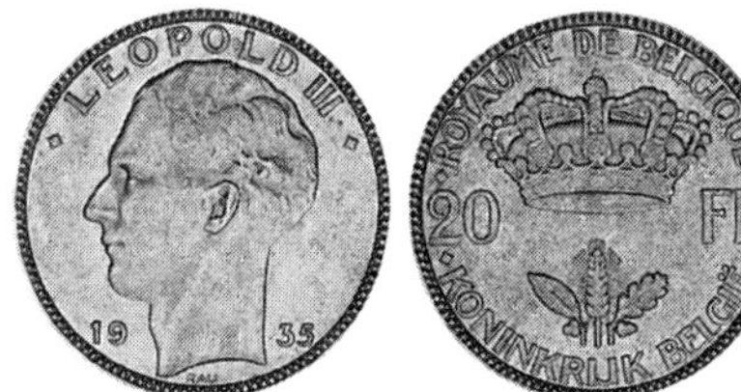

KM# 105 20 FRANCS (20 Frank)
11.0000 g., 0.6800 Silver 0.2405 oz. ASW **Obv:** Head of Leopold II left, neck divides date **Obv. Designer:** Rau **Rev:** Crown above sprig divides denomination **Note:** Both dates exist in position A and B, values are the same. Coins dated 1934 exist with and without umlauts above E in BELGIE.

Date	Mintage	F	VF	XF	Unc	BU
1934	1,250,000	3.00	8.00	12.00	20.00	—
1935	10,760,000	BV	3.50	5.50	8.00	—

KM# 140.1 20 FRANCS (20 Frank)
8.0000 g., 0.8350 Silver 0.2148 oz. ASW, 27 mm. **Obv:** Rampant lion left with shield, denomination below, legend in French **Obv. Legend:** BELGIQUE **Rev:** Helmeted head right, small caduceus divides date at left **Rev. Designer:** Rau **Edge:** Reeded

Date	Mintage	F	VF	XF	Unc	BU
1949	4,600,000	—	3.50	6.00	10.00	—
1950	12,957,000	—	2.50	4.00	7.00	—
1953	3,953,000	—	6.00	9.00	15.00	—
1954	4,835,000	15.00	45.00	80.00	120	—
1955	1,730,000	200	650	900	1,400	—

KM# 140.2 20 FRANCS (20 Frank)
8.0000 g., 0.8350 Silver 0.2148 oz. ASW, 27 mm. **Edge:** Plain **Note:** Medal alignment.

Date	Mintage	F	VF	XF	Unc	BU
1949	Inc. above	15.00	35.00	75.00	125	—
1950	Inc. above	15.00	35.00	75.00	125	—

KM# 141.1 20 FRANCS (20 Frank)
8.0000 g., 0.8350 Silver 0.2148 oz. ASW, 27 mm. **Obv:** Rampant lion left with shield, denomination below, legend in Dutch **Obv. Legend:** BELGIE **Rev:** Helmeted head right, small caduceus divides date at left **Rev. Designer:** Rau **Edge:** Reeded

Date	Mintage	F	VF	XF	Unc	BU
1949	5,545,000	—	3.00	5.00	9.00	—
1950	—	150	500	800	1,200	—
1951	7,885,000	—	2.50	4.00	7.00	—
1953	6,625,000	—	2.50	4.50	8.00	—
1954	5,323,000	12.00	35.00	60.00	100	—
1955	3,760,000	50.00	125	200	275	—

KM# 141.2 20 FRANCS (20 Frank)
8.0000 g., 0.8350 Silver 0.2148 oz. ASW **Edge:** Reeded **Note:** Medal alignment.

Date	Mintage	F	VF	XF	Unc	BU
1949	Inc. above	20.00	35.00	85.00	135	—
1951	Inc. above	15.00	40.00	95.00	160	—

KM# 159 20 FRANCS (20 Frank)
8.5000 g., Nickel-Bronze, 25.65 mm. **Obv:** Head, left **Rev:** Denomination at right above stylized spray, legend in French **Rev. Legend:** BELGIQUE **Designer:** Harry Elstrom

Date	Mintage	F	VF	XF	Unc	BU
1980	60,000,000	—	—	0.70	2.00	—
1980	—	—	4.00	10.00	30.00	—
Note: Medal alignment						
1981	60,000,000	—	—	0.70	2.00	—
1982	54,000,000	—	—	0.70	2.00	—
1989	60,000	—	—	—	6.00	—
Note: In sets only						
1990	60,000	—	—	—	6.00	—
Note: In sets only						
1991	60,000	—	—	—	6.00	—
Note: In sets only						
1992	2,610,000	—	—	0.70	4.00	—
1993	7,540,000	—	—	0.70	3.00	—

KM# 160 20 FRANCS (20 Frank)
8.5000 g., Nickel-Bronze, 25.65 mm. **Obv:** Head, left **Rev:** Denomination at right above stylized spray, legend in Dutch **Rev. Legend:** BELGIE **Designer:** Harry Elstrom

Date	Mintage	F	VF	XF	Unc	BU
1980	60,000,000	—	—	0.70	2.00	—
1980	—	—	4.00	10.00	30.00	—
Note: Medal alignment						
1981	60,000,000	—	—	0.70	2.00	—
1982	54,000,000	—	—	0.70	2.00	—
1989	60,000	—	—	—	6.00	—
Note: In sets only						
1990	60,000	—	—	—	6.00	—
Note: In sets only						
1991	60,000	—	—	—	6.00	—
Note: In sets only						
1992	2,610,000	—	—	0.70	4.00	—
1993	7,540,000	—	—	0.70	3.00	—

KM# 191 20 FRANCS (20 Frank)
8.5000 g., Nickel-Bronze, 25.65 mm. **Ruler:** Albert II **Obv:** Head left, outline around back of head **Rev:** Vertical line divides date and large denomination, legend in French **Rev. Legend:** BELGIQUE **Note:** Mint mark - Angel head. Mintmaster R. Coenen's privy mark - Scale.

Date	Mintage	F	VF	XF	Unc	BU
1994	12,560,000	—	—	0.70	1.00	—
1995	60,000	—	—	—	5.00	—
Note: In sets only						
1996	14,485,000	—	—	—	1.00	—
1997	60,000	—	—	—	5.00	—
Note: In sets only						
1998	6,500,000	—	—	—	3.00	—
1999	60,000	—	—	—	5.00	—
Note: In sets only						
1999 Proof	5,000	Value: 25.00				
Note: Medal alignment; in sets only						
2000	60,000	—	—	—	5.00	—
Note: In sets only						
2000 Proof	5,000	Value: 25.00				
Note: Medal alignment; in sets only						
2001	60,000	—	—	—	4.00	—
Note: In sets only						
2001 Proof	5,000	Value: 25.00				
Note: Medal alignment; in sets only						

KM# 192 20 FRANCS (20 Frank)
8.5000 g., Nickel-Bronze, 25.65 mm. **Ruler:** Albert II **Obv:** Head left, outline around back of head **Rev:** Vertical line divides date and large denomination, legend in Dutch **Rev. Legend:** BELGIE **Note:** Mint mark - Angel head. Mintmaster R. Coenen's privy mark - Scale.

Date	Mintage	F	VF	XF	Unc	BU
1994	12,560,000	—	—	0.70	1.00	—
1995	60,000	—	—	—	5.00	—
Note: In sets only						
1996	3,133,000	—	—	—	1.00	—
1997	60,000	—	—	—	5.00	—
Note: In sets only						
1998	6,500,000	—	—	—	3.00	—
1999	60,000	—	—	—	5.00	—
Note: In sets only						
1999 Proof	5,000	Value: 25.00				
Note: Medal alignment; in sets only						
2000	60,000	—	—	—	5.00	—
Note: In sets only						
2000 Proof	5,000	Value: 25.00				
Note: Medal alignment; in sets only						
2001	60,000	—	—	—	5.00	—
Note: In sets only						
2001 Proof	5,000	Value: 25.00				
Note: Medal alignment; in sets only						

KM# 101.1 20 FRANCS-20 FRANK (Vier / Quatre Belgas)

Nickel **Obv:** Head of Albert, left, legend in French **Obv. Legend:** DES BELGES **Rev:** Crowned arms divide denomination and date **Note:** All dates exist in position A and B, values are the same.

Date	Mintage	F	VF	XF	Unc	BU
1931	3,957,000	20.00	50.00	110	160	175
1932	5,472,000	20.00	50.00	110	160	175

KM# 101.2 20 FRANCS-20 FRANK (Vier / Quatre Belgas)

Nickel **Note:** Medal alignment. Edge varieties exist.

Date	Mintage	F	VF	XF	Unc	BU
1932	Inc. above	65.00	175	400	600	—

KM# 102 20 FRANCS-20 FRANK (Vier / Quatre Belgas)

Nickel **Obv:** Legend in Dutch **Obv. Legend:** DER BELGEN **Note:** All dates exist in position A and B, values are the same.

Date	Mintage	F	VF	XF	Unc	BU
1931	2,600,000	25.00	55.00	120	175	200
1932	6,950,000	15.00	45.00	100	140	175

KM# 106.1 50 FRANCS (50 Frank)

22.0000 g., 0.6800 Silver 0.4810 oz. ASW, 35 mm. **Subject:** Brussels Exposition and Railway Centennial **Obv:** St. Michael slaying dragon (Brussels' patron saint) **Obv. Legend:** DE BELGIQUE **Rev:** Brussels train station, two dates above, legend in French **Rev. Legend:** DE FER BELGES **Edge Lettering:** SOUSLE REGNE DELEOPOLD III **Designer:** Paul Wissaert **Note:** Exists in positions A and B, values are the same.

Date	Mintage	F	VF	XF	Unc	BU
1935	140,000	50.00	90.00	125	265	500

KM# 106.2 50 FRANCS (50 Frank)

22.0000 g., 0.6800 Silver 0.4810 oz. ASW, 35 mm. **Note:** Medal alignment. Exists in positions A and B, values are the same.

Date	Mintage	F	VF	XF	Unc	BU
1935	Inc. above	200	450	600	825	—

KM# 107.1 50 FRANCS (50 Frank)

22.0000 g., 0.6800 Silver 0.4810 oz. ASW, 35 mm. **Obv:** St. Michael slaying dragon (Brussels' patron saint) **Obv. Legend:** BELGIE **Rev:** Brussels railway station, two dates above, legend in Dutch **Rev. Legend:** DER BELGISCHE **Edge Lettering:** ONDER DE REGEERING VAN KONIG LEOPOLD III **Designer:** Paul Wissaert **Note:** Exists in positions A and B, values are the same.

Date	Mintage	F	VF	XF	Unc	BU
1935	140,000	60.00	125	150	225	450

KM# 107.2 50 FRANCS (50 Frank)

22.0000 g., 0.6800 Silver 0.4810 oz. ASW, 35 mm. **Note:** Medal alignment. Exists in positions A and B, values are the same.

Date	Mintage	F	VF	XF	Unc	BU
1935	Inc. above	300	700	900	1,500	—

KM# 121 50 FRANCS (50 Frank)

20.0000 g., 0.8350 Silver 0.5369 oz. ASW **Obv:** Head of Leopold III, left, date below **Rev:** Crown above nine shields dividing denomination, legend in French **Rev. Legend:** BELGIQUE: BELGIE **Designer:** Rau **Note:** Both dates exist in positions A and B, values are the same.

Date	Mintage	F	VF	XF	Unc	BU
1939	1,000,000	BV	8.00	12.00	18.00	—
1940	631,000	7.00	15.00	25.00	35.00	—

KM# 122.2 50 FRANCS (50 Frank)

20.0000 g., 0.8350 Silver 0.5369 oz. ASW **Rev:** Without cross on crown **Note:** Both dates exist in positions A and B, values are the same.

Date	Mintage	F	VF	XF	Unc	BU
1939	Inc. above	8.00	30.00	40.00	55.00	—
1940	Inc. above	8.00	30.00	40.00	55.00	—

KM# 122.3 50 FRANCS (50 Frank)

20.0000 g., 0.8350 Silver 0.5369 oz. ASW **Rev:** Triangle in third arms from left, cross on crown **Note:** Both dates exist in positions A and B, values are the same.

Date	Mintage	F	VF	XF	Unc	BU
1940	Inc. above	15.00	35.00	60.00	85.00	—

KM# 122.4 50 FRANCS (50 Frank)

20.0000 g., 0.8350 Silver 0.5369 oz. ASW **Rev:** Without cross on crown and with triangle in third arms from left **Note:** Both dates exist in positions A and B, values are the same.

Date	Mintage	F	VF	XF	Unc	BU
1940	Inc. above	30.00	90.00	140	200	375

KM# 136.1 50 FRANCS (50 Frank)

12.5000 g., 0.8350 Silver 0.3356 oz. ASW, 30 mm. **Obv:** Rampant lion with shield, left, denomination below, legend in French **Obv. Legend:** BELGIQUE **Rev:** Helmeted head, right, small caduceus divides date at left **Rev. Designer:** Rau **Edge:** Reeded

Date	Mintage	F	VF	XF	Unc	BU
1948	2,000,000	—	BV	4.50	7.00	—
1949	4,354,000	—	BV	4.50	6.00	—
1950	—	200	600	1,000	1,750	—
1951	2,904,000	—	BV	4.50	6.50	—
1954	3,232,000	5.00	12.00	20.00	30.00	—

KM# 136.2 50 FRANCS (50 Frank)

12.5000 g., 0.8350 Silver 0.3356 oz. ASW, 30 mm. **Note:** Medal alignment.

Date	Mintage	F	VF	XF	Unc	BU
1949	Inc. above	10.00	30.00	90.00	175	250

KM# 137 50 FRANCS (50 Frank)

12.5000 g., 0.8350 Silver 0.3356 oz. ASW, 30 mm. **Obv:** Rampant lion with shield left, denomination below, legend in Dutch **Obv. Legend:** BELGIE **Rev:** Helmeted head right, small caduceus divides date at left **Rev. Designer:** Rau **Edge:** Reeded

Date	Mintage	F	VF	XF	Unc	BU
1948	3,000,000	—	BV	4.50	7.00	—
1950	4,110,000	—	BV	4.50	6.00	—
1951	1,698,000	—	BV	4.50	8.00	—
1954	2,978,000	—	BV	4.50	6.50	—

KM# 150.1 50 FRANCS (50 Frank)

12.5000 g., 0.8350 Silver 0.3356 oz. ASW, 29 mm. **Subject:** Brussels World Fair **Obv:** Head of Baudouin, left, within circle, legend in French **Obv. Legend:** DES BELGES **Rev:** World's Fair, Steeple divides date from denomination **Designer:** Carlos van Dionant

Date	Mintage	F	VF	XF	Unc	BU
1958	476,000	—	BV	6.50	10.00	—

KM# 150.2 50 FRANCS (50 Frank)

12.5000 g., 0.8350 Silver 0.3356 oz. ASW, 29 mm. **Note:** Medal alignment.

Date	Mintage	F	VF	XF	Unc	BU
1958	Inc. above	18.00	45.00	100	180	250

KM# 151.1 50 FRANCS (50 Frank)

12.5000 g., 0.8350 Silver 0.3356 oz. ASW, 29 mm. **Obv:** Head of Baudouin, left, within circle, legend in Dutch **Obv. Legend:** DER BELGEN **Rev:** World's Fair, Steeple divides date from denomination **Edge:** Reeded **Designer:** Carlos van Dionant

Date	Mintage	F	VF	XF	Unc	BU
1958	382,000	BV	5.00	7.50	10.00	—

KM# 151.2 50 FRANCS (50 Frank)

12.5000 g., 0.8350 Silver 0.3356 oz. ASW, 29 mm. **Note:** Medal alignment.

Date	Mintage	F	VF	XF	Unc	BU
1958	Inc. above	15.00	35.00	75.00	125	—

KM# 152.1 50 FRANCS (50 Frank)

12.5000 g., 0.8350 Silver 0.3356 oz. ASW, 29 mm. **Subject:** King Baudouin's marriage to Doña Fabiola de Mora y Aragon **Obv:** Conjoined heads of King Baudoin and Dona Fabiola de Mora y Aragon, left **Rev:** Arms flanked by sprays divide Crown and denomination

Date	Mintage	F	VF	XF	Unc	BU
1960	500,000	BV	4.50	6.00	9.00	15.00

KM# 152.2 50 FRANCS (50 Frank)

12.5000 g., 0.8350 Silver 0.3356 oz. ASW, 29 mm. **Note:** Medal alignment.

Date	Mintage	F	VF	XF	Unc	BU
1960	Inc. above	12.50	30.00	60.00	120	200

KM# 168 50 FRANCS (50 Frank)

7.0000 g., Nickel, 22.5 mm. **Obv:** Face left on divided coin **Rev:** Denomination, date at bottom, legend in French **Rev. Legend:** BELGIQUE

Date	Mintage	F	VF	XF	Unc	BU
1987	30,000,000	—	—	2.00	3.00	—
1988	3,500,000	—	—	2.00	6.00	—
1989	15,060,000	—	—	2.00	4.00	—
1990	15,060,000	—	—	2.00	4.00	—
1991	3,500,000	—	—	2.00	5.00	—
1992	15,060,000	—	—	2.00	4.00	—
1993	15,060,000	—	—	2.00	4.00	—

KM# 169 50 FRANCS (50 Frank)

Nickel, 22.5 mm. **Obv:** Face, left, on divided coin **Rev:** Denomination, date at bottom **Rev. Legend:** BELGIE

Date	Mintage	F	VF	XF	Unc	BU
1987	30,000,000	—	—	2.00	3.00	—
1988	3,500,000	—	—	2.00	6.00	—
1989	15,060,000	—	—	2.00	4.00	—
1990	15,060,000	—	—	2.00	4.00	—
1991	3,500,000	—	—	2.00	5.00	—
1992	15,060,000	—	—	2.00	4.00	—
1993	15,060,000	—	—	2.00	4.00	—

KM# 193 50 FRANCS (50 Frank)

7.0500 g., Nickel, 22.5 mm. **Ruler:** Albert II **Obv:** Head left, outline around back of head **Rev:** Vertical line divides large denomination and date, legend in French **Rev. Legend:** BELGIQUE **Note:** Mint mark - Angel head. Mintmaster R. Coenen's privy mark - Scale.

Date	Mintage	F	VF	XF	Unc	BU
1994	5,060,000	—	—	2.00	3.00	—
1995	60,000	—	—	5.00	8.00	—
Note: In sets only						
1996	60,000	—	—	5.00	8.00	—
Note: In sets only						
1997	60,000	—	—	5.00	8.00	—
Note: In sets only						
1998	3,060,000	—	—	3.00	4.50	—
1999	60,000	—	—	5.00	8.00	—
Note: In sets only						
1999 Proof	5,000	Value: 20.00				
Note: Medal alignment; in sets only						
2000	60,000	—	—	5.00	8.00	—
Note: In sets only						
2000 Proof	5,000	Value: 20.00				
Note: Medal alignment; in sets only						
2001	60,000	—	—	—	8.00	—
Note: In sets only						
2001 Proof	5,000	Value: 25.00				
Note: Medal alignment; in sets only						

KM# 194 50 FRANCS (50 Frank)

Nickel, 22.5 mm. **Ruler:** Albert II **Obv:** Head left, outline around back of head **Rev:** Vertical line divides large denomination and date, legend in Dutch **Rev. Legend:** BELGIE **Note:** Mint mark - Angel head. Mintmaster R. Coenen's privy mark - Scale.

Date	Mintage	F	VF	XF	Unc	BU
1994	5,060,000	—	—	2.00	3.00	—
1995	60,000	—	—	5.00	8.00	—
Note: In sets only						
1996	60,000	—	—	5.00	8.00	—
Note: In sets only						
1997	60,000	—	—	5.00	8.00	—
Note: In sets only						
1998	3,060,000	—	—	3.00	4.50	—
1999	60,000	—	—	3.00	8.00	—
Note: In sets only						
1999 Proof	5,000	Value: 25.00				
Note: Medal alignment; in sets only						
2000	60,000	—	—	5.00	8.00	—
Note: In sets only						
2000 Proof	5,000	Value: 25.00				
Note: Medal alignment; in sets only						
2001	60,000	—	—	—	8.00	—
Note: In sets only						
2001 Proof	5,000	Value: 25.00				
Note: Medal alignment; in sets only						

KM# 213.1 50 FRANCS (50 Frank)

7.0200 g., Nickel, 22.78 mm. **Subject:** European Soccer Championship **Obv:** Head of Albert II, left **Rev:** Soccer ball, legend in French **Rev. Legend:** BELGIQUE **Edge:** Coarse reeding

Date	Mintage	F	VF	XF	Unc	BU
2000	500,000	—	—	—	6.00	—

KM# 213.2 50 FRANCS (50 Frank)

Nickel, 22.5 mm. **Note:** Medal alignment.

Date	Mintage	F	VF	XF	Unc	BU
2000	20,000	Value: 22.00				
Note: In the "Euro 2000" sets only						

KM# 214.1 50 FRANCS (50 Frank)

7.0200 g., Nickel, 22.78 mm. **Subject:** European Soccer Championship **Obv:** Head of Albert II, left, rear of head outlined **Rev:** Soccer ball, legend in Dutch **Rev. Legend:** BELGIE **Edge:** Coarse reeding

Date	Mintage	F	VF	XF	Unc	BU
2000	500,000	—	—	4.00	6.00	—

KM# 214.2 50 FRANCS (50 Frank)

Nickel, 22.5 mm. **Note:** Medal alignment.

Date	Mintage	F	VF	XF	Unc	BU
2000	20,000	Value: 22.00				
Note: In the "Euro 2000" sets only						

KM# 138.1 100 FRANCS (100 Frank)

18.0000 g., 0.8350 Silver 0.4832 oz. ASW **Obv:** Crowned arms within wreath divide denomination, legend in French **Obv. Legend:** BELGIQUE **Rev:** Conjoined heads left of Leopold I, Leopold II, Albert I and Leopold III, left, Crown divides date at top, star at bottom

Date	Mintage	F	VF	XF	Unc	BU
1948	1,000,000	—	BV	5.00	10.00	—
1949	106,000	7.50	15.00	40.00	60.00	75.00
1950	2,807,000	—	BV	5.00	9.00	—
1954	2,517,000	—	BV	5.00	10.00	—

KM# 138.2 100 FRANCS (100 Frank)

18.0000 g., 0.8350 Silver 0.4832 oz. ASW **Note:** Medal alignment.

Date	Mintage	F	VF	XF	Unc	BU
1948	Inc. above	10.00	40.00	90.00	220	—
1950	Inc. above	10.00	40.00	90.00	200	—

KM# 139.1 100 FRANCS (100 Frank)

18.0000 g., 0.8350 Silver 0.4832 oz. ASW **Obv:** Crowned arms within wreath divide denomination, legend in Dutch **Obv. Legend:** BELGIE **Rev:** Conjoined heads left of Leopold I, Leopold II, Albert I and Leopold III, left, Crown divides date at top, star at bottom

Date	Mintage	F	VF	XF	Unc	BU
1948	1,000,000	—	BV	5.00	10.00	—
1949	2,271,000	—	BV	5.00	9.00	—
1950	—	300	500	850	1,200	—
1951	4,691,000	—	BV	5.00	9.00	—

KM# 139.2 100 FRANCS (100 Frank)

18.0000 g., 0.8350 Silver 0.4832 oz. ASW **Note:** Medal alignment.

Date	Mintage	F	VF	XF	Unc	BU
1948	Inc. above	10.00	40.00	90.00	200	—
1949	Inc. above	7.50	30.00	75.00	160	—

EURO COINAGE

European Union Issues

KM# 224 EURO CENT

2.2700 g., Copper Plated Steel, 16.2 mm. **Ruler:** Albert II **Obv:** Head left within inner circle, stars 3/4 surround, date below **Obv. Designer:** Jan Alfons Keustermans **Rev:** Denomination and globe **Rev. Designer:** Luc Luycx **Edge:** Plain

Date	Mintage	F	VF	XF	Unc	BU
1999	235,240,000	—	—	—	0.35	0.75
1999 Proof	15,000	Value: 12.00				
2000	40,000	—	—	—	37.50	42.50
2000 Proof	15,000	Value: 15.00				
2001	99,840,000	—	—	—	0.60	1.00
2001 Proof	15,000	Value: 12.00				
2002	140,000	—	—	—	18.50	22.50
2002 Proof	15,000	Value: 15.00				
2003	10,135,000	—	—	—	0.35	0.75
2003 Proof	15,000	Value: 12.00				
2004	180,000,000	—	—	—	0.35	0.75
2004 Proof	—	Value: 12.00				
2005	—	—	—	—	0.35	0.75
2005 Proof	3,000	Value: 12.00				
2006	—	—	—	—	0.35	0.75
2006 Proof	—	Value: 12.00				

KM# 225 2 EURO CENT

3.0300 g., Copper Plated Steel, 18.7 mm. **Ruler:** Albert II **Obv:** Head left within circle, stars 3/4 surround, date below **Obv. Designer:** Jan Alfons Keustermans **Rev:** Denomination and globe **Rev. Designer:** Luc Luycx **Edge:** Grooved

Date	Mintage	F	VF	XF	Unc	BU
1999	40,000	—	—	—	10.00	12.50
1999 Proof	15,000	Value: 15.00				
2000	373,040,000	—	—	—	0.50	1.00
2000 Proof	15,000	Value: 12.00				
2001	40,000	—	—	—	7.00	9.00
Note: Only available in sets at present, circulation strikes not yet released						
2001 Proof	15,000	Value: 15.00				
2002	140,000	—	—	—	3.50	6.50
2002 Proof	15,000	Value: 12.00				
2003	40,135,000	—	—	—	0.50	1.00
2003 Proof	15,000	Value: 12.00				
2004	140,000,000	—	—	—	0.50	1.00
2004 Proof	15,000	Value: 12.00				
2005	—	—	—	—	0.50	1.00
2005 Proof	—	Value: 12.00				
2006	—	—	—	—	0.50	1.00
2006 Proof	—	Value: 12.00				

KM# 226 5 EURO CENT

3.8600 g., Copper Plated Steel, 21.2 mm. **Ruler:** Albert II **Obv:** Head left within circle, stars 3/4 surround, date below **Obv. Designer:** Jan Alfons Keustermans **Rev:** Denomination and globe **Rev. Designer:** Luc Luycx **Edge:** Plain

Date	Mintage	F	VF	XF	Unc	BU
1999	300,040,000	—	—	—	0.75	1.25
1999 Proof	15,000	Value: 12.00				
2000	40,000	—	—	—	10.00	12.50
2000 Proof	15,000	Value: 15.00				
2001	40,000	—	—	—	10.00	12.50
2001 Proof	15,000	Value: 15.00				
2002	140,000	—	—	—	6.00	8.00
2002 Proof	15,000	Value: 15.00				
2003	30,135,000	—	—	—	1.00	1.50
2003 Proof	15,000	Value: 12.00				
2004	97,000,000	—	—	—	1.00	1.50
2004 Proof	—	Value: 12.00				
2005	—	—	—	—	1.00	1.50
2005 Proof	3,000	Value: 12.00				
2006	—	—	—	—	1.00	1.50

KM# 227 10 EURO CENT

4.0700 g., Brass, 19.7 mm. **Ruler:** Albert II **Obv:** Head left within inner circle, stars 3/4 surround, date below **Obv. Designer:** Jan Alfons Keustermans **Rev:** Denomination and map **Rev. Designer:** Luc Luycx **Edge:** Reeded

Date	Mintage	F	VF	XF	Unc	BU
1999	180,990,000	—	—	—	0.75	1.25
1999 Proof	15,000	Value: 12.00				
2000	40,000	—	—	—	10.00	12.50
2000 Proof	15,000	Value: 15.00				
2001	145,790,000	—	—	—	0.75	1.25
2001 Proof	15,000	Value: 12.00				
2002	140,000	—	—	—	6.00	8.00
2002 Proof	15,000	Value: 15.00				
2003	135,000	—	—	—	6.00	8.00
2003 Proof	15,000	Value: 15.00				
2004	20,000,000	—	—	—	1.00	1.50
2004 Proof	—	Value: 12.00				
2005	—	—	—	—	1.00	1.50
2005 Proof	3,000	Value: 12.00				
2006	—	—	—	—	1.00	1.50

KM# 242 10 EURO CENT

4.0700 g., Brass, 19.7 mm. **Ruler:** Albert II **Obv:** King's portrait **Obv. Designer:** Jan Alfons Keustermans **Rev:** Relief Map of Western Europe, stars, lines and value **Rev. Designer:** Luc Luycx **Edge:** Reeded

Date	Mintage	F	VF	XF	Unc	BU
2007	—	—	—	—	1.00	1.50

KM# 228 20 EURO CENT

5.7300 g., Brass, 22.1 mm. **Ruler:** Albert II **Obv:** Head left within circle, stars 3/4 surround, date below **Obv. Designer:** Jan Alfons

Keustermans **Rev:** Denomination and map **Rev. Designer:** Luc Luycx **Edge:** Notched

Date	Mintage	F	VF	XF	Unc	BU
1999	40,000	—	—	—	10.00	12.50
1999 Proof	15,000	Value: 15.00				
2000	181,040,000	—	—	—	0.75	1.25
2000 Proof	15,000	Value: 12.00				
2001	40,000	—	—	—	10.00	12.50
Note: Only available in sets at present, circulation strikes not yet released						
2001 Proof	15,000	Value: 15.00				
2002	104,140,000	—	—	—	1.00	1.50
2002 Proof	15,000	Value: 12.00				
2003	30,135,000	—	—	—	1.25	1.75
2003 Proof	15,000	Value: 12.00				
2004	109,550,000	—	—	—	1.25	1.75
2004 Proof	—	Value: 12.00				
2005	—	—	—	—	1.25	1.75
2005 Proof	3,000	Value: 12.00				
2006	—	—	—	—	1.25	1.75

KM# 243 20 EURO CENT

5.7300 g., Brass, 22.1 mm. **Ruler:** Albert II **Obv:** King's portrait **Obv. Designer:** Jan Alfons Keustermans **Rev:** Relief Map of Western Europe, stars, lines and value **Rev. Designer:** Luc Luycx **Edge:** Notched

Date	Mintage	F	VF	XF	Unc	BU
2007	—	—	—	—	1.25	1.75

KM# 229 50 EURO CENT

7.8100 g., Brass, 24.2 mm. **Ruler:** Albert II **Obv:** Head left within circle, stars 3/4 surround, date below **Obv. Designer:** Jan Alfons Keustermans **Rev:** Denomination and map **Rev. Designer:** Luc Luycx **Edge:** Reeded

Date	Mintage	F	VF	XF	Unc	BU
1999	197,040,000	—	—	—	0.75	1.25
1999 Proof	15,000	Value: 12.00				
2000	40,000	—	—	—	10.00	12.50
2000 Proof	15,000	Value: 15.00				
2001	40,000	—	—	—	10.00	12.50
2001 Proof	15,000	Value: 15.00				
2002	50,040,000	—	—	—	1.00	1.50
2002 Proof	15,000	Value: 12.00				
2003	135,000	—	—	—	1.25	1.75
2003 Proof	15,000	Value: 12.00				
2004	15,000,000	—	—	—	1.25	1.75
2004 Proof	—	Value: 12.00				
2005	—	—	—	—	1.25	1.75
2005 Proof	3,000	Value: 12.00				
2006	—	—	—	—	1.25	1.75

KM# 244 50 EURO CENT

7.8100 g., Brass, 24.2 mm. **Ruler:** Albert II **Obv:** King's portrait **Obv. Designer:** Jan Alfons Keustermans **Rev:** Relief Map of Western Europe, stars, lines and value **Rev. Designer:** Luc Luycx **Edge:** Reeded

Date	Mintage	F	VF	XF	Unc	BU
2007	—	—	—	—	1.25	1.75

KM# 230 EURO

7.5700 g., Bi-Metallic Copper-Nickel center in Brass ring, 23.2 mm. **Ruler:** Albert II **Obv:** Head left within circle, stars 3/4 surround, date below **Obv. Designer:** Jan Alfons Keustermans **Rev:** Denomination and map **Rev. Designer:** Luc Luycx **Edge:** Reeded and plain sections

Date	Mintage	F	VF	XF	Unc	BU
1999	160,040,000	—	—	—	2.50	4.50
1999 Proof	15,000	Value: 15.00				
2000	40,000	—	—	—	12.50	15.00
2000 Proof	15,000	Value: 18.00				
2001	40,000	—	—	—	12.50	15.00
Note: Only available in sets at present, circulation strikes not yet released						
2001 Proof	15,000	Value: 18.00				
2002	90,640,000	—	—	—	3.00	5.00
Note: Only a fraction of the mintage released at present						
2002 Proof	15,000	Value: 15.00				
2003	135,000	—	—	—	3.00	5.00
2003 Proof	15,000	Value: 15.00				
2004	15,000,000	—	—	—	3.00	5.00
2004 Proof	—	Value: 15.00				
2005	—	—	—	—	3.00	5.00
2005 Proof	3,000	Value: 15.00				
2006	—	—	—	—	3.00	5.00

KM# 245 EURO

7.5000 g., Bi-Metallic Copper-Nickel center in Brass ring, 23.2 mm. **Ruler:** Albert II **Obv:** King's portrait **Obv. Designer:** Jan Alfons Keustermans **Rev:** Relief Map of Western Europe, stars, lines and value **Rev. Designer:** Luc Luycx **Edge:** Reeded and plain sections

Date	Mintage	F	VF	XF	Unc	BU
2007	—	—	—	—	3.00	5.00

KM# 231 2 EURO

8.5200 g., Bi-Metallic **Ring Composition:** Copper-Nickel **Center Composition:** Brass, 25.7 mm. **Ruler:** Albert II **Obv:** Head left within circle, stars 3/4 surround, date below **Obv. Designer:** Jan Alfons Keustermans **Rev:** Denomination and map **Rev. Designer:** Luc Luycx **Edge:** Reeded with 2's and stars

Date	Mintage	F	VF	XF	Unc	BU
1999	40,000	—	—	—	12.50	15.00
1999 Proof	15,000	Value: 20.00				
2000	120,040,000	—	—	—	3.50	5.50
2000 Proof	15,000	Value: 18.00				
2001	40,000	—	—	—	12.50	15.00
Note: Only available in sets at present, circulation strikes not yet released						
2001 Proof	15,000	Value: 20.00				
2002	50,140,000	—	—	—	3.75	6.00
2002 Proof	15,000	Value: 18.00				
2003	30,135,000	—	—	—	3.75	6.00
2003 Proof	15,000	Value: 18.00				
2004	65,500,000	—	—	—	3.75	6.00
2004 Proof	—	Value: 18.00				
2005	—	—	—	—	3.75	6.00
2005 Proof	3,000	Value: 18.00				
2006	—	—	—	—	3.75	6.00

KM# 240 2 EURO

8.5200 g., Bi-Metallic **Ring Composition:** Copper-Nickel **Center Composition:** Brass, 25.7 mm. **Ruler:** Albert II **Subject:** Schengen Agreement **Obv:** Albert II of Belgium and Henri of Luxembourg **Rev:** Value and map **Edge:** Reeding over stars

Date	Mintage	F	VF	XF	Unc	BU
2005	6,020,000	—	—	—	5.00	7.50
2005 Proof	3,000	Value: 25.00				

KM# 241 2 EURO

8.5200 g., Bi-Metallic Brass center in Copper-Nickel ring, 25.7 mm. **Ruler:** Albert II **Obv:** Atomic model **Rev:** Value and map **Edge:** Reeding over stars and 2's

Date	Mintage	F	VF	XF	Unc	BU
2006	—	—	—	—	—	3.50

KM# 246 2 EURO

8.5200 g., Bi-Metallic Brass center in Copper-Nickel ring, 25.7 mm. **Ruler:** Albert II **Obv:** King's portrait **Obv. Designer:** Jan Alfons Keustermans **Rev:** Relief Map of Western Europe, stars, lines and value **Rev. Designer:** Luc Luycx **Edge:** Reeded with 2's and stars

Date	Mintage	F	VF	XF	Unc	BU
2007	—	—	—	—	3.75	6.00

KM# 247 2 EURO

8.4500 g., Bi-Metallic **Ring Composition:** Copper Nickel **Center Composition:** Brass, 25.70 mm. **Ruler:** Albert II **Subject:** 50th Anniversary Treaty of Rome **Obv:** Open treaty book **Rev:** Large value at left, modified outline of Europe at right **Edge:** Reeded with stars and 2's

Date	Mintage	F	VF	XF	Unc	BU
2007	—	—	—	—	—	9.00

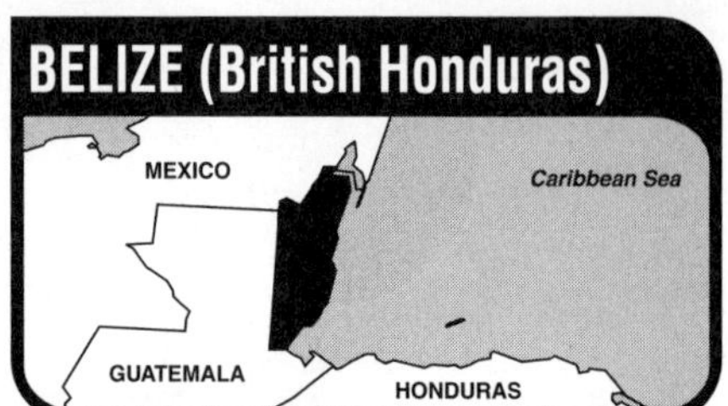

Belize, formerly British Honduras, but now a Constitutional Monarchy within the Commonwealth of Nations, is situated in Central America south of Mexico and east and north of Guatemala, with an area of 8,867 sq. mi. (22,960 sq. km.) and a population of *242,000. Capital: Belmopan. Tourism now augments Belize's economy, in addition to sugar, citrus fruits, chicle and hardwoods which are exported.

The area, site of the ancient Mayan civilization, was sighted by Columbus in 1502, and settled by shipwrecked English seamen in 1638. British buccaneers settled the former capital of Belize in the 17th century. Britain claimed administrative right over the area after the emancipation of Central America from Spain. In 1825, Imperial coins were introduced into the colony and were rated against the Spanish dollar and Honduran currency. It was declared a colony subordinate to Jamaica in 1862 and was established as the separate Crown Colony of British Honduras in 1884. In May, 1885 an order in Council authorized coins for the colony, with the first shipment arriving in July. While the Guatemalan peso was originally the standard of value, in 1894 the colony changed to the gold standard, based on the U.S. gold dollar. The anti-British Peoples United Party, which attained power in 1954, won a constitution, effective in 1964 which established self-government under a British appointed governor. British Honduras became Belize on June 1, 1973, following the passage of a surprise bill by the Peoples United Party, but the constitutional relationship with Britain remained unchanged.

In Dec. 1975, the U.N. General Assembly adopted a resolution supporting the right of the people of Belize to self-determination, and asking Britain and Guatemala to renew their negotiations on the future of Belize. Independence was obtained on Sept. 21, 1981. Elizabeth II is Head of State as Queen of Belize.

RULER

British, until 1981

MINT MARKS

H - Birmingham Mint
No mm - Royal Mint

***NOTE**: From 1975-1985 the Franklin Mint produced coinage in up to 3 different qualities. Qualities of issue are designated in ( ) after each date and are defined as follows:

(M) MATTE - Normal circulation strike or a dull finish produced by sandblasting special uncirculated (polish finish) or proof quality dies.

(U) SPECIAL UNCIRCULATED - Polished or proof-like in appearance without any frosted features.

(P) PROOF - The highest quality obtainable having mirror-like fields and frosted features.

MONETARY SYSTEM

Commencing 1864
100 Cents = 1 Dollar

COMMONWEALTH

DECIMAL COINAGE

KM# 33 CENT

2.7000 g., Bronze, 19.5 mm. **Obv:** Bust of Queen Elizabeth right **Obv. Designer:** Cecil Thomas **Rev:** Denomination within circle, date lower right of circle **Edge:** Smooth **Shape:** Scalloped

Date	Mintage	F	VF	XF	Unc	BU
1973	400,000	—	—	0.10	0.25	0.60
1974	2,000,000	—	—	0.10	0.20	0.50
1975	Inc. above	—	—	0.10	0.15	0.45
1976	3,000,000	—	—	0.10	0.15	0.45

KM# 33a CENT

0.8000 g., Aluminum, 19.5 mm. **Obv:** Bust of Queen Elizabeth right **Rev:** Denomination within circle **Edge:** Smooth, scalloped

Date	Mintage	F	VF	XF	Unc	BU
1976	2,049,999	—	—	0.10	0.25	0.60
1979	2,505,000	—	—	0.10	0.25	0.60
1980	1,505,000	—	—	0.10	0.25	0.60
1982	—	—	—	0.10	0.25	0.60
1983	—	—	—	0.10	0.25	0.60
1986	—	—	—	0.10	0.25	0.60
1987	—	—	—	0.10	0.25	0.60
1989	—	—	—	0.10	0.25	0.60
1991	—	—	—	0.10	0.25	0.60
1992	—	—	—	0.10	0.25	0.60
1994	—	—	—	0.10	0.25	0.60

Date	Mintage	F	VF	XF	Unc	BU
1996	—	—	—	0.10	0.20	0.50
1998	—	—	—	0.10	0.25	0.60
2000	—	—	—	0.10	0.25	0.60
2002	—	—	—	0.10	0.15	0.45

KM# 38 CENT

2.6700 g., Bronze **Obv:** National arms, date below, within wreath **Rev:** Swallow-tailed kite right, denomination above **Edge:** Smooth **Designer:** Michael Rizzello

Date	Mintage	F	VF	XF	Unc	BU
1974FM (M)	225,000	—	—	0.40	0.75	1.50
1974FM (P)	21,000	Value: 1.25				

KM# 46 CENT

Bronze **Obv:** National arms, date below, within wreath **Rev:** Swallow-tailed kite, right, denomination above **Edge:** Smooth **Shape:** Scalloped **Designer:** Michael Rizzello

Date	Mintage	F	VF	XF	Unc	BU
1975FM (M)	118,000	—	—	0.10	0.75	2.00
1975FM (U)	1,095	—	—	0.50	1.00	2.25
1975FM (P)	8,794	Value: 2.00				
1976FM (M)	126,000	—	—	0.10	0.75	2.00
1976FM (U)	759	—	—	0.50	1.00	2.25
1976FM (P)	4,893	Value: 2.00				

KM# 46b CENT

Aluminum **Obv:** National arms, date below, within wreath **Rev:** Swallow-tailed kite, right, denomination above **Edge:** Smooth **Shape:** Scalloped **Designer:** Michael Rizzello

Date	Mintage	F	VF	XF	Unc	BU
1977FM (U)	126,000	—	—	0.10	0.75	1.30
1977FM (P)	2,107	Value: 2.00				
1978FM (U)	125,000	—	—	0.10	0.75	1.30
1978FM (P)	1,671	Value: 2.00				
1979FM (U)	808	—	—	0.50	1.00	2.00
1979FM (P)	1,287	Value: 2.00				
1980FM (U)	761	—	—	0.15	0.75	1.00
1980FM (P)	920	Value: 2.00				
1981FM (U)	297	—	—	1.00	2.00	3.00
1981FM (P)	643	Value: 2.00				

KM# 83 CENT

Aluminum **Rev:** Swallow-tailed kite **Edge:** Smooth **Shape:** Scalloped **Designer:** Michael Rizzello

Date	Mintage	F	VF	XF	Unc	BU
1982FM (U)	—	—	0.15	0.25	1.50	1.75
1982FM (P)	—	Value: 3.00				
1983FM (U)	—	—	0.15	0.25	1.50	1.75
1983FM (P)	—	Value: 3.00				

KM# 90 CENT

Aluminum **Rev:** Swallow-tailed kite, right, denomination above **Rev. Designer:** Michael Rizzello **Edge:** Smooth **Shape:** Scalloped

Date	Mintage	F	VF	XF	Unc	BU
1984FM (U)	—	—	0.15	0.25	1.50	1.75
1984FM (P)	—	Value: 3.00				

KM# 34 5 CENTS

3.6000 g., Nickel-Brass, 20.15 mm. **Obv:** Crowned bust of Queen Elizabeth II right **Obv. Designer:** Cecil Thomas **Rev:** Denomination within circle, date below circle **Edge:** Smooth

Date	Mintage	F	VF	XF	Unc	BU
1973	210,000	—	—	0.50	1.00	2.00
1974	210,000	—	—	0.50	1.00	2.00
1975	420,000	—	—	0.15	0.40	1.00
1976	570,000	—	—	0.15	0.40	1.00
1979	—	—	—	0.15	0.40	1.00

KM# 34a 5 CENTS

1.0700 g., Aluminum, 20.15 mm. **Obv:** Bust of Queen Elizabeth II right **Obv. Designer:** Cecil Thomas **Rev:** Denomination within circle **Edge:** Plain

Date	Mintage	F	VF	XF	Unc	BU
1976	1,000,000	—	—	0.10	0.25	0.60
1979	960,000	—	—	0.10	0.25	0.75
1980	1,040,000	—	—	0.10	0.25	0.60
1986	—	—	—	0.10	0.25	0.60
1987	—	—	—	0.10	0.25	0.60
1989	—	—	—	0.10	0.25	0.60
1991	—	—	—	0.10	0.25	0.60
1992	—	—	—	0.10	0.25	0.60
1993	—	—	—	0.10	0.25	0.60
1994	—	—	—	0.10	0.25	0.60
2000	—	—	—	0.10	0.25	0.60
2002	—	—	—	0.10	0.20	0.45

KM# 39 5 CENTS

Nickel-Brass, 20 mm. **Obv:** National arms, date below, within wreath **Rev:** Fork-tailed flycatchers, denomination above **Edge:** Smooth **Designer:** Michael Rizzello

Date	Mintage	F	VF	XF	Unc	BU
1974FM (M)	50,000	—	—	0.25	1.25	2.50
1974FM (P)	21,000	Value: 2.00				

KM# 47 5 CENTS

3.6000 g., Nickel-Brass, 20 mm. **Obv:** National arms, date below, within wreath **Rev:** Fork-tailed flycatchers, denomination above **Edge:** Smooth **Designer:** Michael Rizzello

Date	Mintage	F	VF	XF	Unc	BU
1975FM (M)	24,000	—	—	0.25	1.50	2.50
1975FM (U)	1,095	—	—	0.50	1.00	2.50
1975FM (P)	8,794	Value: 1.25				
1976FM (M)	25,000	—	—	0.25	1.50	2.50
1976FM (U)	759	—	—	0.50	1.50	2.50
1976FM (P)	4,893	Value: 1.25				

KM# 47b 5 CENTS

Aluminum **Rev:** Fork-tailed flycatcher **Edge:** Smooth

Date	Mintage	F	VF	XF	Unc	BU
1977FM (U)	26,000	—	—	0.10	0.50	0.75
1977FM (P)	2,107	Value: 2.00				
1978FM (U)	25,000	—	—	0.10	0.50	0.75
1978FM (P)	1,671	Value: 2.00				
1979FM (U)	808	—	—	0.15	0.75	1.00
1979FM (P)	1,287	—	—	0.25	1.00	1.50
1980FM (U)	761	—	—	0.15	0.75	1.00
1980FM (P)	920	Value: 2.00				
1981FM (U)	297	—	—	0.15	0.75	1.00
1981FM (P)	643	Value: 2.00				

KM# 64 5 CENTS

1.0000 g., Aluminum, 20.15 mm. **Series:** World Food Day **Obv:** Crowned bust of Queen Elizabeth II, right **Obv. Designer:** Cecil Thomas **Rev:** Denomination, date upper right **Edge:** Smooth

Date	Mintage	F	VF	XF	Unc	BU
1981	—	—	—	0.10	0.35	0.70

KM# 84 5 CENTS

Aluminum **Obv:** National arms within wreath, date below **Rev:** Fork-tailed flycatchers, denomination above **Edge:** Smooth **Designer:** Michael Rizzello

Date	Mintage	F	VF	XF	Unc	BU
1982FM (U)	—	—	0.15	0.35	1.50	2.00
1982FM (P)	—	Value: 3.00				
1983FM (U)	—	—	0.15	0.35	1.50	2.00
1983FM (P)	—	Value: 3.00				

KM# 91 5 CENTS

Aluminum **Designer:** Michael Rizzello

Date	Mintage	F	VF	XF	Unc	BU
1984FM (U)	—	—	0.25	0.50	1.75	2.25
1984FM (P)	—	Value: 3.00				

KM# 35 10 CENTS

2.4000 g., Copper-Nickel, 16.95 mm. **Obv:** Crowned bust of Queen Elizabeth, right **Rev:** Denomination within circle, date below **Edge:** Reeded

Date	Mintage	F	VF	XF	Unc	BU
1974	100,000	—	0.15	0.35	0.60	1.25
1975	200,000	—	0.10	0.25	0.50	1.00
1976	700,000	—	0.10	0.20	0.45	0.75
1979	800,000	—	0.10	0.20	0.40	0.75
1980	—	—	0.10	0.20	0.40	0.75
1981	—	—	0.10	0.20	0.40	0.75
1992	—	—	0.10	0.20	0.40	0.75
2000	—	—	—	0.15	0.40	0.60

KM# 40 10 CENTS

2.4000 g., Copper-Nickel, 16.95 mm. **Obv:** National arms, date below, within wreath **Rev:** Long-tailed hermit, right, denomination above **Edge:** Reeded **Designer:** Michael Rizzello

Date	Mintage	F	VF	XF	Unc	BU
1974FM (M)	27,000	—	—	0.50	2.00	4.00
1974FM (P)	21,000	Value: 1.75				

KM# 48 10 CENTS

2.4000 g., Copper-Nickel, 16.95 mm. **Obv:** National arms, date below, within wreath **Rev:** Long-tailed hermit, right, denomination above **Edge:** Reeded **Designer:** Michael Rizzello

Date	Mintage	F	VF	XF	Unc	BU
1975FM (M)	12,000	—	—	0.25	1.50	2.00
1975FM (U)	1,095	—	—	0.30	2.00	4.00
1975FM (P)	8,794	Value: 1.50				
1976FM (M)	13,000	—	—	0.25	1.50	2.00
1976FM (U)	759	—	—	1.00	2.00	4.00
1976FM (P)	4,893	Value: 1.50				
1977FM (U)	14,000	—	—	0.25	1.50	2.00
1977FM (P)	2,107	Value: 2.00				
1978FM (U)	13,000	—	—	0.25	1.50	1.75
1978FM (P)	1,671	Value: 3.00				
1979FM (U)	808	—	—	1.00	3.00	6.00
1979FM (P)	1,287	Value: 3.00				
1980FM (U)	761	—	—	1.00	3.00	6.00
1980FM (P)	920	Value: 3.00				
1981FM (U)	297	—	—	1.00	3.00	6.00
1981FM (P)	643	Value: 4.00				

KM# 85 10 CENTS

2.4000 g., Copper-Nickel, 16.95 mm. **Rev:** Long-tailed hermit **Edge:** Reeded **Designer:** Michael Rizzello

Date	Mintage	F	VF	XF	Unc	BU
1982FM (U)	—	—	0.25	0.50	2.50	3.50
1982FM (P)	—	Value: 3.50				

Date	Mintage	F	VF	XF	Unc	BU
1983FM (U)	—	—	0.25	0.50	2.50	3.50
1983FM (P)	—	Value: 3.50				

KM# 92 10 CENTS

2.4000 g., Copper-Nickel, 16.95 mm. **Obv:** National arms within wreath, date below **Rev:** Long-tailed hermit, right, denomination above **Edge:** Reeded

Date	Mintage	F	VF	XF	Unc	BU
1984FM (U)	—	—	0.25	0.50	2.50	3.50
1984FM (P)	—	Value: 3.50				

KM# 36 25 CENTS

5.6500 g., Copper-Nickel, 23.6 mm. **Obv:** Crowned bust of Queen Elizabeth II right **Obv. Designer:** Cecil Thomas **Rev:** Denomination within circle, date below **Edge:** Reeded

Date	Mintage	F	VF	XF	Unc	BU
1974	100,000	—	0.35	0.65	1.25	2.50
1975	200,000	—	0.20	0.35	0.75	1.00
1976	790,000	—	0.20	0.35	0.75	1.00
1979	500,000	—	0.20	0.35	0.75	1.00
1980	—	—	0.20	0.35	0.75	1.00
1981	—	—	0.20	0.35	0.75	1.00
1986	—	—	0.20	0.35	0.75	1.00
1987	—	—	0.20	0.35	0.75	1.00
1988	—	—	0.20	0.35	0.75	1.00
1989	—	—	0.20	0.35	0.75	1.00
1991	—	—	0.20	0.35	0.75	1.00
1992	—	—	0.20	0.35	0.75	1.00
1993	—	—	0.20	0.35	0.75	1.00
1994	—	—	0.20	0.35	0.75	1.00
2000	—	—	0.20	0.35	0.75	1.50
2003	—	—	0.20	0.35	0.75	1.50

KM# 41 25 CENTS

Copper-Nickel, 23.6 mm. **Obv:** National arms, date below, within wreath **Rev:** Blue-crowned motmot, left, denomination above **Edge:** Reeded **Designer:** Michael Rizzello

Date	Mintage	F	VF	XF	Unc	BU
1974FM (M)	13,000	—	—	1.00	3.50	5.00
1974FM (P)	21,000	Value: 3.00				

KM# 49 25 CENTS

Copper-Nickel, 23.6 mm. **Obv:** National arms above date within wreath **Rev:** Blue-crowned motmot left, denomination below **Edge:** Reeded **Designer:** Michael Rizzello

Date	Mintage	F	VF	XF	Unc	BU
1975FM (M)	4,716	—	—	0.40	3.00	4.00
1975FM (U)	1,095	—	—	1.00	3.00	4.00
1975FM (P)	8,794	Value: 2.50				
1976FM (M)	5,000	—	—	0.50	4.00	5.00
1976FM (U)	759	—	—	2.00	4.00	6.00
1976FM (P)	4,893	Value: 2.50				
1977FM (U)	5,520	—	—	0.30	3.00	4.00
1977FM (P)	2,107	Value: 2.75				
1978FM (U)	5,458	—	—	0.30	3.00	4.50
1978FM (P)	1,671	Value: 2.75				
1979FM (U)	808	—	—	2.00	4.00	6.00
1979FM (P)	1,287	Value: 3.00				
1980FM (U)	761	—	—	0.40	3.00	4.50
1980FM (P)	920	Value: 3.00				
1981FM (U)	297	—	—	0.40	3.00	6.00
1981FM (P)	643	Value: 3.00				

KM# 86 25 CENTS

Copper-Nickel, 23.6 mm. **Obv:** National arms within wreath, date below **Rev:** Blue-crowned motmot, right, denomination below **Rev. Designer:** Michael Rizzello

Date	Mintage	F	VF	XF	Unc	BU
1982FM (U)	—	—	0.50	1.00	4.00	5.00
1982FM (P)	—	Value: 5.00				
1983FM (U)	—	—	0.50	1.00	4.00	5.00
1983FM (P)	—	Value: 5.00				

KM# 93 25 CENTS

Copper-Nickel, 23.6 mm. **Obv:** National arms within wreath, date below **Rev:** Blue-crowned motmot, right, denomination below **Rev. Designer:** Michael Rizzello **Edge:** Reeded

Date	Mintage	F	VF	XF	Unc	BU
1984FM (U)	—	—	0.50	1.00	4.00	5.00
1984FM (P)	—	Value: 5.00				

KM# 77 25 CENTS

5.6000 g., Copper-Nickel, 23.6 mm. **Subject:** World Forestry Congress **Obv:** Crowned bust of Queen Elizabeth right **Obv. Designer:** Cecil Thomas **Rev:** Denomination within circle, date below **Edge:** Reeded

Date	Mintage	F	VF	XF	Unc	BU
1985	—	—	0.25	0.40	0.85	1.10

KM# 37 50 CENTS

9.0000 g., Copper-Nickel, 27.7 mm. **Obv:** Crowned bust of Queen Elizabeth right **Obv. Designer:** Cecil Thomas **Rev:** Denomination within circle, date below **Edge:** Reeded

Date	Mintage	F	VF	XF	Unc	BU
1974	123,000	—	0.50	1.50	3.00	4.50
1975	Inc. above	—	0.40	0.75	2.00	3.00
1976	312,000	—	0.40	0.75	2.00	3.00
1979	125,000	—	0.50	1.50	3.00	4.50
1980	—	—	0.40	0.75	1.75	2.75
1989	—	—	0.40	0.75	1.75	2.75
1991	—	—	0.50	1.00	2.00	3.00
1992	—	—	0.50	1.00	2.00	3.00
1993	—	—	0.50	1.00	2.00	3.00

KM# 42 50 CENTS

Copper-Nickel, 27.7 mm. **Rev:** Frigate bird **Edge:** Reeded **Designer:** Michael Rizzello

Date	Mintage	F	VF	XF	Unc	BU
1974FM (M)	8,806	—	—	0.40	4.50	—
1974FM (P)	21,000	Value: 3.50				

KM# 50 50 CENTS

Copper-Nickel, 27.7 mm. **Obv:** National arms above date within wreath **Rev:** Frigate birds, denomination above **Edge:** Reeded **Designer:** Michael Rizzello

Date	Mintage	F	VF	XF	Unc	BU
1975FM (M)	2,358	—	—	0.65	6.00	7.00
1975FM (U)	1,095	—	—	0.45	4.50	6.00
1975FM (P)	8,794	Value: 4.00				
1976FM (M)	3,259	—	—	0.55	5.00	6.00
1976FM (U)	759	—	—	2.00	5.00	6.00
1976FM (P)	4,893	Value: 6.00				
1977FM (U)	3,540	—	—	0.45	4.50	6.00
1977FM (P)	2,107	Value: 6.00				
1978FM (U)	2,958	—	—	0.45	4.50	6.00
1978FM (P)	1,671	Value: 6.00				
1979FM (U)	808	—	—	0.55	5.00	7.50
1979FM (P)	1,287	Value: 6.00				
1980FM (U)	761	—	—	0.55	5.00	7.50
1980FM (P)	920	Value: 6.50				
1981FM (U)	297	—	—	0.55	5.00	7.50
1981FM (P)	643	Value: 6.50				

KM# 87 50 CENTS

Copper-Nickel, 27.7 mm. **Obv:** National arms within wreath, date below **Rev:** Frigate birds, denomination above **Rev. Designer:** Michael Rizzello **Edge:** Reeded

Date	Mintage	F	VF	XF	Unc	BU
1982FM (U)	—	—	0.75	1.50	6.50	7.00
1982FM (P)	—	Value: 7.50				
1983FM (U)	—	—	0.75	1.50	6.50	7.00
1983FM (P)	—	Value: 7.50				

KM# 94 50 CENTS

Copper-Nickel, 27.7 mm. **Obv:** National arms within wreath, date below **Rev:** Frigate birds, denomination above **Rev. Designer:** Michael Rizzello **Edge:** Reeded

Date	Mintage	F	VF	XF	Unc	BU
1984FM (U)	—	—	0.75	1.50	6.50	7.00
1984FM (P)	—	Value: 7.50				

KM# 118 50 CENTS

Copper-Nickel **Obv:** New portrait of Queen Elizabeth II **Rev:** Denomination within circle, date below

Date	Mintage	F	VF	XF	Unc	BU
1992	—	—	0.50	1.00	2.00	3.50
1993	—	—	0.50	1.00	2.00	3.50

KM# 43 DOLLAR
Copper-Nickel, 35 mm. **Obv:** National arms above date within wreath **Rev:** Scarlet macaws, denomination above **Edge:** Reeded **Designer:** Michael Rizzello

Date	Mintage	F	VF	XF	Unc	BU
1974FM (M)	6,656	—	—	1.00	9.00	12.00
1974FM (P)	21,000	Value: 6.00				
1975FM (M)	1,182	—	—	1.50	10.00	12.50
1975FM (U)	1,095	—	—	0.75	9.00	12.00
1975FM (P)	8,794	Value: 6.00				
1976FM (M)	1,250	—	—	1.50	10.00	12.50
1976FM (U)	759	—	—	1.25	9.00	12.50
1976FM (P)	4,893	Value: 6.00				
1977FM (U)	1,770	—	—	1.00	9.00	12.00
1977FM (P)	2,107	Value: 6.00				
1978FM (U)	1,708	—	—	1.00	9.00	12.00
1978FM (P)	1,671	Value: 6.00				
1979FM (U)	808	—	—	1.25	9.00	12.00
1979FM (P)	1,287	Value: 6.00				
1980FM (U)	761	—	—	1.25	9.00	12.00
1980FM (P)	920	Value: 6.00				
1981FM (U)	297	—	—	1.50	10.00	12.50
1981FM (P)	643	Value: 8.50				

KM# 88 DOLLAR
Copper-Nickel, 35 mm. **Obv:** National arms within wreath, date below **Rev:** Scarlet macaws, denomination above **Rev. Designer:** Michael Rizzello

Date	Mintage	F	VF	XF	Unc	BU
1982FM (U)	—	—	1.50	3.00	10.00	12.50
1982FM (P)	—	Value: 8.50				
1983FM (U)	—	—	1.50	3.00	10.00	12.50
1983FM (P)	—	Value: 8.50				

KM# 95 DOLLAR
Copper-Nickel, 35 mm. **Obv:** National arms within wreath, date below **Rev:** Scarlet macaws, denomination above **Rev. Designer:** Michael Rizzello

Date	Mintage	F	VF	XF	Unc	BU
1984FM (U)	—	—	1.50	3.00	10.00	12.50
1984FM (P)	—	Value: 8.50				

KM# 99 DOLLAR
8.9000 g., Nickel-Brass, 27 mm. **Obv:** Crowned bust of Queen Elizabeth II right **Obv. Designer:** Raphael Maklouf **Rev:** Columbus' three ships, denomination above, date below **Rev. Designer:** Robert Elderton **Edge:** Alternating reeded and plain **Shape:** 10-sided

Date	Mintage	F	VF	XF	Unc	BU
1990	—	—	—	—	2.25	3.00
1991	—	—	—	—	2.25	3.00
1992	—	—	—	—	2.25	3.00
2000	—	—	—	—	2.25	3.00
2003	—	—	—	—	2.25	3.00

BERMUDA

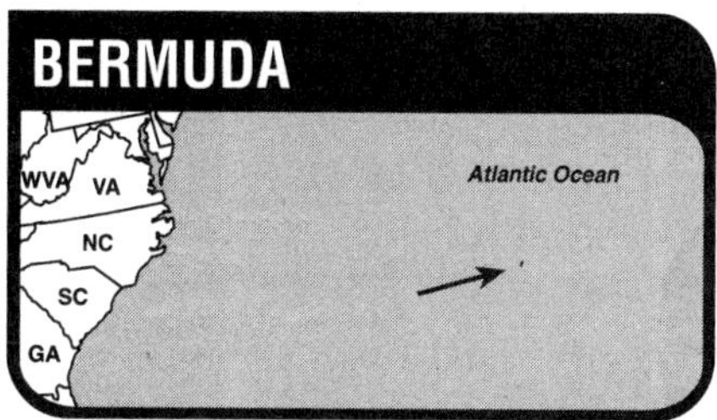

The Parliamentary British Colony of Bermuda, situated in the western Atlantic Ocean 660 miles (1,062 km.) east of North Carolina, has an area of 20.6 sq. mi. (53 sq. km.) and a population of 61,600. Capital: Hamilton. Concentrated essences, beauty preparations, and cut flowers are exported. Most Bermudians derive their livelihood from tourism. The British monarch is the head of state and is represented by a governor.

Bermuda was discovered by Juan de Bermudez, a Spanish navigator, in about 1503. British influence dates from 1609 when a group of Virginia-bound British colonists under the command of Sir George Somers was shipwrecked on the islands for 10 months. The islands were settled in 1612 by 60 British colonists from the Virginia Colony and became a crown colony in 1684. The earliest coins issued for the island were the "Hogge Money" series of 2, 3, 6 and 12 pence, the name derived from the pig in the obverse design, a recognition of the quantity of such animals then found there. The next issue for Bermuda was the Birmingham coppers of 1793; all locally circulating coinage was demonetized in 1842, when the currency of the United Kingdom became standard. Internal autonomy was obtained by the constitution of June 8, 1968.

In February, 1970, Bermuda converted from its former currency, which was sterling, to a decimal currency, the dollar unit which is equal to one U.S. dollar. On July 31, 1972, Bermuda severed its monetary link with the British pound sterling and pegged its dollar to be the same value as the U.S. dollar.

RULER
British

MINT MARKS
CHI - Valcambi, Switzerland
FM - Franklin Mint, U.S.A.*

***NOTE**: From 1975-1985 the Franklin Mint produced coinage in up to 3 different qualities. Qualities of issue are designated in ( ) after each date and are defined as follows:

(M) MATTE - Normal circulation strike or a dull finish produced by sandblasting special uncirculated (polish finish) or proof quality dies.

(U) SPECIAL UNCIRCULATED - Polished or proof-like in appearance without any frosted features.

(P) PROOF - The highest quality obtainable having mirror-like fields and frosted features.

MONETARY SYSTEM
12 Pence = 1 Shilling
20 Shillings = 1 Pound

BRITISH COLONY

POUND STERLING COINAGE

KM# 13 CROWN
28.2800 g., 0.9250 Silver 0.8410 oz. ASW, 38 mm. **Ruler:** Elizabeth II **Subject:** 350th Anniversary - Colony Founding **Obv:** Crowned head right **Obv. Designer:** Cecil Thomas **Rev:** Depicts "Deliverance" and "Patience" ships **Rev. Designer:** N. Silliman

Date	Mintage	F	VF	XF	Unc	BU
1959	100,000	—	BV	13.00	15.00	—
1959 Matte proof	—	Value: 1,000				

Note: Mintage: 6-10

KM# 14 CROWN
22.6200 g., 0.5000 Silver 0.3636 oz. ASW, 36 mm. **Ruler:** Elizabeth II **Obv:** Crowned head right **Obv. Designer:** Cecil Thomas **Rev:** Lion holding shield divides date **Rev. Designer:** George Kruger-Gray **Edge:** Reeded

Date	Mintage	F	VF	XF	Unc	BU
1964	470,000	—	—	BV	6.50	—
1964 Proof	30,000	Value: 8.50				

DECIMAL COINAGE

100 Cents = 1 Dollar

KM# 15 CENT
3.1100 g., Bronze, 19 mm. **Ruler:** Elizabeth II **Obv:** Young bust right **Obv. Designer:** Arnold Machin **Rev:** Wild boar left **Rev. Designer:** Michael Rizzello **Edge:** Smooth

Date	Mintage	F	VF	XF	Unc	BU
1970	5,500,000	—	—	0.10	0.30	0.50
1970 Proof	11,000	Value: 0.50				
1971	4,256,000	—	—	0.10	0.30	0.50
1973	2,144,000	—	—	0.10	0.30	0.50
1974	856,000	—	—	0.10	0.35	0.60
1975	1,000,000	—	—	0.10	0.30	0.50
1976	1,000,000	—	—	0.10	0.30	0.50
1977	2,000,000	—	—	0.10	0.30	0.50
1978	3,160,000	—	—	0.10	0.30	0.50
1980	3,520,000	—	—	0.10	0.30	0.50
1981	3,200,000	—	—	0.10	0.30	0.50
1982	320,000	—	—	0.10	0.30	0.50
1983	800,000	—	—	0.10	0.30	0.50
1983 Proof	6,474	Value: 1.00				
1984	800,000	—	—	0.10	0.30	0.50
1985	800,000	—	—	0.10	0.30	0.50

KM# 44 CENT
Bronze, 19 mm. **Ruler:** Elizabeth II **Obv:** Crowned head right **Obv. Designer:** Raphael Maklouf **Rev:** Wild boar left **Rev. Designer:** Michael Rizzello **Edge:** Smooth

Date	Mintage	F	VF	XF	Unc	BU
1986	1,360,000	—	—	0.10	0.30	0.50
1986 Proof	Inc. above	Value: 2.00				
1987	2,048,000	—	—	0.10	0.30	0.50
1990	1,500,000	—	—	0.10	0.30	0.50

KM# 44a CENT
3.1300 g., Steel, 19 mm. **Ruler:** Elizabeth II **Obv:** Crowned head right **Rev:** Wild boar left **Edge:** Smooth **Note:** Copper coated.

Date	Mintage	F	VF	XF	Unc	BU
1988	2,500,000	—	—	—	2.50	3.50

KM# 44b CENT
Copper Plated Zinc, 19 mm. **Ruler:** Elizabeth II **Obv:** Crowned head right **Rev:** Wild boar left **Edge:** Smooth

Date	Mintage	F	VF	XF	Unc	BU
1991	2,400,000	—	—	0.10	0.25	0.50
1993	1,600,000	—	—	0.10	0.25	0.50
1994	1,440,000	—	—	0.10	0.25	0.50
1995	1,920,000	—	—	0.10	0.25	0.50
1996	3,200,000	—	—	0.10	0.25	0.50
1997	3,400,000	—	—	0.10	0.25	0.50

KM# 107 CENT
Copper Plated Zinc, 19 mm. **Ruler:** Elizabeth II **Obv:** Head with tiara right **Obv. Designer:** Ian Rank-Broadley **Rev:** Wild boar left **Rev. Designer:** Michael Rizzello **Edge:** Smooth

Date	Mintage	F	VF	XF	Unc	BU
1999	2,400,000	—	—	—	0.50	0.75
1999 Proof	2,500	Value: 2.50				
2000	—	—	—	—	0.50	0.75
2000 Proof	—	Value: 2.50				
2001	1,600,000	—	—	—	0.50	0.75
2002	1,120,000	—	—	—	0.50	0.75
2003	800,000	—	—	—	0.50	0.75
2004	1,600,000	—	—	—	0.50	0.75
2005	3,200,000	—	—	—	0.50	0.75

KM# 16 5 CENTS
5.0600 g., Copper-Nickel, 21 mm. **Ruler:** Elizabeth II **Obv:** Young bust right **Obv. Designer:** Arnold Machin **Rev:** Queen angel fish left **Rev. Designer:** Michael Rizzello **Edge:** Smooth

Date	Mintage	F	VF	XF	Unc	BU
1970	2,190,000	—	0.10	0.15	0.50	0.75
1970 Proof	11,000	Value: 0.50				
1974	310,000	—	0.10	0.15	0.50	0.75
1975	500,000	—	0.10	0.15	0.50	0.75
1977	500,000	—	0.10	0.15	0.50	0.75
1979	500,000	—	0.10	0.15	0.50	0.75
1980	1,100,000	—	0.10	0.15	0.50	0.75
1981	900,000	—	0.10	0.15	0.50	0.75
1982	200,000	—	0.10	0.15	0.50	0.75
1983	800,000	—	0.10	0.15	0.50	0.75
1983 Proof	6,474	Value: 1.50				
1984	500,000	—	0.10	0.15	0.50	0.75
1985	—	—	0.10	0.15	0.50	0.75

KM# 45 5 CENTS
2.5400 g., Copper-Nickel, 19.59 mm. **Ruler:** Elizabeth II **Obv:** Crowned head right **Obv. Designer:** Raphael Maklouf **Rev:** Queen angel fish left **Rev. Designer:** Michael Rizzello **Edge:** Plain

Date	Mintage	F	VF	XF	Unc	BU
1986	1,400,000	—	0.10	0.15	0.50	0.75
1986 Proof	Inc. above	Value: 2.50				
1987	1,050,000	—	0.10	0.15	0.50	0.75
1988	700,000	—	0.10	0.15	0.50	0.75
1990	700,000	—	0.10	0.15	0.50	0.75
1993	600,000	—	0.10	0.15	0.50	0.75
1994	1,100,000	—	0.10	0.15	0.50	0.75
1995	700,000	—	0.10	0.15	0.50	0.75
1996	1,500,000	—	0.10	0.15	0.50	0.75
1997	300,000	—	0.10	0.15	0.50	0.75

KM# 108 5 CENTS
5.0600 g., Copper-Nickel, 21 mm. **Ruler:** Elizabeth II **Obv:** Head with tiara right **Obv. Designer:** Ian Rank-Broadley **Rev:** Queen angel fish left **Rev. Designer:** Michael Rizzello **Edge:** Smooth

Date	Mintage	F	VF	XF	Unc	BU
1999	900,000	—	—	—	0.75	1.00
1999 Proof	2,500	Value: 3.50				
2000	1,000,000	—	—	—	0.75	1.00
2000 Proof	—	Value: 3.50				
2001	1,000,000	—	—	—	0.75	1.00
2002	700,000	—	—	—	0.75	1.00
2003	700,000	—	—	—	0.75	1.00
2004	700,000	—	—	—	0.75	1.00
2005	600,000	—	—	—	0.75	1.00

KM# 17 10 CENTS
2.4500 g., Copper-Nickel, 17.8 mm. **Ruler:** Elizabeth II **Obv:** Young bust right **Obv. Designer:** Arnold Machin **Rev:** Bermuda lily **Rev. Designer:** Michael Rizzello **Edge:** Reeded

Date	Mintage	F	VF	XF	Unc	BU
1970	2,500,000	—	0.10	0.15	0.35	0.50
1970 Proof	11,000	Value: 0.50				
1971	2,000,000	—	0.10	0.15	0.35	0.50
1978	500,000	—	0.10	0.15	0.40	0.60
1979	800,000	—	0.10	0.15	0.40	0.60
1980	1,100,000	—	0.10	0.15	0.35	0.50
1981	1,300,000	—	0.10	0.15	0.35	0.50
1982	400,000	—	0.10	0.15	0.40	0.60
1983	1,000,000	—	0.10	0.15	0.35	0.50
1983 Proof	6,474	Value: 2.00				
1984	500,000	—	0.10	0.15	0.40	0.60
1985	—	—	0.10	0.15	0.40	0.60

KM# 46 10 CENTS
Copper-Nickel, 17.8 mm. **Ruler:** Elizabeth II **Obv:** Crowned head right **Obv. Designer:** Raphael Maklouf **Rev:** Bermuda lily **Rev. Designer:** Michael Rizzello **Edge:** Reeded

Date	Mintage	F	VF	XF	Unc	BU
1986	750,000	—	0.10	0.15	0.40	0.60
1986 Proof	Inc. above	Value: 3.50				
1987	2,000,000	—	0.10	0.15	0.40	0.60
1988	720,000	—	0.10	0.15	0.40	0.60
1990	1,500,000	—	0.10	0.15	0.40	0.60
1993	15,000	—	0.10	0.15	0.40	0.60
1994	1,400,000	—	0.10	0.15	0.40	0.60
1995	1,400,000	—	0.10	0.15	0.40	0.60
1996	1,000,000	—	0.10	0.15	0.40	0.60
1997	800,000	—	0.10	0.15	0.40	0.60

KM# 109 10 CENTS
2.4000 g., Copper-Nickel, 17.8 mm. **Ruler:** Elizabeth II **Obv:** Head with tiara right **Obv. Designer:** Ian Rank-Broadley **Rev:** Bermuda lily **Rev. Designer:** Michael Rizzello **Edge:** Reeded

Date	Mintage	F	VF	XF	Unc	BU
1999	1,400,000	—	—	—	0.85	1.00
1999 Proof	2,500	Value: 6.00				
2000	—	—	—	—	0.85	1.00
2000 Proof	—	Value: 6.00				
2001	1,400,000	—	—	—	0.85	1.00
2002	800,000	—	—	—	0.85	1.00
2003	600,000	—	—	—	0.85	1.00
2004	800,000	—	—	—	0.85	1.00
2005	800,000	—	—	—	0.85	1.00

KM# 18 25 CENTS
5.9200 g., Copper-Nickel, 24 mm. **Ruler:** Elizabeth II **Obv:** Young bust right **Obv. Designer:** Arnold Machin **Rev:** Yellow-billed tropical bird **Rev. Designer:** Michael Rizzello **Edge:** Reeded

Date	Mintage	F	VF	XF	Unc	BU
1970	1,500,000	—	0.30	0.50	1.25	1.50
1970 Proof	11,000	Value: 2.00				
1973	1,000,000	—	0.30	0.50	1.25	1.50
1979	570,000	—	0.30	0.50	1.25	1.50
1980	1,120,000	—	0.30	0.50	1.25	1.50
1981	2,200,000	—	0.30	0.50	1.25	1.50
1982	160,000	—	0.30	0.50	1.50	1.75
1983	600,000	—	0.30	0.50	1.25	1.50
1983 Proof	6,474	Value: 2.50				
1984	400,000	—	0.30	0.50	1.25	1.50
1985	—	—	0.30	0.50	1.25	1.50

KM# 32 25 CENTS
Copper-Nickel, 24 mm. **Ruler:** Elizabeth II **Subject:** 375th Anniversary of Bermuda **Obv:** Young bust right **Rev:** Arms of the Bermudas **Edge:** Reeded

Date	Mintage	F	VF	XF	Unc	BU
1984	36,850	—	—	1.50	4.50	—

KM# 33 25 CENTS
Copper-Nickel, 24 mm. **Ruler:** Elizabeth II **Subject:** 375th Anniversary of Bermuda **Obv:** Young bust right **Rev:** City of Hamilton arms **Edge:** Reeded

Date	Mintage	F	VF	XF	Unc	BU
1984	36,850	—	—	1.50	4.50	—

KM# 34 25 CENTS
Copper-Nickel, 24 mm. **Ruler:** Elizabeth II **Subject:** 375th Anniversary of Bermuda **Obv:** Young bust right **Rev:** Town of St. George arms **Edge:** Reeded

Date	Mintage	F	VF	XF	Unc	BU
1984	36,850	—	—	1.50	4.50	—

KM# 35 25 CENTS
Copper-Nickel, 24 mm. **Ruler:** Elizabeth II **Subject:** 375th Anniversary of Bermuda **Obv:** Young bust right **Rev:** Warwick Parish arms **Edge:** Reeded

Date	Mintage	F	VF	XF	Unc	BU
1984	36,850	—	—	1.50	4.50	—

KM# 36 25 CENTS
Copper-Nickel, 24 mm. **Ruler:** Elizabeth II **Subject:** 375th Anniversary of Bermuda **Obv:** Young bust right **Rev:** Smith's Parish arms **Edge:** Reeded

Date	Mintage	F	VF	XF	Unc	BU
1984	36,850	—	—	1.50	4.50	—

KM# 37 25 CENTS
Copper-Nickel, 24 mm. **Ruler:** Elizabeth II **Subject:** 375th Anniversary of Bermuda **Obv:** Young bust right **Rev:** Devonshire Parish arms **Edge:** Reeded

Date	Mintage	F	VF	XF	Unc	BU
1984	36,850	—	—	1.50	4.50	—

KM# 38 25 CENTS
Copper-Nickel, 24 mm. **Ruler:** Elizabeth II **Subject:** 375th Anniversary of Bermuda **Obv:** Young bust right **Rev:** Sandy's Parish arms **Edge:** Reeded

Date	Mintage	F	VF	XF	Unc	BU
1984	36,850	—	—	1.50	4.50	—

KM# 39 25 CENTS
Copper-Nickel, 24 mm. **Ruler:** Elizabeth II **Subject:** 375th Anniversary of Bermuda **Obv:** Young bust right **Rev:** Hamilton Parish arms **Edge:** Reeded

Date	Mintage	F	VF	XF	Unc	BU
1984	36,850	—	—	1.50	4.50	—

KM# 40 25 CENTS
Copper-Nickel, 24 mm. **Ruler:** Elizabeth II **Subject:** 375th Anniversary of Bermuda **Obv:** Young bust right **Rev:** Southampton Parish arms **Edge:** Reeded

Date	Mintage	F	VF	XF	Unc	BU
1984	36,850	—	—	1.50	4.50	—

KM# 41 25 CENTS
Copper-Nickel, 24 mm. **Ruler:** Elizabeth II **Subject:** 375th Anniversary of Bermuda **Obv:** Young bust right **Rev:** Pembroke Parish arms **Edge:** Reeded

Date	Mintage	F	VF	XF	Unc	BU
1984	36,850	—	—	1.50	4.50	—

KM# 42 25 CENTS
Copper-Nickel, 24 mm. **Ruler:** Elizabeth II **Subject:** 375th Anniversary of Bermuda **Obv:** Young bust right **Rev:** Paget Parish arms **Edge:** Reeded

Date	Mintage	F	VF	XF	Unc	BU
1984	36,850	—	—	1.50	4.50	—

KM# 47 25 CENTS
6.0000 g., Copper-Nickel, 24 mm. **Ruler:** Elizabeth II **Subject:** Yellow-billed tropical bird right **Obv:** Crowned head right **Obv. Designer:** Raphael Maklouf **Rev. Designer:** Michael Rizzello **Edge:** Reeded

Date	Mintage	F	VF	XF	Unc	BU
1986	560,000	—	0.30	0.50	1.00	1.50
1986 Proof	2,500	Value: 6.00				
1987	600,000	—	0.30	0.50	1.00	1.50
1988	600,000	—	0.30	0.50	1.00	1.50
1993	480,000	—	0.30	0.50	1.00	1.50
1994	1,040,000	—	0.30	0.50	1.00	1.50
1995	960,000	—	0.30	0.50	1.00	1.50
1996	1,200,000	—	0.30	0.50	1.00	1.50
1997	—	—	0.30	0.50	1.00	1.50
1998	—	—	0.30	0.50	1.00	1.50

KM# 110 25 CENTS
Copper-Nickel, 24 mm. **Ruler:** Elizabeth II **Obv:** Head with tiara right **Obv. Designer:** Ian Rank-Broadley **Rev:** Yellow-billed tropical bird right **Rev. Designer:** Michael Rizzello **Edge:** Reeded

Date	Mintage	F	VF	XF	Unc	BU
1999	800,000	—	—	—	1.50	2.00
1999 Proof	2,500	Value: 10.00				
2000	800,000	—	—	—	1.50	2.00
2000 Proof	—	Value: 9.00				
2001	800,000	—	—	—	1.50	2.00
2002	800,000	—	—	—	1.50	2.00
2003	800,000	—	—	—	1.50	2.00
2004	800,000	—	—	—	1.50	2.00
2005	1,440,000	—	—	—	1.50	2.00

KM# 19 50 CENTS
12.4200 g., Copper-Nickel, 30.5 mm. **Ruler:** Elizabeth II **Obv:** Young bust right **Obv. Designer:** Arnold Machin **Rev:** Arms **Rev. Designer:** Michael Rizzello **Edge:** Reeded

Date	Mintage	F	VF	XF	Unc	BU
1970	1,000,000	—	0.60	0.75	1.00	1.50
1970 Proof	11,000	Value: 2.00				
1978	200,000	—	0.60	0.85	1.25	1.75
1980	60,000	—	0.60	0.85	1.50	2.00
1981	100,000	—	0.60	0.85	1.25	1.75
1982	80,000	—	0.60	0.85	1.50	2.00
1983	60,000	—	0.60	0.85	1.50	2.00
1983 Proof	6,474	Value: 4.50				
1984	40,000	—	0.60	0.85	1.50	2.00
1985	40,000	—	0.60	0.85	1.50	2.00

KM# 48 50 CENTS
12.6000 g., Copper-Nickel, 30.5 mm. **Ruler:** Elizabeth II **Obv:** Crowned head right **Obv. Designer:** Raphael Maklouf **Rev:** National arms **Edge:** Reeded

Date	Mintage	F	VF	XF	Unc	BU
1986	60,000	—	0.60	0.85	1.50	2.00
1986 Proof	Inc. above	Value: 6.00				
1988	60,000	—	0.60	0.85	1.50	2.00

KM# 30 DOLLAR
Nickel-Brass **Ruler:** Elizabeth II **Subject:** Cahow over Bermuda **Obv:** Young bust right **Obv. Designer:** Arnold Machin **Rev:** Bird flying over map

Date	Mintage	F	VF	XF	Unc	BU
1983	250,000	—	—	—	4.00	5.00
1983 Proof	6,474	Value: 7.00				

KM# 56 DOLLAR
7.5600 g., Nickel-Brass, 26 mm. **Ruler:** Elizabeth II **Obv:** Crowned head right **Obv. Designer:** Raphael Maklouf **Rev:** Boat with full sails **Rev. Designer:** Eldon Trimingham III **Edge:** Alternating reeded and plain **Note:** Circulation type.

Date	Mintage	F	VF	XF	Unc	BU
1988	2,000,000	—	—	—	3.00	4.00
1993	15,000	—	—	—	4.00	5.00
Note: In sets only.						
1996	—	—	—	—	3.00	4.00
1997	—	—	—	—	3.00	4.00

KM# 111 DOLLAR
Nickel-Brass, 26 mm. **Ruler:** Elizabeth II **Obv:** Head with tiara right **Obv. Designer:** Rank-Broadley **Rev:** Sailboat **Rev. Designer:** Eldron Trimingham III

Date	Mintage	F	VF	XF	Unc	BU
1999	12,000	—	—	—	3.00	3.50
1999 Proof	2,500	Value: 22.00				
2000	—	—	—	—	3.00	3.50
2000 Proof	—	Value: 22.00				
2001	—	—	—	—	3.00	3.50
2002	12,000	—	—	—	3.00	3.50
2003	12,000	—	—	—	3.00	3.50
2004	12,000	—	—	—	3.00	3.50
2005	240,000	—	—	—	3.00	3.50

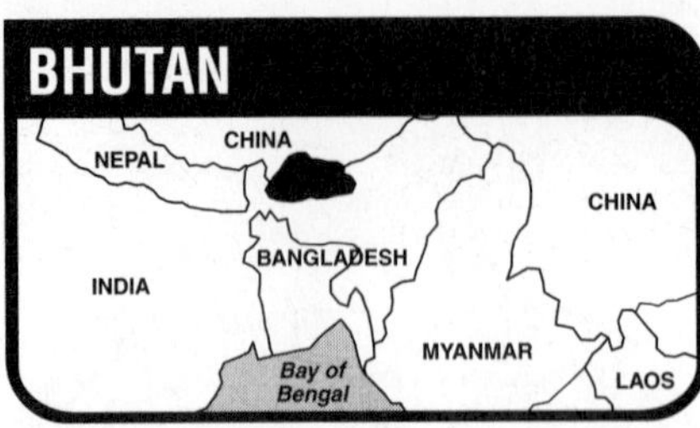

The Kingdom of Bhutan, a landlocked Himalayan country bordered by Tibet and India, has an area of 18,150 sq. mi. (47,000 sq. km.) and a population of *2.03 million. Capital: Thimphu. Virtually the entire population is engaged in agricultural and pastoral activities. Rice, wheat, barley, and yak butter are produced in sufficient quantity to make the country self-sufficient in food. The economy of Bhutan is primitive and many transactions are conducted on a barter basis.

Bhutan's early history is obscure, but is thought to have resembled that of rural medieval Europe. The country was conquered by Tibet in the 9th century, and a dual temporal and spiritual rule developed which operated until the mid-19th century, when the southern part of the country was occupied by the British and annexed to British India. Bhutan was established as a hereditary monarchy in 1907, and in 1910 agreed to British control of its external affairs. In 1949, India and Bhutan concluded a treaty whereby India assumed Britain's role in subsidizing Bhutan and guiding its foreign affairs. In 1971 Bhutan became a full member of the United Nations.

RULERS

Ugyen Wangchuk, 1907-1926
Jigme Wangchuk, 1926-1952
Jigme Dorji Wangchuk, 1952-1972
Jigme Singye Wangchuk, 1972-

CYCLICAL DATES

(1928)

(1950)

OBVERSE LEGENDS

Normal

Modified

KINGDOM

DECIMAL COINAGE

KM# 23.1 PICE

7.0000 g., Bronze, 26.5 mm. **Note:** Similar to KM#23.2.

Date	Mintage	F	VF	XF	Unc	BU
1928	—	22.50	40.00	65.00	100	—

KM# 23.2 PICE

4.9000 g., Bronze, 25.1 mm. **Obv:** Crowned bust, left **Rev:** Coin divided into nine sections, symbol on each section **Note:** Actually struck in 1931.

Date	Mintage	F	VF	XF	Unc	BU
1928	10,000	20.00	35.00	60.00	90.00	—
1928 Proof	—	Value: 100				

KM# A27 PICE

3.3000 g., Bronze **Rev:** Coin divided into nine sections, symbol in each section

Date	Mintage	F	VF	XF	Unc	BU
ND	—	—	—	—	—	—

KM# 27 PICE

2.9000 g., Bronze, 21.28 mm. **Obv:** Square at center, four sections, one symbol in each **Rev:** Coin divided into nine sections, one symbol in each section **Note:** Actually struck in 1951 and 1955. Later strikes of 1955 dates differ in detail because of recut dies.

Date	Mintage	F	VF	XF	Unc	BU
ND	Est. 1,260,000	0.75	1.00	1.50	2.25	—

KM# 29 25 NAYA PAISA

Copper-Nickel **Subject:** 40th Anniversary - Accession of Jigme Wangchuk **Obv:** Crowned bust, left, two dates below **Rev:** Emblem within circle, denomination below

Date	Mintage	F	VF	XF	Unc	BU
1966	10,000	—	0.25	0.50	1.00	2.00
1966 Proof	6,000	Value: 1.50				

KM# 30 50 NAYA PAISA

Copper-Nickel **Subject:** 40th Anniversary - Accession of Jigme Wangchuk **Obv:** Crowned bust, left, dates below **Rev:** Emblem withn circle, denomination below

Date	Mintage	F	VF	XF	Unc	BU
1966	10,000	—	0.35	0.75	1.50	3.00
1966 Proof	6,000	Value: 2.50				

KM# 26 1/2 RUPEE

5.7200 g., Nickel, 24.00 mm. **Obv:** Crowned bust, left, normal legend **Rev:** Coin divided into nine sections, one symbol in each section **Note:** Weight varies: 5.78-5.90 grams.

Date	Mintage	F	VF	XF	Unc	BU
ND(1928)	20,000	2.00	3.00	4.50	7.00	—
Note: Actually struck in 1951						
ND(1950)	202,000	1.50	2.50	3.00	4.50	—
Note: Actually struck in 1955						

KM# 24 1/2 RUPEE

Silver **Obv:** Crowned bust, left **Rev:** Coin divided into nine sections, one symbol in each section **Note:** Weight varies: 5.83-5.85 grams.

Date	Mintage	F	VF	XF	Unc	BU
ND(1928)	50,000	10.00	15.00	22.50	35.00	—
Note: Actually struck in 1929						
ND(1928) Proof	—	Value: 100				

KM# 25 1/2 RUPEE

Silver **Obv:** Legend modified

Date	Mintage	F	VF	XF	Unc	BU
ND(1928)	Inc. above	10.00	15.00	22.50	35.00	—
Note: Actually struck in 1930						

KM# 28 1/2 RUPEE

5.0800 g., Nickel **Obv:** Legend normal

Date	Mintage	F	VF	XF	Unc	BU
ND(1950)	10,000,000	0.75	1.00	1.50	2.25	—
Note: Actually struck in 1967-68						

KM# 31 RUPEE

Copper-Nickel **Subject:** 40th Anniversary - Accession of Jigme Wangchuk **Obv:** Crowned bust, left, dates below **Rev:** Emblem divides date, denomination below

Date	Mintage	F	VF	XF	Unc	BU
1966	10,000	—	0.50	1.00	2.00	4.00
1966 Proof	6,000	Value: 3.50				

KM# 32 3 RUPEE

Copper-Nickel **Subject:** 40th Anniversary - Accession of Jigme Wangchuk **Obv:** Crowned bust, left, dates below **Rev:** Emblem divides date, denomination below

Date	Mintage	F	VF	XF	Unc	BU
1966	5,826	—	—	—	6.00	9.00
1966 Proof	6,000	Value: 7.50				

REFORM COINAGE

Commencing 1974; 100 Chetrums (Paisa) = 1 Ngultrum (Rupee); 100 Ngultrums = 1 Sertum

KM# 37 5 CHETRUMS

1.4800 g., Aluminum, 22 mm. **Obv:** Crowned bust left, date at left **Rev:** Emblem above denomination **Edge:** Plain **Shape:** 4-sided

Date	Mintage	F	VF	XF	Unc	BU
1974	—	—	0.10	0.20	0.50	0.75
1974 Proof	1,000	Value: 1.25				
1975	—	—	0.10	0.15	0.20	0.50
1975 Proof	—	Value: 1.25				

KM# 45 5 CHHERTUM

1.9000 g., Bronze, 17.15 mm. **Obv:** Symbols within circle, date below **Rev:** Symbols within circle, denomination below

Date	Mintage	F	VF	XF	Unc	BU
1979	—	—	0.10	0.20	0.50	0.75
1979 Proof	—	Value: 1.00				

KM# 105 5 CHHERTUM

3.8600 g., Brass, 21.9 mm. **Obv:** Monkey right, date below **Rev:** Effigy of the old "Ma-tam", value below **Edge:** Plain

Date	Mintage	F	VF	XF	Unc	BU
2003	—	—	—	—	0.25	0.50

KM# 38 10 CHETRUMS

2.2700 g., Aluminum, 26 mm. **Obv:** Crowned bust left, date at left **Rev:** Denomination below design **Shape:** Scalloped

Date	Mintage	F	VF	XF	Unc	BU
1974	—	—	0.15	0.25	0.50	1.00
1974 Proof	1,000	Value: 1.50				

KM# 43 10 CHETRUMS

2.3000 g., Aluminum, 26 mm. **Series:** F.A.O. and International Women's Year **Obv:** Emblem above denomination **Rev:** Half figure left, grain sprig on left, date below **Shape:** Scalloped

Date	Mintage	F	VF	XF	Unc	BU
1975	4,000,000	—	0.15	0.25	0.65	1.25
1975 Proof	—	Value: 2.50				

KM# 46 10 CHHERTUM

3.6000 g., Bronze, 20.35 mm. **Obv:** Shell and design within circle, date below **Rev:** Coin divided into nine sections, within circle, symbol in each section, denomination below

Date	Mintage	F	VF	XF	Unc	BU
1979	—	—	0.15	0.30	1.00	1.50
1979 Proof	—	Value: 2.00				

KM# 39 20 CHETRUMS

Aluminum-Bronze, 22 mm. **Series:** F.A.O. **Obv:** Emblem above denomination **Rev:** Rice cultivation **Edge:** Reeded

Date	Mintage	F	VF	XF	Unc	BU
1974	1,194,000	—	0.15	0.25	0.50	0.75
1974 Prooflike	—	—	—	—	1.50	—
Note: In mint sets only						
1974 Proof	1,000	Value: 2.00				

KM# 40.1 25 CHETRUMS

Copper-Nickel **Obv:** Crowned bust, left, date at left **Rev:** Fish above denomination, type I

Date	Mintage	F	VF	XF	Unc	BU
1974	—	—	0.10	0.20	0.75	1.25

KM# 40.2 25 CHETRUMS

Copper-Nickel **Obv:** Crowned bust, left, date at left **Rev:** Fish above denomination, type II **Note:** Bottom of bust closer to rim; upper character at left revised.

Date	Mintage	F	VF	XF	Unc	BU
1974	—	—	0.10	0.20	0.75	1.25
1974 Proof	—	Value: 3.00				
1975	—	—	0.10	0.20	0.75	1.25
1975 Proof	—	Value: 3.00				

KM# 47 25 CHHERTUM

4.6000 g., Copper-Nickel, 21.95 mm. **Obv:** Fish within circle, date below **Rev:** Emblem within circle, denomination below

Date	Mintage	F	VF	XF	Unc	BU
1979	—	—	0.25	0.50	1.25	1.75
1979 Proof	—	Value: 4.00				

KM# 47a 25 CHHERTUM

4.4500 g., Steel, 22.2 mm. **Obv:** Fish within circle, date below **Rev:** Emblem within circle, denomination below **Note:** Aluminum-bronze clad.

Date	Mintage	F	VF	XF	Unc	BU
1979	—	—	—	—	2.50	3.00

KM# 48 50 CHHERTUM

6.9000 g., Copper-Nickel, 25.85 mm. **Obv:** Emblem within circle, date below **Rev:** Coin divided into nine sections within circle, symbol in each section, denomination below

Date	Mintage	F	VF	XF	Unc	BU
1979	—	—	0.25	0.65	1.50	2.00
1979 Proof	—	Value: 5.00				

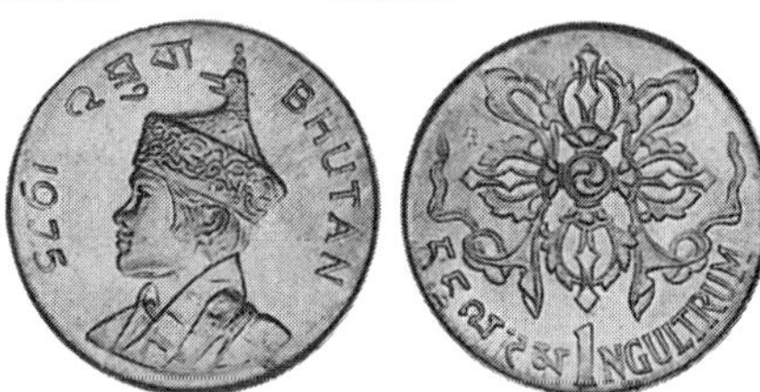

KM# 41 NGULTRUM

Copper-Nickel, 28 mm. **Obv:** Crowned bust, left, date at left **Rev:** Emblem above denomination **Edge:** Reeded security edge

Date	Mintage	F	VF	XF	Unc	BU
1974	—	—	0.20	0.50	1.25	1.75
1974 Proof	1,000	Value: 5.00				
1975	—	—	0.20	0.50	1.25	1.75
1975 Proof	—	Value: 5.00				

KM# 49 NGULTRUM

8.2000 g., Copper-Nickel, 27.95 mm. **Obv:** Emblem within circle, date below **Rev:** Coin divided into nine sections within circle, each has symbol, denomination below

Date	Mintage	F	VF	XF	Unc	BU
1979	—	—	0.30	0.75	2.00	2.75
1979 Proof	—	Value: 5.50				

KM# 49a NGULTRUM

7.9000 g., Copper-Nickel Clad Steel, 27.8 mm. **Obv:** Emblem within circle, date below **Rev:** Coin divided into nine sections within circle, each has symbol, denomination below **Note:** Magnetic

Date	Mintage	F	VF	XF	Unc	BU
1979	—	—	—	—	3.00	3.50

KM# 50 3 NGULTRUMS

Copper-Nickel, 38.5 mm. **Obv:** Crowned head, left, date below **Rev:** National emblem within circle, denomination at right **Edge:** Reeded

Date	Mintage	F	VF	XF	Unc	BU
1979	—	—	1.25	2.50	5.50	—
1979 Proof	—	Value: 8.50				

BIAFRA

On May 30, 1967, the Eastern Region of the Republic of Nigeria, an area occupied principally by the proud and resourceful Ibo tribe, seceded from Nigeria and proclaimed itself the independent Republic of Biafra with Odumegwu Ojukwu as Chief of State. Civil war erupted and raged for 31 months. Casualties, including civilian, were about two million, the majority succumbing to malnutrition and disease. Biafra surrendered to the federal government on January 15, 1970.

MONETARY SYSTEM
12 Pence = 1 Shilling
20 Shillings = 1 Pound

INDEPENDENT REPUBLIC OF BIAFRA

STANDARD COINAGE

KM# 1 3 PENCE
Aluminum

Date	Mintage	F	VF	XF	Unc	BU
1969	—	—	15.00	22.50	35.00	—

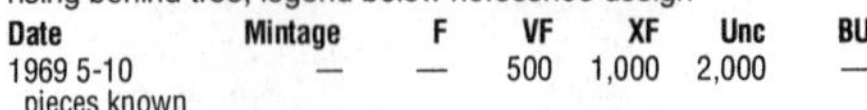

KM# 12 6 PENCE
Aluminum **Obv:** Denomination, date above **Rev:** Radiant sun rising behind tree, legend below horseshoe design

Date	Mintage	F	VF	XF	Unc	BU
1969 5-10 pieces known	—	—	500	1,000	2,000	—

KM# 2 SHILLING
Aluminum, 23.5 mm. **Obv:** Eagle divides denomination and date **Rev:** Radiant sun rising behind tree, legend below horseshoe design

Date	Mintage	F	VF	XF	Unc	BU
1969	—	—	8.00	14.00	25.00	—

KM# 3 SHILLING
Aluminum, 23.5 mm. **Obv:** Eagle divides date and denomination **Rev:** Radiant sun rising behind tree, legend below horseshoe design

Date	Mintage	F	VF	XF	Unc	BU
1969	—	—	—	350	550	—

KM# 4 2-1/2 SHILLING
Aluminum **Obv:** Date and denomination below large cat **Rev:** Rising radiant sun behind tree, legend below horseshoe design

Date	Mintage	F	VF	XF	Unc	BU
1969	—	—	8.00	18.00	40.00	—

BOHEMIA & MORAVIA

Bohemia, a western province in the Czech Republic, was combined with the majority of Moravia in central Czechoslovakia (excluding parts of north and south Moravia which were joined with Silesia in 1938) to form the German protectorate in March, 1939, after the German invasion. Toward the end of war in 1945 the protectorate was dissolved and Bohemia and Moravia once again became part of Czechoslovakia.

MONETARY SYSTEM
100 Haleru = 1 Koruna

GERMAN PROTECTORATE

STANDARD COINAGE

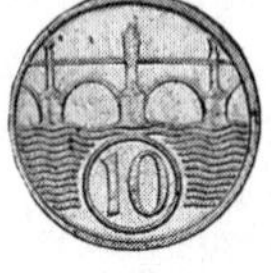

KM# 1 10 HALERU
1.8800 g., Zinc, 17 mm. **Obv:** Czech lion crowned left **Obv. Designer:** Jaroslav Eder **Rev:** Charles bridge in Prague, denomination below **Rev. Designer:** O. Spaniel **Edge:** Plain

Date	Mintage	F	VF	XF	Unc	BU
1940	82,114,000	0.35	0.75	1.50	10.00	13.50
1941	Inc. above	0.25	0.50	1.25	9.00	12.00
1942	Inc. above	0.25	0.50	1.25	9.00	12.00
1943	Inc. above	0.35	0.75	1.50	10.00	13.50
1944	Inc. above	0.75	1.50	3.00	14.00	17.50

KM# 2 20 HALERU
2.6300 g., Zinc, 20 mm. **Obv:** Czech lion crowned left **Obv. Designer:** Jaroslav Eder **Rev:** Wheat ears with sickle, denomination on left **Rev. Designer:** O. Spaniel **Edge:** Plain

Date	Mintage	F	VF	XF	Unc	BU
1940	106,526,000	0.25	0.50	1.25	9.00	12.00
1941	Inc. above	0.25	0.50	1.25	9.00	12.00
1942	Inc. above	0.25	0.50	1.25	9.00	12.00
1943	Inc. above	0.50	0.75	1.50	10.00	13.50
1944	Inc. above	0.50	1.00	2.00	12.00	16.50

KM# 3 50 HALERU
3.7000 g., Zinc, 22 mm. **Obv:** Czech lion crowned **Obv. Designer:** Jaroslav Eder **Rev:** Value within linden branches, wheat ears below **Rev. Designer:** O. Spaniel **Edge:** Milled

Date	Mintage	F	VF	XF	Unc	BU
1940	53,270,000	0.35	0.75	1.50	10.00	13.50
1941	Inc. above	0.35	0.75	1.50	10.00	13.50
1942	Inc. above	0.35	0.75	1.50	10.00	13.50
1943	Inc. above	0.75	1.50	3.00	15.00	20.00
1944	Inc. above	0.75	1.50	3.00	15.00	20.00

KM# 4 KORUNA
4.5000 g., Zinc, 23 mm. **Obv:** Czech lion crowned left **Obv. Designer:** Jaroslav Eder **Rev:** Linden branches divide denomination and date **Rev. Designer:** O. Spaniel **Edge:** Milled

Date	Mintage	F	VF	XF	Unc	BU
1941	102,817,000	0.50	0.75	1.75	12.50	16.50
1942	Inc. above	0.50	0.75	1.75	12.50	16.50
1943	Inc. above	0.50	0.75	1.75	12.50	16.50
1944	Inc. above	0.50	0.75	1.75	12.50	16.50

BOLIVIA

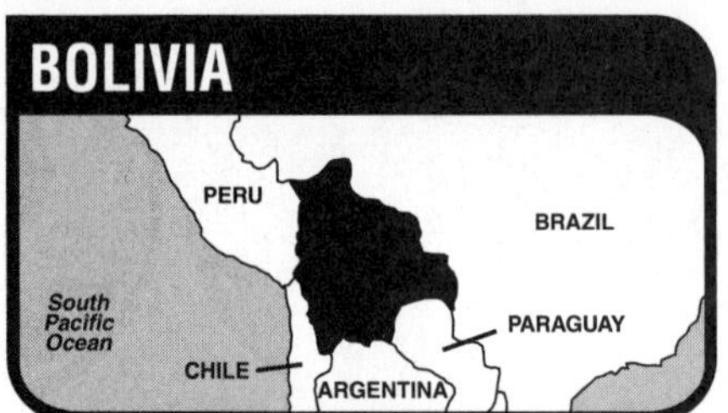

The Republic of Bolivia, a landlocked country in west central South America, has an area of 424,165 sq. mi. (1,098,580 sq. km.) and a population of *8.33 million. Its capitals are: La Paz (administrative) and Sucre (constitutional). Principal exports are tin, zinc, antimony, tungsten, petroleum, natural gas, cotton and coffee.

Much of present day Bolivia was first dominated by the Tiahuanaco Culture ca.400 BC. It had in turn been incorporated into the Inca Empire by 1440AD prior to the arrival of the Spanish, in 1535, who reduced the Indian population to virtual slavery. When Joseph Napoleon was placed upon the throne of occupied Spain in 1809, a fervor of revolutionary activity quickened throughout Alto Peru - culminating in the 1809 Proclamation of Liberty. Sixteen bloody years of struggle ensued before the republic, named for the famed liberator Simon Bolivar, was established on August 6, 1825. Since then Bolivia has survived more than 16 constitutions, 78 Presidents, 3 military juntas and over 160 revolutions.

MINT MARKS
A - Paris
(a) - Paris, privy marks only
CHI - Valcambia
H - Heaton
KN - Kings' Norton

REPUBLIC

REFORM COINAGE

1870 - 1951

KM# 173.1 5 CENTAVOS
Copper-Nickel **Obv:** Arms without shield **Rev:** Caduceus above sprays divides denomination **Note:** Coins dated 1893, 1918 and 1919 medal rotation were struck at the Heaton Mint.

Date	Mintage	F	VF	XF	Unc	BU
1909	4,000,000	1.00	6.00	12.00	20.00	—
1918	530,000	6.00	15.00	40.00	75.00	—
1919	4,370,000	5.00	10.00	20.00	45.00	—

KM# 173.3 5 CENTAVOS
Copper-Nickel **Obv:** State arms within circle, stars below **Rev:** Cornucopia and torch flank date

Date	Mintage	F	VF	XF	Unc	BU
1902	2,000,000	1.00	6.00	15.00	35.00	—
1907(a)	2,000,000	1.00	6.00	15.00	35.00	—
1908	3,000,000	2.00	8.00	20.00	35.00	—
1909	—	3.00	10.00	30.00	60.00	—

KM# 178 5 CENTAVOS
Copper-Nickel **Obv:** State emblem within circle, stars below **Rev:** Caduceus divides denomination, sprays below, date at bottom

Date	Mintage	F	VF	XF	Unc	BU
1935	5,000,000	1.00	2.00	5.00	12.00	—

KM# 174.1 10 CENTAVOS
Copper-Nickel **Obv:** State arms within circle, stars below **Obv. Legend:** REPUBLICA DE BOLIVIA **Rev:** Without privy marks **Note:** Coins dated 1893, 1918 and 1919 medal rotation were struck at the Heaton Mint.

Date	Mintage	F	VF	XF	Unc	BU
1918	1,335,000	3.00	8.00	20.00	45.00	—
1919	6,165,000	2.00	6.00	15.00	35.00	—

KM# 174.3 10 CENTAVOS

Copper-Nickel **Obv:** State emblem within circle, stars below **Rev:** Caduceus divides denomination, sprays below, date at bottom

Date	Mintage	F	VF	XF	Unc	BU
1901	—	20.00	30.00	60.00	100	—
1902	8,500,000	2.00	5.00	12.00	30.00	—
1907/2	4,000,000	6.00	10.00	25.00	50.00	—
1907	Inc. above	2.00	5.00	12.00	30.00	—
1908	6,000,000	2.00	5.00	12.00	30.00	—
1909	8,000,000	2.00	5.00	12.00	30.00	—

KM# 179.1 10 CENTAVOS

Copper-Nickel **Obv:** State emblem within circle, stars below **Rev:** Caduceus divides denomination, sprays below, date at bottom

Date	Mintage	F	VF	XF	Unc	BU
1935	10,000,000	0.50	1.00	2.50	10.00	—
1936	10,000,000	0.50	1.00	2.50	10.00	—

KM# 179.2 10 CENTAVOS

4.5100 g., Copper-Nickel, 22.58 mm. **Obv:** State emblem within circle, stars below **Rev:** Caduceus divides denomination, sprays below, date at bottom

Date	Mintage	F	VF	XF	Unc	BU
1939	—	0.50	1.00	2.50	10.00	—

KM# 179a 10 CENTAVOS

1.7500 g., Zinc, 17.90 mm. **Obv:** State emblem within circle, stars below **Rev:** Caduceus divides denomination, sprays below, date at bottom

Date	Mintage	F	VF	XF	Unc	BU
1942 (p)	10,000,000	0.50	1.00	2.50	10.00	—

KM# 180 10 CENTAVOS

Copper-Nickel, 22.5 mm. **Obv:** State emblem within circle, stars below **Rev:** Caduceus divides denomination, sprays below, date at bottom **Edge:** Reeded

Date	Mintage	F	VF	XF	Unc	BU
1937	20,000,000	0.50	1.00	2.50	10.00	—

KM# 159.2 20 CENTAVOS

4.6000 g., 0.9000 Silver 0.1331 oz. ASW **Obv:** Crossed flags and weapons behind condor topped oval arms, stars below **Obv. Legend:** REPUBLIC BOLIVIANA **Rev:** Denomination within wreath, date below **Note:** Reduced size dates and lettering, bar below CENTS. The small bar usually found below "S" in "9DS" is missing in the 1886-1888 and 1902 dates. Mint mark in monogram.

Date	Mintage	VG	F	VF	XF	Unc
1900PTS MM	170,000	2.75	3.75	8.00	20.00	50.00
1901PTS MM	40,000	3.00	5.00	13.50	28.00	60.00
1901PTS MM/.WM	—	3.00	5.00	16.50	35.00	75.00
1902PTS MM	—	6.50	10.00	20.00	50.00	100
1903PTS MM	10,000	10.00	15.00	30.00	75.00	125
1904PTS MM	—	7.00	12.00	20.00	75.00	150
1907PTS MM	—	45.00	90.00	150	275	475

KM# 176 20 CENTAVOS

4.0000 g., 0.8330 Silver 0.1071 oz. ASW **Obv:** National arms, stars below **Rev:** Denomination within wreath, date below

Date	Mintage	F	VF	XF	Unc	BU
1909H	1,500,000	2.50	5.00	15.00	30.00	—
1909H Proof	—	Value: 500				

KM# 183 20 CENTAVOS

3.2500 g., Zinc, 21.7 mm. **Obv:** State emblem within circle, stars below **Rev:** Caduceus divides denomination, sprays below, date at bottom **Note:** Medal rotation strike.

Date	Mintage	F	VF	XF	Unc	BU
1942 (p)	10,000,000	1.00	2.00	6.00	20.00	—

KM# 175.1 50 CENTAVOS (1/2 Boliviano)

11.5000 g., 0.9000 Silver 0.3327 oz. ASW **Obv:** Crossed flags and weapons behind condor topped oval arms, stars below **Obv. Legend:** REPUBLICA BOLICIANA **Rev:** Denomination within wreath, date below **Note:** Mint mark in monogram.

Date	Mintage	VG	F	VF	XF	Unc
1901/0PTS MM	—	BV	8.00	18.50	37.50	60.00
1901PTS MM	Inc. above	BV	6.00	8.00	20.00	45.00
1902PTS MM	1,530,000	BV	6.00	8.00	20.00	45.00
1903/2PTS MM	690,000	BV	7.00	16.00	37.50	60.00
1903PTS MM	Inc. above	BV	6.00	8.00	20.00	45.00
1904PTS MM	1,290,000	BV	6.00	8.00	20.00	45.00
1905PTS MM	1,690,000	BV	6.00	8.00	20.00	45.00
1905PTS AB	Inc. above	BV	6.00	8.00	20.00	45.00
1906PTS MM	630,000	BV	6.00	10.00	30.00	55.00
1906PTS AB	5,500,000	BV	6.00	8.00	20.00	45.00
1907PTS MM	50,000	BV	7.00	10.00	30.00	55.00
1908PTS MM	—	BV	6.00	8.00	20.00	45.00
1908PTS MM Inverted 8	—	BV	12.00	25.00	50.00	75.00

KM# 177 50 CENTAVOS (1/2 Boliviano)

10.0000 g., 0.8330 Silver 0.2678 oz. ASW **Obv:** National arms, stars below **Rev:** Denomination within wreath, date below

Date	Mintage	VG	F	VF	XF	Unc
1909H	1,400,000	BV	6.00	10.00	25.00	40.00
1909H	—	Value: 350				

KM# 181 50 CENTAVOS (1/2 Boliviano)

Copper-Nickel **Obv:** State emblem within circle, stars below **Rev:** Hand holding torch divides date and denomination **Note:** Most melted upon receipt in Bolivia. Medal rotation strike.

Date	Mintage	F	VF	XF	Unc	BU
1937	8,000,000	10.00	25.00	45.00	75.00	—

KM# 182 50 CENTAVOS (1/2 Boliviano)

8.4500 g., Copper-Nickel, 29.05 mm. **Obv:** State emblem within circle, stars below **Rev:** Caduceus divides denomination, sprays below, date at bottom **Note:** Medal rotation strike.

Date	Mintage	F	VF	XF	Unc	BU
1939	—	0.25	0.50	1.00	5.00	—

KM# 182a.1 50 CENTAVOS (1/2 Boliviano)

Bronze, 24 mm. **Obv:** State emblem within circle, stars below **Rev:** Caduceus divides denomination, sprays below, date at bottom **Note:** Medal rotation strike.

Date	Mintage	F	VF	XF	Unc	BU
1942 (p)	10,000,000	0.35	0.60	1.25	5.00	—

KM# 182a.2 50 CENTAVOS (1/2 Boliviano)

5.0900 g., Bronze, 25 mm. **Obv:** State emblem within circle, stars below **Rev:** Caduceus divides denomination, sprays below, date at bottom **Edge:** Reeded **Note:** Restrike - poor detail. Medal rotation strike.

Date	Mintage	F	VF	XF	Unc	BU
1942	5,310,000	0.25	0.50	1.00	4.00	—

KM# 184 BOLIVIANO

Bronze **Obv:** State emblem within circle, stars below **Rev:** Denomination within wreath, date below **Note:** Medal rotation strike. Mint mark in monogram.

Date	Mintage	F	VF	XF	Unc	BU
1951PTS	10,000,000	0.10	0.20	1.00	3.00	5.00
1951PTS Proof	10	Value: 200				
1951PTS H	15,000,000	0.10	0.20	1.00	3.00	5.00
1951PTS KN	15,000,000	0.25	0.50	1.50	4.00	6.00

KM# 185 5 BOLIVIANOS

Bronze **Obv:** National arms, stars below **Rev:** Denomination within wreath, date below **Note:** Medal rotation strike.

Date	Mintage	F	VF	XF	Unc	BU
1951	7,000,000	0.25	0.50	1.00	3.50	5.50
1951 Proof	—	Value: 200				

Date	Mintage	F	VF	XF	Unc	BU
1951 H	15,000,000	0.25	0.50	1.00	3.50	5.50
1951 KN	15,000,000	0.60	0.90	1.50	4.00	6.00

KM# 186 10 BOLIVIANOS (1 Bolivar)

Bronze **Obv:** Armored bust, right **Rev:** Denomination within wreath, date below **Note:** Medal rotation strike.

Date	Mintage	F	VF	XF	Unc	BU
1951	40,000,000	0.60	1.00	2.00	4.50	6.50
1951 Proof	—	Value: 200				

REFORM COINAGE

1965-1979; 100 Centavos = 1 Peso Boliviano

KM# 187 5 CENTAVOS

Copper Clad Steel **Obv:** State emblem within circle, stars below **Rev:** Denomination, date below **Note:** Medal rotation.

Date	Mintage	F	VF	XF	Unc	BU
1965	10,000,000	0.20	0.30	0.65	1.50	2.00
1970	100,000	0.20	0.30	0.65	2.00	2.50

KM# 188 10 CENTAVOS

Copper Clad Steel **Obv:** State emblem within circle, stars below **Rev:** Denomination, date below **Note:** Medal rotation.

Date	Mintage	F	VF	XF	Unc	BU
1965	10,000,000	0.10	0.25	0.50	1.50	2.00
1967	—	0.10	0.20	0.40	1.00	1.50
1969	5,700,000	0.10	0.20	0.40	1.00	1.50
1971	200,000	0.15	0.25	0.50	1.00	1.50
1972	100,000	0.20	0.40	0.80	1.50	2.00
1973	6,000,000	0.10	0.20	0.40	1.00	1.50

KM# 189 20 CENTAVOS

Nickel Clad Steel **Obv:** State emblem within circle, stars below **Rev:** Denomination, date below **Note:** Medal rotation.

Date	Mintage	F	VF	XF	Unc	BU
1965	5,000,000	0.20	0.40	0.70	2.00	2.50
1967	—	0.20	0.40	0.65	1.75	2.25
1970	400,000	0.20	0.40	0.80	2.50	3.50
1971	400,000	0.20	0.40	0.80	2.50	3.50
1973	5,000,000	0.20	0.40	0.60	1.50	2.00

KM# 193 25 CENTAVOS

Nickel Clad Steel **Obv:** State emblem within circle, stars below **Rev:** Denomination, date below **Note:** Medal rotation.

Date	Mintage	F	VF	XF	Unc	BU
1971	—	0.15	0.30	0.60	1.00	1.50
1972	9,998,000	0.15	0.30	0.60	1.00	1.50

KM# 190 50 CENTAVOS

4.0000 g., Nickel Clad Steel, 24 mm. **Obv:** State emblem within circle, stars below **Rev:** Denomination, date at bottom **Note:** Medal rotation.

Date	Mintage	F	VF	XF	Unc	BU
1965	10,000,000	0.15	0.30	0.65	1.75	2.25
1967	—	0.15	0.30	0.65	1.25	1.75
1972	—	0.15	0.30	0.65	1.25	1.75
1973	5,000,000	0.15	0.30	0.65	1.25	1.75
1974	15,000,000	0.15	0.30	0.65	1.25	1.75
1978	5,000,000	0.15	0.30	0.65	1.25	1.75
1980	3,600,000	0.15	0.30	0.65	1.25	1.75

KM# 192 PESO BOLIVIANOS

6.0000 g., Nickel Clad Steel, 27 mm. **Series:** F.A.O. **Obv:** State emblem within circle, stars below **Rev:** Denomination, date below **Edge:** Reeded **Note:** Medal rotation.

Date	Mintage	F	VF	XF	Unc	BU
1968	10,000,000	0.20	0.40	0.80	1.75	2.50
1969	—	0.20	0.40	0.80	1.75	2.50
1970	10,000,000	0.20	0.40	0.80	1.75	2.50
1972	—	0.20	0.40	0.80	1.75	2.50
1973	5,000,000	0.20	0.40	0.80	1.75	2.50
1974 small date	15,000,000	0.20	0.40	0.80	1.75	2.50
1978	10,000,000	0.20	0.40	0.80	1.75	2.50
1980 large date	2,993,000	0.20	0.40	0.80	1.75	2.50

KM# 191 PESO BOLIVIANOS

6.0000 g., Nickel Clad Steel, 27 mm. **Series:** F.A.O. **Obv:** State emblem within circle, stars below **Rev:** Denomination **Note:** Medal rotation.

Date	Mintage	F	VF	XF	Unc	BU
ND(1968)	40,000	1.50	2.50	3.50	6.50	9.00

KM# 197 5 PESOS BOLIVIANOS

8.5000 g., Nickel Clad Steel, 30 mm. **Obv:** State arms within circle, stars below **Rev:** Denomination, date below **Note:** Medal rotation.

Date	Mintage	F	VF	XF	Unc	BU
1976	20,000,000	0.65	1.25	2.50	5.00	6.50
1978	10,000,000	0.65	1.25	2.50	5.00	6.50
1980	5,231,000	0.65	1.25	2.50	5.00	6.50

KM# 194 100 PESOS BOLIVIANOS

10.0000 g., 0.9330 Silver 0.3000 oz. ASW **Subject:** 150th Anniversary of Independence **Obv:** National arms divide dates **Rev:** Simon Bolivar and Hugo Banzer Suarez left, denomination below **Note:** Medal rotation.

Date	Mintage	F	VF	XF	Unc	BU
ND(1975)	160,000	—	BV	7.00	10.00	—

REFORM COINAGE

1987-; 1,000,000 Peso Bolivianos = 1 Boliviano; 100 Centavos = 1 Boliviano

KM# 200 2 CENTAVOS

1.0000 g., Stainless Steel, 14.01 mm. **Obv:** National arms, star below **Rev:** Denomination within circle, date below **Edge:** Plain

Date	Mintage	F	VF	XF	Unc	BU
1987	20,000,000	—	—	—	0.35	0.50

KM# 201 5 CENTAVOS

Stainless Steel **Obv:** National arms, star below **Rev:** Denomination within circle, date below

Date	Mintage	F	VF	XF	Unc	BU
1987	20,000,000	—	—	—	0.50	0.65

KM# 202 10 CENTAVOS

Stainless Steel **Obv:** National arms, star below **Rev:** Denomination within circle, date below

Date	Mintage	F	VF	XF	Unc	BU
1987	20,000,000	—	—	—	0.65	0.85
1991	23,000,000	—	—	—	0.50	0.65
1995	14,000,000	—	—	—	0.50	0.65
1997	33,000,000	—	—	—	0.50	0.65

KM# 202a 10 CENTAVOS

2.2300 g., Copper Clad Steel, 19.00 mm.

Date	Mintage	F	VF	XF	Unc	BU
1997	—	—	—	—	0.50	0.65

KM# 213 10 CENTAVOS

Copper Clad Steel

Date	Mintage	F	VF	XF	Unc	BU
2001	—	—	—	—	0.50	1.00

KM# 203 20 CENTAVOS

3.2500 g., Stainless Steel, 22 mm. **Obv:** National arms, star below **Rev:** Denomination within circle, date below **Edge:** Plain

Date	Mintage	F	VF	XF	Unc	BU
1987	20,000,000	—	—	—	0.75	1.00
1991	20,000,000	—	—	—	0.65	0.85
1995	14,000,000	—	—	—	0.65	0.85
1997	19,000,000	—	—	—	0.65	0.85

KM# 204 50 CENTAVOS

5.0800 g., Stainless Steel, 24 mm. **Obv:** National arms, star below **Rev:** Denomination within circle, date below **Edge:** Plain

Date	Mintage	F	VF	XF	Unc	BU
1987	15,000,000	—	—	—	1.00	1.25
1991	20,000,000	—	—	—	0.75	1.00
1995	14,000,000	—	—	—	0.75	1.00
1997	15,000,000	—	—	—	0.75	1.00
2001	—	—	—	—	0.75	1.00

KM# 205 BOLIVIANO

Stainless Steel **Obv:** National arms, star below **Rev:** Denomination within circle, date below

Date	Mintage	F	VF	XF	Unc	BU
1987	10,000,000	—	—	—	1.75	2.00
1991	20,000,000	—	—	—	1.00	1.25
1995	9,000,000	—	—	—	1.00	1.25
1997	17,000,000	—	—	—	1.00	1.25

KM# 206.1 2 BOLIVIANOS

Stainless Steel **Obv:** National arms, star below **Rev:** Denomination within circle, date below **Shape:** 11-sided

Date	Mintage	F	VF	XF	Unc	BU
1991	18,000,000	—	—	—	2.00	3.00

KM# 206.2 2 BOLIVIANOS

Stainless Steel, 29 mm. **Obv:** National arms, star below **Rev:** Denomination within circle, date below **Shape:** 11-sided **Note:** Increased size.

Date	Mintage	F	VF	XF	Unc	BU
1995	11,000,000	—	—	—	2.00	3.00
1997	—	—	—	—	2.00	3.00

KM# 212 5 BOLIVIANOS

Center Weight: 5.0000 g. **Center Composition:** Brass Clad Steel, 23 mm. **Obv:** National arms within inner circle **Rev:** Denomination within inner circle **Edge:** Reeded

Date	Mintage	F	VF	XF	Unc	BU
2001	—	—	—	—	3.50	5.00

BOSNIA AND HERZEGOVINA

The Republic of Bosnia and Herzegovina borders Croatia to the north and west, Serbia to the east and Montenegro in the southeast with only 12.4 mi. of coastline. The total land area is 19,735 sq. mi. (51,129 sq. km.). They have a population of *4.34 million. Capital: Sarajevo. Electricity, mining and agriculture are leading industries.

After the defeat of Germany in WWII, during which Bosnia was under the control of Pavelic of Croatia, a new Socialist Republic was formed under Marshall Tito having six constituent republics, all subservient, quite similar to the constitution of the U.S.S.R. Military and civil loyalty was with Tito, not with Moscow. In Jan. 1990, the Yugoslav Government announced a rewriting of the Constitution, abolishing the Communist Party's monopoly of power. Opposition parties were legalized in July 1990. On Oct. 15, 1991 the National Assembly adopted a "Memorandum on Sovereignty", the envisaged Bosnian autonomy within a Yugoslav federation. In March 1992, an agreement was reached under EC auspices by Moslems, Serbs and Croats to set up 3 autonomous ethnic communities under a central Bosnian authority. Independence was declared on April 5, 1992. The 2 Serbian members of government resigned and fighting broke out between all 3 ethnic communities. The Dayton (Ohio) Peace Accord was signed in 1995, which recognized the Federation of Bosnia and Herzegovina and the Srpska (Serbian) Republic. Both governments maintain separate military forces, school systems, etc. The United Nations is currently providing humanitarian aid while a recent peace treaty allowed NATO "Peace Keeping" forces to be deployed in Dec. 1995 replacing the United Nations troops previously acting in a similar role.

MINT MARK

PM - Pobjoy Mint

MONETARY SYSTEM

1 Dinara = 100 Para, 1992-1998

1 Convertible Marka = 100 Convertible Feniga = 1 Deutschemark 1998-

NOTE: German Euros circulate freely.

REPUBLIC

REFORM COINAGE

1998-

KM# 121 5 FENINGA

2.6600 g., Steel, 18 mm. **Obv:** Denomination on map **Rev:** Triangle and stars **Edge:** Reeded

Date	Mintage	F	VF	XF	Unc	BU
2005	—	—	—	—	1.00	1.25

KM# 115 10 FENINGA

3.9000 g., Copper-Plated-Steel, 20 mm. **Obv:** Denomination on map within circle **Rev:** Triangle and stars, date at left, within circle **Edge:** Plain

Date	Mintage	F	VF	XF	Unc	BU
1998	—	—	—	—	0.50	0.75
2000 In mint sets only	—	—	—	—	—	1.00
2004	—	—	—	—	0.50	0.75

KM# 116 20 FENINGA

4.5000 g., Copper-Plated-Steel, 22 mm. **Obv:** Denomination on map within circle **Rev:** Triangle and stars, date at left, within circle

Date	Mintage	F	VF	XF	Unc	BU
1998	—	—	—	—	1.00	1.25
2000 In mint sets only	—	—	—	—	—	1.50
2004	—	—	—	—	1.00	1.25

KM# 117 50 FENINGA

Copper-Plated-Steel **Obv:** Denomination on map within circle **Rev:** Triangle and stars, date at left, within circle

Date	Mintage	F	VF	XF	Unc	BU
1998	—	—	—	—	2.25	2.50
2000 In mint sets only	—	—	—	—	—	3.00

KM# 118 KONVERTIBLE MARKA

4.9000 g., Nickel Plated Steel, 24 mm. **Obv:** Denomination **Rev:** Coat of arms above date **Edge:** Reeded and plain sections

Date	Mintage	F	VF	XF	Unc	BU
2000	—	—	—	—	5.50	6.00
2003	—	—	—	—	5.50	6.00
2006	—	—	—	—	—	5.00

KM# 119 2 KONVERTIBLE MARKA

6.9000 g., Bi-Metallic Copper-Nickel center in Nickel-Brass ring, 25.75 mm. **Obv:** Denomination within circle **Rev:** Dove of peace, date at right, within circle **Edge:** Reeded and plain sections

Date	Mintage	F	VF	XF	Unc	BU
2000	—	—	—	—	13.50	15.00
2002	—	—	—	—	13.50	15.00
2003	—	—	—	—	13.50	15.00

KM# 120 5 KONVERTIBLE MARKA

10.3500 g., Bi-Metallic **Ring Composition:** Copper Nickel **Center Composition:** Brass, 30 mm. **Obv:** Denomination within circle **Rev:** Dove of Peace in flight **Edge:** Reeded

Date	Mintage	F	VF	XF	Unc	BU
2005	—	—	—	—	17.50	20.00

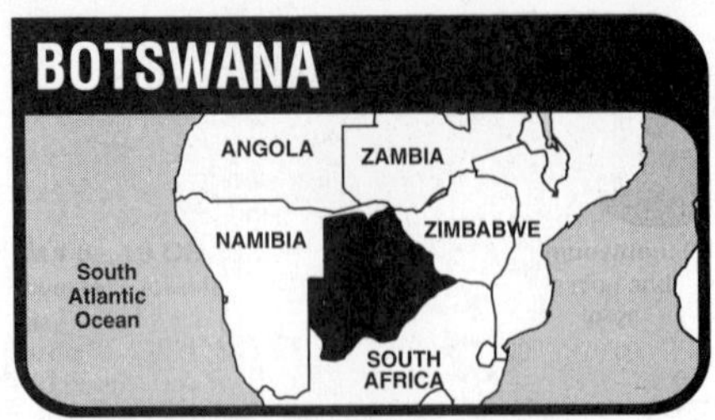

The Republic of Botswana (formerly Bechuanaland), located in south central Africa between Namibia and Zimbabwe, has an area of 224,607 sq. mi. (600,370 sq. km.) and a population of *1.62 million. Capital: Gaborone. Botswana is a member of a Customs Union with South Africa, Lesotho, and Swaziland. The economy is primarily pastoral with a rapidly developing mining industry, of which diamonds, copper and nickel are the chief elements. Meat products and diamonds comprise 85 percent of the exports.

Little is known of the origin of the peoples of Botswana. The early inhabitants, the Bushmen, did not develop a recorded history and are now dying out. The ancestors of the present Botswana residents probably arrived about 1600AD in Bantu migrations from the north and east. Bechuanaland was first united early in the 19th century under Chief Khama III to more effectively resist incursions by the Boer trekkers from Transvaal and by the neighboring Matabeles. As the Boer threat intensified, appeals for protection were made to the British Government, which proclaimed the whole of Bechuanaland a British protectorate in 1885. In 1895, the southern part of the protectorate was annexed to Cape Province. The northern part, known as the Bechuanaland Protectorate, remained under British administration until it became the independent Republic of Botswana on Sept. 30, 1966. Botswana is a member of the Commonwealth of Nations. The president is Chief of State and Head of government.

MINT MARK

B - Berne

MONETARY SYSTEM

100 Cents = 1 Thebe

REPUBLIC

REFORM COINAGE

100 Thebe = 1 Pula

KM# 3 THEBE

0.8000 g., Aluminum, 18.5 mm. **Obv:** National arms, date below **Rev:** Head of Turako, denomination upper right **Edge:** Reeded

Date	Mintage	F	VF	XF	Unc	BU
1976	15,000,000	—	0.10	0.15	0.40	0.75
1976 Proof	26,000	Value: 0.75				
1981 Proof	10,000	Value: 1.00				
1983	5,000,000	—	0.10	0.20	0.45	0.75
1984	5,000,000	—	0.10	0.20	0.45	0.75
1985	—	—	0.10	0.20	0.45	0.75
1987	—	—	0.10	0.20	0.40	0.75
1988	—	—	0.10	0.20	0.40	0.75
1989	—	—	0.10	0.20	0.40	0.75
1991	—	—	0.10	0.20	0.40	0.75

KM# 14 2 THEBE

1.8000 g., Bronze, 17.4 mm. **Subject:** World Food Day **Obv:** National arms above date **Rev:** Millet, denomination at top **Shape:** 12-sided

Date	Mintage	F	VF	XF	Unc	BU
1981	9,990,000	—	0.15	0.25	0.50	0.75
1981 Proof	10,000	Value: 1.00				
1985	—	—	0.15	0.25	0.50	0.75

KM# 4 5 THEBE

2.8000 g., Bronze, 19.5 mm. **Obv:** National arms above date **Rev:** Toko left, denomination at top **Edge:** Reeded

Date	Mintage	F	VF	XF	Unc	BU
1976	3,000,000	—	0.15	0.25	0.50	1.00
1976 Proof	26,000	Value: 1.25				
1977	250,000	—	0.15	0.25	0.50	1.00
1979	200,000	—	0.15	0.25	0.50	1.00
1980	1,000,000	—	0.15	0.25	0.50	1.00
1981	4,990,000	—	0.15	0.25	0.50	1.00
1981 Proof	10,000	Value: 1.50				
1984	2,000,000	—	0.15	0.25	0.50	1.00
1985	—	—	0.15	0.25	0.50	1.00
1988	—	—	0.15	0.25	0.50	1.00
1989	—	—	0.15	0.25	0.50	1.00

KM# 4a.1 5 THEBE

Bronze Clad Steel, 19.5 mm. **Edge:** Plain

Date	Mintage	F	VF	XF	Unc	BU
1991	—	—	0.15	0.25	0.50	1.00

KM# 4a.2 5 THEBE

Bronze Clad Steel, 19.5 mm. **Edge:** Reeded **Note:** Modified design.

Date	Mintage	F	VF	XF	Unc	BU
1996	—	—	0.15	0.25	0.50	1.00

KM# 26 5 THEBE

2.4100 g., Bronze Clad Steel, 16.79 mm. **Obv:** National arms **Rev:** Toko bird **Edge:** Plain **Shape:** 7-sided

Date	Mintage	F	VF	XF	Unc	BU
1998	—	—	0.15	0.25	0.50	1.00

KM# 5 10 THEBE

4.0000 g., Copper-Nickel, 22 mm. **Rev:** South African Oryx right, denomination above **Edge:** Reeded

Date	Mintage	F	VF	XF	Unc	BU
1976	1,500,000	—	0.25	0.40	0.75	1.25
1976 Proof	26,000	Value: 1.50				
1977	500,000	—	0.25	0.40	0.75	1.25
1979	750,000	—	0.25	0.40	0.75	1.25
1980	—	—	0.25	0.40	0.75	1.25
1981	2,590,000	—	0.25	0.40	0.75	1.25
1981 Proof	10,000	Value: 1.75				
1984	4,000,000	—	0.20	0.30	0.60	1.00
1985	—	—	0.20	0.30	0.60	1.00
1989	—	—	0.20	0.30	0.60	1.00

KM# 5a 10 THEBE

3.8000 g., Nickel Clad Steel, 22 mm. **Edge:** Reeded

Date	Mintage	F	VF	XF	Unc	BU
1991	—	—	0.20	0.30	0.60	1.00

KM# 27 10 THEBE

Nickel Clad Steel **Obv:** National arms, date below **Rev:** South African Oryx right, denomination above

Date	Mintage	F	VF	XF	Unc	BU
1998	—	—	0.20	0.30	0.75	1.25

KM# 6 25 THEBE

5.8000 g., Copper-Nickel, 25 mm. **Obv:** National arms with supporters, date below **Rev:** Zebu left, denomination above **Edge:** Reeded

Date	Mintage	F	VF	XF	Unc	BU
1976	1,500,000	—	0.25	0.55	1.50	2.00
1976 Proof	26,000	Value: 2.50				
1977	265,000	—	0.25	0.60	1.75	2.25
1981	740,000	—	0.25	0.60	1.50	2.00
1981 Proof	10,000	Value: 2.50				
1982	400,000	—	0.25	0.60	1.75	2.25
1984	2,000,000	—	0.25	0.55	1.50	2.00
1985	—	—	0.30	0.60	1.50	2.00
1989	—	—	0.30	0.60	1.50	2.00

KM# 6a 25 THEBE

Nickel Clad Steel, 25 mm.

Date	Mintage	F	VF	XF	Unc	BU
1991	—	—	0.30	0.60	1.50	2.00

KM# 28 25 THEBE

3.5000 g., Nickel Clad Steel **Obv:** National arms with supporters, date below **Rev:** Zebu bull, left, denomination above **Shape:** 7-sided

Date	Mintage	F	VF	XF	Unc	BU
1998	—	—	0.30	0.60	1.50	2.00
1999	—	—	0.30	0.60	1.50	2.00

KM# 7 50 THEBE

11.4000 g., Copper-Nickel, 28.5 mm. **Obv:** National arms with supporters, date below **Rev:** African Fish Eagle left, denomination above

Date	Mintage	F	VF	XF	Unc	BU
1976	266,000	—	0.65	1.35	2.25	2.75
1976 Proof	26,000	Value: 3.00				
1977	250,000	—	0.65	1.35	2.25	2.75
1980	—	—	0.65	1.35	2.25	2.75
1981 Proof	10,000	Value: 3.50				
1984	2,000,000	—	0.65	1.35	2.25	2.75
1985	—	—	0.65	1.35	2.25	2.75

KM# 7a 50 THEBE

11.1700 g., Nickel Clad Steel, 28.5 mm.

Date	Mintage	F	VF	XF	Unc	BU
1991	—	—	0.65	1.35	2.25	2.75

KM# 29 50 THEBE

4.8200 g., Nickel Clad Steel **Obv:** National arms with supporters, date below **Rev:** African Fish Eagle left, denomination above

Date	Mintage	F	VF	XF	Unc	BU
1996	—	—	0.50	1.00	2.00	2.50
1998	—	—	0.50	1.00	2.00	2.50

KM# 8 PULA

16.4000 g., Copper-Nickel, 29.5 mm. **Obv:** National arms with supporters, date below **Rev:** Zebra left, denomination above **Shape:** Scalloped

Date	Mintage	F	VF	XF	Unc	BU
1976	166,000	—	1.50	2.50	5.00	6.50
1976 Proof	26,000	Value: 7.00				
1977	500,000	—	1.50	2.50	5.00	6.50
1981	—	—	1.50	2.50	5.00	6.50
1981 Proof	10,000	Value: 7.50				
1985	—	—	1.50	2.50	5.00	6.50
1987	—	—	1.50	2.50	5.00	6.50

KM# 24 PULA

Nickel-Brass **Obv:** National arms with supporters, date below **Rev:** Zebra left, denomination above **Shape:** 7-sided

Date	Mintage	F	VF	XF	Unc	BU
1991	—	—	1.00	1.75	3.50	5.00
1997	—	—	1.00	1.75	3.50	5.00

KM# 25 2 PULA
6.0300 g., Nickel-Brass **Subject:** Wildlife **Obv:** National arms with suppporters, date below **Rev:** Rhinoceros left, denomination above **Shape:** 7-sided

Date	Mintage	F	VF	XF	Unc	BU
1994	—	—	1.75	2.75	5.50	10.00

KM# 25a 2 PULA
Brass **Subject:** Wildlife **Obv:** National arms with supporters, date below **Rev:** Rhinoceros, left, denomination above **Shape:** 7-sided

Date	Mintage	F	VF	XF	Unc	BU
2004	—	—	—	—	2.75	3.50

KM# 30 5 PULA
6.2000 g., Bi-Metallic Copper-Nickel center in Brass ring, 23.4 mm. **Obv:** National arms with supporters, date below, within circle **Rev:** Mophane worm on a mophane leaf, denomination below, within circle **Edge:** Reeded

Date	Mintage	F	VF	XF	Unc	BU
2000	—	—	—	—	6.50	10.00

The Federative Republic of Brazil, which comprises half the continent of South America and is the only Latin American country deriving its culture and language from Portugal, has an area of 3,286,488 sq. mi. (8,511,965 sq. km.) and a population of *169.2 million. Capital: Brasilia. The economy of Brazil is as varied and complex as any in the developing world. Agriculture is a mainstay of the economy, while only 4 percent of the area is under cultivation. Known mineral resources are almost unlimited in variety and size of reserves. A large, relatively sophisticated industry ranges from basic steel and chemical production to finished consumer goods. Coffee, cotton, iron ore and cocoa are the chief exports.

Brazil was discovered and claimed for Portugal by Admiral Pedro Alvares Cabral in 1500. Portugal established a settlement in 1532 and proclaimed the area a royal colony in 1549. During the Napoleonic Wars, Dom Joao VI established the seat of Portuguese government in Rio de Janeiro. When he returned to Portugal, his son Dom Pedro I declared Brazil's independence on Sept. 7, 1822, and became emperor of Brazil. The Empire of Brazil was maintained until 1889 when the federal republic was established. The Federative Republic was established in 1946 by terms of a constitution drawn up by a constituent assembly. Following a coup in 1964 the armed forces retained overall control under a dictatorship until civilian government was restored on March 15, 1985. The current constitution was adopted in 1988.

MINT MARKS

(a) - Paris, privy marks only
A - Berlin 1913
B - Bahia

MONETARY SYSTEM

(1833-1942)
1000 Reis = 1 Mil Reis

(1942-1967)
100 Centavos = 1 Cruzeiro

REPUBLIC

FIRST COINAGE - REIS

1889-1942

KM# 490 20 REIS
7.4900 g., Bronze **Obv:** Star with wreath in background **Rev:** Denomination

Date	Mintage	F	VF	XF	Unc	BU
1901	713,000	1.00	4.50	9.50	20.00	—
1904	850,000	1.00	4.50	9.50	20.00	—
1905	1,075,000	3.50	7.00	14.50	48.00	—
1906	215,000	2.00	5.00	12.00	30.00	—
1908	4,558,000	1.00	4.50	9.50	20.00	—
1909	1,215,000	5.00	10.00	22.00	95.00	—
1910	828,000	1.00	4.50	9.50	20.00	—
1911	1,545,000	1.00	4.50	9.50	20.00	—
1912	480,000	1.00	4.50	9.50	25.00	—

KM# 516.2 20 REIS
Copper-Nickel **Obv:** Denomination at center, dot between "2" and "0" in denomination **Rev:** Bust with cap, right, within 3/4 circle of stars

Date	Mintage	F	VF	XF	Unc	BU
1918	—	0.25	0.50	1.00	4.00	—
1919	2,870,000	0.25	0.50	1.00	4.00	—
1920	825,000	0.25	0.50	1.25	5.00	—
1921	1,020,000	0.25	0.50	1.25	5.00	—
1927	53,000	5.00	10.00	30.00	80.00	—
1935	100	200	450	900	1,500	—

KM# 516.1 20 REIS
Copper-Nickel **Rev:** No dot between "2" and "0" in denomination

Date	Mintage	F	VF	XF	Unc	BU
1918	—	0.25	0.50	2.00	5.00	—
1919	—	0.25	0.50	1.00	4.00	—
1920	—	0.25	0.50	1.25	5.00	—

KM# 491 40 REIS
Bronze **Obv:** Stars at center surrounded by circle of stars **Rev:** Denomination within circle

Date	Mintage	F	VF	XF	Unc	BU
1901	525,000	0.75	2.00	3.00	15.00	—
1907	218,000	0.75	2.00	3.00	15.00	—
1908	4,639,000	0.75	2.00	3.00	15.00	—
1909	4,226,000	0.75	2.00	3.50	17.50	—
1910	848,000	0.75	2.00	4.00	20.00	—
1911	1,660,000	0.75	2.00	4.00	20.00	—
1912	819,000	1.00	2.50	4.50	22.50	—

KM# 517 50 REIS
Copper-Nickel **Obv:** Denomination within circle, date flanked by stars below **Rev:** Liberty head right

Date	Mintage	F	VF	XF	Unc	BU
1918	558,000	0.15	0.35	1.00	6.00	—
1919	558,000	0.15	0.35	1.00	6.00	—
1920	72,000	0.40	1.00	3.50	16.00	—
1921	682,000	0.15	0.35	1.00	6.00	—
1922	176,000	0.40	1.00	3.50	16.00	—
1925	128,000	0.40	1.50	4.00	20.00	—
1926	194,000	0.40	1.50	4.00	20.00	—
1931	20,000	2.00	10.00	40.00	85.00	—
1935	100	125	300	800	1,500	—

KM# 503 100 REIS
5.0000 g., Copper-Nickel, 20.96 mm. **Obv:** National arms, denomination above **Rev:** Liberty bust right **Note:** Roman numeral date.

Date	Mintage	F	VF	XF	Unc	BU
1901	15,775,000	0.40	1.50	3.50	20.00	—

KM# 518 100 REIS
4.9400 g., Copper-Nickel, 21.3 mm. **Obv:** Denomination within circle, date below **Rev:** Liberty bust right

Date	Mintage	F	VF	XF	Unc	BU
1918	600,000	0.40	1.50	3.25	17.50	—
1919	1,219,000	0.40	1.50	3.25	17.50	—
1920	1,251,000	0.40	1.50	3.25	17.50	—
1921	853,000	0.40	1.50	3.25	17.50	—
1922	347,000	0.40	1.50	4.75	20.00	—
1923	956,000	0.40	1.50	4.75	20.00	—
1924	1,478,000	1.00	2.50	8.50	25.00	—
1925	2,502,000	0.30	1.25	2.75	17.00	—
1926	1,807,000	0.50	1.50	4.75	20.00	—
1927	1,451,000	0.30	1.25	2.75	17.00	—
1928	1,514,000	0.30	1.25	2.75	17.00	—
1929	2,503,000	0.30	1.25	2.75	17.00	—
1930	2,398,000	0.30	1.25	2.75	17.00	—
1931	2,500,000	0.25	1.00	2.25	17.00	—
1932	948,000	0.25	1.00	2.25	17.00	—
1933	1,314,000	0.25	1.00	2.25	17.00	—
1934	3,614,000	0.25	1.00	2.25	17.00	—
1935	3,442,000	0.25	1.00	2.25	17.00	—

KM# 527 100 REIS
Copper-Nickel, 21 mm. **Subject:** 400th Anniversary of Colonization **Obv:** Cazique Tibirica **Obv. Designer:** Leopolds Campos **Rev:** Denomination below design **Rev. Designer:** Walter R. Toledo **Edge:** Reeded **Note:** Medal rotation.

Date	Mintage	F	VF	XF	Unc	BU
ND(1932)	1,012,000	0.50	1.00	2.25	6.50	—

KM# 536 100 REIS
4.6200 g., Copper-Nickel, 19 mm. **Obv:** Anchor divides denomination **Obv. Designer:** Walter R. Toledo **Rev:** Admiral Marques Tamandare, founder of Brazilian Navy **Rev. Designer:** Calmon Barreto **Edge:** Plain **Note:** Medal rotation.

Date	Mintage	F	VF	XF	Unc	BU
1936	3,928,000	0.20	0.50	1.50	3.00	—
1937	7,905,000	0.10	0.35	1.00	2.50	—
1938	8,618,000	0.10	0.35	1.00	2.50	—

KM# 544 100 REIS
2.5300 g., Copper-Nickel, 16.87 mm. **Obv:** Denomination within wreath **Rev:** Dr. Getulio Vargas **Edge:** Fluted **Shape:** 16-sided

Date	Mintage	F	VF	XF	Unc	BU
1938	8,106,000	0.10	0.20	0.50	1.50	—
1940	8,797,000	0.10	0.20	0.50	1.50	—
1942	1,285,000	0.10	0.20	0.50	1.50	—

Note: The 1942 issue has a deeper yellow cast due to higher copper content

KM# 504 200 REIS
Copper-Nickel, 25 mm. **Obv:** National arms, denomination above **Rev:** Liberty bust right **Edge:** Plain **Note:** Roman numeral date.

Date	Mintage	F	VF	XF	Unc	BU
1901	12,625,000	0.35	1.00	2.50	15.00	—

KM# 519 200 REIS
7.8200 g., Copper-Nickel, 25 mm. **Obv:** Denomination within circle, date below **Rev:** Liberty bust right

Date	Mintage	F	VF	XF	Unc	BU
1918	625,000	0.35	1.00	2.00	15.00	—
1919	882,000	0.35	1.00	2.00	15.00	—
1920	1,657,000	0.35	1.00	2.00	15.00	—
1921	1,135,000	0.35	1.00	2.00	15.00	—
1922	678,000	0.35	1.00	2.00	15.00	—
1923	1,655,000	0.35	1.00	2.00	15.00	—
1924	1,750,000	0.35	1.00	2.00	15.00	—
1925	2,081,999	0.35	1.00	2.00	15.00	—
1926	324,000	1.00	3.00	8.00	22.50	—
1927	1,806,000	0.35	1.00	2.00	15.00	—
1928	782,000	0.35	1.00	2.00	15.00	—
1929	2,440,000	0.25	1.00	2.00	15.00	—
1930	1,697,000	0.25	1.00	2.00	15.00	—
1931	1,830,000	0.25	1.00	2.00	15.00	—
1932	761,000	0.25	1.00	2.00	15.00	—
1933	173,000	0.35	1.00	2.00	15.00	—
1934	612,000	0.25	1.00	2.00	15.00	—
1935	1,329,000	0.25	1.00	2.00	15.00	—

KM# 528 200 REIS
7.9300 g., Copper-Nickel, 25 mm. **Subject:** 400th Anniversary of Colonization **Obv:** Globe with sash **Obv. Designer:** Calmon Barreto **Rev:** Ship, denomination below, two dates divided at top **Rev. Designer:** Arlindo Bastos **Note:** Medal rotation.

Date	Mintage	F	VF	XF	Unc	BU
ND(1932)	596,000	0.75	1.75	3.50	16.50	—

KM# 537 200 REIS
6.0000 g., Copper-Nickel, 22 mm. **Obv:** Steam engine, date above, denomination below **Rev:** Viscount de Maua, railway builder facing **Edge:** Plain **Designer:** Leopolda Campos **Note:** Medal rotation.

Date	Mintage	F	VF	XF	Unc	BU
1936	2,256,000	0.30	0.75	2.00	8.50	—
1937	6,506,000	0.30	0.75	2.00	8.50	—
1938	5,787,000	0.30	0.75	2.00	8.50	—

KM# 545 200 REIS
3.4400 g., Copper-Nickel, 18.82 mm. **Obv:** Denomination, date below, within wreath **Rev:** Dr. Getulio Vargas left **Edge:** Fluted **Shape:** 18-sided

Date	Mintage	F	VF	XF	Unc	BU
1938	7,666,000	0.20	0.50	0.85	2.75	—
1940	10,161,000	0.15	0.40	0.60	2.25	—

Date	Mintage	F	VF	XF	Unc	BU
1942	1,966,000	0.15	0.40	0.60	2.25	—

Note: The 1942 issue has a yellow cast due to higher copper content

KM# 538 300 REIS
8.0800 g., Copper-Nickel, 25 mm. **Obv:** Harp divides denomination, date above **Obv. Designer:** Walter R. Toledo **Rev:** Composer Antonio Carlos Gomes facing **Rev. Designer:** Calmon Barreto **Edge:** Plain **Note:** Medal rotation.

Date	Mintage	F	VF	XF	Unc	BU
1936	3,029,000	0.30	1.25	4.00	11.50	—
1937	4,507,000	0.30	1.25	4.00	11.50	—
1938	3,753,000	0.30	1.25	4.00	11.50	—

KM# 546 300 REIS
4.5400 g., Copper-Nickel, 20.83 mm. **Obv:** Denomination above date within wreath **Rev:** Dr. Getulio Vargas left **Edge:** Fluted **Shape:** 20-sided

Date	Mintage	F	VF	XF	Unc	BU
1938	12,080,000	0.20	0.35	0.50	2.25	—
1940	8,124,000	0.20	0.35	0.50	2.25	—
1942	2,020,000	0.25	0.40	0.75	3.25	—

Note: The 1942 issue has a yellow cast due to higher copper content

KM# 505 400 REIS
11.7300 g., Copper-Nickel, 30 mm. **Obv:** National arms, denomination above **Rev:** Liberty bust right, circle of stars surround **Edge:** Plain

Date	Mintage	F	VF	XF	Unc	BU
MCMI (1901)	5,531,000	1.50	3.00	8.00	30.00	—

KM# 515 400 REIS
Copper-Nickel **Obv:** National arms, denomination above within circle, date below **Rev:** Liberty bust left

Date	Mintage	F	VF	XF	Unc	BU
1914	646,000	15.00	35.00	75.00	150	—

Note: This is considered a pattern by many authorities

KM# 520 400 REIS
Copper-Nickel **Obv:** Denomination within circle, date below **Rev:** Liberty bust right

Date	Mintage	F	VF	XF	Unc	BU
1918	491,000	0.75	2.00	5.50	18.00	—
1919	891,000	0.75	2.00	5.50	18.00	—
1920	1,521,000	0.75	2.00	5.50	18.00	—

Date	Mintage	F	VF	XF	Unc	BU
1921	871,000	0.50	1.75	5.50	18.00	—
1922	1,275,000	0.50	1.75	5.50	18.00	—
1923	764,000	0.50	1.75	5.50	18.00	—
1925	2,048,000	0.50	1.75	5.50	18.00	—
1926	1,034,000	0.50	1.75	5.50	18.00	—
1927	738,000	0.50	1.75	5.50	18.00	—
1929	869,000	0.50	1.75	5.50	18.00	—
1930	1,030,999	0.50	1.75	5.50	18.00	—
1931	1,431,000	0.50	1.75	5.50	18.00	—
1932	588,000	0.50	1.75	5.50	18.00	—
1935	225,000	0.50	1.75	5.50	18.00	—

KM# 529 400 REIS
Copper-Nickel, 30 mm. **Subject:** 400th Anniversary of Colonization **Obv:** Map divides dates within circle **Obv. Designer:** Walter R. Toledo **Rev:** Lusinian Cross **Rev. Designer:** Basilio Nunes Lusinian Cross **Note:** Medal rotation.

Date	Mintage	F	VF	XF	Unc	BU
ND(1932)	416,000	1.00	2.75	5.50	15.00	—

KM# 539 400 REIS
10.0800 g., Copper-Nickel, 27 mm. **Obv:** Oil lamp, date above, denomination below **Obv. Designer:** Walter R. Toledo **Rev:** Bust of Oswaldo Cruz, Microbiologist, 3/4 left **Rev. Designer:** Calmon Barreto **Note:** Medal rotation.

Date	Mintage	F	VF	XF	Unc	BU
1936	2,079,000	0.50	1.00	2.75	8.50	—
1937	3,111,000	0.50	1.00	2.75	8.50	—
1938	2,681,000	0.50	1.00	2.75	8.50	—

KM# 547 400 REIS
5.4400 g., Copper-Nickel, 23 mm. **Obv:** Denomination above date within wreath **Rev:** Bust of Dr. Getulio Vargas left **Edge:** Fluted **Shape:** 22-sided

Date	Mintage	F	VF	XF	Unc	BU
1938	10,620,000	0.25	0.50	1.00	2.25	—
1940	7,312,000	0.25	0.50	1.00	2.25	—
1942	1,496,000	0.25	0.50	1.50	3.25	—

Note: The 1942 issue has a yellow cast due to higher copper content

KM# 506 500 REIS
5.0000 g., 0.9000 Silver 0.1447 oz. ASW **Obv:** Liberty bust left, date below **Rev:** Denomination at center

Date	Mintage	F	VF	XF	Unc	BU
1906	352,000	BV	2.75	4.75	15.00	—
1907	1,282,000	BV	2.75	4.75	15.00	—
1908	498,000	BV	2.75	4.75	15.00	—
1911	8,000	20.00	35.00	70.00	150	—
1912	Est. 222,000	20.00	40.00	80.00	200	—

KM# 509 500 REIS
5.0000 g., 0.9000 Silver 0.1447 oz. ASW **Obv:** Liberty bust right within circle, date below **Rev:** Denomination within wreath, arms above

Date	Mintage	F	VF	XF	Unc	BU
1912	—	3.00	7.00	14.00	38.00	—

KM# 512 500 REIS
5.0000 g., 0.9000 Silver 0.1447 oz. ASW **Obv:** Liberty bust right within circle of stars, date below **Rev:** Denomination within wreath, arms above

Date	Mintage	F	VF	XF	Unc	BU
1913 A	—	BV	2.50	4.50	15.00	—

KM# 521.1 500 REIS
3.8700 g., Aluminum-Bronze, 23 mm. **Subject:** Independence Centennial **Obv:** Dom Pedro and President Pessoa left **Obv. Designer:** Augusta G. Girardet **Rev:** Denonination at top, dates divided by centennial symbols **Rev. Designer:** Joao da Cruz Vargas

Date	Mintage	F	VF	XF	Unc	BU
ND(1922)	13,744,000	0.25	0.60	1.25	4.75	—

KM# 521.2 500 REIS
Aluminum-Bronze, 23 mm. **Obv:** Dom Pedro and President Pessoa left **Obv. Designer:** Augusta G. Girardet **Rev:** Denomination at top, dates divided by centennial symbols **Rev. Designer:** Joao da Cruz Vargas **Edge:** Reeded **Note:** Error: BBASIL instead of BRASIL.

Date	Mintage	F	VF	XF	Unc	BU
ND(1922)	Inc. above	17.50	35.00	55.00	120	—

KM# 524 500 REIS
3.9500 g., Aluminum-Bronze, 22.73 mm. **Obv:** Denomination within wreath, date below **Rev:** Kneeling liberty figure right

Date	Mintage	F	VF	XF	Unc	BU
1924	7,400,000	0.30	0.75	1.50	7.00	—
1927	2,725,000	0.30	0.75	1.50	7.00	—
1928	9,432,000	0.30	0.75	1.50	7.00	—
1930	146,000	1.00	2.00	3.75	9.00	—

KM# 530 500 REIS
Aluminum-Bronze, 23 mm. **Subject:** 400th Anniversary of Colonization **Obv:** Joao Ramalho, colonist, 3/4 right **Rev:** Clothing divides denomination **Edge:** Reeded **Designer:** Calmon Barreto **Note:** Medal rotation.

Date	Mintage	F	VF	XF	Unc	BU
ND(1932)	34,000	1.50	4.00	11.50	20.00	—

KM# 533 500 REIS
4.0000 g., Aluminum-Bronze, 22 mm. **Obv:** Column divides denomination, date below **Obv. Designer:** Walter R. Toledo **Rev:** Bust of Diego Antonio Feijo Regent of Brazil 1835-1837, 3/4 left **Rev. Designer:** Calmon Barreto **Note:** Medal rotation; wide rim.

Date	Mintage	F	VF	XF	Unc	BU
1935	14,000	2.00	9.00	20.00	40.00	—

KM# 540 500 REIS
5.0000 g., Aluminum-Bronze, 22 mm. **Obv:** Denomination divided by column, date below **Obv. Designer:** Walter R. Toledo **Rev:** Bust of Diego Antonio Feijo 3/4 left **Rev. Designer:** Calmon Barreto **Note:** Medal rotation; thicker planchet.

Date	Mintage	F	VF	XF	Unc	BU
1936	1,326,000	0.60	1.25	4.75	9.00	—
1937	Inc. above	0.60	1.25	4.75	9.00	—
1938	—	0.60	1.25	4.75	9.00	—

KM# 549 500 REIS
5.0000 g., Aluminum-Bronze, 21 mm. **Obv:** Denomination above date within wreath **Rev:** Joaquim Machado de Assis, Author and Poet, 3/4 facing **Designer:** Benedito Ribeiro

Date	Mintage	F	VF	XF	Unc	BU
1939	5,928,000	0.50	1.00	3.00	8.00	—

KM# 507 1000 REIS
10.0000 g., 0.9000 Silver 0.2893 oz. ASW **Obv:** Laureate liberty head left, date below flanked by stars **Rev:** Denomination at center **Edge:** Reeded

Date	Mintage	F	VF	XF	Unc	BU
1906	420,000	BV	6.00	9.00	24.00	—
1907	1,282,000	BV	6.00	9.00	24.00	—
1908	1,624,000	BV	6.00	9.00	24.00	—
1909	816,000	BV	6.00	9.00	24.00	—
1910	2,354,000	BV	6.00	9.00	24.00	—
1911	2,810,000	BV	6.00	9.00	24.00	—
1912	Est. 1,570,000	BV	6.00	9.00	24.00	—

KM# 510 1000 REIS
10.0000 g., 0.9000 Silver 0.2893 oz. ASW **Obv:** Laureate head of Liberty right, circle surrounds, date below **Rev:** Denomination within wreath, arms above

Date	Mintage	F	VF	XF	Unc	BU
1912	Inc. above	BV	6.50	10.00	32.50	—
1913	2,525,000	BV	6.50	10.00	32.50	—

KM# 513 1000 REIS
10.0000 g., 0.9000 Silver 0.2893 oz. ASW, 26 mm. **Obv:** Laureate liberty head right, star circle surrounds, date below **Rev:** Denomination within wreath, arms above **Edge:** Reeded

Date	Mintage	F	VF	XF	Unc	BU
1913 A	—	—	BV	7.00	17.50	—

KM# 522.1 1000 REIS
7.8000 g., Aluminum-Bronze, 26.8 mm. **Subject:** Independence Centennial **Obv:** Dom Pedro and President Pessoa **Obv. Designer:** Augusto G. Girardet **Rev:** Denomination at top, dates divided by centennial symbols **Rev. Designer:** Joao de Cruz Vargas **Edge:** Reeded

Date	Mintage	F	VF	XF	Unc	BU
ND(1922)	16,698,000	0.40	0.60	2.00	6.50	—

KM# 522.2 1000 REIS
Aluminum-Bronze, 25 mm. **Obv:** Dom Pedro and President Pessoa left **Obv. Designer:** Augusto G. Girardet **Rev:** Denomination at top, dates divided by centennial symbols at center **Rev. Designer:** Joao da Cruz Vargas **Edge:** Reeded **Note:** Error: BBASIL instead of BRASIL.

Date	Mintage	F	VF	XF	Unc	BU
ND(1922)	Inc. above	2.50	5.00	10.00	20.00	—

KM# 525 1000 REIS
8.0600 g., Aluminum-Bronze, 26.57 mm. **Obv:** Denomination within wreath, date below, monogram left of knot **Rev:** Kneeling liberty figure right

Date	Mintage	F	VF	XF	Unc	BU
1924	9,354,000	0.50	1.00	2.25	7.50	—
1925	6,205,000	0.50	1.00	2.25	7.50	—
1927	35,817,000	0.50	1.00	2.25	7.50	—
1928	1,899,000	0.50	1.00	2.25	7.50	—
1929	83,000	3.50	14.00	45.00	100	—
1930	45,000	3.50	14.00	45.00	100	—
1931	200,000	1.00	4.50	8.00	16.00	—

KM# 531 1000 REIS
7.0000 g., Aluminum-Bronze, 32 mm. **Subject:** 400th Anniversary of Colonization **Obv:** 3/4 figure of Martin Affonso da Sousa looking left **Obv. Designer:** Leopoldo Campos **Rev:** Denomination encircles arms **Rev. Designer:** Herminio Pereira **Edge:** Reeded **Note:** Medal rotation.

Date	Mintage	F	VF	XF	Unc	BU
ND(1932)	56,000	2.00	4.00	7.50	18.00	—

KM# 534 1000 REIS
8.0000 g., Aluminum-Bronze, 26 mm. **Obv:** Open bible, date above, denomination at top **Obv. Designer:** Walter R. Toledo **Rev:** Head of Jose de Anchieta left **Rev. Designer:** Calmon Barreto **Note:** Medal rotation.

Date	Mintage	F	VF	XF	Unc	BU
1935	138,000	1.00	2.00	4.00	9.00	—

KM# 541 1000 REIS
7.1000 g., Aluminum-Bronze, 24.3 mm. **Obv:** Open bible, date above, denomination at top **Obv. Designer:** Walter R. Toledo **Rev:** Head of Jose de Anchieta left **Rev. Designer:** Calmon Barreto **Edge:** Reeded **Note:** Size reduced. Medal rotation.

Date	Mintage	F	VF	XF	Unc	BU
1936	926,000	0.50	1.00	2.50	7.00	—
1937	Inc. above	0.50	1.00	2.50	7.00	—
1938 LGCB under chin	—	0.50	1.00	2.50	7.00	—

KM# 550 1000 REIS
6.6700 g., Aluminum-Bronze, 23 mm. **Obv:** Denomination above date within wreath **Rev:** Tobias Barreto de Menezes, Philosopher and Poet 3/4 right, BR monogram right of bust, two dates above right shoulder **Designer:** Benedito Ribeiro

Date	Mintage	F	VF	XF	Unc	BU
1939	9,586,000	0.25	0.75	2.00	6.50	—

KM# 508 2000 REIS
20.0000 g., 0.9000 Silver 0.5787 oz. ASW **Obv:** Liberty head left, date below flanked by stars **Rev:** Denomination at center

Date	Mintage	F	VF	XF	Unc	BU
1906	256,000	12.00	13.50	17.50	55.00	—
1907	2,863,000	BV	12.00	14.00	45.00	—
1908	1,707,000	BV	12.00	14.00	45.00	—
1910	585,000	12.00	13.50	17.50	55.00	—
1911	1,929,000	BV	12.00	14.00	45.00	—
1912	741,000	12.00	13.50	17.50	55.00	—

KM# 511 2000 REIS
20.0000 g., 0.9000 Silver 0.5787 oz. ASW **Obv:** Liberty head within circle, date below **Rev:** Denomination within wreath, national arms above

Date	Mintage	F	VF	XF	Unc	BU
1912	Inc. above	12.00	15.00	23.50	58.00	—
1913	395,000	12.00	15.00	25.00	62.00	—

KM# 514 2000 REIS
20.0000 g., 0.9000 Silver 0.5787 oz. ASW **Obv:** Laureate liberty head right within circle, date below **Rev:** Denomination within wreath, national arms above, continuous legend

Date	Mintage	F	VF	XF	Unc	BU
1913 A	—	12.00	14.00	16.50	42.50	—

KM# 523 2000 REIS
7.9000 g., 0.9000 Silver 0.2286 oz. ASW, 26 mm. **Subject:** Independence Centennial **Obv:** Dom Pedro and President Pessoa left **Obv. Designer:** Augusto G. Girardet **Rev:** Two sets of arms, dates below, denomination at bottom **Rev. Designer:** Joao da Cruz Vargas **Edge:** Reeded

Date	Mintage	F	VF	XF	Unc	BU
ND(1922)	1,560,000	—	BV	4.75	9.00	—

KM# 523a 2000 REIS
7.9000 g., 0.5000 Silver 0.1270 oz. ASW, 26 mm. **Edge:** Reeded **Note:** Struck in both .900 and .500 fine silver, but can only be distinguished by analysis (and color), on worn specimens

Date	Mintage	F	VF	XF	Unc	BU
ND(1922)	Inc. above	BV	2.75	3.75	8.50	—

KM# 526 2000 REIS
7.9000 g., 0.5000 Silver 0.1270 oz. ASW **Obv:** Denomination within wreath, date below **Rev:** Laureate liberty head, right, within circle, stars surround

Date	Mintage	F	VF	XF	Unc	BU
1924	9,147,000	BV	2.75	3.75	12.00	—
1925	723,000	BV	2.75	3.75	12.00	—
1926	1,787,000	BV	2.75	3.75	12.00	—
1927	1,008,999	BV	3.00	4.75	14.00	—
1928	1,250,000	BV	2.75	3.75	12.00	—
1929	1,744,000	BV	2.75	3.75	12.00	—
1930	1,240,000	BV	2.75	3.75	12.00	—
1931	546,000	BV	2.75	3.75	12.00	—
1934	938,000	BV	2.75	3.75	12.00	—

KM# 532 2000 REIS
7.9000 g., 0.5000 Silver 0.1270 oz. ASW, 26 mm. **Subject:** 400th Anniversary of Colonization **Obv:** Bust of John III 3/4 right **Obv. Designer:** Leopoldo Campos **Rev:** Arms, denomination above **Rev. Designer:** Arlindo Bastos **Note:** Medal rotation.

Date	Mintage	F	VF	XF	Unc	BU
ND(1932)	695,000	2.75	3.75	7.00	15.00	—

KM# 535 2000 REIS
7.9000 g., 0.5000 Silver 0.1270 oz. ASW, 26 mm. **Obv:** Sword divides denomination, date lower right **Obv. Designer:** Walter R. Toledo **Rev:** Armored head of Duke of Caxias; left, CB below chin **Rev. Designer:** Leopoldo Campos **Edge:** Reeded **Note:** Medal rotation.

Date	Mintage	F	VF	XF	Unc	BU
1935	2,131,000	BV	2.75	3.75	12.50	—

KM# 542 2000 REIS
8.6200 g., Aluminum-Bronze, 26 mm. **Obv:** Hilt divides denomination, date upper right **Obv. Designer:** Walter R. Toledo **Rev:** Armored bust of Duke of Caxias right, crown at left **Rev. Designer:** Leopoldo Campos **Edge:** Plain **Shape:** Round **Note:** Medal rotation.

Date	Mintage	F	VF	XF	Unc	BU
1936	665,000	0.50	1.00	2.00	5.50	—
1937	Inc. above	0.50	1.00	2.00	5.50	—
1938	—	2.50	4.75	11.50	28.00	—

KM# 548 2000 REIS
Aluminum-Bronze, 26.3 mm. **Edge:** Plain **Note:** 24-sided planchet. Medal rotation.

Date	Mintage	F	VF	XF	Unc	BU
1937	—	25.00	50.00	125	300	—
1938	—	0.75	1.50	3.25	7.50	—

KM# 551 2000 REIS
Aluminum-Bronze, 26 mm. **Obv:** Denomination above date within wreath **Rev:** Bust of President Floriano Peixoto facing **Designer:** Orlando Moutinho

Date	Mintage	F	VF	XF	Unc	BU
1939	5,048,000	0.50	1.00	2.00	5.50	—

KM# 543 5000 REIS
10.0000 g., 0.6000 Silver 0.1929 oz. ASW, 26 mm. **Obv:** Wing above denomination **Obv. Designer:** Walter R. Toledo **Rev:** Head of aviation pioneer Alberto Santos Dumont left **Rev. Designer:** Calmon Barreto **Edge:** Reeded **Note:** Medal rotation.

Date	Mintage	F	VF	XF	Unc	BU
1936	1,986,000	BV	4.00	6.00	10.00	—
1937	414,000	BV	4.00	6.00	10.00	—
1938	994,000	BV	4.00	6.00	10.00	—

KM# 496 10000 REIS
8.9645 g., 0.9170 Gold 0.2643 oz. AGW **Obv:** Liberty head left within circle **Rev:** Star with wreath in background

Date	Mintage	F	VF	XF	Unc	BU
1901	111	BV	275	700	1,150	—
1902 Unique	—	—	—	—	—	—
1903	391	BV	275	700	1,150	—
1904	541	BV	275	700	1,150	—
1906	572	BV	275	700	1,150	—
1907	878	BV	265	600	1,100	—
1908	689	BV	265	600	1,100	1,500
1909	1,069	BV	265	600	1,100	1,750
1911	137	265	375	800	1,350	—
1914	969	265	500	1,500	2,400	—
1915	4,314	265	500	1,400	2,000	—
1916	4,720	BV	275	700	1,150	—
1919	526	BV	275	700	1,150	—
1921	2,435	BV	265	600	1,000	—
1922 Rare	6	—	—	—	—	—

KM# 497 20000 REIS

17.9290 g., 0.9170 Gold 0.5286 oz. AGW **Obv:** Liberty head left **Rev:** Stars at center surrounded by circle of stars

Date	Mintage	F	VF	XF	Unc	BU
1901	784	—	BV	700	1,350	1,850
1902	884	—	BV	700	1,350	—
1903	675	—	BV	700	1,350	—
1904	444	—	BV	700	1,350	—
1906	396	BV	550	900	1,600	—
1907	3,310	—	BV	600	1,100	—
1908	6,001,000	—	BV	600	1,100	—
1909	4,427	—	BV	600	1,100	—
1910	5,119	—	BV	600	1,100	1,350
1911	8,467	—	BV	600	1,100	—
1912	4,878	—	BV	600	1,100	—
1913	5,182	—	BV	650	1,200	—
1914	1,980	—	BV	700	1,400	—
1917	2,269	BV	550	800	1,550	—
1918	1,216	BV	550	800	1,550	—
1921	5,924	—	BV	650	1,200	—
1922	2,681	—	BV	800	1,550	—

REFORM COINAGE

1942-1967

100 Centavos = 1 Cruzeiro

KM# 555 10 CENTAVOS

2.8800 g., Copper-Nickel, 17.22 mm. **Obv:** Bust of Getulio Vargas 3/4 left **Rev:** Denomination above line, date below **Edge:** Plain **Note:** KM#555 has a very light yellowish appearance while KM#555a is a deeper yellow.

Date	Mintage	F	VF	XF	Unc	BU
1942	3,826,000	—	0.35	0.50	1.00	—
1943	13,565,000	—	0.25	0.35	0.75	—

KM# 555a.1 10 CENTAVOS

2.9700 g., Aluminum-Bronze, 17.2 mm. **Obv:** Bust left, initial after "Brasil" **Rev:** Denomination above line, date below, initial at end of line above date **Edge:** Plain **Note:** KM#555 has a very light yellowish appearance while KM#555a is a deeper yellow.

Date	Mintage	F	VF	XF	Unc	BU
1943	Inc. above	—	0.25	0.35	0.75	—
1944	12,617,000	—	0.25	0.60	1.00	—
1945	24,674,000	—	0.25	0.60	1.00	—

KM# 555a.2 10 CENTAVOS

2.8400 g., Aluminum-Bronze, 17.2 mm. **Obv:** Bust left **Rev:** Denomination above line, date below **Note:** Without initials.

Date	Mintage	F	VF	XF	Unc	BU
1944	—	—	0.25	0.60	1.00	—
1945	—	—	0.25	0.60	1.00	—
1946	35,159,000	—	0.25	0.60	1.00	—
1947	20,664,000	—	0.25	0.35	0.75	—

KM# 561 10 CENTAVOS

2.9600 g., Aluminum-Bronze, 17.04 mm. **Obv:** Jose Bonifacio de Andrada e Silva, Father of Independence left **Rev:** Denomination above line, date below

Date	Mintage	F	VF	XF	Unc	BU
1947	Inc. above	—	0.15	0.20	0.35	—
1948	45,041,000	—	0.15	0.20	0.35	—
1949	21,763,000	—	0.15	0.20	0.35	—
1950	16,329,999	—	0.15	0.20	0.35	—
1951	15,561,000	—	0.10	0.15	0.35	—
1952	10,966,000	—	0.10	0.20	0.50	—
1953	25,883,000	—	0.10	0.15	0.35	—
1954	17,031,000	—	0.10	0.15	0.35	—
1955	25,172,000	—	0.10	0.15	0.35	—

KM# 564 10 CENTAVOS

1.0200 g., Aluminum, 17.41 mm. **Obv:** National Arms **Rev:** Denomination above line, date below

Date	Mintage	F	VF	XF	Unc	BU
1956	741,000	—	0.10	0.15	0.50	—
1957	25,311,000	—	0.10	0.15	0.25	—
1958	5,813,000	—	0.10	0.15	0.25	—
1959	2,611,000	—	0.10	0.15	0.25	—
1960	624,000	—	0.10	0.15	0.50	—
1961	951,000	—	0.10	0.15	0.50	—

KM# 556 20 CENTAVOS

Copper-Nickel, 20 mm. **Obv:** Bust of Getulio Vargas 3/4 left **Rev:** Denomination above line, date below **Edge:** Plain **Note:** KM#556 has a very light yellowish appearance while KM#556a is a deeper yellow.

Date	Mintage	F	VF	XF	Unc	BU
1942	3,007,000	—	0.25	0.50	1.00	—
1943	13,392,000	—	0.15	0.40	0.75	—

KM# 556a 20 CENTAVOS

4.0000 g., Aluminum-Bronze, 20 mm. **Obv:** Getulio Vargas bust left **Rev:** Denomination above line, date below **Edge:** Plain **Note:** KM#556 has a very light yellowish appearance while KM#556a is a deeper yellow.

Date	Mintage	F	VF	XF	Unc	BU
1943	Inc. above	—	0.15	0.35	0.75	—
1944	12,673,000	—	0.15	0.35	0.75	—
Note: Coins dated 1944 exist with and without designer's initials and straight or curved-back 9 in date						
1945	61,632,000	—	0.15	0.35	0.60	—
1946	31,526,000	—	0.15	0.35	0.60	—
1947	36,422,000	—	0.15	0.35	0.75	—
1948	39,671,000	—	0.15	0.35	0.75	—

KM# 562 20 CENTAVOS

4.0000 g., Aluminum-Bronze, 19.26 mm. **Obv:** Bust of author and lawyer Ruy Barbosa left **Rev:** Denomination above line, date below

Date	Mintage	F	VF	XF	Unc	BU
1948	Inc. above	—	0.15	0.25	0.50	—
1949	24,805,000	—	0.15	0.25	0.50	—
1950	15,145,000	—	0.15	0.25	0.50	—
1951	14,964,000	—	0.15	0.25	0.50	—
1952	10,942,000	—	0.15	0.25	0.50	—
1953	25,585,000	—	0.15	0.25	0.50	—
1954	16,477,000	—	0.15	0.25	0.50	—
1955	25,122,000	—	0.15	0.25	0.50	—
1956	6,716,000	—	0.15	0.25	0.50	—

KM# 565 20 CENTAVOS

Aluminum **Obv:** National arms **Rev:** Denomination above line, date below **Note:** Varieties exist in the thickness of the planchet for year 1956.

Date	Mintage	F	VF	XF	Unc	BU
1956	Inc. above	—	0.10	0.25	0.50	—
1957	27,110,000	—	0.10	0.20	0.40	—
1958	8,552,000	—	0.10	0.20	0.40	—
1959	4,810,000	—	0.10	0.20	0.40	—
1960	510,000	—	0.10	0.25	0.50	—
1961	2,332,000	—	0.10	0.20	0.40	—

KM# 557 50 CENTAVOS

4.7500 g., Copper-Nickel, 21 mm. **Obv:** Bust of Getulio Vargas 3/4 left **Rev:** Denomination above line, date below **Note:** KM#557 has a very light yellowish appearance while KM#557a is a deeper yellow.

Date	Mintage	F	VF	XF	Unc	BU
1942	2,358,000	—	0.40	0.75	1.50	—
1943	13,392,000	—	0.35	0.50	1.00	—

KM# 557a 50 CENTAVOS

4.7500 g., Aluminum-Bronze, 21.3 mm. **Obv:** Getulio Vargas bust left **Rev:** Denomination above line, date below **Edge:** Plain **Note:** KM#557 has a very light yellowish appearance while KM#557a is a deeper yellow.

Date	Mintage	F	VF	XF	Unc	BU
1943	Inc. above	—	0.30	0.50	1.00	—
1944	12,102,000	—	0.30	0.50	1.00	—
1945	73,222,000	—	0.30	0.50	1.00	—
1946	13,941,000	—	0.30	0.50	1.00	—
1947	23,588,000	—	0.20	0.50	1.00	—

KM# 563 50 CENTAVOS

5.0000 g., Aluminum-Bronze, 21.40 mm. **Obv:** Bust of General Eurico Gaspar Dutra left **Rev:** Denomination above line, date below

Date	Mintage	F	VF	XF	Unc	BU
1948	32,023,000	—	0.15	0.25	0.50	—
1949	11,392,000	—	0.15	0.25	0.50	—
1950	7,804,000	—	0.15	0.35	0.75	—
1951	7,523,000	—	0.15	0.35	0.75	—
1952	6,863,000	—	0.15	0.35	0.75	—
1953	17,372,000	—	0.15	0.25	0.50	—
1954	11,353,000	—	0.15	0.25	0.50	—
1955	27,150,000	—	0.15	0.25	0.50	—
1956	32,130,000	—	0.15	0.25	0.50	—

KM# 566 50 CENTAVOS

3.0000 g., Aluminum-Bronze, 17.04 mm. **Obv:** National arms **Rev:** Denomination above line, date below

Date	Mintage	F	VF	XF	Unc	BU
1956	Inc. above	—	0.15	0.25	0.50	—

KM# 569 50 CENTAVOS

1.8300 g., Aluminum, 21.07 mm. **Obv:** National arms **Rev:** Denomination above line, date below

Date	Mintage	F	VF	XF	Unc	BU
1957	49,350,000	—	0.10	0.20	0.35	—
1958	59,815,000	—	0.10	0.20	0.35	—
1959	32,891,000	—	0.10	0.20	0.35	—
1960	15,997,000	—	0.10	0.20	0.35	—
1961	18,456,000	—	0.10	0.20	0.35	—

KM# 558 CRUZEIRO

6.9200 g., Aluminum-Bronze, 22.9 mm. **Obv:** Topographical map **Rev:** Denomination, date at left

Date	Mintage	F	VF	XF	Unc	BU
1942	381,000	—	0.50	1.00	3.50	—
1943	2,728,000	—	0.25	0.50	1.00	—
1944	3,820,000	—	0.25	0.50	1.00	—
1945	32,543,999	—	0.25	0.50	0.75	—
1946	49,794,000	—	0.25	0.50	1.00	—
1947	15,391,000	—	0.25	0.50	1.00	—
1949	7,889,000	—	0.25	0.50	1.00	—
1950	5,163,000	—	0.25	0.50	1.00	—
1951	3,757,000	—	0.25	0.50	1.00	—
1952	1,769,000	—	0.50	1.00	3.50	—
1953	5,195,000	—	0.25	0.50	1.00	—
1954	1,145,000	—	0.25	0.50	1.50	—
1955	1,758,000	—	0.25	0.50	1.00	—
1956	668,000	—	6.00	12.00	20.00	—

KM# 567 CRUZEIRO

4.0300 g., Aluminum-Bronze, 19.03 mm. **Obv:** National arms **Rev:** Denomination above line, date below

Date	Mintage	F	VF	XF	Unc	BU
1956	Inc. above	—	0.20	0.35	0.65	—

KM# 570 CRUZEIRO

2.3800 g., Aluminum, 23.23 mm. **Obv:** National arms **Rev:** Denomination above line, date below

Date	Mintage	F	VF	XF	Unc	BU
1957	11,849,000	—	0.20	0.75	2.50	—
1958	15,443,000	—	0.20	1.00	3.00	—
1959	25,010,000	—	0.20	0.75	2.50	—
1960	35,267,000	—	0.20	0.75	2.50	—
1961	22,181,000	—	0.20	1.00	3.00	—

KM# 559 2 CRUZEIROS

8.3000 g., Aluminum-Bronze, 25 mm. **Obv:** Topographical map **Rev:** Denomination, date at left **Edge:** Reeded

Date	Mintage	F	VF	XF	Unc	BU
1942	276,000	—	0.75	1.50	4.00	—
1943	1,929,000	—	0.25	0.50	1.00	—
1944	3,820,000	—	0.25	0.50	1.00	—
1945	32,543,999	—	0.20	0.40	1.00	—
1946	33,650,000	—	0.20	0.40	1.00	—
1947	9,908,000	—	0.20	0.40	1.00	—
1949	11,252,000	—	0.20	0.40	1.00	—
1950	7,754,000	—	0.25	0.50	1.00	—
1951	390,000	—	0.40	1.00	3.00	—
1952	1,456,000	—	1.00	2.00	5.00	—
1953	3,582,000	—	0.20	0.40	1.00	—
1954	1,197,000	—	0.25	1.00	2.00	—
1955	1,838,000	—	0.20	0.50	1.00	—
1956	253,000	—	2.00	4.00	10.00	—

KM# 568 2 CRUZEIROS

Aluminum-Bronze **Obv:** National arms **Rev:** Denomination above line, date below

Date	Mintage	F	VF	XF	Unc	BU
1956	Inc. above	—	0.20	0.40	1.50	—

KM# 571 2 CRUZEIROS

2.7600 g., Aluminum, 25.26 mm. **Obv:** National arms **Rev:** Denomination above line, date below

Date	Mintage	F	VF	XF	Unc	BU
1957	194,000	—	0.25	0.50	1.50	—
1958	13,687,000	—	0.20	0.30	1.00	—
1959	20,894,000	—	0.20	0.30	1.00	—
1960	19,624,000	—	0.20	0.30	1.00	—
1961	24,924,000	—	0.20	0.30	1.00	—

KM# 560 5 CRUZEIROS

Aluminum-Bronze **Obv:** Topographical map **Rev:** Denomination, date at left

Date	Mintage	F	VF	XF	Unc	BU
1942	115,000	—	1.50	3.50	9.00	—
1943	222,000	—	1.00	2.50	7.00	—

KM# 572 10 CRUZEIROS

2.0000 g., Aluminum **Obv:** Topographical map **Rev:** Large denomination, date below

Date	Mintage	F	VF	XF	Unc	BU
1965	19,656,000	—	0.10	0.20	0.50	—

KM# 573 20 CRUZEIROS

Aluminum **Obv:** Topographical map **Rev:** Large denomination, date below

Date	Mintage	F	VF	XF	Unc	BU
1965	25,930,000	—	0.15	0.25	0.75	—

KM# 574 50 CRUZEIROS

Copper-Nickel **Obv:** Liberty head left **Rev:** Denomination above date

Date	Mintage	F	VF	XF	Unc	BU
1965	18,001,000	—	0.20	0.40	1.50	—

REFORM COINAGE

1967-1985

1000 Old Cruzeiros = 1 Cruzeiro Novo (New);
100 Centavos = 1 (New) Cruzeiro

KM# 575.1 CENTAVO

Stainless Steel **Obv:** Liberty head left **Rev:** Denomination above date

Date	Mintage	F	VF	XF	Unc	BU
1967	57,499,000	—	—	—	0.15	0.25

KM# 575.2 CENTAVO

Stainless Steel **Obv:** Liberty head left **Rev:** Denomination above date **Note:** Thinner planchet.

Date	Mintage	F	VF	XF	Unc	BU
1969	243,855,000	—	—	—	0.15	0.25
1975	—	—	—	0.15	0.30	0.50

KM# 585 CENTAVO

1.8000 g., Stainless Steel, 16.15 mm. **Series:** F.A.O. **Subject:** Sugar Cane **Obv:** Liberty head left **Rev:** Sugar cane, denomination and date to right **Edge:** Plain

Date	Mintage	F	VF	XF	Unc	BU
1975	31,700,000	—	—	0.15	0.25	0.45
1976	18,355,000	—	—	—	0.20	0.45
1977	100,000	—	—	0.15	0.30	0.50
1978	50,000	—	—	0.15	0.30	0.50

KM# 589 CENTAVO

Stainless Steel **Series:** F.A.O. **Subject:** Soja **Obv:** Plants **Rev:** Denomination above date

Date	Mintage	F	VF	XF	Unc	BU
1979	100,000	—	0.15	0.35	1.00	1.25
1980	60,000	—	0.15	0.35	1.00	1.25
1981	100,000	—	0.15	0.35	1.00	1.25
1982	100,000	—	0.15	0.35	1.00	1.25
1983	—	—	0.15	0.35	1.00	1.25

KM# 576.1 2 CENTAVOS

Stainless Steel **Obv:** Liberty head left **Rev:** Denomination above date

Date	Mintage	F	VF	XF	Unc	BU
1967	65,226,000	—	—	—	0.25	0.50

KM# 576.2 2 CENTAVOS

2.2400 g., Stainless Steel, 19.15 mm. **Obv:** Liberty head left **Edge:** Plain **Note:** Thinner planchet.

Date	Mintage	F	VF	XF	Unc	BU
1969	Est. 134,298,000	—	—	—	0.50	0.75
Note: Mintage figure includes coins struck through 1974 dated 1969						
1975	—	—	—	0.25	0.75	1.00

KM# 586 2 CENTAVOS

2.1700 g., Stainless Steel **Series:** F.A.O. **Subject:** Soja **Obv:** Liberty head left **Rev:** Denomination above date, plant at left

Date	Mintage	F	VF	XF	Unc	BU
1975	31,400,000	—	—	0.15	0.25	0.45
1976	18,754,000	—	—	—	0.25	0.45
1977	100,000	—	—	0.20	0.50	0.75
1978	50,000	—	—	0.20	0.50	0.75

KM# 577.1 5 CENTAVOS

Stainless Steel **Obv:** Liberty head left **Rev:** Denomination above date

Date	Mintage	F	VF	XF	Unc	BU
1967	69,304,000	—	—	0.20	0.50	0.75

KM# 577.2 5 CENTAVOS

Stainless Steel **Obv:** Liberty head left **Rev:** Denomination above date **Note:** Thinner planchet.

Date	Mintage	F	VF	XF	Unc	BU
1969	Est. 345,071,000	—	—	0.20	0.50	0.75

Note: Mintage figure includes coins struck through 1974 dated 1969

Date	Mintage	F	VF	XF	Unc	BU
1975	—	—	—	0.20	0.50	0.75

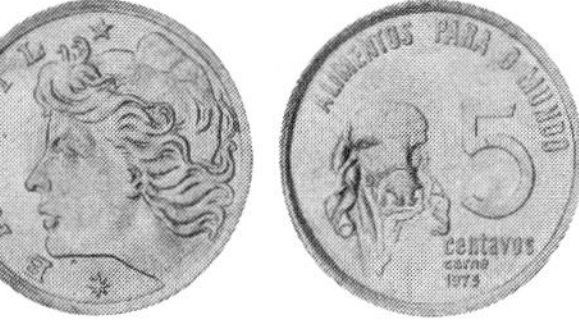

KM# 587.1 5 CENTAVOS

2.6500 g., Stainless Steel, 21 mm. **Series:** F.A.O. **Subject:** Zebu **Obv:** Liberty head left **Rev:** Denomination and date to right of Zebu **Edge:** Plain

Date	Mintage	F	VF	XF	Unc	BU
1975	44,500,000	—	—	0.20	0.50	0.75
1976	134,267,000	—	—	0.20	0.50	0.75
1977	85,360	—	—	0.20	0.65	1.00
1978	34,090,000	—	—	0.20	0.65	1.00

KM# 587.2 5 CENTAVOS

2.6400 g., Stainless Steel, 21.21 mm. **Obv:** Liberty head left **Rev:** Denomination and date to right of Zebu, "5" over wavy lines

Date	Mintage	F	VF	XF	Unc	BU
1975	Inc. above	—	—	0.20	0.50	0.75
1976	Inc. above	—	—	0.20	0.50	0.75
1977	Inc. above	—	—	0.20	0.50	0.75
1978	Inc. above	—	—	0.20	0.65	1.00

KM# 578.1 10 CENTAVOS

Copper-Nickel **Obv:** Liberty head left **Rev:** Oil refinery, denomination and date at right

Date	Mintage	F	VF	XF	Unc	BU
1967	22,420,000	—	—	0.20	0.50	0.75

KM# 578.1a 10 CENTAVOS

Stainless Steel **Obv:** Liberty head left **Rev:** Oil refinery, denomination and date at right

Date	Mintage	F	VF	XF	Unc	BU
1974	114,598,000	—	—	0.20	0.40	0.60
1975	—	—	—	0.20	0.40	0.60
1976	—	—	—	0.20	0.40	0.60
1977	225,213,000	—	—	0.20	0.40	0.60
1978	225,000,000	—	—	0.20	0.40	0.60
1979	100,000	—	—	0.20	0.50	0.75

KM# 578.2 10 CENTAVOS

Copper-Nickel **Obv:** Liberty head left **Rev:** Oil refinery, denomination and date at right **Note:** Thinner planchet.

Date	Mintage	F	VF	XF	Unc	BU
1970	Est. 134,070,000	—	—	0.20	0.40	0.60

Note: Mintage figure includes coins struck through 1974 dated 1970

KM# 579.1a 20 CENTAVOS

Stainless Steel **Obv:** Liberty head left **Rev:** Denomination above date, oil derrick at left

Date	Mintage	F	VF	XF	Unc	BU
1975	102,367,000	—	—	0.20	0.50	0.75
1976	—	—	—	0.20	0.50	0.75
1977	240,001,000	—	—	0.20	0.50	0.75
1978	255,000,000	—	—	0.20	0.50	0.75
1979	116,000	—	—	0.25	0.65	1.00

KM# 579.1 20 CENTAVOS

Copper-Nickel **Obv:** Liberty head left **Rev:** Denomination above date, oil derrick at left **Note:** Thick planchet

Date	Mintage	F	VF	XF	Unc	BU
1967	123,610,000	—	—	0.20	0.50	0.75
1970	—	—	—	0.40	1.00	1.25

KM# 579.2 20 CENTAVOS

Copper-Nickel **Obv:** Liberty head left **Rev:** Denomination above date, oil derrick at left **Note:** Thinner planchet.

Date	Mintage	F	VF	XF	Unc	BU
1970	Est. 384,894,000	—	—	0.20	0.60	0.85

Note: Mintage figure includes coins struck through 1974 dated 1970

KM# 580 50 CENTAVOS

Nickel **Obv:** Liberty head left **Rev:** Freighter at pier divides date and denomination

Date	Mintage	F	VF	XF	Unc	BU
1967	12,987,000	—	0.25	0.50	1.25	1.50

KM# 580a 50 CENTAVOS

7.7400 g., Copper-Nickel, 26.94 mm. **Obv:** Liberty head left **Rev:** Freighter at pier divides date and denomination **Edge:** Reeded **Note:** Varieties of "7" in the date, with serif at top or bottom.

Date	Mintage	F	VF	XF	Unc	BU
1970	503,895,000	—	0.20	0.35	1.00	1.25
1975	—	—	0.20	0.35	1.00	1.25

KM# 580b 50 CENTAVOS

6.7200 g., Stainless Steel, 27 mm. **Obv:** Liberty head left **Rev:** Freighter at pier divides denomination and date **Edge:** Plain **Note:** Varieties of "7" in the date, with serif at top or bottom.

Date	Mintage	F	VF	XF	Unc	BU
1975	79,062,000	—	0.20	0.35	1.00	1.25
1976	—	—	0.20	0.35	1.00	1.25
1977	160,019,000	—	0.20	0.35	1.00	1.25
1978	200,000,000	—	0.20	0.35	1.00	1.25
1979	104,000	—	0.25	0.45	1.25	1.50

KM# 581 CRUZEIRO

Nickel **Obv:** Liberty head left **Rev:** Denomination above date, spray at left

Date	Mintage	F	VF	XF	Unc	BU
1970	Est. 48,930,000	—	0.25	0.50	1.00	1.25

Note: Mintage figure includes coins struck through 1972 dated 1970

Date	Mintage	F	VF	XF	Unc	BU
1970 Proof	18,000	Value: 3.50				

KM# 581a CRUZEIRO

10.0000 g., Copper-Nickel, 28.81 mm. **Obv:** Liberty head left **Rev:** Denomination above date, spray at left

Date	Mintage	F	VF	XF	Unc	BU
1974	—	—	0.20	0.45	1.00	1.25
1975	21,613,000	—	0.20	0.45	1.00	1.25
1976	—	—	0.20	0.45	1.00	1.25
1977	98,000	—	0.25	0.50	1.25	1.50
1978	77,000	—	0.25	0.50	1.25	1.50

KM# 582 CRUZEIRO

Nickel, 29 mm. **Subject:** 150th Anniversary of Independence **Obv:** Pedro I and General Emilio Garrastazu Medici heads left, date below **Rev:** Map above denomination **Edge Lettering:** SESQUICENTENARIO DA INDEPENDENCIA

Date	Mintage	F	VF	XF	Unc	BU
1972	5,600,000	—	0.40	0.85	1.65	2.00

Note: Lettered edge

Date	Mintage	F	VF	XF	Unc	BU
1972	Inc. above	—	0.40	0.85	1.65	2.00

Note: Plain edge; Coins with plain edge are believed by some to be errors

Date	Mintage	F	VF	XF	Unc	BU
1972 Proof	—	Value: 3.50				

Note: Lettered edge

Date	Mintage	F	VF	XF	Unc	BU
1972 Proof	—	Value: 3.50				

Note: Plain edge; Coins with plain edge are believed by some to be errors

KM# 590 CRUZEIRO

3.2800 g., Stainless Steel, 20 mm. **Obv:** Sugar cane **Rev:** Denomination above date, linear design **Edge:** Plain

Date	Mintage	F	VF	XF	Unc	BU
1979	596,000	—	0.15	0.25	0.75	1.00
1980	690,497,000	—	0.15	0.25	0.65	0.85
1981	560,000,000	—	0.15	0.25	0.65	0.85
1982	300,000,000	—	0.15	0.25	0.65	0.85
1983	100,000	—	0.15	0.25	0.75	1.00
1984	62,100,000	—	0.15	0.25	0.65	0.85

KM# 598 CRUZEIRO

3.1000 g., Stainless Steel, 19.9 mm. **Series:** F.A.O. **Obv:** Sugar cane **Rev:** Denomination above date, linear design

Date	Mintage	F	VF	XF	Unc	BU
1985	10,000,000	—	—	0.20	0.50	0.75

KM# 591 5 CRUZEIROS

Stainless Steel, 21.8 mm. **Obv:** Coffee plant **Rev:** Denomination above date, linear design **Edge:** Plain

Date	Mintage	F	VF	XF	Unc	BU
1980	288,200,000	—	0.20	0.35	0.75	1.00
1981	82,000,000	—	0.20	0.35	0.75	1.00
1982	108,000,000	—	0.20	0.35	0.75	1.00
1983	113,400,000	—	0.20	0.35	0.75	1.00
1984	243,000,000	—	0.20	0.35	0.75	1.00

KM# 599 5 CRUZEIROS

4.7000 g., Stainless Steel, 22 mm. **Series:** F.A.O. **Obv:** Coffee plant **Rev:** Denomination above date, linear design

Date	Mintage	F	VF	XF	Unc	BU
1985	10,000,000	—	0.20	0.40	0.85	1.25

KM# 592.1 10 CRUZEIROS

Stainless Steel, 23.9 mm. **Obv:** Map of Brazil **Rev:** Denomination, value, date, linear design

Date	Mintage	F	VF	XF	Unc	BU
1980	100,010,000	—	—	0.50	0.75	1.00
1981	200,000,000	—	—	0.50	0.75	1.00
1982	331,000,000	—	—	0.50	0.75	1.00
1983	390,000,000	—	—	0.50	0.75	1.00
1984	390,000,000	—	—	0.50	0.75	1.00

KM# 592.2 10 CRUZEIROS

5.0000 g., Stainless Steel, 23.9 mm. **Obv:** Map of Brazil **Rev:** Value, date, linear design **Note:** Reduced weight.

Date	Mintage	F	VF	XF	Unc	BU
1985	201,000,000	—	—	0.50	0.75	1.00
1986	—	—	—	0.50	0.75	1.00

KM# 593.1 20 CRUZEIROS
Stainless Steel, 26 mm. **Obv:** Francis of Assisi Church **Rev:** Denomination above date, linear design **Edge:** Plain

Date	Mintage	F	VF	XF	Unc	BU
1981	88,297,000	—	—	0.25	0.85	1.20
1982	158,200,000	—	—	0.20	0.65	0.85
1983	312,000,000	—	—	0.20	0.65	0.85
1984	226,000,000	—	—	0.20	0.65	0.85

KM# 593.2 20 CRUZEIROS
5.9000 g., Stainless Steel, 26 mm. **Obv:** Francis of Assisi Church **Rev:** Denomination above date, linear design **Edge:** Plain **Note:** Reduced weight.

Date	Mintage	F	VF	XF	Unc	BU
1985	205,000,000	—	—	0.20	0.65	0.85
1986	—	—	—	0.20	0.65	0.85

KM# 594.1 50 CRUZEIROS
Stainless Steel **Obv:** Map of Brasilia **Rev:** Denomination above date, linear design **Edge:** Plain

Date	Mintage	F	VF	XF	Unc	BU
1981	57,000,000	—	—	0.35	1.00	1.50
1982	134,000,000	—	—	0.20	0.65	0.85
1983	181,800,000	—	—	0.20	0.65	0.85
1984	292,418,000	—	—	0.20	0.65	0.85

KM# 594.2 50 CRUZEIROS
7.5000 g., Stainless Steel, 27.9 mm. **Obv:** Map **Rev:** Denomination above date, linear design **Note:** Reduced weight.

Date	Mintage	F	VF	XF	Unc	BU
1985	180,000,000	—	—	0.20	0.65	0.85
1986	—	—	—	0.20	0.65	0.85

KM# 595 100 CRUZEIROS
2.2000 g., Stainless Steel, 16.95 mm. **Obv:** National arms **Rev:** Denomination above date

Date	Mintage	F	VF	XF	Unc	BU
1985	162,000,000	—	—	0.20	0.40	0.65
1986	—	—	—	0.20	0.40	0.65

KM# 596 200 CRUZEIROS
2.7000 g., Stainless Steel, 18.9 mm. **Obv:** National arms **Rev:** Denomination above date

Date	Mintage	F	VF	XF	Unc	BU
1985	55,000,000	—	—	0.25	0.50	0.75
1986	—	—	—	0.25	0.50	0.75

KM# 597 500 CRUZEIROS
3.7000 g., Stainless Steel, 20.95 mm. **Obv:** National arms **Rev:** Denomination above date

Date	Mintage	F	VF	XF	Unc	BU
1985	74,000,000	—	—	0.35	1.00	1.25
1986	—	—	—	0.35	1.00	1.25

REFORM COINAGE

1986-1989

1000 Cruzeiros Novos = 1 Cruzado; 100 Centavos = 1 Cruzado

KM# 600 CENTAVO
1.6500 g., Stainless Steel, 14.52 mm. **Obv:** National arms **Rev:** Denomination above date **Edge:** Plain

Date	Mintage	F	VF	XF	Unc	BU
1986	100,000,000	—	—	—	0.15	0.25
1987	1,000,000	—	—	—	0.20	0.35
1988	1,000,000	—	—	—	0.20	0.35

KM# 601 5 CENTAVOS
1.9000 g., Stainless Steel, 15.90 mm. **Obv:** National arms **Rev:** Denomination above date **Edge:** Plain

Date	Mintage	F	VF	XF	Unc	BU
1986	99,282,000	—	—	—	0.15	0.25
1987	1,000,000	—	—	—	0.20	0.35
1988	1,000,000	—	—	—	0.20	0.35

KM# 602 10 CENTAVOS
2.1600 g., Stainless Steel, 16.90 mm. **Obv:** National arms **Rev:** Denomination above date **Edge:** Plain

Date	Mintage	F	VF	XF	Unc	BU
1986	200,000,000	—	—	—	0.15	0.25
1987	245,628,000	—	—	—	0.15	0.25
1988	21,293,000	—	—	—	0.20	0.35

KM# 603 20 CENTAVOS
2.6500 g., Stainless Steel, 18.91 mm. **Obv:** National arms **Rev:** Denomination above date **Edge:** Plain

Date	Mintage	F	VF	XF	Unc	BU
1986	140,000,000	—	—	—	0.20	0.30
1987	157,500,000	—	—	—	0.20	0.30
1988	16,000,000	—	—	—	0.25	0.40

KM# 604 50 CENTAVOS
3.5700 g., Stainless Steel, 20.93 mm. **Obv:** National arms **Rev:** Denomination above date

Date	Mintage	F	VF	XF	Unc	BU
1986	200,000,000	—	—	—	0.35	0.50
1987	201,884,000	—	—	—	0.35	0.50
1988	131,255,000	—	—	—	0.35	0.50

KM# 605 CRUZADO
4.4500 g., Stainless Steel, 22.54 mm. **Obv:** National arms **Rev:** Date divides denomination **Edge:** Plain

Date	Mintage	F	VF	XF	Unc	BU
1986	—	—	—	—	1.00	1.25
1987	383,087,000	—	—	—	0.45	0.65
1988	321,216,000	—	—	—	0.45	0.65

KM# 606 5 CRUZADOS
5.3000 g., Stainless Steel, 25 mm. **Obv:** National arms **Rev:** Date divides denomination **Edge:** Plain

Date	Mintage	F	VF	XF	Unc	BU
1986	—	—	—	—	1.50	1.75
1987	141,000,000	—	—	—	0.65	0.85
1988	291,906,000	—	—	—	0.65	0.85

KM# 607 10 CRUZADOS
6.1400 g., Stainless Steel, 26.82 mm. **Obv:** National arms **Rev:** Date divides denomination **Edge:** Plain

Date	Mintage	F	VF	XF	Unc	BU
1987	131,500,000	—	—	—	1.75	2.00
1988	457,977,000	—	—	—	0.85	1.00

KM# 608 100 CRUZADOS
Stainless Steel **Subject:** Abolition of Slavery Centennial - Male **Obv:** Denomination **Rev:** Outline divides dates on left from head on right

Date	Mintage	F	VF	XF	Unc	BU
ND	200,000	—	—	1.00	3.00	3.50

KM# 609 100 CRUZADOS
Stainless Steel **Subject:** Abolition of Slavery Centennial - Female **Obv:** Denomination **Rev:** Outline divides dates on left from head on right

Date	Mintage	F	VF	XF	Unc	BU
ND	200,000	—	—	1.00	3.00	3.50

KM# 610 100 CRUZADOS
Stainless Steel **Subject:** Abolition of Slavery Centennial - Child **Obv:** Denomination **Rev:** Outline divides dates on left from head on right

Date	Mintage	F	VF	XF	Unc	BU
ND	200,000	—	—	1.00	3.00	3.50

REFORM COINAGE

1989-1990

1000 Old Cruzados = 1 Cruzado Novo

KM# 611 CENTAVO
2.0000 g., Stainless Steel, 16.47 mm. **Obv:** Outlined denomination **Rev:** Farmer, date divides cows at bottom **Edge:** Plain

Date	Mintage	F	VF	XF	Unc	BU
1989	—	—	—	—	0.35	0.50
1990	—	—	—	—	0.35	0.50

KM# 612 5 CENTAVOS
2.2400 g., Stainless Steel, 16.51 mm. **Obv:** Outlined denomination **Rev:** Fisherman, two fish above date at bottom **Edge:** Plain

Date	Mintage	F	VF	XF	Unc	BU
1989	—	—	—	—	0.45	0.60
1990	—	—	—	—	0.45	0.60

KM# 613 10 CENTAVOS
2.4900 g., Stainless Steel, 18.42 mm. **Obv:** Outlined denomination **Rev:** Miner, three diamonds above date at bottom **Edge:** Plain

Date	Mintage	F	VF	XF	Unc	BU
1989	—	—	—	—	0.60	0.75
1990	—	—	—	—	0.60	0.75

KM# 614 50 CENTAVOS
2.8400 g., Stainless Steel, 19.47 mm. **Obv:** Outlined denomination **Rev:** Figure above design, date at bottom **Edge:** Plain

Date	Mintage	F	VF	XF	Unc	BU
1989	—	—	—	—	1.25	1.50
1990	—	—	—	—	1.25	1.50

KM# 615 NOVO CRUZADO
Stainless Steel **Subject:** Centennial of the Republic **Obv:** Denomination **Rev:** Laureate liberty bust 3/4 left divides dates

Date	Mintage	F	VF	XF	Unc	BU
ND(1989)	—	—	—	—	2.00	2.50

REFORM COINAGE

1990-1993

100 Centavos = 1 Cruzeiro; 1 Cruzado Novo = 1 Cruzeiro

KM# 617 CRUZEIRO
Stainless Steel **Obv:** Outlined denomination **Rev:** Date lower right of design

Date	Mintage	F	VF	XF	Unc	BU
1990	—	—	—	—	0.35	0.50

KM# 618.1 5 CRUZEIROS
Stainless Steel, 21.5 mm. **Obv:** Outlined denomination **Rev:** Laborer, date at bottom **Edge:** Plain

Date	Mintage	F	VF	XF	Unc	BU
1990	—	—	—	—	0.45	0.60

KM# 618.2 5 CRUZEIROS
Stainless Steel, 21.5 mm. **Obv:** Outlined denomination **Rev:** Laborer at top, small village above date at bottom **Edge:** Plain **Note:** Thinner planchet.

Date	Mintage	F	VF	XF	Unc	BU
1991	—	—	—	—	0.45	0.60
1992	—	—	—	—	0.45	0.60

KM# 619.1 10 CRUZEIROS
Stainless Steel **Obv:** Outlined denomination **Rev:** Laborer at top, small village above date at bottom

Date	Mintage	F	VF	XF	Unc	BU
1990	—	—	—	—	0.50	0.75

KM# 619.2 10 CRUZEIROS
Stainless Steel **Note:** Thinner planchet.

Date	Mintage	F	VF	XF	Unc	BU
1991	—	—	—	—	0.50	0.75
1992	—	—	—	—	0.50	0.75

KM# 620.1 50 CRUZEIROS
Stainless Steel, 23.5 mm. **Obv:** Outlined denomination **Rev:** Farmer, fish above date below

Date	Mintage	F	VF	XF	Unc	BU
1990	—	—	—	—	0.65	0.85

KM# 620.2 50 CRUZEIROS
Stainless Steel, 23.5 mm. **Obv:** Outlined denomination **Rev:** Farmer, fish above date below **Edge:** Plain **Note:** Thinner planchet.

Date	Mintage	F	VF	XF	Unc	BU
1991	—	—	—	—	0.60	0.80
1992	—	—	—	—	0.60	0.80

KM# 623 100 CRUZEIROS
Stainless Steel, 18 mm. **Obv:** Date left of denomination **Rev:** Manatee **Edge:** Plain

Date	Mintage	F	VF	XF	Unc	BU
1992	—	—	—	—	1.50	2.50
1993	—	—	—	—	1.50	2.50

KM# 624 500 CRUZEIROS
2.6800 g., Stainless Steel, 18.99 mm. **Obv:** Date left of denomination **Rev:** Loggerhead Sea Turtle

Date	Mintage	F	VF	XF	Unc	BU
1992	—	—	—	—	1.50	2.50
1993	—	—	—	—	1.50	2.50

KM# 626 1000 CRUZEIROS
Stainless Steel, 20 mm. **Obv:** Date to left of denomination **Rev:** Fish - Acara **Edge:** Plain

Date	Mintage	F	VF	XF	Unc	BU
1992	—	—	—	—	1.50	2.50
1993	—	—	—	—	1.50	2.50

KM# 625 5000 CRUZEIROS
Stainless Steel **Subject:** 200th Anniversary of Tiradentes' Death **Obv:** Denomination **Rev:** Bust left, two dates below

Date	Mintage	F	VF	XF	Unc	BU
ND	—	—	—	—	2.50	3.50

REFORM COINAGE

1993-1994

1000 Cruzeiros = 1 Cruzeiro Real

KM# 627 5 CRUZEIROS REAIS
Stainless Steel **Obv:** Date to left of denomination **Rev:** Macaw Parrots - Arara, left **Edge:** Plain

Date	Mintage	F	VF	XF	Unc	BU
1993	—	—	—	—	1.50	2.50
1994	—	—	—	—	1.50	2.50

KM# 628 10 CRUZEIROS REAIS
Stainless Steel, 22 mm. **Obv:** Date to left of denomination **Rev:** Anteater - Tamandua, right **Edge:** Plain

Date	Mintage	F	VF	XF	Unc	BU
1993	—	—	—	—	1.50	2.50
1994	—	—	—	—	1.50	2.50

KM# 629 50 CRUZEIROS REAIS
Stainless Steel **Obv:** Date to left of denomination **Rev:** Mother jaguar and cub facing **Edge:** Plain

Date	Mintage	F	VF	XF	Unc	BU
1993	—	—	—	—	1.75	3.00
1994	—	—	—	—	1.75	3.00

KM# 630 100 CRUZEIROS REAIS
Stainless Steel **Obv:** Date to left of denomination **Rev:** Maned wolf right **Edge:** Plain

Date	Mintage	F	VF	XF	Unc	BU
1993	—	—	—	—	1.75	3.00
1994	—	—	—	—	1.75	3.00

REFORM COINAGE

1994-present

2750 Cruzeiros Reais = 1 Real; 100 Centavos = 1 Real

KM# 631 CENTAVO
Stainless Steel, 20 mm. **Obv:** Laureate liberty head left, linear design **Rev:** Denomination above date **Edge:** Plain

Date	Mintage	F	VF	XF	Unc	BU
1994	—	—	—	—	0.35	0.50
1995	—	—	—	—	0.35	0.50
1996	—	—	—	—	0.35	0.50
1997	—	—	—	—	0.35	0.50

KM# 647 CENTAVO
Copper Plated Steel, 17 mm. **Obv:** Cabral bust at right **Rev:** Denomination on linear design at left, 3/4 globe with sash on right, date below **Edge:** Plain

Date	Mintage	F	VF	XF	Unc	BU
1998	—	—	—	—	0.35	0.50
1999	—	—	—	—	0.10	0.20
2000	—	—	—	—	0.10	0.20
2001	—	—	—	—	0.10	0.20
2002	—	—	—	—	0.10	0.20
2003	—	—	—	—	0.10	0.20
2004	—	—	—	—	0.10	0.20

KM# 632 5 CENTAVOS
3.2500 g., Stainless Steel, 21 mm. **Obv:** Laureate liberty head left, linear design **Rev:** Denomination above date **Edge:** Plain

Date	Mintage	F	VF	XF	Unc	BU
1994	—	—	—	—	0.45	0.65
1995	—	—	—	—	0.45	0.65
1996	—	—	—	—	0.45	0.65
1997	—	—	—	—	0.45	0.65

KM# 648 5 CENTAVOS
4.0500 g., Copper Plated Steel, 22 mm. **Obv:** Tiradente bust at right, dove at left **Rev:** Denomination on linear design at left, 3/4 globe with sash on right, date below **Edge:** Plain

Date	Mintage	F	VF	XF	Unc	BU
1998	—	—	—	—	0.45	0.65
1999	—	—	—	—	0.45	0.65
2000	—	—	—	—	0.45	0.65
2001	—	—	—	—	0.45	0.65
2002	—	—	—	—	0.45	0.65
2003	—	—	—	—	0.45	0.65
2004	—	—	—	—	0.45	0.65
2005	—	—	—	—	0.45	0.65

KM# 633 10 CENTAVOS
Stainless Steel, 22 mm. **Obv:** Laureate liberty head, left, lined background **Rev:** Denomiation above date **Edge:** Plain

Date	Mintage	F	VF	XF	Unc	BU
1994	—	—	—	—	0.60	0.80
1995	—	—	—	—	0.60	0.80
1996	—	—	—	—	0.60	0.80
1997	—	—	—	—	0.60	0.80

KM# 641 10 CENTAVOS
Stainless Steel **Series:** F.A.O. **Obv:** Hands holding seedling **Rev:** Denomination above date

Date	Mintage	F	VF	XF	Unc	BU
1995	1,000,000	—	—	—	0.65	0.85

KM# 649.1 10 CENTAVOS
Brass Plated Steel, 20 mm. **Subject:** Pedro I **Obv:** Bust of Pedro, horseman with sword in left hand **Rev:** Denomination **Edge:** Plain
Note: Majority of mintage recalled and melted.

Date	Mintage	F	VF	XF	Unc	BU
1997	—	—	—	—	—	—
1998	—	—	—	—	—	—

KM# 649.2 10 CENTAVOS
4.8500 g., Brass Plated Steel, 20 mm. **Obv:** Bust of Pedro at right, horseman with sword in right hand at left **Rev:** Denomination on linear design at left, 3/4 globe with sash on right, date below **Edge:** Plain

Date	Mintage	F	VF	XF	Unc	BU
1998	—	—	—	—	0.60	0.80
1999	—	—	—	—	0.60	0.80
2000	—	—	—	—	0.60	0.80
2001	—	—	—	—	0.60	0.80
2002	—	—	—	—	0.60	0.80
2003	—	—	—	—	0.60	0.80
2004	—	—	—	—	0.60	0.80

KM# 649.3 10 CENTAVOS
4.8000 g., Brass Plated Steel, 20 mm. **Obv:** Pedro I and horseman **Rev:** Value **Edge:** Reeded

Date	Mintage	F	VF	XF	Unc	BU
2006	—	—	—	—	0.50	0.75

KM# 634 25 CENTAVOS
4.8200 g., Stainless Steel, 23.5 mm. **Obv:** Stylized laureate liberty head left, date below **Rev:** Outlined denomination, linear design **Edge:** Plain

Date	Mintage	F	VF	XF	Unc	BU
1994	—	—	—	—	0.75	1.00
1995	—	—	—	—	0.75	1.00

KM# 642 25 CENTAVOS
Stainless Steel **Series:** F.A.O. **Obv:** Farmer working **Rev:** Outlined denomination, linear design

Date	Mintage	F	VF	XF	Unc	BU
1995	1,000,000	—	—	—	0.80	1.20

KM# 650 25 CENTAVOS
7.6500 g., Brass Plated Steel, 25 mm. **Obv:** Deodoro bust at right, national arms at left **Rev:** Denomination on linear design at left, 3/4 globe with sash on right, date below **Edge:** Reeded

Date	Mintage	F	VF	XF	Unc	BU
1998	—	—	—	—	0.75	1.00
1999	—	—	—	—	0.75	1.00
2000	—	—	—	—	0.75	1.00
2001	—	—	—	—	0.75	1.00
2002	—	—	—	—	0.75	1.00
2003	—	—	—	—	0.75	1.00
2004	—	—	—	—	0.75	1.00

KM# 635 50 CENTAVOS
Stainless Steel, 23 mm. **Obv:** Laureate liberty head left, linear design **Rev:** Denomination above date **Edge:** Plain

Date	Mintage	F	VF	XF	Unc	BU
1994	—	—	—	—	1.25	1.50
1995	—	—	—	—	1.25	1.50

KM# 651 50 CENTAVOS
9.2200 g., Copper-Nickel, 23 mm. **Obv:** Rio Branco bust at right, map at left **Rev:** Denomination on linear design at left, 3/4 globe with sash on right, date below **Edge Lettering:** BRASIL ORDEM E PROGRESSO

Date	Mintage	F	VF	XF	Unc	BU
1998	—	—	—	—	1.25	1.50
1999	—	—	—	—	1.25	1.50
1999 Proof	2,000	—	—	—	—	—
2000	—	—	—	—	1.25	1.50
2001	—	—	—	—	1.25	1.50
2002	—	—	—	—	1.25	1.50
2003	—	—	—	—	1.25	1.50
2005	—	—	—	—	1.25	1.50

KM# 651a 50 CENTAVOS
7.8600 g., Stainless Steel, 23.05 mm. **Obv:** Rio Branco bust at right, map at left **Rev:** Denomination on linear design at left, 3/4 globe with sash on right, date below

Date	Mintage	F	VF	XF	Unc	BU
2002	—	—	—	—	1.25	1.50

KM# 636 REAL
Stainless Steel, 24 mm. **Obv:** Laureate liberty head left, linear design

Date	Mintage	F	VF	XF	Unc	BU
1994	—	—	—	—	2.50	2.75

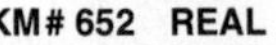

KM# 652 REAL
7.8700 g., Bi-Metallic **Ring Composition:** Brass **Center Composition:** Copper-Nickel, 27 mm. **Obv:** Allegorical portrait left **Rev:** Denomination on linear design at left, 3/4 globe with

sash on right, date below **Edge:** Segmented reeding **Note:** Total coin weight 7.8 grams.

Date	Mintage	F	VF	XF	Unc	BU
1998	—	—	—	—	2.75	3.50
1999	—	—	—	—	2.75	3.50
2000	—	—	—	—	3.00	4.50
2002	—	—	—	—	3.00	4.50

KM# 653 REAL

Bi-Metallic Copper-Nickel center in Brass ring, 27 mm. **Subject:** Universal Declaration of Human Rights **Obv:** Globe **Rev:** Denomination left, globe with sash at right, date below, linear design

Date	Mintage	F	VF	XF	Unc	BU
1998	600,000	—	—	—	2.75	4.00

KM# 652a REAL

7.0000 g., Bi-Metallic **Ring Composition:** Brass-Plated Steel **Center Composition:** Stainless Steel, 26.9 mm. **Obv:** Allegorical portrait **Rev:** Denomination on linear design at left, 3/4 globe with sash on right, date below **Edge:** Segmented reeding

Date	Mintage	F	VF	XF	Unc	BU
2002	—	—	—	—	3.50	4.50
2004	—	—	—	—	3.50	4.50

KM# 656 REAL

7.0000 g., Bi-Metallic **Ring Composition:** Brass-Plated Steel **Center Composition:** Stainless Steel, 26.9 mm. **Subject:** Centennial of Juscelino Kubitschek, president **Obv:** Head left **Obv. Designer:** Alzira Duim **Rev:** Denomination on linear design at left, 3/4 globe with sash on right, date below **Edge:** Segmented reeding

Date	Mintage	F	VF	XF	Unc	BU
2002	50,000,000	—	—	—	3.50	4.50

KM# 668 REAL

6.9100 g., Bi-Metallic Stainless Steel center in Brass plated Stainless Steel ring, 27.1 mm. **Subject:** 40th Anniversary of Central Bank **Obv:** Monument **Rev:** Value on flag **Edge:** Segmented reeding

Date	Mintage	F	VF	XF	Unc	BU
2005	40,000	—	—	—	5.00	6.50

BRITISH HONDURAS

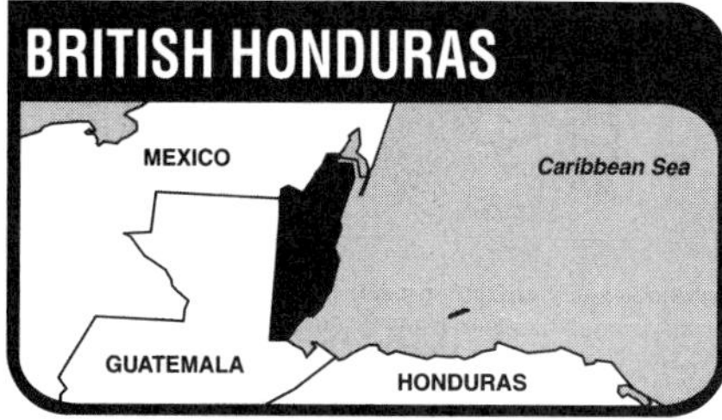

This area, site of the ancient Mayan civilization, was sighted by Columbus in 1502, and settled by shipwrecked English seamen in 1638. British buccaneers settled the former capital of Belize in the 17th century. Britain claimed administrative right over the area after the emancipation of Central America from Spain. In 1825, Imperial coins were introduced into the colony and were rated against the Spanish dollar and Honduran currency. It was declared a colony subordinate to Jamaica in 1862 and was established as the separate Crown Colony of British Honduras in 1884. In May, 1885 an order in Council authorized coins for the colony, with the first shipment arriving in July. While the Guatemalan peso was originally the standard of value, in 1894 the colony changed to the gold standard, based on the U.S. gold dollar. The anti-British Peoples United Party, which attained power in 1954, won a constitution, effective in 1964 which established self-government under a British appointed governor. British Honduras became Belize on June 1, 1973, following the passage of a surprise bill by the Peoples United Party, but the constitutional relationship with Britain remained unchanged. Full independence was achieved in 1981.

MONETARY SYSTEM
100 Cents = 1 Dollar

MINT MARKS
H - Heaton

BRITISH COLONY

DECIMAL COINAGE

KM# 11 CENT

Bronze **Ruler:** Edward VII **Obv:** Bust of King Edward VII right **Obv. Designer:** G.W. DeSaulles **Rev:** Numeric denomination within circle, denomination and date below

Date	Mintage	F	VF	XF	Unc	BU
1904	50,000	6.00	15.00	50.00	90.00	—
1904 Proof	—	Value: 200				
1904 Matte Proof	—	Value: 1,550				
1906	50,000	12.00	27.50	65.00	225	—
1906 Matte Proof	—	Value: 1,050				
1909	25,000	35.00	80.00	150	300	—

KM# 15 CENT

Bronze **Ruler:** George V **Obv:** Bust of King George V left **Obv. Designer:** E.B. MacKennal **Rev:** Numeric denomination within circle, denomination and date below

Date	Mintage	F	VF	XF	Unc	BU
1911	50,000	60.00	100	200	500	—
1912H	50,000	85.00	160	250	600	—
1913	25,000	100	200	300	700	—

KM# 19 CENT

Bronze **Ruler:** George V **Obv:** Bust of King George V left **Obv. Designer:** E.B. MacKennal **Rev:** Numeric denomination within scalloped circle, denomination and date below

Date	Mintage	F	VF	XF	Unc	BU
1914	175,000	3.00	7.50	25.00	120	—
1916H	125,000	3.50	8.50	27.50	125	—
1918	40,000	7.00	15.00	40.00	150	—
1919	50,000	7.00	15.00	40.00	150	—
1924	50,000	7.00	15.00	40.00	125	—
1924 Proof	—	Value: 250				
1926	50,000	5.00	12.00	35.00	125	—
1926 Proof	—	Value: 225				
1936	40,000	2.00	5.00	20.00	65.00	—
1936 Proof	50	Value: 170				

KM# 21 CENT

Bronze **Ruler:** George VI **Obv:** Bust of King George VI left **Obv. Designer:** Percy Metcalf **Rev:** Numeric denomination within scalloped circle, denomination and date below

Date	Mintage	F	VF	XF	Unc	BU
1937	80,000	0.75	4.00	12.00	75.00	—
1937 Proof	—	Value: 170				
1939	50,000	2.00	7.00	20.00	150	—
1939 Proof	—	Value: 100				
1942	50,000	2.00	7.00	20.00	150	—
1942 Proof	—	Value: 125				
1943	100,000	1.00	5.00	15.00	125	—
1943 Proof	—	Value: 150				
1944	100,000	2.00	7.00	20.00	150	—
1944 Proof	—	Value: 200				
1945	130,000	0.75	2.00	7.50	50.00	—
1945 Proof	—	Value: 120				
1947	100,000	0.75	2.50	10.00	70.00	—
1947 Proof	—	Value: 150				

KM# 24 CENT

Bronze **Ruler:** George VI **Obv:** Bust of King George VI left **Obv. Legend:** Without EMPEROR OF INDIA **Obv. Designer:** Percy Metcalf **Rev:** Numeric denomination within scalloped circle, denomination and date below

Date	Mintage	F	VF	XF	Unc	BU
1949	100,000	0.60	1.50	4.00	16.50	—
1949 Proof	—	Value: 135				
1950	100,000	0.40	1.00	2.50	6.50	—
1950 Proof	—	Value: 135				
1951	100,000	0.60	1.50	4.00	16.50	—
1951 Proof	—	Value: 135				

KM# 27 CENT

Bronze **Ruler:** Elizabeth II **Obv:** Head right **Rev:** Numeric denomination within scalloped circle, date and denomination below **Edge:** Plain

Date	Mintage	F	VF	XF	Unc	BU
1954	200,000	0.50	0.75	1.00	5.00	—
1954 Proof	—	Value: 150				

KM# 30 CENT

2.5000 g., Bronze, 19.5 mm. **Ruler:** Elizabeth II **Obv:** Bust of Queen Elizabeth II right **Obv. Designer:** Cecil Thomas **Rev:** Numeric denomination within scalloped circle, date and denomination below **Edge:** Plain **Shape:** Scalloped

Date	Mintage	F	VF	XF	Unc	BU
1956	200,000	0.10	0.25	0.50	3.50	—
1956 Proof	—	Value: 80.00				
1958	400,000	1.00	2.00	9.00	80.00	—
1958 Proof	—	Value: 80.00				
1959	200,000	1.00	2.50	10.00	100	—
1959 Proof	—	Value: 100				
1961	800,000	—	0.15	0.25	0.50	—
1961 Proof	—	Value: 80.00				
1964	300,000	—	0.10	0.30	0.90	—
1965	400,000	—	—	0.10	0.50	—
1966	100,000	—	—	0.10	0.50	—
1967	400,000	—	—	0.10	0.50	—
1968	200,000	—	—	0.10	0.50	—
1969	520,000	—	—	0.10	0.40	—
1970	120,000	—	—	0.10	0.40	—
1971	800,000	—	—	0.10	0.40	—
1972	800,000	—	—	0.10	0.40	—
1973	400,000	—	—	0.10	0.40	—

KM# 14 5 CENTS

Copper-Nickel **Ruler:** Edward VII **Obv:** Bust of King Edward VII right within circle, date below **Obv. Designer:** G.W. DeSaulles **Rev:** Denomination within circle **Edge:** Plain

Date	Mintage	F	VF	XF	Unc	BU
1907	10,000	25.00	50.00	100	250	—
1909	10,000	25.00	50.00	100	250	—

KM# 16 5 CENTS

Copper-Nickel **Ruler:** George V **Obv:** Bust of King George V left within circle, date below **Obv. Designer:** E.B. MacKennal **Rev:** Denomination within circle **Edge:** Plain

Date	Mintage	F	VF	XF	Unc	BU
1911	10,000	25.00	50.00	100	250	—
1912H	20,000	10.00	25.00	55.00	175	—
1912H Proof	—	Value: 550				
1916H	20,000	10.00	25.00	55.00	175	—
1918	20,000	10.00	25.00	55.00	175	—
1919	20,000	8.00	20.00	50.00	160	—
1936	60,000	2.50	5.00	20.00	75.00	—
1936 Proof	50	Value: 450				

KM# 22 5 CENTS

Copper-Nickel **Ruler:** George VI **Obv:** Head of King George VI left **Obv. Designer:** Percy Metcalf **Rev:** Denomination within circle, date below **Edge:** Plain

Date	Mintage	F	VF	XF	Unc	BU
1939	20,000	3.00	6.00	25.00	75.00	—
1939 Proof	—	Value: 275				

KM# 22a 5 CENTS

Nickel-Brass **Ruler:** George VI **Obv:** Head of King George VI left **Obv. Designer:** Percy Metcalf **Rev:** Denomination within circle, date below

Date	Mintage	F	VF	XF	Unc	BU
1942	30,000	5.00	15.00	65.00	200	—
1942 Proof	—	Value: 300				
1943	40,000	2.00	12.00	60.00	190	—
1944	50,000	1.50	10.00	50.00	175	—
1944 Proof	—	Value: 275				
1945	65,000	1.00	5.00	15.00	75.00	—
1945 Proof	—	Value: 150				
1947	40,000	1.50	5.00	15.00	85.00	—
1947 Proof	—	Value: 185				

KM# 25 5 CENTS

Nickel-Brass, 20 mm. **Ruler:** George VI **Obv:** Head of King George VI left **Obv. Legend:** Legend without EMPEROR OF INDIA **Obv. Designer:** Percy Metcalf **Rev:** Denomination within circle, date below **Edge:** Plain

Date	Mintage	F	VF	XF	Unc	BU
1949	40,000	1.50	3.00	10.00	50.00	—
1949 Proof	—	Value: 150				
1950	225,000	0.40	1.00	4.00	30.00	—
1950 Proof	—	Value: 200				
1952	100,000	0.50	2.00	6.00	35.00	—
1952 Proof	—	Value: 250				

KM# 31 5 CENTS

3.6000 g., Nickel-Brass, 20.26 mm. **Ruler:** Elizabeth II **Obv:** Bust of Queen Elizabeth II right **Obv. Designer:** Cecil Thomas **Rev:** Denomination within circle, date below **Edge:** Plain

Date	Mintage	F	VF	XF	Unc	BU
1956	100,000	0.20	0.50	3.00	75.00	—
1956 Proof	—	Value: 125				
1957	100,000	0.30	0.75	1.50	10.00	—
1957 Proof	—	Value: 175				
1958	200,000	0.30	1.00	7.50	90.00	—
1958 Proof	—	Value: 125				
1959	100,000	0.40	2.00	10.00	100	—
1959 Proof	—	Value: 185				
1961	100,000	0.30	0.75	2.50	35.00	—
1961 Proof	—	Value: 120				
1962	200,000	0.15	0.35	0.65	2.00	—
1962 Proof	—	Value: 115				
1963	100,000	0.10	0.20	0.50	1.50	—
1963 Proof	—	Value: 175				
1964	100,000	0.10	0.15	0.35	1.00	—
1965	150,000	—	0.10	0.25	0.75	—
1966	150,000	—	0.10	0.20	0.60	—
1968	200,000	—	0.10	0.15	0.50	—
1969	540,000	—	0.10	0.15	0.50	—
1970	240,000	—	0.10	0.15	0.50	—
1971	450,000	—	0.10	0.15	0.50	—
1972	200,000	—	0.10	0.15	0.50	—
1973	210,000	—	0.10	0.15	0.75	—

KM# 20 10 CENTS

2.3240 g., 0.9250 Silver 0.0691 oz. ASW **Ruler:** George V **Obv:** Bust of King George V left **Obv. Designer:** E.B. MacKennal **Rev:** Denomination within circle, date below **Edge:** Reeded

Date	Mintage	F	VF	XF	Unc	BU
1918	10,000	15.00	25.00	100	350	—
1919	10,000	15.00	25.00	100	350	—
1936	30,000	6.00	12.00	25.00	100	—
1936 Proof	50	Value: 325				

KM# 23 10 CENTS

2.3240 g., 0.9250 Silver 0.0691 oz. ASW **Ruler:** George VI **Obv:** Head of King George VI left **Obv. Designer:** Percy Metcalf **Rev:** Denomination within circle, date below **Edge:** Plain

Date	Mintage	F	VF	XF	Unc	BU
1939	20,000	3.00	7.00	20.00	60.00	—
1939 Proof	—	Value: 300				
1942	10,000	10.00	20.00	60.00	250	—
1943	20,000	3.00	6.00	45.00	250	—
1944	30,000	2.50	5.00	35.00	150	—
1944 Proof	—	Value: 250				
1946	10,000	5.00	12.00	45.00	200	—
1946 Proof	—	Value: 450				

KM# 32 10 CENTS

2.3400 g., Copper-Nickel, 18 mm. **Ruler:** Elizabeth II **Obv:** Bust of Queen Elizabeth II right **Obv. Designer:** Cecil Thomas **Rev:** Denomination within circle, date below **Edge:** Plain

Date	Mintage	F	VF	XF	Unc	BU
1956	100,000	0.45	1.00	2.00	7.50	—
1956 Proof	—	Value: 200				
1959	100,000	0.65	1.50	2.00	7.50	—
1959 Proof	—	Value: 135				
1961	50,000	0.35	0.75	1.25	3.00	—
1961 Proof	—	Value: 135				
1963	50,000	0.20	0.50	0.75	2.00	—
1963 Proof	—	Value: 135				
1964	60,000	0.15	0.25	0.50	1.00	—
1965/6	200,000	5.00	10.00	20.00	40.00	—
1965	Inc. above	—	0.10	0.15	0.50	—
1970	—	—	0.10	0.15	0.75	—

KM# 9 25 CENTS

5.8100 g., 0.9250 Silver 0.1728 oz. ASW **Ruler:** Victoria **Obv:** Head of Queen Victoria left **Rev:** Denomination within circle, date below **Edge:** Plain

Date	Mintage	F	VF	XF	Unc	BU
1901	20,000	20.00	35.00	125	400	—
1901 Proof	30	Value: 650				

KM# 12 25 CENTS

5.8100 g., 0.9250 Silver 0.1728 oz. ASW **Ruler:** Edward VII **Obv:** Bust of King Edward VII right **Obv. Designer:** G.W. DeSaulles **Rev:** Denomination within circle, date below **Edge:** Reeded

Date	Mintage	F	VF	XF	Unc	BU
1906	30,000	15.00	30.00	110	375	—
1907	60,000	10.00	25.00	95.00	325	—

KM# 17 25 CENTS

5.8100 g., 0.9250 Silver 0.1728 oz. ASW **Ruler:** George V **Obv:** Bust of King George V left **Obv. Designer:** E.B. MacKennal **Rev:** Denomination within circle, date below **Edge:** Reeded

Date	Mintage	F	VF	XF	Unc	BU
1911	14,000	25.00	60.00	150	400	—
1919	40,000	8.00	17.50	75.00	250	—

KM# 26 25 CENTS

Copper-Nickel **Ruler:** George VI **Obv:** Head of King George VI left **Obv. Designer:** Percy Metcalf **Rev:** Denomination within circle, date below **Edge:** Reeded

Date	Mintage	F	VF	XF	Unc	BU
1952	75,000	2.00	5.00	50.00	200	—
1952 Proof	—	Value: 250				

KM# 29 25 CENTS

5.6200 g., Copper-Nickel, 23.53 mm. **Ruler:** Elizabeth II **Obv:** Bust of Queen Elizabeth II right **Obv. Designer:** Cecil Thomas **Edge:** Reeded

Date	Mintage	F	VF	XF	Unc	BU
1955	75,000	0.45	1.00	3.50	15.00	—
1955 Proof	—	Value: 150				
1960	75,000	0.45	1.00	5.00	100	—
1960 Proof	—	Value: 250				
1962	50,000	0.30	0.50	1.00	2.50	—
1962 Proof	—	Value: 150				
1963	50,000	0.30	0.50	2.00	7.50	—
1963 Proof	—	Value: 150				
1964	100,000	0.30	0.50	0.75	1.50	—
1965	75,000	—	0.50	1.00	2.00	—
1966	75,000	0.45	1.00	2.00	8.00	—
1968	125,000	0.25	0.50	1.00	2.00	—
1970	—	0.20	0.35	0.75	1.50	—
1971	150,000	0.20	0.30	0.50	1.50	—
1972	200,000	0.20	0.30	0.50	1.50	—
1973	100,000	0.20	0.30	0.60	1.75	—

KM# 10 50 CENTS

11.6200 g., 0.9250 Silver 0.3456 oz. ASW **Ruler:** Victoria **Obv:** Head of Queen Victoria left **Rev:** Denomination within circle, date below

Date	Mintage	F	VF	XF	Unc	BU
1901	10,000	35.00	80.00	400	1,000	—
1901 Proof	30	Value: 1,000				

KM# 13 50 CENTS

11.6200 g., 0.9250 Silver 0.3456 oz. ASW **Ruler:** Edward VII **Obv:** Bust of King Edward VII right **Obv. Designer:** G.W. DeSaulles **Rev:** Denomination within circle, date below

Date	Mintage	F	VF	XF	Unc	BU
1906	15,000	20.00	60.00	225	600	—
1907	19,000	18.00	55.00	170	500	—

KM# 18 50 CENTS

11.6200 g., 0.9250 Silver 0.3456 oz. ASW **Ruler:** George V **Obv:** Bust of King George V left **Obv. Designer:** E.B. MacKennal **Rev:** Denomination within circle, date below

Date	Mintage	F	VF	XF	Unc	BU
1911	12,000	30.00	75.00	250	850	—
1919	40,000	20.00	40.00	150	400	—
1919 Proof	—	Value: 1,250				

KM# 28 50 CENTS

Copper-Nickel **Ruler:** Elizabeth II **Obv:** Bust of Queen Elizabeth II right **Obv. Designer:** Cecil Thomas **Rev:** Denomination within circle, date below

Date	Mintage	F	VF	XF	Unc	BU
1954	75,000	0.30	0.50	1.00	4.00	—
1954 Proof	—	Value: 175				
1962	50,000	0.30	0.50	1.50	5.00	—
1962 Proof	—	Value: 200				
1964	50,000	0.30	0.50	1.50	3.50	—
1965	25,000	1.25	3.00	5.00	22.50	—
1966	25,000	1.00	2.00	4.00	15.00	—
1971	30,000	0.30	0.50	1.50	3.50	—

BRITISH NORTH BORNEO

British North Borneo (now known as *Sabah*), a former British protectorate and crown colony, occupies the northern tip of the island of Borneo. The island of Labuan, which lies 6 miles off the northwest coast of the island of Borneo, was attached to Singapore settlement in 1907. It became an independent settlement of the Straits Colony in 1912 and was incorporated with British North Borneo in 1946. In 1963 it became part of Malaysia.

RULER

British

MINT MARKS

H - Heaton, Birmingham

MONETARY SYSTEM

100 Cents = 1 Straits Dollar

BRITISH PROTECTORATE

STANDARD COINAGE

KM# 1 1/2 CENT

Bronze **Obv:** Denomination within wreath **Rev:** National arms, date below

Date	Mintage	F	VF	XF	Unc	BU
1907H	1,000,000	50.00	135	195	390	—
1907H Proof	—	Value: 700				

KM# 2 CENT

Bronze **Obv:** Denomination within wreath **Rev:** National arms with supporters, date below

Date	Mintage	F	VF	XF	Unc	BU
1907H	1,000,000	50.00	120	230	430	—
1907H Proof	—	Value: 900				

KM# 3 CENT

Copper-Nickel **Obv:** Denomination within circle, date below **Rev:** National arms with supporters

Date	Mintage	F	VF	XF	Unc	BU
1904H	2,000,000	3.50	9.00	18.50	50.00	—
1921H	1,000,000	3.50	9.00	18.50	50.00	—
1935H	1,000,000	2.70	5.00	15.00	40.00	—
1938H	1,000,000	2.70	5.00	15.00	40.00	—
1941H	1,000,000	2.70	5.00	15.00	40.00	—

KM# 4 2-1/2 CENT

Copper-Nickel **Obv:** Denomination within circle, date below **Rev:** National arms with supporters

Date	Mintage	F	VF	XF	Unc	BU
1903H	2,000,000	4.60	14.00	35.00	135	—
1903H Proof	—	Value: 600				
1920H	280,000	11.00	33.00	80.00	210	—

KM# 5 5 CENTS

Copper-Nickel **Obv:** Denomination within circle, date below **Rev:** National arms with supporters

Date	Mintage	F	VF	XF	Unc	BU
1903H	1,000,000	7.00	14.00	26.00	65.00	—
1920H	100,000	11.00	22.00	60.00	110	—
1921H	500,000	5.00	11.00	22.00	65.00	—
1927H	150,000	5.00	11.00	22.00	65.00	—
1928H	150,000	3.00	6.00	16.00	60.00	—
1938H	500,000	2.00	4.00	10.00	27.00	—
1940H	500,000	2.00	4.00	10.00	27.00	—
1941H	1,000,000	2.00	4.00	10.00	27.00	—

KM# 6 25 CENTS

2.8300 g., 0.5000 Silver 0.0455 oz. ASW **Obv:** Denomination within circle, date below **Rev:** National arms with supporters

Date	Mintage	F	VF	XF	Unc	BU
1929H	400,000	35.00	55.00	110	200	—
1929H Proof	—	Value: 500				

BRITISH VIRGIN ISLANDS

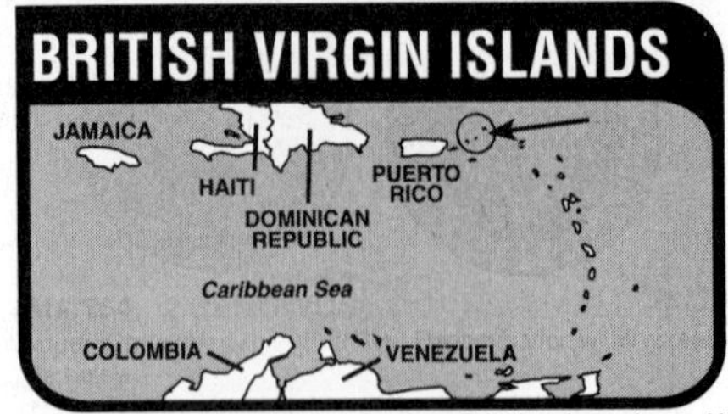

The Colony of the Virgin Islands, a British colony situated in the Caribbean Sea northeast of Puerto Rico and west of the Leeward Islands, has an area of 59 sq. mi. (155 sq. km.) and a population of 13,000. Capital: Road Town. The principal islands of the 36-island group are Tortola, Virgin Gorda, Anegada, and Jost Van Dyke. The chief industries are fishing and stock raising. Fish, livestock and bananas are exported.

The Virgin Islands were discovered by Columbus in 1493, and named by him, Las Virgienes, in honor of St. Ursula and her companions. The British Virgin Islands were formerly part of the administration of the Leeward Islands but received a separate administration as a Crown Colony in 1950. A new constitution promulgated in 1967 provided for a ministerial form of government headed by the Governor.

The Government of the British Virgin Islands issued the first official coinage in its history on June 30, 1973, in honor of 300 years of constitutional government in the islands. U.S. coins and currency continue to be the primary medium of exchange, though the coinage of the British Virgin Islands is legal tender.

***NOTE**: From 1975-1985 the Franklin Mint produced coinage in up to 3 different qualities. Qualities of issue are designated in ( ) after each date and are defined as follows:

(M) MATTE - Normal circulation strike or a dull finish produced by sandblasting special uncirculated (polish finish) or proof quality dies.

(U) SPECIAL UNCIRCULATED - Polished or proof-like in appearance without any frosted features.

(P) PROOF - The highest quality obtainable having mirror-like fields and frosted features.

BRITISH COLONY

STANDARD COINAGE

KM# 1 CENT

Bronze **Ruler:** Elizabeth II **Obv:** Young bust right **Obv. Designer:** Arnold Machin **Rev:** Green-throated Carib and Antillean Crested Hummingbird **Rev. Designer:** Gilroy Roberts

Date	Mintage	F	VF	XF	Unc	BU
1973FM	53,000	—	—	0.10	0.50	1.00
1973FM (P)	181,000	Value: 1.00				
1974FM	22,000	—	—	0.10	0.50	1.00
1974FM (P)	94,000	Value: 1.00				
1975FM (M)	6,000	—	—	0.10	0.75	1.20
1975FM (U)	2,351	—	—	0.10	0.50	1.00
1975FM (P)	32,000	Value: 1.00				
1976FM (M)	12,000	—	—	0.10	0.50	1.00
1976FM (U)	996	—	—	0.10	0.50	1.00
1976FM (P)	15,000	Value: 1.00				
1977FM (M)	500	—	—	0.25	2.00	3.00
1977FM (U)	782	—	—	0.10	0.50	1.00
1977FM (P)	7,218	Value: 1.00				
1978FM (U)	1,443	—	—	0.10	0.50	1.00
1978FM (P)	7,059	Value: 1.00				
1979FM (U)	680	—	—	0.10	0.50	1.00
1979FM (P)	5,304	Value: 1.00				
1980FM (U)	1,007	—	—	0.10	0.50	1.00
1980FM (P)	3,421	Value: 1.00				
1981FM (U)	472	—	—	0.10	0.50	1.00
1981FM (P)	1,124	Value: 1.50				
1982FM (U)	—	—	—	0.10	0.50	1.00
1982FM (P)	—	Value: 1.50				
1983FM (U)	—	—	—	0.10	0.50	1.00
1983FM (P)	—	Value: 1.50				
1984FM (P)	—	Value: 1.50				

KM# 2 5 CENTS

Copper-Nickel, 19.5 mm. **Ruler:** Elizabeth II **Obv:** Young bust right **Obv. Designer:** Arnold Machin **Rev:** Zenaida Doves **Rev. Designer:** Gilroy Roberts

Date	Mintage	F	VF	XF	Unc	BU
1973FM	26,000	—	—	0.15	0.75	1.00
1973FM (P)	181,000	Value: 1.25				
1974FM	18,000	—	—	0.15	0.75	1.00
1974FM (P)	94,000	Value: 1.25				
1975FM (M)	3,800	—	—	0.20	1.00	1.25
1975FM (U)	2,351	—	—	0.15	0.75	1.00
1975FM (P)	32,000	Value: 1.25				
1976FM (M)	4,800	—	—	0.20	1.00	1.25
1976FM (U)	996	—	—	0.15	1.25	1.50
1976FM (P)	15,000	Value: 1.25				
1977FM (M)	500	—	—	0.35	3.50	5.00
1977FM (U)	782	—	—	0.15	1.00	1.25
1977FM (P)	7,218	Value: 1.25				
1978FM (U)	1,443	—	—	0.15	1.00	1.25
1978FM (P)	7,059	Value: 1.25				
1979FM (U)	680	—	—	0.15	1.00	1.25
1979FM (P)	5,304	Value: 1.25				
1980FM (U)	1,007	—	—	0.15	1.00	1.25
1980FM (P)	3,421	Value: 1.25				
1981FM (U)	472	—	—	0.15	1.00	1.25
1981FM (P)	1,124	Value: 1.25				
1982FM (U)	—	—	—	0.15	1.00	1.25
1982FM (P)	—	Value: 1.25				
1983FM (U)	—	—	—	0.15	1.00	1.25
1983FM (P)	—	Value: 1.25				
1984FM (P)	—	Value: 1.25				

KM# 3 10 CENTS

Copper-Nickel **Ruler:** Elizabeth II **Obv:** Young bust right **Obv. Designer:** Arnold Machin **Rev:** Ringed Kingfisher right **Rev. Designer:** Gilroy Roberts

Date	Mintage	F	VF	XF	Unc	BU
1973FM (U)	23,000	—	—	0.20	1.00	1.25
1973FM (P)	181,000	Value: 1.50				
1974FM (U)	13,000	—	—	0.20	1.00	1.25
1974FM (P)	94,000	Value: 1.50				
1975FM (M)	2,000	—	—	0.20	1.25	1.50
1975FM (U)	2,351	—	—	0.20	1.00	1.25
1975FM (P)	32,000	Value: 1.50				
1976FM (M)	3,000	—	—	0.20	1.00	1.25
1976FM (U)	996	—	—	0.20	1.25	1.50
1976FM (P)	15,000	Value: 1.50				
1977FM (M)	500	—	—	0.45	4.00	6.00
1977FM (U)	782	—	—	0.20	1.50	2.00
1977FM (P)	7,218	Value: 1.50				
1978FM (U)	1,443	—	—	0.20	1.25	1.50
1978FM (P)	7,059	Value: 1.50				
1979FM (U)	680	—	—	0.20	1.50	2.00
1979FM (P)	5,304	Value: 1.50				
1980FM (U)	1,007	—	—	0.20	1.50	2.00
1980FM (P)	3,421	Value: 1.50				
1981FM (U)	472	—	—	0.20	2.00	2.50
1981FM (P)	1,124	Value: 1.50				
1982FM (U)	—	—	—	0.20	2.00	2.50
1982FM (P)	—	Value: 1.50				
1983FM (U)	—	—	—	0.20	2.00	2.50
1983FM (P)	—	Value: 1.50				
1984FM (P)	—	Value: 1.50				

KM# 4 25 CENTS

Copper-Nickel **Ruler:** Elizabeth II **Obv:** Young bust right **Obv. Designer:** Arnold Machin **Rev:** Mangrove Cuckoo **Rev. Designer:** Gilroy Roberts

Date	Mintage	F	VF	XF	Unc	BU
1973FM	21,000	—	—	0.30	1.50	1.75
1973FM (P)	181,000	Value: 1.50				
1974FM	12,000	—	—	0.30	1.50	1.75
1974FM (P)	94,000	Value: 2.00				
1975FM (M)	1,000	—	—	0.35	3.00	4.00
1975FM (U)	2,351	—	—	0.30	1.50	1.75
1975FM (P)	32,000	Value: 2.00				
1976FM (M)	2,000	—	—	0.30	2.00	3.00
1976FM (U)	996	—	—	0.30	2.50	3.50
1976FM (P)	15,000	Value: 2.00				
1977FM (M)	500	—	—	0.50	5.00	7.00
1977FM (U)	782	—	—	0.30	2.00	3.00
1977FM (P)	7,218	Value: 2.00				
1978FM (U)	1,443	—	—	0.30	1.75	2.25
1978FM (P)	7,059	Value: 2.00				
1979FM (U)	680	—	—	0.30	2.00	3.00
1979FM (P)	5,304	Value: 2.00				
1980FM (U)	1,007	—	—	0.30	2.00	3.00
1980FM (P)	3,421	Value: 2.00				

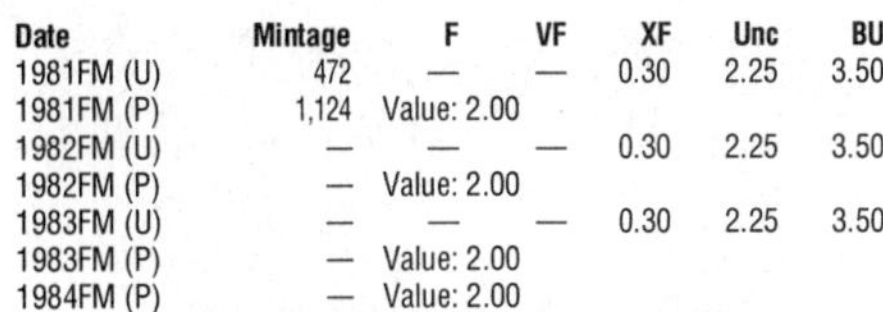

Date	Mintage	F	VF	XF	Unc	BU
1981FM (U)	472	—	—	0.30	2.25	3.50
1981FM (P)	1,124	Value: 2.00				
1982FM (U)	—	—	—	0.30	2.25	3.50
1982FM (P)	—	Value: 2.00				
1983FM (U)	—	—	—	0.30	2.25	3.50
1983FM (P)	—	Value: 2.00				
1984FM (P)	—	Value: 2.00				

KM# 5 50 CENTS

Copper-Nickel **Ruler:** Elizabeth II **Obv:** Young bust right **Obv. Designer:** Arnold Machin **Rev:** Brown Pelican **Rev. Designer:** Gilroy Roberts

Date	Mintage	F	VF	XF	Unc	BU
1973FM	20,000	—	—	0.75	2.00	3.00
1973FM (P)	181,000	Value: 2.50				
1974FM	12,000	—	—	0.75	2.00	3.00
1974FM (P)	94,000	Value: 2.50				
1975FM (M)	1,000	—	—	1.00	5.00	6.00
1975FM (U)	2,351	—	—	0.75	2.50	3.00
1975FM (P)	32,000	Value: 2.50				
1976FM (M)	2,000	—	—	0.75	3.00	4.00
1976FM (U)	996	—	—	0.75	3.50	4.50
1976FM (P)	15,000	Value: 2.50				
1977FM (M)	600	—	—	1.00	6.00	7.50
1977FM (U)	782	—	—	0.75	3.50	4.50
1977FM (P)	7,218	Value: 2.50				
1978FM (U)	1,543	—	—	0.75	2.50	3.00
1978FM (P)	7,059	Value: 2.50				
1979FM (U)	680	—	—	0.75	3.50	4.50
1979FM (P)	5,304	Value: 2.50				
1980FM (U)	1,007	—	—	0.75	3.00	4.00
1980FM (P)	3,421	Value: 2.50				
1981FM (U)	472	—	—	0.75	3.50	5.00
1981FM (P)	1,124	Value: 2.50				
1982FM (U)	—	—	—	0.75	3.50	5.00
1982FM (P)	—	Value: 2.50				
1983FM (U)	—	—	—	0.75	3.50	5.00
1983FM (P)	—	Value: 2.50				
1984FM (P)	—	Value: 2.50				

KM# 6 DOLLAR

Copper-Nickel **Ruler:** Elizabeth II **Obv:** Young bust right **Obv. Designer:** Arnold Machin **Rev:** Magnificent Frigate **Rev. Designer:** Gilroy Roberts

Date	Mintage	F	VF	XF	Unc	BU
1974FM (M)	12,000	—	—	2.00	5.50	7.00
1974FM (U)	—	—	—	—	—	—
1975FM (M)	800	—	—	2.50	8.00	9.00
1975FM (U)	2,351	—	—	2.50	6.50	7.00
1976FM (M)	1,800	—	—	2.50	6.50	7.00
1976FM (U)	996	—	—	2.50	8.00	9.00
1977FM (M)	800	—	—	2.50	8.00	9.00
1977FM (U)	782	—	—	2.50	8.00	9.00
1978FM (U)	1,743	—	—	2.50	6.50	7.00
1979FM (U)	680	—	—	2.50	8.00	9.00
1980FM (U)	1,007	—	—	2.50	6.50	7.00
1981FM (U)	472	—	—	2.50	10.00	11.50
1982FM (U)	—	—	—	2.50	10.00	11.50
1983FM (U)	—	—	—	2.50	10.00	11.50

BRITISH WEST AFRICA

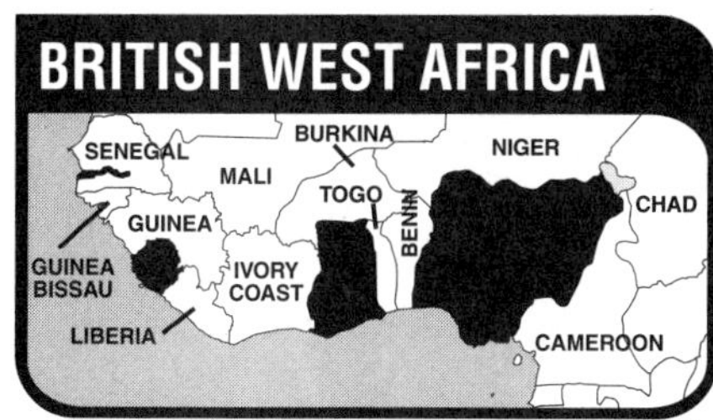

British West Africa was an administrative grouping of the four former British West African colonies of Gambia, Sierra Leone, Nigeria and Gold Coast (now Ghana). All are now independent republics and members of the British Commonwealth of Nations. See separate entries for individual statistics and history.

The Bank of British West Africa became the banker to the Colonial Government in 1894 and held this status until 1912. As such they were responsible for maintaining a proper supply of silver coinage for the colonies.

Through the subsidiary efforts of the Governor of Lagos, Nigeria a specific British West African coinage was put into use between 1907 and 1911. These coins bear the inscription, NIGERIA-BRITISH WEST AFRICA.

The four colonies were supplied with a common coinage and banknotes by the West African Currency Board from 1912 through 1958. This coinage bore the inscription BRITISH WEST AFRICA. The coinage, which includes three denominations of 1936 bearing the name of Edward VIII, is obsolete.

For later coinage see Gambia, Ghana, Sierra Leone and Nigeria.

RULER

British, until 1958

MINT MARKS

G-J.R. Gaunt & Sons, Birmingham
H - Heaton Mint, Birmingham
K, KN - King's Norton, Birmingham
SA - Pretoria, South Africa
No mm - Royal Mint, London

MONETARY SYSTEM

12 Pence = 1 Shilling
20 Shillings = 1 Pound

BRITISH COLONIES

POUND COINAGE

KM# 1 1/10 PENNY
Aluminum **Ruler:** Edward VII **Obv:** Crown above center hole, denomination around hole in English, in Arabic beneath **Obv. Legend:** EDWARD VII KING & EMPEROR **Rev:** Hexagram divides date at bottom **Rev. Legend:** NIGERIA BRITISH WEST AFRICA

Date	Mintage	F	VF	XF	Unc	BU
1907	1,254,000	2.00	4.00	10.00	20.00	35.00
1908	8,363,000	1.00	3.00	6.00	15.00	25.00
1908 Proof	—	Value: 300				

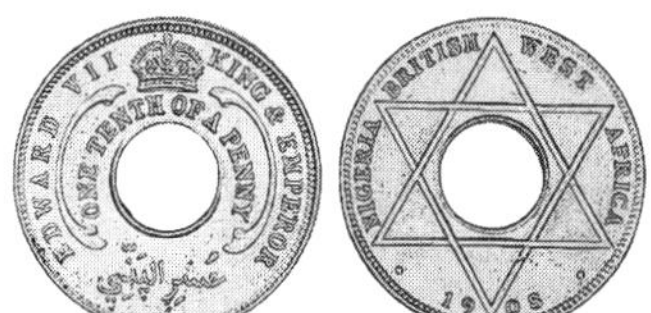

KM# 3 1/10 PENNY
Copper-Nickel **Ruler:** Edward VII **Obv:** Crown above center hole, denomination around hole in English, in Arabic beneath **Obv. Legend:** EDWARD VII KING & EMPEROR **Rev:** Hexagram divides date at bottom **Rev. Legend:** NIGERIA BRITISH WEST AFRICA

Date	Mintage	F	VF	XF	Unc	BU
1908	9,600,000	0.30	0.50	1.00	2.00	3.50
1909	4,800,000	0.40	0.75	1.50	5.00	9.00
1910	7,200,000	0.50	1.00	2.00	7.50	12.50

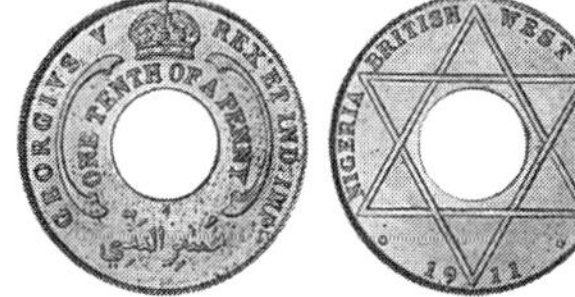

KM# 4 1/10 PENNY
Copper-Nickel **Ruler:** George V **Obv:** Crown above center hole, denomination around hole in English, in Arabic beneath **Obv. Legend:** GEORGIVS V REX ET IND: IMP: **Rev:** Hexagram divides date at bottom **Rev. Legend:** NIGERIA BRITISH WEST AFRICA

Date	Mintage	F	VF	XF	Unc	BU
1911H	7,200,000	1.50	3.50	7.50	15.00	28.00

KM# 7 1/10 PENNY
1.7200 g., Copper-Nickel, 20.5 mm. **Ruler:** George V **Obv:** Crown above center hole, denomination around hole in English, in Arabic beneath **Obv. Legend:** GEORGIVS V REX ET IND: IMP: **Rev:** Hexagram divides date at bottom **Rev. Legend:** BRITISH WEST AFRICA **Edge:** Plain

Date	Mintage	F	VF	XF	Unc	BU
1912H	10,800,000	0.30	0.75	1.50	3.50	7.00
1913	4,632,000	1.00	2.00	3.50	6.50	11.50
1913H	1,080,000	0.30	0.75	1.50	3.50	7.00
1914	1,200,000	3.00	5.00	10.00	22.50	40.00
1914H	20,088,000	0.50	1.25	2.00	5.00	9.00
1915H	10,032,000	0.30	0.75	1.50	5.00	9.00
1916H	480,000	25.00	50.00	75.00	150	175
1917H	9,384,000	2.00	3.00	5.00	15.00	25.00
1919H	912,000	1.25	2.00	4.00	7.50	13.50
1919KN	480,000	10.00	25.00	50.00	75.00	—
1920H	1,560,000	2.00	3.00	5.00	10.00	18.00
1920KN	12,996,000	0.40	1.00	3.00	5.00	9.00
1920KN Proof	—	Value: 125				
1922KN	7,265,000	1.00	1.75	4.50	12.00	20.00
1923KN	12,000,000	0.30	0.75	1.50	5.00	9.00
1925	2,400,000	5.00	10.00	20.00	40.00	70.00
1925H	12,000,000	2.00	3.00	5.00	12.00	20.00
1925KN	12,000,000	0.75	1.50	3.00	8.00	15.00
1926	12,000,000	0.75	1.50	2.50	6.00	10.00
1927	3,984,000	0.20	0.50	1.50	3.00	6.00
1927 Proof	—	Value: 150				
1928	11,760,000	0.20	0.50	1.50	3.00	6.00
1928 Proof	—	Value: 150				
1928H	2,964,000	0.20	0.50	1.50	3.00	6.00
1928KN	3,151,000	2.00	3.00	6.00	15.00	25.00
1930	9,600,000	2.00	3.00	6.00	15.00	25.00
1930 Proof	—	Value: 150				
1931	9,840,000	0.20	0.50	1.00	3.00	6.00
1931 Proof	—	Value: 150				
1932	3,600,000	0.20	0.50	1.50	5.00	9.00
1932 Proof	—	Value: 150				
1933	7,200,000	0.20	0.50	1.50	3.50	7.00
1933 Proof	—	Value: 150				
1934	4,800,000	0.75	1.50	3.00	6.00	10.00
1934 Proof	—	Value: 150				
1935	13,200,000	0.75	1.50	3.00	7.50	12.50
1935 Proof	—	Value: 150				
1936	9,720,000	0.20	0.50	1.00	3.00	6.00
1936 Proof	—	Value: 150				

KM# 14 1/10 PENNY
1.9000 g., Copper-Nickel **Ruler:** Edward VIII **Obv:** Crown above center hole, denomination around hole in English, in Arabic beneath **Obv. Legend:** EDWARDVS VIII REX ET IND: IMP: **Rev:** Hexagram divides date at bottom **Rev. Legend:** BRITISH WEST AFRICA

Date	Mintage	F	VF	XF	Unc	BU
1936	5,880,000	0.25	0.50	1.00	2.50	4.50
1936 Proof	—	Value: 200				
1936H	1,404,000	50.00	75.00	125	250	—
1936H Proof	—	Value: 300				
1936KN	3,000,000	1.00	2.00	3.50	9.00	15.00
1936KN Proof	—	Value: 200				

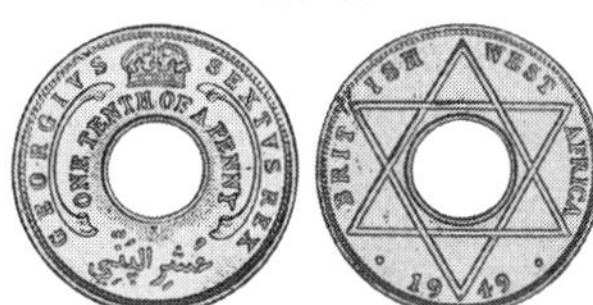

KM# 20 1/10 PENNY
1.8900 g., Copper-Nickel, 20 mm. **Ruler:** George VI **Obv:** Crown above center hole, denomination around hole in English, in Arabic beneath **Obv. Legend:** GEORGIVS VI REX ET IND: IMP: **Rev:** Hexagram divides date at bottom **Rev. Legend:** BRITISH WEST AFRICA

Date	Mintage	F	VF	XF	Unc	BU
1938	12,000,000	0.10	0.25	0.50	1.50	2.50
1938 Proof	—	Value: 125				
1938H	1,596,000	5.00	8.00	12.00	22.50	40.00
1938H Proof	—	Value: 100				
1939	9,840,000	0.25	0.50	1.00	3.50	6.00
1939 Proof	—	Value: 200				
1940	13,920,000	0.25	0.50	1.00	2.00	3.50
1940 Proof	—	Value: 125				
1941	16,560,000	1.00	2.00	4.00	8.00	14.00
1941 Proof	—	Value: 125				
1942	12,360,000	1.00	2.50	4.50	10.00	18.00
1942 Proof	—	Value: 125				
1943	22,560,000	1.00	2.50	5.00	10.00	18.00
1944	10,440,000	1.00	2.50	5.00	10.00	18.00
1944 Proof	—	Value: 150				
1945	25,706,000	0.50	1.00	1.75	6.00	10.00
1945 Proof	—	Value: 125				
1946	2,803,000	1.00	2.00	4.00	9.00	15.00
1946 Proof	—	Value: 125				
1946H	5,004,000	1.00	2.00	4.00	9.00	15.00
1946KN	1,152,000	0.25	0.50	1.00	3.00	5.50
1946KN Proof	—	Value: 125				
1947	4,202,000	0.50	1.00	2.00	5.00	9.00
1947 Proof	—	Value: 125				
1947KN	3,900,000	200	300	500	600	—

KM# 26 1/10 PENNY
Copper-Nickel, 20 mm. **Obv:** Crown above center hole, denomination around hole in English, in Arabic beneath **Obv. Legend:** GEORGIVS SEXTVS REX **Rev:** Hexagram divides date at bottom **Rev. Legend:** BRITISH WEST AFRICA

Date	Mintage	F	VF	XF	Unc	BU
1949H	3,700,000	1.00	2.00	3.00	6.00	10.00
1949KN	3,036,000	1.00	2.00	3.00	5.00	9.00
1950KN	13,200,000	0.25	0.50	1.00	2.50	4.50
1950KN Proof	—	Value: 150				

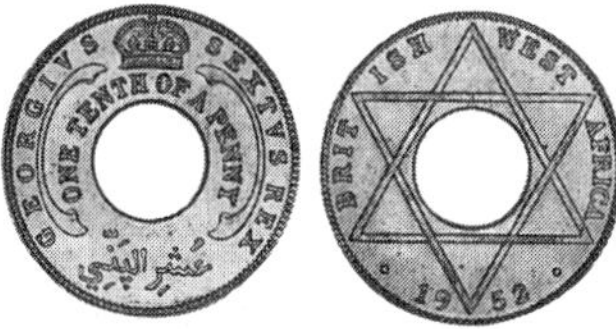

KM# 26a 1/10 PENNY
Bronze, 20 mm. **Obv:** Crown above center hole, denomination around hole in English, in Arabic beneath **Obv. Legend:** GEORGIVS SEXTVS REX **Rev:** Hexagram divides date at bottom **Rev. Legend:** BRITISH WEST AFRICA

Date	Mintage	F	VF	XF	Unc	BU
1952	15,060,000	0.50	1.00	2.00	6.00	10.00
1952 Proof	—	Value: 150				

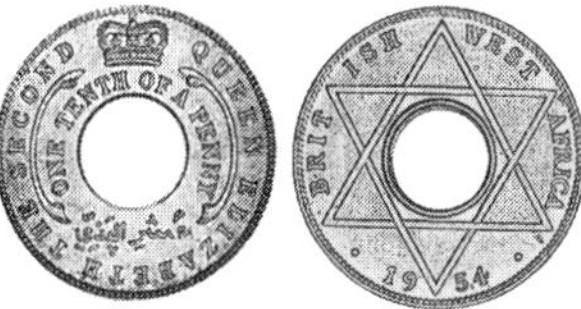

KM# 32 1/10 PENNY
Bronze, 20 mm. **Ruler:** Elizabeth II **Obv:** Crown above center hole, denomination around hole in English, in Arabic beneath **Obv. Legend:** QUEEN ELIZABETH THE SECOND **Rev:** Hexagram divides date at bottom **Rev. Legend:** BRITISH WEST AFRICA

Date	Mintage	F	VF	XF	Unc	BU
1954	4,800,000	0.50	1.00	2.00	4.00	8.00
1954 Proof	—	Value: 150				
1956	2,400,000	100	200	400	700	—
1956 Proof	—	Value: 750				
1957	7,200,000	60.00	120	220	325	—
1957 Proof	—	Value: 600				

KM# 5 1/2 PENNY
Copper-Nickel **Ruler:** George V **Obv:** Crown above center hole, denomination around hole in English, in Arabic beneath **Obv. Legend:** GEORGIVS V REX ET IND: IMP: **Rev:** Hexagram divides date at bottom **Rev. Legend:** NIGERIA BRITISH WEST AFRICA

Date	Mintage	F	VF	XF	Unc	BU
1911H	3,360,000	4.50	12.00	25.00	40.00	75.00

KM# 8 1/2 PENNY

Copper-Nickel, 25.2 mm. **Ruler:** George V **Obv:** Crown above center hole, denomination around hole in English, in Arabic beneath **Obv. Legend:** GEORGIVS V REX ET IND: IMP: **Rev:** Hexagram divides date at bottom **Rev. Legend:** BRITISH WEST AFRICA **Edge:** Plain

Date	Mintage	F	VF	XF	Unc	BU
1912H	3,120,000	2.00	5.00	7.00	20.00	35.00
1913	1,382,000	150	250	325	500	—
1913H	216,000	5.00	10.00	17.50	30.00	55.00
1914	240,000	10.00	20.00	35.00	60.00	110
1914H	586,000	20.00	30.00	50.00	75.00	135
1914K	3,360,000	3.00	6.00	17.50	30.00	55.00
1914K Proof	—	Value: 225				

Note: Issued with East Africa KM#11 in a double (4 pc.) specimen set

Date	Mintage	F	VF	XF	Unc	BU
1915H	3,577,000	1.00	2.00	4.00	15.00	25.00
1916H	4,046,000	1.00	3.00	5.00	15.00	25.00
1917H	214,000	6.00	12.00	28.00	50.00	90.00
1918H	490,000	2.50	5.00	10.00	30.00	55.00
1919H	4,950,000	1.25	2.50	6.00	20.00	35.00
1919KN	3,861,000	1.25	2.50	7.50	25.00	45.00
1920H	26,285,000	1.50	3.00	7.50	15.00	25.00
1920KN	13,844,000	0.50	3.00	8.50	16.50	30.00
1922KN	5,817,000	300	500	750	1,200	—
1927	528,000	20.00	30.00	65.00	135	250
1927 Proof	—	Value: 225				
1929	336,000	6.00	22.00	47.50	95.00	165
1929 Proof	—	Value: 225				
1931	96,000	500	800	1,200	1,500	—
1931 Proof	—	Value: 225				
1932	960,000	2.50	15.00	35.00	55.00	100
1932 Proof	—	Value: 225				
1933	2,122,000	12.00	23.50	55.00	110	200
1933 Proof	—	Value: 225				
1934	1,694,000	2.50	15.00	35.00	75.00	135
1934 Proof	—	Value: 225				
1935	3,271,000	1.00	3.00	18.00	35.00	60.00
1935 Proof	—	Value: 225				
1936	5,400,000	2.50	5.00	18.00	32.00	55.00
1936 Proof	—	Value: 225				

KM# 15 1/2 PENNY

Copper-Nickel, 25.2 mm. **Ruler:** George VI **Obv:** Crown above center hole, denomination around hole in English, in Arabic beneath **Obv. Legend:** GEORGIVS VI REX • ET IND: IMP: **Rev:** Hexagram divides date at bottom **Rev. Legend:** BRITISH WEST AFRICA **Edge:** Plain

Date	Mintage	F	VF	XF	Unc	BU
1936	14,760,000	0.25	0.50	1.00	2.50	4.50
1936 Proof	—	Value: 200				
1936H	2,400,000	1.00	2.00	5.00	12.50	20.00
1936H Proof	—	Value: 200				
1936KN	2,298,000	0.65	1.25	2.25	4.00	7.00
1936KN Proof	—	Value: 200				

KM# 18 1/2 PENNY

5.6600 g., Copper-Nickel, 25.9 mm. **Ruler:** George VI **Obv:** Crown above center hole, denomination around hole in English, in Arabic beneath **Obv. Legend:** GEORGIVS VI REX • ET IND: IMP: **Rev:** Hexagram divides date at bottom **Rev. Legend:** BRITISH WEST AFRICA

Date	Mintage	F	VF	XF	Unc	BU
1937H	4,800,000	0.40	0.85	1.50	4.00	7.00
1937H Proof	—	Value: 125				
1937KN	5,577,000	0.40	0.85	3.00	5.00	9.00
1940KN	2,410,000	2.00	4.00	6.00	15.00	25.00
1940KN Proof	—	Value: 125				
1941H	2,400,000	0.40	2.00	6.00	12.00	20.00
1942	4,800,000	0.40	0.85	4.00	8.50	15.00
1943	3,360,000	0.50	1.00	5.00	10.00	18.00
1944	3,600,000	1.00	3.00	7.00	20.00	35.00
1944 Proof	—	Value: 125				
1946	3,600,000	0.25	1.00	3.00	7.00	12.50
1946 Proof	—	Value: 125				
1947H	15,218,000	0.35	0.75	1.25	5.00	9.00
1947KN	12,000,000	0.40	0.85	2.00	6.00	10.00

KM# 27 1/2 PENNY

Copper-Nickel **Ruler:** Edward VII **Obv:** Crown above center hole, denomination around hole in English, in Arabic beneath **Obv. Legend:** GEORGIVS SEXTVS REX **Rev:** Hexagram divides date at bottom **Rev. Legend:** BRITISH WEST AFRICA

Date	Mintage	F	VF	XF	Unc	BU
1949H	5,909,000	1.50	3.50	12.00	22.00	40.00
1949KN	3,413,000	1.50	3.50	12.00	25.00	45.00
1951	3,468,000	1.50	3.50	12.00	25.00	45.00
1951 Proof	—	Value: 250				

KM# 27a 1/2 PENNY

5.6000 g., Bronze, 25.9 mm. **Obv:** Crown above center hole, denomination around hole in English, in Arabic beneath **Obv. Legend:** GEORGIVS SEXTVS REX **Rev:** Denomination around hole in English, in Arabic beneath **Rev. Legend:** BRITISH WEST AFRICA

Date	Mintage	F	VF	XF	Unc	BU
1952	11,332,000	0.25	0.50	2.50	5.50	9.50
1952 Proof	—	Value: 150				
1952H	27,603,000	0.20	0.35	0.75	2.00	3.50
1952KN	4,800,000	0.50	2.00	5.00	10.00	18.00

KM# 2 PENNY

Copper-Nickel, 30.5 mm. **Ruler:** Edward VII **Obv:** Crown above center hole, denomination around hole in English, in Arabic beneath **Obv. Legend:** EDWARD VII KING & EMPEROR **Rev:** Hexagram, date beneath **Rev. Legend:** NIGERIA BRITISH WEST AFRICA

Date	Mintage	F	VF	XF	Unc	BU
1907	863,000	2.00	5.00	9.00	20.00	35.00
1908	3,217,000	2.00	4.00	8.00	17.50	30.00
1909	960,000	3.50	9.00	28.00	45.00	80.00
1910	2,520,000	2.75	7.00	12.00	25.00	45.00

KM# 6 PENNY

Copper-Nickel, 30.5 mm. **Ruler:** George V **Obv:** Crown above center hole, denomination around hole in English, in Arabic beneath **Obv. Legend:** GEORGIVS V REX ET IND: IMP: **Rev:** Hexagram, date beneath **Rev. Legend:** NIGERIA BRITISH WEST AFRICA

Date	Mintage	F	VF	XF	Unc	BU
1911H	1,920,000	18.00	50.00	100	150	—

KM# 9 PENNY

Copper-Nickel, 30.5 mm. **Ruler:** George V **Obv:** Crown above center hole, denomination around hole in English, in Arabic beneath **Obv. Legend:** GEORGIVS V REX ET IND: IMP: **Rev:** Hexagram, date beneath **Rev. Legend:** BRITISH WEST AFRICA

Date	Mintage	F	VF	XF	Unc	BU
1912H	1,560,000	1.50	3.00	10.00	22.50	40.00
1913	1,680,000	7.50	25.00	45.00	75.00	135
1913H	144,000	5.00	10.00	17.50	35.00	60.00
1914	3,000,000	2.50	5.00	10.00	22.50	40.00
1914H	72,000	35.00	50.00	120	200	—
1915H	3,295,000	1.25	2.00	7.00	15.00	25.00
1916H	3,461,000	1.25	2.00	10.00	20.00	35.00
1917H	444,000	5.00	7.00	24.00	45.00	80.00
1918H	994,000	7.50	15.00	45.00	75.00	135
1919H	21,864,000	1.25	2.50	7.00	15.00	25.00
1919KN	264,000	7.50	25.00	35.00	50.00	90.00
1920H	37,870,000	1.00	1.75	5.50	12.50	22.50
1920KN	20,685,000	1.00	2.00	8.00	17.50	30.00
1922KN	3,971,000	400	750	1,000	1,500	—
1926	8,039,999	2.00	4.00	15.00	30.00	55.00
1927	792,000	25.00	45.00	125	200	—
1927 Proof	—	Value: 225				
1928	6,672,000	2.00	4.00	12.00	25.00	45.00
1928 Proof	—	Value: 225				
1929	636,000	20.00	35.00	65.00	100	—
1929 Proof	—	Value: 225				
1933	2,806,000	2.00	14.00	32.50	65.00	120
1933 Proof	—	Value: 225				
1934	2,640,000	3.50	15.00	35.00	75.00	135
1934 Proof	—	Value: 225				
1935	8,551,000	1.25	12.50	27.50	45.00	80.00
1935 Proof	—	Value: 225				
1936	7,368,000	1.25	3.50	12.00	25.00	45.00
1936 Proof	—	Value: 225				

KM# 16 PENNY

Copper-Nickel, 30.5 mm. **Ruler:** Edward VIII **Obv:** Crown above center hole, denomination around hole in English, in Arabic beneath **Obv. Legend:** EDWARDVS VIII REX ET IND: IMP: **Rev:** Hexagram, date beneath **Rev. Legend:** BRITISH WEST AFRICA **Edge:** Plain

Date	Mintage	F	VF	XF	Unc	BU
1936	7,992,000	0.50	1.00	3.50	7.00	12.50
1936 Proof	—	Value: 250				
1936H	12,600,000	0.35	0.75	1.00	2.25	4.00
1936H Proof	—	Value: 250				
1936KN	12,512,000	0.35	0.75	1.00	2.25	4.00
1936KN Proof	—	Value: 250				

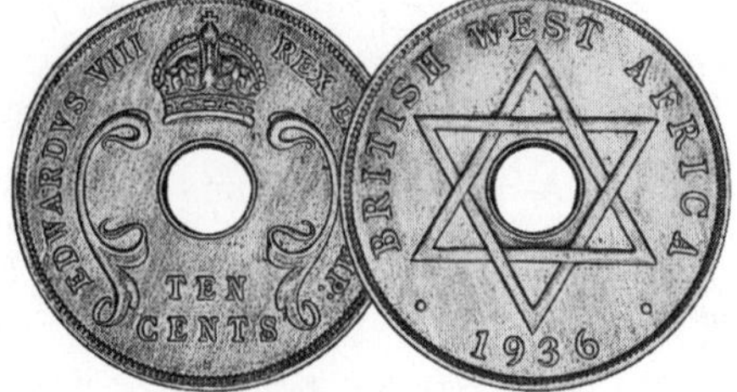

KM# 17 PENNY

Copper-Nickel, 30.5 mm. **Ruler:** Edward VIII **Obv:** Crown above center hole, denomination in English beneath **Obv. Legend:** EDWARDVS VIII REX ET IND: IMP: **Rev:** Hexagram, date beneath **Rev. Legend:** BRITISH WEST AFRICA **Note:** Mule.

Date	Mintage	F	VF	XF	Unc	BU
1936H	—	125	165	225	350	—

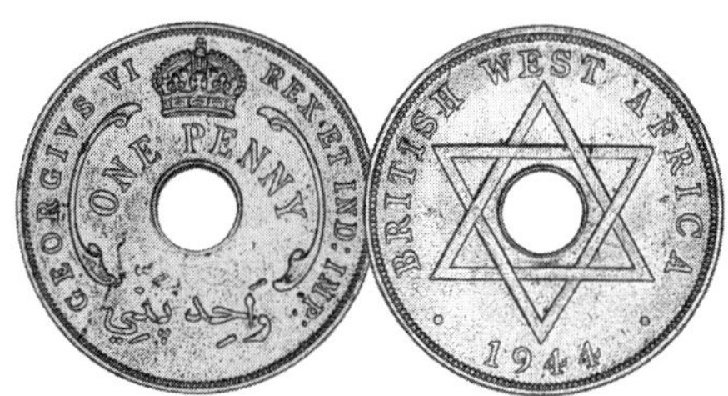

KM# 19 PENNY

9.6500 g., Copper-Nickel, 30.5 mm. **Ruler:** George VI **Obv:** Crown above center hole, denomination around hole in English, in Arabic beneath **Obv. Legend:** GEORGIVS VI REX • ET IND: IMP: **Rev:** Hexagram, date beneath **Rev. Legend:** BRITISH WEST AFRICA **Edge:** Plain

Date	Mintage	F	VF	XF	Unc	BU
1937H	11,999,000	0.50	0.75	1.25	2.00	3.50
1937H Proof	—	Value: 200				
1937KN	11,999,000	0.50	0.75	1.25	2.00	3.50
1937KN Proof	—	Value: 200				
1940	3,840,000	0.50	0.75	1.25	2.00	3.50
1940 Proof	—	—	—	—	—	—
1940H	2,400,000	0.50	0.75	3.00	8.00	14.00
1940KN	2,400,000	0.75	1.50	4.50	10.00	18.00
1941	6,960,000	0.35	0.75	1.25	3.50	6.00
1941 Proof	—	—	—	—	—	—
1942	18,840,000	0.30	0.60	1.00	3.00	5.00
1943	28,920,000	0.30	0.60	1.00	3.00	5.00
1943H	7,140,000	2.00	5.00	10.00	20.00	35.00
1944	19,440,000	0.30	0.60	1.00	4.00	7.00
1945	6,072,000	0.45	0.90	1.75	5.00	9.00
1945 Proof	—	Value: 150				
1945H	9,000,000	1.00	2.00	4.50	10.00	18.00
1945KN	9,557,000	0.75	1.50	3.00	7.00	12.00
1946H	10,446,000	0.85	1.75	3.75	8.00	14.00
1946KN	11,976,000	0.30	0.60	1.00	5.00	9.00
1946SA	1,020,000	250	500	750	1,150	—
1947H	12,443,000	0.30	0.60	1.00	5.00	9.00
1947KN	9,829,000	0.30	0.60	1.00	5.00	9.00
1947SA	58,980,000	0.30	0.60	1.00	4.50	7.50

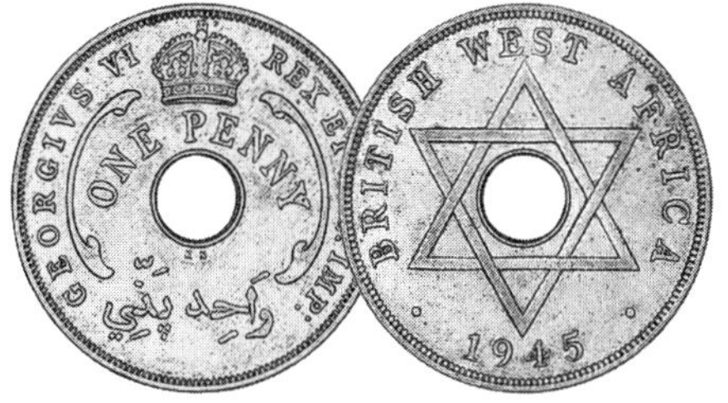

KM# 25 PENNY

Copper-Nickel, 30.5 mm. **Ruler:** George VI **Obv:** Crown above center hole, denomination around hole in English, in Arabic beneath **Obv. Legend:** GEORGIVS VI REX • ET IND: IMP: **Rev:** Hexagram, date beneath **Rev. Legend:** BRITISH WEST AFRICA **Note:** Mule, obverse KM#16, reverse KM#19.

Date	Mintage	F	VF	XF	Unc	BU
1945H	—	2,000	3,000	4,000	6,000	—

KM# 30 PENNY

Copper-Nickel, 30.5 mm. **Obv:** Crown above center hole, denomination around hole in English, in Arabic beneath **Obv. Legend:** GEORGIVS SEXTVS REX **Rev:** Hexagram, date beneath **Rev. Legend:** BRITISH WEST AFRICA

Date	Mintage	F	VF	XF	Unc	BU
1951	1,258,000	7.50	12.50	27.50	45.00	80.00
1951 Proof	—	Value: 250				
1951KN	2,692,000	6.00	10.00	20.00	35.00	60.00

KM# 30a PENNY

Bronze, 30.5 mm. **Obv:** Crown above center hole, denomination around hole in English, in Arabic beneath **Obv. Legend:** GEORGIVS SEXTVS REX **Rev:** Hexagram, date beneath **Rev. Legend:** BRITISH WEST AFRICA

Date	Mintage	F	VF	XF	Unc	BU
1952	10,542,000	0.75	1.50	3.00	8.50	15.00
1952 Proof	—	Value: 175				
1952H	30,794,000	0.20	0.40	0.60	3.00	5.00
1952KN	45,398,000	0.20	0.40	0.60	3.00	5.00
1952KN Proof	—	Value: 175				

KM# 34 PENNY

Bronze, 30.5 mm. **Obv:** Crown above center hole, denomination around hole in English, in Arabic beneath **Obv. Legend:** GEORGIVS SEXTVS REX **Rev:** Hexagram, date beneath **Rev. Legend:** BRITISH WEST AFRICA **Note:** Mule, obverse KM#30, reverse KM#33.

Date	Mintage	F	VF	XF	Unc	BU
1956H	—	50.00	100	175	250	—

KM# 33 PENNY

Bronze, 30.5 mm. **Ruler:** Elizabeth II **Obv:** Crown above center hole, denomination around hole in English, in Arabic beneath **Obv. Legend:** QUEEN ELIZABETH THE SECOND **Rev:** Hexagram, date beneath **Rev. Legend:** BRITISH WEST AFRICA

Date	Mintage	F	VF	XF	Unc	BU
1956H	13,503,000	0.75	1.50	3.50	9.00	16.00
1956KN	13,500,000	0.30	0.60	2.50	8.00	14.00
1957	9,000,000	0.75	1.50	6.00	13.50	25.00
1957 Proof	—	Value: 150				
1957H	5,340,000	1.00	2.50	10.00	20.00	35.00
1957KN	5,600,000	1.00	2.50	8.00	16.00	28.00
1957 N	Inc. above	125	175	250	—	—
Note: Error strike missing the K						
1958	12,200,000	0.75	1.50	6.00	13.50	25.00
1958 Proof	—	Value: 125				
1958KN	Inc. above	0.75	1.50	5.00	10.00	18.00

KM# 10 3 PENCE

1.1438 g., 0.9250 Silver 0.0340 oz. ASW **Ruler:** George V **Obv:** Bust of King George V left **Obv. Legend:** GEORGIVS V D.G.BRITT: OMN:REX F.D.IND:IMP: **Obv. Designer:** E.B. MacKennal **Rev:** Denomination in wreath, date beneath **Rev. Legend:** BRITISH WEST AFRICA

Date	Mintage	F	VF	XF	Unc	BU
1913	240,000	3.50	7.50	45.00	90.00	—
1913 Proof	—	Value: 250				
1913H	496,000	2.00	4.00	15.00	30.00	65.00
1914H	1,560,000	1.00	2.00	12.50	25.00	45.00
1915H	270,000	18.00	25.00	60.00	100	—
1916H	820,000	10.00	15.00	35.00	65.00	—
1917H	3,600,000	1.50	2.50	12.50	25.00	45.00
1918H	1,722,000	1.75	3.50	10.00	20.00	35.00
1919H	19,826,000	1.00	2.00	6.00	15.00	25.00
1919H Proof	—	Value: 200				

KM# 10a 3 PENCE

1.1438 g., 0.5000 Silver 0.0184 oz. ASW **Ruler:** George V **Obv:** Bust of George V facing left **Obv. Legend:** GEORGIVS V D.G.BRITT: OMN:REX F.D.IND:IMP: **Rev:** Denomination in wreath, date beneath **Rev. Legend:** BRITISH WEST AFRICA

Date	Mintage	F	VF	XF	Unc	BU
1920H	3,616,000	25.00	50.00	125	185	—

KM# 10b 3 PENCE

Tin-Brass **Ruler:** George V **Obv:** Bust of George V facing left **Obv. Legend:** GEORGIVS V D.G.BRITT: OMN:REX F.D.IND:IMP: **Rev:** Denomination in wreath, date beneath **Rev. Legend:** BRITISH WEST AFRICA

Date	Mintage	F	VF	XF	Unc	BU
1920KN	19,000,000	1.00	5.00	12.50	25.00	45.00
1920KN Proof	—	Value: 75.00				
1920KN Unique	—	—	—	—	—	—
Note: Mint mark on obverse below bust						
1925	8,800,000	1.50	5.00	20.00	40.00	70.00
1926	1,600,000	10.00	25.00	50.00	85.00	—
1927	800,000	20.00	40.00	100	200	—
1928	1,760,000	10.00	35.00	70.00	125	—
1928 Proof	—	Value: 175				
1933	2,800,000	2.00	4.50	28.00	50.00	70.00
1933 Proof	—	Value: 200				
1934	6,400,000	1.00	12.50	20.00	35.00	60.00
1934 Proof	—	Value: 200				
1935	11,560,000	1.00	12.50	20.00	35.00	60.00
1935 Proof	—	Value: 200				
1936	17,160,000	1.00	3.50	15.00	28.00	50.00
1936 Proof	—	Value: 200				
1936H	1,000,000	15.00	25.00	55.00	85.00	—
1936H Proof	—	Value: 200				
1936KN	2,037,999	10.00	15.00	35.00	65.00	110

KM# 21 3 PENCE

5.2000 g., Copper-Nickel, 21.45 mm. **Ruler:** George VI **Obv:** Bust of George VI left **Obv. Legend:** GEORGIVS VI D.G.BRITT: OMN:REX F.D.IND:IMP: **Obv. Designer:** Percy Metcalf **Rev:** Denomination in wreath, date beneath **Rev. Legend:** BRITISH WEST AFRICA

Date	Mintage	F	VF	XF	Unc	BU
1938H	7,000,000	0.30	0.60	2.50	7.50	12.50
1938H Proof	—	Value: 200				
1938KN	9,056,000	0.35	0.75	2.50	8.00	14.00
1938KN Proof	—	Value: 250				
1939H	16,500,000	0.30	0.60	2.00	5.00	9.00
1939H Proof	—	Value: 300				
1939KN	15,500,000	0.30	0.60	2.00	8.00	14.00
1939KN Proof	—	Value: 200				
1940H	3,862,000	0.50	1.00	2.50	7.50	13.50
1940KN	10,000,000	0.30	0.60	2.00	5.00	9.00
1941H	5,032,000	0.40	0.85	3.50	9.00	16.00
1943H	5,106,000	0.40	0.85	6.00	15.00	25.00
1943KN	9,502,000	0.40	0.85	3.50	9.00	16.00
1944KN	2,536,000	0.40	0.85	6.50	15.00	25.00
1945H	998,000	3.00	5.00	12.00	20.00	35.00
1945KN	3,000,000	0.40	0.85	5.00	12.50	22.00
1946KN	7,488,000	0.40	0.85	3.50	9.00	16.00
1947H	10,000,000	0.35	0.75	3.50	8.00	14.00
1947KN	11,248,000	0.40	0.85	3.50	8.00	14.00

KM# 35 3 PENCE

Copper-Nickel **Ruler:** Elizabeth II **Obv:** Bust of Queen Elizabeth II facing right **Obv. Legend:** QUEEN ELIZABETH THE SECOND **Obv. Designer:** Cecil Thomas **Rev:** Denomination in wreath, date beneath **Rev. Legend:** BRITISH WEST AFRICA

Date	Mintage	F	VF	XF	Unc	BU
1957H	800,000	35.00	60.00	180	300	—

KM# 11 6 PENCE

2.8276 g., 0.9250 Silver 0.0841 oz. ASW **Ruler:** George V **Obv:** Bust of King George V facing left **Obv. Legend:** GEORGIVS V D.G.BRITT: OMN:REX F.D.IND:IMP: **Obv. Designer:** E.B. MacKennal **Rev:** Denomination in wreath, date beneath **Rev. Legend:** BRITISH WEST AFRICA

Date	Mintage	F	VF	XF	Unc	BU
1913	560,000	3.00	5.00	20.00	35.00	60.00
1913 Proof	—	Value: 350				
1913H	400,000	3.00	5.00	20.00	37.50	65.00
1914H	952,000	2.75	5.00	25.00	40.00	70.00
1916H	400,000	5.00	10.00	40.00	60.00	—
1917H	2,400,000	3.00	5.00	20.00	37.50	65.00
1918H	1,160,000	2.00	5.00	20.00	37.50	65.00
1919H	8,676,000	2.00	3.50	11.50	22.00	40.00
1919H Proof	—	Value: 200				

KM# 11a 6 PENCE

2.8276 g., 0.5000 Silver 0.0455 oz. ASW **Ruler:** George V **Obv:** Bust of George V facing left **Obv. Legend:** GEORGIVS V D.G.BRITT: OMN:REX F.D.IND:IMP: **Rev:** Denomination in wreath, date beneath **Rev. Legend:** BRITISH WEST AFRICA

Date	Mintage	F	VF	XF	Unc	BU
1920H	2,948,000	12.50	30.00	100	185	—
1920H Proof	—	Value: 275				

KM# 11b 6 PENCE

Tin-Brass **Ruler:** George V **Obv:** Bust of George V facing left **Obv. Legend:** GEORGIVS V D.G.BRITT: OMN:REX F.D.IND:IMP: **Rev:** Denomination in wreath, date beneath **Rev. Legend:** BRITISH WEST AFRICA

Date	Mintage	F	VF	XF	Unc	BU
1920KN	12,000,000	1.00	5.00	20.00	37.50	65.00
1920KN Proof	—	Value: 125				
1923H	2,000,000	5.00	22.50	60.00	95.00	—
1924	1,000,000	15.00	30.00	100	165	—
1924H	1,000,000	15.00	30.00	100	165	—
1924KN	1,000,000	15.00	30.00	100	165	—
1925	2,800,000	3.50	7.00	35.00	60.00	100
1928	400,000	25.00	50.00	175	250	—
1928 Proof	—	Value: 200				
1933	1,000,000	20.00	40.00	125	185	—
1933 Proof	—	Value: 225				
1935	4,000,000	5.00	12.50	25.00	50.00	90.00
1935 Proof	—	Value: 225				
1936	10,400,000	7.50	15.00	25.00	50.00	90.00
1936 Proof	—	Value: 225				
1936H	480,000	25.00	50.00	125	200	—
1936H Proof	—	Value: 225				
1936KN	2,696,000	15.00	25.00	35.00	70.00	125
1936KN Proof	—	Value: 225				

KM# 22 6 PENCE

3.4900 g., Nickel-Brass **Ruler:** George VI **Obv:** Bust of King George VI left **Obv. Legend:** GEORGIVS VI D.G.BRITT: OMN:REX F.D.IND:IMP: **Obv. Designer:** Percy Metcalf **Rev:** Denomination in wreath, date beneath **Rev. Legend:** BRITISH WEST AFRICA

Date	Mintage	F	VF	XF	Unc	BU
1938	12,114,000	0.50	1.00	2.00	8.00	14.00
1938 Proof	—	Value: 200				
1940	17,829,000	0.75	1.50	3.00	10.00	18.00
1940 Proof	—	Value: 200				
1942	1,600,000	2.50	4.00	10.00	20.00	35.00
1943	10,586,000	0.75	1.75	5.00	11.00	20.00
1944	1,814,000	2.00	3.00	15.00	30.00	55.00
1945	4,000,000	1.00	2.00	12.50	25.00	45.00
1945 Proof	—	Value: 200				
1946	4,000,000	2.50	5.00	25.00	50.00	90.00
1946 Proof	—	Value: 225				
1947	6,120,000	0.50	1.50	5.00	15.00	25.00
1947 Proof	—	Value: 175				

KM# 31 6 PENCE

Nickel-Brass **Ruler:** George VI **Obv:** Bust of King George VI facing left **Obv. Legend:** GEORGIVS VI DIE GRA. BRITT. OMN: REX FID: DEF: **Obv. Designer:** Percy Metcalf **Rev:** Denomination in wreath, date beneath **Rev. Legend:** BRITISH WEST AFRICA

Date	Mintage	F	VF	XF	Unc	BU
1952	2,544,000	—	—	—	300	425
1952 Proof	—	Value: 500				

Note: This type was never released into circulation and the majority of the mintage was melted down at Riverside Metal Company in New Jersey; Approximately 167 pieces avoided the furnace and found their way into the numismatic market

KM# 12 SHILLING

5.6552 g., 0.9250 Silver 0.1682 oz. ASW **Ruler:** George V **Obv:** Bust of King George V facing left **Obv. Legend:** GEORGIVS V D.G.BRITT: OMN:REX F.D.IND:IMP: **Obv. Designer:** E.B. MacKennal **Rev:** Palm tree divides date in circular frame **Rev. Legend:** BRITISH WEST AFRICA

Date	Mintage	F	VF	XF	Unc	BU
1913	8,800,000	3.50	5.00	12.50	22.50	45.00
1913 Proof	—	Value: 400				
1913H	3,540,000	10.00	20.00	55.00	100	—
1914	3,000,000	3.50	5.00	15.00	35.00	65.00
1914H	11,292,000	3.50	5.00	12.50	30.00	55.00
1915H	254,000	20.00	40.00	100	165	—
1916H	11,838,000	3.75	6.00	18.50	35.00	65.00
1917H	15,018,000	3.75	6.00	18.50	35.00	65.00
1918H	9,486,000	3.75	6.50	20.00	40.00	70.00
1918H Proof	—	Value: 200				
1919	2,000,000	10.00	15.00	30.00	55.00	95.00
1919H	992,000	15.00	30.00	65.00	100	—
1919H Proof	—	Value: 200				
1920	828,000	22.50	40.00	100	165	—

KM# 12a SHILLING

Tin-Brass **Ruler:** George V **Obv:** Bust of George V facing left **Obv. Legend:** GEORGIVS V D.G.BRITT: OMN:REX F.D.IND:IMP: **Rev:** Palm tree divides date in circular frame **Rev. Legend:** BRITISH WEST AFRICA

Date	Mintage	F	VF	XF	Unc	BU
1920G	16,000	1,000	2,000	2,500	3,000	—
1920KN	38,800,000	1.50	5.00	12.50	32.50	55.00
1920KN Proof	—	Value: 200				
1920KN Unique	—	—	—	—	—	—

Note: Mint mark on obverse below bust

Date	Mintage	F	VF	XF	Unc	BU
1922KN	32,324,000	2.00	6.50	35.00	70.00	—
1923H	24,384,000	4.00	7.50	25.00	45.00	80.00
1923KN	5,000,000	8.00	15.00	50.00	90.00	—
1924	17,000,000	2.00	6.50	35.00	60.00	110
1924H	9,567,000	10.00	20.00	70.00	125	—
1924KN	7,000,000	7.50	15.00	45.00	80.00	—
1925	19,800,000	4.00	8.00	22.00	45.00	80.00
1926	19,952,000	2.00	5.00	20.00	40.00	70.00
1927	22,248,000	1.50	4.00	18.50	35.00	60.00
1927 Proof	—	Value: 250				
1928	10,000,000	20.00	35.00	75.00	225	—
1928 Proof	—	Value: 300				
1936	70,200,000	3.00	6.50	18.00	32.50	55.00
1936 Proof	—	Value: 225				
1936H	10,920,000	12.50	22.50	45.00	75.00	—
1936KN	14,962,000	2.00	5.00	25.00	42.50	75.00
1936KN Proof	—	Value: 200				

KM# 23 SHILLING

5.6300 g., Nickel-Brass, 23.5 mm. **Ruler:** George VI **Obv:** Bust of King George VI left **Obv. Legend:** GEORGIVS VI D.G.BRITT: OMN:REX F.D.IND:IMP: **Obv. Designer:** Percy Metcalf **Rev:** Palm tree divides date in circular frame **Rev. Legend:** BRITISH WEST AFRICA

Date	Mintage	F	VF	XF	Unc	BU
1938	57,806,000	0.50	1.25	4.50	12.00	20.00
1938 Proof	—	Value: 200				
1939	55,472,000	0.50	1.25	6.50	18.00	30.00
1939 Proof	—	Value: 200				
1940	40,311,000	0.50	1.25	5.50	15.00	25.00
1940 Proof	—	Value: 200				
1942	42,000,000	0.50	1.25	6.50	18.00	30.00
1943	133,600,000	0.50	1.25	5.50	15.00	25.00
1945	8,010,000	1.00	1.50	12.00	25.00	42.00
1945 Proof	—	Value: 200				
1945H	12,864,000	2.00	3.50	18.00	35.00	60.00
1945KN	11,120,000	1.00	2.00	12.00	25.00	42.00
1946	37,350,000	1.00	2.00	18.00	35.00	60.00
1946 Proof	—	Value: 200				
1946H	—	750	1,000	2,000	4,000	—
1947	99,200,000	0.50	1.00	4.50	12.00	20.00
1947 Proof	—	Value: 200				
1947H	10,000,000	1.50	3.00	17.50	30.00	50.00
1947KN	10,384,000	0.50	1.00	6.50	16.50	28.00

KM# 28 SHILLING

Tin-Brass **Ruler:** George VI **Obv:** Bust of King George VI facing left **Obv. Legend:** GEORGIVS VI DIE GRA. BRITT. OMN: REX FID: DEF: **Obv. Designer:** Percy Metcalf **Rev:** Palm tree divides date in circular frame **Rev. Legend:** BRITISH WEST AFRICA

Date	Mintage	F	VF	XF	Unc	BU
1949	70,000,000	0.50	2.50	12.00	25.00	42.00
1949 Proof	—	Value: 175				
1949H	10,000,000	1.25	4.00	12.50	27.50	47.50
1949KN	10,016,000	1.25	4.00	12.50	27.50	47.50
1949KN Proof	—	Value: 200				
1951	35,346,000	1.25	5.00	15.00	30.00	50.00
1951 Proof	—	Value: 175				
1951H	10,000,000	1.25	5.00	15.00	30.00	50.00
1951KN	16,832,000	1.25	5.00	15.00	30.00	50.00
1952	98,654,000	0.50	1.00	3.00	9.00	15.00
1952 Proof	—	Value: 200				
1952KN	41,653,000	0.50	1.00	2.00	6.00	10.00
1952H	44,096,000	0.50	1.00	2.00	7.50	12.50
1952KN Proof	—	Value: 175				

KM# 13 2 SHILLINGS

11.3104 g., 0.9250 Silver 0.3364 oz. ASW **Ruler:** George V **Obv:** Bust of King George V facing left **Obv. Legend:** GEORGIVS V D.G.BRITT: OMN:REX F.D.IND:IMP: **Obv. Designer:** E.B. MacKennal **Rev:** Palm tree divides date in circular frame **Rev. Legend:** BRITISH WEST AFRICA

Date	Mintage	F	VF	XF	Unc	BU
1913	2,100,000	7.00	10.00	17.50	45.00	80.00
1913 Proof	—	Value: 500				
1913H	1,176,000	8.00	15.00	27.50	55.00	95.00
1914	330,000	15.00	50.00	125	200	—
1914H	637,000	10.00	25.00	45.00	75.00	135
1915H	66,000	25.00	60.00	125	185	—
1916H	9,824,000	7.00	15.00	30.00	60.00	110
1917H	1,059,000	15.00	40.00	100	165	—
1917H Proof	—	Value: 300				
1918H	7,294,000	7.00	12.00	30.00	55.00	95.00
1919	2,000,000	8.00	20.00	50.00	85.00	150
1919H	10,866,000	7.00	10.00	40.00	65.00	115
1919H Proof	—	Value: 200				
1920	683,000	30.00	60.00	175	250	—

KM# 13a 2 SHILLINGS

11.3104 g., 0.5000 Silver 0.1818 oz. ASW **Ruler:** George V **Obv:** Bust of George V facing left **Obv. Legend:** GEORGIVS V D.G.BRITT: OMN:REX F.D.IND:IMP: **Rev:** Palm tree divides date in circular frame **Rev. Legend:** BRITISH WEST AFRICA

Date	Mintage	F	VF	XF	Unc	BU
1920H	1,926,000	30.00	55.00	175	275	—

KM# 13b 2 SHILLINGS

Tin-Brass **Ruler:** George V **Obv:** Bust of George V facing left **Obv. Legend:** GEORGIVS V D.G.BRITT: OMN:REX F.D.IND:IMP: **Rev:** Palm tree divides date in circular frame **Rev. Legend:** BRITISH WEST AFRICA

Date	Mintage	F	VF	XF	Unc	BU
1920KN	15,856,000	2.50	5.00	20.00	40.00	70.00
1920KN Proof	—	Value: 250				
1922	10,000,000	3.00	9.00	27.50	55.00	95.00
1922KN	5,500,000	6.00	15.00	45.00	75.00	135
1922KN Proof	—	Value: 250				
1923H	12,696,000	4.00	12.00	37.50	65.00	115
1924	1,500,000	8.00	20.00	55.00	90.00	160
1925	3,700,000	4.00	12.00	40.00	70.00	125
1926	11,500,000	4.50	15.00	50.00	80.00	140
1927	11,100,000	6.00	20.00	65.00	100	185
1927 Proof	—	Value: 250				
1928	7,900,000	1,500	2,000	3,000	5,000	—
1928 Proof	—	Value: 3,000				
1936	32,939,999	5.00	12.00	35.00	60.00	100
1936 Proof	—	Value: 250				
1936H	8,703,000	6.00	18.00	45.00	75.00	130
1936KN	8,794,000	6.00	18.00	45.00	75.00	130

KM# 24 2 SHILLINGS

11.3700 g., Nickel-Brass, 28.51 mm. **Ruler:** George VI **Obv:** Bust of King George VI left **Obv. Legend:** GEORGIVS VI D.G.BRITT: OMN:REX F.D.IND:IMP: **Obv. Designer:** Percy Metcalf **Rev:** Palm tree divides date in circular frame **Rev. Legend:** BRITISH WEST AFRICA

Date	Mintage	F	VF	XF	Unc	BU
1938H	32,000,000	1.00	2.00	6.50	15.00	28.00
1938KN	27,852,000	1.00	2.00	6.50	15.00	28.00

Date	Mintage	F	VF	XF	Unc	BU
Note: Grained edge variety exists, valued at $325						
1939H	5,750,000	2.00	5.00	20.00	35.00	65.00
1939KN	6,250,000	1.00	4.00	16.50	30.00	55.00
1939KN Proof	—	Value: 200				
1942KN	10,000,000	1.25	4.50	17.00	30.00	55.00
1946H	10,500,000	1.25	4.00	12.00	27.50	50.00
1946KN	4,800,000	1.25	7.00	27.00	42.50	80.00
1947H	5,055,000	1.00	6.00	25.00	40.00	75.00
1947KN	4,200,000	1.25	7.00	27.00	42.50	80.00

KM# 29 2 SHILLINGS

Nickel-Brass **Ruler:** George VI **Obv:** Bust of King George VI facing left **Obv. Legend:** GEORGIVS VI DIE GRA. BRITT. OMN: REX FID: DEF: **Obv. Designer:** Percy Metcalf **Rev:** Palm tree divides date in circular frame **Rev. Legend:** BRITISH WEST AFRICA

Date	Mintage	F	VF	XF	Unc	BU
1949H	7,500,000	1.25	7.00	22.00	40.00	75.00
1949KN	7,576,000	1.25	6.00	20.00	35.00	65.00
1951H	6,566,000	1.25	7.00	22.00	40.00	75.00
1951H Proof	—	Value: 250				
1952H	4,410,000	2.00	8.00	22.50	42.00	80.00
1952KN	1,236,000	8.00	20.00	50.00	75.00	145

BRUNEI

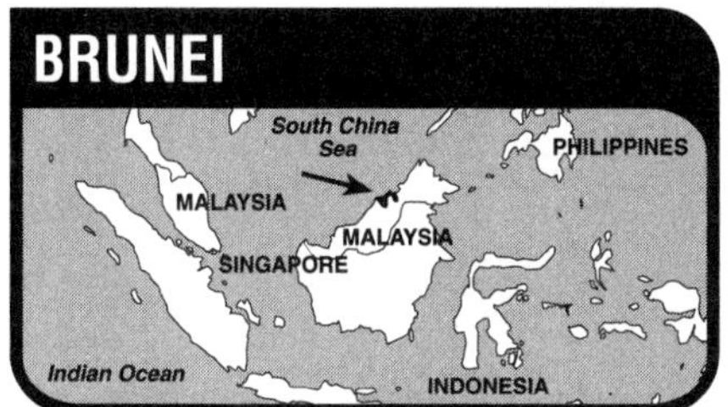

Negara Brunei Darussalam (State of Brunei), an independent sultanate on the northwest coast of the island of Borneo, has an area of 2,226 sq. mi. (5,765 sq. km.) and a population of *326,000. Capital: Bandar Seri Begawan. Crude oil and rubber are exported.

Magellan was the first European to visit Brunei in 1521. It was a powerful state, ruling over northern Borneo and adjacent islands from the 16th to the 19th century. Brunei became a British protectorate in 1888 and a British dependency in 1905. The Constitution of 1959 restored control over internal affairs to the sultan, while delegating responsibility for defense and foreign affairs to Britain. On January 1, 1984 it became independent and is a member of the Commonwealth of Nations.

TITLES

Negri Brunei

RULERS

Sultan Hashim Jalal, 1885-1906
British 1906-1950
Sultan Sir Omar Ali Saifuddin III, 1950-1967
Sultan Hassanal Bolkiah I, 1967-

MONETARY SYSTEM

100 Sen = 1 Dollar

SULTANATE

DECIMAL COINAGE

100 Sen = 1 Dollar (Ringgit)

KM# 4 SEN

Bronze **Ruler:** Sultan Sir Omar Ali Saifuddin III **Obv:** Uniformed head left **Rev:** Native design, denomination below, date at right

Date	Mintage	F	VF	XF	Unc	BU
1967	1,000,000	—	0.20	1.00	1.40	2.00

KM# 9 SEN

Bronze **Ruler:** Sultan Hassanal Bolkiah **Obv:** Head right **Rev:** Native design, denomination below, date at right

Date	Mintage	F	VF	XF	Unc	BU
1968	60,000	—	0.30	1.70	3.50	4.00
1970	140,000	—	0.20	0.60	1.00	1.50
1970 Proof	4,000	Value: 4.00				
1971	400,000	—	0.10	0.25	0.80	1.25

Date	Mintage	F	VF	XF	Unc	BU
1973	120,000	—	0.20	0.80	2.50	3.00
1974	640,000	—	—	0.25	0.80	1.25
1976	140,000	—	—	0.25	0.80	1.25
1977	140,000	—	—	0.25	0.80	1.25

KM# 15 SEN

Bronze **Ruler:** Sultan Hassanal Bolkiah **Obv:** Head right **Rev:** Native design, denomination below, date at right, legend without numeral 'I' in title

Date	Mintage	F	VF	XF	Unc	BU
1977	280,000	—	—	0.25	0.70	1.00
1978	269,000	—	—	0.25	0.70	1.00
1979	250,000	—	0.10	0.50	1.00	1.50
1979 Proof	10,000	Value: 2.00				
1980	260,000	—	—	0.25	0.70	1.00
1981	540,000	—	—	0.25	0.70	1.00
1982	100,000	—	—	2.00	3.00	3.50
1983	500,000	—	—	0.25	0.50	0.75
1984	400,000	—	—	0.25	0.50	0.75
1984 Proof	3,000	Value: 2.00				
1985	200,000	—	—	0.20	0.50	0.75
1985 Proof	—	Value: 2.00				
1986	101,000	—	—	—	0.50	0.75
1986 Proof	7,000	Value: 2.00				

KM# 15a SEN

Copper Clad Steel **Ruler:** Sultan Hassanal Bolkiah **Obv:** Head right **Rev:** Native design, denomination below, date at right, legend without numeral 'I' in title

Date	Mintage	F	VF	XF	Unc	BU
1986	102,000	—	—	—	0.40	0.65
1987	390,000	—	—	—	0.40	0.65
1988	500,000	—	—	—	0.40	0.65
1989	601,000	—	—	—	0.40	0.65
1990	680,000	—	—	—	0.40	0.65
1991	680,000	—	—	—	0.40	0.65
1992	887,000	—	—	—	0.40	0.65
1993	948,000	—	—	—	0.40	0.65

KM# 34 SEN

Copper Clad Steel **Ruler:** Sultan Hassanal Bolkiah **Obv:** Uniformed bust facing **Rev:** Native design denomination below, date at right

Date	Mintage	F	VF	XF	Unc	BU
1993	680,000	—	—	—	0.35	0.50
1994	1,900,000	—	—	—	0.15	0.25
1995	—	—	—	—	—	—
1996	3,044,000	—	—	—	0.15	0.25
2001	576,000	—	—	—	0.35	0.50
2002	804,900	—	—	—	0.35	0.50
2005	—	—	—	—	0.35	0.50

KM# 54 SEN

Copper Clad Steel **Ruler:** Sultan Hassanal Bolkiah **Subject:** 10 Years of Independence **Obv:** Sultan's portrait **Rev:** National arms

Date	Mintage	F	VF	XF	Unc	BU
ND(1994)	—	—	—	—	1.00	1.50

KM# 5 5 SEN

Copper-Nickel **Ruler:** Sultan Sir Omar Ali Saifuddin III **Obv:** Uniformed head left **Rev:** Native design, denomination below, date at right

Date	Mintage	F	VF	XF	Unc	BU
1967	1,500,000	—	0.20	1.20	2.00	2.50

KM# 10 5 SEN

Copper-Nickel **Ruler:** Sultan Hassanal Bolkiah **Obv:** Head right **Rev:** Native design, denomination below, date at right

Date	Mintage	F	VF	XF	Unc	BU
1968	320,000	—	0.15	0.75	1.50	2.00
1970	760,000	—	0.15	0.75	1.50	2.00
1970 Proof	4,000	Value: 4.00				
1971	320,000	—	0.15	0.75	1.50	2.00
1973	128,000	—	0.25	1.50	2.50	3.00
1974	576,000	—	0.15	0.50	1.25	2.00
1976	384,000	—	0.15	0.75	1.50	2.00
1977	384,000	—	0.15	0.75	1.50	2.00

KM# 16 5 SEN

Copper-Nickel **Ruler:** Sultan Hassanal Bolkiah **Obv:** Head right, legend without numeral 'I' in title **Rev:** Native design denomination below, date at right

Date	Mintage	F	VF	XF	Unc	BU
1977	920,000	—	0.10	0.30	0.60	1.00
1978	640,000	—	0.10	0.30	0.60	1.00
1979	650,000	—	0.15	0.45	0.80	1.25
1979 Proof	10,000	Value: 3.00				
1980	640,000	—	0.10	0.30	0.50	0.75
1981	960,000	—	0.10	0.30	0.50	0.75
1982	240,000	—	0.50	1.25	2.25	3.00
1983	1,280,000	—	—	0.10	0.30	0.50
1984	800,000	—	—	0.10	0.30	0.50
1984 Proof	3,000	Value: 3.00				
1985	800,000	—	—	0.10	0.30	0.50
1985 Proof	—	Value: 3.00				
1986	189,000	—	—	—	0.30	0.50
1986 Proof	7,000	Value: 3.00				
1987	960,000	—	—	—	0.30	0.50
1988	820,000	—	—	—	0.30	0.50
1989	1,504,000	—	—	—	0.30	0.50
1990	1,340,000	—	—	—	0.30	0.50
1991	1,340,000	—	—	—	0.30	0.50
1992	1,900,000	—	—	—	0.30	0.50
1993	1,951,000	—	—	—	0.30	0.50

KM# 35 5 SEN

Copper-Nickel **Ruler:** Sultan Hassanal Bolkiah **Obv:** Uniformed bust facing **Rev:** Native design, denomination below, date at right

Date	Mintage	F	VF	XF	Unc	BU
1993	1,340,000	—	—	—	0.50	0.75
1994	2,600,000	—	—	—	0.40	0.65
1996	3,571,000	—	—	—	0.40	0.65
2000	—	—	—	—	0.50	0.75
2001	808,000	—	—	—	0.50	0.75
2002	1,418,178	—	—	—	0.50	0.75
2005	—	—	—	—	0.50	0.75

KM# 55 5 SEN

Copper-Nickel **Ruler:** Sultan Hassanal Bolkiah **Subject:** 10 Years of Independence **Obv:** Sultan's portrait **Rev:** National arms

Date	Mintage	F	VF	XF	Unc	BU
ND(1994)	3,000	—	—	—	1.50	2.00

KM# 6 10 SEN

2.7700 g., Copper-Nickel **Ruler:** Sultan Sir Omar Ali Saifuddin III **Obv:** Military head left **Rev:** Native design, denomination below, date at right

Date	Mintage	F	VF	XF	Unc	BU
1967	3,510,000	—	0.25	1.00	2.00	3.00

KM# 11 10 SEN

Copper-Nickel

Date	Mintage	F	VF	XF	Unc	BU
1968	580,000	—	0.25	0.75	1.50	2.00
1970	1,360,000	—	0.25	0.75	1.50	2.00
1970 Proof	4,000	Value: 4.00				
1971	420,000	—	0.25	0.75	1.30	2.00
1973	300,000	—	0.25	0.75	1.30	2.00
1974	1,410,000	—	0.15	0.55	1.00	1.50
1976	920,000	—	0.15	0.55	1.00	1.50
1977	920,000	—	0.15	0.55	1.00	1.50

KM# 17 10 SEN

Copper-Nickel **Ruler:** Sultan Hassanal Bolkiah **Obv:** Head right, legend without numeral 'I' in title **Rev:** Native design, denomination below, date at right **Edge:** Reeded

Date	Mintage	F	VF	XF	Unc	BU
1977	1,800,000	—	0.10	0.30	0.80	1.25
1978	1,080,000	—	0.10	0.30	0.80	1.25
1979	2,050,000	—	0.10	0.30	0.80	1.25
1979 Proof	10,000	Value: 4.00				
1980	2,840,000	—	—	0.10	0.40	0.65
1981	976,000	—	—	0.10	0.40	0.65
1983	1,080,000	—	—	0.10	0.40	0.65

Date	Mintage	F	VF	XF	Unc	BU
1984	1,400,000	—	—	0.10	0.40	0.65
1984 Proof	3,000	Value: 4.25				
1985	1,540,000	—	—	0.10	0.30	0.50
1985 Proof	—	Value: 4.25				
1986	2,181,000	—	—	—	0.30	0.50
1986 Proof	7,000	Value: 4.25				
1987	2,560,000	—	—	—	0.30	0.50
1988	960,000	—	—	—	0.30	0.50
1989	1,000,000	—	—	—	0.30	0.50
1990	1,800,000	—	—	—	0.30	0.50
1991	1,800,000	—	—	—	0.30	0.50
1992	3,839,000	—	—	—	0.30	0.50
1993	3,973,000	—	—	—	0.30	0.50

KM# 36 10 SEN

Copper-Nickel **Ruler:** Sultan Hassanal Bolkiah **Obv:** Uniformed bust facing **Rev:** Native design, denomination below, date at right

Date	Mintage	F	VF	XF	Unc	BU
1993	1,800,000	—	—	—	0.55	0.85
1994	2,200,000	—	—	—	0.50	0.75
1996	3,618,000	—	—	—	0.50	0.75
2001	164,000	—	—	—	0.65	1.00
2002	476,452	—	—	—	0.65	1.00
2005	—	—	—	—	0.65	1.00

KM# 56 10 SEN

Copper-Nickel **Subject:** 10 Years of Independence **Obv:** Sultan's portrait **Rev:** National arms

Date	Mintage	F	VF	XF	Unc	BU
ND(1994)	3,000	—	—	—	2.00	3.00

KM# 7 20 SEN

Copper-Lead Alloy **Ruler:** Sultan Sir Omar Ali Saifuddin III **Obv:** Uniformed head left **Rev:** Native design, denomination below, date at right

Date	Mintage	F	VF	XF	Unc	BU
1967	2,130,000	—	0.35	1.50	4.00	6.00

KM# 12 20 SEN

5.6500 g., Copper-Nickel, 23.62 mm. **Ruler:** Sultan Hassanal Bolkiah **Obv:** Head right **Rev:** Native design, denomination below, date at right

Date	Mintage	F	VF	XF	Unc	BU
1968	510,000	—	0.20	1.00	3.00	3.50
1970	850,000	—	0.15	0.85	3.00	3.50
1970 Proof	4,000	Value: 4.00				
1971	450,000	—	0.20	1.00	2.00	2.50
1973	450,000	—	0.20	2.00	4.00	4.50
1974	700,000	—	0.15	1.00	2.00	2.50
1976	640,000	—	0.15	1.00	2.00	2.50
1977	640,000	—	0.15	1.00	2.00	2.50

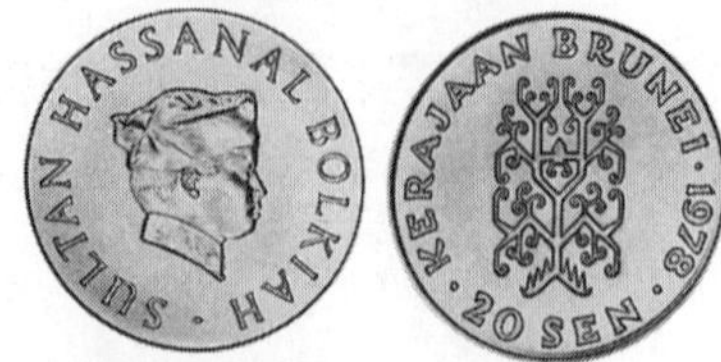

KM# 18 20 SEN

5.4400 g., Copper-Nickel, 23.58 mm. **Ruler:** Sultan Hassanal Bolkiah **Obv:** Head right, legend without numeral 'I' in title **Rev:** Native design, denomination below, date at right

Date	Mintage	F	VF	XF	Unc	BU
1977	1,200,000	—	0.15	0.65	2.00	2.50
1978	720,000	—	0.20	0.75	2.00	2.50
1979	1,060,000	—	0.20	0.75	2.00	2.50
1979 Proof	10,000	Value: 4.50				
1980	1,540,000	—	0.15	0.65	2.00	2.50
1981	2,140,000	—	0.10	0.60	2.00	2.50
1982	120,000	—	2.00	6.00	12.00	15.00
1983	1,350,000	—	0.10	0.35	1.00	1.50
1984	750,000	—	0.10	0.35	1.00	1.50
1984 Proof	3,000	Value: 4.75				

Date	Mintage	F	VF	XF	Unc	BU
1985	1,000,000	—	0.10	0.35	1.00	1.50
1985 Proof	—	Value: 4.75				
1986	2,639,000	—	—	—	1.00	1.50
1986 Proof	7,000	Value: 4.75				
1987	2,400,000	—	—	—	1.00	1.50
1988	560,000	—	—	—	1.00	1.50
1989	500,000	—	—	—	1.00	1.50
1990	720,000	—	—	—	1.00	1.50
1991	725,000	—	—	—	1.00	1.50
1992	2,432,000	—	—	—	1.00	1.50
1993	2,521,000	—	—	—	1.00	1.50

KM# 37 20 SEN

5.6700 g., Copper-Nickel, 23.62 mm. **Ruler:** Sultan Hassanal Bolkiah **Obv:** Uniformed bust facing **Rev:** Native design, denomination below, date at right

Date	Mintage	F	VF	XF	Unc	BU
1993	720,000	—	—	—	1.00	1.50
1994	2,000,000	—	—	—	1.00	1.50
1996	2,767,000	—	—	—	0.75	1.25
2000	—	—	—	—	1.00	1.50
2001	270,647	—	—	—	1.00	1.50
2002	597,272	—	—	—	1.00	1.50
2004	—	—	—	—	1.00	1.50

KM# 57 20 SEN

Copper-Nickel **Subject:** 10 Years of Independence **Obv:** Sultan's portrait **Rev:** National arms

Date	Mintage	F	VF	XF	Unc	BU
ND(1994)	3,000	—	—	—	2.50	3.50

KM# 8 50 SEN

Copper-Nickel **Ruler:** Sultan Sir Omar Ali Saifuddin III **Obv:** Uniformed head left within circle **Rev:** National arms, denomination below, date at right

Date	Mintage	F	VF	XF	Unc	BU
1967	788,000	—	0.75	2.00	5.00	7.00

KM# 13 50 SEN

Copper-Nickel **Ruler:** Sultan Hassanal Bolkiah **Obv:** Head right **Rev:** National arms within circle, denomination below, date at right

Date	Mintage	F	VF	XF	Unc	BU
1968	212,000	—	0.50	2.00	3.00	3.50
1970	300,000	—	0.50	2.00	3.00	3.50
1970 Proof	4,000	Value: 6.50				
1971	320,000	—	0.45	2.00	3.00	3.50
1973	140,000	—	2.00	4.00	6.00	8.00
1974	244,000	—	0.45	2.00	3.00	3.50
1976	240,000	—	0.45	2.00	3.00	3.50
1977	240,000	—	0.45	2.00	3.00	3.50

KM# 19 50 SEN

Copper-Nickel **Ruler:** Sultan Hassanal Bolkiah **Obv:** Head right, legend without numeral 'I' in title **Rev:** National arms within circle, denomination below, date at right

Date	Mintage	F	VF	XF	Unc	BU
1977	499,000	—	0.30	1.10	2.00	2.50
1978	264,000	—	0.30	1.10	2.00	2.50
1979	730,000	—	0.30	1.10	2.00	2.50
1979 Proof	10,000	Value: 6.50				

Date	Mintage	F	VF	XF	Unc	BU
1980	536,000	—	0.30	1.10	2.00	2.50
1981	960,000	—	0.30	1.00	1.50	2.00
1982	136,000	—	2.00	5.00	12.00	14.00
1983	408,000	—	0.30	0.80	1.50	2.00
1984	320,000	—	0.30	0.80	1.50	2.00
1984 Proof	3,000	Value: 6.75				
1985	450,000	—	0.30	0.80	1.50	2.00
1985 Proof	—	—	—	—	—	—
1986	1,067,000	—	—	—	1.50	2.00
1986 Proof	7,000	Value: 6.75				
1987	1,120,000	—	—	—	1.50	2.00
1988	250,000	—	—	—	1.50	2.00
1989	500,000	—	—	—	1.50	2.00
1990	472,000	—	—	—	1.50	2.00
1991	508,000	—	—	—	1.50	2.00
1992	1,072,000	—	—	—	1.50	2.00
1993	1,102,000	—	—	—	1.50	2.00

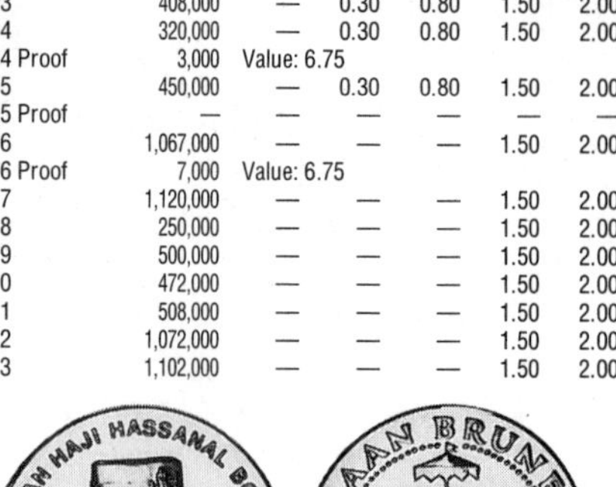

KM# 38 50 SEN

Copper-Nickel, 27.5 mm. **Ruler:** Sultan Hassanal Bolkiah **Obv:** Uniformed bust facing **Rev:** National arms within circle, denomination below, date at right **Edge:** Reeded and security edge

Date	Mintage	F	VF	XF	Unc	BU
1993	472,000	—	—	—	1.50	2.00
1994	600,000	—	—	—	1.50	2.00
1996	458,000	—	—	—	1.50	2.00
2001	50,000	—	—	—	2.50	3.00
2002	1,325	—	—	—	3.50	5.00
2005	—	—	—	—	2.50	3.00

KM# 58 50 SEN

Copper-Nickel **Subject:** 10 Years of Independence **Obv:** Sultan's portrait **Rev:** National arms

Date	Mintage	F	VF	XF	Unc	BU
ND(1994)	3,000	—	—	—	4.50	6.00

KM# 20 DOLLAR

Copper-Nickel **Obv:** Legend without numeral 'I' in title

Date	Mintage	F	VF	XF	Unc	BU
1979 Proof	10,000	Value: 20.00				
1984	5,000	—	—	—	10.00	12.00
1984 Proof	3,000	Value: 22.00				
1985	15,000	—	—	—	8.00	10.00
1985 Proof	10,000	Value: 20.00				
1986	10,000	—	—	—	8.00	10.00
1986 Proof	7,000	Value: 22.00				
1987	2,000	—	—	—	10.00	12.50
1988	2,000	—	—	—	10.00	12.50
1989	2,000	—	—	—	10.00	12.50
1990	3,000	—	—	—	10.00	12.50
1991	3,000	—	—	—	10.00	12.50
1992	—	—	—	—	10.00	12.50

KM# 76 DOLLAR

16.8000 g., Copper-Nickel, 33.3 mm. **Ruler:** Sultan Hassanal Bolkiah **Obv:** Uniformed bust facing **Rev:** Antique cannon **Edge:** Reeded

Date	Mintage	F	VF	XF	Unc	BU
1993	—	—	—	—	10.00	12.50

KM# 23 5 DOLLARS

Copper-Nickel **Ruler:** Sultan Hassanal Bolkiah **Subject:** Year of Hejira 1400 **Obv:** Head right, legend without numeral 'I' in title **Rev:** Denomination below design

Date	Mintage	F	VF	XF	Unc	BU
AH1400 (1980)	10,000	—	5.00	15.00	30.00	35.00

The Republic of Bulgaria, formerly the Peoples Republic of Bulgaria, a Balkan country on the Black Sea in southeastern Europe, has an area of 42,855 sq. mi. (110,910 sq. km.) and a population of *8.31 million. Capital: Sofia. Agriculture remains a key component of the economy but industrialization, particularly heavy industry, has been emphasized since the late 1940s. Machinery, tobacco and cigarettes, wines and spirits, clothing and metals are the chief exports.

The area now occupied by Bulgaria was conquered by the Bulgars, an Asiatic tribe, in the 7th century. Bulgarian kingdoms continued to exist on the Bulgarian peninsula until it came under Turkish rule in 1395. In 1878, after nearly 500 years of Turkish rule, Bulgaria was made a principality under Turkish suzerainty. Union seven years later with Eastern Rumelia created a Balkan state with borders approximating those of present-day Bulgaria. A Bulgarian kingdom, fully independent of Turkey, was proclaimed Sept. 22, 1908. During WWI Bulgaria had been aligned with Germany. After the Armistice certain land concessions were given to Greece and Romania. In 1934 King Boris III suspended all political parties and established a dictatorial monarchy. In 1938 the military began rearming through the aide of the Anglo-French loan. As WW II developed, Bulgaria again supported the Germans but protected their Jewish community. Boris died mysteriously in 1943 and Simeon II became King at the age of six. The country was then ruled by a pro-Nazi regency until it was liberated by Soviet forces in 1944.

The monarchy was abolished and Simeon was ousted by plebiscite in 1946 and Bulgaria became a Peoples Republic on the Soviet pattern. After democratic reforms in 1989 the name was changed to the Republic of Bulgaria.

Coinage of the Peoples Republic features a number of politically oriented commemoratives.

RULERS

Ferdinand I, as Prince, 1887-1908
As King, 1908-1918
Boris III, 1918-1943

MINT MARKS

A - Berlin
(a) Cornucopia & torch - Paris
BP - Budapest
H - Heaton Mint, Birmingham
KB - Kormoczbanya
(p) Poissy - Thunderbolt

MONETARY SYSTEM

100 Stotinki = 1 Lev

PRINCIPALITY

Under Turkish Suzerainty

STANDARD COINAGE

KM# 22.1 STOTINKA

Bronze **Ruler:** Ferdinand I as Prince **Obv:** Crowned arms within circle **Rev:** Denomination above date, within wreath, privy marks and design name below denomination

Date	Mintage	F	VF	XF	Unc	BU
1901	20,000,000	1.25	2.50	7.50	18.00	—

KM# 22.2 STOTINKA

Bronze **Ruler:** Ferdinand I as Prince **Obv:** Crowned arms within circle **Rev:** Denomination above date within wreath, without privy marks and designer name

Date	Mintage	F	VF	XF	Unc	BU
1912	20,000,000	0.75	1.75	6.00	14.00	—

KM# 23.1 2 STOTINKI

2.0100 g., Bronze, 20.14 mm. **Ruler:** Ferdinand I **Obv:** Crowned arms within circle **Rev:** Denomination above date within wreath, privy marks and designer name below denomination

Date	Mintage	F	VF	XF	Unc	BU
1901(a)	40,000,000	1.00	2.00	5.00	12.00	—

KM# 23.2 2 STOTINKI

Bronze **Obv:** Crowned arms within circle **Rev:** Denomination above date within wreath, without privy marks and designer name

Date	Mintage	F	VF	XF	Unc	BU
1912	40,000,000	0.50	1.00	2.20	6.50	—

KM# 24 5 STOTINKI

3.0400 g., Copper-Nickel, 17 mm. **Obv:** Crowned arms within circle **Rev:** Denomination above date within wreath

Date	Mintage	F	VF	XF	Unc	BU
1906	14,000,000	0.20	0.60	2.00	7.00	—
1912	14,000,000	0.20	0.40	1.20	4.00	—
1913	20,000,000	0.20	0.40	1.50	4.00	—
1913 Proof	—	Value: 110				

KM# 24a 5 STOTINKI

Zinc **Obv:** Crowned arms within circle **Rev:** Denomination above date within wreath

Date	Mintage	F	VF	XF	Unc	BU
1917	53,200,000	0.60	1.00	2.50	7.00	—

KM# 25 10 STOTINKI

Copper-Nickel **Obv:** Crowned arms within circle **Rev:** Denomination above date within wreath

Date	Mintage	F	VF	XF	Unc	BU
1906	13,000,000	0.50	1.00	2.50	8.50	—
1912	13,000,000	0.20	0.40	1.75	4.50	—
1912 Proof	—	Value: 110				
1913	20,000,000	0.20	0.40	1.00	2.50	—

KM# 25a 10 STOTINKI

Zinc **Obv:** Crowned arms within circle **Rev:** Denomination above date within wreath

Date	Mintage	F	VF	XF	Unc	BU
1917	59,100,000	0.40	1.00	2.50	6.00	—
1917 Proof	—	Value: 135				

KM# 26 20 STOTINKI

Copper-Nickel **Obv:** Crowned arms within circle **Rev:** Denomination above date within wreath

Date	Mintage	F	VF	XF	Unc	BU
1906	10,000,000	0.50	1.50	3.50	11.00	—
1912	10,000,000	0.20	0.50	1.50	5.50	—
1913	5,000,000	0.20	1.00	2.00	6.00	—
1913	—	—	—	—	—	—

KM# 26a 20 STOTINKI

3.9000 g., Zinc **Obv:** Crowned arms within circle **Rev:** Denomination above date within wreath

Date	Mintage	F	VF	XF	Unc	BU
1917	40,000,000	0.50	1.75	4.00	9.00	—
1917 Proof	—	Value: 130				

KINGDOM

STANDARD COINAGE

KM# 27 50 STOTINKI

2.5000 g., 0.8350 Silver 0.0671 oz. ASW **Obv:** Head right **Rev:** Denomination above date within wreath

Date	Mintage	F	VF	XF	Unc	BU
1910	400,000	1.75	4.00	10.00	22.00	—

KM# 30 50 STOTINKI

2.5000 g., 0.8350 Silver 0.0671 oz. ASW, 18.06 mm. **Obv:** Head left **Rev:** Denomination above date within wreath

Date	Mintage	F	VF	XF	Unc	BU
1912	2,000,000	1.50	2.50	5.00	12.00	—
1913	3,000,000	1.50	2.00	3.50	9.00	—
1916	4,562,000	—	—	260	420	—

Note: Withdrawn from circulation and destroyed possibly only 100 pieces remain; Beware possible counterfeits

KM# 46 50 STOTINKI

Aluminum-Bronze **Obv:** Crowned arms with supporters **Rev:** Denomination above date within wreath

Date	Mintage	F	VF	XF	Unc	BU
1937	60,200,000	0.25	0.50	1.25	4.00	—

KM# 28 LEV

5.0000 g., 0.8350 Silver 0.1342 oz. ASW, 23 mm. **Obv:** Head right **Rev:** Denomination above date within wreath

Date	Mintage	F	VF	XF	Unc	BU
1910	3,000,000	2.75	4.50	9.00	18.00	—

KM# 31 LEV

5.0000 g., 0.8350 Silver 0.1342 oz. ASW **Obv:** Head left **Rev:** Denomination above date within wreath

Date	Mintage	F	VF	XF	Unc	BU
1912	2,000,000	2.75	3.75	6.00	13.00	—
1913	3,500,000	2.75	3.50	5.50	11.00	—
1916	4,569,000	—	—	540	920	—

Note: Withdrawn from circulation and destroyed possibly only 50 pieces remain; Beware possible counterfeits

KM# 35 LEV

Aluminum **Obv:** Crowned arms with supporters on ornate shield **Rev:** Denomination above date within wreath

Date	Mintage	F	VF	XF	Unc	BU
1923	40,000,000	3.00	6.00	15.00	42.00	—

KM# 37 LEV

2.9900 g., Copper-Nickel, 19.7 mm. **Obv:** Crowned arms with supporters on ornate shield **Rev:** Denomination above date within wreath **Edge:** Reeded

Date	Mintage	F	VF	XF	Unc	BU
1925	35,000,000	0.20	0.50	1.25	3.00	—
1925(p)	34,982,000	0.25	0.60	1.50	3.50	—

Note: The Poissy issue bears the thunderbolt mint mark

KM# 37a LEV

Iron **Obv:** Crowned arms with supporters on ornate shield **Rev:** Denomination above date within wreath

Date	Mintage	F	VF	XF	Unc	BU
1941	10,000,000	3.00	7.00	18.00	48.00	—

KM# 29 2 LEVA

10.0000 g., 0.8350 Silver 0.2684 oz. ASW **Obv:** Head right **Rev:** Denomination above date within wreath

Date	Mintage	F	VF	XF	Unc	BU
1910	400,000	5.50	9.00	18.50	48.00	—

KM# 32 2 LEVA

10.0000 g., 0.8350 Silver 0.2684 oz. ASW **Obv:** Head left **Rev:** Denomination above date within wreath

Date	Mintage	F	VF	XF	Unc	BU
1912	1,000,000	5.50	7.00	12.50	20.00	—
1913	500,000	5.50	7.00	14.00	22.00	—
1916	2,286,000	—	—	930	1,850	—

Note: Withdrawn from circulation and destroyed possibly only 30 pieces remain; Beware possible counterfeits

KM# 36 2 LEVA

Aluminum **Obv:** Crowned arms with supporters on ornate shield **Rev:** Denomination above date within wreath

Date	Mintage	F	VF	XF	Unc	BU
1923	20,000,000	3.50	8.00	20.00	60.00	—

KM# 38 2 LEVA

4.9700 g., Copper-Nickel, 22.95 mm. **Obv:** Crowned arms with supporters on ornate shield **Rev:** Denomination above date within wreath

Date	Mintage	F	VF	XF	Unc	BU
1925	20,000,000	0.40	0.80	1.50	4.00	—
1925(p)	20,000,000	0.50	1.00	2.25	5.50	—

Note: The Poissy issue bears the thunderbolt privy mark

KM# 38a 2 LEVA

Iron **Obv:** Crowned arms with supporters on ornate shield **Rev:** Denomination above date within wreath

Date	Mintage	F	VF	XF	Unc	BU
1941	15,000,000	0.75	1.50	8.50	22.50	—

KM# 49 2 LEVA

Iron **Obv:** Crowned arms with supporters **Rev:** Denomination above date within wreath

Date	Mintage	F	VF	XF	Unc	BU
1943	35,000,000	0.75	1.50	12.00	34.00	—

KM# 39 5 LEVA

7.7500 g., Copper-Nickel, 26.13 mm. **Obv:** Denomination above date within wreath **Rev:** Figure on horseback, animals below

Date	Mintage	F	VF	XF	Unc	BU
1930	20,001,000	0.60	1.25	4.00	11.00	—

KM# 39a 5 LEVA

Iron **Obv:** Denomination above date within wreath **Rev:** Figure on horseback, animals below

Date	Mintage	F	VF	XF	Unc	BU
1941	15,000,000	1.00	3.00	8.00	25.00	—

KM# 39b 5 LEVA

Nickel Clad Steel **Obv:** Denomination above date within wreath **Rev:** Figure on horseback, animals below

Date	Mintage	F	VF	XF	Unc	BU
1943	36,000,000	0.50	1.00	3.00	9.00	—

KM# 40 10 LEVA

Copper-Nickel, 30 mm. **Obv:** Denomination above date within wreath **Rev:** Figure on horseback, animals below **Edge:** Reeded

Date	Mintage	F	VF	XF	Unc	BU
1930	15,001,000	0.75	2.00	4.00	10.00	—

KM# 40a 10 LEVA

Iron **Obv:** Denomination above date within wreath **Rev:** Figure on horseback, animals below

Date	Mintage	F	VF	XF	Unc	BU
1941	2,200,000	6.00	12.00	26.00	68.00	—

KM# 40b 10 LEVA

Nickel Clad Steel **Obv:** Denomination above date within wreath **Rev:** Figure on horseback, animals below

Date	Mintage	F	VF	XF	Unc	BU
1943	25,000,000	0.60	1.25	3.00	8.50	—

KM# 33 20 LEVA

6.4516 g., 0.9000 Gold 0.1867 oz. AGW, 21 mm. **Subject:** Declaration of Independence **Obv:** Head left **Rev:** Crowned arms, denomination and date below

Date	Mintage	F	VF	XF	Unc	BU
1912	75,000	BV	185	285	465	—
1912 Proof	Inc. above	Value: 3,000				
1912 Proof; restrike	2,950	Value: 300				

Note: Official restrikes of this type were produced at the Bulgarian Mint in Sophia from 1967-68 and released prior to 2002; These pieces can be distinguished by their thicker more widely spaced edge legends

KM# 41 20 LEVA

4.0000 g., 0.5000 Silver 0.0643 oz. ASW **Obv:** Head left **Rev:** Denomination above date within wreath

Date	Mintage	F	VF	XF	Unc	BU
1930BP	10,016,000	1.50	2.75	4.50	9.00	—

KM# 47 20 LEVA

Copper-Nickel **Obv:** Head left **Rev:** Denomination above date within wreath

Date	Mintage	F	VF	XF	Unc	BU
1940A	6,650,000	0.50	1.00	2.00	7.00	—

KM# 42 50 LEVA

10.0000 g., 0.5000 Silver 0.1607 oz. ASW **Obv:** Head left **Rev:** Denomination above date within wreath

Date	Mintage	F	VF	XF	Unc	BU
1930BP	9,028,000	3.50	5.00	10.00	22.00	—

KM# 44 50 LEVA

10.0000 g., 0.5000 Silver 0.1607 oz. ASW **Obv:** Head left **Rev:** Denomination at top, date below, flower at bottom, grain sprigs flank

Date	Mintage	F	VF	XF	Unc	BU
1934	3,001,000	3.50	5.00	9.50	20.00	—
1934 Proof	—	—	—	—	—	—

KM# 48 50 LEVA

10.0000 g., Copper-Nickel **Obv:** Head left **Rev:** Denomination above date within wreath

Date	Mintage	F	VF	XF	Unc	BU
1940A	12,340,000	0.75	1.50	3.00	8.50	—

KM# 48a 50 LEVA

9.8700 g., Nickel Clad Steel **Obv:** Head left **Rev:** Denomination above date within wreath

Date	Mintage	F	VF	XF	Unc	BU
1943A	15,000,000	1.00	2.00	4.00	9.50	—

KM# 34 100 LEVA

32.2580 g., 0.9000 Gold 0.9334 oz. AGW, 35 mm. **Subject:** Declaration of Independence **Obv:** Head left **Rev:** Crowned arms divide denomination, date below

Date	Mintage	F	VF	XF	Unc	BU
1912	5,000	900	1,000	1,850	3,200	—
1912 Proof	Inc. above	Value: 6,000				
1912 Proof; restrike	1,000	Value: 1,150				

Note: Official restrikes of this type were produced at the Bulgarian Mint in Sophia from 1967-68 and released prior to 2002; These pieces can be distinguished by their thicker more widely spaced edge legends

KM# 43 100 LEVA
20.0000 g., 0.5000 Silver 0.3215 oz. ASW **Obv:** Head, left **Rev:** Denomination above date within wreath

Date	Mintage	F	VF	XF	Unc	BU
1930BP	1,556,000	BV	7.50	12.50	32.00	—

KM# 45 100 LEVA
20.0000 g., 0.5000 Silver 0.3215 oz. ASW **Obv:** Head left **Rev:** Denomination at top, date below, flower at bottom, grain sprigs flank

Date	Mintage	F	VF	XF	Unc	BU
1934	2,506,000	BV	6.75	9.00	16.00	—
1934 Proof	—	—	—	—	—	—
1937	2,207,000	BV	6.75	9.00	16.00	—

PEOPLES REPUBLIC

STANDARD COINAGE

KM# 50 STOTINKA
0.9900 g., Brass, 15.18 mm. **Obv:** National arms within circle **Rev:** Denomination above date at right, grain sprig at left **Edge:** Reeded

Date	Mintage	F	VF	XF	Unc	BU
1951	—	—	—	0.10	0.25	—

KM# 59 STOTINKA
1.0300 g., Brass, 15.20 mm. **Obv:** National arms within circle, date 9 / IX / 1944 on ribbon **Rev:** Denomination above date, grain sprigs flank **Edge:** Reeded

Date	Mintage	F	VF	XF	Unc	BU
1962	—	—	—	0.10	0.25	—
1970	—	—	0.30	0.80	3.00	—

KM# 84 STOTINKA
1.0000 g., Brass, 15.2 mm. **Obv:** National arms within circle, two dates on ribbon, '681-1944 **Rev:** Denomination above date, grain sprigs flank **Edge:** Reeded **Note:** Reeded and security edge varieties exist.

Date	Mintage	F	VF	XF	Unc	BU
1974	—	—	—	0.10	0.15	—
1979 Proof	2,000	Value: 1.50				
1980 Proof	2,000	Value: 1.50				
1981	137	—	—	—	20.00	—
1988	—	—	—	0.10	0.15	—
1989	—	—	—	0.10	0.15	—
1990	—	—	—	0.10	0.15	—

KM# 111 STOTINKA
Brass **Subject:** 1300th Anniversary of Bulgaria

Date	Mintage	F	VF	XF	Unc	BU
1981	—	—	0.10	0.20	0.50	—
1981 Proof	—	Value: 2.00				

KM# 60 2 STOTINKI
2.0000 g., Brass, 18.16 mm. **Obv:** National arms within circle, date 9*IX*1944 on ribbon **Rev:** Denomination above date, grain sprigs flank **Edge:** Reeded

Date	Mintage	F	VF	XF	Unc	BU
1962	—	—	—	0.10	0.25	—

KM# 85 2 STOTINKI
1.9700 g., Brass, 18.1 mm. **Obv:** National arms within circle, two dates on ribbon, '681-1944 **Rev:** Denomination above date at right, grain sprig at left **Edge:** Plain

Date	Mintage	F	VF	XF	Unc	BU
1974	—	—	—	0.10	0.25	—
1979 Proof	2,000	Value: 2.00				
1980 Proof	2,000	Value: 2.00				
1981 Rare	20	—	—	—	—	—
1988	—	—	—	0.10	0.25	—
1989	—	—	—	0.10	0.25	—
1990	—	—	—	0.10	0.25	—

KM# 112 2 STOTINKI
Brass **Subject:** 1300th Anniversary of Bulgaria **Obv:** National arms within circle **Rev:** Denomination above date at right, grain sprig at left

Date	Mintage	F	VF	XF	Unc	BU
1981	—	—	0.10	0.20	0.60	—
1981 Proof	—	Value: 2.50				

KM# 51 3 STOTINKI
2.2400 g., Brass, 19.66 mm. **Obv:** National arms within circle **Rev:** Denomination above date at right, grain sprig at left **Edge:** Reeded

Date	Mintage	F	VF	XF	Unc	BU
1951	—	—	0.10	0.25	0.75	—

KM# 52 5 STOTINKI
2.9700 g., Brass, 22.16 mm. **Obv:** National arms within circle **Rev:** Denomination above date at right, grain sprig at left **Edge:** Reeded

Date	Mintage	F	VF	XF	Unc	BU
1951	—	0.10	0.15	0.25	0.75	—

KM# 61 5 STOTINKI
Brass **Obv:** National arms within circle, date 9 • IX • 1944 on ribbon **Rev:** Denomination above date, grain sprigs flank

Date	Mintage	F	VF	XF	Unc	BU
1962	—	—	0.10	0.20	0.50	—

KM# 86 5 STOTINKI
3.1000 g., Brass, 22.18 mm. **Obv:** National arms within circle, two dates on ribbon '681-1944' **Rev:** Denomination above date, grain sprigs flank **Edge:** Reeded

Date	Mintage	F	VF	XF	Unc	BU
1974	—	—	0.10	0.15	0.25	—
1979 Proof	2,000	Value: 2.00				
1980 Proof	2,000	Value: 2.00				
1988	—	—	—	0.15	0.25	—
1989	—	—	—	0.15	0.25	—
1990	—	—	—	0.15	0.25	—

KM# 113 5 STOTINKI
Brass **Subject:** 1300th Anniversary of Bulgaria **Obv:** National arms within circle **Rev:** Denomination above date within wreath

Date	Mintage	F	VF	XF	Unc	BU
1981	—	—	0.10	0.25	0.75	—
1981 Proof	—	Value: 2.50				

KM# 53 10 STOTINKI
1.8000 g., Copper-Nickel, 16.59 mm. **Obv:** National arms within circle **Rev:** Denomination above date at right, grain sprig at left **Edge:** Reeded

Date	Mintage	F	VF	XF	Unc	BU
1951	—	—	0.10	0.20	0.40	—

KM# 62 10 STOTINKI
1.5900 g., Nickel-Brass, 16.11 mm. **Obv:** National arms within circle, date 9 • IX • 1944 on ribbon **Rev:** Denomination above date within wreath **Edge:** Reeded

Date	Mintage	F	VF	XF	Unc	BU
1962	—	—	0.10	0.20	0.40	—

KM# 87 10 STOTINKI
1.7000 g., Nickel-Brass, 16.10 mm. **Obv:** National arms within circle, two dates on arms, '681-1944' **Rev:** Denomination above date within wreath **Edge:** Reeded

Date	Mintage	F	VF	XF	Unc	BU
1974	—	—	0.10	0.15	0.25	—
1979 Proof	2,000	Value: 3.50				
1980 Proof	2,000	Value: 3.50				
1988	—	—	—	0.15	0.25	—
1989	—	—	—	0.15	0.25	—
1990	—	—	—	0.15	0.25	—

KM# 114 10 STOTINKI
Copper-Nickel **Subject:** 1300th Anniversary of Bulgaria **Obv:** National arms within circle **Rev:** Denomination above date within wreath

Date	Mintage	F	VF	XF	Unc	BU
1981	—	—	0.20	0.50	1.50	—
1981 Proof	—	Value: 3.50				

KM# 55 20 STOTINKI

2.8000 g., Copper-Nickel, 19.49 mm. **Obv:** National arms within circle **Rev:** Denomination above date at right, grain sprig at left **Edge:** Reeded

Date	Mintage	F	VF	XF	Unc	BU
1952	—	1.00	2.50	7.50	20.00	—
1954	—	0.10	0.25	0.75	1.50	—

KM# 63 20 STOTINKI

2.8500 g., Nickel-Brass, 19.62 mm. **Obv:** Date 9 • IX • 1944 on ribbon **Edge:** Reeded

Date	Mintage	F	VF	XF	Unc	BU
1962	—	0.10	0.20	0.30	0.75	—

KM# 88 20 STOTINKI

3.1000 g., Nickel-Brass, 19.59 mm. **Obv:** National arms within circle, two dates on ribbon, '681-1944' **Rev:** Denomination above date within wreath **Edge:** Reeded

Date	Mintage	F	VF	XF	Unc	BU
1974	—	0.10	0.20	0.30	0.60	—
1979 Proof	2,000	Value: 3.50				
1980 Proof	2,000	Value: 3.50				
1988	—	—	—	0.30	0.60	—
Note: Large date (7mm) and small date (5mm) exist						
1989	—	—	—	0.30	0.60	—
1990	—	—	—	0.30	0.60	—

KM# 115 20 STOTINKI

Copper-Nickel **Subject:** 1300th Anniversary of Bulgaria **Obv:** National arms within circle **Rev:** Denomination above date within wreath

Date	Mintage	F	VF	XF	Unc	BU
1981	—	—	0.25	0.65	2.00	—
1981 Proof	—	Value: 4.00				

KM# 54 25 STOTINKI

Copper-Nickel **Obv:** National arms within circle **Rev:** Denomination above date at right, grain sprig at left

Date	Mintage	F	VF	XF	Unc	BU
1951	—	0.10	0.20	0.50	1.00	—

KM# 56 50 STOTINKI

4.0400 g., Copper-Nickel, 22.62 mm. **Obv:** National arms within circle **Rev:** Denomination above date at right, grain sprig at left

Date	Mintage	F	VF	XF	Unc	BU
1959	—	0.10	0.20	0.40	0.80	—

KM# 64 50 STOTINKI

4.1000 g., Nickel-Brass, 23.22 mm. **Obv:** National arms within circle, date 9 • IX • 1944 on ribbon **Rev:** Denomination above date within wreath **Edge:** Reeded

Date	Mintage	F	VF	XF	Unc	BU
1962	—	0.10	0.40	0.65	1.00	—

KM# 89 50 STOTINKI

4.2000 g., Nickel-Brass, 23.3 mm. **Obv:** Two dates on ribbon, '681-1944'

Date	Mintage	F	VF	XF	Unc	BU
1974	—	0.10	0.40	0.65	1.50	—
1979 Proof	2,000	Value: 4.00				
1980 Proof	2,000	Value: 4.00				
1988	—	—	—	0.50	1.00	—
1989	—	—	—	0.50	1.00	—
1990	—	—	—	0.50	1.00	—

KM# 98 50 STOTINKI

Copper-Nickel **Subject:** University Games at Sofia **Obv:** Runner with torch, left, date at lower left **Rev:** Denomination divides arms and date

Date	Mintage	F	VF	XF	Unc	BU
1977	2,000,000	0.20	0.40	0.75	1.50	—

KM# 116 50 STOTINKI

4.0000 g., Copper-Nickel **Subject:** 1300th Anniversary of Bulgaria **Obv:** National arms within circle **Rev:** Denomination above date within wreath

Date	Mintage	F	VF	XF	Unc	BU
1981	—	—	0.30	0.60	1.80	—
1981 Proof	—	Value: 4.00				

KM# 57 LEV

Copper-Nickel **Obv:** National arms within circle, date 9 • IX • 1944 on ribbon **Rev:** Denomination above date within wreath

Date	Mintage	F	VF	XF	Unc	BU
1960	—	0.10	0.25	0.60	1.00	—

KM# 58 LEV

Nickel-Brass **Obv:** National arms within circle **Rev:** Denomination above date, grain sprigs flank

Date	Mintage	F	VF	XF	Unc	BU
1962	—	—	0.50	1.00	1.50	—

KM# 74 LEV

7.7000 g., Nickel-Brass, 27 mm. **Subject:** 25th Anniversary of Socialist Revolution **Obv:** Wide denomination above date, grain sprigs flanking **Rev:** Monument to the fighters of the resistance

Date	Mintage	F	VF	XF	Unc	BU
1969	2,410,196	0.35	0.60	1.25	2.50	—

KM# 76 LEV

Nickel-Brass, 27 mm. **Subject:** 90th Anniversary Liberation From Turks **Obv:** Denomination within wreath, date below **Rev:** Equestrian statue of Alexander II, Czar of Russia, dates flank

Date	Mintage	F	VF	XF	Unc	BU
1969	1,290,373	0.35	0.65	1.50	2.75	—

KM# 90 LEV

Nickel-Brass, 27 mm. **Obv:** Two dates '681-1944' on ribbon

Date	Mintage	F	VF	XF	Unc	BU
1974	—	—	0.50	1.00	2.00	—
1979 Proof	2,000	Value: 6.00				
1980 Proof	2,000	Value: 6.00				
1988	—	—	—	0.75	2.00	—
1989	—	—	—	0.75	2.00	—
1990	—	—	—	0.75	2.00	—

KM# 94 LEV

Bronze, 27 mm. **Subject:** 100th Anniversary of the "April Uprising" Against the Turks **Obv:** Lion above denomination, date at left, circle surrounds **Rev:** Weapons above date within circle

Date	Mintage	F	VF	XF	Unc	BU
1976	300,000	0.35	0.60	1.25	2.50	—
1976 Proof	—	Value: 4.00				

KM# 107 LEV

Copper-Nickel, 27 mm. **Subject:** World Cup Soccer Games in Spain **Obv:** Arms divide date above denomination **Rev:** World Cup trophy **Edge:** Plain

Date	Mintage	F	VF	XF	Unc	BU
1980	220,000	—	0.60	1.25	2.50	—
1980 Proof	30,000	Value: 3.50				

KM# 117 LEV

Copper-Nickel **Subject:** 1300th Anniversary of Bulgaria **Obv:** National arms within circle **Rev:** Denomination above date, grain sprigs flank

Date	Mintage	F	VF	XF	Unc	BU
1981	—	—	0.50	1.00	2.00	—
1981 Proof	—	—	—	—	—	—

KM# 118 LEV
Copper-Nickel, 27 mm. **Subject:** International Hunting Exposition **Obv:** Arms above denomination, grain sprigs flank, date at bottom left **Rev:** Antlered deer head, left, inscription at right

Date	Mintage	F	VF	XF	Unc	BU
1981	250,000	—	0.60	1.25	2.50	—
1981 Proof	50,000	Value: 3.50				

KM# 119 LEV
Copper-Nickel, 31 mm. **Subject:** Russo-Bulgarian Friendship **Obv:** Arms above denomination **Rev:** Flags at top, hands grasped at center, date at bottom **Note:** The same reverse die was used for both Bulgaria 1 Lev, KM#119 and Russia 1 Rouble, KM#189.

Date	Mintage	F	VF	XF	Unc	BU
1981	220,800	—	0.60	1.25	2.50	—
1981 Proof	50,000	Value: 3.50				

KM# 175 LEV
Copper-Nickel, 27 mm. **Series:** 1980 Winter Olympics **Obv:** National arms **Rev:** Hockey player, denomination and date at bottom **Edge:** Reeded

Date	Mintage	F	VF	XF	Unc	BU
1987	—	—	—	—	2.50	—
1987 Proof	300,000	Value: 3.50				

KM# 176 LEV
Copper-Nickel, 27 mm. **Series:** Summer Olympics **Obv:** National arms **Rev:** Sprinters, denomination and date below **Edge:** Reeded

Date	Mintage	F	VF	XF	Unc	BU
1988	—	—	—	—	2.50	—
1988 Proof	300,000	Value: 3.50				

KM# 73 2 LEVA
Copper-Nickel, 30 mm. **Subject:** 1050th Anniversary - Death of Ochridsky, Founder of the First European University **Obv:** Denomination between columns **Rev:** Figure divides dates **Designer:** Krum Danjanov

Date	Mintage	F	VF	XF	Unc	BU
ND(1966)	506,000	—	1.00	2.00	4.00	—

KM# 75 2 LEVA
10.8000 g., Copper-Nickel, 30 mm. **Subject:** 25th Anniversary of Socialist Revolution, September 9, 1944 **Obv:** Large denomination between grain sprigs, date at bottom **Rev:** Monument to the Soviet Soldiers in Plovdiv

Date	Mintage	F	VF	XF	Unc	BU
1969	1,082,210	—	0.75	1.75	3.50	—

KM# 77 2 LEVA
Copper-Nickel, 30 mm. **Subject:** 90th Anniversary - Liberation from Turks **Obv:** Denomination within wreath, date below **Rev:** The Battle on the Orlovo Enesdo (Eagle's nest) by the Russian painter Popov, two dates below

Date	Mintage	F	VF	XF	Unc	BU
1969	756,759	—	0.75	1.75	3.50	—

KM# 80 2 LEVA
Nickel-Brass, 30 mm. **Subject:** 150th Anniversary - Birth of Dobri Chintulov **Obv:** Denomination above date **Rev:** Head facing, two dates below **Designer:** Lubomic Prahof and Dimitar Donowski

Date	Mintage	F	VF	XF	Unc	BU
1972	100,000	—	1.25	2.50	4.50	—

KM# 95.1 2 LEVA
Copper-Nickel, 30 mm. **Subject:** 100th Anniversary of the "April Uprising" Against the Turks **Obv:** Wreath above denomination, date at left, circle surrounds **Rev:** Figure with cannon, date at left, within circle

Date	Mintage	F	VF	XF	Unc	BU
1976	224,800	—	0.75	1.50	3.00	—
1976 Proof	—	Value: 5.00				

KM# 108 2 LEVA
Copper-Nickel, 30 mm. **Subject:** World Cup Soccer Games in Spain **Obv:** Soccer logo **Rev:** National arms within circle divides dates above denomination, grain sprigs flank **Edge:** Plain

Date	Mintage	F	VF	XF	Unc	BU
1980	220,000	—	0.60	1.20	2.50	—
1980 Proof	30,000	Value: 4.50				

KM# 110 2 LEVA
Copper-Nickel, 30 mm. **Subject:** 100th Anniversary - Birth of Yordan Yovkov, Writer **Obv:** Denomination above date **Rev:** Head facing, two dates below **Edge:** Plain

Date	Mintage	F	VF	XF	Unc	BU
1980	200,000	—	1.00	2.50	4.50	—

KM# 120 2 LEVA
Copper-Nickel, 30 mm. **Subject:** International Hunting Exposition **Obv:** National arms above denomination, date bottom left **Rev:** Half figure of hunter with hawk, left

Date	Mintage	F	VF	XF	Unc	BU
1981	250,000	—	0.75	1.50	3.00	—
1981 Proof	50,000	Value: 5.00				

REPUBLIC

STANDARD COINAGE

KM# 199 10 STOTINKI
1.6500 g., Nickel-Brass, 16.16 mm. **Obv:** Ancient lion sculpture left within circle **Rev:** Denomination divides date **Edge:** Reeded

Date	Mintage	F	VF	XF	Unc	BU
1992	—	—	—	—	0.25	0.35

KM# 200 20 STOTINKI
Nickel-Brass **Obv:** Ancient lion sculpture left within circle **Rev:** Denomination divides date

Date	Mintage	F	VF	XF	Unc	BU
1992	—	—	—	—	0.35	0.50

KM# 201 50 STOTINKI
3.0200 g., Nickel-Brass, 19.55 mm. **Obv:** Ancient lion sculpture left within circle **Rev:** Denomination divides date **Edge:** Reeded

Date	Mintage	F	VF	XF	Unc	BU
1992	—	—	—	—	0.50	0.75

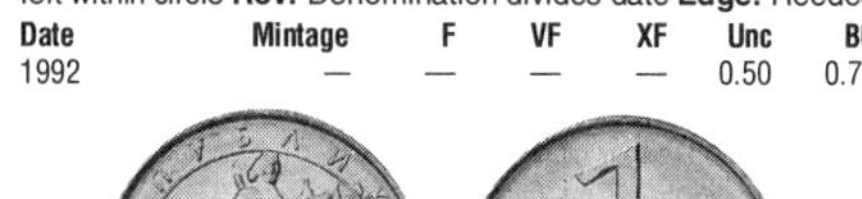

KM# 202 LEV
4.1200 g., Nickel-Brass, 23.19 mm. **Obv:** Madara horseman right within circle **Rev:** Denomination divides symbols, date below **Edge:** Reeded

Date	Mintage	F	VF	XF	Unc	BU
1992	—	—	—	—	0.75	1.00

KM# 203 2 LEVA
5.0800 g., Nickel-Brass, 25.14 mm. **Obv:** Madara horseman right within circle **Rev:** Denomination divides symbols, date below **Edge:** Reeded

Date	Mintage	F	VF	XF	Unc	BU
1992	—	—	—	—	1.25	1.50

KM# 204 5 LEVA
6.0000 g., Nickel-Brass, 27.13 mm. **Obv:** Madara horseman right within circle **Rev:** Denomination divides symbols, date below **Edge:** Reeded

Date	Mintage	F	VF	XF	Unc	BU
1992	—	—	—	—	1.75	2.00

KM# 205 10 LEVA
Copper-Nickel **Obv:** Madara horseman right within circle **Rev:** Denomination divides symbols, date below

Date	Mintage	F	VF	XF	Unc	BU
1992	—	—	—	—	2.50	3.00

KM# 224 10 LEVA
Brass **Obv:** Madara horseman right within circle **Rev:** Denomination divides symbols, date below **Note:** Reduced size and metal change.

Date	Mintage	F	VF	XF	Unc	BU
1997	—	—	—	—	1.25	1.50

KM# 228 20 LEVA
Brass **Obv:** Madara horseman right within circle **Rev:** Denomination divides symbols, date below

Date	Mintage	F	VF	XF	Unc	BU
1997	—	—	—	—	1.50	1.75

KM# 225 50 LEVA
Brass **Obv:** Madara horseman right within circle **Rev:** Denomination divides symbols, date below

Date	Mintage	F	VF	XF	Unc	BU
1997	—	—	—	—	1.75	2.00

REFORM COINAGE

KM# 237 STOTINKA
Brass, 16 mm. **Obv:** Madara horseman right, animal below **Rev:** Denomination above date **Edge:** Plain

Date	Mintage	F	VF	XF	Unc	BU
1999	1,277,500	—	—	—	0.25	0.35
2000	—	—	—	—	0.25	0.35
2002 Proof	10,000	Value: 1.00				

KM# 238 2 STOTINKI
Brass, 18 mm. **Obv:** Madara horseman right, animal below **Rev:** Denomination above date **Edge:** Plain

Date	Mintage	F	VF	XF	Unc	BU
1999	2,048,900	—	—	—	0.35	0.50
2000	—	—	—	—	0.35	0.50
2002 Proof	10,000	Value: 1.50				

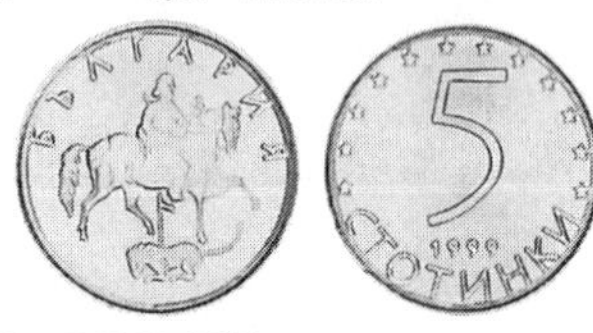

KM# 239 5 STOTINKI
Brass, 20 mm. **Obv:** Madara horseman right, animal below **Rev:** Denomination above date **Edge:** Plain **Note:** Prev. KM#A239.

Date	Mintage	F	VF	XF	Unc	BU
1999	3,453,025	—	—	—	0.50	0.65
2000	—	—	—	—	0.50	0.65
2002 Proof	10,000	Value: 2.00				

KM# 240 10 STOTINKI
Copper-Nickel, 18.5 mm. **Obv:** Madara horseman right, animal below **Rev:** Denomination above date **Edge:** Reeded

Date	Mintage	F	VF	XF	Unc	BU
1999	8,231,400	—	—	—	0.65	0.85
2002 Proof	10,000	Value: 2.50				

KM# 241 20 STOTINKI
Copper-Nickel, 20.5 mm. **Obv:** Madara horseman right, animal below **Rev:** Denomination above date **Edge:** Reeded

Date	Mintage	F	VF	XF	Unc	BU
1999	11,967,500	—	—	—	0.85	1.00
2002 Proof	10,000	Value: 3.00				

KM# 242 50 STOTINKI
Copper-Nickel, 22.5 mm. **Obv:** Madara horseman right, animal below **Rev:** Denomination above date **Edge:** Reeded

Date	Mintage	F	VF	XF	Unc	BU
1999	15,607,000	—	—	—	1.25	1.50
2002 Proof	10,000	Value: 5.00				

KM# 272 50 STOTINKI
Copper-Nickel, 22.5 mm. **Obv:** Stylized Bulgarian arms, lion left, NATO - 2004 under lion **Rev:** Denomination above date **Edge:** Reeded

Date	Mintage	F	VF	XF	Unc	BU
2004	—	—	—	—	2.00	3.00

KM# 274 50 STOTINKI
5.0300 g., Copper-Nickel, 22.6 mm. **Obv:** European Union seated woman allegory **Rev:** Value above date **Edge:** Reeded

Date	Mintage	F	VF	XF	Unc	BU
2005	—	—	—	—	1.25	1.75

KM# 276 50 STOTINKI
5.0000 g., Copper-Zinc-Nickel, 22.5 mm. **Obv:** Value **Rev:** Pillar behind open book **Edge:** Reeded

Date	Mintage	F	VF	XF	Unc	BU
2007	500,000	—	—	—	—	1.50

BURUNDI

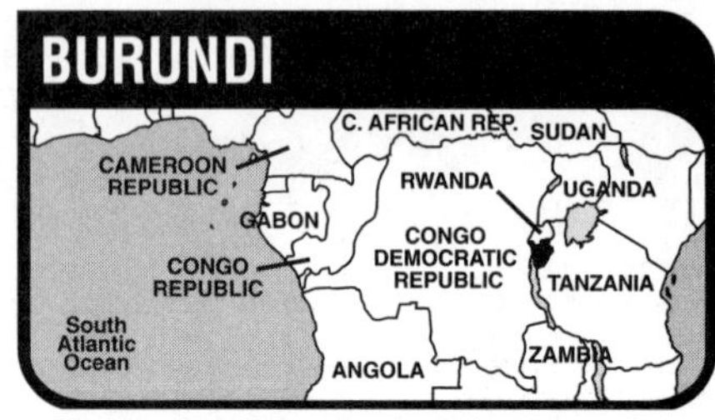

The Republic of Burundi, a landlocked country in central Africa, was a kingdom with a feudalistic society, caste system and Mwami (king) for more than 400 years before independence. It has an area of 10,740 sq. mi. (27,830 sq. km.) and a population of 6.3 million. Capital: Bujumbura. Plagued by poor soil, irregular rainfall and a single-crop economy, coffee, Burundi is barely able to feed itself. Coffee and tea are exported.

Although the area was visited by European explorers and missionaries in the latter half of the 19th century, it wasn't until the 1890s that it, together with Rwanda, fell under European domination as part of German East Africa. Following World War I, the territory was mandated to Belgium by the League of Nations and administered with the Belgian Congo. After World War II it became a U.N. Trust Territory. Limited self-government was established by U.N.-supervised elections in 1961. Burundi gained independence as a kingdom under Mwami Mwambutsa IV on July 1, 1962. The republic was established by military coup in 1966.

NOTE: For earlier coinage see Belgian Congo, and Rwanda and Burundi. For previously listed coinage dated 1966, coins of Mwambutsa IV and Ntare V, refer to *UNUSUAL WORLD COINS*, 3rd edition, Krause Publications, 1992.

RULERS
Mwambutsa IV, 1962-1966
Ntare V, 1966

MINT MARKS
PM - Pobjoy Mint
(b) - Privy Marks, Brussels

MONETARY SYSTEM
100 Centimes = 1 Franc

KINGDOM

STANDARD COINAGE

KM# 6 FRANC
Brass, 23 mm. **Obv:** Denomination within circle, circle with monogram below **Rev:** Arms above date **Edge:** Reeded

Date	Mintage	F	VF	XF	Unc	BU
1965	10,000,000	—	0.75	1.50	3.00	—

REPUBLIC
1966-
STANDARD COINAGE

KM# 18 FRANC
0.8400 g., Aluminum, 19.2 mm. **Obv:** Rising sun above date **Rev:** Denomination

Date	Mintage	F	VF	XF	Unc	BU
1970	10,000,000	2.00	4.50	7.50	17.50	20.00

KM# 19 FRANC
0.8700 g., Aluminum, 18.91 mm. **Obv:** Denomination **Rev:** Arms above date **Edge:** Reeded

Date	Mintage	F	VF	XF	Unc	BU
1976	5,000,000	—	0.30	0.75	1.75	2.50
1980	—	—	0.20	0.65	1.75	2.50
1990PM	—	—	0.15	0.50	1.50	2.00
1993PM	—	—	0.15	0.50	1.50	2.00

KM# 16 5 FRANCS
Aluminum **Obv:** Three stars at center, date below leaves **Rev:** Denomination within wreath

Date	Mintage	F	VF	XF	Unc	BU
1968(b)	2,000,000	—	0.25	0.85	2.00	2.75
1969(b)	2,000,000	—	0.25	0.85	2.00	2.75
1971(b)	2,000,000	—	0.25	0.85	2.00	2.75

KM# 20 5 FRANCS
2.2000 g., Aluminum, 25 mm. **Obv:** Arms above date **Rev:** Denomination

Date	Mintage	F	VF	XF	Unc	BU
1976	2,000,000	—	0.25	0.65	1.75	2.50
1980	—	—	0.25	0.65	1.75	2.50

KM# 17 10 FRANCS
7.8500 g., Copper-Nickel, 28 mm. **Series:** F.A.O. **Subject:** First Anniversary of Republic **Obv:** Date at center **Rev:** Denomination at center **Edge:** Reeded

Date	Mintage	F	VF	XF	Unc	BU
1968	2,000,000	—	0.75	1.50	3.50	4.00
1971	2,000,000	—	0.75	1.50	3.50	4.00

CAMBODIA

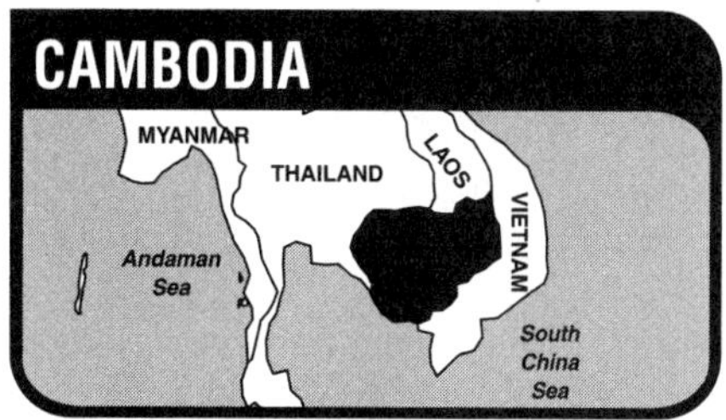

The State of Cambodia, formerly Democratic Kampuchea and the Khmer Republic, a land of paddy fields and forest-clad hills located on the Indo-Chinese peninsula, fronting on the Gulf of Thailand, has an area of 70,238 sq. mi. (181,040 sq. km.) and a population of *11.21 million. Capital: Phnom Penh. Agriculture is the basis of the economy, with rice the chief crop. Native industries include cattle breeding, weaving and rice milling. Rubber, cattle, corn, and timber are exported.

The region was the nucleus of the Khmer empire which flourished from the 5th to the 12th century and attained an excellence in art and architecture still evident in the magnificent ruins at Angkor. The Khmer empire once ruled over much of Southeast Asia, but began to decline in the 13th century as the Thai and Vietnamese invaded the region and attached its territories. At the request of the Cambodian king, a French protectorate attached to Cochin-China was established over the country in 1863, saving it from dissolution, and in 1885, Cambodia was included in the French Union of Indo-China.

France established a constitutional monarchy for Cambodia within the French Union in 1949. The 1954 Geneva Convention resulted in full independence for the Kingdom of Cambodia. King Sihanouk abdicated to his father and won the office of Prime Minister.

Prince Sihanouk was toppled by a bloodless coup led by Lon Nol in March of 1970. Sihanouk moved to Peking to head a government-in-exile. On Oct. 9, 1970, Cambodia became the Khmer Republic, and Lon Nol its President. The government of Lon Nol was in turn toppled, April 17, 1975, by the Khmer Rouge insurgents who took control of the government and renamed the country Democratic Kampuchea.

The Khmer Rouge completely eliminated the economy and created a state without money, exchange or barter while exterminating about 2 million Cambodians. These atrocities were finally halted at the beginning of 1979 when the Vietnamese regulars and Cambodian rebels launched an offensive that drove the Khmer Rouge out of Phnom Penh and the country acquired another new title - The Peoples Republic of Kampuchea.

In 1993 Prince Norodom Sihanouk returned to Kampuchea to lead the Supreme National Council.

RULERS

Kings of Cambodia

Norodom I, 1835-1904
Sisowath, 1904-1927
Sisowath Monivong, 1927-1941
Norodom Sihanouk, 1941-1955
Norodom Suramarit, 1955-1960
Heng Samrin, 1979-1985
Hun Sen, 1985-1991
Norodom Sihanouk, 1991-1993
Chairman, Supreme National Council
King, 1993-

MINT MARKS

(a) - Paris, privy marks only
(k) - Key, Havana, Cuba

MONETARY SYSTEM

(Until 1860)

2 Att = 1 Pe (Pey)
4 Pe = 1 Fuang (Fuong)
8 Fuang = 1 Tical
4 Salong = 1 Tical

(Commencing 1860)

100 Centimes = 1 Franc

INDEPENDENT KINGDOM
DECIMAL COINAGE

KM# 51 10 CENTIMES
Aluminum **Obv:** Bird statue left **Rev:** Denomination within wreath

Date	Mintage	F	VF	XF	Unc	BU
1953(a)	4,000,000	0.25	0.45	0.85	2.00	6.00

KM# 52 20 CENTIMES
Aluminum **Obv:** Two ceremonial bowls **Rev:** Denomination within wreath

Date	Mintage	F	VF	XF	Unc	BU
1953(a)	3,000,000	0.25	0.65	1.50	3.00	5.50

KM# 53 50 CENTIMES
Aluminum **Obv:** Royal emblem **Rev:** Denomination within wreath

Date	Mintage	F	VF	XF	Unc	BU
1953(a)	4,200,000	0.45	0.85	2.00	4.00	6.00

KM# 54 10 SEN
Aluminum, 23 mm. **Obv:** Bird statue left **Rev:** Denomination within wreath

Date	Mintage	F	VF	XF	Unc	BU
1959(a)	1,000,000	0.10	0.20	0.35	1.00	2.00

KM# 55 20 SEN
Aluminum, 27 mm. **Obv:** Two ceremonial bowls **Rev:** Denomination within wreath

Date	Mintage	F	VF	XF	Unc	BU
1959(a)	1,004,000	0.15	0.25	0.60	1.00	1.50

KM# 56 50 SEN
Aluminum **Obv:** Royal emblem **Rev:** Denomination within wreath

Date	Mintage	F	VF	XF	Unc	BU
1959(a)	3,399,000	0.20	0.35	0.75	1.50	2.50

KHMER REPUBLIC

1970 - 1975

DECIMAL COINAGE

KM# 59 RIEL

2.8500 g., Copper-Nickel, 19.42 mm. **Series:** F.A.O. **Obv:** Temple of Angkor Wat **Rev:** Grain bouquet, denomination **Edge:** Reeded

Date	Mintage	F	VF	XF	Unc	BU
1970	5,000,000	—	—	7.50	16.50	22.50

Note: According to the Royal Mint of Great Britain, this coin was minted at the Llantrissant Branch Mint in 1972 but dated 1969. According to the FAO, the coin was to have been dated 1971, but was "not minted" due to the fall of the Cambodian government in 1970. However, this coin was released in limited numbers in 1983. The photograph of the coin, supplied by the FAO, is dated 1970. This type is currently available from many sources in the numismatic market

PEOPLE'S REPUBLIC OF KAMPUCHEA

1979 - 1990

DECIMAL COINAGE

KM# 69 5 SEN

2.4900 g., Aluminum, 20.39 mm. **Obv:** Royal emblem **Rev:** Denomination, date at bottom **Edge:** Plain

Date	Mintage	F	VF	XF	Unc	BU
1979	—	—	0.60	1.25	3.00	4.00

KINGDOM

1993 -

DECIMAL COINAGE

KM# 92 50 RIELS

1.6000 g., Steel, 15.9 mm. **Obv:** Single towered building **Rev:** Denomination within wreath **Edge:** Plain

Date	Mintage	F	VF	XF	Unc	BU
BE2538-1994	—	—	—	—	0.25	0.45

KM# 93 100 RIELS

2.0000 g., Steel, 17.9 mm. **Obv:** Three-towered building **Rev:** Denomination within wreath

Date	Mintage	F	VF	XF	Unc	BU
BE2538-1994	—	—	—	—	0.50	0.85

KM# 94 200 RIELS

2.4000 g., Steel, 19.9 mm. **Obv:** 2 Ceremonial bowls **Rev:** Denomination within wreath

Date	Mintage	F	VF	XF	Unc	BU
BE2538-1994	—	—	—	—	1.00	1.50

KM# 95 500 RIELS

6.5000 g., Bi-Metallic Steel center in Brass ring, 25.8 mm. **Obv:** Royal emblem **Rev:** Denomination within wreath **Edge:** Plain and reeded sections

Date	Mintage	F	VF	XF	Unc	BU
BE2538-1994	—	—	—	—	4.50	6.00

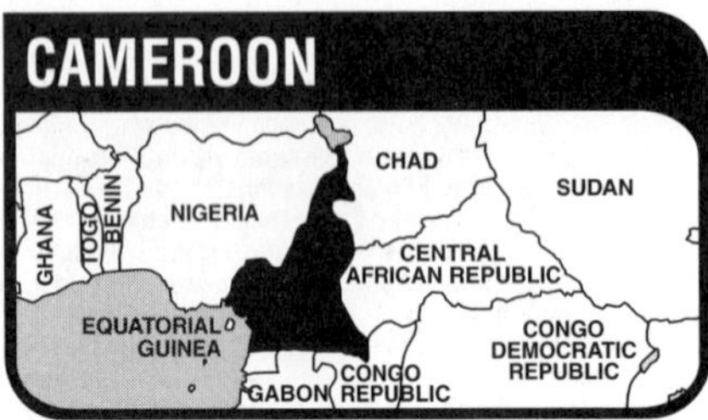

The Republic of Cameroon, located in west-central Africa on the Gulf of Guinea, has an area of 183,569 sq. mi. (475,445 sq. km.) and a population of *15.13 million. Capital: Yaounde. About 90 percent of the labor force is employed on the land; cash crops account for 80 percent of the country's export revenue. Cocoa, coffee, aluminum, cotton, rubber, and timber are exported.

European contact with what is now the United Republic of Cameroon began in the 16th century with the voyage of Portuguese navigator Fernando Po. The following three centuries saw continuous activity by Spanish, Dutch, and British traders and missionaries. The land was spared colonial rule until 1884, when treaties with tribal chiefs brought German domination. In 1919, the League of Nations divided the Cameroons between Great Britain and France, with the larger eastern area going to France. The French and British mandates were converted into United Nations trusteeships in 1946. French Cameroon became the independent Cameroon Republic on Jan. 1, 1960. The federation of East (French) and West (British) Cameroon was established in 1961 when the southern part of British Cameroon voted for reunification with the Cameroon Republic, and the northern part for union with Nigeria Cameroon joined the Commonwealth of Nations in November 1995.

Coins of French Equatorial Africa and of the monetary unions identified as the Equatorial African States and Central African States are also current in Cameroon.

MINT MARKS

(a) - Paris, privy marks only
SA - Pretoria, 1943

MONETARY SYSTEM

100 Centimes = 1 Franc

FRENCH MANDATE

STANDARD COINAGE

KM# 1 50 CENTIMES

2.5300 g., Aluminum-Bronze **Obv:** Laureate head left, date below **Obv. Designer:** A. Patay **Rev:** Spray of branches below denomination

Date	Mintage	F	VF	XF	Unc	BU
1924(a)	4,000,000	1.50	3.50	45.00	100	250
1925(a)	2,500,000	2.00	5.00	50.00	110	275
1926(a)	7,800,000	1.00	2.00	30.00	75.00	200

KM# 4 50 CENTIMES

Bronze, 20.2 mm. **Obv:** Rooster left, monogramed shield top right **Rev:** Cross of Lorraine divides denomination below, date at bottom

Date	Mintage	F	VF	XF	Unc	BU
1943SA	4,000,000	2.00	3.50	12.00	28.00	38.00

KM# 6 50 CENTIMES

Bronze **Obv:** Rooster left, monogramed shield at top right, LIBRE added to legend **Rev:** Cross of Lorraine divides denomination below, date at bottom

Date	Mintage	F	VF	XF	Unc	BU
1943SA	4,000,000	2.50	5.50	12.00	22.00	30.00

KM# 2 FRANC

Aluminum-Bronze, 23 mm. **Obv:** Laureate head left, date below **Obv. Designer:** A. Patay **Rev:** Denomination above three branched spray **Edge:** Reeded

Date	Mintage	F	VF	XF	Unc	BU
1924(a)	3,000,000	2.00	4.00	45.00	100	260
1925(a)	1,722,000	3.00	6.00	60.00	125	285
1926(a)	12,928,000	1.00	2.00	25.00	60.00	150

KM# 5 FRANC

Bronze **Obv:** Rooster left, monogrammed shield top right **Rev:** Cross of Lorraine divides denomination below, date at bottom

Date	Mintage	F	VF	XF	Unc	BU
1943SA	3,000,000	2.50	4.50	17.50	32.00	42.00

KM# 7 FRANC

Bronze **Obv:** Rooster left, monogrammed shield at top right, LIBRE added to legend **Rev:** Cross of Lorraine divides denomination below, date at bottom

Date	Mintage	F	VF	XF	Unc	BU
1943SA	3,000,000	3.50	6.50	20.00	38.00	48.00

KM# 8 FRANC

Aluminum **Obv:** Winged bust left, date below **Obv. Designer:** G.B.L. Bazor **Rev:** Gazelle (gazella Leptoceros), antlers divide denomination

Date	Mintage	F	VF	XF	Unc	BU
1948(a)	8,000,000	0.15	0.35	0.85	1.50	2.50

KM# 3 2 FRANCS

Aluminum-Bronze **Obv:** Laureate head left, date below **Obv. Designer:** A. Patay **Rev:** Denomination above three branch spray

Date	Mintage	F	VF	XF	Unc	BU
1924(a)	500,000	5.00	15.00	100	185	300
1925(a)	100,000	8.00	25.00	160	300	500

KM# 9 2 FRANCS
2.2100 g., Aluminum, 27 mm. **Obv:** Winged bust left, date bilow **Obv. Designer:** G.G. L. Bazor **Rev:** Gazelle (gazella leptoceros), antlers divide denomination

Date	Mintage	F	VF	XF	Unc	BU
1948(a)	5,000,000	0.65	1.25	2.00	4.00	6.00

FRENCH EQUATORIAL AFRICA - CAMEROON

STANDARD COINAGE

KM# 10 5 FRANCS
Aluminum-Bronze **Obv:** Three giant eland **Obv. Designer:** G. B. L. Bazor **Rev:** Denomination

Date	Mintage	F	VF	XF	Unc	BU
1958(a)	30,000,000	0.25	0.50	1.00	3.00	5.00

KM# 11 10 FRANCS
Aluminum-Bronze **Obv:** Three giant eland left, date below **Obv. Designer:** G. B. L. Bazor **Rev:** Denomination within wreath

Date	Mintage	F	VF	XF	Unc	BU
1958(a)	25,000,000	0.25	0.50	1.50	4.00	6.00

KM# 12 25 FRANCS
Aluminum-Bronze **Obv:** Three giant eland left, date below **Obv. Designer:** G. B. L. Bazor **Rev:** Denomination within wreath

Date	Mintage	F	VF	XF	Unc	BU
1958(a)	12,000,000	0.50	1.00	2.00	6.00	8.00

REPUBLIC

STANDARD COINAGE

KM# 13 50 FRANCS
Copper-Nickel, 30 mm. **Subject:** Independence Commemorative **Obv:** Three giant eland left, date above **Obv. Designer:** G. B. L. Bazor **Rev:** Denomination within wreath

Date	Mintage	F	VF	XF	Unc	BU
1960(a)	9,000,000	2.00	3.50	5.50	10.00	12.50

KM# 14 100 FRANCS
12.0000 g., Nickel **Obv:** Three giant eland left **Obv. Designer:** G. B. L. Bazor **Rev:** Denomination, date above **Note:** KM#14 was issued double thick and should not be considered a piefort.

Date	Mintage	F	VF	XF	Unc	BU
1966(a)	4,000,000	1.00	2.00	4.50	10.00	12.50
1967(a)	4,000,000	1.00	2.00	4.50	10.00	12.50
1968(a)	5,000,000	1.00	2.00	4.50	10.00	12.50

KM# 15 100 FRANCS
Nickel **Obv:** Three giant eland left **Obv. Designer:** G. B. L. Bazor **Rev:** Denomination within circle, date below **Note:** Refer also to Equatorial African States and Central African States.

Date	Mintage	F	VF	XF	Unc	BU
1971(a)	9,000,000	2.00	3.00	6.00	12.50	—
1972(a)	3,000,000	2.00	3.00	6.00	12.50	—

KM# 16 100 FRANCS
Nickel **Obv:** Three giant eland left **Obv. Designer:** G. B. L. Bazor **Rev:** Denomination within circle, date below **Note:** Mule

Date	Mintage	F	VF	XF	Unc	BU
1972(a)	4,000,000	6.50	12.50	22.50	45.00	—

KM# 17 100 FRANCS
Nickel **Obv:** Three giant eland left **Obv. Designer:** G. B. L. Bazor **Rev:** Denomination above date, within circle

Date	Mintage	F	VF	XF	Unc	BU
1975(a)	—	1.00	2.00	3.00	5.50	7.00
1980(a)	—	1.00	2.00	3.00	5.50	7.00
1982(a)	—	0.75	1.50	2.50	4.50	6.00
1983(a)	—	0.75	1.50	2.50	4.50	6.00
1984(a)	—	0.75	1.50	2.50	4.50	6.00
1986(a)	—	0.75	1.50	2.50	4.50	6.00

KM# 23 500 FRANCS
10.8900 g., Copper-Nickel, 30.04 mm. **Obv:** Plants divide denomination and date **Rev:** Head 3/4 left

Date	Mintage	F	VF	XF	Unc	BU
1985(a)	—	2.00	3.50	5.50	10.00	12.50
1986(a)	—	2.00	3.50	5.50	10.00	12.50
1988	—	2.00	3.50	5.50	10.00	12.50

CANADA

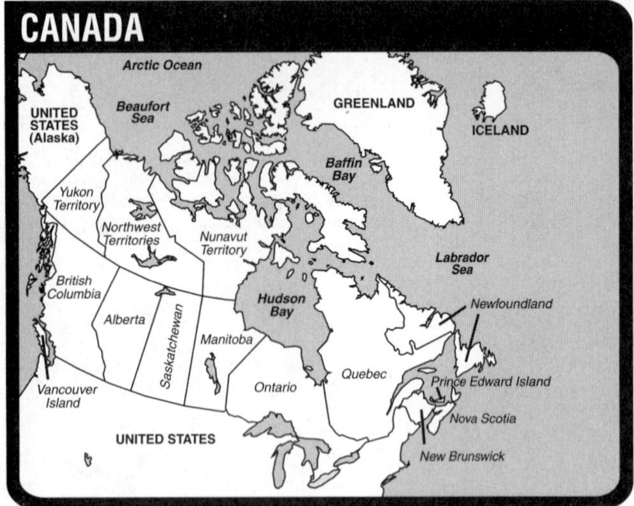

Canada is located to the north of the United States, and spans the full breadth of the northern portion of North America from Atlantic to Pacific oceans, except for the State of Alaska. It has a total area of 3,850,000 sq. mi. (9,971,550 sq. km.) and a population of 30.29 million. Capital: Ottawa.

Jacques Cartier, a French explorer, took possession of Canada for France in 1534, and for more than a century the history of Canada was that of a French colony. Samuel de Champlain helped to establish the first permanent colony in North America, in 1604 at Port Royal, Acadia – now Annapolis Royal, Nova Scotia. Four years later he founded the settlement in Quebec.

The British settled along the coast to the south while the French, motivated by a grand design, pushed into the interior. France's plan for a great American empire was to occupy the Mississippi heartland of the country, and from there to press in upon the narrow strip of English coastal settlements from the west. Inevitably, armed conflict erupted between the French and the British; consequently, Britain acquired Hudson Bay, Newfoundland and Nova Scotia from the French in 1713. British control of the rest of New France was secured in 1763, largely because of James Wolfe's great victory over Montcalm near Quebec in 1759.

During the American Revolution, Canada became a refuge for great numbers of American Royalists, most of whom settled in Ontario, thereby creating an English majority west of the Ottawa River. The ethnic imbalance contravened the effectiveness of the prevailing French type of government, and in 1791 the Constitutional act was passed by the British parliament, dividing Canada at the Ottawa River into two parts, each with its own government: Upper Canada, chiefly English and consisting of the southern section of what is now Ontario; and Lower Canada, chiefly French and consisting principally of the southern section of Quebec. Subsequent revolt by dissidents in both sections caused the British government to pass the Union Act, July 23, 1840, which united Lower and Upper Canada (as Canada East and Canada West) to form the Province of Canada, with one council and one assembly in which the two sections had equal numbers.

The union of the two provinces did not encourage political stability; the equal strength of the French and British made the task of government all but impossible. A further change was made with the passage of the British North American Act, which took effect on July 1, 1867, and established Canada as the first federal union in the British Empire. Four provinces entered the union at first: Upper Canada as Ontario, Lower Canada as Quebec, Nova Scotia and New Brunswick. The Hudson Bay Company's territories were acquired in 1869 out of which were formed the provinces of Manitoba, Saskatchewan and Alberta. British Columbia joined in 1871 and Prince Edward Island in 1873. Canada took over the Arctic Archipelago in 1895. In 1949 Newfoundland came into the confederation.

In the early years, Canada's coins were struck in England at the Royal Mint in London or at the Heaton Mint in Birmingham. Issues struck at the Royal Mint do not bear a mint mark, but those produced by Heaton carry an "H". All Canadian coins have been struck since January 2, 1908, at the Royal Canadian Mints at Ottawa and recently at Winnipeg except for some 1968 pure nickel dimes struck at the U.S. Mint in Philadelphia, and do not bear mint marks. Ottawa's mint mark (C) does not appear on some 20th Century Newfoundland issues, however, as it does on English type sovereigns struck there from 1908 through 1918.

Canada is a member of the Commonwealth of Nations. Elizabeth II is Head of State as Queen of Canada.

RULER
British 1763-

MONETARY SYSTEM
1 Dollar = 100 Cents

CONFEDERATION

CIRCULATION COINAGE

KM# 7 CENT **Weight:** 4.5400 g. **Composition:** Bronze **Ruler:** Victoria **Obverse:** Crowned head left within beaded circle **Obv. Legend:** VICTORIA DEI GRATIA REGINA.

CANADA **Obv. Designer:** Leonard C. Wyon **Reverse:** Denomination and date within beaded circle, chain of leaves surrounds **Edge:** Plain **Size:** 25.5 mm.

Date	Mintage	VG-8	F-12	VF-20	XF-40	MS-60	MS-63	Proof
1901	4,100,000	2.25	4.50	3.00	8.50	35.00	85.00	—

KM# 8 CENT **Weight:** 4.5400 g. **Composition:** Bronze **Ruler:** Edward VII **Obverse:** Kings bust right within beaded circle **Obv. Designer:** G. W. DeSaulles **Reverse:** Denomination above date within circle, chain of leaves surrounds **Edge:** Plain **Size:** 25.5 mm.

Date	Mintage	VG-8	F-12	VF-20	XF-40	MS-60	MS-63	Proof
1902	3,000,000	1.75	2.25	3.50	6.00	25.00	75.00	—
1903	4,000,000	1.75	2.25	3.00	6.00	30.00	80.00	—
1904	2,500,000	2.00	3.50	5.00	8.00	35.00	85.00	—
1905	2,000,000	3.50	6.00	7.50	12.00	45.00	150	—
1906	4,100,000	1.75	2.25	3.00	6.00	35.00	175	—
1907	2,400,000	2.00	3.50	4.50	9.00	35.00	200	—
1907H	800,000	12.00	24.00	30.00	50.00	175	550	—
1908	2,401,506	3.00	3.50	5.00	8.00	30.00	90.00	150
1909	3,973,339	1.75	2.50	3.00	6.00	30.00	100	—
1910	5,146,487	1.75	2.50	3.00	5.00	26.00	70.00	—

KM# 15 CENT **Weight:** 4.5400 g. **Composition:** Bronze **Ruler:** George V **Obverse:** King's bust left **Obv. Designer:** E. B. MacKennal **Reverse:** Denomination above date within beaded circle, chain of leaves surrounds **Edge:** Plain **Size:** 25.5 mm.

Date	Mintage	VG-8	F-12	VF-20	XF-40	MS-60	MS-63	Proof
1911	4,663,486	0.80	1.30	1.75	3.50	25.00	75.00	250

KM# 21 CENT **Weight:** 4.5400 g. **Composition:** Bronze **Ruler:** George V **Obverse:** King's bust left **Obv. Designer:** E. B. MacKennal **Reverse:** Denomination above date within beaded circle, chain of leaves surrounds **Edge:** Plain **Size:** 25.5 mm.

Date	Mintage	VG-8	F-12	VF-20	XF-40	MS-60	MS-63	Proof
1912	5,107,642	0.75	1.50	2.25	3.50	25.00	80.00	—
1913	5,735,405	0.75	1.50	2.25	4.00	23.00	80.00	—
1914	3,405,958	1.00	1.50	2.50	4.00	35.00	125	—
1915	4,932,134	0.75	2.25	3.00	4.00	30.00	100	—
1916	11,022,367	0.50	0.65	1.25	3.00	16.00	50.00	—
1917	11,899,254	0.50	0.65	0.90	2.25	13.00	45.00	—
1918	12,970,798	0.50	0.65	0.90	2.25	12.00	45.00	—
1919	11,279,634	0.50	0.65	0.90	2.25	12.00	45.00	—
1920	6,762,247	0.60	0.75	1.00	2.25	20.00	100	—

Dot below date

KM# 28 CENT **Weight:** 3.2400 g. **Composition:** Bronze **Ruler:** George V **Obverse:** King's bust left **Obv. Designer:** E. B. MacKennal **Reverse:** Denomination above date, leaves flank **Rev. Designer:** Fred Lewis **Edge:** Plain **Size:** 19.10 mm.

Date	Mintage	VG-8	F-12	VF-20	XF-40	MS-60	MS-63	Proof
1920	15,483,923	0.20	0.50	1.00	2.00	15.00	50.00	—
1921	7,601,627	0.50	0.75	1.75	5.00	35.00	200	—
1922	1,243,635	13.00	16.00	21.00	35.00	200	1,200	—
1923	1,019,002	29.00	35.00	40.00	50.00	300	2,000	—
1924	1,593,195	5.00	6.50	8.50	15.00	125	850	—
1925	1,000,622	18.00	21.00	27.00	40.00	200	1,600	—
1926	2,143,372	3.50	4.50	7.00	11.00	100	650	—
1927	3,553,928	1.25	2.00	3.50	6.00	40.00	225	—
1928	9,144,860	0.15	0.30	0.65	1.50	20.00	90.00	—
1929	12,159,840	0.15	0.30	0.65	1.50	20.00	80.00	—
1930	2,538,613	2.00	2.50	4.50	8.50	50.00	225	—
1931	3,842,776	0.65	1.00	2.50	5.50	40.00	200	—
1932	21,316,190	0.15	0.20	0.50	1.50	14.00	45.00	—
1933	12,079,310	0.15	0.30	0.50	1.50	15.00	65.00	—
1934	7,042,358	0.20	0.30	0.75	1.50	14.00	45.00	—
1935	7,526,400	0.20	0.30	0.75	1.50	14.00	45.00	—
1936	8,768,769	0.15	0.30	0.75	1.50	14.00	45.00	—
1936 dot below date; Rare	678,823	—	—	—	—	—	—	—

Note: Only one possible business strike is known to exist. No other examples (or possible business strikes) have ever surfaced.

Date	Mintage	VG-8	F-12	VF-20	XF-40	MS-60	MS-63	Proof
1936 dot below date, specimen, 3 known	—	—	—	—	—	—	—	—

Note: At the David Akers auction of the John Jay Pittman collection (Part 1, 10-97), a gem specimen realized $121,000. At the David Akers auction of the John Jay Pittman collection (Part 3, 10-99), a near choice specimen realized $115,000.

Maple leaf

KM# 32 CENT **Weight:** 3.2400 g. **Composition:** Bronze **Ruler:** George VI **Obverse:** Head left **Obv. Designer:** T. H. Paget **Reverse:** Maple leaf divides date and denomination **Rev. Designer:** George E. Kruger-Gray **Edge:** Plain **Size:** 19.10 mm.

Date	Mintage	VG-8	F-12	VF-20	XF-40	MS-60	MS-63	Proof
1937	10,040,231	0.35	0.50	1.00	2.00	3.00	9.00	—
1938	18,365,608	0.15	0.20	0.35	0.75	3.00	13.00	—
1939	21,600,319	0.10	0.20	0.35	0.70	1.75	5.00	—
1940	85,740,532	0.10	0.15	0.25	0.50	2.25	5.50	—
1941	56,336,011	0.10	0.15	0.25	0.50	8.00	60.00	—
1942	76,113,708	0.10	0.15	0.25	0.50	8.00	60.00	—
1943	89,111,969	0.10	0.15	0.25	0.45	3.50	25.00	—
1944	44,131,216	0.10	0.15	0.30	0.60	12.00	100	—
1945	77,268,591	0.10	0.15	0.20	0.35	3.00	22.00	—
1946	56,662,071	0.10	0.15	0.20	0.35	3.00	7.50	—
1947	31,093,901	0.10	0.15	0.20	0.35	3.00	7.50	—
1947 maple leaf	47,855,448	0.10	0.15	0.20	0.35	3.00	5.00	—

KM# 41 CENT **Weight:** 3.2400 g. **Composition:** Bronze **Ruler:** George VI **Obverse:** Modified legend **Obv. Designer:** T. H. Paget **Rev. Designer:** George E. Kruger-Gray **Edge:** Plain **Size:** 19.10 mm.

Date	Mintage	VG-8	F-12	VF-20	XF-40	MS-60	MS-63	Proof
1948	25,767,779	—	0.15	0.25	0.70	4.00	35.00	—
1949	33,128,933	—	0.10	0.15	0.35	3.00	9.00	—
1950	60,444,992	—	0.10	0.15	0.25	2.00	9.00	—
1951	80,430,379	—	0.10	0.15	0.20	2.00	13.00	—
1952	67,631,736	—	0.10	0.15	0.20	2.00	7.00	—

No strap

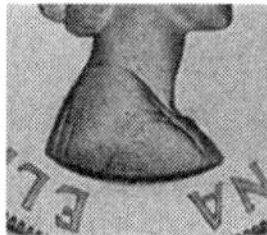
With strap

KM# 49 CENT **Weight:** 3.2400 g. **Composition:** Bronze **Ruler:** Elizabeth II **Obverse:** Laureate bust right **Obv. Designer:** Mary Gillick **Reverse:** Maple leaf divides date and denomination **Rev. Designer:** George E. Kruger-Gray **Size:** 19.10 mm.

Date	Mintage	VG-8	F-12	VF-20	XF-40	MS-60	MS-63	Proof
1953	67,806,016	0.10	0.10	0.10	0.35	0.65	1.50	—
Note: Without strap								
1953	Inc. above	0.50	1.00	1.50	2.50	12.00	55.00	—
Note: With strap								
1954	22,181,760	0.10	0.10	0.10	0.40	2.00	6.00	—
Note: With strap								
1954 Prooflike only	Inc. above	—	—	—	—	250	500	—
Note: Without strap								
1955	56,403,193	—	0.10	0.10	0.20	0.55	1.50	—
Note: With strap								
1955	Inc. above	85.00	125	150	250	600	1,800	—
Note: Without strap								
1956	78,658,535	—	—	—	0.15	0.50	0.90	—
1957	100,601,792	—	—	—	0.10	0.30	0.60	—
1958	59,385,679	—	—	—	0.10	0.30	0.60	—
1959	83,615,343	—	—	—	0.10	0.15	0.30	—
1960	75,772,775	—	—	—	0.10	0.15	0.30	—
1961	139,598,404	—	—	—	—	0.15	0.30	—
1962	227,244,069	—	—	—	—	0.15	0.30	—
1963	279,076,334	—	—	—	—	0.15	0.30	—
1964	484,655,322	—	—	—	—	0.15	0.30	—

KM# 59.1 CENT **Weight:** 3.2400 g. **Composition:** Bronze **Ruler:** Elizabeth II **Obverse:** Queens bust right **Obv. Designer:** Arnold Machin **Reverse:** Maple leaf divides date and denomination **Rev. Designer:** George E. Kruger-Gray **Edge:** Plain **Size:** 19.10 mm.

Date	Mintage	VG-8	F-12	VF-20	XF-40	MS-60	MS-63	Proof
1965	304,441,082	—	—	—	0.40	1.00	4.00	—
Note: Small beads, pointed 5								
1965	Inc. above	—	—	—	—	0.10	0.20	—
Note: Small beads, blunt 5								
1965	Inc. above	—	—	4.50	7.50	18.00	35.00	—
Note: Large beads, pointed 5								
1965	Inc. above	—	—	—	0.10	0.10	0.20	—
Note: Large beads, blunt 5								
1966	184,151,087	—	—	—	—	0.10	0.20	—
1968	329,695,772	—	—	—	—	0.10	0.15	—
1969	335,240,929	—	—	—	—	0.10	0.15	—
1970	311,145,010	—	—	—	—	0.10	0.15	—
1971	298,228,936	—	—	—	—	0.10	0.15	—
1972	451,304,591	—	—	—	—	0.10	0.15	—
1973	457,059,852	—	—	—	—	0.10	0.15	—
1974	692,058,489	—	—	—	—	0.10	0.15	—
1975	642,318,000	—	—	—	—	0.10	0.15	—
1976	701,122,890	—	—	—	—	0.10	0.15	—
1977	453,762,670	—	—	—	—	0.10	0.15	—
1978	911,170,647	—	—	—	—	0.10	0.15	—

KM# 65 CENT **Composition:** Bronze **Ruler:** Elizabeth II **Subject:** Confederation Centennial **Obverse:** Queen's bust right **Obv. Designer:** Arnold Machin **Reverse:** Dove with wings spread, denomination above, two dates below **Rev. Designer:** Alex Coville **Size:** 19.10 mm.

Date	Mintage	VG-8	F-12	VF-20	XF-40	MS-60	MS-63	Proof
ND(1967)	345,140,645	—	—	—	—	0.10	0.20	1.00

KM# 59.2 CENT **Weight:** 3.2400 g. **Composition:** Bronze **Ruler:** Elizabeth II **Obverse:** Queen's bust right **Obv. Designer:** Arnold Machin **Reverse:** Dove with wings spread, denomination above, dates below **Rev. Designer:** George E. Kruger-Gray **Edge:** Plain **Size:** 19.10 mm.

Date	Mintage	VG-8	F-12	VF-20	XF-40	MS-60	MS-63	Proof
1979	754,394,064	—	—	—	—	0.10	0.15	—

KM# 127 CENT **Weight:** 2.8000 g. **Composition:** Bronze **Ruler:** Elizabeth II **Obverse:** Queen's bust right **Obv. Designer:** Arnold Machin **Rev. Designer:** George E. Kruger-Gray **Edge:** Plain **Size:** 19.10 mm. **Note:** Reduced weight.

Date	Mintage	VG-8	F-12	VF-20	XF-40	MS-60	MS-63	Proof
1980	912,052,318	—	—	—	—	0.10	0.15	—
1981	1,209,468,500	—	—	—	—	0.10	0.15	—
1981 Proof	199,000	—	—	—	—	—	—	1.50

KM# 132 CENT **Weight:** 2.5000 g. **Composition:** Bronze **Ruler:** Elizabeth II **Obverse:** Queen's bust right **Obv. Designer:** Arnold Machin **Reverse:** Maple leaf divides date and denomination **Rev. Designer:** George E. Kruger-Gray **Edge:** Plain **Size:** 19.10 mm. **Note:** Reduced weight.

Date	Mintage	VG-8	F-12	VF-20	XF-40	MS-60	MS-63	Proof
1982	911,001,000	—	—	—	—	0.10	0.15	—
1982 Proof	180,908	—	—	—	—	—	—	1.50
1983	975,510,000	—	—	—	—	0.10	0.15	—
1983 Proof	168,000	—	—	—	—	—	—	1.50
1984	838,225,000	—	—	—	—	0.10	0.15	—
1984 Proof	161,602	—	—	—	—	—	—	1.50
1985	771,772,500	—	—	—	3.00	10.00	19.00	—
Note: Pointed 5								
1985	Inc. above	—	—	—	—	0.10	0.15	—
Note: Blunt 5								
1985 Proof	157,037	—	—	—	—	—	—	1.50
Note: Blunt 5								
1986	740,335,000	—	—	—	—	0.10	0.15	—
1986 Proof	175,745	—	—	—	—	—	—	1.50
1987	774,549,000	—	—	—	—	0.10	0.15	—
1987 Proof	179,004	—	—	—	—	—	—	1.50
1988	482,676,752	—	—	—	—	0.10	0.15	—
1988 Proof	175,259	—	—	—	—	—	—	1.50
1989	1,077,347,200	—	—	—	—	0.10	0.15	—
1989 Proof	170,928	—	—	—	—	—	—	1.50

KM# 181 CENT **Weight:** 2.5000 g. **Composition:** Bronze **Ruler:** Elizabeth II **Obverse:** Crowned Queen's head right **Obv. Designer:** Dora dePedery-Hunt **Reverse:** Maple leaf divides date and denomination **Rev. Designer:** George E. Kruger-Gray **Edge:** Plain **Size:** 19.10 mm.

Date	Mintage	VG-8	F-12	VF-20	XF-40	MS-60	MS-63	Proof
1990	218,035,000	—	—	—	—	0.10	0.15	—
1990 Proof	140,649	—	—	—	—	—	—	2.50
1991	831,001,000	—	—	—	—	0.10	0.15	—
1991 Proof	131,888	—	—	—	—	—	—	3.50
1993	752,034,000	—	—	—	—	0.10	0.15	—
1993 Proof	145,065	—	—	—	—	—	—	2.00
1994	639,516,000	—	—	—	—	0.10	0.15	—
1994 Proof	146,424	—	—	—	—	—	—	2.50
1995	624,983,000	—	—	—	—	0.10	0.15	—
1995 Proof	—	—	—	—	—	—	—	2.50
1996	445,746,000	—	—	—	—	0.10	0.15	—
1996 Proof	—	—	—	—	—	—	—	2.50

KM# 204 CENT **Composition:** Bronze **Ruler:** Elizabeth II **Subject:** Confederation 125 **Obverse:** Crowned Queen's head right **Obv. Designer:** Dora dePedery-Hunt **Reverse:** Maple leaf divides date and denomination **Rev. Designer:** George E. Kruger-Gray **Size:** 19.10 mm.

Date	Mintage	VG-8	F-12	VF-20	XF-40	MS-60	MS-63	Proof
ND(1992)	673,512,000	—	—	—	—	0.10	0.15	—
ND(1992) Proof	147,061	—	—	—	—	—	—	2.50

KM# 289 CENT Composition: Copper Plated Steel **Ruler:** Elizabeth II **Obverse:** Crowned head right **Obv. Designer:** Dora dePédery-Hunt **Reverse:** Maple twig design **Rev. Designer:** George E. Kruger-Gray **Edge:** Round and plain **Size:** 19.1 mm.

Date	Mintage	VG-8	F-12	VF-20	XF-40	MS-60	MS-63	Proof
1997	549,868,000	—	—	—	—	0.10	0.15	—
1997 Proof	—	—	—	—	—	—	—	2.75
1998	999,578,000	—	—	—	—	0.10	0.15	—
1998 Proof	—	—	—	—	—	—	—	3.00
1998W	—	—	—	—	—	—	1.75	—
1999P	—	—	—	—	—	—	6.00	—
Note: Plated planchet, set only								
1999	1,089,625,000	—	—	—	—	0.10	0.15	—
1999W	—	—	—	—	—	—	—	—
1999 Proof	—	—	—	—	—	—	—	4.00
2000	771,908,206	—	—	—	—	0.10	0.15	—
2000 Proof	—	—	—	—	—	—	—	4.00
2000W	—	—	—	—	—	—	1.75	—
2001	919,358,000	—	—	—	—	—	0.10	—
2001P Proof	—	—	—	—	—	—	—	5.00
2003	92,219,775	—	—	—	—	—	0.10	—
2003P Proof	—	—	—	—	—	—	—	5.00
2003P	235,936,799	—	—	—	—	—	1.50	—

KM# 445 CENT Composition: Copper Plated Steel **Ruler:** Elizabeth II **Subject:** Elizabeth II Golden Jubilee **Obverse:** Crowned head right, Jubilee commemorative dates 1952-2002 **Obv. Designer:** Dora dePédery-Hunt **Reverse:** Denomination above maple leaves **Rev. Designer:** George E. Kruger-Gray **Edge:** Plain **Size:** 19.1 mm.

Date	Mintage	VG-8	F-12	VF-20	XF-40	MS-60	MS-63	Proof
ND(2002)	—	—	—	—	—	—	0.75	—
ND(2002)P	—	—	—	—	—	—	1.00	—
ND(2002)	—	—	—	—	—	—	—	2.50
Note: In proof sets only								

KM# 490 CENT Composition: Copper Plated Zinc **Ruler:** Elizabeth II **Obverse:** New effigy of Queen Elizabeth II right **Obv. Designer:** Susanna Blunt **Edge:** Plain **Size:** 19.1 mm.

Date	Mintage	MS-63	Proof
2003	56,877,144	0.25	—
2004	653,317,000	0.25	—
2004 Proof	—	—	2.50
2005	759,658,000	0.25	—
2005 Proof	—	—	2.50
2006	1,062,275,000	0.25	—
2006 Proof	—	—	2.50
2007(ml)	—	0.25	—
2007(ml) Proof	—	—	2.50

KM# 2 5 CENTS Weight: 1.1620 g. **Composition:** 0.9250 Silver 0.0346 oz. ASW **Ruler:** Victoria **Obverse:** Head left **Obv. Legend:** VICTORIA DEI GRATIA REGINA. CANADA **Reverse:** Denomination and date within wreath, crown above

Date	Mintage	VG-8	F-12	VF-20	XF-40	MS-60	MS-63	Proof
1901	2,000,000	4.50	6.50	12.00	35.00	150	400	—

KM# 9 5 CENTS Weight: 1.1620 g. **Composition:** 0.9250 Silver 0.0346 oz. ASW **Ruler:** Edward VII **Obv. Designer:** G. W. DeSaulles **Rev. Designer:** Leonard C. Wyon

Date	Mintage	VG-8	F-12	VF-20	XF-40	MS-60	MS-63	Proof
1902	2,120,000	2.25	3.00	4.00	7.00	35.00	55.00	—
1902	2,200,000	2.25	3.25	5.50	11.00	35.00	60.00	—
Note: Large broad H								
1902	Inc. above	7.50	13.00	24.00	40.00	100	175	—
Note: Small narrow H								

KM# 13 5 CENTS Weight: 1.1620 g. **Composition:** 0.9250 Silver 0.0346 oz. ASW **Ruler:** Edward VII **Obverse:** King's bust right **Reverse:** Denomination and date within wreath, crown at top

Date	Mintage	VG-8	F-12	VF-20	XF-40	MS-60	MS-63	Proof
1903	1,000,000	4.00	7.00	17.00	35.00	150	350	—
Note: 22 leaves								
1903H	2,640,000	1.75	3.00	7.00	16.00	100	300	—
Note: 21 leaves								
1904	2,400,000	2.75	4.50	7.00	23.00	175	500	—
1905	2,600,000	1.75	3.00	9.00	16.00	100	225	—
1906	3,100,000	2.25	3.00	6.00	13.00	85.00	225	—
1907	5,200,000	2.25	3.00	4.00	10.00	55.00	150	—
1908	1,220,524	6.00	10.00	23.00	35.00	100	175	—
1909	1,983,725	3.00	6.50	10.00	30.00	175	500	—
Note: Round leaves								
1909	Inc. above	12.00	18.00	35.00	95.00	550	1,300	—
Note: Pointed leaves								
1910	3,850,325	2.25	2.75	5.00	11.00	50.00	95.00	—
Note: Pointed leaves								
1910	Inc. above	15.00	17.00	30.00	85.00	400	1,300	—
Note: Round leaves								

KM# 16 5 CENTS Weight: 1.1620 g. **Composition:** 0.9250 Silver 0.0346 oz. ASW **Ruler:** George V **Obverse:** King's bust left **Obv. Designer:** E. B. MacKennal **Reverse:** Denomination and date within wreath, crown above **Rev. Designer:** Leonard C. Wyon

Date	Mintage	VG-8	F-12	VF-20	XF-40	MS-60	MS-63	Proof
1911	3,692,350	2.00	3.00	6.00	9.00	60.00	100	—

KM# 22 5 CENTS Weight: 1.1620 g. **Composition:** 0.9250 Silver 0.0346 oz. ASW **Ruler:** George V **Obverse:** King's bust left **Obv. Designer:** E. B. MacKennal **Reverse:** Denomination and date within wreath, crown above **Rev. Designer:** Leonard C. Wyon

Date	Mintage	VG-8	F-12	VF-20	XF-40	MS-60	MS-63	Proof
1912	5,863,170	2.00	3.00	5.00	9.00	50.00	150	—
1913	5,488,048	2.00	2.75	4.25	7.50	26.00	50.00	—
1914	4,202,179	2.00	3.00	5.00	9.00	50.00	125	—
1915	1,172,258	11.00	15.00	26.00	50.00	325	600	—
1916	2,481,675	2.75	7.50	13.00	22.00	100	250	—
1917	5,521,373	1.75	2.50	3.00	7.00	30.00	80.00	—
1918	6,052,298	1.75	2.50	3.00	6.50	30.00	65.00	—
1919	7,835,400	1.75	2.50	3.00	6.50	30.00	65.00	—

KM# 22a 5 CENTS Weight: 1.1664 g. **Composition:** 0.8000 Silver 0.0300 oz. ASW **Ruler:** George V **Obv. Designer:** E. B. MacKennal **Rev. Designer:** Leonard C. Wyon **Size:** 15.48 mm.

Date	Mintage	VG-8	F-12	VF-20	XF-40	MS-60	MS-63	Proof
1920	10,649,851	1.75	2.50	3.00	6.50	26.00	50.00	—
1921	2,582,495	2,700	3,000	4,500	6,750	9,500	16,500	—

Note: Approximately 460 known; balance remelted. Stack's A.G. Carter Jr. Sale (12-89) choice BU, finest known, realized $57,200

Near 6 Far 6

KM# 29 5 CENTS Weight: 4.5200 g. **Composition:** Nickel **Ruler:** George V **Obverse:** King's bust left **Obv. Designer:** E. B. MacKennal **Reverse:** Maple leaves divide denomination and date **Rev. Designer:** W. H. J. Blakemore **Size:** 21.2 mm.

Date	Mintage	VG-8	F-12	VF-20	XF-40	MS-60	MS-63	Proof
1922	4,794,119	0.35	1.00	1.75	7.00	45.00	95.00	—
1923	2,502,279	0.40	1.25	5.50	16.00	100	275	—
1924	3,105,839	0.50	1.00	3.75	10.00	85.00	200	—
1925	201,921	55.00	70.00	100	200	1,200	3,600	—
1926 Near 6	938,162	3.00	7.00	16.00	60.00	375	1,300	—
1926 Far 6	Inc. above	100	150	300	600	1,500	4,300	—
1927	5,285,627	0.35	0.65	2.75	15.00	60.00	125	—
1928	4,577,712	0.35	0.65	2.75	15.00	55.00	100	—
1929	5,611,911	0.35	0.65	2.75	15.00	60.00	150	—
1930	3,704,673	0.35	1.50	2.75	15.00	90.00	200	—
1931	5,100,830	0.35	1.50	3.25	18.00	175	475	—
1932	3,198,566	0.35	1.00	3.25	16.00	150	350	—
1933	2,597,867	0.40	1.50	6.00	18.00	175	650	—
1934	3,827,304	0.35	1.00	3.00	16.00	150	375	—
1935	3,900,000	0.35	1.00	2.75	11.00	95.00	250	—
1936	4,400,450	0.35	0.65	1.75	9.00	50.00	100	—

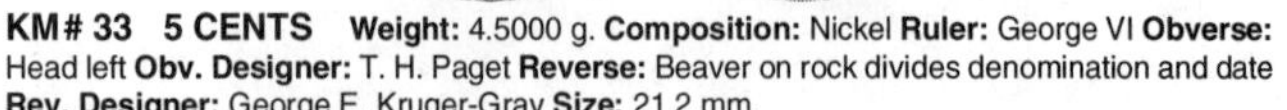

KM# 33 5 CENTS Weight: 4.5000 g. **Composition:** Nickel **Ruler:** George VI **Obverse:** Head left **Obv. Designer:** T. H. Paget **Reverse:** Beaver on rock divides denomination and date **Rev. Designer:** George E. Kruger-Gray **Size:** 21.2 mm.

Date	Mintage	VG-8	F-12	VF-20	XF-40	MS-60	MS-63	Proof
1937 Dot	4,593,263	0.25	0.35	1.25	2.50	9.00	22.00	—
1938	3,898,974	0.30	0.90	2.00	7.00	75.00	150	—
1939	5,661,123	0.25	0.35	1.25	3.00	45.00	80.00	—
1940	13,920,197	0.20	0.30	0.75	2.25	18.00	55.00	—
1941	8,681,785	0.20	0.30	0.75	2.25	23.00	70.00	—
1942 Round	6,847,544	0.20	0.30	0.75	1.75	18.00	35.00	—

KM# 39 5 CENTS **Composition:** Tombac **Ruler:** George VI **Obverse:** Head left **Obv. Designer:** T. H. Paget **Reverse:** Beaver on rock divides denomination and date **Rev. Designer:** George E. Kruger-Gray **Shape:** 12-sided **Size:** 21.2 mm.

Date	Mintage	VG-8	F-12	VF-20	XF-40	MS-60	MS-63	Proof
1942	3,396,234	0.40	0.65	1.25	1.75	3.00	14.00	—

KM# 40a 5 CENTS **Weight:** 4.4000 g. **Composition:** Chrome Plated Steel **Ruler:** George VI **Obverse:** Head left **Reverse:** Torch on "V" divides date **Size:** 21.2 mm.

Date	Mintage	VG-8	F-12	VF-20	XF-40	MS-60	MS-63	Proof
1944	11,532,784	0.10	0.35	0.50	0.90	2.00	7.00	—
1945	18,893,216	0.10	0.20	0.40	0.80	2.00	7.00	—

Dot

Maple leaf

KM# 39a 5 CENTS **Weight:** 4.5000 g. **Composition:** Nickel **Ruler:** George VI **Obverse:** Head left **Obv. Designer:** T. H. Paget **Reverse:** Beaver on rock divides denomination and date **Rev. Designer:** George E. Kruger-Gray **Size:** 21.2 mm.

Date	Mintage	VG-8	F-12	VF-20	XF-40	MS-60	MS-63	Proof
1946	6,952,684	0.10	0.30	0.50	2.00	14.00	32.00	—
1947	7,603,724	0.20	0.30	0.50	1.25	10.00	25.00	—
1947 Dot	Inc. above	12.00	20.00	27.00	60.00	175	300	—
1947 Maple leaf	9,595,124	0.20	0.30	0.45	1.25	10.00	25.00	—

KM# 42 5 CENTS **Weight:** 4.5400 g. **Composition:** Nickel **Ruler:** George VI **Obverse:** Head left, modified legend **Obv. Designer:** T. H. Paget **Reverse:** Beaver on rock divides date and denomination **Rev. Designer:** George E. Kruger-Gray **Size:** 21.2 mm.

Date	Mintage	VG-8	F-12	VF-20	XF-40	MS-60	MS-63	Proof
1948	1,810,789	0.40	0.50	1.00	3.00	18.00	35.00	—
1949	13,037,090	0.20	0.30	0.50	0.75	6.00	12.00	—
1950	11,970,521	0.20	0.30	0.50	0.75	6.00	12.00	—

KM# 42a 5 CENTS **Composition:** Chromium And Nickel-Plated Steel **Ruler:** George VI **Obverse:** Head left **Obv. Designer:** T. H. Paget **Reverse:** Beaver on rock divides date and denomination **Rev. Designer:** George E. Kruger-Gray **Size:** 21.2 mm.

Date	Mintage	VG-8	F-12	VF-20	XF-40	MS-60	MS-63	Proof
1951	4,313,410	0.10	0.25	0.50	0.80	3.50	11.00	—
Note: Low relief; Second "A" in GRATIA points between denticles								
1951	Inc. above	350	525	700	1,000	1,900	3,100	—
Note: High relief; Second "A" in GRATIA points to a denticle								
1952	10,891,148	0.10	0.20	0.45	0.80	3.00	7.50	—

KM# 48 5 CENTS **Weight:** 4.5500 g. **Composition:** Nickel **Ruler:** George VI **Subject:** Nickel Bicentennial **Obverse:** Head left **Obv. Designer:** T. H. Paget **Reverse:** Buildings with center tower divide dates and denomination **Rev. Designer:** Stephen Trenka **Shape:** 12-sided **Size:** 21.2 mm.

Date	Mintage	VG-8	F-12	VF-20	XF-40	MS-60	MS-63	Proof
ND(1951)	9,028,507	0.20	0.30	0.35	0.45	1.75	5.50	—

KM# 50 5 CENTS **Composition:** Chromium And Nickel-Plated Steel **Ruler:** Elizabeth II **Obverse:** Laureate queen's bust, right **Obv. Designer:** Mary Gillick **Reverse:** Beaver on rock divides date and denomination **Rev. Designer:** George E. Kruger-Gray **Shape:** 12-sided **Size:** 21.2 mm.

Date	Mintage	VG-8	F-12	VF-20	XF-40	MS-60	MS-63	Proof
1953	16,635,552	0.10	0.20	0.40	0.90	3.00	7.00	—
Note: Without strap								
1953	Inc. above	300	500	750	900	1,300	2,300	—
Note: Without strap, near leaf								
1953	Inc. above	150	225	300	475	1,100	2,300	—
Note: With strap, far leaf								
1953	Inc. above	0.10	0.20	0.40	0.90	3.50	7.00	—
Note: With strap								
1954	6,998,662	0.10	0.25	0.50	1.00	4.00	8.00	—

KM# 50a 5 CENTS **Weight:** 4.5900 g. **Composition:** Nickel **Ruler:** Elizabeth II **Obverse:** Laureate queen's bust right **Obv. Designer:** Mary Gillick **Reverse:** Beaver on rock divides date and denomination **Rev. Designer:** George E. Kruger-Gray **Size:** 21.2 mm.

Date	Mintage	VG-8	F-12	VF-20	XF-40	MS-60	MS-63	Proof
1955	5,355,028	0.20	0.25	0.40	0.75	3.50	4.50	—
1956	9,399,854	—	0.20	0.30	0.45	2.25	5.00	—
1957	7,387,703	—	—	0.25	0.30	2.00	3.00	—
1958	7,607,521	—	—	0.25	0.30	2.00	3.00	—
1959	11,552,523	—	—	—	0.20	0.70	1.50	—
1960	37,157,433	—	—	—	0.20	0.75	1.50	—
1961	47,889,051	—	—	—	—	0.30	0.80	—
1962	46,307,305	—	—	—	—	0.30	0.80	—

KM# 57 5 CENTS **Composition:** Nickel **Ruler:** Elizabeth II **Obverse:** Laureate queen's bust right **Obv. Designer:** Mary Gillick **Reverse:** Beaver on rock divides date and denomination **Rev. Designer:** George E. Kruger-Gray **Shape:** Round **Size:** 21.2 mm.

Date	Mintage	VG-8	F-12	VF-20	XF-40	MS-60	MS-63	Proof
1963	43,970,320	—	—	—	—	0.20	0.75	—
1964	78,075,068	—	—	—	—	0.20	0.75	—
1964	—	8.00	10.00	12.00	17.00	35.00	100	—
Note: Extra water line								

KM# 60.1 5 CENTS **Weight:** 4.5400 g. **Composition:** Nickel **Ruler:** Elizabeth II **Obverse:** Queen's bust right **Obv. Designer:** Arnold Machin **Reverse:** Beaver on rock divides date and denomination **Rev. Designer:** George E. Kruger-Gray **Size:** 21.2 mm.

Date	Mintage	VG-8	F-12	VF-20	XF-40	MS-60	MS-63	Proof
1965	84,876,018	—	—	—	—	0.20	0.30	—
1966	27,976,648	—	—	—	—	0.20	0.30	—
1968	101,930,379	—	—	—	—	0.20	0.30	—
1969	27,830,229	—	—	—	—	0.20	0.30	—
1970	5,726,010	—	—	—	0.20	0.35	0.75	—
1971	27,312,609	—	—	—	—	0.20	0.30	—
1972	62,417,387	—	—	—	—	0.20	0.30	—
1973	53,507,435	—	—	—	—	0.20	0.30	—
1974	94,704,645	—	—	—	—	0.20	0.30	—
1975	138,882,000	—	—	—	—	0.20	0.30	—
1976	55,140,213	—	—	—	—	0.20	0.30	—
1977	89,120,791	—	—	—	—	0.20	0.30	—
1978	137,079,273	—	—	—	—	0.20	0.30	—

KM# 66 5 CENTS **Composition:** Nickel **Ruler:** Elizabeth II **Subject:** Confederation Centennial **Obverse:** Queen's bust right **Obv. Designer:** Arnold Machin **Reverse:** Snowshoe rabbit bounding left divides dates and denomination **Rev. Designer:** Alex Coville **Size:** 21.2 mm.

Date	Mintage	VG-8	F-12	VF-20	XF-40	MS-60	MS-63	Proof
ND(1967)	36,876,574	—	—	—	—	0.20	0.40	1.00

KM# 60.2 5 CENTS **Composition:** Nickel **Ruler:** Elizabeth II **Obverse:** Queen's bust right **Obv. Designer:** Arnold Machin **Reverse:** Beaver on rock divides date and denomination **Rev. Designer:** George E. Kruger-Gray **Size:** 21.2 mm.

Date	Mintage	VG-8	F-12	VF-20	XF-40	MS-60	MS-63	Proof
1979	186,295,825	—	—	—	—	0.20	0.30	—
1980	134,878,000	—	—	—	—	0.20	0.30	—
1981	99,107,900	—	—	—	—	0.20	0.30	—
1981 Proof	199,000	—	—	—	—	—	—	1.50

KM# 60.2a 5 CENTS **Weight:** 4.6000 g. **Composition:** Copper-Nickel **Ruler:** Elizabeth II **Obverse:** Queen's bust right **Obv. Designer:** Arnold Machin **Reverse:** Beaver on rock divides date and denomination **Rev. Designer:** George E. Kruger-Gray **Size:** 21.2 mm.

Date	Mintage	VG-8	F-12	VF-20	XF-40	MS-60	MS-63	Proof
1982	64,924,400	—	—	—	—	0.20	0.30	—
1982 Proof	180,908	—	—	—	—	—	—	1.50
1983	72,596,000	—	—	—	—	0.20	0.30	—
1983 Proof	168,000	—	—	—	—	—	—	1.50
1984	84,088,000	—	—	—	—	0.20	0.30	—
1984 Proof	161,602	—	—	—	—	—	—	1.50
1985	126,618,000	—	—	—	—	0.20	0.30	—
1985 Proof	157,037	—	—	—	—	—	—	1.50
1986	156,104,000	—	—	—	—	0.20	0.30	—
1986 Proof	175,745	—	—	—	—	—	—	1.50
1987	106,299,000	—	—	—	—	0.15	0.30	—

Date	Mintage	VG-8	F-12	VF-20	XF-40	MS-60	MS-63	Proof
1987 Proof	179,004	—	—	—	—	—	—	1.50
1988	75,025,000	—	—	—	—	0.15	0.30	—
1988 Proof	175,259	—	—	—	—	—	—	1.50
1989	141,570,538	—	—	—	—	0.15	0.30	—
1989 Proof	170,928	—	—	—	—	—	—	1.50

KM# 182 5 CENTS **Weight:** 4.6000 g. **Composition:** Copper-Nickel **Ruler:** Elizabeth II **Obverse:** Crowned head right **Obv. Designer:** Dora dePedery-Hunt **Reverse:** Beaver on rock divides dates and denomination **Rev. Designer:** George E. Kruger-Gray **Edge:** Plain **Size:** 19.55 mm.

Date	Mintage	VG-8	F-12	VF-20	XF-40	MS-60	MS-63	Proof
1990	42,537,000	—	—	—	—	0.15	0.30	—
1990 Proof	140,649	—	—	—	—	—	—	2.50
1991	10,931,000	—	—	—	—	0.30	0.55	—
1991 Proof	131,888	—	—	—	—	—	—	7.00
1993	86,877,000	—	—	—	—	0.15	0.30	—
1993 Proof	143,065	—	—	—	—	—	—	2.50
1994	99,352,000	—	—	—	—	0.15	0.30	—
1994 Proof	146,424	—	—	—	—	—	—	3.00
1995	78,528,000	—	—	—	—	0.15	0.30	—
1995 Proof	50,000	—	—	—	—	—	—	2.50
1996 Far 6	36,686,000	—	—	—	—	0.75	2.25	—
1996 Near 6	Inc. above	—	—	—	—	0.70	2.25	—
1996 Proof	—	—	—	—	—	—	—	6.00
1997	27,354,000	—	—	—	—	0.15	0.30	—
1997 Proof	—	—	—	—	—	—	—	5.00
1998	156,873,000	—	—	—	—	0.15	0.30	—
1998W	—	—	—	—	—	—	1.50	—
1998 Proof	—	—	—	—	—	—	—	5.00
1999	124,861,000	—	—	—	—	0.15	0.30	—
1999W	—	—	—	—	—	—	—	—
1999 Proof	—	—	—	—	—	—	—	5.00
2000	108,514,000	—	—	—	—	0.15	0.30	—
2000W	—	—	—	—	—	—	1.50	—
2000 Proof	—	—	—	—	—	—	—	5.00
2001	30,035,000	—	—	—	—	6.50	12.50	—
2001P Proof	—	—	—	—	—	—	—	10.00
2003	—	—	—	—	—	0.15	0.30	—

KM# 205 5 CENTS **Composition:** Copper-Nickel **Ruler:** Elizabeth II **Subject:** Confederation 125 **Obverse:** Crowned head right **Obv. Designer:** Dora dePedery-Hunt **Reverse:** Beaver on rock divides date and denomination **Rev. Designer:** George E. Kruger-Gray **Size:** 21.2 mm.

Date	Mintage	VG-8	F-12	VF-20	XF-40	MS-60	MS-63	Proof
ND(1992)	53,732,000	—	—	—	—	0.15	0.30	—
ND(1992) Proof	147,061	—	—	—	—	—	—	4.00

KM# 446 5 CENTS **Composition:** Nickel Plated Steel **Ruler:** Elizabeth II **Subject:** Elizabeth II Golden Jubilee **Obverse:** Crowned head right, Jubilee commemorative dates 1952-2002 **Obv. Designer:** Dora dePedery-Hunt **Rev. Designer:** George E. Kruger-Gray **Size:** 21.2 mm. **Note:** Magnetic.

Date	Mintage	MS-63	Proof
ND(2002)P	134,362,000	0.75	—
ND(2002)P Proof	32,642	—	10.00

KM# 491 5 CENTS **Weight:** 3.9300 g. **Composition:** Nickel Plated Steel **Ruler:** Elizabeth II **Obverse:** Crowned head right **Obv. Designer:** Susanna Blunt **Reverse:** Beaver divides date and denomination **Rev. Designer:** George E. Kruger-Gray **Size:** 21.2 mm. **Note:** Magnetic.

Date	Mintage	MS-63	Proof
2003P	61,392,180	1.25	—
2004P	123,085,000	0.50	—
2004P Proof	—	—	2.50
2005P	—	0.50	—
2005P Proof	—	—	2.50
2006P	—	0.50	—
2006P Proof	—	—	2.50
2006(ml)	—	0.50	—
2006(ml) Proof	—	—	2.50

KM# 3 10 CENTS **Weight:** 2.3240 g. **Composition:** 0.9250 Silver 0.0691 oz. ASW **Ruler:** Victoria **Obverse:** Head left **Obv. Legend:** VICTORIA DEI GRATIA REGINA. CANADA **Reverse:** Denomination and date within wreath, crown above **Edge:** Reeded **Size:** 18.03 mm.

Date	Mintage	VG-8	F-12	VF-20	XF-40	MS-60	MS-63	Proof
1901	1,200,000	8.50	18.00	40.00	85.00	225	650	—

KM# 10 10 CENTS **Weight:** 2.3240 g. **Composition:** 0.9250 Silver 0.0691 oz. ASW **Ruler:** Edward VII **Obverse:** Crowned bust right **Obv. Designer:** G. W. DeSaulles **Reverse:** Denomination and date within wreath, crown above **Rev. Designer:** Leonard C. Wyon **Edge:** Reeded **Size:** 18.03 mm.

Date	Mintage	VG-8	F-12	VF-20	XF-40	MS-60	MS-63	Proof
1902	720,000	8.00	16.00	30.00	80.00	325	1,100	—
1902H	1,100,000	4.00	8.00	18.00	40.00	100	250	—
1903	500,000	14.00	30.00	75.00	200	1,000	2,100	—
1903H	1,320,000	7.00	16.00	30.00	65.00	250	550	—
1904	1,000,000	11.00	24.00	45.00	100	325	700	—
1905	1,000,000	6.50	24.00	55.00	100	475	1,100	—
1906	1,700,000	6.50	12.00	30.00	60.00	275	750	—
1907	2,620,000	4.25	11.00	23.00	40.00	200	425	—
1908	776,666	8.00	24.00	55.00	95.00	200	400	—
1909	1,697,200	6.00	18.00	40.00	95.00	375	1,000	—
Note: "Victorian" leaves, similar to 1902-08 coins								
1909	Inc. above	10.00	27.00	55.00	125	500	1,300	—
Note: Broad leaves, similar to 1910-12 coins								
1910	4,468,331	4.00	8.00	18.00	35.00	125	300	—

KM# 17 10 CENTS **Weight:** 2.3240 g. **Composition:** 0.9250 Silver 0.0691 oz. ASW **Ruler:** George V **Obverse:** Crowned bust left **Obv. Designer:** E. B. MacKennal **Reverse:** Denomination and date within wreath, crown above **Rev. Designer:** Leonard C. Wyon **Edge:** Reeded **Size:** 18.03 mm.

Date	Mintage	VG-8	F-12	VF-20	XF-40	MS-60	MS-63	Proof
1911	2,737,584	4.50	11.00	18.00	40.00	100	200	—

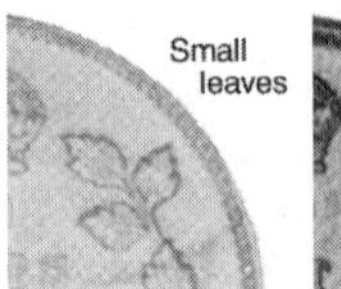

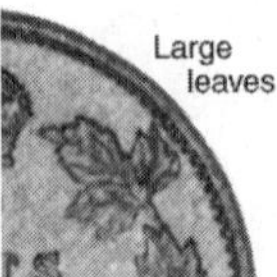

KM# 23 10 CENTS **Weight:** 2.3240 g. **Composition:** 0.9250 Silver 0.0691 oz. ASW **Ruler:** George V **Obverse:** Crowned bust left **Obv. Designer:** E. B. MacKennal **Reverse:** Denomination and date within wreath, crown above **Rev. Designer:** Leonard C. Wyon **Edge:** Reeded **Size:** 18.03 mm.

Date	Mintage	VG-8	F-12	VF-20	XF-40	MS-60	MS-63	Proof
1912	3,235,557	1.75	4.25	9.00	30.00	175	500	—
1913	3,613,937	1.50	2.25	8.50	23.00	125	325	—
Note: Small leaves								
1913	Inc. above	95.00	175	350	900	5,600	20,000	—
Note: Large leaves								
1914	2,549,811	1.50	2.50	8.50	25.00	125	375	—
1915	688,057	6.00	15.00	30.00	100	325	650	—
1916	4,218,114	1.25	2.25	4.00	17.00	75.00	225	—
1917	5,011,988	1.25	1.50	3.00	10.00	50.00	95.00	—
1918	5,133,602	1.25	1.50	3.00	9.00	45.00	80.00	—
1919	7,877,722	1.25	1.50	3.00	9.00	45.00	80.00	—

KM# 23a 10 CENTS **Weight:** 2.3328 g. **Composition:** 0.8000 Silver 0.0600 oz. ASW **Ruler:** George V **Obverse:** Crowned bust left **Obv. Designer:** E. B. MacKennal **Reverse:** Denomination and date within wreath, crown above **Edge:** Reeded **Size:** 18.03 mm.

Date	Mintage	VG-8	F-12	VF-20	XF-40	MS-60	MS-63	Proof
1920	6,305,345	1.00	1.50	3.00	12.00	75.00	125	—
1921	2,469,562	1.25	2.00	6.00	20.00	80.00	225	—
1928	2,458,602	1.00	1.75	4.00	12.00	55.00	125	—
1929	3,253,888	1.00	2.00	3.50	12.00	55.00	100	—
1930	1,831,043	1.00	2.50	4.50	14.00	60.00	125	—
1931	2,067,421	1.00	1.75	4.00	12.00	55.00	100	—
1932	1,154,317	1.50	2.50	9.00	23.00	90.00	225	—
1933	672,368	2.00	4.50	12.00	35.00	175	350	—
1934	409,067	3.00	6.00	22.00	60.00	250	500	—
1935	384,056	3.50	6.00	19.00	60.00	250	500	—
1936	2,460,871	1.00	1.25	3.00	9.00	45.00	80.00	—
1936 Dot on reverse	—	—	—	—	—	—	—	—

Note: Specimen, 4 known; David Akers sale of John Jay Pittman collection, Part 1, 10-97, a gem specimen realized $120,000

KM# 34 10 CENTS **Weight:** 2.3328 g. **Composition:** 0.8000 Silver 0.0600 oz. ASW **Ruler:** George VI **Obverse:** Head left **Obv. Designer:** T. H. Paget **Reverse:** Bluenose sailing left, date at right, denomination below **Rev. Designer:** Emanuel Hahn **Edge:** Reeded **Size:** 18.03 mm.

Date	Mintage	VG-8	F-12	VF-20	XF-40	MS-60	MS-63	Proof
1937	2,500,095	BV	1.00	2.00	3.75	12.00	18.00	—
1938	4,197,323	0.85	1.75	3.25	6.50	40.00	90.00	—
1939	5,501,748	BV	1.25	2.50	5.00	45.00	90.00	—
1940	16,526,470	—	BV	1.50	3.00	15.00	30.00	—
1941	8,716,386	BV	1.25	2.50	6.00	35.00	90.00	—
1942	10,214,011	—	BV	1.25	4.00	30.00	50.00	—
1943	21,143,229	—	BV	1.25	4.00	18.00	35.00	—
1944	9,383,582	—	BV	1.50	4.50	25.00	45.00	—
1945	10,979,570	—	BV	1.25	4.00	18.00	27.00	—
1946	6,300,066	BV	1.00	2.00	4.50	30.00	50.00	—
1947	4,431,926	BV	1.25	2.50	6.00	30.00	50.00	—
1947	9,638,793	—	BV	1.50	3.00	10.00	15.00	—

Note: Maple leaf

KM# 43 10 CENTS **Weight:** 2.3328 g. **Composition:** 0.8000 Silver 0.0600 oz. ASW **Ruler:** George VI **Obverse:** Head left, modified legend **Obv. Designer:** T. H. Paget **Reverse:** Bluenose sailing left, date at right, denomination below **Rev. Designer:** Emanuel Hahn **Size:** 18.03 mm.

Date	Mintage	VG-8	F-12	VF-20	XF-40	MS-60	MS-63	Proof
1948	422,741	2.00	3.50	7.50	13.00	45.00	70.00	—
1949	11,336,172	—	BV	1.00	2.00	9.00	13.00	—
1950	17,823,075	—	—	BV	1.50	8.00	12.00	—
1951	15,079,265	—	—	BV	1.50	6.00	11.00	—
1951	—	—	1.50	2.50	7.00	35.00	60.00	—
Note: Doubled die								
1952	10,474,455	—	—	BV	1.50	5.00	9.00	—

KM# 51 10 CENTS **Weight:** 2.3328 g. **Composition:** 0.8000 Silver 0.0600 oz. ASW **Ruler:** Elizabeth II **Obverse:** Laureate bust right **Obv. Designer:** Mary Gllick **Reverse:** Bluenose sailing left, date at right, denomination below **Rev. Designer:** Emanuel Hahn **Size:** 18.03 mm.

Date	Mintage	VG-8	F-12	VF-20	XF-40	MS-60	MS-63	Proof
1953	17,706,395	—	BV	1.00	1.25	3.00	6.00	—
Note: Without straps								
1953	Inc. above	—	BV	1.00	1.25	5.00	8.00	—
Note: With straps								
1954	4,493,150	—	BV	1.00	2.25	10.00	17.00	—
1955	12,237,294	—	—	BV	1.00	4.50	7.00	—
1956	16,732,844	—	—	BV	1.00	3.00	6.00	—
1956	Inc. above	—	2.25	3.00	4.50	13.00	22.00	—
Note: Dot below date								
1957	16,110,229	—	—	—	BV	2.25	3.00	—
1958	10,621,236	—	—	—	BV	2.25	3.00	—
1959	19,691,433	—	—	—	BV	2.25	3.00	—
1960	45,446,835	—	—	—	BV	1.50	2.25	—
1961	26,850,859	—	—	—	BV	1.00	2.25	—
1962	41,864,335	—	—	—	BV	1.00	1.50	—
1963	41,916,208	—	—	—	BV	1.00	1.50	—
1964	49,518,549	—	—	—	BV	1.00	1.50	—

KM# 61 10 CENTS **Weight:** 2.3328 g. **Composition:** 0.8000 Silver 0.0600 oz. ASW **Ruler:** Elizabeth II **Obverse:** Young bust right **Obv. Designer:** Arnold Machin **Reverse:** Bluenose sailing left, date at right, denomination below **Size:** 18.03 mm.

Date	Mintage	VG-8	F-12	VF-20	XF-40	MS-60	MS-63	Proof
1965	56,965,392	—	—	—	BV	1.00	1.50	—
1966	34,567,898	—	—	—	BV	1.00	1.50	—

KM# 67 10 CENTS **Weight:** 2.3328 g. **Composition:** 0.8000 Silver 0.0600 oz. ASW **Ruler:** Elizabeth II **Subject:** Confederation Centennial **Obverse:** Young bust right **Reverse:** Atlantic mackeral left, denomination above, dates below **Rev. Designer:** Alex Colville **Size:** 18.03 mm.

Date	Mintage	VG-8	F-12	VF-20	XF-40	MS-60	MS-63	Proof
ND(1967)	62,998,215	—	—	—	BV	1.00	1.50	2.00

KM# 67a 10 CENTS **Weight:** 2.3328 g. **Composition:** 0.5000 Silver 0.0375 oz. ASW **Ruler:** Elizabeth II **Subject:** Confederation Centennial **Obverse:** Young bust right **Reverse:** Fish left, denomination above dates below **Size:** 18.03 mm.

Date	Mintage	VG-8	F-12	VF-20	XF-40	MS-60	MS-63	Proof
ND(1967)	Inc. above	—	—	—	BV	0.60	1.50	—

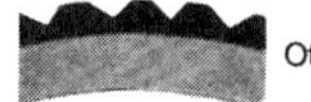
Ottawa

KM# 72 10 CENTS **Weight:** 2.3328 g. **Composition:** 0.5000 Silver 0.0375 oz. ASW **Ruler:** Elizabeth II **Obverse:** Young bust right **Obv. Designer:** Arnold Machin **Reverse:** Bluenose sailing left, date at right, denomination below **Rev. Designer:** Emanuel Hahn **Size:** 18.03 mm.

Date	Mintage	VG-8	F-12	VF-20	XF-40	MS-60	MS-63	Proof
1968	70,460,000	—	—	—	BV	0.60	1.25	—

Note: Ottawa reeding

Ottawa

KM# 72a 10 CENTS **Composition:** Nickel **Ruler:** Elizabeth II **Obverse:** Young bust right **Obv. Designer:** Arnold Machin **Reverse:** Bluenose sailing left, date at right, denomination below **Rev. Designer:** Emanuel Hahn **Size:** 18.03 mm.

Date	Mintage	VG-8	F-12	VF-20	XF-40	MS-60	MS-63	Proof
1968	87,412,930	—	—	—	0.15	0.20	0.35	—

Note: Ottawa reeding

Philadelphia

KM# 73 10 CENTS **Weight:** 2.3300 g. **Composition:** Nickel **Ruler:** Elizabeth II **Obverse:** Young bust right **Obv. Designer:** Arnold Machin **Reverse:** Bluenose sailing left, date at right, denomination below **Rev. Designer:** Emanuel Hahn **Size:** 18.03 mm.

Date	Mintage	VG-8	F-12	VF-20	XF-40	MS-60	MS-63	Proof
1968	85,170,000	—	—	—	0.15	0.25	0.35	—
Note: Philadelphia reeding								
1969	—	—	6,100	8,300	11,000	19,000	—	—
Note: Large date, large ship, 10-20 known								

KM# 77.1 10 CENTS **Weight:** 2.0700 g. **Composition:** Nickel **Ruler:** Elizabeth II **Obverse:** Young bust right **Obv. Designer:** Arnold Machin **Reverse:** Redesigned smaller Bluenose sailing left, date at right, denomination below **Rev. Designer:** Emanuel Hahn **Size:** 18.03 mm.

Date	Mintage	VG-8	F-12	VF-20	XF-40	MS-60	MS-63	Proof
1969	55,833,929	—	—	—	0.15	0.25	0.35	—
1970	5,249,296	—	—	—	0.25	0.40	0.90	—
1971	41,016,968	—	—	—	0.15	0.20	0.35	—
1972	60,169,387	—	—	—	0.15	0.20	0.35	—
1973	167,715,435	—	—	—	0.15	0.20	0.35	—
1974	201,566,565	—	—	—	0.15	0.20	0.35	—
1975	207,680,000	—	—	—	0.15	0.20	0.35	—
1976	95,018,533	—	—	—	0.15	0.20	0.35	—
1977	128,452,206	—	—	—	0.15	0.20	0.35	—
1978	170,366,431	—	—	—	0.15	0.20	0.35	—

KM# 77.2 10 CENTS **Weight:** 2.0700 g. **Composition:** Nickel **Ruler:** Elizabeth II **Obverse:** Smaller young bust right **Obv. Designer:** Arnold Machin **Reverse:** Redesigned smaller Bluenose sailing left, denomination below, date at right **Rev. Designer:** Emanuel Hahn **Size:** 18.03 mm.

Date	Mintage	VG-8	F-12	VF-20	XF-40	MS-60	MS-63	Proof
1979	237,321,321	—	—	—	0.15	0.20	0.35	—
1980	170,111,533	—	—	—	0.15	0.20	0.35	—
1981	123,912,900	—	—	—	0.15	0.20	0.35	—
1981 Proof	199,000	—	—	—	—	—	—	1.50
1982	93,475,000	—	—	—	0.15	0.20	0.35	—
1982 Proof	180,908	—	—	—	—	—	—	1.50
1983	111,065,000	—	—	—	0.15	0.20	0.35	—
1983 Proof	168,000	—	—	—	—	—	—	1.50
1984	121,690,000	—	—	—	0.15	0.20	0.35	—
1984 Proof	161,602	—	—	—	—	—	—	1.50
1985	143,025,000	—	—	—	0.15	0.20	0.35	—
1985 Proof	157,037	—	—	—	—	—	—	1.50
1986	168,620,000	—	—	—	0.15	0.20	0.35	—
1986 Proof	175,745	—	—	—	—	—	—	1.50
1987	147,309,000	—	—	—	0.15	0.20	0.35	—
1987 Proof	179,004	—	—	—	—	—	—	1.50
1988	162,998,558	—	—	—	0.15	0.20	0.35	—
1988 Proof	175,259	—	—	—	—	—	—	1.50
1989	199,104,414	—	—	—	0.15	0.20	0.35	—
1989 Proof	170,528	—	—	—	—	—	—	1.50

KM# 183 10 CENTS **Weight:** 2.1400 g. **Composition:** Nickel **Ruler:** Elizabeth II **Obverse:** Crowned head right **Obv. Designer:** Dora dePedery-Hunt **Reverse:** Bluenose sailing left, date at right, denomination below **Rev. Designer:** Emanuel Hahn **Edge:** Reeded **Size:** 18.03 mm.

Date	Mintage	VG-8	F-12	VF-20	XF-40	MS-60	MS-63	Proof
1990	65,023,000	—	—	—	0.15	0.20	0.35	—
1990 Proof	140,649	—	—	—	—	—	—	2.50

Date	Mintage	VG-8	F-12	VF-20	XF-40	MS-60	MS-63	Proof
1991	50,397,000	—	—	—	0.15	0.30	0.45	—
1991 Proof	131,888	—	—	—	—	—	—	4.00
1993	135,569,000	—	—	—	0.15	0.20	0.35	—
1993 Proof	143,065	—	—	—	—	—	—	2.00
1994	145,800,000	—	—	—	0.15	0.20	0.35	—
1994 Proof	146,424	—	—	—	—	—	—	2.50
1995	123,875,000	—	—	—	0.15	0.20	0.35	—
1995 Proof	50,000	—	—	—	—	—	—	2.50
1996	51,814,000	—	—	—	0.15	0.20	0.35	—
1996 Proof	—	—	—	—	—	—	—	2.50
1997	43,126,000	—	—	—	0.15	0.20	0.35	—
1997 Proof	—	—	—	—	—	—	—	2.50
1998	203,514,000	—	—	—	0.15	0.20	0.35	—
1998W	—	—	—	—	—	—	1.50	—
1998 Proof	—	—	—	—	—	—	—	2.50
1999	258,462,000	—	—	—	0.15	0.20	0.35	—
1999 Proof	—	—	—	—	—	—	—	2.50
2000	159,125,000	—	—	—	0.15	0.20	0.35	—
2000 Proof	—	—	—	—	—	—	—	2.50
2000W	—	—	—	—	—	—	1.50	—

KM# 206 10 CENTS **Composition:** Nickel **Ruler:** Elizabeth II **Subject:** Confederation 125 **Obverse:** Crowned head right **Reverse:** Bluenose sailing left, date at right, denomination below **Size:** 18.03 mm.

Date	Mintage	VG-8	F-12	VF-20	XF-40	MS-60	MS-63	Proof
ND(1992)	174,476,000	—	—	—	—	0.25	0.35	—
ND(1992) Proof	147,061	—	—	—	—	—	—	3.00

KM# 447 10 CENTS **Composition:** Nickel Plated Steel **Ruler:** Elizabeth II **Subject:** Elizabeth II Golden Jubilee **Obverse:** Crowned head right, Jubilee commemorative dates 1952-2002 **Size:** 18 mm.

Date	Mintage	MS-63	Proof
ND(2002)P	251,278,000	1.00	—
ND(2002) Proof	32,642	—	2.50

KM# 492 10 CENTS **Composition:** Nickel Plated Steel **Ruler:** Elizabeth II **Obverse:** Crowned head right **Obv. Designer:** Susanna Blunt **Size:** 18 mm.

Date	Mintage	MS-63	Proof
2003P	—	1.25	—
2004P	211,924,000	0.60	—
2004P Proof	—	—	2.50
2005P	—	0.60	—
2005P Proof	—	—	2.50
2006P	—	0.60	—
2006P Proof	—	—	2.50
2007(ml)	—	0.60	—
2007(ml) Proof	—	—	2.50

KM# 5 25 CENTS **Weight:** 5.8100 g. **Composition:** 0.9250 Silver 0.1728 oz. ASW **Ruler:** Victoria **Obverse:** Crowned head left **Obv. Legend:** VICTORIA DEI GRATIA REGINA. CANADA **Obv. Designer:** Leonard C. Wyon **Reverse:** Denomination and date within wreath, crown above **Size:** 23.88 mm.

Date	Mintage	VG-8	F-12	VF-20	XF-40	MS-60	MS-63	Proof
1901	640,000	12.00	22.00	50.00	150	550	1,200	—

KM# 11 25 CENTS **Weight:** 5.8100 g. **Composition:** 0.9250 Silver 0.1728 oz. ASW **Ruler:** Edward VII **Obverse:** Crowned bust right **Obv. Designer:** G. W. DeSaulles **Reverse:** Denomination and date within wreath, crown above **Size:** 23.4 mm.

Date	Mintage	VG-8	F-12	VF-20	XF-40	MS-60	MS-63	Proof
1902	464,000	10.00	27.00	65.00	175	750	1,900	—
1902H	800,000	6.50	16.00	45.00	100	250	500	—
1903	846,150	15.00	29.00	75.00	200	800	1,900	—
1904	400,000	20.00	55.00	150	350	1,600	5,000	—
1905	800,000	15.00	30.00	100	300	1,400	4,600	—
1906	1,237,843	8.00	21.00	55.00	225	750	1,700	—
Note: Large crown								
1906 Rare	Inc. above	2,500	3,900	6,000	7,500	—	16,000	—
Note: Small crown								
1907	2,088,000	6.50	16.00	55.00	125	425	1,200	—
1908	495,016	15.00	35.00	95.00	200	400	750	—
1909	1,335,929	12.00	26.00	70.00	175	600	1,700	—

KM# 11a 25 CENTS **Weight:** 5.8319 g. **Composition:** 0.9250 Silver 0.1734 oz. ASW **Ruler:** Edward VII **Obverse:** Crowned bust right **Reverse:** Denomination and date within wreath, crown above

Date	Mintage	VG-8	F-12	VF-20	XF-40	MS-60	MS-63	Proof
1910	3,577,569	5.50	16.00	40.00	85.00	275	600	—

KM# 18 25 CENTS **Weight:** 5.8319 g. **Composition:** 0.9250 Silver 0.1734 oz. ASW **Ruler:** George V **Obverse:** Crowned bust left **Obv. Designer:** E. B. MacKennal **Reverse:** Denomination and date within wreath, crown above

Date	Mintage	VG-8	F-12	VF-20	XF-40	MS-60	MS-63	Proof
1911	1,721,341	6.50	18.00	35.00	85.00	250	425	—

KM# 24 25 CENTS **Weight:** 5.8319 g. **Composition:** 0.9250 Silver 0.1734 oz. ASW **Ruler:** George V **Obverse:** Crowned bust left **Obv. Designer:** E. B. MacKennal **Reverse:** Denomination and date within wreath, crown above **Size:** 23.5 mm.

Date	Mintage	VG-8	F-12	VF-20	XF-40	MS-60	MS-63	Proof
1912	2,544,199	5.50	9.00	20.00	55.00	350	1,200	—
1913	2,213,595	3.25	8.50	17.00	50.00	300	950	—
1914	1,215,397	5.00	10.00	23.00	60.00	500	1,600	—
1915	242,382	16.00	45.00	150	425	2,200	6,100	—
1916	1,462,566	3.00	7.50	18.00	40.00	225	700	—
1917	3,365,644	3.00	6.00	12.00	30.00	125	225	—
1918	4,175,649	3.00	5.00	12.00	26.00	95.00	175	—
1919	5,852,262	3.00	5.00	9.50	25.00	95.00	175	—

Dot below wreath

KM# 24a 25 CENTS **Weight:** 5.8319 g. **Composition:** 0.8000 Silver 0.1500 oz. ASW **Ruler:** George V **Obverse:** Crowned bust left **Obv. Designer:** E. B. MacKennal **Reverse:** Denomination and date within wreath, crown below

Date	Mintage	VG-8	F-12	VF-20	XF-40	MS-60	MS-63	Proof
1920	1,975,278	3.00	6.00	12.00	30.00	150	400	—
1921	597,337	11.00	24.00	80.00	225	1,100	2,700	—
1927	468,096	27.00	50.00	100	225	750	1,600	—
1928	2,114,178	3.00	6.00	13.00	35.00	125	325	—
1929	2,690,562	3.00	6.00	13.00	35.00	125	325	—
1930	968,748	3.00	6.00	18.00	40.00	200	500	—
1931	537,815	3.00	6.00	20.00	50.00	200	500	—
1932	537,994	3.00	6.00	25.00	50.00	200	500	—
1933	421,282	3.00	6.50	28.00	65.00	175	325	—
1934	384,350	3.50	9.00	30.00	70.00	225	500	—
1935	537,772	3.50	7.50	22.00	50.00	150	325	—
1936	972,094	3.00	5.00	12.00	21.00	95.00	175	—
1936 Dot	153,322	26.00	65.00	150	300	800	1,800	—
Note: David Akers John Jay Pittman sale Part Three, 10-99, nearly Choice Unc. realized $6,900; considered a possible specimen example								

Maple leaf after date

KM# 35 25 CENTS **Weight:** 5.8319 g. **Composition:** 0.8000 Silver 0.1500 oz. ASW **Ruler:** George VI **Obverse:** Head left **Obv. Designer:** T. H. Paget **Reverse:** Caribou left, denomination above, date at right **Rev. Designer:** Emanuel Hahn **Size:** 23.5 mm.

Date	Mintage	VG-8	F-12	VF-20	XF-40	MS-60	MS-63	Proof
1937	2,690,176	2.50	3.00	4.00	6.00	16.00	35.00	—
1938	3,149,245	2.50	3.00	5.00	10.00	65.00	125	—
1939	3,532,495	2.50	3.50	5.00	7.00	50.00	100	—
1940	9,583,650	—	BV	2.50	3.00	15.00	30.00	—
1941	6,654,672	—	BV	2.50	3.00	16.00	30.00	—
1942	6,935,871	—	BV	2.50	3.00	17.00	45.00	—
1943	13,559,575	—	BV	2.50	3.00	16.00	30.00	—
1944	7,216,237	—	BV	2.50	3.00	26.00	50.00	—
1945	5,296,495	—	BV	2.50	3.00	16.00	45.00	—
1946	2,210,810	BV	2.50	4.00	8.00	45.00	75.00	—
1947	1,524,554	—	BV	4.00	8.00	50.00	95.00	—

Date	Mintage	VG-8	F-12	VF-20	XF-40	MS-60	MS-63	Proof
1947	Inc. above	30.00	40.00	70.00	150	250	500	—
Note: Dot after 7								
1947	4,393,938	—	BV	2.50	3.00	16.00	32.00	—
Note: Maple leaf								

KM# 44 25 CENTS **Weight:** 5.8319 g. **Composition:** 0.8000 Silver 0.1500 oz. ASW **Ruler:** George VI **Obverse:** Head left, modified legend **Obv. Designer:** T. H. Paget **Reverse:** Caribou left, denomination above, date at right **Rev. Designer:** Emanuel Hahn **Size:** 23.5 mm.

Date	Mintage	VG-8	F-12	VF-20	XF-40	MS-60	MS-63	Proof
1948	2,564,424	BV	2.50	3.00	13.00	55.00	75.00	—
1949	7,988,830	—	BV	2.50	3.00	10.00	20.00	—
1950	9,673,335	—	—	BV	2.50	8.00	15.00	—
1951	8,290,719	—	—	BV	2.50	7.00	12.00	—
1952	8,859,642	—	—	BV	2.50	6.00	11.00	—

KM# 52 25 CENTS **Weight:** 5.8319 g. **Composition:** 0.8000 Silver 0.1500 oz. ASW **Ruler:** Elizabeth II **Obverse:** Laureate bust right **Obv. Designer:** Mary Gillick **Reverse:** Caribou left, denomination above, date at right **Rev. Designer:** Emanuel Hahn **Size:** 23.8 mm.

Date	Mintage	VG-8	F-12	VF-20	XF-40	MS-60	MS-63	Proof
1953	10,546,769	—	—	BV	2.50	5.00	10.00	—
Note: Without strap								
1953	Inc. above	—	—	BV	2.50	6.50	18.00	—
Note: With strap								
1954	2,318,891	—	BV	2.50	7.00	25.00	40.00	—
1955	9,552,505	—	—	BV	2.50	6.00	15.00	—
1956	11,269,353	—	—	BV	2.50	3.25	6.50	—
1957	12,770,190	—	—	—	BV		5.00	—
1958	9,336,910	—	—	—	BV		5.00	—
1959	13,503,461	—	—	—	BV		3.50	—
1960	22,835,327	—	—	—	BV		3.50	—
1961	18,164,368	—	—	—	BV		3.50	—
1962	29,559,266	—	—	—	BV		3.50	—
1963	21,180,652	—	—	—	BV		3.00	—
1964	36,479,343	—	—	—	BV		3.00	—

KM# 62 25 CENTS **Weight:** 5.8319 g. **Composition:** 0.8000 Silver 0.1500 oz. ASW **Ruler:** Elizabeth II **Obverse:** Young bust right **Obv. Designer:** Arnold Machin **Reverse:** Caribou left, denomination above, date at right **Rev. Designer:** Emanuel Hahn **Size:** 23.8 mm.

Date	Mintage	VG-8	F-12	VF-20	XF-40	MS-60	MS-63	Proof
1965	44,708,869	—	—	—	BV		BV	—
1966	25,626,315	—	—	—	BV		BV	—

KM# 68 25 CENTS **Weight:** 5.8319 g. **Composition:** 0.8000 Silver 0.1500 oz. ASW **Ruler:** Elizabeth II **Subject:** Confederation Centennial **Obverse:** Young bust right **Reverse:** Lynx striding left divides dates and denomination **Rev. Designer:** Alex Colville **Size:** 23.8 mm.

Date	Mintage	VG-8	F-12	VF-20	XF-40	MS-60	MS-63	Proof
ND(1967)	48,855,500	—	—	—	BV		BV	—

KM# 68a 25 CENTS **Weight:** 5.8319 g. **Composition:** 0.5000 Silver 0.0937 oz. ASW **Ruler:** Elizabeth II **Subject:** Confederation Centennial **Obverse:** Young bust right **Reverse:** Lynx striding left divides dates and denomination **Size:** 23.8 mm.

Date	Mintage	VG-8	F-12	VF-20	XF-40	MS-60	MS-63	Proof
ND(1967)	Inc. above	—	—	—	BV	1.50	2.50	—

KM# 62a 25 CENTS **Weight:** 5.8319 g. **Composition:** 0.5000 Silver 0.0937 oz. ASW **Ruler:** Elizabeth II **Obverse:** Young bust right **Obv. Designer:** Machin **Reverse:** Caribou left, denomination above, date at right **Size:** 23.8 mm.

Date	Mintage	VG-8	F-12	VF-20	XF-40	MS-60	MS-63	Proof
1968	71,464,000	—	—	—	BV	1.50	2.25	—

KM# 62b 25 CENTS **Weight:** 5.0600 g. **Composition:** Nickel **Ruler:** Elizabeth II **Obverse:** Young bust right **Obv. Designer:** Machin **Reverse:** Caribou left, denomination above, date at right **Size:** 23.8 mm.

Date	Mintage	VG-8	F-12	VF-20	XF-40	MS-60	MS-63	Proof
1968	88,686,931	—	—	—	0.30	0.45	0.75	—
1969	133,037,929	—	—	—	0.30	0.45	0.75	—
1970	10,302,010	—	—	—	0.30	1.00	2.00	—
1971	48,170,428	—	—	—	0.30	0.45	0.75	—
1972	43,743,387	—	—	—	0.30	0.45	0.75	—
1973	135,958,589	—	—	—	0.30	0.50	1.00	—
Note: Small bust								
1973	Inc. above	—	60.00	70.00	100	150	500	—
Note: Large bust								
1974	192,360,598	—	—	—	0.30	0.45	0.75	—
1975	141,148,000	—	—	—	0.30	0.45	0.75	—
1976	86,898,261	—	—	—	0.30	0.45	0.75	—
1977	99,634,555	—	—	—	0.30	0.45	0.75	—
1978	176,475,408	—	—	—	0.30	0.45	0.75	—

KM# 81.1 25 CENTS **Composition:** Nickel **Ruler:** Elizabeth II **Subject:** Royal Candian Mounted Police Centennial **Obverse:** Young bust right **Reverse:** Mountie divides dates, denomination above **Rev. Designer:** Paul Cedarberg **Size:** 23.8 mm. **Note:** 120 beads.

Date	Mintage	VG-8	F-12	VF-20	XF-40	MS-60	MS-63	Proof
ND(1973)	134,958,587	—	—	—	0.30	0.55	1.00	—

KM# 81.2 25 CENTS **Composition:** Nickel **Ruler:** Elizabeth II **Subject:** RCMP Centennial **Obverse:** Young bust right **Reverse:** Mountie divides dates, denomination above **Size:** 23.8 mm. **Note:** 132 beads.

Date	Mintage	VG-8	F-12	VF-20	XF-40	MS-60	MS-63	Proof
ND(1973)	Inc. above	40.00	55.00	70.00	85.00	100	200	—

KM# 74 25 CENTS **Weight:** 5.0700 g. **Composition:** Nickel **Ruler:** Elizabeth II **Obverse:** Small young bust right **Obv. Designer:** Machin **Rev. Designer:** Emanuel Hahn **Size:** 23.88 mm.

Date	Mintage	VG-8	F-12	VF-20	XF-40	MS-60	MS-63	Proof
1979	131,042,905	—	—	—	0.30	0.45	0.75	—
1980	76,178,000	—	—	—	0.30	0.45	0.75	—
1981	131,580,272	—	—	—	0.30	0.45	0.75	—
1981 Proof	199,000	—	—	—	—	—	—	2.00
1982	171,926,000	—	—	—	0.30	0.45	0.75	—
1982 Proof	180,908	—	—	—	—	—	—	2.00
1983	13,162,000	—	—	—	0.30	0.75	1.50	—
1983 Proof	168,000	—	—	—	—	—	—	3.00
1984	121,668,000	—	—	—	0.30	0.45	0.75	—
1984 Proof	161,602	—	—	—	—	—	—	2.00
1985	158,734,000	—	—	—	0.30	0.45	0.75	—
1985 Proof	157,037	—	—	—	—	—	—	2.00
1986	132,220,000	—	—	—	0.30	0.45	0.75	—
1986 Proof	175,745	—	—	—	—	—	—	2.00
1987	53,408,000	—	—	—	0.30	0.60	1.25	—
1987 Proof	179,004	—	—	—	—	—	—	2.00
1988	80,368,473	—	—	—	0.30	0.45	1.00	—
1988 Proof	175,259	—	—	—	—	—	—	2.00
1989	119,796,307	—	—	—	0.30	0.45	0.75	—
1989 Proof	170,928	—	—	—	—	—	—	2.00

KM# 184 25 CENTS **Weight:** 5.0700 g. **Composition:** Nickel **Ruler:** Elizabeth II **Obverse:** Crowned head right **Obv. Designer:** Dora dePedery-Hunt **Reverse:** Caribou left, denomination above, date at right **Rev. Designer:** Emanuel Hahn **Size:** 23.88 mm.

Date	Mintage	VG-8	F-12	VF-20	XF-40	MS-60	MS-63	Proof
1990	31,258,000	—	—	—	0.30	0.45	0.90	—
1990 Proof	140,649	—	—	—	—	—	—	2.50
1991	459,000	—	—	2.00	3.00	6.00	12.00	—
1991 Proof	131,888	—	—	—	—	—	—	20.00
1993	73,758,000	—	—	—	0.25	0.35	0.70	—
1993 Proof	143,065	—	—	—	—	—	—	2.00
1994	77,670,000	—	—	—	0.25	0.35	0.70	—
1994 Proof	146,424	—	—	—	—	—	—	3.00
1995	89,210,000	—	—	—	0.25	0.35	0.70	—

Date	Mintage	VG-8	F-12	VF-20	XF-40	MS-60	MS-63	Proof
1995 Proof	50,000	—	—	—	—	—	—	3.00
1996 Proof	—	—	—	—	—	—	—	6.00
1996	28,106,000	—	—	—	—	—	0.70	—
1997	—	—	—	—	—	—	0.70	—
1997 Proof	—	—	—	—	—	—	—	6.00
1998W	—	—	—	—	—	—	5.00	—
1999	258,888,000	—	—	—	—	—	0.75	—
1999 Proof	—	—	—	—	—	—	—	6.00
2000 Proof	—	—	—	—	—	—	—	6.00
2000	434,087,000	—	—	—	—	—	0.75	—
2000W	—	—	—	—	—	—	5.00	—
2001	8,415,000	—	—	—	—	3.00	5.00	—
2001 Proof	—	—	—	—	—	—	—	7.50

KM# 213 25 CENTS **Composition:** Nickel **Series:** 125th Anniversary of Confederation **Subject:** Newfoundland **Reverse:** Fisherman rowing a dory, denomination below **Rev. Designer:** Christopher Newhook **Size:** 23.8 mm.

Date	Mintage	VG-8	F-12	VF-20	XF-40	MS-60	MS-63	Proof
ND(1992)	11,405,000	—	—	—	—	0.35	0.70	—

KM# 203 25 CENTS **Composition:** Nickel **Ruler:** Elizabeth II **Series:** 125th Anniversary of Confederation **Subject:** New Brunswick **Obverse:** Crowned head right **Reverse:** Covered bridge in Newton, denomination below **Rev. Designer:** Ronald Lambert **Size:** 23.8 mm.

Date	Mintage	VG-8	F-12	VF-20	XF-40	MS-60	MS-63	Proof
ND(1992)	12,174,000	—	—	—	—	0.35	0.70	—

KM# 212 25 CENTS **Composition:** Nickel **Ruler:** Elizabeth II **Series:** 125th Anniversary of Confederation **Subject:** Northwest Territories **Obverse:** Crowned head right **Rev. Designer:** Beth McEachen **Size:** 23.8 mm.

Date	Mintage	VG-8	F-12	VF-20	XF-40	MS-60	MS-63	Proof
ND(1992)	12,582,000	—	—	—	—	0.35	0.70	—

KM# 214 25 CENTS **Composition:** Nickel **Ruler:** Elizabeth II **Series:** 125th Anniversary of Confederation **Subject:** Manitoba **Obverse:** Crowned head right **Rev. Designer:** Muriel Hope **Size:** 23.8 mm.

Date	Mintage	VG-8	F-12	VF-20	XF-40	MS-60	MS-63	Proof
ND(1992)	11,349,000	—	—	—	—	0.35	0.70	—

KM# 220 25 CENTS **Composition:** Nickel **Ruler:** Elizabeth II **Series:** 125th Anniversary of Confederation **Subject:** Yukon **Obverse:** Crowned head right **Rev. Designer:** Libby Dulac **Size:** 23.8 mm.

Date	Mintage	VG-8	F-12	VF-20	XF-40	MS-60	MS-63	Proof
ND(1992)	10,388,000	—	—	—	—	0.35	0.70	—

KM# 221 25 CENTS **Composition:** Nickel **Ruler:** Elizabeth II **Series:** 125th Anniversary of Confederation **Subject:** Alberta **Obverse:** Crowned head right **Reverse:** Rock formations in the badlands near Drumhelter, denomination below **Rev. Designer:** Mel Heath **Size:** 23.8 mm.

Date	Mintage	VG-8	F-12	VF-20	XF-40	MS-60	MS-63	Proof
ND(1992)	12,133,000	—	—	—	—	0.35	0.70	—

KM# 222 25 CENTS **Composition:** Nickel **Ruler:** Elizabeth II **Series:** 125th Anniversary of Confederation **Subject:** Prince Edward Island **Obverse:** Crowned head right **Rev. Designer:** Nigel Roe **Size:** 23.8 mm.

Date	Mintage	VG-8	F-12	VF-20	XF-40	MS-60	MS-63	Proof
ND(1992)	13,001,000	—	—	—	—	0.35	0.70	—

KM# 223 25 CENTS **Composition:** Nickel **Ruler:** Elizabeth II **Series:** 125th Anniversary of Confederation **Subject:** Ontario **Obverse:** Crowned head right **Reverse:** Jack pine, denomination below **Rev. Designer:** Greg Salmela **Size:** 23.8 mm.

Date	Mintage	VG-8	F-12	VF-20	XF-40	MS-60	MS-63	Proof
ND(1992)	14,263,000	—	—	—	—	0.35	0.70	—

KM# 231 25 CENTS **Weight:** 5.0300 g. **Composition:** Nickel **Ruler:** Elizabeth II **Series:** 125th Anniversary of Confederation **Subject:** Nova Scotia **Obverse:** Crowned head right **Reverse:** Lighthouse, denomination below **Rev. Designer:** Bruce Wood **Size:** 23.8 mm.

Date	Mintage	VG-8	F-12	VF-20	XF-40	MS-60	MS-63	Proof
ND(1992)	13,600,000	—	—	—	—	0.35	0.70	—

KM# 232 25 CENTS **Composition:** Nickel **Ruler:** Elizabeth II **Series:** 125th Anniversary of Confederation **Subject:** British Columbia **Obverse:** Crowned head right, dates below **Reverse:** Large rock, whales, denomination below **Rev. Designer:** Carla Herrera Egan **Size:** 23.8 mm.

Date	Mintage	VG-8	F-12	VF-20	XF-40	MS-60	MS-63	Proof
ND(1992)	14,001,000	—	—	—	—	0.35	0.70	—

KM# 233 25 CENTS **Composition:** Nickel **Ruler:** Elizabeth II **Series:** 125th Anniversary of Confederation **Subject:** Saskatchewan **Obverse:** Crowned head right **Reverse:** Buildings behind wall, grain stalks on right, denomination below **Rev. Designer:** Brian Cobb **Size:** 23.8 mm.

Date	Mintage	VG-8	F-12	VF-20	XF-40	MS-60	MS-63	Proof
ND(1992)	14,165,000	—	—	—	—	0.35	0.70	—

KM# 234 25 CENTS **Composition:** Nickel **Ruler:** Elizabeth II **Series:** 125th Anniversary of Confederation **Subject:** Quebec **Obverse:** Crowned head right **Reverse:** Boats on water, large rocks in background, denomination below **Rev. Designer:** Romualdas Bukauskas **Size:** 23.8 mm.

Date	Mintage	VG-8	F-12	VF-20	XF-40	MS-60	MS-63	Proof
ND(1992)	13,607,000	—	—	—	—	0.35	0.70	—

KM# 342 25 CENTS **Composition:** Nickel **Ruler:** Elizabeth II **Series:** Millennium **Subject:** January - A Country Unfolds **Obverse:** Crowned head right **Reverse:** Totem pole, portraits **Rev. Designer:** P. Ka-Kin Poon **Size:** 23.8 mm.

Date	Mintage	VG-8	F-12	VF-20	XF-40	MS-60	MS-63	Proof
1999	12,181,200	—	—	—	—	0.50	0.65	—

KM# 343 25 CENTS **Weight:** 5.0900 g. **Composition:** Nickel **Ruler:** Elizabeth II **Series:** Millennium **Subject:** February - Etched in Stone **Obverse:** Crowned head right **Reverse:** Native petroglyphs **Rev. Designer:** L. Springer **Size:** 23.8 mm.

Date	Mintage	VG-8	F-12	VF-20	XF-40	MS-60	MS-63	Proof
1999	14,469,250	—	—	—	—	0.50	0.65	—

KM# 344 25 CENTS **Composition:** Nickel **Ruler:** Elizabeth II **Series:** Millennium **Subject:** March - The Log Drive **Obverse:** Crowned head right **Reverse:** Lumberjack **Rev. Designer:** M. Lavoie **Size:** 23.8 mm.

Date	Mintage	VG-8	F-12	VF-20	XF-40	MS-60	MS-63	Proof
1999	15,033,500	—	—	—	—	0.50	0.65	—

KM# 345 25 CENTS **Weight:** 5.0500 g. **Composition:** Nickel **Ruler:** Elizabeth II **Series:** Millennium **Subject:** April - Our Northern Heritage **Obverse:** Crowned head right **Reverse:** Owl, polar bear **Rev. Designer:** Ken Ojnak Ashevac **Size:** 23.8 mm.

Date	Mintage	VG-8	F-12	VF-20	XF-40	MS-60	MS-63	Proof
1999	15,446,000	—	—	—	—	0.50	0.65	—

KM# 346 25 CENTS **Composition:** Nickel **Ruler:** Elizabeth II **Series:** Millennium **Subject:** May - The Voyageures **Obverse:** Crowned head right **Reverse:** Voyageurs in canoe **Rev. Designer:** S. Mineok **Size:** 23.8 mm.

Date	Mintage	VG-8	F-12	VF-20	XF-40	MS-60	MS-63	Proof
1999	15,566,100	—	—	—	—	0.50	0.65	—

KM# 347 25 CENTS **Weight:** 5.0300 g. **Composition:** Nickel **Ruler:** Elizabeth II **Series:** Millennium **Subject:** June - From Coast to Coast **Obverse:** Crowned head right **Reverse:** 19th-century locomotive **Rev. Designer:** G. Ho **Size:** 23.8 mm.

Date	Mintage	VG-8	F-12	VF-20	XF-40	MS-60	MS-63	Proof
1999	20,432,750	—	—	—	—	0.50	0.65	—

KM# 348 25 CENTS **Composition:** Nickel **Ruler:** Elizabeth II **Series:** Millennium **Subject:** July - A Nation of People **Obverse:** Crowned head right **Reverse:** 6 stylized portraits **Rev. Designer:** M. H. Sarkany **Size:** 23.8 mm.

Date	Mintage	VG-8	F-12	VF-20	XF-40	MS-60	MS-63	Proof
1999	17,321,000	—	—	—	—	0.50	0.65	—

KM# 349 25 CENTS **Weight:** 5.1000 g. **Composition:** Nickel **Ruler:** Elizabeth II **Series:** Millennium **Subject:** August - The Pioneer Spirit **Obverse:** Crowned head right **Reverse:** Hay harvesting **Rev. Designer:** A. Botelho **Size:** 23.8 mm.

Date	Mintage	VG-8	F-12	VF-20	XF-40	MS-60	MS-63	Proof
1999	18,153,700	—	—	—	—	0.50	0.65	—

KM# 350 25 CENTS **Composition:** Nickel **Ruler:** Elizabeth II **Series:** Millennium **Subject:** September - Canada Through a Child's Eye **Obverse:** Crowned head right **Reverse:** Childlike artwork **Rev. Designer:** Claudia Bertrand **Size:** 23.8 mm.

Date	Mintage	VG-8	F-12	VF-20	XF-40	MS-60	MS-63	Proof
1999	31,539,350	—	—	—	—	0.50	0.65	—

KM# 351 25 CENTS **Weight:** 5.1000 g. **Composition:** Nickel **Ruler:** Elizabeth II **Series:** Millennium **Subject:** October - Tribute to the First Nations **Obverse:** Crowned head right **Reverse:** Aboriginal artwork **Rev. Designer:** J. E. Read **Size:** 23.8 mm.

Date	Mintage	VG-8	F-12	VF-20	XF-40	MS-60	MS-63	Proof
1999	32,136,650	—	—	—	—	0.50	0.65	—

KM# 352 25 CENTS **Composition:** Nickel **Ruler:** Elizabeth II **Series:** Millennium **Subject:** November - The Airplane Opens the North **Obverse:** Crowned head right **Reverse:** Bush plane with landing skis **Rev. Designer:** B. R. Brown **Size:** 23.8 mm.

Date	Mintage	VG-8	F-12	VF-20	XF-40	MS-60	MS-63	Proof
1999	27,162,800	—	—	—	—	0.50	0.65	—

KM# 353 25 CENTS **Weight:** 5.0900 g. **Composition:** Nickel **Ruler:** Elizabeth II **Series:** Millennium **Subject:** December - This is Canada **Obverse:** Crowned head right **Reverse:** Eclectic geometric design **Rev. Designer:** J. L. P. Provencher **Size:** 23.8 mm.

Date	Mintage	VG-8	F-12	VF-20	XF-40	MS-60	MS-63	Proof
1999	43,339,200	—	—	—	—	0.50	0.70	—

KM# 373 25 CENTS **Composition:** Nickel **Ruler:** Elizabeth II **Subject:** Health **Obverse:** Crowned head right, denomination below **Reverse:** Ribbon and caduceus, date above **Rev. Designer:** Anny Wassef **Size:** 23.8 mm.

Date	Mintage	VG-8	F-12	VF-20	XF-40	MS-60	MS-63	Proof
2000	35,470,900	—	—	—	—	0.50	0.65	—

KM# 374 25 CENTS **Weight:** 5.1000 g. **Composition:** Nickel **Ruler:** Elizabeth II **Subject:** Freedom **Obverse:** Crowned head right, denomination below **Reverse:** 2 children on maple leaf and rising sun, date above **Rev. Designer:** Kathy Vinish **Size:** 23.8 mm.

Date	Mintage	VG-8	F-12	VF-20	XF-40	MS-60	MS-63	Proof
2000	35,188,900	—	—	—	—	0.50	0.65	—

KM# 375 25 CENTS **Composition:** Nickel **Ruler:** Elizabeth II **Subject:** Family **Obverse:** Crowned head right, denomination below **Reverse:** Wreath of native carvings, date above **Rev. Designer:** Wade Stephen Baker **Size:** 23.8 mm.

Date	Mintage	VG-8	F-12	VF-20	XF-40	MS-60	MS-63	Proof
2000	35,107,700	—	—	—	—	0.50	0.65	—

KM# 376 25 CENTS **Weight:** 5.0800 g. **Composition:** Nickel **Ruler:** Elizabeth II **Subject:** Community **Obverse:** Crowned head right, denomination below **Reverse:** Map on globe, symbols surround, date above **Rev. Designer:** Michelle Thibodeau **Size:** 23.8 mm.

Date	Mintage	VG-8	F-12	VF-20	XF-40	MS-60	MS-63	Proof
2000	35,155,400	—	—	—	—	0.50	0.65	—

KM# 377 25 CENTS **Composition:** Nickel **Ruler:** Elizabeth II **Subject:** Harmony **Obverse:** Crowned head right, denomination below **Reverse:** Maple leaf, date above **Rev. Designer:** Haver Demirer **Size:** 23.8 mm.

Date	Mintage	VG-8	F-12	VF-20	XF-40	MS-60	MS-63	Proof
2000	35,184,200	—	—	—	—	0.50	0.65	—

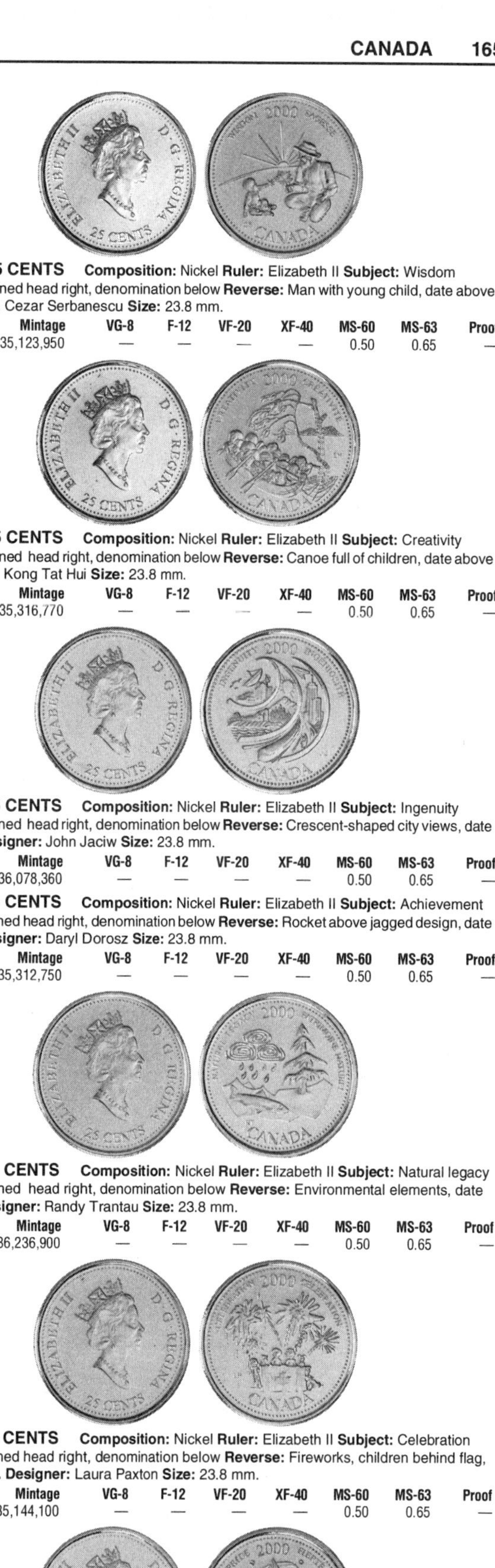

KM# 378 25 CENTS **Composition:** Nickel **Ruler:** Elizabeth II **Subject:** Wisdom **Obverse:** Crowned head right, denomination below **Reverse:** Man with young child, date above **Rev. Designer:** Cezar Serbanescu **Size:** 23.8 mm.

Date	Mintage	VG-8	F-12	VF-20	XF-40	MS-60	MS-63	Proof
2000	35,123,950	—	—	—	—	0.50	0.65	—

KM# 379 25 CENTS **Composition:** Nickel **Ruler:** Elizabeth II **Subject:** Creativity **Obverse:** Crowned head right, denomination below **Reverse:** Canoe full of children, date above **Rev. Designer:** Kong Tat Hui **Size:** 23.8 mm.

Date	Mintage	VG-8	F-12	VF-20	XF-40	MS-60	MS-63	Proof
2000	35,316,770	—	—	—	—	0.50	0.65	—

KM# 380 25 CENTS **Composition:** Nickel **Ruler:** Elizabeth II **Subject:** Ingenuity **Obverse:** Crowned head right, denomination below **Reverse:** Crescent-shaped city views, date above **Rev. Designer:** John Jaciw **Size:** 23.8 mm.

Date	Mintage	VG-8	F-12	VF-20	XF-40	MS-60	MS-63	Proof
2000	36,078,360	—	—	—	—	0.50	0.65	—

KM# 381 25 CENTS **Composition:** Nickel **Ruler:** Elizabeth II **Subject:** Achievement **Obverse:** Crowned head right, denomination below **Reverse:** Rocket above jagged design, date above **Rev. Designer:** Daryl Dorosz **Size:** 23.8 mm.

Date	Mintage	VG-8	F-12	VF-20	XF-40	MS-60	MS-63	Proof
2000	35,312,750	—	—	—	—	0.50	0.65	—

KM# 382 25 CENTS **Composition:** Nickel **Ruler:** Elizabeth II **Subject:** Natural legacy **Obverse:** Crowned head right, denomination below **Reverse:** Environmental elements, date above **Rev. Designer:** Randy Trantau **Size:** 23.8 mm.

Date	Mintage	VG-8	F-12	VF-20	XF-40	MS-60	MS-63	Proof
2000	36,236,900	—	—	—	—	0.50	0.65	—

KM# 383 25 CENTS **Composition:** Nickel **Ruler:** Elizabeth II **Subject:** Celebration **Obverse:** Crowned head right, denomination below **Reverse:** Fireworks, children behind flag, date above **Rev. Designer:** Laura Paxton **Size:** 23.8 mm.

Date	Mintage	VG-8	F-12	VF-20	XF-40	MS-60	MS-63	Proof
2000	35,144,100	—	—	—	—	0.50	0.65	—

KM# 384.2 25 CENTS **Composition:** Nickel **Ruler:** Elizabeth II **Subject:** Pride **Obverse:** Crowned head right, denomination below **Reverse:** Large ribbon 2 with three small maple leaves on large maple leaf, date above **Rev. Designer:** Donald F. Warkentin **Size:** 23.8 mm.

Date	Mintage	VG-8	F-12	VF-20	XF-40	MS-60	MS-63	Proof
2000	50,666,800	—	—	—	—	0.50	0.65	—

KM# 448 25 CENTS **Composition:** Nickel Plated Steel **Ruler:** Elizabeth II **Subject:** Elizabeth II Golden Jubilee **Obverse:** Crowned head right **Size:** 23.9 mm. **Note:** Double-dated 1952-2002.

Date	Mintage	MS-63	Proof
ND(2002)P	152,485,000	2.00	—
ND(2002)P Proof	32,642	—	6.00

KM# 493 25 CENTS **Weight:** 4.4500 g. **Composition:** Nickel Plated Steel **Ruler:** Elizabeth II **Obverse:** Crowned head right **Obv. Designer:** Susanna Blunt **Size:** 23.9 mm.

Date	Mintage	MS-63	Proof
2003P	66,861,633	2.00	—
2003W	—	—	—
2004P	159,465,000	2.50	—
2004P Proof	—	—	5.00
2005P	—	2.50	—
2005P Proof	—	—	5.00
2006P	—	2.50	—
2006P Proof	—	—	5.00
2007(ml)	—	2.50	—
2007(ml) Proof	—	—	5.00

KM# 510 25 CENTS **Weight:** 4.4000 g. **Composition:** Nickel Plated Steel **Ruler:** Elizabeth II **Obverse:** Crowned head right **Reverse:** Red Poppy in center of maple leaf **Edge:** Reeded **Size:** 23.9 mm.

Date	Mintage	MS-63	Proof
2004	28,500,000	5.00	—

KM# 628 25 CENTS **Weight:** 4.4600 g. **Composition:** Nickel Plated Steel **Ruler:** Elizabeth II **Subject:** First Settlement, Ile Ste Croix 1604-2004 **Obverse:** Crowned head right **Reverse:** Sailing ship Bonne-Renommee

Date	Mintage	MS-63	Proof
ND2004P	15,400,000	5.00	—

KM# 535 25 CENTS **Weight:** 4.4300 g. **Composition:** Nickel Plated Steel **Ruler:** Elizabeth II **Subject:** Year of the Veteran **Obverse:** Head right **Reverse:** Profile of young and old soldier **Size:** 23.9 mm.

Date	Mintage	MS-63	Proof
2005P	29,390,000	7.00	—

KM# 530 25 CENTS **Weight:** 4.4300 g. **Composition:** Nickel Plated Steel **Ruler:** Elizabeth II **Subject:** Alberta **Obverse:** Head right **Size:** 23.9 mm.

Date	Mintage	MS-63	Proof
2005P	20,640,000	7.00	—

KM# 531 25 CENTS **Weight:** 4.4300 g. **Composition:** Nickel Plated Steel **Ruler:** Elizabeth II **Subject:** Canada Day **Obverse:** Head right **Reverse:** Beaver, colorized **Size:** 23.9 mm.

Date	Mintage	MS-63	Proof
2005P	58,370	8.50	—

KM# 532 25 CENTS **Weight:** 4.4300 g. **Composition:** Nickel Plated Steel **Ruler:** Elizabeth II **Subject:** Saskatchewan **Obverse:** Head right **Size:** 23.9 mm.

Date	Mintage	MS-63	Proof
2005P	19,290,000	7.00	—

KM# 533 25 CENTS **Weight:** 4.4300 g. **Composition:** Nickel Plated Steel **Ruler:** Elizabeth II **Obverse:** Head right **Reverse:** Stuffed bear in Christmas stocking, colorized **Size:** 23.9 mm.

Date	Mintage	MS-63	Proof
2005P	72,831	10.00	—

KM# 534 25 CENTS **Weight:** 4.4300 g. **Composition:** Nickel Plated Steel **Ruler:** Elizabeth II **Subject:** Toronto Maple Leafs **Obverse:** Head right **Reverse:** Colorized team logo **Size:** 23.9 mm.

Date	Mintage	MS-63	Proof
2006P	—	12.50	—

KM# 6 50 CENTS **Weight:** 11.6200 g. **Composition:** 0.9250 Silver 0.3456 oz. ASW **Ruler:** Victoria **Obverse:** VICTORIA DEI GRATIA REGINA. CANADA **Obv. Designer:** Leonard C. Wyon **Reverse:** Denomination and date within wreath, crown above

Date	Mintage	VG-8	F-12	VF-20	XF-40	MS-60	MS-63	Proof
1901	80,000	55.00	150	225	550	5,700	15,000	—

Victorian leaves

KM# 12 50 CENTS **Weight:** 11.6200 g. **Composition:** 0.9250 Silver 0.3456 oz. ASW **Ruler:** Edward VII **Obverse:** Crowned bust right **Obv. Designer:** G. W. DeSaulles **Reverse:** Denomination and date within wreath, crown above

Date	Mintage	VG-8	F-12	VF-20	XF-40	MS-60	MS-63	Proof
1902	120,000	15.00	35.00	100	250	1,300	3,500	—
1903H	140,000	22.00	45.00	175	450	1,500	3,700	—
1904	60,000	150	200	600	1,000	3,300	9,500	—
1905	40,000	150	275	600	1,400	6,000	15,000	—
1906	350,000	12.00	35.00	95.00	250	1,300	3,500	—
1907	300,000	12.00	35.00	95.00	250	1,400	3,900	—
1908	128,119	21.00	65.00	175	375	1,000	2,000	—
1909	302,118	17.00	60.00	175	475	2,400	7,600	—
1910	649,521	22.00	45.00	175	400	1,600	6,000	—

Note: Victorian leaves

Edwardian leaves

KM# 12a 50 CENTS **Weight:** 11.6638 g. **Composition:** 0.9250 Silver 0.3469 oz. ASW **Ruler:** Edward VII **Obverse:** Crowned bust right **Obv. Designer:** G. W. DeSaulles **Reverse:** Denomination and date within wreath

Date	Mintage	VG-8	F-12	VF-20	XF-40	MS-60	MS-63	Proof
1910	Inc. above	8.00	29.00	85.00	250	1,200	3,300	—

Note: Edwardian leaves

KM# 19 50 CENTS **Weight:** 11.6638 g. **Composition:** 0.9250 Silver 0.3469 oz. ASW **Ruler:** George V **Obverse:** Crowned bust left **Obv. Designer:** E. B. MacKennal **Reverse:** Denomination and date within wreath, crown above

Date	Mintage	VG-8	F-12	VF-20	XF-40	MS-60	MS-63	Proof
1911	209,972	18.00	70.00	250	550	1,400	3,200	—

KM# 25 50 CENTS **Weight:** 11.6638 g. **Composition:** 0.9250 Silver 0.3469 oz. ASW **Ruler:** George V **Obverse:** Crowned bust left, modified legend **Obv. Designer:** E. B. MacKennal **Reverse:** Denomination and date within wreath, crown above

Date	Mintage	VG-8	F-12	VF-20	XF-40	MS-60	MS-63	Proof
1912	285,867	9.00	24.00	100	225	1,100	2,900	—
1913	265,889	9.00	24.00	150	300	1,400	4,800	—
1914	160,128	22.00	55.00	225	550	2,800	7,800	—
1916	459,070	6.00	14.00	55.00	175	650	2,100	—
1917	752,213	5.50	11.00	40.00	100	475	1,100	—
1918	754,989	5.50	10.00	30.00	90.00	400	1,000	—
1919	1,113,429	5.50	10.00	30.00	90.00	375	1,200	—

KM# 25a 50 CENTS **Weight:** 11.6638 g. **Composition:** 0.8000 Silver 0.3000 oz. ASW **Ruler:** George V **Obverse:** Crowned bust left **Obv. Designer:** E. B. MacKennal **Reverse:** Denomination and date within wreath, crown below

Date	Mintage	VG-8	F-12	VF-20	XF-40	MS-60	MS-63	Proof
1920	584,691	5.00	13.00	35.00	125	500	1,800	—
1921	—	22,000	24,000	28,000	32,000	50,000	90,000	—
Note: 75 to 100 known; David Akers John Jay Pittman sale, Part Three, 10-99, Gem Unc. realized $63,250								
1929	228,328	5.00	13.00	35.00	100	475	1,100	—
1931	57,581	11.00	29.00	80.00	225	800	1,800	—
1932	19,213	150	185	375	800	3,600	8,300	—
1934	39,539	15.00	30.00	100	225	650	1,300	—
1936	38,550	15.00	29.00	100	175	500	1,000	—

KM# 36 50 CENTS **Weight:** 11.6638 g. **Composition:** 0.8000 Silver 0.3000 oz. ASW **Ruler:** George VI **Obverse:** Head left **Obv. Designer:** T. H. Paget **Reverse:** Crowned arms with supporters, denomination above, date below **Rev. Designer:** George E. Kruger-Gray **Size:** 30 mm.

Date	Mintage	VG-8	F-12	VF-20	XF-40	MS-60	MS-63	Proof
1937	192,016	BV	5.00	7.00	10.00	30.00	85.00	—
1938	192,018	BV	5.50	10.00	25.00	90.00	400	—
1939	287,976	BV	5.00	8.00	17.00	60.00	250	—
1940	1,996,566	—	—	BV	6.00	27.00	60.00	—
1941	1,714,874	—	—	BV	6.00	27.00	60.00	—
1942	1,974,164	—	—	BV	6.00	27.00	60.00	—
1943	3,109,583	—	—	BV	6.00	27.00	60.00	—
1944	2,460,205	—	—	BV	6.00	27.00	60.00	—
1945	1,959,528	—	—	BV	6.00	30.00	90.00	—
1946	950,235	—	BV	5.00	8.00	60.00	175	—
1946	Inc. above	15.00	28.00	45.00	150	1,100	2,800	—
Note: hoof in 6								
1947	424,885	—	5.00	8.00	12.00	65.00	175	—
Note: straight 7								
1947	Inc. above	—	5.00	9.00	22.00	100	300	—
Note: curved 7								
1947	38,433	18.00	23.00	45.00	70.00	160	275	—
Note: maple leaf, straight 7								
1947	Inc. above	1,000	1,300	1,700	2,200	3,900	7,000	—
Note: maple leaf, curved 7								

KM# 45 50 CENTS **Weight:** 11.6638 g. **Composition:** 0.8000 Silver 0.3000 oz. ASW **Ruler:** George VI **Obverse:** Head left, modified legend **Obv. Designer:** T. H. Paget **Reverse:** Crowned arms with supporters, denomination above, date below **Rev. Designer:** George E. Kruger-Gray

Date	Mintage	VG-8	F-12	VF-20	XF-40	MS-60	MS-63	Proof
1948	37,784	65.00	85.00	100	150	250	350	—
1949	858,991	—	—	BV	7.00	35.00	150	—
1949	Inc. above	10.00	18.00	35.00	60.00	325	750	—
Note: hoof over 9								
1950	2,384,179	6.00	10.00	11.00	35.00	125	225	—
Note: no lines								
1950	Inc. above	—	—	BV	5.00	9.00	30.00	—
Note: lines in 0								
1951	2,421,730	—	—	—	BV	9.00	26.00	—
1952	2,596,465	—	—	—	BV	6.00	18.00	—

KM# 53 50 CENTS **Weight:** 11.6638 g. **Composition:** 0.8000 Silver 0.3000 oz. ASW **Ruler:** Elizabeth II **Obverse:** Laureate bust right **Obv. Designer:** Mary Gillick **Reverse:** Crowned arms with supporters, denomination above, date below

Date	Mintage	VG-8	F-12	VF-20	XF-40	MS-60	MS-63	Proof
1953	1,630,429	—	—	—	BV	7.00	15.00	—
Note: small date								
1953	Inc. above	—	—	BV	5.00	22.00	35.00	—
Note: lg. date, straps								
1953	Inc. above	—	5.00	7.50	14.00	75.00	150	—
Note: lg. date without straps								
1954	506,305	—	BV	5.00	7.00	18.00	35.00	—
1955	753,511	—	—	BV	5.00	15.00	30.00	—
1956	1,379,499	—	—	—	BV	6.00	14.00	—
1957	2,171,689	—	—	—	BV	5.00	10.00	—
1958	2,957,266	—	—	—	BV	5.00	8.50	—

KM# 56 50 CENTS **Weight:** 11.6638 g. **Composition:** 0.8000 Silver 0.3000 oz. ASW **Ruler:** Elizabeth II **Obverse:** Luareate bust right **Obv. Designer:** Mary Gillick **Reverse:** Crown divides date above arms with supporters, denomination at right **Rev. Designer:** Thomas Shingles **Size:** 30 mm.

Date	Mintage	VG-8	F-12	VF-20	XF-40	MS-60	MS-63	Proof
1959	3,095,535	—	—	—	BV	5.00	6.00	—
Note: horizontal shading								
1960	3,488,897	—	—	—	BV		5.00	—
1961	3,584,417	—	—	—	BV		5.00	—
1962	5,208,030	—	—	—	BV		5.00	—
1963	8,348,871	—	—	—	BV		5.00	—
1964	9,377,676	—	—	—	BV		5.00	—

KM# 63 50 CENTS **Weight:** 11.6638 g. **Composition:** 0.8000 Silver 0.3000 oz. ASW **Ruler:** Elizabeth II **Obverse:** Young bust right **Obv. Designer:** Arnold Machin **Reverse:** Crown divides date above arms with supporters, denomination at right **Rev. Designer:** Thomas Shingles

Date	Mintage	VG-8	F-12	VF-20	XF-40	MS-60	MS-63	Proof
1965	12,629,974	—	—	—	BV		5.00	—
1966	7,920,496	—	—	—	BV		5.00	—

KM# 69 50 CENTS **Weight:** 11.6638 g. **Composition:** 0.8000 Silver 0.3000 oz. ASW **Ruler:** Elizabeth II **Subject:** Confederation Centennial **Obverse:** Young bust right **Reverse:** Seated wolf howling divides denomination at top, dates at bottom **Rev. Designer:** Alex Colville **Size:** 29.5 mm.

Date	Mintage	VG-8	F-12	VF-20	XF-40	MS-60	MS-63	Proof
ND(1967)	4,211,392	—	—	—	BV	5.00	6.50	9.00

KM# 75.1 50 CENTS **Composition:** Nickel **Ruler:** Elizabeth II **Obverse:** Young bust right **Obv. Designer:** Arnold Machin **Reverse:** Crown divides date above arms with supporters, denomination at right **Rev. Designer:** Thomas Shingles **Size:** 27.1 mm.

Date	Mintage	VG-8	F-12	VF-20	XF-40	MS-60	MS-63	Proof
1968	3,966,932	—	—	—	0.50	0.65	1.00	—
1969	7,113,929	—	—	—	0.50	0.65	1.00	—
1970	2,429,526	—	—	—	0.50	0.65	1.00	—
1971	2,166,444	—	—	—	0.50	0.65	1.00	—
1972	2,515,632	—	—	—	0.50	0.65	1.00	—
1973	2,546,096	—	—	—	0.50	0.65	1.00	—
1974	3,436,650	—	—	—	0.50	0.65	1.00	—
1975	3,710,000	—	—	—	0.50	0.65	1.00	—
1976	2,940,719	—	—	—	0.50	0.65	1.00	—

KM# 75.2 50 CENTS **Weight:** 8.1000 g. **Composition:** Nickel **Ruler:** Elizabeth II **Obverse:** Small young bust right **Obv. Designer:** Arnold Machin **Reverse:** Crown divides date above arms with supporters, denomination at right **Rev. Designer:** Thomas Shingles **Size:** 27 mm.

Date	Mintage	VG-8	F-12	VF-20	XF-40	MS-60	MS-63	Proof
1977	709,839	—	—	0.50	0.75	1.35	2.00	—

KM# 75.3 50 CENTS **Weight:** 8.1000 g. **Composition:** Nickel **Ruler:** Elizabeth II **Obverse:** Young bust right **Obv. Designer:** Arnold Machin **Reverse:** Crown divides date above arms with supporters, denomination at right, redesigned arms **Rev. Designer:** Thomas Shingles **Size:** 27 mm.

Date	Mintage	VG-8	F-12	VF-20	XF-40	MS-60	MS-63	Proof
1978	3,341,892	—	—	—	0.50	0.65	1.00	—
Note: square jewels								
1978	Inc. above	—	—	1.00	2.50	4.50	6.00	—
Note: round jewels								
1979	3,425,000	—	—	—	0.50	0.65	1.00	—
1980	1,574,000	—	—	—	0.50	0.65	1.00	—
1981	2,690,272	—	—	—	0.50	0.65	1.00	—
1981 Proof	199,000	—	—	—	—	—	—	3.00
1982	2,236,674	—	—	—	30.00	65.00	100	—
Note: small beads								
1982 Proof	180,908	—	—	—	—	—	—	3.00
Note: small beads								
1982	Inc. above	—	—	—	0.50	0.65	1.00	—
Note: large beads								
1983	1,177,000	—	—	—	0.50	0.65	1.00	—
1983 Proof	168,000	—	—	—	—	—	—	3.00
1984	1,502,989	—	—	—	0.50	0.65	1.00	—
1984 Proof	161,602	—	—	—	—	—	—	3.00
1985	2,188,374	—	—	—	0.50	0.65	1.00	—
1985 Proof	157,037	—	—	—	—	—	—	3.00
1986	781,400	—	—	—	0.50	1.00	1.25	—
1986 Proof	175,745	—	—	—	—	—	—	3.00
1987	373,000	—	—	—	0.50	1.00	1.25	—
1987 Proof	179,004	—	—	—	—	—	—	3.50
1988	220,000	—	—	—	0.50	1.00	1.25	—
1988 Proof	175,259	—	—	—	—	—	—	3.00
1989	266,419	—	—	—	0.50	1.00	1.25	—
1989 Proof	170,928	—	—	—	—	—	—	3.00

KM# 185 50 CENTS **Composition:** Nickel **Ruler:** Elizabeth II **Obverse:** Crowned head right **Obv. Designer:** Dora dePedery-Hunt **Reverse:** Crown divides date above arms with supporters, denomination at right **Rev. Designer:** Thomas Shingles **Size:** 27 mm.

Date	Mintage	VG-8	F-12	VF-20	XF-40	MS-60	MS-63	Proof
1990	207,000	—	—	—	0.50	1.00	1.25	—
1990 Proof	140,649	—	—	—	—	—	—	5.00
1991	490,000	—	—	—	0.50	0.85	1.00	—
1991 Proof	131,888	—	—	—	—	—	—	7.00
1993	393,000	—	—	—	0.50	0.85	1.00	—
1993 Proof	143,065	—	—	—	—	—	—	3.00
1994	987,000	—	—	—	0.50	0.75	1.00	—
1994 Proof	146,424	—	—	—	—	—	—	4.00
1995	626,000	—	—	—	0.50	0.75	1.00	—
1995 Proof	50,000	—	—	—	—	—	—	4.00
1996	458,000	—	—	—	0.50	0.65	1.00	—
1996 Proof	—	—	—	—	—	—	—	—

KM# 208 50 CENTS **Composition:** Nickel **Ruler:** Elizabeth II **Subject:** Confederation 125 **Obverse:** Crowned head right **Obv. Designer:** Dora dePedery-Hunt **Reverse:** Crown divides date above arms with supporters, denomination at right **Rev. Designer:** Thomas Shingles **Size:** 27 mm.

Date	Mintage	VG-8	F-12	VF-20	XF-40	MS-60	MS-63	Proof
ND(1992)	445,000	—	—	—	0.50	0.75	1.00	—
ND(1992) Proof	147,061	—	—	—	—	—	—	5.00

KM# 290 50 CENTS **Weight:** 6.9000 g. **Composition:** Nickel **Ruler:** Elizabeth II **Obverse:** Crowned head right **Obv. Designer:** Dora dePedery-Hunt **Reverse:** Redesigned arms **Rev. Designer:** Cathy Bursey-Sabourin **Size:** 27.13 mm.

Date	Mintage	F-12	VF-20	XF-40	AU-50	MS-60	MS-63	Proof
1997	387,000	—	—	0.50	—	0.65	1.00	—
1997 Proof	—	—	—	—	—	—	—	5.00
1998	308,000	—	—	0.50	—	0.65	1.00	—
1998 Proof	—	—	—	—	—	—	—	—
1998W	—	—	—	—	—	—	2.00	—
1999	496,000	—	—	0.50	—	0.65	1.00	—
1999 Proof	—	—	—	—	—	—	—	5.00
2000	559,000	—	—	0.50	—	0.65	1.00	—
2000 Proof	—	—	—	—	—	—	—	5.00
2000W	—	—	—	—	—	—	1.50	—
2001P	—	—	—	—	—	—	1.50	—
2001P Proof	—	—	—	—	—	—	—	5.00
2003P	—	—	—	—	—	—	1.50	—
2003P Proof	—	—	—	—	—	—	—	5.00

KM# 509 50 CENTS **Weight:** 6.9000 g. **Composition:** Nickel Plated Steel **Ruler:** Elizabeth II **Obverse:** Crowned head right **Reverse:** National arms **Edge:** Reeded **Size:** 27.13 mm.

Date	Mintage	MS-63	Proof
ND(2001) P	—	1.50	—

KM# 494 50 CENTS **Weight:** 6.9000 g. **Composition:** Nickel Plated Steel **Ruler:** Elizabeth II **Obverse:** Crowned head right **Obv. Designer:** Susanna Blunt **Rev. Designer:** Cathy Bursey-Sabourin **Size:** 27.13 mm.

Date	Mintage	MS-63	Proof
2003W	—	5.00	—
2003W Proof	—	—	7.50
2004P	—	5.00	—
2004P Proof	—	—	7.50
2005P	—	1.50	—
2005P Proof	—	—	5.00
2006P	—	1.50	—
2006P Proof	—	—	5.00
2006(ml)	—	1.50	—
2007(ml) Proof	—	—	5.00

KM# 30 DOLLAR **Weight:** 23.3276 g. **Composition:** 0.8000 Silver 0.6000 oz. ASW **Ruler:** George V **Subject:** Silver Jubilee **Obverse:** Bust left **Obv. Designer:** Percy Metcalfe **Reverse:** Voyager, date and denomination below **Rev. Designer:** Emanuel Hahn

Date	Mintage	F-12	VF-20	XF-40	AU-50	MS-60	MS-63	Proof
1935	428,707	12.00	18.00	28.00	32.00	37.50	60.00	4,500

KM# 31 DOLLAR **Weight:** 23.3276 g. **Composition:** 0.8000 Silver 0.6000 oz. ASW **Ruler:** George V **Obverse:** Crowned bust left **Obv. Designer:** E. B. MacKennal **Reverse:** Voyageur, date and denomination below **Rev. Designer:** Emanuel Hahn

Date	Mintage	F-12	VF-20	XF-40	AU-50	MS-60	MS-63	Proof
1936	339,600	12.50	14.50	26.00	30.00	35.00	75.00	5,000

Pointed 7 Blunt 7 Maple leaf

KM# 37 DOLLAR **Weight:** 23.3276 g. **Composition:** 0.8000 Silver 0.6000 oz. ASW **Ruler:** George VI **Obverse:** Head left **Obv. Designer:** T. H. Paget **Reverse:** Voyageur, date and denomination below **Rev. Designer:** Emanuel Hahn

Date	Mintage	F-12	VF-20	XF-40	AU-50	MS-60	MS-63	Proof
1937	207,406	9.50	10.00	12.00	22.00	25.00	100	—
1937 Mirror Proof	1,295	—	—	—	—	—	—	650
1937 Matte Proof	Inc. above	—	—	—	—	—	—	250
1938	90,304	25.00	35.00	65.00	80.00	100	175	6,000
1945	38,391	75.00	150	175	225	300	475	2,000
1946	93,055	15.00	25.00	35.00	45.00	95.00	300	1,800
1947		60.00	80.00	150	125	265	1,400	3,500
Note: Pointed 7								
1947	65,595	45.00	60.00	80.00	95.00	125	250	4,500
Note: Blunt 7								
1947	21,135	125	150	175	200	250	475	1,800
Note: Maple leaf								

KM# 38 DOLLAR **Weight:** 23.3276 g. **Composition:** 0.8000 Silver 0.6000 oz. ASW **Ruler:** George VI **Subject:** Royal Visit **Obverse:** Head left **Obv. Designer:** T. H. Paget **Reverse:** Tower at center of building, date and denomination below **Rev. Designer:** Emanuel Hahn

Date	Mintage	F-12	VF-20	XF-40	AU-50	MS-60	MS-63	Proof
1939	1,363,816	—	BV	9.50	10.00	12.00	30.00	—
1939	—	—	—	—	—	—	—	475
Note: Matte specimen								
1939 Proof	—	—	—	—	—	—	—	750
Note: Mirror specimen								

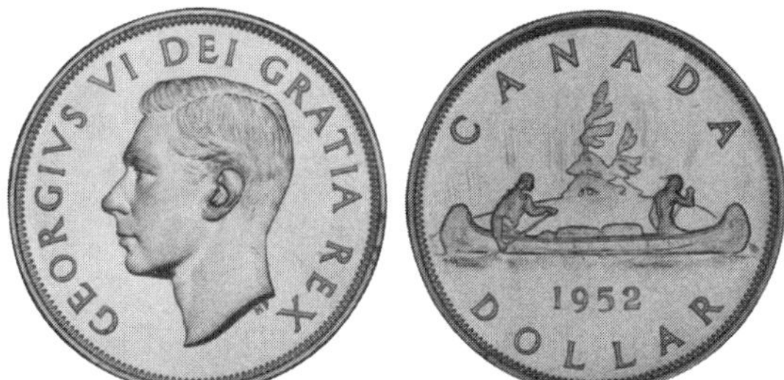

KM# 46 DOLLAR **Weight:** 23.3276 g. **Composition:** 0.8000 Silver 0.6000 oz. ASW **Ruler:** George VI **Obverse:** Head left, modified left legend **Obv. Designer:** T. H. Paget **Reverse:** Voyageur, date and denomination below **Rev. Designer:** Emanuel Hahn

Date	Mintage	F-12	VF-20	XF-40	AU-50	MS-60	MS-63	Proof
1948	18,780	500	600	1,000	1,100	1,300	1,900	3,000
1950	261,002	BV	9.50	10.00	12.00	16.00	50.00	800
Note: With 3 water lines								
1950 Matte Proof	—	—	—	—	—	—	—	—
Note: With 4 water lines, 1 known								
1950	Inc. above	11.00	14.00	21.00	28.00	40.00	90.00	1,500
Note: Arnprior with 2-1/2 water lines								
1951	416,395	BV	9.50	10.00	11.00	13.00	23.00	650
Note: With 3 water lines								
1951	Inc. above	35.00	50.00	60.00	100	175	400	2,000
Note: Arnprior with 1-1/2 water lines								
1952	406,148	BV	9.50	10.00	11.00	12.00	23.00	1,000
Note: With 3 water lines								
1952	Inc. above	11.00	12.00	22.00	30.00	40.00	100	1,250
Note: Arnprior type								
1952	Inc. above	BV	9.50	10.00	11.00	16.50	45.00	—
Note: Without water lines								

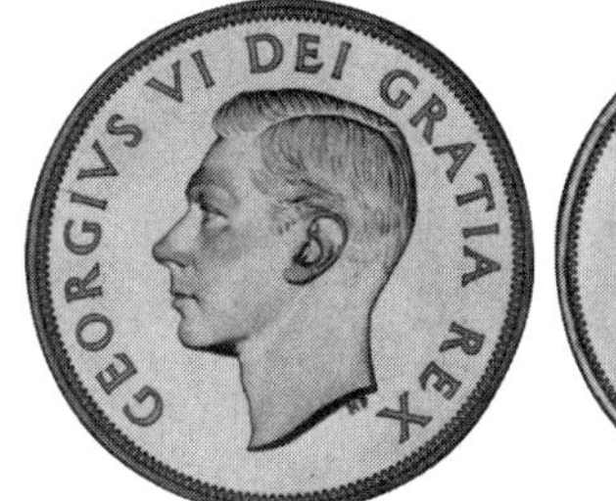

KM# 47 DOLLAR **Weight:** 23.3276 g. **Composition:** 0.8000 Silver 0.6000 oz. ASW **Ruler:** George VI **Subject:** Newfoundland **Obverse:** Head left **Obv. Designer:** T. H. Paget **Reverse:** The "Matthew", John Cabot's ship, date and denomination below **Rev. Designer:** Thomas Shingles

Date	Mintage	F-12	VF-20	XF-40	AU-50	MS-60	MS-63	Proof
1949	672,218	10.00	13.00	16.50	18.50	22.50	27.50	—
1949 Specimen proof	—	—	—	—	—	—	—	1,200

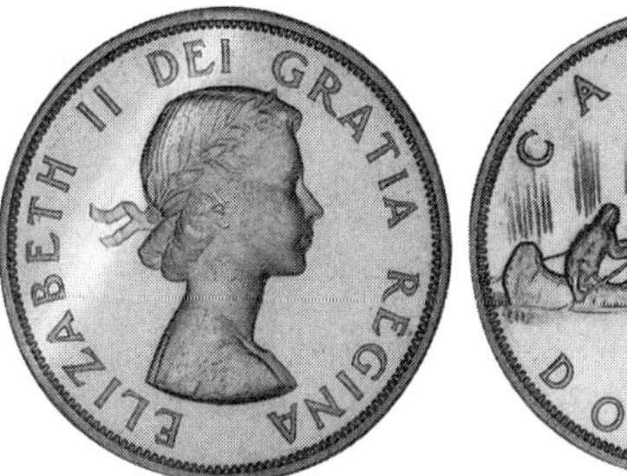

KM# 54 DOLLAR **Weight:** 23.3276 g. **Composition:** 0.8000 Silver 0.6000 oz. ASW **Ruler:** Elizabeth II **Obverse:** Laureate bust right **Obv. Designer:** Mary Gillick **Reverse:** Voyageur, date and denomination below **Rev. Designer:** Emanuel Hahn **Note:** All genuine circulation strike 1955 Arnprior dollars have a die break running along the top of TI in the word GRATIA on the obverse.

Date	Mintage	F-12	VF-20	XF-40	AU-50	MS-60	MS-63	Proof
1953	1,074,578	—	—	BV	9.50	10.00	25.00	400
Note: Without strap, wire rim								
1953	Inc. above	—	—	BV	9.50	10.00	25.00	—
Note: With strap, flat rim								
1954	246,606	BV	9.50	10.00	11.00	16.00	35.00	—
1955	268,105	BV	9.50	10.00	11.00	15.00	29.00	—
Note: With 3 water lines								
1955	Inc. above	45.00	65.00	90.00	100	125	175	—
Note: Arnprior with 1-1/2 water lines* and die break								
1956	209,092	BV	9.50	13.00	16.00	20.00	50.00	—
1957	496,389	—	—	—	BV	9.50	16.00	—
Note: With 3 water lines								
1957	Inc. above	—	BV	9.50	10.00	15.00	35.00	—
Note: With 1 water line								
1959	1,443,502	—	—	—	—		11.00	—
1960	1,420,486	—	—	—	—		11.00	—
1961	1,262,231	—	—	—	—		11.00	—
1962	1,884,789	—	—	—	—		11.00	—
1963	4,179,981	—	—	—	—		9.50	—

KM# 55 DOLLAR **Weight:** 23.3276 g. **Composition:** 0.8000 Silver 0.6000 oz. ASW **Ruler:** Elizabeth II **Subject:** British Columbia **Obverse:** Laureate bust right **Obv. Designer:** Mary Gillick **Reverse:** Totem Pole, dates at left, denomination below **Rev. Designer:** Stephan Trenka

Date	Mintage	F-12	VF-20	XF-40	AU-50	MS-60	MS-63	Proof
ND(1958)	3,039,630	—	—	BV	9.50	10.00	15.00	—

KM# 58 DOLLAR **Weight:** 23.3276 g. **Composition:** 0.8000 Silver 0.6000 oz. ASW **Ruler:** Elizabeth II **Subject:** Charlottetown **Obverse:** Laureate bust right **Reverse:** Design at center, dates at outer edges, denomination below **Rev. Designer:** Dinko Voldanovic **Size:** 36 mm.

Date	Mintage	F-12	VF-20	XF-40	AU-50	MS-60	MS-63	Proof
ND(1964)	7,296,832	—	—	—	—		9.50	—
ND(1964) Specimen proof	Inc. above	—	—	—	—	—	—	250

Small beads Medium beads Large beads

KM# 64.1 DOLLAR **Weight:** 23.3276 g. **Composition:** 0.8000 Silver 0.6000 oz. ASW **Ruler:** Elizabeth II **Obverse:** Young bust right **Obv. Designer:** Arnold Machin **Reverse:** Voyageur, date and denomination below **Rev. Designer:** Emanual Hahn **Size:** 36 mm.

Date	Mintage	F-12	VF-20	XF-40	AU-50	MS-60	MS-63	Proof
1965	10,768,569	—	—	—	—		9.50	—
Note: Small beads, pointed 5								
1965	Inc. above	—	—	—	—		9.50	—
Note: Small beads, blunt 5								
1965	Inc. above	—	—	—	—		9.50	—
Note: Large beads, blunt 5								
1965	Inc. above	—	—	—	—		11.00	—
Note: Large beads, pointed 5								
1965	Inc. above	—	BV	9.50	10.00	12.00	35.00	—
Note: Medium beads, pointed 5								
1966	9,912,178	—	—	—	—		9.50	—
Note: Large beads								
1966	485	—	—	1,200	1,500	1,800	3,300	—
Note: Small beads								

KM# 70 DOLLAR **Weight:** 23.3276 g. **Composition:** 0.8000 Silver 0.6000 oz. ASW **Ruler:** Elizabeth II **Subject:** Confederation Centennial **Obverse:** Young bust right **Obv. Designer:** Arnold Machin **Reverse:** Goose left, dates below, denomination above **Rev. Designer:** Alex Colville **Size:** 36 mm.

Date	Mintage	MS-63	Proof
ND(1967)	6,767,496	11.00	12.00

KM# 76.1 DOLLAR **Composition:** Nickel **Ruler:** Elizabeth II **Obverse:** Young bust right **Obv. Designer:** Arnold Machin **Reverse:** Voyageur, date and denomination below **Rev. Designer:** Emanuel Hahn **Size:** 32 mm.

Date	Mintage	MS-63	P/L	Proof
1968	5,579,714	1.25	—	—
1968	1,408,143	—	1.75	—
1968	—	8.50	—	—
Note: Small island				
1968	—	—	4.00	—
Note: No island				
1968	—	—	25.00	—
Note: Doubled die; exhibits extra water lines				
1969	4,809,313	1.25	—	—
1969	594,258	—	2.00	—
1972	2,676,041	1.50	—	—
1972	405,865	—	2.50	—

KM# 78 DOLLAR **Composition:** Nickel **Ruler:** Elizabeth II **Subject:** Manitoba **Obverse:** Young bust right **Reverse:** Pasque flower divides dates and denomination **Rev. Designer:** Raymond Taylor **Size:** 32 mm.

Date	Mintage	MS-63	P/L	Proof
1970	4,140,058	2.00	—	—
1970	645,869	—	2.50	—

KM# 79 DOLLAR **Composition:** Nickel **Ruler:** Elizabeth II **Subject:** British Columbia **Obverse:** Young bust right **Reverse:** Shield divides dates, denomination below, flowers above **Rev. Designer:** Thomas Shingles **Size:** 32 mm.

Date	Mintage	MS-63	P/L	Proof
1971	4,260,781	2.00	—	—
1971	468,729	—	2.25	—

KM# 82 DOLLAR **Composition:** Nickel **Ruler:** Elizabeth II **Subject:** Prince Edward Island **Obverse:** Young bust right **Reverse:** Building, inscription below divides dates, denomination above **Rev. Designer:** Terry Manning **Size:** 32 mm.

Date	Mintage	MS-63	P/L	Proof
1973	3,196,452	2.00	—	—
1973 (c)	466,881	—	2.50	—

KM# 88 DOLLAR **Composition:** Nickel **Ruler:** Elizabeth II **Subject:** Winnipeg Centennial **Obverse:** Young bust right **Reverse:** Zeros frame pictures, dates below, denomination at bottom **Rev. Designer:** Paul Pederson and Patrick Brindley **Size:** 32 mm.

Date	Mintage	MS-63	P/L	Proof
1974	2,799,363	2.00	—	—
1974 (c)	363,786	—	2.50	—

KM# 76.2 DOLLAR **Weight:** 15.6200 g. **Composition:** Nickel **Ruler:** Elizabeth II **Obverse:** Smaller young bust right **Obv. Designer:** Arnold Machin **Reverse:** Voyageur **Rev. Designer:** Emanuel Hahn **Size:** 32 mm.

Date	Mintage	MS-63	P/L	Proof
1975	3,256,000	1.50	—	—
1975	322,325	—	2.50	—
1976	2,498,204	1.50	—	—
1976	274,106	—	2.50	—

KM# 117 DOLLAR **Composition:** Nickel **Ruler:** Elizabeth II **Obverse:** Young bust right **Obv. Designer:** Arnold Machin **Reverse:** Voyageur modified **Rev. Designer:** Emanuel Hahn **Size:** 32 mm.

Date	Mintage	MS-63	P/L	Proof
1977	1,393,745	2.25	—	—
1977	—	—	2.50	—

KM# 120.1 DOLLAR **Weight:** 15.6200 g. **Composition:** Nickel **Ruler:** Elizabeth II **Obverse:** Young bust right **Obv. Designer:** Arnold Machin **Reverse:** Voyageur, date and denomination below **Rev. Designer:** Emanuel Hahn **Size:** 32.13 mm. **Note:** Modified design.

Date	Mintage	MS-63	Proof
1978	2,948,488	1.50	—
1979	2,954,842	1.50	—
1980	3,291,221	1.50	—
1981	2,778,900	1.50	—
1981 Proof	—	—	—
1982	1,098,500	1.50	—
1982 Proof	180,908	—	5.25
1983	2,267,525	1.50	—
1983 Proof	166,779	—	5.25
1984	1,223,486	1.50	—
1984 Proof	161,602	—	6.00
1985	3,104,092	1.50	—
1985 Proof	153,950	—	7.00
1986	3,089,225	2.00	—
1986 Proof	176,224	—	7.50
1987	287,330	3.50	—
1987 Proof	175,686	—	7.50

KM# 157 DOLLAR **Weight:** 7.0000 g. **Composition:** Aureate-Bronze Plated Nickel **Ruler:** Elizabeth II **Obverse:** Young bust right **Obv. Designer:** Arnold Machin **Reverse:** Loon right, date and denomination below **Rev. Designer:** Robert R. Carmichael **Shape:** 11-sided **Size:** 26.5 mm.

Date	Mintage	MS-63	Proof
1987	205,405,000	2.25	—
1987 Proof	178,120	—	8.00
1988	138,893,539	2.25	—
1988 Proof	175,259	—	6.75
1989	184,773,902	3.00	—
1989 Proof	170,928	—	6.75

KM# 186 DOLLAR **Weight:** 7.0000 g. **Composition:** Aureate-Bronze Plated Nickel **Ruler:** Elizabeth II **Obverse:** Crowned head right **Obv. Designer:** Dora dePedery-Hunt **Reverse:** Loon right, date and denomination **Rev. Designer:** Robert R. Carmichael **Shape:** 11-sided **Size:** 26.5 mm.

Date	Mintage	MS-63	Proof
1990	68,402,000	1.75	—
1990 Proof	140,649	—	7.00
1991	23,156,000	1.75	—
1991 Proof	—	—	13.00
1993	33,662,000	2.00	—
1993 Proof	—	—	6.00
1994	16,232,530	2.00	—
1994 Proof	—	—	7.00
1995	27,492,630	3.00	—
1995 Proof	—	—	7.00
1996	17,101,000	2.00	—
1996 Proof	—	—	7.50
1997	—	5.00	—
1997 Proof	—	—	8.00
1998	—	2.50	—
1998 Proof	—	—	10.00
1998W	—	—	—
1999	—	2.00	—
1999 Proof	—	—	8.00
2000	—	2.00	—
2000 Proof	—	—	8.00
2001	—	2.50	—
2001 Proof	—	—	8.00
2002	—	4.50	—
2002 Proof	—	—	7.50
2003	—	5.50	—
2003 Proof	100,000	—	12.00

KM# 209 DOLLAR **Composition:** Aureate **Ruler:** Elizabeth II **Subject:** Loon right, dates and denomination **Obverse:** Crowned head right **Rev. Designer:** Robert R. Carmichael **Size:** 26.5 mm.

Date	Mintage	MS-63	Proof
ND(1992)	4,242,085	2.00	—
ND(1992) Proof	—	—	8.00

KM# 218 DOLLAR **Composition:** Aureate **Ruler:** Elizabeth II **Subject:** Parliament **Obverse:** Crowned head right, dates below **Reverse:** Backs of three seated figures in front of building, denomination below **Rev. Designer:** Rita Swanson **Size:** 26 mm.

Date	Mintage	MS-63	Proof
ND(1992)	23,915,000	2.25	—
ND(1992) Proof	24,227	—	9.00

KM# 248 DOLLAR **Composition:** Aureate **Ruler:** Elizabeth II **Subject:** War Memorial **Obverse:** Crowned head right, date below **Reverse:** Memorial, denomination at right **Rev. Designer:** R. C. M. Staff **Size:** 26 mm.

Date	Mintage	MS-63	Proof
1994	20,004,830	2.25	—
1994 Proof	54,524	—	7.50

KM# 258 DOLLAR **Weight:** 7.0000 g. **Composition:** Aureate **Ruler:** Elizabeth II **Subject:** Peacekeeping Monument in Ottawa **Obverse:** Crowned head right, date below **Reverse:** Monument, denomination above right **Rev. Designer:** J. K. Harmon, R. G. Henriquez and C. H. Oberlander **Size:** 26 mm. **Note:** Mintage included with KM#186.

Date	Mintage	MS-63	Proof
1995	18,502,750	2.25	—
1995 Proof	43,293	—	7.50

KM# 291 DOLLAR **Composition:** Aureate **Ruler:** Elizabeth II **Subject:** Loon Dollar 10th Anniversary **Obverse:** Crowned head right **Reverse:** Loon in flight left, dates above, denomination below **Rev. Designer:** Jean-Luc Grondin **Size:** 26 mm.

Date	Mintage	MS-63	P/L	Proof
1997	—	—	22.00	—

KM# 467 DOLLAR **Weight:** 7.0000 g. **Composition:** Aureate-Bronze Plated Nickel **Ruler:** Elizabeth II **Subject:** Elizabeth II Golden Jubilee **Obverse:** Crowned head right, Jubilee commemorative dates 1952-2002 **Obv. Designer:** Dora dePédery-Hunt

Date	Mintage	MS-63	Proof
ND(2002)	—	2.50	—
ND(2002) Proof	—	—	8.00

KM# 495 DOLLAR **Weight:** 7.0000 g. **Composition:** Aureate-Bronze Plated Nickel **Ruler:** Elizabeth II **Obverse:** Crowned head right **Obv. Designer:** Susanna Blunt **Rev. Designer:** Robert R. Carmichael **Size:** 26.5 mm.

Date	Mintage	MS-63	Proof
2003	5,102,000	5.50	—
2003	—	—	7.50
2003W	—	7.50	—
2004	3,409,000	3.00	—
2004 Proof	—	—	12.00
2005	—	3.00	—
2005 Proof	—	—	7.50
2006	—	3.00	—
2006 Proof	—	—	7.50
2006(ml)	—	3.00	—
2006(ml) Proof	—	—	7.50

KM# 513 DOLLAR **Weight:** 7.0000 g. **Composition:** Aureate-Bronze Plated Nickel **Ruler:** Elizabeth II **Subject:** Olympics **Obverse:** Crowned head right **Reverse:** Maple leaf, Olympic flame and rings above loon **Edge:** Plain **Shape:** 11-sided **Size:** 26.5 mm.

Date	Mintage	MS-63	Proof
2004	6,526,000	8.00	—

KM# 552 DOLLAR **Weight:** 7.0000 g. **Composition:** Aureate-Bronze Plated Nickel **Ruler:** Elizabeth II **Subject:** Terry Fox **Obverse:** Head right

Date	Mintage	MS-63	Proof
2005	1,290,900	3.50	—

KM# 581 DOLLAR **Weight:** 7.0000 g. **Composition:** 0.9250 Silver 0.2082 oz. ASW **Ruler:** Elizabeth II **Subject:** Lullabies Loonie **Obverse:** Head right **Obv. Designer:** Susanna Blunt **Reverse:** Loon and moon, teddy bear in stars

Date	Mintage	MS-63	Proof
2006	—	3.50	—

KM# 630 DOLLAR **Weight:** 7.0000 g. **Composition:** 0.9250 Silver And Multi-Color Enamel 0.2082 oz. **Ruler:** Elizabeth II **Subject:** Olympic Games **Obverse:** Crowned head right

Date	Mintage	MS-63	Proof
2006	19,956	30.00	—

KM# 270 2 DOLLARS **Weight:** 7.3000 g. **Composition:** Bi-Metallic **Ruler:** Elizabeth II **Obverse:** Crowned head right within circle, date below **Obv. Designer:** Dora dePedery-Hunt **Reverse:** Polar bear right within circle, denomination below **Rev. Designer:** Brent Townsend **Size:** 28 mm.

Date	Mintage	MS-63	Proof
1996	375,483,000	3.25	—
1996 Proof	—	—	10.00
1997	16,942,000	3.25	—
1998	4,926,000	3.25	—
1998W	—	3.25	—
1999	25,130,000	3.25	—
2000	29,847,000	3.25	—
2000W	—	3.25	—
2001	27,008,000	5.00	—
2001 Proof	—	—	12.50
2002	11,910,000	5.00	—
2002 Proof	—	—	12.50
2003	—	5.00	—
2003 Proof	—	—	12.50

KM# 496 2 DOLLARS **Weight:** 7.3000 g. **Composition:** Bi-Metallic **Ruler:** Elizabeth II **Obverse:** Head right **Obv. Designer:** Susanna Blunt **Rev. Designer:** Brent Townsend

Date	Mintage	MS-63	Proof
2003	—	5.00	—
2003W	—	—	18.00
2004	—	5.00	—
2004 Proof	—	—	12.50
2005	—	5.00	—
2005 Proof	—	—	12.50
2006	—	5.00	—
2006 Proof	—	—	12.50

KM# 496a 2 DOLLARS **Weight:** 10.8414 g. **Composition:** 0.9250 Bi-Metallic Gold And Silver 0.3224 oz. **Ruler:** Elizabeth II **Obverse:** Head right **Obv. Designer:** Suanne Blunt **Reverse:** Polar Bear **Edge:** Segmented reeding **Size:** 28 mm.

Date	Mintage	MS-63	Proof
2004 Proof	—	—	25.00

KM# 14 SOVEREIGN **Weight:** 7.9881 g. **Composition:** 0.9170 Gold 0.2355 oz. AGW **Ruler:** Edward VII **Reverse:** St. George slaying dragon, mint mark below horse's rear hooves

Date	Mintage	F-12	VF-20	XF-40	AU-50	MS-60	MS-63
1908C	636	1,250	1,850	2,350	2,600	2,850	4,000
1909C	16,273	200	225	250	285	500	1,600
1910C	28,012	BV	200	225	265	500	3,000

KM# 20 SOVEREIGN **Weight:** 7.9881 g. **Composition:** 0.9170 Gold 0.2355 oz. AGW **Ruler:** George V **Reverse:** St. George slaying dragon, mint mark below horse's rear hooves

Date	Mintage	F-12	VF-20	XF-40	AU-50	MS-60	MS-63
1911C	256,946	—	—	BV	BV	200	250
1911C Specimen	—	—	—	—	—	—	—
1913C	3,715	550	700	950	1,200	1,500	3,000
1914C	14,871	200	225	350	450	600	950
1916C About 20 known	—	8,000	12,500	15,750	17,750	20,000	27,500
Note: Stacks' A.G. Carter Jr. Sale 12-89 Gem BU realized $82,500							
1917C	58,845	—	—	BV	BV	200	750
1918C	106,514	—	—	BV	BV	200	1,100
1919C	135,889	—	—	BV	BV	200	750

KM# 26 5 DOLLARS **Weight:** 8.3592 g. **Composition:** 0.9000 Gold 0.2419 oz. AGW **Ruler:** George V **Obverse:** Crowned bust left **Obv. Designer:** E. B. MacKennal **Reverse:** Arms within wreath, date and denomination below **Rev. Designer:** W. H. J. Blakemore

Date	Mintage	F-12	VF-20	XF-40	AU-50	MS-60	MS-63
1912	165,680	BV	225	250	275	325	800
1913	98,832	BV	225	250	275	325	900
1914	31,122	225	—	350	425	650	3,000

KM# 27 10 DOLLARS **Weight:** 16.7185 g. **Composition:** 0.9000 Gold 0.4837 oz. AGW **Ruler:** George V **Obverse:** Crowned bust left **Obv. Designer:** E. B. MacKennal **Reverse:** Arms within wreath, date and denomination below **Rev. Designer:** W. H. J. Blakemore

Date	Mintage	F-12	VF-20	XF-40	AU-50	MS-60	MS-63
1912	74,759	BV	BV	450	500	800	3,000
1913	149,232	BV	BV	450	500	800	3,000
1914	140,068	BV	450	500	550	1,000	4,000

KM# 484 20 DOLLARS **Composition:** 0.9250 Silver **Ruler:** Elizabeth II **Subject:** Canadian National FA-1 diesel-electric locomotive **Obverse:** Crowned head right **Obv. Designer:** Dora dePédery-Hunt **Rev. Designer:** John Mardon, William Woodruff

Date	Mintage	MS-63	Proof
2003 Proof	15,000	—	40.00

NEWFOUNDLAND

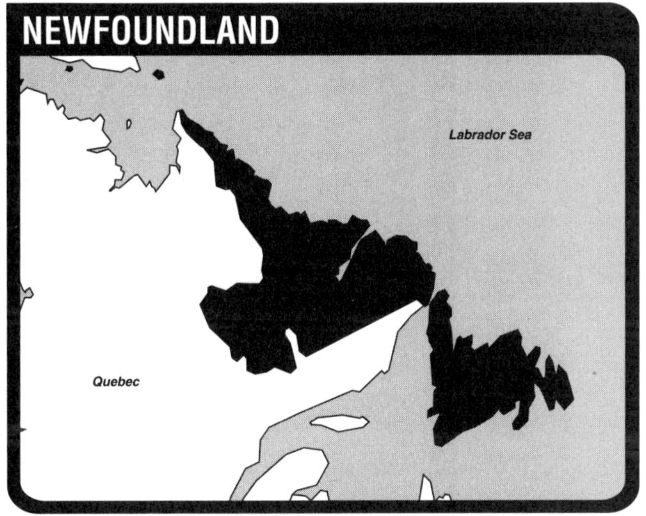

Island which along with Labrador became a province of Canada. Prehistoric inhabitants left evidence of an early presence on the island. Norsemen briefly settled on the island but officially discovered in 1497 by Italian explorer John Cabot. English settlements were sporadic and disputed by France. The English settled along the east coast and the French along the west coast of the island. With the treaty of Utrecht in 1713, it officially became English, but the fishing rights went to France. Controversies continued through the 19th century.

PROVINCE

CIRCULATION COINAGE

KM# 9 LARGE CENT **Composition:** Bronze **Obverse:** Crowned bust right **Obv. Designer:** G.W. DeSaulles **Reverse:** Crown and date within center circle, wreath surrounds, denomination above **Rev. Designer:** Horace Morehen

Date	Mintage	VG-8	F-12	VF-20	XF-40	MS-60	MS-63	Proof
1904H	100,000	7.00	14.00	20.00	55.00	300	700	—
1904H Proof	—	—	—	—	—	—	—	4,000
1907	200,000	2.00	4.00	8.00	30.00	220	650	—
1909	200,000	2.00	4.00	7.00	19.00	100	150	—
1909 Proof	—	—	—	—	—	—	—	400

KM# 16 LARGE CENT **Composition:** Bronze **Obverse:** Crowned bust left **Obv. Designer:** E.B. MacKennal **Reverse:** Crown and date within center circle, wreath surrounds, denomination above **Rev. Designer:** Horace Morehen

Date	Mintage	VG-8	F-12	VF-20	XF-40	MS-60	MS-63	Proof
1913	400,000	1.00	1.50	3.00	7.00	40.00	75.00	—
1917C	702,350	1.00	1.50	3.00	6.00	75.00	200	—
1917C Proof	—	—	—	—	—	—	—	800
1919C	300,000	1.00	2.00	3.00	10.00	175	300	—
1919C Proof	—	—	—	—	—	—	—	1,000
1920C	302,184	1.00	2.00	5.00	18.00	300	1,000	—

Date	Mintage	VG-8	F-12	VF-20	XF-40	MS-60	MS-63	Proof
1929	300,000	1.00	1.50	3.00	6.00	55.00	100	—
1929C Proof	—	—	—	—	—	—	—	1,000
1936	300,000	1.00	1.25	1.75	4.00	28.00	75.00	—

KM# 18 SMALL CENT **Weight:** 3.2000 g. **Composition:** Bronze **Obverse:** Crowned head left **Obv. Designer:** Percy Metcalfe **Reverse:** Pitcher plant divides date, denomination below **Rev. Designer:** Walter J. Newman **Size:** 19 mm.

Date	Mintage	VG-8	F-12	VF-20	XF-40	MS-60	MS-63	Proof
1938	500,000	0.50	0.75	1.50	2.50	16.00	40.00	—
1938 Proof	—	—	—	—	—	—	—	1,000
1940	300,000	1.25	2.00	3.00	10.00	75.00	250	—
1940 Re-engraved date	—	30.00	40.00	125	70.00	500	900	—
1940 Proof	—	—	—	—	—	—	—	1,000
1941C	827,662	0.35	0.45	0.70	2.00	20.00	120	—
1941C Re-engraved date	—	9.00	13.00	30.00	65.00	250	700	—
1942	1,996,889	0.35	0.45	0.70	2.00	30.00	125	—
1943C	1,239,732	0.35	0.45	0.70	2.00	13.50	70.00	—
1944C	1,328,776	1.00	2.00	10.00	30.00	250	550	—
1947C	313,772	0.90	1.65	5.00	12.00	80.00	200	—
1947C Proof	—	—	—	—	—	—	—	2,000

KM# 7 5 CENTS **Weight:** 1.1782 g. **Composition:** 0.9250 Silver 0.0350 oz. ASW **Obverse:** Crowned bust right **Reverse:** Denomination and date within circle

Date	Mintage	VG-8	F-12	VF-20	XF-40	MS-60	MS-63	Proof
1903	100,000	4.00	9.00	18.00	45.00	435	1,350	—
1903 Proof	—	—	—	—	—	—	—	2,000
1904H	100,000	3.00	5.00	14.00	35.00	160	285	—
1904H Proof	—	—	—	—	—	—	—	1,200
1908	400,000	3.00	6.00	11.50	30.00	260	750	—

KM# 13 5 CENTS **Weight:** 1.1782 g. **Composition:** 0.9250 Silver 0.0350 oz. ASW **Obverse:** Crowned bust left **Obv. Designer:** E.B. MacKennal **Reverse:** Denomination and date within circle **Rev. Designer:** G.W. DeSaulles

Date	Mintage	VG-8	F-12	VF-20	XF-40	MS-60	MS-63	Proof
1912	300,000	1.50	2.00	5.00	20.00	125	275	—
1912 Proof	—	—	—	—	—	—	—	2,000
1917C	300,319	1.50	3.00	7.00	25.00	250	650	—
1917C Proof	—	—	—	—	—	—	—	2,000
1919C	100,844	5.00	9.00	25.00	100	950	2,800	—
1919C Proof	—	—	—	—	—	—	—	2,000
1929	300,000	1.50	2.50	3.25	12.00	165	350	—

KM# 19 5 CENTS **Weight:** 1.1782 g. **Composition:** 0.9250 Silver 0.0350 oz. ASW **Obverse:** Crowned head left **Obv. Designer:** Percy Metcalfe **Reverse:** Denomination and date within circle **Rev. Designer:** G.W. DeSaulles

Date	Mintage	VG-8	F-12	VF-20	XF-40	MS-60	MS-63	Proof
1938	100,000	0.85	1.50	2.00	7.00	70.00	225	—
1938 Proof	—	—	—	—	—	—	—	1,000
1940C	200,000	0.85	1.50	2.00	7.00	85.00	300	—
1940C Proof	—	—	—	—	—	—	—	2,000
1941C	621,641	0.65	1.50	2.00	4.00	15.00	35.00	—
1942C	298,348	0.85	1.50	2.00	4.00	17.50	40.00	—
1943C	351,666	0.65	1.00	2.00	4.00	15.00	30.00	—

KM# 19a 5 CENTS **Weight:** 1.1664 g. **Composition:** 0.8000 Silver 0.0300 oz. ASW **Obverse:** Crowned head left **Obv. Designer:** Percy Metcalfe **Reverse:** Denomination and date within circle **Rev. Designer:** G.W. DeSaulles

Date	Mintage	VG-8	F-12	VF-20	XF-40	MS-60	MS-63	Proof
1944C	286,504	1.25	1.75	3.00	7.00	50.00	120	—
1945C	203,828	0.65	1.00	2.00	4.00	14.00	32.00	—
1946C	2,041	200	300	350	400	1,200	1,900	—
1946C Prooflike	—	—	—	—	—	—	2,500	—
1947C	38,400	2.00	3.00	5.00	17.00	65.00	200	—
1947C Prooflike	—	—	—	—	—	—	375	—

KM# 8 10 CENTS **Weight:** 2.3564 g. **Composition:** 0.9250 Silver 0.0701 oz. ASW
Obverse: Crowned bust right **Reverse:** Denomination and date within circle

Date	Mintage	VG-8	F-12	VF-20	XF-40	MS-60	MS-63	Proof
1903	100,000	8.00	25.00	70.00	200	1,200	4,400	—
1903 Proof	—	—	—	—	—	—	—	2,500
1904H	100,000	4.00	10.00	30.00	90.00	200	350	—
1904H Proof	—	—	—	—	—	—	—	1,500

KM# 14 10 CENTS **Weight:** 2.3564 g. **Composition:** 0.9250 Silver 0.0701 oz. ASW
Obverse: Crowned bust left **Obv. Designer:** E.B. MacKennal **Rev. Designer:** G.W. DeSaulles

Date	Mintage	VG-8	F-12	VF-20	XF-40	MS-60	MS-63	Proof
1912	150,000	1.20	3.00	10.00	40.00	165	300	—
1917C	250,805	1.20	3.00	11.00	40.00	400	1,500	—
1919C	54,342	2.00	6.00	18.00	55.00	175	350	—

KM# 20 10 CENTS **Weight:** 2.3564 g. **Composition:** 0.9250 Silver 0.0701 oz. ASW
Obverse: Crowned head left **Obv. Designer:** Percy Metcalfe **Reverse:** Denomination and date within circle **Rev. Designer:** G.W. DeSaulles

Date	Mintage	VG-8	F-12	VF-20	XF-40	MS-60	MS-63	Proof
1938	100,000	1.10	1.75	3.00	11.00	80.00	300	—
1938 Proof	—	—	—	—	—	—	—	2,000
1940	100,000	1.10	1.50	3.00	10.00	80.00	300	—
1940 Proof	—	—	—	—	—	—	—	2,500
1941C	483,630	1.10	1.50	2.20	5.00	40.00	125	—
1942C	293,736	1.10	1.50	2.20	5.00	50.00	130	—
1943C	104,706	1.10	1.50	2.50	6.00	60.00	200	—
1944C	151,471	2.50	3.50	10.00	20.00	200	800	—

KM# 20a 10 CENTS **Weight:** 2.3328 g. **Composition:** 0.8000 Silver 0.0600 oz. ASW
Obverse: Crowned head left **Obv. Designer:** Percy Metcalfe **Rev. Designer:** G.W. DeSaulles

Date	Mintage	VG-8	F-12	VF-20	XF-40	MS-60	MS-63	Proof
1945C	175,833	1.00	1.35	2.25	4.50	45.00	225	—
1946C	38,400	2.00	4.00	10.00	25.00	100	275	—
1946C Proof	—	—	—	—	—	—	—	750
1947C	61,988	1.50	3.00	4.50	14.00	65.00	275	—

KM# 10 20 CENTS **Weight:** 4.7127 g. **Composition:** 0.9250 Silver 0.1401 oz. ASW
Obverse: Crowned bust right **Obv. Designer:** G.W. DeSaulles **Reverse:** Denomination and date within circle **Rev. Designer:** W.H.J. Blakemore

Date	Mintage	VG-8	F-12	VF-20	XF-40	MS-60	MS-63	Proof
1904H	75,000	10.00	30.00	55.00	275	2,500	6,000	—
1904H Proof	—	—	—	—	—	—	—	1,850

KM# 15 20 CENTS **Weight:** 4.7127 g. **Composition:** 0.9250 Silver 0.1401 oz. ASW
Obverse: Crowned bust left **Obv. Designer:** E.B. MacKennal **Reverse:** Denomination and date within circle **Rev. Designer:** W.H.J. Blakemore

Date	Mintage	VG-8	F-12	VF-20	XF-40	MS-60	MS-63	Proof
1912	350,000	2.50	5.00	14.00	55.00	325	850	—
1912 Proof	—	—	—	—	—	—	—	2,500

KM# 17 25 CENTS **Weight:** 5.8319 g. **Composition:** 0.9250 Silver 0.1734 oz. ASW
Obverse: Crowned bust left **Obv. Designer:** E.B. MacKennal **Reverse:** Denomination and date within circle **Rev. Designer:** W.H.J. Blakemore

Date	Mintage	VG-8	F-12	VF-20	XF-40	MS-60	MS-63	Proof
1917C	464,779	3.00	4.00	7.00	17.00	145	300	—
1917C Proof	—	—	—	—	—	—	—	2,500
1919C	163,939	3.00	5.00	14.00	25.00	350	1,250	—
1919C Proof	—	—	—	—	—	—	—	2,500

KM# 11 50 CENTS **Weight:** 11.7800 g. **Composition:** 0.9250 Silver 0.3503 oz. ASW
Obverse: Crowned bust right **Obv. Designer:** G.W. DeSaulles **Rev. Designer:** W.H.J. Blakemore **Size:** 30 mm.

Date	Mintage	VG-8	F-12	VF-20	XF-40	MS-60	MS-63	Proof
1904H	140,000	5.00	6.00	14.00	55.00	275	850	—
1904H Proof	—	—	—	—	—	—	—	5,000
1907	100,000	5.00	6.00	22.00	65.00	350	1,000	—
1908	160,000	5.00	6.00	13.50	50.00	225	700	—
1909	200,000	5.00	12.00	21.00	55.00	300	800	—

KM# 12 50 CENTS **Weight:** 11.7800 g. **Composition:** 0.9250 Silver 0.3503 oz. ASW
Obverse: Crowned bust left **Obv. Designer:** E.B. MacKennal **Reverse:** Denomination and date within circle **Rev. Designer:** W.H.J. Blakemore **Size:** 30 mm.

Date	Mintage	VG-8	F-12	VF-20	XF-40	MS-60	MS-63	Proof
1911	200,000	5.00	6.00	11.00	35.00	200	550	—
1917C	375,560	5.00	6.00	11.00	28.00	145	350	—
1917C Proof	—	—	—	—	—	—	—	2,500
1918C	294,824	5.00	6.00	11.00	28.00	145	350	—
1919C	306,267	5.00	6.00	11.00	30.00	325	1,150	—
1919C Proof	—	—	—	—	—	—	—	2,500

CAPE VERDE

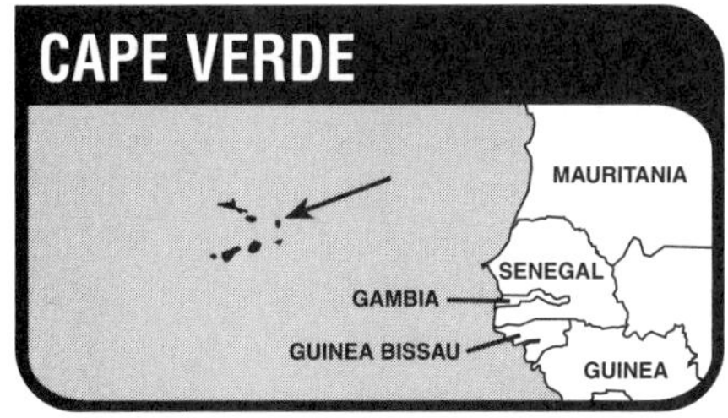

The Republic of Cape Verde, Africa's smallest republic, is located in the Atlantic Ocean, about 370 miles (595 km.) west of Dakar, Senegal, off the coast of Africa. The 14-island republic has an area of 1,557 sq. mi. (4,033 sq. km.) and a population of 435,983. Capital: Praia. The refueling of ships and aircraft is the chief economic function of the country. Fishing is important and agriculture is widely practiced, but the Cape Verdes are not self-sufficient in food. Fish products, salt, bananas, and shellfish are exported.

The date of discovery of the islands is uncertain. Possibly they were visited by Venetian captain Alvise Cadamosto in 1456. Portuguese navigator Diogo Gomes claimed them for Portugal in May of 1460. Settlement began two years later. The early importance and wealth of the islands, which caused them to be attacked by Sir Francis Drake and the Dutch, resulted from the monopoly of the Guinea slave trade granted the inhabitants in 1466. Poverty and famine occasioned by frequent periods of severe drought have marked the history of the country since abolition of the slave trade in 1876.

After 500 years of Portuguese rule, the Cape Verdes became independent on July 5, 1975. At the first general election, all seats of the new national assembly were won by the Party for the Independence of Guinea-Bissau and Cape Verde (PAIGC). The PAIGC linked the two former colonies into one state. Antonio Mascarenhas Monteiro won the first free presidential election in 1991.

RULER

Portuguese, until 1975

MONETARY SYSTEM

100 Centavos = 1 Escudo

PORTUGUESE COLONY

COLONIAL COINAGE

KM# 1 5 CENTAVOS

Bronze **Obv:** Liberty head left **Rev:** Denomination at center, date below

Date	Mintage	F	VF	XF	Unc	BU
1930	1,000,000	0.75	1.50	3.50	10.00	—

KM# 2 10 CENTAVOS

Bronze **Obv:** Denomination at center, date below **Rev:** Liberty head left

Date	Mintage	F	VF	XF	Unc	BU
1930	1,500,000	0.75	1.50	4.00	12.00	—

KM# 3 20 CENTAVOS

Bronze **Obv:** Denomination at center, date below **Rev:** Liberty head left

Date	Mintage	F	VF	XF	Unc	BU
1930	1,500,000	1.00	2.00	5.00	15.00	—

KM# 4 50 CENTAVOS

Nickel-Bronze **Obv:** Liberty head right, long loose hair **Rev:** Encircled arms within wreath, denomination below

Date	Mintage	F	VF	XF	Unc	BU
1930	1,000,000	7.00	30.00	95.00	275	—

KM# 6 50 CENTAVOS

Nickel-Bronze **Obv:** Denomination **Rev:** Miniature crowns above encircled arms, date below

Date	Mintage	F	VF	XF	Unc	BU
1949	1,000,000	0.50	1.00	2.50	6.00	—

KM# 11 50 CENTAVOS

3.4000 g., Bronze, 20 mm. **Obv:** Denomination **Rev:** Miniature crowns above arms, date below

Date	Mintage	F	VF	XF	Unc	BU
1968	1,000,000	0.25	0.50	1.00	2.50	—

KM# 5 ESCUDO

Nickel-Bronze, 26 mm. **Obv:** Liberty head right, long loose hair **Rev:** Encircled arms within wreath, denomination below

Date	Mintage	F	VF	XF	Unc	BU
1930	50,000	15.00	65.00	125	350	—

KM# 7 ESCUDO

Nickel-Bronze, 26 mm. **Obv:** Denomination **Rev:** Miniature crowns above encircled arms, date below

Date	Mintage	F	VF	XF	Unc	BU
1949	500,000	1.25	2.50	5.50	12.50	—

KM# 8 ESCUDO

8.0000 g., Bronze, 26 mm. **Obv:** Denomination **Rev:** Miniature crowns above encircled arms, date below

Date	Mintage	F	VF	XF	Unc	BU
1953	250,000	1.00	5.00	18.00	35.00	—
1968	500,000	0.50	1.00	2.00	5.00	—

KM# 9 2-1/2 ESCUDOS

3.5000 g., Nickel-Bronze, 20 mm. **Obv:** Arms on cross, date below **Rev:** Miniature crowns above arms, denomination below

Date	Mintage	F	VF	XF	Unc	BU
1953	500,000	1.50	8.00	35.00	85.00	—
1967	400,000	0.50	1.00	2.50	8.00	—

KM# 12 5 ESCUDOS

4.4100 g., Nickel-Bronze, 21 mm. **Obv:** Miniature crowns above arms, denomination below **Rev:** Arms on cross, date below

Date	Mintage	F	VF	XF	Unc	BU
1968	200,000	0.75	1.50	3.50	10.00	—

KM# 10 10 ESCUDOS

5.0000 g., 0.7200 Silver 0.1157 oz. ASW **Obv:** Arms on cross, date below **Rev:** Miniature crowns above arms, denomination below

Date	Mintage	F	VF	XF	Unc	BU
1953	400,000	2.00	3.50	6.50	18.00	—

REPUBLIC

DECIMAL COINAGE

KM# 15 20 CENTAVOS

1.3000 g., Aluminum, 21 mm. **Obv:** Emblem within wreath, date below **Rev:** Denomination above fish

Date	Mintage	F	VF	XF	Unc	BU
1977	—	0.10	0.20	0.30	0.65	—
1980	—	0.10	0.20	0.30	0.65	—

KM# 16 50 CENTAVOS

2.1000 g., Aluminum, 24.5 mm. **Obv:** Emblem within wreath, date below **Rev:** Denomination above fish

Date	Mintage	F	VF	XF	Unc	BU
1977	—	0.15	0.25	0.40	0.85	—
1980	—	0.15	0.25	0.40	0.85	—

KM# 17 ESCUDO

4.1000 g., Nickel-Bronze, 23.5 mm. **Series:** F.A.O. **Subject:** Education **Obv:** Emblem within wreath, denomination below, date at bottom **Rev:** Student at desk **Edge:** Reeded

Date	Mintage	F	VF	XF	Unc	BU
1977	1,000,000	0.25	0.50	0.85	1.75	3.00
1980	—	0.25	0.50	0.85	1.75	3.00

KM# 23 ESCUDO
3.9500 g., Brass Plated Steel, 23.5 mm. **Subject:** 10th Anniversary of Independence **Obv:** Emblem within wreath below denomination and date **Rev:** Inscription below building **Edge:** Reeded

Date	Mintage	F	VF	XF	Unc	BU
1985 Proof	—	Value: 350				
1985	—	—	—	0.75	1.50	2.50

KM# 27 ESCUDO
2.5500 g., Brass Plated Steel, 18 mm. **Obv:** Denomination on National emblem, date below **Rev:** Tartaruga Sea Turtle **Edge:** Plain

Date	Mintage	F	VF	XF	Unc	BU
1994	—	—	—	—	1.00	1.25

KM# 18 2-1/2 ESCUDOS
7.0000 g., Nickel-Bronze, 26 mm. **Series:** F.A.O. **Obv:** Emblem within wreath above denomination and date **Rev:** Coffee tree planting

Date	Mintage	F	VF	XF	Unc	BU
1977	1,200,000	0.25	0.50	0.85	1.75	—
1980	—	0.25	0.50	0.85	1.75	3.00
1982	—	0.25	0.50	0.85	1.75	—

KM# 28 5 ESCUDOS
3.9200 g., Copper Plated Steel, 20.97 mm. **Obv:** National emblem to right of denomination, date below **Rev:** Osprey

Date	Mintage	F	VF	XF	Unc	BU
1994	—	—	—	—	2.50	3.00

KM# 31 5 ESCUDOS
3.9600 g., Copper Plated Steel, 20.99 mm. **Obv:** National emblem to right of denomination, date below **Rev:** Flowers - Contra Bruxas

Date	Mintage	F	VF	XF	Unc	BU
1994	—	—	—	—	1.00	1.50

KM# 36 5 ESCUDOS
4.0000 g., Copper Plated Steel, 20.98 mm. **Obv:** National emblem to right of denomination, date below **Rev:** Sailboat - Belmira

Date	Mintage	F	VF	XF	Unc	BU
1994	—	—	—	—	1.00	1.50

KM# 19 10 ESCUDOS
9.0000 g., Copper-Nickel, 28.1 mm. **Obv:** Emblem within wreath above denomination and date **Rev:** Eduardo Mondlane

Date	Mintage	F	VF	XF	Unc	BU
1977	—	0.25	0.50	1.00	2.25	—
1980	—	0.25	0.50	1.00	2.25	—
1982	—	0.20	0.40	0.75	2.00	—

KM# 24 10 ESCUDOS
Copper-Nickel **Subject:** 10th Anniversary of Independence **Obv:** Emblem within wreath below denomination and date **Rev:** Letter design at center, star above

Date	Mintage	F	VF	XF	Unc	BU
1985 Proof	—	Value: 350				
1985	—	—	—	—	2.00	3.00

KM# 29 10 ESCUDOS
4.5100 g., Nickel Plated Steel **Obv:** National emblem, date at left, denomination upper left **Rev:** Brown-headed Kingfisher

Date	Mintage	F	VF	XF	Unc	BU
1994	—	—	—	—	4.00	5.00

KM# 32 10 ESCUDOS
4.5400 g., Nickel Plated Steel, 21.95 mm. **Obv:** National emblem, date at left, denomination upper left **Rev:** Flowers - Lingua De Vaca

Date	Mintage	F	VF	XF	Unc	BU
1994	—	—	—	—	1.50	2.00

KM# 41 10 ESCUDOS
4.5100 g., Nickel Plated Steel **Obv:** National emblem, date at left, denomination upper left **Rev:** Sailship "Carvalho"

Date	Mintage	F	VF	XF	Unc	BU
1994	—	—	—	—	1.50	2.00

KM# 20 20 ESCUDOS
12.0000 g., Copper-Nickel, 31.1 mm. **Obv:** Emblem within wreath above denomination and date **Rev:** Domingos Ramos

Date	Mintage	F	VF	XF	Unc	BU
1977	—	0.35	0.65	1.25	2.75	—
1980	—	0.35	0.65	1.25	2.75	—
1982	—	0.25	0.50	1.00	2.50	—

KM# 30 20 ESCUDOS
5.8000 g., Nickel Plated Steel, 24.94 mm. **Obv:** National emblem, date divided below, denomination at bottom **Rev:** Brown Booby

Date	Mintage	F	VF	XF	Unc	BU
1994	—	—	—	—	4.00	5.00

KM# 33 20 ESCUDOS
5.8000 g., Nickel Plated Steel, 24.93 mm. **Obv:** National emblem, date divided below, denomination at bottom **Rev:** Flowers - Carqueja

Date	Mintage	F	VF	XF	Unc	BU
1994	—	—	—	—	2.00	3.00

KM# 42 20 ESCUDOS
5.8100 g., Nickel Plated Steel, 24.90 mm. **Obv:** National emblem, date divided below, denomination at bottom **Rev:** Sailship "Novas de Alegria"

Date	Mintage	F	VF	XF	Unc	BU
1994	—	—	—	—	2.00	3.00

KM# 21 50 ESCUDOS
16.3000 g., Copper-Nickel, 34.1 mm. **Obv:** Emblem within wreath above denomination and date **Rev:** Head of Amilcar Lopes Cabral left, two dates on right

Date	Mintage	F	VF	XF	Unc	BU
1977	—	1.00	1.50	2.50	4.50	—
1980	—	1.00	1.50	2.50	4.50	—

KM# 37 50 ESCUDOS
7.4000 g., Copper Nickel, 27.89 mm. **Obv:** National emblem divides date, denomination above **Rev:** Cape Verde Sparrow left

Date	Mintage	F	VF	XF	Unc	BU
1994	—	—	—	—	12.00	15.00

KM# 43 50 ESCUDOS
Nickel Plated Steel, 27.99 mm. **Obv:** National emblem divides date, denomination above **Rev:** Sailship "Senhor das Areias"

Date	Mintage	F	VF	XF	Unc	BU
1994	—	—	—	—	5.00	6.00

KM# 44 50 ESCUDOS
5.0000 g., Nickel Plated Steel, 27.89 mm. **Obv:** National emblem **Rev:** Macelina flowers

Date	Mintage	F	VF	XF	Unc	BU
1994	—	—	—	—	5.00	6.00

KM# 25 100 ESCUDOS
Copper-Nickel **Subject:** Papal Visit **Obv:** Emblem within wreath above denomination and date **Rev:** Half figure of Pope

Date	Mintage	F	VF	XF	Unc	BU
1990	—	—	—	—	7.50	9.50

KM# 38 100 ESCUDOS
Bi-Metallic Copper-Nickel center in Bronze ring **Obv:** National emblem divides date, denomination at top, value at bottom **Rev:** Saiao flowers

Date	Mintage	F	VF	XF	Unc	BU
1994	—	—	—	—	8.00	9.00

KM# 38a 100 ESCUDOS
Bi-Metallic Copper-Nickel center in Brass ring **Obv:** National emblem divides date, denomination at top, value at bottom **Rev:** Saiao flowers

Date	Mintage	F	VF	XF	Unc	BU
1994	—	—	—	—	8.00	9.00

KM# 39 100 ESCUDOS
Bi-Metallic Copper-Nickel center in Bronze ring **Obv:** National emblem divides date, denomination at top, value at bottom **Rev:** Raza Lark left within circle **Shape:** 10-sided

Date	Mintage	F	VF	XF	Unc	BU
1994	—	—	—	—	12.50	13.50

KM# 39a 100 ESCUDOS
10.7100 g., Bi-Metallic **Ring Composition:** Brass **Center Composition:** Copper-Nickel, 26 mm. **Obv:** National emblem divides date, denomination at top, value at bottom **Rev:** Calhandra do Ilheu Raso bird

Date	Mintage	F	VF	XF	Unc	BU
1994	—	—	—	—	12.50	13.50

KM# 40 100 ESCUDOS
Bi-Metallic Copper-Nickel center in Bronze ring **Obv:** National emblem divides date, denomination at top, value at bottom **Rev:** Sailship "Madalan"

Date	Mintage	F	VF	XF	Unc	BU
1994	—	—	—	—	9.00	10.00

KM# 40a 100 ESCUDOS
10.9200 g., Bi-Metallic **Ring Composition:** Brass **Center Composition:** Copper-Nickel, 27 mm. **Obv:** National emblem divides date, denomination at top, value at bottom **Rev. Designer:** Sailship "Madalan"

Date	Mintage	F	VF	XF	Unc	BU
1994	—	—	—	—	9.00	10.00

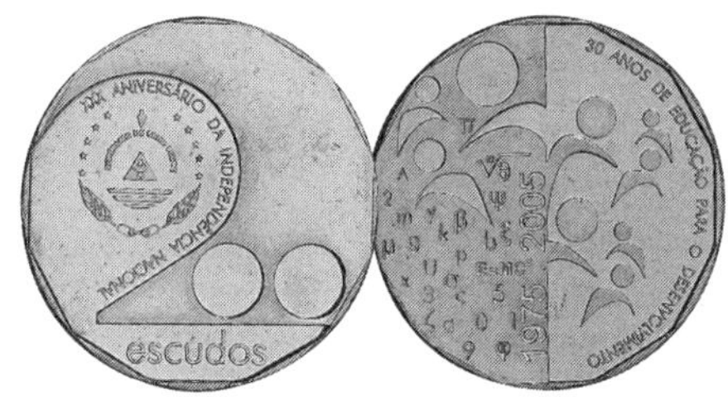

KM# 45 200 ESCUDOS
7.8000 g., Copper-Nickel, 29.5 mm. **Subject:** 30th Anniversary of Independence **Obv:** National arms in number 2 of 200 **Rev:** Symbolic education design **Edge:** Reeded **Shape:** Round

Date	Mintage	F	VF	XF	Unc	BU
2005	—	—	—	—	8.50	10.00

CAYMAN ISLANDS

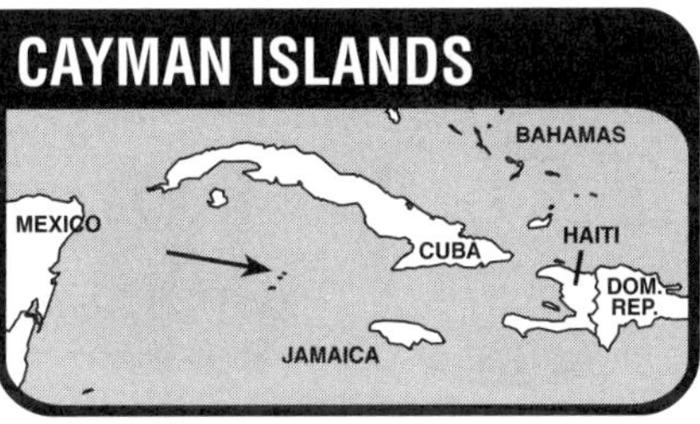

The Cayman Islands is a British Crown Colony situated about 180 miles (280 km) northwest of Jamaica. It consists of three islands: Grand Cayman, Little Cayman, and Cayman Brac. The islands have an area of 102 sq. mi. (259 sq. km.) and a population of 33,200. Capital: George Town. Seafaring, commerce, banking, and tourism are the principal industries. Rope, turtle shells, and sharkskins are exported.

The islands were discovered by Columbus in 1503, and named by him Tortugas (Spanish for turtles') because of the great number of turtles in the nearby waters. Ceded to Britain in 1670, they were colonized from Jamaica by the British and remained dependencies of Jamaica until 1959, when they became a unit territory within the Federation of the West Indies. They became a separate colony when the Federation was dissolved in 1962. Since 1972 a form of self-government has existed, with the Governor responsible for defense and certain other affairs.

While the islands used Jamaican currency for much of their history, the Caymans issued its first national coinage in 1972. The $25 gold and silver commemorative coins issued in 1972 to celebrate the silver wedding anniversary of Queen Elizabeth II and Prince Philip are the first coins in 300 years of Commonwealth coinage to portray a member of the British royal family other than the reigning monarch.

RULER
British

MINT MARKS
CHI - Valcambi
FM - Franklin Mint, U.S.A.*

MONETARY SYSTEM
100 Cents = 1 Dollar

BRITISH COLONY

DECIMAL COINAGE

KM# 1 CENT
2.8700 g., Bronze, 17 mm. **Ruler:** Elizabeth II **Obv:** Young bust right **Rev:** Great Caiman Thrush **Rev. Designer:** Stuart Devlin

Date	Mintage	F	VF	XF	Unc	BU
1972 Proof	11,000	Value: 0.50				
1972	2,155,000	—	—	0.10	0.25	0.75
1973 Proof	9,988	Value: 0.50				
1974 Proof	30,000	Value: 0.50				
1975 Proof	7,175	Value: 0.50				
1976 Proof	3,044	Value: 0.50				
1977	1,800,000	—	—	0.20	0.35	0.90
1977 Proof	1,970	Value: 1.00				
1979FM Proof	4,247	Value: 0.50				
1980FM Proof	1,215	Value: 1.25				
1980FM	—	—	—	0.10	0.25	0.75
1981FM Proof	865	Value: 1.50				
1982	—	—	—	0.10	0.25	0.75
1982FM Proof	589	Value: 1.50				
1983FM Proof	—	Value: 1.50				
1984FM Proof	—	Value: 1.50				
1986	1,000	Value: 1.50				

KM# 87 CENT
2.9500 g., Bronze, 16 mm. **Ruler:** Elizabeth II **Obv:** Crowned bust right **Rev:** Great Caiman Thrush **Rev. Designer:** Stuart Devlin **Edge:** Plain

Date	Mintage	F	VF	XF	Unc	BU
1987	—	—	—	0.10	0.25	0.75
1987 Proof	317	Value: 3.00				
1988 Proof	318	Value: 3.00				
1990	—	—	—	0.10	0.25	0.75

KM# 87a CENT
2.5500 g., Bronze Clad Steel, 17 mm. **Ruler:** Elizabeth II **Obv:** Crowned bust right **Rev:** Great Caiman Thrush **Rev. Designer:** Stuart Devlin

Date	Mintage	F	VF	XF	Unc	BU
1992	—	—	—	0.20	0.50	1.00
1996	—	—	—	0.15	0.35	0.75

KM# 131 CENT
2.5300 g., Bronze Plated Steel, 17 mm. **Ruler:** Elizabeth II **Obv:** Crowned head right **Rev:** Great Caiman thrush **Rev. Designer:** Stuart Devlin

Date	Mintage	F	VF	XF	Unc	BU
1999	—	—	—	0.20	0.50	1.00
2002	—	—	—	—	0.50	1.00
2005	—	—	—	0.20	0.50	1.00

KM# 2 5 CENTS
Copper-Nickel, 18 mm. **Ruler:** Elizabeth II **Obv:** Young bust right **Rev:** Pink-spotted shrimp **Rev. Designer:** Stuart Devlin

Date	Mintage	F	VF	XF	Unc	BU
1972	300,000	—	—	0.10	0.50	1.00
1972 Proof	12,000	Value: 0.75				
1973 Proof	9,988	Value: 0.75				
1973	200,000	—	—	0.30	0.65	1.00
Note: 1973 Business strikes were not released to circulation						
1974 Proof	30,000	Value: 0.75				
1975 Proof	7,175	Value: 0.75				
1976 Proof	3,044	Value: 0.75				
1977 Proof	1,980	Value: 0.75				
1977	600,000	—	—	0.10	0.50	1.00
1979 Proof	4,247	Value: 0.75				
1980 Proof	—	Value: 2.00				
1981 Proof	—	Value: 2.50				
1982 Proof	—	Value: 2.50				
1982	—	—	—	0.10	0.50	1.00
1983 Proof	—	Value: 2.50				

Date	Mintage	F	VF	XF	Unc	BU
1984 Proof	—	Value: 2.50				
1986	1,000	Value: 2.50				

KM# 88 5 CENTS

Copper-Nickel, 18 mm. **Ruler:** Elizabeth II **Obv:** Crowned bust right **Rev:** Pink-spotted shrimp **Rev. Designer:** Stuart Devlin

Date	Mintage	F	VF	XF	Unc	BU
1987	—	—	—	0.10	0.35	1.00
1987 Proof	317	Value: 5.00				
1988 Proof	318	Value: 5.00				
1990	—	—	—	0.10	0.35	1.00

KM# 88a 5 CENTS

2.0000 g., Nickel Clad Steel, 18 mm. **Ruler:** Elizabeth II **Obv:** Crowned bust right **Rev:** Pink-spotted shrimp **Rev. Designer:** Stuart Devlin **Edge:** Plain

Date	Mintage	F	VF	XF	Unc	BU
1992	—	—	—	0.20	0.50	1.00
1996	—	—	—	0.10	0.35	1.00

KM# 132 5 CENTS

2.0000 g., Nickel Clad Steel, 18 mm. **Ruler:** Elizabeth II **Obv:** Crowned head right **Rev:** Pink-spotted shrimp **Rev. Designer:** Stuart Devlin **Edge:** Plain

Date	Mintage	F	VF	XF	Unc	BU
1999	—	—	—	—	0.50	1.00
2002	—	—	—	—	0.50	1.00
2005	—	—	—	—	0.50	1.00

KM# 3 10 CENTS

3.9200 g., Copper-Nickel, 21 mm. **Ruler:** Elizabeth II **Obv:** Young bust right **Rev:** Green Turtle surfacing **Rev. Designer:** Stuart Devlin

Date	Mintage	F	VF	XF	Unc	BU
1972	550,000	—	0.15	0.20	0.50	1.00
1972 Proof	11,000	Value: 1.00				
1973	200,000	—	0.25	0.50	1.00	1.25
Note: 1973 Business strikes were not released to circulation						
1973 Proof	9,988	Value: 1.00				
1974 Proof	30,000	Value: 1.00				
1975 Proof	7,175	Value: 1.00				
1976 Proof	3,044	Value: 1.00				
1977	960,000	—	0.15	0.20	0.50	1.00
1977 Proof	1,980	Value: 1.00				
1979FM Proof	4,247	Value: 1.00				
1980FM Proof	1,215	Value: 3.00				
1981FM Proof	865	Value: 3.00				
1982FM Proof	589	Value: 3.00				
1982	—	—	0.15	0.20	0.50	1.00
1983FM Proof	—	Value: 3.00				
1984FM Proof	—	Value: 3.00				
1986	1,000	Value: 3.00				

KM# 89 10 CENTS

3.8800 g., Copper-Nickel, 21 mm. **Ruler:** Elizabeth II **Obv:** Crowned bust right **Rev:** Green turtle surfacing **Rev. Designer:** Stuart Devlin

Date	Mintage	F	VF	XF	Unc	BU
1987	—	—	0.15	0.20	0.50	1.00
1987 Proof	317	Value: 6.00				
1988 Proof	318	Value: 6.00				
1990	—	—	0.15	0.20	0.50	1.00

KM# 89a 10 CENTS

3.4500 g., Nickel Clad Steel, 21 mm. **Ruler:** Elizabeth II **Obv:** Crowned bust right **Rev:** Green turtle surfacing **Rev. Designer:** Stuart Devlin

Date	Mintage	F	VF	XF	Unc	BU
1992	—	—	0.25	0.40	1.00	1.25
1996	—	—	0.20	0.30	0.75	1.00

KM# 133 10 CENTS

3.4300 g., Nickel Clad Steel, 21 mm. **Ruler:** Elizabeth II **Obv:** Head with tiara right **Rev:** Green turtle surfacing **Rev. Designer:** Stuart Devlin **Edge:** Reeded

Date	Mintage	F	VF	XF	Unc	BU
1999	—	—	0.25	0.40	1.00	1.25
2002	—	—	0.25	0.40	1.00	1.25

KM# 4 25 CENTS

5.6700 g., Copper-Nickel, 24.2 mm. **Ruler:** Elizabeth II **Obv:** Young bust right **Rev:** Schooner sailing right **Rev. Designer:** Stuart Devlin

Date	Mintage	F	VF	XF	Unc	BU
1972	350,000	—	0.35	0.50	1.00	1.25
1972 Proof	11,000	Value: 1.00				
1973	100,000	—	1.00	1.50	2.00	2.50
Note: 1973 Business strikes were not released to circulation						
1973 Proof	9,988	Value: 1.00				
1974 Proof	30,000	Value: 1.00				
1975 Proof	7,175	Value: 1.00				
1976 Proof	3,044	Value: 1.00				
1977 Proof	1,980	Value: 1.00				
1977	520,000	—	0.35	0.50	1.00	1.25
1979FM Proof	4,247	Value: 1.00				
1980FM Proof	1,215	Value: 3.50				
1981FM Proof	865	Value: 4.00				
1982FM Proof	589	Value: 4.00				
1982	—	—	0.35	0.50	1.00	1.25
1983FM Proof	—	Value: 4.00				
1984FM Proof	—	Value: 4.00				
1986 Proof	1,000	Value: 4.00				

KM# 90 25 CENTS

5.7200 g., Copper-Nickel, 24.2 mm. **Ruler:** Elizabeth II **Obv:** Crowned head right **Rev:** Schooner sailing right **Rev. Designer:** Stuart Devlin

Date	Mintage	F	VF	XF	Unc	BU
1987	—	—	0.35	0.50	1.00	1.25
1987 Proof	317	Value: 8.00				
1988 Proof	318	Value: 8.00				
1990	—	—	0.35	0.50	1.00	1.25

KM# 90a 25 CENTS

5.1000 g., Nickel Clad Steel, 24.2 mm. **Ruler:** Elizabeth II **Obv:** Crowned head right **Rev:** Schooner sailing right

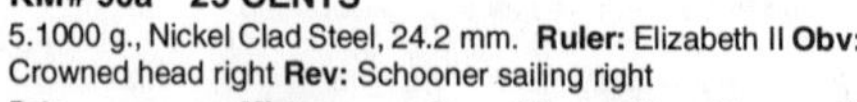

Date	Mintage	F	VF	XF	Unc	BU
1992	—	—	0.45	0.75	1.50	1.75
1996	—	—	0.35	0.60	1.25	1.50

KM# 134 25 CENTS

5.0400 g., Nickel-Clad Steel, 24.2 mm. **Ruler:** Elizabeth II **Obv:** Head with tiara right **Rev:** Schooner sailing right **Rev. Designer:** Stuart Devlin **Edge:** Reeded

Date	Mintage	F	VF	XF	Unc	BU
1999	—	—	—	0.75	1.50	1.75

CENTRAL AFRICAN REPUBLIC

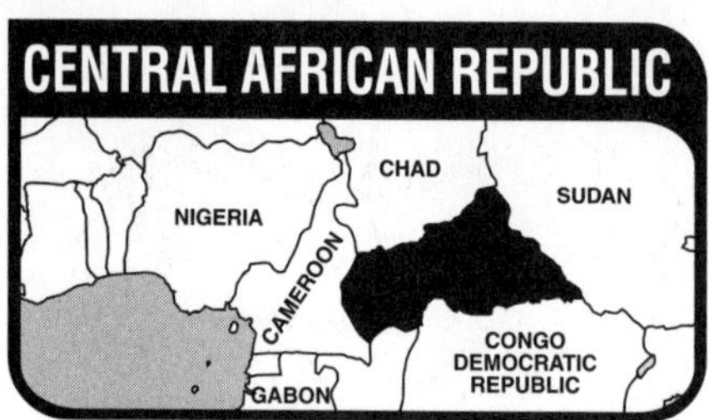

The Central African Republic, a landlocked country in Central Africa, bounded by Chad on the north, Cameroon on the west, Congo (Brazzaville) and Congo Democratic Republic, (formerly Zaire) on the south and the Sudan on the east, has an area of 240,324 sq. mi. (622,984 sq. km.) and a population of 3.2 million. Capital: Bangui. Deposits of uranium, iron ore, manganese and copper remain to be developed. Diamonds, cotton, timber and coffee are exported.

The area that is now the Central African Republic was constituted as the French territory of Ubangi-Shari in 1894. It was united with Chad in 1905 and joined with Middle Congo and Gabon in 1910, becoming one of the four territories of French Equatorial Africa. Upon dissolution of the federation on Dec. 1, 1958, the constituent territories became fully autonomous members of the French Community. Ubangi-Shari proclaimed its complete independence as the Central African Republic on Aug. 13, 1960.

On Jan. 1, 1966, Col. Jean-Bedel Bokassa, Chief of Staff of the Armed Forces, overthrew the government of President David Dacko and assumed power as president of the republic. President Bokassa abolished the constitution of 1959 and dissolved the National Assembly. In 1975 the Congress of the sole political party appointed Bokassa president for life. The republic became a constitutional monarchy on Dec. 4, 1976; President Bokassa was named Emperor Bokassa I. Bokassa was ousted as Central African emperor in a bloodless takeover of the government led by former president David Dacko on Sept. 20, 1979, and the African nation proclaimed once again a republic.

NOTE: For earlier coinage see French Equatorial Africa and Equatorial African States including later coinage as listed in Central African States.

RULERS

French, until 1960

Marshal Jean-Bedel Bokassa, 1976-1979

MINT MARKS

(a) - Paris, privy marks only

MONETARY SYSTEM

100 Centimes = 1 Franc

REPUBLIC

DECIMAL COINAGE

KM# 6 100 FRANCS

7.0000 g., Nickel, 25.5 mm. **Obv:** Three giant eland left **Obv. Designer:** G.B.L. Bazor **Rev:** Denomination within circle

Date	Mintage	F	VF	XF	Unc	BU
1971(a)	2,500,000	5.00	8.00	13.50	28.00	—
1972(a)	3,500,000	5.00	8.00	13.50	28.00	—

KM# 7 100 FRANCS

7.0000 g., Nickel, 25.5 mm. **Obv:** Three giant eland left **Obv. Designer:** G.B.L. Bazor **Rev:** Denomination, date below, within circle

Date	Mintage	F	VF	XF	Unc	BU
1975(a)	—	4.50	7.50	12.50	22.50	—
1976(a)	—	2.00	3.50	6.00	10.00	—
1979(a)	—	6.00	13.50	20.00	35.00	—
1982(a)	—	2.75	4.50	8.00	15.00	—
1983(a)	—	2.75	4.50	9.00	20.00	—
1984(a)	—	2.50	4.00	7.00	11.50	—
1985(a)	—	2.50	4.00	7.00	11.50	—
1988(a)	—	2.50	4.00	7.00	11.50	—
1990(a)	—	2.00	3.50	6.00	10.00	—

Date	Mintage	F	VF	XF	Unc	BU
1996(a)	—	2.00	3.50	6.00	10.00	—
1998(a)	—	2.00	3.50	6.00	10.00	—

KM# 8 100 FRANCS

7.0000 g., Nickel, 25.5 mm. **Obv:** Three giant eland left **Obv. Designer:** G.B.L. Bazor **Rev:** Denomination and date within circle **Rev. Legend:** EMPIRE CENTRAFRICAIN

Date	Mintage	F	VF	XF	Unc	BU
1978(a)	—	40.00	70.00	165	450	825

Note: These were produced during the short-lived reign of dictator Jean-Bedel Bokassa as Emporer

SECOND REPUBLIC

DECIMAL COINAGE

KM# 11 500 FRANCS

Copper-Nickel

Date	Mintage	F	VF	XF	Unc	BU
1985	—	7.50	15.00	30.00	55.00	—
1986	—	7.50	15.00	30.00	55.00	—

CENTRAL AFRICAN STATES

The Central African States, a monetary union comprised of Equatorial Guinea (a former Spanish possession), the former French possessions and now independent states of the Republic of Congo (Brazzaville), Gabon, Central African Republic, Chad and Cameroon, issues a common currency for the member states from a common central bank. The monetary unit, the African Financial Community franc, is tied to and supported by the French franc.

In 1960, an attempt was made to form a union of the newly independent republics of Chad, Congo, Central Africa and Gabon. The proposal was discarded when Chad refused to become a constituent member. The four countries then linked into an Equatorial Customs Unit, to which Cameroon became an associate member in 1961. A more extensive cooperation of the five republics, identified as the Central African Customs and Economic Union, was entered into force at the beginning of 1966.

In 1974 the Central Bank of the Equatorial African States, which had issued coins and paper currency in its own name and with the names of the constituent member nations, changed its name to the Bank of the Central African States. Equatorial Guinea converted to the CFA currency system issuing its first 100 Franc in 1985.

For earlier coinage see French Equatorial Africa.

Country Code Letters

To observe the movement of coinage throughout the states, the country of origin in which the coin is intended to circulate is designated by the following additional code letters:

A = Chad
B = Central African Republic
C = Congo
D = Gabon
E = Cameroon

By 1996 this practice was discontinued as the strategy had proved to be inconclusive.

MONETARY UNION

STANDARD COINAGE

KM# 8 FRANC

1.3000 g., Aluminum, 23 mm. **Obv:** Three giant eland left, date below **Obv. Designer:** G.B.L. Bazor **Rev:** Denomination within wreath

Date	Mintage	F	VF	XF	Unc	BU
1974	3,000,000	0.30	0.60	1.00	2.50	—
1976	4,000,000	0.30	0.60	1.00	2.50	—
1978	1,100,000	0.20	0.40	0.80	2.00	—
1979	250,000	0.20	0.40	0.80	2.00	—
1982	400,000	0.20	0.40	0.80	2.00	—
1985	300,000	0.20	0.40	0.80	2.00	—
1986	300,000	0.20	0.40	0.80	2.00	—
1988	100,000	0.20	0.40	0.80	2.00	—
1990	900,000	0.20	0.40	0.80	2.00	—
1992	300,000	0.20	0.40	0.80	2.00	—
1998(a)	10,000,000	0.20	0.40	0.80	2.00	—

KM# 16 FRANC

1.6100 g., Stainless Steel, 14.9 mm. **Obv:** Value above produce **Rev:** Value **Edge:** Plain

Date	Mintage	F	VF	XF	Unc	BU
2006(a)	—	—	—	—	0.15	0.25

KM# 17 2 FRANCS

2.4300 g., Stainless Steel, 17.9 mm. **Obv:** Value above produce **Rev:** Value **Edge:** Plain

Date	Mintage	F	VF	XF	Unc	BU
2006(a)	—	—	—	—	0.25	0.35

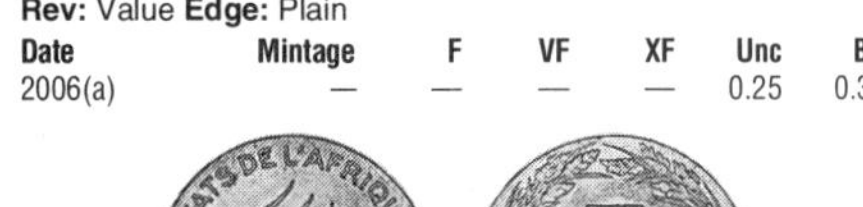

KM# 7 5 FRANCS

3.0000 g., Aluminum-Bronze, 20 mm. **Obv:** Three giant eland left, date below **Obv. Designer:** G.B.L. Bazor **Rev:** Denomination within wreath

Date	Mintage	F	VF	XF	Unc	BU
1973	26,000,000	0.15	0.30	0.60	1.65	—
1975	—	0.15	0.30	0.60	1.65	—
1976	—	0.15	0.30	0.60	1.65	—
1977	—	0.15	0.30	0.60	1.65	—
1978	—	0.15	0.30	0.60	1.65	—
1979	—	0.15	0.30	0.60	1.65	—
1980	—	0.15	0.30	0.60	1.35	—
1981	—	0.15	0.30	0.60	1.35	—
1982	—	0.15	0.30	0.60	1.35	—
1983	—	0.15	0.30	0.60	1.35	—
1984	—	0.15	0.30	0.60	1.35	—
1985	—	0.15	0.30	0.60	1.35	—
1992	—	0.15	0.30	0.60	1.35	—
1996(a)	—	0.15	0.30	0.60	1.25	—
1998(a)	—	0.15	0.30	0.60	1.25	—

KM# 18 5 FRANCS

2.4100 g., Brass, 15.9 mm. **Obv:** Value above produce **Rev:** Value **Edge:** Reeded

Date	Mintage	F	VF	XF	Unc	BU
2006(a)	—	—	—	—	0.50	0.65

KM# 9 10 FRANCS

4.0000 g., Aluminum-Bronze, 23 mm. **Obv:** Three giant eland left, date below **Obv. Designer:** G.B.L. Bazor **Rev:** Denomination within wreath

Date	Mintage	F	VF	XF	Unc	BU
1974	18,500,000	0.20	0.35	0.75	2.00	—
1975	—	0.20	0.35	0.75	2.00	—
1976	—	0.20	0.35	0.75	2.00	—
1977	—	0.20	0.35	0.75	2.00	—
1978	—	0.20	0.35	0.75	2.00	—
1979	—	0.20	0.35	0.75	2.00	—
1980	—	0.20	0.35	0.65	1.35	—
1981	—	0.20	0.35	0.65	1.35	—
1982	—	0.20	0.35	0.65	1.35	—
1983	—	0.20	0.35	0.65	1.35	—
1984	—	0.20	0.35	0.65	1.35	—
1985	—	0.20	0.35	0.65	1.35	—
1992	—	0.20	0.35	0.65	1.35	—
1996	—	0.20	0.35	0.75	1.65	—
1998(a)	—	0.20	0.35	0.75	1.50	—
2003(a)	—	0.20	0.35	0.75	1.50	—

KM# 19 10 FRANCS

3.0000 g., Brass, 17.9 mm. **Obv:** Value above produce **Rev:** Value **Edge:** Reeded

Date	Mintage	F	VF	XF	Unc	BU
2006(a)	—	—	—	—	0.75	—

KM# 10 25 FRANCS

8.0000 g., Aluminum-Bronze, 27.1 mm. **Obv:** Three giant eland left, date below **Obv. Designer:** G.B.L. Bazor **Rev:** Denomination within wreath

Date	Mintage	F	VF	XF	Unc	BU
1975(a)	—	0.50	1.00	1.75	3.00	—
1976(a)	—	0.50	1.00	1.50	2.75	—
1978(a)	—	0.50	1.00	1.50	2.75	—
1982(a)	—	0.35	0.75	1.25	2.50	—
1983(a)	—	0.35	0.75	1.25	2.50	—
1984(a)	—	0.35	0.75	1.25	2.50	—
1985(a)	—	0.35	0.75	1.25	2.50	—
1986(a)	—	0.35	0.75	1.25	2.50	—
1988(a)	—	0.35	0.75	1.25	2.50	—
1990(a)	—	0.35	0.75	1.25	2.50	—
1991(a)	—	0.35	0.75	1.25	2.50	—
1992(a)	—	0.35	0.75	1.25	2.50	—
1996(a)	—	0.35	0.75	1.25	2.50	—
1998(a)	—	0.25	0.50	1.00	2.00	—
2003(a)	—	0.25	0.50	1.00	2.00	—

KM# 20 25 FRANCS

4.2000 g., Brass, 22.7 mm. **Obv:** Value above produce **Rev:** Value **Edge:** Reeded

Date	Mintage	F	VF	XF	Unc	BU
2006(a)	—	—	—	—	1.00	1.25

KM# 11 50 FRANCS

4.7000 g., Nickel, 21.5 mm. **Obv:** Three giant eland left, date below **Obv. Designer:** G.B.L. Bazor **Rev:** Denomination within flower design **Note:** Starting in 1996 an extra flora item was added where the mintmark was formerly located.

Date	Mintage	F	VF	XF	Unc	BU
1976(a) A	10,000,000	2.00	3.50	7.50	12.00	—
1976(a) B	Inc. above	2.00	3.50	7.50	12.00	—
1976(a) C	Inc. above	1.00	2.00	4.00	7.00	—
1976(a) D	Inc. above	1.00	2.00	4.00	7.00	—
1976(a) E	Inc. above	1.00	2.00	4.00	7.50	—
1977(a) A	—	2.00	3.50	7.50	12.00	—
1977(a) B	—	2.00	3.50	7.50	12.00	—
1977(a) C	—	1.00	2.00	4.00	7.00	—
1977(a) D	—	1.00	2.00	4.00	7.00	—
1977(a) E	—	1.00	2.00	4.00	7.50	—
1978(a) A	—	2.00	3.50	7.50	12.00	—
1978(a) B	—	2.00	3.50	7.50	12.00	—
1978(a) C	—	1.00	2.00	4.00	7.00	—
1978(a) D	—	1.00	2.00	4.00	7.00	—
1979(a) B	—	1.00	2.00	4.00	7.50	—
1979(a) E	—	1.00	2.00	4.00	7.50	—
1980(a) A	—	1.50	2.75	5.50	11.50	—
1980(a) C	—	0.75	1.50	3.50	6.00	—
1981(a) C	—	0.75	1.50	3.50	6.00	—
1981(a) D	—	0.85	1.75	3.75	6.50	—
1982(a) A	—	1.50	2.75	5.50	11.50	—
1983(a) B	—	0.75	1.50	3.50	6.00	—
1983(a) D	—	0.75	1.50	3.50	6.00	—
1983(a) E	—	0.75	1.50	3.50	6.00	—
1984(a) A	—	1.50	2.75	5.50	11.50	—
1984(a) B	—	1.50	2.75	5.50	11.50	—
1984(a) C	—	0.75	1.50	3.50	6.00	—
1984(a) D	—	0.75	1.50	3.50	6.00	—
1985(a) A	—	1.50	2.75	5.50	11.50	—
1985(a) B	—	1.50	2.75	5.50	11.50	—
1985(a) D	—	0.75	1.50	3.50	6.00	—
1986(a) B	—	1.50	2.75	5.50	11.50	—
1986(a) E	—	0.85	1.75	3.75	6.50	—
1988(a) B	—	1.50	2.75	5.50	11.50	—
1989(a) A	—	1.50	2.75	5.50	11.50	—
1990(a) B	—	1.50	2.75	5.50	11.50	—
1991(a) A	—	1.50	2.75	5.50	11.50	—
1996(a) Cocoa bean	—	0.75	1.50	3.50	6.00	—
1998(a) Cocoa bean	—	0.75	1.50	3.50	6.00	—
2003(a) Cocoa bean	—	0.75	1.50	3.50	6.00	—

KM# 21 50 FRANCS

4.9000 g., Stainless Steel, 22 mm. **Obv:** Value above produce **Rev:** Value **Edge:** Reeded

Date	Mintage	F	VF	XF	Unc	BU
2006(a)	—	—	—	—	1.25	1.50

KM# 13 100 FRANCS

7.0500 g., Nickel, 25.5 mm. **Obv:** Three giant eland **Rev:** Denomination

Date	Mintage	F	VF	XF	Unc	BU
1992(a)	—	—	—	—	4.50	6.00
1996(a)	—	—	—	—	4.50	6.00
1998(a)	—	—	—	—	4.50	6.00

KM# 15 100 FRANCS

6.0000 g., Bi-Metallic Stainless Steel center in Brass ring, 23.9 mm. **Obv:** Denomination above initials within beaded circle **Rev:** Value above produce **Edge:** Reeded

Date	Mintage	F	VF	XF	Unc	BU
2006(a)	—	—	—	—	5.00	6.50

KM# 12 500 FRANCS

9.0000 g., Nickel, 28 mm. **Obv:** Half figure of woman within circle, date lower right **Rev:** Eland head left divides denomination above **Designer:** P. Lambert

Date	Mintage	F	VF	XF	Unc	BU
1976 A	4,000,000	5.50	8.50	13.50	22.00	—
1976 B	Inc. above	5.50	8.50	13.50	22.00	—
1976 C	Inc. above	4.50	8.00	12.50	20.00	—
1976 D	Inc. above	4.50	8.00	12.50	20.00	—
1976 E	Inc. above	4.50	8.00	12.50	20.00	—
1977 A	—	5.50	8.50	15.00	25.00	—
1977 B	—	5.50	8.50	15.00	25.00	—
1977 C	—	4.50	8.00	12.50	25.00	—
1977 D	—	4.50	8.00	12.50	20.00	—
1977 E	—	3.00	6.00	10.00	16.50	—
1979(a) B	—	3.50	7.00	12.00	18.50	—
1979(a) E	—	3.50	7.00	12.00	18.50	—
1979 D	—	3.50	7.00	12.00	18.50	—
1982 D	—	3.50	7.00	12.00	18.50	—
1984 A	—	3.50	7.00	12.00	18.50	—
1984 B	—	3.50	7.00	12.00	18.50	—
1984 C	—	3.50	7.00	12.00	18.50	—
1984 E	—	3.50	7.00	12.00	18.50	—

KM# 14 500 FRANCS

11.0000 g., Copper-Nickel, 30 mm. **Obv:** Native woman's head half left **Rev:** Plant divides denomination and date **Edge:** Plain

Date	Mintage	F	VF	XF	Unc	BU
1998(a)	—	—	—	—	16.00	18.00

KM# 22 500 FRANCS

8.1000 g., Copper-Nickel, 26 mm. **Obv:** Value above produce **Rev:** Value **Edge:** Segmented reeding and lettering

Date	Mintage	F	VF	XF	Unc	BU
2006(a)	—	—	—	—	8.00	9.50

CENTRAL ASIA

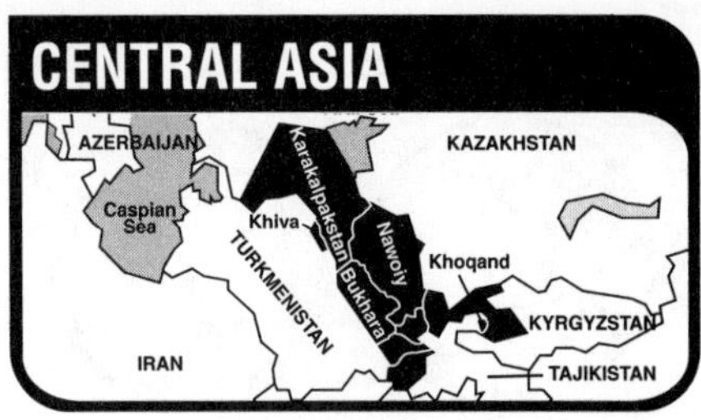

In the several centuries prior to 1500 which witnessed the breakup of the Mongol Empire and the subsequent rise of smaller successor states, no single power or dynasty was able to control the vast expanses of Western and Central Asia. The region known previously as Transoxiana, the land beyond the Oxus River (modern Amu Darya), became the domain of the Shaybanids, then the Janids. The territory ruled by these dynasties had no set borders, which rather expanded and contracted as the fortunes of the rulers ebbed and flowed. At their greatest extent, the khanate took in parts of what are now northern Iran and Afghanistan, as well as part or all of modern Turkmenistan, Uzbekistan, Kazakhstan, Tadzhikistan and Kyrgyzstan. Coins are known to have been struck by virtually every ruler, but some are quite scarce owing to short reigns or the ever-changing political and economic situation.

MINT

Abivard

Akhshi/Akhshikath

اندجان اندگان

Andigan/Andijan

اسفراين

Asfarayin/Isfarayin

استراباد

Astarabad

اوبه

Awbah

بدخشان

Badakhshan

بلخ

Balkh

Bistam

بخارا

Bukhara

Damghan

هراة هرات

Herat

حصر

Hisar

Karmin

Kish

كوفن كوفين

Kufan/Kufin

Langar

ماروار

Marw

مشهد

Mashhad

Nasaf

نمرز نيمروز

Nimruz

نسا

Nisa

قرشي

Qarshi (copper only)

Qayin

قندوز

Qunduz

سبزوار

Sabzavar

سمرقند

Samarqand

تشكند

Tashkand (Tashkent)

ترمذ

Termez

Tun

Turbat

اردو

Urdu (camp mint)

Yazur

BUKHARA

Bukhara, a city and former emirate in southern Russian Turkestan, formed part (Sogdiana) of the Seleucid Empire after the conquest of Alexander the Great and incessantly remained an important region throughout the middle ages, often serving as the capital center for a succession of ruling dynasties of Iranian and Turkish origin until the 19th century. It became virtually a Russian vassal in1868 as a consequence of the Czarist invasion of 1866,following which it gradually became a part of Russian Turkestan and then part of Uzbekistan S.S.R., now Uzbekistan.

RULERS

Russian Vassal,
(since AH1284/1868AD)
Emir Abd al-Ahad,
AH1303-1328 / 1886-1910AD
Emir Sayyid Alim Khan,
AH1329-1339 / 1911-1920AD

MINT NAME

Bukhara Bukhara-yi Sharif

MONETARY SYSTEM

Until AH1322/1905AD: 45 to 64 Pul (Fulus) = 4 Miri = 1 silver Tenga
19 to 21 Tenga = 1 Tilla (gold 4.55 g.)
Until AH1336-1338/1918-1920AD: copper Tenga or Tenga-fulus

Within the protectorate period, Russian currency of Roubles and Kopeks were officially in circulation: 1 silver Tenga = 20 Kopeks

Note: All copper, bronze and brass issues of Bukhara in the 20th century are anonymous. Some silver and gold issues traditionally bear the names of Emirs long since deceased.

Note: Denominations of 1/32 Tenga & Tilla are of very similar design under various rulers, but can be distinguished by date.

Note: Tilla coins are known with a date appearing as "134-", which is actually 1316 with the "1" and "6" stuck close together, appearing as a Persian "4".

Note: Most copper, bronze and brass AH1336-1338 dated coins of 2, 3, 10 and especially 20 Tenga exhibit considerable flat spots, die shifts and other defects. Well-struck specimens with fully struck design demand a considerable premium.

Note: The numerals "0" and "5" have variant forms in Bukhara, including an open "J' – type symbol for "5" instead of a closed symbol:

o O and ◆

5 ل or ل instead of ۵ ۵

KHANATE

Emir Abd Al-Ahad
AH1303-1328/1886-1910AD

HAMMERED COINAGE

KM# 67.2 PUL (Fulus)

Copper **Obv:** Inscription and date **Obv. Inscription:** "Bukhara" **Rev:** Denomination and date

Date	Mintage	Good	VG	F	VF	XF
AH1319	—	—	—	—	—	—

KM# 87 1/32 TENGA (2 Fulus)

Copper **Obv:** Inscription and date **Obv. Inscription:** "zarb Bukhara-yi sharif" **Rev:** Inscription and date **Rev. Inscription:** "Fulus 32" **Note:** Large "32" above Fulus indicates the denomination (1/32 Tenga). Varieties exist. Prev. Y#1.

Date	Mintage	Good	VG	F	VF	XF
AH1322	—	10.00	15.00	20.00	30.00	40.00
AH1324	—	10.00	15.00	20.00	30.00	40.00

KM# 86 1/32 TENGA (2 Fulus)

Copper **Obv:** Inscription and date **Obv. Inscription:** "Fulus Bukhara" **Rev:** "32" in 6-petal ornate cartouche **Note:** Varieties exist on round or irregular flans. Size varies 14-17 mm. Large "32" above Fulus indicates the denomination (1/32 Tenga). Prev. #Y4.1.

Date	Mintage	Good	VG	F	VF	XF
AH1322	—	—	5.00	8.50	16.50	25.00
AH1323	—	—	4.00	7.00	12.00	20.00

Note: Coins exist with denomination error "23"

Date	Mintage	Good	VG	F	VF	XF
AH1324	—	—	4.00	7.00	12.00	20.00
AH1327	—	—	6.00	10.00	18.00	30.00
AH1328	—	—	6.00	10.00	18.00	30.00

KM# 63 TENGA

Silver **Note:** Varieties exist. Weight varies 3.06-3.25 grams; size varies 11-18mm. Die varieties exist with and without date on reverse. Struck in the name of late Emir Haydar. Prev. #Y2.

Date	Mintage	Good	VG	F	VF	XF
AH1319	—	—	10.00	15.00	25.00	60.00
AH1319//1308	—	—	30.00	50.00	75.00	100
AH1319//1311	—	—	30.00	50.00	75.00	100
AH1319 Recut 1311	—	—	10.00	20.00	35.00	60.00
AH1320//1319	—	—	10.00	20.00	35.00	60.00
AH1320//1320	—	—	17.50	30.00	50.00	80.00
AH1321//1320 1321 recut from 1320	—	—	10.00	20.00	35.00	60.00
AH1322	—	—	7.50	15.00	27.50	45.00

Note: Doubled flan errors dated AH1322/1322 consisting of two strikes forged together exist, weighing approximately 6.25 grams

KM# 65 TILLA

4.5500 g., Gold **Note:** Struck in the name of late Ma'sum Ghazi (Emir Shah Murad). Die varieties exist with and without date on reverse. Prev. #Y3.

Date	Mintage	Good	VG	F	VF	XF
AH1319	—	—	115	120	140	185
AH1321	—	—	125	165	250	350
AH1322//1322	—	—	115	120	140	185
AH1324/1324	—	—	115	120	140	185
AH1324//1316	—	—	125	165	250	350
AH1324//1321	—	—	125	165	250	350
AH1325//1325	—	—	115	120	140	185
AH1325//1325	—	—	120	155	225	320

Note: Reverse date recut from 1324

Date	Mintage	Good	VG	F	VF	XF
AH1327	—	—	115	135	200	300
AH1328	—	—	115	135	200	300
AH1328//1292	—	—	175	250	350	500
AH1328//1304	—	—	125	165	250	350
AH1328//1321	—	—	175	250	350	500

Emir Sayyid Alim Khan
AH1329-1339/1911-1920AD

HAMMERED COINAGE

KM# A63 1/32 TENGA (2 Fulus)

Copper **Obv. Inscription:** "Fulus Bukhara" **Rev:** "32" in a 6-petal ornate cartouche **Note:** Size varies 12-14 mm. Similar to KM#86. "32" indicates denomination (1/32 Tenga). Numerous die varieties exist including placement of date for 1332 with date inside or below Fulus.

Date	Mintage	Good	VG	F	VF	XF
AH1329	—	—	6.00	12.00	20.00	35.00
AH1330	—	—	4.00	7.00	15.00	22.50

Note: Date appearing as "1335" is actually "1330" with small circle instead of dot for zero

Date	Mintage	Good	VG	F	VF	XF
AH1331	—	—	5.00	8.50	16.50	25.00
AH1332	—	—	4.00	7.00	15.00	22.50
AH1333	—	—	6.00	12.00	20.00	35.00

Note: Exists with denomination errors 21, 201, 22, 31, etc.

Date	Mintage	Good	VG	F	VF	XF
AH13-33 Divided date	—	—	8.00	15.00	25.00	40.00
ND	—	—	12.50	25.00	40.00	75.00

KM# 42 2 FULUS

Copper **Obv:** Inscription and date **Obv. Inscription:** "Fulus Bukhara" **Rev:** "2" in 6-petal ornate cartouche **Note:** Many varieties exist, including placement of date for 1332 and 1333 with date inside or below Fulu. Size varies: 11-14mm. Prev. #Y4.

Date	Mintage	Good	VG	F	VF	XF
AH1330	—	—	15.00	27.50	45.00	70.00
AH1332	—	—	7.50	14.00	22.50	35.00

Note: This date exists with denomination error "6" and with "2" engraved above "32"

Date	Mintage	Good	VG	F	VF	XF
AH1333	—	—	15.00	20.00	45.00	70.00
AH13-33 Divided date	—	—	20.00	35.00	50.00	75.00
ND	—	—	20.00	35.00	50.00	75.00

Note: With 2 above crescent in circle resembling an Arabic "4"

KM# 44 4 FULUS

Copper **Obv:** Sanah and date, inscription below **Obv. Inscription:** "Bukhara" **Rev. Inscription:** "Chahar Fulus" **Note:** Size varies: 14-16 mm. Die varieties exist. Prev. #Y5.

Date	Mintage	Good	VG	F	VF	XF
AH1334	—	—	5.00	8.50	16.50	25.00
AH1335	—	—	30.00	50.00	80.00	125

KM# 45 8 FULUS

Copper **Obv:** Inscription, date below double line **Obv. Inscription:** "Bukhara" **Rev. Inscription:** "Hasht Fulus" **Note:** Size varies: 15-18mm. Die varieties exist. Prev. #YA5.

Date	Mintage	Good	VG	F	VF	XF
AH1335	—	—	5.00	8.50	16.50	25.00

KM# A6 1/2 TENGA

Copper, 14 mm. **Obv. Inscription:** Inscription and date in hextagonal frame **Rev:** "zarb Buhkhara" **Rev. Inscription:** "fulus nim tangah" **Note:** Prev. #Y6.

Date	Mintage	Good	VG	F	VF	XF
AH1336	—	—	15.00	30.00	50.00	100

KM# 46.1 TENGA

Copper **Obv:** Inscription and date in dotted circle **Obv. Inscription:** "zarb Bukhara" **Rev. Inscription:** "fulus yak tangah" **Note:** Size varies 13-16mm. Small round or irregular flans, no border. Die varieties exist.

Date	Mintage	Good	VG	F	VF	XF
AH1336	—	—	20.00	35.00	55.00	80.00

KM# 46.2 TENGA

Copper **Obv:** Inscription and date in beaded circle **Obv. Inscription:** "zarb Bukhara" **Rev. Inscription:** "fulus yak tangah" **Note:** Size varies 17-20mm. Large round or irregular flans, irregular flans are scarcer than round flans. Many varieties exist. Prev. #Y6a.

Date	Mintage	Good	VG	F	VF	XF
AH1336	—	—	6.00	12.00	20.00	35.00
AH1337	—	—	6.00	12.00	20.00	35.00

Note: This date exists with 5-rayed (outlined and full), and 6-rayed (outlined) star on obverse

Date	Mintage	Good	VG	F	VF	XF
	—	—	10.00	17.50	30.00	50.00

Note: Overstruck on 4 or 8 Fulus, KM#44 and 45

Date	Mintage	Good	VG	F	VF	XF
AH1337	—	—	10.00	17.50	30.00	50.00

Note: Overstruck on 8 Fulus KM#45

Date	Mintage	Good	VG	F	VF	XF
AH1338	—	—	75.00	100	135	185

KM# 47 2 TENGA

Bronze **Obv:** Inscription and date in dotted circle **Obv. Inscription:** "zarb bukhara" **Rev. Inscription:** "fulus du tangah" **Note:** Size varies 22-23mm. Varieties with upright and oblique milled edge exist, both years exist with 5-rayed (outlined and full), and 6-rayed (outlined) star on obverse. Prev. #Y7.

Date	Mintage	Good	VG	F	VF	XF
AH1336	—	—	6.00	12.00	25.00	55.00
AH1337	—	—	6.00	12.00	25.00	55.00

Note: Also exists without star (rare)

KM# 48 3 TENGA

Bronze **Obv:** Inscription and date **Obv. Inscription:** "zarb Bukhara" **Rev. Inscription:** "fulus se tangah" **Note:** Greek meander circle both sides. Varieties with upright and oblique milled edge exist. Size varies 24-26mm. Prev. #Y8.

Date	Mintage	Good	VG	F	VF	XF
AH1336	—	—	6.00	12.00	25.00	50.00
AH1337	—	—	6.00	12.00	25.00	50.00

Note: Exists with 5-rayed outlined and full (whole or broken) star on obverse

Date	Mintage	Good	VG	F	VF	XF
AH1337	—	—	—	—	—	—

Note: Struck on small 23 mm and thin 2 Tenga flan

KM# 49 4 TENGA

Bronze, 30 mm. **Obv:** Inscription and date **Obv. Inscription:** "zarb Bukhara" **Rev. Inscription:** "fulus chahar tangah" **Note:** Floral design circle on both sides. Prev. #Y9.

Date	Mintage	Good	VG	F	VF	XF
AH1336 Rare	—	—	—	—	—	—

Note: This denomination was officially announced for circulation, but its production in quantity was reduced as it was considered excessive and economically senseless

KM# 50 5 TENGA

Bronze **Obv:** Inscription and date in almond-shaped inner border **Obv. Inscription:** "zarb Bukhara" **Rev. Inscription:** "fulus panj tangah" **Note:** Greek meander circle on both sides. Varieties exist with upright and oblique milled edge. Size varies 28-30mm. Prev. #Y10.

Date	Mintage	Good	VG	F	VF	XF
AH1336	—	—	25.00	40.00	65.00	100
AH1337	—	—	25.00	40.00	65.00	100

KM# 53 10 TENGA

Brass, 29 mm. **Obv:** Inscription and date **Obv. Inscription:** "zarb Bukhara" **Rev:** Inscription and date **Rev. Inscription:** "yakdah tangah" **Note:** Square frames on both sides vary in size, varieties exist with upright and oblique milled edge. Reverse date varies in position and arrangement (full or divided dates with different combinations). Prev. #Y11.

Date	Mintage	Good	VG	F	VF	XF
AH1337//1337	—	—	8.00	15.00	25.00	40.00

Note: With chain border on both sides

Date	Mintage	Good	VG	F	VF	XF
AH1337//1337	—	—	12.50	22.50	40.00	60.00

Note: With branch border (similar to 20 Tenga) on obverse

Date	Mintage	Good	VG	F	VF	XF
AH1337//1338	—	—	10.00	17.50	32.50	50.00
AH1338//1338	—	—	30.00	45.00	80.00	125

KM# 51.1 20 TENGA

Bronze Or Brass **Obv:** Inscription and date in crescent, 6-pointed circled star above **Obv. Inscription:** "zarb Bukharayi sharif" **Rev:** Inscription and date within 6-pointed star **Rev. Inscription:** "bist tangah" **Note:** Varieties exist with upright and oblique milled edge, obverse date varies in position and arrangement (full or divided dates with different combinations). Prev. KM#51 and #Y12.

Date	Mintage	Good	VG	F	VF	XF
AH1337	—	—	22.50	35.00	50.00	85.00

Note: Dated on both sides

Date	Mintage	Good	VG	F	VF	XF
AH1337	—	—	27.50	45.00	75.00	110

Note: Dated reverse only

KM# 51.2 20 TENGA

Brass, 33 mm. **Obv:** Inscription (mintname in error without second alif) and date in crescent, 6-pointed circled star above **Obv. Inscription:** "zarb Bukhari sharif" **Rev:** Inscription and date within 6-pointed star **Rev. Inscription:** "bist tangah"

Date	Mintage	Good	VG	F	VF	XF
AH1337	—	—	40.00	55.00	80.00	120

Note: Dated on both sides

KM# A65 TILLA

4.5500 g., Gold **Note:** Struck in the name of late Ma'sum Ghazi (Emir Shah Murad).

Date	Mintage	Good	VG	F	VF	XF
AH1329	—	—	95.00	110	135	185
AH1330	—	—	150	250	350	500
AH1331	—	—	120	180	250	350

KHIVA

Khwarezm (Khiva), a historical region, once a great kingdom under the names of Chorasmia, Khwarezm and Gurganj (Urgench), is located in the lower stream and the delta of the Amu Darya River, east of the Caspian Sea and south of the Aral Sea. Russia established relations with Khwarezm (Khiva Khanate) in the 17th century, occupied it in 1873, and annexed it in 1875. Revolution concentrated Russia's preoccupation elsewhere during 1917 and Khiva seized this opportunity to declare its independence. It was able to sustain this status for a scant two years. By 1919 the Soviet regime had reestablished control over the region and extinguished the independent state. In AH1338/1920AD it was proclaimed Khorezm People's Soviet Republic and later became part of the Uzbekistan S.S.R. (Qaraqalpaq Autonomous Republic), now Uzbekistan.

RULERS

Russian Vassals
(since AH1290 / 1873AD)
Sayyid Muhammad Rahim
AH1282-1328 / 1865-910AD
Isfandiyar
AH1328-1336 / 1910-1918AD
Sayyid Abdullah
Normally in AH1337-1338 / 1919-1920AD
Actual ruler – Muhammad Qurban Sardar (Junaid Khan)
AH1334-1338 / 1916-1920AD

MINT NAMES

خوارزم

Khwarezm

دار الاسلام خوارزم

Dar al-Islam Khwarezm

Note: All copper, bronze and brass issues of Khiva (Khorezm, Khwarezm) in the 20th century are anonymous, except the silver Tenga Y#8, which bears the name of a Khan, long since deceased.

MONETARY SYSTEM

24 to 32 Pul (Fulus) = 4 Shahi = 1 silver Tenga
about 20 Tenga = 1 Tilla (gold 4.55 g.)

AH1337-1338 / 1918-1920AD: copper Tenga or Tenga-fulus

Within the protectorate period, Russian currency of Rubles and Kopeks were officially in circulation : 1 silver Tenga was equivalent to 20 Kopeks.

Note: Denomination of Pul are of similar design under various rulers, but can be distinguished by date.
2 ½ & 5 Tenga: Ornamentation, size and design of borders and die rotation vary considerably. Crudely engraved dies with mostly simplified design are known struck on cast flans. Cast specimens exist.

Note: 50, 200 & 1000 Roubles coins with crude inscriptions are modern fantasies.

KHANATE

Sayyid Muhammad Rahim

AH1282-1328 / 1865-1910 AD

HAMMERED COINAGE

Y# 3.1 PUL (Fulus)

Copper **Obv:** Inscription in circle **Obv. Inscription:** "Khwarezm" **Rev:** Inscription, date appears as "3" above "1" or "2" above "2" **Rev. Inscription:** "fulus" **Note:** Oblong or irregular flans.

Date	Mintage	Good	VG	F	VF	XF
AH1322	—	5.00	8.00	20.00	35.00	—
AH1323	—	5.00	8.00	20.00	35.00	—
AH1324	—	5.00	8.00	20.00	35.00	—
AH1325	—	5.00	8.00	20.00	35.00	—
AH1326	—	5.00	8.00	20.00	35.00	—

Isfandiyar

AH1328-1336 / 1910-1918 AD

HAMMERED COINAGE

Y# 3.2 PUL (Fulus)

Copper **Obv:** Inscription in circle **Obv. Inscription:** "Khwarezm" **Rev:** Inscription, date appears as "3" above "1" or "2" above "2" **Rev. Inscription:** "fulus" **Note:** Oblong or irregular flans, similar to Y#3.1.

Date	Mintage	Good	VG	F	VF	XF
AH1328	—	5.00	8.00	20.00	35.00	—
AH1329	—	5.00	8.00	20.00	35.00	—

Sayyid Abdullah and Junaid Khan

AH1337-1338 / 1919-1920 AD

HAMMERED COINAGE

Y# A9.1 TENGA

Copper **Obv:** Inscription and date in dotted or reeded circle **Obv. Inscription:** "zarb Khwarezm" **Rev:** Rising sun and crescent, inscription below **Rev. Inscription:** "fulus bir tangah" **Note:** Size varies: 17-19 mm.

Date	Mintage	Good	VG	F	VF	XF
AH1337	—	—	75.00	120	200	400

Y# A9.2 TENGA

Copper **Obv:** Inscription and date in dotted or reeded circle **Obv. Inscription:** "zarb Khwarezm" **Rev:** No crescent above rising sun **Rev. Inscription:** "fulus bir tangah" **Note:** Die varieties exist with different border patterns and date above or below mint name. Crudely struck specimens with Tajik inscription "fulus yak tangah" (instead of the Uzbek "bir tangah") are modern forgeries. Size varies: 17-19mm.

Date	Mintage	Good	VG	F	VF	XF
AH1337	—	—	60.00	100	150	250

Y# 8 TENGA

2.2800 g., Silver **Note:** Struck in the name of Sayyid Muhammad Rahim; die varieties exist.

Date	Mintage	Good	VG	F	VF	XF
AH1337//1337	—	—	250	400	600	850

Note: The estimated number known to exist does not exceed 20 pieces

Y# 9.1 2-1/2 TENGA

Copper Or Bronze **Obv:** Inscription and date **Obv. Inscription:** "zarb Dar al-Islam Khwarezm" **Rev:** Rising sun and crescent, inscription below **Rev. Inscription:** "fulus iki yarim tangah" **Note:** Die varieties exist. Number of sun rays vary from 7 to 13. Date above mint name and strikes with additional date on reverse exist.

Date	Mintage	Good	VG	F	VF	XF
AH1337	—	—	30.00	45.00	75.00	120

Y# 9.2 2-1/2 TENGA

Bronze Or Brass **Obv:** Inscription and date **Obv. Inscription:** "zarb Dar al-Islam Khwarezm" **Rev:** Full sun and crescent, inscription below **Rev. Inscription:** "fulus iki yarim tangah" **Note:** Many die varieties exist. Number of sun rays vary from 8 to 18, date above or below mintname. Strikes with additional date on reverse exist. Size varies 20-22mm.

Date	Mintage	Good	VG	F	VF	XF
AH1337	—	—	30.00	45.00	75.00	120

Note: Rare 1337 strikes over Russian Kopek Y#9.2 are known

Y# 9.3 2-1/2 TENGA
Bronze Or Brass **Obv:** Inscription and date **Obv. Inscription:** "zarb Dar al-Islam Khwarezm" **Rev:** Full sun and crescent, modified inscription below **Rev. Inscription:** "iki yarim tangah fulus" **Note:** Many die varieties exist. Number of sun rays vary from 10-13. Size varies 20-22mm.

Date	Mintage	Good	VG	F	VF	XF
AH1337	—	—	25.00	40.00	70.00	—
Note: Date above or below mint name						
AH1338	—	—	150	250	400	—
Note: Date below mint name						

Y# 10.1 5 TENGA
Copper Or Bronze, 30 mm. **Obv:** Inscription and date **Obv. Inscription:** "zarb Dar al-Islam Khwarezm" **Rev:** Rising sun and crescent, inscription below **Rev. Inscription:** "fulus besh tangah"

Date	Mintage	Good	VG	F	VF	XF
AH1337 Rare	—	—	—	—	—	—

Y# 10.2 5 TENGA
Copper Or Bronze **Obv:** Inscription and date **Obv. Inscription:** "zarb Dar al-Islam Khwarezm" **Rev:** Full sun and crescent, inscription below **Rev. Inscription:** "fulus besh tangah" **Note:** Many die varieties exist. Number of sun rays vary from 9-20, date above or below mint name. Strikes with additional date on reverse exist. Size varies 29-32mm.

Date	Mintage	Good	VG	F	VF	XF
AH1337	—	—	25.00	40.00	70.00	125

Y# 10.3 5 TENGA
Bronze Or Brass **Obv:** Inscription and date **Obv. Inscription:** "zarb Dar al-Islam Khwarezm" **Rev:** Full sun and crescent, modified inscription below **Rev. Inscription:** "besh tangah fulus" **Note:** Many die varieties exist. Number of sun rays vary from 9-18, date appears above or below mint name. Strikes with additional date on reverse exist. Size varies 29-32mm.

Date	Mintage	Good	VG	F	VF	XF
AH1337	—	—	20.00	35.00	60.00	90.00
Note: Rare 1337 strikes over Russian 3 Kopek Y#11.2 are known						
AH1338	—	—	35.00	55.00	80.00	120

Y# 11.1 15 TENGA
Bronze **Obv:** Inscription and date **Obv. Inscription:** "zarb Dar al-Islam Khwarezm" **Rev:** Inscription and date in crescent, 6-pointed circled star above **Rev. Inscription:** "on besh tangah fulus" **Note:** Size varies 28-31mm.

Date	Mintage	Good	VG	F	VF	XF
AH1338	—	—	120	200	350	600
Note: Struck on flans of 5 Tenga with obverse of 5 Tenga; In an attempt to replace 5 Tenga by 15 Tenga due to inflation, flans of 5 Tenga with obverse dies of 5 Tenga were used first; Confusion due to the similar size led to production and usage of special broader flans (see Y#11.2)						

Y# 11.2 15 TENGA
Bronze **Obv. Inscription:** "zarb Dar al-Islam Khwarezm" **Rev:** Inscription and date in crescent, 6-pointed circled star above **Rev. Inscription:** "on besh tangah fulus" **Note:** Struck on broad flans. Strikes with or without date above mint name on obverse exist. Die varieties with different rim patterns on reverse exist. Size varies 32-34mm.

Date	Mintage	Good	VG	F	VF	XF
AH1338	—	—	100	175	250	400

KHOREZM PEOPLE'S SOVIET REPUBLIC
AH1338-1343 / 1920-1924 AD

HAMMERED COINAGE

Y# 15.1 20 ROUBLES
Copper Or Bronze **Obv:** Inscription and date, star above, legend around **Obv. Legend:** "zarb fulus Khwarezm shuralar qarari ilan" **Obv. Inscription:** "yigirma manat" **Rev:** Divided arms above, inscription (in Russian) below **Note:** Die varieties exist. Both dates have 6 points in obverse star. Size varies 25-26mm.

Date	Mintage	Good	VG	F	VF	XF
AH1338	—	—	25.00	40.00	70.00	100
AH1339	—	—	40.00	70.00	100	150

Y# 15.2 20 ROUBLES
Copper Or Bronze **Obv:** Inscription and date, star above, legend around **Obv. Legend:** "zarb fulus Khwarezm shuralar qarari ilan" **Obv. Inscription:** "yigirma manat" **Rev:** Crossed arms above, denomination "20 / RUB" (in Russian) below **Note:** Die varieties exist. Size varies 25-26mm.

Date	Mintage	Good	VG	F	VF	XF
AH1338	—	—	30.00	50.00	80.00	120
Note: 6 points in obverse star						
AH1339	—	—	20.00	35.00	50.00	80.00
Note: Varieties exist with 6 or 8 points in obverse star, with 8 stars much scarcer						

Y# 16.1 25 ROUBLES
Bronze Or Brass **Obv:** Inscription and date above, legend below (starting on the right with "Khwarezm") **Obv. Legend:** "zarb fulus Khwarezm shuralar qarari ilan" **Obv. Inscription:** "yigirma besh manat" **Rev:** Arms in center, crescent and star above, denomination "25 RUBLES" (in Russian) around **Note:** Many die varieties exist with different arms design. Varieties exist with 8, 12, 16 or 18 points in reverse star. The strike with inverted "R" has 12 points in star. Size varies 24-26mm.

Date	Mintage	Good	VG	F	VF	XF
AH1339	—	—	17.50	30.00	40.00	75.00
AH1339	—	—	50.00	70.00	100	175
Note: With inverted Russian "R" in "Rubles"						

Y# 16.2 25 ROUBLES
Bronze Or Brass **Obv:** Inscription and date above, legend below (starting on the right with "shuralar") **Obv. Legend:** "zarb fulus Khwarezm shuralar qarari ilan" **Obv. Inscription:** "yigirma besh manat" **Rev:** Arms in center, crescent and star above, denomination "25 Rubles" (in Russian) around **Note:** Many die varieties exist with different arms design. Varieties exist with 8, 12, 16 or 18 points in reverse star. The strike with inverted "R" has 12 points in star. Size varies 24-26mm.

Date	Mintage	Good	VG	F	VF	XF
AH1339	—	—	17.50	25.00	40.00	70.00
AH1339	—	—	50.00	70.00	100	175
Note: With inverted Russian "R" in "Rubles"						

Y# 17 100 ROUBLES
Bronze **Obv:** Crescent and star in center, inscription and date above, legend below **Obv. Legend:** "zarb fulus Khwarezm shuralar qarari ilan" **Obv. Inscription:** "yuz manat" **Rev:** Denomination "100 Rubles" (in Russian), arms below **Note:** Die varieties exist. Varieties exist with 6 or 8 points in obverse star. Size varies 20-22.

Date	Mintage	Good	VG	F	VF	XF
AH1339	—	—	22.50	40.00	60.00	90.00

Y# 18 500 ROUBLES
Bronze, 24 mm. **Obv:** Inscription in center, 12-pointed star and date above, legend around **Obv. Legend:** "zarb fulus Khwarezmjumhuriyeti" **Obv. Inscription:** "500 / besh yuz manat / 500" **Rev:** Arms with two stars above, "Rubles" (in Russian) / "500" below **Note:** Genuine specimens appear like the pictured coin, no die varieties exist.

Date	Mintage	Good	VG	F	VF	XF
AH1339	—	—	100	175	250	350

Y# 19.1 500 ROUBLES
Bronze Or Brass **Obv:** Inscription (in one word) in center, star and divided date above, legend around **Obv. Legend:** "zarb fulus jumhuriyeti Khwarezm" **Obv. Inscription:** "beshyuz manat" **Rev:** Arms with two stars above, "Rubles" (in Russian) / "500" below **Note:** Die varieties exist. Varieties exist with 8 or 17 points in obverse star, the later is much scarcer. Size varies 18-20mm.

Date	Mintage	Good	VG	F	VF	XF
AH1339	—	—	20.00	35.00	50.00	80.00

Y# 19.2 500 ROUBLES

Bronze Or Brass **Obv:** Inscription (in 2 words) in center, star and divided date above, legend around **Obv. Legend:** "zarb fulus jumhuriyeti Khwarezm" **Obv. Inscription:** "besh yuz manat" **Rev:** Arms with two stars above, "Rubles" (in Russian) / "500" below **Note:** Die varieties exist. Two varieties of the arms design exist. Size varies 18-20mm.

Date	Mintage	Good	VG	F	VF	XF
AH1339	—	—	17.50	25.00	40.00	70.00

Note: Varieties exist with 5, 6, 8, 12 or 16 points in obverse star

Date	Mintage	Good	VG	F	VF	XF
AH1340	—	—	22.50	40.00	60.00	90.00

Note: Varieties exist with 5 or 6 points in obverse star

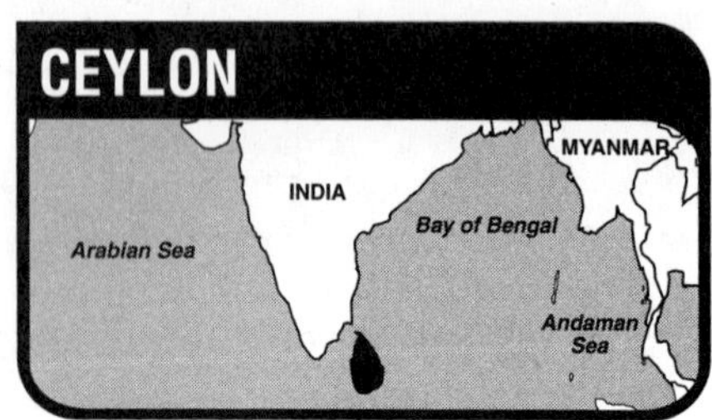

The earliest known inhabitants of Ceylon, the Veddahs, were subjugated by the Sinhalese from northern India in the 6th century B.C. Sinhalese rule was maintained until 1408, after which the island was controlled by China for 30 years. The Portuguese came to Ceylon in 1505 and maintained control of the coastal area for 150 years. The Dutch supplanted them in 1658, which were in turn supplanted by the British who seized the Dutch colonies in 1796, and made them a Crown Colony in 1802. In 1815, the British conquered the independent Kingdom of Kandy in the central part of the island. Constitutional changes in 1931 and 1946 granted the Ceylonese a measure of autonomy and a parliamentary form of government. Britain granted Ceylon independence as a self-governing state within the British Commonwealth on Feb. 4, 1948. On May 22, 1972, the Ceylonese adopted a new Constitution, which declared Ceylon to be the Republic of Sri Lanka –'Resplendent Island'

RULER

British, 1796-1948

BRITISH COLONY

DECIMAL COINAGE

100 Cents = 1 Rupee

KM# 90 1/4 CENT

Copper **Ruler:** Victoria **Obv:** Head left within circle **Obv. Legend:** QUEEN VICTORIA **Rev:** Tree within circle

Date	Mintage	F	VF	XF	Unc	BU
1901	216,000	1.50	3.00	5.00	12.00	—
1901 Proof	—	Value: 125				

KM# 100 1/4 CENT

Copper **Ruler:** Edward VII **Obv:** Crowned bust right **Rev:** Tree within circle, date below, denomination above

Date	Mintage	F	VF	XF	Unc	BU
1904	103,000	2.50	5.00	10.00	22.00	—
1904 Proof	—	Value: 150				

KM# 91 1/2 CENT

2.3600 g., Copper, 18.3 mm. **Ruler:** Victoria **Obv:** Head left within circle **Obv. Legend:** QUEEN VICTORIA **Rev:** Tree within circle

Date	Mintage	F	VF	XF	Unc	BU
1901	2,020,000	1.25	2.50	4.00	10.00	—

KM# 101 1/2 CENT

Copper **Ruler:** Edward VII **Obv:** Crowned bust right **Rev:** Tree within circle, date below, denomination above

Date	Mintage	F	VF	XF	Unc	BU
1904	2,012,000	1.00	2.00	5.00	12.00	—
1904 Proof	—	Value: 120				
1905	1,000,000	1.50	3.00	6.00	15.00	—
1905 Proof	—	Value: 120				
1906	3,056,000	1.00	2.00	5.00	12.00	—
1906 Proof	—	Value: 120				
1908	1,000,000	1.50	3.00	6.00	15.00	—
1908 Proof	—	Value: 200				
1909	3,000,000	1.00	2.00	5.00	12.00	—
1909 Proof	—	Value: 120				

KM# 106 1/2 CENT

Copper **Ruler:** George V **Obv:** Crowned bust left **Rev:** Tree within circle, date below, denomination above

Date	Mintage	F	VF	XF	Unc	BU
1912	5,008,000	1.25	2.75	4.00	10.00	—
1912 Proof	—	Value: 120				
1914	2,000,000	1.25	2.75	6.00	12.00	—
1914 Proof	—	Value: 120				
1917	2,000,000	1.50	3.00	6.00	12.00	—
1917 Proof	—	Value: 120				
1926	5,000,000	0.50	1.00	2.00	5.00	—
1926 Proof	—	Value: 120				

KM# 110 1/2 CENT

Copper **Ruler:** George VI **Obv:** Crowned head left **Rev:** Tree within circle, date below, denomination above

Date	Mintage	F	VF	XF	Unc	BU
1937	3,026,000	0.30	0.85	1.50	3.50	—
1937 Proof	—	Value: 175				
1940	5,080,000	0.25	0.65	1.25	3.00	—

KM# 92 CENT

Copper **Ruler:** Victoria **Obv:** Head left within circle **Obv. Legend:** QUEEN VICTORIA **Rev:** Tree within circle

Date	Mintage	F	VF	XF	Unc	BU
1901	1,014,000	2.50	5.00	10.00	22.00	—

KM# 102 CENT

Copper **Ruler:** Edward VII **Obv:** Crowned bust right **Rev:** Tree within circle, date below, denomination above

Date	Mintage	F	VF	XF	Unc	BU
1904	2,529,000	1.00	2.00	4.00	8.00	—
1904 Proof	—	Value: 125				
1905	1,509,000	1.25	2.25	5.00	10.00	—
1905 Proof	—	Value: 125				
1906	1,751,000	1.25	2.25	5.00	10.00	—
1906 Proof	—	Value: 125				
1908	—	1.00	2.00	4.00	8.00	—
1908 Proof	—	Value: 225				
1909	2,500,000	1.00	2.00	4.00	8.00	—
1909 Proof	—	Value: 125				
1910	8,236,000	0.50	1.00	2.50	5.00	—
1910 Proof	—	Value: 125				

KM# 107 CENT

4.5700 g., Copper, 23 mm. **Ruler:** George V **Obv:** Crowned bust left **Rev:** Tree within circle, date below, denomination above

Date	Mintage	F	VF	XF	Unc	BU
1912	5,855,000	0.50	1.00	2.00	4.00	—
1912 Proof	—	Value: 115				
1914	6,000,000	0.50	1.00	2.25	5.00	—
1914 Proof	—	Value: 115				
1917	1,000,000	1.00	1.75	3.00	8.00	—
1917 Proof	—	Value: 115				
1920	2,000,000	0.50	1.00	2.25	5.00	—
1920 Proof	—	Value: 115				
1922	2,930,000	0.50	1.00	2.25	5.00	—
1922 Proof	—	Value: 115				
1923	2,500,000	0.50	1.00	2.25	5.00	—
1923 Proof	—	Value: 115				
1925	7,490,000	0.35	0.75	1.50	3.50	—
1925 Proof	—	Value: 115				
1926	3,750,000	0.35	0.75	1.50	3.50	—
1926 Proof	—	Value: 115				
1928	2,500,000	0.35	0.75	1.50	4.00	—
1928 Proof	—	Value: 115				
1929	5,000,000	0.35	0.75	1.50	3.50	—
1929 Proof	—	Value: 115				

KM# 111 CENT

4.6400 g., Copper, 22 mm. **Ruler:** George VI **Obv:** Crowned head left, PM below neck at right **Rev:** Tree within circle, date below, denomination above **Note:** High relief. Thickness: 1.73mm.

Date	Mintage	F	VF	XF	Unc	BU
1937	4,538,000	0.25	0.50	1.25	3.00	—
1937 Proof	—	Value: 100				
1940	10,190,000	0.15	0.30	1.00	2.00	—
1940 Proof	—	Value: 75.00				
1942	20,780,000	0.15	0.30	1.00	2.00	—

KM# 111a CENT

2.3600 g., Bronze, 22.35 mm. **Ruler:** George VI **Obv:** Crowned head left **Rev:** Tree within circle, date below, denomination above **Note:** Low relief. Thin planchet, .87mm.

Date	Mintage	F	VF	XF	Unc	BU
1942	Inc. above	0.15	0.30	0.75	1.75	—
1942 Proof	—	Value: 75.00				
1943	43,705,000	0.15	0.30	0.50	1.00	—
1945	34,100,000	0.15	0.35	0.60	1.20	—
1945 Proof	—	Value: 20.00				

Note: Frozen year 1945, restruck until 1962

KM# 117 2 CENTS

2.5400 g., Nickel-Brass, 18 mm. **Ruler:** George VI **Obv:** Crowned head left **Rev:** Denomination above date **Shape:** Scalloped

Date	Mintage	F	VF	XF	Unc	BU
1944	30,165,000	0.10	0.25	0.50	1.25	—

KM# 119 2 CENTS
2.5500 g., Brass, 18 mm. **Ruler:** George VI **Obv:** Crowned head left, legend without EMPEROR OF INDIA **Rev:** Denomination above date **Shape:** Scalloped

Date	Mintage	F	VF	XF	Unc	BU
1951	15,000,000	0.10	0.25	0.75	1.75	—
1951 Proof	150	Value: 20.00				

KM# 124 2 CENTS
Brass **Ruler:** Elizabeth II **Obv:** Laureate bust right **Rev:** Denomination above date **Shape:** Scalloped

Date	Mintage	F	VF	XF	Unc	BU
1955	37,131,000	0.10	0.15	0.25	0.65	—
1957	38,200,000	0.10	0.15	0.25	0.65	—
1957 Proof	—	Value: 75.00				

KM# 103 5 CENTS
Copper-Nickel, 18 mm. **Ruler:** Edward VII **Obv:** Crowned bust right **Rev:** Denomination above date **Shape:** Square

Date	Mintage	F	VF	XF	Unc	BU
1909	2,000,000	1.50	3.00	5.00	17.00	—
1910	4,000,000	1.00	2.00	3.50	12.00	—

KM# 108 5 CENTS
3.6600 g., Copper-Nickel, 18 mm. **Ruler:** George V **Obv:** Crowned bust left **Rev:** Denomination above date **Shape:** 4-sided

Date	Mintage	F	VF	XF	Unc	BU
1912 H	4,000,000	0.75	1.50	3.00	10.00	—
1920	6,000,000	0.50	1.00	2.00	7.00	—
1926	3,000,000	0.75	1.50	4.00	12.50	—

KM# 113.1 5 CENTS
Nickel-Brass, 18 mm. **Ruler:** George VI **Obv:** Crowned head left **Rev:** Denomination above date **Shape:** Square

Date	Mintage	F	VF	XF	Unc	BU
1942	12,752,000	0.35	0.75	1.50	4.50	—
1942 Proof	—	Value: 50.00				
1943	Inc. above	0.35	0.75	1.50	4.50	—
1943 Proof	—	Value: 50.00				

KM# 113.2 5 CENTS
Nickel-Brass, 18 mm. **Ruler:** George VI **Obv:** Crowned head left **Rev:** Denomination above date **Note:** Thin planchet.

Date	Mintage	F	VF	XF	Unc	BU
1944	18,064,000	0.20	0.35	0.70	2.00	—
1945	31,192,000	0.15	0.30	0.60	1.75	—
1945 Proof	—	Value: 60.00				

Note: Varieties exist in bust, denomination and legend placement for 1945; The date was frozen at 1945 and these coins were struck until 1962

KM# 120 5 CENTS
Nickel-Brass, 18 mm. **Ruler:** George VI **Obv:** Crowned head left, legend without EMPEROR OF INDIA **Rev:** Denomination above date **Shape:** Square

Date	Mintage	F	VF	XF	Unc	BU
1951 Proof	150	Value: 20.00				
1951 Proof, restrike	—	Value: 12.00				

KM# 97 10 CENTS
1.1664 g., 0.8000 Silver 0.0300 oz. ASW **Ruler:** Edward VII **Obv:** Crowned bust right **Rev:** Plant divides denomination above date

Date	Mintage	F	VF	XF	Unc	BU
1902	1,000,000	1.00	2.75	6.00	20.00	—
1902 Proof	—	Value: 150				
1903	1,000,000	1.00	2.75	6.00	20.00	—
1903 Proof	—	Value: 150				
1907	500,000	2.50	5.00	15.00	25.00	—
1908	1,500,000	1.00	2.75	6.00	15.00	—
1909	1,000,000	1.00	2.75	6.00	15.00	—
1910	2,000,000	1.00	2.75	6.00	15.00	—

KM# 104 10 CENTS
1.1664 g., 0.8000 Silver 0.0300 oz. ASW **Ruler:** George V **Obv:** Crowned bust left **Rev:** Plant divides denomination, date below

Date	Mintage	F	VF	XF	Unc	BU
1911	1,000,000	1.00	1.75	5.00	12.00	—
1912	1,000,000	1.25	2.00	6.00	15.00	—
1913	2,000,000	1.00	1.50	4.00	10.00	—
1914	2,000,000	1.00	1.50	4.00	10.00	—
1914 Proof	—	Value: 150				
1917	879,000	1.00	2.50	7.50	17.50	—
1917 Proof	—	Value: 150				

KM# 104a 10 CENTS
1.1664 g., 0.5500 Silver 0.0206 oz. ASW **Ruler:** George V **Obv:** Crowned bust left **Rev:** Plant divides denomination, date below

Date	Mintage	F	VF	XF	Unc	BU
1919 B	750,000	1.50	3.50	10.00	20.00	—
1919 B Proof	—	Value: 150				
1920 B	3,059,000	1.00	2.50	6.00	15.00	—
1920 B Proof	—	Value: 150				
1921 B	1,583,000	0.75	1.75	5.00	10.00	—
1921 Proof	—	Value: 150				
1922	282,000	1.75	3.50	10.00	25.00	—
1922 Proof	—	Value: 150				
1924	1,508,000	0.75	1.75	4.00	10.00	—
1924 Proof	—	Value: 150				
1925	1,500,000	0.75	1.75	4.00	10.00	—
1925 Proof	—	Value: 150				
1926	1,500,000	0.75	1.75	4.00	10.00	—
1926 Proof	—	Value: 150				
1927	1,500,000	0.75	1.75	4.00	10.00	—
1927 Proof	—	Value: 150				
1928	1,500,000	0.75	1.75	4.00	10.00	—
1928 Proof	—	Value: 150				

KM# 112 10 CENTS
1.1664 g., 0.8000 Silver 0.0300 oz. ASW, 15.5 mm. **Ruler:** George VI **Obv:** Crowned head left **Rev:** Plant divides denomination, date below **Edge:** Reeded

Date	Mintage	F	VF	XF	Unc	BU
1941	16,271,000	0.65	1.00	2.50	6.00	—

KM# 118 10 CENTS
Nickel-Brass, 23 mm. **Ruler:** George VI **Obv:** Crowned head left **Rev:** Denomination above date **Shape:** Scalloped

Date	Mintage	F	VF	XF	Unc	BU
1944	30,500,000	0.25	0.50	1.00	3.00	—
1944 Proof	—	Value: 90.00				

KM# 121 10 CENTS
4.1400 g., Nickel-Brass, 23 mm. **Ruler:** George VI **Obv:** Crowned head left, legend without EMPEROR OF INDIA **Rev:** Denomination above date **Shape:** Scalloped

Date	Mintage	F	VF	XF	Unc	BU
1951	34,760,000	0.10	0.20	0.40	1.25	—
1951 Proof	150	Value: 15.00				
1951 Proof, restrike	—	Value: 4.00				

Note: Frozen year 1951; restruck until 1962. Royal Mint strikes (1959-62) differ slightly in the formation of native inscriptions

KM# 98 25 CENTS
2.9160 g., 0.8000 Silver 0.0750 oz. ASW **Ruler:** Edward VII **Obv:** Crowned bust right **Rev:** Plant divides denomination, date below

Date	Mintage	F	VF	XF	Unc	BU
1902	400,000	4.00	8.00	20.00	40.00	—
1902 Proof	—	Value: 150				
1903	400,000	4.00	8.00	20.00	40.00	—
1903 Proof	—	Value: 150				
1907	120,000	7.50	20.00	30.00	50.00	—
1908	400,000	4.00	8.00	15.00	35.00	—
1909	400,000	4.00	8.00	15.00	35.00	—
1910	800,000	2.00	5.00	10.00	20.00	—

KM# 105 25 CENTS
2.9160 g., 0.8000 Silver 0.0750 oz. ASW **Ruler:** George V **Obv:** Crowned bust left **Rev:** Plant divides denomination, date below

Date	Mintage	F	VF	XF	Unc	BU
1911	400,000	3.00	6.00	12.00	30.00	—
1911 Proof	—	Value: 175				
1913	1,200,000	1.50	2.50	7.50	17.50	—
1913 Proof	—	Value: 175				
1914	400,000	3.00	6.00	12.00	25.00	—
1914 Proof	—	Value: 175				
1917	300,000	4.00	8.00	15.00	35.00	—
1917 Proof	—	Value: 175				

KM# 105a 25 CENTS
2.9160 g., 0.5500 Silver 0.0516 oz. ASW **Ruler:** George V **Obv:** Crowned bust left **Rev:** Plant divides denomination, date below

Date	Mintage	F	VF	XF	Unc	BU
1919 B Proof	—	Value: 150				
1919 B	1,400,000	1.25	3.00	7.50	15.00	—
1920 B Proof	—	Value: 150				
1920 B	1,600,000	1.25	3.00	7.50	15.00	—
1921 B	600,000	3.50	7.50	15.00	30.00	—
1921 B Proof	—	Value: 150				
1922 Proof	—	Value: 150				
1922	1,211,000	1.25	3.25	7.50	15.00	—
1925 Proof	—	Value: 150				

Date	Mintage	F	VF	XF	Unc	BU
1925	1,004,000	1.25	3.50	7.50	15.00	—
1926 Proof	—	Value: 150				
1926	1,000,000	1.25	3.50	7.50	15.00	—

KM# 115 25 CENTS

2.7400 g., Nickel-Brass, 19.3 mm. **Ruler:** George VI **Obv:** Crowned head left **Rev:** Crown at top divides date, denomination below **Note:** Frozen date 1943, restruck until 1951.

Date	Mintage	F	VF	XF	Unc	BU
1943	13,920,000	0.25	0.50	1.00	2.50	—

KM# 122 25 CENTS

Nickel-Brass **Ruler:** George VI **Obv:** Legend without EMPEROR OF INDIA **Rev:** Crown divides date at top, denomination below

Date	Mintage	F	VF	XF	Unc	BU
1951	25,940,000	0.10	0.30	0.60	1.75	—
1951 Proof	150	Value: 20.00				
1951 Proof, restrike	—	Value: 4.00				

Note: Frozen year 1951; restruck until 1962. Royal Mint strikes (1959-62) differ in numerals 9 and 5

KM# 99 50 CENTS

5.8319 g., 0.8000 Silver 0.1500 oz. ASW **Ruler:** Edward VII **Obv:** Crowned bust right **Rev:** Plant divides denomination, date below

Date	Mintage	F	VF	XF	Unc	BU
1902	200,000	5.00	10.00	30.00	70.00	—
1902 Proof	—	Value: 175				
1903	800,000	3.00	8.00	18.00	35.00	—
1903 Proof	—	Value: 175				
1910	200,000	7.00	13.00	30.00	60.00	—

KM# 109 50 CENTS

5.8319 g., 0.8000 Silver 0.1500 oz. ASW **Ruler:** George V **Obv:** Crowned bust left **Rev:** Plant divides denomination, date below

Date	Mintage	F	VF	XF	Unc	BU
1913	400,000	7.00	13.00	30.00	60.00	—
1913 Proof	—	Value: 175				
1914	200,000	5.00	15.00	30.00	60.00	—
1914 Proof	—	Value: 175				
1917	1,073,000	2.50	5.00	10.00	20.00	—
1917 Proof	—	Value: 175				

KM# 109a 50 CENTS

5.8319 g., 0.5500 Silver 0.1031 oz. ASW **Ruler:** George V **Obv:** Crowned bust left **Rev:** Plant divides denomination, date below

Date	Mintage	F	VF	XF	Unc	BU
1919 B	750,000	1.65	3.50	7.00	16.00	—
1919 B Proof	—	Value: 120				
1920 B	800,000	1.65	3.50	7.00	16.00	—
1920 B Proof	—	Value: 120				
1921 B	800,000	1.65	3.50	7.00	16.00	—
1921 B Proof	—	Value: 120				

Date	Mintage	F	VF	XF	Unc	BU
1922	1,040,000	1.65	3.50	7.00	16.00	—
1922 Proof	—	Value: 120				
1924	1,010,000	1.65	3.50	7.00	16.00	—
1924 Proof	—	Value: 120				
1925	500,000	2.00	5.00	10.00	20.00	—
1925 Proof	—	Value: 120				
1926	500,000	2.00	5.00	10.00	20.00	—
1926 Proof	—	Value: 120				
1927	500,000	2.00	5.00	10.00	20.00	—
1927 Proof	—	Value: 120				
1928	500,000	2.00	5.00	10.00	20.00	—
1928 Proof	—	Value: 120				
1929	500,000	2.00	5.00	10.00	20.00	—
1929 Proof	—	Value: 120				

KM# 114 50 CENTS

5.8319 g., 0.8000 Silver 0.1500 oz. ASW **Ruler:** George VI **Obv:** Crowned head left **Rev:** Plant divides denomination, date below

Date	Mintage	F	VF	XF	Unc	BU
1942	662,000	2.50	4.50	9.00	18.50	—

KM# 116 50 CENTS

5.5400 g., Nickel-Brass **Ruler:** George VI **Obv:** Crowned head left **Rev:** Crown divides date above denomination **Note:** Frozen date 1943, restruck until 1951.

Date	Mintage	F	VF	XF	Unc	BU
1943	8,600,000	0.35	0.75	1.50	3.50	—

KM# 123 50 CENTS

5.4900 g., Nickel-Brass **Ruler:** George VI **Obv:** Crowned head left, legend without EMPEROR OF INDIA **Rev:** Crown divides date above denomination

Date	Mintage	F	VF	XF	Unc	BU
1951	19,980,000	0.20	0.35	0.75	1.75	—
1951 Proof	150	Value: 20.00				
1951 Proof, restrike	—	Value: 5.00				

Note: Frozen year 1951; restruck until 1962. Royal Mint strikes (1959-62) differ slightly in the formation of native inscriptions

BRITISH COMMONWEALTH

DECIMAL COINAGE

100 Cents = 1 Rupee

KM# 125 RUPEE

Copper-Nickel, 28 mm. **Ruler:** Elizabeth II **Subject:** 2,500 Years of Buddhism **Obv:** Date and design at center, denomination at left **Rev:** Temple above 2500, design in background **Rev. Designer:** B. R. Sindall

Date	Mintage	F	VF	XF	Unc	BU
1957	2,000,000	0.50	1.00	2.00	3.00	—
1957 Proof	1,800	Value: 12.00				

KM# 126 5 RUPEES

28.2757 g., 0.9250 Silver 0.8409 oz. ASW, 39 mm. **Ruler:** Elizabeth II **Subject:** 2,500 Years of Buddhism **Obv:** Flowers and date at center, denomination at left **Rev:** 2500 within inner circle of flower, circle of animals surround, ducks encircle them **Rev. Designer:** B. R. Sindall

Date	Mintage	F	VF	XF	Unc	BU
1957	500,000	11.50	13.50	17.50	30.00	35.00
1957 Proof	1,800	Value: 75.00				

Note: 258,000 returned in 1962 to be melted at The Royal Mint

DECIMAL COINAGE

KM# 127 CENT

0.7000 g., Aluminum, 16 mm. **Ruler:** Elizabeth II **Obv:** Denomination at center, date below **Rev:** Crowned arms

Date	Mintage	F	VF	XF	Unc	BU
1963	33,000,000	—	—	—	0.10	0.20
1965	12,000,000	—	—	0.10	0.15	0.25
1967	10,000,000	—	—	0.10	0.15	0.25
1968	22,505,000	—	—	—	0.10	0.20
1969	10,000,000	—	—	—	0.10	0.20
1970	15,000,000	—	—	—	0.10	0.20
1971	55,000,000	—	—	—	0.10	0.20
1971 Proof	20,000	Value: 0.50				

KM# 128 2 CENTS

0.7600 g., Aluminum, 18.3 mm. **Ruler:** Elizabeth II **Obv:** Denomination at center, date below **Rev:** Crowned arms **Shape:** Scalloped

Date	Mintage	F	VF	XF	Unc	BU
1963	26,000,000	—	—	0.10	0.15	0.25
1965	7,000,000	—	—	0.10	0.15	0.25
1967	15,000,000	—	—	0.10	0.15	0.25
1968	15,000,000	—	—	0.10	0.15	0.25
1970	13,000,000	—	—	0.10	0.15	0.25
1971	45,000,000	—	—	0.10	0.15	0.25
1971 Proof	20,000	Value: 1.00				

KM# 129 5 CENTS

3.2000 g., Nickel-Brass, 18 mm. **Ruler:** Elizabeth II **Obv:** Denomination at center, date below **Rev:** Crowned arms **Shape:** 4-sided

Date	Mintage	F	VF	XF	Unc	BU
1963	16,000,000	—	0.10	0.15	0.25	0.35
1965	9,000,000	—	0.10	0.15	0.25	0.35
1968	12,000,000	—	0.10	0.15	0.25	0.35
1969	2,500,000	—	0.10	0.20	0.40	0.60
1970	7,000,000	—	0.10	0.15	0.25	0.35
1971	32,000,000	—	0.10	0.15	0.25	0.35
1971 Proof	20,000	Value: 1.50				

KM# 130 10 CENTS
4.1200 g., Nickel-Brass, 23 mm. **Ruler:** Elizabeth II **Obv:** Denomination at center, date below **Rev:** Crowned arms **Shape:** Scalloped

Date	Mintage	F	VF	XF	Unc	BU
1963	14,000,000	—	0.10	0.15	0.25	0.35
1965	3,000,000	—	0.10	0.15	0.35	0.50
1969	6,000,000	—	0.10	0.15	0.25	0.35
1971	29,000,000	—	0.10	0.15	0.20	0.30
1971 Proof	20,000	Value: 1.25				

KM# 131 25 CENTS
Copper-Nickel, 18 mm. **Ruler:** Elizabeth II **Obv:** Denomination at center, date below **Rev:** Crowned arms

Date	Mintage	F	VF	XF	Unc	BU
1963	30,000,000	—	0.10	0.20	0.40	0.55
1965	8,000,000	—	0.10	0.25	0.50	0.65
1971 Proof	20,000	Value: 1.50				
1971	24,000,000	—	0.10	0.15	0.30	0.45

KM# 132 50 CENTS
Copper-Nickel, 21.5 mm. **Ruler:** Elizabeth II **Obv:** Denomination at center, date below **Rev:** Crowned arms

Date	Mintage	F	VF	XF	Unc	BU
1963	15,000,000	0.10	0.20	0.35	0.75	1.00
1965	7,000,000	0.10	0.20	0.35	0.75	1.00
1971 Proof	20,000	Value: 2.50				
1971	4,000,000	0.25	0.50	0.75	1.50	1.75
1972	—	0.25	0.50	0.75	1.50	1.75

KM# 133 RUPEE
7.1000 g., Copper-Nickel, 25.3 mm. **Ruler:** Elizabeth II **Obv:** Denomination above date **Rev:** Crowned arms

Date	Mintage	F	VF	XF	Unc	BU
1963	20,000,000	0.10	0.20	0.40	1.00	1.25
1965	5,000,000	0.15	0.25	0.50	1.25	1.50
1969	2,500,000	0.15	0.25	0.50	1.75	2.00
1971 Proof	20,000	Value: 4.50				
1971	5,000,000	0.15	0.25	0.50	1.50	1.75

KM# 134 2 RUPEES
Copper-Nickel **Ruler:** Elizabeth II **Series:** F.A.O. **Obv:** Large denomination above date **Rev:** King Parakramabahu I (1153-1186) between wheat stalks

Date	Mintage	F	VF	XF	Unc	BU
1968	500,000	0.50	1.50	2.25	3.50	5.00

CHAD

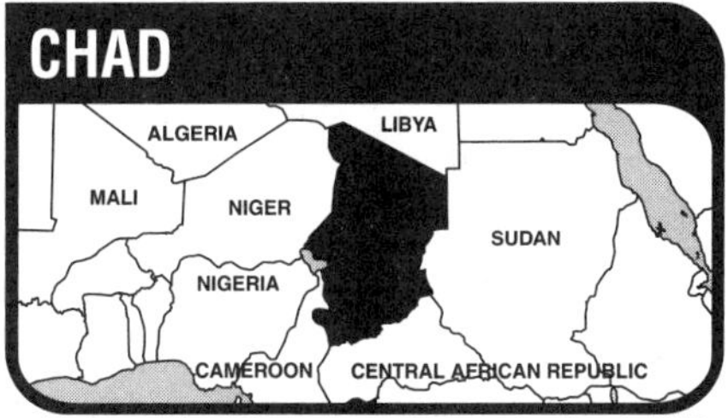

The Republic of Chad, a landlocked country of central Africa, is the largest country of former French Equatorial Africa. It has an area of 495,755 sq. mi. (1,284,000 sq. km.) and a population of *7.27 million. Capital: N'Djamena. An expanding livestock industry produces camels, cattle and sheep. Cotton (the chief product), ivory and palm oil are important exports.

Although supposedly known to Ptolemy, the Chad area was first visited by white men in 1823. Exaggerated estimates of its economic importance led to a race for its possession (1890-93), which resulted in the territory being divided by treaty between Great Britain, France and Germany. As a consequence of World War I, the German area was mandated to France in 1919. Chad was absorbed into the colony of French Equatorial Africa, as part of Ubangi-Shari, in 1910 and became a separate colony in 1920. Upon dissolution of French Equatorial Africa in 1959, the component states became autonomous members of the French Union. Chad became an independent republic on Aug. 11, 1960.

NOTE: For earlier and related coinage see French Equatorial Africa and the Equatorial African States. For later coinage see Central African States.

MINT MARKS
(a) - Paris, privy marks only
(b) = Brussels
NI - Numismatic Italiana, Arezzo, Italy

COMMEMORATIVE EDGE INSCRIPTIONS
1960 LIBERTE PROGRESS SOLIDARITE
1970/REPUBLIQUE DU TCHAD

REPUBLIC

DECIMAL COINAGE

KM# 2 100 FRANCS
7.0000 g., Nickel, 25.5 mm. **Obv:** Three Giant Eland left **Rev:** Denomination within circle, date below **Designer:** G.B.L. Bazor

Date	Mintage	F	VF	XF	Unc	BU
1971(a)	5,000,000	10.00	17.50	27.50	45.00	—
1972(a)	5,000,000	10.00	17.50	27.50	45.00	—

KM# 3 100 FRANCS
7.0000 g., Nickel, 25.5 mm. **Obv:** Three Giant Eland **Rev:** Denomination and date within circle **Designer:** G.B.L. Bazor

Date	Mintage	F	VF	XF	Unc	BU
1975(a)	—	10.00	15.00	22.00	35.00	—
1978(a)	—	12.00	20.00	28.00	45.00	—
1980(a)	—	10.00	17.50	25.00	40.00	—
1982(a)	—	10.00	15.00	22.00	35.00	—
1984(a)	—	10.00	15.00	22.00	35.00	—
1985(a)	—	10.00	14.00	20.00	30.00	—
1988(a)	—	10.00	14.00	20.00	30.00	—
1990(a)	—	10.00	14.00	20.00	30.00	—
1991(a)	—	—	—	—	—	—

KM# 13 500 FRANCS
Copper-Nickel **Obv:** Plants divide date and denomination **Rev:** Woman's head 3/4 left

Date	Mintage	F	VF	XF	Unc	BU
1985(a)	—	15.00	22.00	35.00	50.00	—

CHILE

The Republic of Chile, a ribbon-like country on the Pacific coast of southern South America, has an area of 292,135 sq. mi. (756,950 sq. km.) and a population of *15.21 million. Capital: Santiago. Historically, the economic base of Chile has been the rich mineral deposits of its northern provinces. Copper has accounted for more than 75 percent of Chile's export earnings in recent years. Other important mineral exports are iron ore, iodine and nitrate of soda. Fresh fruits and vegetables, as well as wine are increasingly significant in inter-hemispheric trade.

Diego de Almargo was the first Spaniard to attempt to wrest Chile from the Incas and Araucanian tribes in 1536. He failed, and was followed by Pedro de Valdivia, a favorite of Pizarro, who founded Santiago in 1541. When the Napoleonic Wars involved Spain, leaving the constituent parts of the Spanish Empire to their own devices, Chilean patriots formed a national government and proclaimed the country's independence, Sept. 18, 1810. Independence however, was not secured until Feb. 12, 1818, after a bitter struggle led by Bernardo O'Higgins and San Martin. Despite a long steady history of monetary devaluation, reflected in declining weight and fineness in its currency, Chile developed a strong democracy. This was displaced when rampant inflation characterized chaotic and subsequently repressive governments in the mid to late 20th century.

RULER
Spanish until 1818

MINT MARK
So - Santiago

MONETARY SYSTEM
16 Reales = 1 Escudo

REPUBLIC

DECIMAL COINAGE

KM# 161 CENTAVO
Copper **Obv:** Liberty head left **Rev:** Denomination within wreath, date below

Date	Mintage	F	VF	XF	Unc	BU
1904	970,000	0.75	1.50	3.00	8.00	—
1908	174,000	1.50	3.00	9.00	16.00	—
1991 Rare	—	—	—	—	—	—
Note: Error for 1919						
1919	173,000	1.25	2.50	8.50	15.00	—

KM# 164 2 CENTAVOS

Copper **Obv:** Liberty head left **Rev:** Denomination within wreath, date below

Date	Mintage	F	VF	XF	Unc	BU
1919	147,000	1.50	3.00	6.00	17.50	—

KM# 162 2-1/2 CENTAVOS (Dos I Medio)

Copper **Obv:** Liberty head left **Rev:** Denomination within wreath

Date	Mintage	F	VF	XF	Unc	BU
1904	277,000	3.50	7.50	20.00	50.00	—
1906	161,000	4.50	10.00	22.00	55.00	—
1907	262,000	3.50	7.50	20.00	45.00	—
Note: Varieties exist for 1907 dated coins						
1908	201,000	3.00	7.00	19.00	45.00	—

KM# 155.2 5 CENTAVOS

1.0000 g., 0.5000 Silver 0.0161 oz. ASW, 14 mm. **Obv:** Defiant Condor on rock left, 0.5 below condor **Obv. Designer:** O. Roty **Rev:** Denomination above date within wreath **Note:** Varieties exist with 0.5, 0.5., 0/5.5., 0,5 or 05. below condor.

Date	Mintage	F	VF	XF	Unc	BU
1901/801	2,109,000	3.00	6.00	15.00	32.50	—
Note: With 05.						
1901/891	Inc. above	3.00	6.00	15.00	32.50	—
1901/896	Inc. above	3.00	6.00	15.00	32.50	—
1904/891/9	—	3.50	7.50	15.00	37.50	—
1904/894	2,527,000	3.50	7.50	15.00	37.50	—
1904/1	Inc. above	3.50	7.00	15.00	37.50	—
Note: With 0.5						
1904	Inc. above	2.00	5.00	10.00	27.50	—
Note: With 05.						
1906/4	713,000	5.00	10.00	25.00	45.00	—
1906	Inc. above	2.00	5.00	10.00	27.50	—
1907	2,791,000	2.00	3.00	8.00	22.50	—
Note: Exists with both 0.5 and 0.5. obverse varieties						
1907.	Inc. above	2.00	3.00	8.00	22.50	—
1909/899	—	2.50	5.00	12.00	27.50	—

KM# 155.2a 5 CENTAVOS

1.0000 g., 0.4000 Silver 0.0129 oz. ASW **Obv:** Defiant Condor on rock left **Obv. Designer:** O. Roty **Rev:** Denomination above date within wreath **Note:** Without fineness below condor.

Date	Mintage	F	VF	XF	Unc	BU
1908/1	—	2.50	5.00	10.00	22.50	—
1908/2	—	2.50	5.00	10.00	22.50	—
1908	3,642,000	2.00	3.00	7.00	18.00	—
1909/1	1,177,000	2.00	4.00	9.00	20.00	—
1909/2	—	2.00	4.00	9.00	20.00	—
1909/8	Inc. above	2.00	4.00	9.00	20.00	—
1909	Inc. above	2.00	5.00	9.00	20.00	—
1910/01	1,587,000	2.00	3.00	7.00	18.00	—
1910	Inc. above	2.00	3.00	7.00	18.00	—
1911	847,000	2.00	4.00	9.00	20.00	—
1913/1	—	2.50	5.00	10.00	22.50	—
1913/2	2,573,000	3.00	7.00	15.00	35.00	—
Note: Varieties exist with a dot below 1 in date for 1913						
1913	Inc. above	2.00	3.00	7.00	18.00	—
Note: Varieties exist with a dot below 1 in date for 1913						
1919	Inc. below	1.50	3.00	7.00	18.00	—
Note: With and without dash below second 9 in date						

KM# 155.3 5 CENTAVOS

1.0000 g., 0.4500 Silver 0.0145 oz. ASW **Obv:** Defiant Condor on rock left, 0.45 below condor **Obv. Designer:** O. Roty **Rev:** Denomination above date within wreath

Date	Mintage	F	VF	XF	Unc	BU
1915/1	—	1.50	3.50	6.00	16.50	—
1915	2,250,000	1.50	3.00	5.00	15.00	—
Note: 1915 exists with flat and curved top on 5						
1916/1	4,337,000	1.50	3.50	6.00	16.50	—
1916/5	Inc. above	1.50	3.50	6.00	16.50	—
1916	Inc. above	1.50	3.00	5.00	15.00	—
1919/1	1,494,000	3.00	7.00	15.00	35.00	—
Note: With dash below second 9 in date						
1919/2	Inc. above	2.00	4.00	8.00	22.50	—
1919/5	Inc. above	2.00	4.00	8.00	22.50	—
1919	Inc. above	3.00	5.00	10.00	22.50	—

KM# 165 5 CENTAVOS

Copper-Nickel **Obv:** Defiant Condor on rock left, without designer's name O. ROTY at bottom **Obv. Designer:** O. Roty **Rev:** Denomination above date within wreath **Note:** Varieties exist.

Date	Mintage	F	VF	XF	Unc	BU
1920	718,000	1.00	1.50	3.00	12.00	—
1921	2,406,000	0.60	1.25	2.00	7.00	—
1922	3,872,000	0.60	1.25	2.00	7.00	—
1923	2,150,000	0.60	1.25	2.00	7.00	—
1925	994,000	0.60	1.25	2.00	7.00	—
Note: Obverse variety known with dot to left of right wing tip.						
1926	594,000	1.50	2.50	3.00	9.00	—
1927	1,276,000	0.50	1.00	2.00	6.00	—
1928	5,197,000	0.50	1.00	2.00	6.00	—
1933	3,000,000	5.00	10.00	25.00	55.00	—
1934	Inc. above	0.25	0.50	1.00	3.00	—
1936	2,000,000	0.25	0.50	1.00	3.00	—
1937	2,000,000	0.25	0.50	1.00	3.00	—
1938	2,000,000	0.25	0.50	1.00	3.00	—

KM# 156.2 10 CENTAVOS

2.0000 g., 0.5000 Silver 0.0321 oz. ASW, 17 mm. **Obv:** Defiant Condor on rock left, 0.5 below condor **Obv. Designer:** O. Roty **Rev:** Denomination above date within wreath **Note:** Obverse varieties exist with 0.5, 0,5, 0.5. or 0.5/9 below condor. Struck by law of January 19, 1899.

Date	Mintage	F	VF	XF	Unc	BU
1901/891	Inc. above	17.50	30.00	55.00	150	—
1901/896	—	17.50	30.00	55.00	150	—
1904/896	—	2.00	3.50	7.00	16.50	—
1904/899	779,000	2.00	3.50	7.00	16.50	—
1906	139,000	2.50	4.50	8.50	18.00	—
1907/2	—	2.50	4.50	8.50	18.00	—
1907/807	—	2.50	4.50	8.50	18.00	—
1907	3,151,000	2.00	3.50	7.00	16.50	—
Note: Exists with both 0.5 and 0.5. obverse varieties						

KM# 156.2a 10 CENTAVOS

1.5000 g., 0.4000 Silver 0.0193 oz. ASW **Obv:** Defiant Condor on rock left **Obv. Designer:** O. Roty **Rev:** Denomination above date within wreath **Note:** Varieties exist.

Date	Mintage	F	VF	XF	Unc	BU
1908/1	—	1.50	3.00	6.00	15.00	—
1908	4,149,000	1.00	2.00	4.50	12.00	—
1908/inverted 6	—	1.50	3.00	6.00	15.00	—
1909/8	2,964,000	1.50	3.00	6.00	15.00	—
1909	Inc. above	1.00	2.00	4.50	12.00	—
1913	1,269,000	1.50	3.00	6.00	15.00	—
1919/8	—	3.00	6.00	12.00	25.00	—
1919	883,000	2.50	5.00	10.00	20.00	—
1920/5	—	1.50	3.00	6.00	18.00	—
1920	2,109,000	1.00	2.00	4.50	12.00	—

KM# 156.3 10 CENTAVOS

1.5000 g., 0.4500 Silver 0.0217 oz. ASW **Obv:** Defiant Condor on rock left, 0.45 below condor **Obv. Designer:** O. Roty **Rev:** Denomination above date within wreath

Date	Mintage	F	VF	XF	Unc	BU
1915	1,620,000	1.00	1.50	3.00	7.50	—
1916	2,855,000	1.00	1.50	3.00	7.50	—
1917/1	—	2.00	3.50	7.00	18.00	—
1917	736,000	1.50	2.50	5.00	14.00	—
1918/5	—	2.00	3.50	7.00	18.00	—
1918	Inc. above	1.50	2.50	5.00	14.00	—
1919/3	—	2.00	3.50	7.00	18.00	—

KM# 166 10 CENTAVOS

3.0800 g., Copper-Nickel, 19.7 mm. **Obv:** Defiant Condor on rock left, without designer's name O. ROTY at bottom **Obv. Designer:** O. Roty **Rev:** Denomination above date within wreath **Edge:** Plain

Date	Mintage	F	VF	XF	Unc	BU
1920	451,000	1.50	3.50	7.00	15.00	—
1921	2,654,000	0.50	0.75	1.50	3.00	—
1922	4,017,000	0.50	0.75	1.50	3.00	—
1923	3,356,000	0.50	0.75	7.00	16.50	—
1924	1,445,000	0.50	0.75	1.50	3.00	—
1925	2,665,000	0.50	0.75	1.50	3.00	—
1927	523,000	1.00	2.00	3.50	7.00	—
1928	3,052,000	0.50	0.75	1.50	3.00	—
1932	1,500,000	1.00	2.00	3.50	7.00	—
1933/2	5,800,000	0.75	1.00	2.00	4.00	—
1933 Over reversed 3	—	0.50	1.00	2.00	5.00	—
1933	Inc. above	0.25	0.50	1.00	2.00	—
1934	900,000	0.50	0.75	1.50	3.00	—
1935	1,500,000	0.50	0.75	1.50	3.00	—
1936	3,300,000	0.25	0.50	1.00	2.00	—
1937 Over reversed 3	—	0.50	1.00	2.00	5.00	—
1937	2,000,000	0.25	0.50	1.00	2.00	—
1938 Over reversed 3	—	0.50	1.00	2.00	5.00	—
1938	5,000,000	0.25	0.50	1.00	2.00	—
1939 Over reversed 3	—	0.50	1.00	2.00	5.00	—
1939	1,200,000	0.25	0.50	1.00	2.00	—
1940	6,100,000	0.25	0.50	1.00	2.00	—
1941	900,000	1.00	2.00	3.00	6.00	—

KM# 151.2 20 CENTAVOS

4.0000 g., 0.5000 Silver 0.0643 oz. ASW, 21.5 mm. **Obv:** Defiant Condor on rock left, 0.5 below condor **Obv. Designer:** O. Roty **Rev:** Denomination above date within wreath **Note:** Obverse varieties with 0.5 or 0.5. exist. Issued by law of January 19, 1899.

Date	Mintage	F	VF	XF	Unc	BU
1906/806	—	2.50	6.00	12.00	25.00	—
1906/896	866,000	2.50	6.00	12.00	25.00	—
1906	Inc. above	2.00	5.00	10.00	20.00	—
1907/807	—	2.00	5.00	10.00	20.00	—
1907/895	7,625,000	2.00	5.00	10.00	20.00	—
1907	Inc. above	1.50	4.00	10.00	20.00	—

KM# 151.3 20 CENTAVOS

3.0000 g., 0.4000 Silver 0.0386 oz. ASW **Obv:** Defiant Condor on rock left, without 0.5 below condor **Obv. Designer:** O. Roty **Rev:** Denomination above date within wreath

Date	Mintage	F	VF	XF	Unc	BU
1907/807	—	1.50	3.50	8.00	16.50	—
1907	1,201,000	1.00	3.00	7.00	15.00	—
1908/808	—	1.50	3.50	8.00	16.50	—

Date	Mintage	F	VF	XF	Unc	BU
1908	5,869,000	0.85	3.00	6.00	12.50	—
1909	1,080,000	0.85	3.00	6.00	12.50	—
1913/1	3,507,000	1.00	4.00	8.00	20.00	—
1913/50	Inc. above	1.00	4.00	8.00	20.00	—
1913	Inc. above	1.50	4.00	8.00	20.00	—
1919	3,749,000	0.85	3.00	6.00	12.50	—
1920	4,189,000	0.85	3.00	6.00	12.50	—

KM# 151.4 20 CENTAVOS

3.0000 g., 0.4500 Silver 0.0434 oz. ASW **Obv:** Defiant Condor on rock left, 0.45 below condor's wing, O'Roty at bottom **Obv. Designer:** O. Roty **Rev:** Denomination above date within wreath

Date	Mintage	F	VF	XF	Unc	BU
1916	3,377,000	2.00	4.00	8.00	20.00	—

KM# 167.1 20 CENTAVOS

4.5000 g., Copper-Nickel, 22.68 mm. **Obv:** Without designer's name O. ROTY at bottom **Rev:** Denomination and date within wreath, large numeral **Edge:** Plain

Date	Mintage	F	VF	XF	Unc	BU
1920	499,000	1.00	2.50	5.50	15.00	—
1921	6,547,000	0.35	1.00	3.00	7.00	—
1922	8,261,000	0.35	1.00	3.00	7.00	—
1923	5,439,000	0.35	1.00	3.00	7.00	—
1924	16,096,000	0.35	1.00	3.00	7.00	—
1925	9,830,000	0.35	1.00	3.00	7.00	—
Note: Varieties exist with dot under 5 in date for 1925						
1929	9,685,000	0.35	1.00	3.00	7.00	—

KM# 167.3 20 CENTAVOS

4.2700 g., Copper-Nickel, 22.5 mm. **Obv:** Defiant Condor on rock left, with designer's name O. ROTY at bottom **Rev:** Denomination above date within wreath

Date	Mintage	F	VF	XF	Unc	BU
1932 Over reversed 3	—	0.50	1.00	2.00	6.50	—
1932	—	0.35	0.75	1.25	5.00	—
1933 Over reversed 3X	—	1.00	1.50	2.50	7.00	—
1933/ Reversed 33	1,000,000	1.00	1.50	2.50	7.00	—
1933	Inc. above	0.35	0.75	1.25	5.00	—
1937 Over reversed 3	—	1.00	1.50	2.50	7.00	—
1937	—	0.35	0.75	1.25	5.00	—
1938	3,043,000	0.35	0.75	1.25	5.00	—
1939 3/reversed 3	5,283,000	1.00	1.50	2.50	7.00	—
1939	Inc. above	0.35	0.75	1.25	3.50	—
1940	9,300,000	0.35	0.75	1.25	3.00	—
1941	3,000,000	0.35	0.75	1.25	3.50	—

KM# 167.4 20 CENTAVOS

Copper-Nickel **Obv:** With designer's name O. ROTY at bottom **Rev:** Denomination and date within wreath

Date	Mintage	F	VF	XF	Unc	BU
1929	Inc. above	1.00	2.50	5.00	10.00	—

KM# 167.2 20 CENTAVOS

4.4900 g., Copper-Nickel **Obv:** Without designer's name **Rev:** Denomination and date within wreath, small numeral

Date	Mintage	F	VF	XF	Unc	BU
1932	—	0.50	1.00	2.00	6.00	—
1932 Over reversed 3	—	0.75	1.50	3.00	8.00	—
1933 Over reversed 3X	—	0.50	1.00	2.00	5.00	—
1933/ Reversed 33	59,000,000	0.50	1.00	2.00	5.00	—
1933	Inc. above	0.35	0.75	1.25	3.50	—

KM# 177 20 CENTAVOS

2.9200 g., Copper, 18 mm. **Obv:** Armored bust of General Bernardo O'Higgins right, Thenot on truncation **Rev:** Denomination above date

Date	Mintage	F	VF	XF	Unc	BU
1942	30,000,000	0.15	0.25	1.00	4.00	—
1943	396,000,000	0.15	0.25	1.00	4.00	—
1944	29,100,000	0.15	0.25	1.00	4.00	—
1945	11,400,000	0.15	0.25	1.00	4.00	—
1946	13,800,000	0.15	0.25	1.00	4.00	—
1947	15,700,000	0.15	0.25	1.00	4.00	—
1948	15,200,000	0.15	0.25	1.00	4.00	—
1949	14,700,000	0.15	0.25	1.00	4.00	—
1950	15,200,000	0.15	0.25	1.00	4.00	—
1951	14,700,000	0.15	0.25	1.00	4.00	—
1952	15,500,000	0.15	0.25	1.00	4.00	—
1953	7,800,000	0.15	0.25	1.00	4.00	—

KM# 163 40 CENTAVOS

6.0000 g., 0.4000 Silver 0.0772 oz. ASW **Obv:** Defiant Condor on rock, left **Obv. Designer:** O. Roty **Rev:** Denomination above date within wreath

Date	Mintage	F	VF	XF	Unc	BU
1907	56,000	20.00	40.00	80.00	195	—
1908/6	—	7.00	14.00	28.00	55.00	—
1908	1,452,000	6.00	12.00	25.00	50.00	—

KM# 160 50 CENTAVOS

10.0000 g., 0.7000 Silver 0.2250 oz. ASW **Obv:** Defiant Condor on rock left **Obv. Designer:** O. Roty **Rev:** Denomination above date within wreath **Note:** Varieties with 0.7 or 0.7. exist.

Date	Mintage	F	VF	XF	Unc	BU
1902	2,022,000	6.00	12.00	22.50	50.00	—
1903	1,111,000	6.00	12.00	22.50	50.00	—
1905	1,075,000	6.00	12.00	22.50	50.00	—

KM# 178 50 CENTAVOS

Copper **Obv:** Bust of General Bernardo O'Higgins right, Thenot on truncation **Rev:** Denomination above date **Edge:** Plain

Date	Mintage	F	VF	XF	Unc	BU
1942	4,715,000	1.00	2.00	5.00	10.00	—

KM# 152.2 PESO

20.0000 g., 0.7000 Silver 0.4501 oz. ASW, 35 mm. **Obv:** Defiant Condor on rock, left, 0.7 below right wing **Obv. Designer:** O. Roty **Rev:** Denomination above date within wreath

Date	Mintage	F	VF	XF	Unc	BU
1902	178,000	12.00	25.00	60.00	125	—
1903	372,000	9.00	18.00	38.00	80.00	—
1905	429,000	9.00	18.00	38.00	80.00	—

KM# 152.3 PESO

12.0000 g., 0.9000 Silver 0.3472 oz. ASW, 31.5 mm. **Obv:** Defiant Condor on rock, left, 0.9 below right wing **Obv. Designer:** O. Roty **Rev:** Denomination above date within wreath

Date	Mintage	F	VF	XF	Unc	BU
1910	2,166,000	5.50	7.50	12.50	28.00	—

KM# 152.4 PESO

9.0000 g., 0.7200 Silver 0.2083 oz. ASW, 27.5 mm. **Obv:** Defiant Condor on rock, left, 0.72 below right wing **Obv. Designer:** O. Roty **Rev:** Denomination above date within wreath

Date	Mintage	F	VF	XF	Unc	BU
1915	6,032,000	3.75	5.50	8.00	18.00	—
1917	3,033,000	4.00	6.50	12.00	25.00	—

KM# 152.5 PESO

9.0000 g., 0.5000 Silver 0.1447 oz. ASW, 29 mm. **Obv:** Defiant Condor on rock, left, 0.5 below right wing **Obv. Designer:** O. Roty **Rev:** Denomination above date within wreath

Date	Mintage	F	VF	XF	Unc	BU
1921	2,287,000	2.75	3.75	7.50	16.00	—
1922	2,718,000	2.75	3.75	7.50	16.00	—

KM# 152.6 PESO

9.0000 g., 0.5000 Silver 0.1447 oz. ASW **Obv:** Defiant Condor on rock left, 0.5 below right wing **Rev:** Date and denomination within wreath **Note:** Struck with medal rotation.

Date	Mintage	F	VF	XF	Unc	BU
1924	1,748,000	2.75	3.75	7.50	16.00	—
1925	2,037,000	2.75	3.75	7.50	16.00	—
Note: Varieties of 1925 dated coins exist with flat and curved tops						

KM# A171.1 PESO

9.0000 g., 0.5000 Silver 0.1447 oz. ASW **Obv:** Defiant Condor on rock left, 0.5 below right wing **Rev:** Date and denomination within wreath **Note:** A mule, with 0.5 and without mint mark on obverse.

Date	Mintage	F	VF	XF	Unc	BU
1927	—	15.00	30.00	45.00	90.00	—

KM# 171.1 PESO

9.0000 g., 0.5000 Silver 0.1447 oz. ASW **Obv:** Defiant Condor on rock left, 0.5 below right wing **Obv. Designer:** O. Roty **Rev:** Denomination above date within wreath

Date	Mintage	F	VF	XF	Unc	BU
1927So	3,890,000	4.00	6.00	10.00	20.00	—

KM# 171.2 PESO

9.0000 g., 0.5000 Silver 0.1447 oz. ASW **Obv:** Defiant Condor on rock left, 0.5 below right wing **Rev:** Date and denomination within wreath, thick numeral **Note:** Varieties 0.5 and 0,5 exist. Total of 2,431,608 pieces dated 1921-1927 were melted down in 1932.

Date	Mintage	F	VF	XF	Unc	BU
1927So	—	4.00	6.00	10.00	20.00	—

KM# 174 PESO

6.0000 g., 0.4000 Silver 0.0772 oz. ASW, 26 mm. **Obv:** Defiant Condor on rock left **Obv. Designer:** O. Roty **Rev:** Denomination above date within wreath

Date	Mintage	F	VF	XF	Unc	BU
1932	4,000,000	1.75	2.75	5.00	10.00	—

KM# 176.1 PESO

Copper-Nickel, 29 mm. **Obv:** Defiant Condor on rock left **Obv. Designer:** O. Roty **Rev:** Denomination above date within wreath

Date	Mintage	F	VF	XF	Unc	BU
1933	29,976,000	0.35	0.75	1.75	3.50	—

KM# 176.2 PESO

Copper-Nickel, 29 mm. **Obv:** Defiant Condor on rock left, O ROTY incuse on rock base **Obv. Designer:** O. Roty **Rev:** Denomination above date within wreath

Date	Mintage	F	VF	XF	Unc	BU
1940	150,000	2.00	3.00	6.00	12.00	—

KM# 179 PESO

7.3900 g., Copper, 25 mm. **Obv:** Armored bust of General Bernardo O'Higgins right **Rev:** Denomination above date

Date	Mintage	F	VF	XF	Unc	BU
1942	15,150,000	0.10	0.35	2.00	9.00	—
1943	16,900,000	0.10	0.35	2.00	9.00	—
1944	12,050,000	0.10	0.35	2.00	9.00	—
1945	7,600,000	0.10	0.35	2.00	9.00	—
1946	2,050,000	0.10	0.35	5.00	15.00	—
1947	2,200,000	0.10	0.35	5.00	15.00	—
1948	5,900,000	0.10	0.25	2.00	5.00	—
1949	7,100,000	0.10	0.20	1.00	4.00	—
1950	7,250,000	0.10	0.20	1.00	4.00	—
1951	8,150,000	0.10	0.20	1.00	4.00	—
1952	10,400,000	0.10	0.20	1.00	4.00	—
1953 Short top 5	17,200,000	0.10	0.20	1.00	3.00	—
1953 Long top 5	Inc. above	0.10	0.20	1.00	3.00	—
1954	7,566,000	0.10	0.20	1.00	3.00	—

KM# 179a PESO

2.0000 g., Aluminum, 25 mm. **Obv:** Armored bust, right **Rev:** Denomination above date

Date	Mintage	F	VF	XF	Unc	BU
1954	43,550,000	0.10	0.15	0.50	1.50	—
1954 Proof	—	Value: 25.00				
1955	69,050,000	0.10	0.15	0.50	1.50	—
1956	58,250,000	0.10	0.15	0.50	1.50	—
1956 Proof	—	Value: 25.00				
1957	49,250,000	0.10	0.15	0.50	1.50	—
1958	29,900	0.10	0.15	0.50	1.50	—

KM# 172 2 PESOS

18.0000 g., 0.5000 Silver 0.2893 oz. ASW **Obv:** Defiant Condor on rock left **Obv. Designer:** O. Roty **Rev:** Denomination above date within wreath **Note:** Obverse varieties 0.5 and 0,5 with curved top and flat top 5 exist. 459,510 pieces were melted down in 1932.

Date	Mintage	F	VF	XF	Unc	BU
1927	1,060,000	BV	4.50	9.00	20.00	—

KM# 159 5 PESOS

2.9955 g., 0.9170 Gold 0.0883 oz. AGW, 16.5 mm. **Obv:** Head left **Rev:** Plumed arms with supporters

Date	Mintage	F	VF	XF	Unc	BU
1911	1,399	—	—	200	350	—

KM# 173.1 5 PESOS

25.0000 g., 0.9000 Silver 0.7234 oz. ASW **Obv:** Defiant Condor on rock, left, 0.9 below right wing **Obv. Designer:** O. Roty **Rev:** Denomination above date within wreath, narrow 5, width = 2.5mm

Date	Mintage	F	VF	XF	Unc	BU
1927	965,000	11.00	14.00	22.50	50.00	250

KM# 173.2 5 PESOS

25.0000 g., 0.9000 Silver 0.7234 oz. ASW **Obv:** Defiant Condor on rock left, 0.9 below right wing **Rev:** Denomination and date within wreath, wide numeral, width = 3mm **Note:** Varieties 0.9 and 0,9 exist. 436,510 pieces of KM#173.1 and #173.2 were melted down in 1932.

Date	Mintage	F	VF	XF	Unc	BU
1927	Inc. above	11.00	14.00	22.50	50.00	—

KM# 180 5 PESOS

Aluminum **Obv:** Condor in flight **Rev:** Denomination above date flanked by grain sprigs

Date	Mintage	F	VF	XF	Unc	BU
1956	1,600,000	0.15	0.35	0.50	1.25	—

KM# 157 10 PESOS

5.9910 g., 0.9170 Gold 0.1766 oz. AGW, 21 mm. **Obv:** Head left **Rev:** Plumed arms with supporters

Date	Mintage	F	VF	XF	Unc	BU
1901	1,651,000	—	BV	160	200	—

KM# 181 10 PESOS

2.9600 g., Aluminum, 28 mm. **Obv:** Condor in flight **Rev:** Denomination above date, grain sprigs flank

Date	Mintage	F	VF	XF	Unc	BU
1956	13,100,000	0.15	0.35	0.50	0.75	1.50
1957	28,800,000	0.15	0.35	0.50	0.75	1.50
1958	44,500,000	0.15	0.35	0.50	0.75	1.50
1959	10,220,000	0.25	0.50	1.00	1.50	2.50

KM# 158 20 PESOS

11.9821 g., 0.9170 Gold 0.3532 oz. AGW, 27 mm. **Obv:** Head left **Rev:** Plumed arms with supporters

Date	Mintage	F	VF	XF	Unc	BU
1906	41,000	—	—	BV	300	—
1907	12,000	—	—	BV	300	—
1908	26,000	—	—	BV	300	—
1910	28,000	—	—	BV	300	320
1911	17,000	—	—	BV	300	320
1913/11	18,000	—	—	BV	300	320
1913	Inc. above	—	—	BV	300	320
1914	22,000	—	—	BV	300	320
1915	65,000	—	—	BV	300	320
1916	36,000	—	—	BV	300	320
1917	717,000	—	—	BV	300	320

KM# 168 20 PESOS

4.0679 g., 0.9000 Gold 0.1177 oz. AGW **Obv:** Head left, date below **Rev:** Arms with supporters, denomination above

Date	Mintage	F	VF	XF	Unc	BU
1926	85,000	—	—	BV	120	—
1958	500	BV	100	140	220	—
1959	25,000	—	—	BV	110	—
1961	20,000	—	—	BV	110	—
1964	—	—	—	BV	110	—
1976	99,000	—	—	BV	110	—
1977	38,000	—	—	BV	110	—
1979	30,000	—	—	BV	110	—
1980	30,000	—	—	BV	110	—

KM# 169 50 PESOS

10.1698 g., 0.9000 Gold 0.2943 oz. AGW **Obv:** Head left, date below **Rev:** Coat of arms, denomination above

Date	Mintage	F	VF	XF	Unc	BU
1926	126,000	—	—	BV	250	260
1958	10,000	—	—	BV	250	260
1961	20,000	—	—	BV	250	260
1962	30,000	—	—	BV	250	260
1965	—	—	—	BV	250	260
1966	—	—	—	BV	250	260
1967	—	—	—	BV	250	260
1968	—	—	—	BV	250	260
1969	—	—	—	BV	250	260
1970	—	—	—	—	650	—
1974	—	—	—	BV	250	260

KM# 170 100 PESOS

20.3397 g., 0.9000 Gold 0.5885 oz. AGW **Obv:** Head left, date below **Rev:** Coat of arms, denomination above

Date	Mintage	F	VF	XF	Unc	BU
1926	678,000	—	—	BV	500	520

KM# 175 100 PESOS

20.3397 g., 0.9000 Gold 0.5885 oz. AGW **Obv:** Head left, date below, revised bust and legend style **Rev:** Coat of arms, denomination above, revised legend style

Date	Mintage	F	VF	XF	Unc	BU
1932	9,315	—	BV	510	540	—
1946	260,000	—	—	BV	500	515
1947	540,000	—	—	BV	500	515
1948	420,000	—	—	BV	500	515
1949	310,000	—	—	BV	500	515
1950	20,000	—	—	BV	500	515
1951	145,000	—	—	BV	500	515
1952	245,000	—	—	BV	500	515
1953	175,000	—	—	BV	500	515
1954	190,000	—	—	BV	500	515
1955	150,000	—	—	BV	500	515
1956	60,000	—	—	BV	500	515
1957	40,000	—	—	BV	500	515
1958	157,000	—	—	BV	500	515
1959	90,000	—	—	BV	500	515
1960	200,000	—	—	BV	500	515
1961	295,000	—	—	BV	500	515
1962	260,000	—	—	BV	500	515
1963	210,000	—	—	BV	500	515
1964	—	—	—	BV	500	515
1968	—	—	—	BV	500	515
1969	—	—	—	BV	500	515
1970	—	—	—	BV	500	515
1971	—	—	—	BV	500	515
1972	—	—	—	BV	500	515
1973	—	—	—	BV	500	515
1974	—	—	—	BV	500	515
1976	172,000	—	—	BV	500	515
1977	25,000	—	—	BV	500	515
1979	100,000	—	—	BV	500	515
1980	50,000	—	—	BV	500	515

REFORM COINAGE

10 Pesos = 1 Centesimo; 100 Centesimos = 1 Escudo

KM# 192 1/2 CENTESIMO

Aluminum **Obv:** Condor in flight **Rev:** Denomination above date, grain sprigs flank

Date	Mintage	F	VF	XF	Unc	BU
1962	3,750,000	—	0.10	0.30	0.50	1.50
1962 Proof	—	Value: 10.00				
1963	8,100,000	—	0.10	0.30	0.50	1.50

KM# 189 CENTESIMO

Aluminum **Obv:** Condor in flight **Rev:** Denomination above date, grain sprigs flank

Date	Mintage	F	VF	XF	Unc	BU
1960	20,160,000	—	0.50	1.00	2.00	3.00
1960 Proof	—	Value: 45.00				
1961	Inc. above	—	0.50	1.00	2.00	3.00
1962	26,320,000	—	0.50	1.00	2.00	3.00
1963	27,100,000	—	0.50	1.00	2.00	3.00
1963 Proof	—	Value: 45.00				

KM# 193 2 CENTESIMOS

3.0700 g., Aluminum-Bronze, 20 mm. **Obv:** Condor in flight **Rev:** Denomination above date, grain sprigs flank **Edge:** Plain

Date	Mintage	F	VF	XF	Unc	BU
1960	2,050,000	—	—	—	50.00	—
Note: Not released for circulation						
1960 Proof	—	Value: 50.00				
1964	2,050,000	—	—	0.10	2.00	3.00
1965	32,550,000	—	—	0.10	2.00	3.00
1966	31,800,000	—	—	0.10	2.00	3.00
1967	34,750,000	—	—	0.10	2.00	3.00
1967 Proof	—	Value: 50.00				
1968	29,400,000	—	—	0.10	2.00	3.00
1969	—	—	—	—	3.00	5.00
1969 Proof	—	Value: 50.00				
1970	20,250,000	—	—	0.10	2.00	3.00

KM# 190 5 CENTESIMOS

4.1200 g., Aluminum-Bronze, 23.14 mm. **Obv:** Condor in flight **Rev:** Denomination above date, grain sprigs flank

Date	Mintage	F	VF	XF	Unc	BU
1960	—	—	—	—	75.00	—
Note: Not released for circulation						
1960 Proof	—	Value: 100				
1961	12,000	—	2.50	5.00	10.00	15.00
1962	—	—	2.00	4.00	10.00	15.00
1964	16,628,000	—	0.10	0.15	2.00	3.00
1965	27,680,000	—	0.10	0.15	2.00	3.00
1966	32,360,000	—	0.10	0.15	2.00	3.00
1966 Proof	—	Value: 50.00				
1967	19,680,000	—	0.10	0.15	2.00	3.00
1968	4,400,000	—	0.10	0.15	2.00	3.00
1968 Proof	—	Value: 50.00				
1969	13,200,000	—	—	—	5.00	7.00
1969 Proof	—	Value: 50.00				
1970	30,680,000	—	0.10	0.15	2.00	3.00
1971	16,080,000	—	0.10	0.15	2.00	3.00

KM# 191 10 CENTESIMOS

8.1000 g., Aluminum-Bronze, 27.17 mm. **Obv:** Condor in flight **Rev:** Denomination above date, grain sprigs flank

Date	Mintage	F	VF	XF	Unc	BU
1960 Proof	—	Value: 70.00				
1960	—	—	2.00	4.00	10.00	15.00
1961	1,915,000	—	0.10	1.00	4.00	6.00
1962	1,480,000	—	0.10	0.20	2.00	3.00
1963 Small date	10,980,000	—	0.10	0.20	2.00	3.00
1964	27,070,000	—	0.10	0.20	2.00	3.00
1965	49,480,000	—	0.10	0.20	2.00	3.00
1966	60,680,000	—	0.10	0.20	2.00	3.00
1967	27,520,000	—	0.10	0.25	2.00	3.00
1967 Proof	—	Value: 50.00				
1968	8,040,000	—	0.10	0.20	2.00	3.00
1969	15,660,000	—	—	—	5.00	7.00
1970 Large date	42,080,000	—	0.10	0.20	1.00	2.00

KM# 194 10 CENTESIMOS

2.5400 g., Aluminum-Bronze, 18.10 mm. **Obv:** Armored bust of Bernardo O'Higgins, right **Rev:** Arms above denomination, date at left **Edge:** Plain

Date	Mintage	F	VF	XF	Unc	BU
1971	99,700,000	—	—	0.10	0.15	0.25

KM# 195 20 CENTESIMOS

3.0000 g., Aluminum-Bronze, 19.97 mm. **Obv:** Bust of Jose Manuel Balmaceda left **Rev:** Arms above denomination, date at left **Edge:** Plain

Date	Mintage	F	VF	XF	Unc	BU
1971	89,200,000	—	—	0.10	0.20	0.35
1972	—	—	0.10	0.20	1.00	1.50

KM# 196 50 CENTESIMOS

Aluminum-Bronze **Obv:** Bust of Manuel Rodriguez right **Rev:** Arms above denomination, date at left

Date	Mintage	F	VF	XF	Unc	BU
1971	58,300,000	—	0.10	0.15	0.25	0.45

KM# 197 ESCUDO

2.7400 g., Copper-Nickel, 18.90 mm. **Obv:** Bust of Jose Miguel Carrera 3/4 facing **Rev:** Arms above denomination, date at left **Edge:** Reeded

Date	Mintage	F	VF	XF	Unc	BU
1971	160,900,000	—	0.10	0.20	0.40	0.60
1972	Inc. above	—	0.10	0.20	0.40	0.60
1972 Proof	—	Value: 50.00				

KM# 199 5 ESCUDOS

4.5100 g., Copper-Nickel, 23.03 mm. **Obv:** Lautaro, Araucanian Indian, upriser against Spain **Rev:** Arms above denomination, date at left

Date	Mintage	F	VF	XF	Unc	BU
1971	—	—	0.10	0.25	0.75	1.25
1972	—	—	0.10	0.25	0.75	1.25
1972 Proof	—	Value: 50.00				

KM# 199a 5 ESCUDOS

Aluminum **Obv:** Lautaro, Araucanian Indian, upriser against Spain **Rev:** Arms above denomination, date at left

Date	Mintage	F	VF	XF	Unc	BU
1972	—	—	0.10	0.15	0.20	0.50

KM# 200 10 ESCUDOS

2.1000 g., Aluminum, 24.93 mm. **Obv:** Defiant Condor on rock left **Rev:** Denomination above date within wreath **Edge:** Plain

Date	Mintage	F	VF	XF	Unc	BU
1974	33,750,000	—	0.10	0.15	0.35	0.50
1974 Proof	—	Value: 50.00				
1975	31,600,000	—	—	—	—	—

Note: Although recorded with mintage, no examples are known with this date

KM# 201 50 ESCUDOS

4.0000 g., Nickel-Brass, 21.48 mm. **Obv:** Defiant Condor on rock left **Obv. Designer:** O. Roty **Rev:** Denomination above date within wreath **Shape:** 12-sided

Date	Mintage	F	VF	XF	Unc	BU
1974	5,700,000	—	0.15	0.25	0.60	0.85
1975	20,300,000	—	0.15	0.20	0.50	0.75

KM# 202 100 ESCUDOS

5.0100 g., Nickel-Brass, 23.5 mm. **Obv:** Defiant Condor on rock left **Obv. Designer:** O. Roty **Rev:** Denomination above date within wreath **Shape:** 12-sided

Date	Mintage	F	VF	XF	Unc	BU
1974	32,100,000	—	0.20	0.35	0.75	1.00
1975	65,600,000	—	0.20	0.35	0.75	1.00

REFORM COINAGE

100 Centavos = 1 Peso; 1000 Old Escudos = 1 Peso

KM# 203 CENTAVO

2.0000 g., Aluminum, 24.93 mm. **Obv:** Defiant Condor on rock left **Obv. Designer:** O. Roty **Rev:** Denomination above date within wreath **Edge:** Plain

Date	Mintage	F	VF	XF	Unc	BU
1975	2,000,000	—	0.10	0.15	0.50	0.75

KM# 204 5 CENTAVOS

Aluminum-Bronze **Obv:** Defiant Condor on rock left **Obv. Designer:** O. Roty **Rev:** Denomination above date within wreath **Shape:** 12-sided

Date	Mintage	F	VF	XF	Unc	BU
1975	5,400,000	—	—	0.10	0.25	0.75
1976	6,600,000	—	—	—	—	—

Note: Although recorded with mintage, no examples are known with this date

KM# 204a 5 CENTAVOS

Aluminum **Obv:** Defiant Condor on rock left **Rev:** Date and denomination within wreath **Shape:** 12-sided

Date	Mintage	F	VF	XF	Unc	BU
1976	5,000,000	—	—	0.10	0.25	0.75

KM# 205 10 CENTAVOS

Aluminum-Bronze **Obv:** Defiant Condor on rock left **Obv. Designer:** O. Roty **Rev:** Denomination above date within wreath **Shape:** 12-sided

Date	Mintage	F	VF	XF	Unc	BU
1975	8,600,000	—	—	0.10	0.25	0.75
1976	9,000,000	—	—	—	—	—

Note: Although recorded with mintage, no examples are known with this date

KM# 205a 10 CENTAVOS

2.0200 g., Aluminum, 23.75 mm. **Obv:** Defiant Condor on rock left **Obv. Designer:** O. Roty **Rev:** Denomination above date within wreath **Shape:** 12-sided

Date	Mintage	F	VF	XF	Unc	BU
1976	6,600,000	—	—	0.10	0.25	0.50
1977	57,800,000	—	—	0.10	0.25	0.50
1978	58,050,000	—	—	0.10	0.25	0.50
1979	101,950,000	—	—	0.10	0.25	0.50

KM# 206 50 CENTAVOS

4.1300 g., Copper-Nickel, 22.17 mm. **Obv:** Defiant Condor on rock left **Obv. Designer:** O. Roty **Rev:** Denomination above date within wreath

Date	Mintage	F	VF	XF	Unc	BU
1975	38,000,000	—	—	0.10	0.25	0.50
1976	1,000,000	—	0.50	1.00	2.00	3.00
1977	10,000,000	—	—	0.10	0.25	0.50

KM# 206a 50 CENTAVOS

3.9500 g., Aluminum-Bronze, 22.06 mm. **Obv:** Defiant Condor on rock left **Obv. Designer:** O. Roty **Rev:** Denomination above date within wreath

Date	Mintage	F	VF	XF	Unc	BU
1978	19,250,000	—	—	0.10	0.25	0.60
1979	28,000,000	—	—	0.10	0.25	0.60

KM# 207 PESO

Copper-Nickel, 24 mm. **Obv:** Armored bust of Bernardo O'Higgins right **Obv. Legend:** BERNARDO O'HIGGINS **Rev:** Denomination above date within wreath

Date	Mintage	F	VF	XF	Unc	BU
1975	51,000,000	—	0.10	0.15	0.25	0.35

KM# 208 PESO

5.1100 g., Copper-Nickel, 24 mm. **Obv:** Armored bust of Bernardo O'Higgins right **Obv. Legend:** LIBERTADOR. B. O'HIGGINS **Rev:** Denomination above date within wreath

Date	Mintage	F	VF	XF	Unc	BU
1976	30,000,000	—	—	0.10	0.25	0.35
1977	20,000,000	—	—	0.10	0.25	0.35

KM# 208a PESO

Aluminum-Bronze, 24 mm. **Obv:** Armored bust of Bernardo O'Higgins right **Rev:** Denomination above date within wreath

Date	Mintage	F	VF	XF	Unc	BU
1978	39,706,000	—	—	0.10	0.25	0.35
1979	63,000,000	—	—	0.10	0.25	0.35

KM# 216.1 PESO

2.0000 g., Aluminum-Bronze, 17 mm. **Obv:** Armored bust right **Rev:** Denomination above date within wreath **Note:** Reduced size. Wide date.

Date	Mintage	F	VF	XF	Unc	BU
1981	40,000,000	—	—	0.10	0.20	0.30
1984	60,000,000	—	—	0.10	0.20	0.30
1985	20,000,000	—	—	0.10	0.20	0.30
1986	45,000,000	—	—	0.10	0.20	0.30
1987	80,000,000	—	—	0.10	0.20	0.30

KM# 216.2 PESO

2.0100 g., Aluminum-Bronze, 16.98 mm. **Obv:** Armored bust, right **Rev:** Denomination above date within wreath **Edge:** Plain **Note:** Narrow date.

Date	Mintage	F	VF	XF	Unc	BU
1988	105,000,000	—	—	0.10	0.20	0.30
1989	205,000,000	—	—	0.10	0.20	0.30
1990	140,000,000	—	—	0.10	0.20	0.30
1991	140,000,000	—	—	0.10	0.20	0.30
1992	—	—	—	0.10	0.20	0.30

KM# 231 PESO

0.7000 g., Aluminum, 16.32 mm. **Obv:** Gen. Bernardo O'Higgins bust right **Obv. Legend:** REPUBLICA - DE CHILE **Rev:** Denomination above date within wreath **Edge:** Plain **Shape:** 8-sided **Note:** Varieties exist.

Date	Mintage	F	VF	XF	Unc	BU
1992So Wide date	—	—	—	—	0.10	0.20
1992So Narrow date	—	—	—	—	0.10	0.20
1993So Narrow date	—	—	—	—	0.10	0.20
1994So	—	—	—	—	0.10	0.20
1995So	—	—	—	—	0.10	0.20
1996So	—	—	—	—	0.10	0.20
1997So	—	—	—	—	0.10	0.20
1998So	—	—	—	—	0.10	0.20
1999So	—	—	—	—	0.10	0.20
2000So	—	—	—	—	0.10	0.20
2001So	—	—	—	—	0.10	0.20
2002So	—	—	—	—	0.10	0.20
2003So	—	—	—	—	0.10	0.20
2004So	—	—	—	—	0.10	0.20
2005So	—	—	—	—	0.10	0.20
2006So	—	—	—	—	0.10	0.20

KM# 209 5 PESOS
6.9400 g., Copper-Nickel, 25.8 mm. **Subject:** 3rd Anniversary of New Government **Obv:** Winged figure with upraised arms, broken chain on wrists **Rev:** Denomination above date within wreath

Date	Mintage	F	VF	XF	Unc	BU
1976	2,100,000	—	0.15	0.25	2.00	3.50
1977	28,300,000	—	0.15	0.25	2.00	3.00
1978	11,704,000	—	0.15	0.25	2.00	3.00
1980	8,200,000	—	0.15	0.25	2.00	3.00

KM# 217.1 5 PESOS
2.7000 g., Nickel-Brass, 19 mm. **Obv:** Winged figure with arms upraised, broken chain on wrists **Rev:** Denomination above date within wreath **Note:** Wide date.

Date	Mintage	F	VF	XF	Unc	BU
1981	17,000,000	—	—	0.10	0.50	0.75
1982	20,000,000	—	—	0.10	0.50	0.75
1984	12,000,000	—	—	0.10	0.50	0.75
1985	16,000,000	—	—	0.10	0.50	0.75
1986	16,000,000	—	—	0.10	0.50	0.75
1987	8,000,000	—	—	0.10	0.50	0.75

KM# 217.2 5 PESOS
2.7800 g., Nickel-Brass **Obv:** Winged figure with arms upraised, broken chain on wrists **Rev:** Denomination above date within wreath **Note:** Narrow date.

Date	Mintage	F	VF	XF	Unc	BU
1988	27,000,000	—	—	0.10	0.50	0.75
1989	32,000,000	—	—	0.10	0.50	0.75
1990	23,000,000	—	—	0.10	0.50	0.75

KM# 229 5 PESOS
2.7500 g., Nickel-Brass **Obv:** Armored bust of Bernardo O'Higgins right **Rev:** Denomination above date within wreath

Date	Mintage	F	VF	XF	Unc	BU
1990	8,000,000	—	—	0.10	0.50	0.75
1991	2,000,000	—	—	0.10	0.50	0.75
1992	—	—	—	0.10	0.50	0.75

KM# 232 5 PESOS
2.1600 g., Aluminum-Bronze, 16.02 mm. **Obv:** Gen. Bernardo O'Higgins bust right **Obv. Legend:** REPUBLICA - DE CHILE **Rev:** Denomination above date within wreath **Edge:** Plain **Shape:** 8-sided **Note:** Varieties exist.

Date	Mintage	F	VF	XF	Unc	BU
1992So Wide date	—	—	—	0.10	0.35	0.60
1993So Narrow date	—	—	—	0.10	0.35	0.60
1994So Narrow date	—	—	—	0.10	0.35	0.60
1995So Narrow date	—	—	—	0.10	0.35	0.60
1996So Narrow date	—	—	—	0.10	0.35	0.60
1997So Narrow date	—	—	—	0.10	0.35	0.60
1998So Narrow date	—	—	—	0.10	0.35	0.60
1999So Narrow date	—	—	—	0.10	0.35	0.60
2000So Narrow date	—	—	—	0.10	0.35	0.60
2001So Narrow date	—	—	—	0.10	0.35	0.60
2001 (sa) Wide date	—	—	—	0.15	0.50	0.75
Note: Without name of sculptor						
2002So Narrow date	—	—	—	0.10	0.35	0.60
2002So Narrow date	—	—	—	0.15	0.50	0.75
2003So	—	—	—	0.10	0.35	0.60
2004So	—	—	—	0.10	0.35	0.60
2005So	—	—	—	0.10	0.35	0.60
2006So	—	—	—	0.10	0.35	0.60

KM# 210 10 PESOS
9.0000 g., Copper-Nickel, 28 mm. **Subject:** 3rd Anniversary of New Government **Obv:** Winged figure with arms upraised, broken chains on wrists **Rev:** Denomination above date within wreath

Date	Mintage	F	VF	XF	Unc	BU
1976	2,100,000	—	0.10	0.20	1.25	1.50
1977	30,000,000	—	0.10	0.20	1.00	1.25
1978	20,004,000	—	0.10	0.20	1.00	1.25
1979	7,000,000	—	0.10	0.20	1.00	1.25
1980	20,000,000	—	0.10	0.20	1.00	1.25

KM# 218.1 10 PESOS
3.5000 g., Nickel-Brass, 21 mm. **Obv:** Winged figure with arms upraised, broken chain on wrists **Rev:** Denomination above date within wreath **Note:** Wide date, narrow rim.

Date	Mintage	F	VF	XF	Unc	BU
1981	55,000,000	—	0.10	0.20	0.50	0.75
1982	45,000,000	—	0.10	0.20	0.50	0.75
1984	30,000,000	—	0.10	0.20	0.50	0.75
1985	400,000	—	0.50	1.50	3.50	5.00
1986 Narrow date	25,000,000	—	0.10	0.20	0.50	0.75
1986 Wide date	Inc. above	—	0.10	0.20	0.50	0.75
1987	8,000,000	—	0.10	0.20	0.50	0.75

KM# 218.2 10 PESOS
Nickel-Brass **Obv:** Winged figure with arms upraised, broken chain on wrists **Rev:** Denomination above date within wreath **Note:** Narrow date.

Date	Mintage	F	VF	XF	Unc	BU
1988	45,000,000	—	0.10	0.20	0.50	0.75
1989	73,000,000	—	0.10	0.20	0.50	0.75

KM# 218.3 10 PESOS
Nickel-Brass **Obv:** Winged figure with arms upraised, broken chain on wrists **Rev:** Denomination above date within wreath **Note:** Wide rim.

Date	Mintage	F	VF	XF	Unc	BU
1990	10,000,000	—	0.10	0.20	0.50	0.75

KM# 228.1 10 PESOS
Nickel-Brass **Obv:** Small bust of Bernardo O'Higgins right, wide rim **Rev:** Denomination above date within wreath

Date	Mintage	F	VF	XF	Unc	BU
1990	5,000,000	—	0.10	0.20	0.50	0.75

KM# 228.2 10 PESOS
3.5500 g., Nickel-Brass, 20.92 mm. **Obv:** Gen. Bernardo O'Higgins bust right **Obv. Legend:** REPUBLICA - DE CHILE **Rev:** Denomination above date within sprays **Edge:** Reeded **Note:** All 9's are curl tail 9's except for the 1999 date, these are straight tail 9's. Normal rim.

Date	Mintage	F	VF	XF	Unc	BU
1990So	25,000,000	—	0.10	0.20	0.50	0.65
1991So	—	—	0.10	0.20	0.50	0.65
1992So	—	—	0.10	0.20	0.50	0.65
1993So	—	—	0.10	0.20	0.50	0.65
1994So	—	—	0.10	0.20	0.50	0.65
1995So	—	—	0.10	0.20	0.50	0.65
1996So	—	—	0.10	0.20	0.50	0.65
1997So	—	—	0.10	0.20	0.50	0.65
1998So	—	—	0.10	0.20	0.50	0.65
1999So	—	—	0.10	0.20	0.50	0.65
2000So	—	—	0.10	0.20	0.50	0.65
2002So	—	—	0.10	0.20	0.50	0.65
2003So	—	—	0.10	0.20	0.50	0.65
2004So	—	—	0.10	0.20	0.50	0.65
2005So	—	—	0.10	0.20	0.50	0.65
2006So	—	—	0.10	0.20	0.50	0.65
2007So	—	—	0.10	0.20	0.50	0.65

KM# 219.1 50 PESOS
7.0000 g., Aluminum-Bronze, 25.71 mm. **Obv:** Armored bust right **Rev:** Denomination above date within wreath **Shape:** 10-sided **Note:** Wide date.

Date	Mintage	F	VF	XF	Unc	BU
1981	12,000,000	—	0.25	0.50	1.25	1.50
1982	14,000,000	—	0.25	0.50	1.25	1.50
1985	400,000	—	0.60	1.50	3.50	5.00
1986	1,000,000	—	0.25	0.50	1.25	1.50
1987	4,000,000	—	0.25	0.50	1.25	1.50

KM# 219.2 50 PESOS
7.0000 g., Aluminum-Bronze, 25.40 mm. **Obv:** Gen. Bernardo O'Higgins bust right **Obv. Legend:** REPUBLICA - DE CHILE **Rev:** Denomination above date within sprays **Edge:** Plain **Shape:** 10-sided **Note:** Narrow date.

Date	Mintage	F	VF	XF	Unc	BU
1988So	4,800,000	—	0.25	0.50	1.25	1.50
1989So	4,000,000	—	0.25	0.50	1.25	1.50
1991So	10,845,000	—	0.25	0.50	1.25	1.50
1992So	—	—	0.25	0.50	1.25	1.50
1993So	—	—	0.25	0.50	1.25	1.50
1994So	—	—	0.25	0.50	1.25	1.50
1995So	—	—	0.25	0.50	1.25	1.50
1996So	—	—	0.25	0.50	1.25	1.50
1997So	—	—	0.25	0.50	1.25	1.50
1998So	—	—	0.25	0.50	1.25	1.50
1999So	—	—	0.25	0.50	1.25	1.50
2000So	—	—	0.25	0.50	1.25	1.50
2001So	—	—	0.25	0.50	1.25	1.50
2002So	—	—	0.25	0.50	1.25	1.50
2005So	—	—	0.25	0.50	1.00	1.25
2006So	—	—	0.25	0.50	1.00	1.25

KM# 226.1 100 PESOS
Aluminum-Bronze, 26.8 mm. **Obv:** Coat of arms **Rev:** Denomination above date within wreath **Edge:** POR LA RAZON O LA FUERZA **Note:** Wide date with pointed 9.

Date	Mintage	F	VF	XF	Unc	BU
1981	10,000,000	—	0.50	0.75	2.50	3.00
1984	8,000,000	—	0.50	0.75	2.50	3.00
1985	15,000,000	—	0.50	0.75	2.50	3.00
1986	11,000,000	—	0.50	0.75	2.50	3.00
1987	15,000,000	—	0.50	0.75	2.50	3.00

KM# 226.2 100 PESOS
Aluminum-Bronze, 26.8 mm. **Obv:** Coat of arms **Rev:** Denomination above date within wreath **Edge:** POR LA RAZON O LA FUERZA **Note:** Narrow date with curved 9.

Date	Mintage	F	VF	XF	Unc	BU
1989	20,000,000	—	0.50	0.75	2.50	3.00
1991	4,320,000	—	0.50	0.75	2.50	3.00
1992	—	—	0.50	0.75	2.50	3.00
1993	—	—	0.50	0.75	2.50	3.00
1994	—	—	0.50	0.75	2.50	3.00
1995	—	—	0.50	0.75	2.50	3.00
1996	—	—	0.50	0.75	2.50	3.00
1997	—	—	0.50	0.75	2.50	3.00
1998	—	—	0.50	0.75	2.50	3.00
1999	—	—	0.50	0.75	2.50	3.00
2000	—	—	0.50	0.75	2.50	3.00

KM# 236 100 PESOS
7.5800 g., Bi-Metallic Copper-nickel center in Brass ring, 23.43 mm. **Subject:** Native people **Obv:** Bust of native Mapuche girl facing **Obv. Legend:** REPUBLICA DE CHILE - PUEBLOS ORIGINARIOS **Rev:** National arms above denomination **Edge:** Segmented reeding

Date	Mintage	F	VF	XF	Unc	BU
2001So	—	—	—	—	2.50	3.00
2003So	—	—	—	—	2.50	3.00
2004So	—	—	—	—	2.50	3.00
2005So	—	—	—	—	2.50	3.00
2006So	—	—	—	—	2.50	3.00

KM# 235 500 PESOS
6.6000 g., Bi-Metallic Aluminum-bronze center in Copper-nickel ring, 25.9 mm. **Subject:** Cardinal Raul Silva Henriquez **Obv:** Bust of Henriquez within inner ring facing left **Rev:** Denomination above date within wreath **Edge:** Reeded

Date	Mintage	F	VF	XF	Unc	BU
2000So	—	—	—	—	6.00	6.50
2000So Proof	—	—	—	—	—	—
2001So	—	—	—	—	6.00	6.50
2002So 4.1mm date	—	—	—	—	6.00	6.50
2002So 5.2mm date	—	—	—	—	6.00	6.50
2003So	—	—	—	—	6.00	6.50

CHINA

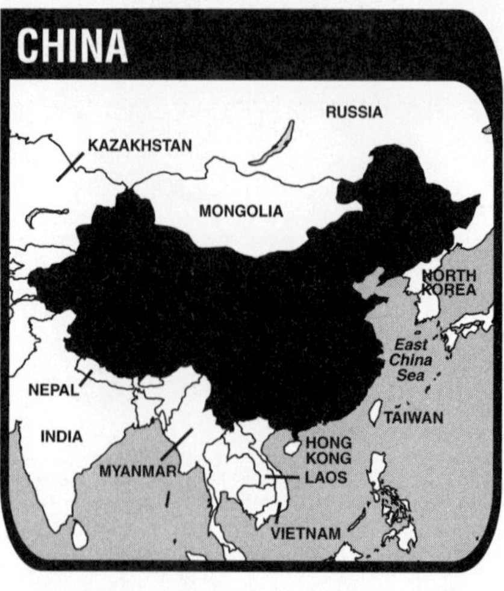

Before 1912, China was ruled by an imperial government. The republican administration which replaced it was itself supplanted on the Chinese mainland by a communist government in 1949, but it has remained in control of Taiwan and other offshore islands in the China Sea with a land area of approximately 14,000 square miles and a population of more than 14 million. The People's Republic of China administers some 3.7 million square miles and an estimated 1.19 billion people. This communist government, officially established on October 1, 1949, was admitted to the United Nations, replacing its nationalist predecessor, the Republic of China, in 1971.

Cast coins in base metals were used in China many centuries before the Christian era, but locally struck coinages of the western type in gold, silver, copper and other metals did not appear until 1888.In spite of the relatively short time that modern coins have been in use, the number of varieties is exceptionally large.

Both Nationalist and Communist China, as well as the pre-revolutionary Imperial government and numerous provincial or other agencies, including some foreign-administered agencies and governments, have issued coins in China. Most of these have been in dollar (yuan) or dollar-fraction denominations, based on the internationally used dollar system, but coins in tael denominations were issued in the 1920's and earlier. The striking of coins nearly ceased in the late 1930's through the 1940's due to the war effort and a period of uncontrollable inflation while vast amounts of paper currency were issued by the Nationalist, Communist and Japanese occupation institutions.

EMPERORS
Obverse Types

KUANG-HSÜ 光緒

Te Tsung 1875-1908 德宗

Type A

光緒通寶
Kuang-hsü T'ung-pao (Guangxu)

Type B

光緒重寶
Kuang-hsü Chung-pao

Type C

光緒元寶
Kuang-hsü Yuan-pao

Kuang-hsü - When the previous emperor died, his mother, the Empress Dowager Tz'u-hsi, chose her four-year-old nephew, born August 14, 1871, as emperor. She adopted the boy so that she could act as regent and on February 25, 1875, the young prince ascended the throne, taking the reign title of Kuang-hsü. In 1898 he tried to assert himself and collected a group of progressive officials around him. He issued a series of edicts for revamping of the military, abolition of civil service examinations, improvement of agriculture and restructuring of administrative procedures. During Kuang-hsü's reign (1875-1908) the Empress Dowager totally dominated the government. She confined the emperor to his palace and spread rumors that he was deathly ill. Foreign powers let it be known they would not take kindly to the Emperor's death. This saved his life but thereafter he had no power over the government. On November 15, 1908, Tz'u-hsi died under highly suspicious circumstances and the usually healthy emperor was announced as having died the previous day.

HSÜAN-T'UNG 1908-1911

Type A

宣統
Hsüan-t'ung T'ung-pao (Xuantong)

Hsuan-t'ung - The last emperor of the Ch'ing dynasty in China and Japan's puppet emperor, under the assumed name of K'ang-te, in Manchoukuo from 1934 to 1945, was born on February 7, 1906. He succeeded to the throne at the age of three on November 14, 1908. He reigned under a regency for three years but on February 12, 1912, was forced to abdicate the throne. He was permitted to continue living in the palace in Peking until he left secretly in 1924. On March 9, 1932, he was installed as president, and from 1934 to 1945 was emperor of Manchoukuo under the reign title of K'ang-te. He was taken prisoner by the Russians in August of 1945 and returned to China as a war criminal in 1950. He was pardoned in 1959 and went to live in Peking where he worked in the repair shop of a botanical garden. He died peacefully in Peking in 1967.

Although Hsüan-t'ung became Emperor in 1908, all the coins of his reign are based on an Accession year of 1909.

HUNG-HSIEN 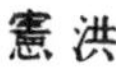

(Yuan Shih-k'ai) 宣統通
Dec. 15, 1915 - March 21, 1916

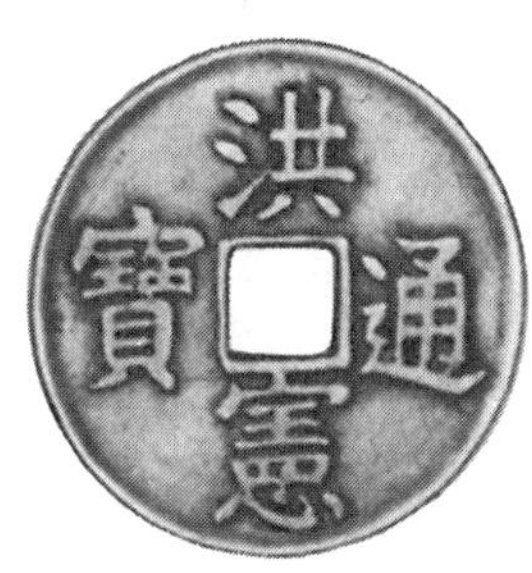

憲洪 通寶

Hung-hsien T'ung-pao

Hung-hsien (more popularly known as Yuan Shih-K'ai). Born in 1859 in Honan Province, he was the first Han Chinese to hold a viceroyalty and become a grand councillor without any academic qualifications. In 1885 he was made Chinese commissioner at Seoul. During the Boxer Rebellion of 1900, the division under his command was the only remnant of China's army to survive. He enjoyed the trust and support of the dowager empress, Tz'u-hsi, and at her death he was stripped of all his offices. However, when the tide of the revolution threatened to engulf the Manchus Yuan appeared as the only man who could lead the country to peace and unity. Both the Emperor and the provisional president recommended that Yuan be the first president of China. He contrived to make himself president for life and boldly tried to create a new imperial dynasty in 1915-1916. He died of uremia on June 6, 1916.

NOTE: For other legend types refer to Rebel Issues listed after Yunnan-Szechuan.

NUMERALS

NUMBER	CONVENTIONAL	FORMAL	COMMERCIAL
1	一 元	壹 弌	〡
2	二	弍 貳	〢
3	三	叁 弎	〣
4	四	肆	〤
5	五	伍	〥
6	六	陸	〦
7	七	柒	〧
8	八	捌	〨
9	九	玖	〩
10	十	拾 什	十
20	十 二 or 廿	拾貳	〢十
25	五 十 二 or 五廿	伍拾貳	〢十〥
30	十 三 or 卅	拾叁	〣十
100	百 一	佰壹	〡百
1,000	千 一	仟壹	〡千
10,000	萬 一	萬壹	〡万
100,000	萬十 億 一	萬拾 億壹	十万
1,000,000	萬百一	萬佰壹	〡百万

NOTE: This table has been adapted from *Chinese Bank Notes* by Ward Smith and Brian Matravers.

MONETARY UNITS

Dollar Amounts		
DOLLAR *(Yuan)*	元 or 員	圓 or 圜
HALF DOLLAR *(Pan Yuan)*	圓 半	元中
50¢ *(Chiao/Hao)*	角伍	毫伍
10¢ *(Chiao/Hao)*	角壹	毫壹
1¢ *(Fen/Hsien)*	分壹	仙壹

COPPER AND CASH COIN AMOUNTS

COPPER *(Mei)*	枚	CASH *(Wen)*	文

Tael Amounts	
1 TAEL *(Liang)*	兩
HALF TAEL *(Pan Liang)*	兩半
5 MACE *(Wu Ch'ien)*	錢伍
1 MACE *(I Ch'ien)*	錢壹
1 CANDEREEN *(I Fen)*	分壹

COMMON PREFIXES

COPPER *(T'ung)*	銅	GOLD *(Chin)*	金
SILVER *(Yin)*	銀	Ku Ping *(Tael)**	平庫

NOTE: This table has been adapted from Chinese Bank Notes by Ward Smith and Brian Matravers.

MONETARY SYSTEM

Cash Coin System

800-1600 Cash = 1 Tael
400 Sinkiang 'red' cash = 1 Tael

In theory, 1000 cash were equal to a tael of silver, but in actuality the rate varied from time to time and place to place.

Dollar System

10 Cash (Wen, Ch'ien) = 1 Cent (Fen, Hsien)
10 Cents = 1 Chiao (Hao)
100 Cents = 1 Dollar (Yuan)
1 Dollar = 0.72 Tael

Imperial silver coins normally bore no denomination, but were inscribed with their weights as follows:

1 Dollar = 7 Mace and 2 Candareens
50 Cents = 3 Mace and 6 Candareens
20 Cents = 1 Mace and 4.4 Candareens
10 Cents = 7.2 Candareens
5 Cents = 3.6 Candareens

NOTE: *Candareen* is spelled *Candarin* and misspelled as *Caindarin* on Kirin Province Imperial coinage.

Tael System

10 Li = 1 Fen (Candareen)
10 Fen (Candareen) = 1 Ch'ien (Mace)
10 Ch'ien (Mace) = 1 Liang (Tael)

DATING

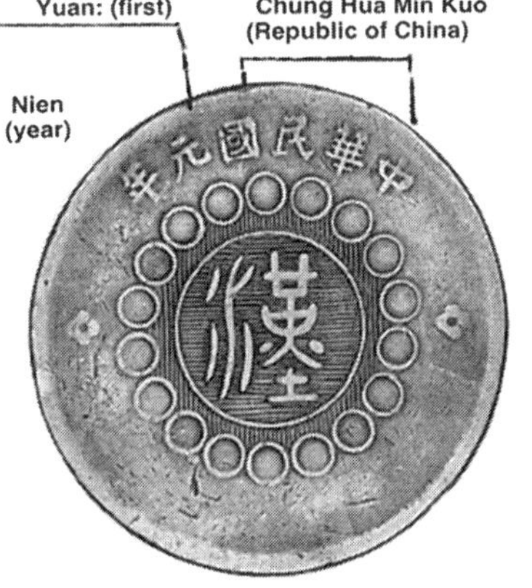

Most struck Chinese coins are dated by year within a given period, such as the regnal eras or the republican periods. A 1907 issue, for example, would be dated in the 33rd year of the Kuang Hsu era (1875 + 33 - 1 = 1907) or a 1926 issue is dated in the 15th year of the Republic (1912 + 15 - 1 = 1926). The mathematical discrepancy in both instances is accounted for by the fact that the first year is included in the elapsed time. Modern Chinese Communist coins are dated in western numerals using the western calendar, but earlier issues use conventional Chinese numerals. The coins of the Republic of China (Taiwan) are also dated in the year of the Republic, which is added to equal the calendar year. Still another method is a 60-year, repeating cycle, outlined in the table below. The date is shown by the combination of two characters, the first from the top row and the second from the column at left. In this catalog, when a cyclical date is used, the abbreviation CD appears before the AD date.

Dates not in parentheses are those which appear on the coins. For undated coins, dates appearing in parentheses are the years in which the coin was actually minted. Undated coins for which the year of minting is unknown are listed with ND (No Date) in the date or year column.

CYCLICAL DATES

	庚	辛	壬	癸	甲	乙	丙	丁	戊	己
戌	1850 1910		1862 1922		1874 1934		1886 1946		1838 1898	
亥		1851 1911		1863 1923		1875 1935		1887 1947		1839 1899
子	1840 1900		1852 1912		1864 1924		1876 1936		1888 1948	
丑		1841 1901		1853 1913		1865 1925		1877 1937		1889 1949
寅	1830 1890		1842 1902		1854 1914		1866 1926		1878 1938	
卯		1831 1891		1843 1903		1855 1915		1867 1927		1879 1939
辰	1880 1940		1832 1892		1844 1904		1856 1916		1868 1928	
巳		1881 1941		1833 1893		1845 1905		1857 1917		1869 1929
午	1870 1930		1882 1942		1834 1894		1846 1906		1858 1918	
未		1871 1931		1883 1943		1835 1895		1847 1907		1859 1919
申	1860 1920		1872 1932		1884 1944		1836 1896		1848 1908	
酉		1861 1921		1873 1933		1885 1945		1837 1897		1849 1909

NOTE: This table has been adapted from *Chinese Bank Notes* by Ward Smith and Brian Matravers.

GRADING

Chinese coins should not be graded entirely by western standards. In addition to Fine, Very Fine, Extremely Fine (XF), and Uncirculated, the type of strike should be considered weak, medium or sharp strike. China had no rigid minting rules as we know them. For instance, Kirin (Jilin) and Sinkiang (Xinjiang) Provinces used some dies made of iron - hence, they wore out rapidly. Some communist army issues were apparently struck by crude hand methods on soft dies (it is hard to find two coins of the same die!). In general, especially for some minor coins, dies were used until they were worn well beyond western standards. Subsequently, one could have an uncirculated coin struck from worn dies with little of the design or letters still visible, but still uncirculated! All prices quoted are for well-struck (sharp struck), well-centered specimens. Most silver coins can be found from very fine to uncirculated. Some copper coins are difficult to find except in poorer grades.

REFERENCES

The following references have been used for this section:

K - Edward Kann - Illustrated Catalog of Chinese Coins.

Hsu - T.K. Hsu - Illustrated Catalog of Chinese Coins, 1981 edition.

W - A.M. Tracey Woodward - The Minted Ten-Cash Coins of China.

NOTE: The die struck 10 and 20 Cash coins are often found silver plated. This was not done at the mint. They were apparently plated to be passed to the unwary as silver coins.

CH'ING DYNASTY

Manchu, 1644 - 1911

GENERAL CAST COINAGE

C# 1-19.1 CASH

Cast Brass, 19 mm. **Ruler:** Hsüan-t'ung **Obv. Inscription:** Hsüan-t'ung T'ung-pao **Rev:** Manchu inscription **Rev. Inscription:** Boo-ciowan

Date	Mintage	Good	VG	F	VF	XF
ND(1909-11)	—	5.50	7.00	10.00	15.00	—

STANDARD UNIFIED GENERAL COINAGE

A Central mint opened at Tientsin in 1905, was made responsible for producing most of the dies for the Tai Ch'ing Hu Poo coinage and for the 1910 and 1911 unified coinage. The mint was burned down in 1912 but resumed operations in 1914 with Yuan Shih-k'ai dollar issues. It continued producing dies for selected branch mints until 1921. It was superseded as the Central mint of China by Nanking in 1927 and by the new Nationalist Government mint at Shanghai in 1933.

Y# 7 CASH

Brass **Ruler:** Kuang-hsü **Obv. Legend:** "Kuang-hsü" **Rev:** Dragon **Note:** Struck.

Date	Mintage	VG	F	VF	XF	Unc
CD1908	—	1.00	3.00	6.00	12.00	—

Y# 18 CASH

Brass **Ruler:** Hsüan-t'ung **Obv. Legend:** "Hsüan-t'ung" **Rev:** Dragon **Note:** Struck.

Date	Mintage	VG	F	VF	XF	Unc
CD1909	—	25.00	50.00	85.00	135	—

Note: Inc. Y25

Y# 25 CASH

Brass **Obv. Inscription:** Tai-ch'ing T'ung-pi

Date	Mintage	VG	F	VF	XF	Unc
ND(1909)	92,126,000	1.00	1.50	2.00	3.00	—

Y# 8 2 CASH

Copper **Ruler:** Kuang-hsü **Obv. Inscription:** Tai-ch'ing T'ung-pi **Rev:** Dragon

Date	Mintage	VG	F	VF	XF	Unc
CD1905 Hu-pu	—	2.50	4.50	10.00	17.50	—
CD1906 Hu-pu	—	3.00	6.00	10.00	25.00	—

Y# 8.1 2 CASH

Copper **Ruler:** Kuang-hsü **Obv:** Four dots divide legend **Obv. Inscription:** Tai-ch'ing T'ung-pi **Rev:** Dragon

Date	Mintage	VG	F	VF	XF	Unc
CD1907	—	7.00	18.00	25.00	40.00	—

Y# A18 2 CASH

Copper **Ruler:** Hsüan-t'ung **Obv. Inscription:** Hsüan-t'ung

Date	Mintage	VG	F	VF	XF	Unc
CD1909 Rare	13,353,000	—	—	—	—	—

Y# 3 5 CASH

Copper **Ruler:** Kuang-hsü **Obv. Inscription:** Kuang-hsü Yüan-pao **Rev:** Dragon **Rev. Legend:** HU POO

Date	Mintage	VG	F	VF	XF	Unc
ND(1903-05) Hu-pu	3,671,000	7.00	14.00	21.00	35.00	—

Y# 9 5 CASH

Copper **Ruler:** Kuang-hsü **Obv. Inscription:** Tai-ch'ing T'ung-pi **Rev:** Dragon; smaller legend **Rev. Legend:** Kuang-hsü

Date	Mintage	VG	F	VF	XF	Unc
CD1905	—	5.00	10.00	20.00	35.00	—
CD1906 Rare	—	—	—	—	—	—

Y# 9.1 5 CASH

Copper **Ruler:** Kuang-hsü **Obv:** Four dots divide legend **Obv. Legend:** Kuang-hsü **Obv. Inscription:** Tai-ch'ing T'ung-pi **Rev:** Dragon

Date	Mintage	VG	F	VF	XF	Unc
CD1907	—	16.50	40.00	75.00	125	—

Y# 19 5 CASH

Copper **Ruler:** Hsüan-t'ung **Obv. Legend:** Hsüan-t'ung

Date	Mintage	VG	F	VF	XF	Unc
CD1909	2,170,000	—	—	850	1,200	—

Y# 4 10 CASH

Copper **Ruler:** Kuang-hsü **Obv. Inscription:** Kuang-hsü Yüan-pao **Rev:** Side view dragon **Rev. Legend:** HU POO

Date	Mintage	VG	F	VF	XF	Unc
ND(1903-05)	281,171,000	0.65	2.00	3.50	6.00	25.00

Y# 4.1 10 CASH

Copper **Ruler:** Kuang-hsü **Rev:** Side view dragon; different rosettes; smaller legend **Rev. Legend:** HU POO

Date	Mintage	VG	F	VF	XF	Unc
ND(1903-05)	Inc. above	0.35	1.00	2.00	5.00	20.00

Y# 10 10 CASH

Copper **Ruler:** Kuang-hsü **Obv. Inscription:** Tai-ch'ing T'ung-pi **Rev:** Side view dragon **Rev. Legend:** Kuang-hsü Nien-tsao TAI-CHING-TI-KUO...

Date	Mintage	VG	F	VF	XF	Unc
CD1905	Inc. above	0.50	1.50	3.00	5.00	25.00

Y# 10.1 10 CASH

Copper **Ruler:** Kuang-hsü **Obv. Inscription:** Tai-ch'ing T'ung-pi **Rev:** Different dragon; larger legend **Rev. Legend:** TAI-CHING-TI-KUO...

Date	Mintage	VG	F	VF	XF	Unc
CD1905	—	10.00	25.00	65.00	110	200

Y# 10.2 10 CASH

Copper **Ruler:** Kuang-hsü **Obv. Inscription:** Tai-ch'ing T'ung-pi **Rev:** Dragon **Rev. Legend:** Kuang-hsü Nien-tsao TAI-CHING-TI-KUO

Date	Mintage	VG	F	VF	XF	Unc
CD1906	—	0.25	0.75	1.50	3.00	20.00

Y# 10.3 10 CASH

Copper **Ruler:** Kuang-hsü **Obv:** Without dots **Obv. Inscription:** Tai-ch'ing T'ung-pi **Rev:** Dragon; legend without dot after "KUO" **Rev. Legend:** Kuang-hsü Nien-tsao TAI-CHING-TI-KUO

Date	Mintage	VG	F	VF	XF	Unc
CD1907	—	0.35	1.00	2.00	4.50	18.00

Y# 10.4 10 CASH

Copper **Ruler:** Kuang-hsü **Obv. Inscription:** Tai-ch'ing T'ung-pi **Rev:** Dragon; legend with dot after "KUO" **Rev. Legend:** Kuang-hsü Nien-tsao TAI-CHING-TI-KUO.

Date	Mintage	VG	F	VF	XF	Unc
CD1907	—	0.35	1.00	2.00	4.50	18.00

Y# 10.4a 10 CASH

Brass **Ruler:** Kuang-hsü **Obv:** Without dots **Obv. Inscription:** Tai-ch'ing T'ung-pi **Rev:** Dragon **Rev. Legend:** Kuang-hsü Nien-tsao TAI-CHING-TI-KUO.

Date	Mintage	VG	F	VF	XF	Unc
CD1907	—	1.85	5.50	20.00	35.00	80.00

Y# 10.5 10 CASH

Copper **Ruler:** Kuang-hsü **Obv:** Four dots divide legend **Obv. Inscription:** Tai-ch'ing T'ung-pi **Rev:** Dragon **Rev. Legend:** Kuang-hsü Nien-tsao TAI-CHING-TI-KUO.

Date	Mintage	VG	F	VF	XF	Unc
CD1907	—	0.35	1.00	2.00	4.50	18.00

Y# 10.5a 10 CASH

Brass **Ruler:** Kuang-hsü **Obv. Inscription:** Tai-ch'ing T'ung-pi **Rev:** Dragon **Rev. Legend:** Kuang-hsü Nien-tsao TAI-CHING-TI-KUO.

Date	Mintage	VG	F	VF	XF	Unc
CD1907	—	1.85	5.50	15.00	30.00	85.00

Y# 20 10 CASH

Copper **Ruler:** Hsüan-t'ung **Obv. Inscription:** Tai-ch'ing T'ung-pi **Rev:** Waves below dragon **Rev. Legend:** Hsüan-t'ung Nien-tsao TAI-CHING-TI-KUO.

Date	Mintage	VG	F	VF	XF	Unc
CD1909	—	0.35	1.00	2.00	4.00	22.50

Y# 20.1 10 CASH
Copper **Ruler:** Hsüan-t'ung **Obv. Inscription:** Tai-ch'ing T'ung-pi **Rev:** Rosette below dragon, "U" of "KUO" inverted "A" **Rev. Legend:** Hsüan-t'ung Nien-tsao TAI-CHING-TI-KUO.

Date	Mintage	VG	F	VF	XF	Unc
CD1909	—	1.85	5.50	12.00	25.00	60.00

Note: Although this coin bears no indication of its origin, it was minted in the Manchurian Provinces ca.1922

Y# 20x 10 CASH
Copper **Ruler:** Hsüan-t'ung **Obv:** Rosette in center **Obv. Inscription:** Tai-ch'ing T'ung-pi **Rev:** Dragon **Rev. Legend:** Hsüan-t'ung Nien-tsao TAI-CHING-TI-KUO.

Date	Mintage	VG	F	VF	XF	Unc
CD1909	—	3.50	10.00	20.00	30.00	80.00

Note: Although this coin bears no indication of its origin, it was minted in Kirin Province

Y# 27 10 CASH
Bronze **Ruler:** Hsüan-t'ung **Obv:** Dragon **Obv. Inscription:** Tai-ch'ing T'ung-pi **Rev. Legend:** Hsüan-t'ung...

Date	Mintage	VG	F	VF	XF	Unc
3(1911)	95,585,000	0.85	2.50	4.00	8.00	90.00
3(1911) Proof; Rare	—	—	—	—	—	—

Y# 27a 10 CASH
Brass **Ruler:** Hsüan-t'ung **Obv:** Dragon **Obv. Inscription:** Tai-ch'ing T'ung-pi **Rev. Legend:** Hsüan-t'ung...

Date	Mintage	VG	F	VF	XF	Unc
3(1911)	—	12.00	30.00	45.00	95.00	150

Y# 5 20 CASH
Copper, 32 mm. **Ruler:** Kuang-hsü **Obv. Inscription:** Kuang-hsü Yüan-pao **Rev:** Dragon **Rev. Legend:** HU POO

Date	Mintage	VG	F	VF	XF	Unc
ND(1903)	—	0.50	1.00	2.00	3.00	—

Y# 5.1 20 CASH
Copper, 32 mm. **Ruler:** Kuang-hsü **Obv:** Four-point rosette in center **Obv. Inscription:** Kuang-hsü Yüan-pao **Rev:** Dragon **Rev. Legend:** HU POO

Date	Mintage	VG	F	VF	XF	Unc
ND(1903)	—	2.50	6.00	12.00	25.00	—

Y# 5.2 20 CASH
Copper, 32 mm. **Ruler:** Kuang-hsü **Obv. Inscription:** Kuang-hsü Yüan-pao **Rev:** Head of dragon and clouds redesigned **Rev. Legend:** HU POO

Date	Mintage	VG	F	VF	XF	Unc
ND(1903) Restrike	—	2.50	6.00	12.00	25.00	—

Note: Y#5-5.2 were struck at the Wuchang Mint in 1917 from unused dies prepared in 1903

Y# 5a 20 CASH
Copper, 32 mm. **Ruler:** Kuang-hsü **Obv. Inscription:** Kuang-hsü Yüan-pao **Rev:** Dragon in circle of dots **Rev. Legend:** HU POO

Date	Mintage	VG	F	VF	XF	Unc
ND(1903-05)	—	30.00	50.00	85.00	125	—

Y# 11 20 CASH
Copper, 32 mm. **Ruler:** Kuang-hsü **Obv. Inscription:** Tai-ch'ing T'ung-pi **Rev:** Dragon **Rev. Legend:** Kuang-hsü Nien-tsao, TAI-CHING-TI-KUO

Date	Mintage	VG	F	VF	XF	Unc
CD1905	—	12.50	30.00	50.00	75.00	—

Y# 11.1 20 CASH
Copper, 32 mm. **Ruler:** Kuang-hsü **Obv. Inscription:** Tai-ch'ing T'ung-pi **Rev:** Dragon **Rev. Legend:** Kuang-hsü Nien-tsao, TAI-CHING-TI-KUO

Date	Mintage	VG	F	VF	XF	Unc
CD1906	—	12.50	30.00	50.00	75.00	—

Y# 11.3a 20 CASH
Brass, 32 mm. **Ruler:** Kuang-hsü **Obv. Inscription:** Tai-ch'ing T'ung-pi **Rev:** Dragon **Rev. Legend:** Kuang-hsü Nien-tsao, TAI-CHING-TI-KUO

Date	Mintage	VG	F	VF	XF	Unc
CD1907	—	3.50	8.00	15.00	30.00	—

Y# 11.2 20 CASH
Copper, 32 mm. **Ruler:** Kuang-hsü **Obv:** Dots around date **Obv. Inscription:** Tai-ch'ing T'ung-pi **Rev:** Dragon **Rev. Legend:** Kuang-hsü Nien-tsao, TAI-CHING-TI-KUO **Note:** 1.2-1.7 mm. thick.

Date	Mintage	VG	F	VF	XF	Unc
CD1907	—	0.60	1.50	2.00	4.00	—

Y# 11.3 20 CASH
Copper, 32 mm. **Ruler:** Kuang-hsü **Obv. Inscription:** Tai-ch'ing T'ung-pi **Rev:** Dragon **Rev. Legend:** Kuang-hsü Nien-tsao, TAI-CHING-TI-KUO **Note:** 2.0-2.3 mm. thick.

Date	Mintage	VG	F	VF	XF	Unc
CD1907	—	2.50	6.00	12.00	25.00	—

Y# 21 20 CASH
Brass, 32 mm. **Ruler:** Hsüan-t'ung **Obv. Inscription:** Tai-ch'ing T'ung-pi **Rev:** With dot between "KUO" and COPPER; six waves beneath dragon **Rev. Legend:** Hsüan-t'ung Nien-tsao, TAI-CHING-TI-KUO...

Date	Mintage	VG	F	VF	XF	Unc
CD1909	—	1.00	2.50	5.00	10.00	—

Y# 21.1 20 CASH
Copper, 32 mm. **Ruler:** Hsüan-t'ung **Obv. Inscription:** Tai-ch'ing T'ung-pi **Rev:** With dot between "KUO" and "COPPER"; six waves beneath dragon **Rev. Legend:** Hsüan-t'ung Nien-tsao, TAI-CHING-TI-KUO... **Note:** 1.2-1.7 mm. thick.

Date	Mintage	VG	F	VF	XF	Unc
CD1909	—	1.25	3.00	6.00	10.00	—

Y# 21.2 20 CASH
Copper, 32 mm. **Ruler:** Hsüan-t'ung **Obv. Inscription:** Tai-ch'ing T'ung-pi **Rev:** Without dot between "KUO" and "COPPER"; six waves beneath dragon **Rev. Legend:** Hsüan-t'ung Nien-tsao, TAI-CHING-TI-KUO... **Note:** 2.0-2.3 mm. thick.

Date	Mintage	VG	F	VF	XF	Unc
CD1909	—	1.25	3.00	6.00	10.00	—

Y# 21.3 20 CASH

Copper, 32 mm. **Ruler:** Hsüan-t'ung **Obv. Inscription:** Tai-ch'ing T'ung-pi **Rev:** Without dot between "KUO" and "COPPER"; rosette beneath dragon **Rev. Legend:** Hsüan-t'ung Nien-tsao, TAI-CHING-TI-KUO...

Date	Mintage	VG	F	VF	XF	Unc
CD1909 Restrike	—	6.00	15.00	40.00	70.00	—

Note: Although this coin bears no indication of its origin, it was minted in the Manchurian Provinces ca.1922

Y# 21.4 20 CASH

Copper, 32 mm. **Ruler:** Hsüan-t'ung **Obv. Inscription:** Tai-ch'ing T'ung-pi **Rev:** Without dot between "KUO" and "COPPER"; dot below dragon's chin **Rev. Legend:** Hsüan-t'ung Nien-tsao, TAI-CHING-TI-KUO...

Date	Mintage	VG	F	VF	XF	Unc
CD1909 Restrike	—	3.50	8.50	16.00	30.00	—

Note: Although this coin bears no indication of its origin, it was minted in the Manchurian Provinces ca.1922

Y# 21.5 20 CASH

Copper, 32 mm. **Ruler:** Hsüan-t'ung **Obv:** Inner circle of large dots **Obv. Inscription:** Tai-ch'ing T'ung-pi **Rev:** Without dot between "KUO" and "COPPER"; five crude waves beneath dragon with redesigned forehead; inner circle of large dots **Rev. Legend:** Hsüan-t'ung Nien-tsao, TAI-CHING-TI-KUO...

Date	Mintage	VG	F	VF	XF	Unc
CD1909	—	1.25	3.00	6.00	30.00	100

K# 215 10 CENTS

2.7000 g., 0.8200 Silver 0.0712 oz. ASW **Ruler:** Kuang-hsü **Obv. Inscription:** Tai-ch'ing T'ung-pi **Rev:** Dragon **Rev. Legend:** Kuang-hsü Nien-tsao, TAI-CHING-TI-KUO...

Date	Mintage	VG	F	VF	XF	Unc
CD1907	—	150	250	500	850	2,000

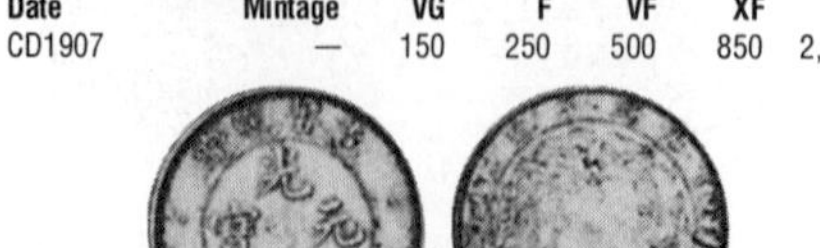

Y# 12 10 CENTS

2.7000 g., 0.8200 Silver 0.0712 oz. ASW **Ruler:** Kuang-hsü **Obv. Inscription:** Kuang-hsü Yüan-pao **Rev:** Dragon **Rev. Legend:** Kuang-hsü Nien-tsao, TAI-CHING-TI-KUO...

Date	Mintage	VG	F	VF	XF	Unc
ND(1908)	—	12.00	30.00	40.00	120	300

K# 222 10 CENTS

3.2000 g., 0.6500 Silver 0.0669 oz. ASW **Ruler:** Hsüan-t'ung **Obv. Inscription:** Tai-ch'ing Yin-pi **Rev:** Dragon **Rev. Legend:** Hsüan-t'ung Nien-tsao

Date	Mintage	VG	F	VF	XF	Unc
ND(1910)	—	80.00	120	200	400	1,000
ND(1910) Proof	—	Value: 1,500				

Y# 28 10 CENTS

2.7000 g., Silver **Ruler:** Hsüan-t'ung **Obv. Legend:** Hsüan-t'ung **Obv. Inscription:** Tai-ch'ing Yin-pi **Rev:** Dragon **Rev. Legend:** Hsüan-t'ung Nien-tsao

Date	Mintage	VG	F	VF	XF	Unc
3(1911)	—	10.00	20.00	40.00	85.00	235

Note: Refer to Hunan Republic 10 Cents, K#762

K# 214 20 CENTS

5.5000 g., 0.8200 Silver 0.1450 oz. ASW **Ruler:** Kuang-hsü **Obv. Inscription:** Tai-ch'ing Yin-pi **Rev:** Dragon **Rev. Legend:** Kuang-hsü Nien-tsao, TAI-CHING-TI-KUO...

Date	Mintage	VG	F	VF	XF	Unc
CD1907	—	200	400	650	1,100	2,500

Y# 13 20 CENTS

5.3000 g., 0.8200 Silver 0.1397 oz. ASW **Ruler:** Kuang-hsü **Obv. Inscription:** Kuang-hsü Yüan-pao **Rev:** Dragon **Rev. Legend:** Kuang-hsü Nien-tsao, TAI-CHING-TI-KUO...

Date	Mintage	VG	F	VF	XF	Unc
ND(1908)	—	20.00	60.00	100	150	400

K# 217w 20 CENTS

5.3000 g., 0.8200 Silver 0.1397 oz. ASW **Ruler:** Kuang-hsü **Obv. Inscription:** Kuang-hsü Yüan-pao **Rev:** Dragon **Rev. Legend:** Kuang-hsü Nien-tsao, TAI-CHING-TI-KUO... with "COPPER COIN" (error)

Date	Mintage	VG	F	VF	XF	Unc
ND(1908) Rare	—	—	—	—	—	—

Y# 29 20 CENTS

5.4000 g., 0.8200 Silver 0.1424 oz. ASW **Ruler:** Hsüan-t'ung **Obv. Legend:** Hsüan-t'ung **Obv. Inscription:** Tai-ch'ing Yin-pi **Rev:** Dragon

Date	Mintage	VG	F	VF	XF	Unc
3(1911)	—	45.00	85.00	150	300	500

K# 221 25 CENTS

6.7000 g., 0.8000 Silver 0.1723 oz. ASW **Ruler:** Hsüan-t'ung **Obv. Legend:** Hsüan-t'ung Nien-tsao **Obv. Inscription:** Tai-ch'ing Yin-pi **Rev:** Dragon

Date	Mintage	VG	F	VF	XF	Unc
ND(1910)	1,410,000	65.00	200	400	750	1,200
ND(1910) Proof	—	Value: 3,000				

K# 213 50 CENTS

13.6000 g., 0.8600 Silver 0.3760 oz. ASW **Ruler:** Kuang-hsü **Obv. Inscription:** Tai-ch'ing Yin-pi **Rev:** Dragon **Rev. Legend:** Kuang-hsü Nien-tsao, TAI-CHING-TI-KUO...

Date	Mintage	VG	F	VF	XF	Unc
CD1907	—	500	800	1,200	2,000	4,500

Y# 23 50 CENTS

13.4000 g., 0.8000 Silver 0.3446 oz. ASW **Ruler:** Hsüan-t'ung **Obv. Inscription:** Tai-ch'ing Yin-pi **Rev:** Dragon **Rev. Legend:** Hsüan-t'ung Nien-tsao

Date	Mintage	VG	F	VF	XF	Unc
ND(1910)	1,571,000	65.00	100	200	350	900
ND(1910) Proof	—	Value: 2,000				

Y# 30 50 CENTS

13.4000 g., 0.8000 Silver 0.3446 oz. ASW **Ruler:** Hsüan-t'ung **Obv. Legend:** Hsüan-t'ung **Obv. Inscription:** Tai-ch'ing Yin-pi **Rev:** Dragon

Date	Mintage	VG	F	VF	XF	Unc
3(1911)	Inc. above	500	900	1,500	2,500	6,000
3(1911) Proof	—	Value: 8,000				

K# 212 DOLLAR

26.9000 g., 0.9000 Silver 0.7783 oz. ASW **Ruler:** Kuang-hsü **Obv. Inscription:** Tai-ch'ing Yin-pi **Rev:** Dragon **Rev. Legend:** Kuang-hsü Nien-tsao, TAI-CHING-TI-KOU...

Date	Mintage	VG	F	VF	XF	Unc
CD1907	—	1,000	1,500	2,500	5,000	10,000

Y# 14 DOLLAR
26.9000 g., 0.9000 Silver 0.7783 oz. ASW **Ruler:** Kuang-hsü **Obv. Inscription:** Kuang-hsü Yüan-pao **Rev:** Dragon **Rev. Legend:** Kuang-hsü Nien-tsao, TAI-CHING-TI-KOU...

Date	Mintage	VG	F	VF	XF	Unc
ND(1908)	—	20.00	50.00	100	150	900

K# 219 DOLLAR
26.9000 g., 0.9000 Silver 0.7783 oz. ASW **Ruler:** Hsüan-t'ung **Obv. Inscription:** Tai-ch'ing Yin-pi **Rev:** Dragon **Rev. Legend:** Hsüan-t'ung Nien-tsao

Date	Mintage	VG	F	VF	XF	Unc
ND(1910)	—	400	800	1,500	2,500	5,000
ND(1910) Proof	—	Value: 7,000				

Y# 31 DOLLAR
26.9000 g., 0.9000 Silver 0.7783 oz. ASW **Ruler:** Hsüan-t'ung **Obv. Legend:** Hsüan-t'ung **Obv. Inscription:** Tai-ch'ing Yin-pi **Rev:** Dragon

Date	Mintage	VG	F	VF	XF	Unc
3(1911)	77,153,000	15.00	25.00	37.50	75.00	450

Note: Struck at the Tientsin, Nanking, and Wuchang Mints without distinctive marks

Y# 31.1 DOLLAR
26.9000 g., 0.9000 Silver 0.7783 oz. ASW **Ruler:** Hsüan-t'ung **Obv. Legend:** Hsüan-t'ung **Obv. Inscription:** Tai-ch'ing Yin-pi **Rev:** Dragon; "dot" after "DOLLAR"

Date	Mintage	VG	F	VF	XF	Unc
3(1911)	Inc. above	20.00	40.00	80.00	200	1,000

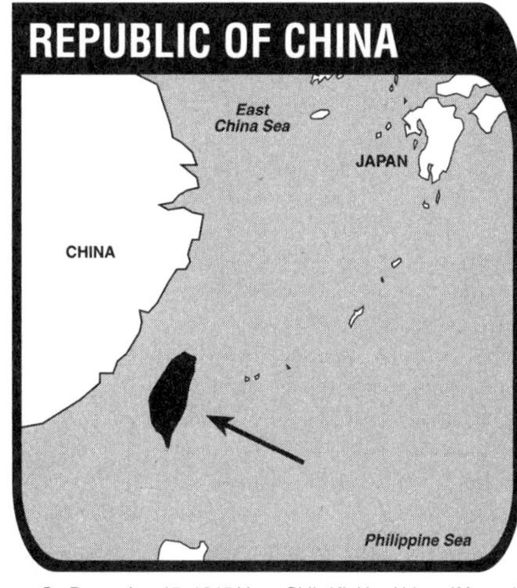

On December 15, 1915 Yuan Shih-K'ai had himself formally chosen and proclaimed emperor. Opposition developed within China and among various foreign powers. A rebellion broke out in Yünnan and spread to other southern provinces. Opposition was so great that Yuan rescinded the monarchy on March 21, 1916. On June 6th he died.

REPUBLIC

STANDARD COINAGE

Y# 301 10 CASH (10 Wen)
Copper **Obv:** Crossed flags, florals at left and right **Rev:** Double circle with small rosettes separating legend **Mint:** Nanking

Date	Mintage	VG	F	VF	XF	Unc
ND(ca.1912)	—	0.20	0.50	0.75	1.50	15.00

Y# 301a 10 CASH (10 Wen)
Brass **Obv:** Crossed flags, florals at left and right **Rev:** Double circle with small rosettes separating legend

Date	Mintage	VG	F	VF	XF	Unc
ND(ca.1912)	—	—	—	—	—	—

Y# 301.1 10 CASH (10 Wen)
Copper **Obv:** Second character from right in bottom legend is rounded **Rev:** Double circle with three dots separating legend

Date	Mintage	VG	F	VF	XF	Unc
ND(ca.1912)	—	0.35	1.00	2.00	5.00	22.00

Y# 301.2 10 CASH (10 Wen)
Copper **Obv:** Second character from right in bottom legend is rounded **Rev:** Double circle with two dots separating legend

Date	Mintage	VG	F	VF	XF	Unc
ND(ca.1912)	—	0.20	0.50	1.00	2.50	16.00

Y# 301.3 10 CASH (10 Wen)
Copper **Obv:** Small star on flag **Rev:** Double circle with six-pointed stars separating legend **Mint:** Nanking

Date	Mintage	VG	F	VF	XF	Unc
ND(ca.1912)	—	0.25	0.75	1.50	3.00	18.00

Y# 301.4 10 CASH (10 Wen)
Copper **Obv:** Large star on flag extending to edges of flag **Rev:** Double circle with six-pointed stars separating legend

Date	Mintage	VG	F	VF	XF	Unc
ND(ca.1912)	—	3.50	10.00	15.00	25.00	65.00

Y# 301.4a 10 CASH (10 Wen)
Brass **Obv:** Large star on flag extending to edges of flag **Rev:** Double circle with six-pointed stars separating legend

Date	Mintage	VG	F	VF	XF	Unc
ND(ca.1912)	—	—	—	—	—	—

Y# 301.5 10 CASH (10 Wen)
Copper **Obv:** Flower wtih many stems **Rev:** Single circle

Date	Mintage	VG	F	VF	XF	Unc
ND(ca.1912)	—	0.25	0.75	1.50	3.00	20.00

Y# 301.6 10 CASH (10 Wen)
Copper **Obv:** Flower wtih fewer stems **Rev:** Single circle

Date	Mintage	VG	F	VF	XF	Unc
ND(ca.1912)	—	0.25	0.75	1.50	3.00	20.00

Y# 309 10 CASH (10 Wen)
Copper **Mint:** Tientsin

Date	Mintage	VG	F	VF	XF	Unc
ND(1914-17)	—	3.50	10.00	20.00	40.00	120

Note: Pieces with L. GIORGI near rim are patterns

Y# 307 10 CASH (10 Wen)
Copper **Obv:** One large rosette on either side **Rev:** Slender leaves and short ribbon **Mint:** Taiyüan

Date	Mintage	VG	F	VF	XF	Unc
ND(1919)	421,138,000	0.20	0.50	1.00	3.00	14.00

Y# 307a 10 CASH (10 Wen)
Copper **Obv:** Crossed flags, three rosettes on either side, ornate right flag **Rev:** Long ribbon

Date	Mintage	VG	F	VF	XF	Unc
ND(1919)	Inc. above	0.40	1.00	2.00	4.00	12.50

Y# 307a.1 10 CASH (10 Wen)
6.6400 g., Copper, 28.05 mm. **Obv:** Crossed flags, three rosettes on either side, ornate right flag **Rev:** Short ribbon and smaller wheat ears

Date	Mintage	VG	F	VF	XF	Unc
ND(1919)	Inc. above	3.50	10.00	20.00	40.00	100

Y# 307b 10 CASH (10 Wen)
Brass **Obv:** Crossed flags, three rosettes at either side, ornate right flag **Rev:** Long ribbon

Date	Mintage	VG	F	VF	XF	Unc
ND(1919)	—	—	—	—	—	—

Y# 307.1 10 CASH (10 Wen)
Copper **Rev:** Larger leaves and longer ribbon

Date	Mintage	VG	F	VF	XF	Unc
ND(1919)	Inc. above	3.50	10.00	20.00	40.00	100

Y# 302 10 CASH (10 Wen)
Copper **Rev:** Vine above leaf at 12-o'clock; wreath tied at bottom; M-shaped leaves at base of wheat ears **Mint:** Anhwei

Date	Mintage	VG	F	VF	XF	Unc
ND(ca.1920)	—	0.20	0.60	1.50	3.00	18.00

Y# 302a 10 CASH (10 Wen)
Brass **Obv:** Crossed flags, florals at left and right **Rev:** Vine above leaf at 12-o'clock; wreath tied at bottom; M-shaped leaves at base of wheat ears

Date	Mintage	VG	F	VF	XF	Unc
ND(ca.1920)	—	—	—	—	—	—

Y# 302.1 10 CASH (10 Wen)
Copper **Obv:** Crossed flags, florals at left and right **Rev:** Vine above leaf at 12-o'clock, wreath tied at bottom; M-shaped leaves at base of larger wheat ears

Date	Mintage	VG	F	VF	XF	Unc
ND(ca.1920)	—	0.35	1.00	3.50	6.50	20.00

Y# 302.2 10 CASH (10 Wen)
Copper **Rev:** Vine beneath leaf at 12-o'clock; wreath not tied at bottom; without M-shaped leaves at base of wheat ears

Date	Mintage	VG	F	VF	XF	Unc
ND(ca.1920)	—	0.50	1.50	4.00	8.00	22.00

Y# 302.3 10 CASH (10 Wen)
Copper **Rev:** Leaves pointing clockwise

Date	Mintage	VG	F	VF	XF	Unc
ND(ca.1920)	—	10.00	30.00	40.00	60.00	115

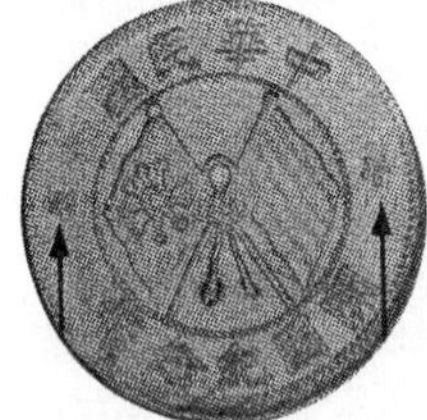

Y# 303 10 CASH (10 Wen)
Copper **Obv:** Crossed flags, small star-shaped rosettes at left and right **Rev:** Small 4-petaled rosettes separating legend

Date	Mintage	VG	F	VF	XF	Unc
ND(ca.1920)	—	0.20	0.50	1.00	2.00	15.00

Y# 303a 10 CASH (10 Wen)
Brass **Obv:** Crossed flags, stars replace rosettes at left and right **Rev:** Small 4-petaled rosettes separating legend

Date	Mintage	VG	F	VF	XF	Unc
ND(ca.1920)	—	0.50	1.50	4.00	10.00	22.50

Y# 303.1 10 CASH (10 Wen)
Copper **Obv:** Crossed flags, left flag's star in relief, small star-shaped rosettes at left and right **Rev:** Small 4-petaled rosettes separating legend

Date	Mintage	VG	F	VF	XF	Unc
ND(ca.1920)	—	0.20	0.50	1.00	2.00	15.00

Y# 303.3 10 CASH (10 Wen)
Copper **Obv:** Large rosettes replace stars **Rev:** Stars separating legend

Date	Mintage	VG	F	VF	XF	Unc
ND(ca.1920)	—	1.00	3.00	6.25	12.50	25.00

Y# 303.4 10 CASH (10 Wen)
Copper **Obv:** Crossed flags, very small pentagonal rosettes at left and right

Date	Mintage	VG	F	VF	XF	Unc
ND(ca.1920)	—	0.25	0.75	1.50	3.00	15.00

Y# 303.4a 10 CASH (10 Wen)
Brass **Obv:** Crossed flags, very small pentagonal rosettes at left and right **Rev:** Stars separating legend

Date	Mintage	VG	F	VF	XF	Unc
ND(ca.1920)	—	1.00	3.00	6.25	12.50	25.00

Y# 303.5 10 CASH (10 Wen)
Brass **Obv:** Crossed flags, three large rosettes at left and right **Rev:** Stars separate legend

Date	Mintage	VG	F	VF	XF	Unc
ND(ca.1920)	—	—	—	—	—	—

Y# 304 10 CASH (10 Wen)
Copper **Obv:** Circled flags flanked by pentagonal rosettes **Mint:** Anhwei

Date	Mintage	VG	F	VF	XF	Unc
ND(ca.1920)	—	3.75	11.50	21.50	42.50	85.00

Y# 305 10 CASH (10 Wen)
Copper **Rev:** Chrysanthemum **Mint:** Changsha

Date	Mintage	VG	F	VF	XF	Unc
ND(ca.1920)	—	5.00	15.00	25.00	50.00	115

Y# 306a 10 CASH (10 Wen)

Copper **Obv:** Crossed flags, five characters in lower legend

Date	Mintage	VG	F	VF	XF	Unc
ND(ca.1920)	—	1.75	5.00	12.00	25.00	65.00

Y# 306b 10 CASH (10 Wen)

Brass **Obv:** Crossed flags, five characters in lower legend

Date	Mintage	VG	F	VF	XF	Unc
ND(ca.1920)	—	0.35	1.00	2.50	5.00	18.00

Y# 306.1 10 CASH (10 Wen)

Copper **Obv:** Crossed flags, florals at left and right **Rev:** Wheat ear design within circle **Mint:** Changsha

Date	Mintage	VG	F	VF	XF	Unc
ND(ca.1920)	—	0.20	0.50	1.25	3.00	14.00

Y# 306.1b 10 CASH (10 Wen)

Copper **Obv:** Crossed flags, florals at left and right **Rev:** Thin leaf blade between lower wheat ears

Date	Mintage	VG	F	VF	XF	Unc
ND(ca.1920)	—	1.75	5.00	7.50	14.00	30.00

Y# 306.2 10 CASH (10 Wen)

Copper **Obv:** Crossed flags, florals at left and right, dot on either side of upper legend **Rev:** Wheat ear design within circle

Date	Mintage	VG	F	VF	XF	Unc
ND(ca.1920)	—	0.35	1.00	2.00	3.50	15.00

Y# 306.2b 10 CASH (10 Wen)

Brass **Obv:** Crossed flags, florals at left and right, dot on either side of upper legend **Rev:** Thin leaf blade between lower wheat ears

Date	Mintage	VG	F	VF	XF	Unc
ND(ca.1920)	—	0.45	1.25	3.00	5.00	15.00

Y# 306.3 10 CASH (10 Wen)

Copper **Obv:** Star between flags **Rev:** Wheat ear design within circle

Date	Mintage	VG	F	VF	XF	Unc
ND(ca.1920)	—	6.50	20.00	40.00	75.00	—

Y# 306.4 10 CASH (10 Wen)

Copper **Obv:** Elongated rosettes, different characters in bottom legend **Rev:** Thin leaf blade between lower wheat ears

Date	Mintage	VG	F	VF	XF	Unc
ND(ca.1920)	—	9.00	27.50	55.00	85.00	215

Y# 311 10 CASH (10 Wen)

Copper **Mint:** Kalgan

Date	Mintage	VG	F	VF	XF	Unc
13 (1924)	—	65.00	175	350	500	850

Y# 308 20 CASH (20 Wen)

Copper, 32.3 mm. **Obv:** Crossed flags **Rev:** Value in sprays **Mint:** Taiyüan

Date	Mintage	VG	F	VF	XF	Unc
8 (1919)	200,861,000	0.50	1.50	3.00	7.50	30.00

Y# 308b 20 CASH (20 Wen)

Cast Brass **Obv:** Crossed flags **Rev:** Value in sprays

Date	Mintage	Good	VG	F	VF	XF
8(1919)	—	10.00	15.00	18.50	27.50	—

Note: A "warlord" issue; refer to note under Szechuan - Republic

Y# 308a 20 CASH (20 Wen)

Copper **Obv:** Crossed flags **Rev:** Value in sprays

Date	Mintage	VG	F	VF	XF	Unc
10 (1921)	Inc. above	0.35	1.00	2.50	6.00	30.00

Y# 310 20 CASH (20 Wen)

Copper **Obv:** Crossed flags **Rev:** Value in sprays **Mint:** Tientsin

Date	Mintage	VG	F	VF	XF	Unc
ND(ca.1921)	—	5.00	15.00	30.00	70.00	135

Note: Some sources date these 20 Cash pieces bearing crossed flags ca.1912, but many were not struck until the 1920s; this coin is usually found weakly struck and lightweight

Y# 312 20 CASH (20 Wen)

Copper **Obv:** Crossed flags **Rev:** Value in sprays **Mint:** Kalgan

Date	Mintage	VG	F	VF	XF	Unc
13 (1924)	—	3.50	10.00	30.00	70.00	135

Note: This coin is usually found weakly struck

HSU# 9 20 CASH (20 Wen)

Copper **Obv:** Crossed flags **Rev:** Value in sprays **Note:** Nationalist commemorative.

Date	Mintage	VG	F	VF	XF	Unc
ND(1927-28)	—	75.00	225	400	650	900

HSU# 445a 500 CASH (500 Wen)
Copper **Subject:** Nationalist Commemorative **Obv:** Crossed flags **Rev:** Value in sprays

Date	Mintage	VG	F	VF	XF	Unc
ND(1927/8) Rare	12	—	—	—	—	—

Y# 323 1/2 CENT (1/2 Fen)
Bronze **Mint:** Tientsin

Date	Mintage	VG	F	VF	XF	Unc
5 (1916)	1,789,000	1.75	5.00	10.00	20.00	45.00

Y# 346 1/2 CENT (1/2 Fen)
Bronze

Date	Mintage	VG	F	VF	XF	Unc
25 (1936)	64,720,000	0.25	0.75	1.50	3.00	7.50
28 (1939) Rare	—	—	—	—	—	—

Y# 347 CENT
Copper

Date	Mintage	VG	F	VF	XF	Unc
25 (1936)	311,780,000	0.15	0.40	0.75	1.75	2.50
26 (1937)	307,198,000	0.15	0.45	1.00	1.50	3.00
27 (1938)	12,000,000	1.00	3.00	5.00	8.00	16.00
28 (1939)	75,000,000	0.65	2.00	4.00	7.00	15.00

Y# 324 CENT (1 Fen)
Bronze **Mint:** Tientsin

Date	Mintage	VG	F	VF	XF	Unc
5 (1916)	—	1.75	5.00	10.00	20.00	50.00

Note: Pieces with "L. GIORGI" near rim are patterns

Y# 353 CENT (1 Fen)
Brass **Note:** Shi Kwan Cent.

Date	Mintage	VG	F	VF	XF	Unc
28(1939)	—	13.50	40.00	60.00	120	200

Y# 355 CENT (1 Fen)
Aluminum

Date	Mintage	VG	F	VF	XF	Unc
29 (1940)	150,000,000	—	0.10	0.25	0.50	1.50

Y# 357 CENT (1 Fen)
Brass

Date	Mintage	VG	F	VF	XF	Unc
29 (1940)	50,000,000	0.25	0.75	1.00	2.00	4.00

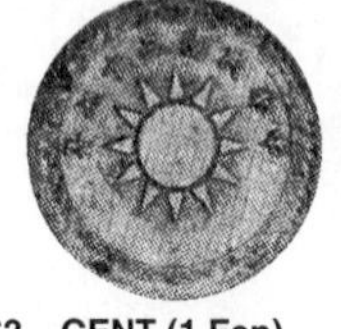

Y# 363 CENT (1 Fen)
Bronze

Date	Mintage	VG	F	VF	XF	Unc
37 (1948)	—	1.50	4.00	10.00	15.00	20.00

Y# 325a 2 CENTS (2 Fen)
Bronze

Date	Mintage	VG	F	VF	XF	Unc
22(1933)	—	13.50	40.00	60.00	95.00	150

Y# 354 2 CENTS (2 Fen)
Brass

Date	Mintage	VG	F	VF	XF	Unc
28(1939)	300,000,000	3.50	10.00	15.00	25.00	50.00

Y# 358 2 CENTS (2 Fen)
Brass

Date	Mintage	VG	F	VF	XF	Unc
29(1940)	—	0.20	0.50	1.00	1.50	2.00
30(1941) Rare	—	—	—	—	—	—

Y# 348 5 CENTS (5 Fen)
3.0700 g., Nickel, 18.5 mm.

Date	Mintage	VG	F	VF	XF	Unc
25(1936)	72,844,000	0.35	1.00	1.50	3.00	6.00
27(1938)	34,325,000	0.75	2.50	4.50	8.00	15.00
28(1939)	6,000,000	3.50	10.00	15.00	25.00	50.00

Y# 348.1 5 CENTS (5 Fen)
Nickel **Rev:** A mint mark below spade (Vienna)

Date	Mintage	VG	F	VF	XF	Unc
25(1936)	20,000,000	0.35	1.00	2.00	3.50	15.00

Y# 348.2 5 CENTS (5 Fen)
Nickel **Obv:** Character "P'ing" on both sides of portrait

Date	Mintage	VG	F	VF	XF	Unc
25 (1936)	—	17.50	50.00	80.00	125	175

Y# 348.3 5 CENTS (5 Fen)
Nickel **Obv:** Character "Ch'ing" on both sides of portrait

Date	Mintage	VG	F	VF	XF	Unc
25 (1936)	—	17.50	50.00	80.00	125	175

Y# 356 5 CENTS (5 Fen)
1.1000 g., Aluminum

Date	Mintage	VG	F	VF	XF	Unc
29(1940)	350,000,000	0.20	0.50	1.00	2.50	4.00

Y# 359 5 CENTS (5 Fen)
Copper-Nickel

Date	Mintage	VG	F	VF	XF	Unc
29(1940)	57,000,000	0.10	0.25	1.50	2.50	5.00
30(1941)	96,000,000	0.10	0.25	1.50	2.50	6.00

K# 602 10 CENTS (1 Chiao)
2.3000 g., Silver, 18 mm. **Subject:** Sun Yat-sen Founding of the Republic **Obv:** Bust left within circle **Rev:** Two 5-pointed stars dividing legend at top **Note:** vertical reeding

Date	Mintage	VG	F	VF	XF	Unc
ND(1912)	—	65.00	200	500	700	1,250

K# 602b 10 CENTS (1 Chiao)
2.3000 g., Silver, 18 mm. **Subject:** Sun Yat-sen Founding of the Republic **Obv:** Bust left within circle **Rev:** Two 5-pointed stars dividing legend at top **Edge:** Engrailed with circles

Date	Mintage	VG	F	VF	XF	Unc
ND(1912)	—	—	—	700	850	1,500

Y# 326 10 CENTS (1 Chiao)
2.7000 g., 0.7000 Silver 0.0608 oz. ASW

Date	Mintage	VG	F	VF	XF	Unc
3 (1914)	—	2.00	5.00	10.00	20.00	70.00
3 (1914) Specimen	—	Value: 500				
5 (1916)	—	6.50	20.00	35.00	60.00	125
5 (1916) Specimen	—	Value: 750				

Y# 334 10 CENTS (1 Chiao)
Silver **Subject:** Unadopted design of national emblem

Date	Mintage	VG	F	VF	XF	Unc
15 (1926)	—	2.00	5.00	12.00	25.00	60.00

Y# 339 10 CENTS (1 Chiao)
2.5000 g., Silver, 18 mm. **Subject:** Death of Sun Yat-sen

Date	Mintage	VG	F	VF	XF	Unc
16 (1927)	—	10.00	25.00	40.00	70.00	145

Y# 349 10 CENTS (1 Chiao)
Nickel, 21 mm.

Date	Mintage	VG	F	VF	XF	Unc
25(1936)	73,866,000	0.20	0.60	1.00	3.00	7.50
27(1938)	110,203,000	0.65	2.00	4.25	8.00	20.00
28(1939)	68,000,000	0.50	1.50	3.50	10.00	27.50

Y# 349a 10 CENTS (1 Chiao)
Non-Magnetic Nickel Alloy

Date	Mintage	VG	F	VF	XF	Unc
25(1936)	1,000,000	6.00	18.00	30.00	40.00	65.00

Note: All of the Y#349 coins were supposed to have been minted in pure nickel at the Shanghai Mint; However, in 1936 a warlord had the Tientsin Mint produce about one million 10 Cent pieces of heavily alloyed nickel; The result is that the Shanghai pieces are attracted to a magnet while the Tientsin pieces are not

Y# 349.1 10 CENTS (1 Chiao)
Nickel **Rev:** Mint mark A below spade (Vienna Mint)

Date	Mintage	VG	F	VF	XF	Unc
25(1936)A	60,000,000	0.35	1.00	2.00	8.00	25.00

Y# 360 10 CENTS (1 Chiao)
Copper-Nickel, 21 mm. **Edge:** Reeded

Date	Mintage	VG	F	VF	XF	Unc
29(1940)	68,000,000	0.20	0.50	2.50	8.00	15.00
30(1941)	254,000,000	0.20	0.50	1.50	2.50	5.00
31(1942)	10,000,000	8.50	25.00	60.00	80.00	120

Y# 360.1 10 CENTS (1 Chiao)
Copper-Nickel **Edge:** Plain

Date	Mintage	VG	F	VF	XF	Unc
29(1940) Rare	Inc. above	—	—	—	—	—
30(1941)	Inc. above	0.65	2.00	7.50	10.00	15.00

Y# 317 20 CENTS (2 Chiao)
5.2000 g., Silver, 23 mm. **Subject:** Founding of the Republic

Date	Mintage	VG	F	VF	XF	Unc
ND(1912)	155,000	6.50	15.00	20.00	38.00	85.00

Y# 327 20 CENTS (2 Chiao)
5.4000 g., 0.7000 Silver 0.1215 oz. ASW, 22.88 mm.

Date	Mintage	VG	F	VF	XF	Unc
3 (1914)	—	2.25	3.50	6.00	12.00	70.00
3 (1914) Specimen	—	Value: 250				
5 (1916)	—	2.25	3.50	6.00	15.00	90.00
5 (1916) Specimen	—	Value: 500				
9 (1920)	—	45.00	100	275	500	1,000

Y# 335 20 CENTS (2 Chiao)
5.2000 g., Silver **Subject:** Unadopted design of national emblem

Date	Mintage	VG	F	VF	XF	Unc
15 (1926)	—	3.50	10.00	15.00	30.00	80.00

Y# 340 20 CENTS (2 Chiao)
5.3000 g., Silver, 23 mm. **Subject:** Death of Sun Yat-sen

Date	Mintage	VG	F	VF	XF	Unc
16(1927)	—	6.50	15.00	25.00	40.00	100

Y# 350 20 CENTS (20 Fen)
6.0500 g., Nickel, 24.06 mm.

Date	Mintage	VG	F	VF	XF	Unc
25(1936)	49,620,000	0.20	0.50	2.50	6.00	10.00
27(1938)	61,248,000	0.35	1.00	2.00	7.00	12.00
28(1939)	38,000,000	0.65	2.00	5.00	10.00	15.00

Y# 350.1 20 CENTS (20 Fen)
Nickel **Rev:** Mint mark A below spade (Vienna Mint)

Date	Mintage	VG	F	VF	XF	Unc
25(1936)A	40,000,000	0.35	1.00	2.00	3.50	6.00

Y# 361 20 CENTS (20 Fen)
Copper-Nickel

Date	Mintage	VG	F	VF	XF	Unc
31(1942)	32,300,000	0.15	0.40	1.00	2.25	4.00

Y# 328 50 CENTS (1/2 Yuan)
13.6000 g., 0.7000 Silver 0.3061 oz. ASW

Date	Mintage	VG	F	VF	XF	Unc
3 (1914)	—	8.50	25.00	45.00	75.00	250
3 (1914) Specimen	—	Value: 1,000				

Y# 362 50 CENTS (1/2 Yuan)
9.0600 g., Copper-Nickel, 28 mm. **Edge:** Reeded

Date	Mintage	VG	F	VF	XF	Unc
31(1942)	57,000,000	0.50	1.50	3.00	7.50	15.00
32(1943)	4,000,000	1.25	3.50	9.50	17.50	30.00

Y# 318 DOLLAR (Yuan)
26.9000 g., 0.9000 Silver 0.7783 oz. ASW, 39 mm. **Subject:** Sun Yat-sen Founding of the Republic **Obv:** Sun Yat-sen facing left **Rev:** Two five-pointed stars dividing legend at top

Date	Mintage	VG	F	VF	XF	Unc
ND(1912)	—	50.00	150	300	450	850

Y# 318.1 DOLLAR (Yuan)
26.9000 g., 0.9000 Silver 0.7783 oz. ASW, 39 mm. **Obv:** Dot below ear

Date	Mintage	VG	F	VF	XF	Unc
ND(1912)	—	—	—	—	—	—

Note: For similar issue with rosettes see Y#318a.1 (1927)

Y# 319 DOLLAR (Yuan)
27.3000 g., 0.9000 Silver 0.7899 oz. ASW, 39 mm. **Obv:** Sun Yat-sen facing left

Date	Mintage	VG	F	VF	XF	Unc
ND(1912)	—	35.00	100	285	400	650

Y# 320 DOLLAR (Yuan)
26.5000 g., Silver, 39 mm. **Subject:** Li Yüan-hung Founding of Republic **Rev. Designer:** Chu Tse-fang

Date	Mintage	VG	F	VF	XF	Unc
ND(1912)	—	150	450	900	1,500	2,000

Y# 320.1 DOLLAR (Yuan)
26.5000 g., Silver, 39 mm. **Rev. Legend:** OE for OF

Date	Mintage	VG	F	VF	XF	Unc
ND(1912)	—	175	550	1,100	1,800	—

Y# 320.2 DOLLAR (Yuan)
26.5000 g., Silver **Rev. Legend:** CIIINA for CHINA

Date	Mintage	VG	F	VF	XF	Unc
ND(1912)	—	175	550	1,100	1,800	—

Y# 321 DOLLAR (Yuan)
26.5000 g., Silver, 39 mm. **Subject:** Li Yüan-hung Founding of Republic

Date	Mintage	VG	F	VF	XF	Unc
ND(1912)	—	50.00	100	150	200	600

Y# 321.1 DOLLAR (Yuan)
26.5000 g., Silver, 39 mm. **Rev:** H of "THE" in legend engraved as I I

Date	Mintage	VG	F	VF	XF	Unc
ND(1912)	—	50.00	100	170	250	650

Y# 322 DOLLAR (Yuan)
26.7000 g., 0.9000 Silver 0.7726 oz. ASW, 39 mm. **Subject:** Yüan Shih-kai Founding of Republic **Designer:** Luigi Giorgi **Note:** 2.8mm thickness.

Date	Mintage	VG	F	VF	XF	Unc
ND (1914)	20,000	100	175	300	450	600

Y# 322.1 DOLLAR (Yuan)
26.7000 g., 0.9000 Silver 0.7726 oz. ASW, 39 mm. **Subject:** Yüan Shih-kai Founding of Republic **Note:** 3.25mm thickness.

Date	Mintage	VG	F	VF	XF	Unc
ND(ca.1918)	—	100	175	300	450	600

Note: A restrike made about 1918 for collectors

Y# 329 DOLLAR (Yuan)
26.4000 g., 0.8900 Silver 0.7554 oz. ASW **Subject:** Yüan Shih-kai **Obv:** Six characters above head **Note:** Vertical reeding.

Date	Mintage	VG	F	VF	XF	Unc
3 (1914)	—	10.00	12.50	16.00	25.00	50.00

Y# 329.1 DOLLAR (Yuan)
26.4000 g., 0.8900 Silver 0.7554 oz. ASW **Note:** Edge engrailed with circles.

Date	Mintage	VG	F	VF	XF	Unc
3 (1914)	—	15.00	60.00	150	1,000	2,200

Y# 329.2 DOLLAR (Yuan)
26.4000 g., 0.8900 Silver 0.7554 oz. ASW **Edge:** Ornamented with alternating T's

Date	Mintage	VG	F	VF	XF	Unc
3	—	15.00	60.00	150	1,000	2,200

Y# 329.3 DOLLAR (Yuan)
26.4000 g., 0.8900 Silver 0.7554 oz. ASW **Edge:** Plain

Date	Mintage	VG	F	VF	XF	Unc
3 (1914)	—	15.00	40.00	75.00	500	800

Y# 329.4 DOLLAR (Yuan)
26.4000 g., 0.8900 Silver 0.7554 oz. ASW **Note:** Tiny circle in ribbon bow. This is a mint mark, but it is not clear what mint is indicated.

Date	Mintage	VG	F	VF	XF	Unc
3 (1914)	—	12.00	20.00	40.00	85.00	200

Y# 332 DOLLAR (Yuan)
26.8000 g., Silver, 39 mm. **Ruler:** Hung-hsien **Subject:** Inauguration of Hung-hsien Regime **Obv:** Bust of Hung-hsien in military uniform with plumed hat facing **Rev:** Winged dragon left **Designer:** Luigi Giorgi **Note:** K#663.

Date	Mintage	VG	F	VF	XF	Unc
ND (1916)	—	100	400	700	1,000	1,500

Y# 329.6 DOLLAR (Yuan)
26.4000 g., 0.8900 Silver 0.7554 oz. ASW **Obv:** Seven characters above head

Date	Mintage	VG	F	VF	XF	Unc
8 (1919)	—	11.00	13.00	18.50	45.00	135
9 (1920)	—	10.00	12.00	14.50	22.50	50.00
10 (1921)	—	10.00	12.00	14.50	22.50	50.00

K# 676 DOLLAR (Yuan)
26.5000 g., Silver, 39 mm. **Subject:** President Hsu Shih-chang **Edge:** Reeded

Date	Mintage	VG	F	VF	XF	Unc
10 (1921)	—	125	250	500	900	1,650

K# 676.1 DOLLAR (Yuan)
26.5000 g., Silver, 39 mm. **Edge:** Plain

Date	Mintage	VG	F	VF	XF	Unc
10 (1921)	—	200	500	800	1,500	2,500

K# 677 DOLLAR (Yuan)
26.7000 g., Silver, 39 mm. **Obv:** Bust of President Tsao Kun facing

Date	Mintage	VG	F	VF	XF	Unc
ND (1923)	50,000	125	250	500	850	1,500

K# 678 DOLLAR (Yuan)
26.7000 g., Silver, 39 mm. **Obv:** Bust of President Tsao Kun in military uniform facing

Date	Mintage	VG	F	VF	XF	Unc
ND (1923)	—	—	—	500	850	1,500

Y# 336 DOLLAR (Yuan)
26.8000 g., Silver **Subject:** Unadopted design of national emblem **Rev:** Value in small characters

Date	Mintage	VG	F	VF	XF	Unc
12 (1923)	—	200	500	900	1,500	2,500

Y# 336.1 DOLLAR (Yuan)
26.8000 g., Silver **Subject:** Unadopted design of national emblem **Rev:** Value in large characters

Date	Mintage	VG	F	VF	XF	Unc
12 (1923)	—	250	500	1,000	2,750	4,500

K# 683 DOLLAR (Yuan)
Silver, 39 mm. **Obv:** Bust of President Tuan Chi-jui facing

Date	Mintage	VG	F	VF	XF	Unc
ND (1924)	—	125	200	450	800	1,500

K# 690 DOLLAR (Yuan)
26.5000 g., Silver, 39 mm. **Obv:** Bust of General Chu Yu-pu facing

Date	Mintage	VG	F	VF	XF	Unc
ND (1927)	—	—	—	5,000	12,000	25,000

Y# 318a.1 DOLLAR (Yuan)
27.0000 g., 0.8900 Silver 0.7726 oz. ASW **Obv:** Bust of Sun Yat-sen left **Rev:** Two rosettes dividing legend at top **Edge:** Incuse reeding

Date	Mintage	VG	F	VF	XF	Unc
ND(1927)	—	10.00	12.00	14.00	17.50	35.00

Y# 318a.2 DOLLAR (Yuan)
27.0000 g., 0.8900 Silver 0.7726 oz. ASW **Edge:** Reeding in relief

Date	Mintage	VG	F	VF	XF	Unc
ND(1927)	—	10.00	12.00	14.00	17.50	35.00

Note: Varieties exist with errors in the English legend. For similar coins with 5-pointed stars dividing legends, see Y#318 (1912). In 1949 the Canton Mint restruck Memento dollars. There are modern restrikes in red copper and brass.

K# 609 DOLLAR (Yuan)
27.0000 g., Silver **Obv:** Bust of Sun Yat-sen **Rev:** Sun Yat-sen Memorial

Date	Mintage	VG	F	VF	XF	Unc
16(1927)	480	750	1,500	3,000	5,000	9,500

Y# 344 DOLLAR (Yuan)

26.7000 g., 0.8800 Silver 0.7554 oz. ASW **Obv:** Bust of Sun Yat-sen left **Rev:** 3 wild geese flying above junk, rising sun

Date	Mintage	VG	F	VF	XF	Unc
21(1932)	2,260,000	100	175	300	400	600

Y# 345 DOLLAR (Yuan)

26.7000 g., 0.8800 Silver 0.7554 oz. ASW **Rev:** Without birds above junk or rising sun

Date	Mintage	VG	F	VF	XF	Unc
22(1933)	46,400,000	10.00	12.50	15.00	20.00	50.00
23(1934)	128,740,000	10.00	12.00	14.00	16.00	30.00

Note: In 1949, three U.S. mints restruck a total of 30 million "Junk Dollars" dated Year 23.

Y# 324a FEN

Bronze

Date	Mintage	VG	F	VF	XF	Unc
22 (1933)	—	2.75	8.00	15.00	30.00	100

Shortly after World War I the greatest external threat to the territorial integrity of China was posed by Japan, which urgently needed room for an expanding population and raw materials for its industrial and military machines, and which recognized the necessity of controlling all of China if it was to realize its plan of dominating the rest of the Asiatic and South Sea countries. The Japanese had large investments in Manchuria (a name given by non-Chinese to the three northeastern provinces of China), which allowed them privileges that compromised Chinese sovereignty. The educated of China were not reconciled to Japan's growing power in Manchuria, and the resultant friction occasioned a series of vexing incidents, which Japan decided to circumvent by direct action. On the night of Sept. 18-19, 1931, with a contrived incident for an excuse, Japanese forces seized the city of Mukden (Shenyang), and within a few weeks completely demolished Chinese power north of the Great Wall.

In Feb. 1932, after the Japanese occupation of Manchuria, they set up Manchoukuo as an independent republic. Jehol (Rehe) was occupied by the Japanese in 1933 and added to Manchoukuo. Manchoukuo was established as an empire in 1934 with the deposed Manchu emperor Hsuan T'ung (the late Henry Pu Yi) as the puppet emperor K'ang Te. Lacking the means to face the Japanese armies in the field, the Chinese could only trade space for time.

Not content with confining its control of China to the areas north of the Great Wall, the Japanese launched a major campaign in 1937, and by the fall of 1938 had occupied in addition to Manchuria the provinces of Hopei (Hebei) and Chahar, most of the port cities, and the major cities as far west as Hankow (Hankou), now part of Wuhan. In addition, they dominated or threatened the provinces of Suiyuan, Shansi (Shanxi) and Shantung (Shandong).

Still the Chinese did not yield. The struggle was prolonged until the advent of World War II, which brought about the defeat of Japan and the return of the puppet states to Chinese control.

As the victorious Japanese armies swept deeper into China, Japan established central banks under control of the Bank of Japan in the conquered provinces for the purpose of establishing control over banking and finance in the puppet states, and eventually in all of China. These included the Chi Tung Bank, which had its main office in Tientsin (Tianjin) with branches in Peking (Beijing), Chinan (Jinan) and Tangshan, the Federal Reserve Bank of China with its main office in Peking (Beijing) and branches in 37 other cities; and the Hua Hsing Bank with its main office in Shanghai and two branches. The puppet states of Manchukuo, previously detailed in this introduction, and Mengchiang, which comprised a greater part of Inner Mongolia, were also major coin-issuing entities.

EAST HOPEI

AUTONOMOUS

The Chi Tung Bank was the banking institution of the "East Hopei Anti-Comintern Autonomous Government" established by the Japanese in 1936 to undermine the political position of China in the northwest provinces. It issued both coins and notes between 1937 and 1939 with a restraint uncharacteristic of the puppet banks of the China-Japanese puppet states.

ANTI-COMINTERN AUTONOMOUS GOVERNMENT

STANDARD COINAGE

Y# 516 5 LI

Copper **Issuer:** Chi Tung Bank **Obv:** Japanese character "first" **Rev:** Value in grain stalks

Date	Mintage	VG	F	VF	XF	Unc
26(1937)	—	8.00	20.00	40.00	70.00	200

Y# 517 FEN

Copper **Issuer:** Chi Tung Bank **Obv:** Japanese character "first" **Rev:** Value in grain stalks

Date	Mintage	VG	F	VF	XF	Unc
26(1937)	—	2.50	6.00	12.00	18.00	60.00

Y# 518 5 FEN

Copper-Nickel **Issuer:** Chi Tung Bank **Obv:** Japanese character "first" **Rev:** Value in grain stalks

Date	Mintage	VG	F	VF	XF	Unc
26(1937)	—	2.00	5.00	9.00	13.00	50.00

Y# 519 CHIAO

Copper-Nickel **Issuer:** Chi Tung Bank **Obv:** T'ien-ning Pagoda in Peking **Rev:** Value in grain stalks

Date	Mintage	VG	F	VF	XF	Unc
26(1937)	—	2.00	5.00	9.00	13.00	45.00

Y# 520 2 CHIAO

Copper-Nickel **Issuer:** Chi Tung Bank **Obv:** T'ien-ning Pagoda in Peking **Rev:** Value in grain stalks

Date	Mintage	VG	F	VF	XF	Unc
26(1937)	—	2.50	6.00	12.00	20.00	70.00

MANCHOUKUO

(Manchukuo)

The former Japanese puppet state of Manchoukuo (largely Manchuria), comprising the northeastern Chinese provinces of Fengtien (Liaoning), Kirin (Jilin), Heilungkiang (Heilongjiang) and Jehol (Rehe), had an area of 503,143 sq. mi. (1,303,134 sq. km.) and a population of 43.3 million. Capital: Changchun, renamed Hsinking. The area is rich in fertile soil, timber and mineral resources, including coal, iron and gold.

Until the closing years of the 19th century when Chinese influence became predominant, Manchuria was chiefly a domain of the tribal Manchus and their Mongol allies. Coincident with the rise of Chinese influence, foreign imperialistic powers began to appreciate the value of the area to their expansionist philosophy. Japan, overpopulated and poor in resources, desired it as a source of raw materials and for increased living area. Russia wanted it as the eastern terminus of the Trans-Siberian railway that was to unite its Asian empire. The inevitable conflict of Japanese, Chinese and Russian interests required that one or more of the powers be eliminated. After eliminating Russia in their war of 1904-05, Japan eliminated China on the night of Sept. 18, 1931, when, on the pretext of a contrived incident, it moved militarily to seize control of the Three Eastern Provinces. Early in 1932 Japan declared Manchuria independent by virtue of a voluntary separatist movement and established the state of Manchoukuo. To give the puppet state an aura of legitimacy, the deposed emperor of the former Manchu dynasty was recalled from retirement and designated "chief executive". The area was restored to China at the end of World War II.

RULERS

Ta T'ung, 1932-1934
K'ang Te, 1934-1945

The puppet emperor under the assumed name of K'ang Te was previously the last emperor of China (P'u-yi, or Hsuan T'ung, 1909-11).

MONETARY SYSTEM

10 Li = 1 Fen
10 Fen = 1 Chiao

IDENTIFICATION OF REIGN CHARACTERS

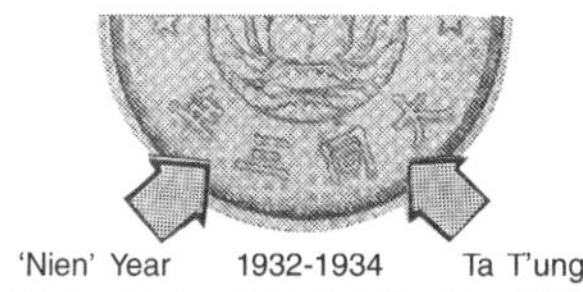

'Nien' Year 1932-1934 Ta T'ung

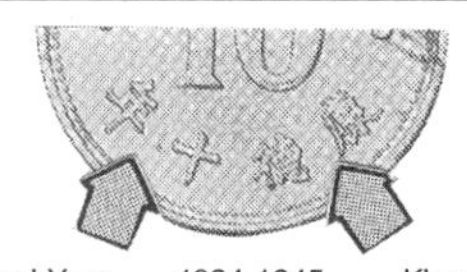

'Nien' Year 1934-1945 K'ang Te

DATE ABBREVIATIONS

TT - Ta T'ung
KT - K'ang Te

GREEK RIM BORDER VARIETIES

Narrow Design Wide Design

MARKET VALUATIONS

Uncirculated aluminum coins without any planchet defects are worth up to twice the market valuations given.

JAPANESE OCCUPATION

STANDARD COINAGE

Y# 1 5 LI

Bronze **Ruler:** Ta-t'ung **Obv:** Flag **Rev:** Value in floral sprays

Date	Mintage	VG	F	VF	XF	Unc
TT 2(1933)	—	16.00	40.00	70.00	100	200
TT 3(1934)	—	3.00	8.00	18.00	30.00	60.00

Y# 5 5 LI

Bronze **Ruler:** K'ang-te **Obv:** Character Yuan for "first", flag **Rev:** Value in floral sprays

Date	Mintage	VG	F	VF	XF	Unc
KT 1(1934)	—	2.50	6.00	15.00	20.00	50.00
KT 2(1935)	—	2.50	6.00	15.00	20.00	50.00
KT 3(1936)	—	12.00	27.50	42.50	60.00	110
KT 4(1937)	—	3.00	8.00	20.00	25.00	55.00
KT 6(1939)	—	75.00	150	200	275	375

Y# 2 FEN

5.0100 g., Bronze, 23.97 mm. **Ruler:** Ta-t'ung **Obv:** Flag **Rev:** Value in floral sprays

Date	Mintage	VG	F	VF	XF	Unc
TT 2(1933)	—	1.50	4.00	8.00	16.00	50.00
TT 3(1934)	—	1.25	3.00	6.00	10.00	40.00

Y# 6 FEN

Bronze **Ruler:** K'ang-te **Obv:** Character Yuan for "first", flag **Rev:** Value in floral sprays

Date	Mintage	VG	F	VF	XF	Unc
KT 1(1934)	—	0.80	2.00	6.00	12.00	30.00
KT 2(1935)	—	0.80	2.00	6.00	10.00	20.00
KT 3(1936)	—	0.80	2.00	6.00	10.00	20.00
KT 4(1937)	—	0.80	2.00	6.00	10.00	20.00
KT 5(1938)	—	0.80	2.00	6.00	10.00	20.00
KT 6(1939)	—	0.80	2.00	6.00	12.00	30.00

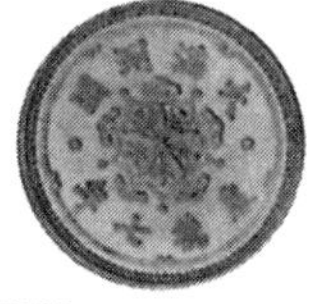

Y# 9 FEN

Aluminum, 19 mm. **Ruler:** K'ang-te **Obv:** National symbol **Rev:** Value in floral wreath

Date	Mintage	VG	F	VF	XF	Unc
KT 6(1939)	—	0.30	0.80	1.50	4.00	10.00
KT 7(1940)	—	0.30	0.80	1.50	4.00	10.00
KT 8(1941)	—	0.30	0.80	1.50	4.00	10.00
KT 9(1942)	—	0.30	0.80	1.50	4.00	10.00
KT 10(1943)	—	0.30	0.80	1.50	4.00	10.00

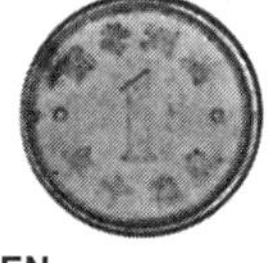

Y# 13 FEN

Aluminum **Ruler:** K'ang-te **Obv:** Legend around large "1" **Rev:** Floral wreath

Date	Mintage	VG	F	VF	XF	Unc
KT 10(1943)	—	0.70	1.50	4.00	10.00	20.00
KT 11(1944)	—	0.70	1.50	4.00	10.00	20.00

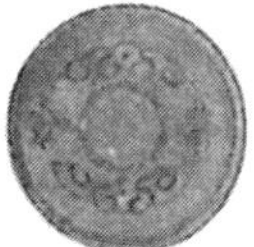

Y# 13a FEN

Red Fiber **Ruler:** K'ang-te **Obv:** Legend around large "1" **Rev:** Floral wreath

Date	Mintage	Good	VG	F	VF	XF
KT 12(1945)	—	4.00	6.00	9.00	18.00	30.00

Y# 13a.1 FEN

Brown Fiber **Ruler:** K'ang-te **Obv:** Legend around large "1" **Rev:** Floral wreath

Date	Mintage	Good	VG	F	VF	XF
KT 12(1945)	—	4.00	6.00	14.00	30.00	40.00

Y# 3 5 FEN

3.5000 g., Copper-Nickel **Ruler:** Ta-t'ung **Obv:** Lotus flower **Rev:** Pearl above value between facing dragons

Date	Mintage	VG	F	VF	XF	Unc
TT 2(1933)	—	0.70	1.50	4.00	10.00	30.00
TT 3(1934)	—	0.30	0.80	2.00	4.00	20.00

Y# 7 5 FEN

Copper-Nickel **Ruler:** K'ang-te **Rev:** Pearl above value between facing dragons

Date	Mintage	VG	F	VF	XF	Unc
KT 1(1934)	—	0.50	1.25	3.00	6.00	12.00
Note: Character Yuan for "first".						
KT 2(1935)	—	0.50	1.25	3.00	6.00	12.00
KT 3(1936)	—	0.50	1.25	3.00	6.00	12.00

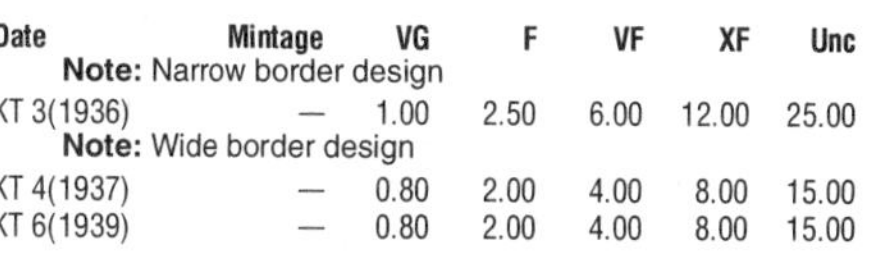

Date	Mintage	VG	F	VF	XF	Unc
Note: Narrow border design						
KT 3(1936)	—	1.00	2.50	6.00	12.00	25.00
Note: Wide border design						
KT 4(1937)	—	0.80	2.00	4.00	8.00	15.00
KT 6(1939)	—	0.80	2.00	4.00	8.00	15.00

Y# 11 5 FEN

Aluminum **Ruler:** K'ang-te **Obv:** Legend around large "5" **Rev:** National symbol above value in floral sprays

Date	Mintage	VG	F	VF	XF	Unc
KT 7 (1940)	—	0.50	1.25	3.00	6.00	12.00
KT 8 (1941)	—	0.30	0.80	1.50	4.00	8.00
KT 9 (1942)	—	0.30	0.80	1.50	4.00	8.00
KT 10 (1943)	—	0.30	0.80	1.50	4.00	8.00

Y# A13 5 FEN

Aluminum **Ruler:** K'ang-te **Obv:** Legend around small "5" **Rev:** Wreath

Date	Mintage	VG	F	VF	XF	Unc
KT 10 (1943)	—	0.80	2.00	5.00	10.00	25.00
KT 11 (1944)	—	0.80	2.00	5.00	10.00	25.00

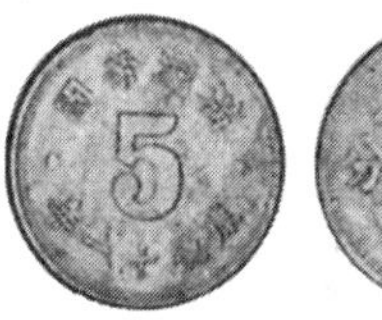

Y# A13a 5 FEN

Red Fiber **Ruler:** K'ang-te **Obv:** Legend around small "5" **Rev:** Wreath

Date	Mintage	VG	F	VF	XF	Unc
KT 11 (1944)	—	5.00	9.00	18.00	30.00	—
KT 12 (1945)	—	85.00	115	150	—	—

Y# A13a.1 5 FEN

Brown Fiber **Ruler:** K'ang-te **Obv:** Legend around small "5" **Rev:** Floral wreath

Date	Mintage	VG	F	VF	XF	Unc
KT 11 (1944)	—	10.00	20.00	30.00	50.00	—

Y# 4 CHIAO (10 Fen)

Copper-Nickel **Ruler:** Ta-t'ung **Obv:** Lotus flower **Rev:** Pearl above value between facing dragons

Date	Mintage	VG	F	VF	XF	Unc
TT 2 (1933)	—	1.25	3.00	6.00	14.00	30.00
TT 3 (1934)	—	0.60	1.50	4.00	8.00	25.00

Y# 8 CHIAO (10 Fen)

Copper-Nickel **Ruler:** K'ang-te **Rev:** Pearl above value between facing dragons

Date	Mintage	VG	F	VF	XF	Unc
KT 1 (1934)	—	0.60	1.50	4.00	6.00	16.00
Note: Character Yuan for "first".						
KT 2 (1935)	—	0.60	1.50	4.00	6.00	16.00
KT 5 (1938)	—	0.60	1.50	4.00	6.00	16.00
KT 6 (1939)	—	0.60	1.50	4.00	6.00	16.00
KT 6 (1939) Proof	—	—	—	—	—	—

Y# 10 CHIAO (10 Fen)

Copper-Nickel **Ruler:** K'ang-te **Obv:** Dragon head facing **Rev:** National symbol above value in floral sprays

Date	Mintage	VG	F	VF	XF	Unc
KT 7 (1940)	—	4.00	6.00	10.00	20.00	50.00

Y# 12 CHIAO (10 Fen)

Aluminum **Ruler:** K'ang-te **Obv:** Legend around "10" on "Fundo" weight outline **Rev:** National symbol above value in floral sprays

Date	Mintage	VG	F	VF	XF	Unc
KT 7 (1940)	—	0.70	1.50	4.00	6.00	16.00
KT 8 (1941)	—	0.70	1.50	4.00	6.00	16.00
KT 9 (1942)	—	0.70	1.50	4.00	6.00	16.00
KT 10 (1943)	—	115	275	400	500	600

Y# 14 CHIAO (10 Fen)

Aluminum **Ruler:** K'ang-te **Rev:** Legend around large "10"

Date	Mintage	VG	F	VF	XF	Unc
KT 10 (1943)	—	1.25	3.00	6.00	10.00	25.00

MENG CHIANG

As Japanese troops moved into North China in 1937, the political situation became fluid in several provinces bordering on Manchoukuo, which were sometimes referred to as Inner Mongolia. On September 27, 1937, the Chanan Bank was established. As the situation became more settled the Japanese effected the merger of two local banks with the Bank of Chanan under a new title, Meng Chiang (Mongolian Borderlands or Mongol Territory) Bank. The Meng Chiang Bank was organized on November 27 and opened on December 1, 1937, with headquarters in Kalgan (Zhangjiakou) and branch offices in about a dozen locations throughout the region. Its notes were declared the exclusive currency for the area. The bank closed at the end of the war.

JAPANESE OCCUPATION

STANDARD COINAGE

Y# 521 5 CHIAO

Copper-Nickel **Obv:** Legend in floral design **Rev:** Value in facing dragons

Date	Mintage	VG	F	VF	XF	Unc
27(1938)	—	1.75	3.50	6.50	12.00	28.00

PROVISIONAL GOVT. OF CHINA

In late 1937 the Japanese North China Expeditionary Army established the "Provisional Government of China" at Peking (Beijing).

FEDERAL RESERVE BANK

The Federal Reserve Bank of China was opened in 1938 by Japanese military authorities in Peking (Beijing). It was the puppet financial agency of the Japanese in northeast China. The puppet bank issued both coins and currency, but in modest amounts.

JAPANESE OCCUPATION

STANDARD COINAGE

Y# 523 FEN

Aluminum **Issuer:** Federal Reserve Bank **Obv:** Legend around FR Bank symbol **Rev:** Temple of Heaven

Date	Mintage	VG	F	VF	XF	Unc
30 (1941)	—	0.20	0.50	1.00	2.50	7.00
31 (1942)	—	0.20	0.50	1.00	2.00	6.00
32 (1943)	—	1.25	3.00	6.00	10.00	30.00

Y# 524 5 FEN

Aluminum **Issuer:** Federal Reserve Bank **Obv:** Legend around FR Bank symbol **Rev:** Temple of Heaven **Note:** The 5 Fen pieces were struck on thick (1 gram) and thin (.8 gram) planchets.

Date	Mintage	VG	F	VF	XF	Unc
30 (1941)	—	0.35	0.75	2.00	4.00	10.00
31 (1942)	—	0.40	1.00	2.50	5.00	15.00
32 (1943)	—	1.50	3.50	7.50	15.00	45.00

Y# 525 CHIAO

Aluminum, 22 mm. **Issuer:** Federal Reserve Bank **Obv:** Legend around FR Bank symbol **Rev:** Temple of Heaven **Note:** The 1 Chiao pieces were struck on thick (1.5 gram), thin (1.2 gram), and very thin (1.0 gram) planchets.

Date	Mintage	VG	F	VF	XF	Unc
30 (1941)	—	0.15	0.40	1.00	2.00	6.00
31 (1942)	—	0.15	0.40	1.00	2.00	6.00
32 (1943)	—	0.60	1.50	3.00	6.50	20.00

The Peoples Republic of China, located in eastern Asia, has an area of 3,696,100 sq. mi. (9,596,960 sq. km.) (including Manchuria and Tibet) and a population of *1.20 billion. Capital: Peking (Beijing). The economy is based on agriculture, mining, and manufacturing. Textiles, clothing, metal ores, tea and rice are exported.

China's ancient civilization began in east-central Henan's Huayang county, 2800-2300 B.C. The warring feudal states comprising early China were first united under Emperor Ch'in Shih (246-210 B.C.) who gave China its name and first central government. Subsequent dynasties alternated brilliant cultural achievements with internal disorder until the Empire was brought down by the revolution of 1911, and the Republic of China installed in its place. Chinese culture attained a pre-eminence in art, literature and philosophy, but a traditional backwardness in industry and administration ill prepared China for the demands of 19th century Western expansionism which exposed it to military and political humiliations, and mandated a drastic revision of political practice in order to secure an accommodation with the modern world.

The Republic of 1911 barely survived the stress of World War I, and was subsequently all but shattered by the rise of nationalism and the emergence of the Chinese Communist movement. Moscow, which practiced a policy of cooperation between Communists and other parties in movements for national liberation, sought to establish an entente between the Chinese Communist Party and the Kuomintang ('National Peoples Party') of Sun Yat-sen. The ensuing cooperation was based on little more than the hope each had of using the other.

An increasingly uneasy association between the Kuomintang and the Chinese Communist Party developed and continued until April 12, 1927, when Chiang Kai-shek, Sun Yat-sen's political heir, instituted a bloody purge to stamp out the Communists within the Kuomintang and the government and virtually paralyzed their ranks throughout China. Some time after the mid-1927 purges, the Chinese Communist Party turned to armed force to resist Chiang Kai-shek and during the period of 1930-34 acquired control over large parts of Kiangsi (Jiangxi), Fukien (Fujian), Hunan and Hupeh (Hubei). The Nationalist Nanking government responded with a series of campaigns against the soviet power bases and, by October of 1934, succeeded in driving the remnants of the Communist army to a refuge in Shensi (Shaanxi) Province. There the Communists reorganized under the leadership of Mao Tse-tung, defeated the Nationalist forces, and on Sept. 21, 1949, established the Peoples Republic of China. Thereafter relations between Russia and Communist China steadily deteriorated until 1958, when China emerged as an independent center of Communist power.

MONETARY SYSTEM

After 1949

10 Fen (Cents) = 1 Jiao

10 Jiao = 1 Renminbi Yuan

MINT MARKS

(b) - Beijing (Peking)

(s) - Shanghai

(y) - Shenyang (Mukden)

OBVERSE LEGENDS

ZHONGHUA RENMIN GONGHEGUO

(Peoples Republic of China)

ZHONGGUO RENMIN YINHANG

(Peoples Bank of China)

PEOPLES REPUBLIC

STANDARD COINAGE

KM# 1 FEN

0.6500 g., Aluminum, 18 mm. **Obv:** National emblem **Rev:** Denomination above wreath, date below **Note:** Previous #Y 1.

Date	Mintage	F	VF	XF	Unc	BU
1955	—	0.20	0.50	1.50	5.00	—
1956	—	0.40	1.00	2.50	7.50	—
1957	—	0.60	1.50	3.50	10.00	—
1958	—	0.10	0.25	0.75	2.50	—
1959	—	0.10	0.25	0.75	2.50	—
1961	—	0.10	0.25	0.75	2.50	—
1963	—	0.10	0.25	0.50	1.50	—
1964	—	0.10	0.25	0.50	1.00	—
1971	—	0.10	0.25	0.50	1.00	—
1972	—	0.10	0.25	0.50	1.00	—
1973	—	0.10	0.25	0.50	1.50	—
1974	—	0.10	0.25	0.50	1.00	—
1975	500,000	0.10	0.25	0.50	1.00	—
1976	—	—	0.10	0.25	0.50	—
1977	—	—	0.10	0.25	0.50	—
1978	—	—	0.10	0.25	0.50	—
1979	—	—	0.25	1.00	5.00	—
1980	—	—	0.10	0.25	0.50	—
1980 Proof	—	Value: 1.00				
1981	—	—	0.10	0.25	0.50	—
1981 Proof	—	Value: 1.00				
1982	—	—	—	0.25	0.50	—
1982 Proof	—	Value: 1.00				
1983	2,412,000	—	—	0.10	0.25	—
1983 Proof	—	Value: 1.00				
1984	3,283,000	—	—	0.10	0.25	—
1984 Proof	—	Value: 1.00				
1985	—	—	—	0.10	0.25	—
1985 Proof	—	Value: 1.00				
1986	—	—	—	0.10	0.25	—
1986 Proof	—	Value: 1.00				
1987	—	—	—	0.10	0.25	—
1991	—	—	—	0.10	0.25	—
1991 Proof	—	Value: 1.00				
1992	—	—	—	0.10	0.25	—
1992 Proof	—	Value: 1.00				
1993	—	—	—	—	0.75	—
Note: In sets only						
1993 Proof	—	Value: 1.00				
1994	—	—	—	—	0.75	—
Note: In sets only						
1994 Proof	—	Value: 1.00				
1995	—	—	—	—	0.75	—

Date	Mintage	F	VF	XF	Unc	BU
Note: In sets only						
1995 Proof	—	Value: 1.00				
1996	—	—	—	—	0.75	—
Note: In sets only						
1996 Proof	—	Value: 1.00				
1997	—	—	—	0.10	0.25	—

KM# 2 2 FEN

1.0500 g., Aluminum, 21 mm. **Obv:** National emblem **Rev:** Denomination above wreath, date below **Note:** Previous #Y 2.

Date	Mintage	F	VF	XF	Unc	BU
1956	—	0.10	0.25	0.75	1.50	—
1959	—	0.20	0.50	1.00	4.00	—
1960	—	0.20	0.50	1.00	4.00	—
1961	—	0.10	0.25	0.75	1.50	—
1962	—	0.10	0.25	0.75	1.50	—
1963	—	0.10	0.25	0.75	1.50	—
1964	—	0.10	0.25	0.50	1.25	—
1974	—	0.10	0.25	0.50	1.50	—
1975	—	0.10	0.25	0.50	1.00	—
1976	—	0.10	0.25	0.50	1.00	—
1977	360,000	0.10	0.25	0.50	0.75	—
1978	—	0.10	0.20	0.40	0.60	—
1979	—	0.10	0.20	0.40	0.60	—
1980	—	0.10	0.20	0.40	0.60	—
1980 Proof	—	Value: 1.00				
1981	—	0.10	0.20	0.40	0.60	—
1981 Proof	—	Value: 1.00				
1982	—	0.10	0.20	0.40	0.60	—
1982 Proof	—	Value: 1.00				
1983	1,790,000	—	0.10	0.20	0.35	—
1983 Proof	—	Value: 1.00				
1984	1,963,000	—	0.10	0.20	0.35	—
1984 Proof	—	Value: 1.00				
1985	—	—	0.10	0.20	0.35	—
1985 Proof	—	Value: 1.00				
1986	—	—	0.15	0.35	0.75	—
1986 Proof	—	Value: 1.00				
1987	—	—	0.10	0.20	0.35	—
1988	—	—	0.10	0.20	0.35	—
1989	—	—	0.10	0.20	0.35	—
1990	—	—	0.10	0.20	0.35	—
1991	—	—	0.10	0.20	0.35	—
1991 Proof	—	Value: 1.00				
1992	—	—	0.10	0.20	0.35	—
1992 Proof	—	Value: 1.00				
1993	—	—	—	—	0.75	—
Note: In sets only						
1993 Proof	—	Value: 1.00				
1994	—	—	—	—	0.75	—
Note: In sets only						
1994 Proof	—	Value: 1.00				
1995	—	—	—	—	0.75	—
Note: In sets only						
1995 Proof	—	Value: 1.00				
1996	—	—	—	—	0.75	—
Note: In sets only						
1996 Proof	—	Value: 1.00				

KM# 3 5 FEN

1.6000 g., Aluminum, 24 mm. **Obv:** National emblem **Rev:** Denomination above wreath, date below **Note:** Previous #Y 3.

Date	Mintage	F	VF	XF	Unc	BU
1955	—	0.30	0.75	2.00	10.00	—
1956	—	0.15	0.35	0.75	2.00	—
1957	—	0.15	0.35	0.75	2.50	—
1974	—	0.15	0.25	0.50	1.50	—
1975	—	0.15	0.25	0.50	1.50	—
1976	350,000	0.15	0.25	0.50	0.75	—
1979	—	0.15	0.50	1.25	10.00	—
1980	—	0.15	0.25	0.50	0.75	—
1980 Proof	—	Value: 1.00				
1981	—	0.15	0.25	0.50	0.75	—
1981 Proof	—	Value: 1.00				
1982	—	0.15	0.25	0.50	0.75	—
1982 Proof	—	Value: 1.00				
1983	484,000	—	0.15	0.25	0.45	—
1983 Proof	—	Value: 1.00				
1984	600,000	—	0.15	0.25	0.45	—
1984 Proof	—	Value: 1.00				
1985	—	—	0.15	0.25	0.45	—
1985 Proof	—	Value: 1.00				
1986	—	—	0.15	0.25	0.45	—
1986 Proof	—	Value: 1.00				
1987	—	—	0.15	0.25	0.45	—
1988	—	—	0.15	0.25	0.45	—
1989	—	—	0.15	0.25	0.45	—
1990	—	—	0.15	0.25	0.45	—
1991	—	—	0.15	0.25	0.45	—
1991 Proof	—	Value: 1.00				
1992	—	—	0.15	0.25	0.45	—
1992 Proof	—	Value: 1.00				
1993	—	—	—	—	0.75	—
Note: In sets only						
1993 Proof	—	Value: 1.00				
1994	—	—	—	—	0.75	—
Note: In sets only						
1994 Proof	—	Value: 1.00				
1995	—	—	—	—	0.75	—
Note: In sets only						
1995 Proof	—	Value: 1.00				
1996	—	—	—	—	0.75	—
Note: In sets only						
1996 Proof	—	Value: 1.00				

KM# 15 JIAO

2.6000 g., Copper-Zinc, 20 mm. **Obv:** National emblem **Rev:** Denomination above wreath, date below **Note:** Previous #Y 24.

Date	Mintage	F	VF	XF	Unc	BU
1980	—	—	—	—	0.50	—
1980 Proof	—	Value: 1.00				
1981	—	—	—	—	0.50	—
1981 Proof	—	Value: 1.00				
1982 Proof	—	Value: 1.00				
1983	3,100,000	—	—	—	0.50	—
1983 Proof	—	Value: 1.00				
1984	3,500,000	—	—	—	0.50	—
1984 Proof	—	Value: 1.00				
1985 Proof	—	Value: 1.00				
1985	—	—	—	—	0.50	—
1986 Proof	—	Value: 1.00				

KM# 155 JIAO

Brass **Series:** 6th National Games **Subject:** Gymnast **Obv:** Stylized torch divides date below **Rev:** Gymnast above date, denomination at left **Note:** Previous #Y 148.

Date	Mintage	F	VF	XF	Unc	BU
1987	10,570,000	—	—	1.00	2.00	3.00

KM# 156 JIAO

Brass **Series:** 6th National Games **Subject:** Soccer **Obv:** Stylized torch divides date below **Rev:** Soccer player divides date and denomination **Note:** Previous #Y 149.

Date	Mintage	F	VF	XF	Unc	BU
1987	Inc. above	—	—	1.00	2.00	3.00

KM# 157 JIAO

Brass **Series:** 6th National Games **Subject:** Volleyball **Obv:** Stylized torch divides date below **Rev:** Volleyball player, date below, denomination at right **Note:** Previous #Y 150.

Date	Mintage	F	VF	XF	Unc	BU
1987	Inc. above	—	—	1.00	2.00	3.00

KM# 335 JIAO

Aluminum, 22.5 mm. **Obv:** National emblem, date below **Rev:** Peony blossom, denomination at right **Note:** Previous Y # 328.

Date	Mintage	F	VF	XF	Unc	BU
1991	—	—	—	—	0.50	—
1991 Proof	—	Value: 1.00				
1992	—	—	—	—	0.50	—
1992 Proof	—	Value: 1.00				
1993	—	—	—	—	0.50	—
1993 Proof	—	Value: 1.00				
1994	—	—	—	—	0.50	—
1994 Proof	—	Value: 1.00				
1995	—	—	—	—	0.50	—
1995 Proof	—	Value: 1.00				
1996	—	—	—	—	0.50	—
1996 Proof	—	Value: 1.00				
1997	—	—	—	—	0.50	—
1998	—	—	—	—	0.50	—
1999	—	—	—	—	0.50	—
1999 Proof	—	Value: 1.00				

KM# 1210 JIAO

1.1200 g., Aluminum, 19 mm. **Obv:** Denomination, date below **Rev:** Orchid **Rev. Legend:** ZHONGGUA RENMIN YINHANG **Edge:** Plain **Note:** Previous Y # 1068.

Date	Mintage	F	VF	XF	Unc	BU
1999	—	—	—	—	0.50	—
2000	—	—	—	—	0.50	—
2001	—	—	—	—	0.50	—
2002	—	—	—	—	0.50	—
2003	—	—	—	—	0.50	—

KM# 16 2 JIAO

4.1500 g., Copper-Zinc, 23 mm. **Obv:** National emblem **Rev:** Denomination above wreath, date below **Note:** Previous #Y 25.

Date	Mintage	F	VF	XF	Unc	BU
1980	—	—	—	—	0.60	—
1980 Proof	—	Value: 1.25				
1981	—	—	—	—	0.60	—
1981 Proof	—	Value: 1.25				
1982 Proof	—	Value: 1.25				
1983	4,200,000	—	—	—	0.60	—
1983 Proof	—	Value: 1.25				
1984	2,500,000	—	—	—	0.60	—
1984 Proof	—	Value: 1.25				
1985 Proof	—	Value: 1.25				
1986 Proof	—	Value: 1.25				

KM# 17 5 JIAO

6.0000 g., Copper-Zinc, 26 mm. **Obv:** National emblem **Rev:** Denomination above wreath, date below **Note:** Previous #Y 26.

Date	Mintage	F	VF	XF	Unc	BU
1980	—	—	—	—	0.75	—
1980 Proof	—	Value: 1.50				
1981	—	—	—	—	0.75	—
1981 Proof	—	Value: 1.50				
1982 Proof	—	Value: 1.50				
1983	3,000,000	—	—	—	0.75	—
1983 Proof	—	Value: 1.50				
1984	3,500,000	—	—	—	0.75	—
1984 Proof	—	Value: 1.50				
1985	—	—	—	—	0.75	—
1985 Proof	—	Value: 1.50				
1986 Proof	—	Value: 1.50				

KM# 336 5 JIAO

3.8300 g., Brass, 20.5 mm. **Obv:** National emblem, date below **Rev:** Denomination above flowers **Edge:** Segmented reeding **Note:** Previous Y # 329.

Date	Mintage	F	VF	XF	Unc	BU
1991	—	—	—	—	1.00	—
1991 Proof	—	Value: 1.50				
1992	—	—	—	—	1.00	—
1992 Proof	—	Value: 1.50				
1993	—	—	—	—	1.00	—
1993 Proof	—	Value: 1.50				
1994	—	—	—	—	1.00	—
1994 Proof	—	Value: 1.50				
1995	—	—	—	—	1.00	—
1995 Proof	—	Value: 1.50				
1996	—	—	—	—	1.00	—
1996 Proof	—	Value: 1.50				
1997	—	—	—	—	1.00	—
1998	—	—	—	—	1.00	—
1999	—	—	—	—	1.00	—
2000	—	—	—	—	1.00	—
2001	—	—	—	—	1.00	—

KM# 1411 5 JIAO

3.8000 g., Brass, 20.5 mm. **Obv:** Denomination **Rev:** Flower **Rev. Legend:** ZHONGGUA RENMIN YINHANG **Edge:** Reeded and plain sections **Note:** Previous Y # 1106.

Date	Mintage	F	VF	XF	Unc	BU
2002	—	—	—	—	1.50	—
2003	—	—	—	—	1.50	—
2005	—	—	—	—	1.50	—

KM# 18 YUAN

9.3000 g., Copper-Nickel, 30 mm. **Obv:** National emblem, date below **Rev:** Great wall **Note:** Previous #Y 27.

Date	Mintage	F	VF	XF	Unc	BU
1980	—	—	—	—	2.00	—
1980 Proof	—	Value: 3.00				
1981	—	—	—	—	2.00	—
1981 Proof	—	Value: 3.00				
1982 Proof	—	Value: 3.00				
1983	3,100,000	—	—	—	2.00	—
1983 Proof	—	Value: 3.00				
1984	4,100,000	—	—	—	2.00	—
1984 Proof	—	Value: 3.00				
1985	—	—	—	—	2.00	—
1985 Proof	—	Value: 3.00				
1986 Proof	—	Value: 3.00				

KM# 104 YUAN

Copper-Nickel **Subject:** 35th Anniversary - Peoples Republic **Obv:** National emblem above buildings, dates below **Rev:** Republic figures **Note:** Previous #Y 85.

Date	Mintage	F	VF	XF	Unc	BU
ND(1984)	20,410,000	—	—	—	6.00	—
ND(1984) Proof	—	Value: 7.50				

KM# 105 YUAN

Copper-Nickel **Subject:** 35th Anniversary - Peoples Republic **Obv:** National emblem **Rev:** Dancers **Note:** Previous #Y 86.

Date	Mintage	F	VF	XF	Unc	BU
ND(1984)	Inc. above	—	—	—	6.00	—
ND(1984) Proof	—	Value: 7.50				

KM# 106 YUAN

Copper-Nickel **Subject:** 35th Anniversary - Peoples Republic **Obv:** National emblem above buildings, dates below **Rev:** Monument amid cranes in flight **Note:** Previous #Y 87.

Date	Mintage	F	VF	XF	Unc	BU
ND(1984)	Inc. above	—	—	—	6.00	—
ND(1984) Proof	—	Value: 7.50				

KM# 110 YUAN

Copper-Nickel **Subject:** 20th Anniversary - Tibet Autonomous Region **Obv:** National emblem, date below **Rev:** Potala Palace **Note:** Previous #Y 96.

Date	Mintage	F	VF	XF	Unc	BU
1985	2,612,000	—	—	3.00	8.50	—
1985 Proof	10,000	Value: 12.00				

KM# 111 YUAN

Copper-Nickel **Subject:** 30th Anniversary - Xinjiang Autonomous Region **Note:** Previous #Y 109.

Date	Mintage	F	VF	XF	Unc	BU
1985	4,500,000	—	—	2.00	6.00	—
1985 Proof	10,000	Value: 12.00				

KM# 130 YUAN

Copper-Nickel **Subject:** Year of Peace **Obv:** National emblem, date below **Rev:** Seated woman with doves **Note:** Previous #Y 151.

Date	Mintage	F	VF	XF	Unc	BU
1986	27,048,000	—	—	—	5.00	—

KM# 158 YUAN

Copper-Nickel **Subject:** 40th Anniversary - Mongolian Autonomous Region **Obv:** Building, date below **Rev:** Riders, sheep below, denomination at left **Note:** Previous #Y 140.

Date	Mintage	F	VF	XF	Unc	BU
1987	9,054,000	—	—	2.00	6.00	—

KM# 180 YUAN

Copper-Nickel **Subject:** 30th Anniversary - Kwangsi Autonomous Region **Obv:** Mountains and water, inscription and date below **Rev:** Native dancers, denomination at right, two dates upper left **Note:** Previous #Y 198.

Date	Mintage	F	VF	XF	Unc	BU
1988	4,072,000	—	—	—	7.00	—

KM# 181 YUAN

Copper-Nickel **Subject:** 30th Anniversary - Ningxia Autonomous Region **Rev:** Women with plants, denomination at right, within circle, dates below **Note:** Previous #Y 211.

Date	Mintage	F	VF	XF	Unc	BU
1988	1,560,000	—	—	—	15.00	—

KM# 182 YUAN

Copper-Nickel **Subject:** 40th Anniversary - Peoples Bank **Obv:** National emblem, date below **Rev:** Building divides dates **Note:** Previous #Y 212.

Date	Mintage	F	VF	XF	Unc	BU
1988	2,068,000	—	—	8.00	50.00	—

KM# 220 YUAN

Copper-Nickel **Subject:** 40th Anniversary - Peoples Republic **Obv:** National emblem above buildings, date below **Rev:** Music score divides artistic year and dates **Note:** Previous Y# 204.

Date	Mintage	F	VF	XF	Unc	BU
1989	2,000,000	—	—	—	4.00	—

KM# 266 YUAN

Nickel Clad Steel **Series:** XI Asian Games **Obv:** Building, Roman numerals above, inscription and date below **Rev:** Sword Dancer, panda dancer at left, denomination at right **Note:** Previous Y# 264.

Date	Mintage	F	VF	XF	Unc	BU
1990	25,608,000	—	—	—	4.00	—

KM# 264 YUAN

Nickel Clad Steel **Series:** 11th Asian Games - Beijing 1990 **Obv:** Building, Roman numeral above, inscription and date below **Rev:** Female archer, denomination above, panda archer below **Note:** Previous # Y 256.

Date	Mintage	F	VF	XF	Unc	BU
1990	Inc. above	—	—	—	4.00	—

KM# 338 YUAN

Nickel Clad Steel, 25 mm. **Subject:** Planting Trees Festival **Rev:** Head of young woman **Note:** Previous Y# 279.

Date	Mintage	F	VF	XF	Unc	BU
1991	10,000,000	—	—	—	2.25	—

KM# 339 YUAN

Nickel Clad Steel, 25 mm. **Subject:** Planting Trees Festival **Obv:** Trees, inscription, and numbers within circle **Rev:** Monument on globe divides birds in flight, date below **Note:** Previous Y# 280.

Date	Mintage	F	VF	XF	Unc	BU
1991	10,000,000	—	—	—	2.25	—

KM# 340 YUAN

Nickel Clad Steel, 25 mm. **Subject:** Planting Trees Festival **Obv:** Trees,inscription, and numbers within circle **Rev:** Seedling, date below **Note:** Previous Y# 281.

Date	Mintage	F	VF	XF	Unc	BU
1991	10,000,000	—	—	—	2.25	—

KM# 341 YUAN

5.9100 g., Nickel Plated Steel, 25 mm. **Subject:** 70th Anniversary of the Founding of the Chinese Communist Party **Obv:** National emblem, date below **Rev:** House of Shanghai **Note:** Previous Y# 284.

Date	Mintage	F	VF	XF	Unc	BU
1991	30,000,000	—	—	—	2.25	—

KM# 342 YUAN

5.8100 g., Nickel Plated Steel, 25 mm. **Subject:** 70th Anniversary of the Founding of the Chinese Communist Party **Rev:** House in Tsun-i (Zunyi), Kweichow Province **Note:** Previous Y# 285.

Date	Mintage	F	VF	XF	Unc	BU
1991	30,000,000	—	—	—	2.25	—

KM# 343 YUAN

5.8400 g., Nickel Plated Steel, 25 mm. **Subject:** 70th Anniversary of the Founding of the Chinese Communist Party - Meeting in Tiananmen Square, 1978 **Obv:** National emblem, date below **Rev:** Flags, monument, and building **Note:** Previous Y# 286.

Date	Mintage	F	VF	XF	Unc	BU
1991	30,000,000	—	—	—	2.25	—

KM# 344 YUAN

Nickel Plated Steel, 25 mm. **Subject:** 1st Women's World Football Cup **Obv:** Conjoined soccer balls, artistic woman design on top **Rev:** Goalie, date at right **Note:** Previous Y# 316.

Date	Mintage	F	VF	XF	Unc	BU
1991	10,000,000	—	—	—	2.50	—

KM# 345 YUAN

Nickel Plated Steel, 25 mm. **Subject:** 1st Women's World Football Cup **Obv:** Conjoined soccer balls, artistic woman design on top **Rev:** Player, soccer ball background, date at lower right **Note:** Previous Y# 317.

Date	Mintage	F	VF	XF	Unc	BU
1991	10,000,000	—	—	—	2.50	—

KM# 337 YUAN

Nickel Clad Steel, 25 mm. **Obv:** National emblem, date below **Rev:** Denomination above flowers **Note:** Previous Y # 330.

Date	Mintage	F	VF	XF	Unc	BU
1991	—	—	—	—	1.50	—
1991 Proof	—	Value: 2.50				
1992	—	—	—	—	1.50	—
1992 Proof	—	Value: 2.50				
1993	—	—	—	—	1.50	—
1993 Proof	—	Value: 2.50				
1994	—	—	—	—	1.50	—
1994 Proof	—	Value: 2.50				
1995	—	—	—	—	1.50	—
1995 Proof	—	Value: 2.50				
1996	—	—	—	—	1.50	—
1996 Proof	—	Value: 2.50				
1997	—	—	—	—	1.50	—
1997 Proof	—	Value: 2.50				
1998	—	—	—	—	1.50	—

Date	Mintage	F	VF	XF	Unc	BU
1998 Proof	—	Value: 2.50				
1999	—	—	—	—	1.50	—
1999 Proof	—	Value: 2.50				

KM# 390 YUAN

Nickel Clad Steel, 25 mm. **Subject:** 10th Anniversary - Constitution **Obv:** National emblem, date below **Rev:** Constitution, denomination at right, dates and flower below **Note:** Previous Y # 364.

Date	Mintage	F	VF	XF	Unc	BU
1992	10,000,000	—	—	—	2.50	—

KM# 470 YUAN

Nickel Clad Steel, 25 mm. **Subject:** 100th Birthday of Soong Ching Ling - Second Wife of Sun Yat-sen **Obv:** Building, date below **Rev:** Bust of Ching-ling, 1892-1981, half left, revolutionary stateswoman **Note:** Previous Y # 365.

Date	Mintage	F	VF	XF	Unc	BU
1993	10,448,000	—	—	—	3.50	—
1993 Proof	—	Value: 5.00				

KM# 471 YUAN

Nickel Clad Steel, 25 mm. **Subject:** 100th Anniversary - Birth of Chairman Mao **Obv:** Buildings and mountains, date below **Rev:** Mao's head, left **Note:** Previous Y # 399.

Date	Mintage	F	VF	XF	Unc	BU
1993	20,000,000	—	—	—	3.50	—
1993 Prooflike	—	—	—	—	5.00	—

KM# 610 YUAN

Nickel Clad Steel, 25 mm. **Series:** Children's Year **Subject:** Project Hope **Obv:** National emblem, date below **Rev:** Two children, denomination lower left **Note:** Previous Y # 455.

Date	Mintage	F	VF	XF	Unc	BU
1994	—	—	—	—	2.50	—

KM# 880 YUAN

6.0500 g., Nickel Plated Steel, 25 mm. **Obv:** Zhu De's home in Sichuan, date below **Rev:** Marshal Zhu De, 3/4 left **Edge:** Lettered **Edge Lettering:** "ZHONGGUO" twice **Mint:** Shanghai **Note:** Previous Y # 1124.

Date	Mintage	F	VF	XF	Unc	BU
1996	580,000	—	—	—	3.50	—

KM# 1212 YUAN
6.1000 g., Nickel Plated Steel, 24.9 mm. **Obv:** Denomination, date below **Rev:** Chrysanthemum **Rev. Legend:** ZHONGGUA RENMIN YINHANG **Edge:** "RMB" three times **Note:** Previous Y # 1069.

Date	Mintage	F	VF	XF	Unc	BU
1999	—	—	—	—	1.50	—
2000	—	—	—	—	1.50	—
2001	—	—	—	—	2.00	—
2002	—	—	—	—	2.00	—
2003	—	—	—	—	2.00	—
2004	—	—	—	—	2.00	—
2006	—	—	—	—	2.00	—

KM# 1465 YUAN
6.8500 g., Brass, 25 mm. **Obv:** Value **Rev:** Celebrating child and ram **Edge:** Lettered **Edge Lettering:** "R M B" three times **Mint:** Shanghai **Note:** Previous Y # 1125.

Date	Mintage	F	VF	XF	Unc	BU
2003	—	—	—	—	5.00	—

KM# 1574 YUAN
5.9600 g., Nickel Clad Steel, 25 mm. **Obv:** Building **Rev:** Bust of Chenyun **Edge:** Lettered **Note:** Previous Y # 1208.

Date	Mintage	F	VF	XF	Unc	BU
2005	—	—	—	—	3.50	—

KM# 1775 YUAN
6.7500 g., Brass, 25 mm. **Subject:** 29th Olympics **Obv:** Stylized Olympics logo **Rev:** Cartoon swimmer **Edge:** Reeded **Mint:** Shenyang **Note:** Previous Y # 1256.

Date	Mintage	F	VF	XF	Unc	BU
2008 (2006)(y)	—	—	—	—	—	6.00

KM# 1776 YUAN
6.7500 g., Brass, 25 mm. **Subject:** 29th Olympics **Obv:** Stylized Olympics logo **Rev:** Cartoon Weight Lifter **Edge:** Reeded **Mint:** Shanghai **Note:** Previous Y # 1257.

Date	Mintage	F	VF	XF	Unc	BU
2008 (2006)	—	—	—	—	—	6.00

KM# 1363 5 YUAN
12.8000 g., Brass, 30 mm. **Subject:** 50th Anniversary - Chinese Occupation of Tibet **Obv:** National emblem **Rev:** Potala Palace, value and two dancers **Edge:** Reeded **Mint:** Shenyang **Note:** Previous Y # 1126.

Date	Mintage	F	VF	XF	Unc	BU
2001(y)	10,000,000	—	—	—	7.00	—

KM# 1461 5 YUAN
12.8000 g., Brass, 30 mm. **Obv:** National emblem **Rev:** Chaotian Temple in Beigang Taiwan **Edge:** Reeded **Mint:** Shenyang **Note:** Previous Y # 1127.

Date	Mintage	F	VF	XF	Unc	BU
2003	10,000,000	—	—	—	7.00	—

KM# 1462 5 YUAN
12.8000 g., Brass, 30 mm. **Obv:** National emblem **Rev:** Chikan Tower on Treasure Island Taiwan **Edge:** Reeded **Mint:** Shenyang **Note:** Previous Y # 1128.

Date	Mintage	F	VF	XF	Unc	BU
2003(y)	10,000,000	—	—	—	7.00	—

KM# 1463 5 YUAN
12.8000 g., Brass, 30 mm. **Subject:** Chaotian Temple in Beijing **Obv:** State emblem **Rev:** Buildings **Edge:** Reeded **Note:** Previous Y # 1230.

Date	Mintage	F	VF	XF	Unc	BU
2003	10,000,000	—	—	—	7.00	—

KM# 1526 5 YUAN
12.7000 g., Brass, 30 mm. **Obv:** National emblem **Rev:** Peking Man bust and discovery site view **Edge:** Reeded **Note:** Previous Y # 1201.

Date	Mintage	F	VF	XF	Unc	BU
2004	6,000,000	—	—	—	6.00	—

KM# 1527 5 YUAN
12.7000 g., Brass, 30 mm. **Obv:** National emblem **Rev:** Pavillion and bridge **Edge:** Reeded **Note:** Previous Y # 1202.

Date	Mintage	F	VF	XF	Unc	BU
2004	6,000,000	—	—	—	6.00	—

KM# 1576 5 YUAN
12.9200 g., Brass, 30 mm. **Obv:** National emblem **Rev:** Lijiang building **Edge:** Reeded **Note:** Previous Y # 1209.

Date	Mintage	F	VF	XF	Unc	BU
2005	—	—	—	—	6.00	—

KM# 1578 5 YUAN
12.9200 g., Brass, 30 mm. **Obv:** National emblem **Rev:** Green City Hall **Edge:** Reeded **Note:** Previous Y # 1210.

Date	Mintage	F	VF	XF	Unc	BU
2005	—	—	—	—	6.00	—

KM# 1577 5 YUAN
12.8000 g., Brass, 30 mm. **Subject:** "Taiwan" **Obv:** State emblem **Rev:** Tower and terrace **Edge:** Reeded **Note:** Previous Y # 1231.

Date	Mintage	F	VF	XF	Unc	BU
2005	—	—	—	—	6.00	—

KM# 1300 10 YUAN
7.8000 g., Bi-Metallic Copper-Nickel center in Brass ring, 25.5 mm. **Obv:** Rocket and city view above wheel **Rev:** Number two and eye above map of China **Edge:** Segmented reeding **Note:** Previous Y # 1123.

Date	Mintage	F	VF	XF	Unc	BU
2000	—	—	—	—	8.00	—

TAIWAN

REPUBLIC

STANDARD COINAGE

Y# 531 CHIAO
Bronze **Obv:** Bust of Sun Yat-sen left **Rev:** Map, symbols on sides

Date	Mintage	F	VF	XF	Unc	BU
38(1949)	157,600,000	0.15	0.30	1.00	4.00	5.00

Y# 533 CHIAO

1.1400 g., Aluminum, 19 mm. **Obv:** Bust of Sun Yat-sen left **Rev:** Map, symbols on sides **Edge:** Reeded

Date	Mintage	F	VF	XF	Unc	BU
44(1955)	583,980,000	—	0.10	0.15	1.00	1.50

Y# 545 CHIAO

1.1000 g., Aluminum **Obv:** Single-heart orchid **Rev:** Two Chinese symbols

Date	Mintage	F	VF	XF	Unc	BU
56(1967)	89,999,000	—	0.10	0.15	0.75	1.00
59(1970)	30,000,000	—	0.10	0.25	1.00	1.25
60(1971)	19,925,000	—	0.20	0.40	1.50	2.00
61(1972)	11,141,000	0.10	0.40	0.60	2.00	2.50
62(1973)	111,400,000	—	—	0.10	0.75	1.00
63(1974)	71,930,000	—	0.10	0.25	1.00	1.25

Y# 534 2 CHIAO

1.8000 g., Aluminum, 22.9 mm. **Obv:** Bust of Sun Yat-sen left **Rev:** Map, symbols at sides **Edge:** Smooth

Date	Mintage	F	VF	XF	Unc	BU
39(1950)	327,495,000	—	0.10	0.50	3.00	3.50

Y# 532 5 CHIAO

5.0000 g., 0.7200 Silver 0.1157 oz. ASW **Obv:** Bust of Sun Yat-sen left **Rev:** Map, symbols at sides

Date	Mintage	F	VF	XF	Unc	BU
38(1949)	—	1.85	2.25	3.75	5.50	7.00

Y# 535 5 CHIAO

Brass, 27 mm. **Obv:** Bust of Sun Yat-sen left **Rev:** Map, symbols at sides **Edge:** Reeded

Date	Mintage	F	VF	XF	Unc	BU
43(1954)	279,624,000	—	0.10	0.25	1.00	1.50

Y# 546 5 CHIAO

3.4000 g., Brass, 22.5 mm. **Obv:** Mayling orchid **Edge:** Reeded

Date	Mintage	F	VF	XF	Unc	BU
56(1967)	109,999,000	—	0.10	0.15	0.50	0.75
59(1970)	6,010,000	0.15	0.30	0.60	1.25	1.50
60(1971)	4,434,000	0.20	0.40	0.80	1.50	1.75
61(1972)	21,171,000	—	0.10	0.20	1.00	1.25
62(1973)	88,840,000	—	0.10	0.20	1.00	1.25
69(1980)	3,972,000	—	0.10	0.20	1.00	1.25
70(1981)	100,000,000	—	0.10	0.20	1.00	1.25

Y# 550 1/2 YUAN

3.0000 g., Bronze, 18 mm. **Obv:** Orchid **Rev:** Value and Chinese symbols **Edge:** Plain

Date	Mintage	F	VF	XF	Unc	BU
70(1981)	103,800,000	—	0.10	0.20	1.00	1.25
70(1981) Proof	—	Value: 10.00				
75(1986)	22,000,000	—	0.10	0.20	1.00	1.25

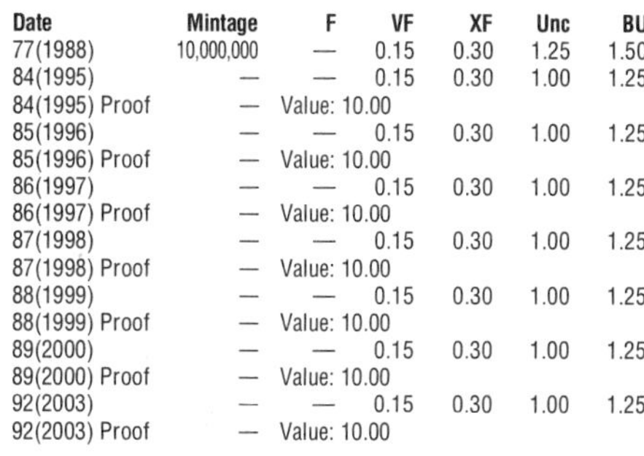

Date	Mintage	F	VF	XF	Unc	BU
77(1988)	10,000,000	—	0.15	0.30	1.25	1.50
84(1995)	—	—	0.15	0.30	1.00	1.25
84(1995) Proof	—	Value: 10.00				
85(1996)	—	—	0.15	0.30	1.00	1.25
85(1996) Proof	—	Value: 10.00				
86(1997)	—	—	0.15	0.30	1.00	1.25
86(1997) Proof	—	Value: 10.00				
87(1998)	—	—	0.15	0.30	1.00	1.25
87(1998) Proof	—	Value: 10.00				
88(1999)	—	—	0.15	0.30	1.00	1.25
88(1999) Proof	—	Value: 10.00				
89(2000)	—	—	0.15	0.30	1.00	1.25
89(2000) Proof	—	Value: 10.00				
92(2003)	—	—	0.15	0.30	1.00	1.25
92(2003) Proof	—	Value: 10.00				

Y# 536 YUAN

5.9300 g., Copper-Nickel-Zinc, 25 mm. **Obv:** Plum blossom **Rev:** Orchid **Edge:** Reeded

Date	Mintage	F	VF	XF	Unc	BU
49(1960)	321,717,000	—	0.10	0.20	0.50	0.65
59(1970)	48,800,000	0.10	0.20	0.50	1.00	1.25
60(1971)	41,532,000	0.10	0.20	0.50	1.00	1.25
61(1972)	105,309,000	—	0.10	0.20	0.50	0.65
62(1973)	353,924,000	—	0.10	0.20	0.50	0.65
63(1974)	535,605,000	—	0.10	0.20	0.50	0.65
64(1975)	456,874,000	—	0.10	0.20	0.50	0.65
65(1976)	634,497,000	—	0.10	0.20	0.50	0.65
66(1977)	116,900,000	—	0.10	0.20	0.50	0.65
67(1978)	104,245,000	—	0.10	0.20	0.50	0.65
68(1979)	—	0.10	0.20	0.50	0.80	1.00
69(1980)	113,900,000	—	0.10	0.20	0.50	0.65

Y# A537 YUAN

Silver **Subject:** 50th Anniversary of the Republic **Obv:** Chiang Kai-shek left **Rev:** Value at center within flower wreath

Date	Mintage	F	VF	XF	Unc	BU
50(1961)	—	—	—	—	285	325

Note: This coin was released accidentally or was released and quickly withdrawn and is very scarce today

Y# 543 YUAN

Copper-Nickel **Subject:** 80th Birthday of Chiang Kai-shek **Obv:** Bust of Chiang Kai-shek **Rev:** Chinese value in center

Date	Mintage	F	VF	XF	Unc	BU
55(1966)	—	0.25	0.35	0.50	1.00	1.50

Y# 547 YUAN

Copper-Nickel-Zinc, 25 mm. **Series:** F.A.O. **Obv:** Orchid **Rev:** Farmer in field, value below **Edge:** Reeded

Date	Mintage	F	VF	XF	Unc	BU
58(1969)	10,000,000	0.25	0.35	0.50	1.00	1.50

Y# 551 YUAN

3.8000 g., Bronze, 19.92 mm. **Obv:** Bust of Chiang Kai-shek left **Rev:** Chinese value in center, 1 below **Edge:** Reeded

Date	Mintage	F	VF	XF	Unc	BU
70(1981)	1,080,000,000	—	—	0.10	0.15	0.25
70(1981) Proof	—	Value: 12.50				
71(1982)	780,000,000	—	—	0.10	0.15	0.25
72(1983)	420,000,000	—	—	0.10	0.15	0.25
73(1984)	110,000,000	—	—	0.10	0.15	0.25
74(1985)	200,000,000	—	—	0.10	0.15	0.25
75(1986)	200,000,000	—	—	0.10	0.15	0.25
76(1987)	110,000,000	—	—	0.10	0.15	0.25
77(1988)	40,000,000	—	—	0.20	0.50	0.65
81(1992)	—	—	—	0.15	0.25	0.35
82(1993)	—	—	—	0.15	0.25	0.35
83(1994)	—	—	—	0.15	0.25	0.35
84(1995)	—	—	—	0.15	0.25	0.35
84(1995) Proof	—	Value: 12.50				
85(1996)	—	—	—	0.15	0.25	0.35
85(1996) Proof	—	Value: 12.50				
86(1997)	—	—	—	0.15	0.25	0.35
86(1997) Proof	—	Value: 12.50				
87(1998)	—	—	—	0.15	0.30	0.35
87(1998) Proof	—	Value: 12.50				
88(1999)	—	—	—	0.15	0.30	0.35
88(1999) Proof	—	Value: 12.50				
89(2000)	—	—	—	0.15	0.30	0.35
89(2000) Proof	—	Value: 12.50				
92(2003)	—	—	—	0.15	0.30	0.45
92(2003) Proof	—	Value: 12.50				

Y# 537 5 YUAN

Copper-Nickel **Obv:** Bust of Sun Yat-sen left **Rev:** Mausoleum in Nanking **Edge:** Reeded

Date	Mintage	F	VF	XF	Unc	BU
54(1965)	—	0.35	0.75	1.50	5.00	6.50

Y# 548 5 YUAN

9.5000 g., Copper-Nickel, 28.9 mm. **Obv:** Bust of Chiang Kai-shek left **Rev:** Chinese symbols in center **Edge:** Reeded

Date	Mintage	F	VF	XF	Unc	BU
59(1970)	12,360,000	0.20	0.40	0.80	1.50	2.00
60(1971)	20,575,000	0.20	0.35	0.50	1.00	1.50
61(1972)	27,998,000	0.20	0.35	0.50	1.00	1.50
62(1973)	50,122,000	0.20	0.35	0.50	0.80	1.25
63(1974)	418,068,000	0.20	0.35	0.50	0.80	1.25
64(1975)	39,520,000	0.20	0.35	0.50	0.80	1.25
65(1976)	140,000,000	0.20	0.35	0.50	0.80	1.25
66(1977)	50,260,000	0.20	0.35	0.50	0.80	1.25
67(1978)	78,082,000	0.20	0.35	0.50	0.80	1.25
68(1979)	—	0.20	0.35	0.50	0.80	1.25
69(1980)	273,000,000	0.20	0.35	0.50	0.80	1.25
70(1981)	162,000,000	0.20	0.35	0.50	0.80	1.25

Y# 552 5 YUAN

Copper-Nickel **Obv:** Bust of Chiang Kai-shek left **Rev:** Chinese symbols in center, 5 below

Date	Mintage	F	VF	XF	Unc	BU
70(1981)	522,432,000	—	0.15	0.20	0.50	0.75
70(1981) Proof	—	Value: 12.50				
71(1982)	6,600,000	—	0.15	0.20	0.50	0.75

Date	Mintage	F	VF	XF	Unc	BU
72(1983)	34,000,000	—	0.15	0.20	0.50	0.75
73(1984)	280,000,000	—	0.15	0.20	0.50	0.75
77(1988)	200,000,000	—	0.15	0.20	0.50	0.75
78(1989)	—	—	0.15	0.20	0.50	0.75
84(1995)	—	—	0.15	0.25	0.50	0.75
84(1995) Proof	—	Value: 12.50				
85(1996)	—	—	0.15	0.25	0.50	0.75
85(1996) Proof	—	Value: 12.50				
86(1997)	—	—	0.15	0.25	0.50	0.75
86(1997) Proof	—	Value: 12.50				
87(1998)	—	—	0.15	0.25	0.50	0.75
87(1998) Proof	—	Value: 12.50				
88(1999)	—	—	0.15	0.25	0.50	0.75
88(1999) Proof	—	Value: 12.50				
89(2000)	—	—	0.15	0.25	0.50	0.75
89(2000) Proof	—	Value: 12.50				
92(2003)	—	—	0.15	0.25	0.50	0.75
92(2003) Proof	—	Value: 12.50				

Y# 538 10 YUAN

Copper-Nickel, 26 mm. **Obv:** Bust of Sun Yat-sen left **Rev:** Mausoleum in Nanking

Date	Mintage	F	VF	XF	Unc	BU
54(1965)	—	0.50	1.00	2.00	6.00	7.50

Y# 553 10 YUAN

7.5000 g., Copper-Nickel, 26 mm. **Obv:** Bust of Chiang Kai-shek left **Rev:** Chinese symbols in center, 10 below

Date	Mintage	F	VF	XF	Unc	BU
70(1981)	123,000,000	—	0.30	0.45	0.75	1.00
70(1981) Proof	—	Value: 15.00				
71(1982)	361,000,000	—	0.30	0.45	0.75	1.00
72(1983)	196,000,000	—	0.30	0.45	0.75	1.00
73(1984)	220,000,000	—	0.30	0.45	0.75	1.00
74(1985)	200,000,000	—	0.30	0.45	0.75	1.00
75(1986)	100,000,000	—	0.30	0.45	0.75	1.00
76(1987)	90,000,000	—	0.30	0.45	0.75	1.00
77(1988)	100,000,000	—	0.30	0.45	0.75	1.00
78(1989)	—	—	0.30	0.45	0.75	1.00
79(1990)	—	—	0.30	0.45	0.75	1.00
80(1991)	—	—	0.30	0.45	0.75	1.00
81(1992)	—	—	0.30	0.45	0.75	1.00
82(1993)	—	—	0.30	0.45	0.75	1.00
83(1994)	—	—	0.30	0.45	0.75	1.00
84(1995)	—	—	0.25	0.45	0.75	1.00
84(1995) Proof	—	Value: 15.00				
85(1996)	—	—	0.25	0.45	0.75	1.00
85(1996) Proof	—	Value: 15.00				
86(1997)	—	—	0.25	0.45	0.75	1.00
86(1997) Proof	—	Value: 15.00				
87(1998)	—	—	0.25	0.45	0.75	1.00
87(1998) Proof	—	Value: 15.00				
88(1999)	—	—	0.25	0.45	0.75	1.00
88(1999) Proof	—	Value: 15.00				
89(2000)	—	—	0.25	0.45	0.75	1.00
89(2000) Proof	—	Value: 15.00				
92(2003)	—	—	0.25	0.45	0.75	1.00
92(2003) Proof	—	Value: 15.00				

Y# 555 10 YUAN

Copper-Nickel, 26 mm. **Subject:** 50th Anniversary - Taiwan's Liberation from Japan **Obv:** Map with dates flanking **Rev:** Chinese symbols in center, 10 below

Date	Mintage	F	VF	XF	Unc	BU
84(1995)	—	—	—	—	2.50	3.00

Y# 558 10 YUAN

Copper-Nickel, 26 mm. **Subject:** 50th Anniversary - Taiwan Yuan (Dollar) **Obv:** Coins **Rev:** Anniversary dates above denomination **Edge:** Reeded

Date	Mintage	F	VF	XF	Unc	BU
88(1999)	30,000,000	—	—	—	2.75	3.50

Y# 560 10 YUAN

7.5000 g., Copper-Nickel, 26 mm. **Subject:** Year of the Dragon **Obv:** Stylized dragon above denomination **Rev:** Dragon

Date	Mintage	F	VF	XF	Unc	BU
89(2000)	—	—	—	—	3.00	3.50

Y# 567 10 YUAN

7.4300 g., Copper-Nickel, 26 mm. **Subject:** 90th Anniversary of the Republic **Obv:** Bust of Sun Yat-sen facing **Rev:** Holographic design and denomination **Edge:** Reeded

Date	Mintage	F	VF	XF	Unc	BU
90 (2001)	30,000,000	—	—	—	2.50	3.00

Y# 539 50 YUAN

17.1000 g., 0.7500 Silver 0.4123 oz. ASW **Obv:** Bust of Sun Yat-sen left **Rev:** Chinese symbols in center, bird above, deer below

Date	Mintage	F	VF	XF	Unc	BU
54(1965)	—	—	—	12.50	25.00	32.50

Y# 554 50 YUAN

Brass **Obv:** Orchid burst **Rev:** Chinese symbols center, 50 below, flower wreath circle

Date	Mintage	F	VF	XF	Unc	BU
81-1992 (1992)	—	—	0.50	1.00	3.50	4.00
82-1993 (1993)	—	—	0.50	1.00	3.50	4.00
84-1995 (1995)	—	—	0.50	1.00	3.50	4.00
84-1995 (1995) Proof	—	—	—	—	—	—
85-1996 (1996)	—	—	0.50	1.00	3.50	4.00
85-1996 (1996) Proof	—	—	—	—	—	—
86-1997 (1997)	—	—	0.50	1.00	3.50	4.00
86-1997 (1997) Proof	—	—	—	—	—	—
87-1998 (1998)	—	—	0.50	1.00	3.50	4.00
87-1998 (1998) Proof	—	—	—	—	—	—
88-1999 (1999)	—	—	0.50	1.00	3.50	4.00
88-1999 (1999) Proof	—	—	—	—	—	—
89-2000 (2000)	—	—	0.50	1.00	3.50	4.00
89-2000 (2000) Proof	—	—	—	—	—	—

Y# 556 50 YUAN

Bi-Metallic Brass center in Copper-Nickel ring **Obv:** Parliament building **Rev:** Value left, Chinese symbols at bottom

Date	Mintage	F	VF	XF	Unc	BU
84-1995 (1995)	—	—	—	—	5.75	6.50
84-1995 (1995) Proof	—	—	—	—	—	—
85-1996 (1996)	—	—	—	—	5.75	6.50
85-1996 (1996) Proof	—	—	—	—	—	—
86-1997 (1997)	—	—	—	—	5.75	6.50
86-1997 (1997) Proof	—	—	—	—	—	—
87-1998 (1998)	—	—	—	—	5.75	6.50
87-1998 (1998) Proof	—	—	—	—	—	—
88-1999 (1999)	—	—	—	—	5.75	6.50
88-1999 (1999) Proof	—	—	—	—	—	—
89-2000 (2000)	—	—	—	—	5.75	6.50
89-2000 (2000) Proof	—	—	—	—	—	—

Y# 568 50 YUAN

10.0000 g., Brass, 28 mm. **Obv:** Bust **Rev:** Denomination above latent image denomination **Edge:** Reeding and denomination **Mint:** Central Mint of China

Date	Mintage	F	VF	XF	Unc	BU
91-2002	—	—	—	—	7.50	10.00
92-2003	—	—	—	—	7.50	10.00
92-2003 Proof	—	Value: 20.00				

COLOMBIA

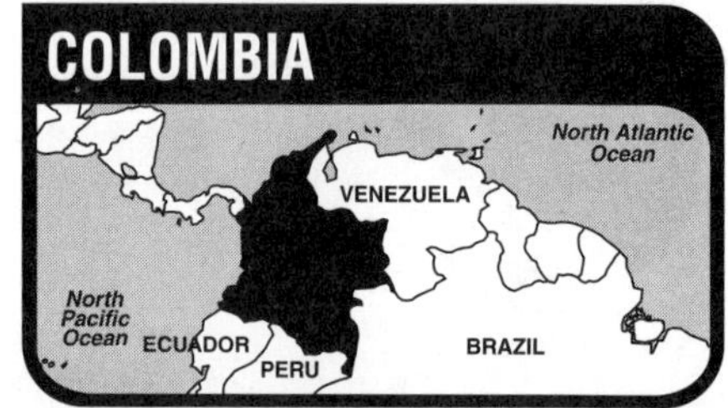

The Republic of Colombia, in the northwestern corner of South America, has an area of 440,831 sq. mi. (1,138,910 sq. km.) and a population of*42.3 million. Capital: Bogota. The economy is primarily agricultural with a mild, rich coffee being the chief crop. Colombia has the world's largest platinum deposits and important reserves of coal, iron ore, petroleum and limestone; other precious metals and emeralds are also mined. Coffee, crude oil, bananas, sugar and emeralds are exported.

The northern coast of present Colombia was one of the first parts of the American continent to be visited by Spanish navigators. At Darien in Panama is the site of the first permanent European settlement on the American mainland in 1510. New Granada, as Colombia was known until 1861, stemmed from the settlement of Santa Marta in 1525. New Granada was established as a Spanish colony in 1549. Independence was declared in 1810, and secured in 1819 when Simon Bolivar united Colombia, Venezuela, Panama and Ecuador as the Republic of Gran Colombia. Venezuela withdrew from the Republic in 1829; Ecuador in 1830; and Panama in 1903.

MINT MARKS

A, M – Medellin (capital), Antioquia (state)
B - BOGOTA
(D) Denver, USA
H – Birmingham (Heaton & Sons)
(m) - Medellin, w/o mint mark
(Mo) - Mexico City
NI - Numismatica Italiana, Arezzo, Italy
mint marks stylized in wreath

(P) - Philadelphia
(S) - San Francisco, USA.
(W) - Waterbury, CT (USA, Scoville mint)

REPUBLIC

INFLATIONARY COINAGE

P/M - Papel Moneda

Beginning about 1886, Colombia fell victim to rampant printing press inflation and a debased, vanishing coinage. Left without solid backing, the peso gradually fell until it was worth 1 centavo of the old silver-based currency. The copper-nickel 1, 2, and 5 peso p/m coins reflected this inflation, and later circulated at par with the newer 1, 2, and 5 centavo coins.

KM# A279 PESO (Papel Moneda)

2.0000 g., Copper-Nickel **Obv:** Liberty head right **Rev:** Denomination, p/m below, within wreath

Date	Mintage	F	VF	XF	Unc	BU
1907 AM	2,860,000	1.25	3.50	13.50	37.50	—
1907 AM Proof	—	Value: 85.00				
1910 AM	1,205,000	3.50	9.00	17.50	45.00	—
1911 AM	2,816,000	2.75	7.50	17.50	45.00	—
1912 AM	6,094,000	2.00	7.00	16.50	40.00	—
1912 H Without crossbar	2,000,000	1.50	3.75	12.50	37.50	—
1912 H With crossbar	Inc. above	1.50	3.75	12.50	37.50	—
1913 AM	306,000	6.50	12.50	22.50	55.00	—
1914 AM	552,000	6.00	10.00	18.50	42.50	—
1916/4 AM	234,000	11.00	20.00	37.50	70.00	—
1916 AM	Inc. above	11.00	20.00	37.50	70.00	—

KM# B279 2 PESOS (Papel Moneda)

3.0000 g., Copper-Nickel **Obv:** Liberty head right, date below **Rev:** Denomination, p/m below, within wreath **Note:** Date varieties exist.

Date	Mintage	F	VF	XF	Unc	BU
1907 AM	4,161,000	1.75	3.75	15.00	37.50	—
1907 AM Proof	—	Value: 100				
1910/07 AM	1,189,000	7.50	13.50	25.00	47.50	—
1910 AM	Inc. above	6.75	12.50	22.00	42.50	—
1914 AM	1,000,000	4.50	11.00	23.50	47.50	—

KM# 279 5 PESOS (Papel Moneda)

4.0000 g., Copper-Nickel **Obv:** Liberty head right, date below **Rev:** Denomination, p/m below, within wreath

Date	Mintage	F	VF	XF	Unc	BU
1907 AM	6,143,000	2.50	9.00	20.00	40.00	—
1907 AM Proof	—	Value: 115				
1909 AM	4,000,000	2.75	8.50	18.50	40.00	—
1912 H	2,000,000	3.00	6.50	13.50	30.00	—
1912 AM	1,897,000	3.75	9.50	22.50	47.50	—
1913 AM	Inc. above	3.00	8.50	22.50	47.50	—
1914 AM	Inc. above	10.00	20.00	38.50	67.50	—

DECIMAL COINAGE

100 Centavos = 1 Peso

KM# 275 CENTAVO

2.0000 g., Copper-Nickel **Obv:** Liberty head right **Rev:** Denomination within wreath **Note:** Erratically punched final two digits of date are common on these issues, especially 1935-1948. A very faint "17" is often observable beneath the final two digits on many dates of this type.

Date	Mintage	F	VF	XF	Unc	BU
1918	430,000	6.00	15.00	35.00	125	—
1919	Inc. above	8.00	25.00	60.00	140	—
1920(D)	7,540,000	6.50	13.50	32.00	120	—
1921(D)	12,460,000	6.50	12.50	30.00	60.00	—
1933(P)	3,000,000	0.50	3.00	5.00	10.00	—
1935(P)	5,000,000	0.50	3.00	7.00	15.00	—
1936	1,540,000	2.00	5.00	15.00	45.00	—
1938(P)	7,920,000	0.25	0.50	2.00	6.00	—
1941B	1,000,000	0.50	1.00	3.00	10.00	—
1946B	2,096,000	0.35	0.75	2.50	6.50	—
1947/17B	1,835,000	1.00	3.50	6.00	12.00	—
1947/37B	Inc. above	1.00	3.50	6.00	12.00	—
1947/6B	Inc. above	1.00	3.50	6.00	12.00	—
1947B	Inc. above	0.50	1.00	2.00	5.00	—
1948/38B	1,139,000	1.00	3.50	6.00	12.00	—
1948B	Inc. above	0.50	1.00	2.00	5.00	—

KM# 205 CENTAVO

2.0000 g., Bronze, 17 mm. **Obv:** Liberty cap within wreath **Rev:** Coffee bean sprigs flank denomination, cornucopia above **Note:** Several date varieties exist.

Date	Mintage	F	VF	XF	Unc	BU
1942	1,000,000	1.00	2.00	4.50	12.50	—
1942B	Inc. above	1.00	3.50	9.00	28.00	—
1943	—	0.50	1.00	2.50	7.00	—
1943B	4,515,000	0.50	1.00	2.50	7.00	—
1944B	4,515,000	0.35	0.65	1.50	5.00	—
1945B	3,769,000	0.50	1.00	2.50	7.00	—
1945B over reversed B	—	0.35	0.65	1.50	5.00	—
1948B	585,000	0.50	1.00	3.00	10.00	—
1949B	4,255,000	0.35	0.65	1.50	5.00	—
1950B	5,827,000	0.45	0.75	2.50	8.00	—
1951B	Inc. above	0.35	0.65	1.75	5.50	—
1957	2,500,000	0.25	0.45	0.75	2.00	—
1958	590,000	0.25	0.45	1.00	2.25	—
1959	2,677,000	0.15	0.25	0.50	1.25	—
1960	2,500,000	0.15	0.25	0.50	1.25	—
1961 Widely spaced date	3,673,000	0.15	0.25	0.50	1.25	—
1961 Narrowly spaced date	Inc. above	0.15	0.25	0.45	1.00	—
1962	4,065,000	0.15	0.25	0.50	1.25	—
1963	1,845,000	0.15	0.25	0.75	2.00	—
1964/44	3,165,000	0.50	1.50	2.50	5.00	—
1964	Inc. above	0.15	0.25	0.50	1.25	—
1965 Large date	5,510,000	0.15	0.25	0.45	1.00	—
1965 Small date	Inc. above	0.15	0.25	0.45	1.00	—
1966	3,910,000	0.15	0.25	0.50	1.25	—

KM# 275a CENTAVO

2.0000 g., Nickel Clad Steel, 17 mm. **Obv:** Liberty head right **Rev:** Denomination within wreath **Note:** Erratically punched final two digits of date are common on these issues.

Date	Mintage	F	VF	XF	Unc	BU
1952/12B	—	0.20	0.50	1.50	4.00	—
1952B	Inc. above	0.10	0.15	0.75	3.00	—
1954B	5,080,000	0.10	0.15	0.50	2.00	—
1956	1,315,000	0.10	0.20	1.00	5.00	—
1957	900,000	0.35	0.75	2.50	7.50	—
1958/48	—	0.35	0.75	2.00	6.00	—
1958	1,596,000	0.20	0.45	1.00	3.00	—

KM# 218 CENTAVO

Bronze **Subject:** Uprising Sesquicentennial **Obv:** Liberty cap within wreath **Rev:** Coffee bean sprigs flank denomination, cornucopia above **Note:** This and the other issues in the uprising commemorative series offer the usual design of the period with the dates 1810-1960 added at the bottom of the obverse.

Date	Mintage	F	VF	XF	Unc	BU
ND(1960)	500,000	0.60	1.50	3.00	8.00	—

KM# 205a CENTAVO

Copper Clad Steel, 17 mm. **Obv:** Liberty cap within wreath **Rev:** Coffee bean sprigs flank denomination, cornucopia above **Note:** Several date varieties exist.

Date	Mintage	F	VF	XF	Unc	BU
1967	5,730,000	—	0.10	0.15	0.45	—
1968	7,390,000	—	0.10	0.15	0.45	—
1969	6,870,000	—	0.10	0.15	0.45	—
1970	3,839,000	—	0.10	0.20	0.60	—
1971	3,020,000	—	0.10	0.20	0.60	—
1972	3,100,000	—	0.10	0.20	0.60	—
1973	—	—	—	0.10	0.35	—
1974	2,000,000	—	—	0.10	0.35	—
1975	1,000,000	—	—	0.10	0.35	—
1976	1,000,000	—	—	0.10	0.35	—
1977	900,000	—	0.10	0.15	0.45	—
1978	224,000	—	0.10	0.20	0.65	—

KM# 198 2 CENTAVOS

3.0000 g., Copper-Nickel **Obv:** Liberty head right, date below **Rev:** Denomination within wreath **Note:** Erratically punched final two digits exist for 1946-1947. A very faint "17" is often observable beneath the final two digits on many dates of this type.

Date	Mintage	F	VF	XF	Unc	BU
1918	930,000	7.00	15.00	30.00	80.00	—
1919	Inc. above	16.50	30.00	60.00	135	—
1920	3,855,000	3.00	6.50	18.50	50.00	—
1921(D)	11,145,000	2.50	5.00	15.00	40.00	—
1922 10 pieces known	—	1,350	2,800	—	—	—
1933(P)	3,500,000	0.50	1.50	4.00	10.00	—
1935(P)	2,500,000	0.35	1.00	3.50	8.00	—
1938(P)	3,872,000	0.35	1.00	3.25	7.00	—
1941B	500,000	1.00	2.00	7.00	20.00	—
1942B	500,000	1.50	2.50	8.00	16.50	—
1946/36B	2,593,000	1.00	2.50	6.00	12.50	—
1946B	Inc. above	0.75	1.50	4.75	11.00	—
1947/3B	1,337,000	0.75	1.50	4.00	10.00	—
1947/36B	Inc. above	0.75	1.50	4.00	10.00	—
1947B	Inc. above	0.35	1.00	3.00	8.00	—

KM# 210 2 CENTAVOS

3.0300 g., Bronze, 19.04 mm. **Obv:** Liberty cap within wreath, date below **Rev:** Coffee bean sprigs flank denomination, cornucopia above **Mint:** Bogota

Date	Mintage	F	VF	XF	Unc	BU
1948B	2,648,000	0.35	1.00	4.00	10.00	—
1949B	1,278,000	0.75	2.00	7.00	15.00	—
1950B	2,285,000	0.75	1.50	7.00	18.00	—

KM# 211 2 CENTAVOS

3.1000 g., Aluminum-Bronze **Obv:** Head left, date below, divided legend **Rev:** Denomination within wreath

Date	Mintage	F	VF	XF	Unc	BU
1952B Small date	5,038,000	0.15	0.25	0.50	2.00	—
1965/3	1,830,000	0.10	0.20	0.40	1.00	—
1965 Large date	Inc. above	0.15	0.25	0.50	2.00	—

KM# 214 2 CENTAVOS

2.9300 g., Aluminum-Bronze **Obv:** Head left, date below, continuous legend **Rev:** Denomination within wreath **Mint:** Bogota

Date	Mintage	F	VF	XF	Unc	BU
1955 Large date	2,513,000	0.15	0.30	1.00	3.00	—
1955B Large date	Inc. above	0.15	0.30	0.75	2.00	—
1959 Small date	4,609,000	0.10	0.20	0.50	1.50	—

KM# 219 2 CENTAVOS

Aluminum-Bronze **Subject:** Uprising Sesquicentennial **Obv:** Head left, date below **Rev:** Denomination within wreath **Mint:** Bogota

Date	Mintage	F	VF	XF	Unc	BU
ND(1960)	250,000	1.00	2.00	3.00	8.00	—

KM# 190 2-1/2 CENTAVOS

Copper-Nickel **Obv:** Liberty cap within circle **Rev:** Denomination within circle **Mint:** Waterbury

Date	Mintage	F	VF	XF	Unc	BU
1902(W)	Est. 400,000	—	—	500	900	—

KM# 184 5 CENTAVOS

Copper-Nickel **Obv:** Head left **Rev:** Large denomination, sprays flank **Mint:** Waterbury

Date	Mintage	F	VF	XF	Unc	BU
1902(W)	Est. 400,000	—	—	650	1,000	—

KM# 191 5 CENTAVOS

1.2500 g., 0.6660 Silver 0.0268 oz. ASW **Obv:** Head left, date below **Rev:** Small denomination within two cornucopias **Edge:** Plain **Mint:** Philadelphia

Date	Mintage	F	VF	XF	Unc	BU
1902(P)	400,000	0.75	1.50	3.50	8.00	—

KM# 199 5 CENTAVOS

4.0000 g., Copper-Nickel **Obv:** Head right, date below **Rev:** Denomination within wreath **Note:** Varieties exist. Erratically punched final two digits of date are common on these issues, especially 1935-1950. A very faint "17" is often observable beneath the final two digits on many dates of this type.

Date	Mintage	F	VF	XF	Unc	BU
1918	767,000	11.00	25.00	50.00	100	—
1919	1,926,000	16.50	30.00	65.00	125	—
1920	2,062,000	11.00	25.00	50.00	100	—
1920H	—	10.00	27.50	45.00	100	—
1921	1,574,000	16.50	30.00	65.00	125	—
1921H	—	16.50	30.00	65.00	125	—
1922	2,623,000	16.50	30.00	65.00	125	—
1922H	—	16.50	30.00	65.00	125	—
1924	120,000	18.50	35.00	70.00	125	—
1933(P)	2,000,000	1.00	2.00	6.00	15.00	—
1935/24	1,616,000	5.00	12.00	30.00	60.00	—
1935(P)	10,000,000	0.75	1.75	3.50	10.00	—
1936	—	45.00	75.00	150	350	—
1938B	2,000,000	1.00	2.50	5.50	13.00	—
1938	3,867,000	2.00	3.75	8.00	15.00	—
1938 Large 38 in date	Inc. above	2.00	4.50	10.00	20.00	—
1939/5	2,000,000	1.75	3.00	6.00	13.00	—
1939	Inc. above	0.75	1.50	3.50	8.00	—
1941	—	2.50	5.50	9.00	23.00	—
1941B	500,000	3.00	6.00	10.00	25.00	—
1946(P) (S) Small date	40,000,000	0.20	0.50	1.00	3.00	—
1946(m) Large date	3,330,000	2.00	4.00	8.50	23.00	—
1949B	2,750,000	0.45	1.00	2.50	6.00	—
1950B Large 50 in date	3,611,000	6.00	12.00	25.00	45.00	—
1950B Small 50 in date	Inc. above	0.45	1.00	3.00	6.00	—

KM# 206 5 CENTAVOS

4.0200 g., Bronze, 21 mm. **Obv:** Liberty cap within wreath, date below **Rev:** Coffee bean sprigs flank denomination, cornucopia above **Note:** Some coins of 1942-1956 have weak "B" mint mark.

Date	Mintage	F	VF	XF	Unc	BU
1942	—	2.00	4.00	12.00	30.00	—
1942B	800,000	1.00	2.50	4.50	12.00	—
1943	—	5.00	9.00	18.00	35.00	—
1943B	6,053,000	0.75	1.50	3.00	10.00	—
1944	—	0.75	1.50	3.00	10.00	—
1944B	9,013,000	0.75	1.50	3.00	10.00	—
1945/4	—	0.75	1.50	3.00	10.00	—
1945	—	0.75	1.50	3.00	10.00	—
1945B	11,101,000	0.25	0.75	1.25	4.00	—
1946/5	—	1.25	3.50	4.50	12.50	—
1946	—	0.50	1.25	2.00	7.00	—
1952	—	1.25	2.50	3.50	10.00	—
1952B	3,985,000	0.15	0.40	1.00	2.50	—
1953B	5,180,000	0.10	0.25	0.75	2.00	—
1954B	1,159,000	0.10	0.25	0.75	2.00	—
1955B	6,819,000	0.10	0.25	0.75	2.00	—
1956	8,772,000	0.10	0.25	0.50	1.00	—
1956B	—	0.75	1.50	4.50	12.50	—
1957	8,912,000	0.10	0.25	0.75	2.00	—
1958	15,016,000	0.10	0.25	0.50	1.50	—
1959	14,271,000	0.10	0.25	0.50	1.50	—
1960/660	11,716,000	0.25	0.75	1.00	2.25	—
1960/70	Inc. above	0.25	0.75	1.00	2.25	—
1960	Inc. above	0.10	0.25	0.50	1.25	—
1961	11,200,000	0.10	0.25	0.50	1.25	—
CD1962	10,928,000	—	0.10	0.35	1.00	—
1963/53	15,113,000	—	—	—	—	—
1963	Inc. above	—	0.10	0.35	1.00	—
1964	9,336,000	—	0.10	0.35	1.00	—
1965	6,460,000	—	0.10	0.35	1.00	—
1966	7,170,000	—	0.10	0.35	1.00	—

KM# 206a 5 CENTAVOS

3.2300 g., Copper Clad Steel, 21.29 mm. **Obv:** Liberty cap within wreath, date below **Rev:** Coffee bean sprigs flank denomination, cornucopia above **Note:** Varieties exist for 1967, 1970, and 1973.

Date	Mintage	F	VF	XF	Unc	BU
1967	10,280,000	—	—	0.10	1.00	—
1968	8,900,000	—	—	0.10	1.00	—
1969	17,800,000	—	—	0.10	1.00	—
1970	14,842,000	—	—	0.10	0.50	—
1971	10,730,000	—	—	0.10	0.50	—
1972	10,170,000	—	—	0.10	0.50	—
1973	10,525,000	—	—	0.10	0.50	—
1974	5,310,000	—	—	0.10	0.50	—
1975	5,631,000	—	—	0.10	0.50	—
1976	3,009,000	—	—	0.10	0.50	—
1977	2,000,000	—	—	0.10	0.50	—
1978	468,000	—	—	0.10	0.50	—
1979	8,087,000	—	—	—	—	—

KM# 220 5 CENTAVOS

Bronze **Subject:** Uprising Sesquicentennial **Obv:** Liberty cap within wreath **Rev:** Coffee bean sprigs flank denomination, cornucopia above

Date	Mintage	F	VF	XF	Unc	BU
ND(1960)	400,000	1.75	3.50	7.50	25.00	—

KM# 196.1 10 CENTAVOS

2.5000 g., 0.9000 Silver 0.0723 oz. ASW **Obv:** Simon Bolivar head right, date below **Rev:** Arms and value **Note:** Varieties exist.

Date	Mintage	F	VF	XF	Unc	BU
1911	5,065,000	1.00	1.75	10.00	25.00	—
1913	8,305,000	1.00	1.75	9.00	20.00	—
1914	3,840,000	1.00	1.75	10.00	25.00	—
1920	2,149,000	1.00	1.75	10.00	25.00	—
1934B B on obverse	140,000	3.00	7.00	18.00	40.00	—
1934/24	Inc. above	6.25	13.50	28.00	60.00	—
1934	Inc. above	6.00	12.50	28.00	60.00	—
1937B	—	5.00	11.50	22.50	45.00	—
1938/7B	2,055,000	1.75	3.75	6.50	20.00	—
1938B Wide date	Inc. above	1.00	2.00	4.00	10.00	—

Date	Mintage	F	VF	XF	Unc	BU
1938 Narrow date	Inc. above	1.00	2.00	4.00	10.00	—
1940	450,000	1.50	2.50	4.50	15.00	—
1941	4,415,000	1.00	1.50	3.00	8.00	—
1942	3,140,000	5.00	10.00	16.50	38.00	—
1942B B on reverse	Inc. above	1.00	1.50	3.00	7.50	—

KM# 196.2 10 CENTAVOS

2.5000 g., 0.9000 Silver 0.0723 oz. ASW **Obv:** Simon Bolivar head right **Rev:** National arms recut

Date	Mintage	F	VF	XF	Unc	BU
1920	Inc. above	2.00	6.00	12.00	30.00	—

KM# 207.1 10 CENTAVOS

2.5000 g., 0.5000 Silver 0.0402 oz. ASW **Obv:** Francisco de Paula Santander head right **Rev:** Denomination within wreath, mint mark at bottom **Designer:** Gilroy Roberts

Date	Mintage	F	VF	XF	Unc	BU
1945B	4,830,000	0.75	1.50	3.50	9.00	—
1945 B-B	—	—	—	—	—	—
1945 Backwards B	—	1.00	2.00	4.00	10.00	—
1946/5B	—	0.65	1.50	4.50	13.00	—
1946B	—	0.65	1.50	4.50	13.00	—
1947/5B	7,366,000	1.50	3.00	5.00	15.00	—
1947/6B	Inc. above	1.50	3.00	5.00	15.00	—
1947B	Inc. above	1.50	3.00	5.00	15.00	—

KM# 207.2 10 CENTAVOS

2.5000 g., 0.5000 Silver 0.0402 oz. ASW **Obv:** Head of Santander right, date below **Rev:** Denomination within wreath, mint mark at top **Designer:** Gilroy Roberts **Note:** Varieties exist. Almost all dies for 1946-1951 show at least faint traces of overdating from 1945. Coins with absolutely no underdate, and those with very bold underdate, are generally worth more to advanced specialists.

Date	Mintage	F	VF	XF	Unc	BU
1947/5B	Inc. above	2.00	4.00	7.50	20.00	—
1947B	Inc. above	2.00	4.00	7.50	20.00	—
1948/5B	3,629,000	0.75	1.50	5.00	15.00	—
1948B	Inc. above	0.65	1.25	3.00	10.00	—
1949/5B	5,923,000	3.00	6.50	12.50	28.00	—
1949B	Inc. above	0.65	1.25	2.25	8.00	—
1950B	6,783,000	0.65	1.50	2.75	9.00	—
1951/5B	5,185,000	0.65	1.50	2.75	9.00	—
1951B	Inc. above	0.65	1.25	2.25	8.00	—
1952B	1,060,000	1.25	2.25	4.50	13.00	—

KM# 212.1 10 CENTAVOS

Copper-Nickel, 18 mm. **Obv:** Arms above date **Rev:** Head of Chief Calarca right divides denomination **Mint:** Bogota

Date	Mintage	F	VF	XF	Unc	BU
1952B	6,035,000	0.35	1.00	3.50	15.00	—
1953B	6,985,000	0.25	0.50	1.50	6.00	—

KM# 212.2 10 CENTAVOS

2.3300 g., Copper-Nickel, 18.5 mm. **Obv:** Arms above date **Rev:** Head of Chief Calarca right divides denomination **Mint:** Bogota **Note:** Varieties exist.

Date	Mintage	F	VF	XF	Unc	BU
1954B	13,006,000	0.20	0.50	1.25	3.00	—
1955B	9,968,000	0.20	0.50	1.25	3.00	—
1956	36,010,000	0.10	0.20	0.50	1.50	—
1956B	—	0.10	0.20	0.50	1.50	—
1958	41,695,000	—	—	—	—	—
1959	36,653,000	0.10	0.20	0.50	1.50	—
1960	32,290,000	0.10	0.20	0.50	2.00	—
1961	17,780,000	0.10	0.20	0.50	2.00	—
1962	8,930,000	0.10	0.20	0.50	2.00	—
1963	37,540,000	0.10	0.20	0.50	1.50	—
1964	61,672,000	0.10	0.20	0.50	1.50	—
1965	12,804,000	0.10	0.25	0.75	3.00	—
1966 Large date	23,544,000	0.10	0.20	0.50	1.50	—

KM# 221 10 CENTAVOS
Copper-Nickel **Subject:** Uprising Sesquicentennial **Obv:** Arms above two dates **Rev:** Head of Chief Calarca right divides denomination

Date	Mintage	F	VF	XF	Unc	BU
ND(1960)	1,000,000	1.00	2.00	3.50	8.00	—

KM# 226 10 CENTAVOS
2.5100 g., Nickel Clad Steel, 18.3 mm. **Obv:** Head of Santander right, date below **Rev:** Denomination within circular wreath

Date	Mintage	F	VF	XF	Unc	BU
1967	26,980,000	—	0.10	0.20	1.00	—
1968	23,670,000	—	0.10	0.20	1.00	—
1969	29,450,000	—	0.10	0.20	1.00	—

KM# 236 10 CENTAVOS
2.5200 g., Nickel Clad Steel, 18.3 mm. **Obv:** Head of Santander right, date below **Rev:** Denomination within wreath

Date	Mintage	F	VF	XF	Unc	BU
1969	Inc. above	—	0.10	0.20	1.00	—
1970	38,935,000	—	0.10	0.20	1.00	—
1971	53,314,000	—	0.10	0.20	1.00	—

KM# 243 10 CENTAVOS
Nickel Clad Steel, 18.3 mm. **Obv:** Legend divided after REPUBLICA

Date	Mintage	F	VF	XF	Unc	BU
1970	—	—	—	—	—	—
1971	—	—	—	—	—	—

KM# 253 10 CENTAVOS
2.5200 g., Nickel Clad Steel, 18.4 mm. **Obv:** Head right, date below, continuous legend **Rev:** Denomination within wreath **Note:** Varieties exist.

Date	Mintage	F	VF	XF	Unc	BU
1972	58,000,000	—	0.10	0.15	0.35	—
1973	46,549,000	—	0.10	0.15	0.35	—
1974	49,740,000	—	0.10	0.15	0.35	—
1975	46,037,000	—	0.10	0.15	0.35	—
1976	46,084,000	—	0.10	0.15	0.35	—
1977	8,127,000	—	0.10	0.15	0.35	—
1978	97,081,000	—	0.10	0.15	0.35	—
1980	18,929,000	—	0.10	0.15	0.35	—

KM# 197 20 CENTAVOS
5.0000 g., 0.9000 Silver 0.1447 oz. ASW **Obv:** Head of Simon Bolivar right, date below **Rev:** Arms, denomination above

Date	Mintage	F	VF	XF	Unc	BU
1911	1,206,000	2.00	3.50	7.50	17.50	—
1913	1,630,000	2.00	3.50	7.50	22.50	—
1914	2,560,000	2.00	3.50	9.00	25.00	—
1920 Wide date	1,242,000	2.50	6.00	12.50	32.50	—
1920 Narrow date	Inc. above	2.50	6.00	12.50	32.50	—
1921	372,000	7.00	15.00	35.00	85.00	—
1922	45,000	30.00	55.00	85.00	225	—
1933B	330,000	3.50	7.50	15.00	35.00	—
Note: Mint mark on obverse						
1933B	Inc. above	12.50	25.00	45.00	125	—
Note: Mint mark on reverse						
1933B	Inc. above	5.00	10.00	20.00	50.00	—
Note: Mint mark on both sides						
1938/1	1,410,000	4.00	8.00	17.00	35.00	—
1938	Inc. above	2.25	5.00	10.00	22.00	—
1941	—	2.50	6.00	12.00	28.00	—
1942	155,000	9.00	20.00	32.50	65.00	—
1942B	Inc. above	2.00	3.50	7.50	20.00	—
Note: Mint mark on reverse						

KM# 208.1 20 CENTAVOS
5.0000 g., 0.5000 Silver 0.0804 oz. ASW **Obv:** Francisco de Paula Santander **Rev:** Mint mark in field below CENTAVOS **Designer:** Gilroy Roberts

Date	Mintage	F	VF	XF	Unc	BU
1945B	1,675,000	1.25	3.00	7.00	15.00	—
1945BB	Inc. above	6.00	12.00	25.00	50.00	—
Note: 1945BB has extra B on wreath at bottom						
1946/5B	6,599,000	1.25	2.50	6.50	15.00	—
1946B	Inc. above	1.50	3.00	9.00	20.00	—
1947/5B	9,708,000	3.00	6.00	12.00	28.00	—
1947B	—	3.00	6.00	12.00	28.00	—

KM# 208.3 20 CENTAVOS
5.0000 g., 0.5000 Silver 0.0804 oz. ASW **Obv:** Francisco de Paula Santander **Rev:** Without mint mark **Designer:** Gilroy Roberts

Date	Mintage	F	VF	XF	Unc	BU
1946(m)	—	3.00	7.50	15.00	32.50	—
1946/5(m)	—	3.75	9.50	16.50	37.50	—
1947(m)	1,748,000	5.00	8.50	15.00	35.00	—

KM# 208.2 20 CENTAVOS
5.0000 g., 0.5000 Silver 0.0804 oz. ASW **Obv:** Francisco de Paula Santander **Rev:** Mint mark on wreath at top **Designer:** Gilroy Roberts **Note:** Almost all dies for 1946-1951 show at least faint traces of overdating from 1945. Coins with absolutely no underdate, and those with very bold underdate, are generally worth more to advanced specialists. Varieties exist.

Date	Mintage	F	VF	XF	Unc	BU
1947/5B	Inc. above	5.00	10.00	20.00	50.00	—
1948/5B	Inc. above	1.25	3.00	5.00	12.00	—
1948B	Inc. above	1.50	3.00	5.00	14.00	—
1949/5B	403,000	3.75	8.50	17.50	45.00	—
1949B	Inc. above	2.50	5.00	10.00	32.50	—
1950/45B	1,899,000	2.75	6.75	15.00	50.00	—
1950B	Inc. above	2.75	6.00	13.50	37.50	—
1951/45B	7,498,000	1.25	3.00	6.50	13.50	—
1951B	Inc. above	1.25	3.00	6.00	12.50	—

KM# 213 20 CENTAVOS
5.0000 g., 0.3000 Silver 0.0482 oz. ASW **Obv:** Arms, date below **Rev:** Bust of Simon Bolivar left, divides denomination

Date	Mintage	F	VF	XF	Unc	BU
1952B Rare	3,887	—	—	—	—	—
1953B	17,819,000	1.00	1.50	3.50	7.50	—

KM# 215.1 20 CENTAVOS
Copper-Nickel, 23.4 mm. **Obv:** Head of Simon Bolivar right, small date below **Rev:** Denomination above arms, half circle of stars below

Date	Mintage	F	VF	XF	Unc	BU
1956	39,778,000	0.10	0.15	0.50	1.50	—
1959	55,519,000	0.10	0.15	0.50	1.50	—

KM# 215.2 20 CENTAVOS
4.9300 g., Copper-Nickel, 23.4 mm. **Obv:** Head of Simon Bolivar right, large date below **Rev:** Denomination above arms, half circle of stars below

Date	Mintage	F	VF	XF	Unc	BU
1963	12,035,000	—	0.10	0.50	1.50	—
1964	29,075,000	—	0.10	0.50	1.50	—
1965	19,180,000	0.10	0.25	0.75	2.50	—

KM# 215.3 20 CENTAVOS
Copper-Nickel, 23.4 mm. **Obv:** Head of Simon Bolivar right, medium date **Rev:** Denomination above arms, half circle of stars below

Date	Mintage	F	VF	XF	Unc	BU
1966	23,060,000	0.10	0.15	0.50	1.50	—

KM# 222 20 CENTAVOS
Copper-Nickel **Subject:** Uprising Sesquicentennial **Obv:** Head right divides dates below **Rev:** Denomination above arms, half circle of stars below

Date	Mintage	F	VF	XF	Unc	BU
ND(1960)	500,000	0.75	1.50	3.00	8.00	—

KM# 224 20 CENTAVOS
Copper-Nickel **Obv:** Arms above denomination **Rev:** Bust of Jorge Eliecer Gaitan left, date below

Date	Mintage	F	VF	XF	Unc	BU
1965	1,000,000	—	0.10	0.50	1.50	—

KM# 227 20 CENTAVOS
Nickel Clad Steel **Obv:** Head of Santander right, large date and continuous legend **Rev:** Denomination within wreath

Date	Mintage	F	VF	XF	Unc	BU
1967	15,720,000	—	0.10	0.20	1.00	—
1968	26,680,000	—	0.10	0.20	1.00	—
1969	22,470,000	—	0.10	0.20	1.00	—

KM# 237 20 CENTAVOS
Nickel Clad Steel **Obv:** Refined detailed portrait of Santander right, with smaller date and legend **Rev:** Denomination within wreath

Date	Mintage	F	VF	XF	Unc	BU
1969	Inc. above	—	—	—	—	—
1970	44,358,000	—	0.10	0.20	1.00	—

KM# 245 20 CENTAVOS
Nickel Clad Steel **Obv:** Head right, legend divided after REPUBLICA DE **Rev:** Denomination within wreath

Date	Mintage	F	VF	XF	Unc	BU
1971	77,526,000	—	—	0.10	0.35	—

KM# 246.1 20 CENTAVOS
Nickel Clad Steel **Obv:** Head right, date below, legend continuous **Rev:** Denomination within wreath **Note:** Varieties exist with and without dots.

Date	Mintage	F	VF	XF	Unc	BU
1971	Inc. above	—	—	0.10	0.35	—
1972	41,891,000	—	—	0.10	0.35	—
1973/1	41,440,000	—	—	0.10	0.35	—
1973	Inc. above	—	—	0.15	0.50	—
1974/1	45,941,000	—	—	0.35	1.00	—
1974	Inc. above	—	—	0.10	0.35	—
1975	28,635,000	—	—	0.10	0.35	—
1976	29,590,000	—	—	0.10	0.35	—
1977	2,054,000	—	—	0.15	0.50	—
1978	10,630,000	—	—	0.10	0.35	—

KM# 246.2 20 CENTAVOS
Nickel Clad Steel **Obv:** Head right, date below, smaller letters in legend **Rev:** Wreath with larger 20 and smaller CENTAVOS

Date	Mintage	F	VF	XF	Unc	BU
1979	16,655,000	—	—	0.10	0.20	—

KM# 267 25 CENTAVOS
Aluminum-Bronze **Obv:** Head of Simon Bolivar right, date below **Rev:** Denomination within lines

Date	Mintage	F	VF	XF	Unc	BU
1979	88,874,000	—	0.10	0.15	0.25	—
1980	46,168,000	—	0.10	0.15	0.25	—

KM# 186.2 50 CENTAVOS
12.5000 g., 0.8350 Silver 0.3356 oz. ASW **Obv:** Liberty head left, incuse lettering on headband, date below **Rev:** Denomination above arms **Edge Lettering:** DIOS LEI LIBERTAD **Mint:** Bogota **Note:** Similar to KM#186.1a.

Date	Mintage	VG	F	VF	XF	Unc
1906	446,000	6.50	13.50	25.00	40.00	75.00
1907	1,126,000	5.50	8.50	15.00	30.00	60.00
1908/7	871,000	20.00	30.00	45.00	65.00	135
1908	Inc. above	6.00	10.00	18.00	35.00	70.00

KM# 192 50 CENTAVOS
12.5000 g., 0.8350 Silver 0.3356 oz. ASW **Obv:** Liberty head left, date below **Rev:** Denomination above arms **Mint:** Philadelphia

Date	Mintage	F	VF	XF	Unc	BU
1902(P)	960,000	13.50	27.50	50.00	125	—

KM# 193.1 50 CENTAVOS
12.5000 g., 0.9000 Silver 0.3617 oz. ASW **Obv:** Simon Bolivar, sharper featured head right, date below **Rev:** Denomination above arms, left wing and flags far from legend **Note:** Struck at Birmingham and Bogota mints. Date varieties exist.

Date	Mintage	F	VF	XF	Unc	BU
1912	1,207,000	6.00	12.50	35.00	75.00	—
1912 Proof; rare	—	—	—	—	—	—
1913	417,000	6.00	12.50	35.00	75.00	—
1914 Closed 4	769,000	7.00	15.00	40.00	85.00	—
1915 Small date	946,000	6.00	12.50	30.00	70.00	—
1915 Small date; Proof; rare	—	—	—	—	—	—
1915 Large date	Inc. above	—	—	—	—	—
1915 Proof; rare	—	—	—	—	—	—
1916 Small date	1,060,000	5.00	10.00	22.50	50.00	—
1917 Normal 7	99,000	10.00	20.00	45.00	90.00	—
1917 Foot on 7	Inc. above	10.00	20.00	45.00	90.00	—
1917 Curved top	Inc. above	10.00	20.00	50.00	100	—
1918	400,000	5.00	10.00	25.00	75.00	—
1919	Inc. above	15.00	25.00	40.00	85.00	—
1922	150,000	10.00	15.00	30.00	75.00	—
1923	150,000	10.00	15.00	30.00	75.00	—
1931/21B	—	5.00	10.00	22.50	50.00	—
1931B	700,000	5.00	10.00	22.50	50.00	—
1931	Inc. above	65.00	120	185	350	—
1932/12B	300,000	8.00	14.00	30.00	75.00	—
1932/22B	Inc. above	7.00	15.00	35.00	80.00	—
1932B	Inc. above	5.00	10.00	22.50	50.00	—
1932 Flat top 3, no B	Inc. above	20.00	30.00	45.00	90.00	—
1933/13B	1,000,000	5.00	10.00	20.00	45.00	—
1933/23B	Inc. above	5.00	10.00	25.00	50.00	—
1933B	Inc. above	BV	5.00	10.00	28.00	—

KM# 193.2 50 CENTAVOS
12.5000 g., 0.9000 Silver 0.3617 oz. ASW **Obv:** Simon Bolivar, sharper featured head right, date below **Rev:** Denomination above arms, larger letters, left wing and flags close to legend **Mint:** Medellin **Note:** Date varieties exist.

Date	Mintage	F	VF	XF	Unc	BU
1914 Open 4	—	5.00	10.00	30.00	80.00	—
1915/4 Large date	—	45.00	75.00	125	200	—
1915 Large date	—	55.00	100	150	250	—
1918/4	—	10.00	20.00	35.00	75.00	—
1918	—	5.00	10.00	25.00	65.00	—
1919/8	—	7.50	15.00	30.00	70.00	—
1919	—	7.50	15.00	30.00	70.00	—
1921	300,000	7.50	15.00	30.00	70.00	—
1922	—	5.00	10.00	25.00	65.00	—
1932/22M	1,200,000	20.00	40.00	70.00	145	—
1932M	Inc. above	BV	5.00	15.00	30.00	—
1932 Round top 3, no M	Inc. above	18.00	35.00	60.00	125	—
1933M	800,000	BV	7.50	25.00	50.00	—
1933/23 Round top 3s, no M	Inc. above	15.00	25.00	35.00	75.00	—

KM# 274 50 CENTAVOS
12.5000 g., 0.9000 Silver 0.3617 oz. ASW **Obv:** Simon Bolivar, rounded featured head right, date below **Rev:** Denomination above arms **Note:** Struck at the Philadelphia and San Francisco mints.

Date	Mintage	F	VF	XF	Unc	BU
1916(P)	1,300,000	BV	7.50	25.00	50.00	—
1917(P)	142,000	6.00	18.00	37.50	75.00	—
1921(P)	1,000,000	BV	6.00	20.00	45.00	—
1922(P)	3,000,000	BV	5.00	15.00	40.00	—
1934(S)	10,000,000	BV	5.00	15.00	40.00	—

KM# 209 50 CENTAVOS
12.5000 g., 0.5000 Silver 0.2009 oz. ASW **Obv:** Simon Bolivar armored bust left, date below **Rev:** Denomination within circular wreath **Mint:** Bogota

Date	Mintage	F	VF	XF	Unc	BU
1947/6B	1,240,000	4.50	7.00	20.00	50.00	—
1947B	Inc. above	10.00	15.00	30.00	75.00	—
1948/6B	707,000	4.50	7.00	20.00	50.00	—
1948B/B inverted B	Inc. above	25.00	40.00	60.00	120	—
1948B	Inc. above	7.50	12.50	25.00	65.00	—

KM# 217 50 CENTAVOS
12.5600 g., Copper-Nickel **Obv:** Denomination below arms **Rev:** Head of Simon Bolivar right, date below **Note:** Various sizes of date exist.

Date	Mintage	F	VF	XF	Unc	BU
1958	3,596,000	0.15	0.50	1.25	3.50	—
1958 Medal Rotation	Inc. above	6.00	12.00	22.00	40.00	—
1959	13,466,000	0.15	0.30	1.00	3.00	—
1959 Medal Rotation	Inc. above	2.00	3.50	6.00	10.00	—
1960	4,360,000	0.15	0.30	1.50	4.00	—
1961	3,260,000	0.15	0.30	1.50	4.00	—
1962	2,336,000	0.15	0.30	1.50	4.00	—
1963	4,098,000	0.15	0.30	1.00	3.00	—
1964	9,274,000	0.15	0.30	1.00	3.00	—
1965	5,800,000	0.15	0.30	1.00	3.00	—
1966	2,820,000	0.15	0.30	1.00	3.00	—

KM# 223 50 CENTAVOS
Copper-Nickel **Subject:** Uprising Sesquicentennial **Obv:** Denomination below arms **Rev:** Head right, two dates below

Date	Mintage	F	VF	XF	Unc	BU
ND(1960)	200,000	1.50	3.00	7.50	15.00	—

KM# 225 50 CENTAVOS
Copper-Nickel, 30.5 mm. **Obv:** Arms and denomination **Rev:** Jorge Eliecer Gaitan bust left, date below

Date	Mintage	F	VF	XF	Unc	BU
1965	600,000	0.10	0.20	0.50	1.50	—

KM# 228 50 CENTAVOS
Nickel Clad Steel, 30 mm. **Obv:** Head of Francisco de Paula Santander right, date below **Rev:** Denomination within circular wreath

Date	Mintage	F	VF	XF	Unc	BU
1967	3,460,000	0.10	0.15	0.25	1.00	—
1968	5,460,000	0.10	0.15	0.25	1.00	—
1969	1,590,000	0.10	0.15	0.25	1.00	—

KM# 244.1 50 CENTAVOS

Nickel Clad Steel **Obv:** Head right, flat truncation, date below **Rev:** Denomination within wreath, 5 far from wreath **Shape:** 12-sided **Note:** Date varieties exist.

Date	Mintage	F	VF	XF	Unc	BU
1970	30,906,000	—	0.10	0.15	0.50	—
1971	32,650,000	—	0.10	0.15	0.50	—
1972	25,290,000	—	0.10	0.15	0.50	—
1973	8,060,000	—	0.10	0.15	0.50	—
1974	19,541,000	—	0.10	0.15	0.50	—
1975	4,325,000	—	0.10	0.15	0.60	—
1976	13,181,000	—	0.10	0.15	0.45	—
1977	10,413,000	—	0.10	0.15	0.45	—
1978	10,736,000	—	0.10	0.15	0.45	—

KM# 244.3 50 CENTAVOS

Nickel Clad Steel **Obv:** Head right, angled truncation, date below **Rev:** Denomination within wreath, 5 far from wreath **Shape:** Twelve sided **Note:** Mule.

Date	Mintage	F	VF	XF	Unc	BU
1979	—	10.00	20.00	30.00	50.00	—

KM# 244.2 50 CENTAVOS

Nickel Clad Steel **Obv:** Head right, angled truncation, date below **Rev:** Denomination within wreath, 5 close to wreath **Shape:** 12-sided **Note:** Various sizes of dates exist.

Date	Mintage	F	VF	XF	Unc	BU
1979	22,584,000	—	0.10	0.15	0.45	—
1980	16,433,000	—	0.10	0.15	0.45	—
1982	10,107,000	—	0.10	0.15	0.45	—

KM# 216 PESO

25.0000 g., 0.9000 Silver 0.7234 oz. ASW, 37 mm. **Subject:** 200th Anniversary of Popayan Mint **Obv:** Arms above denomination **Rev:** Monument, sprays flank, date above **Mint:** Mexico City

Date	Mintage	F	VF	XF	Unc	BU
ND(1956)(Mo)	12,000	BV	10.00	15.00	25.00	—

KM# 229 PESO

Copper-Nickel, 30 mm. **Obv:** Head of Simon Bolivar right, date below **Rev:** Denomination within circular wreath **Shape:** 10-sided

Date	Mintage	F	VF	XF	Unc	BU
1967	4,000,000	0.15	0.30	0.50	1.00	—

KM# 258.1 PESO

Copper-Nickel, 25.3 mm. **Obv:** Bust of Simon Bolivar 3/4 facing, small date below **Rev:** Denomination, ears of corn flank

Date	Mintage	F	VF	XF	Unc	BU
1974	56,020,000	—	0.10	0.15	0.50	—
1975 medium date	117,714,000	—	0.10	0.15	0.40	—
1976	98,728,000	—	0.10	0.15	0.40	—

KM# 258.2 PESO

Copper-Nickel **Obv:** Bust of Simon Bolivar 3/4 facing, large date below **Rev:** Denomination, ears of corn flank

Date	Mintage	F	VF	XF	Unc	BU
1976	Inc. above	—	0.10	0.15	0.40	—
1977	62,083,000	—	0.10	0.15	0.40	—
1978	48,624,000	—	0.10	0.15	0.40	—
1979	83,908,000	—	0.10	0.15	0.40	—
1980	93,406,000	—	0.10	0.15	0.40	—
1981	65,219,000	—	0.10	0.15	0.40	—

KM# 263 2 PESOS

7.5000 g., Bronze, 23.8 mm. **Obv:** Bust of Simon Bolivar 3/4 facing, date below **Rev:** Denomination within wreath **Note:** Varieties exist.

Date	Mintage	F	VF	XF	Unc	BU
1977	76,661,000	0.10	0.15	0.25	0.50	—
1978	69,575,000	0.10	0.15	0.25	0.50	—
1979	56,537,000	0.10	0.15	0.25	0.50	—
1980	108,521,000	0.10	0.15	0.25	0.50	—
1981	40,368,000	0.10	0.15	0.25	0.50	—
1983	8,358,000	0.10	0.15	0.25	0.50	—
1987	—	0.10	0.15	0.25	0.50	—
1988	16,200,000	0.10	0.15	0.25	0.50	—

KM# 194 2-1/2 PESOS

3.9940 g., 0.9170 Gold 0.1177 oz. AGW **Obv:** Native, date below **Rev:** Arms and denomination

Date	Mintage	F	VF	XF	Unc	BU
1913	18,000	—	BV	100	125	—

KM# 200 2-1/2 PESOS

3.9940 g., 0.9170 Gold 0.1177 oz. AGW **Obv:** Simon Bolivar large head right, date below **Rev:** Arms and denomination

Date	Mintage	F	VF	XF	Unc	BU
1919A	—	—	BV	100	115	—
Note: Two varieties, with large or small first 1 in date						
1919B	—	—	—	—	—	—
1919	34,000	—	BV	100	115	—
1920/19A	—	—	BV	100	115	—
1920A	—	—	BV	100	115	—
1920	34,000	—	BV	110	150	—

KM# 203 2-1/2 PESOS

3.9940 g., 0.9170 Gold 0.1177 oz. AGW **Obv:** Simon Bolivar small head, MEDELLIN below, date at bottom **Rev:** Arms and denomination

Date	Mintage	F	VF	XF	Unc	BU
1924	—	—	BV	100	120	—
1925 Rare	—	—	—	—	—	—
1927	—	—	BV	100	125	—
1928	14,000	—	BV	120	175	—
1929 Rare	—	—	—	—	—	—

KM# 195.2 5 PESOS

7.9881 g., 0.9170 Gold 0.2355 oz. AGW **Obv:** Native, date below **Rev:** Arms and denomination **Note:** Medallic die rotation.

Date	Mintage	F	VF	XF	Unc	BU
1913	Inc. above	—	—	BV	200	210
1917	43,000	—	—	BV	200	210
1918	Inc. above	—	—	BV	200	210
1919	Inc. above	—	—	BV	200	210

KM# 195.1 5 PESOS

7.9881 g., 0.9170 Gold 0.2355 oz. AGW **Obv:** Native, date below **Rev:** Arms and denomination **Note:** Various rotations of dies exist.

Date	Mintage	F	VF	XF	Unc	BU
1913	17,000	—	—	200	225	—
1918/3	423,000	—	—	BV	215	—
1918	Inc. above	—	—	BV	215	—
1919	2,181,000	—	—	BV	200	210
1919 Long-tail 9	Inc. above	—	—	BV	200	210
1919 Dot over 9	Inc. above	—	—	BV	215	—

KM# 201.1 5 PESOS

7.9881 g., 0.9170 Gold 0.2355 oz. AGW **Obv:** Simon Bolivar, large head right **Rev:** Arms and denomination **Note:** 1920A dated coins come with mint mark centered or on right side of coat of arms; 1923B dated coins come with B on the left or right of coat of arms. The 1923B mint mark to right carries a 25% premium in value. Various rotations of dies exist.

Date	Mintage	F	VF	XF	Unc	BU
1919	Inc. above	—	—	BV	200	210
Note: Narrow or wide dates, with multiple varieties of numeral alignment						
1919A	Inc. above	—	—	BV	200	210
Note: Narrow or wide date						
1919B	—	—	—	BV	200	210
1920	870,000	—	—	BV	200	210
1920A	Inc. above	—	—	BV	200	210
Note: Placement of A below coat of arms varies						
1920B	108,000	—	—	BV	200	210
Note: Placement of B varies						
1921A	—	—	—	—	—	—
1922B	29,000	—	—	BV	200	210
Note: Two varieties known, with B touching or separated from coat of arms						
1923B	74,000	—	—	BV	200	210
1924B	705,000	—	—	BV	200	210
Note: Placement of B varies						

KM# 201.2 5 PESOS

7.9881 g., 0.9170 Gold 0.2355 oz. AGW **Obv:** Simon Bolivar, large head **Rev:** Arms and denomination **Note:** Medallic die rotation.

Date	Mintage	F	VF	XF	Unc	BU
1920	Inc. above	—	—	BV	200	210

KM# 204 5 PESOS

7.9881 g., 0.9170 Gold 0.2355 oz. AGW **Obv:** Simon Bolivar, small head, MEDELLIN below, date at bottom **Rev:** Arms and denomination **Note:** 1924 dated coins have several varieties in size of 2 and 4. 1925 dated coins exist with an Arabic and a Spanish style 5. 1930 dated coins have three varieties in size and placement of 3.

Date	Mintage	F	VF	XF	Unc	BU
1924 Large 2	120,000	—	—	BV	200	210
1924 Large 4	Inc. above	—	—	BV	200	210
1924 Small 4	Inc. above	—	—	BV	200	210
1924 MFDELLIN	Inc. above	—	—	BV	200	220
1925/4	668,000	—	—	BV	200	210
1925 MFDELLIN	Inc. above	—	—	BV	200	210
Note: Wide or narrow date						
1925 MFDFLLIN	Inc. above	—	—	BV	200	210
Note: Wide or narrow date						
1926	383,000	—	—	BV	200	210
1926 MFDFLLIN	Inc. above	—	—	BV	200	210
1926 MFDFLLIN	Inc. above	—	—	BV	200	210
Note: With large 6 in date						
1927 MFDFLLIN	365,000	—	—	BV	200	210
Note: Wide or narrow date						
1928 MFDFLLIN	314,000	—	—	BV	200	210
Note: Narrow or wide date with large or normal 2						
1929 MFDFLLIN	321,000	—	—	BV	200	210
Note: Narrow or wide date						
1930 MFDFLLIN	502,000	—	—	BV	200	210
Note: Varieties known with aligned date or dropped 3 in date						

KM# 230 5 PESOS

Copper-Nickel, 34 mm. **Subject:** International Eucharistic Congress **Obv:** Denomination within wheat stalks, date below **Rev:** Design within circle, within square, at center

Date	Mintage	F	VF	XF	Unc	BU
1968B	660,000	0.25	0.50	0.75	1.75	—

KM# 247 5 PESOS

Nickel Clad Steel, 30 mm. **Subject:** 6th Pan-American Games in Cali **Obv:** Torches flank denomination at center, date below **Rev:** Games logo

Date	Mintage	F	VF	XF	Unc	BU
1971	2,000,000	0.15	0.35	0.60	1.50	—

KM# 268 5 PESOS

Bronze, 26.3 mm. **Obv:** Seated figure right **Rev:** Denomination and buildings

Date	Mintage	F	VF	XF	Unc	BU
1980	146,268,000	0.15	0.35	0.60	1.25	—
1.981	9,148,000	0.15	0.35	0.60	1.25	—
1.982	—	0.15	0.35	0.75	1.50	—
1983	84,107,000	0.15	0.35	0.60	1.25	—
1985	—	0.15	0.35	0.60	1.25	—
1986	14,700,000	0.15	0.35	0.60	1.25	—
1987	—	0.15	0.35	0.60	1.25	—
1988 Small date	45,000,000	0.15	0.35	0.60	1.25	—
1988 Large inverted date	Inc. above	0.15	0.35	0.60	1.25	—
1989	—	0.15	0.35	0.60	1.25	—

KM# 280 5 PESOS

2.6000 g., Copper-Aluminum-Nickel, 17.3 mm. **Obv:** Arms above date **Rev:** Denomination within wreath **Note:** Varieties exist, such as 1989 where some have 72 beads on the obverse and reverse and some have 66 beads.

Date	Mintage	F	VF	XF	Unc	BU
1989	—	—	—	—	0.50	0.75
1990	—	—	—	—	0.50	0.75
1991	—	—	—	—	0.50	0.75
1992	—	—	—	—	0.35	0.65
1993	—	—	—	—	0.35	0.65

KM# 202 10 PESOS

15.9761 g., 0.9170 Gold 0.4710 oz. AGW **Obv:** Head of Simon Bolivar right, date below **Rev:** Arms and denomination

Date	Mintage	F	VF	XF	Unc	BU
1919	101,000	—	BV	400	425	—
1924B	55,000	—	BV	400	425	—
Note: Varieties with aligned date and dropped 4 in date						

KM# 270 10 PESOS

9.9600 g., Copper-Nickel-Zinc, 28 mm. **Obv:** Figure on horseback and standing, date at left **Rev:** Map showing San Andreas Island and Providencia, denomination below **Note:** Date varieties exist.

Date	Mintage	F	VF	XF	Unc	BU
1.981	104,554,000	—	0.15	0.25	1.25	—
1.982	83,605,000	—	0.15	0.25	1.25	—
1983	104,051,000	—	0.15	0.25	1.25	—
1985	80,000,000	—	0.15	0.25	1.25	—
1988	50,700,000	—	0.15	0.25	1.25	—
1989	—	—	0.15	0.25	1.25	—

KM# 281.1 10 PESOS

3.3000 g., Copper-Nickel-Zinc, 18.75 mm. **Obv:** Flagged arms, date below **Rev:** Denomination within wreath, wide 10 (5mm) - wreath nearly touches beads in rim **Edge:** Reeded **Note:** Varieties exist.

Date	Mintage	F	VF	XF	Unc	BU
1989	—	—	—	—	0.75	1.00
1990	—	—	—	—	0.75	1.00
1991	—	—	—	—	0.75	1.00
1992	—	—	—	—	0.50	0.75
1993	—	—	—	—	0.50	0.75
1994	—	—	—	—	0.50	0.75

KM# 281.2 10 PESOS

3.3000 g., Copper-Nickel-Zinc, 18.75 mm. **Obv:** Flagged arms, date below **Rev:** Narrow 10 (4.5mm) - wreath is 1 mm away from beads in rim

Date	Mintage	F	VF	XF	Unc	BU
1993	—	—	—	3.00	7.00	—
1994	—	—	—	3.00	7.00	—

KM# 271 20 PESOS

Aluminum-Bronze, 25 mm. **Obv:** Vase, date below **Rev:** Denomination within wreath **Note:** 1985 and 1988 coins exist with large and small dates.

Date	Mintage	F	VF	XF	Unc	BU
1982	—	—	0.15	0.20	0.30	0.50
1984	64,066,000	—	0.15	0.20	0.30	0.50
1985	100,690,000	—	0.15	0.20	0.30	0.50
1986	18,300,000	—	0.15	0.20	0.30	0.50
1987	—	—	0.15	0.20	0.30	0.50
1988	72,000,000	—	0.15	0.20	0.30	0.50
1989	—	—	0.15	0.20	0.30	0.50

KM# 282.1 20 PESOS

3.6000 g., Copper-Aluminum-Nickel, 20.25 mm. **Obv:** Flagged arms above date, 72 beads circle around the rim **Rev:** Denomination within wreath **Note:** Varieties exist.

Date	Mintage	F	VF	XF	Unc	BU
1989	—	—	—	—	0.75	1.00
1990	—	—	—	—	0.75	1.00
1991	—	—	—	—	0.75	1.00
1992	—	—	—	—	0.75	1.00
1993	—	—	—	—	0.75	1.00
1994	—	—	—	—	0.75	1.00

KM# 282.2 20 PESOS

3.6000 g., Copper-Aluminum-Nickel, 20.25 mm. **Obv:** Flagged arms, 68 beads circle around the rim **Rev:** Denomination within wreath

Date	Mintage	F	VF	XF	Unc	BU
1994	—	—	—	—	0.50	0.75
2003	—	—	—	—	0.50	0.75

KM# 294 20 PESOS

2.0000 g., Brass, 17.2 mm. **Obv:** Simon Bolivar left **Rev:** Value **Edge:** Reeded

Date	Mintage	F	VF	XF	Unc	BU
2004	—	—	—	—	0.15	0.25

KM# 272 50 PESOS

8.4000 g., Copper-Nickel, 26.8 mm. **Subject:** National Constitution **Obv:** Arms above denomination, sprigs flank date below **Rev:** Building, stars below, within circle

Date	Mintage	F	VF	XF	Unc	BU
1986	14,900,000	—	—	—	1.25	1.50
1987 Large date	—	—	—	—	1.25	1.50
1988 Small date	100,000,000	—	—	—	1.25	1.50
1989	—	—	—	—	1.25	1.50

KM# 283.1 50 PESOS

4.5000 g., Copper-Nickel-Zinc, 21.8 mm. **Obv:** Flagged arms above date **Rev:** Denomination within wreath, 66 beads circle around rim **Note:** Varieties exist.

Date	Mintage	F	VF	XF	Unc	BU
1989	—	—	—	—	1.00	1.25
1990	—	—	—	—	1.00	1.25
1991	—	—	—	—	1.00	1.25
1992	—	—	—	—	1.00	1.25
1993	—	—	—	—	1.00	1.25
1994	—	—	—	—	1.00	1.25

KM# 283.2 50 PESOS

4.5000 g., Copper-Nickel-Zinc, 21.8 mm. **Obv:** Flagged arms, date below **Rev:** Denomination within wreath, 72 beads circle around rim

Date	Mintage	F	VF	XF	Unc	BU
1990	—	—	—	—	1.00	1.25
1994	—	—	—	—	1.00	1.25
2003	—	—	—	—	1.00	1.25
2005	—	—	—	—	1.00	1.25

KM# 285.1 100 PESOS
Brass **Obv:** Flagged arms above date **Rev:** Denomination within wreath, numerals 4.5mm tall

Date	Mintage	F	VF	XF	Unc	BU
1992	—	—	—	—	1.75	2.00
1993	—	—	—	—	1.75	2.00
1994	—	—	—	—	1.75	2.00
1995	—	—	—	—	1.75	2.00

KM# 285.2 100 PESOS
Brass **Obv:** Flagged arms above date **Rev:** Denomination within wreath, numerals 6mm tall **Note:** Edge varieties exist.

Date	Mintage	F	VF	XF	Unc	BU
1994	—	—	—	—	1.75	2.00
1995	—	—	—	—	1.75	2.00

KM# 287 200 PESOS
7.1000 g., Copper-Zinc-Nickel, 24.8 mm. **Obv:** Denomination within lined circle, date below **Rev:** Quimbaya artwork

Date	Mintage	F	VF	XF	Unc	BU
1994	—	—	—	—	1.50	2.00
1995	—	—	—	—	1.50	2.00
1996	—	—	—	—	1.50	2.00

KM# 286 500 PESOS
7.4000 g., Bi-Metallic Aluminum-Bronze center in Copper-Nickel ring, 23.8 mm. **Obv:** Guacari tree within circle **Rev:** Denomination within circle, date below **Edge:** Segmented reeding

Date	Mintage	F	VF	XF	Unc	BU
1993	—	—	—	—	4.00	4.50
1994	—	—	—	—	4.00	4.50
1995	—	—	—	—	4.00	4.50
1996	—	—	—	—	4.00	4.50
1997	—	—	—	—	4.00	4.50
2002	—	—	—	—	4.00	4.50
2003	—	—	—	—	4.00	4.50
2004	—	—	—	—	4.00	4.50
2005	—	—	—	—	4.00	4.50

KM# 288 1000 PESOS
Copper-Aluminum-Nickel **Obv:** Armored bust 3/4 facing **Rev:** Head right, arms divide dates above, denomination below **Edge:** Reeded and lettered **Edge Lettering:** CULTURA SINU MIL PESOS

Date	Mintage	F	VF	XF	Unc	BU
1996	—	—	—	—	3.75	4.00
1997	—	—	—	—	3.75	4.00
1998	—	—	—	—	3.75	4.00

KM# 293 5000 PESOS
15.3000 g., Nickel **Subject:** 50th Anniversary - Organization of American States **Obv:** Denomination, date below **Rev:** Circle of flags

Date	Mintage	F	VF	XF	Unc	BU
1998	—	—	—	—	5.50	6.50

COMOROS

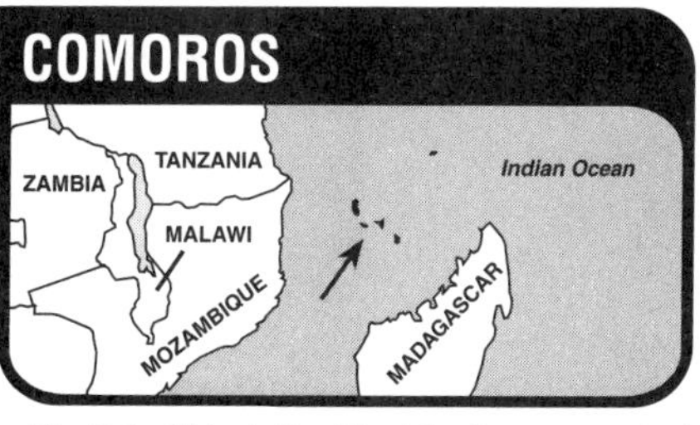

The Federal Islamic Republic of the Comoros, a volcanic archipelago located in the Mozambique Channel of the Indian Ocean 300 miles (483 km.) northwest of Madagascar, has an area of 719 sq. mi. (2,171 sq. km.) and a population of *714,000. Capital: Moroni. The economy of the islands is based on agriculture. There are practically no mineral resources. Vanilla, essence for perfumes, copra, and sisal are exported.

Ancient Phoenician traders were probably the first visitors to the Comoro Islands, but the first detailed knowledge of the area was gathered by Arab sailors. Arab dominion and culture were firmly established when the Portuguese, Dutch, and French arrived in the 16th century. In 1843 a Malagasy ruler ceded the island of Mayotte to France; the other three principal islands of the archipelago-Anjouan, Moheli, and Grand Comore came under French protection in 1886. The islands were joined administratively with Madagascar in 1912. The Comoros became partially autonomous, with the status of a French overseas territory, in 1946, and achieved complete internal autonomy in 1961. On Dec. 31, 1975, after 133 years of French association, the Comoro Islands became the independent Republic of the Comoros.

Mayotte retained the option of determining its future ties and in 1976 voted to remain French. Its present status is that of a French Territorial Collectivity. French currency now circulates there.

TITLES

دولة انجزنجية

Daulat Anjazanchiyah

RULERS
French, 1886-1975

MINT MARKS
(a) - Paris, privy marks only
A - Paris

MONETARY SYSTEM
100 Centimes = 1 Franc

FEDERAL ISLAMIC REPUBLIC

BANQUE CENTRAL COINAGE

KM# 15 5 FRANCS
3.8500 g., Aluminum, 31 mm. **Subject:** World Fisheries Conference **Obv:** Trees surround denomination, date upper right **Rev:** Coelacanth fish left

Date	Mintage	F	VF	XF	Unc	BU
1984(a)	1,010,000	0.25	0.50	1.50	6.00	10.00
1992(a)	—	0.25	0.50	1.50	6.00	10.00

KM# 17 10 FRANCS
3.9100 g., Aluminum-Bronze, 22.4 mm. **Obv:** Half moon with four stars vertical from point to point **Rev:** Denomination above date

Date	Mintage	F	VF	XF	Unc	BU
1992(a)	—	—	—	—	1.65	2.00

KM# 14 25 FRANCS
3.9700 g., Nickel, 20 mm. **Series:** F.A.O. **Obv:** Chickens **Rev:** Denomination above date

Date	Mintage	F	VF	XF	Unc	BU
1981(a)	1,000,000	1.50	3.00	6.00	16.00	—
1982(a)	2,007,000	0.20	0.40	0.80	2.00	4.00

KM# 14a 25 FRANCS
Steel, 20 mm. **Series:** F.A.O. **Obv:** Chickens **Rev:** Denomination abovwe date

Date	Mintage	F	VF	XF	Unc	BU
2001(a) Horseshoe	—	0.20	0.40	0.80	2.00	—

KM# 16 50 FRANCS
6.0300 g., Stainless Steel, 23.93 mm. **Obv:** Building with tall tower **Rev:** Moon and stars above denomination, date below

Date	Mintage	F	VF	XF	Unc	BU
1990(a)	—	0.50	0.80	1.50	2.50	3.50
1994(a)	—	0.50	0.80	1.50	2.50	3.50
2001(a)	—	0.50	0.80	1.50	2.50	3.50

KM# 18 100 FRANCS
10.0000 g., Nickel, 28 mm. **Subject:** Circulation Type **Obv:** Denomination, moon and stars above, date below **Rev:** Boat and fish **Edge:** Plain

Date	Mintage	F	VF	XF	Unc	BU
1999(a)	—	—	—	—	3.50	5.00
2003	—	—	—	—	3.50	5.00

INSTITUT D'EMISSION COINAGE

KM# 9 50 FRANCS
6.0900 g., Nickel, 24.1 mm. **Subject:** Independence of Republic **Obv:** Building with tall tower **Rev:** Half moon on cross above denomination, date below

Date	Mintage	F	VF	XF	Unc	BU
1975(a)	1,200,000	0.40	0.75	1.25	2.25	3.00

KM# 13 100 FRANCS
Nickel **Series:** F.A.O. **Obv:** Half moon and stars above denomination, date below **Rev:** Boat and fish

Date	Mintage	F	VF	XF	Unc	BU
1977(a)	1,500,000	0.60	1.00	2.00	3.75	5.00

FRENCH COLONIAL

DECIMAL COINAGE

KM# 4 FRANC
0.9000 Aluminum **Obv:** Winged Liberty bust left, cargo ships in background, date below **Obv. Designer:** G.B.L. Bazor **Rev:** Trees surrounding denomination

Date	Mintage	F	VF	XF	Unc	BU
1964(a)	500,000	0.15	0.25	0.40	1.25	4.00

KM# 5 2 FRANCS
2.2100 g., Aluminum, 27.1 mm. **Obv:** Winged Liberty bust left, date below, cargo ships in background **Obv. Designer:** G.B.L. Bazor **Rev:** Trees surround denomination

Date	Mintage	F	VF	XF	Unc	BU
1964(a)	600,000	0.15	0.25	0.50	1.50	5.00

KM# 6 5 FRANCS
3.7300 g., Aluminum, 31.1 mm. **Obv:** Winged Liberty bust left, date below, cargo ships in background **Obv. Designer:** G.B.L. Bazor **Rev:** Trees surround denomination

Date	Mintage	F	VF	XF	Unc	BU
1964(a)	1,000,000	0.20	0.40	0.65	2.00	6.00

KM# 7 10 FRANCS
3.0100 g., Aluminum-Bronze **Obv:** Winged Liberty bust left, date below, cargo ships in background **Obv. Designer:** G.B.L. Bazor **Rev:** Plants on mantle with shells flanking, denomination at center, fish below

Date	Mintage	F	VF	XF	Unc	BU
1964(a)	600,000	0.20	0.50	1.00	2.50	4.00

KM# 8 20 FRANCS
3.8900 g., Aluminum-Bronze, 23.8 mm. **Obv:** Winged Liberty bust left, date below, cargo ships in background **Obv. Designer:** G.B.L. Bazor **Rev:** Plants on mantle, shells flank, denomination at center, fish below

Date	Mintage	F	VF	XF	Unc	BU
1964(a)	500,000	0.30	0.65	1.25	3.00	6.00

CONGO FREE STATE

In ancient times the territory comprising former Zaire was occupied by Negrito peoples (Pygmies) pushed into the mountains by Bantu and Nilotic invaders. The interior was first explored by the American correspondent Henry Stanley, who was subsequently commissioned by King Leopold II of Belgium to conclude development treaties with the local chiefs. The Berlin conference of 1885 awarded the area to Leopold, who administered and exploited it as his private property until it was annexed to Belgium in 1908.

For later issues, see Belgian Congo.

RULER
Leopold II

ROYAL DOMAIN
1865-1908

STANDARD COINAGE

KM# 9 5 CENTIMES
Copper-Nickel **Ruler:** Leopold II **Obv:** Crowned monograms surround center hole, within circle **Rev:** Hole at center of radiant star, denomination above, date below

Date	Mintage	F	VF	XF	Unc	BU
1906	100,000	5.00	10.00	25.00	60.00	—
1908/6	—	—	—	—	—	—
1908	180,000	4.00	8.00	20.00	50.00	—

KM# 10 10 CENTIMES
Copper-Nickel **Ruler:** Leopold II **Obv:** Hole at center of crowned monograms within circle **Rev:** Hole at center of radiant star, denomination above, date below

Date	Mintage	F	VF	XF	Unc	BU
1906	100,000	5.00	12.00	35.00	90.00	—
1908	800,000	3.00	8.00	30.00	80.00	—

KM# 11 20 CENTIMES
Copper-Nickel **Ruler:** Leopold II **Obv:** Hole at center of crowned monograms within circle **Rev:** Hole at center of radiant star, denomination above, date below

Date	Mintage	F	VF	XF	Unc	BU
1906	100,000	5.00	12.00	40.00	110	—
1908	400,000	4.00	8.00	35.00	95.00	—

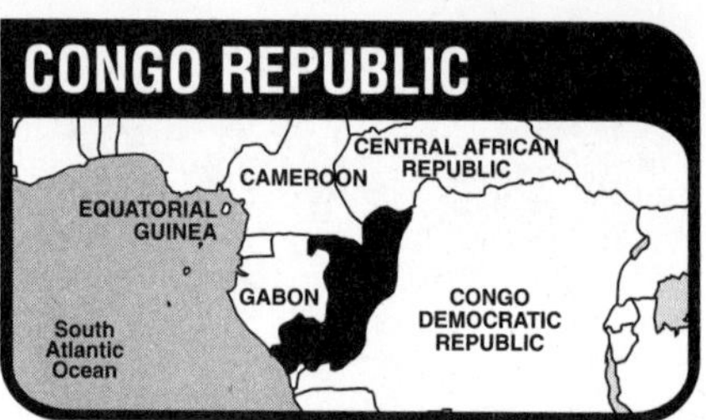

The Republic of the Congo (formerly the Peoples Republic of the Congo), located on the equator in west-central Africa, has an area of 132,047 sq. mi. (342,000 sq. km.) and a population of *2.98 million. Capital: Brazzaville. Agriculture forestry, mining, and food processing are the principal industries. Timber, industrial diamonds, potash, peanuts, and cocoa beans are exported.

The Portuguese were the first Europeans to explore the Congo (Brazzaville) area, 14th century. They conducted a slave trade with the tribal kingdoms of Teke, Loango, and Kongo without attempting developmental colonization. French influence was established in 1883 when the king of Teke signed a treaty with Savorgnan de Brazza, thereby placing his kingdom under the protection of France. While a French protectorate, the area was known as Middle Congo. In 1910 Middle Congo became a part of French Equatorial Africa, which also included Gabon, Ubangi-Shari (now the Central African Republic), and Chad. Following World War II, during which it was an important center of Free French activities, the Middle Congo was given a large measure of internal autonomy, and its inhabitants were made French citizens. Upon approval of the constitution of the Fifth French Republic, 1958, it became a member of the new French Community. On Aug. 15, 1960, Middle Congo became the independent Republic of the Congo-Brazzaville. In Jan. 1970 the country's name was changed to Peoples Republic of the Congo. A new constitution which asserts the government's advocacy of socialism was adopted in 1973.

In June and July of 1992, a new 125-member National Assembly was elected. Later that year a new president, Pascal Lissouba was elected. In November, President Lissouba dismissed the previous government and dissolved the National Assembly. A new 23-member government, including members of the opposition, was formed in December, 1992, and the name was changed to Republique du Congo.

NOTE: For earlier and related coinage see French Equatorial Africa and the Equatorial African States. For later coinage see Central African States.

RULER
French until 1960

MINT MARK
(a) - Paris, privy marks only

MONETARY SYSTEM
100 Centimes = 1 Franc

PEOPLE'S REPUBLIC
Republique Populaire du Congo

DECIMAL COINAGE

KM# 1 100 FRANCS
Nickel **Obv:** Three Giant Eland left **Obv. Designer:** G.B.L. Bazor **Rev:** Denomination within circle, date below

Date	Mintage	F	VF	XF	Unc	BU
1971(a)	2,700,000	8.00	15.00	25.00	40.00	—
1972(a)	2,500,000	8.00	15.00	25.00	40.00	—

KM# 2 100 FRANCS
Nickel **Obv:** Three Giant Eland left **Obv. Designer:** G.B.L. Bazor **Rev:** Denomination within circle, date below

Date	Mintage	F	VF	XF	Unc	BU
1975(a)	—	4.00	8.00	16.50	30.00	—
1982(a)	—	2.50	4.50	8.00	12.50	—
1983(a)	—	2.50	5.00	8.00	12.50	—
1985(a)	—	2.00	3.00	6.00	10.00	—
1990(a)	—	2.00	3.00	4.00	6.00	—

KM# 4 500 FRANCS
Copper-Nickel **Obv:** Plants divide date and denomination, within octagon **Rev:** Inscription lower right of woman's head 3/4 left, within octagon

Date	Mintage	F	VF	XF	Unc	BU
1985(a)	—	3.50	6.50	10.00	18.50	—
1986(a)	—	3.50	6.50	10.00	18.50	—

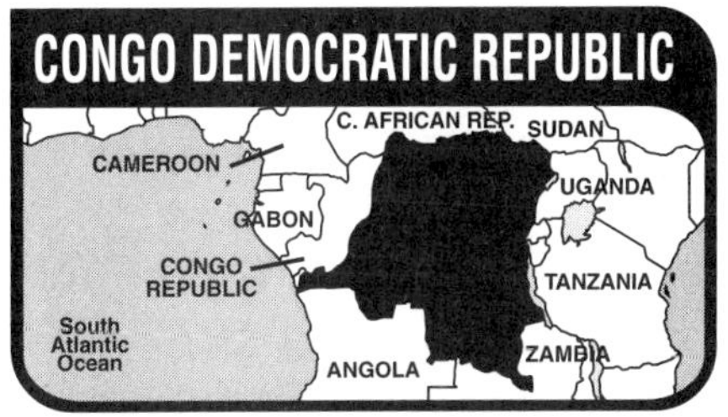

The Democratic Republic of the Congo (formerly the Republic of Zaire, and earlier the Belgian Congo), located in the south-central part of Africa, has an area of 905,568 sq. mi. (2,345,410 sq. km.) and a population of *47.4 million. Capital: Kinshasa. The mineral-rich country produces copper, tin, diamonds, gold, zinc, cobalt and uranium.

In ancient times the territory comprising former Zaire was occupied by Negrito peoples (Pygmies) pushed into the mountains by Bantu and Nilotic invaders. The interior was first explored by the American correspondent Henry Stanley, who was subsequently commissioned by King Leopold II of Belgium to conclude development treaties with the local chiefs. The Berlin conference of 1885 awarded the area to Leopold, who administered and exploited it as his private property until it was annexed to Belgium in 1908. Belgium received the mandate for the German territory of Ruanda-Urundi as a result of the international treaties after WWI. During World War II, Belgian Congolese troops fought on the side of the Allies, notably in Ethiopia. Following the eruption of bloody independence riots in 1959, Belgium granted the Belgian Congo independence as the Republic of the Congo on June 30, 1960. The nation officially changed its name to Zaire on Oct. 27, 1971, and following a Civil War in 1997 changed its name to the "Democratic Republic of the Congo."

MINT MARKS
(b) – Brussels, privy marks only

REPUBLIC
1960 - 1971
DECIMAL COINAGE

KM# 1 10 FRANCS
3.2700 g., Aluminum, 29.8 mm. **Obv:** Denomination above date **Rev:** Lion face **Note:** Most recalled and melted.

Date	Mintage	F	VF	XF	Unc	BU
1965(b)	Est. 100,000,000	0.60	1.50	3.00	7.00	10.00

REFORM COINAGE
100 Sengis = 1 Likuta; 100 Makuta (plural of Likuta) = 1 Zaire

KM# 7 10 SENGIS
0.7000 g., Aluminum, 17 mm. **Obv:** Denomination within circle **Rev:** Leopard crouching on branch, date below **Edge:** Reeded

Date	Mintage	F	VF	XF	Unc	BU
1967 Proof	—	—	—	—	—	—
1967	90,996,000	—	0.15	0.45	1.00	3.00

KM# 8 LIKUTA
1.2700 g., Aluminum, 20.9 mm. **Obv:** Denomination within circle **Rev:** Arms above date

Date	Mintage	F	VF	XF	Unc	BU
1967 Proof	—	—	—	—	—	—
1967	49,180,000	—	0.15	0.50	1.25	—

KM# 9 5 MAKUTA
6.4100 g., Copper-Nickel, 25 mm. **Obv:** Denomination within circle **Rev:** Bust of President Mobutu 3/4 left, date below

Date	Mintage	F	VF	XF	Unc	BU
1967 Proof	—	—	—	—	—	—
1967	2,470,000	0.25	0.50	1.00	3.00	—

DEMOCRATIC REPUBLIC
1998 -
REFORM COINAGE
Congo Francs replace Zaire; July 1998

KM# 76 25 CENTIMES
0.8800 g., Aluminum, 19.90 mm. **Obv:** Lion left **Rev:** Weasel **Edge:** Plain

Date	Mintage	F	VF	XF	Unc	BU
2002	—	—	—	—	0.75	1.00

KM# 77 25 CENTIMES
0.8500 g., Aluminum, 20 mm. **Obv:** Lion left **Rev:** Ram right, looking left **Edge:** Plain

Date	Mintage	F	VF	XF	Unc	BU
2002	—	—	—	—	0.75	1.00

KM# 83 25 CENTIMES
1.3000 g., Aluminum, 20 mm. **Obv:** Lion left **Rev:** Wild dog leaping right **Edge:** Plain

Date	Mintage	F	VF	XF	Unc	BU
2002	—	—	—	—	0.75	1.00

KM# 75 50 CENTIMES
2.2000 g., Aluminum, 26.97 mm. **Obv:** Lion left **Rev:** Soccer player right, bumping ball with head **Edge:** Plain

Date	Mintage	F	VF	XF	Unc	BU
2002	—	—	—	—	1.25	1.50

KM# 78 50 CENTIMES
2.1600 g., Aluminum, 27 mm. **Obv:** Lion left **Rev:** Giraffe right, looking left **Edge:** Plain

Date	Mintage	F	VF	XF	Unc	BU
2002	—	—	—	—	1.25	1.50

KM# 79 50 CENTIMES
2.2000 g., Aluminum, 26.92 mm. **Obv:** Lion left **Rev:** Gorilla facing, looking left **Edge:** Plain

Date	Mintage	F	VF	XF	Unc	BU
2002	—	—	—	—	1.00	1.25

KM# 80 50 CENTIMES
2.1600 g., Aluminum, 27 mm. **Obv:** Lion left **Rev:** Butterfly **Edge:** Plain

Date	Mintage	F	VF	XF	Unc	BU
2002	—	—	—	—	1.50	1.75

KM# 123 50 CENTIMES
3.9200 g., Stainless Steel, 22.3 mm. **Obv:** Lion left above denomination **Rev:** Verney L. Camereon **Edge:** Plain

Date	Mintage	F	VF	XF	Unc	BU
2002	—	—	—	—	1.00	1.25

KM# 81 FRANC
4.5700 g., Brass, 20.31 mm. **Obv:** Lion left **Rev:** Turtle **Edge:** Plain

Date	Mintage	F	VF	XF	Unc	BU
2002	—	—	—	—	1.25	1.50

KM# 82 FRANC
4.5200 g., Brass, 20.32 mm. **Obv:** Lion left **Rev:** Chicken **Edge:** Plain

Date	Mintage	F	VF	XF	Unc	BU
2002	—	—	—	—	1.50	1.75

KM# 156 FRANC
5.0000 g., Nickel Clad Steel, 24.8 mm. **Subject:** 25th Anniversary - Pope John Paul II's Visit **Obv:** Lion left **Rev:** Pope John Paul II as a priest in 1946 **Edge:** Plain

Date	Mintage	F	VF	XF	Unc	BU
2004	—	—	—	—	2.00	2.50

KM# 157 FRANC
5.0000 g., Nickel Clad Steel, 24.8 mm. **Subject:** 25th Anniversary - Pope John Paul II's Visit **Obv:** Lion left **Rev:** Pope John Paul II as a Cardinal in 1967 **Edge:** Plain

Date	Mintage	F	VF	XF	Unc	BU
2004	—	—	—	—	2.00	2.50

KM# 158 FRANC
5.0000 g., Nickel Clad Steel, 24.8 mm. **Subject:** 25th Anniversary - Pope John Paul II's Visit **Obv:** Lion left **Rev:** Pope John Paul II as newly elected pope in 1978 **Edge:** Plain

Date	Mintage	F	VF	XF	Unc	BU
2004	—	—	—	—	2.00	2.50

KM# 159 FRANC
5.0000 g., Nickel Clad Steel, 24.8 mm. **Subject:** 25th Anniversary - Pope John Paul II's Visit **Obv:** Lion left **Rev:** Pope John Paul II wearing a mitre **Edge:** Plain

Date	Mintage	F	VF	XF	Unc	BU
2004	—	—	—	—	2.00	2.50

KM# 174 FRANC
6.0000 g., Copper-Nickel, 21 mm. **Obv:** Lion left **Rev:** African Golden Cat right **Edge:** Plain

Date	Mintage	F	VF	XF	Unc	BU
2004	5,000	—	—	—	7.25	9.00

COOK ISLANDS

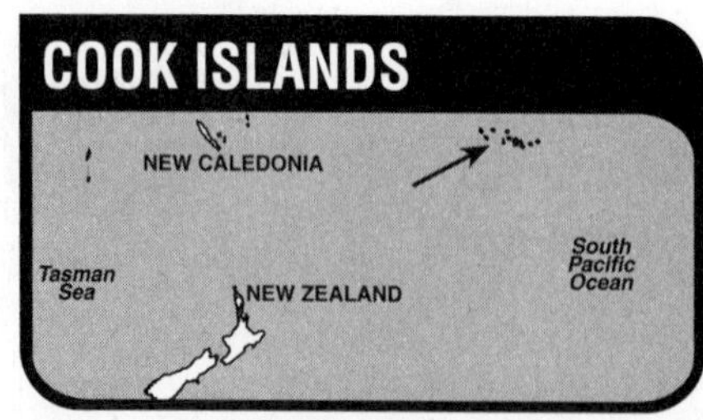

Cook Islands, a self-governing dependency of New Zealand consisting of 15 islands, is located in the South Pacific Ocean about 2,000 miles (3,218 km.) northeast of New Zealand. It has an area of 93 sq. mi. (234 sq. km.) and a population of 17,185. Capital: Avarua. The United States claims the islands of Danger, Manahiki, Penrhyn, and Rakahanga atolls. Citrus and canned fruits and juices, copra, clothing, jewelry, and mother-of-pearl shell are exported.

Spanish navigator Alvaro de Mendada first sighted the islands in 1595. Portuguese navigator Pedro Fernandes de Quieros landed on Rakahanga in 1606. English navigator Capt. James Cook sailed to the islands on three occasions: 1773, 1774 and 1777. He named them Hervey Islands, in honor of Augustus John Hervey, a lord of the Admiralty. The islands were declared a British protectorate in 1888, and were annexed to New Zealand in 1901. They were granted internal self-government in 1965. New Zealand provides an annual subsidy and retains responsibility for defense and foreign affairs.

RULER
British

MINT MARKS
(b) - British Royal Mint
FM - Franklin Mint, U.S.A. *
PM - Pobjoy Mint

***NOTE**: From 1975-1985 the Franklin Mint produced coinage in up to three different qualities. Qualities of issue are designated in () after each date and are defined as follows:

(M) MATTE - Normal circulation strike or a dull finish produced by sandblasting special uncirculated (polish finish) or proof quality dies.

(U) SPECIAL UNCIRCULATED - Polished or proof-like in appearance without any frosted features.

(P) PROOF - The highest quality obtainable having mirror-like fields and frosted features.

MONETARY SYSTEM

(Until 1967)
12 Pence = 1 Shilling
20 Shillings = 1 Pound

(Commencing 1967)
100 Cents = 1 Dollar

DEPENDENCY OF NEW ZEALAND

DECIMAL COINAGE

KM# 1 CENT
Bronze **Ruler:** Elizabeth II **Obv:** Young bust right, date below **Rev:** Taro leaf, denomination at right **Rev. Designer:** James Berry

Date	Mintage	F	VF	XF	Unc	BU
1972 Proof	17,000	Value: 0.50				
1972	117,000	—	—	0.10	0.20	0.35
1973 Proof	13,000	Value: 0.50				
1973	8,500	—	—	0.10	0.20	0.35
1974 Proof	7,300	Value: 0.50				
1974	300,000	—	—	0.10	0.20	0.35
1975FM (M)	1,000	—	—	—	0.50	0.65
1975FM (P)	21,000	Value: 0.50				
1975FM (U)	2,251	—	—	—	0.20	0.35
1975	429,000	—	—	0.10	0.20	0.35
1976FM (M)	1,001	—	—	—	0.50	0.65
1976FM (P)	18,000	Value: 0.50				
1976FM (U)	1,066	—	—	—	0.20	0.35
1977FM (M)	1,171	—	—	—	0.50	0.65
1977FM (P)	5,986	Value: 0.50				
1977FM (U)	1,002	—	—	—	0.20	0.35
1979FM (U)	500	—	—	—	1.00	1.25
1979FM (M)	1,000	—	—	—	0.50	0.65
1979FM (P)	4,058	Value: 0.50				
1983 Proof	10,000	Value: 0.50				
1983	—	—	—	0.10	0.20	0.35

KM# 1a CENT
Bronze **Ruler:** Elizabeth II **Obv:** Young bust right, date below **Rev:** Taro leaf, denomination **Edge Lettering:** 1728 • CAPT. JAMES COOK • 1978

Date	Mintage	F	VF	XF	Unc	BU
1978FM (U)	767	—	—	—	0.75	1.00
1978FM (M)	1,000	—	—	—	0.85	1.15
1978FM (P)	6,287	Value: 0.50				

KM# 1b CENT
Bronze **Ruler:** Elizabeth II **Subject:** Wedding of Prince Charles and Lady Diana **Obv:** Young bust right **Edge Lettering:** THE ROYAL WEDDING 29 JULY 1981

Date	Mintage	F	VF	XF	Unc	BU
1981FM (M)	1,000	—	—	—	0.50	0.65
1981FM (P)	9,205	Value: 0.40				
1981FM (U)	1,100	—	—	—	0.50	0.65

KM# 419 CENT
1.4400 g., Aluminum, 21.9 mm. **Ruler:** Elizabeth II **Obv:** Crowned head right, date below **Rev:** Bust of Capt. James Cook right, denomination below **Edge:** Plain

Date	Mintage	F	VF	XF	Unc	BU
2003	—	—	—	—	1.25	1.50

KM# 420 CENT
1.4400 g., Aluminum, 21.9 mm. **Ruler:** Elizabeth II **Obv:** Crowned head right, date below **Rev:** Collie dog right, denomination below **Edge:** Plain

Date	Mintage	F	VF	XF	Unc	BU
2003	—	—	—	—	0.75	1.00

KM# 421 CENT
1.4400 g., Aluminum, 21.9 mm. **Ruler:** Elizabeth II **Obv:** Crowned head right, date below **Rev:** Pointer dog right, denomination above **Edge:** Plain

Date	Mintage	F	VF	XF	Unc	BU
2003	—	—	—	—	0.75	1.00

KM# 422 CENT
1.4400 g., Aluminum, 21.9 mm. **Ruler:** Elizabeth II **Obv:** Crowned head right, date below **Rev:** Rooster right, denomination above **Edge:** Plain

Date	Mintage	F	VF	XF	Unc	BU
2003	—	—	—	—	0.75	1.00

KM# 423 CENT
1.4400 g., Aluminum, 22 mm. **Ruler:** Elizabeth II **Obv:** Crowned head right, date below **Rev:** Monkey on branch, denomination at left **Edge:** Plain

Date	Mintage	F	VF	XF	Unc	BU
2003	—	—	—	—	0.75	1.00

KM# 2 2 CENTS
Bronze **Ruler:** Elizabeth II **Obv:** Young bust right, date below **Rev:** Pineapple, denomination at right **Rev. Designer:** James Berry

Date	Mintage	F	VF	XF	Unc	BU
1972 Proof	17,000	Value: 0.75				
1972	63,000	—	0.10	0.15	0.30	0.50
1973 Proof	13,000	Value: 0.75				
1973	8,500	—	0.15	0.20	0.40	0.60
1974 Proof	7,300	Value: 0.75				
1974	120,000	—	0.10	0.15	0.30	0.50
1975FM (P)	21,000	Value: 0.75				
1975FM (U)	2,251	—	—	—	0.30	0.50
1975FM (M)	1,000	—	—	—	0.50	0.75
1975	129,000	—	0.10	0.15	0.25	0.45
1976FM (M)	1,001	—	—	—	0.75	1.00
1976FM (P)	18,000	Value: 0.75				
1976FM (U)	1,066	—	—	—	0.30	0.50
1977FM (M)	1,171	—	—	—	0.75	1.00
1977FM (P)	5,986	Value: 0.75				
1977FM (U)	1,002	—	—	—	0.30	0.50
1979FM (U)	500	—	—	—	0.30	0.50
1979FM (M)	1,000	—	—	—	0.75	1.00
1979FM (P)	4,058	Value: 0.75				
1983 Proof	10,000	Value: 0.75				
1983	—	—	0.10	0.15	0.25	0.45

KM# 2a 2 CENTS

Bronze **Ruler:** Elizabeth II **Obv:** Young bust right **Rev:** Pineapple, denomination at right **Edge Lettering:** 1728 • CAPT. JAMES COOK • 1978

Date	Mintage	F	VF	XF	Unc	BU
1978FM (U)	767	—	—	—	0.85	1.15
1978FM (M)	1,000	—	—	—	0.75	1.00
1978FM (P)	6,287	Value: 0.50				

KM# 2b 2 CENTS

Bronze **Ruler:** Elizabeth II **Subject:** Wedding of Prince Charles and Lady Diana **Obv:** Young bust right, date below **Edge Lettering:** THE ROYAL WEDDING 29 JULY 1981

Date	Mintage	F	VF	XF	Unc	BU
1981FM (M)	1,000	—	—	—	0.75	1.00
1981FM (P)	9,205	Value: 0.50				
1981FM (U)	1,100	—	—	—	0.75	1.00

KM# 3 5 CENTS

Copper-Nickel, 19.41 mm. **Ruler:** Elizabeth II **Obv:** Young bust right, date below **Rev:** Hibiscus, denomination below **Rev. Designer:** James Berry

Date	Mintage	F	VF	XF	Unc	BU
1972 Proof	17,000	Value: 1.00				
1972	32,000	—	0.10	0.20	0.40	0.60
1973 Proof	13,000	Value: 1.00				
1973	8,500	—	0.15	0.25	0.50	0.75
1974 Proof	7,300	Value: 1.00				
1974	80,000	—	0.10	0.20	0.40	0.60
1975FM (P)	21,000	Value: 0.85				
1975FM (U)	2,251	—	—	—	0.40	0.60
1975FM (M)	1,000	—	—	—	1.00	1.25
1975	89,000	—	0.10	0.20	0.40	0.60
1976FM (M)	1,001	—	—	—	1.00	1.25
1976FM (P)	18,000	Value: 0.85				
1976FM (U)	1,066	—	—	—	0.40	0.60
1977FM (M)	1,171	—	—	—	1.00	1.25
1977FM (P)	5,986	Value: 1.00				
1977FM (U)	1,002	—	—	—	0.40	0.60
1979FM (U)	500	—	—	—	0.40	0.60
1979FM (M)	1,000	—	—	—	1.00	1.25
1979FM (P)	4,058	Value: 1.00				
1983 Proof	10,000	Value: 1.00				
1983	—	—	0.10	0.20	0.40	0.60

KM# 3a 5 CENTS

Copper-Nickel **Ruler:** Elizabeth II **Obv:** Young bust right, date below **Rev:** Hibiscus, denomination below **Edge Lettering:** 1728 • CAPT. JAMES COOK • 1978

Date	Mintage	F	VF	XF	Unc	BU
1978FM (U)	767	—	—	—	0.75	1.00
1978FM (M)	1,000	—	—	—	1.00	1.25
1978FM (P)	6,287	Value: 0.50				

KM# 3b 5 CENTS

Copper-Nickel, 19.41 mm. **Ruler:** Elizabeth II **Subject:** Wedding of Prince Charles and Lady Diana **Obv:** Young bust right, date below **Edge Lettering:** THE ROYAL WEDDING 29 JULY 1981

Date	Mintage	F	VF	XF	Unc	BU
1981FM (M)	1,000	—	—	—	1.00	1.25
1981FM (P)	9,205	Value: 0.50				
1981FM (U)	1,100	—	—	—	1.00	1.25

KM# 33 5 CENTS

Copper-Nickel, 19.41 mm. **Ruler:** Elizabeth II **Obv:** Crowned head right, date below **Rev:** Hibiscus **Rev. Designer:** James Berry

Date	Mintage	F	VF	XF	Unc	BU
1987 Proof	—	Value: 1.00				
1987	—	—	—	0.15	0.35	0.50
1988 Proof	—	Value: 1.00				
1988	—	—	—	0.15	0.35	0.50
1992 Proof	—	Value: 1.00				
1992	—	—	—	0.15	0.35	0.50
1994 Proof	200	Value: 1.50				
1994	20,000	—	—	0.15	0.35	0.50

KM# 369 5 CENTS

4.4300 g., Nickel Clad Steel, 24.05 mm. **Ruler:** Elizabeth II **Subject:** F.A.O. **Obv:** Head with tiara right, date below **Rev:** Statue of Tangaroa divides denomination **Rev. Designer:** James Berry **Edge:** Plain

Date	Mintage	F	VF	XF	Unc	BU
2000 Proof	—	Value: 3.50				
2000	—	—	—	—	1.00	1.50

KM# 4 10 CENTS

Copper-Nickel, 23.6 mm. **Ruler:** Elizabeth II **Obv:** Young bust right, date below **Rev:** Orange, denomination above **Rev. Designer:** James Berry

Date	Mintage	F	VF	XF	Unc	BU
1972 Proof	17,000	Value: 1.25				
1972	35,000	—	0.10	0.20	0.65	0.85
1973 Proof	13,000	Value: 1.25				
1973	59,000	—	0.10	0.20	0.65	0.85
1974 Proof	7,300	Value: 1.25				
1974	50,000	—	0.10	0.20	0.50	0.85
1975FM (P)	21,000	Value: 1.25				
1975FM (U)	2,251	—	—	—	0.50	0.85
1975FM (M)	1,000	—	—	—	1.25	1.50
1975	59,000	—	0.10	0.20	0.50	0.85
1976FM (M)	1,001	—	—	—	1.25	1.50
1976FM (P)	18,000	Value: 1.25				
1976FM (U)	1,066	—	—	—	0.50	0.65
1977FM (M)	1,171	—	—	—	1.25	1.50
1977FM (P)	5,986	Value: 1.25				
1977FM (U)	1,002	—	—	—	0.50	0.65
1983 Proof	10,000	Value: 1.25				
1983	—	—	0.10	0.20	0.50	0.65

KM# 4a 10 CENTS

Copper-Nickel, 23.6 mm. **Ruler:** Elizabeth II **Obv:** Young bust right, date below **Rev:** Orange, denomination above **Edge Lettering:** 1728 • CAPT. JAMES COOK • 1978

Date	Mintage	F	VF	XF	Unc	BU
1978FM (U)	767	—	—	—	1.25	1.50
1978FM (M)	1,000	—	—	—	1.25	1.50
1978FM (P)	6,287	Value: 1.00				

KM# 4b 10 CENTS

Copper-Nickel, 23.6 mm. **Ruler:** Elizabeth II **Series:** F.A.O. **Obv:** Young bust right, date below **Rev:** Orange, denomination above

Date	Mintage	F	VF	XF	Unc	BU
1979FM (U)	500	—	—	—	1.50	1.75
1979FM (M)	9,000	—	—	—	1.00	1.25
1979FM (P)	4,058	Value: 1.25				

KM# 4c 10 CENTS

Copper-Nickel, 23.6 mm. **Ruler:** Elizabeth II **Subject:** Wedding of Prince Charles and Lady Diana **Obv:** Young bust right, date below **Edge Lettering:** THE ROYAL WEDDING 29 JULY 1981

Date	Mintage	F	VF	XF	Unc	BU
1981FM (M)	1,000	—	—	—	1.25	1.50
1981FM (P)	9,205	Value: 0.75				
1981FM (U)	1,100	—	—	—	1.25	1.50

KM# 34 10 CENTS

5.6800 g., Copper-Nickel, 23.6 mm. **Ruler:** Elizabeth II **Obv:** Crowned head right, date below **Rev:** Orange, denomination above **Rev. Designer:** James Berry

Date	Mintage	F	VF	XF	Unc	BU
1987 Proof	—	Value: 1.25				
1987	—	—	—	0.20	0.50	0.75
1988 Proof	—	Value: 1.25				
1988	—	—	—	0.20	0.50	0.75
1992 Proof	—	Value: 1.25				
1992	—	—	—	0.20	0.50	0.75
1994 Proof	200	Value: 1.75				
1994	20,000	—	—	0.20	0.50	0.75

KM# 5 20 CENTS

Copper-Nickel, 28.52 mm. **Ruler:** Elizabeth II **Obv:** Young bust right, date below **Rev:** Fairy Tern right, denomination below **Rev. Designer:** James Berry

Date	Mintage	F	VF	XF	Unc	BU
1972 Proof	17,000	Value: 1.50				
1972	31,000	—	0.20	0.40	0.75	1.00
1973 Proof	13,000	Value: 1.50				
1973	49,000	—	0.20	0.40	0.75	1.00
1974 Proof	7,300	Value: 1.50				
1974	5,500	—	0.20	0.45	0.85	1.25
1975FM (M)	1,000	—	—	—	1.50	1.75
1975FM (P)	21,000	Value: 1.50				
1975FM (U)	2,251	—	—	—	0.85	1.25
1975	60,000	—	0.20	0.40	0.75	1.00
1983 Proof	10,000	Value: 1.50				
1983	—	—	0.20	0.40	0.85	1.25

KM# 14 20 CENTS

Copper-Nickel, 28.52 mm. **Ruler:** Elizabeth II **Obv:** Young bust right, date below **Rev:** Two Pacific Triton shells, denomination lower right **Rev. Designer:** James Berry

Date	Mintage	F	VF	XF	Unc	BU
1976FM (M)	1,001	—	—	—	1.50	1.75
1976FM (P)	18,000	Value: 1.50				
1976FM (U)	1,066	—	—	—	1.00	1.25
1977FM (M)	1,171	—	—	—	1.50	1.75
1977FM (P)	5,986	Value: 1.50				
1977FM (U)	1,002	—	—	—	1.00	1.25
1979FM (U)	500	—	—	—	2.00	1.50
1979FM (M)	1,000	—	—	—	1.50	1.75
1979FM (P)	4,058	Value: 1.50				

KM# 14a 20 CENTS

Copper-Nickel, 28.52 mm. **Ruler:** Elizabeth II **Obv:** Young bust right, date below **Rev:** Shells, denomination at right **Edge Lettering:** 1728 • CAPT. JAMES COOK • 1978

Date	Mintage	F	VF	XF	Unc	BU
1978FM (P)	6,287	Value: 1.50				
1978FM (U)	767	—	—	—	2.00	2.50
1978FM (M)	1,000	—	—	—	1.50	1.75

KM# 14b 20 CENTS

Copper-Nickel, 28.52 mm. **Ruler:** Elizabeth II **Subject:** Wedding of Prince Charles and Lady Diana **Obv:** Young bust right, date below **Rev:** Shells, denomination at right **Edge Lettering:** THE ROYAL WEDDING 29 JULY 1981

Date	Mintage	F	VF	XF	Unc	BU
1981FM (M)	1,000	—	—	—	1.50	1.75
1981FM (P)	9,205	Value: 1.00				
1981FM (U)	1,100	—	—	—	1.50	1.75

KM# 35 20 CENTS

11.3100 g., Copper-Nickel, 28.52 mm. **Ruler:** Elizabeth II **Obv:** Crowned head right, date below **Rev:** Fairy Tern, denomination below **Rev. Designer:** James Berry

Date	Mintage	F	VF	XF	Unc	BU
1987 Proof	—	Value: 1.50				
1987	—	—	—	0.25	0.75	1.00
1988 Proof	—	Value: 1.50				
1988	—	—	—	0.25	0.75	1.00

Date	Mintage	F	VF	XF	Unc	BU
1992 Proof	—	Value: 1.50				
1992	—	—	—	0.25	0.75	1.00
1994 Proof	200	Value: 2.00				
1994	20,000	—	—	0.25	0.75	1.00

KM# 6.1 50 CENTS

Copper-Nickel, 31.75 mm. **Ruler:** Elizabeth II **Obv:** Young bust right, date below **Obv. Designer:** Machin **Rev:** Bonito fish, denomination upper left **Rev. Designer:** James Berry

Date	Mintage	F	VF	XF	Unc	BU
1972 Proof	17,000	Value: 3.00				
1972	31,000	—	—	0.65	1.25	2.00
1973 Proof	13,000	Value: 3.00				
1973	19,000	—	—	0.65	1.25	2.00
1974 Proof	7,300	Value: 3.00				
1974	10,000	—	—	0.65	1.25	2.00
1975FM (M)	1,000	—	—	—	2.00	3.00
1975FM (P)	21,000	Value: 2.50				
1975FM (U)	2,251	—	—	—	1.50	2.00
1975	19,000	—	—	0.65	1.25	2.00
1976FM (M)	1,001	—	—	—	2.00	3.00
1976FM (P)	18,000	Value: 2.50				
1976FM (U)	1,066	—	—	—	1.50	2.00
1977FM (M)	1,171	—	—	—	2.00	3.00
1977FM (P)	5,986	Value: 3.00				
1977FM (U)	1,002	—	—	—	1.50	2.00
1983 Proof	10,000	Value: 3.50				
1983	—	—	—	0.65	1.25	2.00

KM# 6.2 50 CENTS

Copper-Nickel, 31.75 mm. **Ruler:** Elizabeth II **Obv:** Young bust right, date below **Edge Lettering:** 1728 • CAPT. JAMES COOK • 1978

Date	Mintage	F	VF	XF	Unc	BU
1978FM (P)	6,287	Value: 2.00				
1978FM (U)	767	—	—	—	2.00	3.00
1978FM (M)	1,000	—	—	—	2.00	3.00

KM# 6.3 50 CENTS

Copper-Nickel, 31.75 mm. **Ruler:** Elizabeth II **Series:** F.A.O. **Obv:** Young bust right, date below **Rev:** F.A.O. logo, Bonito fish, denomination upper left

Date	Mintage	F	VF	XF	Unc	BU
1979FM (P)	4,058	Value: 2.25				
1979FM (U)	500	—	—	—	2.50	3.50
1979FM (M)	9,000	—	—	0.75	1.25	2.00

KM# 6.4 50 CENTS

Copper-Nickel, 31.75 mm. **Ruler:** Elizabeth II **Subject:** Wedding of Prince Charles and Lady Diana **Obv:** Young bust right, date below **Edge Lettering:** THE ROYAL WEDDING 29 JULY 1981

Date	Mintage	F	VF	XF	Unc	BU
1981FM (M)	1,000	—	—	—	2.00	3.00
1981FM (P)	9,205	Value: 1.50				
1981FM (U)	1,100	—	—	—	2.00	3.00

KM# 36 50 CENTS

13.5400 g., Copper-Nickel, 31.75 mm. **Ruler:** Elizabeth II **Obv:** Crowned head right, date below **Rev:** Bonito fish, denomination upper left **Rev. Designer:** James Berry

Date	Mintage	F	VF	XF	Unc	BU
1987	—	—	—	0.65	1.50	2.00
1987 Proof	—	Value: 2.00				
1992	—	—	—	0.65	1.50	2.00

KM# 41 50 TENE

13.6000 g., Copper-Nickel, 31.75 mm. **Ruler:** Elizabeth II **Obv:** Crowned head right, date below **Rev:** Hawksbill turtle right, denomination above **Rev. Designer:** Horst Hahne

Date	Mintage	F	VF	XF	Unc	BU
1988	60,000	—	—	0.50	2.00	3.50
1988 Proof	1,000	Value: 3.50				
1992 Proof	—	Value: 3.50				
1992	—	—	—	—	2.00	3.50
1994	20,000	—	—	—	2.00	3.50
1994 Proof	200	Value: 4.00				

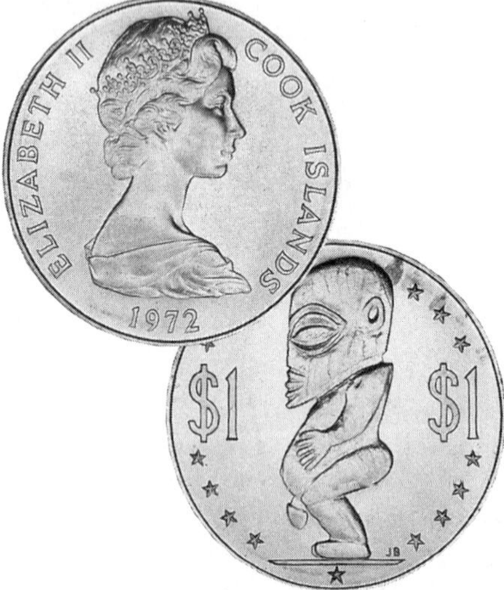

KM# 7 DOLLAR

27.2000 g., Copper-Nickel, 38.5 mm. **Ruler:** Elizabeth II **Obv:** Young bust right, date below **Rev:** Tangaroa, Polynesian God of Creation, divides denominations **Rev. Designer:** James Berry

Date	Mintage	F	VF	XF	Unc	BU
1972 Proof	27,000	Value: 4.00				
1972	31,000	—	1.00	1.50	2.50	4.00
1973 Proof	13,000	Value: 6.00				
1973	49,000	—	1.00	1.50	2.50	4.00
1974 Proof	7,300	Value: 6.00				
1974	20,000	—	1.00	1.50	2.50	4.00
1975FM (M)	1,000	—	—	—	4.50	6.00
1975FM (P)	21,000	Value: 6.00				
1975FM (U)	2,251	—	—	—	3.50	5.00
1975	29,000	—	1.00	1.50	2.50	4.00
1976FM (M)	1,001	—	—	—	4.50	6.00
1976FM (P)	18,000	Value: 5.00				
1976FM (U)	1,066	—	—	—	4.50	6.00
1977FM (M)	1,171	—	—	—	4.50	6.00
1977FM (P)	5,986	Value: 6.50				
1977FM (U)	1,002	—	—	—	4.50	6.00
1979FM (P)	4,058	Value: 6.50				
1979FM (U)	500	—	—	—	5.50	7.00
1979FM (M)	1,000	—	—	—	4.50	6.00
1983 Proof	10,000	Value: 5.00				
1983	—	—	1.00	1.50	3.50	5.00

KM# 7a DOLLAR

27.2000 g., Copper-Nickel, 38.5 mm. **Ruler:** Elizabeth II **Obv:** Young bust right, date below **Rev:** Tangaroa, Polynesian God of Creation, divides denominations **Edge Lettering:** 1728 • CAPT. JAMES COOK • 1978

Date	Mintage	F	VF	XF	Unc	BU
1978FM (P)	6,287	Value: 5.50				
1978FM (U)	767	—	—	—	6.00	7.50
1978FM (M)	1,000	—	—	—	6.00	7.50

KM# 7b DOLLAR

27.2000 g., Copper-Nickel, 38.5 mm. **Ruler:** Elizabeth II **Subject:** Wedding of Prince Charles and Lady Diana **Obv:** Young bust right, date below **Rev:** Tangaroa, Polynesian God of Creation, divides denominations **Edge Lettering:** THE ROYAL WEDDING 29 JULY 1981

Date	Mintage	F	VF	XF	Unc	BU
1981FM (M)	1,000	—	—	—	5.00	6.50
1981FM (P)	9,205	Value: 5.00				
1981FM (U)	1,100	—	—	—	5.00	6.50

KM# 37 DOLLAR

Copper-Nickel, 28.52 mm. **Ruler:** Elizabeth II **Obv:** Crowned head right, date below **Rev:** Tangaroa statue divides denominations **Rev. Designer:** James Berry **Shape:** Scalloped

Date	Mintage	F	VF	XF	Unc	BU
1987 Proof	—	Value: 4.50				
1987	—	—	—	1.00	2.50	3.50
1988 Proof	—	Value: 4.50				
1988	—	—	—	1.00	2.50	3.50
1992 Proof	—	Value: 4.50				
1992	—	—	—	1.00	2.50	3.50
1994 Proof	200	Value: 5.50				
1994	20,000	—	—	1.00	2.50	3.50

KM# 416 DOLLAR

10.7500 g., Copper-Nickel, 28.5 mm. **Ruler:** Elizabeth II **Obv:** Queen's new portrait **Rev:** Tangaroa statue and value **Edge:** Scalloped

Date	Mintage	F	VF	XF	Unc	BU
2003	—	—	—	—	2.50	3.00

KM# 38 2 DOLLARS

Copper-Nickel, 28.52 mm. **Ruler:** Elizabeth II **Obv:** Crowned head right, date below **Rev:** Kumete table, morter and pestle from Atiu Island, denomination above **Rev. Designer:** Horst Hahne **Shape:** 3-sided

Date	Mintage	F	VF	XF	Unc	BU
1987 Proof	—	Value: 6.00				
1987	—	—	—	2.25	3.50	5.00
1988 Proof	—	Value: 6.00				
1988	—	—	—	2.25	3.50	5.00
1992 Proof	—	Value: 6.00				
1992	—	—	—	2.25	3.25	4.50
1994 Proof	200	Value: 6.50				
1994	20,000	—	—	2.25	3.25	4.50

KM# 417 2 DOLLARS

7.5500 g., Copper-Nickel, 26 mm. **Ruler:** Elizabeth II **Obv:** Crowned bust right, new portrait **Rev:** Mortar and pestle from Atiu Island **Edge:** Triangular

Date	Mintage	F	VF	XF	Unc	BU
2003	—	—	—	—	3.00	3.50

KM# 39 5 DOLLARS

Aluminum-Bronze, 31.51 mm. **Ruler:** Elizabeth II **Obv:** Crowned head right, date below **Rev:** Conch shell, denomination above **Rev. Designer:** Horst Hahne **Shape:** 12-sided

Date	Mintage	F	VF	XF	Unc	BU
1987 Proof	—	Value: 9.00				
1987	—	—	—	3.50	5.50	7.50
1988 Proof	—	Value: 9.00				
1988	—	—	—	3.50	5.50	7.50
1992 Proof	—	Value: 9.00				
1992	—	—	—	3.50	5.50	7.50
1994 Proof	200	Value: 12.00				
1994	20,000	—	—	3.50	5.50	7.50

KM# 418 5 DOLLARS

14.0000 g., Aluminum-Bronze, 31.5 mm. **Ruler:** Elizabeth II **Obv:** Crowned bust right, new portrait **Rev:** Conch shell and value **Shape:** 12-sided

Date	Mintage	F	VF	XF	Unc	BU
2003	—	—	—	—	6.00	8.00

The Republic of Costa Rica, located in southern Central America between Nicaragua and Panama, has an area of 19,730 sq. mi. (51,100 sq. km.) and a population of 3.4 million. Capital: San Jose. Agriculture predominates; tourism and coffee, bananas, beef and sugar contribute heavily to the country's export earnings.

Costa Rica was discovered by Christopher Columbus in 1502, during his last voyage to the New World, and was a colony of Spain from 1522 until independence in 1821. Established as a republic in 1848, Costa Rica adopted democratic reforms in the 1870's and 80's. Today, Costa Rica remains a model of orderly democracy in Latin America, although, like most of the hemisphere - its economy is in stress.

MINT MARKS

CR - San Jose 1825-1947
(P) – Philadelphia, 1905-1961
(L) – London, 1937, 1948

ISSUING BANK INITIALS - MINTS

BCCR - Philadelphia 1951-1958,1961
BICR - Philadelphia 1935
BNCR - London 1937,1948
BNCR - San Jose 1942-1947
GCR - Philadelphia 1905-1908,1929
GCR - San Jose 1917-1941

KEY TO MINT IDENTIFICATION

Key Letter	Mint
(a)	Armant Metalurgica, Santiago, Chile
(c)	Casa de Moneda, Mexico City Mint
(cc)	Casa de Moneda, Brazil
(co)	Colombia Republican Banko
(g)	Guatemala Mint
(i)	Italcambio Mint
(p) or (P)	Philadelphia Mint, USA
®	RCM – Royal Canadian Mint
(rm)	Royal Mint, London
(s)	San Francisco
(sj)	San Jose
(sm)	Sherrit Mint, Toronto
(v)	Vereingte Deutsche Metallwerke, Karlsruhe
(w)	Westain, Toronto

ASSAYERS' INITIALS

CY – Carlos Yglesias, 1902
JCV – Jesus Cubrero Vargas, 1903
GCR – Gobierno de Costa Rica

MONETARY SYSTEM

8 Reales = 1 Peso
16 Pesos = 8 Escudos = 1 Onza

REPUBLIC

REFORM COINAGE

1897, 100 Centimos = 1 Colon

KM# 144 2 CENTIMOS

1.0000 g., Copper-Nickel **Obv:** Large numeral above date **Rev:** Denomination above sprays **Edge:** Plain

Date	Mintage	F	VF	XF	Unc	BU
1903(P)	630,000	0.50	1.00	2.25	5.00	8.50

Note: 274,342 of this type were used as blanks for KM178 in 1942.

KM# 145 5 CENTIMOS

1.0000 g., 0.9000 Silver 0.0289 oz. ASW **Obv:** National arms, date below **Rev:** Denomination within wreath **Edge:** Reeded

Date	Mintage	F	VF	XF	Unc	BU
1905(P)	500,000	BV	0.75	2.00	6.00	—
1910(P)	400,000	BV	0.75	2.00	7.50	—
1912(P)	540,000	BV	0.75	1.50	5.00	—
1914(P)	510,000	BV	0.75	1.50	5.50	—

KM# 146 10 CENTIMOS

2.0000 g., 0.9000 Silver 0.0579 oz. ASW **Obv:** National arms, date below **Rev:** Denomination within wreath

Date	Mintage	F	VF	XF	Unc	BU
1905(P)	400,000	0.80	1.25	3.00	10.00	—
1910(P)	400,000	0.80	1.25	3.00	12.00	—
1912(P)	270,000	0.80	1.25	3.00	12.00	—
1914(P)	150,000	0.85	1.50	4.00	15.00	—

KM# 143 50 CENTIMOS

10.0000 g., 0.9000 Silver 0.2893 oz. ASW **Obv:** National arms, date below **Rev:** Denomination within wreath

Date	Mintage	F	VF	XF	Unc	BU
1902 CY	120,000	15.00	30.00	60.00	135	—
1903 JCV	380,000	10.00	20.00	40.00	90.00	—

Note: Of the total mintage for this date, San Jose Mint struck 132,140 in 1903 and Philadelphia Mint struck an additional 250,000 in 1904 with the 1903 date; the two strikings are indistinguishable.

Date	Mintage	F	VF	XF	Unc	BU
1914(P) GCR	200,000	—	—	1,250	2,000	—

Note: Most coins dated 1914 were later counterstamped UN COLON/ 1923; See KM#164.

KM# 139 2 COLONES

1.5560 g., 0.9000 Gold 0.0450 oz. AGW **Obv:** National arms **Rev:** Bust of Colombus right

Date	Mintage	F	VF	XF	Unc	BU
1915(P)	5,000	BV	50.00	75.00	125	—
1916(P)	5,000	BV	55.00	75.00	150	—
1921(P)	3,000	BV	65.00	100	200	—
1922(P)	13,000	BV	45.00	60.00	100	—
1926(P)	15,000	BV	45.00	60.00	85.00	—
1928(P)	25,000	BV	45.00	55.00	80.00	—

REFORM COINAGE

1917, 100 Centavos = 1 Colon

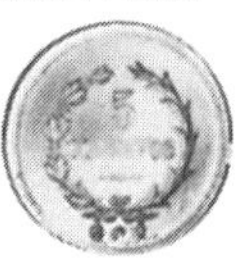

KM# 147 5 CENTAVOS

1.0000 g., Brass **Obv:** National arms, date below **Rev:** Denomination within wreath **Edge:** Plain

Date	Mintage	F	VF	XF	Unc	BU
1917(sj)	400,000	3.00	10.00	22.00	75.00	—
1918(sj)	1,000,000	1.25	4.00	10.00	40.00	—
1919(sj)	500,000	1.25	4.50	12.00	35.00	—

KM# 148 10 CENTAVOS

2.0000 g., 0.5000 Silver 0.0321 oz. ASW **Obv:** National arms, date below **Rev:** Denomination within wreath **Edge:** Reeded

Date	Mintage	F	VF	XF	Unc	BU
1917(sj)	100,000	1.00	2.00	3.25	6.50	9.50

KM# 149.1 10 CENTAVOS

2.0000 g., Brass **Obv:** National arms, date below **Rev:** Denomination within wreath, GCR at lower right

Date	Mintage	F	VF	XF	Unc	BU
1917 GCR	500,000	1.50	5.00	13.50	60.00	—

KM# 149.2 10 CENTAVOS

2.0000 g., Brass **Obv:** National arms, date below **Rev:** Denomination within wreath, GCR at bottom center

Date	Mintage	F	VF	XF	Unc	BU
1917 GCR	Inc. above	3.50	8.00	20.00	70.00	—
1918 GCR	900,000	1.25	3.00	10.00	40.00	—
1919 GCR	250,000	1.75	4.50	13.50	50.00	—

KM# 150 50 CENTAVOS

10.0000 g., 0.5000 Silver 0.1607 oz. ASW **Obv:** National arms
Note: All but 10 examples of the 1917 issue and the complete 1918 mintage were counterstamped UN COLON/1923. See KM#165.

Date	Mintage	F	VF	XF	Unc	BU
1917 GCR	9,400	—	—	1,250	2,500	—
1918 GCR	30,000	—	—	—	—	—

COUNTERSTAMPED COINAGE

Type VIII • 1923

In the financially stressful years between 1914 and 1925 many Latin American countries saw their currencies lose much of its former purchasing power. Governments reacted in several ways: In Peru, Chile, Brazil and most of Central America, this took the form of devaluing their monetary unit relative to such standards as the U.S. dollar and Swiss franc. Costa Rica began issuing coins of .500 fine silver and brass to replace the .900 fine silver issues of the past. A decree of 1923 also made provisions for the old .900 fine silver coins to be revalued, doubling their previous face values, by dated counterstamping conducted at the San Jose Mint through 1923 and into 1924.

Obverse counterstamp: 1923 in 11mm circle.

Reverse counterstamp: 50/CENTIMOS in 11mm circle.

NOTE: The total mintage for KM#154-159 was 1,866,000 pieces.

KM# 159 50 CENTIMOS

6.3000 g., 0.7500 Silver 0.1519 oz. ASW, 25 mm.
Counterstamp: Type VIII **Obv:** Liberty cap and flags above shield turned 1/4 right, date within circle on shield, spray and date below **Rev:** Denomination within circle, wreath surrounds **Note:** Counterstamped on 25 Centavos, KM#130.

CS Date	Host Date	Good	VG	F	VF	XF
1923	1889HEATON	—	2.25	3.00	5.00	8.50
1923	1890/80HEATON	—	2.50	3.75	7.00	10.00
1923	1890HEATON	—	2.25	3.00	5.00	8.50
1923	1892HEATON	—	2.25	3.00	5.00	8.50
1923	1893HEATON	—	2.00	2.75	4.50	7.50

KM# 154 50 CENTIMOS

6.4000 g., 0.9030 Silver 0.1858 oz. ASW **Counterstamp:** Type VIII **Note:** Counterstamped on 1/4 Peso, KM#103.

CS Date	Host Date	Good	VG	F	VF	XF
1923	1850 JB	200	400	700	—	—

KM# 156 50 CENTIMOS

6.2500 g., 0.7500 Silver 0.1507 oz. ASW **Counterstamp:** Type VIII **Note:** Counterstamped on 25 Centavos, KM#106.

CS Date	Host Date	Good	VG	F	VF	XF
1923	1865 GW	25.00	40.00	60.00	100	—
1923	1875 GW	20.00	30.00	40.00	80.00	—
1923	1864 GW	75.00	150	300	500	—

KM# 157 50 CENTIMOS

6.2500 g., 0.7500 Silver 0.1507 oz. ASW **Counterstamp:** Type VIII **Obv:** Liberty cap and flags above shield turned 3/4 right, date within circle on shield **Rev:** Denomination within circle, wreath surrounds, G.W. 9 DS. **Note:** Counterstamped on 25 Centavos, KM#127.1.

CS Date	Host Date	Good	VG	F	VF	XF
1923	1887 GW	—	3.50	6.00	9.50	15.00
1923	1886 GW	—	3.50	6.00	9.50	15.00

KM# 158 50 CENTIMOS
6.2500 g., 0.7500 Silver 0.1507 oz. ASW **Counterstamp:** Type VIII **Obv:** Date within circle, spray below **Rev:** Denomination within circle, wreath surrounds, 9Ds G.W. **Note:** Counterstamped on 25 Centavos, KM#127.2.

CS Date	Host Date	Good	VG	F	VF	XF
1923	1887 GW	—	3.50	6.00	9.50	15.00
1923	1886 GW	—	4.00	8.00	15.00	25.00

KM# 155 50 CENTIMOS
6.2500 g., 0.0750 Silver 0.0151 oz. ASW **Counterstamp:** Type VIII **Note:** Counterstamped on 25 Centavos, KM#105.

CS Date	Host Date	Good	VG	F	VF	XF
1923	1864 GW	150	325	550	—	—

COUNTERSTAMPED COINAGE

Type IX • 1923

Obverse counterstamp: 1923 in 14mm circle.

Reverse counterstamp: UN/COLON in 14mm circle.

NOTE: The total mintage for KM#162-164 was 421,810 pieces. Host dates of 1867 GW, 1870 GW and 1872 GW are listed, but no examples are currently known to exist.

KM# 165 COLON
10.0000 g., 0.5000 Silver 0.1607 oz. ASW **Counterstamp:** Type IX **Obv:** Denomination on shield, date below **Rev:** Date within circle, wreath surrounds **Note:** Counterstamped on 50 Centimos, KM#150. For KM#165 the mintage were: 1917 host 9,390 pieces; 1918 host 28,800 pieces.

CS Date	Host Date	Good	VG	F	VF	XF
1923	1917 GCR	—	—	10.00	17.50	25.00
1923	1918 GCR	—	—	10.00	20.00	30.00

KM# 162 COLON
12.5000 g., 0.7500 Silver 0.3014 oz. ASW **Counterstamp:** Type IX **Note:** Counterstamped on 50 Centavos, KM#112.

CS Date	Host Date	Good	VG	F	VF	XF
1923	1866/5 GW	25.00	40.00	75.00	—	—
1923	1865 GW	25.00	40.00	75.00	—	—
1923	1867 GW	100	200	—	—	—
1923	1870 GW	150	—	—	—	—
1923	1872 GW	200	—	—	—	—
1923	1875 GW	25.00	40.00	75.00	—	—

KM# 163 COLON (Un)
12.5000 g., 0.7500 Silver 0.3014 oz. ASW **Counterstamp:** Type IX **Obv:** Date within circle, wreath surrounds **Rev:** Liberty cap and flags above shield, turned 3/4 right, denomination within circle on shield **Note:** Counterstamped on 50 Centavos, KM#124.

CS Date	Host Date	Good	VG	F	VF	XF
1923	1880 GW	—	6.50	10.00	25.00	50.00
1923	1885 GW	—	6.50	10.00	25.00	50.00
1923	1886 GW	—	9.00	17.50	30.00	60.00
1923	1887 GW	—	6.50	10.00	27.50	55.00
1923	1890 GW	—	6.50	10.00	27.50	55.00

KM# 164 COLON (Un)
10.0000 g., 0.9000 Silver 0.2893 oz. ASW **Counterstamp:** Type IX **Obv:** Date within circle, wreath surrounds **Rev:** Denomination within circle on shield **Note:** Counterstamped on 50 Centimos, KM#143.

CS Date	Host Date	Good	VG	F	VF	XF
1923	1902 CY	—	5.00	9.00	13.50	22.50
1923	1903 JCV	—	4.00	6.50	10.00	17.50
1923	1914 GCR	—	5.00	9.00	13.50	20.00

REFORM COINAGE

1920, 100 Centimos = 1 Colon

KM# 151 5 CENTIMOS
1.0000 g., Brass **Obv:** National arms, date below **Rev:** Denomination within wreath, G.C.R. lower right **Edge:** Plain

Date	Mintage	F	VF	XF	Unc	BU
1920	500,000	1.25	4.00	12.50	27.50	—
1921	500,000	2.00	5.00	15.00	37.50	—
1922	500,000	1.25	4.00	10.00	25.00	—
1936	1,500,000	0.40	0.75	2.00	7.50	—
1938	1,000,000	0.50	1.25	4.00	13.50	—
1940	1,300,000	0.40	0.75	1.50	7.50	—
1941	1,000,000	0.50	1.25	3.50	15.00	—

KM# 169 5 CENTIMOS
1.0000 g., Bronze **Obv:** National arms, date below **Rev:** Denomination within wreath, G.C.R. lower right

Date	Mintage	F	VF	XF	Unc	BU
1929(P)	1,500,000	0.60	1.25	3.00	6.25	11.00

KM# 178 5 CENTIMOS
1.0000 g., Copper-Nickel **Obv:** National arms, date below **Rev:** Denomination within wreath, star below divides B.N. at left from C.R. at right

Date	Mintage	F	VF	XF	Unc	BU
1942	274,000	0.65	1.00	3.00	8.50	—

Note: Struck over 2 Centimos, KM#144. Overstrikes with clear evidence of the undertype command a 10-15% premium.

KM# 179 5 CENTIMOS
1.0000 g., Brass **Obv:** National arms, date below **Rev:** Denomination within wreath, star below divides B.N. at left from C.R. at right

Date	Mintage	F	VF	XF	Unc	BU
1942	1,730,000	0.20	0.60	1.25	8.50	—
1942 Prooflike	—	Value: 35.00				

Note: Struck from specially polished dies.

Date	Mintage	F	VF	XF	Unc	BU
1943	1,000,000	0.20	1.00	3.00	8.50	—
1946	1,000,000	0.20	1.15	3.50	9.00	—
1946 Proof	—	Value: 100				
1947	3,000,000	0.10	0.45	1.00	3.50	—

KM# A184 5 CENTIMOS
1.0000 g., Copper-Nickel **Obv:** National arms, date below **Rev:** Denomination within wreath, star below divides B.C. at left from C.R. at right **Note:** Struck in Philadelphia 1951-52.

Date	Mintage	F	VF	XF	Unc	BU
1951(P)	3,000,000	0.35	0.75	1.50	2.75	5.00

KM# 184.1 5 CENTIMOS
1.0000 g., Copper-Nickel **Obv:** National arms, ribbon above, date below **Rev:** Denomination within wreath, B.C.C.R. below **Note:** Struck in Philadelphia, 1952.

Date	Mintage	F	VF	XF	Unc	BU
1951(P)	7,000,000	0.10	0.15	0.40	1.00	—

KM# 184.2 5 CENTIMOS
1.0100 g., Copper-Nickel, 14.99 mm. **Obv:** Small ships, 7 stars on arms, no flag on near ship, date below **Rev:** Denomination within wreath, B.C.C.R. below **Note:** Varieties exist for shields of each date.

Date	Mintage	F	VF	XF	Unc	BU
1969	20,000,000	—	—	0.10	0.15	—
1976 Proof	5,000	Value: 2.50				
1976	—	—	—	0.10	0.15	—
1978	7,520,000	—	—	0.10	0.15	—

KM# 184.3 5 CENTIMOS
1.0200 g., Copper-Nickel, 14.98 mm. **Obv:** Large ships, 7 stars on arms, flag on near ship, date below arms **Rev:** Denomination within wreath, B.C.C.R. below **Note:** Dies vary for each date.

Date	Mintage	F	VF	XF	Unc	BU
1972(g)	12,550,000	—	—	0.10	0.15	—
1973(g)	20,000,000	—	—	0.10	0.15	—
1976(g)	15,000,000	—	—	0.10	0.15	—

KM# 152 10 CENTIMOS
2.0000 g., Brass **Obv:** National arms, date below **Rev:** Denomination within wreath, G.C.R. at lower right

Date	Mintage	F	VF	XF	Unc	BU
1920 GCR	850,000	0.75	2.00	6.50	35.00	—
1921 GCR	750,000	1.00	2.50	10.00	47.50	—
1922 GCR	750,000	0.75	2.00	6.50	35.00	—

KM# 170 10 CENTIMOS
2.0000 g., Bronze **Obv:** National arms, date below **Rev:** Denomination within wreath, G.C.R. at bottom

Date	Mintage	F	VF	XF	Unc	BU
1929(P) GCR	500,000	1.00	2.00	5.00	22.50	—

KM# 174 10 CENTIMOS
Brass **Obv:** National arms, date below **Rev:** Denomination within wreath, G.C.R. below

Date	Mintage	F	VF	XF	Unc	BU
1936(sj)	750,000	0.35	0.65	3.00	10.00	—
1941(sj)	500,000	0.50	1.50	5.00	15.00	—

KM# 180 10 CENTIMOS
2.0000 g., Brass **Obv:** National arms, date below **Rev:** Denomination within wreath, B.N. - C.R. divided below

Date	Mintage	F	VF	XF	Unc	BU
1942(sj)	1,000,000	0.30	0.60	2.00	8.00	—
1943(sj)	500,000	0.35	0.75	3.50	12.00	—
1946(sj)	500,000	0.65	1.25	4.00	13.50	—
1947(sj)	1,500,000	0.25	0.50	1.50	5.50	—

Note: Edge varieties exist on 1947 strikes

KM# 185.1 10 CENTIMOS

2.0000 g., Copper-Nickel **Obv:** Small ships, 5 stars in shield, date below arms **Rev:** Denomination within wreath, B.C.C.R. below

Date	Mintage	F	VF	XF	Unc	BU
1951(P)	2,500,000	0.10	0.20	0.70	1.25	—

Note: Struck in 1952

KM# 185.1a 10 CENTIMOS

1.7500 g., Stainless Steel, 18 mm. **Obv:** National arms, date below **Rev:** Denomination within wreath, B.C.C.R. below

Date	Mintage	F	VF	XF	Unc	BU
1953(P)	5,290,000	—	—	0.10	0.75	—
1958(P)	10,470,000	—	—	0.10	0.25	—
Note: Struck in 1959						
1967(s)	5,500,000	—	—	0.10	0.25	—

KM# 185.2 10 CENTIMOS

2.0200 g., Copper-Nickel, 17.91 mm. **Obv:** Small ships, 7 stars in field, date below arms **Rev:** Denomination within wreath, B.C.C.R. below **Note:** Dies vary for each date

Date	Mintage	F	VF	XF	Unc	BU
1969(s)	10,000,000	—	—	0.10	0.15	—
1976(sm)	40,000,000	—	—	0.10	0.15	—
1976 Proof	5,000	Value: 2.50				

KM# 185.2b 10 CENTIMOS

2.0200 g., Nickel Clad Steel, 17.97 mm. **Obv:** National arms **Rev:** Denomination within wreath, B.C.C.R. below

Date	Mintage	F	VF	XF	Unc	BU
1979(sm)	10,000,000	—	—	0.10	0.15	—

KM# 185.2a 10 CENTIMOS

Aluminum, 18 mm. **Obv:** National arms, small ships, 7 stars in field **Rev:** Denomination within wreath, B.C.C.R. below

Date	Mintage	F	VF	XF	Unc	BU
1982(v)	40,000,000	—	—	0.10	0.15	—

KM# 185.3 10 CENTIMOS

1.9700 g., Copper-Nickel, 17.98 mm. **Obv:** Large ships, 7 stars in field, date below arms **Rev:** Denomination within wreath B.C.C.R. below

Date	Mintage	F	VF	XF	Unc	BU
1972(g)	20,000,000	—	—	0.10	0.15	—
1975(g)	5,000,000	—	—	0.10	0.15	—

KM# 168 25 CENTIMOS

3.4500 g., 0.6500 Silver 0.0721 oz. ASW **Obv:** National arms, date below **Rev:** Denomination within wreath, G.C.R. below at right **Edge:** Reeded

Date	Mintage	F	VF	XF	Unc	BU
1924	1,340,000	1.25	2.25	5.00	12.50	18.50

Note: Typical examples of KM#168 are weak at centers, fully struck up XF and Unc pieces command a 50% premium.

KM# 171 25 CENTIMOS

3.4500 g., Copper-Nickel **Obv:** National arms, date below **Rev:** Denomination within wreath, B.I.C.R. below **Edge:** Incuse lettered

Date	Mintage	F	VF	XF	Unc	BU
1935(P)	1,200,000	0.25	0.75	2.50	15.00	—

KM# 175 25 CENTIMOS

3.3300 g., Copper-Nickel **Obv:** National arms, date below **Rev:** Denomination within wreath, B.N.C.R. below

Date	Mintage	F	VF	XF	Unc	BU
1937(L)	1,600,000	0.25	0.75	1.75	8.00	—
1937(L) Proof	—	Value: 100				
1948(L)	9,200,000	0.10	0.20	0.40	1.25	—
1948(L) Proof	—	—	—	—	—	—

KM# 181 25 CENTIMOS

3.5000 g., Yellow Brass **Obv:** National arms, date below **Rev:** Denomination within wreath, star divides B.N. from C.R. below **Edge:** Reeded

Date	Mintage	F	VF	XF	Unc	BU
1944(sj)	800,000	0.50	1.00	3.25	11.00	16.50
1945(sj)	1,200,000	0.50	1.00	2.50	8.50	15.00
1946(sj)	1,200,000	0.50	1.00	2.75	9.00	12.50

KM# 181a 25 CENTIMOS

3.5000 g., Red Brass **Obv:** National arms, date below **Rev:** Denomination within wreath, star below divides B.N. and C.R. **Edge:** Reeded

Date	Mintage	F	VF	XF	Unc	BU
1945(sj)	Inc. above	2.00	4.00	10.00	20.00	35.00

KM# 188.1 25 CENTIMOS

3.4600 g., Copper-Nickel, 23.03 mm. **Obv:** Small ships, 7 stars on arms, date below **Rev:** Denomination within wreath, B.C.C.R. below **Note:** Dies vary for each date.

Date	Mintage	F	VF	XF	Unc	BU
1967(L)	4,000,000	—	—	0.10	0.50	—
1969	4,000,000	—	—	0.10	0.50	—
1974(v)	—	—	—	0.10	0.30	—
1976(sm)	12,000,000	—	—	0.10	0.30	—
1976 Proof	5,000	Value: 2.50				
1978(a)	10,000,000	—	—	0.10	0.30	—

KM# 188.1a 25 CENTIMOS

Nickel Clad Steel **Obv:** National arms, date below **Rev:** Denomination within wreath, B.C.C.R. below **Note:** Beaded rims.

Date	Mintage	F	VF	XF	Unc	BU
1980(sm)	30,000,000	—	—	0.10	0.25	—

KM# 188.1b 25 CENTIMOS

Aluminum **Obv:** National arms, date below **Rev:** Denomination within wreath, B.C.C.R. below **Edge:** Plain

Date	Mintage	F	VF	XF	Unc	BU
1982(r)	30,000,000	—	—	0.10	0.25	—

KM# 188.3 25 CENTIMOS

1.0500 g., Aluminum, 17 mm. **Obv:** National arms, date below **Rev:** Denomination within wreath, B.C.C.R. below **Edge:** Reeded **Note:** Reduced size. Dies vary for each date.

Date	Mintage	F	VF	XF	Unc	BU
1983(r)	60,000,000	—	—	0.10	0.20	—
1986(c)	60,000,000	—	—	0.10	0.20	—
1989(c)	60,000,000	—	—	0.10	0.20	—

KM# 172 50 CENTIMOS

6.2500 g., Copper-Nickel, 25.02 mm. **Obv:** National arms, date below **Rev:** Denomination within wreath, B.I.C.R. below

Date	Mintage	F	VF	XF	Unc	BU
1935(P)	700,000	0.50	2.00	8.00	30.00	—

KM# 176 50 CENTIMOS

Copper-Nickel **Obv:** National arms, date below **Rev:** Denomination within wreath, B.N.C.R. below

Date	Mintage	F	VF	XF	Unc	BU
1937(L)	600,000	0.30	1.00	3.00	15.00	—
1937(L) Proof	—	Value: 150				

KM# 182 50 CENTIMOS

6.8900 g., Copper-Nickel, 26 mm. **Obv:** National arms, date below **Rev:** Denomination within wreath, B.N.C.R. below **Edge Lettering:** -BNCR- (repeated)

Date	Mintage	F	VF	XF	Unc	BU
1948(L)	4,000,000	0.15	0.25	0.50	2.00	—
1948(L) Proof	—	—	—	—	—	—

KM# 189.1 50 CENTIMOS

Copper-Nickel, 26 mm. **Obv:** Small ships, 7 stars on shield, date below arms **Rev:** Denomination within wreath, B.C.C.R. below **Note:** Medal rotation.

Date	Mintage	F	VF	XF	Unc	BU
1965(L)	1,000,000	—	0.10	0.25	1.00	—

KM# 189.3 50 CENTIMOS

7.2900 g., Copper-Nickel, 26 mm. **Obv:** National arms, date below **Rev:** Denomination within wreath, B.C.C.R. below, large 50 **Edge Lettering:** -BCCR- (repeated) **Note:** Dies vary for each date - the main varieties are an open or closed "5" in "50", or large and small dates.

Date	Mintage	F	VF	XF	Unc	BU
1968(P)	2,000,000	—	0.10	0.15	0.50	—
1970(P)	4,000,000	—	0.10	0.15	0.35	—
1976(sm)	6,000,000	—	0.10	0.15	0.35	—
1976 Proof	5,000	Value: 2.50				
1978(v)	10,000,000	—	0.10	0.15	0.35	—

KM# 189.2 50 CENTIMOS

7.0100 g., Copper-Nickel, 26 mm. **Obv:** Large ships, 7 stars in shield, date below arms **Rev:** Denomination within wreath, B.C.C.R. below, large 50

Date	Mintage	F	VF	XF	Unc	BU
1972(g) Large date	4,000,000	—	0.10	0.15	0.35	—
1975(g) Large date	524,000	—	0.10	0.15	0.35	—
1975 Small date	Inc. above	—	0.10	0.15	0.35	—

KM# 209.1 50 CENTIMOS

2.1800 g., Stainless Steel, 19.11 mm. **Obv:** Large ships, letters incuse on ribbon, date below arms **Rev:** Denomination within wreath, B.C.C.R. below, thick 50 **Edge:** Plain

Date	Mintage	F	VF	XF	Unc	BU
1982(c)	12,000,000	—	—	0.10	0.25	—
1983(c)	24,000,000	—	—	0.10	0.25	—
1990(c)	24,000,000	—	—	0.10	0.25	—

KM# 209.2 50 CENTIMOS

2.2000 g., Stainless Steel, 18.95 mm. **Obv:** Small ships, letters in relief on ribbon **Rev:** Denomination within wreath

Date	Mintage	F	VF	XF	Unc	BU
1984(L)	42,000,000	—	—	0.10	0.25	—

KM# 173 COLON

10.0000 g., Copper-Nickel, 29 mm. **Obv:** National arms, date below **Rev:** Denomination within wreath, B.I.C.R below **Edge:** Incuse BICR; plain **Note:** Beaded rims.

Date	Mintage	F	VF	XF	Unc	BU
1935(P)	350,000	0.75	2.00	8.00	50.00	—

Note: Struck in 1936.

KM# 177 COLON

Copper-Nickel, 29 mm. **Obv:** National arms, date below **Rev:** Denomination within wreath, B.N.C.R. below **Edge Lettering:** -BNCR- (repeated)

Date	Mintage	F	VF	XF	Unc	BU
1937(L)	300,000	0.50	1.25	5.00	25.00	—
1937(L) Proof	—	Value: 200				

Date	Mintage	F	VF	XF	Unc	BU
1948(L)	1,350,000	0.20	0.40	0.75	2.00	—
1948(L) Proof	—	—	—	—	—	—

KM# 186.1 COLON

8.6670 g., Stainless Steel, 29 mm. **Obv:** Small ships, 5 stars in shield, date below **Rev:** Denomination within wreath, B.C.C.R. below **Edge Lettering:** -BCCR- (repeated)

Date	Mintage	F	VF	XF	Unc	BU
1954(P)	987,000	0.20	0.35	1.00	10.00	—

KM# 186.1a COLON

10.0000 g., Copper-Nickel, 29 mm. **Obv:** National arms, date below **Rev:** Denomination within wreath, B.C.C.R. below

Date	Mintage	F	VF	XF	Unc	BU
1961(P)	1,000,000	0.10	0.20	0.50	2.00	—

KM# 186.2 COLON

10.3200 g., Copper-Nickel, 29 mm. **Obv:** Small ships, 7 stars in shield, date below **Rev:** Denomination within wreath, B.C.C.R. below **Edge Lettering:** -BCCR- (repeated)

Date	Mintage	F	VF	XF	Unc	BU
1965(v)	1,000,000	0.10	0.20	0.40	1.00	—
1968(P)	2,000,000	0.10	0.20	0.30	0.65	—
1970(P)	2,000,000	0.10	0.20	0.30	0.65	—
1974(v)	2,000,000	0.10	0.20	0.30	0.65	—
1978(v)	10,000,000	0.10	0.20	0.30	0.65	—

KM# 186.3 COLON

9.7400 g., Copper-Nickel, 29 mm. **Obv:** Large ships, 7 stars in shield, date below **Rev:** Denomination within wreath, B.C.C.R. below

Date	Mintage	F	VF	XF	Unc	BU
1972(g)	2,000,000	0.10	0.20	0.30	0.65	—
1975(g)	1,028,000	0.10	0.20	0.30	0.65	—

KM# 186.4 COLON

9.7400 g., Copper-Nickel, 29 mm. **Obv:** Small ships, 7 stars in shield **Rev:** Denomination within wreath, large "1" **Edge Lettering:** -BCCR- (repeated) **Note:** Dies vary for each date.

Date	Mintage	F	VF	XF	Unc	BU
1976(sm)	12,000,000	0.10	0.20	0.30	0.65	—
1976(sm) Proof	5,000	Value: 2.50				
1977(sm)	22,000,000	0.10	0.20	0.30	0.65	—

KM# 210.1 COLON

3.2000 g., Stainless Steel, 21 mm. **Obv:** Large ships, letters incuse on ribbon, date below arms **Rev:** Denomination within wreath, B.C.C.R. below

Date	Mintage	F	VF	XF	Unc	BU
1982(cc)	12,000,000	—	—	0.15	0.35	—
1983(cc)	24,000,000	—	—	0.15	0.35	—
1984(L)	60,000,000	—	—	0.15	0.35	—
1991(cc)	30,000,000	—	—	0.15	0.35	—

KM# 210.2 COLON

3.2000 g., Stainless Steel, 21 mm. **Obv:** Small ships, letters in relief on ribbon, date below arms **Rev:** Denomination within wreath, B.C.C.R. below **Note:** Varieties exist with a "slim 1" in the value for 1984 & 1989, and a "fat 1" in the value for 1993 & 1994.

Date	Mintage	F	VF	XF	Unc	BU
1984(L)	Inc. above	—	—	0.15	0.35	—
1989(c)	50,000,000	—	—	0.15	0.35	—
1993(sm)	50,000,000	—	—	0.15	0.35	—
1994(v)	15,000,000	—	—	0.15	0.35	—

KM# 233 COLON

2.7800 g., Brass, 15.04 mm. **Obv:** National arms, date below **Rev:** Denomination above spray, B.C.C.R. below

Date	Mintage	F	VF	XF	Unc	BU
1998(a)	—	—	—	1.50	3.50	—

KM# 183 2 COLONES

Copper-Nickel, 32 mm. **Obv:** National arms, date below **Rev:** Denomination within wreath, B.N.C.R. below **Edge Lettering:** -BNCR- (repeated)

Date	Mintage	F	VF	XF	Unc	BU
1948(L)	1,380,000	0.50	0.75	1.25	3.00	—
1948(L) Proof	—	Value: 250				

KM# 187.1 2 COLONES

12.0000 g., Stainless Steel, 32 mm. **Obv:** National arms with small ships, 5 stars in shield, date below arms **Rev:** Denomination within wreath, B.C.C.R. below **Edge Lettering:** -BCCR- (repeated)

Date	Mintage	F	VF	XF	Unc	BU
1954(P)	1,028,000	0.25	0.50	2.00	15.00	—

KM# 187.1a 2 COLONES
Copper-Nickel, 32 mm. **Obv:** National arms, date below **Rev:** Denomination within wreath, B.C.C.R. below **Edge Lettering:** -BCCR- (repeated)

Date	Mintage	F	VF	XF	Unc	BU
1961(P)	1,000,000	0.15	0.30	0.50	1.25	—

KM# 187.2 2 COLONES
Copper-Nickel, 32 mm. **Obv:** Small ships, 7 stars in shield, date below arms **Rev:** Denomination within wreath, B.C.C.R. below **Edge Lettering:** -BCCR- (repeated) **Note:** Dies vary for each date.

Date	Mintage	F	VF	XF	Unc	BU
1968(L)	2,000,000	0.15	0.30	0.45	1.00	—
1970(P)	1,000,000	0.15	0.30	0.45	1.25	—
1972(v)	2,000,000	0.15	0.30	0.45	1.00	—
1978(v)	10,000,000	0.15	0.30	0.45	1.00	—

KM# 211.1 2 COLONES
4.2500 g., Stainless Steel, 23.1 mm. **Obv:** Large ships, letters incuse on ribbon, date below arms **Rev:** Denomination within wreath, B.C.C.R. below

Date	Mintage	F	VF	XF	Unc	BU
1982(cc)	12,000,000	—	—	0.20	0.60	—
1983(cc)	24,000,000	—	—	0.20	0.60	—

KM# 211.2 2 COLONES
4.2500 g., Stainless Steel, 23.1 mm. **Obv:** Small ship, letters in relief on ribbon, date below arms **Rev:** Denomination within wreath, B.C.C.R. below

Date	Mintage	F	VF	XF	Unc	BU
1984(L)	72,000,000	—	—	0.20	0.60	—

KM# 214.1 5 COLONES
7.2500 g., Stainless Steel, 25.9 mm. **Obv:** Small ship, letters in relief on ribbon, date below arms **Rev:** Denomination above spray, B.C.C.R. below, thick '5' on lined background

Date	Mintage	F	VF	XF	Unc	BU
1983(cc)	24,000,000	—	0.10	0.25	0.75	—
1989(v)	20,000,000	—	0.10	0.25	0.75	—

KM# 214.2 5 COLONES
7.2500 g., Stainless Steel, 25.9 mm. **Obv:** Large ship, letters incuse on ribbon **Rev:** Numeral on lined background, B.C.C.R. below sprays

Date	Mintage	F	VF	XF	Unc	BU
1985(cc)	25,000,000	—	0.10	0.25	0.75	—

KM# 214.3 5 COLONES
7.2500 g., Nickel Clad Steel, 25.9 mm. **Obv:** Small ship, letters in relief on ribbon **Rev:** Numeral on lined bakground, B.C.C.R. below sprays

Date	Mintage	F	VF	XF	Unc	BU
1993(L)	20,000,000	—	0.10	0.25	0.75	1.25

KM# 227 5 COLONES
4.0300 g., Brass Plated Steel, 21.5 mm. **Obv:** National arms, date below **Obv. Legend:** REPUBLICA DE COSTA RICA **Rev:** Denomination above sprays, B.C.C.R. below **Edge:** Segmented reeding

Date	Mintage	F	VF	XF	Unc	BU
1995(w)	15,000,000	—	—	0.25	0.75	—

KM# 227a 5 COLONES
4.0000 g., Brass, 21.6 mm. **Obv:** National arms, large date below **Rev:** Denomination above spray, B.C.C.R. below, large letters in legends **Edge:** Segmented reeding

Date	Mintage	F	VF	XF	Unc	BU
1997(a)	—	—	—	—	0.50	—

KM# 227a.1 5 COLONES
4.0000 g., Brass, 21.6 mm. **Obv:** National arms, date below, smaller letters in legend and smaller date, shield is outlined **Obv. Legend:** REPUBLICA DE COSTA RICA **Rev:** Denomination above sprays, B.C.C.R. below, smaller letters in legend **Edge:** Segmented reeding

Date	Mintage	F	VF	XF	Unc	BU
1999(co)	—	—	—	—	0.65	—

KM# 227a.2 5 COLONES
4.0000 g., Brass, 21.6 mm. **Obv:** National arms, date below, large letters in legend, large date, shield is not outlined **Rev:** Denomination above spray, B.C.C.R. below, large letters in legend, thick '5' **Edge:** Segmented reeding

Date	Mintage	F	VF	XF	Unc	BU
2001(a)	—	—	—	—	0.65	—

KM# 227a.3 5 COLONES
Brass, 21.6 mm. **Obv:** National arms, date below, thin numeral, large letters in legends **Edge:** Segmented reeding

Date	Mintage	F	VF	XF	Unc	BU
2001	—	—	—	—	0.65	—

KM# 227b 5 COLONES
0.9000 g., Aluminum, 21.4 mm. **Obv:** National arms **Obv. Legend:** REPUBLICA DE COSTA RICA **Rev:** Denomination above sprays, B.C.C.R. **Edge:** Plain

Date	Mintage	F	VF	XF	Unc	BU
2005	—	—	—	—	—	0.50

KM# 204 10 COLONES
Nickel, 32 mm. **Subject:** 25th Anniversary of the Central Bank **Obv:** National arms, denomination below **Rev:** Two dates above tree at center

Date	Mintage	F	VF	XF	Unc	BU
ND(1975)(v)	495,115	1.00	2.00	5.00	10.00	—
ND(1975)(v) Proof	5,000	Value: 15.00				

KM# 215.1 10 COLONES
8.4500 g., Stainless Steel, 28.3 mm. **Obv:** Small ship, letters in relief on ribbon, date below arms **Rev:** Denomination above spray, B.C.C.R. below, thick number on lined background

Date	Mintage	F	VF	XF	Unc	BU
1983(v)	12,000,000	—	0.20	0.35	1.25	—
1992(v)	25,000,000	—	0.20	0.35	1.25	—

KM# 215.2 10 COLONES
8.4500 g., Stainless Steel, 28.3 mm. **Obv:** Large ship, letters incuse on ribbon, date below arms **Rev:** Denomination above spray, B.C.C.R. below, thick number on lined background

Date	Mintage	F	VF	XF	Unc	BU
1985(cc)	20,000,000	—	0.20	0.35	1.25	—

KM# 228 10 COLONES
4.0200 g., Brass Plated Steel, 23.5 mm. **Obv:** National arms, date below **Rev:** Denomination above spray, B.C.C.R. below, thick 1 in numeral **Edge:** Segmented reeding

Date	Mintage	F	VF	XF	Unc	BU
1995(w)	15,000,000	—	—	0.35	1.25	—
2002	—	—	—	0.35	1.25	—

KM# 203 5 COLONES
Nickel **Subject:** 25th Anniversary of the Central Bank **Obv:** National arms, denomination below **Rev:** Plants with two dates at right

Date	Mintage	F	VF	XF	Unc	BU
ND(1975)	2,000,000	—	0.15	0.35	1.25	—
ND(1975) Proof	5,000	Value: 2.00				

KM# 228a 10 COLONES
5.0500 g., Brass, 23.5 mm. **Obv:** National arms, date below, large letters in legend and date, shield outlined **Obv. Legend:** REPUBLICA DE COSTA RICA **Rev:** Denomination above sprays, B.C.C.R. below, thick 1 in numeral **Edge:** Segmented reeding

Date	Mintage	F	VF	XF	Unc	BU
1997(a)	—	—	—	—	1.00	—
2002(a)	—	—	—	—	1.00	—

KM# 228a.1 10 COLONES
5.0000 g., Brass, 23.5 mm. **Obv:** National arms and date below, small letters in legend **Rev:** Thin "1" in value above spray, B.C.C.R. below. Legends smaller than on KM#228a. **Edge:** Segmented reeding

Date	Mintage	F	VF	XF	Unc	BU
1999(co)	—	—	—	—	1.15	—

KM# 228.2 10 COLONES
5.0000 g., Brass, 23.5 mm. **Obv:** National arms, date below, large legend and date, shield not outlined **Rev:** Denomination above spray, B.C.C.R. below **Edge:** Segmented reeding

Date	Mintage	F	VF	XF	Unc	BU
2002	—	—	—	—	1.15	—

KM# 228b 10 COLONES
1.1300 g., Aluminum, 22.97 mm. **Obv:** National arms **Obv. Legend:** REPUBLICA DE COSTA RICA **Rev:** Denomination above sprays, B.C.C.R. **Edge:** Plain

Date	Mintage	F	VF	XF	Unc	BU
2005	—	—	—	—	—	0.75

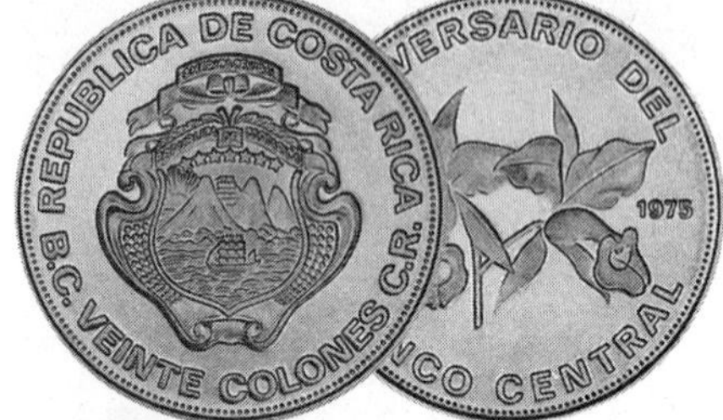

KM# 205 20 COLONES
Nickel, 36 mm. **Subject:** 25th Anniversary of the Central Bank **Obv:** National arms above denomination **Rev:** Flowers divide dates **Edge:** Reeded

Date	Mintage	F	VF	XF	Unc	BU
ND(1975)(v)	1,995,111	1.00	1.50	2.50	5.00	—
ND(1975)(v) Proof	5,000	Value: 9.00				

KM# 216.1 20 COLONES
9.7000 g., Stainless Steel, 31.25 mm. **Obv:** Letters in relief on ribbon, date below arms **Rev:** Denomination above spray, B.C.C.R. below, thick numerals on patterned background

Date	Mintage	F	VF	XF	Unc	BU
1983(v)	16,000,000	—	0.35	0.65	1.75	—

KM# 216.2 20 COLONES
9.7000 g., Stainless Steel, 31.25 mm. **Obv:** Letters incuse on ribbon, date below arms **Rev:** Denomination above spray, B.C.C.R. below, thick numerals on patterned background

Date	Mintage	F	VF	XF	Unc	BU
1985(cc)	25,000,000	—	0.35	0.65	1.75	—

KM# 216.3 20 COLONES
9.7500 g., Nickel Plated Steel, 31.25 mm. **Obv:** National arms, date below, letters in relief on ribbons **Rev:** Denomination above spray, B.C.C.R. below, numerals on patterned background

Date	Mintage	F	VF	XF	Unc	BU
1994(sm)	10,000,000	—	0.35	0.65	1.75	—

KM# 229 25 COLONES
Brass Plated Steel **Obv:** National arms, date below **Rev:** Denomination above spray, B.C.C.R. below **Edge:** Segmented reeding

Date	Mintage	F	VF	XF	Unc	BU
1995	—	—	—	—	2.50	—

KM# 229a 25 COLONES
7.0000 g., Brass, 25.4 mm. **Obv:** National arms **Obv. Legend:** REPUBLICA DE COSTA RICA **Rev:** Value above sprays, B.C.C.R. below **Edge:** Segmented reeding

Date	Mintage	F	VF	XF	Unc	BU
2001(a)	—	—	0.50	1.00	2.50	—
2003	—	—	0.50	1.00	2.50	—

KM# 229a.1 25 COLONES
7.0000 g., Brass **Obv:** National arms, date below **Rev:** Value above sprays, B.C.C.R. below **Edge:** Plain

Date	Mintage	F	VF	XF	Unc	BU
2005	—	—	—	—	2.50	—

KM# 231 50 COLONES
7.8000 g., Brass, 27.5 mm. **Obv:** National arms, large date below, shield outlined **Obv. Legend:** REPUBLICA DE COSTA RICA **Rev:** Value above spray **Rev. Legend:** B. C. C. R. **Edge:** Segmented reeding

Date	Mintage	F	VF	XF	Unc	BU
1997(a)	—	—	—	—	3.00	—
2002(a)	—	—	—	—	3.00	—

KM# 231.1 50 COLONES
7.8000 g., Brass, 27.5 mm. **Obv:** National arms, date below, small letters and numerals in legend and date **Obv. Legend:** REPUBLICA DE COSTA RICA **Rev:** Value above spray, smaller letters in legend **Rev. Legend:** B. C. C. R. **Edge:** Segmented reeding

Date	Mintage	F	VF	XF	Unc	BU
1999	—	—	—	—	3.00	—

KM# 231.2 50 COLONES
7.8000 g., Brass, 27.5 mm. **Obv:** National arms, date below, large legend and date, shield not outlined **Obv. Legend:** REPUBLICA DE COSTA RICA **Rev:** Value over spray **Rev. Legend:** B. C. C. R. **Edge:** Segmented reeding

Date	Mintage	F	VF	XF	Unc	BU
2003	—	—	—	—	3.00	—

KM# 231b 50 COLONES
Brass Plated Steel **Obv:** National arms above date **Rev:** Value above sprays, B.C.C.R. below **Edge:** Segmented reeding

Date	Mintage	F	VF	XF	Unc	BU
2006	—	—	—	—	3.50	—

KM# 224 100 COLONES
Nickel **Obv:** National arms, denomination below **Rev:** Bust of President Dr. Oscar Arias S. divides dates

Date	Mintage	F	VF	XF	Unc	BU
1987(sm)	25,000	—	—	—	7.50	—

KM# 230 100 COLONES
Brass Plated Steel **Obv:** National arms above date **Rev:** Denomination above spray, B.C.C.R. below **Edge:** Segmented reeding

Date	Mintage	F	VF	XF	Unc	BU
1995(w)	—	—	—	—	4.50	—

KM# 230a 100 COLONES
Brass **Obv:** National arms, date below, large letters in legend and date, shield outlined **Rev:** Value above spray, B.C.C.R. below **Edge:** Segmented reeding

Date	Mintage	F	VF	XF	Unc	BU
1997(a)	—	—	—	—	4.50	—
1998(a)	—	—	—	—	4.50	—

KM# 230a.1 100 COLONES
9.0000 g., Brass, 29.5 mm. **Obv:** National arms, date below, small letters in legend **Rev:** Denomination above spray, B.C.C.R. below, small letters in legend **Edge:** Segmented reeding

Date	Mintage	F	VF	XF	Unc	BU
1999(co)	—	—	—	—	4.50	—

KM# 240 100 COLONES
9.1000 g., Brass, 29.5 mm. **Obv:** New design with much smaller legend and date **Rev:** Value **Edge:** Segmented reeding

Date	Mintage	F	VF	XF	Unc	BU
2000(a)	—	—	—	—	4.50	—

KM# 240a 100 COLONES
Brass Plated Steel **Obv:** National arms above date **Rev:** Value above sprays **Edge:** Reeded

Date	Mintage	F	VF	XF	Unc	BU
2006	—	—	—	—	4.50	—

KM# 236 500 COLONES
9.8000 g., Brass **Subject:** 50 Years - Central Bank **Obv:** National arms, date below **Rev:** Bank building, value below

Date	Mintage	F	VF	XF	Unc	BU
2000(a) Proof	500	Value: 10.00				
2000(a)	5,000,000	—	—	—	2.50	3.50

KM# 239.1 500 COLONES
11.0000 g., Copper-Aluminum-Nickel, 32.9 mm. **Obv:** National arms **Obv. Legend:** REPUBLICA DE COSTA RICA **Rev:** Value above sprays, B.C.C.R. below, thick numerals **Edge:** Segmented reeding

Date	Mintage	F	VF	XF	Unc	BU
2003(a)	—	—	—	2.00	3.00	—
2005	—	—	—	2.00	3.00	—

KM# 239.2 500 COLONES
Brass, 32.9 mm. **Obv:** National arms, date below **Obv. Legend:** REPUBLICA DE COSTA RICA **Rev:** Denomination above sprays, B.C.C.R. below, thin numerals **Edge:** Segmented reeding

Date	Mintage	F	VF	XF	Unc	BU
2003	100	—	—	120	200	—

KM# 239.1a 500 COLONES
Brass Plated Steel **Obv:** National arms, date below **Rev:** Value above sprays, B.C.C.R. below **Edge:** Segmented reeding

Date	Mintage	F	VF	XF	Unc	BU
2006	—	—	—	120	200	—

The island of Crete (Kriti), located 60 miles southeast of the Peloponnesus, was the center of a brilliant civilization that flourished before the advent of Greek culture. After being conquered by the Romans, Byzantines, Moslems and Venetians, Crete became part of the Turkish Empire in 1669. As a consequence of the Greek Revolution of the1820s, it was ceded to Egypt. Egypt returned the island to the Turks in 1840, and they ceded it to Greece in 1913, after the Second Balkan War.

RULER
Prince George, 1898-1906

MINT MARKS
A - Paris
(a) - Paris (privy marks only)

GREEK ADMINISTRATION

STANDARD COINAGE

KM# 1 LEPTON
Bronze, 15 mm. **Ruler:** Prince George **Obv:** Crown **Rev:** Denomination within wreath

Date	Mintage	F	VF	XF	Unc	BU
1901A	1,710,717	6.00	12.00	27.50	100	200

KM# 2 2 LEPTA
Bronze **Ruler:** Prince George **Obv:** Crown **Rev:** Denomination within wreath

Date	Mintage	F	VF	XF	Unc	BU
1901A	707,000	6.00	12.50	40.00	175	250

KM# 6 50 LEPTA
2.5000 g., 0.8350 Silver 0.0671 oz. ASW **Ruler:** Prince George **Obv:** Head right **Rev:** Crowned arms, denomination below

Date	Mintage	F	VF	XF	Unc	BU
1901(a)	600,000	25.00	55.00	135	750	1,000

KM# 7 DRACHMA
5.0000 g., 0.8350 Silver 0.1342 oz. ASW **Ruler:** Prince George **Obv:** Head right **Rev:** Crowned, mantled and supported arms, denomination below

Date	Mintage	F	VF	XF	Unc	BU
1901(a)	500,000	35.00	60.00	200	2,500	3,500

KM# 8 2 DRACHMAI
10.0000 g., 0.8350 Silver 0.2684 oz. ASW **Ruler:** Prince George **Obv:** Head right **Rev:** Crowned, mantled and supported arms, denomination below

Date	Mintage	F	VF	XF	Unc	BU
1901(a)	175,000	75.00	150	800	7,500	10,000

KM# 9 5 DRACHMAI
25.0000 g., 0.9000 Silver 0.7234 oz. ASW **Ruler:** Prince George **Obv:** Head right **Rev:** Crowned, mantled and supported arms, denomination below

Date	Mintage	F	VF	XF	Unc	BU
1901(a)	150,000	100	200	1,200	10,000	20,000

The Republic of Croatia, (Hrvatska) bordered on the west by the Adriatic Sea and the northeast by Hungary, has an area of 21,829 sq. mi. (56,538 sq. km.) and a population of 4.7 million. Capital: Zagreb.

The country was attached to the Kingdom of Hungary until Dec. 1, 1918, when it joined with the Serbs and Slovenes to form the Kingdom of the Serbs, Croats and Slovenes, which changed its name to the Kingdom of Yugoslavia on Oct. 3, 1929. On April 6, 1941, Hitler, angered by the coup d'etat that overthrew the pro-Nazi regime of regent Prince Paul, sent the Nazi armies crashing across the Yugoslav borders from Germany, Hungary, Romania and Bulgaria. Within a week the army of the Balkan Kingdom was prostrate and broken. Yugoslavia was dismembered to reward Hitler's Balkan allies. Croatia, reconstituted as a nominal kingdom, was given to the administration of an Italian princeling, who wisely decided to remain in Italy. By 1947 it was again totally part of the 6 Yugoslav Socialist Republics.

Croatia proclaimed their independence from Yugoslavia on Oct. 8, 1991.

Local Serbian forces, supported by the Yugoslav Federal Army, had developed a military stronghold and proclaimed an independent "SRPSKEKRAJINA" State in the area around Knin, located in southern Croatia having an estimated population of 350,000 Croat Serbs. In September 1995, Croat forces overwhelmed Croat Serb forces ending the short life of their proclaimed Serbian Republic.

NOTE: Coin dates starting with 1994 are followed with a period. Example: 1994.

MONETARY SYSTEM
100 Banica = 1 Kuna

The word kunas', related to the Russian Kunitsa, which means marten, reflects the use of furs for money in medieval Eastern Europe.

KINGDOM

DECIMAL COINAGE

KM# 1 KUNA
Zinc **Note:** Similar to 2 Kune, KM#2.

Date	Mintage	F	VF	XF	Unc	BU
1941 Rare	—	—	—	—	—	—

Note: Possibly unique

KM# 2 2 KUNE

2.2600 g., Zinc, 19.1 mm. **Edge:** Plain **Designer:** Ivan Kerdic **Note:** Medal rotation

Date	Mintage	F	VF	XF	Unc	BU
1941	—	3.00	22.00	28.00	42.00	—
1941 Proof	—	Value: 80.00				

KM# A3 500 KUNA

9.9500 g., 0.9000 Gold 0.2879 oz. AGW **Obv:** Ante Pavelió, date below **Rev:** Denomination above arms within braided circle **Designer:** Ivan Kerdic

Date	Mintage	F	VF	XF	Unc	BU
1941	170	—	1,750	2,250	3,000	—

KM# B3 500 KUNA

9.9500 g., 0.9000 Gold 0.2879 oz. AGW **Obv:** Kneeling figure with sheaf of grain, date below **Rev:** Denomination above arms within braided circle

Date	Mintage	F	VF	XF	Unc	BU
1941	—	—	—	—	3,400	—

REPUBLIC

REFORM COINAGE

May 30, 1994 - 1000 Dinara = 1 Kuna; 100 Lipa = 1 Kuna

For the circulating minor coins, the reverse legend (name of item) is in Croatian for odd dated years and Latin for even dated years.

KM# 3 LIPA

0.8000 g., Aluminum, 16 mm. **Obv:** Denomination above crowned arms **Obv. Legend:** REPUBLIKA HRVATSKA **Rev:** Ears of corn, date below **Rev. Legend:** KUKURUZ **Edge:** Plain **Designer:** Kuzma Kovacic

Date	Mintage	F	VF	XF	Unc	BU
1993	57,834,100	—	—	0.20	0.50	—
1993 Proof	17,000	Value: 1.00				
1995.	7,101,000	—	—	0.20	0.50	—
1995. With dot	—	—	—	0.20	0.50	—
1995. With dot, Proof	4,000	Value: 2.00				
1997.	5,019,000	—	—	0.20	0.50	—
1997. Proof	—	Value: 1.00				
1999.	8,000,000	—	—	0.20	0.50	—
1999. Proof	2,000	Value: 1.50				
2001.	2,000,000	—	—	0.20	0.50	—
2001. Proof	1,000	Value: 2.50				
2003.	1,500,000	—	—	0.20	0.50	—
2003. Proof	1,000	Value: 2.50				
2005.	—	—	—	0.20	0.50	—
2005. Proof	—	Value: 2.00				

KM# 12 LIPA

0.7000 g., Aluminum, 17 mm. **Obv:** Denomination above crowned arms **Obv. Legend:** REPUBLIKA HRVATSKA **Rev:** Ears of corn, date below **Rev. Legend:** ZEA MAYS **Edge:** Plain

Date	Mintage	F	VF	XF	Unc	BU
1994.	2,003,097	—	—	0.40	1.00	—
1994. Proof	4,000	Value: 2.00				
1996.	2,000,000	—	—	0.40	1.00	—
1996. Proof	5,000	Value: 1.00				
1998.	2,000,000	—	—	0.40	1.00	—
1998. Proof	2,000	Value: 2.50				
2000.	2,000,000	—	—	0.40	1.00	—
2000. Proof	1,000	Value: 2.50				
2002.	3,000,000	—	—	0.40	1.00	—
2002. Proof	1,000	Value: 2.50				
2004.	2,000,000	—	—	0.40	1.00	—

Date	Mintage	F	VF	XF	Unc	BU
2004. Proof	2,000	Value: 1.50				
2006	—	—	—	0.40	1.00	—

KM# 13 LIPA

Aluminum, 17 mm. **Obv:** Denomination above crowned arms **Rev:** Ears of corn, date below **Rev. Legend:** FAO

Date	Mintage	F	VF	XF	Unc	BU
ND(1995)	1,000,000	—	—	0.30	1.00	—
ND(1995) Proof	5,000	Value: 1.50				

KM# 4 2 LIPE

0.9000 g., Aluminum, 18.97 mm. **Obv:** Denomination above crowned arms on half braid **Obv. Legend:** REPUBLIKA HRVATSKA **Rev:** Grapevine, date below **Rev. Legend:** VINOVA LOZA **Edge:** Plain

Date	Mintage	F	VF	XF	Unc	BU
1993	17,958,962	—	—	0.40	1.00	—
1993 Proof	17,000	Value: 2.00				
1995. With dot	7,498,000	—	—	0.40	1.00	—
1995. With dot, Proof	4,000	Value: 2.00				
1997.	4,996,000	—	—	0.40	1.00	—
1997. Proof	2,000	Value: 2.50				
1999.	8,000,000	—	—	0.40	1.00	—
1999. Proof	2,000	Value: 2.50				
2001.	2,986,000	—	—	0.40	1.00	—
2001. Proof	1,000	Value: 3.00				
2003.	2,000,000	—	—	0.40	1.00	—
2003. Proof	1,000	Value: 3.00				
2005.	—	—	—	0.40	1.00	—
2005. Proof	—	Value: 3.00				

KM# 14 2 LIPE

0.9200 g., Aluminum, 19 mm. **Obv:** Denomination above crowned arms on half braid **Obv. Legend:** REPUBLIKA HRVATSKA **Rev:** Grapevine, date below **Rev. Legend:** VITIS VINIFERA **Edge:** Plain **Designer:** Kuzma Kovacic

Date	Mintage	F	VF	XF	Unc	BU
1994.	2,000,163	—	—	0.80	2.00	—
1994. Proof	4,000	Value: 2.25				
1996.	2,006,000	—	—	0.80	2.00	—
1996. Proof	5,000	Value: 2.25				
1998.	2,000,000	—	—	0.80	2.00	—
1998. Proof	2,000	Value: 2.50				
2000.	2,000,000	—	—	0.80	2.00	—
2000, Proof	1,000	Value: 3.00				
2002.	2,000,000	—	—	0.80	2.00	—
2002. Proof	1,000	Value: 3.00				
2004.	2,000,000	—	—	0.80	2.00	—
2004. Proof	2,000	Value: 2.50				
2006	—	—	—	0.80	2.00	—

KM# 36 2 LIPE

0.9400 g., Aluminum, 18.97 mm. **Subject:** Olympics **Obv:** Denomination above crowned arms on half braid **Rev:** Olympic logo, torch above date below **Edge:** Plain

Date	Mintage	F	VF	XF	Unc	BU
1996.	1,000,000	—	—	0.30	0.60	—
1996. Proof	5,000	Value: 1.00				

KM# 5 5 LIPA

2.5400 g., Brass Plated Steel, 17.99 mm. **Obv:** Denomination above crowned arms **Obv. Legend:** REPUBLIKA HRVATSKA **Rev:** Oak leaves, date below **Rev. Legend:** HRAST LUZNJAK **Edge:** Plain **Designer:** Kuzma Kovacic

Date	Mintage	F	VF	XF	Unc	BU
1993	42,686,969	—	—	0.40	1.50	—
1993 Proof	17,000	Value: 2.00				
1995. With dot	17,308,000	—	—	0.40	1.00	—
1995. Proof	4,000	Value: 3.00				
1997.	29,964,000	—	—	0.40	1.00	—
1997. Proof	2,000	Value: 3.50				
1999.	25,402,000	—	—	0.40	1.00	—
1999. Proof	2,000	Value: 3.50				
2001.	6,598,000	—	—	0.40	1.00	—
2001. Proof	1,000	Value: 4.00				
2003.	13,000,000	—	—	0.40	1.00	—
2003. Proof	2,000	Value: 3.50				
2005.	—	—	—	0.40	1.00	—
2005. Proof	—	Value: 3.50				
2007	—	—	—	0.40	1.00	—

KM# 15 5 LIPA

2.4200 g., Brass Plated Steel, 17.99 mm. **Obv:** Denomination above crowned arms **Obv. Legend:** REPUBLIKA HRVATSKA **Rev:** Oak leaves, date below **Rev. Legend:** QUERCUS ROBUR **Edge:** Plain **Designer:** Kuzma Kovacic

Date	Mintage	F	VF	XF	Unc	BU
1994.	2,005,346	—	—	0.80	2.00	—
1994. Proof	4,000	Value: 2.25				
1996.	2,004,000	—	—	0.80	2.00	—
1996. Proof	5,000	Value: 2.50				
1998.	2,000,000	—	—	0.80	2.00	—
1998. Proof	2,000	Value: 3.00				
2000.	4,500,000	—	—	0.80	2.00	—
2000. Proof	1,000	Value: 4.00				
2002.	3,500,000	—	—	0.80	2.00	—
2002. Proof	1,000	Value: 4.00				
2004.	2,000,000	—	—	0.80	2.00	—
2004. Proof	2,000	Value: 3.00				
2006	—	—	—	0.80	2.00	—

KM# 37 5 LIPA

Brass Plated Steel, 18 mm. **Subject:** Olympics **Obv:** Denomination above crowned arms **Rev:** Olympic logo, torch above, date below **Designer:** Kuzma Kovacic

Date	Mintage	F	VF	XF	Unc	BU
1996.	900,000	—	—	0.60	1.25	—
1996. Proof	5,000	Value: 2.00				

KM# 6 10 LIPA

3.3200 g., Brass Plated Steel, 20 mm. **Obv:** Denomination above crowned arms **Obv. Legend:** REPUBLIKA HRVATSKA **Rev:** Tobacco plant, date below **Rev. Legend:** DUHAN **Edge:** Plain **Designer:** Kuzma Kovacic

Date	Mintage	F	VF	XF	Unc	BU
1993	63,689,778	—	—	0.40	1.50	—
1993 Proof	17,000	Value: 3.00				
1995. With dot	26,335,500	—	—	0.40	1.50	—
1995. With dot, Proof	4,000	Value: 4.00				
1997.	39,995,500	—	—	0.40	1.50	—
1997. Proof	1,000	Value: 4.50				
1999.	49,500,000	—	—	0.40	1.50	—
1999. Proof	2,000	Value: 4.50				
2001.	31,500,000	—	—	0.40	1.50	—
2001. Proof	1,000	Value: 5.00				
2003.	12,000,000	—	—	0.40	1.50	—
2003. Proof	1,000	Value: 5.00				
2005.	—	—	—	0.40	1.50	—
2005. Proof	—	Value: 5.00				

KM# 16 10 LIPA

Brass Plated Steel, 20 mm. **Obv:** Denomination above crowned arms on half braid **Obv. Legend:** REPUBLIKA HRVATSKA **Rev:**

Tobacco plant, date below **Rev. Legend:** NICOTIANA TABACUM **Edge:** Plain **Designer:** Kuzma Kovacic

Date	Mintage	F	VF	XF	Unc	BU
1994.	2,000,127	—	—	0.80	2.50	—
1994. Proof	4,000	Value: 4.00				
1996.	2,000,000	—	—	0.80	2.50	—
1996. Proof	5,000	Value: 3.50				
1998.	2,000,000	—	—	0.80	2.50	—
1998. Proof	2,000	Value: 4.50				
2000.	3,000,000	—	—	0.80	2.50	—
2000. Proof	1,000	Value: 5.00				
2002.	2,000,000	—	—	0.80	2.50	—
2002. Proof	1,000	Value: 5.00				
2004.	2,000,000	—	—	0.80	2.50	—
2004. Proof	2,000	Value: 4.50				
2006	—	—	—	0.80	2.50	—

KM# 38 10 LIPA

Brass, 20 mm. **Subject:** 50th Anniversary - UN **Obv:** Denomination above crowned arms above half braid **Rev:** UN logo, dates below **Designer:** Kuzma Kovacic

Date	Mintage	F	VF	XF	Unc	BU
ND(1995)	900,000	—	—	0.50	1.20	—
ND(1995)	5,000	Value: 4.00				

KM# 7 20 LIPA

2.9000 g., Nickel Plated Steel, 18.5 mm. **Obv:** Denomination above crowned arms on half braid **Obv. Legend:** REPUBLIKA HRVATSKA **Rev:** Olive branch, date below **Rev. Legend:** MASLINA **Edge:** Plain **Designer:** Kuzma Kovacic

Date	Mintage	F	VF	XF	Unc	BU
1993	25,206,442	—	—	0.50	1.50	—
1993 Proof	17,000	Value: 3.00				
1995. With dot	—	—	—	0.50	1.50	—
1995.	39,718,500	—	—	0.50	1.50	—
1995. Proof	4,000	Value: 4.00				
1997.	9,999,000	—	—	0.45	1.50	—
1997. Proof	2,000	Value: 4.50				
1999.	33,500,000	—	—	0.45	1.50	—
1999. Proof	2,000	Value: 4.50				
2001.	23,000,000	—	—	0.45	1.50	—
2001. Proof	1,000	Value: 5.00				
2003.	12,500,000	—	—	0.45	1.50	—
2003. Proof	1,000	Value: 5.00				
2005.	—	—	—	0.45	1.50	—
2005. Proof	—	Value: 5.00				

KM# 17 20 LIPA

2.8800 g., Nickel Plated Steel, 18.5 mm. **Obv:** Denomination above crowned arms on half braid **Obv. Legend:** REPUBLIKA HRVATSKA **Rev:** Olive branch, date below **Rev. Legend:** OLEA EUROPAEA **Edge:** Plain

Date	Mintage	F	VF	XF	Unc	BU
1994.	2,072,862	—	—	0.80	2.50	—
1994. Proof	4,000	Value: 3.00				
1996.	2,000,000	—	—	0.80	2.50	—
1996. Proof	5,000	Value: 4.00				
1998.	2,000,000	—	—	0.80	2.50	—
1998. Proof	2,000	Value: 4.50				
2000.	2,000,000	—	—	0.80	2.50	—
2000. Proof	1,000	Value: 5.00				
2002.	2,000,000	—	—	0.80	2.50	—
2002. Proof	1,000	Value: 5.00				
2004.	2,000,000	—	—	0.80	2.50	—
2004. Proof	2,000	Value: 4.50				
2006	—	—	—	0.80	2.50	—

KM# 18 20 LIPA

2.9000 g., Nickel Plated Steel, 18.5 mm. **Subject:** F.A.O. **Obv:** Denomination above crowned arms on half braid **Rev:** Olive branch, date below **Designer:** Kuzma Kovacic

Date	Mintage	F	VF	XF	Unc	BU
ND(1995)	1,000,000	—	—	0.50	1.50	—
ND(1995) Proof	5,000	Value: 4.50				

KM# 8 50 LIPA

3.6500 g., Nickel Plated Steel, 20.5 mm. **Obv:** Denomination above crowned arms on half braid **Obv. Legend:** REPUBLIKA HRVATSKA **Rev:** Flowers, date below **Rev. Legend:** VELEBITSKA DEGENIJA **Edge:** Plain **Designer:** Kuzma Kovacic

Date	Mintage	F	VF	XF	Unc	BU
1993	51,456,267	—	—	0.60	1.50	—
1993 Proof	17,000	Value: 4.00				
1995. With dot	23,077,000	—	—	0.60	1.50	—
1995. With dot, Proof	4,000	Value: 4.50				
1997.	1,473,000	—	—	0.60	1.50	—
1997. Proof	2,000	Value: 5.00				
1999.	1,000,000	—	—	0.60	1.50	—
1999. Proof	2,000	Value: 5.00				
2001.	5,500,000	—	—	0.60	1.50	—
2001. Proof	1,000	Value: 5.50				
2003.	8,000,000	—	—	0.60	1.50	—
2003. Proof	1,000	Value: 5.50				
2005.	—	—	—	0.60	1.50	—
2005. Proof	—	Value: 5.00				

KM# 19 50 LIPA

3.6500 g., Nickel Plated Steel, 20.5 mm. **Obv:** Denomination above crowned arms on half braid **Obv. Legend:** REPUBLIKA HRVATSKA **Rev:** Flowers, date below **Rev. Legend:** DEGENIA VELEBITICA **Edge:** Plain **Designer:** Kuzma Kovacic

Date	Mintage	F	VF	XF	Unc	BU
1994.	2,001,131	—	—	0.80	2.50	—
1994. Proof	4,000	Value: 4.00				
1996.	2,000,000	—	—	0.80	2.50	—
1996. Proof	5,000	Value: 4.00				
1998.	2,000,000	—	—	0.80	2.50	—
1998. Proof	2,000	Value: 4.50				
2000.	3,500,000	—	—	0.80	2.50	—
2000. Proof	1,000	Value: 5.00				
2002.	2,000,000	—	—	0.80	2.50	—
2002. Proof	1,000	Value: 5.00				
2004.	2,000,000	—	—	0.80	2.50	—
2004. Proof	2,000	Value: 4.50				
2006	—	—	—	0.80	2.50	—

KM# 39 50 LIPA

3.6500 g., Nickel Plated Steel, 20.5 mm. **Subject:** European soccer **Obv:** Denomination above crowned arms on half braid **Rev:** Checkered shield, soccer ball at bottom, date above **Designer:** Kuzma Kovacic

Date	Mintage	F	VF	XF	Unc	BU
1996.	900,000	—	—	0.40	1.50	—
1996. Proof	5,000	Value: 4.00				

KM# 9.1 KUNA

5.0000 g., Copper-Nickel, 22.5 mm. **Obv:** Marten back of numeral, arms divide branches below **Obv. Legend:** REPUBLIKA HRVATSKA **Rev:** Nightingale left, two dates **Rev. Legend:** SLAVUJ **Edge:** Reeded **Designer:** Kusma Kovacic

Date	Mintage	F	VF	XF	Unc	BU
1993	49,913,770	—	—	0.75	1.65	1.75
1993 Proof	17,000	Value: 3.00				
1995. With dot	32,707,000	—	—	0.75	1.65	1.75
1995. With dot, Proof	4,000	Value: 3.50				
1997.	6,205,000	—	—	0.75	1.65	1.75
1997. Proof	2,000	Value: 4.00				
2001.	1,000,000	—	—	0.75	1.65	2.00
2001. Proof	1,000	Value: 4.50				
2003.	2,000,000	—	—	0.75	1.65	2.00
2003. Proof	1,000	Value: 4.50				
2005.	—	—	—	0.75	1.65	2.00
2005. Proof	—	Value: 4.50				

KM# 9.2 KUNA

4.9300 g., Copper-Nickel, 22.5 mm. **Obv:** Crowned arms flanked by sprays, denomination above on marten **Rev:** Nightingale, left, '1994' above, date below **Edge:** Reeded

Date	Mintage	F	VF	XF	Unc	BU
1999.	18,000,000	—	—	0.75	1.75	—
1999. Proof	2,000	Value: 4.00				

KM# 20.1 KUNA

5.0000 g., Copper-Nickel, 22.5 mm. **Obv:** Marten back of numeral, arms divide branches below **Rev:** Nightingale left, date below **Rev. Legend:** Error spelling "LUSCINNIA" MEGARHYNCHOS **Designer:** Kuzma Kovacic **Note:** Formerly KM-20

Date	Mintage	F	VF	XF	Unc	BU
1994.	2,000,133	—	—	0.50	2.00	—
1994. Proof	4,000	Value: 4.00				
1996.	—	—	—	—	—	—
2002.	—	—	—	—	—	2.00

KM# 20.2 KUNA

5.0000 g., Copper-Nickel, 22.5 mm. **Obv:** Marten back of numeral, arms divide branches below **Obv. Legend:** REPUBLIKA HRVATSKA **Rev:** Nightingale left, date below **Rev. Legend:** Correct spelling "LUSCINIA" MEGARHYNCHOS **Edge:** Reeded **Designer:** Kuzma Kovacic

Date	Mintage	F	VF	XF	Unc	BU
1996.	2,000,000	—	—	1.00	3.00	—
1996. Proof	5,000	Value: 5.00				
1998.	2,000,000	—	—	1.00	3.00	—
1998. Proof	1,000	Value: 5.00				
2000.	2,000,000	—	—	1.00	3.00	—
2000. Proof	1,000	Value: 5.00				
2002.	1,000,000	—	—	1.00	3.00	—
2002. Proof	1,000	Value: 5.00				
2006	—	—	—	1.00	3.00	—

KM# 40 KUNA

Copper-Nickel, 22.5 mm. **Subject:** Olympics **Obv:** Marten back of numeral, arms divide branches below **Rev:** Olympic logo, torch above, date below

Date	Mintage	F	VF	XF	Unc	BU
1996.	1,000,000	—	—	0.40	1.50	—
1996. Proof	5,000	Value: 3.00				

KM# 10 2 KUNE

6.2000 g., Copper-Nickel, 24.5 mm. **Obv:** Marten back of numeral, arms divide branches below **Obv. Legend:** REPUBLIKA HRVATSKA **Rev:** Bluefin tuna right, date below **Rev. Legend:** TUNJ **Edge:** Reeded **Designer:** Kuzma Kovacic

Date	Mintage	F	VF	XF	Unc	BU
1993	19,774,119	—	—	1.00	2.00	—
1993 Proof	17,000	Value: 4.50				
1995. With dot	9,304,000	—	—	1.00	2.00	—
1995. With dot, Proof	4,000	Value: 5.50				
1997.	1,305,000	—	—	1.00	2.00	—
1997. Proof	1,000	Value: 6.00				
1999.	2,500,000	—	—	1.00	2.00	—
1999. Proof	2,000	Value: 6.00				
2001.	1,250,000	—	—	1.00	2.00	—
2001. Proof	1,000	Value: 6.50				

Date	Mintage	F	VF	XF	Unc	BU
2003.	7,250,000	—	—	1.00	2.00	—
2003. Proof	1,000	Value: 6.50				
2005.	—	—	—	1.00	2.00	—
2005. Proof	—	Value: 6.50				

KM# 21 2 KUNE

6.2000 g., Copper-Nickel, 24.5 mm. **Obv:** Marten back of numeral, arms divide branches below **Obv. Legend:** REPUBLIKA HRVATSKA **Rev:** Bluefin tuna right, date below **Rev. Legend:** THUNNUS - THYNNUS **Edge:** Reeded **Designer:** Kuzma Kovacic

Date	Mintage	F	VF	XF	Unc	BU
1994.	2,000,758	—	—	1.50	3.00	—
1994. Proof	4,000	Value: 5.00				
1996.	2,000,000	—	—	1.50	3.00	—
1996. Proof	5,000	Value: 4.50				
1998.	2,000,000	—	—	1.50	3.00	—
1998. Proof	1,000	Value: 5.50				
2000.	2,000,000	—	—	1.50	3.00	—
2000. Proof	1,000	Value: 6.00				
2002.	1,000,000	—	—	1.50	3.00	—
2002. Proof	1,000	Value: 6.00				
2004.	2,000,000	—	—	1.50	3.00	—
2004. Proof	2,000	Value: 5.50				
2006	—	—	—	1.50	3.00	—

KM# 22 2 KUNE

6.2000 g., Copper-Nickel, 24.5 mm. **Obv:** Marten back of numeral, arms divide branches below **Rev:** Bluefin tuna right, date below **Rev. Legend:** FAO **Designer:** Kuzma Kovacic

Date	Mintage	F	VF	XF	Unc	BU
ND(1995)	500,000	—	—	0.60	2.00	—
ND(1995) Proof	5,000	Value: 5.50				

KM# 11 5 KUNA

7.5000 g., Copper-Nickel, 26.7 mm. **Obv:** Marten back of numeral, arms divide branches below **Obv. Legend:** REPUBLIKA HRVATSKA **Rev:** Brown bear left, date below **Rev. Legend:** MRKI MEDVJRD **Edge:** Reeded

Date	Mintage	F	VF	XF	Unc	BU
1993	4,989,300	—	—	1.50	5.00	7.00
1993 Proof	17,000	Value: 6.50				
1995. With dot	3,724,000	—	—	1.50	5.00	7.00
1995. With dot, Proof	4,000	Value: 7.50				
1997.	1,165,000	—	—	1.50	5.00	7.00
1997. Proof	2,000	Value: 7.50				
1999.	4,000,000	—	—	1.50	5.00	7.00
1999. Proof	2,000	Value: 7.50				
2001.	17,300,000	—	—	1.50	5.00	8.00
2001. Proof	1,000	Value: 8.00				
2003.	1,000,000	—	—	1.50	5.00	8.00
2003. Proof	1,000	Value: 8.00				
2005.	—	—	—	1.50	5.00	8.00
2005. Proof	—	Value: 8.00				

KM# 23 5 KUNA

7.5000 g., Copper-Nickel, 26.7 mm. **Obv:** Marten back of numeral, arms divide branches below **Obv. Legend:** REPUBLIKA HRVATSKA **Rev:** Brown bear left, date below **Rev. Legend:** URSUS ARCTOS **Edge:** Reeded

Date	Mintage	F	VF	XF	Unc	BU
1994.	2,001,442	—	—	2.00	—	7.00
1994. Proof	4,000	Value: 7.50				
1996.	2,000,000	—	—	2.00	—	7.00
1996. Proof	5,000	Value: 7.50				
1998. Proof	—	Value: 7.50				
2000.	7,700,000	—	—	2.00	—	7.00
2000. Proof	1,000	Value: 9.00				
2002.	2,000,000	—	—	2.00	5.00	7.50
2002. Proof	1,000	Value: 9.00				
2004.	2,000,000	—	—	2.00	5.00	7.50
2004. Proof	2,000	Value: 8.00				
2006	—	—	—	2.00	5.00	7.50

KM# 24 5 KUNA

Copper-Nickel, 26.7 mm. **Subject:** 500th Anniversary - Senj **Obv:** Denomination on square divides arms above from shield below, circle surrounds **Rev:** Anniversary dates on symbol within circle

Date	Mintage	F	VF	XF	Unc	BU
1994.	1,000,000	—	—	—	3.50	—
1994. Proof	5,000	Value: 8.00				

KM# 66 25 KUNA

Bi-Metallic Brass center in Copper-Nickel ring, 31 mm. **Subject:** 10th Anniversary of International Recognition **Obv:** Denomination in 3-D on outlined marten within circle, arms divide sprays below **Rev:** National map **Edge:** Plain **Shape:** 12-sided

Date	Mintage	F	VF	XF	Unc	BU
ND(2002)	200,000	—	—	—	8.50	—

KM# 78 25 KUNA

12.6500 g., Bi-Metallic, 31 mm. **Subject:** Croatian European Union Candidacy **Obv:** Denomination in 3-D on outlined marten within circle, arms divide sprays below **Rev:** Joined squares within circle of stars **Edge:** Plain **Shape:** 12-sided

Date	Mintage	F	VF	XF	Unc	BU
ND (2004)	30,000	—	—	—	10.00	—
ND (2004) Proof	—	Value: 25.00				

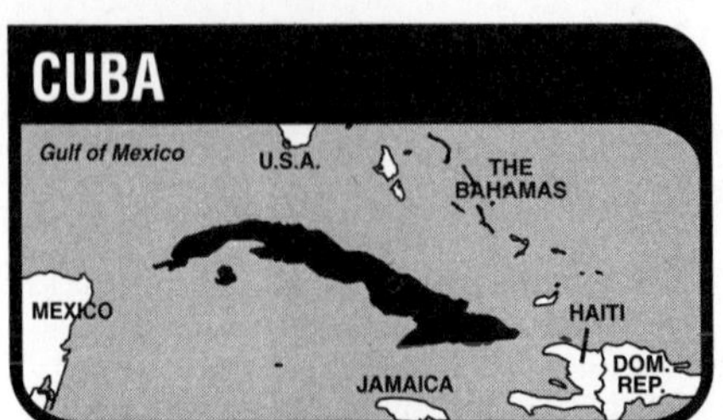

The Republic of Cuba, situated at the northern edge of the Caribbean Sea about 90 miles (145 km.) south of Florida, has an area of 42,804 sq. mi. (110,860 sq. km.) and a population of *11.2 million. Capital: Havana. The Cuban economy is based on the cultivation and refining of sugar, which provides 80 percent of export earnings.

Discovered by Columbus in 1492 and settled by Diego Velasquez in the early 1500s, Cuba remained a Spanish possession until 1898, except for a brief British occupancy of Havana in 1762-63. Cuban attempts to gain freedom were crushed, even while Spain was granting independence to its other American possessions. Ten years of warfare, 1868-78, between Spanish troops and Cuban rebels exacted guarantees of rights which were never implemented. The final revolt, begun in 1895, evoked American sympathy, and with the aid of U.S. troops independence was proclaimed on May 20, 1902. Fulgencio Batista seized the government in 1952 and established a dictatorship. Opposition to Batista, led by Fidel Castro, drove him into exile on Jan. 1, 1959. A communist-type, 25-member collective leadership headed by Castro was inaugurated in March, 1962.

RULER

Spanish, until 1898

MINT MARK

Key - Havana, 1977-

MONETARY SYSTEM

100 Centavos = 1 Peso

FIRST REPUBLIC

1902 - 1962

DECIMAL COINAGE

KM# 9.1 CENTAVO

2.5200 g., Copper-Nickel **Obv:** National arms within wreath, denomination below **Rev:** Roman denomination within circle of star, date below, 2.5 G. 250M

Date	Mintage	F	VF	XF	Unc	BU
1915	9,396,000	—	1.00	2.00	40.00	200
1915 Proof	200	Value: 450				
1916	9,318,000	—	1.00	2.00	50.00	175
1916 Proof	104	Value: 950				
1920	19,378,000	—	1.50	3.00	50.00	175
1938	2,000,000	—	2.50	6.00	75.00	210

KM# 9.2a CENTAVO

Brass **Obv:** National arms within wreath, denomination below **Rev:** Roman denomination within circle of star, 2.3 GR. 300M

Date	Mintage	F	VF	XF	Unc	BU
1943	20,000,000	—	0.40	1.25	7.00	75.00

KM# 9.2 CENTAVO

2.5500 g., Copper-Nickel **Obv:** National arms within wreath, denomination below **Rev:** Roman denomination within circle of star, 2.5 GR. 250M

Date	Mintage	F	VF	XF	Unc	BU
1946	50,000,000	—	0.20	1.00	4.00	60.00
1961	100,000,000	—	0.25	0.60	1.50	5.00

KM# 26 CENTAVO

Brass, 17 mm. **Subject:** Birth of Jose Marti Centennial **Obv:** Star on triangular shield divides denomination **Rev:** Bust, left **Designer:** Esteban Valderrama

Date	Mintage	F	VF	XF	Unc	BU
1953	50,000,000	—	0.15	0.75	12.00	60.00
1953 Proof; Rare	100	—	—	—	—	—

KM# 30 CENTAVO

Copper-Nickel, 17 mm. **Obv:** Star on triangular shield divides denomination **Rev:** Bust of Jose Marti left, date at left **Designer:** Esteban Valderrama

Date	Mintage	F	VF	XF	Unc	BU
1958	50,000,000	—	0.15	0.75	45.00	140

KM# A10 2 CENTAVOS

Copper-Nickel **Obv:** National arms within wreath, denomination below **Rev:** Roman denomination within circle of star, date below

Date	Mintage	F	VF	XF	Unc	BU
1915	6,090,000	—	1.25	3.00	40.00	175
1915 Proof	150	Value: 500				
1916	5,322,000	—	1.25	3.50	45.00	180
1916 Proof	100	Value: 1,000				

KM# 11.1 5 CENTAVOS

4.9000 g., Copper-Nickel, 21 mm. **Obv:** National arms within wreath above denomination **Rev:** Roman denomination within circle of star, date below, 5.0 G. 250M

Date	Mintage	F	VF	XF	Unc	BU
1915	5,096,000	—	1.50	4.00	50.00	200
1915 Proof	150	Value: 600				
1916	1,714,000	—	1.50	5.00	50.00	210
1916 Proof	100	Value: 1,000				
1920	10,000,000	—	1.50	4.50	60.00	225

KM# 11.2 5 CENTAVOS

Copper-Nickel, 21 mm. **Obv:** National arms within wreath, denomination below **Rev:** Roman denomination within circle of star, 5.0 G 250M **Note:** No period after G

Date	Mintage	F	VF	XF	Unc	BU
1920	—	—	1.75	5.00	100	400

KM# 11.3 5 CENTAVOS

5.0000 g., Copper-Nickel, 21 mm. **Obv:** National arms within wreath, denomination below **Rev:** Roman denomination within circle of star, date below, 5 GR. 250M **Note:** Prev. KM #11.2.

Date	Mintage	F	VF	XF	Unc	BU
1943	Inc. above	7.50	15.00	20.00	35.00	70.00
1946	40,000,000	—	0.50	0.75	5.00	45.00
1960	20,000,000	—	0.75	1.25	15.00	70.00
1961	70,000,000	—	0.15	0.40	1.00	2.00

KM# 11.3a 5 CENTAVOS

5.0000 g., Brass **Rev:** 4.6 GR. 300M **Note:** Prev. KM#11.2a.

Date	Mintage	F	VF	XF	Unc	BU
1943	6,000,000	—	1.00	3.50	20.00	60.00

KM# A12 10 CENTAVOS

2.5000 g., 0.9000 Silver 0.0723 oz. ASW, 17.8 mm. **Obv:** National arms within wreath, denomination below **Rev:** Star

Date	Mintage	F	VF	XF	Unc	BU
1915	5,690,000	1.50	4.00	12.00	100	450
1915 Proof	125	Value: 1,500				
1916	560,000	7.00	20.00	75.00	500	2,000
1916 Proof	50	Value: 1,750				
1920	3,090,000	2.50	6.00	20.00	200	650
1948	5,120,000	—	1.25	2.00	9.00	20.00
1949	9,880,000	—	1.25	1.75	9.00	20.00

KM# 23 10 CENTAVOS

2.5000 g., 0.9000 Silver 0.0723 oz. ASW, 18 mm. **Subject:** 50th Year of Republic **Obv:** Two dates left of flag, tower at right, denomination below **Rev:** Star above tree, spoked wheel below **Designer:** Juan J. Sicre

Date	Mintage	F	VF	XF	Unc	BU
1952	10,000,000	—	1.25	2.50	4.50	20.00

KM# 13.2 20 CENTAVOS

5.0000 g., 0.9000 Silver 0.1447 oz. ASW, 23 mm. **Obv:** National arms within wreath, denomination below **Rev:** Low relief star, date below **Note:** Coins with high relief stars normally exhibit a weak key and palm tree on the reverse. Coins with low relief stars tend to exhibit much more distinct lines in the valleys running towards the center of the star.

Date	Mintage	F	VF	XF	Unc	BU
1915 Coarse reeding	Inc. above	2.25	5.00	15.00	60.00	300
1915 Fine reeding	Inc. above	15.00	50.00	175	1,400	4,000
1916	2,535,000	2.50	6.50	18.00	300	875
1916 Proof	50	Value: 3,200				
1920	6,130,000	—	3.00	8.00	50.00	325
1932	184,000	22.00	75.00	300	1,000	1,750
1948	6,830,000	—	2.00	3.00	10.00	30.00
1949	13,170,000	—	2.00	3.00	10.00	30.00

KM# 13 20 CENTAVOS

5.0000 g., 0.9000 Silver 0.1447 oz. ASW, 23 mm. **Obv:** National arms within wreath **Rev:** High relief star

Date	Mintage	F	VF	XF	Unc	BU
1915 Fine reeding	—	3.00	8.00	35.00	245	800
1915 Coarse reeding	—	75.00	225	450	1,000	2,000
1915 Proof	125	Value: 2,000				

KM# 24 20 CENTAVOS

5.0000 g., 0.9000 Silver 0.1447 oz. ASW, 23 mm. **Subject:** 50th Year of Republic **Obv:** Two dates left of flag, tower at right, denomination below **Rev:** Star above tree, spoked wheel below **Designer:** Juan J. Sicre

Date	Mintage	F	VF	XF	Unc	BU
1952	8,700,000	—	2.25	3.00	6.50	35.00

KM# 27 25 CENTAVOS

6.2500 g., 0.9000 Silver 0.1808 oz. ASW, 24 mm. **Subject:** Centennial - Birth of Jose Marti **Obv:** Liberty cap on post, denomination at right **Rev:** Bust, left **Designer:** Esteban Valderrama

Date	Mintage	F	VF	XF	Unc	BU
1953	19,000,000	—	2.50	3.50	7.00	20.00
1953 Proof; Rare	—	—	—	—	—	—

KM# 14 40 CENTAVOS

10.0000 g., 0.9000 Silver 0.2893 oz. ASW **Obv:** National arms within wreath, denomination below **Rev:** High relief star, date below

Date	Mintage	F	VF	XF	Unc	BU
1915	2,633,000	4.50	12.00	25.00	300	750
1915 Proof	100	Value: 1,300				
1920	540,000	15.00	50.00	120	500	1,300
1920 Proof; Rare	—	—	—	—	—	—

KM# 14.2 40 CENTAVOS

10.0000 g., 0.9000 Silver 0.2893 oz. ASW **Obv:** National arms within wreath, denomination below **Rev:** Medium relief star, date below

Date	Mintage	F	VF	XF	Unc	BU
1915	Inc. above	30.00	100	275	1,250	1,750

KM# 14.3 40 CENTAVOS

10.0000 g., 0.9000 Silver 0.2893 oz. ASW **Obv:** National arms within wreath, denomination below **Rev:** Low relief star, date below **Note:** Coins with high relief stars normally exhibit a weak key and palm tree on the reverse. Coins with low relief stars tend to exhibit much more distinct lines in the valleys running towards the center of the star.

Date	Mintage	F	VF	XF	Unc	BU
1915	Inc. above	5.50	15.00	35.00	200	750
1916	188,000	18.00	75.00	400	1,250	2,500
1916 Proof	50	Value: 2,500				
1920	Inc. above	20.00	75.00	175	700	3,000

KM# 25 40 CENTAVOS

10.0000 g., 0.9000 Silver 0.2893 oz. ASW, 28 mm. **Subject:** 50th Year of Republic **Obv:** Two dates left of flag, tower at right, denomination below **Rev:** Star abovetree, spoked wheel below **Designer:** Juan J. Sicre

Date	Mintage	F	VF	XF	Unc	BU
1952	1,250,000	—	4.00	6.00	25.00	75.00

KM# 28 50 CENTAVOS

12.5000 g., 0.9000 Silver 0.3617 oz. ASW, 31 mm. **Subject:** Centennial - Birth of Jose Marti **Obv:** Inscription on scroll, denomination at right **Rev:** Bust, left **Designer:** Esteban Valderrama

Date	Mintage	F	VF	XF	Unc	BU
ND(1953)	2,000,000	—	5.00	8.00	20.00	60.00
ND(1953) Proof; Rare	—	—	—	—	—	—

KM# 15.1 PESO

26.7295 g., 0.9000 Silver 0.7734 oz. ASW **Obv:** National arms within wreath, denomination below **Rev:** High relief star, date below

Date	Mintage	F	VF	XF	Unc	BU
1915	1,976,000	9.00	20.00	60.00	300	2,000
1915 Proof	100	Value: 2,000				

KM# 15.2 PESO

26.7295 g., 0.9000 Silver 0.7734 oz. ASW **Obv:** National arms within wreath, denomination below **Rev:** Low relief star, date below **Note:** Coins with high relief stars normally exhibit a weak key and palm tree on the reverse. Coins with low relief stars tend to exhibit much more distinct lines in the valleys running towards the center of the star.

Date	Mintage	F	VF	XF	Unc	BU
1915	Inc. above	75.00	225	600	2,500	8,500
1916	843,000	10.00	20.00	70.00	1,000	3,800
1916 Proof	50	Value: 3,500				
1932	3,550,000	—	11.00	28.00	175	750
1933	6,000,000	—	10.00	20.00	125	235
1934	3,000,000	—	11.00	30.00	150	275

KM# 16 PESO

1.6718 g., 0.9000 Gold 0.0484 oz. AGW **Obv:** National arms within wreath, denomination below **Rev:** Head of Jose Marti right, date below

Date	Mintage	F	VF	XF	Unc	BU
1915	6,850	50.00	100	150	275	600
1915 Proof	140	Value: 1,750				
1916	11,000	50.00	100	150	300	700
1916 Proof	100	Value: 2,500				

KM# 22 PESO

26.7295 g., 0.9000 Silver 0.7734 oz. ASW **Obv:** National arms within wreath at right, denomination at left **Rev:** Laureate bust right, date lower right **Note:** Known as the "ABC" Peso.

Date	Mintage	F	VF	XF	Unc	BU
1934	7,000,000	11.00	25.00	60.00	225	600
1934 Matte proof	—	Value: 5,250				
1935	12,500,000	11.00	25.00	55.00	200	575
1936	16,000,000	11.00	25.00	65.00	250	750
1937	11,500,000	85.00	250	550	1,100	3,500
1938	10,800,000	10.00	22.50	45.00	150	525
1939	9,200,000	10.00	22.50	45.00	150	425

KM# 29 PESO

26.7295 g., 0.9000 Silver 0.7734 oz. ASW, 38 mm. **Subject:** Centennial of Jose Marti **Obv:** Radiant sun rising above water, denomination below **Rev:** Bust left, two dates **Designer:** Esteban Valderrama

Date	Mintage	F	VF	XF	Unc	BU
ND(1953)	1,000,000	—	BV	12.50	40.00	200
ND(1953) Proof; Rare	—	—	—	—	—	—

KM# 17 2 PESOS

3.3436 g., 0.9000 Gold 0.0967 oz. AGW **Obv:** National arms within wreath, denomination below **Rev:** Head right, date below

Date	Mintage	F	VF	XF	Unc	BU
1915	10,000	85.00	95.00	175	500	1,000
1915 Proof	100	Value: 3,000				
1916	150,000	BV	85.00	95.00	200	450
1916 Proof; Rare	8	—	—	—	—	—

KM# 18 4 PESOS

6.6872 g., 0.9000 Gold 0.1935 oz. AGW **Obv:** National arms within wreath, denomination below **Rev:** Head right, date below

Date	Mintage	F	VF	XF	Unc	BU
1915	6,300	165	185	375	1,100	1,600
1915 Proof	100	Value: 3,000				
1916	129,000	BV	165	185	500	750
1916 Proof	90	Value: 4,500				

KM# 19 5 PESOS

8.3592 g., 0.9000 Gold 0.2419 oz. AGW **Obv:** National arms within wreath, denomination below **Rev:** Head right, date below

Date	Mintage	F	VF	XF	Unc	BU
1915	696,000	—	BV	215	250	475
1915 Proof	—	Value: 3,200				
1916	1,132,000	—	—	BV	220	450
1916 Proof	—	Value: 6,500				

Note: American Numismatic Rarities Eliasberg sale 4-05, Proof 65 realized $13,800.

KM# 20 10 PESOS

16.7185 g., 0.9000 Gold 0.4837 oz. AGW **Obv:** National arms within wreath, denomination below **Rev:** Head right, date below

Date	Mintage	F	VF	XF	Unc	BU
1915	95,000	—	BV	425	575	800
1915 Proof	—	Value: 7,500				
Proof	—	—	—	—	—	—
1916	1,169,000	—	BV	BV	425	750
1916 Proof, Rare	—	—	—	—	—	—

Note: David Akers John Jay Pittman sale 8-99 very choice Proof realized $19,550, choice Proof realized $14,950. American Numismatic Rarities Eliasberg sale 4-05, Proof 62 realized $29,900.

KM# 21 20 PESOS

33.4370 g., 0.9000 Gold 0.9675 oz. AGW **Subject:** Jose Marti **Obv:** National arms within wreath, denomination below **Rev:** Head right, date below

Date	Mintage	F	VF	XF	Unc	BU
1915	57,000	—	BV	850	1,500	3,000
1915 Proof; Rare	—	—	—	—	—	—

Note: David Akers John Jay Pittman sale 8-99 very choice proof 1915 realized $11,500.

Date	Mintage	F	VF	XF	Unc	BU
1916 Proof; Rare	10	—	—	—	—	—

Note: David Akers John Jay Pittman sale 8-99 nearly choice Proof 1916 realized $43,125.

SECOND REPUBLIC

1962 - Present

DECIMAL COINAGE

KM# 33.1 CENTAVO

0.7300 g., Aluminum **Obv:** National arms within wreath, denomination below **Rev:** Roman denomination within circle of star, date below **Rev. Legend:** PATRIA Y LIBERTAD

Date	Mintage	F	VF	XF	Unc	BU
1963	200,020,000	—	0.10	0.30	0.60	1.25
1966	50,000,000	—	0.10	0.40	0.80	1.75
1967	—	—	—	—	—	—
1969	50,000,000	—	0.10	0.40	0.80	1.75
1970	50,000,000	—	0.10	0.40	0.80	1.75
1971	49,960,000	—	0.40	0.80	1.50	3.00
1972	100,000,000	—	0.10	0.40	0.80	1.75
1978	50,000,000	—	0.10	0.40	0.80	1.75
1979	100,000,000	—	0.10	0.40	0.80	1.75
1981	—	—	0.10	0.40	0.80	1.75
1982	—	—	0.10	0.40	0.80	1.75

KM# 33.2 CENTAVO

Aluminum **Obv:** National arms within wreath, denomination below **Rev:** Roman denomination within circle of star, date below **Rev. Legend:** PATRIA O MUERTE

Date	Mintage	F	VF	XF	Unc	BU
1983	—	—	0.10	0.40	0.80	1.75
1984	—	—	0.10	0.40	0.80	1.75
1985	—	—	0.10	0.40	0.80	1.75
1986	—	—	0.10	0.40	0.80	1.75
1987	—	—	0.10	0.40	0.80	1.75
1988	—	—	0.10	0.40	0.80	1.75

KM# 33.3 CENTAVO

0.7500 g., Aluminum, 16.76 mm. **Obv:** Cuban arms within wreath, denomination below **Rev:** Roman denomination within circle of star, date below **Edge:** Plain

Date	Mintage	F	VF	XF	Unc	BU
1998	—	—	0.10	0.40	0.80	1.75
2001	—	—	0.10	0.40	0.80	1.75
2002	—	—	0.10	0.40	0.80	1.75
2003	—	—	0.10	0.40	0.80	1.75
2004	—	—	0.10	0.40	0.80	1.75
2005	—	—	0.10	0.40	0.80	1.75

KM# 104.2 2 CENTAVOS

1.0000 g., Aluminum **Obv:** National arms within wreath, denomination below **Rev:** Roman denomination within circle of star, date below **Note:** Large lettered legends, short edge denticles on both sides of coin

Date	Mintage	F	VF	XF	Unc	BU
1983	Inc. above	—	0.10	0.20	0.50	1.00
1984	—	—	0.10	0.25	1.00	2.00
1985	—	—	0.10	0.20	0.50	1.00
1986	—	—	0.10	0.20	0.50	1.00

KM# 104.1 2 CENTAVOS

Aluminum **Obv:** National arms within wreath, denomination below **Rev:** Roman denomination within circle of star, date below **Note:** Small lettered legends, long edge denticles on both sides of coin

Date	Mintage	F	VF	XF	Unc	BU
1983	3,996,000	—	0.10	0.25	1.00	2.00

KM# 34 5 CENTAVOS
Aluminum, 21 mm. **Obv:** National arms within wreath, denomination below **Rev:** Roman denomination within circle of star, date below

Date	Mintage	F	VF	XF	Unc	BU
1963	80,000,000	—	0.10	0.25	0.75	1.50
1966	50,000,000	—	0.15	0.35	1.50	3.00
1968	—	—	0.15	0.35	1.50	3.00
1969	—	—	0.25	0.50	2.50	5.00
1971	100,020,000	—	0.10	0.25	0.75	1.50
1972	100,000,000	—	0.10	0.25	0.75	1.50
2001	—	—	0.10	0.25	0.75	1.50
2002	—	—	0.10	0.25	0.75	1.50
2003	—	—	0.10	0.25	0.75	1.50
2004	—	—	0.10	0.25	0.75	1.50
2006	—	—	0.10	0.25	0.75	1.50

KM# 31 20 CENTAVOS
Copper-Nickel, 24 mm. **Subject:** Jose Marti **Obv:** National arms within wreath, denomination below **Rev:** Bust left, date lower left

Date	Mintage	F	VF	XF	Unc	BU
1962	83,860,000	—	1.00	1.50	3.00	6.00
1968	25,750,000	—	1.25	2.00	4.00	8.00

KM# 35.1 20 CENTAVOS
2.0000 g., Aluminum, 24 mm. **Obv:** Cuban arms within wreath, denomination below **Rev:** Roman denomination within circle of star, date below

Date	Mintage	F	VF	XF	Unc	BU
1969	25,000,000	—	1.00	1.50	2.50	5.00
1970	29,560,000	0.35	1.25	1.75	4.00	—
1971	25,000,000	—	1.00	1.50	2.50	5.00
1972	—	—	1.00	1.50	2.50	5.00
2002	—	—	0.50	1.00	2.00	4.00
2003	—	—	0.50	1.00	2.00	4.00
2005	—	—	0.50	1.00	2.00	4.00
2006	—	—	0.50	1.00	2.00	4.00

KM# 35.2 20 CENTAVOS
Aluminum, 24 mm. **Obv:** National arms, revised shield **Rev:** Roman denomination within circle of star, date below

Date	Mintage	F	VF	XF	Unc	BU
ND	—	4.00	7.00	10.00	15.00	—

KM# 32 40 CENTAVOS
9.6000 g., Copper-Nickel **Subject:** Camilo Cienfuegos Gornaran **Obv:** National arms within wreath, denomination below **Rev:** Uniformed bust right, date at left

Date	Mintage	F	VF	XF	Unc	BU
1962	15,250,000	—	3.00	5.00	7.00	12.00

KM# 622 PESO
11.3000 g., Copper-Nickel, 30 mm. **Subject:** AIDS **Obv:** National arms within wreath, denomination below **Rev:** AIDS ribbon on silhouette before world map

Date	Mintage	F	VF	XF	Unc	BU
1998	50,000	—	—	—	15.00	—

KM# 346 3 PESOS
9.0000 g., Copper-Nickel, 26.3 mm. **Subject:** Ernesto Che Guevara **Obv:** National arms within wreath, denomination below **Rev:** Head facing, date below

Date	Mintage	F	VF	XF	Unc	BU
1990	4,050,000	—	—	3.00	6.00	8.00

KM# 346a 3 PESOS
8.2000 g., Nickel Clad Steel, 26.3 mm. **Obv:** National arms within wreath, denomination below **Rev:** Head facing, date below

Date	Mintage	F	VF	XF	Unc	BU
1992	—	—	—	3.00	6.00	8.00
1992 Proof	500	Value: 25.00				
1995	—	—	—	3.00	6.00	8.00
2002	—	—	—	2.50	5.00	7.00

VISITOR'S COINAGE

KM# 409 CENTAVO
Copper-Nickel **Obv:** Stag, date below **Rev:** Palm tree within logo and denomination

Date	Mintage	F	VF	XF	Unc	BU
1988	—	—	0.50	1.50	3.00	—

KM# 410 CENTAVO
Aluminum **Obv:** Palm tree within logo **Rev:** Denomination

Date	Mintage	F	VF	XF	Unc	BU
1988	—	—	0.50	1.50	5.00	—

KM# 411 5 CENTAVOS
Copper-Nickel **Obv:** Mollusk and date **Rev:** Palm tree within logo, denomination

Date	Mintage	F	VF	XF	Unc	BU
1981	—	0.45	0.75	2.00	4.00	—

KM# 412.1 5 CENTAVOS
Copper-Nickel **Obv:** Mollusk and date **Rev:** Palm tree within logo, denomination

Date	Mintage	F	VF	XF	Unc	BU
1981	—	0.45	0.75	2.00	4.00	—

KM# 412.2 5 CENTAVOS
Copper-Nickel **Obv:** Mollusk and date **Rev:** Palm tree within logo, denomination

Date	Mintage	F	VF	XF	Unc	BU
1981	—	0.45	0.75	2.00	4.00	—

KM# 412.3 5 CENTAVOS
Copper-Nickel **Obv:** Mollusk and date **Rev:** Palm tree within logo, small 5

Date	Mintage	F	VF	XF	Unc	BU
1989	—	0.35	0.50	1.50	3.00	—

KM# 412.3a 5 CENTAVOS
Stainless Steel **Obv:** Palm tree within logo, denomination **Rev:** Mollusk and date

Date	Mintage	F	VF	XF	Unc	BU
1989	—	—	1.00	3.00	6.00	—

KM# 413 5 CENTAVOS
Aluminum **Obv:** Palm tree within logo, date below **Rev:** Denomination

Date	Mintage	F	VF	XF	Unc	BU
1988	—	0.50	1.00	3.00	5.00	—

KM# 414 10 CENTAVOS
Copper-Nickel **Obv:** Hummingbird in flight right, date below **Rev:** Palm tree within logo, denomination

Date	Mintage	F	VF	XF	Unc	BU
1981	—	—	0.65	2.00	4.00	5.00

KM# 415.1 10 CENTAVOS
Copper-Nickel **Obv:** Hummingbird in flight right, date below **Rev:** Palm tree within logo, large "10"

Date	Mintage	F	VF	XF	Unc	BU
1981	—	0.50	1.00	3.00	5.00	7.00

KM# 415.2 10 CENTAVOS
Copper-Nickel **Obv:** Hummingbird in flight right, date below **Rev:** Palm tree within logo, small "10"

Date	Mintage	F	VF	XF	Unc	BU
1981	—	—	0.65	2.00	4.00	15.00

KM# 416 10 CENTAVOS
Aluminum **Obv:** Palm tree within logo, date below **Rev:** Denomination

Date	Mintage	F	VF	XF	Unc	BU
1988	—	—	0.65	2.00	4.00	—

KM# 415.2a 10 CENTAVOS
Stainless Steel **Obv:** Hummingbird in flight right **Rev:** Palm tree within logo, small 10

Date	Mintage	F	VF	XF	Unc	BU
1989	—	—	1.25	4.00	9.00	80.00

KM# 415.3 10 CENTAVOS
Copper-Nickel **Obv:** Hummingbird in flight right **Rev:** Palm tree within logo, denomination **Note:** Reduced size.

Date	Mintage	F	VF	XF	Unc	BU
1989	—	—	1.25	4.50	10.00	—

KM# 417 25 CENTAVOS
6.3200 g., Copper-Nickel **Obv:** Flower, date below **Rev:** Palm tree within logo, denomination

Date	Mintage	F	VF	XF	Unc	BU
1981	—	0.50	1.00	2.50	6.00	—

KM# 418.1 25 CENTAVOS
Copper-Nickel **Obv:** Flower, date below **Rev:** Palm tree within logo, large 25

Date	Mintage	F	VF	XF	Unc	BU
1981	—	—	1.00	3.00	7.00	—

KM# 418.2 25 CENTAVOS
Copper-Nickel **Obv:** Flower, date below **Rev:** Palm tree within logo, small 25

Date	Mintage	F	VF	XF	Unc	BU
1989	—	—	1.00	3.00	7.00	—

KM# 418.2a 25 CENTAVOS
Stainless Steel **Obv:** Flower and date **Rev:** Palm tree within logo, denomination

Date	Mintage	F	VF	XF	Unc	BU
1989	—	—	2.00	5.50	12.00	—

KM# 419 25 CENTAVOS
Aluminum **Obv:** Palm tree within logo, date below **Rev:** Denomination

Date	Mintage	F	VF	XF	Unc	BU
1988	—	—	0.75	2.50	5.00	—

KM# 420 50 CENTAVOS
Copper-Nickel **Obv:** Palm tree within logo, date below **Rev:** Denomination and logo

Date	Mintage	F	VF	XF	Unc	BU
1981	—	—	2.50	7.50	15.00	—

Note: Varieties exist in the number of lines below the palm tree.

KM# 461 50 CENTAVOS
Copper-Nickel **Obv:** Palm tree within logo, denomination **Rev:** Denomination and logo

Date	Mintage	F	VF	XF	Unc	BU
1989	—	—	5.00	15.00	30.00	—

KM# 421 PESO
Copper-Nickel **Obv:** Lighthouse **Rev:** Palm tree within logo, denomination

Date	Mintage	F	VF	XF	Unc	BU
1981	—	—	4.00	12.00	24.00	—

KM# 580 PESO
Copper-Nickel **Obv:** Lighthouse **Rev:** Palm tree within logo, denomination

Date	Mintage	F	VF	XF	Unc	BU
1989	—	—	4.00	12.00	24.00	—

PESO CONVERTIBLE SERIES

KM# 729 CENTAVO
1.7000 g., Copper Plated Steel, 15 mm. **Obv:** National arms within wreath, denomination below **Rev:** Tower and denomination **Edge:** Reeded

Date	Mintage	F	VF	XF	Unc	BU
2000	—	—	—	—	3.00	—
2002	—	—	—	—	3.00	—

KM# 733 CENTAVO
0.7500 g., Aluminum, 16.75 mm. **Obv:** Cuban arms **Rev:** Tower and denomination **Edge:** Plain

Date	Mintage	F	VF	XF	Unc	BU
2001	—	—	—	—	2.00	—
2002	—	—	—	—	2.00	—

Date	Mintage	F	VF	XF	Unc	BU
2003	—	—	—	—	2.00	—
2005	—	—	—	—	2.00	—

KM# 575.1 5 CENTAVOS
2.6300 g., Nickel-Plated Steel, 17.9 mm. **Obv:** National arms within wreath, denomination and date below **Rev:** Casa Colonial, denomination above **Note:** Medal alignment

Date	Mintage	F	VF	XF	Unc	BU
1994	—	—	—	—	1.00	—

KM# 575.2 5 CENTAVOS
2.6500 g., Nickel-Plated Steel, 18 mm. **Obv:** National arms **Rev:** Casa Colonial **Note:** Coin alignment, recut designs.

Date	Mintage	F	VF	XF	Unc	BU
1996	—	—	—	—	1.00	—
1998	—	—	—	—	1.00	—
1999	—	—	—	—	1.00	—
2000	—	—	—	—	1.00	—
2002	—	—	—	—	1.00	—
2006	—	—	—	—	1.00	—

KM# 576.1 10 CENTAVOS
Nickel-Bonded Steel, 20 mm. **Obv:** National arms within wreath, denomination and date below **Rev:** Castillo de la Fuerza, denomination above **Note:** Medal alignment.

Date	Mintage	F	VF	XF	Unc	BU
1994	—	—	—	—	2.00	—

KM# 576.2 10 CENTAVOS
3.9400 g., Nickel Plated Steel **Obv:** National arms **Rev:** Castillo de la Fuerza **Note:** Coin alignment, recut designs.

Date	Mintage	F	VF	XF	Unc	BU
1996	—	—	—	—	2.00	—
1999	—	—	—	—	2.00	—
2000	—	—	—	—	2.00	—
2002	—	—	—	—	2.00	—

KM# 577.1 25 CENTAVOS
Nickel Bonded Steel, 23 mm. **Obv:** National arms within wreath, denomination and date below **Rev:** Trinidad, denomination upper right **Note:** Medal alignment. Prev. KM#577.

Date	Mintage	F	VF	XF	Unc	BU
1994	—	—	—	—	3.00	—

KM# 577.2 25 CENTAVOS
5.7000 g., Nickel Plated Steel, 23 mm. **Obv:** National arms **Rev:** Trinidad **Note:** Coin alignment.

Date	Mintage	F	VF	XF	Unc	BU
1998	—	—	—	—	3.00	—
2000	—	—	—	—	3.00	—
2001	—	—	—	—	3.00	—
2002	—	—	—	—	3.00	—
2003	—	—	—	—	3.00	—
2006	—	—	—	—	3.00	—

KM# 578.1 50 CENTAVOS
7.5000 g., Nickel Plated Steel, 25 mm. **Obv:** National arms within wreath, denomination and date below **Rev:** Cathedral of Havana, denomination above **Note:** Medal alignment.

Date	Mintage	F	VF	XF	Unc	BU
1994	—	—	—	—	5.00	—

KM# 578.2 50 CENTAVOS
7.5000 g., Nickel Plated Steel, 25 mm. **Obv:** Cuban arms **Rev:** Havana Cathedral **Note:** Coin alignment.

Date	Mintage	F	VF	XF	Unc	BU
2002	—	—	—	—	5.00	—

KM# 579.1 PESO
8.5000 g., Nickel Plated Steel, 27 mm. **Obv:** National arms within wreath, denomination and date below **Rev:** Guama, denomination upper left **Note:** Medal alignment.

Date	Mintage	F	VF	XF	Unc	BU
1994	—	—	—	—	5.00	—

KM# 579.2 PESO
8.5000 g., Nickel Plated Steel, 27 mm. **Obv:** National arms **Rev:** Guama **Note:** Coin alignment.

Date	Mintage	F	VF	XF	Unc	BU
1998	—	—	—	—	5.00	—
2000	—	—	—	—	5.00	—
2001	—	—	—	—	5.00	—

KM# 730 5 PESOS
4.4600 g., Bi-Metallic Nickel Plated Steel center in Brass Plated Steel ring, 23 mm. **Obv:** National arms within wreath, denomination below **Rev:** Bust right, denomination at right, within circle **Edge:** Reeded **Note:** Medal alignment.

Date	Mintage	F	VF	XF	Unc	BU
1999	—	—	—	—	25.00	—

CURACAO

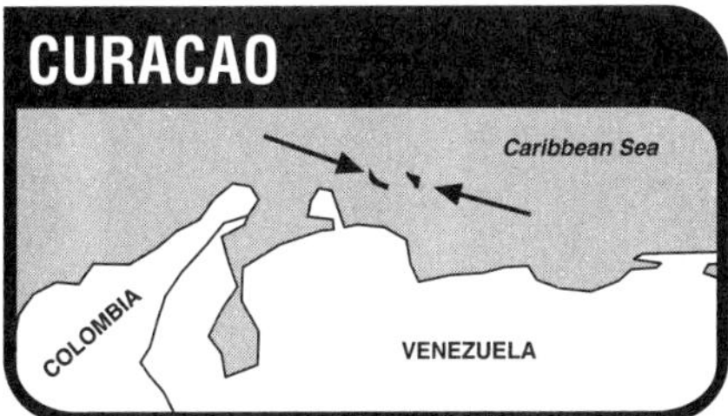

The island of Curacao, the largest of the six islands that comprise the Netherlands Antilles, which is an autonomous part of the Kingdom of the Netherlands located in the Caribbean Sea 40 miles off the coast of Venezuela, has an area of 173 sq. mi. (472 sq. km.) and a population of 127,900. Capital: Willemstad. The chief industries are banking and tourism. Salt, phosphates and cattle are exported.

Curacao was discovered by Spanish navigator Alonsode Ojeda in 1499 and was settled by Spain in 1527. The Dutch West India Company took the island from Spain in 1634 and administered it until 1787, when it was surrendered to the United Netherlands. The Dutch held it thereafter except for two periods during the Napoleonic Wars, 1800-1803 and 1807-16, when it was occupied by the British. During World War II, Curacao refined 60 percent of the oil used by the Allies; the refineries were protected by U.S. troops after Germany invaded the Netherlands in1940.

During the second occupation of the Napoleonic period, the British created an emergency coinage for Curacao by cutting the Spanish dollar into 5 equal segments and countermarking each piece with a rosette indent.

MINT MARKS
D - Denver
P - Philadelphia
(u) - Utrecht

KINGDOM OF NETHERLANDS

1816

MONETARY REFORM
15 Realen = 1 Peso, 1818-22
7 Stuivers = 1 Reaal, 1822-27
10 Stuivers = 1 Franc, 1822-27
5 Francs = 1 Dollar
20 Stuivers = 1 Gulden, 1827-99
2/5 Peso = 1 Gulden, 1827-96
5/7 Peso = 1 Gulden, 1896-97
1 Peso = 1 Gulden, 1897-99

MODERN COINAGE

100 Cents = 1 Gulden

KM# 39 CENT
2.5000 g., Bronze, 19 mm. **Obv:** Rampant lion left within circle, date below **Rev:** Denomination within wreath **Edge:** Reeded

Date	Mintage	F	VF	XF	Unc	BU
1942P	2,500,000	1.25	2.50	5.00	10.00	25.00

Note: This coin was also circulated in Suriname. For similar coins dated 1943P & 1957-1960, see Suriname.

KM# 41 CENT
Bronze **Obv:** Rampant lion left within circle, date below **Rev:** Denomination within wreath

Date	Mintage	F	VF	XF	Unc	BU
1944D	3,000,000	1.00	2.00	5.00	12.00	20.00
1947 (u) Proof	80	Value: 50.00				
1947 (u)	1,500,000	2.00	3.25	7.00	15.00	30.00

KM# 42 2-1/2 CENTS
4.0000 g., Bronze, 23 mm. **Obv:** Rampant lion left within circle, date below **Rev:** Denomination within wreath **Edge:** Reeded

Date	Mintage	F	VF	XF	Unc	BU
1944D	1,000,000	1.00	2.00	5.00	12.00	20.00
1947 (u) Proof	80	Value: 50.00				
1947 (u)	500,000	1.25	3.00	6.50	15.00	25.00
1948 (u)	1,000,000	1.00	2.00	5.00	12.00	20.00
1948 (u) Proof	75	Value: 50.00				

KM# 40 5 CENTS
4.5000 g., Copper-Nickel, 18 mm. **Obv:** Flower within inner circle **Rev:** Denomination within circle divides date at sides, shells at corners of coin **Edge:** Plain

Date	Mintage	F	VF	XF	Unc	BU
1943	8,595,000	1.25	2.50	4.00	8.50	19.00

Note: The above piece does not bear either a palm tree privy mark or a mint mark, but it was struck expressly for use in Curacao and Surinam. This homeland type of KM#153 was last issued in the Netherlands in 1940

KM# 47 5 CENTS
4.4800 g., Copper-Nickel, 18 mm. **Obv:** Flower within inner circle **Rev:** Denomination within circle divides date at sides, shells at corners **Shape:** 4-sided

Date	Mintage	F	VF	XF	Unc	BU
1948 Proof	75	Value: 50.00				
1948	1,000,000	1.25	2.50	6.00	12.00	20.00

KM# 37 10 CENTS
1.4000 g., 0.6400 Silver 0.0288 oz. ASW, 15 mm. **Obv:** Head left **Rev:** Denomination and date within wreath **Edge:** Reeded

Date	Mintage	F	VF	XF	Unc	BU
1941P	800,000	4.00	9.00	18.00	36.00	50.00
1942P	1,500,100	3.00	7.00	16.00	32.00	45.00
1943P	4,500,000	2.50	6.00	15.00	30.00	40.00

Note: Both these coins were also circulated in Surinam. For coins dated 1942P, see Surinam.

KM# 38 25 CENTS
3.5800 g., 0.6400 Silver 0.0737 oz. ASW, 19 mm. **Obv:** Head left **Rev:** Denomination above date within wreath **Edge:** Reeded

Date	Mintage	F	VF	XF	Unc	BU
1941P	1,100,000	3.00	6.00	12.50	25.00	35.00
1943/1P	2,500,000	45.00	90.00	175	220	350
1943P	Inc. above	1.75	4.00	7.50	15.00	25.00

Note: Both coins were also circulated in Surinam. For similar coins dated 1943, 1944 & 1945-P with acorn mint mark, see Netherlands.

KM# 36 1/10 GULDEN
1.4000 g., 0.6400 Silver 0.0288 oz. ASW **Obv:** Head left **Rev:** Crowned arms divide denomination, date below

Date	Mintage	F	VF	XF	Unc	BU
1901 Proof	40	Value: 250				
1901	300,000	10.00	20.00	40.00	85.00	140

KM# 43 1/10 GULDEN
1.4000 g., 0.6400 Silver 0.0288 oz. ASW, 15 mm. **Obv:** Head left **Rev:** Denomination, date below **Edge:** Reeded

Date	Mintage	F	VF	XF	Unc	BU
1944D	1,500,000	1.25	3.50	7.50	15.00	30.00
1947 Proof	80	Value: 70.00				
1947	1,000,000	1.25	3.50	7.50	12.50	25.00

KM# 48 1/10 GULDEN
1.4000 g., 0.6400 Silver 0.0288 oz. ASW, 15 mm. **Obv:** Head left **Rev:** Denomination, date below **Edge:** Reeded

Date	Mintage	F	VF	XF	Unc	BU
1948	1,000,000	1.25	3.50	7.50	12.50	25.00
1948 Proof	75	Value: 70.00				

KM# 44 1/4 GULDEN
3.5800 g., 0.6400 Silver 0.0737 oz. ASW, 18.8 mm. **Obv:** Head left **Rev:** Denomination, date below **Edge:** Reeded

Date	Mintage	F	VF	XF	Unc	BU
1944D	1,500,000	1.50	3.75	8.50	17.50	35.00
1947 (u) Proof	80	Value: 80.00				
1947 (u)	1,000,000	1.50	3.50	7.50	12.50	25.00

KM# 45 GULDEN
10.0000 g., 0.7200 Silver 0.2315 oz. ASW, 28 mm. **Obv:** Head left **Edge Lettering:** GOD * ZU * MET * ONS *

Date	Mintage	F	VF	XF	Unc	BU
1944D	500,000	5.00	15.00	25.00	50.00	75.00

KM# 46 2-1/2 GULDEN
25.0000 g., 0.7200 Silver 0.5787 oz. ASW, 38 mm. **Obv:** Head left **Rev:** Crowned arms divide denomination, date belw **Edge Lettering:** GOD * ZU * MET * ONS *

Date	Mintage	F	VF	XF	Unc	BU
1944D	200,000	—	BV	8.50	12.50	20.00

Note: 60,000 coins melted down after minting.

CYPRUS

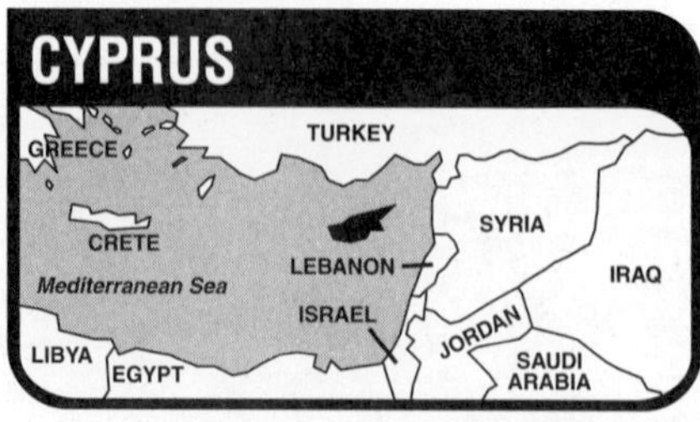

The island of Cyprus lies in the eastern Mediterranean Sea 44 miles (71 km.) south of Turkey and 60 miles (97 km.) off the Syrian coast. It is the third largest island in the Mediterranean Sea, having an area of 3,572 sq. mi. (9,251 sq. km.) and a population of 736,636. Capital: Nicosia. Agriculture, light manufacturing and tourism are the chief industries. Citrus fruit, potatoes, footwear and clothing are exported

The importance of Cyprus dates from the Bronze Age when it was desired as a principal source of copper (from which the island derived its name) and as a strategic trading center. It was during this period that large numbers of Greeks settled on the island and gave it the predominantly Greek character. Its role as an international marketplace made it a prime disseminator of the then prevalent cultures, a role that still influences the civilization of Western man. Because of its fortuitous position and influential role, Cyprus was conquered by a succession of empires: the Assyrian, Egyptian, Persian, Macedonian, Ptolemaic, Roman and Byzantine. It was taken from Isaac Comnenus by Richard the Lion-Heart in 1191, sold to the Templar Knights and for the following 7 centuries was ruled by the Franks, the Venetians and the Ottomans. During the Ottoman period Cyprus acquired its Turkish community (18 percent of its population). In 1878 the island fell into British hands and was made a crown colony of Britain in 1925. Finally, on Aug. 16, 1960, it became an independent republic.

In 1964, the ethnic Turks withdrew from active participation in the government. Turkish forces invaded Cyprus in 1974, gained control of 40 percent of the island and forcibly separated the Greek and Turkish communities. In 1983, Turkish Cypriots proclaimed their own state in northern Cyprus, which remains without international recognition.

Cyprus is a member of the Commonwealth of Nations. The president is Chief of State and Head of Government. Cyprus is also a member of the European Union.

RULER
British, until 1960

MINT MARKS
no mint mark - Royal Mint, London, England
H - Birmingham, England

MONETARY SYSTEM
9 Piastres = 1 Shilling
20 Shillings = 1 Pound

BRITISH COLONY

PIASTRE COINAGE

KM# 1.2 1/4 PIASTRE
Bronze, 21 mm. **Obv:** Crowned head left **Rev:** Denomination within circle

Date	Mintage	F	VF	XF	Unc	BU
1901	72,000	20.00	50.00	100	200	—

KM# 8 1/4 PIASTRE
Bronze **Obv:** Crowned bust right **Rev:** Denomination within circle, date below **Shape:** 12-sided

Date	Mintage	F	VF	XF	Unc	BU
1902	72,000	20.00	30.00	50.00	150	—
1905	422,000	10.00	30.00	40.00	100	—
1908	36,000	50.00	100	200	350	—

KM# 16 1/4 PIASTRE
Bronze **Obv:** Crowned bust left **Rev:** Denomination within circle, date below

Date	Mintage	F	VF	XF	Unc	BU
1922	72,000	10.00	25.00	40.00	100	—
1926 Proof	—	Value: 365				
1926	360,000	5.00	10.00	20.00	65.00	—

KM# 11 1/2 PIASTRE
Bronze **Obv:** Crowned bust right **Rev:** Denomination within circle, date at right

Date	Mintage	F	VF	XF	Unc	BU
1908	36,000	80.00	200	400	600	—

KM# 17 1/2 PIASTRE
Bronze **Obv:** Crowned bust left **Rev:** Denomination within circle, date at right

Date	Mintage	F	VF	XF	Unc	BU
1922	36,000	40.00	80.00	150	300	—
1927 Proof	—	Value: 375				
1927	108,000	10.00	20.00	50.00	120	—
1930	180,000	10.00	20.00	50.00	100	—
1930 Proof	—	Value: 365				
1931 Proof	—	Value: 425				
1931	90,000	15.00	30.00	80.00	140	—

KM# 20 1/2 PIASTRE
Copper-Nickel, 19.4 mm. **Obv:** Crowned bust left **Rev:** Denomination, date at right **Shape:** Scalloped

Date	Mintage	F	VF	XF	Unc	BU
1934 Proof	—	Value: 325				
1934	1,440,000	0.75	2.50	6.50	20.00	—

KM# 22 1/2 PIASTRE
Copper-Nickel, 19.4 mm. **Obv:** Crowned head left **Rev:** Denomination, date at right **Shape:** Scalloped

Date	Mintage	F	VF	XF	Unc	BU
1938 Proof	—	Value: 325				
1938	1,080,000	0.35	2.00	5.00	12.50	—

KM# 22a 1/2 PIASTRE
2.5000 g., Bronze, 19.4 mm. **Obv:** Crowned head left **Rev:** Denomination, date at right **Shape:** Scalloped

Date	Mintage	F	VF	XF	Unc	BU
1942	1,080,000	2.00	4.00	10.00	25.00	—

Note: A large portion of the mintage was destroyed during WWII

Date	Mintage	F	VF	XF	Unc	BU
1942 Proof	—	Value: 400				
1943	1,620,000	0.25	1.00	2.50	15.00	—
1944	2,160,000	0.25	1.00	2.50	12.50	—
1945 Proof	—	Value: 200				
1945	1,080,000	0.25	1.00	2.50	15.00	—

KM# 29 1/2 PIASTRE
Bronze, 19.4 mm. **Obv:** Crowned head left **Rev:** Denomination, date at right **Shape:** Scalloped

Date	Mintage	F	VF	XF	Unc	BU
1949 Proof	—	Value: 150				
1949	1,080,000	0.15	0.35	1.00	3.50	—

KM# 12 PIASTRE
Bronze **Obv:** Crowned bust right **Rev:** Denomination within circle, date at right

Date	Mintage	F	VF	XF	Unc	BU
1908	27,000	100	200	350	700	—

KM# 18 PIASTRE

Bronze **Obv:** Crowned bust left **Rev:** Denomination within circle, date at right

Date	Mintage	F	VF	XF	Unc	BU
1922	54,000	15.00	50.00	150	300	—
1927 Proof	—	Value: 400				
1927	127,000	10.00	20.00	60.00	150	—
1930	96,000	10.00	25.00	100	200	—
1930 Proof	—	Value: 400				
1931 Proof	—	Value: 725				
1931	45,000	20.00	50.00	100	200	—

KM# 21 PIASTRE

Copper-Nickel **Obv:** Crowned bust left **Rev:** Denomination, date at right **Shape:** Scalloped

Date	Mintage	F	VF	XF	Unc	BU
1934 Proof	—	Value: 325				
1934	1,440,000	1.00	2.50	6.50	16.50	—

KM# 23 PIASTRE

Copper-Nickel **Obv:** Crowned head left **Rev:** Denomination, date at right **Shape:** Scalloped

Date	Mintage	F	VF	XF	Unc	BU
1938 Proof	—	Value: 325				
1938	2,700,000	0.60	1.50	3.00	12.50	—

KM# 23a PIASTRE

5.2200 g., Bronze **Obv:** Crowned head left **Rev:** Denomination, date at right

Date	Mintage	F	VF	XF	Unc	BU
1942 Proof	—	Value: 225				
1942	1,260,000	1.00	2.00	5.00	20.00	—
1943	2,520,000	0.50	1.00	2.50	15.00	—
1944	3,240,000	0.50	1.00	2.50	10.00	—
1945 Proof	—	Value: 200				
1945	1,080,000	0.60	1.50	3.00	20.00	—
1946 Proof	—	Value: 200				
1946	1,080,000	0.60	1.50	3.00	20.00	—

KM# 30 PIASTRE

Bronze **Obv:** Crowned head left **Obv. Legend:** Legend ends ...DEI GRATIA REX **Rev:** Denomination, date at right **Shape:** Scalloped

Date	Mintage	F	VF	XF	Unc	BU
1949 Proof	—	Value: 150				
1949	1,080,000	0.25	0.75	2.00	4.00	—

KM# 4 3 PIASTRES

1.8851 g., 0.9250 Silver 0.0561 oz. ASW **Obv:** Crowned and veiled bust left **Rev:** Crown over denomination divides date, circle surrounds

Date	Mintage	F	VF	XF	Unc	BU
1901 Proof	—	Value: 800				
1901	300,000	8.00	25.00	50.00	100	—

KM# 5 4-1/2 PIASTRES

2.8276 g., 0.9250 Silver 0.0841 oz. ASW, 19 mm. **Obv:** Crowned and veiled bust left **Rev:** Crowned arms divide date, denomination below

Date	Mintage	F	VF	XF	Unc	BU
1901 Proof	—	Value: 950				
1901	400,000	10.00	20.00	40.00	100	—

KM# 15 4-1/2 PIASTRES

2.8276 g., 0.9250 Silver 0.0841 oz. ASW, 19 mm. **Obv:** Crowned bust left **Rev:** Crowned arms divide date, denomination below

Date	Mintage	F	VF	XF	Unc	BU
1921	600,000	5.00	10.00	30.00	80.00	—

KM# 24 4-1/2 PIASTRES

2.8276 g., 0.9250 Silver 0.0841 oz. ASW, 19 mm. **Obv:** Crowned head left **Obv. Designer:** Percy Metcalfe **Rev:** Two stylized rampant lions left, denomination and date 3/4 surround **Rev. Designer:** George E. Kruger-Gray

Date	Mintage	F	VF	XF	Unc	BU
1938 Proof	—	Value: 400				
1938	192,000	2.00	6.00	15.00	30.00	—

KM# 6 9 PIASTRES

5.6552 g., 0.9250 Silver 0.1682 oz. ASW **Obv:** Crowned and veiled bust left **Rev:** Crowned arms divide date, denomination below

Date	Mintage	F	VF	XF	Unc	BU
1901 Proof	—	Value: 1,250				
1901	600,000	15.00	40.00	100	200	—

KM# 9 9 PIASTRES

5.6552 g., 0.9250 Silver 0.1682 oz. ASW **Obv:** Crowned bust right **Rev:** Crowned arms divide date, denomination below

Date	Mintage	F	VF	XF	Unc	BU
1907	60,000	35.00	100	275	500	—

KM# 13 9 PIASTRES

5.6552 g., 0.9250 Silver 0.1682 oz. ASW **Obv:** Crowned bust left **Rev:** Crowned arms divide date, denomination below

Date	Mintage	F	VF	XF	Unc	BU
1913	50,000	40.00	125	300	600	—
1919	400,000	5.00	10.00	30.00	100	—
1921	490,000	5.00	10.00	30.00	100	—

KM# 25 9 PIASTRES

5.6552 g., 0.9250 Silver 0.1682 oz. ASW **Obv:** Crowned head left **Obv. Designer:** Percy Metcalfe **Rev:** Two stylized rampant lions left, date at right, denomination below **Rev. Designer:** George E. Kruger-Gray

Date	Mintage	F	VF	XF	Unc	BU
1938 Proof	—	Value: 400				
1938	504,000	5.00	8.00	12.00	30.00	—
1940 Proof	—	Value: 400				
1940	800,000	2.75	5.00	10.00	27.50	—

KM# 27 SHILLING

5.6300 g., Copper-Nickel **Obv:** Crowned head left **Obv. Designer:** Percy Metcalfe **Rev:** Two stylized rampant lions left, date below, denomination above **Rev. Designer:** George E. Kruger-Gray

Date	Mintage	F	VF	XF	Unc	BU
1947 Proof	—	Value: 300				
1947	1,440,000	2.00	4.00	10.00	30.00	—

KM# 31 SHILLING

Copper-Nickel **Obv:** Crowned head left **Obv. Legend:** Legend ends; DEI GRATIA REX **Obv. Designer:** Percy Metcalfe **Rev:** Two stylized rampant lions left, date below, denomination above **Rev. Designer:** George E. Kruger-Gray

Date	Mintage	F	VF	XF	Unc	BU
1949 Proof	—	Value: 300				
1949	1,440,000	2.00	4.00	10.00	30.00	—

KM# 7 18 PIASTRES

11.3104 g., 0.9250 Silver 0.3364 oz. ASW **Obv:** Crowned and veiled bust left **Rev:** Crowned arms divide date and denomination below

Date	Mintage	F	VF	XF	Unc	BU
1901 Proof	—	Value: 2,500				
1901	200,000	40.00	150	300	500	—

KM# 10 18 PIASTRES
11.3104 g., 0.9250 Silver 0.3364 oz. ASW **Obv:** Crowned bust right **Rev:** Crowned arms divide date and denomination below

Date	Mintage	F	VF	XF	Unc	BU
1907	20,000	80.00	225	485	1,250	—

KM# 14 18 PIASTRES
11.3104 g., 0.9250 Silver 0.3364 oz. ASW **Obv:** Crowned bust left **Rev:** Crowned arms divide date and denomination below

Date	Mintage	F	VF	XF	Unc	BU
1913	25,000	70.00	140	350	650	—
1921	155,000	25.00	60.00	150	350	—

KM# 26 18 PIASTRES
11.3104 g., 0.9250 Silver 0.3364 oz. ASW **Obv:** Crowned head left **Obv. Designer:** Percy Metcalfe **Rev:** Two stylized rampant lions left, date and denomination 3/4 surround **Rev. Designer:** George E. Kruger-Gray

Date	Mintage	F	VF	XF	Unc	BU
1938 Proof	—	Value: 450				
1938	200,000	5.50	20.00	30.00	50.00	—
1940 Proof	—	Value: 450				
1940	100,000	15.00	30.00	50.00	80.00	—

KM# 28 2 SHILLING
4.0000 g., Copper-Nickel, 28.3 mm. **Obv:** Crowned head left **Obv. Designer:** Percy Metcalfe **Rev:** Two stylized rampant lions left, date below, denomination above **Rev. Designer:** George E. Kruger-Gray

Date	Mintage	F	VF	XF	Unc	BU
1947 Proof	—	Value: 400				
1947	720,000	2.00	4.00	10.00	35.00	—

KM# 32 2 SHILLING
Copper-Nickel, 28.3 mm. **Obv:** Crowned head left **Obv. Designer:** Percy Metcalfe **Rev:** Two stylized rampant lions left, date below, denomination above **Rev. Designer:** George E. Kruger-Gray

Date	Mintage	F	VF	XF	Unc	BU
1949 Proof	—	Value: 400				
1949	720,000	4.00	8.00	15.00	40.00	—

KM# 19 45 PIASTRES
28.2759 g., 0.9250 Silver 0.8409 oz. ASW, 38 mm. **Subject:** 50th Anniversary of British Rule **Obv:** Crowned bust left **Obv. Designer:** E.B. MacKennal **Rev:** Two stylized rampant lions left, date at right, denomination below **Rev. Designer:** George E. Kruger-Gray

Date	Mintage	F	VF	XF	Unc	BU
ND(1928) Proof	517	Value: 550				
ND(1928)	80,000	25.00	35.00	60.00	150	—

DECIMAL COINAGE

50 Mils = 1 Shilling; 20 Shillings = 1 Pound; 1000 Mils = 1 Pound

KM# 33 3 MILS
2.8000 g., Bronze, 20 mm. **Obv:** Crowned bust right **Rev:** Flying fish divides date and denomination

Date	Mintage	F	VF	XF	Unc	BU
1955 Proof	2,000	Value: 2.50				
1955	6,250,000	—	—	0.10	0.25	—

KM# 34 5 MILS
Bronze **Obv:** Crowned bust right **Rev:** Standing figure with open arms, date and denomination below

Date	Mintage	F	VF	XF	Unc	BU
1955 Proof	2,000	Value: 3.00				
1955	10,000,000	—	0.15	0.25	0.40	—
1956 Proof	—	Value: 300				
1956	2,950,000	—	0.15	0.30	0.50	—

KM# 35 25 MILS
Copper-Nickel **Obv:** Crowned bust right **Rev:** Bulls head above denomination, date below

Date	Mintage	F	VF	XF	Unc	BU
1955 Proof	2,000	Value: 3.00				
1955	2,500,000	—	0.25	0.35	1.00	—

KM# 36 50 MILS
Copper-Nickel **Obv:** Crowned bust right **Rev:** Fern leaves divide denomination, date below

Date	Mintage	F	VF	XF	Unc	BU
1955 Proof	2,000	Value: 3.00				
1955	4,000,000	—	0.35	0.50	1.00	—

KM# 37 100 MILS
Copper-Nickel, 28 mm. **Obv:** Crowned bust right **Rev:** Stylized ancient merchant ship, denomination upper left, date below

Date	Mintage	F	VF	XF	Unc	BU
1955 Proof	2,000	Value: 4.50				
1955	2,500,000	—	0.50	0.75	1.50	—
1957 Proof	—	Value: 440				
Note: All but 10,000 of 1957 issue were melted down.						
1957	Est. 500,000	—	10.00	15.00	50.00	—

REPUBLIC

DECIMAL COINAGE

50 Mils = 1 Shilling; 20 Shillings = 1 Pound; 1000 Mils = 1 Pound

KM# 38 MIL
Aluminum, 18.5 mm. **Obv:** Shielded arms within wreath, date above **Rev:** Denomination within wreath **Shape:** 12-sided

Date	Mintage	F	VF	XF	Unc	BU
1963 Proof	25,000	Value: 1.00				
1963	5,000,000	—	—	—	0.15	—
1971	500,000	—	—	0.10	0.25	—
1972 Proof	—	Value: 2.00				
1972	500,000	—	—	0.10	0.25	—

KM# 39 5 MILS
5.7400 g., Bronze **Obv:** Shielded arms within wreath, date above **Rev:** Stylized ancient merchant ship, denomination upper left

Date	Mintage	F	VF	XF	Unc	BU
1963 Proof	25,000	Value: 1.25				
1963	12,000,000	—	—	0.10	0.35	—
1970	2,500,000	—	—	0.10	1.00	—
1971	2,500,000	—	—	0.10	0.35	—
1972	2,500,000	—	—	0.10	0.35	—
1973	5,000,000	—	—	0.10	0.35	—
1974	2,500,000	—	—	0.10	0.35	—
1976	2,000,000	—	—	0.10	0.35	—
1977	2,000,000	—	—	0.10	0.35	—
1978	2,000,000	—	—	0.10	0.35	—
1979	2,000,000	—	—	0.10	0.35	—
1980 Proof	—	Value: 2.50				
1980	4,000,000	—	—	0.10	0.35	—

KM# 50.1 5 MILS
1.2000 g., Aluminum, 20 mm. **Obv:** Shielded arms within wreath, date above **Rev:** Stylized ancient merchant ship, denomination upper left **Shape:** 12-sided

Date	Mintage	F	VF	XF	Unc	BU
1981	12,500,000	—	—	—	0.25	—

KM# 50.2 5 MILS
1.2000 g., Aluminum, 20 mm. **Obv:** Shielded arms within wreath, date above **Rev:** Stylized ancient merchant ship, denomination upper left **Shape:** 12-sided

Date	Mintage	F	VF	XF	Unc	BU
1982 Proof	—	Value: 2.00				
1982	15,000,000	—	—	—	0.25	—

KM# 40 25 MILS
2.8000 g., Copper-Nickel, 19.4 mm. **Obv:** Shielded arms within wreath, date above **Rev:** Cedar of Lebanon, denomination at left

Date	Mintage	F	VF	XF	Unc	BU
1963 Proof	25,000	Value: 1.50				
1963	2,500,000	—	0.10	0.15	0.45	—
1968	1,500,000	—	0.10	0.15	2.00	—
1971	1,000,000	—	0.10	0.15	0.45	—
1972	500,000	—	0.10	0.15	0.50	—
1973	1,000,000	—	0.10	0.15	0.45	—
1974	1,000,000	—	0.10	0.15	0.45	—
1976	2,000,000	—	0.10	0.15	0.45	—
1977	500,000	—	0.10	0.15	0.45	—
1978	500,000	—	0.10	0.15	0.45	—
1979	1,000,000	—	0.10	0.15	0.45	—
1980	2,000,000	—	0.10	0.15	0.45	—
1981	3,000,000	—	0.10	0.15	0.45	—
1982 Proof	—	Value: 3.00				
1982	1,000,000	—	0.10	0.15	0.45	—

KM# 41 50 MILS
5.6000 g., Copper-Nickel, 23.5 mm. **Obv:** Shielded arms within wreath, date above **Rev:** Grape cluster above denomination

Date	Mintage	F	VF	XF	Unc	BU
1963 Proof	25,000	Value: 1.75				
1963	2,800,000	—	0.20	0.30	1.00	—
1970	500,000	—	0.20	0.35	2.00	—
1971	500,000	—	0.20	0.35	1.25	—
1972	750,000	—	0.20	0.30	1.00	—
1973	750,000	—	0.20	0.30	1.00	—
1974	1,500,000	—	0.20	0.30	1.00	—
1976	1,500,000	—	0.20	0.30	1.00	—
1977	500,000	—	0.20	0.30	1.00	—
1978	500,000	—	0.20	0.30	3.00	—
1979	1,000,000	—	0.20	0.30	1.00	—
1980	3,000,000	—	0.20	0.30	1.00	—
1981	4,000,000	—	0.20	0.30	1.00	—
1982 Proof	—	Value: 3.50				
1982	2,000,000	—	0.20	0.30	1.00	—

KM# 42 100 MILS
11.3000 g., Copper-Nickel, 28.45 mm. **Obv:** Shielded arms within wreath, date above **Rev:** Cyprus Mouflon left, denomination below

Date	Mintage	F	VF	XF	Unc	BU
1963 Proof	25,000	Value: 2.50				
1963	1,750,000	—	0.40	0.70	2.00	3.00
1971	500,000	—	0.50	0.75	2.00	3.00
1973	750,000	—	0.40	0.70	2.00	3.00
1974	1,000,000	—	0.50	0.75	2.00	3.00
1976	1,500,000	—	0.40	0.70	2.00	3.00
1977	500,000	—	0.50	0.75	2.00	3.00
1978	1,000,000	—	0.50	0.75	2.00	3.00
1979	1,000,000	—	0.40	0.70	2.00	3.00
1980	1,000,000	—	0.40	0.70	2.00	3.00
1981	2,000,000	—	0.40	0.70	2.00	3.00
1982 Proof	—	Value: 5.00				
1982	2,000,000	—	0.40	0.70	2.00	3.00

KM# 43 500 MILS
Copper-Nickel **Series:** F.A.O. **Obv:** Double cornucopia, as on the ancient coins of Ptolemy II **Rev:** Figure holding tray of fruit, denomination at right **Designer:** Antis Ioannides

Date	Mintage	F	VF	XF	Unc	BU
1970	80,000	—	1.50	4.50	10.00	—

KM# 44 500 MILS
Copper-Nickel **Obv:** Shielded arms within wreath, date above **Rev:** Hercules, denomination at right

Date	Mintage	F	VF	XF	Unc	BU
1975	500,000	—	1.25	1.75	4.00	—
1977 Proof	—	Value: 15.00				
1977	300,000	—	1.25	1.75	5.00	—

KM# 45 500 MILS
Copper-Nickel **Subject:** Refugees, denomination and date at right **Obv:** Shielded arms within wreath, date above

Date	Mintage	F	VF	XF	Unc	BU
1976	25,000	—	1.25	2.00	4.00	—

KM# 48 500 MILS
Copper-Nickel **Subject:** Human Rights **Obv:** Flame within wreath divides dates **Rev:** Stylized crying dove above denomination

Date	Mintage	F	VF	XF	Unc	BU
ND(1978)	50,000	—	1.25	2.00	4.00	—

KM# 49 500 MILS
Copper-Nickel **Series:** Summer Olympic Games **Obv:** Shielded arms within wreath, date above **Rev:** Olympic logo divides date and denomination, sprays surround

Date	Mintage	F	VF	XF	Unc	BU
1980	50,000	—	1.25	2.50	6.50	—

KM# 46 POUND
Copper-Nickel, 38.5 mm. **Obv:** Shielded arms within wreath, date above **Rev:** Refugees, date and denomination at right **Note:** Refugee Commemorative.

Date	Mintage	F	VF	XF	Unc	BU
1976	25,000	—	2.00	2.50	5.50	—

REFORM COINAGE

100 Cents = 1 Pound

KM# 52 HALF CENT
Aluminum **Obv:** Shielded arms within wreath, date below **Rev:** Cyclamen, denomination at right **Shape:** 12-sided

Date	Mintage	F	VF	XF	Unc	BU
1983 Proof	6,250	Value: 1.50				
1983	10,000,000	—	—	0.10	0.15	0.25

KM# 53.1 CENT
Nickel-Brass **Obv:** Shielded arms within wreath, date below **Rev:** Stylized bird on a branch, value number surrounded by single line

Date	Mintage	F	VF	XF	Unc	BU
1983	15,000,000	—	—	0.10	0.20	0.30
1983 Proof	6,250	Value: 1.50				

KM# 53.2 CENT
Nickel-Brass **Obv:** Shielded arms within wreath, date below **Rev:** Stylized bird on a branch, value number surrounded by double line

Date	Mintage	F	VF	XF	Unc	BU
1985	5,000,000	—	—	0.10	0.20	0.30
1987	5,000,000	—	—	0.10	0.20	0.30
1988	5,000,000	—	—	0.10	0.20	0.30
1990	4,000,000	—	—	0.10	0.20	0.30

KM# 53.3 CENT
2.0300 g., Nickel-Brass, 16.48 mm. **Obv:** Shielded arms within altered wreath, date below **Rev:** Stylized bird on a branch, denomination at left **Edge:** Plain

Date	Mintage	F	VF	XF	Unc	BU
1991	4,000,000	—	—	0.10	0.20	0.30
1992	4,000,000	—	—	0.10	0.20	0.30
1993	7,000,000	—	—	0.10	0.20	0.30
1994	10,000,000	—	—	0.10	0.20	0.30
1996	12,000,000	—	—	0.10	0.20	0.30
1998	15,000,000	—	—	0.10	0.20	0.30
2003	5,000,000	—	—	0.10	0.20	0.30
2004	—	—	—	0.10	0.20	0.30

KM# 54.1 2 CENTS
Nickel-Brass, 19 mm. **Obv:** Shielded arms within wreath, date below **Rev:** Stylized goats, value number surrounded by single line

Date	Mintage	F	VF	XF	Unc	BU
1983 Proof	6,250	Value: 1.50				
1983	12,000,000	—	—	0.15	0.25	0.35

KM# 54.2 2 CENTS
Nickel-Brass, 19 mm. **Obv:** Shielded arms within wreath, date below **Rev:** Stylized goats; value number surrounded by double line

Date	Mintage	F	VF	XF	Unc	BU
1985	8,000,000	—	—	0.15	0.25	0.35
1988	5,150,000	—	—	0.15	0.25	0.35
1990	4,000,000	—	—	0.15	0.25	0.35

KM# 54.3 2 CENTS
2.5800 g., Nickel-Brass, 18.95 mm. **Obv:** Shielded arms within altered wreath, date below **Rev:** Stylized goats, denomination upper right **Edge:** Plain

Date	Mintage	F	VF	XF	Unc	BU
1991	4,000,000	—	—	0.15	0.25	0.35
1992	4,000,000	—	—	0.15	0.25	0.35
1993	4,000,000	—	—	0.15	0.25	0.35
1994	10,000,000	—	—	0.15	0.25	0.35
1996	12,000,000	—	—	0.15	0.25	0.35
1998	10,000,000	—	—	0.15	0.25	0.35
2003	5,000,000	—	—	0.15	0.25	0.35
2004	—	—	—	0.15	0.25	0.35

KM# 55.1 5 CENTS
Nickel-Brass, 22 mm. **Obv:** Shielded arms within wreath, date below **Rev:** Stylized bulls head, value number surrounded by single line **Note:** REV: Value number surrounded by single line

Date	Mintage	F	VF	XF	Unc	BU
1983 Proof	6,250	Value: 2.00				
1983	15,000,000	—	—	0.20	0.50	0.75

KM# 55.2 5 CENTS
Nickel-Brass, 22 mm. **Obv:** Shielded arms within wreath, date below **Rev:** Value number surrounded by double line

Date	Mintage	F	VF	XF	Unc	BU
1985	5,000,000	—	—	0.20	0.50	0.75
1987	5,000,000	—	—	0.20	0.50	0.75
1988	5,060,000	—	—	0.20	0.50	0.75
1990	—	—	—	0.20	0.50	0.75

KM# 55.3 5 CENTS
3.8000 g., Nickel-Brass, 20.37 mm. **Obv:** Altered wreath around arms **Rev:** Stylized bulls head above denomination **Edge:** Plain

Date	Mintage	F	VF	XF	Unc	BU
1991	4,000,000	—	—	0.20	0.50	0.75
1992	4,000,000	—	—	0.20	0.50	0.75
1993	5,000,000	—	—	0.20	0.50	0.75
1994	8,000,000	—	—	0.20	0.50	0.75
1998	1,000,000	—	—	0.20	0.50	0.75
2001	15,000,000	—	—	0.20	0.50	0.75
2004	—	—	—	0.20	0.50	0.75

KM# 56.1 10 CENTS
Nickel-Brass **Obv:** Shielded arms within wreath, date below **Rev:** Decorative vase, value number surrounded by single line

Date	Mintage	F	VF	XF	Unc	BU
1983 Proof	6,250	Value: 3.00				
1983	10,000,000	—	—	0.35	0.75	1.00

KM# 56.2 10 CENTS
Nickel-Brass **Obv:** Shielded arms within wreath, date below **Rev:** Value number framed by double line

Date	Mintage	F	VF	XF	Unc	BU
1985	5,000,000	—	—	0.35	0.75	1.00
1988	5,035,000	—	—	0.35	0.75	1.00
1990	4,000,000	—	—	0.35	0.75	1.00

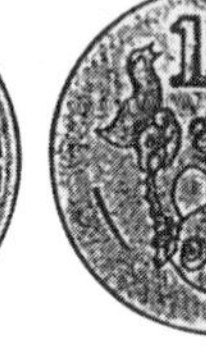

KM# 56.3 10 CENTS
5.5700 g., Nickel-Brass, 24.4 mm. **Obv:** Altered wreath around arms **Rev:** Decorative vase, denomination above

Date	Mintage	F	VF	XF	Unc	BU
1991	4,000,000	—	—	0.35	0.75	1.00
1992	3,000,000	—	—	0.35	0.75	1.00
1993	3,000,000	—	—	0.35	0.75	1.00
1994	8,000,000	—	—	0.35	0.75	1.00
1998	5,000,000	—	—	0.35	0.75	1.00
2002	10,000,000	—	—	0.35	0.75	1.00
2004	—	—	—	0.35	0.75	1.00

KM# 57.1 20 CENTS
Nickel-Brass, 27 mm. **Obv:** Shielded arms within wreath, date below **Rev:** Value number framed by single line

Date	Mintage	F	VF	XF	Unc	BU
1983 Proof	6,200	Value: 5.00				
1983	10,000,000	—	—	0.50	2.00	3.50

KM# 57.2 20 CENTS
Nickel-Brass, 27 mm. **Obv:** Shielded arms within wreath, date below **Rev:** Value number framed by double line

Date	Mintage	F	VF	XF	Unc	BU
1985	5,040,000	—	—	0.50	2.50	3.00
1988	1,000,000	—	—	0.50	2.50	3.00

KM# 62.1 20 CENTS
Bronze, 27 mm. **Obv:** Shielded arms within wreath, date below **Rev:** Head left, denomination at right

Date	Mintage	F	VF	XF	Unc	BU
1989 Proof	—	Value: 30.00				
1989	2,000,000	—	—	—	1.00	1.50
1990	3,000,000	—	—	—	1.00	1.50

KM# 62.2 20 CENTS
7.7500 g., Nickel-Brass, 27 mm. **Obv:** Altered wreath around arms **Rev:** Head left, denomination at right

Date	Mintage	F	VF	XF	Unc	BU
1991	4,000,000	—	—	—	1.00	1.50
1992	3,000,000	—	—	—	1.00	1.50
1993	4,000,000	—	—	—	1.00	1.50
1994	8,000,000	—	—	—	1.00	1.50
1998	5,000,000	—	—	—	1.00	1.50
2001	15,000,000	—	—	—	1.00	1.50
2004	—	—	—	—	1.00	1.50

KM# 58 50 CENTS
Copper-Nickel, 32 mm. **Series:** F.A.O. **Subject:** Forestry **Obv:** Shielded arms within wreath, date above **Rev:** Goddess Diana in the shape of a stylized tree, denomination at right

Date	Mintage	F	VF	XF	Unc	BU
1985	33,000	—	2.00	4.00	15.00	20.00

KM# 66 50 CENTS
7.0000 g., Copper-Nickel, 26.11 mm. **Subject:** Abduction of Europa **Obv:** National arms, date below **Rev:** Female figure riding bull right within square, denomination below **Edge:** Plain **Shape:** 7-sided

Date	Mintage	F	VF	XF	Unc	BU
1991 narrow date	3,005,000	—	—	—	2.50	3.25
1993 wide date	300,000	—	—	—	2.50	3.25
1994 wide date	500,000	—	—	—	2.50	3.25
1996	5,000,000	—	—	—	2.50	3.25
1998	5,000,000	—	—	—	2.50	3.25
2002	7,000,000	—	—	—	2.50	3.25
2004	—	—	—	—	2.50	3.25

EURO COINAGE

European Union Issues

KM# 78 EURO CENT
2.2700 g., Copper Plated Steel, 16.20 mm. **Obv:** Two Mouflons **Rev:** Large value at left, globe at lower right **Edge:** Plain

Date	Mintage	F	VF	XF	Unc	BU
2008	—	—	—	—	0.35	0.50

KM# 79 2 EURO CENT
3.0300 g., Copper Plated Steel, 18.70 mm. **Obv:** Two Mouflons **Rev:** Large value at left, globe at lower right **Edge:** Plain

Date	Mintage	F	VF	XF	Unc	BU
2008	—	—	—	—	0.50	0.75

KM# 80 5 EURO CENT

3.8600 g., Copper Plated Steel, 21.20 mm. **Obv:** Two Mouflons **Rev:** Large value at left, globe at lower right **Edge:** Plain

Date	Mintage	F	VF	XF	Unc	BU
2008	—	—	—	—	1.00	1.25

KM# 81 10 EURO CENT

4.0700 g., Brass, 19.70 mm. **Obv:** Early sailing boat **Rev:** Modified outline of Europe at left, large value at right

Date	Mintage	F	VF	XF	Unc	BU
2008	—	—	—	—	1.25	1.50

KM# 82 20 EURO CENT

5.7300 g., Brass, 22.10 mm. **Obv:** Early sailing boat **Rev:** Modified outline of Europe at left, large value at right **Edge:** Notched

Date	Mintage	F	VF	XF	Unc	BU
2008	—	—	—	—	1.50	2.00

KM# 83 50 EURO CENT

7.8100 g., Brass, 24.20 mm. **Obv:** Early sailing boat **Rev:** Modified outline of Europe at left, large value at right **Edge:** Reeded

Date	Mintage	F	VF	XF	Unc	BU
2008	—	—	—	—	2.00	2.50

KM# 84 EURO

7.5000 g., Bi-Metallic **Ring Composition:** Brass **Center Composition:** Copper Nickel, 23.20 mm. **Obv:** Ancient statue wearing a cross found in Soloi **Rev:** Large value at left, modified outline of Europe at right **Edge:** Segmented reeding

Date	Mintage	F	VF	XF	Unc	BU
2008	—	—	—	—	3.50	5.00

KM# 85 2 EURO

8.5200 g., Bi-Metallic, 25.70 mm. **Obv:** Ancient statue wearing a cross found in Soloi **Rev:** Large value at left, modified outline of Europe at right

Date	Mintage	F	VF	XF	Unc	BU
2008	—	—	—	—	5.00	7.00

CZECH REPUBLIC

The Czech Republic was formerly united with Slovakia as Czechoslovakia. It is bordered in the west by Germany, to the north by Poland, to the east by Slovakia and to the south by Austria. It consists of 3 major regions: Bohemia, Moravia and Silesia and has an area of 30,450 sq. mi. (78,864 sq. km.) and a population of 10.4 million. Capital: Prague (Praha). Agriculture and livestock are chief occupations while coal deposits are the main mineral resources.

The Czech lands were united with the Slovaks to form the Czechoslovak State, which came into existence on Oct. 28, 1918 upon the dissolution of the Austrian-Hungarian Empire. In 1938, this territory was broken up for the benefit of Germany, Poland, and Hungary by the Munich (Munchen) Agreement. In March 1939 the German influenced Slovak government proclaimed Slovakia independent. Germany incorporated the Czech lands into the Third Reich as the "Protectorate of Bohemia and Moravia." A Czech government-in-exile was set up in London in July 1940. The Soviets and USA forces liberated the area by May 1945. Communist influence increased steadily while pressure for liberalization culminated in the overthrow of the Stalinist leader Antonin Novotny and his associates in 1968. The Communist Party then introduced far reaching reforms which resulted in warnings from Moscow (Moskva), followed by occupation and stationing of Soviet forces. Mass demonstrations for reform began again in Nov. 1989 and the Federal Assembly abolished the Communist Party's sole right to govern. The new government formed was the Czech and Slovak Federal Republic. A movement for Democratic Slovakia was apparent in the June 1992 elections and on December 31, 1992, the CSFR was dissolved and the two new republics came into being on Jan. 1, 1993.

NOTE: For earlier issues see Czechoslovakia, Bohemia and Moravia or Slovakia listings.

MINT MARKS

(c) - castle = Hamburg
(cr) - cross = British Royal Mint
(l) - leaf = Royal Canadian
(m) - crowned *b* or *CM* = Jablonec nad Nisou
(mk) - *MK* in circle = Kremnica
(o) - broken circle = Vienna (Wien)

MONETARY SYSTEM

1 Czechoslovak Koruna (Kcs) = 1 Czech Koruna (Kc)
1 Koruna = 100 Haleru

REPUBLIC

STANDARD COINAGE

KM# 6 10 HALERU

0.6000 g., Aluminum, 15.5 mm. **Obv:** Crowned Czech lion left, date below **Rev:** Denomination and stylized river **Edge:** Plain **Designer:** Jiri Pradler **Note:** Two varieties of mint marks exist for 1994.

Date	Mintage	F	VF	XF	Unc	BU
1993(m)	94,902,000	—	—	—	0.20	—
1993(c)	100,000,000	—	—	—	0.20	—
Note: 200 pieces destroyed						
1994(m)	53,127,024	—	—	—	0.20	—
1994(c) In sets only	2,500	—	—	—	2.50	—
1994(m) Proof, dull	2,000	—	—	—	—	—
1994(m) Proof, bright	27,500	—	—	—	—	—
1995(m)	106,918,596	—	—	—	0.20	—
1996(m)	61,498,678	—	—	—	0.20	—
1997(m)	40,968,395	—	—	—	0.20	—
Note: 85,778 pieces destroyed						
1997(m) Proof	1,500	Value: 3.50				
1998(m)	41,027,073	—	—	—	0.20	—
1998(m) Proof	2,600	Value: 2.00				
1999(m)	54,428,800	—	—	—	0.20	—
1999(m) Proof	2,000	Value: 2.00				
2000(m)	52,497,440	—	—	—	0.20	—
2000(m) Proof	2,500	Value: 2.00				
2001(m)	40,525,000	—	—	—	0.20	—
2001(m) Proof	2,500	Value: 2.00				
2002(m)	81,496,000	—	—	—	0.20	—
2002(m) Proof	3,490	Value: 2.00				
2003(m)	3,022,350	—	—	—	0.20	—
2003(m) Proof	3,000	Value: 2.00				

Date	Mintage	F	VF	XF	Unc	BU
2004(m)	—	—	—	—	—	—
2004(m) Proof	3,000	Value: 2.00				

KM# 2.2 20 HALERU

Aluminum, 17 mm. **Obv:** Crowned Czech lion **Rev:** Linden leaf and value, "h" above flat line, closed 2 in denomination **Designer:** Jaroslav Bejvl **Note:** Coin alignment.

Date	Mintage	F	VF	XF	Unc	BU
1993(m)	Inc. above	—	—	—	4.00	—

KM# 2.1 20 HALERU

0.7400 g., Aluminum, 17 mm. **Obv:** Crowned Czech lion left, date above **Rev:** Linden leaf within denomination; closed 2, "h" above flat line **Edge:** Milled **Designer:** Jaroslav Bejvl **Note:** Medallic coin alignment.

Date	Mintage	F	VF	XF	Unc	BU
1993(c)	80,000,000	—	—	—	0.30	—
1993(m)	30,558,000	—	—	—	0.30	—
1994(c)	9,310,000	—	—	—	0.30	—
1994(m)	81,291,201	—	—	—	0.30	—
1994(m) Proof, dull	2,500	—	—	—	3.00	—
1994(m) Proof, bright	17,500	—	—	—	1.00	—
1995(c)	450,000	—	—	—	1.75	—
1995(m)	80,960,374	—	—	—	0.30	—
1996(m)	61,086,142	—	—	—	0.30	—
1997(m)	51,013,450	—	—	—	0.30	—
Note: 78,835 pieces destroyed						
1997(m) Proof	1,500	Value: 5.00				

KM# 2.3 20 HALERU

0.7400 g., Aluminum **Obv:** Crowned Czech lion left, date above **Rev:** Open 2 in denomination, "h" above angle line **Note:** Medal alignment.

Date	Mintage	F	VF	XF	Unc	BU
1998(m)	51,135,904	—	—	—	0.30	—
1998(m) Proof	2,600	Value: 3.00				
1999(m)	20,820,612	—	—	—	0.30	—
1999(m) Proof	2,000	Value: 3.00				
2000(m)	31,466,085	—	—	—	0.30	—
2000(m) Proof	2,500	Value: 3.00				
2001(m)	44,425,000	—	—	—	0.30	—
2001(m) Proof	2,500	Value: 3.00				
2002(m)	20,000	—	—	—	0.30	—
2002(m) Proof	3,490	Value: 3.00				
2003(m)	22,200	—	—	—	0.30	—
2003(m) Proof	3,000	Value: 3.00				
2004(m)	—	—	—	—	—	—
2004(m) Proof	3,000	Value: 3.00				

KM# 3.1 50 HALERU

0.9000 g., Aluminum, 19 mm. **Obv:** Crowned Czech lion left, date below **Rev:** Large denomination **Edge:** Part plain, part milled repeated **Designer:** Vladimir Oppl **Note:** Prev. KM#3.

Date	Mintage	F	VF	XF	Unc	BU
1993(c)	70,003,000	—	—	—	0.50	—
Note: 201 pieces destroyed						
1993(m)	30,474,000	—	—	—	0.50	—
1994(m)	21,109,425	—	—	—	0.50	—
Note: Open and closed 9 varieties exist in date						
1994(m) Proof, dull	2,500	—	—	—	3.00	—
1994(m) Proof, bright	27,500	—	—	—	1.00	—
1995(m)	30,940,000	—	—	—	0.50	—
1996(m)	35,904,000	—	—	—	0.50	—
1997(m)	25,713,443	—	—	—	0.50	—
Note: 35,610 pieces destroyed						
1997(m) Proof	1,500	Value: 5.00				
1998(m)	25,000	—	—	—	0.50	—
1998(m) Proof	2,600	Value: 3.00				
1999(m)	21,024,800	—	—	—	0.50	—
Note: 8,687 pieces destroyed						
1999(m) Proof	2,000	Value: 3.00				
2000(m)	15,753,440	—	—	—	0.50	—
2000(m) Proof	2,500	Value: 3.00				
2001(m)	21,425,000	—	—	—	0.50	—
2001(m) Proof	2,500	Value: 3.00				

KM# 3.2 50 HALERU

0.9000 g., Aluminum, 19 mm. **Subject:** Outlined lettering and larger mint mark **Obv:** Crowned Czech lion right, date below **Rev:** Large denomination

Date	Mintage	F	VF	XF	Unc	BU
2001(m)	21,425,000	—	—	—	0.50	—
2001(m) Proof	2,500	Value: 3.00				
2002(m)	26,246,298	—	—	—	0.50	—
2002(m) Proof	3,490	Value: 3.00				
2003(m)	41,548,000	—	—	—	0.50	—
2003(m) Proof	3,000	Value: 3.00				
2004(m)	931,145	—	—	—	0.50	—
2004(m) Proof	4,000	Value: 3.00				
2005(m)	36,800	—	—	—	0.50	—
2005(m) Proof	3,000	Value: 3.00				
2006(m)	40,000	—	—	—	0.50	—
2006(m) Proof	3,500	Value: 3.00				
2007(m)	—	—	—	—	0.50	—
2007(m) Proof	—	Value: 3.00				
2008(m)	—	—	—	—	0.50	—
2008(m) Proof	—	Value: 3.00				

KM# 7 KORUNA

Nickel Clad Steel, 20 mm. **Obv:** Crowned Czech lion left, date below **Rev:** Denomination above crown **Edge:** Milled **Designer:** Jarmila Truhlikova-Spevakova **Note:** Two varieties of mint marks exist for 1996. 2000-03 have two varieties in the artisit monogram.

Date	Mintage	F	VF	XF	Unc	BU
1993(l)	102,431,000	—	—	—	0.60	—
1994(m)	52,162,620	—	—	—	0.60	—
1995(m)	40,668,280	—	—	—	0.60	—
1996(m)	35,344,913	—	—	—	0.60	—
Note: Figure 1 with and without serif, three varieties of designer's signature.						
1997(m)	15,055,501	—	—	—	0.60	—
1997(m) Proof	1,500	Value: 6.50				
1998(m)	25,000	—	—	—	0.60	—
1998(m) Proof	2,600	Value: 4.00				
Note: 90 pieces destroyed.						
1999(m)	24,904	—	—	—	0.60	—
1999(m) Proof	2,000	Value: 4.00				
2000(m)	15,568,697	—	—	—	0.60	—
2000(m) Proof	2,500	Value: 4.00				
2001(m)	15,938,353	—	—	—	0.60	—
2001(m) Proof	2,500	Value: 4.00				
2002(m)	26,244,666	—	—	—	0.60	—
2002(m) Proof	3,490	Value: 4.00				
2003(m)	36,877,440	—	—	—	0.60	—
2003(m) Proof	3,000	Value: 4.00				
2004(m)	30,500	—	—	—	0.60	—
2004(m) Proof	4,000	Value: 4.00				
2005(m)	—	—	—	—	0.60	—
2005(m) Proof	3,000	Value: 6.00				
2006(m)	35,864	—	—	—	0.60	—
2006(m) Proof	2,500	Value: 6.00				
2007(m)	—	—	—	—	0.60	—
2007(m) Proof	—	Value: 6.00				
2008(m)	—	—	—	—	0.60	—
2008(m) Proof	—	Value: 6.00				

KM# 8 5 KORUN

4.8000 g., Nickel Plated Steel, 23 mm. **Obv:** Crowned Czech lion left, date below **Rev:** Large denomination, Charles bridge and linden leaf **Edge:** Plain **Designer:** Jiri Harcuba

Date	Mintage	F	VF	XF	Unc	BU
1993(l)	70,001,000	—	—	—	1.00	—
1994(l)	14,400,000	—	—	—	1.00	—
1994(m)	30,475,491	—	—	—	1.00	—
1995(m)	20,155,218	—	—	—	1.00	—
Note: Two varieties of figure 5 and designer's signature.						
1996(m)	5,053,730	—	—	—	1.00	—
1997(m)	40,000	—	—	—	1.00	—
1997(m) Proof	1,500	Value: 10.00				
1998(m)	25,000	—	—	—	1.00	—
Note: 10,207 pieces destroyed						
1998(m) Proof	2,600	Value: 6.00				
Note: 90 Pieces destroyed.						
1999(m)	29,490	—	—	—	1.00	—
1999(m) Proof	2,000	Value: 6.00				
2000(m)	26,431	—	—	—	1.00	—
2000(m) Proof	2,500	Value: 6.00				
2001(m)	25,000	—	—	—	1.00	—
2001(m) Proof	2,500	Value: 6.00				
2002(m)	21,344,995	—	—	—	1.00	—
2002(m) Proof	3,490	Value: 6.00				
2003(m)	22,000	—	—	—	1.00	—
2003(m) Proof	3,000	Value: 6.00				
2004(m)	34,940	—	—	—	1.00	—
2004(m) Proof	4,000	Value: 6.00				
2005(m)	—	—	—	—	1.00	—
2005(m) Proof	3,000	Value: 6.00				
2006(m)	25,000	—	—	—	1.00	—
2006(m) Proof	2,500	Value: 6.00				
2007(m)	—	—	—	—	1.00	—
2007(m) Proof	—	Value: 6.00				
2008(m)	—	—	—	—	1.00	—
2008(m) Proof	—	Value: 6.00				

KM# 4 10 KORUN

7.6200 g., Copper Plated Steel, 24.5 mm. **Obv:** Crowned Czech lion left, date below **Rev:** Brno Cathedral, denomination below **Edge:** Milled **Designer:** Ladislav Kozak **Note:** Position of designer's initials on reverse change during the 1995 strike.

Date	Mintage	F	VF	XF	Unc	BU
1993(c)	70,001,000	—	—	—	2.00	—
1993(c) Small 10	1,000	25.00	75.00	150	250	—
1994(m)	20,677,220	—	—	—	1.50	—
1994(m) bright	30,000	—	—	—	2.00	—
1995(m)	152,388	—	—	—	1.50	—
1995(m) LK below	20,530,459	—	—	—	1.50	—
1996(m)	20,644,143	—	—	—	1.50	—
1997(m)	48,215	—	—	—	1.50	—
1997(m) Proof	1,500	Value: 12.00				
1998(m)	25,000	—	—	—	1.50	—
Note: 142,465 pieces melted.						
1998(m) Proof	2,600	Value: 7.00				
Note: 90 pieces melted.						
1999(m)	29,490	—	—	—	1.50	—
Note: 2,036 pieces melted.						
1999(m) Proof	2,000	Value: 7.00				
2000(m)	25,000	—	—	—	1.50	—
2000(m) Proof	2,500	Value: 7.00				
2001(m)	25,000	—	—	—	1.50	—
2001(m) Proof	2,500	Value: 7.00				
2002(m)	20,156	—	—	—	1.50	—
2002(m) Proof	3,490	Value: 7.00				
2003(m)	18,747,000	—	—	—	1.50	—
2003(m) Proof	3,000	Value: 7.00				
2004(m)	2,255,740	—	—	—	1.50	—
2004(m) Proof	4,000	Value: 7.00				
2005(m)	—	—	—	—	1.50	—
2005(m) Proof	3,000	Value: 7.00				
2006(m)	—	—	—	—	1.50	—
2006(m) Proof	2,500	Value: 7.00				
2007(m)	—	—	—	—	1.50	—
2007(m) Proof	—	Value: 7.00				
2008(m)	—	—	—	—	1.50	—
2008(m) Proof	—	Value: 7.00				

KM# 42 10 KORUN

7.5200 g., Copper Plated Steel, 24.5 mm. **Subject:** Year 2000 **Obv:** Crowned Czech lion left, date below **Rev:** Clock works above denomination, within circle **Rev. Designer:** Ladislav Kozak **Edge:** Reeded

Date	Mintage	F	VF	XF	Unc	BU
2000	10,032,799	—	—	—	1.50	—
2000 Proof	2,500	Value: 7.50				

KM# 5 20 KORUN

8.4300 g., Brass Plated Steel, 26 mm. **Obv:** Crowned Czech lion left, date below **Rev:** St. Wenceslas (Duke Vaclav) on horse **Edge:** Plain **Shape:** 13-sided **Designer:** Vladimir Oppl **Note:** Two varieties of mint marks and style of 9's exist for 1997.

Date	Mintage	F	VF	XF	Unc	BU
1993(c)	55,001,000	—	—	1.00	3.00	—
1994(c)	100,000	—	—	—	3.50	—
1995(m)	101,837	—	—	—	2.50	—
1996(m)	101,150	—	—	—	2.50	—
1997(m)	8,091,219	—	—	—	2.50	—
1997(m) Proof	1,500	Value: 16.50				
1998(m)	15,725,000	—	—	—	2.50	—
Note: 41,786 pieces destroyed.						
1998(m) Proof	2,600	Value: 10.00				
Note: 90 pieces destroyed						
1999(m)	26,274,900	—	—	—	2.50	—
Note: 1,422 pieces destroyed.						
1999(m) Proof	2,000	Value: 10.00				
2000(m)	5,694,581	—	—	—	—	—
2000(m) Proof	2,500	—	—	—	—	—
2001(m)	25,000	—	—	—	2.50	—
2001(m) Proof	2,500	Value: 10.00				
2002(m)	20,996,500	—	—	—	2.50	—
2002(m) Proof	3,490	Value: 10.00				
2003(m)	22,000	—	—	—	2.50	—
2003(m) Proof	3,000	Value: 10.00				
2004(m)	8,249,507	—	—	—	2.50	—
2004(m) Proof	4,000	Value: 10.00				
2005(m)	—	—	—	—	2.50	—
2005(m) Proof	3,000	Value: 10.00				
2006(m)	—	—	—	—	2.50	—
2006(m) Proof	2,500	Value: 10.00				
2007(m)	—	—	—	—	2.50	—
2007(m) Proof	—	Value: 10.00				
2008(m)	—	—	—	—	2.50	—
2008(m) Proof	—	Value: 10.00				

KM# 43 20 KORUN

8.4300 g., Brass Plated Steel, 26 mm. **Subject:** Year 2000 **Obv:** Crowned Czech lion left, date below **Rev:** Astrolab and denomination within circle **Edge:** Plain **Shape:** 13-sided **Designer:** Vladimir Oppl

Date	Mintage	F	VF	XF	Unc	BU
2000	10,015,000	—	—	—	2.50	—
2000 Proof	2,500	Value: 10.00				

KM# 1 50 KORUN

9.7000 g., Bi-Metallic Brass plated Steel center in Copper plated Steel ring, 27.5 mm. **Obv:** Crowned Czech lion left **Rev:** Prague city view **Edge:** Plain **Designer:** Ladislav Kozak

Date	Mintage	F	VF	XF	Unc	BU
1993(c)	35,001,000	—	—	2.50	7.50	—
1994(c)	100,000	—	—	—	9.00	—
1995(m)	102,977	—	—	—	9.00	—
1996(m)	103,073	—	—	—	9.00	—
1997(m)	40,002	—	—	—	9.00	—
1997(m) Proof	1,500	Value: 35.00				
1998(m)	25,000	—	—	—	9.00	—
Note: 2,600 pieces destroyed.						
1998(m) Proof	2,600	Value: 20.00				
Note: 90 pieces destroyed						
1999(m)	29,490	—	—	—	9.00	—
1999(m) Proof	2,000	Value: 20.00				
2000(m)	26,436	—	—	—	9.00	—
2000(m) Proof	2,500	Value: 20.00				
2001(m)	16,000	—	—	—	9.00	—
2001(m) Proof	2,500	Value: 20.00				
2002(m)	16,771	—	—	—	9.00	—

Date	Mintage	F	VF	XF	Unc	BU
2002(m) Proof	3,490	Value: 20.00				
2003(m)	22,000	—	—	—	9.00	—
2003(m) Proof	3,000	Value: 20.00				
2004(m)	34,555	—	—	—	9.00	—
2004(m) Proof	4,000	Value: 20.00				
2005(m)	—	—	—	—	9.00	—
2005(m) Proof	3,000	Value: 20.00				
2006(m)	—	—	—	—	9.00	—
2006(m) Proof	2,500	Value: 20.00				
2007(m)	—	—	—	—	9.00	—
2007(m) Proof	—	Value: 20.00				
2008(m)	—	—	—	—	9.00	—
2008(m) Proof	—	Value: 20.00				

CZECHOSLOVAKIA

The Republic of Czechoslovakia, founded at the end of World War I, was part of the old Austrian-Hungarian Empire. It had an area of 49,371 sq. mi. (127,870 sq. km.) and a population of 15.6 million. Capital: Prague (Praha).

Czechoslovakia proclaimed itself a republic on Oct. 28, 1918, with Tomas G. Masaryk as President. Hitler's rise to power in Germany provoked Czechoslovakia's German minority in the Sudetenland to agitate for autonomy. At Munich (Munchen) in Sept. of 1938, France and Britain, seeking to avoid World War II, forced the cession of the Sudetenland to Germany. In March, 1939, Germany invaded Czechoslovakia and established the "protectorate of Bohemia and Moravia". Bohemia is a historic province in northwest Czechoslovakia that includes the city of Prague, one of the oldest continually occupied sites in Europe. Moravia is an area of considerable mineral wealth in central Czechoslovakia. Slovakia, a province in southeastern Czechoslovakia under Nazi influence was constituted as a republic. The end of World War II saw the re-established independence of Czechoslovakia, while bringing it within the Russian sphere of influence. On Feb. 23-25, 1948, the Communists seized control of the government in a coup d'etat, and adopted a constitution making the country a 'people's republic'. A new constitution adopted June 11, 1960, converted the country into a 'socialist republic', which lasted until 1989. On Nov. 11, 1989, demonstrations against the communist government began and in Dec. of that same year, communism was overthrown, and the Czech and Slovak Federal Republic was formed. In 1993 the CSFR split into the Czech Republic and The Republic of Slovakia.

NOTE: For additional listings see Bohemia and Moravia, Czech Republic and Slovakia.

MINT MARKS

(k) - Kremnica

(l) - Leningrad

MONETARY SYSTEM

100 Haleru = 1 Koruna

REPUBLIC

DECIMAL COINAGE

KM# 5 2 HALERE

2.0000 g., Zinc, 17 mm. **Obv:** Czech lion with Slovak shield **Rev:** Charles Bridge in Praha, denomination below **Edge:** Plain **Designer:** O. Spaniel

Date	Mintage	F	VF	XF	Unc	BU
1923	2,700,000	3.00	5.00	10.00	16.00	—
1924	17,300,000	2.25	3.50	5.00	9.00	—
1925	2,000,000	3.00	5.00	7.50	17.00	—

KM# 6 5 HALERU

1.6600 g., Bronze, 16 mm. **Obv:** Czech lion with Slovak shield, date below **Rev:** Charles Bridge in Praha, denomination below **Edge:** Plain **Designer:** O. Spaniel

Date	Mintage	F	VF	XF	Unc	BU
1923	37,800,000	0.20	0.30	0.50	2.00	—
1924	10	—	—	2,500	5,000	—
Note: There are two varieties of the number 4 in 1924 dated coins: with and without seraphs						
1925	12,000,000	0.20	0.30	0.50	2.50	—
1926	1,084,000	1.50	4.00	20.00	60.00	—
1927	8,916,000	0.25	0.35	0.75	2.50	—
1928	5,320,000	0.30	0.45	0.75	2.50	—
1929	12,680,000	0.25	0.35	0.75	2.50	—

Date	Mintage	F	VF	XF	Unc	BU
1930	5,000,000	0.35	3.50	15.00	50.00	—
1931	7,448,000	0.25	0.35	0.75	2.50	—
1932	3,556,000	0.65	3.50	12.00	35.00	—
1938	14,244,000	0.25	0.35	0.75	2.00	—

KM# 3 10 HALERU

1.9600 g., Bronze, 18 mm. **Obv:** Czech lion with Slovak shield, date below **Rev:** Charles Bridge of Praha, denomination below **Edge:** Plain

Date	Mintage	F	VF	XF	Unc	BU
1922	6,000,000	0.30	0.45	1.00	2.75	—
1923	24,000,000	0.25	0.35	0.75	2.00	—
1924	5,320,000	0.30	0.45	1.00	3.00	—
1925	24,680,000	0.25	0.35	0.60	2.25	—
1926	10,000,000	0.25	0.35	0.75	2.25	—
1927	10,000,000	0.25	0.35	0.75	2.25	—
1928	14,290,000	0.25	0.35	0.75	2.25	—
1929	5,710,000	1.25	2.50	10.00	25.00	—
1930	6,980,000	0.30	0.45	1.00	2.50	—
1931	6,740,000	0.30	0.45	1.00	2.50	—
1932	11,280,000	0.25	0.35	0.75	2.00	—
1933	4,190,000	1.50	3.50	12.00	25.00	—
1934	13,200,000	0.25	0.35	0.75	2.00	—
1935	3,420,000	1.50	3.50	12.00	25.00	—
1936	8,560,000	0.25	0.35	0.75	2.00	—
1937	20,200,000	0.25	0.35	0.75	2.00	—
1938	21,400,000	0.25	0.35	0.75	2.00	—

KM# 1 20 HALERU

3.3300 g., Copper-Nickel, 20 mm. **Obv:** Czech lion with Slovak shield, date below **Rev:** Sheaf with sickle, linden branch, denomination at left **Edge:** Plain **Designer:** O. Spaniel

Date	Mintage	F	VF	XF	Unc	BU
1921	40,000,000	0.25	0.35	0.60	2.50	—
1922	9,100,000	0.25	0.35	0.60	2.50	—
1924	20,931,000	0.25	0.35	0.60	2.50	—
1925	4,244,000	1.50	3.40	12.00	25.00	—
1926	14,825,000	0.25	0.35	0.60	2.50	—
1927	11,757,000	0.25	0.35	0.60	2.50	—
1928	14,018,000	0.25	0.35	0.60	2.50	—
1929	4,225,000	0.30	0.50	1.25	3.50	—
1930	—	1.00	2.00	5.00	14.00	—
1931	5,000,000	0.30	0.40	0.75	3.00	—
1933	Inc. above	9.00	25.00	80.00	160	—
1937	8,208,000	0.25	0.35	0.60	2.50	—
1938	18,787,000	0.25	0.35	0.60	2.50	—

KM# 16 25 HALERU

4.0000 g., Copper-Nickel, 21 mm. **Obv:** Czech lion with Slovak shield, date below **Rev:** Large denomination **Edge:** Milled **Designer:** O. Spaniel

Date	Mintage	F	VF	XF	Unc	BU
1932	—	—	1,250	2,250	3,000	—
1933	22,711,000	0.50	1.00	2.00	4.00	—

KM# 2 50 HALERU

5.0000 g., Copper-Nickel, 22 mm. **Obv:** Czech lion with Slovak shield, date below **Rev:** Linden branches and wheat sprigs bound with ribbon **Edge:** Milled **Designer:** O. Spaniel

Date	Mintage	F	VF	XF	Unc	BU
1921	3,000,000	0.25	0.50	1.00	3.00	—
1922	37,000,000	0.20	0.40	0.60	2.50	—
1924	10,000,000	0.20	0.40	0.60	3.00	—
1925	1,415,000	0.50	1.00	2.50	10.00	—
1926	1,585,000	3.50	9.00	20.00	45.00	—
1927	2,000,000	0.50	1.00	2.00	9.00	—
1931	6,000,000	0.25	0.50	1.00	2.50	—

KM# 4 KORUNA

6.6600 g., Copper-Nickel, 25 mm. **Obv:** Czech lion with Slovak shield, date below **Rev:** Woman with sheaf and sickle, denomination at left **Edge:** Milled **Designer:** O. Spaniel

Date	Mintage	F	VF	XF	Unc	BU
1922	50,000,000	0.30	0.50	0.75	2.00	—
1923	15,385,000	0.30	0.50	0.75	2.00	—
1924	21,041,000	0.30	0.50	0.75	2.00	—
1925	8,574,000	0.40	0.60	1.25	4.00	—
1929	5,000,000	0.50	0.75	1.25	3.50	—
1930	5,000,000	0.40	0.60	1.25	5.00	—
1937	3,806,000	0.40	0.60	1.00	3.00	—
1938	8,582,000	0.40	0.60	1.00	3.00	—

KM# 10 5 KORUN

10.0000 g., Copper-Nickel, 30 mm. **Obv:** Czech lion with Slovak shield, date below **Rev:** Industrial factory and large value

Date	Mintage	F	VF	XF	Unc	BU
1925	16,474,500	1.50	2.50	3.50	9.00	—
1926	8,912,000	1.75	2.75	4.00	10.00	—
1927	4,613,500	8.00	20.00	80.00	160	—

KM# 11 5 KORUN

7.0000 g., 0.5000 Silver 0.1125 oz. ASW, 27 mm. **Obv:** Czech lion with Slovak shield, date below **Rev:** Industrial factory and large value **Edge:** Plain with crosses and waves **Designer:** Ota Gutfreud

Date	Mintage	F	VF	XF	Unc	BU
1928	1,710,000	2.00	3.00	5.00	10.00	—
Note: Edge varieties exist for 1928						
1929	12,861,000	1.65	2.50	4.00	8.50	—
1930	10,429,000	1.65	2.50	4.00	8.50	—
1931	2,000,000	3.00	5.00	15.00	45.00	—
1932	1,000,000	5.00	7.50	20.00	60.00	—

KM# 11a 5 KORUN

7.0000 g., Nickel, 27 mm. **Obv:** Czech lion with Slovak shield, date below **Rev:** Industrial factory and large value **Designer:** O. Guttfreund

Date	Mintage	F	VF	XF	Unc	BU
1937	36,000	400	900	1,850	3,500	—
1938	17,200,000	1.25	2.50	4.00	6.50	—

KM# 12 10 KORUN

10.0000 g., 0.7000 Silver 0.2250 oz. ASW, 30 mm. **Subject:** 10th Anniversary of Independence **Obv:** Denomination above state shield within circle, dates below **Rev:** Bust right **Edge:** Milled **Designer:** O. Spaniel

Date	Mintage	F	VF	XF	Unc	BU
ND(1928)	1,000,000	3.00	4.50	7.00	11.50	—

KM# 15 10 KORUN

10.0000 g., 0.7000 Silver 0.2250 oz. ASW, 30 mm. **Obv:** State emblem, date below **Rev:** Republic holding linden tree, denomination above **Edge:** Milled **Designer:** J. Horejc

Date	Mintage	F	VF	XF	Unc	BU
1930	4,949,000	3.00	4.00	7.00	11.50	—
1931	6,689,000	2.85	3.75	6.00	10.00	—
1932	11,447,500	BV	3.50	5.00	9.00	—
1933	915,000	350	850	1,750	3,000	—

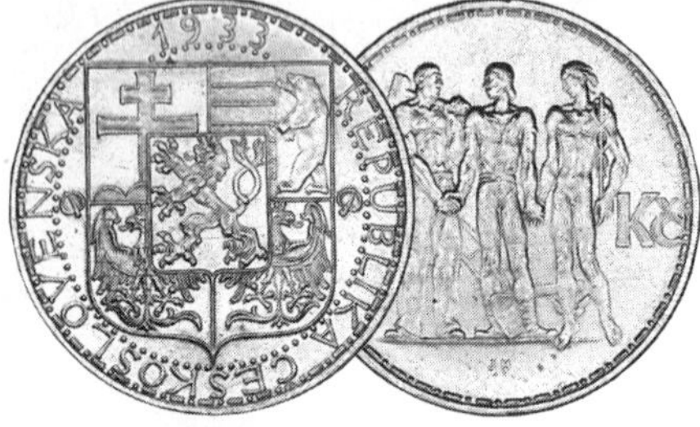

KM# 17 20 KORUN

12.0000 g., 0.7000 Silver 0.2701 oz. ASW, 34 mm. **Obv:** State emblem, date above **Rev:** Three figures: Industry, Agriculture, and Business, divide denomination **Edge:** Plain with crosses and waves **Designer:** J. Horejc

Date	Mintage	F	VF	XF	Unc	BU
1933	2,280,000	—	4.50	7.50	14.00	—
1934	3,280,000	—	4.50	7.50	14.00	—

KM# 18 20 KORUN

12.0000 g., 0.7000 Silver 0.2701 oz. ASW, 34 mm. **Subject:** Death of President Masaryk **Obv:** Denomination above state emblem **Obv. Designer:** J. Horejc **Rev:** Bust right, dates at left **Rev. Designer:** O. Spaniel **Edge:** Plain with crosses and waves

Date	Mintage	F	VF	XF	Unc	BU
ND(1937)	1,000,000	—	4.00	7.00	11.50	—

TRADE COINAGE

KM# 7 DUKAT

3.4900 g., 0.9860 Gold 0.1106 oz. AGW **Subject:** 5th Anniversary of the Republic **Obv:** Shield with Czech lion and Slovak shield **Obv. Designer:** J. Benda **Rev:** Duke Wenceslas (Vaclav) half-length figure facing **Rev. Designer:** O. Spaniel **Edge:** Milled **Note:** Serially numbered below the duke. The number is in the die.

Date	Mintage	F	VF	XF	Unc	BU
1923	1,000	—	1,000	2,500	5,000	—

KM# 8 DUKAT

3.4900 g., 0.9860 Gold 0.1106 oz. AGW **Obv:** Czech lion with Slovak shield, date below **Obv. Designer:** J. Benda **Rev:** Duke Wenceslas (Vaclav) half-length figure facing **Rev. Designer:** O. Spaniel **Edge:** Milled **Note:** Similar to KM#7 but without serial numbers.

Date	Mintage	F	VF	XF	Unc	BU
1923	61,861	—	BV	100	125	—
1924	32,814	—	BV	100	125	—
1925	66,279	—	BV	100	125	—
1926	58,669	—	BV	100	125	—
1927	25,774	—	BV	100	125	—
1928	18,983	—	BV	100	135	—
1929	10,253	—	BV	100	165	—
1930	11,338	—	BV	100	165	—
1931	43,482	—	BV	100	125	—
1932	26,617	—	BV	100	125	—
1933	57,597	—	BV	100	125	—
1934	9,729	—	100	120	175	—
1935	13,178	—	BV	100	135	—
1936	14,566	—	BV	100	135	—
1937	324	—	—	2,400	3,000	—
1938	56	—	—	1,750	16,500	—
1939	276	—	—	—	8,000	—

Note: Czech reports show mintage of 20 for Czechoslovakia and 256 for state of Slovakia

Date	Mintage	F	VF	XF	Unc	BU
1951	500	—	—	2,400	3,000	—

KM# 9 2 DUKATY

6.9800 g., 0.9860 Gold 0.2213 oz. AGW, 25 mm. **Obv:** Czech lion with Slovak shield, denomination divides date below **Obv. Designer:** J. Benda **Rev:** Duke Wenceslas (Vaclav) half-length figure facing **Rev. Designer:** O. Spaniel **Edge:** Milled

Date	Mintage	F	VF	XF	Unc	BU
1923	4,000	—	200	300	400	—
1929	3,262	—	200	300	400	—
1930	Inc. above	—	200	375	500	—
1931	2,994	—	200	300	400	—
1932	5,496	—	200	300	400	—
1933	4,671	—	200	300	400	—
1934	2,403	—	200	325	450	—
1935	2,577	—	200	300	450	—
1936	819	—	300	600	900	—
1937	8	—	—	—	60,000	—
1938	186	—	—	—	8,000	—

Note: Czech reports show mintage of 14 for Czechoslovakia and 172 for state of Slovakia

Date	Mintage	F	VF	XF	Unc	BU
1951	200	—	—	—	5,000	—

KM# 13 5 DUKATU

17.4500 g., 0.9860 Gold 0.5532 oz. AGW, 34 mm. **Obv:** Czech lion with Slovak shield, denomination and date below **Obv. Designer:** J. Benda **Rev:** Duke Wenceslas (Vaclav) on horseback right **Rev. Designer:** O. Spaniel **Edge:** Milled

Date	Mintage	F	VF	XF	Unc	BU
1929	1,827	—	475	650	975	—
1930	543	—	500	1,000	1,500	—
1931	1,528	—	475	650	975	—
1932	1,827	—	475	650	975	—
1933	1,752	—	475	650	975	—
1934	1,101	—	475	650	975	—
1935	1,037	—	475	650	975	—
1936	728	—	—	4,200	5,000	—
1937 Rare	4	—	—	—	—	—
1938	56	—	—	—	20,000	—

Note: Czech reports show mintage of 12 for Czechoslovakia and 44 for state of Slovakia

Date	Mintage	F	VF	XF	Unc	BU
1951	100	—	—	—	10,000	—

KM# 14 10 DUKATU

34.9000 g., 0.9860 Gold 1.1063 oz. AGW, 42 mm. **Obv:** Czech lion with Slovak shield, denomination and date below **Obv. Designer:** J. Benda **Rev:** Duke Wenceslas (Vaclav) on horseback right **Rev. Designer:** O. Spaniel

Date	Mintage	F	VF	XF	Unc	BU
1929	1,564	—	975	1,700	2,250	—
1930	394	—	1,000	3,000	4,000	—
1931	1,239	—	975	1,700	2,250	—
1932	1,035	—	975	1,700	2,250	—
1933	1,780	—	975	1,700	2,250	—
1934	1,298	—	975	1,900	2,500	—
1935	600	—	1,000	2,000	3,000	—
1936	633	—	1,100	2,500	3,500	—
1937 Rare	34	—	—	—	—	—
1938	192	—	—	—	45,000	—
1951	100	—	—	—	17,500	—

Note: Czech reports show mintage of 20 for Czechoslovakia and 172 for state of Slovakia.

POST WAR COINAGE

KM# 20 20 HALERU

2.0000 g., Bronze, 18 mm. **Obv:** Czech lion with Slovak shield, date below **Rev:** Sheaf with sickle, linden branch, denomination at left **Edge:** Plain **Designer:** O. Spaniel

Date	Mintage	F	VF	XF	Unc	BU
1947	—	65.00	125	200	300	—
1948	24,340,000	0.10	0.15	0.40	1.50	—
1949	25,660,000	0.10	0.15	0.40	1.50	—
1950	11,132,000	0.10	0.15	0.40	2.00	—

KM# 31 20 HALERU

0.5300 g., Aluminum, 16 mm. **Obv:** Czech lion with Slovak shield, date below **Rev:** Wheat sheaf, sickle, linden branch, denomination at left **Edge:** Plain **Designer:** O. Spaniel

Date	Mintage	F	VF	XF	Unc	BU
1951	46,800,000	0.10	0.15	0.25	1.00	—
1952	80,340,000	0.10	0.15	0.25	1.00	—

KM# 21 50 HALERU

Bronze, 20 mm. **Obv:** Czech lion with Slovak shield, date below **Rev:** Linden branches and wheat sprigs bound with ribbon **Edge:** Plain **Designer:** O. Spaniel

Date	Mintage	F	VF	XF	Unc	BU
1947	50,000,000	0.15	0.25	0.40	1.00	—
1948	20,000,000	0.15	0.25	0.40	1.50	—
1949	12,715,000	0.15	0.25	0.40	2.00	—
1950	17,415,000	0.15	0.25	0.40	1.80	—

KM# 32 50 HALERU
Aluminum, 18 mm. **Obv:** Czech lion with Slovak shield, date below **Rev:** Linden branches and wheat sprigs bound with ribbon **Edge:** Plain **Designer:** O. Spaniel

Date	Mintage	F	VF	XF	Unc	BU
1951	60,000,000	0.15	0.35	0.50	0.75	—
1952	60,000,000	0.25	0.45	0.60	1.00	—
1953	34,920,000	1.00	2.50	6.00	10.00	—

KM# 19 KORUNA
Copper-Nickel, 21 mm. **Obv:** Czech lion with Slovak shield, date below **Rev:** Woman with sheaf and sickle, denomination at left **Edge:** Milled **Designer:** Otakar Spaniel

Date	Mintage	F	VF	XF	Unc	BU
1946	88,000,000	0.15	0.25	0.50	1.00	—
1947	12,550,000	1.50	2.50	3.75	6.50	—

Note: Varieties exist for "4" in 1946 strikes

KM# 22 KORUNA
1.3400 g., Aluminum, 21 mm. **Obv:** Czech lion with Slovak shield, date below **Rev:** Woman with sheaf and sickle, denomination at left **Edge:** Milled **Designer:** O. Spaniel

Date	Mintage	F	VF	XF	Unc	BU
1947	—	150	450	1,000	2,000	—
Note: Counterfeits, with prooflike fields, are known.						
1950	62,190,000	0.20	0.35	0.45	1.00	—
1951	61,395,000	0.20	0.35	0.45	1.25	—
1952	101,105,000	0.20	0.30	0.40	0.80	—
1953	73,905,000	0.40	0.75	1.75	4.50	—

KM# 23 2 KORUNY
Copper-Nickel, 23.5 mm. **Obv:** Czech lion with Slovak shield, date below **Rev:** Juraj Janosik bust right, wearing hat, denomination at right **Edge:** Milled **Designer:** J. Wagner

Date	Mintage	F	VF	XF	Unc	BU
1947	20,000,000	0.20	0.40	0.60	1.25	—
1948	20,476,000	0.20	0.40	0.60	1.50	—

KM# 34 5 KORUN
Aluminum, 23 mm. **Obv:** Czech lion with Slovak shield, date below **Rev:** Industrial factory and large value **Designer:** O. Guttfreund

Date	Mintage	F	VF	XF	Unc	BU
1951	—	—	300	700	1,500	—
Note: Not released for circulation. Almost the entire mintage was melted						
1952	40,715,000	25.00	50.00	90.00	140	—

Note: Weakly struck counterfeits are known

PEOPLES REPUBLIC

DECIMAL COINAGE

KM# 35 HALER
0.4900 g., Aluminum, 16 mm. **Obv:** Czech lion with Slovak shield, date below **Rev:** Large denomination within linden wreath, star above **Edge:** Plain

Date	Mintage	F	VF	XF	Unc	BU
1953	188,885,000	—	—	0.10	0.25	—
1954	—	—	—	0.10	0.25	—
1955	—	—	—	0.15	0.50	—
1956	—	—	—	0.10	0.25	—
1957	—	—	—	0.10	0.25	—
1958	—	0.10	0.25	0.35	0.75	—
1959	—	—	—	0.15	0.50	—
1960	—	—	—	0.10	0.25	—

KM# 36 3 HALERE
0.6500 g., Aluminum, 18 mm. **Obv:** Czech lion with Slovak shield, date below **Rev:** Large denomination within linden wreath, star above **Edge:** Plain

Date	Mintage	F	VF	XF	Unc	BU
1953	90,001,000	—	0.10	0.15	0.30	—
1954	Inc. above	—	0.10	0.15	0.30	—

KM# 37 5 HALERU
Aluminum, 20 mm. **Obv:** Czech lion with Slovak shield, date below **Rev:** Large denomination within linden wreath, star above **Edge:** Plain

Date	Mintage	F	VF	XF	Unc	BU
1953	160,233,000	0.10	0.15	0.25	0.50	—
1954	Inc. above	0.10	0.15	0.25	0.50	—
1955	Inc. above	1.50	3.50	30.00	120	—

KM# 38 10 HALERU
Aluminum, 22 mm. **Obv:** Czech lion with Slovak shield, date below **Rev:** Large denomination within linden wreath, star above

Date	Mintage	F	VF	XF	Unc	BU
1953	—	0.10	0.15	1.00	5.00	—
Note: Unknown Mint-125 notches in milled edge						
1953	160,000	0.10	0.15	1.00	5.00	—
Note: Leningrad Mint-133 notches in milled edge						
1954	—	0.25	0.50	2.00	7.00	—
1955	—	0.50	2.50	12.00	50.00	—
1956	—	0.10	0.15	1.00	5.00	—
1958	—	2.00	5.00	25.00	70.00	—

KM# 39 25 HALERU
1.4600 g., Aluminum, 24 mm. **Obv:** Czech lion with Slovak shield, date below **Rev:** Large denomination within linden wreath, star above

Date	Mintage	F	VF	XF	Unc	BU
1953	215,002,000	0.10	0.20	0.30	4.00	—
Note: Kremnica Mint - 134 notches in milled edge						
1953	Inc. above	0.30	0.50	0.60	6.00	—
Note: Leningrad Mint - 145 notches in milled edge						
1954	Inc. above	9.00	18.00	35.00	140	—

KM# 46 KORUNA
4.0000 g., Aluminum-Bronze, 23 mm. **Obv:** Czech lion with Slovak shield, date below **Rev:** Woman kneeling planting linden tree, denomination at left **Rev. Designer:** M. Uchitilova-Kucova **Edge:** Milled

Date	Mintage	F	VF	XF	Unc	BU
1957	137,000,000	0.20	0.30	0.45	5.00	—
1958	Inc. above	0.20	0.30	0.45	7.00	—
1959	Inc. above	0.15	0.25	0.35	4.50	—
1960	Inc. above	0.15	0.25	0.35	4.50	—

SOCIALIST REPUBLIC

DECIMAL COINAGE

KM# 51 HALER
0.5200 g., Aluminum, 16 mm. **Obv:** Czech lion with socialist shield within shield, date below **Rev:** Denomination within linden wreath, star above **Edge:** Plain

Date	Mintage	F	VF	XF	Unc	BU
1962	20,056,000	—	—	0.10	0.15	—
1963	Inc. above	—	—	0.10	0.15	—
1986	3,360,000	—	—	—	1.00	—

KM# 52 3 HALERE
0.6400 g., Aluminum, 18 mm. **Obv:** Czech lion with socialist shield within shield, date below **Rev:** Denomination within linden wreath, star above **Edge:** Plain

Date	Mintage	F	VF	XF	Unc	BU
1962	Inc. below	100	150	200	280	—
Note: Counterfeits, with prooflike fields, are known.						
1963	5,130,000	—	—	0.10	0.15	—

KM# 53 5 HALERU
Aluminum, 20 mm. **Obv:** Czech lion with socialist shield within shield, date below **Rev:** Denomination within linden wreath, star above **Edge:** Plain

Date	Mintage	F	VF	XF	Unc	BU
1962	55,150,000	—	0.10	0.15	0.25	—
1963	Inc. above	—	0.10	0.15	0.25	—
1966	Inc. above	—	0.10	0.15	0.25	—
1967	20,770,000	—	0.10	0.15	0.25	—
1970	5,090,000	—	0.10	0.15	0.20	—
1972	10,090,000	—	0.10	0.15	0.20	—
1973	10,140,000	—	0.10	0.15	0.20	—
1974	15,510,000	—	0.10	0.15	0.20	—
1975	15,510,000	—	0.10	0.15	0.20	—
1976	15,550,000	—	0.10	0.15	0.20	—

KM# 86 5 HALERU
Aluminum, 16.2 mm. **Obv:** Czech lion with socialist shield within shield, date below **Rev:** Large denomination, star above **Edge:** Plain **Designer:** F. David

Date	Mintage	F	VF	XF	Unc	BU
1977	26,710,000	—	—	0.10	0.25	—
1978	51,110,000	—	—	0.10	0.25	—
1979	72,380,000	—	—	0.10	0.25	—
1980	50,600	—	—	—	0.25	—
Note: In sets only						
1981	66,160	—	—	—	0.50	—
Note: In sets only						
1982	53,847	—	—	—	1.00	—

Date	Mintage	F	VF	XF	Unc	BU
Note: In sets only						
1983	60,000	—	—	—	0.50	—
Note: In sets only						
1984	39,957	—	—	—	0.75	—
Note: In sets only						
1985	39,791	—	—	—	0.75	—
Note: In sets only						
1986	20,020,000	—	—	0.10	0.25	—
1987	520,000	—	—	0.10	0.35	—
1988	8,029,999	—	—	0.10	0.25	—
1989	110,000	—	—	0.10	0.50	—
1990	13,950,000	—	—	0.10	0.25	—

KM# 49.1 10 HALERU

Aluminum **Obv:** Star above Czech lion with socialist shield within shield **Rev:** Large denomination within linden wreath, star above

Date	Mintage	F	VF	XF	Unc	BU
1961	314,480,000	—	0.10	0.20	0.35	—
1962	Inc. above	—	0.10	0.20	0.35	—
1963	Inc. above	—	0.10	0.20	0.35	—
1964	Inc. above	—	0.10	0.20	0.35	—
1965	Inc. above	—	0.10	0.20	0.35	—
1966	Inc. above	—	0.10	0.20	0.35	—
1967	46,990,000	—	0.10	0.20	0.35	—
1968	37,275,000	—	0.10	0.20	0.35	—
1969	80,000,000	—	0.10	0.15	0.35	—
1970	50,005,000	—	0.10	0.20	0.35	—
1971	30,450,000	—	0.10	0.20	0.35	—

KM# 49.2 10 HALERU

Aluminum, 22 mm. **Obv:** Star above Czech lion with socialist shield within shield, flat-top 3 in date below **Rev:** Denomination within linden wreath, star above **Note:** Obverse muled from 50 Haleru, KM 55.1.

Date	Mintage	F	VF	XF	Unc	BU
1963	Est. 3,600	12.50	25.00	60.00	150	—

Note: Weakly struck counterfeits are known.

KM# 80 10 HALERU

Aluminum, 18.2 mm. **Obv:** Czech lion with socialist shield within shield, fat date below **Rev:** Large thick denomination, star above **Designer:** F. David **Note:** Varieties exist.

Date	Mintage	F	VF	XF	Unc	BU
1974	11,470,000	—	—	0.10	0.25	—
1975	41,002,000	—	—	0.10	0.25	—
1976	182,000,000	—	—	0.10	0.25	—
1977	151,760,000	—	—	0.10	0.25	—
1978	62,620,000	—	—	0.10	0.25	—
1979	30,240,000	—	—	0.10	0.25	—
1980	31,280,000	—	—	0.10	0.25	—
1981	43,616,160	—	—	0.10	0.25	—
1982	74,568,847	—	—	0.10	0.25	—
1983	50,560,000	—	—	0.10	0.25	—
1984	40,369,957	—	—	0.10	0.25	—
1985	92,929,791	—	—	0.10	0.25	—
1986	87,260,000	—	—	0.10	0.25	—
1987	30,030,000	—	—	0.10	0.25	—
1988	47,479,999	—	—	0.10	0.25	—
1989	50,300,000	—	—	0.10	0.25	—
1990	25,220,000	—	—	0.10	0.25	—

KM# 74 20 HALERU

Brass, 19.5 mm. **Obv:** Czech lion with socialist shield within shield, thick date below **Rev:** Large thick denomination, star above **Designer:** F. David **Note:** Varieties exist.

Date	Mintage	F	VF	XF	Unc	BU
1972	25,820,000	—	0.10	0.20	0.40	—
1973	39,095,000	—	0.10	0.20	0.40	—

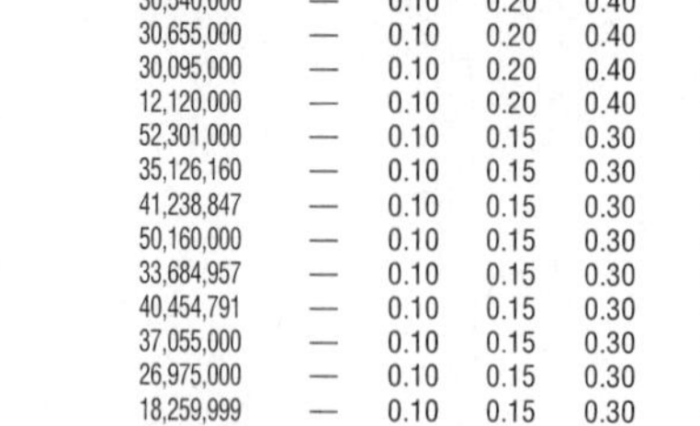

Date	Mintage	F	VF	XF	Unc	BU
1974	24,795,000	—	0.10	0.20	0.40	—
1975	30,025,000	—	0.10	0.20	0.40	—
1976	30,540,000	—	0.10	0.20	0.40	—
1977	30,655,000	—	0.10	0.20	0.40	—
1978	30,095,000	—	0.10	0.20	0.40	—
1979	12,120,000	—	0.10	0.20	0.40	—
1980	52,301,000	—	0.10	0.15	0.30	—
1981	35,126,160	—	0.10	0.15	0.30	—
1982	41,238,847	—	0.10	0.15	0.30	—
1983	50,160,000	—	0.10	0.15	0.30	—
1984	33,684,957	—	0.10	0.15	0.30	—
1985	40,454,791	—	0.10	0.15	0.30	—
1986	37,055,000	—	0.10	0.15	0.30	—
1987	26,975,000	—	0.10	0.15	0.30	—
1988	18,259,999	—	0.10	0.15	0.30	—
1989	29,980,000	—	0.10	0.15	0.30	—
1990	15,030,000	—	0.10	0.15	0.30	—

KM# 54 25 HALERU

Aluminum, 24 mm. **Obv:** Czech lion with socialist shield within shield, date below **Rev:** Large denomination within linden wreath, star above **Edge:** Milled **Note:** This denomination ceased to be legal tender in 1972.

Date	Mintage	F	VF	XF	Unc	BU
1962	69,880,000	0.10	0.15	0.20	0.35	—
1963	Inc. above	0.10	0.15	0.20	0.35	—
1964	Inc. above	0.10	0.15	0.20	0.35	—

KM# 55.1 50 HALERU

Bronze, 21.5 mm. **Obv:** Czech lion with socialist shield within shield, date below **Rev:** Large denomination within linden wreath, star above

Date	Mintage	F	VF	XF	Unc	BU
1963	80,560,000	0.10	0.20	0.30	0.45	—
1964	Inc. above	0.10	0.20	0.30	0.45	—
1965	Inc. above	0.10	0.20	0.30	0.45	—
1969	9,876,000	0.10	0.20	0.30	0.45	—
1970	31,536,000	0.10	0.20	0.30	0.40	—
1971	20,800,000	0.10	0.20	0.30	0.40	—

KM# 55.2 50 HALERU

Bronze, 21.5 mm. **Obv:** Czech lion with socialist shield within shield, small date, without dots **Rev:** Value within linden wreath, star above **Note:** Obverse muled with 10 Haleru, KM 49.1.

Date	Mintage	F	VF	XF	Unc	BU
1969	—	12.50	22.50	40.00	75.00	—

KM# 89 50 HALERU

Copper-Nickel, 20.8 mm. **Obv:** Czech lion with socialist shield within shield, thick date below **Rev:** Thick denomination, star above **Edge:** Milled **Designer:** F. David **Note:** Date varieties exist.

Date	Mintage	F	VF	XF	Unc	BU
1977	Est. 5	—	—	500	1,000	—
1978	40,480,000	—	—	0.10	0.50	—
1979	76,116,000	—	—	0.10	0.50	—
1980	51,000	—	—	—	1.50	—
Note: In sets only						
1981	66,000	—	—	—	1.50	—
Note: In sets only						
1982	14,261,847	—	—	0.10	0.50	—
1983	16,168,000	—	—	0.10	0.50	—
1984	16,207,957	—	—	0.10	0.50	—
1985	10,467,791	—	—	0.10	0.50	—
1986	10,020,000	—	—	0.10	0.50	—
1987	5,138,000	—	—	0.10	0.50	—
1988	5,089,999	—	—	0.10	0.50	—
1989	13,030,000	—	—	0.10	0.50	—
1990	7,742,000	—	—	0.10	0.50	—

KM# 50 KORUNA

Aluminum-Bronze, 23 mm. **Obv:** Czech lion with socialist shield within shield, date below **Rev:** Woman planting linden tree, denomination at left **Rev. Designer:** Marie Uchytilova-Kucova **Edge:** Milled **Note:** Date varieties exist.

Date	Mintage	F	VF	XF	Unc	BU
1961	146,964,000	—	0.15	0.30	0.60	—
1962	Inc. above	—	0.15	0.30	0.60	—
1963	Inc. above	—	0.15	0.30	0.60	—
1964	Inc. above	—	0.15	0.30	0.60	—
1965	Inc. above	—	0.15	0.30	0.60	—
1966	Inc. above	0.40	0.65	0.90	1.25	—
1967	7,924,000	—	0.15	0.30	0.60	—
1968	10,696,000	—	0.15	0.30	0.60	—
1969	21,820,000	—	0.15	0.30	0.60	—
1970	31,036,000	—	0.15	0.30	0.60	—
1971	10,152,000	—	0.15	0.30	0.60	—
1975	6,657,000	—	0.15	0.30	0.60	—
1976	14,211,000	—	0.15	0.30	0.60	—
1977	10,434,000	—	0.15	0.30	0.75	—
1979	Inc. below	—	0.15	0.30	0.75	—
1980	24,513,000	—	0.15	0.30	0.75	—
1981	7,179,000	—	0.15	0.30	0.75	—
1982	17,162,847	—	0.15	0.30	0.75	—
1983	4,758,000	—	0.15	0.30	0.75	—
1984	9,732,957	—	0.15	0.30	0.75	—
1985	10,545,751	—	0.15	0.30	0.75	—
1986	2,789,000	—	0.15	0.30	0.75	—
1987	30,000	—	—	—	2.50	—
Note: In sets only						
1988	29,999	—	—	—	2.50	—
Note: In sets only						
1989	1,038,000	—	0.15	0.30	0.75	—
1990	19,368,000	—	0.15	0.30	0.75	—

KM# 75 2 KORUNY

Copper-Nickel, 24 mm. **Obv:** Czech lion with socialist shield within shield, date below **Rev:** Star above hammer and sickle, large value at right **Edge:** Plain with crosses and waves **Designer:** J. Nalepa

Date	Mintage	F	VF	XF	Unc	BU
1972	20,344,000	—	0.25	0.45	1.00	—
1973	21,087,000	—	0.25	0.45	1.00	—
Note: 1973 date exists with edge of 5 Korun KM#60, value: $15.00						
1974	27,957,000	—	0.25	0.45	1.00	—
1975	35,094,000	—	0.25	0.45	1.00	—
1976	1,100,000	—	0.25	0.45	1.00	—
1977	4,201,000	—	0.25	0.65	1.50	—
1980	14,943,000	—	0.25	0.35	0.75	—
1981	17,264,000	—	0.25	0.35	0.75	—
1982	8,108,000	—	0.25	0.35	0.75	—
1983	10,190,000	—	0.25	0.35	0.75	—
1984	8,634,000	—	0.25	0.35	0.75	—
1985	6,772,000	—	0.25	0.35	0.75	—
1986	10,262,000	—	0.25	0.35	0.75	—
1987 In mint sets only	30,000	—	—	—	2.50	—
1988 In mint sets only	30,000	—	—	—	2.50	—
1989	9,092,000	—	0.25	0.35	0.75	—
1990	10,672,000	—	0.25	0.35	0.75	—

KM# 57 3 KORUNY

5.5800 g., Copper-Nickel, 23.5 mm. **Obv:** Czech lion with socialist shield within shield, date below **Obv. Designer:** Zdenek Kolarsky **Rev:** Branch of five linden leaves within banner, large value at right **Rev. Designer:** E. Hajek **Edge:** Plain with lime leaves and waves

Date	Mintage	F	VF	XF	Unc	BU
1965	15,000,000	—	0.50	1.00	2.50	—
1966	Inc. above	—	0.50	1.00	2.50	—
1968	7,000,000	—	0.45	0.85	2.00	—
1969	10,080,000	—	0.40	0.75	1.50	—

KM# 60 5 KORUN
7.2200 g., Copper-Nickel, 26 mm. **Obv:** Czech lion with socialist shield within shield, date below **Rev:** Geometric design and large denomination **Edge:** Plain with rhombs and waves **Designer:** J. Harcuba

Date	Mintage	F	VF	XF	Unc	BU
1966	6,383,000	—	0.75	1.00	2.00	—
Note: 1966 varieties on obverse of coin: large date: no space between letter B in REPUBLIC and coat of arms; small date: space between letter B in REPUBLIC and coat of arms; plain edge: no ornamental inscription on edge (error coin). So far there has been no indication of any of the varieties as being scarce						
1967	4,544,000	—	—	0.75	1.50	—
1968	14,120,000	—	—	0.75	1.50	—
1969	Inc. above	0.75	1.50	5.00	9.00	—
Note: Date in semi-circle						
1969	5,486,000	—	—	0.75	1.50	—
Note: Straight date						
1970	10,073,000	—	—	0.75	1.50	—
1973	15,620,000	—	—	0.75	1.25	—
Note: Two variations in 3 of date						
1974	20,053,000	—	—	0.75	1.25	—
Note: Three variations in 4 of date						
1975	17,158,000	—	—	0.75	1.25	—
1978	5,317,000	—	—	0.75	1.25	—
1979	9,219,000	—	—	0.75	1.25	—
1980	12,559,000	—	—	0.75	1.25	—
1981	8,620,160	—	—	0.75	1.25	—
1982	6,903,847	—	—	0.75	1.25	—
1983	6,704,000	—	—	0.75	1.25	—
1984	6,856,957	—	—	0.75	1.25	—
1985	6,763,791	—	—	0.75	1.25	—
1986	20,000	—	—	—	35.00	—
Note: In sets only						
1987	30,000	—	—	—	7.00	—
Note: In sets only						
1988	29,999	—	—	—	5.00	—
1989	5,039,000	—	—	0.75	1.25	—
1990	2,783,000	—	—	0.75	1.25	—

CZECH SLOVAK FEDERAL REPUBLIC

DECIMAL COINAGE

KM# 149 HALER
0.7900 g., Aluminum, 16 mm. **Obv:** CSFR above quartered shield, linden leaves flanking, date below **Rev:** Denomination within linden wreath **Edge:** Plain

Date	Mintage	F	VF	XF	Unc	BU
1991	55,000	—	—	—	2.50	—
1992	50,000	—	—	—	2.50	—

KM# 150 5 HALERU
0.7500 g., Aluminum, 16.2 mm. **Obv:** CSFR above quartered shield, linden leaves flanking, date below **Obv. Designer:** Miroslav Ronai **Rev:** Large, thick, denomination **Rev. Designer:** Frantisek David **Edge:** Plain

Date	Mintage	F	VF	XF	Unc	BU
1991	10,055,000	—	—	0.10	0.25	—
1992	50,000	—	—	—	2.00	—
Note: In sets only						

KM# 146 10 HALERU
Aluminum, 18.2 mm. **Obv:** CSFR above quartered shield, linden leaves flanking, date below **Obv. Designer:** Miroslav Ronai **Rev:** Large, thick denomination **Rev. Designer:** Frantisek David

Date	Mintage	F	VF	XF	Unc	BU
1991	40,055,000	—	—	—	0.50	—
1992	45,050,000	—	—	—	0.50	—

KM# 143 20 HALERU
Aluminum-Bronze, 19.5 mm. **Obv:** CSFR above quartered shield, linden leaves flanking, date below **Obv. Designer:** Miroslav Ronai **Rev:** Large, thick denomination **Rev. Designer:** Frantisek David **Edge:** Milled

Date	Mintage	F	VF	XF	Unc	BU
1991	41,105,000	—	—	0.20	0.50	—
1992	35,050,000	—	—	0.20	0.50	—

KM# 144 50 HALERU
Copper-Nickel, 20.8 mm. **Obv:** CSFR above quartered shield, linden leaves flanking, date below **Obv. Designer:** Miroslav Ronai **Rev:** Large, thick denomination **Rev. Designer:** Frantisek David **Edge:** Milled

Date	Mintage	F	VF	XF	Unc	BU
1991	24,463,000	—	—	0.35	0.75	—
1992	15,062,000	—	—	0.35	0.75	—

KM# 151 KORUNA
4.0800 g., Copper-Aluminum, 23 mm. **Obv:** CSFR above quartered shield, linden leaves flanking, date below **Obv. Designer:** Miroslav Ronai **Rev:** Female planting linden tree, denomination at left **Rev. Designer:** Marie Uchytilova-Kucova **Edge:** Reeded

Date	Mintage	F	VF	XF	Unc	BU
1991	20,056,000	—	—	0.50	1.00	—
1992	20,387,000	—	—	0.50	1.00	—

KM# 148 2 KORUNY
Copper-Nickel, 24 mm. **Obv:** CSFR above quartered shield, linden leaves flanking, date below **Obv. Designer:** Miroslav Ronai **Rev:** Linden leaf, large value at right **Rev. Designer:** Josef Nalepa **Edge:** Plain with wave x wave

Date	Mintage	F	VF	XF	Unc	BU
1991(k)	25,201,000	—	—	0.60	1.25	—
1991(l)	20,000,000	—	—	0.60	1.25	—
1992	1,051,000	—	—	—	1.25	—

KM# 152 5 KORUN
Copper-Nickel, 26 mm. **Obv:** CSFR above quartered shield, linden leaves flanking, date below **Obv. Designer:** Jarmila Truhlikova-Spevakova **Rev:** Geometric design, large value **Rev. Designer:** Drahomir Zobek **Edge:** Eight plain and eight milled areas

Date	Mintage	F	VF	XF	Unc	BU
1991(k)	18,564,000	—	—	0.75	2.00	—
1991(l)	10,000,750	—	—	—	—	—
1992	50,000	—	—	2.50	6.00	—
Note: In sets only						

KM# 139.1 10 KORUN
Nickel-Bronze, 24.5 mm. **Obv:** CSFR above quartered shield, date below, denomination at left **Obv. Designer:** J. Truhlikova-Spevakova **Rev:** Bust right, dates at left **Rev. Designer:** M. Ronai **Edge:** Eight plain and eight milled areas **Note:** Designer initials (MR) below bust, four varieties exist.

Date	Mintage	F	VF	XF	Unc	BU
1990	9,990,000	—	—	2.00	7.00	—
1993	2,500,000	—	—	2.00	6.00	—

KM# 139.2 10 KORUN
Nickel-Bronze, 24.5 mm. **Obv:** CSFR above shield, date below, denomination at left **Obv. Designer:** J. Truhlikova-Spevakova **Rev:** Tomas G. Masaryk bust, right, dates at left **Rev. Designer:** M. Ronai **Note:** Designer name below bust: RONAI.

Date	Mintage	F	VF	XF	Unc	BU
1990	Inc. above	—	2.00	5.00	10.00	—

KM# 153 10 KORUN
Nickel-Bronze, 24.5 mm. **Obv:** CSFR above quartered shield, date below, denomination at left **Obv. Designer:** J. Truhlikova-Spevakova **Rev:** Uniformed bust left, dates at right **Rev. Designer:** D. Zobek

Date	Mintage	F	VF	XF	Unc	BU
1991	10,036,000	—	—	2.00	5.00	—
1993	2,500,000	—	—	2.50	6.00	—

KM# 159 10 KORUN
Nickel-Bronze, 24.5 mm. **Obv:** CSFR above quartered shield, date below, denomination at left **Obv. Designer:** J. Truhlikova-Spevakova **Rev:** Bust right, dates at left **Rev. Designer:** J. Uprka **Edge:** Eight plain and eight milled areas

Date	Mintage	F	VF	XF	Unc	BU
1992	5,050,000	—	—	2.00	5.00	—

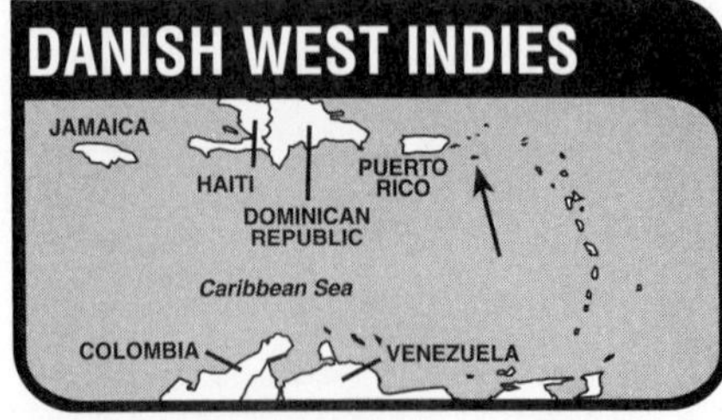

The Danish West Indies (now the U.S. organized unincorporated territory of the Virgin Islands of the United States) consisted of the islands of St. Thomas, St. John, St. Croix, and 62 islets in the Caribbean Sea roughly 40 miles (64 km.) east of Puerto Rico. The islands have a combined area of 133 sq. mi. (352 sq. km.) and a population of *106,000. Capital: Charlotte Amalie. Tourism is the principal industry. Watch movements, costume jewelry, pharmaceuticals, and rum are exported.

The Virgin Islands were discovered by Columbus, in 1493, during his second voyage to America. During the 17th century, individual islands, actually the peaks of a submerged mountain range, were held by Spain, Holland, England, France and Denmark. These islands were also the favorite resorts of the buccaneers operating in the Caribbean and the coastal waters of eastern North America. Control of most of the 100-island group finally passed to Denmark, with England securing the easterly remainder. The Danish islands had their own coinage from the early 18th century, based on but unequal to, Denmark's homeland system. In the late 18th and early 19th centuries, Danish minor copper and silver coinage augmented the islands currency. The Danish islands were purchased by the United States in 1917 for $25 million, mainly to forestall their acquisition by Germany and because they command the Anegada Passage into the Caribbean Sea, a strategic point on the defense perimeter of the Panama Canal.

RULER

Danish, until 1917

MINTMASTERS' INITIALS

Letter	Date	Name
P, VBP	1893-1918	Vilhelm Burchard Poulsen

MONEYERS' INITIALS

Letter	Date	Name
GJ	1901-1933	(Knud) Gunnar Jensen
AH	1908-1924	Andreas Frederik Vilhelm Hansen

MONETARY SYSTEM

(1904-1934)
5 Bit = 1 Cent
100 Bit = 1 Franc
5 Francs = 1 Daler

DANISH COLONY

DECIMAL COINAGE

20 Cents = 1 Franc

KM# 74 1/2 CENT (2-1/2 Bit)

Bronze **Ruler:** Christian IX **Obv:** Crowned monogram above date **Rev:** Denominations divided by trident, caduceus and sickle **Note:** Mintmaster's initial: P. Moneyer's initials: GJ.

Date	Mintage	F	VF	XF	Unc	BU
1905(h)	190,000	2.75	5.50	12.50	33.50	—
1905(h) Prooflike	—	—	—	—	—	—

Note: Specimen strike

KM# 75 CENT (5 Bit)

Bronze, 23 mm. **Ruler:** Christian IX **Rev:** Denominations divided by trident, caduceus and sickle **Note:** Mintmaster's initial: P. Moneyer's initials: GJ.

Date	Mintage	F	VF	XF	Unc	BU
1905(h)	500,000	3.50	7.50	20.00	57.50	—

KM# 83 CENT (5 Bit)

Bronze **Obv:** Crowned monogram above date **Rev:** Denominations divided by trident, caduceus and sickle **Note:** Mintmaster's initials: VBP. Moneyer's initials: AH-GJ.

Date	Mintage	F	VF	XF	Unc	BU
1913(h)	200,000	9.00	17.50	40.00	90.00	—

KM# 76 2 CENTS (10 Bit)

Bronze **Ruler:** Christian IX **Obv:** Crowned monogram above date **Rev:** Denominations divided by trident, caduceus and sickle **Note:** Mintmaster's initial: P. Moneyer's initials: GJ.

Date	Mintage	F	VF	XF	Unc	BU
1905(h)	150,000	5.00	13.50	30.00	72.50	—
1905(h) Prooflike	20	—	—	—	—	—

Note: Specimen strike

KM# 77 5 CENTS (25 Bit)

Nickel **Ruler:** Christian IX **Obv:** Crowned monogram above date **Rev:** Denominations divided by trident, caduceus and sickle **Note:** Mintmaster's initial: P. Moneyer's initials: GJ.

Date	Mintage	F	VF	XF	Unc	BU
1905(h)	199,000	3.00	7.50	18.50	64.00	—
1905(h) Prooflike	20	—	—	—	—	—

Note: Specimen strike

KM# 78 10 CENTS (50 Bit)

2.5000 g., 0.8000 Silver 0.0643 oz. ASW **Ruler:** Christian IX **Obv:** Head left **Rev:** Plant divides denominations **Note:** Mintmaster's initial: P. Moneyer's initials: GJ.

Date	Mintage	F	VF	XF	Unc	BU
1905(h)	175,000	4.00	8.50	18.50	65.00	—
1905(h) Prooflike	20	—	—	—	—	—

Note: Specimen strike

KM# 79 20 CENTS (1 Franc)

5.0000 g., 0.8000 Silver 0.1286 oz. ASW **Ruler:** Christian IX **Obv:** Uniformed bust left **Rev:** Three liberty figures divide denominations, date below **Note:** Mintmaster's initial: P. Moneyer's initials: GJ.

Date	Mintage	F	VF	XF	Unc	BU
1905(h)	150,000	12.50	27.50	70.00	140	—
1905(h) Prooflike	20	—	—	—	—	—

Note: Specimen strike

KM# 81 20 CENTS (1 Franc)

5.0000 g., 0.8000 Silver 0.1286 oz. ASW **Obv:** Head left **Rev:** Three liberty figures divide denominations, date below **Note:** Mintmaster's initial: P. Moneyer's initials: GJ.

Date	Mintage	F	VF	XF	Unc	BU
1907(h)	101,000	15.00	35.00	87.50	180	—
1907(h) Prooflike	10	—	—	—	—	—

Note: Specimen strike

KM# 80 40 CENTS (2 Francs)

10.0000 g., 0.8000 Silver 0.2572 oz. ASW **Ruler:** Christian IX **Note:** Mintmaster's initial: P. Moneyer's initials: GJ.

Date	Mintage	F	VF	XF	Unc	BU
1905(h)	38,000	30.00	60.00	160	335	—
1905(h) Prooflike	20	—	—	—	—	—

Note: Specimen strike

KM# 82 40 CENTS (2 Francs)

10.0000 g., 0.8000 Silver 0.2572 oz. ASW **Obv:** Head left **Rev:** Three liberty figures divide denominations, date below **Note:** Mintmaster's initial: P. Moneyer's initials: GJ.

Date	Mintage	F	VF	XF	Unc	BU
1907(h)	25,000	55.00	115	235	440	—
1907(h) Prooflike	10	—	—	—	—	1,100

Note: Specimen strike

KM# 72 4 DALER (20 Francs)

6.4516 g., 0.9000 Gold 0.1867 oz. AGW **Ruler:** Christian IX **Obv:** Head left **Rev:** Seated liberty figure divides denominations **Note:** Mintmaster's initial: P. Moneyer's initials: GJ.

Date	Mintage	F	VF	XF	Unc	BU
1904(h)	121,000	165	250	400	665	—
1905(h)	Inc. above	175	275	425	785	—

KM# 73 10 DALER (50 Francs)

16.1290 g., 0.9000 Gold 0.4667 oz. AGW **Ruler:** Christian IX **Obv:** Head left **Rev:** Seated liberty figure divides denominations, date below **Note:** Mintmaster's initial: P. Moneyer's initials: GJ.

Date	Mintage	F	VF	XF	Unc	BU
1904(h)	2,005	1,250	2,000	4,275	7,000	—

DANZIG

Danzig is an important seaport on the northern coast of Poland with access to the Baltic Sea. It has at different times belonged to the Teutonic Knights, Pomerania, Russia, and Prussia. It was part of the Polish Kingdom from 1587-1772.

Danzig (Gdansk) was a free city from 1919 to 1939 during which most of its modern coinage was made.

MONETARY SYSTEM

Until 1923
100 Pfennig = 1 Mark

Commencing 1923
100 Pfennig = 1 Gulden

FREE CITY

STANDARD COINAGE

KM# 140 PFENNIG
1.6300 g., Bronze, 17.03 mm. **Obv:** Denomination **Rev:** Arms divide date

Date	Mintage	F	VF	XF	Unc	BU
1923	4,000,000	1.00	3.00	5.00	10.00	18.00
1923 Proof	—	Value: 60.00				
1926	1,500,000	1.50	4.00	8.00	16.00	35.00
1929	1,000,000	2.50	7.50	12.00	20.00	40.00
1930	2,000,000	1.25	3.50	6.50	12.00	22.00
1937	3,000,000	1.25	3.50	6.50	12.00	22.00

KM# 141 2 PFENNIG
Bronze **Obv:** Denomination **Rev:** Arms divide date

Date	Mintage	F	VF	XF	Unc	BU
1923	1,000,000	1.75	4.50	7.50	15.00	35.00
1923 Proof	—	Value: 75.00				
1926	1,750,000	1.75	4.50	7.50	15.00	35.00
1937	500,000	2.75	6.50	12.50	20.00	40.00

KM# 142 5 PFENNIG
Copper-Nickel **Obv:** Denomination **Rev:** Arms divide date within snowflake design

Date	Mintage	F	VF	XF	Unc	BU
1923	3,000,000	1.25	2.75	6.00	12.50	22.50
1923 Proof	—	Value: 100				
1928	1,000,000	3.50	8.50	16.00	30.00	60.00
1928 Proof	—	Value: 175				

KM# 151 5 PFENNIG
Aluminum-Bronze **Obv:** Denomination **Rev:** Turbot left, date below

Date	Mintage	F	VF	XF	Unc	BU
1932	4,000,000	1.50	2.50	10.00	20.00	35.00

KM# 143 10 PFENNIG
Copper-Nickel **Obv:** Denomination **Rev:** Arms divide date within snowflake design

Date	Mintage	F	VF	XF	Unc	BU
1923	5,000,000	2.50	3.50	9.00	18.00	37.50
1923 Proof	—	Value: 125				

KM# 152 10 PFENNIG
Aluminum-Bronze **Obv:** Denomination **Rev:** Codfish (godus morrhua) left, date below

Date	Mintage	F	VF	XF	Unc	BU
1932	5,000,000	1.75	2.75	10.00	20.00	36.00

KM# 144 1/2 GULDEN
2.5000 g., 0.7500 Silver 0.0603 oz. ASW **Obv:** Date divided by shielded arms, denomination above **Rev:** Ship at sea

Date	Mintage	F	VF	XF	Unc	BU
1923	1,000,000	7.50	20.00	35.00	75.00	—
1923 Proof	—	Value: 150				
1927	400,000	17.50	35.00	75.00	140	—
1927 Proof	—	Value: 250				

KM# 153 1/2 GULDEN
Nickel **Obv:** Crowned vertical crosses **Rev:** Denomination above date

Date	Mintage	F	VF	XF	Unc	BU
1932	1,400,000	8.00	25.00	37.50	70.00	—

KM# 145 GULDEN
5.0000 g., 0.7500 Silver 0.1206 oz. ASW **Obv:** Ship and star divide denomination **Rev:** Shielded arms with supporters, star above, date below

Date	Mintage	F	VF	XF	Unc	BU
1923	2,500,000	12.50	27.50	40.00	95.00	—
1923 Proof	—	Value: 200				

KM# 154 GULDEN
Nickel **Obv:** Large numeric denomination within circle **Rev:** Arms divide date

Date	Mintage	F	VF	XF	Unc	BU
1932	2,500,000	8.00	25.00	35.00	60.00	90.00

KM# 146 2 GULDEN
10.0000 g., 0.7500 Silver 0.2411 oz. ASW **Obv:** Ship and star divide denomination **Rev:** Shielded arms with supporters, star above, date below

Date	Mintage	F	VF	XF	Unc	BU
1923	1,250,000	30.00	70.00	125	245	—
1923 Proof	—	Value: 325				

KM# 155 2 GULDEN
10.0000 g., 0.5000 Silver 0.1607 oz. ASW **Obv:** Ship afloat within circle, denomination below **Rev:** Shielded arms with supporters, date above

Date	Mintage	F	VF	XF	Unc	BU
1932	1,250,000	100	150	200	375	—

KM# 147 5 GULDEN
25.0000 g., 0.7500 Silver 0.6028 oz. ASW **Obv:** Marienkirche within circle **Rev:** Shielded arms with supporters, denomination below, star above

Date	Mintage	F	VF	XF	Unc	BU
1923	700,000	65.00	135	225	475	—
1923 Proof	—	Value: 550				
1927	160,000	150	250	385	675	—
1927 Proof	—	Value: 1,000				

KM# 156 5 GULDEN
14.8200 g., 0.5000 Silver 0.2382 oz. ASW **Obv:** Marienkirche within circle, denomination below **Rev:** Shielded arms with supporters, date above

Date	Mintage	F	VF	XF	Unc	BU
1932	430,000	125	225	350	950	—

KM# 157 5 GULDEN
14.8200 g., 0.5000 Silver 0.2382 oz. ASW **Obv:** Grain elevator by harbor within circle, denomination below **Rev:** Shielded arms with supporters, date above

Date	Mintage	F	VF	XF	Unc	BU
1932	430,000	150	350	850	1,500	—

KM# 158 5 GULDEN
Nickel **Obv:** Ship with three crowns asea, numeric denomination at left, circle surrounds, denomination below circle, date at right **Rev:** Arms with supporters on oval shield

Date	Mintage	F	VF	XF	Unc	BU
1935	800,000	120	180	265	500	—

KM# 159 10 GULDEN
Nickel **Obv:** Town hall tower, numeric denomination at right, circle surrounds, denomination below, date at right **Rev:** Arms with supporters on oval shield

Date	Mintage	F	VF	XF	Unc	BU
1935	380,000	300	500	750	1,400	—

DENMARK

The Kingdom of Denmark (Danmark), a constitutional monarchy located at the mouth of the Baltic Sea, has an area of 16,639 sq. mi. (43,070 sq. km.) and a population of 5.2 million. Capital: Copenhagen. Most of the country is arable. Agriculture is conducted by large farms served by cooperatives. The largest industries are food processing, iron and metal, and shipping. Machinery, meats (chiefly bacon), dairy products and chemicals are exported.

Denmark, a great power during the Viking period of the 9th-11th centuries, conducted raids on western Europe and England, and in the 11th century united England, Denmark and Norway under the rule of King Canute. Despite a struggle between the crown and the nobility (13th-14th centuries) which forced the King to grant a written constitution, Queen Margaret (Margrethe) (1387-1412) succeeded in uniting Denmark, Norway, Sweden, Finland and Greenland under the Danish crown, placing all of the Nordic countries under the rule of Denmark. An unwise alliance with Napoleon caused the loss of Norway to Sweden in 1814. In the following years a liberal movement was fostered, which succeeded in making Denmark a constitutional monarchy in 1849.

In 1864, Denmark lost Schleswig and Holstein to Prussia. In 1920, Denmark regained North-Schleswig by plebiscite.

The present decimal system of currency was introduced in 1874. As a result of a referendum held September 28, 2000, the currency of the European Monetary Union, the Euro, will not be introduced in Denmark in the foreseeable future.

RULERS

Christian IX, 1863-1906
Frederik VIII, 1906-1912
Christian X, 1912-1947
Frederik IX, 1947-1972
Margrethe II, 1972—

MINT MARKS

(h) - Copenhagen, heart

MINT OFFICIALS' INITIALS

Copenhagen

Letter	Date	Name
*P, VBP	1893-1918	Vilhelm Buchard Poulsen
HCN	1919-1927	Hans Christian Nielsen
N	1927-1955	Niels Peter Nielsen
C	1956-1971	Alfred Frederik Christiansen
S	1971-1978	Vagn Sorensen
B	1978-1981	Peter M Bjarno
R, NR	1982-1989	N. Norregaard Rasmussen
LG	1989-2001	Laust Grove

NOTE: The letter P was only used on Danish West Indies coins and on Denmark, KM#802.

MONEYERS' INITIALS

Copenhagen

Letter	Date	Name
GI, GJ	1901-1933	Knud Gunnar Jensen
AH	1908-1924	Andreas Frederik Vilhelm Hansen
HS, S	1933-1968	Harald Salomon
B	1968-1983	Frode Bahnsen
A	1986-	Johan Alkjaer (designer)
HV	1986-	Hanne Varming (sculptor)
JP	1989-	Jan Petersen

MONETARY SYSTEM

100 Øre = 1 Krone

KINGDOM

DECIMAL COINAGE

100 Øre = 1 Krone; 1874-present

KM# 792.2 ORE

2.0000 g., Bronze **Ruler:** Christian IX **Obv:** Crowned monogram **Rev:** Denomination above porpoise and barley stalk

Date	Mintage	F	VF	XF	Unc	BU
1902/802(h) VBP	2,977,000	2.75	4.50	10.00	32.50	—
1902(h) VBP	Inc. above	1.75	2.75	6.50	28.00	—
1904/804(h) VBP	4,962,000	1.75	3.50	6.25	20.00	—
1904(h) VBP	Inc. above	1.25	2.25	4.75	18.00	—

KM# 804 ORE

2.0000 g., Bronze **Ruler:** Frederik VIII **Obv:** Denomination within circle, date and initials VBP below **Rev:** Crowned F8F monogram, initials GJ at lower right **Rev. Legend:** "THE KINGDOM OF DENMARK"

Date	Mintage	F	VF	XF	Unc	BU
1907(h) VBP, GJ	5,975,000	1.25	2.75	5.50	16.00	—
1909(h) VBP, GJ	2,985,000	1.25	2.75	5.50	18.50	—
1910(h) VBP; GJ	2,994,000	1.75	4.50	12.00	30.00	—
1912(h) VBP; GJ	3,006,000	1.25	3.75	8.00	25.00	—

KM# 812.1 ORE

2.0000 g., Bronze **Ruler:** Christian X **Obv:** Crowned CX monogram, initials VBP and mint mark at lower left, date and initials GJ at lower right **Rev:** Thick denomination, ornaments flanking

Date	Mintage	F	VF	XF	Unc	BU
1913(h) VBP; GJ	5,011,000	1.00	1.50	2.00	6.00	—
1915(h) VBP; GJ	4,940,000	1.35	2.25	3.75	10.00	—
1916(h) VBP; GJ	2,439,000	1.35	2.75	5.00	14.00	—
1917(h) VBP; GJ	4,564,000	16.00	25.00	45.00	90.00	—

KM# 812.1a ORE

1.7400 g., Iron **Ruler:** Christian X **Obv:** Crowned CX monogram, initials VBP and mint mark at lower left, date and initials GJ at lower right **Rev:** Thick denomination, ornaments flanking

Date	Mintage	F	VF	XF	Unc	BU
1918(h) VBP; GJ	6,776,000	2.00	5.50	20.00	65.00	—

KM# 812.2 ORE

2.0000 g., Bronze **Ruler:** Christian X **Obv:** Crowned CX monogram, initials HCN and mint mark at lower left, date and initials GJ at lower right **Rev:** Value, ornaments flanking

Date	Mintage	F	VF	XF	Unc	BU
1919(h) HCN; GJ	4,586,000	1.00	1.50	4.00	8.50	—
1920(h) HCN; GJ	2,367,000	6.00	12.50	30.00	60.00	—
1921(h) HCN; GJ	3,121,000	1.35	2.25	3.25	8.50	—
1922(h) HCN; GJ	3,267,000	1.75	2.50	4.00	9.50	—
1923(h) HCN; GJ	2,938,000	1.75	2.50	3.75	8.50	—

KM# 812.2a ORE

1.7400 g., Iron **Ruler:** Christian X **Obv:** Crowned CX monogram, initials HCN and mint mark at lower left, date and initials GJ at lower right **Rev:** Value, ornaments flanking

Date	Mintage	F	VF	XF	Unc	BU
1919(h) HCN; GJ	931,000	5.00	15.00	42.50	110	—

KM# 826.1 ORE

1.9000 g., Bronze **Ruler:** Christian X **Obv:** Crowned CXC monogram within title "KING OF DENMARK", initials GJ below **Rev:** Country name and date above center hole, denomination, mint mark, and initials HCN below

Date	Mintage	F	VF	XF	Unc	BU
1926(h) HCN; GJ	1,572,000	3.00	6.50	20.00	65.00	—
1927(h) HCN; GJ	Inc. above	0.10	0.30	4.50	25.00	—

KM# 826.2 ORE

1.9000 g., Bronze **Ruler:** Christian X **Obv:** Crowned CXC monogram within title "KING OF DENMARK", initials GJ below **Rev:** Country name and date above center hole, denomination, mint mark, and initial N below **Note:** For coins dated 1941 refer to Faeroe Islands listings.

Date	Mintage	F	VF	XF	Unc	BU
1927(h) N; GJ	Inc. above	4.00	11.00	30.00	90.00	—
1928(h) N; GJ	29,691,000	0.10	0.25	2.75	12.50	—
1929(h) N; GJ	5,172,000	0.10	0.25	2.75	17.50	—
1930(h) N; GJ	5,306,000	0.10	0.20	2.75	20.00	—
1932(h) N; GJ	5,089,000	0.10	0.20	2.75	18.00	—
1933(h) N; GJ	2,095,000	0.25	1.50	5.50	35.00	—
1934(h) N; GJ	3,665,000	—	0.15	1.00	10.00	25.00
1935(h) N; GJ	5,668,000	—	0.15	1.00	7.00	—
1936(h) N; GJ	5,584,000	—	0.15	0.40	4.00	—
1937(h) N; GJ	6,877,000	—	0.15	0.40	3.25	—
1938(h) N; GJ	3,850,000	—	0.15	0.40	2.50	—
1939(h) N; GJ	5,662,000	—	0.15	0.30	2.50	—
1940(h) N; GJ	1,965,000	—	0.15	0.30	2.00	—

KM# 832 ORE

1.6000 g., Zinc **Ruler:** Christian X **Obv:** Crowned monogram divides date, mint mark and initials N-S below **Rev:** Oak and beech leaves divide value

Date	Mintage	F	VF	XF	Unc	BU
1941(h) N; S	21,570,000	0.10	0.30	9.00	40.00	—
1942(h) N; S	6,997,000	0.10	0.30	9.00	40.00	—
1943(h) N; S	15,082,000	0.10	0.30	9.00	40.00	—
1944(h) N; S	11,981,000	0.10	0.30	9.00	40.00	—
1945(h) N; S	916,000	1.00	2.00	20.00	60.00	—
1946(h) N; S	712,000	3.00	7.50	25.00	75.00	—

KM# 839.1 ORE

1.6000 g., Zinc, 16 mm. **Ruler:** Frederik IX **Obv:** Crowned F IX R monogram and date **Rev:** Mint mark, initials N-S below value

Date	Mintage	F	VF	XF	Unc	BU
1948(h) N; S	460,000	1.00	2.25	9.50	55.00	—
1949(h) N; S	2,513,000	0.35	0.80	3.50	45.00	—
1950(h) N; S	9,453,000	0.25	0.40	3.25	40.00	—
1951(h) N; S	2,931,000	0.35	1.00	3.50	55.00	—
1952(h) N; S	7,626,000	0.15	0.30	2.25	30.00	—
1953(h) N; S	11,994,000	0.10	0.20	2.25	30.00	—
1954(h) N; S	12,642,000	0.10	0.20	2.25	25.00	—
1955(h) N; S	14,177,000	0.10	0.20	1.75	25.00	—

KM# 839.2 ORE

1.6000 g., Zinc, 16 mm. **Ruler:** Frederik IX **Obv:** Crowned FIXR monogram and date **Rev:** Mint mark, initials C-S below value

Date	Mintage	F	VF	XF	Unc	BU
1956(h) C; S	20,211,000	0.10	0.20	0.80	7.00	—
1957(h) C; S	20,900,000	0.10	0.20	0.80	7.00	—
1958(h) C; S	16,021,000	—	0.10	0.60	6.00	—
1959(h) C; S	15,929,000	—	0.10	0.60	6.00	—
1960(h) C; S	23,982,000	—	0.10	0.60	4.00	—
1961(h) C; S	18,986,000	—	0.10	0.50	3.00	—
1962(h) C; S	16,992,000	—	0.10	0.50	1.75	—
1963(h) C; S	28,986,000	—	0.10	0.40	1.75	—
1964(h) C; S	21,971,000	—	0.10	0.40	1.75	—
1965(h) C; S	29,943,000	—	0.10	0.30	1.75	—
1966(h) C; S	35,907,000	—	0.10	0.20	1.75	—
1967(h) C; S	32,959,000	—	0.10	0.20	1.75	—
1968(h) C; S	21,889,000	—	—	0.20	0.80	—
1969(h) C; S	29,243,000	—	—	0.10	0.80	—
1970(h) C; S	22,970,000	—	—	0.10	0.50	—
1971(h) C; S	21,983,000	—	—	0.10	0.50	—

KM# 839.3 ORE

1.6000 g., Zinc, 16 mm. **Ruler:** Frederik IX **Obv:** Crowned F IX R monogram and date **Rev:** Mint mark, initials C-S below value

Date	Mintage	F	VF	XF	Unc	BU
1972(h) S; S	13,000,000	—	—	0.10	0.60	—

KM# 846 ORE

1.8000 g., Bronze **Ruler:** Frederik IX **Obv:** Crowned F IX R monogram, date **Rev:** Two barley stalks around value, initials below **Note:** Never released for circulation, see note at 2 Ore, KM#847.

Date	Mintage	F	VF	XF	Unc	BU
1960(h) C; S	8,990,000	—	—	1.00	1.50	—
1962(h) C; S	Inc. above	—	—	1.00	1.50	—
1963(h) C; S	9,980,000	—	—	1.00	1.50	—
1964(h) C; S	2,990,000	—	—	1.00	1.50	—

KM# 793.2 2 ORE

4.0000 g., Bronze **Ruler:** Christian IX **Obv:** Crowned monogram **Rev:** Denomination above porpoise and barley stalk

Date	Mintage	F	VF	XF	Unc	BU
1902/802(h) VBP	3,502,000	3.00	6.00	12.00	45.00	—
1902(h) VBP	Inc. above	1.50	3.00	6.00	37.50	—
1906(h) VBP	2,498,000	3.50	10.00	22.50	45.00	—

KM# 805 2 ORE

4.0000 g., Bronze **Ruler:** Frederik VIII **Obv:** Denomination within circle, date and initials VBP below **Rev:** Crowned F8F monogram, initials GJ at lower right

Date	Mintage	F	VF	XF	Unc	BU
1907(h) VBP; GJ	2,502,000	1.50	3.00	12.00	32.50	—

Date	Mintage	F	VF	XF	Unc	BU
1909(h) VBP; GJ	2,485,000	2.25	5.00	20.00	70.00	—
1912(h) VBP; GJ	2,480,000	2.25	5.00	14.00	45.00	—

KM# 813.1 2 ORE

4.0000 g., Bronze **Ruler:** Christian X **Obv:** Crowned CX monogram, initials VBP and mint mark at lower left, date and initials GJ at lower right **Rev:** Value, ornament flanking

Date	Mintage	F	VF	XF	Unc	BU
1913(h) VBP; GJ	373,000	27.50	50.00	85.00	220	—
1914(h) VBP; GJ	2,126,000	2.25	4.00	6.50	25.00	—
1915(h) VBP; GJ	2,485,000	1.75	4.00	6.50	27.50	—
1916(h) VBP; GJ	1,383,000	2.75	4.00	7.50	30.00	—
1917(h) VBP; GJ	1,837,000	14.00	27.50	45.00	100	135

KM# 813.1a 2 ORE

3.4700 g., Iron **Ruler:** Christian X **Obv:** Crowned CX monogram, initials VBP and mint mark at lower left, date and initials GJ at lower right **Rev:** Value, ornament flanking

Date	Mintage	F	VF	XF	Unc	BU
1918(h) VBP; GJ	4,160,999	2.25	7.50	30.00	90.00	—

KM# 813.2 2 ORE

4.0000 g., Bronze **Ruler:** Christian X **Obv:** Crowned CX monogram, initials HCN and mint mark at lower left, date and initials GJ at lower right **Rev:** Thick denomination, ornaments flanking

Date	Mintage	F	VF	XF	Unc	BU
1919(h) HCN; GJ	5,503,000	6.00	12.00	27.50	60.00	—
1920(h) HCN; GJ	2,528,000	1.00	1.50	3.50	22.50	—
1921(h) HCN; GJ	2,158,000	3.25	5.00	8.50	20.00	—
1923(h) HCN; GJ	2,625,000	2.25	4.00	7.00	20.00	—

KM# 813.2a 2 ORE

3.4700 g., Iron **Ruler:** Christian X **Obv:** Crowned CX monogram, initials HCN and mint mark at lower left, date and initials GJ at lower right **Rev:** Value, ornament flanking

Date	Mintage	F	VF	XF	Unc	BU
1919(h) HCN; GJ	1,944,000	20.00	45.00	100	250	—

KM# 827.1 2 ORE

3.8000 g., Bronze **Ruler:** Christian X **Obv:** Crowned CXC monogram within title "KING OF DENMARK", initials GJ below **Rev:** Country name and date above center hole, denomination, mint mark, and initials HCN below

Date	Mintage	F	VF	XF	Unc	BU
1926(h) HCN; GJ	301,000	42.50	80.00	250	1,050	—
1927(h) HCN; GJ	15,359,000	0.10	0.20	3.25	25.00	—

KM# 827.2 2 ORE

3.8000 g., Bronze **Ruler:** Christian X **Obv:** Crowned CXC monogram within title "KING OF DENMARK", initials GJ below **Rev:** Country name and date above center hole, denomination, mint mark, and initial N below **Note:** For coins dated 1941 refer to Faeroe Islands listings.

Date	Mintage	F	VF	XF	Unc	BU
1927(h) N; GJ	Inc. above	1.00	2.25	55.00	190	290
1928(h) N; GJ	5,758,000	0.10	0.20	2.50	22.50	50.00
1929(h) N; GJ	6,817,000	0.10	0.20	2.50	42.50	—
1930(h) N; GJ	2,327,000	0.75	1.50	8.50	80.00	—
1931(h) N; GJ	5,135,000	0.10	0.20	2.25	30.00	55.00
1932(h) N; GJ	Inc. above	1.25	2.25	35.00	150	—
1934(h) N; GJ	756,000	0.50	1.00	8.00	42.50	—
1935(h) N; GJ	1,391,000	0.10	0.20	2.00	27.50	—
1936(h) N; GJ	2,973,000	0.10	0.20	1.00	25.00	—
1937(h) N; GJ	3,437,000	0.10	0.20	1.00	12.50	—
1938(h) N; GJ	2,177,000	—	0.10	0.50	5.50	—
1939(h) N; GJ	3,165,000	—	0.10	0.50	3.25	—
1940(h) N; GJ	1,582,000	—	0.10	0.50	2.25	—

KM# 833 2 ORE

1.2000 g., Aluminum **Ruler:** Christian X **Obv:** Crowned CX monogram and date within title: "KING OF DENMARK"; mint mark and initials N-S below **Rev:** Oak and beach leaves divide value

Date	Mintage	F	VF	XF	Unc	BU
1941(h) N; S	26,205,000	0.10	0.60	2.25	14.00	—
1941(h) N; S Proof	—	Value: 150				

KM# 833a 2 ORE

3.2000 g., Zinc **Ruler:** Christian X **Obv:** Crowned CX monogram divides date, mint mark and initials N-S below **Rev:** Oak and beach leaves divide value

Date	Mintage	F	VF	XF	Unc	BU
1942(h) N; S	12,934,000	0.10	0.40	10.00	55.00	—
1943(h) N; S	9,603,000	0.10	0.40	10.00	55.00	—
1944(h) N; S	6,069,000	0.10	0.40	10.00	55.00	—
1945(h) N; S	329,000	4.25	8.50	45.00	120	—
1947(h) N; S	589,000	1.50	3.00	22.50	90.00	—

KM# 840.1 2 ORE

3.2000 g., Zinc, 20.8 mm. **Ruler:** Frederik IX **Obv:** Crowned F IX R monogram and date **Rev:** Mint mark, initials N-S below value

Date	Mintage	F	VF	XF	Unc	BU
1948(h) N; S	1,927,000	0.40	1.00	6.50	55.00	—
1949(h) N; S	1,603,000	3.75	14.50	60.00	250	—
1950(h) N; S	4,544,000	0.75	1.35	6.50	60.00	—
1951(h) N; S	3,766,000	1.50	2.50	12.50	95.00	—
1952(h) N; S	4,874,000	0.10	0.20	2.50	45.00	—
1953(h) N; S	8,112,000	0.10	0.20	2.50	35.00	—
1954(h) N; S	6,497,000	0.10	0.20	2.50	25.00	—
1955(h) N; S	6,968,000	—	0.10	1.50	15.00	—

KM# 840.2 2 ORE

3.2000 g., Zinc, 20.8 mm. **Ruler:** Frederik IX **Obv:** Crowned FR monogram divides date, IX below **Rev:** Mint mark, initials C-S below value

Date	Mintage	F	VF	XF	Unc	BU
1956(h) C; S	10,004,000	—	0.10	1.00	7.50	—
1957(h) C; S	15,329,000	—	0.10	1.00	6.00	—
1958(h) C; S	8,119,999	—	0.10	1.00	5.00	—
1959(h) C; S	10,462,000	—	0.10	1.00	4.00	—
1960(h) C; S	16,504,000	—	0.10	0.80	3.00	—
1961(h) C; S	15,504,000	—	0.10	0.80	2.50	—
1962(h) C; S	10,980,000	—	0.10	0.80	2.50	—
1963(h) C; S	19,470,000	—	0.10	0.30	1.50	—
1964(h) C; S	15,411,000	—	0.10	0.30	1.00	—
1965(h) C; S	20,173,000	—	0.10	0.20	1.00	—
1966(h) C; S	21,949,000	—	0.10	0.20	1.00	—
1967(h) C; S	22,439,000	—	0.10	0.20	1.00	—
1968(h) C; S	17,632,000	—	—	0.10	0.80	—
1969(h) C; S	29,276,000	—	—	0.10	0.80	—
1970(h) C; S	23,864,000	—	—	0.10	0.50	—
1971(h) C; S	35,811,000	—	—	0.10	0.50	—

KM# 847 2 ORE

3.6000 g., Bronze **Ruler:** Frederik IX **Obv:** Crowned F IX R monogram, date **Rev:** Two barley stalks around value, mint mark and initials C-S below **Note:** KM#847 was never released for circulation. Together with the 4 dates of 1 Øre, KM#846, they were sold as a 10 coin set to collectors by the mint. Approximately 100,000 sets were sold, remaining coins were melted. The date 1963 was produced eclusively

Date	Mintage	F	VF	XF	Unc	BU
1960(h) C; S	Inc. above	—	—	1.00	1.50	—
1962(h) C; S	Inc. above	—	—	1.00	1.50	—
1963(h) C; S	100,000	—	—	1.00	1.50	—
1964(h) C; S	3,990,000	—	—	1.00	1.50	—
1965(h) C; S	11,980,000	—	—	1.00	1.50	—
1966(h) C; S	12,000,000	—	—	1.00	1.50	—

KM# 840.3 2 ORE

3.2000 g., Zinc **Ruler:** Frederik IX **Obv:** Crowned F IX R monogram and date **Rev:** Mint mark, initials S-S below value

Date	Mintage	F	VF	XF	Unc	BU
1972(h) S; S	6,496,000	—	0.15	0.30	0.85	—

KM# 794.2 5 ORE

8.0000 g., Bronze **Ruler:** Christian IX **Obv:** Crowned monogram **Rev:** Value above porpoise and barley stalk

Date	Mintage	F	VF	XF	Unc	BU
1902(h) VBP	601,000	12.50	25.00	47.50	140	—
1904(h) VBP	397,000	25.00	50.00	125	275	—
1906(h) VBP	1,000,000	17.50	40.00	85.00	200	—

KM# 806 5 ORE

8.0000 g., Bronze **Ruler:** Frederik VIII **Obv:** Crowned F VIII F monogram, initials VBP at lower right **Rev:** Value within circle, date and initials VP below

Date	Mintage	F	VF	XF	Unc	BU
1907(h) VBP; GJ	1,000,000	8.00	15.00	40.00	95.00	—
1908(h) VBP; GJ	1,198,000	9.00	17.00	45.00	105	—
1912(h) VBP; GJ	999,000	10.00	19.00	50.00	120	160

KM# 814.1 5 ORE

8.0000 g., Bronze **Ruler:** Christian X **Obv:** Crowned CX monogram, initials VBP and mint mark lower at left, date and initials GJ at lower right **Rev:** Thick value, ornaments flanking

Date	Mintage	F	VF	XF	Unc	BU
1913(h) VBP; GJ	216,000	60.00	110	150	275	425
1914(h) VBP; GJ	785,000	8.00	16.00	20.00	45.00	—
1916(h) VBP; GJ	887,000	10.00	20.00	30.00	60.00	—
1917(h) VBP; GJ	494,000	12.50	30.00	50.00	100	250

KM# 814.1a 5 ORE

6.9400 g., Iron **Ruler:** Christian X **Obv:** Crowned CX monogram, initials VBP and mint mark at lower left, date and initials GJ at lower right **Rev:** Value, ornament flanking

Date	Mintage	F	VF	XF	Unc	BU
1918(h) VBP; GJ	1,918,000	8.00	16.00	45.00	140	—

KM# 814.2 5 ORE

8.0000 g., Bronze **Ruler:** Christian X **Obv:** Crowned CX monogram, initials HCN and mint mark at lower left, date and initials GJ at lower right **Rev:** Thick value, ornaments flanking

Date	Mintage	F	VF	XF	Unc	BU
1919(h) HCN; GJ	994,000	3.25	5.50	8.50	22.50	—
1920(h) HCN; GJ	2,618,000	7.00	13.50	22.50	45.00	—
1921(h) HCN; GJ	3,248,000	4.50	8.00	11.50	25.00	—
1923(h) HCN; GJ	369,000	85.00	175	240	425	—

KM# 814.2a 5 ORE

6.9400 g., Iron **Ruler:** Christian X **Obv:** Crowned CX monogram, initials HCN and mint mark at lower left, date and initials GJ at lower right **Rev:** Value, ornament flanking

Date	Mintage	F	VF	XF	Unc	BU
1919(h) HCN; GJ	1,034,999	25.00	75.00	140	300	—

KM# 828.1 5 ORE

7.6000 g., Bronze, 27.4 mm. **Ruler:** Christian X **Obv:** Crowned CXC monogram within title "KING OF DENMARK", initials GJ below **Rev:** Country name and date above center hole, denomination, mint mark, and initials HCN below

Date	Mintage	F	VF	XF	Unc	BU
1927(h) HCN; GJ	7,129,000	0.10	0.25	3.50	30.00	—

KM# 828.2 5 ORE

7.6000 g., Bronze **Ruler:** Christian X **Obv:** Crowned CXC monogram within title "KING OF DENMARK", initials GJ below **Rev:** Country name and date above center hole, denomination, mint mark, and initial N below **Note:** For coins dated 1941 refer to Faeroe Islands.

Date	Mintage	F	VF	XF	Unc	BU
1927(h) N; GJ	Inc. above	4.00	8.00	90.00	700	1,000
1928(h) N; GJ	4,685,000	0.10	0.40	3.50	32.50	—
1929(h) N; GJ	1,387,000	0.30	0.60	5.00	75.00	—
1930(h) N; GJ	1,339,000	0.40	0.80	15.00	80.00	—
1932(h) N; GJ	1,010,999	0.30	0.60	9.50	75.00	100
1932(h) N; GJ Proof	—	Value: 150				
1934(h) N; GJ	524,000	0.30	0.60	8.00	55.00	—
1935(h) N; GJ	1,124,000	2.25	4.50	27.50	125	—
1936(h) N; GJ	1,091,000	0.20	0.40	3.25	37.50	—
1937(h) N; GJ	1,209,000	0.20	0.40	1.50	25.00	—
1938(h) N; GJ	1,093,000	0.40	1.00	2.25	15.00	—
1939(h) N; GJ	1,402,000	0.15	0.20	0.50	4.25	—
1940(h) N; GJ	2,735,000	0.15	0.20	0.50	4.25	—

KM# 834 5 ORE

2.4000 g., Aluminum **Ruler:** Christian X **Obv:** Crowned CX monogram divides date, mint mark and initials N-S below **Rev:** Oak and beech leaves divide value

Date	Mintage	F	VF	XF	Unc	BU
1941(h) N; S	16,984,000	0.10	1.00	3.75	20.00	—
1941(h) N; S Proof	—	Value: 150				

KM# 834a 5 ORE

6.4000 g., Zinc **Ruler:** Christian X **Obv:** Crowned CX monogram and date within title: "KING OF DENMARK"; mint mark and initials N-S below **Rev:** Value between oak and beech leaves

Date	Mintage	F	VF	XF	Unc	BU
1942(h) N; S	2,963,000	1.50	3.00	30.00	90.00	—
1943(h) N; S	4,522,000	0.50	1.75	22.50	75.00	—
1944(h) N; S	3,744,000	0.60	2.00	22.50	75.00	—
1945(h) N; S	864,000	4.00	10.00	45.00	125	—

KM# 843.1 5 ORE

6.4000 g., Zinc **Ruler:** Frederik IX **Obv:** Crowned FIXR monogram, IX, and date **Rev:** Mint mark, initials N-S below value

Date	Mintage	F	VF	XF	Unc	BU
1950(h) N; S	657,000	6.00	12.50	50.00	120	—
1951(h) N; S Straight 5	1,858,000	1.25	3.00	14.00	60.00	—
1951(h) N; S Slant 5	Inc. above	1.00	2.50	12.00	55.00	—
1952(h) N; S	3,562,000	0.60	1.00	6.50	35.00	—
1953(h) N; S	5,944,000	0.60	1.00	4.50	30.00	—
1954(h) N; S	3,060,000	0.40	1.25	4.00	25.00	—
1955(h) N; S	2,314,000	1.00	2.00	6.00	25.00	—

KM# 843.2 5 ORE

6.4000 g., Zinc **Ruler:** Frederik IX **Obv:** Crowned FR monogram, IX below, divides date **Rev:** Mint mark, initials C-S below value

Date	Mintage	F	VF	XF	Unc	BU
1956(h) C; S	5,888,000	0.40	1.25	2.75	11.00	—
1957(h) C; S	8,606,000	0.20	0.50	1.50	6.50	—
1958(h) C; S	9,598,000	0.20	0.50	1.50	5.50	—
1959(h) C; S	6,110,000	0.10	0.20	1.00	5.50	—
1960(h) C; S	11,800,000	0.10	0.20	1.00	3.50	—
1961(h) C; S	8,995,000	0.20	0.40	1.00	2.75	—
1962(h) C; S	9,729,000	0.10	0.20	0.80	2.75	—
1963(h) C; S	8,980,000	0.10	0.20	0.80	2.50	—
1964(h) C; S	6,738,000	0.75	1.25	3.50	7.00	—

KM# 848.1 5 ORE

6.0000 g., Bronze, 24 mm. **Ruler:** Frederik IX **Obv:** Crowned FR monogram, IX below, divides date **Rev:** Two barley stalks around denomination, initials C-S below

Date	Mintage	F	VF	XF	Unc	BU
1960(h) C; S	3,760,000	0.10	0.25	1.25	6.00	—
1962(h) C; S	5,873,000	0.25	0.75	2.25	20.00	—
1963(h) C; S	23,287,000	—	0.10	0.50	2.75	—
1964(h) C; S	41,521,000	—	0.10	0.50	2.75	—
1965(h) C; S	14,229,000	—	0.10	0.50	2.75	—
1966(h) C; S	23,410,000	—	0.10	0.50	2.75	—
1967(h) C; S	15,094,000	—	0.10	0.50	2.75	—
1968(h) C; S	16,105,000	—	0.10	0.40	1.75	—
1969(h) C; S	23,594,000	—	0.10	0.30	1.00	—
1970(h) C; S	26,176,000	—	—	0.10	1.00	—
1971(h) C; S	10,076,000	—	—	0.10	1.00	—

KM# 848.2 5 ORE

6.0000 g., Bronze, 24 mm. **Ruler:** Frederik IX **Obv:** Crowned F IX R monogram, date **Rev:** Two barley stalks around value, initials S-S below

Date	Mintage	F	VF	XF	Unc	BU
1972(h) S; S	27,938,000	—	—	0.10	1.00	—

KM# 859.1 5 ORE

1.6000 g., Copper Clad Iron, 15.5 mm. **Ruler:** Margrethe II **Obv:** Crowned MIIR monogram divides date; mint mark, initials S-B **Rev:** "DANMARK" above denomination

Date	Mintage	F	VF	XF	Unc	BU
1973(h) S; B	75,138,000	—	—	0.10	0.70	—
1974(h) S; B	71,796,000	—	—	0.10	0.70	—
1975(h) S; B	45,004,000	—	—	0.10	0.70	—
1976(h) S; B	73,296,000	—	—	0.10	0.70	—
1977(h) S; B	74,066,000	—	—	0.10	0.70	—
1978(h) S; B	52,425,000	—	—	0.10	0.70	—

KM# 859.2 5 ORE

1.6000 g., Copper Clad Iron, 15.5 mm. **Ruler:** Margrethe II **Obv:** Crowned MIIR monogram divides date; mint mark, initials B-B **Rev:** "DANMARK" above denomination

Date	Mintage	F	VF	XF	Unc	BU
1979(h) B; B	58,953,000	—	—	0.10	0.70	—
1980(h) B; B	54,362,000	—	—	0.10	0.70	—
1981(h) B; B	52,201,000	—	—	0.10	0.35	—

KM# 859.3 5 ORE

1.6000 g., Copper Clad Iron, 15.5 mm. **Ruler:** Margrethe II **Obv:** Crowned MIIR monogram divides date; mint mark, initials R-B **Rev:** "DANMARK" above value

Date	Mintage	F	VF	XF	Unc	BU
1982(h) R; B	74,296,000	—	—	0.10	0.30	—
1983(h) R; B	70,655,000	—	—	0.10	0.30	—
1984(h) R; B	27,599,000	—	—	0.10	0.30	—
1985(h) R; B	56,676,000	—	—	0.10	0.30	—
1986(h) R; B	62,496,000	—	—	0.10	0.30	—
1987(h) R; B	71,798,000	—	—	0.10	0.30	—
1988(h) R; B	48,925,000	—	—	0.10	0.30	—

KM# 795.2 10 ORE

1.4500 g., 0.4000 Silver 0.0186 oz. ASW **Ruler:** Christian IX **Obv:** Head right **Rev:** Denomination above porpoise and barley stalk, star at top

Date	Mintage	F	VF	XF	Unc	BU
1903/803(h) VBP	3,007,000	4.50	8.00	15.00	35.00	—
1903(h) VBP	Inc. above	3.00	6.00	12.00	27.50	—
1904(h) VBP	2,449,000	20.00	30.00	47.50	95.00	—
1905(h) VBP	1,571,000	2.50	5.00	10.00	27.50	—

KM# 807 10 ORE

1.4500 g., 0.4000 Silver 0.0186 oz. ASW **Ruler:** Frederik VIII **Obv:** Head left, initials GJ below **Rev:** Value, date, mint mark, initials VBP within circle, lily ornamentation surrounds

Date	Mintage	F	VF	XF	Unc	BU
1907(h) VBP; GJ	3,068,000	3.25	5.50	11.50	30.00	50.00
1910(h) VBP; GJ	2,530,000	3.25	5.50	10.00	27.50	—
1911(h) VBP; GJ	579,000	27.50	45.00	70.00	140	—
1912(h) VBP; GJ	1,951,000	3.75	7.00	12.00	30.00	—

KM# 818.1 10 ORE

1.4500 g., 0.4000 Silver 0.0186 oz. ASW **Ruler:** Christian X **Obv:** Crowned CX monogram, initials VBP and mint mark at lower left, date and initials GJ at lower right **Rev:** Value, ornaments flanking

Date	Mintage	F	VF	XF	Unc	BU
1914(h) VBP; GJ	2,128,000	4.00	7.00	11.00	22.50	35.00
1915(h) VBP; GJ	915,000	5.50	10.00	14.00	25.00	—
1916(h) VBP; GJ	2,699,000	4.00	7.00	11.50	20.00	—
1917(h) VBP; GJ	6,003,000	2.25	4.00	6.00	12.50	—
1918(h) VBP; GJ	5,042,000	1.35	2.50	4.25	4.00	—

KM# 818.2 10 ORE

1.4500 g., 0.4000 Silver 0.0186 oz. ASW **Ruler:** Christian X **Obv:** Crowned CX monogram, initials HCN and mint mark at lower left, date and initials GJ at lower right **Rev:** Value, ornament flanking

Date	Mintage	F	VF	XF	Unc	BU
1919(h) HCN; GJ	10,184,000	1.00	1.50	2.75	4.75	—

KM# 818.2a 10 ORE

1.5000 g., Copper-Nickel, 15 mm. **Ruler:** Christian X **Obv:** Crowned CX monogram, initials HCN and mint mark at lower left, date and initials GJ at lower right **Rev:** Value, ornaments flanking

Date	Mintage	F	VF	XF	Unc	BU
1920(h) HCN; GJ	10,234,000	2.75	4.00	9.50	40.00	—
1921(h) HCN; GJ	8,064,000	2.75	3.75	8.00	32.50	—
1922(h) HCN; GJ	3,065,000	20.00	30.00	50.00	95.00	—
1923(h) HCN; GJ	1,790,000	325	475	650	900	—

KM# 822.1 10 ORE

3.0000 g., Copper-Nickel **Ruler:** Christian X **Obv:** Crowned CXR monogram around center hole, date, mint mark and initials HCN-GJ below hole **Rev:** Center hole flanked by spiral ornamentation dividing value

Date	Mintage	F	VF	XF	Unc	BU
1924(h) HCN; GJ	14,661,000	0.25	1.50	3.00	20.00	—
1925(h) HCN; G	8,678,000	0.30	1.50	8.00	40.00	—
1925(h) HCN; GJ	—	—	—	—	—	—
1926(h) HCN; GJ	4,107,000	0.30	1.50	8.00	45.00	—

KM# 822.2 10 ORE

3.0000 g., Copper-Nickel **Ruler:** Christian X **Obv:** Crowned CXR monogram around center hole, date, mint mark and initial N-GJ below hole **Rev:** Center hole flanked by spiral ornamentation dividing value **Note:** For coins dated 1941 without mint mark or initials refer to Faeroe Islands listings.

Date	Mintage	F	VF	XF	Unc	BU
1929(h) N; GJ	5,037,000	0.75	1.25	8.00	45.00	—
1931(h) N; GJ Large N	Inc. above	1.35	2.50	11.00	55.00	—
1931(h) N; GJ Small N	3,054,000	1.35	2.50	11.00	55.00	—
1933(h) N; GJ	1,274,000	7.50	15.00	35.00	90.00	—
1934(h) N; GJ	2,013,000	1.00	2.50	8.00	30.00	—
1935(h) N; GJ	2,848,000	1.35	2.50	7.00	27.50	—
1936(h) N; GJ	3,320,000	1.35	2.50	6.00	45.00	—
1937(h) N; GJ	2,234,000	1.00	1.75	6.00	20.00	—
1938(h) N; GJ	2,991,000	1.75	3.00	5.50	17.50	—
1939(h) N; GJ	2,973,000	1.00	2.00	5.50	17.50	—
1940(h) N; GJ	2,998,000	0.50	1.00	2.00	12.50	—
1941(h) N; GJ	748,000	2.75	4.50	8.00	20.00	—
1946(h) N; GJ	460,000	2.50	4.25	6.00	10.00	—
1947(h) N; GJ	1,292,000	85.00	115	170	230	—

KM# 822.2a 10 ORE

2.4000 g., Zinc **Ruler:** Christian X **Obv:** Crowned CXR monogram around center hole, date, mint mark and initials N-GJ below hole **Rev:** Center hole flanked by spiral ornamentation dividing value

Date	Mintage	F	VF	XF	Unc	BU
1941(h) N; GJ	7,706,000	1.00	2.00	14.00	40.00	—
1942(h) N; GJ	8,676,000	1.00	2.00	14.00	40.00	—
1943(h) N; GJ	2,181,000	1.75	3.25	15.00	42.50	—
1944(h) N; GJ	7,994,000	1.35	2.50	10.00	32.50	—
1945(h) N; GJ	1,280,000	45.00	70.00	110	225	325

KM# 841.1 10 ORE

3.0000 g., Copper-Nickel, 18 mm. **Ruler:** Frederik IX **Obv:** Crowned FIXR monogram divides date, oak and beech branches below **Rev:** Denomination, country name, mint mark, initials N-S

Date	Mintage	F	VF	XF	Unc	BU
1948(h) N; S	5,317,000	0.20	0.60	4.00	25.00	—
1949(h) N; S	7,595,000	0.10	0.20	3.00	22.50	—
1950(h) N; S	6,886,000	0.10	0.20	3.00	20.00	—
1951(h) N; S	8,763,000	0.10	0.20	4.00	30.00	—
1952(h) N; S	6,810,000	0.10	0.20	3.00	22.50	—
1953(h) N; S	11,946,000	0.10	0.20	3.00	20.00	—
1954(h) N; S	19,739,000	—	0.10	1.50	10.00	—
1955(h) N; S	17,623,000	—	0.10	1.50	10.00	—

KM# 841.2 10 ORE

3.0000 g., Copper-Nickel, 18 mm. **Ruler:** Frederik IX **Obv:** Crowned FIXR monogram divides date, oak and beech branches below **Rev:** Denomination, country name, mint mark, initials C-S

Date	Mintage	F	VF	XF	Unc	BU
1956(h) C; S	12,323,000	—	0.10	2.25	12.50	—
1957(h) C; S	13,227,000	—	0.10	1.00	6.50	—
1958(h) C; S	10,870,000	—	0.10	1.00	6.50	—
1959(h) C; S	1,255,000	30.00	45.00	65.00	140	—
1960(h) C; S	5,107,000	0.10	0.30	1.00	4.25	—

KM# 849.1 10 ORE

3.0000 g., Copper-Nickel, 18 mm. **Ruler:** Frederik IX **Obv:** Crowned FIXR monogram divides date, mint mark and initials C-S below **Rev:** Denomination, country name above oak branches

Date	Mintage	F	VF	XF	Unc	BU
1960(h) C; S	Inc. above	0.10	0.30	0.75	4.00	—
1961(h) C; S	20,258,000	—	0.15	0.40	5.00	—
1962(h) C; S	12,785,000	—	0.15	0.40	5.00	—
1963(h) C; S	17,171,000	—	0.15	0.40	4.00	—
1964(h) C; S	14,282,000	—	0.15	0.40	3.25	—
1965(h) C; S	21,857,000	—	0.15	0.40	3.25	—
1966(h) C; S	24,160,000	—	0.15	0.20	2.75	—
1967(h) C; S	21,544,000	—	0.15	0.20	1.75	—
1968(h) C; S	7,586,000	—	0.15	0.20	1.50	—
1969(h) C; S	31,534,000	—	—	0.10	1.00	—
1970(h) C; S	37,813,000	—	—	0.10	0.30	—
1971(h) C; S	17,719,000	—	—	0.10	0.30	—

KM# 849.2 10 ORE

3.0000 g., Copper-Nickel, 18 mm. **Ruler:** Frederik IX **Obv:** Crowned FIXR above mint mark and initials S-S **Rev:** Value, country name above oak branches

Date	Mintage	F	VF	XF	Unc	BU
1972(h) S; S	46,959,000	—	—	0.10	0.30	—

KM# 860.1 10 ORE

3.0000 g., Copper-Nickel, 18 mm. **Ruler:** Margrethe II **Obv:** Crowned MIIR monogram divides date, mint mark and initials S-B below **Rev:** Value flanked by oak leaves

Date	Mintage	F	VF	XF	Unc	BU
1973(h) S; B	37,538,000	—	—	0.10	0.30	—
1974(h) S; B	38,570,000	—	—	0.10	0.30	—
1975(h) S; B	62,633,000	—	—	0.10	0.50	—
1976(h) S; B	64,358,999	—	—	0.10	0.50	—
1977(h) S; B	61,994,000	—	—	0.10	0.50	—
1978(h) S; B	30,302,000	—	—	0.10	0.50	—

KM# 860.2 10 ORE

3.0000 g., Copper-Nickel, 18 mm. **Ruler:** Margrethe II **Obv:** Crowned MIIR monogram divides date, mint mark and initials B-B below **Rev:** Value flanked by oak leaves

Date	Mintage	F	VF	XF	Unc	BU
1979(h) B; B	10,224,000	—	—	0.10	0.30	—
1980(h) B; B	37,233,000	—	—	0.10	0.30	—
1981(h) B; B	51,565,000	—	—	0.10	0.20	—

KM# 860.3 10 ORE

3.0000 g., Copper-Nickel, 18 mm. **Ruler:** Margrethe II **Obv:** Crowned MIIR monogram divides date, mint mark and initials R-B below **Rev:** Value flanked by oak leaves

Date	Mintage	F	VF	XF	Unc	BU
1982(h) R; B	40,195,000	—	—	0.10	0.20	—
1983(h) R; B	35,634,000	—	—	0.10	0.20	—
1984(h) R; B	17,828,000	—	—	0.10	0.20	—
1985(h) R; B	29,317,000	—	—	0.10	0.20	—
1986(h) R; B	46,254,000	—	—	0.10	0.20	—
1987(h) R; B	27,898,000	—	—	0.10	0.20	—
1988(h) R; B	29,400,000	—	—	0.10	0.20	—

KM# 796.2 25 ORE

2.4200 g., 0.6000 Silver 0.0467 oz. ASW **Ruler:** Christian IX **Obv:** Head right **Rev:** Value above porpoise and barley stalk, star at top

Date	Mintage	F	VF	XF	Unc	BU
1904(h) VBP	1,922,000	15.00	30.00	45.00	105	—
1905/805(h) VBP	1,722,000	10.00	17.50	40.00	70.00	—
1905(h) VBP	Inc. above	7.00	12.50	30.00	57.50	—

KM# 808 25 ORE

2.4200 g., 0.6000 Silver 0.0467 oz. ASW **Ruler:** Frederik VIII **Obv:** Head left, initials GJ below **Rev:** Value, date, mint mark, initials VBP within circle, lily ornamentation surrounds

Date	Mintage	F	VF	XF	Unc	BU
1907(h) VBP; GJ	2,009,000	6.00	11.00	20.00	50.00	—
1911(h) VBP; GJ	2,015,000	6.00	11.00	20.00	50.00	—

KM# 815.1 25 ORE

2.4200 g., 0.6000 Silver 0.0467 oz. ASW **Ruler:** Christian X **Obv:** Crowned CX monogram, initials VBP and mint mark lower left, date and initials GJ lower right **Rev:** Value, ornaments flanking

Date	Mintage	F	VF	XF	Unc	BU
1913(h) VBP; GJ	2,016,000	4.00	7.50	12.50	25.00	—
1914(h) VBP; GJ	347,000	95.00	150	210	325	—
1915(h) VBP; GJ	2,862,000	3.25	6.00	10.00	20.00	—
1916(h) VBP; GJ	938,000	10.00	16.00	27.50	40.00	—
1917(h) VBP; GJ	1,354,000	42.50	70.00	105	170	—
1918(h) VBP; GJ	2,089,999	6.00	9.50	15.00	23.00	—

KM# 815.2 25 ORE

2.4200 g., 0.6000 Silver 0.0467 oz. ASW **Ruler:** Christian X **Obv:** Crowned CX monogram, initials HCN and mint mark lower left, date and initials GJ lower right **Rev:** Value, ornament flanking

Date	Mintage	F	VF	XF	Unc	BU
1919(h) HCN; GJ	9,295,000	1.25	2.00	3.00	6.00	—

KM# 815.2a 25 ORE

2.4000 g., Copper-Nickel **Ruler:** Christian X **Obv:** Crowned CX monogram, initials HCN and mint mark lower left, date and initials GJ lower right **Rev:** Value, ornament flanking

Date	Mintage	F	VF	XF	Unc	BU
1920(h) HCN; GJ	12,288,000	3.00	5.00	16.00	50.00	—
1921(h) HCN; GJ	9,444,000	2.50	4.00	16.00	50.00	—
1922(h) HCN; GJ	5,701,000	32.50	45.00	65.00	110	—

KM# 823.1 25 ORE

4.5000 g., Copper-Nickel **Ruler:** Christian X **Obv:** Crowned CXR monogram around center hole, date, mint mark and initials HCN-GJ below hole **Rev:** Center hole flanked by designs divide value

Date	Mintage	F	VF	XF	Unc	BU
1924(h) HCN; GJ	8,035,000	0.30	1.75	4.50	17.50	—
1925(h) HCN; GJ	1,906,000	5.00	9.00	20.00	70.00	240
1926(h) HCN; GJ	2,659,000	1.50	2.75	8.00	50.00	—

KM# 823.2 25 ORE

4.5000 g., Copper-Nickel **Ruler:** Christian X **Obv:** Crowned CXR monogram around center hole, date, mint mark and initials N-GJ below hole **Rev:** Center hole flanked by spiral ornamentations dividing value **Note:** For coins dated 1941 refer to Faeroe Islands listings.

Date	Mintage	F	VF	XF	Unc	BU
1929(h) N; GJ	886,000	1.75	3.75	10.00	50.00	—
1930(h) N; GJ	3,423,000	2.25	4.50	15.00	60.00	—
1932(h) N; GJ	846,000	8.50	12.50	22.50	75.00	—
1933(h) N; GJ	479,000	30.00	42.50	60.00	140	—
1934(h) N; GJ	1,660,000	2.75	5.50	15.00	55.00	—
1935(h) N; GJ	1,032,000	12.50	25.00	42.50	95.00	—
1936(h) N; GJ	1,453,000	1.75	2.75	7.50	37.50	—
1937(h) N; GJ	1,612,000	3.25	5.50	9.50	25.00	—
1938(h) N; GJ	1,794,000	2.75	4.00	8.00	25.00	—
1939(h) N; GJ	1,972,000	12.50	22.50	37.50	75.00	—
1940(h) N; GJ	1,356,000	1.35	2.25	4.00	15.00	—
1946(h) N; GJ	2,323,000	1.25	2.75	4.00	10.00	—
1947(h) N; GJ	1,751,000	5.00	10.00	16.00	25.00	—

KM# 823.2a 25 ORE

3.6000 g., Zinc **Ruler:** Christian X **Obv:** Crowned CXR monogram around center hole, date, mint mark and initials N-GJ below hole **Rev:** Center hole flanked by spiral ornamentations dividing value

Date	Mintage	F	VF	XF	Unc	BU
1941(h) N; GJ	15,332,000	4.00	7.50	20.00	50.00	—
1942(h) N; GJ	997,000	1.50	3.50	12.50	40.00	—
1943(h) N; GJ	5,784,000	4.00	9.00	20.00	45.00	—
1944(h) N; GJ	10,665,000	1.50	4.00	12.50	40.00	60.00
1945(h) N; GJ	4,543,000	2.50	5.00	12.50	40.00	60.00

KM# 842.1 25 ORE

4.5000 g., Copper-Nickel, 23 mm. **Ruler:** Frederik IX **Obv:** Crowned FIXR monogram divides value, oak and beech branches below **Rev:** Value, country name, mint mark, initials N-S

Date	Mintage	F	VF	XF	Unc	BU
1948(h) N; S	1,853,000	2.25	5.00	10.00	55.00	—
1949(h) N; S	15,000,000	0.20	0.50	2.25	17.50	—
1950(h) N; S	13,771,000	0.20	0.50	3.75	30.00	—
1951(h) N; S	5,045,000	0.20	0.50	4.50	35.00	—
1952(h) N; S	2,017,999	0.75	3.00	14.00	45.00	—
1953(h) N; S	9,553,000	0.20	0.50	2.25	11.00	—
1954(h) N; S	11,337,000	0.20	0.50	1.50	6.50	—
1955(h) N; S	6,385,000	0.20	0.50	1.50	6.50	—

KM# 842.2 25 ORE

4.5000 g., Copper-Nickel, 23 mm. **Ruler:** Frederik IX **Obv:** Crowned FIXR monogram divides date, oak and beech branches below **Rev:** Value, country name, mint mark, initials C-S

Date	Mintage	F	VF	XF	Unc	BU
1956(h) C; S	10,228,000	0.20	0.50	1.00	5.50	—
1957(h) C; S	7,421,000	0.20	0.50	0.75	4.50	—
1958(h) C; S	3,600,000	0.30	0.60	1.00	5.00	—
1959(h) C; S	2,211,000	2.25	4.25	7.00	11.00	20.00
1960(h) C; S	3,453,000	0.30	0.60	1.25	6.00	—

KM# 850 25 ORE

4.5000 g., Copper-Nickel, 23 mm. **Ruler:** Frederik IX **Obv:** Crowned FIXR monogram divides date, oak and beech branches below **Rev:** Value, country name, mint mark, initials C-S

Date	Mintage	F	VF	XF	Unc	BU
1960(h) C; S	Inc. above	6.50	11.00	15.00	27.50	—
1961(h) C; S	20,860,000	0.20	0.35	1.00	6.00	—
1962(h) C; S	12,563,000	0.20	0.35	1.00	5.00	—
1964(h) C; S	6,175,000	0.20	0.35	1.00	5.00	—
1965(h) C; S	13,492,000	0.20	0.35	1.00	5.00	—
1966(h) C; S	50,220,000	0.20	0.35	1.00	5.00	—
1967(h) C; S	87,468,000	6.00	12.50	16.00	27.50	—

KM# 855.1 25 ORE

4.3000 g., Copper-Nickel, 23 mm. **Ruler:** Frederik IX **Obv:** Crowned F IX R monogram, date below, to left of center hole, beech branch to right, initials C-S and mint mark at bottom **Rev:** Value, country name and 2 stalks of barley around center hole

Date	Mintage	F	VF	XF	Unc	BU
1966(h) C; S	Inc. above	—	0.20	0.40	3.00	—
1967(h) C; S	Inc. above	—	0.20	0.40	2.50	—
1968(h) C; S	39,142,000	—	0.20	0.40	1.50	—
1969(h) C; S	16,974,000	—	0.20	0.40	1.25	—
1970(h) C; S	5,393,000	—	—	0.20	0.80	—
1971(h) C; S	12,725,000	—	—	0.20	0.70	—

KM# 855.2 25 ORE

4.3000 g., Copper-Nickel, 23 mm. **Ruler:** Frederik IX **Obv:** Crowned F IX R monogram and date to left of center hole, beech branch to right, initial S-S and mint mark at bottom **Rev:** Value, country name and 2 stalks of barley around center hole

Date	Mintage	F	VF	XF	Unc	BU
1972(h) S; S	31,422,000	—	—	0.20	0.50	—

KM# 861.1 25 ORE

4.3000 g., Copper-Nickel, 23 mm. **Ruler:** Margrethe II **Obv:** Crowned MIIR monogram to left, oak branch to right of center hole, date above, mint mark and initials S-B below **Rev:** Denomination divided by center hole, stylized stalks flank

Date	Mintage	F	VF	XF	Unc	BU
1973(h) S; B	30,834,000	—	—	0.20	0.50	—
1974(h) S; B	22,178,000	—	—	0.20	0.50	—
1975(h) S; B	28,798,000	—	—	0.20	0.50	—
1976(h) S; B	48,388,000	—	—	0.20	0.50	—
1977(h) S; B	32,238,999	—	—	0.20	0.50	—
1978(h) S; B	17,444,000	—	—	0.20	0.50	—

KM# 861.2 25 ORE

4.3000 g., Copper-Nickel, 23 mm. **Ruler:** Margrethe II **Obv:** Crowned MIIR monogram to left, oak branch to right of center hole, date above, mint mark and initials B-B below **Rev:** Value divided by center hole, stylized stalks flank

Date	Mintage	F	VF	XF	Unc	BU
1979(h) B; B	24,261,000	—	—	0.20	0.50	—
1980(h) B; B	30,448,000	—	—	0.20	0.50	—
1981(h) B; B	1,427,000	—	—	0.20	0.50	—

KM# 861.3 25 ORE

4.3000 g., Copper-Nickel, 23 mm. **Ruler:** Margrethe II **Obv:** Crowned MIIR monogram to left, oak branch to right of center hole, date above, mint mark and initials B-B below **Rev:** Value divided by center hole, stylized stalks flank

Date	Mintage	F	VF	XF	Unc	BU
1982(h) R; B	24,671,000	—	—	0.20	0.50	—
1983(h) R; B	32,706,000	—	—	0.20	0.50	—
1984(h) R; B	22,882,000	—	—	0.20	0.50	—
1985(h) R; B	29,048,000	—	—	0.20	0.50	—
1986(h) R; B	53,496,000	—	—	0.20	0.50	—
1987(h) R; B	30,575,000	—	—	0.20	0.50	—
1988(h) R; B	23,370,000	—	—	0.20	0.50	—

KM# 868.1 25 ORE

2.8000 g., Bronze, 17.5 mm. **Ruler:** Margrethe II **Obv:** Large crown divides date above, initial to right of country **Rev:** Denomination, small heart above, mint mark and initials LG-JP below **Note:** Beginning in 1996 and ending with 1998, the words "DANMARK" and "ØRE" have raised edges. Heart mint mark under "ØRE"; Prev. KM#868.

Date	Mintage	F	VF	XF	Unc	BU
1990 LG; JP; A	109,084,000	—	—	—	0.40	—
1991 LG; JP; A	102,162,000	—	—	—	0.40	—
1992 LG; JP; A	6,293,000	—	—	—	1.25	—
1993 LG; JP; A	14,756,000	—	—	—	0.40	—
1994 LG; JP; A	35,750,000	—	—	—	0.40	—
1995 LG; JP; A	40,000,000	—	—	—	0.40	—
1996 LG; JP; A	46,760,000	—	—	—	0.15	—
1997 LG; JP; A	30,306,000	—	—	—	0.15	—
1998 LG; JP; A	17,200,000	—	—	—	0.15	—
1999 LG; JP; A	18,748,000	—	—	—	0.15	—
2000 LG; JP; A	14,500,000	—	—	—	0.15	—
2001 LG; JP; A	10,530,000	—	—	—	0.15	—

KM# 868.2 25 ORE

2.8000 g., Bronze, 17.5 mm. **Ruler:** Margrethe II **Obv:** Large crown divides date above **Rev:** Denomination, small heart above **Edge:** Plain **Note:** Without initials

Date	Mintage	F	VF	XF	Unc	BU
2002	12,000,000	—	—	—	0.15	—
2003	17,590,000	—	—	—	0.15	—
2004 Proof	3,000	Value: 12.00				
2004	7,040,304	—	—	—	0.15	—
2005 Proof	—	Value: 12.00				
2005	—	—	—	—	0.15	—
2006 Proof	—	Value: 12.00				
2006	—	—	—	—	0.15	—
2007	—	—	—	—	0.15	—

KM# 866.1 50 ORE

4.3000 g., Bronze **Ruler:** Margrethe II **Obv:** Date above large crown, country name below, initial A to right **Rev:** Large heart above value, mint mark and initials NR-JP below **Note:** Heart mint mark under the word "Øre".

Date	Mintage	F	VF	XF	Unc	BU
1989 NR; JP; A	92,236,000	—	—	—	0.50	—

KM# 866.2 50 ORE

4.3000 g., Bronze **Ruler:** Margrethe II **Obv:** Large crown divides date above, initial to right of country name **Rev:** Large heart above value, mint mark and initials LG-JP below **Note:** Beginning in 1996 and ending with 1998, the words "DANMARK" and "ØRE" have raised edges. Heart mint mark under the word "ØRE".

Date	Mintage	F	VF	XF	Unc	BU
1990 LG; JP; A	63,518,000	—	—	—	0.50	—
1991 LG; JP; A	11,115,000	—	—	—	0.50	—
1992 LG; JP; A	14,397,000	—	—	—	0.50	—
1993 LG; JP; A	14,328,000	—	—	—	0.50	—
1994 LG; JP; A	25,055,000	—	—	—	0.35	—
1995 LG; JP; A	15,988,000	—	—	—	0.35	—
1996 LG; JP; A	11,536,000	—	—	—	0.35	—
1997 LG; JP; A	15,574,000	—	—	—	0.25	—
1998 LG; JP; A	13,120,000	—	—	—	0.25	—
1999 LG; JP; A	14,186,000	—	—	—	0.25	—
2000 LG; JP; A	15,500,000	—	—	—	0.25	—
2001 LG; JP; A	12,270,000	—	—	—	0.25	—

KM# 831.1 1/2 KRONE

3.0000 g., Aluminum-Bronze **Ruler:** Christian X **Obv:** Crowned CXC monogram, date, mint mark, and initials HCN-GJ **Rev:** Value above, country name below large crown

Date	Mintage	F	VF	XF	Unc	BU
1924(h) HCN; GJ	2,150,000	4.00	9.00	17.50	72.50	—
1925(h) HCN; GJ	3,432,000	4.00	9.00	20.00	80.00	—
1926(h) HCN; GJ	716,000	11.50	25.00	40.00	95.00	—

KM# 831.2 1/2 KRONE

3.0000 g., Aluminum-Bronze **Ruler:** Christian X **Obv:** Crowned CXC monogram, date, mint mark, and initial N-GJ **Rev:** Value above, country name below large crown

Date	Mintage	F	VF	XF	Unc	BU
1939(h) N; GJ	226,000	70.00	100	130	200	—
1940(h) N; GJ	1,871,000	4.50	8.50	12.50	22.50	—

KM# 819 KRONE

7.5000 g., 0.8000 Silver 0.1929 oz. ASW **Ruler:** Christian X **Obv:** Head of Christian X, right, with titles, date, mint mark and initials AH at neck, and VBP at date **Rev:** Crowned royal arms with porpoise to left, barley stalk to right, value below

Date	Mintage	F	VF	XF	Unc	BU
1915(h) VBP; AH	1,410,000	2.75	5.00	8.00	22.50	—
1916(h) VBP; AH	992,000	3.75	8.00	15.00	27.50	—

KM# 824.1 KRONE

6.5000 g., Aluminum-Bronze, 25.5 mm. **Ruler:** Christian X **Obv:** Crowned CXC monogram, date, mint mark, and initials HCN-GJ **Rev:** Denomination above large crown, country name below

Date	Mintage	F	VF	XF	Unc	BU
1924(h) HCN; GJ	999,000	170	450	1,000	2,400	—
1925(h) HCN; GJ	6,314,000	2.00	8.50	40.00	105	—
1926(h) HCN; GJ	2,706,000	2.00	8.50	42.50	110	—

KM# 824.2 KRONE

6.5000 g., Aluminum-Bronze, 25.5 mm. **Ruler:** Christian X **Obv:** Crowned CXC monogram, date, mint mark, and initials N-GJ **Rev:** Denomination above large crown, country name below

Date	Mintage	F	VF	XF	Unc	BU
1929(h) N; GJ	501,000	8.00	15.00	85.00	210	—
1930(h) N; GJ	540,000	22.50	42.50	115	340	—
1931(h) N; GJ	540,000	9.00	20.00	60.00	190	—
1934(h) N; GJ	529,000	6.50	11.50	40.00	150	265
1935(h) N; GJ	505,000	35.00	50.00	100	230	—

Date	Mintage	F	VF	XF	Unc	BU
1936(h) N; GJ	558,000	10.00	20.00	60.00	185	—
1938(h) N; GJ	407,000	17.50	27.50	55.00	170	270
1939(h) N; GJ	1,517,000	2.75	4.50	10.00	50.00	—
1940(h) N; GJ	1,496,000	2.75	5.00	90.00	55.00	—
1941(h) N; GJ	661,000	10.00	20.00	60.00	250	—

KM# 835 KRONE

6.5000 g., Aluminum-Bronze, 25.5 mm. **Ruler:** Christian X **Obv:** Head right, with titles, mint mark, initials N-S **Rev:** Value divided by stalk of wheat and oats crossed, date

Date	Mintage	F	VF	XF	Unc	BU
1942(h) N; S	3,952,000	2.00	3.25	10.00	55.00	—
1943(h) N; S	798,000	12.50	32.50	100	350	—
1944(h) N; S	1,760,000	2.00	4.00	17.50	72.50	—
1945(h) N; S	2,581,000	2.00	3.00	8.00	55.00	—
1946(h) N; S	4,321,000	2.00	3.00	5.00	32.50	—
1947(h) N; S	5,060,000	2.00	2.50	3.00	12.50	—

KM# 837.1 KRONE

6.5000 g., Aluminum-Bronze, 25.5 mm. **Ruler:** Frederik IX **Obv:** Head right, titles, mint mark, initials N-S **Rev:** Crowned royal arms divide date, value above

Date	Mintage	F	VF	XF	Unc	BU
1947(h) N; S	Inc. above	3.00	6.00	11.50	30.00	—
1948(h) N; S	4,248,000	2.00	3.00	6.50	14.00	—
1949(h) N; S	1,300,000	4.25	8.50	18.00	45.00	—
1952(h) N; S	2,124,000	3.00	5.00	10.00	24.00	—
1953(h) N; S	573,000	4.25	7.00	13.00	26.00	—
1954(h) N; S	584,000	14.00	22.50	45.00	75.00	140
1955(h) N; S	1,359,000	5.50	8.75	13.00	25.00	—

KM# 837.2 KRONE

6.5000 g., Aluminum-Bronze, 25.5 mm. **Ruler:** Frederik IX **Obv:** Head right, titles, mint mark, initials C-S **Rev:** Crowned royal arms divide date, value above

Date	Mintage	F	VF	XF	Unc	BU
1956(h) C; S	2,858,000	1.75	2.75	4.00	8.00	—
1957(h) C; S	10,896,000	0.60	1.00	1.50	4.00	—
1958(h) C; S	1,507,000	1.00	1.75	2.25	4.25	—
1959(h) C; S	243,000	15.00	25.00	30.00	42.50	—
1960(h) C; S	100	—	—	3,000	3,750	—

Note: 1960 dated coins were not released into circulation, however, approximately 50 pieces did eventually make their way into the collector's market in 1969.

KM# 851.1 KRONE

6.8000 g., Copper-Nickel, 25.5 mm. **Ruler:** Frederik IX **Obv:** Older head right, titles, mint mark, initials C-S **Rev:** Crowned and quartered royal arms divide date, value above

Date	Mintage	F	VF	XF	Unc	BU
1960(h) C; S	1,000,000	1.00	1.50	2.75	9.00	—
1961(h) C; S	10,348,000	—	0.50	1.75	14.00	—
1962(h) C; S	27,068,000	—	0.50	1.75	12.00	—
1963(h) C; S	32,083,000	—	0.50	1.50	6.50	—
1964(h) C; S	5,984,000	—	0.50	1.50	6.50	—
1965(h) C; S	13,799,000	—	0.50	1.25	7.00	—
1966(h) C; S	10,890,000	—	0.50	1.25	5.00	—
1967(h) C; S	18,304,000	—	0.50	1.25	5.00	—
1968(h) C; S	8,212,999	—	0.50	1.00	3.75	—
1969(h) C; S	9,597,000	—	0.50	1.00	2.00	—
1970(h) C; S	9,460,000	—	—	0.50	2.00	—
1971(h) C; S	13,985,000	—	—	0.50	2.00	—

KM# 851.2 KRONE

6.8000 g., Copper-Nickel, 25.5 mm. **Ruler:** Frederik IX **Obv:** Older head right, titles, mint mark, initials S-S **Rev:** Crowned royal arms divide date, value above

Date	Mintage	F	VF	XF	Unc	BU
1972(h) S; S	21,019,000	—	—	0.40	1.25	—

KM# 862.1 KRONE

6.8000 g., Copper-Nickel, 25.5 mm. **Ruler:** Margrethe II **Obv:** Head right, with titles, mint mark, initials S-B **Rev:** Crowned and quartered royal arms divide date, value below

Date	Mintage	F	VF	XF	Unc	BU
1973(h) S; B	18,268,000	—	—	0.40	1.00	—
Note: Narrow rim (0.7mm)						
1973(h) S; B	Inc. above	—	—	0.40	1.00	—
Note: Wide rim (1.1mm)						
1974(h) S; B	17,742,000	—	—	0.40	0.80	—
1975(h) S; B	20,136,000	—	—	0.40	0.80	—
1976(h) S; B	28,049,000	—	—	0.40	0.80	—
1977(h) S; B	25,685,000	—	—	0.40	0.80	—
1978(h) S; B	11,286,000	—	—	0.40	0.80	—

KM# 862.2 KRONE

6.8000 g., Copper-Nickel, 25.5 mm. **Ruler:** Margrethe II **Obv:** Head right, with titles, mint mark, initials S-B **Rev:** Crowned and quartered royal arms divide date, value below

Date	Mintage	F	VF	XF	Unc	BU
1979(h) B; B	25,216,000	—	—	0.35	0.80	—
1980(h) B; B	25,825,000	—	—	0.35	0.80	—
1981(h) B; B	8,889,000	—	—	0.35	0.80	—

KM# 862.3 KRONE

6.8000 g., Copper-Nickel, 25.5 mm. **Ruler:** Margrethe II **Obv:** Head right with titles, mint mark, initials **Rev:** Crowned and quartered royal arms divide date, value below

Date	Mintage	F	VF	XF	Unc	BU
1982(h) R; B	5,011,000	—	—	0.35	0.80	—
1983(h) R; B	13,946,000	—	—	0.35	0.80	—
1984(h) R; B	36,439,000	—	—	0.35	0.70	—
1985(h) R; B	10,843,000	—	—	0.35	0.70	—
1986(h) R; B	12,556,000	—	—	0.35	0.70	—
1987(h) R; B	20,120,000	—	—	0.35	0.70	—
1988(h) R; B	32,073,999	—	—	0.35	0.70	—
1989(h) R; B	15,704,000	—	—	0.35	0.70	—

KM# 873.1 KRONE

3.6000 g., Copper-Nickel **Ruler:** Margrethe II **Obv:** Wave design surrounds center hole, value above, hearts flank **Rev:** 3 crowned MII monograms around center hole, date, mint mark, and initials LG-JP-A below **Note:** Prev. KM#873.

Date	Mintage	F	VF	XF	Unc	BU
1992 LG; JP; A	81,621,000	—	—	—	0.60	—
1993 LG; JP; A	15,844,000	—	—	—	0.60	—
1994 LG; JP; A	23,658,000	—	—	—	0.60	—
1995 LG; JP; A	34,966,000	—	—	—	0.60	—
1996 LG; JP; A	10,081,000	—	—	—	0.60	—
1997 LG; JP; A	10,121,807	—	—	—	0.60	—
1998 LG; JP; A	13,100,000	—	—	—	0.60	—
1999 LG; JP; A	6,479,000	—	—	—	0.60	—
2000 LG; JP; A	21,500,000	—	—	—	0.60	—
2001 LG; JP; A	14,640,000	—	—	—	0.60	—

KM# 873.2 KRONE

3.6000 g., Copper-Nickel, 20.29 mm. **Ruler:** Margrethe II **Obv:** 3 crowned MII monograms around center hole, date below **Rev:** Design surounds center hole, value above, hearts flank **Edge:** Reeded **Note:** Without initials

Date	Mintage	F	VF	XF	Unc	BU
2002	9,000,000	—	—	—	0.40	—
2003	5,231,000	—	—	—	0.40	—
2004 Proof	3,000	Value: 18.00				
2004	16,139,596	—	—	—	0.40	—
2005	—	—	—	—	0.40	—
2005 Proof	—	Value: 18.00				
2006 Proof	—	Value: 18.00				
2006	—	—	—	—	0.40	—
2007	—	—	—	—	40.00	—

KM# 802 2 KRONER

15.0000 g., 0.8000 Silver 0.3858 oz. ASW, 31 mm. **Ruler:** Christian IX **Subject:** 40th Anniversary of Reign **Obv:** Armored bust right, with titles and anniversary dates, date and "P" below bust **Rev:** Seated woman holding royal shield; flying dove to the left; Motto: "With God for honor and justice"; value in exergue **Designer:** Gunnar Jensen

Date	Mintage	F	VF	XF	Unc	BU
1903(h) P; GJ	103,000	7.00	15.00	35.00	60.00	120

KM# 803 2 KRONER

15.0000 g., 0.8000 Silver 0.3858 oz. ASW, 31 mm. **Ruler:** Frederik VIII **Subject:** Death of Christian IX and Accession of Frederik VIII **Obv:** Armored bust left with titles, motto, date, initials VBP **Rev:** Bust left with titles, date of death, value, initials GJ **Designer:** Gunnar Jensen

Date	Mintage	F	VF	XF	Unc	BU
1906(h) VBP GJ	151,000	6.00	9.00	30.00	55.00	110

KM# 811 2 KRONER

15.0000 g., 0.8000 Silver 0.3858 oz. ASW, 31 mm. **Ruler:** Christian X **Subject:** Death of Frederik VIII and Accession of Christian X **Obv:** Head right with initials AH at neck, date, mint mark and initials VBP below **Rev:** Head right with initials AH, value below, date of death **Designer:** Gunnar Jensen **Note:** Coin rotation.

Date	Mintage	F	VF	XF	Unc	BU
1912(h) VBP; AH	102,000	8.00	17.50	37.50	70.00	125

KM# 820 2 KRONER

15.0000 g., 0.8000 Silver 0.3858 oz. ASW, 31 mm. **Ruler:** Christian X **Obv:** Head right with initials AH at neck, date, mint mark and initial VBP below **Rev:** Crowned royal arms, porpoise and barley stalk flanking, value below

Date	Mintage	F	VF	XF	Unc	BU
1915(h) AH	657,000	15.00	27.50	45.00	80.00	—
1916(h) AH	402,000	10.00	13.50	20.00	40.00	—

KM# 821 2 KRONER
15.0000 g., 0.8000 Silver 0.3858 oz. ASW, 31 mm. **Ruler:** Christian X **Subject:** Silver Wedding Anniversary **Obv:** Heads of Christian X and Queen Alexandrine right, initials GJ **Rev:** Crowned arms within anniversary dates, initials HCN, denomination below **Designer:** Gunnar Jensen

Date	Mintage	F	VF	XF	Unc	BU
1923(h) HCN; GJ	203,000	—	—	15.00	30.00	60.00

KM# 825.1 2 KRONER
13.0000 g., Aluminum-Bronze, 31 mm. **Ruler:** Christian X **Obv:** Crowned CXC monogram, date, mint mark, and initials HCN-GJ **Rev:** Denomination above large crown, country name below

Date	Mintage	F	VF	XF	Unc	BU
1924(h) HCN; GJ	1,138,000	25.00	160	550	1,800	—
1925(h) HCN; GJ	3,248,000	2.50	15.00	50.00	125	—
1926(h) HCN; GJ	1,126,000	2.50	15.00	50.00	175	—

KM# 825.2 2 KRONER
13.0000 g., Aluminum-Bronze, 31 mm. **Ruler:** Christian X **Obv:** Crowned CXC monogram, date, mint mark, and initials N-GJ **Rev:** Denomination above large crown, country name below

Date	Mintage	F	VF	XF	Unc	BU
1936(h) N; GJ	400,000	7.00	17.00	75.00	330	—
1938(h) N; GJ	191,000	17.50	27.50	105	275	—
1939(h) N; GJ	723,000	2.00	3.75	10.00	45.00	—
1940(h) N; GJ	743,000	7.00	12.00	25.00	70.00	—
1941(h) N; GJ	129,000	40.00	65.00	225	475	—

KM# 829 2 KRONER
15.0000 g., 0.8000 Silver 0.3858 oz. ASW, 31 mm. **Ruler:** Christian X **Subject:** King's 60th Birthday **Obv:** Head right, date, mint mark, initials AH at neck, N below **Rev:** Draped and supported national arms, value below, initials HS, two dates at top **Designer:** Andreas Hansen

Date	Mintage	F	VF	XF	Unc	BU
1930(h) N; AH/HS	303,000	—	—	8.00	14.00	30.00

KM# 830 2 KRONER
15.0000 g., 0.8000 Silver 0.3858 oz. ASW, 31 mm. **Ruler:** Christian X **Subject:** 25th Anniversary of Reign **Obv:** Head right, mint mark and initials N-S below **Rev:** Crowned royal arms, value below **Designer:** Andreas Hansen

Date	Mintage	F	VF	XF	Unc	BU
ND(1937)(h) N; S	209,000	—	—	9.00	18.00	40.00

KM# 836 2 KRONER
15.0000 g., 0.8000 Silver 0.3858 oz. ASW, 31 mm. **Ruler:** Christian X **Subject:** King's 75th Birthday **Obv:** Head right, mint mark and initials N-S below **Rev:** Dates of birth and 75th birthday year within wreath, legend around, denomination below **Rev. Legend:** "IN ONE WITH HIS PEOPLE IN SORROW AND VICTORY" **Designer:** Harald Salomon

Date	Mintage	F	VF	XF	Unc	BU
ND(1945)(h) N; S	157,000	—	—	12.00	24.00	65.00

KM# 838.1 2 KRONER
13.0000 g., Aluminum-Bronze, 31.4 mm. **Ruler:** Frederik IX **Obv:** Head right, mint mark and initials N-S below **Rev:** Crowned royal arms divide date, value above

Date	Mintage	F	VF	XF	Unc	BU
1947(h) N; S	1,151,000	2.25	4.50	12.50	40.00	—
1948(h) N; S	857,000	1.75	3.00	8.00	32.50	—
1949(h) N; S	272,000	4.50	9.50	30.00	85.00	—
1951(h) N; S	1,576,000	1.35	2.25	4.50	22.50	—
1952(h) N; S	1,958,000	1.00	2.00	5.00	20.00	—
1953(h) N; S	432,000	2.25	4.50	12.50	45.00	—
1954(h) N; S	716,000	2.25	4.00	9.50	37.50	—
1955(h) N; S	457,000	3.75	6.50	11.00	37.50	—

KM# 838.2 2 KRONER
13.0000 g., Aluminum-Bronze, 31.4 mm. **Ruler:** Frederik IX **Obv:** Head right, mint mark and initials C-S below **Rev:** Crowned royal arms divide date, value above

Date	Mintage	F	VF	XF	Unc	BU
1956(h) C; S	1,444,000	2.00	3.25	5.50	11.50	—
1957(h) C; S	2,610,000	1.50	2.25	3.50	7.00	—
1958(h) C; S	2,605,000	1.50	2.25	3.25	8.00	—
1959(h) C; S	192,000	17.50	25.00	35.00	55.00	—

KM# 844 2 KRONER
15.0000 g., 0.8000 Silver 0.3858 oz. ASW, 31 mm. **Ruler:** Frederik IX **Subject:** Foundation for the Campaign against Tuberculosis in Greenland **Obv:** Conjoined heads right, date, mint mark and initials N-S below **Rev:** Map of Greenland, country name in Greenlandic language, denomination below **Designer:** Harald Salomon **Note:** Greenland Commemorative.

Date	Mintage	F	VF	XF	Unc	BU
1953(h) N; S	152,000	—	6.50	17.50	40.00	200

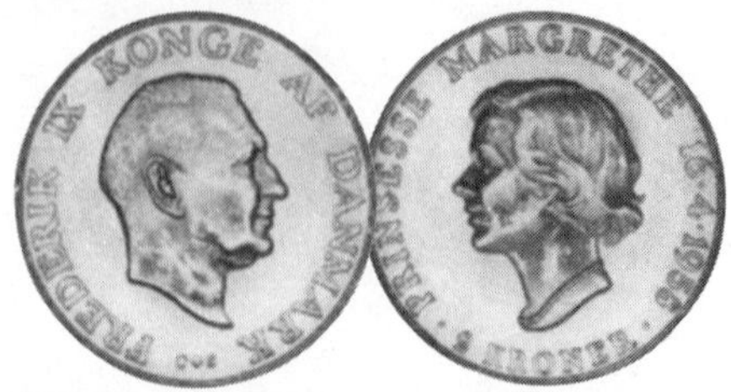

KM# 845 2 KRONER
15.0000 g., 0.8000 Silver 0.3858 oz. ASW, 31 mm. **Ruler:** Frederik IX **Subject:** Princess Margrethe's 18th Birthday **Obv:** Head right with titles, mint mark and initials C-S below **Obv. Designer:** Harald Salomon **Rev:** Head left, date of 18th birthday, value below **Rev. Designer:** Harold Salomon

Date	Mintage	F	VF	XF	Unc	BU
ND(1958)(h) C; S	301,000	—	—	8.50	17.50	30.00

KM# 874.1 2 KRONER
Copper-Nickel **Ruler:** Margrethe II **Obv:** 3 crowned MII monograms around center hole, date and initials LG-JP-A below **Rev:** Design surrounds center hole, denomination above, hearts flank **Note:** Prev. KM#874.

Date	Mintage	F	VF	XF	Unc	BU
1992 LG; JP; A	41,648,000	—	—	—	0.75	—
1993 LG; JP; A	43,864,000	—	—	—	0.75	—
1994 LG; JP; A	27,629,000	—	—	—	0.75	—
1995 LG; JP; A	19,850,000	—	—	—	0.75	—
1996 LG; JP; A	2,884,000	—	—	—	0.75	—
1997 LG; JP; A	25,874,000	—	—	—	0.75	—
1998 LG; JP; A	4,360,000	—	—	—	0.75	—
1999 LG; JP; A	20,608,000	—	—	—	0.60	—
2000 LG; JP; A	10,400,000	—	—	—	0.60	—
2001 LG; JP; A	11,180,000	—	—	—	0.60	—

KM# 874.2 2 KRONER
5.9400 g., Copper-Nickel, 24.37 mm. **Ruler:** Margrethe II **Obv:** 3 crowned MII monograms around center hole, date and initials LGpJP-A below **Rev:** Wave design surrounds center hole, denomination above, hearts flank **Edge:** Reeded and plain sections **Note:** Without initials

Date	Mintage	F	VF	XF	Unc	BU
2002	60,159,000	—	—	—	0.60	—
2004 Proof	3,000	Value: 22.00				
2004	7,381,531	—	—	—	0.60	—
2005	—	—	—	—	0.60	—
2005 Proof	—	Value: 22.00				
2006 Proof	—	Value: 22.00				
2006	—	—	—	—	0.60	—
2007	—	—	—	—	0.60	—

KM# 852 5 KRONER
17.0000 g., 0.8000 Silver 0.4372 oz. ASW, 33 mm. **Ruler:** Frederik IX **Subject:** Silver Wedding Anniversary **Obv:** Conjoined heads right, within titles **Rev:** Crowned double FI monogram, silver anniversary dates above, 2 barley stalks, value, mint mark and initials C-S below

Date	Mintage	F	VF	XF	Unc	BU
ND(1960)(h) C; S	410,000	—	6.50	8.00	15.00	32.50

KM# 853.1 5 KRONER
15.0000 g., Copper-Nickel, 33 mm. **Ruler:** Frederik IX **Obv:** Head right, titles, mint mark and initials C-S **Rev:** Crowned and quartered arms divide date within two oak branches, value above

Date	Mintage	F	VF	XF	Unc	BU
1960(h) C; S	6,418,000	—	2.25	4.00	17.50	—
1961(h) C; S	9,744,000	—	2.25	4.00	22.50	—
1962(h) C; S	2,073,999	—	2.75	4.50	27.50	50.00
1963(h) C; S	709,000	—	2.75	4.50	30.00	45.00
1964(h) C; S	1,443,000	—	2.25	4.00	25.00	40.00
1965(h) C; S	2,574,000	—	2.25	2.50	20.00	35.00
1966(h) C; S	4,370,000	—	2.00	2.25	12.50	—
1967(h) C; S	1,864,000	—	2.00	2.25	9.00	—

Date	Mintage	F	VF	XF	Unc	BU
1968(h) C; S	4,131,999	—	2.00	2.00	9.00	—
1969(h) C; S	72,000	2.25	4.50	7.50	15.00	—
1970(h) C; S	2,246,000	—	—	2.00	4.00	—
1971(h) C; S	4,767,000	—	—	2.00	3.50	—

KM# 853.2 5 KRONER

15.0000 g., Copper-Nickel, 33 mm. **Ruler:** Frederik IX **Obv:** Head right, mint mark and initials S-S **Rev:** Crowned and quartered arms divide date within two oak branches, value above

Date	Mintage	F	VF	XF	Unc	BU
1972(h) S; S	2,599,000	—	—	2.00	3.25	—

KM# 854 5 KRONER

17.0000 g., 0.8000 Silver 0.4372 oz. ASW, 33 mm. **Ruler:** Frederik IX **Subject:** Wedding of Princess Anne Marie **Obv:** Head right, mint mark and initials C-S **Rev:** Head left within title and wedding date

Date	Mintage	F	VF	XF	Unc	BU
1964(h) C; S	359,000	—	—	7.50	15.00	—

KM# 863.1 5 KRONER

15.0000 g., Copper-Nickel, 33 mm. **Ruler:** Margrethe II **Obv:** Head right, mint mark and initial S-B below **Rev:** Crowned and quartered royal arms divide date and oak leaves, value below

Date	Mintage	F	VF	XF	Unc	BU
1973(h) S; B	3,774,000	—	—	2.00	4.00	—
Note: Narrow rim (1.0mm)						
1973(h) S; B	Inc. above	—	—	2.00	4.00	—
Note: Wide rim (1.5mm)						
1974(h) S; B	5,239,000	—	—	2.00	4.00	—
1975(h) S; B	5,810,000	—	—	3.50	8.00	—
1976(h) S; B	7,651,000	—	—	2.00	5.00	—
1977(h) S; B	6,885,000	—	—	2.00	5.00	—
1978(h) S; B	2,984,000	—	—	2.00	5.00	—

KM# 863.2 5 KRONER

15.0000 g., Copper-Nickel, 33 mm. **Ruler:** Margrethe II **Obv:** Head right, mint mark and initials B-B below **Rev:** Crowned and quartered royal arms divide date and oak leaves, value below

Date	Mintage	F	VF	XF	Unc	BU
1979(h) B; B	2,861,000	—	—	2.00	4.00	—
1980(h) B; B	3,622,000	—	—	2.50	6.50	—
1981(h) B; B	1,057,000	—	—	2.00	4.00	—

KM# 863.3 5 KRONER

15.0000 g., Copper-Nickel, 33 mm. **Ruler:** Margrethe II **Obv:** Head right, mint mark and initials R-B below **Rev:** Crowned and quartered royal arms divide date and oak leaves, value below

Date	Mintage	F	VF	XF	Unc	BU
1982(h) R; B	1,002,000	—	—	2.50	6.50	—
1983(h) R; B	1,044,000	—	—	2.00	3.50	—
1984(h) R; B	713,000	—	—	2.00	4.00	—
1985(h) R; B	621,000	—	—	2.00	4.00	—
1986(h) R; B	1,042,000	—	—	2.00	3.50	—
1987(h) R; B	611,000	—	—	2.00	3.50	—
1988(h) R; B	648,000	—	—	2.00	3.50	—

KM# 869.1 5 KRONER

9.2000 g., Copper-Nickel, 28 mm. **Ruler:** Margrethe II **Obv:** 3 crowned MII monograms around center hole, date and initials LG-JP-A below **Rev:** Wave design surrounds center hole, denomination above, hearts flank **Note:** Large and small date varieties exist.

Date	Mintage	F	VF	XF	Unc	BU
1990 LG; JP; A	46,745,000	—	—	—	2.25	—
1991 LG; JP; A	3,752,000	—	—	—	2.25	—
1992 LG; JP; A	2,426,000	—	—	—	2.25	—
1993 LG; JP; A	1,538,000	—	—	—	2.25	—
1994 LG; JP; A	7,920,000	—	—	—	2.25	—
1995 LG; JP; A	5,850,000	—	—	—	2.25	—
1997 LG; JP; A	5,258,000	—	—	—	2.00	—
1998 LG; JP; A	6,450,000	—	—	—	2.00	—
1999 LG; JP; A	4,786,000	—	—	—	2.00	—
2000 LG; JP; A	2,800,000	—	—	—	2.00	—
2001 LG; JP; A	5,700,000	—	—	—	2.00	—

KM# 869.2 5 KRONER

9.2500 g., Copper Nickel, 28.52 mm. **Ruler:** Margrethe II **Obv:** 3 crowned MII monograms around center hole, date and initials LG-JP-A below **Rev:** Wave design surrounds center hole, denomination above, hearts flank **Edge:** Reeded **Note:** Without initials

Date	Mintage	F	VF	XF	Unc	BU
2002	5,980,000	—	—	—	2.00	—
2004 Proof	3,000	Value: 25.00				
2004	1,415,925	—	—	—	2.00	—
2005	—	—	—	—	2.00	—
2005 Proof	—	Value: 25.00				
2006 Proof	—	Value: 25.00				
2006	—	—	—	—	2.00	—
2007	—	—	—	—	2.00	—

KM# 809 10 KRONER

4.4803 g., 0.9000 Gold 0.1296 oz. AGW **Ruler:** Frederik VIII **Obv:** Head left with titles **Rev:** Draped crowned national arms above date, value, mint mark and initials VBP

Date	Mintage	F	VF	XF	Unc	BU
1908(h) VBP; GJ	308,000	—	120	130	150	—
1909(h) VBP; GJ	153,000	—	120	135	160	—

KM# 816 10 KRONER

4.4803 g., 0.9000 Gold 0.1296 oz. AGW **Ruler:** Christian X **Obv:** Head right with title, date, mint mark, initials VBP. Initials AH at neck **Rev:** Draped crowned national arms above date, value, mint mark and initials VBP

Date	Mintage	F	VF	XF	Unc	BU
1913(h) AH/ GJ	312,000	—	120	130	150	—
1917(h) AH/ GJ	132,000	—	120	140	165	—

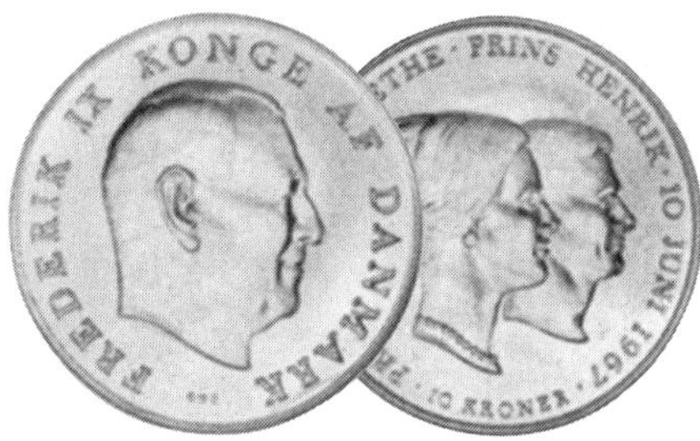

KM# 856 10 KRONER

20.4000 g., 0.8000 Silver 0.5247 oz. ASW **Ruler:** Frederik IX **Subject:** Wedding of Princess Margrethe **Obv:** Head right with titles, mint mark, initials C-S **Rev:** Heads of Prince and Princess right, value below

Date	Mintage	F	VF	XF	Unc	BU
ND(1967)(h) C; S	419,000	—	—	8.00	16.00	50.00
Note: 78,383 pieces were melted.						

KM# 857 10 KRONER

20.4000 g., 0.8000 Silver 0.5247 oz. ASW **Ruler:** Frederik IX **Subject:** Wedding of Princess Benedikte **Obv:** Head right, mint mark and initials C-S below **Rev:** Head left, value below

Date	Mintage	F	VF	XF	Unc	BU
ND(1968)(h) C; S	254,000	—	—	8.50	17.50	55.00
Note: 42,923 were melted.						

KM# 858 10 KRONER

20.4000 g., 0.8000 Silver 0.5247 oz. ASW **Ruler:** Margrethe II **Subject:** Death of Frederik IX and Accession of Margrethe II **Obv:** Head right, motto, titles, mint mark and initials S-B **Rev:** Head right with titles, date of death, value below

Date	Mintage	F	VF	XF	Unc	BU
1972(h) S; S	402,000	—	—	7.50	11.00	20.00

KM# 864.1 10 KRONER

12.5000 g., Copper-Nickel, 28 mm. **Ruler:** Margrethe II **Obv:** Head right with tiara, mint mark and initials B-B below **Rev:** Large 10 on horizontal grid, two rye stalks flanking, date above

Date	Mintage	F	VF	XF	Unc	BU
1979(h) B; B	76,801,000	—	—	2.00	5.00	—
1981(h) B; B	10,520,000	—	2.50	5.00	13.00	—

KM# 864.2 10 KRONER

12.5000 g., Copper-Nickel, 28 mm. **Ruler:** Margrethe II **Obv:** Head right with tiara, mint mark and initials R-B below **Rev:** Large 10 on horizontal grid, two rye stalks flanking, date above

Date	Mintage	F	VF	XF	Unc	BU
1982(h) R; B	1,065,000	—	2.50	5.00	13.50	—
1983(h) R; B	1,123,000	—	2.50	5.00	13.50	—
1984(h) R; B	748,000	—	3.00	6.00	16.00	22.50
1985(h) R; B	720,000	—	3.00	6.00	16.00	22.50
1987(h) R; B	719,000	—	2.50	4.75	13.50	20.00
1988(h) R; B	718,000	—	2.25	4.50	12.50	—

KM# 865 10 KRONER

12.5000 g., Copper-Nickel, 28 mm. **Ruler:** Margrethe II **Subject:** Crown Prince's 18th Birthday **Obv:** Head with tiara right, mint mark and initials R-A below **Rev:** Head left, date of 18th birthday, value below **Edge:** Plain

Date	Mintage	F	VF	XF	Unc	BU
ND(1986)(h) R; A	1,090,351	—	—	5.00	14.00	—
ND(1986)(h) R; A Proof	2,000	—	—	—	—	—

Note: In folder

KM# 867.1 10 KRONER

7.0000 g., Aluminum-Bronze, 23.4 mm. **Ruler:** Margrethe II **Obv:** Head with tiara right, titles, date, initials NR-JP-A **Rev:** Crowned arms within ornaments, value below **Edge:** Plain

Date	Mintage	F	VF	XF	Unc	BU
1989 NR; JP; A	38,346,000	—	—	—	4.00	—

KM# 867.2 10 KRONER

7.0000 g., Aluminum-Bronze, 23.4 mm. **Ruler:** Margrethe II **Obv:** Head with tiara right, titles, date, initials LG-JP-A **Rev:** Crowned arms within ornaments, value below **Edge:** Plain

Date	Mintage	F	VF	XF	Unc	BU
1990 LG; JP; A	12,193,000	—	—	—	4.00	—
1991 LG; JP; A	1,065,000	—	—	—	6.00	—
1992 LG; JP; A	484,000	—	—	4.00	8.00	—
1993 LG; JP; A	1,069,000	—	—	3.00	6.00	—

KM# 877 10 KRONER

7.0000 g., Aluminum-Bronze, 23.4 mm. **Ruler:** Margrethe II **Obv:** New portrait right, date below **Rev:** Crowned arms within ornaments, value below **Edge:** Plain **Note:** Beginning with strikes in 1995 and ending in 1998, letters and numbers on reverse have raised edges.

Date	Mintage	F	VF	XF	Unc	BU
1994 LG; JP; A	4,058,000	—	—	—	5.00	—
1995 LG; JP; A	9,461,000	—	—	—	5.00	—
1997 LG; JP; A	3,725,000	—	—	—	5.00	—
1998 LG; JP; A	6,000,000	—	—	—	4.25	—
1999 LG; JP; A	4,034,749	—	—	—	4.25	—

KM# 887.1 10 KRONER

7.0000 g., Aluminum-Bronze, 23.4 mm. **Ruler:** Margrethe II **Obv:** Crowned head right within inner circle, date, initials LG-JP-A below, mint mark after II in title **Obv. Designer:** Mogens Moller **Rev:** Crowned arms within inner circle above denomination **Edge:** Plain

Date	Mintage	F	VF	XF	Unc	BU
2001 LG; JP; A	4,800,000	—	—	—	3.00	—

KM# 887.2 10 KRONER

7.1000 g., Aluminum-Bronze, 23.31 mm. **Ruler:** Margrethe II **Obv:** Crowned head right, mint mark after II in title **Obv. Legend:** MARGRETHE II - DANMARKS DRONNING **Obv. Designer:** Mogens Moller **Rev:** Crowned arms and denomination **Edge:** Plain **Note:** Without initials

Date	Mintage	F	VF	XF	Unc	BU
2002	7,299,900	—	—	—	3.00	—

KM# 896 10 KRONER

6.9500 g., Aluminum-Bronze, 23.39 mm. **Ruler:** Margrethe II **Obv:** Head right within circle, date below **Obv. Legend:** MARGRETHE II - DANMARKS DRONNING **Rev:** Crowned arms above denomination **Edge:** Plain **Designer:** Mogens Moller

Date	Mintage	F	VF	XF	Unc	BU
2004 Proof	—	Value: 30.00				
2004	5,835,426	—	—	—	2.75	—
2005 Proof	—	Value: 30.00				
2005	—	—	—	—	2.75	—
2006 Proof	—	Value: 30.00				
2006	—	—	—	—	2.75	—
2007	—	—	—	—	2.75	—

KM# 898 10 KRONER

7.0000 g., Aluminum-Bronze, 23.4 mm. **Ruler:** Margrethe II **Subject:** Hans Christian Andersen's Ugly duckling story **Obv:** Head right within circle, date below **Rev:** Swan and reflection on water within circle, value below **Rev. Designer:** Hans Pauli Olsen **Edge:** Plain

Date	Mintage	F	VF	XF	Unc	BU
2005	1,200,000	—	—	—	3.25	—

KM# 900 10 KRONER

7.0000 g., Aluminum-Bronze, 23.4 mm. **Ruler:** Margrethe II **Subject:** Hans Christian Andersen's Little Mermaid **Obv:** Head right within circle, date below **Rev:** Little Mermaid **Rev. Designer:** Tina Maria Nielsen **Edge:** Plain

Date	Mintage	F	VF	XF	Unc	BU
2005	1,200,000	—	—	—	3.25	—

KM# 903 10 KRONER

7.1000 g., Aluminum-Bronze, 23.31 mm. **Ruler:** Margrethe II **Subject:** H.C. Andersen's "The Snow Queen" **Obv:** Head right within circle, date below **Obv. Legend:** MARGRETHE II - DANMARKS DRONNING **Rev:** Stylized figures **Rev. Designer:** Bjørn Nørgaard **Edge:** Plain

Date	Mintage	F	VF	XF	Unc	BU
2006	1,200,000	—	—	—	3.25	—

KM# 916 10 KRONER

7.1000 g., Aluminum-Bronze, 23.31 mm. **Ruler:** Margrethe II **Subject:** Polar Year **Obv:** Crowned bust right **Obv. Legend:** MARGRETHE II - DANMARKS DRONNING **Rev:** Polar bear facing, walking on ice flow **Rev. Legend:** POLARÅR 2007-2009 **Edge:** Plain

Date	Mintage	F	VF	XF	Unc	BU
2007(h)	1,200,000	—	—	—	3.00	—

KM# 817.1 20 KRONER

8.9606 g., 0.9000 Gold 0.2593 oz. AGW **Ruler:** Christian X **Obv:** Head right with title, date, mint mark, initials VBP, initials AH at neck **Rev:** Crowned and mantled arms above date, value, mint mark and initials VBP

Date	Mintage	F	VF	XF	Unc	BU
1913(h) AH/GJ	815,000	—	230	245	270	—
1914(h) AH/GJ	920,000	—	230	245	270	—
1915(h) AH/GJ	532,000	—	235	250	275	—
1916(h) AH/GJ	1,401,000	—	235	250	275	—
1917(h) AH/GJ	Inc. above	—	235	250	275	—

KM# 817.2 20 KRONER

8.9606 g., 0.9000 Gold 0.2593 oz. AGW **Ruler:** Christian X **Obv:** Head right with title, date, mint mark, and initials HCN, initials AH at neck **Rev:** Crowned and mantled arms above date, value, mint mark, and initials HCN **Note:** 1926-1927 dated 20 Kroners were not released for circulation.

Date	Mintage	F	VF	XF	Unc	BU
1926(h) HCN	358,000	—	—	3,000	6,000	—
1927(h) HCN	Inc. above	—	—	3,000	6,000	—

KM# 817.3 20 KRONER

8.9606 g., 0.9000 Gold 0.2593 oz. AGW **Ruler:** Christian X **Obv:** Head right with title, date, mint mark, and initials HCN. Initials AH at neck **Rev:** Crowned and mantled arms above date, value, mint mark and initials HCN **Note:** The 1930-1931 dated 20 Kroners were not released for circulation.

Date	Mintage	F	VF	XF	Unc	BU
1930(h) N	1,285,000	—	—	3,000	6,000	—
1931(h) N	Inc. above	—	—	3,000	6,000	—

KM# 870 20 KRONER

9.3000 g., Aluminum-Bronze **Ruler:** Margrethe II **Subject:** 50th Birthday of Queen Margrethe **Obv:** Head with hat right, mint mark after 2 in legend, initials LG left of shoulder **Rev:** Large crown above daisy flower divides dates, value below **Edge:** Alternate reeded and plain sections **Designer:** Jan Petersen

Date	Mintage	F	VF	XF	Unc	BU
ND(1990)(h) LG	1,101,000	—	—	—	6.00	—

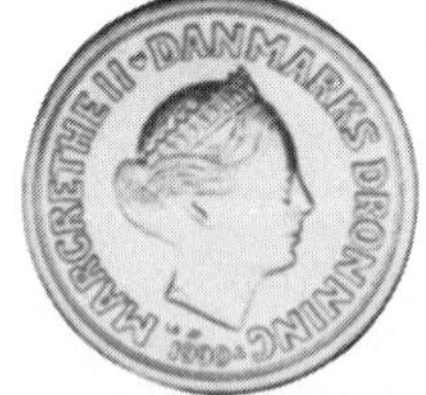

KM# 871 20 KRONER

9.3000 g., Aluminum-Bronze **Ruler:** Margrethe II **Obv:** Head with tiara right, titles, date, initials LG-JP-A, mint mark after II in legend **Rev:** Crowned arms within ornaments and value **Edge:** Alternate reeded and plain sections **Note:** Large and small date varieties exist.

Date	Mintage	F	VF	XF	Unc	BU
1990(h) LG; JP ; A	34,368,000	—	—	—	7.00	—
1991(h) LG; JP; A	11,563,000	—	—	—	8.00	—
1993(h) LG; JP; A	674,000	—	—	—	9.00	—

KM# 875 20 KRONER

9.3000 g., Aluminum-Bronze **Ruler:** Margrethe II **Subject:** Silver Wedding Anniversary **Obv:** Heads of Prince Henrik and Margrethe II facing each other, anniversary dates below **Rev:** Fairy tale house, mint mark and initials LG at lower left, denomination at left **Edge:** Alternate reeded and plain sections **Designer:** Jan Petersen

Date	Mintage	F	VF	XF	Unc	BU
ND(1992)(h) LG	994,000	—	—	—	6.00	—

KM# 878 20 KRONER
9.3000 g., Aluminum-Bronze **Ruler:** Margrethe II **Obv:** New portrait right, date, mint mark and initials LG-JP-A below **Rev:** Crowned arms within ornament and value **Edge:** Alternating reeded and plain sections **Note:** Strikes dated 1996 and 1998 have letters and numbers on reverse with raised edges.

Date	Mintage	F	VF	XF	Unc	BU
1994(h) LG, JP; A	2,565,000	—	—	—	6.50	—
1996(h) LG, JP; A	8,651,000	—	—	—	6.00	—
1998(h) LG, JP; A	4,000,000	—	—	—	6.00	—
1999(h) LG, JP; A	4,133,363	—	—	—	6.00	—

KM# 879 20 KRONER
9.3000 g., Aluminum-Bronze **Ruler:** Margrethe II **Subject:** 1000 Years of Danish Coinage **Obv:** Head with cloche left, inner legend in runic letters **Rev:** Large crown on cross, mint mark and initials LG **Edge:** Alternate reeded and plain sections **Designer:** Jan Petersen

Date	Mintage	F	VF	XF	Unc	BU
ND(1995)(h) LG; JP; A	1,000,000	—	—	—	6.00	—

KM# 881 20 KRONER
9.3000 g., Aluminum-Bronze **Ruler:** Margrethe II **Subject:** Wedding of Prince Joachim **Obv:** New portrait right, mint mark after II in legend, initials LG below at date **Rev:** Schackenborg castle at center, value below **Edge:** Alternate reeded and plain sections **Designer:** Jan Petersen

Date	Mintage	F	VF	XF	Unc	BU
1995(h) LG, JP	1,000,000	—	—	—	6.00	—

Note: Although dated 1995, this coin was minted at the end of the year and included in a 1996 mint set.

KM# 883 20 KRONER
9.3000 g., Aluminum-Bronze **Ruler:** Margrethe II **Subject:** 25th Anniversary - Queen's Reign **Obv:** Full-length portrait, mint mark and initials LG **Rev:** Crowned arms within anniversary date and value **Edge:** Alternate reeded and plain sections **Designer:** Jan Petersen

Date	Mintage	F	VF	XF	Unc	BU
ND(1997)(h) LG; JP	1,000,000	—	—	—	6.00	—

KM# 885 20 KRONER
9.3600 g., Aluminum-Bronze **Ruler:** Margrethe II **Subject:** 60th Birthday of Queen Margrethe II **Obv:** Bust right **Rev:** Crown divides dates above daisy flowers, denomination below **Edge:** Alternating reeded and plain sections **Designer:** Mogens Moeller

Date	Mintage	F	VF	XF	Unc	BU
ND(2000)(h) LG	1,000,000	—	—	—	5.75	—

KM# 888.1 20 KRONER
9.3000 g., Aluminum-Bronze **Ruler:** Margrethe II **Obv:** Crowned head right within circle, date and initials LG-JP-A below, mint mark after II in legend **Rev:** Crowned arms within ornaments and value **Edge:** Alternate reeded and plain sections **Designer:** Mogens Moller

Date	Mintage	F	VF	XF	Unc	BU
2001(h) LG; JP; A	2,900,000	—	—	—	5.25	—

KM# 888.2 20 KRONER
9.3000 g., Aluminum-Bronze, 26.9 mm. **Ruler:** Margrethe II **Obv:** Crowned head right within circle, mint mark after II in legend **Rev:** Crowned arms within ornaments and value **Edge:** Alternate reeded and plain sections **Designer:** Mogens Møller **Note:** Without initials.

Date	Mintage	F	VF	XF	Unc	BU
2002	5,500,000	—	—	—	5.25	—
2004	—	—	—	—	5.25	—

KM# 889 20 KRONER
9.3000 g., Aluminum-Bronze, 26.8 mm. **Ruler:** Margrethe II **Subject:** Danish Towers **Obv:** Head right within circle date below, mint mark after II in legend **Rev:** Aarhus City Hall **Rev. Designer:** Lis Nogel **Edge:** Reeded and plain sections

Date	Mintage	F	VF	XF	Unc	BU
2002	1,000,000	—	—	—	5.25	—
2003	—	—	—	—	—	—

KM# 890 20 KRONER
9.3000 g., Aluminum-Bronze, 26.8 mm. **Ruler:** Margrethe II **Subject:** Danish towers **Obv:** Head right within circle, mint mark and date **Rev:** Copenhagen Old Stock Exchange spire with four intertwined dragon tails **Rev. Designer:** Karin Lorentzen **Edge:** Alternate reeded and plain sections

Date	Mintage	F	VF	XF	Unc	BU
2003	1,000,000	—	—	—	5.25	—

KM# 891 20 KRONER
9.3000 g., Aluminum-Bronze, 26.94 mm. **Ruler:** Margrethe II **Obv:** Head right within circle, mint mark and date **Obv. Legend:** MARGRETHE II - DANMARKS DRONNING **Rev:** Crowned arms above denomination **Rev. Designer:** Mogens M?ller **Edge:** Alternate reeded and plain sections

Date	Mintage	F	VF	XF	Unc	BU
2003	5,720,000	—	—	—	5.25	—
2004	6,922,182	—	—	—	5.25	—
2004 Proof	3,000	Value: 40.00				
2005	—	—	—	—	5.25	—
2005 Proof	—	Value: 45.00				
2006	—	—	—	—	5.25	—
2006 Proof	—	Value: 45.00				
2007	—	—	—	—	5.25	—

KM# 892 20 KRONER
9.3100 g., Aluminum-Bronze, 26.8 mm. **Ruler:** Margrethe II **Subject:** Danish towers **Obv:** Head right within circle, mint mark and date **Rev:** Christiansborg Castle (parliament) tower and Danish flag **Rev. Designer:** Hans Pauli Olsen **Edge:** Alternate reeded and plain sections

Date	Mintage	F	VF	XF	Unc	BU
2003	1,000,000	—	—	—	5.25	—

KM# 893 20 KRONER
9.3100 g., Aluminum-Bronze, 26.8 mm. **Ruler:** Margrethe II **Subject:** Danish towers **Obv:** Head right within circle, date below **Rev:** Gåsetårnet tower **Rev. Designer:** Tina Maria Nielsen **Edge:** Alternate reeded and plain sections

Date	Mintage	F	VF	XF	Unc	BU
2004	1,200,000	—	—	—	5.25	—

KM# 894 20 KRONER
9.3100 g., Aluminum-Bronze, 26.8 mm. **Ruler:** Margrethe II **Subject:** Crown Prince's Wedding **Obv:** Head right within circle, date below **Rev:** Crown Prince Frederik and Crown Princess Mary **Rev. Designer:** Karin Lorentzen **Edge:** Alternate reeded and plain sections

Date	Mintage	F	VF	XF	Unc	BU
2004	1,200,000	—	—	—	5.25	—

KM# 897 20 KRONER
Aluminum-Bronze, 26.8 mm. **Ruler:** Margrethe II **Subject:** Danish towers **Obv:** Head right within circle, date below **Rev:** Svaneke water tower, Bornholm **Rev. Designer:** Morten Straede **Edge:** Alternate reeded and plain sections

Date	Mintage	F	VF	XF	Unc	BU
2004	1,200,000	—	—	—	5.25	—

KM# 899 20 KRONER
9.3000 g., Aluminum-Bronze, 26.8 mm. **Ruler:** Margrethe II **Subject:** Danish Towers **Obv:** Head right within circle, date below **Rev:** Landet Kirke, with elements from the story of Elvira Madigan and Sixten Sparre, including a revolver among leaves of chestnut-trees **Rev. Designer:** Øivind Nygaard **Edge:** Segmented reeding

Date	Mintage	F	VF	XF	Unc	BU
2005	1,200,000	—	—	—	5.25	—

KM# 901 20 KRONER

9.3000 g., Aluminum-Bronze, 26.94 mm. **Ruler:** Margrethe II **Subject:** Danish Towers **Obv:** Head right within circle, date below **Obv. Legend:** MARGRETHE II - DANMARKS DRONNING **Rev:** Lighthouse of Nolsoy (Faeroe Islands) **Rev. Designer:** Hans Pauli Olsen **Edge:** Alternate plain and reeded segments

Date	Mintage	F	VF	XF	Unc	BU
2005	1,200,000	—	—	—	5.25	—

KM# 902 20 KRONER

9.3300 g., Aluminum-Bronze, 26.8 mm. **Ruler:** Margrethe II **Subject:** Danish Towers **Obv:** Head right within circle, date below **Rev:** Grasten Castle Bell Tower **Rev. Designer:** Sys Hindsbo **Edge:** Segmented reeding

Date	Mintage	F	VF	XF	Unc	BU
2006(h)	1,200,000	—	—	—	5.25	—

KM# 913 20 KRONER

9.3000 g., Aluminum-Bronze, 26.94 mm. **Ruler:** Margrethe II **Subject:** Danish Towers **Obv:** Margrethe II **Obv. Legend:** MARGRETHE II - DANMARKS DRONNING **Rev:** The Greenland Cairns: Nukaritt/Three Brothers **Rev. Legend:** TRE BRØDRE **Rev. Designer:** Niels Motzfeldt **Edge:** Alternate plain and reeded segments

Date	Mintage	F	VF	XF	Unc	BU
2006	1,200,000	—	—	—	5.25	—

KM# 920 20 KRONER

9.3000 g., Aluminum-Bronze, 26.94 mm. **Ruler:** Margrethe II **Series:** Danish ships **Obv:** Crowned bust right **Obv. Legend:** MARGRETHE II - DANMARKS DRONNING **Rev:** Sailing ship Jylland **Rev. Legend:** FREGATTEN - JYLLAND **Edge:** Alternate plain and reeded segments

Date	Mintage	F	VF	XF	Unc	BU
2007(h)	—	—	—	—	—	4.50

KM# 921 20 KRONER

9.3000 g., Aluminum-Bronze, 26.94 mm. **Ruler:** Margrethe II **Series:** Danish ships **Obv:** Crowned bust right **Obv. Legend:** MARGRETHE II - DANMARKS DRONNING **Rev:** Ship Vaedderen, route map in background **Rev. Legend:** VAEDDEREN **Edge:** Alternate plain and reeded segments

Date	Mintage	F	VF	XF	Unc	BU
2007(h)	—	—	—	—	—	4.50

DJIBOUTI

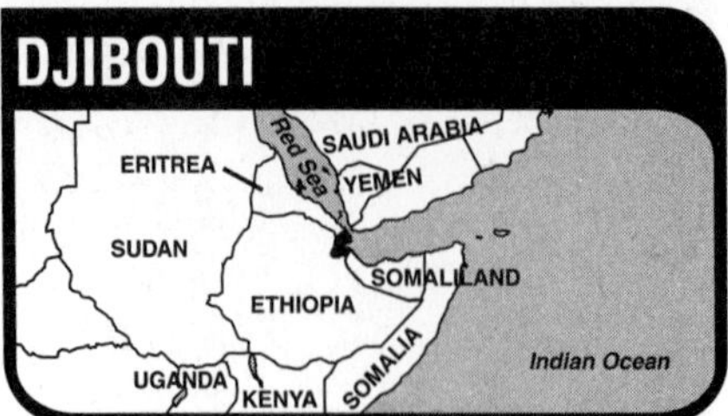

The Republic of Djibouti (formerly French Somaliland and the French Overseas Territory of Afars and Issas), located in northeast Africa at the Bab el Mandeb Strait connecting the Suez Canal and the Red Sea with the Gulf of Aden and the Indian Ocean, has an area of 8,950 sq. mi. (22,000 sq. km.) and a population of 421,320. Capital: Djibouti. The tiny nation has less than one sq. mi. of arable land, and no natural resources except salt, sand, and camels. The commercial activities of the transshipment port of Djibouti and the Addis Abada-Djibouti railroad are the basis of the economy. Salt, fish and hides are exported.

French interest in former French Somaliland began in 1839 with concessions obtained by a French naval lieutenant from the provincial sultans. French Somaliland was made a protectorate in 1884 and its boundaries were delimited by the Franco-British and Ethiopian accords of 1887 and 1897. It became a colony in 1896 and a territory within the French Union in 1946. In 1958 it voted to join the new French Community as an overseas territory, and reaffirmed that choice by a referendum in March, 1967. Its name was changed from French Somaliland to the French Territory of Afars and Issas on July 5, 1967.

The French Tricolor, which had flown over the strategically important territory for 115 years, was lowered for the last time on June 27, 1977, when French Afars and Issas became Africa's 49th independent state, under the name of the Republic of Djibouti.

Djibouti, a seaport and capital city of the Republic of Djibouti (and formerly of French Somaliland and French Afars and Issas) is located on the east coast of Africa at the southernmost entrance to the Red Sea. The capital was moved from Obok to Djibouti in 1892 and established as the transshipment point for Ethiopia's foreign trade via the Franco-Ethiopian railway linking Djibouti and Addis Ababa.

RULER

French, until 1977

REPUBLIC

STANDARD COINAGE

KM# 20 FRANC

1.3000 g., Aluminum, 23 mm. **Obv:** National arms within wreath, date below **Rev:** Giant eland head with headdress facing, divides denomination, shell on fish flank below

Date	Mintage	F	VF	XF	Unc	BU
1977(a)	300,000	0.50	0.75	1.50	3.00	5.00
1996(a)	—	0.50	0.75	1.50	3.00	5.00
1997(a)	350	—	—	—	16.00	18.00
Note: In sets only						
1999(a)	1,800	—	—	—	7.00	9.00
Note: In sets only						

KM# 21 2 FRANCS

2.2000 g., Aluminum, 27.1 mm. **Obv:** National arms within wreath, date below **Rev:** Giant eland head with headdress facing, divides denomination, shell on fish flank below

Date	Mintage	F	VF	XF	Unc	BU
1977(a)	200,000	0.75	1.00	1.75	3.50	5.50
1991(a)	—	0.75	1.00	1.75	3.50	5.50
1996(a)	—	0.75	1.00	1.75	3.50	5.50
1997(a)	350	—	—	—	16.00	18.00
Note: In sets only						
1999(a)	1,800	—	—	—	7.00	9.00
Note: In sets only						

KM# 22 5 FRANCS

3.7500 g., Aluminum, 31.1 mm. **Obv:** National arms within wreath, date below **Rev:** Giant eland head with headdress facing, divides denomination, shell on fish flank below

Date	Mintage	F	VF	XF	Unc	BU
1977(a)	400,000	0.75	1.25	2.00	4.00	6.00
1986(a)	—	0.75	1.00	1.75	3.50	5.50
1989(a)	—	0.75	1.00	1.75	3.50	5.50
1991(a)	—	0.75	1.00	1.75	3.50	5.50
1996(a)	—	0.75	1.00	1.75	3.50	5.50
1997(a)	350	—	—	—	16.00	18.00
Note: In sets only						
1999(a)	1,800	—	—	—	7.00	9.00
Note: In sets only						

KM# 23 10 FRANCS

3.0000 g., Aluminum-Bronze, 20 mm. **Obv:** National arms within wreath, date below **Rev:** Boats on water, denomination above **Note:** Varieties exist.

Date	Mintage	F	VF	XF	Unc	BU
1977(a)	600,000	0.45	0.85	1.50	3.00	5.00
1983(a)	—	0.50	1.00	1.75	3.50	5.50
1989(a)	—	0.45	0.75	1.25	2.50	4.50
1991(a)	—	0.45	0.75	1.25	2.50	4.50
1996(a)	—	0.45	0.75	1.25	2.50	4.50
1997(a)	350	—	—	—	16.00	18.00
Note: In sets only						
1999(a)	1,800	—	—	—	7.00	9.00
Note: In sets only						

KM# 34 10 FRANCS

3.4000 g., Copper-Nickel, 20.9 mm. **Obv:** National arms **Rev:** Chimpanzee **Edge:** Plain

Date	Mintage	F	VF	XF	Unc	BU
2003	—	—	—	—	1.50	2.50

KM# 24 20 FRANCS

4.0000 g., Aluminum-Bronze, 23.5 mm. **Obv:** National arms within wreath, date below **Rev:** Boats on water, denomination above **Note:** Varieties exist.

Date	Mintage	F	VF	XF	Unc	BU
1977(a)	700,000	0.50	1.00	1.50	3.00	5.00
1982(a)	—	0.50	1.00	1.75	3.50	5.50
1983(a)	—	0.50	1.00	1.50	3.00	5.00
1986(a)	—	0.45	0.75	1.25	2.50	4.50
1991(a)	—	0.45	0.75	1.25	2.50	4.50
1996(a)	—	0.45	0.75	1.25	2.50	4.50
1997(a)	350	—	—	—	16.00	18.00
Note: In sets only						
1999(a)	1,800	—	—	—	7.00	9.00
Note: In sets only						

KM# 25 50 FRANCS

7.0500 g., Copper-Nickel, 25.7 mm. **Obv:** National arms within wreath, date below **Rev:** Pair of dromedary camels right, denomination above

Date	Mintage	F	VF	XF	Unc	BU
1977(a)	1,500,000	0.75	1.50	3.00	6.00	9.00
1982(a)	—	0.75	1.50	3.00	6.00	9.00
1983(a)	—	0.50	1.00	2.25	6.00	9.00
1986(a)	—	0.50	1.00	2.25	6.00	9.00
1989(a)	—	0.50	1.00	2.25	6.00	9.00
1991(a)	—	0.50	1.00	2.25	6.00	9.00
1997(a)	350	—	—	—	16.00	18.00
Note: In sets only						
1999(a)	1,800	—	—	—	7.00	9.00
Note: In sets only						

KM# 26 100 FRANCS

12.0000 g., Copper-Nickel, 30 mm. **Obv:** National arms within wreath, date below **Rev:** Pair of dromedary camels right, denomination above

Date	Mintage	F	VF	XF	Unc	BU
1977(a)	1,500,000	1.00	2.00	3.00	7.50	10.00
1983(a)	—	1.00	2.50	3.50	8.00	10.00
1991(a)	—	1.00	1.75	2.75	7.50	8.00
1996(a)	—	1.00	1.75	2.25	7.00	8.00
1997(a)	350	—	—	—	18.00	20.00
Note: In sets only						
1999(a)	1,800	—	—	—	8.00	10.00
Note: In sets only						
2004(a)	—	—	—	2.25	7.00	9.00

KM# 27 500 FRANCS

Aluminum-Bronze **Obv:** National arms within wreath, date below **Rev:** Denomination within sprays

Date	Mintage	F	VF	XF	Unc	BU
1989(a)	—	3.00	4.00	6.00	10.00	12.00
1991(a)	—	3.00	4.00	6.00	10.00	12.00
1997(a)	350	—	—	—	18.00	20.00
Note: In sets only						
1999(a)	1,800	—	—	—	12.00	15.00
Note: In sets only						

DOMINICAN REPUBLIC

The Dominican Republic, which occupies the eastern two-thirds of the island of Hispaniola, has an area of 18,704 sq. mi. (48,734 sq. km.) and a population of 7.9 million. Capital: Santo Domingo. The largely agricultural economy produces sugar, coffee, tobacco and cocoa. Tourism and casino gaming are also a rising source of revenue.

Columbus discovered Hispaniola in 1492, and named it La Isla Espanola - 'the Spanish Island'. Santo Domingo, the oldest white settlement in the Western Hemisphere, was the base from which Spain conducted its exploration of the New World. Later, French buccaneers settled the western third of Hispaniola, naming the colony St. Dominique, which in 1697, was ceded to France by Spain. In 1804, following a bloody revolt by former slaves, the French colony became the Republic of Haiti - mountainous country'. The Spanish called their part of Hispaniola Santo Domingo. In 1822, the Haitians conquered the entire island and held it until 1844, when Juan Pablo Duarte, the national hero of the Dominican Republic, drove them out of Santo Domingo and established an independent Dominican Republic. The republic returned voluntarily to Spanish dominion from 1861 to 1865, after being rejected by France, Britain and the United States. Independence was reclaimed in 1866.

MINT MARKS

(c) - Stylized maple leaf, Royal Canadian Mint
Mo – Mexico City
(o) - CHI in oval - Valcambi, Chiasso, Italy
(t) - Tower, Tower Mint, London

MONETARY SYSTEM

100 Centavos = 1 Peso Oro

REPUBLIC

REFORM COINAGE

1937

100 Centavos = 1 Peso Oro

KM# 17 CENTAVO

3.1100 g., Bronze **Obv:** National arms **Rev:** Palm tree divides denomination and weight, date below

Date	Mintage	F	VF	XF	Unc	BU
1937	1,000,000	0.50	1.50	7.50	75.00	100
1937 Proof	—	Value: 350				
1939	2,000,000	0.50	1.25	5.00	40.00	60.00
1941	2,000,000	0.25	0.50	3.00	12.00	25.00
1942	2,000,000	0.25	0.50	3.00	15.00	30.00
1944	5,000,000	0.20	0.50	1.50	10.00	20.00
1947	3,000,000	0.20	0.50	1.00	8.00	15.00
1949	3,000,000	0.20	0.40	1.00	8.00	15.00
1951	3,000,000	0.20	0.35	0.75	8.00	15.00
1952	3,000,000	0.20	0.35	0.75	8.00	15.00
1955	3,000,000	0.15	0.35	0.75	6.00	12.00
1956	3,000,000	0.15	0.35	0.75	6.00	12.00
1957	5,000,000	0.10	0.25	0.75	5.00	10.00
1959	5,000,000	0.10	0.25	0.75	5.00	10.00
1961	5,000,000	0.10	0.20	0.50	2.00	5.00
1961 10 known; Proof	—	Value: 500				

KM# 25 CENTAVO

Bronze **Subject:** 100th Anniversary - Restoration of the Republic **Obv:** National arms, date below **Rev:** Taino Indian divides denomination and weight, date below **Rev. Designer:** T. H. Paget

Date	Mintage	F	VF	XF	Unc	BU
1963	13,000,000	—	—	0.10	0.40	0.80

KM# 31 CENTAVO

3.0200 g., Bronze **Obv:** National arms **Rev:** Profile of native princess left divides denomination and weight, date below

Date	Mintage	F	VF	XF	Unc	BU
1968	5,000,000	—	—	0.10	0.20	0.50
1971	6,000,000	—	—	0.10	0.20	0.50
1972	3,000,000	—	—	0.10	0.20	0.50
1972 Proof	500	Value: 15.00				
1975	500,000	—	0.10	0.20	0.30	0.60

KM# 32 CENTAVO

3.0200 g., Bronze **Series:** F.A.O. **Obv:** National arms, date below **Rev:** Profile of native princess left divides denomination and weight, date below **Rev. Designer:** T. H. Paget

Date	Mintage	F	VF	XF	Unc	BU
1969	5,000,000	—	—	0.10	0.30	0.60

KM# 40 CENTAVO

Bronze **Subject:** Centennial - Death of Juan Pablo Duarte **Obv:** National arms, two dates below **Rev:** Bust facing divides denomination and weight, date below

Date	Mintage	F	VF	XF	Unc	BU
1976	3,995,000	—	—	0.10	0.20	0.50
1976 Proof	5,000	Value: 1.00				

KM# 48 CENTAVO

Bronze **Subject:** Death of Juan Pablo Duarte **Obv:** National arms without memorial legend **Rev:** Bust facing divides denomination and weight, date below

Date	Mintage	F	VF	XF	Unc	BU
1978	2,995,000	—	—	0.10	0.15	0.30
1978 Proof	5,000	Value: 2.00				
1979	2,985,000	—	—	0.10	0.15	0.30
1979 Proof	500	Value: 15.00				
1980	200,000	—	—	0.10	0.15	0.30
1980 Proof	3,000	Value: 1.00				
1981 Proof	3,000	Value: 1.00				

Note: KM#48a previously listed here has been moved to the Pattern section

KM# 64 CENTAVO

2.0000 g., Copper Plated Zinc, 19.1 mm. **Subject:** Human Rights **Obv:** National arms, denomination at left, date below **Rev:** Bust of Caonabo right

Date	Mintage	F	VF	XF	Unc	BU
1984Mo	10,000,000	—	—	—	0.25	0.50
1984Mo Proof	1,600	Value: 1.50				
1986	18,067,000	—	—	—	0.25	0.50
1986 Proof	1,600	Value: 1.50				
1987	15,000,000	—	—	—	0.25	0.50
1987(t) Proof	1,600	Value: 1.50				

KM# 18 5 CENTAVOS

Copper-Nickel, 21 mm. **Obv:** National arms **Rev:** Profile of native princess left divides denomination and weight, date below **Rev. Designer:** T. H. Paget

Date	Mintage	F	VF	XF	Unc	BU
1937	2,000,000	1.00	1.75	5.00	50.00	65.00
1937 Proof	—	Value: 600				
1939	200,000	5.00	15.00	60.00	350	400
1951	2,000,000	0.75	1.25	2.00	20.00	35.00
1956	1,000,000	0.20	0.50	0.80	3.50	5.00
1959	1,000,000	0.20	0.50	0.80	3.50	5.00
1961	4,000,000	0.10	0.20	0.35	0.75	1.25
1961 10 known; Proof	—	Value: 700				
1971	440,000	0.20	0.40	0.60	1.50	2.05
1972	2,000,000	0.10	0.15	0.20	0.40	0.90
1972 Proof	500	Value: 15.00				
1974	5,000,000	—	—	0.10	0.40	0.90
1974 Proof	500	Value: 15.00				

KM# 26 5 CENTAVOS

Copper-Nickel, 21 mm. **Subject:** 100th Anniversary - Restoration of the Republic **Obv:** National arms, two dates below **Rev:** Profile of native princess left divides denomination and weight, date below **Rev. Designer:** T. H. Paget

Date	Mintage	F	VF	XF	Unc	BU
1963	4,000,000	—	0.10	0.15	0.60	1.25

KM# 41 5 CENTAVOS

Copper-Nickel, 41 mm. **Subject:** Centennial - Death of Juan Pablo Duarte **Obv:** National arms, two dates below **Rev:** Bust facing divides denomination and weight, date below

Date	Mintage	F	VF	XF	Unc	BU
1976	5,595,000	—	—	0.10	0.50	1.00
1976 Proof	5,000	Value: 2.00				

KM# 49 5 CENTAVOS

Copper-Nickel, 21 mm. **Obv:** National arms without memorial legend **Rev:** Bust facing divides denomination and weight, date below

Date	Mintage	F	VF	XF	Unc	BU
1978	1,996,000	—	—	0.10	0.35	0.90
1978 Proof	5,000	Value: 1.50				
1979	2,988,000	—	—	0.10	0.35	0.90
1979 Proof	500	Value: 15.00				
1980	5,300,000	—	—	0.10	0.35	0.90
1980 Proof	3,000	Value: 2.00				
1981	4,500,000	—	—	0.10	0.35	0.90
1981 Proof	3,000	Value: 2.00				

Note: KM#49a previously listed here has been moved to the Pattern section

KM# 59 5 CENTAVOS

5.0000 g., Copper Nickel, 21 mm. **Subject:** Human Rights **Obv:** National arms, date below **Rev:** Conjoined busts right, denomination above

Date	Mintage	F	VF	XF	Unc	BU
1983	3,998,000	—	—	0.10	0.30	0.90
1983(t) Proof	1,600	Value: 2.00				
1984Mo	10,000,000	—	—	0.10	0.30	0.90
1984Mo Proof	1,600	Value: 2.00				
1986	12,898,000	—	—	0.10	0.30	0.90
1986 Proof	1,600	Value: 2.00				
1987	10,000,000	—	—	0.10	0.30	0.90
1987(t) Proof	1,700	Value: 2.00				

KM# 69 5 CENTAVOS

Nickel Clad Steel, 21 mm. **Subject:** Native Culture **Obv:** National arms, date below **Rev:** Native drummer, denomination at left

Date	Mintage	F	VF	XF	Unc	BU
1989	50,000,000	—	—	—	0.35	0.90

KM# 19 10 CENTAVOS

2.5000 g., 0.9000 Silver 0.0723 oz. ASW, 17.9 mm. **Obv:** National arms **Rev:** Profile of native princess left divides denomination and weight

Date	Mintage	F	VF	XF	Unc	BU
1937	1,000,000	BV	2.00	5.00	40.00	60.00
1937 Proof	—	Value: 700				
1939	150,000	5.00	15.00	40.00	300	350
1942	2,000,000	1.25	2.00	3.00	30.00	40.00

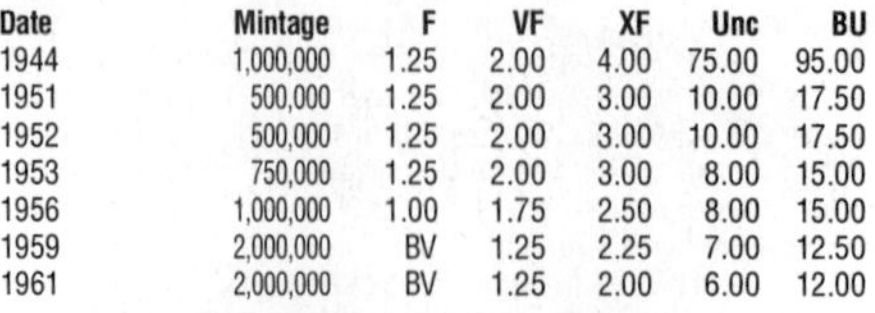

Date	Mintage	F	VF	XF	Unc	BU
1944	1,000,000	1.25	2.00	4.00	75.00	95.00
1951	500,000	1.25	2.00	3.00	10.00	17.50
1952	500,000	1.25	2.00	3.00	10.00	17.50
1953	750,000	1.25	2.00	3.00	8.00	15.00
1956	1,000,000	1.00	1.75	2.50	8.00	15.00
1959	2,000,000	BV	1.25	2.25	7.00	12.50
1961	2,000,000	BV	1.25	2.00	6.00	12.00

KM# 19a 10 CENTAVOS

2.4900 g., Copper-Nickel, 17.9 mm. **Obv:** National arms **Rev:** Profile of native princess left divides denomination and weight, date below **Edge:** Plain

Date	Mintage	F	VF	XF	Unc	BU
1967	10,000,000	—	—	0.15	0.50	1.00
1973	8,000,000	—	—	0.15	0.50	1.00
1973 Proof	500	Value: 20.00				
1975	8,000,000	—	—	0.15	0.50	1.00

KM# 27 10 CENTAVOS

2.5000 g., 0.6500 Silver 0.0522 oz. ASW, 17.9 mm. **Subject:** 100th Anniversary - Restoration of the Republic **Obv:** National arms **Rev:** Profile of native princess left divides denomination and weight **Rev. Designer:** T. H. Paget

Date	Mintage	F	VF	XF	Unc	BU
1963	4,000,000	—	BV	1.00	2.00	3.00

KM# 42 10 CENTAVOS

Copper-Nickel, 17.9 mm. **Subject:** Centennial - Death of Juan Pablo Duarte **Obv:** National arms **Rev:** Bust facing, date below

Date	Mintage	F	VF	XF	Unc	BU
1976	5,595,000	—	—	0.10	0.75	1.50
1976 Proof	5,000	Value: 2.00				

KM# 50 10 CENTAVOS

2.5600 g., Copper-Nickel, 17.9 mm. **Obv:** National arms **Rev:** Bust facing divides denomination and weight, date below

Date	Mintage	F	VF	XF	Unc	BU
1978	3,000,000	—	—	0.10	0.50	1.00
1978 Proof	5,000	Value: 2.00				
1979	4,020,000	—	—	0.10	0.50	1.00
1979 Proof	500	Value: 20.00				
1980	4,400,000	—	—	0.10	0.35	1.00
1980 Proof	3,000	Value: 3.00				
1981	6,000,000	—	—	0.10	0.35	1.00
1981 Proof	3,000	Value: 3.00				

Note: KM#50a previously listed here has been moved to the Pattern section

KM# 60 10 CENTAVOS

2.5000 g., Copper-Nickel, 17.9 mm. **Subject:** Human Rights **Obv:** National arms, date below **Rev:** Head left, denomination above

Date	Mintage	F	VF	XF	Unc	BU
1983	4,998,000	—	—	0.10	0.35	0.90
1983(t)	4,000,000	—	—	0.10	0.35	0.90
1983(t) Proof	1,600	Value: 2.50				
1984Mo	15,000,000	—	—	0.10	0.25	0.75
Note: Coarse reeding						
1984Mo Proof	1,600	Value: 2.50				
Note: Coarse reeding						
1986	15,515,000	—	—	0.10	0.25	0.75
1986 Proof	1,600	Value: 2.50				
1987	20,000,000	—	—	0.10	0.25	0.75
1987(t) Proof	1,700	Value: 2.50				

KM# 70 10 CENTAVOS

Nickel Clad Steel, 17.9 mm. **Obv:** National arms, date below **Rev:** Indigenous fruits and vegetables divide denomination

Date	Mintage	F	VF	XF	Unc	BU
1989	40,000,000	—	—	—	0.40	0.90
1991	3,500,000	—	—	—	0.40	0.90

KM# 20 25 CENTAVOS

6.2500 g., 0.9000 Silver 0.1808 oz. ASW, 24 mm. **Obv:** National arms **Rev:** Profile of native princess left divides denomination and weight, date below **Rev. Designer:** T. H. Paget

Date	Mintage	F	VF	XF	Unc	BU
1937	560,000	BV	5.00	15.00	65.00	75.00
1937 Proof	—	Value: 1,000				
1939	160,000	5.00	15.00	50.00	500	650
1942	560,000	2.50	4.00	10.00	100	125
1944	400,000	2.50	4.00	8.00	100	125
1947	400,000	2.50	4.00	8.00	80.00	100
1951	400,000	2.50	4.00	8.00	80.00	100
1952	400,000	BV	3.00	5.00	12.50	15.00
1956	400,000	BV	2.50	4.00	10.00	12.50
1960	600,000	BV	2.50	4.00	10.00	12.50
1961	800,000	BV	2.50	4.00	10.00	12.50

KM# 20a.1 25 CENTAVOS

6.2500 g., Copper Nickel, 24 mm. **Obv:** National arms **Rev:** Profile of native princess left divides denomination and weight, date below **Rev. Designer:** T. H. Paget **Edge:** Plain

Date	Mintage	F	VF	XF	Unc	BU
1967	5,000,000	—	0.10	0.20	0.75	1.00
1972	800,000	—	0.10	0.40	1.00	1.50
1972 Proof	500	Value: 20.00				

KM# 20a.2 25 CENTAVOS

5.9500 g., Copper-Nickel, 24 mm. **Obv:** National arms **Rev:** Profile of native princess left divides denomination and weight, date below **Rev. Designer:** T. H. Paget **Edge:** Reeded

Date	Mintage	F	VF	XF	Unc	BU
1974	2,000,000	—	0.10	0.40	1.00	1.50
1974 Proof	500	Value: 20.00				

KM# 28 25 CENTAVOS

6.2500 g., 0.6500 Silver 0.1306 oz. ASW, 24 mm. **Subject:** 100th Anniversary - Restoration of the Republic **Obv:** National arms, two dates below **Rev:** Profile of native princess left divides denomination and weight, date below **Rev. Designer:** T. H. Paget

Date	Mintage	F	VF	XF	Unc	BU
1963	2,400,000	—	BV	2.00	3.00	5.00

KM# 43 25 CENTAVOS

Copper-Nickel, 24 mm. **Subject:** Centennial - Death of Juan Pablo Duarte **Obv:** National arms, two dates below **Rev:** Bust facing divides denomination and weight, date below

Date	Mintage	F	VF	XF	Unc	BU
1976	3,195,000	—	0.10	0.40	1.00	1.50
1976 Proof	5,000	Value: 2.50				

KM# 51 25 CENTAVOS

6.2700 g., Copper-Nickel, 24 mm. **Obv:** National arms without memorial legend **Rev:** Bust facing divides denomination and weight, date below

Date	Mintage	F	VF	XF	Unc	BU
1978	996,000	—	—	0.35	0.75	1.00
1978 Proof	5,000	Value: 3.00				
1979	2,089,000	—	—	0.15	0.50	0.75
1979 Proof	500	Value: 25.00				
1980	2,600,000	—	—	0.15	0.50	0.75
1980 Proof	3,000	Value: 3.00				
1981	3,200,000	—	—	0.15	0.50	0.75
1981 Proof	3,000	Value: 3.00				

Note: KM#51a previously listed here has been moved to the Pattern section

KM# 61.1 25 CENTAVOS

6.2500 g., Copper-Nickel, 24 mm. **Subject:** Human Rights **Obv:** National arms, date below, denomination at left **Rev:** Profiles of the Mirabel sisters left, Patria, Minerva & Maria Teresa, human rights martyrs murdered 25.11.1960 by Trujillo **Edge:** Fine reeding **Note:** Medal rotation.

Date	Mintage	F	VF	XF	Unc	BU
1983	793,000	—	0.10	0.20	0.50	1.00
1983(t)	5,000	—	—	—	2.50	4.00
1983(t) Proof	1,600	Value: 8.00				
1984Mo Coarse reeding	6,400,000	—	—	0.15	0.40	1.00
1984Mo Proof; coarse reeding	1,600	Value: 8.00				

KM# 61.2 25 CENTAVOS

6.2500 g., Copper-Nickel, 24 mm. **Subject:** Human Rights **Obv:** National arms, date below, denomination at left **Rev:** Profiles of the Mirabel sisters left, Patria, Minerva and Maria Teresa, human rights martyrs murdered 25.11.1960 by Trujillo **Edge:** Fine reeding **Note:** Coin rotation.

Date	Mintage	F	VF	XF	Unc	BU
1986 Coarse reeding	10,132,000	—	—	0.15	0.40	1.00
1986 Proof	1,600	Value: 8.00				
1987	6,000,000	—	—	0.15	0.40	1.00
1987(t) Proof	1,700	Value: 8.00				

KM# 71.1 25 CENTAVOS

Nickel Clad Steel, 24 mm. **Subject:** Native Culture **Obv:** National arms, date below **Rev:** Two oxen pulling cart, denomination above

Date	Mintage	F	VF	XF	Unc	BU
1989 Coarse reeding	16,000,000	—	—	—	0.60	1.25
1991 Fine reeding	38,000,000	—	—	—	0.60	1.25

KM# 71.2 25 CENTAVOS

Nickel Clad Steel, 24 mm. **Subject:** Native Culture **Obv:** National arms, date below **Rev:** Two oxen pulling cart, denomination above **Edge:** Coarse reeding **Note:** Obverse and reverse legends and designs in beaded circle. Varieties exist.

Date	Mintage	F	VF	XF	Unc	BU
1990	20,000,000	—	—	—	0.60	1.25

KM# 21 1/2 PESO

12.5000 g., 0.9000 Silver 0.3617 oz. ASW, 30.5 mm. **Obv:** National arms **Rev:** Profile of native princess left divides denomination and weight **Rev. Designer:** T. H. Paget

Date	Mintage	F	VF	XF	Unc	BU
1937	500,000	BV	7.50	12.50	70.00	100
1937 Proof	—	Value: 1,500				
1944	100,000	BV	15.00	40.00	400	450
1947	200,000	BV	10.00	30.00	350	500
1951	200,000	BV	7.50	15.00	150	200
1952	140,000	BV	7.50	12.50	70.00	100
1959	100,000	BV	6.00	10.00	40.00	75.00
1960	100,000	BV	6.00	9.00	30.00	55.00
1961	400,000	BV	5.00	7.00	25.00	50.00

KM# 21a.1 1/2 PESO

Copper-Nickel, 30.5 mm. **Obv:** National arms **Rev:** Profile of native princess left divides denomination and weight **Rev. Designer:** T.H. Pajet **Edge:** Plain

Date	Mintage	F	VF	XF	Unc	BU
1967	1,500,000	—	0.20	0.40	1.50	3.00
1968	600,000	—	0.30	0.50	2.50	5.00

KM# 29 1/2 PESO

12.5000 g., 0.6500 Silver 0.2612 oz. ASW, 30.5 mm. **Subject:** 100th Anniversary - Restoration of the Republic **Obv:** National arms **Rev:** Profile of native princess left divides denomination and weight **Rev. Designer:** T. H. Paget

Date	Mintage	F	VF	XF	Unc	BU
1963	300,000	—	BV	4.50	7.50	9.00

KM# 21a.2 1/2 PESO

Copper-Nickel, 30.5 mm. **Obv:** National arms **Rev:** Profile of native princess left divides denomination and weight **Edge:** Reeded

Date	Mintage	F	VF	XF	Unc	BU
1973	600,000	—	0.20	0.40	1.50	2.00
1973 Proof	500	Value: 30.00				
1975	600,000	—	0.20	0.40	1.50	2.00

KM# 44 1/2 PESO

Copper-Nickel, 30.5 mm. **Subject:** Centennial - Death of Juan Pablo Duarte **Obv:** National arms, two dates below **Rev:** Bust facing divides denomination and weight, date below

Date	Mintage	F	VF	XF	Unc	BU
1976	195,000	—	0.20	0.40	1.50	2.00
1976 Proof	5,000	Value: 3.00				

KM# 52 1/2 PESO

12.3800 g., Copper-Nickel, 30.5 mm. **Obv:** National arms without memorial legend **Rev:** Bust facing divides denomination and weight, date below

Date	Mintage	F	VF	XF	Unc	BU
1978	296,000	—	0.20	0.40	1.50	2.00
1978 Proof	5,000	Value: 4.00				
1979	967,000	—	0.20	0.40	1.50	2.00
1979 Proof	500	Value: 30.00				
1980	1,000,000	—	0.20	0.40	1.50	2.00
1980 Proof	3,000	Value: 5.00				
1981	1,300,000	—	0.20	0.40	1.50	2.00
1981 Proof	3,000	Value: 5.00				

Note: KM#52a previously listed here has been moved to the Pattern section

KM# 62.1 1/2 PESO

12.5000 g., Copper-Nickel, 30.5 mm. **Subject:** Human Rights **Obv:** National arms, date below, denomination at left **Rev:** Three profiles right **Edge:** Fine reeding **Note:** Medal rotation.

Date	Mintage	F	VF	XF	Unc	BU
1983	393,000	—	0.20	0.40	1.50	2.00
1983(t)	5,000	—	—	—	4.00	5.00
1983(t) Proof	1,600	Value: 15.00				
1984Mo Coarse reeding	3,200,000	—	0.20	0.40	1.50	2.00
1984Mo Proof; coarse reeding	1,600	Value: 15.00				

KM# 62.2 1/2 PESO

12.5000 g., Copper-Nickel, 30.5 mm. **Subject:** Human Rights **Obv:** National arms, date below, denomination at left **Rev:** Three profiles right **Edge:** Fine reeding **Note:** Coin rotation.

Date	Mintage	F	VF	XF	Unc	BU
1986	5,225,000	—	0.20	0.40	2.00	1.50
1986 Proof	1,600	Value: 15.00				
1987	3,000,000	—	0.20	0.40	2.00	1.50
1987(t) Proof	1,700	Value: 15.00				

KM# 73.1 1/2 PESO

Nickel Clad Steel, 30.5 mm. **Subject:** National Culture **Obv:** National arms **Rev:** Beacon at Colon

Date	Mintage	F	VF	XF	Unc	BU
1989	8,000,000	—	—	—	2.00	3.00

KM# 73.2 1/2 PESO

Nickel-Clad Steel, 30.5 mm. **Subject:** National Culture **Obv:** National arms, date below **Rev:** Beacon at Colon, denomination at left

Date	Mintage	F	VF	XF	Unc	BU
1990	1,500,000	—	—	—	2.00	3.00

KM# 22 PESO

26.7000 g., 0.9000 Silver 0.7726 oz. ASW **Obv:** National arms **Rev:** HP below head of native princess left **Rev. Designer:** T. H. Paget

Date	Mintage	F	VF	XF	Unc	BU
1939	15,000	15.00	45.00	200	1,500	—
1939 Proof	—	Value: 2,250				
1952	20,000	BV	10.00	12.00	16.00	30.00

KM# 23 PESO
26.7000 g., 0.9000 Silver 0.7726 oz. ASW, 38 mm. **Subject:** 25th Anniversary of Trujillo Regime **Obv:** National arms **Rev:** Bust right divides date and denomination **Note:** 30,550 officially melted following Trujillo's assassination in 1961.

Date	Mintage	F	VF	XF	Unc	BU
1955	50,000	10.00	12.00	15.00	25.00	35.00

KM# 45 PESO
Copper-Nickel **Subject:** Centennial - Death of Juan Pablo Duarte **Obv:** National arms, two dates below **Rev:** Bust facing divides denomination and weight, date below

Date	Mintage	F	VF	XF	Unc	BU
1976	25,000	—	—	1.00	2.00	4.00
1976 Proof	5,000	Value: 7.50				

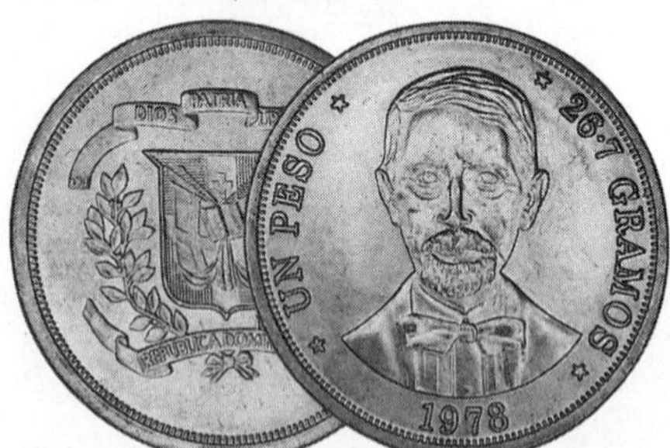

KM# 53 PESO
Copper-Nickel **Obv:** National arms without memorial legend **Rev:** Bust facing divides denomination and weight, date below

Date	Mintage	F	VF	XF	Unc	BU
1978	35,000	—	—	1.00	2.00	4.00
1978 Proof	5,000	Value: 7.50				
1979	45,000	—	—	1.00	2.00	4.00
1979 Proof	500	Value: 35.00				
1980	20,000	—	—	1.00	2.00	4.00
1980 Proof	3,000	Value: 6.50				
1981 Proof	3,000	Value: 6.50				

Note: KM#53a previously listed here has been moved to the Pattern section

KM# 63.1 PESO
16.9000 g., Copper Nickel, 33.2 mm. **Subject:** Human Rights **Obv:** National arms, date below, denomination at left **Rev:** Three profiles right **Edge:** Fine reeding **Shape:** 10-sided **Note:** Medal rotation.

Date	Mintage	F	VF	XF	Unc	BU
1983	5,000	—	—	—	6.00	12.00
1983(t)	93,000	—	—	1.00	2.50	4.00
1983(t) Proof	1,600	Value: 15.00				
1984Mo Coarse reeding	120,000	—	—	1.00	2.50	4.00
1984Mo Proof; coarse reeding	1,600	Value: 15.00				

KM# 63.2 PESO
16.9000 g., Copper-Nickel, 33.2 mm. **Subject:** Human Rights **Obv:** National arms, date below, denomination at left **Rev:** Three profiles right **Edge:** Fine reeding **Shape:** 10-sided **Note:** Coin rotation.

Date	Mintage	F	VF	XF	Unc	BU
1986	—	—	—	1.00	2.50	4.00

KM# 65 PESO
Nickel Bonded Steel **Subject:** 15th Central American and Caribbean Games **Obv:** National arms, date below, denomination at left **Rev:** St. George and coat of arms **Shape:** Round

Date	Mintage	F	VF	XF	Unc	BU
1986	100,000	—	—	1.00	3.00	5.00
1986 Proof	2,000	Value: 15.00				

KM# 80.1 PESO
Copper-Zinc, 25 mm. **Subject:** Juan Pablo Duarte **Obv:** National arms and denomination **Rev:** DUARTE on bust 3/4 left, date below **Shape:** 11-sided **Note:** Coin die alignment.

Date	Mintage	F	VF	XF	Unc	BU
1991	40,000,000	—	—	—	2.00	2.50
1992	35,000,000	—	—	—	2.00	2.50

KM# 80.2 PESO
6.4900 g., Copper-Zinc, 25 mm. **Subject:** Juan Pablo Duarte **Obv:** National arms and denomination **Rev:** DUARTE below bust, date below **Note:** Coin die alignment.

Date	Mintage	F	VF	XF	Unc	BU
1992	35,000,000	—	—	—	2.00	2.50
1993	40,000,000	—	—	—	2.00	2.50
2000	—	—	—	—	2.00	2.50
2002	—	—	—	—	2.00	2.50
2005	—	—	—	—	2.00	2.50

KM# 89 5 PESOS
5.9500 g., Bi-Metallic Stainless Steel center in Brass ring, 23 mm. **Subject:** Sanchez **Obv:** National arms and denomination **Rev:** Portrait facing within circle, date below **Edge:** Segmented reeding

Date	Mintage	F	VF	XF	Unc	BU
2002	—	—	—	—	2.50	3.00
2005	—	—	—	—	2.50	3.00
2007	—	—	—	—	2.50	3.00

KM# 106 10 PESOS
8.0500 g., Bi-Metallic Brass center in Copper-Nickel ring, 26.93 mm. **Obv:** Value at left of national arms **Obv. Legend:** • REPUBLICA DOMINICANA • **Rev:** Bust of General Mella facing **Rev. Legend:** BANCO CENTRAL DE LA REPUBLICA DOMINICANA **Edge:** Segmented reeding

Date	Mintage	F	VF	XF	Unc	BU
2005	—	—	—	—	6.00	8.00

East Africa was an administrative grouping of five separate British territories: Kenya, Uganda, the Sultanate of Zanzibar and British Somaliland.

The common interest of Kenya, Tanganyika and Uganda invited cooperation in economic matters and consideration of political union. The territorial governors, organized as the East Africa High Commission, met periodically to administer such common activities as taxation, industrial development and education. The authority of the Commission did not infringe upon the constitution and internal autonomy of the individual colonies. A common coinage and banknotes, which were also legal tender in Aden, were provided for use of the member colonies by the East Africa Currency Board. The coinage through 1919 had the legend "East Africa and Uganda Protectorate".

NOTE: For later coinage see Kenya, Tanzania and Uganda.

RULER
British

MINT MARKS
A - Ackroyd & Best, Morley
I - Bombay Mint
H - Heaton Mint, Birmingham, England
K, KN - King's Norton Mint, Birmingham, England
SA - Pretoria Mint, South Africa
No mint mark – British Royal Mint, London

EAST AFRICA AND UGANDA PROTECTORATES

DECIMAL COINAGE

50 Cents = 1 Shilling; 100 Cents = 1 Florin

KM# 6 1/2 CENT
Aluminum **Ruler:** Edward VII **Edge:** Plain

Date	Mintage	F	VF	XF	Unc	BU
1908	900,000	15.00	25.00	60.00	90.00	—

KM# 6a 1/2 CENT
Copper-Nickel **Ruler:** Edward VII **Obv:** Center hole divides crown and denomination, fleurs flank **Rev:** Tusks flank center hole, denomination above, circle surrounds **Edge:** Plain

Date	Mintage	F	VF	XF	Unc	BU
1909	900,000	6.00	12.00	35.00	60.00	95.00

KM# 5 CENT

Aluminum **Ruler:** Edward VII **Obv:** Center hole divides crown and denomination, fleurs flank **Rev:** Tusks flank center hole, denomination above, circle surrounds **Edge:** Plain

Date	Mintage	F	VF	XF	Unc	BU
1907	6,948,000	5.00	10.00	30.00	50.00	—
1908	2,871,000	8.00	16.00	35.00	60.00	—

KM# 5a CENT

2.8800 g., Copper-Nickel **Ruler:** Edward VII **Obv:** Center hole divides crown and denomination, fleurs flank **Rev:** Tusks flank center hole, denomination above, circle surrounds **Edge:** Plain

Date	Mintage	F	VF	XF	Unc	BU
1909	25,000,000	0.50	1.25	3.00	7.00	—
1910	6,000,000	0.50	1.25	4.00	12.00	—

KM# 7 CENT

Copper-Nickel **Ruler:** George V **Obv:** Center hole divides crown and denomination, fleurs flank **Rev:** Tusks flank center hole, denomination above, circle surrounds **Edge:** Plain

Date	Mintage	F	VF	XF	Unc	BU
1911H	25,000,000	0.25	1.00	5.00	15.00	—
1912H	20,000,000	0.25	1.00	3.00	8.00	—
1913	4,529,000	0.75	1.50	8.00	20.00	—
1914 S	6,000,000	0.75	1.75	5.00	15.00	—
1914H	2,500,000	1.00	3.00	8.00	20.00	—
1916H	1,824,000	1.25	4.00	10.00	25.00	—
1917H	3,176,000	0.75	2.00	5.00	15.00	—
1918H	10,000,000	0.50	1.00	3.25	12.00	—

KM# A11 5 CENTS

Copper-Nickel **Ruler:** Edward VII

Date	Mintage	F	VF	XF	Unc	BU
1907 Rare	—	—	—	—	—	—

KM# 11 5 CENTS

Copper-Nickel **Ruler:** George V **Obv:** Center hole divides crown and denomination, fleurs flank **Rev:** Tusks flank center hole, denomination above, circle surrounds **Edge:** Plain

Date	Mintage	F	VF	XF	Unc	BU
1913H	300,000	1.50	4.00	20.00	35.00	—
1914K	1,240,000	0.75	3.25	12.00	22.50	—
1914K Proof	—	Value: 200				

Note: The 1914K was issued with British West Africa KM#8 in a double (4 pieces) Specimen Set

Date	Mintage	F	VF	XF	Unc	BU
1919H	200,000	10.00	15.00	40.00	120	—

KM# 2 10 CENTS

Copper-Nickel **Ruler:** Edward VII **Obv:** Center hole divides crown and denomination, fleurs flank **Rev:** Tusks flank center hole, denomination above, circle surrounds **Edge:** Plain

Date	Mintage	F	VF	XF	Unc	BU
1906	—	1,000	1,500	2,000	3,000	—
1907	1,000,000	1.50	4.00	16.00	30.00	50.00
1910	500,000	4.00	8.00	35.00	60.00	—

KM# 8 10 CENTS

Copper-Nickel **Ruler:** George V **Obv:** Center hole divides crown and denomination, fleurs flank **Rev:** Tusks flank center hole, denomination above, circle surrounds **Edge:** Plain

Date	Mintage	F	VF	XF	Unc	BU
1911H	1,250,000	2.00	5.00	25.00	40.00	—
1912H	1,050,000	2.00	5.00	30.00	55.00	—
1913	50,000	75.00	150	300	500	—
1918H	400,000	10.00	20.00	80.00	150	—

KM# 3 25 CENTS

2.9160 g., 0.8000 Silver 0.0750 oz. ASW **Ruler:** Edward VII **Obv:** Bust of King Edward VII right **Obv. Designer:** G.W. DeSaulles **Rev:** Lion and mountains within 3/4 circle with fleur ends, denomination and date below **Edge:** Reeded

Date	Mintage	F	VF	XF	Unc	BU
1906	400,000	3.00	7.00	35.00	60.00	—
1910H	200,000	4.00	8.00	50.00	90.00	—

KM# 10 25 CENTS

2.9160 g., 0.8000 Silver 0.0750 oz. ASW **Ruler:** George V **Obv:** Bust of King George V left **Obv. Designer:** E.B. MacKennal **Rev:** Lion and mountains within 3/4 circle with fleur ends, date and denomination below **Edge:** Reeded

Date	Mintage	F	VF	XF	Unc	BU
1912	180,000	4.00	15.00	45.00	80.00	—
1913	300,000	3.50	10.00	35.00	60.00	—
1914H	80,000	20.00	35.00	60.00	100	—
1914H Proof	—	Value: 400				
1918H	40,000	150	300	500	900	—

KM# 4 50 CENTS

5.8319 g., 0.8000 Silver 0.1500 oz. ASW **Ruler:** Edward VII **Obv:** Bust of King Edward VII right **Obv. Designer:** G.W. DeSaulles **Rev:** Lion and mountains within circle with fleur ends, denomination and date below **Edge:** Reeded

Date	Mintage	F	VF	XF	Unc	BU
1906	200,000	4.50	30.00	80.00	140	—
1906 Proof	—	Value: 400				
1909	100,000	15.00	50.00	155	300	—
1910	100,000	10.00	45.00	110	225	—

KM# 9 50 CENTS

5.8319 g., 0.8000 Silver 0.1500 oz. ASW **Ruler:** George V **Obv:** Bust of King George V left **Obv. Designer:** E.B. MacKennal **Rev:** Lion and mountains within circle with fleur ends, denomination and date below **Edge:** Reeded

Date	Mintage	F	VF	XF	Unc	BU
1911	150,000	7.50	35.00	85.00	140	—
1911 Proof	—	Value: 250				
1912	100,000	8.00	45.00	125	200	—
1913	200,000	5.00	30.00	65.00	135	—
1914H	180,000	5.00	30.00	65.00	135	—
1918H	60,000	60.00	200	350	500	—
1919	100,000	250	350	900	1,500	—

BRITISH COLONIES

DECIMAL COINAGE

50 Cents = 1 Shilling; 100 Cents = 1 Florin

KM# 12 CENT

Copper-Nickel **Ruler:** George V **Obv:** Center hole divides crown and denomination, fleurs flank **Rev:** Tusks flank center hole, denomination above, circle surrounds **Edge:** Plain

Date	Mintage	F	VF	XF	Unc	BU
1920H	Est. 2,908,000	30.00	60.00	110	225	—

Note: Only about 30% of the total mintage was released into circulation

Date	Mintage	F	VF	XF	Unc	BU
1920H Proof; 20-30 pcs	—	Value: 300				
1920	—	—	—	—	750	—
1921	920,000	—	—	—	3,000	—

Note: Not released for circulation

KM# 13 5 CENTS

Copper-Nickel **Ruler:** George V **Obv:** Center hole divides crown and denomination, fleurs flank **Rev:** Tusks flank center hole, denomination above, circle surrounds **Edge:** Plain

Date	Mintage	F	VF	XF	Unc	BU
1920H	Est. 550,000	75.00	250	300	425	—

Note: Only about 30% of the total mintage was released into circulation

Date	Mintage	F	VF	XF	Unc	BU
1920H Proof; 20-30 pcs	—	Value: 475				

KM# 14 10 CENTS

Copper-Nickel **Ruler:** George V **Obv:** Center hole divides crown and denomination, fleurs flank **Rev:** Tusks flank center hole, denomination above, circle surrounds **Edge:** Plain

Date	Mintage	F	VF	XF	Unc	BU
1920H	Est. 700,000	120	150	225	375	—
1920H Proof	—	Value: 600				

Note: 20-30 pcs

KM# 15 25 CENTS

2.9160 g., 0.5000 Silver 0.0469 oz. ASW **Ruler:** George V **Obv:** Bust of King George V left **Obv. Designer:** E.B. MacKennal **Rev:** Lion and mountains within circle with fleur ends, date and denomination below **Edge:** Reeded

Date	Mintage	F	VF	XF	Unc	BU
1920H	748,000	25.00	35.00	75.00	150	—
1920H Proof	—	Value: 250				

Note: 20-30 pieces

KM# 16 50 CENTS

5.8319 g., 0.5000 Silver 0.0937 oz. ASW **Ruler:** George V **Obv:** Bust of King George V left **Obv. Designer:** E.B. MacKennal **Rev:**

Lion and mountains within circle with fleur ends, date and denomination below **Edge:** Reeded **Note:** Not released for circulation.

Date	Mintage	F	VF	XF	Unc	BU
1920A	12,000	1,500	2,000	3,000	4,000	—
1920H	62,000	500	1,000	1,500	2,500	—
1920H Proof	—	Value: 600				

Note: 20-30 pieces

KM# 17 FLORIN

11.6638 g., 0.5000 Silver 0.1875 oz. ASW **Ruler:** George V **Obv:** Bust of King George V left **Obv. Designer:** E.B. MacKennal **Rev:** Lion and mountains within circle with fleur ends, denomination and date below **Edge:** Reeded

Date	Mintage	F	VF	XF	Unc	BU
1920	1,479,000	15.00	75.00	200	325	—
1920A	542,000	200	500	1,100	2,000	—
1920H	9,689,000	12.50	60.00	125	275	—
1920H Proof	—	Value: 800				
Note: 20-30 pieces						
1921	2	—	—	—	4,500	—

REFORM COINAGE

Commencing May 1921

100 Cents = 1 Shilling

KM# 22 CENT

1.9100 g., Bronze **Ruler:** George V **Obv:** Center hole divides crown and denomination, fleurs flank **Rev:** Tusks flank center hole, denomination above, circle surrounds **Edge:** Plain

Date	Mintage	F	VF	XF	Unc	BU
1922	8,250,000	0.25	1.00	8.00	15.00	22.00
1922H	43,750,000	0.25	0.50	3.50	6.50	9.00
1923	50,000,000	0.25	0.50	3.50	6.50	9.00
1924	Inc. above	0.25	0.75	5.00	10.00	15.00
1924H	17,500,000	0.25	0.75	4.00	8.00	11.00
1924KN	10,720,000	0.25	0.75	4.00	8.00	11.00
1924KN Proof	—	Value: 125				
1925	6,000,000	50.00	100	225	350	—
1925KN	6,780,000	2.00	4.00	18.00	35.00	52.00
1927	10,000,000	0.25	0.75	5.00	10.00	15.00
1927 Proof	—	Value: 125				
1928H	12,000,000	0.25	0.75	4.00	8.00	11.00
1928KN	11,764,000	0.50	2.00	8.00	18.00	27.00
1928KN Proof	—	Value: 125				
1930	15,000,000	0.25	0.75	2.50	5.00	8.00
1930 Proof	—	Value: 125				
1935	10,000,000	0.25	0.50	1.75	3.50	6.00

KM# 29 CENT

1.9500 g., Bronze **Ruler:** George VI **Obv:** Center hole divides crown and denomination, fleurs flank **Rev:** Tusks flank center hole, denomination above, circle surrounds **Edge:** Plain

Date	Mintage	F	VF	XF	Unc	BU
1942	25,000,000	0.10	0.25	1.25	2.50	4.00
1942I	15,000,000	0.15	0.30	1.50	3.00	5.00

KM# 32 CENT

1.7000 g., Bronze **Ruler:** George VI **Obv:** Center hole divides crown and denomination, fleurs flank **Obv. Legend:** ET IND. IMP. dropped from legend **Rev:** Tusks flank center hole, denomination above, circle surrounds **Edge:** Plain

Date	Mintage	F	VF	XF	Unc	BU
1949	4,000,000	0.35	0.75	2.00	4.00	7.00
1949 Proof	—	Value: 125				
1950	16,000,000	0.10	0.25	1.25	2.50	5.00
1950 Proof	—	Value: 150				
1951H	9,000,000	0.10	0.25	1.25	2.50	5.00
1951H Proof	—	Value: 125				
1951KN	11,140,000	0.10	0.25	1.25	2.50	5.00
1951KN Proof	—	Value: 125				
1952	7,000,000	0.10	0.25	1.25	2.50	5.00
1952 Proof	—	Value: 150				
1952H	13,000,000	0.10	0.25	1.25	2.50	5.00
1952H Proof	—	Value: 125				
1952KN	5,230,000	0.10	0.35	1.50	5.00	8.00

KM# 35 CENT

2.0000 g., Bronze, 20 mm. **Ruler:** Elizabeth II **Obv:** Center hole divides crown and denomination, fleurs flank **Rev:** Tusks flank center hole, denomination above, circle surrounds **Edge:** Plain

Date	Mintage	F	VF	XF	Unc	BU
1954	8,000,000	0.10	0.25	0.85	2.50	5.00
1954 Proof	—	Value: 150				
1955	5,000,000	0.10	0.25	0.50	1.75	3.00
1955H	6,384,000	0.10	0.20	0.65	1.75	3.00
1955KN	4,000,000	0.10	0.20	0.65	1.75	3.00
1956H	15,616,000	0.10	0.15	0.30	1.25	3.00
1956KN	9,680,000	0.10	0.20	0.40	1.25	3.00
1957	15,000,000	0.10	0.20	0.65	1.75	3.00
1957H	5,000,000	1.50	3.00	6.00	15.00	21.00
1957KN	Inc. above	0.10	0.20	0.65	1.75	3.00
1959H	10,000,000	0.10	0.20	0.40	1.25	2.00
1959KN	10,000,000	0.10	0.20	0.40	1.25	2.00
1961	1,800,000	0.15	0.40	2.00	3.50	5.00
1961 Proof	—	Value: 100				
1961H	1,800,000	0.15	0.40	2.00	3.50	5.00
1962H	10,320,000	0.10	0.20	0.40	1.25	2.00

KM# 18 5 CENTS

6.2400 g., Bronze, 25.3 mm. **Ruler:** George V **Edge:** Plain

Date	Mintage	F	VF	XF	Unc	BU
1921	1,000,000	2.00	4.00	15.00	32.00	50.00
1922	2,500,000	0.50	1.25	4.50	12.50	15.00
1923	2,400,000	0.50	1.25	6.00	15.00	18.00
1923 Proof	—	Value: 150				
1924	4,800,000	0.50	1.00	5.00	15.00	21.00
1925	6,600,000	0.50	1.00	4.00	10.00	15.00
1925 Proof	—	Value: 125				
1928	1,200,000	1.50	3.00	10.00	25.00	35.00
1928 Proof	—	Value: 150				
1933	5,000,000	0.50	1.00	5.00	10.00	15.00
1934	3,910,000	0.50	1.00	7.50	15.00	21.00
1934 Proof	—	Value: 150				
1935	5,800,000	0.50	1.00	5.00	10.00	15.00
1935 Proof	—	Value: 150				
1936	1,000,000	2.00	15.00	30.00	50.00	—

KM# 23 5 CENTS

Bronze, 26 mm. **Ruler:** Edward VIII **Obv:** Center hole divides crown and denomination, fleurs flank **Rev:** Tusks flank center hole, denomination above, circle surrounds **Edge:** Plain

Date	Mintage	F	VF	XF	Unc	BU
1936H	3,500,000	0.25	0.50	2.00	5.50	9.00
1936H Proof	—	Value: 150				
1936KN	2,150,000	0.25	0.50	2.00	5.50	9.00
1936KN Proof	—	Value: 150				

KM# 25.1 5 CENTS

6.3200 g., Bronze **Ruler:** George VI **Obv:** Center hole divides crown and denomination, fleurs flank **Rev:** Tusks flank center hole, denomination above, circle surrounds **Edge:** Plain **Note:** Thick flan.

Date	Mintage	F	VF	XF	Unc	BU
1937H	3,000,000	0.50	1.00	2.00	4.00	7.00
1937KN	3,000,000	0.50	1.00	2.00	6.00	10.00
1939H	2,000,000	0.50	1.00	5.00	13.50	20.00
1939KN	2,000,000	0.50	1.00	5.00	13.50	20.00
1941	—	3.00	10.00	25.00	40.00	65.00
1941I	20,000,000	0.50	1.00	2.00	5.00	8.00

KM# 25.2 5 CENTS

5.6700 g., Bronze **Ruler:** George VI **Obv:** Center hole divides crown and denomination, fleurs flank **Rev:** Tusks flank center hole, denomination above, circle surrounds **Edge:** Plain **Note:** Thin flan, reduced weight.

Date	Mintage	F	VF	XF	Unc	BU
1941I	Inc. above	0.50	1.00	2.00	5.00	8.00
1942	16,000,000	0.50	1.00	2.00	4.00	7.00
1942SA	4,120,000	1.00	6.00	15.00	30.00	42.00
1943SA	17,880,000	Value: 3.00				

KM# 25.3 5 CENTS

Bronze **Ruler:** George VI **Edge:** Plain **Note:** Similar to KM#25.2, but hole not punched.

Date	Mintage	F	VF	XF	Unc	BU
1942	—	—	—	—	100	—

KM# 33 5 CENTS

5.7700 g., Bronze **Ruler:** George VI **Obv:** Center hole divides crown and denomination, fleurs flank **Obv. Legend:** ET IND. IMP. dropped from legend **Rev:** Tusks flank center hole, denomination above, circle surrounds **Edge:** Plain

Date	Mintage	F	VF	XF	Unc	BU
1949	4,000,000	0.25	0.50	3.00	6.00	10.00
1949 Proof	—	Value: 175				
1951H	6,000,000	0.25	0.50	2.00	5.00	8.00
1951H Proof	—	Value: 175				
1952	11,200,000	0.20	0.40	1.00	3.00	6.00
1952 Proof	—	Value: 200				

KM# 37 5 CENTS

5.7700 g., Bronze **Ruler:** Elizabeth II **Obv:** Center hole divides crown and denomination, fleurs flank **Rev:** Tusks flank center hole, denomination above, circle surrounds **Edge:** Plain

Date	Mintage	F	VF	XF	Unc	BU
1955	2,000,000	0.10	0.25	0.75	2.00	3.50
1955 Proof	—	Value: 150				
1955H	4,000,000	0.20	0.50	1.25	3.50	5.00
1955H Proof	—	Value: 150				
1955KN	2,000,000	0.35	0.80	2.50	5.00	8.00
1956H	3,000,000	0.15	0.35	1.00	3.00	5.00
1956KN	3,000,000	3.00	5.00	8.00	10.00	15.00
1956KN Proof	—	Value: 125				
1957H	5,000,000	0.10	0.25	0.75	2.00	3.50
1957KN	5,000,000	0.10	0.25	0.75	2.00	3.50
1961H	4,000,000	0.15	0.35	1.00	3.00	5.50
1963	12,600,000	—	0.10	0.30	0.75	1.50
1963 Proof	—	Value: 150				

KM# 39 5 CENTS

5.6900 g., Bronze **Ruler:** Elizabeth II **Obv:** Fleurs flank center hole, country name below, denomination above and right **Rev:** Tusks flank center hole, denomination above, circle surrounds **Edge:** Plain **Note:** Post-independence issue.

Date	Mintage	F	VF	XF	Unc	BU
1964	7,600,000	—	0.10	0.20	0.50	0.85

KM# 19 10 CENTS
11.1400 g., Bronze **Ruler:** George V **Obv:** Center hole divides crown and denomination, fleurs flank **Rev:** Tusks flank center hole, denomination above, circle surrounds **Edge:** Plain

Date	Mintage	F	VF	XF	Unc	BU
1921	130,000	5.00	20.00	45.00	80.00	—
1922	7,120,000	1.00	3.00	8.00	20.00	—
1923	1,200,000	1.25	4.00	20.00	40.00	—
1924	4,900,000	0.65	2.25	14.00	25.00	—
1925	4,800,000	0.65	2.25	14.00	25.00	—
1927	2,000,000	0.75	2.50	12.50	20.00	—
1928	3,800,000	0.75	2.50	15.00	30.00	—
1928 Proof	—	Value: 175				
1933	6,260,000	0.75	2.50	6.50	17.50	—
1934	3,649,000	0.75	2.50	15.00	30.00	—
1935	7,300,000	0.65	2.00	8.00	18.00	—
1936	500,000	1.50	15.00	30.00	50.00	—

KM# 24 10 CENTS
10.7400 g., Bronze, 30.5 mm. **Ruler:** Edward VIII **Obv:** Center hole divides crown and denomination, fleurs flank **Rev:** Tusks flank center hole, denomination above, circle surrounds **Edge:** Plain **Note:** For listing of mule dated 1936H with obverse of KM#24 and reverse of British West Africa KM#16 refer to British West Africa listings.

Date	Mintage	F	VF	XF	Unc	BU
1936	2,000,000	1.00	3.50	8.00	25.00	40.00
1936 Proof	—	Value: 200				
1936H	4,330,000	0.25	0.50	1.50	6.50	10.00
1936H Proof	—	Value: 325				
1936KN	4,142,000	0.25	0.50	1.50	6.50	10.00
1936KN Proof	—	Value: 145				

KM# 24a 10 CENTS
Copper-Nickel **Ruler:** Edward VIII **Obv:** Center hole divides crown and denomination, fleurs flank **Rev:** Tusks flank center hole, denomination above, circle surrounds **Edge:** Plain

Date	Mintage	F	VF	XF	Unc	BU
1936KN	—	—	—	—	—	—

KM# 26.1 10 CENTS
11.3400 g., Bronze **Ruler:** George VI **Obv:** Center hole divides crown and denomination, fleurs flank **Rev:** Tusks flank center hole, denomination above, circle surrounds **Edge:** Plain **Note:** Thick flan.

Date	Mintage	F	VF	XF	Unc	BU
1937	2,000,000	0.25	0.75	2.50	6.00	9.00
1937 Proof	—	Value: 175				
1937H	2,500,000	0.25	0.75	2.50	8.00	13.00
1937H Proof	—	Value: 175				
1937KN	2,500,000	0.25	0.75	2.50	8.00	13.00
1937KN Proof	—	Value: 175				
1939H	2,000,000	0.25	0.70	5.50	15.00	21.00
1939KN	2,029,999	0.25	0.70	5.50	12.50	16.00
1939KN Proof	—	Value: 175				
1941I	15,682,000	0.35	1.00	6.00	15.00	23.00
1941I Proof	—	Value: 175				
1941	—	0.50	1.50	7.50	16.00	21.00
1941 Proof	—	Value: 175				

KM# 26.2 10 CENTS
Bronze **Ruler:** George VI **Obv:** Center hole divides crown and denomination, fleurs flank **Rev:** Tusks flank center hole, denomination above, circle surrounds **Edge:** Plain **Note:** Thin flan, reduced weight.

Date	Mintage	F	VF	XF	Unc	BU
1942	12,000,000	0.20	0.50	1.75	4.00	7.00
1942I	4,317,000	3.00	5.00	12.00	20.00	28.00
1942 Proof	—	Value: 175				
1943SA	14,093,000	0.25	0.50	4.50	10.00	15.00
1945SA	5,000,000	0.25	0.50	5.00	12.50	16.00

KM# 34 10 CENTS
9.5000 g., Bronze **Ruler:** George VI **Obv:** Center hole divides crown and denomination, fleurs flank **Obv. Legend:** ET IND. IMP. dropped from legend **Rev:** Tusks flank center hole, denomination above, circle surrounds **Edge:** Plain

Date	Mintage	F	VF	XF	Unc	BU
1949	4,000,000	0.25	2.50	5.00	15.00	21.00
1949 Proof	—	Value: 175				
1950	8,000,000	0.20	0.40	1.75	4.00	7.00
1950 Proof	—	Value: 200				
1951	14,500,000	0.20	0.40	1.25	3.00	6.00
1951 Proof	—	Value: 175				
1952	15,800,000	0.20	0.40	1.25	3.00	6.00
1952 Proof	—	Value: 250				
1952H	2,000,000	3.00	5.00	10.00	20.00	30.00

KM# 38 10 CENTS
9.3600 g., Bronze **Ruler:** Elizabeth II **Obv:** Center hole divides crown and denomination, fleurs flank **Rev:** Tusks flank center hole, denomination above, circle surrounds **Edge:** Plain

Date	Mintage	F	VF	XF	Unc	BU
1956	6,001,000	0.35	1.00	2.50	10.00	15.00
1956 Proof	—	Value: 175				
1964H Rare	—	—	—	—	—	—

KM# 40 10 CENTS
9.4000 g., Bronze **Ruler:** Elizabeth II **Obv:** Fleurs flank center hole, country name below, denomination above and right **Rev:** Tusks flank center hole, denomination above, circle surrounds **Edge:** Plain **Note:** Post-independence issue.

Date	Mintage	F	VF	XF	Unc	BU
1964H	10,002,000	0.10	0.15	0.30	1.00	1.50

KM# 20 50 CENTS
3.8879 g., 0.2500 Silver 0.0312 oz. ASW **Ruler:** George V **Obv:** Crowned bust of King George V left **Obv. Designer:** E.B. MacKennal **Rev:** Lion and mountains within 3/4 circle with fleur ends, date below divides denominations **Edge:** Reeded

Date	Mintage	F	VF	XF	Unc	BU
1921	6,200,000	1.00	5.00	17.50	30.00	—
1922	Inc. above	1.00	4.00	16.00	27.50	—
1923	396,000	5.00	18.00	55.00	80.00	—
1924	1,000,000	2.00	14.00	25.00	40.00	—

KM# 27 50 CENTS
3.8879 g., 0.2500 Silver 0.0312 oz. ASW **Ruler:** George VI **Obv:** Crowned head of King George VI left **Obv. Designer:** Percy Metcalfe **Rev:** Lion and mountains within 3/4 circle with fleur ends, date and denomination below and right **Edge:** Reeded

Date	Mintage	F	VF	XF	Unc	BU
1937H	4,000,000	0.75	1.25	5.50	12.50	—
1937H Proof	—	Value: 275				
1942H	5,000,000	0.75	1.25	9.00	20.00	—
1943I	2,000,000	1.50	5.00	17.50	30.00	—
1944SA	1,000,000	2.00	6.00	18.00	32.50	—

KM# 30 50 CENTS
3.8900 g., Copper-Nickel **Ruler:** George VI **Obv:** Crowned head of King George VI left **Obv. Legend:** ET INDIA IMPERATOR dropped from legend **Obv. Designer:** Percy Metcalfe **Rev:** Lion and mountains within 3/4 circle with fleur ends, date divides denominations below **Edge:** Reeded

Date	Mintage	F	VF	XF	Unc	BU
1948	7,290,000	0.20	0.40	2.00	6.00	10.00
1948 Proof	—	Value: 250				
1949	12,960,000	0.15	0.30	1.50	5.00	10.00
1949 Proof	—	Value: 325				
1952KN	2,000,000	0.20	0.40	2.00	7.50	10.00

KM# 36 50 CENTS
Copper-Nickel **Ruler:** Elizabeth II **Obv:** Crowned bust right **Obv. Designer:** Cecil Thomas **Rev:** Lion and mountains within 3/4 circle with fleur ends, date divides denominations below **Edge:** Reeded **Note:** The KHN mint marks above exist because the master dies were produced with both the KN and H mint marks for use at either mint. Each mint was required to remove the other's mint mark before striking, but this was not always meticulously done. When one or the other mint mark was not fully removed a weak trace would remain creating the appearance of a wide space K N with a weak H in the middle or an H flanked by a weak K and N, in the field below the lion.

Date	Mintage	F	VF	XF	Unc	BU
1954	3,720,000	0.15	0.35	1.00	4.00	8.00
1954 Proof	—	Value: 225				
1955H	1,600,000	1.00	3.00	6.00	15.00	8.00
1955H Proof	—	Value: 225				
1955KHN	—	10.00	20.00	55.00	85.00	8.00
1955KN	—	0.15	0.35	1.75	5.00	8.00
1956H	2,000,000	0.15	0.25	1.25	4.00	8.00
1956H Proof	—	Value: 225				
1956KHN	—	10.00	20.00	35.00	65.00	8.00
1956KN	2,000,000	0.15	0.35	1.75	5.00	8.00
1958H	2,600,000	0.15	0.40	2.00	5.00	8.00
1960	4,000,000	0.10	0.25	1.25	4.00	8.00
1962KN	4,000,000	0.15	0.35	1.75	5.00	8.00
1963	6,000,000	0.10	0.25	1.25	4.00	8.00

KM# 21 SHILLING

7.7759 g., 0.2500 Silver 0.0625 oz. ASW, 27.8 mm. **Ruler:** George V **Obv:** Bust of King George V left **Obv. Designer:** E.B. MacKennal **Edge:** Reeded

Date	Mintage	F	VF	XF	Unc	BU
1921	6,141,000	1.50	5.75	18.00	30.00	—
1921H	4,240,000	1.75	3.00	25.00	40.00	—
1922	18,858,000	1.25	2.25	13.00	28.00	—
1922H	20,052,000	1.25	2.25	13.00	28.00	—
1923	4,000,000	5.00	10.00	30.00	45.00	—
1924	44,604,000	1.00	2.00	7.00	18.00	—
1925	28,405,000	1.00	2.00	7.00	20.00	—
1925 Proof	—	Value: 250				

KM# 28.1 SHILLING

7.7759 g., 0.2500 Silver 0.0625 oz. ASW **Ruler:** George VI **Obv:** Crowned head of King George VI left **Obv. Designer:** Percy Metcalfe **Rev:** Lion and mountains within 3/4 circle with fleur ends, date divides denominations below **Edge:** Reeded **Note:** REV; Type I, thin rim and short milling, EAST AFRICA further from edge than Type II, larger loop on right side of coin below diamond in legend. Edge reeding spaced out

Date	Mintage	F	VF	XF	Unc	BU
1937H	7,672,000	1.00	2.00	12.50	22.00	25.00
1937H Proof	—	Value: 300				
1941I	7,000,000	1.25	2.25	14.00	28.00	—
1942H	4,430,000	1.25	2.25	14.00	28.00	—
1942H Proof	—	Value: 300				
1944H	10,000,000	1.25	2.25	17.00	32.00	—

KM# 28.2 SHILLING

7.7759 g., 0.2500 Silver 0.0625 oz. ASW **Ruler:** George VI **Obv:** Crowned head left **Rev:** Type II, thicker rim and larger milling, EAST AFRICA and leaves very near the edge, small leaf (loop) under diamond on right side **Edge:** Reeded

Date	Mintage	F	VF	XF	Unc	BU
1941I Rare	—	—	—	—	—	—

KM# 28.3 SHILLING

7.7759 g., 0.2500 Silver 0.0625 oz. ASW **Ruler:** George VI **Obv:** Crowned head left **Rev:** Type III, retouched central image, especially tuft of grass in front of lion **Edge:** Reeded

Date	Mintage	F	VF	XF	Unc	BU
1942I	3,900,000	1.00	2.00	13.00	25.00	—
1943I	—	500	750	1,200	1,500	—

Note: 25-50 pieces

KM# 28.4 SHILLING

7.7759 g., 0.2500 Silver 0.0625 oz. ASW **Ruler:** George VI **Obv:** Crowned head left **Rev:** Lion and mountains within 3/4 circle with fleur ends, date divides denominations below **Edge:** Reeded **Note:** Obverse and reverse as KM#28.1, edge reeding close. For more in-depth comparison of these reverse variety types, see The Guidebook and Catalogue of British Commonwealth Coins, 1649-1971, 3rd Edition, Remick, J. Winnipeg, Regency Coin and Stamp, 1971.

Date	Mintage	F	VF	XF	Unc	BU
1944SA	5,820,000	1.25	2.25	17.00	30.00	—
1945SA	10,080,000	1.25	2.25	13.00	27.50	—
1946SA	18,260,000	1.00	2.00	12.00	20.00	—

KM# 31 SHILLING

7.8100 g., Copper-Nickel, 27.8 mm. **Ruler:** George VI **Obv:** Crowned head of King George VI left **Obv. Legend:** ET INDIA IMPERATOR dropped from legend **Obv. Designer:** Percy Metcalfe **Rev:** Lion and mountains within 3/4 circle with fleur ends, date and denomination below **Edge:** Reeded

Date	Mintage	F	VF	XF	Unc	BU
1948	19,704,000	0.50	0.90	2.00	6.50	12.00
1949	38,318,000	0.50	0.90	2.00	6.50	12.00
1949 Proof	—	Value: 250				
1949H	12,584,000	0.50	0.90	2.25	7.50	12.50
1949KN	15,060,000	0.50	0.90	3.25	7.50	12.50
1950	56,362,000	0.35	0.60	1.50	5.00	12.00
1950 Proof	—	Value: 250				
1950H	12,416,000	0.50	0.90	3.25	6.00	12.00
1950KN	10,040,000	0.40	0.70	2.00	5.00	12.00
1952	55,605,000	0.35	0.60	1.50	5.00	12.00
1952 Proof	—	Value: 175				
1952H	8,023,999	0.35	0.60	1.75	5.00	12.00
1952KN	9,360,000	0.35	0.60	1.75	5.00	12.00

EAST CARIBBEAN STATES

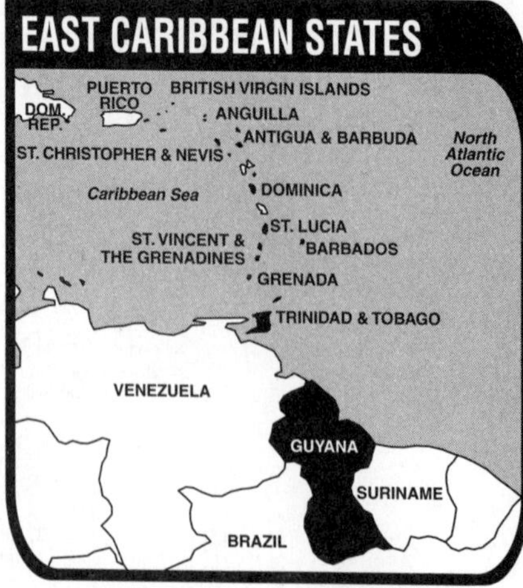

The East Caribbean States, formerly the British Caribbean Territories (Eastern Group), formed a currency board in 1950 to provide the constituent territories of Trinidad & Tobago, Barbados, British Guiana (now Guyana), British Virgin Islands, Anguilla, St. Kitts, Nevis, Antigua, Dominica, St. Lucia, St. Vincent and Grenada with a common currency, thereby permitting withdrawal of the regular British Pound currency. This was dissolved in 1965 and after the breakup, the East Caribbean Territories, a grouping including Barbados, the Leeward and Windward Islands, came into being. Coinage of the dissolved 'Eastern Group' continues to circulate. Paper currency of the East Caribbean Authority was first issued in 1965 and although Barbados withdrew from the group they continued using them prior to 1973 when Barbados issued a decimal coinage.

A series of 4-dollar coins tied to the FAO coinage program were released in 1970 under the name of the Caribbean Development Bank by eight loosely federated island groupings in the eastern Caribbean. These issues are listed individually in this volume under Antigua, Barbados, Dominica, Grenada, Montserrat, St. Kitts, St. Lucia and St. Vincent.

BRITISH CARIBBEAN TERRITORIES

STANDARD COINAGE

100 Cents = 1 British West Indies Dollar

KM# 1 1/2 CENT

5.6300 g., Bronze, 20.4 mm. **Ruler:** Elizabeth II **Obv:** Crowned bust right **Rev:** Denomination above date

Date	Mintage	F	VF	XF	Unc	BU
1955	500,000	0.30	0.50	1.00	2.50	—
1955 Proof	2,000	Value: 3.00				
1958	200	0.50	0.75	1.50	3.00	—
1958 Proof	20	Value: 145				

KM# 2 CENT

5.6400 g., Bronze **Ruler:** Elizabeth II **Obv:** Crowned bust right **Rev:** Denomination within wreath, date below

Date	Mintage	F	VF	XF	Unc	BU
1955	8,000,000	0.15	0.25	0.60	1.00	—
1955 Proof	2,000	Value: 3.00				
1957	3,000,000	0.15	0.25	1.75	3.00	—
1957 Proof	—	Value: 100				
1958	1,500,000	0.35	0.50	4.50	7.50	—
1958 Proof	20	Value: 165				
1959	500,000	0.40	0.60	6.00	20.00	—
1959 Proof	—	Value: 100				
1960	2,500,000	0.15	0.25	0.60	1.25	—
1960 Proof	—	Value: 100				
1961	2,280,000	0.25	0.35	0.75	1.25	—
1961 Proof	—	Value: 100				
1962	2,000,000	0.15	0.25	0.50	1.25	—
1962 Proof	—	Value: 100				
1963	750,000	0.45	0.70	1.20	2.50	—
1963 Proof	—	Value: 100				
1964	2,500,000	—	—	0.20	0.35	—
1964 Proof	—	Value: 100				
1965	4,800,000	—	—	0.20	0.35	—
1965 Prooflike	—	—	—	—	0.75	—
1965 Proof	—	Value: 5.00				

KM# 3 2 CENTS

9.5500 g., Bronze, 30.5 mm. **Ruler:** Elizabeth II **Obv:** Crowned bust right **Rev:** Denomination within wreath, date below

Date	Mintage	F	VF	XF	Unc	BU
1955	5,500,000	0.15	0.25	0.50	1.00	—
1955 Proof	2,000	Value: 3.00				
1957	1,250,000	0.15	0.25	1.25	2.50	—
1957 Proof	—	Value: 110				
1958	1,250,000	0.15	0.25	2.50	5.00	—
1958 Proof	20	Value: 185				
1960	750,000	0.15	0.25	1.75	3.50	—
1960 Proof	—	Value: 110				
1961	788,000	0.15	0.25	1.75	3.50	—
1961 Proof	—	Value: 110				
1962	1,060,000	0.10	0.20	0.30	0.85	—
1962 Proof	—	Value: 110				
1963	250,000	0.50	0.75	1.50	5.00	—
1963 Proof	—	Value: 110				
1964	1,188,000	0.10	0.20	0.30	0.75	—
1964 Proof	—	Value: 110				
1965	2,001,000	—	0.10	0.20	0.45	—
1965 Prooflike	—	—	—	—	0.75	—
1965 Proof	—	Value: 5.00				

KM# 4 5 CENTS

Nickel-Brass, 21 mm. **Ruler:** Elizabeth II **Obv:** Crowned head right **Rev:** Sir Francis Drake's Golden Hind divides denomination, date below

Date	Mintage	F	VF	XF	Unc	BU
1955	8,600,000	0.15	0.25	0.60	1.25	—
1955 Proof	2,000	Value: 4.50				
1956	2,000,000	0.15	0.25	0.60	1.00	—
1956 Proof	—	Value: 300				
1960	1,000,000	0.20	0.30	0.90	1.50	—
1960 Proof	—	Value: 150				
1962	1,300,000	0.15	0.25	0.50	1.00	—
1962 Proof	—	Value: 150				
1963	200,000	0.25	0.35	1.20	2.00	—
1963 Proof	—	Value: 150				
1964	1,350,000	—	0.10	0.30	0.75	—
1964 Proof	—	Value: 150				
1965	2,400,000	—	0.10	0.20	0.50	—
1965 Prooflike	—	—	—	—	0.75	—
1965 Proof	—	Value: 5.00				

KM# 5 10 CENTS

2.5900 g., Copper-Nickel, 18 mm. **Ruler:** Elizabeth II **Obv:** Crowned head right **Rev:** Sir Francis Drake's Golden Hind divides denomination, date below

Date	Mintage	F	VF	XF	Unc	BU
1955	5,000,000	0.15	0.25	0.45	0.75	—
1955 Proof	2,000	Value: 4.50				
1956	4,000,000	0.15	0.25	0.45	0.75	—
1956 Proof	—	Value: 175				
1959	2,000,000	0.15	0.25	0.60	1.00	—
1959 Proof	—	Value: 175				
1961	1,260,000	0.20	0.30	0.50	1.00	—
1961 Proof	—	Value: 175				
1962	1,200,000	0.15	0.25	0.50	1.00	—
1962 Proof	—	Value: 175				
1964	1,400,000	0.10	0.20	0.35	0.65	—
1965	3,200,000	0.10	0.20	0.30	0.50	—
1965 Prooflike	—	—	—	—	0.75	—
1965 Proof	—	Value: 5.00				

KM# 6 25 CENTS

6.5100 g., Copper-Nickel **Ruler:** Elizabeth II **Obv:** Crowned bust right **Rev:** Sir Francis Drake's Golden Hind divides denomination, date below

Date	Mintage	F	VF	XF	Unc	BU
1955	7,000,000	0.35	0.50	0.70	1.00	—
1955 Proof	2,000	Value: 6.50				
1957	800,000	0.75	1.00	2.25	4.50	—
1957 Proof	—	Value: 225				
1959	1,000,000	0.35	0.50	1.25	2.25	—
1959 Proof	—	Value: 225				
1961	744,000	0.50	0.75	2.50	5.00	—
1961 Proof	—	Value: 225				
1962	480,000	0.25	0.50	1.25	2.50	—
1962 Proof	—	Value: 225				
1963	480,000	0.25	0.50	1.25	2.50	—
1963 Proof	—	Value: 225				
1964	480,000	0.25	0.50	1.00	1.75	—
1964 Proof	—	Value: 225				
1965	1,280,000	0.25	0.50	0.75	1.00	—
1965 Prooflike	—	—	—	—	1.50	—
1965 Proof	—	Value: 7.50				

KM# 7 50 CENTS

13.0000 g., Copper-Nickel, 30 mm. **Ruler:** Elizabeth II **Obv:** Crowned bust right **Rev:** Figure and horseheads above shielded arms and circular pictures, denomination and date divided below

Date	Mintage	F	VF	XF	Unc	BU
1955	1,500,000	1.00	1.50	2.00	3.50	5.00
1955 Proof	2,000	Value: 12.50				
1965	100,000	2.00	5.00	7.50	15.00	—
1965 Prooflike	—	—	—	—	7.50	—
1965 Proof	—	Value: 10.00				

EAST CARIBBEAN STATES

STANDARD COINAGE

100 Cents = 1 Dollar

KM# 10 CENT

0.9000 g., Aluminum, 18.4 mm. **Ruler:** Elizabeth II **Obv:** Young bust right **Rev:** Wreath divides denomination, date upper right **Shape:** Scalloped **Note:** Prev. KM#1.

Date	Mintage	F	VF	XF	Unc	BU
1981	—	—	—	—	0.20	0.30
1981 Proof	5,000	Value: 1.25				
1983	—	—	—	—	0.20	0.30
1984	—	—	—	—	0.20	0.30
1986	—	—	—	—	0.20	0.30
1986 Proof	2,500	Value: 1.25				
1987	—	—	—	—	0.20	0.30
1989	—	—	—	—	0.20	0.30
1991	—	—	—	—	0.20	0.30
1992	—	—	—	—	0.20	0.30
1993	—	—	—	—	0.20	0.30
1994	—	—	—	—	0.20	0.30
1995	—	—	—	—	0.20	0.30
1996	—	—	—	—	0.20	0.30
1997	—	—	—	—	0.20	0.30
1998	—	—	—	—	0.20	0.30
1999	—	—	—	—	0.20	0.30
2000	—	—	—	—	0.20	0.30

KM# 34 CENT

1.0300 g., Aluminum, 18.42 mm. **Ruler:** Elizabeth II **Obv:** Crowned head right **Obv. Designer:** Ian Rank-Broadley **Rev:** Denomination **Edge:** Plain

Date	Mintage	F	VF	XF	Unc	BU
2002	—	—	—	—	0.20	0.30
2004	—	—	—	—	0.20	0.30

KM# 11 2 CENTS

1.1000 g., Aluminum, 18.25 mm. **Ruler:** Elizabeth II **Obv:** Young bust right **Rev:** Wreath divides denomination, date upper right **Shape:** Square **Note:** Prev. KM#2.

Date	Mintage	F	VF	XF	Unc	BU
1981	—	—	—	0.10	0.25	0.35
1981 Proof	5,000	Value: 1.50				
1984	—	—	—	0.10	0.25	0.35
1986	—	—	—	0.10	0.25	0.35
1986 Proof	2,500	Value: 1.50				
1987	—	—	—	0.10	0.25	0.35
1989	—	—	—	0.10	0.25	0.35
1991	—	—	—	0.10	0.25	0.35
1992	—	—	—	0.10	0.25	0.35
1993	—	—	—	0.10	0.25	0.35
1994	—	—	—	0.10	0.25	0.35
1995	—	—	—	0.10	0.25	0.35
1996	—	—	—	0.10	0.25	0.35
1997	—	—	—	0.10	0.25	0.35
1998	—	—	—	0.10	0.25	0.35
1999	—	—	—	0.10	0.25	0.35
2000	—	—	—	0.10	0.25	0.35

KM# 35 2 CENTS

1.4200 g., Aluminum, 21.46 mm. **Ruler:** Elizabeth II **Obv:** Crowned head right **Obv. Designer:** Ian Rank-Broadley **Rev:** Denomination **Edge:** Plain

Date	Mintage	F	VF	XF	Unc	BU
2002	—	—	—	—	0.25	0.35

KM# 12 5 CENTS

1.3100 g., Aluminum, 23.1 mm. **Ruler:** Elizabeth II **Obv:** Young bust right **Rev:** Wreath divides denomination, date upper right **Shape:** Scalloped **Note:** Prev. KM#3.

Date	Mintage	F	VF	XF	Unc	BU
1981	—	—	—	0.10	0.30	0.45
1981 Proof	5,000	Value: 2.25				
1984	—	—	—	0.10	0.30	0.45
1986	—	—	—	0.10	0.30	0.45
1986 Proof	2,500	Value: 2.25				
1987	—	—	—	0.10	0.30	0.45
1989	—	—	—	0.10	0.30	0.45
1991	—	—	—	0.10	0.30	0.45
1992	—	—	—	0.10	0.30	0.45
1993	—	—	—	0.10	0.30	0.45
1994	—	—	—	0.10	0.30	0.45
1995	—	—	—	0.10	0.30	0.45
1996	—	—	—	0.10	0.30	0.45
1997	—	—	—	0.10	0.30	0.45
1998	—	—	—	0.10	0.30	0.45
1999	—	—	—	0.10	0.30	0.45
2000	—	—	—	0.10	0.30	0.45

KM# 36 5 CENTS

1.7400 g., Aluminum, 23.11 mm. **Ruler:** Elizabeth II **Obv:** Crowned head right **Obv. Designer:** Ian Rank-Broadley **Rev:** Denomination **Edge:** Plain

Date	Mintage	F	VF	XF	Unc	BU
2002	—	—	—	—	0.30	0.45

KM# 13 10 CENTS

2.6000 g., Copper-Nickel, 18.1 mm. **Ruler:** Elizabeth II **Obv:** Young bust right **Rev:** Sir Francis Drake's Golden Hind, denomination below and left, date at right **Note:** Prev. KM#4.

Date	Mintage	F	VF	XF	Unc	BU
1981	—	—	0.10	0.15	0.40	0.60
1981 Proof	5,000	Value: 3.00				
1986	—	—	0.10	0.15	0.40	0.60
1986 Proof	2,500	Value: 3.00				
1987	—	—	0.10	0.15	0.40	0.60
1989	—	—	0.10	0.15	0.40	0.60
1991	—	—	0.10	0.15	0.40	0.60
1992	—	—	0.10	0.15	0.40	0.60
1993	—	—	0.10	0.15	0.40	0.60
1994	—	—	0.10	0.15	0.40	0.60
1995	—	—	0.10	0.15	0.40	0.60
1996	—	—	0.10	0.15	0.40	0.60
1997	—	—	0.10	0.15	0.40	0.60
1998	—	—	0.10	0.15	0.40	0.60

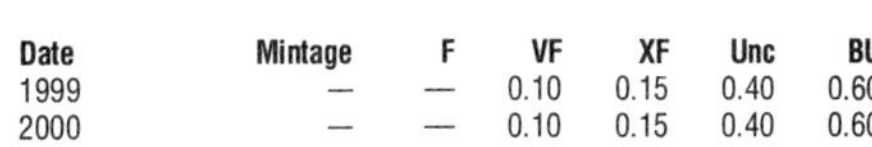

Date	Mintage	F	VF	XF	Unc	BU
1999	—	—	0.10	0.15	0.40	0.60
2000	—	—	0.10	0.15	0.40	0.60

KM# 37 10 CENTS

Copper-Nickel, 18.06 mm. **Ruler:** Elizabeth II **Obv:** Crowned head right **Obv. Designer:** Ian Rank-Broadley **Rev:** Sir Francis Drake's Golden Hind and denomination **Edge:** Reeded

Date	Mintage	F	VF	XF	Unc	BU
2002	—	—	—	—	0.40	0.60

KM# 14 25 CENTS

6.5000 g., Copper-Nickel, 24 mm. **Ruler:** Elizabeth II **Obv:** Young bust right **Rev:** Sir Francis Drake's Golden Hind, divides denomination, date at right **Note:** Prev. KM#5.

Date	Mintage	F	VF	XF	Unc	BU
1981	—	—	0.15	0.20	0.50	0.75
1981 Proof	5,000	Value: 4.00				
1986	—	—	0.15	0.20	0.50	0.75
1986 Proof	2,500	Value: 4.00				
1987	—	—	0.15	0.20	0.50	0.75
1989	—	—	0.15	0.20	0.50	0.75
1991	—	—	0.15	0.20	0.50	0.75
1992	—	—	0.15	0.20	0.50	0.75
1993	—	—	0.15	0.20	0.50	0.75
1994	—	—	0.15	0.20	0.50	0.75
1995	—	—	0.15	0.20	0.50	0.75
1996	—	—	0.15	0.20	0.50	0.75
1997	—	—	0.15	0.20	0.50	0.75
1998	—	—	0.15	0.20	0.50	0.75
1999	—	—	0.15	0.20	0.50	0.75
2000	—	—	0.15	0.20	0.50	0.75

KM# 38 25 CENTS

6.4800 g., Copper-Nickel, 23.98 mm. **Ruler:** Elizabeth II **Obv:** Crowned head right **Obv. Designer:** Ian Rank-Broadley **Rev:** Sir Francis Drake's Golden Hind and denomination **Edge:** Reeded

Date	Mintage	F	VF	XF	Unc	BU
2002	—	—	—	—	0.50	0.75

KM# 15 DOLLAR

8.2000 g., Aluminum-Bronze, 26.9 mm. **Ruler:** Elizabeth II **Obv:** Young bust right **Rev:** Sir Francis Drake's Golden Hind divides denomination, date at right **Note:** Prev. KM#6.

Date	Mintage	F	VF	XF	Unc	BU
1981	—	—	0.50	0.75	1.50	2.50
1981 Proof	5,000	Value: 8.00				
1986	—	—	0.50	0.75	1.50	2.50
1986 Proof	2,500	Value: 8.00				

KM# 20 DOLLAR

7.9300 g., Copper-Nickel, 27.5 mm. **Ruler:** Elizabeth II **Obv:** Young bust right **Rev:** Sir Francis Drake's Golden Hind divides denomination, date at right **Shape:** 10-sided **Note:** Prev. KM#11.

Date	Mintage	F	VF	XF	Unc	BU
1989	—	—	—	—	2.25	3.25
1991	—	—	—	—	2.25	3.25
1992	—	—	—	—	2.25	3.25
1993	—	—	—	—	2.25	3.25
1994	—	—	—	—	2.25	3.25
1995	—	—	—	—	2.25	3.25
1996	—	—	—	—	2.25	3.25

Date	Mintage	F	VF	XF	Unc	BU
1997	—	—	—	—	2.00	3.00
1998	—	—	—	—	2.00	3.00
1999	—	—	—	—	2.00	3.00
2000	—	—	—	—	2.00	3.00

KM# 39 DOLLAR

7.9800 g., Copper-Nickel, 26.5 mm. **Ruler:** Elizabeth II **Obv:** Crowned head right **Obv. Designer:** Ian Rank-Broadley **Rev:** Sir Francis Drake's Golden Hind and denomination **Edge:** Alternating plain and reeded

Date	Mintage	F	VF	XF	Unc	BU
2002	—	—	—	—	2.00	3.00

EAST TIMOR

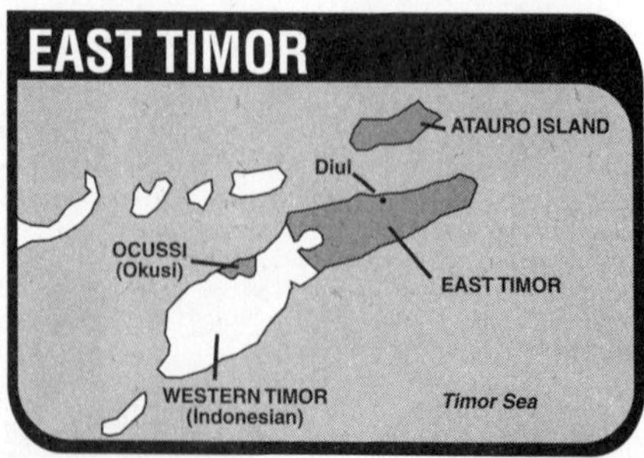

East Timor, population: 522,433, area: 7332 sq. miles, capital: Dili, is primarily located on the eastern half of the island of Timor, just northwest of Australia at the eastern end of the Indonesian archipelago. Formerly a Portuguese colony, Timor declared its independence from Portugal on November 28, 1975. After nine short days of fledgling autonomy, a guerilla faction sympathetic to the Indonesian territorial claim to East Timor seized the government. On July 17, 1976 the Provisional government enacted a law, which dissolved the free republic and made East Timor the 24th province of Indonesia. Violent rule and civil unrest plagued the province, with great loss of life and extreme damage to property and natural resources until independence was again achieved with United Nations assistance during a period from 1999 to 2002. Emerging as the Democratic Republic of Timor-Leste and commonly known as East Timor the country has worked, with international assistance to rebuild its decimated infrastructure. Natural resources waiting to be tapped include rich oil reserves, though current exports are most dependent on coffee, sandalwood and marble. The first coins of the new republic were issued in 2003.

DEMOCRATIC REPUBLIC OF TIMOR-LESTE

DECIMAL COINAGE

KM# 1 CENTAVO

3.1000 g., Nickel Clad Steel, 17 mm. **Obv:** Nautilus above date **Rev:** Denomination within circle **Edge:** Plain

Date	Mintage	F	VF	XF	Unc	BU
2003 Proof	12,500	Value: 7.00				
2003	1,500,000	—	—	—	1.50	2.50
2004	1,500,000	—	—	—	1.50	2.50

KM# 2 5 CENTAVOS

4.0500 g., Nickel Clad Steel, 18.8 mm. **Obv:** Rice plant above date **Rev:** Denomination within circle **Edge:** Plain

Date	Mintage	F	VF	XF	Unc	BU
2003 Proof	12,500	Value: 9.00				
2003	1,500,000	—	—	—	2.00	3.00
2004	1,500,000	—	—	—	2.00	3.00

KM# 3 10 CENTAVOS

5.1100 g., Nickel Clad Steel, 20.8 mm. **Obv:** Rooster left above date **Rev:** Denomination within circle **Edge:** Plain

Date	Mintage	F	VF	XF	Unc	BU
2003 Proof	12,500	Value: 12.00				
2003	2,500,000	—	—	—	2.50	4.00
2004	2,500,000	—	—	—	2.50	4.00

KM# 4 25 CENTAVOS

5.8700 g., Copper-Zinc-Nickel, 21.3 mm. **Obv:** Sail boat above date **Rev:** Denomination within circle **Edge:** Reeded

Date	Mintage	F	VF	XF	Unc	BU
2003 Proof	12,500	Value: 15.00				
2003	1,500,000	—	—	—	3.50	5.00
2004	1,500,000	—	—	—	3.50	5.00

KM# 5 50 CENTAVOS

6.5000 g., Copper-Zinc-Nickel, 25 mm. **Obv:** Coffee plant with beans above date **Rev:** Denomination within circle **Edge:** Reeded

Date	Mintage	F	VF	XF	Unc	BU
2003 Proof	12,500	Value: 20.00				
2003	1,000,000	—	—	—	5.00	7.00
2004	1,000,000	—	—	—	5.00	7.00

ECUADOR

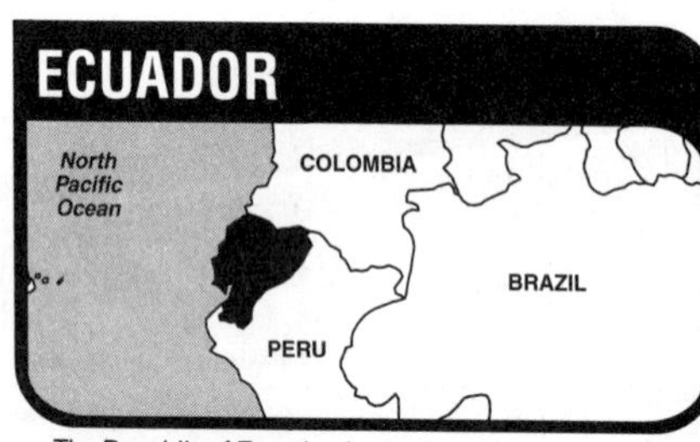

The Republic of Ecuador, located astride the equator on the Pacific Coast of South America, has an area of 105,037 sq. mi. (283,560 sq. km.) and a population of 10.9 million. Capital: Quito. Agriculture is the mainstay of the economy but there are appreciable deposits of minerals and petroleum. It is one of the world's largest exporters of bananas and balsa wood. Coffee, cacao, sugar and petroleum are also valuable exports.

Ecuador was first sighted in 1526 by Francisco Pizarro. Conquest was undertaken by Sebastian de Benalcazar, who founded Quito in 1534. Ecuador was part of the Viceroyalty of New Granada through the 16th and 17th centuries. After previous attempts to attain independence were crushed, Antonio Sucre, the able lieutenant of Bolivar, secured Ecuador's freedom in the Battle of Pinchincha, May 24, 1822. It then joined Venezuela and Colombia in a confederation known as Gran Colombia, and became an independent republic when it left the confederacy in 1830.

MINT MARKS

BIRMm - Birmingham, Heaton
Birmingham - Birmingham
D - Denver
H - Heaton, Birmingham
HF - LeLocle (Swiss)
LIMA - Lima
Mo - Mexico
PHILA.U.S.A. - Philadelphia
PHILADELPHIA - Philadelphia
PHILA - Philadelphia

MONETARY SYSTEM

10 Centavos = 1 Decimo
10 Decimos = 1 Sucre
25 Sucres = 1 Condor

REPUBLIC

DECIMAL COINAGE

10 Centavos = 1 Decimo; 10 Decimos = 1 Sucre;
25 Sucres = 1 Condor

KM# 57 1/2 CENTAVO (Medio)

Copper-Nickel **Obv:** Flag draped arms, date below **Rev:** Denomination within laurels

Date	Mintage	F	VF	XF	Unc	BU
1909H	4,000,000	4.00	9.00	20.00	40.00	—

KM# 58 CENTAVO (Un)

Copper-Nickel **Obv:** Flag draped arms, date below **Rev:** Denomination within laurels

Date	Mintage	F	VF	XF	Unc	BU
1909H	3,000,000	4.50	10.00	22.00	45.00	—

KM# 67 CENTAVO (Un)

6.2500 g., Bronze **Obv:** Flag draped arms, date below **Rev:** Denomination within laurels

Date	Mintage	F	VF	XF	Unc	BU
1928	2,016,000	1.00	2.00	7.50	25.00	—

KM# 59 2 CENTAVOS (Dos)

Copper-Nickel **Obv:** Flag draped arms, date below **Rev:** Denomination within laurels

Date	Mintage	F	VF	XF	Unc	BU
1909H	2,500,000	5.00	12.00	25.00	60.00	—
1909H Proof	—	Value: 200				

KM# 61 2-1/2 CENTAVOS

Copper-Nickel **Obv:** Flag draped arms, date below **Rev:** Denomination within laurels

Date	Mintage	F	VF	XF	Unc	BU
1917	1,600,000	6.00	15.00	55.00	175	—

KM# 68 2-1/2 CENTAVOS

Nickel **Obv:** Flag draped arms, date below **Rev:** Denomination within laurels

Date	Mintage	F	VF	XF	Unc	BU
1928	4,000,000	2.00	4.00	20.00	50.00	—

KM# 55.1 1/2 DECIMO (Medio)

1.2500 g., 0.9000 Silver 0.0362 oz. ASW **Obv:** Head of Sucre left **Rev:** Flag-draped arms, denomination upper left

Date	Mintage	F	VF	XF	Unc	BU
1902/892LIMA JF	1,000,000	1.00	2.00	8.50	20.00	—
1902/802LIMA JF	Inc. above	1.00	2.00	8.50	20.00	—
1902LIMA JF	Inc. above	0.75	1.50	6.00	20.00	—
1905/805LIMA JF	500,000	3.00	5.00	15.00	40.00	—
1905/2LIMA JF	Inc. above	3.50	6.00	18.00	50.00	—
1905LIMA JF	Inc. above	0.75	1.50	7.00	15.00	—
1912/05LIMA FG	20,000	3.00	6.00	18.00	50.00	—
1912LIMA FG	Inc. above	0.75	1.50	6.00	15.00	—
1912LIMA FG	Inc. above	2.00	3.00	8.50	20.00	—

Note: FCUADOH (obverse error)

KM# 55.2 1/2 DECIMO (Medio)

1.2500 g., 0.9000 Silver 0.0362 oz. ASW **Obv:** Head of Sucre left, date below **Rev:** Modified flag draped arms, denomination upper left

Date	Mintage	F	VF	XF	Unc	BU
1915BIRMm	2,000,000	0.75	1.25	5.00	10.00	—
1915BIRMm Proof	—	Value: 200				

KM# 60.1 5 CENTAVOS (Cinco)

Copper-Nickel **Obv:** Flag draped arms with tails on flagpoles pointing outward, date below **Rev:** Denomination within laurels

Date	Mintage	F	VF	XF	Unc	BU
1909H	2,000,000	4.50	10.00	30.00	80.00	—

KM# 60.2 5 CENTAVOS (Cinco)

Copper-Nickel **Obv:** Flag draped arms with tails on flagpoles pointing downward, date below **Rev:** Denomination within laurels **Note:** Thin planchet.

Date	Mintage	F	VF	XF	Unc	BU
1917	1,200,000	8.50	25.00	80.00	200	—
1918	7,980,000	4.00	8.50	17.50	75.00	—

KM# 63 5 CENTAVOS (Cinco)

Copper-Nickel **Obv:** Flag draped arms, date below **Rev:** Denomination within laurels

Date	Mintage	F	VF	XF	Unc	BU
1919	12,000,000	1.00	2.00	8.00	15.00	—
Note: 3 berries to left of "C" on reverse						
1919	Inc. above	1.25	2.50	20.00	40.00	—
Note: 4 berries loose to left of "C" on reverse						
1919	Inc. above	1.25	2.50	20.00	40.00	—
Note: 4 berries tight to left of "C" on reverse						

KM# 65 5 CENTAVOS (Cinco)

Copper-Nickel **Obv:** Flag draped arms, date below **Rev:** Head right within wreath, denomination below

Date	Mintage	F	VF	XF	Unc	BU
1924H	10,000,000	2.00	5.00	15.00	35.00	—

KM# 69 5 CENTAVOS (Cinco)

Nickel **Obv:** Flag draped arms, date below **Rev:** Head right within wreath, denomination below

Date	Mintage	F	VF	XF	Unc	BU
1928	16,000,000	1.00	2.00	3.00	6.50	—

KM# 75 5 CENTAVOS (Cinco)

Nickel **Obv:** Flag draped arms, date below **Rev:** Denomination within wreath

Date	Mintage	F	VF	XF	Unc	BU
1937HF	15,000,000	0.10	0.20	0.75	2.00	—

KM# 75a 5 CENTAVOS (Cinco)

Brass **Obv:** Flag draped arms, date below **Rev:** Denomination within wreath

Date	Mintage	F	VF	XF	Unc	BU
1942	2,000,000	1.00	2.00	6.00	15.00	—
1944D	3,000,000	1.00	2.00	5.00	10.00	—

KM# 75b 5 CENTAVOS (Cinco)

1.9400 g., Copper-Nickel, 17.1 mm. **Obv:** Flag draped arms **Rev:** Denomination within wreath

Date	Mintage	F	VF	XF	Unc	BU
1946	40,000,000	—	—	0.40	1.00	—

KM# 75c 5 CENTAVOS (Cinco)

Nickel Clad Steel **Obv:** Flag draped arms, date below **Rev:** Denomination within wreath

Date	Mintage	F	VF	XF	Unc	BU
1970	—	—	—	0.15	0.50	—
1970	—	—	—	—	—	—
Note: ECADOR (obverse legend error)						

KM# 50.3 DECIMO (Un)

2.5000 g., 0.9000 Silver 0.0723 oz. ASW **Obv:** Head left, legend without "LEY" **Rev. Legend:** Flag draped arms

Date	Mintage	VG	F	VF	XF	Unc
1902LIMA JF	519,000	—	1.75	4.50	10.00	22.00
Note: With JR below fasces on reverse						
1902LIMA JF	Inc. above	—	1.75	4.50	10.00	22.00
Note: Without JR below fasces on reverse						
1902LIMA JF/TF	—	—	1.50	3.00	10.00	20.00
1905LIMA JF	250,000	—	1.50	3.00	10.00	20.00
1912LIMA FG	30,000	—	3.00	6.00	15.00	35.00

KM# 50.4 DECIMO (Un)

2.5000 g., 0.9000 Silver 0.0723 oz. ASW **Obv:** Head of Sucre left, date below **Rev:** Flag draped arms, denomination upper left

Date	Mintage	VG	F	VF	XF	Unc
1915BIRMm	1,000,000	—	BV	1.25	2.00	7.00
1915BIRMm Proof	—	Value: 300				

KM# 50.5 DECIMO (Un)

2.5000 g., 0.9000 Silver 0.0723 oz. ASW **Obv:** Head of Sucre left **Rev:** Flag draped arms

Date	Mintage	VG	F	VF	XF	Unc
1916PHILA	2,000,000	—	BV	1.25	2.00	7.00

KM# 62 10 CENTAVOS (Diez)

Copper-Nickel **Obv:** Flag draped arms, date below **Rev:** Denomination within wreath

Date	Mintage	F	VF	XF	Unc	BU
1918	1,000,000	10.00	20.00	40.00	90.00	—

KM# 64 10 CENTAVOS (Diez)

Copper-Nickel **Obv:** Flag draped arms, date below **Rev:** Denomination within wreath

Date	Mintage	F	VF	XF	Unc	BU
1919	2,000,000	2.00	4.00	10.00	25.00	—
1919 Proof	—	Value: 300				

KM# 66 10 CENTAVOS (Diez)

Copper-Nickel **Obv:** Flag draped arms, date below **Rev:** Head of Bolivar left within wreath, denomination below **Note:** The H mint mark is very small and is located above the date.

Date	Mintage	F	VF	XF	Unc	BU
1924H	5,000,000	1.25	2.50	7.50	20.00	—
1924H Proof	—	Value: 100				

KM# 70 10 CENTAVOS (Diez)

Nickel **Obv:** Flag draped arms, date below **Rev:** Head of Bolivar right within wreath, denomination below

Date	Mintage	F	VF	XF	Unc	BU
1928	16,000,000	1.00	2.00	6.50	20.00	—

KM# 76 10 CENTAVOS (Diez)

Nickel **Obv:** Flag draped arms **Rev:** Denomination in wreath

Date	Mintage	F	VF	XF	Unc	BU
1937HF	7,500,000	0.25	0.50	1.00	3.50	—

KM# 76a 10 CENTAVOS (Diez)

Brass **Obv:** Flag draped arms, date below **Rev:** Denomination within wreath

Date	Mintage	F	VF	XF	Unc	BU
1942	5,000,000	0.60	1.00	5.00	15.00	—

KM# 76b 10 CENTAVOS (Diez)

Copper-Nickel **Obv:** Flag draped arms, date below **Rev:** Denomination within wreath

Date	Mintage	F	VF	XF	Unc	BU
1946	40,000,000	0.10	0.15	0.25	1.00	—

KM# 76c 10 CENTAVOS (Diez)

2.8000 g., Nickel Clad Steel, 19.3 mm. **Obv:** Flag draped arms, date below **Rev:** Denomination within wreath **Note:** Varieties exist.

Date	Mintage	F	VF	XF	Unc	BU
1964	20,000,000	—	—	0.20	0.75	—
1968	15,000,000	—	—	0.20	0.75	—
1972	20,000,000	—	—	0.15	0.65	—

KM# 76d 10 CENTAVOS (Diez)

Copper-Nickel Clad Steel **Obv:** Flag draped arms, date below **Rev:** Denomination within wreath

Date	Mintage	F	VF	XF	Unc	BU
1976	10,000,000	—	—	0.15	0.65	—

KM# 51.3 2 DECIMOS (Dos)

5.0000 g., 0.9000 Silver 0.1447 oz. ASW **Obv:** Head of Sucre left **Rev:** Flag-draped arms, legend without "LEI"

Date	Mintage	F	VF	XF	Unc	BU
1912/18 FG	50,000	5.00	12.50	30.00	75.00	—
1912 FG	Inc. above	2.75	6.00	20.00	50.00	—
1914 FG LIMA.	110,000	3.00	7.00	14.50	40.00	—
1914 FG LIMA	Inc. above	2.50	5.50	11.50	30.00	—
1915 FG	157,000	5.00	15.00	50.00	100	—
Note: Small "R" below fasces on reverse						

KM# 51.4 2 DECIMOS (Dos)
5.0000 g., 0.9000 Silver 0.1447 oz. ASW **Obv:** Head of Sucre left **Rev:** Flag-draped arms, mint name in legend below **Rev. Legend:** ...PHILADELPHIA...

Date	Mintage	F	VF	XF	Unc	BU
1914 TF	2,500,000	2.25	3.50	7.50	15.00	—
1916 TF	1,000,000	2.25	3.50	7.50	15.00	—

KM# 77.1 20 CENTAVOS
3.9000 g., Nickel, 21 mm. **Obv:** Flag draped arms, date below **Rev:** Denomination within wreath

Date	Mintage	F	VF	XF	Unc	BU
1937HF	7,500,000	0.25	0.50	1.00	5.00	—

KM# 77.1a 20 CENTAVOS
3.7200 g., Brass, 21 mm. **Obv:** Flag draped arms, date below **Rev:** Denomination within wreath

Date	Mintage	F	VF	XF	Unc	BU
1942	5,000,000	0.60	1.00	6.00	15.00	—
1944 D	15,000,000	0.40	0.75	4.00	10.00	—

KM# 77.1b 20 CENTAVOS
Copper Nickel, 21 mm. **Obv:** Flag draped arms **Rev:** Denomination within wreath

Date	Mintage	F	VF	XF	Unc	BU
1946	30,000,000	0.25	0.75	2.00	5.00	—

KM# 77.1c 20 CENTAVOS
Nickel Clad Steel, 21 mm. **Obv:** Flag draped arms, date below **Rev:** Denomination within wreath

Date	Mintage	F	VF	XF	Unc	BU
1959	14,400,000	—	—	0.20	1.00	—
1962	14,400,000	—	—	0.20	1.00	—
1966	24,000,000	—	—	0.20	1.00	—
1969	24,000,000	—	—	0.20	1.00	—
1971	12,000,000	—	—	0.20	1.00	—
1972	48,432,000	—	—	0.20	1.00	—

KM# 77.2 20 CENTAVOS
Copper-Nickel, 21 mm. **Obv:** Modified flag draped arms, date below **Rev:** Denomination within wreath

Date	Mintage	F	VF	XF	Unc	BU
1974	19,562,000	—	—	0.15	0.50	—

KM# 77.2a 20 CENTAVOS
Nickel Coated Steel, 21 mm. **Obv:** Flag draped arms, date below **Rev:** Denomination within wreath

Date	Mintage	F	VF	XF	Unc	BU
1975	52,437,000	—	—	0.15	0.35	—
1978	37,500,000	—	—	0.15	0.35	—
1980	18,000,000	—	—	0.15	0.35	—
1981	21,000,000	—	—	0.15	0.35	—

KM# 71 50 CENTAVOS (Cincuenta)
2.5000 g., 0.7200 Silver 0.0579 oz. ASW **Obv:** Head of Sucre left, date below **Rev:** Flag draped arms, denomination above, mint name below **Rev. Legend:** ...PHILA•U•S•A...

Date	Mintage	F	VF	XF	Unc	BU
1928	1,000,000	1.50	3.00	15.00	40.00	—
1930	155,000	2.00	5.00	25.00	60.00	—

KM# 81 50 CENTAVOS (Cincuenta)
4.9200 g., Nickel Clad Steel **Obv:** Flag draped arms, date below **Rev:** Denomination within wreath

Date	Mintage	F	VF	XF	Unc	BU
1963	20,000,000	—	0.15	0.25	0.85	—
1971	5,000,000	—	0.15	0.25	0.85	—
1974	—	—	0.15	0.25	0.85	—
1975	—	—	0.15	0.25	0.85	—
1977	40,000,000	—	0.10	0.20	0.75	—
1979	25,000,000	—	0.10	0.20	0.75	—
1982	20,000,000	—	0.10	0.20	0.75	—

KM# 87 50 CENTAVOS (Cincuenta)
Nickel Clad Steel **Obv:** Modified flag draped arms, date below **Rev:** Denomination within wreath

Date	Mintage	F	VF	XF	Unc	BU
1985	30,000,000	—	0.10	0.20	0.40	—

KM# 90 50 CENTAVOS (Cincuenta)
Nickel Clad Steel **Obv:** Flag draped arms, date below **Rev:** Denomination within square **Note:** The circulation strikes were withdrawn from circulation and remelted. Approximately 100,000 pieces were released.

Date	Mintage	F	VF	XF	Unc	BU
1988	—	—	—	—	0.30	—
1988 Proof	25	—	—	—	—	—

KM# 72 SUCRE (Un)
5.0000 g., 0.7200 Silver 0.1157 oz. ASW **Obv:** Head of Sucre left, date below **Rev:** Flag draped arms, denomination above, mint name in legend below **Rev. Legend:** ...PHILA•U•S•A...

Date	Mintage	F	VF	XF	Unc	BU
1928	3,000,000	2.00	4.00	12.50	35.00	—
1930	400,000	3.00	10.00	30.00	70.00	—
1934	2,000,000	BV	2.00	10.00	30.00	—

KM# 78.1 SUCRE (Un)
Nickel, 26.5 mm. **Obv:** Flag draped arms, date below **Rev:** Head of Sucre left within wreath, denomination below

Date	Mintage	F	VF	XF	Unc	BU
1937 HF	9,000,000	0.50	1.00	2.00	7.00	—

KM# 78.2 SUCRE (Un)
Nickel, 25.9 mm. **Obv:** Flag draped arms **Rev:** Head of Sucre left

Date	Mintage	F	VF	XF	Unc	BU
1946	18,000,000	0.40	0.60	0.80	2.00	—

KM# 78a SUCRE (Un)
Copper-Nickel, 26 mm. **Obv:** Different ship in flag draped arms, date below **Rev:** Head of Sucre left within wreath, denozmination below

Date	Mintage	F	VF	XF	Unc	BU
1959	8,400,000	0.25	0.50	0.65	1.00	—
1959 Proof	—	Value: 250				

KM# 78b SUCRE (Un)
Nickel Clad Steel, 26 mm. **Obv:** Flag draped arms, date below **Rev:** Head left within wreath, denomination below **Note:** Ship in arms similar to KM#78

Date	Mintage	F	VF	XF	Unc	BU
1964	20,000,000	—	0.10	0.25	0.75	—
1970	24,000,000	—	0.10	0.25	0.75	—
1971	8,092,000	—	0.10	0.25	0.75	—
1974	40,308,000	—	0.10	0.25	0.50	—
1978	32,000,000	—	0.10	0.25	0.50	—
1979	32,000,000	—	0.10	0.25	0.50	—
1980	110,000,000	—	0.10	0.25	0.50	—
1981	70,000,000	—	0.10	0.25	0.50	—

KM# 83 SUCRE (Un)
Nickel Clad Steel, 26 mm. **Obv:** Modified flag draped arms, date below **Rev:** Head left within wreath, denomination below **Note:** Ship in arms similar to KM #78

Date	Mintage	F	VF	XF	Unc	BU
1974	32,000,000	—	0.10	0.20	0.40	—
1975	32,000,000	—	0.10	0.20	0.40	—
1975 Proof	—	Value: 150				
1977	32,000,000	—	0.10	0.20	0.35	—

KM# 85.1 SUCRE (Un)
Nickel Clad Steel, 26 mm. **Obv:** Modified coat of arms **Rev:** Large head right within wreath

Date	Mintage	F	VF	XF	Unc	BU
1985	—	—	—	—	0.50	—

KM# 85.2 SUCRE (Un)
Nickel Clad Steel, 26 mm. **Obv:** Flag draped arms, date below **Rev:** Small head left within wreath, denomination below

Date	Mintage	F	VF	XF	Unc	BU
1986	—	—	—	—	0.50	—

KM# 89 SUCRE (Un)
Nickel Clad Steel **Obv:** Flag draped arms, date below **Rev:** Head left within wreath, denomination below **Note:** The 1988 circulation

strikes were reportedly withdrawn from circulation and remelted. Approximately 100,000 pieces were released.

Date	Mintage	F	VF	XF	Unc	BU
1988	—	—	—	—	0.40	—
1988 Proof	25	—	—	—	—	—
1990	—	—	—	—	0.40	—
1992	—	—	—	—	0.40	—

KM# 73 2 SUCRES (Dos)

10.0000 g., 0.7200 Silver 0.2315 oz. ASW **Obv:** Head of Sucre left, date below **Rev:** Flag draped arms, denomination above, mint name below **Rev. Legend:** ...PHILA•U•S•A...

Date	Mintage	F	VF	XF	Unc	BU
1928	500,000	3.50	10.00	30.00	70.00	—
1930	100,000	7.00	25.00	50.00	90.00	—

KM# 80 2 SUCRES (Dos)

10.0000 g., 0.7200 Silver 0.2315 oz. ASW **Obv:** Head of Sucre left, date below **Rev:** Flag draped arms, denomination above

Date	Mintage	F	VF	XF	Unc	BU
1944Mo	1,000,000	3.50	5.00	8.00	16.00	—

KM# 82 2 SUCRES (Dos)

Copper-Nickel **Obv:** Flag draped arms, date below **Rev:** Head 3/4 facing, divides denomination **Note:** Not released to circulation. All but approximatley 35 pieces remelted.

Date	Mintage	F	VF	XF	Unc	BU
1973	2,000,000	—	—	200	300	—

KM# 79 5 SUCRES (Cinco)

25.0000 g., 0.7200 Silver 0.5787 oz. ASW **Obv:** Head of Sucre left, date below **Rev:** Flag draped arms, denomination above

Date	Mintage	F	VF	XF	Unc	BU
1943Mo	1,000,000	—	BV	8.50	16.50	27.50
1944Mo	2,600,000	—	BV	8.00	14.00	22.50

KM# 84 5 SUCRES (Cinco)

Copper-Nickel **Obv:** Flag draped arms, date below **Rev:** Head of Sucre left within wreath, denomination below

Date	Mintage	F	VF	XF	Unc	BU
1973	500	—	—	—	1,200	—

Note: Only 7 pieces were distributed to Ecuadorian government officials, while 8 pieces (5 of these cancelled) reside in the Central Bank Collection; the remaining 485 pieces have been remelted

KM# 91 5 SUCRES (Cinco)

5.2900 g., Nickel Clad Steel, 22 mm. **Obv:** Flag draped arms, date below **Rev:** Denomination within lines, design in background **Note:** The 1988 circulation strikes were reportedly withdrawn from circulation and remelted. Approximately 100,000 pieces were released.

Date	Mintage	F	VF	XF	Unc	BU
1988	—	—	—	—	0.50	—
1988 Proof	25	—	—	—	—	—
1991	—	—	—	—	0.50	—

KM# 92.1 10 SUCRES (Diez)

Nickel Clad Steel, 24 mm. **Obv:** Flag draped arms, date below **Rev:** Denomination to right of statuette **Note:** Similar to KM#92.2 but small arms and letters. The circulation strikes were withdrawn from circulation and remelted. Approximately 100,000 pieces were released.

Date	Mintage	F	VF	XF	Unc	BU
1988	—	—	—	—	1.00	—
1988 Proof	25	—	—	—	—	—

KM# 92.2 10 SUCRES (Diez)

6.1700 g., Nickel Clad Steel, 24 mm. **Obv:** Flag draped arms, date below, large arms and letters **Rev:** Denomination to right of statuette

Date	Mintage	F	VF	XF	Unc	BU
1991	—	—	—	—	1.00	—

KM# 94.1 20 SUCRES

Nickel Clad Steel, 26 mm. **Obv:** Flag draped arms, date below **Rev:** Denomination to right of small monument **Note:** The circulation strikes were withdrawn from circulation and remelted. Approximately 100,000 pieces released.

Date	Mintage	F	VF	XF	Unc	BU
1988	—	—	—	—	1.75	—
1988 Proof	25	—	—	—	—	—

KM# 94.2 20 SUCRES

Nickel Clad Steel, 26 mm. **Obv:** Modified coat of arms **Rev:** Denomination to right of small monument

Date	Mintage	F	VF	XF	Unc	BU
1991	—	—	—	—	1.75	—

KM# 93 50 SUCRES

Nickel Clad Steel, 29 mm. **Obv:** Flag draped arms, date below **Rev:** Denomination to left of native mask **Note:** The 1988 circulation strikes were withdrawn from circulation and remelted. Approximately 100,000 pieces released.

Date	Mintage	F	VF	XF	Unc	BU
1988 Narrow date	—	—	—	—	3.00	—
Note: 141 denticles in obverse border						
1988 Proof	25	—	—	—	—	—
1991 Wide date	—	—	—	—	3.00	—
Note: 141 denticles in obverse border						
1991 Narrow date	—	—	—	—	3.00	—
Note: 161 denticles in obverse border						

KM# 96 100 SUCRES

Bi-Metallic Bronze plated Steel center in Nickel plated Steel ring, 19 mm. **Subject:** National Bicentennial **Obv:** Flag draped arms within circle, date below **Rev:** Bust left within circle, denomination below

Date	Mintage	F	VF	XF	Unc	BU
1995	—	—	0.35	0.55	2.00	3.00

KM# 101 100 SUCRES

3.6000 g., Bi-Metallic Brass clad steel center in Stainless Steel ring, 19.9 mm. **Subject:** 70th Anniversary - Central Bank **Obv:** Bust of Antonio Jose de Sucre left within circle, dates below **Rev:** Denomination within circle, grain sprigs flank

Date	Mintage	F	VF	XF	Unc	BU
ND(1997)	—	—	0.25	0.50	2.00	3.00

KM# 97 500 SUCRES

Bi-Metallic Bronze plated Steel center in Nickel plated Steel ring, 21.5 mm. **Subject:** State Reform **Obv:** Flag draped arms within circle, date below **Rev:** Isidro Ayora facing within circle, denomination below

Date	Mintage	F	VF	XF	Unc	BU
1995	—	—	—	—	3.00	4.00

KM# 102 500 SUCRES

5.7500 g., Bi-Metallic Aluminumn-Bronze center in Copper-Nickel ring, 21.5 mm. **Subject:** 70th Anniversary - Central Bank

Obv: Isidro Ayora head facing within circle, dates below **Rev:** Denomination within circle, grain sprigs flank

Date	Mintage	F	VF	XF	Unc	BU
ND(1997)	—	—	—	—	3.00	4.00

KM# 99 1000 SUCRES

Bi-Metallic Brass center in Stainless Steel ring, 23.5 mm. **Obv:** Flag draped arms within circle, date below **Rev:** Eugenio Espejo head right within circle, denomination below

Date	Mintage	F	VF	XF	Unc	BU
1996	—	—	—	—	5.00	6.00

KM# 103 1000 SUCRES

7.1900 g., Bi-Metallic Aluminumn-Bronze center in Copper-Nickel ring, 23.9 mm. **Subject:** 70th Anniversary - Central Bank **Obv:** Eugenio Espejo head right within circle, dates below **Rev:** Denomination within circle, grain sprigs flank

Date	Mintage	F	VF	XF	Unc	BU
ND(1997)	—	—	—	—	5.00	6.00

KM# 74 CONDOR (Un)

8.3592 g., 0.9000 Gold 0.2419 oz. AGW **Obv:** Head of Bolivar left, date below **Rev:** Flag draped arms, denomination above, mint name below **Rev. Legend:** ...BIRMINGHAM... **Note:** 5,000 were released into circulation; the remainder are held as the Central Bank gold reserve.

Date	Mintage	F	VF	XF	Unc	BU
1928	20,000	—	BV	220	350	425

REFORM COINAGE

100 Centavos = 1 Dollar

KM# 104 CENTAVO (Un)

2.5200 g., Brass, 19 mm. **Obv:** Map of the Americas within circle **Rev:** Denomination **Edge:** Plain

Date	Mintage	F	VF	XF	Unc	BU
2000	—	—	—	—	0.20	0.40
2003	—	—	—	—	0.20	0.40
2004	—	—	—	—	0.20	0.40

KM# 104a CENTAVO (Un)

2.4200 g., Copper Plated Steel, 19 mm. **Obv:** Map of the Americas **Rev:** Denomination **Edge:** Plain

Date	Mintage	F	VF	XF	Unc	BU
2003	—	—	—	—	0.30	0.50

KM# 105 5 CENTAVOS (Cinco)

5.0000 g., Steel, 21.2 mm. **Subject:** Juan Montalvo **Obv:** Bust 3/4 facing and arms **Rev:** Denomination **Edge:** Plain

Date	Mintage	F	VF	XF	Unc	BU
2000	—	—	—	—	0.50	0.75

KM# 106 10 CENTAVOS (Diez)

2.2400 g., Steel, 17.9 mm. **Subject:** Eugenio Espejo **Obv:** Bust 3/4 left and arms **Rev:** Denomination **Edge:** Plain

Date	Mintage	F	VF	XF	Unc	BU
2000	—	—	—	—	0.75	1.00

KM# 107 25 CENTAVOS

5.6500 g., Steel, 24.2 mm. **Subject:** Jose Joaquin De Olmedo **Obv:** Bust facing and arms **Rev:** Denomination **Edge:** Reeded

Date	Mintage	F	VF	XF	Unc	BU
2000	—	—	—	—	1.00	1.50

KM# 108 50 CENTAVOS (Cincuenta)

11.3200 g., Steel, 30.6 mm. **Subject:** Eloy Alfaro **Obv:** Head at left 3/4 facing and arms **Rev:** Denomination **Edge:** Reeded

Date	Mintage	F	VF	XF	Unc	BU
2000	—	—	—	2.00	5.00	6.50

KM# 110 SUCRE (Un)

11.2500 g., Nickel Clad Steel, 30.5 mm. **Obv:** Denomination **Rev:** Antonio Jose De Sucre and small national arms **Edge:** Reeded

Date	Mintage	F	VF	XF	Unc	BU
2000	—	—	—	—	5.00	6.50

EGYPT

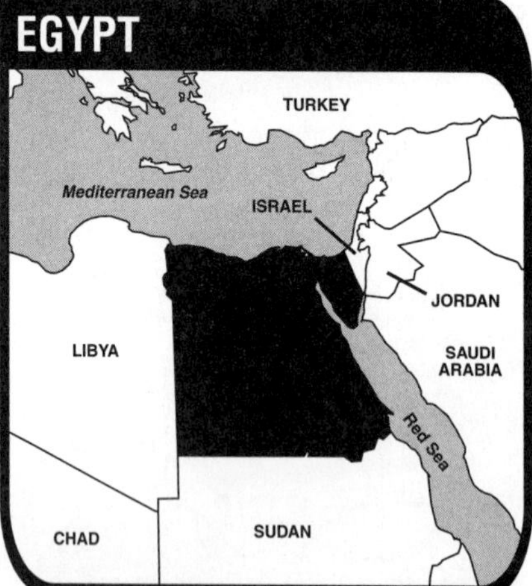

The Arab Republic of Egypt, located on the northeastern corner of Africa, has an area of 385,229 sq. mi. (1,1001,450 sq. km.) and a population of 62.4 million. Capital: Cairo. Although Egypt is an almost rainless expanse of desert, its economy is predominantly agricultural. Cotton, rice and petroleum are exported. Other main sources of income are revenues from the Suez Canal, remittances of Egyptian workers abroad and tourism.

Egyptian history dates back to about 3000 B.C. when the empire was established by uniting the upper and lower kingdoms. Following its 'Golden Age' (16th to 13th centuries B.C.), Egypt was conquered by Persia (525 B.C.) and Alexander the Great (332 B.C.). The Ptolemies, descended from one of Alexander's generals, ruled until the suicide of Cleopatra (30 B.C.) when Egypt became the private domain of the Roman emperor, and subsequently part of the Byzantine world. Various Muslim dynasties ruled Egypt from 641 on, including Ayyubid Sultans to 1250 and Mamluks to 1517, when it was conquered by the Ottoman Turks, interrupted by the occupation of Napoleon (1798-1801). A semi-independent dynasty was founded by Muhammad Ali in 1805 which lasted until 1952. Turkish rule became increasingly casual, permitting Great Britain to inject its influence by purchasing shares in the Suez Canal. British troops occupied Egypt in 1882, becoming the de facto rulers. On Dec. 14, 1914, Egypt was made a protectorate of Britain. British occupation ended on Feb. 28, 1922, when Egypt became a sovereign, independent kingdom. The monarchy was abolished and a republic proclaimed on June 18, 1953.

On Feb. 1, 1958, Egypt and Syria formed the United Arab Republic. Yemen joined on March 8 in an association known as the United Arab States. Syria withdrew from the United Arab Republic on Sept. 29, 1961, and on Dec. 26 Egypt dissolved its ties with Yemen in the United Arab States. On Sept. 2, 1971, Egypt finally shed the name United Arab Republic in favor of the Arab Republic of Egypt.

RULERS

British, 1882-1922

Kingdom, 1922-1953

Ahmed Fuad I, 1922-1936
Farouk, 1936-1952
Fuad II, 1952-1953

Republic, 1953-

MONETARY SYSTEM

(1885-1916)

10 Ushr-al-Qirsh = 1 Piastre

(Commencing 1916)

10 Milliemes = 1 Piastre (Qirsh)
100 Piastres = 1 Pound (Gunayh)

MINT MARKS

Egyptian coins issued prior to the advent of the British Protectorate series of Sultan Hussein Kamil introduced in 1916 were very similar to Turkish coins of the same period. They can best be distinguished by the presence of the Arabic word *Misr* Egypt) on the reverse, which generally appears immediately above the Muslim accession date of the ruler, which is presented in Arabic numerals. Each coin is individually dated according to the regnal years.

BP - Budapest, Hungary
H - Birmingham, England
KN - King's Norton, England

ENGRAVER

W - Emil Weigand, Berlin

INITIAL LETTERS

Letters, symbols and numerals were placed on coins during the reigns of Mustafa II (1695) until Selim III (1789). They have been observed in various positions but the most common position being over *bin* in the third row of the obverse. In Egypt these letters and others used on the Paras (Medins) above the word *duribe* on the reverse during this period.

REGNAL YEAR IDENTIFICATION

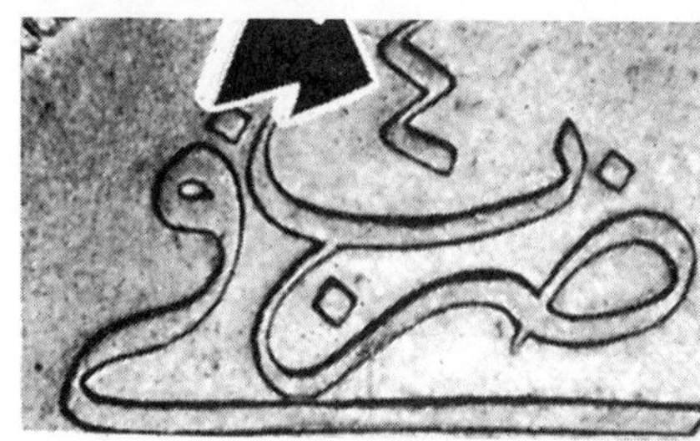

4
Duriba fi

Misr **Accession Date**

DENOMINATIONS

Para

Qirsh

NOTE: The unit of value on coins of this period is generally presented on the obverse immediately below the toughra, as shown in the illustrations above.

Piastres 1916-1933

Milliemes

Piastres 1934 –

TITLES

المصرية

al-Mamlaka al-Misriya

(The Kingdom of Egypt)

U.A.R. EGYPT

The legend illustrated is *Jumhuriyat Misr* al-*Arabiyya* which translates to 'The Arab Republic of Egypt'. Similar legends are found on the modern issues of Syria.

OTTOMAN EMPIRE
Resumed

Abdul Hamid II
AH1293-1327/1876-1909AD

REFORM COINAGE

KM# 287 1/40 QIRSH

Bronze **Obv:** Tughra **Rev:** Legend

Date	Mintage	F	VF	XF	Unc	BU
AH1293/27 (1901)	1,200,000	1.50	4.00	11.00	18.00	—
AH1293/29 (1903)	2,000,000	1.00	3.00	6.00	15.00	—
AH1293/31 (1905) H	2,400,000	1.00	3.00	6.00	15.00	—
AH1293/32 (1906) H	Inc. below	1.00	4.00	11.00	18.00	—
AH1293/33 (1907) H	1,200,000	1.00	4.00	11.00	18.00	—
AH1293/35 (1909) H	1,200,000	2.00	5.00	7.00	15.00	—

KM# 288 1/20 QIRSH

3.1200 g., Bronze **Obv:** Tughra **Rev:** Legend

Date	Mintage	F	VF	XF	Unc	BU
AH1293/27 (1901)	1,402,000	1.00	3.00	5.00	12.00	—
AH1293/29 (1903)	3,200,000	1.00	3.00	5.00	12.00	—
AH1293/31 (1905) H	3,000,000	1.00	3.00	5.00	12.00	—
AH1293/32 (1906) H	Inc. below	1.00	3.00	5.00	12.00	—
AH1293/33 (1907) H	1,400,000	2.00	3.00	7.00	15.00	—
AH1293/35 (1909) H	1,400,000	3.00	6.00	12.00	20.00	—

KM# 289 1/10 QIRSH

1.7200 g., Copper-Nickel **Obv:** Tughra **Rev:** Denomination

Date	Mintage	F	VF	XF	Unc	BU
AH1293/27-35(1901) Proof	—	Value: 100				

Note: Above value for common date proof

Date	Mintage	F	VF	XF	Unc	BU
AH1293/27 (1901)	3,010,000	1.00	2.00	5.00	10.00	—
AH1293/28 (1902)	6,000,000	1.00	2.00	5.00	10.00	—
AH1293/29 (1903)	1,500,000	1.00	3.00	6.00	15.00	—
AH1293/30 (1904)	1,000,000	1.00	3.00	6.00	15.00	—
AH1293/31 (1905) H	3,000,000	1.00	3.00	6.00	15.00	—
AH1293/32 (1906) H	Inc. below	1.00	3.00	6.00	15.00	—
AH1293/33 (1907) H	2,000,000	1.00	3.00	5.00	10.00	—
AH1293/35 (1909) H	2,000,000	1.25	5.00	12.00	20.00	—

KM# 290 2/10 QIRSH

2.3900 g., Copper-Nickel **Obv:** Tughra **Rev:** Denomination

Date	Mintage	F	VF	XF	Unc	BU
AH1293/27 (1901)	1,002,000	1.00	5.00	12.00	20.00	—
AH1293/28 (1902)	2,000,000	1.00	5.00	12.00	20.00	—
AH1293/29 (1903)	1,500,000	1.00	5.00	12.00	20.00	—
AH1293/30 (1904)	—	3.00	12.00	22.00	40.00	—
AH1293/31 (1905) H	1,000,000	1.00	5.00	12.00	20.00	—
AH1293/33 (1907) H	1,500,000	1.00	5.00	12.00	20.00	—
AH1293/35 (1909) H	750,000	2.00	10.00	20.00	35.00	—

KM# 291 5/10 QIRSH

3.9100 g., Copper-Nickel

Date	Mintage	F	VF	XF	Unc	BU
AH1293/27 (1901)	4,999,000	0.30	5.00	11.00	20.00	—
AH1293/29 (1903)	12,000,000	0.30	2.00	6.00	12.00	—
AH1293/30 (1904)	2,000,000	0.50	4.00	12.00	25.00	—
AH1293/33 (1907) H	1,000,000	2.00	9.00	22.50	40.00	—
AH1293/27-33 (1908) Proof	—	Value: 145				

Note: Above value for common date proof

KM# 292 QIRSH

1.4000 g., 0.8330 Silver 0.0375 oz. ASW **Obv:** Tughra

Date	Mintage	F	VF	XF	Unc	BU
AH1293/27-33 (1901) Proof	—	Value: 135				

Note: Above value for common date proof

Date	Mintage	F	VF	XF	Unc	BU
AH1293/27 (1901) W	200,000	1.25	7.00	15.00	27.50	—
AH1293/29 (1903) W	100,000	1.50	7.00	16.00	30.00	—
AH1293/29 (1903) H	100,000	1.25	5.00	12.00	25.00	—
AH1293/33 (1907) H	100,000	1.25	5.00	12.00	25.00	—

KM# 299 QIRSH

Copper-Nickel **Obv:** Tughra **Rev:** Stars surround legend

Date	Mintage	F	VF	XF	Unc	BU
AH1293/27 (1901)	999,000	2.00	12.00	32.00	50.00	—
AH1293/29 (1903)	3,500,000	2.00	5.00	15.00	30.00	—
AH1293/30 (1904)	500,000	2.50	14.00	35.00	55.00	—
AH1293/33 (1907) H	1,000,000	2.00	8.00	21.00	40.00	—

KM# 293 2 QIRSH

2.8000 g., 0.8330 Silver 0.0750 oz. ASW, 19 mm. **Obv:** Flower to right of tughra **Rev:** Denomination

Date	Mintage	F	VF	XF	Unc	BU
AH1293/17-33 (1901) Proof	—	Value: 145				

Note: Above value for common date of proof

Date	Mintage	F	VF	XF	Unc	BU
AH1293/27 (1901) W	1,000,000	2.00	8.00	21.00	35.00	—
AH1293/29 (1903) W	450,000	2.00	10.00	25.00	45.00	—
AH1293/29 (1903) H	1,250,000	2.00	6.00	15.00	30.00	—
AH1293/30 (1904) H	500,000	3.00	10.00	22.00	40.00	—
AH1293/31 (1905) H	Inc. above	3.00	10.00	22.00	40.00	—
AH1293/33 (1907) H	450,000	2.00	10.00	22.00	35.00	—

KM# 294 5 QIRSH

7.0000 g., 0.8330 Silver 0.1875 oz. ASW **Obv:** Flower at right of toughra

Date	Mintage	F	VF	XF	Unc	BU
AH1293/27 (1901) W	448,000	5.00	12.50	30.00	50.00	—
AH1293/29 (1903) W	600,000	5.00	10.00	30.00	50.00	—
AH1293/29 (1903) H	3,465,000	5.00	10.00	30.00	50.00	—
(1904) H	—	—	—	—	—	—
AH1293/30 (1904) H	1,213,000	5.00	10.00	32.50	60.00	—
AH1293/31 (1905) H	1,959,000	5.00	10.00	32.50	60.00	—
(1906) H	—	—	—	—	—	—
AH1293/32 (1906) H	Inc. above	5.00	10.00	30.00	50.00	—
AH1293/33 (1907) H	2,800,000	3.00	7.50	30.00	50.00	—

KM# 295 10 QIRSH

14.0000 g., 0.8330 Silver 0.3749 oz. ASW **Obv:** Flower at right of tughra **Rev:** Denomination

Date	Mintage	F	VF	XF	Unc	BU
AH1293/27-33 (1901) Proof	—	Value: 435				

Note: Above value for common date of proof

Date	Mintage	F	VF	XF	Unc	BU
AH1293/27 (1901) W	250,000	15.00	50.00	95.00	150	—
AH1293/29 (1903) W	Est. 2,450,000	8.00	25.00	60.00	100	—
AH1293/29 (1903) H	2,950,000	8.00	25.00	65.00	100	—
AH1293/30 (1904) H	1,000,000	8.00	25.00	65.00	100	—
AH1293/31 (1905) H	1,250,000	10.00	28.00	65.00	150	—
AH1293/32 (1906) H	Inc. below	8.00	16.00	65.00	100	—
AH1293/33 (1907) H	2,400,000	8.00	16.50	65.00	100	—

KM# 282 10 QIRSH

0.8544 g., 0.8750 Gold 0.0240 oz. AGW **Obv:** Al-Ghazi at right of tughra **Rev:** Denomination

Date	Mintage	F	VF	XF	Unc	BU
AH1293/34 (1908)	5,000	60.00	150	250	450	—

KM# 296 20 QIRSH

28.0000 g., 0.8330 Silver 0.7499 oz. ASW **Obv:** Tughra **Rev:** Legend within wreath

Date	Mintage	F	VF	XF	Unc	BU
AH1293/27-33(1901) Proof	—	Value: 825				

Note: Above value for common date of proof

Date	Mintage	F	VF	XF	Unc	BU
AH1293/27 (1901) W	25,000	17.50	70.00	250	500	—
AH1293/29 (1903) W	50,000	15.00	60.00	200	425	—
AH1293/29 (1903) H	425,000	12.00	50.00	180	400	—
AH1293/30 (1904) H	200,000	12.00	55.00	200	400	—
AH1293/31 (1905) H	250,000	12.00	55.00	200	400	—
AH1293/32 (1906) H	Inc. below	12.00	55.00	200	400	—
AH1293/33 (1907) H	300,000	12.00	45.00	175	350	—

Muhammad V
AH1327-1332/1909-1914AD
MILLED COINAGE

KM# 300 1/40 QIRSH
Bronze **Obv:** Tughra **Rev:** Denomination

Date	Mintage	F	VF	XF	Unc	BU
AH1327/2 (1910) H	2,000,000	1.50	3.00	10.00	25.00	—
AH1327/3 (1911) H	2,000,000	1.50	3.00	10.00	25.00	—
AH1327/4 (1911) H	1,200,000	1.50	3.00	10.00	25.00	—
AH1327/6 (1913) H	1,200,000	1.00	2.00	8.00	20.00	—

KM# 301 1/20 QIRSH
Bronze **Obv:** Tughra **Rev:** Denomination

Date	Mintage	F	VF	XF	Unc	BU
AH1327/2 (1910) H	2,000,000	1.00	5.00	11.00	18.00	—
AH1327/3 (1911) H	2,000,000	1.50	5.00	15.00	25.00	—
AH1327/4 (1911) H	2,400,000	1.00	5.00	11.00	18.00	—
AH1327/6 (1913) H	1,400,000	0.75	4.00	11.00	18.00	—

KM# 302 1/10 QIRSH
Copper-Nickel **Obv:** Tughra **Rev:** Denomination

Date	Mintage	F	VF	XF	Unc	BU
AH1327/2-6 (1910) H Proof	—	Value: 110				
Note: Above value for common date of proof						
AH1327/2 (1910) H	3,000,000	3.00	6.00	15.00	25.00	—
AH1327/3 (1911)	1,000,000	5.00	12.00	30.00	50.00	—
AH1327/4 (1911) H	3,000,000	1.00	2.00	5.00	12.50	—
AH1327/6 (1913) H	3,000,000	0.75	1.50	3.00	12.50	—

KM# 303 2/10 QIRSH
2.4200 g., Copper-Nickel **Obv:** Tughra within wreath **Rev:** Denomination

Date	Mintage	F	VF	XF	Unc	BU
AH1327/2 (1910) H	1,000,000	2.00	6.00	15.00	25.00	—
AH1327/3 (1911)	500,000	3.00	10.00	15.00	35.00	—
AH1327/4 (1911) H	1,000,000	2.00	6.00	15.00	25.00	—
AH1327/6 (1913) H	1,000,000	1.25	6.00	15.00	25.00	—
AH1327/2-6 (1914) H Proof	—	Value: 120				
Note: Above value for common date of proof						

KM# 304 5/10 QIRSH
Copper-Nickel **Obv:** Tughra within wreath **Rev:** Denomination

Date	Mintage	F	VF	XF	Unc	BU
AH1327/2 (1910) H	2,131,000	2.50	12.00	20.00	50.00	—
AH1327/3 (1911)	1,000,000	5.00	22.00	45.00	75.00	—
AH1327/4 (1911) H	3,327,000	1.00	5.00	11.00	25.00	—
AH1327/6 (1913) H	3,000,000	1.00	5.00	11.00	25.00	—

KM# 305 QIRSH
1.4000 g., 0.8330 Silver 0.0375 oz. ASW **Obv:** Tughra **Rev:** Denomination

Date	Mintage	F	VF	XF	Unc	BU
AH1327/2 (1910) H	251,000	2.00	6.00	18.00	28.00	—
AH1327/3 (1911) H	171,000	2.25	6.00	18.00	35.00	—

KM# 306 QIRSH
Copper-Nickel **Obv:** Tughra within wreath **Rev:** Denomination within circle of stars

Date	Mintage	F	VF	XF	Unc	BU
AH1327/2 (1910) H	1,000,000	2.00	7.00	18.00	35.00	—
AH1327/3 (1911)	300,000	20.00	40.00	95.00	150	—
AH1327/4 (1911) H	500,000	4.00	15.00	40.00	65.00	—
AH1327/6 (1913) H	2,500,000	2.00	4.00	8.00	20.00	—

KM# 307 2 QIRSH
2.8000 g., 0.8330 Silver 0.0750 oz. ASW **Obv:** Tughra, spray below **Rev:** Denomination within wreath

Date	Mintage	F	VF	XF	Unc	BU
AH1327/2 (1910) H	250,000	5.00	15.00	45.00	90.00	—
AH1327/3 (1911) H	300,000	5.00	15.00	45.00	90.00	—

KM# 308 5 QIRSH
7.0000 g., 0.8330 Silver 0.1875 oz. ASW **Obv:** Tughra above spray **Rev:** Denomination within wreath

Date	Mintage	F	VF	XF	Unc	BU
AH1327/2-6 (1910) H Proof	—	Value: 350				
Note: Above value for common date of proof						
AH1327/2 (1910) H	574,000	10.00	40.00	90.00	150	—
AH1327/3 (1911) H	2,400,000	5.00	20.00	40.00	70.00	—
AH1327/4 (1911) H	1,351,000	6.00	22.00	40.00	85.00	—
AH1327/6 (1913) H	7,400,000	4.00	15.00	27.00	55.00	—

KM# 309 10 QIRSH
14.0000 g., 0.8330 Silver 0.3749 oz. ASW **Obv:** Tughra, spray below **Rev:** Denomination within wreath

Date	Mintage	F	VF	XF	Unc	BU
AH1327/2-6 (1910) H Proof	—	Value: 475				
Note: Above value for common date of proof						
AH1327/2 (1910) H	300,000	20.00	50.00	110	200	—
AH1327/3 (1911) H	1,300,000	8.00	25.00	75.00	115	—
AH1327/4 (1911) H	300,000	10.00	50.00	110	200	—
AH1327/6 (1913) H	4,212,000	6.00	15.00	35.00	80.00	—

KM# 310 20 QIRSH
28.0000 g., 0.8330 Silver 0.7499 oz. ASW **Obv:** Tughra, spray below **Rev:** Denomination within wreath

Date	Mintage	F	VF	XF	Unc	BU
AH1327/2-6 (1910) H Proof	—	Value: 950				
Note: Above value for common date of proof						
AH1327/2 (1910) H	75,000	35.00	65.00	210	500	—
AH1327/3 (1911) H	600,000	22.50	65.00	100	325	—
AH1327/4 (1911) H	100,000	30.00	55.00	135	425	—
AH1327/6 (1913) H	875,000	21.50	32.50	70.00	300	—

BRITISH PROTECTORATE
AH1333-1341 / 1914-1922AD

Hussein Kamil
As Sultan, AH1333-1336/1914-1917AD
OCCUPATION COINAGE

French

KM# 312 1/2 MILLIEME
Bronze **Obv:** Tughra, date below **Rev:** Dates below denominations **Note:** Accession date: AH1333.

Date	Mintage	F	VF	XF	Unc	BU
AH1335-1917	4,000,000	1.35	5.00	12.50	25.00	—

KM# 313 MILLIEME
Copper-Nickel **Obv:** Center hole divides date and legend **Rev:** Center hole divides denomination, date below **Note:** Accession date: AH1333.

Date	Mintage	F	VF	XF	Unc	BU
AH1335-1917H	12,000,000	0.40	2.00	7.00	12.00	—
AH1335-1917	4,002,000	1.25	4.00	11.00	20.00	—

KM# 314 2 MILLIEMES
Copper-Nickel **Obv:** Center hole divides date **Rev:** Center hole divides denomination, date below **Note:** Accession date: AH1333.

Date	Mintage	F	VF	XF	Unc	BU
AH1335-1916H	300,000	1.25	8.00	15.00	30.00	—
AH1335-1917H	9,000,000	0.40	2.00	5.00	14.00	—
AH1335-1917	3,006,000	1.00	4.00	12.00	22.00	—

KM# 315 5 MILLIEMES
4.7500 g., Copper-Nickel **Obv:** Center hole divides dates **Rev:** Center hole divides denomination **Note:** Accession date: AH1333.

Date	Mintage	F	VF	XF	Unc	BU
AH1335-1916H	3,000,000	1.35	5.50	10.00	20.00	—
AH1335-1916	3,000,000	2.00	5.00	10.00	20.00	—
AH1335-1917H	37,000,000	0.60	1.50	2.50	8.00	—
AH1335-1917	6,776,000	1.00	2.50	6.00	15.00	—

KM# 316 10 MILLIEMES
Copper-Nickel **Obv:** Center hole divides dates **Rev:** Center hole divides denomination **Note:** Accession date: AH1333.

Date	Mintage	F	VF	XF	Unc	BU
AH1335-1916	1,006,999	2.00	6.00	18.00	35.00	—
AH1335-1916H	1,000,000	1.50	6.00	18.00	35.00	—
AH1335-1917	1,010,999	2.00	6.00	18.00	35.00	—
AH1335-1917H	6,000,000	0.75	2.00	7.00	15.00	—
AH1335-1917KN	4,000,000	1.25	3.00	8.00	20.00	—

KM# 317.1 2 PIASTRES
2.8000 g., 0.8330 Silver 0.0750 oz. ASW **Obv:** Text above date and sprays **Rev:** Denomination, legend within wreath **Note:** Accession date: AH1333.

Date	Mintage	F	VF	XF	Unc	BU
AH1335-1916	2,505,000	2.00	6.00	15.00	30.00	—
AH1335-1917	4,461,000	1.50	4.50	10.00	20.00	—

KM# 317.2 2 PIASTRES
2.8000 g., 0.8330 Silver 0.0750 oz. ASW **Obv:** Without inner circle **Rev:** Without inner circle **Note:** Accession date: AH1333.

Date	Mintage	F	VF	XF	Unc	BU
AH1335-1917H	2,180,000	1.50	4.00	8.00	15.00	—

KM# 318.1 5 PIASTRES
7.0000 g., 0.8330 Silver 0.1875 oz. ASW **Obv:** Text within wreath **Rev:** Denomination within wreath **Note:** Accession date: AH1333.

Date	Mintage	F	VF	XF	Unc	BU
AH1335-1916	6,000,000	3.50	9.00	20.00	35.00	—
AH1335-1917	9,218,000	2.75	5.00	17.50	32.00	—

KM# 318.2 5 PIASTRES
7.0000 g., 0.8330 Silver 0.1875 oz. ASW **Obv:** Without inner circle **Rev:** WIthout inner circle **Note:** Accession date: AH1333.

Date	Mintage	F	VF	XF	Unc	BU
AH1335-1917H	5,036,000	3.50	9.00	22.00	45.00	—
AH1335-1917H Proof	—	Value: 325				

KM# 319 10 PIASTRES
14.0000 g., 0.8330 Silver 0.3749 oz. ASW **Obv:** Text above date within wreath **Rev:** Denomination within wreath, dates below **Note:** Accession date: AH1333.

Date	Mintage	F	VF	XF	Unc	BU
AH1335-1916	2,900,000	6.00	15.00	40.00	95.00	—
AH1335-1917	4,859,000	6.00	12.00	22.00	85.00	—

KM# 320 10 PIASTRES
14.0000 g., 0.8330 Silver 0.3749 oz. ASW **Obv:** Text above date within wreath, without inner circle **Rev:** Denomination within wreath, without inner circle **Note:** Accession date: AH1333.

Date	Mintage	F	VF	XF	Unc	BU
AH1335-1917H	2,000,000	6.00	15.00	45.00	100	—

KM# 321 20 PIASTRES
28.0000 g., 0.8330 Silver 0.7499 oz. ASW **Obv:** Text above date within wreath **Rev:** Denomination within wreath, dates below **Note:** Accession date: AH1333.

Date	Mintage	F	VF	XF	Unc	BU
AH1335-1916	1,500,000	12.00	25.00	85.00	160	—
AH1335-1917	840,000	12.00	20.00	95.00	180	—
AH1335-1917 Proof	—	Value: 750				

KM# 322 20 PIASTRES
28.0000 g., 0.8330 Silver 0.7499 oz. ASW **Obv:** Without inner circle **Rev:** Without inner circle **Note:** Accession date: AH1333.

Date	Mintage	F	VF	XF	Unc	BU
AH1335-1917H	250,000	22.00	65.00	155	300	—

KM# 324 100 PIASTRES
8.5000 g., 0.8750 Gold 0.2391 oz. AGW **Obv:** Text above date within wreath **Rev:** Denomination within wreath, dates below **Note:** Accession date: AH1333.

Date	Mintage	F	VF	XF	Unc	BU
AH1335-1916	10,000	—	BV	220	325	—
AH1335-1916 Proof	—	Value: 1,500				

Note: Restrikes may exist

Fuad I

As Sultan, AH1336-1341/1917-1922AD

OCCUPATION COINAGE

French

KM# 325 2 PIASTRES
2.8000 g., 0.8330 Silver 0.0750 oz. ASW **Obv:** Text above date **Rev:** Denomination and dates **Note:** Accession date: AH1335.

Date	Mintage	F	VF	XF	Unc	BU
AH1338-1920H	2,820,000	37.50	110	200	365	—

KM# 326 5 PIASTRES
7.0000 g., 0.8330 Silver 0.1875 oz. ASW **Obv:** Text above date **Rev:** Denomination and dates **Note:** Accession date: AH1335.

Date	Mintage	F	VF	XF	Unc	BU
AH1338-1920H	1,000,000	17.50	55.00	165	340	—

KM# 327 10 PIASTRES
14.0000 g., 0.8330 Silver 0.3749 oz. ASW **Obv:** Text above date **Rev:** Denomination and dates **Note:** Accession date: AH1335.

Date	Mintage	F	VF	XF	Unc	BU
AH1338-1920H	500,000	17.50	65.00	200	350	—

KM# 328 20 PIASTRES
28.0000 g., 0.8330 Silver 0.7499 oz. ASW **Obv:** Text above date **Rev:** Denomination and dates **Note:** Accession date: AH1335.

Date	Mintage	F	VF	XF	Unc	BU
AH1338-1920H Rare	2	—	—	—	—	—

KINGDOM

AH1341-1372 / 1922-1952AD

Fuad I

As King, AH1341-1355/1922-1936AD

DECIMAL COINAGE

KM# 330 1/2 MILLIEME
Bronze **Obv:** Bust right **Rev:** Denomination, dates above

Date	Mintage	F	VF	XF	Unc	BU
AH1342-1924H	3,000,000	2.00	5.00	14.00	25.00	—
AH1342-1924H Proof	—	Value: 120				

KM# 343 1/2 MILLIEME

Bronze **Obv:** Uniformed bust left **Rev:** Dates above denomination

Date	Mintage	F	VF	XF	Unc	BU
AH1348-1929BP	1,000,000	6.00	20.00	30.00	50.00	—
AH1351-1932H	1,000,000	3.00	20.00	30.00	50.00	—
AH1351-1932H Proof	—	Value: 160				

KM# 331 MILLIEME

Bronze **Obv:** Bust right **Rev:** Denomination divides dates

Date	Mintage	F	VF	XF	Unc	BU
AH1342-1924H	6,500,000	1.25	3.00	6.00	15.00	—

KM# 344 MILLIEME

4.2400 g., Bronze **Obv:** Uniformed bust left **Rev:** Denomination divides dates

Date	Mintage	F	VF	XF	Unc	BU
AH1348-1929BP	4,500,000	1.50	4.00	10.00	20.00	—
AH1351-1932H	2,500,000	0.50	1.25	6.00	15.00	—
AH1351-1932H Proof	—	Value: 120				
AH1352-1933H	5,110,000	1.25	3.00	6.00	15.00	—
AH1354-1935H	18,000,000	0.20	0.50	2.00	8.00	—

KM# 332 2 MILLIEMES

Copper-Nickel **Obv:** Bust right **Rev:** Denomination divides dates

Date	Mintage	F	VF	XF	Unc	BU
AH1342-1924H	4,500,000	1.25	3.00	10.00	20.00	—
AH1342-1924H Proof	—	Value: 120				

KM# 345 2 MILLIEMES

Copper-Nickel **Obv:** Uniformed bust left **Rev:** Denomination divides dates

Date	Mintage	F	VF	XF	Unc	BU
AH1348-1929BP	Est. 3,500,000	0.40	1.00	3.00	10.00	—

KM# 356 2-1/2 MILLIEMES

Copper-Nickel **Obv:** Uniformed bust left **Rev:** Denomination divides dates **Shape:** 8-sided

Date	Mintage	F	VF	XF	Unc	BU
AH1352-1933	4,000,000	1.25	7.00	10.00	30.00	—

KM# 333 5 MILLIEMES

Copper-Nickel **Obv:** Bust right **Rev:** Denomination divides dates

Date	Mintage	F	VF	XF	Unc	BU
AH1342-1924	6,000,000	1.25	6.00	17.50	28.00	—

KM# 346 5 MILLIEMES

Copper-Nickel **Obv:** Uniformed bust left **Rev:** Denomination divides dates

Date	Mintage	F	VF	XF	Unc	BU
AH1348-1929BP	4,000,000	0.75	5.00	14.00	25.00	—
AH1352-1933H	3,000,000	1.50	4.00	18.00	35.00	—
AH1354-1935H	8,000,000	0.80	1.00	6.00	12.50	—
AH1354-1935H Proof	—	Value: 120				

KM# 334 10 MILLIEMES

5.1900 g., Copper-Nickel **Obv:** Bust right **Rev:** Denomination divides dates

Date	Mintage	F	VF	XF	Unc	BU
AH1342-1924	2,000,000	2.00	15.00	30.00	50.00	—

KM# 347 10 MILLIEMES

5.2200 g., Copper-Nickel **Obv:** Uniformed bust left **Rev:** Denomination divides dates

Date	Mintage	F	VF	XF	Unc	BU
AH1348-1929BP	1,500,000	1.35	8.50	20.00	38.00	—
AH1352-1933H	1,500,000	1.35	8.50	25.00	45.00	—
AH1354-1935H	4,000,000	0.75	3.00	11.50	20.00	—

KM# 335 2 PIASTRES

2.8000 g., 0.8330 Silver 0.0750 oz. ASW **Obv:** Bust right **Rev:** Denomination above center circle, dates flank below

Date	Mintage	F	VF	XF	Unc	BU
AH1342-1923H	2,500,000	2.00	6.00	11.00	35.00	—

KM# 348 2 PIASTRES

2.8000 g., 0.8330 Silver 0.0750 oz. ASW **Obv:** Uniformed bust left **Rev:** Denomination above center circle, dates flank below

Date	Mintage	F	VF	XF	Unc	BU
AH1348-1929BP	500,000	2.00	5.00	11.00	20.00	—

Note: Edge varieties exist

KM# 336 5 PIASTRES

7.0000 g., 0.8330 Silver 0.1875 oz. ASW **Obv:** Bust right **Rev:** Denomination above center circle, dates flank below

Date	Mintage	F	VF	XF	Unc	BU
AH1341-1923H	1,800,000	3.50	10.00	30.00	60.00	—
AH1341-1923	800,000	4.50	15.00	35.00	60.00	—
AH1341-1923H Proof	—	Value: 250				

KM# 349 5 PIASTRES

7.0000 g., 0.8330 Silver 0.1875 oz. ASW **Obv:** Uniformed bust left **Rev:** Denomination above center circle, dates flank below

Date	Mintage	F	VF	XF	Unc	BU
AH1348-1929BP	800,000	4.50	15.00	35.00	65.00	—
AH1352-1933	1,300,000	3.50	7.50	25.00	55.00	—
AH1352-1933 Proof	—	Value: 250				

KM# 337 10 PIASTRES

14.0000 g., 0.8330 Silver 0.3749 oz. ASW, 32.5 mm. **Obv:** Bust right **Rev:** Denomination above center circle, dates flank below

Date	Mintage	F	VF	XF	Unc	BU
AH1341-1923	400,000	7.00	22.50	70.00	120	—
AH1341-1923H	1,000,000	7.00	22.50	60.00	100	—
AH1341-1923H Proof	—	Value: 450				

KM# 350 10 PIASTRES

14.0000 g., 0.8330 Silver 0.3749 oz. ASW **Obv:** Uniformed bust left **Rev:** Denomination above center circle, dates flank below

Date	Mintage	F	VF	XF	Unc	BU
AH1348-1929BP	400,000	6.50	20.00	55.00	100	—
AH1352-1933	Est. 350,000	6.50	20.00	55.00	100	—
AH1352-1933 Proof	—	Value: 475				

KM# 338 20 PIASTRES

28.0000 g., 0.8330 Silver 0.7499 oz. ASW **Obv:** Bust right **Rev:** Denomination above center circle, dates flank below

Date	Mintage	F	VF	XF	Unc	BU
AH1341-1923	100,000	20.00	60.00	210	425	—
AH1341-1923H	50,000	20.00	70.00	240	425	—
AH1341-1923H Proof	—	Value: 875				

KM# 339 20 PIASTRES
1.7000 g., 0.8750 Gold 0.0478 oz. AGW **Obv:** Bust right **Rev:** Denomination above center inscription, dates flank below

Date	Mintage	F	VF	XF	Unc	BU
AH1341-1923	65,000	50.00	85.00	145	325	—

KM# 351 20 PIASTRES
1.7000 g., 0.8750 Gold 0.0478 oz. AGW **Obv:** Bust left

Date	Mintage	F	VF	XF	Unc	BU
AH1348 Proof	—	—	—	—	—	—
AH1348-1929	—	45.00	65.00	85.00	125	—
AH1349-1930	—	45.00	65.00	85.00	125	—
AH1349-1930 Proof	—	—	—	—	—	—

KM# 352 20 PIASTRES
28.0000 g., 0.8330 Silver 0.7499 oz. ASW **Obv:** Uniformed bust left **Rev:** Denomination above center circle, dates flank below

Date	Mintage	F	VF	XF	Unc	BU
AH1348-1929BP	50,000	15.00	70.00	165	350	—
AH1352-1933	25,000	12.50	70.00	150	300	—
AH1352-1933 Proof	—	—	—	—	—	—

KM# 340 50 PIASTRES
4.2500 g., 0.8750 Gold 0.1196 oz. AGW **Obv:** Bust right **Rev:** Denomination above inscription, dates flank

Date	Mintage	F	VF	XF	Unc	BU
AH1341-1923	18,000	BV	115	135	175	—

KM# 353 50 PIASTRES
4.2500 g., 0.8750 Gold 0.1196 oz. AGW **Obv:** Bust left **Rev:** Denomination above inscription, dates flank below

Date	Mintage	F	VF	XF	Unc	BU
AH1348-1929	—	BV	120	145	185	—
AH1348-1929 Proof	—	—	—	—	—	—
AH1349-1930	—	BV	115	135	165	—
AH1349-1930 Proof	—	—	—	—	—	—

KM# 341 100 PIASTRES
8.5000 g., 0.8750 Gold 0.2391 oz. AGW **Obv:** Bust right **Rev:** Denomination above center circle, dates flank below

Date	Mintage	F	VF	XF	Unc	BU
AH1340-1922	25,000	BV	215	235	275	—

KM# 354 100 PIASTRES
8.5000 g., 0.8750 Gold 0.2391 oz. AGW **Obv:** Bust left

Date	Mintage	F	VF	XF	Unc	BU
AH1348-1929	—	BV	220	245	295	—
AH1349-1930	—	BV	215	235	275	—
AH1349-1930 Proof	—	—	—	—	—	—

KM# 342 500 PIASTRES
42.5000 g., 0.8750 Gold 1.1956 oz. AGW **Obv:** Bust right **Rev:** Denomination above center circle, dates flank below

Date	Mintage	F	VF	XF	Unc	BU
AH1340-1922	1,800	—	—	1,100	1,450	—
AH1340-1922 Proof	—	Value: 1,650				

Note: Circulation coins were struck in both red and yellow gold

KM# 355 500 PIASTRES
42.5000 g., 0.8750 Gold 1.1956 oz. AGW **Obv:** Uniformed bust left **Rev:** Denomination above center circle, dates flank below

Date	Mintage	F	VF	XF	Unc	BU
AH1348-1929	—	—	—	1,100	1,350	—
AH1349-1930	—	—	—	1,100	1,350	—
AH1351-1932	—	—	—	1,100	1,350	—
AH1351-1932 Proof	—	Value: 1,650				

Farouk
AH1355-1372/1936-1952AD
DECIMAL COINAGE

KM# 357 1/2 MILLIEME
Bronze **Obv:** Uniformed bust looking left **Rev:** Denomination, dates below

Date	Mintage	F	VF	XF	Unc	BU
AH1357-1938	4,000,000	1.50	5.00	9.00	18.00	—
AH1357-1938 Proof	—	Value: 100				

KM# 358 MILLIEME
Bronze **Obv:** Uniformed bust looking left **Rev:** Denomination, dates below

Date	Mintage	F	VF	XF	Unc	BU
AH1357-1938	26,240,000	0.20	0.50	2.00	7.00	—
AH1357-1938 Proof	—	Value: 120				
AH1364-1945	10,000,000	1.25	7.00	26.00	50.00	—
AH1366-1947	—	1.25	7.00	26.00	50.00	—
AH1369-1950	5,000,000	0.40	1.00	3.00	10.00	—
AH1369-1950 Proof	—	Value: 85.00				

KM# 362 MILLIEME
3.9600 g., Copper-Nickel, 18.1 mm.

Date	Mintage	F	VF	XF	Unc	BU
AH1357-1938	3,500,000	1.00	3.50	8.00	15.00	—

KM# 359 2 MILLIEMES
2.5100 g., Copper-Nickel **Obv:** Uniformed bust looking left **Rev:** Denomination divides dates

Date	Mintage	F	VF	XF	Unc	BU
AH1357-1938	2,500,000	1.50	4.00	14.00	25.00	—
AH1357-1938 Proof	—	Value: 140				

KM# 360 5 MILLIEMES
Bronze **Obv:** Uniformed bust looking left **Rev:** Denomination divides dates **Shape:** Scalloped

Date	Mintage	F	VF	XF	Unc	BU
AH1357-1938	—	0.40	1.00	3.00	10.00	—
AH1357-1938 Proof	—	Value: 65.00				
AH1362-1943	—	0.40	1.00	3.00	10.00	—

KM# 363 5 MILLIEMES
4.0000 g., Copper-Nickel **Obv:** Uniformed bust looking left **Rev:** Denomination divides dates

Date	Mintage	F	VF	XF	Unc	BU
AH1357-1938	7,000,000	0.40	1.00	4.00	10.00	—
AH1357-1938 Proof	—	Value: 75.00				
AH1360-1941	11,500,000	0.20	1.00	4.00	8.00	—

KM# 361 10 MILLIEMES
5.7000 g., Bronze **Obv:** Uniformed bust looking left **Rev:** Denomination divides dates **Shape:** Scalloped

Date	Mintage	F	VF	XF	Unc	BU
AH1357-1938	—	0.40	1.00	4.00	10.00	—
AH1357-1938 Proof	—	Value: 140				
AH1362-1943	—	—	0.75	4.00	10.00	—

KM# 364 10 MILLIEMES
5.5500 g., Copper-Nickel, 23 mm. **Obv:** Uniformed bust looking left **Rev:** Denomination divides dates

Date	Mintage	F	VF	XF	Unc	BU
AH1357-1938	3,500,000	0.40	1.00	5.00	12.50	—
AH1357-1938 Proof	—	Value: 85.00				
AH1360-1941	5,322,000	0.40	1.00	5.00	12.50	—

KM# 365 2 PIASTRES
2.8000 g., 0.8330 Silver 0.0750 oz. ASW

Date	Mintage	F	VF	XF	Unc	BU
AH1356-1937	500,000	1.25	1.75	3.00	8.00	—
Note: Fine and coarse edge reeding exist						
AH1356-1937 Proof	—	Value: 300				
AH1358-1939	500,000	1.50	4.00	10.00	75.00	—
AH1358-1939 Proof	—	Value: 200				
AH1361-1942	10,000,000	1.25	1.75	4.00	10.00	—
Note: Normal and flat rim varieties exist for AH1361 coins						

KM# 369 2 PIASTRES
2.8000 g., 0.5000 Silver 0.0450 oz. ASW **Obv:** Uniformed bust left **Rev:** Denomination and dates within tasseled wreath **Shape:** 6-sided

Date	Mintage	F	VF	XF	Unc	BU
AH1363-1944	32,000	0.85	1.45	2.75	5.50	—

KM# 366 5 PIASTRES
7.0000 g., 0.8330 Silver 0.1875 oz. ASW, 25.92 mm. **Obv:** Uniformed bust left **Edge:** Security

Date	Mintage	F	VF	XF	Unc	BU
AH1356-1937	—	2.75	3.75	6.50	15.00	—
AH1356-1937 Proof	—	Value: 275				
AH1358-1939	8,000,000	2.75	3.75	6.50	15.00	—
AH1358-1939 Proof	—	Value: 275				

KM# 367 10 PIASTRES
14.0000 g., 0.8330 Silver 0.3749 oz. ASW

Date	Mintage	F	VF	XF	Unc	BU
AH1356-1937	2,800,000	5.50	9.00	17.50	35.00	—
AH1356-1937 Proof	—	Value: 375				
AH1358-1939	2,850,000	5.50	9.00	17.50	35.00	—
AH1358-1939 Proof	—	Value: 300				

KM# 368 20 PIASTRES
28.0000 g., 0.8330 Silver 0.7499 oz. ASW **Obv:** Uniformed bust looking left **Rev:** Denomination and dates within tasseled wreath

Date	Mintage	F	VF	XF	Unc	BU
AH1356-1937	—	12.00	26.00	50.00	90.00	—
AH1356-1937 Proof	—	Value: 1,000				
AH1358-1939	—	12.00	26.00	50.00	90.00	—
AH1358-1939 Proof	—	Value: 1,200				

KM# 370 20 PIASTRES
1.7000 g., 0.8750 Gold 0.0478 oz. AGW **Subject:** Royal Wedding **Obv:** Uniformed bust looking left **Rev:** Dates within circle, denomination above, decorative vine surrounds

Date	Mintage	F	VF	XF	Unc	BU
AH1357-1938	20,000	BV	65.00	90.00	125	145

KM# 371 50 PIASTRES
4.2500 g., 0.8750 Gold 0.1196 oz. AGW **Subject:** Royal Wedding **Obv:** Uniformed bust looking left **Rev:** Dates within circle, denomination above, decorative vine surrounds

Date	Mintage	F	VF	XF	Unc	BU
AH1357-1938	10,000	BV	120	150	250	—

KM# 372 100 PIASTRES
8.5000 g., 0.8750 Gold 0.2391 oz. AGW **Subject:** Royal Wedding **Obv:** Uniformed bust looking left **Rev:** Dates within circle, denomination above, decorative vine surrounds

Date	Mintage	F	VF	XF	Unc	BU
AH1357-1938	5,000	—	BV	220	300	—
Note: Circulation coins were struck in both red and yellow gold						

FIRST REPUBLIC
AH1373-1378 / 1953-1958AD

DECIMAL COINAGE

KM# 375 MILLIEME
Aluminum-Bronze **Obv:** Denomination divides dates **Rev:** Small sphinx with outlined base

Date	Mintage	F	VF	XF	Unc	BU
AH1373-1954	—	—	8.00	17.00	35.00	—
AH1374-1954	—	—	3.00	12.00	25.00	—
AH1374-1955	—	—	2.00	7.00	15.00	—
AH1375-1955	—	—	2.00	7.00	15.00	—
AH1375-1956	—	—	2.00	7.00	15.00	—

KM# 376 MILLIEME
Aluminum-Bronze **Obv:** Denomination divides dates **Rev:** Small sphinx without base outlined

Date	Mintage	F	VF	XF	Unc	BU
AH1373-1954	—	—	—	—	—	—
AH1374-1954	—	—	2.00	7.00	15.00	—
AH1374-1955	—	—	1.00	2.00	5.00	—
AH1375-1955	—	—	1.00	2.00	5.00	—
AH1375-1956	—	—	1.50	4.00	10.00	—
AH1376-1957	—	—	—	—	—	—

KM# 377.1 MILLIEME
Aluminum-Bronze **Rev:** Large sphinx; without outlined base
Note: Prev. KM#377.

Date	Mintage	F	VF	XF	Unc	BU
AH1375-1956	—	—	0.50	2.00	4.00	—
AH1376-1957	—	—	0.75	2.50	5.00	—
AH1377-1958	—	—	0.75	2.50	5.00	—

KM# 377.2 MILLIEME
Aluminum-Bronze **Obv:** Denomination divides dates **Rev:** Small sphinx without outlined base

Date	Mintage	F	VF	XF	Unc	BU
AH1376-1957BP	—	—	0.75	1.50	5.00	—
AH1377-1958BP	—	—	0.75	1.50	5.00	—

KM# 378 5 MILLIEMES
Aluminum-Bronze **Obv:** Denomination divides dates **Rev:** Small sphinx with outlined base

Date	Mintage	F	VF	XF	Unc	BU
AH1373-1954	—	—	5.00	10.00	35.00	—
AH1374-1954	—	—	4.00	8.00	25.00	—
AH1374-1955	—	—	10.00	20.00	50.00	—
AH1375-1956	—	—	3.00	6.00	15.00	—

KM# 379 5 MILLIEMES
Aluminum-Bronze **Obv:** Denomination divides dates **Rev:** Large sphinx

Date	Mintage	F	VF	XF	Unc	BU
AH1376-1957	—	—	2.00	4.00	10.00	—
AH1377-1957	—	—	2.00	4.00	10.00	—
AH1377-1958	—	—	2.00	4.00	10.00	—

Thin "milliemes"

Thick "milliemes"

KM# 380.1 10 MILLIEMES
Aluminum-Bronze **Obv:** Denomination divides dates **Rev:** Small sphinx with base outlined **Note:** Thin milliemes.

Date	Mintage	F	VF	XF	Unc	BU
AH1373-1954	—	—	5.00	12.00	25.00	—

KM# 380.2 10 MILLIEMES
Aluminum-Bronze **Obv:** Denomination divides date **Rev:** Small sphinx with base outlined **Note:** Thick Milliemes.

Date	Mintage	F	VF	XF	Unc	BU
AH1374-1954	—	—	4.00	10.00	20.00	—
AH1374-1955	—	—	3.00	7.00	15.00	—

KM# 381 10 MILLIEMES
4.7400 g., Aluminum-Bronze, 23.0 mm. **Rev:** Large sphinx
Note: Exists also with eagle, 2 stars.

Date	Mintage	F	VF	XF	Unc	BU
AH1374-1955	—	—	50.00	85.00	150	—
AH1375-1956	—	—	3.00	7.00	15.00	—
AH1376-1957	—	—	2.00	6.00	12.00	—
AH1377-1958	—	—	2.00	6.00	12.00	—

KM# 382 5 PIASTRES
3.5000 g., 0.7200 Silver 0.0810 oz. ASW **Obv:** Denomination within wings **Rev:** Small Sphinx with outlined base **Note:** Die varieties exist which appear to be lacking outlined base of Sphinx.

Date	Mintage	F	VF	XF	Unc	BU
AH1375-1956	—	BV	1.50	3.00	8.00	—
AH1376-1956	—	1.50	3.00	5.00	10.00	—
AH1376-1957	—	BV	1.50	3.00	8.00	—

KM# 383 10 PIASTRES
7.0000 g., 0.6250 Silver 0.1407 oz. ASW **Obv:** Denomination within wings **Rev:** Large sphinx

Date	Mintage	F	VF	XF	Unc	BU
AH1374-1955	1,408,000	2.00	4.00	9.00	18.00	—

Note: Varieties in date sizes exist

KM# 383a 10 PIASTRES
7.0000 g., 0.7200 Silver 0.1620 oz. ASW **Obv:** Denomination within wings **Rev:** Sphinx, dates

Date	Mintage	F	VF	XF	Unc	BU
AH1375-1956	—	BV	3.50	7.00	15.00	—
AH1376-1957	—	BV	3.50	6.00	12.00	—

KM# 384 20 PIASTRES
14.0000 g., 0.7200 Silver 0.3241 oz. ASW **Obv:** Denomination within wings

Date	Mintage	F	VF	XF	Unc	BU
AH1375-1956	—	BV	5.50	9.00	18.00	—

KM# 385 25 PIASTRES
17.5000 g., 0.7200 Silver 0.4051 oz. ASW, 35 mm. **Subject:** Suez Canal Nationalization **Obv:** Denomination and dates above wings **Rev:** Headquarter building in Port Said **Rev. Designer:** A. Wahba

Date	Mintage	F	VF	XF	Unc	BU
AH1375-1956	258,000	BV	6.50	10.00	20.00	—

KM# 389 25 PIASTRES
17.5000 g., 0.7200 Silver 0.4051 oz. ASW, 35 mm. **Subject:** National Assembly Inauguration **Obv:** Denomination and dates above wings **Rev:** Radiant sun behind building **Rev. Designer:** A. Wahba

Date	Mintage	F	VF	XF	Unc	BU
AH1376-1957	246,000	BV	6.00	9.00	17.00	—

KM# 388 5 POUNDS
42.5000 g., 0.8750 Gold 1.1956 oz. AGW **Subject:** 3rd and 5th Anniversaries of Revolution **Obv:** Denomination and dates above wings **Rev:** Horse, chariot, and archer

Date	Mintage	F	VF	XF	Unc	BU
AH1374-1955	—	—	—	1,125	1,350	—
AH1377-1957	—	—	—	1,150	1,400	—

Note: Struck in red and yellow gold

UNITED ARAB REPUBLIC
AH1378-1391 / 1958-1971AD
DECIMAL COINAGE

KM# 393 MILLIEME
Aluminum-Bronze **Obv:** Denomination divides dates, legend above **Rev:** Eagle with shield on breast

Date	Mintage	F	VF	XF	Unc	BU
AH1380-1960	—	—	0.10	0.15	0.30	—
AH1386-1966 Proof	—	Value: 3.00				

KM# 403 2 MILLIEMES
Aluminum-Bronze **Obv:** Denomination divides dates, legend above **Rev:** Eagle with shield on breast

Date	Mintage	F	VF	XF	Unc	BU
AH1381-1962	—	—	0.15	0.35	0.65	—
AH1386-1966 Proof	—	Value: 3.00				

KM# 394 5 MILLIEMES
Aluminum-Bronze **Obv:** Denomination divides dates, legend above **Rev:** Eagle with shield on breast

Date	Mintage	F	VF	XF	Unc	BU
AH1380-1960	—	—	0.15	0.45	0.85	—
AH1386-1966 Proof	—	Value: 3.00				

KM# 410 5 MILLIEMES
Aluminum

Date	Mintage	F	VF	XF	Unc	BU
AH1386-1967	—	—	0.15	0.40	0.75	—

KM# 395 10 MILLIEMES
Aluminum-Bronze **Obv:** Denomination divides dates, legend above **Obv. Legend:** Misr **Rev:** Eagle with shield on breast

Date	Mintage	F	VF	XF	Unc	BU
AH1378-1958	—	—	15.00	20.00	40.00	—
AH1380-1960	16,079,999	—	0.80	1.20	2.25	—
AH1386-1966 Proof	—	Value: 4.00				

KM# 396 10 MILLIEMES
Aluminum-Bronze **Obv:** Denomination divides dates, legend above, without Misr above denomination **Rev:** Eagle with shield on breast

Date	Mintage	F	VF	XF	Unc	BU
AH1378-1958 Proof	—	Value: 300				
AH1378-1958	—	—	15.00	25.00	40.00	—

KM# 411 10 MILLIEMES
Aluminum **Obv:** Denomination divides dates **Rev:** Eagle with shield on breast

Date	Mintage	F	VF	XF	Unc	BU
AH1386-1967	—	—	0.15	0.35	0.75	—

KM# 390 20 MILLIEMES
Aluminum-Bronze, 24 mm. **Subject:** Agriculture and Industrial Fair in Cairo **Obv:** Denomination divides dates, legend above **Rev:** Symbols of agriculture and industry

Date	Mintage	F	VF	XF	Unc	BU
AH1378-1958	—	—	0.75	1.50	5.00	—

KM# 397 5 PIASTRES
3.5000 g., 0.7200 Silver 0.0810 oz. ASW **Obv:** Denomination divides dates, legend above **Rev:** Eagle with shield on breast

Date	Mintage	F	VF	XF	Unc	BU
AH1380-1960	—	—	1.75	3.00	5.00	—
AH1386-1966	—	Value: 8.00				

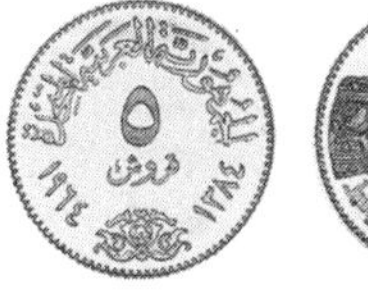

KM# 404 5 PIASTRES
2.5000 g., 0.7200 Silver 0.0579 oz. ASW **Subject:** Diversion of the Nile **Obv:** Denomination divides dates, legend above **Rev:** Sadd el-Ali Dam, Nile River basin scene

Date	Mintage	F	VF	XF	Unc	BU
AH1384-1964	500,000	—	1.25	2.50	4.00	—
AH1384-1964 Proof	2,000	Value: 8.00				

KM# 412 5 PIASTRES

Copper-Nickel, 25 mm. **Obv:** Denomination divides dates, legend above **Rev:** Eagle with shield on breast

Date	Mintage	F	VF	XF	Unc	BU
AH1387-1967	10,800,000	—	0.50	0.75	1.50	—

Note: Edge varieties, narrow and gapped milling, exist

KM# 414 5 PIASTRES

Copper-Nickel **Subject:** International Industrial Fair **Obv:** Denomination, legend above **Rev:** Globe with cogwheel section around, dates below

Date	Mintage	F	VF	XF	Unc	BU
AH1388-1968	500,000	—	0.75	1.00	2.50	—

KM# 417 5 PIASTRES

Copper-Nickel, 25 mm. **Subject:** 50th Anniversary - International Labor Organization **Obv:** Denomination, legend **Rev:** Hands holding open-ended wrenches within wreath, dates divided below

Date	Mintage	F	VF	XF	Unc	BU
AH1389-1969	500,000	—	0.75	1.00	2.50	—

KM# 392 10 PIASTRES

7.0000 g., 0.7200 Silver 0.1620 oz. ASW, 24 mm. **Subject:** First Anniversary of U.A.R. Founding **Obv:** Denomination divides dates, legend above **Rev:** Eagle with shield on breast

Date	Mintage	F	VF	XF	Unc	BU
AH1378-1959	—	—	3.25	6.00	17.50	—

KM# 398 10 PIASTRES

7.0000 g., 0.7200 Silver 0.1620 oz. ASW **Obv:** Denomination divides dates, legend above **Rev:** Eagle with shield on breast

Date	Mintage	F	VF	XF	Unc	BU
AH1380-1960	500,000	—	3.00	4.50	7.50	—
AH1386-1966 Proof	—	Value: 12.50				

KM# 405 10 PIASTRES

5.0000 g., 0.7200 Silver 0.1157 oz. ASW **Subject:** Diversion of the Nile **Obv:** Denomination divides dates, legend above **Rev:** Sadd el-Ali Dam, Nile River basin scene

Date	Mintage	F	VF	XF	Unc	BU
AH1384-1964	500,000	—	2.50	3.50	6.00	—
AH1384-1964 Proof	2,000	Value: 12.50				

KM# 413 10 PIASTRES

Copper-Nickel, 27 mm. **Obv:** Denomination divides dates, legend above **Rev:** Eagle with shield on breast

Date	Mintage	F	VF	XF	Unc	BU
AH1387-1967	13,200,000	—	0.60	0.90	2.00	—

KM# 419 10 PIASTRES

Copper-Nickel **Subject:** Cairo International Agricultural Fair **Obv:** Denomination divides dates, legend above **Rev:** Grain sprig above globe and name

Date	Mintage	F	VF	XF	Unc	BU
AH1389-1969	1,000,000	—	0.75	1.25	3.00	—

KM# 418 10 PIASTRES

Copper-Nickel **Series:** F.A.O. **Obv:** Denomination divides dates, legend above **Rev:** People with oxen, eagle above, logo below

Date	Mintage	F	VF	XF	Unc	BU
ND(1970)	500,000	—	0.75	1.25	3.50	—

KM# 420 10 PIASTRES

Copper-Nickel **Subject:** 50 Years - Banque Misr **Obv:** Crowned head within wreath left of denomination and date **Rev:** Sun above building

Date	Mintage	F	VF	XF	Unc	BU
AH1390-1970	500,000	—	0.60	1.00	2.00	—

KM# 421.1 10 PIASTRES

Copper-Nickel **Subject:** Cairo International Industrial Fair **Obv:** Denomination **Rev:** Ship within cogwheel, dates in box below

Date	Mintage	F	VF	XF	Unc	BU
AH1390-1970	500,000	—	0.60	1.00	3.25	—

KM# 421.2 10 PIASTRES

6.0200 g., Copper-Nickel, 27 mm. **Subject:** Cairo International Industrial Fair **Obv:** New shorter Arabic inscriptions, denomination at center **Rev:** Ship within cogwheel, dates in box below

Date	Mintage	F	VF	XF	Unc	BU
AH1391-1971	500,000	—	0.60	1.00	2.75	—

KM# 399 20 PIASTRES

14.0000 g., 0.7200 Silver 0.3241 oz. ASW **Obv:** Denomination divides dates, legend above **Rev:** Eagle with shield on breast

Date	Mintage	F	VF	XF	Unc	BU
AH1380-1960	400,000	—	7.00	15.00	25.00	—
AH1386-1966 Proof	—	Value: 32.50				

KM# 400 25 PIASTRES

17.5000 g., 0.7200 Silver 0.4051 oz. ASW **Subject:** 3rd Year of National Assembly **Obv:** Denomination and dates above wings **Rev:** Radiant sun back of building, hand on book in front

Date	Mintage	F	VF	XF	Unc	BU
AH1380-1960	250,000	—	6.50	9.00	18.00	—

KM# 406 25 PIASTRES

10.0000 g., 0.7200 Silver 0.2315 oz. ASW **Subject:** Diversion of the Nile **Obv:** Denomination divides dates, legend above **Rev:** Sadd el-Ali Dam, Nile River basin scene

Date	Mintage	F	VF	XF	Unc	BU
AH1384-1964	250,000	—	3.75	5.50	9.50	—
AH1384-1964 Proof	2,000	Value: 35.00				

KM# 422 25 PIASTRES

6.0000 g., 0.7200 Silver 0.1389 oz. ASW **Subject:** President Nasser **Obv:** Head of President Nasser right

Date	Mintage	F	VF	XF	Unc	BU
AH1390-1970	700,000	—	2.50	4.00	6.50	—

ARAB REPUBLIC

AH1391- / 1971- AD

DECIMAL COINAGE

KM# A423 MILLIEME

Aluminum **Obv:** Denomination divides dates, legend above **Rev:** Eagle with shield on breast

Date	Mintage	F	VF	XF	Unc	BU
AH1392-1972	—	—	0.10	0.30	0.50	—

KM# A425 5 MILLIEMES
Aluminum **Obv:** Denomination divides dates, legend above **Rev:** Eagle with shield on breast

Date	Mintage	F	VF	XF	Unc	BU
AH1392-1972	16,000,000	—	0.20	0.50	2.50	—

KM# A424 5 MILLIEMES
Aluminum **Obv:** Denomination divides dates, legend above **Rev:** Corn ears and grain sprigs encircle figure below sun **Note:** Mule - Obverse of KM#A425 and reverse of KM#433.

Date	Mintage	F	VF	XF	Unc	BU
AH1392-1972	—	—	10.00	20.00	45.00	—

KM# 432 5 MILLIEMES
2.0000 g., Brass, 18 mm. **Obv:** Denomination divides dates, legend above **Rev:** Eagle with shield on breast

Date	Mintage	F	VF	XF	Unc	BU
AH1393-1973	—	—	0.10	0.15	0.30	—

KM# A433 5 MILLIEMES
Aluminum, 18 mm. **Obv:** Denomination divides dates, legend above **Rev:** Eagle with shield on breast **Note:** Mule - Obverse of KM#433 and reverse of KM#A425.

Date	Mintage	F	VF	XF	Unc	BU
AH1393-1973	—	—	10.00	20.00	45.00	—

KM# 433 5 MILLIEMES
Aluminum **Series:** F.A.O. **Obv:** Denomination divides dates, legend above **Rev:** Corn ears and grain sprigs encircle figure below sun

Date	Mintage	F	VF	XF	Unc	BU
AH1393-1973	10,000,000	—	0.10	0.20	0.35	—

KM# 434 5 MILLIEMES
2.0000 g., Brass, 18 mm. **Obv:** Denomination divides dates, legend above **Rev:** Nefertiti head right and grain sprig **Note:** Mule.

Date	Mintage	F	VF	XF	Unc	BU
AH1393-1973	—	—	5.00	10.00	20.00	—

KM# 445 5 MILLIEMES
4.0000 g., Brass, 18 mm. **Series:** International Women's Year **Obv:** Denomination divides dates, legend above **Rev:** Nefertiti head right and grain sprig

Date	Mintage	F	VF	XF	Unc	BU
AH1395-1975	10,000,000	—	0.10	0.15	0.30	—

KM# 462 5 MILLIEMES
Brass, 18 mm. **Series:** F.A.O. **Obv:** Denomination divides dates, legend above **Rev:** People, animals, and building

Date	Mintage	F	VF	XF	Unc	BU
AH1397-1977	5,000,000	—	0.10	0.20	0.50	—

KM# 463 5 MILLIEMES
Brass **Subject:** 1971 Corrective Revolution **Obv:** Denomination divides dates, legend above **Rev:** City scene

Date	Mintage	F	VF	XF	Unc	BU
AH1397-1977	2,500,000	—	0.10	0.20	0.50	—
AH1399-1979	2,500,000	—	0.10	0.20	0.50	—

KM# A426 10 MILLIEMES
Aluminum, 21 mm.

Date	Mintage	F	VF	XF	Unc	BU
AH1392-1972	20,000,000	—	0.50	2.00	6.00	—

Note: Two varieties of edge letterings exist

KM# 435 10 MILLIEMES
3.2000 g., Brass, 21 mm.

Date	Mintage	F	VF	XF	Unc	BU
AH1393-1973	—	—	0.10	0.25	0.50	—
AH1396-1976	—	—	0.75	1.50	3.00	—

KM# 446 10 MILLIEMES
3.2000 g., Brass, 21 mm. **Series:** F.A.O. **Obv:** Denomination divides dates, legend above **Rev:** Family scene

Date	Mintage	F	VF	XF	Unc	BU
AH1395-1975	10,000,000	—	0.10	0.20	0.35	—

KM# 449 10 MILLIEMES
3.1100 g., Brass, 21 mm. **Series:** F.A.O. **Obv:** Denomination divides dates, legend above **Rev:** Osiris seated, wheat ear at right

Date	Mintage	F	VF	XF	Unc	BU
AH1396-1976	10,000,000	—	0.10	0.20	0.30	—

KM# 464 10 MILLIEMES
3.2800 g., Brass, 21 mm. **Series:** F.A.O. **Obv:** Denomination divides dates, legend above **Rev:** Various laborers surround center design

Date	Mintage	F	VF	XF	Unc	BU
AH1397-1977	10,000,000	—	0.10	0.20	0.85	—

KM# 465 10 MILLIEMES
Brass, 21 mm. **Subject:** 1971 Corrective Revolution **Obv:** Denomination divides dates, legend above **Rev:** Date and denomination left of head

Date	Mintage	F	VF	XF	Unc	BU
AH1397-1977	2,500,000	—	0.10	0.20	0.65	—
AH1399-1979	2,500,000	—	0.20	0.40	1.00	—

KM# 476 10 MILLIEMES
Brass, 21 mm. **Series:** F.A.O. **Obv:** Denomination divides dates, legend above **Rev:** Woman looking into microscope

Date	Mintage	F	VF	XF	Unc	BU
AH1398-1978	2,000,000	—	0.10	0.20	0.80	—

KM# 483 10 MILLIEMES
Brass, 21 mm. **Series:** International Year of the Child **Obv:** Denomination divides dates, legend above **Rev:** Seated woman and child

Date	Mintage	F	VF	XF	Unc	BU
AH1399-1979	2,000,000	—	0.10	0.20	0.65	—

KM# 498 10 MILLIEMES
Aluminum-Bronze, 21 mm. **Subject:** Sadat's Corrective Revolution **Obv:** Fist raised holding grain stalk **Rev:** Denomination divides dates, legend above

Date	Mintage	F	VF	XF	Unc	BU
AH1400-1980	2,500,000	—	0.10	0.25	1.00	—

KM# 499 10 MILLIEMES
Aluminum-Bronze, 21 mm. **Series:** F.A.O.

Date	Mintage	F	VF	XF	Unc	BU
AH1400-1980	2,000,000	—	0.10	0.20	0.60	—

KM# 553.1 PIASTRE
Aluminum-Bronze, 18 mm. **Obv:** Christian date left of denomination, tughra above **Rev:** Pyramids

Date	Mintage	F	VF	XF	Unc	BU
AH1404-1984	—	—	—	0.15	0.35	—

KM# 553.2 PIASTRE
Aluminum-Bronze, 18 mm. **Obv:** Islamic date left of denomination, tughra above **Rev:** Pyramids

Date	Mintage	F	VF	XF	Unc	BU
AH1404-1984	—	—	—	0.15	0.35	—

KM# 500 2 PIASTRES
4.9000 g., Aluminum-Bronze, 21 mm.

Date	Mintage	F	VF	XF	Unc	BU
AH1400-1980	—	—	0.20	0.30	0.60	—

KM# 554.1 2 PIASTRES
4.9000 g., Aluminum-Bronze, 21 mm. **Obv:** Christian date left of denomination

Date	Mintage	F	VF	XF	Unc	BU
AH1404-1984	—	—	—	0.20	0.50	—

KM# 554.2 2 PIASTRES
4.9000 g., Aluminum-Bronze, 21 mm. **Obv:** Islamic date left of denomination

Date	Mintage	F	VF	XF	Unc	BU
AH1404-1984	—	—	—	0.20	0.50	—

KM# A427 5 PIASTRES
4.5100 g., Copper-Nickel, 24.5 mm. **Subject:** 25th Anniversary of UNICEF

Date	Mintage	F	VF	XF	Unc	BU
AH1392-1972	500,000	—	0.75	1.00	3.00	—

Note: Error in spelling "UNICFE".

KM# A428 5 PIASTRES
4.5000 g., Copper-Nickel, 25 mm. **Obv:** Denomination divides dates, legend above **Rev:** Islamic falcon

Date	Mintage	F	VF	XF	Unc	BU
AH1392-1972	—	—	0.50	0.75	2.00	—

KM# 436 5 PIASTRES
Copper-Nickel, 25 mm. **Subject:** Cairo State Fair **Obv:** Denomination divides dates, legend above **Rev:** Stylized design

Date	Mintage	F	VF	XF	Unc	BU
AH1393-1973	500,000	—	0.60	0.75	2.25	—

KM# 437 5 PIASTRES
Copper-Nickel, 25 mm. **Subject:** 75th Anniversary - National Bank of Egypt **Obv:** Denomination divides dates, legend above **Rev:** Bank building in front of globe at left

Date	Mintage	F	VF	XF	Unc	BU
AH1393-1973	1,000,000	—	0.60	0.75	2.00	—

KM# A441 5 PIASTRES
4.5500 g., Copper-Nickel, 25 mm. **Subject:** First Anniversary - October War **Obv:** Denomination divides dates, legend above **Rev:** Soldier with gun facing right

Date	Mintage	F	VF	XF	Unc	BU
AH1394-1974	2,000,000	—	0.60	0.75	2.00	—

KM# 447 5 PIASTRES
4.4600 g., Copper-Nickel, 25 mm. **Series:** International Women's Year **Obv:** Denomination divides dates, legend above **Rev:** Bust of Nefertiti right, grain sprig at left

Date	Mintage	F	VF	XF	Unc	BU
AH1395-1975	2,000,000	—	0.50	0.65	1.25	—

KM# 451 5 PIASTRES
Copper-Nickel, 25 mm. **Subject:** 1976 Cairo Trade Fair **Obv:** Denomination divides dates, legend above **Rev:** Legend forms square around design, florals flank

Date	Mintage	F	VF	XF	Unc	BU
AH1396-1976	500,000	—	0.60	0.75	2.00	—

KM# 450 5 PIASTRES
Copper-Nickel, 25 mm. **Obv:** Denomination divides dates, legend above **Rev:** Islamic falcon **Note:** Mule.

Date	Mintage	F	VF	XF	Unc	BU
AH1396-1976	—	—	5.00	10.00	20.00	—

KM# 466 5 PIASTRES
Copper-Nickel, 25 mm. **Subject:** 1971 Corrective Revolution

Date	Mintage	F	VF	XF	Unc	BU
AH1397-1977	1,000,000	—	0.50	0.60	1.50	—
AH1399-1979	—	—	0.50	0.60	1.25	—

KM# 467 5 PIASTRES
Copper-Nickel, 25 mm. **Subject:** 50th Anniversary - Textile Industry **Obv:** Crowned head within wreath at right of denomination and dates **Rev:** Figure between dates

Date	Mintage	F	VF	XF	Unc	BU
AH1397-1977	1,000,000	—	0.50	0.75	1.65	—

KM# 468 5 PIASTRES
Copper-Nickel, 25 mm. **Series:** F.A.O. **Obv:** Denomination divides dates, legend above **Rev:** People, animals, and building

Date	Mintage	F	VF	XF	Unc	BU
AH1397-1977	—	—	0.50	0.75	1.65	—

Note: Edge varieties exist with narrow and wide milling

KM# 477 5 PIASTRES
Copper-Nickel, 25 mm. **Subject:** Portland Cement **Obv:** Denomination divides dates, legend above **Rev:** Cement factory, dates at top

Date	Mintage	F	VF	XF	Unc	BU
AH1398-1978	500,000	—	0.50	0.75	1.65	—

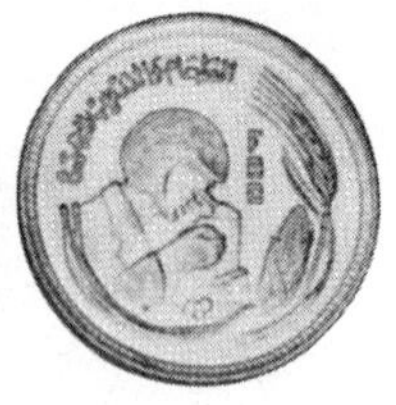

KM# 478 5 PIASTRES
4.4600 g., Copper-Nickel, 25 mm. **Series:** F.A.O. **Obv:** Denomination divides dates, legend above **Rev:** Woman looking into microscope

Date	Mintage	F	VF	XF	Unc	BU
AH1398-1978	1,000,000	—	0.50	0.75	1.65	—

KM# 484 5 PIASTRES
Copper-Nickel, 25 mm. **Series:** International Year of the Child **Obv:** Denomination divides dates, legend above **Rev:** Woman seated with child

Date	Mintage	F	VF	XF	Unc	BU
AH1399-1979	1,000,000	—	0.50	0.75	1.65	—

KM# 501 5 PIASTRES
Copper-Nickel, 25 mm. **Subject:** Applied Professions **Obv:** Denomination divides dates, legend above **Rev:** Various professions depicted, date and shield below

Date	Mintage	F	VF	XF	Unc	BU
AH1400-1980	500,000	—	0.50	0.75	1.35	—

KM# 502 5 PIASTRES
Copper-Nickel, 25 mm. **Subject:** Sadat's Corrective Revolution of May 15, 1971 **Obv:** Denomination divides dates, legend above **Rev:** Raised fist holding stalk of grain

Date	Mintage	F	VF	XF	Unc	BU
AH1400-1980	1,000,000	—	0.50	0.75	1.75	—

KM# 555.1 5 PIASTRES
Aluminum-Bronze **Obv:** Christian date left of denomination, tughra above **Rev:** Pyramids

Date	Mintage	F	VF	XF	Unc	BU
AH1404-1984	—	—	—	0.25	0.75	—

Note: Varieties exist with wide and narrow rims

KM# 555.2 5 PIASTRES
Aluminum-Bronze **Obv:** Islamic date left of denomination, tughra above **Rev:** Pyramids

Date	Mintage	F	VF	XF	Unc	BU
AH1404-1984	—	—	—	0.25	0.75	—

KM# 622.1 5 PIASTRES
4.9100 g., Aluminum-Bronze, 23.39 mm. **Obv:** Tughra below dates and denomination, denomination not shaded **Rev:** Pyramids **Edge:** Reeded

Date	Mintage	F	VF	XF	Unc	BU
AH1404-1984	—	—	—	0.25	0.85	—

KM# 622.2 5 PIASTRES
Aluminum-Bronze, 23 mm. **Obv:** Denomination shaded, tughra below **Rev:** Pyramids

Date	Mintage	F	VF	XF	Unc	BU
AH1404-1984	—	—	—	0.25	0.85	—

KM# 731 5 PIASTRES
Brass, 21 mm. **Obv:** Denomination divides dates, legend above **Rev:** Decorated vase

Date	Mintage	F	VF	XF	Unc	BU
AH1413-1992	—	—	—	—	0.50	0.75

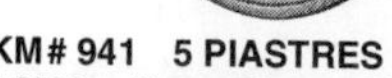

KM# 941 5 PIASTRES
1.9500 g., Brass, 18 mm. **Obv:** Denomination divides dates below, legend above **Rev:** Antique pottery vase **Edge:** Plain

Date	Mintage	F	VF	XF	Unc	BU
AH1425-2004	—	—	—	—	1.50	—

KM# 429 10 PIASTRES
Copper-Nickel, 27 mm. **Subject:** Cairo International Fair **Obv:** Denomination, legend **Rev:** Dates in box below ship with mast

Date	Mintage	F	VF	XF	Unc	BU
AH1392-1972	500,000	—	0.60	1.00	2.50	—

KM# 430 10 PIASTRES
Copper-Nickel, 27 mm. **Rev:** Islamic falcon

Date	Mintage	F	VF	XF	Unc	BU
AH1392-1972	—	—	0.60	1.00	4.00	—

KM# 431 10 PIASTRES
Copper-Nickel, 27 mm. **Obv:** Denomination divides dates, legend above **Rev:** Islamic falcon **Note:** Mule.

Date	Mintage	F	VF	XF	Unc	BU
AH1392-1972	—	—	5.50	17.50	27.50	—

Note: Wide and narrow inscriptions exist for obverse

KM# 442 10 PIASTRES
Copper-Nickel, 27 mm. **Subject:** First Anniversary - October War **Obv:** Denomination divides dates, legend above **Rev:** Wreath above 3/4 figure of soldier, dates below

Date	Mintage	F	VF	XF	Unc	BU
AH1394-1974	2,000,000	—	0.60	1.00	4.00	—

KM# 448 10 PIASTRES
6.0000 g., Copper-Nickel, 27 mm. **Series:** F.A.O. **Obv:** Denomination divides dates, legend above **Rev:** Family scene

Date	Mintage	F	VF	XF	Unc	BU
AH1395-1975	2,000,000	—	0.60	1.00	4.00	—

KM# 452 10 PIASTRES
Copper-Nickel, 27 mm. **Subject:** Reopening of the Suez Canal **Obv:** Denomination divides dates, legend above **Rev:** Canal scene

Date	Mintage	F	VF	XF	Unc	BU
AH1396-1976	5,000,000	—	0.60	1.00	4.00	—

Note: Wide and narrow inscriptions exist for the obverse

KM# 469 10 PIASTRES
Copper-Nickel, 27 mm. **Series:** F.A.O. **Obv:** Denomination divides dates, legend above **Rev:** Various laborers surround center design

Date	Mintage	F	VF	XF	Unc	BU
AH1397-1977	1,000,000	—	0.60	1.00	3.00	—

KM# 470 10 PIASTRES
5.9500 g., Copper-Nickel, 27 mm. **Subject:** 1971 Corrective Revolution **Obv:** Denomination divides dates, legend above **Rev:** Date and denomination left of head

Date	Mintage	F	VF	XF	Unc	BU
AH1397-1977	1,000,000	—	0.50	0.85	3.00	—
AH1399-1979	1,000,000	—	0.50	0.85	3.00	—

KM# 471 10 PIASTRES
Copper-Nickel, 27 mm. **Subject:** 20th Anniversary - Economic Union

Date	Mintage	F	VF	XF	Unc	BU
AH1397-1977	1,000,000	—	0.50	0.85	3.00	—

KM# 479 10 PIASTRES
Copper-Nickel, 27 mm. **Subject:** Cairo International Fair **Obv:** Denomination divides dates, legend above **Rev:** Legend forms square around design at top

Date	Mintage	F	VF	XF	Unc	BU
AH1398-1978	—	—	0.50	0.85	3.50	—

KM# 485 10 PIASTRES
Copper-Nickel, 27 mm. **Subject:** 25th Anniversary of Abbasia Mint **Obv:** Denomination divides dates, legend above **Rev:** Dates at top corners of building, cogwheel design above

Date	Mintage	F	VF	XF	Unc	BU
AH1399-1979	1,000,000	—	0.50	0.85	3.00	—

KM# 486 10 PIASTRES
Copper-Nickel, 27 mm. **Subject:** National Education Day **Obv:** Denomination divides dates, legend above **Rev:** Teachers, back to back and students, wreath in background

Date	Mintage	F	VF	XF	Unc	BU
AH1399-1979	1,000,000	—	0.50	0.85	3.00	—

KM# 503 10 PIASTRES
Copper-Nickel, 27 mm. **Subject:** Doctor's Day **Obv:** Denomination divides dates, legend above **Rev:** Seated Egyptian healer with staff left

Date	Mintage	F	VF	XF	Unc	BU
AH1400-1980	1,000,000	—	0.50	1.00	3.00	—

KM# 504 10 PIASTRES
Copper-Nickel, 27 mm. **Subject:** Egyptian-Israeli Peace Treaty **Obv:** Denomination divides dates, legend above **Rev:** Anwar Sadat at right facing left, dove of peace, hand with quill signing treaty

Date	Mintage	F	VF	XF	Unc	BU
AH1400-1980	1,000,000	—	1.00	2.00	4.50	—

KM# 505 10 PIASTRES
Copper-Nickel, 27 mm. **Series:** F.A.O.

Date	Mintage	F	VF	XF	Unc	BU
AH1400-1980	1,000,000	—	0.50	1.00	3.00	—

KM# 506 10 PIASTRES
Copper-Nickel, 27 mm. **Series:** F.A.O. **Subject:** Sadat's Corrective Revolution of May 15, 1971 **Obv:** Denomination divides dates, legend above **Rev:** Raised fist with grain stalk

Date	Mintage	F	VF	XF	Unc	BU
AH1400-1980	1,000,000	—	0.50	1.00	3.00	—
AH1401-1981	—	—	0.60	1.20	3.50	—

KM# 520 10 PIASTRES
Copper-Nickel, 27 mm. **Subject:** Scientist's Day **Obv:** Denomination, seated figure at left **Rev:** Cogwheel center of spray below sun and satellite dish

Date	Mintage	F	VF	XF	Unc	BU
AH1401-1981	—	—	0.50	1.00	3.00	—

KM# 521 10 PIASTRES
6.1200 g., Copper-Nickel, 27 mm. **Subject:** 25th Anniversary - Trade Unions **Obv:** Denomination divides dates, legend above **Rev:** Half cogwheel above shield

Date	Mintage	F	VF	XF	Unc	BU
AH1402-1981	—	—	1.00	2.00	4.50	—

KM# 599 10 PIASTRES

Copper-Nickel, 27 mm. **Subject:** 50th Anniversary of Egyptian Products Co. **Obv:** Denomination divides dates, legend above **Rev:** Head within crowned wreath at top, triangle in background

Date	Mintage	F	VF	XF	Unc	BU
AH1402-1982	—	—	0.50	1.00	3.00	—

KM# 556 10 PIASTRES

4.4900 g., Copper-Nickel, 24.81 mm. **Obv:** Denomination divides dates, legend above **Rev:** Mohamad Ali Mosque **Edge:** Reeded

Date	Mintage	F	VF	XF	Unc	BU
AH1404-1984	—	—	—	0.50	1.00	—

KM# 570 10 PIASTRES

Copper-Nickel, 25 mm. **Subject:** 25th Anniversary - National Planning Institute **Obv:** Arabic legends, dates below **Rev:** Shield divides dates

Date	Mintage	F	VF	XF	Unc	BU
AH1405-1985	100,000	—	—	—	2.00	—

KM# 573 10 PIASTRES

Copper-Nickel, 25 mm. **Subject:** 60th Anniversary - Egyptian Parliament **Obv:** Arabic legends, dates below **Rev:** Dates above building

Date	Mintage	F	VF	XF	Unc	BU
AH1405-1985	250,000	—	—	—	2.00	—

KM# 675 10 PIASTRES

Copper-Nickel, 25 mm. **Subject:** 1973 October War **Obv:** Tughra below dates, denomination at right **Rev:** Figure with flag left, building at right, dates below

Date	Mintage	F	VF	XF	Unc	BU
AH1410-1989	250,000	—	—	—	2.00	—

KM# 732 10 PIASTRES

Brass, 23 mm. **Obv:** Denomination divides dates, legend above **Rev:** Mohamad Ali Mosque

Date	Mintage	F	VF	XF	Unc	BU
AH1413-1992	—	—	—	—	2.00	—

KM# 922 10 PIASTRES

4.5200 g., Copper-Nickel, 24.8 mm. **Subject:** National Women's Council **Obv:** Value **Rev:** Woman standing next to Sphinx **Edge:** Reeded

Date	Mintage	F	VF	XF	Unc	BU
AH1425-2004	—	—	—	—	1.50	—

KM# 507 20 PIASTRES

10.0500 g., Copper-Nickel, 30.04 mm. **Obv:** Denomination divides dates, legend above **Rev:** Eagle with shield on breast **Edge:** Reeded

Date	Mintage	F	VF	XF	Unc	BU
AH1400-1980	—	—	0.75	1.00	3.00	—

KM# 557 20 PIASTRES

6.0000 g., Copper-Nickel, 27 mm. **Obv:** Denomination divides dates, legend above **Obv. Legend:** Mohammad Ali Mosque **Rev:** Mohammad Ali Mosque

Date	Mintage	F	VF	XF	Unc	BU
AH1404-1984	—	—	—	0.70	2.00	—

KM# 596 20 PIASTRES

6.0000 g., Copper-Nickel, 27 mm. **Subject:** 25th Anniversary - Cairo International Airport **Obv:** Arabic legends, dates below **Rev:** Birds in flight, wings and tails form diamond at center

Date	Mintage	F	VF	XF	Unc	BU
AH1405-1985	50,000	—	—	—	5.00	—

KM# 597 20 PIASTRES

Copper-Nickel, 27 mm. **Subject:** Professions **Obv:** Arabic legends, dates below **Rev:** People doing various jobs

Date	Mintage	F	VF	XF	Unc	BU
AH1406-1985	100,000	—	—	—	3.00	—

KM# 606 20 PIASTRES

Copper-Nickel, 27 mm. **Subject:** Warrior's Day **Obv:** Arabic legends, dates below **Rev:** Torch on crossed swords within wreath

Date	Mintage	F	VF	XF	Unc	BU
AH1406-1986	50,000	—	—	—	5.00	—

KM# 607 20 PIASTRES

Copper-Nickel, 27 mm. **Subject:** Census **Obv:** Arabic legends, dates below **Rev:** City scene

Date	Mintage	F	VF	XF	Unc	BU
AH1407-1986	500,000	—	—	—	3.00	—

KM# 652 20 PIASTRES

Copper-Nickel, 27 mm. **Subject:** Investment Bank **Obv:** Tughra divides dates **Rev:** Design in center of toothed circle, within circle

Date	Mintage	F	VF	XF	Unc	BU
AH1407-1987	250,000	—	—	—	5.00	—

KM# 646 20 PIASTRES

Copper-Nickel, 27 mm. **Subject:** Police Day **Obv:** Arabic legends, dates below **Rev:** Eagle with wings spread on pedestal within wreath

Date	Mintage	F	VF	XF	Unc	BU
AH1408-1988	250,000	—	—	—	5.00	—

KM# 650 20 PIASTRES

Copper-Nickel, 27 mm. **Subject:** Dedication of Cairo Opera House **Obv:** Arabic legends, dates below **Rev:** Building

Date	Mintage	F	VF	XF	Unc	BU
AH1409-1988	250,000	—	—	—	5.00	—

KM# 676 20 PIASTRES

6.0000 g., Copper-Nickel, 27 mm. **Subject:** 1973 October War **Obv:** Tughra below denomination and dates **Rev:** Figure with flag at left, building at right, dates below **Edge:** Reeded

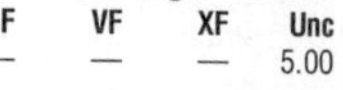

Date	Mintage	F	VF	XF	Unc	BU
AH1410-1989	250,000	—	—	—	5.00	—

KM# 685 20 PIASTRES
Copper-Nickel, 27 mm. **Subject:** National Health Insurance **Obv:** Denomination and dates within circle at top **Rev:** People within half moon design at left, rock in background, dates below

Date	Mintage	F	VF	XF	Unc	BU
AH1409-1989	250,000	—	—	—	5.00	—

KM# 690 20 PIASTRES
Copper-Nickel, 25 mm. **Subject:** Cairo Subway **Obv:** Four patterned tiles divide dates **Rev:** Designs within circles flank 3/4 wreath surrounding train

Date	Mintage	F	VF	XF	Unc	BU
AH1409-1989	250,000	—	—	—	5.00	—

KM# 733 20 PIASTRES
Copper-Nickel, 25 mm. **Subject:** Mosque **Obv:** Denomination divides dates **Rev. Designer:** Buildings with towers

Date	Mintage	F	VF	XF	Unc	BU
AH1413-1992	—	—	—	—	2.50	—

KM# 923 20 PIASTRES
6.0000 g., Copper-Nickel, 26.8 mm. **Subject:** National Women's Council **Obv:** Value **Rev:** Woman standing next to Sphinx **Edge:** Reeded

Date	Mintage	F	VF	XF	Unc	BU
AH1425-2004	—	—	—	—	2.50	—

KM# 438 25 PIASTRES
6.0000 g., 0.7200 Silver 0.1389 oz. ASW **Subject:** 75th Anniversary - National Bank of Egypt **Obv:** Denomination divides dates **Rev:** National Bank building, globe at back, divides dates

Date	Mintage	F	VF	XF	Unc	BU
AH1393-1973	100,000	—	4.00	6.00	9.00	—

KM# 734 25 PIASTRES
Copper-Nickel **Obv:** Chain surrounds center hole, dates below **Rev:** Chain surrounds center hole, denomination below

Date	Mintage	F	VF	XF	Unc	BU
AH1413-1993	—	—	—	—	2.75	—

KM# 939 50 PIASTRES
6.4400 g., Aluminum-Bronze, 24.8 mm. **Obv:** Value **Rev:** Cleopatra left **Edge:** Reeded

Date	Mintage	F	VF	XF	Unc	BU
AH1426-2005	—	—	—	—	2.00	—

KM# 942 50 PIASTRES
6.5000 g., Brass, 25 mm. **Rev:** Queen Cleopatra VII **Edge:** Reeded

Date	Mintage	F	VF	XF	Unc	BU
AH1426-2005	—	—	—	—	4.00	—

KM# 942a 50 PIASTRES
6.5100 g., Brass, 22.99 mm. **Obv:** Value **Rev:** Queen Cleopatra VII bust left **Edge:** Reeded

Date	Mintage	F	VF	XF	Unc	BU
AH1428-2007	—	—	—	—	—	—

KM# 940 POUND
8.5000 g., Bi-Metallic Brass center in Copper-Nickel ring, 25.1 mm. **Obv:** Value **Rev:** King Tutankhaman's gold mask **Edge:** Reeded

Date	Mintage	F	VF	XF	Unc	BU
AH1426-2005	—	—	—	—	3.00	5.00
AH1428-2007	—	—	—	—	3.00	5.00

EL SALVADOR

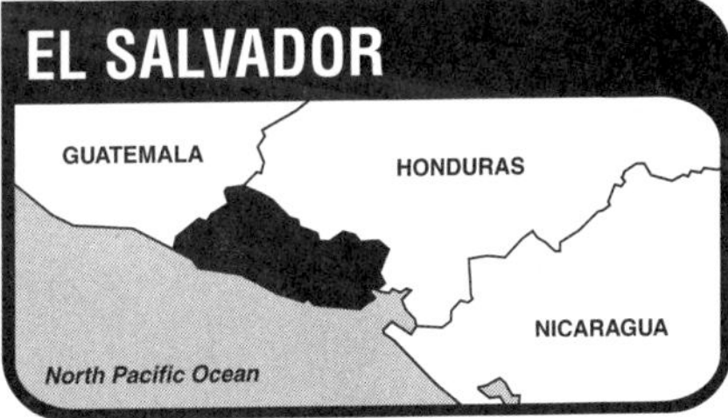

The Republic of El Salvador, a Central American country bordered by Guatemala, Honduras and the Pacific Ocean, has an area of 8,124 sq. mi. (21,040 sq. km.) and a population of 6.0 million. Capital: San Salvador. This most intensely cultivated of Latin America countries produces coffee (the major crop), sugar and balsam for export. Gold, silver and other metals are largely unexploited.

The first Spanish attempt to subjugate the area was undertaken in 1523 by Pedro de Alvarado, Cortes' lieutenant. He was forced to retreat by Indian forces, but returned in 1525 and succeeded in bringing the region under control of the Captaincy General of Guatemala. In 1821, El Salvador and the other Central American provinces jointly declared independence from Spain. In 1823, the Republic of Central America was formed by the five Central American states; this federation dissolved in 1839. El Salvador then became an independent republic in 1841.

Since 1960, El Salvador has been a part of the Central American Common Market. During the 1980's El Salvador went through a 12 year Civil War that ended in 1992 with the signing of a United Nations-sponsored Peace Accord. Free elections, with full participation of all political parties, were held in 1994, 1997 and 1999. Armando Calderon-Sol was elected president in 1994 for a 5-year term and Francisco Flores was elected in 1999 for a 5-year term as well.

MINT MARKS

C.A.M. - Central American Mint, San Salvador
H - Heaton Mint, Birmingham
S - San Francisco
Mo - Mexico
(a) - British Royal Mint, England
(b) - Denver Mint, USA
(c) - Deutsche Nickel A.G., Germany
(d) - Guatemala City Mint, Guatemala
(e) - Mexico City Mint, Mexico
(f) - San Francisco Mint, USA
(g) - Sherrit Mint, Canada
(h) - Vereingte Deutsche Metall, Germany
(i) - Royal Canadian Mint, Canada
(P) – Philadelphia Mint, USA

NOTE: The Monetary Integration Law of November 2000 resulted in the elimination of the Colon coinage and notes by early October 2002. No new coins are expected to be minted.

REPUBLIC OF EL SALVADOR

DECIMAL COINAGE

100 Centavos = 1 Peso

KM# 120 1/4 REAL
3.2000 g., Bronze **Obv:** Flag draped arms within wreath, liberty cap on top, swords above cap **Rev:** Denomination and date within wreath **Note:** The decimal value of this coin was about 3 Centavos. It was apparently struck in response to the continuing use of the Reales monetary system in rural areas.

Date	Mintage	F	VF	XF	Unc	BU
1909	—	20.00	40.00	75.00	150	—

KM# 106 CENTAVO
2.5000 g., Copper-Nickel **Obv:** Head of Francisco Morazan left, date below **Obv. Legend:** REPUBLICA DEL SALVADOR **Rev:** Denomination within wreath **Note:** Medal rotation.

Date	Mintage	F	VF	XF	Unc	BU
1913H	2,500,000	1.50	3.50	6.00	40.00	—

KM# 127 CENTAVO
2.5000 g., Copper-Nickel **Obv:** Head of Francisco Morazan left, date below **Rev:** Denomination within wreath **Note:** Medal rotation.

Date	Mintage	F	VF	XF	Unc	BU
1915(P)	5,000,000	1.25	4.50	12.50	35.00	—
1919(P)	1,000,000	2.25	7.00	20.00	60.00	—
1920(P)	1,490,000	1.50	6.00	15.00	40.00	—
1925(f)	200,000	4.00	12.00	25.00	70.00	—
1926(f)	400,000	3.00	10.00	20.00	55.00	—
1928S	5,000,000	1.25	7.00	16.00	40.00	—
Note: Varieties exist with large or small "S"						
1936(P)	2,500,000	1.25	4.50	12.50	35.00	—

KM# 107 3 CENTAVOS
3.3000 g., Copper-Nickel **Obv:** Head of Francisco Morazan left **Obv. Legend:** REPUBLICA DEL SALVADOR **Rev:** Denomination within wreath **Note:** Medal rotation.

Date	Mintage	F	VF	XF	Unc	BU
1913H	1,000,000	2.00	8.00	20.00	65.00	125

KM# 128 3 CENTAVOS
3.5000 g., Copper Nickel **Obv:** Head of Francisco Morazan left, date below **Rev:** Denomination within wreath **Note:** Medal rotation.

Date	Mintage	F	VF	XF	Unc	BU
1915(P)	2,700,000	2.00	8.00	20.00	65.00	200

KM# 121 5 CENTAVOS
1.2500 g., 0.8350 Silver 0.0336 oz. ASW **Obv:** Arms **Rev:** Denomination within wreath

Date	Mintage	F	VF	XF	Unc	BU
1911	1,000,000	3.00	10.00	20.00	45.00	—

KM# 124 5 CENTAVOS
1.2500 g., 0.8350 Silver 0.0336 oz. ASW **Obv:** Flag draped triangular arms within wreath **Rev:** Denomination within wreath

Date	Mintage	F	VF	XF	Unc	BU
1914(P)	2,000,000	3.00	7.00	15.00	35.00	—
1914(P) Proof	20	Value: 750				

KM# 129 5 CENTAVOS
5.0000 g., Copper-Nickel **Obv:** Head of Francisco Morazan left, date below **Rev:** Denomination within wreath **Note:** Medal rotation.

Date	Mintage	F	VF	XF	Unc	BU
1915(P)	2,500,000	2.25	6.00	15.00	60.00	—
1916(P)	1,500,000	2.50	7.00	20.00	65.00	—
1917(P)	1,000,000	3.00	8.00	20.00	70.00	—
1918/7(P)	1,000,000	2.50	7.00	20.00	60.00	—
1918(P)	Inc. above	2.50	7.00	17.50	70.00	—
1919/8(P)	—	2.50	7.00	17.50	70.00	—
1919(P)	2,000,000	2.50	7.00	17.50	70.00	—
1920(P)	2,000,000	1.75	4.50	10.00	50.00	—
1921(f)	1,780,000	2.00	5.00	12.00	55.00	—
1925(f)	4,000,000	1.25	3.50	10.00	55.00	—

KM# 122 10 CENTAVOS
2.5000 g., 0.8350 Silver 0.0671 oz. ASW **Obv:** Flag draped arms, liberty cap on top, dates below **Rev:** Denomination within wreath

Date	Mintage	F	VF	XF	Unc	BU
1911	1,000,000	3.00	7.00	15.00	65.00	—

KM# 125 10 CENTAVOS
2.5000 g., 0.8350 Silver 0.0671 oz. ASW **Obv:** Flag draped triangular arms within wreath, dates below **Rev:** Denomination within wreath

Date	Mintage	F	VF	XF	Unc	BU
1914(P)	1,500,000	2.50	6.50	12.50	45.00	—
1914(P) Proof	20	Value: 750				

KM# 123 25 CENTAVOS
6.2500 g., 0.8350 Silver 0.1678 oz. ASW **Obv:** Flag draped arms, liberty cap above, dates below **Rev:** Denomination within wreath

Date	Mintage	F	VF	XF	Unc	BU
1911	600,000	5.00	9.00	18.00	50.00	—

KM# 126 25 CENTAVOS
6.2500 g., 0.8350 Silver 0.1678 oz. ASW **Obv:** Flag draped triangular arms within wreath, dates below **Rev:** Denomination within wreath

Date	Mintage	F	VF	XF	Unc	BU
1914(P) 15 DE SEPT DE 1821	1,400,000	5.50	6.50	10.00	30.00	—
1914(P) 15 SET DE 1821	Inc. above	5.50	6.50	10.00	30.00	—
1914(P) Proof	20	Value: 1,500				

KM# 115.1 PESO (Colon)
25.0000 g., 0.9000 Silver 0.7234 oz. ASW **Obv:** Arms **Obv. Legend:** REPUBLICA DEL SALVADOR **Rev:** Columbus bust left

Date	Mintage	F	VF	XF	Unc	BU
1904C.A.M.	600,000	10.00	15.00	30.00	160	—
1908C.A.M.	1,600,000	10.00	14.00	28.00	140	—
1911C.A.M.	500,000	10.00	15.00	30.00	150	—
1914C.A.M.	700,000	—	—	—	625	—

Note: 1914 struck at the Brussels mint, but then remelted

KM# 115.2 PESO (Colon)
25.0000 g., 0.9000 Silver 0.7234 oz. ASW **Obv:** Flag draped arms, liberty cap and swords above, dates below **Rev:** Columbus bust left, denomination below, heavier portrait (wider right shoulder) **Note:** Struck at United States mints.

Date	Mintage	F	VF	XF	Unc	BU
1904C.A.M. (f)	400,000	12.00	20.00	40.00	250	—
1909C.A.M. (f)	690,000	11.00	17.50	32.50	200	—
1911C.A.M. (P) (S)	1,020,000	10.00	15.00	30.00	175	—
Note: Of the total mintage, 510,993 struck at Philadelphia Mint (P), and 511,108 were struck at San Francisco Mint (f)						
1914C.A.M. (P)	2,100,000	10.00	15.00	30.00	175	425
1914C.A.M. Proof	Est. 20	Value: 3,000				

REFORM COINAGE

100 Centavos = 1 Colon

KM# 133 CENTAVO
2.5000 g., Copper-Nickel **Obv:** Head of Francisco Morazan right **Rev:** Denomination within wreath **Note:** Medal rotation.

Date	Mintage	F	VF	XF	Unc	BU
1940(P)	1,000,000	2.00	6.00	15.00	45.00	—

KM# 135.1 CENTAVO
2.5000 g., Bronze, 15 mm. **Obv:** Head of Francisco Morazan left, date below **Rev:** Denomination within wreath

Date	Mintage	F	VF	XF	Unc	BU
1942(f)	5,000,000	0.20	0.50	1.00	4.50	—
Note: Struck in 1943						
1943(f)	5,000,000	0.20	0.50	1.00	4.50	—
Note: Struck in 1944						
1945(P)	5,000,000	0.20	0.40	0.75	3.50	—
1947(f)	5,000,000	0.20	0.50	1.00	4.00	—
1951(f)	10,000,000	0.10	0.30	0.75	2.50	—
1952(f)	10,000,000	0.10	0.20	0.40	2.00	—
Note: Struck in 1953						
1956(P)	10,000,000	0.10	0.20	0.40	2.00	—
Note: Struck in 1957						
1966	5,000,000	—	—	0.10	0.75	—
1968 (f)	5,000,000	—	—	0.10	0.75	—
1969 (b)	5,000,000	—	—	0.10	0.75	—
1972 (f)	20,000,000	—	—	0.10	0.50	—

KM# 135.1a CENTAVO
2.5000 g., Bronze Clad Steel **Obv:** Head of Francisco Morazan left **Rev:** Denomination within wreath **Note:** Prev. KM#135d. Medal rotation.

Date	Mintage	F	VF	XF	Unc	BU
1989(h)	36,000,000	—	—	0.10	0.20	0.35
1992(h)	—	—	—	0.10	0.20	0.35

KM# 135.2 CENTAVO
2.5000 g., Brass **Obv:** Head of Francisco Morazan left **Rev:** Denomination within wreath **Note:** Prev. KM#135a. Medal rotation.

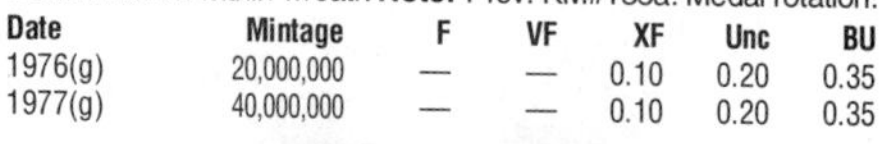

Date	Mintage	F	VF	XF	Unc	BU
1976(g)	20,000,000	—	—	0.10	0.20	0.35
1977(g)	40,000,000	—	—	0.10	0.20	0.35

KM# 135.2a CENTAVO
2.5000 g., Copper-Zinc **Obv:** DH monogram at truncation, smaller Morazan portrait **Rev:** Denomination in wreath, SM at right base of 1 **Note:** Previously KM#135c.

Date	Mintage	F	VF	XF	Unc	BU
1981(d)	50,000,000	—	—	0.10	0.20	0.35

KM# 135.2b CENTAVO
2.5000 g., Copper Clad Steel **Obv:** DH monogram at truncation, smaller Morazan portrait **Rev:** Denomination in wreath, SM at right base of 1 **Note:** Prev. KM#135b.

Date	Mintage	F	VF	XF	Unc	BU
1986 (a)	30,000,000	—	—	0.10	0.20	0.35

KM# A154 CENTAVO
1.5000 g., Brass Plated Steel, 15 mm. **Obv:** Head of Francisco Morazan left **Rev:** Denomination in wreath

Date	Mintage	F	VF	XF	Unc	BU
1988(h) Proof	—	Value: 50.00				

KM# 135.2c CENTAVO
2.5000 g., Brass Clad Steel **Obv:** DH monogram at truncation, smaller portrait **Rev:** Denomination in wreath, SM at right base of 1

Date	Mintage	F	VF	XF	Unc	BU
1995(a)	—	—	—	0.10	0.20	0.35

KM# 147 2 CENTAVOS
2.6000 g., Nickel-Brass **Obv:** Head of Francisco Morazan left **Rev:** Denomination within wreath **Note:** Medal rotation.

Date	Mintage	F	VF	XF	Unc	BU
1974(a)	10,002,000	—	0.10	0.20	1.00	—
1974(a)	2,000	Value: 30.00				

Note: In proof sets only

KM# 148 3 CENTAVOS

4.0000 g., Nickel-Brass, 19 mm. **Obv:** Head of Francisco Morazan left **Rev:** Denomination within wreath **Note:** Medal rotation.

Date	Mintage	F	VF	XF	Unc	BU
1974(a)	10,002,000	0.10	0.15	0.20	1.00	—
1974(a)	2,000	Value: 35.00				

Note: In proof sets only

KM# 134 5 CENTAVOS

5.0000 g., Copper-Nickel, 23 mm. **Obv:** Head of Francisco Morazan left **Rev:** Denomination within wreath **Note:** Medal rotation.

Date	Mintage	F	VF	XF	Unc	BU
1939	—	—	—	—	—	—
1940(P)	800,000	1.00	3.00	10.00	30.00	—
1951	2,000,000	0.75	2.00	6.00	15.00	—
1956	8,000,000	0.10	0.15	0.25	1.00	—
1959	6,000,000	0.10	0.15	0.25	1.00	—
1963	10,000,000	—	0.10	0.15	0.50	—
1966	6,000,000	0.10	0.15	0.25	0.75	—
1967 (f)	10,000,000	—	0.10	0.15	0.50	—
1972 (f)	10,000,000	—	0.10	0.15	0.50	—
1974 (g)	10,002,000	—	0.10	0.15	0.50	—
1974 (g)	2,000	Value: 35.00				

Note: In proof sets only

KM# 134a 5 CENTAVOS

5.0000 g., Nickel-Silver, 23 mm. **Obv:** Head of Francisco Morazan left, date below **Rev:** Denomination within wreath

Date	Mintage	F	VF	XF	Unc	BU
1944(f)	5,000,000	0.25	0.50	1.50	5.00	—
1948(f)	3,000,000	0.25	0.50	1.00	2.50	—
1950(f)	2,000,000	0.25	0.50	1.50	5.00	—
1952(f)	4,000,000	0.20	0.35	0.75	4.00	—

Note: Half the total mintage was struck in 1952, the remainder in 1953

KM# 149 5 CENTAVOS

5.0000 g., Copper-Nickel Clad Steel, 23 mm. **Obv:** Head of Francisco Morazan left, date below **Rev:** Denomination within wreath **Note:** Medal rotation.

Date	Mintage	F	VF	XF	Unc	BU
1975 (a)	15,000,000	—	0.10	0.15	0.30	0.50
1975	2,000	Value: 40.00				
Note: In proof sets only						
1986 (h)	30,000,000	—	0.10	0.15	0.30	0.50

KM# 149a 5 CENTAVOS

5.0000 g., Nickel Clad Steel, 23 mm. **Obv:** Head of Francisco Morazan left **Rev:** Denomination within wreath

Date	Mintage	F	VF	XF	Unc	BU
1976 (g)	15,000,000	—	0.10	0.15	0.30	0.50
1984 (a)	15,000,000	—	0.10	0.15	0.30	0.50

KM# 149b 5 CENTAVOS

5.0000 g., Copper-Nickel-Zinc, 23 mm. **Obv:** Head of Francisco Morazan left **Rev:** Denomination within wreath **Note:** Previously KM#149a.

Date	Mintage	F	VF	XF	Unc	BU
1977(h)	26,000,000	—	0.10	0.15	0.30	0.50

KM# 154 5 CENTAVOS

2.0000 g., Stainless Steel, 17 mm. **Obv:** Head of Francisco Morazan left, date below **Rev:** Denomination within wreath

Date	Mintage	F	VF	XF	Unc	BU
1987(h)	30,000,000	—	0.10	0.15	0.30	0.50
1987(h) Proof	—	Value: 50.00				
1999(h)	—	—	0.10	0.15	0.30	0.50

KM# 154a 5 CENTAVOS

2.0000 g., Copper-Nickel Clad Steel **Obv:** Head of Francisco Morazan left **Rev:** Denomination within wreath **Note:** Medal rotation.

Date	Mintage	F	VF	XF	Unc	BU
1991 (h)	—	—	0.10	0.15	0.30	0.50
1998 (c)	—	—	0.10	0.15	0.30	0.50

KM# 154b 5 CENTAVOS

2.0000 g., Nickel Clad Steel, 17 mm. **Obv:** Head of Francisco Morazan left, date below **Rev:** Denomination within wreath **Note:** Medal rotation.

Date	Mintage	F	VF	XF	Unc	BU
1992 (g)	—	—	0.10	0.15	0.30	0.50
1993 (g)	—	—	0.10	0.15	0.30	0.50
1994 (h)	—	—	0.10	0.15	0.30	0.50
1994(h) Proof	—	Value: 40.00				
1995 (g)	—	—	0.10	0.15	0.30	0.50
1998	—	—	0.10	0.15	0.30	0.50
1999	—	—	0.10	0.15	0.30	0.50

KM# 130 10 CENTAVOS

7.0000 g., Copper-Nickel, 26 mm. **Obv:** Head of Francisco Morazan left, date below **Rev:** Denomination within wreath **Note:** Medal rotation.

Date	Mintage	F	VF	XF	Unc	BU
1921(f)	2,000,000	4.50	10.00	30.00	200	300
1925(f)	2,000,000	5.00	12.50	55.00	—	—
1940(f)	500,000	6.50	15.00	40.00	90.00	—
1951(f)	1,000,000	1.00	3.50	12.50	30.00	—
1967(f)	2,000,000	—	0.10	0.50	2.00	—
1968(b)	3,000,000	—	0.10	0.40	1.25	—
1969(b)	3,000,000	—	0.10	0.40	1.25	—
1972(f)	7,000,000	—	0.10	0.25	1.00	—

KM# 130a 10 CENTAVOS

7.0000 g., Copper-Nickel-Zinc, 26 mm. **Obv:** Head of Francisco Morazan left **Rev:** Denomination within wreath

Date	Mintage	F	VF	XF	Unc	BU
1952(f)	2,000,000	0.15	0.25	0.75	4.00	—
Note: Of the 2,000,000 struck, 336,000 were struck in 1952 and the remaining 1,664,000 struck in 1953						
1985 Mo	15,000,000	—	0.10	0.15	0.30	—

KM# 150 10 CENTAVOS

7.0000 g., Copper-Nickel Clad Steel, 26 mm. **Obv:** Head of Francisco Morazan left date below **Rev:** Denomination within wreath **Note:** Medal rotation.

Date	Mintage	F	VF	XF	Unc	BU
1975(a)	15,000,000	—	0.15	0.25	0.50	—
1975(a)	2,000	Value: 35.00				

Note: In proof sets only

KM# 150a 10 CENTAVOS

7.0000 g., Copper-Nickel-Zinc, 26 mm. **Obv:** Head of Francisco Morazan left **Rev:** Denomination within wreath **Note:** Medal rotation.

Date	Mintage	F	VF	XF	Unc	BU
1977(h)	24,000,000	—	0.10	0.20	0.45	—
1977(h) Proof	—	Value: 40.00				

KM# 155 10 CENTAVOS

3.0000 g., Stainless Steel, 20 mm. **Obv:** Head of Francisco Morazan left date below **Rev:** Denomination within wreath **Note:** Medal rotation.

Date	Mintage	F	VF	XF	Unc	BU
1987 (h)	30,000,000	—	0.10	0.20	0.40	0.60
1987(h) Proof	—	Value: 50.00				
1999 (i)	—	—	0.10	0.20	0.40	0.60

KM# 155a 10 CENTAVOS

Nickel Clad Steel **Obv:** Head of Francisco Morazan left **Rev:** Denomination within wreath **Note:** Medal rotation.

Date	Mintage	F	VF	XF	Unc	BU
1992 (a)	—	—	0.10	0.20	0.40	0.60
1993 (g)	—	—	0.10	0.20	0.40	0.60
1994 (h)	—	—	0.10	0.20	0.40	0.60
1994 Proof	—	Value: 40.00				

KM# 155b 10 CENTAVOS

Copper-Nickel Clad Steel **Obv:** Head of Francisco Morazan left **Rev:** Denomination within wreath

Date	Mintage	F	VF	XF	Unc	BU
1995 (c)	—	—	0.10	0.20	0.40	0.60
1998 (c)	—	—	0.10	0.20	0.40	0.60
1999	—	—	0.10	0.20	0.40	0.60

KM# 136 25 CENTAVOS

7.5000 g., 0.9000 Silver 0.2170 oz. ASW **Obv:** Head of Francisco Morazan left, date below **Rev:** Denomination within wreath

Date	Mintage	F	VF	XF	Unc	BU
1943	1,000,000	3.00	4.00	8.00	16.00	—
1944	1,000,000	3.00	4.00	8.00	16.00	—

KM# 137 25 CENTAVOS

2.5000 g., 0.9000 Silver 0.0723 oz. ASW **Obv:** Head of Jose Matias Delgado left, date below **Rev:** Denomination within wreath **Designer:** Gilroy Roberts

Date	Mintage	F	VF	XF	Unc	BU
1953	14,000,000	1.00	1.50	2.50	4.50	—

KM# 139 25 CENTAVOS

2.5000 g., Nickel, 17.8 mm. **Obv:** Head of Jose Matias Delgado left, date below **Rev:** Denomination within wreath

Date	Mintage	F	VF	XF	Unc	BU
1970 (a)	14,000,000	—	0.10	0.20	0.60	0.80
1973 (g)	28,000,000	—	0.10	0.20	0.50	0.75

Date	Mintage	F	VF	XF	Unc	BU
1975 (g)	20,000,000	—	0.10	0.20	0.50	0.75
1977 (a)	22,400,000	—	0.10	0.20	0.50	0.75

KM# 139a 25 CENTAVOS

2.5000 g., Copper-Nickel **Obv:** Head of Jose Matias Delgado left **Rev:** Denomination within wreath

Date	Mintage	F	VF	XF	Unc	BU
1986Mo	21,000,000	—	0.10	0.20	0.50	0.75
1986Mo Proof	—	Value: 50.00				

KM# 157 25 CENTAVOS

4.0000 g., Stainless Steel, 22.5 mm. **Obv:** Head of Jose Matias Delgado left, date below **Rev:** Denomination within wreath **Note:** Medal rotation.

Date	Mintage	F	VF	XF	Unc	BU
1988 (h)	20,000,000	—	0.10	0.20	0.50	0.75
1988(h) Proof	—	Value: 50.00				
1999 (i)	—	—	0.10	0.20	0.50	0.75

KM# 157a 25 CENTAVOS

4.0000 g., Copper-Nickel Clad Steel **Obv:** Bust of Jose Matias Delgado left **Rev:** Denomination

Date	Mintage	F	VF	XF	Unc	BU
1992(c)	—	—	0.10	0.20	0.50	0.75
1995(c)	—	—	0.10	0.20	0.50	0.75

KM# 157b 25 CENTAVOS

4.0000 g., Nickel Clad Steel **Obv:** Head of Jose Matias Delgado left, date below **Rev:** Denomination within wreath **Note:** Medal rotation.

Date	Mintage	F	VF	XF	Unc	BU
1993 (a)	—	—	0.10	0.20	0.50	0.75
1994 (g)	—	—	0.10	0.20	0.50	0.75
1998	—	—	0.10	0.20	0.50	0.75
1999	—	—	0.10	0.20	0.50	0.75

KM# 138 50 CENTAVOS

5.0000 g., 0.9000 Silver 0.1447 oz. ASW **Obv:** Head of Jose Matias Delgado left, date below **Rev:** Denomination within wreath **Designer:** Gilroy Roberts

Date	Mintage	F	VF	XF	Unc	BU
1953	3,000,000	2.00	3.00	4.00	8.00	—

KM# 140.1 50 CENTAVOS

5.0000 g., Nickel, 20 mm. **Obv:** Head of Jose Matias Delgado left, date below **Rev:** Denomination within wreath **Note:** 1.65 millimeters thick.

Date	Mintage	F	VF	XF	Unc	BU
1970(a)	3,000,000	—	0.20	0.30	0.60	0.80

KM# 140.2 50 CENTAVOS

5.1000 g., Nickel, 20 mm. **Obv:** Head of Jose Matias Delgado left **Rev:** Denomination **Note:** Two millimeters thick.

Date	Mintage	F	VF	XF	Unc	BU
1977(a)	1,500,000	—	0.20	0.30	0.60	0.80

KM# 131 COLON

25.0000 g., 0.9000 Silver 0.7234 oz. ASW, 37 mm. **Subject:** 400th Anniversary - San Salvador **Obv:** Flags flank triangular arms within wreath, denomination below **Obv. Designer:** Ignacio Cortes **Rev:** Alvarado and Quinonez busts left, dates above **Rev. Designer:** Jose C. Tovar

Date	Mintage	F	VF	XF	Unc	BU
ND(1925)Mo	2,000	50.00	90.00	135	225	—

KM# 153 COLON

9.2500 g., Copper-Nickel, 29 mm. **Obv:** Head of Christopher Columbus left, date below **Rev:** Denomination within wreath

Date	Mintage	F	VF	XF	Unc	BU
1984Mo	10,000,000	—	0.50	1.00	2.50	3.50
1984Mo Proof	—	Value: 125				
1985Mo	20,000,000	—	0.50	1.00	2.50	3.50
1985Mo Proof	—	Value: 200				

KM# 156 COLON

6.0000 g., Stainless Steel, 25 mm. **Obv:** Head of Christopher Columbus left, date below **Rev:** Denomination within wreath

Date	Mintage	F	VF	XF	Unc	BU
1988 (h)	30,000,000	—	0.40	0.80	2.25	3.00
1988 (h) Proof	—	Value: 50.00				
1999 (i)	—	—	—	0.80	2.25	3.00

KM# 156a COLON

6.0000 g., Copper-Nickel Clad Steel, 25 mm. **Obv:** Head of Christopher Columbus left **Rev:** Denomination within wreath **Note:** Medal rotation.

Date	Mintage	F	VF	XF	Unc	BU
1991(h)	—	—	0.40	0.80	2.25	3.00

KM# 156b COLON

6.0000 g., Nickel Clad Steel, 25 mm. **Obv:** Head of Christopher Columbus left **Rev:** Denomination within wreath **Note:** Medal rotation.

Date	Mintage	F	VF	XF	Unc	BU
1993 (a)	—	—	0.40	0.80	2.25	3.00
1994 (g)	—	—	0.40	0.80	2.25	3.00
1995 (h)	—	—	0.40	0.80	2.25	3.00
1998	—	—	0.40	0.80	2.25	3.00
1999	—	—	0.40	0.80	2.25	3.00

KM# 162 5 COLONES

7.5000 g., Bi-Metallic Bronze Plated Steel center in Nickel-plated Steel ring, 26 mm. **Obv:** Columbus' ships sailing west on world map within circle, date below **Rev:** Denomination within circle, wreath surrounds **Edge:** Segmented reeding **Note:** Viridian mint. Not released for circulation.

Date	Mintage	F	VF	XF	Unc	BU
1997	—	—	—	—	—	—

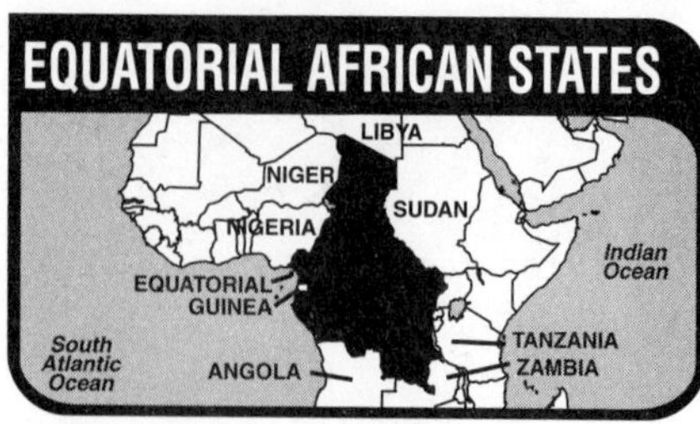

For historical background, see the introduction to Central African States.

CURRENCY UNION

DECIMAL COINAGE

100 Centimes = 1 Franc

KM# 6 FRANC

Aluminum **Obv:** Three giant eland left, date below **Rev:** Denomination within wreath **Designer:** G. B. L. Bazor

Date	Mintage	F	VF	XF	Unc	BU
1969(a)	2,500,000	0.25	0.65	1.00	2.25	—
1971(a)	3,000,000	0.25	0.65	1.00	2.25	—

KM# 1 5 FRANCS

Aluminum-Bronze **Obv:** Three giant eland left **Rev:** Denomination within wreath **Designer:** G. B. L. Bazor

Date	Mintage	F	VF	XF	Unc	BU
1961(a)	10,000,000	0.35	1.00	1.50	2.50	—
1962(a)	5,000,000	0.35	1.00	1.50	2.50	—

KM# 1a 5 FRANCS

Aluminum-Nickel-Bronze **Obv:** Three giant eland left, date below **Rev:** Denomination within wreath **Designer:** G. B. L. Bazor

Date	Mintage	F	VF	XF	Unc	BU
1965(a)	7,000,000	0.35	1.00	1.50	3.00	—
1967(a)	4,000,000	0.35	1.00	1.25	2.50	—
1968(a)	5,000,000	0.35	1.00	1.25	2.50	—
1970(a)	9,000,000	0.35	1.00	1.25	2.50	—
1972(a)	5,000,000	0.35	1.00	1.25	2.50	—
1973(a)	5,010,000	0.35	1.00	1.25	2.50	—

KM# 2 10 FRANCS

Aluminum-Bronze **Obv:** Three giant eland left **Rev:** Denomination within wreath **Designer:** G. B. L. Bazor

Date	Mintage	F	VF	XF	Unc	BU
1961(a)	10,000,000	0.40	1.00	1.75	3.00	—
1962(a)	5,000,000	0.40	1.00	1.75	3.00	—

KM# 2a 10 FRANCS

Aluminum-Nickel-Bronze **Obv:** Three giant eland left, date below **Rev:** Denomination within wreath **Designer:** G. B. L. Bazor

Date	Mintage	F	VF	XF	Unc	BU
1965(a)	7,000,000	1.00	1.75	2.75	5.00	—
1967(a)	10,000,000	0.40	1.00	1.75	3.00	—
1968(a)	2,000,000	1.50	2.25	3.50	6.00	—
1969(a)	10,000,000	0.40	1.00	1.75	3.00	—
1972(a)	5,000,000	0.40	1.00	1.75	3.00	—
1973(a)	5,000,000	0.75	1.50	2.50	4.50	—

KM# 4 25 FRANCS

Aluminum-Bronze **Obv:** Three giant eland left, date below **Obv. Designer:** G.B.L. Bazor **Rev:** Denomination within wreath

Date	Mintage	F	VF	XF	Unc	BU
1962(a)	6,000,000	0.50	1.25	2.25	4.00	—

KM# 4a 25 FRANCS
Aluminum-Nickel-Bronze **Obv:** Three giant eland left, date below **Obv. Designer:** G.B.L. Bazor **Rev:** Denomination, within wreath

Date	Mintage	F	VF	XF	Unc	BU
1970(a)	3,019,000	0.50	1.25	2.25	4.00	—
1972(a)	5,000,000	0.50	1.25	2.00	3.00	—

KM# 3 50 FRANCS
Copper-Nickel, 30.7 mm. **Obv:** Three giant eland left, date below **Obv. Designer:** G.B.L. Bazor **Rev:** Denomination within wreath

Date	Mintage	F	VF	XF	Unc	BU
1961(a)	5,000,000	2.00	4.00	6.00	10.00	—
1963(a)	5,000,000	2.00	4.00	6.00	10.00	—

KM# 5 100 FRANCS
11.7100 g., Nickel, 25.2 mm. **Obv:** Three giant eland left **Obv. Designer:** G.B.L. Bazor **Rev:** Denomination, date above **Note:** KM#5 was issued double thick and should not be considered a piefort.

Date	Mintage	F	VF	XF	Unc	BU
1966(a)	6,000,000	2.00	4.00	7.00	12.00	—
1967(a)	5,800,000	2.00	4.00	7.00	12.00	—
1968(a)	6,200,000	2.00	4.00	7.00	12.00	—

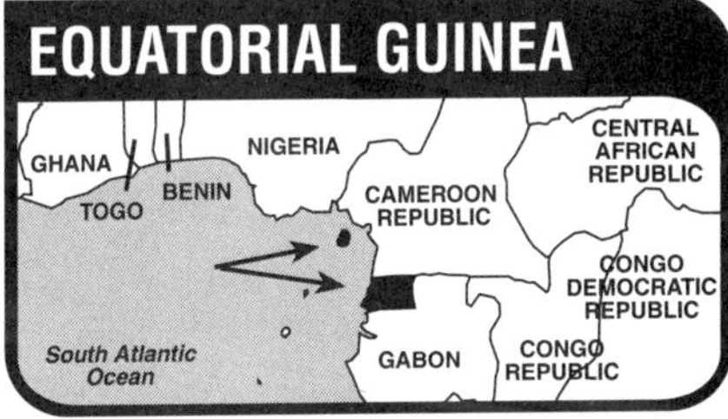

The Republic of Equatorial Guinea (formerly Spanish Guinea) consists of Rio Muni, located on the coast of West-Central Africa between Cameroon and Gabon, and the off-shore islands of Fernando Po, Annobon, Corisco, Elobey Grande and Elobey Chico. The equatorial country has an area of 10,831 sq. mi. (28,050 sq. km.) and a population of 420,293. Capital: Malabo. The economy is based on agriculture and forestry. Cacao, wood and coffee are exported.

Fernando Po was discovered between 1474 and 1496 by Portuguese navigators charting a route to the spice islands of the Far East. Portugal retained control of it and the adjacent islands until 1778 when they, together with trading rights to the African coast between the Ogooue and Niger Rivers, were ceded to Spain. Fernando Po was administered, with Spanish consent, by the British from 1827 to 1844 when it was reclaimed by Spain. Mainland Rio Muni was granted to Spain by the Berlin Conference of 1885. The name of the colony was changed from Spanish Guinea to Equatorial Guinea in Dec. of 1963. Independence was attained on Oct. 12, 1968.

Equatorial Guinea converted to the CFA currency system as issued for the Central African States issuing its first 100 Franc denomination in 1985.

NOTE: The 1969 coinage carries the actual minting date in the stars at the sides of the large date.

MINT MARK
(a) - Paris, privy marks only

REPUBLIC

PESETA COINAGE

KM# 1 PESETA
3.4200 g., Aluminum-Bronze, 19.5 mm. **Edge:** Reeded

Date	Mintage	F	VF	XF	Unc	BU
1969(69)	—	0.35	0.75	1.25	2.50	—

KM# 2 5 PESETAS
4.9000 g., Copper-Nickel, 22 mm. **Edge:** Reeded

Date	Mintage	F	VF	XF	Unc	BU
1969(69)	—	0.75	1.50	2.50	8.00	—

KM# 3 25 PESETAS
Copper-Nickel, 24 mm. **Obv:** Crossed tusks, date below **Rev:** Denomination at left, shielded arms at right, stars above arms

Date	Mintage	F	VF	XF	Unc	BU
1969(69)	—	1.50	2.50	6.50	12.00	—

KM# 5 25 PESETAS
5.0000 g., 0.9990 Silver 0.1606 oz. ASW **Subject:** World Bank **Obv:** Crossed tusks divide arms above and denomination below **Rev:** Banner crosses globe

Date	Mintage	F	VF	XF	Unc	BU
1970 Proof	2,475	Value: 10.00				

KM# 6 25 PESETAS
5.0000 g., 0.9990 Silver 0.1606 oz. ASW **Subject:** United Nations **Obv:** Crossed tusks divide arms above and denomination below **Rev:** UN logo

Date	Mintage	F	VF	XF	Unc	BU
1970 Proof	2,475	Value: 10.00				

KM# 4 50 PESETAS
Copper-Nickel **Obv:** Head right, date below **Rev:** Denomination at left, arms at right

Date	Mintage	F	VF	XF	Unc	BU
1969(69)	—	2.00	3.00	7.50	15.00	—

REFORM COINAGE

1975-1980

KM# 32 EKUELE
Brass **Obv:** Head left, date below **Rev:** Assorted tools divide denomination **Note:** Withdrawn from circulation.

Date	Mintage	F	VF	XF	Unc	BU
1975	3,000,000	1.00	2.00	3.00	5.00	7.00

KM# 33 5 EKUELE
Copper-Nickel **Obv:** Head left, date below **Rev:** Figures on split shields divide denomination **Note:** Withdrawn from circulation.

Date	Mintage	F	VF	XF	Unc	BU
1975	2,800,000	1.00	2.00	3.50	6.00	8.00

KM# 34 10 EKUELE
Copper-Nickel **Obv:** Head left, date below **Rev:** Rooster within shield divides denomination **Note:** Withdrawn from circulation.

Date	Mintage	F	VF	XF	Unc	BU
1975	1,300,000	1.50	2.50	4.50	9.00	12.00

REFORM COINAGE

1980-1982

KM# 50 EKUELE
Aluminum-Bronze **Obv:** T. E. Nkogo head right, date below **Rev:** Denomination at left, shielded arms at right, stars above arms **Note:** Two digit incuse date within star to left of date on obverse

Date	Mintage	F	VF	XF	Unc	BU
1980(80)	Est. 200,000	—	—	—	60.00	65.00

KM# 51 5 BIPKWELE
Copper-Nickel **Obv:** T. E. Nkogo right **Rev:** Value and arms **Note:** Two digit incuse date within star to left of date on obverse

Date	Mintage	F	VF	XF	Unc	BU
1980(80)	Est. 200,000	—	65.00	125	175	—

KM# 52 25 BIPKWELE
6.3800 g., Copper-Nickel **Obv:** T. E. Nkogo head right, date below **Rev:** Denomination at left, arms at right **Note:** Two digit incuse date within star to left of date on obverse

Date	Mintage	F	VF	XF	Unc	BU
1980(80)	Est. 200,000	—	15.00	25.00	45.00	50.00
1981	Est. 800,000	—	—	—	—	—

KM# 53 50 BIPKWELE
Copper-Nickel **Obv:** T. E. Nkogo right **Rev:** Value and arms **Note:** Two digit incuse date within star to left of date on obverse

Date	Mintage	F	VF	XF	Unc	BU
1980(80)	Est. 200,000	—	—	—	50.00	55.00
1981	Est. 500,000	—	—	—	—	—

REFORM COINAGE

1985-

KM# 62 5 FRANCOS
Aluminum-Bronze **Obv:** Three Giant Eland left **Obv. Designer:** G.B.L. Bazor **Rev:** Denomination above date

Date	Mintage	F	VF	XF	Unc	BU
1985(a)	—	—	2.50	4.50	8.00	15.00

KM# 60 25 FRANCOS
Aluminum-Bronze **Obv:** Three Giant Eland left **Obv. Designer:** G.B.L. Bazor **Rev:** Denomination above date

Date	Mintage	F	VF	XF	Unc	BU
1985(a)	—	—	3.50	7.00	15.00	25.00

KM# 64 50 FRANCOS
Nickel **Obv:** Three Giant Eland left **Obv. Designer:** G.B.L. Bazor **Rev:** Denomination above date

Date	Mintage	F	VF	XF	Unc	BU
1985(a)	—	—	8.00	16.00	28.00	—
1986(a)	—	—	6.00	12.00	20.00	30.00

KM# 59 100 FRANCOS
Nickel **Obv:** Three Giant Eland left **Obv. Designer:** G.B.L. Bazor **Rev:** Denomination above date

Date	Mintage	F	VF	XF	Unc	BU
1985(a)	—	—	10.00	20.00	35.00	—
1986(a)	—	—	7.00	14.00	25.00	—

ERITREA

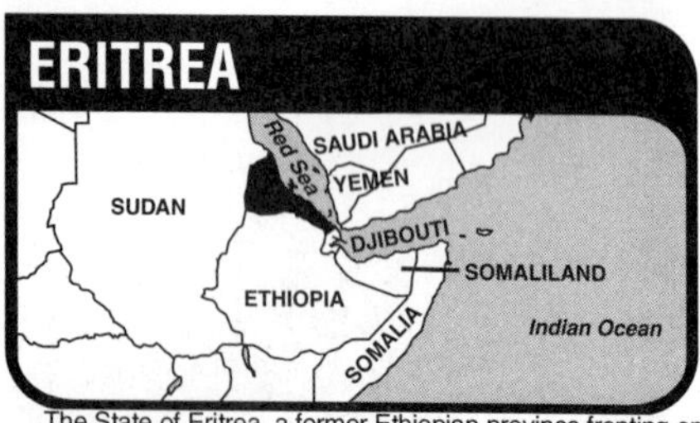

The State of Eritrea, a former Ethiopian province fronting on the Red Sea, has an area of 45,300 sq. mi. (117,600 sq. km.) and a population of 3.6 million. It was an Italian colony from 1889 until its incorporation into Italian East Africa in 1936. It was under the British Military Administration from 1941 to Sept. 15, 1952, when the United Nations designated it an autonomous unit within the federation of Ethiopia and Eritrea. On Nov. 14, 1962, it was annexed with Ethiopia. In 1991 the Eritrean Peoples Liberation Front extended its control over the entire territory of Eritrea. Following 2 years of provisional government, Eritrea held a referendum on independence in May 1993. Overwhelming popular approval led to the proclamation of an independent Republic of Eritrea on May 24.

RULERS
Vittorio Emanuele III, 1900-1945

MINT MARKS
M - Milan
PM - Pobjoy
R – Rome

MONETARY SYSTEM
100 Centesimi = 1 Lira
5 Lire = 1 Tallero
100 Cents = 1 Nakfa (from 1997)

ITALIAN COLONY

COLONIAL COINAGE

KM# 5 TALLERO
28.0668 g., 0.8350 Silver 0.7534 oz. ASW, 40 mm. **Ruler:** Vittorio Emanuele III **Obv:** Bust with loose hair right, date at right **Rev:** Crowned imperial eagle with shield on breast

Date	Mintage	F	VF	XF	Unc	BU
1918R	510,000	40.00	100	300	650	1,000

REPUBLIC

DECIMAL COINAGE

100 Cents = 1 Dollar

KM# 43 CENT
2.2000 g., Nickel Clad Steel, 17 mm. **Obv:** Red-fronted gazelle right, divides denomination **Rev:** Soldiers with flag, date at left **Designer:** Clarence Holbert

Date	Mintage	F	VF	XF	Unc	BU
1997	—	—	—	—	0.50	1.00

KM# 44 5 CENTS
2.7000 g., Nickel Clad Steel, 18.9 mm. **Obv:** Leopard on log divides denomination **Rev:** Soldiers with flag, date at left **Designer:** Clarence Holbert

Date	Mintage	F	VF	XF	Unc	BU
1997	—	—	—	—	0.75	1.50

KM# 45 10 CENTS
3.3000 g., Nickel Clad Steel, 20.95 mm. **Obv:** Ostrich left divides denomination **Rev:** Soldiers with flag, date at left **Designer:** Clarence Holbert

Date	Mintage	F	VF	XF	Unc	BU
1997	—	—	—	—	1.00	1.75

KM# 46 25 CENTS
5.8000 g., Nickel Clad Steel, 23 mm. **Obv:** Grevy's zebra left divides denomination **Rev:** Soldiers with flag, date at left **Designer:** Clarence Holbert

Date	Mintage	F	VF	XF	Unc	BU
1997	—	—	—	—	1.25	2.00

KM# 47 50 CENTS
7.8000 g., Nickel Clad Steel, 24.95 mm. **Obv:** Greater Kudu left divides denomination **Rev:** Soldiers with flag, date at left **Designer:** Clarence Holbert

Date	Mintage	F	VF	XF	Unc	BU
1997	—	—	—	—	1.50	2.25

KM# 48 100 CENTS
10.3000 g., Nickel Clad Steel, 26.2 mm. **Obv:** African elephant and calf left, divide denomination **Rev:** Soldiers with flag, date at left **Designer:** Clarence Holbert

Date	Mintage	F	VF	XF	Unc	BU
1997	—	—	—	—	2.00	3.00

ESTONIA

The Republic of Estonia (formerly the Estonian Soviet Socialist Republic of the U.S.S.R.) is the northernmost of the three Baltic States in Eastern Europe. It has an area of 17,462 sq. mi. (45,100 sq. km.) and a population of 1.6 million. Capital: Tallinn. Agriculture and dairy farming are the principal industries. Butter, eggs, bacon, timber and petroleum are exported.

This small and ancient Baltic state had enjoyed but two decades of independence since the 13th century until the present time. After having been conquered by the Danes, the Livonian Knights, the Teutonic Knights of Germany (who reduced the people to serfdom), the Swedes, the Poles and Russia, Estonia declared itself an independent republic on Feb. 24, 1918 but was not freed until Feb. 1919. The peace treaty was signed Feb. 2, 1920. Shortly after the start of World War II, it was again occupied by Russia and incorporated as the 16th state of the U.S.S.R Germany occupied the tiny state from 1941 to 1944, after which it was retaken by Russia. Most of the nations of the world, including the United States and Great Britain, did not recognize Estonia's incorporation into the Soviet Union.

The coinage, issued during the country's brief independence, is obsolete.

On August 20, 1991, the Parliament of the Estonian Soviet Socialist Republic voted to reassert the republic's independence.

REPUBLIC

1918 - 1941

REPUBLIC COINAGE

KM# 1 MARK
Copper-Nickel, 18 mm. **Obv:** Three Czech lions left divide date **Rev:** Denomination **Edge:** Milled

Date	Mintage	F	VF	XF	Unc	BU
1922	5,025,000	3.00	4.00	7.00	15.00	—

KM# 1a MARK
2.6000 g., Nickel-Bronze, 18 mm. **Obv:** Three Czech lions left divide date **Rev:** Denomination **Edge:** Milled

Date	Mintage	F	VF	XF	Unc	BU
1924	1,985,000	3.00	6.00	10.00	20.00	—

KM# 5 MARK
Nickel-Bronze **Obv:** Three Czech lions left divide date **Rev:** Denomination

Date	Mintage	F	VF	XF	Unc	BU
1926	3,979,000	5.00	8.00	15.00	30.00	—

KM# 2 3 MARKA
Copper-Nickel **Obv:** Three Czech lions left divide date **Rev:** Denomination

Date	Mintage	F	VF	XF	Unc	BU
1922	2,089,000	3.00	6.00	8.00	14.00	—

KM# 2a 3 MARKA
Nickel-Bronze **Obv:** Three Czech lions left divide date **Rev:** Denomination

Date	Mintage	F	VF	XF	Unc	BU
1925	1,134,000	5.00	8.00	15.00	30.00	—

KM# 6 3 MARKA
Nickel-Bronze **Obv:** Three Czech lions on shield within wreath **Rev:** Denomination, date below

Date	Mintage	F	VF	XF	Unc	BU
1926	903,000	25.00	50.00	80.00	150	—

KM# 3 5 MARKA
5.0000 g., Copper-Nickel, 23 mm. **Obv:** Three Czech lions left divide date **Rev:** Denomination **Edge:** Milled

Date	Mintage	F	VF	XF	Unc	BU
1922	3,983,000	5.00	8.00	10.00	20.00	—

KM# 3a 5 MARKA
5.0000 g., Nickel-Bronze, 23 mm. **Obv:** Three Czech lions left divide date **Rev:** Denomination **Edge:** Milled

Date	Mintage	F	VF	XF	Unc	BU
1924	1,335,000	5.00	8.00	15.00	25.00	—

KM# 7 5 MARKA
Nickel-Bronze **Obv:** Three Czech lions on shield within wreath **Rev:** Denomination above date

Date	Mintage	F	VF	XF	Unc	BU
1926	1,038,000	75.00	150	200	350	—

KM# 4 10 MARKA
6.0000 g., Nickel-Bronze, 26 mm. **Obv:** Three Czech lions left divide date **Rev:** Denomination **Edge:** Milled

Date	Mintage	F	VF	XF	Unc	BU
1925	2,200,000	7.00	12.00	20.00	40.00	—

KM# 8 10 MARKA
Nickel-Bronze **Obv:** Three Czech lions on shield within wreath **Rev:** Denomination above date

Date	Mintage	F	VF	XF	Unc	BU
1926	2,789,000	650	1,000	1,500	2,000	—

Note: Most of this issue was melted down; Not released to circulation

REFORM COINAGE

100 Senti = 1 Kroon

KM# 10 SENT
2.0000 g., Bronze, 17 mm. **Obv:** Three Czech lions left above date **Rev:** Denomination, oak leaves in background **Edge:** Plain

Date	Mintage	F	VF	XF	Unc	BU
1929	23,553,000	1.00	2.00	3.00	4.00	—

KM# 19.1 SENT
2.0000 g., Bronze, 16 mm. **Obv:** Three Czech lions left above date **Rev:** Denomination **Edge:** Plain **Note:** 1mm thick planchet.

Date	Mintage	F	VF	XF	Unc	BU
1939	5,000,000	4.00	8.00	15.00	35.00	—

KM# 19.2 SENT
Bronze **Obv:** Three Czech lions left divide date **Rev:** Denomination **Note:** 0.9mm thick planchet.

Date	Mintage	F	VF	XF	Unc	BU
1939	Inc. above	6.00	10.00	15.00	35.00	—

KM# 15 2 SENTI
3.5000 g., Bronze, 19 mm. **Obv:** Three Czech lions left above date **Rev:** Denomination **Edge:** Plain

Date	Mintage	F	VF	XF	Unc	BU
1934	5,838,000	2.00	3.00	6.00	10.00	—

KM# 11 5 SENTI
3.5000 g., Bronze, 23.3 mm. **Obv:** Three Czech lions left above date **Rev:** Denomination **Edge:** Plain

Date	Mintage	F	VF	XF	Unc	BU
1931	11,000,000	2.00	3.00	8.00	15.00	—

KM# 12 10 SENTI
Nickel-Bronze, 18 mm. **Obv:** Three Czech lions within shield divide date **Rev:** Denomination **Edge:** Plain

Date	Mintage	F	VF	XF	Unc	BU
1931	4,089,000	2.00	3.00	10.00	17.00	—

KM# 17 20 SENTI
3.9200 g., Nickel-Bronze, 21 mm. **Obv:** Three Czech lions within shield divide date **Rev:** Denomination **Edge:** Plain

Date	Mintage	F	VF	XF	Unc	BU
1935	4,250,000	4.00	6.00	12.00	20.00	—

KM# 9 25 SENTI
Nickel-Bronze **Obv:** Three Czech lions within shield, wreath surrounds **Rev:** Denomination above date

Date	Mintage	F	VF	XF	Unc	BU
1928	2,025,000	6.00	9.00	25.00	40.00	—

KM# 18 50 SENTI
7.5000 g., Nickel-Bronze, 27.5 mm. **Obv:** Three Czech lions within shield divide date **Rev:** Denomination **Edge:** Plain

Date	Mintage	F	VF	XF	Unc	BU
1936	1,256,000	6.00	9.00	17.00	35.00	—

KM# 14 KROON
6.0000 g., 0.5000 Silver 0.0964 oz. ASW, 26 mm. **Subject:** 10th Singing Festival **Obv:** Three Czech lions within shield, wreath surrounds, date below **Obv. Designer:** Gunther Reidorf **Rev:** Harp divides dates, denomination below **Rev. Designer:** Georg Vestenberg

Date	Mintage	F	VF	XF	Unc	BU
1933	350,000	15.00	25.00	40.00	60.00	90.00

KM# 16 KROON
5.9600 g., Aluminum-Bronze, 25 mm. **Obv:** Three Czech lions within shield, wreath surrounds, date below **Rev:** Ship of Vikings, denomination below **Edge:** Plain **Note:** 1990 restrikes which exist are private issues.

Date	Mintage	F	VF	XF	Unc	BU
1934	3,304,000	5.00	8.00	14.00	40.00	60.00

KM# 20 2 KROONI
12.0000 g., 0.5000 Silver 0.1929 oz. ASW, 30 mm. **Subject:** Toompea Fortress at Tallinn **Obv:** Three Czech lions within shield, wreath surrounds, date below **Rev:** Castle denomination below **Edge:** Milled

Date	Mintage	F	VF	XF	Unc	BU
1930	1,276,000	6.00	9.00	16.00	40.00	70.00

KM# 13 2 KROONI
12.0000 g., 0.5000 Silver 0.1929 oz. ASW, 30 mm. **Subject:** Tercentenary - University of Tartu **Obv:** Three Czech lions within shield, wreath surrounds, date below **Obv. Designer:** Gunther Reidorf **Rev:** University building, denomination below **Rev. Designer:** Georg Vestenberg **Edge:** Plain

Date	Mintage	F	VF	XF	Unc	BU
1932	100,000	15.00	25.00	35.00	60.00	80.00

MODERN REPUBLIC

1991 - present

STANDARD COINAGE

KM# 21 5 SENTI
1.2900 g., Brass, 15.9 mm. **Obv:** Three Czech lions left divide date **Rev:** Denomination **Edge:** Plain

Date	Mintage	F	VF	XF	Unc	BU
1991	—	—	—	—	0.30	—
1992	—	—	—	—	0.30	—
1995	—	—	—	—	0.30	—

KM# 22 10 SENTI

1.8500 g., Copper-Aluminum-Nickel, 17.1 mm. **Obv:** Three Czech lions left divide date **Rev:** Denomination **Edge:** Plain

Date	Mintage	F	VF	XF	Unc	BU
1991	—	—	—	—	0.50	—
1992	—	—	—	—	0.50	—
1994	—	—	—	—	0.50	—
1996	—	—	—	—	0.50	—
1997	—	—	—	—	0.50	—
1998	—	—	—	—	0.50	—
2002	—	—	—	—	0.50	0.75
2006	—	—	—	—	0.50	0.75

KM# 23 20 SENTI

2.2700 g., Brass, 18.9 mm. **Obv:** Three Czech lions left divide date **Rev:** Denomination **Edge:** Plain

Date	Mintage	F	VF	XF	Unc	BU
1992	—	—	—	—	1.00	—
1996	—	—	—	—	1.00	—

KM# 23a 20 SENTI

2.0000 g., Nickel Plated Steel, 18.9 mm. **Obv:** Three Czech lions left divide date **Rev:** Denomination **Edge:** Plain

Date	Mintage	F	VF	XF	Unc	BU
1997	—	—	—	—	1.00	—
1999	—	—	—	—	1.00	—
2003	—	—	—	—	0.65	1.00
2004	—	—	—	—	0.65	1.00
2006	—	—	—	—	0.65	1.00

KM# 24 50 SENTI

2.9000 g., Brass, 19.5 mm. **Obv:** Three Czech lions left divide date **Rev:** Denomination **Edge:** Plain

Date	Mintage	F	VF	XF	Unc	BU
1992	—	—	—	—	1.50	—
2004	—	—	—	—	1.00	1.25
2006	—	—	—	—	1.00	1.25

KM# 28 KROON

5.4400 g., Copper-Nickel, 23.5 mm. **Obv:** Three Czech lions within shield divide date **Rev:** Large, thick denomination **Edge:** Plain

Date	Mintage	F	VF	XF	Unc	BU
1992	20,000	—	—	—	—	—
Note: In sets only						
1993	—	—	—	—	2.00	—
1995	—	—	—	—	2.00	—

KM# 35 KROON

5.0000 g., Brass, 23.5 mm. **Obv:** Three Czech lions within shield divide date **Rev:** Large, thick denomination **Edge:** Three reeded and plain sections

Date	Mintage	F	VF	XF	Unc	BU
1998	—	—	—	—	1.50	—
2000	—	—	—	—	1.50	—
2001	—	—	—	—	1.50	1.75
2003	—	—	—	—	1.50	1.75

KM# 36 KROON

Brass, 23.5 mm. **Obv:** Bird above date **Rev:** Festival building and denomination

Date	Mintage	F	VF	XF	Unc	BU
1999	100,000	—	—	—	6.00	—

KM# 29 5 KROONI

7.1000 g., Brass, 26.2 mm. **Subject:** 75th Anniversary - Declaration of Independence **Obv:** Three Czech lions within shield divide date **Rev:** Small deer right, denomination at right **Edge:** Plain

Date	Mintage	F	VF	XF	Unc	BU
1993	—	—	—	—	4.00	7.00
1993 Prooflike	—	Value: 6.00				

KM# 30 5 KROONI

7.1000 g., Brass, 26.1 mm. **Subject:** 75th Anniversary - Estonian National Bank **Obv:** Three Czech lions within shield divide date **Rev:** Denomination on design **Edge:** Plain

Date	Mintage	F	VF	XF	Unc	BU
1994	—	—	—	—	4.00	—

ETHIOPIA

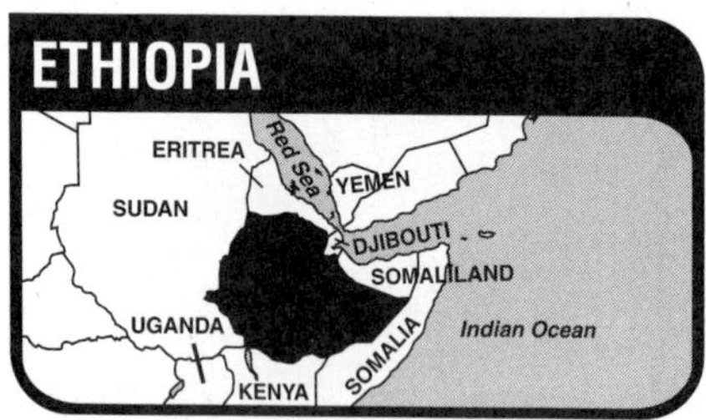

The People's Federal Republic of Ethiopia (formerly the Peoples Democratic Republic and the Empire of Ethiopia), Africa's oldest independent nation, faces the Red Sea in East-Central Africa. The country has an area of 424,214 sq. mi. (1,004,390 sq. km.) and a population of 56 million people who are divided among 40 tribes that speak some 270 languages and dialects. Capital: Addis Ababa. The economy is predominantly agricultural and pastoral. Gold and platinum are mined and petroleum fields are being developed. Coffee, oilseeds, hides and cereals are exported.

Legend claims that Menelik I, the son born to Solomon, King of Israel, by the Queen of Sheba, settled in Axum in North Ethiopia to establish the dynasty, which reigned with only brief interruptions until 1974. Modern Ethiopian history began with the reign of Emperor Menelik II (1889-1913) under whose guidance the country emerged from medieval isolation. Progress continued throughout the reigns of Menelik's daughter, Empress Zauditu, and her successor Emperor Haile Selassie I who was coronated in 1930. Ethiopia was invaded by Italy in 1935, and together with Italian Somaliland and Eritrea became part of Italian East Africa. Victor Emmanuel III, as declared by Mussolini, would be Ethiopia's emperor as well as a king of Italy. Liberated by British and Ethiopian troops in 1941, Ethiopia reinstated Haile Selassie I to the throne. The 225th consecutive Solomonic ruler was deposed by a military committee on Sept 12, 1974. In July 1976 Ethiopia's military provisional government referred to the country as Socialist Ethiopia. After establishing a new regime in 1991, Ethiopia became a federated state and is now the Federal Republic of Ethiopia. Following 2 years of provisional government, the province of Eritrea held a referendum on independence in May 1993 leading to the proclamation of its independence on May 24.

No coins, patterns or presentation pieces are known bearing Emperor Lij Yasu's likeness or titles. Coins of Menelik II were struck during this period with dates frozen.

RULERS

Menelik II, 1889-1913
Lij Yasu, 1913-1916
Zauditu, Empress, 1916-1930
Haile Selassie I
1930-36, 1941-1974
Victor Emmanuel III, of Italy
1936-1941

MINT MARKS

A - Paris
(a) - Paris, privy marks only
(b)

Coinage of Menelik II, 1889-1913

NOTE: The first national issue coinage, dated 1887 and 1888 E.E., carried a cornucopia, A, and fasces on the reverse. Subsequent dates have a torch substituted for the fasces, the A being dropped. All issues bearing these marks were struck at the Paris Mint. Coins without mint marks were struck in Addis Ababa.

MONETARY SYSTEM

(Until about 1903)
40 Besa = 20 Gersh = 1 Birr
(After 1903)
32 Besa = 16 Gersh = 1 Birr

DATING

Ethiopian coinage is dated by the Ethiopian Era calendar (E.E.), which commenced 7 years and 8 months after the advent of A.D. dating.

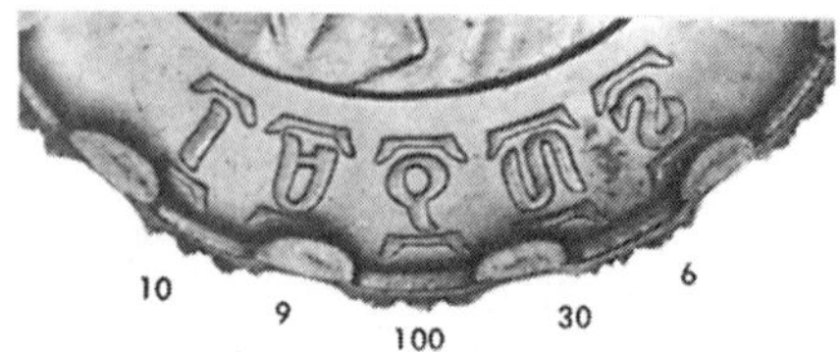

EXAMPLE

1900 (10 and 9 = 19 x 100)
36 (Add 30 and 6)
1936 E.E.
8 (Add)
1943/4 AD

EMPIRE OF ETHIOPIA

REFORM COINAGE

KM# 12 GERSH

1.4038 g., 0.8350 Silver 0.0377 oz. ASW, 16.5 mm. **Ruler:** Menelik II EE1882-1906 / 1889-1913AD **Obv:** Crowned bust right **Rev:** Crowned lion left, left foreleg raised holding ribboned cross

Date	Mintage	F	VF	XF	Unc	BU
EE1895A	44,789,000	2.00	3.50	10.00	20.00	—

Note: Struck between 1903-1928

KM# 3 1/4 BIRR

7.1088 g., 0.8350 Silver 0.1908 oz. ASW, 25 mm. **Ruler:** Menelik II EE1882-1906 / 1889-1913AD **Obv:** Crowned bust right **Rev:** Crowned lion left, left foreleg raised holding ribboned cross

Date	Mintage	F	VF	XF	Unc	BU
EE1895A	821,000	5.00	15.00	45.00	100	—

Note: Struck between 1903 and 1925

KM# 19 BIRR

28.0750 g., 0.8350 Silver 0.7537 oz. ASW, 40 mm. **Ruler:** Menelik II EE1882-1906 / 1889-1913AD **Obv:** Crowned bust right **Rev:** Crowned lion left, right foreleg raised holding ribboned cross

Date	Mintage	F	VF	XF	Unc	BU
EE1895	459,000	25.00	90.00	250	500	—

Note: Struck in 1901, 1903 and 1904

EE1895 Proof — Value: 1,200

KM# 20 1/2 WERK

3.5000 g., 0.9000 Gold 0.1013 oz. AGW, 18 mm. **Ruler:** Empress Zauditu EE1909-1923 / 1916-1930AD **Obv:** Crowned bust left, laurels below **Rev:** St. George on horseback slaying the dragon

Date	Mintage	F	VF	XF	Unc	BU
EE1923	—	250	500	900	1,500	—

KM# 21 WERK

7.0000 g., 0.9000 Gold 0.2025 oz. AGW, 21 mm. **Ruler:** Empress Zauditu EE1909-1923 / 1916-1930AD **Obv:** Crowned bust left, laurels below **Rev:** St. George on horseback slaying the dragon

Date	Mintage	F	VF	XF	Unc	BU
EE1923	—	500	750	1,500	2,500	—

DECIMAL COINAGE

100 Santeems (Cents) = 1 Birr (Dollar)

100 Matonas = 100 Santeems

KM# 27 MATONA

Copper **Ruler:** Haile Selassie I EE1923-1929 / 1930-1936AD **Obv:** Crowned head right **Rev:** Crowned lion right, right foreleg raised holding ribboned cross

Date	Mintage	F	VF	XF	Unc	BU
EE1923	1,250,000	1.50	2.50	8.00	16.00	22.00

Note: Struck by ICI in Birmingham, England. Other denominations in the Matona series were struck in Addis Ababa

KM# 32 CENT (Ande Santeem)

Copper, 17 mm. **Ruler:** Haile Selassie I EE1923-1929 / 1930-36AD; Second Reign, EE1936-1966 / 1943-74AD **Obv:** Bust left, date below **Rev:** Crowned lion right, right foreleg raised holding ribboned cross **Designer:** Gilroy Roberts

Date	Mintage	F	VF	XF	Unc	BU
EE1936	20,000,000	—	0.10	0.20	1.00	2.00

Note: Struck at Philadelphia, Birmingham and the Royal Mint, London between 1944 and 1975 with the date EE1936 frozen

KM# 28.1 5 MATONAS

Copper **Ruler:** Haile Selassie I EE1923-1929 / 1930-1936AD **Obv:** Crowned head right **Rev:** Crowned lion right, right foreleg raised holding ribboned cross **Edge:** Plain

Date	Mintage	F	VF	XF	Unc	BU
EE1923	1,363,000	2.00	3.50	6.00	20.00	25.00

KM# 28.2 5 MATONAS

Copper **Ruler:** Haile Selassie I EE1923-1929 / 1930-1936AD **Obv:** Crowned head right **Rev:** Crowned lion right, right foreleg raised holding ribboned cross **Edge:** Reeded

Date	Mintage	F	VF	XF	Unc	BU
EE1923	Inc. above	3.00	4.50	8.00	25.00	40.00

KM# 33 5 CENTS (Amist Santeem)

Copper, 20 mm. **Ruler:** Haile Selassie I EE1923-1929 / 1930-36AD; Second Reign, EE1936-1966 / 1943-74AD **Obv:** Bust left, date below **Rev:** Crowned lion right, right foreleg raised holding ribboned cross **Designer:** Gilroy Roberts

Date	Mintage	F	VF	XF	Unc	BU
EE1936	219,000,000	—	0.10	0.20	0.50	1.50

Note: Struck between 1944-1962 in Philadelphia and 1964-1966 in Birmingham

KM# 29 10 MATONAS

Nickel **Ruler:** Haile Selassie I EE1923-1929 / 1930-1936AD **Obv:** Crowned bust right **Rev:** Crowned lion right, right foreleg raised holding ribboned cross

Date	Mintage	F	VF	XF	Unc	BU
EE1923	936,000	1.50	2.50	4.50	12.50	—

KM# 34 10 CENTS (Assir Santeem)

Copper, 23 mm. **Ruler:** Haile Selassie I EE1923-1929 / 1930-36AD; Second Reign, EE1936-1966 / 1943-74AD **Obv:** Bust left, date below **Rev:** Crowned lion right, right foreleg raised holding ribboned cross **Designer:** Gilroy Roberts

Date	Mintage	F	VF	XF	Unc	BU
EE1936	348,998,000	—	0.10	0.25	1.00	2.00

Note: Struck between 1945-1963 in Philadelphia, 1964-1966 in Birmingham and 1974-1975 in London

KM# 30 25 MATONAS

Nickel **Ruler:** Haile Selassie I EE1923-1929 / 1930-1936AD **Obv:** Crowned head right **Rev:** Crowned lion right, right foreleg raised holding ribboned cross

Date	Mintage	F	VF	XF	Unc	BU
EE1923	2,742,000	1.25	2.00	5.00	10.00	—

KM# 35 25 CENTS (Haya Amist Santeem)

Copper, 26 mm. **Ruler:** Haile Selassie I EE1923-1929 / 1930-36AD; Second Reign, EE1936-1966 / 1943-74AD **Obv:** Bust left, date below **Rev:** Crowned lion right, right foreleg raised holding ribboned cross **Designer:** Gilroy Roberts

Date	Mintage	F	VF	XF	Unc	BU
EE1936	10,000,000	5.00	10.00	20.00	45.00	60.00

Note: 421,500 issued and 1952 withdrawn and replaced by KM#36

KM# 36 25 CENTS (Haya Amist Santeem)

Copper, 25.5 mm. **Ruler:** Haile Selassie I EE1923-1929 / 1930-36AD; Second Reign, EE1936-1966 / 1943-74AD **Obv:** Bust left, date below **Rev:** Crowned lion right, right foreleg raised holding ribboned cross **Shape:** Scalloped **Designer:** Gilroy Roberts

Date	Mintage	F	VF	XF	Unc	BU
EE1936	30,000,000	0.25	0.50	1.00	4.00	8.00

Note: Issued in 1952 and 1953. Crude and refined edges

KM# 31 50 MATONAS

7.1100 g., Nickel **Ruler:** Haile Selassie I EE1923-1929 / 1930-1936AD **Obv:** Crowned head right **Rev:** Crowned lion right, right foreleg raised holding ribboned cross

Date	Mintage	F	VF	XF	Unc	BU
EE1923	1,621,000	1.50	3.00	8.00	15.00	—

KM# 37 50 CENTS (Hamsa Santeem)

7.0307 g., 0.8000 Silver 0.1808 oz. ASW **Ruler:** Haile Selassie I EE1923-1929 / 1930-36AD; Second Reign, EE1936-1966 / 1943-74AD **Obv:** Bust left, date below **Rev:** Crowned lion right, right foreleg raised holding ribboned cross **Designer:** Gilroy Roberts

Date	Mintage	F	VF	XF	Unc	BU
EE1936	30,000,000	3.00	5.00	12.00	25.00	—

Note: Struck in 1944-1945

KM# 37a 50 CENTS (Hamsa Santeem)

7.0307 g., 0.7000 Silver 0.1582 oz. ASW **Ruler:** Haile Selassie I EE1923-1929 / 1930-36AD; Second Reign, EE1936-1966 / 1943-74AD **Obv:** Bust left, date below **Rev:** Crowned lion right, right foreleg raised holding ribboned cross

Date	Mintage	F	VF	XF	Unc	BU
EE1936	20,434,000	2.50	4.50	12.00	25.00	—

Note: Struck in 1947

PEOPLES DEMOCRATIC REPUBLIC

We have two varieties for KM#43.1 to KM#46.1. One was minted at the British Royal Mint, the other at the Berlin Mint. The main difference is where the lion's chin whiskers end above the date (easiest to see on the 2nd, 3rd and 4th characters).

British Royal Mint

Berlin Mint

DECIMAL COINAGE

100 Santeems (Cents) = 1 Birr (Dollar)

100 Matonas = 100 Santeems

KM# 43.1 CENT

0.6000 g., Aluminum, 17 mm. **Series:** F.A.O. **Obv:** Small lion head right, uniform chin whiskers **Rev:** Farmer with two oxen, denomination above **Designer:** Stuart Devlin

Date	Mintage	F	VF	XF	Unc	BU
EE1969	35,034,000	0.20	0.30	0.50	1.00	—

KM# 43.2 CENT

0.6000 g., Aluminum, 17 mm. **Obv:** Small lion head right, two long chin whiskers at left nearly touch date **Rev:** Farmer with two oxen, denomination above

Date	Mintage	F	VF	XF	Unc	BU
EE1969	Inc. above	0.25	0.35	0.65	1.25	—

KM# 44.1 5 CENTS

3.0000 g., Copper-Zinc, 20 mm. **Obv:** Small lion head right, uniform chin whiskers **Rev:** Denomination left of figure **Designer:** Stuart Devlin

Date	Mintage	F	VF	XF	Unc	BU
EE1969	201,275,000	0.20	0.30	0.50	1.00	—

KM# 44.2 5 CENTS

3.0000 g., Copper-Zinc, 20 mm. **Obv:** Lion head right, date below **Rev:** Denomination left of figure

Date	Mintage	F	VF	XF	Unc	BU
EE1969	Inc. above	0.25	0.35	0.65	1.25	—

KM# 45.1 10 CENTS

4.5000 g., Copper-Zinc, 23 mm. **Obv:** Small lion head right, uniform chin whiskers **Rev:** Mountain Nyala, denomination at right **Designer:** Stuart Devlin

Date	Mintage	F	VF	XF	Unc	BU
EE1969	202,722,000	0.20	0.30	0.60	1.50	3.00

KM# 45.2 10 CENTS

4.5000 g., Copper-Zinc, 23 mm. **Obv:** Small lion head, two long chin whiskers at left nearly touch date **Rev:** Mountain Nyala and denomination

Date	Mintage	F	VF	XF	Unc	BU
EE1969	Inc. above	0.25	0.40	0.75	1.75	3.00

KM# 46.1 25 CENTS

3.7000 g., Copper-Nickel, 21.45 mm. **Obv:** Small lion head right, uniform chin whiskers **Rev:** Man and woman with arms raised divide denomination **Edge:** Reeded **Designer:** Stuart Devlin

Date	Mintage	F	VF	XF	Unc	BU
EE1969	44,983,000	0.20	0.30	0.60	1.25	2.00

KM# 46.2 25 CENTS

3.7000 g., Copper-Nickel, 21.45 mm. **Obv:** Small lion head, two long chin whiskers at left nearly touch date **Rev:** Man and woman with arms raised divide denomination

Date	Mintage	F	VF	XF	Unc	BU
EE1969	Inc. above	0.25	0.40	0.75	1.50	—

KM# 47.1 50 CENTS

6.0000 g., Copper-Nickel, 25 mm. **Obv:** Small lion head right, uniform chin whiskers **Rev:** People of the Republic, denomination above **Designer:** Stuart Devlin

Date	Mintage	F	VF	XF	Unc	BU
EE1969	27,772,000	0.40	0.75	1.25	3.00	—

KM# 47.2 50 CENTS

6.0000 g., Copper-Nickel, 25 mm. **Obv:** Small lion head, two long chin whiskers at left nearly touch date **Rev:** People of the republic, denomination above

Date	Mintage	F	VF	XF	Unc	BU
EE1969	Inc. above	0.50	0.85	1.50	3.00	—

FAEROE ISLANDS

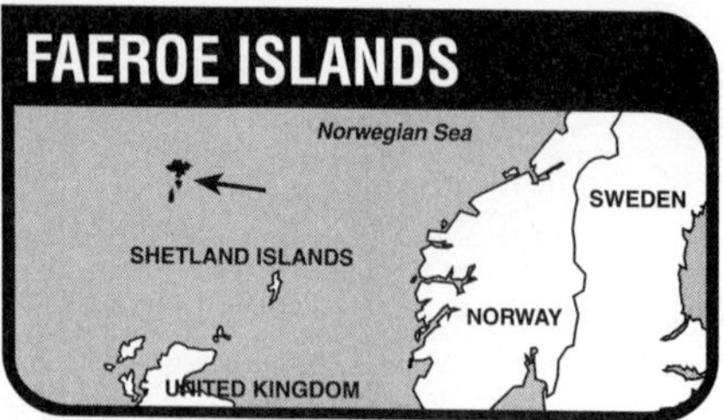

The Faeroe Islands, a self-governing community within the kingdom of Denmark, are situated in the North Atlantic between Iceland and the Shetland Islands. The 17 inhabited islands and numerous islets and reefs have an area of 540 sq. mi. (1,400 sq. km.)and a population of 46,000. Capital: Thorshavn. The principal industries are fishing and livestock. Fish and fish products are exported.

While it is thought that Irish hermits lived on the islands in the 7th and 8th centuries, the present inhabitants are descended from 6th century Norse settlers. The Faeroe Islands became a Norwegian fief in 1035 and became Danish in 1380 when Norway and Denmark were united. They have ever since remained in Danish possession and were granted self-government (except for an appointed governor-general) with their own legislature, executive and flag in 1948.

The islands were occupied by British troops during World War II, after the German occupation of Denmark. The Faeroe island coinage was struck in London during World War II.

RULER

Danish

MONETARY SYSTEM

100 Øre = 1 Krone

DANISH STATE

DECIMAL COINAGE

KM# 1 ORE

Bronze **Obv:** Center hole divides date and denomination **Rev:** Center hole within crowned monogram

Date	Mintage	F	VF	XF	Unc	BU
1941	Est. 200,000	20.00	40.00	60.00	90.00	—

Note: Also struck in 1942 with 1941 dies

1941 Proof	—	Value: 565

KM# 2 2 ORE

Bronze **Obv:** Center hole divides date and denomination **Rev:** Center hole within crowned monogram

Date	Mintage	F	VF	XF	Unc	BU
1941	Est. 200,000	5.00	10.00	22.50	55.00	—

Note: Also struck in 1942 with 1941 dies

1941 Proof	—	Value: 565

KM# 3 5 ORE

Bronze **Obv:** Center hole divides date and denomination **Rev:** Center hole within crowned monogram

Date	Mintage	F	VF	XF	Unc	BU
1941	Est. 200,000	4.00	8.00	18.50	55.00	—

Note: Also struck in 1942 with 1941 dies

1941 Proof	—	Value: 565

KM# 4 10 ORE

Copper-Nickel **Obv:** Center hole divides crowned monogram, date below **Rev:** Center hole with ornaments divides denomination

Date	Mintage	F	VF	XF	Unc	BU
1941	Est. 300,000	5.50	11.00	25.00	80.00	—

Note: Also struck in 1942 with 1941 dies

1941 Proof	—	Value: 585

KM# 5 25 ORE

Copper-Nickel **Obv:** Center hole divides crowned monogram, date below **Rev:** Center hole with ornaments divides denominatio

Date	Mintage	F	VF	XF	Unc	BU
1941	Est. 250,000	7.00	12.50	30.00	95.00	—

Note: Also struck in 1942 with 1941 dies

1941 Proof	—	Value: 585

FALKLAND ISLANDS

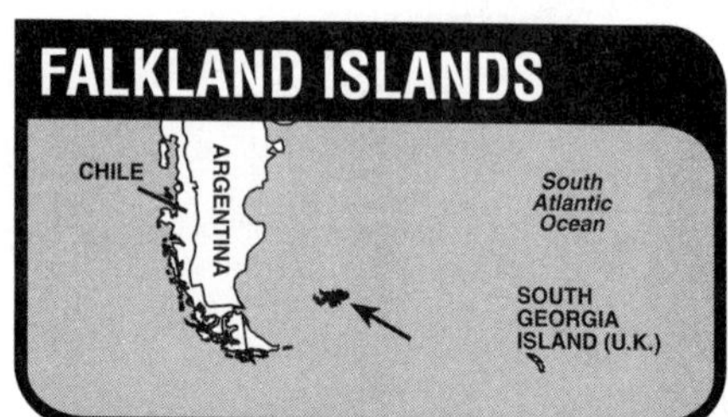

The Colony of the Falkland Islands and Dependencies, a British colony located in the South Atlantic about 500 miles north-east of Cape Horn, has an area of 4,700 sq. mi. (12,170 sq. km.) and a population of 2,121. East Falkland, West Falkland, South Georgia, and South Sandwich are the largest of the 200 islands. Capital: Stanley. Sheep grazing is the main industry. Wool, whale oil, and seal oil are exported.

The Falklands were discovered by British navigator John Davis (Davys) in 1592, and named by Capt. John Strong - for Vis-count Falkland, treasurer of the British navy - in 1690. French navigator Louis De Bougainville established the first settlement, at Port Louis, in 1764. The following year Capt. John Byron claimed the islands for Britain and left a small party at Saunders Island. Spain later forced the French and British to abandon their settlements but did not implement its claim to the islands. In 1829 the Republic of Buenos Aires, which claimed to have inherited the Spanish rights, sent Louis Vernet to develop a colony on the islands. In 1831 he seized three American sealing vessels, whereupon the men of the corvette, the U.S.S. Lexington, destroyed his settlement and proclaimed the Falklands to be 'free of all governance'. Britain, which had never renounced its claim, then re-established its settlement in 1833.

RULER

British

MONETARY SYSTEM

100 Pence = 1 Pound

BRITISH COLONY

DECIMAL COINAGE

KM# 1 1/2 PENNY

1.7820 g., Bronze, 17.14 mm. **Ruler:** Elizabeth II **Obv:** Young bust right **Rev:** Salmon behind denomination, date at right **Designer:** William Gardner

Date	Mintage	F	VF	XF	Unc	BU
1974	140,000	—	—	0.10	0.35	0.50
1974 Proof	23,000	Value: 1.50				
1980	—	—	—	0.10	0.25	0.50
1980 Proof	10,000	Value: 1.50				
1982	—	—	—	0.10	0.25	0.50
1982 Proof	—	Value: 1.50				
1983	—	—	—	0.10	0.25	0.50

KM# 2 PENNY

3.6000 g., Bronze, 20.3 mm. **Ruler:** Elizabeth II **Obv:** Young bust right **Rev:** Gentoo penguins flank denomination, date below **Designer:** William Gardner

Date	Mintage	F	VF	XF	Unc	BU
1974	96,000	—	0.10	0.20	0.60	1.00
1974 Proof	23,000	Value: 2.00				
1980	—	—	0.10	0.20	0.60	1.00
1980 Proof	10,000	Value: 2.00				
1982	—	—	0.10	0.20	0.60	1.00
1982 Proof	—	Value: 2.00				
1983	—	—	0.10	0.20	0.60	1.00
1985	—	—	0.10	0.20	0.60	1.00
1987	111,000	—	—	0.20	0.60	1.00
1987 Proof	—	Value: 2.50				
1992	—	—	0.10	0.20	0.60	1.00
1992 Proof	—	Value: 2.50				

KM# 2a PENNY

Copper Plated Steel, 20.3 mm. **Ruler:** Elizabeth II **Obv:** Young bust right **Rev:** Denomination divides penguins, date below

Date	Mintage	F	VF	XF	Unc	BU
1998	2,500	—	—	—	0.50	0.75
1999	—	—	—	—	0.50	0.75
1999 Proof	2,500	Value: 2.00				

KM# 130 PENNY

Bronze Plated Steel **Ruler:** Elizabeth II **Obv:** Head with tiara right **Obv. Legend:** QUEEN ELIZABETH THE SECOND **Rev:** Two Gentoo penguins flank value **Rev. Legend:** FALKLAND ISLANDS

Date	Mintage	F	VF	XF	Unc	BU
2004	—	—	—	—	0.50	0.75

KM# 3 2 PENCE

7.1000 g., Bronze, 25.9 mm. **Ruler:** Elizabeth II **Obv:** Young bust right **Rev:** Upland goose, wings open, denomination above, date at right **Designer:** William Gardner

Date	Mintage	F	VF	XF	Unc	BU
1974	72,000	—	0.10	0.15	0.50	2.00
1974 Proof	23,000	Value: 3.00				
1980	—	—	0.10	0.15	0.50	2.00
1980 Proof	10,000	Value: 3.00				
1982	—	—	0.10	0.15	0.50	2.00
1982 Proof	—	Value: 3.00				
1983	—	—	0.10	0.15	0.50	2.00
1985	—	—	0.10	0.15	0.50	2.00
1987	106,000	—	—	0.15	0.50	2.00
1987 Proof	—	Value: 3.50				
1992	—	—	0.10	0.15	0.50	2.00
1992 Proof	—	Value: 3.50				

KM# 3a 2 PENCE

Copper Plated Steel, 25.9 mm. **Ruler:** Elizabeth II **Obv:** Young bust right **Rev:** Upland goose, wings open, denomination above, date at right

Date	Mintage	F	VF	XF	Unc	BU
1998	—	—	—	—	0.35	1.00
1999	—	—	—	—	0.35	1.00
1999 Proof	2,500	Value: 3.00				

KM# 131 2 PENCE

Bronze Plated Steel **Ruler:** Elizabeth II **Obv:** Head with tiara right **Obv. Legend:** QUEEN ELIZABETH THE SECOND **Rev:** Upland goose alighting, value above **Rev. Legend:** FALKLAND ISLANDS

Date	Mintage	F	VF	XF	Unc	BU
2004	—	—	—	—	0.50	1.00

KM# 4.1 5 PENCE

5.6500 g., Copper-Nickel, 23.6 mm. **Ruler:** Elizabeth II **Obv:** Young bust right **Rev:** Blackbrowed albatross in flight, denomination and date below **Designer:** William Gardner

Date	Mintage	F	VF	XF	Unc	BU
1974	67,000	—	0.10	0.25	0.75	1.00
1974 Proof	23,000	Value: 3.50				
1980	—	—	0.10	0.25	0.75	1.00
1980 Proof	10,000	Value: 4.00				
1982	—	—	0.10	0.25	0.75	1.00
1982 Proof	—	Value: 4.00				
1983	—	—	0.10	0.25	0.75	1.00
1985	—	—	0.10	0.20	0.75	1.00
1987	5,000	—	—	0.25	0.75	1.00
1987 Proof	—	Value: 4.50				
1992	—	—	0.10	0.25	0.75	1.00
1992 Proof	—	Value: 4.50				

KM# 4.2 5 PENCE

Copper-Nickel, 18 mm. **Ruler:** Elizabeth II **Obv:** Young bust right **Rev:** Blackbrowed albatross in flight, denomination and date below **Designer:** William Gardner

Date	Mintage	F	VF	XF	Unc	BU
1998	—	—	—	—	0.75	1.00
1999	—	—	—	—	0.75	1.00
1999 Proof	2,500	Value: 4.00				

KM# 132 5 PENCE

Copper-Nickel **Ruler:** Elizabeth II **Obv:** Head with tiara right **Obv. Legend:** QUEEN ELIZABETH THE SECOND **Rev:** Blackbrowed Albatross in flight, value below **Rev. Legend:** FALKLAND - ISLANDS

Date	Mintage	F	VF	XF	Unc	BU
2004	—	—	—	—	0.75	1.00

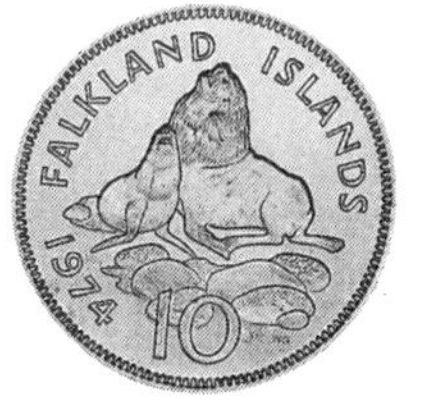

KM# 5.1 10 PENCE

11.3100 g., Copper-Nickel, 28.5 mm. **Ruler:** Elizabeth II **Obv:** Young bust right **Rev:** Ursine seal with cub, denomination below, date at left **Designer:** William Gardner

Date	Mintage	F	VF	XF	Unc	BU
1974	87,000	—	0.20	0.40	1.50	3.50
1974 Proof	23,000	Value: 5.00				
1980	—	—	0.20	0.40	1.50	3.50
1980 Proof	10,000	Value: 5.00				
1982	—	—	0.20	0.40	1.50	3.50
1982 Proof	—	Value: 5.00				
1983	—	—	0.20	0.40	1.50	3.50
1985	—	—	0.20	0.40	1.50	3.50
1987	4,000	—	—	0.40	1.50	3.50
1987 Proof	—	Value: 5.50				
1992	—	—	0.20	0.40	1.50	3.50
1992 Proof	—	Value: 5.50				

KM# 5.2 10 PENCE

Copper-Nickel, 24.5 mm. **Ruler:** Elizabeth II **Obv:** Young bust right **Rev:** Ursine seal with cub, denomination below, date at left **Designer:** William Gardner

Date	Mintage	F	VF	XF	Unc	BU
1998	—	—	—	—	1.50	3.00
1999	—	—	—	—	1.50	3.00
1999 Proof	2,500	Value: 5.00				

KM# 133 10 PENCE

Copper-Nickel **Ruler:** Elizabeth II **Obv:** Head with tiara right **Obv. Legend:** QUEEN ELIZABETH THE SECOND **Rev:** Ursine seal with cub, value below **Rev. Legend:** FALKLAND ISLANDS

Date	Mintage	F	VF	XF	Unc	BU
2004	—	—	—	—	1.50	3.00

KM# 17 20 PENCE

5.0000 g., Copper-Nickel, 21.95 mm. **Ruler:** Elizabeth II **Obv:** Young bust right **Rev:** Romney marsh sheep left, denomination above **Shape:** 7-sided **Designer:** William Gardner

Date	Mintage	F	VF	XF	Unc	BU
1982	—	—	0.40	0.65	2.00	4.00
1982 Proof	—	Value: 5.00				
1983	—	—	0.40	0.65	2.00	4.00
1985	—	—	0.40	0.65	2.00	4.00
1987	4,250	—	0.40	0.65	2.00	4.00
1987 Proof	—	Value: 5.50				
1992	—	—	0.40	0.65	2.00	4.00
1992 Proof	—	Value: 5.50				
1998	—	—	0.40	0.65	2.00	4.00
1999	—	—	—	—	2.00	4.00
1999 Proof	2,500	Value: 5.00				

KM# 134 20 PENCE

Copper-Nickel **Ruler:** Elizabeth II **Obv:** Head with tiara right **Obv. Legend:** QUEEN ELIZABETH THE SECOND **Rev:** Romney marsh sheep standing left, value above **Rev. Legend:** FALKLAND ISLANDS **Edge:** Plain **Shape:** 7-sided

Date	Mintage	F	VF	XF	Unc	BU
2004	—	—	—	—	2.00	4.00

KM# 10 50 PENCE

Copper-Nickel, 38.5 mm. **Ruler:** Elizabeth II **Subject:** Queen's Silver Jubilee **Obv:** Young bust right, dates at left **Rev:** Sheep above ship on shield within wreath, denomination below

Date	Mintage	F	VF	XF	Unc	BU
ND(1977)	100,000	—	1.00	1.50	3.00	4.50

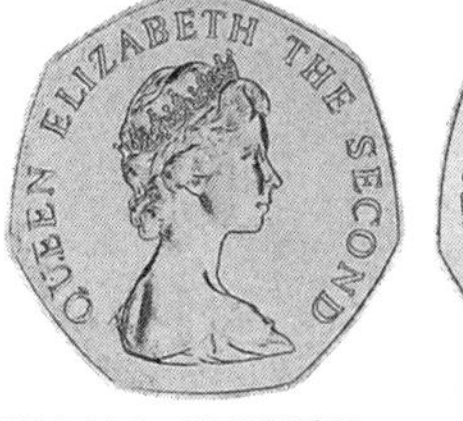

KM# 14.1 50 PENCE

13.6500 g., Copper-Nickel, 30 mm. **Ruler:** Elizabeth II **Obv:** Young bust right **Rev:** Falkland Island fox (extinct), date at right, denomination above **Shape:** 7-sided

Date	Mintage	F	VF	XF	Unc	BU
1980	—	—	1.00	2.00	5.00	7.50
1980 Proof	—	Value: 8.00				
1982	—	—	1.00	2.00	5.00	7.50
1982 Proof	—	Value: 8.00				
1983	—	—	1.00	2.00	5.00	7.50
1985	—	—	1.00	2.00	5.00	7.50
1987	4,000	—	1.00	2.00	5.00	7.50
1987 Proof	—	Value: 9.00				
1992	—	—	1.00	2.00	5.00	7.50
1992 Proof	—	Value: 9.00				
1995	—	—	—	2.00	5.00	7.50

KM# 14.2 50 PENCE

Copper-Nickel, 27.3 mm. **Ruler:** Elizabeth II **Obv:** Young bust right **Rev:** Falkland Island fox (extinct) **Shape:** 7-sided **Note:** Reduced size.

Date	Mintage	F	VF	XF	Unc	BU
1998	—	—	—	2.00	5.00	7.50
1999	—	—	—	2.00	5.00	7.50
1999 Proof	2,500	Value: 8.00				

KM# 135 50 PENCE

Copper-Nickel **Ruler:** Elizabeth II **Obv:** Young bust right

Date	Mintage	F	VF	XF	Unc	BU
2004	—	—	—	—	5.00	7.50

KM# 24 POUND

9.5000 g., Nickel-Brass, 22.5 mm. **Ruler:** Elizabeth II **Obv:** Crowned bust right **Rev:** State shield, date and denomination **Edge Lettering:** DESIRE THE RIGHT

Date	Mintage	F	VF	XF	Unc	BU
1987	—	—	—	—	3.50	—
1987 Proof	2,500	Value: 12.50				
1992	—	—	—	—	3.50	—
1992 Proof	—	Value: 12.50				
1999	—	—	—	—	3.50	—
1999 Proof	2,500	Value: 12.50				

KM# 136 POUND

Nickel-Brass **Ruler:** Elizabeth II **Obv:** Crowned bust right

Date	Mintage	F	VF	XF	Unc	BU
2004	—	—	—	—	3.50	5.00

KM# 137 2 POUNDS

11.9800 g., Bi-Metallic Copper - Nickel center in Nickel-Brass ring **Ruler:** Elizabeth II **Obv:** Head with tiara right **Obv. Legend:** QUEEN ELIZABETH THE SECOND **Rev:** Sun and map surrounded by wildlife **Edge:** Reeded and lettered **Edge Lettering:** 30 YEARS OF FALKLAND ISLANDS COINAGE

Date	Mintage	F	VF	XF	Unc	BU
2004	—	—	—	5.00	10.00	12.00

FIJI ISLANDS

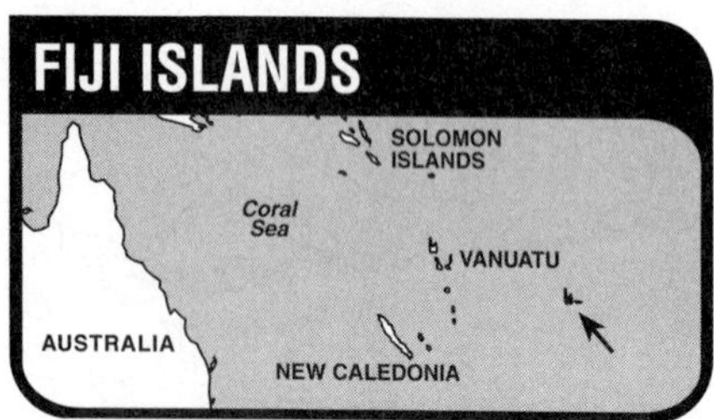

The Republic of Fiji, consists of about 320 islands located in the southwestern Pacific 1,100 miles (1,770 km.) north of New Zealand. The islands have a combined area of 7,056 sq. mi. (18,274 sq. km.) and a population of 772,891. Capital: Suva. Fiji's economy is based on agriculture and mining. Sugar, coconut products, manganese, and gold are exported.

The first European to sight Fiji was the Dutch navigator Abel Tasman in 1643 and the islands were visited by British naval captain James Cook in 1774. The first complete survey of the island was conducted by the United States in 1840. Settlement by mercenaries from Tonga, and traders attracted by the sandalwood trade, began in 1801. Following a lengthy period of intertribal warfare, the islands were unconditionally ceded to Great Britain in 1874 by King Cakobau. Fiji became a sovereign and independent nation on Oct. 10, 1970, the 96th anniversary of the cession of the islands to Queen Victoria.

Fiji was declared a Republic in 1987 following two military coups. It left the British Commonwealth and Queen Elizabeth ceased to be the Head of State. A new constitution was introduced in 1991. The country returned to the Commonwealth in 1997 with a revised constitution. Fiji is a member of the Commonwealth of Nations, but has been subject to periodic short suspensions.

RULER

British until 1970

MINT MARKS

(c) - Australian Mint, Canberra
(H) – The Mint, Birmingham
(I) – Royal Mint, Llatrisant
(o) - Royal Canadian Mint, Ottawa
S - San Francisco, U.S.A.

MONETARY SYSTEM

12 Pence = 1 Shilling
2 Shillings = 1 Florin
20 Shillings = 1 Pound

REPUBLIC

British Administration until 1970

POUND STERLING COINAGE

KM# 1 1/2 PENNY

Copper-Nickel **Ruler:** George V **Obv:** Crown above center hole **Rev:** Center hole divides date, denomination above

Date	Mintage	F	VF	XF	Unc	BU
1934	96,000	0.75	1.75	4.00	15.00	20.00
1934 Proof	—	—	—	—	—	—

KM# 14 1/2 PENNY

Copper-Nickel **Ruler:** George VI **Obv:** Crown above center hole **Rev:** Center hole divides date, denomination above

Date	Mintage	F	VF	XF	Unc	BU
1940	24,000	2.50	7.50	12.50	30.00	50.00
1940 Proof	—	Value: 350				
1941	96,000	0.75	1.50	4.00	10.00	20.00
1941 Proof	—	Value: 200				

KM# 14a 1/2 PENNY

Brass **Ruler:** George VI **Obv:** Crown above center hole **Rev:** Center hole divides date, denomination above

Date	Mintage	F	VF	XF	Unc	BU
1942S	250,000	—	0.35	2.50	10.00	20.00
1943S	250,000	—	0.35	2.50	12.50	20.00

KM# 16 1/2 PENNY

Copper-Nickel **Ruler:** George VI **Obv:** Crown above center hole, EMPEROR dropped from legend **Rev:** Center hole divides date, denomination above

Date	Mintage	F	VF	XF	Unc	BU
1949	96,000	—	0.50	2.00	7.50	12.50
1949	—	Value: 210				
1950	115,000	—	0.35	1.50	6.00	10.00
1950 Proof	—	Value: 230				
1951	115,000	—	0.35	1.50	5.00	7.50
1951 Proof	—	Value: 190				
1952	228,000	—	0.25	0.75	1.50	2.00
1952 Proof	—	—	—	—	—	—

KM# 20 1/2 PENNY

Copper-Nickel **Obv:** Crown above center hole **Rev:** Center hole divides date, denomination above

Date	Mintage	F	VF	XF	Unc	BU
1954	228,000	—	0.25	0.50	1.00	1.50
1954 Proof	—	Value: 180				

KM# 2 PENNY

Copper-Nickel, 26 mm. **Ruler:** George V **Obv:** Crown above center hole **Rev:** Center hole divides date, denomination below

Date	Mintage	F	VF	XF	Unc	BU
1934	480,000	0.50	1.00	5.00	12.50	22.50
1934 Proof	—	—	—	—	—	—
1935	240,000	0.65	1.25	5.00	15.00	25.00
1935 Proof	—	—	—	—	—	—
1936	240,000	0.65	1.25	5.00	17.50	27.50
1936 Proof	—	—	—	—	—	—

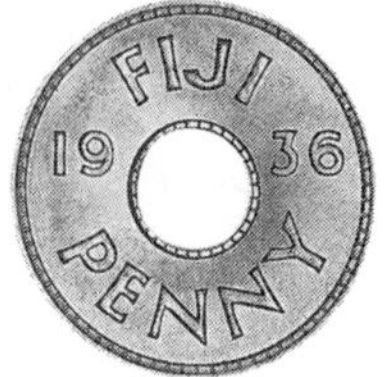

KM# 6 PENNY

Copper-Nickel, 26 mm. **Ruler:** Edward VIII **Obv:** Crown above center hole **Rev:** Center hole divides date, denomination below

Date	Mintage	F	VF	XF	Unc	BU
1936	120,000	0.50	1.00	2.00	4.00	7.50
1936 Proof	—	Value: 225				

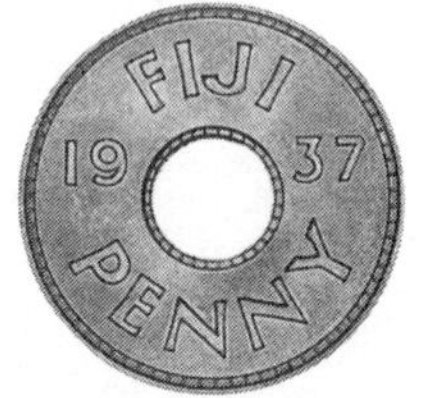

KM# 7 PENNY

Copper-Nickel, 26 mm. **Ruler:** George VI **Obv:** Crown above center hole **Rev:** Center hole divides date, denomination below

Date	Mintage	F	VF	XF	Unc	BU
1937	360,000	0.50	1.00	3.00	7.50	12.50
1937 Proof	—	Value: 225				
1940	144,000	1.50	3.00	15.00	45.00	75.00
1940 Proof	—	Value: 225				
1941	228,000	0.50	1.00	2.00	10.00	15.00
1941 Proof	—	Value: 225				
1945	240,000	1.00	2.00	6.00	15.00	25.00
1945 Proof	—	Value: 225				

KM# 7a PENNY

Brass, 26 mm. **Ruler:** George VI **Obv:** Crown above center hole **Rev:** Center hole divides date, denomination below

Date	Mintage	F	VF	XF	Unc	BU
1942S	1,000,000	0.25	1.00	3.50	10.00	20.00
1943S	1,000,000	0.25	1.00	3.50	7.50	20.00

KM# 17 PENNY

6.5000 g., Copper-Nickel, 26 mm. **Ruler:** George VI **Obv:** Crown above center hole, "EMPEROR" dropped from legend **Rev:** Center hole divides date, denomination below

Date	Mintage	F	VF	XF	Unc	BU
1949	120,000	0.25	0.50	1.00	4.50	7.50
1949 Proof	—	Value: 325				
1950	58,000	1.50	3.50	12.50	65.00	100
1950 Proof	—	Value: 200				
1952	230,000	0.25	0.50	1.00	3.75	7.00
1952 Proof	—	Value: 175				

KM# 21 PENNY

6.6400 g., Copper-Nickel, 26 mm. **Ruler:** Elizabeth II **Obv:** Crown above center hole **Rev:** Center hole divides date, denomination below

Date	Mintage	F	VF	XF	Unc	BU
1954	511,000	0.20	0.50	1.00	3.00	4.50
1954 Proof	—	Value: 175				
1955	230,000	0.20	0.50	1.25	5.00	9.00
1955 Proof	—	Value: 175				
1956	230,000	0.20	0.50	1.25	3.50	7.50
1956 Proof	—	Value: 175				
1957	360,000	0.10	0.25	0.75	3.00	7.00
1957 Proof	—	Value: 175				
1959	864,000	—	0.20	0.35	2.00	3.50
1959 Proof	—	Value: 175				
1961	432,000	0.15	0.35	0.50	1.25	3.00
1961 Proof	—	Value: 175				
1963	432,000	0.15	0.35	0.50	1.25	3.00
1963 Proof	—	Value: 175				
1964	864,000	—	0.15	0.25	0.85	2.00
1964 Proof	—	Value: 150				
1965	1,440,000	—	—	0.20	0.75	2.00
1966	720,000	—	—	0.20	0.85	2.50
1967	720,000	—	—	0.20	0.75	1.50
1968	720,000	—	—	0.20	0.75	1.50

KM# 15 THREEPENCE

6.1700 g., Nickel-Brass, 21.19 mm. **Ruler:** George VI **Obv:** Crowned head left **Rev:** Native dwelling, date above, denomination below **Shape:** 12-sided

Date	Mintage	F	VF	XF	Unc	BU
1947	450,000	1.50	2.50	6.00	20.00	45.00
1947 Proof	—	Value: 190				

KM# 18 THREEPENCE

Nickel-Brass **Ruler:** George VI **Obv:** Crowned head left, EMPEROR dropped from legend **Rev:** Native dwelling, date above, denomination below **Shape:** 12-sided

Date	Mintage	F	VF	XF	Unc	BU
1950	450,000	0.50	1.00	4.00	15.00	25.00
1950 Proof	—	Value: 190				
1952	400,000	0.50	1.00	5.00	22.50	35.00
1952 Proof	—	Value: 190				

KM# 22 THREEPENCE

Nickel-Brass **Ruler:** Elizabeth II **Obv:** Crowned head right **Rev:** Native dwelling, date above, denomination below **Shape:** 12-sided

Date	Mintage	F	VF	XF	Unc	BU
1955	400,000	0.50	1.00	4.00	17.50	35.00
1955 Proof	—	Value: 130				
1956	200,000	0.50	1.00	4.00	20.00	40.00
1956 Proof	—	Value: 155				
1958	200,000	0.50	1.00	4.00	20.00	40.00
1958 Proof	—	Value: 140				
1960	240,000	0.25	0.50	3.00	8.50	15.00
1960 Proof	—	Value: 125				
1961	240,000	0.25	0.50	1.25	6.00	12.50
1961 Proof	—	Value: 125				
1963	240,000	0.15	0.30	0.75	5.00	10.00
1963 Proof	—	Value: 115				
1964	240,000	0.15	0.30	0.50	2.00	5.00
1965	800,000	—	0.15	0.25	1.50	3.50
1967	800,000	—	0.15	0.25	1.50	3.50

KM# 3 SIXPENCE

2.8276 g., 0.5000 Silver 0.0455 oz. ASW, 19.5 mm. **Ruler:** George V **Obv:** Crowned bust left **Rev:** Sea turtle divides date, denomination below

Date	Mintage	F	VF	XF	Unc	BU
1934	160,000	1.25	2.50	10.00	35.00	45.00
1934 Proof	—	Value: 450				
1935	120,000	1.50	3.50	12.50	45.00	55.00
1935 Proof	—	Value: 350				
1936	40,000	2.00	4.00	15.00	55.00	70.00
1936 Proof	—	Value: 350				

KM# 8 SIXPENCE

2.8276 g., 0.5000 Silver 0.0455 oz. ASW, 19.5 mm. **Ruler:** George VI **Obv:** Crowned head left **Rev:** Sea turtle divides date, denomination below

Date	Mintage	F	VF	XF	Unc	BU
1937	40,000	2.00	4.00	16.00	50.00	75.00
1937 Proof	—	Value: 400				

KM# 11 SIXPENCE

2.8276 g., 0.5000 Silver 0.0455 oz. ASW, 19.5 mm. **Ruler:** George VI **Obv:** Smaller head **Rev:** Sea turtle divides date, denomination below

Date	Mintage	F	VF	XF	Unc	BU
1938	40,000	2.00	4.00	13.50	45.00	60.00
1938 Proof	—	Value: 500				
1940	40,000	2.00	4.00	13.50	45.00	60.00
1940 Proof	—	Value: 350				
1941	40,000	3.00	8.00	20.00	60.00	85.00
1941 Proof	—	Value: 350				

KM# 11a SIXPENCE

2.8276 g., 0.9000 Silver 0.0818 oz. ASW, 19.5 mm. **Ruler:** George VI **Obv:** Crowned head left **Rev:** Sea turtle divides date, denomination below

Date	Mintage	F	VF	XF	Unc	BU
1942S	400,000	—	1.25	2.50	7.50	10.00
1943S	400,000	—	1.25	2.50	7.50	10.00

KM# 19 SIXPENCE

Copper-Nickel, 19.5 mm. **Ruler:** Elizabeth II **Obv:** Crowned head right **Rev:** Sea turtle divides date, denomination below

Date	Mintage	F	VF	XF	Unc	BU
1953	800,000	0.25	0.50	1.00	3.00	7.50
1953 Proof	—	Value: 210				
1958	400,000	0.25	0.50	1.50	4.50	8.00
1958 Proof	—	Value: 200				
1961	400,000	0.25	0.50	1.00	3.50	7.00
1961 Proof	—	Value: 200				
1962	400,000	0.25	0.50	1.00	3.00	7.00
1962 Proof	—	Value: 200				
1965	800,000	0.15	0.30	1.00	2.50	6.00
1967	800,000	0.15	0.30	1.00	2.50	6.00

KM# 4 SHILLING

5.6552 g., 0.5000 Silver 0.0909 oz. ASW, 23.5 mm. **Ruler:** George V **Obv:** Crowned bust left **Rev:** Outrigger divides dates, denomination above

Date	Mintage	F	VF	XF	Unc	BU
1934	360,000	1.50	4.00	14.50	60.00	75.00
1934 Proof	—	Value: 650				
1935	180,000	1.50	4.00	14.50	75.00	90.00
1935 Proof	—	Value: 550				
1936	140,000	1.50	6.00	15.50	75.00	90.00
1936 Proof	—	—	—	—	—	—

KM# 9 SHILLING

5.6552 g., 0.5000 Silver 0.0909 oz. ASW, 23.5 mm. **Ruler:** George VI **Obv:** Crowned head left **Rev:** Outrigger divides dates, denomination above

Date	Mintage	F	VF	XF	Unc	BU
1937	40,000	1.50	7.00	17.50	80.00	100
1937 Proof	—	Value: 500				

KM# 12 SHILLING

5.6552 g., 0.5000 Silver 0.0909 oz. ASW, 23.5 mm. **Ruler:** George VI **Obv:** Smaller head **Rev:** Outrigger divides date, denomination above

Date	Mintage	F	VF	XF	Unc	BU
1938	40,000	1.50	7.00	17.50	80.00	100
1938 Proof	—	Value: 450				
1941	40,000	1.50	7.00	17.50	80.00	100
1941 Proof	—	Value: 450				

KM# 12a SHILLING

5.6552 g., 0.9000 Silver 0.1636 oz. ASW, 23.5 mm. **Ruler:** George VI **Obv:** Crowned head left **Rev:** Outrigger divides date, denomination above

Date	Mintage	F	VF	XF	Unc	BU
1942S	500,000	—	2.50	3.50	7.50	10.00
1943S	500,000	—	2.50	3.50	7.50	10.00

KM# 23 SHILLING

Copper-Nickel, 23.5 mm. **Ruler:** Elizabeth II **Obv:** Crowned head right **Rev:** Outrigger divides date, denomination above

Date	Mintage	F	VF	XF	Unc	BU
1957	400,000	0.50	0.75	2.00	10.00	12.50
1957 Proof	—	Value: 350				
1958	400,000	0.50	0.75	2.25	10.00	12.50
1958 Proof	—	Value: 300				
1961	200,000	0.75	1.00	2.25	7.50	10.00
1961 Proof	—	Value: 275				
1962	400,000	0.35	0.75	1.25	4.00	6.50
1962 Proof	—	Value: 250				
1965	800,000	0.25	0.50	0.75	2.00	3.50

KM# 5 FLORIN

11.3104 g., 0.5000 Silver 0.1818 oz. ASW **Ruler:** George V **Obv:** Crowned bust left **Rev:** Shield of arms divides date, denomination below

Date	Mintage	F	VF	XF	Unc	BU
1934	200,000	2.50	4.50	17.50	125	145
1934 Proof	—	Value: 750				
1935	50,000	2.75	9.00	20.00	190	210
1935 Proof	—	Value: 700				
1936	65,000	2.75	9.00	20.00	170	190
1936 Proof	—	Value: 725				

KM# 10 FLORIN

11.3104 g., 0.5000 Silver 0.1818 oz. ASW **Ruler:** George VI **Obv:** Crowned head left **Rev:** Shield of arms divides date, denomination below

Date	Mintage	F	VF	XF	Unc	BU
1937	30,000	2.65	7.00	17.50	150	170
1937 Proof	—	Value: 850				

KM# 13 FLORIN

11.3104 g., 0.5000 Silver 0.1818 oz. ASW **Ruler:** George VI **Obv:** Smaller head **Rev:** Shield of arms divides dates, denomination below

Date	Mintage	F	VF	XF	Unc	BU
1938	20,000	4.00	12.00	25.00	185	215
1938 Proof	—	Value: 750				
1941	20,000	4.00	12.00	25.00	185	215
1941 Proof	—	Value: 775				
1945	100,000	9.00	20.00	35.00	230	275
1945 Proof	—	Value: 750				

KM# 13a FLORIN

11.3104 g., 0.9000 Silver 0.3273 oz. ASW **Ruler:** George VI **Obv:** Crowned head left **Rev:** Shield of arms divides date, denomination below

Date	Mintage	F	VF	XF	Unc	BU
1942S	250,000	—	4.50	6.00	12.50	17.50
1943S	250,000	—	4.50	6.50	15.00	20.00

Note: BU coins must display full face of leopard at top of arms

KM# 24 FLORIN

Copper-Nickel **Ruler:** Elizabeth II **Obv:** Crowned head right **Rev:** Shield of arms divides date, denomination below

Date	Mintage	F	VF	XF	Unc	BU
1957	300,000	0.50	1.00	4.00	15.00	20.00
1957 Proof	—	Value: 375				
1958	220,000	0.50	1.00	4.00	15.00	20.00
1958 Proof	—	Value: 375				
1962	200,000	0.25	0.50	2.00	10.00	15.00
1962 Proof	—	Value: 375				
1964	200,000	0.25	0.50	1.50	5.00	10.00
1964 Proof	—	Value: 400				
1965	400,000	0.25	0.50	1.00	3.00	5.00

DECIMAL COINAGE

100 Cents = 1 Dollar

KM# 27 CENT

1.9000 g., Bronze, 17.5 mm. **Ruler:** Elizabeth II **Rev:** Tanoa kava bowl divides denomination **Rev. Designer:** Ken Payne

Date	Mintage	F	VF	XF	Unc	BU
1969(h)	11,000,000	—	—	0.10	0.20	1.00
1969 Proof	10,000	Value: 0.50				
1973(c)	3,000,000	—	—	0.10	0.50	2.00
1975(c)	2,064,000	—	—	0.10	0.50	1.00
1976(c)	—	—	—	0.10	0.50	1.00
(c)	2,005,000	—	—	0.10	0.50	1.00
1983(c)	3,000,000	—	—	0.10	0.50	1.00
1983 Proof	3,000	Value: 1.00				
1984(c)	2,295,000	—	—	0.10	0.35	1.00
1985(c)	—	—	—	0.10	0.35	1.00

KM# 39 CENT

1.9000 g., Bronze, 17.5 mm. **Ruler:** Elizabeth II **Series:** F.A.O. **Obv:** Young bust right **Rev:** Rice plant at left, denomination at right

Date	Mintage	F	VF	XF	Unc	BU
1977(c)	3,000,000	—	—	0.10	0.50	1.50
1978(c)	3,032,000	—	—	0.10	0.50	1.50
1978 Proof	2,000	Value: 2.50				
1979(c)	2,500,000	—	—	0.10	2.00	4.00
1980(c)	314,000	—	—	0.10	0.50	1.50
1980 Proof	2,500	Value: 1.50				
1981(c)	4,040,000	—	—	0.10	0.50	1.00
1982(c)	5,000,000	—	—	0.10	0.50	1.00
1982 Proof	3,000	Value: 1.00				

KM# 49 CENT

1.9000 g., Bronze, 17.5 mm. **Ruler:** Elizabeth II **Obv:** Crowned head right, date at right **Rev:** Tanoa kava bowl divides denomination **Rev. Designer:** Ken Payne

Date	Mintage	F	VF	XF	Unc	BU
1986(c)	3,400,000	—	—	0.10	0.50	1.00
1987(c)	3,400,000	—	—	0.15	0.50	1.00

KM# 49a CENT

1.5400 g., Copper Plated Zinc, 17.5 mm. **Ruler:** Elizabeth II **Obv:** Crowned head right, date at right **Rev:** Tanoa kava bowl divides denomination

Date	Mintage	F	VF	XF	Unc	BU
1990(o)	8,500,000	—	—	0.10	0.25	0.75
1992(o)	16,200,000	—	—	0.10	0.25	0.75
1994(o)	7,800,000	—	—	—	0.25	0.75
1995(o)	6,000,000	—	—	—	0.25	2.00
1997(o)	12,000,000	—	—	—	0.25	1.00
1999(o)	14,000,000	—	—	—	0.25	0.75
2001	—	—	—	—	0.20	0.65
2002(o)	5,880,000	—	—	—	0.20	0.65
2003(o)	8,030,000	—	—	—	0.20	0.65
(o)	8,840,000	—	—	—	0.20	0.65
2005(o)	9,720,000	—	—	—	0.20	0.65

KM# 28 2 CENTS

3.8500 g., Bronze, 21.1 mm. **Ruler:** Elizabeth II **Obv:** Young bust right, date at right **Rev:** Palm fan and denomination **Rev. Designer:** Ken Payne

Date	Mintage	F	VF	XF	Unc	BU
1969(h)	8,000,000	—	—	0.10	0.50	0.75
1969 Proof	10,000	Value: 0.75				
1973(c)	2,110,000	—	0.10	0.15	0.75	2.50
1975(c)	1,500,000	—	0.10	0.15	0.75	1.50
1976(c)	1,004,999	—	0.10	0.15	0.75	1.50
1977	1,250,000	—	—	0.10	0.75	1.50
1978(c)	1,502,000	—	—	0.10	0.75	1.50
1978 Proof	2,000	Value: 3.50				
1979(c)	500,000	—	—	0.10	2.50	5.00
1980(c)	4,019,999	—	—	0.10	1.00	1.75
1980 Proof	2,500	Value: 2.50				
1981(c)	3,250,000	—	—	0.10	1.00	2.00
1982(c)	4,000,000	—	—	0.10	1.00	1.75
1982 Proof	3,000	Value: 2.00				
1983(c)	3,000,000	—	—	0.10	0.75	1.75
1983 Proof	3,000	Value: 1.50				
1984(c)	1,845,000	—	—	0.10	0.75	1.75
1985(c)	1,700,000	—	—	0.10	0.75	2.00

KM# 50 2 CENTS

3.8500 g., Bronze, 21.1 mm. **Ruler:** Elizabeth II **Obv:** Crowned head right, date at right **Rev:** Palm fan and denomination **Rev. Designer:** Ken Payne

Date	Mintage	F	VF	XF	Unc	BU
1986(c)	1,700,000	—	—	0.15	0.75	1.50
1987(c)	1,700,000	—	—	0.15	0.75	1.50

KM# 50a 2 CENTS

3.8500 g., Copper Plated Zinc, 21.1 mm. **Ruler:** Elizabeth II **Obv:** Crowned head right, date at right **Rev:** Palm fan and denomination

Date	Mintage	F	VF	XF	Unc	BU
1990(o)	5,500,000	—	—	—	0.75	1.00
1992(o)	10,000,000	—	—	—	0.50	1.00
1994(o)	6,000,000	—	—	—	0.35	2.00
1995(o)	5,000,000	—	—	—	0.35	1.00
2001(o)	2,830,000	—	—	—	0.30	0.85
2002(o)	5,000,000	—	—	—	0.30	0.85
2003(o)	6,410,000	—	—	—	0.30	0.85
2004(o)	7,050,000	—	—	—	0.30	0.85
2005(o)	7,760,000	—	—	—	0.30	0.85

KM# 29 5 CENTS

2.8000 g., Copper-Nickel, 19.35 mm. **Ruler:** Elizabeth II **Obv:** Young bust right, date at right **Rev:** Fijian drum - lali divides denomination **Rev. Designer:** Ken Payne

Date	Mintage	F	VF	XF	Unc	BU
1969(l)	9,200,000	—	0.10	0.20	0.75	1.00
1969 Proof	10,000	Value: 0.75				
1973(c)	600,000	—	0.10	0.30	1.50	2.00
1974(c)	608,000	—	0.10	0.30	1.25	2.00
1975(c)	1,008,000	—	0.10	0.20	1.00	2.00
1976(c)	1,205,000	—	0.10	0.20	1.00	2.00
1977	960,000	—	0.10	0.20	1.00	2.00
1978(c)	880,000	—	0.10	0.20	1.00	2.00
1978 Proof	2,000	Value: 5.00				
1979(c)	1,500,000	—	0.10	0.25	2.00	4.50
1980(c)	2,506,000	—	0.10	0.15	1.00	1.50
1980 Proof	2,500	Value: 3.50				
1981(c)	1,980,000	—	0.10	0.15	1.00	1.50
1982(c)	2,700,000	—	0.10	0.15	1.00	1.50
1982 Proof	3,000	Value: 3.00				
1983(c)	3,000,000	—	0.10	0.15	1.00	1.50
1983 Proof	3,000	Value: 2.00				
1984(c)	5,005,000	—	0.10	0.20	1.00	1.50

KM# 51 5 CENTS

2.8000 g., Copper-Nickel, 19.35 mm. **Ruler:** Elizabeth II **Obv:** Crowned head right, date at right **Rev:** Fijian drum - lali divides denomination **Rev. Designer:** Ken Payne

Date	Mintage	F	VF	XF	Unc	BU
1986(c)	1,200,000	—	0.10	0.20	1.00	1.50
1987(c)	1,200,000	—	0.10	0.20	1.00	2.00

KM# 51a 5 CENTS

2.3700 g., Nickel Bonded Steel, 19.35 mm. **Ruler:** Elizabeth II **Obv:** Crowned head right **Rev:** Fijian drum - lali divides denomination

Date	Mintage	F	VF	XF	Unc	BU
1990(o)	4,000,000	—	—	—	1.00	1.50
1992(o)	7,700,000	—	—	—	0.75	1.00
1994(o)	500,000	—	—	—	0.75	1.00
1995	—	—	—	—	0.75	2.50
1997(l)	4,000,000	—	—	—	0.75	1.00
1998(l)	3,000,000	—	—	—	0.75	1.00
1999(l)	3,000,000	—	—	—	0.75	1.00
2000(l)	3,000,000	—	—	—	0.75	1.00

KM# 77 5 CENTS

Nickel Bonded Steel, 19.35 mm. **Ruler:** Elizabeth II **Series:** F.A.O. **Subject:** Harvest From the Sea **Obv:** Crowned head right, date at right **Rev:** Fish, F.A.O. logo below denomination

Date	Mintage	F	VF	XF	Unc	BU
1995(o)	300,000	—	—	—	1.00	1.50

KM# 30 10 CENTS

5.6000 g., Copper-Nickel, 23.6 mm. **Ruler:** Elizabeth II **Rev:** Throwing club - ula tava tava **Rev. Designer:** Ken Payne

Date	Mintage	F	VF	XF	Unc	BU
1969	3,500,000	—	0.20	0.40	1.00	1.50
1969 Proof	10,000	Value: 1.00				
1973	750,000	—	0.20	0.50	2.50	4.00
1975	752,000	—	0.20	0.50	1.75	3.00
1976	805,000	—	0.20	0.50	1.50	2.50
1977	240,000	—	0.25	0.65	1.50	2.50
1978	664,000	—	0.20	0.50	1.50	2.50
1978 Proof	2,000	Value: 6.00				
1979	702,000	—	0.20	0.50	1.50	2.50
1980	1,000,000	—	0.15	0.30	1.50	2.50
1980 Proof	2,500	Value: 4.50				
1981	1,200,000	—	0.20	0.50	1.25	2.00
1982	1,500,000	—	0.20	0.50	1.25	2.00
1982 Proof	3,000	Value: 4.00				
1983	3,003,000	—	0.25	0.65	1.25	2.00
1983 Proof	3,000	Value: 3.00				
1984	5,000,000	—	0.25	0.65	1.25	2.00
1985	660,000	—	0.20	0.50	1.25	2.00

KM# 52 10 CENTS

5.6000 g., Copper-Nickel, 23.6 mm. **Ruler:** Elizabeth II **Obv:** Crowned head right, date at right **Rev:** Throwing club - ula tava tava divides denomination **Rev. Designer:** Ken Payne

Date	Mintage	F	VF	XF	Unc	BU
1986(c)	740,000	—	0.20	0.40	1.50	2.25
1987(c)	740,000	—	0.20	0.40	1.50	2.25

KM# 52a 10 CENTS

4.7600 g., Nickel Bonded Steel, 23.6 mm. **Ruler:** Elizabeth II **Obv:** Crowned head right **Rev:** Throwing club - ula tava tava

Date	Mintage	F	VF	XF	Unc	BU
1990	2,000,000	—	—	—	1.25	1.75
1992	31,640,000	—	—	—	1.25	1.75
1994	1,000,000	—	—	—	1.25	1.75
1995	736,000	—	—	—	1.25	2.00
1996	1,000,000	—	—	—	1.25	2.50
1997	2,000,000	—	—	—	1.00	1.50
1998(l)	2,000,000	—	—	—	1.00	1.25
1999(l)	2,000,000	—	—	—	1.00	1.25
2000(l)	1,340,000	—	—	—	1.00	1.25

KM# 31 20 CENTS

11.2500 g., Copper-Nickel, 28.5 mm. **Ruler:** Elizabeth II **Obv:** Young bust right, date at right **Rev:** Tabua on braided sennit cord divides denomination **Rev. Designer:** Ken Payne

Date	Mintage	F	VF	XF	Unc	BU
1969	2,000,000	—	0.30	0.80	1.50	2.00
1969 Proof	10,000	Value: 1.75				
1973	250,000	—	0.35	1.00	2.25	3.00
1974	252,000	—	0.35	0.75	2.00	2.75
1975	352,000	—	0.35	0.75	3.00	4.50
1976	405,000	—	0.25	0.65	1.75	2.25
1977	200,000	—	0.35	0.75	3.50	4.00
1978	406,000	—	0.25	0.50	1.75	2.25
1978 Proof	2,000	Value: 8.00				
1979	500,000	—	0.25	0.60	1.75	2.25
1980	1,014,000	—	0.25	0.60	1.75	2.25
1980 Proof	2,500	Value: 6.50				
1981	1,200,000	—	0.25	0.60	1.75	2.25
1982	1,500,000	—	0.25	0.60	1.50	2.00
1982 Proof	3,000	Value: 6.00				
1983	3,003,000	—	0.35	0.75	1.50	2.00
1983 Proof	3,000	Value: 5.00				
1984	5,005,000	—	0.35	0.75	1.50	2.00
1985	240,000	—	0.20	0.35	1.75	2.25

KM# 53 20 CENTS

11.2500 g., Copper-Nickel, 28.5 mm. **Ruler:** Elizabeth II **Obv:** Crowned head right, date at right **Rev:** Tabua on braided sennit cord divides denomination **Rev. Designer:** Ken Payne

Date	Mintage	F	VF	XF	Unc	BU
1986(c)	360,000	—	0.25	0.60	2.00	2.50
1987(c)	360,000	—	0.25	0.60	2.00	2.50

KM# 53a 20 CENTS

11.2500 g., Nickel Bonded Steel, 28.5 mm. **Ruler:** Elizabeth II **Obv:** Crowned head right **Rev:** Tabua on braided sennit cord divides denomination

Date	Mintage	F	VF	XF	Unc	BU
1990	1,500,000	—	0.20	0.35	1.50	2.00
1992	1,000,000	—	0.20	0.35	1.75	3.50
1994	500,000	—	0.20	0.35	1.50	3.00
1995	200,000	—	0.20	0.35	1.50	2.00
1996(l)	1,000,000	—	0.20	0.35	1.25	1.50
1997(l)	153,000	—	0.20	0.35	1.50	3.00
1998	1,000,000	—	0.20	0.35	1.25	1.50
1999(l)	1,000,000	—	0.20	0.35	1.25	1.50
2000(l)	1,000,000	—	0.20	0.35	1.25	1.50

KM# 95 20 CENTS

11.2400 g., Copper-Nickel, 28.5 mm. **Ruler:** Elizabeth II **Obv:** Crowned head right, date at right **Obv. Designer:** Raphael Maklouf **Rev:** South Pacific Games flame logo **Edge:** Reeded

Date	Mintage	F	VF	XF	Unc	BU
2003	1,540,000	—	—	—	1.50	2.50

KM# 36 50 CENTS

15.5500 g., Copper-Nickel, 31.5 mm. **Ruler:** Elizabeth II **Obv:** Young bust right, date at right **Rev:** Sailing canoe - Takia, denomination below **Shape:** 12-sided

Date	Mintage	F	VF	XF	Unc	BU
1975	1,000,000	—	0.75	1.50	4.00	6.50
1976	805,000	—	0.50	1.00	2.00	3.50
1978	4,006	—	1.25	2.00	5.00	6.50
1978 Proof	2,000	Value: 13.00				
1979(c)	258,000	—	0.75	1.00	5.00	6.50
1980	316,000	—	0.75	1.00	2.00	3.50
1980 Proof	2,500	Value: 11.50				
1981	511,000	—	0.75	1.00	4.00	7.00
1982	1,000,000	—	0.75	1.00	3.00	5.00
1982 Proof	3,000	Value: 10.00				
1983	3,000,000	—	0.65	1.00	2.50	4.00
1983 Proof	3,000	Value: 9.00				
1984	5,000,000	—	0.65	1.00	2.25	3.50

KM# 44 50 CENTS

15.5500 g., Copper-Nickel, 31.5 mm. **Ruler:** Elizabeth II **Series:** F.A.O. **Subject:** First Indians in Fiji Centennial **Obv:** Young bust right, date at right **Rev:** Rice plants, denomination and date at right **Shape:** 12-sided

Date	Mintage	F	VF	XF	Unc	BU
1979	258,000	—	—	—	2.50	—
1979 Proof	6,004	Value: 7.50				

KM# 45 50 CENTS

15.5500 g., Copper-Nickel, 31.5 mm. **Ruler:** Elizabeth II **Subject:** 10th Anniversary of Independence **Obv:** Arms with supporters, date below **Rev:** Prince Charles 3/4 facing, denomination below **Rev. Designer:** Michael Rizzello **Shape:** 12-sided

Date	Mintage	F	VF	XF	Unc	BU
1980	10,000	—	—	—	2.50	—

KM# 54 50 CENTS

15.5500 g., Copper-Nickel, 31.5 mm. **Ruler:** Elizabeth II **Obv:** Crowned head right, date at right **Rev:** Sailing canoe - Takia, denomination below **Shape:** 12-sided

Date	Mintage	F	VF	XF	Unc	BU
1986(c)	160,000	—	0.75	1.00	2.00	4.00
1987(c)	160,000	—	0.50	0.75	2.00	4.00

KM# 54a 50 CENTS

13.4300 g., Nickel Bonded Steel, 31.5 mm. **Ruler:** Elizabeth II **Obv:** Crowned head right **Rev:** Sailing canoe - Takia, denomination below **Shape:** 12-sided

Date	Mintage	F	VF	XF	Unc	BU
1990(o)	800,000	—	—	0.60	1.75	2.50
1992(o)	280,000	—	—	0.60	1.75	2.50
1994(o)	480,000	—	—	0.60	1.50	2.50
1995(l)	480,000	—	—	0.60	1.50	2.50
1996(l)	560,000	—	—	0.60	1.50	2.50
1997(l)	536,000	—	—	0.60	1.50	2.50
1998(l)	536,000	—	—	0.60	1.50	2.50
1999(l)	536,000	—	—	0.60	1.50	2.50
2000(l)	536,000	—	—	0.60	1.50	2.50

KM# 32 DOLLAR

Copper-Nickel, 38.5 mm. **Ruler:** Elizabeth II **Obv:** Young bust right **Rev:** Arms with supporters, date below

Date	Mintage	F	VF	XF	Unc	BU
1969	70,000	—	—	1.00	3.00	—
1969 Proof	10,000	Value: 3.50				
1976	5,007	—	1.00	2.00	5.00	—

KM# 73 DOLLAR

8.0400 g., Brass **Ruler:** Elizabeth II **Obv:** Crowned head right, date at right **Rev:** "Saqamoli" drinking vessel, denomination above

Date	Mintage	F	VF	XF	Unc	BU
1995	5,000,000	—	—	1.00	2.00	3.50
1996(I)	1,000,000	—	—	1.00	2.00	3.50
1997(I)	1,000,000	—	—	1.00	2.00	3.50
1998(I)	1,000,000	—	—	1.00	2.00	3.50
1999(I)	1,000,000	—	—	1.00	2.00	3.50
2000(I)	1,000,000	—	—	1.00	2.00	3.50

FINLAND

The Republic of Finland, the third northernmost state of the European continent, has an area of 130,559 sq. mi. (338,127 sq. km.) and a population of 5.1 million. Capital: Helsinki. Lumbering, shipbuilding, metal and woodworking are the leading industries. Paper, timber, wood pulp, plywood and metal products are exported.

The Finns, who probably originated in the Volga region of Russia, took Finland from the Lapps late in the 7th century. They were conquered in the 12th century by Eric IX of Sweden, and brought into contact with Western Christendom. In 1809, Sweden was conquered by Alexander I of Russia, and the peace terms gave Finland to Russia which became a grand duchy, with autonomy, within the Russian Empire until Dec. 6, 1917, when, shortly after the Bolshevik revolution it declared its independence. After a brief but bitter civil war between the Russian communists and Finnish nationalists in which the Whites (nationalists) were victorious, a new constitution was adopted, and on Dec. 6, 1917 Finland was established as a republic. In 1939 Soviet troops attacked Finland over disputed territorial concessions which were later granted in the peace treaty of 1940. When the Germans invaded Russia, Finland became involved and in the Armistice of 1944 lost the Petsamo area to the Soviets.

RULER

Nicholas II, 1894-1917

MONETARY SYSTEM

100 Pennia = 1 Markka

Commencing 1963

100 Old Markka = 1 New Markka

MINT MARKS

H - Birmingham 1921
Heart (h) - Copenhagen 1922
No mm – Helsinki

MINT OFFICIALS' INITIALS

Letter	Date	Name
H	1948-1958	Peippo Uolevi Helle
H-M	1990	Raimo Heino & Raimo Makkonen
K	1976-1983	Timo Koivuranta
K-H	1977, 1979	Timo Koivuranta & Heikki Haivaoja (Designer)
K-M	1983	Timo Koivuranta & Pertti Makinen
K-N	1978	Timo Koivuranta & Antti Neuvonen
K-T	1982	Timo Koivuranta & Erja Tielinen
L	1885-1912	Johan Conrad Lihr
L	1948	Vesa Uolevi Liuhto
L-M	1991	Arto Lappalainen & Raimo Makkonen
L-M	2000	Maija Lavonen & Raimo Makkonen
M	1987	Raimo Makkonen
M-G	1998	Raimo Makkonen & Henrik Gummerus
M-L	1997	Raimo Makkonen & Tero Lounas
M-L-L	1995	Raimo Makkonen & Arto Lappalainen & Marita Lappalainen
M-L-M	1989	Marjo Lahtinen & Raimo Makkonen
M-M	2004, 2006	Pertti Mäkinen & Raimo Makkonen
M-O	1998	Raimo Makkonen & Harri Ojala
M-S	1992, 1997	Raimo Makkonen & Erkki Salmela
N	1983-1987	Tapio Nevalainen
P-M	1989-1991, 1994-1995, 1997, 2000	Reijo Paavilainen & Raimo Makkonen
P-M	2003	Matti Peltokangas & Raimo Makkonen
P-N	1985	Reijo Paavilainen & Tapio Nevalainen
P-V-M	1999	Juhani Pallasmaa, Jukka Veistola & Raimo Makkonen
R-M	1999	Jarkko Roth & Raimo Makkonen
S	1912-1947	Isak Gustaf Sundell
S	1958-1975	Allan Alarik Soiniemi
S-H	1967-1971	Allan Alarik Soiniemi & Heikki Haivaoja (Designer)
S-J	1960	Allan Alarik Soiniemi & Toivo Jaatinen
S-M	1995	Terho Sakki & Raimo Makkonen
S-M	2003	Anneli Sijriläinen & Raimo Makkonen
T-M	1996, 2000	Erja Tielinen & Raimo Makkonen
W-M	2002	Erkki Vainio & Hannu Veijalainen & Raimo Makkonen

GRAND DUCHY

DECIMAL COINAGE

KM# 13 PENNI

1.2800 g., Copper, 15 mm. **Ruler:** Nicholas II **Obv:** Crowned monogram **Rev:** Denomination and date **Designer:** Aleksander Fadejev

Date	Mintage	F	VF	XF	Unc	BU
1901	1,520,000	0.75	1.25	2.50	8.00	—
1902	1,000,000	0.75	1.25	5.00	12.00	—
1903	1,145,000	0.75	1.25	5.00	12.00	—
Note: Small 3						
1903	Inc. above	1.50	2.50	10.00	20.00	—
Note: Large 3						
1904	500,000	2.50	5.00	10.00	20.00	—
1905	1,390,000	0.50	1.00	2.00	6.00	—
1906	1,020,000	0.50	1.00	2.00	5.00	—
1907	2,490,000	0.75	1.25	2.50	4.00	—
Note: Normal 7						
1907	Inc. above	0.30	0.75	1.75	4.00	—
Note: Without serif on 7 arm						
1908	950,000	0.50	1.00	3.00	7.00	—
1909	3,060,000	0.25	0.65	1.25	2.50	—
1911	2,550,000	0.25	0.65	1.25	2.50	—
1912	2,450,000	0.25	0.65	1.25	2.50	—
1913	1,650,000	0.25	0.65	1.25	3.00	—
1914	1,900,000	0.25	0.65	1.25	3.50	—
1915	2,250,000	0.25	0.65	1.25	2.50	—
1916	3,040,000	0.25	0.50	1.00	2.00	—

KM# 15 5 PENNIA

6.4000 g., Copper, 25 mm. **Ruler:** Nicholas II **Obv:** Crowned monogram **Rev:** Denomination and date **Designer:** Aleksander Fadejev

Date	Mintage	F	VF	XF	Unc	BU
1901	990,000	1.00	5.00	15.00	80.00	—
1905	620,000	2.00	10.00	40.00	125	—
1906	960,000	1.00	5.00	20.00	100	—
1907	770,000	2.00	10.00	75.00	150	—
1908	1,660,000	0.75	2.50	15.00	50.00	—
1910	60,000	25.00	50.00	120	250	—
1911	1,050,000	0.75	2.50	6.00	30.00	—
1912	460,000	1.50	5.00	25.00	75.00	—
1913	1,060,000	0.65	1.25	4.00	15.00	—
1914	820,000	0.65	1.25	3.00	15.00	—
1915	2,080,000	0.30	0.75	3.00	10.00	—
1916	4,470,000	0.30	0.75	3.00	10.00	—
1917	4,070,000	0.30	0.75	3.00	10.00	—

KM# 14 10 PENNIA

12.8000 g., Copper, 30 mm. **Ruler:** Nicholas II **Obv:** Crowned monogram **Rev:** Denomination and date within wreath **Designer:** Aleksander Fadejev

Date	Mintage	F	VF	XF	Unc	BU
1905	500,000	2.00	10.00	70.00	175	—
1907	503,000	2.00	10.00	70.00	175	—
1908	320,000	1.50	10.00	35.00	100	—
1909	180,000	3.00	20.00	100	225	—
1910	241,000	1.50	7.50	35.00	100	—
1911	370,000	1.00	5.00	20.00	60.00	—
1912	191,000	1.50	7.50	25.00	100	—
1913	150,000	2.50	10.00	50.00	150	—
1914	605,000	0.75	1.50	10.00	30.00	—
1915	420,000	0.50	1.00	5.00	15.00	—
1916	1,952,000	0.50	1.00	3.00	10.00	—
1917	1,600,000	0.75	1.50	4.00	12.00	—

KM# 6.2 25 PENNIA

1.2747 g., 0.7500 Silver 0.0307 oz. ASW, 16 mm. **Ruler:** Nicholas II **Obv:** Crowned imperial double eagle with sceptre and orb **Rev:** Denomination and date within wreath **Designer:** Aleksander Fadejev **Note:** Dentilated border.

Date	Mintage	F	VF	XF	Unc	BU
1901 L	993,000	1.00	2.00	8.00	35.00	—
1902 L	210,000	3.00	10.00	30.00	100	—
1906 L	281,000	2.00	5.00	15.00	60.00	—
1907 L	590,000	1.00	2.00	5.00	25.00	—
1908 L	340,000	1.00	2.50	20.00	50.00	—
1909 L	1,099,000	0.75	1.50	5.00	15.00	—
1910 L	392,000	2.50	5.00	15.00	50.00	—
1913 S	832,000	0.50	1.00	1.50	3.00	—
1915 S	2,400,000	0.50	0.75	1.00	1.50	—
1916 S	6,392,000	0.50	0.75	1.00	1.50	—
1917 S	5,820,000	0.50	0.75	1.00	1.50	—

KM# 2.2 50 PENNIA

2.5494 g., 0.7500 Silver 0.0615 oz. ASW, 18.6 mm. **Ruler:** Nicholas II **Obv:** Crowned imperial double eagle with sceptre and orb **Rev:** Denomination and date within wreath **Designer:** Aleksander Fadejev **Note:** Dentilated border.

Date	Mintage	F	VF	XF	Unc	BU
1907 L	260,000	1.00	5.00	30.00	90.00	—
1908 L	353,000	0.90	2.00	10.00	30.00	—
1911 L	616,000	0.85	1.25	2.50	5.00	—
1914 S	600,000	0.85	1.00	1.50	4.00	—
1915 S	1,000,000	0.85	1.00	1.50	2.50	—
1916 S	4,752,000	0.85	1.00	1.50	2.50	—
1917 S	3,972,000	0.85	1.00	1.50	2.50	—

KM# 3.2 MARKKA

5.1828 g., 0.8680 Silver 0.1446 oz. ASW, 24 mm. **Ruler:** Nicholas II **Obv:** Crowned imperial double eagle holding orb and scepter, fineness around (text in Finnish) **Rev:** Denomination and date within wreath **Designer:** Aleksander Fadejev **Note:** Obverse text translates to: "94.48 pieces from one pound of fine silver." Dentilated border.

Date	Mintage	F	VF	XF	Unc	BU
1907 L	350,000	6.00	8.00	10.00	25.00	—
1908 L	153,000	8.00	12.00	25.00	50.00	—
1915 S	1,212,000	5.00	7.00	10.00	12.00	—

KM# 7.2 2 MARKKAA

10.3657 g., 0.8680 Silver 0.2893 oz. ASW, 27.5 mm. **Ruler:** Nicholas II **Obv:** Crowned imperial double eagle holding orb and scepter, fineness around (Finnish text) **Rev:** Denomination and date within wreath **Designer:** Aleksander Fadejev **Note:** Obverse text translates to: "47.24 pieces from one pound of fine silver." Dentilated border.

Date	Mintage	F	VF	XF	Unc	BU
1905 L	24,000	100	170	500	1,200	—
1906 L	225,000	12.00	17.00	50.00	80.00	—
1907 L	125,000	15.00	25.00	75.00	250	—
1908 L	124,000	15.00	25.00	50.00	75.00	—

KM# 8.2 10 MARKKAA

3.2258 g., 0.9000 Gold 0.0933 oz. AGW, 18.9 mm. **Ruler:** Nicholas II **Obv:** Crowned imperial double eagle holding orb and scepter **Rev:** Denomination and date within circle, fineness around **Note:** Regal issues

Date	Mintage	F	VF	XF	Unc	BU
1904 L	102,000	250	350	400	500	—
1905 L	43,000	1,500	2,000	2,800	3,000	—
1913 S	396,000	100	150	175	200	—

KM# 9.2 20 MARKKAA
6.4516 g., 0.9000 Gold 0.1867 oz. AGW, 21.3 mm. **Ruler:** Nicholas II **Obv:** Crowned imperial double eagle holding orb and scepter **Rev:** Denomination and date within circle, fineness around **Note:** Regal issues.

Date	Mintage	F	VF	XF	Unc	BU
1903 L	112,000	170	185	210	230	—
1904 L	188,000	170	185	200	220	—
1910 L	201,000	170	185	200	220	—
1911 L	161,000	170	185	200	220	—
1912 L	881,000	2,500	4,500	6,000	7,000	—
1912 S	Inc. above	170	185	200	220	—
1913 S	214,000	170	185	200	220	—

CIVIL WAR COINAGE

Kerenski Government Issue

KM# 16 PENNI
1.2800 g., Copper, 15 mm. **Ruler:** Nicholas II

Date	Mintage	F	VF	XF	Unc	BU
1917	1,650,000	0.25	0.75	1.00	1.50	—

KM# 17 5 PENNIA
6.4000 g., Copper, 25 mm. **Ruler:** Nicholas II **Obv:** Imperial double eagle holding royal orb and scepter, shield on breast within circle **Rev:** Denomination above date

Date	Mintage	F	VF	XF	Unc	BU
1917	Inc. above	0.30	0.75	3.00	7.00	—

KM# 18 10 PENNIA
12.8000 g., Copper, 30 mm. **Ruler:** Nicholas II

Date	Mintage	F	VF	XF	Unc	BU
1917	Inc. above	0.50	1.00	4.00	10.00	—

KM# 19 25 PENNIA
1.2747 g., 0.7500 Silver 0.0307 oz. ASW, 16 mm. **Ruler:** Nicholas II **Obv:** Crown above eagle removed

Date	Mintage	F	VF	XF	Unc	BU
1917 S	2,310,000	—	BV	1.00	1.50	—

KM# 20 50 PENNIA
2.5494 g., 0.7500 Silver 0.0615 oz. ASW, 18.6 mm. **Ruler:** Nicholas II **Obv:** Imperial double eagle holding royal orb and scepter, shield on breast **Rev:** Denomination and date within wreath **Note:** No crown above eagle

Date	Mintage	F	VF	XF	Unc	BU
1917 S	570,000	—	BV	1.25	2.00	—

CIVIL WAR COINAGE

Liberated Finnish Government Issue

KM# 21 5 PENNIA
2.5000 g., Copper, 17.9 mm. **Obv:** Flag and 3 trumpets within wreath, wreath knot centered between 9 and 1 of date below **Obv. Legend:** • KANSAN TYÖ, KANSAN VALTA • - SUOMI - FINLAND **Rev:** Large value flanked by flower heads **Note:** Prev. KM#21.1. For previously listed KM#21.2, refer to Unusual World Coins, X#B1.

Date	Mintage	F	VF	XF	Unc	BU
1918	35,000	20.00	30.00	45.00	60.00	—

REPUBLIC

DECIMAL COINAGE

KM# 23 PENNI
1.0000 g., Copper, 14 mm. **Rev:** Denomination flanked by rosettes **Designer:** Isak Sundell

Date	Mintage	F	VF	XF	Unc	BU
1919	1,200,000	0.25	0.65	1.75	3.00	—
1920	720,000	0.25	0.65	1.75	3.00	—
1921	510,000	0.35	1.00	2.00	4.00	—
1922	1,060,000	0.25	0.65	1.75	3.00	—
1923	990,000	0.25	0.65	1.75	3.00	—
1924	2,180,000	0.25	0.65	1.75	3.00	—

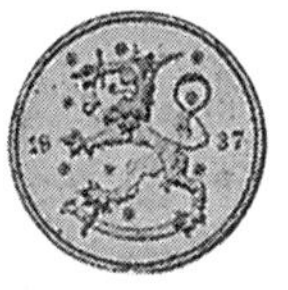

KM# 22 5 PENNIA
2.5000 g., Copper, 18 mm. **Obv:** Rampant lion left with sword divides date **Rev:** Rosettes flank denomination **Designer:** Isak Sundell

Date	Mintage	F	VF	XF	Unc	BU
1918	4,270,000	0.10	0.25	1.00	4.00	—
1919	4,640,000	0.10	0.25	1.00	4.00	—
1920	7,710,000	0.10	0.25	1.00	3.00	—
1921	5,910,000	0.10	0.25	1.00	3.00	—
1922	8,540,000	0.10	0.25	1.00	3.00	—
1927	1,520,000	0.75	1.50	3.50	15.00	—
1928	2,110,000	0.25	0.50	1.50	8.00	—
1929	1,500,000	0.25	0.50	1.50	8.00	—
1930	2,140,000	0.75	1.25	3.00	12.00	—
1932	2,130,000	0.15	0.50	1.00	4.00	—
1934	2,180,000	0.15	0.50	1.00	4.00	—
1935	1,610,000	0.15	0.35	1.00	3.00	—
1936	2,610,000	0.15	0.35	1.00	3.00	—
1937	3,830,000	0.10	0.25	1.00	3.00	—
1938	4,300,000	0.10	0.25	1.00	3.00	—
1939	2,270,000	0.10	0.25	1.00	3.00	—
1940	1,610,000	0.25	0.50	1.50	5.00	—

KM# 64.1 5 PENNIA
1.2700 g., Copper, 16 mm. **Obv:** Rosette above center hole flanked by leaves dividing date below **Rev:** Center hole divides denomination, rosettes flank **Designer:** Isak Sundell **Note:** Punched center hole.

Date	Mintage	F	VF	XF	Unc	BU
1941	5,950,000	0.10	0.20	0.50	1.25	—
1942	4,280,000	0.10	0.20	0.50	1.25	—
1943	1,530,000	0.10	0.50	1.25	2.50	—

KM# 64.2 5 PENNIA
Copper, 16 mm. **Designer:** Isak Sundell **Note:** Without punched center hole. These issues were not authorized by the government and any that exist were illegally removed from the mint.

Date	Mintage	F	VF	XF	Unc	BU
1941	Inc. above	25.00	30.00	70.00	100	—
1942	Inc. above	25.00	30.00	70.00	100	—
1943	Inc. above	50.00	70.00	100	125	—

KM# 24 10 PENNIA
5.0000 g., Copper, 22 mm. **Obv:** Rampant lion left, holding sword, divides date **Designer:** Isak Sundell

Date	Mintage	F	VF	XF	Unc	BU
1919	3,670,000	0.10	0.25	1.00	5.00	—
1920	2,380,000	0.10	0.25	1.00	5.00	—
1921	3,970,000	0.10	0.25	1.00	5.00	—
1922	2,180,000	0.10	0.25	2.00	7.00	—
1923	910,000	1.00	2.00	10.00	30.00	—
1924	1,350,000	0.25	0.50	3.00	12.00	—
1926	1,690,000	0.25	0.50	2.00	10.00	—
1927	1,330,000	0.50	1.00	5.00	15.00	—
1928	1,006,000	0.50	1.00	2.50	10.00	—
1929	1,560,000	0.35	0.85	2.00	7.00	—
1930	650,000	0.75	1.50	7.00	15.00	—
1931	1,040,000	1.00	2.00	10.00	30.00	—
1934	1,680,000	0.35	0.85	2.00	7.00	—
1935	1,690,000	0.15	0.25	1.00	5.00	—
1936	2,009,999	0.15	0.25	1.00	5.00	—
1937	2,420,000	0.10	0.25	0.50	3.50	—
1938	2,940,000	0.10	0.25	0.50	3.50	—
1939	2,100,000	0.10	0.25	0.50	3.50	—
1940	2,009,999	0.25	0.50	1.00	5.00	—

KM# 33.1 10 PENNIA
2.5500 g., Copper, 18.5 mm. **Obv:** Rosette above center hole flanked by leaves dividing date below **Rev:** Center hole divides denomination, rosettes flank **Designer:** Isak Sundell

Date	Mintage	F	VF	XF	Unc	BU
1941	3,610,000	0.10	0.25	0.50	1.25	—
1942	4,970,000	0.10	0.25	0.50	1.25	—
1943	1,860,000	0.25	0.75	1.50	2.50	—

KM# 33.2 10 PENNIA
2.6000 g., Copper, 18.5 mm. **Obv:** Rosette above center hole flanked by leaves dividing date below **Rev:** Center hole divides denomination, rosettes flank **Designer:** Isak Sundell **Note:** Without punched center hole. These issues were not authorized by the government and any that exist were illegally removed from the mint.

Date	Mintage	F	VF	XF	Unc	BU
1941	Inc. above	20.00	30.00	50.00	75.00	—
1942	Inc. above	20.00	30.00	50.00	75.00	—
1943	Inc. above	30.00	50.00	70.00	100	—

KM# 34.2 10 PENNIA
Iron **Obv:** Sprigs divide date, rosette above **Rev:** Rosettes and denomination **Designer:** Isak Sundell **Note:** Without punched center hole. These issues were not authorized by the government and any that exist were illegally removed from the mint.

Date	Mintage	F	VF	XF	Unc	BU
1943	Inc. above	30.00	50.00	70.00	100	—
1944	Inc. above	30.00	50.00	70.00	100	—
1945	Inc. above	50.00	70.00	100	150	—

KM# 34.1 10 PENNIA
1.1200 g., Iron, 16 mm. **Obv:** Rosette above center hole flanked by leaves dividing date below **Rev:** Center hole flanked by rosettes divides denomination **Designer:** Isak Sundell **Note:** Reduced planchet size.

Date	Mintage	F	VF	XF	Unc	BU
1943	1,430,000	0.10	0.25	1.00	5.00	—
1944	3,040,000	0.10	0.25	1.00	5.00	—
1945	1,810,000	0.25	0.50	2.00	10.00	—

KM# 25 25 PENNIA
1.2700 g., Copper-Nickel, 16 mm. **Obv:** Rampant lion left holding sword divides date **Rev:** Denomination flanked by grain sprigs **Designer:** Isak Sundell

Date	Mintage	F	VF	XF	Unc	BU
1921 H	20,096,000	0.10	0.25	1.00	3.00	—
1925 S	1,250,000	0.50	1.50	15.00	25.00	—
1926 S	2,820,000	0.40	1.25	5.00	12.00	—
1927 S	1,120,000	0.50	1.50	10.00	20.00	—
1928 S	2,920,000	0.40	1.00	5.00	12.00	—
1929 S	200,000	2.00	4.00	25.00	50.00	—
1930 S	1,090,000	0.50	1.50	5.00	15.00	—
1934 S	1,260,000	0.40	0.75	3.00	10.00	—
1935 S	2,190,000	0.30	0.50	2.00	8.00	—
1936 S	2,300,000	0.20	0.40	2.00	5.00	—
1937 S	4,019,999	0.20	0.40	1.00	3.00	—
1938 S	4,500,000	0.20	0.40	1.00	3.00	—
1939 S	2,712,000	0.20	0.40	1.00	3.00	—
1940 S	4,840,000	0.15	0.30	0.75	2.00	—

KM# 25a 25 PENNIA
1.2700 g., Copper, 16 mm. **Obv:** Rampant lion left divides date **Rev:** Grain sprigs flank denomination **Designer:** Isak Sundell

Date	Mintage	F	VF	XF	Unc	BU
1940 S	72,000	0.50	1.00	5.00	20.00	—
1941 S	5,980,000	0.10	0.35	2.00	5.00	—
1942 S	6,464,000	0.10	0.35	2.00	5.00	—
1943 S	4,912,000	0.25	0.50	2.00	7.00	—

KM# 25b 25 PENNIA
Iron, 16 mm. **Obv:** Rampant lion left divides dates **Rev:** Grain sprigs flank denomination **Designer:** Isak Sundell

Date	Mintage	F	VF	XF	Unc	BU
1943 S	2,700,000	0.15	0.50	3.00	12.00	—
1944 S	5,480,000	0.15	0.50	2.00	8.00	—
Note: Small closed 4's						
1944 S	Inc. above	0.15	0.50	2.00	8.00	—
Note: Large open 4's						
1945 S	6,810,000	0.25	0.75	3.00	12.00	—

KM# 26 50 PENNIA
2.5500 g., Copper-Nickel, 18.5 mm. **Obv:** Rampant lion left divides date **Designer:** Isak Sundell

Date	Mintage	F	VF	XF	Unc	BU
1921 H	10,072,000	0.15	0.30	1.00	3.00	—
1923 S	6,000,000	0.25	1.00	3.00	12.00	—
1929 S	984,000	1.00	2.00	15.00	40.00	—
1934 S	612,000	1.00	2.50	15.00	40.00	—
1935 S	610,000	1.00	2.50	10.00	35.00	—
1936 S	1,520,000	0.30	0.50	3.00	12.00	—
1937 S	2,350,000	0.15	0.25	1.00	5.00	—
1938 S	2,330,000	0.15	0.25	1.00	5.00	—
1939 S	1,280,000	0.15	0.25	1.00	5.00	—
1940 S	3,152,000	0.15	0.25	1.00	3.00	—

KM# 26a 50 PENNIA
2.5500 g., Copper, 18.5 mm. **Obv:** Rampant lion left divides date **Rev:** Grain sprigs flank denomination **Designer:** Isak Sundell

Date	Mintage	F	VF	XF	Unc	BU
1940 S	480,000	1.25	2.50	8.00	20.00	—
1941 S	3,860,000	0.15	0.40	3.00	8.00	—
1942 S	5,900,000	0.15	0.40	3.00	8.00	—
1943 S	3,140,000	0.25	0.50	3.00	8.00	—

KM# 26b 50 PENNIA
2.2500 g., Iron, 18.5 mm. **Obv:** Rampant lion left divides date **Rev:** Grain sprigs flank denomination **Designer:** Isak Sundell

Date	Mintage	F	VF	XF	Unc	BU
1943 S	1,580,000	0.25	0.50	5.00	20.00	—
1944 S	7,600,000	0.15	0.40	3.00	12.00	—
1945 S	4,700,000	0.15	0.40	3.00	15.00	—
1946 S	2,632,000	0.30	0.50	3.00	15.00	—
1947 S	1,748,000	0.50	2.00	10.00	25.00	—
1948 L	1,112,000	3.00	10.00	20.00	35.00	—

KM# 27 MARKKA
5.1000 g., Copper-Nickel, 24 mm. **Designer:** Isak Sundell

Date	Mintage	F	VF	XF	Unc	BU
1921 H	10,048,000	1.00	2.00	3.00	10.00	—
1922 Heart	10,000,000	1.00	2.00	5.00	15.00	—
1923 S	1,780,000	10.00	20.00	35.00	70.00	—
1924 S	3,270,000	5.00	10.00	20.00	40.00	—

KM# 30 MARKKA
4.0000 g., Copper-Nickel, 21 mm. **Obv:** Rampant lion left divides date **Rev:** Denomination flanked by branches **Designer:** Isak Sundell **Note:** Reduced size.

Date	Mintage	F	VF	XF	Unc	BU
1928 S	3,000,000	0.15	1.00	5.00	20.00	—
1929 S	3,862,000	0.15	1.00	5.00	20.00	—
1930 S	10,284,000	0.15	1.00	5.00	15.00	—
1931 S	2,830,000	0.15	1.00	5.00	15.00	—
1932 S	4,140,000	0.15	1.00	5.00	15.00	—
1933 S	4,032,000	0.15	1.00	5.00	15.00	—
1936 S	562,000	1.00	3.00	15.00	50.00	—
1937 S	4,930,000	0.15	1.00	3.00	6.00	—
1938 S	4,410,000	0.15	1.00	3.00	6.00	—
1939 S	3,070,000	0.15	1.00	3.00	6.00	—
1940 S	3,372,000	0.15	1.00	3.00	6.00	—

Note: Coins dated 1928S, 1929S and 1930S are known to be restruck on 1921-24, KM#27 coins; 1928S: 2 or 3 known

KM# 30a MARKKA
4.0000 g., Copper, 21 mm. **Obv:** Rampant lion left divides date **Rev:** Denomination flanked by branches **Designer:** Isak Sundell

Date	Mintage	F	VF	XF	Unc	BU
1940 S	84,000	1.50	3.50	8.00	20.00	—
1941 S	8,970,000	0.15	0.50	2.00	8.00	—
1942 S	11,200,000	0.15	0.50	2.00	8.00	—
1943 S	7,460,000	0.15	0.50	2.00	8.00	—
1949 H	250	3,000	4,000	6,000	8,000	—
Note: Counterfeits exist						
1950 H	320,000	0.50	1.00	3.00	10.00	—
1951 H	4,630,000	0.25	0.50	2.00	8.00	—

KM# 30b MARKKA
3.5000 g., Iron, 21 mm. **Obv:** Rampant lion left divides date **Rev:** Branches flank denomination **Designer:** Isak Sundell

Date	Mintage	F	VF	XF	Unc	BU
1943 S	7,460,000	0.15	0.25	5.00	20.00	—
1944 S	12,830,000	0.15	0.25	5.00	20.00	—
1945 S	21,950,000	0.15	0.25	5.00	20.00	—
1946 S	2,630,000	0.15	0.30	5.00	20.00	—
1947 S	1,750,000	0.25	0.50	5.00	25.00	—
1948 L	20,500,000	0.15	0.25	3.00	10.00	—
1949 H	17,358,000	0.15	0.25	2.00	8.00	—
1950 H	14,654,000	0.15	0.25	2.00	7.00	—
1951 H	21,414,000	0.15	0.25	2.00	7.00	—
1952 H	5,410,000	0.25	0.50	5.00	20.00	—

KM# 36 MARKKA
1.1500 g., Iron, 16 mm. **Obv:** Four joined loops form design, date below **Rev:** Grasped hands flank denomination **Designer:** Peippo Uolevi Helle

Date	Mintage	F	VF	XF	Unc	BU
1952	22,050,000	0.15	0.35	1.00	7.00	—
1953	28,618,000	0.15	0.35	1.00	7.00	—

KM# 36a MARKKA
1.1500 g., Nickel Plated Iron, 16 mm. **Obv:** Four joined loops form design, date below **Rev:** Grasped hands flank denomination **Designer:** Peippo Uolevi Helle

Date	Mintage	F	VF	XF	Unc	BU
1953	6,000,000	5.00	8.00	15.00	25.00	—
1954	36,400,000	—	0.10	0.25	0.50	—
1955	38,100,000	—	0.10	0.25	0.50	—
1956	35,600,000	—	0.10	0.25	1.00	—
1957	29,100,000	—	0.10	0.25	0.50	—
1958	19,940,000	0.10	0.20	0.35	0.70	—
1959	23,920,000	—	0.10	0.25	0.50	—
Note: Thick letters						
1959	Inc. above	—	0.10	0.25	1.00	—
Note: Thin letters						
1960	22,020,000	—	0.10	0.25	0.50	—
1961	32,220,000	—	0.10	0.25	0.50	—
1962	29,040,000	—	0.10	0.25	0.50	—

KM# 31 5 MARKKAA
4.5000 g., Aluminum-Bronze, 23 mm. **Obv:** Wreath divides denomination **Rev:** Shielded arms within wreath divide date **Designer:** Isak Sundell

Date	Mintage	F	VF	XF	Unc	BU
1928 S	580,000	50.00	80.00	150	350	—
1929 S	Inc. above	50.00	80.00	150	350	—
1930 S	592,000	1.00	3.00	40.00	100	—
1931 S	3,090,000	1.00	2.00	20.00	40.00	—
1932 S	964,000	10.00	25.00	200	400	—
1933 S	1,050,000	1.00	3.00	30.00	100	—
1935 S	440,000	2.00	5.00	30.00	100	—
1936 S	470,000	2.00	5.00	30.00	100	—
1937 S	1,032,000	1.00	3.00	20.00	40.00	—
1938 S	912,000	1.00	3.00	20.00	40.00	—
1939 S	752,000	1.00	3.00	20.00	40.00	—
1940 S	820,000	2.00	5.00	25.00	50.00	—
1941 S	1,452,000	1.00	3.00	12.00	25.00	—
1942 S	1,390,000	1.00	2.00	10.00	20.00	—
1946 S	618,000	5.00	10.00	30.00	100	—

KM# 31a 5 MARKKAA
4.5500 g., Brass, 23 mm. **Obv:** Denomination divided by wreath **Rev:** Shielded arms within wreath divides date below **Designer:** Isak Sundell

Date	Mintage	F	VF	XF	Unc	BU
1946 S	5,538,000	0.50	1.00	2.00	7.00	—
1947 S	6,550,000	1.00	2.00	3.00	12.00	—
1948 L	8,210,000	0.50	1.00	2.00	10.00	—
1949 H	11,014,000	2.00	5.00	10.00	20.00	—
Note: Thin H						
1949 H	Inc. above	1.00	2.00	3.00	7.00	—
Note: Wide H						
1950 H	4,760,000	0.50	1.00	3.00	7.00	—
1951 H	7,800,000	0.50	1.00	2.00	5.00	—
1952 H	1,210,000	3.00	8.00	15.00	30.00	—

KM# 37 5 MARKKAA
2.5500 g., Iron, 18 mm. **Obv:** Four joined loops form design, date below **Rev:** Grasped hands flank denomination **Designer:** Peippo Uolevi Helle

Date	Mintage	F	VF	XF	Unc	BU
1952	10,820,000	0.20	0.35	2.00	8.00	—
1953	9,772,000	0.20	0.35	3.00	10.00	—

KM# 37a 5 MARKKAA
2.5500 g., Nickel Plated Iron, 18 mm. **Obv:** Four joined loops form design, date below **Rev:** Grasped hands flank denomination **Designer:** Peippo Uolevi Helle

Date	Mintage	F	VF	XF	Unc	BU
1953	Inc. above	60.00	100	130	200	—
1954	6,696,000	—	0.20	1.00	5.00	—
1955	9,894,000	—	0.20	1.00	5.00	—
1956	8,220,000	—	0.20	1.00	5.00	—
1957	4,276,000	—	0.20	1.00	5.00	—
1958	3,300,000	—	0.20	1.00	7.00	—
1959	5,874,000	—	0.20	1.00	5.00	—
1960	3,066,000	0.10	0.25	1.00	5.00	—
1961	7,254,000	0.10	0.25	0.50	3.00	—
1962	4,542,000	0.50	2.00	5.00	8.00	—

KM# 63 10 MARKKAA
8.0000 g., Aluminum-Bronze, 27 mm. **Obv:** Wreath divides denomination **Rev:** Shielded arms within wreath divide date below **Designer:** Isak Sundell

Date	Mintage	F	VF	XF	Unc	BU
1928 S	730,000	3.00	15.00	70.00	200	—
1929 S	Inc. above	2.00	8.00	50.00	150	—
1930 S	260,000	1.00	5.00	35.00	100	—
1931 S	1,530,000	1.00	3.00	20.00	90.00	—
1932 S	1,010,000	1.00	2.50	10.00	70.00	—
1934 S	154,000	2.00	8.00	50.00	120	—
1935 S	81,000	3.00	12.00	70.00	180	—
1936 S	304,000	2.00	8.00	50.00	100	—
1937 S	181,000	1.50	5.00	20.00	90.00	—
1938 S	631,000	1.00	3.00	15.00	60.00	—
1939 S	133,000	5.00	10.00	30.00	75.00	—

KM# 38 10 MARKKAA
3.0000 g., Aluminum-Bronze, 20 mm. **Obv:** Rampant lion left within circle, date below **Rev:** Tree right of denomination **Designer:** Peippo Uolevi Helle

Date	Mintage	F	VF	XF	Unc	BU
1952 H	6,390,000	0.20	1.00	5.00	12.00	—
1953 H	22,650,000	0.15	0.35	1.00	5.00	—
1954 H	2,452,000	0.50	1.00	5.00	15.00	—
1955 H	2,342,000	0.20	0.50	5.00	12.00	—
1956 H	4,240,000	0.20	0.40	3.00	10.00	—
1958 H	3,292,000	3.00	10.00	20.00	35.00	—
Note: Thin 1						
1958 H	Inc. above	0.20	0.40	3.00	8.00	—
Note: Wide 1						
1960 S	740,000	2.00	5.00	10.00	20.00	—
1961 S	3,580,000	2.00	5.00	10.00	20.00	—
Note: Wide 1						
1961 S	Inc. above	0.20	0.50	2.00	5.00	—
1962 S	1,852,000	0.30	1.00	3.00	7.00	—

Note: The "1" in the denomination on all 1952 to 1956 issues is the thin variety; 1960 issues are the wide variety, and 1961's and 1962's are thin; Varieties exist in root length of tree

KM# 32 20 MARKKAA
13.0000 g., Aluminum-Bronze, 31 mm. **Obv:** Wreath divides denomination **Rev:** Shielded arms within wreath divide date below **Designer:** Isak Sundell

Date	Mintage	F	VF	XF	Unc	BU
1931 S	16,000	20.00	30.00	50.00	75.00	—
1932 S	14,000	30.00	40.00	60.00	90.00	—
1934 S	390,000	2.00	10.00	50.00	100	—
1935 S	250,000	2.00	10.00	50.00	100	—
1936 S	110,000	3.00	15.00	50.00	150	—
1937 S	510,000	1.50	5.00	15.00	50.00	—
1938 S	360,000	1.50	5.00	15.00	50.00	—
1939 S	960,000	1.00	2.00	6.00	20.00	—

KM# 39 20 MARKKAA

4.5000 g., Aluminum-Bronze, 25.5 mm. **Obv:** Rampant lion left within circle, date below **Rev:** Tree right of denomination **Designer:** Peippo Uolevi Helle

Date	Mintage	F	VF	XF	Unc	BU
1952 H	83,000	7.00	10.00	20.00	40.00	—
1953 H	2,880,000	0.25	0.50	3.00	15.00	—
1954 H	17,034,000	0.15	0.50	2.00	10.00	—
1955 H	2,800,000	0.25	0.50	5.00	15.00	—
1956 H	2,540,000	0.25	0.50	5.00	15.00	—
1957 H	1,050,000	0.50	1.00	8.00	20.00	—
1958 H	515,000	2.50	5.00	20.00	40.00	—
1959 S	1,580,000	0.25	0.50	5.00	15.00	—
1960 S	3,850,000	0.15	0.50	3.00	10.00	—
1961 S	4,430,000	0.15	0.50	3.00	10.00	—
1962 S	2,280,000	0.15	0.50	3.00	8.00	—

KM# 40 50 MARKKAA

5.5000 g., Aluminum-Bronze, 25 mm. **Obv:** Rampant lion left within circle, date below **Rev:** Tree right of denomination **Designer:** Peippo Uolevi Helle

Date	Mintage	F	VF	XF	Unc	BU
1952 H	991,000	2.00	5.00	20.00	40.00	—
1953 H	10,300,000	0.25	0.50	3.00	10.00	—
1954 H	1,170,000	2.00	5.00	20.00	40.00	—
1955 H	583,000	2.50	5.00	25.00	50.00	—
1956 H	792,000	2.00	5.00	20.00	40.00	—
1958 H	242,000	25.00	40.00	60.00	75.00	—
1960 S	110,000	25.00	50.00	75.00	100	—
1961 S	1,811,000	1.00	2.00	5.00	15.00	—
1962 S	405,000	2.00	4.00	15.00	25.00	—

KM# 28 100 MARKKAA

4.2105 g., 0.9000 Gold 0.1218 oz. AGW, 18.5 mm. **Obv:** Rampant lion left divides date **Rev:** Denomination flanked by sprigs **Designer:** Isak Sundell

Date	Mintage	F	VF	XF	Unc	BU
1926 S	50,000	—	950	1,150	1,300	—

KM# 41 100 MARKKAA

5.2000 g., 0.5000 Silver 0.0836 oz. ASW, 24 mm. **Obv:** Shielded arms above date **Rev:** Denomination surrounded by trees and tree tops **Designer:** Peippo Uolevi Helle

Date	Mintage	F	VF	XF	Unc	BU
1956 H	3,012,000	—	BV	1.50	3.00	—
1957 H	3,012,000	—	BV	1.50	3.00	—
1958 H	1,704,000	BV	2.00	5.00	8.00	—
1959 S	1,270,000	5.00	7.50	18.00	25.00	—
1960 S	290,000	3.50	7.00	12.00	18.00	—

KM# 29 200 MARKKAA

8.4210 g., 0.9000 Gold 0.2437 oz. AGW, 22.5 mm. **Obv:** Rampant lion left divides date **Rev:** Denomination flanked by sprigs **Designer:** Isak Sundell

Date	Mintage	F	VF	XF	Unc	BU
1926 S	50,000	—	1,300	1,800	2,000	—

KM# 42 200 MARKKAA

8.3000 g., 0.5000 Silver 0.1334 oz. ASW, 27.5 mm. **Obv:** Shielded arms above date **Rev:** Denomination surrounded by trees and tree tops **Designer:** Peippo Uolevi Helle

Date	Mintage	F	VF	XF	Unc	BU
1956 H	1,552,000	—	BV	3.00	7.00	—
1957 H	2,157,000	—	BV	3.00	7.00	—
1958 H	1,477,000	BV	2.50	5.00	10.00	—
1958 S	34,000	400	600	750	850	—
1959 S	70,000	25.00	40.00	55.00	70.00	—

KM# 35 500 MARKKAA

12.0000 g., 0.5000 Silver 0.1929 oz. ASW, 32 mm. **Obv:** Wreath divides denomination **Rev:** Olympic logo above date **Designer:** Aarre Aaltonen and Matti Visanti

Date	Mintage	F	VF	XF	Unc	BU
1951 H	19,000	200	300	375	425	—
1952 H	586,000	20.00	28.00	40.00	50.00	—

REFORM COINAGE

100 Old Markka = 1 New Markka 1963

KM# 44 PENNI

1.6000 g., Copper, 15.8 mm. **Obv:** Four joined loops form design, date below **Rev:** Grasped hands flank denomination **Designer:** Peippo Uolevi Helle

Date	Mintage	F	VF	XF	Unc	BU
1963	171,333,000	—	0.15	0.25	1.50	—
Note: Struck at Leningrad Mint						
1964	49,300,000	—	0.15	0.50	2.00	—
1965	43,112,000	—	0.15	0.50	2.00	—
1966	36,880,000	—	0.15	0.50	2.00	—
1967	62,792,000	—	0.15	0.50	2.00	—
1968	73,416,000	—	—	0.50	2.00	—
1969	51,748,000	—	—	0.50	2.00	—

KM# 44a PENNI

0.4500 g., Aluminum, 15.8 mm. **Obv:** Four joined loops form design, date below **Rev:** Grasped hands flank denomination **Designer:** Peippo Uolevi Helle

Date	Mintage	F	VF	XF	Unc	BU
1969	28,524,000	—	—	0.50	2.00	—
1970	85,140,000	—	—	0.20	1.00	—
1971	70,240,000	—	—	0.20	1.00	—
1972	95,096,000	—	—	0.20	1.00	—
1973	115,532,000	—	—	0.20	0.50	—
1974	100,132,000	—	—	0.20	0.50	—
1975	111,906,000	—	—	0.20	0.50	—
1976	34,965,000	—	—	0.20	0.50	—
1977	61,393,000	—	—	0.20	0.50	—
1978	90,132,000	—	—	0.20	0.50	—
1979	33,388,000	—	—	0.20	0.50	—

KM# 45 5 PENNIA

2.6000 g., Copper, 18.5 mm. **Obv:** Four joined loops form design, date below **Rev:** Grasped hands flank denomination **Designer:** Peippo Uolevi Helle

Date	Mintage	F	VF	XF	Unc	BU
1963	60,320,000	—	0.15	0.50	1.50	—
1964	4,634,000	0.50	1.00	5.00	15.00	—
1965	10,264,000	—	0.15	0.50	2.00	—
1966	8,064,000	—	0.15	0.50	3.00	—
1967	9,968,000	—	0.15	0.50	2.00	—
1968	6,144,000	—	0.15	0.50	2.00	—
1969	3,598,000	—	0.15	0.50	2.00	—
1970	13,772,000	—	0.15	0.25	1.00	—
1971	20,010,000	—	—	0.25	1.00	—
1972	24,122,000	—	—	0.25	1.00	—
1973	25,644,000	—	—	0.25	1.00	—
1974	21,530,000	—	—	0.25	1.00	—
1975	25,010,000	—	—	0.25	1.00	—
1976	25,551,000	—	—	0.25	1.00	—
1977	1,489,000	—	0.10	0.50	1.50	—

KM# 45a 5 PENNIA

0.8000 g., Aluminum, 18 mm. **Obv:** Four joined loops form design, date below **Rev:** Grasped hands flank denomination **Designer:** Peippo Uolevi Helle

Date	Mintage	F	VF	XF	Unc	BU
1977	30,552,000	—	—	0.15	0.50	—
1978	26,112,000	—	—	0.15	0.50	—
1979	40,042,000	—	—	0.15	0.50	—
1980	60,026,000	—	—	0.15	0.50	—
1981	2,044,000	—	0.20	0.40	1.00	—
1982	10,012,000	—	—	0.25	0.75	—
1983	33,885,000	—	—	—	0.25	—
1984	25,001,000	—	—	—	0.25	—
1985	25,000,000	—	—	—	0.25	—
1986	20,000,000	—	—	—	0.25	—
1987	2,020,000	—	—	—	0.25	—
1988	33,005,000	—	—	—	0.15	—
1989	2,200,000	—	—	—	0.50	—
1990	2,506,000	—	—	—	0.50	—

KM# 46 10 PENNIA

3.0000 g., Aluminum-Bronze, 20 mm. **Obv:** Rampant lion left, date below **Rev:** Tree right of denomination **Designer:** Peippo Uolevi Helle

Date	Mintage	F	VF	XF	Unc	BU
1963 S	38,420,000	—	0.15	0.50	1.50	—
1964 S	6,926,000	—	0.15	1.00	3.00	—
1965 S	4,524,000	—	0.15	0.50	3.00	—
1966 S	3,094,000	—	0.15	0.50	2.00	—
1967 S	1,050,000	0.15	0.30	3.00	10.00	—
1968 S	3,004,000	—	0.15	0.25	1.50	—
1969 S	5,046,000	—	—	0.20	1.50	—
1970 S	3,996,000	—	—	0.20	1.50	—
1971 S	15,026,000	—	—	0.10	1.00	—
1972 S	19,900,000	—	—	0.10	1.00	—
1973 S	9,196,000	—	—	0.10	1.00	—
1974 S	8,930,000	—	—	0.10	1.00	—
1975 S	15,064,000	—	—	0.10	0.50	—
1976 K	10,063,000	—	—	0.10	0.50	—
1977 K	10,043,000	—	—	0.10	0.50	—
1978 K	10,062,000	—	—	0.10	0.50	—
1979 K	13,072,000	—	—	0.10	0.50	—
1980 K	23,654,000	—	—	0.10	0.50	—
1981 K	30,036,000	—	—	0.10	0.50	—
1982 K	35,548,000	—	—	0.10	0.50	—

KM# 46a 10 PENNIA

1.0000 g., Aluminum, 20 mm. **Obv:** Rampant lion left, date below **Rev:** Tree right of denomination **Designer:** Peippo Uolevi Helle

Date	Mintage	F	VF	XF	Unc	BU
1983 K	6,320,000	—	—	0.25	1.00	—
1983 N	4,191,000	—	—	0.25	1.00	—
1984 N	20,061,000	—	—	0.10	0.50	—
1985 N	20,000,000	—	—	0.10	0.50	—
1986 N	15,000,000	—	—	0.10	0.50	—
1987 M	8,654,000	—	—	0.25	1.00	—
1987 N	1,400,000	—	—	0.25	1.00	—
1988 M	23,197,000	—	—	0.10	0.50	—
1989 M	2,400,000	—	—	0.25	0.50	—
1990 M	2,254,000	—	—	0.25	0.50	—

KM# 65 10 PENNIA

1.8000 g., Copper-Nickel, 16.3 mm. **Obv:** Flower pods and stems, date at right **Rev:** Denomination to right of honeycombs **Designer:** Antti Neuvonen

Date	Mintage	F	VF	XF	Unc	BU
1990 M	338,100,000	—	—	0.10	0.15	—
1991 M	263,899,000	—	—	0.10	0.15	—

Date	Mintage	F	VF	XF	Unc	BU
1992 M	136,131,000	—	—	0.10	0.15	—
1993 M	56,206,000	—	—	0.10	0.15	—
1994 M	59,946,000	—	—	0.10	0.15	—
1994 M Proof	5,000	Value: 7.00				
1995 M	85,000,000	—	—	0.10	0.15	—
1995 M Proof	3,000	Value: 7.00				
1996 M	123,000,000	—	—	0.10	0.15	—
1996 M Proof	1,200	Value: 7.00				
1997 M	43,406,000	—	—	0.10	0.15	—
1997 M Proof	2,000	Value: 7.00				
1998 M	95,322,000	—	—	0.10	0.15	—
1998 M Proof	2,000	Value: 7.00				
1999 M	46,375,000	—	—	0.10	0.15	—
1999 M Proof	—	Value: 7.00				
2000 M	114,903,000	—	—	—	0.15	—
2000 M Proof	—	Value: 7.00				
2001 M Proof	—	Value: 7.00				
2001 M	25,000,000	—	—	—	1.00	—

KM# 47 20 PENNIA

4.5000 g., Aluminum-Bronze, 22.5 mm. **Obv:** Rampant lion left, date below **Rev:** Tree right of denomination **Designer:** Peippo Uolevi Helle

Date	Mintage	F	VF	XF	Unc	BU
1963 S	39,970,000	—	0.15	0.20	1.50	—
1964 S	4,248,000	0.50	1.00	2.50	5.00	—
1965 S	5,704,000	0.10	0.50	1.00	3.00	—
1966 S	4,085,000	0.10	0.50	1.00	3.00	—
1967 S	1,716,000	0.10	0.50	1.00	3.00	—
1968 S	1,330,000	0.10	0.50	1.00	3.00	—
1969 S	201,000	0.50	1.00	2.00	4.00	—
1970 S	230,000	0.50	1.00	2.00	3.50	—
1971 S	5,150,000	—	0.25	0.50	1.00	—
Note: Some coins dated 1971 are magnetic and command a higher premium						
1972 S	10,001,000	—	0.25	0.50	1.00	—
1973 S	9,462,000	—	0.25	0.50	1.00	—
1974 S	12,705,000	—	0.25	0.50	1.00	—
1975 S	12,068,000	—	0.25	0.50	1.00	—
1976 K	20,058,000	—	0.25	0.50	1.00	—
1977 K	10,063,000	—	0.25	0.50	1.00	—
1978 K	10,014,000	—	0.25	0.50	1.00	—
1979 K	7,513,000	—	0.25	0.50	1.00	—
1980 K	20,047,000	—	—	0.25	0.50	—
1981 K	30,002,000	—	—	0.25	0.50	—
1982 K	35,050,000	—	—	0.25	0.50	—
1983 K	7,113,000	—	—	0.25	0.50	—
1983 N	12,889,000	—	—	0.25	0.50	—
1984 N	20,029,000	—	—	0.25	0.50	—
1985 N	15,004,000	—	—	0.25	0.50	—
1986 N	20,001,000	—	—	0.25	0.50	—
1987 M	25,670,000	—	—	0.25	0.50	—
1987 N	1,200,000	—	0.25	0.50	1.00	—
1988 M	13,853,000	—	—	0.25	0.50	—
1989 M	40,695,000	—	—	0.25	0.50	—
1990 M	9,168,000	—	—	0.25	0.50	—

KM# 48 50 PENNIA

5.5000 g., Aluminum-Bronze, 25.0 mm. **Obv:** Rampant lion left, date below **Rev:** Tree right of denomination **Designer:** Peippo Uolevi Helle

Date	Mintage	F	VF	XF	Unc	BU
1963 S	17,316,000	—	0.20	0.50	3.00	—
1964 S	3,101,000	—	0.25	3.00	10.00	—
1965 S	1,667,000	—	0.20	2.00	5.00	—
1966 S	1,051,000	—	0.20	2.00	5.00	—
1967 S	400,000	0.25	0.50	2.00	5.00	—
1968 S	816,000	—	0.25	1.00	4.00	—
1969 S	1,341,000	—	0.20	0.50	3.00	—
1970 S	2,250,000	—	0.20	0.50	2.00	—
1971 S	10,003,000	—	0.20	0.50	1.50	—
Note: Some coins dated 1971 are magnetic and command a higher premium						
1972 S	7,892,000	—	0.20	0.50	1.50	—
1973 S	5,428,000	—	0.20	0.50	1.50	—
1974 S	5,049,000	—	0.20	0.50	1.50	—
1975 S	4,305,000	—	0.20	0.50	1.50	—
1976 K	7,022,000	—	0.20	0.50	1.50	—
1977 K	8,077,000	—	0.20	0.50	1.50	—
1978 K	8,048,000	—	0.20	0.50	1.50	—
1979 K	8,004,000	—	0.20	0.50	1.50	—
1980 K	5,349,000	—	0.20	0.50	1.50	—
1981 K	20,031,000	—	0.20	0.50	1.00	—
1982 K	5,042,000	—	0.20	0.50	1.00	—
1983 K	4,043,999	—	—	0.25	1.00	—
1983 N	1,016,000	—	0.20	0.50	1.50	—
1984 N	3,006,000	—	—	0.25	1.00	—
1985 N	10,000,000	—	—	0.25	1.00	—
1986 N	9,002,000	—	—	0.25	1.00	—
1987 N	700,000	—	0.30	0.75	1.50	—
1987 M	4,305,000	—	—	0.25	1.00	—
1988 M	14,735,000	—	—	0.25	1.00	—
1989 M	10,651,000	—	—	0.25	1.00	—
1990 M	5,391,000	—	—	0.50	2.00	—

KM# 66 50 PENNIA

3.3000 g., Copper-Nickel, 19.7 mm. **Obv:** Polar bear, date below **Rev:** Denomination above flower heads **Designer:** Antti Neuvonen

Date	Mintage	F	VF	XF	Unc	BU
1990 M	70,459,000	—	—	0.20	0.75	—
1991 M	90,480,000	—	—	0.20	0.75	—
1992 M	58,996,000	—	—	0.20	0.75	—
1993 M	10,066,000	—	—	0.20	0.75	—
1994 M	3,005,000	—	—	0.20	0.75	—
1994 M Proof	5,000	Value: 8.00				
1995 M	1,048,000	—	—	0.20	0.75	—
1995 M Proof	3,000	Value: 8.00				
1996 M	17,000,000	—	—	0.20	0.75	—
1996 M Proof	1,200	Value: 8.00				
1997 M	524,000	—	—	0.20	0.75	—
1997 M Proof	2,000	Value: 8.00				
1998 M	3,345,500	—	—	0.20	0.75	—
1998 M Proof	2,000	Value: 8.00				
1999 M	100,000	—	—	0.20	0.75	—
1999 M Proof	—	Value: 8.00				
2000 M	100,000	—	—	0.20	0.75	—
2000 M Proof	—	Value: 8.00				
2001 M Proof	—	Value: 8.00				
2001 M	200,000	—	—	0.20	0.75	1.50

KM# 49 MARKKA

6.4000 g., 0.3500 Silver 0.0720 oz. ASW, 24 mm. **Obv:** Rampant lion left, date below **Obv. Designer:** Olof Eriksson **Rev:** Stylized fir trees with denomination in center **Rev. Designer:** Heikki Haivaoja **Edge Lettering:** SUOMI FINLAND

Date	Mintage	F	VF	XF	Unc	BU
1964 S	9,999,000	BV	1.20	2.00	5.00	—
1965 S	15,107,000	—	BV	1.50	4.00	—
1966 S	15,183,000	—	BV	1.50	3.00	—
1967 S	6,249,000	—	BV	1.50	3.00	—
1968 S	3,063,000	—	BV	1.50	3.00	—

KM# 49a MARKKA

6.1000 g., Copper-Nickel, 24 mm. **Obv:** Rampant lion left, date below **Obv. Designer:** Olof Eriksson **Rev:** Denomination flanked by stylized fir trees **Rev. Designer:** Heikki Haivaoja **Edge Lettering:** SUOMI FINLAND

Date	Mintage	F	VF	XF	Unc	BU
1969 S	1,308,000	0.25	0.50	1.00	2.00	—
1970 S	12,255,000	—	0.35	0.50	1.00	—
1971 S	19,676,000	—	0.35	0.50	1.00	—
1972 S	19,885,000	—	0.35	0.50	1.00	—
1973 S	17,060,000	—	0.35	0.50	1.00	—
1974 S	18,065,000	—	0.35	0.50	1.00	—
1975 S	11,523,000	—	0.35	0.50	1.00	—
1976 K	12,048,000	—	0.35	0.50	1.00	—
1977 K	10,077,000	—	0.35	0.50	1.00	—
1978 K	10,022,000	—	0.35	0.50	1.00	—
1979 K	11,311,000	—	0.35	0.50	1.00	—
1980 K	19,306,000	—	—	0.35	0.75	—
1981 K	32,003,000	—	—	0.35	0.75	—
1982 K	30,001,000	—	—	0.35	0.75	—
1983 K	8,074,999	—	—	0.35	0.75	—
1983 N	11,927,000	—	—	0.35	0.75	—
1984 N	15,000,000	—	—	0.35	0.75	—
1985 N	19,001,000	—	—	0.35	0.75	—
1986 N	10,000,000	—	—	0.35	0.75	—
1987 M	9,303,000	—	—	0.35	0.75	—
1987 N	700,000	—	0.50	1.00	2.00	—
1988 M	27,535,000	—	—	0.35	0.75	—
1989 M	37,520,000	—	—	0.35	0.75	—
1990 M	50,305,000	—	—	0.35	0.75	—
1991 M	15,026,000	—	—	0.35	0.75	—
1992 M	3,628,000	—	—	0.35	0.75	—
1993 M	1,036,000	—	—	0.50	1.00	—

KM# 76 MARKKA

4.9000 g., Aluminum-Bronze, 22 mm. **Obv:** Rampant lion left within circle, date below **Rev:** Ornaments flank denomination within circle

Date	Mintage	F	VF	XF	Unc	BU
1993 M	91,588,000	—	—	0.35	0.75	—
1994 M	152,011,000	—	—	0.35	0.75	—
1994 M Proof	5,000	Value: 10.00				
1995 M	40,008,000	—	—	0.35	0.75	—
1995 M Proof	3,000	Value: 10.00				
1996 M	21,000,000	—	—	0.35	0.75	—
1996 M Proof	1,200	Value: 10.00				
1997 M	23,775,200	—	—	0.35	0.75	—
1997 M Proof	2,000	Value: 10.00				
1998 M	33,955,200	—	—	0.35	0.75	—
1998 M Proof	2,000	Value: 10.00				
1999 M	100,000	—	—	0.35	0.75	—
1999 M Proof	—	Value: 10.00				
2000 M	100,000	—	—	0.35	0.75	—
2000 M Proof	—	Value: 10.00				
2001 M Proof	—	Value: 10.00				
2001 M	200,000	—	—	0.35	0.75	—

KM# 106 MARKKA

6.1000 g., Copper-Nickel, 24 mm. **Subject:** Remembrance Markka **Obv:** Rampant lion with sword left **Rev:** Denomination and pine tree **Edge:** Plain **Designer:** Antti Neuvonen **Note:** This coin is encased in acrylic resin and sealed in a display card.

Date	Mintage	F	VF	XF	Unc	BU
2001 N-M	500,000	—	—	—	5.00	6.50

KM# 53 5 MARKKAA

8.0000 g., Aluminum-Bronze, 26.3 mm. **Obv:** Icebreaker "Varma", date below **Rev:** Stylized flock of birds **Edge Lettering:** REPUBLIKEN FINLAND SUOMEN TASAVALTA **Designer:** Heikki Häiväoja

Date	Mintage	F	VF	XF	Unc	BU
1972 S	400,000	1.50	2.00	2.50	4.00	—
1973 S	2,188,000	—	1.25	2.00	3.00	—
1974 S	300,000	—	1.25	2.00	3.00	—
1975 S	300,000	—	1.25	2.00	3.00	—
1976 K	400,000	—	1.25	2.00	3.00	—
1977 K	300,000	—	1.25	2.00	3.00	—
1978 K	300,000	—	1.25	2.00	3.00	—

KM# 57 5 MARKKAA

8.0000 g., Aluminum-Bronze, 26.3 mm. **Obv:** Icebreaker "Urho", date below **Rev:** Stylized flock of birds with denomination at top **Designer:** Heikki Häiväoja

Date	Mintage	F	VF	XF	Unc	BU
1979 K	2,005,000	—	—	1.50	2.25	—
1980 K	501,000	—	1.50	2.00	3.00	—
1981 K	1,009,000	—	—	1.50	2.25	—
1982 K	3,004,000	—	—	1.50	2.25	—
1983 K	8,776,000	—	—	1.50	2.25	—
1983 N	11,230,000	—	—	1.50	2.25	—
1984 N	15,001,000	—	—	1.50	2.25	—
1985 N	8,005,000	—	—	1.50	2.25	—
1986 N	5,006,000	—	—	1.50	2.25	—
1987 N	660,000	—	1.50	2.00	3.00	—
1987 M	2,348,000	—	—	1.50	2.25	—
1988 M	3,042,000	—	—	1.50	2.25	—
1989 M	10,175,000	—	—	1.50	2.25	—
1990 M	9,925,000	—	—	1.50	2.25	—
1991 M	9,910,000	—	—	2.00	3.00	—
1992 M	547,000	—	—	2.00	3.00	—
1993 M	911,000	—	—	2.00	3.00	—

KM# 73 5 MARKKAA

5.5000 g., Copper-Aluminum-Nickel, 24.5 mm. **Obv:** Lake Saimaa ringed seal, date below **Rev:** Denomination, dragonfly and lily pad leaves

Date	Mintage	F	VF	XF	Unc	BU
1992 M	800,000	—	—	—	3.50	6.00
1993 M	46,034,000	—	—	—	2.00	5.00
1994 M	19,003,000	—	—	—	2.00	5.00
1994 M Proof	5,000	Value: 12.00				
1995 M	9,016,000	—	—	—	2.50	5.00
1995 M Proof	3,000	Value: 12.00				
1996 M	7,000,000	—	—	—	2.50	5.00
1996 M Proof	1,200	Value: 12.00				
1997 M	537,700	—	—	2.00	3.00	5.00
1997 M Proof	2,000	Value: 12.00				
1998 M	813,650	—	—	—	2.50	5.00
1998 M Proof	2,000	Value: 12.00				
1999 M	100,000	—	—	—	2.50	5.00
1999 M Proof	—	Value: 12.00				
2000 M	100,000	—	—	—	2.50	5.00
2000 M Proof	—	Value: 12.00				
2001 M Proof	—	Value: 12.00				
2001 M	200,000	—	—	—	4.00	6.00

KM# 77 10 MARKKAA

8.8000 g., Bi-Metallic Brass center in Copper-Nickel ring, 27.25 mm. **Obv:** Capercaillie bird within circle, date above **Rev:** Denomination and branches

Date	Mintage	F	VF	XF	Unc	BU
1993 M	30,002,000	—	—	2.00	3.50	5.00
1994 M	19,979,000	—	—	2.00	3.50	5.00
1994 M Proof	5,000	Value: 18.00				
1995 M	4,008,000	—	—	2.00	3.50	5.00
1995 M Proof	3,000	Value: 18.00				
1996 M	3,300,000	—	—	2.00	3.50	5.00
1996 M Proof	1,200	Value: 18.00				
1997 M	917,607	—	—	2.00	3.50	5.00
1997 M Proof	2,000	Value: 18.00				
1998 M	797,713	—	—	2.00	3.50	5.00
1998 M Proof	2,000	Value: 18.00				
1999 M	100,000	—	—	3.00	5.00	6.00
1999 M Proof	—	Value: 18.00				
2000 M	100,000	—	—	3.00	5.00	6.00
2000 M Proof	—	Value: 18.00				
2001 M Proof	—	Value: 18.00				
2001 M	200,000	—	—	3.00	5.00	6.00

KM# 82 10 MARKKAA

8.0000 g., Bi-Metallic Brass center in Copper-Nickel ring, 27.25 mm. **Subject:** European Unity **Obv:** Swan in flight within circle, date upper right **Rev:** Denomination and branches **Designer:** Pertti Mäkinen and Antti Neuvonen

Date	Mintage	F	VF	XF	Unc	BU
1995 M	500,000	—	—	2.50	4.50	6.00

EURO COINAGE

European Union Issues

KM# 98 EURO CENT

2.2700 g., Copper Plated Steel, 16.3 mm. **Obv:** Rampant lion left surrounded by stars, date at left **Obv. Designer:** Heikki Häiväoja **Rev:** Denomination and globe **Rev. Designer:** Luc Luycx **Edge:** Plain

Date	Mintage	F	VF	XF	Unc	BU
1999	8,100,000	—	—	—	1.25	—
1999 Proof	—	—	—	—	—	—
2000	7,600,000	—	—	—	3.50	—
2000 Proof	—	—	—	—	—	—
2001	500,000	—	—	—	10.00	—
2001 Proof	—	—	—	—	—	—
2002	659,000	—	—	—	5.00	—
2002 Proof	16,000	Value: 15.00				
2003	6,790,000	—	—	—	5.00	—
2003 Proof	—	Value: 15.00				
2004	9,690,000	—	—	—	5.00	—
2004 Proof	—	Value: 15.00				
2005	5,800,000	—	—	—	5.00	—
2005 Proof	—	Value: 15.00				
2006	—	—	—	—	5.00	—
2006 Proof	—	Value: 15.00				
2007	—	—	—	—	5.00	—
2008	—	—	—	—	5.00	—

KM# 99 2 EURO CENT

3.0000 g., Copper Plated Steel, 18.7 mm. **Obv:** Rampant lion surrounded by stars, date at left **Obv. Designer:** Heikki Häiväoja **Rev:** Denomination and globe **Rev. Designer:** Luc Luycx **Edge:** Grooved

Date	Mintage	F	VF	XF	Unc	BU
1999	1,785,000	—	—	—	1.25	—
1999 Proof	—	—	—	—	—	—
2000	13,937,000	—	—	—	3.50	—
2000 Proof	—	—	—	—	—	—
2001	500,000	—	—	—	10.00	—
2001 Proof	—	—	—	—	—	—
2002	659,000	—	—	—	5.00	—
2002 Proof	16,000	Value: 15.00				
2003	6,790,000	—	—	—	5.00	—
2003 Proof	—	Value: 15.00				
2004	8,024,000	—	—	—	5.00	—
2004 Proof	—	Value: 15.00				
2005	5,800,000	—	—	—	5.00	—
2005 Proof	—	Value: 15.00				
2006	—	—	—	—	5.00	—
2006 Proof	—	Value: 15.00				
2007	—	—	—	—	5.00	—
2008	—	—	—	—	5.00	—

KM# 100 5 EURO CENT

3.9400 g., Copper Plated Steel, 19.66 mm. **Obv:** Rampant lion left surrounded by stars, date at left **Obv. Designer:** Heikki Häiväoja **Rev:** Denomination and globe **Rev. Designer:** Luc Luycx **Edge:** Plain

Date	Mintage	F	VF	XF	Unc	BU
1999	63,380,000	—	—	—	1.00	—
1999 Proof	—	—	—	—	—	—
2000	56,660,000	—	—	—	1.00	—
2000 Proof	—	—	—	—	—	—
2001 Proof	—	—	—	—	—	—
2001	213,756,000	—	—	—	0.50	—
2002 Proof	16,000	Value: 15.00				
2002	101,824,000	—	—	—	0.50	—
2003	790,000	—	—	—	1.00	—
2003 Proof	—	Value: 15.00				
2004	629,000	—	—	—	1.00	—
2004 Proof	—	Value: 15.00				
2005	800,000	—	—	—	1.00	—
2005 Proof	—	Value: 15.00				
2006	—	—	—	—	1.00	—
2006 Proof	—	Value: 15.00				
2007	—	—	—	—	1.00	—
2008	—	—	—	—	1.00	—

KM# 101 10 EURO CENT

4.0000 g., Brass, 19.7 mm. **Obv:** Rampant lion left surrounded by stars, date at left **Obv. Designer:** Heikki Häiväoja **Rev:** Denomination and map **Rev. Designer:** Luc Luycx **Edge:** Reeded

Date	Mintage	F	VF	XF	Unc	BU
1999	133,520,000	—	—	—	1.25	—
1999 Proof	—	—	—	—	—	—
2000	167,449,000	—	—	—	1.75	—
2000 Proof	—	—	—	—	—	—
2001	14,730,000	—	—	—	10.00	—
2001 Proof	—	—	—	—	—	—
2002	1,499,000	—	—	—	2.50	—
2002 Proof	16,000	Value: 18.00				
2003	790,000	—	—	—	2.50	—
2003 Proof	—	Value: 18.00				
2004	629,000	—	—	—	2.50	—
2004 Proof	—	Value: 18.00				
2005	800,000	—	—	—	2.50	—
2005 Proof	—	Value: 18.00				
2006	1,000,000	—	—	—	2.50	—
2006 Proof	—	Value: 18.00				

KM# 126 10 EURO CENT

4.0000 g., Brass, 19.7 mm. **Obv:** Rampant lion surrounded by stars **Obv. Designer:** Heikki Häiväoja **Rev:** Relief map of Western Europe, stars, lines and value **Rev. Designer:** Luc Luycx **Edge:** Reeded

Date	Mintage	F	VF	XF	Unc	BU
2007	—	—	—	—	2.50	—
2008	—	—	—	—	—	—

KM# 102 20 EURO CENT

5.7300 g., Brass, 22.2 mm. **Obv:** Rampant lion left surrounded by stars, date at left **Obv. Designer:** Heikki Häiväoja **Rev:** Denomination and map **Rev. Designer:** Luc Luycx **Edge:** Notched

Date	Mintage	F	VF	XF	Unc	BU
1999	42,350,000	—	—	—	1.25	—
1999 Proof	—	—	—	—	—	—
2000	500,000	—	—	—	12.00	—
2000 Proof	—	—	—	—	—	—
2001	121,763,000	—	—	—	1.75	—
2001 Proof	—	—	—	—	—	—
2002	100,759,000	—	—	—	1.75	—
2002 Proof	16,000	Value: 20.00				
2003	790,000	—	—	—	1.75	—
2003 Proof	—	Value: 20.00				
2004	629,000	—	—	—	1.75	—
2004 Proof	—	Value: 20.00				
2005	800,000	—	—	—	1.75	—
2005 Proof	—	Value: 20.00				
2006	1,000,000	—	—	—	1.75	—
2006 Proof	—	Value: 20.00				

KM# 127 20 EURO CENT

5.7300 g., Brass, 22.2 mm. **Obv:** Rampant lion surrounded by stars **Obv. Designer:** Heikki Häiväoja **Rev:** Relief map of Western Europe, stars, lines and value **Rev. Designer:** Luc Luycx **Edge:** Notched

Date	Mintage	F	VF	XF	Unc	BU
2007	—	—	—	—	1.75	—
2008	—	—	—	—	—	—

KM# 103 50 EURO CENT

7.8100 g., Brass, 24.2 mm. **Obv:** Rampant lion left surrounded by stars, date at left **Obv. Designer:** Heikki Häiväoja **Rev:** Denomination and map **Rev. Designer:** Luc Luycx **Edge:** Reeded

Date	Mintage	F	VF	XF	Unc	BU
1999	20,696,000	—	—	—	1.75	—
1999 Proof	—	—	—	—	—	—
2000	67,097,000	—	—	—	1.50	—
2000 Proof	—	—	—	—	—	—
2001	4,432,000	—	—	—	7.50	—
2001 Proof	—	—	—	—	—	—
2002	1,147,000	—	—	—	5.00	—
2002 Proof	16,000	Value: 22.00				
2003	790,000	—	—	—	5.00	—
2003 Proof	—	Value: 22.00				
2004	629,000	—	—	—	5.00	—
2004 Proof	—	Value: 22.00				
2005	4,800,000	—	—	—	5.00	—
2005 Proof	—	Value: 22.00				
2006	6,850,000	—	—	—	5.00	—
2006 Proof	—	Value: 22.00				

KM# 128 50 EURO CENT

7.8100 g., Brass, 24.2 mm. **Obv:** Rampant lion surrounded by stars **Obv. Designer:** Heikki Häiväoja **Rev:** Relief map of Western Europe, stars, lines and value **Rev. Designer:** Luc Luycx **Edge:** Reeded

Date	Mintage	F	VF	XF	Unc	BU
2007	—	—	—	—	5.00	—
2008	—	—	—	—	—	—

KM# 104 EURO

7.5000 g., Bi-Metallic Copper-nickel center in Brass ring, 23.2 mm. **Obv:** 2 flying swans, date below, surrounded by stars on outer ring **Obv. Designer:** Pertti Mäkinen **Rev:** Denomination and map **Rev. Designer:** Luc Luycx **Edge:** Reeded and plain sections

Date	Mintage	F	VF	XF	Unc	BU
1999	16,210,000	—	—	—	5.00	—
1999 Proof	—	—	—	—	—	—
2000	36,639,000	—	—	—	5.00	—
2000 Proof	—	—	—	—	—	—
2001	13,862,000	—	—	—	3.00	—
2001 Proof	—	—	—	—	—	—
2002	14,114,000	—	—	—	6.50	—
2002 Proof	16,000	Value: 25.00				
2003	790,000	—	—	—	6.50	—
2003 Proof	—	Value: 25.00				
2004	5,529,000	—	—	—	6.50	—
2004 Proof	—	Value: 25.00				
2005	7,935,000	—	—	—	6.50	—
2005 Proof	—	Value: 25.00				
2006	1,705,000	—	—	—	6.50	—
2006 Proof	—	Value: 25.00				

KM# 129 EURO

7.5000 g., Bi-Metallic Copper-Nickel center in Brass ring, 23.2 mm. **Obv:** 2 flying swans surrounded by stars on outer ring **Obv. Designer:** Pertti Mäekinen **Rev:** Relief map of western Europe, stars, lines and value **Rev. Designer:** Luc Luycx **Edge:** Reeded and plain sections

Date	Mintage	F	VF	XF	Unc	BU
2007	—	—	—	—	6.50	—
2008	—	—	—	—	—	—

KM# 105 2 EURO

8.5200 g., Bi-Metallic Brass center in Copper-nickel ring, 25.6 mm. **Obv:** 2 cloudberry flowers surrounded by stars on outer ring **Obv. Designer:** Raimo Heino **Rev:** Denomination and map **Rev. Designer:** Luc Luycx **Edge:** Reeded and lettered **Edge Lettering:** SUOMI FINLAND

Date	Mintage	F	VF	XF	Unc	BU
1999	16,090,000	—	—	—	4.00	—
1999 Proof	—	—	—	—	—	—
2000	8,680,000	—	—	—	4.00	—
2000 Proof	—	—	—	—	—	—
2001	29,132,000	—	—	—	4.00	—
2001 Proof	—	—	—	—	—	—
2002	1,386,000	—	—	—	7.50	—
2002 Proof	16,000	Value: 30.00				
2003	9,080,000	—	—	—	5.00	—
2003 Proof	—	Value: 30.00				
2004	10,029,000	—	—	—	5.00	—
2004 Proof	—	Value: 30.00				
2005	10,800,000	—	—	—	5.00	—
2005 Proof	—	Value: 30.00				
2006	11,000,000	—	—	—	5.00	—
2006 Proof	—	Value: 30.00				

KM# 114 2 EURO

8.5200 g., Bi-Metallic, 25.6 mm. **Subject:** EU Expansion **Obv:** Stylized flower **Obv. Designer:** Pertti Mäkinen **Rev:** Denomination and map **Rev. Designer:** Luc Luycx **Edge:** Reeded and lettered

Date	Mintage	F	VF	XF	Unc	BU
2004	1,000,000	—	—	—	10.00	11.50

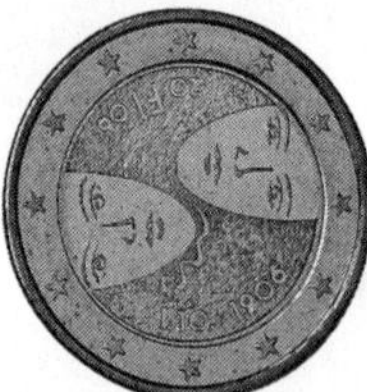

KM# 125 2 EURO

8.5200 g., Bi-Metallic Brass center in Copper-Nickel ring, 25.6 mm. **Obv:** Two faces **Obv. Designer:** Pertti Mäkinen **Rev:** Value and map **Rev. Designer:** Luc Luycx **Edge:** Reeded and lettered **Edge Lettering:** "SUOMI FINLAND" **Note:** Centennial of Universal Suffrage

Date	Mintage	F	VF	XF	Unc	BU
ND (2006) M-M	2,500,000	—	—	—	6.00	7.50

KM# 130 2 EURO

8.5200 g., Bi-Metallic Brass center in Copper-nickel ring, 25.6 mm. **Obv:** 2 cloudberry flowers surrounded by stars on outer ring **Obv. Designer:** Raimo Heino **Rev:** Relief map of Western Europe, stars, lines and value **Rev. Designer:** Luc Luycx **Edge:** Reeded and lettered **Edge Lettering:** SUOMI FINLAND

Date	Mintage	F	VF	XF	Unc	BU
2007	—	—	—	—	6.00	7.50

KM# 138 2 EURO

8.3200 g., Bi-Metallic Coper-Nickel center in Brass ring, 25.72 mm. **Subject:** 50th Anniversary Treaty of Rome **Obv:** Open treaty book **Rev:** Large value at left, modified outline of Europe at right **Edge:** Reeded and lettered

Date	Mintage	F	VF	XF	Unc	BU
2007	—	—	—	—	7.00	9.00

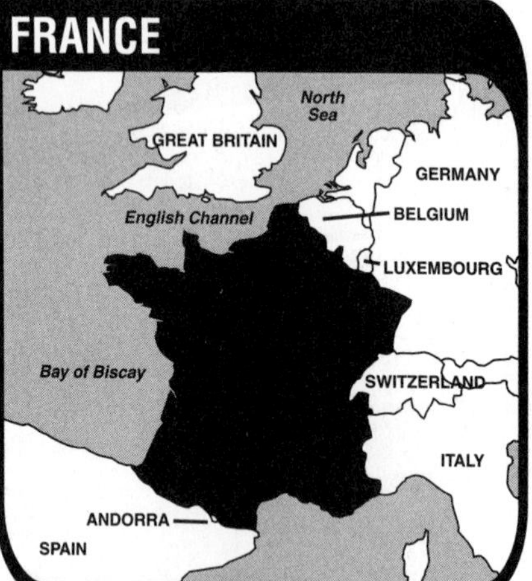

The French Republic, largest of the West European nations, has an area of 210,026 sq. mi. (547,030 sq. km.) and a population of 58.1 million. Capital: Paris. Agriculture, manufacturing, tourist industry and financial services are the most important elements of France's diversified economy. Textiles and clothing, steel products, machinery and transportation equipment, chemicals, pharmaceuticals, nuclear electricity, agricultural products and wine are exported.

France, the Gaul of ancient times, emerged from the Renaissance as a modern centralized national state which reached its zenith during the reign of Louis XIV (1643-1715) when it became an absolute monarchy and the foremost power in Europe. Although his reign marks the golden age of French culture, the domestic abuses and extravagance of Louis XIV plunged France into a series of costly wars. This, along with a system of special privileges granted the nobility and other favored groups, weakened the monarchy and brought France to bankruptcy. This laid the way for the French Revolution of 1789-99 that shook Europe and affected the whole world.

The monarchy was abolished and the First Republic formed in 1793. The new government fell in 1799 to a coup led by Napoleon Bonaparte who, after declaring himself First Consul for life, in 1804 had himself proclaimed Emperor of France and King of Italy.

Napoleon's military victories made him master of much of Europe, but his disastrous Russian campaign of 1812 initiated a series of defeats that led to his abdication in 1814 and exile to the island of Elba. The monarchy was briefly restored under Louis XVIII. Napoleon returned to France in March 1815, but his efforts to uphold his power were totally crushed at the battle of Waterloo. He was exiled to the island of St. Helena where he died in 1821.

The monarchy under Louis XVIII was again restored in 1815, but the ultra reactionary regime of Charles X (1824-30) was overthrown by a liberal revolution and Louis Philippe of Orleans replaced him as monarch. The monarchy was ousted by the Revolution of 1848 and the Second Republic proclaimed. Louis Napoleon Bonaparte (nephew of Napoleon I) was elected president of the Second Republic. He was proclaimed emperor in 1852. As Napoleon III, he gave France two decades of prosperity under a stable, autocratic regime, but led it to defeat in the Franco-Prussian War of 1870, after which the Third Republic was established.

The Third Republic endured until 1940 and the capitulation of France to the swiftly maneuvering German forces. Marshal Philippe Petain formed a puppet government that sued for peace and ruled unoccupied France until 1942 from Vichy. Meanwhile, General Charles de Gaulle escaped to London where he formed a wartime government in exile and the Free French army. De Gaulle's provisional exile government was officially recognized by the Allies after the liberation of Paris in 1944, and De Gaulle, who had been serving as head of the provisional government, tacitly maintained that position. In October 1945, the people overwhelmingly rejected a return to the prewar government, thus paving the way for the formation of the Fourth Republic in 1947 just after the dismissal of De Gaulle, at grips with a coalition of rival parties, the Communists especially.

In actual operation, the Fourth Republic was remarkably like the Third, with the National Assembly the focus of power causing a constant governmental instability. The later years of the Fourth Republic were marked by a burst of industrial expansion unmatched in modern French history. The growth rate, however, was marred by a two colonial wars, nagging inflationary trend that weakened the franc and undermined the betterment of the people's buying power. This and the Algerian conflict led to the recall of De Gaulle to power, the adoption of a new constitution vesting strong powers in the executive, and the establishment in 1959 of the current Fifth Republic.

RULERS

Third Republic, 1871-1940
Vichy State, 1940-1944
De Gaulle's Provisional Govt., 1944-1946
Fourth Republic, 1947-1958
Fifth Republic, 1959—

MINT MARKS AND PRIVY MARKS

In addition to the date and mint mark which are customary on western civilization coinage, most coins manufactured by the French Mints contain two or three small 'Marks or Differents' as the French call them. These privy marks represent the men responsible for the dies which struck the coins. One privy mark is sometimes for the Engraver General (since 1880 the title is Chief Engraver). The other privy mark is the signature of the Mint Director of each mint; another one is the different' of the local engraver. Three other marks appeared at the end of Louis XIV's reign: one for the Director General of Mints, one for the General Engineer of Mechanical edge-marking, one identifying over struck coins in 1690-1705 and in 1715-1723. Equally amazing and unique is that sometimes the local assayer's or Judge-custody's 'different' or 'secret pellet' appears. Since 1880 this privy mark has represented the office rather than the personage of both the Administration of Coins & Medals and the Mint Director, and a standard privy mark has been used (cornucopia).

For most dates these privy marks are important though minor features for advanced collectors or local researchers. During some issue dates, however, the marks changed. To be even more accurate sometimes the marks changed when the date didn't, even though it should have. These coins can be attributed to the proper mintage report only by considering the privy marks. Previous references (before G. Sobin and F. Droulers) have by and large ignored these privy marks. It is entirely possible that unattributed varieties may exist for any privy mark transition. All transition years which may have two or three varieties or combinations of privy marks have the known attribution indicated after the date (if it has been confirmed).

ENGRAVER GENERAL'S PRIVY MARKS

Mark	Desc.	Date	Name
	Torch	1896-1930	Henry Patey
	Wing	1931-Oct. 1958	Lucien Bazor
	Owl	1958-74	Raymond Joly
	Dolphin	1974-94	Rousseau
	Bee	1994-	Pierre Rodier

MINT DIRECTOR'S PRIVY MARKS

Some modern coins struck from dies produced at the Paris Mint have the 'A' mint mark. In the absence of a mint mark, the cornucopia privy mark serves to attribute a coin to Paris design.

A – Paris, Central Mint

B – Beaumont – Le Roger

Cornucopia 1943-58

(b) – Brussels

Legend ending BD, see PAU

C - Castelsarrasin

C	Cornucopia	1914, 1943-46

Thunderbolt (tb) - Poissy

	Cornucopia	1922-24

Star (s) - Madrid

★		1916

MONETARY SYSTEM

(Commencing 1960)
1 Old Franc = 1 New Centime
100 New Centimes = 1 New Franc

MODERN REPUBLICS
1870-

DECIMAL COINAGE

KM# 840 CENTIME

1.0000 g., Bronze, 15 mm. **Obv:** Liberty head right **Rev:** Denomination above date within wreath **Designer:** Dupuis **Note:** Without mint mark or privy mark.

Date	Mintage	F	VF	XF	Unc	BU
1901	1,000,000	1.00	2.00	15.00	35.00	50.00
1902	1,000,000	0.75	1.50	4.00	15.00	—
1903	2,000,000	0.50	1.50	3.00	15.00	—
1904	1,000,000	0.75	1.50	4.00	15.00	—
1908	4,500,000	2.00	4.00	10.00	20.00	—
1909	1,500,000	3.00	5.00	12.00	30.00	50.00
1910	1,500,000	10.00	20.00	40.00	100	185
1911	5,000,000	0.25	0.75	1.50	5.00	—
1912	2,000,000	0.50	1.00	2.00	7.00	—
1913	1,500,000	0.50	1.00	2.00	7.00	—
1914	1,000,000	0.75	1.50	3.00	9.50	—
1916	1,996,000	0.50	1.00	2.00	6.50	—
1919	2,407,000	0.25	0.75	1.50	4.00	—
1920	2,594,000	0.25	0.75	1.50	4.00	—

KM# 841 2 CENTIMES

2.0000 g., Bronze, 20.2 mm. **Obv:** Liberty head right **Rev:** Denomination and date within wreath **Designer:** Dupuis **Note:** Without mint mark or privy mark.

Date	Mintage	F	VF	XF	Unc	BU
1901	1,000,000	1.00	2.50	4.00	11.50	55.00
1902	750,000	1.50	3.50	5.50	15.00	—
1903	750,000	1.50	3.50	5.50	16.50	—
1904	500,000	2.00	4.50	7.50	18.50	60.00
1907	250,000	10.00	25.00	55.00	130	200
1908	3,500,000	0.35	0.75	2.00	6.00	—
1909	1,750,000	6.00	12.00	30.00	50.00	90.00
1910	1,750,000	0.50	1.00	5.00	12.50	—
1911	5,000,000	0.15	0.50	1.25	5.00	—
1912	1,500,000	0.25	1.00	2.00	7.00	—
1913	1,750,000	0.25	1.00	2.00	7.00	—
1914	2,000,000	0.15	0.50	1.25	5.00	—
1916	500,000	0.75	1.50	3.00	9.00	—
1919	902,000	0.50	1.00	2.00	6.00	—
1920	598,000	0.75	1.50	3.00	8.00	—

KM# 842 5 CENTIMES

5.0000 g., Bronze, 25.1 mm. **Obv:** Liberty head right **Rev:** Republic protecting her child, denomination at right, date below **Designer:** Dupuis **Note:** Without mint mark.

Date	Mintage	F	VF	XF	Unc	BU
1901 (c)	6,000,000	1.75	3.50	15.00	55.00	75.00
1902	7,900,000	1.75	3.50	10.00	50.00	70.00
1903	2,879,000	5.00	10.00	25.00	75.00	100
1904	8,000,000	1.00	3.00	6.50	25.00	50.00
1905	2,100,000	6.00	16.00	45.00	115	225
1906	8,394,000	0.75	2.50	6.00	24.00	50.00
1907	7,900,000	0.75	2.50	6.00	24.00	50.00
1908	6,090,000	2.00	4.00	12.00	32.00	75.00
1909	8,000,000	0.75	2.50	6.00	25.00	50.00
1910	4,000,000	1.50	2.50	9.00	50.00	85.00
1911	15,386,000	0.25	0.75	1.75	9.00	—
1912	20,000,000	0.25	0.75	1.75	9.00	—
1913	12,603,000	0.25	0.75	1.75	9.00	—
1914	7,000,000	0.25	0.75	1.75	9.00	—
1915	6,032,000	0.25	0.75	1.75	9.00	—
1916	41,531,000	0.25	0.75	1.75	7.50	—
1916 (s)	Inc. above	0.25	0.75	1.75	7.50	—
1917	16,963,000	0.25	0.75	1.75	7.50	—
1920	8,151,999	2.00	4.00	9.00	28.00	—
1921	142,000	250	450	850	1,350	—

KM# 865 5 CENTIMES

3.0000 g., Copper-Nickel, 17 mm. **Obv:** Monogram within wreath divided by center hole, liberty cap above **Rev:** Denomination divided by plant and center hole **Designer:** Lindaver

Date	Mintage	F	VF	XF	Unc	BU
1914 Rare	—	—	—	—	—	—
1917	10,458,000	1.00	1.75	4.00	18.00	40.00
1918	35,592,000	0.25	0.75	1.75	4.50	—
1919	43,848,000	0.25	0.75	1.75	4.00	—
1920	51,321,000	0.25	0.50	1.75	3.50	—

KM# 875 5 CENTIMES

2.0000 g., Copper-Nickel, 17 mm. **Obv:** Monogram divided by center hole, liberty cap above, wreath surrounds **Rev:** Denomination divided by plant and center hole, date below **Designer:** Lindaver

Date	Mintage	F	VF	XF	Unc	BU
1920	Inc. above	5.00	15.00	28.00	75.00	150
1921	32,908,000	0.25	0.50	1.75	4.00	—
1922	31,700,000	0.25	0.50	1.75	4.00	—
1922 (tb)	17,717,000	1.50	2.50	5.00	13.50	—
1923	23,322,000	0.50	1.50	2.00	6.50	—
1923 (tb)	45,097,000	0.25	0.50	1.00	3.50	—
1924	47,018,000	0.25	0.50	1.00	3.50	—
1924 (tb)	21,210,000	0.50	1.50	2.00	5.50	—
1925	66,837,999	0.25	0.50	1.00	2.50	—
1926	19,820,000	0.25	1.50	2.00	5.50	—
1927	6,066,000	2.50	8.50	25.00	70.00	—
1930	31,902,000	0.20	0.50	1.00	2.25	—
1931	34,711,000	0.20	0.50	1.00	2.25	—
1932	31,112,000	0.20	0.50	1.00	2.25	—
1933	12,970,000	1.00	1.75	4.00	10.00	—
1934	27,144,000	0.30	0.65	2.00	5.00	—
1935	57,221,000	0.25	0.50	1.00	2.25	—
1936	64,340,999	0.15	0.25	0.75	2.25	—
1937	26,329,000	0.15	0.25	0.75	2.25	—
1938	21,614,000	0.15	0.25	0.75	2.25	—

KM# 875a 5 CENTIMES

1.5000 g., Nickel-Bronze, 17 mm. **Obv:** Center hole divides monogram, liberty cap above, wreath surrounds **Rev:** Center hole and plant divide denomination, date below **Designer:** Lindaver

Date	Mintage	F	VF	XF	Unc	BU
.1938.	26,330,000	0.15	0.50	1.00	3.00	—
.1938. star	Inc. above	100	200	300	425	—
.1939.	52,673,000	0.10	0.25	0.75	2.00	—

KM# 843 10 CENTIMES

10.0000 g., Bronze, 30 mm. **Obv:** Liberty head right **Rev:** Republic protecting her child **Designer:** Dupuis **Note:** Without mint mark.

Date	Mintage	F	VF	XF	Unc	BU
1901 (c)	2,700,000	1.50	3.00	20.00	50.00	75.00
1902	3,800,000	0.75	1.75	6.50	25.00	—
1903	3,650,000	0.75	1.75	6.50	25.00	—
1904	3,800,000	0.75	1.75	6.50	25.00	—
1905	950,000	25.00	50.00	125	275	—
1906	3,000,000	2.00	5.00	12.00	40.00	65.00
1907	4,000,000	0.75	1.75	4.50	20.00	—
1908	3,500,000	0.75	1.75	4.50	20.00	—
1909	2,933,000	0.75	1.75	4.50	25.00	—
1910	3,567,000	0.75	1.75	4.50	20.00	—
1911	7,903,000	0.50	1.25	2.75	12.00	—
1912	9,500,000	0.50	1.25	2.75	12.00	—
1913	9,000,000	0.50	1.25	2.75	12.00	—
1914	6,000,000	0.75	1.75	3.50	14.00	—
1915	4,362,000	0.50	1.25	2.75	12.00	—
1916	22,477,000	0.25	0.75	1.50	7.00	—
1916 (s)	Inc. above	0.25	0.75	1.50	7.00	—
1917	11,914,000	0.25	0.75	1.50	7.00	—
1920	4,119,000	1.50	3.00	10.00	40.00	65.00
1921	1,896,000	8.00	16.00	40.00	85.00	140

KM# 866 10 CENTIMES

4.0000 g., Nickel, 21.3 mm. **Obv:** Monogram divided by center hole, liberty cap above, wreath surrounds **Rev:** Denomination divided by plant and center hole, date below **Designer:** Lindaver

Date	Mintage	F	VF	XF	Unc	BU
1914 dash	3,972	400	700	1,000	1,600	—

KM# 866a 10 CENTIMES

4.0000 g., Copper-Nickel, 21.3 mm. **Obv:** Center hole divides monogram, liberty cap above, wreath surrounds **Rev:** Center hole and plant divides denomination, date below **Designer:** Lindaver **Note:** Varieties with small and large hole exist.

Date	Mintage	F	VF	XF	Unc	BU
1917	8,170,999	0.75	1.50	3.50	20.00	—
1918	30,605,000	0.25	0.50	1.00	3.50	—
1919	33,488,999	0.25	0.50	1.00	3.50	—
1920	38,845,000	0.25	0.50	1.00	3.50	—
1921	42,768,000	0.10	0.35	0.75	2.50	—
1922	23,033,000	0.35	0.75	1.25	4.00	—
1922 (tb)	12,412,000	0.75	1.50	2.50	6.50	—
1923	18,701,000	0.50	1.00	2.00	4.50	—
1923 (tb)	30,016,000	0.25	0.50	1.00	3.00	—
1924	43,949,000	0.10	0.35	0.75	2.00	—
1924 (tb)	13,591,000	1.50	4.50	12.50	40.00	65.00
1925	46,266,000	0.10	0.35	0.75	2.00	—
1926	25,660,000	0.25	0.50	1.00	3.00	—
1927	16,203,000	0.40	0.75	1.25	4.00	—
1928	6,967,000	1.00	2.50	8.00	28.00	55.00
1929	24,531,000	0.10	0.35	1.00	2.00	—
1930	22,146,000	0.10	0.35	1.00	2.00	—
1931	49,107,000	0.10	0.35	1.00	2.00	—
1932	30,317,000	0.10	0.35	1.00	2.00	—
1933	13,042,000	0.35	0.75	1.50	4.00	—
1934	24,067,000	0.10	0.50	1.00	2.00	—
1935	47,487,000	0.10	0.50	1.00	2.00	—
1936	57,738,000	0.10	0.50	1.00	2.00	—
1937	25,308,000	0.10	0.50	1.00	2.00	—
1938	17,063,000	0.25	0.75	1.75	4.50	—

KM# 889.1 10 CENTIMES

3.0000 g., Nickel-Bronze, 21.3 mm. **Obv:** Monogram divided by center hole, liberty cap above, wreath surrounds **Rev:** Denomination divided by plant and center hole, date below **Designer:** Lindaver

Date	Mintage	F	VF	XF	Unc	BU
.1938.	24,151,000	0.25	0.50	1.00	2.00	—
1.938.	Inc. above	—	—	—	—	—
.1939.	62,269,000	0.15	0.30	0.65	1.75	—

KM# 889.2 10 CENTIMES

Nickel-Bronze, 21.3 mm. **Obv:** Center hole divides monogram, liberty cap above **Rev:** Center hole and plant divide denomination **Note:** Thin flan: 1.35-1.45mm thickness

Date	Mintage	F	VF	XF	Unc	BU
.1939.	Inc. above	0.10	0.20	0.50	1.25	—

KM# 898.1 10 CENTIMES

Zinc, 21 mm. **Obv:** Grain sprigs flank center hole **Rev:** Center hole divides denomination, oak leaves flank, date below **Note:** Issued for Vichy French State, thickness 1.5 mm. Varieties exist w/o hole.

Date	Mintage	F	VF	XF	Unc	BU
1941	70,860,000	0.35	0.65	1.50	6.00	—
1942	139,598,000	0.30	0.60	1.25	4.00	—
1943	48,957,600	1.00	2.00	4.00	15.00	—

KM# 898.2 10 CENTIMES

2.5000 g., Zinc, 21.3 mm. **Obv:** Grain sprigs flank center hole **Rev:** Center hole divides denomination, oak leaves flank, date below **Designer:** Atelier de Paris **Note:** Thin flan, 1.3mm.

Date	Mintage	F	VF	XF	Unc	BU
1941	Inc. above	0.25	0.50	1.25	3.00	—
1942	Inc. above	0.20	0.40	1.00	2.25	—
1943	Inc. above	0.75	1.50	2.75	6.00	—

KM# 895 10 CENTIMES

Zinc **Rev:** Without dash below MES in C MES

Date	Mintage	F	VF	XF	Unc	BU
1941	235,875,000	1.00	2.00	6.00	15.00	—

KM# 896 10 CENTIMES

Zinc **Obv:** Monogram within wreath divided by center hole, liberty cap above **Rev:** Center hole within wreath divides denomination, date below, dash below MES in C MES

Date	Mintage	F	VF	XF	Unc	BU
1941	Inc. above	0.75	1.25	4.00	10.00	—

KM# 897 10 CENTIMES

Zinc, 21 mm. **Obv:** Monogram within wreath divided by center hole, liberty cap above **Rev:** Center hole within wreath divides denomination, dot before and after date below

Date	Mintage	F	VF	XF	Unc	BU
.1941.	Inc. above	0.25	0.50	1.00	4.00	—
1941.	Inc. above	0.25	0.50	1.00	4.00	—

KM# 903 10 CENTIMES

1.5000 g., Zinc, 17 mm. **Obv:** Grain sprigs flank center hole **Rev:** Center hole divides denomination, oak leaves flank, date below **Designer:** Atelier de Paris **Note:** Reduced size.

Date	Mintage	F	VF	XF	Unc	BU
1943	24,638,000	0.25	0.75	2.50	7.00	—
1944	58,463,000	0.25	0.50	2.00	5.00	—

KM# 906.1 10 CENTIMES

Zinc, 17 mm. **Obv:** Monogram divided by center hole, liberty cap above, wreath surrounds **Rev:** Center hole and plant divide denomination, date below **Note:** Reduced size.

Date	Mintage	F	VF	XF	Unc	BU
1945	38,174,000	1.00	1.75	3.25	12.00	—
1946 Rare	—	—	—	—	—	—

KM# 906.2 10 CENTIMES

Zinc **Obv:** Monogram divided by center hole, liberty cap above, wreath surrounds **Rev:** Center hole and plant divide denomination

Date	Mintage	F	VF	XF	Unc	BU
1945B	7,246,000	1.50	3.00	6.00	16.00	—
1946B	10,566,000	2.50	5.00	10.00	25.00	—

KM# 906.3 10 CENTIMES

Zinc **Obv:** Monogram divided by center hole, liberty cap above, wreath surrounds **Rev:** Center hole and plant divide denomination

Date	Mintage	F	VF	XF	Unc	BU
1945C	8,379,000	2.00	4.00	8.00	20.00	45.00

KM# 899 20 CENTIMES

3.5000 g., Zinc, 24 mm. **Obv:** Grain sprigs flank center hole **Rev:** Center hole divides denomination, oak leaves flank, date below **Designer:** Atelier **Note:** Issued for Vichy French State.

Date	Mintage	F	VF	XF	Unc	BU
1941	54,044,000	1.00	2.00	4.00	17.00	—

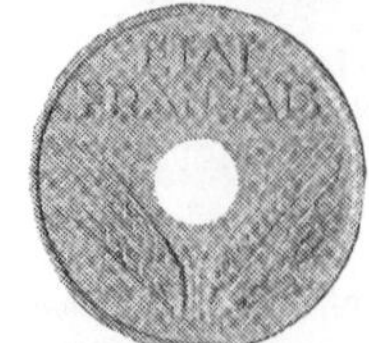

KM# 900.1 20 CENTIMES

3.5000 g., Zinc **Obv:** Grain sprigs flank center hole **Rev:** Center hole divides denomination, oak leaves flank, date below **Designer:** Atelier **Note:** Thick flan.

Date	Mintage	F	VF	XF	Unc	BU
1941	31,397,000	1.00	2.00	4.00	15.00	—
1942	112,868,000	0.50	1.00	2.00	7.00	—
1943	64,138,000	0.75	1.50	2.50	8.50	—

KM# 900.2 20 CENTIMES

3.0000 g., Zinc **Obv:** Grain sprigs flank center hole **Rev:** Center hole divides denomination, leaves flank **Note:** Thin flan. Struck at Paris Mint.

Date	Mintage	F	VF	XF	Unc	BU
1941	Inc. above	0.50	0.75	2.00	8.50	—
1942	Inc. above	0.50	0.75	2.00	7.50	—
1943	Inc. above	0.50	0.75	2.00	6.50	—
1944	5,250,000	15.00	30.00	80.00	165	—

KM# 900.2a 20 CENTIMES

3.0000 g., Iron **Obv:** Grain sprigs flank center hole **Rev:** Center hole divides denomination, leaves flank **Designer:** Atelier

Date	Mintage	F	VF	XF	Unc	BU
1944	695,000	25.00	50.00	150	185	250

KM# 907.1 20 CENTIMES

Zinc **Obv:** Monogram divided by center hole, liberty cap above, wreath surrounds **Rev:** Center hole and plant divide denomination, date below **Note:** Fourth Republic.

Date	Mintage	F	VF	XF	Unc	BU
1945	6,003,000	2.00	4.00	9.00	22.00	—
1946	2,662,000	8.00	18.00	35.00	70.00	140

KM# 907.2 20 CENTIMES

3.0000 g., Zinc, 24 mm. **Obv:** Monogram divided by center hole, liberty cap above, wreath surrounds **Rev:** Center hole and plant divide denomination, date below **Designer:** Lindaver

Date	Mintage	F	VF	XF	Unc	BU
1945B	100,000	85.00	165	285	470	—
1946B Rare	5,525,000	75.00	150	260	450	—

KM# 907.3 20 CENTIMES

Zinc **Obv:** Monogram divided by center hole, liberty cap above, wreath surrounds **Rev:** Center hole and plant divide denomination, date below

Date	Mintage	F	VF	XF	Unc	BU
1945C	299,000	20.00	40.00	85.00	150	220

KM# 855 25 CENTIMES

7.0000 g., Nickel, 24 mm. **Obv:** Laureate liberty head left **Rev:** Denomination and date flanked by cornucopias **Designer:** Patey **Note:** Without mint mark.

Date	Mintage	F	VF	XF	Unc	BU
1903	16,000,000	0.25	1.00	2.00	11.50	—

KM# 856 25 CENTIMES

7.0000 g., Nickel, 24 mm. **Obv:** Laureate bust left **Rev:** Oak leaves divide date and denomination, column with axe head on top at left **Shape:** 22-sided **Designer:** Patey

Date	Mintage	F	VF	XF	Unc	BU
1904	16,000,000	0.25	0.75	2.00	13.50	—
1905	8,000,000	0.50	1.50	3.50	20.00	—

KM# 867 25 CENTIMES

5.0400 g., Nickel, 24 mm. **Obv:** Monogram divided by center hole, liberty cap above, wreath surrounds **Rev:** Center hole and plant divide denomination, dash under "MES" in denomination **Designer:** Lindaver

Date	Mintage	F	VF	XF	Unc	BU
1914	941,000	1.50	3.00	7.00	22.50	—
1915	535,000	2.50	4.00	8.00	32.00	—
1916	100,000	15.00	30.00	60.00	120	—
1917	65,000	30.00	50.00	85.00	185	375

KM# 867a 25 CENTIMES

5.0000 g., Copper-Nickel, 24 mm. **Obv:** Monogram divided by center hole, liberty cap above, wreath surrounds **Rev:** Without dash under "MES" in denomination **Edge:** Plain **Designer:** Lindaver **Note:** Varieties: Edges reeded on 1920, 1929, 1931, different hole.

Date	Mintage	F	VF	XF	Unc	BU
1917	3,085,000	2.00	4.00	12.00	22.00	—
1918	18,330,000	0.25	0.50	1.50	3.50	—
1919	5,106,000	1.00	2.00	3.00	7.00	—
1920	18,108,000	0.15	0.50	1.00	3.00	—
1921	18,531,000	0.15	0.50	1.00	3.00	—
1922	17,766,000	0.15	0.50	1.00	3.00	—
1923	19,718,000	0.15	0.50	1.00	3.00	—
1924	24,535,000	0.15	0.50	1.00	3.00	—
1925	17,807,000	0.15	0.50	1.00	3.00	—
1926	13,226,000	0.15	0.50	1.00	3.00	—
1927	13,465,000	0.15	0.50	1.00	3.00	—
1928	9,960,000	0.25	0.50	1.50	3.50	—
1929	12,887,000	0.15	0.50	1.00	2.50	—
1930	28,363,000	0.15	0.50	1.00	2.50	—
1931	22,121,000	0.15	0.50	1.00	2.50	—
1932	30,364,000	0.15	0.50	1.00	2.50	—
1933	28,562,000	0.15	0.50	1.00	2.50	—
1936	4,657,000	1.50	3.00	8.00	18.00	—
1937	7,780,000	0.25	0.50	1.50	3.50	—

KM# 867b 25 CENTIMES

4.1600 g., Nickel-Bronze, 24 mm. **Obv. Designer:** Monogram divided by center hole, liberty cap above, wreath surrounds **Rev:** Center hole and plant divide denomination, date below **Edge:** Plain **Note:** Listings below appear with a period before and after the date.

Date	Mintage	F	VF	XF	Unc	BU
1938	5,170,000	0.25	0.50	1.00	2.50	—
1939	42,964,000	0.15	0.35	0.75	1.50	—
Note: Thick flan (1.55mm)						
1939	Inc. above	0.15	0.35	0.75	1.50	—
Note: Thin flan (1.35mm)						
1940	3,446,000	6.00	12.00	18.00	35.00	—

KM# 854 50 CENTIMES

2.5000 g., 0.8350 Silver 0.0671 oz. ASW, 18 mm. **Obv:** Figure sowing seed **Rev:** Leafy branch divides date and denomination **Designer:** Louis Oscar Roty **Note:** Without mint mark.

Date	Mintage	F	VF	XF	Unc	BU
1901	4,960,000	2.00	4.00	12.00	45.00	90.00
1902	3,778,000	2.50	5.00	15.00	55.00	80.00

Date	Mintage	F	VF	XF	Unc	BU
1903	2,222,000	12.00	25.00	50.00	150	200
1904	4,000,000	1.50	3.50	10.00	45.00	90.00
1905	2,381,000	5.00	9.00	20.00	100	200
1906	2,679,000	2.50	5.00	15.00	55.00	85.00
1907	7,332,000	1.50	3.50	10.00	30.00	—
1908	14,304,000	1.00	1.50	4.00	15.00	—
1909	9,900,000	1.00	1.50	4.00	15.00	—
1910	15,923,000	BV	1.25	3.00	10.00	—
1911	1,330,000	20.00	50.00	110	200	—
1912	16,000,000	BV	1.00	1.50	5.00	—
1913	14,000,000	BV	1.00	1.50	5.00	—
1914	9,657,000	BV	1.00	1.50	6.00	—
1915	20,893,000	BV	1.00	1.25	3.00	—
1916	52,963,000	BV	1.00	1.25	2.50	—
1917	48,629,000	BV	1.00	1.25	2.50	—
1918	36,492,000	BV	1.00	1.25	2.50	—
1919	24,299,000	BV	1.00	1.25	2.50	—
1920	8,509,000	1.00	1.50	3.00	6.00	—

KM# 884 50 CENTIMES

2.0000 g., Aluminum-Bronze, 18 mm. **Obv:** Denomination within circle **Rev:** Mercury seated left, caduceus at left, shield on right, date below **Designer:** Domard F. **Note:** Varieties for 1924: Closed and open 4's.

Date	Mintage	F	VF	XF	Unc	BU
1921	8,692,000	0.75	2.00	6.00	18.00	—
1922	86,226,000	0.15	0.25	1.00	4.00	—
1923	119,584,000	0.15	0.25	0.75	2.50	—
1924	97,036,000	0.15	0.25	1.00	3.00	—
1925	48,017,000	0.25	0.50	1.25	5.00	—
1926	46,447,000	0.25	0.50	1.25	5.00	—
1927	23,703,000	0.75	1.50	3.00	8.50	—
1928	10,329,000	0.75	2.00	5.00	16.00	—
1929	6,669,000	2.50	6.00	12.50	25.00	60.00

KM# 894.1 50 CENTIMES

2.0000 g., Aluminum-Bronze, 18 mm. **Obv:** Laureate head left **Rev:** Denomination above date, cornucopias flank **Designer:** Pierre Alexandre Morlon

Date	Mintage	F	VF	XF	Unc	BU
1931	62,775,000	0.15	0.25	1.00	3.00	—
1932 Closed 9	Inc. above	0.15	0.25	0.50	2.00	—
1932 Open 9	108,839,000	0.15	0.25	0.50	2.00	—
1933 Closed 9	Inc. above	0.15	0.25	0.75	3.00	—
1933 Open 9	41,937,000	0.15	0.25	0.75	3.00	—
1936	16,602,000	0.50	1.00	2.00	5.00	—
1937	43,950,000	0.15	0.25	0.75	3.00	—
1938	55,707,000	0.15	0.25	0.75	3.00	—
1939	96,594,000	0.15	0.25	0.50	2.00	—
1940	10,854,000	0.50	1.00	2.00	5.00	—
1941	82,958,000	0.15	0.25	1.00	3.00	—
1947	Est. 2,170,000	60.00	125	225	350	—

Note: 1947 date was struck for colonial use in Africa

KM# 894.1a 50 CENTIMES

Aluminum, 18 mm. **Obv:** Laureate liberty head left **Rev:** Cornucopias flank denomination and date **Note:** Without mint mark. Thick and thin planchets exist.

Date	Mintage	F	VF	XF	Unc	BU
1941	129,758,000	0.15	0.25	0.50	2.00	—
1944	9,898,000	0.50	1.00	2.50	6.00	—
1945	26,224,000	0.15	0.25	1.00	3.00	—
1946	24,605,000	0.15	0.25	1.00	3.00	—
1947	51,744,000	0.15	0.25	0.60	2.00	—

KM# 894.2a 50 CENTIMES

0.7000 g., Aluminum, 18 mm. **Obv:** Laureate liberty head left **Rev:** Cornucopias flank denomination and date **Designer:** Morlon

Date	Mintage	F	VF	XF	Unc	BU
1944B	20,000	—	—	—	—	—
Note: Reported, not confirmed						
1945B	6,357,000	0.50	1.00	3.00	8.00	—
1946B	29,344,000	0.15	0.25	1.00	4.00	—
1947B	18,504,000	2.00	5.00	10.00	20.00	—

KM# 894.3a 50 CENTIMES

Aluminum, 18 mm. **Obv:** Laureate liberty head left **Rev:** Cornucopias flank denomination and date

Date	Mintage	F	VF	XF	Unc	BU
1944C	17,220,000	—	—	—	—	—
Note: Reported, not confirmed						
1945C	2,968,000	1.00	3.00	6.00	12.00	—

KM# 894.2 50 CENTIMES

Aluminum-Bronze, 18 mm. **Obv:** Laureate liberty head left **Rev:** Cornucopias flank denomination and date

Date	Mintage	F	VF	XF	Unc	BU
1939B	6,200,000	0.50	1.00	2.50	10.00	—

KM# 914.1 50 CENTIMES

Aluminum, 18 mm. **Obv:** Double bit axe, grain sprigs flank **Rev:** Denomination above date, oak leaves flank **Designer:** Lucien Bazor **Note:** Without mint mark. Vichy French State. Thick and thin planchets exist.

Date	Mintage	F	VF	XF	Unc	BU
1942	50,134,000	0.15	0.25	0.75	2.00	—
1943	84,462,000	0.15	0.25	0.75	1.50	—
1944	57,410,000	1.50	3.00	6.00	18.00	—

KM# 914.2 50 CENTIMES

0.8000 g., Aluminum, 18 mm. **Obv:** Grain sprigs flank double bit axe **Rev:** Denomination above date, oak leaves flank **Designer:** Bazor

Date	Mintage	F	VF	XF	Unc	BU
1943B	21,916,000	5.00	10.00	28.00	50.00	70.00
1944B	27,334,000	1.50	3.00	7.00	15.00	25.00

KM# 914.3 50 CENTIMES

Aluminum, 18 mm. **Obv:** Grain sprigs flank double bit axe **Rev:** Denomination above date, oak leaves flank

Date	Mintage	F	VF	XF	Unc	BU
1944C Small C	27,213,000	2.00	4.00	8.00	26.00	40.00
1944C Large C	Inc. above	—	—	—	—	—

KM# 914.4 50 CENTIMES

Aluminum, 18 mm. **Obv:** Grain sprigs flank double bit axe **Rev:** Denomination above date, oak leaves flank **Note:** Without mint mark. Thin flan. Struck at Paris Mint.

Date	Mintage	F	VF	XF	Unc	BU
1942	—	0.15	0.25	1.00	2.50	—
1943	—	0.15	0.25	0.50	1.25	—

KM# 844.1 FRANC

5.0000 g., 0.8350 Silver 0.1342 oz. ASW, 23 mm. **Obv:** Figure sowing seed **Rev:** Leafy branch divides date and denomination **Designer:** Louis Oscar Roty **Note:** Without mint mark.

Date	Mintage	F	VF	XF	Unc	BU
1901	6,200,000	Value: 140				
1902	6,000,000	2.00	4.00	20.00	75.00	130
1903	472,000	40.00	80.00	325	650	1,000
1904	7,000,000	2.00	4.00	17.50	75.00	130
1905	6,004,000	2.00	4.00	15.00	65.00	110
1906	1,908,000	6.00	20.00	40.00	100	175
1907	2,563,000	4.00	9.00	30.00	90.00	150
1908	3,961,000	2.50	5.00	20.00	65.00	110
1909	10,924,000	2.00	2.50	5.00	22.00	75.00
1910	7,725,000	2.00	2.50	5.00	22.00	75.00
1911	5,542,000	2.25	3.00	12.00	45.00	90.00
1912	10,001,000	2.00	2.50	5.00	22.00	75.00
1913	13,654,000	2.00	2.50	4.00	18.00	50.00
1914	14,361,000	2.00	2.50	3.50	15.00	45.00
1915	47,955,000	BV	1.85	2.25	5.50	—
1916	92,029,000	—	BV	2.00	3.50	—
1917	57,153,000	—	BV	2.00	3.50	—
1918	50,112,000	—	BV	2.00	3.50	—
1919	46,112,000	—	BV	2.00	3.50	—
1920	19,322,000	BV	1.85	2.50	5.50	—

KM# 844.2 FRANC

5.0000 g., 0.8350 Silver 0.1342 oz. ASW, 23 mm. **Obv:** Figure sowing seed **Rev:** Leafy branch divides date and denomination **Designer:** Louis Oscar Roty

Date	Mintage	F	VF	XF	Unc	BU
1914C	43,000	135	250	350	500	700

KM# 876 FRANC

4.0900 g., Aluminum-Bronze, 23 mm. **Obv:** Value **Obv. Legend:** CHAMBRES • DE • COMMERCE • DE • FRANCE **Rev:** Mercury seated left **Rev. Legend:** COMMERCE - INDUSTRIE **Edge:** Reeded **Designer:** Domard **Note:** Without mint mark. Chamber of Commerce.

Date	Mintage	F	VF	XF	Unc	BU
1920	590,000	3.00	5.00	12.50	32.00	—
1921	54,572,000	0.25	0.50	1.50	5.50	—
1922	111,343,000	0.15	0.25	1.00	4.50	—
1923	140,138,000	0.15	0.25	1.00	3.50	—
1924 Closed 4	Inc. above	0.35	0.60	2.00	6.50	—
1924 Open 4	87,715,000	0.15	0.25	1.00	4.50	—
1925	36,523,000	0.25	0.50	1.50	5.50	—
1926	1,580,000	3.00	8.00	20.00	45.00	75.00
1927	11,330,000	0.50	1.50	3.50	8.50	—

KM# 885 FRANC

4.0000 g., Aluminum-Bronze, 23 mm. **Obv:** Laureate head left **Rev:** Cornucopias flank denomination and date **Edge:** Plain **Designer:** Pierre Alexandre Morlon

Date	Mintage	F	VF	XF	Unc	BU
1931	15,504,000	0.25	0.50	2.00	6.50	—
1932	29,768,000	0.15	0.25	1.00	4.00	—
1933	15,356,000	0.25	0.50	2.00	6.50	—
1934	17,286,000	0.25	0.50	2.00	5.00	—
1935	1,166,000	6.00	15.00	25.00	60.00	100
1936	23,817,000	0.15	0.25	1.00	4.00	—
1937	30,940,000	0.15	0.25	1.00	3.00	—
1938	66,165,000	0.15	0.25	1.00	2.50	—
1939	48,434,000	0.15	0.25	1.00	3.00	—
1940	25,525,000	0.15	0.25	1.00	3.50	—
1941	34,705,000	0.15	0.25	1.00	3.00	—

KM# 902.1 FRANC

Aluminum, 23 mm. **Obv:** Double bit axe, grain sprigs flank **Rev:** Denomination above date, oak leaves flank **Designer:** Lucien Bazor **Note:** Without mint mark. Vichy French State Issues. Thick and thin planchets exist.

Date	Mintage	F	VF	XF	Unc	BU
1942	152,144,000	0.25	0.50	1.50	4.00	—
1942 Without LB	Inc. above	—	—	—	—	—
1943	205,564,000	0.10	0.25	1.00	2.50	—
1943 Thin flan	Inc. above	0.10	0.25	1.00	2.50	—
1944	50,605,000	0.50	1.25	2.00	10.00	—

KM# 902.2 FRANC

1.2800 g., Aluminum, 23 mm. **Obv:** Grain sprigs flank double bit axe **Rev:** Leaves flank denomination, date below

Date	Mintage	F	VF	XF	Unc	BU
1943B	68,082,000	5.00	9.00	28.00	80.00	120
1944B	13,622,000	1.50	3.00	12.00	25.00	—
1944 large C	74,859,000	0.50	1.50	3.50	12.50	—
1944 small C	—	50.00	100	200	400	600

KM# 902.3 FRANC

Aluminum, 23 mm. **Obv:** Grain sprigs flank double bit axe **Rev:** Leaves flank denomination, date below

Date	Mintage	F	VF	XF	Unc	BU
1944 Large C	74,859,000	0.25	0.75	1.50	5.50	—
1944 Small C	Inc. above	15.00	30.00	70.00	325	—

KM# 885a.1 FRANC

1.3000 g., Aluminum, 23 mm. **Obv:** Laureate head left **Rev:** Cornucopias flank denomination and date **Edge:** Plain **Designer:** Morlon **Note:** Thick and thin planchets exist.

Date	Mintage	F	VF	XF	Unc	BU
1941	60,877,000	0.10	0.20	1.00	4.00	—
1943	4,400	1,200	1,500	2,250	4,000	6,000
1944	22,608,000	0.10	0.20	1.50	5.00	—
1945	61,780,000	0.10	0.15	0.50	2.00	—
1946	52,516,000	0.10	0.15	0.25	2.00	—
1947	110,448,000	0.10	0.15	0.25	2.00	—
1948	96,092,000	0.10	0.15	0.25	2.00	—

Date	Mintage	F	VF	XF	Unc	BU
1949	41,090,000	0.10	0.15	0.25	2.00	—
1950	27,882,000	0.10	0.15	0.50	2.50	—
1957	16,497,000	0.10	0.15	0.75	3.00	—
1958	21,197,000	0.10	0.15	0.75	3.00	—
1959	41,985,000	0.10	0.15	0.25	1.25	—

KM# 885a.2 FRANC

Aluminum, 23 mm. **Obv:** Laureate head left **Rev:** Cornucopias flank denomination and date

Date	Mintage	F	VF	XF	Unc	BU
1945B	4,251,000	1.00	3.50	9.00	28.00	75.00
1946B	26,493,000	0.10	0.20	1.50	5.00	—
1947B	31,562,000	0.10	0.20	1.00	4.00	—
1948B	45,481,000	0.10	0.20	1.00	3.50	—
1949B	35,840,000	0.10	0.20	1.00	4.00	—
1950B	18,800,000	1.00	2.00	3.50	15.00	—
1957B	63,976,000	0.10	0.20	1.00	4.00	—
1958B	13,412,000	0.25	0.75	2.00	5.50	—

KM# 885a.3 FRANC

Aluminum, 23 mm. **Obv:** Laureate head left **Rev:** Cornucopias flank denomination and date

Date	Mintage	F	VF	XF	Unc	BU
1944C	33,600,000	0.50	1.50	3.50	12.00	—
1945C	5,220,000	1.50	3.50	9.00	25.00	60.00

KM# 885b FRANC

Zinc, 23 mm. **Obv:** Laureate head left **Rev:** Cornucopias flank denomination and date **Note:** Struck for colonial use in Africa.

Date	Mintage	F	VF	XF	Unc	BU
1943A	Est. 17,000	750	1,100	1,700	3,200	—

KM# 845.1 2 FRANCS

10.0000 g., 0.8350 Silver 0.2684 oz. ASW, 27 mm. **Obv:** Figure sowing seed **Rev:** Leafy branch divides denomination and date **Designer:** Louis Oscar Roty **Note:** Without mint mark.

Date	Mintage	F	VF	XF	Unc	BU
1901	1,860,000	6.50	18.00	50.00	150	275
1902	2,000,000	6.50	18.00	50.00	125	210
1904	1,500,000	7.50	18.00	40.00	175	250
1905	2,000,000	6.50	18.00	50.00	150	225
1908	2,502,000	3.75	6.00	20.00	75.00	100
1909	1,000,000	8.00	18.00	35.00	175	250
1910	2,190,000	3.75	6.00	20.00	75.00	100
1912	1,000,000	7.00	18.00	40.00	125	200
1913	500,000	15.00	25.00	45.00	150	225
1914	5,719,000	BV	3.75	7.00	25.00	50.00
1915	13,963,000	—	BV	4.00	18.00	—
1916	17,887,000	—	BV	4.00	18.00	—
1917	16,555,000	—	BV	4.00	18.00	—
1918	12,026,000	—	BV	4.00	18.00	—
1919	9,261,000	—	BV	4.00	15.00	—
1920	3,014,000	BV	4.00	7.00	25.00	—

KM# 845.2 2 FRANCS

10.0000 g., 0.8352 Silver 0.2685 oz. ASW, 27 mm. **Obv:** Figure sowing seed **Rev:** Leafy branch divides date and denomination

Date	Mintage	F	VF	XF	Unc	BU
1914C	462,000	9.00	16.00	35.00	65.00	160
1914C Matte Proof	—	Value: 650				

KM# 877 2 FRANCS

8.0000 g., Aluminum-Bronze, 27 mm. **Subject:** French Chamber of Commerce **Obv:** Denomination within circle **Rev:** Mercury seated left, caduceus at left, shield on right, date below **Note:** Without mint mark.

Date	Mintage	F	VF	XF	Unc	BU
1920	14,363,000	6.00	15.00	40.00	90.00	—
1921	Inc. above	0.75	1.50	3.00	12.50	—
1922	29,463,000	0.50	1.00	2.00	7.50	—
1923	43,960,000	0.50	1.00	2.00	7.50	—
1924 Open 4	29,631,000	0.50	1.00	2.00	7.50	—
1924 Closed 4	Inc. above	0.65	1.50	3.00	10.00	—
1925/3	31,607,000	0.75	1.75	4.00	12.50	—
1925	Inc. above	0.50	1.00	2.00	8.00	—
1926	2,962,000	7.00	18.00	50.00	100	—
1927	1,678,000	100	150	300	700	—

KM# 886 2 FRANCS

8.0000 g., Aluminum-Bronze, 27 mm. **Obv:** Laureate head left **Rev:** Denomination and date flanked by cornucopias **Designer:** Pierre Alexandre Morlon

Date	Mintage	F	VF	XF	Unc	BU
1931	1,717,000	3.00	6.00	12.00	35.00	—
1932	8,943,000	0.75	1.50	3.00	10.00	—
1933	8,413,000	0.75	1.50	3.00	10.00	—
1934	6,896,000	1.25	2.50	6.00	12.00	—
1935	298,000	12.00	20.00	40.00	90.00	—
1936	12,394,000	0.25	1.00	2.00	6.00	—
1937	11,055,000	0.25	1.00	2.00	6.00	—
1938	28,072,000	0.20	0.50	1.00	5.00	—
1939	25,403,000	0.20	0.50	1.00	5.00	—
1940	9,716,000	1.00	2.00	3.50	10.00	—
1941	16,684,000	0.25	1.00	2.00	6.00	—

KM# 886a.1 2 FRANCS

Aluminum, 27 mm. **Obv:** Laureate head left **Rev:** Denomination and date flanked by cornucopias

Date	Mintage	F	VF	XF	Unc	BU
1941	Inc. above	0.25	0.50	1.00	3.00	—
1944	7,224,000	0.75	1.50	4.00	12.00	—
1945	16,636,000	0.50	1.00	2.50	7.00	—
1946	34,930,000	0.20	0.50	1.00	3.50	—
1947	78,984,000	0.20	0.30	1.00	2.50	—
1948	32,354,000	0.20	0.50	1.00	3.50	—
1949	13,683,000	0.25	0.50	1.00	2.50	—
1950	12,191,000	0.25	0.50	1.00	2.50	—
1958	9,906,000	0.20	0.50	1.00	3.50	—
1959	17,774,000	0.20	0.50	1.00	3.50	—

KM# 904.1 2 FRANCS

Aluminum, 27 mm. **Obv:** Double bit axe, grain sprigs flank **Rev:** Oak leaves flank denomination, date below **Designer:** Lucien Bazor **Note:** Without mint mark. Issued for Vichy French State.

Date	Mintage	F	VF	XF	Unc	BU
1943	106,997,000	0.20	0.50	1.00	6.00	—
1944	25,546,000	0.75	1.50	3.50	8.00	—

KM# 904.2 2 FRANCS

2.2000 g., Aluminum, 27 mm. **Obv:** Grain sprigs flank double bit axe **Rev:** Oak leaves flank denomination, date below **Designer:** Bazor

Date	Mintage	F	VF	XF	Unc	BU
1943B	34,131,000	3.50	7.00	15.00	25.00	—
1944B	10,298,000	1.50	3.00	6.00	18.00	—

KM# 904.3 2 FRANCS

Aluminum, 27 mm. **Obv:** Grain sprigs flank double bit axe **Rev:** Oak leaves flank denomination, date below

Date	Mintage	F	VF	XF	Unc	BU
1944C	19,470,000	1.25	2.50	5.00	18.00	—

KM# 905 2 FRANCS

8.1500 g., Brass, 27 mm. **Obv:** FRANCE within wreath **Rev:** Large denomination above date **Note:** Without mint mark. Issued during Allied Occupation for circulation in Algeria and France.

Date	Mintage	F	VF	XF	Unc	BU
1944	50,000,000	1.00	2.00	5.00	25.00	60.00

KM# 886a.2 2 FRANCS

2.2000 g., Aluminum, 27 mm. **Obv:** Laureate head left **Rev:** Denomination and date flanked by cornucopias **Designer:** Morlon

Date	Mintage	F	VF	XF	Unc	BU
1944B	170,000	—	—	—	—	—
1945B	1,726,000	3.00	7.00	15.00	35.00	—
1946B	6,018,000	2.00	4.00	8.00	20.00	—
1947B	26,220,000	0.20	0.50	1.00	3.50	—
1948B	39,090,000	0.20	0.50	1.00	3.00	—
1949B	23,955,000	0.20	0.50	1.00	3.50	—
1950B	18,185,000	0.50	1.00	3.00	5.00	—

KM# 886a.3 2 FRANCS

Aluminum, 27 mm. **Obv:** Laureate head left **Rev:** Denomination and date flanked by cornucopias

Date	Mintage	F	VF	XF	Unc	BU
1945C	1,165,000	5.00	10.00	25.00	65.00	110

KM# 887 5 FRANCS

6.0000 g., Nickel, 23.7 mm. **Obv:** Head right, date below **Rev:** Denomination flanked by grain sprigs **Designer:** L. Bazor **Note:** Without mint mark.

Date	Mintage	F	VF	XF	Unc	BU
1933 (a)	105,029,373	0.75	1.50	3.50	9.00	—

KM# 888 5 FRANCS

12.0000 g., Nickel, 31 mm. **Obv:** Laureate head left **Rev:** Denomination above date within sectioned wreath **Designer:** Larrillier **Note:** Without mint mark.

Date	Mintage	F	VF	XF	Unc	BU
1933 (a)	56,686,000	0.25	0.75	2.50	8.00	—
1935 (a)	54,164,000	0.25	0.75	2.50	8.00	—
1936 (a)	117,000	400	700	1,200	1,850	—
1937 (a)	157,000	35.00	60.00	120	225	—
1938 (a)	4,977,000	12.00	25.00	50.00	120	—
1939 (a)	—	700	1,200	2,000	4,000	—

KM# 888a.1 5 FRANCS

12.0000 g., Aluminum-Bronze, 31 mm. **Obv:** Laureate head left **Rev:** Denomination above date within sectioned wreath **Designer:** Larrillier **Note:** Struck for Colonial use in Algeria.

Date	Mintage	F	VF	XF	Unc	BU
1938 (a)	10,144,000	6.00	10.00	18.00	85.00	120
1939 (a)	Inc. above	2.50	5.00	12.00	30.00	60.00
1940 (a)	38,758,000	1.00	2.00	3.50	10.00	40.00

KM# 888a.2 5 FRANCS

Aluminum-Bronze, 31 mm. **Obv:** Laureate head left **Rev:** Denomination above date within sectioned wreath **Note:** Struck for Colonial use in Africa.

Date	Mintage	F	VF	XF	Unc	BU
1945 (a) Open 9	13,044,000	1.00	2.00	4.00	11.00	—
1946 (a) Open 9	21,790,000	1.00	2.00	4.00	11.00	—
1947 (a)	2,662,000	165	400	600	1,200	—

Note: Date exists with both open and closed 9's.

KM# 888a.3 5 FRANCS

Aluminum-Bronze, 31 mm. **Obv:** Laureate head left **Rev:** Denomination above date within sectioned wreath

Date	Mintage	F	VF	XF	Unc	BU
1945C Open 9	Inc. above	3.00	7.00	15.00	30.00	—
1946C Open 9	Inc. above	5.00	15.00	30.00	60.00	—

KM# 888b.1 5 FRANCS

3.5000 g., Aluminum, 31.5 mm. **Obv:** Laureate head left **Rev:** Denomination above date within sectioned wreath **Edge:** Plain **Designer:** Lavrillier **Note:** Without mint mark.

Date	Mintage	F	VF	XF	Unc	BU
1945 (a) Open 9	95,399,000	0.20	0.35	1.50	6.00	—
1946 (a) Open 9	61,332,000	0.20	0.35	1.50	6.00	—
1947 (a) Open 9	46,576,000	0.20	0.35	1.50	6.00	—
1947 (a) Closed 9	Inc. above	0.20	0.35	1.50	6.00	—
1948 (a) Open 9	104,473,000	1.00	3.00	6.00	12.50	—
1948 (a) Closed 9	Inc. above	5.00	10.00	30.00	50.00	—
1949 (a) Closed 9	203,252,000	0.20	0.35	0.75	3.00	—
1950 (a) Closed 9	128,372,000	0.20	0.35	0.75	3.00	—
1952 (a) Closed 9	4,000,000	20.00	40.00	100	225	—

KM# 888b.2 5 FRANCS

Aluminum, 31 mm. **Obv:** Laureate head left **Rev:** Denomination above date within sectioned wreath

Date	Mintage	F	VF	XF	Unc	BU
1945B Open 9	6,043,000	1.50	3.00	5.00	15.00	—
1946B Open 9	13,360,000	0.75	1.50	3.00	12.00	—
1947B Open 9	30,839,000	0.50	1.00	2.50	8.00	—
1947B Closed 9	Inc. above	0.50	1.00	2.50	8.00	—
1948B Open 9	28,047,000	20.00	40.00	100	175	—
B Closed 9	Inc. above	20.00	40.00	100	175	—
1949B Closed 9	48,414,000	0.50	1.00	2.50	8.00	—
1950B Closed 9	28,952,000	0.75	1.50	3.50	9.00	—

KM# 888b.3 5 FRANCS

Aluminum, 31 mm. **Obv:** Laureate head left **Rev:** Denomination above date within sectioned wreath

Date	Mintage	F	VF	XF	Unc	BU
1945C Open 9	2,208,000	7.00	15.00	28.00	60.00	85.00
1946C Open 9	1,269,000	8.00	18.00	38.00	75.00	95.00

KM# 901 5 FRANCS

4.0000 g., Copper-Nickel, 22 mm. **Obv:** Double bit axe divides denomination, date below **Rev:** Head with collar left **Designer:** Bazor **Note:** Without mint mark.

Date	Mintage	F	VF	XF	Unc	BU
1941 (a)	13,782,000	65.00	100	150	250	400

Note: Never released into circulation.

KM# 846 10 FRANCS

3.2258 g., 0.9000 Gold 0.0933 oz. AGW

Date	Mintage	F	VF	XF	Unc	BU
1901	2,100,000	—	BV	90.00	125	180
1901	2,100,000	—	BV	90.00	125	180
1905	1,426,000	—	BV	90.00	125	180
1905	1,426,000	—	BV	90.00	125	180
1906	3,665,000	—	BV	90.00	125	180
1907	3,364,000	—	BV	90.00	125	180
1908	1,650,000	—	BV	90.00	125	180
1909	599,000	—	BV	90.00	220	400
1910	2,110,000	—	BV	90.00	125	180
1911	1,881,000	—	BV	90.00	125	180
1912	1,756,000	—	BV	90.00	150	200
1914	3,041,000	—	BV	85.00	120	180

KM# 878 10 FRANCS

10.0000 g., 0.6800 Silver 0.2186 oz. ASW, 28 mm. **Designer:** Turin **Note:** Without mint mark.

Date	Mintage	F	VF	XF	Unc	BU
1929	16,292,000	BV	3.50	5.50	12.00	—
1930	36,986,000	BV	3.00	4.50	9.00	—
1931	35,468,000	BV	3.00	4.50	9.00	—
1932	40,288,000	BV	3.00	3.50	7.00	—
1933	31,146,000	BV	3.00	3.50	7.00	—
1934	52,001,000	BV	3.00	3.50	7.00	—
1936	—	—	—	—	—	—
1937	52,000	65.00	125	250	360	500
1938	14,090,000	BV	3.00	6.00	12.50	—
1939	8,298,999	3.00	4.00	8.00	17.50	—

KM# 908.1 10 FRANCS

7.0000 g., Copper-Nickel, 26 mm. **Obv:** Laureate head right, long leaves and short leaves **Rev:** Denomination above date, inscription below, grain columns flank **Edge:** Reeded **Designer:** Turin **Note:** Large head.

Date	Mintage	F	VF	XF	Unc	BU
1945 (ll)	6,557,000	0.25	0.75	2.00	6.00	—
1945 (sl)	Inc. above	15.00	30.00	50.00	90.00	140
1946 (ll)	24,409,000	185	300	400	—	—
1946 (sl)	Inc. above	0.25	0.50	2.00	5.00	—
1947	41,627,000	0.25	0.50	1.00	3.00	—

KM# 908.2 10 FRANCS

Copper-Nickel, 26 mm. **Obv:** Laureate head right **Rev:** Denomination above date, inscription below, grain columns flank **Edge:** Reeded **Note:** Large head

Date	Mintage	F	VF	XF	Unc	BU
1946B (ll)	8,452,000	20.00	35.00	50.00	85.00	—
1946B (sl)	Inc. above	0.25	0.75	2.00	6.00	—
1947B	17,188,000	0.25	0.50	2.00	5.00	—

KM# 909.1 10 FRANCS

Copper-Nickel, 26 mm. **Obv:** Laureate head right, small head **Rev:** Denomination above date, inscription below, grain columns flank **Note:** Without mint mark.

Date	Mintage	F	VF	XF	Unc	BU
1947	Inc. above	0.30	0.75	1.50	3.50	—
1948	155,945,000	0.20	0.35	0.75	2.00	—
1949	118,149,000	0.20	0.35	0.75	2.00	—

KM# 909.2 10 FRANCS

7.0000 g., Copper-Nickel, 26 mm. **Obv:** Large head **Rev:** Denomination above date, inscription below, grain columns flank **Designer:** Turin

Date	Mintage	F	VF	XF	Unc	BU
1947B	Inc. above	1.00	2.50	6.00	17.00	—
1948B	40,500,000	0.35	0.75	2.00	4.00	—
1949B	29,518,000	0.35	0.75	2.00	4.00	—

KM# 915.1 10 FRANCS

3.0000 g., Aluminum-Bronze, 20 mm. **Obv:** Head left **Rev:** Denomination above date at right, rooster above laurel leaves at left **Edge:** Plain **Designer:** Georges Guiraud **Note:** Without mint mark.

Date	Mintage	F	VF	XF	Unc	BU
1950	13,534,000	0.35	0.65	1.50	5.00	—
1951	153,689,000	0.20	0.35	0.75	2.00	—
1952	76,810,000	0.20	0.35	0.75	2.00	—
1953	46,272,000	0.25	0.50	0.75	2.50	—
1954	2,207,000	4.00	12.00	30.00	50.00	—
1955	47,466,000	0.20	0.35	0.75	2.50	—
1956	2,570,000	—	—	—	—	—
Note: Reported, not confirmed.						
1957	26,351,000	0.50	1.00	2.00	4.50	—
1958 (w)	27,213,000	0.50	1.00	2.00	4.50	—
1959	125,000	—	—	—	—	—
Note: Reported, not confirmed.						

KM# 915.2 10 FRANCS

Aluminum-Bronze, 20 mm. **Obv:** Head left **Rev:** Rooster above laurel sprig, denominaton at right **Designer:** Georges Guiraud

Date	Mintage	F	VF	XF	Unc	BU
1950B	4,808,000	1.00	3.00	6.00	17.50	—
1951B	106,866,000	0.20	0.35	0.75	2.00	—
1952B	72,346,000	0.20	0.35	0.75	2.00	—
1953B	36,466,000	0.25	0.50	1.00	3.00	—
1954B	21,634,000	0.75	1.50	3.50	7.00	—
1958B	1,500,000	—	—	—	—	—
Note: Reported, not confirmed.						

KM# 847 20 FRANCS

6.4516 g., 0.9000 Gold 0.1867 oz. AGW **Edge Lettering:** DIEU PROTEGE LA FRANCE

Date	Mintage	F	VF	XF	Unc	BU
1901A	2,643,000	—	—	BV	200	325
1901A	2,643,000	—	—	BV	200	325
1902A	2,394,000	—	—	BV	200	325
1902A	2,394,000	—	—	BV	200	325
1903A	4,405,000	—	—	BV	200	325
1904A	7,706,000	—	—	BV	200	325
1905A	9,158,000	—	—	BV	200	325
1906A	14,613,000	—	—	BV	200	325

KM# 857 20 FRANCS

6.4516 g., 0.9000 Gold 0.1867 oz. AGW **Obv:** Oak leaf wreath encircles liberty head right **Rev:** Rooster divides denomination, date below **Edge Lettering:** LIBERTE EGALITE FRATERNITE **Note:** All dates from 1907-1914 have been officially restruck.

Date	Mintage	F	VF	XF	Unc	BU
1906	—	—	—	BV	200	315
1907	17,716,000	—	—	BV	200	315
1908	6,721,000	—	—	BV	200	315
1909	9,637,000	—	—	BV	200	315
1910	5,779,000	—	—	BV	200	315
1911	5,346,000	—	—	BV	200	315
1912	10,332,000	—	—	BV	200	315
1913	12,163,000	—	—	BV	200	315
1914	6,518,000	—	—	BV	200	315

KM# 879 20 FRANCS

20.0000 g., 0.6800 Silver 0.4372 oz. ASW, 35 mm. **Obv:** Laureate head right, long and short leaves **Rev:** Denomination above date, inscription below, grain columns flank **Designer:** P. Turin **Note:** Without mint mark.

Date	Mintage	F	VF	XF	Unc	BU
1929 (ll)	3,234,000	BV	6.50	9.00	35.00	75.00
1932 Only 1 known	—	—	—	—	—	—
1933 (sl)	—	BV	6.00	7.00	18.00	40.00
Note: Counterfeits exist in bronze-aluminum with thin silver sheath.						
1933 (ll)	Inc. above	BV	6.00	7.00	18.00	40.00
1934 (sl)	11,785,000	BV	6.00	10.00	30.00	45.00
1936 (sl)	48,000	200	300	450	700	—
1937 (sl)	1,189,000	10.00	15.00	25.00	50.00	85.00
1938 (sl)	10,910,000	BV	6.00	7.50	20.00	35.00
1939 (sl)	3,918	1,000	2,000	2,750	4,500	—

KM# 916.1 20 FRANCS

4.0000 g., Aluminum-Bronze, 23.5 mm. **Obv:** Head left, "GEORGES GUIRAUD" behind head **Rev:** Denomination above date at right, rooster above laurel branch at left **Edge:** Plain

Date	Mintage	F	VF	XF	Unc	BU
1950	5,779,000	0.50	1.00	2.50	7.00	—
Note: 3 plumes						
1950	—	125	200	350	700	—
Note: 4 plumes						

KM# 916.2 20 FRANCS

Aluminum-Bronze, 23 mm. **Obv:** Head left **Rev:** Rooster above laurel sprig, denomination at right

Date	Mintage	F	VF	XF	Unc	BU
1950B	—	1.50	3.00	7.00	20.00	—
Note: 3 plumes						
1950B	—	40.00	85.00	150	225	—
Note: 4 plumes						

KM# 917.1 20 FRANCS

Aluminum-Bronze, 23 mm. **Obv:** Head left, "G. GUIRAUD" behind head **Rev:** Denomination above date at right, rooster above laurel branch at left **Note:** Without mint mark.

Date	Mintage	F	VF	XF	Unc	BU
1950	120,656,000	2.00	6.00	12.00	40.00	—
Note: 3 plumes						
1950	Inc. above	0.25	0.40	1.00	2.50	—
Note: 4 plumes						
1951	97,922,000	0.25	0.40	1.00	2.50	—
Note: 4 plumes						
1952	130,281,000	0.25	0.40	1.00	2.50	—
Note: 4 plumes						
1953	60,158,000	0.30	0.50	1.00	2.50	—
Note: 4 plumes						

KM# 917.2 20 FRANCS

Aluminum-Bronze, 23 mm. **Obv:** "G. GUIRAUD" behind head **Rev:** Rooster above laurel sprig, denomination at right

Date	Mintage	F	VF	XF	Unc	BU
1950B	43,355,000	25.00	35.00	50.00	135	—
Note: 3 plumes						
1950B	Inc. above	0.50	1.00	3.00	6.50	—

Date	Mintage	F	VF	XF	Unc	BU
Note: 4 plumes						
1951B	46,815,000	0.30	0.50	1.75	3.50	—
Note: 4 plumes						
1952B	54,381,000	0.30	0.50	1.75	3.50	—
Note: 4 plumes						
1953B	42,410,000	0.30	0.50	1.75	3.50	—
Note: 4 plumes						
1954B	1,573,000	125	200	350	800	—
Note: 4 plumes						

KM# 831 50 FRANCS

16.1290 g., 0.9000 Gold 0.4667 oz. AGW **Obv:** Standing Genius writing the Constitution, rooster at right, fasces at left **Rev:** Denomination above date within circular wreath

Date	Mintage	F	VF	XF	Unc	BU
1904A	20,000	425	575	950	1,650	—

KM# 918.1 50 FRANCS

8.0000 g., Aluminum-Bronze, 27 mm. **Obv:** Head left **Rev:** Denomination above date at right, rooster above laurel branch at left **Edge:** Plain **Designer:** Georges Guiraud **Note:** Without mint mark.

Date	Mintage	F	VF	XF	Unc	BU
1950	600,000	75.00	150	350	625	—
1951	68,630,000	0.50	1.00	2.25	5.50	—
1952	74,212,000	0.50	1.00	2.25	5.50	—
1953	63,172,000	0.50	1.00	2.25	5.50	—
1954	997,000	15.00	35.00	65.00	110	—
1958 (w)	501,000	25.00	50.00	85.00	240	—

KM# 918.2 50 FRANCS

Aluminum-Bronze, 27 mm. **Obv:** Head left **Rev:** Rooster above laurel, denomination at right

Date	Mintage	F	VF	XF	Unc	BU
1950B Rare	—	—	—	—	—	—
1951B	11,829,000	0.75	1.50	3.00	9.00	—
1952B	13,432,000	1.00	2.00	5.00	15.00	—
1953B	23,376,000	0.65	1.25	2.50	8.00	—
1954B	6,531,000	3.00	5.50	11.50	30.00	—

KM# 832 100 FRANCS

32.2581 g., 0.9000 Gold 0.9334 oz. AGW **Obv:** Standing Genius writing the Constitution, rooster on right, fasces on left **Rev:** Denomination above date within circular wreath **Edge Lettering:** DIEU PROTEGE LA FRANCE

Date	Mintage	F	VF	XF	Unc	BU
1901A	10,000	—	—	BV	950	1,500
1901A	10,000	—	—	BV	950	1,500
1902A	10,000	—	—	BV	950	1,500
1902A	10,000	—	—	BV	950	1,500
1903A	10,000	—	—	BV	950	1,500
1904A	20,000	—	—	BV	950	1,500
1905A	10,000	—	—	BV	950	1,500
1906A	30,000	—	—	BV	950	1,500

KM# 858 100 FRANCS

32.2581 g., 0.9000 Gold 0.9334 oz. AGW **Obv:** Standing Genius writing the constitution, rooster on right, column on the left **Rev:** Denomination and date within wreath **Edge Lettering:** LIBERTE EGALITE FRATERNITE

Date	Mintage	F	VF	XF	Unc	BU
1907A	20,000	—	—	BV+5%	950	1,150
1908A	23,000	—	—	BV+5%	950	1,150
1909A	20,000	—	—	BV+5%	950	1,150
1910A	20,000	—	—	BV+5%	950	1,150
1911A	30,000	—	—	BV+5%	950	1,150
1912A	20,000	—	—	BV+5%	950	1,150
1913A	30,000	—	—	BV+5%	950	1,150
1914A Rare	1,281	—	—	—	—	—

KM# 880 100 FRANCS

6.5500 g., 0.9000 Gold 0.1895 oz. AGW **Obv:** Winged head left **Rev:** Denomination above grain sprig, date below, laurel and oak branches flank **Note:** Without mint mark.

Date	Mintage	F	VF	XF	Unc	BU
1929	50	—	—	2,500	4,000	—
1932	Est. 50	—	—	3,250	4,750	—
1933	Est. 300	—	—	1,650	2,500	—
1934 Rare	—	—	—	—	—	—
1935	6,102,000	—	—	BV+5%	350	750
1936	7,689,000	—	—	BV+5%	350	750

KM# 919.1 100 FRANCS

6.0000 g., Copper-Nickel, 24 mm. **Obv:** Liberty bust with torch right **Rev:** Denomination above date at left, grain sprigs at right **Edge:** Reeded **Designer:** R. Cochet

Date	Mintage	F	VF	XF	Unc	BU
1954	97,285,000	0.50	1.00	2.50	7.00	—
1955	152,517,000	0.25	0.75	1.50	4.50	—
1956	7,578,000	2.00	5.00	8.00	30.00	—
1957	11,312,000	1.50	3.00	6.00	18.00	—
1958 (w)	3,256,000	2.50	5.50	12.50	35.00	—
1958 (o)	Inc. above	20.00	40.00	90.00	175	—

KM# 919.2 100 FRANCS

Copper-Nickel, 24 mm. **Obv:** Liberty bust with torch right **Rev:** Denomination and date left of grain sprigs

Date	Mintage	F	VF	XF	Unc	BU
1954B	86,261,000	0.50	1.25	2.50	5.00	—
1955B	136,585,000	0.25	0.75	1.50	3.50	—
1956B	19,154,000	1.00	2.00	4.50	10.00	—
1957B	25,702,000	1.00	2.00	4.50	12.50	—
1958B	54,072,000	1.00	2.00	4.50	11.50	—

REFORM COINAGE

Commencing 1960

1 Old Franc = 1 New Centime; 100 New Centimes = 1 New Franc

KM# 928 CENTIME

1.6500 g., Chrome-Steel, 15 mm. **Obv:** Cursive legend surrounds grain sprig **Rev:** Cursive denomination, date at top **Edge:** Plain **Designer:** Atelier de Paris **Note:** 1991-1993 dated coins, non-Proof, exist in both coin and medal alignment. Values given here are for medal alignment examples. Pieces struck in coin alignment have been traded for as much as $50.00.

Date	Mintage	F	VF	XF	Unc	BU
1962	34,200,000	—	—	0.10	0.25	0.35
1963	16,811,000	—	0.10	0.15	0.35	0.50
1964	22,654,000	—	—	0.10	0.25	0.35
1965	47,799,000	—	—	0.10	0.25	0.35
1966	19,688,000	—	—	0.10	0.25	0.35
1967	52,308,000	—	—	0.10	0.25	0.35
1968	40,890,000	—	—	0.10	0.25	0.35
1969	35,430,000	—	—	0.10	0.25	0.35
1970	29,600,000	—	—	0.10	0.25	0.35
1971	3,082,000	—	—	0.10	0.25	0.35
1972	1,014,999	—	0.10	0.15	0.35	0.50
1973	1,806,000	—	0.10	0.15	0.35	0.50
1974	7,949,000	—	—	0.10	0.25	0.35
1975	771,000	—	0.10	0.25	1.00	1.50
1976	4,482,000	—	—	0.10	0.25	0.35
1977	6,425,000	—	—	0.10	0.25	0.35
1978	1,236,000	—	0.10	0.15	0.35	0.50
1979	2,213,000	—	—	0.10	0.25	0.35
1980	60,000	—	—	—	1.00	1.50
1981	50,000	—	—	—	1.00	1.50
1982	69,000	—	—	—	1.00	1.50
1983	101,000	—	—	—	1.00	1.50
1984	50,000	—	—	—	1.00	1.50
1985	20,000	—	—	—	1.00	1.50
1986	48,000	—	—	—	1.00	1.50
Note: In sets only						
1987	100,000	—	—	—	1.00	1.50
1988	100,000	—	—	—	1.00	1.50
1989	83,000	—	—	—	1.00	1.50
1990	15,000	—	—	—	1.00	1.50
1991	5,000	—	—	—	1.00	1.50
1991 Proof	10,000	Value: 2.00				
1992	85,000	—	—	—	1.00	1.50
1992 Proof	15,000	Value: 2.00				
1993	40,000	—	—	—	1.00	1.50
1993 Proof	10,000	Value: 2.00				
1994 bee	20,000	—	—	—	1.00	1.50
1994 fish	10,000	—	—	—	1.00	1.50
1995	25,000	—	—	—	1.00	1.50
1995 Proof	10,000	Value: 2.00				
1996	17,000	—	—	—	1.00	1.50
1996 Proof	8,000	Value: 2.00				
1997	15,000	—	—	—	1.00	1.50
Note: In sets only						
1997 Proof	10,000	Value: 2.00				
1998	—	—	—	—	1.00	1.50
Note: In sets only						
1998 Proof	—	Value: 2.00				
1999	—	—	—	—	1.00	1.50
Note: In sets only						
1999 Proof	—	Value: 2.00				
2000	—	—	—	—	1.00	1.50
Note: In sets only						
2000 Proof	—	Value: 2.00				
2001 Proof	—	Value: 2.00				
2001	—	—	—	—	1.00	1.50
Note: In sets only						

KM# 928a CENTIME

2.5000 g., 0.7500 Gold 0.0603 oz. AGW **Obv:** Cursive legend surrounds grain sprig, medallic alignment **Rev:** Cursive denomination, date above, medallic alignment **Edge:** Plain **Note:** Last Centime.

Date	Mintage	F	VF	XF	Unc	BU
2000	25,000	—	—	—	—	55.00
2001	Est. 7,492	—	—	—	—	110

KM# 927 5 CENTIMES

Chrome-Steel **Obv:** Cursive legend surrounds grain sprig **Rev:** Cursive denomination, date above

Date	Mintage	F	VF	XF	Unc	BU
1961	39,000,000	0.10	0.20	0.50	2.00	3.00
1962	166,360,000	0.10	0.15	0.20	0.75	1.00
1963	71,900,000	0.10	0.20	0.40	1.00	1.50
1964	126,480,000	0.10	0.15	0.30	0.75	1.00

KM# 933 5 CENTIMES

2.0000 g., Copper-Aluminum-Nickel, 17 mm. **Obv:** Liberty bust left **Obv. Designer:** Henri Lagriffoul **Rev:** Denomination above date, grain sprig below, laurel branch at left **Rev. Designer:** Adrien Dieudonne **Edge:** Plain **Note:** 1991-1993 dated coins, non-Proof exist in both coin and medal alignment.

Date	Mintage	F	VF	XF	Unc	BU
1966	502,512,000	—	—	—	0.10	0.15
1967	11,747,000	—	—	0.10	0.25	0.35

Date	Mintage	F	VF	XF	Unc	BU
1968	110,395,000	—	—	—	0.10	0.15
1969	94,955,000	—	—	—	0.10	0.15
1970	58,900,000	—	—	—	0.10	0.15
1971	93,190,000	—	—	—	0.10	0.15
1972	100,515,000	—	—	—	0.10	0.15
1973	100,344,000	—	—	—	0.10	0.15
1974	103,890,000	—	—	—	0.10	0.15
1975	95,835,000	—	—	—	0.10	0.15
1976	148,395,000	—	—	—	0.10	0.15
1977	115,285,000	—	—	—	0.10	0.15
1978	189,804,000	—	—	—	0.10	0.15
1979	180,000,000	—	—	—	0.10	0.15
1980	180,010,000	—	—	—	0.10	0.15
1981	134,974,000	—	—	—	0.10	0.15
1982	138,000,000	—	—	—	0.10	0.15
1983	132,000,000	—	—	—	0.10	0.15
1984	150,000,000	—	—	—	0.10	0.15
1985	170,000,000	—	—	—	0.10	0.15
1986	280,000,000	—	—	—	0.10	0.15
1987	310,000,000	—	—	—	0.10	0.15
1988	200,000,000	—	—	—	0.10	0.15
1989	84,000	—	—	—	1.00	1.50
1990	79,992,000	—	—	—	0.20	0.30
1991	49,994,000	—	—	—	0.20	0.30
1991 Proof	10,000	Value: 1.00				
1992	179,996,000	—	—	—	0.20	0.30
1992 Proof	15,000	Value: 1.00				
1993	154,988,000	—	—	—	0.20	0.30
1993 Proof	10,000	Value: 1.00				
1994	—	—	—	—	0.20	0.30
1994 fish	60,000,000	—	—	—	0.20	0.30
1994 fish Proof	10,000	—	—	—	—	—
1994 bee	59,996,000	—	—	—	0.20	0.30
1995	129,991,999	—	—	—	0.20	0.30
1995 Proof	10,000	Value: 1.00				
1996	139,990,000	—	—	—	0.20	0.30
1996 Proof	8,000	Value: 1.00				
1997	199,995,000	—	—	—	0.20	0.30
1997 Proof	10,000	Value: 1.00				
1998	300,084,000	—	—	—	0.20	0.30
1998 Proof	—	Value: 1.00				
1999	—	—	—	—	1.50	2.50
Note: In sets only						
1999 Proof	—	Value: 1.00				
2000	—	—	—	—	1.50	2.50
Note: In sets only						
2000 Proof	—	Value: 1.00				
2001 Proof	—	Value: 1.00				
2001	—	—	—	—	1.50	2.50
Note: In sets only						

KM# 929 10 CENTIMES

3.0000 g., Copper-Aluminum-Nickel, 20 mm. **Obv:** Liberty bust left **Obv. Designer:** Henri Lagriffoul **Rev:** Denomination above date, grain sprig below, laurel branch at left **Rev. Designer:** Adrien Dieudonne **Edge:** Plain **Note:** Without mint mark. 1991-1993 dated coins, non-Proof, exist in both coin and medal alignment.

Date	Mintage	F	VF	XF	Unc	BU
1962	29,100,000	—	—	0.10	0.40	0.60
1963	217,601,000	—	—	—	0.10	0.15
1964	93,409,000	—	—	0.10	0.20	0.30
1965	41,220,000	—	—	0.10	0.30	0.50
1966	16,428,999	—	0.10	0.15	0.40	0.60
1967	196,728,000	—	—	—	0.10	0.15
1968	111,700,000	—	—	—	0.10	0.15
1969	129,530,000	—	—	—	0.10	0.15
1970	77,020,000	—	—	—	0.10	0.15
1971	26,280,000	—	—	—	0.10	0.15
1972	45,700,000	—	—	—	0.10	0.15
1973	58,000,000	—	—	—	0.10	0.15
1974	91,990,000	—	—	—	0.10	0.15
1975	74,450,000	—	—	—	0.10	0.15
1976	137,320,000	—	—	—	0.10	0.15
1977	140,110,000	—	—	—	0.10	0.15
1978	154,360,000	—	—	—	0.10	0.15
1979	140,000,000	—	—	—	0.10	0.15
1980	140,010,000	—	—	—	0.10	0.15
1981	135,000,000	—	—	—	0.10	0.15
1982	110,000,000	—	—	—	0.10	0.15
1983	150,000,000	—	—	—	0.10	0.15
1984	200,000,000	—	—	—	0.10	0.15
1985	170,000,000	—	—	—	0.10	0.15
1986	150,000,000	—	—	—	0.10	0.15
1987	150,000,000	—	—	—	0.10	0.15
1988	145,000,000	—	—	—	0.10	0.15
1989	179,984,000	—	—	—	0.10	0.15
1990	179,992,000	—	—	—	0.10	0.15
1991	179,986,000	—	—	—	0.10	0.15
1991 Proof	10,000	Value: 1.00				
1992	179,996,000	—	—	—	0.10	0.15
1992 Proof	15,000	Value: 1.00				
1993	154,988,000	—	—	—	0.10	0.15
1993 Proof	10,000	Value: 1.00				
1994	—	—	—	—	0.10	0.15
1994 Fish	103,000,000	—	—	—	0.10	0.15
1994 Fish Proof	10,000	Value: 1.00				
1994 Bee	76,988,000	—	—	—	0.10	0.15
1995	169,996,000	—	—	—	0.10	0.15
1995 Proof	10,000	Value: 1.00				
1996	179,981,000	—	—	—	0.10	0.15
1996 Proof	8,000	Value: 1.00				
1997	551,991,000	—	—	—	0.10	0.15
1997 Proof	10,000	Value: 1.00				
1998	350,000,000	—	—	—	0.10	0.15
1998 Proof	—	Value: 1.00				
1999	—	—	—	—	2.00	3.00
Note: In sets only						
1999 Proof	—	Value: 1.00				
2000	60,000,000	—	—	—	0.10	0.15
2000 Proof	—	Value: 1.00				
2001 Proof	—	Value: 1.00				
2001	—	—	—	—	2.00	—
Note: In sets only						

KM# 930 20 CENTIMES

4.0000 g., Copper-Aluminum-Nickel, 23.5 mm. **Obv:** Liberty bust left **Obv. Designer:** Henri Lagriffoul **Rev:** Denomination above date, grain sprig below, laurel branch at left **Rev. Designer:** Adrien Dieudonne **Edge:** Plain **Note:** Without mint mark. 1991-1993 dated coins, non-Proof, exist in both coin and medal alignment.

Date	Mintage	F	VF	XF	Unc	BU
1962	48,200,000	—	—	0.10	0.40	0.60
1963	190,330,000	—	—	0.10	0.30	0.50
1964	127,521,000	—	—	0.10	0.30	0.50
1965	27,024,000	—	0.10	0.20	0.40	0.60
1966	21,762,000	—	0.10	0.20	0.40	0.60
1967	138,780,000	—	—	0.10	0.15	0.25
1968	77,408,000	—	—	0.10	0.20	0.30
1969	50,570,000	—	—	0.10	0.20	0.30
1970	70,040,000	—	—	0.10	0.15	0.25
1971	31,080,000	—	—	0.10	0.15	0.25
1972	39,740,000	—	—	0.10	0.15	0.25
1973	45,240,000	—	—	0.10	0.15	0.25
1974	54,250,000	—	—	0.10	0.15	0.25
1975	40,570,000	—	—	0.10	0.15	0.25
1976	117,610,000	—	—	—	0.10	0.15
1977	100,340,000	—	—	—	0.10	0.15
1978	125,015,000	—	—	—	0.10	0.15
1979	70,000,000	—	—	—	0.10	0.15
1980	20,010,000	—	—	0.10	0.15	0.25
1981	125,000,000	—	—	—	0.10	0.15
1982	150,000,000	—	—	—	0.10	0.15
1983	110,000,000	—	—	—	0.10	0.15
1984	200,000,000	—	—	—	0.10	0.15
1985	150,000,000	—	—	—	0.10	0.15
1986	40,000,000	—	—	—	0.10	0.15
1987	60,000,000	—	—	—	0.10	0.15
1988	220,000,000	—	—	—	0.10	0.15
1989	139,985,000	—	—	—	0.10	0.15
1990	49,990,000	—	—	—	0.10	0.15
1991	39,992,000	—	—	—	0.10	0.15
1991 1 Proof	10,000	Value: 1.00				
1992	89,985,000	—	—	—	0.10	0.15
1992 1 Proof	15,000	Value: 1.00				
1993	10,990,000	—	—	—	0.10	0.15
1993 1 Proof	10,000	Value: 1.00				
1994	—	—	—	—	0.10	0.15
1994 Fish	60,000,000	—	—	—	0.10	0.15
1994 Fish Proof	10,000	Value: 1.00				
1994 Bee	79,900,000	—	—	—	0.10	0.15
1995	109,995,000	—	—	—	0.10	0.15
1995 Proof	10,000	Value: 1.00				
1996	139,987,000	—	—	—	0.10	0.15
1996 Proof	8,000	Value: 1.00				
1997	436,216,500	—	—	—	0.10	0.15
1997 Proof	10,000	Value: 1.00				
1998	—	—	—	—	2.00	3.00
Note: In sets only						
1998 Proof	—	Value: 1.00				
1999	—	—	—	—	2.00	3.00
Note: In sets only						
1999 Proof	—	Value: 1.00				
2000	85,385,000	—	—	—	0.10	0.15
2000 Proof	—	Value: 1.00				
2001 Proof	—	Value: 1.00				
2001	—	—	—	—	2.00	—
Note: In sets only						

KM# 939.1 50 CENTIMES

4.5000 g., Aluminum-Bronze, 19.5 mm. **Obv:** Liberty bust left, 3 folds in collar **Obv. Designer:** Henri Lagriffoul **Rev:** Denomination above date, grain sprig below, laurel branch at left **Rev. Designer:** Adrien Dieudonne **Edge:** Reeded

Date	Mintage	F	VF	XF	Unc	BU
1962	37,560,000	0.30	0.60	1.50	3.00	5.00
1963	62,482,000	0.20	0.40	1.00	2.00	3.00

KM# 939.2 50 CENTIMES

Aluminum-Bronze, 25 mm. **Obv:** 4 folds in collar **Rev:** Denomination above grain sprig, laurel at left

Date	Mintage	F	VF	XF	Unc	BU
1962	Inc. above	30.00	70.00	120	170	275
1963	Inc. above	0.20	0.40	1.00	2.00	3.00
1964	41,471,000	0.45	0.90	2.00	6.00	9.00

KM# 931.1 1/2 FRANC

4.5000 g., Nickel, 19.5 mm. **Obv:** The seed sower **Rev:** Laurel divides denomination and date **Edge:** Reeded **Designer:** Louis Oscar Roty **Note:** Without mint mark.

Date	Mintage	F	VF	XF	Unc	BU
1965	184,834,000	—	—	0.15	0.30	0.50
Note: Small legends						
1965	Inc. above	—	—	0.15	0.30	0.50
Note: Large legends						
1966	88,890,000	—	—	0.15	0.30	0.50
1967	28,394,000	—	—	0.15	0.40	0.60
1968	57,548,000	—	—	0.15	0.30	0.50
1969	47,144,000	—	—	0.15	0.30	0.50
1970	42,298,000	—	—	0.15	0.30	0.50
1971	36,068,000	—	—	0.15	0.30	0.50
1972	42,302,000	—	—	0.15	0.30	0.50
1972	Inc. above	25.00	50.00	100	150	—
Note: Without "O. ROTY"						
1973	48,372,000	—	—	0.15	0.30	0.60
1974	37,072,000	—	—	0.15	0.30	0.50
1975	22,803,000	—	—	0.15	0.40	0.60
1976	115,314,000	—	—	0.15	0.30	0.50
1977	131,644,000	—	—	0.15	0.30	0.50
1978	63,360,000	—	—	0.15	0.30	0.50
1979	51,000	—	—	—	0.50	0.75
1980	60,000	—	—	—	0.50	0.75
Note: In sets only						
1981	50,000	—	—	—	0.50	0.75
1982	78,000	—	—	—	0.50	0.75
1983	50,000,000	—	—	0.15	0.30	0.50
1984	80,000,000	—	—	0.15	0.30	0.50
1985	50,000,000	—	—	—	1.50	2.50
1986	110,000,000	—	—	—	1.50	2.50
1987	50,000,000	—	—	—	0.30	0.50
1988	100,000	—	—	—	0.40	0.60
1989	83,000	—	—	—	0.40	0.60
1990	15,000	—	—	—	0.40	0.60
1991	49,988,000	—	—	—	0.40	0.60
Note: Exists in both coin and medal alignment						
1992	29,968,000	—	—	—	0.40	0.60
Note: Exists in both coin and medal alignment						
1993	24,972,000	—	—	—	0.40	0.60
1994 Fish	10,000,000	—	—	—	0.40	0.60
1994 Bee	29,972,000	—	—	—	0.40	0.60
1995	29,976,000	—	—	—	0.40	0.60
1996	55,978,000	—	—	—	0.40	0.60
1997	99,976,000	—	—	—	0.40	0.60
1998	—	—	—	—	2.00	3.00
Note: In sets only						
1999	—	—	—	—	2.00	3.00
Note: In sets only						
2000	75,000,000	—	—	—	0.40	0.60
2001	—	—	—	—	2.00	3.00
Note: In sets only						

KM# 931.2 1/2 FRANC

4.5000 g., Nickel, 19.5 mm. **Obv:** Modified sower, engraver's signature: "O. ROTY" preceded by "D'AP" **Rev:** Laurel divides date and denomination **Edge:** Plain

Date	Mintage	F	VF	XF	Unc	BU
1991	—	—	—	—	0.40	0.60
1991 Proof	10,000	Value: 1.50				
1992	—	—	—	—	0.40	0.60
1992 Proof	15,000	Value: 1.50				
1993	—	—	—	—	0.40	0.60
1993 Proof	10,000	Value: 1.50				
1994 Fish	—	—	—	—	0.40	0.60

Date	Mintage	F	VF	XF	Unc	BU
1994 Fish Proof	10,000	Value: 1.50				
1994 Bee	—	—	—	—	0.40	0.60
1995	—	—	—	—	0.40	0.60
1995 Proof	10,000	Value: 1.50				
1996	—	—	—	—	0.40	0.60
1996 Proof	8,000	Value: 1.50				
1997	—	—	—	—	0.40	0.60
1997 Proof	10,000	Value: 1.50				
1998 Proof	—	Value: 1.50				
1999 Proof	—	Value: 1.50				
2000	—	—	—	—	0.40	0.60
2000 Proof	—	Value: 1.50				
2001 Proof	—	Value: 1.50				
2001	—	—	—	—	0.40	0.60

KM# 925.1 FRANC

6.0000 g., Nickel, 24 mm. **Obv:** The seed sower **Obv. Designer:** Louis Oscar Roty **Rev:** Laurel branch divides denomination and date **Edge:** Reeded **Note:** Without mint mark.

Date	Mintage	F	VF	XF	Unc	BU
1960	406,375,000	—	—	0.20	0.40	0.60
1961	119,611,000	—	—	0.20	0.40	0.60
1962	14,014,000	—	—	0.25	0.50	0.75
1964	77,425,000	—	—	0.20	0.40	0.60
1965	44,252,000	—	—	0.20	0.40	0.60
1966	38,038,000	—	—	0.20	0.40	0.60
1967	11,322,000	—	—	0.25	0.50	0.75
1968	51,550,000	—	—	0.20	0.40	0.60
1969	70,595,000	—	—	0.20	0.40	0.60
1970	42,560,000	—	—	0.20	0.40	0.60
1971	42,475,000	—	—	0.20	0.40	0.60
1972	48,250,000	—	—	0.20	0.40	0.60
1973	70,000,000	—	—	0.20	0.40	0.60
1974	82,235,000	—	—	0.20	0.40	0.60
1975	101,685,000	—	—	0.20	0.40	0.60
1976	192,520,000	—	—	0.20	0.40	0.60
1977	230,085,000	—	—	0.20	0.40	0.60
1978	136,580,000	—	—	0.20	0.40	0.60
1979	51,000	—	—	—	3.00	5.00
1980	60,000	—	—	—	3.00	5.00
Note: In sets only						
1981	50,000	—	—	—	3.00	5.00
1982	92,000	—	—	—	3.00	5.00
1983	101,000	—	—	—	3.00	5.00
1984	50,000	—	—	—	3.00	5.00
1985	7,002,000	—	—	—	2.00	3.00
1986	48,000	—	—	—	3.00	5.00
1987	100,000	—	—	—	2.50	4.00
1988	100,000	—	—	—	2.50	4.00
1989	83,000	—	—	—	3.00	5.00
1990	15,000	—	—	—	4.00	6.00
1991	54,988,000	—	—	—	0.40	0.60
Note: Exists in both coin and medal alignment						
1992	30,000,000	—	—	—	0.40	0.60
Note: Exists in both coin and medal alignment						
1993	20,000	—	—	—	4.00	6.00
1994 Bee	4,792,000	—	—	—	0.40	0.60
1995	15,000	—	—	—	0.40	0.60
1996	—	—	—	—	3.00	5.00
Note: In sets only						
1997	—	—	—	—	3.00	5.00
Note: In sets only						
1998	—	—	—	—	3.00	5.00
Note: In sets only						
1999	80,432,000	—	—	—	0.40	0.60
2000	—	—	—	—	3.00	5.00
Note: In sets only						
2001	20,000,000	—	—	—	0.40	0.60

KM# 963 FRANC

6.0000 g., Nickel, 24 mm. **Subject:** 30th Anniversary of Fifth Republic **Obv:** Head right **Rev:** Denomination within six sided wreath, dates below

Date	Mintage	F	VF	XF	Unc	BU
1988	49,921,000	—	—	—	1.00	2.00

KM# 967 FRANC

6.0000 g., Nickel, 24 mm. **Subject:** 200th Anniversary of Estates General **Obv:** Denomination within wreath, date below **Rev:** Three figure monument

Date	Mintage	F	VF	XF	Unc	BU
1989	5,010,000	—	—	—	2.50	4.50

KM# 925.2 FRANC

6.0000 g., Nickel, 24 mm. **Obv:** Modified sower, engraver's signature: O. ROTY, preceded by D'AP **Rev:** Laurel divides date and denomination **Edge:** Plain

Date	Mintage	F	VF	XF	Unc	BU
1991	—	—	—	—	0.40	0.60
1991 Proof	10,000	Value: 2.50				
1992	—	—	—	—	0.40	0.60
1992 Proof	15,000	Value: 2.50				
1993	—	—	—	—	0.40	0.60
1993 Proof	10,000	Value: 2.50				
1994 Bee	—	—	—	—	0.40	0.60
1994 Fish Proof	10,000	Value: 2.50				
1995	35,000	—	—	—	0.40	0.60
1995 Proof	10,000	Value: 2.50				
1996	5,000	—	—	—	0.40	0.60
1996 Proof	8,000	Value: 2.50				
1997	15,000	—	—	—	0.40	0.60
1997 Proof	—	Value: 2.50				
1998 Proof	—	Value: 2.50				
1999 Proof	—	Value: 2.50				
2000	—	—	—	—	0.40	0.60
2000 Proof	—	Value: 2.50				
2001 Proof	—	Value: 2.50				
2001	—	—	—	—	0.40	0.60

KM# 1004.1 FRANC

6.0000 g., Nickel, 24 mm. **Subject:** 200th Anniversary of French Republic **Obv:** Liberty bust left **Rev:** Denomination within wreath, date below

Date	Mintage	F	VF	XF	Unc	BU
1992	30,000,000	—	—	—	1.25	2.00

KM# 1133 FRANC

6.0000 g., Nickel, 24 mm. **Subject:** 200th Anniversary of Institute of France **Obv:** Institut de France building divides denomination, date below **Rev:** Framed arms, date below, branches flank three sides

Date	Mintage	F	VF	XF	Unc	BU
1995	4,976,000	—	—	—	1.50	2.00

KM# 1160 FRANC

6.0000 g., Nickel, 24 mm. **Subject:** 100th Anniversary - Birth of Jacques Rueff **Obv:** Head at right facing **Rev:** Figure at center, flanked by branches, divides denomination

Date	Mintage	F	VF	XF	Unc	BU
1996	2,976,000	—	—	—	1.50	2.50

KM# 942.1 2 FRANCS

7.5000 g., Nickel, 26.5 mm. **Obv:** The seed sower **Rev:** Denomination on branches, date below **Edge:** Plain **Designer:** Louis Oscar Roty

Date	Mintage	F	VF	XF	Unc	BU
1979	130,000,000	—	—	0.40	0.65	1.00
1980	100,010,000	—	—	0.40	0.65	1.00
1981	120,000,000	—	—	0.40	0.65	1.00
1982	90,000,000	—	—	0.40	0.65	1.00
1983	90,000,000	—	—	0.40	0.65	1.00
1984	50,000	—	—	—	0.75	1.25
1985	20,000	—	—	—	2.00	3.00
1986	48,000	—	—	—	2.00	3.00
1987	100,000	—	—	—	0.75	1.25
1988	100,000	—	—	—	0.75	1.25
1989	83,000	—	—	—	0.75	1.25
1990	15,000	—	—	—	0.75	1.25
1994 Fish	—	—	—	—	0.75	1.25
1994 Bee	—	—	—	—	14.00	20.00
1995	—	—	—	—	0.75	1.25
1996	—	—	—	—	0.75	1.25
1997	—	—	—	—	0.75	1.25
1998	—	—	—	—	0.75	1.25
1999	—	—	—	—	0.75	1.25
2000	—	—	—	—	0.75	1.25
2001 Bee	—	—	—	—	0.75	1.25

KM# 942.2 2 FRANCS

7.5000 g., Nickel, 26.5 mm. **Obv:** The seed sower **Rev:** Denomination on branches, date below **Edge:** Plain

Date	Mintage	F	VF	XF	Unc	BU
1991	5,000	—	—	—	—	—
1991 Proof	10,000	Value: 3.50				
1992	15,000	—	—	—	0.75	1.25
1992 Proof	85,000	Value: 3.50				
1993	40,000	—	—	—	0.75	1.25
1993 Proof	10,000	Value: 3.50				
1994 Fish	9,870,000	—	—	—	0.75	1.25
1994 Fish Proof	10,000	Value: 3.50				
1994 Bee	20,000	—	—	—	0.75	1.25
1995	20,000	—	—	—	0.75	1.25
1995 Proof	10,000	Value: 3.50				
1996	11,980,000	—	—	—	0.75	1.25
1996 Proof	8,000	Value: 3.50				
1997	9,990,000	—	—	—	0.75	1.25
1997 Proof	10,000	Value: 3.50				
1998	45,000,000	—	—	—	0.75	1.25
1998 Proof	—	Value: 3.50				
1999 Proof	—	Value: 3.50				
2000	25,000,000	—	—	—	0.75	1.25
2000 Proof	—	Value: 3.50				
2001 Proof	—	Value: 3.50				
2001	—	—	—	—	0.75	1.25

KM# 1062 2 FRANCS

7.5000 g., Nickel, 26.5 mm. **Obv:** Bust with hat facing, double cross in background **Obv. Designer:** Emile Rousseau **Rev:** Denomination on branches, date below **Edge:** Reeded

Date	Mintage	F	VF	XF	Unc	BU
1993	30,000,000	—	—	—	1.00	1.50

KM# 1119 2 FRANCS

7.5000 g., Nickel, 26.5 mm. **Obv:** Head of Louis Pasteur facing, building at left **Obv. Designer:** Pierre Rodier **Rev:** Denomination to right of bottles, date below

Date	Mintage	F	VF	XF	Unc	BU
1995	9,975,000	—	—	—	2.00	2.75

KM# 1187 2 FRANCS

7.5000 g., Nickel, 26.5 mm. **Obv:** Georges Guynemer, WWI ace fighter pilot, looking left, date below **Obv. Designer:** Pierre Rodier **Rev:** Guynemer's stork emblem below denomination

Date	Mintage	F	VF	XF	Unc	BU
1997	—	—	—	—	2.25	3.00

KM# 1213 2 FRANCS

7.5000 g., Nickel, 26.5 mm. **Subject:** 50th Anniversary-Declaration of Human Rights **Obv:** Rene Cassin head right, initials above inscription, dates and building below **Obv. Designer:** Pierre Rodier **Rev:** Denomination on world globe, laurel spray and date below

Date	Mintage	F	VF	XF	Unc	BU
1998	—	—	—	—	2.25	3.00

KM# 926 5 FRANCS

12.0000 g., 0.8350 Silver 0.3221 oz. ASW, 19 mm. **Obv:** Figure sowing seed **Rev:** Branches divide denomination and date **Edge Lettering:** LIBERTE EGALITE FRATERNITE **Designer:** Louis Oscar Roty

Date	Mintage	F	VF	XF	Unc	BU
1960	55,182,000	—	—	BV	5.00	6.50
1961	15,630,000	—	—	BV	5.00	6.50
1962	42,500,000	—	—	BV	5.00	6.50
1963	37,936,000	—	—	BV	5.00	6.50
1964	32,378,000	—	—	BV	5.00	6.50
1965	5,156,000	—	—	BV	6.00	7.50
1966	5,017,000	—	—	BV	6.00	7.50
1967	502,000	—	BV	6.00	12.00	15.00
1968	557,000	—	—	BV	10.00	12.50
1969	504,000	—	—	BV	10.00	12.50

KM# 926a.1 5 FRANCS

10.0000 g., Nickel Clad Copper-Nickel, 29 mm. **Obv:** The seed sower **Rev:** Branches divide denomination and date **Edge:** Reeded **Designer:** Raymond Joly

Date	Mintage	F	VF	XF	Unc	BU
1970	57,890,000	—	—	1.00	1.25	1.75
1971	142,204,000	—	—	1.00	1.25	1.75
1972	45,492,000	—	—	1.00	1.50	2.25
1973	45,079,000	—	—	1.00	1.25	1.75
1974	26,888,000	—	—	1.00	1.25	1.75
1975	16,712,000	—	—	1.00	1.25	1.75
1976	1,662,000	—	1.00	1.25	2.00	3.00
1977	485,000	—	1.00	1.50	2.25	3.50
1978	30,022,000	—	—	1.00	1.25	1.75
1979	51,000	—	—	2.00	3.50	5.50
1980	60,000	—	—	—	5.00	7.50
Note: In sets only						
1981	50,000	—	—	2.00	3.00	5.50
1982	60,000	—	—	2.00	3.50	5.50
1983	101,000	—	—	2.00	3.50	5.50
1984	49,000	—	—	2.00	3.50	5.50
1985	20,000	—	—	2.00	6.00	9.00
1986	48,000	—	—	—	5.00	7.50
Note: In sets only						
1987	20,000,000	—	—	—	1.65	2.50
1988	100,000	—	—	—	1.65	2.85
1989	83,000	—	—	—	1.65	3.00
1990	14,990,000	—	—	—	1.65	2.50
1991	7,488,000	—	—	—	1.65	2.50
1992	9,966,000	—	—	—	1.65	2.50
1993	14,970,000	—	—	—	1.65	2.50
1994 Bee	6,000,000	—	—	—	1.65	2.50
1994 Fish	3,990,000	—	—	—	1.65	2.50
1995	19,986,000	—	—	—	1.65	2.50
1996	12,000	—	—	3.00	5.00	7.50
1997	—	—	—	—	5.00	7.50
Note: In sets only						
1998	—	—	—	—	5.00	7.50
Note: In sets only						
1999	—	—	—	—	5.00	7.50
Note: In sets only						
2000	—	—	—	—	5.00	7.50
Note: In sets only						
2001	—	—	—	—	5.00	7.50
Note: In sets only						

KM# 968 5 FRANCS

10.0000 g., Copper-Nickel, 29 mm. **Subject:** Centennial - Erection of Eiffel Tower **Obv:** Base of tower, denomination above **Obv. Designer:** Joaquin Jimenez **Rev:** Eiffel Tower, dates at right **Rev. Designer:** Frederic Soubert

Date	Mintage	F	VF	XF	Unc	BU
1989	9,774,000	—	—	—	6.50	9.00

KM# 926a.2 5 FRANCS

6.5000 g., Nickel Clad Copper-Nickel, 29 mm. **Obv:** Modified sower, engraver's signature: "O. ROTY" preceded by "D'AP" **Rev:** Branches divide date and denomination **Edge:** Plain

Date	Mintage	F	VF	XF	Unc	BU
1991	7,490,000	—	—	—	1.65	2.50
1991 Proof	10,000	Value: 6.50				
1992	9,986,000	—	—	—	1.65	2.50
1992 Proof	15,000	Value: 6.50				
1993	14,990,000	—	—	—	1.65	2.50
1993 Proof	10,000	Value: 6.50				
1994 Fish	6,000,000	—	—	—	1.65	2.50
1994 Fish Proof	10,000	Value: 6.50				
1994 Bee	3,990,000	—	—	—	1.65	2.50
1995	20,006,000	—	—	—	1.65	2.50
1995 Proof	—	Value: 6.50				
1996	17,000	—	—	—	1.65	2.50
1996 Proof	8,000	Value: 6.50				
1997	15,000	—	—	—	1.65	2.50
1997 Proof	—	Value: 6.50				
1998 Proof	—	Value: 6.50				
1999 Proof	—	Value: 6.50				
2000	—	—	—	—	1.65	2.50
2000 Proof	—	Value: 6.50				
2001 Proof	—	Value: 6.50				
2001	—	—	—	—	1.65	2.50

KM# 1006 5 FRANCS

10.0000 g., Copper-Nickel, 29 mm. **Obv:** Denomination within design **Obv. Designer:** E. Rousseau **Rev:** Bust of Pierre Mendes France facing

Date	Mintage	F	VF	XF	Unc	BU
1992	10,000,000	—	—	—	4.50	6.00

KM# 1063 5 FRANCS

10.0000 g., Nickel Clad Copper-Nickel, 29 mm. **Obv:** Head of Voltaire the poet 3/4 facing **Obv. Designer:** P. Rodier **Rev:** Quill divides building and date from denomination **Edge:** Reeded

Date	Mintage	F	VF	XF	Unc	BU
1994	15,000,000	—	—	—	4.00	5.00

KM# 1155 5 FRANCS

10.0500 g., Nickel Clad Steel, 29 mm. **Obv:** Denomination and date within wreath **Rev:** Hercules group design **Edge:** Reeded **Designer:** Augustine Dupr?

Date	Mintage	F	VF	XF	Unc	BU
1996	4,976,000	—	—	—	4.50	6.00

KM# 932 10 FRANCS

25.0000 g., 0.9000 Silver 0.7234 oz. ASW, 37 mm. **Obv:** Denomination and date within wreath **Rev:** Hercules group **Designer:** Augustine Dupré **Note:** Without mint mark.

Date	Mintage	F	VF	XF	Unc	BU
1965	8,051,000	—	BV	10.00	12.50	15.00
1966	9,800,000	—	BV	10.00	12.50	15.00
1967	10,100,000	—	BV	10.00	12.50	15.00
1968	3,887,000	—	BV	12.00	14.00	17.50
1969	761,000	—	BV	14.00	16.00	20.00
1970	5,013,000	—	BV	10.00	12.50	15.00
1971	513,000	—	BV	14.00	18.00	22.50
1972	915,000	—	BV	12.00	14.00	17.50
1973	207,000	—	BV	14.00	20.00	25.00

KM# 940 10 FRANCS

10.0000 g., Nickel-Brass, 26 mm. **Rev:** High tension towers and electric transmission wires, denomination at center **Edge Lettering:** Incuse, LIBERTÉ, EGALITÉ, FRATERNITÉ **Designer:** Georges Mathieu

Date	Mintage	F	VF	XF	Unc	BU
1974	22,447,000	—	—	1.50	2.00	2.50
1975	59,013,000	—	—	1.50	2.00	2.50
1976	104,093,000	—	—	1.50	2.00	2.50
1977	100,028,000	—	—	1.50	2.00	2.50
1978	97,590,000	—	—	1.50	2.00	2.50

Date	Mintage	F	VF	XF	Unc	BU
1979	110,000,000	—	—	1.50	2.00	2.50
1980	80,010,000	—	—	1.50	2.00	2.50
1981	50,000	—	—	—	2.75	3.75
1982	74,000	—	—	—	2.75	3.75
1983	101,000	—	—	—	2.75	3.75
1984	39,988,000	—	—	1.50	2.00	2.50
1985	30,000,000	—	—	1.50	2.00	2.50
1987	Est. 50,000,000	—	—	—	2.50	2.50

KM# 950 10 FRANCS
10.0000 g., Nickel-Bronze, 26 mm. **Subject:** 100th Anniversary - Death of Leon Gambetta **Obv:** Denomination and date, flags in background **Obv. Designer:** E. Rousseau **Rev:** Head left

Date	Mintage	F	VF	XF	Unc	BU
1982	3,045,000	—	—	2.50	4.00	5.00

KM# 952 10 FRANCS
Nickel-Bronze, 26 mm. **Subject:** 200th Anniversary - Montgolfier Balloon **Obv:** Denomination and date below balloon basket **Rev:** Balloon, figures and date below **Designer:** D. Ponce

Date	Mintage	F	VF	XF	Unc	BU
1983	3,001,000	—	—	2.50	4.00	5.00

KM# 953 10 FRANCS
Nickel-Bronze, 26 mm. **Subject:** 200th Anniversary - Birth of Stendhal **Obv:** Head 3/4 facing **Obv. Designer:** J. Mauriel **Rev:** Quill, branch, book, and buildings divide date and denomination

Date	Mintage	F	VF	XF	Unc	BU
1983	2,951,000	—	—	2.50	4.00	5.00

KM# 954 10 FRANCS
Nickel-Bronze, 26 mm. **Subject:** 200th Anniversary - Birth of Francois Rude **Obv:** Head 3/4 right, RF below **Obv. Designer:** J. P. Gendis **Rev:** Armed figure divides denomination and date

Date	Mintage	F	VF	XF	Unc	BU
1984	10,000,000	—	—	2.50	3.50	4.50

KM# 956 10 FRANCS
Nickel-Bronze, 26 mm. **Subject:** Centennial - Death of Victor Hugo **Obv:** Denomination above armed figures, quill and book at right, date below **Obv. Designer:** C. Lesot **Rev:** Head facing

Date	Mintage	F	VF	XF	Unc	BU
1985	10,000,000	—	—	2.50	3.50	4.50

KM# 959 10 FRANCS
6.5000 g., Nickel, 21 mm. **Obv:** Designs divide denomination and date **Rev:** Madam Republic head, map in background **Designer:** Joaquin Jimenez

Date	Mintage	F	VF	XF	Unc	BU
1986	110,015,000	—	—	3.00	10.00	12.00

Note: Recalled and melted, no longer legal tender

KM# 958 10 FRANCS
6.5000 g., Nickel, 21 mm. **Subject:** 100th Anniversary - Birth of Robert Schuman **Obv:** Rooster at left, denomination right **Obv. Designer:** Lobbay **Rev:** Half head right

Date	Mintage	F	VF	XF	Unc	BU
1986	9,961,000	—	—	3.00	6.50	7.50

KM# 961d 10 FRANCS
Nickel-Bronze, 21 mm. **Subject:** Millennium of King Capet and France **Obv:** Denomination and date within circle **Rev:** Crowned figure standing at center, rosettes in background

Date	Mintage	F	VF	XF	Unc	BU
1987	70,000,000	—	—	3.00	6.50	9.00

KM# 964.1 10 FRANCS
6.5000 g., Bi-Metallic Nickel center in Aluminum-Bronze ring, 23 mm. **Subject:** Spirit of Bastille **Obv:** Winged figure divides RF within circle **Rev:** Patterned denomination above date within circle **Edge:** Plain or Reeded **Designer:** Atelier de Paris

Date	Mintage	F	VF	XF	Unc	BU
1988	100,000,000	—	—	2.50	6.00	7.50
1989	249,980,000	—	—	2.50	6.00	7.50
1990	250,000,000	—	—	2.50	6.00	7.50
1991	249,987,000	—	—	2.50	6.00	7.50

Note: Exist in both medal and coin alignment

Date	Mintage	F	VF	XF	Unc	BU
1992	99,966,000	—	—	2.50	6.00	7.50

Note: Exist in both medal and coin alignment

Date	Mintage	F	VF	XF	Unc	BU
1995	15,000	—	—	6.00	10.00	12.50
1996	12,000	—	—	6.00	10.00	12.50
2000	28,065,000	—	—	2.50	6.00	7.50

KM# 965 10 FRANCS
Aluminum-Bronze, 26 mm. **Subject:** 100th Anniversary - Birth of Roland Garros **Obv:** Denomination below wings **Rev:** Dates and plane above head right **Designer:** H. Duetthe

Date	Mintage	F	VF	XF	Unc	BU
1988	30,000,000	—	—	2.50	4.00	5.00

KM# 964.2 10 FRANCS
Aluminum-Bronze, 23 mm. **Obv:** Winged figure divides RF **Rev:** Patterned denomination above date **Edge:** Plain

Date	Mintage	F	VF	XF	Unc	BU
1991	—	—	—	—	—	—

Note: Exists in both medal and coin alignment.

Date	Mintage	F	VF	XF	Unc	BU
1991 Proof	10,000	Value: 15.00				
1992	—	—	—	—	6.00	7.50

Note: Exists in both medal and coin alignment.

Date	Mintage	F	VF	XF	Unc	BU
1992 Proof	15,000	Value: 15.00				
1993	20,000	—	—	—	6.00	7.50
1993 Proof	10,000	Value: 15.00				
1994 Bee	20,000	—	—	—	6.00	7.50
1994 Fish Proof	10,000	Value: 15.00				
1995	25,000	—	—	—	6.00	7.50
1995 Proof	10,000	Value: 15.00				
1996	17,000	—	—	—	6.00	7.50
1996 Proof	8,000	Value: 15.00				
1997	15,000	—	—	—	6.00	7.50
1997 Proof	10,000	Value: 15.00				
1998	—	—	—	—	6.00	7.50
1998 Proof	—	Value: 15.00				
1999	—	—	—	—	6.00	7.50
1999 Proof	—	Value: 15.00				
2000	—	—	—	—	6.00	7.50
2000 Proof	—	Value: 15.00				
2001 Proof	—	Value: 15.00				
2001	—	—	—	—	6.00	7.50

KM# 1008.2 20 FRANCS
9.0000 g., Tri-Metallic Copper-Aluminum-Nickel center plug, Nickel inner ring, Copper-Aluminum-Nickel outer ring, 27 mm. **Obv:** Mont St. Michel **Rev:** Patterned denomination above date **Edge:** 5 milled bands, reeded or plain

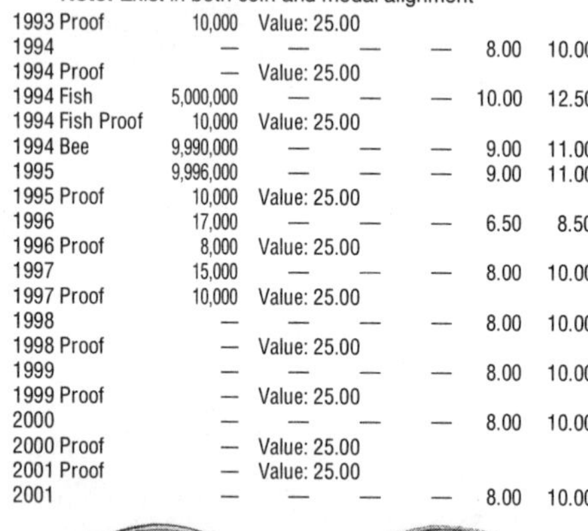

Date	Mintage	F	VF	XF	Unc	BU
1992	Inc. above	—	—	—	6.50	8.50

Note: Open V in outer ring, exist in both coin and medal alignment

Date	Mintage	F	VF	XF	Unc	BU
1992 Proof	15,000	Value: 25.00				
1992	59,986,000	—	—	—	6.50	8.50

Note: Closed V in outer ring, exist in both coin and medal alignment

Date	Mintage	F	VF	XF	Unc	BU
1993	54,990,000	—	—	—	7.00	9.00

Note: Exist in both coin and medal alignment

Date	Mintage	F	VF	XF	Unc	BU
1993 Proof	10,000	Value: 25.00				
1994	—	—	—	—	8.00	10.00
1994 Proof	—	Value: 25.00				
1994 Fish	5,000,000	—	—	—	10.00	12.50
1994 Fish Proof	10,000	Value: 25.00				
1994 Bee	9,990,000	—	—	—	9.00	11.00
1995	9,996,000	—	—	—	9.00	11.00
1995 Proof	10,000	Value: 25.00				
1996	17,000	—	—	—	6.50	8.50
1996 Proof	8,000	Value: 25.00				
1997	15,000	—	—	—	8.00	10.00
1997 Proof	10,000	Value: 25.00				
1998	—	—	—	—	8.00	10.00
1998 Proof	—	Value: 25.00				
1999	—	—	—	—	8.00	10.00
1999 Proof	—	Value: 25.00				
2000	—	—	—	—	8.00	10.00
2000 Proof	—	Value: 25.00				
2001 Proof	—	Value: 25.00				
2001	—	—	—	—	8.00	10.00

KM# 1008.1 20 FRANCS
Tri-Metallic Copper-Aluminum-Nickel center plug%2C Nickel inner ring%2C Copper-Aluminum-Nickel outer ring, 27 mm. **Obv:** Mont St. Michel **Rev:** Patterned denomination above date within circle **Edge:** 4 milled bands

Date	Mintage	F	VF	XF	Unc	BU
1992	Inc. above	—	—	—	15.00	18.00

Note: Open V in outer ring

Date	Mintage	F	VF	XF	Unc	BU
1992	60,000,000	—	—	—	15.00	18.00

Note: Closed V in outer ring

KM# 1016 20 FRANCS
Tri-Metallic Aluminum-Bronze center plug, Nickel inner ring, Copper-Aluminum-Nickel outer ring, 27 mm. **Subject:** Mediterranean Games **Obv:** Tower of Adge **Rev:** Denomination flanked by laurels, wavy design below, rings divide date at bottom

Date	Mintage	F	VF	XF	Unc	BU
1993	5,001,000	—	—	—	10.00	12.00

KM# 1036 20 FRANCS
Tri-Metallic Aluminum-Bronze center plug, Nickel inner ring, Copper-Aluminum-Nickel outer ring, 26.8 mm. **Subject:** Founder of Modern Day Olympics - Pierre de Coubertin **Obv:**

Head left, 'RF' below, torch at right **Rev:** Building at left, denomination and date divided by Olympic logo at right

Date	Mintage	F	VF	XF	Unc	BU
1994	15,000,000	—	—	—	10.00	12.00

EURO COINAGE

European Union Issues

KM# 1282 EURO CENT

2.2700 g., Copper Plated Steel, 16.3 mm. **Obv:** Human face **Obv. Designer:** Fabienne Courtiade **Rev:** Denomination and globe **Rev. Designer:** Luc Luycx **Edge:** Plain

Date	Mintage	F	VF	XF	Unc	BU
1999	794,054,000	—	—	—	0.35	0.50
1999 Proof	15,000	Value: 10.00				
2000	605,267,000	—	—	—	0.35	0.50
2000 Proof	15,000	Value: 10.00				
2001	300,681,580	—	—	—	0.35	0.50
2001 Proof	15,000	Value: 10.00				
2002	200,000	—	—	—	7.50	10.00
2002 Proof	40,000	Value: 8.00				
2003 Proof	20,000	Value: 10.00				
2003	160,175,000	—	—	—	1.00	1.50
2004	400,000,000	—	—	—	0.35	0.50
2005	240,200,000	—	—	—	0.35	0.50
2006	—	—	—	—	0.35	0.50
2007	—	—	—	—	0.35	0.50

KM# 1283 2 EURO CENT

3.0300 g., Copper-Plated-Steel, 18.7 mm. **Obv:** Human face **Obv. Designer:** Fabienne Courtiade **Rev:** Denomination and globe **Rev. Designer:** Luc Luycx **Edge:** Grooved

Date	Mintage	F	VF	XF	Unc	BU
1999	702,104,000	—	—	—	0.50	0.75
1999 Proof	Est. 15,000	Value: 10.00				
2000	510,155,000	—	—	—	0.50	0.75
2000 Proof	15,000	Value: 10.00				
2001	249,101,580	—	—	—	0.50	0.75
2001 Proof	15,000	Value: 10.00				
2002	100,000	—	—	—	10.00	12.50
Note: In sets only						
2002 Proof	40,000	Value: 8.00				
2003 Proof	20,000	Value: 10.00				
2003	160,175,000	—	—	—	1.25	2.00
2004	300,000,000	—	—	—	—	1.00
2005	260,200,000	—	—	—	—	1.00
2006	—	—	—	—	—	1.00
2007	—	—	—	—	—	1.00

KM# 1284 5 EURO CENT

3.8600 g., Copper-Plated-Steel, 21.2 mm. **Obv:** Human face **Obv. Designer:** Fabienne Courtiade **Rev:** Denomination and globe **Rev. Designer:** Luc Luycx **Edge:** Plain

Date	Mintage	F	VF	XF	Unc	BU
1999	616,227,000	—	—	—	0.75	1.25
1999 Proof	Est. 15,000	Value: 12.00				
2000	280,099,000	—	—	—	0.75	1.25
2000 Proof	15,000	Value: 12.00				
2001	217,324,477	—	—	—	0.75	1.25
2001 Proof	15,000	Value: 12.00				
2002	186,400,000	—	—	—	0.75	1.25
2002 Proof	15,000	Value: 10.00				
2003	101,175,000	—	—	—	1.00	1.50
2003 Proof	20,000	Value: 12.00				
2004	60,000,000	—	—	—	—	1.25
2005	20,200,000	—	—	—	—	1.25
2006	—	—	—	—	—	1.25
2007	—	—	—	—	—	1.25

KM# 1285 10 EURO CENT

4.0700 g., Brass, 19.7 mm. **Obv:** The seed sower divides date and RF **Obv. Designer:** Laurent Jorb **Rev:** Denomination and map **Rev. Designer:** Luc Luycx **Edge:** Reeded

Date	Mintage	F	VF	XF	Unc	BU
1999	447,284,600	—	—	—	0.75	1.25
1999 Proof	15,000	Value: 12.00				
2000	297,467,000	—	—	—	0.75	1.25
2000 Proof	15,000	Value: 12.00				
2001	144,513,261	—	—	—	1.25	2.00
2001 Proof	15,000	Value: 12.00				
2002	206,700,000	—	—	—	0.75	1.25
2002 Proof	40,000	Value: 10.00				
2003 Proof	20,000	Value: 12.00				
2003	180,875,000	—	—	—	1.25	2.00
2004	—	—	—	—	—	1.50
2005	45,000,000	—	—	—	—	1.50
2006	—	—	—	—	—	1.50

KM# 1410 10 EURO CENT

4.0700 g., Brass, 19.7 mm. **Obv:** Sower **Obv. Designer:** Laurent Jorb **Rev:** Relief map of Western Europe, stars, lines and value **Rev. Designer:** Luc Luycx **Edge:** Reeded

Date	Mintage	F	VF	XF	Unc	BU
2007	—	—	—	—	—	1.50

KM# 1286 20 EURO CENT

5.7300 g., Brass, 22.2 mm. **Obv:** The seed sower divides date and RF **Obv. Designer:** Laurent Jorb **Rev:** Denomination and map **Rev. Designer:** Luc Luycx **Edge:** Notched

Date	Mintage	F	VF	XF	Unc	BU
1999	454,326,200	—	—	—	1.00	1.50
1999 Proof	15,000	Value: 14.00				
2000	148,988,600	—	—	—	1.25	2.00
2000 Proof	15,000	Value: 14.00				
2001	256,342,108	—	—	—	1.00	1.50
2001 Proof	15,000	Value: 14.00				
2002	192,100,000	—	—	—	1.00	1.50
2002 Proof	40,000	Value: 12.00				
2003	100,000	—	—	—	6.50	9.50
2003 Proof	20,000	Value: 14.00				
2004	—	—	—	—	—	1.50
2005	—	—	—	—	—	1.50
2006	—	—	—	—	—	1.50

KM# 1411 20 EURO CENT

5.7300 g., Brass, 22.2 mm. **Obv:** Sower **Obv. Designer:** Laurent Jorb **Rev:** Relief map of Western Europe, stars, lines and value **Rev. Designer:** Luc Luycx **Edge:** Notched

Date	Mintage	F	VF	XF	Unc	BU
2007	—	—	—	—	—	1.50

KM# 1287 50 EURO CENT

7.8100 g., Brass, 24.2 mm. **Obv:** The seed sower divides date and RF **Obv. Designer:** Laurent Jorb **Rev:** Denomination and map **Rev. Designer:** Luc Luycx **Edge:** Reeded

Date	Mintage	F	VF	XF	Unc	BU
1999	150,788,600	—	—	—	1.50	2.25
1999 Proof	15,000	Value: 15.00				
2000	179,531,000	—	—	—	1.25	2.00
2000 Proof	15,000	Value: 15.00				
2001	276,287,274	—	—	—	1.25	2.00
2001 Proof	15,000	Value: 15.00				
2002	226,500,000	—	—	—	1.25	2.00
2002 Proof	40,000	Value: 14.00				
2003 Proof	20,000	Value: 15.00				
2003	100,000	—	—	—	7.50	11.50
2004	—	—	—	—	—	2.00
2005	—	—	—	—	—	2.00
2006	—	—	—	—	—	2.00

KM# 1412 50 EURO CENT

7.8100 g., Brass, 24.2 mm. **Obv:** Sower **Obv. Designer:** Laurent Jorb **Rev:** Relief map of Western Europe, stars, lines and value **Rev. Designer:** Luc Luycx **Edge:** Reeded

Date	Mintage	F	VF	XF	Unc	BU
2007	—	—	—	—	—	2.00

KM# 1288 EURO

7.5000 g., Bi-Metallic Copper-Nickel center in Brass ring, 23.3 mm. **Obv:** Stylized tree divides RF within circle, date below **Obv. Designer:** Joaquin Jimenez **Rev:** Denomination and map **Rev. Designer:** Luc Luycx **Edge:** Reeded and plain sections

Date	Mintage	F	VF	XF	Unc	BU
1999	301,085,000	—	—	—	2.50	3.75
1999 Proof	15,000	Value: 18.00				
2000	297,305,000	—	—	—	2.50	3.75
2000 Proof	15,000	Value: 18.00				
2001	150,251,624	—	—	—	2.75	4.00
2001 Proof	15,000	Value: 18.00				
2002	129,400,000	—	—	—	2.50	3.75
2002 Proof	40,000	Value: 16.00				
2003 Proof	20,000	Value: 18.00				
2003	100,000	—	—	—	8.00	12.50
2004	—	—	—	—	—	2.50
2005	—	—	—	—	—	2.50
2006	—	—	—	—	—	2.50

KM# 1289 2 EURO

8.5200 g., Bi-Metallic Brass center in Copper-Nickel ring, 25.6 mm. **Obv:** Stylized tree divides RF within circle, date below **Obv. Designer:** Joaquin Jimenez **Rev:** Denomination and map **Rev. Designer:** Luc Luycx **Edge:** Reeding with 2's and stars

Date	Mintage	F	VF	XF	Unc	BU
1999	56,730,000	—	—	—	4.50	7.00
1999 Proof	15,000	Value: 20.00				
2000	171,155,000	—	—	—	3.75	6.00
2000 Proof	15,000	Value: 20.00				
2001	237,950,793	—	—	—	3.75	6.00
2001 Proof	15,000	Value: 20.00				
2002	153,700,000	—	—	—	3.75	6.00
2002 Proof	40,000	Value: 18.00				
2003 Proof	20,000	Value: 20.00				
2003	100,000	—	—	—	8.50	13.50
2004	—	—	—	—	—	5.00
2005	—	—	—	—	—	5.00
2006	—	—	—	—	—	5.00

KM# 1414 2 EURO

8.5200 g., Bi-Metallic Brass center in Copper-Nickel ring, 25.6 mm. **Obv:** Stylized tree **Obv. Designer:** Joaquin Jimenez **Rev:** Relief map of Western Europe, stars, lines and value **Rev. Designer:** Luc Luycx **Edge:** Reeding with 2's and stars

Date	Mintage	F	VF	XF	Unc	BU
2007	—	—	—	—	—	6.00

FRENCH AFARS & ISSAS

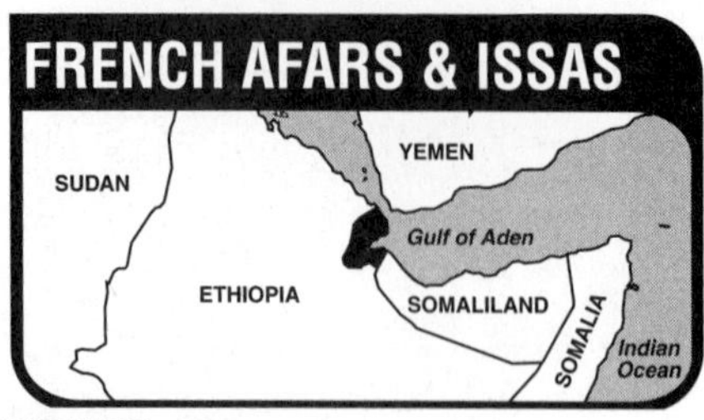

MINT MARK
- Paris (privy marks only)

MONETARY SYSTEM
100 Centimes = 1 Franc

NOTE
For later coinage, see Djibouti
For earlier coinage, see French Somaliland

FRENCH COLONY

DECIMAL COINAGE

KM# 16 FRANC
1.3000 g., Aluminum, 24 mm. **Obv:** Winged bust left, date below **Obv. Designer:** G.B.L. Bazor **Rev:** Lyre antelope divides denomination

Date	Mintage	F	VF	XF	Unc	BU
1969(a)	100,000	1.00	2.00	3.50	6.00	—
1971(a)	100,000	1.00	2.00	3.50	6.00	—
1975(a)	300,000	0.75	1.25	2.00	3.00	—

KM# 13 2 FRANCS
2.2000 g., Aluminum, 27 mm. **Obv:** Winged bust left, date below **Obv. Designer:** G.B.L. Bazor **Rev:** Lyre antelope divides denomination

Date	Mintage	F	VF	XF	Unc	BU
1968(a)	100,000	1.00	2.00	3.50	6.00	—
1975(a)	180,000	0.75	1.50	2.50	5.00	—

KM# 14 5 FRANCS
3.8000 g., Aluminum, 31.1 mm. **Obv:** Winged bust left, date below **Obv. Designer:** G.B.L. Bazor **Rev:** Lyre antelope divides denomination

Date	Mintage	F	VF	XF	Unc	BU
1968(a)	100,000	1.00	2.00	3.50	6.00	—
1975(a)	300,000	0.75	1.25	2.00	4.00	—

KM# 17 10 FRANCS
3.0000 g., Aluminum-Bronze, 20 mm. **Obv:** Winged bust left, date below **Obv. Designer:** G.B.L. Bazor **Rev:** Dhow, ocean liner, denomination above

Date	Mintage	F	VF	XF	Unc	BU
1969(a)	100,000	1.50	3.00	6.00	9.00	—
1970(a)	300,000	1.00	2.00	4.00	7.00	—
1975(a)	360,000	0.75	1.50	3.00	5.00	—

KM# 15 20 FRANCS
4.1000 g., Aluminum-Bronze, 23.6 mm. **Obv:** Winged bust left, date below **Obv. Designer:** G.B.L. Bazor **Rev:** Dhow, ocean liner, denomination above

Date	Mintage	F	VF	XF	Unc	BU
1968(a)	300,000	1.50	2.50	4.50	8.00	—
1975(a)	300,000	1.25	2.00	4.00	7.00	—

KM# 18 50 FRANCS
7.0000 g., Copper Nickel, 25.5 mm. **Obv:** Hooded head left, date below **Obv. Designer:** R. Joly **Rev:** Pair of dromedary camels, denomination above

Date	Mintage	F	VF	XF	Unc	BU
1970(a)	600,000	1.50	3.00	6.00	10.00	12.00
1975(a)	180,000	1.50	3.00	6.00	10.00	12.00

KM# 19 100 FRANCS
11.9000 g., Copper-Nickel, 30 mm. **Obv:** Hooded head left, date below **Obv. Designer:** R. Joly **Rev:** Pair of dromedary camels, denomination below

Date	Mintage	F	VF	XF	Unc	BU
1970(a)	600,000	2.50	4.00	7.00	11.50	15.00
1975(a)	400,000	2.50	4.50	7.50	12.50	16.00

FRENCH EQUATORIAL AFRICA

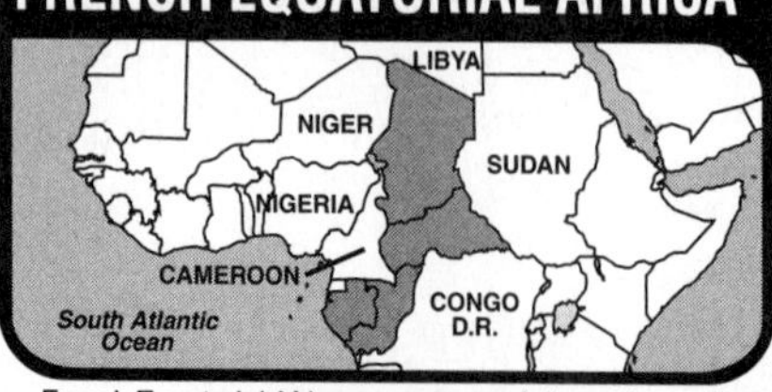

French Equatorial Africa, an area consisting of four self governing dependencies (Middle Congo, Ubangi-Shari, Chad and Gabon) in West-Central Africa, had an area of 969,111 sq. mi. (2,509,987 sq. km.). Capital: Brazzaville. The area, rich in natural resources, exported cotton, timber, coffee, cacao, diamonds and gold.

Little is known of the history of these parts of Africa prior to French occupation - which began with no thought of territorial acquisition. France's initial intent was simply to establish a few supply stations along the west coast of Africa to service the warships assigned to combat the slave trade in the early part of the 19th century. French settlement began in 1839. Gabon (then Gabun) and the Middle Congo were secured between 1885 and 1891; Chad and Ubangi-Shari between 1894 and 1897. The four colonies were joined to form French Equatorial Africa in 1910. The dependencies were changed from colonies to territories within the French Union in 1946, and all the inhabitants were made French citizens. In 1958 they voted to become autonomous republics within the new French Community, and attained full independence in 1960.

For later coinage see Central African States, Congo Peoples Republic, Gabon and Chad.

RULER
French, until 1960

MINT MARKS
(a) - Paris, privy marks only
(t) - Poissy, privy marks only, thunderbolt
SA - Pretoria (1942-1943)

ENGRAVERS' INITIALS
GLS – Steynberg

MONETARY SYSTEM
100 Centimes = 1 Franc

FRENCH COLONY

DECIMAL COINAGE

KM# 3 5 CENTIMES
Aluminum-Bronze **Note:** Similar to 10 Centimes, KM#4.

Date	Mintage	F	VF	XF	Unc	BU
1943	Est. 44,000,000	90.00	150	325	650	800

Note: Not released for circulation

KM# 4 10 CENTIMES
Aluminum-Bronze

Date	Mintage	F	VF	XF	Unc	BU
1943	Est. 13,000,000	75.00	100	160	375	500

Note: Not released for circulation

KM# 5 25 CENTIMES
Aluminum-Bronze **Note:** Similar to 10 Centimes, KM#4.

Date	Mintage	F	VF	XF	Unc	BU
1943	Est. 4,160,000	200	350	550	850	1,000

Note: Not released for circulation

KM# 1 50 CENTIMES
Brass **Rev:** Double cross divides denomination, date below

Date	Mintage	F	VF	XF	Unc	BU
1942SA	8,000,000	1.50	3.00	8.00	20.00	25.00

KM# 1a 50 CENTIMES
Bronze **Rev:** Double cross divides denomination

Date	Mintage	F	VF	XF	Unc	BU
1943SA	16,000,000	1.25	2.50	7.00	18.00	25.00

KM# 2 FRANC
Brass **Obv:** Rooster, small shield above **Rev:** Double cross divides denomination, date below

Date	Mintage	F	VF	XF	Unc	BU
1942SA	3,000,000	2.00	3.50	10.00	22.50	30.00

KM# 2a FRANC
Bronze **Obv:** Rooster left, small shield above **Rev:** Double cross divides denomination

Date	Mintage	F	VF	XF	Unc	BU
1943SA	6,000,000	1.75	2.75	9.00	20.00	30.00

KM# 6 FRANC
Aluminum, 23 mm. **Obv:** Winged bust left, date below **Obv. Designer:** G.B.L. Bazor **Rev:** Loder's gazelle divides denomination

Date	Mintage	F	VF	XF	Unc	BU
1948(a)	15,000,000	0.15	0.25	0.50	2.00	—

KM# 7 2 FRANCS
Aluminum **Obv:** Winged bust left, date below **Obv. Designer:** G.B.L. Bazor **Rev:** Loder's gazelle divides denomination

Date	Mintage	F	VF	XF	Unc	BU
1948(a)	5,040,000	0.25	0.50	1.50	4.00	—

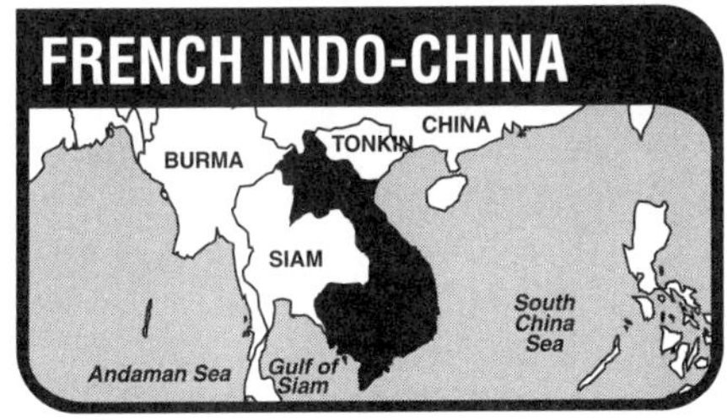

French Indo-China, made up of the protectorates of Annam, Tonkin, Cambodia and Laos and the colony of Cochin-China was located on the Indo-Chinese peninsula of Southeast Asia. The colony had an area of 286,194 sq. mi. (741,242 sq. km.). and a population of 30 million. Principal cities: Saigon, Haiphong, Vientiane, Pnom-Penh and Hanoi.

The forebears of the modern Indo-Chinese people originated in the Yellow River Valley of Northern China. From there, they were driven into the Indo-Chinese peninsula by the Han Chinese. The Chinese followed southward in the second century B.C., conquering the peninsula and ruling it until 938, leaving a lingering heritage of Chinese learning and culture. Indo-Chinese independence was basically maintained until the arrival of the French in the mid-19th century who established control over all of Vietnam, Laos and Cambodia. Activities directed toward obtaining self-determination accelerated during the Japanese occupation of World War II. The dependencies were changed from colonies to territories within the French Union in 1946, and all the inhabitants were made French citizens.

In Aug. of 1945, an uprising erupted involving the French and Vietnamese Nationalists, culminated in the French military disaster at Dien Bien Phu (May, 1954) and the subsequent Geneva Conference that brought an end to French colonial rule in Indo-China.

For later coinage see Kampuchea, Laos and Vietnam.

RULER

French, until 1954

MINT MARKS

A - Paris
(a) - Paris, privy marks only
B - Beaumont-le-Roger
C - Castlesarrasin
H - Heaton, Birmingham
(p) - Thunderbolt - Poissy
S - San Francisco, U.S.A.
None - Osaka, Japan
None - Hanoi, Tonkin

MONETARY SYSTEM

5 Sapeques = 1 Cent
100 Cents = 1 Piastre

FRENCH COLONY

STANDARD COINAGE

KM# 6 2 SAPEQUE

Bronze

Date	Mintage	F	VF	XF	Unc	BU
1901A	4,843,000	2.50	7.50	15.00	45.00	100
1902A	2,500,000	7.50	20.00	40.00	125	200

KM# 25 1/4 CENT

Zinc **Obv:** Square surrounds center hole, grain sprigs flank, date below **Rev:** Square around center hole, corners section coin, denomination divided by hole **Note:** Lead counterfeits dated 1941 and 1942 are known.

Date	Mintage	F	VF	XF	Unc	BU
1941	—	12.00	25.00	35.00	—	—
1942	221,800,000	8.00	15.00	35.00	75.00	100
1943	279,450,000	15.00	35.00	55.00	125	150
1944	46,122,000	100	180	250	750	1,250

KM# 20 1/2 CENT

Bronze, 21 mm. **Obv:** Center hole divides RF, liberty cap above, wreath surrounds **Rev:** Denomination divided by grain sprigs around center hole, date below

Date	Mintage	F	VF	XF	Unc	BU
1935(a)	26,365,000	0.25	0.50	2.00	10.00	—
1936(a)	23,635,000	0.25	0.50	2.00	10.00	—
1937(a)	10,244,000	0.50	1.50	5.00	15.00	—
1938(a)	16,665,000	0.25	0.75	2.50	12.00	—
1939(a)	17,305,000	0.25	0.75	2.50	12.00	—
1940(a)	11,218,000	4.00	8.00	20.00	40.00	75.00

KM# 20a 1/2 CENT

Zinc, 21 mm. **Obv:** Center hole divides RF, liberty cap above, wreath surrounds **Rev:** Denomination divided by center hole and grain sprigs

Date	Mintage	F	VF	XF	Unc	BU
1939(a)	185,000	200	400	600	900	—
1940(a)	Inc. above	350	500	800	1,200	—

KM# 8 CENT

7.5100 g., Bronze, 27.5 mm. **Obv:** Center hole within statue, denomination below **Rev:** Symbols at four sides of center hole within circle, date below

Date	Mintage	F	VF	XF	Unc	BU
1901	9,750,000	2.00	3.00	7.50	25.00	—
1902	6,050,000	4.00	7.00	15.00	50.00	—
1903	8,000,000	2.50	4.00	8.00	30.00	—
1906	2,000,000	15.00	20.00	35.00	100	—

KM# 12.1 CENT

Bronze, 26 mm. **Obv:** Center hole within statue, denomination below, mint mark "A" for Paris mint **Rev:** Symbols at four sides of center hole within circle, date below

Date	Mintage	F	VF	XF	Unc	BU
1908	3,000,000	10.00	20.00	55.00	235	350
1909	5,000,000	20.00	40.00	80.00	275	—
1910	7,703,000	2.00	5.00	15.00	35.00	—
1911	15,234,000	0.75	3.00	10.00	20.00	—
1912	17,027,000	0.75	2.00	7.50	20.00	—
1913	3,945,000	2.00	7.00	18.00	45.00	—
1914	11,027,000	0.75	3.00	15.00	30.00	—
1916	1,312,000	8.00	15.00	30.00	65.00	—
1917	9,762,000	1.00	4.00	10.00	20.00	—
1918	2,372,000	6.00	12.50	25.00	50.00	—
1919	9,148,000	1.00	4.00	7.50	20.00	—
1920	18,305,000	0.75	3.00	5.00	12.50	—
1921	14,272,000	0.75	2.00	3.00	10.00	—
1922	8,850,000	1.00	3.00	5.00	20.00	—
1923	1,079,000	40.00	90.00	180	350	—
1926	11,672,000	0.75	2.00	4.00	15.00	—
1927	3,328,000	5.00	15.00	35.00	70.00	—
1930	4,682,000	1.25	2.75	5.00	15.00	—
1931	5,318,000	30.00	85.00	200	550	—
Note: Torch privy mark						
1931	Inc. above	60.00	120	300	800	—
Note: Wing privy mark						
1937	8,902,000	1.50	3.00	6.00	25.00	—
1938	15,499,000	1.00	2.00	4.00	16.00	—
1939	17,589,000	1.00	2.00	4.00	16.00	—

KM# 12.2 CENT

Bronze, 26 mm. **Obv:** No mint mark at bottom, (San Francisco mint) **Rev:** Four symbols surround center hole **Note:** Without mint mark.

Date	Mintage	F	VF	XF	Unc	BU
1920	13,290,000	2.00	4.00	10.00	25.00	—
1921	1,710,000	15.00	70.00	180	350	—

KM# 12.3 CENT

Bronze, 26 mm. **Obv:** Center hole within statue, denomination below **Rev:** Four symbols surround center hole

Date	Mintage	F	VF	XF	Unc	BU
1922(p)	9,476,000	1.00	1.75	5.00	12.00	—
1923(p)	35,524,000	0.50	0.75	1.50	7.50	—

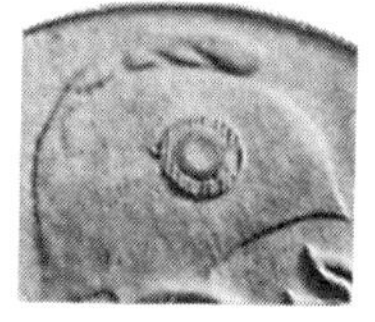

Type I

KM# 24.1 CENT

Zinc **Obv:** Wreath surrounds center hole, liberty cap above, denomination below **Rev:** Center hole divides denomination, wreath surrounds, date below **Note:** Vichy Government issue. Type 1: Circles on Phrygian cap.

Date	Mintage	F	VF	XF	Unc	BU
1940	1,990,000	10.00	16.00	40.00	75.00	—

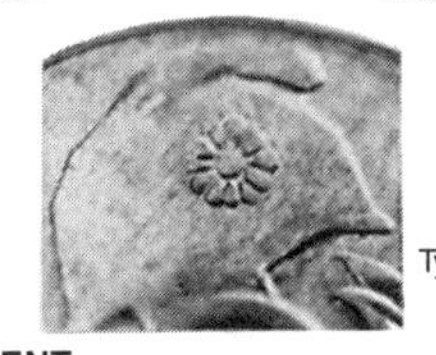

Type II

KM# 24.2 CENT

Zinc **Obv:** Wreath surrounds center hole, liberty cap above, denomination below **Rev:** Center hole divides denomination, wreath surrounds, date below **Note:** Vichy Government issue. Type 2: Rosette on Phrygian cap, variety 2 with 12 petals.

Date	Mintage	F	VF	XF	Unc	BU
1940	150,000	18.00	35.00	70.00	140	—

KM# 24.3 CENT

Zinc **Obv:** Wreath surrounds, cap above, denomination below **Rev:** Wreath surrounds center hole, denomination divided **Note:** Vichy Government issue. Type 2: Rosette on Phrygian cap. Variety 2: 11 petals.

Date	Mintage	F	VF	XF	Unc	BU
1940	2,360,000	8.00	18.00	35.00	70.00	—
1941	2,500,000	7.00	16.00	25.00	70.00	—

KM# 26 CENT

Aluminum **Obv:** Center hole flanked by leafy sprays, date below **Rev:** Denomination left and top of center hole **Note:** Edge varieties exist - plain, grooved, and partially grooved.

Date	Mintage	F	VF	XF	Unc	BU
1943	15,000,000	0.75	2.00	4.00	8.00	—

KM# 18 5 CENTS

5.0000 g., Copper-Nickel, 24 mm. **Obv:** Cornucopias flank center hole, laureate head left above **Rev:** Center hole within wreath divides denomination, date below **Designer:** A. Patey **Note:** 1.6 mm thick; prev. KM#18.1.

Date	Mintage	F	VF	XF	Unc	BU
1923(a)	1,611,000	5.00	10.00	20.00	40.00	—
1924(a)	3,389,000	6.00	12.00	24.00	45.00	—
1925(a)	6,000,000	5.00	10.00	20.00	35.00	—
1930(a) Torch	4,000,000	5.00	10.00	20.00	35.00	—
1937(a) Wing	10,000,000	2.00	5.00	10.00	20.00	—
1938(a)	1,480,000	15.00	30.00	75.00	160	—
1938(a) Proof	—	Value: 275				

KM# 18.1a 5 CENTS
4.0000 g., Nickel-Brass, 24 mm. **Obv:** Cornucopias flank center hole, laureate head left above **Rev:** Center hole divides denomination, wreath surrounds, date below **Note:** 1.3 mm thick.

Date	Mintage	F	VF	XF	Unc	BU
1938(a)	50,569,000	0.75	2.00	5.00	12.00	—
1939(a)	38,501,000	0.75	2.00	5.00	12.00	—

KM# 27 5 CENTS
Aluminum **Note:** Vichy Government issue. Edge varieties exist: reeded - rare, plain, grooved, and partially grooved.

Date	Mintage	F	VF	XF	Unc	BU
1943A	10,000,000	1.00	2.00	5.00	10.00	—

KM# 30.1 5 CENTS
Aluminum **Obv:** Bust right holding laurel, date below **Rev:** Plant divides denomination

Date	Mintage	F	VF	XF	Unc	BU
1946(a)	28,000,000	0.25	0.60	1.00	5.00	—

KM# 30.2 5 CENTS
Aluminum **Obv:** Bust right holding laurel, date below **Rev:** Plant divide denomination

Date	Mintage	F	VF	XF	Unc	BU
1946B	22,000,000	0.25	0.60	1.00	5.00	—

KM# 9 10 CENTS
2.7000 g., 0.8350 Silver 0.0725 oz. ASW **Obv:** Liberty seated left with fasces **Rev:** Denomination within wreath **Rev. Legend:** TITRE 0.835. POIDS 2 GR. 7 **Designer:** Barre

Date	Mintage	F	VF	XF	Unc	BU
1901	2,950,000	7.00	25.00	60.00	200	350
1902	7,050,000	4.00	12.00	30.00	125	—
1903	1,300,000	12.00	30.00	80.00	325	—
1908	1,000,000	50.00	100	200	575	725
1909	1,000,000	30.00	75.00	130	425	—
1910	2,689,000	25.00	60.00	100	350	—
1911	2,311,000	25.00	40.00	80.00	325	—
1912	2,500,000	25.00	35.00	70.00	275	—
1913	4,847,000	7.50	12.50	30.00	125	—
1914	2,667,000	10.00	30.00	60.00	175	—
1916	2,000,000	10.00	30.00	60.00	185	—
1917	1,500,000	25.00	50.00	100	300	—
1919	1,500,000	30.00	60.00	125	350	—

KM# 14 10 CENTS
3.0000 g., 0.4000 Silver 0.0386 oz. ASW **Obv:** Liberty seated, date below **Rev:** Denomination within wreath, without fineness indicated **Designer:** Barre **Note:** Without mint mark.

Date	Mintage	F	VF	XF	Unc	BU
1920	10,000,000	10.00	20.00	50.00	120	150

KM# 16.1 10 CENTS
2.7000 g., 0.6800 Silver 0.0590 oz. ASW **Obv:** Liberty seated, date below **Rev:** Denomination within wreath **Rev. Legend:** TITRE 0.680 POIDS 2 GR. 7 **Designer:** Barre

Date	Mintage	F	VF	XF	Unc	BU
1921A	12,516,000	1.50	3.00	9.00	25.00	30.00
1922A	22,381,000	1.50	3.00	9.00	20.00	25.00
1923A	21,755,000	1.50	3.00	9.00	20.00	25.00
1924A	2,816,000	4.00	9.00	25.00	60.00	80.00
1925A	4,909,000	2.00	5.00	15.00	35.00	50.00
1927A	6,471,000	2.50	7.00	17.50	40.00	60.00
1928A	1,593,000	40.00	100	200	480	750
1929A	5,831,000	1.50	3.00	10.00	30.00	50.00
1930A	6,608,000	1.50	3.00	7.50	30.00	50.00
1931A Proof	100	Value: 400				

KM# 16.2 10 CENTS
2.7000 g., 0.6800 Silver 0.0590 oz. ASW **Obv:** Liberty seated left, date below **Rev:** Denomination within wreath **Rev. Legend:** TITRE 0.680 POIDS 2 GR. 7 **Designer:** Barre

Date	Mintage	F	VF	XF	Unc	BU
1937(a)	25,000,000	1.00	1.50	3.00	8.00	10.00

KM# 21.1 10 CENTS
Nickel, 18 mm. **Obv:** Bust right holding laurel, date without dots **Obv. Designer:** P. Turin **Rev:** Plant divides denomination **Note:** These coins are magnetic.

Date	Mintage	F	VF	XF	Unc	BU
1939(a)	16,841,000	0.50	1.00	2.00	8.00	10.00
1940(a)	25,505,000	0.50	1.00	1.00	8.00	10.00

KM# 21.1a 10 CENTS
3.0000 g., Copper-Nickel, 17.96 mm. **Obv:** Date without dots **Rev:** Plant divides denomination **Edge:** Reeded **Designer:** P. Turin **Note:** These coins are not magnetic.

Date	Mintage	F	VF	XF	Unc	BU
1939(a)	—	45.00	100	100	375	—
Note: Mintage included in KM#21.2						
1941S	50,000,000	0.50	1.00	3.00	8.00	—

KM# 21.2 10 CENTS
Copper-Nickel, 18 mm. **Obv:** Date between two dots **Rev:** Plant divides denomination **Designer:** P. Turin **Note:** These coins are not magnetic.

Date	Mintage	F	VF	XF	Unc	BU
.1939.(a)	2,237,000	65.00	140	250	475	—

KM# 28.1 10 CENTS
Aluminum, 23 mm. **Obv:** Bust right holding laurel, date below **Obv. Designer:** P. Turin **Rev:** Plant divides denomination

Date	Mintage	F	VF	XF	Unc	BU
1945(a)	40,170,000	0.25	0.50	1.00	4.50	—

KM# 28.2 10 CENTS
Aluminum, 23 mm. **Obv:** Bust right holding laurel, date below **Obv. Designer:** P. Turin **Rev:** Plant divides denomination

Date	Mintage	F	VF	XF	Unc	BU
1945B	9,830,000	1.00	2.00	5.00	12.50	—

KM# 10 20 CENTS
5.4000 g., 0.8350 Silver 0.1450 oz. ASW **Designer:** Barre

Date	Mintage	F	VF	XF	Unc	BU
1901	1,375,000	20.00	50.00	100	300	—
1902	3,525,000	7.50	15.00	40.00	175	—
1903	675,000	50.00	100	150	600	—
1908	500,000	100	250	400	850	—
1909	500,000	100	200	350	850	—
1911	2,340,000	7.50	15.00	35.00	120	—
1912	160,000	100	200	400	900	1,100
1913	1,252,000	50.00	100	150	400	—
1914	2,500,000	7.50	15.00	25.00	120	—
1916	1,000,000	20.00	45.00	120	280	—

KM# 13 20 CENTS
0.8350 Silver **Obv:** KM#10 **Rev:** KM#3a **Note:** Mule.

Date	Mintage	F	VF	XF	Unc	BU
1909	—	100	250	650	1,000	1,400

KM# 15 20 CENTS
6.0000 g., 0.4000 Silver 0.0772 oz. ASW **Rev:** Without fineness indicated **Note:** Without mint mark.

Date	Mintage	F	VF	XF	Unc	BU
1920	4,000,000	12.50	25.00	50.00	125	—

KM# 17.1 20 CENTS
5.4000 g., 0.6800 Silver 0.1181 oz. ASW **Obv:** Seated liberty left, date below **Rev:** Denomination within wreath **Rev. Legend:** TITRE O.680 POIDS 5 GR. 4 **Designer:** Barre

Date	Mintage	F	VF	XF	Unc	BU
1921A	3,663,000	4.00	10.00	20.00	40.00	—
1922A	5,812,000	3.00	6.00	12.00	25.00	—
1923A	7,109,000	3.00	6.00	12.00	25.00	—
1924A	1,400,000	8.00	20.00	40.00	90.00	—
1925A	2,556,000	6.00	15.00	30.00	75.00	—
1927A	3,245,000	4.00	10.00	20.00	40.00	—
1928A	794,000	15.00	40.00	80.00	225	—
1929A	644,000	20.00	50.00	100	275	—
1930A	5,576,000	3.00	6.00	12.00	25.00	—

KM# 17.2 20 CENTS
5.4000 g., 0.6800 Silver 0.1181 oz. ASW **Obv:** Liberty seated, date below **Rev:** Denomination within wreath **Rev. Legend:** TITRE O.680 POIDS 5 GR. 4 **Designer:** Barre

Date	Mintage	F	VF	XF	Unc	BU
1937(a)	17,500,000	1.75	2.50	6.00	12.00	—

KM# 23 20 CENTS
Nickel, 24 mm. **Obv:** Bust right holding laurel, date below **Obv. Designer:** P. Turin **Rev:** Plant divides denomination **Note:** Magnetic coin with security edge.

Date	Mintage	F	VF	XF	Unc	BU
1939(a)	344,500	15.00	30.00	40.00	125	—

KM# 23a.1 20 CENTS
Copper-Nickel, 24 mm. **Obv:** Bust right holding laurel, date below **Obv. Designer:** P. Turin **Rev:** Plant divides denomination **Edge:** Reeded **Note:** Non-magnetic coin.

Date	Mintage	F	VF	XF	Unc	BU
1939(a)	14,676,000	0.50	1.00	2.00	10.00	—
Note: Date between dots						

KM# 23a.2 20 CENTS
Copper-Nickel, 24 mm. **Obv:** Bust right holding laurel, date below **Obv. Designer:** P. Turin **Rev:** Plant divides denomination **Edge:** Reeded **Note:** Non-magnetic coin.

Date	Mintage	F	VF	XF	Unc	BU
1941S	25,000,000	0.50	1.00	2.00	5.00	—
Note: Date between dots						

KM# 29.1 20 CENTS
Aluminum **Obv:** Bust right holding laurel, date below **Obv. Designer:** P. Turin **Rev:** Plant divides denomination

Date	Mintage	F	VF	XF	Unc	BU
1945(a)	15,412,000	0.50	1.00	2.50	10.00	—

KM# 29.2 20 CENTS
Aluminum **Obv:** Bust right holding laurel, date below **Obv. Designer:** P. Turin **Rev:** Plant divides denomination

Date	Mintage	F	VF	XF	Unc	BU
1945B	6,665,000	2.00	4.00	8.00	25.00	—

KM# 29.3 20 CENTS
Aluminum **Obv:** Bust right holding laurel, date below **Obv. Designer:** P. Turin **Rev:** Plant divides denomination

Date	Mintage	F	VF	XF	Unc	BU
1945C	22,423,000	0.50	1.00	3.00	15.00	—

KM# 4a.2 50 CENTS
13.5000 g., 0.9000 Silver 0.3906 oz. ASW **Obv:** Liberty seated, date below **Rev:** Denomination within wreath **Rev. Legend:** TITRE 0.900. POIDS 13 GR. 5 **Designer:** Barre

Date	Mintage	F	VF	XF	Unc	BU
1936(a)	4,000,000	5.50	6.50	12.00	25.00	—

KM# 31 50 CENTS
12.4700 g., Copper-Nickel **Obv:** Liberty seated, date below **Rev:** Denomination within wreath **Rev. Legend:** BRONZE DE NICKEL **Designer:** Barre

Date	Mintage	F	VF	XF	Unc	BU
1946(a)	32,292,000	2.00	4.00	9.00	25.00	—

KM# 5a.1 PIASTRE
27.0000 g., 0.9000 Silver 0.7812 oz. ASW **Obv:** Liberty seated left with fasces **Rev:** Denomination within wreath **Rev. Legend:** TITRE 0.900 POIDS 27 GR. **Designer:** Barre

Date	Mintage	F	VF	XF	Unc	BU
1901A	3,150,000	11.50	15.00	25.00	150	275
1902A	3,327,000	11.50	15.00	25.00	150	275
1903A	10,077,000	11.50	13.50	12.00	110	—
1904A	5,751,000	11.50	15.00	20.00	130	—
1905A	3,561,000	11.50	15.00	20.00	130	—
1906A	10,194,000	11.50	13.50	20.00	110	—
1907A	14,062,000	11.50	13.50	20.00	110	—
1908A	13,986,000	11.50	13.50	20.00	110	—
1909A	9,201,000	11.50	13.50	15.00	100	—
1910A	761,000	25.00	40.00	120	320	450
1913A	3,244,000	11.50	15.00	22.50	100	—
1924A	2,831,000	11.50	13.50	22.50	150	—
1925A	2,882,000	11.50	13.50	22.50	150	—
1926A	6,383,000	11.50	13.50	20.00	110	—
1927A	8,183,999	11.50	13.50	20.00	85.00	100
1928A	5,290,000	11.50	13.50	20.00	110	—

KM# 5a.2 PIASTRE
27.0000 g., 0.9000 Silver 0.7812 oz. ASW **Rev:** Denomination within wreath **Designer:** Barre **Note:** Without mint mark.

Date	Mintage	F	VF	XF	Unc	BU
1921	4,850,000	12.00	20.00	40.00	125	175
1922	1,150,000	13.50	30.00	75.00	250	325

KM# 5a.3 PIASTRE
27.0000 g., 0.9000 Silver 0.7812 oz. ASW **Rev:** Denomination within wreath **Designer:** Barre

Date	Mintage	F	VF	XF	Unc	BU
1921H	3,580,000	12.00	20.00	40.00	150	—
1922H	7,420,000	11.50	13.50	20.00	100	—

KM# 19 PIASTRE
20.0000 g., 0.9000 Silver 0.5787 oz. ASW **Obv:** Laureate head left **Rev:** Denomination and date within keyhole shape wreath

Date	Mintage	F	VF	XF	Unc	BU
1931(a)	16,000,000	10.00	20.00	50.00	110	—

FEDERATED STATES

French Union

STANDARD COINAGE

KM# 32.1 PIASTRE
Copper-Nickel, 34.5 mm. **Obv:** Bust right holding laurel, date below **Obv. Designer:** P. Turin **Rev:** Grain sprigs below denomination **Note:** Security edge.

Date	Mintage	F	VF	XF	Unc	BU
1946(a)	2,520,000	7.50	12.50	20.00	85.00	135
1947(a)	261,000	15.00	35.00	75.00	160	300

KM# 32.2 PIASTRE
18.1300 g., Copper-Nickel, 34.5 mm. **Obv:** Bust right holding laurel, date below **Obv. Designer:** P. Turin **Rev:** Denomination above plants **Edge:** Reeded **Note:** Similar coins dated 1946 with reverse legend: INDOCHINE - FRANCAISE are Essais.

Date	Mintage	F	VF	XF	Unc	BU
1947(a)	54,480,000	2.00	4.00	7.50	10.00	30.00

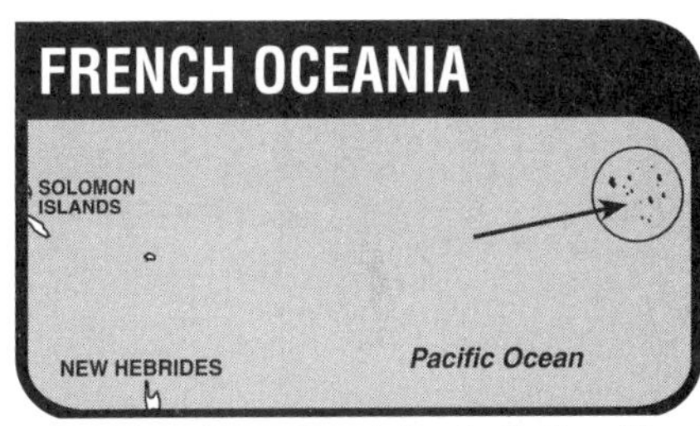

The Colony of French Oceania (now the Territory of French Polynesia), comprising 130 basalt and coral islands scattered among five archipelagoes in the South Pacific, had an area of 1,544 sq. mi. (3,999 sq. km.). Capital: Papeete. The colony produced phosphates, copra and vanilla.

Tahiti of the Society Islands, the hub of French Oceania, was visited by Capt. Cook in 1769 and by Capt. Bligh on the Bounty 1788-89. The Society Islands were claimed by France in 1768, and in 1903 grouped with the Marquesas Islands, the Tuamotu Archipelago, the Gambier Islands and the Austral Islands under a single administrative head located at Papeete, Tahiti, to form the colony of French Oceania.

RULER
French

MINT MARKS
(a) - Paris, privy marks only
(b)

MONETARY SYSTEM
100 Centimes = 1 Franc

FRENCH OVERSEAS TERRITORY

DECIMAL COINAGE

KM# 1 50 CENTIMES
Aluminum **Obv:** Seated Liberty with torch and cornucopia right, date below **Obv. Designer:** G.B.L. Bazor **Rev:** Inscription and island scene divide denomination

Date	Mintage	F	VF	XF	Unc	BU
1949(a)	795,000	0.50	0.75	1.50	3.00	6.50

KM# 2 FRANC
1.3100 g., Aluminum, 23.4 mm. **Obv. Designer:** G.B.L. Bazor

Date	Mintage	F	VF	XF	Unc	BU
1949(a)	2,000,000	0.20	0.35	1.00	2.00	3.00

KM# 3 2 FRANCS
Aluminum, 31 mm. **Obv:** Seated Liberty with torch and cornucopia right, date below **Obv. Designer:** G.B.L. Bazor

Date	Mintage	F	VF	XF	Unc	BU
1949(a)	1,000,000	0.40	0.60	1.25	2.50	4.00

KM# 4 5 FRANCS
Aluminum **Obv:** Seated Liberty with torch and cornucopia right, date below **Obv. Designer:** G.B.L. Bazor **Rev:** Inscription and island scene divide denomination

Date	Mintage	F	VF	XF	Unc	BU
1952	2,000,000	0.50	0.75	1.50	3.50	5.50

FRENCH POLYNESIA

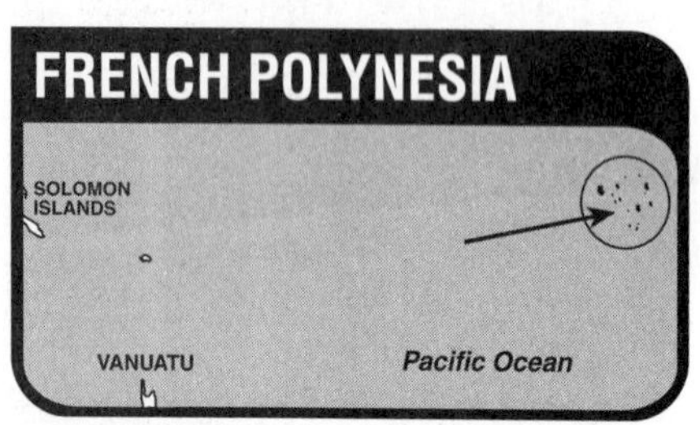

The Territory of French Polynesia (formerly French Oceania) has an area of 1,544 sq. mi. (3,941 sq. km.) and a population of 220,000. It is comprised of the same five archipelagoes that were grouped administratively to form French Oceania.

The colony of French Oceania became the Territory of French Polynesia by act of the French National Assembly in March, 1957. In Sept. of 1958 it voted in favor of the new constitution of the Fifth Republic, thereby electing to remain within the new French Community.

Picturesque, mountainous Tahiti, the setting of many tales of adventure and romance, is one of the most inspiringly beautiful islands in the world. Robert Louis Stevenson called it 'God's sweetest works'. It was there that Paul Gaugin, one of the pioneers of the Impressionist movement, painted the brilliant, exotic pictures that later made him famous. The arid coral atolls of Tuamotu comprise the most economically valuable area of French Polynesia. Pearl oysters thrive in the warm, limpid lagoons, and extensive portions of the atolls are valuable phosphate rock.

RULER
French

MINT MARKS
(a) - Paris, privy marks only
(b)

MONETARY SYSTEM
100 Centimes = 1 Franc

FRENCH OVERSEAS TERRITORY

DECIMAL COINAGE

KM# 1 50 CENTIMES
Aluminum **Obv:** Seated Liberty with torch and cornucopia right, date below **Obv. Designer:** G.B.L. Bazor **Rev:** Legend and island scene divides denomination

Date	Mintage	F	VF	XF	Unc	BU
1965(a)	400,000	0.10	0.25	0.50	1.50	4.50

KM# 2 FRANC
Aluminum **Obv:** Seated Liberty with torch and cornucopia right, date below **Obv. Designer:** G.B.L. Bazor **Rev:** Legend and island scene divide denomination

Date	Mintage	F	VF	XF	Unc	BU
1965(a)	3,300,000	—	0.10	0.20	0.75	2.50

KM# 11 FRANC
1.3000 g., Aluminum, 23 mm. **Obv:** Seated Liberty with torch and cornucopia right, date below, legend added flanking figure's feet **Obv. Legend:** I. E. O. M. **Obv. Designer:** G.B.L. Bazor **Rev:** Legend and island scene divide denomination

Date	Mintage	F	VF	XF	Unc	BU
1975(a)	2,000,000	—	0.10	0.15	0.45	2.50
1977(a)	2,000,000	—	0.10	0.15	0.45	1.75
1979(a)	1,500,000	—	0.10	0.15	0.45	1.25
1981(a)	2,000,000	—	0.10	0.15	0.45	1.25
1982(a)	1,000,000	—	0.10	0.15	0.45	1.25
1983(a)	2,200,000	—	0.10	0.15	0.45	1.25
1984(a)	1,500,000	—	0.10	0.15	0.45	1.25
1985(a)	2,000,000	—	0.10	0.15	0.45	1.25
1986(a)	2,000,000	—	0.10	0.15	0.45	1.25
1987(a)	2,000,000	—	0.10	0.15	0.45	1.25
1989(a)	1,000,000	—	0.10	0.15	0.45	1.25
1990(a)	1,500,000	—	0.10	0.15	0.45	1.00
1991(a)	1,400,000	—	0.10	0.15	0.35	1.00
1992(a)	800,000	—	0.10	0.15	0.35	1.00
1993(a)	2,300,000	—	0.10	0.15	0.35	1.00
1994(a)	1,000,000	—	0.10	0.15	0.30	1.00
1995(a)	1,000,000	—	0.10	0.15	0.30	1.00
1996(a)	2,700,000	—	0.10	0.15	0.30	1.00
1997(a)	1,100,000	—	0.10	0.15	0.25	0.75
1998(a)	1,600,000	—	0.10	0.15	0.25	0.75
1999(a)	2,600,000	—	0.10	0.15	0.25	0.75
2000(a)	3,000,000	—	0.10	0.15	0.25	0.75
2001(a)	2,900,000	—	—	—	0.50	1.00
2002(a)	1,600,000	—	—	—	0.50	1.00
2003(a)	4,200,000	—	—	—	0.50	1.00

KM# 3 2 FRANCS
Aluminum **Obv:** Seated Liberty with torch and cornucopia right, date below **Obv. Designer:** G.B.L. Bazor **Rev:** Legend and island scene divide denomination

Date	Mintage	F	VF	XF	Unc	BU
1965(a)	1,750,000	—	0.10	0.25	1.00	2.50

KM# 10 2 FRANCS
2.7000 g., Aluminum, 27 mm. **Obv:** Seated Liberty with torch and cornucopia right, date below, legend added flanking figure's feet **Obv. Legend:** I. E. O. M. **Obv. Designer:** G.B.L. Bazor **Rev:** Legend and island scene divide denomination

Date	Mintage	F	VF	XF	Unc	BU
1973(a)	400,000	—	0.10	0.25	0.75	3.00
1975(a)	1,000,000	—	0.10	0.25	0.75	2.00
1977(a)	1,000,000	—	0.10	0.25	0.75	2.00
1979(a)	2,000,000	—	0.10	0.25	0.75	1.75
1982(a)	1,000,000	—	0.10	0.25	0.75	1.75
1983(a)	1,500,000	—	0.10	0.25	0.75	1.75
1984(a)	1,200,000	—	0.10	0.25	0.75	1.75
1985(a)	1,400,000	—	0.10	0.25	0.75	1.50
1986(a)	1,500,000	—	0.10	0.25	0.75	1.50
1987(a)	1,000,000	—	0.10	0.25	0.75	1.50
1988(a)	500,000	—	0.10	0.25	0.75	1.50
1989(a)	1,000,000	—	0.10	0.25	0.75	1.50
1990(a)	1,500,000	—	0.10	0.25	0.75	1.50
1991(a)	1,500,000	—	0.10	0.25	0.60	1.50
1992(a)	—	—	0.10	0.25	0.60	1.25
1993(a)	1,400,000	—	0.10	0.25	0.50	1.25
1995(a)	1,200,000	—	0.10	0.20	0.40	1.25
1996(a)	2,200,000	—	0.10	0.20	0.40	1.25
1997(a)	1,300,000	—	0.10	0.20	0.40	1.25
1998(a)	600,000	—	0.10	0.20	0.40	1.25
1999(a)	2,800,000	—	0.10	0.20	0.40	1.00
2000(a)	1,600,000	—	0.10	0.20	0.40	1.00
2001(a)	2,400,000	—	—	—	0.75	1.50
2002(a)	2,500,000	—	—	—	0.75	1.50
2003(a)	3,200,000	—	—	—	0.75	1.50

KM# 4 5 FRANCS
3.7500 g., Aluminum, 31 mm. **Obv:** Seated Liberty with torch and cornucopia right, date below **Obv. Designer:** G.B.L. Bazor **Rev:** Legend and island scene divide denomination

Date	Mintage	F	VF	XF	Unc	BU
1965(a)	1,520,000	0.10	0.25	0.50	1.75	3.50

KM# 12 5 FRANCS
3.7500 g., Aluminum, 31 mm. **Obv:** Seated Liberty with torch and cornucopia right, date below, legend added flanking figure's feet **Obv. Legend:** I. E. O. M. **Obv. Designer:** G.B.L. Bazor **Rev:** Legend and island divide denomination

Date	Mintage	F	VF	XF	Unc	BU
1975(a)	500,000	0.10	0.20	0.40	1.25	3.25
1977(a)	500,000	0.10	0.20	0.40	1.25	2.25
1982(a)	500,000	0.10	0.20	0.40	1.25	2.25
1983(a)	800,000	0.10	0.20	0.40	1.25	2.00
1984(a)	600,000	0.10	0.20	0.40	1.25	2.00
1985(a)	—	0.10	0.20	0.40	1.25	2.00
1986(a)	600,000	0.10	0.20	0.40	1.25	2.00
1987(a)	400,000	0.10	0.20	0.40	1.25	1.75
1988(a)	400,000	0.10	0.20	0.40	1.25	1.75
1989(a)	—	0.10	0.20	0.40	1.25	1.75
1990(a)	500,000	0.10	0.20	0.40	1.25	1.75
1991(a)	700,000	0.10	0.20	0.40	1.00	1.50
1992(a)	500,000	0.10	0.20	0.40	1.00	1.50
1993(a)	400,000	0.10	0.20	0.35	0.85	1.25
1994(a)	500,000	0.10	0.20	0.35	0.70	1.25
1996(a)	100,000	0.10	0.20	0.35	0.75	1.25
1997(a)	500,000	0.10	0.20	0.35	0.85	1.25
1998(a)	800,000	0.10	0.20	0.35	0.70	1.25
1999(a)	600,000	0.10	0.20	0.35	0.65	1.25
2000(a)	900,000	—	—	—	0.50	1.00
2001(a)	1,600,000	—	—	—	1.00	2.00
2002(a)	400,000	—	—	—	1.00	2.00
2003(a)	1,000,000	—	—	—	1.00	2.00

KM# 5 10 FRANCS
Nickel **Obv:** Capped head left, date below **Obv. Designer:** R. Joly **Rev:** Native art above denomination **Rev. Designer:** A. Guzman

Date	Mintage	F	VF	XF	Unc	BU
1967(a)	1,000,000	0.25	0.50	0.75	1.85	4.75

KM# 8 10 FRANCS
6.0000 g., Nickel, 24 mm. **Obv:** Capped head left, date and legend below **Obv. Legend:** I. E. O. M. **Obv. Designer:** R. Joly **Rev:** Native art, denomination below **Rev. Designer:** A. Guzman

Date	Mintage	F	VF	XF	Unc	BU
1972(a)	300,000	0.25	0.50	0.75	2.75	4.50
1973(a)	400,000	0.25	0.50	0.75	2.75	3.00
1975(a)	1,000,000	0.25	0.50	0.75	1.75	2.75
1979(a)	500,000	0.25	0.50	0.75	1.75	2.75
1982(a)	500,000	0.25	0.50	0.75	1.75	2.75
1983(a)	1,000,000	0.25	0.50	0.75	1.75	2.75
1984(a)	800,000	0.25	0.50	0.75	1.75	2.75
1985(a)	800,000	0.25	0.50	0.75	1.75	2.75
1986(a)	800,000	0.25	0.50	0.75	1.75	2.50
1991(a)	600,000	0.25	0.50	0.75	1.50	2.50
1992(a)	400,000	0.25	0.50	0.75	1.25	2.50
1993(a)	600,000	0.25	0.50	0.75	1.25	2.25
1995(a)	500,000	0.25	0.50	0.70	1.00	2.00
1996(a)	300,000	0.25	0.50	0.70	1.00	2.00
1997(a)	300,000	0.25	0.50	0.70	1.00	2.00
1998(a)	1,000,000	0.25	0.45	0.65	0.85	1.75
1999(a)	2,000,000	0.25	0.45	0.65	0.85	1.75
2000(a)	1,200,000	0.25	0.45	0.65	0.85	1.75
2001(a)	500,000	—	—	—	1.25	2.75
2002(a)	600,000	—	—	—	1.25	2.75
2003(a)	1,000,000	—	—	—	1.25	2.75

KM# 6 20 FRANCS
10.0000 g., Nickel, 28.3 mm. **Obv:** Capped head left, date below **Obv. Designer:** R. Joly **Rev:** Flowers, vanilla shoots, bread fruit **Rev. Designer:** A. Guzman

Date	Mintage	F	VF	XF	Unc	BU
1967(a)	750,000	0.35	0.75	1.25	3.00	4.50
1969(a)	250,000	0.35	1.00	2.00	7.00	9.00
1970(a)	500,000	0.35	0.75	1.25	3.25	3.75

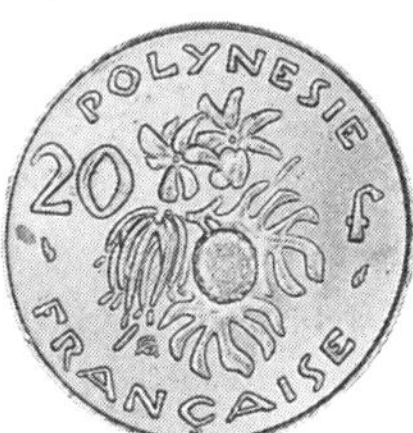

KM# 9 20 FRANCS
10.0000 g., Nickel, 28.3 mm. **Obv:** Capped head left, date and legend below **Obv. Legend:** I. E. O. M. **Obv. Designer:** R. Joly **Rev:** Flowers, vanilla shoots, bread fruit **Rev. Designer:** A. Guzman

Date	Mintage	F	VF	XF	Unc	BU
1972(a)	300,000	0.30	0.50	1.00	3.00	5.50
1973(a)	300,000	0.30	0.50	1.00	3.00	4.50
1975(a)	700,000	0.30	0.50	1.00	2.25	3.50
1977(a)	350,000	0.35	0.75	1.50	4.50	7.50
1979(a)	500,000	0.30	0.50	1.00	2.25	3.50
1983(a)	800,000	0.30	0.50	1.00	2.25	3.50
1984(a)	600,000	0.30	0.50	1.00	2.25	3.50
1986(a)	400,000	0.30	0.50	1.00	2.25	3.00
1988(a)	250,000	0.30	0.50	1.00	2.25	3.00
1991(a)	—	0.30	0.50	1.00	2.00	3.00
1992(a)	—	0.30	0.50	1.00	2.00	3.00
1993(a)	—	0.30	0.50	1.00	1.75	2.50
1995(a)	—	0.30	0.50	1.00	1.75	2.50
1996(a)	—	0.30	0.50	0.85	1.50	2.25
1997(a)	—	0.30	0.50	0.85	1.50	2.25
1998(a)	—	0.30	0.50	0.85	1.35	2.00
1999(a)	—	0.30	0.50	0.85	1.35	2.00
2000(a)	—	—	—	—	1.25	1.75
2001(a)	500,000	—	—	—	1.75	3.25
2002(a)	—	—	—	—	1.75	3.25
2003(a)	700,000	—	—	—	1.75	3.00

KM# 7 50 FRANCS
15.0000 g., Nickel, 33 mm. **Obv:** Capped head left, date below **Obv. Designer:** R. Joly **Rev:** Denomination above Moorea Harbor **Rev. Designer:** A. Guzman

Date	Mintage	F	VF	XF	Unc	BU
1967(a)	600,000	0.60	1.00	2.00	5.00	8.00

KM# 13 50 FRANCS
15.0000 g., Nickel, 33 mm. **Obv:** Capped head left, date and legend below **Obv. Legend:** I. E. O. M. **Obv. Designer:** R. Joly **Rev:** Denomination above Moorea Harbor **Rev. Designer:** A. Guzman

Date	Mintage	F	VF	XF	Unc	BU
1975(a)	500,000	0.60	0.80	1.25	4.00	7.50
1982(a)	500,000	0.60	0.80	1.25	4.00	6.00
1985(a)	Inc. above	0.60	0.80	1.25	4.00	6.00
1988(a)	125,000	0.60	0.80	1.25	4.00	7.00
1991(a)	—	0.60	0.80	1.25	3.50	5.00
1995(a)	—	0.60	0.75	1.20	2.00	3.00
1996(a)	—	0.60	0.75	1.00	1.50	2.50
1998(a)	—	0.60	0.75	1.00	1.50	2.50
1999(a)	—	0.60	0.75	1.00	1.50	2.50
2000(a)	—	—	—	—	1.50	2.50
2001(a)	300,000	—	—	—	2.00	4.00
2002(a)	—	—	—	—	2.00	4.00
2003(a)	240,000	—	—	—	2.00	4.00

KM# 14 100 FRANCS
10.0000 g., Nickel-Bronze, 30 mm. **Obv:** Capped head left, date below **Obv. Designer:** R. Joly **Rev:** Denomination above Moorea Harbor **Rev. Designer:** A. Guzman

Date	Mintage	F	VF	XF	Unc	BU
1976(a)	2,000,000	1.20	1.50	2.00	4.00	9.00
1979(a)	150	—	—	—	—	—
1982(a)	1,000,000	1.20	1.50	2.25	5.00	8.50
1984(a)	500,000	1.20	1.50	2.25	5.00	8.00
1986(a)	400,000	1.20	1.50	2.25	5.00	8.00
1987(a)	500,000	1.20	1.50	2.25	5.00	8.00
1988(a)	500,000	1.20	1.50	2.25	5.00	7.50
1991(a)	—	1.20	1.50	2.25	4.25	7.00
1992(a)	—	1.20	1.50	2.25	4.00	7.00
1995(a)	—	1.20	1.50	2.25	3.50	6.50
1996(a)	—	1.20	1.50	2.00	3.00	6.50
1997(a)	—	1.20	1.50	2.00	3.00	6.00
1998(a)	—	1.00	1.25	1.75	2.50	5.00
1999(a)	—	—	—	—	2.50	5.00
2000(a)	—	—	—	—	2.00	3.50
2001(a)	200,000	—	—	—	3.00	5.00
2002(a)	—	—	—	—	3.00	5.00
2003(a)	600,000	—	—	—	2.75	5.00

FRENCH SOMALILAND

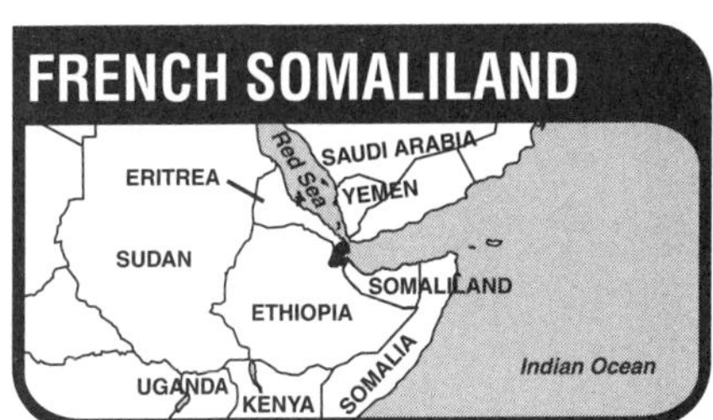

French Somaliland is located in northeast Africa at the Bab el Mandeb Strait connecting the Suez Canal and the Red Sea with the Gulf of Aden and the Indian Ocean. French interest in French Somaliland began in 1839 with concessions obtained by a French naval lieutenant from the provincial sultans. French Somaliland was made a protectorate in 1884 and its boundaries were delimited by the Franco-British and Ethiopian accords of 1887 and 1897. It became a colony in 1896 and a territory within the French Union in 1946.

NOTE: For later coinage see French Afars & Issas.

MINT MARK
(a) - Paris (privy marks only)

MONETARY SYSTEM
100 Centimes = 1 Franc

FRENCH OVERSEAS TERRITORY

DECIMAL COINAGE

KM# 4 FRANC
Aluminum **Obv:** Winged head left, date below **Obv. Designer:** G.B.L. Bazor **Rev:** Lyre antelope divides denomination

Date	Mintage	F	VF	XF	Unc	BU
1948(a)	200,000	6.50	12.50	25.00	45.00	75.00
1949(a)	Inc. above	8.00	15.00	30.00	60.00	95.00

KM# 8 FRANC
1.3000 g., Aluminum, 22.8 mm. **Obv:** Winged head left, date below **Obv. Designer:** G.B.L. Bazor **Rev:** Lyre antelope divides denomination

Date	Mintage	F	VF	XF	Unc	BU
1959(a)	500,000	0.25	0.50	1.50	3.00	5.00
1965(a)	200,000	0.35	0.60	2.00	4.00	6.00

KM# 5 2 FRANCS
Aluminum **Obv:** Winged head left, date below **Obv. Designer:** G.B.L. Bazor **Rev:** Lyre antelope divides denomination

Date	Mintage	F	VF	XF	Unc	BU
1948(a)	200,000	6.50	12.50	25.00	60.00	80.00
1949(a)	Inc. above	8.00	15.00	30.00	70.00	—

KM# 9 2 FRANCS
2.2000 g., Aluminum **Obv:** Winged head left, date below **Obv. Designer:** G.B.L. Bazor **Rev:** Lyre antelope divides denomination

Date	Mintage	F	VF	XF	Unc	BU
1959(a)	200,000	0.25	0.75	2.50	5.00	7.00
1965(a)	240,000	0.25	0.75	2.50	5.00	7.00

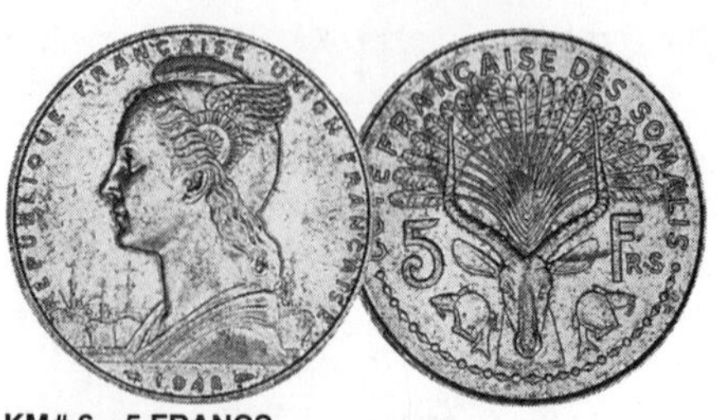

KM# 6 5 FRANCS
Aluminum **Obv:** Winged head left, date below **Obv. Designer:** G.B.L. Bazor **Rev:** Lyre antelope divides denomination

Date	Mintage	F	VF	XF	Unc	BU
1948(a)	500,000	5.00	10.00	25.00	45.00	75.00

KM# 10 5 FRANCS
3.6600 g., Aluminum **Obv:** Winged head left, date below **Obv. Designer:** G.B.L. Bazor **Rev:** Lyre antelope divides denomination

Date	Mintage	F	VF	XF	Unc	BU
1959(a)	500,000	0.25	0.75	2.50	5.50	7.50
1965(a)	200,000	0.25	0.75	3.00	6.50	8.50

KM# 7 20 FRANCS
3.9600 g., Aluminum-Bronze **Obv:** Winged head left, date below **Obv. Designer:** G.B.L. Bazor **Rev:** Dhow, ocean liner, denomination above

Date	Mintage	F	VF	XF	Unc	BU
1952(a)	500,000	1.25	2.50	4.50	10.00	12.00

KM# 12 20 FRANCS
Aluminum-Bronze **Obv:** Winged head left, date below **Obv. Designer:** G.B.L. Bazor **Rev:** Dhow, ocean liner, denomination above

Date	Mintage	F	VF	XF	Unc	BU
1965(a)	200,000	1.00	2.00	4.00	8.00	10.00

FRENCH WEST AFRICA

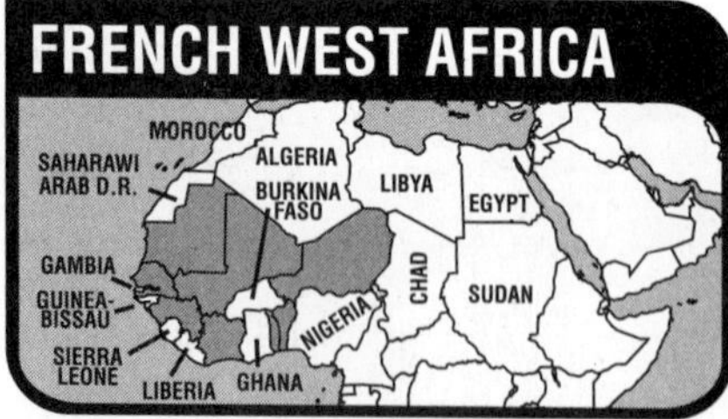

French West Africa (Afrique Occidentale Francaise), a former federation of French colonial territories on the northwest coast of Africa, had an area of 1,831,079 sq. mi. (4,742,495 sq. km.) and a population of about 17.4 million. Capital: Dakar. The constituent territories were Mauritania, Senegal, Dahomey, French Sudan, Ivory Coast, Upper Volta, Niger, French Guinea, and later on the mandated area of Togo. Peanuts, palm kernels, cacao, coffee and bananas were exported.

Prior to the mid-19th century, France, as the other European states, maintained establishments on the west coast of Africa for the purpose of trading in slaves and gum, but made no serious attempt at colonization. From 1854 onward, the coastal settlements were gradually extended into the interior until, by the opening of the 20th century, acquisition ended and organization and development began. French West Africa was formed in 1895 by grouping the several colonies under one administration (at Dakar) while retaining a large measure of autonomy to each of the constituent territories. The inhabitants of French West Africa were made French citizens in 1946. With the exception of French Guinea, all of the colonies voted in 1958 to become autonomous members of the new French Community. French Guinea voted to become the fully independent Republic of Guinea. The present-day independent states are members of the "Union Monetaire Ouest-Africaine". For later coinage see West African States.

RULERS
French

MINT MARKS
(a) - Paris, privy marks only
(L) – London

MONETARY SYSTEM
100 Centimes = 1 Franc
5 Francs = 1 Unit

FRENCH COLONIES
COLONIAL COINAGE

KM# 1 50 CENTIMES
Aluminum-Bronze **Obv:** Laureate head left **Rev:** Cornucopias flank denomination and date

Date	Mintage	F	VF	XF	Unc	BU
1944(L)	10,000,000	2.00	4.00	15.00	28.00	32.00
1944(L) Proof	—	Value: 200				

KM# 2 FRANC
Aluminum-Bronze **Obv:** Laureate head left **Rev:** Cornucopias flank denomination and date

Date	Mintage	F	VF	XF	Unc	BU
1944(L)	15,000,000	1.00	2.00	10.00	20.00	24.00
1944(L) Proof	—	Value: 250				

KM# 3 FRANC
Aluminum **Obv:** Winged head left, date below **Rev:** Rhim gazelle facing divides denomination **Designer:** G. B. L. Bazor

Date	Mintage	F	VF	XF	Unc	BU
1948(a)	30,110,000	0.15	0.20	2.00	4.00	5.00
1955(a)	5,200,000	0.20	0.35	1.00	3.00	4.00

KM# 4 2 FRANCS
2.2400 g., Aluminum, 27 mm. **Obv:** Winged head left, date below **Rev:** Rhim gazelle facing divides denomination **Designer:** G. B. L. Bazor

Date	Mintage	F	VF	XF	Unc	BU
1948(a)	12,665,000	0.20	0.30	0.50	1.75	2.75
1955(a)	1,400,000	0.25	0.40	5.00	12.00	14.00

KM# 5 5 FRANCS
Aluminum-Bronze **Obv:** Head left divides date above **Rev:** Rhim gazelle facing, divides denomination **Rev. Designer:** G.B.L. Bazor

Date	Mintage	F	VF	XF	Unc	BU
1956(a)	85,000,000	0.35	0.50	1.00	2.50	5.00

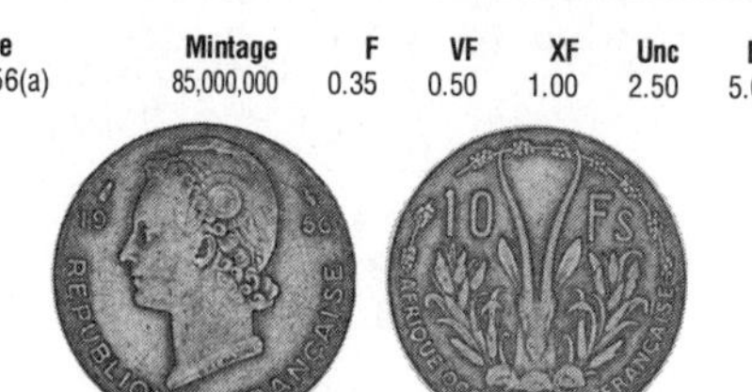

KM# 6 10 FRANCS
Aluminum-Bronze, 23.5 mm. **Obv:** Head left, divides date above **Rev:** Rhim gazelle facing divides denomination **Rev. Designer:** G.B.L. Bazor

Date	Mintage	F	VF	XF	Unc	BU
1956(a)	20,000,000	0.50	1.00	1.50	3.50	6.00

KM# 8 10 FRANCS
3.9200 g., Aluminum-Bronze, 23.9 mm. **Obv:** Fish divides denomination **Rev:** Rhim gazelle facing, date below **Rev. Designer:** G.B.L. Bazor **Note:** Issued for circulation in French West Africa, including Togo.

Date	Mintage	F	VF	XF	Unc	BU
1957(a)	30,000,000	0.50	1.00	1.50	3.00	5.00

KM# 7 25 FRANCS
Aluminum-Bronze **Obv:** Head left divides date above **Rev:** Rhim gazelle facing, divides denomination **Rev. Designer:** G.B.L. Bazor

Date	Mintage	F	VF	XF	Unc	BU
1956(a)	37,877,000	0.50	1.00	2.00	5.50	8.00

KM# 9 25 FRANCS
Aluminum-Bronze **Obv:** Fish divides denomination **Rev:** Rhim gazelle facing, date below **Rev. Designer:** G.B.L. Bazor **Note:** Also issued for circulation in Togo

Date	Mintage	F	VF	XF	Unc	BU
1957(a)	30,000,000	0.50	1.00	2.00	5.00	7.00

GABON

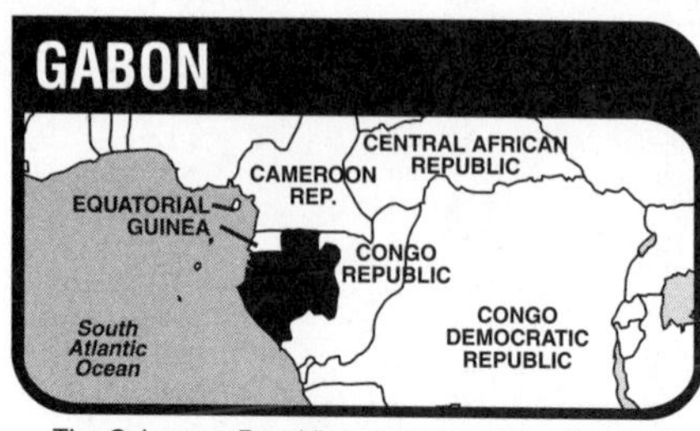

The Gabonese Republic, a member of the French Community, straddles the equator on the west coast of Africa. The hot and humid rain forest country has an area of 103,347 sq. mi. (267,670 sq. km.) and a population of 1.2 million, almost all of Bantu origin. Capital: Libreville. Extravagantly rich in resources, Gabon exports crude oil, manganese ore, gold and timbers.

Gabon was first visited by Portuguese navigator Diego Cam in the 15th century. Dutch, French and British traders, lured by the rich stands of hard woods and oil palms, quickly followed. The French founded their first settlement on the left bank of the Gabon River in 1839 and established their presence by signing treaties with the tribal chiefs. After gradually extending their influence into the interior during the last half of the 19th century, France occupied Gabon in 1885 and, in 1910, organized it as one of the four territories of French Equatorial Africa. It became an autonomous republic within the French Union in 1946, and on Aug. 17, 1960, became a completely independent republic within the new French Community.

For earlier coinage see French Equatorial Africa, Central African States and the Equatorial African States.

MINT MARKS

(a) - Paris, privy marks only
(t) - Poissy, privy marks only, thunderbolt

REPUBLIC

DECIMAL COINAGE

KM# 12 100 FRANCS
Nickel, 25 mm. **Obv:** Three great eland left **Obv. Designer:** G.B.L. Bazor **Rev:** Denomination within circle, date below

Date	Mintage	F	VF	XF	Unc	BU
1971(a)	1,300,000	4.50	9.00	17.50	25.00	—
1972(a)	2,000,000	4.50	9.00	17.50	25.00	—

KM# 13 100 FRANCS
Nickel, 25 mm. **Obv:** Three great eland left **Obv. Designer:** G.B.L. Bazor **Rev:** Denomination within circle, date below

Date	Mintage	F	VF	XF	Unc	BU
1975(a)	—	2.00	4.00	7.50	15.00	22.00
1977(a)	—	3.00	6.50	12.50	24.00	30.00
1978(a)	—	2.50	4.50	9.00	18.50	26.00
1982(a)	—	1.75	3.50	6.50	10.00	15.00
1983(a)	—	1.75	3.50	6.50	10.00	15.00
1984(a)	—	1.75	3.50	6.50	10.00	15.00
1985(a)	—	1.75	3.50	6.50	10.00	15.00

KM# 14 500 FRANCS
Copper-Nickel **Obv:** Leafy plants divide denomination and date **Rev:** Head left, inscription at right

Date	Mintage	F	VF	XF	Unc	BU
1985(a)	—	4.00	7.00	12.00	20.00	—

GAMBIA

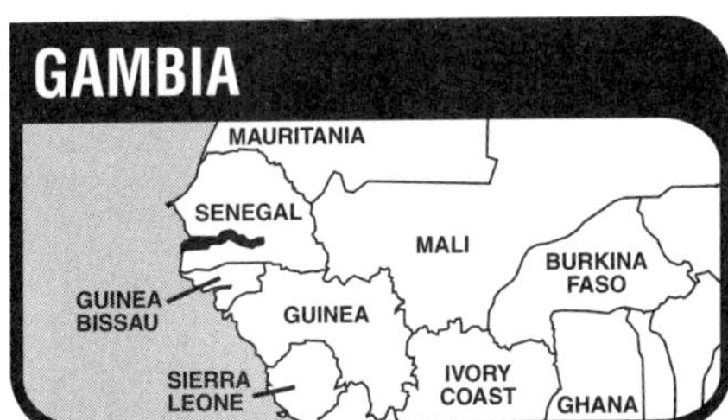

The Republic of The Gambia, occupies a strip of land 7 miles (11km.) to 20 miles (32 km.) wide and 200 miles (322 km.) long encompassing both sides of West Africa's Gambia River, and completely surrounded by Senegal. The republic, one of Africa's smallest countries, has an area of 4,127 sq. mi. (11,300 sq. km.) and a population of 989,273. Capital: Banjul. Agriculture and tourism are the principal industries. Peanuts constitute 95 per cent of export earnings.

The Gambia was once part of the great empires of Ghana and Songhay. When Portuguese gold seekers and slave traders visited The Gambia in the 15th century, it was part of the Kingdom of Mali. In 1588 the territory became, through purchase, the first British colony in Africa. English slavers established Fort James, the first settlement, on a small island a dozen miles up the Gambia River in 1664. After alternate periods of union with Sierra Leone and existence as a separate colony The Gambia became a British colony in 1888. On Feb. 18, 1965, The Gambia achieved independence as a constitutional monarchy within the Commonwealth of Nations, with Elizabeth II as Head of State as Queen of The Gambia. It became a republic on April 24, 1970, remaining a member of the Commonwealth, but with the president as Chief of State and Head of Government.

Together with Senegal, The Gambia formed a confederation on February 1, 1982. This confederation was officially dissolved on September 21, 1989. In July, 1994 a military junta took control of The Gambia and disbanded its elected government.

For earlier coinage see British West Africa.

RULER

British until 1970

MONETARY SYSTEM

12 Pence = 1 Shilling
20 Shillings = 1 Pound

COLONIAL

STERLING COINAGE

KM# 1 PENNY
Bronze, 25.5 mm. **Obv:** Young bust right **Obv. Designer:** Arnold Machin **Rev:** Sailing vessel, denomination at right **Edge:** Smooth

Date	Mintage	F	VF	XF	Unc	BU
1966	3,600,000	—	0.20	0.40	1.00	1.25
1966 Proof	6,600	Value: 1.00				

KM# 2 3 PENCE
Nickel-Brass, 21.5 mm. **Obv:** Young bust right **Obv. Designer:** Arnold Machin **Rev:** Double-spurred francolin, denomination above **Edge:** Smooth

Date	Mintage	F	VF	XF	Unc	BU
1966	2,000,000	—	0.30	0.50	1.50	2.00
1966 Proof	6,600	Value: 1.50				

KM# 3 6 PENCE
2.7700 g., Copper-Nickel, 19.5 mm. **Obv:** Young bust right **Obv. Designer:** Arnold Machin **Rev:** Peanuts divide denomination **Edge:** Reeded

Date	Mintage	F	VF	XF	Unc	BU
1966	1,500,000	—	0.30	0.50	1.75	2.00
1966 Proof	6,600	Value: 1.75				

KM# 4 SHILLING
5.8000 g., Copper-Nickel, 23.5 mm. **Obv:** Young bust right **Obv. Designer:** Arnold Machin **Rev:** Oil palm, denomination above **Edge:** Reeded

Date	Mintage	F	VF	XF	Unc	BU
1966	2,500,000	—	0.50	0.80	2.00	2.50
1966 Proof	6,600	Value: 2.00				

KM# 5 2 SHILLINGS
Copper-Nickel, 28.3 mm. **Obv:** Young bust right **Rev:** African domestic ox divides denomination **Edge:** Reeded

Date	Mintage	F	VF	XF	Unc	BU
1966	1,600,000	—	0.75	1.50	2.50	3.00
1966 Proof	6,600	Value: 2.50				

KM# 6 4 SHILLINGS
Copper-Nickel, 34 mm. **Obv:** Young bust right **Obv. Designer:** Arnold Machin **Rev:** Slender-snouted crocodile, denomination at right **Edge:** Reeded

Date	Mintage	F	VF	XF	Unc	BU
1966	800,000	—	1.50	2.50	5.50	10.00
1966 Proof	6,600	Value: 8.00				

KM# 7 8 SHILLINGS
Copper-Nickel **Obv:** Young bust right **Obv. Designer:** Arnold Machin **Rev:** Hippopotamus, denomination above

Date	Mintage	F	VF	XF	Unc	BU
1970	25,000	—	2.00	4.00	12.00	17.50

REPUBLIC

DECIMAL COINAGE

100 Bututs = 1 Dalasi

KM# 8 BUTUT
1.8000 g., Bronze, 17.15 mm. **Obv:** President's bust left **Obv. Designer:** Michael Rizzello **Rev:** Peanuts, denomination at right

Date	Mintage	F	VF	XF	Unc	BU
1971	12,449,000	—	—	0.10	0.20	0.30
1971 Proof	32,000	Value: 0.50				
1973	3,000,000	—	—	0.10	0.25	0.35
1974	19,060,000	—	0.25	0.50	1.50	2.00

KM# 14 BUTUT
Bronze **Series:** F.A.O. **Obv:** President's bust left **Obv. Designer:** Michael Rizzello **Rev:** Peanuts, denomination at right

Date	Mintage	F	VF	XF	Unc	BU
1974	26,062,000	—	—	0.10	0.20	0.30
1985	4,500,000	—	—	0.15	0.25	0.35

KM# 54 BUTUT
Copper Plated Steel, 17.6 mm. **Obv:** National arms, date below **Rev:** Peanuts, denomination at right

Date	Mintage	F	VF	XF	Unc	BU
1998	—	—	—	—	0.20	0.30

KM# 9 5 BUTUTS
3.5500 g., Bronze, 20.3 mm. **Obv:** President's bust left **Obv. Designer:** Michael Rizzello **Rev:** Sailing vessel, denomination at right

Date	Mintage	F	VF	XF	Unc	BU
1971	5,400,000	—	—	0.10	0.35	0.50
1971 Proof	32,000	Value: 0.60				

KM# 55 5 BUTUTS
Copper Plated Steel **Obv:** National arms, date below **Rev:** Sailboat, denomination at right

Date	Mintage	F	VF	XF	Unc	BU
1998	—	—	—	—	0.35	0.50

KM# 10 10 BUTUTS
6.2000 g., Nickel-Brass, 25.9 mm. **Obv:** President's bust left **Obv. Designer:** Michael Rizzello **Rev:** Double-spurred francolin, denomination at right

Date	Mintage	F	VF	XF	Unc	BU
1971	3,000,000	—	0.15	0.35	1.50	2.00
1971 Proof	32,000	Value: 2.00				

KM# 56 10 BUTUTS
Brass Plated Steel, 26 mm. **Obv:** National arms, date below **Rev:** Double-spurred francolin, denomination at right

Date	Mintage	F	VF	XF	Unc	BU
1998	—	—	—	—	1.00	1.50

KM# 11 25 BUTUTS
5.6500 g., Copper-Nickel, 23.6 mm. **Obv:** President's bust left **Obv. Designer:** Michael Rizzello **Rev:** Oil palm, denomination above

Date	Mintage	F	VF	XF	Unc	BU
1971	3,040,000	—	0.15	0.30	0.75	1.00
1971 Proof	32,000	Value: 1.25				

KM# 57 25 BUTUTS
4.9700 g., Copper-Nickel, 23.9 mm. **Obv:** National arms, date below **Rev:** Oil palm, denomination above

Date	Mintage	F	VF	XF	Unc	BU
1998	—	—	—	—	1.00	1.25

KM# 12 50 BUTUTS
11.3000 g., Copper-Nickel, 28.5 mm. **Obv:** President's bust left **Obv. Designer:** Michael Rizzello **Rev:** African domestic ox divides denomination

Date	Mintage	F	VF	XF	Unc	BU
1971	1,700,000	—	0.35	0.65	1.75	2.50
1971 Proof	32,000	Value: 1.75				

KM# 58 50 BUTUTS
Copper-Nickel, 28.8 mm. **Obv:** National arms, date below **Rev:** African domestic ox divides denomination

Date	Mintage	F	VF	XF	Unc	BU
1998	—	—	—	—	1.50	2.00

KM# 13 DALASI
Copper-Nickel **Obv:** President's bust left **Obv. Designer:** Michael Rizzello **Rev:** Slender-snouted crocodile, denomination at right

Date	Mintage	F	VF	XF	Unc	BU
1971	1,300,000	—	2.00	3.50	8.00	10.00
1971 Proof	32,000	Value: 5.00				

KM# 29 DALASI
12.2000 g., Copper-Nickel, 30.8 mm. **Obv:** President's bust left **Obv. Designer:** Michael Rizzello **Rev:** Slender-snouted crocodile, denomination at right **Edge:** Reeded, smooth alternating edge **Shape:** 7-sided

Date	Mintage	F	VF	XF	Unc	BU
1987	—	—	1.75	2.75	6.00	7.50

KM# 59 DALASI
8.8100 g., Copper Nickel, 28 mm. **Obv:** National arms, date below **Rev:** Slender-snouted crocodile, denomination at right **Shape:** 7-sided

Date	Mintage	F	VF	XF	Unc	BU
1998	—	—	1.75	2.75	6.00	7.50

GEORGIA

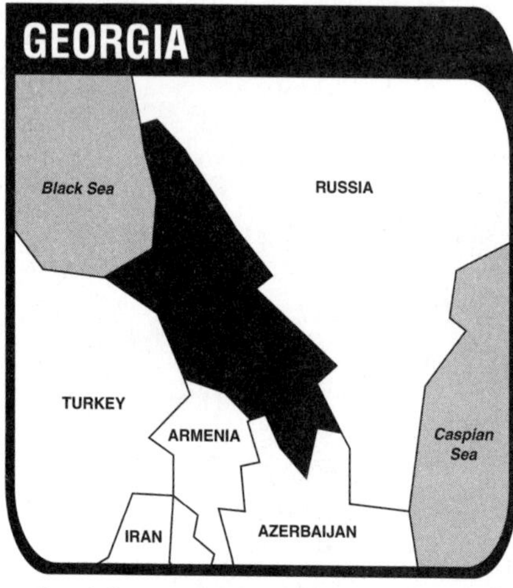

Georgia (formerly the Georgian Social Democratic Republic under the U.S.S.R.), is bounded by the Black Sea to the west and by Turkey, Armenia and Azerbaijan. It occupies the western part of Transcaucasia covering an area of 26,900 sq. mi. (69,700 sq. km.) and a population of 5.7 million. Capitol: Tbilisi. Hydro-electricity, minerals, forestry and agriculture are the chief industries.

After the Russian Revolution the Georgians, Armenians, and Azerbaijanis formed the short-lived Transcaucasian Federal Republic on Sept. 20, 1917, which broke up into three independent republics on May 26, 1918. A Germano-- Georgian treaty was signed on May 28, 1918, followed by a Turko-Georgian peace treaty on June 4. The end of WW I and the collapse of the central powers allowed free elections.

On May 20, 1920, Soviet Russia concluded a peace treaty, recognizing its independence, but later invaded on Feb. 11, 1921 and a soviet republic was proclaimed. On March 12, 1922 Stalin included Georgia in a newly formed Transcaucasian Soviet Federated Socialist Republic. On Dec. 5, 1936 the T.S.F.S.R. was dissolved and Georgia became a direct member of the U.S.S.R. The collapse of the U.S.S.R. allowed full transition to independence and on April 9, 1991 a unanimous vote declared the republic an independent state based on its original treaty of independence of May 1918.

REPUBLIC

STANDARD COINAGE

100 Thetri = 1 Lari

KM# 89 50 THETRI
6.5200 g., Copper-Nickel, 24 mm. **Obv:** National arms **Rev:** Value **Edge:** Reeded and lettered

Date	Mintage	F	VF	XF	Unc	BU
2006	—	—	—	—	3.00	4.00

KM# 90 LARI
7.8500 g., Copper-Nickel, 26.2 mm. **Obv:** National arms **Rev:** Value **Edge:** Reeded and lettered

Date	Mintage	F	VF	XF	Unc	BU
2006	—	—	—	—	5.00	6.50

KM# 94 2 LARI
8.0600 g., Bi-Metallic **Ring Composition:** Copper Nickel **Center Composition:** Brass, 26.99 mm. **Obv:** National arms **Rev:** Large value **Edge:** Reeded and lettered

Date	Mintage	F	VF	XF	Unc	BU
2006	—	—	—	—	7.50	9.00

KM# 91 2 LARI
8.0500 g., Bi-Metallic Brass center in Copper-Nickel ring, 27 mm. **Obv:** National arms **Rev:** Value **Edge:** Reeded and lettered

Date	Mintage	F	VF	XF	Unc	BU
2006	—	—	—	—	6.00	7.50

INDEPENDENT STATE (C.I.S.)

STANDARD COINAGE

100 Thetri = 1 Lari

KM# 76 THETRI
1.3500 g., Stainless Steel, 14.9 mm. **Obv:** Stylized candelabra design divides date within circle **Rev:** Denomination above grapes **Edge:** Smooth

Date	Mintage	F	VF	XF	Unc	BU
1993	—	—	—	—	0.25	0.35

KM# 77 2 THETRI
1.8500 g., Stainless Steel, 17.4 mm. **Obv:** Stylized candelabra divides date within circle **Rev:** Stylized eagle above denomination **Edge:** Smooth

Date	Mintage	F	VF	XF	Unc	BU
1993	—	—	—	—	0.35	0.50

KM# 78 5 THETRI
2.4500 g., Stainless Steel, 19.9 mm. **Obv:** Stylized candelabra divides date within circle **Rev:** Stylized lion above denomination **Edge:** Smooth

Date	Mintage	F	VF	XF	Unc	BU
1993	—	—	—	—	0.75	1.00

KM# 79 10 THETRI
2.9500 g., Stainless Steel, 21.9 mm. **Obv:** Stylized candelabra divides date within circle **Rev:** St. Mamas riding lion right, denomination **Edge:** Smooth

Date	Mintage	F	VF	XF	Unc	BU
1993	—	—	—	—	1.25	1.50

KM# 80 20 THETRI
4.9500 g., Stainless Steel, 25 mm. **Obv:** Stylized candelabra divides date within circle **Rev:** Red Deer left, denomination **Edge:** Smooth

Date	Mintage	F	VF	XF	Unc	BU
1993	—	—	—	—	1.50	2.00

KM# 81 50 THETRI
2.4500 g., Brass, 19 mm. **Obv:** Stylized candelabra divides date within circle **Rev:** Stylized griffin left, above denomination **Edge:** Smooth

Date	Mintage	F	VF	XF	Unc	BU
1993	—	—	—	—	2.00	2.50

KM# 85 10 LARI
10.6000 g., Bi-Metallic Copper-Nickel center in Brass ring, 26 mm. **Subject:** State System: 3000 Years **Obv:** Denomination within circle **Rev:** Eagle above lion within circle **Edge:** Reeding over "GEORGIA . TEN LARI"

Date	Mintage	F	VF	XF	Unc	BU
2000	1,000	—	—	—	18.00	20.00

GERMAN EAST AFRICA

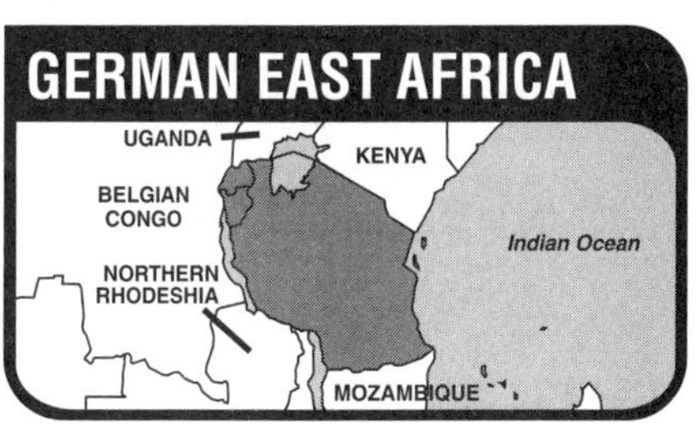

German East Africa (Tanganyika), located on the coast of east-central Africa between British East Africa (now Kenya) and Portuguese East Africa (now Mozambique), had an area of 362,284 sq. mi. (938,216 sq. km.) and a population of about 6 million. Capital: Dar es Salaam. Chief products prior to German control were ivory and slaves; after German control, sisal, coffee, and rubber. Germany acquired control of the area by treaties with coastal chiefs in 1884, established it as a protectorate in 1891, and proclaimed it the Colony of German East Africa in 1897. After World War I, Tanganyika was entrusted to Great Britain as a League of Nations mandate, and after World War II as a United Nations trust territory. Tanganyika became an independent nation within the British Commonwealth on Dec. 9, 1961. Coins dated up until 1902 were issued by the German East Africa Company. From 1904 onwards, the government issued coins.

NOTE: For later coinage see East Africa.

TITLE

Sharaka(t) Almania

RULER
Wilhelm II, 1888-1918

MINT MARKS
A - Berlin
J - Hamburg
T - Tabora

MONETARY SYSTEM
Until 1904
64 Pesa = 1 Rupie
Commencing 1904
100 Heller = 1 Rupie

COLONY

STANDARD COINAGE

German East Africa Company

1891-

KM# 3 1/4 RUPIE
2.9160 g., 0.9170 Silver 0.0860 oz. ASW **Ruler:** Wihelm II **Obv:** Armored bust left **Rev:** Shielded arms, denomination below

Date	Mintage	F	VF	XF	Unc	BU
1901	350,000	6.00	18.00	45.00	140	160

KM# 4 1/2 RUPIE
5.8319 g., 0.9170 Silver 0.1719 oz. ASW **Ruler:** Wihelm II **Obv:** Armored bust left **Rev:** Shielded arms, denomination below

Date	Mintage	F	VF	XF	Unc	BU
1901	215,000	15.00	40.00	100	240	300

KM# 2 RUPIE

11.6638 g., 0.9170 Silver 0.3439 oz. ASW **Ruler:** Wihelm II **Obv:** Armored bust left **Rev:** Shielded arms, denomination below

Date	Mintage	F	VF	XF	Unc	BU
1901	319,000	12.50	25.00	75.00	175	225
1902	151,000	20.00	40.00	125	450	550

STANDARD COINAGE

1904-

KM# 6 1/2 HELLER

Bronze **Ruler:** Wihelm II **Obv:** Crown with ribbon above date **Rev:** Denomination within wreath

Date	Mintage	F	VF	XF	Unc	BU
1904A	1,201,000	2.00	6.00	10.00	35.00	50.00
1905A	7,192,000	2.25	5.25	9.00	32.50	45.00
1905J	4,000,000	2.25	5.25	9.00	32.50	45.00
1906J	6,000,000	1.25	3.50	6.50	28.00	40.00
1906J Proof	—	Value: 250				

KM# 7 HELLER

Bronze **Ruler:** Wihelm II **Obv:** Crown with ribbon above date **Rev:** Denomination within wreath

Date	Mintage	F	VF	XF	Unc	BU
1904A	10,256,000	0.75	2.25	4.00	20.00	30.00
1904A Proof	—	Value: 125				
1904J	2,500,000	0.75	2.25	7.00	25.00	35.00
1905A	3,760,000	0.75	2.25	7.00	25.00	35.00
1905A Proof	—	Value: 125				
1905J	7,556,000	0.75	2.25	4.00	25.00	35.00
1906A	3,004,000	0.75	2.25	7.00	25.00	40.00
1906A Proof	—	Value: 200				
1906J	1,962,000	0.75	2.25	7.00	30.00	50.00
1907J	17,790,000	0.75	1.50	4.00	20.00	25.00
1908J	12,205,000	0.75	1.50	4.00	20.00	25.00
1908J Proof	—	Value: 135				
1909J	1,698,000	2.50	7.50	15.00	35.00	50.00
1909J Proof	—	Value: 135				
1910J	5,096,000	0.75	1.50	4.00	20.00	25.00
1910J Proof	—	Value: 135				
1911J	6,420,000	0.75	1.50	4.00	20.00	25.00
1911J Proof	—	Value: 135				
1912J	7,012,000	0.75	1.50	4.00	25.00	40.00
1912J Proof	—	Value: 135				
1913A	—	0.75	1.50	4.00	20.00	30.00
1913A Proof	—	Value: 135				
1913J	5,186,000	0.75	1.50	4.00	20.00	30.00
1913J Proof	—	Value: 150				

KM# 11 5 HELLER

Bronze **Ruler:** Wihelm II **Obv:** Crown with ribbon above date **Rev:** Denomination within wreath

Date	Mintage	F	VF	XF	Unc	BU
1908J	600,000	20.00	45.00	85.00	550	650
1908J Proof	—	Value: 1,200				
1909J	756,000	22.00	50.00	90.00	550	650
1909J Proof	60	Value: 1,200				

KM# 13 5 HELLER

Copper-Nickel **Ruler:** Wihelm II **Obv:** Center hole divides date, crown with ribbon above, legend below **Rev:** Center hole divides denomination, sprigs flank

Date	Mintage	F	VF	XF	Unc	BU
1913A	1,000,000	6.00	15.00	25.00	55.00	100
1913A Proof	—	Value: 250				
1913J	1,000,000	6.00	15.00	25.00	60.00	100
1913J Proof	—	Value: 250				
1914J	1,000,000	5.00	12.00	22.00	50.00	100
1914J Proof	—	Value: 250				

KM# 14.1 5 HELLER

Brass **Ruler:** Wihelm II **Obv:** Crown with ribbon above date, oval base on crown **Rev:** Denomination within wreath **Note:** 1-1/2 -2mm thick. Tabora emergency issue.

Date	Mintage	F	VF	XF	Unc	BU
1916T	30,000	10.00	20.00	40.00	80.00	150

KM# 14.2 5 HELLER

Brass **Ruler:** Wihelm II **Obv:** Crown with ribbon above date, flat base on crown **Rev:** Denomination within wreath **Note:** 1mm or less thick.

Date	Mintage	F	VF	XF	Unc	BU
1916T	Inc. above	4.00	12.00	30.00	60.00	100

KM# 12 10 HELLER

Copper-Nickel **Ruler:** Wihelm II **Obv:** Center hole divides date, crown with ribbon above, legend below **Rev:** Center hole divides denomination, sprigs flank

Date	Mintage	F	VF	XF	Unc	BU
1908J	—	5.00	15.00	30.00	90.00	125
1908J Proof	—	Value: 350				
1909J	1,990,000	3.00	10.00	20.00	80.00	125
1909J Proof	—	Value: 275				
1910J	500,000	3.00	10.00	20.00	80.00	150
1910J Proof	—	Value: 275				
1911A	500,000	5.00	15.00	35.00	100	150
1911A Proof	—	Value: 300				
1914J	200,000	10.00	30.00	60.00	125	200
1914 Proof	—	Value: 285				

Obverse A - Large crown

Obverse B - Small crown

Reverse A
Curles tip on second L

Reverse B
Pointed tips on L's

Reverse C
Curled tips on L's

KM# 15 20 HELLER

Copper **Ruler:** Wihelm II **Obv:** Crown with ribbon above date **Rev:** Denomination within wreath **Note:** Tabora Emergency Coinage.

Date	Mintage	F	VF	XF	Unc	BU
1916T	300,000	6.00	10.00	20.00	85.00	100
Note: Obverse A and reverse A						
1916T	Inc. above	125	200	350	—	—
Note: Obverse A and reverse B						
1916T	Inc. above	60.00	85.00	140	—	—
Note: Obverse B and reverse A						
1916T	Inc. above	6.00	10.00	20.00	60.00	80.00
Note: Obverse B and reverse B						
1916T Rare	Inc. above	—	—	—	—	—
Note: Obverse A and reverse C						
1916T Rare	Inc. above	—	—	—	—	—
Note: Obverse B and reverse C						

KM# 15a 20 HELLER

Brass **Ruler:** Wihelm II **Obv:** Crown with ribbon above date **Rev:** Denomination within wreath **Note:** Tabora Emergency Issue.

Date	Mintage	F	VF	XF	Unc	BU
1916T	1,600,000	6.00	10.00	20.00	75.00	90.00
Note: Obverse A and reverse A; Curled tip on second L						
1916T	Inc. above	7.00	12.50	25.00	85.00	100
Note: Obverse A and reverse B; Pointed tips on L's						
1916T	Inc. above	7.00	12.50	25.00	85.00	100
Note: Obverse B and reverse A; Curled tip on second L						
1916T	Inc. above	6.00	10.00	20.00	65.00	80.00
Note: Obverse B and reverse B; Pointed tips on L's						
1916T	Inc. above	10.00	30.00	45.00	125	150
Note: Obverse A and reverse C; Curled tips on L's						
1916T	Inc. above	12.00	35.00	50.00	135	150
Note: Obverse B and reverse C; Curled tips on L's						

KM# 8 1/4 RUPIE

2.9160 g., 0.9170 Silver 0.0860 oz. ASW **Ruler:** Wihelm II **Obv:** Armored bust left **Rev:** Shielded arms, denomination below

Date	Mintage	F	VF	XF	Unc	BU
1904A	300,000	5.00	12.00	37.50	110	150
1904A Proof	—	Value: 300				
1906A	300,000	5.00	12.00	37.50	110	150
1906A Proof	—	Value: 300				
1906J	100,000	20.00	60.00	125	300	400
1907J	200,000	10.00	25.00	75.00	200	275
1907J Proof	—	Value: 375				
1909A	300,000	6.00	13.50	40.00	185	225
1910J	600,000	5.00	12.00	37.50	110	140
1910J Proof	—	Value: 350				
1912J	400,000	6.00	13.50	40.00	120	175
1912J Proof	—	Value: 350				
1913A	200,000	6.50	14.50	42.50	135	225
1913A Proof	—	Value: 350				
1913J	400,000	5.00	12.00	37.50	110	140
1913J Proof	—	Value: 300				
1914J	200,000	6.50	14.50	42.50	125	200
1914J Proof	—	Value: 300				

KM# 9 1/2 RUPIE
5.8319 g., 0.9170 Silver 0.1719 oz. ASW **Ruler:** Wihelm II **Obv:** Armored bust left **Rev:** Shielded arms, denomination below

Date	Mintage	F	VF	XF	Unc	BU
1904A	400,000	15.00	40.00	95.00	275	300
1904A Proof	—	Value: 450				
1906A	50,000	125	225	350	750	1,000
1906A Proof	—	Value: 1,000				
1906J	50,000	125	225	350	750	1,000
1907J	140,000	20.00	50.00	125	300	350
1907J Proof	—	Value: 550				
1909A	100,000	30.00	65.00	150	350	500
1910J	300,000	20.00	40.00	100	250	275
1910J Proof	—	Value: 450				
1912J	200,000	15.00	40.00	95.00	250	300
1913A	100,000	20.00	45.00	110	300	400
1913J	200,000	15.00	40.00	95.00	200	250
1914J	100,000	20.00	45.00	100	285	350

KM# 10 RUPIE
11.6638 g., 0.9170 Silver 0.3439 oz. ASW **Ruler:** Wihelm II **Obv:** Armored bust left **Rev:** Shielded arms, denomination below

Date	Mintage	F	VF	XF	Unc	BU
1904A	1,000,000	11.50	22.50	45.00	130	150
1904A Proof	—	Value: 425				
1905A	300,000	15.00	27.50	60.00	185	250
1905A Proof	—	Value: 450				
1905J	1,000,000	11.50	22.50	45.00	130	160
1905J Proof	—	Value: 400				
1906A	950,000	11.50	22.50	45.00	130	160
1906J	700,000	15.00	27.50	65.00	175	200
1907J	880,000	9.00	15.00	45.00	180	200
1908J	500,000	12.50	25.00	55.00	190	225
1908J Proof	—	Value: 450				
1909A	200,000	15.00	27.50	65.00	275	350
1910J	270,000	9.00	15.00	45.00	200	275
1911A	300,000	12.50	25.00	55.00	175	250
1911A Proof	—	Value: 450				
1911J	1,400,000	9.00	15.00	45.00	150	175
1911J Proof	—	Value: 400				
1912J	300,000	12.50	25.00	55.00	165	250
1912J Proof	—	Value: 450				
1913A	400,000	12.50	25.00	55.00	160	225
1913J	1,400,000	9.00	15.00	45.00	150	175
1913J Proof	—	Value: 400				
1914J	500,000	11.50	22.50	50.00	175	250

KM# 16.1 15 RUPIEN
7.1680 g., 0.7500 Gold 0.1728 oz. AGW **Ruler:** Wihelm II **Obv:** Crowned imperial eagle, right arabesque ends below "T" of "OSTAFRIKA" **Rev:** Elephant roaring right above date **Note:** Tabora Emergency Issue.

Date	Mintage	F	VF	XF	Unc	BU
1916T	9,803	650	950	1,400	2,350	2,850

KM# 16.2 15 RUPIEN
7.1680 g., 0.7500 Gold 0.1728 oz. AGW **Ruler:** Wihelm II **Obv:** Crowned imperial eagle above denomination, right arabesque ends below first "A" of "OSTAFRIKA" **Rev:** Elephant roaring right above date **Note:** Tabora Emergency Issue.

Date	Mintage	F	VF	XF	Unc	BU
1916T	6,395	675	1,000	1,500	2,350	2,850

Although the origin of the German Empire can be traced to the Treaty of Verdun that ceded Charlemagne's lands east of the Rhine to German Prince Louis, it was for centuries little more than a geographic expression, con- sisting of hundreds of effectively autonomous big and little states. Nominally the states owed their allegiance to the Holy Roman Emperor, who was also a German king, but as the Emperors exhibited less and less concern for Germany the actual power devolved on the lords of the individual states. The fragmentation of the empire climaxed with the tragic denouement of the Thirty Years War, 1618-48, which devastated much of Germany, destroyed its agriculture and medieval commercial eminence and ended the attempt of the Hapsburgs to unify Germany. Deprived of administrative capacity by a lack of resources, the imperial authority became utterly powerless. At this time Germany contained an estimated 1,800 individual states, some with a population of as little as 300. The German Empire of recent history (the creation of Bis- marck) was formed on April 14, 1871, when the king of Prussia became German Emperor William I. The new empire comprised 4 kingdoms, 6 grand duchies, 12 duchies and principalities, 3 free cities and the nonautonomous province of Alsace-Lorraine. The states had the right to issue gold and silver coins of higher value than 1 Mark; coins of 1 Mark and under were general issues of the empire.

MINT MARKS
A - Berlin, 1750-date
D - Munich (Germany), 1872-date
E - Muldenhutten (Germany), 1887-1953
F - Stuttgart (Germany) 1872-date
G - Karlsruhe (Germany) 1872-date
J - Hamburg (Germany) 1873-date

MONETARY SYSTEM

After the German unification in 1871 when the old Thaler system was abandoned in favor of the Mark system (100 Pfennig = 1 Mark) the Vereinsthaler continued to circulate as a legal tender 3 Mark coin, and the double Thaler as a 6 Mark coin until 1908. In 1908 the Vereinsthalers were officially demonetized and the Thaler coinage was replaced by the new 3 Mark coin which had the same specifications as the old Vereinsthaler. The double Thaler coinage was not replaced as there was no great demand for a 6 Mark coin. Until the 1930's the German public continued to refer to the 3 Mark piece as a "Thaler".

Commencing 1871
100 Pfennig = 1 Mark

VERRECHNUNGS & GUTSCHRIFTS TOKENS

These were metallic indebtedness receipts used for commercial and banking purposes due to the lack of available subsidiary coinage. These tokens could be redeemed in sufficient quantities.

ANHALT-DESSAU

Anhalt-Dessau was part of the 1252 division that included Zerbst and Köthen. In 1396, Anhalt-Zerbst was divided into Anhalt-Zerbst and Anhalt-Dessau. In 1508, Anhalt-Zerbst was absorbed into Anhalt-Dessau. The latter was given to the eldest son of Joachim Ernst in the division of 1603. As other lines became extinct, they fell to Anhalt-Dessau, which united all territories of the dynasty in 1863. The last ruler was forced to give up power at the end of World War I. Anhalt area: 2314 km. Capital: Dessau.

RULERS
Friedrich I, 1871-1904
Friedrich II, 1904-1918
Ernst, 1918

MINT MARK
A – Berlin Mint, 1839-1914

DUCHY

REFORM COINAGE

KM# 27 2 MARK
11.1110 g., 0.9000 Silver 0.3215 oz. ASW, 28 mm. **Ruler:** Friedrich II **Obv:** Head left **Rev:** Crowned imperial German eagle, shield on breast **Edge:** Reeded

Date	Mintage	F	VF	XF	Unc	BU
1901A	—	150	325	600	1,200	1,600
1904A	50,000	150	375	600	1,000	1,400
1904A Proof	150	Value: 1,750				

KM# 29 3 MARK
16.6670 g., 0.9000 Silver 0.4823 oz. ASW, 33 mm. **Ruler:** Friedrich II **Obv:** Head left **Rev:** Crowned imperial German eagle, shield on breast **Edge Lettering:** GOTT MIT UNS

Date	Mintage	F	VF	XF	Unc	BU
1909A	100,000	35.00	75.00	150	300	400
1911A	100,000	40.00	85.00	165	325	400
Common date Proof	—	Value: 550				
Common date Proof	—	Value: 400				

KM# 30 3 MARK
16.6670 g., 0.9000 Silver 0.4823 oz. ASW, 33 mm. **Ruler:** Friedrich II **Subject:** Silver Wedding Anniversary **Obv:** Jugate heads left **Rev:** Crowned imperial German eagle, shield on breast **Edge Lettering:** GOTT MIT UNS

Date	Mintage	F	VF	XF	Unc	BU
1914A	200,000	25.00	60.00	85.00	100	160
1914A Proof	1,000	Value: 325				

KM# 31 5 MARK
27.7770 g., 0.9000 Silver 0.8037 oz. ASW, 38 mm. **Ruler:** Friedrich II **Subject:** Silver Wedding Anniversary **Obv:** Jugate heads left **Rev:** Crowned imperial German eagle, shield on breast **Edge Lettering:** GOTT MIT UNS

Date	Mintage	F	VF	XF	Unc	BU
1901A	—	450	750	1,400	2,700	3,750
1914A	30,000	65.00	180	285	450	650
1914A Proof	1,000	Value: 1,000				

KM# 25 10 MARK
3.9820 g., 0.9000 Gold 0.1152 oz. AGW **Ruler:** Friedrich I **Obv:** Head right **Obv. Legend:** FRIEDRICH HERZOG VON ANHALT **Rev:** Crowned imperial German eagle **Rev. Legend:** DEUTSCHES REICH date 10 MARK

Date	Mintage	F	VF	XF	Unc	BU
1901A	20,000	750	1,200	1,700	2,700	3,500
1901A Proof	200	Value: 4,250				

KM# 26 20 MARK
7.9650 g., 0.9000 Gold 0.2305 oz. AGW **Ruler:** Friedrich I **Obv:** Small head right **Obv. Legend:** FRIEDRICH HERZOG VON ANHALT **Rev:** Crowned imperial German eagle **Rev. Legend:** DEUTSCHES REICH date ZWEI MARK

Date	Mintage	F	VF	XF	Unc	BU
1901A	15,000	750	1,200	1,700	2,700	3,500
1901A Proof	200	Value: 4,250				

KM# 28 20 MARK
7.9650 g., 0.9000 Gold 0.2305 oz. AGW **Ruler:** Friedrich II **Obv:** Head left **Rev:** Crowned imperial German eagle, shield on breast **Edge Lettering:** GOTT MIT UNS

Date	Mintage	F	VF	XF	Unc	BU
1904A	25,000	600	1,000	1,400	2,500	3,500
1904A Proof	200	Value: 3,750				

BADEN

The earliest rulers of Baden, in the southwestern part of Germany along the Rhine, descended from the dukes of Zähringen in the late 11th century. The first division of the territory occurred in 1190, when separate lines of margraves were established in Baden and in Hachberg. Immediately prior to its extinction in 1418, Hachberg was sold back to Baden, which underwent several minor divisions itself during the next century. Baden acquired most of the countship of Sponheim from Electoral Pfalz near the end of the 15th century. In 1515, the most significant division of the patrimony took place, in which the Baden-Baden and Baden-(Pforzheim) Durlach lines were established.

Although Baden-Durlach was founded upon the division of Baden in 1515, the youngest son of Christoph I did not begin ruling in his own right until the demise of his father. This part of Baden was called Pforzheim until 1565, when the margrave moved his seat from the former to Durlach, located to the west and nearer the Rhine. After the male line of Baden-Baden failed in 1771 and the two parts of Baden were reunited, the fortunes of the margraviate continued to grow. Karlsruhe, near Durlach, was developed into a well-planned capital city. The ruler was given the rank of elector in 1803, only to be raised to grand duke three years later. The grand duchy came to an end in 1918, but had by this time become one of the largest states in Germany.

RULERS
Friedrich I, Prince Regent 1852-1856,
Grand Duke 1856-1907
Friedrich II, 1907-1918

GRAND DUCHY

REFORM COINAGE

KM# 269 2 MARK
11.1110 g., 0.9000 Silver 0.3215 oz. ASW, 28 mm. **Ruler:** Friedrich I as Grand Duke **Obv:** Head left **Obv. Legend:** FRIEDRICH GROSHERZOG VON BADEN **Rev:** Crowned imperial German eagle **Rev. Legend:** DEUTSCHES REICH date ZWEI MARK

Date	Mintage	F	VF	XF	Unc	BU
1901G	401,322	40.00	90.00	329	1,200	2,250
1901G Proof	—	Value: 3,000				
1902G	5,368	275	700	1,500	4,000	6,000
1902G Proof	—	Value: 5,500				

KM# 271 2 MARK
11.1110 g., 0.9000 Silver 0.3215 oz. ASW, 28 mm. **Ruler:** Friedrich I as Grand Duke **Subject:** 50th Year of Reign **Obv:** Head right **Rev:** Crowned imperial German eagle, shield on breast

Date	Mintage	F	VF	XF	Unc	BU
1902	375,018	12.00	25.00	35.00	50.00	70.00

KM# 272 2 MARK
11.1110 g., 0.9000 Silver 0.3215 oz. ASW, 28 mm. **Ruler:** Friedrich I as Grand Duke **Obv:** Head right **Rev:** Crowned imperial German eagle, shield on breast

Date	Mintage	F	VF	XF	Unc	BU
1902G	198,250	25.00	60.00	100	250	400
1903G	493,989	20.00	45.00	90.00	250	350
1904G	1,121,754	20.00	40.00	80.00	250	350
1905G	609,835	20.00	45.00	70.00	175	300
1906G	107,549	45.00	90.00	225	900	1,400
1907G	913,024	20.00	40.00	65.00	150	225

KM# 276 2 MARK
11.1110 g., 0.9000 Silver 0.3215 oz. ASW, 28 mm. **Ruler:** Friedrich I as Grand Duke **Subject:** Golden Wedding Anniversary **Obv:** Heads of royal couple right **Rev:** Crowned imperial German eagle, shield on breast

Date	Mintage	F	VF	XF	Unc	BU
1906	350,000	15.00	25.00	35.00	60.00	70.00
1906 Matte proof	200	—	—	—	—	—

KM# 278 2 MARK
11.1110 g., 0.9000 Silver 0.3215 oz. ASW, 28 mm. **Ruler:** Friedrich I as Grand Duke **Subject:** Death of Friedrich **Obv:** Head right **Rev:** Crowned imperial German eagle, shield on breast

Date	Mintage	F	VF	XF	Unc	BU
1907	350,000	20.00	50.00	70.00	90.00	100
1907 Proof	—	Value: 150				

KM# 283 2 MARK
11.1110 g., 0.9000 Silver 0.3215 oz. ASW, 28 mm. **Ruler:** Friedrich II **Obv:** Head left **Rev:** Crowned imperial German eagle, shield on breast

Date	Mintage	F	VF	XF	Unc	BU
1911G	72,000	125	250	400	750	1,000
1913G	937,050	100	250	400	700	1,000
(1911-1913) Proof	—	Value: 1,200				

KM# 280 3 MARK
16.6670 g., 0.9000 Silver 0.4823 oz. ASW, 33 mm. **Ruler:** Friedrich II **Obv:** Head left **Rev:** Crowned imperial German eagle, shield on breast

Date	Mintage	F	VF	XF	Unc	BU
1908G	304,927	12.00	25.00	35.00	100	135
1909G	760,716	12.00	25.00	35.00	75.00	135
1910G	674,640	12.00	25.00	35.00	75.00	135
1911G	382,033	12.00	25.00	35.00	75.00	135
1912G	835,199	12.00	25.00	35.00	75.00	135
1914G	412,804	12.00	25.00	35.00	70.00	135
1915G	169,533	20.00	50.00	75.00	225	250
(1908-1915)G Proof	—	Value: 225				

KM# 268 5 MARK
27.7770 g., 0.9000 Silver 0.8037 oz. ASW, 38 mm. **Ruler:** Friedrich I as Grand Duke **Obv:** Head left **Obv. Legend:** FRIEDRICH GROSHERZOG VON BADEN **Rev:** Crowned imperial German eagle **Rev. Legend:** DEUTSCHES REICH date FUNF MARK

Date	Mintage	F	VF	XF	Unc	BU
1901G	128,131	30.00	90.00	350	2,000	3,800
1902G	42,708	35.00	90.00	350	2,000	4,000
(1891-1902)G Proof	—	Value: 5,000				

KM# 273 5 MARK
27.7770 g., 0.9000 Silver 0.8037 oz. ASW, 38 mm. **Ruler:** Friedrich I as Grand Duke **Subject:** 50th Year of Reign **Obv:** Head right **Rev:** Crowned imperial German eagle, shield on breast

Date	Mintage	F	VF	XF	Unc	BU
1902	50,024	45.00	90.00	150	225	300
1902 Proof	—	Value: 625				

KM# 274 5 MARK
27.7770 g., 0.9000 Silver 0.8037 oz. ASW, 38 mm. **Ruler:** Friedrich I as Grand Duke **Obv:** Head right **Rev:** Crowned imperial German eagle, shield on breast **Edge Lettering:** GOTT MIT UNS **Note:** Varieties exist.

Date	Mintage	F	VF	XF	Unc	BU
1902G	128,100	35.00	60.00	150	600	1,200
1903G	439,105	20.00	50.00	140	600	1,000
1904G	237,914	20.00	50.00	140	600	1,000
1907G	243,821	20.00	50.00	140	600	850
(1902-1907)G Proof	—	Value: 1,250				

KM# 277 5 MARK
27.7770 g., 0.9000 Silver 0.8037 oz. ASW, 38 mm. **Ruler:** Friedrich I as Grand Duke **Subject:** Golden Wedding Anniversary **Obv:** Jugate busts right **Rev:** Crowned imperial German eagle, shield on breast

Date	Mintage	F	VF	XF	Unc	BU
1906	60,000	40.00	80.00	145	220	325
1906 Proof	—	Value: 400				

KM# 279 5 MARK
27.7770 g., 0.9000 Silver 0.8037 oz. ASW, 38 mm. **Ruler:** Friedrich I as Grand Duke **Subject:** Death of Friedrich **Obv:** Head right **Rev:** Crowned imperial German eagle, shield on breast

Date	Mintage	F	VF	XF	Unc	BU
1907	60,000	60.00	125	175	250	350
1907 Proof	—	Value: 425				

KM# 281 5 MARK
27.7770 g., 0.9000 Silver 0.8037 oz. ASW, 38 mm. **Ruler:** Friedrich II **Obv:** Head left **Rev:** Crowned imperial German eagle, shield on breast

Date	Mintage	F	VF	XF	Unc	BU
1908G	184,000	40.00	60.00	200	700	1,100
1913G	244,000	30.00	50.00	175	450	900
(1908-1913)G Proof	—	Value: 1,300				

KM# 267 10 MARK
3.9820 g., 0.9000 Gold 0.1152 oz. AGW **Ruler:** Friedrich I as Grand Duke **Obv:** Head left **Obv. Legend:** FRIEDRICH GROSHERZOG VON BADEN **Rev:** Crowned imperial German eagle **Rev. Legend:** DEUTSCHES REICH date 10 MARK

Date	Mintage	F	VF	XF	Unc	BU
1901G	91,248	145	250	350	500	600
1901G Proof	—	Value: 1,700				

KM# 275 10 MARK
3.9820 g., 0.9000 Gold 0.1152 oz. AGW **Ruler:** Friedrich I as Grand Duke **Obv:** Head right **Rev:** Crowned imperial German eagle, shield on breast

Date	Mintage	F	VF	XF	Unc	BU
1902G	30,409	175	300	450	750	1,250
1903G	109,450	125	200	265	450	700
1904G	149,240	115	200	245	400	700
1905G	95,932	125	200	265	500	700
1906G	120,902	125	200	245	400	700
1907G	121,902	115	200	245	400	700
(1902-1907)G Proof	—	Value: 2,000				

KM# 282 10 MARK
3.9820 g., 0.9000 Gold 0.1152 oz. AGW **Ruler:** Friedrich II **Obv:** Head right **Rev:** Crowned imperial German eagle, shield on breast

Date	Mintage	F	VF	XF	Unc	BU
1909G	86,000	225	500	650	950	1,300
1910G	60,649	225	500	650	950	1,300
1911G	29,488	2,000	4,000	5,000	6,750	8,000
1912G	25,975	700	1,000	1,600	2,000	3,000
1913G	41,567	500	700	850	1,250	2,000
(1909-1913)G Proof	—	Value: 2,000				

KM# 284 20 MARK
7.9650 g., 0.9000 Gold 0.2305 oz. AGW **Ruler:** Friedrich II **Obv:** Head left **Rev:** Crowned imperial German eagle, shield on breast

Date	Mintage	F	VF	XF	Unc	BU
1911G	190,836	BV	215	240	320	425
1912G	311,063	BV	215	240	320	425
1913G	85,374	BV	215	250	350	425
1914G	280,520	BV	215	240	320	425
(1911-1914)G Proof	—	Value: 1,750				

BAVARIA

(Bayern)

Located in south Germany. In 1180 the Duchy of Bavaria was given to the Count of Wittelsbach by the emperor. He is the ancestor of all who ruled in Bavaria until 1918. Primogeniture was proclaimed in 1506 and in 1623 the dukes of Bavaria were given the electoral right. Bavaria, which had been divided for the various heirs, was reunited in 1799. The title of king was granted to Bavaria in 1805. Captial: München, population-- 1905: 6,524,372.

RULERS

Otto, 1886-1913, Prince Regent Luitpold, 1886-1912
Ludwig III, 1913-1918

MINT MARKS

D - Munich

KINGDOM

REFORM COINAGE

KM# 913 2 MARK
11.1110 g., 0.9000 Silver 0.3215 oz. ASW, 28 mm. **Ruler:** Otto Prince Regent Luitpold **Obv:** Head left **Obv. Legend:** OTTO KOENIG VON BAYERN **Rev:** Crowned imperial German eagle **Rev. Legend:** DEUTSCHES REICH, ZWEI MARK **Edge:** Reeded **Note:** Open and closed curl varieties exist. Prev. KM#511.

Date	Mintage	F	VF	XF	Unc	BU
1901D	829,064	12.00	28.00	55.00	135	300
1902D	1,340,789	10.00	22.00	45.00	120	300
1903D	1,406,067	10.00	22.00	45.00	110	275
1904D	2,320,238	9.00	20.00	40.00	100	275
1905D	1,406,100	10.00	22.00	45.00	100	275
1906D	1,054,500	10.00	22.00	55.00	120	325
1907D	2,106,712	9.00	20.00	35.00	100	275
1908D	632,700	10.00	22.00	45.00	95.00	300
1912D	213,652	12.00	28.00	60.00	125	400
1913D	97,698	40.00	80.00	160	250	475

KM# 997 2 MARK

11.1110 g., 0.9000 Silver 0.3215 oz. ASW **Ruler:** Otto Prince Regent Luitpold **Subject:** 90th Birthday of Prince Regent Luitpold **Obv:** Head right **Rev:** Crowned imperial eagle, shield on breast **Edge:** Reeded **Note:** Prev. KM#516.

Date	Mintage	F	VF	XF	Unc	BU
1911D	640,000	12.00	22.00	35.00	55.00	75.00
1911D Proof	—	Value: 125				

KM# 1002 2 MARK

11.1110 g., 0.9000 Silver 0.3215 oz. ASW, 28 mm. **Ruler:** Ludwig III **Obv:** Head left **Rev:** Crowned imperial eagle, shield on breast **Note:** Prev. KM#519.

Date	Mintage	F	VF	XF	Unc	BU
1914D	573,533	30.00	50.00	110	185	300
1914D Proof	—	Value: 450				

KM# 996 3 MARK

16.6670 g., 0.9000 Silver 0.4823 oz. ASW, 33 mm. **Ruler:** Otto Prince Regent Luitpold **Obv:** Head left **Rev:** Crowned imperial eagle, shield on breast **Edge Lettering:** GOTT MIT UNS **Note:** Prev. KM#515

Date	Mintage	F	VF	XF	Unc	BU
1908D	680,529	12.00	20.00	35.00	60.00	125
1909D	827,460	10.00	18.00	30.00	50.00	125
1910D	1,496,091	10.00	18.00	30.00	50.00	125
1911D	843,437	12.00	20.00	35.00	60.00	125
1912D	1,013,650	12.00	20.00	35.00	60.00	125
1913D	713,275	12.00	20.00	35.00	60.00	125
1913D Proof	—	Value: 125				

KM# 998 3 MARK

16.6670 g., 0.9000 Silver 0.4823 oz. ASW, 33 mm. **Ruler:** Otto Prince Regent Luitpold **Subject:** 90th Birthday of Prince Regent Luitpold **Obv:** Head right **Rev:** Crowned imperial eagle, shield on breast **Edge Lettering:** GOTT MIT UNS **Note:** Prev. KM#517.

Date	Mintage	F	VF	XF	Unc	BU
1911D	639,721	12.00	22.00	35.00	50.00	65.00
1911D Proof	—	Value: 125				

KM# 1005 3 MARK

16.6670 g., 0.9000 Silver 0.4823 oz. ASW, 33 mm. **Ruler:** Ludwig III **Obv:** Head left **Rev:** Crowned imperial eagle, shield on breast **Edge Lettering:** GOTT MIT UNS **Note:** Prev. KM#520.

Date	Mintage	F	VF	XF	Unc	BU
1914D	717,460	17.50	32.50	50.00	75.00	130
1914D Proof	—	Value: 250				

KM# 1010 3 MARK

16.6670 g., 0.9000 Silver 0.4823 oz. ASW, 33 mm. **Ruler:** Ludwig III **Subject:** Golden Wedding Anniversary **Obv:** Jugate heads right **Rev:** Crowned imperial eagle, shield on breast **Note:** Prev. KM#523.

Date	Mintage	F	VF	XF	Unc	BU
1918D	130	—	12,500	26,000	32,000	45,000

KM# 915 5 MARK

27.7770 g., 0.9000 Silver 0.8037 oz. ASW, 38 mm. **Ruler:** Otto **Obv:** Head left **Obv. Legend:** OTTO KOENIG VON BAYERN **Rev:** Crowned imperial German eagle **Rev. Legend:** DEUTSCHES REICH, FUNF MARK **Edge Lettering:** GOTT MIT UNS **Note:** Varieties in the hair locks and curls exist. Prev. KM#512.1-512.4.

Date	Mintage	F	VF	XF	Unc	BU
1901D	295,371	14.00	25.00	85.00	300	550
1902D	506,049	14.00	25.00	65.00	250	500
1903D	1,012,097	14.00	25.00	65.00	250	450
1904D	548,340	16.00	30.00	70.00	250	450
1906D	70,249	35.00	75.00	200	1,100	2,000
1907D	752,653	14.00	20.00	50.00	200	425
1908D	576,579	14.00	20.00	50.00	200	425
1913D	520,000	14.00	20.00	40.00	120	275
(1901-1913)D Proof	—	Value: 800				

KM# 999 5 MARK

27.7770 g., 0.9000 Silver 0.8037 oz. ASW, 38 mm. **Ruler:** Otto Prince Regent Luitpold **Subject:** 90th Birthday of Prince Regent Luitpold **Obv:** Head right **Rev:** Crowned imperial eagle, shield on breast **Note:** Prev. KM#518.

Date	Mintage	F	VF	XF	Unc	BU
1911D	160,000	25.00	65.00	95.00	170	225
1911D Proof	—	Value: 275				

KM# 1007 5 MARK

27.7770 g., 0.9000 Silver 0.8037 oz. ASW, 38 mm. **Ruler:** Ludwig III **Obv:** Head left **Note:** Prev. KM#521.

Date	Mintage	F	VF	XF	Unc	BU
1914D	142,600	40.00	90.00	175	250	375

KM# 994 10 MARK

3.9820 g., 0.9000 Gold 0.1152 oz. AGW **Ruler:** Otto **Obv:** Head left **Obv. Legend:** OTTO KOENIG V. BAYERN **Rev:** Crowned imperial German eagle **Rev. Legend:** DEUTSCHES REICH **Note:** Prev. KM#514.

Date	Mintage	F	VF	XF	Unc	BU
1901D	140,639	110	135	190	275	425
1902D	70,308	110	135	190	275	425
1903D	534,426	110	130	190	275	425
1904D	210,112	110	130	185	275	425
1905D	281,231	110	130	185	275	425
1906D	140,512	110	135	200	300	425
1907D	211,211	110	130	195	275	425
1909D	208,970	110	130	195	275	425
1910D	140,753	110	130	195	275	425
1911D	71,616	110	135	215	325	425
1912D	140,874	110	135	200	300	425
(1901-1912)D Proof	71,616,140,874	Value: 1,000				

KM# 920 20 MARK

7.9650 g., 0.9000 Gold 0.2305 oz. AGW **Ruler:** Otto **Obv:** Head left **Obv. Legend:** OTTO KOENIG VON BAYERN **Rev:** Type III **Rev. Legend:** DEUTSCHES REICH **Edge Lettering:** GOTT MIT UNS **Note:** Prev. KM#513.

Date	Mintage	F	VF	XF	Unc	BU
1905D	501,000	BV	210	225	275	375
1905D Proof	—	Value: 1,600				
1913D	310,778	Value: 30,000				
1913D Proof	—	Value: 35,000				

KM# 1009 20 MARK

7.9650 g., 0.9000 Gold 0.2305 oz. AGW **Ruler:** Ludwig III **Obv:** Head left **Rev:** Crowned imperial eagle, shield on breast **Note:** Prev. KM#522. Never officially released.

Date	Mintage	F	VF	XF	Unc	BU
1914D	532,851	—	2,000	2,800	3,300	4,250
1914D Proof	—	Value: 4,500				

BREMEN

Established at about the same time as the bishopric in 787, Bremen was under the control of the bishops and archbishops until joining the Hanseatic League in 1276. Archbishop Albrecht II granted the mint right to the city in 1369, but this was not formalized by imperial decree until 1541. In 1646, Bremen was raised to free imperial status and continued to strike its own coins into the early 20th century. The city lost its free imperial status in 1803 and was controlled by France from 1806 until 1813. Regaining it independence in 1815, Bremen joined the North German Confederation in 1867 and the German Empire in 1871. Since 1369, there was practically continuous coinage until 1907.

FREE CITY

REGULAR COINAGE

KM# 250 2 MARK
11.1110 g., 0.9000 Silver 0.3215 oz. ASW, 28 mm. **Obv:** Key on crowned shield with supporters **Rev:** Crowned imperial eagle, shield on breast, date at right, denomination below **Edge:** Reeded

Date	Mintage	F	VF	XF	Unc	BU
1904 J	100,000	30.00	70.00	100	150	225
1904 J Proof	200	Value: 400				

KM# 251 5 MARK
27.7770 g., 0.9000 Silver 0.8037 oz. ASW, 38 mm. **Obv:** Key on crowned shield with supporters **Rev:** Crowned imperial eagle, shield on breast, date at right, denomination below **Edge Lettering:** GOTT MIT UNS

Date	Mintage	F	VF	XF	Unc	BU
1906 J	40,846	85.00	200	300	450	550
1906 J Proof	600	Value: 1,000				

KM# 253 10 MARK
3.9820 g., 0.9000 Gold 0.1152 oz. AGW **Obv:** Key on crowned shield with supporters **Rev:** Crowned imperial eagle, shield on breast, date at right, denomination below

Date	Mintage	F	VF	XF	Unc	BU
1907 J	20,006	425	850	1,250	1,700	2,500
1907 J Proof	—	Value: 2,800				

KM# 252 20 MARK
7.9650 g., 0.9000 Gold 0.2305 oz. AGW **Edge Lettering:** GOTT MIT UNS

Date	Mintage	F	VF	XF	Unc	BU
1906 J	20,122	425	850	1,150	1,750	2,500
1906 J Proof	—	Value: 2,800				

BRUNSWICK-WOLFENBUTTEL

(Braunschweig-Wolfenbüttel)

Located in north-central Germany. Wolfenbüttel was annexed to Brunswick in 1257. One of the five surviving sons of Albrecht II founded the first line in Wolfenbüttel in 1318. A further division in Wolfenbüttel and Lüneburg was undertaken in 1373. Another division occurred in 1495, but the Wolfenbüttel duchy survived in the younger line. Heinrich IX was forced out of his territory during the religious wars of the mid-sixteenth century by Duke Johann Friedrich I of Saxony and Landgrave Philipp of Hessen in 1542, but was restored to his possessions in 1547. Duke Friedrich Ulrich was forced to cede the Grubenhagen lands, which had been acquired by Wolfenbüttel in 1596, to Lüneburg in 1617. When the succession died out in 1634, the lands and titles fell to the cadet line in Dannenberg. The line became extinct once again and passed to Brunswick-Bevern in 1735 from which a new succession of Wolfenbüttel dukes descended. The ducal family was beset by continual personal and political tragedy during the nineteenth century. Two of the dukes were killed in battles with Napoleon, the territories were occupied by the French and became part of the Kingdom of Westphalia, another duke was forced out by a revolt in 1823. From 1884 until 1913, Brunswick-Wolfenbüttel was governed by Prussia and then turned over to the only surviving (of 3) prince of Brunswick who married the only daughter of Kaiser Wilhelm II. His reign was short, however, as he was forced to abdicate at the end of World War I.

RULERS
Prussian rule, 1884-1913
Ernst August, 1913-1918

DUCHY

REFORM COINAGE

KM# 1161 3 MARK
16.6670 g., 0.9000 Silver 0.4823 oz. ASW, 33 mm. **Ruler:** Ernst August **Subject:** Ernst August Wedding and Accession **Obv:** Jugate heads right **Rev:** Crowned imperial eagle, shield on breast **Edge Lettering:** GOTT MIT UNS

Date	Mintage	F	VF	XF	Unc	BU
1915A	1,700	600	1,200	2,000	2,750	3,500
1915A Proof	—	Value: 3,750				

KM# 1162 3 MARK
16.6670 g., 0.9000 Silver 0.4823 oz. ASW, 33 mm. **Ruler:** Ernst August **Subject:** Ernst August Wedding and Accession **Obv:** Jugate heads right **Obv. Legend:** U LUNEB added **Rev:** Crowned imperial eagle, shield on breast

Date	Mintage	F	VF	XF	Unc	BU
1915A	31,634	50.00	120	200	275	375
1915A Proof	—	Value: 450				

KM# 1163 5 MARK
27.7770 g., 0.9000 Silver 0.8037 oz. ASW, 38 mm. **Ruler:** Ernst August **Subject:** Ernst August Wedding and Accession **Obv:** Jugate heads right **Rev:** Crowned imperial eagle, shield on breast **Edge Lettering:** GOTT MIT UNS

Date	Mintage	F	VF	XF	Unc	BU
1915A	1,400	800	1,750	3,000	3,750	4,500
1915A Proof	—	Value: 4,750				

KM# 1164 5 MARK
27.7770 g., 0.9000 Silver 0.8037 oz. ASW, 38 mm. **Ruler:** Ernst August **Subject:** Ernst August Wedding and Accession **Obv:** Jugate heads right **Obv. Legend:** U. LUNEB added **Rev:** Crowned imperial eagle, shield on breast

Date	Mintage	F	VF	XF	Unc	BU
1915A	8,600	185	400	700	1,200	1,500
1915A Proof	—	Value: 1,600				

HAMBURG

The city of Hamburg is located on the Elbe River about 75 miles (125 kilometers) from the North Sea. Tradition states that it was founded by Charlemagne in the early 9th century. At first, the town was controlled by the archbishopric of Bremen and Hamburg (see Bremen). In 1110, Hamburg and the territory of Holstein came under the rule of Count Adolf I of Schauenburg (Schaumburg, ruled 1106-1128), which inaugurated a period stretching for four centuries in which the Holstein dynasty exercised authority over the city. Hamburg joined with Lübeck in 1241 to form the first partnership in what was to become the Hanseatic League. Count Adolf VI of Schauenburg (1290-1315) gave civic autonomy to Hamburg in 1292 and leased the mint right to the citizens the next year. Local *hohlpfennige* had already been struck fifty years previous. From this early time, the city struck an almost continuous series of coins throughout the centuries up to World War I. In 1510, Hamburg was granted the status of a Free City of the Empire, although it had actually been free for about 250 years. It was occupied by the French during the period of the Napoleonic Wars. In 1866, Hamburg joined the North German Confederation and became a part of the German Empire in 1871.

FREE CITY

REFORM COINAGE

KM# 294 2 MARK
11.1110 g., 0.9000 Silver 0.3215 oz. ASW, 28 mm. **Obv:** Helmeted arms with lion supporters **Obv. Legend:** FREIE UND HANSESTADT HAMBURG **Rev:** Crowned imperial eagle **Rev. Legend:** DEUTSCHES REICH 1899, ZWEI MARK below **Edge:** Reeded

Date	Mintage	F	VF	XF	Unc	BU
1901J	482,408	15.00	25.00	60.00	200	300
1902J	778,880	12.50	25.00	60.00	200	300
1903J	817,215	12.50	25.00	50.00	200	300
1904J	1,248,330	12.50	25.00	50.00	180	300
1905J	204,040	35.00	65.00	125	550	1,000
1906J	1,224,910	12.50	25.00	50.00	180	300
1907J	1,225,503	12.50	25.00	50.00	180	300
1908J	367,750	12.50	30.00	55.00	180	325
1911J	204,250	12.50	30.00	55.00	180	325
1912J	78,500	20.00	50.00	110	300	600
1913J	105,325	12.50	30.00	65.00	180	550
1914J	327,758	10.00	25.00	50.00	140	300
(1901-1914)J Proof	—	Value: 400				

KM# 296 3 MARK
16.6670 g., 0.9000 Silver 0.4823 oz. ASW, 33 mm. **Obv:** Three tower castle on helmeted shield with supporters **Rev:** Crowned

imperial eagle, shield on breast **Edge Lettering:** GOTT MIT UNS

Date	Mintage	F	VF	XF	Unc	BU
1908J	408,475	12.50	25.00	40.00	80.00	130
1909J	1,388,892	12.50	25.00	40.00	80.00	130
1910J	525,500	12.50	25.00	40.00	80.00	130
1911J	922,000	12.50	25.00	40.00	80.00	130
1912J	491,088	12.50	25.00	40.00	80.00	130
1913J	343,200	12.50	25.00	40.00	80.00	130
1914J	575,111	12.50	25.00	40.00	80.00	130
(1908-1914) Proof	—	Value: 250				

KM# 293 5 MARK

27.7770 g., 0.9000 Silver 0.8037 oz. ASW, 38 mm. **Obv:** Helmeted arms with lion supporters **Obv. Legend:** FREIE UND HANSESTADT HAMBURG **Rev:** Crowned imperial eagle **Rev. Legend:** DEUTSCHES REICH 1907, FUNF MARK below **Edge Lettering:** GOTT MIT UNS

Date	Mintage	F	VF	XF	Unc	BU
1901J	171,603	20.00	40.00	100	500	900
1902J	294,034	17.50	35.00	80.00	400	800
1903J	588,535	17.50	35.00	75.00	275	450
1904J	318,640	16.00	32.00	75.00	275	550
1907J	325,534	16.00	32.00	75.00	275	550
1908J	457,794	16.00	32.00	75.00	220	400
1913J	326,800	16.00	32.00	60.00	165	250
(1901-1913)J Proof	—	Value: 1,500				

KM# 292 10 MARK

3.9820 g., 0.9000 Gold 0.1152 oz. AGW **Obv:** Helmeted arms with lion supporters **Obv. Legend:** FREIE UND HANSESTADT HAMBURG **Rev:** Crowned imperial eagle, type II **Rev. Legend:** DEUTSCHES REICH

Date	Mintage	F	VF	XF	Unc	BU
1901J	81,891	110	150	175	385	500
1902J	40,763	120	225	350	650	1,000
1903J	229,786	110	150	175	350	500
1905J	164,000	110	150	175	350	500
1906J	163,347	110	150	175	350	500
1907J	111,373	110	150	175	350	500
1908J	31,685	150	300	450	800	1,300
1909J	122,245	110	150	175	350	500
1909J Proof	—	Value: 1,600				
1910J	40,598	120	225	300	600	1,000
1910J Proof	—	Value: 2,000				
1911J	75,000	115	175	250	300	800
1911J Proof	—	Value: 6,000				
1912J	47,775	145	245	350	500	1,000
1912J Proof	—	Value: 2,000				
1913J	40,937	145	245	300	400	1,000
1913J Proof	—	Value: 2,000				

KM# 295 20 MARK

7.9650 g., 0.9000 Gold 0.2305 oz. AGW **Obv:** Helmeted arms with lion supporters **Obv. Legend:** FREIE UND HANSESTADT HAMBURG **Rev:** Crowned imperial eagle, type III **Rev. Legend:** DEUTSCHES REICH **Edge Lettering:** GOTT MIT UNS

Date	Mintage	F	VF	XF	Unc	BU
1908J Rare	14	—	—	—	75,000	—
1913J	491,133	—	BV	210	220	275
1913J Proof	—	Value: 1,000				

HESSE-DARMSTADT

(Hessen-Darmstadt)

Founded by the youngest of Philipp I's four sons upon the death of their father in 1567, Hesse-Darmstadt was one of the two main branches of the family which survived past the beginning of the 17th century. The Countship of Hanau-Lichtenberg was through marriage when the male line failed in 1736. Ludwig X was forced to cede that territory to France in 1801. In 1803, Darmstadt acquired part of the Palatinate, the city of Friedberg, part of the city of Mainz, and the Duchy of Westphalia in a general settlement with France. The Landgrave was elevated to the status of Grand Duke in 1806 and reacquired Hesse-Homburg, which got its souveranity back in 1816. In 1815 the Congress of Vienna awarded Hesse-Darmstadt the city of Worms and all of Mainz. These were relinquished, along with Hesse-Homburg, to Prussia in 1866 and Hesse-Darmstadt was called just Hesse from 1867 onwards. Hesse became part of the German Empire in 1871, but ceased to exist as a semi-sovereign state at the end of World War I.

RULER

Ernst Ludwig, 1892-1918

GRAND DUCHY

REFORM COINAGE

Grossherzogtum within the German Empire

KM# 372 2 MARK

11.1110 g., 0.9000 Silver 0.3215 oz. ASW, 28 mm. **Ruler:** Ernst Ludwig **Subject:** 400th Birthday of Philipp the Magnanimous **Obv:** Jugate heads left, dates below **Rev:** Crowned imperial eagle with shield on breast **Edge:** Reeded

Date	Mintage	F	VF	XF	Unc	BU
1904	100,000	30.00	65.00	100	150	200
1904 Proof	2,250	Value: 400				

Note: Obverse matte, reverse polished

KM# 375 3 MARK

16.6670 g., 0.9000 Silver 0.4823 oz. ASW, 33 mm. **Ruler:** Ernst Ludwig **Obv:** Head left **Rev:** Crowned imperial eagle, shield on breast **Edge Lettering:** GOTT MIT UNS

Date	Mintage	F	VF	XF	Unc	BU
1910A	200,000	50.00	100	175	400	550
1910A Proof	Est. 500	Value: 750				

KM# 376 3 MARK

16.6670 g., 0.9000 Silver 0.4823 oz. ASW, 33 mm. **Ruler:** Ernst Ludwig **Subject:** 25-Year Jubilee **Obv:** Head left **Rev:** Crowned imperial eagle, shield on breast **Note:** All minted pieces are proof. Values in circulated grades are for impaired proofs.

Date	Mintage	F	VF	XF	Unc	BU
1917A	1,333	—	3,400	5,200	7,000	9,500
1917A Proof	Inc. above	Value: 9,500				

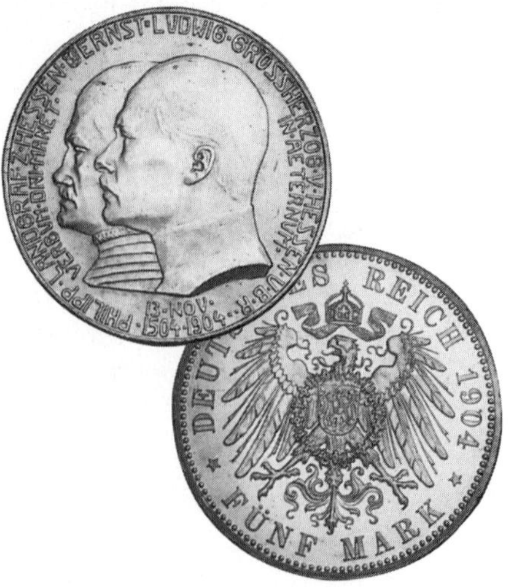

KM# 373 5 MARK

27.7770 g., 0.9000 Silver 0.8037 oz. ASW, 38 mm. **Ruler:** Ernst Ludwig **Subject:** 400th birthday of Philipp the Magnanimous **Obv:** Jugate heads left, dates below **Rev:** Crowned imperial eagle, shield on breast **Edge Lettering:** GOTT MIT UNS

Date	Mintage	F	VF	XF	Unc	BU
1904	40,000	70.00	140	260	370	500
1904 Proof	700	Value: 750				

Note: Obverse matte, reverse polished

KM# 371 20 MARK

7.9650 g., 0.9000 Gold 0.2305 oz. AGW **Ruler:** Ernst Ludwig **Obv:** Head left **Obv. Legend:** ERNST LUDWIG GROSHERZOG VON HESSEN **Rev:** Crowned imperial eagle, shield on breast **Rev. Legend:** DEUTSCHES REICH date, 20 MARK below **Edge Lettering:** GOTT MIT UNS

Date	Mintage	F	VF	XF	Unc	BU
1901A	80,000	250	460	800	1,600	2,500
1901A Proof	600	Value: 3,200				
1903A	40,000	250	460	800	1,600	2,500
1903A Proof	100	Value: 3,200				

KM# 374 20 MARK

7.9650 g., 0.9000 Gold 0.2305 oz. AGW **Ruler:** Ernst Ludwig **Obv:** Head left **Obv. Legend:** ERNST LUDWIG GROSSHERZOG VON HESSEN **Rev:** Crowned imperial eagle, shield on breast **Rev. Legend:** DEUTSCHES REICH date, 20 MARK below **Edge Lettering:** GOTT MIT UNS

Date	Mintage	F	VF	XF	Unc	BU
1905A	45,000	300	420	600	1,200	1,400
1905A Proof	200	Value: 2,400				
1906A	85,000	210	360	460	1,000	1,400
1906A Proof	199	Value: 2,250				
1908A	40,000	250	400	750	1,200	1,400
1908A Proof	—	Value: 2,250				
1911A	150,000	210	360	550	1,000	1,400
1911A Proof	—	Value: 2,250				

LIPPE-DETMOLD

After the division of 1613, the Counts of Lippe-Detmold, as the senior branch of the family, ruled over the largest portion of Lippe (see), a small patrimony in northwestern Germany. In 1620, Lippe-Sternberg became extinct and its lands and titles reverted to Lippe-Detmold. The younger brother of Hermann Adolf founded the line of Lippe-Sternberg-Schwalenberg (Biesterfeld) in 1652, which lasted into the 20th century. In 1720, the count was raised to the rank of prince, but did not use the title until 1789. Lippe joined the North German Confederation in 1866 and became part of the German Empire in 1871. Prince Alexander was declared insane and placed under a regency during his entire reign. There ensued a ten-year testamentary dispute between the Lippe-Biesterfeld and the Schaumburg-Lippe lines over the succession to the childless Alexander - a Wilhelmine cause célèbre. Leopold (V) of the Biesterfeld line gained the principality in 1905, but was forced to abdicate in 1918, at the end of World War I. In

1947, Lippe was absorbed by the German state of North Rhine-Westphalia.

RULERS
Alexander, 1895-1905
Leopold IV, 1905-1918

MINT MARK
A - Berlin mint, 1843-1918

PRINCIPALITY

REFORM COINAGE

KM# 270 2 MARK
11.1110 g., 0.9000 Silver 0.3215 oz. ASW, 28 mm. **Ruler:** Leopold IV **Obv:** Head left **Rev:** Crowned imperial eagle, shield on breast **Edge:** Reeded

Date	Mintage	F	VF	XF	Unc	BU
1906A	20,000	125	250	350	500	650
1906A Proof	1,100	Value: 750				

KM# 275 3 MARK
16.6670 g., 0.9000 Silver 0.4823 oz. ASW, 33 mm. **Ruler:** Leopold IV **Obv:** Head left **Rev:** Crowned imperial eagle, shield on breast **Edge Lettering:** GOTT MIT UNS

Date	Mintage	F	VF	XF	Unc	BU
1913A	15,000	150	300	450	600	750
1913A Proof	100	Value: 900				

LUBECK

The original settlement was called Liubice, the capital of a Slavic principality. It was located at the confluence of the Schwartau with the Trave Rivers and contained a castle with a merchant town on a harbor. The town was burned down in 1138 and Count Adolf II of Holstein (1128-64) refounded the city four miles (6.5 kilometers) up the Trave in 1143. Duke Heinirich III the Lion of Saxony (1153-80) forced Adolf II to relinquish Lübeck to him as his feudal overlord. Heinrich III no sooner had the city in his possession when a fire destroyed it. Heinrich III began rebuilding it in 1159 and this is now considered the traditional date of it founding. As the city and its trade on the Baltic grew in importance, special rights and privileges were granted to it in 1188 by Emperor Friedrich I Barbarossa. In 1226, Friedrich II raised Lübeck to the status of a free imperial city and a long period of self-government began. From about 1190 and into the 13th century, an imperial mint operated in the town. Although Lübeck was granted the mint right in 1188, reiterated in 1226 and 1340, its earliest civic coinage only began about 1350. The commercial importance of the city became even greater when it joined with Hamburg in 1241 to form the nucleus of what was to become the Hanseatic League. In 1358, the member cities of the League, which had grown very powerful during the preceding century, elected Lübeck as the administrative capital. By the beginning of the 15th century, the city was second only to Cologne as the largest in northern Germany.

The Protestant Reformation swept through Lübeck in 1529-30 (see Bishopric) and changes came rapidly as the governing city council was removed from office, only to be replaced by a revolutionary *burgomeister*, Jürgen Wullenwever. An unsuccessful war ensued against Denmark, Sweden and the Netherlands and caused the city to lose its powerful position in northern Europe. This began the dismemberment of the Hanseatic League and even a victorious war against Sweden during 1563-1570 was not enough to prevent the decline of Lübeck's fortunes. The demise of the League in 1630, during the Thirty Years' War, may have actually been beneficial to the city as it was able to remain neutral during the long years of struggle throughout Germany. The city was able to regain much of its lost economic power during the 18th century, partly due to increased trade with Russia through its new Baltic port of St. Petersburg. Lübeck's economy was completely ruined, however, during the Napoleonic Wars (1792-1815). Occupied by the French from 1811 to 1813, it was restored as a free city in the latter year. After 1815, the city was a member of the German Confederation and joined the North German Confederation in 1866. It remained a free city as part of the German Empire from 1871 until the end of World War I in 1918. However, its status as a self-governing entity, which had begun in 1226, did not end until 1937, when it was made a part of the province of Schleswig-Holstein.

FREE CITY

REFORM COINAGE

KM# 210 2 MARK
11.1110 g., 0.9000 Silver 0.3215 oz. ASW, 28 mm. **Obv:** Double imperial eagle with divided shield on breast **Rev:** Crowned imperial eagle, shield on breast **Edge:** Reeded

Date	Mintage	F	VF	XF	Unc	BU
1901A	25,000	100	200	300	475	600
1901A Proof	—	Value: 700				

KM# 212 2 MARK
11.1110 g., 0.9000 Silver 0.3215 oz. ASW, 28 mm. **Obv:** Double imperial eagle with divided shield on breast **Edge:** Reeded **Designer:** Crowned imperial eagle, shield on breast

Date	Mintage	F	VF	XF	Unc	BU
1904A	25,000	45.00	85.00	135	225	325
1904A Proof	200	Value: 400				
1905A	25,000	45.00	85.00	135	225	325
1905A Proof	178	Value: 400				
1906A	25,000	45.00	85.00	135	225	325
1906A Proof	200	Value: 400				
1907A	25,000	45.00	85.00	135	225	325
1907A Proof	—	Value: 400				
1911A	25,000	45.00	85.00	135	225	325
1911A Proof	—	Value: 400				
1912A	25,000	45.00	85.00	135	225	325
1912A Proof	—	Value: 400				

KM# 215 3 MARK
16.6670 g., 0.9000 Silver 0.4823 oz. ASW, 33 mm. **Obv:** Double imperial eagle with divided shield on breast **Rev:** Crowned imperial eagle, shield on breast **Edge Lettering:** GOTT MIT UNS

Date	Mintage	F	VF	XF	Unc	BU
1908	33,334	25.00	70.00	125	200	300
1909A	33,334	25.00	70.00	125	200	300
1910A	33,334	25.00	70.00	125	200	300
1911A	33,334	25.00	70.00	125	200	300
1912A	34,000	25.00	70.00	125	200	300
1913A	30,000	25.00	70.00	125	200	300
1914A	10,000	35.00	85.00	150	250	250
(1908-1914)A Proof	—	Value: 400				

KM# 213 5 MARK
27.7770 g., 0.9000 Silver 0.8037 oz. ASW, 38 mm. **Obv:** Double imperial eagle with divided shield on breast **Rev:** Crowned imperial eagle, shield on breast

Date	Mintage	F	VF	XF	Unc	BU
1904A	10,000	120	275	400	550	900
1904A Proof	200	Value: 1,300				

Date	Mintage	F	VF	XF	Unc	BU
1907A	10,000	120	275	400	575	900
1908A	10,000	120	300	425	600	900
1913A	6,000	120	300	450	650	900

KM# 211 10 MARK
3.9820 g., 0.9000 Gold 0.1152 oz. AGW **Obv:** Double imperial eagle with divided shield on breast **Rev:** Crowned imperial eagle, shield on breast **Edge Lettering:** ~ * ~

Date	Mintage	F	VF	XF	Unc	BU
1901A	10,000	375	850	1,200	1,650	2,300
1901A Proof	200	Value: 2,700				
1904A	10,000	375	850	1,200	1,650	2,300
1904A Proof	130	Value: 2,700				

KM# 214 10 MARK
3.9820 g., 0.9000 Gold 0.1152 oz. AGW **Obv:** Double imperial eagle with divided shield on breast **Rev:** Crowned imperial eagle, shield on breast **Edge:** ~ * ~

Date	Mintage	F	VF	XF	Unc	BU
1905A	10,000	300	800	1,200	1,650	2,250
1905A Proof	247	Value: 2,750				
1906A	10,000	300	800	1,200	1,650	2,250
1906A Proof	216	Value: 3,000				
1909A	10,000	300	800	1,200	1,650	2,250
1909A Proof	—	Value: 2,750				
1910A	10,000	300	800	1,200	1,650	2,250
1910A Proof	—	Value: 3,000				

MECKLENBURG-SCHWERIN

The Duchy of Mecklenburg was divided in 1592 to form the branches of Mecklenburg-Schwerin and Mecklenburg-Güstrow. During the Thirty Years' War, the several dukes of the Mecklenburg states sided with the Protestant forces against the emperor. Albrecht von Wallenstein, Duke of Friedland and imperial general, ousted the Mecklenburg dukes from their territories in 1628. The rightful rulers were each restored to their lands in 1632. In 1658, Mecklenburg-Schwerin was divided by the four sons of Adolf Friedrich into the lines of Mecklenburg-Schwerin, Mecklenburg-Grabow, Mecklenburg-Mirow (extinct in 1675) and Mecklenburg-Strelitz (see). Mecklenburg-Schwerin and Mecklenburg-Güstrow fell extinct in the male line in 1692 and 1695 respectively, becoming a source of dispute between Mecklenburg-Grabow and Mecklenburg-Strelitz. Both parties finally agreed to a settlement in 1701 which awarded about eighty percent of all Mecklenburg territory to Grabow, which became the main Schwerin line, and the rest to Strelitz. No coinage was produced for Mecklenburg-Schwerin from 1708 until 1750. In 1815, the Congress of Vienna elevated the ruler to the rank of Grand Duke. Mecklenburg-Schwerin became a part of the German Empire in 1871. The last grand duke abdicated at the end of World War I in 1918.

RULER
Friedrich Franz IV, 1897-1918

MINT MARKS
A - Berlin mint, 1852-1915

GRAND DUCHY

REFORM COINAGE

KM# 330 2 MARK
11.1110 g., 0.9000 Silver 0.3215 oz. ASW, 28 mm. **Ruler:** Friedrich Franz IV **Subject:** Grand Duke Coming of Age **Obv:** Head right **Rev:** Crowned imperial eagle, shield on breast **Edge:** Reeded

Date	Mintage	F	VF	XF	Unc	BU
1901A	50,000	125	300	500	1,100	1,500
1901A Proof	1,000	Value: 1,800				

KM# 333 2 MARK
11.1110 g., 0.9000 Silver 0.3215 oz. ASW, 28 mm. **Ruler:** Friedrich Franz IV **Subject:** Friedrich Franz IV Wedding **Obv:** Jugate heads left **Rev:** Crowned imperial eagle, shield on breast **Edge:** Reeded

Date	Mintage	F	VF	XF	Unc	BU
1904A	100,000	18.00	40.00	65.00	100	150
1904A Proof	6,000	Value: 225				

KM# 340 3 MARK
16.6670 g., 0.9000 Silver 0.4823 oz. ASW, 33 mm. **Ruler:** Friedrich Franz IV **Subject:** 100 Years as Grand Duchy **Obv:** Uniformed jugate busts left **Rev:** Crowned imperial eagle, shield on breast within circle **Edge Lettering:** GOTT MIT UNS

Date	Mintage	F	VF	XF	Unc	BU
1915A	33,334	50.00	100	175	250	350
1915A Proof	—	Value: 500				

KM# 334 5 MARK
27.7770 g., 0.9000 Silver 0.8037 oz. ASW, 38 mm. **Ruler:** Friedrich Franz IV **Subject:** Friedrich Franz IV Wedding **Obv:** Jugate heads left **Rev:** Crowned imperial eagle, shield on breast **Edge Lettering:** GOTT MIT UNS

Date	Mintage	F	VF	XF	Unc	BU
1904A	40,000	45.00	100	175	250	375
1904A Proof	2,500	Value: 600				

KM# 341 5 MARK
27.7770 g., 0.9000 Silver 0.8037 oz. ASW, 38 mm. **Ruler:** Friedrich Franz IV **Subject:** 100 Years as Grand Duchy **Obv:** Uniformed jugate busts left **Rev:** Crowned imperial eagle, shield on breast within circle **Edge Lettering:** GOTT MIT UNS

Date	Mintage	F	VF	XF	Unc	BU
1915A	10,000	135	375	500	900	1,200
1915A Proof	—	Value: 1,250				

KM# 331 10 MARK
3.9820 g., 0.9000 Gold 0.1152 oz. AGW **Ruler:** Friedrich Franz IV **Subject:** Grand Duke Coming of Age **Obv:** Head right **Rev:** Crowned imperial eagle, shield on breast, type III **Edge:** ~ * ~

Date	Mintage	F	VF	XF	Unc	BU
1901A	10,000	750	1,600	2,700	4,000	6,000
1901A Proof	200	Value: 7,000				

KM# 332 20 MARK
7.9650 g., 0.9000 Gold 0.2305 oz. AGW **Ruler:** Friedrich Franz IV **Subject:** Grand Duke Coming of Age **Obv:** Head right **Rev:** Crowned imperial eagle, shield on breast, type III **Edge Lettering:** GOTT MIT UNS

Date	Mintage	F	VF	XF	Unc	BU
1901A	5,000	1,000	2,700	4,200	5,750	8,000
1901A Proof	200	Value: 8,500				

MECKLENBURG-STRELITZ

The Duchy of Mecklenburg-Strelitz was the youngest branch of the dynasty established when Mecklenburg-Schwerin was divided in 1658. Like its parent senior line, Mecklenburg-Strelitz became a grand duchy in 1815 as enacted by the Congress of Vienna. It became a constituent part of the German Empire in 1871, but all sovereignty ended with the conclusion of World War I in 1918.

RULERS
Friedrich Wilhelm, 1860-1904
Adolf Friedrich V, 1904-1914
Adolf Friedrich VI, 1914-1918

GRAND DUCHY

REFORM COINAGE

KM# 115 2 MARK
11.1110 g., 0.9000 Silver 0.3215 oz. ASW, 28 mm. **Ruler:** Adolph Friedrich V **Obv:** Head left **Rev:** Crowned imperial eagle, shield on breast **Edge:** Reeded

Date	Mintage	F	VF	XF	Unc	BU
1905A	10,000	150	350	575	850	1,200
1905A Proof	2,500	Value: 1,200				

KM# 120 3 MARK
16.6670 g., 0.9000 Silver 0.4823 oz. ASW, 33 mm. **Ruler:** Adolph Friedrich V **Obv:** Head left **Rev:** Crowned imperial eagle, shield on breast **Edge Lettering:** GOTT MIT UNS

Date	Mintage	F	VF	XF	Unc	BU
1913A	7,000	250	500	950	1,600	2,400
1913A Proof	—	Value: 2,600				

KM# 116 10 MARK
3.9820 g., 0.9000 Gold 0.1152 oz. AGW **Ruler:** Adolph Friedrich V **Obv:** Head left **Rev:** Crowned imperial eagle, shield on breast **Edge:** ~ * ~

Date	Mintage	F	VF	XF	Unc	BU
1905A	1,000	1,750	3,000	5,000	6,500	8,000
1905A Proof	150	Value: 9,000				

KM# 117 20 MARK
7.9650 g., 0.9000 Gold 0.2305 oz. AGW **Ruler:** Adolph Friedrich V **Obv:** Head left **Rev:** Crowned imperial eagle, shield on breast, type III **Edge Lettering:** GOTT MIT UNS

Date	Mintage	F	VF	XF	Unc	BU
1905A	1,000	2,000	4,250	6,500	8,500	12,000
1905A Proof	160	Value: 13,000				

OLDENBURG

The county of Oldenburg was situated on the North Sea-coast, to the east of the principality of East Friesland. It was originally part of the old duchy of Saxony and the first recorded lord ruled from the beginning of the 11th century. The first count was named in 1091 and had already acquired the county of Delmenhorst prior to that time. The first identifiable Oldenburg coinage was struck in the first half of the 13th century. Oldenburg was divided into Oldenburg and Delmenhorst in 1270, but the two lines were reunited by marriage five generations later. Through another marriage to the heiress of the duchy of Schleswig and county of Holstein, the royal house of Denmark descended through the Oldenburg line beginning in 1448, while a junior branch continued as counts of Oldenburg. The lordship of Jever was added to the county's domains in 1575. In 1667, the last count died without a direct heir and Oldenburg reverted to Denmark until 1773. In the following year, Oldenburg was given to the bishop of Lübeck, of the Holstein-Gottorp line, and raised to the status of a duchy. Oldenburg was occupied several times during the Napoleonic Wars and became a grand duchy in 1829. In 1817, Oldenburg acquired the principality of Birkenfeld from Prussia and struck coins in denominations used there. World War I spelled the end of temporal power for the Grand Duke in 1918, but the title has continued up to the present time. Grand Duke Anton Günther was born in 1923.

RULER
Friedrich August, 1900-1918

MINT MARK
A - Berlin mint, 1891-1901

GRAND DUCHY

REFORM COINAGE

KM# 202 2 MARK
11.1110 g., 0.9000 Silver 0.3215 oz. ASW, 28 mm. **Ruler:** Friedrich August **Obv:** Head left **Obv. Legend:** FRIEDRICH AUGUST GROSSHERZOG V. OLDENBURG **Rev:** Crowned imperial eagle with wreathed arms on breast **Rev. Legend:** DEUTSCHES REICH date, ZWEI MARK below **Edge:** Reeded

Date	Mintage	F	VF	XF	Unc	BU
1901A	75,000	100	225	400	900	1,500
1901A Proof	260	Value: 2,000				

KM# 203 5 MARK

27.7770 g., 0.9000 Silver 0.8037 oz. ASW, 38 mm. **Ruler:** Friedrich August **Obv:** Head left **Obv. Legend:** FRIEDRICH AUGUST GROSSHERZOG V. OLDENBURG **Rev:** Crowned imperial eagle with wreathed arms on breast **Rev. Legend:** DEUTSCHES REICH date, FUNF MARK below **Edge Lettering:** GOTT ~ MIT ~ UNS

Date	Mintage	F	VF	XF	Unc	BU
1901A	10,000	350	800	1,500	3,750	5,500
1901A Proof	170	Value: 6,000				

PRUSSIA

(Preussen)

Elector Friedrich III of Brandenburg-Prussia (1688-1713) was accorded the title of "King in Prussia" in 1701 as a reward for his support of Austria during the War of the Spanish Succession. Under successive strong leaders, Prussia gained increasing importance and added to its territories to become one of the leading countries of Europe in the course of the 18th century. As part of the reforms instituted by Friedrich II, the system of single letter mintmarks representing specific mints replaced the traditional incorporation of mint officials' symbols and/or initials as part of coin designs. Some of these very same mintmarks are still in use on modern German coins up to the present day. During the Napoleonic Wars (1792-1815), Prussia was allied with Saxony and they were soundly defeated at Jena in 1806. Prussia was forced to cede large portions of its territory at the time, but played a large part in the final defeat of Napoleon. The Congress of Vienna awarded Prussia part of Pomerania, the northern half of Saxony, much of Westphalia and the Rhineland, thus making it the largest state in Germany and a major power in European affairs. After defeating Denmark in 1864 and Austria in 1866, Prussia acquired Schleswig-Holstein, Hannover, Hesse-Cassel, Nassau and Frankfurt am Main. By this time, Prussia encompassed a large part of German territory and its population included two-thirds of all the German people. By winning the Franco-Prussian War (1870-71), Prussia became the pivotal state in the unification of Germany in 1871. King Wilhelm I was proclaimed Kaiser (Emperor) of all Germany, but World War I brought an end to both the Empire and the Kingdom of Prussia in 1918.

NOTE: For coins of Neuchatel previously listed here, see Switzerland.

RULER

Wilhelm II, 1888-1918

MINT MARK

A - Berlin = Prussia, East Friesland, East Prussia, Posen

KINGDOM

REFORM COINAGE

KM# 522 2 MARK

11.1110 g., 0.9000 Silver 0.3215 oz. ASW, 28 mm. **Ruler:** Wilhelm II **Obv:** Head right **Obv. Legend:** WILHELM II DEUTSCHER KAISER KONIG V. PREUSSEN **Rev:** Crowned imperial eagle **Rev. Legend:** DEUTSCHES REICH date, ZWEI MARK below **Edge:** Reeded

Date	Mintage	F	VF	XF	Unc	BU
1901	398,486	70.00	160	300	1,000	2,000
1901 Proof	—	Value: 3,000				

Date	Mintage	F	VF	XF	Unc	BU
1902	3,948,323	7.50	16.00	55.00	100	275
1903	4,078,709	7.50	16.00	55.00	100	275
1904A	9,981,031	7.50	16.00	55.00	100	250
1905A	6,423,135	7.00	15.00	50.00	100	275
1905A Proof	620	Value: 600				
1906A	4,000,000	7.00	15.00	50.00	100	300
1906A Proof	85	Value: 600				
1907A	8,085,264	7.00	15.00	50.00	100	250
1908A	2,389,550	7.00	15.00	45.00	100	300
1911A	1,181,475	10.00	22.00	55.00	110	300
1912A	732,813	12.00	28.00	58.00	125	325

KM# 525 2 MARK

11.1110 g., 0.9000 Silver 0.3215 oz. ASW, 28 mm. **Ruler:** Wilhelm II **Subject:** 200 Years - Kingdom of Prussia **Obv:** Friedrich I, Wilhelm II left **Rev:** Crowned imperial eagle with shield on breast **Edge:** Reeded

Date	Mintage	F	VF	XF	Unc	BU
1901A	2,600,000	7.50	15.00	22.00	35.00	50.00
1901A Proof	—	Value: 125				

KM# 532 2 MARK

11.1110 g., 0.9000 Silver 0.3215 oz. ASW, 28 mm. **Ruler:** Wilhelm II **Subject:** 100 Years - Defeat of Napoleon **Obv:** Eagle with snake in talons, denomination below **Rev:** Figure on horseback surrounded by people **Edge:** Reeded

Date	Mintage	F	VF	XF	Unc	BU
1913A	1,500,000	7.50	15.00	22.00	40.00	50.00
1913A Proof	—	Value: 125				

KM# 533 2 MARK

11.1110 g., 0.9000 Silver 0.3215 oz. ASW, 28 mm. **Ruler:** Wilhelm II **Subject:** 25th Year of Reign **Obv:** Uniformed bust right **Rev:** Crowned imperial eagle with shield on breast **Edge:** Reeded

Date	Mintage	F	VF	XF	Unc	BU
1913A	1,500,000	7.50	15.00	22.00	40.00	50.00
1913A Proof	5,000	Value: 125				

KM# 527 3 MARK

16.6670 g., 0.9000 Silver 0.4823 oz. ASW, 33 mm. **Ruler:** Wilhelm II **Obv:** Head right **Rev:** Crowned imperial eagle with shield on breast **Edge Lettering:** GOTT MIT UNS

Date	Mintage	F	VF	XF	Unc	BU
1908A	2,858,666	7.00	14.00	24.00	90.00	135
1909A	6,343,745	7.00	14.00	24.00	90.00	135
1910A	5,590,624	7.00	14.00	24.00	90.00	135
1911A	3,241,770	7.00	14.00	24.00	90.00	135
1912A	4,626,330	7.00	14.00	24.00	85.00	135
(1908-1912)A Proof	—	Value: 250				

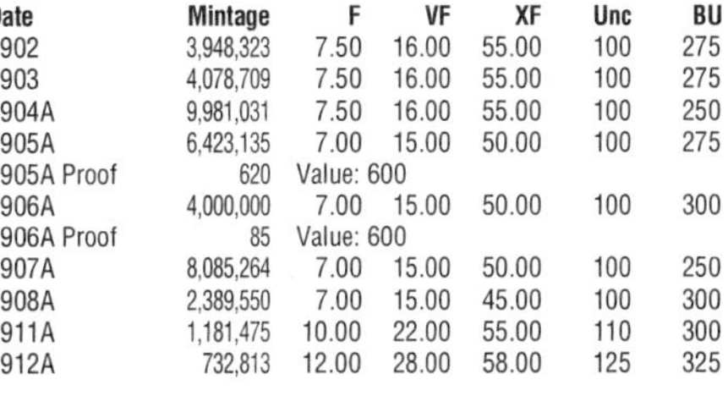

KM# 530 3 MARK

16.6670 g., 0.9000 Silver 0.4823 oz. ASW, 33 mm. **Ruler:** Wilhelm II **Subject:** Berlin University **Obv:** Friedrich Wilhelm III and Wilhelm II left divide dates **Rev:** Crowned imperial eagle with shield on breast **Edge Lettering:** GOTT MIT UNS

Date	Mintage	F	VF	XF	Unc	BU
1910A	200,000	22.00	55.00	85.00	125	225
1910A Proof	2,000	Value: 325				

KM# 531 3 MARK

16.6670 g., 0.9000 Silver 0.4823 oz. ASW, 33 mm. **Ruler:** Wilhelm II **Subject:** Breslau University **Obv:** Friedrich Wilhelm III, Wilhelm II left within circle **Rev:** Crowned imperial eagle with shield on breast **Edge Lettering:** GOTT MIT UNS

Date	Mintage	F	VF	XF	Unc	BU
1911A	400,000	18.00	45.00	70.00	85.00	200
1911A Proof	—	Value: 300				

KM# 534 3 MARK

16.6670 g., 0.9000 Silver 0.4823 oz. ASW, 33 mm. **Ruler:** Wilhelm II **Subject:** 100 Years - Defeat of Napoleon **Obv:** Eagle with snake in talons, denomination below **Rev:** Figure on horseback surrounded by people **Edge Lettering:** GOTT MIT UNS

Date	Mintage	F	VF	XF	Unc	BU
1913A	3,000,000	8.00	20.00	25.00	40.00	60.00
1913A Proof	—	Value: 150				

KM# 535 3 MARK

16.6670 g., 0.9000 Silver 0.4823 oz. ASW, 33 mm. **Ruler:** Wilhelm II **Subject:** 25th Year of Reign **Obv:** Uniformed bust right **Rev:** Crowned imperial eagle with shield on breast **Edge Lettering:** GOTT MIT UNS

Date	Mintage	F	VF	XF	Unc	BU
1913A	1,000,000	8.00	20.00	25.00	40.00	60.00
1913A Proof	6,000	Value: 130				

KM# 538 3 MARK
16.6670 g., 0.9000 Silver 0.4823 oz. ASW, 33 mm. **Ruler:** Wilhelm II **Obv:** Uniformed bust right **Rev:** Crowned imperial eagle with shield on breast **Edge Lettering:** GOTT MIT UNS

Date	Mintage	F	VF	XF	Unc	BU
1914A	2,022,000	10.00	20.00	25.00	70.00	200
1914A Proof	—	Value: 300				

KM# 539 3 MARK
16.6670 g., 0.9000 Silver 0.4823 oz. ASW, 33 mm. **Ruler:** Wilhelm II **Subject:** Centenary - Absorption of Mansfeld **Obv:** St. George slaying the dragon **Rev:** Crowned imperial eagle with shield on breast **Edge Lettering:** GOTT MIT UNS

Date	Mintage	F	VF	XF	Unc	BU
1915A	30,000	220	400	600	1,100	1,300
1915A Proof	—	Value: 1,500				

KM# 523 5 MARK
27.7770 g., 0.9000 Silver 0.8037 oz. ASW, 38 mm. **Ruler:** Wilhelm II **Obv:** Head right **Obv. Legend:** WILHELM II DEUTSCHER KAISER KONIG V. PREUSSEN **Rev:** Crowned imperial eagle, type III **Rev. Legend:** DEUTSCHES REICH date, FUNF MARK below **Edge Lettering:** GOTT MIT UNS

Date	Mintage	F	VF	XF	Unc	BU
1901A	667,990	9.00	20.00	80.00	450	1,100
1902A	1,950,840	8.00	17.50	80.00	300	1,000
1903A	3,855,795	8.00	17.50	80.00	300	900
1904A	2,060,410	8.00	17.50	95.00	300	850
1906A	230,963	20.00	40.00	130	1,000	1,750
1907A	2,103,338	8.00	16.00	65.00	200	600
1908A	2,230,579	8.00	16.00	60.00	250	600
(1891-1908)A Common date proof	—	Value: 1,500				

KM# 526 5 MARK
27.7770 g., 0.9000 Silver 0.8037 oz. ASW, 38 mm. **Ruler:** Wilhelm II **Subject:** 200 Years - Kingdom of Prussia **Obv:** Friedrich I, Wilhelm II left **Rev:** Crowned imperial eagle with shield on breast **Edge Lettering:** GOTT MIT UNS

Date	Mintage	F	VF	XF	Unc	BU
1901A	460,000	30.00	50.00	80.00	110	150
1901A Proof	—	Value: 275				

KM# 536 5 MARK
27.7770 g., 0.9000 Silver 0.8037 oz. ASW, 38 mm. **Ruler:** Wilhelm II **Obv:** Uniformed bust right **Rev:** Crowned imperial eagle, shield on breast

Date	Mintage	F	VF	XF	Unc	BU
1913A	1,961,712	14.00	28.00	40.00	150	250
1914A	1,587,179	13.00	24.00	35.00	150	250
(1913-1914)A Proof	—	Value: 1,000				

KM# 520 10 MARK
3.9820 g., 0.9000 Gold 0.1152 oz. AGW **Ruler:** Wilhelm II **Obv:** Head right **Obv. Legend:** WILHELM II DEUTSCHER KAISER KONIG V. PREUSSEN **Rev:** Crowned imperial eagle, type III **Rev. Legend:** DEUTSCHES REICH date, 10 MARK below **Edge:** ~ * ~

Date	Mintage	F	VF	XF	Unc	BU
1901A	701,930	BV	110	125	250	400
1901A Proof	—	Value: 1,300				
1902A	270,911	BV	135	185	275	425
1902A Proof	—	Value: 1,300				
1903A	1,684,979	BV	110	125	250	400
1903A Proof	—	Value: 1,300				
1904A	1,178,129	BV	110	125	250	400
1905A	1,072,513	BV	110	125	250	400
1905A Proof	117	Value: 1,300				
1906A	541,970	BV	115	135	265	425
1906A Proof	150	Value: 1,300				
1907A	812,698	BV	110	125	250	400
1907A Proof	—	Value: 1,300				
1909A	531,934	BV	115	135	265	425
1909A Proof	—	Value: 1,300				
1910A	803,111	BV	110	125	250	400
1911A	270,798	BV	130	180	275	400
1911A Proof	—	Value: 1,300				
1912A	542,372	BV	110	125	250	400
1912A Proof	—	Value: 1,300				

KM# 521 20 MARK
7.9650 g., 0.9000 Gold 0.2305 oz. AGW **Ruler:** Wilhelm II **Obv:** Head right **Obv. Legend:** WILHELM II DEUTSCHER KAISER KONIG V. PREUSSEN **Rev:** Crowned imperial eagle, type III **Rev. Legend:** DEUTSCHES REICH date, 20 MARK below

Date	Mintage	F	VF	XF	Unc	BU
1901A	5,188,340	—	BV	BV+10%	245	400
1901A Proof	—	Value: 1,400				
1902A	4,138,128	—	BV	BV+10%	245	400
1902A Proof	—	Value: 1,400				
1903A	2,870,073	—	BV	BV+10%	245	400
1903A Proof	—	Value: 1,400				
1904A	3,452,625	—	BV	BV+10%	245	400
1904A Proof	—	Value: 1,250				
1905A	4,220,793	—	BV	BV+10%	245	400
1905A Proof	287	Value: 1,250				
1905J	920,784	BV+5%	BV+10%	190	300	400
1906A	7,788,922	—	BV	BV+10%	250	400
1906A Proof	124	Value: 1,250				
1906J	101,808	BV+5%	290	380	600	400
1907A	2,576,286	—	BV	BV+10%	245	400
1907A Proof	—	Value: 1,250				
1908A	3,274,168	—	BV	BV+10%	245	400
1908A Proof	—	Value: 1,200				
1909A	5,212,836	—	BV	BV+10%	245	400
1909J	350,128	BV+5%	BV+10%	225	300	400
1909A Proof	—	Value: 1,200				
1909J Proof	—	Value: 1,750				
1910A	8,645,549	—	BV	BV+10%	245	400
1910J	753,217	—	BV	BV+10%	245	400
1911A	4,745,790	—	BV	BV+10%	245	400
1912A	5,569,398	—	BV	BV+10%	245	400
1912J	502,530	BV+3%	BV+5%	225	300	400
1913A	6,102,730	—	BV	160	245	400
1913A Proof	—	Value: 1,000				

KM# 537 20 MARK
7.9650 g., 0.9000 Gold 0.2305 oz. AGW **Ruler:** Wilhelm II **Obv:** Uniformed bust right **Rev:** Crowned imperial eagle with shield on breast

Date	Mintage	F	VF	XF	Unc	BU
1913A	—	BV	BV+5%	220	250	300
1913A Proof	—	Value: 1,500				
1914A	2,136,861	BV	BV+5%	220	250	300
1914A Proof	—	Value: 1,500				
1915A	1,268,055	—	1,100	1,400	2,000	2,500

REUSS-OBERGREIZ

The other branch of the division of 1635, Obergreiz went through a number of consolidations and further divisions. Upon the extinction of the Ruess-Untergreiz linein 1768, the latter passed to Reuss-Obergreiz and this line continued on into the 20th century, obtaining the rank of count back in 1673 and that of prince in 1778.

RULERS
Heinrich XXII, 1859-1902
Heinrich XXIV, 1902-1918

PRINCIPALITY

REFORM COINAGE

KM# 128 2 MARK
11.1110 g., 0.9000 Silver 0.3215 oz. ASW, 28 mm. **Ruler:** Heinrich XXII **Obv:** Head right **Obv. Legend:** HEINRICH XXII v. G. G. ALT. L. SOUV. FRUST REUSS **Rev:** Crowned imperial eagle with shield on breast **Rev. Legend:** DEUTSCHES REICH date, ZWEI MARK below **Edge:** Reeded

Date	Mintage	F	VF	XF	Unc	BU
1901A	10,000	125	225	375	700	1,000
1901A Proof	—	Value: 1,100				

KM# 130 3 MARK
16.6670 g., 0.9000 Silver 0.4823 oz. ASW, 33 mm. **Ruler:** Heinrich XXIV **Obv:** Head right **Rev:** Crowned imperial eagle with shield on breast

Date	Mintage	F	VF	XF	Unc	BU
1909A	10,000	140	285	450	800	1,200
1909A Proof	400	Value: 1,500				

SAXE-ALTENBURG

(Sachsen-Neu-Altenburg)

A new line was established at Altenburg when the Duke of Saxe-Hildburghausen exchanged Hildburghausen for Altenburg in 1826. This line lasted until the end of World War I, when the last duke was forced to abdicate.

RULERS
Ernst I, 1853-1908
Ernst II, 1908-1918

MINT MARK
A – Berlin Mint, 1886-1918

DUCHY

REFORM COINAGE

KM# 144 2 MARK
11.1110 g., 0.9000 Silver 0.3215 oz. ASW, 28 mm. **Ruler:** Ernst I **Subject:** Ernst 75th Birthday **Obv:** Head right **Rev:** Crowned imperial eagle with shield on breast **Edge:** Reeded

Date	Mintage	F	VF	XF	Unc	BU
1901A	50,000	120	250	450	750	1,000
1901A Proof	500	Value: 1,250				

KM# 145 5 MARK
27.7770 g., 0.9000 Silver 0.8037 oz. ASW, 38 mm. **Ruler:** Ernst I **Subject:** Ernst 75th Birthday **Obv:** Head right **Rev:** Crowned imperial eagle with shield on breast **Edge Lettering:** GOTT MIT UNS

Date	Mintage	F	VF	XF	Unc	BU
1901A	20,000	200	425	700	1,400	2,000
1901A Proof	500	Value: 2,250				

KM# 147 5 MARK
27.7770 g., 0.9000 Silver 0.8037 oz. ASW, 38 mm. **Ruler:** Ernst I **Subject:** Ernst's 50th Year of Reign **Obv:** Head right, date and sprays below **Rev:** Crowned imperial eagle with shield on breast **Edge Lettering:** GOTT MIT UNS

Date	Mintage	F	VF	XF	Unc	BU
1903A	20,000	100	200	325	500	700
1903A Proof	300	Value: 750				

SAXE-COBURG-GOTHA

(Sachsen-Coburg-Gotha)

Upon the extinction of the ducal line in Saxe-Gotha-Altenburg in 1826, Gotha was assigned to Saxe-Coburg-Saalfeld and Saxe-Meiningen received Saalfeld. The resulting duchy became called Saxe-Coburg-Gotha. Albert, the son of Ernst I and younger brother of Ernst II, married Queen Victoria of Great Britain and the British royal dynastic name was that of Saxe-Coburg-Gotha. Their son, Alfred was made the Duke of Edinburgh and succeeded his uncle, Ernst II, as Duke of Saxe-Coburg-Gotha. Alfred's older brother, Eduard Albert, followed their mother as King Edward VII (1901-1910). The last duke of Saxe-Coburg-Gotha was Alfred's nephew, Karl Eduard, forced to abdicate in 1918 as a result of World War I, which was fought in part against his cousin, King George V.

RULER
Karl Eduard, 1900-1918

MINT MARK
A – Berlin Mint, 1886-1911

DUCHY

REFORM COINAGE

KM# 152 2 MARK
11.1110 g., 0.9000 Silver 0.3215 oz. ASW, 28 mm. **Ruler:** Karl Eduard **Obv:** Head right **Edge:** Reeded

Date	Mintage	F	VF	XF	Unc	BU
1905A	10,000	135	285	600	1,100	1,300
1905A Proof	2,000	Value: 1,400				
1911A Proof	100	Value: 14,000				

KM# 153 5 MARK
27.7770 g., 0.9000 Silver 0.8037 oz. ASW, 38 mm. **Ruler:** Karl Eduard **Obv:** Head right **Rev:** Crowned imperial eagle with shield on breast **Edge Lettering:** GOTT MIT UNS

Date	Mintage	F	VF	XF	Unc	BU
1907A	10,000	325	750	1,150	1,750	2,200
1907A Proof	—	Value: 2,750				

KM# 154 10 MARK
3.9820 g., 0.9000 Gold 0.1152 oz. AGW **Ruler:** Karl Eduard **Obv:** Head right **Rev:** Crowned imperial eagle with shield on breast **Edge:** ~ * ~

Date	Mintage	F	VF	XF	Unc	BU
1905A	10,000	650	1,200	1,800	2,250	3,250
1905A Proof	489	Value: 4,000				

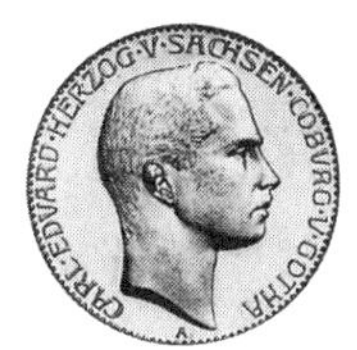

KM# 155 20 MARK
7.9650 g., 0.9000 Gold 0.2305 oz. AGW **Ruler:** Karl Eduard **Obv:** Head, right **Rev:** Crowned imperial eagle with shield on breast, type I **Edge Lettering:** GOTT MIT UNS

Date	Mintage	F	VF	XF	Unc	BU
1905A	10,000	700	1,350	2,000	2,800	3,500
1905A Proof	484	Value: 4,500				

SAXE-MEININGEN

(Sachsen-Meiningen)

The duchy of Saxe-Meiningen was located in Thuringia (Thüringen), sandwiched between Saxe-Weimar-Eisenach on the west and north and the enclave of Schmalkalden belonging to Hesse-Cassel on the east. It was founded upon the division of the Ernestine line in Saxe-Gotha in 1680. In 1735, due to an exchange of some territory, the duchy became known as Saxe-Coburg-Meiningen. In 1826, Saxe-Coburg-Gotha assigned Saalfeld to Saxe-Meiningen. The duchy came under the strong influence of Prussia from 1866, when Bernhard II was forced to abdicate because of his support of Austria. The last duke was forced to give up his sovereign power at the end of World War I in 1918.

RULERS
Georg II, 1866-1914
Bernhard III, 1914-1918

DUCHY

REFORM COINAGE

KM# 196 2 MARK
11.1110 g., 0.9000 Silver 0.3215 oz. ASW, 28 mm. **Ruler:** Georg II **Subject:** Duke's 75th Birthday **Obv:** Head right **Rev:** Crowned imperial eagle with shield on breast **Edge:** Reeded

Date	Mintage	F	VF	XF	Unc	BU
1901D	20,000	100	250	400	750	1,000
1901D Proof	—	Value: 1,250				

KM# 198 2 MARK
11.1110 g., 0.9000 Silver 0.3215 oz. ASW, 28 mm. **Ruler:** Georg II **Obv:** Head left, long beard **Rev:** Crowned imperial eagle with shield on breast **Edge:** Reeded

Date	Mintage	F	VF	XF	Unc	BU
1902D	20,000	250	800	1,100	2,200	3,000

KM# 199 2 MARK
11.1110 g., 0.9000 Silver 0.3215 oz. ASW, 28 mm. **Ruler:** Georg II **Obv:** Head left, short beard **Rev:** Crowned imperial eagle with shield on breast

Date	Mintage	F	VF	XF	Unc	BU
1902D	Inc. above	100	200	350	750	1,250
1913D	5,000	150	275	600	1,250	1,750
1913D Proof	—	Value: 1,600				

KM# 206 2 MARK
11.1110 g., 0.9000 Silver 0.3215 oz. ASW, 28 mm. **Ruler:** Bernhard III **Subject:** Death of Georg II **Obv:** Head left, long beard **Rev:** Crowned imperial eagle with shield on breast **Edge:** Reeded

Date	Mintage	F	VF	XF	Unc	BU
1915	30,000	35.00	75.00	150	220	325

KM# 203 3 MARK
16.6670 g., 0.9000 Silver 0.4823 oz. ASW, 33 mm. **Ruler:** Georg II **Obv:** Head left, long beard **Rev:** Crowned imperial eagle with shield on breast **Edge Lettering:** GOTT MIT UNS

Date	Mintage	F	VF	XF	Unc	BU
1908D	35,000	35.00	110	165	250	350
1908D Proof	—	Value: 500				
1913D	20,000	35.00	110	165	300	400
1913D Proof	—	Value: 550				

KM# 207 3 MARK

16.6670 g., 0.9000 Silver 0.4823 oz. ASW, 33 mm. **Ruler:** Bernhard III **Subject:** Death of Georg II **Obv:** Head left, long beard **Rev:** Crowned imperial eagle with shield on breast **Edge Lettering:** GOTT MIT UNS

Date	Mintage	F	VF	XF	Unc	BU
1915	30,000	30.00	70.00	150	220	325
1915 Proof	—	Value: 400				

KM# 197 5 MARK

27.7770 g., 0.9000 Silver 0.8037 oz. ASW, 38 mm. **Ruler:** Georg II **Subject:** Duke's 75th Birthday **Obv:** Head right, long beard **Rev:** Crowned imperial eagle with shield on breast **Edge Lettering:** GOTT MIT UNS

Date	Mintage	F	VF	XF	Unc	BU
1901D	20,000	85.00	325	500	1,000	1,600
1901D Proof	—	Value: 2,000				

KM# 200 5 MARK

27.7770 g., 0.9000 Silver 0.8037 oz. ASW, 38 mm. **Ruler:** Georg II **Obv:** Long beard **Rev:** Crowned imperial eagle with shield on breast **Edge Lettering:** GOTT MIT UNS

Date	Mintage	F	VF	XF	Unc	BU
1902D	20,000	60.00	200	350	1,000	1,250

KM# 201 5 MARK

27.7770 g., 0.9000 Silver 0.8037 oz. ASW, 38 mm. **Ruler:** Georg II **Obv:** Head left, long beard **Rev:** Crowned imperial eagle with shield on breast

Date	Mintage	F	VF	XF	Unc	BU
1902D	Inc. above	60.00	175	450	1,200	1,800
1908D	60,000	50.00	160	275	850	1,350

KM# 202 10 MARK

3.9820 g., 0.9000 Gold 0.1152 oz. AGW **Ruler:** Georg II **Obv:** Head left, long beard **Rev:** Crowned imperial eagle with shield on breast **Edge:** ~ * ~

Date	Mintage	F	VF	XF	Unc	BU
1902D	2,000	900	2,000	3,000	4,000	5,500
1902D Proof	—	Value: 6,000				

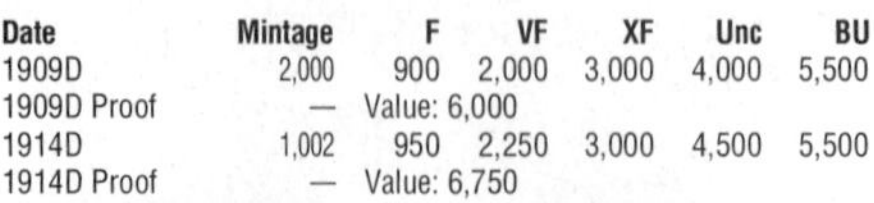

Date	Mintage	F	VF	XF	Unc	BU
1909D	2,000	900	2,000	3,000	4,000	5,500
1909D Proof	—	Value: 6,000				
1914D	1,002	950	2,250	3,000	4,500	5,500
1914D Proof	—	Value: 6,750				

KM# 195 20 MARK

7.9650 g., 0.9000 Gold 0.2305 oz. AGW **Ruler:** Georg II **Obv:** Head left, short beard **Obv. Legend:** GEORG HERZOG VON SACHSEN MEININGEN **Rev:** Crowned imperial eagle, type III **Rev. Legend:** DEUTSCHES REICH date, 20 MARK below

Date	Mintage	F	VF	XF	Unc	BU
1905D	1,000	3,000	5,000	7,500	12,500	15,000
1905D Proof	—	Value: 15,000				

KM# 205 20 MARK

7.9650 g., 0.9000 Gold 0.2305 oz. AGW **Ruler:** Georg II **Obv:** Head left, long beard **Rev:** Crowned imperial eagle with shield on breast **Edge Lettering:** GOTT MIT UNS

Date	Mintage	F	VF	XF	Unc	BU
1910D	1,004	1,500	3,000	4,750	6,000	7,500
1910D Proof	—	Value: 8,500				
1914D	1,000	1,500	3,000	4,750	6,000	7,500
1914D Proof	—	Value: 8,500				

SAXE-WEIMAR-EISENACH

(Sachsen-Weimar-Eisenach)

When the death of the duke of Saxe-Eisenach in 1741 heralded the extinction of that line, its possessions reverted to Saxe-Weimar, which henceforth was known as Saxe-Weimar-Eisenach. Because of the strong role played by the duke during the Napoleonic Wars, Saxe-Weimar-Eisenach was raised to the rank of a grand duchy in 1814 and granted the territory of Neustadt, taken from Saxony. The last grand duke abdicated at the end of World War I.

RULERS

Karl Alexander, 1853-1901
Wilhelm Ernst, 1901-1918

MINT MARK

A – Berlin Mint, 1840-1915

GRAND DUCHY

REFORM COINAGE

Y# 170 2 MARK

11.1110 g., 0.9000 Silver 0.3215 oz. ASW, 28 mm. **Ruler:** Wilhelm Ernst **Obv:** Head left **Rev:** Crowned imperial eagle with shield on breast **Edge:** Reeded

Date	Mintage	F	VF	XF	Unc	BU
1901A	100,000	125	300	450	850	1,300
1901A Proof	—	Value: 1,500				

Y# 172 2 MARK

11.1110 g., 0.9000 Silver 0.3215 oz. ASW, 28 mm. **Ruler:** Wilhelm Ernst **Subject:** Grand Duke's First Marriage - Caroline **Obv:** Jugate heads left **Rev:** Crowned imperial eagle with shield on breast **Edge:** Reeded

Date	Mintage	F	VF	XF	Unc	BU
1903A	40,000	35.00	60.00	100	160	225
1903A Proof	Est. 1,000	Value: 250				

Y# 174 2 MARK

11.1110 g., 0.9000 Silver 0.3215 oz. ASW, 28 mm. **Ruler:** Wilhelm Ernst **Subject:** Jena University 350th Anniversary **Obv:** Johan Friedrich I the Magnanimous 3/4 right **Rev:** Crowned imperial eagle with shield on breast **Edge:** Reeded

Date	Mintage	F	VF	XF	Unc	BU
1908	50,000	25.00	55.00	110	135	200

Y# 176 3 MARK

16.6670 g., 0.9000 Silver 0.4823 oz. ASW, 33 mm. **Ruler:** Wilhelm Ernst **Subject:** Grand Duke's Second Marriage - Feodora **Obv:** Jugate heads left **Rev:** Crowned imperial eagle with shield on breast **Edge Lettering:** GOTT MIT UNS

Date	Mintage	F	VF	XF	Unc	BU
1910	133,000	20.00	40.00	85.00	120	160
1910A Proof	—	Value: 250				

Y# 177 3 MARK

16.6670 g., 0.9000 Silver 0.4823 oz. ASW, 33 mm. **Ruler:** Wilhelm Ernst **Subject:** Centenary of Grand Duchy **Obv:** Wilhelm Ernst and Carl August right **Rev:** Crowned imperial eagle with shield on breast **Edge Lettering:** GOTT MIT UNS

Date	Mintage	F	VF	XF	Unc	BU
1915A	50,000	25.00	50.00	140	150	250
1915A Proof	200	Value: 400				

Y# 173 5 MARK

27.7770 g., 0.9000 Silver 0.8037 oz. ASW, 38 mm. **Ruler:** Wilhelm Ernst **Subject:** Grand Duke's First Marriage - Caroline **Obv:** Jugate heads left **Rev:** Crowned imperial eagle with shield on breast **Edge Lettering:** GOTT MIT UNS

Date	Mintage	F	VF	XF	Unc	BU
1903A	24,000	60.00	125	225	375	500
1903A Proof	Est. 1,000	Value: 625				

Y# 175 5 MARK

27.7770 g., 0.9000 Silver 0.8037 oz. ASW, 38 mm. **Ruler:** Wilhelm Ernst **Subject:** Jena University 350th Anniversary **Obv:** Johan Friedrich I the Magnanimous 3/4 right **Rev:** Crowned imperial eagle with shield on breast **Edge Lettering:** GOTT MIT UNS

Date	Mintage	F	VF	XF	Unc	BU
1908	40,000	60.00	110	200	300	375
1908 Proof	—	Value: 750				

Y# 171 20 MARK

7.9650 g., 0.9000 Gold 0.2305 oz. AGW **Ruler:** Wilhelm Ernst **Subject:** Golden Wedding of Carl Alexander **Obv:** Head left **Rev:** Crowned imperial eagle with shield on breast **Edge Lettering:** GOTT MIT UNS

Date	Mintage	F	VF	XF	Unc	BU
1901A	5,000	1,100	2,200	3,000	4,000	5,000
1901A Proof	—	Value: 6,500				

SAXONY

Saxony, located in southeast Germany was founded in 850. The first coinage was struck c. 990. It was divided into two lines in 1464. The electoral right was obtained by the elder line in 1547. During the time of the Reformation, Saxony was one of the more powerful states in central Europe. It became a kingdom in 1806. At the Congress of Vienna in 1815, they were forced to cede half its territories to Prussia.

RULERS

Albert, 1873-1902
Georg, 1902-1904
Friedrich August III, 1904-1918

MINT MARK

L - Leipzig

KINGDOM

REFORM COINAGE

KM# 1245 2 MARK

11.1110 g., 0.9000 Silver 0.3215 oz. ASW **Ruler:** Albert **Edge:** Reeded **Note:** Similar to KM#185.

Date	Mintage	F	VF	XF	Unc	BU
1901E	439,724	12.50	55.00	110	300	1,000
1902E	542,762	10.00	55.00	110	275	800
1902E Proof	—	Value: 1,750				

KM# 1255 2 MARK

11.1110 g., 0.9000 Silver 0.3215 oz. ASW, 28 mm. **Ruler:** Georg **Subject:** Death of Albert **Obv:** Head right **Rev:** Crowned imperial eagle with shield on breast **Edge:** Reeded

Date	Mintage	F	VF	XF	Unc	BU
1902E	167,625	15.00	40.00	65.00	125	175
1902E Proof	250	Value: 225				

KM# 1257 2 MARK

11.1110 g., 0.9000 Silver 0.3215 oz. ASW, 28 mm. **Ruler:** Georg **Obv:** Head right **Rev:** Crowned imperial eagle with shield on breast

Date	Mintage	F	VF	XF	Unc	BU
1903E	745,551	30.00	60.00	140	250	550
1903E Proof	50	Value: 800				
1904E	1,265,533	17.50	50.00	100	200	500
1904E Proof	—	Value: 750				

KM# 1261 2 MARK

11.1110 g., 0.9000 Silver 0.3215 oz. ASW, 28 mm. **Ruler:** Friedrich August III **Subject:** Death of Georg **Obv:** Head right **Rev:** Crowned imperial eagle with shield on breast **Edge:** Reeded

Date	Mintage	F	VF	XF	Unc	BU
1904E	150,000	15.00	40.00	90.00	120	160
1904E Proof	55	Value: 250				

KM# 1263 2 MARK

11.1110 g., 0.9000 Silver 0.3215 oz. ASW, 28 mm. **Ruler:** Friedrich August III **Obv:** Head right **Rev:** Crowned imperial eagle with shield on breast **Edge:** Reeded

Date	Mintage	F	VF	XF	Unc	BU
1905E	558,951	20.00	45.00	75.00	160	275
1905E Proof	100	Value: 500				
1906E	558,750	20.00	45.00	75.00	160	275
1907E	1,112,519	20.00	45.00	70.00	155	275
1908E	335,689	20.00	45.00	70.00	155	275
1911E	186,250	20.00	45.00	75.00	200	300
1912E	167,625	20.00	45.00	75.00	200	300
1914E	298,000	20.00	45.00	70.00	125	275
(1905-1914)E Proof	—	Value: 500				

KM# 1268 2 MARK

11.1110 g., 0.9000 Silver 0.3215 oz. ASW, 28 mm. **Ruler:** Friedrich August III **Subject:** 500th Anniversary - Leipzig University **Obv:** Crown Prince Friedrich the Pugnacious and Friedrich August III left **Rev:** Crowned imperial eagle with shield on breast **Edge:** Reeded

Date	Mintage	F	VF	XF	Unc	BU
1909	125,000	15.00	35.00	65.00	100	130
1909 Proof	300	Value: 225				

KM# 1267 3 MARK

16.6670 g., 0.9000 Silver 0.4823 oz. ASW, 33 mm. **Ruler:** Friedrich August III **Obv:** Head right **Rev:** Crowned imperial eagle with shield on breast **Edge Lettering:** GOTT MIT UNS

Date	Mintage	F	VF	XF	Unc	BU
1908E	276,073	10.00	22.00	40.00	100	135
1909E	1,196,719	10.00	20.00	35.00	80.00	135
1910E	745,000	10.00	20.00	35.00	90.00	135
1911E	581,250	10.00	20.00	35.00	90.00	135
1912E	378,750	10.00	20.00	35.00	90.00	135
1913E	306,500	10.00	20.00	35.00	90.00	135
(1908-1913)E Proof	—	Value: 325				

KM# 1275 3 MARK

16.6670 g., 0.9000 Silver 0.4823 oz. ASW, 33 mm. **Ruler:** Friedrich August III **Subject:** Battle of Leipzig Centennial **Obv:** Monument divides date above **Rev:** Crowned imperial eagle with shield on breast **Edge Lettering:** GOTT MIT UNS

Date	Mintage	F	VF	XF	Unc	BU
1913E	999,999	12.00	18.00	28.00	40.00	55.00
1913E Proof	17,000	Value: 200				

KM# 1276 3 MARK

16.6670 g., 0.9000 Silver 0.4823 oz. ASW, 33 mm. **Ruler:** Friedrich August III **Subject:** Jubilee of Reformation **Obv:** Friederich the Wise right, Protector of Martin Luther **Rev:** Crowned imperial eagle with shield on breast **Edge Lettering:** GOTT MIT UNS

Date	Mintage	F	VF	XF	Unc	BU
1917E Proof	100	Value: 75,000				

KM# 1246 5 MARK

27.7770 g., 0.9000 Silver 0.8037 oz. ASW, 38 mm. **Ruler:** Albert **Obv:** Head right **Obv. Legend:** ALBERT KOENIG VON SACHSEN **Rev:** Crowned imperial eagle **Rev. Legend:** DEUTSCHES REICH date, FUNF MARK below **Edge Lettering:** GOTT MIT UNS

Date	Mintage	F	VF	XF	Unc	BU
1901E	156,450	25.00	55.00	300	750	1,500
1901E Proof	—	Value: 2,750				
1902E	168,200	20.00	45.00	275	650	1,200
1902E Proof	—	Value: 2,750				

KM# 1256 5 MARK
27.7770 g., 0.9000 Silver 0.8037 oz. ASW, 38 mm. **Ruler:** Georg **Subject:** Death of Albert **Obv:** Head right **Rev:** Crowned imperial eagle with shield on breast **Edge Lettering:** GOTT MIT UNS

Date	Mintage	F	VF	XF	Unc	BU
1902E	100,000	30.00	65.00	125	300	325
1902E Proof	250	Value: 600				

KM# 1258 5 MARK
27.7770 g., 0.9000 Silver 0.8037 oz. ASW, 38 mm. **Ruler:** Georg **Obv:** Head right **Rev:** Crowned imperial eagle with shield on breast **Edge Lettering:** GOTT MIT UNS

Date	Mintage	F	VF	XF	Unc	BU
1903E	536,298	25.00	50.00	175	550	1,000
1903E Proof	50	Value: 1,500				
1904E	290,643	30.00	60.00	175	650	1,000
1904E Proof	—	Value: 1,500				

KM# 1262 5 MARK
27.7770 g., 0.9000 Silver 0.8037 oz. ASW, 38 mm. **Ruler:** Friedrich August III **Subject:** Death of Georg **Obv:** Head right **Rev:** Crowned imperial eagle with shield on breast **Edge Lettering:** GOTT MIT UNS

Date	Mintage	F	VF	XF	Unc	BU
1904E	37,200	45.00	150	225	350	450
1904E Proof	70	Value: 800				

KM# 1266 5 MARK
27.7770 g., 0.9000 Silver 0.8037 oz. ASW, 38 mm. **Ruler:** Friedrich August III **Obv:** Head right **Rev:** Crowned imperial eagle with shield on breast

Date	Mintage	F	VF	XF	Unc	BU
1907E	398,043	20.00	40.00	90.00	300	500
1908E	317,301	20.00	40.00	85.00	250	500
1914E	298,000	17.50	35.00	80.00	200	325
1914E Proof	—	Value: 1,500				

KM# 1269 5 MARK
27.7770 g., 0.9000 Silver 0.8037 oz. ASW, 38 mm. **Ruler:** Friedrich August III **Subject:** 500th Anniversary - Leipzig University **Obv:** Crown Prince Friedrich the Pugracious and Friederich August III left **Rev:** Crowned imperial eagle with shield on breast **Edge Lettering:** GOTT MIT UNS

Date	Mintage	F	VF	XF	Unc	BU
1909	50,000	50.00	100	190	275	350
1909 Proof	300	Value: 525				

KM# 1247 10 MARK
3.9820 g., 0.9000 Gold 0.1152 oz. AGW **Ruler:** Albert **Rev:** Crowned imperial eagle, type III **Edge:** ~ * ~

Date	Mintage	F	VF	XF	Unc	BU
1901E	74,767	115	175	250	500	650
1902E	37,413	115	175	250	500	700
1902E Proof	—	Value: 2,000				

KM# 1259 10 MARK
3.9820 g., 0.9000 Gold 0.1152 oz. AGW **Ruler:** Georg **Obv:** Head right **Rev:** Crowned imperial eagle with shield on breast **Edge:** ~ * ~

Date	Mintage	F	VF	XF	Unc	BU
1903E	283,822	120	210	350	600	1,000
1903E Proof	100	Value: 2,250				
1904E	149,260	120	210	350	600	1,000
1904E Proof	—	Value: 2,000				

KM# 1264 10 MARK
3.9820 g., 0.9000 Gold 0.1152 oz. AGW **Ruler:** Friedrich August III **Obv:** Head right **Rev:** Crowned imperial eagle with shield on breast **Edge:** ~ * ~

Date	Mintage	F	VF	XF	Unc	BU
1905E	111,994	125	250	325	500	750
1905E Proof	100	Value: 2,000				
1906E	75,093	125	250	325	500	750
1906E Proof	—	Value: 2,000				
1907E	112,000	125	250	325	500	750
1907E Proof	111,878	Value: 2,000				
1909E	112,070	125	250	325	500	750
1910E	75,185	125	250	325	500	750
1910E Proof	—	Value: 2,000				
1911E	37,622	125	250	325	500	750
1912E	75,252	125	250	325	500	750
1912E Proof	—	Value: 2,250				

KM# 1260 20 MARK
7.9650 g., 0.9000 Gold 0.2305 oz. AGW **Ruler:** Georg **Obv:** Head right **Rev:** Crowned imperial eagle with shield on breast, type III **Edge Lettering:** GOTT MIT UNS

Date	Mintage	F	VF	XF	Unc	BU
1903E	250,000	BV	215	320	450	550
1903E Proof	—	Value: 2,500				

KM# 1265 20 MARK
7.9650 g., 0.9000 Gold 0.2305 oz. AGW **Ruler:** Friedrich August III **Obv:** Head right **Rev:** Crowned imperial eagle with shield on breast

Date	Mintage	F	VF	XF	Unc	BU
1905E	500,173	BV	220	400	500	600
1905E Proof	86	Value: 1,500				
1913E	121,002	BV	225	500	600	750
1914E	325,246	BV	220	375	450	550
1914E Proof	—	Value: 1,750				

SCHAUMBURG-LIPPE

The tiny countship of Schaumburg-Lippe, with an area of only 131 square miles (218 square kilometers) in northwest Germany, was surrounded by the larger states of Brunswick-Lüneburg-Calenberg, an enclave of Hesse-Cassel, and the bishopric of Minden (part of Brandenburg-Prussia from 1648). It was founded in 1640 when Schaumburg-Gehmen was divided between Hesse-Cassel and Lippe-Alverdissen. The two became known as Schaumburg-Hessen and Schaumburg-Lippe. Philipp II, the youngest son of Count Simon VI of Lippe came into the possession of Alverdissen and Lipperode upon his father's death in 1613. In 1640, he also inherited half of Schaumburg-Bückeburg, becoming the first Count of Schaumburg-Lippe. A separate line of Schaumburg-Alverdissen was established in 1681 and, upon the extinction of the elder line in 1777, the lands and titles devolved onto Alverdissen, becoming the ruling line in the countship. In 1806, the count was raised to the rank of prince and Schaumburg-Lippe was incorporated into the Rhine Confederation. It became a part of the German Confederation in 1815 and joined the North German Confederation in 1866. The principality became a member state in the German Empire in 1871. The last sovereign prince resigned as a result of World War I.

RULERS
Albrecht Georg, 1893-1911
Adolf II Bernhard, 1911-1918

MINT MARK
A - Berlin mint, 1858-1911

PRINCIPALITY

REFORM COINAGE

Y# 203 2 MARK
11.1110 g., 0.9000 Silver 0.3215 oz. ASW, 28 mm. **Ruler:** Albrecht Georg **Subject:** Death of Prince Georg **Obv:** Head left **Obv. Legend:** GEORG FURST ZU SCHAUMBURG-LIPPE **Rev:** Crowned imperial eagle with shield on breast **Rev. Legend:** DEUTSCHES REICH date, ZWEI MARK below **Edge:** Reeded

Date	Mintage	F	VF	XF	Unc	BU
1904A	5,000	200	400	500	850	950
1904A Proof	200	Value: 1,750				

Y# 206 3 MARK
16.6670 g., 0.9000 Silver 0.4823 oz. ASW, 33 mm. **Ruler:** Albrecht Georg **Subject:** Death of Prince Georg **Obv:** Head left **Rev:** Crowned imperial eagle with shield on breast **Edge Lettering:** GOTT MIT UNS

Date	Mintage	F	VF	XF	Unc	BU
1911A	50,000	30.00	65.00	100	250	300
1911A Proof	—	Value: 325				

Y# 204 5 MARK
27.7770 g., 0.9000 Silver 0.8037 oz. ASW, 38 mm. **Ruler:** Albrecht Georg **Subject:** Death of Prince Georg **Obv:** Head left **Obv. Legend:** GEORG FURST ZU SCHAUMBURG-LIPPE **Rev:** Crowned imperial eagle with shield on breast **Rev. Legend:** DEUTSCHES REICH date, FUNF MARK below **Edge Lettering:** GOTT MIT UNS

Date	Mintage	F	VF	XF	Unc	BU
1904A	3,000	350	775	1,250	2,400	3,000
1904A Proof	200	Value: 3,500				

Y# 205 20 MARK
7.9650 g., 0.9000 Gold 0.2305 oz. AGW **Ruler:** Albrecht Georg **Subject:** Death of Prince Georg **Obv:** Head left **Obv. Legend:** GEORG FURST ZU SCHAUMBURG-LIPPE **Rev:** Crowned imperial eagle with shield on breast **Rev. Legend:** DEUTSCHES REICH date, 20 MARK below **Edge Lettering:** GOTT MIT UNS

Date	Mintage	F	VF	XF	Unc	BU
1904A	5,500	750	1,600	2,400	3,250	4,000
1904A Proof	132	Value: 5,000				

SCHWARZBURG-SONDERSHAUSEN

As the elder main line of Schwarzburg established in 1552, the counts of Schwarzburg-Sondershausen controlled their scattered territories from the castle of Sondershausen in northern Thuringia (Thüringen), 10 miles (16 kilometers) southeast of Nordhausen. Count Christian Wilhelm I was raised to the rank of prince in 1697 and the line descended from him until it finally became extinct in 1909. All titles and territories then passed to Schwarzburg-Rudolstadt.

RULER
Karl Günther, 1880-1909

Arms: See under Schwarzburg

CROSS REFERENCES:

F = Ernst Fischer, *Die Münzen des Hauses Schwarzburg,* **Heidelberg, 1904.**

R = Ernst Helmuth von Bethe, *Schwarzburger Münzen und Medaillen: Sammlung des Schlossmuseums in Rudolstadt,* **Halle (Saale), 1903.**

MINT MARK
A - Berlin mint, 1846-1909

PRINCIPALITY

REFORM COINAGE

KM# 152 2 MARK
11.1110 g., 0.9000 Silver 0.3215 oz. ASW, 28 mm. **Ruler:** Karl Günther **Subject:** 25th Anniversary of Reign **Obv:** Head right, leafy spray below **Rev:** Crowned German imperial eagle with shield on breast **Edge:** Reeded **Note:** Thick rim. Prev. Y#211.

Date	Mintage	F	VF	XF	Unc	BU
1905	13,000	45.00	90.00	160	250	325
1905 Proof	5,000	Value: 300				

KM# 153 2 MARK
11.1110 g., 0.9000 Silver 0.3215 oz. ASW, 28 mm. **Ruler:** Karl Günther **Subject:** 25th Anniversary of Reign **Obv:** Head right, leafy spray below **Rev:** Crowned German imperial eagle with shield on breast **Note:** Thin rim. Previous Y#211a.

Date	Mintage	F	VF	XF	Unc	BU
1905	62,000	25.00	50.00	95.00	150	225
1905 Proof	5,000	Value: 300				

KM# 154 3 MARK
16.6670 g., 0.9000 Silver 0.4823 oz. ASW, 33 mm. **Ruler:** Karl Günther **Subject:** Death of Karl Gunther **Obv:** Head right **Rev:** Crowned German imperial eagle with shield on breast **Edge Lettering:** GOTT MIT UNS **Note:** Previous Y#212.

Date	Mintage	F	VF	XF	Unc	BU
1909A	70,000	30.00	60.00	100	175	300
1909A Proof	200	Value: 450				

WALDECK

The former Countship of Waldeck was located in the western part of the German Empire, bordered by the Landgraviate of Hesse-Cassel on the east and south, the Duchy of Westphalia on the west and the Bishopric of Paderborn on the north. Arolsen was the seat of the counts and they traced their line of descent from a branch of the counts of Schwalenberg beginning in the early 11th century. Waldeck underwent several divisions over the centuries, the first such significant occurrence having taken place in 1474 with the establishment of Waldeck-Wildungen and Waldeck-Eisenberg. The latter was further divided into Waldeck-Eisenberg and Waldeck-Neu-Landau in 1539, but the former inherited Wildungen when the elder branch of the family became extinct in 1598. The line at Neu-Landau failed after two generations and reverted to Eisenberg the previous year (1597). A new line at Wildungen was established from Eisenberg in 1598 as well, but this, too, fell extinct in 1692, only ten years after the count having been raised to the rank of prince.

Waldeck-Eisenberg had received the Countship of Pyrmont in 1625 and became known as Waldeck-Pyrmont (see) upon the permanent unification of the two countships in 1668.

WALDECK-PYRMONT

The Count of Waldeck-Eisenberg inherited the Countship of Pyrmont, located between Lippe and Hannover, in 1625, thus creating an entity which encompassed about 672 square miles (1120 square kilometers). Waldeck and Pyrmont were permanently united in 1668, thus continuing the Eisenberg line as Waldeck-Pyrmont from that date. The count was raised to the rank of prince in 1712 and the unification of the two territories was confirmed in 1812. Waldeck-Pyrmont joined the German Confederation in 1815 and the North German Confederation in 1867. The prince renounced his sovereignty on 1 October of that year and Waldeck-Pyrmont was incorporated into Prussia. However, coinage was struck into the early 20th century for Waldeck-Pyrmont as a member of the German Empire. The hereditary territorial titles were lost along with the war in 1918. Some coins were struck for issue in Pyrmont only in the 18th through 20th centuries and those are listed separately under that name.

RULER
Friedrich, 1893-1918 (d.1946)

MINT OFFICIALS
AW - Albert Welle, mintmaster in Arolsen 1827-1840
FW, F*w, W, .W. – Friedrich Welle

MINT MARKS
A - Berlin mint, 1842-1903
B - Hannover mint, 1867

PRINCIPALITY

REFORM COINAGE

Y# 213 5 MARK
27.7770 g., 0.9000 Silver 0.8037 oz. ASW, 38 mm. **Ruler:** Friedrich **Obv:** Head left **Rev:** Crowned imperial eagle with shield on breast **Edge Lettering:** GOTT MIT UNS

Date	Mintage	F	VF	XF	Unc	BU
1903A	2,000	—	3,000	4,000	5,000	7,500
1903A Proof	300	Value: 8,000				

Y# 214 20 MARK
7.9650 g., 0.9000 Gold 0.2305 oz. AGW **Ruler:** Friedrich **Obv:** Head left **Rev:** Crowned imperial eagle with shield on breast **Edge Lettering:** GOTT MIT UNS

Date	Mintage	F	VF	XF	Unc	BU
1903A	2,000	2,400	4,000	6,500	110,000	13,000
1903A Proof	150	Value: 14,000				

WURTTEMBERG

Located in South Germany, between Baden and Bavaria, Württemberg takes its name from the ancestral castle of the ruling dynasty. The early countship was located in the old duchy of Swabia, most of which was given to Count Ulrich II (1265-79) in 1268 by Conradin von Hohenstaufen. Ulrich's son, Eberhard II (1279-1325) moved the seat of his rule to Stuttgart. Württemberg obtained the mint right in 1374 and joined the Swabian monetary union two years later. The countship was divided into the lines of Württemberg-Urach and Württemberg-Stuttgart in 1441 and the elder Urach branch was raised to the rank of duke in 1495. It became extinct in the following year and the younger line in Württemberg-Stuttgart inherited the lands and ducal title. A cadet line of the family had been established in Mömpelgard in 1473 and, when the Württemberg-Stuttgart line fell extinct in 1593, the primacy of the dynasty fell to Württemberg-Mömpelgard. The latter took the Stuttgart title and spun off several cadet branches in Neustadt, Neuenburg and Weiltingen-Brenz. Meanwhile, the duke in Stuttgart succumbed to the French advances under Napoleon. Land west of the Rhine was exchanged with France for territories in and around Reutlingen, Heilbronn and seven other towns in 1802. More territories were added in Swabia at the expense of Austria in 1805. Napoleon elevated the duke to the status of elector in 1803 and then to king in 1806. Even more land was given to Württemberg that year, doubling the kingdom's size, and it joined the Confederation of the Rhine. At the close of the Napoleonic Wars (1792-1815), Württemberg joined the German Confederation, but sided with Austria in its war with Prussia in 1866. It sided with Prussia against France in 1870 and became a member of the German Empire in 1871. King Wilhelm II was forced to abdicate at the end of World War I in 1918.

RULER
Wilhelm II, 1891-1918

MINT MARKS
C, CT - Christophstal Mint
F - Freudenstadt Mint
S - Stuttgart Mint
T - Tübingen Mint

KINGDOM

REFORM COINAGE

KM# 631 2 MARK
11.1110 g., 0.9000 Silver 0.3215 oz. ASW, 28 mm. **Ruler:** Wilhelm II **Obv:** Head right **Obv. Legend:** WILHELM II KOENIG VON WUERTTEMBERG **Rev:** Crowned imperial eagle with shield on breast **Rev. Legend:** DEUTSCHES REICH date, ZWEI MARK below **Edge:** Reeded

Date	Mintage	F	VF	XF	Unc	BU
1901F	591,927	9.00	19.00	45.00	125	300
1902F	815,620	8.00	17.00	45.00	125	350
1903F	811,383	9.00	19.00	45.00	125	300
1904F	1,988,177	8.00	15.00	35.00	100	275
1905F	609,835	9.00	20.00	40.00	100	300
1906F	1,504,620	9.00	20.00	40.00	100	325
1907F	1,504,497	8.00	15.00	35.00	100	275
1908F	451,370	8.00	22.00	45.00	125	275
1912F	251,224	8.00	15.00	35.00	100	200
1913F	5,675	8.00	17.00	45.00	125	300
1914F	5,962	8.00	17.00	40.00	100	225
(1901-1914) Proof	—	Value: 275				

KM# 635 3 MARK
16.6670 g., 0.9000 Silver 0.4823 oz. ASW, 33 mm. **Ruler:** Wilhelm II **Obv:** Head right **Rev:** Crowned imperial eagle with shield on breast **Edge Lettering:** GOTT MIT UNS

Date	Mintage	F	VF	XF	Unc	BU
1908F	300,000	10.00	20.00	30.00	70.00	135
1909F	1,906,698	10.00	20.00	30.00	65.00	135
1910F	837,230	10.00	20.00	30.00	65.00	135
1911F	424,820	10.00	20.00	30.00	65.00	135
1912F	849,100	10.00	17.50	25.00	60.00	135
1913F	267,700	10.00	20.00	30.00	75.00	150
1914F	733,121	10.00	17.50	25.00	60.00	110
(1908-1914)F Proof	—	Value: 300				

KM# 636 3 MARK
16.6670 g., 0.9000 Silver 0.4823 oz. ASW, 33 mm. **Ruler:** Wilhelm II **Subject:** Silver Wedding Anniversary **Obv:** Conjoined heads right, normal bar in "H" of "CHARLOTTE" **Rev:** Crowned imperial eagle with shield on breast **Edge Lettering:** GOTT MIT UNS

Date	Mintage	F	VF	XF	Unc	BU
1911F	493,000	12.00	18.00	35.00	45.00	65.00
1911F Proof	—	Value: 150				

KM# 637 3 MARK
16.6670 g., 0.9000 Silver 0.4823 oz. ASW, 33 mm. **Ruler:** Wilhelm II **Subject:** Silver Wedding Anniversary **Obv:** High bar in "H" of "CHARLOTTE" **Rev:** Crowned imperial eagle with shield on breast **Edge Lettering:** GOTT MIT UNS

Date	Mintage	F	VF	XF	Unc	BU
1911F	7,000	140	300	475	700	800
1911F Proof	—	Value: 1,200				

KM# 638 3 MARK
16.6670 g., 0.9000 Silver 0.4823 oz. ASW, 33 mm. **Ruler:** Wilhelm II **Subject:** 25th Year of Reign **Obv:** Head right **Rev:** Crowned imperial eagle with shield on breast **Edge Lettering:** GOTT MIT UNS **Note:** 5,650 were melted.

Date	Mintage	F	VF	XF	Unc	BU
1916F Proof	1,000	Value: 8,500				

KM# 632 5 MARK
27.7770 g., 0.9000 Silver 0.8037 oz. ASW, 38 mm. **Ruler:** Wilhelm II **Obv:** Head right **Obv. Legend:** WILHELM II KOENIG VON WUERTTEMBERG **Rev:** Crowned imperial eagle with shield on breast **Rev. Legend:** DEUTSCHES REICH date, FUNF MARK below **Edge Lettering:** GOTT MIT UNS

Date	Mintage	F	VF	XF	Unc	BU
1901F	210,700	15.00	35.00	90.00	600	1,100
1902F	360,889	15.00	35.00	90.00	400	1,200
1903F	722,182	15.00	30.00	75.00	375	900
1904F	391,317	15.00	30.00	75.00	375	900
1906F	45,000	25.00	65.00	200	1,200	2,000
1906F Proof	50	Value: 2,750				
1907F	436,321	15.00	30.00	65.00	300	650
1908F	521,716	15.00	30.00	55.00	250	500
1913F	341,200	15.00	30.00	50.00	200	375
(1901-1913)F Proof	—	Value: 1,300				

KM# 633 10 MARK
3.9820 g., 0.9000 Gold 0.1152 oz. AGW **Ruler:** Wilhelm II **Obv:** Head right **Obv. Legend:** WILHELM II KOENIG VON WUERTTEMBERG **Rev:** Crowned imperial eagle with shield on breast **Rev. Legend:** DEUTSCHES REICH **Edge:** ~ * ~

Date	Mintage	F	VF	XF	Unc	BU
1901F	110,262	110	135	175	300	550
1902F	50,112	125	150	200	400	700
1903F	180,402	110	125	175	300	550
1903F Proof	—	Value: 1,750				
1904F	349,631	110	125	175	300	550
1904F Proof	—	Value: 1,750				
1905F	199,312	110	125	175	300	500
1905F Proof	—	Value: 1,750				
1906F	100,164	110	125	175	300	560
1906F Proof	50	Value: 1,760				
1907F	149,921	110	125	175	300	500
1907F Proof	—	Value: 1,750				
1909F	100,189	110	125	175	300	500
1909F Proof	—	Value: 1,750				
1910F	150,229	110	125	175	300	500
1910F Proof	—	Value: 1,750				
1911F	50,337	140	275	350	600	800
1911F Proof	—	Value: 1,750				
1912F	49,353	140	275	335	600	800
1912F Proof	—	Value: 1,750				
1913F	50,038	140	275	375	600	800
1913F Proof	—	Value: 1,750				

KM# 634 20 MARK
7.9650 g., 0.9000 Gold 0.2305 oz. AGW **Ruler:** Wilhelm II **Obv:** Head right **Obv. Legend:** WILHELM II KOENIG VON WUERTTEMBERG **Rev:** Crowned imperial eagle with shield on breast **Rev. Legend:** DEUTSCHES REICH date, 20 MARK below **Edge Lettering:** GOTT MIT UNS

Date	Mintage	F	VF	XF	Unc	BU
1905F	500,594	—	BV	215	250	350
1905F Proof	—	Value: 2,000				
1913F	42,687	5,000	12,500	25,000	40,000	55,000
1913F Proof	—	Value: 70,000				
1914F	552,684	1,750	2,750	3,750	5,000	6,000
1914F Proof	—	Value: 8,000				

1871-1918

Germany, a nation of north-central Europe which from1871 to 1945 was, successively, an empire, a republic and a totalitarian state, attained its territorial peak as an empire when it comprised a 208,780 sq. mi. (540,740 sq. km.) homeland and an overseas colonial empire.

As the power of the Roman Empire waned, several war-like tribes residing in northern Germany moved south and west, invading France, Belgium, England, Italy and Spain. In 800 A.D. the Frankish king Charlemagne, who ruled most of France and Germany, was crowned Emperor of the Holy Roman Empire, a loose federation of an estimated 1,800 German States that lasted until 1806. Modern Germany was formed from the eastern part of Charlemagne's empire.

After 1812, the German States were reduced to a federation of 32, of which Prussia was the strongest. In 1871, Prussian chancellor Otto von Bismarck united the German States into an empire ruled by William I, the Prussian king. The empire initiated a colonial endeavor and became one of the world's greatest powers. Germany disintegrated as a result of World War I.

It was reestablished as the Weimar Republic. The humiliation of defeat, economic depression, poverty and discontent gave rise to Adolf Hitler, 1933, who reconstituted Germany as the Third Reich and after initial diplomatic and military triumphs, expanded his goals beyond Europe into Africa and USSR which led it into final disaster in World War II, ending on VE Day, May 7, 1945.

RULERS
Wilhelm II, 1888-1918

MINT MARKS
- A - Berlin
- D - Munich
- E - Muldenhutten (1887-1953)
- F - Stuttgart
- G - Karlsruhe
- J - Hamburg

MONETARY SYSTEM
(Until 1923)
100 Pfennig = 1 Mark

(Commencing 1945)
100 Pfennig = 1 Mark

EMPIRE

STANDARD COINAGE

KM# 10 PFENNIG

2.0200 g., Copper **Ruler:** Wilhelm II **Obv:** Denomination, date at right **Rev:** Crowned imperial eagle with shield on breast **Note:** Struck from 1890-1916.

Date	Mintage	F	VF	XF	Unc	BU
1901A	21,045,000	0.20	1.25	4.00	22.00	25.00
1901D	5,337,000	0.50	2.00	9.00	40.00	45.00
1901E	1,397,000	1.00	6.00	27.50	80.00	100
1901F	2,925,000	0.60	4.00	17.50	60.00	80.00
1901G	1,977,000	2.50	9.00	32.50	110	130
1901J	2,011,000	4.00	12.50	40.00	180	225
1902A	7,474,000	0.50	2.00	4.00	25.00	30.00
1902D	2,811,000	0.60	3.50	6.00	40.00	45.00
1902E	1,183,000	1.00	6.00	25.00	110	130
1902F	1,250,000	1.00	6.00	20.00	100	120
1902G	881,000	4.00	22.50	60.00	200	230
1902J	150	475	1,600	2,200	5,000	6,000
1903A	12,690,000	0.20	1.00	4.00	30.00	35.00
1903D	3,140,000	0.80	2.00	8.00	40.00	50.00
1903E	1,956,000	1.50	3.00	10.00	50.00	60.00
1903F	2,945,000	0.80	2.00	10.00	45.00	55.00
1903G	1,377,000	3.00	6.00	25.00	100	125
1903J	2,832,000	1.00	4.00	20.00	60.00	80.00
1904A	28,625,000	0.20	1.00	3.00	25.00	30.00
1904D	4,118,000	0.80	2.00	8.00	40.00	45.00
1904E	2,778,000	1.00	3.00	9.00	40.00	50.00
1904F	4,520,000	1.00	3.00	8.00	40.00	50.00
1904G	3,232,000	2.00	6.00	18.00	80.00	90.00
1904J	4,467,000	1.00	2.50	10.00	40.00	50.00
1905A	19,631,000	0.20	1.00	3.50	18.00	22.00
1905D	6,084,000	0.50	2.00	5.50	30.00	35.00
1905E	3,564,000	0.50	2.00	5.50	30.00	35.00
1905E	Inc. above	—	—	2,500	—	—
Note: Cross under denomination						
1905F	4,153,000	0.80	3.00	6.50	40.00	45.00
1905G	3,051,000	0.80	3.00	18.00	70.00	80.00
1905J	4,085,000	1.00	5.00	12.00	55.00	65.00
1906A	46,921,000	0.20	0.80	2.50	18.00	20.00
1906D	5,633,000	0.20	0.80	5.00	30.00	35.00
1906E	7,278,000	0.20	0.80	5.00	20.00	25.00
1906F	7,173,000	0.20	0.80	5.00	25.00	30.00
1906G	5,194,000	0.20	0.80	5.00	40.00	45.00
1906J	3,622,000	0.20	1.00	6.00	45.00	55.00
1907A	33,711,000	0.20	0.80	1.50	14.00	16.00
1907D	14,691,000	0.20	1.00	2.00	20.00	23.00
1907E	3,719,000	0.20	1.50	5.00	20.00	25.00
1907F	7,026,000	0.20	1.00	3.00	20.00	23.00
1907G	3,052,000	0.20	1.50	6.00	30.00	35.00
1907J	6,722,000	0.20	1.50	6.00	20.00	25.00
1908A	21,922,000	0.20	0.60	1.25	12.00	15.00
1908D	10,629,000	0.20	0.80	2.25	20.00	23.00
1908E	3,400,000	0.20	1.50	5.00	22.00	26.00
1908F	6,112,000	0.20	1.50	5.00	22.00	26.00
1908G	3,663,000	0.20	2.00	6.00	40.00	45.00
1908J	5,581,000	0.20	1.50	5.00	22.00	26.00
1909A	21,430,000	0.20	0.75	3.00	20.00	23.00
1909D	2,814,000	0.20	1.25	7.00	55.00	65.00
1909E	2,562,000	1.00	3.00	8.00	45.00	50.00
1909F	2,425,000	1.50	4.00	10.00	50.00	60.00
1909G	1,220,000	1.50	5.00	12.00	80.00	90.00
1909J	1,634,000	1.50	5.00	11.00	80.00	90.00
1910A	10,761,000	0.20	0.75	2.50	15.00	18.00
1910D	4,221,000	0.20	1.00	3.00	20.00	24.00
1910E	1,600,000	0.50	3.00	5.00	38.00	42.00
1910F	3,009,000	0.30	2.00	6.00	30.00	35.00
1910G	1,834,000	0.50	3.00	16.00	85.00	95.00
1910J	2,450,000	0.50	3.00	9.00	60.00	70.00
1911A	38,172,000	0.20	0.75	2.00	14.00	16.00
1911D	8,657,000	0.20	1.00	3.00	20.00	23.00
1911E	5,236,000	0.20	1.00	3.00	20.00	23.00
1911F	5,780,000	0.20	1.00	3.00	20.00	23.00
1911G	2,075,000	0.20	1.50	5.00	35.00	40.00
1911J	5,594,000	0.20	1.00	3.00	15.00	18.00
1912A	42,693,000	0.10	0.75	1.50	10.00	13.00
1912D	10,173,000	0.10	0.80	2.00	12.00	15.00
1912E	5,689,000	0.10	0.80	2.50	13.00	16.00
1912F	7,441,000	0.10	0.80	3.00	13.00	16.00
1912G	5,526,000	0.10	0.80	3.00	15.00	20.00
1912J	5,615,000	0.10	0.80	3.00	25.00	30.00
1913A	32,671,000	0.10	0.50	2.00	10.00	13.00
1913D	8,161,000	0.20	1.00	3.00	12.00	15.00
1913E	2,258,000	1.00	2.00	4.00	20.00	23.00
1913F	6,620,000	0.20	1.00	3.00	14.00	16.00
1913G	3,209,000	0.20	1.00	2.00	25.00	30.00
1913J	1,456,000	0.10	5.00	11.00	45.00	50.00
1914A	9,976,000	0.20	0.80	2.00	8.00	10.00
1914D	1,842,000	0.20	1.25	2.50	14.00	17.00
1914E	2,926,000	0.30	2.00	3.00	15.00	18.00
1914F	3,316,000	0.20	1.00	2.00	15.00	18.00
1914G	2,100,000	0.20	1.75	2.50	15.00	18.00
1914J	4,368,000	0.20	1.75	2.50	15.00	18.00
1915A	14,738,000	0.10	0.75	1.50	8.00	10.00
1915D	1,771,000	0.20	1.00	2.50	20.00	22.00
1915E	2,779,000	0.20	1.00	3.50	20.00	22.00
1915F	1,411,000	0.20	1.00	4.00	25.00	30.00
1915G	2,041,000	0.20	1.00	4.00	25.00	30.00
1915J	2,981,000	0.20	1.00	4.00	20.00	25.00
1916A	5,960,000	0.20	0.75	2.50	10.00	12.00
1916D	5,401,000	0.20	1.00	4.00	25.00	30.00
1916E	818,000	1.00	6.00	8.00	35.00	40.00
1916F	1,104,000	0.80	3.00	8.00	35.00	40.00
1916G	671,000	1.50	6.00	20.00	60.00	70.00
1916J	898,000	1.00	5.00	10.00	50.00	55.00
1901-16 Common date proof	—	Value: 100				

KM# 24 PFENNIG

Aluminum **Ruler:** Wilhelm II **Obv:** Denomination, date at right **Rev:** Crowned imperial eagle with shield on breast

Date	Mintage	F	VF	XF	Unc	BU
1916G	—	—	260	380	8,000	1,000
1917A	27,159,000	0.15	0.75	2.00	6.00	8.00
1917A Proof	—	Value: 90.00				
1917D	6,940,000	0.15	0.75	2.50	10.00	12.00
1917E	3,862,000	0.50	2.00	5.00	15.00	18.00
1917E Proof	—	Value: 90.00				
1917F	5,125,000	0.25	2.00	3.00	10.00	12.00
1917G	3,139,000	0.25	2.00	4.00	10.00	13.00
1917G Proof	—	Value: 90.00				
1917J	4,182,000	0.50	2.50	3.00	24.00	28.00
1917J Proof	—	Value: 90.00				
1918A	—	—	2,000	3,000	4,000	5,000
1918D	318,000	10.00	20.00	45.00	100	125
1918F	—	—	2,500	4,000	—	—
Note: The 1918F 1 Pfennigs are from the burned-out ruins of the Stuttgart Mint destroyed in World War II						
1916-18 Common date proof	—	Value: 90.00				

KM# 16 2 PFENNIG

3.3000 g., Copper **Ruler:** Wilhelm II **Obv:** Denomination, date at right **Rev:** Crowned imperial eagle with shield on breast

Date	Mintage	F	VF	XF	Unc	BU
1904A	5,414,000	0.20	1.00	5.00	25.00	30.00
1904D	1,404,000	0.50	2.00	10.00	30.00	35.00
1904E	744,000	2.00	6.00	16.00	70.00	80.00
1904F	1,002,000	0.20	3.50	12.00	45.00	55.00
1904G	495,000	3.00	7.00	28.00	140	160
1904J	44,000	2.00	11.00	25.00	180	200
1905A	5,172,000	0.10	0.50	2.50	20.00	22.00
1905D	1,570,000	0.20	2.00	10.00	30.00	35.00
1905E	924,000	0.40	3.50	12.00	55.00	65.00
1905F	1,115,000	0.40	3.00	10.00	60.00	70.00
1905G	1,030,000	0.40	3.50	16.00	80.00	100
1905J	1,609,000	0.40	3.00	12.00	90.00	100
1906A	8,459,000	0.20	1.00	5.00	30.00	35.00
1906D	3,539,000	0.20	1.75	6.00	35.00	40.00
1906E	2,055,000	0.20	1.50	7.50	40.00	45.00
1906F	2,840,000	0.20	1.50	6.50	35.00	40.00
1906G	1,527,000	0.40	2.00	12.00	80.00	90.00
1906J	1,908,000	0.40	2.00	12.00	60.00	70.00
1907A	13,468,000	0.10	0.50	3.00	16.00	20.00
1907D	1,921,000	0.20	0.75	4.50	28.00	30.00
1907E	744,000	0.50	2.50	8.00	55.00	65.00
1907F	1,059,000	0.20	2.50	12.00	70.00	80.00
1907G	610,000	0.50	3.00	12.00	70.00	80.00
1907J	952,000	0.20	2.50	10.00	60.00	65.00
1908A	5,421,000	0.10	1.00	4.00	20.00	25.00
1908D	1,407,000	0.10	2.00	7.00	25.00	30.00
1908E	745,000	1.00	3.00	10.00	50.00	55.00
1908F	1,003,000	0.10	3.00	10.00	50.00	55.00
1908G	610,000	0.25	4.00	14.00	70.00	80.00
1908J	817,000	0.10	3.00	12.00	60.00	70.00
1910A	5,421,000	0.20	1.00	5.00	18.00	22.00
1910D	1,407,000	0.50	2.00	8.00	30.00	35.00
1910E	745,000	1.00	4.50	10.00	55.00	60.00
1910F	1,003,000	0.40	2.00	8.00	50.00	55.00
1910G	517,000	0.40	3.00	15.00	90.00	110
1910J	568,000	0.40	3.00	15.00	80.00	90.00
1911A	8,187,000	0.20	1.00	3.00	17.00	20.00
1911D	2,100,000	0.20	2.00	4.00	22.00	26.00
1911E	1,133,000	0.50	3.00	5.00	26.00	30.00
1911F	1,490,000	0.40	2.00	4.00	22.00	26.00
1911G	1,313,000	0.40	2.00	6.00	30.00	35.00
1911J	1,883,000	0.40	2.00	4.00	22.00	26.00
1912A	13,580,000	0.20	0.75	3.00	18.00	20.00
1912D	3,109,000	0.30	1.00	4.00	22.00	26.00
1912E	1,808,000	0.30	2.00	5.00	22.00	26.00
1912F	2,366,000	0.30	1.00	6.00	22.00	26.00
1912G	1,395,000	0.50	2.50	7.50	50.00	60.00
1912J	1,605,000	0.50	2.00	6.00	30.00	35.00
1913A	4,212,000	0.20	0.75	3.00	16.00	18.00
1913D	2,525,000	0.20	1.00	6.00	24.00	28.00
1913E	413,000	0.50	3.00	12.00	65.00	75.00
1913F	1,602,000	0.40	2.00	12.00	60.00	70.00
1913G	741,000	1.50	9.00	13.00	70.00	80.00
1913J	1,254,000	0.40	2.00	9.00	60.00	70.00
1914A	5,350,000	0.10	1.00	3.00	14.00	16.00
1914E	1,201,000	1.00	5.00	8.00	40.00	45.00
1914F	158,000	12.00	45.00	90.00	300	325
1914G	610,000	2.00	9.00	25.00	120	140
1914J	817,000	0.10	6.00	17.00	70.00	80.00
1915A	3,897,000	0.40	1.00	3.00	12.00	15.00
1915D	1,407,000	0.40	2.00	6.00	20.00	25.00
1915E	288,000	3.00	15.00	28.00	50.00	60.00
1915F	904,000	0.20	2.00	7.00	25.00	30.00
1916A	3,524,000	0.20	1.00	3.00	12.00	14.00
1916D	915,000	0.40	1.50	8.00	18.00	22.00
1916E	484,000	1.00	3.50	10.00	32.00	36.00
1916F	651,000	0.25	1.50	5.00	20.00	25.00
1916G	397,000	1.00	3.50	14.00	50.00	60.00
1916J	531,000	0.50	2.50	12.00	40.00	50.00
1904-16 Common date proof	—	Value: 150				

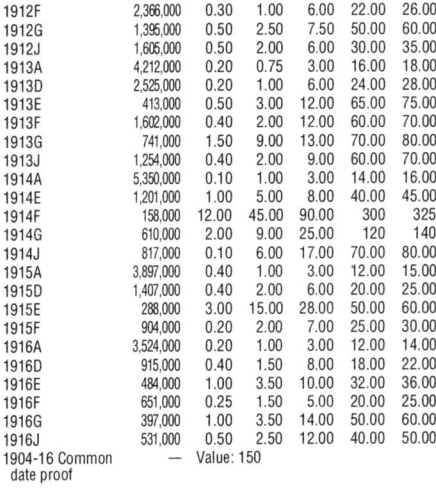

KM# 11 5 PFENNIG

2.4700 g., Copper-Nickel, 18 mm. **Ruler:** Wilhelm II **Obv:** Denomination, date at right **Rev:** Crowned imperial eagle with shield on breast **Note:** Struck from 1890-1915.

Date	Mintage	F	VF	XF	Unc	BU
1901A	8,155,000	0.20	0.60	5.00	40.00	50.00
1901D	2,779,000	0.20	1.50	12.00	75.00	85.00
1901E	1,492,000	0.40	2.50	12.00	100	120
1901F	1,810,000	0.40	2.50	10.00	90.00	110
1901G	915,000	0.50	3.50	35.00	300	350
1901J	1,226,000	0.50	3.50	25.00	150	170
1902A	8,949,000	0.20	0.75	5.00	40.00	50.00
1902D	2,812,000	0.40	2.50	12.00	90.00	110
1902E	1,120,000	1.00	3.50	12.00	70.00	80.00
1902F	1,800,000	1.00	3.00	11.00	60.00	70.00
1902G	1,220,000	1.50	6.00	25.00	150	170
1902J	1,636,000	1.50	6.00	20.00	130	150
1903A	5,932,000	0.20	4.00	6.00	70.00	80.00
1903D	1,406,000	0.60	2.00	15.00	100	120
1903E	1,114,000	0.80	3.50	18.00	80.00	100
1903F	1,209,000	1.00	4.00	20.00	175	225
1903G	610,000	2.00	9.00	55.00	275	300
1903J	817,000	1.00	6.00	45.00	225	250
1904A	6,791,000	0.20	6.00	10.00	65.00	75.00
1904D	1,408,000	1.00	2.50	15.00	80.00	100
1904E	746,000	1.50	6.00	20.00	130	150
1904F	1,006,000	1.00	3.50	20.00	100	120
1904G	610,000	2.00	8.00	25.00	300	350
1904J	818,000	1.00	5.00	28.00	200	225
1905A	8,129,000	0.20	0.75	2.50	35.00	45.00
1905D	2,109,000	0.20	1.00	6.00	80.00	90.00
1905E	1,117,000	0.40	1.75	7.00	60.00	70.00
1905F	1,505,000	0.20	1.00	6.00	70.00	80.00
1905G	915,000	1.00	3.00	16.00	130	145
1905J	1,226,000	0.60	2.50	12.00	120	135
1906A	18,970,000	0.20	0.75	2.00	25.00	35.00
1906D	4,922,000	0.20	1.00	5.00	40.00	50.00
1906E	2,605,000	0.20	1.25	5.00	45.00	55.00
1906F	3,512,000	0.20	1.00	5.00	50.00	60.00
1906G	2,136,000	0.50	2.00	15.00	130	150
1906J	2,859,000	0.20	1.75	13.00	130	150
1907A	11,930,000	0.20	0.75	2.25	20.00	25.00
1907D	2,113,000	0.20	1.00	5.00	40.00	50.00
1907E	1,517,000	0.30	1.75	5.00	40.00	50.00
1907F	1,845,000	0.30	1.75	5.00	40.00	45.00
1907G	915,000	1.00	2.50	6.00	60.00	80.00
1907J	1,636,000	0.50	2.00	5.00	45.00	50.00
1908A	22,114,000	0.20	0.50	2.50	18.00	20.00
1908D	4,991,000	0.20	1.00	3.00	20.00	25.00
1908E	2,919,000	0.30	1.50	5.00	35.00	40.00
1908/7F	5,124,000	30.00	60.00	80.00	125	150
1908F	Inc. above	0.50	1.50	5.00	40.00	50.00
1908G	3,357,000	0.50	2.00	8.00	70.00	80.00
1908J	3,264,000	0.50	2.00	10.00	110	130
1909A	5,797,000	0.40	1.50	9.00	60.00	70.00
1909D	2,753,000	0.60	2.50	14.00	110	130
1909E	984,000	1.50	4.50	18.00	120	140
1909F	252,000	2.00	18.00	50.00	250	300
1909/8J	1,632,000	1.00	5.00	5.00	45.00	50.00
1909J	Inc. above	1.00	9.00	28.00	170	190
1910A	7,344,000	0.20	0.50	3.00	25.00	30.00
1910D	2,814,000	0.20	0.80	6.00	40.00	50.00
1910E	1,290,000	0.20	1.00	9.00	60.00	70.00
1910F	1,721,000	0.20	1.50	11.00	65.00	75.00
1910G	1,222,000	0.30	1.75	20.00	120	130
1910J	152,000	30.00	42.50	70.00	150	175

Date	Mintage	F	VF	XF	Unc	BU
1911A	15,660,000	0.20	0.50	1.50	10.00	12.00
1911D	2,221,000	0.20	1.00	2.50	15.00	18.00
1911E	1,770,000	0.40	2.00	3.00	15.00	18.00
1911F	2,714,000	0.40	2.00	3.00	15.00	18.00
1911G	1,833,000	0.40	1.00	2.50	15.00	18.00
1911J	3,116,000	0.20	1.00	2.00	18.00	22.00
1912A	19,320,000	0.20	0.80	2.00	12.00	15.00
1912D	4,015,000	0.20	0.80	2.50	16.00	18.00
1912E	2,568,000	0.20	1.00	2.50	20.00	25.00
1912F	3,679,000	0.20	1.00	2.50	22.00	25.00
1912G	2,440,000	0.20	1.00	3.00	30.00	35.00
1912J	3,020,000	0.20	1.00	2.50	20.00	25.00
1913A	15,506,000	0.20	0.50	1.50	12.00	15.00
1913D	5,519,000	0.20	0.50	2.00	15.00	18.00
1913E	2,373,000	0.50	2.00	3.00	17.00	20.00
1913F	2,054,000	0.50	2.00	3.00	17.00	20.00
1913G	1,221,000	1.00	5.00	9.00	70.00	80.00
1913J	253,000	10.00	16.00	35.00	160	180
1914A	23,605,000	0.20	0.50	1.00	9.00	10.00
1914D	3,014,000	0.20	0.80	1.50	12.00	15.00
1914E	1,710,000	0.20	1.00	3.50	12.00	15.00
1914F	2,206,000	0.20	1.00	2.50	18.00	22.00
1914G	1,218,000	0.20	1.00	3.00	20.00	25.00
1914J	3,235,000	0.20	1.00	2.50	20.00	25.00
1915D	3,516,000	0.10	1.00	2.00	18.00	22.00
1915E	834,000	1.00	8.00	13.00	60.00	70.00
1915F	1,894,000	0.10	2.00	5.00	35.00	40.00
1915G	894,000	0.50	7.00	18.00	70.00	80.00
1915J	1,669,000	0.10	6.00	14.00	60.00	70.00
1901-15 Common date proof	—	Value: 120				

KM# 19 5 PFENNIG

2.5100 g., Iron **Obv:** Denomination, date below **Rev:** Crowned imperial eagle with shield on breast

Date	Mintage	F	VF	XF	Unc	BU
1915A	34,631,000	0.20	0.50	3.00	15.00	20.00
1915D	2,021,000	2.00	7.00	13.00	60.00	70.00
1915E	4,670,000	1.00	4.00	9.00	40.00	45.00
1915F	3,500,000	0.80	3.00	6.00	35.00	40.00
1915G	3,676,000	0.80	3.00	6.00	35.00	40.00
1915J	2,100,000	1.50	6.00	12.00	50.00	60.00
1916A	51,003,000	0.20	0.50	2.50	12.00	15.00
1916D	19,590,000	0.20	0.50	3.00	18.00	22.00
1916E	2,271,000	2.00	6.00	15.00	50.00	60.00
1916F	10,479,000	0.20	0.80	5.00	25.00	30.00
1916G	5,599,000	0.50	1.50	5.50	35.00	40.00
1916J	10,253,000	0.30	1.00	4.00	30.00	35.00
1917A	87,315,000	0.10	0.30	1.50	12.00	15.00
1917D	19,581,000	0.20	1.00	2.50	14.00	17.00
1917E	11,092,000	0.50	1.00	3.00	18.00	20.00
1917F	10,930,000	0.20	0.50	3.50	20.00	22.00
1917F	—	600	1,000	1,600	2,250	2,500
Note: Mule with Polish reverse of Y#5, see Poland						
1917G	6,720,000	0.20	1.00	4.00	18.00	22.00
1917J	11,686,000	0.20	1.00	4.50	20.00	25.00
1918A	223,516,000	0.10	0.50	1.00	6.00	8.00
1918D	29,130,000	0.10	0.50	1.00	8.00	10.00
1918E	23,600,000	0.20	1.00	2.00	10.00	14.00
1918F	24,598,000	0.10	0.30	1.25	10.00	12.00
1918G	12,697,000	0.20	1.00	2.00	10.00	14.00
1918J	20,240,000	0.10	0.50	1.00	8.00	10.00
1919A	112,102,000	0.10	0.50	0.75	6.00	8.00
1919D	41,163,000	0.10	0.50	1.00	8.00	10.00
1919E	20,608,000	0.10	0.50	1.00	8.00	10.00
1919F	32,700,000	0.10	0.50	1.00	8.00	10.00
1919G	13,925,000	0.20	1.00	2.00	15.00	20.00
1919J	16,249,000	0.50	1.50	6.00	15.00	20.00
1920A	80,300,000	0.10	0.40	1.00	5.00	8.00
1920D	25,502,000	0.10	0.50	1.00	6.00	9.00
1920E	11,646,000	0.50	1.00	3.00	25.00	30.00
1920F	24,300,000	0.10	0.40	1.00	10.00	12.00
1920G	10,244,000	0.10	0.50	1.25	16.00	18.00
1920J	16,857,000	0.20	0.30	1.00	14.00	16.00
1921A	143,418,000	0.10	0.20	0.75	7.00	9.00
1921D	38,133,000	0.10	0.20	1.00	7.00	9.00
1921E	21,104,000	0.50	1.00	3.50	25.00	30.00
1921F	24,800,000	0.10	0.20	1.00	8.00	10.00
1921G	21,289,000	0.10	0.20	1.00	8.00	10.00
1921J	28,928,000	0.15	1.00	2.50	8.00	10.00
1922A Rare	89,062,000	—	—	—	—	—
1922D	31,240,000	0.10	0.20	0.50	12.00	14.00
1922E	19,156,000	0.50	1.00	8.00	20.00	25.00
1922F	16,436,000	0.10	0.20	1.00	12.00	14.00
1922G	19,708,000	0.10	0.25	1.00	8.00	10.00
1922J	16,820,000	0.10	0.20	1.25	15.00	18.00
1915-22 Common date proof	—	Value: 110				

KM# 12 10 PFENNIG

3.7200 g., Copper-Nickel, 21.11 mm. **Ruler:** Wilhelm II **Obv:** Denomination, date at right **Rev:** Crowned imperial eagle with shield on breast **Note:** Struck from 1890-1916.

Date	Mintage	F	VF	XF	Unc	BU
1901A	10,200,000	0.20	1.00	8.00	70.00	—
1901D	3,259,000	1.00	4.00	22.00	150	—
1901E	1,863,000	1.00	5.00	20.00	170	—
1901F	2,594,000	1.00	5.00	16.00	130	—
1901G	1,527,000	2.00	17.00	60.00	280	—
1901J	1,225,000	2.00	14.00	60.00	280	—
1902A	5,878,000	0.20	1.00	4.00	60.00	—
1902D	1,406,000	0.20	1.00	15.00	120	—
1902E	502,000	1.00	5.00	45.00	280	—
1902F	1,003,000	0.20	1.00	15.00	110	—
1902G	610,000	0.20	10.00	50.00	280	—
1902J	815,000	1.50	8.00	30.00	220	—
1903A	5,131,000	0.20	0.50	5.00	90.00	—
1903D	1,406,000	0.40	1.00	15.00	150	—
1903E	988,000	0.40	1.00	15.00	120	—
1903F	1,003,000	0.50	2.00	22.00	175	—
1903G	610,000	2.00	8.00	50.00	250	—
1903J	816,000	1.50	6.00	45.00	250	—
1904A	5,189,000	0.20	0.50	4.00	70.00	—
1904D	1,056,000	0.20	1.50	14.00	140	—
1904E	559,000	0.20	1.50	14.00	130	—
1904F	753,000	0.20	1.50	16.00	180	—
1904G	457,000	2.00	10.00	50.00	280	—
1904J	612,000	2.00	8.00	40.00	250	—
1905A	8,650,000	0.20	0.50	3.00	48.00	—
1905A Proof	250	Value: 100				
1905D	1,846,000	0.20	1.00	6.00	100	—
1905E	980,000	0.40	1.50	16.00	150	—
1905F	1,310,000	0.40	1.50	16.00	150	—
1905G	642,000	1.50	8.00	50.00	250	—
1905J	1,430,000	1.50	8.00	40.00	220	—
1906A	14,470,000	0.20	0.50	4.00	50.00	—
1906D	4,132,000	0.20	1.00	5.00	80.00	—
1906E	2,189,000	0.20	1.00	6.00	80.00	—
1906F	2,953,000	0.20	1.00	6.00	75.00	—
1906G	1,952,000	1.00	5.00	40.00	260	—
1906J	2,042,000	1.00	5.00	30.00	220	—
1907A	17,971,000	0.20	0.50	2.00	25.00	—
1907D	2,813,000	0.20	1.00	3.00	40.00	—
1907E	2,291,000	0.20	1.00	3.00	45.00	—
1907F	3,206,000	0.20	1.00	6.00	60.00	—
1907G	1,889,000	0.50	2.00	15.00	140	—
1907J	2,750,000	0.40	1.00	12.00	90.00	—
1908A	20,410,000	0.20	0.50	2.00	35.00	—
1908D	6,773,000	0.20	1.00	2.00	28.00	—
1908E	2,490,000	0.20	1.00	5.00	80.00	—
1908F	3,535,000	0.20	1.00	5.00	80.00	—
1908G	1,708,000	0.40	2.00	15.00	130	—
1908J	2,649,000	0.20	1.00	12.00	90.00	—
1909A	2,270,000	0.40	1.00	8.00	80.00	—
1909D	966,000	0.60	2.00	15.00	120	—
1909E	806,000	1.00	3.00	13.00	130	—
1909F	780,000	3.00	12.00	36.00	180	—
1909G	980,000	2.00	9.00	40.00	240	—
1909J	725,000	3.00	15.00	60.00	350	—
1910A	3,734,000	0.20	6.00	2.00	30.00	—
1910D	1,406,000	0.30	1.00	4.00	35.00	—
1910E	300,000	2.50	10.00	28.00	160	—
1910F	1,003,000	0.50	2.00	12.00	60.00	—
1910G	610,000	2.50	10.00	33.00	220	—
1911A	13,554,000	0.10	0.50	1.50	25.00	—
1911D	2,508,000	0.20	0.80	2.50	25.00	—
1911E	2,246,000	0.30	0.80	3.00	30.00	—
1911F	2,235,000	0.30	0.80	3.00	30.00	—
1911G	1,678,000	0.20	1.50	6.00	45.00	—
1911J	3,062,000	0.20	0.80	3.00	38.00	—
1912A	21,312,000	0.10	0.40	2.00	18.00	—
1912D	6,988,000	0.20	0.80	2.00	24.00	—
1912E	2,649,000	0.20	0.80	3.00	28.00	—
1912F	3,787,000	0.10	0.40	3.00	22.00	—
1912G	2,441,000	0.40	0.40	4.00	30.00	—
1912J	2,730,000	0.10	0.40	4.00	30.00	—
1913A	13,466,000	0.10	0.50	1.00	18.00	—
1913D	3,164,000	0.20	0.80	2.00	22.00	—
1913E	1,478,000	0.20	1.00	2.50	25.00	—
1913F	1,991,000	0.20	1.00	2.50	30.00	—
1913G	1,373,000	0.20	1.50	4.00	35.00	—
1913J	1,550,000	0.20	1.50	4.00	35.00	—
1914A	18,570,000	0.10	0.50	2.00	18.00	—
1914D	2,301,000	0.10	0.50	2.00	22.00	—
1914E	3,478,000	0.10	0.60	3.00	22.00	—
1914F	4,515,000	0.20	1.00	2.50	25.00	—
1914G	2,689,000	0.20	1.00	3.00	30.00	—
1914J	1,589,000	0.20	0.50	3.00	28.00	—
1915A	10,639,000	0.10	0.50	2.00	18.00	—
1915D	2,277,000	0.10	0.50	3.00	22.00	—
1915E	1,027,000	0.20	1.00	3.00	30.00	—
1915F	1,508,000	0.20	1.00	3.00	30.00	—
1915G	363,000	30.00	100	180	380	—
1915J	2,677,000	0.50	1.00	5.00	30.00	—
1916D	1,128,000	0.50	1.00	5.00	30.00	—
1901-16 Common date proof	—	Value: 80.00				

KM# 20 10 PFENNIG

3.6000 g., Iron **Obv:** Denomination, date below **Rev:** Crowned imperial eagle with shield on breast, beaded border

Date	Mintage	F	VF	XF	Unc	BU
1916A	69,143,000	0.20	0.60	1.50	8.00	—
1916D	11,609,000	0.20	0.60	1.50	12.00	—
1916E	8,280,000	0.30	1.00	2.50	12.00	—
1916F	7,473,000	0.30	2.00	4.50	15.00	—
1916G	5,878,000	0.30	2.00	4.50	18.00	—
1916J	11,683,000	0.30	1.00	2.50	15.00	—
1916 Rare	—	180	220	—	—	—
1917A	53,198,000	0.20	0.60	1.50	4.00	—
1917D	16,370,000	0.20	0.60	1.50	5.00	—
1917E	9,182,000	0.30	1.00	3.00	7.00	—
1917F	11,341,000	0.20	1.50	3.00	7.00	—
1917F	—	—	—	—	—	—
Note: Mule with Polish reverse of Y#6, see Poland						
1917G	7,088,000	0.30	1.50	8.00	25.00	—
1917J	9,205,000	0.30	1.00	8.00	25.00	—
1918D	42,000	0.50	1,250	2,400	—	—
1921A	16,265,000	0.80	3.00	8.00	33.00	—
1922D	—	2.00	6.00	12.00	45.00	—
1922E	2,235,000	10.00	30.00	60.00	200	—
1922F	1,928,000	2.00	6.00	12.00	45.00	—
1922G	1,358,000	10.00	30.00	60.00	200	—
1922J	2,420,000	2.00	6.00	15.00	60.00	—
1922	—	40.00	130	200	—	—
Note: There are several 1915A patterns for this type						
1916-22 Common date proof	—	Value: 95.00				

KM# 25 10 PFENNIG

Zinc **Ruler:** Wilhelm II **Rev:** Crowned imperial eagle with shield on breast, beaded border

Date	Mintage	F	VF	XF	Unc	BU
1917A	—	90.00	180	380	—	—
1917	—	90.00	180	380	—	—

KM# 26 10 PFENNIG

Zinc **Obv:** Denomination, date below **Rev:** Crowned imperial eagle with shield on breast **Note:** Weight varies: 3.10-3.60 grams. Without mint mark. Variations in planchet thickness exist.

Date	Mintage	F	VF	XF	Unc	BU
1917	75,073,000	0.10	0.20	1.00	8.00	—
1918	202,008,000	0.10	0.20	1.00	8.00	—
1918 Proof	28	Value: 300				
1919	147,800,000	0.10	0.20	1.00	8.00	—
1919 Proof	50	Value: 100				
1920	223,019,000	0.10	0.20	1.00	6.00	—
1920 Proof	40	Value: 100				
1921	319,334,000	0.10	0.20	1.00	4.00	—
1921 Proof	24	Value: 300				
1922	274,499,000	0.10	0.20	1.00	8.00	—
1922 Proof	12	Value: 400				

KM# 18 25 PFENNIG

4.0200 g., Nickel **Ruler:** Wilhelm II **Obv:** Crowned imperial eagle with shield on breast **Rev:** Denomination within wreath

Date	Mintage	F	VF	XF	Unc	BU
1909A	962,000	3.00	9.00	15.00	33.00	—
1909D	1,406,000	3.00	9.00	12.00	22.00	—
1909E	250,000	15.00	33.00	48.00	110	—
1909F	400,000	3.00	11.00	20.00	55.00	—
1909G	610,000	5.00	13.00	20.00	55.00	—
1909J	10,000	220	500	1,000	2,500	—
1910A	9,522,000	2.00	6.00	10.00	22.00	—
1910D	1,408,000	4.00	11.00	22.00	70.00	—
1910E	1,242,000	5.00	14.00	23.00	70.00	—
1910F	1,605,000	3.00	9.00	20.00	60.00	—
1910G	330,000	3.00	9.00	20.00	70.00	—
1910J	1,561,000	3.00	9.00	17.00	50.00	—
1911A	3,179,000	2.50	8.00	14.00	25.00	—
1911D	506,000	5.00	14.00	28.00	60.00	—
1911E	747,000	4.00	11.00	22.00	70.00	—
1911G	892,000	4.00	11.00	22.00	70.00	—
1911J	516,000	6.00	11.00	26.00	80.00	—
1912A	2,590,000	3.00	9.00	12.00	35.00	—
1912D	900,000	4.50	12.00	15.00	45.00	—
1912F	1,003,000	4.50	12.00	15.00	45.00	—

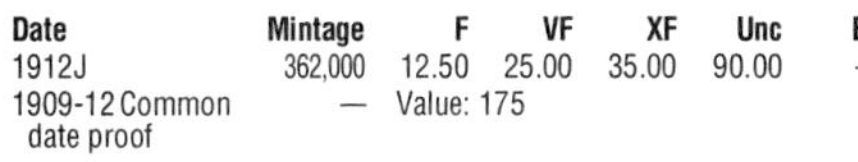

Date	Mintage	F	VF	XF	Unc	BU
1912J	362,000	12.50	25.00	35.00	90.00	—
1909-12 Common date proof	—	Value: 175				

KM# 15 50 PFENNIG

2.7770 g., 0.9000 Silver 0.0804 oz. ASW **Ruler:** Wilhelm II **Obv:** Denomination within wreath **Rev:** Crowned imperial eagle with shield on breast within wreath

Date	Mintage	F	VF	XF	Unc	BU
1901A	194,000	160	300	400	650	750
1902F	95,000	250	300	500	850	1,000
1902F Proof	—	Value: 800				
1903A	384,000	130	220	280	500	600
1901-03 Common date proof	—	Value: 500				

KM# 17 1/2 MARK

2.7770 g., 0.9000 Silver 0.0804 oz. ASW, 20 mm. **Obv:** Denomination within wreath **Rev:** Crowned imperial eagle with shield on breast within wreath **Note:** Some coins dated from 1918-19 were issued with a black finish to prevent hoarding.

Date	Mintage	F	VF	XF	Unc	BU
1905A	37,766,000	0.85	1.25	2.50	22.00	—
1905D	7,636,000	0.85	1.25	3.00	33.00	—
1905E	4,908,000	0.85	1.25	3.00	30.00	—
1905F	6,310,000	0.85	1.25	4.00	28.00	—
1905G	3,886,000	1.00	4.00	6.00	45.00	—
1905J	6,316,000	1.00	3.00	9.00	75.00	—
1906A	29,754,000	0.80	1.50	3.00	25.00	—
1906D	11,977,000	0.90	2.00	4.00	30.00	—
1906E	5,821,000	0.90	2.00	4.00	30.00	—
1906F	8,036,000	1.00	3.00	6.00	30.00	—
1906G	4,273,000	1.00	3.00	6.00	30.00	—
1906J	2,179,000	2.00	8.00	25.00	250	—
1907A	14,168,000	0.80	1.25	3.00	85.00	—
1907D	2,884,000	0.90	1.50	4.50	33.00	—
1907E	600,000	2.00	10.00	28.00	90.00	—
1907F	1,202,000	1.50	5.00	20.00	165	—
1907G	927,000	1.50	4.00	30.00	165	—
1907J	3,268,000	1.00	3.00	18.00	110	—
1908A	5,018,000	0.90	3.00	15.00	100	—
1908D	400,000	5.00	15.00	50.00	200	—
1908E	591,000	3.00	10.00	18.00	140	—
1908F	1,000	2,000	5,000	8,000	10,000	—
1908G	675,000	3.00	30.00	60.00	500	—
1808/7J	1,309,000	3.00	30.00	60.00	500	—
1908J	Inc. above	3.00	26.00	100	1,200	—
1909A	5,404,000	0.85	2.00	9.00	100	—
1909/5D	1,001,000	1.00	4.00	20.00	120	—
1909D	Inc. above	1.00	4.00	20.00	120	—
1909E	745,000	3.00	9.00	20.00	120	—
1909F	999,000	1.00	4.00	20.00	130	—
1909G	607,000	4.00	15.00	24.00	400	—
1909J	816,000	3.00	10.00	20.00	180	—
1911A	2,710,000	1.00	2.00	9.00	90.00	—
1911/05D	703,000	1.00	3.00	12.00	85.00	—
1911D	Inc. above	1.00	3.00	12.00	85.00	—
1911E	376,000	1.00	4.00	14.00	70.00	—
1911F	502,000	3.00	9.00	22.00	140	—
1911G	610,000	3.00	9.00	22.00	110	—
1911J	418,000	5.00	15.00	40.00	380	—
1912A	2,709,000	1.00	3.00	9.00	45.00	—
1912/5D	703,000	3.00	10.00	20.00	60.00	—
1912D	Inc. above	3.00	10.00	20.00	60.00	—
1912E	369,000	3.00	10.00	30.00	170	—
1912F	501,000	4.00	12.00	22.00	170	—
1912J	399,000	11.00	30.00	60.00	350	—
1913A	5,419,000	0.90	2.00	7.00	25.00	—
1913/05D	1,406,000	1.00	3.00	9.00	30.00	—
1913D	Inc. above	1.00	3.00	9.00	30.00	—
1913E	745,000	2.00	5.00	10.00	55.00	—
1913F	1,003,000	1.50	4.00	8.00	55.00	—
1913G	610,000	3.00	9.00	18.00	80.00	—
1913J	817,000	3.00	10.00	20.00	140	—
1914A	13,525,000	0.85	1.50	4.00	24.00	—
1914/05D	328,000	3.00	10.00	25.00	50.00	—
1914D	Inc. above	3.00	10.00	25.00	50.00	—
1914J	2,292,000	1.00	3.00	10.00	70.00	—
1915A	13,015,000	0.85	1.25	4.00	11.00	—
1915/05D	5,117,000	0.90	1.50	3.00	10.00	—
1915D	Inc. above	0.85	1.25	5.00	12.00	—
1915E	3,308,000	0.85	1.25	3.00	12.00	—
1915F	5,309,000	0.85	1.25	3.00	12.00	—
1915G	2,730,000	0.85	2.00	6.00	18.00	—
1915J	2,285,000	0.85	2.00	4.00	18.00	—
1916A	9,750,000	0.85	1.25	3.00	14.00	—
1916/616D	4,397,000	0.90	1.50	3.00	10.00	—
1916/05D	Inc. above	0.90	1.50	3.00	10.00	—
1916/5D	Inc. above	0.90	1.50	3.00	10.00	—
1916D	Inc. above	0.90	2.00	7.00	15.00	—
1916E	1,640,000	0.90	2.00	7.00	10.00	—
1916F	2,410,000	0.90	2.00	7.00	15.00	—
1916G	1,779,000	1.00	3.00	8.00	30.00	—
1916J	1,464,000	1.00	3.00	8.00	35.00	—
1917A	14,692,000	0.85	1.25	3.00	10.00	—
1917/05D	979,000	0.90	2.00	5.00	16.00	—
1917D	Inc. above	0.90	2.00	5.00	16.00	—
1917E	1,561,000	0.90	1.50	3.00	10.00	—
1917F	450,000	3.00	10.00	30.00	220	—
1917G	619,000	3.00	10.00	30.00	180	—
1917J	1,039,000	1.50	5.00	10.00	30.00	—
1918A	14,622,000	0.85	1.25	3.00	10.00	—
1918/05D	3,670,000	0.90	1.50	3.00	10.00	—
1918D	Inc. above	0.90	1.50	3.00	10.00	—
1918E	2,807,000	1.50	5.00	12.00	25.00	—
1918E Proof	19	—	—	—	—	—
1918F	4,010,000	3.00	9.00	20.00	80.00	—
1918G	1,032,000	2.00	6.00	14.00	60.00	—
1918J	3,452,000	1.50	5.00	12.00	30.00	—
1919A	9,124,000	0.85	1.25	4.00	12.00	—
1919/1619D	2,195,000	0.90	1.50	5.00	15.00	—
1919/05D	Inc. above	0.90	1.50	5.00	15.00	—
1919D	Inc. above	2.00	6.00	12.00	50.00	—
1919E	1,767,000	2.00	6.00	12.00	25.00	—
1919F	1,559,000	3.00	9.00	18.00	80.00	—
1919J	1,875,000	2.00	6.00	22.00	35.00	—
1905-19 Common date proof	—	Value: 150				

KM# 14 MARK

5.5500 g., 0.9000 Silver 0.1606 oz. ASW **Ruler:** Wilhelm II **Obv:** Denomination within wreath **Rev:** Crowned imperial eagle with shield on breast **Note:** Struck from 1890-1916.

Date	Mintage	F	VF	XF	Unc	BU
1901A	3,821,000	2.00	6.00	20.00	50.00	—
1901/800D	914,000	2.50	5.00	12.00	35.00	—
1901/801D	915,000	2.50	5.00	12.00	35.00	—
1901D	Inc. above	2.00	6.00	20.00	50.00	—
1901E	484,000	3.00	10.00	20.00	250	—
1901F	802,000	2.00	6.00	18.00	220	—
1901G	579,000	3.00	10.00	40.00	320	—
1901J	531,000	3.50	12.00	45.00	320	—
1902A	5,222,000	1.75	5.00	14.00	150	—
1902D	1,546,000	1.75	4.00	14.00	120	—
1902E	819,000	2.50	9.00	30.00	300	—
1902F	953,000	2.00	7.00	30.00	200	—
1902G	270,000	5.00	20.00	60.00	800	—
1902J	898,000	3.00	10.00	40.00	800	—
1903A	3,965,000	1.65	4.00	12.00	100	—
1903/803D	914,000	1.75	5.00	12.00	60.00	—
1903D	Inc. above	1.75	5.00	12.00	60.00	—
1903E	485,000	3.00	9.00	33.00	280	—
1903F	652,000	3.00	8.00	25.00	250	—
1903G	614,000	3.00	8.00	45.00	400	—
1903J	531,000	3.50	10.00	30.00	1,000	—
1904A	3,243,000	1.65	3.00	12.00	100	—
1904D	1,761,000	1.65	3.50	16.00	60.00	—
1904E	931,000	1.65	4.00	20.00	200	—
1904F	1,255,000	1.65	4.00	18.00	120	—
1904G	664,000	2.50	8.00	26.00	200	—
1904J	1,021,000	2.50	8.00	35.00	1,000	—
1905A	10,303,000	1.65	3.50	14.00	50.00	—
1905D	1,759,000	1.65	4.00	15.00	100	—
1905E	931,000	2.00	5.00	22.00	170	—
1905F	Inc. above	—	—	—	—	—
1905G	860,000	2.00	6.00	20.00	280	—
1905J	1,021,000	2.50	7.00	35.00	750	—
1906A	5,414,000	1.65	3.50	11.00	150	—
1906D	1,412,000	1.65	4.00	11.00	110	—
1906E	745,000	2.50	9.00	22.00	220	—
1906F	2,257,000	1.75	5.00	16.00	120	—
1906G	609,000	3.00	11.00	40.00	400	—
1906G Proof	—	—	—	—	—	—
1906J	372,000	5.00	15.00	50.00	2,000	—
1907A	9,201,000	1.65	2.50	5.00	55.00	—
1907D	2,387,000	1.65	2.75	9.00	50.00	—
1907E	1,265,000	1.65	3.00	11.00	80.00	—
1907F	1,704,000	1.65	3.00	8.00	65.00	—
1907G	1,035,000	1.25	4.00	12.00	130	—
1907J	1,833,000	1.75	5.00	25.00	350	—
1908A	4,338,000	1.65	3.00	9.00	85.00	—
1908D	1,126,000	1.65	3.00	9.00	60.00	—
1908E	596,000	2.50	7.00	18.00	100	—
1908F	802,000	1.65	5.00	15.00	85.00	—
1908G	488,000	2.50	9.00	24.00	210	—
1908J	653,000	2.50	8.00	30.00	420	—
1909A	4,151,000	1.65	5.00	13.00	200	—
1909D	1,968,000	1.65	5.00	12.00	75.00	—
1909E	Inc. below	40.00	120	180	420	—
1909G	854,000	3.00	10.00	24.00	170	—
1909J	53,000	85.00	175	285	650	—
1910A	5,870,000	1.65	3.50	12.00	55.00	—
1910D	1,406,000	1.75	4.00	6.00	50.00	—
1910E	1,050,000	1.75	5.00	12.00	80.00	—
1910F	1,631,000	1.75	5.00	10.00	70.00	—
1910G	610,000	2.00	7.00	22.00	170	—
1910J	1,094,000	2.50	8.00	30.00	330	—
1911A	5,693,000	1.65	3.00	9.00	60.00	—
1911D	126,000	8.00	30.00	48.00	170	—
1911E	738,000	1.75	5.00	8.00	60.00	—
1911F	773,000	2.50	9.00	50.00	900	—
1911G	305,000	3.50	11.00	40.00	100	—
1911J	812,000	2.50	9.00	35.00	100	—
1912A	2,439,000	1.65	2.50	6.00	70.00	—
1912D	632,000	1.75	4.00	10.00	100	—
1912E	708,000	2.00	5.00	10.00	70.00	—
1912F	502,000	2.00	6.00	16.00	145	—
1912J	409,000	5.00	25.00	50.00	750	—
1913F	450,000	5.00	15.00	30.00	130	—
1913G	275,000	15.00	40.00	60.00	180	—
1913J	368,000	7.00	20.00	40.00	270	—
1914A	11,304,000	1.65	2.25	4.00	15.00	—
1914/9D	3,515,000	1.65	2.50	6.00	18.00	—
1914D	Inc. above	1.65	2.50	6.00	18.00	—
1914E	2,235,000	1.65	3.00	7.00	18.00	—
1914F	2,300,000	1.65	2.25	3.75	15.00	—
1914G	1,911,000	1.65	4.00	8.00	20.00	—
1914J	2,978,000	1.65	4.00	8.00	18.00	—
1915A	13,817,000	1.65	2.25	4.00	15.00	—
1915D	4,218,000	1.65	3.00	5.00	15.00	—
1915E	2,235,000	1.65	3.00	5.00	15.00	—
1915F	2,911,000	1.65	3.00	9.00	20.00	—
1915G	1,749,000	1.65	3.00	6.00	15.00	—
1915J	1,634,000	1.75	4.00	8.00	15.00	—
1916F	306,000	10.00	30.00	45.00	90.00	—
1901-16 Common date proof	—	Value: 150				

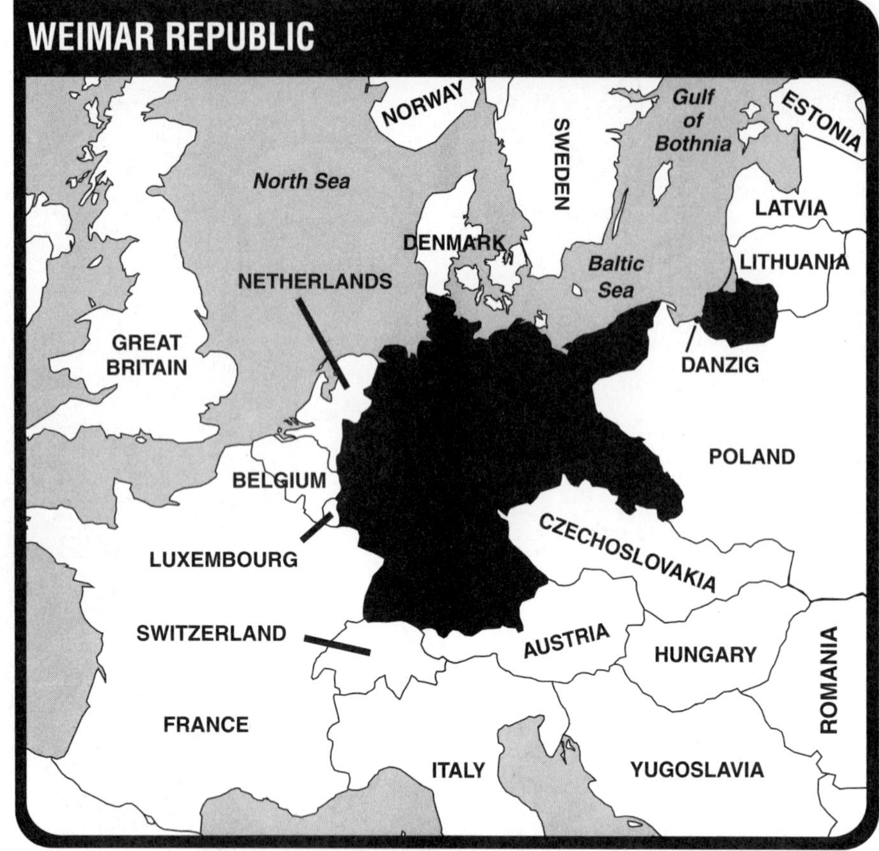

1919-1933

The Imperial German government disintegrated in a flurry of royal abdications as World War I ended. Desperate German parliamentarians, fearful of impending anarchy and civil war, hastily declared a German Republic. The new National Assembly, which was convened Feb. 6, 1919 in Weimar had to establish a legal government, draft a constitution, and then conclude a peace treaty with the Allies. Friedrich Ebert was elected as Reichs President. The harsh terms of the peace treaty imposed on Germany were economically and psychologically unacceptable to the German population regardless of political persuasion and the problem of German treaty compliance was to plague the Republic until the worldwide Great Depression of 1929. The new constitution paid less attention to fundamental individual rights and concentrated more power in the President and Central Government to insure a more stable social and economic order. The German bureaucracy survived the transition intact and had a stifling effect on the democratic process. The army started training large numbers of reservists in conjunction with the U.S.S.R. thereby circumventing treaty limitations on the size of the German military.

New anti-democratic ideologies were forming. Communism and Fascism were spreading. The National Socialist German Workers Party, under Hitler's leadership, incorporated the ever-present anti-Semitism into a new virulent Nazi Catechism.

In spite of the historic German inflation, the French occupation of the Rhineland, and the loss of vast territories and resources, the republic survived. By 1929 the German economy had been restored to its pre-war level. Much of the economic gains however were dependent on the extensive assistance provided by the U.S.A. and collapsed along with the world economy in 1929. Even during the good times, the Republic was never able to muster any loyal public support or patriotism. By 1930, Nationalists, Nazis, and Communists held nearly half of the Reichstag seats and the government was forced to rely more and more on presidential decrees as the only means to effectuate policy. In 1932, the Nazis won 230 Reichstag seats. As head of the largest party, Hitler claimed the right to form the next government. President Hindenburg's opposition forced a second election in which the Nazis lost 34 seats. Von Papen, however, convinced Hindenburg to name Hitler Chancellor by arguing that Hitler could be controlled! Hitler formed his cabinet and immediately began consolidating his power and laying the groundwork for the Third Reich.

MONETARY SYSTEM

(During 1923-1924)
100 Rentenpfennig = 1 Rentenmark

(Commencing 1924)
100 Reichspfennig = 1 Reichsmark

WEIMAR REPUBLIC

MARK COINAGE

1922-1923

KM# 27 50 PFENNIG

Aluminum, 23 mm. **Obv:** Denomination above date **Rev:** Sheaf behind inscription

Date	Mintage	F	VF	XF	Unc	BU
1919A	7,173,000	0.25	1.00	3.50	20.00	25.00
1919D	791,000	5.00	11.00	22.00	70.00	90.00
1919E	930,000	2.00	6.00	15.00	60.00	80.00
1919E Proof	35	Value: 350				
1919F	160,000	10.00	20.00	40.00	120	150
1919G	660,000	2.00	4.00	10.00	40.00	48.00
1919J	800,000	5.00	10.00	24.00	70.00	85.00
1920A	119,793,000	0.10	0.50	1.00	7.00	10.00
1920D	28,306,000	0.10	0.50	1.50	9.00	12.00
1920E	14,400,000	0.25	1.00	2.50	12.00	15.00
1920E Proof	226	Value: 150				
1920F	10,932,000	0.25	1.00	2.50	12.00	15.00
1920G	5,040,000	0.25	1.00	3.00	20.00	25.00
1920J	15,423,000	0.25	1.00	3.00	12.00	15.00
1921A	184,468,000	0.10	0.15	0.50	3.00	5.00
1921D	48,729,000	0.10	0.15	0.75	6.00	8.00
1921E	31,210,000	0.15	1.00	2.00	10.00	12.00
1921E Proof	332	Value: 115				
1921F	46,950,000	0.10	0.15	0.75	10.00	12.00
1921G	19,107,000	0.10	0.25	1.00	6.00	8.00
1921J	28,013,000	0.10	0.25	1.00	6.00	8.00
1922A	145,215,000	0.10	0.25	1.00	6.00	8.00
1922D	58,019,000	0.10	0.25	1.00	6.00	8.00
1922E	33,930,000	0.15	1.00	2.00	10.00	14.00
1922E Proof	333	Value: 115				
1922F	33,000,000	0.10	0.25	1.00	6.00	8.00
1922G	36,745,000	0.10	0.25	1.00	6.00	8.00
1922J	36,202,000	0.10	0.25	1.00	6.00	8.00

KM# 28 3 MARK

Aluminum **Obv:** Denomination above date **Rev:** Eagle **Edge:** Reeded

Date	Mintage	F	VF	XF	Unc	BU
1922A	15,497,000	0.25	2.50	7.00	14.00	20.00
1922A Proof	—	Value: 85.00				
1922E	2,000	60.00	100	200	600	700
1922E Proof	1,000	Value: 300				
1922F Rare	—	—	—	—	—	—

KM# 29 3 MARK

2.0300 g., Aluminum **Subject:** 3rd Anniversary Weimar Constitution

Date	Mintage	F	VF	XF	Unc	BU
1922A	32,514,000	0.25	1.00	3.00	10.00	12.00
1922D	8,441,000	140	200	300	800	1,000
1922D Proof	—	Value: 1,100				
1922E	2,440,000	0.50	2.00	4.00	12.00	15.00
1922E Proof	22,000	Value: 50.00				
1922F	6,023,000	2.00	6.00	12.00	35.00	45.00
1922G	3,655,000	0.50	2.00	4.00	12.00	15.00
1922J	4,896,000	0.50	2.00	4.00	12.00	15.00
1923E	2,060,000	6.00	12.00	25.00	70.00	80.00
1923E Proof	2,291	Value: 75.00				
1923F	—	300	650	1,000	2,250	2,750

Note: The 1923F 3 Mark pieces are from the burned-out ruin of the Stuttgart Mint, destroyed in World War II

KM# 35 200 MARK

1.0000 g., Aluminum, 23 mm. **Obv:** Denomination above date **Rev:** Eagle

Date	Mintage	F	VF	XF	Unc	BU
1923A	174,900,000	0.15	0.50	0.75	2.00	3.00
1923A Proof	—	Value: 125				
1923D	35,189,000	0.20	0.50	1.00	2.20	3.00
1923D Proof, unique	—	—	—	—	—	—
1923E	11,250,000	0.20	1.00	3.00	7.00	9.00
1923E Proof	4,095	Value: 100				
1923F	20,090,000	0.25	0.75	2.00	3.00	4.00
1923F Proof	—	Value: 125				
1923G	24,923,000	0.25	0.75	2.00	3.00	4.00
1923G Proof	—	Value: 125				
1923J	16,258,000	0.20	1.00	3.00	7.00	9.00
1923J Proof	—	Value: 125				

KM# 36 500 MARK

1.6700 g., Aluminum **Obv:** Denomination above date **Rev:** Eagle

Date	Mintage	F	VF	XF	Unc	BU
1923A	59,278,000	0.20	1.00	1.50	5.00	6.00
1923A Proof	—	Value: 125				
1923D	13,683,000	0.25	1.00	3.00	5.00	7.00
1923D Proof	—	Value: 125				
1923E	2,128,000	2.00	5.00	12.00	30.00	35.00
1923E Proof	2,053	Value: 100				
1923F	7,963,000	0.25	1.00	3.00	8.00	9.00
1923F Proof	—	Value: 125				
1923G	4,404,000	0.25	1.75	6.00	14.00	16.00
1923G Proof	—	Value: 125				
1923J	1,008,000	10.00	20.00	40.00	90.00	100
1923J Proof	—	Value: 250				

RENTENMARK COINAGE

1923-1929

KM# 30 RENTENPFENNIG

2.0000 g., Bronze **Obv:** Denomination within circle **Rev:** Wheat sheaf divides date

Date	Mintage	F	VF	XF	Unc	BU
1923A	12,629,000	0.25	1.00	3.00	15.00	16.00
1923D	Est. 2,314,000	0.25	2.00	7.00	30.00	33.00
1923E	2,200,000	1.00	3.00	8.00	30.00	33.00
1923F	160,000	2.00	8.00	24.00	80.00	90.00
1923G	1,004,000	1.00	4.00	8.00	30.00	33.00
1923J	1,470,000	2.00	8.00	20.00	85.00	100
1924A	55,273,000	25.00	0.50	3.00	12.00	14.00
1924D	17,540,000	25.00	1.50	4.00	15.00	17.00
1924E	6,838,000	1.00	1.50	6.00	24.00	27.00
1924F	10,347,000	1.00	2.50	6.00	24.00	27.00
1924G	7,366,000	1.00	3.00	9.00	30.00	33.00
1924J	11,024,000	1.00	2.50	6.00	24.00	26.00
1925A	—	750	1,250	2,500	—	—
1929F	—	150	250	500	1,000	1,200
1923-29 Common date proof	—	Value: 120				

KM# 31 2 RENTENPFENNIG

3.3000 g., Bronze, 20 mm. **Obv:** Denomination within circle **Rev:** Wheat sheaf divides date

Date	Mintage	F	VF	XF	Unc	BU
1923A	8,587,000	0.20	1.00	3.00	20.00	22.00
1923D	1,490,000	0.20	1.00	6.00	35.00	40.00
1923F	Inc. above	1.00	3.50	9.00	35.00	45.00
1923G	Inc. above	1.00	2.00	10.00	40.00	50.00
1923J	Inc. above	2.00	6.00	15.00	70.00	80.00
1924A	80,864,000	0.20	0.50	1.00	8.00	10.00
1924D	19,899,000	0.25	1.00	3.00	15.00	17.00
1924E	6,595,000	0.25	1.00	3.00	15.00	17.00
1924F	14,969,000	0.25	1.00	3.00	15.00	17.00
1924G	10,349,000	0.25	1.00	4.00	18.00	20.00
1924J	21,196,000	0.25	1.00	3.00	15.00	17.00
1923-24 Common date proof	—	Value: 140				

KM# 32 5 RENTENPFENNIG

2.5200 g., Aluminum-Bronze

Date	Mintage	F	VF	XF	Unc	BU
1923A	3,083,000	1.00	3.00	10.00	50.00	55.00
1923D	Inc. below	1.00	3.00	12.00	60.00	65.00
1923F	Inc. below	35.00	70.00	120	300	320
1923G	Inc. below	10.00	25.00	50.00	200	220
1924A	171,966,000	0.25	1.00	3.00	20.00	24.00
1924D	31,163,000	0.25	1.00	5.00	28.00	30.00
1924E	12,206,000	0.25	1.00	6.00	30.00	33.00
1924F	29,032,000	0.25	1.00	5.00	30.00	33.00
1924G	19,217,000	0.25	1.00	6.00	30.00	33.00
1924J	32,332,000	0.25	1.00	5.00	25.00	27.00
1925F 1 known	—	—	5,000	—	—	—
1923-25 Common date proof	—	Value: 160				

KM# 33 10 RENTENPFENNIG

3.9200 g., Aluminum-Bronze, 21 mm. **Obv:** Denomination within square, oak leaf on each side **Rev:** Six grain sprigs form center triangle above date

Date	Mintage	F	VF	XF	Unc	BU
1923A	Inc. below	0.25	3.00	10.00	30.00	33.00
1923D	Inc. below	0.50	6.00	12.00	48.00	53.00
1923F	Inc. below	70.00	100	180	400	420
1923G	Inc. below	2.50	15.00	25.00	120	140
1924A	169,956,000	0.25	1.00	3.00	15.00	17.00
1924D	33,894,000	0.25	1.00	4.00	18.00	20.00
1924E	18,679,000	0.25	1.50	4.50	22.00	24.00
1924F	42,237,000	0.25	1.50	5.00	22.00	24.00
1924F Proof	—	Value: 160				
1924G	18,758,000	0.25	1.50	5.00	22.00	25.00
1924J	33,928,000	0.25	1.50	6.00	25.00	28.00
1925F	13,000	900	1,500	2,000	—	—
1923-1925 Common date proof	—	Value: 160				

KM# 34 50 RENTENPFENNIG

5.1700 g., Aluminum-Bronze **Obv:** Denomination within square, oak leaf on each side **Rev:** Six grain sprigs form center triangle above date

Date	Mintage	F	VF	XF	Unc	BU
1923A	451,000	10.00	20.00	32.00	80.00	90.00
1923D	192,000	15.00	30.00	48.00	180	200
1923F	120,000	40.00	90.00	125	420	450
1923G	120,000	20.00	40.00	55.00	220	240
1923J	4,000	500	800	1,600	2,500	2,800
1924A	117,365,000	5.00	12.00	20.00	60.00	70.00
1924D	30,971,000	6.00	15.00	25.00	80.00	90.00
1924E	14,668,000	6.00	15.00	25.00	80.00	90.00
1924F	21,968,000	10.00	15.00	25.00	85.00	100
1924G	13,349,000	12.00	22.00	36.00	130	150
1924J	17,252,000	10.00	20.00	35.00	100	120
1923-24 Common date proof	—	Value: 225				

REICHSMARK COINAGE

1924-1938

KM# 37 REICHSPFENNIG

2.0000 g., Bronze **Obv:** Denomination within circle **Rev:** Wheat sheaf divides date

Date	Mintage	F	VF	XF	Unc	BU
1924A	13,496,000	0.20	0.50	1.00	10.00	11.00
1924D	6,206,000	0.20	0.50	1.00	12.00	13.00
1924E	1,100,000	100	250	400	850	900
1924F	2,650,000	0.20	0.50	1.00	12.00	13.00
1924G	5,100,000	0.25	0.75	3.00	15.00	16.00
1924J	24,400,000	0.20	0.50	1.00	12.00	13.00
1925A	40,925,000	0.20	0.50	1.00	5.00	10.00
1925D	1,558,000	5.00	15.00	35.00	100	120
1925E	10,460,000	0.20	0.50	1.00	10.00	11.00
1925F	5,673,000	0.20	0.50	1.00	10.00	11.00
1925G	13,502,000	0.20	0.50	1.00	10.00	11.00
1925J	30,300,000	0.20	0.50	1.00	10.00	11.00
1927A	4,671,000	0.30	1.00	3.00	18.00	19.00
1927D	4,203,000	0.30	1.00	3.00	18.00	19.00
1927E	8,000,000	0.30	1.00	3.00	18.00	19.00
1927F	2,350,000	0.50	2.00	10.00	35.00	37.00
1927G	3,236,000	0.50	2.00	8.00	30.00	32.00
1928A	19,300,000	0.20	0.50	1.00	10.00	11.00
1928D	10,200,000	0.20	0.50	1.00	11.00	12.00
1928F	8,672,000	0.20	0.50	1.00	12.00	13.00
1928G	3,764,000	0.50	2.00	5.00	24.00	26.00
1929A	37,170,000	0.20	0.50	1.00	6.00	10.00
1929D	9,337,000	0.20	0.50	1.00	6.00	10.00
1929E	6,600,000	0.20	0.50	1.00	6.00	11.00
1929F	3,150,000	0.20	0.50	1.50	6.00	11.00
1929G	1,986,000	0.20	0.75	3.00	13.00	15.00
1930A	40,997,000	0.20	0.50	1.00	8.00	10.00
1930D	6,441,000	0.20	0.50	1.00	10.00	12.00
1930E	1,412,000	6.00	15.00	40.00	140	160
1930F	6,415,000	0.20	0.50	1.50	10.00	11.00
1930G	5,017,000	0.20	0.50	1.00	10.00	11.00
1931A	38,481,000	0.20	0.50	3.00	8.00	10.00
1931D	5,998,000	0.20	0.50	1.00	11.00	12.00
1931E	12,800,000	0.20	0.50	2.50	14.00	16.00
1931F	12,591,000	0.20	0.50	1.00	11.00	12.00
1931G	2,622,000	0.20	0.50	8.00	30.00	33.00
1932A	17,096,000	0.20	0.75	2.50	20.00	24.00
1933A	37,846,000	0.20	0.50	1.00	8.00	10.00
1933E	2,945,000	0.30	2.00	8.00	30.00	33.00
1933F	5,023,000	0.20	0.50	1.00	11.00	12.00
1934A	51,214,000	0.20	0.50	1.00	7.00	9.00
1934D	7,408,000	0.20	0.50	1.00	10.00	12.00
1934E	4,628,000	0.50	3.50	10.00	35.00	40.00
1934F	5,667,000	0.20	0.50	1.00	11.00	13.00
1934G	2,450,000	0.20	0.50	3.00	15.00	17.00
1934J	4,271,000	0.20	0.50	3.00	15.00	17.00
1935A	35,894,000	0.20	0.50	1.00	7.00	9.00
1935D	15,489,000	0.20	0.50	1.00	8.00	10.00
1935E	8,351,000	0.20	0.50	2.00	11.00	14.00
1935F	12,094,000	0.20	0.50	1.50	8.00	10.00
1935G	7,454,000	0.20	0.50	1.00	11.00	14.00
1935J	8,505,000	0.20	0.50	1.00	10.00	12.00
1936A	Est. 50,949,000	0.20	0.50	1.00	7.00	8.00
1936D	12,262,000	0.20	0.50	1.00	9.00	10.00
1936E	2,576,000	0.50	3.00	7.00	30.00	33.00
1936F	6,915,000	0.20	0.50	1.00	10.00	12.00
1936G	Est. 2,940,000	0.20	0.50	1.00	11.00	13.00
1936J	Est. 5,421,000	0.20	0.50	1.00	11.00	13.00
1924-36 Common date proof	—	Value: 85.00				

KM# 38 2 REICHSPFENNIG

3.3400 g., Bronze **Obv:** Denomination within circle **Rev:** Wheat sheaf divides date

Date	Mintage	F	VF	XF	Unc	BU
1923F Proof	—	Value: 4,500				
1924A	19,620,000	0.20	0.50	1.00	10.00	12.00
1924D	3,482,000	0.30	1.00	2.00	20.00	22.00
1924E	4,253,000	0.30	2.00	5.00	25.00	28.00
1924F	4,567,000	0.30	0.60	1.50	15.00	17.00
1924G	7,560,000	0.30	0.60	1.50	15.00	17.00
1924J	7,489,000	0.30	0.50	1.00	15.00	17.00
1925A	22,433,000	0.20	0.50	1.00	7.00	8.00
1925D	2,412,000	0.20	1.00	4.00	30.00	32.00
1925E	5,414,000	0.30	0.60	2.00	18.00	20.00
1925F	4,851,000	0.30	0.60	2.00	18.00	20.00
1925G	2,456,000	2.00	7.00	15.00	75.00	80.00
1936A	3,220,000	0.50	2.00	5.00	24.00	26.00
1936D	6,525,000	0.20	0.50	1.50	8.00	10.00
1936E	573,000	5.00	12.00	22.00	80.00	90.00
1936F	3,100,000	0.20	0.60	4.00	23.00	25.00
1923-36 Common date proof	—	Value: 90.00				

KM# 75 4 REICHSPFENNIG

Bronze **Obv:** Large denomination within circle, date at right **Rev:** Eagle

Date	Mintage	F	VF	XF	Unc	BU
1932A	27,101,000	—	9.00	15.00	35.00	40.00
1932A Proof	—	Value: 150				
1932D	7,055,000	—	12.00	18.00	40.00	50.00
1932D Proof	—	Value: 150				
1932E	3,729,000	—	15.00	23.00	45.00	55.00
1932E Proof	—	Value: 150				
1932F	5,022,000	—	12.00	18.00	48.00	60.00
1932F Proof	—	Value: 150				
1932G	3,050,000	—	15.00	25.00	80.00	100
1932G Proof	—	Value: 150				
1932J	4,094,000	—	12.00	18.00	65.00	75.00
1932J Proof	—	Value: 150				

KM# 39 5 REICHSPFENNIG

2.5400 g., Aluminum-Bronze **Obv:** Denomination within square, oak leaf on each side **Rev:** Six grain sprigs form center triangle above date

Date	Mintage	F	VF	XF	Unc	BU
1924A	14,469,000	0.30	0.60	3.00	20.00	22.00
1924D	8,139,000	0.50	1.00	4.00	20.00	23.00
1924E	5,976,000	0.50	1.00	5.00	25.00	28.00
1924E Proof, Rare	166	—	—	—	—	—
1924F	3,134,000	0.50	1.00	4.00	25.00	28.00
1924G	4,790,000	0.50	1.00	7.00	30.00	33.00
1924J	2,200,000	0.50	2.00	10.00	40.00	44.00
1925A	85,239,000	0.20	0.50	2.50	13.00	15.00
1925D	39,750,000	0.20	0.50	2.50	15.00	17.00
1925E	17,554,000	0.20	1.00	4.00	18.00	20.00
1925E Proof, Rare	61	—	—	—	—	—
1925F Large 5	20,990,000	6.00	14.00	28.00	130	150
1925F Small 5	Inc. above	0.20	0.50	4.00	25.00	28.00
1925G	10,232,000	0.20	1.00	5.00	26.00	30.00
1925J	10,950,000	0.50	4.00	9.00	40.00	45.00
1926A	22,377,000	0.50	1.00	5.00	30.00	35.00
1926E	5,990,000	10.00	25.00	50.00	260	290
1926E Proof, Rare	33	—	—	—	—	—
1926F	2,871,000	5.00	16.00	38.00	190	220
1930A	7,418,000	0.30	3.00	6.00	25.00	30.00
1935A	19,178,000	0.20	0.50	1.00	10.00	12.00
1935D	5,480,000	0.20	0.50	2.00	12.00	14.00
1935E	2,384,000	0.30	0.60	3.00	20.00	22.00
1935F	4,585,000	0.20	0.50	2.00	16.00	18.00
1935G	2,652,000	0.30	3.00	6.00	20.00	22.00
1935J	2,614,000	0.30	3.00	6.00	24.00	26.00
1936A	36,992,000	0.20	0.30	1.00	10.00	12.00

Date	Mintage	F	VF	XF	Unc	BU
1936D	8,108,000	0.20	0.50	2.00	12.00	14.00
1936E	2,981,000	0.20	0.60	3.00	18.00	20.00
1936F	6,643,000	0.20	0.60	3.00	15.00	17.00
1936G	2,274,000	0.20	0.60	3.00	18.00	20.00
1936J	4,470,000	0.20	0.60	3.00	18.00	20.00
1924-36 Common date proof	—	Value: 100				

KM# 40 10 REICHSPFENNIG

4.0500 g., Aluminum-Bronze, 21 mm. **Obv:** Denomination within square, oak leaf on each side **Rev:** Six grain sprigs form center triangle above date

Date	Mintage	F	VF	XF	Unc	BU
1924A	20,883,000	0.20	1.00	6.00	32.00	35.00
1924D	9,639,000	0.20	1.00	9.00	52.00	60.00
1924E	5,185,000	0.20	1.00	6.00	35.00	40.00
1924E Proof, Rare	166	—	—	—	—	—
1924F	2,758,000	1.00	9.00	28.00	160	180
1924G	4,363,000	0.30	2.00	11.00	70.00	85.00
1924J	3,993,000	0.30	2.00	11.00	70.00	85.00
1925A	102,319,000	0.20	0.50	2.00	15.00	20.00
1925D	36,853,000	0.20	1.00	4.00	28.00	32.00
1925E	18,700,000	0.30	2.00	9.00	45.00	52.00
1925E Proof, Rare	61	—	—	—	—	—
1925F	12,516,000	0.20	3.00	15.00	55.00	62.00
1925G	10,360,000	0.30	4.00	15.00	60.00	70.00
1925J	8,755,000	1.00	5.00	17.00	80.00	90.00
1926A	14,390,000	0.30	2.00	10.00	50.00	55.00
1926G	1,481,000	2.00	10.00	28.00	130	150
1928A	2,308,000	2.00	6.00	12.00	45.00	60.00
1928G	Inc. below	50.00	120	200	600	700
1929A	25,712,000	0.20	1.00	2.00	22.00	25.00
1929D	7,049,000	0.20	1.00	2.00	35.00	40.00
1929E	3,138,000	0.30	2.00	12.00	75.00	90.00
1929F	3,740,000	0.30	2.00	12.00	65.00	75.00
1929G	2,729,000	0.30	4.00	18.00	90.00	100
1929J	4,086,000	0.30	2.00	12.00	75.00	85.00
1930A	7,540,000	0.20	1.00	3.00	20.00	24.00
1930D	2,148,000	0.30	2.00	5.00	35.00	40.00
1930E	2,090,000	1.00	4.00	13.00	90.00	110
1930F	2,006,000	1.00	4.00	13.00	60.00	75.00
1930G	1,542,000	2.00	5.00	20.00	100	130
1930J	1,637,000	2.00	4.00	12.00	100	120
1931A	9,661,000	0.30	2.00	4.00	25.00	35.00
1931D	664,000	15.00	35.00	70.00	180	200
1931F	1,482,000	7.50	20.00	45.00	150	180
1931G	38,000	170	260	430	1,600	2,000
1932A	4,528,000	0.30	2.00	4.00	24.00	28.00
1932D	2,812,000	0.50	4.00	10.00	50.00	60.00
1932E	1,491,000	2.50	5.00	12.00	75.00	90.00
1932F	1,806,000	3.00	8.00	15.00	90.00	115
1932G	137,000	350	850	1,250	2,000	2,500
1933A	1,349,000	15.00	25.00	45.00	170	200
1933G	1,046,000	5.00	15.00	30.00	80.00	100
1933J	1,634,000	3.00	9.00	20.00	60.00	75.00
1934A	3,200,000	0.30	1.00	6.00	30.00	35.00
1934D	1,252,000	2.00	7.00	18.00	110	125
1934E	Inc. below	18.00	35.00	65.00	180	215
1934F	100,000	12.00	30.00	55.00	170	205
1934G	150,000	15.00	40.00	75.00	290	335
1935A	35,890,000	0.20	0.50	2.00	15.00	17.00
1935D	8,960,000	0.20	0.50	2.00	18.00	20.00
1935E	5,966,000	0.20	0.50	2.00	20.00	22.00
1935F	7,944,000	0.20	0.30	1.50	18.00	20.00
1935G	4,847,000	0.20	0.50	3.00	20.00	22.00
1935J	8,995,000	0.20	0.50	3.00	16.00	18.00
1936A	24,527,000	0.20	0.80	2.00	18.00	20.00
1936D	8,092,000	0.20	1.00	3.00	23.00	25.00
1936E	2,441,000	0.20	1.00	6.00	28.00	31.00
1936F	4,889,000	0.20	1.00	3.00	24.00	27.00
1936G	1,715,000	0.20	3.00	12.00	50.00	56.00
1936J	1,632,000	0.50	4.00	18.00	70.00	80.00
1924-36 Common date proof	—	Value: 100				

KM# 41 50 REICHSPFENNIG

Aluminum-Bronze **Obv:** Denomination within square, oak leaf on each side **Rev:** Six grain sprigs form center triangle above date

Date	Mintage	F	VF	XF	Unc	BU
1924A	801,000	700	1,200	2,000	3,000	3,500
1924A	—	Value: 4,000				
1924E	Inc. below	1,650	3,000	4,500	5,500	6,500
1924F	55,000	3,200	7,000	10,000	17,000	20,000
1924F Proof	—	Value: 22,500				

Note: Peus Auction #324 4-89 proof realized $10,360

Date	Mintage	F	VF	XF	Unc	BU
1924G	11,000	6,000	12,000	18,000	25,000	30,000
1924G Proof	—	Value: 15,000				
1925E	1,805,000	900	1,400	2,250	3,750	4,250
1925E Proof	196	Value: 5,500				
1925F	—	6,000	12,000	18,000	25,000	30,000
1925F Proof	—	Value: 35,000				

Note: Peus Auction #324 4-89 proof realized $23,830. Kurdfälzische Munzhandlung Mannheim 6-91 proof realized $37,600

KM# 49 50 REICHSPFENNIG

3.5100 g., Nickel **Obv:** Eagle within circle, leaf spray below **Rev:** Denomination within lined circle, oak leaves and acorns above

Date	Mintage	F	VF	XF	Unc	BU
1927A	16,309,000	2.00	3.00	7.00	23.00	25.00
1927D	2,228,000	3.00	7.00	15.00	65.00	75.00
1927E	1,070,000	4.00	9.00	18.00	70.00	80.00
1927F	1,940,000	2.50	6.00	12.00	60.00	70.00
1927G	1,756,000	5.00	15.00	25.00	100	120
1927J	4,056,000	2.50	6.00	12.00	60.00	70.00
1928A	43,864,000	0.80	2.00	4.00	18.00	20.00
1928D	14,088,000	1.00	3.00	6.00	30.00	35.00
1928E	8,618,000	1.00	3.00	6.00	30.00	35.00
1928F	9,954,000	1.00	3.00	6.00	30.00	35.00
1928G	6,177,000	1.00	3.50	7.00	40.00	50.00
1928J	6,565,000	1.00	3.00	6.00	40.00	50.00
1929A	10,298,000	1.00	3.00	7.00	40.00	50.00
1929D	1,965,000	2.00	6.00	15.00	70.00	85.00
1929F	1,162,000	9.00	20.00	45.00	150	170
1930A	4,128,000	1.00	4.00	8.00	40.00	48.00
1930D	1,406,000	4.00	8.00	15.00	75.00	88.00
1930E	745,000	20.00	35.00	70.00	220	250
1930F	320,000	50.00	100	140	360	420
1930G	610,000	18.00	40.00	80.00	250	280
1930J	526,000	20.00	50.00	100	280	320
1931A	5,624,000	1.00	4.00	8.00	21.00	24.00
1931D	1,125,000	2.00	7.00	16.00	32.00	35.00
1931F	1,484,000	2.00	6.00	15.00	30.00	33.00
1931G	60,000	190	290	420	900	1,000
1931J	291,000	45.00	120	200	400	500
1932E	598,000	40.00	90.00	150	400	500
1932G	96,000	800	1,300	1,900	2,900	3,500
1933G	333,000	55.00	120	180	430	475
1933J	654,000	45.00	100	155	360	390
1935A	6,390,000	1.00	4.00	9.00	32.00	36.00
1935D	2,812,000	3.00	7.00	15.00	42.00	48.00
1935E	745,000	10.00	25.00	40.00	130	150
1935F	2,006,000	3.00	6.00	12.00	40.00	50.00
1935G	650,000	15.00	35.00	48.00	140	180
1935J	1,635,000	3.00	14.00	34.00	100	120
1936A	7,696,000	2.00	4.00	10.00	25.00	35.00
1936D	844,000	7.00	20.00	42.00	155	175
1936E	1,190,000	7.00	20.00	40.00	165	190
1936F	602,000	9.00	25.00	52.00	180	220
1936G	936,000	6.00	18.00	35.00	110	130
1936J	490,000	30.00	70.00	120	260	290
1937A	10,842,000	1.00	2.50	5.00	12.00	14.00
1937D	2,814,000	1.00	4.00	12.00	36.00	40.00
1937F	1,700,000	1.00	4.00	12.00	36.00	40.00
1937J	300,000	60.00	120	200	380	420
1938E	1,200,000	8.00	15.00	30.00	110	125
1938G	1,299,000	7.00	13.00	26.00	90.00	105
1938J	1,333,000	7.00	13.00	26.00	90.00	105
1927-38 Common date proof	—	Value: 200				

KM# 42 MARK

5.0000 g., 0.5000 Silver 0.0804 oz. ASW **Obv:** Denomination above date **Rev:** Eagle

Date	Mintage	F	VF	XF	Unc	BU
1924A	75,536,000	5.00	12.00	24.00	65.00	75.00
1924D	17,099,000	6.00	13.00	26.00	75.00	90.00
1924E	12,293,000	7.00	16.00	32.00	170	190
1924E Proof	115	Value: 275				
1924F	16,550,000	6.00	13.00	26.00	120	140
1924G	10,065,000	7.00	15.00	30.00	160	190
1924J	13,481,000	6.00	12.00	25.00	110	130
1925A	13,878,000	14.00	28.00	56.00	270	290
1925D	6,100,000	9.00	20.00	40.00	130	150
1924-25 Common date proof	—	Value: 250				

KM# 43 3 MARK

15.0000 g., 0.5000 Silver 0.2411 oz. ASW, 30 mm. **Obv:** Denomination above date **Rev:** Eagle

Date	Mintage	F	VF	XF	Unc	BU
1924A	24,386,000	16.00	40.00	80.00	110	130
1924D	3,769,000	20.00	45.00	90.00	280	320
1924E	3,353,000	20.00	42.00	80.00	280	320
1924E Proof	115	Value: 450				
1924F	4,518,000	20.00	40.00	80.00	200	230
1924G	2,745,000	25.00	50.00	100	300	340
1924J	3,677,000	20.00	40.00	80.00	220	250
1925D	2,558,000	40.00	100	200	700	790
1924-25 Common date proof	—	Value: 280				

KM# 44 REICHSMARK

5.0000 g., 0.5000 Silver 0.0804 oz. ASW **Obv:** Eagle above date **Rev:** Denomination within wreath

Date	Mintage	F	VF	XF	Unc	BU
1925A	34,527,000	5.00	12.00	24.00	50.00	55.00
1925A Proof	600	Value: 380				
1925D	13,854,000	6.00	16.00	28.00	60.00	70.00
1925E	6,460,000	8.00	20.00	32.00	110	125
1925F	8,035,000	8.00	17.00	27.00	135	155
1925G	4,520,000	9.00	23.00	38.00	120	140
1925J	6,800,000	9.00	22.00	36.00	115	135
1926A	35,555,000	8.00	17.00	26.00	95.00	110
1926D	4,424,000	10.00	21.00	38.00	120	140
1926E	3,225,000	14.00	32.00	70.00	230	260
1926E Proof	31	Value: 450				
1926F	3,045,000	12.00	30.00	50.00	190	210
1926G	3,410,000	14.00	32.00	55.00	240	260
1926J	1,290,000	50.00	110	180	480	540
1927A	364,000	250	390	600	1,300	1,400
1927F	1,959,000	40.00	70.00	110	280	310
1927J	2,451,000	30.00	55.00	100	240	265

KM# 45 2 REICHSMARK

10.0000 g., 0.5000 Silver 0.1607 oz. ASW, 28 mm. **Obv:** Eagle above date **Rev:** Denomination within wreath

Date	Mintage	F	VF	XF	Unc	BU
1925A	16,145,000	8.00	16.00	24.00	80.00	90.00
1925D	2,272,000	10.00	20.00	32.00	120	135
1925E	1,971,000	12.00	25.00	43.00	160	175
1925E Proof	101	Value: 350				
1925F	2,414,000	11.00	23.00	37.00	100	115
1925G	929,000	15.00	32.00	65.00	210	230
1925J	2,326,000	10.00	20.00	32.00	96.00	110
1926A	31,645,000	8.00	16.00	25.00	70.00	80.00
1926D	11,322,000	8.00	16.00	25.00	80.00	90.00
1926E	5,107,000	11.00	23.00	45.00	170	190
1926E Proof	30	—	750	—	—	—
1926F	7,115,000	8.00	16.00	32.00	105	120
1926G	5,171,000	10.00	20.00	42.00	150	170
1926J	5,305,000	10.00	18.00	38.00	115	130
1927A	6,399,000	12.00	25.00	40.00	135	150
1927D	466,000	800	1,200	2,000	5,000	6,000
1927E	373,000	200	325	700	1,400	1,600
1927E Proof	53	Value: 3,000				
1927F	502,000	60.00	200	300	950	1,100
1927J	540,000	45.00	100	185	500	580
1931D	2,109,000	20.00	36.00	53.00	160	180
1931E	1,118,000	26.00	50.00	85.00	240	270
1931F	1,505,000	22.00	40.00	65.00	190	230
1931G	915,000	30.00	55.00	100	250	300
1931J	1,226,000	30.00	55.00	100	520	600
1925-31 Common date proof	—	Value: 300				

KM# 46 3 REICHSMARK
15.0000 g., 0.5000 Silver 0.2411 oz. ASW, 30 mm. **Subject:** 1000th Year of the Rhineland **Obv:** Armored figure behind shield divides date, right arm raised **Rev:** Denomination within wreath **Designer:** Wackerle

Date	Mintage	F	VF	XF	Unc	BU
1925A	3,052,000	25.00	45.00	55.00	100	110
1925A Proof	—	Value: 200				
1925D	1,123,000	25.00	50.00	60.00	110	125
1925D Proof	—	Value: 240				
1925E	441,000	25.00	55.00	65.00	120	145
1925E Proof	229	Value: 250				
1925F	173,000	30.00	60.00	75.00	135	155
1925F Proof	—	Value: 280				
1925G	300,000	30.00	55.00	70.00	115	130
1925G Proof	—	Value: 240				
1925J	492,000	30.00	55.00	70.00	115	130
1925J Proof	—	Value: 240				

KM# 48 3 REICHSMARK
15.0000 g., 0.5000 Silver 0.2411 oz. ASW, 30 mm. **Subject:** 700 Years of Freedom for Lubeck **Obv:** Denomination within circle, leaf spray below **Rev:** Double-headed eagle on shield within circle, dates above

Date	Mintage	F	VF	XF	Unc	BU
1926A	200,000	60.00	110	180	240	260
1926A Proof	—	Value: 300				

KM# 50 3 REICHSMARK
15.0000 g., 0.5000 Silver 0.2411 oz. ASW, 30 mm. **Subject:** 100th Anniversary of Bremerhaven **Obv:** Eagle on shield within scalloped design **Rev:** Shield divides date below ship

Date	Mintage	F	VF	XF	Unc	BU
1927A	150,000	70.00	130	190	270	290
1927A Proof	—	Value: 360				

KM# 52 3 REICHSMARK
15.0000 g., 0.5000 Silver 0.2411 oz. ASW, 30 mm. **Subject:** 1000th Anniversary - Founding of Nordhausen **Obv:** Large denomination within scalloped design **Rev:** Heinrich I and Mathilde **Designer:** Maxmillian Dasio

Date	Mintage	F	VF	XF	Unc	BU
1927A	100,000	60.00	120	190	260	290
1927A Proof	—	Value: 500				

KM# 53 3 REICHSMARK
15.0000 g., 0.5000 Silver 0.2411 oz. ASW, 30 mm. **Subject:** 400th Anniversary - Philipps University in Marburg **Obv:** Eagle, denomination below **Rev:** Arms of Philip I the Magnanimous **Designer:** Maxmillian Dasio

Date	Mintage	F	VF	XF	Unc	BU
1927A	130,000	60.00	115	160	240	265
1927A Proof	—	Value: 290				

KM# 54 3 REICHSMARK
15.0000 g., 0.5000 Silver 0.2411 oz. ASW, 30 mm. **Subject:** 450th Anniversary - Tubingen University **Obv:** Eagle, denomination below **Rev:** Count Eberhard the Bearded left

Date	Mintage	F	VF	XF	Unc	BU
1927F	50,000	190	380	520	720	760
1927F Proof	—	Value: 980				

KM# 57 3 REICHSMARK
15.0000 g., 0.5000 Silver 0.2411 oz. ASW, 30 mm. **Subject:** 900th Anniversary - Founding of Naumburg **Obv:** Eagle above denomination **Rev:** Margrave Hermann, City Founder

Date	Mintage	F	VF	XF	Unc	BU
1928A	100,000	70.00	115	170	230	250
1928A Matte proof	—	Value: 480				

KM# 58 3 REICHSMARK
15.0000 g., 0.5000 Silver 0.2411 oz. ASW, 30 mm. **Subject:** 400th Anniversary - Death of Albrecht Durer **Obv:** Eagle above denomination **Rev:** Head left within circle, date below **Designer:** Nida Rumelin

Date	Mintage	F	VF	XF	Unc	BU
1928D	50,000	150	330	530	710	750
1928D Matte proof	—	Value: 900				

KM# 59 3 REICHSMARK
15.0000 g., 0.5000 Silver 0.2411 oz. ASW, 30 mm. **Subject:** 1000th Anniversary - Founding of Dinkelsbuhl **Obv:** Eagle above denomination **Rev:** Shield below figure holding sickle and sheaf, towers flank, date is divided in fourths by the above **Designer:** Karl Roth

Date	Mintage	F	VF	XF	Unc	BU
1928D	40,000	250	500	750	900	1,000
1928D Proof	—	Value: 1,400				
1928D Matte proof	—	Value: 2,250				

KM# 65 3 REICHSMARK
15.0000 g., 0.5000 Silver 0.2411 oz. ASW, 30 mm. **Subject:** 1000th Anniversary - Meissen **Obv:** Eagle within circle, denomination below **Rev:** Central figure holding shields on poles divides date, five crosses above

Date	Mintage	F	VF	XF	Unc	BU
1929E	200,000	30.00	50.00	75.00	115	125
1929E Proof	—	Value: 330				

KM# 62 3 REICHSMARK
15.0000 g., 0.5000 Silver 0.2411 oz. ASW, 30 mm. **Subject:** Waldeck-Prussia Union **Obv:** Imperial eagle above denomination **Rev:** Eagle with wings lowered holds shield at left, date below **Designer:** Kruschker

Date	Mintage	F	VF	XF	Unc	BU
1929A	170,000	55.00	125	175	250	270
1929A Proof	—	Value: 450				

KM# 63 3 REICHSMARK
15.0000 g., 0.5000 Silver 0.2411 oz. ASW, 30 mm. **Subject:** 10th Anniversary - Weimar Constitution **Obv:** Paul von Hindenburg **Rev:** Hand with two fingers raised within circle, dates below **Designer:** Rudolf Bosselt

Date	Mintage	F	VF	XF	Unc	BU
1929A	1,421,000	20.00	35.00	65.00	80.00	70.00
1929A Proof	—	Value: 250				
1929A Matte proof	—	—	—	—	—	—
1929D	499,000	20.00	40.00	75.00	90.00	98.00
1929D Proof	—	Value: 250				
1929E	122,000	24.00	50.00	85.00	100	110
1929E Proof	—	Value: 280				
1929F	370,000	20.00	40.00	80.00	95.00	105
1929F Proof	—	Value: 280				
1929G	256,000	20.00	40.00	80.00	95.00	105
1929G Proof	—	Value: 280				
1929J	342,000	20.00	40.00	75.00	90.00	105
1929J Proof	—	Value: 280				

KM# 60 3 REICHSMARK
15.0000 g., 0.5000 Silver 0.2411 oz. ASW, 30 mm. **Subject:** 200th Anniversary - Birth of Gotthold Lessing **Obv:** Small eagle, denomination below **Rev:** Head left divides dates **Designer:** Rudolf Bosselt

Date	Mintage	F	VF	XF	Unc	BU
1929A	217,000	25.00	50.00	80.00	130	140
1929A Proof	—	Value: 290				

Date	Mintage	F	VF	XF	Unc	BU
1929D	56,000	30.00	55.00	85.00	145	155
1929D Proof	—	Value: 330				
1929E	30,000	30.00	65.00	95.00	160	170
1929E Proof	—	Value: 330				
1929F	40,000	25.00	45.00	90.00	140	150
1929F Proof	—	Value: 330				
1929G	24,000	25.00	40.00	85.00	160	170
1929G Proof	—	Value: 330				
1929J	33,000	25.00	40.00	85.00	150	160
1929J Proof	—	Value: 330				

KM# 67 3 REICHSMARK

15.0000 g., 0.5000 Silver 0.2411 oz. ASW, 30 mm. **Subject:** Graf Zeppelin Flight **Obv:** Eagle, denomination below **Rev:** Zeppelin across globe, date below

Date	Mintage	F	VF	XF	Unc	BU
1930A	542,000	35.00	65.00	90.00	140	150
1930A Proof	—	Value: 325				
1930D	141,000	35.00	70.00	95.00	150	160
1930D Proof	—	Value: 360				
1930E	75,000	45.00	90.00	125	170	185
1930E Proof	—	Value: 360				
1930F	100,000	35.00	70.00	95.00	145	155
1930F Proof	—	Value: 325				
1930G	61,000	45.00	90.00	125	170	185
1930G Proof	—	Value: 360				
1930J	82,000	50.00	100	115	155	170
1930J Proof	—	Value: 360				

KM# 69 3 REICHSMARK

15.0000 g., 0.5000 Silver 0.2411 oz. ASW, 30 mm. **Subject:** 700th Anniversary - Death of Von Der Vogelweide **Obv:** Eagle on shield, design in background **Rev:** Robed figure with tablet, harp and shield at left, birds at right, date below **Rev. Designer:** Grienauer

Date	Mintage	F	VF	XF	Unc	BU
1930A	163,000	35.00	55.00	95.00	120	130
1930A Proof	—	Value: 290				
1930A Matte proof	—	Value: 500				
1930D	42,000	35.00	65.00	100	140	150
1930D Proof	—	Value: 290				
1930E	22,000	37.50	75.00	120	160	175
1930E Proof	—	Value: 290				
1930F	30,000	37.50	85.00	110	200	220
1930F Proof	—	Value: 290				
1930G	18,000	45.00	80.00	130	175	190
1930G Proof	—	Value: 290				
1930J	25,000	45.00	80.00	120	165	180
1930J Proof	—	Value: 290				

KM# 70 3 REICHSMARK

15.0000 g., 0.5000 Silver 0.2411 oz. ASW, 30 mm. **Subject:** Liberation of Rhineland **Obv:** Eagle on shield, design in background **Rev:** Eagle left on bridge divides date

Date	Mintage	F	VF	XF	Unc	BU
1930A	1,734,000	25.00	48.00	65.00	100	110
1930A Proof	—	Value: 240				
1930A Matte proof	—	—	—	—	—	—
1930D	450,000	25.00	55.00	75.00	120	135
1930D Proof	—	Value: 240				
1930E	38,000	75.00	120	200	330	360
1930E Proof	—	Value: 450				
1930F	321,000	35.00	60.00	90.00	110	125

Date	Mintage	F	VF	XF	Unc	BU
1930F Proof	—	Value: 240				
1930G	195,000	35.00	65.00	100	130	145
1930G Proof	—	Value: 240				
1930J	261,000	35.00	60.00	90.00	120	135
1930J Proof	—	Value: 240				

KM# 72 3 REICHSMARK

15.0000 g., 0.5000 Silver 0.2411 oz. ASW, 30 mm. **Subject:** 300th Anniversary - Magdeburg Rebuilding **Obv:** Eagle on shield, scalloped design in background **Rev:** Shield divides dates above city scene

Date	Mintage	F	VF	XF	Unc	BU
1931A	100,000	90.00	170	255	340	370
1931A Proof	—	Value: 450				

KM# 73 3 REICHSMARK

15.0000 g., 0.5000 Silver 0.2411 oz. ASW, 30 mm. **Subject:** Centenary - Death of von Stein **Obv:** Eagle divides dates, denomination below **Rev:** Head left, name below

Date	Mintage	F	VF	XF	Unc	BU
1931A	150,000	55.00	120	180	240	260
1931A Proof	—	Value: 380				

KM# 74 3 REICHSMARK

15.0000 g., 0.5000 Silver 0.2411 oz. ASW, 30 mm. **Obv:** Eagle above date **Rev:** Denomination within wreath

Date	Mintage	F	VF	XF	Unc	BU
1931A	13,324,000	130	260	360	660	750
1931D	2,232,000	160	300	400	790	900
1931E	2,235,000	190	330	430	1,050	1,200
1931F	2,357,000	160	300	400	730	860
1931G	1,468,000	190	360	490	1,160	1,320
1931J	1,115,000	230	330	460	1,140	1,300
1932A	2,933,000	140	260	400	730	860
1932D	1,986,000	150	280	460	900	1,050
1932F	653,000	230	430	880	2,100	2,600
1932G	210,000	500	900	1,700	4,500	5,800
1932J	1,336,000	190	320	470	970	1,060
1933G	152,000	900	1,750	3,100	7,200	9,000

Note: Less than 10 percent of issue was released

Date	Mintage	F	VF	XF	Unc	BU
1931-33 Common date proof	—	Value: 1,400				

KM# 76 3 REICHSMARK

15.0000 g., 0.5000 Silver 0.2411 oz. ASW, 30 mm. **Subject:** Centenary - Death of Goethe **Obv:** Eagle divides dates, denomination below **Rev:** Head left, name below

Date	Mintage	F	VF	XF	Unc	BU
1932A	217,000	35.00	80.00	110	160	175
1932A Proof	—	Value: 240				
1932D	56,000	40.00	80.00	115	180	195
1932D Proof	—	Value: 240				

Date	Mintage	F	VF	XF	Unc	BU
1932E	30,000	45.00	85.00	125	200	220
1932E Proof	—	Value: 280				
1932F	40,000	35.00	80.00	115	180	195
1932F Proof	—	Value: 240				
1932F Matte proof	—	Value: 600				
1932G	24,000	45.00	85.00	125	200	220
1932G Proof	—	Value: 320				
1932J	33,000	45.00	80.00	115	180	195
1932J Proof	—	Value: 280				

KM# 47 5 REICHSMARK

25.0000 g., 0.5000 Silver 0.4019 oz. ASW, 37 mm. **Subject:** 1000th Year of the Rhineland **Obv:** Armored figure behind shield divides date, right arm raised **Rev:** Denomination within wreath **Designer:** Wackerle

Date	Mintage	F	VF	XF	Unc	BU
1925A	684,000	50.00	95.00	125	210	225
1925A Proof	—	Value: 600				
1925D	452,000	50.00	95.00	140	240	265
1925D Proof	—	Value: 700				
1925E	204,000	55.00	110	160	255	285
1925E Proof	226	Value: 700				
1925F	212,000	55.00	105	150	245	275
1925F Proof	—	Value: 700				
1925G	89,000	60.00	120	170	300	350
1925G Proof	—	Value: 700				
1925J	43,000	95.00	190	290	520	580
1925J Proof	—	Value: 800				

KM# 51 5 REICHSMARK

25.0000 g., 0.5000 Silver 0.4019 oz. ASW, 37 mm. **Subject:** 100th Anniversary - Bremerhaven **Obv:** Eagle on shield, scalloped design in background **Rev:** Crowned shield divides date below ship

Date	Mintage	F	VF	XF	Unc	BU
1927A	50,000	220	420	580	760	850
1927A Proof	—	Value: 980				

KM# 55 5 REICHSMARK

25.0000 g., 0.5000 Silver 0.4019 oz. ASW, 37 mm. **Subject:** 450th Anniversary - University of Tubingen **Rev:** Bust left within circle

Date	Mintage	F	VF	XF	Unc	BU
1927F	40,000	130	290	550	720	850
1927F Proof	—	Value: 1,100				

KM# 56 5 REICHSMARK

25.0000 g., 0.5000 Silver 0.4019 oz. ASW, 37 mm. **Obv:** Eagle within circle, denomination below **Rev:** Oaktree divides date

Date	Mintage	F	VF	XF	Unc	BU
1927A	7,926,000	35.00	90.00	140	260	280
1927D	1,471,000	40.00	100	160	340	370
1927E	1,100,000	50.00	120	175	430	470
1927F	700,000	50.00	130	220	550	630
1927G	759,000	60.00	160	260	880	1,000
1927J	1,006,000	50.00	125	190	480	520
1928A	15,466,000	40.00	100	135	290	320
1928D	4,613,000	45.00	110	145	400	440
1928E	2,310,000	60.00	130	190	520	580
1928F	3,771,000	50.00	120	160	420	480
1928G	1,923,000	65.00	145	180	450	500
1928J	2,450,000	60.00	125	170	430	490
1929A	6,730,000	45.00	100	130	300	330
1929D	2,020,000	50.00	130	190	490	535
1929E	860,000	140	320	540	1,650	1,900
1929F	814,000	70.00	175	260	760	850
1929G	950,000	90.00	190	290	880	990
1929J	779,000	90.00	190	300	800	890
1930A	3,790,000	60.00	120	170	410	440
1930D	606,000	175	450	600	1,700	1,900
1930E	354,000	500	1,550	2,200	5,100	5,700
1930F	630,000	300	650	930	1,650	1,800
1930G	367,000	600	1,350	1,850	4,600	5,100
1930J	740,000	300	660	880	1,800	2,000
1931A	14,651,000	40.00	100	140	270	300
1931D	3,254,000	50.00	120	165	385	420
1931E	2,245,000	60.00	135	180	450	490
1931F	4,152,000	50.00	120	165	385	420
1931G	1,620,000	75.00	190	330	950	1,080
1931J	3,092,000	60.00	140	210	460	500
1932A	32,303,000	40.00	100	140	270	300
1932D	8,556,000	45.00	115	160	300	340
1932E	4,013,000	55.00	125	180	320	360
1932F	5,019,000	50.00	120	170	310	350
1932G	3,504,000	60.00	150	220	500	570
1932J	3,752,000	60.00	150	220	520	590
1933J	423,000	700	1,400	2,600	5,400	6,000
1933J Proof	—	Value: 6,500				
1927-33 Common date proof	—	Value: 900				

KM# 66 5 REICHSMARK

25.0000 g., 0.5000 Silver 0.4019 oz. ASW, 37 mm. **Subject:** 1000th Anniversary - Meissen **Obv:** Eagle **Rev:** Central figure holding shields on poles divides date, five crosses above

Date	Mintage	F	VF	XF	Unc	BU
1929E	120,000	160	250	400	550	600
1929E Proof	—	Value: 1,000				

KM# 61 5 REICHSMARK

25.0000 g., 0.5000 Silver 0.4019 oz. ASW, 37 mm. **Subject:** 200th Anniversary - Birth of Gotthold Lessing **Obv:** Small eagle, denomination below **Rev:** Head left divides date

Date	Mintage	F	VF	XF	Unc	BU
1929A	87,000	60.00	100	145	255	275
1929A Proof	—	Value: 600				
1929D	22,000	60.00	110	160	280	310
1929D Proof	—	Value: 670				
1929E	12,000	60.00	125	200	300	330
1929E Proof	—	Value: 670				
1929F	16,000	60.00	120	180	290	320
1929F Proof	—	Value: 670				
1929G	9,760	80.00	150	225	350	400
1929G Proof	—	Value: 800				
1929J	13,000	70.00	130	210	330	360
1929J Proof	—	Value: 670				

KM# 64 5 REICHSMARK

25.0000 g., 0.5000 Silver 0.4019 oz. ASW, 37 mm. **Subject:** 10th Anniversary - Weimar Constitution **Obv:** Hand with two fingers raised, dates below **Rev:** Head left, denomination above

Date	Mintage	F	VF	XF	Unc	BU
1929A	325,000	55.00	100	160	260	290
1929A Proof	—	Value: 500				
1929D	84,000	60.00	120	180	290	330
1929D Proof	—	Value: 500				
1929E	45,000	70.00	140	200	320	360
1929E Proof	—	Value: 500				
1929F	60,000	70.00	130	190	350	380
1929F Proof	—	Value: 500				
1929G	37,000	70.00	140	200	370	410
1929G Proof	—	Value: 500				
1929J	49,000	70.00	130	190	350	380
1929J Proof	—	Value: 500				

KM# 68 5 REICHSMARK

25.0000 g., 0.5000 Silver 0.4019 oz. ASW, 37 mm. **Subject:** Graf Zeppelin Flight **Obv:** Eagle, denomination below **Rev:** Zeppelin across globe, date below

Date	Mintage	F	VF	XF	Unc	BU
1930A	217,000	70.00	120	190	300	330
1930A Proof	—	Value: 500				
1930A Matte proof	—	—	—	—	—	—
1930D	56,000	75.00	130	200	325	360
1930D Proof	—	Value: 700				
1930E	30,000	80.00	160	210	350	390
1930E Proof	—	Value: 550				
1930F	40,000	75.00	140	200	340	380
1930F Proof	—	Value: 500				
1930G	24,000	85.00	160	235	350	390
1930G Proof	—	Value: 660				
1930J	33,000	80.00	150	220	340	380
1930J Proof	—	Value: 660				

KM# 71 5 REICHSMARK

25.0000 g., 0.5000 Silver 0.4019 oz. ASW, 37 mm. **Subject:** Liberation of Rhineland **Obv:** Eagle on shield, design in background **Rev:** Eagle left on bridge divides date

Date	Mintage	F	VF	XF	Unc	BU
1930A	325,000	70.00	125	190	310	340
1930A Proof	—	Value: 500				
1930D	84,000	70.00	135	220	375	400
1930D Proof	—	Value: 550				
1930E	45,000	80.00	150	275	420	450
1930E Proof	—	Value: 500				
1930F	60,000	70.00	135	235	400	440
1930F Proof	—	Value: 500				
1930G	37,000	90.00	170	280	440	490
1930G Proof	—	Value: 670				
1930J	49,000	80.00	150	250	420	460
1930J Proof	—	Value: 620				

KM# 77 5 REICHSMARK

25.0000 g., 0.5000 Silver 0.4019 oz. ASW, 37 mm. **Subject:** Centenary - Death of Goethe **Obv:** Eagle divides dates, denomination below **Rev:** Head left, name below

Date	Mintage	F	VF	XF	Unc	BU
1932A	11,000	950	2,300	2,850	3,450	3,800
1932A Proof	—	Value: 4,500				
1932D	2,812	1,000	2,400	3,000	3,800	4,200
1932D Proof	—	Value: 5,000				
1932E	1,490	1,000	2,500	3,150	4,200	4,500
1932E Proof	—	Value: 5,000				
1932F	2,006	1,000	2,400	3,000	4,000	4,500
1932F Proof	—	Value: 5,000				
1932G	1,220	1,050	2,550	3,200	4,250	4,750
1932G Proof	—	Value: 5,000				
1932J	1,634	1,000	2,450	3,100	4,100	4,500
1932J Proof	—	Value: 5,000				

1933-1945

A wide range of factors, such as humiliation of defeat, economic depression, poverty, and a pervasive feeling of discontent aided Hitler in his climb to power. After the unsuccessful Putsch (uprising against the Bavarian Government) in 1923, Hitler was imprisoned in Landsberg Fortress. While imprisoned Hitler dictated his book *"Mein Kampf"* which became the cornerstone of Nazism espousing Hitler's irrational ideology and the manipulation of power without moral constraint as the basis of strategy.

Master propagandist Josef Goebbels tried to attract the sympathetic attention of the German public. The usual tactic was to have Hitler promise all things to all people provided that they in turn would pledge to him their complete faith and obedience.

Once in power, coercion was used to elicit the appearance of unanimous endorsement. Public works and military rearmament helped overcome the depression. It took the Nazis only about two years to consolidate their system politically. The combined terrorism of the storm troops and the police forces, including the Gestapo, stifled potential opposition. By 1935, Nazi affiliated organizations controlled all German cultural, professional, and economic fields, assuring strict compliance with the party line.

With the passage of the Nurnberg Laws in 1935, the more ominous aspects of Nazi anti-Semitism came to light. Jews were deprived of their citizenship and forbidden to marry non-Jews. This was followed by confiscation of property and the required wearing of the Star of David for identification purposes, eventually culminating in the mass deportation to concentration and death camps.

By 1936, unemployment was virtually eliminated and economic production was up to 1929 levels. All sources of information were under the control of Josef Goebbels, while all police power was in the hands of Heinrich Himmler. Himmler's Gestapo would silence Germans who were not convinced by Goebbel's propaganda machine. Usually the implied threat was enough. The majority of Germans did not suffer any ill effects at first and national pride stirred once again.

Hitler's audacity in foreign affairs met with success due to the trend of appeasement by the western powers. First, Germany withdrew from the League of Nations and the World Disarmament Council. In 1935, the Saar voted to return to Germany and Hitler renounced the reviled 1921 peace treaty and related pacts. In 1936, German forces reoccupied the Rhineland. In 1938, Austria was annexed and at the Munich Conference, which excluded Czechoslovakia, Great Britain and France agreed that the Sudetenland was to become German territory. In 1939, Slovakia became an independent Nazi Puppet State and the "Protectorate" of Bohemia and Moravia was established. Next came the German-Soviet non-aggression pact, which secretly divided up Poland between the two totalitarian powers. Great Britain and France finally declared war when Poland was invaded. The years of 1939-1942 were a period of impressive victories for Germany's well-trained and equipped forces. However, when Hitler expanded his war beyond Western Europe by invading Africa and Russia and declaring war on the U.S.A., it started the chain of events, which would culminate in the total and final German defeat

THIRD REICH

STANDARD COINAGE

KM# 89 REICHSPFENNIG

2.0100 g., Bronze, 17.43 mm. **Obv:** Eagle above swastika within wreath **Rev:** Denomination, oak leaves below

Date	Mintage	F	VF	XF	Unc	BU
1936A	—	2.00	5.50	15.00	50.00	75.00
Note: Mintage included with KM#37						
1936E	150,000	27.50	55.00	110	165	275
1936F	4,600,000	25.00	50.00	90.00	200	300
1936G	—	15.00	25.00	60.00	110	200
Note: Mintage included with KM#37						
1936J	—	10.00	22.50	50.00	100	125
Note: Mintage included with KM#37						
1937A	67,180,000	0.20	0.35	1.00	3.50	6.00
1937D	14,060,000	0.20	0.35	1.25	6.00	12.00
1937E	10,700,000	0.20	0.40	1.25	6.00	12.00
1937F	11,058,000	0.20	0.40	1.25	6.00	12.00
1937G	4,250,000	0.20	0.40	2.50	6.00	14.00
1937J	6,714,000	0.20	0.40	1.25	6.00	12.00
1938A	75,707,000	0.15	0.35	0.50	5.00	9.00
1938B	2,378,000	0.50	4.00	6.50	15.00	30.00
1938D	13,930,000	0.15	0.35	0.60	6.00	9.00
1938E	14,503,000	0.15	0.35	0.60	6.00	9.00
1938F	11,714,000	0.15	0.35	0.60	6.00	9.00
1938G	8,390,000	0.15	0.35	1.25	6.00	11.00
1938J	15,458,000	0.15	0.35	0.60	6.00	9.00
1939A	97,541,000	0.15	0.35	0.60	4.00	9.00
1939B	22,732,000	0.20	0.40	0.90	6.00	11.00
1939D	20,760,000	0.15	0.30	0.60	5.00	9.00
1939E	12,478,000	0.15	0.35	0.60	6.00	11.00
1939F	12,482,000	0.15	0.35	0.60	5.00	9.00
1939G	12,250,000	0.15	0.35	0.60	5.00	9.00
1939J	8,368,000	0.15	0.35	0.60	6.00	11.00
1940A	27,094,000	0.15	0.35	0.60	5.00	10.00
1940F	7,850,000	0.20	0.45	1.25	7.00	12.00
1940G	3,875,000	1.00	4.00	11.00	20.00	35.00
1940J	7,450,000	0.60	2.75	4.50	10.00	20.00
1936-1940 Common date proof	—	Value: 140				

KM# 97 REICHSPFENNIG

1.8100 g., Zinc, 17 mm. **Obv:** Eagle above swastika within wreath **Rev:** Denomination, oak leaves below

Date	Mintage	F	VF	XF	Unc	BU
1940A	223,948,000	0.15	0.25	1.00	5.00	8.00
1940B	62,198,000	0.15	0.25	1.00	5.00	8.00
1940D	43,951,000	0.15	0.25	1.00	5.00	8.00
1940E	20,749,000	0.25	1.00	4.50	11.00	17.50
1940F	33,854,000	0.15	0.25	1.00	6.00	10.00
1940G	20,165,000	0.15	0.25	1.00	6.00	12.00
1940J	24,459,000	0.15	0.25	1.00	6.00	10.00
1941A	281,618,000	0.15	0.20	0.50	4.00	7.00
1941B	62,285,000	0.20	1.00	1.50	5.00	7.00
1941D	73,745,000	0.15	0.20	0.60	5.00	7.00
1941E	49,041,000	0.15	0.50	1.50	8.50	15.00
1941F	51,017,000	0.15	0.20	0.60	5.00	8.00
1941G	44,810,000	0.15	0.50	1.00	7.50	10.00
1941J	57,625,000	0.15	0.20	0.60	6.00	10.00
1942A	558,877,000	0.15	0.20	0.50	5.00	6.00
1942B	124,740,000	0.15	0.25	1.00	6.00	7.00
1942D	134,145,000	0.15	0.20	0.60	6.00	7.00
1942E	84,674,000	0.20	1.25	2.00	8.00	10.00
1942F	90,788,000	0.15	0.20	0.60	6.00	7.00
1942G	59,858,000	0.15	0.20	0.60	6.00	9.00
1942J	122,934,000	0.15	0.50	1.00	6.00	7.00
1943A	372,401,000	0.15	0.20	0.50	6.00	7.00
1943B	79,315,000	0.15	0.50	0.90	6.00	7.00
1943D	91,629,000	0.15	0.20	0.50	6.00	7.00
1943E	34,191,000	0.50	2.25	6.50	12.00	18.00
1943F	70,269,000	0.15	0.50	0.90	6.00	7.00
1943G	24,688,000	0.20	1.25	2.00	8.00	11.00
1943J	37,695,000	0.20	1.25	2.00	6.00	7.00
1944A	124,421,000	0.15	0.50	1.50	5.00	7.00
1944B	87,850,000	0.25	1.00	1.75	6.00	9.00
1944D	56,755,000	0.25	1.00	2.00	7.00	10.00
1944E	41,729,000	0.25	1.75	4.00	12.00	18.00
1944F	15,580,000	0.50	3.50	6.50	17.50	25.00
1944G	34,967,000	0.15	0.60	1.50	6.00	11.00
1945A	17,145,000	0.50	2.50	7.00	20.00	30.00
1945E	6,800,000	45.00	60.00	100	175	275
1940-1945 Common date proof	—	Value: 140				

KM# 90 2 REICHSPFENNIG

3.3400 g., Bronze, 20.11 mm. **Obv:** Eagle above swastika within wreath **Rev:** Denomination, oak leaves below

Date	Mintage	F	VF	XF	Unc	BU
1936A	Inc. below	0.60	3.50	10.00	40.00	50.00
1936D	Inc. below	0.60	3.50	8.00	30.00	35.00
1936F	3,100,000	5.00	15.00	40.00	100	160
1937A	34,404,000	0.20	0.60	1.25	7.00	11.00
1937D	9,016,000	0.20	0.60	1.25	7.00	11.00
1937E	Inc. below	12.50	17.50	35.00	70.00	110
1937F	7,487,000	0.20	0.60	1.75	8.00	12.00
1937G	490,000	2.00	7.50	14.00	40.00	50.00
1937J	450,000	2.00	7.50	14.00	30.00	35.00
1938A	27,264,000	0.20	0.30	0.60	6.00	9.00
1938B	2,714,000	1.50	3.50	8.00	30.00	40.00
1938D	8,770,000	0.20	0.35	1.00	6.00	9.00
1938E	5,450,000	0.35	1.00	2.00	7.00	10.00
1938F	10,090,000	0.20	0.35	1.00	6.00	9.00
1938G	3,685,000	0.20	0.35	5.50	15.00	22.00
1938J	7,243,000	0.20	0.35	1.25	7.00	13.00
1939A	37,348,000	0.20	0.35	1.00	6.00	9.00
1939B	9,361,000	0.20	0.35	1.00	6.00	9.00
1939D	7,555,000	0.20	0.35	1.00	6.00	9.00
1939E	6,650,000	0.35	1.00	2.00	7.00	11.00
1939F	7,019,000	0.20	0.35	1.00	6.00	10.00
1939G	4,885,000	0.20	0.35	1.25	9.00	15.00
1939J	6,996,000	0.20	0.35	1.25	7.00	10.00
1940A	22,681,000	0.20	0.35	1.00	8.00	12.00
1940D	3,855,000	0.60	2.50	5.50	20.00	25.00
1940E	3,412,000	2.00	8.00	12.50	20.00	30.00
1940G	1,161,000	40.00	80.00	120	225	375
1940J	2,357,000	1.50	7.00	13.50	35.00	50.00
1936-1940 Common date proof	—	Value: 175				

KM# 91 5 REICHSPFENNIG

2.5300 g., Aluminum-Bronze **Obv:** Eagle above swastika within wreath **Rev:** Denomination, oak leaves below

Date	Mintage	F	VF	XF	Unc	BU
1936A	Inc. below	30.00	65.00	90.00	130	180
1936D	Inc. below	30.00	65.00	90.00	160	225
1936G	Inc. below	50.00	90.00	150	300	375
1937A	29,700,000	0.50	1.00	2.00	7.00	10.00
1937D	4,992,000	0.50	1.00	2.00	12.50	20.00
1937E	4,474,000	0.50	1.50	3.50	20.00	30.00
1937F	2,092,000	0.50	1.00	6.00	20.00	40.00
1937G	2,749,000	2.50	6.50	12.50	35.00	50.00
1937J	6,991,000	0.50	2.50	5.00	20.00	30.00
1938A	54,012,000	0.50	2.50	4.00	9.00	12.50
1938B	3,447,000	0.50	2.00	4.00	15.00	20.00
1938D	17,708,000	0.50	1.00	2.00	8.00	10.00
1938E	8,602,000	0.50	1.00	4.00	12.00	20.00
1938F	8,147,000	0.50	1.00	2.00	10.00	20.00
1938G	7,323,000	0.50	1.00	2.00	10.00	20.00
1938J	7,646,000	0.50	1.00	2.00	10.00	20.00
1939A	35,337,000	0.50	1.00	2.00	7.00	10.00
1939B	8,313,000	0.50	1.00	1.50	7.00	10.00
1939D	8,304,000	0.50	1.50	2.00	7.50	12.00
1939E	5,138,000	0.50	1.50	2.00	7.50	12.00
1939F	10,339,000	0.50	1.00	1.50	7.00	10.00
1939G	4,266,000	0.50	2.50	6.50	15.00	22.00
1939J	4,177,000	0.50	2.00	6.50	12.50	22.00
1936-1939 Common date proof	—	Value: 150				

KM# 100 5 REICHSPFENNIG

2.5000 g., Zinc, 19 mm. **Obv:** Imperial eagle above swastika within wreath **Rev:** Denomination, oak leaves below

Date	Mintage	F	VF	XF	Unc	BU
1940A	174,684,000	0.20	0.25	0.75	6.00	8.00
1940B	63,469,000	0.25	1.00	1.50	6.00	8.00
1940D	44,364,000	0.25	1.00	1.50	6.00	8.00
1940E	25,800,000	0.30	1.00	3.50	7.00	10.00
1940F	31,381,000	0.25	1.00	2.00	7.00	10.00
1940G	24,148,000	0.25	1.00	2.75	8.00	15.00
1940J	30,518,000	0.25	1.00	2.00	7.00	10.00
1941A	246,216,000	0.20	0.25	0.75	5.00	7.00
1941B	60,297,000	0.20	0.40	1.75	7.50	10.00
1941D	51,100,000	0.20	0.40	1.75	7.50	10.00
1941E	26,354,000	0.20	0.40	1.75	7.50	10.00
1941F	36,725,000	0.20	0.40	1.75	7.50	10.00
1941G	21,276,000	0.20	0.40	2.00	8.50	12.00
1941J	52,872,000	0.20	0.40	2.00	7.50	10.00
1942A	161,042,000	0.20	0.25	0.75	6.00	9.00
1942B	12,405,000	0.25	1.50	4.50	10.00	15.00
1942D	15,486,000	0.20	0.45	2.25	8.00	12.00
1942E	8,800,000	6.00	15.00	20.00	40.00	50.00
1942F	24,662,000	0.20	0.35	1.50	8.00	12.00
1942G	12,749,000	0.20	0.40	2.25	10.00	15.00
1943A	46,830,000	0.20	0.50	1.75	7.00	10.00
1943B	833,000	30.00	50.00	75.00	160	200
1943D	13,650,000	0.20	0.50	3.50	9.00	13.00
1943E	16,581,000	2.00	6.00	10.00	20.00	25.00
1943F	9,891,000	0.25	1.00	2.50	8.00	12.00
1943G	7,237,000	0.20	0.75	2.25	9.00	15.00
1944A	23,699,000	3.50	12.50	25.00	40.00	50.00
1944D	26,340,000	0.25	1.25	2.50	7.00	10.00
1944E	19,720,000	0.50	2.50	5.00	10.00	14.00
1944F	6,853,000	0.25	1.50	2.75	8.00	12.00
1944G	3,540,000	100	200	275	400	500
1940-1944 Common date proof	—	Value: 225				

KM# 92 10 REICHSPFENNIG

4.0300 g., Aluminum-Bronze **Obv:** Eagle above swastika within wreath **Rev:** Denomination, oak leaves below

Date	Mintage	F	VF	XF	Unc	BU
1936A	Inc. below	20.00	40.00	60.00	100	120
1936E	245,000	90.00	150	200	300	375
1936G	129,000	175	225	300	450	700
1937A	36,830,000	0.50	1.00	2.25	12.00	20.00
1937D	6,882,000	0.50	2.00	3.50	12.00	22.00
1937E	3,786,000	2.00	9.00	18.00	45.00	60.00
1937F	5,934,000	1.00	2.50	6.00	25.00	40.00
1937G	2,131,000	1.00	5.50	9.00	30.00	60.00
1937J	4,439,000	1.00	2.00	5.00	20.00	30.00
1938A	70,068,000	0.50	1.00	2.00	7.00	12.00
1938B	7,852,000	1.00	2.00	4.50	15.00	20.00
1938D	16,990,000	0.50	1.00	2.00	9.00	16.00
1938E	10,739,000	0.50	2.00	2.50	10.00	18.00
1938F	12,307,000	0.50	2.00	2.75	11.00	18.00
1938G	8,584,000	0.50	2.00	3.00	12.00	22.00
1938J	10,389,000	0.50	2.00	2.75	12.00	20.00
1939A	40,171,000	0.50	2.00	2.25	9.00	15.00
1939B	7,814,000	0.50	2.00	2.25	10.00	16.00
1939D	11,307,000	0.50	2.00	2.25	12.00	20.00
1939E	5,079,000	1.00	2.00	6.50	15.00	20.00
1939F	6,993,000	0.50	2.00	3.00	12.00	20.00
1939G	5,532,000	1.00	4.50	9.00	16.00	22.00
1939J	5,557,000	0.50	2.00	2.50	12.00	20.00
1936-1939 Common date proof	—	Value: 175				

KM# 101 10 REICHSPFENNIG

3.5200 g., Zinc, 21 mm. **Obv:** Eagle above swastika within wreath **Rev:** Denomination, oak leaves below

Date	Mintage	F	VF	XF	Unc	BU
1940A	212,948,000	0.20	0.40	1.75	8.00	15.00
1940B	76,274,000	0.20	0.75	3.00	12.00	20.00
1940D	45,434,000	0.20	0.75	2.50	12.00	20.00
1940E	34,350,000	0.20	0.75	2.50	12.00	25.00
1940F	27,603,000	0.20	1.50	6.00	17.50	40.00
1940G	27,308,000	0.20	1.50	8.00	25.00	50.00
1940J	41,678,000	0.20	1.25	2.50	12.00	25.00
1941A	240,284,000	0.20	0.40	1.50	7.00	14.00
1941B	70,747,000	0.20	0.75	3.00	9.00	15.00
1941D	77,560,000	0.20	0.75	3.50	12.00	20.00
1941E	36,548,000	0.20	0.75	3.50	12.00	20.00
1941F	42,834,000	0.20	0.75	3.50	12.00	20.00
1941G	28,765,000	0.20	2.25	9.00	25.00	40.00
1941J	30,525,000	0.20	0.75	2.50	12.00	25.00
1942A	184,545,000	0.20	0.30	0.75	9.00	15.00
1942B	16,329,000	1.00	3.00	12.00	30.00	50.00
1942D	40,852,000	0.20	1.25	3.50	12.00	25.00
1942E	18,334,000	1.00	2.00	12.00	30.00	50.00
1942F	32,690,000	0.20	0.50	3.50	12.00	25.00
1942G	20,295,000	1.00	2.00	12.00	35.00	60.00
1942J	29,957,000	0.50	1.75	3.50	12.00	25.00
1943A	157,357,000	0.20	1.50	2.50	9.00	15.00
1943B	11,940,000	2.50	7.50	14.00	30.00	60.00
1943D	17,304,000	0.25	1.75	4.50	16.00	25.00
1943E	10,445,000	2.50	7.50	14.00	35.00	60.00
1943F	24,804,000	0.25	2.50	5.00	20.00	25.00
1943G	3,618,000	4.00	14.00	35.00	80.00	150
1943J	1,821,000	25.00	45.00	85.00	200	300
1944A	84,164,000	0.20	1.00	2.50	10.00	15.00
1944B	40,781,000	0.50	1.50	2.50	12.00	20.00
1944D	30,369,000	0.50	1.50	2.50	12.00	20.00
1944E	29,963,000	0.50	2.00	4.50	12.00	20.00
1944F	19,639,000	0.50	2.50	5.00	14.00	25.00
1944G	13,023,000	0.75	3.50	10.00	30.00	50.00
1945A	7,112,000	5.00	12.50	30.00	90.00	150
1945E	4,897,000	15.00	35.00	80.00	140	200
1940-1945 Common date proof	—	Value: 250				

KM# 87 50 REICHSPFENNIG

Aluminum **Obv:** Eagle above date **Rev:** Denomination, oak leaves below

Date	Mintage	F	VF	XF	Unc	BU
1935A	75,912,000	1.00	2.25	9.00	35.00	80.00
1935A Proof	—	Value: 250				
1935D	19,688,000	1.00	2.25	12.00	60.00	100
1935D Proof	—	Value: 250				
1935E	10,418,000	1.00	3.50	12.00	60.00	100
1935E Proof	—	Value: 250				
1935F	14,061,000	1.00	2.25	12.00	60.00	100
1935F Proof	—	Value: 250				
1935G	0,540,000	2.00	4.50	14.00	65.00	110
1935G Proof	—	Value: 250				
1935J	11,438,000	2.00	4.50	14.00	65.00	110
1935J Proof	—	Value: 250				

KM# 95 50 REICHSPFENNIG

Nickel **Obv:** Eagle above swastika within wreath **Rev:** Denomination within circle, oak leaves and acorns below

Date	Mintage	F	VF	XF	Unc	BU
1938A	5,051,000	17.50	32.50	42.50	55.00	75.00
1938B	1,124,000	25.00	40.00	50.00	80.00	100
1938D	1,260,000	25.00	40.00	55.00	80.00	100
1938E	949,000	25.00	40.00	60.00	100	125
1938F	1,210,000	15.00	30.00	50.00	90.00	125
1938G	460,000	30.00	70.00	90.00	160	225
1938J	730,000	30.00	90.00	120	225	300
1939A	15,037,000	20.00	30.00	40.00	50.00	60.00
1939B	2,826,000	20.00	35.00	45.00	60.00	90.00
1939D	3,648,000	17.50	35.00	45.00	60.00	90.00
1939E	1,924,000	17.50	35.00	50.00	85.00	100
1939F	2,602,000	17.50	35.00	50.00	70.00	90.00
1939G	1,565,000	17.50	35.00	75.00	130	170
1939J	2,114,000	17.50	35.00	60.00	100	120
1938-1939 Common date proof	—	Value: 275				

KM# 96 50 REICHSPFENNIG

1.3400 g., Aluminum **Obv:** Eagle above swastika within wreath **Rev:** Denomination, oak leaves below

Date	Mintage	F	VF	XF	Unc	BU
1939A	5,000,000	2.50	6.00	20.00	65.00	100
1939B	5,482,000	2.50	6.00	20.00	65.00	100
1939D	600,000	6.00	16.00	35.00	120	170
1939E	2,000,000	2.50	6.00	25.00	70.00	110
1939F	3,600,000	2.50	11.00	30.00	70.00	120
1939G	560,000	12.50	22.50	60.00	150	200
1939J	1,000,000	12.50	22.50	50.00	150	200
1940A	56,128,000	2.50	4.50	11.00	35.00	50.00
1940B	10,016,000	5.00	9.00	25.00	70.00	100
1940D	13,800,000	8.00	15.00	30.00	100	150
1940E	5,618,000	8.00	15.00	30.00	100	150
1940F	6,663,000	5.00	10.00	25.00	65.00	100
1940G	5,616,000	15.00	27.00	55.00	130	200
1940J	7,335,000	8.00	15.00	30.00	100	150
1941A	31,263,000	5.00	9.00	20.00	65.00	100
1941B	4,291,000	3.00	10.00	25.00	80.00	110
1941D	7,200,000	2.00	10.00	25.00	80.00	110
1941E	3,806,000	5.00	15.00	27.50	85.00	125
1941F	5,128,000	2.50	10.00	25.00	65.00	100
1941G	3,091,000	10.00	20.00	40.00	110	150
1941J	4,165,000	10.00	20.00	35.00	110	150
1942A	11,580,000	2.00	5.00	10.00	30.00	50.00
1942B	2,876,000	5.00	12.00	25.00	70.00	100
1942D	2,247,000	2.00	20.00	35.00	80.00	120
1942E	3,810,000	5.00	20.00	40.00	110	150
1942F	5,133,000	2.00	15.00	30.00	80.00	120
1942G	1,400,000	10.00	25.00	70.00	125	200
1943A	29,325,000	2.00	5.00	10.00	30.00	40.00
1943B	8,229,000	2.00	5.00	10.00	25.00	40.00
1943D	5,315,000	2.00	7.00	16.00	50.00	75.00
1943G	2,892,000	10.00	20.00	50.00	110	180
1943J	4,166,000	5.00	9.00	14.00	30.00	45.00
1944B	5,622,000	2.50	8.00	12.00	50.00	70.00
1944D	4,886,000	7.50	16.00	40.00	100	130
1944F	3,739,000	5.00	10.00	20.00	75.00	100
1944G	1,190,000	60.00	100	180	400	600
1940-1944 Common date proof	—	Value: 275				

KM# 78 REICHSMARK

4.8500 g., Nickel **Obv:** Denomination within wreath, date below **Rev:** Eagle

Date	Mintage	F	VF	XF	Unc	BU
1933A	6,030,000	1.00	2.75	8.00	35.00	45.00
1933D	4,562,000	1.00	3.50	10.00	35.00	45.00
1933E	3,500,000	2.50	7.50	10.00	25.00	45.00
1933F	1,400,000	4.00	8.50	16.00	45.00	65.00
1933G	2,000,000	2.50	10.00	20.00	90.00	130
1934A	52,345,000	1.00	1.75	3.00	10.00	15.00
1934D	30,597,000	1.00	1.75	5.00	16.00	22.00

Date	Mintage	F	VF	XF	Unc	BU
1934E	15,135,000	1.00	3.00	7.00	16.00	22.00
1934F	23,672,000	1.00	2.75	5.00	15.00	20.00
1934G	13,252,000	1.50	5.00	10.00	20.00	25.00
1934J	16,820,000	1.00	3.50	7.50	16.00	20.00
1935A	57,896,000	1.00	2.50	5.00	12.50	15.00
1935J	3,621,000	10.00	15.00	30.00	110	150
1936A	20,287,000	1.25	4.50	8.00	20.00	25.00
1936D	4,940,000	2.50	7.50	15.00	40.00	50.00
1936E	3,200,000	10.00	15.00	35.00	110	150
1936F	2,075,000	20.00	30.00	50.00	110	150
1936G	620,000	30.00	75.00	150	225	275
1936J	2,975,000	7.50	15.00	30.00	110	150
1937A	49,976,000	1.00	1.75	3.00	9.00	13.00
1937D	10,529,000	2.00	5.00	10.00	20.00	30.00
1937E	2,926,000	4.00	12.50	22.50	50.00	70.00
1937F	6,221,000	4.00	12.50	22.50	65.00	90.00
1937G	2,143,000	3.00	9.00	16.00	45.00	70.00
1937J	4,721,000	3.00	9.00	16.00	60.00	90.00
1938A	9,829,000	2.00	5.00	12.00	30.00	45.00
1938E	2,073,000	5.00	18.00	35.00	90.00	130
1938F	2,739,000	6.00	20.00	25.00	75.00	100
1938G	4,381,000	15.00	35.00	70.00	140	225
1938J	1,269,000	30.00	65.00	100	160	250
1939A	52,150,000	6.00	12.50	16.00	40.00	50.00
1939B	9,836,000	60.00	110	160	275	375
1939D	12,522,000	10.00	22.50	37.50	80.00	100
1939E	6,570,000	25.00	40.00	70.00	130	160
1939F	10,033,000	15.00	25.00	45.00	110	150
1939G	5,475,000	70.00	140	200	350	450
1939J	8,478,000	20.00	40.00	60.00	120	175
1933-1939 Common date proof	—	Value: 250				

KM# 79 2 REICHSMARK

8.0000 g., 0.6250 Silver 0.1607 oz. ASW, 27 mm. **Subject:** 450th Anniversary - Birth of Martin Luther **Obv:** Eagle above denomination **Rev:** Head left, dates below

Date	Mintage	F	VF	XF	Unc	BU
1933A	542,000	10.00	22.50	30.00	50.00	70.00
1933A Proof	—	Value: 250				
1933D	141,000	12.00	25.00	35.00	60.00	75.00
1933D Proof	—	Value: 250				
1933E	75,000	15.00	30.00	40.00	60.00	90.00
1933E Proof	—	Value: 275				
1933F	100,000	12.00	25.00	35.00	60.00	80.00
1933F Proof	—	Value: 275				
1933G	61,000	16.00	30.00	42.00	75.00	120
1933G Proof	—	Value: 275				
1933J	82,000	12.00	25.00	40.00	60.00	85.00
1933J Proof	—	Value: 265				

KM# 81 2 REICHSMARK

8.0000 g., 0.6250 Silver 0.1607 oz. ASW, 27 mm. **Subject:** 1st Anniversary - Nazi Rule March 21, 1933 **Obv:** Eagle divides dates, denomination below **Rev:** Potsdam Garrison Church

Date	Mintage	F	VF	XF	Unc	BU
1934A	2,710,000	4.50	10.00	22.00	50.00	90.00
1934A Proof	—	Value: 250				
1934D	703,000	5.50	12.00	28.00	70.00	110
1934D Proof	—	Value: 250				
1934E	373,000	7.50	16.50	40.00	100	130
1934E Proof	—	Value: 250				
1934F	502,000	6.00	12.00	32.50	75.00	110
1934F Proof	—	Value: 250				
1934G	305,000	7.00	15.00	45.00	110	140
1934G Proof	—	Value: 250				
1934J	409,000	7.00	15.00	40.00	100	120
1934J Proof	—	Value: 250				

KM# 84 2 REICHSMARK

8.0000 g., 0.6250 Silver 0.1607 oz. ASW, 27 mm. **Subject:** 175th Anniversary - Birth of Schiller **Obv:** Eagle, oak leaves flank, denomination below **Rev:** Head left, date below **Designer:** Hubert Zimmerman

Date	Mintage	F	VF	XF	Unc	BU
1934F	300,000	40.00	70.00	90.00	120	145
1934F Proof	—	Value: 250				

KM# 93 2 REICHSMARK

8.0000 g., 0.6250 Silver 0.1607 oz. ASW, 27 mm. **Subject:** Swastika-Hindenburg Issue **Obv:** Eagle above swastika within wreath **Rev:** Large head, right

Date	Mintage	F	VF	XF	Unc	BU
1936D	840,000	4.00	7.00	20.00	60.00	90.00
1936E	Inc. below	9.00	28.00	45.00	110	170
1936G	Inc. below	8.00	18.00	30.00	80.00	140
1936J	Inc. below	30.00	70.00	160	400	550
1937A	23,425,000	2.50	3.00	4.50	11.00	16.00
1937D	6,190,000	2.50	3.00	4.50	16.00	20.00
1937E	3,725,000	2.50	3.50	6.00	22.00	30.00
1937F	5,015,000	2.50	3.00	6.00	16.00	22.00
1937G	1,913,000	2.50	4.50	10.00	30.00	45.00
1937J	2,756,000	2.50	3.50	5.50	20.00	35.00
1938A	13,201,000	2.50	3.00	5.00	11.00	20.00
1938B	13,163,000	2.50	3.00	5.00	15.00	22.00
1938D	3,711,000	2.50	3.00	5.00	16.00	30.00
1938E	4,731,000	2.50	3.00	5.00	16.00	30.00
1938F	1,882,000	3.00	4.00	6.50	20.00	40.00
1938G	2,313,000	2.50	3.00	5.50	17.00	30.00
1938J	2,306,000	2.50	3.50	5.50	17.00	30.00
1939A	26,855,000	2.25	3.00	4.50	11.00	15.00
1939B	3,522,000	2.50	3.25	5.50	14.00	30.00
1939D	5,357,000	2.50	3.25	5.00	14.00	25.00
1939E	251,000	15.00	30.00	45.00	100	160
1939F	3,180,000	2.50	3.25	5.50	14.00	30.00
1939G	2,305,000	2.50	3.50	7.50	20.00	40.00
1939J	3,414,000	2.50	3.25	7.00	17.50	30.00
1936-1939 Common date proof	—	Value: 225				

KM# 80 5 REICHSMARK

13.8800 g., 0.9000 Silver 0.4016 oz. ASW, 29 mm. **Subject:** 450th Anniversary - Birth of Martin Luther **Obv:** Eagle, denomination below **Rev:** Head left, dates below

Date	Mintage	F	VF	XF	Unc	BU
1933A	108,000	60.00	100	150	200	275
1933A Proof	—	Value: 400				
1933D	28,000	60.00	125	175	200	300
1933D Proof	—	Value: 450				
1933E	12,000	80.00	145	190	225	300
1933E Proof	—	Value: 450				
1933F	20,000	60.00	125	160	200	300
1933F Proof	—	Value: 525				
1933G	12,000	100	175	250	300	400
1933G Proof	—	Value: 550				
1933J	16,000	85.00	145	180	250	350
1933J Proof	—	Value: 550				

KM# 82 5 REICHSMARK

13.8800 g., 0.9000 Silver 0.4016 oz. ASW, 29 mm. **Subject:** 1st Anniversary - Nazi Rule **Obv:** Eagle divides date, denomination below **Rev:** Potsdam Garrison Church

Date	Mintage	F	VF	XF	Unc	BU
1934A	2,168,000	10.00	12.00	40.00	100	120
1934D	562,000	10.00	15.00	45.00	120	140
1934E	298,000	10.00	18.00	50.00	150	180
1934F	401,000	10.00	14.00	40.00	120	160
1934G	244,000	10.00	20.00	50.00	160	190
1934J	327,000	10.00	18.00	45.00	160	190

Date	Mintage	F	VF	XF	Unc	BU
1934 Proof	—	Value: 300				

Note: Impaired proofs are common and valued around $200

KM# 83 5 REICHSMARK

13.8800 g., 0.9000 Silver 0.4016 oz. ASW, 29 mm. **Subject:** 1st Anniversary - Nazi Rule **Obv:** Eagle divides date, denomination below **Rev:** Potsdam Garrison Church, date 21 MARZ 1933 dropped

Date	Mintage	F	VF	XF	Unc	BU
1934A	14,526,000	5.00	6.00	10.00	35.00	40.00
1934D	6,303,000	5.00	6.00	13.00	40.00	50.00
1934E	2,739,000	5.00	7.00	15.00	55.00	65.00
1934F	4,844,000	5.00	6.00	13.00	40.00	50.00
1934G	2,304,000	5.00	7.50	15.00	55.00	65.00
1934J	4,294,000	5.00	6.50	14.00	50.00	60.00
1935A	23,407,000	4.00	5.00	9.00	30.00	40.00
1935D	3,539,000	5.00	6.50	14.00	40.00	50.00
1935E	2,476,000	5.00	7.50	15.00	55.00	65.00
1935F	2,177,000	5.00	7.50	17.50	50.00	70.00
1935G	1,966,000	5.00	7.50	16.00	65.00	75.00
1935J	1,425,000	6.00	10.00	22.50	90.00	110
1934-1935 Common date proof	—	Value: 275				

KM# 85 5 REICHSMARK

13.8800 g., 0.9000 Silver 0.4016 oz. ASW, 29 mm. **Subject:** 175th Anniversary - Birth of Schiller **Obv:** Eagle, oak leaves flank, denomination below **Rev:** Head left, dates below

Date	Mintage	F	VF	XF	Unc	BU
1934F	100,000	150	200	285	425	475
1934F Proof	—	Value: 750				

KM# 86 5 REICHSMARK

13.8800 g., 0.9000 Silver 0.4016 oz. ASW, 29 mm. **Subject:** Hindenburg issue **Obv:** Eagle divides date, denomination below **Rev:** Large head, right

Date	Mintage	F	VF	XF	Unc	BU
1935A	19,325,000	4.00	5.00	9.00	16.00	20.00
1935D	6,596,000	4.00	6.00	9.00	20.00	25.00
1935E	3,260,000	4.00	6.00	11.00	25.00	30.00
1935F	4,372,000	4.00	6.00	9.00	25.00	30.00
1935G	2,371,000	4.00	6.50	12.50	35.00	45.00
1935J	2,830,000	4.00	6.50	12.50	40.00	60.00
1936A	30,611,000	4.00	5.50	9.00	16.00	20.00
1936D	7,032,000	4.00	6.00	9.00	20.00	25.00
1936E	3,320,000	4.00	6.00	11.00	25.00	30.00
1936F	4,926,000	4.00	6.00	11.00	25.00	30.00
1936G	2,734,000	4.00	6.50	15.00	50.00	70.00
1936J	3,706,000	4.00	6.50	14.00	40.00	50.00
1935-1936 Common date proof	—	Value: 250				

KM# 94 5 REICHSMARK
13.8800 g., 0.9000 Silver 0.4016 oz. ASW, 29 mm. **Subject:** Swastika-Hindenburg Issue **Obv:** Eagle above swastika within wreath **Rev:** Large head, right

Date	Mintage	F	VF	XF	Unc	BU
1936A	8,430,000	4.00	6.00	10.00	20.00	30.00
1936D	1,872,000	4.00	7.00	14.00	30.00	40.00
1936E	870,000	5.00	8.00	16.00	35.00	50.00
1936F	1,732,000	4.00	7.00	14.00	40.00	50.00
1936G	743,000	5.00	9.00	20.00	65.00	80.00
1936J	640,000	8.00	18.00	30.00	80.00	110
1937A	6,662,000	4.00	6.00	9.00	20.00	30.00
1937D	2,173,000	4.00	6.00	10.00	25.00	35.00
1937E	1,490,000	5.00	8.00	14.00	30.00	50.00
1937F	1,578,000	4.00	7.50	14.00	35.00	45.00
1937G	1,472,000	5.00	8.00	14.00	35.00	45.00
1937J	2,191,000	4.00	6.00	12.50	30.00	40.00
1938A	6,789,000	4.00	6.00	9.00	20.00	25.00
1938D	1,304,000	4.00	6.00	12.50	25.00	35.00
1938E	425,000	5.00	8.00	14.00	40.00	60.00
1938F	740,000	4.00	6.50	12.50	40.00	60.00
1938G	861,000	4.00	7.50	14.00	40.00	60.00
1938J	1,302,000	4.00	6.50	12.50	30.00	40.00
1939A	3,428,000	4.00	7.50	12.50	25.00	40.00
1939B	1,942,000	5.00	8.00	14.00	25.00	50.00
1939D	1,216,000	7.00	11.00	18.00	40.00	50.00
1939E	1,320,000	15.00	20.00	40.00	80.00	110
1939F	1,060,000	7.50	12.50	25.00	70.00	100
1939G	567,000	12.50	20.00	35.00	100	140
1939J	1,710,000	5.00	10.00	20.00	60.00	75.00
1936-1939 Common date proof	—	Value: 250				

MILITARY COINAGE

WWII

KM# 98 5 REICHSPFENNIG
Zinc **Note:** Circulated only in occupied territories.

Date	Mintage	F	VF	XF	Unc	BU
1940A	—	15.00	20.00	30.00	60.00	90.00
1940B	3,020,000	100	160	325	550	750
1940D	—	30.00	45.00	75.00	120	190
1940E	2,445,000	100	200	325	550	750
1940F	—	200	300	425	675	900
1940G	—	6,000	10,000	—	—	—
1940J	—	100	225	325	500	750
1941A	—	300	500	800	1,500	2,500
1941F	—	5,000	10,000	—	—	—
1940-1941 Common date proof	—	Value: 850				

KM# 99 10 REICHSPFENNIG
Zinc **Rev:** Eagle head above center hole, denomination below **Note:** Circulated only in occupied territories.

Date	Mintage	F	VF	XF	Unc	BU
1940A	—	15.00	20.00	30.00	50.00	80.00
1940B	840,000	200	325	650	950	1,250
1940D	—	5,000	6,000	10,000	15,000	20,000
1940E	5,100,000	3,000	4,500	6,000	10,000	12,000
1940F	—	300	450	1,250	1,750	2,250
1940G	150,000	100	125	225	400	550
1940J	—	400	900	1,400	2,500	2,750
1941A	—	600	1,000	1,800	2,500	2,750
1941F 2 known	—	—	12,000	—	15,000	—
1940-1941 Proof	—	Value: 1,150				

ALLIED OCCUPATION

POST WW II COINAGE

KM# A102 REICHSPFENNIG
Zinc **Obv:** Modified design, swastika and wreath removed **Rev:** Eagle missing tail feathers

Date	Mintage	F	VF	XF	Unc	BU
1944D	—	—	—	10,000	—	—

Note: Possibly a pattern, only one known

KM# A103 REICHSPFENNIG
Zinc **Obv:** Eagle above date **Rev:** Denomination

Date	Mintage	F	VF	XF	Unc	BU
1945F	2,984,000	6.00	12.00	20.00	40.00	60.00
1946F	1,633,000	20.00	40.00	70.00	140	165
1946G	1,500,000	40.00	70.00	110	170	225
1945-1946 Common date proof	—	Value: 250				

KM# A105 5 REICHSPFENNIG
Zinc **Obv:** Eagle, date below **Rev:** Denomination

Date	Mintage	F	VF	XF	Unc	BU
1947A	—	3.00	7.50	15.00	40.00	55.00
1947D	16,528,000	3.00	5.00	7.00	20.00	40.00
1948A	—	5.00	12.50	20.00	45.00	70.00
1948E	7,666,000	150	300	400	700	850
1947-1948 Proof	—	Value: 250				

KM# A104 10 REICHSPFENNIG
Zinc **Obv:** Eagle **Rev:** Denomination

Date	Mintage	F	VF	XF	Unc	BU
1945F	5,942,000	4.50	7.50	15.00	35.00	60.00
1946F	3,738,000	15.00	25.00	35.00	90.00	120
1946G	1,600,000	40.00	70.00	120	200	300
1947A	—	4.50	10.00	20.00	35.00	65.00
1947E	2,612,000	250	350	575	775	950
1947F	1,269,000	2.00	4.00	9.00	20.00	28.00
1948A	—	5.00	18.00	22.50	35.00	55.00
1948F	19,579,000	2.00	4.00	9.00	30.00	40.00
1946-1948 Common date proof	—	Value: 225				

GERMANY-FEDERAL REPUBLIC

1949-

The Federal Republic of Germany, located in north-central Europe, has an area of 137,744 sq. mi. (356,910sq. km.) and a population of 81.1 million. Capital: Berlin. The economy centers about one of the world's foremost industrial establishments. Machinery, motor vehicles, iron, steel, yarns and fabrics are exported.

During the post-Normandy phase of World War II, Allied troops occupied the western German provinces of Schleswig-Holstein, Hamburg, Lower Saxony, Bremen, North Rhine-Westphalia, Hesse, Rhineland-Palatinate, Baden-Wurttemberg, Bavaria and Saarland. The conquered provinces were divided into American, British and French occupation zones. Five eastern German provinces were occupied and administered by the forces of the Soviet Union.

The post-World War II division of Germany was ended Oct. 3, 1990, when the German Democratic Republic (East Germany) ceased to exist and its five constituent provinces were formally admitted to the Federal Republic of Germany. An election Dec. 2, 1990, chose representatives to the united federal parliament (Bundestag), which then conducted its opening session in Berlin in the old Reichstag building. Berlin is again the capital of a United Germany.

MINT MARKS

A - Berlin
D - Munich
F - Stuttgart
G - Karlsruhe
J - Hamburg

MONETARY SYSTEM

100 Pfennig = 1 Deutsche Mark (DM)

FEDERAL REPUBLIC

STANDARD COINAGE

KM# A101 PFENNIG

Bronze Clad Steel, 16.5 mm. **Obv. Legend:** BANK DEUTSCHER LÄNDER

Date	Mintage	F	VF	XF	Unc	BU
1948D	46,325,000	—	0.50	15.00	40.00	—
1948F	68,203,000	—	0.50	8.00	32.50	—
1948F Proof	250	Value: 150				
1948G	45,604,000	—	0.50	15.00	60.00	—
1948J	79,304,000	—	0.50	15.00	50.00	—
1949D	99,863,000	—	0.50	6.00	27.50	—
1949D Proof	—	Value: 100				
1949F	70,900,000	—	0.50	6.00	22.50	—
1949F Proof	250	Value: 60.00				
1949G	70,950,000	—	0.50	10.00	40.00	—
1949J	101,932,000	—	0.50	6.00	27.50	—
1949J Proof	—	Value: 85.00				

KM# 105 PFENNIG

2.0000 g., Copper Plated Steel, 16.5 mm. **Obv:** Five oak leaves, date below **Obv. Legend:** BUNDES REPUBLIK DEUTSCHLAND **Rev:** Denomination

Date	Mintage	F	VF	XF	Unc	BU
1950D	772,592,000	—	—	0.10	2.00	—
1950F	898,277,000	—	—	0.10	2.00	—
1950F Proof	620	Value: 27.50				
1950G	515,673,000	—	—	0.10	3.00	—
1950G Proof	1,800	Value: 5.00				
1950J	784,424,000	—	—	0.10	2.00	—
1950J Proof	—	Value: 12.00				
1966D	65,063,000	—	—	0.10	3.00	—
1966F	75,031,000	—	—	0.10	3.00	—
1966F Proof	100	Value: 35.00				
1966G	48,261,000	—	—	0.10	5.00	—
1966G Proof	3,070	Value: 4.00				
1966J	66,842,000	—	—	0.10	3.00	—
1966J Proof	1,000	Value: 8.00				
1967D	39,082,000	—	0.10	2.00	8.00	—
1967F	45,003,000	—	0.10	1.50	8.00	—
1967F Proof	1,500	Value: 6.00				
1967G	20,787,000	—	0.20	4.50	17.00	—
1967G Proof	4,500	Value: 3.50				
1967J	42,583,000	—	0.10	1.50	8.00	—
1967J Proof	1,500	Value: 8.00				
1968D	32,796,999	—	0.10	1.50	7.00	—
1968F	26,338,000	—	0.10	1.50	7.00	—
1968F Proof	3,000	Value: 5.00				
1968G	20,382,000	—	0.10	1.50	8.00	—
1968G Proof	6,023	Value: 4.00				
1968J	23,414,000	—	0.10	1.50	8.00	—
1968J Proof	2,000	Value: 6.50				
1969D	78,177,000	—	—	0.10	1.00	—
1969F	90,172,000	—	—	0.10	1.00	—
1969F Proof	5,100	Value: 1.50				
1969G	61,836,000	—	—	0.10	2.00	—
1969G Proof	8,700	Value: 1.25				
1969J	80,221,000	—	—	0.10	1.00	—
1969J Proof	5,000	Value: 1.50				
1970D	91,151,000	—	—	0.10	1.00	—
1970F	105,236,000	—	—	0.10	1.00	—
1970F Proof	5,240	Value: 1.50				
1970G	82,421,000	—	—	0.10	1.00	—
1970G Proof	10,200	Value: 1.00				
1970 Small J	93,455,000	—	—	0.10	1.00	—
1970 Large J	Inc. above	—	—	0.10	1.00	—
1970J Proof	5,000	Value: 1.50				
1971D	116,612,000	—	—	0.10	0.50	—
1971D Proof	8,000	Value: 1.00				
1971F	157,393,000	—	—	0.10	0.50	—
1971F Proof	8,000	Value: 1.00				
1971G	77,674,000	—	—	0.10	1.00	—
1971G Proof	10,200	Value: 1.00				
1971J	120,218,000	—	—	0.10	0.50	—
1971J Proof	8,000	Value: 1.00				
1972D	90,696,000	—	—	0.10	0.25	—
1972D Proof	8,000	Value: 1.00				
1972F	105,006,000	—	—	0.10	0.25	—
1972F Proof	8,000	Value: 1.00				
1972G	60,660,000	—	—	0.10	0.25	—
1972G Proof	10,000	Value: 1.00				
1972J	93,492,000	—	—	0.10	0.25	—
1972J Proof	8,000	Value: 1.00				
1973D	38,976,000	—	—	0.10	0.25	—
1973D Proof	9,000	Value: 1.00				
1973F	45,006,000	—	—	0.10	0.25	—
1973F Proof	9,000	Value: 1.00				
1973G	25,811,000	—	—	0.10	0.25	—
1973G Proof	9,000	Value: 1.00				
1973J	40,057,000	—	—	0.10	0.25	—
1973J Proof	9,000	Value: 1.00				
1974D	90,951,000	—	—	0.10	0.25	—
1974D Proof	35,000	Value: 0.40				
1974F	105,091,000	—	—	0.10	0.25	—
1974F Proof	35,000	Value: 0.40				
1974G	60,548,000	—	—	0.10	0.25	—
1974G Proof	35,000	Value: 0.40				
1974J	93,527,000	—	—	0.10	0.25	—
1974J Proof	35,000	Value: 0.40				
1975D	91,053,000	—	—	0.10	0.25	—
1975D Proof	43,000	Value: 0.40				
1975F	105,007,000	—	—	0.10	0.25	—
1975F Proof	43,000	Value: 0.40				
1975G	60,704,000	—	—	0.10	0.25	—
1975G Proof	43,000	Value: 0.40				
1975J	93,495,000	—	—	0.10	0.25	—
1975J Proof	43,000	Value: 0.40				
1976D	130,227,000	—	—	0.10	0.25	—
1976D Proof	43,000	Value: 0.40				
1976F	150,037,000	—	—	0.10	0.25	—
1976F Proof	43,000	Value: 0.40				
1976G	86,586,000	—	—	0.10	0.25	—
1976G Proof	43,000	Value: 0.40				
1976J	133,500,000	—	—	0.10	0.25	—
1976J Proof	43,000	Value: 0.40				
1977D	143,000,000	—	—	0.10	0.25	—
1977D Proof	52,000	Value: 0.40				
1977F	165,000,000	—	—	0.10	0.25	—
1977F Proof	51,000	Value: 0.40				
1977G	95,201,000	—	—	0.10	0.25	—
1977G Proof	51,000	Value: 0.40				
1977J	146,788,000	—	—	0.10	0.25	—
1977J Proof	51,000	Value: 0.40				
1978D	156,000,000	—	—	0.10	0.25	—
1978D Proof	54,000	Value: 0.40				
1978F	180,000,000	—	—	0.10	0.25	—
1978F Proof	54,000	Value: 0.40				
1978G	103,800,000	—	—	0.10	0.25	—
1978G Proof	54,000	Value: 0.40				
1978J	160,200,000	—	—	0.10	0.25	—
1978J Proof	54,000	Value: 0.40				
1979D	156,000,000	—	—	0.10	0.25	—
1979D Proof	89,000	Value: 0.40				
1979F	180,000,000	—	—	0.10	0.25	—
1979F Proof	89,000	Value: 0.40				
1979G	103,800,000	—	—	0.10	0.25	—
1979G Proof	89,000	Value: 0.40				
1979J	160,200,000	—	—	0.10	0.25	—
1979J Proof	89,000	Value: 0.40				
1980D	200,080,000	—	—	0.10	0.25	—
1980D Proof	110,000	Value: 0.40				
1980F	200,620,000	—	—	0.10	0.25	—
1980F Proof	110,000	Value: 0.40				
1980G	71,940,000	—	—	0.10	0.25	—
1980G Proof	110,000	Value: 0.40				
1980J	143,110,000	—	—	0.10	0.25	—
1980J Proof	110,000	Value: 0.40				
1981D	169,550,000	—	—	0.10	0.25	—
1981D Proof	91,000	Value: 0.40				
1981F	274,010,000	—	—	0.10	0.25	—
1981F Proof	91,000	Value: 0.40				
1981G	178,010,000	—	—	0.10	0.25	—
1981G Proof	91,000	Value: 0.40				
1981J	189,090,000	—	—	0.10	0.25	—
1981J Proof	91,000	Value: 0.40				
1982D	130,090,000	—	—	0.10	0.20	—
1982D Proof	78,000	Value: 0.40				
1982F	108,390,000	—	—	0.10	0.20	—
1982F Proof	78,000	Value: 0.40				
1982G	77,740,000	—	—	0.10	0.20	—
1982G Proof	78,000	Value: 0.40				
1982J	124,720,000	—	—	0.10	0.20	—
1982J Proof	78,000	Value: 0.40				
1983D	46,800,000	—	—	0.10	0.20	—
1983D Proof	75,000	Value: 0.40				
1983F	54,000,000	—	—	0.10	0.20	—
1983F Proof	75,000	Value: 0.40				
1983G	31,140,000	—	—	0.10	0.20	—

Date	Mintage	F	VF	XF	Unc	BU
1983G Proof	75,000	Value: 0.40				
1983J	48,060,000	—	—	0.10	0.20	—
1983J Proof	75,000	Value: 0.40				
1984D	58,500,000	—	—	0.10	0.20	—
1984D Proof	64,000	Value: 0.40				
1984F	67,500,000	—	—	0.10	0.20	—
1984F Proof	64,000	Value: 0.40				
1984G	38,900,000	—	—	0.10	0.20	—
1984G Proof	64,000	Value: 0.40				
1984J	60,100,000	—	—	0.10	0.20	—
1984J Proof	64,000	Value: 0.40				
1985D	19,500,000	—	—	0.10	0.20	—
1985D Proof	56,000	Value: 0.40				
1985F	22,500,000	—	—	0.10	0.20	—
1985F Proof	54,000	Value: 0.40				
1985G	13,000,000	—	—	—	0.10	—
1985G Proof	55,000	Value: 0.40				
1985J	20,000,000	—	—	—	0.10	—
1985J Proof	54,000	Value: 0.40				
1986D	39,000,000	—	—	—	0.10	—
1986D Proof	44,000	Value: 0.40				
1986F	45,000,000	—	—	—	0.10	—
1986F Proof	44,000	Value: 0.40				
1986G	25,900,000	—	—	—	0.10	—
1986G Proof	44,000	Value: 0.40				
1986J	40,100,000	—	—	—	0.10	—
1986J Proof	44,000	Value: 0.40				
1987D	6,500,000	—	—	—	0.10	—
1987D Proof	45,000	Value: 0.40				
1987F	7,500,000	—	—	—	0.10	—
1987F Proof	45,000	Value: 0.40				
1987G	4,330,000	—	—	—	0.10	—
1987G Proof	45,000	Value: 0.40				
1987J	6,680,000	—	—	—	0.10	—
1987J Proof	45,000	Value: 0.40				
1988D	52,000,000	—	—	—	0.10	—
1988D Proof	45,000	Value: 0.40				
1988F	60,000,000	—	—	—	0.10	—
1988F Proof	45,000	Value: 0.40				
1988G	34,600,000	—	—	—	0.10	—
1988G Proof	45,000	Value: 0.40				
1988J	53,400,000	—	—	—	0.10	—
1988J Proof	45,000	Value: 0.40				
1989D	104,000,000	—	—	—	0.10	—
1989D Proof	45,000	Value: 0.40				
1989F	120,000,000	—	—	—	0.10	—
1989F Proof	45,000	Value: 0.40				
1989G	69,200,000	—	—	—	0.10	—
1989G Proof	45,000	Value: 0.40				
1989J	106,800,000	—	—	—	0.10	—
1989J Proof	45,000	Value: 0.40				
1990D	169,000,000	—	—	—	0.10	—
1990D Proof	45,000	Value: 0.40				
1990F	195,000,000	—	—	—	0.10	—
1990F Proof	45,000	Value: 0.40				
1990G	112,450,000	—	—	—	0.10	—
1990G Proof	45,000	Value: 0.40				
1990J	173,550,000	—	—	—	0.10	—
1990J Proof	45,000	Value: 0.40				
1991A	260,000,000	—	—	—	0.10	—
1991A Proof	45,000	Value: 0.40				
1991D	273,000,000	—	—	—	0.10	—
1991D Proof	45,000	Value: 0.40				
1991F	312,000,000	—	—	—	0.10	—
1991F Proof	45,000	Value: 0.40				
1991G	182,000,000	—	—	—	0.10	—
1991G Proof	45,000	Value: 0.40				
1991J	273,000,000	—	—	—	0.10	—
1991J Proof	45,000	Value: 0.40				
1992A	40,000,000	—	—	—	0.10	—
1992A Proof	45,000	Value: 0.40				
1992D	42,000,000	—	—	—	0.10	—
1992D Proof	45,000	Value: 0.40				
1992F	48,000,000	—	—	—	0.10	—
1992F Proof	45,000	Value: 0.40				
1992G	28,000,000	—	—	—	0.10	—
1992G Proof	45,000	Value: 0.40				
1992J	42,000,000	—	—	—	0.10	—
1992J Proof	45,000	Value: 0.40				
1993A	40,000,000	—	—	—	0.10	—
1993A Proof	45,000	Value: 0.40				
1993D	42,000,000	—	—	—	0.10	—
1993D Proof	45,000	Value: 0.40				
1993F	48,000,000	—	—	—	0.10	—
1993F Proof	45,000	Value: 0.40				
1993G	28,000,000	—	—	—	0.10	—
1993G Proof	45,000	Value: 0.40				
1993J	42,000,000	—	—	—	0.10	—
1993J Proof	45,000	Value: 0.40				
1994A	100,000,000	—	—	—	0.10	—
1994A Proof	45,000	Value: 0.40				
1994D	105,000,000	—	—	—	0.10	—
1994D Proof	45,000	Value: 0.40				
1994F	120,000,000	—	—	—	0.10	—
1994F Proof	45,000	Value: 0.40				
1994G	70,000,000	—	—	—	0.10	—
1994G Proof	45,000	Value: 0.40				
1994J	105,000,000	—	—	—	0.10	—
1994J Proof	45,000	Value: 0.40				
1995A	100,000,000	—	—	—	0.15	—
1995A Proof	45,000	Value: 0.45				
1995D	105,000,000	—	—	—	0.15	—
1995D Proof	45,000	Value: 0.45				
1995F	120,000,000	—	—	—	0.15	—
1995F Proof	45,000	Value: 0.45				
1995G	70,000,000	—	—	—	0.15	—
1995G Proof	45,000	Value: 0.45				
1995J	105,000,000	—	—	—	0.15	—
1995J Proof	45,000	Value: 0.45				
1996A	80,000,000	—	—	—	0.20	—
1996A Proof	45,000	Value: 0.50				
1996D	84,000,000	—	—	—	0.20	—
1996D Proof	45,000	Value: 0.50				
1996F	96,000,000	—	—	—	0.20	—
1996F Proof	45,000	Value: 0.50				
1996G	56,000,000	—	—	—	0.20	—
1996G Proof	45,000	Value: 0.50				
1996J	84,000,000	—	—	—	0.20	—
1996J Proof	45,000	Value: 0.50				
1997A	70,000	—	—	—	1.75	—
Note: In sets only						
1997A Proof	45,000	Value: 2.00				
1997D	70,000	—	—	—	1.75	—
Note: In sets only						
1997D Proof	45,000	Value: 2.00				
1997F	70,000	—	—	—	1.75	—
Note: In sets only						
1997F Proof	45,000	Value: 2.00				
1997G	70,000	—	—	—	1.75	—
Note: In sets only						
1997G Proof	45,000	Value: 2.00				
1997J	70,000	—	—	—	1.75	—
Note: In sets only						
1997J Proof	45,000	Value: 2.00				
1998A	70,000	—	—	—	1.75	—
Note: In sets only						
1998A Proof	45,000	Value: 2.00				
1998D	70,000	—	—	—	1.75	—
Note: In sets only						
1998D Proof	45,000	Value: 2.00				
1998F	70,000	—	—	—	1.75	—
Note: In sets only						
1998F Proof	45,000	Value: 2.00				
1998G	70,000	—	—	—	1.75	—
Note: In sets only						
1998G Proof	45,000	Value: 2.00				
1998J	70,000	—	—	—	1.75	—
Note: In sets only						
1998J Proof	45,000	Value: 2.00				
1999A	70,000	—	—	—	1.75	—
Note: In sets only						
1999A Proof	45,000	Value: 2.00				
1999D	70,000	—	—	—	1.75	—
Note: In sets only						
1999D Proof	45,000	Value: 2.00				
1999F	70,000	—	—	—	1.75	—
Note: In sets only						
1999F Proof	45,000	Value: 2.00				
1999G	70,000	—	—	—	1.75	—
Note: In sets only						
1999G Proof	45,000	Value: 2.00				
1999J	70,000	—	—	—	1.75	—
Note: In sets only						
1999J Proof	45,000	Value: 2.00				
2000A	20,000	—	—	—	1.75	—
Note: In sets only						
2000A Proof	45,000	Value: 2.00				
2000D	20,000	—	—	—	1.75	—
Note: In sets only						
2000D Proof	45,000	Value: 2.00				
2000F	20,000	—	—	—	1.75	—
Note: In sets only						
2000F Proof	45,000	Value: 2.00				
2000G	20,000	—	—	—	1.75	—
Note: In sets only						
2000G Proof	45,000	Value: 2.00				
2000J	20,000	—	—	—	1.75	—
Note: In sets only						
2000J Proof	45,000	Value: 2.00				
2001A	130,000	—	—	—	5.00	—
Note: In sets only						
2001A Proof	78,000	Value: 5.00				
2001D	130,000	—	—	—	5.00	—
Note: In sets only						
2001D Proof	78,000	Value: 5.00				
2001F	130,000	—	—	—	5.00	—
Note: In sets only						
2001F Proof	78,000	Value: 5.00				
2001G	130,000	—	—	—	5.00	—
Note: In sets only						
2001G Proof	78,000	Value: 5.00				
2001J	130,000	—	—	—	5.00	—
Note: In sets only						
2001J Proof	78,000	Value: 5.00				

KM# 106 2 PFENNIG

Bronze, 19.25 mm. **Obv:** Five oak leaves, date below **Rev:** Denomination

Date	Mintage	F	VF	XF	Unc	BU
1950D	26,263,000	—	0.10	2.50	12.00	—
1950D Proof	—	Value: 50.00				
1950F	30,278,000	—	0.10	2.00	10.00	—
1950F Proof	200	—	—	—	—	—
1950G	17,151,000	—	0.10	25.00	75.00	—
1950G Proof	—	Value: 90.00				
1950J	27,216,000	—	0.10	2.50	12.00	—
1950J Proof	—	Value: 40.00				
1958D	19,440,000	—	0.10	3.00	14.00	—
1958F	24,122,000	—	0.10	2.00	10.00	—
1958F Proof	100	—	—	—	—	—
1958G	15,255,000	—	0.10	4.00	18.00	—
1958J	21,250,000	—	0.10	2.00	10.00	—
1959D	19,690,000	—	0.10	2.00	10.00	—
1959F	25,017,000	—	0.10	1.50	10.00	—
1959F Proof	75	—	—	—	—	—
1959G	12,899,000	—	0.10	3.00	14.00	—
1959J	25,482,000	—	0.10	2.00	10.00	—
1960D	21,979,000	—	0.10	1.50	9.00	—
1960F	13,060,000	—	—	0.10	10.00	—
1960F Proof	75	—	—	—	—	—
1960G	5,657,000	—	0.10	2.00	18.00	—
1960J	17,799,000	—	0.10	2.00	10.00	—
1961D	26,662,000	—	0.10	1.50	9.00	—
1961F	24,990,000	—	0.10	1.50	8.00	—
1961G	18,060,000	—	0.10	1.50	9.00	—
1961J	22,147,000	—	0.10	1.50	8.00	—
1962D	21,297,000	—	0.10	1.50	9.00	—
1962F	42,189,000	—	0.10	1.00	6.00	—
1962G	17,297,000	—	0.10	2.00	12.00	—
1962J	30,706,000	—	0.10	1.00	8.00	—
1963D	7,648,000	—	0.10	2.00	10.00	—
1963F	18,299,000	—	0.10	1.50	9.00	—
1963G	35,838,000	—	0.10	1.50	8.00	—
1963G Proof	—	—	—	—	—	—
1963J	42,884,000	—	0.10	1.50	6.00	—
1964D	20,336,000	—	0.10	1.50	10.00	—
1964F	31,400,000	—	0.10	1.50	7.00	—
1964G	18,431,000	—	0.10	1.50	8.00	—
1964G Proof	Est. 600	Value: 12.00				
1964J	13,370,000	—	0.10	1.50	8.00	—
1965D	48,541,000	—	0.10	1.00	4.00	—
1965F	27,000,000	—	0.10	1.00	6.00	—
1965F Proof	Est. 80	Value: 70.00				
1965G	13,584,000	—	0.10	1.50	7.00	—
1965G Proof	1,200	Value: 5.00				
1965J	33,397,000	—	0.10	1.00	4.00	—
1966D	65,077,000	—	—	0.50	3.00	—
1966F	52,543,000	—	—	0.50	3.00	—
1966F Proof	100	Value: 80.00				
1966G	40,804,000	—	—	0.50	3.00	—
1966G Proof	3,070	Value: 5.50				
1966J	46,754,000	—	—	0.50	3.00	—
1966J Proof	1,000	Value: 40.00				
1967D	25,997,000	—	0.10	1.00	6.00	—
1967F	30,004,000	—	0.10	1.00	5.00	—
1967F Proof	1,500	Value: 7.00				
1967G	6,280,000	—	0.10	1.50	10.00	—
1967G Proof	4,500	Value: 4.50				
1967J	26,725,000	—	0.10	1.00	6.00	—
1967J Proof	1,500	Value: 10.00				
1968D	19,523,000	—	0.10	1.00	5.00	—
1968G	15,357,000	—	0.10	1.00	6.00	—
1968G Proof	3,651	Value: 4.00				
1968J	—	—	200	400	600	—
Note: A 1968J error of 1963J exists with coin alignment						
1969J	—	—	200	400	600	—

KM# 106a 2 PFENNIG

2.9000 g., Bronze Clad Steel, 19.25 mm. **Obv:** Five oak leaves, date below **Rev:** Denomination

Date	Mintage	F	VF	XF	Unc	BU
1967G Proof	520	Value: 950				
1968D	19,523,000	—	—	0.50	2.50	—
1968F	30,000,000	—	—	0.50	2.50	—
1968F Proof	3,000	Value: 6.00				
1968G	13,004,000	—	—	0.50	2.50	—
1968G Proof	2,372	Value: 4.00				
1968J	20,026,000	—	—	0.25	2.00	—
1968J Proof	2,000	Value: 7.50				
1969D	39,012,000	—	—	0.25	1.00	—
1969D Proof	—	Value: 1.25				

Date	Mintage	F	VF	XF	Unc	BU
1969F	45,029,000	—	—	0.25	1.00	—
1969F Proof	5,100	Value: 1.25				
1969G	32,156,999	—	—	0.25	1.00	—
1969G Proof	8,700	Value: 1.25				
1969J	40,102,000	—	—	0.25	1.00	—
1969J Proof	5,000	Value: 2.50				
1970D	45,525,000	—	—	0.10	0.25	—
1970F	73,851,000	—	—	0.10	0.25	—
1970F Proof	5,140	Value: 1.25				
1970G	30,330,000	—	—	0.10	0.25	—
1970G Proof	10,200	Value: 1.25				
1970 Small J	46,730,000	—	—	0.10	0.25	—
1970 Large J	Inc. above	—	—	0.10	0.25	—
1970J Proof	5,000	Value: 1.75				
1971D	71,755,000	—	—	0.10	0.25	—
1971D Proof	8,000	Value: 1.25				
1971F	82,765,000	—	—	0.10	0.25	—
1971F Proof	8,000	Value: 1.25				
1971G	47,850,000	—	—	0.10	0.25	—
1971G Proof	10,000	Value: 1.25				
1971J	73,641,000	—	—	0.10	0.25	—
1971J Proof	8,000	Value: 1.25				
1972D	52,403,000	—	—	0.10	0.25	—
1972D Proof	8,000	Value: 1.00				
1972F	60,272,000	—	—	0.10	0.25	—
1972F Proof	8,000	Value: 1.00				
1972G	34,864,000	—	—	0.10	0.25	—
1972G Proof	10,000	Value: 1.00				
1972J	53,673,000	—	—	0.10	0.25	—
1972J Proof	8,000	Value: 1.00				
1973D	26,190,000	—	—	0.10	0.25	—
1973D Proof	9,000	Value: 1.00				
1973F	30,160,000	—	—	0.10	0.25	—
1973F Proof	9,000	Value: 1.00				
1973G	17,379,000	—	—	0.10	0.25	—
1973G Proof	9,000	Value: 1.00				
1973J	26,830,000	—	—	0.10	0.25	—
1973J Proof	9,000	Value: 1.00				
1974D	58,667,000	—	—	0.10	0.25	—
1974D Proof	35,000	Value: 0.50				
1974F	67,596,000	—	—	0.10	0.25	—
1974F Proof	35,000	Value: 0.50				
1974G	39,007,000	—	—	0.10	0.25	—
1974G Proof	35,000	Value: 0.50				
1974J	60,195,000	—	—	0.10	0.25	—
1974J Proof	35,000	Value: 0.50				
1975D	58,634,000	—	—	0.10	0.25	—
1975D Proof	43,000	Value: 0.50				
1975F	67,685,000	—	—	0.10	0.25	—
1975F Proof	43,000	Value: 0.50				
1975G	39,391,000	—	—	0.10	0.25	—
1975G Proof	43,000	Value: 0.50				
1975J	60,207,000	—	—	0.10	0.25	—
1975J Proof	43,000	Value: 0.50				
1976D	78,074,000	—	—	0.10	0.25	—
1976D Proof	43,000	Value: 0.50				
1976F	90,130,000	—	—	0.10	0.25	—
1976F Proof	43,000	Value: 0.50				
1976G	51,988,000	—	—	0.10	0.25	—
1976G Proof	43,000	Value: 0.50				
1976J	80,145,000	—	—	0.10	0.25	—
1976J Proof	43,000	Value: 0.50				
1977D	84,516,000	—	—	0.10	0.20	—
1977D Proof	51,000	Value: 0.40				
1977F	97,504,000	—	—	0.10	0.20	—
1977F Proof	51,000	Value: 0.40				
1977G	56,276,000	—	—	0.10	0.20	—
1977G Proof	51,000	Value: 0.40				
1977J	86,888,000	—	—	0.10	0.20	—
1977J Proof	51,000	Value: 0.40				
1978D	84,500,000	—	—	0.10	0.20	—
1978D Proof	54,000	Value: 0.40				
1978F	97,500,000	—	—	0.10	0.20	—
1978F Proof	54,000	Value: 0.40				
1978G	56,225,000	—	—	0.10	0.20	—
1978G Proof	54,000	Value: 0.40				
1978J	86,775,000	—	—	0.10	0.20	—
1978J Proof	54,000	Value: 0.40				
1979D	91,000,000	—	—	0.10	0.20	—
1979D Proof	89,000	Value: 0.40				
1979F	105,000,000	—	—	0.10	0.20	—
1979F Proof	89,000	Value: 0.40				
1979G	60,550,000	—	—	0.10	0.20	—
1979G Proof	89,000	Value: 0.40				
1979J	93,480,000	—	—	0.10	0.20	—
1979J Proof	89,000	Value: 0.40				
1980D	93,360,000	—	—	0.10	0.20	—
1980D Proof	110,000	Value: 0.40				
1980F	120,360,000	—	—	0.10	0.20	—
1980F Proof	110,000	Value: 0.40				
1980G	50,830,000	—	—	0.10	0.20	—
1980G Proof	110,000	Value: 0.40				
1980J	102,260,000	—	—	0.10	0.20	—
1980J Proof	110,000	Value: 0.40				
1981D	93,910,000	—	—	0.10	0.20	—
1981D Proof	91,000	Value: 0.40				
1981F	83,710,000	—	—	0.10	0.20	—
1981F Proof	91,000	Value: 0.40				
1981G	89,850,000	—	—	0.10	0.20	—
1981G Proof	91,000	Value: 0.40				
1981J	87,250,000	—	—	0.10	0.20	—
1981J Proof	91,000	Value: 0.40				
1982D	64,390,000	—	—	0.10	0.20	—
1982D Proof	78,000	Value: 0.40				
1982F	36,870,000	—	—	0.10	0.20	—
1982F Proof	78,000	Value: 0.40				
1982G	58,590,000	—	—	0.10	0.20	—
1982G Proof	78,000	Value: 0.40				
1982J	57,690,000	—	—	0.10	0.20	—
1982J Proof	78,000	Value: 0.40				
1983D	71,500,000	—	—	0.10	0.20	—
1983D Proof	75,000	Value: 0.40				
1983F	82,500,000	—	—	0.10	0.20	—
1983F Proof	75,000	Value: 0.40				
1983G	47,575,000	—	—	0.10	0.20	—
1983G Proof	75,000	Value: 0.40				
1983J	73,425,000	—	—	0.10	0.20	—
1983J Proof	75,000	Value: 0.40				
1984D	58,500,000	—	—	0.10	0.20	—
1984D Proof	64,000	Value: 0.40				
1984F	67,500,000	—	—	0.10	0.20	—
1984F Proof	64,000	Value: 0.40				
1984G	38,900,000	—	—	0.10	0.20	—
1984G Proof	64,000	Value: 0.40				
1984J	60,100,000	—	—	0.10	0.20	—
1984J Proof	64,000	Value: 0.40				
1985D	19,500,000	—	0.10	1.00	3.00	—
1985D Proof	56,000	Value: 0.40				
1985F	22,500,000	—	0.25	1.00	3.00	—
1985F Proof	54,000	Value: 0.40				
1985G	13,000,000	0.25	0.75	2.50	8.00	—
1985G Proof	55,000	Value: 0.40				
1985J	20,000,000	0.25	0.50	2.00	7.00	—
1985J Proof	54,000	Value: 0.40				
1986D	39,000,000	—	—	—	0.25	—
1986D Proof	44,000	Value: 0.40				
1986F	45,000,000	—	—	—	0.25	—
1986F Proof	44,000	Value: 0.40				
1986G	25,900,000	—	—	—	0.50	—
1986G Proof	44,000	Value: 0.40				
1986J	40,100,000	—	—	—	0.25	—
1986J Proof	44,000	Value: 0.40				
1987D	6,500,000	0.50	1.00	2.50	5.00	—
1987D Proof	45,000	Value: 0.40				
1987F	7,500,000	0.50	1.00	2.50	5.00	—
1987F Proof	45,000	Value: 0.40				
1987G	4,330,000	0.75	1.25	2.75	6.00	—
1987G Proof	45,000	Value: 0.40				
1987J	6,680,000	0.50	1.00	2.50	5.00	—
1987J Proof	45,000	Value: 0.40				
1988D	52,000,000	—	—	—	0.25	—
1988D Proof	45,000	Value: 0.40				
1988F	60,000,000	—	—	—	0.25	—
1988F Proof	45,000	Value: 0.40				
1988G	34,600,000	—	—	—	0.25	—
1988G Proof	45,000	Value: 0.40				
1988J	53,400,000	—	—	—	0.25	—
1988J Proof	45,000	Value: 0.40				
1989D	52,000,000	—	—	—	0.25	—
1989D Proof	45,000	Value: 0.40				
1989F	60,000,000	—	—	—	0.25	—
1989F Proof	45,000	Value: 0.40				
1989G	34,600,000	—	—	—	0.25	—
1989G Proof	45,000	Value: 0.40				
1989J	53,400,000	—	—	—	0.25	—
1989J Proof	45,000	Value: 0.40				
1990D	71,500,000	—	—	—	0.25	—
1990D Proof	45,000	Value: 0.40				
1990F	82,500,000	—	—	—	0.25	—
1990F Proof	45,000	Value: 0.40				
1990G	47,570,000	—	—	—	0.25	—
1990G Proof	45,000	Value: 0.40				
1990J	73,420,000	—	—	—	0.25	—
1990J Proof	45,000	Value: 0.40				
1991A	115,000,000	—	—	—	0.25	—
1991A Proof	45,000	Value: 0.40				
1991D	120,750,000	—	—	—	0.25	—
1991D Proof	45,000	Value: 0.40				
1991F	138,000,000	—	—	—	0.25	—
1991F Proof	45,000	Value: 0.40				
1991G	80,500,000	—	—	—	0.25	—
1991G Proof	45,000	Value: 0.40				
1991J	120,750,000	—	—	—	0.25	—
1991J Proof	45,000	Value: 0.40				
1992A	60,000,000	—	—	—	0.25	—
1992A Proof	45,000	Value: 0.40				
1992D	63,000,000	—	—	—	0.25	—
1992D Proof	45,000	Value: 0.40				
1992F	72,000,000	—	—	—	0.25	—
1992F Proof	45,000	Value: 0.40				
1992G	42,000,000	—	—	—	0.25	—
1992G Proof	45,000	Value: 0.40				
1992J	63,000,000	—	—	—	0.25	—
1992J Proof	45,000	Value: 0.40				
1993A	10,000,000	—	0.25	1.00	4.00	—
1993A Proof	45,000	Value: 0.40				
1993D	10,500,000	—	0.25	1.00	4.00	—
1993D Proof	45,000	Value: 0.40				
1993F	12,000,000	—	0.25	1.00	4.00	—
1993F Proof	45,000	Value: 0.40				
1993G	7,000,000	—	0.25	1.00	4.00	—
1993G Proof	45,000	Value: 0.40				
1993J	10,000,000	—	0.25	1.00	4.00	—
1993J Proof	45,000	Value: 0.40				
1994A	55,000,000	—	—	—	0.15	—
1994A Proof	45,000	Value: 0.40				
1994D	57,750,000	—	—	—	0.15	—
1994D Proof	45,000	Value: 0.40				
1994F	66,000,000	—	—	—	0.15	—
1994F Proof	45,000	Value: 0.40				
1994G	38,500,000	—	—	—	0.25	—
1994G Proof	45,000	Value: 0.40				
1994J	57,750,000	—	—	—	0.15	—
1994J Proof	45,000	Value: 0.40				
1995A	1,000,000,000	—	—	—	0.15	—
1995A Proof	45,000	Value: 0.45				
1995D	105,000,000	—	—	—	0.15	—
1995D Proof	45,000	Value: 0.45				
1995F	120,000,000	—	—	—	0.15	—
1995F Proof	45,000	Value: 0.45				
1995G	70,000,000	—	—	—	0.25	—
1995G Proof	45,000	Value: 0.45				
1995J	105,000,000	—	—	—	0.15	—
1995J Proof	45,000	Value: 0.45				
1996A	40,000,000	—	—	—	0.20	—
1996A Proof	45,000	Value: 0.50				
1996D	42,000,000	—	—	—	0.20	—
1996D Proof	45,000	Value: 0.50				
1996F	48,000,000	—	—	—	0.20	—
1996F Proof	45,000	Value: 0.50				
1996G	28,000,000	—	—	—	0.25	—
1996G Proof	45,000	Value: 0.50				
1996J	42,000,000	—	—	—	0.20	—
1996J Proof	45,000	Value: 0.50				
1997A	70,000	—	—	—	1.75	—
Note: In sets only						
1997A Proof	45,000	Value: 2.00				
1997D	70,000	—	—	—	1.75	—
Note: In sets only						
1997D Proof	45,000	Value: 2.00				
1997F	70,000	—	—	—	1.75	—
Note: In sets only						
1997F Proof	45,000	Value: 2.00				
1997G	70,000	—	—	—	1.75	—
Note: In sets only						
1997G Proof	45,000	Value: 2.00				
1997J	70,000	—	—	—	1.75	—
Note: In sets only						
1997J Proof	45,000	Value: 2.00				
1998A	70,000	—	—	—	1.75	—
Note: In sets only						
1998A Proof	45,000	Value: 2.00				
1998D	70,000	—	—	—	1.75	—
Note: In sets only						
1998D Proof	45,000	Value: 2.00				
1998F	70,000	—	—	—	1.75	—
Note: In sets only						
1998F Proof	45,000	Value: 2.00				
1998G	70,000	—	—	—	1.75	—
Note: In sets only						
1998G Proof	45,000	Value: 2.00				
1998J	70,000	—	—	—	1.75	—
Note: In sets only						
1998J Proof	45,000	Value: 2.00				
1999A	70,000	—	—	—	1.75	—
Note: In sets only						
1999A Proof	45,000	Value: 2.00				
1999D	70,000	—	—	—	1.75	—
Note: In sets only						
1999D Proof	45,000	Value: 2.00				
1999F	70,000	—	—	—	1.75	—
Note: In sets only						
1999F Proof	45,000	Value: 2.00				
1999G	70,000	—	—	—	1.75	—
Note: In sets only						
1999G Proof	45,000	Value: 2.00				
1999J	70,000	—	—	—	1.75	—
Note: In sets only						
1999J Proof	45,000	Value: 2.00				
2000A	70,000	—	—	—	1.75	—
Note: In sets only						
2000A Proof	45,000	Value: 2.00				
2000D	70,000	—	—	—	1.75	—
Note: In sets only						
2000D Proof	45,000	Value: 2.00				
2000F	70,000	—	—	—	1.75	—
Note: In sets only						
2000F Proof	45,000	Value: 2.00				
2000G	70,000	—	—	—	1.75	—
Note: In sets only						
2000G Proof	45,000	Value: 2.00				
2000J	70,000	—	—	—	1.75	—
Note: In sets only						
2000J Proof	45,000	Value: 2.00				
2001A	130,000	—	—	—	5.00	—
Note: In sets only						
2001A Proof	78,000	Value: 5.00				
2001D	130,000	—	—	—	5.00	—
Note: In sets only						
2001D Proof	78,000	Value: 5.00				
2001F	130,000	—	—	—	5.00	—
Note: In sets only						
2001F Proof	78,000	Value: 5.00				
2001G	130,000	—	—	—	5.00	—
Note: In sets only						

Date	Mintage	F	VF	XF	Unc	BU
2001G Proof	78,000	Value: 5.00				
2001J	130,000	—	—	—	5.00	—

Note: In sets only

Date	Mintage	F	VF	XF	Unc	BU
2001J Proof	78,000	Value: 5.00				

KM# 102 5 PFENNIG

Bronze Clad Steel, 18.5 mm. **Obv:** Five oak leaves, date below **Obv. Legend:** BANK DEUTSCHER LÄNDER **Rev:** Denomination

Date	Mintage	F	VF	XF	Unc	BU
1949D	60,026,000	0.25	1.00	10.00	45.00	—
1949D Proof	—	Value: 150				
1949F	66,081,999	0.25	1.00	7.50	35.00	—
1949F Proof	250	Value: 85.00				
1949G	57,356,000	0.25	1.50	12.50	50.00	—
1949J	68,977,000	0.25	1.00	10.00	40.00	—
1949J Proof	—	Value: 85.00				

KM# 107 5 PFENNIG

3.0000 g., Brass Plated Steel, 18.5 mm. **Obv:** Five oak leaves, date below **Obv. Legend:** BUNDES REPUBLIK DEUTSCHLAND **Rev:** Denomination

Date	Mintage	F	VF	XF	Unc	BU
1950D	271,962,000	—	—	1.50	5.00	—
1950F	362,880,000	—	—	1.50	5.00	—
1950F Proof	500	Value: 65.00				
1950G	180,492,000	—	—	1.50	5.00	—
1950G Proof	1,800	Value: 25.00				
1950J Large J	285,283,000	—	—	1.50	5.00	—
1950J Small J	Inc. above	—	—	1.50	5.00	—
1966D	26,036,000	—	—	1.50	8.50	—
1966F	30,047,000	—	—	1.50	8.50	—
1966F Proof	100	Value: 60.00				
1966G	17,333,000	—	—	1.50	8.50	—
1966G Proof	3,070	Value: 7.50				
1966J	26,741,000	—	—	1.50	8.50	—
1966J Proof	1,000	Value: 17.50				
1967D	10,418,000	—	—	1.50	8.50	—
1967F	12,012,000	—	—	1.50	8.50	—
1967F Proof	1,500	Value: 15.00				
1967G	1,736,000	0.50	2.50	7.00	25.00	—
1967G Proof	4,500	Value: 7.50				
1967J	10,706,000	—	—	1.50	8.50	—
1967J Proof	1,500	Value: 15.00				
1968D	13,047,000	—	—	1.00	6.00	—
1968F	15,026,000	—	—	1.00	5.00	—
1968F Proof	3,000	Value: 9.00				
1968G	13,855,000	—	—	1.00	7.00	—
1968G Proof	6,023	Value: 6.00				
1968J	13,362,000	—	—	1.00	7.00	—
1968J Proof	2,000	Value: 15.00				
1969D	23,488,000	—	—	0.50	2.50	—
1969F	27,046,000	—	—	0.50	2.50	—
1969F Proof	5,000	Value: 3.00				
1969G	15,631,000	—	—	0.50	3.00	—
1969G Proof	8,700	Value: 2.50				
1969J	24,120,000	—	—	0.50	2.50	—
1969J Proof	5,000	Value: 2.00				
1970D	39,940,000	—	—	0.10	1.00	—
1970F	45,517,000	—	—	0.10	1.00	—
1970F Proof	5,140	Value: 2.50				
1970G	27,638,000	—	—	0.10	1.00	—
1970G Proof	10,200	Value: 1.50				
1970J	40,873,000	—	—	0.10	1.00	—
1970J Proof	5,000	Value: 2.50				
1971D	57,345,000	—	—	0.10	1.00	—
1971D Proof	8,000	Value: 1.50				
1971F	66,426,000	—	—	0.10	1.00	—
1971F Proof	8,000	Value: 1.50				
1971G	38,284,000	—	—	0.10	1.00	—
1971G Proof	10,000	Value: 1.50				
1971J	58,566,000	—	—	0.10	1.00	—
1971J Proof	8,000	Value: 1.50				
1972D	52,325,000	—	—	0.10	1.00	—
1972D Proof	8,000	Value: 1.50				
1972F	60,292,000	—	—	0.10	1.00	—
1972F Proof	8,000	Value: 1.50				
1972G	34,719,000	—	—	0.10	1.00	—
1972G Proof	10,000	Value: 1.50				
1972J	54,218,000	—	—	0.10	1.00	—
1972J Proof	8,000	Value: 1.50				
1973D	15,596,000	—	—	0.10	1.00	—
1973D Proof	9,000	Value: 1.50				
1973F	18,039,000	—	—	0.10	1.00	—
1973F Proof	9,000	Value: 1.50				
1973G	10,391,000	—	—	0.10	1.00	—
1973G Proof	9,000	Value: 1.50				
1973J	16,035,000	—	—	0.10	1.00	—
1973J Proof	9,000	Value: 1.50				
1974D	15,769,000	—	—	0.10	1.00	—
1974D Proof	35,000	Value: 0.50				
1974F	18,143,000	—	—	0.10	1.00	—
1974F Proof	35,000	Value: 0.50				
1974G	10,508,000	—	—	0.10	1.00	—
1974G Proof	35,000	Value: 0.50				
1974J	16,055,000	—	—	0.10	1.00	—
1974J Proof	35,000	Value: 0.50				
1975D	15,715,000	—	—	0.10	1.00	—
1975D Proof	43,000	Value: 0.50				
1975F	18,013,000	—	—	0.10	0.35	—
1975F Proof	43,000	Value: 0.50				
1975G	10,466,000	—	—	0.10	0.35	—
1975G Proof	43,000	Value: 0.50				
1975J	16,201,000	—	—	0.10	0.35	—
1975J Proof	43,000	Value: 0.50				
1976D	47,091,000	—	—	0.10	0.35	—
1976D Proof	43,000	Value: 0.50				
1976F	54,370,000	—	—	0.10	0.35	—
1976F Proof	43,000	Value: 0.50				
1976G	31,367,000	—	—	0.10	0.35	—
1976G Proof	43,000	Value: 0.50				
1976J	48,321,000	—	—	0.10	0.35	—
1976J Proof	43,000	Value: 0.50				
1977D	52,159,000	—	—	0.10	0.35	—
1977D Proof	51,000	Value: 0.45				
1977F	60,124,000	—	—	0.10	0.35	—
1977F Proof	51,000	Value: 0.45				
1977G	34,600,000	—	—	0.10	0.35	—
1977G Proof	51,000	Value: 0.45				
1977J	53,481,000	—	—	0.10	0.35	—
1977J Proof	51,000	Value: 0.45				
1978D	41,600,000	—	—	0.10	0.35	—
1978D Proof	54,000	Value: 0.45				
1978F	48,000,000	—	—	0.10	0.35	—
1978F Proof	54,000	Value: 0.45				
1978G	27,680,000	—	—	0.10	0.35	—
1978G Proof	54,000	Value: 0.45				
1978J	42,720,000	—	—	0.10	0.35	—
1978J Proof	54,000	Value: 0.45				
1979D	41,600,000	—	—	0.10	0.20	—
1979D Proof	89,000	Value: 0.40				
1979F	48,000,000	—	—	0.10	0.20	—
1979F Proof	89,000	Value: 0.40				
1979G	27,680,000	—	—	0.10	0.20	—
1979G Proof	89,000	Value: 0.40				
1979J	42,711,000	—	—	0.10	0.20	—
1979J Proof	89,000	Value: 0.40				
1980D	39,880,000	—	—	0.10	0.20	—
1980D Proof	110,000	Value: 0.40				
1980F	53,270,000	—	—	0.10	0.20	—
1980F Proof	110,000	Value: 0.40				
1980G	43,070,000	—	—	0.10	0.20	—
1980G Proof	110,000	Value: 0.40				
1980J	59,130,000	—	—	0.10	0.20	—
1980J Proof	110,000	Value: 0.40				
1981D	82,250,000	—	—	0.10	0.20	—
1981D Proof	91,000	Value: 0.40				
1981F	84,910,000	—	—	0.10	0.20	—
1981F Proof	91,000	Value: 0.40				
1981G	41,910,000	—	—	0.10	0.20	—
1981G Proof	91,000	Value: 0.40				
1981J	49,290,000	—	—	0.10	0.20	—
1981J Proof	91,000	Value: 0.40				
1982D	57,500,000	—	—	0.10	0.20	—
1982D Proof	78,000	Value: 0.40				
1982F	53,290,000	—	—	0.10	0.20	—
1982F Proof	78,000	Value: 0.40				
1982G	23,750,000	—	—	0.10	0.20	—
1982G Proof	78,000	Value: 0.40				
1982J	62,000,000	—	—	0.10	0.20	—
1982J Proof	78,000	Value: 0.40				
1983D	46,800,000	—	—	0.10	0.20	—
1983D Proof	75,000	Value: 0.40				
1983F	54,000,000	—	—	0.10	0.20	—
1983F Proof	75,000	Value: 0.40				
1983G	31,140,000	—	—	0.10	0.20	—
1983G Proof	75,000	Value: 0.40				
1983J	48,060,000	—	—	0.10	0.20	—
1983J Proof	75,000	Value: 0.40				
1984D	36,400,000	—	—	0.10	0.20	—
1984D Proof	64,000	Value: 0.40				
1984F	42,000,000	—	—	0.10	0.20	—
1984F Proof	64,000	Value: 0.40				
1984G	24,200,000	—	—	0.10	0.20	—
1984G Proof	64,000	Value: 0.40				
1984J	37,400,000	—	—	0.10	0.20	—
1984J Proof	64,000	Value: 0.40				
1985D	15,600,000	—	—	0.10	0.50	—
1985D Proof	56,000	Value: 0.50				
1985F	18,000,000	—	—	0.10	0.50	—
1985F Proof	54,000	Value: 0.50				
1985G	10,400,000	—	—	0.10	0.50	—
1985G Proof	55,000	Value: 0.50				
1985J	16,000,000	—	—	0.10	0.50	—
1985J Proof	54,000	Value: 0.50				
1986D	36,400,000	—	—	—	0.25	—
1986D Proof	44,000	Value: 0.40				
1986F	42,000,000	—	—	—	0.25	—
1986F Proof	44,000	Value: 0.40				
1986G	24,200,000	—	—	—	0.25	—
1986G Proof	44,000	Value: 0.40				
1986J	37,400,000	—	—	—	0.25	—
1986J Proof	44,000	Value: 0.40				
1987D	52,000,000	—	—	—	0.25	—
1987D Proof	45,000	Value: 0.40				
1987F	60,000,000	—	—	—	0.25	—
1987F Proof	45,000	Value: 0.40				
1987G	34,600,000	—	—	—	0.25	—
1987G Proof	45,000	Value: 0.40				
1987J	53,400,000	—	—	—	0.25	—
1987J Proof	45,000	Value: 0.40				
1988D	52,400,000	—	—	—	0.25	—
1988D Proof	45,000	Value: 0.40				
1988F	72,000,000	—	—	—	0.25	—
1988F Proof	45,000	Value: 0.40				
1988G	41,500,000	—	—	—	0.25	—
1988G Proof	45,000	Value: 0.40				
1988J	64,099,999	—	—	—	0.25	—
1988J Proof	45,000	Value: 0.40				
1989D	93,600,000	—	—	—	0.25	—
1989D Proof	45,000	Value: 0.40				
1989F	108,000,000	—	—	—	0.25	—
1989F Proof	45,000	Value: 0.40				
1989G	62,280,000	—	—	—	0.25	—
1989G Proof	45,000	Value: 0.40				
1989J	96,120,000	—	—	—	0.25	—
1989J Proof	45,000	Value: 0.40				
1990A	70,000,000	—	—	—	0.10	—
1990D	93,600,000	—	—	—	0.10	—
1990D Proof	45,000	Value: 0.40				
1990F	108,000,000	—	—	—	0.10	—
1990F Proof	45,000	Value: 0.40				
1990G	62,280,000	—	—	—	0.10	—
1990G Proof	45,000	Value: 0.40				
1990J	96,120,000	—	—	—	0.10	—
1990J Proof	45,000	Value: 0.40				
1991A	128,000,000	—	—	—	0.10	—
1991A Proof	45,000	Value: 0.40				
1991D	134,400,000	—	—	—	0.10	—
1991D Proof	45,000	Value: 0.40				
1991F	153,600,000	—	—	—	0.10	—
1991F Proof	45,000	Value: 0.40				
1991G	89,600,000	—	—	—	0.10	—
1991G Proof	45,000	Value: 0.40				
1991J	134,400,000	—	—	—	0.10	—
1991J Proof	45,000	Value: 0.40				
1992A	28,000,000	—	—	—	0.10	—
1992A Proof	45,000	Value: 0.40				
1992D	29,400,000	—	—	—	0.10	—
1992D Proof	45,000	Value: 0.40				
1992F	33,600,000	—	—	—	0.10	—
1992F Proof	45,000	Value: 0.40				
1992G	19,600,000	—	—	—	0.10	—
1992G Proof	45,000	Value: 0.40				
1992J	29,400,000	—	—	—	0.10	—
1992J Proof	45,000	Value: 0.40				
1993A	36,000,000	—	—	—	0.10	—
1993A Proof	45,000	Value: 0.40				
1993D	37,800,000	—	—	—	0.10	—
1993D Proof	45,000	Value: 0.40				
1993F	43,200,000	—	—	—	0.10	—
1993F Proof	45,000	Value: 0.40				
1993G	25,200,000	—	—	—	0.10	—
1993G Proof	45,000	Value: 0.40				
1993J	37,800,000	—	—	—	0.10	—
1993J Proof	45,000	Value: 0.40				
1994A	38,000,000	—	—	—	0.10	—
1994A Proof	45,000	Value: 0.40				
1994D	39,900,000	—	—	—	0.10	—
1994D Proof	45,000	Value: 0.40				
1994F	45,600,000	—	—	—	0.10	—
1994F Proof	45,000	Value: 0.40				
1994G	26,600,000	—	—	—	0.10	—
1994G Proof	45,000	Value: 0.40				
1994J	39,900,000	—	—	—	0.10	—
1994J Proof	45,000	Value: 0.40				
1995A	48,000,000	—	—	—	0.15	—
1995A Proof	45,000	Value: 0.45				
1995D	50,400,000	—	—	—	0.15	—
1995D Proof	45,000	Value: 0.45				
1995F	57,600,000	—	—	—	0.15	—
1995F Proof	45,000	Value: 0.45				
1995G	33,600,000	—	—	—	0.15	—
1995G Proof	45,000	Value: 0.45				
1995J	50,400,000	—	—	—	0.15	—
1995J Proof	45,000	Value: 0.45				
1996A	48,000,000	—	—	—	0.20	—
1996A Proof	45,000	Value: 0.50				
1996D	50,400,000	—	—	—	0.20	—
1996D Proof	45,000	Value: 0.50				
1996F	57,600,000	—	—	—	0.20	—
1996F Proof	45,000	Value: 0.50				
1996G	33,600,000	—	—	—	0.20	—
1996G Proof	45,000	Value: 0.50				
1996J	50,400,000	—	—	—	0.20	—
1996J Proof	45,000	Value: 0.50				
1997A	70,000	—	—	—	1.75	—

Note: In sets only

Date	Mintage	F	VF	XF	Unc	BU
1997A Proof	45,000	Value: 2.00				
1997D	70,000	—	—	—	1.75	—

Date	Mintage	F	VF	XF	Unc	BU
Note: In sets only						
1997D Proof	45,000	Value: 2.00				
1997F	70,000	—	—	—	1.75	—
Note: In sets only						
1997F Proof	45,000	Value: 2.00				
1997G	70,000	—	—	—	1.75	—
Note: In sets only						
1997G Proof	45,000	Value: 2.00				
1997J	70,000	—	—	—	1.75	—
Note: In sets only						
1997J Proof	45,000	Value: 2.00				
1998A	70,000	—	—	—	1.75	—
Note: In sets only						
1998A Proof	45,000	Value: 2.00				
1998D	70,000	—	—	—	1.75	—
Note: In sets only						
1998D Proof	45,000	Value: 2.00				
1998F	70,000	—	—	—	1.75	—
Note: In sets only						
1998F Proof	45,000	Value: 2.00				
1998G	70,000	—	—	—	1.75	—
Note: In sets only						
1998G Proof	45,000	Value: 2.00				
1998J	70,000	—	—	—	1.75	—
Note: In sets only						
1998J Proof	45,000	Value: 2.00				
1999A	70,000	—	—	—	1.75	—
Note: In sets only						
1999A Proof	45,000	Value: 2.00				
1999D	70,000	—	—	—	1.75	—
Note: In sets only						
1999D Proof	45,000	Value: 2.00				
1999F	70,000	—	—	—	1.75	—
Note: In sets only						
1999F Proof	45,000	Value: 2.00				
1999G	70,000	—	—	—	1.75	—
Note: In sets only						
1999G Proof	45,000	Value: 2.00				
1999J	70,000	—	—	—	1.75	—
Note: In sets only						
1999J Proof	45,000	Value: 2.00				
2000A	45,000	—	—	—	1.75	—
Note: In sets only						
2000A Proof	70,000	Value: 2.00				
2000D	45,000	—	—	—	1.75	—
Note: In sets only						
2000D Proof	70,000	Value: 2.00				
2000F	45,000	—	—	—	1.75	—
Note: In sets only						
2000F Proof	70,000	Value: 2.00				
2000G	45,000	—	—	—	1.75	—
Note: In sets only						
2000G Proof	70,000	Value: 2.00				
2000J	45,000	—	—	—	1.75	—
Note: In sets only						
2000J Proof	70,000	Value: 2.00				
2001A	130,000	—	—	—	5.00	—
Note: In sets only						
2001A Proof	78,000	Value: 5.00				
2001D	130,000	—	—	—	5.00	—
Note: In sets only						
2001D Proof	78,000	Value: 5.00				
2001F	130,000	—	—	—	5.00	—
Note: In sets only						
2001F Proof	78,000	Value: 5.00				
2001G	130,000	—	—	—	5.00	—
Note: In sets only						
2001G Proof	78,000	Value: 5.00				
2001J	130,000	—	—	—	5.00	—
Note: In sets only						
2001J Proof	78,000	Value: 5.00				

KM# 103 10 PFENNIG

Brass Clad Steel, 21.5 mm. **Obv:** Five oak leaves, date below **Obv. Legend:** BANK DEUTSCHER LÄNDER **Rev:** Denomination

Date	Mintage	F	VF	XF	Unc	BU
1949D	140,558,000	—	0.50	7.50	30.00	—
1949D Proof	—	Value: 150				
1949F	120,932,000	—	0.50	10.00	35.00	—
1949F Proof	250	Value: 140				
1949G	82,933,000	—	1.00	10.00	40.00	—
1949J Large J	154,095,000	—	0.50	7.50	30.00	—
1949J Proof	—	Value: 60.00				
1949J Small J	Inc. above	—	0.50	7.50	32.00	—
1949J Proof	—	Value: 60.00				

KM# 108 10 PFENNIG

4.0000 g., Brass Plated Steel, 21.5 mm. **Obv:** Five oak leaves, date below **Obv. Legend:** BUNDES REPUBLIK DEUTSCHLAND **Rev:** Denomination **Edge:** Plain

Date	Mintage	F	VF	XF	Unc	BU
1950D	393,209,000	—	—	0.50	4.00	—
1950F	584,340,000	—	—	0.50	4.00	—
1950F Proof	500	Value: 45.00				
1950G	309,045,000	—	0.20	1.00	8.00	—
1950G Proof	1,800	Value: 5.00				
1950J	402,452,000	—	—	0.50	4.00	—
1950J Proof	—	Value: 20.00				
1966D	31,220,000	—	0.20	1.50	8.00	—
1966F	36,097,000	—	0.20	1.50	8.00	—
1966F Proof	100	Value: 75.00				
1966G	25,338,000	—	0.20	1.50	9.00	—
1966G Proof	3,070	Value: 7.50				
1966J	32,116,000	—	0.20	1.50	8.00	—
1966J Proof	1,000	Value: 12.50				
1967D	15,632,000	—	0.20	3.00	10.00	—
1967F	18,049,000	—	0.20	2.00	9.00	—
1967F Proof	1,500	Value: 15.00				
1967G	1,518,000	0.20	2.00	7.00	30.00	—
1967G Proof	4,500	Value: 7.50				
1967J	16,050,999	—	0.20	3.00	10.00	—
1967J Proof	1,500	Value: 12.50				
1968D	5,207,000	—	0.20	2.00	10.00	—
1968F	6,010,000	—	0.20	2.00	8.00	—
1968F Proof	3,000	Value: 10.00				
1968G	12,384,000	—	0.15	1.50	7.00	—
1968G Proof	6,023	Value: 5.00				
1968J	5,422,000	—	0.20	2.00	10.00	—
1968J Proof	2,000	Value: 10.00				
1969D	41,693,000	—	—	0.15	2.00	—
1969F	48,084,000	—	—	0.15	2.00	—
1969F Proof	5,000	Value: 3.00				
1969G	48,760,000	—	—	0.15	2.00	—
1969G Proof	8,700	Value: 2.50				
1969J	42,756,000	—	—	0.15	2.00	—
1969J Proof	5,000	Value: 2.50				
1970D	54,085,000	—	—	0.15	2.00	—
1970F	60,086,000	—	—	0.15	2.00	—
1970F Proof	5,140	Value: 3.00				
1970G	35,900,000	—	—	0.15	1.00	—
1970G Proof	10,200	Value: 2.00				
1970J	40,115,000	—	—	0.15	1.00	—
1970J Proof	5,000	Value: 2.50				
1971D	54,022,000	—	—	0.15	0.25	—
1971D Proof	8,000	Value: 2.50				
1971F	92,534,000	—	—	0.15	0.25	—
1971F Proof	8,000	Value: 2.50				
1971G	88,614,000	—	—	0.15	0.25	—
1971G Proof	10,000	Value: 2.00				
1971 Small J	65,622,000	—	—	0.15	0.25	—
1971 Large J	Inc. above	—	—	0.15	0.25	—
1971J Proof	8,000	Value: 1.50				
1972D	104,345,000	—	—	0.15	0.25	—
1972D Proof	8,000	Value: 1.50				
1972F	110,177,000	—	—	0.15	0.25	—
1972F Proof	8,000	Value: 1.50				
1972G	71,766,000	—	—	0.15	0.25	—
1972G Proof	10,000	Value: 1.50				
1972J	96,991,000	—	—	0.15	0.25	—
1972J Proof	8,000	Value: 1.50				
1973D	26,052,000	—	—	0.15	0.25	—
1973D Proof	9,000	Value: 1.50				
1973F	30,070,000	—	—	0.15	0.25	—
1973F Proof	9,000	Value: 1.50				
1973G	17,294,000	—	—	0.15	0.25	—
1973G Proof	9,000	Value: 1.50				
1973J	26,774,000	—	—	0.15	0.25	—
1973J Proof	9,000	Value: 1.50				
1974D	15,707,000	—	—	0.15	0.25	—
1974D Proof	35,000	Value: 0.75				
1974F	18,135,000	—	—	0.15	0.25	—
1974F Proof	35,000	Value: 0.75				
1974G	10,450,000	—	—	0.15	0.25	—
1974G Proof	35,000	Value: 0.75				
1974J	16,056,000	—	—	0.15	0.25	—
1974J Proof	35,000	Value: 0.75				
1975D	15,654,000	—	—	0.15	0.25	—
1975D Proof	43,000	Value: 0.75				
1975F	18,043,000	—	—	0.15	0.25	—
1975F Proof	43,000	Value: 0.75				
1975G	10,403,000	—	—	0.15	0.25	—
1975G Proof	43,000	Value: 0.75				
1975J	16,111,000	—	—	0.15	0.25	—
1975J Proof	43,000	Value: 0.75				
1976D	65,200,000	—	—	0.15	0.25	—
1976D Proof	43,000	Value: 0.75				
1976F	75,282,000	—	—	0.15	0.25	—
1976F Proof	43,000	Value: 0.75				
1976G	43,372,000	—	—	0.15	0.25	—
1976G Proof	43,000	Value: 0.75				
1976J	66,930,000	—	—	0.15	0.25	—
1976J Proof	43,000	Value: 0.75				
1977D	64,989,000	—	—	0.10	0.20	—
1977D Proof	51,000	Value: 0.50				
1977F	75,052,000	—	—	0.10	0.20	—
1977F Proof	51,000	Value: 0.50				
1977G	43,300,000	—	—	0.10	0.20	—
1977G Proof	51,000	Value: 0.50				
1977J	66,800,000	—	—	0.10	0.20	—
1977J Proof	51,000	Value: 0.50				
1978D	91,000,000	—	—	0.10	0.20	—
1978D Proof	54,000	Value: 0.50				
1978F	105,000,000	—	—	0.10	0.20	—
1978F Proof	54,000	Value: 0.50				
1978G	60,590,000	—	—	0.10	0.20	—
1978G Proof	54,000	Value: 0.50				
1978J	93,490,000	—	—	0.10	0.20	—
1978J Proof	54,000	Value: 0.50				
1979D	104,000,000	—	—	0.10	0.20	—
1979D Proof	89,000	Value: 0.50				
1979F	120,000,000	—	—	0.10	0.20	—
1979F Proof	89,000	Value: 0.50				
1979G	69,200,000	—	—	0.10	0.20	—
1979G Proof	89,000	Value: 0.50				
1979J	106,800,000	—	—	0.10	0.20	—
1979J Proof	89,000	Value: 0.50				
1980D	65,450,000	—	—	0.10	0.20	—
1980D Proof	110,000	Value: 0.50				
1980F	122,780,000	—	—	0.10	0.20	—
1980F Proof	110,000	Value: 0.50				
1980G	75,410,000	—	—	0.10	0.20	—
1980G Proof	110,000	Value: 0.50				
1980J	70,960,000	—	—	0.10	0.20	—
1980J Proof	110,000	Value: 0.50				
1981D	135,200,000	—	—	0.10	0.20	—
1981D Proof	91,000	Value: 0.50				
1981F	117,410,000	—	—	0.10	0.20	—
1981F Proof	91,000	Value: 0.50				
1981G	69,440,000	—	—	0.10	0.20	—
1981G Proof	91,000	Value: 0.50				
1981J	138,360,000	—	—	0.10	0.20	—
1981J Proof	91,000	Value: 0.50				
1982D	74,690,000	—	—	0.10	0.20	—
1982D Proof	78,000	Value: 0.50				
1982F	85,140,000	—	—	0.10	0.20	—
1982F Proof	78,000	Value: 0.50				
1982G	50,840,000	—	—	0.10	0.20	—
1982G Proof	78,000	Value: 0.50				
1982J	80,620,000	—	—	0.10	0.20	—
1982J Proof	78,000	Value: 0.50				
1983D	33,800,000	—	—	0.10	0.20	—
1983D Proof	75,000	Value: 0.50				
1983F	39,000,000	—	—	0.10	0.20	—
1983F Proof	75,000	Value: 0.50				
1983G	22,490,000	—	—	0.10	0.20	—
1983G Proof	75,000	Value: 0.50				
1983J	34,710,000	—	—	0.10	0.20	—
1983J Proof	75,000	Value: 0.50				
1984D	52,000,000	—	—	0.10	0.20	—
1984D Proof	64,000	Value: 0.50				
1984F	60,000,000	—	—	0.10	0.20	—
1984G Proof	64,000	Value: 0.50				
1984G	34,600,000	—	—	0.10	0.20	—
1984G Proof	64,000	Value: 0.50				
1984J	53,400,000	—	—	0.10	0.20	—
1984J Proof	64,000	Value: 0.50				
1985D	78,000,000	—	—	—	0.15	—
1985D Proof	56,000	Value: 0.50				
1985F	90,000,000	—	—	—	0.15	—
1985F Proof	54,000	Value: 0.50				
1985G	51,900,000	—	—	—	0.15	—
1985G Proof	55,000	Value: 0.50				
1985J	80,100,000	—	—	—	0.15	—
1985J Proof	54,000	Value: 0.50				
1986D	41,600,000	—	—	—	0.15	—
1986D Proof	44,000	Value: 0.50				
1986F	48,000,000	—	—	—	0.15	—
1986F Proof	44,000	Value: 0.50				
1986G	27,700,000	—	—	—	0.15	—
1986G Proof	44,000	Value: 0.50				
1986J	42,700,000	—	—	—	0.15	—
1986J Proof	44,000	Value: 0.15				
1987D	58,500,000	—	—	—	0.10	—
1987D Proof	45,000	Value: 0.15				
1987F	67,500,000	—	—	—	0.10	—
1987F Proof	45,000	Value: 0.15				
1987G	38,900,000	—	—	—	0.10	—
1987G Proof	45,000	Value: 0.50				
1987J	60,100,000	—	—	—	0.15	—
1987J Proof	45,000	Value: 0.50				
1988D	109,200,000	—	—	—	0.15	—
1988D Proof	45,000	Value: 0.50				
1988F	126,000,000	—	—	—	0.15	—
1988F Proof	45,000	Value: 0.50				
1988G	72,700,000	—	—	—	0.15	—
1988G Proof	45,000	Value: 0.50				
1988J	112,100,000	—	—	—	0.15	—
1988J Proof	45,000	Value: 0.50				
1989D	119,600,000	—	—	—	0.15	—
1989D Proof	45,000	Value: 0.50				
1989F	138,000,000	—	—	—	0.15	—

Date	Mintage	F	VF	XF	Unc	BU
1989F Proof	45,000	Value: 0.50				
1989G	79,580,000	—	—	—	0.15	—
1989G Proof	45,000	Value: 0.50				
1989J	122,820,000	—	—	—	0.15	—
1989J Proof	45,000	Value: 0.50				
1990A	100,000,000	—	—	—	0.15	—
1990D	156,000,000	—	—	—	0.15	—
1990D Proof	45,000	Value: 0.50				
1990F	180,000,000	—	—	—	0.15	—
1990F Proof	45,000	Value: 0.50				
1990G	103,800,000	—	—	—	0.15	—
1990G Proof	45,000	Value: 0.50				
1990J	160,200,000	—	—	—	0.15	—
1990J Proof	45,000	Value: 0.50				
1991A	170,000,000	—	—	—	0.15	—
1991A Proof	45,000	Value: 0.40				
1991D	178,550,000	—	—	—	0.15	—
1991D Proof	45,000	Value: 0.40				
1991F	204,000,000	—	—	—	0.15	—
1991F Proof	45,000	Value: 0.40				
1991G	119,000,000	—	—	—	0.15	—
1991G Proof	45,000	Value: 0.40				
1991J	178,500,000	—	—	—	0.15	—
1991J Proof	45,000	Value: 0.40				
1992A	80,000,000	—	—	—	0.10	—
1992A Proof	45,000	Value: 0.40				
1992D	84,000,000	—	—	—	0.10	—
1992D Proof	45,000	Value: 0.40				
1992F	96,000,000	—	—	—	0.10	—
1992F Proof	45,000	Value: 0.40				
1992G	56,000,000	—	—	—	0.10	—
1992G Proof	45,000	Value: 0.40				
1992J	84,000,000	—	—	—	0.10	—
1992J Proof	45,000	Value: 0.40				
1993A	80,000,000	—	—	—	0.10	—
1993A Proof	45,000	Value: 0.40				
1993D	84,000,000	—	—	—	0.10	—
1993D Proof	45,000	Value: 0.40				
1993F	96,000,000	—	—	—	0.10	—
1993F Proof	45,000	Value: 0.40				
1993G	56,000,000	—	—	—	0.10	—
1993G Proof	45,000	Value: 0.40				
1993J	84,000,000	—	—	—	0.10	—
1993J Proof	45,000	Value: 0.40				
1994A	100,000,000	—	—	—	0.10	—
1994A Proof	45,000	Value: 0.40				
1994D	105,000,000	—	—	—	0.10	—
1994D Proof	45,000	Value: 0.40				
1994F	120,000,000	—	—	—	0.10	—
1994F Proof	45,000	Value: 0.40				
1994G	70,000,000	—	—	—	0.10	—
1994G Proof	45,000	Value: 0.40				
1994J	105,000,000	—	—	—	0.10	—
1994J Proof	45,000	Value: 0.40				
1995A	110,000,000	—	—	—	0.15	—
1995A Proof	45,000	Value: 0.45				
1995D	115,000,000	—	—	—	0.15	—
1995D Proof	45,000	Value: 0.45				
1995F	132,000,000	—	—	—	0.15	—
1995F Proof	45,000	Value: 0.45				
1995G	77,000,000	—	—	—	0.15	—
1995G Proof	45,000	Value: 0.45				
1995J	115,500,000	—	—	—	0.15	—
1995J Proof	45,000	Value: 0.45				
1996A	90,000,000	—	—	—	0.20	—
1996A Proof	45,000	Value: 0.50				
1996D	94,500,000	—	—	—	0.20	—
1996D Proof	45,000	Value: 0.50				
1996F	108,000,000	—	—	—	0.20	—
1996F Proof	45,000	Value: 0.50				
1996G	63,000,000	—	—	—	0.20	—
1996G Proof	45,000	Value: 0.50				
1996J	94,500,000	—	—	—	0.20	—
1996J Proof	45,000	Value: 0.50				
1997A	70,000	—	—	—	1.75	—
Note: In sets only						
1997A Proof	45,000	Value: 2.00				
1997D	70,000	—	—	—	1.75	—
Note: In sets only						
1997D Proof	45,000	Value: 2.00				
1997F	70,000	—	—	—	1.75	—
Note: In sets only						
1997F Proof	45,000	Value: 2.00				
1997G	70,000	—	—	—	1.75	—
Note: In sets only						
1997G Proof	45,000	Value: 2.00				
1997J	70,000	—	—	—	1.75	—
Note: In sets only						
1997J Proof	45,000	Value: 2.00				
1998A	—	—	—	—	1.75	—
1998A Proof	—	Value: 2.00				
1998D	—	—	—	—	1.75	—
1998D Proof	—	Value: 2.00				
1998F	70,000	—	—	—	1.75	—
Note: In sets only						
1998F Proof	45,000	Value: 2.00				
1998G	—	—	—	—	1.75	—
1998G Proof	—	Value: 2.00				
1998J	—	—	—	—	1.75	—
1998J Proof	—	Value: 2.00				
1999A	—	—	—	—	1.75	—
1999A Proof	—	Value: 2.00				
1999D	—	—	—	—	1.75	—
1999D Proof	—	Value: 2.00				
1999F	70,000	—	—	—	1.75	—
Note: In sets only						
1999F Proof	45,000	Value: 2.00				
1999G	—	—	—	—	1.75	—
1999G Proof	—	Value: 2.00				
1999J	—	—	—	—	1.75	—
1999J Proof	—	Value: 2.00				
2000A	70,000	—	—	—	1.75	—
Note: In sets only						
2000A Proof	45,000	Value: 2.00				
2000D	70,000	—	—	—	1.75	—
Note: In sets only						
2000D Proof	45,000	Value: 2.00				
2000F	70,000	—	—	—	1.75	—
Note: In sets only						
2000F Proof	45,000	Value: 2.00				
2000G	70,000	—	—	—	1.75	—
Note: In sets only						
2000G Proof	45,000	Value: 2.00				
2000J	70,000	—	—	—	1.75	—
Note: In sets only						
2000J Proof	45,000	Value: 2.00				
2001A	130,000	—	—	—	5.00	—
Note: In sets only						
2001A Proof	78,000	Value: 5.00				
2001D	130,000	—	—	—	5.00	—
Note: In sets only						
2001D Proof	78,000	Value: 5.00				
2001F	130,000	—	—	—	5.00	—
Note: In sets only						
2001F Proof	78,000	Value: 5.00				
2001G	130,000	—	—	—	5.00	—
Note: In sets only						
2001G Proof	78,000	Value: 5.00				
2001J	130,000	—	—	—	5.00	—
Note: In sets only						
2001J Proof	78,000	Value: 5.00				

KM# 104 50 PFENNIG

3.5000 g., Copper-Nickel, 20 mm. **Obv:** Denomination **Obv. Legend:** BANK DEUTSCHER LÄNDER **Rev:** Woman planting an oak seedling, date below

Date	Mintage	F	VF	XF	Unc	BU
1949D	39,108,000	—	0.75	4.50	45.00	—
1949F	45,118,000	—	0.50	3.00	35.00	—
1949F Proof	200	Value: 125				
1949G	25,924,000	—	0.75	5.00	55.00	—
1949J	42,303,000	—	0.75	3.50	35.00	—
1949J Proof	—	Value: 135				
1950G	30,000	—	350	475	750	—

Note: The 1950G dated coin was restruck without authorization by a mint official using genuine dies - quantity unknown

KM# 109.1 50 PFENNIG

3.5000 g., Copper-Nickel, 20 mm. **Obv:** Denomination **Obv. Legend:** BUNDESREPUBLIK DEUTSCHLAND **Rev:** Woman planting an oak seedling **Edge:** Reeded

Date	Mintage	F	VF	XF	Unc	BU
1950D	100,735,000	—	0.50	0.75	7.00	—
1950F	143,510,000	—	0.50	0.75	7.00	—
1950F Proof	450	Value: 85.00				
1950G	66,421,000	—	0.50	1.50	12.00	—
1950G Proof	1,800	Value: 5.00				
1950J	102,736,000	—	0.50	0.75	9.00	—
1950J Proof	—	Value: 25.00				
1966D	8,327,999	—	0.50	1.00	15.00	—
1966F	9,605,000	—	0.50	1.00	15.00	—
1966F Proof	100	Value: 125				
1966G	5,543,000	—	0.50	1.50	15.00	—
1966G Proof	3,070	Value: 10.00				
1966J	8,569,000	—	1.00	7.00	35.00	—
1966J Proof	1,000	Value: 20.00				
1967D	5,207,000	—	0.50	1.00	15.00	—
1967F	6,005,000	—	0.50	1.00	15.00	—
1967F Proof	1,500	Value: 18.00				
1967G	1,843,000	—	1.00	5.00	22.00	—
1967G Proof	4,500	Value: 15.00				
1967J	10,684,000	—	0.50	1.50	20.00	—
1967J Proof	1,500	Value: 18.00				
1968D	7,809,000	—	0.50	1.50	12.00	—
1968F	3,000,000	—	0.50	1.50	12.00	—
1968F Proof	3,000	Value: 15.00				
1968G	6,818,000	—	0.50	1.50	12.00	—
1968G Proof	6,023	Value: 8.00				
1968J	2,672,000	—	1.00	5.00	30.00	—
1968J Proof	2,000	Value: 15.00				
1969D	14,561,000	—	0.45	0.55	2.50	—
1969F	16,804,000	—	0.45	0.55	2.50	—
1969F Proof	5,000	Value: 4.00				
1969G	9,704,000	—	0.45	0.55	2.50	—
1969G Proof	8,700	Value: 3.50				
1969J	14,969,000	—	0.45	0.55	2.50	—
1969J Proof	5,000	Value: 10.00				
1970D	25,294,000	—	0.45	0.55	1.50	—
1970F	26,455,000	—	0.45	0.55	1.50	—
1970F Proof	5,140	Value: 3.50				
1970G	11,955,000	—	0.45	0.55	1.50	—
1970G Proof	10,200	Value: 3.00				
1970J	10,683,000	—	0.45	0.55	1.50	—
1970J Proof	5,000	Value: 3.50				
1971D	23,393,000	—	0.45	0.55	1.25	—
1971D Proof	8,000	Value: 3.00				
1971F	29,746,000	—	0.45	0.55	1.25	—
1971F Proof	8,000	Value: 3.00				
1971G	15,556,000	—	0.45	0.55	1.25	—
1971G Proof	10,000	Value: 3.00				
1971 Large J	24,044,000	—	0.45	0.55	1.25	—
1971 Small J	Inc. above	—	0.45	0.55	1.25	—
1971J Proof	8,000	Value: 3.00				

KM# 109.2 50 PFENNIG

3.5000 g., Copper-Nickel, 20 mm. **Obv:** Denomination **Rev:** Woman planting an oak seedling **Edge:** Plain **Note:** Counterfeits of 1972 dated coins with reeded edges exist.

Date	Mintage	F	VF	XF	Unc	BU
1972D	26,008,000	—	—	0.45	0.60	—
1972D Proof	8,000	Value: 2.00				
1972F	30,043,000	—	—	0.45	0.60	—
1972F Proof	8,000	Value: 2.00				
1972G	17,337,000	—	—	0.45	0.60	—
1972G Proof	10,000	Value: 2.00				
1972J	26,707,000	—	—	0.45	0.60	—
1972J Proof	8,000	Value: 2.00				
1973D	7,810,000	—	—	0.45	1.00	—
1973D Proof	9,000	Value: 2.00				
1973F	8,994,000	—	—	0.45	0.60	—
1973F Proof	9,000	Value: 2.00				
1973G	5,201,000	—	—	0.45	0.60	—
1973G Proof	9,000	Value: 2.00				
1973J	8,010,999	—	—	0.45	0.60	—
1973J Proof	9,000	Value: 2.00				
1974D	18,264,000	—	—	0.45	1.00	—
1974D Proof	35,000	Value: 1.00				
1974 Large F	21,036,000	—	—	0.45	1.00	—
1974 Small F	Inc. above	—	—	0.45	1.00	—
1974F Proof	35,000	Value: 1.00				
1974G	12,159,000	—	—	0.45	1.50	—
1974G Proof	35,000	Value: 1.00				
1974J	18,752,000	—	—	0.45	1.00	—
1974J Proof	35,000	Value: 1.00				
1975D	13,055,000	—	—	0.45	1.00	—
1975D Proof	43,000	Value: 1.00				
1975F	15,003,000	—	—	0.45	1.00	—
1975F Proof	43,000	Value: 1.00				
1975G	8,675,000	—	—	0.45	1.50	—
1975G Proof	43,000	Value: 1.00				
1975J	13,379,000	—	—	0.45	1.00	—
1975J Proof	43,000	Value: 1.00				
1976D	10,411,000	—	—	0.45	0.60	—
1976D Proof	43,000	Value: 1.00				
1976F	12,048,000	—	—	0.45	0.60	—
1976F Proof	43,000	Value: 1.00				
1976G	6,653,000	—	—	0.45	1.25	—
1976G Proof	43,000	Value: 1.00				
1976J	10,716,000	—	—	0.45	0.60	—
1976J Proof	43,000	Value: 1.00				
1977D	10,400,000	—	—	0.45	0.60	—
1977D Proof	51,000	Value: 0.75				
1977F	12,000,000	—	—	0.45	0.60	—
1977F Proof	51,000	Value: 0.75				
1977G	6,921,000	—	—	0.45	1.00	—
1977G Proof	51,000	Value: 0.75				
1977J	10,708,000	—	—	0.45	0.60	—
1977J Proof	51,000	Value: 0.75				
1978D	10,400,000	—	—	0.45	1.00	—
1978D Proof	54,000	Value: 0.75				
1978F	12,000,000	—	—	0.45	0.60	—
1978F Proof	54,000	Value: 0.75				
1978G	6,640,000	—	—	0.45	1.00	—
1978G Proof	54,000	Value: 0.75				
1978J	10,680,000	—	—	0.45	0.60	—
1978J Proof	54,000	Value: 0.75				
1979D	10,400,000	—	—	0.45	1.00	—
1979D Proof	89,000	Value: 0.75				
1979F	12,000,000	—	—	0.45	0.60	—
1979F Proof	89,000	Value: 0.75				

Date	Mintage	F	VF	XF	Unc	BU
1979G	6,920,000	—	—	0.45	1.00	—
1979G Proof	89,000	Value: 0.75				
1979J	10,680,000	—	—	0.45	0.60	—
1979J Proof	89,000	Value: 0.75				
1980D	23,250,000	—	—	0.45	0.60	—
1980D Proof	110,000	Value: 0.75				
1980F	17,440,000	—	—	0.45	0.60	—
1980F Proof	110,000	Value: 0.75				
1980G	22,460,000	—	—	0.45	1.00	—
1980G Proof	110,000	Value: 0.75				
1980J	24,030,000	—	—	0.45	0.60	—
1980J Proof	110,000	Value: 0.75				
1981D	17,900,000	—	—	0.45	1.25	—
1981D Proof	91,000	Value: 0.75				
1981F	29,810,000	—	—	0.45	1.25	—
1981F Proof	91,000	Value: 0.75				
1981G	10,880,000	—	—	0.45	1.50	—
1981G Proof	91,000	Value: 0.75				
1981J	24,140,000	—	—	0.45	1.25	—
1981J Proof	91,000	Value: 0.75				
1982D	21,540,000	—	—	0.45	1.25	—
1982D Proof	78,000	Value: 0.75				
1982F	28,900,000	—	—	0.45	1.25	—
1982F Proof	78,000	Value: 0.75				
1982G	19,710,000	—	—	0.45	1.50	—
1982G Proof	78,000	Value: 0.75				
1982J	17,210,000	—	—	0.45	1.25	—
1982J Proof	78,000	Value: 0.75				
1983D	20,800,000	—	—	0.45	1.25	—
1983D Proof	75,000	Value: 0.75				
1983F	24,000,000	—	—	0.45	1.25	—
1983F Proof	75,000	Value: 0.75				
1983G	13,840,000	—	—	0.45	1.50	—
1983G Proof	75,000	Value: 0.75				
1983J	21,360,000	—	—	0.45	1.25	—
1983J Proof	75,000	Value: 0.75				
1984D	11,700,000	—	—	0.45	1.50	—
1984D Proof	64,000	Value: 0.75				
1984F	13,500,000	—	—	0.45	1.50	—
1984F Proof	64,000	Value: 0.75				
1984G	7,800,000	—	—	0.45	1.50	—
1984G Proof	64,000	Value: 0.75				
1984J	12,000,000	—	—	0.45	1.50	—
1984J Proof	64,000	Value: 0.75				
1985D	15,700,000	—	—	0.45	1.50	—
1985D Proof	56,000	Value: 0.75				
1985F	18,000,000	—	—	0.45	1.50	—
1985F Proof	54,000	Value: 0.75				
1985G	10,400,000	—	—	0.45	1.50	—
1985G Proof	55,000	Value: 0.75				
1985J	16,100,000	—	—	0.45	1.50	—
1985J Proof	54,000	Value: 0.75				
1986D	2,100,000	—	1.00	2.00	8.00	—
1986D Proof	44,000	Value: 0.75				
1986F	2,400,000	—	1.00	2.00	7.00	—
1986F Proof	44,000	Value: 0.75				
1986G	1,400,000	1.00	2.00	4.00	10.00	—
1986G Proof	44,000	Value: 0.75				
1986J	2,100,000	—	1.50	3.50	12.50	—
1986J Proof	44,000	Value: 0.75				
1987D	520,000	2.00	5.00	10.00	30.00	—
1987D Proof	45,000	Value: 0.75				
1987F	600,000	1.00	3.00	6.00	15.00	—
1987F Proof	45,000	Value: 0.75				
1987G	350,000	2.50	5.00	8.00	28.00	—
1987G Proof	45,000	Value: 0.75				
1987J	530,000	1.00	3.00	6.00	15.00	—
1987J Proof	45,000	Value: 0.75				
1988D	4,160,000	—	—	0.50	2.00	—
1988D Proof	45,000	Value: 0.75				
1988F	4,800,000	—	—	0.50	2.00	—
1988F Proof	45,000	Value: 0.75				
1988G	2,770,000	—	—	1.00	3.00	—
1988G Proof	45,000	Value: 0.75				
1988J	4,300,000	—	—	0.50	2.00	—
1988J Proof	45,000	Value: 0.75				
1989D	36,400,000	—	—	—	0.50	—
1989D Proof	45,000	Value: 0.75				
1989F	42,000,000	—	—	—	0.50	—
1989F Proof	45,000	Value: 0.75				
1989G	24,220,000	—	—	—	0.50	—
1989G Proof	45,000	Value: 0.75				
1989J	37,380,000	—	—	—	0.50	—
1989J Proof	45,000	Value: 0.75				
1990A	150,000,000	—	—	—	0.50	—
1990D	58,500,000	—	—	—	0.50	—
1990D Proof	45,000	Value: 0.75				
1990F	67,500,000	—	—	—	0.50	—
1990F Proof	45,000	Value: 0.75				
1990G	38,920,000	—	—	—	0.50	—
1990G Proof	45,000	Value: 0.75				
1990J	60,070,000	—	—	—	0.50	—
1990J Proof	45,000	Value: 0.75				
1991A	22,000,000	—	—	—	0.50	—
1991A Proof	45,000	Value: 0.75				
1991D	23,100,000	—	—	—	0.50	—
1991D Proof	45,000	Value: 0.75				
1991F	26,400,000	—	—	—	0.50	—
1991F Proof	45,000	Value: 0.75				
1991G	15,400,000	—	—	—	0.50	—
1991G Proof	45,000	Value: 0.75				
1991J	23,100,000	—	—	—	0.50	—
1991J Proof	45,000	Value: 0.75				
1992A	18,000,000	—	—	—	0.50	—
1992A Proof	45,000	Value: 0.75				
1992D	18,900,000	—	—	—	0.50	—
1992D Proof	45,000	Value: 0.75				
1992F	21,600,000	—	—	—	0.50	—
1992F Proof	45,000	Value: 0.75				
1992G	12,600,000	—	—	—	1.00	—
1992G Proof	45,000	Value: 0.75				
1992J	18,900,000	—	—	—	0.50	—
1992J Proof	45,000	Value: 0.75				
1993A	16,000,000	—	—	—	0.50	—
1993A Proof	45,000	Value: 0.75				
1993D	16,800,000	—	—	—	0.50	—
1993D Proof	45,000	Value: 0.75				
1993F	19,200,000	—	—	—	0.50	—
1993F Proof	45,000	Value: 0.75				
1993G	11,200,000	—	—	—	1.50	—
1993G Proof	45,000	Value: 0.75				
1993J	16,800,000	—	—	—	0.50	—
1993J Proof	45,000	Value: 0.75				
1994A	7,500,000	—	—	—	1.50	—
1994A Proof	45,000	Value: 0.75				
1994D	Est. 7,875,000	—	—	—	3.00	—
1994D Proof	45,000	Value: 0.75				
1994F	9,000,000	—	—	—	1.50	—
1994F Proof	45,000	Value: 0.75				
1994G	5,250,000	—	—	—	1.50	—
1994G Proof	45,000	Value: 0.75				
1994J	7,875,000	—	—	—	1.00	—
1994J Proof	45,000	Value: 0.75				
1995A	1,300,000	—	—	—	2.25	—
1995A Proof	45,000	Value: 6.00				
1995D	1,365,000	—	—	—	2.25	—
1995D Proof	45,000	Value: 6.00				
1995F	20,000	—	—	—	90.00	—
1995F Proof	45,000	Value: 12.00				
1995G	20,000	—	—	—	100	—
1995G Proof	45,000	Value: 12.00				
1995J	150,000	—	—	—	14.00	—
1995J Proof	45,000	Value: 12.00				
1996A	50,000	—	—	—	12.00	—
Note: In sets only						
1996A Proof	45,000	Value: 13.50				
1996D	50,000	—	—	—	12.00	—
Note: In sets only						
1996D Proof	45,000	Value: 13.50				
1996F	50,000	—	—	—	12.00	—
Note: In sets only						
1996F Proof	45,000	Value: 13.50				
1996G	50,000	—	—	—	12.00	—
Note: In sets only						
1996G Proof	45,000	Value: 13.50				
1996J	50,000	—	—	—	12.00	—
Note: In sets only						
1996J Proof	45,000	Value: 13.50				
1997A	70,000	—	—	—	4.75	—
Note: In sets only						
1997A Proof	45,000	Value: 5.00				
1997D	70,000	—	—	—	4.75	—
Note: In sets only						
1997D Proof	45,000	Value: 5.00				
1997F	70,000	—	—	—	4.75	—
Note: In sets only						
1997F Proof	45,000	Value: 5.00				
1997G	70,000	—	—	—	4.75	—
Note: In sets only						
1997G Proof	45,000	Value: 5.00				
1997J	70,000	—	—	—	4.75	—
Note: In sets only						
1997J Proof	45,000	Value: 5.00				
1998A	70,000	—	—	—	4.75	—
Note: In sets only						
1998A Proof	45,000	Value: 5.00				
1998D	70,000	—	—	—	4.75	—
Note: In sets only						
1998D Proof	45,000	Value: 5.00				
1998F	70,000	—	—	—	4.75	—
Note: In sets only						
1998F Proof	45,000	Value: 5.00				
1998G	70,000	—	—	—	4.75	—
Note: In sets only						
1998G Proof	45,000	Value: 5.00				
1998J	70,000	—	—	—	4.75	—
Note: In sets only						
1998J Proof	45,000	Value: 5.00				
1999A	70,000	—	—	—	4.75	—
Note: In sets only						
1999A Proof	45,000	Value: 5.00				
1999D	70,000	—	—	—	4.75	—
Note: In sets only						
1999D Proof	45,000	Value: 5.00				
1999F	70,000	—	—	—	4.75	—
Note: In sets only						
1999F Proof	45,000	Value: 5.00				
1999G	70,000	—	—	—	4.75	—
Note: In sets only						
1999G Proof	45,000	Value: 5.00				
1999J	70,000	—	—	—	4.75	—
Note: In sets only						
1999J Proof	45,000	Value: 5.00				
2000A	70,000	—	—	—	5.00	—
Note: In sets only						
2000A Proof	45,000	Value: 5.00				
2000D	70,000	—	—	—	5.00	—
Note: In sets only						
2000D Proof	45,000	Value: 5.00				
2000F	70,000	—	—	—	5.00	—
Note: In sets only						
2000F Proof	45,000	Value: 5.00				
2000G	70,000	—	—	—	5.00	—
Note: In sets only						
2000G Proof	45,000	Value: 5.00				
2000J	70,000	—	—	—	5.00	—
Note: In sets only						
2000J Proof	45,000	Value: 5.00				
2001A	130,000	—	—	—	10.00	—
Note: In sets only						
2001A Proof	78,000	Value: 10.00				
2001D	130,000	—	—	—	10.00	—
Note: In sets only						
2001D Proof	78,000	Value: 10.00				
2001F	130,000	—	—	—	10.00	—
Note: In sets only						
2001F Proof	78,000	Value: 10.00				
2001G	130,000	—	—	—	10.00	—
Note: In sets only						
2001G Proof	78,000	Value: 10.00				
2001J	130,000	—	—	—	10.00	—
Note: In sets only						
2001J Proof	78,000	Value: 10.00				

KM# 110 MARK

5.5000 g., Copper-Nickel, 23.5 mm. **Obv:** Eagle **Rev:** Denomination flanked by oak leaves, date below

Date	Mintage	F	VF	XF	Unc	BU
1950D	60,467,000	—	1.50	12.00	75.00	—
1950D Proof	—	Value: 200				
1950F	69,183,000	—	1.50	12.00	70.00	—
1950F Proof	150	Value: 450				
1950G	39,826,000	—	2.00	15.00	110	—
1950G Proof	Est. 200	Value: 375				
1950J	61,483,000	—	1.00	10.00	65.00	—
1950J Proof	—	Value: 200				
1954D	5,202,000	2.00	8.00	100	425	—
1954D Proof	—	Value: 925				
1954F	6,000,000	2.50	10.00	200	650	—
1954F Proof	175	Value: 1,000				
1954G	3,459,000	4.00	25.00	450	1,900	—
1954G Proof	15	Value: 2,250				
1954J	5,341,000	1.50	7.00	55.00	400	—
1954J Proof	—	Value: 1,000				
1955D	3,093,000	2.00	9.00	125	550	—
1955D Proof	—	Value: 900				
1955F	4,909,000	1.00	6.00	50.00	500	—
1955F Proof	Est. 20	Value: 750				
1955G	2,500,000	4.00	40.00	400	1,650	—
1955G Proof	—	Value: 2,750				
1955J	5,294,000	1.00	6.00	50.00	220	—
1955J Proof	—	Value: 650				
1956D	13,231,000	1.00	4.00	35.00	325	—
1956D Proof	—	Value: 525				
1956F	14,700,000	1.00	4.00	35.00	375	—
1956F Proof	100	Value: 500				
1956G	8,362,000	1.00	4.00	35.00	275	—
1956G Proof	—	Value: 650				
1956J	11,478,000	1.00	5.00	40.00	220	—
1956J Proof	—	Value: 850				
1957D	6,820,000	1.00	5.00	75.00	325	—
1957D Proof	100	Value: 475				
1957F	6,390,000	1.00	5.00	75.00	325	—
1957F Proof	100	Value: 485				
1957G	3,841,000	2.50	10.00	145	800	—
1957G Proof	27	Value: 1,350				
1957J	6,632,000	1.00	6.00	100	500	—
1957J Proof	200	Value: 385				
1958D	4,150,000	1.00	4.00	40.00	275	—
1958D Proof	200	Value: 400				
1958F	4,109,000	1.00	5.00	45.00	375	—
1958F Proof	100	Value: 525				
1958G	3,460,000	2.50	8.00	135	1,100	—
1958G Proof	20	Value: 2,100				
1958J	4,656,000	1.00	5.00	50.00	500	—
1958J Proof	37	Value: 850				
1959D	10,409,000	—	2.00	20.00	225	—
1959D Proof	40	Value: 850				
1959F	11,972,000	—	2.00	20.00	225	—
1959F Proof	100	Value: 475				
1959G	6,921,000	1.00	5.00	40.00	375	—
1959G Proof	20	Value: 2,100				
1959J	10,691,000	1.00	4.00	35.00	650	—
1959J Proof	25	Value: 1,250				

Date	Mintage	F	VF	XF	Unc	BU
1960D	5,453,000	—	2.00	25.00	750	—
1960D Proof	100	Value: 550				
1960F	5,709,000	—	2.00	25.00	250	—
1960F Proof	100	Value: 800				
1960G	3,632,000	1.00	6.00	50.00	600	—
1960G Proof	100	Value: 650				
1960J	5,612,000	2.50	8.00	200	750	—
1960J Proof	36	Value: 1,650				
1961D	7,536,000	—	2.00	20.00	275	—
1961D Proof	60	Value: 800				
1961F	6,029,000	—	2.00	20.00	175	—
1961F Proof	50	Value: 800				
1961G	4,843,000	1.00	6.00	50.00	475	—
1961G Proof	70	Value: 700				
1961J	7,483,000	1.50	7.00	75.00	850	—
1961J Proof	28	Value: 1,000				
1962D	10,327,000	—	1.50	15.00	400	—
1962D Proof	40	Value: 800				
1962F	11,122,000	—	1.50	10.00	125	—
1962F Proof	45	Value: 750				
1962G	6,054,000	—	2.00	25.00	800	—
1962G Proof	100	Value: 550				
1962J	10,822,000	—	2.00	17.50	220	—
1962J Proof	28	Value: 1,100				
1963D	12,624,000	—	1.00	10.00	110	—
1963D Proof	40	Value: 550				
1963F	18,292,000	—	1.50	15.00	135	—
1963F Proof	45	Value: 650				
1963G	11,253,000	—	1.50	12.50	165	—
1963G Proof	200	Value: 300				
1963J	15,906,000	—	1.50	15.00	200	—
1963J Proof	28	Value: 1,200				
1964D	8,048,000	—	0.85	4.00	100	—
1964D Proof	30	Value: 1,000				
1964F	12,796,000	—	0.85	4.00	90.00	—
1964F Proof	25	Value: 1,900				
1964G	3,465,000	—	2.00	20.00	250	—
1964G Proof	368	Value: 275				
1964J	6,958,000	—	0.85	4.00	85.00	—
1964J Proof	33	Value: 900				
1965D	9,388,000	—	0.75	3.00	37.50	—
1965F	9,013,000	—	0.75	3.00	40.00	—
1965F Proof	Est. 80	Value: 175				
1965G	6,232,000	—	0.75	3.00	47.50	—
1965G Proof	1,200	Value: 65.00				
1965J	8,023,999	—	0.75	3.00	55.00	—
1966D	11,717,000	—	0.75	3.00	42.50	—
1966F	11,368,000	—	0.75	3.00	42.50	—
1966F Proof	100	Value: 200				
1966G	7,799,000	—	0.75	3.00	55.00	—
1966G Proof	3,070	Value: 45.00				
1966J	12,030,000	—	0.75	3.00	42.50	—
1966J Proof	1,000	Value: 85.00				
1967D	13,017,000	—	0.75	3.00	32.50	—
1967F	7,500,000	—	0.75	5.00	100	—
1967F Proof	1,500	Value: 95.00				
1967G	4,324,000	—	0.75	3.00	55.00	—
1967G Proof	4,500	Value: 50.00				
1967J	13,357,000	—	0.75	3.00	40.00	—
1967J Proof	1,500	Value: 85.00				
1968D	1,303,000	—	1.00	10.00	65.00	—
1968F	1,500,000	—	0.75	4.00	40.00	—
1968F Proof	3,000	Value: 65.00				
1968G	5,198,000	—	1.50	7.00	60.00	—
1968G Proof	6,023	Value: 35.00				
1968J	1,338,000	1.00	12.50	145	375	—
1968J Proof	2,000	Value: 85.00				
1969D	13,025,000	—	0.75	1.50	22.00	—
1969F	15,021,000	—	0.75	1.50	20.00	—
1969F Proof	5,000	Value: 15.00				
1969G	8,665,000	—	0.75	1.50	32.50	—
1969G Proof	8,700	Value: 14.50				
1969J	13,370,000	—	0.75	1.50	25.00	—
1969J Proof	5,000	Value: 18.00				
1970D	17,928,000	—	0.75	1.00	20.00	—
1970F	19,408,000	—	0.75	1.00	25.00	—
1970F Proof	5,140	Value: 15.00				
1970G	20,386,000	—	0.75	1.00	32.50	—
1970G Proof	10,200	Value: 9.00				
1970J	10,707,000	—	0.75	1.00	20.00	—
1970J Proof	5,000	Value: 15.00				
1971D	24,513,000	—	0.75	1.00	10.00	—
1971D Proof	8,000	Value: 8.00				
1971F	28,275,000	—	0.75	1.00	10.00	—
1971F Proof	8,000	Value: 8.00				
1971G	16,375,000	—	0.75	1.00	12.50	—
1971G Proof	10,000	Value: 8.00				
1971J	25,214,000	—	0.75	1.00	10.00	—
1971J Proof	8,000	Value: 8.00				
1972D	20,904,000	—	0.75	1.00	10.00	—
1972D Proof	8,000	Value: 7.00				
1972F	24,086,000	—	0.75	1.00	10.00	—
1972F Proof	8,000	Value: 7.00				
1972G	13,868,000	—	0.75	1.00	10.00	—
1972G Proof	10,000	Value: 7.00				
1972J	21,360,000	—	0.75	1.00	10.00	—
1972J Proof	8,000	Value: 7.00				
1973D	14,327,000	—	0.75	1.00	6.00	—
1973D Proof	9,000	Value: 5.00				
1973F	16,591,999	—	0.75	1.00	6.00	—
1973F Proof	9,000	Value: 5.00				
1973G	10,409,000	—	0.75	1.00	6.00	—
1973G Proof	9,000	Value: 5.00				
1973J	14,704,000	—	0.75	1.00	6.00	—
1973J Proof	9,000	Value: 5.00				
1974D	20,876,000	—	0.75	1.00	6.00	—
1974D Proof	35,000	Value: 4.00				
1974F	24,057,000	—	0.75	1.00	6.00	—
1974F Proof	35,000	Value: 4.00				
1974G	13,931,000	—	0.75	1.00	6.00	—
1974G Proof	35,000	Value: 4.00				
1974J	21,440,000	—	0.75	1.00	6.00	—
1974J Proof	35,000	Value: 4.00				
1975D	18,241,000	—	0.75	1.00	6.00	—
1975D Proof	43,000	Value: 4.00				
1975F	21,059,000	—	0.75	1.00	6.00	—
1975F Proof	43,000	Value: 4.00				
1975G	12,142,000	—	0.75	1.00	6.50	—
1975G Proof	43,000	Value: 4.00				
1975J	18,770,000	—	0.75	1.00	6.00	—
1975J Proof	43,000	Value: 4.00				
1976D	15,670,000	—	0.75	1.00	6.00	—
1976D Proof	43,000	Value: 4.00				
1976F	18,105,000	—	0.75	1.00	6.00	—
1976F Proof	43,000	Value: 4.00				
1976G	10,382,000	—	0.75	1.00	6.00	—
1976G Proof	43,000	Value: 4.00				
1976J	16,046,000	—	0.75	1.00	6.00	—
1976J Proof	43,000	Value: 4.00				
1977D	20,801,000	—	0.75	0.85	3.00	—
1977D Proof	51,000	Value: 2.00				
1977F	24,026,000	—	0.75	0.85	3.00	—
1977F Proof	51,000	Value: 2.00				
1977G	13,849,000	—	0.75	0.85	3.00	—
1977G Proof	51,000	Value: 2.00				
1977J	21,416,000	—	0.75	0.85	3.00	—
1977J Proof	51,000	Value: 2.00				
1978D	15,600,000	—	0.75	0.85	2.00	—
1978D Proof	54,000	Value: 1.25				
1978F	18,000,000	—	0.75	0.85	2.00	—
1978F Proof	54,000	Value: 1.25				
1978G	10,380,000	—	0.75	0.85	2.00	—
1978G Proof	54,000	Value: 1.25				
1978J	16,020,000	—	0.75	0.85	2.00	—
Note: Error with coin alignment exists						
1978J Proof	54,000	Value: 1.25				
1979D	18,200,000	—	0.75	0.85	2.00	—
1979D Proof	89,000	Value: 1.25				
1979F	21,000,000	—	0.75	0.85	2.00	—
1979F Proof	89,000	Value: 1.25				
1979G	12,110,000	—	0.75	0.85	2.00	—
1979G Proof	89,000	Value: 1.25				
1979J	18,690,000	—	0.75	0.85	2.00	—
1979J Proof	89,000	Value: 1.25				
1980D	24,330,000	—	—	0.75	0.90	—
1980D Proof	110,000	Value: 1.00				
1980F	9,670,000	—	—	0.75	0.90	—
1980F Proof	110,000	Value: 1.00				
1980G	8,540,000	—	—	0.75	0.90	—
1980G Proof	110,000	Value: 1.00				
1980J	16,010,000	—	—	0.75	0.90	—
1980J Proof	110,000	Value: 1.00				
1981D	21,150,000	—	—	1.50	4.00	—
1981D Proof	91,000	Value: 1.00				
1981F	25,910,000	—	—	1.50	4.00	—
1981F Proof	91,000	Value: 1.00				
1981G	14,090,000	—	—	1.50	4.00	—
1981G Proof	91,000	Value: 1.00				
1981J	18,800,000	—	—	1.50	4.00	—
1981J Proof	91,000	Value: 1.00				
1982D	20,590,000	—	—	1.50	4.00	—
1982D Proof	78,000	Value: 1.00				
1982F	22,990,000	—	—	1.50	4.00	—
1982F Proof	78,000	Value: 1.00				
1982G	14,900,000	—	—	1.50	4.00	—
1982G Proof	78,000	Value: 1.00				
1982J	11,520,000	—	—	1.50	4.00	—
1982J Proof	78,000	Value: 1.00				
1983D	18,200,000	—	—	1.50	4.00	—
1983D Proof	75,000	Value: 1.00				
1983F	21,000,000	—	—	1.50	4.00	—
1983F Proof	75,000	Value: 1.00				
1983G	12,100,000	—	—	1.50	4.00	—
1983G Proof	75,000	Value: 1.00				
1983J	18,690,000	—	—	1.50	4.00	—
1983J Proof	75,000	Value: 1.00				
1984D	8,400,000	—	—	1.50	4.00	—
1984D Proof	64,000	Value: 1.50				
1984F	9,700,000	—	—	1.50	4.00	—
1984F Proof	64,000	Value: 1.50				
1984G Proof	64,000	Value: 1.50				
1984G	5,600,000	—	—	1.50	4.00	—
1984J	8,700,000	—	—	1.50	4.00	—
1984J Proof	64,000	Value: 1.50				
1985D	11,700,000	—	—	1.50	4.00	—
1985D Proof	56,000	Value: 1.50				
1985F	13,500,000	—	—	1.50	4.00	—
1985F Proof	54,000	Value: 1.50				
1985G	7,800,000	—	—	1.50	4.00	—
1985G Proof	55,000	Value: 1.50				
1985J	12,000,000	—	—	1.50	4.00	—
1985J Proof	54,000	Value: 1.50				
1986D	10,400,000	—	—	1.50	5.00	—
1986D Proof	44,000	Value: 1.50				
1986F	12,000,000	—	—	1.50	5.00	—
1986F Proof	44,000	Value: 1.50				
1986G	6,900,000	—	—	1.50	5.00	—
1986G Proof	44,000	Value: 1.50				
1986J	10,700,000	—	—	1.50	5.00	—
1986J Proof	44,000	Value: 1.50				
1987D	3,120,000	—	3.50	7.50	15.00	—
1987D Proof	45,000	Value: 1.50				
1987F	3,600,000	—	3.50	7.50	15.00	—
1987F Proof	45,000	Value: 1.50				
1987G	2,080,000	—	3.50	7.50	15.00	—
1987G Proof	45,000	Value: 1.50				
1987J	3,200,000	—	3.50	7.50	15.00	—
1987J Proof	45,000	Value: 1.50				
1988D	20,800,000	—	—	0.75	2.00	—
1988D Proof	45,000	Value: 1.50				
1988F	24,000,000	—	—	0.75	2.00	—
1988F Proof	45,000	Value: 1.50				
1988G	13,800,000	—	—	0.75	2.00	—
1988G Proof	45,000	Value: 1.50				
1988J	21,400,000	—	—	0.75	2.00	—
1988J Proof	45,000	Value: 1.50				
1989D	39,000,000	—	—	—	1.00	—
1989D Proof	45,000	Value: 1.50				
1989F	45,000,000	—	—	—	1.00	—
1989F Proof	45,000	Value: 1.50				
1989G	25,950,000	—	—	—	1.00	—
1989G Proof	45,000	Value: 1.50				
1989J	40,050,000	—	—	—	1.00	—
1989J Proof	45,000	Value: 1.50				
1990A	55,000,000	—	—	—	1.00	—
1990D	77,740,000	—	—	—	1.00	—
1990D Proof	45,000	Value: 1.50				
1990F	89,700,000	—	—	—	1.00	—
1990F Proof	45,000	Value: 1.50				
1990G	51,720,000	—	—	—	1.00	—
1990G Proof	45,000	Value: 1.50				
1990J	79,830,000	—	—	—	1.00	—
1990J Proof	45,000	Value: 1.50				
1991A	30,000,000	—	—	—	1.00	—
1991A Proof	45,000	Value: 1.50				
1991D	31,500,000	—	—	—	1.00	—
1991D Proof	45,000	Value: 1.50				
1991F	36,000,000	—	—	—	1.00	—
1991F Proof	45,000	Value: 1.50				
1991G	21,000,000	—	—	—	1.00	—
1991G Proof	45,000	Value: 1.50				
1991J	31,500,000	—	—	—	1.00	—
1991J Proof	45,000	Value: 1.50				
1992A	30,000,000	—	—	—	1.00	—
1992A Proof	45,000	Value: 1.50				
1992D	31,500,000	—	—	—	1.00	—
1992D Proof	45,000	Value: 1.50				
1992F	36,000,000	—	—	—	1.00	—
1992F Proof	45,000	Value: 1.50				
1992G	21,000,000	—	—	—	1.00	—
1992G Proof	45,000	Value: 1.50				
1992J	31,500,000	—	—	—	1.00	—
1992J Proof	45,000	Value: 1.50				
1993A	8,000,000	—	—	—	1.00	—
1993A Proof	45,000	Value: 1.50				
1993D	8,400,000	—	—	—	1.00	—
1993D Proof	45,000	Value: 1.50				
1993F	9,600,000	—	—	—	1.00	—
1993F Proof	45,000	Value: 1.50				
1993G	5,600,000	—	—	—	1.00	—
1993G Proof	45,000	Value: 1.50				
1993J	8,400,000	—	—	—	1.00	—
1993J Proof	45,000	Value: 1.50				
1994A	18,000,000	—	—	—	1.00	—
1994A Proof	45,000	Value: 1.50				
1994D	18,900,000	—	—	—	1.00	—
1994D Proof	45,000	Value: 1.50				
1994F	21,800,000	—	—	—	1.00	—
1994F Proof	45,000	Value: 1.50				
1994G	12,800,000	—	—	—	1.00	—
1994G Proof	45,000	Value: 1.50				
1994J	18,900,000	—	—	—	1.00	—
1994J Proof	45,000	Value: 1.50				
1995A	20,000	—	—	—	70.00	—
Note: In sets only						
1995A Proof	45,000	Value: 20.00				
1995D	20,000	—	—	—	70.00	—
Note: In sets only						
1995D Proof	45,000	Value: 20.00				
1995F	20,000	—	—	—	70.00	—
Note: In sets only						
1995F Proof	45,000	Value: 20.00				
1995G	20,000	—	—	—	70.00	—
Note: In sets only						
1995G Proof	45,000	Value: 20.00				
1995J	100,000	—	—	—	18.00	—
1995J Proof	45,000	Value: 20.00				
1996A	50,000	—	—	—	12.50	—
Note: In sets only						
1996A Proof	45,000	Value: 14.00				
1996D	50,000	—	—	—	12.50	—
Note: In sets only						
1996D Proof	45,000	Value: 14.00				
1996F	50,000	—	—	—	12.50	—
Note: In sets only						
1996F Proof	45,000	Value: 14.00				

Date	Mintage	F	VF	XF	Unc	BU
1996G	50,000	—	—	—	12.50	—
Note: In sets only						
1996G Proof	45,000	Value: 14.00				
1996J	50,000	—	—	—	12.50	—
Note: In sets only						
1996J Proof	45,000	Value: 14.00				
1997A	70,000	—	—	—	4.75	—
Note: In sets only						
1997A Proof	45,000	Value: 5.00				
1997D	70,000	—	—	—	4.75	—
Note: In sets only						
1997D Proof	45,000	Value: 5.00				
1997F	70,000	—	—	—	4.75	—
Note: In sets only						
1997F Proof	45,000	Value: 5.00				
1997G	70,000	—	—	—	4.75	—
Note: In sets only						
1997G Proof	45,000	Value: 5.00				
1997J	70,000	—	—	—	4.75	—
Note: In sets only						
1997J Proof	45,000	Value: 5.00				
1998A	70,000	—	—	—	4.75	—
Note: In sets only						
1998A Proof	45,000	Value: 5.00				
1998D	70,000	—	—	—	4.75	—
Note: In sets only						
1998D Proof	45,000	Value: 5.00				
1998F	70,000	—	—	—	4.75	—
Note: In sets only						
1998F Proof	45,000	Value: 5.00				
1998G	70,000	—	—	—	4.75	—
Note: In sets only						
1998G Proof	45,000	Value: 5.00				
1998J	70,000	—	—	—	4.75	—
Note: In sets only						
1998J Proof	45,000	Value: 5.00				
1999A	70,000	—	—	—	4.75	—
Note: In sets only						
1999A Proof	45,000	Value: 5.00				
1999D	70,000	—	—	—	4.75	—
Note: In sets only						
1999D Proof	45,000	Value: 5.00				
1999F	70,000	—	—	—	4.75	—
Note: In sets only						
1999F Proof	45,000	Value: 5.00				
1999G	70,000	—	—	—	4.75	—
Note: In sets only						
1999G Proof	45,000	Value: 5.00				
1999J	70,000	—	—	—	4.75	—
Note: In sets only						
1999J Proof	45,000	Value: 5.00				
2000A	70,000	—	—	—	5.00	—
Note: In sets only						
2000A Proof	45,000	Value: 5.00				
2000D	70,000	—	—	—	5.00	—
Note: In sets only						
2000D Proof	45,000	Value: 5.00				
2000F	70,000	—	—	—	5.00	—
Note: In sets only						
2000F Proof	45,000	Value: 5.00				
2000G	70,000	—	—	—	5.00	—
Note: In sets only						
2000G Proof	45,000	Value: 5.00				
2000J	70,000	—	—	—	5.00	—
Note: In sets only						
2000J Proof	45,000	Value: 5.00				
2001A	130,000	—	—	—	15.00	—
Note: In sets only						
2001A Proof	78,000	Value: 15.00				
2001D	130,000	—	—	—	15.00	—
Note: In sets only						
2001D Proof	78,000	Value: 15.00				
2001F	130,000	—	—	—	15.00	—
Note: In sets only						
2001F Proof	78,000	Value: 15.00				
2001G	130,000	—	—	—	15.00	—
Note: In sets only						
2001G Proof	78,000	Value: 15.00				
2001J	130,000	—	—	—	15.00	—
Note: In sets only						
2001J Proof	78,000	Value: 15.00				

KM# 111 2 MARK

7.0000 g., Copper-Nickel, 26.75 mm. **Obv:** Eagle **Rev:** Denomination flanked by leaves, grapes, and grain sprigs, date above

Date	Mintage	F	VF	XF	Unc	BU
1951D	19,564,000	—	25.00	30.00	100	—
1951D Proof	200	Value: 450				
1951F	22,609,000	—	25.00	30.00	100	—
1951F Proof	150	Value: 500				
1951G	Est. 13,012,000	—	50.00	75.00	200	—
Note: The 1951G dated coin was restruck without authorization by a mint official using genuine dies - quantity unknown						
1951G Proof	33	Value: 1,200				
1951J	20,104,000	—	25.00	30.00	100	—
1951J Proof	180	Value: 450				

KM# 116 2 MARK

7.0000 g., Copper-Nickel, 26.75 mm. **Subject:** Max Planck **Obv:** Eagle above denomination **Rev:** Head left, dates below

Date	Mintage	F	VF	XF	Unc	BU
1957D	7,452,000	—	2.00	6.00	65.00	—
1957D Proof	350	Value: 235				
1957F	6,337,000	—	2.00	6.00	65.00	—
1957F Proof	100	Value: 325				
1957G	2,598,000	—	3.00	7.50	135	—
1957G Proof	56	Value: 600				
1957J	11,210,000	—	2.00	6.00	60.00	—
1957J Proof	370	Value: 175				
1958D	12,623,000	—	1.50	5.00	50.00	—
1958D Proof	1,240	Value: 85.00				
1958F	16,825,000	—	1.50	4.00	45.00	—
1958F Proof	300	Value: 200				
1958G	10,744,000	—	1.50	4.00	45.00	—
1958G Proof	45	Value: 700				
1958J	9,408,000	—	1.50	4.00	45.00	—
1958J Proof	100	Value: 400				
1959D	1,020,000	—	4.00	15.00	240	—
1959D Proof	38	Value: 1,150				
1959F	203,000	—	15.00	60.00	425	—
1959F Proof	24	Value: 1,850				
1960D	3,535,000	—	1.50	4.00	35.00	—
1960D Proof	100	Value: 325				
1960F	3,692,000	—	1.50	4.00	35.00	—
1960F Proof	50	Value: 600				
1960G	2,695,000	—	2.00	4.00	35.00	—
1960G Proof	130	Value: 300				
1960J	4,676,000	—	1.50	4.00	35.00	—
1960J Proof	36	Value: 800				
1961D	3,918,000	—	1.50	4.00	35.00	—
1961D Proof	50	Value: 600				
1961F	3,872,000	—	1.50	4.00	35.00	—
1961F Proof	46	Value: 650				
1961G	2,776,000	—	2.00	4.00	35.00	—
1961G Proof	100	Value: 325				
1961J	2,940,000	—	1.50	4.00	35.00	—
1961J Proof	28	Value: 800				
1962D	4,105,000	—	2.00	6.00	35.00	—
1962D Proof	50	Value: 600				
1962F	3,344,000	—	2.00	6.00	35.00	—
1962F Proof	42	Value: 625				
1962G	1,800,000	—	2.00	6.00	45.00	—
1962G Proof	130	Value: 300				
1962J	3,609,000	—	2.00	6.00	25.00	—
1962J Proof	28	Value: 750				
1963D	4,411,000	—	1.50	4.00	25.00	—
1963D Proof	40	Value: 650				
1963F	3,752,000	—	1.50	4.00	25.00	—
1963F Proof	47	Value: 600				
1963G	3,448,000	—	1.50	4.00	25.00	—
1963G Proof	200	Value: 350				
1963J	7,348,000	—	1.50	4.00	25.00	—
1963J Proof	32	Value: 700				
1964D	5,205,000	—	1.50	4.00	20.00	—
1964D Proof	40	Value: 650				
1964F	4,834,000	—	1.50	4.00	20.00	—
1964F Proof	36	Value: 800				
1964G	3,044,000	5.00	10.00	25.00	125	—
1964G Proof	368	Value: 150				
1964J	2,681,000	—	1.50	4.00	20.00	—
1964J Proof	43	Value: 600				
1965D	3,903,000	—	1.50	2.50	15.00	—
1965D Proof	35	Value: 800				
1965F	4,045,000	—	1.50	2.50	15.00	—
1965F Proof	300	Value: 250				
1965G	2,599,000	—	1.50	2.50	15.00	—
1965G Proof	8,233	Value: 5.00				
1965J	4,006,999	—	1.50	2.50	15.00	—
Note: Error exists without edge inscription						
1965J Proof	36	Value: 750				
1966D	5,855,000	—	1.50	2.50	12.00	—
1966D Proof	20	Value: 900				
1966F	3,750,000	—	1.50	2.50	12.00	—
1966F Proof	450	Value: 250				
1966G	3,895,000	—	1.50	2.50	12.00	—
1966G Proof	3,070	Value: 20.00				
1966J	6,014,000	—	1.50	2.50	12.00	—
1966J Proof	1,000	Value: 35.00				
1967D	3,254,000	—	1.50	2.50	12.00	—
1967D Proof	20	Value: 900				
1967F	3,758,000	—	1.50	2.50	12.00	—
1967F Proof	1,600	Value: 32.00				
1967G	1,878,000	—	1.50	4.00	16.50	—
1967G Proof	5,363	Value: 28.00				
1967J	6,684,000	—	1.25	2.50	12.00	—
1967J Proof	1,500	Value: 32.00				
1968D	4,166,000	—	1.50	2.50	15.00	—
1968D Proof	30	Value: 850				
1968F	1,050,000	—	2.00	5.00	20.00	—
1968F Proof	3,100	Value: 22.00				
1968G	3,060,000	—	2.00	2.50	12.00	—
1968G Proof	6,023	Value: 15.00				
1968J	939,000	—	2.00	4.00	20.00	—
1968J Proof	2,000	Value: 28.00				
1969D	2,602,000	—	2.00	2.50	15.00	—
1969F	3,005,000	—	2.00	2.50	15.00	—
1969F Proof	5,100	Value: 6.00				
1969G	1,754,000	—	2.00	2.50	16.50	—
1969G Proof	8,700	Value: 6.00				
1969J	2,680,000	—	2.00	2.50	10.00	—
1969J Proof	5,000	Value: 6.00				
1970D	5,203,000	—	1.50	2.00	4.00	—
1970F	6,018,000	—	1.50	2.00	4.00	—
1970F Proof	5,140	Value: 7.50				
1970G	3,461,000	—	1.50	2.00	4.00	—
1970G Proof	10,000	Value: 5.00				
1970J	5,691,000	—	1.50	2.00	4.00	—
1970J Proof	5,000	Value: 6.00				
1971D	8,451,000	—	1.00	1.25	3.00	—
1971D Proof	8,000	Value: 5.00				
1971F	10,017,000	—	1.00	1.25	3.00	—
1971F Proof	8,000	Value: 5.00				
1971G	5,631,000	—	1.00	1.25	3.00	—
1971G Proof	10,000	Value: 5.00				
1971J	8,786,000	—	1.00	1.25	3.00	—
1971J Proof	8,000	Value: 6.00				

KM# 124 2 MARK

7.0000 g., Copper-Nickel Clad Nickel, 26.75 mm. **Subject:** Konrad Adenauer **Obv:** Eagle above denomination **Rev:** Head left, dates below

Date	Mintage	F	VF	XF	Unc	BU
1969D	7,001,000	—	—	1.50	3.00	—
1969F	7,006,000	—	—	1.50	3.00	—
1969G	7,010,000	—	—	1.50	3.00	—
1969J	7,000,000	—	—	1.50	3.00	—
1970D	7,318,000	—	—	1.50	3.00	—
1970F	8,422,000	—	—	1.50	3.00	—
1970G	4,844,000	—	—	1.50	3.00	—
1970J	7,476,000	—	—	1.50	3.00	—
1971D	7,287,000	—	—	1.50	3.00	—
1971F	8,400,000	—	—	1.50	3.00	—
1971G	4,848,000	—	—	1.50	3.00	—
1971J	7,476,000	—	—	1.50	3.00	—
1972D	7,286,000	—	—	1.50	3.00	—
1972D Proof	8,000	Value: 4.50				
1972F	8,392,000	—	—	1.50	3.00	—
1972F Proof	8,000	Value: 4.50				
1972G	4,848,000	—	—	1.50	3.00	—
1972G Proof	10,000	Value: 4.50				
1972J	7,476,000	—	—	1.50	3.00	—
1972J Proof	8,000	Value: 4.50				
1973D	10,393,000	—	—	1.50	3.00	—
1973D Proof	9,000	Value: 4.50				
1973F	11,015,000	—	—	1.50	3.00	—
Note: Errors exist without edge inscription						
1973F Proof	9,000	Value: 4.50				
1973G	9,022,000	—	—	1.50	3.00	—
1973G Proof	9,000	Value: 4.50				
1973J	12,272,000	—	—	1.50	3.00	—
Note: Errors with coin alignment exist						
1973J Proof	9,000	Value: 4.50				
1974D	5,151,000	—	—	1.50	3.00	—
1974D Proof	35,000	Value: 2.25				
1974F	5,894,000	—	—	1.50	3.00	—
1974F Proof	35,000	Value: 2.25				
1974G	3,790,000	—	—	1.50	3.00	—
1974G Proof	35,000	Value: 2.25				
1974J	5,282,000	—	—	1.50	3.00	—
1974J Proof	35,000	Value: 2.25				
1975D	4,553,000	—	—	1.50	2.50	—
1975D Proof	43,000	Value: 2.25				
1975F	5,270,000	—	—	1.50	2.50	—
1975F Proof	43,000	Value: 2.25				
1975G	3,035,000	—	—	1.50	2.50	—
1975G Proof	43,000	Value: 2.25				
1975J	4,673,000	—	—	1.50	2.50	—
1975J Proof	43,000	Value: 2.25				
1976D	4,576,000	—	—	1.50	2.50	—
1976D Proof	43,000	Value: 2.25				

Date	Mintage	F	VF	XF	Unc	BU
1976F	5,257,000	—	—	1.50	2.50	—
1976F Proof	43,000	Value: 2.25				
1976G	3,028,000	—	—	1.50	2.50	—
1976G Proof	43,000	Value: 2.25				
1976J	4,673,000	—	—	1.50	2.50	—
1976J Proof	43,000	Value: 2.25				
1977D	5,906,000	—	—	1.50	2.50	—
1977D Proof	51,000	Value: 2.00				
1977F	6,765,000	—	—	1.50	2.50	—
1977F Proof	51,000	Value: 2.00				
1977G	3,892,000	—	—	1.50	2.50	—
1977G Proof	51,000	Value: 2.00				
1977J	6,007,000	—	—	1.50	2.50	—
1977J Proof	51,000	Value: 2.00				
1978D	3,304,000	—	—	1.50	2.50	—
1978D Proof	54,000	Value: 2.00				
1978F	3,804	—	—	1.50	2.50	—
1978F Proof	54,000	Value: 2.00				
1978G	2,217,000	—	—	1.50	2.50	—
1978G Proof	54,000	Value: 2.00				
1978J	3,392,000	—	—	1.50	2.50	—
1978J Proof	54,000	Value: 2.00				
1979D	3,209,000	—	—	1.50	2.50	—
1979D Proof	89,000	Value: 2.00				
1979F	3,689,000	—	—	1.50	2.50	—
1979F Proof	89,000	Value: 2.00				
1979G	2,165,000	—	—	1.50	2.50	—
1979G Proof	89,000	Value: 2.00				
1979J	3,293,000	—	—	1.50	2.50	—
1979J Proof	89,000	Value: 2.00				
1980D	10,810,000	—	—	1.50	2.00	—
1980D Proof	110,000	Value: 2.00				
1980F	8,910,000	—	—	1.50	2.00	—
1980F Proof	110,000	Value: 2.00				
1980G	1,170,000	—	—	1.50	2.00	—
1980G Proof	110,000	Value: 2.00				
1980J	4,670,000	—	—	1.50	2.00	—
1980J Proof	110,000	Value: 2.00				
1981D	8,180,000	—	—	1.50	2.00	—
1981D Proof	91,000	Value: 2.00				
1981F	7,690,000	—	—	1.50	2.00	—
1981F Proof	91,000	Value: 2.00				
1981G	7,070,000	—	—	1.50	2.00	—
1981G Proof	91,000	Value: 2.00				
1981J	8,289,999	—	—	1.50	2.00	—
1981J Proof	91,000	Value: 2.00				
1982D	9,220,000	—	—	1.50	2.00	—
1982D Proof	78,000	Value: 2.00				
1982F	11,260,000	—	—	1.50	2.00	—
1982F Proof	78,000	Value: 2.00				
1982G	6,640,000	—	—	1.50	2.00	—
1982G Proof	78,000	Value: 2.00				
1982J	9,790,000	—	—	1.50	2.00	—
1982J Proof	78,000	Value: 2.00				
1983D	1,560,000	—	—	1.50	2.00	—
1983D Proof	75,000	Value: 2.00				
1983F	1,800,000	—	—	1.50	2.00	—
1983F Proof	75,000	Value: 2.00				
1983G	1,030,000	—	—	1.50	2.00	—
1983G Proof	75,000	Value: 2.00				
1983J	1,600,000	—	—	1.50	2.00	—
1983J Proof	75,000	Value: 2.00				
1984D	52,000	—	2.00	4.50	8.50	—
1984D Proof	64,000	Value: 2.00				
1984F	60,000	—	2.00	4.50	8.50	—
1984F Proof	64,000	Value: 2.00				
1984G	35,000	—	3.00	6.00	11.50	—
1984G Proof	64,000	Value: 2.00				
1984J	53,000	—	2.00	4.50	8.50	—
1984J Proof	64,000	Value: 2.00				
1985D	2,600,000	—	—	—	2.00	—
1985D Proof	56,000	Value: 2.25				
1985F	3,000,000	—	—	—	1.75	—
1985F Proof	54,000	Value: 2.25				
1985G	1,730,000	—	—	—	1.75	—
1985G Proof	55,000	Value: 2.25				
1985J	2,670,000	—	—	—	1.75	—
1985J Proof	54,000	Value: 2.25				
1986D	2,600,000	—	—	—	1.75	—
1986D Proof	44,000	Value: 2.25				
1986F	3,000,000	—	—	—	1.75	—
1986F Proof	44,000	Value: 2.25				
1986G	1,730,000	—	—	—	1.75	—
1986G Proof	44,000	Value: 2.25				
1986J	2,670,000	—	—	—	1.75	—
1986J Proof	44,000	Value: 2.25				
1987D	4,420,000	—	—	—	1.75	—
1987D Proof	45,000	Value: 2.25				
1987F	5,100,000	—	—	—	1.75	—
1987F Proof	45,000	Value: 2.25				
1987G	2,940,000	—	—	—	1.75	—
1987G Proof	45,000	Value: 2.25				
1987J	4,540,000	—	—	—	1.75	—
1987J Proof	45,000	Value: 2.25				

KM# A127 2 MARK

7.0000 g., Copper-Nickel Clad Nickel, 26.75 mm. **Subject:** Theodor Heuss **Obv:** Eagle above denomination **Rev:** Head left, dates below

Date	Mintage	F	VF	XF	Unc	BU
1970D	7,317,000	—	—	1.50	3.00	—
1970F	8,426,000	—	—	1.50	3.00	—
1970G	4,844,000	—	—	1.50	3.00	—
1970J	7,476,000	—	—	1.50	3.00	—
1971D	7,280,000	—	—	1.50	3.00	—
1971F	8,403,000	—	—	1.50	3.00	—
1971G	4,841,000	—	—	1.50	3.00	—
1971J	7,476,000	—	—	1.50	3.00	—
1972D	7,288,000	—	—	1.50	3.00	—
1972D Proof	8,000	Value: 4.50				
1972F	8,401,000	—	—	1.50	3.00	—
1972F Proof	8,000	Value: 4.50				
1972G	4,859,000	—	—	1.50	3.00	—
1972G Proof	10,000	Value: 4.50				
1972J	7,476,000	—	—	1.50	3.00	—
1972J Proof	8,000	Value: 4.50				
1973D	10,379,000	—	—	1.50	3.00	—
1973D Proof	9,000	Value: 4.50				
1973F	11,018,000	—	—	1.50	3.00	—
1973F Proof	9,000	Value: 4.50				
1973G	8,975,000	—	—	1.50	3.00	—
1973G Proof	9,000	Value: 4.50				
1973J	12,360,000	—	—	1.50	3.00	—
1973J Proof	9,000	Value: 4.50				
1974D	5,147,000	—	—	1.50	3.00	—
1974D Proof	35,000	Value: 2.00				
1974F	5,899,000	—	—	1.50	3.00	—
1974F Proof	35,000	Value: 2.00				
1974G	3,820,000	—	—	1.50	3.00	—
1974G Proof	35,000	Value: 2.00				
1974J	5,280,000	—	—	1.50	3.00	—
1974J Proof	35,000	Value: 2.00				
1975D	4,623,000	—	—	1.50	2.00	—
1975D Proof	43,000	Value: 2.00				
1975F	5,251,000	—	—	1.50	2.00	—
1975F Proof	43,000	Value: 2.00				
1975G	3,034,000	—	—	1.50	2.00	—
1975G Proof	43,000	Value: 2.00				
1975J	4,675,000	—	—	1.50	2.00	—
1975J Proof	43,000	Value: 2.00				
1976D	4,546,000	—	—	1.50	2.00	—
1976D Proof	43,000	Value: 2.00				
1976F	5,259,000	—	—	1.50	2.00	—
1976F Proof	43,000	Value: 2.00				
1976G	3,028,000	—	—	1.50	2.00	—
1976G Proof	43,000	Value: 2.00				
1976J	4,681,000	—	—	1.50	2.00	—
1976J Proof	43,000	Value: 2.00				
1977D	5,857,000	—	—	1.50	2.00	—
1977D Proof	51,000	Value: 1.75				
1977F	6,752,000	—	—	1.50	2.00	—
1977F Proof	51,000	Value: 1.75				
1977G	3,892,000	—	—	1.50	2.00	—
1977G Proof	51,000	Value: 1.75				
1977J	6,009,000	—	—	1.50	2.00	—
1977J Proof	51,000	Value: 1.75				
1978D	3,804,000	—	—	1.50	2.00	—

Note: Errors without edge inscription exist

Date	Mintage	F	VF	XF	Unc	BU
1978D Proof	54,000	Value: 1.75				
1978F	3,804,000	—	—	1.50	2.00	—
1978F Proof	54,000	Value: 1.75				
1978G	2,217,000	—	—	1.50	2.00	—
1978G Proof	54,000	Value: 1.75				
1978J	3,392,000	—	—	1.50	2.00	—
1978J Proof	54,000	Value: 1.75				
1979D	3,209,000	—	—	1.50	2.00	—
1979D Proof	89,000	Value: 1.75				
1979F	3,689,000	—	—	1.50	2.00	—
1979F Proof	89,000	Value: 1.75				
1979G	2,165,000	—	—	1.50	2.00	—
1979G Proof	89,000	Value: 1.75				
1979J	3,293,000	—	—	1.50	2.00	—
1979J Proof	89,000	Value: 1.75				
1980D	2,000,000	—	—	1.50	1.75	—
1980D Proof	110,000	Value: 1.75				
1980F	2,300,000	—	—	1.50	1.75	—
1980F Proof	110,000	Value: 1.75				
1980G	1,300,000	—	—	1.50	1.75	—
1980G Proof	110,000	Value: 1.75				
1980J	2,000,000	—	—	1.50	1.75	—
1980J Proof	110,000	Value: 1.75				
1981D	2,000,000	—	—	1.50	1.75	—
1981D Proof	91,000	Value: 1.75				
1981F	2,300,000	—	—	1.50	1.75	—
1981F Proof	91,000	Value: 1.75				
1981G	1,300,000	—	—	1.50	1.75	—
1981G Proof	91,000	Value: 1.75				
1981J	2,000,000	—	—	1.50	1.75	—
1981J Proof	91,000	Value: 1.75				
1982D	3,100,000	—	—	1.50	1.75	—
1982D Proof	78,000	Value: 1.75				
1982F	3,600,000	—	—	1.50	1.75	—
1982F Proof	78,000	Value: 1.75				
1982G	2,100,000	—	—	1.50	1.75	—
1982G Proof	78,000	Value: 1.75				
1982J	3,200,000	—	—	1.50	1.75	—
1982J Proof	78,000	Value: 1.75				
1983D	1,560,000	—	—	1.50	1.75	—
1983D Proof	75,000	Value: 1.75				
1983F	1,800,000	—	—	1.50	1.75	—
1983F Proof	75,000	Value: 1.75				
1983G	1,030,000	—	—	1.50	1.75	—
1983G Proof	75,000	Value: 1.75				
1983J	1,600,000	—	—	1.50	1.75	—
1983J Proof	75,000	Value: 1.75				
1984D	52,000	—	2.00	4.50	8.50	—
1984D Proof	64,000	Value: 2.00				
1984F	60,000	—	2.00	4.50	8.50	—
1984F Proof	64,000	Value: 2.00				
1984G	35,000	—	3.00	6.00	11.50	—
1984G Proof	64,000	Value: 2.00				
1984J	53,000	—	2.00	4.50	8.50	—
1984J Proof	64,000	Value: 2.00				
1985D	2,600,000	—	—	—	1.75	—
1985D Proof	56,000	Value: 2.25				
1985F	3,000,000	—	—	—	1.75	—
1985F Proof	54,000	Value: 2.25				
1985G	1,730,000	—	—	—	1.75	—
1985G Proof	55,000	Value: 2.25				
1985J	2,670,000	—	—	—	1.75	—
1985J Proof	54,000	Value: 2.25				
1986D	2,600,000	—	—	—	1.75	—
1986D Proof	44,000	Value: 2.25				
1986F	3,000,000	—	—	—	1.75	—
1986F Proof	44,000	Value: 2.25				
1986G	1,730,000	—	—	—	1.75	—
1986G Proof	44,000	Value: 2.25				
1986J	2,670,000	—	—	—	1.75	—
1986J Proof	44,000	Value: 2.25				
1987D	4,420,000	—	—	—	1.75	—
1987D Proof	45,000	Value: 2.25				
1987F	5,100,000	—	—	—	1.75	—
1987F Proof	45,000	Value: 2.25				
1987G	2,940,000	—	—	—	1.75	—
1987G Proof	45,000	Value: 2.25				
1987J	4,540,000	—	—	—	1.75	—
1987J Proof	45,000	Value: 2.25				

KM# 149 2 MARK

7.0000 g., Copper-Nickel Clad Nickel, 26.75 mm. **Subject:** Dr. Kurt Schumacher **Obv:** Eagle above denomination **Rev:** Head 3/4 left divides dates

Date	Mintage	F	VF	XF	Unc	BU
1979D	3,209,000	—	—	1.50	2.00	—
1979D Proof	89,000	Value: 1.75				
1979F	3,689,000	—	—	1.50	2.00	—
1979F Proof	89,000	Value: 1.75				
1979G	2,165,000	—	—	1.50	2.00	—
1979G Proof	89,000	Value: 1.75				
1979J	3,293,000	—	—	1.50	2.00	—
1979J Proof	89,000	Value: 1.75				
1980D	2,000,000	—	—	1.50	2.00	—
1980D Proof	110,000	Value: 1.75				
1980F	2,300,000	—	—	1.50	2.00	—
1980F Proof	110,000	Value: 1.75				
1980G	1,300,000	—	—	1.50	2.00	—
1980G Proof	110,000	Value: 1.75				
1980J	2,000,000	—	—	1.50	2.00	—
1980J Proof	110,000	Value: 1.75				
1981D	2,000,000	—	—	1.50	2.00	—
1981D Proof	91,000	Value: 1.75				
1981F	2,000,000	—	—	1.50	2.00	—

Note: Errors without edge inscription exist

Date	Mintage	F	VF	XF	Unc	BU
1981F Proof	91,000	Value: 1.75				
1981G	1,300,000	—	—	1.50	2.00	—
1981G Proof	91,000	Value: 1.75				
1981J	2,000,000	—	—	1.50	2.00	—
1981J Proof	91,000	Value: 1.75				
1982D	3,100,000	—	—	1.50	2.00	—
1982D Proof	78,000	Value: 1.75				
1982F	3,600,000	—	—	1.50	2.00	—
1982F Proof	78,000	Value: 1.75				
1982G	2,100,000	—	—	1.50	2.00	—
1982G Proof	78,000	Value: 1.75				
1982J	3,200,000	—	—	1.50	2.00	—
1982J Proof	78,000	Value: 1.75				
1983D	1,560,000	—	—	1.50	2.00	—

Date	Mintage	F	VF	XF	Unc	BU
1983D Proof	75,000	Value: 1.75				
1983F	1,800,000	—	—	1.50	2.00	—
1983F Proof	75,000	Value: 1.75				
1983G	1,030,000	—	—	1.50	2.00	—
1983G Proof	75,000	Value: 1.75				
1983J	1,600,000	—	—	1.50	2.00	—
1983J Proof	75,000	Value: 1.75				
1984D	52,000	—	2.00	4.50	8.50	—
1984D Proof	64,000	Value: 1.75				
1984F	60,000	—	2.00	4.50	8.50	—
1984F Proof	64,000	Value: 1.75				
1984G	35,000	—	3.00	6.00	11.50	—
1984G Proof	64,000	Value: 1.75				
1984J	53,000	—	2.00	4.50	8.50	—
1984J Proof	64,000	Value: 1.75				
1985D	2,600,000	—	—	—	1.75	—
1985D Proof	56,000	Value: 2.25				
1985F	3,000,000	—	—	—	1.75	—
1985F Proof	54,000	Value: 2.25				
1985G	1,730,000	—	—	—	1.75	—
1985G Proof	55,000	Value: 2.25				
1985J	2,670,000	—	—	—	1.75	—
1985J Proof	54,000	Value: 2.25				
1986D	2,600,000	—	—	—	1.75	—
1986D Proof	44,000	Value: 2.25				
1986F	3,000,000	—	—	—	1.75	—
1986F Proof	44,000	Value: 2.25				
1986G	1,730,000	—	—	—	1.75	—
1986G Proof	44,000	Value: 2.25				
1986J	2,670,000	—	—	—	1.75	—
1986J Proof	44,000	Value: 2.25				
1987D	4,420,000	—	—	—	1.75	—
1987D Proof	45,000	Value: 2.25				
1987F	5,100,000	—	—	—	1.75	—
1987F Proof	45,000	Value: 2.25				
1987G	2,940,000	—	—	—	1.75	—
1987G Proof	45,000	Value: 2.25				
1987J	4,540,000	—	—	—	1.75	—
1987J Proof	45,000	Value: 2.25				
1988D	5,850,000	—	—	—	1.75	—
1988D Proof	45,000	Value: 2.25				
1988F	6,750,000	—	—	—	1.75	—
1988F Proof	45,000	Value: 2.25				
1988G	3,890,000	—	—	—	1.75	—
1988G Proof	45,000	Value: 2.25				
1988J	6,010,000	—	—	—	1.75	—
1988J Proof	45,000	Value: 2.25				
1989D	10,400,000	—	—	—	1.75	—
1989D Proof	45,000	Value: 2.25				
1989F	12,000,000	—	—	—	1.75	—
1989F Proof	45,000	Value: 2.25				
1989G	6,920,000	—	—	—	1.75	—
1989G Proof	45,000	Value: 2.25				
1989J	10,680,000	—	—	—	1.75	—
1989J Proof	45,000	Value: 2.25				
1990D	18,370,000	—	—	—	1.75	—
1990D Proof	45,000	Value: 2.25				
1990F	21,200,000	—	—	—	1.75	—
1990F Proof	45,000	Value: 2.25				
1990G	12,220,000	—	—	—	1.75	—
1990G Proof	45,000	Value: 2.25				
1990J	18,870,000	—	—	—	1.75	—
1990J Proof	45,000	Value: 2.25				
1991A	4,000,000	—	—	—	1.75	—
1991A Proof	45,000	Value: 2.25				
1991D	4,200,000	—	—	—	1.75	—
1991D Proof	45,000	Value: 2.25				
1991F	4,800,000	—	—	—	1.75	—
1991F Proof	45,000	Value: 2.25				
1991G	2,800,000	—	—	—	1.75	—
1991G Proof	45,000	Value: 2.25				
1991J	4,200,000	—	—	—	1.75	—
1991J Proof	45,000	Value: 2.25				
1992A	7,330,000	—	—	—	1.75	—
1992A Proof	45,000	Value: 2.25				
1992D	7,700,000	—	—	—	1.75	—
1992D Proof	45,000	Value: 2.25				
1992F	8,800,000	—	—	—	1.75	—
1992F Proof	45,000	Value: 2.25				
1992G	5,130,000	—	—	—	1.75	—
1992G Proof	45,000	Value: 2.25				
1992J	7,700,000	—	—	—	1.75	—
1992J Proof	45,000	Value: 2.25				
1993A	600,000	—	—	3.00	7.00	—
1993A Proof	45,000	Value: 2.25				
1993D	630,000	—	—	3.00	7.00	—
1993D Proof	45,000	Value: 2.25				
1993F	720,000	—	—	3.00	7.00	—
1993F Proof	45,000	Value: 2.25				
1993G	420,000	—	—	4.00	10.00	—
1993G Proof	45,000	Value: 2.25				
1993J	630,000	—	—	3.00	7.00	—
1993J Proof	45,000	Value: 2.25				

KM# 170 2 MARK

7.0000 g., Copper-Nickel Clad Nickel, 26.75 mm. **Subject:** Ludwig Erhard **Obv:** Eagle above denomination **Rev:** Head facing divides dates

Date	Mintage	F	VF	XF	Unc	BU
1988D	5,850,000	—	—	—	1.65	—
1988D Proof	45,000	Value: 2.00				
1988F	6,750,000	—	—	—	1.65	—
1988F Proof	45,000	Value: 2.00				
1988G	3,890,000	—	—	—	1.65	—
1988G Proof	45,000	Value: 2.00				
1988J	6,010,000	—	—	—	1.65	—
1988J Proof	45,000	Value: 2.00				
1989D	10,400,000	—	—	—	1.65	—
1989D Proof	45,000	Value: 2.00				
1989F	12,000,000	—	—	—	1.65	—
1989F Proof	45,000	Value: 2.00				
1989G	6,920,000	—	—	—	1.65	—
1989G Proof	45,000	Value: 2.00				
1989J	10,680,000	—	—	—	1.65	—
1989J Proof	45,000	Value: 2.00				
1990D	18,370,000	—	—	—	1.65	—
1990D Proof	45,000	Value: 2.00				
1990F	21,200,000	—	—	—	1.65	—
1990F Proof	45,000	Value: 2.00				
1990G	12,220,000	—	—	—	1.65	—
1990G Proof	45,000	Value: 2.00				
1990J	18,870,000	—	—	—	1.65	—
1990J Proof	45,000	Value: 2.00				
1991A	4,000,000	—	—	—	1.65	—
1991A Proof	45,000	Value: 2.00				
1991D	4,200,000	—	—	—	1.65	—
1991D Proof	45,000	Value: 2.00				
1991F	4,800,000	—	—	—	1.65	—
1991F Proof	45,000	Value: 2.00				
1991G	2,800,000	—	—	—	1.65	—
Note: Errors without edge inscription exist						
1991G Proof	45,000	Value: 2.00				
1991J	4,200,000	—	—	—	1.65	—
1991J Proof	45,000	Value: 2.00				
1992A	7,330,000	—	—	—	1.75	—
1992A Proof	45,000	Value: 2.25				
1992D	7,700,000	—	—	—	1.75	—
1992D Proof	45,000	Value: 2.25				
1992F	8,800,000	—	—	—	1.75	—
1992F Proof	45,000	Value: 2.25				
1992G	5,130,000	—	—	—	1.75	—
1992G Proof	45,000	Value: 2.25				
1992J	7,700,000	—	—	—	1.75	—
1992J Proof	45,000	Value: 2.25				
1993A	600,000	—	—	3.00	7.00	—
1993A Proof	45,000	Value: 2.25				
1993D	630,000	—	—	3.00	7.00	—
1993D Proof	45,000	Value: 2.25				
1993F	720,000	—	—	3.00	7.00	—
1993F Proof	45,000	Value: 2.25				
1993G	420,000	—	—	4.00	10.00	—
1993G Proof	45,000	Value: 2.25				
1993J	630,000	—	—	3.00	7.00	—
1993J Proof	45,000	Value: 2.25				
1994A	5,000,000	—	—	—	1.75	—
1994A Proof	45,000	Value: 2.25				
1994D	5,250,000	—	—	—	1.75	—
1994D Proof	45,000	Value: 2.25				
1994F	6,000,000	—	—	—	1.75	—
1994F Proof	45,000	Value: 2.25				
1994G	3,500,000	—	—	—	1.75	—
1994G Proof	45,000	Value: 2.25				
1994J	5,250,000	—	—	—	1.75	—
1994J Proof	45,000	Value: 2.25				
1995A	1,595,000	—	—	—	3.50	—
1995A Proof	45,000	Value: 17.50				
1995D	20,000	—	—	—	60.00	—
Note: In sets only						
1995D Proof	45,000	Value: 17.50				
1995F	20,000	—	—	—	60.00	—
Note: In sets only						
1995F Proof	45,000	Value: 17.50				
1995G	920,000	—	—	—	6.00	—
1995G Proof	45,000	Value: 17.50				
1995J	20,000	—	—	—	60.00	—
Note: In sets only						
1995J Proof	45,000	Value: 17.50				
1996A	—	—	—	—	5.00	—
1996A Proof	45,000	Value: 6.00				
1996D	—	—	—	—	5.00	—
1996D Proof	45,000	Value: 6.00				
1996F	—	—	—	—	5.00	—
1996F Proof	45,000	Value: 6.00				
1996G	—	—	—	—	5.00	—
1996G Proof	45,000	Value: 6.00				
1996J	—	—	—	—	5.00	—
1996J Proof	45,000	Value: 6.00				
1997A	70,000	—	—	—	4.25	—
Note: In sets only						
1997A Proof	45,000	Value: 5.00				
1997D	70,000	—	—	—	4.25	—
Note: In sets only						
1997D Proof	45,000	Value: 5.00				
1997F	70,000	—	—	—	4.25	—
Note: In sets only						
1997F Proof	45,000	Value: 5.00				
1997G	70,000	—	—	—	4.25	—
Note: In sets only						
1997G Proof	45,000	Value: 5.00				
1997J	70,000	—	—	—	4.25	—
Note: In sets only						
1997J Proof	45,000	Value: 5.00				
1998A	70,000	—	—	—	4.25	—
Note: In sets only						
1998A Proof	45,000	Value: 5.00				
1998D	70,000	—	—	—	4.25	—
Note: In sets only						
1998D Proof	45,000	Value: 5.00				
1998F	70,000	—	—	—	4.25	—
Note: In sets only						
1998F Proof	45,000	Value: 5.00				
1998G	70,000	—	—	—	4.25	—
Note: In sets only						
1998G Proof	45,000	Value: 5.00				
1998J	70,000	—	—	—	4.25	—
Note: In sets only						
1998J Proof	45,000	Value: 5.00				
1999A	70,000	—	—	—	4.25	—
Note: In sets only						
1999A Proof	45,000	Value: 5.00				
1999D	70,000	—	—	—	4.25	—
Note: In sets only						
1999D Proof	45,000	Value: 5.00				
1999F	70,000	—	—	—	4.25	—
Note: In sets only						
1999F Proof	45,000	Value: 5.00				
1999G	70,000	—	—	—	4.75	—
Note: In sets only						
1999G Proof	45,000	Value: 5.00				
1999J	70,000	—	—	—	4.75	—
Note: In sets only						
1999J Proof	45,000	Value: 5.00				
2000A	70,000	—	—	—	5.00	—
Note: In sets only						
2000A Proof	45,000	Value: 5.00				
2000D	70,000	—	—	—	5.00	—
Note: In sets only						
2000D Proof	45,000	Value: 5.00				
2000F	70,000	—	—	—	5.00	—
Note: In sets only						
2000F Proof	45,000	Value: 5.00				
2000G	70,000	—	—	—	5.00	—
Note: In sets only						
2000G Proof	45,000	Value: 5.00				
2000J	70,000	—	—	—	5.00	—
Note: In sets only						
2000J Proof	45,000	Value: 5.00				
2001A	130,000	—	—	—	10.00	—
Note: In sets only						
2001A Proof	78,000	Value: 10.00				
2001D	130,000	—	—	—	10.00	—
Note: In sets only						
2001D Proof	78,000	Value: 10.00				
2001F	130,000	—	—	—	10.00	—
Note: In sets only						
2001F Proof	78,000	Value: 10.00				
2001G	130,000	—	—	—	10.00	—
Note: In sets only						
2001G Proof	78,000	Value: 10.00				
2001J	130,000	—	—	—	10.00	—
Note: In sets only						
2001J Proof	78,000	Value: 10.00				

KM# 175 2 MARK

7.0000 g., Copper-Nickel Clad Nickel, 26.75 mm. **Subject:** Franz Joseph Strauss **Obv:** Eagle above denomination **Rev:** Head left divides dates

Date	Mintage	F	VF	XF	Unc	BU
1990D	18,370,000	—	—	—	1.75	—
1990D Proof	45,000	Value: 2.25				
1990F	21,200,000	—	—	—	1.75	—
1990F Proof	45,000	Value: 2.25				
1990G	12,220,000	—	—	—	1.75	—
1990G Proof	45,000	Value: 2.25				
1990J	18,870,000	—	—	—	1.75	—

Date	Mintage	F	VF	XF	Unc	BU
1990J Proof	45,000	Value: 2.25				
1991A	4,000,000	—	—	—	1.75	—
1991A Proof	45,000	Value: 2.25				
1991D	4,200,000	—	—	—	1.75	—
1991D Proof	45,000	Value: 2.25				
1991F	4,800,000	—	—	—	1.75	—
1991F Proof	45,000	Value: 2.25				
1991G	2,800,000	—	—	—	1.75	—
1991G Proof	45,000	Value: 2.25				
1991J	4,200,000	—	—	—	1.75	—
1991J Proof	45,000	Value: 2.25				
1992A	7,330,000	—	—	—	1.75	—
1992A Proof	45,000	Value: 2.25				
1992D	7,700,000	—	—	—	1.75	—
1992D Proof	45,000	Value: 2.25				
1992F	8,800,000	—	—	—	1.75	—
1992F Proof	45,000	Value: 2.25				
1992G	5,130,000	—	—	—	1.75	—
1992G Proof	45,000	Value: 2.25				
1992J	7,700,000	—	—	—	1.75	—
1992J Proof	45,000	Value: 2.25				
1993A	600,000	—	—	3.00	7.00	—
1993A Proof	45,000	Value: 2.25				
1993D	630,000	—	—	3.00	7.00	—
1993D Proof	45,000	Value: 2.25				
1993F	720,000	—	—	3.00	7.00	—
1993F Proof	45,000	Value: 2.25				
1993G	420,000	—	—	4.00	10.00	—
1993G Proof	45,000	Value: 2.25				
1993J	630,000	—	—	3.00	7.00	—
1993J Proof	45,000	Value: 2.25				
1994A	5,000,000	—	—	—	1.75	—
1994A Proof	45,000	Value: 2.25				
1994D	5,250,000	—	—	—	1.75	—
1994D Proof	45,000	Value: 2.25				
1994F	6,000,000	—	—	—	1.75	—
1994F Proof	45,000	Value: 2.25				
1994G	3,500,000	—	—	—	1.75	—
1994G Proof	45,000	Value: 2.25				
1994J	5,250,000	—	—	—	1.75	—
1994J Proof	45,000	Value: 2.25				
1995A	1,595,000	—	—	—	3.50	—
1995A Proof	45,000	Value: 17.50				
1995D	20,000	—	—	—	60.00	—
Note: In sets only						
1995D Proof	45,000	Value: 17.50				
1995F	20,000	—	—	—	60.00	—
Note: In sets only						
1995F Proof	45,000	Value: 17.50				
1995G	620,000	—	—	—	7.00	—
1995G Proof	45,000	Value: 17.50				
1995J	20,000	—	—	—	60.00	—
Note: In sets only						
1995J Proof	45,000	Value: 17.50				
1996A	—	—	—	—	5.00	—
1996A Proof	45,000	Value: 6.00				
1996D	—	—	—	—	5.00	—
1996D Proof	45,000	Value: 6.00				
1996F	—	—	—	—	5.00	—
1996F Proof	45,000	Value: 6.00				
1996G	—	—	—	—	5.00	—
1996G Proof	45,000	Value: 6.00				
1996J	—	—	—	—	5.00	—
1996J Proof	45,000	Value: 6.00				
1997A	70,000	—	—	—	4.25	—
Note: In sets only						
1997A Proof	45,000	Value: 5.00				
1997D	70,000	—	—	—	4.25	—
Note: In sets only						
1997D Proof	45,000	Value: 5.00				
1997F	70,000	—	—	—	4.25	—
Note: In sets only						
1997F Proof	45,000	Value: 5.00				
1997G	70,000	—	—	—	4.25	—
Note: In sets only						
1997G Proof	45,000	Value: 5.00				
1997J	70,000	—	—	—	4.25	—
Note: In sets only						
1997J Proof	45,000	Value: 5.00				
1998A	70,000	—	—	—	4.25	—
Note: In sets only						
1998A Proof	45,000	Value: 5.00				
1998D	70,000	—	—	—	4.25	—
Note: In sets only						
1998D Proof	45,000	Value: 5.00				
1998F	70,000	—	—	—	4.25	—
Note: In sets only						
1998F Proof	45,000	Value: 5.00				
1998G	70,000	—	—	—	4.25	—
Note: In sets only						
1998G Proof	45,000	Value: 5.00				
1998J	70,000	—	—	—	4.25	—
Note: In sets only						
1998J Proof	45,000	Value: 5.00				
1999A	70,000	—	—	—	4.25	—
Note: In sets only						
1999A Proof	45,000	Value: 5.00				
1999D	70,000	—	—	—	4.25	—
Note: In sets only						
1999D Proof	45,000	Value: 5.00				
1999F	70,000	—	—	—	4.25	—
Note: In sets only						
1999F Proof	45,000	Value: 5.00				
1999G	70,000	—	—	—	4.25	—
Note: In sets only						
1999G Proof	45,000	Value: 5.00				
1999J	70,000	—	—	—	4.25	—
Note: In sets only						
1999J Proof	45,000	Value: 5.00				
2000A	70,000	—	—	—	5.00	—
Note: In sets only						
2000A Proof	45,000	Value: 5.00				
2000D	70,000	—	—	—	5.00	—
Note: In sets only						
2000D Proof	45,000	Value: 5.00				
2000F	70,000	—	—	—	5.00	—
Note: In sets only						
2000F Proof	45,000	Value: 5.00				
2000G	70,000	—	—	—	5.00	—
Note: In sets only						
2000G Proof	45,000	Value: 5.00				
2000J	70,000	—	—	—	5.00	—
Note: In sets only						
2000J Proof	45,000	Value: 5.00				
2001A	130,000	—	—	—	10.00	—
Note: In sets only						
2001A Proof	78,000	Value: 10.00				
2001D	130,000	—	—	—	10.00	—
Note: In sets only						
2001D Proof	78,000	Value: 10.00				
2001F	130,000	—	—	—	10.00	—
Note: In sets only						
2001F Proof	78,000	Value: 10.00				
2001G	130,000	—	—	—	10.00	—
Note: In sets only						
2001G Proof	78,000	Value: 10.00				
2001J	130,000	—	—	—	10.00	—
Note: In sets only						
2001J Proof	78,000	Value: 10.00				

KM# 183 2 MARK

7.0000 g., Copper-Nickel Clad Nickel, 26.75 mm. **Subject:** Willy Brandt **Obv:** Eagle above denomination **Rev:** Head facing divides dates

Date	Mintage	F	VF	XF	Unc	BU
1994A	5,000,000	—	—	—	2.00	—
1994A Proof	45,000	Value: 2.50				
1994D	5,250,000	—	—	—	2.00	—
1994D Proof	45,000	Value: 2.50				
1994F	6,000,000	—	—	—	2.00	—
1994F Proof	45,000	Value: 2.50				
1994G	3,600,000	—	—	—	2.00	—
1994G Proof	45,000	Value: 2.50				
1994J	5,250,000	—	—	—	2.00	—
1994J Proof	45,000	Value: 2.50				
1995A	1,595,000	—	—	—	3.50	—
1995A Proof	45,000	Value: 17.50				
1995D	20,000	—	—	—	65.00	—
Note: In sets only						
1995D Proof	45,000	Value: 17.50				
1995F	20,000	—	—	—	65.00	—
Note: In sets only						
1995F Proof	45,000	Value: 17.50				
1995G	1,220,000	—	—	—	4.50	—
1995G Proof	45,000	Value: 17.50				
1995J	75,000	—	—	—	30.00	—
1995J Proof	45,000	Value: 17.50				
1996A	—	—	—	—	5.50	—
1996A Proof	45,000	Value: 6.50				
1996D	—	—	—	—	5.50	—
1996D Proof	45,000	Value: 6.50				
1996F	—	—	—	—	5.50	—
1996F Proof	45,000	Value: 6.50				
1996G	—	—	—	—	5.50	—
1996G Proof	45,000	Value: 6.50				
1996J	—	—	—	—	5.50	—
1996J Proof	45,000	Value: 6.50				
1997A	70,000	—	—	—	4.25	—
Note: In sets only						
1997A Proof	45,000	Value: 5.00				
1997D	70,000	—	—	—	4.25	—
Note: In sets only						
1997D Proof	45,000	Value: 5.00				
1997F	70,000	—	—	—	4.25	—
Note: In sets only						
1997F Proof	45,000	Value: 5.00				
1997G	70,000	—	—	—	4.25	—
Note: In sets only						
1997G Proof	45,000	Value: 5.00				
1997J	70,000	—	—	—	4.25	—
Note: In sets only						
1997J Proof	45,000	Value: 5.00				
1998A	70,000	—	—	—	4.25	—
Note: In sets only						
1998A Proof	45,000	Value: 5.00				
1998D	70,000	—	—	—	4.25	—
Note: In sets only						
1998D Proof	45,000	Value: 5.00				
1998F	70,000	—	—	—	4.25	—
Note: In sets only						
1998F Proof	45,000	Value: 5.00				
1998G	70,000	—	—	—	4.25	—
Note: In sets only						
1998G Proof	45,000	Value: 5.00				
1998J	70,000	—	—	—	4.25	—
Note: In sets only						
1998J Proof	45,000	Value: 5.00				
1999A	70,000	—	—	—	4.25	—
Note: In sets only						
1999A Proof	45,000	Value: 5.00				
1999D	70,000	—	—	—	4.25	—
Note: In sets only						
1999D Proof	45,000	Value: 5.00				
1999F	70,000	—	—	—	4.25	—
Note: In sets only						
1999F Proof	45,000	Value: 5.00				
1999G	70,000	—	—	—	4.25	—
Note: In sets only						
1999G Proof	45,000	Value: 5.00				
1999J	70,000	—	—	—	4.25	—
Note: In sets only						
1999J Proof	45,000	Value: 5.00				
2000A	70,000	—	—	—	5.00	—
Note: In sets only						
2000A Proof	45,000	Value: 5.00				
2000D	70,000	—	—	—	5.00	—
Note: In sets only						
2000D Proof	45,000	Value: 5.00				
2000F	70,000	—	—	—	5.00	—
Note: In sets only						
2000F Proof	45,000	Value: 5.00				
2000G	70,000	—	—	—	5.00	—
Note: In sets only						
2000G Proof	45,000	Value: 5.00				
2000J	70,000	—	—	—	5.00	—
Note: In sets only						
2000J Proof	45,000	Value: 5.00				
2001A	130,000	—	—	—	10.00	—
Note: In sets only						
2001A Proof	78,000	Value: 10.00				
2001D	130,000	—	—	—	10.00	—
Note: In sets only						
2001D Proof	78,000	Value: 10.00				
2001F	130,000	—	—	—	10.00	—
Note: In sets only						
2001F Proof	78,000	Value: 10.00				
2001G	130,000	—	—	—	10.00	—
Note: In sets only						
2001G Proof	78,000	Value: 10.00				
2001J	130,000	—	—	—	10.00	—
Note: In sets only						
2001J Proof	78,000	Value: 10.00				

KM# 112.1 5 MARK

11.2000 g., 0.6250 Silver 0.2250 oz. ASW, 29 mm. **Obv:** Denomination above date **Rev:** Large eagle

Date	Mintage	F	VF	XF	Unc	BU
1951D	20,600,000	—	4.00	15.00	65.00	—
1951D Proof	—	Value: 425				
1951F	24,000,000	—	4.00	15.00	75.00	—
1951F Proof	280	Value: 350				
1951G	13,840,000	—	4.00	20.00	125	—
1951G Proof	—	Value: 950				
1951J	21,360,000	—	4.00	15.00	60.00	—
1951J Proof	—	Value: 245				
1956D	1,092,000	2.00	15.00	60.00	275	—
1956D Proof	—	Value: 1,500				
1956F	1,200,000	—	10.00	75.00	475	—
1956F Proof	23	Value: 2,500				
1956J	1,068,000	—	10.00	50.00	250	—
1956J Proof	—	Value: 2,750				
1957D	566,000	—	10.00	65.00	300	—
1957D Proof	—	—	—	—	—	—
1957F	2,100,000	—	7.50	50.00	300	—
1957F Proof	—	Value: 2,500				
1957G	692,000	—	10.00	75.00	650	—
1957G Proof	—	Value: 3,500				
1957J	1,630,000	—	7.50	35.00	225	—
1957J Proof	—	—	—	—	—	—
1958D	1,226,000	—	7.50	30.00	150	—

Date	Mintage	F	VF	XF	Unc	BU
1958D Proof	—	—	—	—	—	—
1958F	600,000	2.00	20.00	145	800	—
1958F Proof	100	Value: 1,350				
1958G	1,557,000	—	7.50	28.00	140	—
1958G Proof	—	—	—	—	—	—
1958J	60,000	—	1,100	2,500	4,250	—
1958J Proof	—	Value: 7,000				
1959D	496,000	—	10.00	45.00	325	—
1959D Proof	—	Value: 1,250				
1959G	692,000	—	15.00	45.00	285	—
1959G Proof	—	Value: 1,500				
1959J	713,000	—	8.00	40.00	300	—
1959J Proof	—	Value: 2,000				
1960D	1,040,000	—	7.00	20.00	110	—
1960D Proof	—	Value: 1,250				
1960F	1,576,000	—	7.00	20.00	135	—
1960F Proof	50	Value: 1,250				
1960G	692,000	—	7.00	22.00	125	—
1960G Proof	—	Value: 750				
1960J	1,618,000	—	7.00	18.00	90.00	—
1960J Proof	—	—	—	—	—	—
1961D	1,040,000	—	4.50	20.00	100	—
1961D Proof	—	Value: 450				
1961F	824,000	—	4.50	22.00	200	—
1961F Proof	—	Value: 2,200				
1961J	518,000	—	6.00	28.00	165	—
1961J Proof	—	Value: 3,000				
1963D	2,080,000	—	4.50	15.00	60.00	—
1963D Proof	—	—	—	—	—	—
1963F	1,254,000	—	4.50	18.00	75.00	—
1963F Proof	—	Value: 2,500				
1963G	600,000	—	7.50	20.00	90.00	—
1963G Proof	Est. 100	Value: 500				
1963J	2,136,000	—	4.50	15.00	60.00	—
1963J Proof	—	Value: 3,000				
1964D	456,000	—	15.00	50.00	175	—
1964D Proof	—	Value: 3,250				
1964F	2,646,000	—	4.50	15.00	60.00	—
1964F Proof	—	Value: 2,500				
1964G	1,649,000	—	4.50	15.00	60.00	—
1964G Proof	Est. 600	Value: 450				
1964J	1,335,000	—	4.00	15.00	65.00	—
1964J Proof	—	Value: 2,750				
1965D	4,354,000	—	4.00	12.50	30.00	—
1965D Proof	—	Value: 4,000				
1965F	4,050,000	—	4.00	8.00	30.00	—
1965F Proof	Est. 80	Value: 1,000				
1965G	2,335,000	—	4.00	7.00	25.00	—
1965G Proof	8,233	Value: 50.00				
1965J	3,605,000	—	4.00	7.00	25.00	—
1965J Proof	—	Value: 3,250				
1966D	5,200,000	—	4.00	7.00	22.50	—
1966D Proof	—	Value: 4,000				
1966F	6,000,000	—	4.00	7.00	22.50	—
1966F Proof	100	Value: 1,000				
1966G	3,460,000	—	4.00	7.00	22.50	—
1966G Proof	3,070	Value: 50.00				
1966J	5,340,000	—	4.00	7.00	22.50	—
1966J Proof	1,000	Value: 125				
1967D	3,120,000	—	4.00	7.00	22.50	—
1967D Proof	—	Value: 4,000				
1967F	3,598,000	—	4.00	7.00	22.50	—
1967F Proof	1,500	Value: 110				
1967G	1,406,000	—	4.00	7.00	25.00	—
1967G Proof	4,500	Value: 40.00				
1967J	3,204,000	—	4.00	7.00	22.50	—
Note: Errors exist with coin alignment						
1967J Proof	1,500	Value: 100				
1968D	1,300,000	—	4.00	10.00	35.00	—
1968D Proof	—	Value: 4,000				
1968F	1,497,000	—	4.00	10.00	35.00	—
1968F Proof	3,000	Value: 125				
1968G	1,535,000	—	4.00	10.00	35.00	—
1968G Proof	6,023	Value: 50.00				
1968J	1,335,000	—	4.00	10.00	35.00	—
1968J Proof	2,000	Value: 125				
1969D	2,080,000	—	4.00	7.00	20.00	—
1969D Proof	—	Value: 35.00				
1969F	2,395,000	—	4.00	7.00	20.00	—
1969F Proof	5,000	Value: 35.00				
1969G	3,484,000	—	4.00	7.00	20.00	—
1969G Proof	8,700	Value: 30.00				
1969J	2,136,000	—	4.00	7.00	20.00	—
1969J Proof	5,000	Value: 30.00				
1970D	2,000,000	—	4.00	7.00	20.00	—
1970D Proof	—	Value: 30.00				
1970F	1,995,000	—	4.00	7.00	20.00	—
1970F Proof	5,140	Value: 25.00				
1970G	6,000,000	—	3.50	4.50	10.00	—
1970G Proof	10,200	Value: 22.00				
1970J	4,000,000	—	3.50	4.50	10.00	—
1970J Proof	5,000	Value: 25.00				
1971D	4,000,000	—	3.50	4.50	10.00	—
1971D Proof	8,000	Value: 22.00				
1971F	3,993,000	—	3.50	4.50	10.00	—
1971F Proof	8,000	Value: 22.00				
1971G	6,010,000	—	3.50	4.50	10.00	—
1971G Proof	10,000	Value: 22.00				
1971J	6,000,000	—	3.50	4.50	10.00	—
1971J Proof	8,000	Value: 22.00				
1972D	3,000,000	—	3.50	4.50	12.00	—
1972D Proof	8,000	Value: 22.00				
1972F	8,992,000	—	3.50	4.50	10.00	—
1972F Proof	8,100	Value: 22.00				
1972G	4,999,000	—	3.50	4.50	10.00	—
1972G Proof	10,000	Value: 22.00				
1972J	6,000,000	—	3.50	4.50	10.00	—
1972J Proof	8,000	Value: 22.00				
1973D	3,380,000	—	3.50	4.50	10.00	—
1973D Proof	9,000	Value: 22.00				
1973F	3,891,000	—	3.50	4.50	8.50	—
1973F Proof	9,100	Value: 22.00				
1973G	2,240,000	—	3.50	4.50	8.50	—
1973G Proof	9,000	Value: 22.00				
1973J	5,571,000	—	3.50	4.50	8.50	—
1973J Proof	9,000	Value: 22.00				
1974D	4,594,000	—	3.50	4.50	8.50	—
1974D Proof	35,000	Value: 22.00				
1974F	6,514,000	—	3.50	4.50	8.50	—
1974F Proof	35,000	Value: 22.00				
1974G	3,708,000	—	3.50	4.50	8.50	—
1974G Proof	35,000	Value: 22.00				
1974J	2,968,000	—	3.50	4.50	8.50	—
1974J Proof	35,000	Value: 22.00				

KM# 112.3 5 MARK

11.2000 g., 0.6250 Silver 0.2250 oz. ASW, 29 mm. **Obv:** Denomination **Rev:** Large eagle **Note:** Error. With edge lettering: GRUSS DICH DEUTSCHLAND AUS HERZENSGRUND.

Date	Mintage	F	VF	XF	Unc	BU
1957J	Inc. above	—	1,250	1,650	2,400	—

KM# 112.2 5 MARK

11.2000 g., 0.6250 Silver 0.2250 oz. ASW, 29 mm. **Obv:** Denomination **Rev:** Large eagle **Note:** Uninscribed plain edge errors.

Date	Mintage	F	VF	XF	Unc	BU
1959D	Inc. above	—	65.00	125	200	—
1959J	Inc. above	—	65.00	125	200	—
1963J	Inc. above	—	65.00	125	200	—
1964F	Inc. above	—	65.00	125	200	—
1964G	Inc. above	—	—	—	—	—
1965F	Inc. above	—	65.00	125	200	—
1965J	Inc. above	—	—	—	—	—
1965G	Inc. above	—	65.00	125	200	—
1966F	Inc. above	—	125	250	350	—
1966G	Inc. above	—	65.00	125	200	—
Note: Errors without edge inscription exist with coin alignment						
1967D	Inc. above	—	125	250	350	—
1967G	Inc. above	—	65.00	125	200	—
1969F	Inc. above	—	—	—	—	—
1970F	Inc. above	—	—	—	—	—
1970G	Inc. above	—	—	—	—	—
1971F	Inc. above	—	—	—	—	—
1972F	Inc. above	—	—	—	—	—
1973F	Inc. above	—	—	—	—	—
1974F	Inc. above	—	—	—	—	—

KM# 112.4 5 MARK

11.2000 g., 0.6250 Silver 0.2250 oz. ASW, 29 mm. **Obv:** Denomination **Rev:** Large eagle **Note:** Error. With edge lettering: ALLE MENSCHEN WERDEN BRUDER.

Date	Mintage	F	VF	XF	Unc	BU
1970F	—	—	1,250	1,650	2,400	—

KM# 140.1 5 MARK

10.0000 g., Copper-Nickel Clad Nickel, 29 mm. **Obv:** Denomination within rounded square **Rev:** Eagle above date

Date	Mintage	F	VF	XF	Unc	BU
1975D	65,663,000	—	—	3.50	4.50	—
Note: Error strikes exist without edge inscription						
1975D Proof	43,000	Value: 7.00				
1975F	75,002,000	—	—	3.50	4.50	—
Note: Error strikes exist without edge inscription						
1975F Proof	43,000	Value: 7.00				
1975G	43,297,000	—	—	3.50	4.50	—
1975G Proof	43,000	Value: 7.00				
1975J	67,372,000	—	—	3.50	4.50	—
1975J Proof	43,000	Value: 7.00				
1976D	7,821,000	—	—	3.50	5.00	—
1976D Proof	43,000	Value: 7.00				
1976F	9,072,000	—	—	3.50	5.00	—
1976F Proof	43,000	Value: 7.00				
1976G	5,784,000	—	—	3.50	5.00	—
1976G Proof	43,000	Value: 7.00				
1976J	8,068,000	—	—	3.50	5.00	—
1976J Proof	43,000	Value: 7.00				
1977D	8,321,000	—	—	3.50	5.00	—
1977D Proof	51,000	Value: 6.00				
1977F	9,612,000	—	—	3.50	5.00	—
1977F Proof	51,000	Value: 6.00				
1977G	5,746,000	—	—	3.50	5.00	—
1977G Proof	51,000	Value: 6.00				
1977J	8,577,000	—	—	3.50	5.00	—
1977J Proof	51,000	Value: 6.00				
1978D	7,854,000	—	—	3.50	5.00	—
1978D Proof	54,000	Value: 6.00				
1978F	9,054,000	—	—	3.50	5.00	—
1978F Proof	54,000	Value: 6.00				
1978G	5,244,000	—	—	3.50	5.00	—
1978G Proof	54,000	Value: 6.00				
1978J	8,064,000	—	—	3.50	5.00	—
1978J Proof	54,000	Value: 6.00				
1979D	7,889,000	—	—	3.50	5.00	—
1979D Proof	89,000	Value: 6.00				
1979F	9,089,000	—	—	3.50	5.00	—
1979F Proof	89,000	Value: 6.00				
1979G	5,279,000	—	—	3.50	5.00	—
1979G Proof	89,000	Value: 6.00				
1979J	8,099,000	—	—	3.50	5.00	—
1979J Proof	89,000	Value: 6.00				
1980D	8,300,000	—	—	3.50	5.00	—
1980D Proof	110,000	Value: 6.00				
1980F	9,640,000	—	—	3.50	5.00	—
1980F Proof	110,000	Value: 6.00				
1980G	5,500,000	—	—	3.50	5.00	—
1980G Proof	110,000	Value: 6.00				
1980J	8,500,000	—	—	3.50	5.00	—
1980J Proof	110,000	Value: 6.00				
1981D	8,300,000	—	—	3.50	5.00	—
1981D Proof	91,000	Value: 7.00				
1981F	9,600,000	—	—	3.50	5.00	—
1981F Proof	91,000	Value: 7.00				
1981G	5,500,000	—	—	3.50	5.00	—
1981G Proof	91,000	Value: 7.00				
1981J	8,500,000	—	—	3.50	5.00	—
1981J Proof	91,000	Value: 7.00				
1982D	8,900,000	—	—	3.50	5.00	—
1982D Proof	78,000	Value: 7.00				
1982F	10,300,000	—	—	3.50	5.00	—
1982F Proof	78,000	Value: 7.00				
1982G	5,990,000	—	—	3.50	5.00	—
1982G Proof	78,000	Value: 7.00				
1982J	9,100,000	—	—	3.50	5.00	—
1982J Proof	78,000	Value: 7.00				
1983D	6,240,000	—	—	3.50	5.00	—
1983D Proof	75,000	Value: 9.00				
1983F	7,200,000	—	—	3.50	5.00	—
1983F Proof	75,000	Value: 9.00				
1983G	4,152,000	—	—	3.50	5.00	—
1983G Proof	75,000	Value: 9.00				
1983J	6,408,000	—	—	3.50	5.00	—
1983J Proof	75,000	Value: 9.00				
1984D	6,000,000	—	—	3.50	5.00	—
1984D Proof	64,000	Value: 9.00				
1984F	6,900,000	—	—	3.50	5.00	—
1984F Proof	64,000	Value: 9.00				
1984G	4,000,000	—	—	3.50	5.00	—
1984G Proof	64,000	Value: 9.00				
1984J	6,100,000	—	—	3.50	5.00	—
1984J Proof	64,000	Value: 9.00				
1985D	4,900,000	—	—	3.50	6.00	—
1985D Proof	56,000	Value: 10.00				
1985F	5,700,000	—	—	3.50	6.00	—
1985F Proof	54,000	Value: 10.00				
1985G	3,300,000	—	—	3.50	6.00	—
1985G Proof	55,000	Value: 10.00				
1985J	5,100,000	—	—	3.50	6.00	—
1985J Proof	54,000	Value: 10.00				
1986D	4,900,000	—	—	3.50	7.00	—
1986D Proof	44,000	Value: 20.00				
1986F	5,700,000	—	—	3.50	7.00	—
1986F Proof	44,000	Value: 20.00				
1986G	3,300,000	—	—	3.50	7.00	—
1986G Proof	44,000	Value: 25.00				
1986J	5,100,000	—	—	3.50	7.00	—
1986J Proof	44,000	Value: 20.00				
1987D	6,760,000	—	—	3.50	6.00	—
1987D Proof	45,000	Value: 10.00				
1987F	7,800,000	—	—	3.50	6.00	—
1987F Proof	45,000	Value: 10.00				
1987G	4,500,000	—	—	3.50	6.00	—
1987G Proof	45,000	Value: 10.00				
1987J	6,940,000	—	—	3.50	6.00	—
1987J Proof	45,000	Value: 10.00				
1988D	11,960,000	—	—	—	5.00	—
1988D Proof	45,000	Value: 12.00				
1988F	13,800,000	—	—	—	5.00	—
1988F Proof	45,000	Value: 12.00				
1988G	7,960,000	—	—	—	5.00	—
1988G Proof	45,000	Value: 12.00				
1988J	12,280,000	—	—	—	5.00	—
1988J Proof	45,000	Value: 12.00				
1989D	17,160,000	—	—	—	5.00	—
1989D Proof	45,000	Value: 12.00				
1989F	19,800,000	—	—	—	5.00	—
1989F Proof	45,000	Value: 12.00				
1989G	11,420,000	—	—	—	5.00	—
1989G Proof	45,000	Value: 12.00				
1989J	17,620,000	—	—	—	5.00	—
1989J Proof	45,000	Value: 12.00				
1990D	20,900,000	—	—	—	5.00	—
1990D Proof	45,000	Value: 10.00				
1990F	24,120,000	—	—	—	5.00	—
1990F Proof	45,000	Value: 10.00				
1990G	13,910,000	—	—	—	5.00	—
1990G Proof	45,000	Value: 10.00				

Date	Mintage	F	VF	XF	Unc	BU
1990J	21,470,000	—	—	—	5.00	—
1990J Proof	45,000	Value: 10.00				
1991A	18,000,000	—	—	—	5.00	—
1991A Proof	45,000	Value: 7.00				
1991D	18,900,000	—	—	—	5.00	—
1991D Proof	45,000	Value: 7.00				
1991F	21,600,000	—	—	—	5.00	—
1991F Proof	45,000	Value: 7.00				
1991G	12,600,000	—	—	—	5.00	—
1991G Proof	45,000	Value: 7.00				
1991J	18,900,000	—	—	—	5.00	—
1991J Proof	45,000	Value: 7.00				
1992A	16,000,000	—	—	—	5.00	—
1992A Proof	45,000	Value: 7.00				
1992D	16,800,000	—	—	—	5.00	—
1992D Proof	45,000	Value: 7.00				
1992F	19,200,000	—	—	—	5.00	—
1992F Proof	45,000	Value: 7.00				
1992G	11,200,000	—	—	—	5.00	—
1992G Proof	45,000	Value: 7.00				
1992J	16,800,000	—	—	—	5.00	—
1992J Proof	45,000	Value: 7.00				
1993A	3,200,000	—	—	—	6.00	—
1993A Proof	45,000	Value: 10.00				
1993D	3,380,000	—	—	—	6.00	—
1993D Proof	45,000	Value: 10.00				
1993F	3,840,000	—	—	—	6.00	—
1993F Proof	45,000	Value: 10.00				
1993G	2,240,000	—	—	—	6.00	—
1993G Proof	45,000	Value: 10.00				
1993J	3,360,000	—	—	—	6.00	—
1993J Proof	45,000	Value: 10.00				
1994A	4,000,000	—	—	—	5.00	—
1994A Proof	45,000	Value: 10.00				
1994D	4,200,000	—	—	—	5.00	—
1994D Proof	45,000	Value: 10.00				
1994F	4,800,000	—	—	—	5.00	—
1994F Proof	45,000	Value: 10.00				
1994G	2,800,000	—	—	—	5.00	—
1994G Proof	45,000	Value: 10.00				
1994J	4,200,000	—	—	—	5.00	—
1994J Proof	45,000	Value: 10.00				
1995A	20,000	—	—	—	80.00	—
Note: In sets only						
1995A Proof	45,000	Value: 30.00				
1995D	20,000	—	—	—	80.00	—
Note: In sets only						
1995D Proof	45,000	Value: 30.00				
1995F	20,000	—	—	—	80.00	—
Note: In sets only						
1995F Proof	45,000	Value: 30.00				
1995G	20,000	—	—	—	80.00	—
Note: In sets only						
1995G Proof	45,000	Value: 30.00				
1995J	20,000	—	—	—	80.00	—
Note: In sets only						
1995J Proof	45,000	Value: 30.00				
1996A	50,000	—	—	—	15.00	—
Note: In sets only						
1996A Proof	45,000	Value: 17.50				
1996D	50,000	—	—	—	15.00	—
Note: In sets only						
1996D Proof	45,000	Value: 17.50				
1996F	50,000	—	—	—	15.00	—
Note: In sets only						
1996F Proof	45,000	Value: 17.50				
1996G	50,000	—	—	—	15.00	—
Note: In sets only						
1996G Proof	45,000	Value: 17.50				
1996J	50,000	—	—	—	15.00	—
Note: In sets only						
1996J Proof	45,000	Value: 17.50				
1997A	70,000	—	—	—	6.00	—
Note: In sets only						
1997A Proof	45,000	Value: 7.00				
1997D	70,000	—	—	—	6.00	—
Note: In sets only						
1997D Proof	45,000	Value: 7.00				
1997F	70,000	—	—	—	6.00	—
Note: In sets only						
1997F Proof	45,000	Value: 7.00				
1997G	70,000	—	—	—	6.00	—
Note: In sets only						
1997G Proof	45,000	Value: 7.00				
1997J	70,000	—	—	—	6.00	—
Note: In sets only						
1997J Proof	45,000	Value: 7.00				
1998A	70,000	—	—	—	6.00	—
Note: In sets only						
1998A Proof	45,000	Value: 7.00				
1998D	70,000	—	—	—	6.00	—
Note: In sets only						
1998D Proof	45,000	Value: 7.00				
1998F	70,000	—	—	—	6.00	—
Note: In sets only						
1998F Proof	45,000	Value: 7.00				
1998G	70,000	—	—	—	6.00	—
Note: In sets only						
1998G Proof	45,000	Value: 7.00				
1998J	70,000	—	—	—	6.00	—
Note: In sets only						
1998J Proof	45,000	Value: 7.00				
1999A	70,000	—	—	—	6.00	—
Note: In sets only						
1999A Proof	45,000	Value: 7.00				
1999D	70,000	—	—	—	6.00	—
Note: In sets only						
1999D Proof	45,000	Value: 7.00				
1999F	70,000	—	—	—	6.00	—
Note: In sets only						
1999F Proof	45,000	Value: 7.00				
1999G	70,000	—	—	—	6.00	—
Note: In sets only						
1999G Proof	45,000	Value: 7.00				
1999J	70,000	—	—	—	6.00	—
Note: In sets only						
1999J Proof	45,000	Value: 7.00				
2000A	70,000	—	—	—	15.00	—
Note: In sets only						
2000A Proof	45,000	Value: 15.00				
2000D	70,000	—	—	—	15.00	—
Note: In sets only						
2000D Proof	45,000	Value: 15.00				
2000F	70,000	—	—	—	15.00	—
Note: In sets only						
2000F Proof	45,000	Value: 15.00				
2000G	70,000	—	—	—	15.00	—
Note: In sets only						
2000G Proof	45,000	Value: 15.00				
2000J	70,000	—	—	—	15.00	—
Note: In sets only						
2000J Proof	45,000	Value: 15.00				
2001A	130,000	—	—	—	30.00	—
Note: In sets only						
2001A Proof	78,000	Value: 30.00				
2001D	130,000	—	—	—	30.00	—
Note: In sets only						
2001D Proof	78,000	Value: 30.00				
2001F	130,000	—	—	—	30.00	—
Note: In sets only						
2001F Proof	78,000	Value: 30.00				
2001G	130,000	—	—	—	30.00	—
Note: In sets only						
2001G Proof	78,000	Value: 30.00				
2001J	130,000	—	—	—	30.00	—
Note: In sets only						
2001J Proof	78,000	Value: 30.00				

KM# 140.2 5 MARK

5.4400 g., Copper-Nickel Clad Nickel, 29 mm. **Obv:** Denomination within rounded square **Rev:** Eagle **Note:** Thin variety.

Date	Mintage	F	VF	XF	Unc	BU
1975J	—	—	—	90.00	150	—
Note: Illegally produced by a German Mint official						

KM# 140.3 5 MARK

10.0000 g., Copper-Nickel Clad Nickel, 29 mm. **Obv:** Denomination within rounded square **Rev:** Eagle **Note:** Errors without edge inscription.

Date	Mintage	F	VF	XF	Unc	BU
1975D	—	—	—	—	—	—
1975F	—	—	—	—	—	—

COMMEMORATIVE COINAGE

KM# 113 5 MARK

11.2000 g., 0.6250 Silver 0.2250 oz. ASW, 29 mm. **Subject:** Centenary - Nurnberg Museum **Obv:** Eagle below legend **Rev:** Mosaic eagle divides dates

Date	Mintage	F	VF	XF	Unc	BU
1952D	199,000	—	500	700	800	1,200
1952D Proof	1,345	Value: 4,000				

KM# 114 5 MARK

11.2000 g., 0.6250 Silver 0.2250 oz. ASW, 29 mm. **Subject:** 150th Anniversary - Death of Friedrich von Schiller **Obv:** Eagle above denomination **Rev:** Head with high collar right **Edge Lettering:** SE10 EIN16 EIN16 EIN16

Date	Mintage	F	VF	XF	Unc	BU
1955F	199,000	—	260	400	700	800
1955F Proof	1,217	Value: 1,850				

KM# 115 5 MARK

11.2000 g., 0.6250 Silver 0.2250 oz. ASW, 29 mm. **Subject:** 300th Anniversary - Birth of Ludwig von Baden **Obv:** Eagle above denomination, date below **Rev:** Bust, right

Date	Mintage	F	VF	XF	Unc	BU
1955G	198,000	—	260	400	600	600
1955G Proof	Est. 2,000	Value: 1,750				
Note: This coin was restruck without authorization by a mint official using genuine dies - quantity unknown						

KM# 117 5 MARK

11.2000 g., 0.6250 Silver 0.2250 oz. ASW, 29 mm. **Subject:** Centenary - Death of Joseph Freiherr von Eichendorff **Obv:** Eagle divides date at top, denomination below **Rev:** Head with high collar left, dates below

Date	Mintage	F	VF	XF	Unc	BU
1957J	198,000	—	200	380	500	600
1957J Proof	2,000	Value: 1,800				

KM# 118.1 5 MARK

11.2000 g., 0.6250 Silver 0.2250 oz. ASW, 29 mm. **Subject:** 150th Anniversary - Death of Johann Gottlieb Fichte, philosopher **Obv:** Eagle divides date above denomination **Rev:** Head with high collar left, dates below

Date	Mintage	F	VF	XF	Unc	BU
1964J	495,000	—	50.00	75.00	125	—
1964J Proof	5,000	Value: 800				

KM# 118.2 5 MARK

11.2000 g., 0.6250 Silver 0.2250 oz. ASW, 29 mm. **Obv:** Eagle above denomination **Rev:** Head with high collar left **Note:** Error. Plain edge.

Date	Mintage	F	VF	XF	Unc	BU
1964J	—	—	250	500	900	—

KM# 119.1 5 MARK

11.2000 g., 0.6250 Silver 0.2250 oz. ASW, 29 mm. **Subject:** 250th Anniversary - Death of Gottfried Wilhelm Leibniz, philosopher **Obv:** Eagle divides date above, denomination below **Rev:** Head 3/4 facing, dates below

Date	Mintage	F	VF	XF	Unc	BU
1966D	1,940,000	—	7.00	12.00	15.00	20.00
1966D Proof	60,000	Value: 110				

KM# 119.2 5 MARK

11.2000 g., 0.6250 Silver 0.2250 oz. ASW, 29 mm. **Obv:** Eagle divides date, denomination below **Rev:** Head 3/4 facing, dates **Note:** Error. Plain edge.

Date	Mintage	F	VF	XF	Unc	BU
1966D	—	—	225	425	700	—

KM# 120.1 5 MARK

11.2000 g., 0.6250 Silver 0.2250 oz. ASW, 29 mm. **Subject:** Wilhelm and Alexander von Humboldt **Obv:** Eagle above denomination dividing date **Rev:** Conjoined heads; one left and one facing

Date	Mintage	F	VF	XF	Unc	BU
1967F	2,000,000	—	9.00	12.00	15.00	20.00
1967F Proof	60,000	Value: 140				

KM# 120.2 5 MARK

11.2000 g., 0.6250 Silver 0.2250 oz. ASW, 29 mm. **Obv:** Eagle **Rev:** Conjoined heads; one left and one facing **Note:** Error. Plain edge.

Date	Mintage	F	VF	XF	Unc	BU
1967F	—	—	225	425	700	—

KM# 121 5 MARK

11.2000 g., 0.6250 Silver 0.2250 oz. ASW, 29 mm. **Subject:** 150th Anniversary - Birth of Friedrich Raiffeisen **Obv:** Eagle above denomination and date **Rev:** Bust 3/4 facing, dates below

Date	Mintage	F	VF	XF	Unc	BU
1968J	3,860,000	—	3.00	4.50	6.00	8.00
1968J Proof	140,000	Value: 40.00				

KM# 122 5 MARK

11.2000 g., 0.6250 Silver 0.2250 oz. ASW, 29 mm. **Subject:** 500th Anniversary - Death of Johannes Gutenberg **Obv:** Denomination divides date, eagle above **Rev:** Bust 3/4 right, dates below

Date	Mintage	F	VF	XF	Unc	BU
1968G	2,900,000	—	3.50	7.00	9.00	11.00
1968G Proof	100,000	Value: 70.00				

KM# 123.1 5 MARK

11.2000 g., 0.6250 Silver 0.2250 oz. ASW, 29 mm. **Subject:** 150th Anniversary - Birth of Max von Pettenkofer **Obv:** Stylized eagle, denomination above **Rev:** Face 3/4 left, dates below

Date	Mintage	F	VF	XF	Unc	BU
1968D	2,900,000	—	3.50	7.00	9.00	11.00
1968D Proof	100,000	Value: 50.00				

KM# 123.2 5 MARK

11.2000 g., 0.6250 Silver 0.2250 oz. ASW, 29 mm. **Obv:** Stylized eagle, denomination above **Rev:** Face 3/4 left **Note:** Polished devices.

Date	Mintage	F	VF	XF	Unc	BU
1968D Proof	—	Value: 300				

KM# 125.1 5 MARK

11.2000 g., 0.6250 Silver 0.2250 oz. ASW, 29 mm. **Subject:** 150th Anniversary - Birth of Theodor Fontane, writer, poet **Obv:** Eagle divides date, denomination below **Rev:** Head left

Date	Mintage	F	VF	XF	Unc	BU
1969G	2,830,000	—	3.50	7.00	9.00	11.00
1969G Proof	170,000	Value: 35.00				

KM# 125.2 5 MARK

11.2000 g., 0.6250 Silver 0.2250 oz. ASW, 29 mm. **Obv:** Eagle divides date, denomination below **Rev:** Head left **Note:** Error. Incomplete nose and hair.

Date	Mintage	F	VF	XF	Unc	BU
1969G Proof	—	Value: 140				

KM# 126.1 5 MARK

11.2000 g., 0.6250 Silver 0.2250 oz. ASW, 29 mm. **Subject:** 375th Anniversary - Death of Gerhard Mercator **Obv:** Eagle, denomination divides date below **Rev:** Bust with long beard 3/4 right

Date	Mintage	F	VF	XF	Unc	BU
1969F	5,004,000	—	—	—	5.00	6.00
1969F Proof	200,000	Value: 20.00				

KM# 126.2 5 MARK

11.2000 g., 0.6250 Silver 0.2250 oz. ASW, 29 mm. **Obv:** Eagle, denomination divides date below **Rev:** Bust with long beard 3/4 right **Note:** Error. Plain edge.

Date	Mintage	F	VF	XF	Unc	BU
1969F	—	—	250	450	750	—

KM# 126.3 5 MARK

11.2000 g., 0.6250 Silver 0.2250 oz. ASW, 29 mm. **Obv:** Eagle, denomination divides date below **Rev:** Bust with long beard 3/4 right **Note:** Error. With edge lettering: Einigkeit und Recht und Freiheit.

Date	Mintage	F	VF	XF	Unc	BU
1969F	—	—	600	1,000	1,600	—

KM# 126.4 5 MARK

11.2000 g., 0.6250 Silver 0.2250 oz. ASW, 29 mm. **Obv:** Eagle, denomination divides date below **Rev:** Bust with long beard 3/4 right **Note:** Error. With long "R" in "MERCATOR".

Date	Mintage	F	VF	XF	Unc	BU
1969F	—	—	25.00	55.00	100	—

KM# 127 5 MARK

11.2000 g., 0.6250 Silver 0.2250 oz. ASW, 29 mm. **Subject:** 200th Anniversary - Birth of Ludwig van Beethoven, composer **Obv:** Eagle, denomination divides date below **Rev:** Head left, dates below

Date	Mintage	F	VF	XF	Unc	BU
1970F	5,000,000	—	—	3.50	6.00	7.00
1970F Proof	200,000	Value: 18.00				

KM# 128.1 5 MARK

11.2000 g., 0.6250 Silver 0.2250 oz. ASW, 29 mm. **Subject:** Foundation of German Empire, 1871 **Obv:** Eagle divides date above legend, denomination below **Rev:** Reichstag building

Date	Mintage	F	VF	XF	Unc	BU
1971G	5,000,000	—	3.50	5.00	6.00	7.00
1971G Proof	200,000	Value: 20.00				

KM# 128.2 5 MARK

11.2000 g., 0.6250 Silver 0.2250 oz. ASW, 29 mm. **Obv:** Eagle divides date above legend **Rev:** Reichstag building **Note:** Error. With weak window details.

Date	Mintage	F	VF	XF	Unc	BU
1971F Proof	—	Value: 100				

KM# 129 5 MARK

11.2000 g., 0.6250 Silver 0.2250 oz. ASW, 29 mm. **Subject:** 500th Anniversary - Birth of Albrecht Durer **Obv:** Eagle above inscription, date and denomination below **Rev:** Initials above name and dates

Date	Mintage	F	VF	XF	Unc	BU
1971D	8,000,000	—	—	—	4.00	6.00
1971D Proof	200,000	Value: 27.50				

KM# 136 5 MARK

11.2000 g., 0.6250 Silver 0.2250 oz. ASW, 29 mm. **Subject:** 500th Anniversary - Birth of Nicholas Copernicus **Obv:** Eagle in grid form, denomination divides date below **Rev:** Sun at center of rings, planet names descend from top towards center

Date	Mintage	F	VF	XF	Unc	BU
1973J	8,000,000	—	—	—	6.00	7.00
1973J Proof	250,000	Value: 12.00				

KM# 137 5 MARK

11.2000 g., 0.6250 Silver 0.2250 oz. ASW, 29 mm. **Subject:** 125th Anniversary - Frankfurt Parliament **Obv:** Denomination below stylized eagle divides date **Rev:** Date at center of Parliament building

Date	Mintage	F	VF	XF	Unc	BU
1973G	8,000,000	—	—	—	6.00	7.00
1973G Proof	250,000	Value: 12.00				

KM# 138 5 MARK
11.2000 g., 0.6250 Silver 0.2250 oz. ASW, 29 mm. **Subject:** 25th Anniversary - Constitutional Law **Obv:** Fat eagle above date divided by denomination **Rev:** Symbol divides dates

Date	Mintage	F	VF	XF	Unc	BU
1974F	8,000,000	—	—	—	6.00	7.00
1974F Proof	250,000	Value: 12.00				

KM# 139 5 MARK
11.2000 g., 0.6250 Silver 0.2250 oz. ASW, 29 mm. **Subject:** 250th Anniversary - Birth of Immanuel Kant, philosopher **Obv:** Legend divides eagle and denomination **Rev:** Bust at left facing right, name and dates at right

Date	Mintage	F	VF	XF	Unc	BU
1974D	8,000,000	—	—	—	6.00	7.00
1974D Proof	250,000	Value: 14.00				

KM# 141 5 MARK
11.2000 g., 0.6250 Silver 0.2250 oz. ASW, 29 mm. **Subject:** 50th Anniversary - Death of Friedrich Ebert **Obv:** Eagle above denomination, date at right **Rev:** Head left, dates at left

Date	Mintage	F	VF	XF	Unc	BU
1975J	8,000,000	—	—	—	6.00	7.00
1975J Proof	250,000	Value: 14.00				

KM# 142.1 5 MARK
11.2000 g., 0.6250 Silver 0.2250 oz. ASW, 29 mm. **Subject:** European Monument Protection Year **Obv:** Eagle divides date at top, denomination below **Rev:** Patterned designs and two line inscription with date **Note:** 2.1 mm thick.

Date	Mintage	F	VF	XF	Unc	BU
1975F	8,000,000	—	—	—	6.00	7.00
1975F Proof	250,000	Value: 12.00				

KM# 142.2 5 MARK
5.3000 g., 0.6250 Silver 0.1065 oz. ASW, 29 mm. **Obv:** Eagle divides date at top **Rev:** Patterned design **Note:** 1.4 mm thick.

Date	Mintage	F	VF	XF	Unc	BU
1975F	Inc. above	—	—	—	10.00	11.00

KM# 143 5 MARK
5.3000 g., 0.6250 Silver 0.1065 oz. ASW, 29 mm. **Subject:** Centenary - Birth of Albert Schweitzer **Obv:** Eagle above denomination **Rev:** Head facing, dates at right

Date	Mintage	F	VF	XF	Unc	BU
1975G	8,000,000	—	—	—	6.00	7.00
1975G Proof	250,000	Value: 14.00				

KM# 144 5 MARK
5.3000 g., 0.6250 Silver 0.1065 oz. ASW, 29 mm. **Subject:** 300th Anniversary - Death of von Grimmelshausen **Obv:** Eagle above denomination, date at left **Rev:** Mythic figure with book left, dates divided above

Date	Mintage	F	VF	XF	Unc	BU
1976D	8,000,000	—	—	—	6.00	7.00
1976D Proof	250,000	Value: 18.00				

KM# 145 5 MARK
5.3000 g., 0.6250 Silver 0.1065 oz. ASW, 29 mm. **Subject:** 200th Anniversary - Birth of Carl Friedrich Gauss **Obv:** Eagle above date and denomination **Rev:** Head 3/4 facing, dates at right

Date	Mintage	F	VF	XF	Unc	BU
1977J	8,000,000	—	—	—	6.00	7.00
1977J Proof	250,000	Value: 18.00				

KM# 146 5 MARK
5.3000 g., 0.6250 Silver 0.1065 oz. ASW, 29 mm. **Subject:** 200th Anniversary - Birth of Heinrich von Kleist **Obv:** Eagle above denomination **Rev:** Bust 3/4 left, dates below

Date	Mintage	F	VF	XF	Unc	BU
1977G	8,000,000	—	—	—	6.00	7.00
1977G Proof	250,000	Value: 16.00				

KM# 147 5 MARK
5.3000 g., 0.6250 Silver 0.1065 oz. ASW, 29 mm. **Subject:** 100th Anniversary - Birth of Gustav Stresemann **Obv:** Eagle above denomination **Rev:** Head left, dates at left

Date	Mintage	F	VF	XF	Unc	BU
1978D	8,000,000	—	—	—	6.00	7.00
1978D Proof	250,000	Value: 14.00				

KM# 148 5 MARK
5.3000 g., 0.6250 Silver 0.1065 oz. ASW, 29 mm. **Subject:** 225th Anniversary - Death of Balthasar Neumann **Obv:** Eagle above denomination **Rev:** Interior of Vierzehnheiligen

Date	Mintage	F	VF	XF	Unc	BU
1978F	8,000,000	—	—	—	6.00	7.00
1978F Proof	259,000	Value: 12.00				

KM# 150 5 MARK
5.3000 g., 0.6250 Silver 0.1065 oz. ASW, 29 mm. **Subject:** 150th Anniversary - German Archaeological Institute **Obv:** Denomination divides date, eagle above

Date	Mintage	F	VF	XF	Unc	BU
1979J	8,000,000	—	—	—	6.00	7.00
1979J Proof	250,000	Value: 14.00				

KM# 151 5 MARK
10.0000 g., Copper-Nickel Clad Nickel, 29 mm. **Subject:** 100th Anniversary - Birth of Otto Hahn **Obv:** Stylized eagle above legend **Rev:** Symbols of Hahn's studies in chemistry, name and dates below

Date	Mintage	F	VF	XF	Unc	BU
1979G	5,000,000	—	—	3.50	5.00	6.00
1979G Proof	350,000	Value: 11.00				

KM# 152 5 MARK
10.0000 g., Copper-Nickel Clad Nickel, 29 mm. **Subject:** 750th Anniversary - Death of von der Vogelweide **Obv:** Eagle above date divided by denomination **Rev:** Sleeping half figure with paper, dates below

Date	Mintage	F	VF	XF	Unc	BU
1980D	5,000,000	—	—	3.50	5.00	6.00
1980D Proof	350,000	Value: 11.50				

KM# 153 5 MARK
10.0000 g., Copper-Nickel Clad Nickel, 29 mm. **Subject:** 100th Anniversary - Cologne Cathedral **Obv:** Eagle, narrow design **Rev:** Cathedral

Date	Mintage	F	VF	XF	Unc	BU
1980F	5,000,000	—	—	4.00	5.00	6.00
1980F Proof	350,000	Value: 13.50				

KM# 154 5 MARK
10.0000 g., Copper-Nickel Clad Nickel, 29 mm. **Subject:** 200th Anniversary - Death of Gotthold Ephraim Lessing **Obv:** Denomination divides date below eagle **Rev:** Bust in silhouette left

Date	Mintage	F	VF	XF	Unc	BU
1981J	6,500,000	—	—	—	4.00	5.00
1981J Proof	350,000	Value: 10.00				

KM# 155 5 MARK

10.0000 g., Copper-Nickel Clad Nickel, 29 mm. **Subject:** 150th Anniversary - Death of Carl vom Stein **Obv:** Eagle in relief, denomination divides date below **Rev:** Bust 3/4 facing, dates at right

Date	Mintage	F	VF	XF	Unc	BU
1981G	6,500,000	—	—	—	4.00	5.00
1981G Proof	350,000	Value: 10.00				

KM# 156 5 MARK

10.0000 g., Copper-Nickel Clad Nickel, 29 mm. **Subject:** 150th Anniversary - Death of Johann Wolfgang von Goethe **Obv:** Eagle above denomination, date at right **Rev:** Head right, dates below

Date	Mintage	F	VF	XF	Unc	BU
1982D	8,000,000	—	—	—	4.00	5.00
1982D Proof	350,000	Value: 11.50				

KM# 157 5 MARK

10.0000 g., Copper-Nickel Clad Nickel, 29 mm. **Subject:** 10th Anniversary - U.N. Environmental Conference **Obv:** Eagle above denomination **Rev:** Stylized figure in center of design, date above

Date	Mintage	F	VF	XF	Unc	BU
1982F	8,000,000	—	—	—	4.00	5.00
1982F Proof	350,000	Value: 10.00				

KM# 158 5 MARK

10.0000 g., Copper-Nickel Clad Nickel, 29 mm. **Subject:** 100th Anniversary - Death of Karl Marx **Obv:** Eagle in relief above denomination **Rev:** Head 3/4 facing, dates below

Date	Mintage	F	VF	XF	Unc	BU
1983J	8,000,000	—	—	—	4.00	5.00
1983J Proof	350,000	Value: 10.00				

KM# 159 5 MARK

10.0000 g., Copper-Nickel Clad Nickel, 29 mm. **Subject:** 500th Anniversary - Birth of Martin Luther **Obv:** Eagle, denomination below divides date **Rev:** Inscription covers head 3/4 right

Date	Mintage	F	VF	XF	Unc	BU
1983G	8,000,000	—	—	—	4.00	5.00
1983G Proof	350,000	Value: 12.00				

KM# 160 5 MARK

10.0000 g., Copper-Nickel Clad Nickel, 29 mm. **Subject:** 150th Anniversary - German Customs Union **Obv:** Eagle, denomination divides date below **Rev:** Horses and carriage

Date	Mintage	F	VF	XF	Unc	BU
1984D	8,000,000	—	—	—	4.00	5.00
1984D Proof	350,000	Value: 11.50				

KM# 161 5 MARK

10.0000 g., Copper-Nickel Clad Nickel, 29 mm. **Subject:** 175th Anniversary - Birth of Felix Bartholdy **Obv:** Eagle above denomination **Rev:** 3/4 figure looking left, left hand on hip, music score in background

Date	Mintage	F	VF	XF	Unc	BU
1984J	8,000,000	—	—	—	4.00	5.00
1984J Proof	350,000	Value: 12.50				

KM# 162 5 MARK

10.0000 g., Copper-Nickel Clad Nickel, 29 mm. **Subject:** European Year of Music **Obv:** Stylized eagle in circle at left, denomination at right, date above **Rev:** Circle at left holds stars and outline of face in harp, music notes at right

Date	Mintage	F	VF	XF	Unc	BU
1985F	8,000,000	—	—	—	4.00	5.00
1985F Proof	350,000	Value: 11.50				

KM# 163 5 MARK

10.0000 g., Copper-Nickel Clad Nickel, 29 mm. **Subject:** 150th Anniversary - German Railroad **Obv:** Stylized eagle above denomination **Rev:** Spoked wheel design

Date	Mintage	F	VF	XF	Unc	BU
1985G	8,000,000	—	—	—	4.00	5.00
1985G Proof	350,000	Value: 10.00				

KM# 164 5 MARK

10.0000 g., Copper-Nickel Clad Nickel, 29 mm. **Subject:** 600th Anniversary - Heidelberg University **Obv:** Denomination divides date below eagle **Rev:** Crowned rampant lion left within legend

Date	Mintage	F	VF	XF	Unc	BU
1986D	8,000,000	—	—	—	4.00	5.00
1986D Proof	350,000	Value: 10.00				

KM# 165 5 MARK

10.0000 g., Copper-Nickel Clad Nickel, 29 mm. **Subject:** 200th Anniversary - Death of Frederick the Great **Obv:** Eagle above denomination **Rev:** Uniformed bust left, dates below

Date	Mintage	F	VF	XF	Unc	BU
1986F	8,000,000	—	—	—	4.00	5.00
1986F Proof	350,000	Value: 12.50				

KM# 130 10 MARK

15.5000 g., 0.6250 Silver 0.3114 oz. ASW, 33 mm. **Series:** Munich Olympics **Obv:** Artistic eagle, denomination below **Rev:** "In Deutschland" with spiraling symbol

Date	Mintage	F	VF	XF	Unc	BU
1972D	2,500,000	—	—	—	7.50	10.00
1972D Proof	125,000	Value: 26.00				
1972F	2,375,000	—	—	—	7.50	10.00
1972F Proof	125,000	Value: 26.00				
1972G	2,500,000	—	—	—	7.50	10.00
1972G Proof	125,000	Value: 26.00				
1972J	2,500,000	—	—	—	7.50	10.00
1972J Proof	125,000	Value: 26.00				

KM# 131 10 MARK

15.5000 g., 0.6250 Silver 0.3114 oz. ASW, 33 mm. **Series:** Munich Olympics **Obv:** Eagle above denomination **Rev:** Schleife (knot)

Date	Mintage	F	VF	XF	Unc	BU
1972D	5,000,000	—	—	—	7.50	10.00
1972D Proof	125,000	Value: 20.00				
1972F	4,875,000	—	—	—	7.50	10.00
1972F Proof	125,000	Value: 20.00				
1972G	5,000,000	—	—	—	7.50	10.00
1972G Proof	125,000	Value: 20.00				
1972J	5,000,000	—	—	—	7.50	10.00
1972J Proof	125,000	Value: 20.00				

KM# 132 10 MARK

15.5000 g., 0.6250 Silver 0.3114 oz. ASW, 33 mm. **Series:** Munich Olympics **Obv:** Eagle above denomination **Rev:** Athletes kneeling

Date	Mintage	F	VF	XF	Unc	BU
1972D	5,000,000	—	—	—	7.00	9.00
1972D Proof	150,000	Value: 16.00				
1972F	4,850,000	—	—	—	7.00	9.00
1972F Proof	150,000	Value: 16.00				
1972G	5,000,000	—	—	—	7.00	9.00
1972G Proof	150,000	Value: 16.00				
1972J	5,000,000	—	—	—	7.00	9.00
1972J Proof	150,000	Value: 16.00				

KM# 133 10 MARK

15.5000 g., 0.6250 Silver 0.3114 oz. ASW, 33 mm. **Series:** Munich Olympics **Obv:** Eagle above denomination **Rev:** Stadium - aerial view

Date	Mintage	F	VF	XF	Unc	BU
1972D	5,000,000	—	—	—	7.00	9.00
1972D Proof	150,000	Value: 16.00				
1972F	4,850,000	—	—	—	7.00	9.00
1972F Proof	150,000	Value: 16.00				
1972G	5,000,000	—	—	—	7.00	9.00
1972G Proof	150,000	Value: 16.00				
1972J	5,000,000	—	—	—	7.00	9.00
1972J Proof	150,000	Value: 16.00				

KM# 134.1 10 MARK

15.5000 g., 0.6250 Silver 0.3114 oz. ASW, 33 mm. **Series:** Munich Olympics **Obv:** Eagle above denomination **Rev:** "In Munchen" - with spiral symbol **Edge:** Lettering separated by periods

Date	Mintage	F	VF	XF	Unc	BU
1972D	2,500,000	—	—	—	7.50	10.00
1972D Proof	150,000	Value: 20.00				
1972F	2,350,000	—	—	—	7.50	10.00
1972F Proof	150,000	Value: 20.00				
1972G	2,500,000	—	—	—	7.50	10.00
1972G Proof	150,000	Value: 20.00				
1972J	2,500,000	—	—	—	7.50	10.00
1972J Proof	150,000	Value: 20.00				

KM# 134.2 10 MARK

15.5000 g., 0.6250 Silver 0.3114 oz. ASW, 33 mm. **Obv:** Eagle above denomination **Rev:** Spiral design **Edge:** Lettering separated by arabesques **Note:** Error.

Date	Mintage	F	VF	XF	Unc	BU
1972D	—	—	—	—	2,760	—
1972F	—	—	—	—	2,760	—
1972G	—	—	—	—	2,760	—
1972J	600	—	200	300	550	—

KM# 135 10 MARK

15.5000 g., 0.6250 Silver 0.3114 oz. ASW, 33 mm. **Series:** Munich Olympics **Obv:** Eagle above denomination **Rev:** Olympic Flame, spiral symbol above, rings divide date below

Date	Mintage	F	VF	XF	Unc	BU
1972D	5,000,000	—	—	—	7.00	9.00
1972D Proof	150,000	Value: 16.00				
1972F	4,850,000	—	—	—	7.00	9.00
1972F Proof	150,000	Value: 16.00				
1972G	5,000,000	—	—	—	7.00	9.00
1972G Proof	150,000	Value: 16.00				
1972J	5,000,000	—	—	—	7.00	9.00
1972J Proof	150,000	Value: 16.00				

EURO COINAGE

European Union Issues

KM# 207 EURO CENT

2.2700 g., Copper Plated Steel, 16.3 mm. **Obv:** Oak leaves **Obv. Designer:** Rolf Lederbogen **Rev:** Denomination and globe **Rev. Designer:** Luc Luycx **Edge:** Plain

Date	Mintage	F	VF	XF	Unc	BU
2002A	770,000,000	—	—	—	0.35	—
2002A Proof	130,000	Value: 1.00				
2002D	805,350,000	—	—	—	0.35	—
2002D Proof	130,000	Value: 1.00				
2002F	902,660,000	—	—	—	0.35	—
2002F Proof	130,000	Value: 1.00				
2002G	537,100,000	—	—	—	0.35	—
2002G Proof	130,000	Value: 1.00				
2002J	833,100,000	—	—	—	0.35	—
2002J Proof	130,000	Value: 1.00				
2003A	180,000	—	—	—	4.50	—
2003A Proof	150,000	Value: 1.00				
2003D	180,000	—	—	—	4.50	—
2003D Proof	150,000	Value: 1.00				
2003F	180,000	—	—	—	4.50	—
2003F Proof	150,000	Value: 1.00				
2003G	180,000	—	—	—	4.50	—
2003G Proof	150,000	Value: 1.00				
2003J	180,000	—	—	—	4.50	—
2003J Proof	150,000	Value: 1.00				
2004A	—	—	—	—	2.50	—
2004A Proof	—	Value: 1.00				
2004D	—	—	—	—	2.50	—
2004D Proof	—	Value: 1.00				
2004F	—	—	—	—	2.50	—
2004F Proof	—	Value: 1.00				
2004G	—	—	—	—	2.50	—
2004G Proof	—	Value: 1.00				
2004J	—	—	—	—	2.50	—
2004J Proof	—	Value: 1.00				
2005A	—	—	—	—	0.35	—
2005A Proof	—	Value: 1.00				
2005D	—	—	—	—	0.35	—
2005D Proof	—	Value: 1.00				
2005F	—	—	—	—	0.35	—
2005F Proof	—	Value: 1.00				
2005G	—	—	—	—	0.35	—
2005G Proof	—	Value: 1.00				
2005J	—	—	—	—	0.35	—
2005J Proof	—	Value: 1.00				
2006A	—	—	—	—	0.35	—
2006A Proof	—	Value: 1.00				
2006D	—	—	—	—	0.35	—
2006D Proof	—	Value: 1.00				
2006F	—	—	—	—	0.35	—
2006F Proof	—	Value: 1.00				
2006G	—	—	—	—	0.35	—
2006G Proof	—	Value: 1.00				
2006J	—	—	—	—	0.35	—
2006J Proof	—	Value: 1.00				
2007A	—	—	—	—	0.35	—
2007A Proof	—	Value: 1.00				
2007D	—	—	—	—	0.35	—
2007D Proof	—	Value: 1.00				
2007F	—	—	—	—	0.35	—
2007F Proof	—	Value: 1.00				
2007G	—	—	—	—	0.35	—
2007G Proof	—	Value: 1.00				
2007J	—	—	—	—	0.35	—
2007J Proof	—	Value: 1.00				
2008A	—	—	—	—	0.35	—
2008A Proof	—	Value: 1.00				
2008D	—	—	—	—	0.35	—
2008D Proof	—	Value: 1.00				
2008F	—	—	—	—	0.35	—
2008F Proof	—	Value: 1.00				
2008G	—	—	—	—	0.35	—
2008G Proof	—	Value: 1.00				
2008J	—	—	—	—	0.35	—
2008J Proof	—	Value: 1.00				

KM# 208 2 EURO CENT

3.0000 g., Copper Plated Steel, 18.7 mm. **Obv:** Oak leaves **Obv. Designer:** Rolf Lederbogen **Rev:** Denomination and globe **Rev. Designer:** Luc Luycx **Edge:** Grooved

Date	Mintage	F	VF	XF	Unc	BU
2002A	460,000,000	—	—	—	0.50	—
2002A Proof	130,000	Value: 1.50				
2002D	436,100,000	—	—	—	0.50	—
2002D Proof	130,000	Value: 1.50				
2002F	495,960,000	—	—	—	0.50	—
2002F Proof	130,000	Value: 1.50				
2002G	311,900,000	—	—	—	0.50	—
2002G Proof	130,000	Value: 1.50				
2002J	419,274,000	—	—	—	0.50	—
2002J Proof	130,000	Value: 1.50				
2003A	100,000,000	—	—	—	0.50	—
2003A Proof	150,000	Value: 1.50				
2003D	151,855,000	—	—	—	0.50	—
2003D Proof	150,000	Value: 1.50				
2003F	175,400,000	—	—	—	0.50	—
2003F Proof	150,000	Value: 1.50				
2003G	80,200,000	—	—	—	0.50	—
2003G Proof	150,000	Value: 1.50				
2003J	168,681,000	—	—	—	0.50	—
2003J Proof	150,000	Value: 1.50				
2004A	—	—	—	—	0.50	—
2004A Proof	—	Value: 1.50				
2004D	—	—	—	—	0.50	—
2004D Proof	—	Value: 1.50				
2004F	—	—	—	—	0.50	—
2004F Proof	—	Value: 1.50				
2004G	—	—	—	—	0.50	—
2004G Proof	—	Value: 1.50				
2004J	—	—	—	—	0.50	—
2004J Proof	—	Value: 1.50				
2005A	—	—	—	—	0.50	—
2005A Proof	—	Value: 1.50				
2005D	—	—	—	—	0.50	—
2005D Proof	—	Value: 1.50				
2005F	—	—	—	—	0.50	—
2005F Proof	—	Value: 1.50				
2005G	—	—	—	—	0.50	—
2005G Proof	—	Value: 1.50				
2005J	—	—	—	—	0.50	—
2005J Proof	—	Value: 1.50				
2006A	—	—	—	—	0.50	—
2006A Proof	—	Value: 1.50				
2006D	—	—	—	—	0.50	—
2006D Proof	—	Value: 1.50				
2006F	—	—	—	—	0.50	—
2006F Proof	—	Value: 1.50				
2006G	—	—	—	—	0.50	—
2006G Proof	—	Value: 1.50				
2006J	—	—	—	—	0.50	—
2006J Proof	—	Value: 1.50				
2007A	—	—	—	—	0.50	—
2007A Proof	—	Value: 1.50				
2007D	—	—	—	—	0.50	—
2007D Proof	—	Value: 1.50				
2007F	—	—	—	—	0.50	—
2007F Proof	—	Value: 1.50				
2007G	—	—	—	—	0.50	—
2007G Proof	—	Value: 1.50				
2007J	—	—	—	—	0.50	—
2007J Proof	—	Value: 1.50				
2008A	—	—	—	—	0.50	—
2008A Proof	—	Value: 1.50				
2008D	—	—	—	—	0.50	—
2008D Proof	—	Value: 1.50				
2008F	—	—	—	—	0.50	—
2008F Proof	—	Value: 1.50				
2008G	—	—	—	—	0.50	—
2008G Proof	—	Value: 1.50				
2008J	—	—	—	—	0.50	—
2008J Proof	—	Value: 1.50				

KM# 209 5 EURO CENT

3.8600 g., Copper Plated Steel, 21.2 mm. **Obv:** Oak leaves **Obv. Designer:** Rolf Lederbogen **Rev:** Denomination and globe **Rev. Designer:** Luc Luycx **Edge:** Plain

Date	Mintage	F	VF	XF	Unc	BU
2002A	475,000,000	—	—	—	0.75	—
2002A Proof	130,000	Value: 2.00				
2002D	495,700,000	—	—	—	0.75	—
2002D Proof	130,000	Value: 2.00				
2002F	563,710,000	—	—	—	0.75	—
2002F Proof	130,000	Value: 2.00				
2002G	328,400,000	—	—	—	0.75	—
2002G Proof	130,000	Value: 2.00				
2002J	501,850,000	—	—	—	0.75	—
2002J Proof	130,000	Value: 2.00				
2003A	180,000	—	—	—	4.50	—
2003A Proof	150,000	Value: 2.00				
2003D	180,000	—	—	—	4.50	—
2003D Proof	150,000	Value: 2.00				
2003F	180,000	—	—	—	4.50	—
2003F Proof	150,000	Value: 2.00				
2003G	180,000	—	—	—	4.50	—
2003G Proof	150,000	Value: 2.00				
2003J	180,000	—	—	—	4.50	—
2003J Proof	150,000	Value: 2.00				
2004A	—	—	—	—	2.50	—
2004A Proof	—	Value: 2.00				
2004D	—	—	—	—	2.50	—
2004D Proof	—	Value: 2.00				
2004F	—	—	—	—	2.50	—
2004F Proof	—	Value: 2.00				
2004G	—	—	—	—	2.50	—
2004G Proof	—	Value: 2.00				
2004J	—	—	—	—	2.50	—
2004J Proof	—	Value: 2.00				
2005A	—	—	—	—	0.75	—
2005A Proof	—	Value: 2.00				
2005D	—	—	—	—	0.75	—
2005D Proof	—	Value: 2.00				
2005F	—	—	—	—	0.75	—
2005F Proof	—	Value: 2.00				
2005G	—	—	—	—	0.75	—
2005G Proof	—	Value: 2.00				
2005J	—	—	—	—	0.75	—
2005J Proof	—	Value: 2.00				
2006A	—	—	—	—	0.75	—
2006A Proof	—	Value: 2.00				
2006D	—	—	—	—	0.75	—
2006D Proof	—	Value: 2.00				
2006F	—	—	—	—	0.75	—
2006F Proof	—	Value: 2.00				

Date	Mintage	F	VF	XF	Unc	BU
2006G	—	—	—	—	0.75	—
2006G Proof	—	Value: 2.00				
2006J	—	—	—	—	0.75	—
2006J Proof	—	Value: 2.00				
2007A	—	—	—	—	0.75	—
2007A Proof	—	Value: 2.00				
2007D	—	—	—	—	0.75	—
2007D Proof	—	Value: 2.00				
2007F	—	—	—	—	0.75	—
2007F Proof	—	Value: 2.00				
2007G	—	—	—	—	0.75	—
2007G Proof	—	Value: 2.00				
2007J	—	—	—	—	0.75	—
2007J Proof	—	Value: 2.00				
2008A	—	—	—	—	0.75	—
2008A Proof	—	Value: 2.00				
2008D	—	—	—	—	0.75	—
2008D Proof	—	Value: 2.00				
2008F	—	—	—	—	0.75	—
2008F Proof	—	Value: 2.00				
2008G	—	—	—	—	0.75	—
2008G Proof	—	Value: 2.00				
2008J	—	—	—	—	0.75	—
2008J Proof	—	Value: 2.00				

KM# 210 10 EURO CENT

4.0000 g., Brass, 19.7 mm. **Obv:** Brandenburg Gate **Obv. Designer:** Reinhard Heinsdorff **Rev:** Denomination and map **Rev. Designer:** Luc Luycx **Edge:** Reeded

Date	Mintage	F	VF	XF	Unc	BU
2002A	696,000,000	—	—	—	0.75	—
2002A Proof	130,000	Value: 2.00				
2002D	722,050,000	—	—	—	0.75	—
2002D Proof	130,000	Value: 2.00				
2002F	788,860,000	—	—	—	0.75	—
2002F Proof	130,000	Value: 2.00				
2002G	545,500,000	—	—	—	0.75	—
2002G Proof	130,000	Value: 2.00				
2002J	694,150,000	—	—	—	0.75	—
2002J Proof	130,000	Value: 2.00				
2003A	15,000,000	—	—	—	1.25	—
2003A Proof	150,000	Value: 2.00				
2003D	9,000,000	—	—	—	1.25	—
2003D Proof	150,000	Value: 2.00				
2003F	1,500,000	—	—	—	1.50	—
2003F Proof	150,000	Value: 2.00				
2003G	9,450,000	—	—	—	1.25	—
2003G Proof	150,000	Value: 2.00				
2003J	89,405,000	—	—	—	1.25	—
2003J Proof	150,000	Value: 2.00				
2004A	—	—	—	—	1.25	—
2004A Proof	—	Value: 2.00				
2004D	—	—	—	—	1.25	—
2004D Proof	—	Value: 2.00				
2004F	—	—	—	—	1.25	—
2004F Proof	—	Value: 2.00				
2004G	—	—	—	—	1.25	—
2004G Proof	—	Value: 2.00				
2004J	—	—	—	—	1.25	—
2004J Proof	—	Value: 2.00				
2005A	—	—	—	—	1.25	—
2005A Proof	—	Value: 2.00				
2005D	—	—	—	—	1.25	—
2005D Proof	—	Value: 2.00				
2005F	—	—	—	—	1.25	—
2005F Proof	—	Value: 2.00				
2005G	—	—	—	—	1.25	—
2005G Proof	—	Value: 2.00				
2005J	—	—	—	—	1.25	—
2005J Proof	—	Value: 2.00				
2006A	—	—	—	—	1.25	—
2006A Proof	—	Value: 2.00				
2006D	—	—	—	—	1.25	—
2006D Proof	—	Value: 2.00				
2006F	—	—	—	—	1.25	—
2006F Proof	—	Value: 2.00				
2006G	—	—	—	—	1.25	—
2006G Proof	—	Value: 2.00				
2006J	—	—	—	—	1.25	—
2006J Proof	—	Value: 2.00				

KM# 254 10 EURO CENT

4.0000 g., Brass, 19.7 mm. **Obv:** Brandenburg Gate **Obv. Designer:** Reinhard Heinsdorff **Rev:** Relief map of Western Europe, stars, lines and value **Rev. Designer:** Luc Luycx **Edge:** Reeded

Date	Mintage	F	VF	XF	Unc	BU
2007A	—	—	—	—	1.25	—
2007A Proof	—	Value: 2.00				
2007D	—	—	—	—	1.25	—
2007D Proof	—	Value: 2.00				
2007F	—	—	—	—	1.25	—
2007F Proof	—	Value: 2.00				
2007G	—	—	—	—	1.25	—
2007G Proof	—	Value: 2.00				
2007J	—	—	—	—	1.25	—
2007J Proof	—	Value: 2.00				
2008A	—	—	—	—	1.25	—
2008A Proof	—	Value: 2.00				
2008D	—	—	—	—	1.25	—
2008D Proof	—	Value: 2.00				
2008F	—	—	—	—	1.25	—
2008F Proof	—	Value: 2.00				
2008G	—	—	—	—	1.25	—
2008G Proof	—	Value: 2.00				
2008J	—	—	—	—	1.25	—
2008J Proof	—	Value: 2.00				

KM# 211 20 EURO CENT

5.7300 g., Brass, 22.2 mm. **Obv:** Brandenburg Gate **Obv. Designer:** Reinhard Heinsdorff **Rev:** Denomination and map **Rev. Designer:** Luc Luycx **Edge:** Notched

Date	Mintage	F	VF	XF	Unc	BU
2002A	378,000,000	—	—	—	1.00	—
2002A Proof	130,000	Value: 3.00				
2002D	367,100,000	—	—	—	1.00	—
2002D Proof	130,000	Value: 3.00				
2002F	423,760,000	—	—	—	1.00	—
2002F Proof	130,000	Value: 3.00				
2002G	252,100,000	—	—	—	1.00	—
2002G Proof	130,000	Value: 3.00				
2002J	441,000,000	—	—	—	1.00	—
2002J Proof	130,000	Value: 3.00				
2003A	42,000,000	—	—	—	1.00	—
2003A Proof	150,000	Value: 3.00				
2003D	24,100,000	—	—	—	1.00	—
2003D Proof	150,000	Value: 3.00				
2003F	82,000,000	—	—	—	1.00	—
2003F Proof	150,000	Value: 3.00				
2003G	24,829,000	—	—	—	1.00	—
2003G Proof	150,000	Value: 3.00				
2003J	180,000	—	—	—	4.50	—
2003J Proof	150,000	Value: 3.00				
2004A	—	—	—	—	2.50	—
2004A Proof	—	Value: 3.00				
2004D	—	—	—	—	2.50	—
2004D Proof	—	Value: 3.00				
2004F	—	—	—	—	2.50	—
2004F Proof	—	Value: 3.00				
2004G	—	—	—	—	2.50	—
2004G Proof	—	Value: 3.00				
2004J	—	—	—	—	2.50	—
2004J Proof	—	Value: 3.00				
2005A	—	—	—	—	1.00	—
2005A Proof	—	Value: 3.00				
2005D	—	—	—	—	1.00	—
2005D Proof	—	Value: 3.00				
2005F	—	—	—	—	1.00	—
2005F Proof	—	Value: 3.00				
2005G	—	—	—	—	1.00	—
2005G Proof	—	Value: 3.00				
2005J	—	—	—	—	1.00	—
2005J Proof	—	Value: 3.00				
2006A	—	—	—	—	1.00	—
2006A Proof	—	Value: 3.00				
2006D	—	—	—	—	1.00	—
2006D Proof	—	Value: 3.00				
2006F	—	—	—	—	1.00	—
2006F Proof	—	Value: 3.00				
2006G	—	—	—	—	1.00	—
2006G Proof	—	Value: 3.00				
2006J	—	—	—	—	1.00	—
2006J Proof	—	Value: 3.00				

KM# 255 20 EURO CENT

5.7300 g., Brass, 22.2 mm. **Obv:** Brandenburg Gate **Obv. Designer:** Reinhard Heinsdorff **Rev:** Relief map of Western Europe, stars, lines and value **Rev. Designer:** Luc Luycx **Edge:** Notched

Date	Mintage	F	VF	XF	Unc	BU
2007A	—	—	—	—	1.00	—
2007A Proof	—	Value: 3.00				
2007D	—	—	—	—	1.00	—
2007D Proof	—	Value: 3.00				
2007F	—	—	—	—	1.00	—
2007F Proof	—	Value: 3.00				
2007G	—	—	—	—	1.00	—
2007G Proof	—	Value: 3.00				
2007J	—	—	—	—	1.00	—
2007J Proof	—	Value: 3.00				
2008A	—	—	—	—	1.00	—
2008A Proof	—	Value: 3.00				
2008D	—	—	—	—	1.00	—
2008D Proof	—	Value: 3.00				
2008F	—	—	—	—	1.00	—
2008F Proof	—	Value: 3.00				
2008G	—	—	—	—	1.00	—
2008G Proof	—	Value: 3.00				
2008J	—	—	—	—	1.00	—
2008J Proof	—	Value: 3.00				

KM# 212 50 EURO CENT

7.8100 g., Brass, 24.2 mm. **Obv:** Brandenburg Gate **Obv. Designer:** Reinhard Heinsdorff **Rev:** Denomination and map **Rev. Designer:** Luc Luycx **Edge:** Reeded

Date	Mintage	F	VF	XF	Unc	BU
2002A	337,600,000	—	—	—	1.75	—
2002A Proof	130,000	Value: 4.00				
2002D	370,340,000	—	—	—	1.75	—
2002D Proof	130,000	Value: 4.00				
2002F	432,000,000	—	—	—	1.75	—
2002F Proof	130,000	Value: 4.00				
2002G	257,860,000	—	—	—	1.75	—
2002G Proof	130,000	Value: 4.00				
2002J	375,467,000	—	—	—	1.75	—
2002J Proof	130,000	Value: 4.00				
2003A	180,000	—	—	—	4.50	—
2003A Proof	150,000	Value: 4.00				
2003D	180,000	—	—	—	4.50	—
2003D Proof	150,000	Value: 4.00				
2003F	180,000	—	—	—	4.50	—
2003F Proof	150,000	Value: 4.00				
2003G	180,000	—	—	—	4.50	—
2003G Proof	150,000	Value: 4.00				
2003J	54,400,000	—	—	—	1.75	—
2003J Proof	150,000	Value: 4.00				
2004A	—	—	—	—	1.75	—
2004A Proof	—	Value: 4.00				
2004D	—	—	—	—	1.75	—
2004D Proof	—	Value: 4.00				
2004F	—	—	—	—	1.75	—
2004F Proof	—	Value: 4.00				
2004G	—	—	—	—	1.75	—
2004G Proof	—	Value: 4.00				
2004J	—	—	—	—	1.75	—
2004J Proof	—	Value: 4.00				
2005A	—	—	—	—	1.50	—
2005A Proof	—	Value: 4.00				
2005D	—	—	—	—	1.50	—
2005D Proof	—	Value: 4.00				
2005F	—	—	—	—	1.50	—
2005F Proof	—	Value: 4.00				
2005G	—	—	—	—	1.50	—
2005G Proof	—	Value: 4.00				
2005J	—	—	—	—	1.50	—
2005J Proof	—	Value: 4.00				
2006A	—	—	—	—	1.50	—
2006A Proof	—	Value: 4.00				
2006D	—	—	—	—	1.50	—
2006D Proof	—	Value: 4.00				
2006F	—	—	—	—	1.50	—
2006F Proof	—	Value: 4.00				
2006G	—	—	—	—	1.50	—
2006G Proof	—	Value: 4.00				
2006J	—	—	—	—	1.50	—
2006J Proof	—	Value: 4.00				

KM# 256 50 EURO CENT

7.8100 g., Brass, 24.2 mm. **Obv:** Brandenburg Gate **Obv. Designer:** Reinhard Heinsdorff **Rev:** Relief map of Western Europe, stars, lines and value **Rev. Designer:** Luc Luycx **Edge:** Reeded

Date	Mintage	F	VF	XF	Unc	BU
2007A	—	—	—	—	1.50	—
2007A Proof	—	Value: 4.00				
2007D	—	—	—	—	1.50	—
2007D Proof	—	Value: 4.00				
2007F	—	—	—	—	1.50	—
2007F Proof	—	Value: 4.00				
2007G	—	—	—	—	1.50	—
2007G Proof	—	Value: 4.00				
2007J	—	—	—	—	1.50	—
2007J Proof	—	Value: 4.00				
2008A	—	—	—	—	1.50	—
2008A Proof	—	Value: 4.00				
2008D	—	—	—	—	1.50	—
2008D Proof	—	Value: 4.00				
2008F	—	—	—	—	1.50	—
2008F Proof	—	Value: 4.00				
2008G	—	—	—	—	1.50	—
2008G Proof	—	Value: 4.00				
2008J	—	—	—	—	1.50	—
2008J Proof	—	Value: 4.00				

KM# 213 EURO
7.5000 g., Bi-Metallic Copper-Nickel center in Brass ring, 23.3 mm. **Obv:** Stylized eagle **Obv. Designer:** Heinz Sneschana Russewa-Hover **Rev:** Denomination over map **Rev. Designer:** Luc Luycx **Edge:** Three normally reeded and three very finely reeded sections

Date	Mintage	F	VF	XF	Unc	BU
2002A	367,750,000	—	—	—	2.50	—
2002A Proof	130,000	Value: 6.50				
2002D	372,700,000	—	—	—	2.50	—
2002D Proof	130,000	Value: 6.50				
2002F	440,910,000	—	—	—	2.50	—
2002F Proof	130,000	Value: 6.50				
2002G	266,975,000	—	—	—	2.50	—
2002G Proof	130,000	Value: 6.50				
2002J	433,000,000	—	—	—	2.50	—
2002J Proof	130,000	Value: 6.50				
2003A	36,750,000	—	—	—	2.50	—
2003A Proof	150,000	Value: 6.50				
2003D	180,000	—	—	—	5.50	—
2003D Proof	150,000	Value: 6.50				
2003F	375,000	—	—	—	5.50	—
2003F Proof	150,000	Value: 6.50				
2003G	180,000	—	—	—	5.50	—
2003G Proof	150,000	Value: 6.50				
2003J	975,000	—	—	—	2.50	—
2003J Proof	150,000	Value: 6.50				
2004A	—	—	—	—	2.50	—
2004A Proof	—	Value: 6.50				
2004D	—	—	—	—	2.50	—
2004D Proof	—	Value: 6.50				
2004F	—	—	—	—	2.50	—
2004F Proof	—	Value: 6.50				
2004G	—	—	—	—	2.50	—
2004G Proof	—	Value: 6.50				
2004J	—	—	—	—	2.50	—
2004J Proof	—	Value: 6.50				
2005A	—	—	—	—	2.50	—
2005A Proof	—	Value: 5.00				
2005D	—	—	—	—	2.50	—
2005D Proof	—	Value: 5.00				
2005F	—	—	—	—	2.50	—
2005F Proof	—	Value: 5.00				
2005G	—	—	—	—	2.50	—
2005G Proof	—	Value: 5.00				
2005J	—	—	—	—	2.50	—
2005J Proof	—	Value: 5.00				
2006A	—	—	—	—	2.50	—
2006A Proof	—	Value: 5.00				
2006D	—	—	—	—	2.50	—
2006D Proof	—	Value: 5.00				
2006F	—	—	—	—	2.50	—
2006F Proof	—	Value: 5.00				
2006G	—	—	—	—	2.50	—
2006G Proof	—	Value: 5.00				
2006J	—	—	—	—	2.50	—
2006J Proof	—	Value: 5.00				

KM# 257 EURO
7.5000 g., Bi-Metallic Copper-Nickel center in Brass ring, 23.3 mm. **Obv:** Stylized eagle **Obv. Designer:** Heinz Sneschana Russewa-Hover **Rev:** Relief map of Western Europe, stars, lines and value **Rev. Designer:** Luc Luycx **Edge:** Three normally reeded and three very finely reeded sections

Date	Mintage	F	VF	XF	Unc	BU
2007A	—	—	—	—	2.50	—
2007A Proof	—	Value: 5.00				
2007D	—	—	—	—	2.50	—
2007D Proof	—	Value: 5.00				
2007F	—	—	—	—	2.50	—
2007F Proof	—	Value: 5.00				
2007G	—	—	—	—	2.50	—
2007G Proof	—	Value: 5.00				
2007J	—	—	—	—	2.50	—
2007J Proof	—	Value: 5.00				
2008A	—	—	—	—	2.50	—
2008A Proof	—	Value: 5.00				
2008D	—	—	—	—	2.50	—
2008D Proof	—	Value: 5.00				
2008F	—	—	—	—	2.50	—
2008F Proof	—	Value: 5.00				
2008G	—	—	—	—	2.50	—
2008G Proof	—	Value: 5.00				
2008J	—	—	—	—	2.50	—
2008J Proof	—	Value: 5.00				

KM# 214 2 EURO
8.5200 g., Bi-Metallic Brass center in Copper-Nickel ring, 25.6 mm. **Obv:** Stylized eagle **Obv. Designer:** Heinz Sneschana Russewa-Hover **Rev:** Denomination and map **Rev. Designer:** Luc Luycx **Edge:** Reeded and "EINIGKEIT UND RECHT UND FREIHEIT"

Date	Mintage	F	VF	XF	Unc	BU
2002A	238,775,000	—	—	—	4.50	—
2002A Proof	130,000	Value: 12.50				
2002D	231,400,000	—	—	—	4.50	—
2002D Proof	130,000	Value: 12.50				
2002F	264,610,000	—	—	—	4.50	—
2002F Proof	130,000	Value: 12.50				
2002G	181,050,000	—	—	—	4.50	—
2002G Proof	130,000	Value: 12.50				
2002J	257,718,000	—	—	—	4.50	—
2002J Proof	130,000	Value: 12.50				
2003A	20,475,000	—	—	—	4.50	—
2003A Proof	150,000	Value: 12.50				
2003D	30,300,000	—	—	—	4.50	—
2003D Proof	150,000	Value: 12.50				
2003F	74,000,000	—	—	—	4.50	—
2003F Proof	150,000	Value: 12.50				
2003G	13,950,000	—	—	—	4.50	—
2003G Proof	150,000	Value: 12.50				
2003J	6,450,000	—	—	—	4.50	—
2003J Proof	150,000	Value: 12.50				
2004A	—	—	—	—	4.50	—
2004A Proof	—	Value: 12.50				
2004D	—	—	—	—	4.50	—
2004D Proof	—	Value: 12.50				
2004F	—	—	—	—	4.50	—
2004F Proof	—	Value: 12.50				
2004G	—	—	—	—	4.50	—
2004G Proof	—	Value: 12.50				
2004J	—	—	—	—	4.50	—
2004J Proof	—	Value: 12.50				
2005A	—	—	—	—	4.50	—
2005A Proof	—	Value: 10.00				
2005D	—	—	—	—	4.50	—
2005D Proof	—	Value: 10.00				
2005F	—	—	—	—	4.50	—
2005F Proof	—	Value: 10.00				
2005G	—	—	—	—	4.50	—
2005G Proof	—	Value: 10.00				
2005J	—	—	—	—	4.50	—
2005J Proof	—	Value: 10.00				
2006A	—	—	—	—	4.50	—
2006A Proof	—	Value: 10.00				
2006D	—	—	—	—	4.50	—
2006D Proof	—	Value: 10.00				
2006	—	—	—	—	4.50	—
2006F Proof	—	Value: 10.00				
2006G	—	—	—	—	4.50	—
2006G Proof	—	Value: 10.00				
2006J	—	—	—	—	4.50	—
2006J Proof	—	Value: 10.00				

KM# 253 2 EURO
8.5200 g., Bi-Metallic Brass center in Copper-Nickel ring **Obv:** Towered city gate **Obv. Legend:** BUNDESREPUBLIK DEUTSCHLAND **Obv. Inscription:** SCHLESWIG- / HOLSTEIN **Rev:** Denomination over map

Date	Mintage	F	VF	XF	Unc	BU
2006A	6,000,000	—	—	—	5.00	—
2006A Proof	70,000	Value: 10.00				
2006D	6,300,000	—	—	—	5.00	—
2006D Proof	70,000	Value: 10.00				
2006F	7,250,000	—	—	—	5.00	—
2006F Proof	70,000	Value: 10.00				
2006G	4,200,000	—	—	—	5.00	—
2006G Proof	70,000	Value: 10.00				
2006J	6,300,000	—	—	—	5.00	—
2006J Proof	70,000	Value: 10.00				

KM# 258 2 EURO
8.5200 g., Bi-Metallic Brass center in Copper-Nickel ring, 25.6 mm. **Obv:** Stylized eagle **Obv. Designer:** Heinz Sneschana Russewa-Hover **Rev:** Relief map of Western Europe, stars, lines and value **Rev. Designer:** Luc Luycx **Edge:** Reeded and lettered **Edge Lettering:** EINIGKEIT UND RECHT UND FREIHEIT

Date	Mintage	F	VF	XF	Unc	BU
2007A	—	—	—	—	4.50	—
2007A Proof	—	Value: 10.00				
2007D	—	—	—	—	4.50	—
2007D Proof	—	Value: 10.00				
2007F	—	—	—	—	4.50	—
2007F Proof	—	Value: 10.00				
2007G	—	—	—	—	4.50	—
2007G Proof	—	Value: 10.00				
2007J	—	—	—	—	4.50	—
2007J Proof	—	Value: 10.00				
2008A	—	—	—	—	4.50	—
2008A Proof	—	Value: 10.00				
2008D	—	—	—	—	4.50	—
2008D Proof	—	Value: 10.00				
2008F	—	—	—	—	4.50	—
2008F Proof	—	Value: 10.00				
2008G	—	—	—	—	4.50	—
2008G Proof	—	Value: 10.00				
2008J	—	—	—	—	4.50	—
2008J Proof	—	Value: 10.00				

KM# 259 2 EURO
8.4500 g., Bi-Metallic Brass center in Copper-Nickel ring, 25.72 mm. **Subject:** 50th Anniversary Treaty of Rome **Obv:** Large value at left, modified outline of Europe at right **Rev:** Open Treaty book **Edge:** Reeded and lettered **Edge Lettering:** EINIGKEIT UND RECHT UND FREIHEIT

Date	Mintage	F	VF	XF	Unc	BU
2007F	—	—	—	—	—	9.00

KM# 260 2 EURO
8.4000 g., Bi-Metallic Brass center in Copper-Nickel ring, 25.72 mm. **Obv:** Large value at left, modified outline of Europe at right **Obv. Legend:** BUNDESREPUBLIK DEUTSCHLAND **Rev:** City buildings **Edge:** Reeded and lettered **Edge Lettering:** EINIGKEIT UND RECHT UND FREIHEIT

Date	Mintage	F	VF	XF	Unc	BU
2007F	—	—	—	—	—	9.00

1949-1990

The German Democratic Republic, formerly East Germany, was located on the great north European plain, had an area of 41,768 sq. mi. (108,330 sq. km.) and a population of 16.6 million. The figures included East Berlin, which had been incorporated into the G.D.R. Capital: East Berlin. The economy was highly industrialized. Machinery, transport equipment chemicals, and lignite were exported.

During the closing days of World War II in Europe, Soviet troops advancing into Germany from the east occupied the German provinces of Mecklenburg, Brandenburg, Lusatia, Saxony and Thuringia. These five provinces comprised the occupation zone administered by the Soviet Union after the cessation of hostilities. The other three zones were administered by the U.S., Great Britain and France. Under the Potsdam agreement, questions affecting Germany as a whole were to be settled by the commanders of the occupation zones acting jointly and by unanimous decision. When Soviet intransigence rendered the quadripartite commission inoperable, the three western zones were united to form the Federal Republic of Germany, May 23, 1949. Thereupon the Soviet Union dissolved its occupation zone and established it as the Democratic Republic of Germany, Oct. 7, 1949.

The post-WW II division of Germany was ended Oct. 3,1990, when the German Democratic Republic (East Germany) ceased to exist and its five constituent provinces were formally admitted to the Federal Republic of Germany. An election Dec. 2, 1990, chose representatives to the united federal parliament (Bundestag), which then conducted its opening session in Berlin in the old Reichstag building.

MARKS
A - Berlin
E - Muldenhutten

MONETARY SYSTEM
100 Pfennig = 1 Mark

DEMOCRATIC REPUBLIC

STANDARD COINAGE

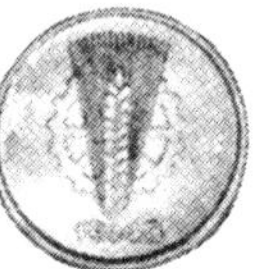

KM# 1 PFENNIG
Aluminum **Obv:** Denomination **Rev:** Cogwheel back of grain sprig

Date	Mintage	F	VF	XF	Unc	BU
1948A	243,000,000	—	1.00	9.00	40.00	70.00
1949A	Inc. above	—	1.00	8.00	35.00	45.00
1949E	55,200,000	—	11.50	50.00	250	325
1950A	—	—	1.00	8.00	35.00	45.00
1950E	—	—	6.00	20.00	75.00	100

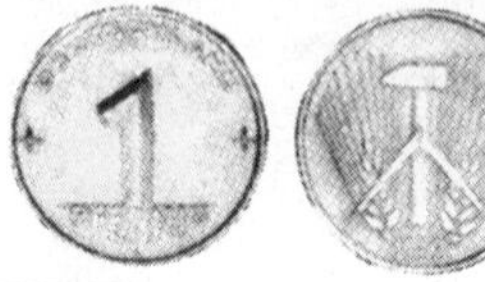

KM# 5 PFENNIG

Aluminum **Obv:** Denomination **Rev:** Grain sprigs back of hammer and protractor

Date	Mintage	F	VF	XF	Unc	BU
1952A	297,213,000	—	0.50	3.00	7.00	9.00
1952E	49,296,000	—	5.00	10.00	40.00	55.00
1953A	114,002,000	—	1.00	3.00	8.00	12.00
1953E	50,876,000	—	4.00	15.00	50.00	65.00

KM# 8.1 PFENNIG

Aluminum, 17 mm. **Obv:** State emblem **Rev:** Denomination flanked by oak leaves, date below

Date	Mintage	F	VF	XF	Unc	BU
1960A	101,808,000	—	0.25	0.75	3.00	4.00
1961A	101,776,000	—	0.25	0.75	3.00	4.00
1962A	81,459,000	—	0.25	0.75	3.00	4.00
1963A	101,402,000	—	0.25	0.75	3.00	4.00
1964A	98,967,000	—	0.25	0.75	3.00	4.00
1965A	38,585,000	—	3.00	15.00	40.00	60.00
1968A	813,680,000	—	0.25	0.80	2.50	3.00
1972A	4,801,000	—	3.00	10.00	20.00	25.00
1973A	5,518,000	—	3.00	8.00	20.00	25.00
1975A	202,752,000	—	0.25	0.75	2.50	3.00

KM# 8.2 PFENNIG

0.7000 g., Aluminum, 17 mm. **Obv:** State emblem, smaller design features **Rev:** Denomination flanked by leaves, smaller design features

Date	Mintage	F	VF	XF	Unc	BU
1977A	61,560,000	—	0.10	0.25	2.00	3.00
1978A	200,050,000	—	0.10	0.20	1.00	2.00
1979A	100,640,000	—	0.10	0.20	1.00	2.00
1979A Proof	—	Value: 45.00				
1980A	153,000,000	—	0.10	0.20	1.00	2.00
1980A Proof	—	Value: 45.00				
1981A	200,436,000	—	0.10	0.20	1.00	2.00
1981A Proof	40	—	—	—	1.00	2.00
1982A	99,200,000	—	0.10	0.20	1.00	2.00
1982A Proof	2,500	Value: 10.00				
1983A	150,000,000	—	0.10	0.20	1.00	2.00
1983A Proof	2,550	Value: 18.00				
1984A	137,600,000	—	0.10	0.20	1.00	2.00
1984A Proof	3,015	Value: 4.50				
1985A	125,060,000	—	0.10	0.20	1.00	2.00
1985A Proof	2,816	Value: 4.50				
1986A	73,900,000	—	0.10	0.20	1.00	2.00
1986A Proof	2,800	Value: 4.50				
1987A	50,015,000	—	0.10	0.20	1.00	2.00
1987A Proof	2,345	Value: 4.50				
1988A	75,450,000	—	0.10	0.20	1.00	2.00
1988A Proof	2,300	Value: 4.50				
1989A	84,410,000	—	0.10	0.20	1.00	2.00
1989A Proof	2,300	Value: 4.50				
1990A	15,670,000	—	0.10	2.00	5.00	10.00

KM# 2 5 PFENNIG

Aluminum **Obv:** Denomination **Rev:** Cogwheel back of grain sprig

Date	Mintage	F	VF	XF	Unc	BU
1948A	205,072,000	—	2.50	6.00	50.00	75.00
1949A	Inc. above	—	2.50	6.00	60.00	100
1950A	Inc. above	—	2.50	6.00	40.00	65.00

KM# 6 5 PFENNIG

Aluminum **Obv:** Denomination **Rev:** Grain sprigs flank hammer and protractor, date below

Date	Mintage	F	VF	XF	Unc	BU
1952A	113,397,000	—	2.00	5.00	10.00	13.00
1952E	24,024,000	—	3.50	9.00	35.00	45.00
1953A	40,994,000	—	2.00	6.50	15.00	20.00
1953E	28,665,000	—	5.00	17.50	90.00	120

KM# 9.1 5 PFENNIG

Aluminum, 19 mm. **Obv:** State emblem **Rev:** Denomination flanked by oak leaves, date below

Date	Mintage	F	VF	XF	Unc	BU
1968A	282,303,000	—	0.50	1.00	2.50	3.00
1972A	51,462,000	—	0.50	1.00	2.00	3.00
1975A	84,710,000	—	0.50	1.00	2.00	3.00

KM# 9.2 5 PFENNIG

1.0000 g., Aluminum, 19 mm. **Obv:** State emblem, smaller design features **Rev:** Denomination flanked by oak leaves, smaller design features **Note:** Varieties exist.

Date	Mintage	F	VF	XF	Unc	BU
1976A 2 known	—	—	—	—	—	—
1978A	43,257,000	—	0.15	0.25	1.00	2.00
1979A	46,194,000	—	0.15	0.25	1.00	2.00
1979A Proof	—	Value: 45.00				
1980A	31,977,000	—	0.15	0.25	1.00	2.00
1980A Proof	—	Value: 45.00				
1981A	33,101,999	—	0.15	0.25	1.00	2.00
1981A Proof	40	—	—	—	—	—
1982A	916,000	—	10.00	35.00	25.00	35.00
1982A Proof	2,500	Value: 10.00				
1983A	100,890,000	—	0.15	0.25	1.00	2.00
1983A Proof	2,550	Value: 18.00				
1984A	Est. 6,000	—	—	—	30.00	40.00
1984A Proof	3,015	Value: 4.50				
1985A	1,000,000	—	1.50	6.50	15.00	18.00
1985A Proof	2,816	Value: 4.50				
1986A	1,000,000	—	1.50	6.50	10.00	15.00
1986A Proof	2,800	Value: 4.50				
1987A	Est. 20,000	—	—	—	12.50	16.00
1987A Proof	2,345	Value: 4.50				
1988A	35,930,000	—	0.15	0.25	1.00	2.00
1988A Proof	2,300	Value: 4.50				
1989A	21,550,000	—	0.15	0.25	1.00	2.00
1989A Proof	2,300	Value: 4.50				
1990A	50,640,000	—	0.15	0.25	1.00	2.00

KM# 3 10 PFENNIG

Aluminum **Obv:** Denomination **Rev:** Cogwheel back of grain sprigs **Note:** Also exists with medallic die rotation (1950E).

Date	Mintage	F	VF	XF	Unc	BU
1948A	216,537,000	—	2.50	19.00	75.00	100
1949A	Inc. above	—	2.50	15.00	70.00	90.00
1950A	Inc. above	—	2.50	10.00	70.00	90.00
1950E	16,000,000	—	15.00	150	800	1,000

KM# 7 10 PFENNIG

Aluminum **Obv:** Denomination **Rev:** Grain sprigs flank hammer and protractor, date below

Date	Mintage	F	VF	XF	Unc	BU
1952A	70,427,000	—	2.00	12.00	60.00	80.00
1952E	21,498,000	—	10.00	30.00	300	400
1953A	18,611,000	—	3.50	18.00	75.00	100
1953E	11,500,000	—	15.00	70.00	400	550

KM# 10 10 PFENNIG

1.5000 g., Aluminum, 21 mm. **Obv:** State emblem **Rev:** Denomination divides leaf and date

Date	Mintage	F	VF	XF	Unc	BU
1963A	21,063,000	—	7.00	30.00	60.00	80.00
1965A	55,313,000	—	1.00	2.00	3.00	4.00
1967A	96,955,000	—	0.15	1.00	3.00	4.00
1968A	207,461,000	—	0.15	1.00	2.00	3.00
1970A	13,387,000	—	0.15	1.00	3.00	5.00
1971A	66,617,999	—	0.15	1.00	2.00	3.00
1972A	5,702,000	—	0.50	3.00	8.00	10.00
1973A	11,257,000	—	0.15	1.00	3.00	4.00
1978A	40,000,000	—	0.15	1.00	2.00	3.00
1979A	54,665,000	—	0.15	1.00	2.00	3.00
1979A Proof	—	Value: 45.00				
1980A	20,664,000	—	0.15	1.00	3.00	4.00
1980A Proof	—	Value: 45.00				
1981A	40,704,000	—	0.15	1.00	2.00	3.00
1981A Proof	40	—	—	—	—	—
1982A	40,212,000	—	0.15	1.00	3.00	4.00
1982A Proof	2,500	Value: 10.00				
1983A	40,699,000	—	0.15	10.00	50.00	75.00
1983A Proof	2,550	Value: 20.00				
1984A	Est. 12,000	—	—	10.00	25.00	35.00
Note: Issued in sets only, remainder unaccountable						
1984A Proof	3,015	Value: 4.50				
1985A	1,010,000	—	0.35	4.50	12.00	15.00
1985A Proof	2,816	Value: 4.50				
1986A	1,000,000	—	0.35	4.50	12.00	15.00
1986A Proof	2,800	Value: 4.50				
1987A	Est. 20,000	—	—	7.00	12.00	15.00
Note: Issued in sets only, remainder unaccountable						
1987A Proof	2,345	Value: 4.50				
1988A	10,705,000	—	0.15	1.00	2.00	3.00
1988A Proof	2,300	Value: 4.50				
1989A	37,640,000	—	0.15	1.00	2.00	3.00
1989A Proof	2,300	Value: 4.50				
1990A	Est. 14,000	—	—	—	17.00	25.00
Note: Issued in sets only, remainder unaccountable						

KM# 11 20 PFENNIG

5.4000 g., Brass, 22.3 mm. **Obv:** State emblem **Rev:** Denomination above date **Note:** Ribbon width varieties exist.

Date	Mintage	F	VF	XF	Unc	BU
1969	167,168,000	—	0.25	2.00	5.00	7.00
1971	24,563,000	—	0.25	3.00	6.00	7.00
1972A	5,007,000	—	1.00	4.00	10.00	12.00
1973A	2,524,000	—	1.00	4.50	10.00	12.00
1974A	7,458,000	—	1.00	2.50	8.00	10.00
1979A	293,000	—	1.00	3.00	7.50	9.00
1979A Proof	—	Value: 50.00				
1980A	2,190,000	—	1.00	3.00	20.00	30.00
1980A Proof	—	Value: 50.00				
1981A	983,000	—	1.00	4.00	9.00	12.00
1981A Proof	40	—	—	—	—	—
1982A	10,458,000	—	1.00	4.00	9.00	12.00
1982A Proof	2,500	Value: 12.50				
1983A	25,809,000	—	1.00	2.00	3.00	5.00
1983A Proof	2,550	Value: 25.00				
1984A	25,009,000	—	1.00	2.00	3.00	5.00
1984A Proof	3,015	Value: 5.50				
1985A	1,559,000	—	1.00	3.00	8.00	12.00
1985A Proof	2,816	Value: 5.50				
1986A	1,147,000	—	1.00	4.00	10.00	15.00
1986A Proof	2,800	Value: 5.50				
1987A	Est. 20,000	—	4.00	6.00	10.00	15.00
Note: Issued in sets only, remainder unaccountable						
1987A Proof	2,345	Value: 5.50				
1988A	Est. 15,000	—	4.00	6.00	10.00	15.00
Note: Issued in sets only, remainder unaccountable						
1988A Proof	2,300	Value: 5.50				
1989A	14,690,000	—	0.20	1.00	2.00	3.00
1989A Proof	2,300	Value: 5.50				
1990A	Est. 14,000	—	—	—	15.00	20.00
Note: Issued in sets only, remainder unaccountable						

KM# 4 50 PFENNIG

3.3800 g., Aluminum-Bronze **Obv:** Denomination above date **Rev:** Man and cart in front of buildings with tall smokestacks

Date	Mintage	F	VF	XF	Unc	BU
1949A	Inc. below	—	—	7,500	8,000	10,000
1950A	67,703,000	—	3.50	10.00	70.00	300
Note: Some authorities believe the 1949-dated piece is a pattern						

KM# 12.1 50 PFENNIG

Aluminum, 23 mm. **Obv:** Small state emblem

Date	Mintage	F	VF	XF	Unc	BU
1958A	101,606,000	—	1.00	3.00	8.00	10.00

KM# 12.2 50 PFENNIG

1.9000 g., Aluminum, 23 mm. **Obv:** State emblem **Rev:** Denomination divides date and leaf **Note:** Inscription varieties exist.

Date	Mintage	F	VF	XF	Unc	BU
1968A	19,860,000	—	1.00	2.00	4.00	5.00
1971A	35,829,000	—	1.00	2.00	3.00	4.00
1972A	8,117,000	—	1.00	2.00	4.50	5.50
1973A	6,530,000	—	1.00	2.00	6.00	8.00
1979A	1,026,999	—	1.00	2.00	6.00	8.00
1979A Proof	—	—	—	—	—	—
1980A	1,118,000	—	5.00	10.00	15.00	20.00
1980A Proof	—	—	—	—	—	—
1981A	10,546,000	—	1.00	3.00	5.00	7.00
1981A Proof	40	—	—	—	—	—
1982A	79,832,000	—	0.35	0.75	2.50	3.00
1982A Proof	2,500	Value: 12.50				
1983A	1,309,000	—	1.00	3.00	8.00	12.00
1983A Proof	2,550	Value: 25.00				
1984A	Est. 5,000	—	—	—	30.00	40.00
1984A Proof	3,015	Value: 5.50				
1985A	1,565,000	—	1.00	3.00	10.00	15.00
1985A Proof	2,816	Value: 5.50				
1986A	776,000	—	1.00	3.00	10.00	15.00
1986A Proof	2,800	Value: 5.50				
1987A	Est. 21,000	—	5.00	10.00	15.00	20.00
Note: Issued in sets only, remainder unaccountable						
1987A Proof	2,345	Value: 5.50				
1988A	Est. 15,000	—	6.00	12.00	15.00	20.00
Note: Issued in sets only, remainder unaccountable						
1988A Proof	2,300	Value: 5.50				
1989A	31,000	—	1.00	3.00	8.00	12.00
1989A Proof	2,300	Value: 5.50				
1990A	Est. 14,000	—	—	—	15.00	20.00
Note: Issued in sets only, remainder unaccountable						

KM# 13 MARK

Aluminum **Obv:** State emblem **Rev:** Large, thick denomination flanked by leaves, date below

Date	Mintage	F	VF	XF	Unc	BU
1956A	112,108,000	—	1.00	3.00	9.00	12.00
1962A	45,920,000	—	1.00	4.00	8.00	12.00
1963A	31,910,000	—	1.00	2.50	8.00	12.00

KM# 35.1 MARK

Aluminum **Obv:** State emblem **Rev:** Large 1 flanked by oak leaves

Date	Mintage	F	VF	XF	Unc	BU
1972A	30,288,000	—	1.00	4.00	5.00	8.00

KM# 35.2 MARK

2.4000 g., Aluminum, 25 mm. **Obv:** State emblem **Rev:** Large, thick denomination flanked by leaves, small date below

Date	Mintage	F	VF	XF	Unc	BU
1973A	6,972,000	—	1.00	4.00	10.00	12.00
1975A	32,094,000	—	1.00	2.00	5.00	7.00
1977A	119,813,000	—	0.50	1.00	2.00	3.00
1978A	18,824,000	—	0.50	1.00	2.00	3.00
1979A	1,002,999	—	1.00	2.00	7.50	10.00
1979A Proof	—	—	—	—	—	—
1980A	1,069,000	—	5.00	10.00	15.00	20.00
1980A Proof	—	—	—	—	—	—
1981A	1,006,000	—	1.00	3.00	7.50	10.00
1981A Proof	40	—	—	—	—	—
1982A	51,619,000	—	0.50	1.00	2.00	3.00
1982A Proof	2,500	Value: 25.00				
1983A	1,065,000	—	1.00	2.00	7.50	10.00
1983A Proof	2,550	Value: 30.00				
1984A	Est. 5,000	—	—	—	40.00	50.00
1984A Proof	3,015	Value: 7.50				
1985A	1,128,000	—	1.00	2.00	7.50	10.00
1985A Proof	2,816	Value: 7.50				
1986A	1,000,000	—	1.00	2.00	7.50	10.00
1986A Proof	2,800	Value: 7.50				
1987A	Est. 21,000	—	8.00	12.00	18.00	22.00
Note: Issued in sets only, remainder unaccountable						
1987A Proof	2,345	Value: 7.50				
1988A	Est. 15,000	—	—	—	15.00	20.00
Note: Issued in sets only, remainder unaccountable						
1988A Proof	2,300	Value: 7.50				
1989A	33,000	—	2.00	10.00	15.00	20.00
1989A Proof	2,300	Value: 7.50				
1990A	Est. 14,000	—	—	—	20.00	25.00
Note: Issued in sets only, remainder unaccountable						

KM# 14 2 MARK

Aluminum **Obv:** State emblem **Rev:** Large denomination flanked by leaves, date below

Date	Mintage	F	VF	XF	Unc	BU
1957A	77,961,000	—	2.00	4.00	8.00	10.00

KM# 48 2 MARK

3.0000 g., Aluminum, 27 mm. **Obv:** State emblem **Rev:** Large denomination flanked by leaves, date below

Date	Mintage	F	VF	XF	Unc	BU
1972A	—	—	—	—	—	—
Note: 3 pieces known						
1974A	5,790,000	—	2.00	5.00	12.00	15.00
1975A	32,464,000	—	2.00	2.00	9.00	10.00
1977A	27,859,000	—	2.00	5.00	8.00	10.00
1978A	23,415,000	—	2.00	5.00	8.00	10.00
1979A	985,000	—	2.00	5.00	8.00	10.00
1979A Proof	—	—	—	—	—	—
1980A	1,018,999	—	2.00	5.00	9.00	12.00
1980A Proof	—	—	—	—	—	—
1981A	939,000	—	2.00	5.00	8.00	10.00
1981A Proof	40	—	—	—	—	—
1982A	60,488,000	—	1.00	2.00	3.00	4.00
1982A Proof	2,500	Value: 55.00				
1983A	1,030,000	—	1.00	2.00	6.00	8.00
1983A Proof	2,550	Value: 75.00				
1984A	Est. 6,000	—	—	—	30.00	40.00
1984A Proof	3,015	Value: 20.00				
1985A	1,310,000	—	3.00	6.00	10.00	15.00
1985A Proof	2,816	Value: 20.00				
1986A	1,000,000	—	3.00	6.00	10.00	15.00
1986A Proof	2,800	Value: 20.00				
1987A	Est. 30,000	—	8.00	12.00	18.00	22.00
Note: Issued in sets only, remainder unaccountable						
1987A Proof	2,345	Value: 20.00				
1988A	Est. 15,000	—	8.00	12.00	18.00	22.00
Note: Issued in sets only, remainder unaccountable						
1988A Proof	2,300	Value: 20.00				
1989A	46,000	—	5.00	10.00	15.00	20.00
1989A Proof	2,300	Value: 20.00				
1990A	Est. 14,000	—	—	—	30.00	40.00
Note: Issued in sets only, remainder unaccountable						

KM# 19.1 5 MARK

9.7000 g., Copper-Nickel, 29 mm. **Subject:** 125th Anniversary of Birth of Robert Koch, doctor **Obv:** State emblem **Rev:** Head left

Date	Mintage	F	VF	XF	Unc	BU
1968	100,000	—	—	10.00	20.00	30.00

KM# 19.2 5 MARK

9.7000 g., Copper-Nickel, 29 mm. **Obv:** State emblem **Rev:** Head left **Note:** Error: plain edge.

Date	Mintage	F	VF	XF	Unc	BU
1968	—	—	—	—	400	450

KM# 22.1 5 MARK

Nickel-Bronze, 29 mm. **Subject:** 20th Anniversary D.D.R **Obv:** State emblem **Rev:** Denomination, date at left

Date	Mintage	F	VF	XF	Unc	BU
1969	50,222,000	—	—	3.00	4.50	7.50
Note: 10% nickel and 90% copper						

KM# 22.1a 5 MARK

Copper-Nickel, 29 mm. **Obv:** State emblem **Rev:** Denomination, date at left

Date	Mintage	F	VF	XF	Unc	BU
1969	12,741	—	50.00	60.00	70.00	80.00
Note: 25% nickel and 75% copper						

KM# 22.2 5 MARK

Nickel-Bronze, 29 mm. **Obv:** State emblem **Rev:** Denomination, date at left **Note:** Error: plain edge.

Date	Mintage	F	VF	XF	Unc	BU
1969	—	—	—	—	120	150

KM# 22.3 5 MARK

Nickel-Bronze, 29 mm. **Obv:** State emblem **Rev:** Denomination, date at left **Note:** Error: Mongolian inscription and dates on edge.

Date	Mintage	F	VF	XF	Unc	BU
1969	—	—	—	—	—	—

KM# 29 5 MARK

9.7000 g., Copper-Nickel, 29 mm. **Subject:** Brandenburg Gate

Date	Mintage	F	VF	XF	Unc	BU
1971A	4,000,000	—	—	3.00	10.00	20.00
1979A	32,000	—	—	10.00	25.00	35.00
1979A Proof	2,500	—	—	—	—	—
1980A	30,000	—	—	10.00	15.00	20.00
1980A Proof	2,500	—	—	—	—	—
1981A	30,000	—	—	10.00	15.00	20.00
1981A Proof	2,500	—	—	—	—	—
1982A	28,000	—	—	10.00	15.00	25.00
1982A Proof	2,500	Value: 200				
1983A	3,000	—	—	—	900	1,100
1984A	28,000	—	—	25.00	40.00	60.00
1984A Proof	3,015	Value: 120				
1985A	3,000	—	—	—	900	1,100
1986A	28,000	—	—	50.00	110	125
1986A Proof	2,800	Value: 140				
1987A	220,000	—	—	10.00	15.00	20.00
1987A Proof	6,424	Value: 80.00				
1988A	28,000	—	—	12.00	15.00	35.00
1988A Proof	2,300	Value: 125				
1989A	28,000	—	—	121	25.00	35.00
1989A Proof	2,405	Value: 125				
1990A	50,000	—	—	12.00	25.00	35.00

KM# 37 5 MARK

9.7000 g., Copper-Nickel, 29 mm. **Subject:** City of Meissen **Obv:** State emblem, denomination **Rev:** City scene

Date	Mintage	F	VF	XF	Unc	BU
1972A	3,500,000	—	—	4.00	10.00	12.00
1981A Proof	40	Value: 2,750				
1983A	28,000	—	—	150	180	200
1983A Proof	2,550	Value: 400				

KM# 36.1 5 MARK

9.7000 g., Copper-Nickel, 29 mm. **Subject:** 75th Anniversary - Death of Johannes Brahms **Obv:** State emblem, denomination **Rev:** Name, musical score, dates

Date	Mintage	F	VF	XF	Unc	BU
1972	55,000	—	—	15.00	20.00	25.00

KM# 36.2 5 MARK

9.7000 g., Copper-Nickel, 29 mm. **Obv:** State emblem, denomination **Rev:** Musical score, name and dates **Note:** Error: Double edge inscription.

Date	Mintage	F	VF	XF	Unc	BU
1972	—	—	—	—	475	575

KM# 43 5 MARK

9.7000 g., Copper-Nickel, 29 mm. **Subject:** 125th Anniversary - Birth of Otto Lilienthal, aviation pioneer **Obv:** State emblem, denomination **Rev:** Plane divides dates

Date	Mintage	F	VF	XF	Unc	BU
1973	100,000	—	—	40.00	50.00	60.00

KM# 49 5 MARK

9.7000 g., Copper-Nickel, 29 mm. **Subject:** Centenary - Death of Philipp Reis, physicist, telephone inventor **Obv:** State emblem, denomination **Rev:** Telephone and telegraph divided by name, dates at bottom

Date	Mintage	F	VF	XF	Unc	BU
1974	100,000	—	—	—	20.00	30.00

KM# 54 5 MARK

9.7000 g., Copper-Nickel, 29 mm. **Subject:** 100th Anniversary - Birth of Thomas Mann, writer **Obv:** State emblem, denomination **Rev:** Head left, dates below

Date	Mintage	F	VF	XF	Unc	BU
1975	100,000	—	—	15.00	20.00	25.00

KM# 55 5 MARK

9.7000 g., Copper-Nickel, 29 mm. **Subject:** International Women's Year **Obv:** State emblem, denomination **Rev:** Profiles of three women right

Date	Mintage	F	VF	XF	Unc	BU
1975	250,000	—	—	15.00	20.00	25.00

KM# 60 5 MARK

9.7000 g., Copper-Nickel, 29 mm. **Subject:** 200th Anniversary - Birth of Ferdinand von Schill, military officer **Obv:** State emblem, denomination **Rev:** Hat divides dates above sword and name

Date	Mintage	F	VF	XF	Unc	BU
1976	100,000	—	—	20.00	28.00	35.00

KM# 64 5 MARK

9.7000 g., Copper-Nickel, 29 mm. **Subject:** 125th Anniversary - Death of Friedrich Ludwig Jahn, father of German gymnastics **Obv:** State emblem, denomination **Rev:** Bust 3/4 facing, dates below

Date	Mintage	F	VF	XF	Unc	BU
1977	90,000	—	—	30.00	40.00	50.00
1977 Proof	10,000	Value: 80.00				

KM# 67 5 MARK

9.7000 g., Copper-Nickel, 29 mm. **Subject:** 175th Anniversary - Death of Friedrich Klopstock, poet **Obv:** State emblem, denomination **Rev:** Bust left

Date	Mintage	F	VF	XF	Unc	BU
1978	96,000	—	—	30.00	40.00	50.00
1978 Proof	4,500	Value: 100				

KM# 68 5 MARK

9.7000 g., Copper-Nickel, 29 mm. **Subject:** Anti-Apartheid Year **Obv:** Denomination, date below small state emblem at left **Rev:** Raised clenched fist

Date	Mintage	F	VF	XF	Unc	BU
1978A	196,000	—	—	20.00	25.00	30.00
1978A Proof	4,000	Value: 110				

KM# 72 5 MARK

9.7000 g., Copper-Nickel, 29 mm. **Subject:** 100th Anniversary - Birth of Albert Einstein, physicist **Obv:** State emblem, denomination **Rev:** Head 3/4 right

Date	Mintage	F	VF	XF	Unc	BU
1979	56,000	—	—	55.00	80.00	95.00
1979 Proof	4,500	Value: 120				

KM# 76 5 MARK

9.7000 g., Copper-Nickel, 29 mm. **Subject:** 75th Anniversary - Death of Adolph von Menzel **Obv:** State emblem, denomination **Rev:** Bust left divides dates

Date	Mintage	F	VF	XF	Unc	BU
1980	55,000	—	—	35.00	50.00	60.00
1980 Proof	5,500	Value: 110				

KM# 79 5 MARK

9.7000 g., Copper-Nickel, 29 mm. **Subject:** 450th Anniversary - Death of Tilman Riemenschneider, sculptor **Obv:** State emblem, denomination **Rev:** Bust 3/4 facing, divides dates

Date	Mintage	F	VF	XF	Unc	BU
1981	55,000	—	—	40.00	60.00	70.00
1981 Proof	5,500	Value: 110				

KM# 84 5 MARK

9.7000 g., Copper-Nickel, 29 mm. **Subject:** 200th Anniversary - Birth of Friedrich Frobel **Obv:** State emblem, denomination **Rev:** Three children with building blocks, dates below

Date	Mintage	F	VF	XF	Unc	BU
1982	55,000	—	—	40.00	60.00	75.00
1982 Proof	5,500	Value: 100				

KM# 85 5 MARK

9.7000 g., Copper-Nickel-Zinc, 29 mm. **Subject:** Goethe's Weimar Cottage **Obv:** Small state emblem, denomination **Rev:** Cottage

Date	Mintage	F	VF	XF	Unc	BU
1982A	245,000	—	—	25.00	35.00	42.00
1982A Proof	5,500	Value: 100				
Note: House and trees frosted						
1982A Proof	210	Value: 3,000				
Note: House only frosted						

KM# 86 5 MARK

9.7000 g., Copper-Nickel-Zinc, 29 mm. **Subject:** Wartburg Castle **Obv:** State emblem, denomination **Rev:** Castle **Designer:** Heinz Rodewald

Date	Mintage	F	VF	XF	Unc	BU
1982A	245,000	—	—	25.00	40.00	45.00
1982A Proof	5,500	Value: 90.00				
1983A	10,000	—	—	—	400	450

KM# 89 5 MARK

9.7000 g., Copper-Nickel, 29 mm. **Subject:** Wittenberg Church **Obv:** Small state emblem, denomination **Rev:** Church **Designer:** Heinz Rodewald

Date	Mintage	F	VF	XF	Unc	BU
1983A	245,000	—	—	25.00	40.00	50.00
1983A Proof	5,500	Value: 80.00				

KM# 90 5 MARK

9.7000 g., Copper-Nickel, 29 mm. **Subject:** Martin Luther's birthplace **Obv:** State emblem, denomination **Rev:** House **Designer:** Heinz Rodewald

Date	Mintage	F	VF	XF	Unc	BU
1983A	245,000	—	—	25.00	40.00	50.00
1983A Proof	5,500	Value: 90.00				

KM# 91 5 MARK

Copper-Nickel-Zinc, 29 mm. **Subject:** 125th Anniversary - Birth of Max Planck **Obv:** State emblem, denomination **Rev:** Head right, dates below **Rev. Designer:** Dietrich Dorfstedoer

Date	Mintage	F	VF	XF	Unc	BU
1983	56,000	—	—	32.00	45.00	55.00
1983 Proof	4,200	Value: 100				

KM# 96 5 MARK

9.7000 g., Copper-Nickel, 29 mm. **Subject:** Leipzig Old City Hall **Obv:** State emblem, denomination **Rev:** City hall building

Date	Mintage	F	VF	XF	Unc	BU
1984A	245,000	—	—	25.00	40.00	50.00
1984A Proof	5,500	Value: 70.00				

KM# 97 5 MARK

9.7000 g., Copper-Nickel, 29 mm. **Subject:** Thomas Church of Leipzig **Obv:** State emblem, denomination **Rev:** Church

Date	Mintage	F	VF	XF	Unc	BU
1984A	245,000	—	—	25.00	40.00	50.00
1984A Proof	5,500	Value: 70.00				

KM# 98 5 MARK

9.7000 g., Copper-Nickel, 29 mm. **Subject:** 150th Anniversary - Death of Adolf Freiherr von Lutzow **Obv:** State emblem, denomination **Rev:** Three uniformed figures on horses

Date	Mintage	F	VF	XF	Unc	BU
1984A	55,000	—	—	55.00	70.00	80.00
1984A Proof	5,000	Value: 110				

KM# 102 5 MARK

9.7000 g., Copper-Nickel, 29 mm. **Subject:** Restoration of Dresden Women's Church **Obv:** State emblem divides date above six line inscription, denomination below **Rev:** Church buildings, date above

Date	Mintage	F	VF	XF	Unc	BU
1985A	245,000	—	—	25.00	35.00	40.00
1985A Proof	8,476	Value: 70.00				

KM# 103 5 MARK

9.7000 g., Copper-Nickel, 29 mm. **Subject:** Restoration of Dresden Zwinger **Obv:** State emblem, denomination **Rev:** Building

Date	Mintage	F	VF	XF	Unc	BU
1985A	245,000	—	—	25.00	35.00	45.00
1985A Proof	5,500	Value: 70.00				

KM# 104 5 MARK

9.7000 g., Copper-Nickel, 29 mm. **Subject:** 225th Anniversary - Death of Caroline Neuber **Obv:** State emblem, denomination **Rev:** Caroline on stage, 1697-1760

Date	Mintage	F	VF	XF	Unc	BU
1985A	56,000	—	—	75.00	90.00	100
1985A Proof	4,000	Value: 150				

KM# 110 5 MARK

9.7000 g., Copper-Nickel, 29 mm. **Subject:** Potsdam - Sanssouci Palace **Obv:** State emblem, denomination **Rev:** Palace

Date	Mintage	F	VF	XF	Unc	BU
1986A	296,000	—	—	9.00	12.00	17.50
1986A Proof	4,200	Value: 100				

KM# 111 5 MARK

9.7000 g., Copper-Nickel, 29 mm. **Subject:** Potsdam - New Palace **Obv:** State emblem, denomination **Rev:** Palace buildings

Date	Mintage	F	VF	XF	Unc	BU
1986A	296,000	—	—	9.00	12.00	17.50
1986A Proof	4,200	Value: 100				

KM# 112 5 MARK

9.7000 g., Copper-Nickel, 29 mm. **Subject:** 175th Anniversary - Death of Heinrich von Kleist **Obv:** State emblem, denomination **Rev:** Bust left looking forward divides dates

Date	Mintage	F	VF	XF	Unc	BU
1986A	56,000	—	—	130	150	180
1986A Proof	4,000	Value: 200				

KM# 114 5 MARK

9.7000 g., Copper-Zinc-Nickel, 29 mm. **Subject:** Berlin - Nikolai Quarter **Obv:** State emblem, denomination **Rev:** Buildings with two towers

Date	Mintage	F	VF	XF	Unc	BU
1987A	496,000	—	—	8.00	12.00	15.00
1987A Proof	4,200	Value: 75.00				

KM# 115 5 MARK

9.7000 g., Copper-Zinc-Nickel, 29 mm. **Subject:** Berlin - Red City Hall **Obv:** State emblem, denomination **Rev:** City hall building

Date	Mintage	F	VF	XF	Unc	BU
1987A	496,000	—	—	8.00	12.00	15.00
1987A Proof	4,200	Value: 75.00				

KM# 116 5 MARK
9.7000 g., Copper-Zinc-Nickel, 29 mm. **Subject:** Berlin - Universal Time Clock **Obv:** State emblem, denomination **Rev:** Universal clock

Date	Mintage	F	VF	XF	Unc	BU
1987A	496,000	—	—	8.00	12.00	15.00
1987A Proof	4,200	Value: 75.00				

KM# 120 5 MARK
9.7000 g., Copper-Nickel, 29 mm. **Subject:** Germany's First Railroad **Obv:** State emblem, denomination **Rev:** Train engine, tower in background

Date	Mintage	F	VF	XF	Unc	BU
1988A	496,000	—	—	8.00	9.00	12.50
1988A Proof	4,200	Value: 130				

KM# 121 5 MARK
9.7000 g., Copper-Nickel, 29 mm. **Subject:** Port City of Rostock **Obv:** State emblem, denomination **Rev:** Ships in port

Date	Mintage	F	VF	XF	Unc	BU
1988A	496,000	—	—	8.00	9.00	12.50
1988A Proof	4,200	Value: 120				

KM# 122 5 MARK
9.7000 g., Copper-Nickel, 29 mm. **Subject:** 50th Anniversary - Death of Ernst Barlach **Obv:** State emblem, denomination **Rev:** Full-length figure playing horn, dates at right

Date	Mintage	F	VF	XF	Unc	BU
1988A	56,000	—	—	50.00	65.00	80.00
1988A Proof	4,000	Value: 175				

KM# 129 5 MARK
9.7000 g., Copper-Zinc-Nickel, 29 mm. **Subject:** Katharinen Kirche in Zwickau **Obv:** State emblem, denomination **Rev:** Church **Rev. Designer:** Wilfried Klink

Date	Mintage	F	VF	XF	Unc	BU
1989A	496,000	—	—	7.00	9.00	11.50
1989A Proof	4,200	Value: 110				

KM# 130 5 MARK
9.7000 g., Copper-Zinc-Nickel, 29 mm. **Subject:** Marien Kirche in Muhlhausen **Obv:** State emblem, denomination **Rev:** Church and city scene **Rev. Designer:** Heinz Rodewald

Date	Mintage	F	VF	XF	Unc	BU
1989A	496,000	—	—	7.00	9.00	11.50
1989A Proof	4,200	Value: 110				

KM# 131 5 MARK
9.7000 g., Copper-Zinc-Nickel, 29 mm. **Subject:** 100th Anniversary - Birth of Carl von Ossietzky **Obv:** State emblem, denomination **Rev:** Bust left, dates at right

Date	Mintage	F	VF	XF	Unc	BU
1989A	56,000	—	—	60.00	75.00	90.00
1989A Proof	4,000	Value: 200				

KM# 135 5 MARK
9.7000 g., Copper-Zinc-Nickel, 29 mm. **Subject:** Zeughaus Museum **Obv:** State emblem, denomination **Rev:** Museum

Date	Mintage	F	VF	XF	Unc	BU
1990A	496,000	—	—	7.00	8.00	10.00
1990A Proof	4,200	Value: 100				

KM# 133 5 MARK
9.7000 g., Copper-Zinc-Nickel, 29 mm. **Subject:** 100th Anniversary - Birth of Kurt Tucholsky **Obv:** State emblem, denomination **Rev:** Head facing, dates below

Date	Mintage	F	VF	XF	Unc	BU
1990A	51,000	—	—	40.00	60.00	70.00
1990A Proof	4,000	Value: 125				

KM# 134 5 MARK
9.7000 g., Copper-Zinc-Nickel, 29 mm. **Subject:** 500 Years of Postal Service **Obv:** State emblem, denomination **Rev:** Antique car

Date	Mintage	F	VF	XF	Unc	BU
1990A	496,000	—	—	7.00	9.00	11.00
1990A Proof	4,200	Value: 100				

GHANA

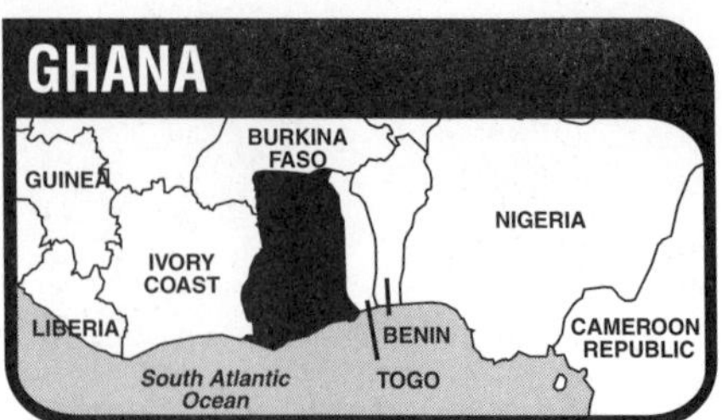

The Republic of Ghana, a member of the Commonwealth of Nations situated on the West Coast of Africa between Ivory Coast and Togo, has an area of 92,100 sq. mi. (238,540 sq. km.) and a population of 14 million, almost entirely African. Capital: Accra. Cocoa (the major crop), coconuts, palm kernels and coffee are exported. Mining, second in importance to agriculture, is concentrated on gold, manganese and industrial diamonds.

The state of Ghana, comprising the Gold Coast and British Togoland, obtained independence on March 6, 1957, becoming the first Negro African colony to do so. On July I, 1960, Ghana adopted a republican constitution, changing from a ministerial to a presidential form of government. The government was overthrown, the constitution suspended and the National Assembly dissolved by the Ghanaian army and police on Feb. 24, 1966. The government was returned to civilian authority in Oct. 1969, but was again seized by military officers in a bloodless coup on Jan. 13, 1972, but 3 further coups occurred in 1978, 1979 and 1981. The latter 2 coups were followed by suspension of the constitution and banning of political parties. A new constitution, which allowed multiparty politics, was approved in April 1992.

Ghana's monetary denomination of Cedi' is derived from the word 'sedie' meaning cowrie, a shell money commonly employed by coastal tribes.

MONETARY SYSTEM
12 Pence = 1 Shilling

REPUBLIC

STANDARD COINAGE

KM# 1 1/2 PENNY
Bronze **Obv:** Dr. Kwame Nkrumah head right **Rev:** Date divided by star, denomination below **Designer:** P. K. K. Quaidoo

Date	Mintage	F	VF	XF	Unc	BU
1958	32,200,000	—	0.10	0.25	0.50	1.50
1958 Proof	20,000	Value: 0.75				

KM# 2 PENNY
Bronze **Obv:** Dr. Kwame Nkrumah head right **Rev:** Date divided by star, denomination below **Designer:** P. K. K. Quaidoo

Date	Mintage	F	VF	XF	Unc	BU
1958	60,000,000	—	0.15	0.35	0.75	1.75
1958 Proof	20,000	Value: 1.00				

KM# 3 3 PENCE
Copper Nickel, 19.5 mm. **Obv:** Dr. Kwame Nkrumah head right **Rev:** Date divided by star, denomination below **Shape:** Scalloped **Designer:** P. K. K. Quaidoo

Date	Mintage	F	VF	XF	Unc	BU
1958	25,200,000	—	0.20	0.45	1.00	2.00
1958 Proof	20,000	Value: 1.50				

KM# 4 6 PENCE

2.2600 g., Copper Nickel **Obv:** Head of Dr. Kwame Nkrumah right **Rev:** Date divided by star, denomination below **Designer:** P. K. K. Quaidoo

Date	Mintage	F	VF	XF	Unc	BU
1958	15,200,000	—	0.20	0.45	1.00	2.00
1958 Proof	—	Value: 1.50				

KM# 5 SHILLING

Copper Nickel, 21 mm. **Obv:** Dr. Kwame Nkrumah head right **Rev:** Date divided by star, denomination below **Designer:** P. K. K. Quaidoo

Date	Mintage	F	VF	XF	Unc	BU
1958	34,400,000	—	0.25	0.50	1.75	3.50
1958 Proof	20,000	Value: 2.50				

KM# 6 2 SHILLING

Copper Nickel, 26.5 mm. **Obv:** Dr. Kwame Nkrumah head right **Rev:** Date divided by star, denomination below **Designer:** P. K. K. Quaidoo

Date	Mintage	F	VF	XF	Unc	BU
1958	72,700,000	—	0.35	0.75	2.25	4.50
1958 Proof	20,000	Value: 3.50				

DECIMAL COINAGE

KM# 12 1/2 PESEWA

Bronze, 20.3 mm. **Obv:** Bush drums **Rev:** Star divides date and denomination

Date	Mintage	F	VF	XF	Unc	BU
1967	30,000,000	—	0.10	0.20	0.50	0.75
1967 Proof	2,000	Value: 1.00				

KM# 13 PESEWA

Bronze, 25.5 mm. **Obv:** Bush drums **Rev:** Star divides date and denomination

Date	Mintage	F	VF	XF	Unc	BU
1967	30,000,000	—	0.15	0.25	0.60	0.85
1967 Proof	2,000	Value: 1.25				
1975	50,250,000	—	0.10	0.20	0.50	0.75
1979	50,000,000	—	0.10	0.20	0.50	0.75

KM# 14 2-1/2 PESEWAS

3.2000 g., Copper-Nickel, 19.5 mm. **Obv:** Cocoa beans within circle **Rev:** Rampant lion at center of quartered shield dividing date and denomination **Shape:** Scalloped

Date	Mintage	F	VF	XF	Unc	BU
1967	6,000,000	—	0.10	0.20	0.75	1.25
1967 Proof	2,000	Value: 1.50				

KM# 8 5 PESEWAS

Copper-Nickel **Obv:** Dr. Kwame Nkrumah head right **Rev:** Star divides date and denomination **Shape:** Scalloped

Date	Mintage	F	VF	XF	Unc	BU
1965	30,000,000	—	0.20	0.35	1.25	2.25

KM# 15 5 PESEWAS

Copper-Nickel, 19.5 mm. **Obv:** Cocoa beans within circle **Rev:** Rampant lion at center of quartered shield dividing date and denomination

Date	Mintage	F	VF	XF	Unc	BU
1967	30,000,000	—	0.15	0.25	0.75	1.25
1967 Proof	2,000	Value: 2.00				
1973	8,000,000	—	0.15	0.25	0.75	1.25
1975	20,000,000	—	0.15	0.25	0.75	1.25

KM# 9 10 PESEWAS

Copper-Nickel **Obv:** Dr. Kwame Nkrumah head right **Rev:** Star divides date and denomination

Date	Mintage	F	VF	XF	Unc	BU
1965	50,000,000	—	0.25	0.50	1.25	2.00

KM# 16 10 PESEWAS

5.5700 g., Copper-Nickel, 13.5 mm. **Obv:** Cocoa beans within circle **Rev:** Rampant lion at center of quartered shield dividing date and denomination

Date	Mintage	F	VF	XF	Unc	BU
1967	13,200,000	—	0.20	0.40	1.50	2.00
1967 Proof	2,000	Value: 2.50				
1975	20,000,000	—	0.20	0.40	1.25	1.75
1979	5,500,000	—	0.20	0.40	1.25	1.75

KM# 17 20 PESEWAS

Copper-Nickel, 28.5 mm. **Obv:** Cocoa beans within circle **Rev:** Rampant lion at center of quartered shield dividing date and denomination

Date	Mintage	F	VF	XF	Unc	BU
1967	25,800,000	—	0.25	0.50	1.75	2.50
1967 Proof	2,000	Value: 3.00				
1979	5,000,000	—	0.25	0.50	1.75	2.50

KM# 10 25 PESEWAS

8.6500 g., Copper-Nickel **Obv:** Head of Dr. Kwame Nkrumah right **Rev:** Star divides date and denomination

Date	Mintage	F	VF	XF	Unc	BU
1965	60,100,000	—	0.35	0.75	2.00	3.50

KM# 11 50 PESEWAS

Copper-Nickel **Obv:** Dr. Kwame Nkrumah head right **Rev:** Star divides date and denomination

Date	Mintage	F	VF	XF	Unc	BU
1965	18,200,000	—	0.75	1.50	3.50	5.00

KM# 18 50 PESEWAS

12.3600 g., Brass **Series:** F.A.O. **Obv:** Cocoa beans within circle **Rev:** Rampant lion at center of quartered shield dividing date and denomination

Date	Mintage	F	VF	XF	Unc	BU
1979	60,000,000	—	0.45	0.75	2.25	3.50

KM# 24 50 PESEWAS

Brass **Obv:** Cocoa beans within circle **Rev:** Rampant lion at center of quartered shield dividing date and denomination

Date	Mintage	F	VF	XF	Unc	BU
1984	10,000,000	—	0.10	0.25	0.60	1.00

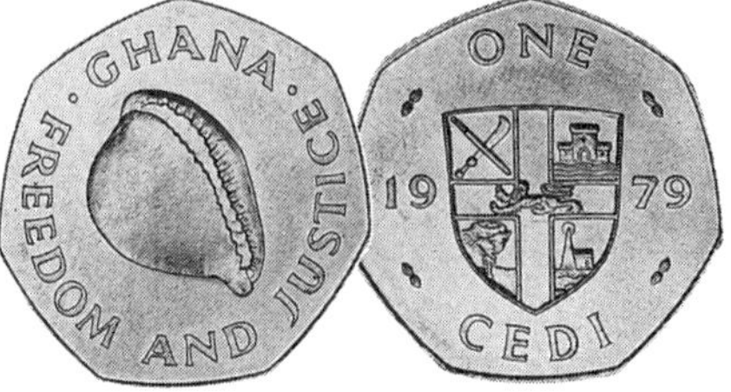

KM# 19 CEDI

11.9000 g., Brass, 30 mm. **Series:** F.A.O. **Obv:** Cowrie shell **Rev:** Rampant lion at center of quartered shield dividing date and denomination

Date	Mintage	F	VF	XF	Unc	BU
1979	160,000,000	—	0.35	0.85	3.00	7.50

KM# 25 CEDI

2.2400 g., Brass, 19.2 mm. **Obv:** Cowrie shell **Rev:** Rampant lion at center of quartered shield dividing date and denomination

Date	Mintage	F	VF	XF	Unc	BU
1984	40,000,000	—	0.10	0.25	1.50	3.00

KM# 26 5 CEDIS

Brass **Obv:** Bush drums **Rev:** Rampant lion at center of quartered shield dividing date and denomination

Date	Mintage	F	VF	XF	Unc	BU
1984	88,920,000	—	0.10	0.20	0.50	0.75

KM# 33 5 CEDIS
Brass Plated Steel **Obv:** Bush drums **Rev:** Rampant lion at center of quartered shield dividing date and denomination

Date	Mintage	F	VF	XF	Unc	BU
1991	—	—	0.10	0.20	0.50	0.75

KM# 29 10 CEDIS
3.5000 g., Nickel Clad Steel, 21.8 mm. **Obv:** Cocoa beans within circle **Rev:** Rampant lion at center of quartered shield dividing date and denomination **Shape:** 7-sided

Date	Mintage	F	VF	XF	Unc	BU
1991	—	—	—	0.35	0.75	1.25

KM# 36 10 CEDIS
4.4100 g., Copper-Nickel, 22.9 mm. **Obv:** National arms divides date and denomination **Rev:** Gorilla family **Edge:** Plain

Date	Mintage	F	VF	XF	Unc	BU
2003	—	—	—	—	1.50	2.00

KM# 30 20 CEDIS
5.4000 g., Nickel Clad Steel, 24.5 mm. **Obv:** Cowrie shell **Rev:** Rampant lion at center of quartered shield dividing date and denomination

Date	Mintage	F	VF	XF	Unc	BU
1991	—	—	—	0.35	1.50	3.00
1995	—	—	—	0.35	1.50	3.00

KM# 31 50 CEDIS
Copper-Nickel, 27.4 mm. **Obv:** Bush drums **Rev:** Rampant lion at center of quartered shield dividing date and denomination

Date	Mintage	F	VF	XF	Unc	BU
1991	—	—	—	1.00	2.25	3.50

KM# 31a 50 CEDIS
7.4000 g., Nickel Plated Steel, 27.4 mm. **Obv:** Bush drums **Rev:** Rampant lion at center of quartered shield dividing date and denomination

Date	Mintage	F	VF	XF	Unc	BU
1995	—	—	—	1.00	2.25	3.50
1997	—	—	—	1.00	2.25	3.50
1999	—	—	—	1.00	2.25	3.50

KM# 32 100 CEDIS
6.9000 g., Bi-Metallic Brass center in Copper-Nickel ring, 25 mm. **Obv:** Cocoa beans within circle **Rev:** Rampant lion at center of quartered shield dividing date and denomination, circle surrounds

Date	Mintage	F	VF	XF	Unc	BU
1991	—	—	—	1.75	3.50	4.75
1997	—	—	—	1.50	3.25	4.50
1999	—	—	—	1.50	3.25	4.50

KM# 35 200 CEDIS
Nickel Plated Steel **Obv:** Cowrie shell **Rev:** Rampant lion at center of quartered shield dividing date and denomination **Shape:** 7-sided

Date	Mintage	F	VF	XF	Unc	BU
1996	—	—	—	—	4.00	5.00
1998	—	—	—	—	4.00	5.00

Note: Fields frosted but not center design

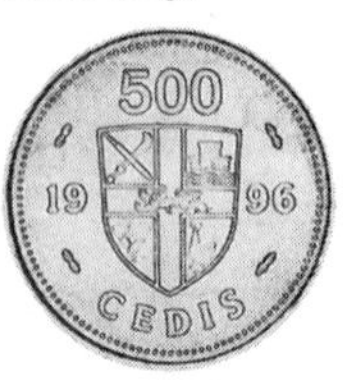

KM# 34 500 CEDIS
9.1700 g., Nickel-Brass **Obv:** Bush drums **Rev:** Rampant lion at center of quartered shield dividing date and denomination

Date	Mintage	F	VF	XF	Unc	BU
1996	—	—	—	—	4.75	5.50
1998	—	—	—	—	4.75	5.50

REFORM COINAGE

2007-

KM# 37 PESEWA
1.8200 g., Copper Clad Steel, 16.97 mm. **Obv:** National arms **Obv. Legend:** GHANA **Rev:** Modern arch bridge **Edge:** Plain

Date	Mintage	F	VF	XF	Unc	BU
2007	—	—	—	—	—	0.75

KM# 38 5 PESEWAS
2.5200 g., Nickel Clad Steel, 17.98 mm. **Obv:** National arms **Obv. Legend:** GHANA **Rev:** Native male blowing horn **Edge:** Plain

Date	Mintage	F	VF	XF	Unc	BU
2007	—	—	—	—	—	1.25

KM# 39 10 PESEWAS
3.2200 g., Nickel Clad Steel, 20.43 mm. **Obv:** National arms **Obv. Legend:** GHANA **Rev:** Open book, pen **Edge:** Reeded

Date	Mintage	F	VF	XF	Unc	BU
2007	—	—	—	—	—	2.50

KM# 40 20 PESEWAS
4.3600 g., Nickel Clad Steel, 23.47 mm. **Obv:** National arms **Obv. Legend:** GHANA **Rev:** Split open fruit **Edge:** Plain

Date	Mintage	F	VF	XF	Unc	BU
2007	—	—	—	—	—	3.50

KM# 41 50 PESEWAS
6.0800 g., Nickel, 26.40 mm. **Obv:** National arms **Obv. Legend:** GHANA **Rev:** 1/2 length figure of native woman facing **Edge:** Reeded

Date	Mintage	F	VF	XF	Unc	BU
2007	—	—	—	—	—	6.00

KM# 42 CEDI
7.3000 g., Bi-Metallic Brass center in Nickel Clad Steel ring, 27.98 mm. **Obv:** National arms **Obv. Legend:** GHANA **Rev:** Balance scale in sprays **Edge:** Segmented reeding

Date	Mintage	F	VF	XF	Unc	BU
2007	—	—	—	—	—	10.00

GIBRALTAR

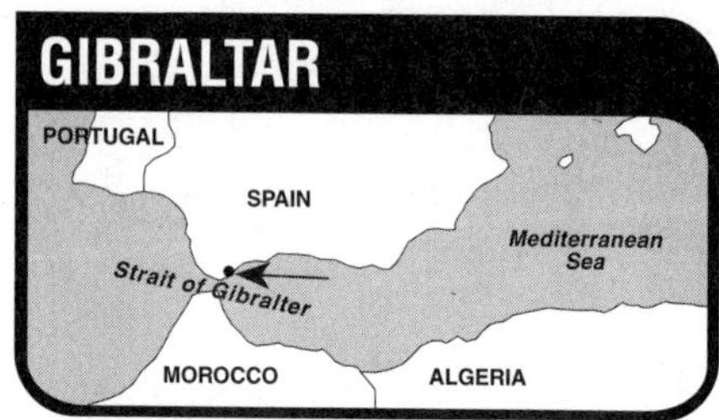

The British Colony of Gibraltar, located at the southernmost point of the Iberian Peninsula, has an area of 2.25 sq. mi. (6.5 sq. km.) and a population of 29,651. Capital (and only town): Gibraltar. Aside from its strategic importance as guardian of the western entrance to the Mediterranean Sea, Gibraltar is also a free port and a British naval base.

Gibraltar, rooted in Greek mythology as one of the Pillars of Hercules, has long been a coveted stronghold. Moslems took it from Spain and fortified it in 711. Spain retook it in 1309, lost it again to the Moors in 1333 and retook it in 1462. After 1540 Spain strengthened its defenses and held it until the War of the Spanish Succession when it was captured by a combined British and Dutch force in 1704. Britain held it against the Franco-Spanish attacks of 1704-05 and through the historic Great Siege of 1779-83.Recently Spain has attempted to discourage British occupancy by harassment and economic devices. In 1967, Gibraltar's inhabitants voted 12,138 to 44 to remain under British rule.

Gibraltar's celebrated Barbary Ape, the last monkey to be found in a wild state in Europe, is featured on the colony's first decimal crown, released in 1971.

RULERS
British

MINT MARKS
PM - Pobjoy Mint
PMM – Pobjoy Mint (only appears on coins dated 2000)

NOTE: ALL coins for 1988 –2003 include the PM mint mark except the 2000 dated circulation pieces which instead have PMM.

MINT PRIVY MARKS
U - Unc finish

DIE MARKS
1988: AA-AE
1989: AA-AF
1990: AA-AB
1991: AA
1992: AA-BB
1993: AA-BB
1994-1999: AA

MONETARY SYSTEM
4 Farthings = 1 Penny
12 Pence = 1 Shilling
2 Shillings = 1 Florin
5 Shillings = 1 Crown
20 Shillings = 1 Pound

BRITISH COLONY

CROWN COINAGE

1967-1970

KM# 4 CROWN
Copper-Nickel, 38.5 mm. **Ruler:** Elizabeth II **Obv:** Young bust right **Obv. Designer:** Arnold Machin **Rev:** Key below castle divides date, denomination below

Date	Mintage	F	VF	XF	Unc	BU
1967	125,000	—	1.00	2.00	5.00	—
1968	40,000	—	1.25	2.50	6.00	—
1969	40,000	—	1.25	2.50	6.00	—
1970	45,000	—	1.25	2.50	6.00	—

DECIMAL COINAGE

100 Pence = 1 Pound

KM# 20 PENNY
3.5700 g., Bronze, 20.5 mm. **Ruler:** Elizabeth II **Obv:** Crowned head right **Obv. Designer:** Raphael Maklouf **Rev:** Barbary partridge divides denomination **Rev. Designer:** Alfred Ryman

Date	Mintage	F	VF	XF	Unc	BU
1988 AA	—	—	—	—	0.35	0.50
1988 AB	—	—	—	—	0.35	0.50
1988 AC	—	—	—	—	0.35	0.50
1988 AD	—	—	—	—	0.35	0.50
1988 AE	—	—	—	—	0.35	0.50
1989 AA	—	—	—	—	0.35	0.50
1989 AB	—	—	—	—	0.35	0.50
1989 AC	—	—	—	—	0.35	0.50
1989 AD	—	—	—	—	0.35	0.50
1989 AE	—	—	—	—	0.35	0.50
1989 AF	—	—	—	—	0.35	0.50
1990 AA	—	—	—	—	0.35	0.50
1990 AB	—	—	—	—	0.35	0.50
1991 AA	—	—	—	—	0.35	0.50
1992 AA	—	—	—	—	0.35	0.50
1992 BB	—	—	—	—	0.35	0.50
1993 AA	—	—	—	—	0.35	0.50
1993 BB	—	—	—	—	0.35	0.50
1994 AA	—	—	—	—	0.35	0.50
1995 AA	—	—	—	—	0.35	0.50
1995 AB	—	—	—	—	0.35	0.50

KM# 20a PENNY
3.5600 g., Bronze Plated Steel, 20.29 mm. **Ruler:** Elizabeth II **Obv:** Crowned head right **Rev:** Barbary partridge left divides denomination **Edge:** Plain

Date	Mintage	F	VF	XF	Unc	BU
1995 AA	—	—	—	—	0.35	0.50
1995PM AB	—	—	—	—	0.35	0.50
1996 AA	—	—	—	—	0.35	0.50
1997 AA	—	—	—	—	0.35	0.50

KM# 773 PENNY
3.5200 g., Bronze Plated Steel, 20.4 mm. **Ruler:** Elizabeth II **Obv:** Head with tiara right **Obv. Designer:** Ian Rank-Broadley **Rev:** Barbary partridge left divides denomination

Date	Mintage	F	VF	XF	Unc	BU
1998 AA	—	—	—	—	0.35	0.50
1999 AA	—	—	—	—	0.35	0.50
2000PMM AA	—	—	—	—	0.35	0.50
2001 AA	—	—	—	—	0.35	0.50
2002 AA	—	—	—	—	0.35	0.50
2003 AA	—	—	—	—	0.35	0.50

KM# 1046 PENNY
3.5400 g., Copper-Plated-Steel, 20.02 mm. **Ruler:** Elizabeth II **Subject:** 300th Anniversary **Obv:** Crowned bust right **Rev:** Monkey **Edge:** Plain

Date	Mintage	F	VF	XF	Unc	BU
2004	—	—	—	—	0.30	0.50

KM# 21 2 PENCE
7.1500 g., Bronze, 25.83 mm. **Ruler:** Elizabeth II **Obv:** Crowned head right **Obv. Designer:** Raphael Maklouf **Rev:** Lighthouse on Europa Point, denomination **Rev. Designer:** Alfred Ryman **Edge:** Plain

Date	Mintage	F	VF	XF	Unc	BU
1988 AA	—	—	—	—	0.50	0.75
1988 AB	—	—	—	—	0.50	0.75
1988 AC	—	—	—	—	0.50	0.75
1988 AD	—	—	—	—	0.50	0.75
1988 AE	—	—	—	—	0.50	0.75
1989 AA	—	—	—	—	0.50	0.75
1989 AB	—	—	—	—	0.50	0.75
1989 AC	—	—	—	—	0.50	0.75
1989 AD	—	—	—	—	0.50	0.75
1989 AE	—	—	—	—	0.50	0.75
1989 AF	—	—	—	—	0.50	0.75
1990 AA	—	—	—	—	0.50	0.75
1990 AB	—	—	—	—	0.50	0.75
1991 AA	—	—	—	—	0.50	0.75
1991 AB	—	—	—	—	0.50	0.75
1992 AA	—	—	—	—	0.50	0.75
1992 BB	—	—	—	—	0.50	0.75
1993 AA	—	—	—	—	0.50	0.75
1993 BB	—	—	—	—	0.50	0.75
1994 AA	—	—	—	—	0.50	0.75
1995 AA	—	—	—	—	0.50	0.75

KM# 21a 2 PENCE
Bronze Plated Steel, 26 mm. **Ruler:** Elizabeth II **Obv:** Crowned head right **Rev:** Lighthouse on Europa Point, denomination

Date	Mintage	F	VF	XF	Unc	BU
1995 AB	—	—	—	—	0.50	0.65
1995 AA	—	—	—	—	0.50	0.75
1996 AA	—	—	—	—	0.50	0.75
1997 AA	—	—	—	—	0.50	0.75

KM# 774 2 PENCE
Bronze Plated Steel, 20.4 mm. **Ruler:** Elizabeth II **Obv:** Head with tiara right **Obv. Designer:** Ian Rank-Broadley

Date	Mintage	F	VF	XF	Unc	BU
1998 AA	—	—	—	—	0.50	0.85
1999 AA	—	—	—	—	0.50	0.85
2000 AA	—	—	—	—	0.50	0.85
2001PM AB	—	—	—	—	0.50	0.85
2001 AA	—	—	—	—	0.50	0.85

KM# 1044 2 PENCE
7.0400 g., Copper-Plated-Steel, 25.4 mm. **Ruler:** Elizabeth II **Subject:** 200th Anniversary **Obv:** Crowned bust right **Rev:** Four old keys **Edge:** Plain

Date	Mintage	F	VF	XF	Unc	BU
2004	—	—	—	—	0.50	0.65

KM# 22 5 PENCE
3.2400 g., Copper-Nickel, 23.6 mm. **Ruler:** Elizabeth II **Obv:** Crowned head right **Obv. Designer:** Raphael Maklouf **Rev:** Barbary ape divides denomination **Rev. Designer:** Alfred Ryman

Date	Mintage	F	VF	XF	Unc	BU
1988 AA	—	—	—	—	0.85	1.50
1989 AA	—	—	—	—	0.85	1.50
1989 AB	—	—	—	—	0.85	1.50
1989PM AC	—	—	—	—	0.85	1.50
1990 AA	—	—	—	—	0.85	1.50
1990 AB	—	—	—	—	0.85	1.50

KM# 22a 5 PENCE
3.1000 g., Copper-Nickel, 18 mm. **Ruler:** Elizabeth II **Obv:** Crowned head right **Rev:** Barbary ape divides denomination **Note:** Reduced size.

Date	Mintage	F	VF	XF	Unc	BU
1990 AA	—	—	—	—	0.60	1.00
1990 AB	—	—	—	—	0.60	1.00
1991 AA	—	—	—	—	0.60	1.00
1992 AA	—	—	—	—	0.60	1.00
1992 AB	—	—	—	—	0.60	1.00
1993 AA	—	—	—	—	0.60	1.00
1993 AB	—	—	—	—	0.60	1.00
1994 AA	—	—	—	—	0.60	1.00
1995 AA	—	—	—	—	0.60	1.00
1996 AA	—	—	—	—	0.60	1.00
1997 AA	—	—	—	—	0.60	1.00

KM# 775 5 PENCE
3.1000 g., Copper-Nickel, 18 mm. **Ruler:** Elizabeth II **Obv:** Head with tiara right **Obv. Designer:** Ian Rank-Broadley **Rev:** Barbary Ape left divides denomination

Date	Mintage	F	VF	XF	Unc	BU
1998 AA	—	—	—	—	0.60	0.75
1999 AA	—	—	—	—	0.60	0.75
2000	—	—	—	—	0.60	0.75
2001	—	—	—	—	0.60	0.75

KM# 1049 5 PENCE
3.2500 g., Copper-Nickel, 18 mm. **Ruler:** Elizabeth II **Subject:** Tercentenary 1704-2004 **Obv:** Elizabeth II **Rev:** British Royal Sceptre **Edge:** Reeded

Date	Mintage	F	VF	XF	Unc	BU
2004PM	—	—	—	—	—	1.50

KM# 23.1 10 PENCE
11.5000 g., Copper-Nickel, 28.5 mm. **Ruler:** Elizabeth II **Obv:** Crowned head right **Obv. Designer:** Raphael Maklouf **Rev:** Moorish castle, denomination **Rev. Designer:** Alfred Ryman

Date	Mintage	F	VF	XF	Unc	BU
1988 AA	—	—	—	—	1.00	1.25
1988 AB	—	—	—	—	1.00	1.25
1989 AA	—	—	—	—	1.00	1.25
1989PM AB	—	—	—	—	1.00	1.25
1989PM AC	—	—	—	—	1.00	1.25
1989PM AD	—	—	—	—	1.00	1.25

Date	Mintage	F	VF	XF	Unc	BU
1990 AA	—	—	—	—	1.00	1.25
1990 AB	—	—	—	—	1.00	1.25
1990 AC	—	—	—	—	1.00	1.25
1991 AA	—	—	—	—	1.00	1.25
1991 AB	—	—	—	—	1.00	1.25

KM# 23.2 10 PENCE
6.5000 g., Copper-Nickel, 24.5 mm. **Ruler:** Elizabeth II **Obv:** Crowned head right **Obv. Designer:** Raphael Maklouf **Rev:** Moorish castle, denomination **Rev. Designer:** Alfred Ryman **Edge:** Reeded **Note:** Reduced size.

Date	Mintage	F	VF	XF	Unc	BU
1994 AA	—	—	—	—	1.00	1.25

KM# 112 10 PENCE
6.5000 g., Copper-Nickel, 24.5 mm. **Ruler:** Elizabeth II **Obv:** Crowned head right **Obv. Designer:** Raphael Maklouf **Rev:** Europort

Date	Mintage	F	VF	XF	Unc	BU
1992 AA	—	—	—	—	0.75	1.00
1993 AA	—	—	—	—	0.75	1.00
1995 AA	—	—	—	—	0.75	1.00
1996 AA	—	—	—	—	0.75	1.00
1996PM BB	—	—	—	—	0.75	1.00
1997 AA	—	—	—	—	0.75	1.00

KM# 776 10 PENCE
6.5000 g., Copper-Nickel, 24.5 mm. **Ruler:** Elizabeth II **Obv:** Head with tiara right, date below **Obv. Designer:** Ian Rank-Broadley **Rev:** Denomination below building

Date	Mintage	F	VF	XF	Unc	BU
1998 AA	—	—	—	—	1.00	1.25
1999 AA	—	—	—	—	1.00	1.25
2000	—	—	—	—	1.00	1.25
2001	—	—	—	—	1.00	1.25

KM# 1047 10 PENCE
6.4200 g., Copper-Nickel, 24.4 mm. **Ruler:** Elizabeth II **Subject:** 300th Anniversary **Obv:** Elizabeth II **Rev:** Three military officers planning Operation Torch 1942 **Edge:** Reeded

Date	Mintage	F	VF	XF	Unc	BU
2004	—	—	—	—	0.75	1.00

KM# 16 20 PENCE
5.0000 g., Copper-Nickel, 21.4 mm. **Ruler:** Elizabeth II **Obv:** Crowned head right **Obv. Designer:** Raphael Maklouf **Rev:** Our Lady of Europa, a polychrome wood statue, two-feet tall, from the 16th century **Rev. Designer:** Alfred Ryman **Shape:** 7-sided

Date	Mintage	F	VF	XF	Unc	BU
1988 AA	—	—	—	—	1.50	2.00
1988 AB	—	—	—	—	1.50	2.00
1988 AC	—	—	—	—	1.50	2.00
1988 AA Proof	—	—	—	—	—	—
1989 AA	—	—	—	—	1.50	2.00
1990 AA	—	—	—	—	1.50	2.00
1991 AA	—	—	—	—	1.50	2.00
1992 AA	—	—	—	—	1.50	2.00
1993 AA	—	—	—	—	1.50	2.00
1994 AA	—	—	—	—	1.50	2.00
1995 AA	—	—	—	—	1.50	2.00
1995 AA Proof	—	—	—	—	—	—

Date	Mintage	F	VF	XF	Unc	BU
1996 AA	—	—	—	—	1.50	2.00
1997 AA	—	—	—	—	1.50	2.00

KM# 777 20 PENCE
5.0000 g., Copper-Nickel, 21.4 mm. **Ruler:** Elizabeth II **Obv:** Head with tiara right, date below **Obv. Designer:** Ian Rank-Broadley **Rev:** Our Lady of Europa, denomination below and right **Rev. Designer:** Alfred Ryman **Shape:** 7-sided

Date	Mintage	F	VF	XF	Unc	BU
1998 AA	—	—	—	—	1.50	2.00
1999 AA	—	—	—	—	1.50	2.00
2000 AA	—	—	—	—	1.50	2.00
2001 AA	—	—	—	—	1.50	2.00

KM# 1048 20 PENCE
4.9400 g., Copper-Nickel, 21.4 mm. **Ruler:** Elizabeth II **Subject:** 300th Anniversary **Obv:** Crowned buat right **Rev:** Neanderthal skull found in Gibraltar in 1848 **Edge:** Plain **Shape:** 7-sided

Date	Mintage	F	VF	XF	Unc	BU
2004	—	—	—	—	1.00	1.50

KM# 5 25 NEW PENCE
Copper-Nickel, 38.5 mm. **Ruler:** Elizabeth II **Obv:** Young bust right, date below **Obv. Designer:** Arnold Machin **Rev:** Barbary ape left, denomination below **Rev. Designer:** Christopher Ironside

Date	Mintage	F	VF	XF	Unc	BU
1971	75,000	—	—	2.00	6.00	14.00

KM# 6 25 NEW PENCE
Copper-Nickel, 38.5 mm. **Ruler:** Elizabeth II **Subject:** 25th Wedding Anniversary **Obv:** Young bust right **Obv. Designer:** Arnold Machin **Rev:** Arms of Queen Elizabeth II and Prince Philip, date and denomination below **Rev. Designer:** Stuart Devlin

Date	Mintage	F	VF	XF	Unc	BU
1972	70,000	—	—	1.50	3.50	5.00

KM# 10 25 NEW PENCE
Copper-Nickel, 38.5 mm. **Ruler:** Elizabeth II **Subject:** Queen's Silver Jubilee **Obv:** Young bust right **Obv. Designer:** Arnold Machin **Rev:** Shield within wreath of apes and laurel, denomination below

Date	Mintage	F	VF	XF	Unc	BU
1977	65,000	—	—	1.50	3.50	5.00

KM# 17 50 PENCE
13.4000 g., Copper-Nickel, 30 mm. **Ruler:** Elizabeth II **Obv:** Crowned head right **Obv. Designer:** Raphael Maklouf **Rev:** Denomination in wreath of Candytuft flowers (Iberis Gibraltarica) **Rev. Designer:** Alfred Ryman **Shape:** 7-sided

Date	Mintage	F	VF	XF	Unc	BU
1988 AA	30,000	—	—	—	2.00	2.50
1988 AB	—	—	—	—	2.00	2.50
1989 AA	—	—	—	—	2.00	2.50
1989 AB	—	—	—	—	2.00	2.50

KM# 39 50 PENCE
13.4000 g., Copper-Nickel, 30 mm. **Ruler:** Elizabeth II **Obv:** Crowned head right **Obv. Designer:** Raphael Maklouf **Rev:** Dolphins surround denomination **Shape:** 7-sided

Date	Mintage	F	VF	XF	Unc	BU
1990 AA	—	—	—	—	4.50	6.00
1991 AA	—	—	—	—	4.50	6.00
1992 AA	—	—	—	—	4.50	6.00
1993 AA	—	—	—	—	4.50	6.00
1994 AA	—	—	—	—	4.50	6.00
1995 AA	—	—	—	—	4.50	6.00
1996 AA	—	—	—	—	4.50	6.00
1997	—	—	—	—	4.00	6.00

KM# 778 50 PENCE
8.0000 g., Copper-Nickel, 27.3 mm. **Ruler:** Elizabeth II **Obv:** Head with tiara right **Obv. Designer:** Ian Rank-Broadley **Rev:** Dolphins surround denomination **Edge:** Plain **Shape:** 7-sided

Date	Mintage	F	VF	XF	Unc	BU
1998PM AA	—	—	—	—	4.50	5.50
1999PM AA	—	—	—	—	4.50	5.50
2000PM AA	—	—	—	—	4.50	5.50
2001 AA	—	—	—	—	4.50	5.50
2001 AB	—	—	—	—	4.50	5.50

KM# 1050 50 PENCE
8.0000 g., Copper-Nickel, 27.3 mm. **Ruler:** Elizabeth II **Subject:** Tercentenary 1704-2004 **Obv:** Elizabeth II **Rev:** HMS Victory sailing past Gibraltar **Edge:** Plain **Shape:** Seven sided

Date	Mintage	F	VF	XF	Unc	BU
2004PM	—	—	—	—	—	3.00

KM# 18 POUND
9.5000 g., Nickel-Brass, 22.5 mm. **Ruler:** Elizabeth II **Obv:** Crowned head right **Obv. Designer:** Raphael Maklouf **Rev:** Gibraltar castle and key **Rev. Designer:** Alfred Ryman

Date	Mintage	F	VF	XF	Unc	BU
1988 AA	—	—	—	—	3.50	4.50
1988PM AB	—	—	—	—	3.50	4.50
1990 AA	—	—	—	—	3.50	4.50
1991 AA	—	—	—	—	3.50	4.50
1991 AC	—	—	—	—	3.50	4.50
1992 AA	—	—	—	—	3.50	4.50
1993 AA	—	—	—	—	3.50	4.50
1996 AA	—	—	—	—	3.50	4.50
1997 AA	—	—	—	—	3.50	4.50

KM# 32 POUND
9.5000 g., Nickel-Brass, 22.5 mm. **Ruler:** Elizabeth II **Subject:** 150th Anniversary of Gibraltar Coinage **Obv:** Crowned head right **Obv. Designer:** Raphael Maklouf **Rev:** Gibraltar castle and key within circle

Date	Mintage	F	VF	XF	Unc	BU
1989 AA	—	—	—	—	4.00	5.00

KM# 191 POUND
Nickel-Brass, 22.5 mm. **Ruler:** Elizabeth II **Subject:** Referendum of 1967 **Obv:** Crowned head right **Obv. Designer:** Raphael Maklouf **Rev:** Gibraltar arms above Rock of Gibraltar with Union Jack background

Date	Mintage	F	VF	XF	Unc	BU
1993 AA	—	—	—	—	4.50	5.50

KM# 324 POUND
9.5000 g., Nickel-Brass, 22.5 mm. **Ruler:** Elizabeth II **Subject:** 40th Anniversary - Queen Elizabeth II's 1st Royal Visit to Gibraltar **Obv:** Crowned head right **Obv. Designer:** Raphael Maklouf **Rev:** Luxury liner at sea

Date	Mintage	F	VF	XF	Unc	BU
1994 AA	—	—	—	—	7.50	9.00

KM# 340 POUND
9.5000 g., Nickel-Brass, 22.5 mm. **Ruler:** Elizabeth II **Subject:** National Day, 50th Anniversary of the U.N. **Obv:** Crowned head right **Obv. Designer:** Raphael Maklouf **Rev:** Rock of Gibraltar

Date	Mintage	F	VF	XF	Unc	BU
1995 AA	—	—	—	—	3.50	5.00

KM# 869 POUND
9.5000 g., Nickel-Brass, 22.5 mm. **Ruler:** Elizabeth II **Obv:** Head with tiara right **Obv. Designer:** Ian Rank-Broadley **Rev:** Gibraltar castle and key

Date	Mintage	F	VF	XF	Unc	BU
1998 AA	—	—	—	—	3.50	4.50
1999 AA	—	—	—	—	3.50	4.50
2000PMM AA	—	—	—	—	3.50	4.50
2001 AA	—	—	—	—	3.50	4.50
2001 AB	—	—	—	—	3.50	4.50
2002 AC	—	—	—	—	3.50	4.50

KM# 1036 POUND
9.5000 g., Nickel-Brass, 22 mm. **Ruler:** Elizabeth II **Subject:** 1700th Anniversary - Death of St. George **Obv:** Bust with tiara right **Rev:** St. George and the dragon **Edge:** Reeded

Date	Mintage	F	VF	XF	Unc	BU
2003	—	—	—	—	9.00	10.00

KM# 1051 POUND
9.5000 g., Nickel-Brass, 22.5 mm. **Ruler:** Elizabeth II **Subject:** Tercentenary 1704-2004 **Obv:** Elizabeth II **Rev:** Old cannon set for a downhill target **Edge:** Reeded

Date	Mintage	F	VF	XF	Unc	BU
2004PM	—	—	—	—	—	4.00

KM# 24 2 POUNDS
Virenium **Ruler:** Elizabeth II **Obv:** Crowned head right **Obv. Designer:** Raphael Maklouf **Rev:** Cannon in fortress tunnel **Rev. Designer:** Alfred Ryman

Date	Mintage	F	VF	XF	Unc	BU
1988 AA	—	—	—	—	7.50	8.50
1989 AA	—	—	—	—	7.50	8.50
1990 AA	—	—	—	—	7.50	8.50
1991 AA	—	—	—	—	7.50	8.50
1993 AA	—	—	—	—	7.50	8.50
1995 AA	—	—	—	—	7.50	8.50
1995 AB	—	—	—	—	7.50	8.50
1995 AC	—	—	—	—	7.50	8.50
1996 AA	—	—	—	—	7.50	8.50

KM# 970 2 POUNDS
Bi-Metallic Steel Copper-Nickel center in Brass ring, 28.4 mm. **Ruler:** Elizabeth II **Subject:** Bicentennial of the Union Jack **Obv:** Head with tiara right **Obv. Designer:** Ian Rank-Broadley **Rev:** Standing Britannia wearing flag as a cape **Edge:** Reeded

Date	Mintage	F	VF	XF	Unc	BU
2001 AA	—	—	—	—	10.00	12.00

KM# 1043 2 POUNDS
12.0600 g., Bi-Metallic Copper-Nickel center in Brass ring, 28.3 mm. **Ruler:** Elizabeth II **Obv:** Head with tiara right **Obv. Designer:** Ian Rank-Broadley **Rev:** Old cannon **Edge:** Reeded

Date	Mintage	F	VF	XF	Unc	BU
2003PM	—	—	—	—	10.00	12.00

KM# 1057 2 POUNDS
9.5000 g., Nickel-Brass, 22.5 mm. **Ruler:** Elizabeth II **Subject:** Tercentenary 1704-2004 **Obv:** Elizabeth II **Rev:** Old cannon set for a downhill target **Edge:** Reeded

Date	Mintage	F	VF	XF	Unc	BU
2004PM	—	—	—	—	—	4.00

GREAT BRITAIN

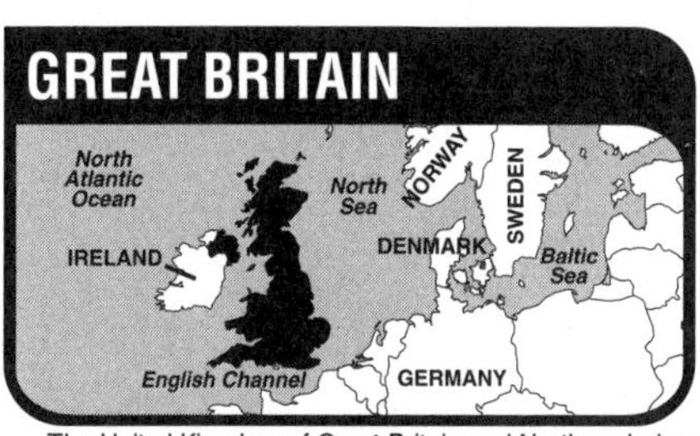

The United Kingdom of Great Britain and Northern Ireland, located off the northwest coast of the European continent, has an area of 94,227 sq. mi. (244,820 sq. km.) and a population of 54 million. Capital: London. The economy is based on industrial activity and trading. Machinery, motor vehicles, chemicals, and textile yarns and fabrics are exported.

After the departure of the Romans, who brought Britain into a more active relationship with Europe, it fell prey to invaders from Scandinavia and the Low Countries who drove the original Britons into Scotland and Wales, and established a profusion of kingdoms that finally united in the 11th century under the Danish King Canute. Norman rule, following the conquest of 1066, stimulated the development of those institutions, which have since distinguished British life. Henry VIII (1509-47) turned Britain from continental adventuring and faced it to the sea - a decision that made Britain a world power during the reign of Elizabeth I (1558-1603). Strengthened by the Industrial Revolution and the defeat of Napoleon, 19th century Britain turned to the remote parts of the world and established a colonial empire of such extent and prosperity that the world has never seen its like. World Wars I and II sealed the fate of the Empire and relegated Britain to a lesser role in world affairs by draining her resources and inaugurating a worldwide movement toward national self-determination in her former colonies.

By the mid-20th century, most of the territories formerly comprising the British Empire had gained independence, and the empire had evolved into the Commonwealth of Nations, an association of equal and autonomous states, which enjoy special trade interests. The Commonwealth is presently composed of 54 member nations, including the United Kingdom. All recognize the British monarch as head of the Commonwealth. Sixteen continue to recognize the British monarch as Head of State. They are: United Kingdom, Antigua and Barbuda, Australia, Bahamas, Barbados, Belize, Canada, Grenada, Jamaica, New Zealand, Papua New Guinea, St. Christopher & Nevis, Saint Lucia, Saint Vincent and the Grenadines, Solomon Islands, and Tuvalu. Elizabeth II is personally, and separately, the Queen of the sovereign, independent countries just mentioned. There is no other British connection between the several individual, national sovereignties, except that High Commissioners represent them each instead of ambassadors in each others' countries.

RULERS

Victoria, 1837-1901
Edward VII, 1901-1910
George V, 1910-1936
Edward VIII, 1936
George VI, 1936-1952
Elizabeth II, 1952--

MINT MARKS

H - Heaton
KN - King's Norton

MONETARY SYSTEM

Colloquial Denomination Terms

Ha'penny = 1/2 Penny
Tanner = 6 Pence
Bob = 1 Shilling
Half a Crown (Half a Dollar) = 2 Shillings 6 Pence
Dollar = 5 Shillings
Half a quid = 10 Shillings
Quid = 1 Pound
Tenner = 10 Pounds
Pony = 20 Pounds

(Until 1970)

4 Farthings = 1 Penny
12 Pence = 1 Shilling
2 Shillings = 1 Florin
5 Shillings = 1 Crown
20 Shillings = 1 Pound (Sovereign)
21 Shillings = 1 Guinea
½ Sovereign = 10 Shillings (i.e. ½ Pound)
1 Sovereign = 1 Pound

NOTE: Proofs exist for many dates of British coins in the 19th and early 20th centuries and for virtually all coins between 1926 and 1964. Those not specifically listed here are extremely rare.

NOTE: Pound Coinage - Strictly red, original mint luster coins in the copper series command premiums.

KINGDOM

Resumed

PRE-DECIMAL COINAGE

KM# 791 1/3 FARTHING

0.9500 g., Bronze **Ruler:** Edward VII **Obv:** Head right **Rev:** Denomination and date within crowned oak wreath **Note:** Homeland style struck for Malta.

Date	Mintage	F	VF	XF	Unc	BU
1902	288,000	2.50	5.00	10.00	35.00	—

KM# 823 1/3 FARTHING

0.9500 g., Bronze **Ruler:** George V **Obv:** Head left **Rev:** Crowned value within oak wreath **Note:** Homeland style struck for Malta.

Date	Mintage	F	VF	XF	Unc	BU
1913	288,000	2.50	5.00	10.00	35.00	—

KM# 788.2 FARTHING

2.8000 g., Bronze, 20 mm. **Ruler:** Victoria **Obv:** Mature draped bust left **Obv. Legend:** VICTORIA. DEI. GRA. BRITT. REGINA. FID. DEF. IND. IMP. **Obv. Designer:** Thomas Brock **Rev:** Britannia seated right **Note:** Blackened finish.

Date	Mintage	F	VF	XF	Unc	BU
1901	8,016,000	0.45	0.75	3.00	17.00	—

KM# 792 FARTHING

2.8000 g., Bronze, 20 mm. **Ruler:** Edward VII **Obv:** Head right **Rev:** Britannia seated right

Date	Mintage	F	VF	XF	Unc	BU
1902	5,125,000	0.50	1.50	5.00	25.00	—
1903	5,331,000	0.50	1.50	5.50	25.00	—
1903 Proof	—	Value: 1,250				
Note: Shield heraldically colored						
1904	3,629,000	1.50	2.50	8.00	30.00	—
1905	4,077,000	0.50	1.25	5.50	25.00	—
1906	5,340,000	0.50	1.25	5.50	25.00	—
1907	4,399,000	0.50	1.25	5.50	25.00	—
1908	4,265,000	0.50	1.25	5.50	25.00	—
1909	8,852,000	0.50	1.25	5.50	25.00	—
1910	2,598,000	1.00	3.00	8.00	35.00	—

KM# 808.1 FARTHING

2.8000 g., Bronze, 20 mm. **Ruler:** George V **Obv:** Head left **Obv. Designer:** Bertram MacKennal **Rev:** Britannia seated right

Date	Mintage	F	VF	XF	Unc	BU
1911	5,197,000	0.60	1.00	3.00	21.00	—
1912	7,670,000	0.35	0.75	2.25	20.00	—
1913	4,184,000	0.50	0.75	2.25	20.00	—
1914	6,127,000	0.35	0.75	2.25	20.00	—
1915	7,129,000	0.50	0.75	4.50	22.00	—
1916	10,993,000	0.35	0.75	2.00	20.00	—
1917	21,435,000	0.15	0.35	1.50	20.00	—
1918	19,363,000	0.75	1.50	9.50	27.00	—

KM# 808.2 FARTHING

2.8000 g., Bronze, 20 mm. **Ruler:** George V **Obv:** Head left **Obv. Designer:** Bertram MacKennal **Rev:** Britannia seated right **Note:** Bright finish.

Date	Mintage	F	VF	XF	Unc	BU
1918	Inc. above	0.20	0.40	1.00	12.50	—
1919	15,089,000	0.20	0.40	1.00	12.50	—
1920	11,481,000	0.20	0.40	1.00	13.50	—
1921	9,469,000	0.20	0.40	1.00	14.00	—
1922	9,957,000	0.20	0.40	1.00	14.00	—
1923	8,034,000	0.20	0.40	1.00	14.00	—
1924	8,733,000	0.20	0.40	1.00	14.00	—
1924 Specimen	2	—	—	—	—	1,500
1925	12,635,000	0.20	0.40	1.00	14.00	—

KM# 825 FARTHING

2.8000 g., Bronze, 20 mm. **Ruler:** George V **Obv:** Head left, modified effigy **Obv. Designer:** Bertram MacKennal **Rev:** Britannia seated right

Date	Mintage	F	VF	XF	Unc	BU
1926	9,792,000	0.15	0.40	1.00	6.50	—
1926 Proof	—	Value: 850				
1927	7,868,000	0.15	0.40	1.00	6.50	—
1927 Proof	—	Value: 550				
1928	11,626,000	0.15	0.35	1.00	6.50	—
1928 Proof	—	Value: 450				
1929	8,419,000	0.15	0.35	1.00	6.50	—
1929 Proof	—	Value: 450				
1930	4,195,000	0.25	0.50	1.00	6.50	—
1930 Proof	—	Value: 450				
1931	6,595,000	0.15	0.35	1.00	6.50	—
1931 Proof	—	Value: 450				
1932	9,293,000	0.15	0.35	1.00	6.50	—
1932 Proof	—	Value: 450				
1933	4,560,000	0.15	0.35	1.00	6.50	—
1933 Proof	—	Value: 450				
1934	3,053,000	0.35	0.75	2.00	10.00	—
1934 Proof	—	Value: 450				
1935	2,227,000	1.00	2.00	3.00	7.50	—
1935 Proof	—	Value: 450				
1936	9,734,000	0.15	0.35	1.00	5.00	—
1936 Proof	—	Value: 450				

KM# 843 FARTHING

2.8000 g., Bronze, 20 mm. **Ruler:** George VI **Obv:** Head left **Obv. Designer:** T. H. Paget **Rev:** Wren left

Date	Mintage	F	VF	XF	Unc	BU
1937	8,131,000	0.15	0.25	0.50	5.00	—
1937 Matte Proof	—	Value: 1,500				
Note: There are reportedly 3-4 pieces known of this variety struck specifically for use in photographs						
1937 Proof	26,000	Value: 11.00				
1938	7,450,000	0.15	0.30	0.60	7.50	—
1938 Proof	—	Value: 425				
1939	31,440,000	0.10	0.25	0.50	5.00	—
1939 Proof	—	Value: 425				
1940	18,360,000	0.10	0.25	0.50	5.00	—
1940 Proof	—	Value: 425				
1941	27,312,000	0.10	0.25	0.50	4.50	—
1941 Proof	—	Value: 425				
1942	28,858,000	0.10	0.20	0.50	4.50	—
1942 Proof	—	Value: 425				
1943	33,345,999	0.10	0.15	0.50	4.50	—
1943 Proof	—	Value: 450				
1944	25,138,000	0.10	0.15	0.50	4.50	—
1944 Proof	—	Value: 450				
1945	23,736,000	0.10	0.20	0.50	4.50	—
1945 Proof	—	Value: 450				
1946	24,365,000	0.10	0.20	0.50	4.50	—
1946 Proof	—	Value: 450				
1947	14,746,000	0.10	0.20	0.50	4.50	—
1947 Proof	—	Value: 450				
1948	16,622,000	0.10	0.20	0.50	4.50	—
1948 Proof	—	Value: 450				

KM# 867 FARTHING

Bronze, 20 mm. **Ruler:** George VI **Obv:** Head left **Obv. Legend:** Without IND IMP **Obv. Designer:** T. H. Paget **Rev:** Wren left

Date	Mintage	F	VF	XF	Unc	BU
1949	8,424,000	0.10	0.20	0.50	6.50	—
1949 Proof	—	Value: 450				
1950	10,325,000	0.10	0.20	0.50	6.50	—
1950 Matte Proof	—	Value: 1,500				
Note: There are reportedly 3-4 known of this variety, struck specifically for use in photographs						
1950 Proof	18,000	Value: 13.00				
1951	14,016,000	0.10	0.20	0.50	7.00	—
1951 Matte Proof	—	Value: 1,500				
Note: There are reportedly 3-4 known of this variety, struck specifically for use in photographs						
1951 Proof	20,000	Value: 20.00				
1952	5,251,000	0.10	0.20	0.50	6.00	—
1952 Proof	—	Value: 550				

KM# 881 FARTHING

Bronze, 20 mm. **Ruler:** Elizabeth II **Obv:** Laureate bust right **Obv. Designer:** Mary Gillick **Rev:** Wren left

Date	Mintage	F	VF	XF	Unc	BU
1953	6,131,000	0.15	0.25	0.50	3.00	—
1953 Proof	40,000	Value: 8.00				
1953 Matte Proof	—	Value: 1,500				
Note: There are reportedly 1-2 known of this variety, struck specifically for use in photographs						

KM# 895 FARTHING

Bronze, 20 mm. **Ruler:** Elizabeth II **Obv:** Laureate bust right **Obv. Legend:** Without BRITT OMN **Obv. Designer:** Mary Gillick **Rev:** Wren left

Date	Mintage	F	VF	XF	Unc	BU
1954	6,566,000	0.10	0.15	0.50	5.00	—
1954 Proof	—	Value: 450				
1955	5,779,000	0.10	0.15	0.50	5.00	—
1955 Proof	—	Value: 450				
1956	1,997,000	0.25	0.50	3.00	7.50	—
1956 Proof	—	Value: 450				

KM# 789 1/2 PENNY

5.7000 g., Bronze, 25.5 mm. **Ruler:** Victoria **Obv:** Mature draped bust left **Obv. Legend:** VICTORIA. DEI. GRA. BRITT. REGINA FID. DEF. IND. IMP. **Obv. Designer:** Thomas Brock **Rev:** Britannia seated right

Date	Mintage	F	VF	XF	Unc	BU
1901	11,127,000	2.25	4.50	18.00	30.00	—
1901 Proof	—	Value: 900				

KM# 793.1 1/2 PENNY

Bronze, 25.5 mm. **Ruler:** Edward VII **Obv:** Head right **Rev:** Britannia seated right, low horizon line

Date	Mintage	F	VF	XF	Unc	BU
1902	13,673,000	6.50	20.00	75.00	180	—

KM# 793.2 1/2 PENNY

5.2000 g., Bronze, 25.5 mm. **Ruler:** Edward VII **Obv:** Head right **Rev:** Britannia seated right, high horizon line

Date	Mintage	F	VF	XF	Unc	BU
1902	Inc. above	0.95	2.50	10.00	35.00	—
1903	11,451,000	0.95	2.50	10.00	40.00	—
1904	8,131,000	1.50	4.50	16.50	50.00	—
1905	10,125,000	0.95	2.50	10.00	40.00	—
1906	11,101,000	0.95	2.50	10.00	35.00	—
1907	16,849,000	0.95	2.50	10.00	35.00	—
1908	16,620,999	0.95	2.50	10.00	35.00	—
1909	8,279,000	0.95	2.50	10.00	45.00	—
1910	10,770,000	0.95	2.50	10.00	40.00	—

KM# 809 1/2 PENNY
5.4000 g., Bronze, 25.5 mm. **Ruler:** George V **Obv:** Head left **Obv. Designer:** Bertram MacKennal **Rev:** Britannia seated right

Date	Mintage	F	VF	XF	Unc	BU
1911	12,571,000	0.75	1.50	9.00	35.00	—
1912	21,186,000	0.75	1.25	9.00	35.00	—
1913	17,476,000	0.75	1.75	12.00	35.00	—
1914	20,289,000	0.75	1.50	9.00	35.00	—
1915	21,563,000	0.75	1.50	9.00	35.00	—
1916	39,386,000	0.75	1.50	5.00	35.00	—
1917	38,245,000	0.75	1.50	5.00	35.00	—
1918	22,321,000	0.75	1.50	5.00	35.00	—
1919	28,104,000	0.75	1.50	5.00	35.00	—
1920	35,147,000	0.75	1.50	5.00	35.00	—
1921	28,027,000	0.75	1.50	5.00	35.00	—
1922	10,735,000	1.00	2.00	7.00	35.00	—
1923	12,266,000	0.75	1.50	5.00	35.00	—
1924	13,971,000	1.00	2.00	7.00	35.00	—
1924 Specimen	2	—	—	—	—	1,800
1925	12,216,000	1.00	2.00	7.00	35.00	—

KM# 824 1/2 PENNY
Bronze, 25.5 mm. **Ruler:** George V **Obv:** Head left, modified effigy **Obv. Designer:** Bertram MacKennal **Rev:** Britannia seated right

Date	Mintage	F	VF	XF	Unc	BU
1925	Inc. above	1.50	4.00	8.00	60.00	—
1926	6,712,000	1.50	4.00	8.00	35.00	—
1926 Proof	—	Value: 900				
1927	15,590,000	0.75	1.50	5.00	35.00	—
1927 Proof	—	Value: 600				

KM# 837 1/2 PENNY
Bronze, 25.5 mm. **Ruler:** George V **Obv:** Smaller head left **Obv. Designer:** Bertram MacKennal **Rev:** Britannia seated right

Date	Mintage	F	VF	XF	Unc	BU
1928	20,935,000	0.25	0.50	2.50	25.00	—
1928 Proof	—	Value: 550				
1929	25,680,000	0.25	0.50	2.50	25.00	—
1929 Proof	—	Value: 550				
1930	12,533,000	0.25	0.50	2.50	25.00	—
1930 Proof	—	Value: 550				
1931	16,138,000	0.25	0.50	2.50	25.00	—
1931 Proof	—	Value: 550				
1932	14,448,000	0.25	0.50	2.50	25.00	—
1932 Proof	—	Value: 550				
1933	10,560,000	0.25	0.50	2.50	25.00	—
1933 Proof	—	Value: 550				
1934	7,704,000	0.50	1.00	4.00	25.00	—
1934 Proof	—	Value: 600				
1935	12,180,000	0.25	0.50	2.50	25.00	—
1935 Proof	—	Value: 500				
1936	23,009,000	0.25	0.50	2.50	19.00	—
1936 Proof	—	Value: 500				

KM# 844 1/2 PENNY
Bronze, 25.5 mm. **Ruler:** George VI **Obv:** Head left **Rev:** The Golden Hind **Designer:** T. H. Paget

Date	Mintage	F	VF	XF	Unc	BU
1937	24,504,000	0.25	0.35	0.50	7.00	—
1937 Proof	26,000	Value: 11.00				
1937 Matte Proof	Est. 4	Value: 1,250				
1938	40,320,000	0.25	0.50	1.00	10.00	—
1938 Proof	—	Value: 500				
1939	28,925,000	0.25	0.50	2.00	12.00	—
1939 Proof	—	Value: 500				
1940	32,162,000	0.25	0.50	3.00	14.00	—
1940 Proof	—	Value: 500				
1941	45,120,000	0.20	0.50	1.00	7.50	—
1941 Proof	—	Value: 500				
1942	71,909,000	0.10	0.20	0.60	7.50	—
1942 Proof	—	Value: 500				
1943	76,200,000	0.10	0.25	0.75	7.50	—
1943 Proof	—	Value: 550				
1944	81,840,000	0.10	0.25	0.75	7.50	—
1944 Proof	—	Value: 550				
1945	57,000,000	0.10	0.25	1.00	9.00	—
1945 Proof	—	Value: 550				
1946	22,726,000	0.20	0.50	2.50	12.00	—
1946 Proof	—	Value: 550				
1947	21,266,000	0.10	0.25	1.50	10.00	—
1947 Proof	—	Value: 600				
1948	26,947,000	0.10	0.25	0.90	7.50	—
1948 Proof	—	Value: 600				

KM# 868 1/2 PENNY
Bronze, 25.5 mm. **Ruler:** George VI **Obv:** Head left **Obv. Legend:** Without IND IMP **Rev:** The Golden Hind **Designer:** T. H. Paget

Date	Mintage	F	VF	XF	Unc	BU
1949	24,744,000	0.10	0.25	4.00	15.00	—
1949 Proof	—	Value: 550				
1950	24,154,000	0.10	0.25	3.00	12.00	—
1950 Proof	18,000	Value: 12.00				
1950 Matte Proof	—	Value: 1,250				
Note: There are reportedly 1-2 known of this variety, struck specifically for use in photographs						
1951	14,868,000	0.25	0.50	5.00	24.00	—
1951 Proof	20,000	Value: 15.00				
1951 Matte Proof	—	Value: 1,250				
Note: There are reportedly 1-2 known of this variety, struck specifically for use in photographs						
1952	33,278,000	0.10	0.25	1.00	10.00	—
1952 Proof	—	Value: 550				

KM# 882 1/2 PENNY
Bronze, 25.5 mm. **Ruler:** Elizabeth II **Obv:** Laureate bust right **Obv. Designer:** Mary Gillick **Rev:** The Golden Hind **Rev. Designer:** T. H. Paget

Date	Mintage	F	VF	XF	Unc	BU
1953	8,926,000	0.20	0.40	1.00	5.00	—
1953 Proof	40,000	Value: 13.00				
1953 Matte Proof	—	Value: 1,250				
Note: There are reportedly 1-2 known of this variety, struck specifically for use in photographs						

KM# 896 1/2 PENNY
5.6000 g., Bronze, 25.44 mm. **Ruler:** Elizabeth II **Obv:** Laureate bust right **Obv. Legend:** Without BRITT OMN **Rev:** The Golden Hind **Edge:** Plain

Date	Mintage	F	VF	XF	Unc	BU
1954	19,375,000	0.10	0.25	1.50	4.00	—
1954 Proof	—	Value: 500				
1955	18,799,000	0.10	0.25	1.25	3.50	—
1955 Proof	—	Value: 500				
1956	21,799,000	0.15	0.50	1.25	3.50	—
1956 Proof	—	Value: 500				
1957	43,684,000	0.10	0.25	0.50	3.50	—
1957 Proof	—	Value: 450				
1958	62,318,000	—	0.10	0.20	2.00	—
1958 Proof	—	Value: 450				
1959	79,176,000	—	0.10	0.15	1.50	—
1959 Proof	—	Value: 450				
1960	41,340,000	—	0.10	0.15	1.50	—
1960 Proof	—	Value: 450				
1962	41,779,000	—	—	0.10	1.00	—
1962 Proof	—	Value: 500				
1963	45,036,000	—	—	0.10	1.00	—
1963 Proof	—	Value: 500				
1964	78,583,000	—	—	0.10	1.00	—
1964 Proof	—	Value: 500				
1965	98,083,000	—	—	—	1.00	—
1965 Proof	—	—	—	—	—	—
Note: Reported, not confirmed						
1966	95,289,000	—	—	—	0.55	—
1966 Proof	—	—	—	—	—	—
Note: Reported, not confirmed						
1967	146,491,000	—	—	—	0.55	—
1967 Proof	—	—	—	—	—	—
Note: Reported, not confirmed						
1970 Proof	750,000	Value: 3.50				

KM# 790 PENNY
9.4500 g., Bronze, 30.8 mm. **Ruler:** Victoria **Obv:** Mature draped bust left **Obv. Legend:** VICTORIA. DEI. GRA. BRITT. REGINA. FID. DEF IND. IMP. **Obv. Designer:** Thomas Brock **Rev:** Britannia seated right

Date	Mintage	F	VF	XF	Unc	BU
1901	22,206,000	0.45	1.50	15.00	35.00	—
1901 Proof	—	—	—	—	—	—

KM# 794.1 PENNY
9.4500 g., Bronze, 30.8 mm. **Ruler:** Edward VII **Obv:** Head right **Rev:** Britannia seated right, low sea level

Date	Mintage	F	VF	XF	Unc	BU
1902	26,977,000	5.00	20.00	100	180	—

KM# 794.2 PENNY
Bronze, 30.8 mm. **Ruler:** Edward VII **Obv:** Head right **Rev:** Britannia seated right, high sea level

Date	Mintage	F	VF	XF	Unc	BU
1902	Inc. above	1.25	3.50	12.50	50.00	—
1903	21,415,000	1.25	5.00	26.00	70.00	—
1904	12,913,000	1.25	7.00	50.00	120	—
1905	17,784,000	1.25	7.00	40.00	95.00	—
1906	37,990,000	1.25	5.00	26.00	95.00	—
1907	47,322,000	1.25	5.00	27.00	95.00	—
1908	31,506,000	0.95	5.00	23.00	80.00	—
1908 Matte Proof; Rare	3	—	—	—	—	—
1909	19,617,000	1.25	5.00	27.00	80.00	—
1910	29,549,000	0.75	4.50	22.00	80.00	—

KM# 810 PENNY

9.4500 g., Bronze, 30.8 mm. **Ruler:** George V **Obv:** Head left **Obv. Legend:** GEORGIVS V DEI GRA: BRITT: OMN: REX FID: DEF: IND: IMP: **Obv. Designer:** Bertram MacKennal **Rev:** Britannia seated right **Note:** Fully struck and orginal mint lustre coins command a premium.

Date	Mintage	F	VF	XF	Unc	BU
1911	23,079,000	0.80	2.50	16.00	50.00	—
1912	48,306,000	0.80	2.50	17.00	50.00	—
1912H	16,800,000	1.00	8.00	75.00	230	—
1913	65,497,000	0.80	3.00	22.00	75.00	—
1914	50,821,000	0.80	2.50	17.00	50.00	—
1915	47,311,000	0.80	2.50	17.00	50.00	—
1916	86,411,000	0.80	2.50	17.00	50.00	—
1917	107,905,000	0.80	2.50	17.00	50.00	—
1918	84,227,000	0.80	2.50	17.00	50.00	—
1918H	2,573,000	4.00	30.00	250	650	—
1918KN	Inc. above	4.50	40.00	375	1,100	—
1919	113,761,000	0.80	2.50	17.00	50.00	—
1919H	4,526,000	1.25	13.00	275	800	—
1919KN	Inc. above	4.00	25.00	400	1,400	—
1920	124,693,000	0.80	2.50	17.00	50.00	—
1921	129,717,999	0.80	2.50	17.00	50.00	—
1922	16,347,000	0.80	4.00	20.00	50.00	—
1922	—	—	2,500	—	7,500	—
Note: Reverse of 1927						
1922 Specimen	2	—	—	—	—	15,000
Note: Reverse of 1927						
1926	4,499,000	2.50	7.00	30.00	100	—
1926 Proof	—	Value: 1,500				

KM# 826 PENNY

Bronze, 30.8 mm. **Ruler:** George V **Obv:** Modified head left **Obv. Designer:** Bertram MacKennal **Rev:** Britannia seated right

Date	Mintage	F	VF	XF	Unc	BU
1926	—	20.00	125	1,200	2,500	—
1926 Proof	—	—	—	—	—	—
Note: Reported, not confirmed						
1927	60,990,000	0.35	0.75	8.00	30.00	—
1927 Proof	—	Value: 1,350				

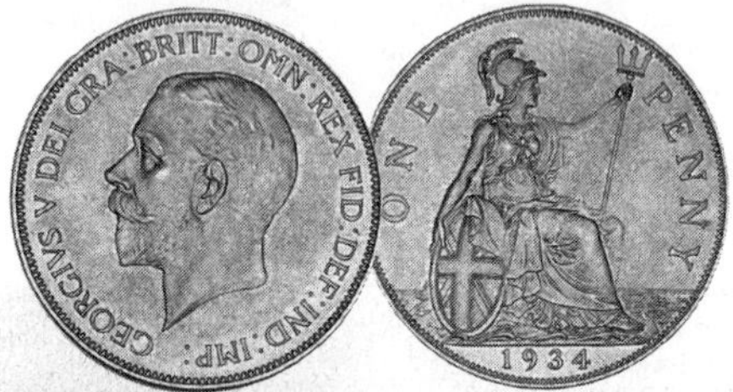

KM# 838 PENNY

Bronze, 30.8 mm. **Ruler:** George V **Obv:** Smaller head left **Obv. Designer:** Bertram MacKennal **Rev:** Britannia seated right

Date	Mintage	F	VF	XF	Unc	BU
1928	50,178,000	0.25	0.50	8.00	30.00	—
1928 Proof	—	Value: 1,350				
1929	49,133,000	0.25	0.50	8.00	30.00	—
1929 Proof	—	Value: 1,350				
1930	29,098,000	0.35	1.50	15.00	35.00	—
1930 Proof	—	Value: 1,350				
1931	19,843,000	0.35	1.50	15.00	35.00	—
1931 Proof	—	Value: 1,350				
1932	8,278,000	1.00	4.50	20.00	70.00	—
1932 Proof	—	Value: 1,500				
1933 Rare	Est. 7	—	—	—	70,000	—
1933 Proof	—	—	—	—	—	—
Note: Reported, not confirmed						
1934	13,966,000	0.50	4.00	20.00	60.00	—
1934 Proof	—	Value: 1,500				
1935	56,070,000	0.25	0.50	5.00	30.00	—
1935 Proof	—	Value: 1,250				
1936	154,296,000	0.25	0.40	5.00	25.00	—
1936 Proof	—	Value: 1,250				

KM# 845 PENNY

9.4500 g., Bronze, 30.8 mm. **Ruler:** George VI **Obv:** Head left **Obv. Designer:** T. H. Paget **Rev:** Britannia seated right

Date	Mintage	F	VF	XF	Unc	BU
1937	88,896,000	0.20	0.35	1.00	7.50	—
1937 Proof	26,000	Value: 19.00				
1937 Matte Proof	Est. 4	Value: 2,500				
1938	121,560,000	0.20	0.35	1.00	10.00	—
1938 Proof	—	Value: 1,000				
1939	55,560,000	0.25	0.50	4.00	15.00	—
1939 Proof	—	Value: 1,000				
1940	42,284,000	0.25	0.50	7.50	30.00	—
1940 Proof	—	Value: 1,100				
1944	42,600,000	0.25	0.50	6.00	20.00	—
1944 Proof	—	Value: 1,000				
1945	79,531,000	0.20	0.35	5.00	19.00	—
1945 Proof	—	Value: 1,000				
1946	66,855,999	0.20	0.35	5.00	19.00	—
1946 Proof	—	Value: 1,000				
1947	52,220,000	0.15	0.25	0.75	7.50	—
1947 Proof	—	Value: 1,500				
1948	63,961,000	0.15	0.25	0.75	7.50	—
1948 Proof	—	Value: 1,250				

KM# 869 PENNY

Bronze, 30.8 mm. **Ruler:** George VI **Obv:** Head left **Obv. Legend:** without IND: IMP: **Obv. Designer:** T. H. Paget **Rev:** Britannia seated right

Date	Mintage	F	VF	XF	Unc	BU
1949	14,324,000	0.20	0.35	0.75	7.50	—
1949 Proof	—	Value: 1,200				
1950	240,000	3.00	6.00	20.00	55.00	—
1950 Matte Proof	—	Value: 2,500				
Note: There are reportedly 1-2 known of this variety, struck specifically for use in photography						
1950 Proof	18,000	Value: 40.00				
1951	120,000	3.00	13.00	35.00	60.00	—
1951 Matte Proof	—	Value: 2,500				
Note: There are reportedly 1-2 known of this variety, struck specifically for use in photography						
1951 Proof	20,000	Value: 50.00				
1952 Unique	—	—	—	—	—	75,000

KM# 883 PENNY

9.4400 g., Bronze, 30.8 mm. **Ruler:** Elizabeth II **Obv:** Laureate bust right **Rev:** Britannia seated right

Date	Mintage	F	VF	XF	Unc	BU
1953	1,308,000	0.75	1.25	5.00	14.00	—
1953 Proof	40,000	Value: 20.00				
1953 Matte Proof; Rare	—	Value: 2,500				
Note: There are reportedly 1-2 known of this variety, struck specifically for use in photography						

KM# 897 PENNY

9.4000 g., Bronze, 30.72 mm. **Ruler:** Elizabeth II **Obv:** Laureate bust right **Obv. Legend:** without BRITT: OMN: **Rev:** Britannia seated right **Edge:** Plain

Date	Mintage	F	VF	XF	Unc	BU
1954 1 Known	—	—	—	—	—	—
1961	48,313,000	—	0.10	0.15	1.50	—
1961 Proof	—	Value: 700				
1962	143,309,000	—	—	0.10	1.00	—
1962 Proof	—	Value: 700				
1963	125,236,000	—	—	0.10	1.00	—
1963 Proof	—	Value: 700				
1964	153,294,000	—	—	—	0.55	—
1964 Proof	—	Value: 750				
1965	121,310,000	—	—	—	0.55	—
1966	165,739,000	—	—	—	0.55	—
1967	654,564,000	—	—	—	0.30	—
1970 Proof	750,000	Value: 5.00				

KM# 777 3 PENCE

1.4138 g., 0.9250 Silver 0.0420 oz. ASW, 16 mm. **Ruler:** Victoria **Obv:** Mature draped bust left **Obv. Designer:** Thomas Brock **Rev:** Crowned denomination divides date within oak wreath

Date	Mintage	F	VF	XF	Unc	BU
1901	6,100,000	1.00	2.00	6.00	25.00	—
1901 Prooflike	8,976	—	—	—	50.00	60.00

KM# 797.1 3 PENCE

1.4138 g., 0.9250 Silver 0.0420 oz. ASW, 16 mm. **Ruler:** Edward VII **Obv:** Head right **Rev:** Crowned denomination divides date within oak wreath **Note:** The prooflike coins come with a mirror or satin finish.

Date	Mintage	F	VF	XF	Unc	BU
1902	8,287,000	1.00	4.00	8.00	20.00	—
1902 Prooflike	8,976	—	—	—	35.00	50.00
1902 Matte Proof	15,000	Value: 40.00				
1903	5,235,000	2.00	5.00	25.00	70.00	—
1903 Prooflike	8,976	—	—	—	35.00	50.00
1904	3,630,000	5.00	12.00	45.00	175	—
1904 Prooflike	8,876	—	—	—	35.00	50.00

KM# 797.2 3 PENCE

1.4138 g., 0.9250 Silver 0.0420 oz. ASW, 16 mm. **Ruler:** Edward VII **Obv:** Head right **Rev:** Crowned denomination divides date within oak wreath **Note:** The below Prooflike listings can be of mirror or satin-like finish, which are more difficult to separate from the currency strikes, especially for the years 1903-1906.

Date	Mintage	F	VF	XF	Unc	BU
1904	Inc. above	4.00	8.50	35.00	100	—
1905	3,563,000	2.50	7.50	28.00	75.00	—
1905 Prooflike	8,976	—	—	—	35.00	50.00
1906	3,174,000	3.00	8.50	35.00	100	—
1906 Prooflike	8,800	—	—	—	35.00	50.00
1907	4,841,000	1.50	5.00	28.00	50.00	—
1907 Prooflike	11,000	—	—	—	35.00	50.00
1908	8,176,000	1.50	3.00	15.00	50.00	—
1908 Prooflike	8,760	—	—	—	35.00	50.00
1909	4,054,999	1.50	5.50	27.00	70.00	—
1909 Prooflike	1,983	—	—	—	45.00	75.00
1910	4,565,000	0.75	1.50	15.00	30.00	—
1910 Prooflike	1,140	—	—	—	50.00	80.00

KM# 813 3 PENCE

1.4138 g., 0.9250 Silver 0.0420 oz. ASW, 16 mm. **Ruler:** George V **Obv:** Head left **Obv. Designer:** Bertram MacKennal **Rev:** Crowned denomination divides date within oak wreath

Date	Mintage	F	VF	XF	Unc	BU
1911	5,843,000	0.75	1.25	5.00	24.00	—
1911 Prooflike	1,991	—	—	—	60.00	70.00
1911 Proof	6,007	Value: 65.00				
1912	8,934,000	0.75	1.25	5.00	24.00	—
1912 Prooflike	1,246	—	—	—	60.00	70.00
1913	7,144,000	0.75	1.25	5.00	24.00	—
1913 Prooflike	1,228	—	—	—	60.00	70.00
1914	6,735,000	0.75	1.25	5.00	22.00	—
1914 Prooflike	982	—	—	—	60.00	70.00
1915	5,452,000	0.75	1.25	5.00	22.00	—
1915 Prooflike	1,293	—	—	—	60.00	70.00
1916	18,556,000	0.65	1.00	3.00	15.00	—
1916 Prooflike	1,128	—	—	—	60.00	70.00
1917	21,664,000	0.65	1.00	3.00	15.00	—
1917 Prooflike	1,237	—	—	—	60.00	70.00
1918	20,632,000	0.65	1.00	4.50	15.00	—
1918 Prooflike	1,375	—	—	—	60.00	70.00
1919	16,846,000	0.65	1.00	4.50	15.00	—
1919 Prooflike	1,258	—	—	—	60.00	70.00
1920	16,704,999	0.65	1.00	3.00	20.00	—
1920 Prooflike	1,399	—	—	—	60.00	70.00

KM# 813a 3 PENCE

1.4138 g., 0.5000 Silver 0.0227 oz. ASW, 16 mm. **Ruler:** George V **Obv:** Head left **Obv. Designer:** Bertram MacKennal **Rev:** Crowned denomination divides date within oak wreath

Date	Mintage	F	VF	XF	Unc	BU
1920	Inc. above	—	1.00	3.00	18.00	—
1921	8,751,000	—	1.00	3.00	30.00	—
1921 Prooflike	1,386	—	—	—	50.00	60.00
1922	7,981,000	—	1.00	7.00	30.00	—
1922 Prooflike	1,373	—	—	—	50.00	60.00
1923 Prooflike	1,430	—	—	—	50.00	60.00
1924 Prooflike	1,515	—	—	—	50.00	60.00
1924 Satin specimen	2	—	—	—	—	2,500
1925	3,733,000	0.75	2.00	14.00	35.00	—
1925 Prooflike	1,438	—	—	—	50.00	60.00
1926	4,109,000	1.25	4.00	16.50	45.00	—
1926 Prooflike	1,504	—	—	—	50.00	60.00
1927 Prooflike	1,690	—	—	—	50.00	60.00

KM# 831 3 PENCE

1.4138 g., 0.5000 Silver 0.0227 oz. ASW, 16 mm. **Ruler:** George V **Obv:** Head left **Obv. Designer:** Bertram MacKennal **Rev:** Three oak leaves and acorns divided

Date	Mintage	F	VF	XF	Unc	BU
1927 Proof	15,000	Value: 50.00				
1927 Matte Proof	—	Value: 2,000				

Note: There are reportedly 3-4 known of this variety, struck specifically for use in photographs

Date	Mintage	F	VF	XF	Unc	BU
1928	1,302,000	1.75	3.50	14.50	45.00	—
1928 Proof	—	Value: 500				
1930	1,319,000	1.50	3.00	14.00	40.00	—
1930 Proof	—	Value: 500				
1931	6,252,000	BV	0.50	1.25	12.00	—
1931 Proof	—	Value: 500				
1932	5,887,000	BV	0.60	1.75	12.50	—
1932 Proof	—	Value: 500				
1933	5,579,000	BV	0.60	1.75	12.50	—
1933 Proof	—	Value: 500				
1934	7,406,000	BV	0.50	1.25	12.00	—
1934 Proof	—	Value: 500				
1935	7,028,000	BV	0.50	1.25	12.00	—
1935 Proof	—	Value: 500				
1936	3,239,000	BV	0.60	1.75	13.00	—
1936 Proof	—	Value: 500				

KM# 848 3 PENCE

1.4138 g., 0.5000 Silver 0.0227 oz. ASW, 16 mm. **Ruler:** George VI **Obv:** Head left **Obv. Designer:** T. H. Paget **Rev:** St. George shield on Tudor rose divides date **Rev. Designer:** George Krueger-Gray

Date	Mintage	F	VF	XF	Unc	BU
1937	8,148,000	BV	0.50	1.25	7.00	—
1937 Proof	26,000	Value: 15.00				
1937 Matte Proof; Rare	—	—	—	—	—	—

Note: There are reportedly 2-4 known of this variety, struck specifically for use in photography

Date	Mintage	F	VF	XF	Unc	BU
1938	6,402,000	BV	0.50	1.25	10.00	—
1938 Proof	—	Value: 500				
1939	1,356,000	BV	1.50	8.50	25.00	—
1939 Proof	—	Value: 500				
1940	7,914,000	BV	0.60	2.50	18.00	—
1940 Proof	—	Value: 500				
1941	7,979,000	BV	0.60	4.00	20.00	—
1941 Proof	—	Value: 500				
1942	4,144,000	1.00	5.00	15.00	50.00	—
1942 Proof	—	Value: 500				
1943	1,379,000	1.00	5.00	24.00	60.00	—
1943 Proof	—	Value: 500				
1944	2,005,999	2.25	10.00	40.00	100	—
1944 Proof	—	Value: 600				
1945 Rare	320,000	—	—	—	—	—

Note: Issue melted, only one known

KM# 849 3 PENCE

Nickel-Brass **Ruler:** George VI **Obv:** Head left **Obv. Designer:** T. H. Paget **Rev:** Thrift plant (allium porrum) **Rev. Designer:** Frances Madge Kitchener **Shape:** 12-sided

Date	Mintage	F	VF	XF	Unc	BU
1937	45,708,000	0.25	0.40	2.00	10.00	—
1937 Proof	26,000	Value: 17.50				
1937 Matte Proof ; Rare	—	—	—	—	—	—

Note: There are reportedly 2-4 known of this variety, struck specifically for use in photography

Date	Mintage	F	VF	XF	Unc	BU
1938	14,532,000	0.40	0.80	6.00	25.00	—
1938 Proof	—	Value: 450				
1939	5,603,000	0.40	1.50	10.00	50.00	—
1939 Proof	—	Value: 450				
1940	12,636,000	0.25	0.50	5.00	20.00	—
1940 Proof	—	Value: 450				
1941	60,239,000	0.25	0.40	2.50	14.00	—
1941 Proof	—	Value: 450				
1942	103,214,000	0.25	0.40	2.50	12.00	—
1942 Proof	—	—	—	—	—	—
1943	101,702,000	0.25	0.40	2.50	12.00	—
1943 Proof	—	—	—	—	—	—
1944	69,760,000	0.25	0.40	2.50	12.00	—
1944 Proof	—	—	—	—	—	—
1945	33,942,000	0.25	0.50	2.50	18.00	—
1945 Proof	—	—	—	—	—	—
1946	621,000	4.00	17.50	125	550	—
1946 Proof	—	Value: 900				
1948	4,230,000	0.60	1.50	8.00	55.00	—
1948 Proof	—	Value: 750				

KM# 873 3 PENCE

6.8000 g., Nickel-Brass **Ruler:** George VI **Obv:** Head left **Obv. Legend:** without IND IMP **Obv. Designer:** T. H. Paget **Rev:** Thrift plant (allium porrum) **Rev. Designer:** Frances Madge Kitchener

Date	Mintage	F	VF	XF	Unc	BU
1949	464,000	4.00	17.50	125	500	—
1949 Proof	—	Value: 850				
1950	1,600,000	1.00	3.00	15.00	85.00	—
1950 Proof	18,000	Value: 35.00				
1950 Matte Proof; Rare	—	—	—	—	—	—

Note: There are reportedly 2-4 known of this variety, struck specifically for use in photography

Date	Mintage	F	VF	XF	Unc	BU
1951	1,184,000	1.00	3.00	20.00	110	—
1951 Proof	20,000	Value: 40.00				
1951 Matte Proof; Rare	—	Value: 1,800				

Note: There are reportedly 2-4 known of this variety, struck specifically for use in photography

Date	Mintage	F	VF	XF	Unc	BU
1952	25,494,000	0.25	0.50	5.00	19.00	—
1952 Proof	—	Value: 650				

KM# 886 3 PENCE

Nickel-Brass **Ruler:** Elizabeth II **Obv:** Laureate bust right **Obv. Designer:** Mary Gillick **Rev:** Crowned portcullis **Rev. Designer:** William Gardner

Date	Mintage	F	VF	XF	Unc	BU
1953	30,618,000	0.25	0.50	0.75	6.00	—
1953 Proof	40,000	Value: 12.00				
1953 Matte Proof; Rare	—	—	—	—	—	—

Note: There are reportedly 2-4 known of this variety, struck specifically for use in photography

KM# 900 3 PENCE

Nickel-Brass **Ruler:** Elizabeth II **Obv:** Laureate bust right **Obv. Legend:** without BRITT OMN **Obv. Designer:** Mary Gillick **Rev:** Crowned portcullis **Rev. Designer:** William Gardner **Shape:** 12-sided

Date	Mintage	F	VF	XF	Unc	BU
1954	41,720,000	—	0.25	0.50	10.00	—
1954 Proof	—	Value: 400				
1955	41,075,000	—	—	0.75	10.00	—
1955 Proof	—	Value: 400				
1956	36,902,000	—	—	1.25	10.00	—
1956 Proof	—	Value: 400				
1957	24,294,000	—	—	0.50	5.00	—
1957 Proof	—	Value: 400				
1958	20,504,000	—	1.00	2.25	8.00	—
1958 Proof	—	Value: 400				
1959	28,499,000	—	—	0.50	6.50	—
1959 Proof	—	Value: 400				
1960	83,078,000	—	—	0.40	6.50	—
1960 Proof	—	Value: 400				
1961	41,102,000	—	—	0.25	2.50	—
1961 Proof	—	Value: 400				
1962	47,242,000	—	—	0.25	1.50	—
1962 Proof	—	Value: 400				
1963	35,280,000	—	—	0.25	1.50	—
1963 Proof	—	Value: 400				
1964	47,440,000	—	—	0.25	1.50	—
1964 Proof	—	—	—	—	—	—
1965	23,907,000	—	—	0.25	1.50	—
1965 Proof	—	—	—	—	—	—
1966	55,320,000	—	—	0.25	0.50	—
1966 Proof	—	—	—	—	—	—
1967	49,000,000	—	0.15	0.25	0.50	—
1967 Proof	—	—	—	—	—	—
1970 Proof	750,000	Value: 3.50				

KM# 779 6 PENCE

3.0100 g., 0.9250 Silver 0.0895 oz. ASW, 19.5 mm. **Ruler:** Victoria **Obv:** Mature draped bust left **Obv. Legend:** VICTORIA. DEI. GRA. BRITT. REGINA. FID. DEF. IND. IMP. **Obv. Designer:** Thomas Brock **Rev:** Crowned denomination within oak wreath

Date	Mintage	F	VF	XF	Unc	BU
1901	5,109,000	4.00	8.00	25.00	50.00	—

KM# 799 6 PENCE

3.0100 g., 0.9250 Silver 0.0895 oz. ASW, 19.5 mm. **Ruler:** Edward VII **Obv:** Head right **Rev:** Crowned denomination within oak wreath, date below

Date	Mintage	F	VF	XF	Unc	BU
1902	6,356,000	5.00	10.00	30.00	50.00	—
1902 Matte Proof	15,000	Value: 50.00				
1903	5,411,000	5.00	10.00	30.00	100	—
1904	4,487,000	6.00	15.00	65.00	200	—
1905	4,236,000	5.00	12.00	35.00	135	—
1906	7,641,000	4.00	10.00	30.00	100	—
1907	8,734,000	5.00	10.00	35.00	100	—

Date	Mintage	F	VF	XF	Unc	BU
1908	6,739,000	5.00	12.00	40.00	160	—
1909	6,584,000	5.00	10.00	35.00	100	—
1910	12,491,000	5.00	8.50	25.00	65.00	—

KM# 815 6 PENCE

3.0100 g., 0.9250 Silver 0.0895 oz. ASW, 19.5 mm. **Ruler:** George V **Obv:** Head left **Obv. Designer:** Bertram MacKennal **Rev:** Lion atop crown dividing date

Date	Mintage	F	VF	XF	Unc	BU
1911	9,165,000	2.00	8.00	18.00	50.00	—
1911 Proof	6,007	Value: 55.00				
1912	10,984,000	4.00	10.00	25.00	75.00	—
1913	7,500,000	5.00	12.00	45.00	80.00	—
1914	22,715,000	2.00	8.00	18.00	35.00	—
1915	15,695,000	2.00	8.00	18.00	35.00	—
1916	22,207,000	2.00	8.00	18.00	35.00	—
1917	7,725,000	5.00	15.00	30.00	85.00	—
1918	27,559,000	2.00	8.00	18.00	35.00	—
1919	13,375,000	4.00	10.00	20.00	42.50	—
1920	14,136,000	4.00	10.00	25.00	55.00	—

KM# 815a.1 6 PENCE

2.8276 g., 0.5000 Silver 0.0455 oz. ASW, 19.5 mm. **Ruler:** George V **Obv:** Head left **Obv. Designer:** Bertram MacKennal **Rev:** Lion atop crown dividing date **Note:** Narrow rim.

Date	Mintage	F	VF	XF	Unc	BU
1920	Inc. above	2.00	4.00	18.00	55.00	—
1921	30,340,000	2.00	4.00	12.00	35.00	—
1922	16,879,000	2.00	5.00	15.00	38.00	—
1923	6,383,000	3.00	6.00	20.00	90.00	—
1924	17,444,000	2.00	4.00	12.00	35.00	—
1924 Satin specimen	2	—	—	—	—	1,600
1925	12,721,000	2.00	4.00	15.00	35.00	—

KM# 815a.2 6 PENCE

2.8276 g., 0.5000 Silver 0.0455 oz. ASW, 19.5 mm. **Ruler:** George V **Obv:** Head left **Obv. Designer:** Bertram MacKennal **Rev:** Lion atop crown dividing date **Note:** Wide rim.

Date	Mintage	F	VF	XF	Unc	BU
1925	Inc. above	2.00	4.00	18.00	35.00	—
1926	21,810,000	2.00	4.00	18.00	35.00	—

KM# 828 6 PENCE

2.8276 g., 0.5000 Silver 0.0455 oz. ASW, 19.5 mm. **Ruler:** George V **Obv:** Modified head left **Obv. Designer:** Bertram MacKennal **Rev:** Lion atop crown divides date

Date	Mintage	F	VF	XF	Unc	BU
1926	Inc. above	BV	3.00	10.00	35.00	—
1927	8,925,000	2.00	4.00	15.00	35.00	—
1927 Proof	—	Value: 1,000				

KM# 832 6 PENCE

2.8276 g., 0.5000 Silver 0.0455 oz. ASW, 19.5 mm. **Ruler:** George V **Obv:** Head left **Obv. Designer:** Bertram MacKennal **Rev:** Six oak leaves and acorns divided **Note:** Varieties in edge milling exist.

Date	Mintage	F	VF	XF	Unc	BU
1927 Proof	15,000	Value: 35.00				
1927 Matte Proof; Rare	—	—	—	—	2,000	—

Note: There are reportedly 3-4 known of this variety, struck specifically for use in photographs

Date	Mintage	F	VF	XF	Unc	BU
1928	23,123,000	BV	2.00	7.50	22.00	—
1928 Proof	—	Value: 500				
1929	28,319,000	BV	2.00	7.00	22.00	—
1929 Proof	—	Value: 500				
1930	16,990,000	BV	2.00	7.00	25.00	—
1930 Proof	—	Value: 500				
1931	16,873,000	2.00	3.00	8.00	30.00	—
1931 Proof	—	Value: 500				
1932	9,406,000	2.00	4.00	17.00	50.00	—
1932 Proof	—	Value: 500				
1933	22,185,000	2.00	3.00	8.00	25.00	—
1933 Proof	—	Value: 500				
1934	9,304,000	2.00	3.00	10.00	35.00	—
1934 Proof	—	Value: 500				
1935	13,996,000	BV	2.00	7.50	22.00	—
1935 Proof	—	Value: 500				
1936	24,380,000	BV	2.00	7.50	22.00	—
1936 Proof	—	Value: 500				

KM# 852 6 PENCE

2.8276 g., 0.5000 Silver 0.0455 oz. ASW, 19.5 mm. **Ruler:** George VI **Obv:** Head left **Obv. Designer:** T. H. Paget **Rev:** Crowned monogram divides date **Rev. Designer:** George Krueger-Gray

Date	Mintage	F	VF	XF	Unc	BU
1937	22,303,000	—	BV	1.50	10.00	—
1937 Proof	26,000	Value: 18.00				
1937 Matte Proof; Rare	—	—	—	—	—	—

Note: There are reportedly 3-4 known of this variety, struck specifically for use in photographs

Date	Mintage	F	VF	XF	Unc	BU
1938	13,403,000	BV	1.25	7.00	23.00	—
1938 Proof	—	Value: 450				
1939	28,670,000	—	BV	3.00	15.00	—
1939 Proof	—	Value: 450				
1940	20,875,000	—	BV	3.00	15.00	—
1940 Proof	—	Value: 450				
1941	23,087,000	—	BV	3.00	10.00	—
1941 Proof	—	Value: 450				
1942	44,943,000	—	BV	1.50	10.00	—
1942 Proof	—	Value: 450				
1943	46,927,000	—	BV	1.50	10.00	—
1943 Proof	—	Value: 450				
1944	36,953,000	—	BV	1.50	10.00	—
1944 Proof	—	Value: 450				
1945	39,939,000	—	BV	1.50	10.00	—
1945 Proof	—	Value: 500				
1946	43,466,000	—	BV	1.50	10.00	—
1946 Proof	—	Value: 500				

KM# 862 6 PENCE

Copper-Nickel, 19.5 mm. **Ruler:** George VI **Obv:** Head left **Obv. Designer:** T. H. Paget **Rev:** Crowned monogram divides date **Rev. Designer:** George Krueger-Gray

Date	Mintage	F	VF	XF	Unc	BU
1947	29,993,000	—	0.20	0.50	10.00	—
1947 Proof	—	Value: 450				
1948	88,324,000	—	0.20	1.50	7.50	—
1948 Proof	—	Value: 600				

KM# 875 6 PENCE

Copper-Nickel, 19.5 mm. **Ruler:** George VI **Obv:** Head left **Rev:** Crowned monogram divides date **Rev. Legend:** without IND IMP **Rev. Designer:** T. H. Paget

Date	Mintage	F	VF	XF	Unc	BU
1949	41,336,000	—	0.20	1.50	10.00	—
1949 Proof	—	Value: 500				
1950	32,741,999	—	0.20	1.50	10.00	—
1950 Proof	18,000	Value: 15.00				
1950 Matte Proof; Rare	—	—	—	—	—	—

Note: There are reportedly 3-4 known of this variety, struck specifically for use in photographs

Date	Mintage	F	VF	XF	Unc	BU
1951	40,399,000	—	0.20	3.50	19.00	—
1951 Proof	20,000	Value: 16.00				
1951 Matte Proof; Rare	—	—	—	—	—	—

Note: There are reportedly 3-4 known of this variety, struck specifically for use in photographs

Date	Mintage	F	VF	XF	Unc	BU
1952	1,012,999	1.25	7.50	30.00	75.00	—
1952 Proof	—	Value: 1,500				

KM# 889 6 PENCE

Copper-Nickel, 19.5 mm. **Ruler:** Elizabeth II **Obv:** Laureate bust right **Obv. Designer:** Mary Gillick **Rev:** Flora; leek, rose, thistle and shamrock **Rev. Designer:** F. G. Fuller and Cecil Thomas

Date	Mintage	F	VF	XF	Unc	BU
1953	70,324,000	—	0.15	0.50	4.00	—
1953 Proof	40,000	Value: 7.50				
1953 Matte Proof; Rare	—	—	—	—	—	—

Note: There are reportedly 3-4 known of this variety, struck specifically for use in photographs

KM# 903 6 PENCE

Copper-Nickel, 19.5 mm. **Ruler:** Elizabeth II **Obv:** Laureate bust right **Obv. Legend:** Without BRITT OMN **Obv. Designer:** Mary Gillick **Rev:** Flora; leek, rose, thistle and shamrock **Rev. Designer:** F. G. Fuller and Cecil Thomas

Date	Mintage	F	VF	XF	Unc	BU
1954	105,241,000	—	0.15	0.50	6.00	—
1954 Proof	—	Value: 425				
1955	109,930,000	—	0.15	0.35	4.00	—
1955 Proof	—	Value: 425				
1956	109,842,000	—	0.15	0.35	4.00	—
1956 Proof	—	Value: 425				
1957	105,654,000	—	0.15	0.35	3.50	—
1957 Proof	—	Value: 425				
1958	123,519,000	—	0.15	0.35	3.00	—
1958 Proof	—	Value: 425				
1959	93,089,000	—	0.15	0.35	3.00	—
1959 Proof	—	Value: 425				
1960	103,283,000	—	0.15	0.35	3.00	—
1960 Proof	—	Value: 425				
1961	115,052,000	—	0.15	0.35	3.00	—
1961 Proof	—	Value: 425				
1962	166,484,000	—	0.15	0.35	1.75	—
1962 Proof	—	Value: 425				
1963	120,056,000	—	0.15	0.30	1.50	—
1963 Proof	—	Value: 425				
1964	152,336,000	—	0.15	0.25	1.50	—
1964 Proof	—	—	—	—	—	—

Note: Reported, not confirmed

Date	Mintage	F	VF	XF	Unc	BU
1965	129,644,000	—	0.10	0.20	1.50	—
1965 Proof	—	—	—	—	—	—

Note: Reported, not confirmed

Date	Mintage	F	VF	XF	Unc	BU
1966	175,676,000	—	0.10	0.20	1.50	—
1966 Proof	—	—	—	—	—	—

Note: Reported, not confirmed

Date	Mintage	F	VF	XF	Unc	BU
1967	240,788,000	—	0.10	0.20	1.50	—
1967 Proof	—	—	—	—	—	—

Note: Reported, not confirmed

Date	Mintage	F	VF	XF	Unc	BU
1970 Proof	750,000	Value: 3.50				

KM# 780 SHILLING

5.6552 g., 0.9250 Silver 0.1682 oz. ASW, 23.5 mm. **Ruler:** Victoria **Obv:** Mature draped bust left **Obv. Legend:** VICTORIA. DEI. GRA. BRITT. REGINA. FID. DEF. IND. IMP. **Obv. Designer:** Thomas Brock **Rev:** Crowned shields of England, Scotland and Ireland **Rev. Designer:** Edward Paynter

Date	Mintage	F	VF	XF	Unc	BU
1901	3,426,000	4.00	10.00	55.00	75.00	—

KM# 800 SHILLING

5.6552 g., 0.9250 Silver 0.1682 oz. ASW, 23.5 mm. **Ruler:** Edward VII **Obv:** Head right **Rev:** Lion atop crown dividing date

Date	Mintage	F	VF	XF	Unc	BU
1902	7,890,000	5.00	15.00	50.00	80.00	—
1902 Matte Proof	15,000	Value: 90.00				

Date	Mintage	F	VF	XF	Unc	BU
1903	2,061,999	8.00	20.00	125	500	—
1904	2,040,000	8.00	15.00	125	400	—
1905	488,000	65.00	180	900	4,000	—
1906	10,791,000	5.00	11.00	60.00	200	—
1907	14,083,000	5.00	11.00	90.00	225	—
1908	3,807,000	10.00	21.00	150	700	—
1909	5,665,000	10.00	21.00	175	550	—
1910	26,547,000	3.00	10.00	65.00	150	—

KM# 816 SHILLING

5.6552 g., 0.9250 Silver 0.1682 oz. ASW, 23.5 mm. **Ruler:** George V **Obv:** Head left **Obv. Designer:** Bertram MacKennal **Rev:** Lion atop crown dividing date **Note:** Fully struck 1914-1918 pieces command a premium.

Date	Mintage	F	VF	XF	Unc	BU
1911	20,066,000	2.50	4.50	20.00	75.00	—
1911 Proof	6,007	Value: 90.00				
1912	15,594,000	3.00	6.00	30.00	100	—
1913	9,002,000	4.00	8.00	45.00	125	—
1914	23,416,000	2.50	4.00	25.00	45.00	—
1915	39,279,000	2.50	3.50	20.00	45.00	—
1916	35,862,000	2.50	3.50	20.00	40.00	—
1917	22,203,000	2.50	4.00	25.00	50.00	—
1918	34,916,000	2.50	3.50	20.00	40.00	—
1919	10,824,000	3.00	6.00	30.00	65.00	—

KM# 816a SHILLING

5.6552 g., 0.5000 Silver 0.0909 oz. ASW, 23.5 mm. **Ruler:** George V **Obv:** Head left **Obv. Designer:** Bertram MacKennal **Rev:** Lion atop crown dividing date

Date	Mintage	F	VF	XF	Unc	BU
1920	22,825,000	2.00	4.00	27.00	50.00	—
1921	22,649,000	2.50	6.00	30.00	70.00	—
1922	27,216,000	2.00	4.00	27.00	60.00	—
1923	14,575,000	2.00	3.50	27.00	50.00	—
1924	9,250,000	2.00	5.00	30.00	70.00	—
1924	2	—	—	—	—	2,500
Note: Satin specimen						
1925	5,419,000	4.00	8.00	45.00	125	—
1926	22,516,000	2.00	5.00	27.00	85.00	—

KM# 829 SHILLING

5.6552 g., 0.5000 Silver 0.0909 oz. ASW, 23.5 mm. **Ruler:** George V **Obv:** Modified head left **Obv. Designer:** Bertram MacKennal **Rev:** Lion atop crown dividing date

Date	Mintage	F	VF	XF	Unc	BU
1926	Inc. above	1.50	3.50	27.00	50.00	—
1927	9,262,000	1.50	4.00	25.00	50.00	—

KM# 833 SHILLING

5.6552 g., 0.5000 Silver 0.0909 oz. ASW, 23.5 mm. **Ruler:** George V **Obv:** Head left **Obv. Designer:** Bertram MacKennal **Rev:** Lion atop crown

Date	Mintage	F	VF	XF	Unc	BU
1927	Inc. above	1.50	3.00	15.00	50.00	—
1927 Proof	15,000	Value: 50.00				
1927 Matte Proof	—	Value: 2,500				
Note: There are reportedly 1-2 of this variety, struck specifically for use in photographs						
1928	18,137,000	BV	2.00	11.00	30.00	—
1928 Proof	—	Value: 900				
1929	19,343,000	BV	2.00	10.00	30.00	—
1929 Proof	—	Value: 900				
1930	3,137,000	2.50	6.00	23.00	70.00	—
1930 Proof	—	Value: 900				
1931	6,994,000	2.00	3.50	11.00	25.00	—
1931 Proof	—	Value: 900				
1932	12,168,000	2.00	3.50	11.00	25.00	—
1932 Proof	—	Value: 800				
1933	11,512,000	1.50	3.00	10.00	25.00	—
1933 Proof	—	Value: 800				
1934	6,138,000	2.00	5.50	18.00	65.00	—
1934 Proof	—	Value: 900				

Date	Mintage	F	VF	XF	Unc	BU
1935	9,183,000	1.50	3.00	10.00	25.00	—
1935 Proof	—	Value: 800				
1936	11,911,000	1.50	2.50	8.00	25.00	—
1936 Proof	—	Value: 800				

KM# 853 SHILLING

5.6552 g., 0.5000 Silver 0.0909 oz. ASW, 23.5 mm. **Ruler:** George VI **Obv:** Head left **Obv. Designer:** T. H. Paget **Rev:** Lion atop crown dividing date **Rev. Designer:** George Krueger-Gray

Date	Mintage	F	VF	XF	Unc	BU
1937	8,359,000	—	BV	2.50	10.00	—
1937 Proof	26,000	Value: 15.00				
1937 Matte Proof	—	Value: 2,000				
Note: There are reportedly 1-2 known of this variety, struck specifically for use in photographs						
1938	4,833,000	—	BV	7.50	35.00	—
1938 Proof	—	Value: 650				
1939	11,053,000	—	BV	3.00	17.50	—
1939 Proof	—	Value: 600				
1940	11,099,000	—	BV	2.50	13.00	—
1940 Proof	—	Value: 600				
1941	11,392,000	—	BV	2.00	13.00	—
1941 Proof	—	Value: 600				
1942	17,454,000	—	BV	2.00	13.00	—
1942 Proof	—	Value: 600				
1943	11,404,000	—	BV	2.00	13.00	—
1943 Proof	—	Value: 600				
1944	11,587,000	—	BV	2.00	13.00	—
1944 Proof	—	Value: 650				
1945	15,143,000	—	BV	1.50	10.00	—
1945 Proof	—	Value: 750				
1946	18,664,000	—	BV	1.50	6.00	—
1946 Proof	—	Value: 750				

KM# 854 SHILLING

5.6552 g., 0.5000 Silver 0.0909 oz. ASW, 23.5 mm. **Ruler:** George VI **Obv:** Head left **Obv. Designer:** T. H. Paget **Rev:** Scottish crest; lion seated atop crown holding sword and scepter divides date, shields flank **Rev. Designer:** George Krueger-Gray

Date	Mintage	F	VF	XF	Unc	BU
1937	6,749,000	—	BV	1.75	10.00	—
1937 Proof	26,000	Value: 15.00				
1937 Matte Proof	—	Value: 2,000				
Note: There are reportedly 1-2 known of this variety, struck specifically for use in photographs						
1938	4,798,000	—	BV	6.00	35.00	—
1938 Proof	—	Value: 650				
1939	10,264,000	—	BV	3.00	17.00	—
1939 Proof	—	Value: 600				
1940	9,913,000	—	BV	2.50	13.00	—
1940 Proof	—	Value: 600				
1941	8,086,000	—	BV	3.00	13.00	—
1941 Proof	—	Value: 600				
1942	13,677,000	—	BV	2.00	13.00	—
1942 Proof	—	Value: 600				
1943	9,824,000	—	BV	2.00	13.00	—
1943 Proof	—	Value: 650				
1944	10,990,000	—	BV	2.00	13.00	—
1944 Proof	—	Value: 650				
1945	15,106,000	—	BV	1.50	10.00	—
1945 Proof	—	Value: 750				
1946	16,382,000	—	BV	1.50	10.00	—
1946 Proof	—	Value: 750				

KM# 863 SHILLING

Copper-Nickel, 23.5 mm. **Ruler:** George VI **Obv:** Head left **Obv. Designer:** T. H. Paget **Rev:** English crest; lion atop crown dividing date **Rev. Designer:** George Krueger-Gray

Date	Mintage	F	VF	XF	Unc	BU
1947	12,121,000	0.10	0.25	1.00	10.00	—
1947 Proof	—	Value: 600				
1948	45,577,000	0.10	0.20	1.00	10.00	—
1948 Proof	—	Value: 750				

KM# 864 SHILLING

Copper-Nickel, 23.5 mm. **Ruler:** George VI **Obv:** Head left **Obv. Designer:** T. H. Paget **Rev:** Scottish crest; lion seated atop crown holding sword and scepter divides date, shields flank **Rev. Designer:** George Krueger-Gray

Date	Mintage	F	VF	XF	Unc	BU
1947	12,283,000	0.10	0.25	1.00	10.00	—
1947 Proof	—	Value: 600				
1948	45,352,000	0.10	0.20	1.00	10.00	—
1948 Proof	—	Value: 750				

KM# 876 SHILLING

Copper-Nickel, 23.5 mm. **Ruler:** George VI **Obv:** Head left **Obv. Designer:** T. H. Paget **Rev:** English crest; lion atop crown dividing date **Rev. Designer:** George Krueger-Gray

Date	Mintage	F	VF	XF	Unc	BU
1949	19,328,000	0.10	0.25	1.50	22.00	—
1949 Proof	—	Value: 600				
1950	19,244,000	0.10	0.25	1.50	22.00	—
1950 Proof	18,000	Value: 22.00				
1950 Matte Proof	—	Value: 1,600				
Note: There are reportedly 1-2 known of this variety, struck specifically for use in photographs						
1951	9,957,000	0.10	0.25	3.50	24.00	—
1951 Proof	20,000	Value: 22.00				
1951 Matte Proof	—	Value: 1,600				
Note: There are reportedly 1-2 known of this variety, struck specifically for use in photographs						
1952 Proof; Rare	—	—	—	—	—	—
Note: There are reportedly 1-2 known of this variety.						

KM# 877 SHILLING

Copper-Nickel, 23.5 mm. **Ruler:** George VI **Obv:** Head left **Obv. Designer:** T. H. Paget **Rev:** Scottish crest; lion seated atop crown holding sword and scepter divides date, shields flank **Rev. Designer:** George Krueger-Gray

Date	Mintage	F	VF	XF	Unc	BU
1949	21,243,000	0.10	0.25	1.50	22.00	—
1949 Proof	—	Value: 600				
1950	14,300,000	0.10	0.25	1.50	22.00	—
1950 Proof	18,000	Value: 22.00				
1950 Matte Proof	—	Value: 1,600				
Note: There are reportedly 1-2 known of this variety, struck specifically for use in photographs						
1951	10,961,000	0.10	0.25	3.50	24.00	—
1951 Proof	20,000	Value: 22.00				
1951 Matte Proof	—	Value: 1,600				
Note: There are reportedly 1-2 known of this variety, struck specifically for use in photographs						

KM# 890 SHILLING

Copper-Nickel, 23.5 mm. **Ruler:** Elizabeth II **Obv:** Laureate bust right **Obv. Designer:** Mary Gillick **Rev:** Crowned English shield divides date **Rev. Designer:** William Gardner

Date	Mintage	F	VF	XF	Unc	BU
1953	41,943,000	—	0.15	0.50	7.00	—
1953 Proof	40,000	Value: 14.00				
1953 Matte Proof	—	Value: 1,600				
Note: There are reportedly 1-2 known of this variety, struck specifically for use in photographs						

KM# 891 SHILLING

Copper-Nickel, 23.5 mm. **Ruler:** Elizabeth II **Obv:** Laureate bust right **Obv. Designer:** Mary Gillick **Rev:** Crowned Scottish shield divides date **Rev. Designer:** William Gardner

Date	Mintage	F	VF	XF	Unc	BU
1953	20,664,000	—	0.15	0.50	7.50	—
1953 Proof	40,000	Value: 14.00				
1953 Matte Proof	—	Value: 1,600				

Note: There are reportedly 1-2 known of this variety, struck specifically for use in photographs

KM# 904 SHILLING

Copper-Nickel, 23.5 mm. **Ruler:** Elizabeth II **Obv:** Laureate bust right **Obv. Legend:** without BRITT OMN **Obv. Designer:** Mary Gillick **Rev:** Crowned English shield divides date **Rev. Designer:** William Gardner

Date	Mintage	F	VF	XF	Unc	BU
1954	30,162,000	—	0.15	0.50	6.50	—
1954 Proof	—	Value: 600				
1955	45,260,000	—	0.15	0.50	6.50	—
1955 Proof	—	Value: 600				
1956	44,970,000	—	0.15	0.50	10.00	—
1956 Proof	—	Value: 600				
1957	42,774,000	—	0.15	0.50	6.00	—
1957 Proof	—	Value: 600				
1958	14,392,000	0.25	0.50	3.00	30.00	—
1958 Proof	—	Value: 650				
1959	19,443,000	—	0.15	0.40	6.00	—
1959 Proof	—	Value: 600				
1960	27,028,000	—	0.15	0.35	4.00	—
1960 Proof	—	Value: 600				
1961	39,817,000	—	0.15	0.35	2.50	—
1961 Proof	—	Value: 600				
1962	36,704,000	—	0.15	0.25	1.75	—
1962 Proof	—	Value: 600				
1963	49,434,000	—	—	0.25	1.25	—
1963 Proof	—	Value: 600				
1964	8,591,000	—	—	0.25	1.25	—
1964 Proof	—	—	—	—	—	—
Note: Reported, not confirmed						
1965	9,216,000	—	—	0.25	1.25	—
1965 Proof	—	—	—	—	—	—
Note: Reported, not confirmed						
1966	15,002,000	—	—	0.25	1.25	—
1966 Proof	—	—	—	—	—	—
Note: Reported, not confirmed						
1970 Proof	750,000	Value: 5.00				

KM# 905 SHILLING

5.6000 g., Copper-Nickel, 23.5 mm. **Ruler:** Elizabeth II **Obv:** Laureate bust right **Obv. Designer:** Mary Gillick **Rev:** Crowned Scottish shield divides date **Rev. Designer:** William Gardner

Date	Mintage	F	VF	XF	Unc	BU
1954	26,772,000	—	0.15	0.25	6.50	—
1954 Proof	—	Value: 600				
1954 Matte Proof; Rare	Est. 2	—	—	—	—	—
1955	27,951,000	—	0.15	0.35	8.00	—
1955 Proof	—	Value: 600				
1956	42,854,000	—	0.15	1.00	12.00	—
1956 Proof	—	Value: 600				
1957	17,960,000	—	0.25	3.50	30.00	—
1957 Proof	—	Value: 650				
1958	40,823,000	—	0.15	0.50	6.00	—
1958 Proof	—	Value: 600				
1959	1,012,999	0.50	1.00	3.50	35.00	—
1959 Proof	—	Value: 650				
1960	14,376,000	—	0.15	0.50	5.00	—
1960 Proof	—	Value: 600				
1961	2,763,000	—	0.20	1.00	14.00	—
1961 Proof	—	Value: 600				
1962	17,475,000	—	0.15	0.25	3.50	—
1962 Proof	—	Value: 600				
1963	32,299,999	—	0.15	0.25	1.25	—
1963 Proof	—	Value: 600				
1964	5,239,000	—	0.15	0.25	2.00	—
1964 Proof	—	—	—	—	—	—
Note: Reported, not confirmed						
1965	2,774,000	—	0.15	0.25	1.75	—
1965 Proof	—	—	—	—	—	—
Note: Reported, not confirmed						
1966	15,604,000	—	0.15	0.25	1.25	—
1966 Proof	—	—	—	—	—	—
Note: Reported, not confirmed						
1970 Proof	750,000	Value: 3.00				

KM# 781 FLORIN (Two Shillings)

11.3104 g., 0.9250 Silver 0.3364 oz. ASW, 28.3 mm. **Ruler:** Victoria **Obv:** Mature draped bust left **Obv. Legend:** VICTORIA. DEI. GRA. BRITT. REGINA. FID. DEF. IND.IMP. **Obv. Designer:** Thomas Brock **Rev:** Crowned shields of England, Scotland and Ireland

Date	Mintage	F	VF	XF	Unc	BU
1901	2,649,000	6.00	12.00	60.00	125	—

KM# 801 FLORIN (Two Shillings)

11.3104 g., 0.9250 Silver 0.3364 oz. ASW, 28.3 mm. **Ruler:** Edward VII **Obv:** Head right **Rev:** Britannia standing looking right

Date	Mintage	F	VF	XF	Unc	BU
1902	2,190,000	8.00	20.00	60.00	120	—
1902 Matte Proof	15,000	Value: 120				
1903	995,000	18.00	40.00	125	425	—
1904	2,770,000	18.00	40.00	175	475	—
1905	1,188,000	100	225	750	1,500	—
1906	6,910,000	10.00	25.00	100	425	—
1907	5,948,000	10.00	30.00	125	450	—
1908	3,280,000	18.00	50.00	225	650	—
1909	3,483,000	18.00	50.00	225	650	—
1910	5,651,000	10.00	20.00	90.00	300	—

KM# 817 FLORIN (Two Shillings)

11.3104 g., 0.9250 Silver 0.3364 oz. ASW, 28.3 mm. **Ruler:** George V **Obv:** Head left **Obv. Designer:** Bertram MacKennal **Rev:** Cross of crowned shield, sceptres in angles **Note:** Fully struck examples are scarce

Date	Mintage	F	VF	XF	Unc	BU
1911	5,951,000	5.00	10.00	40.00	100	—
1911 Proof	6,007	Value: 110				
1912	8,572,000	5.00	12.00	55.00	110	—
1913	4,545,000	6.50	15.00	75.00	150	—
1914	21,253,000	BV	6.00	35.00	60.00	—
1915	12,358,000	4.75	8.00	45.00	110	—
1916	21,064,000	BV	6.00	28.00	70.00	—
1917	11,182,000	4.75	7.00	30.00	85.00	—
1918	29,212,000	BV	6.00	28.00	65.00	—
1919	9,469,000	5.00	12.00	30.00	100	—

KM# 817a FLORIN (Two Shillings)

11.3104 g., 0.5000 Silver 0.1818 oz. ASW, 28.3 mm. **Ruler:** George V **Obv:** Head left **Obv. Designer:** Bertram MacKennal **Rev:** Cross of crowned shields, sceptres in angles

Date	Mintage	F	VF	XF	Unc	BU
1920	15,388,000	2.75	6.00	35.00	110	—
1921	34,864,000	2.75	5.50	30.00	100	—
1922	23,861,000	2.65	4.50	28.00	55.00	—
1923	21,547,000	2.50	4.00	23.00	45.00	—
1924	4,582,000	3.50	7.00	45.00	100	—
1924 Satin specimen	2	—	—	—	—	2,500
1925	1,404,000	25.00	50.00	175	380	—
1926	5,125,000	3.00	8.50	40.00	110	—

KM# 834 FLORIN (Two Shillings)

11.3104 g., 0.5000 Silver 0.1818 oz. ASW, 28.3 mm. **Ruler:** George V **Obv:** Head left **Obv. Designer:** Bertram MacKennal **Rev:** Cross of crowned sceptres, shields in angles

Date	Mintage	F	VF	XF	Unc	BU
1927 Proof	15,000	Value: 75.00				
1927 Matte Proof	—	Value: 3,500				
Note: There are reportedly 3-4 known of this variety, struck specifically for use in photographs						
1928	11,088,000	BV	3.00	11.50	25.00	—
1928 Proof	—	Value: 900				
1929	16,397,000	BV	3.00	11.50	25.00	—
1929 Proof	—	Value: 950				
1930	5,734,000	BV	5.00	12.50	37.50	—
1930 Proof	—	Value: 1,350				
1931	6,556,000	BV	5.00	11.50	45.00	—
1931 Proof	—	Value: 900				
1932	717,000	20.00	85.00	225	600	—
1932 Proof	—	Value: 2,000				
1933	8,685,000	BV	3.00	11.50	30.00	—
1933 Proof	—	Value: 900				
1935	7,541,000	BV	3.00	11.50	25.00	—
1935 Proof	—	Value: 900				
1936	9,897,000	BV	2.75	11.50	25.00	—
1936 Proof	—	Value: 900				

KM# 855 FLORIN (Two Shillings)

11.3104 g., 0.5000 Silver 0.1818 oz. ASW, 28.3 mm. **Ruler:** George VI **Obv:** Head left **Obv. Designer:** T. H. Paget **Rev:** Crowned tudor rose, thistle, letter 'G', and shamrock, letter 'R' flanking **Rev. Designer:** George Krueger-Gray

Date	Mintage	F	VF	XF	Unc	BU
1937	13,007,000	—	BV	3.00	13.00	—
1937 Proof	26,000	Value: 18.00				
1937 Matte Proof; Rare	—	—	—	—	—	—
Note: There are reportedly 1-2 known of this variety, struck specifically for use in photographs						
1938	7,909,000	BV	2.75	10.00	30.00	—
1938 Proof	—	Value: 850				
1939	20,851,000	—	BV	4.50	18.00	—
1939 Proof	—	Value: 800				
1940	18,700,000	—	BV	4.50	12.00	—
1940 Proof	—	Value: 800				
1941	24,451,000	—	BV	4.50	12.00	—
1941 Proof	—	Value: 800				
1942	39,895,000	—	BV	3.00	10.00	—
1942 Proof	—	Value: 750				
1943	26,712,000	—	BV	3.00	10.00	—
1943 Proof	—	Value: 500				
1944	27,560,000	—	BV	3.00	10.00	—
1944 Proof	—	Value: 600				
1945	25,858,000	—	BV	3.00	10.00	—
1945 Proof	—	Value: 800				
1946	22,300,000	—	BV	3.00	10.00	—
1946 Proof	—	Value: 800				

KM# 865 FLORIN (Two Shillings)

Copper-Nickel, 28.3 mm. **Ruler:** George VI **Obv:** Head left **Obv. Designer:** T. H. Paget **Rev:** Crowned tudor rose, thistle, letter 'G', and shamrock, letter 'R' flanking **Rev. Designer:** George Krueger-Gray

Date	Mintage	F	VF	XF	Unc	BU
1947	22,910,000	0.20	0.35	1.00	10.00	—
1947 Proof	—	Value: 650				
1948	67,554,000	0.20	0.35	1.00	10.00	—
1948 Proof	—	Value: 700				

KM# 878 FLORIN (Two Shillings)

Copper-Nickel, 28.3 mm. **Ruler:** George VI **Obv:** Head left **Obv. Legend:** without IND IMP **Obv. Designer:** T. H. Paget **Rev:** Crowned tudor rose, thistle, letter 'G', and shamrock, letter 'R' flanking **Rev. Designer:** George Krueger-Gray

Date	Mintage	F	VF	XF	Unc	BU
1949	28,615,000	0.20	0.35	1.00	18.00	—
1949 Proof	—	Value: 700				
1950	24,357,000	0.20	0.35	1.00	20.00	—
1950 Proof	18,000	Value: 25.00				
1950 Matte Proof; Rare	—	—	—	—	—	—
Note: There are reportedly 1-2 known of this variety, struck specifically for use in photographs						
1951	27,412,000	0.20	0.75	4.00	25.00	—
1951 Proof	20,000	Value: 30.00				
1951 Matte Proof; Rare	—	—	—	—	—	—

Note: There are reportedly 1-2 known of this variety, struck specifically for use in photographs

KM# 892 FLORIN (Two Shillings)

Copper-Nickel, 28.3 mm. **Ruler:** Elizabeth II **Obv:** Laureate bust right **Obv. Designer:** Mary Gillick **Rev:** Tudor rose at center, thistle and shamrock wreath surround **Rev. Designer:** F. G. Fuller and Cecil Thomas

Date	Mintage	F	VF	XF	Unc	BU
1953	11,959,000	0.25	0.50	1.00	8.00	—
1953 Proof	40,000	Value: 15.00				
1953 Matte Proof; Rare	—	—	—	—	—	—

Note: There are reportedly 1-2 known of this variety, struck specifically for use in photographs

KM# 906 FLORIN (Two Shillings)

Copper-Nickel, 28.3 mm. **Ruler:** Elizabeth II **Obv:** Laureate bust right **Obv. Legend:** without BRITT OMN **Obv. Designer:** Mary Gillick **Rev:** Tudor rose at center, thistle and shamrock wreath surround **Rev. Designer:** F. G. Fuller and Cecil Thomas

Date	Mintage	F	VF	XF	Unc	BU
1954	13,085,000	0.20	0.50	5.50	65.00	—
1954 Proof	—	Value: 600				
1955	25,887,000	0.20	0.50	2.00	6.00	—
1955 Proof	—	Value: 600				
1956	47,824,000	0.20	0.30	1.00	6.00	—
1956 Proof	—	Value: 600				
1957	33,070,999	0.20	0.40	5.00	65.00	—
1957 Proof	—	Value: 700				
1958	9,565,000	0.25	1.25	5.00	30.00	—
1958 Proof	—	Value: 700				
1959	14,080,000	0.25	0.50	5.00	40.00	—
1959 Proof	—	Value: 650				
1960	13,832,000	—	0.20	1.25	6.00	—
1960 Proof	—	Value: 600				
1961	37,735,000	—	0.20	1.00	5.00	—
1961 Proof	—	Value: 600				
1962	35,148,000	—	0.20	0.75	5.00	—
1962 Proof	—	Value: 600				
1963	26,471,000	—	0.20	0.75	5.00	—
1963 Proof	—	Value: 600				
1964	16,539,000	—	0.20	0.50	5.00	—
1965	48,163,000	—	0.20	0.50	4.50	—
1966	83,999,000	—	0.20	0.30	2.50	—
1967	39,718,000	—	0.20	0.30	2.00	—
1970 Proof	750,000	Value: 6.50				

KM# 782 1/2 CROWN

14.1380 g., 0.9250 Silver 0.4204 oz. ASW, 32.3 mm. **Ruler:** Victoria **Obv:** Mature draped bust left **Obv. Designer:** Thomas Brock **Rev:** Crowned and quartered spade shield within wreath **Rev. Legend:** FID. DEF. IND. IMP., HALF date CROWN below

Date	Mintage	F	VF	XF	Unc	BU
1901	1,577,000	16.00	27.00	65.00	150	—

KM# 802 1/2 CROWN

14.1380 g., 0.9250 Silver 0.4204 oz. ASW, 32.3 mm. **Ruler:** Edward VII **Obv:** Head right **Rev:** Crowned and quartered shield within Garter band **Note:** Particular attention should be given to quality of detail in hair and beard on obverse.

Date	Mintage	F	VF	XF	Unc	BU
1902	1,316,000	15.00	40.00	70.00	160	—
1902 Matte Proof	15,000	Value: 170				
1903	275,000	100	275	850	2,800	—
1904	710,000	50.00	200	700	1,800	—
1905	166,000	250	700	2,400	6,500	—
1906	2,886,000	20.00	45.00	200	650	—
1907	3,694,000	20.00	45.00	200	700	—
1908	1,759,000	25.00	50.00	500	1,100	—
1909	3,052,000	20.00	45.00	400	825	—
1910	2,558,000	15.00	35.00	175	500	—

KM# 818.1 1/2 CROWN

14.1380 g., 0.9250 Silver 0.4204 oz. ASW, 32.3 mm. **Ruler:** George V **Obv:** Head left **Obv. Designer:** Bertram MacKennal **Rev:** Crowned and quartered shield within Garter band **Note:** Fully struck World War I (1914-1918) specimens command a premium.

Date	Mintage	F	VF	XF	Unc	BU
1911	2,915,000	6.00	18.00	60.00	125	—
1911 Proof	6,007	Value: 125				
1912	4,701,000	7.00	25.00	65.00	225	—
1913	4,090,000	8.50	30.00	75.00	225	—
1914	18,333,000	BV	10.00	28.00	100	—
1915	32,433,000	BV	10.00	28.00	95.00	—
1916	29,530,000	BV	10.00	28.00	95.00	—
1917	11,172,000	6.00	15.00	45.00	95.00	—
1918	29,080,000	BV	10.00	28.00	65.00	—
1919	10,267,000	6.00	15.00	45.00	85.00	—

KM# 818.1a 1/2 CROWN

14.1380 g., 0.5000 Silver 0.2273 oz. ASW, 32.3 mm. **Ruler:** George V **Obv:** Head left **Obv. Designer:** Bertram MacKennal **Rev:** Crowned shield within Garter rose, crown touches shield **Note:** Fully struck coins command a premium.

Date	Mintage	F	VF	XF	Unc	BU
1920	17,983,000	5.00	8.00	25.00	75.00	—
1921	23,678,000	6.00	10.00	30.00	85.00	—
1922	16,396,999	5.50	8.00	35.00	100	—

KM# 818.2 1/2 CROWN

14.1380 g., 0.5000 Silver 0.2273 oz. ASW, 32.3 mm. **Ruler:** George V **Obv:** Head left **Obv. Designer:** Bertram MacKennal **Rev:** Crowned shield within Garter band, groove between crown and shield **Note:** Fully struck coins command a premium.

Date	Mintage	F	VF	XF	Unc	BU
1922	Inc. above	4.00	8.00	25.00	100	—
1923	26,309,000	3.50	5.00	15.00	50.00	—
1924	5,866,000	6.00	10.00	35.00	100	—
1924 Satin specimen	Est. 2	—	—	—	—	3,500
1925	1,413,000	23.00	50.00	300	550	—
1926	4,474,000	5.00	10.00	35.00	150	—

KM# 830 1/2 CROWN

14.1380 g., 0.5000 Silver 0.2273 oz. ASW, 32.3 mm. **Ruler:** George V **Obv:** Modified head left, larger beads **Obv. Designer:** Bertram MacKennal **Rev:** Crowned shield within Garter band

Date	Mintage	F	VF	XF	Unc	BU
1926	Inc. above	5.00	10.00	45.00	125	—
1927	6,838,000	4.50	7.00	28.00	70.00	—

KM# 835 1/2 CROWN

14.1380 g., 0.5000 Silver 0.2273 oz. ASW, 32.3 mm. **Ruler:** George V **Obv:** Head left **Obv. Designer:** Bertram MacKennal **Rev:** Quartered shield flanked by crowned monograms

Date	Mintage	F	VF	XF	Unc	BU
1927 Proof	15,000	Value: 60.00				
1927 Matte Proof; Rare	—	—	—	—	—	—

Note: There are reportedly 1-2 known of this variety, struck specifically for use in photographs

Date	Mintage	F	VF	XF	Unc	BU
1928	18,763,000	BV	5.00	11.00	35.00	—
1928 Proof	—	Value: 1,000				
1929	17,633,000	BV	5.00	11.00	35.00	—
1929 Proof	—	Value: 1,000				
1930	810,000	10.00	45.00	175	550	—
1930 Proof	—	Value: 1,400				
1931	11,264,000	BV	5.00	11.00	35.00	—
1931 Proof	—	Value: 1,000				
1932	4,794,000	4.00	8.00	17.50	75.00	—
1932 Proof	—	Value: 1,100				
1933	10,311,000	BV	5.00	11.00	35.00	—
1933 Proof	—	Value: 1,000				
1934	2,422,000	4.50	10.00	25.00	100	—
1934 Proof	—	Value: 1,100				
1935	7,022,000	BV	5.00	11.00	28.00	—
1935 Proof	—	Value: 900				
1936	7,039,000	BV	3.25	9.00	25.00	—
1936 Proof	—	Value: 900				

KM# 856 1/2 CROWN

14.1380 g., 0.5000 Silver 0.2273 oz. ASW, 32.3 mm. **Ruler:** George VI **Obv:** Head left **Obv. Designer:** T. H. Paget **Rev:** Quartered shield flanked by crowned monograms **Rev. Designer:** George Krueger-Gray

Date	Mintage	F	VF	XF	Unc	BU
1937	9,106,000	—	BV	4.50	19.00	—
1937 Proof	26,000	Value: 20.00				
1937 Matte Proof; Rare	—	—	—	—	—	—

Note: There are reportedly 1-2 known of this variety, struck specifically for use in photographs

Date	Mintage	F	VF	XF	Unc	BU
1938	6,426,000	—	BV	10.00	35.00	—
1938 Proof	—	Value: 1,000				
1939	15,479,000	—	BV	5.50	19.00	—
1939 Proof	—	Value: 900				
1940	17,948,000	—	BV	5.50	19.00	—
1940 Proof	—	Value: 900				
1941	15,774,000	—	BV	5.50	19.00	—
1941 Proof	—	Value: 900				
1942	31,220,000	—	BV	3.50	10.00	—
1942 Proof	—	Value: 900				
1943	15,463,000	—	BV	3.50	19.00	—
1943 Proof	—	Value: 650				
1944	15,255,000	—	BV	3.50	10.00	—
1944 Proof	—	Value: 800				
1945	19,849,000	—	BV	3.50	10.00	—
1945 Proof	—	Value: 800				
1946	22,725,000	—	BV	3.50	10.00	—
1946 Proof	—	Value: 800				

KM# 866 1/2 CROWN

Copper-Nickel, 32.3 mm. **Ruler:** George VI **Obv:** Head left **Obv. Designer:** T. H. Paget **Rev:** Quartered shield flanked by crowned monograms **Rev. Designer:** George Krueger-Gray

Date	Mintage	F	VF	XF	Unc	BU
1947	21,910,000	0.25	0.50	1.00	10.00	—
1947 Proof	—	Value: 750				
1948	71,165,000	0.25	0.50	1.00	10.00	—
1948 Proof	—	Value: 1,000				

KM# 879 1/2 CROWN

Copper-Nickel, 32.3 mm. **Ruler:** George VI **Obv:** Head left **Obv. Designer:** T. H. Paget **Rev:** Quartered shield flanked by crowned monograms **Rev. Legend:** without IND IMP **Rev. Designer:** George Krueger-Gray

Date	Mintage	F	VF	XF	Unc	BU
1949	28,273,000	0.25	0.50	1.25	16.00	—
1949 Proof	—	Value: 900				
1950	28,336,000	0.25	0.50	3.00	22.50	—
1950 Proof	18,000	Value: 25.00				
1950 Matte Proof; Rare	—	—	—	—	—	—

Note: There are reportedly 1-2 known of this variety, struck specifically for use in photographs

Date	Mintage	F	VF	XF	Unc	BU
1951	9,004,000	0.50	0.75	1.50	35.00	—
1951 Proof	20,000	Value: 30.00				

Date	Mintage	F	VF	XF	Unc	BU
1951 Matte Proof; Rare	—	—	—	—	—	—

Note: There are reportedly 1-2 known of this variety, struck specifically for use in photographs

Date	Mintage	F	VF	XF	Unc	BU
1952	Est. 1	—	50,000	—	—	—
1952 Proof	Est. 1	Value: 80,000				

KM# 893 1/2 CROWN

Copper-Nickel, 32.3 mm. **Ruler:** Elizabeth II **Obv:** Laureate bust right **Obv. Designer:** Mary Gillick **Rev:** Crowned quartered shield flanked by initials, 'ER' **Rev. Designer:** F. G. Fuller and Cecil Thomas

Date	Mintage	F	VF	XF	Unc	BU
1953	4,333,000	0.50	0.75	1.75	10.50	—
1953 Proof	40,000	Value: 15.00				
1953 Matte Proof; Rare	—	—	—	—	—	—

Note: There are reportedly 1-2 known of this variety, struck specifically for use in photographs

KM# 907 1/2 CROWN

14.0000 g., Copper-Nickel, 32.3 mm. **Ruler:** Elizabeth II **Obv:** Laureate bust right **Obv. Legend:** without BRITT OMN **Obv. Designer:** Mary Gillick **Rev:** Crowned quartered shield flanked by initials, 'ER' **Rev. Designer:** F. G. Fuller and Cecil Thomas

Date	Mintage	F	VF	XF	Unc	BU
1954	11,615,000	0.50	0.75	4.00	50.00	—
1954 Proof	—	Value: 850				
1955	23,629,000	0.25	0.50	1.00	10.00	—
1955 Proof	—	Value: 800				
1956	33,935,000	0.25	0.50	0.75	13.00	—
1956 Proof	—	Value: 800				
1957	34,201,000	0.25	0.50	0.75	8.50	—
1957 Proof	—	Value: 800				
1958	15,746,000	0.25	0.75	3.50	30.00	—
1958 Proof	—	Value: 900				
1959	9,029,000	0.75	1.25	6.00	60.00	—
1959 Proof	—	Value: 900				
1960	19,929,000	0.25	0.50	0.75	7.00	—
1960 Proof	—	Value: 800				
1961	25,888,000	0.25	0.50	0.75	5.00	—
1961 Prooflike	—	—	—	—	15.00	—
1961 Proof	—	Value: 900				
1962	24,013,000	0.25	0.50	0.75	5.00	—
1962 Proof	—	—	—	—	—	—
1963	17,625,000	0.25	0.50	0.75	5.00	—
1963 Proof	—	—	—	—	—	—
1964	5,974,000	0.25	0.50	0.75	6.00	—
1965	9,778,000	0.20	0.30	0.50	5.00	—
1966	13,375,000	0.20	0.30	0.50	1.50	—
1967	33,058,000	0.20	0.30	0.50	1.50	—
1970 Proof	750,000	Value: 6.50				

KM# 803 CROWN

28.2759 g., 0.9250 Silver 0.8409 oz. ASW, 38.61 mm. **Ruler:** Edward VII **Obv:** Head right **Rev:** St. George slaying the dragon

Date	Mintage	F	VF	XF	Unc	BU
1902	256,000	50.00	75.00	125	250	—
1902 Matte Proof	15,000	Value: 250				

KM# 836 CROWN

28.2759 g., 0.5000 Silver 0.4545 oz. ASW, 38.61 mm. **Ruler:** George V **Obv:** Head left **Obv. Designer:** Bertram MacKennal **Rev:** Date divided above crown within wreath

Date	Mintage	F	VF	XF	Unc	BU
1927 Proof	15,000	Value: 275				
1927 Matte Proof; Rare	—	—	—	—	—	—

Note: There are reportedly 1-2 known of this variety, struck specifically for use in photographs

Date	Mintage	F	VF	XF	Unc	BU
1928	9,034	100	150	225	450	—
1928 Proof	—	Value: 2,500				
1929	4,994	100	160	250	475	—
1929 Proof	—	Value: 2,500				
1930	4,847	100	160	250	475	—
1930 Proof	—	Value: 2,500				
1931	4,056	110	170	280	500	—
1931 Proof	—	Value: 2,500				
1932	2,395	180	275	425	1,100	—
1932 Proof	—	Value: 3,500				
1933	7,132	100	150	225	475	—
1933 Proof	—	Value: 2,500				
1934	932	1,250	2,000	3,000	6,000	—
1934 Proof	—	Value: 6,000				
1936	2,473	180	275	425	1,100	—
1936 Proof	—	Value: 4,000				

KM# 842 CROWN

28.2759 g., 0.5000 Silver 0.4545 oz. ASW, 38.61 mm. **Ruler:** George V **Subject:** Silver Jubilee **Obv:** Head left **Obv. Designer:** Bertram MacKennal **Rev:** St. George slaying the dragon **Rev. Designer:** Percy Metcalfe

Date	Mintage	F	VF	XF	Unc	BU
1935	715,000	10.00	15.00	20.00	50.00	—

Note: Incused edge lettering

Date	Mintage	F	VF	XF	Unc	BU
1935 Proof	—	Value: 400				

Note: Raised edge lettering

Date	Mintage	F	VF	XF	Unc	BU
1935	—	—	—	—	85.00	—

Note: Specimen in box of issue

Date	Mintage	F	VF	XF	Unc	BU
1935	Inc. above	—	250	500	1,000	—

Note: (Error) Edge lettering: MEN.ANNO-REGNIXXV

KM# 842a CROWN

0.9250 Silver, 38.61 mm. **Ruler:** George V **Subject:** Silver Jubilee **Obv:** Head left **Obv. Designer:** Bertram MacKennal **Rev:** St. George slaying the dragon

Date	Mintage	F	VF	XF	Unc	BU
1935	2,500	Value: 2,200				

Note: Raised edge lettering

Date	Mintage	F	VF	XF	Unc	BU
1935 Proof	—	Value: 1,500				

Note: (Error) Edge lettering: DECUS ANNO REGNI TUTAMEN•XXV•

KM# 857 CROWN

0.5000 Silver, 38.61 mm. **Ruler:** George VI **Obv:** Head left **Obv. Designer:** T. H. Paget **Rev:** Crowned, quartered shield with supporters **Rev. Designer:** George Krueger-Gray

Date	Mintage	F	VF	XF	Unc	BU
1937	419,000	8.00	12.00	25.00	50.00	—
1937 Proof	26,000	Value: 60.00				
1937 Proof	—	Value: 1,200				
Note: Frosted cameo relief; V.I.P. issue						
1937 Matte Proof; Rare	—	—	—	—	—	—
Note: 1-2 pieces known						

KM# 880 CROWN

Copper-Nickel, 38.61 mm. **Ruler:** George VI **Subject:** Festival of Britain **Obv:** Head left **Obv. Designer:** T. H. Paget **Rev:** St. George slaying the dragon **Rev. Designer:** Pistrucci

Date	Mintage	F	VF	XF	Unc	BU
1951 Prooflike	2,004,000	—	—	—	22.50	—
1951 Proof	—	Value: 25.00				
1951 Proof	—	Value: 800				
Note: Frosted cameo relief; V.I.P. issue; 30-50 pieces known						
1951 Matte Proof	—	Value: 3,500				
Note: 1-2 pieces known						

KM# 894 CROWN

Copper-Nickel, 38.61 mm. **Ruler:** Elizabeth II **Subject:** Coronation of Queen Elizabeth II **Obv:** Queen on horseback left, crowned monograms flank **Obv. Designer:** Gilbert Ledward **Rev:** Crown at center of cross formed by Rose, shamrock, leek and thistle, shields in angles **Rev. Designer:** F. G. Fuller and Cecil Thomas **Edge Lettering:** FAITH AND TRUTH I WILL BEAR UNTO YOU

Date	Mintage	F	VF	XF	Unc	BU
1953	5,963,000	—	—	7.50	15.00	—
1953 Proof	40,000	Value: 45.00				
1953 Proof	—	Value: 800				
Note: 20-30 pieces; V.I.P. issue						
1953 Matte Proof	—	Value: 3,500				
Note: 1-2 pieces						

KM# 909 CROWN

Copper-Nickel, 38.61 mm. **Ruler:** Elizabeth II **Subject:** British Exhibition in New York **Obv:** Laureate bust right **Obv. Designer:** Mary Gillick **Rev:** Crown at center of cross formed by Rose, shamrock, leek and thistle, shields in angles **Rev. Designer:** F. G. Fuller and Cecil Thomas

Date	Mintage	F	VF	XF	Unc	BU
1960	1,024,000	—	—	6.00	12.00	—
1960 Prooflike	70,000	—	—	—	35.00	—
1960 Proof	—	Value: 750				
Note: V.I.P. issue; 30-50 pieces						

KM# 910 CROWN

Copper-Nickel, 38.61 mm. **Ruler:** Elizabeth II **Subject:** Winston Churchill **Obv:** Laureate bust right **Obv. Designer:** Mary Gillick **Rev:** Head right **Rev. Designer:** Oscar Neman

Date	Mintage	F	VF	XF	Unc	BU
1965	9,640,000	—	—	0.65	2.00	—
1965 Specimen	—	—	—	—	1,200	—
Note: Satin finish						

DECIMAL COINAGE

1971-1981, 100 New Pence = 1 Pound; 1982, 100 Pence = 1 Pound

KM# 914 1/2 NEW PENNY

1.7820 g., Bronze, 17.14 mm. **Ruler:** Elizabeth II **Obv:** Young bust right **Obv. Designer:** Arnold Machin **Rev:** Crown **Rev. Designer:** Christopher Ironside

Date	Mintage	F	VF	XF	Unc	BU
1971	1,394,188,000	—	—	0.10	0.20	—
1971 Proof	350,000	Value: 1.00				
1972 Proof	150,000	Value: 3.00				
1973	365,680,000	—	—	0.15	0.40	—
1973 Proof	100,000	Value: 1.00				
1974	365,448,000	—	—	0.15	0.35	—
1974 Proof	100,000	Value: 1.00				
1975	197,600,000	—	—	0.15	0.45	—
1975 Proof	100,000	Value: 1.00				
1976	412,172,000	—	—	0.15	0.35	—
1976 Proof	100,000	Value: 1.00				
1977	66,368,000	—	—	0.15	0.20	—
1977 Proof	194,000	Value: 1.00				
1978	59,532,000	—	—	0.15	0.20	—
1978 Proof	88,000	Value: 1.00				
1979	219,132,000	—	—	0.15	0.20	—
1979 Proof	81,000	Value: 1.00				
1980	202,788,000	—	—	0.15	0.20	—
1980 Proof	143,000	Value: 1.00				
1981	46,748,000	—	—	0.15	0.40	—
1981 Proof	100,000	Value: 1.00				

KM# 926 1/2 PENNY

1.7820 g., Bronze, 17.14 mm. **Ruler:** Elizabeth II **Obv:** Bust right **Obv. Designer:** Arnold Machin **Rev:** "HALF PENNY" above crown and fraction **Rev. Designer:** Christopher Ironside **Note:** Denomination now demonetized.

Date	Mintage	F	VF	XF	Unc	BU
1982	190,752,000	—	—	0.15	0.20	—
1982 Proof	107,000	Value: 1.00				
1983	7,600,000	—	—	0.25	0.55	—
1983 Proof	108,000	Value: 1.50				
1984	Est. 159,000	—	—	—	2.00	—
Note: In sets only						
1984 Proof	107,000	Value: 2.50				

KM# 915 NEW PENNY

3.5600 g., Bronze, 20.32 mm. **Ruler:** Elizabeth II **Obv:** Young bust right **Obv. Designer:** Arnold Machin **Rev:** Crowned portocullis **Rev. Designer:** Christopher Ironside

Date	Mintage	F	VF	XF	Unc	BU
1971	1,521,666,000	—	—	0.15	0.20	—
1971 Proof	350,000	Value: 1.25				
1972 Proof	150,000	Value: 3.00				
1973	280,196,000	—	—	0.15	0.40	—
1973 Proof	100,000	Value: 1.25				
1974	330,892,000	—	—	0.15	0.40	—
1974 Proof	100,000	Value: 1.25				
1975	221,604,000	—	—	0.15	0.50	—

Date	Mintage	F	VF	XF	Unc	BU
1975 Proof	100,000	Value: 1.25				
1976	300,160,000	—	—	0.15	0.30	—
1976 Proof	100,000	Value: 1.25				
1977	285,430,000	—	—	0.15	0.20	—
1977 Proof	194,000	Value: 1.25				
1978	292,770,000	—	—	0.15	0.45	—
1978 Proof	88,000	Value: 1.25				
1979	459,000,000	—	—	0.15	0.20	—
1979 Proof	81,000	Value: 1.25				
1980	416,304,000	—	—	0.15	0.20	—
1980 Proof	143,000	Value: 1.25				
1981	301,800,000	—	—	0.15	0.25	—
1981 Proof	100,000	Value: 1.25				

KM# 927 PENNY

3.5600 g., Bronze, 20.32 mm. **Ruler:** Elizabeth II **Obv:** Young bust right **Obv. Designer:** Arnold Machin **Rev:** Crowned portcullis **Rev. Designer:** Christopher Ironside

Date	Mintage	F	VF	XF	Unc	BU
1982	100,292,000	—	—	0.15	0.20	—
1982 Proof	107,000	Value: 1.25				
1983	243,002,000	—	—	0.15	0.40	—
1983 Proof	108,000	Value: 1.25				
1984	154,760,000	—	—	0.20	1.25	—
1984 Proof	107,000	Value: 1.25				

KM# 935 PENNY

3.5600 g., Bronze, 20.32 mm. **Ruler:** Elizabeth II **Obv:** Crowned head right **Obv. Designer:** Raphael Maklouf **Rev:** Crowned portcullis **Rev. Designer:** Christopher Ironside **Note:** Queen's head reduced size.

Date	Mintage	F	VF	XF	Unc	BU
1985	200,605,000	—	—	0.15	0.35	—
1985 Proof	102,000	Value: 1.25				
1986	369,989,000	—	—	0.15	0.35	—
1986 Proof	125,000	Value: 1.25				
1987	499,946,000	—	—	0.15	0.25	—
1987 Proof	89,000	Value: 1.25				
1988	793,492,000	—	—	0.15	0.25	—
1988 Proof	125,000	Value: 1.25				
1989	658,142,000	—	—	0.15	0.25	—
1989 Proof	100,000	Value: 1.25				
1990	529,048,000	—	—	0.15	0.25	—
1990 Proof	100,000	Value: 1.25				
1991	206,458,000	—	—	0.15	0.25	—
1991 Proof	—	Value: 1.25				
1992	—	—	—	—	0.50	—
Note: In sets only						
1992 Proof	—	Value: 1.75				

KM# 935a PENNY

Copper Plated Steel, 20.32 mm. **Ruler:** Elizabeth II **Obv:** Crowned head right **Obv. Designer:** Raphael Maklouf **Rev:** Crowned portcullis **Rev. Designer:** Christopher Ironside

Date	Mintage	F	VF	XF	Unc	BU
1992	253,867,000	—	—	0.15	0.25	—
1993	602,590,000	—	—	0.15	0.25	—
1993 Proof	—	Value: 1.25				
1994	843,834,000	—	—	0.15	0.25	—
1994 Proof	—	Value: 1.25				
1995	303,314,000	—	—	0.15	0.25	—
1995 Proof	—	Value: 1.25				
1996	723,840,000	—	—	—	0.25	—
1996 Proof	—	Value: 1.25				
1997	396,874,000	—	—	—	0.25	—
1997 Proof	—	Value: 1.25				

KM# 986 PENNY

3.5900 g., Copper Plated Steel, 20.34 mm. **Ruler:** Elizabeth II **Obv:** Head with tiara right **Obv. Designer:** Ian Rank-Broadley **Rev:** Crowned portcullis **Rev. Designer:** Christopher Ironside **Edge:** Plain

Date	Mintage	F	VF	XF	Unc	BU
1998	739,770,000	—	—	—	0.20	—
1998 Proof	Est. 100,000	Value: 3.25				
1999	891,392,000	—	—	—	0.20	—
2000	1,060,364,000	—	—	—	0.20	—
2001	928,802,000	—	—	—	0.20	—
2002	601,446,000	—	—	—	0.20	—
2003	539,436,000	—	—	—	0.20	—
2004	739,764,000	—	—	—	0.20	—
2004 Proof	—	Value: 3.25				
2005	584,916,000	—	—	—	0.20	—
2005 Proof	—	Value: 3.25				
2006	—	—	—	—	0.20	—
2006 Proof	—	Value: 3.25				
2007	—	—	—	—	0.20	—
2007 Proof	—	Value: 3.25				

KM# 916 2 NEW PENCE

7.1200 g., Bronze, 25.91 mm. **Ruler:** Elizabeth II **Obv:** Young bust right **Obv. Designer:** Arnold Machin **Rev:** Welsh plumes and crown **Rev. Designer:** Christopher Ironside

Date	Mintage	F	VF	XF	Unc	BU
1971	1,454,856,000	—	—	0.10	0.20	—
1971 Proof	350,000	Value: 1.50				
1972 Proof	150,000	Value: 3.50				
1973 Proof	100,000	Value: 3.50				
1974 Proof	100,000	Value: 3.50				
1975	145,545,000	—	—	0.15	0.40	—
1975 Proof	100,000	Value: 1.50				
1976	181,379,000	—	—	0.15	0.30	—
1976 Proof	100,000	Value: 1.50				
1977	109,281,000	—	—	0.15	0.20	—
1977 Proof	194,000	Value: 1.50				
1978	189,658,000	—	—	0.15	0.40	—
1978 Proof	88,000	Value: 1.50				
1979	260,200,000	—	—	0.15	0.25	—
1979 Proof	81,000	Value: 1.50				
1980	408,527,000	—	—	0.15	0.25	—
1980 Proof	143,000	Value: 1.50				
1981	353,191,000	—	—	0.15	0.25	—
1981 Proof	100,000	Value: 1.50				

KM# 928 2 PENCE

7.1200 g., Bronze, 25.91 mm. **Ruler:** Elizabeth II **Obv:** Young bust right **Obv. Designer:** Arnold Machin **Rev:** Welsh plumes and crown **Rev. Designer:** Christopher Ironside

Date	Mintage	F	VF	XF	Unc	BU
1982	205,000	—	—	—	1.00	—
Note: In sets only						
1982 Proof	107,000	Value: 1.50				
1983	631,000	—	—	—	1.00	—
Note: In sets only						
1983 Proof	108,000	Value: 1.50				
1984	159,000	—	—	—	1.50	—
Note: In sets only						
1984 Proof	107,000	Value: 1.50				

KM# 936 2 PENCE

7.1200 g., Bronze, 25.91 mm. **Ruler:** Elizabeth II **Obv:** Crowned head right **Obv. Designer:** Raphael Maklouf **Rev:** Welsh plumes and crown **Rev. Designer:** Christopher Ironside

Date	Mintage	F	VF	XF	Unc	BU
1985	107,113,000	—	—	0.15	0.25	—
1985 Proof	102,000	Value: 1.50				
1986	168,968,000	—	—	0.15	0.50	—
1986 Proof	125,000	Value: 1.50				
1987	218,101,000	—	—	0.15	0.25	—
1987 Proof	89,000	Value: 1.50				
1988	419,889,000	—	—	0.15	0.25	—
1988 Proof	125,000	Value: 1.50				
1989	359,226,000	—	—	0.15	0.25	—
1989 Proof	100,000	Value: 1.50				
1990	204,500,000	—	—	0.15	0.25	—
1990 Proof	100,000	Value: 1.50				
1991	86,625,000	—	—	0.15	0.25	—
1991 Proof	—	Value: 1.50				
1992	—	—	—	—	0.50	—
Note: In sets only						
1992 Proof	—	Value: 2.00				

KM# 936a 2 PENCE

Copper Plated Steel, 25.91 mm. **Ruler:** Elizabeth II **Obv:** Crowned head right **Obv. Designer:** Raphael Maklouf **Rev:** Welsh plumes and crown **Rev. Designer:** Christopher Ironside

Date	Mintage	F	VF	XF	Unc	BU
1992	102,247,000	—	—	0.15	0.25	—
1993	235,674,000	—	—	0.15	0.25	—
1993 Proof	—	Value: 1.50				
1994	531,628,000	—	—	0.10	0.25	—
1994 Proof	—	Value: 1.50				
1995	124,482,000	—	—	0.10	0.25	—
1995 Proof	—	Value: 1.50				
1996	296,278,000	—	—	0.10	0.25	—
1996 Proof	—	Value: 1.50				
1997	496,116,000	—	—	0.10	0.25	—
1997 Proof	—	Value: 1.50				

KM# 987 2 PENCE

7.1400 g., Copper Plated Steel, 25.86 mm. **Ruler:** Elizabeth II **Obv:** Head with tiara right **Obv. Designer:** Ian Rank-Broadley **Rev:** Welsh plumes and crown **Rev. Designer:** Christopher Ironside **Edge:** Plain

Date	Mintage	F	VF	XF	Unc	BU
1998	115,154,000	—	—	—	0.25	—
1998 Proof	Est. 100,000	Value: 3.25				
1999	353,816,000	—	—	—	0.25	—
1999 Proof	—	Value: 3.25				
2000	536,643,000	—	—	—	0.25	—
2001	551,886,000	—	—	—	0.25	—
2002	168,556,000	—	—	—	0.25	—
2004	356,396,000	—	—	—	0.25	—
2003	260,225,000	—	—	—	0.25	—
2004 Proof	—	Value: 3.25				
2005	243,325,000	—	—	—	0.25	—
2005 Proof	—	Value: 3.25				
2006	—	—	—	—	0.25	—
2006 Proof	—	Value: 3.25				
2007	—	—	—	—	0.25	—
2007 Proof	—	Value: 3.25				

KM# 987a 2 PENCE

Bronze, 25.91 mm. **Ruler:** Elizabeth II **Obv:** Head with tiara right **Obv. Designer:** Ian Rank-Broadley **Rev:** Welsh plumes and crown **Rev. Designer:** Christopher Ironside

Date	Mintage	F	VF	XF	Unc	BU
1998	98,676,000	—	—	—	0.25	—
1999	460,000,000	—	—	—	0.25	—
1999 Proof	79,401	Value: 2.50				
Note: In sets only						
2000 Proof	—	—	—	—	—	—
2001	—	—	—	—	0.25	—
2001 Proof	Est. 100,000	Value: 2.50				
2002 Proof	—	Value: 2.50				
2003 Proof	—	Value: 2.50				
2004 Proof	100,000	Value: 2.50				

KM# 911 5 NEW PENCE

5.6500 g., Copper-Nickel, 23.59 mm. **Ruler:** Elizabeth II **Obv:** Young bust right **Obv. Designer:** Arnold Machin **Rev:** Crowned thistle **Rev. Designer:** Christopher Ironside

Date	Mintage	F	VF	XF	Unc	BU
1968	98,868,000	—	—	0.15	0.30	—
1969	120,270,000	—	—	0.15	0.40	—
1970	225,949,000	—	—	0.15	0.40	—
1971	81,783,000	—	—	0.15	0.45	—
1971 Proof	350,000	Value: 1.75				
1972 Proof	150,000	Value: 3.50				
1973 Proof	100,000	Value: 3.50				
1974 Proof	100,000	Value: 3.50				
1975	141,539,000	—	—	0.15	0.30	—
1975 Proof	100,000	Value: 1.50				
1976 Proof	100,000	Value: 3.50				
1977	24,308,000	—	—	0.15	0.35	—
1977 Proof	194,000	Value: 1.50				
1978	61,094,000	—	—	0.15	0.50	—
1978 Proof	88,000	Value: 1.50				
1979	155,456,000	—	—	0.15	0.30	—
1979 Proof	81,000	Value: 1.50				
1980	220,566,000	—	—	0.15	0.30	—
1980 Proof	143,000	Value: 1.50				
1981 Proof	100,000	Value: 1.75				

KM# 929 5 PENCE

5.6500 g., Copper-Nickel, 23.59 mm. **Ruler:** Elizabeth II **Obv:** Young bust right **Obv. Designer:** Arnold Machin **Rev:** Crowned thistle **Rev. Designer:** Christopher Ironside

Date	Mintage	F	VF	XF	Unc	BU
1982	205,000	—	—	—	2.25	—
Note: In sets only						

Date	Mintage	F	VF	XF	Unc	BU
1982 Proof	107,000	Value: 1.75				
1983	637,000	—	—	—	1.75	—
Note: In sets only						
1983 Proof	108,000	Value: 1.75				
1984	159,000	—	—	—	1.75	—
Note: In sets only						
1984 Proof	107,000	Value: 1.50				

KM# 937 5 PENCE

5.6500 g., Copper-Nickel, 23.59 mm. **Ruler:** Elizabeth II **Obv:** Crowned head right **Obv. Designer:** Raphael Maklouf **Rev:** Modified design, Five Pence is away from the edge **Rev. Designer:** Christopher Ironside

Date	Mintage	F	VF	XF	Unc	BU
1985	178,000	—	—	—	2.00	—
Note: In sets only						
1985 Proof	102,000	Value: 1.50				
1986	167,000	—	—	—	1.00	—
Note: In sets only						
1986 Proof	125,000	Value: 1.50				
1987	48,220,000	—	—	0.15	0.30	—
1987 Proof	89,000	Value: 1.75				
1988	120,745,000	—	—	0.15	0.30	—
1988 Proof	125,000	Value: 1.75				
1989	101,406,000	—	—	0.15	0.30	—
1989 Proof	100,000	Value: 1.75				
1990	—	—	—	—	2.50	—
Note: In sets only						
1990 Proof	—	Value: 2.75				

KM# 937b 5 PENCE

3.2500 g., Copper-Nickel, 18 mm. **Ruler:** Elizabeth II **Obv:** Crowned head right **Obv. Designer:** Raphael Maklouf **Rev:** Crowned thistle **Rev. Designer:** Christopher Ironside **Note:** Reduced size. Varieties in thickness and edge milling exist.

Date	Mintage	F	VF	XF	Unc	BU
1990	1,634,976,000	—	—	—	0.35	—
1990 Proof	—	Value: 2.00				
1991	724,979,000	—	—	—	0.35	—
1991 Proof	—	Value: 2.00				
1992	453,174,000	—	—	—	0.35	—
1992 Proof	—	Value: 2.00				
1993	56,945	—	—	—	1.25	—
Note: In sets only						
1993 Proof	—	Value: 2.00				
1994	93,602,000	—	—	—	0.35	—
1994 Proof	—	Value: 2.00				
1995	183,384,000	—	—	—	0.35	—
1995 Proof	—	Value: 2.00				
1996	302,902,000	—	—	—	0.35	—
1996 Proof	—	Value: 2.00				
1997	236,596,000	—	—	—	0.35	—
1997 Proof	—	Value: 2.00				

KM# 988 5 PENCE

3.2500 g., Copper-Nickel, 18 mm. **Ruler:** Elizabeth II **Obv:** Head with tiara right **Obv. Designer:** Ian Rank-Broadley **Rev:** Crowned thistle

Date	Mintage	F	VF	XF	Unc	BU
1998	217,376,000	—	—	—	0.30	—
1998 Proof	Est. 100,000	Value: 3.25				
1999	195,490,000	—	—	—	0.30	—
1999 Proof	79,401	Value: 3.00				
2000	388,506,000	—	—	—	0.30	—
2000 Proof	Est. 100,000	Value: 3.00				
2001	320,330,000	—	—	—	0.30	—
2001 Proof	Est. 100,000	Value: 3.00				
2002	219,258,000	—	—	—	0.30	—
2002 Proof	—	Value: 3.00				
2003	333,230,000	—	—	—	0.30	—
2003 Proof	—	Value: 3.00				
2004	271,810,000	—	—	—	0.30	—
2004 Proof	100,000	Value: 3.00				
2005	264,412,000	—	—	—	0.30	—
2005 Proof	—	Value: 3.00				
2006	—	—	—	—	0.30	—
2006 Proof	—	Value: 3.00				
2007 Proof	—	Value: 3.00				
2007	—	—	—	—	0.30	—

KM# 912 10 NEW PENCE

11.3100 g., Copper-Nickel, 28.5 mm. **Ruler:** Elizabeth II **Obv:** Young bust right **Obv. Designer:** Arnold Machin **Rev:** Crowned lion prancing left

Date	Mintage	F	VF	XF	Unc	BU
1968	336,143,000	—	—	0.25	0.50	—
1969	314,008,000	—	—	0.25	0.55	—
1970	133,571,000	—	—	0.25	0.65	—
1971	63,205,000	—	—	0.25	0.90	—
1971 Proof	350,000	Value: 1.75				
1972 Proof	150,000	Value: 3.75				
1973	152,174,000	—	—	0.25	0.50	—
1973 Proof	100,000	Value: 1.75				
1974	92,741,000	—	—	0.25	0.50	—
1974 Proof	100,000	Value: 1.75				
1975	181,559,000	—	—	0.25	0.50	—
1975 Proof	100,000	Value: 1.75				
1976	228,220,000	—	—	0.25	0.50	—
1976 Proof	100,000	Value: 1.75				
1977	59,323,000	—	—	0.25	0.60	—
1977 Proof	194,000	Value: 1.75				
1978 Proof	88,000	Value: 5.25				
1979	115,457,000	—	—	0.25	0.60	—
1979 Proof	81,000	Value: 1.75				
1980	88,650,000	—	—	0.25	0.65	—
1980 Proof	143,000	Value: 1.75				
1981	3,487,000	—	0.25	0.50	1.75	—
1981 Proof	100,000	Value: 1.75				

KM# 930 10 PENCE

11.3100 g., Copper-Nickel, 28.5 mm. **Ruler:** Elizabeth II **Obv:** Young bust right **Obv. Designer:** Arnold Machin **Rev:** Crowned lion prancing left **Rev. Designer:** Christopher Ironside

Date	Mintage	F	VF	XF	Unc	BU
1982	205,000	—	—	—	2.75	—
Note: In sets only						
1982 Proof	107,000	Value: 1.75				
1983	637,000	—	—	—	2.75	—
Note: In sets only						
1983 Proof	108,000	Value: 1.75				
1984	159,000	—	—	—	2.00	—
Note: In sets only						
1984 Proof	107,000	Value: 1.75				

KM# 938 10 PENCE

11.3100 g., Copper-Nickel, 28.5 mm. **Ruler:** Elizabeth II **Obv:** Crowned head right **Obv. Designer:** Raphael Maklouf **Rev:** Modified design, Ten Pence is away from the edge **Rev. Designer:** Christopher Ironside

Date	Mintage	F	VF	XF	Unc	BU
1985	178,000	—	—	—	2.75	—
Note: In sets only						
1985 Proof	102,000	Value: 1.75				
1986	167,000	—	—	—	1.75	—
Note: In sets only						
1986 Proof	125,000	Value: 1.75				
1987	172,000	—	—	—	2.75	—
Note: In sets only						
1987 Proof	89,000	Value: 2.75				
1988	134,000	—	—	—	2.75	—
Note: In sets only						
1988 Proof	125,000	Value: 2.75				
1989	78,000	—	—	—	3.50	—
Note: In sets only						
1989 Proof	100,000	Value: 2.75				
1990	—	—	—	—	3.50	—
Note: In sets only						
1990 Proof	100,000	Value: 2.75				
1991	—	—	—	—	3.50	—
Note: In sets only						
1991 Proof	—	Value: 2.75				
1992	—	—	—	—	2.75	—
Note: In sets only						
1992 Proof	—	Value: 3.50				

KM# 938b 10 PENCE

6.5000 g., Copper-Nickel, 24.5 mm. **Ruler:** Elizabeth II **Obv:** Crowned head right **Rev:** Crowned lion prancing left **Note:** Reduced size. Varieties in thickness and edge milling exist.

Date	Mintage	F	VF	XF	Unc	BU
1992	1,413,455,000	—	—	0.25	0.50	—
1992 Proof	—	Value: 2.75				
1993	—	—	—	—	1.00	—
Note: In sets only						
1993 Proof	—	Value: 1.75				
1994	—	—	—	—	1.00	—
Note: In sets only						
1994 Proof	—	Value: 1.75				
1995	43,259,000	—	—	—	1.00	—
1995 Proof	—	Value: 1.75				
1996	118,738,000	—	—	—	1.00	—
1996 Proof	—	Value: 1.75				
1997	99,196,000	—	—	—	1.00	—
1997 Proof	—	Value: 1.75				

KM# 989 10 PENCE

6.5000 g., Copper-Nickel, 24.5 mm. **Ruler:** Elizabeth II **Obv:** Head with tiara right **Obv. Designer:** Ian Rank-Broadley **Rev:** Crowned lion prancing left **Rev. Designer:** Christopher Ironside

Date	Mintage	F	VF	XF	Unc	BU
1998	—	—	—	—	1.25	—
Note: In sets only						
1998 Proof	—	Value: 4.50				
Note: In sets only						
1999	136,492	—	—	—	1.25	—
Note: In sets only						
1999 Proof	79,401	Value: 3.25				
Note: In sets only						
2000	134,727,000	—	—	—	0.40	—
2000 Proof	Est. 100,000	Value: 3.25				
2001	82,081,000	—	—	—	0.40	—
2001 Proof	Est. 100,000	Value: 3.25				
2002	80,934,000	—	—	—	0.40	—
2002 Proof	—	Value: 3.25				
2003	88,118,000	—	—	—	0.40	—
2003 Proof	—	Value: 3.25				
2004	99,602,000	—	—	—	0.40	—
2004 Proof	100,000	Value: 3.25				
2005	89,839,000	—	—	—	0.40	—
2005 Proof	—	Value: 3.25				
2006	—	—	—	—	0.40	—
2006 Proof	—	Value: 3.25				
2007	—	—	—	—	0.40	—
2007 Proof	—	Value: 3.25				

KM# 931 20 PENCE

5.0000 g., Copper-Nickel, 21.4 mm. **Ruler:** Elizabeth II **Obv:** Young bust right **Obv. Designer:** Arnold Machin **Rev:** Crowned rose **Rev. Designer:** William Gardner **Shape:** 7-sided

Date	Mintage	F	VF	XF	Unc	BU
1982	740,815,000	—	—	0.45	0.65	—
1982 Proof	107,000	Value: 4.50				
1983	158,463,000	—	—	0.45	0.65	—
1983 Proof	108,000	Value: 2.25				
1984	65,351,000	—	—	0.45	0.65	—
1984 Proof	107,000	Value: 2.25				

KM# 939 20 PENCE

5.0000 g., Copper-Nickel, 21.4 mm. **Ruler:** Elizabeth II **Obv:** Crowned head right **Obv. Designer:** Raphael Maklouf **Rev:** Crowned rose **Rev. Designer:** William Gardner **Shape:** 7-sided

Date	Mintage	F	VF	XF	Unc	BU
1985	74,274,000	—	—	0.45	0.75	—
1985 Proof	102,000	Value: 4.50				
1986	167,000	—	—	—	1.00	—
Note: In sets only						
1986 Proof	125,000	Value: 4.50				
1987	137,450,000	—	—	0.45	0.75	—
1987 Proof	89,000	Value: 4.50				
1988	38,038,000	—	—	0.45	0.75	—
1988 Proof	125,000	Value: 5.00				
1989	132,014,000	—	—	0.45	0.75	—
1989 Proof	100,000	Value: 5.00				
1990	88,098,000	—	—	0.45	0.75	—
1990 Proof	100,000	Value: 5.00				
1991	35,901,000	—	—	0.45	1.00	—
1991 Proof	—	Value: 5.00				
1992	31,205,000	—	—	0.45	1.00	—
1992 Proof	—	Value: 5.00				
1993	123,124,000	—	—	0.45	0.75	—
1993 Proof	—	Value: 5.00				
1994	67,131,000	—	—	0.45	1.00	—
1994 Proof	—	Value: 5.00				
1995	102,005,000	—	—	0.45	0.75	—
1995 Proof	—	Value: 5.00				
1996	83,164,000	—	—	0.45	0.75	—
1996 Proof	—	Value: 5.00				
1997	89,519,000	—	—	0.45	0.75	—
Note: Variations in portrait exist						
1997 Proof	—	Value: 5.00				

KM# 990 20 PENCE

5.0000 g., Copper-Nickel, 21.4 mm. **Ruler:** Elizabeth II **Obv:** Head with tiara right **Obv. Designer:** Ian Rank-Broadley **Rev:** Crowned rose **Rev. Designer:** William Gardner **Shape:** 7-sided

Date	Mintage	F	VF	XF	Unc	BU
1998	76,965,000	—	—	—	0.60	—
1998 Proof	Est. 100,000	Value: 3.50				
1999	73,478,750	—	—	—	0.60	—
1999 Proof	79,401	Value: 3.00				
2000	136,418,750	—	—	—	0.60	—
2000 Proof	Est. 100,000	Value: 3.25				
2001	148,122,500	—	—	—	0.60	—
2001 Proof	Est. 100,000	Value: 3.25				
2002	93,360,000	—	—	—	0.60	—
2002 Proof	100,000	Value: 3.25				
2003	153,383,750	—	—	—	0.60	—
2003 Proof	—	Value: 3.25				
2004	120,212,500	—	—	—	0.60	—
2004 Proof	100,000	Value: 3.25				
2005	104,016,000	—	—	—	0.60	—
2005 Proof	—	Value: 3.25				
2006	—	—	—	—	0.60	—
2006 Proof	—	Value: 3.25				
2007	—	—	—	—	0.60	—
2007 Proof	—	Value: 3.25				

KM# 913 50 NEW PENCE

13.5000 g., Copper-Nickel, 30 mm. **Ruler:** Elizabeth II **Obv:** Young bust right **Obv. Designer:** Arnold Machin **Rev:** Britannia seated right **Rev. Designer:** Christopher Ironside **Shape:** 7-sided

Date	Mintage	F	VF	XF	Unc	BU
1969	188,400,000	—	—	1.25	2.50	—
1970	19,461,000	—	—	1.25	3.50	—
1971 Proof	350,000	Value: 3.50				
1972 Proof	150,000	Value: 6.50				
1974 Proof	100,000	Value: 3.00				
1975 Proof	100,000	Value: 3.00				
1976	43,747,000	—	—	1.75	3.50	—
1976 Proof	100,000	Value: 2.50				
1977	49,536,000	—	—	1.75	3.50	—
1977 Proof	194,000	Value: 2.50				
1978	72,005,000	—	—	1.75	3.50	—
1978 Proof	88,000	Value: 2.75				
1979	58,680,000	—	—	1.75	2.25	—
1979 Proof	81,000	Value: 2.75				
1980	89,086,000	—	—	1.75	2.25	—
1980 Proof	143,000	Value: 2.50				
1981	74,003,000	—	—	1.75	2.25	—
1981 Proof	100,000	Value: 2.50				

KM# 918 50 PENCE

13.5000 g., Copper-Nickel, 30 mm. **Ruler:** Elizabeth II **Subject:** Britain's entry into E.E.C **Obv:** Young bust right **Obv. Designer:** Arnold Machin **Rev:** Denomination and date at center of nine clasped hands **Rev. Designer:** David Wynne **Shape:** 7-sided

Date	Mintage	F	VF	XF	Unc	BU
1973	89,775,000	—	—	1.25	2.00	—
1973 Proof	357,000	Value: 5.50				

KM# 932 50 PENCE

13.5000 g., Copper-Nickel, 30 mm. **Ruler:** Elizabeth II **Obv:** Young bust right **Obv. Designer:** Arnold Machin **Rev:** Britannia seated right **Rev. Designer:** Christopher Ironside **Shape:** 7-sided

Date	Mintage	F	VF	XF	Unc	BU
1982	51,312,000	—	—	1.25	1.75	—
1982 Proof	107,000	Value: 2.50				
1983	62,825,000	—	—	1.25	2.00	—
1983 Proof	125,000	Value: 2.50				
1984	Est. 107,000	—	—	—	2.75	—
Note: In sets only						
1984 Proof	125,000	Value: 2.50				

KM# 940.1 50 PENCE

13.5000 g., Copper-Nickel, 30 mm. **Ruler:** Elizabeth II **Obv:** Crowned head right **Obv. Designer:** Raphael Maklouf **Rev:** Britannia seated right **Rev. Designer:** Christopher Ironside **Shape:** 7-sided

Date	Mintage	F	VF	XF	Unc	BU
1985	682,100	—	—	1.25	5.50	—
1985 Proof	102,000	Value: 2.75				
1986	167,000	—	—	—	2.75	—
Note: In sets only						
1986 Proof	125,000	Value: 2.75				
1987	172,000	—	—	—	2.75	—
Note: In sets only						
1987 Proof	89,000	Value: 2.75				
1988	134,000	—	—	—	2.75	—
Note: In sets only						
1988 Proof	125,000	Value: 3.50				
1989	78,000	—	—	—	3.50	—
Note: In sets only						
1989 Proof	100,000	Value: 2.75				
1990	—	—	—	—	3.50	—
Note: In sets only						
1990 Proof	100,000	Value: 6.00				
1991	—	—	—	—	3.50	—
Note: In sets only						
1991 Proof	—	Value: 6.50				
1992	—	—	—	—	3.50	—
Note: In sets only						
1992 Proof	—	Value: 6.50				
1993	—	—	—	—	3.50	—
Note: In sets only						
1993 Proof	—	Value: 3.50				
1995	—	—	—	—	2.75	—
Note: In sets only						
1995 Proof	—	Value: 3.50				
1996	—	—	—	—	2.75	—
Note: In sets only						
1996 Proof	—	Value: 3.50				
1997	—	—	—	—	2.75	—
Note: In sets only						
1997 Proof	—	Value: 3.50				

KM# 963 50 PENCE

13.5000 g., Copper-Nickel, 30 mm. **Ruler:** Elizabeth II **Subject:** British Presidency of European Council of Ministers **Obv:** Crowned head right **Obv. Designer:** Raphael Maklouf **Rev:** Stars on conference table **Shape:** 7-sided

Date	Mintage	F	VF	XF	Unc	BU
ND(1992)	109,000	—	—	—	5.75	—
ND(1992) Proof	Est. 100,000	Value: 13.50				

KM# 966 50 PENCE

13.5000 g., Copper-Nickel, 30 mm. **Ruler:** Elizabeth II **Subject:** 50th Anniversary of Normandy Invasion **Obv:** Crowned head right **Obv. Designer:** Raphael Maklouf **Rev:** Boats and planes **Rev. Designer:** John Mills **Shape:** 7-sided

Date	Mintage	F	VF	XF	Unc	BU
1994	6,706,000	—	—	—	2.50	—
1994 Proof	—	Value: 11.50				

KM# 940.2 50 PENCE

8.0000 g., Copper-Nickel, 27.3 mm. **Ruler:** Elizabeth II **Obv:** Crowned head right **Obv. Designer:** Raphael Maklouf **Rev:** Britannia seated right **Rev. Designer:** Christopher Ironside **Shape:** 7-sided **Note:** Reduced size.

Date	Mintage	F	VF	XF	Unc	BU
1997	456,364,000	—	—	—	2.50	—
1997 Proof	—	Value: 3.50				

KM# 991 50 PENCE

8.0000 g., Copper-Nickel, 27.3 mm. **Ruler:** Elizabeth II **Obv:** Head with tiara right **Obv. Designer:** Ian Rank-Broadley **Rev:** Britannia seated right **Rev. Designer:** Christopher Ironside **Shape:** 7-sided

Date	Mintage	F	VF	XF	Unc	BU
1998	74,350,500	—	—	—	1.75	—
1998 Proof	Est. 100,000	Value: 2.50				
1999	29,905,000	—	—	—	1.75	—
1999 Proof	79,401	Value: 2.50				
2000	39,172,000	—	—	—	1.75	—
2000 Proof	Est. 100,000	Value: 2.50				
2001	84,999,500	—	—	—	1.75	—
2001 Proof	Est. 100,000	Value: 2.50				
2002	23,907,500	—	—	—	1.75	—
2002 Proof	—	Value: 2.50				
2003	26,557,030	—	—	—	1.75	—
2003 Proof	—	Value: 2.50				
2004	Est. 33,478,000	—	—	—	1.75	—
2004 Proof	100,000	Value: 2.50				
2005	30,254,500	—	—	—	1.75	—
2005 Proof	—	Value: 2.50				
2006	—	—	—	—	1.75	—
2006 Proof	—	Value: 2.50				
2007	—	—	—	—	1.75	—
2007 Proof	—	Value: 2.50				

KM# 992 50 PENCE
8.0000 g., Copper-Nickel, 27.3 mm. **Ruler:** Elizabeth II **Subject:** 25th Anniversary - Britain in the Common Market **Obv:** Head with tiara right **Obv. Designer:** Ian Rank-Broadley **Rev:** Bouquet of stars **Rev. Designer:** John Mills **Shape:** 7-sided

Date	Mintage	F	VF	XF	Unc	BU
1998	4,967,000	—	—	—	2.75	—
1998 Proof	Est. 100,000	Value: 9.50				

KM# 996 50 PENCE
8.0000 g., Copper-Nickel, 27.3 mm. **Ruler:** Elizabeth II **Subject:** National Health Service **Obv:** Head with tiara right **Obv. Designer:** Ian Rank-Broadley **Rev:** Radiant hands within circle **Rev. Designer:** David Cornell **Shape:** 7-sided

Date	Mintage	F	VF	XF	Unc	BU
1998	5,001,000	—	—	—	2.75	—
1998	—	—	—	—	7.00	—
Note: In folder						
1998 Proof	—	Value: 12.00				

KM# 1004 50 PENCE
8.0000 g., Copper-Nickel, 27.3 mm. **Ruler:** Elizabeth II **Subject:** Public Library **Obv:** Head with tiara right **Obv. Designer:** Ian Rank-Broadley **Rev:** Open book above building, CDs in pediment **Edge:** Plain edge **Shape:** 7-sided

Date	Mintage	F	VF	XF	Unc	BU
2000	Est. 5,000,000	—	—	—	2.75	—
2000 Proof	100,000	Value: 12.50				

KM# 1036 50 PENCE
8.0000 g., Copper-Nickel, 27.3 mm. **Ruler:** Elizabeth II **Subject:** Woman's Suffrage **Obv:** Head with tiara right **Obv. Designer:** Ian Rank-Broadley **Rev:** Standing woman with banner **Edge:** Plain **Shape:** 7-sided

Date	Mintage	F	VF	XF	Unc	BU
2003	Est. 5,000,000	—	—	—	2.50	—
2003 Proof	—	Value: 9.50				

KM# 1047 50 PENCE
8.0000 g., Copper-Nickel, 27.3 mm. **Ruler:** Elizabeth II **Subject:** The First Four Minute Mile **Obv:** Head with tiara right **Obv. Designer:** Ian Rank-Broadley **Rev:** Running legs, stop watch and value **Edge:** Plain

Date	Mintage	F	VF	XF	Unc	BU
2004	Est. 5,000,000	—	—	—	5.00	6.00
2004 Proof	100,000	Value: 7.50				

KM# 1050 50 PENCE
8.0000 g., Copper-Nickel, 27.3 mm. **Ruler:** Elizabeth II **Obv:** Head with tiara right **Obv. Designer:** Ian Rank-Broadley **Rev:** Text from the first English dictionary by Samuel Johnson **Edge:** Plain

Date	Mintage	F	VF	XF	Unc	BU
2005	36,125,000	—	—	—	2.50	3.50
2005 Proof	50,000	Value: 6.00				

KM# 1057 50 PENCE
8.0000 g., Copper-Nickel, 27.3 mm. **Ruler:** Elizabeth II **Obv:** Head with tiara right **Obv. Designer:** Ian Rank-Broadley **Rev:** Victoria Cross obverse and reverse views **Edge:** Plain **Shape:** 7-sided

Date	Mintage	F	VF	XF	Unc	BU
2006	—	—	—	—	5.00	6.00
2006 Proof	50,000	Value: 7.50				

KM# 1058 50 PENCE
8.0000 g., Copper-Nickel, 27.3 mm. **Ruler:** Elizabeth II **Obv:** Head with tiara right **Obv. Designer:** Ian Rank-Broadley **Rev:** Heroic Act scene with cross shape in background **Edge:** Plain **Shape:** 7-sided

Date	Mintage	F	VF	XF	Unc	BU
2006	—	—	—	—	5.00	6.00
2006 Proof	50,000	Value: 7.50				

KM# 1073 50 PENCE
8.0000 g., Copper-Nickel, 27.3 mm. **Ruler:** Elizabeth II **Subject:** Centennial of Scouting **Obv:** Bust right **Rev:** Fleur de Lis Scouting emblem superimposed on globe **Edge:** Plain **Shape:** 7-sided

Date	Mintage	F	VF	XF	Unc	BU
2007	—	—	—	—	—	5.00
2007 Proof	50,000	Value: 7.50				

KM# 933 POUND
9.5000 g., Nickel-Brass, 22.5 mm. **Ruler:** Elizabeth II **Obv:** Young bust right **Obv. Designer:** Arnold Machin **Rev:** Shield of Great Britain within the Garter, crowned and supported **Rev. Designer:** Eric Sewell **Edge Lettering:** DECUS ET TUTAMEN

Date	Mintage	F	VF	XF	Unc	BU
1983	443,054,000	—	—	2.25	4.00	5.50
1983 Proof	108,000	Value: 6.00				

KM# 934 POUND
9.5000 g., Nickel-Brass, 22.5 mm. **Ruler:** Elizabeth II **Obv:** Young bust right **Obv. Designer:** Arnold Machin **Rev:** Scottish thistle **Rev. Designer:** Leslie Durbin **Edge Lettering:** NEMO ME IMPUNE LACESSIT

Date	Mintage	F	VF	XF	Unc	BU
1984	146,257,000	—	—	2.25	4.00	5.50
1984 Proof	107,000	Value: 6.00				

KM# 941 POUND
9.5000 g., Nickel-Brass, 22.5 mm. **Ruler:** Elizabeth II **Obv:** Crowned head right **Obv. Designer:** Raphael Maklouf **Rev:** Welsh leek, crown encircles **Rev. Designer:** Leslie Durbin **Edge Lettering:** PLEIDIOL WYF I'M GWLAD

Date	Mintage	F	VF	XF	Unc	BU
1985	228,431,000	—	—	2.00	3.50	5.00
1985 Proof	102,000	Value: 6.00				
1990	97,269,000	—	—	2.00	4.00	5.50
1990 Proof	100,000	Value: 6.00				

KM# 946 POUND
9.5000 g., Nickel-Brass, 22.5 mm. **Ruler:** Elizabeth II **Obv:** Crowned head right **Obv. Designer:** Raphael Maklouf **Rev:** Northern Ireland - Blooming flax, crown encircles **Rev. Designer:** Leslie Durbin **Edge Lettering:** DECUS ET TUTAMEN

Date	Mintage	F	VF	XF	Unc	BU
1986	10,410,000	—	—	2.00	4.00	5.50
1986 Proof	125,000	Value: 6.00				
1991	38,444,000	—	—	2.00	4.00	5.50
1991 Proof	—	Value: 6.00				

KM# 948 POUND
9.5000 g., Nickel-Brass, 22.5 mm. **Ruler:** Elizabeth II **Obv:** Crowned head right **Obv. Designer:** Raphael Maklouf **Rev:** Oak tree, crown encircles **Rev. Designer:** Leslie Durbin **Edge Lettering:** DECUS ET TUTAMEN

Date	Mintage	F	VF	XF	Unc	BU
1987	39,299,000	—	—	—	3.50	5.00
1987 Proof	125,000	Value: 6.00				
1992	36,320,000	—	—	—	4.00	5.50
1992 Proof	—	Value: 6.00				

KM# 954 POUND
9.5000 g., Nickel-Brass, 22.5 mm. **Ruler:** Elizabeth II **Obv:** Crowned head right **Obv. Designer:** Raphael Maklouf **Rev:** Crowned shield of the United Kingdom **Rev. Designer:** Derek Carringe **Edge Lettering:** DECUS ET TUTAMEN

Date	Mintage	F	VF	XF	Unc	BU
1988	7,119,000	—	—	—	4.00	5.50
1988 Proof	Est. 125,000	Value: 7.00				

KM# 959 POUND
9.5000 g., Nickel-Brass, 22.5 mm. **Ruler:** Elizabeth II **Obv:** Crowned head right **Obv. Designer:** Raphael Maklouf **Rev:** Scottish thistle, crown encircles **Rev. Designer:** Leslie Durbin **Edge Lettering:** NEMO ME IMPUNE LACESSIT

Date	Mintage	F	VF	XF	Unc	BU
1989	70,581,000	—	—	—	4.00	5.50
1989 Proof	100,000	Value: 6.00				

KM# 964 POUND

9.5000 g., Nickel-Brass, 22.5 mm. **Ruler:** Elizabeth II **Obv:** Crowned head right **Obv. Designer:** Raphael Maklouf **Rev:** Shield of Great Britain with Garter, crowned and supported **Rev. Designer:** Eric Sewell **Edge Lettering:** DECUS ET TUTAMEN

Date	Mintage	F	VF	XF	Unc	BU
1993	114,745,000	—	—	—	4.00	5.50
1993 Proof	—	Value: 6.00				

KM# 967 POUND

9.5000 g., Nickel-Brass, 22.5 mm. **Ruler:** Elizabeth II **Obv:** Crowned head right **Obv. Designer:** Raphael Maklouf **Rev:** Scottish arms; rampant lion left within circle **Rev. Designer:** Norman Sillman **Edge Lettering:** NEMO ME IMPUNE LACESSIT

Date	Mintage	F	VF	XF	Unc	BU
1994	29,753,000	—	—	2.00	3.50	6.00
1994 Proof	—	Value: 6.00				

KM# 969 POUND

9.5000 g., Nickel-Brass, 22.5 mm. **Ruler:** Elizabeth II **Obv:** Crowned head right **Obv. Designer:** Raphael Maklouf **Rev:** Welsh Dragon left **Rev. Designer:** Norman Sillman **Edge Lettering:** PLEIDIOL WYF I'M GWLAD

Date	Mintage	F	VF	XF	Unc	BU
1995	34,504,000	—	—	2.50	5.50	8.00
1995 Proof	100,000	Value: 7.00				

KM# 972 POUND

9.5000 g., Nickel-Brass, 22.5 mm. **Ruler:** Elizabeth II **Obv:** Crowned head right **Obv. Designer:** Raphael Maklouf **Rev:** Celtic Cross **Rev. Designer:** Norman Sillman **Edge Lettering:** DECUS ET TUTAMEN

Date	Mintage	F	VF	XF	Unc	BU
1996	89,886,000	—	—	—	3.50	5.00
1996 Proof	Est. 100,000	Value: 6.00				

KM# 975 POUND

9.5000 g., Nickel-Brass, 22.5 mm. **Ruler:** Elizabeth II **Obv:** Crowned head right **Obv. Designer:** Raphael Maklouf **Rev:** Plantagenet lions **Rev. Designer:** Norman Sillman **Edge Lettering:** DECUS ET TUTAMEN

Date	Mintage	F	VF	XF	Unc	BU
1996	—	—	—	—	—	—
Note: Counterfeit date						
1997	57,117,450	—	—	—	3.50	6.00
1997 Proof	Est. 100,000	Value: 6.00				

KM# 993 POUND

9.5000 g., Nickel-Brass, 22.5 mm. **Ruler:** Elizabeth II **Obv:** Head with tiara right **Obv. Designer:** Ian Rank-Broadley **Rev:** Shield of Great Britain within Garter, crowned and supported **Rev. Designer:** Eric Sewell **Edge Lettering:** DECUS ET TUTAMEN

Date	Mintage	F	VF	XF	Unc	BU
1998	Est. 100,000	—	—	—	8.50	10.00
Note: In sets only						
2003	61,596,500	—	—	—	5.00	6.00
2003 Proof	—	Value: 7.50				

KM# 998 POUND

9.5000 g., Nickel-Brass, 22.5 mm. **Ruler:** Elizabeth II **Obv:** Head with tiara right **Obv. Designer:** Ian Rank-Broadley **Rev:** Scottish lion within circle **Rev. Designer:** Norman Sillman **Edge Lettering:** NEMO ME IMPUNE LACESSTT

Date	Mintage	F	VF	XF	Unc	BU
1999	—	—	—	2.00	3.50	7.50
1999 Proof	Est. 100,000	Value: 6.00				

KM# 1005 POUND

9.5000 g., Nickel-Brass, 22.5 mm. **Ruler:** Elizabeth II **Obv:** Head with tiara right **Obv. Designer:** Ian Rank-Broadley **Rev:** Welsh dragon left **Rev. Designer:** Norman Sillman **Edge:** Reeded and lettered **Edge Lettering:** PLEIDOL WYF I'M GWLAD

Date	Mintage	F	VF	XF	Unc	BU
2000	109,496,500	—	—	—	3.50	7.00
2000 Proof	Est. 100,000	Value: 6.00				

KM# 1013 POUND

9.5000 g., Nickel-Brass, 22.5 mm. **Ruler:** Elizabeth II **Subject:** Northern Ireland **Obv:** Head with tiara right **Obv. Designer:** Ian Rank-Broadley **Rev:** Celtic style cross **Rev. Designer:** Norman Sillman **Edge:** Reeding **Edge Lettering:** DECUS ET TUTAMEN

Date	Mintage	F	VF	XF	Unc	BU
2001	58,093,731	—	—	—	4.00	5.00
2001 Proof	—	Value: 6.00				

KM# 1030 POUND

9.5000 g., Nickel-Brass, 22.5 mm. **Ruler:** Elizabeth II **Obv:** Head with tiara right **Obv. Designer:** Ian Rank-Broadley **Rev:** Three lions **Rev. Designer:** Norman Sillman **Edge:** Reeded **Edge Lettering:** DECUS ET TUTAMEN

Date	Mintage	F	VF	XF	Unc	BU
2002	77,818,000	—	—	—	5.00	6.00
2002 Proof	100,000	Value: 6.00				

KM# 1048 POUND

9.5000 g., Nickel-Brass, 22.5 mm. **Ruler:** Elizabeth II **Obv:** Head with tiara right **Obv. Designer:** Ian Rank-Broadley **Rev:** "Forth Rail Bridge" in Scotland **Edge:** Reeded and lettered **Edge Lettering:** "NEMO ME IMPUNE LACESSIT"

Date	Mintage	F	VF	XF	Unc	BU
2004	39,162,000	—	—	—	6.00	7.50
2004 Proof	100,000	Value: 9.00				

KM# 1051 POUND

9.5000 g., Nickel-Brass, 22.5 mm. **Ruler:** Elizabeth II **Obv:** Head with tiara right **Obv. Designer:** Ian Rank-Broadley **Rev:** Menai Bridge in Wales **Edge:** Reeded and lettered **Edge Lettering:** "PLEIDOL WYF I'M GWLAD"

Date	Mintage	F	VF	XF	Unc	BU
2005	70,763,000	—	—	—	5.00	6.00
2005 Proof	50,000	Value: 5.00				

KM# 1059 POUND

9.5000 g., Nickel-Brass, 22.5 mm. **Ruler:** Elizabeth II **Obv:** Head with tiara right **Obv. Designer:** Ian Rank-Broadley **Rev:** Egyptian Arch Bridge at Newry, Northern Ireland **Edge:** Reeded and lettered

Date	Mintage	F	VF	XF	Unc	BU
2006	—	—	—	—	8.00	9.00
2006 Proof	50,000	Value: 10.00				

KM# 1074 POUND

9.5000 g., Nickel-Brass, 22.5 mm. **Ruler:** Elizabeth II **Obv:** Head with tiara right **Obv. Designer:** Ian Rank-Broadley **Rev:** Gateshead Millennium Bridge **Edge:** Reeded and lettered

Date	Mintage	F	VF	XF	Unc	BU
2007	—	—	—	—	7.00	8.00
2007 Proof	50,000	Value: 10.00				

KM# 976 2 POUNDS

12.0000 g., Bi-Metallic Copper-Nickel center in Nickel-Brass ring, 28.35 mm. **Ruler:** Elizabeth II **Obv:** Crowned head right **Obv. Designer:** Raphael Maklouf **Rev:** Celtic designs within circle **Rev. Designer:** Bruce Rushin **Edge Lettering:** STANDING ON THE SHOULDERS OF GIANTS

Date	Mintage	F	VF	XF	Unc	BU
1997	13,735,000	—	—	—	7.50	12.50
1997 Proof	Est. 100,000	Value: 13.00				

KM# 994 2 POUNDS

12.0000 g., Bi-Metallic Copper-Nickel center in Nickel-Brass ring, 28.35 mm. **Ruler:** Elizabeth II **Obv:** Head with tiara right within circle **Obv. Designer:** Ian Rank-Broadley **Rev:** Celtic design within circle **Rev. Designer:** Bruce Rushin **Edge Lettering:** STANDING ON THE SHOULDERS OF GIANTS

Date	Mintage	F	VF	XF	Unc	BU
1998	91,110,375	—	—	—	6.00	8.50
1998 Proof	Est. 100,000	Value: 10.00				
1999	38,652,000	—	—	—	6.00	8.50
1999 Proof	—	Value: 10.00				
2000	25,770,000	—	—	—	6.00	8.50
2000 Proof	—	Value: 10.00				
2001	37,843,500	—	—	—	6.00	8.50

Date	Mintage	F	VF	XF	Unc	BU
2001 Proof	—	Value: 10.00				
2002	15,521,000	—	—	—	6.00	8.50
2002 Proof	—	Value: 10.00				
2003	21,830,250	—	—	—	6.00	8.50
2003 Proof	—	Value: 10.00				
2004	13,904,500	—	—	—	6.00	8.50
2004 Proof	100,000	Value: 10.00				
2005	20,507,000	—	—	—	6.00	8.50
2005 Proof	—	Value: 10.00				
2006	—	—	—	—	6.00	8.50
2006 Proof	—	Value: 10.00				
2007 Proof	—	Value: 10.00				
2007	—	—	—	—	6.00	8.50

KM# 1014 2 POUNDS
11.9700 g., Bi-Metallic Copper-Nickel center in Nickel-Brass ring, 28.4 mm. **Ruler:** Elizabeth II **Subject:** First Transatlantic Radio Transmission **Obv:** Head with tiara right within circle **Obv. Designer:** Ian Rank-Broadley **Rev:** Symbolic design **Rev. Designer:** Robert Evans **Edge:** Reeded and inscribed **Edge Lettering:** WIRELESS BRIDGES THE ATLANTIC... MARCONI... 1901

Date	Mintage	F	VF	XF	Unc	BU
2001	5,000,000	—	—	—	6.00	7.00
2001 Proof	—	Value: 10.00				

KM# 1019 2 POUNDS
32.4500 g., 0.9584 Silver 0.9998 oz. ASW, 40 mm. **Ruler:** Elizabeth II **Subject:** Britannia Bullion **Obv:** Head with tiara right **Obv. Designer:** Ian Rank-Broadley **Rev:** Stylized "Britannia and the Lion" **Edge:** Reeded

Date	Mintage	F	VF	XF	Unc	BU
2001	100,000	—	—	—	25.00	30.00
2001 Proof	10,000	Value: 55.00				

KM# 1031 2 POUNDS
12.0000 g., Bi-Metallic Copper-Nickel center in Nickel-Brass ring, 28.4 mm. **Ruler:** Elizabeth II **Subject:** 17th Commonwealth Games - Manchester, England **Obv:** Head with tiara right **Obv. Designer:** Ian Rank-Broadley **Rev:** Runner breaking ribbon at finish line, national flag of England in circle behind athlete **Rev. Designer:** Matthew Bonaccorsi **Edge:** Reeded and lettered **Edge Lettering:** SPIRIT OF FRIENDSHIP MANCHESTER 2002

Date	Mintage	F	VF	XF	Unc	BU
2002	—	—	—	—	6.00	7.00
2002 Proof	—	Value: 8.75				

KM# 1032 2 POUNDS
12.0000 g., Bi-Metallic Copper-Nickel center in Nickel-Brass ring, 28.4 mm. **Ruler:** Elizabeth II **Subject:** 17th Commonwealth Games - Manchester, England **Obv:** Head with tiara right **Obv. Designer:** Ian Rank-Broadley **Rev:** Runner breaking ribbon at finish line, national flag of Scotland in circle behind athlete **Rev. Designer:** Matthew Bonaccorsi **Edge:** Reeded and lettered

Date	Mintage	F	VF	XF	Unc	BU
2002	—	—	—	—	5.00	6.00
2002 Proof	—	Value: 8.75				

KM# 1033 2 POUNDS
12.0000 g., Bi-Metallic Copper-Nickel center in Nickel-Brass ring, 28.4 mm. **Ruler:** Elizabeth II **Subject:** 17th Commonwealth Games - Manchester, England **Obv:** Head with tiara right **Obv. Designer:** Ian Rank-Broadley **Rev:** Runner breaking ribbon at finish line, national flag of Wales in circle behind athlete **Rev. Designer:** Matthew Bonaccorsi **Edge:** Reeded and lettered **Edge Lettering:** SPIRIT OF FRIENDSHIP MANCHESTER 2002

Date	Mintage	F	VF	XF	Unc	BU
2002	—	—	—	—	6.00	7.00
2002 Proof	—	Value: 8.75				

KM# 1034 2 POUNDS
12.0000 g., Bi-Metallic Copper-Nickel center in Nickel-Brass ring, 28.4 mm. **Ruler:** Elizabeth II **Subject:** 17th Commonwealth Games - Manchester, England **Obv:** Head with tiara right **Obv. Designer:** Ian Rank-Broadley **Rev:** Runner breaking ribbon at finish line, national flag of Northern Ireland in circle behind athlete **Rev. Designer:** Matthew Bonaccorsi **Edge:** Reeded and lettered **Edge Lettering:** SPIRIT OF FRIENDSHIP MANCHESTER 2002

Date	Mintage	F	VF	XF	Unc	BU
2002	—	—	—	—	6.00	7.00
2002 Proof	—	Value: 8.75				

KM# 1037 2 POUNDS
12.0000 g., Bi-Metallic Copper-Nickel center in Nickel-Brass ring, 28.4 mm. **Ruler:** Elizabeth II **Subject:** 50th Anniversary of the Discovery of DNA **Obv:** Head with tiara right **Obv. Designer:** Ian Rank-Broadley **Rev:** DNA Double Helix **Rev. Designer:** John Mills **Edge:** Reeded and inscribed **Edge Lettering:** DEOXYRIBONUCLEIC ACID

Date	Mintage	F	VF	XF	Unc	BU
ND(2003)	—	—	—	—	7.00	8.00
ND(2003) Proof	—	Value: 10.00				

KM# 1049 2 POUNDS
12.0000 g., Bi-Metallic Nickel-Brass center in Copper-Nickel ring, 28.4 mm. **Ruler:** Elizabeth II **Subject:** Richard Trevithick, Inventor of the First Steam Locomotive **Obv:** Head with tiara right **Obv. Designer:** Ian Rank-Broadley **Rev:** First steam locomotive **Edge:** Reeded and lettered **Edge Lettering:** 2004 R. TREVITHICK 1804 INVENTION-INDUSTRY-PROGRESS

Date	Mintage	F	VF	XF	Unc	BU
2004	—	—	—	—	7.50	8.50
2004 Proof	100,000	Value: 10.00				

KM# 1052 2 POUNDS
12.0000 g., Bi-Metallic Nickel-Brass center in Copper-Nickel ring, 28.4 mm. **Ruler:** Elizabeth II **Subject:** 400th Anniversary - The Gunpowder Plot **Obv:** Head with tiara right **Obv. Designer:** Ian Rank-Broadley **Rev:** Circular design of Royal scepters, swords and crosiers **Rev. Designer:** Peter Forster **Edge:** Reeded and lettered **Edge Lettering:** REMEMBER REMEMBER THE FIFTH OF NOVEMBER

Date	Mintage	F	VF	XF	Unc	BU
ND(2005)	—	—	—	—	6.00	7.00
ND(2005) Proof	50,000	Value: 9.00				

KM# 1060 2 POUNDS
12.0000 g., Bi-Metallic Copper-Nickel center in Nickel-Brass ring, 28.4 mm. **Ruler:** Elizabeth II **Subject:** 200th Birthday of Engineer Isambard Kingdom Brunel **Obv:** Head with tiara right **Obv. Designer:** Ian Rank-Broadley **Rev:** Isambard Brunel **Edge:** Lettered

Date	Mintage	F	VF	XF	Unc	BU
2006	—	—	—	—	16.00	18.00
2006 Proof	50,000	Value: 35.00				

KM# 1061 2 POUNDS
12.0000 g., Bi-Metallic Copper-Nickel center in Nickel-Brass ring, 28.4 mm. **Ruler:** Elizabeth II **Subject:** Engineering Achievements of Isambard Kingdom Brunel **Obv:** Head with tiara right **Obv. Designer:** Ian Rank-Broadley **Rev:** Paddington Station structural supports **Edge:** Lettered

Date	Mintage	F	VF	XF	Unc	BU
2006	—	—	—	—	16.00	17.50
2006 Proof	50,000	Value: 20.00				

KM# 1075 2 POUNDS
12.0000 g., Bi-Metallic Copper-Nickel center in Brass ring, 28.4 mm. **Ruler:** Elizabeth II **Subject:** 200th Anniversary of the Abolition of the Slave Trade **Obv:** Bust right **Rev:** Chain crossing 1807 date **Edge:** Reeded and lettered

Date	Mintage	F	VF	XF	Unc	BU
2007	—	—	—	—	—	6.00
2007 Proof	50,000	Value: 9.00				

KM# 1076 2 POUNDS
12.0000 g., Bi-Metallic Copper-Nickel center in Brass ring, 28.4 mm. **Ruler:** Elizabeth II **Subject:** 300th Anniversary of the Act of Union of England and Scotland **Obv:** Bust right **Rev:** Combination of British and Scottish arms **Edge:** Reeded and lettered

Date	Mintage	F	VF	XF	Unc	BU
2007	—	—	—	—	—	6.00
2007 Proof	50,000	Value: 9.00				

SOVEREIGN COINAGE

KM# 784 1/2 SOVEREIGN

3.9940 g., 0.9170 Gold 0.1177 oz. AGW **Ruler:** Victoria **Obv:** Mature draped bust left **Obv. Legend:** VICTORIA • DEI • GRA • BRITT • REGINA • FID • DEF • IND • IMP • **Obv. Designer:** Thomas Brock **Rev:** St. George slaying the dragon right

Date	Mintage	F	VF	XF	Unc	BU
1901	2,037,999	BV	BV	110	170	—

KM# 804 1/2 SOVEREIGN

3.9940 g., 0.9170 Gold 0.1177 oz. AGW **Ruler:** Edward VII **Obv:** Head right **Rev:** St. George slaying the dragon

Date	Mintage	F	VF	XF	Unc	BU
1902	4,244,000	—	BV	110	130	—
1902 Proof	15,000	Value: 225				
1903	2,522,000	—	BV	110	130	—
1904	1,717,000	—	BV	110	130	—
1905	3,024,000	—	BV	110	130	—
1906	4,245,000	—	BV	110	130	—
1907	4,233,000	—	BV	110	130	—
1908	3,997,000	—	BV	110	130	—
1909	4,011,000	—	BV	110	130	—
1910	5,024,000	—	BV	110	130	—

KM# 819 1/2 SOVEREIGN

3.9940 g., 0.9170 Gold 0.1177 oz. AGW **Ruler:** George V **Obv:** Head left **Obv. Designer:** Bertram MacKennal **Rev:** St. George slaying the dragon

Date	Mintage	F	VF	XF	Unc	BU
1911	6,104,000	—	BV	110	130	—
1911 Proof	3,764	Value: 350				
1912	6,224,000	—	BV	110	130	—
1913	6,094,000	—	BV	110	130	—
1914	7,251,000	—	BV	110	130	—
1915	2,043,000	—	BV	110	130	—

KM# 785 SOVEREIGN

7.9881 g., 0.9170 Gold 0.2355 oz. AGW **Ruler:** Victoria **Obv:** Mature draped bust left **Obv. Legend:** VICTORIA • DEI • GRA • BRITT • REGINA • FID • DEF • IND • IMP • **Obv. Designer:** Thomas Brock **Rev:** St. George slaying the dragon

Date	Mintage	F	VF	XF	Unc	BU
1901	1,579,000	—	—	BV	235	—

KM# 805 SOVEREIGN

7.9881 g., 0.9170 Gold 0.2355 oz. AGW **Ruler:** Edward VII **Obv:** Head right **Rev:** St. George slaying the dragon

Date	Mintage	F	VF	XF	Unc	BU
1902	4,738,000	—	—	BV	220	—
1902 Proof	15,000	Value: 350				
1903	8,889,000	—	—	BV	220	—
1904	10,041,000	—	—	BV	220	—
1905	5,910,000	—	—	BV	220	—
1906	10,467,000	—	—	BV	220	—
1907	18,459,000	—	—	BV	220	—
1908	11,729,000	—	—	BV	220	—
1909	12,157,000	—	—	BV	220	—
1910	22,380,000	—	—	BV	220	—

KM# 820 SOVEREIGN

7.9881 g., 0.9170 Gold 0.2355 oz. AGW **Ruler:** George V **Obv:** Head left **Obv. Designer:** Bertram MacKennal **Rev:** St. George slaying the dragon

Date	Mintage	F	VF	XF	Unc	BU
1911	30,044,000	—	—	BV	230	—
1911 Proof	3,764	Value: 800				
1912	30,318,000	—	—	BV	230	—
1913	24,540,000	—	—	BV	230	—
1914	11,501,000	—	—	BV	230	—
1915	20,295,000	—	—	BV	230	—
1916	1,554,000	—	—	BV	230	—
1917	1,014,999	3,000	3,500	6,500	12,000	—
1925	4,406,000	—	—	BV	230	—

KM# 859 SOVEREIGN

7.9881 g., 0.9170 Gold 0.2355 oz. AGW **Ruler:** George VI **Obv:** Head left **Obv. Designer:** T. H. Paget **Rev:** St. George slaying the dragon

Date	Mintage	F	VF	XF	Unc	BU
1937 Proof	5,500	Value: 2,000				
1937 Matte Proof; Unique	—	—	—	—	—	—

KM# 908 SOVEREIGN

7.9881 g., 0.9170 Gold 0.2355 oz. AGW **Ruler:** Elizabeth II **Obv:** Laureate bust right **Obv. Designer:** Mary Gillick **Rev:** St. George slaying the dragon

Date	Mintage	F	VF	XF	Unc	BU
1957	2,072,000	—	—	BV	230	—
1957 Proof	—	—	—	—	—	—
1958	8,700,000	—	—	BV	230	—
1958 Proof	—	—	—	—	—	—
1959	1,358,000	—	—	BV	230	—
1959 Proof	—	—	—	—	—	—
1962	3,000,000	—	—	BV	230	—
1962 Proof	—	—	—	—	—	—
1963	7,400,000	—	—	BV	230	—
1963 Proof	—	—	—	—	—	—
1964	3,000,000	—	—	BV	230	—
1965	3,800,000	—	—	BV	230	—
1966	7,050,000	—	—	BV	230	—
1967	5,000,000	—	—	BV	230	—
1968	4,203,000	—	—	BV	230	—

KM# 919 SOVEREIGN

7.9881 g., 0.9170 Gold 0.2355 oz. AGW **Ruler:** Elizabeth II **Obv:** Young bust right **Obv. Designer:** Arnold Machin **Rev:** St. George slaying the dragon

Date	Mintage	F	VF	XF	Unc	BU
1974	5,003,000	—	—	BV	BV	230
1976	4,150,000	—	—	BV	BV	230
1978	6,550,000	—	—	BV	BV	230
1979	9,100,000	—	—	BV	BV	230
1979 Proof	50,000	Value: 175				
1980	5,100,000	—	—	BV	BV	230
1980 Proof	91,000	Value: 175				
1981	5,000,000	—	—	BV	BV	230
1981 Proof	33,000	Value: 175				
1982	2,950,000	—	—	BV	BV	230
1982 Proof	23,000	Value: 175				
1983 Proof	21,000	Value: 175				
1984 Proof	20,000	Value: 175				

KM# 806 2 POUNDS

15.9761 g., 0.9170 Gold 0.4710 oz. AGW **Ruler:** Edward VII **Obv:** Head right **Rev:** St. George slaying the dragon

Date	Mintage	F	VF	XF	Unc	BU
1902	46,000	BV	BV	475	700	—
1902 Proof	8,066	Value: 750				

Note: Proof issues with mint mark S below right rear hoof of horse were struck at Sydney, refer to Australia listings

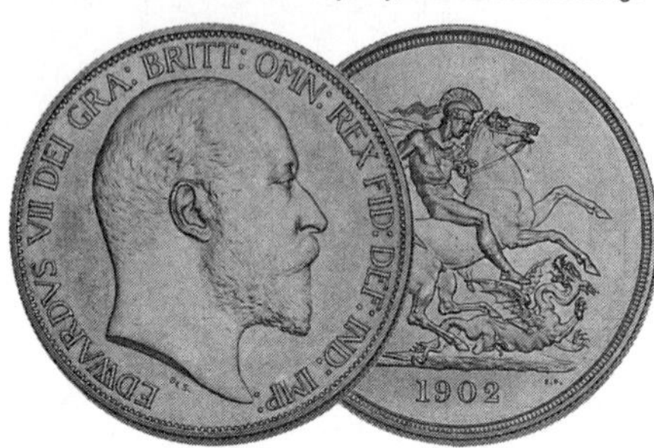

KM# 807 5 POUNDS

39.9403 g., 0.9170 Gold 1.1775 oz. AGW **Ruler:** Edward VII **Obv:** Head right **Rev:** St. George slaying the dragon

Date	Mintage	F	VF	XF	Unc	BU
1902	Est. 35,000	—	BV	1,100	1,500	—

Note: 27,000 pieces were melted

Date	Mintage	F	VF	XF	Unc	BU
1902 Proof	8,066	Value: 1,400				

Note: Proof issues with mint mark S below right rear hoof of horse were struck at Sydney, refer to Australia listings

TRADE COINAGE

Britannia Issues

Issued to facilitate British trade in the Orient, the reverse design incorporated the denomination in Chinese characters and Malay script.

This issue was struck at the Bombay (B) and Calcutta (C) Mints in India, except for 1925 and 1930 issues which were struck at London. Through error the mint marks did not appear on some early (1895-1900) issues as indicated.

KM# T5 DOLLAR

26.9568 g., 0.9000 Silver 0.7800 oz. ASW **Obv:** Britannia standing **Rev:** Oriental designs on cross **Designer:** G. W. de Saulles **Note:** Miltmark is located within the top of the trident held by Britannia.

Date	Mintage	F	VF	XF	Unc	BU
1901B	Inc. above	15.00	20.00	25.00	60.00	—
1901C	1,514,000	25.00	45.00	100	200	—
1901B Proof	Inc. above	Value: 800				
1901/0B	25,680,000	40.00	60.00	100	200	—
1902B	30,404,000	15.00	20.00	25.00	60.00	—
1902C	1,267,000	25.00	45.00	80.00	175	—
1902B Proof	Inc. above	Value: 800				
1902C Proof	Inc. above	Value: 800				
1903/2B	3,956,000	12.00	25.00	40.00	75.00	—
1903B	Inc. above	12.00	20.00	—	60.00	—
1903B Proof	Inc. above	Value: 800				

Date	Mintage	F	VF	XF	Unc	BU
1904/898B	649,000	50.00	80.00	125	200	—
1904/3B	Inc. above	30.00	50.00	100	225	—
1904/0B	Inc. above	80.00	125	175	300	—
1904B	Inc. above	40.00	60.00	100	250	—
1904B Proof	Inc. above	Value: 700				
1907B	1,946,000	12.00	20.00	25.00	60.00	—
1908/3B	6,871,000	40.00	60.00	100	175	—
1908/7B	Inc. above	35.00	50.00	90.00	125	—
1908B	Inc. above	12.00	20.00	25.00	60.00	—
1908B Proof	Inc. above	Value: 700				
1909/8B	5,954,000	30.00	45.00	80.00	125	—
1909B	Inc. above	12.00	20.00	25.00	60.00	—
1910/00B	553,000	40.00	60.00	100	175	—
1910B	Inc. above	12.00	20.00	25.00	60.00	—
1911/00B	—	30.00	50.00	100	150	—
1911B	37,471,000	12.00	20.00	25.00	60.00	—
1912B	5,672,000	12.00	20.00	25.00	60.00	—
1912B Proof	Inc. above	Value: 800				
1913/2B	—	100	150	250	700	—
1913B	1,567,000	30.00	60.00	125	300	—
1913B Proof	Inc. above	Value: 800				
1921B	5	—	—	—	15,000	—
Note: Original mintage 50,211						
1921B Proof; restrike	—	Value: 4,500				
1925	6,870,000	15.00	20.00	25.00	70.00	—
1929/1B	5,100,000	30.00	50.00	80.00	200	—
1929B	Inc. above	12.00	20.00	25.00	60.00	—
1929B Proof	Inc. above	Value: 800				
1930B	10,400,000	12.00	20.00	25.00	60.00	—
1930B Proof	Inc. above	Value: 800				
1930	6,660,000	12.00	20.00	25.00	60.00	—
1934B	17,335,000	75.00	150	200	500	—
1934B Proof	Inc. above	Value: 3,500				
1934B Proof; restrike	20	Value: 3,000				
1935B	Est. 25	1,000	1,500	2,500	15,000	—
Note: Original mintage 6,811,995						
1935B Proof	20	Value: 7,500				
1935B Proof; restrike	20	Value: 4,000				

The Hellenic (Greek) Republic is situated in southeastern Europe on the southern tip of the Balkan Peninsula. The republic includes many islands, the most important of which are Crete and the Ionian Islands. Greece (including islands) has an area of 50,944 sq. mi. (131,940 sq. km.) and a population of 10.3 million. Capital: Athens. Greece is still largely agricultural. Tobacco, cotton, fruit and wool are exported.

Greece, the Mother of Western civilization, attained the peak of its culture in the 5th century B.C., when it contributed more to government, drama, art and architecture than any other people to this time. Greece fell under Roman domination in the 2nd and 1st centuries B.C., becoming part of the Byzantine Empire until Constantinople fell to the Crusaders in 1202. With the fall of Constantinople to the Turks in 1453, Greece became part of the Ottoman Empire. Independence from Turkey was won with the revolution of 1821-27. In 1833, Greece was established as a monarchy, with sovereignty guaranteed by Britain, France and Russia. After a lengthy power struggle between the monarchist forces and democratic factions, Greece was proclaimed a republic in 1925. The monarchy was restored in 1935 and reconfirmed by a plebiscite in 1946. The Italians invaded Greece via Albania on Oct. 28, 1940 but were driven back well within the Albanian border. Germany began their invasion in April 1941 and quickly overran the entire country and drove off a British Expeditionary force by the end of April. King George II and his new government went into exile. The German-Italian occupation of Greece lasted until Oct. 1944 after which only German troops remained until the end of the occupation. On April 21, 1967, a military junta took control of the government and suspended the constitution. King Constantine II made an unsuccessful attempt against the junta in the fall of 1968 and consequently fled to Italy. The monarchy was formally abolished by plebiscite, Dec. 8, 1974, and Greece was established as the Hellenic Republic, the third republic in Greek history.

RULERS

George I, 1863-1913
Constantine I, 1913-1917, 1920-1922
Alexander I, 1917-1920
George II, 1922-1923, 1935-1947
Paul I, 1947-1964
Constantine II, 1964-1973

MINT MARKS

(a) - Paris, privy marks only
A - Paris
B - Vienna
BB - Strassburg
H - Heaton, Birmingham
K - Bordeaux
KN - King's Norton
(p) - Poissy – Thunderbolt
Anthemion – Greek National Mint, Athens

MONETARY SYSTEM

Commencing 1831
100 Lepta = 1 Drachma

KINGDOM

DECIMAL COINAGE

KM# 62 5 LEPTA

Nickel **Ruler:** George I **Obv:** Crown right of center hole **Rev:** Owl on amphora left of center hole **Rev. Designer:** Ch. Pillet

Date	Mintage	F	VF	XF	Unc	BU
1912(a)	25,053,000	0.75	3.00	7.50	65.00	150

KM# 63 10 LEPTA

Nickel, 21 mm. **Ruler:** George I **Obv:** Crown right of center hole **Rev:** Owl on amphora left of center hole **Rev. Designer:** Ch. Pillet

Date	Mintage	F	VF	XF	Unc	BU
1912(a)	28,973,000	0.75	3.00	7.50	70.00	125

KM# 66.1 10 LEPTA

1.5200 g., Aluminum **Ruler:** George II **Obv:** Crown above date **Rev:** Olive branch, denomination **Note:** 1.77mm thick.

Date	Mintage	F	VF	XF	Unc	BU
1922(p)	120,000,000	1.00	2.00	9.00	40.00	60.00

KM# 66.2 10 LEPTA

1.6500 g., Aluminum **Ruler:** Constantine I **Obv:** Crown above date **Rev:** Olive branch, denomination **Note:** 2.2mm thick.

Date	Mintage	F	VF	XF	Unc	BU
1922(p)	—	3.00	10.00	20.00	80.00	150

KM# 64 20 LEPTA

Nickel **Ruler:** George I **Obv:** Crowned, mantled shield right of center hole **Rev:** Athena standing at left of center hole, olive branch at right

Date	Mintage	F	VF	XF	Unc	BU
1912(a)	10,145,000	0.75	2.00	8.50	80.00	125

KM# 65 50 LEPTA

Copper-Nickel **Ruler:** Constantine I **Obv:** Crowned, mantled shield right of center hole **Rev:** Olive branch below center hole **Designer:** George Jakobicles **Note:** Most of these were melted and only 30 - 40 of each piece are known to exist.

Date	Mintage	F	VF	XF	Unc	BU
1921H	1,000,000	—	1,500	3,500	6,500	9,000
1921KN	1,524,000	—	4,000	7,000	10,000	17,500

KM# 60 DRACHMA

5.0000 g., 0.8350 Silver 0.1342 oz. ASW **Ruler:** George I **Obv:** Head left **Rev:** Mythological figure Thetis with shield of Achilles, seated on sea horse

Date	Mintage	F	VF	XF	Unc	BU
1910(a)	4,570,000	7.50	15.00	45.00	200	400
1911(a)	1,881,000	9.00	20.00	55.00	450	800

KM# 61 2 DRACHMAI

10.0000 g., 0.8350 Silver 0.2684 oz. ASW **Ruler:** George I **Obv:** Head left **Rev:** Mythological figure Thetis with shield of Achilles seated on sea horse

Date	Mintage	F	VF	XF	Unc	BU
1911(a)	1,500,000	10.00	30.00	80.00	1,500	2,500

REPUBLIC

DECIMAL COINAGE

KM# 67 20 LEPTA

1.7300 g., Copper-Nickel **Obv:** Denomination above date **Rev:** Athena head left

Date	Mintage	F	VF	XF	Unc	BU
1926	20,000,000	0.75	1.50	5.00	20.00	60.00

KM# 68 50 LEPTA

2.8900 g., Copper-Nickel **Obv:** Denomination above date **Rev:** Athena head left

Date	Mintage	F	VF	XF	Unc	BU
1926	20,000,000	0.45	1.00	4.50	20.00	60.00
1926B (1930)	20,000,000	0.45	1.00	4.50	30.00	75.00

KM# 69 DRACHMA

5.0300 g., Copper-Nickel, 23 mm. **Obv:** Denomination above date **Rev:** Athena head left

Date	Mintage	F	VF	XF	Unc	BU
1926	15,000,000	0.45	1.00	5.00	35.00	75.00
1926B	20,000,000	0.45	1.00	5.00	50.00	100

KM# 70 2 DRACHMAI

Copper-Nickel, 27 mm. **Obv:** Denomination above date **Rev:** Athena head left

Date	Mintage	F	VF	XF	Unc	BU
1926	22,000,000	1.00	2.00	9.00	50.00	100

KM# 71.1 5 DRACHMAI

Nickel **Obv:** Phoenix and flames **Rev:** Denomination within wreath **Note:** LONDON MINT: In second set of berries on left only 1 berry will have a dot on it.

Date	Mintage	F	VF	XF	Unc	BU
1930	23,500,000	0.75	1.50	8.00	80.00	150
1930 Proof	—	Value: 2,500				

KM# 71.2 5 DRACHMAI

Nickel **Obv:** Phoenix and flames **Rev:** Denomination within wreath **Note:** BRUSSELLS MINT: 2 berries will have dots.

Date	Mintage	F	VF	XF	Unc	BU
1930	1,500,000	1.50	3.50	20.00	150	350

KM# 72 10 DRACHMAI

7.0000 g., 0.5000 Silver 0.1125 oz. ASW, 25 mm. **Obv:** Grain sprig divides denomination **Rev:** Demeter head left

Date	Mintage	F	VF	XF	Unc	BU
1930	7,500,000	5.00	10.00	30.00	370	600
1930 Proof	—	Value: 3,000				

KM# 73 20 DRACHMAI

11.3100 g., 0.5000 Silver 0.1818 oz. ASW, 28.43 mm. **Obv:** Prow of ancient ship **Rev:** Neptune head right

Date	Mintage	F	VF	XF	Unc	BU
1930	11,500,000	6.00	12.50	28.00	250	400
1930 Proof	—	Value: 3,000				

KINGDOM

DECIMAL COINAGE

KM# 77 5 LEPTA

0.8500 g., Aluminum, 20.5 mm. **Obv:** Center hole within crowned wreath **Rev:** Grain sprigs left of center hole

Date	Mintage	F	VF	XF	Unc	BU
1954	15,000,000	—	0.20	0.50	4.00	10.00
1971	1,002,000	0.20	0.50	1.00	5.00	10.00

Note: 1971 dated coins have smaller hole at center

KM# 78 10 LEPTA

Aluminum **Obv:** Center hole within crowned wreath **Rev:** Olives above center hole, double denomination below

Date	Mintage	F	VF	XF	Unc	BU
1954	48,000,000	—	0.15	0.45	4.00	10.00
1959	20,000,000	—	0.15	0.45	4.00	10.00
1964	12,000,000	—	0.15	0.45	4.00	7.00
1965	—	—	—	—	6.50	—
Note: In sets only						
1965 Proof	4,987	Value: 10.00				

Date	Mintage	F	VF	XF	Unc	BU
1966	20,000,000	—	0.15	0.45	4.00	7.00
1969	20,000,000	—	0.15	0.45	4.00	7.00
1971	5,922,000	—	0.35	1.00	5.00	8.00

Note: Small center hole

KM# 102 10 LEPTA

Aluminum **Obv:** Soldier and Phoenix **Rev:** Trident between two dolphins

Date	Mintage	F	VF	XF	Unc	BU
1973	2,742,000	—	0.20	1.00	5.00	7.00

KM# 79 20 LEPTA

Aluminum, 24 mm. **Obv:** Center hole within crowned wreath **Rev:** Olive branch left of center hole

Date	Mintage	F	VF	XF	Unc	BU
1954	24,000,000	—	0.15	0.50	4.00	10.00
1959	20,000,000	—	0.15	0.50	4.00	10.00
1964	8,000,000	—	0.15	0.50	3.50	6.50
1966	15,000,000	—	0.15	0.50	3.50	6.50
1969	20,000,000	—	0.15	0.50	3.50	6.50
1971	4,108,000	—	0.35	1.00	4.00	7.00

Note: Small center hole

KM# 104 20 LEPTA

Aluminum **Obv:** Soldier in front of phoenix, anniversary date below **Rev:** Olive branch, denomination

Date	Mintage	F	VF	XF	Unc	BU
1973	2,718,000	—	0.20	0.60	5.00	7.00

KM# 80 50 LEPTA

Copper-Nickel, 18 mm. **Ruler:** Paul I **Obv:** Head left **Rev:** Crowned arms with supporters

Date	Mintage	F	VF	XF	Unc	BU
1954	37,228,000	0.15	0.25	1.25	35.00	85.00
1957	5,108,000	1.00	5.00	50.00	210	450
1957 Proof	—	Value: 2,000				
1959	10,160,000	0.15	0.25	5.00	60.00	150
1962	20,500,000	0.15	0.25	1.50	8.00	75.00
Note: Plain edge						
1962	Inc. above	0.15	0.25	1.50	8.00	75.00
Note: Serrated edge						
1964	20,000,000	0.15	0.25	1.50	8.00	75.00
1965	—	—	—	—	6.50	—
Note: In sets only						
1965 Proof	4,987	Value: 12.50				

KM# 88 50 LEPTA

Copper-Nickel, 18 mm. **Ruler:** Constantine II **Obv:** Head left **Rev:** Crowned arms with supporters **Designer:** Vassos Phalireas

Date	Mintage	F	VF	XF	Unc	BU
1966	30,000,000	0.20	0.50	1.00	5.50	25.00
1966 Proof	—	Value: 1,500				
1970	10,160,000	0.30	0.60	1.50	6.00	27.50

KM# 97.1 50 LEPTA

Copper-Nickel **Ruler:** Constantine II **Obv:** Small head left **Rev:** Soldier in front of Phoenix **Designer:** Vassos Philareas

Date	Mintage	F	VF	XF	Unc	BU
1971	10,999,000	—	0.10	0.15	4.00	20.00
1973	9,342,000	—	0.20	0.50	5.00	22.00

KM# 97.2 50 LEPTA

Copper-Nickel **Ruler:** Constantine II **Obv:** Large head left **Rev:** Soldier in front of Phoenix **Designer:** Vassos Philareas

Date	Mintage	F	VF	XF	Unc	BU
1973	Inc. above	—	0.20	0.50	5.00	15.00

KM# 81 DRACHMA

Copper-Nickel, 20.8 mm. **Ruler:** Paul I **Obv:** Head left **Rev:** Crowned arms with supporters

Date	Mintage	F	VF	XF	Unc	BU
1954	24,091,000	0.15	0.25	0.75	50.00	100
1957	8,151,000	1.00	5.00	50.00	150	400
1957 Proof	—	Value: 2,500				
1959	10,180,000	0.15	0.25	2.00	50.00	150
1962	20,060,000	0.25	1.00	2.00	8.00	100
1965	—	—	—	—	6.50	—
Note: In sets only						
1965 Proof	4,987	Value: 12.50				

KM# 89 DRACHMA

Copper-Nickel **Ruler:** Constantine II **Obv:** Head left **Rev:** Crowned arms with supporters **Designer:** Vassos Philareas

Date	Mintage	F	VF	XF	Unc	BU
1966	20,000,000	—	0.15	0.45	4.50	12.00
1966 Proof	—	Value: 1,250				
1967	20,000,000	—	0.15	0.45	4.50	12.00
1970	7,001,000	—	0.50	1.00	7.00	16.00
1970 Proof	—	Value: 1,500				

KM# 98 DRACHMA

Copper-Nickel **Ruler:** Constantine II **Obv:** Head left **Rev:** Soldier in front of Phoenix **Designer:** Vassos Phalireas

Date	Mintage	F	VF	XF	Unc	BU
1971	11,985,000	—	0.20	0.75	4.50	12.00
1973	8,196,000	—	0.25	1.00	5.50	14.00

KM# 82 2 DRACHMAI

Copper-Nickel **Ruler:** Paul I **Obv:** Head left **Rev:** Crowned arms with supporters

Date	Mintage	F	VF	XF	Unc	BU
1954	12,609,000	0.50	0.75	1.50	30.00	125
1957	10,171,000	1.00	5.00	50.00	150	400
1957 Proof	—	Value: 3,000				
1959	5,000,000	1.00	2.00	25.00	225	650
1962	10,096,000	0.50	0.75	2.50	10.00	60.00
1965	—	—	—	—	5.50	—
Note: In sets only						
1965 Proof	4,987	Value: 12.50				

KM# 90 2 DRACHMAI
Copper-Nickel **Ruler:** Constantine II **Obv:** Head left **Rev:** Crowned arms with supporters **Designer:** Vassos Phalireas

Date	Mintage	F	VF	XF	Unc	BU
1966	10,000,000	0.15	0.25	0.50	4.50	12.00
1966 Proof	—	Value: 1,400				
1967	10,000,000	0.15	0.25	0.50	5.00	12.00
1970	7,000,000	0.50	1.00	2.00	8.00	18.00
1970 Proof	—	Value: 2,000				

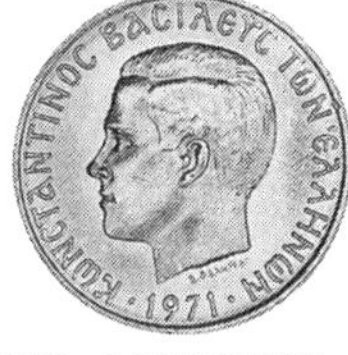

KM# 99 2 DRACHMAI
Copper-Nickel, 22.9 mm. **Ruler:** Constantine II **Obv:** Head left **Rev:** Soldier in front of Phoenix **Designer:** Vassos Phalireas

Date	Mintage	F	VF	XF	Unc	BU
1971	9,998,000	0.15	0.25	0.75	4.50	12.00
1973	7,972,000	0.20	0.50	1.50	5.50	14.00

KM# 83 5 DRACHMAI
Copper-Nickel **Ruler:** Paul I

Date	Mintage	F	VF	XF	Unc	BU
1954	21,000,000	0.25	0.50	1.50	25.00	50.00
1965	—	—	—	—	5.50	—

Note: In sets only

Date	Mintage	F	VF	XF	Unc	BU
1965 Proof	4,987	Value: 15.00				

KM# 91 5 DRACHMAI
Copper-Nickel, 27.5 mm. **Ruler:** Constantine II **Obv:** Head left **Rev:** Crowned arms with supporters **Designer:** Vassos Phalireas

Date	Mintage	F	VF	XF	Unc	BU
1966	12,000,000	0.15	0.25	1.00	6.00	20.00
1966	—	Value: 1,250				
1970	5,000,000	0.50	1.00	3.00	10.00	22.00

KM# 100 5 DRACHMAI
Copper-Nickel **Ruler:** Constantine II **Obv:** Head left **Rev:** Soldier in front of Phoenix **Designer:** Vassos Phalireas

Date	Mintage	F	VF	XF	Unc	BU
1971	4,014,000	0.25	0.50	2.00	6.00	15.00
1973	3,166,000	0.25	0.50	1.50	5.50	15.00

KM# 84 10 DRACHMAI
Nickel, 30 mm. **Ruler:** Paul I **Obv:** Head left **Rev:** Crowned arms with supporters

Date	Mintage	F	VF	XF	Unc	BU
1959	20,000,000	0.30	0.50	2.00	16.00	50.00
1959 Proof	—	Value: 2,000				
1965	—	—	—	—	5.50	—

Note: In sets only

Date	Mintage	F	VF	XF	Unc	BU
1965 Proof	4,987	Value: 15.00				

KM# 96 10 DRACHMAI
Copper-Nickel **Ruler:** Constantine II **Obv:** Head left **Rev:** Crowned arms with supporters **Designer:** Vassos Phalireas

Date	Mintage	F	VF	XF	Unc	BU
1968	40,000,000	0.25	0.50	0.75	5.50	15.00

KM# 101 10 DRACHMAI
7.5400 g., Copper-Nickel, 29.9 mm. **Ruler:** Constantine II **Obv:** Head left **Rev:** Soldier in front of Phoenix **Designer:** Vassos Phalireas

Date	Mintage	F	VF	XF	Unc	BU
1971	502,000	0.25	0.50	1.00	7.50	16.00
1973	541,000	0.50	1.00	2.50	8.00	18.00

KM# 85 20 DRACHMAI
7.5000 g., 0.8350 Silver 0.2013 oz. ASW, 26.2 mm. **Ruler:** Paul I **Obv:** Head left **Rev:** Selene, moon goddess

Date	Mintage	F	VF	XF	Unc	BU
1960	20,000,000	—	—	BV	7.00	16.00
1960 Proof	—	Value: 2,000				
1965	—	—	—	—	8.00	18.00
1965 Proof	4,987	Value: 18.00				

KM# 111.3 20 DRACHMAI
Copper-Nickel **Ruler:** Constantine II **Obv:** Soldier in front of Phoenix **Rev:** Selene, wide rim with continuous wave design at rear hoof

Date	Mintage	F	VF	XF	Unc	BU
1973	Inc. above	0.50	1.00	2.00	10.00	15.00

KM# 111 20 DRACHMAI
Copper-Nickel **Ruler:** Constantine II **Obv:** Soldier in front of Phoenix **Rev:** Selene, narrow rim with faint veil or no veil **Note:** Possible varieties exist; narrow rim with faint veil or no veil / wide rim with heavy veil and broken wave design at rear hoof.

Date	Mintage	F	VF	XF	Unc	BU
1973	3,092,000	0.50	1.00	2.00	8.50	11.50

KM# 86 30 DRACHMAI
18.0000 g., 0.8350 Silver 0.4832 oz. ASW, 34 mm. **Ruler:** Paul I **Subject:** Centennial - Five Greek Kings **Edge Lettering:** Greek text

Date	Mintage	F	VF	XF	Unc	BU
ND(1963)	3,000,000	—	BV	7.50	10.00	12.00

KM# 87 30 DRACHMAI
12.0000 g., 0.8350 Silver 0.3221 oz. ASW, 30.3 mm. **Ruler:** Constantine II **Subject:** Constantine and Anne-Marie Wedding **Edge Lettering:** Greek text

Date	Mintage	F	VF	XF	Unc	BU
1964	1,000,000	—	BV	5.00	9.00	12.00

Note: Berne: small edge lettering, BØ below epaulette

Date	Mintage	F	VF	XF	Unc	BU
1964	1,000,000	—	BV	5.00	8.00	12.00

Note: Kongsberg: large edge lettering, BØ on top of shoulder

Date	Mintage	F	VF	XF	Unc	BU
1964 Proof	—	Value: 3,500				

KM# 93 50 DRACHMAI
12.5000 g., 0.8350 Silver 0.3356 oz. ASW **Ruler:** Constantine II **Subject:** April 21, 1967 Revolution **Obv:** Crowned shield with supporters **Rev:** Soldier in front of Phoenix

Date	Mintage	F	VF	XF	Unc	BU
1967(1970)	100,000	—	—	25.00	75.00	100

REPUBLIC

DECIMAL COINAGE

KM# 103 10 LEPTA
1.0900 g., Aluminum **Obv:** Phoenix above flame **Rev:** Pair of dolphins flank trident

Date	Mintage	F	VF	XF	Unc	BU
1973	15,134,472	—	0.10	0.50	2.00	5.00

KM# 113 10 LEPTA
Aluminum **Obv:** Arms within wreath **Rev:** Charging bull right

Date	Mintage	F	VF	XF	Unc	BU
1976	2,043,000	—	0.10	0.30	2.00	5.00
1978	791,000	0.50	1.00	2.50	5.00	10.00
1978 Proof	20,000	Value: 5.00				

KM# 105 20 LEPTA
Aluminum **Obv:** Phoenix with date below **Rev:** Olive branch, denomination

Date	Mintage	F	VF	XF	Unc	BU
1973	15,265,797	—	0.20	0.50	2.50	5.00

KM# 114 20 LEPTA
Aluminum **Obv:** Arms within wreath **Rev:** Stallion's head left

Date	Mintage	F	VF	XF	Unc	BU
1976	2,506,000	—	0.15	0.40	2.50	5.00
1978	803,000	0.45	1.00	2.50	5.00	10.00
1978 Proof	20,000	Value: 5.00				

KM# 106 50 LEPTA
Nickel-Brass, 18 mm. **Obv:** Phoenix and flame **Rev:** Ornamental plume

Date	Mintage	F	VF	XF	Unc	BU
1973	55,231,898	—	—	0.15	1.00	3.00

KM# 115 50 LEPTA
2.5200 g., Nickel-Brass, 18 mm. **Subject:** Markos Botsaris **Obv:** Denomination **Rev:** Bust left

Date	Mintage	F	VF	XF	Unc	BU
1976	51,016,000	—	—	0.15	1.00	—
1978	12,010,000	—	—	0.15	1.00	—
1978 Proof	20,000	Value: 8.00				
1980	6,682,000	—	—	0.15	1.25	—
1982	3,365,000	—	—	0.15	1.25	—
1984	1,208,000	—	—	0.15	1.25	—
1986	—	—	—	0.15	1.25	—

KM# 107 DRACHMA
Nickel-Brass, 21 mm. **Obv:** Phoenix and flame **Rev:** Owl left of denomination

Date	Mintage	F	VF	XF	Unc	BU
1973	45,218,431	—	0.75	1.50	3.00	6.00

KM# 116 DRACHMA
Nickel-Brass, 21 mm. **Subject:** Konstantinos Kanaris **Obv:** Full masted ship at sea **Rev:** Bust left

Date	Mintage	F	VF	XF	Unc	BU
1976	102,060,000	—	—	0.15	1.00	3.00
Note: Varieties exist						
1978	21,200,000	—	—	0.15	1.00	2.00
1978 Proof	20,000	Value: 8.00				
1980	52,503,000	—	—	0.15	1.00	2.00
1982	54,186,000	—	—	0.15	1.00	2.00
1984	33,665,000	—	—	0.15	1.00	2.00
1986	17,901,000	—	—	0.15	1.00	3.00

KM# 150 DRACHMA
2.8000 g., Copper, 18 mm. **Subject:** Lascarina Bouboulina, 1783-1825 **Obv:** Full masted ship at sea **Rev:** Bust left

Date	Mintage	F	VF	XF	Unc	BU
1988(an)	36,707,000	—	—	—	0.50	1.00
1990(an)	—	—	—	—	0.50	1.00
1992	—	—	—	—	0.50	1.00
1993	—	—	—	—	10.00	15.00
Note: In sets only						
1993 Proof	—	Value: 45.00				
1994	—	—	—	—	0.50	1.00
1998	—	—	—	—	0.50	1.00
2000	—	—	—	—	0.50	1.00

KM# 108 2 DRACHMAI
Nickel-Brass **Obv:** Phoenix and flame **Rev:** Owl left of denomination

Date	Mintage	F	VF	XF	Unc	BU
1973	51,163,812	—	0.75	1.50	4.00	7.00

KM# 117 2 DRACHMAI
Nickel-Brass, 24 mm. **Subject:** Georgios Karaiskakis **Obv:** Crossed rifles with branch **Rev:** Bust left

Date	Mintage	F	VF	XF	Unc	BU
1976	92,401,000	—	—	0.25	1.00	2.00
1978	16,772,000	—	—	0.25	1.00	2.00
1978 Proof	20,000	Value: 8.00				
1980	45,955,000	—	—	0.25	1.00	2.00

KM# 130 2 DRACHMES
Nickel-Brass, 24 mm. **Subject:** Georgios Karaiskakis **Obv:** Crossed rifles and branch **Rev:** Bust left

Date	Mintage	F	VF	XF	Unc	BU
1982	64,414,000	—	—	0.20	1.00	2.00
1984	37,861,000	—	—	0.20	1.00	2.00
1986	21,019,000	—	—	0.20	1.00	2.00

KM# 151 2 DRACHMES
3.8000 g., Copper, 21 mm. **Subject:** Manto Mavrogenous, 1797-1840 - independence hero **Obv:** Ship's wheel, scope and anchor **Rev:** Bust facing looking right

Date	Mintage	F	VF	XF	Unc	BU
1988(an)	36,707,000	—	—	—	0.50	1.00
1990	—	—	—	—	0.50	1.00
1992	—	—	—	—	0.50	1.00
1993	—	—	—	—	10.00	15.00
Note: In sets only						
1993 Proof	—	Value: 45.00				
1994	—	—	—	—	0.50	1.00
1998	—	—	—	—	0.50	1.00
2000	—	—	—	—	0.50	1.00

KM# 109.1 5 DRACHMAI
Copper-Nickel, 25 mm. **Obv:** Phoenix and flame **Rev:** Pegasus rearing right **Note:** Denomination spelling ends with I.

Date	Mintage	F	VF	XF	Unc	BU
1973	33,957,473	0.75	1.25	2.00	4.00	10.00

KM# 109.2 5 DRACHMAI
Copper-Nickel, 25 mm. **Obv:** Phoenix and flame **Rev:** Pegasus rearing right **Note:** Denomination spelling ends with A.

Date	Mintage	F	VF	XF	Unc	BU
1973	Inc. above	1.00	2.00	4.00	10.00	15.00

KM# 118 5 DRACHMAI
Copper-Nickel, 22.5 mm. **Subject:** Aristotle **Obv:** Denomination **Rev:** Head left

Date	Mintage	F	VF	XF	Unc	BU
1976	85,187,000	—	0.20	0.35	1.00	2.00
1978	17,404,000	—	0.20	0.35	1.00	3.00
1978 Proof	20,000	Value: 8.00				
1980	33,701,000	—	0.20	0.35	1.00	2.00

KM# 131 5 DRACHMES
5.5500 g., Copper-Nickel, 22.46 mm. **Subject:** Aristotle **Obv:** Denomination **Rev:** Head left **Edge:** Plain

Date	Mintage	F	VF	XF	Unc	BU
1982	42,647,000	—	0.20	0.35	1.00	2.00
1984	29,778,000	—	0.20	0.35	1.00	2.00
1986	16,730,000	—	0.20	0.35	1.00	2.00
1988	30,273,000	—	—	0.30	0.75	1.50
1990	—	—	—	0.30	0.75	1.50
1992	—	—	—	0.30	0.75	1.50
1993	—	—	—	—	10.00	15.00
Note: In sets only						
1993 Proof	—	Value: 50.00				
1994	—	—	—	—	0.75	1.50
1998	—	—	—	—	0.75	1.50
1999	—	—	—	—	0.75	1.50
2000	—	—	—	—	0.75	1.50

KM# 110 10 DRACHMAI
7.5500 g., Copper-Nickel **Obv:** Phoenix and flame **Rev:** Pegasus rearing right

Date	Mintage	F	VF	XF	Unc	BU
1973	22,599,848	1.00	1.50	2.50	6.00	10.00

KM# 119 10 DRACHMAI
7.5400 g., Copper-Nickel, 25.95 mm. **Subject:** Democritus **Obv:** Atom design **Rev:** Head left **Edge:** Plain

Date	Mintage	F	VF	XF	Unc	BU
1976	76,816,000	—	0.25	0.50	1.00	5.00
1978	14,637,000	—	0.25	0.50	1.00	5.00

Date	Mintage	F	VF	XF	Unc	BU
1978 Proof	20,000	Value: 10.00				
1980	28,733,000	—	0.25	0.50	1.00	5.00

KM# 132 10 DRACHMES
7.6000 g., Copper-Nickel, 26 mm. **Obv:** Atom design **Rev:** Head of Democritus left

Date	Mintage	F	VF	XF	Unc	BU
1982	35,539,000	—	0.25	0.50	1.00	2.00
1984	23,802,000	—	0.25	0.50	1.00	2.00
1986	24,441,000	—	0.25	0.50	1.00	2.00
1988	16,869,000	—	0.20	0.45	1.00	2.00
1990	—	—	0.20	0.45	1.00	2.00
1992	—	—	0.20	0.45	1.00	2.00
1993	—	—	—	—	15.00	20.00
Note: In sets only						
1993 Proof	—	Value: 60.00				
1994	—	—	0.20	0.45	1.00	2.00
1998	—	—	0.20	0.45	1.00	2.00
2000	—	—	—	—	1.00	2.00
2002	—	—	0.25	0.50	1.25	2.50

KM# 112 20 DRACHMAI
Copper-Nickel, 29 mm. **Subject:** Athena **Obv:** Phoenix and flame **Rev:** Helmeted head left

Date	Mintage	F	VF	XF	Unc	BU
1973	20,650,087	0.35	0.50	1.00	2.00	5.00

KM# 120 20 DRACHMAI
Copper-Nickel, 29 mm. **Subject:** Pericles **Obv:** The Parthenon **Rev:** Helmeted head left **Edge Lettering:** In Greek

Date	Mintage	F	VF	XF	Unc	BU
1976	53,167,500	—	0.30	0.50	1.25	5.00
1978	65,353,000	—	0.30	0.50	1.50	5.00
1978 Proof	20,000	Value: 10.00				
1980	17,562,000	—	0.30	0.50	1.25	5.00

KM# 133 20 DRACHMES
Copper-Nickel, 28.8 mm. **Subject:** Pericles **Obv:** The Parthenon **Rev:** Helmeted head left **Edge Lettering:** In Greek

Date	Mintage	F	VF	XF	Unc	BU
1982	24,299,000	—	0.30	0.50	1.00	3.00
1984	13,412,000	—	0.30	0.50	1.25	3.50
1986	10,553,000	—	0.30	0.50	1.00	3.00
1988	16,196,000	—	—	0.50	1.00	3.00

KM# 154 20 DRACHMES
7.0000 g., Nickel-Bronze, 24.5 mm. **Subject:** Dionysios Solomos, composer of National Anthem **Obv:** Olive branch right of lined field **Rev:** Bust looking right

Date	Mintage	F	VF	XF	Unc	BU
1990(an)	—	—	—	—	1.25	2.50
1992	—	—	—	—	1.25	2.50
1993	—	—	—	—	15.00	20.00
Note: In sets only						
1993 Proof	—	Value: 85.00				
1994	—	—	—	—	1.25	2.50
1998(an)	—	—	—	—	1.25	2.50
2000	—	—	—	—	1.25	2.50

KM# 124 50 DRACHMAI
Copper-Nickel **Subject:** Solon the Archon of Athens **Obv:** Denomination above waves and date **Rev:** Head left

Date	Mintage	F	VF	XF	Unc	BU
1980(an)	32,250,999	0.50	0.75	1.50	3.50	6.00

KM# 134 50 DRACHMES
11.9600 g., Copper-Nickel, 31 mm. **Subject:** Solon the Archon of Athens **Obv:** Denomination above waves and date **Rev:** Head left **Note:** Obv: Denomination in modern Greek

Date	Mintage	F	VF	XF	Unc	BU
1982(an)	18,899,000	0.40	0.60	1.00	1.50	3.00
1984(an)	11,411,000	0.40	0.60	1.00	1.50	3.00

KM# 147 50 DRACHMES
9.2000 g., Nickel-Brass, 27.6 mm. **Subject:** Homer **Obv:** Ancient sailing boat **Rev:** Head left

Date	Mintage	F	VF	XF	Unc	BU
1986(an)	12,078,000	—	0.50	1.00	2.50	5.00
1988(an)	23,589,000	—	—	0.75	1.50	3.00
1990(an)	—	—	—	0.75	1.75	3.50
1992	—	—	—	0.75	1.75	3.50
1993	—	—	—	—	20.00	25.00
Note: In sets only						
1993 Proof	—	Value: 70.00				
1994	—	—	—	0.75	1.75	3.50
1998	—	—	—	—	1.75	3.50
1999	—	—	—	—	1.75	3.50
2000	—	—	—	—	1.75	3.50

KM# 164 50 DRACHMES
Brass, 27 mm. **Series:** 150th Anniversary of the Constitution **Subject:** Dimitrios Kallergis **Obv:** Bust 3/4 left **Rev:** Center of Parliament Building

Date	Mintage	F	VF	XF	Unc	BU
ND(1994)(an)	7,500,000	—	—	—	3.00	5.00

KM# 168 50 DRACHMES
Brass, 27 mm. **Series:** 150th Anniversary of the Constitution **Subject:** Makrygiannis **Obv:** Bust 3/4 left **Rev:** Center of Parliament Building

Date	Mintage	F	VF	XF	Unc	BU
ND(1994)(an)	7,500,000	—	—	—	3.00	5.00

KM# 159 100 DRACHMES
10.2000 g., Brass, 29.3 mm. **Subject:** Macedonia - Alexander the Great **Obv:** Radiant design within circle **Rev:** Head right

Date	Mintage	F	VF	XF	Unc	BU
1990(an)	—	—	—	—	2.35	4.50
1992	—	—	—	—	2.35	4.50
1993	—	—	—	—	20.00	25.00
Note: In sets only						
1993 Proof	—	Value: 85.00				
1994	—	—	—	—	2.35	4.50
1998	—	—	—	—	2.35	4.50
2000	—	—	—	—	2.35	4.50

KM# 169 100 DRACHMES
9.8700 g., Brass, 29.48 mm. **Subject:** VI Universal Track Championship Games **Obv:** Ancient city view and track **Rev:** Runner and track **Edge:** Alternating reeded and smooth sections

Date	Mintage	F	VF	XF	Unc	BU
1997(an)	5,000,000	—	—	—	2.75	5.00

KM# 170 100 DRACHMES
9.8500 g., Brass, 29.45 mm. **Subject:** 13th World Basketball Championships **Obv:** Cup in ball design **Rev:** Four basketball players in action **Edge:** Segmented reeding

Date	Mintage	F	VF	XF	Unc	BU
1998(an)	—	—	—	—	4.50	6.50

KM# 173 100 DRACHMES

10.0000 g., Brass, 29.4 mm. **Obv:** Ancient wrestlers **Rev:** Modern wrestlers **Edge:** Reeded and plain sections

Date	Mintage	F	VF	XF	Unc	BU
1999	—	—	—	—	3.50	5.50

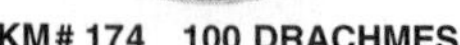

KM# 174 100 DRACHMES

10.0000 g., Brass, 29.4 mm. **Obv:** Statue of Atlas **Rev:** Weight lifter **Edge:** Reeded and plain sections

Date	Mintage	F	VF	XF	Unc	BU
1999	—	—	—	—	3.50	5.50

EURO COINAGE

European Union Issues

The Greek Euro coinage series contains the denomination in Lepta as well.

KM# 181 EURO CENT

2.2700 g., Copper Plated Steel, 16.2 mm. **Subject:** Euro Coinage **Obv:** Ancient Athenian trireme **Obv. Designer:** George Stamatopoulos **Rev:** Denomination and globe **Rev. Designer:** Luc Luycx **Edge:** Plain

Date	Mintage	F	VF	XF	Unc	BU
2002	88,000,000	—	—	—	0.35	—
2002 F in star	15,000,000	—	—	—	1.25	—
2003	7,000,000	—	—	—	0.35	—
2003 Proof	—	—	—	—	—	—
2004	45,000,000	—	—	—	0.35	—
2005	—	—	—	—	0.35	—
2006	—	—	—	—	0.35	—
2007	—	—	—	—	0.35	—

KM# 182 2 EURO CENT

3.0300 g., Copper Plated Steel, 18.7 mm. **Subject:** Euro Coinage **Obv:** Corvette sailing ship **Obv. Designer:** George Stamatopoulos **Rev:** Denomination and globe **Rev. Designer:** Luc Luycx **Edge:** Grooved

Date	Mintage	F	VF	XF	Unc	BU
2002	172,000,000	—	—	—	0.50	—
2002 F in star	18,000,000	—	—	—	1.00	—
2003	9,000,000	—	—	—	0.50	—
2003 Proof	—	—	—	—	—	—
2004	25,000,000	—	—	—	0.50	—
2005	—	—	—	—	0.50	—
2006	—	—	—	—	0.50	—
2007	—	—	—	—	0.50	—

KM# 183 5 EURO CENT

3.8600 g., Copper Plated Steel, 21.2 mm. **Subject:** Euro Coinage **Obv:** Freighter **Obv. Designer:** George Stamatopoulos **Rev:** Denomination and globe **Rev. Designer:** Luc Luycx **Edge:** Plain

Date	Mintage	F	VF	XF	Unc	BU
2002	288,000,000	—	—	—	1.00	—
2002 F in star	18,000,000	—	—	—	1.25	—
2003	400,000	—	—	—	1.00	—
2003 Proof	—	—	—	—	—	—
2004	250,000	—	—	—	1.00	—
2005	—	—	—	—	1.00	—
2006	—	—	—	—	1.00	—
2007	—	—	—	—	1.00	—

KM# 184 10 EURO CENT

4.0700 g., Brass, 19.7 mm. **Subject:** Euro Coinage **Obv:** Bust of Rhgas Feriaou's half right **Obv. Designer:** George Stamatopoulos **Rev:** Denomination and map **Rev. Designer:** Luc Luycx **Edge:** Reeded

Date	Mintage	F	VF	XF	Unc	BU
2002	257,000,000	—	—	—	1.25	—
2002 F in star	24,000,000	—	—	—	2.00	—
2003	330,000	—	—	—	1.25	—
2003 Proof	—	—	—	—	—	—
2004	—	—	—	—	1.25	—
2005	—	—	—	—	1.25	—
2006	—	—	—	—	1.25	—

KM# 211 10 EURO CENT

4.0700 g., Brass, 19.7 mm. **Subject:** Euro Coinage **Obv:** Bust of Rhgas Feriaou's half right **Obv. Designer:** George Stamatopoulos **Rev:** Relief map of Western Europe, stars, lines and value **Rev. Designer:** Luc Luycx **Edge:** Reeded

Date	Mintage	F	VF	XF	Unc	BU
2007	—	—	—	—	1.25	—

KM# 185 20 EURO CENT

5.7300 g., Brass, 22.1 mm. **Subject:** Euro Coinage **Obv:** Bust of John Kapodistrias half right **Obv. Designer:** George Stamatopoulos **Rev:** Denomination and map **Rev. Designer:** Luc Luycx **Edge:** Notched

Date	Mintage	F	VF	XF	Unc	BU
2002	370,000,000	—	—	—	1.25	—
2002 E in star	21,000,000	—	—	—	2.25	—
2003	330,000	—	—	—	1.25	—
2003 Proof	—	—	—	—	—	—
2004	400,000	—	—	—	1.25	—
2005	—	—	—	—	1.25	—
2006	—	—	—	—	1.25	—

KM# 212 20 EURO CENT

5.7300 g., Brass, 22.1 mm. **Subject:** Euro Coinage **Obv:** Bust of John Kapodistrias' half right **Obv. Designer:** George Stamatopoulos **Rev:** Relief map of Western Europe, stars, lines and value **Rev. Designer:** Luc Luycx **Edge:** Notched

Date	Mintage	F	VF	XF	Unc	BU
2007	—	—	—	—	1.25	—

KM# 186 50 EURO CENT

7.8100 g., Brass, 24.2 mm. **Subject:** Euro Coinage **Obv:** Bust of El. Venizelos half left **Obv. Designer:** George Stamatopoulos **Rev:** Denomination and map **Rev. Designer:** Luc Luycx **Edge:** Reeded

Date	Mintage	F	VF	XF	Unc	BU
2002	145,000,000	—	—	—	1.50	—
2002 F in star	18,000,000	—	—	—	2.50	—
2003	330,000	—	—	—	1.50	—
2003 Proof	—	—	—	—	—	—
2004	400,000	—	—	—	1.50	—
2005	—	—	—	—	1.50	—
2006	—	—	—	—	1.50	—

KM# 213 50 EURO CENT

7.8100 g., Brass, 24.2 mm. **Subject:** Euro Coinage **Obv:** Bust of El. Venizelos half left **Obv. Designer:** George Stamatopoulos **Rev:** Relief map of Western Europe, stars, lines and value **Rev. Designer:** Luc Luycx **Edge:** Reeded

Date	Mintage	F	VF	XF	Unc	BU
2007	—	—	—	—	1.50	—

KM# 187 EURO

7.5000 g., Bi-Metallic Copper-Nickel center in Brass ring, 23.2 mm. **Subject:** Euro Coinage **Obv:** Ancient Athenian coin design **Obv. Designer:** George Stamatopoulos **Rev:** Denomination and map **Rev. Designer:** Luc Luycx **Edge:** Reeded and plain sections

Date	Mintage	F	VF	XF	Unc	BU
2002	118,000,000	—	—	—	4.00	—
2002 S in star	15,000,000	—	—	—	6.00	—
2003	1,650,000	—	—	—	7.50	—
2003 Proof	—	—	—	—	—	—
2004	10,000,000	—	—	—	5.00	—
2005	—	—	—	—	5.00	—
2006	—	—	—	—	5.00	—

KM# 214 EURO

7.5000 g., Bi-Metallic Copper-Nickel center in Brass ring, 23.2 mm. **Subject:** Euro Coinage **Obv:** Ancient Athenian coin design **Obv. Designer:** George Stamatopoulos **Rev:** Relief map of Western Europe, stars, lines and value **Rev. Designer:** Luc Luycx **Edge:** Reeded and plain sections

Date	Mintage	F	VF	XF	Unc	BU
2007	—	—	—	—	4.00	—

KM# 188 2 EURO

8.5200 g., Bi-Metallic Brass center in Copper-Nickel ring, 25.7 mm. **Subject:** Euro Coinage **Obv:** Europa seated on a bull **Obv. Designer:** George Stamatopoulos **Rev:** Denomination and map **Rev. Designer:** Luc Luycx **Edge:** Reeded with Greek letters and stars

Date	Mintage	F	VF	XF	Unc	BU
2002	162,000,000	—	—	—	4.00	—
2002 S in star	6,000,000	—	—	—	6.50	—
2003	540,000	—	—	—	4.00	—
2003 Proof	—	—	—	—	—	—
2004	—	—	—	—	—	—
Note: In sets only						
2005	—	—	—	—	4.00	—
2006	—	—	—	—	4.00	—

KM# 209 2 EURO

8.5200 g., Bi-Metallic **Ring Composition:** Copper Nickel **Center Composition:** Brass, 25.7 mm. **Subject:** 2004 Olympics **Obv:** Discus thrower **Rev:** Denomination and map **Edge:** Reeded and lettered **Edge Lettering:** Greek

Date	Mintage	F	VF	XF	Unc	BU
2004	50,000,000	—	—	—	4.00	6.00

KM# 215 2 EURO

8.5200 g., Bi-Metallic Brass center in Copper-Nickel ring, 25.7 mm. **Subject:** Euro Coinage **Obv:** Europa seated on a bull **Obv. Designer:** George Stamatopoulos **Rev:** Relief map of Western Europe, stars, lines and value **Rev. Designer:** Luc Luycx **Edge:** Reeded with Greek letters and stars

Date	Mintage	F	VF	XF	Unc	BU
2007	15,000	—	—	—	—	9.00
Note: In sets only						

KM# 216 2 EURO

8.5500 g., Bi-Metallic Brass center in Copper-Nickel ring, 25.72 mm. **Subject:** 50th Anniversary - Treaty of Rome **Obv:** Open treaty book **Rev:** Large value at left, modified outline of Europe at right **Edge:** Reeded and lettered

Date	Mintage	F	VF	XF	Unc	BU
2007	—	—	—	—	—	9.00

GREENLAND

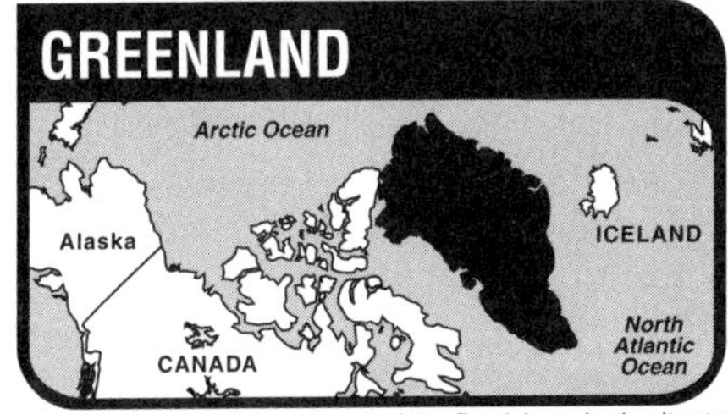

Greenland, an integral part of the Danish realm is situated between the North Atlantic Ocean and the Polar Sea, almost entirely within the Arctic Circle. An island nation, it has an area of 840,000 sq. mi. (2,175,600 sq. km.) and a population of 57,000. Capital: Nuuk (formerly Godthaab). Greenland is the world's only source of natural cryolite, a fluoride of sodium and aluminum important in making aluminum. Fish products and minerals are exported.

Eric the Red discovered Greenland in 982 and established the first settlement in 986. Greenland was a republic until 1261, when the sovereignty of Norway was extended to the island. The original colony was abandoned about 1400 when increasing cold interfered with the breeding of cattle. Successful recolonization was undertaken by Denmark in 1721. In 1921 Denmark extended its claim to include the entire island, and made it a colony of the crown in 1924. The island's colonial status was abolished by amendment to the Danish constitution on June 5, 1953, and Greenland became an integral part of the Kingdom of Denmark. The last Greenlandic coins were withdrawn on July 1, 1967, and since then, Danish coins have been used. Greenland has had home rule since May 1, 1979.

RULERS
Danish

MINT MARKS
Heart (h) Copenhagen (Kobenhavn)

MINTMASTERS' INITIALS
HCN - Hans Christian Nielsen, 1919-1927
C - Alfred Kristian Frederik Christiansen, 1956-1971
GJ - Knud Gunnar Jensen, 1901-1933
S - Harald Salomon, 1933-1968

MONETARY SYSTEM
100 Øre = 1 Krone

DANISH COLONY

MILLED COINAGE

KM# 5 25 ORE
Copper-Nickel **Obv:** Crowned arms of Denmark **Obv. Legend:** GRØNLANDS STYRELSE **Rev:** Polar bear walking left, date below divided by 'GS', denomination above

Date	Mintage	F	VF	XF	Unc	BU
1926(h) HCN GJ	310,000	4.00	7.00	12.50	38.50	52.50

Note: This coin was withdrawn from circulation during 1940 and sent to the United States to be holed to avoid confusion with the Danish 1 Krone coin

KM# 7 50 ORE
Aluminum-Bronze **Obv:** Crowned arms of Denmark **Obv. Legend:** GR?NLANDS STYRELSE **Rev:** Polar bear walking left, denomination above, date below divided by 'GS'

Date	Mintage	F	VF	XF	Unc	BU
1926(h) HCN CJ	195,837	6.00	9.50	15.00	38.50	60.00

KM# 8 KRONE
Aluminum-Bronze **Obv:** Crowned arms of Denmark **Obv. Legend:** GRØNLANDS STYRELSE **Rev:** Polar bear walking left, denomination above, date below divided by 'GS'

Date	Mintage	F	VF	XF	Unc	BU
1926(h) HCN CJ	286,982	4.50	10.00	18.00	58.50	70.00

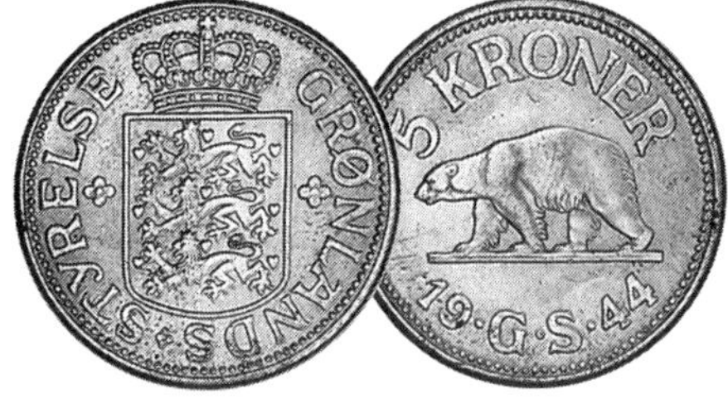

KM# 9 5 KRONER
Brass **Obv:** Crowned arms of Denmark **Obv. Legend:** GRØNLANDS STYRELSE **Rev:** Polar bear walking left, denomination above, date below divided by "GS" **Rev. Designer:** Gilroy Roberts **Note:** Mainly struck for use by American forces in Greenland during WWII, when 5 Kroner was equal to one U.S. dollar.

Date	Mintage	F	VF	XF	Unc	BU
1944	100,000	40.00	60.00	85.00	130	160

Note: Struck at the Philadelphia Mint; Without mintmark

DANISH COLONY

MILLED COINAGE

KM# 6 25 ORE
Copper-Nickel **Obv:** Crowned arms of Denmark **Rev:** Hole at center of polar bear, left, denomination above, date below divided by 'GS' **Note:** Center hole added to KM#5.

Date	Mintage	F	VF	XF	Unc	BU
1926(h) HCN GJ	31,716	20.00	40.00	75.00	125	—

Note: The hole was added 1940/41 in New York to avoid confusion with the 1 Krone coins of Denmark

DANISH STATE

1953-1979

MILLED COINAGE

KM# 10 KRONE
Aluminum-Bronze, 27.3 mm. **Issuer:** Royal Greenland Trade Company **Obv:** Crowned arms of Denmark and Greenland, date below **Obv. Legend:** DEN KONGELIGE GRØNLANDSKE HANDEL **Rev:** Denomination within flower spray

Date	Mintage	F	VF	XF	Unc	BU
1957(h) C S	100,209	8.00	12.50	22.50	58.00	75.00

KM# 10a KRONE
Copper-Nickel, 27.3 mm. **Issuer:** Royal Greenland Trade Company **Obv:** Crowned arms of Denmark and Greenland **Rev:** Denomination within floral wreath

Date	Mintage	F	VF	XF	Unc	BU
1960(h) C S	108,500	3.75	7.50	12.50	22.50	—
1964(h) C S	110,000	8.00	15.00	20.00	30.00	—

GRENADA

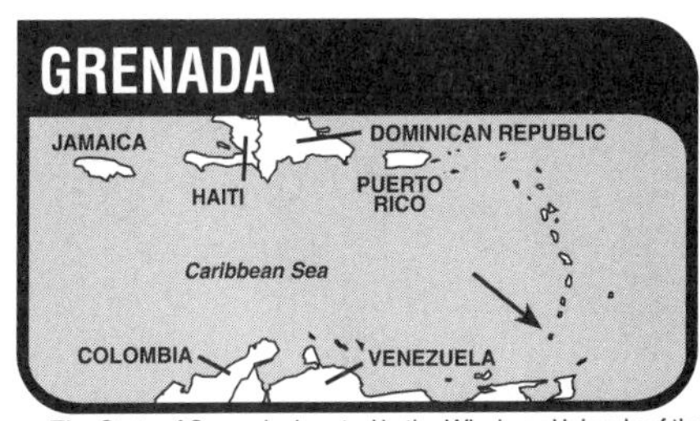

The State of Grenada, located in the Windward Islands of the Caribbean Sea 90 miles (145 km.) north of Trinidad, has(with Carriacou and Petit Martinique) an area of 133 sq. mi. (344 sq. km.) and a population of 94,000. Capital: St.George's. Grenada is the smallest independent nation in the Western Hemisphere. The economy is based on agriculture and tourism. Sugar, coconuts, nutmeg, cocoa and bananas are exported.

Columbus discovered Grenada in 1498 during his third voyage to the Americas. Spain failed to colonize the island, and in 1627 granted it to the British who sold it to the French who colonized it in 1650. Grenada was captured by the British in 1763, retaken by the French in 1779, and finally ceded to the British in 1783. In 1958 Grenada joined the Federation of the West Indies, which was dissolved in 1962. In 1967 it became an internally self-governing British associated state. Full independence was attained on Feb. 4, 1974. Grenada is a member of the Commonwealth of Nations. The prime minister is the Head of Government. Elizabeth II is Head of State as Queen of Grenada.

The early coinage of Grenada consists of cut and countermarked pieces of Spanish or Spanish Colonial Reales, which were valued at 11 Bits. In 1787 8 Reales coins were cut into 11 triangular pieces and countermarked with an incuse G. Later in 1814 large denomination cut pieces were issued being 1/2, 1/3 or 1/6 cuts and countermarked with a TR, incuse G and a number 6, 4,2, or 1 indicating the value in bitts.

RULERS
British

INDEPENDENT STATE

Commonwealth of Nations

MODERN COINAGE

KM# 15 4 DOLLARS
Copper-Nickel, 38.5 mm. **Series:** F.A.O. **Obv:** Cocoa beans within oval **Rev:** Sugar cane and banana tree branch

Date	Mintage	F	VF	XF	Unc	BU
1970	13,000	—	6.00	10.00	20.00	30.00
1970 Proof	2,000	Value: 35.00				

KM# 16 10 DOLLARS
Copper-Nickel **Subject:** Royal Visit **Obv:** Crowned bust right **Rev:** Arms with supporters within circle

Date	Mintage	F	VF	XF	Unc	BU
1985	Est. 100,000	—	—	4.50	9.00	—

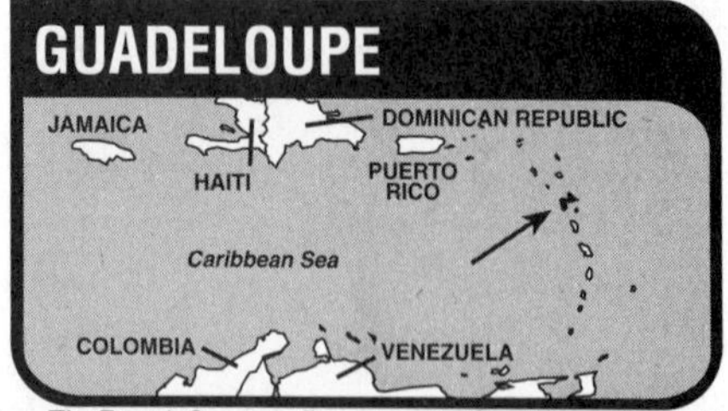

The French Overseas Department of Guadeloupe, located in the Leeward Islands of the West Indies about 300 miles (493 km.) southeast of Puerto Rico, has an area of 687 sq. mi. (1,780 sq. km.) and a population of 306,000. Actually it is two islands separated by a narrow saltwater stream: volcanic Basse-Terre to the west and the flatter limestone formation of Grande-Terre to the east. Capital: Basse-Terre, on the island of that name. The principal industries are agriculture, the distillation of liquors, and tourism. Sugar, bananas, and rum are exported.

Guadeloupe was discovered by Columbus in 1493 and settled in 1635 by two Frenchmen, L'Olive and Duplessis, who took possession in the name of the French Company of the Islands of America. When repeated efforts by private companies to colonize the island failed, it was relinquished to the French crown in 1674, and established as a dependency of Martinique. The British occupied the island on two occasions, 1759-63 and 1810-16, before it passed permanently to France. A colony until 1946 Guadeloupe was then made an overseas territory of the FrenchUnion. In 1958 it voted to become an Overseas Department within the new French Community.

The well-known R.F. in garland oval countermark of the French Government is only legitimate if on a French Colonies 12 deniers 1767 C#4. Two other similar but incuse RF countermarks are on cut pieces in the values of 1 and 4 escalins. Contemporary and modern counterfeits are known of both these types.

RULER

French 1816-

MONETARY SYSTEM

100 Centimes = 1 Franc

FRENCH COLONY

MODERN COINAGE

KM# 45 50 CENTIMES

Copper-Nickel **Obv:** Armored head left within circle **Obv. Designer:** A. Patay **Rev:** Sugar cane stalk divides date and denomination **Shape:** 18-sided

Date	Mintage	F	VF	XF	Unc	BU
1903	600,000	16.00	35.00	85.00	240	500
1921	600,000	12.00	30.00	75.00	185	400

KM# 46 FRANC

Copper-Nickel **Obv:** Armored head left within circle **Obv. Designer:** A. Patay **Rev:** Sugar cane stalk divides date and denomination **Note:** 20-sided.

Date	Mintage	F	VF	XF	Unc	BU
1903	700,000	20.00	40.00	90.00	250	550
1921	700,000	15.00	30.00	80.00	200	450

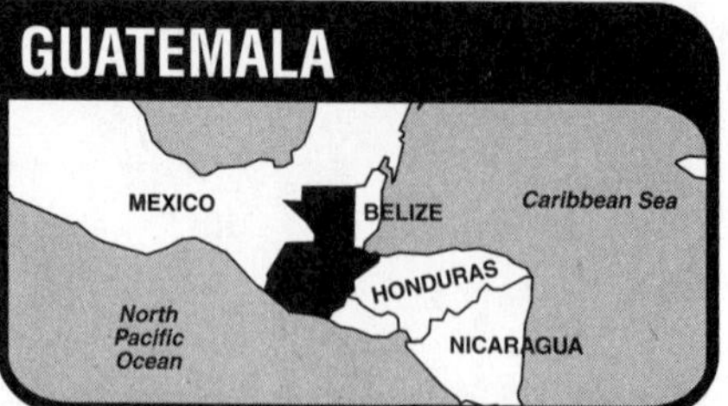

The Republic of Guatemala, the northernmost of the five Central American republics, has an area of 42,042 sq. mi. (108,890 sq. km.) and a population of 10.7 million. Capital: Guatemala City. The economy of Guatemala is heavily dependent on agriculture, however, the country is rich in nickel resources which are being developed. Coffee, cotton and bananas are exported.

Guatemala, once the site of an ancient Mayan civilization, was conquered by Pedro de Alvarado, the resourceful lieutenant of Cortes who undertook the conquest from Mexico. Cruel but strategically skillful, he progressed rapidly along the Pacific coastal lowlands to the highland plain of Quetzaltenango where the decisive battle for Guatemala was fought. After routing the Indian forces, he established the city of Guatemala in 1524. The Spanish Captaincy-General of Guatemala included all Central America but Panama. Guatemala declared its independence of Spain in 1821 and was absorbed into the Mexican empire of Augustin Iturbide (1822-23). From 1823 to 1839 Guatemala was a constituent state of the Central American Republic. Upon dissolution of that confederation, Guatemala proclaimed itself an independent republic. Like El Salvador, Guatemala suffered from internal strife between right-wing, US-backed military government and leftist indigenous peoples from ca. 1954 to ca. 1997.

MINT MARKS

H, (H) - Heaton, Birmingham
(KN) – Birmingham, King's Norton Mint
(L) – London, Royal Mint
(P) – Philadelphia, USA
NG - ??? 1992
(S) – San Francisco, USA

REPUBLIC

STANDARD COINAGE

8 Reales = 1 Peso

KM# 175 1/4 REAL

Copper-Nickel **Obv:** Sun above three mountains **Rev:** Denomination within wreath, 5 stars below **Note:** Medal rotation.

Date	Mintage	F	VF	XF	Unc	BU
1901H	5,056,000	0.25	0.45	1.00	2.50	—

KM# 176 1/2 REAL (Medio)

Copper-Nickel **Obv:** Justice seated left **Rev:** Quetzal with scroll and weapons within thick wreath **Note:** Medal rotation.

Date	Mintage	F	VF	XF	Unc	BU
1901(H)	6,652,000	0.35	0.65	1.25	2.75	—

KM# 177 REAL

Copper-Nickel, 21 mm. **Obv:** Justice seated left **Rev:** National arms, thick wreath **Note:** Medal rotation.

Date	Mintage	F	VF	XF	Unc	BU
1901(H)	7,388,000	0.20	0.35	1.20	4.00	—
1910(H)	4,000,000	0.25	0.40	1.25	5.00	—
1911(H)	2,000,000	0.25	0.45	1.35	5.00	—
1912(H)	8,000,000	0.20	0.35	1.00	3.00	—

PROVISIONAL COINAGE

1915-1923

KM# 230 12-1/2 CENTAVOS

Copper **Obv:** Word at center divides flower **Rev:** Denomination within circle

Date	Mintage	F	VF	XF	Unc	BU
1915	6,000,000	0.75	1.25	3.50	12.50	—

KM# 231 25 CENTAVOS

Copper **Obv:** Word at center divides flower **Rev:** Denomination within circle

Date	Mintage	F	VF	XF	Unc	BU
1915	4,000,000	0.75	1.25	5.00	15.00	—

KM# 232.1 50 CENTAVOS

Aluminum-Bronze **Obv:** Flower design **Rev:** Denomination within circle **Note:** Thin numerals in denomination.

Date	Mintage	F	VF	XF	Unc	BU
1922	3,803,000	0.80	1.50	5.50	17.50	—

KM# 232.2 50 CENTAVOS

Aluminum-Bronze **Obv:** Flower design **Rev:** Denomination within circle **Note:** Thick numerals in denomination.

Date	Mintage	F	VF	XF	Unc	BU
1922	Inc. above	0.80	1.50	5.50	17.50	—

KM# 233 PESO

Aluminum-Bronze **Subject:** Miguel Garcia Granados **Obv:** Bust left **Rev:** Denomination

Date	Mintage	F	VF	XF	Unc	BU
1923	1,477,000	1.50	2.50	8.50	28.00	—

KM# 234 5 PESOS

Aluminum-Bronze **Subject:** Justo Rufino Barrios **Obv:** Bust right **Rev:** Denomination

Date	Mintage	F	VF	XF	Unc	BU
1923	440,000	2.00	4.00	16.00	48.00	—

KM# 234a 5 PESOS

Copper **Subject:** Justo Rufino Barrios **Obv:** Bust right **Rev:** Denomination

Date	Mintage	F	VF	XF	Unc	BU
1923	Inc. above	2.00	4.00	16.00	48.00	—

REFORM COINAGE

100 Centavos = 1 Quetzal

KM# 248.1 1/2 CENTAVO (Medio)

Brass **Obv:** National arms **Rev:** Denomination

Date	Mintage	F	VF	XF	Unc	BU
1932(L)	6,000,000	0.15	0.50	2.00	5.00	—
1932(L) Proof	—	Value: 200				

KM# 248.2 1/2 CENTAVO (Medio)

Brass **Obv:** National arms **Rev:** Denomination, center dot

Date	Mintage	F	VF	XF	Unc	BU
1946	640,000	0.75	1.75	3.75	15.00	—

KM# 237 CENTAVO (Un)

Copper **Obv:** Incuse legend on scroll **Rev:** Denomination

Date	Mintage	F	VF	XF	Unc	BU
1925	357,000	4.50	7.50	20.00	40.00	—

KM# 237a CENTAVO (Un)

Bronze **Obv:** National arms **Rev:** Denomination

Date	Mintage	F	VF	XF	Unc	BU
1925	Inc. above	5.00	8.00	15.00	40.00	—

KM# 247 CENTAVO (Un)

Copper **Obv:** National arms **Rev:** Denomination

Date	Mintage	F	VF	XF	Unc	BU
1929(L)	500,000	2.00	3.00	8.00	25.00	—
1929(L) Proof	—	—	—	—	—	—

KM# 249 CENTAVO (Un)

Brass, 20.3 mm. **Obv:** National arms **Rev:** Denomination

Date	Mintage	F	VF	XF	Unc	BU
1932(L)	3,000,000	0.40	1.00	350	11.50	—
1932(L) Proof	—	—	—	—	—	—
1933(L)	1,500,000	0.60	1.50	4.50	12.50	—
1933(L) Proof	—	—	—	—	—	—
1934(L)	1,000,000	0.50	1.25	4.50	12.50	—
1934(L) Proof	—	—	—	—	—	—
1936(L)	1,500,000	0.40	1.00	4.50	12.50	—
1936(L) Proof	—	—	—	—	—	—
1938/7(L)	1,000,000	0.40	1.00	5.00	14.00	—
1938(L)	Inc. above	0.40	1.00	4.50	12.50	—
1938(L) Proof	—	—	—	—	—	—
1939(L)	1,500,000	0.50	1.25	4.50	10.00	—
1939(L) Proof	—	—	—	—	—	—
1946	539,000	—	0.15	0.75	6.00	—
1947	1,121,000	—	0.15	0.35	3.50	—
1948	1,651,000	—	0.15	0.35	4.50	—
1949	1,022,000	—	0.15	0.45	5.00	—

KM# 251 CENTAVO (Un)

3.0000 g., Brass, 20 mm. **Obv:** Bird with shield above date **Rev:** Branch right of denomination

Date	Mintage	F	VF	XF	Unc	BU
1943(P)	450,000	3.00	6.00	10.00	30.00	—
1944(S)	2,049,999	0.50	1.25	2.50	8.00	—

KM# 254 CENTAVO (Un)

Brass, 22 mm. **Subject:** Fray Bartolome de las Casas **Obv:** National arms **Rev:** Bust left

Date	Mintage	F	VF	XF	Unc	BU
1949	1,091,000	—	0.15	0.35	5.00	—
1950	3,663,000	—	0.15	0.25	1.75	—
1951	3,586,000	—	0.25	5.00	25.00	—
1952	1,445,000	—	0.15	0.30	20.00	—
1953	2,214,000	—	0.15	0.25	5.00	—
1954	1,455,000	—	0.15	0.30	2.25	—

KM# 259 CENTAVO (Un)

2.9400 g., Nickel-Brass, 21 mm. **Subject:** Fray Bartolome de las Casas **Obv:** National arms **Rev:** Larger bust left

Date	Mintage	F	VF	XF	Unc	BU
1954(KN)	10,000,000	—	—	0.15	3.00	—
1957(KN)	1,600,000	—	0.15	0.25	1.00	—
1958(KN)	2,000,000	—	0.15	0.25	2.00	—

KM# 260 CENTAVO (Un)

2.9900 g., Brass, 21 mm. **Subject:** Fray Bartolome de las Casas **Obv:** National arms **Rev:** Bust left **Note:** Larger obverse lettering

Date	Mintage	F	VF	XF	Unc	BU
1958	10,001,000	—	—	0.15	2.00	—
1961	1,826,000	—	—	0.15	1.00	—
1963	4,926,000	—	—	0.15	1.00	—
1964	4,280,000	—	—	0.15	1.00	—

KM# 265 CENTAVO (Un)

2.4500 g., Brass, 19 mm. **Subject:** Fray Bartolome de las Casas **Obv:** National arms **Rev:** Bust left **Note:** Size reduced. Varieties in size and style of date exist.

Date	Mintage	F	VF	XF	Unc	BU
1965	3,845,000	—	—	0.15	1.00	—
1966	6,100,000	—	—	0.15	1.00	—
1967	6,400,000	—	—	0.15	1.00	—
1968	2,590,000	—	—	0.15	1.00	—
1969	13,780,000	—	—	0.15	1.00	—
1970	10,511,000	—	—	0.15	1.00	—

KM# 273 CENTAVO (Un)

2.4400 g., Brass **Subject:** Fray Bartolome de las Casas **Obv:** National arms **Rev:** Bust left **Note:** Smaller date and lettering.

Date	Mintage	F	VF	XF	Unc	BU
1972	11,500,000	—	—	0.15	0.25	—
1973	12,000,000	—	—	0.15	0.25	—

KM# 275.1 CENTAVO (Un)

2.4700 g., Brass, 19.1 mm. **Subject:** Fray Bartolome de las Casas **Obv:** National arms **Rev:** Bust left, larger head **Note:** Larger date and lettering; no dots left and right of date.

Date	Mintage	F	VF	XF	Unc	BU
1974	10,000,000	—	—	0.15	0.25	—
1975	15,000,000	—	—	0.15	0.25	—
1976	15,230,000	—	—	0.15	0.25	—
1977	30,000,000	—	—	0.15	0.25	—
1978	30,000,000	—	—	0.15	0.25	—
1979	30,000,000	—	—	0.15	0.25	—

KM# 275.2 CENTAVO (Un)

2.5500 g., Brass, 18 mm. **Obv:** National arms **Rev:** Bust left, smaller head **Note:** Smaller legend and date. Dots left and right of date

Date	Mintage	F	VF	XF	Unc	BU
1979	Inc. above	—	—	0.15	0.25	—
1980	20,000,000	—	—	0.15	0.25	—
1984	20,000,000	—	—	0.15	0.25	—

KM# 275.3 CENTAVO (Un)

2.5600 g., Brass, 18.97 mm. **Rev:** Fray Bartolome de las Casas, smaller head **Edge:** Plain **Note:** Smaller legend and date. Dots left and right of date.

Date	Mintage	F	VF	XF	Unc	BU
1985	—	—	—	0.15	0.25	—
1986	—	—	—	0.15	0.25	—
1987	50,000,000	—	—	0.15	0.25	—
1988	51,400,000	—	—	0.15	0.25	—
1989	—	—	—	0.15	0.25	—
1990	—	—	—	0.15	0.25	—
1991	—	—	—	0.15	0.25	—
1992	—	—	—	0.15	0.25	—

KM# 275.4 CENTAVO (Un)

Brass **Obv:** National arms, legend on scroll in relief **Rev:** Bust left **Note:** Varieties exist.

Date	Mintage	F	VF	XF	Unc	BU
1981	30,000,000	—	—	0.15	0.25	—
1982	30,000,000	—	—	0.15	0.25	—

KM# 275.5 CENTAVO (Un)

2.5500 g., Brass **Subject:** Fray Bartolome de las Casas **Obv:** National arms **Rev:** Head left, modified portrait

Date	Mintage	F	VF	XF	Unc	BU
1993	—	—	—	0.15	0.25	—
1994	—	—	—	0.15	0.25	—
1995	—	—	—	0.15	0.25	—

KM# 282 CENTAVO (Un)

0.8000 g., Aluminum, 18.92 mm. **Subject:** Fray Bartolome de las Casas **Obv:** National arms **Rev:** Bust left **Edge:** Plain **Shape:** 7-sided

Date	Mintage	F	VF	XF	Unc	BU
1999	—	—	—	0.15	0.25	—

KM# 250 2 CENTAVOS (Dos)

Brass **Obv:** National arms **Rev:** Denomination

Date	Mintage	F	VF	XF	Unc	BU
1932(L)	3,000,000	0.50	1.25	10.00	35.00	—
1932(L) Proof	—	—	—	—	—	—

KM# 252 2 CENTAVOS (Dos)

6.0000 g., Brass **Obv:** Bird with shield above date **Rev:** Branch right of denomination

Date	Mintage	F	VF	XF	Unc	BU
1943(P)	150,000	3.50	7.50	15.00	45.00	—
1944(S)	1,100,000	0.60	2.00	8.00	25.00	—

KM# 238.1 5 CENTAVOS

1.6667 g., 0.7200 Silver 0.0386 oz. ASW **Obv:** National arms **Rev:** Bird on pillar, engraver's initials 'JAC' below "Centavos"

Date	Mintage	F	VF	XF	Unc	BU
1925	573,000	3.00	5.75	15.00	35.00	—
1944	1,026,000	BV	1.25	5.00	15.00	—

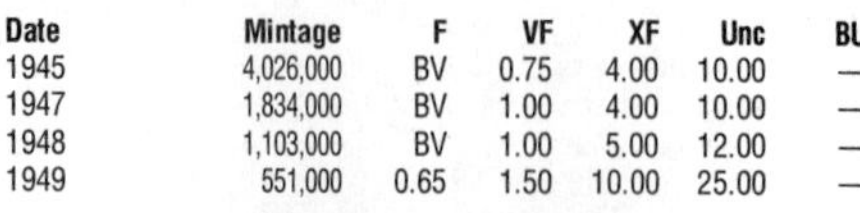

Date	Mintage	F	VF	XF	Unc	BU
1945	4,026,000	BV	0.75	4.00	10.00	—
1947	1,834,000	BV	1.00	4.00	10.00	—
1948	1,103,000	BV	1.00	5.00	12.00	—
1949	551,000	0.65	1.50	10.00	25.00	—

KM# 238.2 5 CENTAVOS

1.6667 g., 0.7200 Silver 0.0386 oz. ASW **Obv:** National arms, short-tailed quetzal **Rev:** Bird on pillar, without engraver's initials

Date	Mintage	F	VF	XF	Unc	BU
1928(L)	1,000,000	BV	1.00	10.00	35.00	—
1928(L) Proof	—	Value: 400				
1929(L)	1,000,000	BV	1.00	4.00	12.00	—
1929(L) Proof	—	—	—	—	—	—
1932(L)	2,000,000	BV	1.00	4.00	10.00	—
1932(L) Proof	—	—	—	—	—	—
1933(L)	600,000	BV	1.00	5.00	15.00	—
1933(L) Proof	—	—	—	—	—	—
1934(L)	1,200,000	BV	1.00	4.00	10.00	—
1934(L) Proof	—	—	—	—	—	—
1937(L)	400,000	BV	1.00	4.00	10.00	—
1937(L) Proof	—	—	—	—	—	—
1938(L)	300,000	0.65	1.50	5.00	15.00	—
1938(L) Proof	—	—	—	—	—	—
1943(P)	900,000	BV	0.75	4.00	10.00	—

KM# 255 5 CENTAVOS

1.6667 g., 0.7200 Silver 0.0386 oz. ASW **Obv:** National arms **Rev:** Kapok tree **Note:** Varieties exist with and without dashes.

Date	Mintage	F	VF	XF	Unc	BU
1949	305,000	0.65	1.50	7.00	25.00	—

KM# 257.1 5 CENTAVOS

1.6667 g., 0.7200 Silver 0.0386 oz. ASW **Obv:** National arms **Rev:** Kapok tree

Date	Mintage	F	VF	XF	Unc	BU
1950	453,000	BV	1.00	4.00	10.00	—
1951	1,032,000	BV	1.00	2.00	8.00	—
1952	913,000	BV	1.00	2.00	7.00	—
1953	447,000	BV	1.00	2.00	7.00	—
1954	520,000	BV	1.00	3.00	9.00	—
1955	2,061,999	BV	1.00	1.50	3.00	—
1956	1,301,000	BV	1.00	1.50	3.00	—
1957	2,941,000	BV	1.00	1.50	2.50	—

SMALL DATE

LARGE DATE

KM# 257.2 5 CENTAVOS

1.6670 g., 0.7200 Silver 0.0386 oz. ASW **Obv:** National arms **Rev:** Kapok tree **Note:** Small crude date and large crude dates.

Date	Mintage	F	VF	XF	Unc	BU
1958 Small date	3,025,000	BV	0.75	1.00	2.50	—
1958 Large date	Inc. above	BV	1.00	1.75	3.50	—
1959	232,000	BV	1.00	1.50	2.00	—

KM# 257.3 5 CENTAVOS

1.6670 g., 0.7200 Silver 0.0386 oz. ASW **Obv:** National arm, short-tailed quetzal **Obv. Legend:** Kapok tree

Date	Mintage	F	VF	XF	Unc	BU
1958 Small date	—	BV	1.00	1.75	3.50	—
1958 Large date	—	BV	1.00	1.75	3.50	—

KM# 261 5 CENTAVOS

1.6670 g., 0.7200 Silver 0.0386 oz. ASW **Obv:** National arms **Rev:** Kapok tree, level ground

Date	Mintage	F	VF	XF	Unc	BU
1960	4,770,000	—	BV	0.65	1.25	—
1961	6,756,000	—	BV	0.65	1.25	—
1964	1,529,000	—	BV	0.65	1.25	—

KM# 266.1 5 CENTAVOS

Copper-Nickel, 16 mm. **Obv:** National arms **Rev:** Kapok tree **Note:** Coins Dated 1965 are smaller with curved tails in the "9" & "6", while dates for 1967-1970 have straight tails in the "9" & "6".

Date	Mintage	F	VF	XF	Unc	BU
1965 Small date	1,642,000	—	0.15	0.50	4.00	—
1967 Large date	2,800,000	—	—	0.15	0.35	—
1968 Large date	4,030,000	—	—	0.15	0.35	—
1969 Large date	7,210,000	—	—	0.15	0.35	—
1970 Large date	8,121,000	—	—	0.15	0.35	—

KM# 266.2 5 CENTAVOS

Copper-Nickel, 16 mm. **Obv:** National arms, dashes before and after legend **Rev:** Kapok tree **Note:** Coins dates 1966 are smaller with curved tails in the "9" & "6".

Date	Mintage	F	VF	XF	Unc	BU
1966 Small date	3,600,000	—	—	0.15	0.35	—

KM# 270 5 CENTAVOS

1.6000 g., Copper-Nickel, 16 mm. **Obv:** Legend on scroll incuse, small shield and quetzal **Obv. Legend:** Kapok tree

Date	Mintage	F	VF	XF	Unc	BU
1971	8,270,000	—	—	0.15	0.35	—
1974	10,575,000	—	—	0.15	0.35	—
1975	10,000,000	—	—	0.15	0.35	—
1976	6,000,000	—	—	0.15	0.35	—
1977	20,000,000	—	—	0.15	0.35	—

KM# 276.1 5 CENTAVOS

Copper-Nickel, 16 mm. **Obv:** National arms, large shield and quetzal **Rev:** Kapok tree

Date	Mintage	F	VF	XF	Unc	BU
1977	Inc. above	—	—	0.15	0.35	—
1978	15,000,000	—	—	0.15	0.30	—
1979	12,000,000	—	—	0.15	0.30	—

KM# 276.2 5 CENTAVOS

Copper-Nickel, 16 mm. **Obv:** Legend on scroll in relief **Rev:** Kapok tree

Date	Mintage	F	VF	XF	Unc	BU
1980	8,000,000	—	—	0.15	0.30	—

KM# 276.3 5 CENTAVOS

Copper-Nickel, 16 mm. **Obv:** National arms **Rev:** Kapok tee modified

Date	Mintage	F	VF	XF	Unc	BU
1981	8,000,000	—	—	0.15	0.30	—
1985	—	—	—	0.15	0.30	—

KM# 276.4 5 CENTAVOS

2.6900 g., Copper-Nickel, 16 mm. **Obv:** National arms, legend on scroll incuse **Obv. Legend:** REPUBLICA DE GUATEMALA • 1986 • **Rev:** Kapok tree smaller, less ground below **Edge:** Reeded **Note:** Varieties exist.

Date	Mintage	F	VF	XF	Unc	BU
1985	—	—	—	0.15	0.30	—
1986 Large date	—	—	—	0.15	0.30	—
1986 Small date	—	—	—	—	—	—
1987	25,000,000	—	—	0.15	0.30	—
1988	21,800,000	—	—	0.15	0.30	—
1989	—	—	—	0.15	0.30	—
1990	—	—	—	0.15	0.30	—
1991	—	—	—	0.15	0.30	—
1992	—	—	—	0.15	0.30	—
1993	—	—	—	0.15	0.30	—
1994	—	—	—	0.15	0.30	—
1996	—	—	—	0.15	0.30	—
1998	—	—	—	0.15	0.30	—

KM# 276.5 5 CENTAVOS

Copper-Nickel, 16 mm. **Obv:** National arms, smaller lettering **Rev:** Kapok tree

Date	Mintage	F	VF	XF	Unc	BU
1995	—	—	—	0.15	0.30	—

KM# 276.6 5 CENTAVOS

1.6000 g., Copper-Nickel, 16 mm. **Obv:** National arms, smaller sized emblem, no dots by date **Obv. Legend:** REPUBLICA DE GUATEMALA 1997 **Rev:** Kapok tree center, value at right, ground below **Note:** Varieties exist.

Date	Mintage	F	VF	XF	Unc	BU
1997	—	—	—	0.15	0.30	—
1998	—	—	—	0.15	0.30	—
2000	—	—	—	0.15	0.30	—

KM# 239.1 10 CENTAVOS

3.3333 g., 0.7200 Silver 0.0772 oz. ASW **Obv:** National arms **Rev:** Bird on engraved pillar, engraver's initials below "CENTAVOS" **Note:** Varieties exist.

Date	Mintage	F	VF	XF	Unc	BU
1925	573,000	3.50	6.50	15.00	35.00	—
1944	155,000	1.25	3.50	10.00	20.00	—
1945	1,499,000	BV	1.25	2.00	5.00	—
1947	471,000	BV	1.50	3.00	10.00	—
1948	324,000	BV	1.50	2.00	7.00	—
1949	145,000	BV	2.00	4.50	10.00	—

KM# 239.2 10 CENTAVOS

3.3333 g., 0.7200 Silver 0.0772 oz. ASW **Obv:** National arms, short-tailed quetzal **Rev:** Bird on engraved pillar, without engraver's initials

Date	Mintage	F	VF	XF	Unc	BU
1928(L)	500,000	BV	2.50	5.00	30.00	—
1928(L) Proof	—	Value: 250				
1929(L)	500,000	BV	2.00	3.50	25.00	—
1929(L) Proof	—	—	—	—	—	—
1932(L)	500,000	BV	2.00	3.50	15.00	—
1932(L) Proof	—	—	—	—	—	—
1933(L)	650,000	BV	1.75	3.00	18.00	—
1933(L) Proof	—	—	—	—	—	—
1934(L)	300,000	BV	1.75	3.00	18.00	—
1934(L) Proof	—	—	—	—	—	—
1936(L)	200,000	BV	2.50	6.00	20.00	—
1936(L) Proof	—	—	—	—	—	—
1938(L)	150,000	1.25	3.00	6.00	18.00	—
1938(L) Proof	—	—	—	—	—	—
1943(P)	600,000	BV	1.25	3.00	10.00	—

KM# 239.3 10 CENTAVOS

3.3333 g., 0.7200 Silver 0.0772 oz. ASW **Obv:** National arms **Rev:** Quetzal on pillar, with engraver's initials **Note:** Mintage included above, in KM#239.1. Varieties exist.

Date	Mintage	F	VF	XF	Unc	BU
1947	—	BV	3.00	4.00	10.00	—

KM# 256.1 10 CENTAVOS

3.3333 g., 0.7200 Silver 0.0772 oz. ASW **Obv:** National arms **Rev:** Small monolith

Date	Mintage	F	VF	XF	Unc	BU
1949	281,000	BV	2.50	5.00	15.00	—
1950	550,000	BV	1.50	3.00	7.00	—
1951	263,000	BV	2.50	5.00	15.00	—
1952	307,000	BV	1.50	3.00	7.00	—
1953	388,000	BV	1.50	3.00	7.00	—
1955	896,000	BV	1.50	3.00	7.00	—
1956	501,000	BV	1.50	5.00	15.00	—
1958	1,528,000	BV	1.50	3.00	8.00	—

KM# 256.2 10 CENTAVOS
3.3333 g., 0.7200 Silver 0.0772 oz. ASW **Obv:** National arms **Rev:** Larger monolith

Date	Mintage	F	VF	XF	Unc	BU
1957	1,123,000	BV	1.25	2.00	3.00	—
1958	Inc. above	BV	1.50	2.50	5.00	—
1958	Inc. above	6.00	12.00	22.50	40.00	—

Note: Medallic die alignment

KM# 256.3 10 CENTAVOS
3.3333 g., 0.7200 Silver 0.0772 oz. ASW **Obv:** National arms **Rev:** Small monolith

Date	Mintage	F	VF	XF	Unc	BU
1958	Inc. above	BV	1.25	2.00	3.00	—
1959	461,000	BV	1.25	2.00	3.00	—
1959	Inc. above	6.00	12.00	22.50	37.50	—

Note: Medallic die alignment

KM# 262 10 CENTAVOS
3.3333 g., 0.7200 Silver 0.0772 oz. ASW **Obv:** National arms **Rev:** Monolith

Date	Mintage	F	VF	XF	Unc	BU
1960	1,743,000	BV	1.50	2.00	2.50	—
1961	2,647,000	BV	1.50	2.00	2.50	—
1964	965,000	BV	1.50	2.00	2.50	—

KM# 267 10 CENTAVOS
2.8500 g., Copper-Nickel, 21 mm. **Obv:** National arms **Rev:** Monolith **Note:** Varieties of curved and straight "9" in date exist.

Date	Mintage	F	VF	XF	Unc	BU
1965	2,227,000	—	0.15	0.25	0.75	—
1966	1,550,000	—	0.15	0.35	0.85	—
1967	3,120,000	—	0.15	0.25	0.75	—
1968	3,220,000	—	0.15	0.25	0.75	—
1969	3,530,000	—	0.15	0.25	0.75	—
1970	4,153,000	—	0.15	0.25	0.75	—

KM# 271.1 10 CENTAVOS
Copper-Nickel, 21 mm. **Obv:** National arms, small wreath **Rev:** Monolith

Date	Mintage	F	VF	XF	Unc	BU
1971	4,580,000	—	0.15	0.25	0.75	—

KM# 271.2 10 CENTAVOS
Copper-Nickel, 21 mm. **Obv:** National arms, large wreath **Rev:** Monolith

Date	Mintage	F	VF	XF	Unc	BU
1971	Inc. above	—	0.15	0.25	0.75	—
1973	—	—	0.15	0.25	0.75	—

KM# 274 10 CENTAVOS
3.1700 g., Copper-Nickel, 21 mm. **Obv:** National arms **Rev:** Monolith

Date	Mintage	F	VF	XF	Unc	BU
1974	3,500,000	—	0.15	0.25	0.75	—
1975 Dots flank date	6,000,000	—	0.15	0.25	0.75	—

KM# 277.1 10 CENTAVOS
Copper-Nickel, 21 mm. **Obv:** National arms **Rev:** Monolith **Note:** Wide rim toothed border.

Date	Mintage	F	VF	XF	Unc	BU
1976	2,000,000	—	0.15	0.25	0.75	—
1977	5,000,000	—	0.15	0.25	0.75	—

KM# 277.2 10 CENTAVOS
Copper-Nickel, 21 mm. **Obv:** National arms **Rev:** Monolith **Note:** Round beads instead of toothed border.

Date	Mintage	F	VF	XF	Unc	BU
1978	8,500,000	—	0.15	0.25	0.75	—
1979	11,000,000	—	0.15	0.25	0.75	—

KM# 277.3 10 CENTAVOS
Copper-Nickel, 21 mm. **Obv:** Legend on scroll in relief, quetzal in silhouette **Rev:** Monolith, front view

Date	Mintage	F	VF	XF	Unc	BU
1980	5,000,000	—	0.15	0.25	0.75	—
1981	4,000,000	—	0.15	0.25	0.75	—

KM# 277.4 10 CENTAVOS
3.1400 g., Copper-Nickel, 21 mm. **Obv:** Quetzal is solid **Rev:** Monolith, larger

Date	Mintage	F	VF	XF	Unc	BU
1983	20,000,000	—	0.15	0.25	0.75	—
1986	—	—	0.15	0.25	0.75	—

KM# 277.5 10 CENTAVOS
3.2000 g., Copper-Nickel, 21 mm. **Obv:** National arms **Rev:** Monolith, larger **Note:** Varieties exist with fine and coarse characters.

Date	Mintage	F	VF	XF	Unc	BU
1986	—	—	0.15	0.25	0.75	—
1987	17,000,000	—	0.15	0.25	0.75	—
1988	13,250,000	—	0.15	0.25	0.75	—
1989	—	—	0.15	0.25	0.75	—
1990	—	—	0.15	0.25	0.75	—
1991	—	—	0.15	0.25	0.75	—
1992	—	—	0.15	0.25	0.75	—
1993	—	—	0.15	0.25	0.75	—
1994	—	—	0.15	0.25	0.75	—

KM# 277.6 10 CENTAVOS
3.2000 g., Copper-Nickel, 21 mm. **Obv:** National arms **Obv. Legend:** Smaller letters in REPUBLICA DE GUATEMALA **Rev:** Monolith **Note:** Varieties exist.

Date	Mintage	F	VF	XF	Unc	BU
1995	—	—	0.15	0.25	0.75	—
1996	—	—	0.15	0.25	0.75	—
1997	—	—	0.15	0.25	0.75	—
1998	—	—	0.15	0.25	0.75	—
2000	—	—	0.15	0.25	0.75	—

KM# 240.1 1/4 QUETZAL
8.3333 g., 0.7200 Silver 0.1929 oz. ASW **Obv:** National arms **Rev:** Quetzal on pillar **Edge:** Lettered

Date	Mintage	F	VF	XF	Unc	BU
1925(P)	1,160,000	4.50	9.00	25.00	50.00	75.00

KM# 240.2 1/4 QUETZAL
8.3333 g., 0.7200 Silver 0.1929 oz. ASW **Obv:** National arms, without NOBLES below scroll **Rev:** Quetzal atop engraved pillar

Date	Mintage	F	VF	XF	Unc	BU
1925 (P)	Inc. above	37.50	75.00	175	400	—

KM# 243.1 1/4 QUETZAL
8.3333 g., 0.7200 Silver 0.1929 oz. ASW, 27 mm. **Obv:** National arms **Rev:** Quetzal on pillar, larger design **Edge Lettering:** REPUBLICA DE GUATEMALA AMERICA CENTRAL

Date	Mintage	F	VF	XF	Unc	BU
1926(L)	2,000,000	3.00	6.00	15.00	65.00	—
1926(L) Proof	—	—	—	—	—	—
1928(L)	400,000	3.50	5.50	10.00	55.00	70.00
1928(L) Proof	—	—	—	—	—	—
1929(L)	400,000	3.50	6.00	12.50	45.00	55.00
1929(L) Proof	—	—	—	—	—	—

KM# 243.2 1/4 QUETZAL
8.3333 g., 0.7200 Silver 0.1929 oz. ASW, 27 mm. **Obv:** National arms **Rev:** Quetzal atop engraved pillar **Edge:** Reeded

Date	Mintage	F	VF	XF	Unc	BU
1946	203,000	3.50	6.50	13.50	22.00	30.00
1947	134,000	4.00	8.00	12.50	20.00	30.00
1948	129,000	4.00	7.50	12.00	20.00	30.00
1949/8	25,000	5.25	10.00	16.50	30.00	40.00
1949	Inc. above	12.50	27.50	55.00	100	—

KM# 253 25 CENTAVOS
8.3333 g., 0.7200 Silver 0.1929 oz. ASW, 27 mm. **Obv:** Quetzal and map of the state **Rev:** Government buildings

Date	Mintage	F	VF	XF	Unc	BU
1943(P)	900,000	3.00	6.00	12.00	45.00	55.00

Note: 150,000 of total mintage struck in 1943, remainder struck in 1944

KM# 258 25 CENTAVOS
8.3333 g., 0.7200 Silver 0.1929 oz. ASW, 27 mm. **Obv:** National arms **Rev:** Head left **Note:** Denticulated rims.

Date	Mintage	F	VF	XF	Unc	BU
1950	81,000	3.50	6.00	12.00	30.00	40.00
1951	11,000	8.50	17.50	27.50	70.00	80.00
1952	112,000	BV	3.50	7.00	15.00	25.00

Date	Mintage	F	VF	XF	Unc	BU
1954	246,000	BV	3.50	6.00	12.00	17.50
1955	409,000	BV	3.50	6.00	12.00	17.50
1956	342,000	BV	3.50	6.00	12.00	17.50
1957	257,000	BV	3.25	5.50	10.00	14.00
1958	394,000	BV	3.25	5.50	10.00	14.00
1959/8	277,000	BV	3.25	5.50	10.00	14.00
1959	Inc. above	BV	3.50	6.50	12.50	20.00

KM# 263 25 CENTAVOS
8.3333 g., 0.7200 Silver 0.1929 oz. ASW, 27 mm.

Date	Mintage	F	VF	XF	Unc	BU
1960	560,000	BV	2.75	3.25	6.00	—
1960	Inc. above	20.00	50.00	100	175	—

Note: Planchet size and weight vary in 1960 type as well as density of reeding; Medallic die alignment

Date	Mintage	F	VF	XF	Unc	BU
1961	750,000	BV	2.75	3.25	6.00	—
1962	—	—	BV	3.25	6.00	—
1963	1,100,000	—	BV	3.00	5.50	—
1964	299,000	BV	2.75	3.25	6.00	—

KM# 268 25 CENTAVOS
8.0500 g., Copper-Nickel, 27 mm. **Obv:** National arms **Rev:** Head left **Edge Lettering:** REPUBLICA DE GUATEMALA C. A.

Date	Mintage	F	VF	XF	Unc	BU
1965	1,178,000	0.15	0.25	0.60	1.75	—
1966	910,000	0.15	0.25	0.60	1.75	—

KM# 269 25 CENTAVOS
Copper-Nickel, 27 mm. **Obv:** National arms **Rev:** Head left, modified design **Edge Lettering:** REPUBLICA DE GUATEMALA C. A.

Date	Mintage	F	VF	XF	Unc	BU
1967 Small date	1,140,000	0.15	0.25	0.60	1.75	—
1968 Medium date	1,540,000	0.15	0.25	0.60	1.50	—
1969 Large date	2,069,000	0.15	0.25	0.60	1.50	—
1970 Large date	2,501,000	0.15	0.25	0.60	1.50	—

KM# 272 25 CENTAVOS
Copper-Nickel, 27 mm. **Obv:** Smaller arms, legend on scroll incuse **Rev:** Head left

Date	Mintage	F	VF	XF	Unc	BU
1971	2,850,000	0.15	0.25	0.50	1.00	—
1975	1,592,000	0.15	0.25	0.50	1.00	—
1976	2,000,000	0.15	0.25	0.50	1.00	—

KM# 278.1 25 CENTAVOS
7.9000 g., Copper-Nickel, 27 mm. **Obv:** National arms **Rev:** Large head left

Date	Mintage	F	VF	XF	Unc	BU
1977	2,000,000	0.15	0.25	0.65	1.25	—
1978	4,400,000	0.15	0.25	0.45	1.00	—
1979	5,400,000	0.15	0.25	0.45	1.00	—

KM# 278.2 25 CENTAVOS
Copper-Nickel, 27 mm. **Obv:** National arms, legend on scroll in relief **Rev:** Small head left **Note:** Wide rim

Date	Mintage	F	VF	XF	Unc	BU
1981	1,600,000	0.15	0.25	0.50	1.00	—

KM# 278.4 25 CENTAVOS
Copper-Nickel, 27 mm. **Obv:** National arms, quetzal is solid **Rev:** Head left **Note:** Narrow rim.

Date	Mintage	F	VF	XF	Unc	BU
1982	2,000,000	0.15	0.25	0.50	1.00	—

KM# 278.3 25 CENTAVOS
Copper-Nickel, 27 mm. **Obv:** National arms, legend on scroll incuse **Rev:** Small head left

Date	Mintage	F	VF	XF	Unc	BU
1984	2,000,000	0.15	0.25	0.50	1.00	—

KM# 278.5 25 CENTAVOS
8.0300 g., Copper-Nickel, 27 mm. **Obv:** National arms **Rev:** Large head left **Edge Lettering:** REPUBLICA DE GUATEMALA C. A. **Note:** Varieties exist in number of wing feathers and details on head.

Date	Mintage	F	VF	XF	Unc	BU
1985	—	0.15	0.25	0.35	0.85	—
1986	—	0.15	0.25	0.35	0.85	—
1987	13,316,000	0.15	0.25	0.35	0.85	—
1988	6,600,000	0.15	0.25	0.35	0.85	—
1989	—	0.15	0.25	0.35	0.85	—
1990	—	0.15	0.25	0.35	0.85	—
1991	—	0.15	0.25	0.35	0.85	—
1992	—	0.15	0.25	0.35	0.85	—
1993	—	0.15	0.25	0.35	0.85	—
1994	—	0.15	0.25	0.35	0.85	—
1995	—	0.15	0.25	0.35	0.85	—

KM# 278.6 25 CENTAVOS
8.0900 g., Copper-Nickel, 27 mm. **Obv:** Smaller design with wider rims **Rev:** Head left, smaller design with wider rims **Edge Lettering:** REPUBLICA DE GUATEMALA CA **Note:** Varieties exist.

Date	Mintage	F	VF	XF	Unc	BU
1996	—	0.15	0.25	0.35	0.85	—
1997	—	0.15	0.25	0.35	0.85	—
1998	—	0.15	0.25	0.35	0.85	—

KM# 264 50 CENTAVOS
12.0000 g., 0.7200 Silver 0.2778 oz. ASW, 30.95 mm. **Obv:** National arms **Rev:** Whitenun orchid (lycaste skinneri var. alba) **Rev. Legend:** MONJA BLANCA FLOR NACIONAL **Edge:** Reeded

Date	Mintage	F	VF	XF	Unc	BU
1962	1,983,000	—	BV	3.00	6.00	9.00

Date	Mintage	F	VF	XF	Unc	BU
1963/2	350,000	3.50	7.50	12.50	20.00	25.00
1963	Inc. above	—	—	3.00	6.00	9.00

KM# 283 50 CENTAVOS
5.5400 g., Brass, 24.2 mm. **Obv:** National arms **Rev:** Whitenun orchid (lycaste skinneri var. alba orchidaceae) **Edge:** Reeded

Date	Mintage	F	VF	XF	Unc	BU
1998	—	—	—	0.50	1.25	1.75
2001	—	—	—	0.50	1.25	1.75

KM# 241.1 1/2 QUETZAL
16.6667 g., 0.7200 Silver 0.3858 oz. ASW **Obv:** National arms **Rev:** Quetzal on engraved pillar

Date	Mintage	F	VF	XF	Unc	BU
1925(P)	400,000	18.50	30.00	65.00	225	300

KM# 241.2 1/2 QUETZAL
16.6667 g., 0.7200 Silver 0.3858 oz. ASW **Obv:** Without NOBLES below scroll **Rev:** Quetzal on pillar

Date	Mintage	F	VF	XF	Unc	BU
1925 (P)	Inc. above	70.00	120	250	550	—

KM# 242 QUETZAL
33.3333 g., 0.7200 Silver 0.7716 oz. ASW **Obv:** National arms **Rev:** Quetzal on engraved pillar

Date	Mintage	F	VF	XF	Unc	BU
1925(P)	Est. 10,000	475	675	1,150	2,200	—

Note: 7,000 pieces were withdrawn and remelted in 1927 and 1928. Of those remaining, an additonal unknown quantity was melted in 1932, leaving somewhat less than 3000 survivors of this type.

KM# 284 QUETZAL
11.1000 g., Brass, 28.9 mm. **Obv:** National arms **Rev:** PAZ above stylized dove **Edge:** Reeded

Date	Mintage	F	VF	XF	Unc	BU
1999	—	—	—	1.00	2.50	3.00
2000 Small letters	—	—	—	1.00	2.50	3.00
2001 Small letters	—	—	—	1.00	2.50	3.00

KM# 244 5 QUETZALES
8.3592 g., 0.9000 Gold 0.2419 oz. AGW **Obv:** National arms **Rev:** Quetzal atop engraved pillar

Date	Mintage	F	VF	XF	Unc	BU
1926(P)	48,000	BV	225	275	350	—

KM# 245 10 QUETZALES
16.7185 g., 0.9000 Gold 0.4837 oz. AGW **Obv:** National arms **Rev:** Quetzal atop engraved pillar

Date	Mintage	F	VF	XF	Unc	BU
1926(P)	18,000	BV	460	500	750	—

KM# 246 20 QUETZALES
33.4370 g., 0.9000 Gold 0.9675 oz. AGW **Obv:** National arms **Rev:** Quetzal atop engraved pillar

Date	Mintage	F	VF	XF	Unc	BU
1926(P)	49,000	BV	BV	900	1,100	—

GUERNSEY

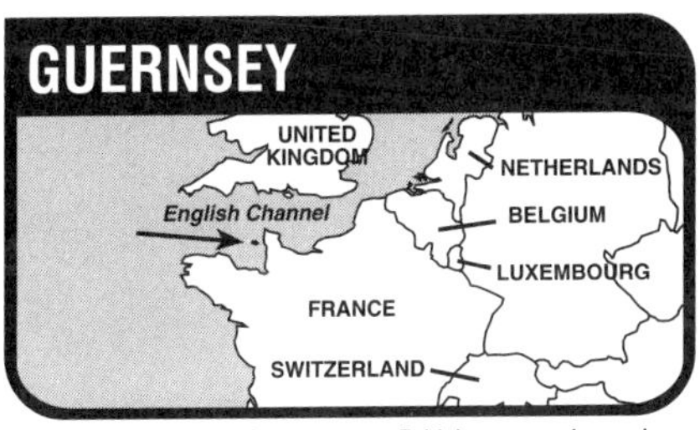

The Bailiwick of Guernsey, a British crown dependency located in the English Channel 30 miles (48 km.) west of Normandy, France, has an area of 30 sq. mi. (194 sq. km.)(including the isles of Alderney, Jethou, Herm, Brechou, and Sark), and a population of 54,000. Capital: St. Peter Port. Agriculture and cattle breeding are the main occupations.

Militant monks from the duchy of Normandy established the first permanent settlements on Guernsey prior to the Norman invasion of England, but the prevalence of prehistoric monuments suggests an earlier occupancy. The island, the only part of the duchy of Normandy belonging to the British crown, has been a possession of Britain since the Norman Conquest of 1066. During the Anglo-French wars, the harbors of Guernsey were employed in the building and out-fitting of ships for the English privateers preying on French shipping. Guernsey is administered by its own laws and customs. Unless the island is mentioned specifically, acts passed by the British Parliament are not applicable to Guernsey. During World War II, German troops occupied the island from June 30, 1940 till May 9,1945.

RULERS
British

MINT MARKS
H - Heaton, Birmingham

MONETARY SYSTEM
8 Doubles = 1 Penny
12 Pence = 1 Shilling
5 Shillings = 1 Crown
20 Shillings = 1 Pound

1 Stem

3 Stems

BRITISH DEPENDENCY

STANDARD COINAGE

KM# 10 DOUBLE
Bronze **Obv:** National arms **Rev:** Value, date

Date	Mintage	F	VF	XF	Unc	BU
1902H	84,000	0.25	0.60	2.50	6.00	—
1902H Proof	—	Value: 250				
1903H	112,000	0.25	0.50	2.25	5.00	—
1911H	45,000	0.50	1.50	4.00	12.00	—

KM# 11 DOUBLE
Bronze **Obv:** Arms **Rev:** Denomination above date

Date	Mintage	F	VF	XF	Unc	BU
1911H	90,000	0.30	1.20	3.00	10.00	—
1914H	45,000	1.50	3.00	6.00	12.00	—
1929H	79,000	0.30	0.85	2.50	5.50	—
1933H	96,000	0.30	0.85	2.50	5.50	—
1938H	96,000	0.30	0.85	2.50	5.50	—

KM# 9 2 DOUBLES
3.6200 g., Bronze, 22 mm. **Obv:** National arms **Rev:** Value, date

Date	Mintage	F	VF	XF	Unc	BU
1902H	18,000	4.50	9.00	18.00	30.00	—
1902H Proof	—	Value: 250				
1903H	18,000	6.00	12.50	22.00	35.00	—
1906H	18,000	6.00	12.50	22.00	35.00	—
1908H	18,000	6.00	12.50	22.00	35.00	—
1911H	29,000	4.50	9.00	15.00	27.50	—

KM# 12 2 DOUBLES
Bronzed Copper **Obv:** Arms **Rev:** Denomination above date

Date	Mintage	F	VF	XF	Unc	BU
1914H	29,000	4.50	9.00	18.50	27.50	—
1914H Proof	—	Value: 125				
1917H	15,000	20.00	35.00	70.00	155	—
1918H	57,000	1.25	2.50	9.00	15.00	—
1920H	57,000	1.25	2.50	9.00	15.00	—
1929H	79,000	0.35	1.25	6.00	10.00	—

KM# 5 4 DOUBLES
4.8400 g., Bronze, 26.10 mm. **Obv:** National arms **Rev:** Value, date **Note:** Varieties exist.

Date	Mintage	F	VF	XF	Unc	BU
1902H	105,000	1.50	3.00	5.00	22.00	—
1902H Proof	—	Value: 250				
1903H	52,000	1.50	3.00	9.00	25.00	—
1906H	52,000	1.50	3.00	9.00	25.00	—
1908H	26,000	3.00	7.50	15.00	30.00	—
1910H	52,000	1.50	3.00	9.00	25.00	—
1910H Proof	—	Value: 250				
1911H	52,000	2.25	4.50	13.50	27.50	—

KM# 13 4 DOUBLES
4.7600 g., Bronze **Obv:** Arms **Rev:** Denomination above date

Date	Mintage	F	VF	XF	Unc	BU
1914H	209,000	0.75	1.50	4.50	24.00	—
1918H	157,000	0.75	1.50	6.00	27.00	—
1920H	157,000	0.45	1.25	4.50	18.00	—
1945H	96,000	0.45	1.25	4.50	10.00	—
1949H	19,000	1.50	3.00	12.00	20.00	—

KM# 15 4 DOUBLES
4.8200 g., Bronze **Obv:** Arms **Rev:** Guernsey lily

Date	Mintage	F	VF	XF	Unc	BU
1956	240,000	0.25	0.45	0.75	2.00	3.50
1956 Proof	2,100	Value: 4.00				
1966 Proof	10,000	Value: 2.00				

KM# 7 8 DOUBLES
8.3400 g., Bronze, 31.13 mm. **Obv:** National arms within 3/4 wreath **Rev:** Value, date within wreath

Date	Mintage	F	VF	XF	Unc	BU
1902H	235,000	2.50	4.50	12.00	29.00	—
1902H Proof	—	Value: 250				
1903H	118,000	1.00	4.00	11.00	27.00	—
1910H	91,000	1.25	4.00	12.50	35.00	—
1910H Proof	—	Value: 250				
1911H	78,000	6.00	17.00	40.00	80.00	—

KM# 14 8 DOUBLES
10.1400 g., Bronze **Obv:** Arms within wreath **Rev:** Denomination and date within wreath

Date	Mintage	F	VF	XF	Unc	BU
1914H	157,000	1.00	3.00	8.00	23.00	—
1914H Proof	—	Value: 150				
1918H	157,000	1.50	4.00	11.00	27.00	—
1920H	157,000	1.00	2.00	6.00	15.00	—
1920H Proof	—	Value: 150				
1934H	124,000	1.00	2.00	6.00	18.00	—
1934H Proof	500	Value: 175				
1938H	120,000	0.50	1.50	4.00	9.00	—
1938H Proof	—	Value: 250				
1945H	192,000	0.40	0.85	2.00	5.50	—
1947H	240,000	0.30	0.60	2.25	5.00	—
1949H	230,000	0.30	0.60	2.25	5.00	—

KM# 16 8 DOUBLES

Bronze **Ruler:** Elizabeth II **Obv:** Arms **Rev:** Three flowered lily

Date	Mintage	F	VF	XF	Unc	BU
1956	500,000	0.10	0.20	0.50	1.25	2.50
1956 Proof	2,100	Value: 4.00				
1959	500,000	0.10	0.20	0.50	1.25	2.50
1959 Proof	—	—	—	—	—	—
1966 Proof	10,000	Value: 3.50				

KM# 17 3 PENCE

Copper Nickel, 21 mm. **Ruler:** Elizabeth II **Obv:** Arms **Rev:** Guernsey cow (bos primigenius taurus) right **Shape:** Scalloped **Note:** Thin flan.

Date	Mintage	F	VF	XF	Unc	BU
1956	500,000	0.10	0.20	0.50	1.50	2.00
1956 Proof	2,100	Value: 4.00				

KM# 18 3 PENCE

Copper Nickel, 21 mm. **Ruler:** Elizabeth II **Obv:** Arms **Rev:** Guernsey cow (bos primigenius taurus) right **Shape:** Scalloped **Note:** Thick flan.

Date	Mintage	F	VF	XF	Unc	BU
1959	500,000	0.10	0.20	0.50	1.50	2.00
1959 Proof	—	Value: 150				
1966 Proof	10,000	Value: 2.00				

KM# 19 10 SHILLING

Copper Nickel **Ruler:** Elizabeth II **Series:** 90th Anniversary - Norman Conquest **Subject:** William I **Obv:** Young bust right **Rev:** Crowned bust left **Shape:** 4-sided **Designer:** Arnold Machin

Date	Mintage	F	VF	XF	Unc	BU
1966	300,000	—	1.00	1.25	1.75	—
1966 Proof	10,000	Value: 3.00				

DECIMAL COINAGE

100 Pence = 1 Pound

KM# 20 1/2 NEW PENNY

Bronze, 17.14 mm. **Ruler:** Elizabeth II **Obv:** Arms **Rev:** Denomination and date

Date	Mintage	F	VF	XF	Unc	BU
1971	2,066,000	—	—	0.15	0.30	0.50
1971 Proof	10,000	Value: 1.00				

KM# 21 NEW PENNY

3.5500 g., Bronze, 20.3 mm. **Ruler:** Elizabeth II **Obv:** Arms **Rev:** Gannet in flight

Date	Mintage	F	VF	XF	Unc	BU
1971	1,922,000	—	—	0.15	0.45	1.00
1971 Proof	10,000	Value: 1.00				

KM# 27 PENNY

3.5500 g., Bronze, 20.3 mm. **Ruler:** Elizabeth II **Obv:** Arms **Rev:** Gannet in flight

Date	Mintage	F	VF	XF	Unc	BU
1977	640,000	—	—	0.15	0.45	1.00
1979	2,400,000	—	—	0.15	0.45	1.00
1979 Proof	20,000	Value: 1.00				
1981 Proof	10,000	Value: 2.00				

KM# 40 PENNY

3.6500 g., Bronze, 20.3 mm. **Ruler:** Elizabeth II **Obv:** Crowned head right, small arms at left **Rev:** Edible crab **Rev. Designer:** Robert Elderton **Edge:** Plain

Date	Mintage	F	VF	XF	Unc	BU
1985	60,000	—	—	0.15	0.50	1.00
1985 Proof	2,500	Value: 2.00				
1986	1,010,000	—	—	0.15	0.50	1.00
1986 Proof	2,500	Value: 2.00				
1987	5,000	—	—	0.15	0.50	1.00
1987 Proof	2,500	Value: 2.00				
1988	500,000	—	—	0.15	0.50	1.00
1988 Proof	2,500	Value: 2.00				
1989	1,000,000	—	—	0.15	0.50	1.00
1989 Proof	2,500	Value: 2.00				
1990	5,000	—	—	0.15	0.50	1.00
1990 Proof	700	Value: 4.00				

KM# 40a PENNY

3.5500 g., Copper Plated Steel, 20.3 mm. **Ruler:** Elizabeth II **Obv:** Crowned head right, small arms at left **Rev:** Chancre crab **Rev. Designer:** Robert Elderton

Date	Mintage	F	VF	XF	Unc	BU
1992	—	—	—	—	0.35	1.00
Note: In sets only						
1992 Proof	—	Value: 5.00				
1994	750,000	—	—	—	0.35	1.00
1997	2,000,000	—	—	—	0.35	1.00
1997 Proof	—	Value: 5.00				

KM# 89 PENNY

3.5300 g., Copper Plated Steel, 20.3 mm. **Ruler:** Elizabeth II **Obv:** Head with tiara right **Obv. Designer:** Ian Rank-Broadley **Rev:** Edible crab **Rev. Designer:** Robert Elderton **Edge:** Plain

Date	Mintage	F	VF	XF	Unc	BU
1998	—	—	—	—	0.50	0.75
2003	1,302,600	—	—	—	0.35	1.00
2006	1,731,000	—	—	—	0.35	0.75

KM# 22 2 NEW PENCE

7.1000 g., Bronze, 25.9 mm. **Ruler:** Elizabeth II **Obv:** Arms **Rev:** Windmill from Sark

Date	Mintage	F	VF	XF	Unc	BU
1971	1,680,000	—	—	0.15	0.35	0.50
1971 Proof	10,000	Value: 1.00				

KM# 28 2 PENCE

7.1000 g., Bronze, 25.9 mm. **Ruler:** Elizabeth II **Obv:** Arms **Rev:** Windmill from Sark

Date	Mintage	F	VF	XF	Unc	BU
1977	700,000	—	—	0.15	0.25	0.45
1979	2,400,000	—	—	0.15	0.25	0.45
1979 Proof	20,000	Value: 1.00				
1981 Proof	10,000	Value: 2.00				

KM# 41 2 PENCE

7.2000 g., Bronze, 25.80 mm. **Ruler:** Elizabeth II **Obv:** Crowned head right, small arms at left **Rev:** Guernsey cows **Rev. Designer:** Robert Elderton **Edge:** Plain

Date	Mintage	F	VF	XF	Unc	BU
1985	60,000	—	—	0.20	0.75	2.00
1985 Proof	2,500	Value: 50.00				
1986	510,000	—	—	0.20	0.75	2.00
1986 Proof	2,500	Value: 2.00				
1987	5,000	—	—	0.20	0.75	2.00
1987 Proof	2,500	Value: 2.00				
1988	500,000	—	—	0.20	0.75	2.00
1988 Proof	2,500	Value: 2.00				
1989	500,000	—	—	0.20	0.75	2.00
1989 Proof	2,500	Value: 2.00				
1990	380,000	—	—	0.20	0.75	2.00
1990 Proof	700	Value: 4.00				

KM# 41a 2 PENCE

7.2000 g., Copper Plated Steel, 25.9 mm. **Ruler:** Elizabeth II **Obv:** Crowned head right, small arms at left **Rev:** Guernsey cows **Rev. Designer:** Robert Elderton **Edge:** Plain

Date	Mintage	F	VF	XF	Unc	BU
1992	—	—	—	—	0.30	1.00
Note: In sets only						
1992 Proof	—	Value: 5.00				
1996	500,000	—	—	—	0.30	1.00
1997	—	—	—	—	0.30	1.00
Note: In sets only						
1997 Proof	—	Value: 5.00				

KM# 23 5 NEW PENCE

5.6500 g., Copper-Nickel, 23.6 mm. **Ruler:** Elizabeth II **Obv:** Arms **Rev:** Guernsey lily **Rev. Designer:** Arnold Machin

Date	Mintage	F	VF	XF	Unc	BU
1968	800,000	—	0.15	0.25	0.45	0.65
1971 Proof	10,000	Value: 1.00				

KM# 29 5 PENCE

5.6500 g., Copper-Nickel, 23.6 mm. **Ruler:** Elizabeth II **Obv:** Arms **Rev:** Guernsey lily **Rev. Designer:** Arnold Machin

Date	Mintage	F	VF	XF	Unc	BU
1977	250,000	—	—	0.20	0.45	0.65
1979	200,000	—	—	0.20	0.45	0.65
1979 Proof	20,000	Value: 2.00				
1981 Proof	10,000	Value: 3.00				
1982	200,000	—	—	0.20	0.45	0.65

KM# 42.1 5 PENCE

5.6500 g., Copper-Nickel, 23.6 mm. **Ruler:** Elizabeth II **Obv:** Crowned head right, small arms at left **Rev:** Sailboats **Rev. Designer:** Robert Elderton

Date	Mintage	F	VF	XF	Unc	BU
1985	35,000	—	—	0.20	0.45	0.65
1985 Proof	2,500	Value: 2.50				

Date	Mintage	F	VF	XF	Unc	BU
1986	100,000	—	—	0.20	0.45	0.65
1986 Proof	2,500	Value: 2.50				
1987	300,000	—	—	0.20	0.45	0.65
1987 Proof	2,500	Value: 2.50				
1988	405,000	—	—	0.20	0.45	0.65
1988 Proof	2,500	Value: 2.50				
1989	5,000	—	—	0.20	0.50	0.75
1989 Proof	2,500	Value: 2.50				
1990	Est. 2,520	—	—	—	0.60	0.85
Note: In sets only						
1990 Proof	700	Value: 5.00				

KM# 42.2 5 PENCE

3.2600 g., Copper-Nickel, 18 mm. **Obv:** Crowned head right, small arms at left **Rev:** Sailboats **Rev. Designer:** Robert Elderton **Note:** Reduced size

Date	Mintage	F	VF	XF	Unc	BU
1990	2,400,000	—	—	0.20	0.45	0.65
1990 Proof	700	Value: 5.00				
1992	1,300,000	—	—	—	0.50	0.75
1992 In proof sets only	—	Value: 6.00				
1997	—	—	—	—	0.50	0.75
1997 Proof	—	Value: 5.00				

KM# 24 10 NEW PENCE

11.3000 g., Copper-Nickel, 28.5 mm. **Ruler:** Elizabeth II **Obv:** Arms **Rev:** Guernsey cow **Rev. Designer:** Arnold Machin

Date	Mintage	F	VF	XF	Unc	BU
1968	600,000	—	0.20	0.40	1.50	2.00
1970	300,000	—	0.20	0.40	1.50	2.00
1971 Proof	10,000	Value: 2.00				

KM# 30 10 PENCE

11.3000 g., Copper-Nickel, 28.5 mm. **Ruler:** Elizabeth II **Obv:** Arms **Rev:** Guernsey cow **Rev. Designer:** Arnold Machin

Date	Mintage	F	VF	XF	Unc	BU
1977	480,000	—	—	0.25	1.00	2.00
1979	659,000	—	—	0.25	1.00	2.00
1979 Proof	20,000	Value: 2.00				
1981 Proof	10,000	Value: 3.00				
1982	200,000	—	—	0.35	1.25	2.00
1984	400,000	—	—	0.25	1.00	2.00

KM# 43.1 10 PENCE

11.3000 g., Copper-Nickel, 28.5 mm. **Ruler:** Elizabeth II **Obv:** Crowned head right, small arms at left **Rev:** Tomato plant **Rev. Designer:** Robert Elderton

Date	Mintage	F	VF	XF	Unc	BU
1985	110,000	—	—	0.25	0.60	0.85
1985 Proof	2,500	Value: 2.50				
1986	300,000	—	—	0.25	0.60	0.85
1986 Proof	2,500	Value: 6.00				
1987	250,000	—	—	0.25	0.60	0.85
1987 Proof	2,500	Value: 2.50				
1988	300,000	—	—	0.25	0.60	0.85
1988 Proof	2,500	Value: 2.50				
1989	200,000	—	—	0.25	0.60	0.85
1989 Proof	2,500	Value: 2.50				

Date	Mintage	F	VF	XF	Unc	BU
1990	3,500	—	—	0.25	0.60	0.85
1990 Proof	700	Value: 5.00				

KM# 43.2 10 PENCE

Copper-Nickel, 24.5 mm. **Obv:** Crowned head right, small arms at left **Rev:** Tomato plant **Rev. Designer:** Robert Elderton **Note:** Reduced size.

Date	Mintage	F	VF	XF	Unc	BU
1992	3,500,000	—	—	—	0.60	0.85
1992 Proof	—	Value: 6.00				
1997	—	—	—	—	0.60	0.85
Note: In sets only						
1997 Proof	—	Value: 6.00				

KM# 149 10 PENCE

6.4400 g., Copper-Nickel, 24.5 mm. **Ruler:** Elizabeth II **Obv:** Crowned head right **Obv. Designer:** Ian Rank-Broadley **Rev:** Tomato plant **Rev. Designer:** Robert Elderton **Edge:** Reeded

Date	Mintage	F	VF	XF	Unc	BU
2003	32,600	—	—	—	0.60	0.85
2006	26,000	—	—	—	0.60	0.85

KM# 38 20 PENCE

5.1000 g., Copper-Nickel, 21.4 mm. **Ruler:** Elizabeth II **Obv:** Arms **Rev:** Guernsey milk can **Shape:** 7-sided

Date	Mintage	F	VF	XF	Unc	BU
1982	500,000	—	—	0.45	0.90	1.25
1983	500,000	—	—	0.45	0.90	1.25

KM# 44 20 PENCE

5.1000 g., Copper-Nickel, 21.4 mm. **Ruler:** Elizabeth II **Obv:** Crowned head right, small arms at left **Rev:** Island map within cogwheel **Rev. Designer:** Robert Elderton **Shape:** 7-sided

Date	Mintage	F	VF	XF	Unc	BU
1985	35,000	—	—	0.45	0.85	1.20
1985 Proof	2,500	Value: 3.00				
1986	10,000	—	—	0.45	0.85	1.20
1986 Proof	2,500	Value: 3.00				
1987	5,000	—	—	0.45	0.85	1.20
1987 Proof	2,500	Value: 3.00				
1988	5,000	—	—	0.45	0.85	1.20
1988 Proof	2,500	Value: 3.00				
1989	93,000	—	—	0.45	0.85	1.20
1989 Proof	2,500	Value: 3.00				
1990	113,000	—	—	0.45	0.85	1.20
1990 Proof	700	Value: 6.00				
1992	800,000	—	—	—	1.00	1.50
1992 Proof	—	Value: 7.00				
1997	—	—	—	—	1.00	1.50
1997 Proof	—	Value: 3.00				

KM# 90 20 PENCE

5.1000 g., Copper-Nickel, 21.4 mm. **Ruler:** Elizabeth II **Obv:** Head with tiara right, small arms at left **Obv. Designer:** Ian Rank-Broadley **Rev:** Island map within cogwheel **Rev. Designer:** Robert Elderton **Shape:** 7-sided

Date	Mintage	F	VF	XF	Unc	BU
1999	800,000	—	—	—	0.90	1.25
1999 Proof	—	Value: 3.00				
2003	732,600	—	—	—	0.90	1.25
2006	16,250	—	—	—	0.90	1.25

KM# 25 50 NEW PENCE

13.5000 g., Copper-Nickel, 30 mm. **Obv:** Arms **Rev:** Ducal cap of the Duke of Normandy **Shape:** 7-sided

Date	Mintage	F	VF	XF	Unc	BU
1969	200,000	—	1.00	1.50	2.50	3.50
1970	200,000	—	1.00	1.50	2.50	3.50
1971 Proof	10,000	Value: 4.00				

KM# 34 50 PENCE

13.5000 g., Copper-Nickel, 30 mm. **Ruler:** Elizabeth II **Obv:** Arms **Rev:** Ducal cap of the Duke of Normandy **Shape:** 7-sided

Date	Mintage	F	VF	XF	Unc	BU
1979 Proof	20,000	Value: 4.50				
1981	200,000	—	—	0.90	1.45	2.25
1981 Proof	10,000	Value: 5.50				
1982	150,000	—	—	0.90	1.45	2.25
1983	200,000	—	—	0.90	1.45	2.25
1984	200,000	—	—	0.90	1.45	2.25

KM# 45.1 50 PENCE

13.5000 g., Copper-Nickel, 30 mm. **Ruler:** Elizabeth II **Obv:** Crowned head right, small shield at left **Rev:** Freesia flowers **Rev. Designer:** Robert Elderton **Shape:** 7-sided

Date	Mintage	F	VF	XF	Unc	BU
1985	35,000	—	—	0.90	1.45	2.25
1985 Proof	2,500	Value: 4.00				
1986	10,000	—	—	0.90	1.45	2.25
1986 Proof	2,500	Value: 4.00				
1987	5,000	—	—	0.90	1.45	2.25
1987 Proof	2,500	Value: 4.50				
1988	6,000	—	—	0.90	1.45	2.25
1988 Proof	2,500	Value: 4.50				
1989	55,000	—	—	0.90	1.45	2.25
1989 Proof	2,500	Value: 4.50				
1990	80,000	—	—	0.90	1.45	2.25
1990 Proof	700	Value: 7.50				
1992	65,000	—	—	—	2.00	3.00
1992 Proof	—	Value: 7.50				
1997 Proof	—	Value: 7.50				

KM# 45.2 50 PENCE

Copper-Nickel, 27.3 mm. **Ruler:** Elizabeth II **Obv:** Crowned head right, small shield at left **Obv. Designer:** Ian Rank-Broadley **Rev:** Freesia flowers **Rev. Designer:** Robert Elderton **Shape:** 7-sided

Date	Mintage	F	VF	XF	Unc	BU
1997	1,000,000	—	—	—	1.75	2.75
1997 Proof	—	Value: 8.50				

KM# 145 50 PENCE

7.9700 g., Copper-Nickel, 27.3 mm. **Ruler:** Elizabeth II **Subject:** Coronation Jubilee **Obv:** Head with tiara right **Obv. Designer:** Ian Rank-Broadley **Rev:** Queen on horseback **Edge:** Plain **Shape:** 7-sided

Date	Mintage	F	VF	XF	Unc	BU
2003	—	—	—	—	1.50	2.50

KM# 146 50 PENCE

7.9700 g., Copper-Nickel, 27.3 mm. **Ruler:** Elizabeth II **Subject:** Coronation Jubilee **Obv:** Head with tiara right **Rev:** Queen on throne **Edge:** Plain **Shape:** 7-sided

Date	Mintage	F	VF	XF	Unc	BU
2003	—	—	—	—	1.50	2.50

KM# 147 50 PENCE

7.9700 g., Copper-Nickel, 27.3 mm. **Ruler:** Elizabeth II **Subject:** Coronation Jubilee **Obv:** Head with tiara right **Rev:** Crown **Edge:** Plain **Shape:** 7-sided

Date	Mintage	F	VF	XF	Unc	BU
2003	—	—	—	—	1.50	2.50
2006	—	—	—	—	1.50	2.50

KM# 148 50 PENCE

7.9700 g., Copper-Nickel, 27.3 mm. **Ruler:** Elizabeth II **Subject:** Coronation Jubilee **Obv:** Head with tiara right **Rev:** Crowned ERII monogram **Edge:** Plain **Shape:** 7-sided

Date	Mintage	F	VF	XF	Unc	BU
2003	—	—	—	—	1.50	2.50

KM# 156 50 PENCE

7.9700 g., Copper-Nickel, 27.3 mm. **Ruler:** Elizabeth II **Obv:** Head with tiara right **Rev:** Crossed flowers **Edge:** Plain **Shape:** 7-sided

Date	Mintage	F	VF	XF	Unc	BU
2003	—	—	—	—	1.75	2.75
2006	19,000	—	—	—	1.75	2.75

KM# 37 POUND

7.9000 g., Nickel-Brass, 22 mm. **Ruler:** Elizabeth II **Obv:** Arms **Rev:** Guernsey lily

Date	Mintage	F	VF	XF	Unc	BU
1981	200,000	—	1.80	2.00	3.50	4.50
1981 Proof	10,000	Value: 5.00				

KM# 39 POUND

Nickel-Brass, 22.5 mm. **Ruler:** Elizabeth II **Obv:** Arms **Rev:** H.M.S. Crescent

Date	Mintage	F	VF	XF	Unc	BU
1983	269,000	—	1.80	2.00	3.50	4.50

KM# 46 POUND

Nickel-Brass, 22.5 mm. **Ruler:** Elizabeth II **Obv:** Crowned head right, small shield at left **Rev:** Design divides denomination

Date	Mintage	F	VF	XF	Unc	BU
1985	35,000	—	—	1.75	2.50	3.50
1985 Proof	2,500	Value: 6.50				
1986	10,000	—	—	1.75	2.50	3.50
1986 Proof	2,500	Value: 6.50				
1987	5,000	—	—	1.75	2.50	3.50
1987 Proof	2,500	Value: 6.50				
1988	5,000	—	—	1.75	2.50	3.50
1988 Proof	2,500	Value: 6.50				
1989	5,000	—	—	1.75	2.50	3.50
1989 Proof	2,500	Value: 6.50				
1990	3,500	—	—	1.75	2.50	3.50
1990 Proof	700	Value: 10.00				
1992	—	—	—	—	3.50	5.00
Note: In sets only						
1992 Proof	—	Value: 12.50				
1997	—	—	—	—	3.50	5.00
Note: In sets only						
1997 Proof	—	Value: 12.50				

KM# 110 POUND

9.5000 g., Nickel-Brass, 22.5 mm. **Ruler:** Elizabeth II **Subject:** Circulation Type **Obv:** Head with tiara right **Obv. Designer:** Ian Rank-Broadley **Rev:** Denomination **Edge:** Reeded

Date	Mintage	F	VF	XF	Unc	BU
2001	175,000	—	—	—	2.50	3.50
2003	46,600	—	—	—	2.50	3.50
2006	11,000	—	—	—	2.50	3.50

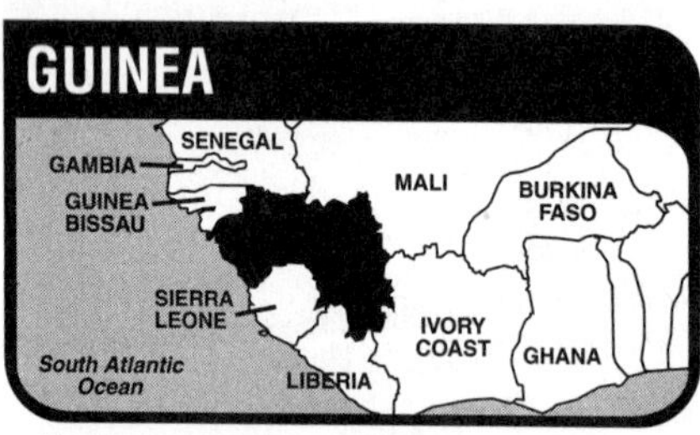

KM# 83 2 POUNDS

12.0000 g., Bi-Metallic Copper-Nickel center in Nickel-Brass ring, 28.35 mm. **Ruler:** Elizabeth II **Obv:** Head with tiara right **Obv. Designer:** Ian Rank-Broadley **Rev:** Latent image arms on cross **Edge:** BAILIWICK OF GUERNSEY

Date	Mintage	F	VF	XF	Unc	BU
1998	Est. 150,000	—	—	—	8.50	10.00
2003	19,600	—	—	—	8.50	10.00
2006	9,500	—	—	—	8.50	10.00

GUINEA

The Republic of Guinea, situated on the Atlantic Coast of Africa between Sierra Leone and Guinea-Bissau, has an area of 94,964 sq. mi. (245,860 sq. km.) and a population of 6.4 million. Capital: Conakry. Although Guinea contains one-third of the world's reserves of bauxite and significant deposits of iron ore, gold and diamonds, the economy is still dependent on agriculture, aluminum, bananas, copra and coffee are exported.

The coast of Guinea was known to Portuguese navigators of the 15th century but was seldom visited by European traders of the 16th-18th centuries because of its dangerous coastal waters. French penetration of the area began in the mid-19th century with the entering into of protectorate treaties with several of the coastal chiefs. After a long struggle with Guinea's native leader Samory Toure, France secured the area and until 1890 administered it as a part of Senegal. In 1895 the colony (Guinee Francais) became an autonomous part of the federation of French West Africa. The inhabitants were extended French citizenship in 1946 when the colony became an overseas territory of the French Union. Guinea became an independent republic on Oct. 2, 1958, when it declined to enter the new French Community.

MONETARY SYSTEM

100 Centimes = 1 Franc

REPUBLIC

DECIMAL COINAGE

KM# 4 FRANC

Copper-Nickel **Obv:** Head of Ahmed Sekou Toure left **Rev:** Feathers flank denomination within wreath

Date	Mintage	F	VF	XF	Unc	BU
1962	—	1.25	2.00	3.50	7.00	15.00
1962 Proof	—	Value: 50.00				

KM# 1 5 FRANCS

Aluminum-Bronze **Obv:** Head of Ahmed Sekou Toure right **Rev:** Palm trees flank denomination

Date	Mintage	F	VF	XF	Unc	BU
1959	—	2.75	4.75	12.00	22.50	—

KM# 5 5 FRANCS

Copper-Nickel, 20 mm. **Obv:** Head right **Rev:** Denomination within wreath, coconuts below **Note:** Mules with two obverses exist.

Date	Mintage	F	VF	XF	Unc	BU
1962	—	1.25	2.00	3.00	6.50	12.50
1962 Proof	—	Value: 70.00				

KM# 2 10 FRANCS

Aluminum-Bronze **Obv:** Head of Ahmed Sekou Toure left **Rev:** Denomination above spray

Date	Mintage	F	VF	XF	Unc	BU
1959	—	5.00	20.00	50.00	90.00	—

KM# 6 10 FRANCS

Copper-Nickel, 22 mm. **Obv:** Head of Ahmed Sekou Toure left **Rev:** Denomination within wreath

Date	Mintage	F	VF	XF	Unc	BU
1962	—	1.75	2.75	6.00	12.00	25.00
1962 Proof	—	Value: 85.00				

KM# 3 25 FRANCS

Aluminum-Bronze **Obv:** Head of Ahmed Sekou Toure right **Rev:** Palm trees flank denomination

Date	Mintage	F	VF	XF	Unc	BU
1959	—	10.00	50.00	110	200	—

KM# 7 25 FRANCS

Copper-Nickel **Obv:** Head of Ahmed Sekou Toure right **Rev:** Denomination within wreath

Date	Mintage	F	VF	XF	Unc	BU
1962	—	2.50	4.00	7.50	15.00	30.00
1962 Proof	—	Value: 120				

KM# 8 50 FRANCS

Copper-Nickel **Obv:** Head of Ahmed Sekou Toure left **Rev:** Denomination within wreath **Note:** Not released into circulation.

Date	Mintage	F	VF	XF	Unc	BU
1969	4,000	—	—	35.00	55.00	85.00

DECIMAL COINAGE

100 Cauris = 1 Syli

KM# 42 50 CAURIS
Aluminum **Obv:** Cowrie shell **Rev:** Denomination within wreath
Note: Nkrumah

Date	Mintage	F	VF	XF	Unc	BU
1971	—	1.00	2.00	3.50	6.00	—

KM# 43 SYLI
Aluminum **Obv:** Bust facing **Rev:** Denomination within wreath

Date	Mintage	F	VF	XF	Unc	BU
1971	—	2.00	3.00	5.50	12.50	—

KM# 44 2 SYLIS
Aluminum **Obv:** Head left **Rev:** Denomination within wreath

Date	Mintage	F	VF	XF	Unc	BU
1971	—	1.00	2.00	5.00	10.00	—

KM# 45 5 SYLIS
2.2700 g., Aluminum **Obv:** Head left **Rev:** Denomination within wreath

Date	Mintage	F	VF	XF	Unc	BU
1971	—	1.25	2.25	5.50	11.50	—

REFORM COINAGE

KM# 56 FRANC
1.4400 g., Brass Clad Steel, 15.50 mm. **Obv:** Shield with rifle and sword crossed on branch held by bird above **Rev:** Palm branch right of denomination **Edge:** Plain

Date	Mintage	F	VF	XF	Unc	BU
1985	—	0.10	0.20	0.40	1.00	—

KM# 53 5 FRANCS
2.0000 g., Brass Clad Steel, 17.5 mm. **Obv:** Shield with rifle and sword crossed on branch held by bird above **Rev:** Palm branch right of denomination

Date	Mintage	F	VF	XF	Unc	BU
1985	—	0.10	0.20	0.40	1.00	—

KM# 52 10 FRANCS
2.9500 g., Brass Clad Steel, 20.4 mm. **Obv:** Shield with rifle and sword crossed on branch held by bird above **Rev:** Palm branch right of denomination

Date	Mintage	F	VF	XF	Unc	BU
1985	—	0.20	0.40	0.80	1.25	—

KM# 60 25 FRANCS
4.9500 g., Brass, 22.5 mm. **Obv:** Shield with rifle and sword crossed on branch held by bird above **Rev:** Palm branch right of denomination

Date	Mintage	F	VF	XF	Unc	BU
1987	—	0.20	0.40	0.85	1.75	—

KM# 63 50 FRANCS
Copper-Nickel **Obv:** Without sword and rifle **Rev:** Leaves right of denomination

Date	Mintage	F	VF	XF	Unc	BU
1994	—	0.30	0.60	1.25	2.75	—

GUINEA-BISSAU

The Republic of Guinea-Bissau, formerly Portuguese Guinea, an overseas province on the west coast of Africa between Senegal and Guinea, has an area of 13,948 sq. mi. (36,120 sq. km.) and a population of 1.1 million. Capital: Bissau. The country has undeveloped deposits of oil and bauxite. Peanuts, oil-palm kernels and hides are exported.

Portuguese Guinea was discovered by Portuguese navigator, Nuno Tristao, in 1446. Trading rights in the area were granted to Cape Verde islanders but few prominent posts were established before 1851, and they were principally coastal installations. The chief export of this colony's early period was slaves for South America, a practice that adversely affected trade with the native people and retarded subjection of the interior. Territorial disputes with France delayed final demarcation of the colony's frontiers until 1905.

The African Party for the Independence of Guinea-Bissau was founded in 1956, and several years later began a guerrilla warfare that grew in effectiveness until 1974, when the rebels controlled most of the colony. Portugal's costly overseas wars in her African territories resulted in a military coup in Portugal in April 1974, which appreciably brightened the prospects for freedom for Guinea-Bissau. In August 1974, the Lisbon government signed an agreement granting independence to Portuguese Guinea effective Sept. 10, 1974. The new republic took the name of Guinea-Bissau.

RULER
Portuguese until 1974

PORTUGUESE GUINEA

DECIMAL COINAGE

KM# 1 5 CENTAVOS
Bronze **Obv:** Denomination above date **Rev:** Liberty head left

Date	Mintage	F	VF	XF	Unc	BU
1933	100,000	30.00	60.00	90.00	165	—

KM# 2 10 CENTAVOS
Bronze **Obv:** Denomination above date **Rev:** Liberty head left

Date	Mintage	F	VF	XF	Unc	BU
1933	250,000	28.00	85.00	500	1,000	—

KM# 12 10 CENTAVOS
Aluminum **Obv:** Denomination above date **Rev:** Divided shield with crowned towers and small shields above on lined circle

Date	Mintage	F	VF	XF	Unc	BU
1973	100,000	4.00	8.00	15.00	30.00	40.00

KM# 3 20 CENTAVOS
Bronze **Obv:** Denomination above date **Rev:** Liberty head left

Date	Mintage	F	VF	XF	Unc	BU
1933	350,000	4.00	8.50	35.00	65.00	100

KM# 13 20 CENTAVOS
Bronze **Obv:** Denomination above date **Rev:** Crowned towers and small shields above divided shield on lined circle

Date	Mintage	F	VF	XF	Unc	BU
1973	100,000	3.00	6.00	15.00	30.00	40.00

KM# 4 50 CENTAVOS
Nickel-Bronze **Obv:** Laureate head right **Rev:** Shield on lined circle within wreath

Date	Mintage	F	VF	XF	Unc	BU
1933	600,000	15.00	50.00	200	450	—

KM# 6 50 CENTAVOS
Bronze, 23 mm. **Subject:** 500th Anniversary of Discovery **Obv:** Denomination within circle, dates below **Rev:** Crowned towers above divided shield on lined circle

Date	Mintage	F	VF	XF	Unc	BU
ND(1946)	2,000,000	1.00	3.00	15.00	30.00	40.00

KM# 8 50 CENTAVOS
Bronze **Obv:** Denomination **Rev:** Towers above divided shield on lined circle

Date	Mintage	F	VF	XF	Unc	BU
1952	10,000,000	0.35	0.75	2.00	5.00	8.00

KM# 5 ESCUDO
Nickel-Bronze **Obv:** Laureate head right **Rev:** Shield on lined circle within wreath

Date	Mintage	F	VF	XF	Unc	BU
1933	800,000	7.50	22.50	200	450	—

KM# 7 ESCUDO
Bronze, 27 mm. **Subject:** 500th Anniversary of Discovery **Obv:** Denomination within circle **Rev:** Crowned towers and small shields above divided shield on lined circle

Date	Mintage	F	VF	XF	Unc	BU
ND(1946)	2,000,000	0.75	2.00	6.00	16.00	28.00

KM# 14 ESCUDO
Bronze **Obv:** Denomination **Rev:** Crowned towers and small shields above divided shield on lined circle

Date	Mintage	F	VF	XF	Unc	BU
1973	250,000	6.50	12.50	22.50	40.00	55.00

KM# 9 2-1/2 ESCUDOS
3.4100 g., Copper-Nickel **Obv:** Shield on lined circle at center of cross **Rev:** Crowned towers and small shields above divided shield on lined circle

Date	Mintage	F	VF	XF	Unc	BU
1952	3,010,000	0.50	1.50	3.00	7.00	10.00

KM# 15 5 ESCUDOS
Copper-Nickel **Obv:** Shield on lined circle at center of cross **Rev:** Crowned towers and small shields above divided shield on lined circle

Date	Mintage	F	VF	XF	Unc	BU
1973	800,000	2.50	5.00	10.00	20.00	28.00

KM# 10 10 ESCUDOS
5.0000 g., 0.7200 Silver 0.1157 oz. ASW **Obv:** Shield on lined circle at center of cross **Rev:** Crowned towers and small shields above divided shield on lined circle

Date	Mintage	F	VF	XF	Unc	BU
1952	1,200,000	4.00	18.00	70.00	140	180

KM# 16 10 ESCUDOS
Copper-Nickel **Obv:** Shield on lined circle at center of cross **Rev:** Crowned towers and small shields above divided shield on lined circle

Date	Mintage	F	VF	XF	Unc	BU
1973	1,700,000	3.00	10.00	20.00	40.00	55.00

KM# 11 20 ESCUDOS
10.0000 g., 0.7200 Silver 0.2315 oz. ASW **Obv:** Shield on lined circle at center of cross, date below **Rev:** Crowned towers and small shields above divided shield on lined circle

Date	Mintage	F	VF	XF	Unc	BU
1952	750,000	6.00	15.00	45.00	90.00	—

REPUBLIC

DECIMAL COINAGE

KM# 17 50 CENTAVOS
2.2000 g., Aluminum **Series:** F.A.O. **Obv:** National arms **Rev:** Palm tree left of denomination

Date	Mintage	F	VF	XF	Unc	BU
1977	6,000,000	2.00	3.00	4.50	8.00	10.00

KM# 17a 50 CENTAVOS
6.0000 g., Aluminum-Bronze, 25 mm. **Obv:** National arms **Rev:** Palm tree left of denomination **Note:** Struck on KM#19 planchet.

Date	Mintage	F	VF	XF	Unc	BU
1977	—	—	—	—	—	—

KM# 18 PESO
4.0200 g., Aluminum-Bronze **Series:** F.A.O. **Obv:** National arms **Rev:** Denomination below bouquet

Date	Mintage	F	VF	XF	Unc	BU
1977	7,000,000	2.25	3.50	5.50	9.00	12.00

KM# 19 2-1/2 PESOS
6.0400 g., Aluminum-Bronze **Series:** F.A.O. **Obv:** National arms **Rev:** Tree divides denomination

Date	Mintage	F	VF	XF	Unc	BU
1977	4,000,000	2.25	4.50	6.50	10.00	15.00

KM# 20 5 PESOS
8.0000 g., Copper-Nickel **Series:** F.A.O. **Obv:** National arms **Rev:** Denomination above bouquet

Date	Mintage	F	VF	XF	Unc	BU
1977	6,000,000	2.50	5.00	7.00	11.50	16.00

KM# 21 20 PESOS
12.6500 g., Copper-Nickel **Series:** F.A.O. **Obv:** National arms **Rev:** Plants left of denomination

Date	Mintage	F	VF	XF	Unc	BU
1977	2,500,000	4.00	6.50	11.50	18.00	25.00

GUYANA

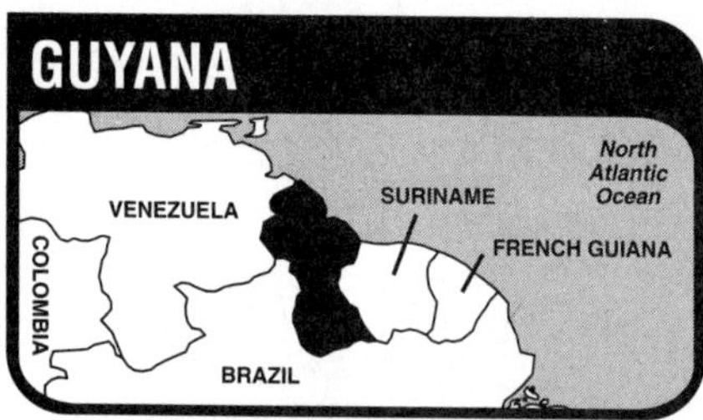

The Cooperative Republic of Guyana, is situated on the northeast coast of South America, has an area of 83,000 sq. mi. (214,970 sq. km.) and a population of 729,000. Capital: Georgetown. The economy is basically agrarian. Sugar, rice and bauxite are exported.

The original area of Essequibo and Demerary, which included present-day Suriname, French Guiana, and parts of Brazil and Venezuela was sighted by Columbus in 1498. The first European settlement was made late in the 16th century by the Dutch, however, the region was claimed for the British by Sir Walter Raleigh during the reign of Elizabeth I. For the next 150 years, possession alternated between the Dutch and the British, with a short interval of French control. The British exercised de facto control after 1796 over the Dutch colonies of Essequibo, Demerary and Berbice. They were not ceded to them by the Dutch until 1814. From 1803 to 1831, Essequibo and Demerary were administered separately from Berbice. The three colonies were united in the British Crown Colony of British Guiana in 1831. British Guiana won internal self-government in 1952 and full independence, under the traditional name of Guyana, on May 26,1966. Guyana became a republic on Feb. 23, 1970. It is a member of the Commonwealth of Nations. The president is the Chief of State. The prime minister is the Head of Government. Guyana is a member of the Caribbean Community and Common Market (CARICOM).

RULER
British, until 1966

***NOTE**: From 1975-1985 the Franklin Mint produced coinage in up to 3 different qualities. Qualities of issue are designated in ( ) after each date and are defined as follows:

(M) MATTE - Normal circulation strike or a dull finish produced by sandblasting special uncirculated (polish finish) or proof quality dies.

(U) SPECIAL UNCIRCULATED - Polished or proof-like in appearance without any frosted features.

(P) PROOF - The highest quality obtainable having mirror-like fields and frosted features.

BRITISH GUIANA AND WEST INDIES

STERLING COINAGE

KM# 26 4 PENCE

1.8851 g., 0.9250 Silver 0.0561 oz. ASW **Obv:** Head left **Rev:** Crowned denomination within wreath

Date	Mintage	F	VF	XF	Unc	BU
1901	60,000	5.00	10.00	22.50	55.00	70.00

KM# 27 4 PENCE

1.8851 g., 0.9250 Silver 0.0561 oz. ASW **Obv:** Crowned bust right **Obv. Designer:** G.W. DeSaulles **Rev:** Crowned denomination within wreath

Date	Mintage	F	VF	XF	Unc	BU
1903	60,000	5.00	10.00	22.50	55.00	70.00
1903 Matte proof	—	Value: 450				
1908	30,000	5.00	12.50	40.00	90.00	100
1909	36,000	5.00	12.50	40.00	90.00	100
1910	66,000	5.00	10.00	40.00	85.00	100

KM# 28 4 PENCE

1.8851 g., 0.9250 Silver 0.0561 oz. ASW **Obv:** Crowned bust left **Obv. Designer:** E.B. MacKennal **Rev:** Crowned denomination within wreath

Date	Mintage	F	VF	XF	Unc	BU
1911	30,000	8.00	25.00	70.00	115	130
1913	30,000	8.00	25.00	70.00	115	130
1916	30,000	8.00	25.00	70.00	115	130

BRITISH GUIANA

STERLING COINAGE

KM# 29 4 PENCE

1.8851 g., 0.9250 Silver 0.0561 oz. ASW **Obv:** Crowned bust left **Obv. Designer:** E.B. MacKennal **Rev:** Crowned denomination within wreath

Date	Mintage	F	VF	XF	Unc	BU
1917	72,000	5.00	12.50	40.00	90.00	100
1917 Matte proof	—	Value: 450				
1918	210,000	1.25	3.50	15.00	55.00	65.00
1921	90,000	5.00	10.00	27.50	70.00	85.00
1923	12,000	20.00	45.00	85.00	160	180
1925	30,000	8.00	20.00	50.00	100	125
1926	30,000	8.00	20.00	50.00	100	125
1931	15,000	10.00	25.00	60.00	120	140
1931 Proof	—	Value: 175				
1935	36,000	3.00	12.50	50.00	175	200
1935 Proof	—	Value: 175				
1936	63,000	1.75	2.50	10.00	30.00	45.00
1936 Proof	—	Value: 225				

KM# 30 4 PENCE

1.8851 g., 0.9250 Silver 0.0561 oz. ASW **Obv:** Crowned head left **Obv. Designer:** Percy Metcalf **Rev:** Crowned denomination within wreath

Date	Mintage	F	VF	XF	Unc	BU
1938	30,000	8.00	20.00	50.00	100	125
1938 Proof	—	Value: 175				
1939	48,000	1.75	2.50	7.50	20.00	30.00
1939 Proof	—	Value: 175				
1940	90,000	1.25	2.00	3.50	18.50	25.00
1940 Proof	—	Value: 175				
1941	120,000	1.25	1.75	3.00	12.50	17.50
1941 Proof	—	Value: 175				
1942	180,000	1.25	1.75	3.00	12.50	17.50
1942 Proof	—	Value: 175				
1943	240,000	1.25	1.75	2.50	8.00	12.00
1943 Proof	—	Value: 400				

KM# 30a 4 PENCE

1.8851 g., 0.5000 Silver 0.0303 oz. ASW **Obv:** Head left **Obv. Designer:** Percy Metcalf **Rev:** Crowned denomination within wreath

Date	Mintage	F	VF	XF	Unc	BU
1944	90,000	0.85	1.25	2.50	8.00	10.00
1945	120,000	0.65	1.00	2.00	7.00	9.00
1945 Proof	—	Value: 200				

REPUBLIC

DECIMAL COINAGE

KM# 31 CENT

1.5300 g., Nickel-Brass, 15.99 mm. **Obv:** Denomination within circle **Rev:** Stylized lotus flower **Edge:** Plain

Date	Mintage	F	VF	XF	Unc	BU
1967	6,000,000	—	—	0.10	0.25	0.35
1967 Proof	5,100	Value: 2.00				
1969	4,000,000	—	—	0.10	0.25	0.35
1970	6,000,000	—	—	0.10	0.25	0.35
1971	4,000,000	—	—	0.10	0.25	0.35
1972	4,000,000	—	—	0.10	0.25	0.35
1973	4,000,000	—	—	0.10	0.25	0.35
1974	11,000,000	—	—	0.10	0.20	0.30
1975	—	—	—	0.10	0.25	0.35
1976	—	—	—	0.10	0.25	0.35
1977	16,000,000	—	—	0.10	0.20	0.30
1978	10,450,000	—	—	0.10	0.20	0.30
1979	—	—	—	0.10	0.20	0.30
1980	12,000,000	—	—	0.10	0.20	0.30
1981	10,000,000	—	—	0.10	0.20	0.30
1982	8,000,000	—	—	0.10	0.20	0.30
1983	12,000,000	—	—	0.10	0.20	0.30
1985	8,000,000	—	—	0.10	0.20	0.30
1987	6,000,000	—	—	0.10	0.20	0.30
1988	80,000	—	—	0.15	0.50	0.75
1989	—	—	—	0.10	0.20	0.30
1991	—	—	—	0.10	0.20	0.30
1992	—	—	—	0.10	0.20	0.30

KM# 37 CENT

Nickel-Brass, 16 mm. **Subject:** 10th Anniversary of Independence **Obv:** Helmeted and supported arms **Rev:** Manatee

Date	Mintage	F	VF	XF	Unc	BU
1976FM (M)	15,000	—	—	0.15	1.00	3.00
1976FM (U)	50	—	—	—	—	—
1976FM (P)	28,000	Value: 1.50				
1977FM (M)	—	—	—	—	3.00	4.50
1977FM (U)	15,000	—	—	0.20	1.00	3.00
1977FM (P)	7,215	Value: 1.50				
1978FM (M)	—	—	—	—	3.00	4.50
1978FM (U)	15,000	—	—	0.20	1.00	3.00
1978FM (P)	5,044	Value: 1.50				
1979FM (U)	15,000	—	—	0.20	1.00	3.00
1979FM (P)	3,547	Value: 1.50				
1980FM (U)	30,000	—	—	0.20	1.00	3.00
1980FM (P)	2,763	Value: 1.75				

KM# 32 5 CENTS

Nickel-Brass, 19.5 mm. **Obv:** Denomination within circle **Rev:** Stylized lotus flower **Note:** Varieties exist.

Date	Mintage	F	VF	XF	Unc	BU
1967	4,600,000	—	—	0.10	0.30	0.40
1967 Proof	5,100	Value: 2.00				
1972	1,200,000	—	—	0.10	0.35	0.45
1974	3,000,000	—	—	0.10	0.35	0.45
1975	—	—	—	0.10	0.35	0.45
1976	—	—	—	0.10	0.35	0.45
1977	1,500,000	—	—	0.10	0.35	0.45
1978	2,000	—	—	1.25	4.00	6.00
1979	—	—	—	0.30	1.00	1.50
1980	1,000,000	—	—	0.10	0.35	0.45
1981	1,000,000	—	—	0.10	0.35	0.45
1982	2,000,000	—	—	0.10	0.30	0.40
1985	3,000,000	—	—	0.10	0.30	0.40
1986	4,000,000	—	—	0.10	0.30	0.40
1987	3,000,000	—	—	0.10	0.30	0.40
1988	2,000,000	—	—	0.10	0.30	0.40
1989	—	—	—	0.10	0.30	0.40
1990	—	—	—	0.10	0.30	0.40
1991	—	—	—	0.10	0.30	0.40
1992	—	—	—	0.10	0.30	0.40

KM# 38 5 CENTS

Nickel-Brass, 19.5 mm. **Subject:** 10th Anniversary of Independence **Obv:** Helmeted and supported arms **Rev:** Jaguar (panthera onca)

Date	Mintage	F	VF	XF	Unc	BU
1976FM (M)	15,000	—	—	0.20	1.75	5.00
1976FM (U)	50	—	—	—	—	—
1976FM (P)	28,000	Value: 1.75				
1977FM (M)	—	—	—	—	3.00	5.00
1977FM (U)	15,000	—	—	0.20	1.75	5.00
1977FM (P)	7,215	Value: 2.00				
1978FM (M)	—	—	—	—	5.00	6.50
1978FM (U)	15,000	—	—	0.20	1.75	5.00
1978FM (P)	5,044	Value: 2.00				
1979FM (U)	15,000	—	—	0.20	1.75	5.00
1979FM (P)	3,547	Value: 2.25				
1980FM (U)	30,000	—	—	0.20	1.75	5.00
1980FM (P)	2,763	Value: 2.50				

KM# 33 10 CENTS

2.7500 g., Copper-Nickel, 18 mm. **Obv:** Denomination within circle **Rev:** Helmeted and supported arms **Edge:** Reeded

Date	Mintage	F	VF	XF	Unc	BU
1967	4,000,000	—	0.10	0.20	0.35	0.50
1967 Proof	5,100	Value: 2.50				
1973	1,500,000	—	0.10	0.20	0.40	0.60
1974	1,700,000	—	0.10	0.20	0.40	0.60
1976	—	—	0.10	0.20	0.40	0.60
1977	4,000,000	—	0.10	0.20	0.40	0.60
1978	2,010,000	—	0.10	0.20	0.40	0.60
1979	—	—	0.10	0.20	0.40	0.60
1980	1,000,000	—	0.10	0.20	0.40	0.60
1981	1,000,000	—	0.10	0.20	0.40	0.60
1982	2,000,000	—	0.10	0.20	0.35	0.50
1985	3,000,000	—	0.10	0.20	0.35	0.50
1986	4,000,000	—	0.10	0.20	0.35	0.50
1987	3,000,000	—	0.10	0.20	0.35	0.50
1988	2,000,000	—	0.10	0.20	0.35	0.50
1989	—	—	0.10	0.20	0.35	0.50
1990	—	—	0.10	0.20	0.35	0.50
1991	—	—	0.10	0.20	0.35	0.50
1992	—	—	0.10	0.20	0.35	0.50

KM# 39 10 CENTS

Copper-Nickel, 18 mm. **Subject:** 10th Anniversary of Independence **Obv:** Helmeted and supported arms **Rev:** Squirrel Monkey

Date	Mintage	F	VF	XF	Unc	BU
1976	2,006,000	—	—	0.25	1.50	3.00
1976FM (M)	10,000	—	—	0.25	1.50	3.00
1976FM (U)	50	—	—	—	—	—
1976FM (P)	28,000	Value: 3.00				
1977	1,500,000	—	—	0.25	1.50	3.00
1977FM (M)	—	—	—	—	8.00	10.00
1977FM (U)	10,000	—	—	0.25	1.50	3.00
1977FM (P)	7,215	Value: 3.00				
1978FM (M)	—	—	—	—	8.00	10.00
1978FM (U)	10,000	—	—	0.25	1.50	3.00
1978FM (P)	5,044	Value: 3.00				
1979FM (U)	10,000	—	—	0.25	1.50	3.00
1979FM (P)	3,547	Value: 3.00				
1980FM (U)	20,000	—	—	0.25	1.50	3.00
1980FM (P)	2,763	Value: 4.00				

KM# 34 25 CENTS

4.2900 g., Copper-Nickel, 20.42 mm. **Obv:** Denomination within circle **Rev:** Helmeted and supported arms **Edge:** Plain

Date	Mintage	F	VF	XF	Unc	BU
1967	3,500,000	—	0.15	0.25	0.60	0.75
1967 Proof	5,100	Value: 2.50				
1972	1,000,000	—	0.15	0.25	0.65	0.85
1974	4,000,000	—	0.15	0.25	0.65	0.85
1975	—	—	0.15	0.25	0.65	0.85
1976	—	—	0.15	0.25	0.65	0.85
1977	4,000,000	—	0.15	0.25	0.65	0.85
1978	2,006,000	—	0.15	0.25	0.65	0.85
1981	1,000,000	—	0.15	0.25	0.65	0.85
1982	1,500,000	—	0.15	0.25	0.65	0.85
1984	1,000,000	—	0.15	0.25	0.65	0.85
1985	2,000,000	—	0.15	0.25	0.60	0.75
1986	4,000,000	—	0.15	0.25	0.60	0.75
1987	3,000,000	—	0.15	0.25	0.60	0.75
1988	4,000,000	—	0.15	0.25	0.60	0.75
1989	—	—	0.15	0.25	0.60	0.75
1990	—	—	0.15	0.25	0.60	0.75
1991	—	—	0.15	0.25	0.60	0.75
1992	—	—	0.15	0.25	0.60	0.75

KM# 40 25 CENTS

Copper-Nickel, 21.5 mm. **Subject:** 10th Anniversary of Independence **Obv:** Helmeted and supported arms **Rev:** Harpy Eagle

Date	Mintage	F	VF	XF	Unc	BU
1976FM (M)	4,000	—	—	0.30	2.50	3.50
1976FM (U)	50	—	—	—	—	—
1976FM (P)	28,000	Value: 3.00				
1977	2,000,000	—	0.15	0.25	2.00	3.50
1977FM (M)	—	—	—	—	10.00	12.00
1977FM (U)	4,000	—	—	0.30	4.00	5.00
1977FM (P)	7,215	Value: 3.00				
1978FM (M)	—	—	—	—	10.00	12.00
1978FM (U)	4,000	—	—	0.30	4.00	5.00
1978FM (P)	5,044	Value: 3.50				
1979FM (U)	4,000	—	—	0.30	4.00	5.00
1979FM (P)	3,547	Value: 3.50				
1980FM (U)	8,437	—	—	0.30	4.00	5.00
1980FM (P)	2,763	Value: 4.50				

KM# 35 50 CENTS

Copper-Nickel **Obv:** Denomination within circle **Rev:** Helmeted and supported arms

Date	Mintage	F	VF	XF	Unc	BU
1967	1,000,000	—	0.25	0.35	0.75	1.25
1967 Proof	5,100	Value: 3.50				

KM# 41 50 CENTS

Copper-Nickel, 25 mm. **Subject:** 10th Anniversary of Independence **Obv:** Helmeted and supported arms **Rev:** Hoatzin

Date	Mintage	F	VF	XF	Unc	BU
1976FM (M)	2,000	—	—	0.40	5.00	6.00
1976FM (U)	50	—	—	—	—	—
1976FM (P)	28,000	Value: 4.00				
1977FM (M)	—	—	—	—	20.00	22.50
1977FM (U)	2,000	—	—	0.40	5.00	6.00
1977FM (P)	7,215	Value: 4.00				
1978FM (M)	—	—	—	—	20.00	22.50
1978FM (U)	2,000	—	—	0.40	5.00	6.00
1978FM (P)	5,044	Value: 4.50				
1979FM (U)	2,000	—	—	0.40	5.00	6.00
1979FM (P)	3,547	Value: 4.50				
1980FM (U)	4,437	—	—	0.40	3.50	5.00
1980FM (P)	2,763	Value: 5.50				

KM# 36 DOLLAR

Copper-Nickel, 35.5 mm. **Series:** F.A.O. **Obv:** Bulls head left of denomination **Rev:** Head left **Rev. Designer:** Patrick Munroe **Note:** Cuffy, slave who organized a revolt on 23 Feb. 1763, which was the first step towards independence.

Date	Mintage	F	VF	XF	Unc	BU
1970	500,000	—	0.50	1.75	4.00	5.00
1970 Proof	5,000	Value: 6.00				

KM# 42 DOLLAR

Copper-Nickel, 35.5 mm. **Series:** F.A.O. **Subject:** 10th Anniversary of Independence **Obv:** Helmeted and supported arms **Rev:** Common Caiman

Date	Mintage	F	VF	XF	Unc	BU
1976FM (M)	600	—	—	0.50	6.00	7.00
1976FM (U)	50	—	—	—	—	—
1976FM (P)	28,000	Value: 7.00				
1977FM (M)	—	—	—	—	30.00	32.50
1977FM (U)	500	—	—	0.50	6.00	7.00
1977FM (P)	7,215	Value: 7.50				
1978FM (M)	—	—	—	—	30.00	32.50
1978FM (U)	500	—	—	0.50	6.00	7.00
1978FM (P)	5,044	Value: 8.00				
1979FM (U)	500	—	—	0.50	6.00	7.00
1979FM (P)	3,547	Value: 8.00				
1980FM (U)	1,437	—	—	0.50	6.00	7.00
1980FM (P)	2,763	Value: 8.50				

KM# 50 DOLLAR

2.4000 g., Copper Plated Steel, 16.96 mm. **Obv:** Helmeted and supported arms **Obv. Designer:** Sean Thomas **Rev:** Hand gathering rice **Rev. Designer:** Jean Thomas **Edge:** Reeded

Date	Mintage	F	VF	XF	Unc	BU
1996	—	—	—	—	0.50	0.65
2001	—	—	—	0.30	0.50	0.65
2002	—	—	—	0.30	0.50	0.65

KM# 51 5 DOLLARS

3.7800 g., Copper Plated Steel, 20.5 mm. **Obv:** Helmeted and supported arms **Rev:** Sugar cane **Rev. Designer:** Selayn Cambridge **Edge:** Reeded

Date	Mintage	F	VF	XF	Unc	BU
1996	—	—	—	—	0.75	1.00
2002	—	—	—	—	0.75	1.00
2005	—	—	—	—	0.75	1.00

KM# 52 10 DOLLARS

5.0000 g., Nickel Plated Steel, 23 mm. **Obv:** Helmeted and supported arms **Rev:** Gold mining scene **Rev. Designer:** Ignatias Adams **Edge:** Reeded **Shape:** 7-sided

Date	Mintage	F	VF	XF	Unc	BU
1996	—	—	—	—	1.25	1.50
2007	—	—	—	—	1.25	1.50

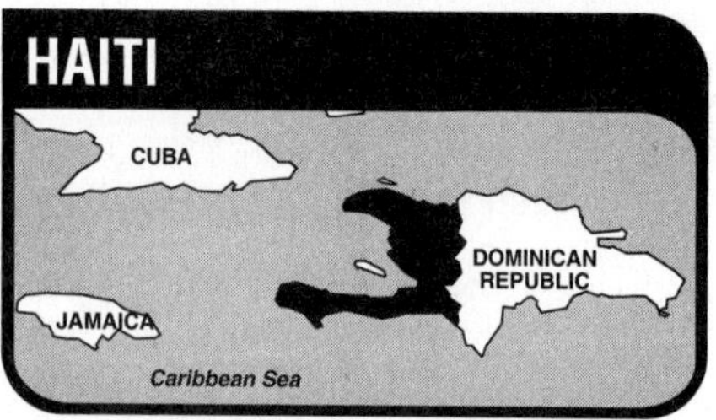

The Republic of Haiti, which occupies the western one-third of the island of Hispaniola in the Caribbean Sea between Puerto Rico and Cuba, has an area of 10,714 sq. mi. (27,750 sq. km.) and a population of 6.5 million. Capital: Port-au-Prince. The economy is based on agriculture; but light manufacturing and tourism are increasingly important. Coffee, bauxite, sugar, essential oils and handicrafts are exported.

Columbus discovered Hispaniola in 1492. Spain colonized the island, making Santo Domingo the base for exploration of the Western Hemisphere. The area that is now Haiti was ceded to France by Spain in 1697. Slaves brought from Africa to work the coffee and sugar cane plantations made it one of the richest colonies of the French Empire. A slave revolt in the 1790's led to the establishment of the Republic of Haiti in1804, making it the oldest Black republic in the world and the second oldest republic (after the United States) in the Western Hemisphere.

The French language is used on Haitian coins although it is spoken by only about 10% of the populace. A form of Creole is the language of the Haitians.

MINT MARKS

A - Paris
(a) - Paris, privy marks only
HEATON - Birmingham
R - Rome
(w) = Waterbury (Connecticut, USA) (Scoville Mfg. Co.)
(p) – Philadelphia (U.S.A. mint)

MONETARY SYSTEM

100 Centimes = 1 Gourde

REPUBLIC
1863 -
DECIMAL COINAGE

100 Centimes = 1 Gourde

KM# 53 5 CENTIMES

Copper-Nickel **Obv:** President Pierre Nord Alexis left **Rev:** National arms

Date	Mintage	F	VF	XF	Unc	BU
1904(w)	2,000,000	1.00	5.00	15.00	30.00	40.00
1904(w) Proof	—	Value: 90.00				
1905(w)	20,000,000	0.75	3.00	10.00	25.00	30.00
1905(w) Proof	—	Value: 100				

KM# 52 5 CENTIMES

Copper-Nickel **Obv:** National arms **Rev:** Denomination above date **Note:** Struck at the Scovill Mfg. Co., Waterbury, Connecticut; design incorporates Paris privy and mint director's marks.

Date	Mintage	F	VF	XF	Unc	BU
1904(w)	—	3.00	10.00	20.00	55.00	65.00
1904(w) Proof	—	Value: 120				

KM# 57 5 CENTIMES

Copper-Nickel **Obv:** President Dumarsais Estime left **Rev:** National arms

Date	Mintage	F	VF	XF	Unc	BU
1949(p)	10,000,000	0.25	0.75	2.00	6.00	7.50

KM# 59 5 CENTIMES

Copper-Zinc-Nickel **Obv:** President Paul Eugene Magloire left

Date	Mintage	F	VF	XF	Unc	BU
1953(p)	3,000,000	0.25	0.35	0.65	1.50	2.00

KM# 62 5 CENTIMES

Copper-Nickel, 20 mm. **Obv:** President Francois Duvalier left **Rev:** National arms **Designer:** Gilroy Roberts

Date	Mintage	F	VF	XF	Unc	BU
1958(p)	15,000,000	—	—	0.10	0.25	0.50
1970	5,000,000	—	—	0.10	0.20	0.45

KM# 119 5 CENTIMES

2.7000 g., Copper-Nickel, 20 mm. **Series:** F.A.O. **Obv:** President Jean-Claude Duvalier left **Rev:** National arms

Date	Mintage	F	VF	XF	Unc	BU
1975	16,000,000	—	—	0.10	0.20	0.45

KM# 145 5 CENTIMES

Copper-Nickel **Series:** F.A.O. **Obv:** Head right, small logo at left **Rev:** Woman and child **Note:** Denomination as 0.05 Gourdes.

Date	Mintage	F	VF	XF	Unc	BU
1981R	15,000	—	0.10	0.75	1.00	1.50

KM# 154 5 CENTIMES

3.1000 g., Copper-Nickel-Zinc, 19.9 mm. **Subject:** Charlemagne Peralte, national hero **Obv:** Bust facing **Rev:** National arms

Date	Mintage	F	VF	XF	Unc	BU
1986	—	—	—	—	0.25	0.40

KM# 154a 5 CENTIMES

Nickel Plated Steel, 19.9 mm. **Subject:** Charlemagne Peralte, national hero **Obv:** Bust facing **Rev:** National arms

Date	Mintage	F	VF	XF	Unc	BU
1995	—	—	—	—	0.25	0.40
1997	—	—	—	—	0.25	0.40

KM# 54 10 CENTIMES

Copper-Nickel **Obv:** President Pierre Nord Alexis left **Rev:** National arms

Date	Mintage	F	VF	XF	Unc	BU
1906(w)	10,000,000	1.00	3.00	7.00	20.00	25.00
1906(w) Proof	—	Value: 100				

KM# 58 10 CENTIMES

3.7800 g., Copper-Nickel, 22.70 mm. **Obv:** President Dumarsais Estime left **Rev:** National arms

Date	Mintage	F	VF	XF	Unc	BU
1949(p)	5,000,000	0.50	2.00	6.00	15.00	17.50

KM# 60 10 CENTIMES

Copper-Zinc-Nickel **Obv:** President Paul Eugene Magloire left **Rev:** National arms

Date	Mintage	F	VF	XF	Unc	BU
1953(p)	1,500,000	—	0.25	1.00	5.00	7.50

KM# 63 10 CENTIMES

Copper-Zinc-Nickel, 22.5 mm. **Obv:** President Francois Duvalier left **Rev:** National arms **Designer:** Gilroy Roberts

Date	Mintage	F	VF	XF	Unc	BU
1958(p)	7,500,000	—	0.10	0.15	0.35	0.50
1970	2,500,000	—	—	0.10	0.20	0.40

KM# 120 10 CENTIMES

Copper-Nickel, 23 mm. **Series:** F.A.O. **Obv:** President Jean-Claude Duvalier left **Rev:** National arms

Date	Mintage	F	VF	XF	Unc	BU
1975	12,000,000	—	—	0.10	0.20	0.40
1983	2,000,000	—	—	0.10	0.30	0.50

KM# 146 10 CENTIMES

Copper-Nickel **Series:** F.A.O. **Obv:** Head right, small logo at left **Rev:** Sun above farmer in field on tractor **Note:** Denomination as 0.10 Gourdes.

Date	Mintage	F	VF	XF	Unc	BU
1981R	15,000	—	0.10	0.35	1.00	1.25

KM# 55 20 CENTIMES

Copper-Nickel **Obv:** President Pierre Nord Alexis left **Rev:** National arms

Date	Mintage	F	VF	XF	Unc	BU
1907(w)	5,000,000	2.00	6.00	15.00	35.00	40.00
1907(w) Proof	—	Value: 125				
1908(w)	—	—	—	—	—	—

Note: Reported, not confirmed

KM# 61 20 CENTIMES

Nickel-Silver **Obv:** President Paul Eugene Magliore left **Rev:** National arms

Date	Mintage	F	VF	XF	Unc	BU
1956(p)	2,500,000	0.60	1.00	2.00	5.00	6.50

KM# 77 20 CENTIMES

Nickel-Silver **Obv:** President Francois Duvalier left **Rev:** National arms

Date	Mintage	F	VF	XF	Unc	BU
1970	1,000,000	—	0.25	0.35	0.85	1.00

KM# 100 20 CENTIMES

Copper-Nickel, 26 mm. **Series:** F.A.O. **Obv:** President Jean-Claude Duvalier left **Rev:** National arms

Date	Mintage	F	VF	XF	Unc	BU
1972	1,500,000	—	0.10	0.25	1.00	1.25

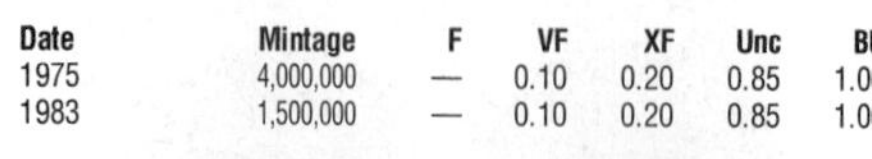

Date	Mintage	F	VF	XF	Unc	BU
1975	4,000,000	—	0.10	0.20	0.85	1.00
1983	1,500,000	—	0.10	0.20	0.85	1.00

KM# 147 20 CENTIMES

Copper-Nickel, 26.2 mm. **Series:** F.A.O. **Obv:** Head right, small logo at left **Rev:** Harvesters **Note:** Denomination as 0.20 Gourdes.

Date	Mintage	F	VF	XF	Unc	BU
1981R	15,000	—	0.10	0.45	1.25	1.40

KM# 152 20 CENTIMES

7.5400 g., Copper-Nickel, 26.15 mm. **Subject:** Charlemagne Peralte, national hero **Obv:** Bust facing **Rev:** National arms **Edge:** Plain **Note:** No accent marks on obverse legend.

Date	Mintage	F	VF	XF	Unc	BU
1986	2,500,000	—	0.10	0.20	0.65	0.95
1989	—	—	0.10	0.20	0.65	0.95
1991	—	—	0.10	0.20	0.65	0.95

KM# 152a 20 CENTIMES

Nickel Plated Steel, 26.2 mm. **Subject:** Charlemagne Peralte, national hero **Obv:** Bust facing **Rev:** National arms **Note:** Accent marks on E and Is in obverse legend.

Date	Mintage	F	VF	XF	Unc	BU
1995	—	—	—	—	0.75	1.00
2000	—	—	—	—	0.75	1.00

KM# 56 50 CENTIMES

9.7300 g., Copper-Nickel, 29 mm. **Obv:** President Pierre Nord Alexis left **Rev:** National arms

Date	Mintage	F	VF	XF	Unc	BU
1907(w)	2,000,000	1.00	5.50	15.00	45.00	50.00
1907(w) Proof	—	Value: 250				
1908(w)	800,000	1.25	10.00	30.00	55.00	60.00
1908(w) Proof	—	Value: 300				

KM# 101 50 CENTIMES

Copper-Nickel **Series:** F.A.O. **Obv:** President Jean-Claude Duvalier left **Rev:** National arms

Date	Mintage	F	VF	XF	Unc	BU
1972	600,000	—	0.10	0.25	1.50	2.00

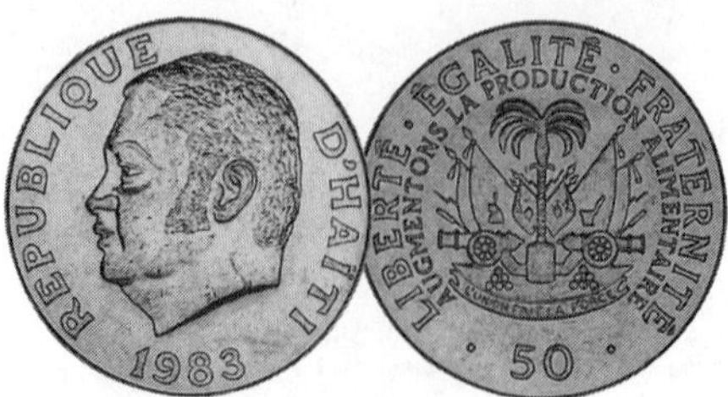

KM# 101a 50 CENTIMES

Copper-Nickel-Zinc **Obv:** Head left **Rev:** National arms **Note:** Varieties exist.

Date	Mintage	F	VF	XF	Unc	BU
1975	1,200,000	—	0.10	0.20	1.00	1.50
1979	2,000,000	—	0.10	0.20	1.00	1.50
1983	1,000,000	—	0.10	0.20	1.00	1.50
1985	—	—	—	—	0.75	1.00

KM# 148 50 CENTIMES

Copper-Nickel **Series:** F.A.O. **Obv:** Head right, small logo at left **Rev:** Plants **Note:** Denomination as 0.50 Gourdes.

Date	Mintage	F	VF	XF	Unc	BU
1981R	15,000	—	0.15	0.65	1.75	2.00

KM# 153 50 CENTIMES

9.8500 g., Copper-Nickel, 28.97 mm. **Subject:** Charlemagne Peralte, national hero **Obv:** Bust facing **Rev:** National arms **Edge:** Plain **Note:** No accent marks on obverse legend.

Date	Mintage	F	VF	XF	Unc	BU
1986	2,000,000	—	0.10	0.25	1.00	1.50
1989	—	—	0.10	0.25	1.00	1.50
1991	—	—	0.10	0.25	1.00	1.50

KM# 153a 50 CENTIMES

Nickel Plated Steel, 29 mm. **Subject:** Charlemagne Peralte, national hero **Obv:** Bust facing **Rev:** National arms **Note:** Accent marks on obverse legend.

Date	Mintage	F	VF	XF	Unc	BU
1995	—	—	0.10	0.25	1.25	1.50
1999	—	—	0.10	0.25	1.25	1.50

KM# 155 GOURDE

6.3000 g., Brass Plated Steel, 23 mm. **Obv:** Citadelle de Roi Christophe **Shape:** 7-sided

Date	Mintage	F	VF	XF	Unc	BU
1995	—	—	—	—	1.75	2.00
2000	—	—	—	—	1.75	2.00
2003	—	—	—	—	1.75	2.00

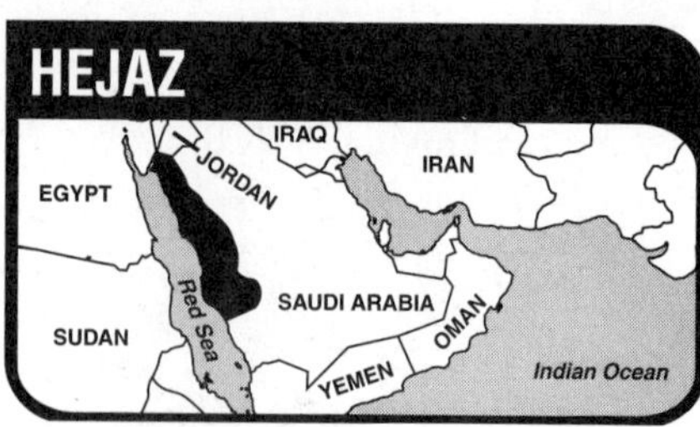

Hejaz, a province of Saudi Arabia and a former vilayet of the Ottoman Empire, occupies an 800-mile long (1,287km.) coastal strip between Nejd and the Red Sea. The province was a Turkish dependency until freed in World War I. Husain Ibn Ali, Amir of Mecca, opposed the Turkish control and, with the aid of Lawrence of Arabia, wrested much of Hejaz from the Turks and in 1916 assumed the title of King of Hejaz. Abd Al-Aziz Bin Sa'ud, of Nejd conquered Hejaz in 1925, and in 1926 combined it and Nejd into a single kingdom.

TITLES

Hal-Hejaz

RULERS

al Husain Ibn Ali, AH1334-42/1916-24AD
Abd Al-Aziz Bin Sa'ud, AH1343-1373/1925-1953AD

MONETARY SYSTEM

40 Para = 1 Piastre (Ghirsh)
20 Piastres = 1 Riyal
100 Piastres = 1 Dinar

KINGDOM

COUNTERMARKED COINAGE

Minor Coins

Following the defeat of the Ottomans in 1916, Turkish 10, 20 and 40 Para coins of Muhammed V and 40 Para coins of Muhammed VI were countermarked al-Hejaz in Arabic. The countermark was applied to the obverse side effacing the Ottoman Sultan's toughra, and thus refuting Turkish rule in Hejaz.

Countermarks on the reverse are rare errors. The 10 Para of Muhammed V and 10 and 20 Para (billon) of Abdul Mejid and Mahmud II exist with a smaller, 6-milimeter countermark. These are probably unofficial. Other host coins are considered controversial.

KM# 2 10 PARA

Nickel **Countermark:** Hejaz **Obv:** Reshat **Note:** Large countermark on Turkey 10 Para, KM#760. Accession date: 1327.

CM Date	Host Date	Good	VG	F	VF	XF
ND(1327)	AH1327//2-7 Rare	—	—	—	—	—
ND(AH1327)	AH1327//7 Rare	—	—	—	—	—

KM# 3 20 PARA

Nickel **Countermark:** "Hejaz" **Note:** Countermark on Turkey 20 Para, KM#761. Accession date: 1327.

CM Date	Host Date	Good	VG	F	VF	XF
ND(1327)	AH1327//2	5.00	9.00	20.00	40.00	—
ND(1327)	AH1327//3	4.00	7.00	15.00	30.00	—
ND(1327)	AH1327//4	3.00	6.00	12.00	25.00	—
ND(1327)	AH1327//5	3.00	6.00	12.00	25.00	—
ND(1327)	AH1327//6	3.00	6.00	12.00	25.00	—
ND(1327)	AH1327//x p.y. obliterated	2.00	5.00	10.00	20.00	—

KM# 4 40 PARA

Nickel **Countermark:** "Hejaz" **Obv:** El Ghazi **Note:** Countermark on Turkey 40 Para, KM#766. Accession date: 1327.

CM Date	Host Date	Good	VG	F	VF	XF
ND(1327)	AH1327//3	6.00	10.00	20.00	40.00	—
ND(1327)	AH1327//4	3.00	6.00	12.00	25.00	—
ND(1327)	AH1327//5	3.00	6.00	12.00	25.00	—
ND(1327)	AH1327//x p.y. obliterated	2.00	5.00	10.00	20.00	—

KM# 5 40 PARA

Copper-Nickel **Countermark:** "Hejaz" **Note:** Countermark on Turkey 40 Para, KM#779. Accession date: 1327.

CM Date	Host Date	Good	VG	F	VF	XF
ND(1327)	AH1327//8	4.00	6.00	12.00	25.00	—
ND(1327)	AH1327//9	20.00	30.00	75.00	150	—
ND(1327)	AH1327//x p.y. obliterated	3.00	6.00	10.00	20.00	—

KM# 6 40 PARA

Copper-Nickel **Countermark:** "Hejaz" **Note:** Countermark on Turkey 40 Para, KM#828. Accession date: 1336.

CM Date	Host Date	Good	VG	F	VF	XF
ND(1326)	AH1336//4	50.00	75.00	150	250	—
ND(1326)	AH1336//x	40.00	50.00	100	200	—

COUNTERMARKED COINAGE

Silver Coins

Silver coins of various sizes were also countermarked al-Hejaz. The most common host coins include the Maria Theresa Thaler of Austria, and 5, 10, and 20 Kurush or Qirsh of Turkey and Egypt. The countermark occurs in various sizes and styles of script. These countermarks may have been applied by local silversmiths to discourage re-exportation of the badly needed hard currency and silver of known fineness.

Some crown-sized examples exist with both the al-Hejaz and Nejd countermarks. The authenticity of the silver countermarked coins has long been discussed, and it is likely that most were privately produced. Other host coins are considered controversial.

KM# 10 5 PIASTRES

Silver **Countermark:** "Hejaz" **Note:** Countermark on Turkey 5 Kurush, KM#750. Accession date: 1327.

CM Date	Host Date	Good	VG	F	VF	XF
(1916-20)	ND(AH1327//1-7)	100	125	200	400	—

KM# 11 5 PIASTRES

Silver **Countermark:** "Hejaz" **Note:** Countermark on Turkey 5 Kurush, KM#771. Accession date: 1327.

CM Date	Host Date	Good	VG	F	VF	XF
(1916-20)	ND(AH1327//7-9)	100	125	200	400	—

KM# 12 5 PIASTRES

Silver **Countermark:** "Hejaz" **Note:** Countermark on Egypt 5 Qirsh, KM#308. Accession date: 1327.

CM Date	Host Date	Good	VG	F	VF	XF
(1916-20)	ND(AH1327// 2H-4H, 6H)	100	125	200	400	—

KM# 13 10 PIASTRES

Silver **Countermark:** "Hejaz" **Note:** Countermark on Turkey 10 Kurush, KM#751. Accession date: 1327.

CM Date	Host Date	Good	VG	F	VF	XF
(1916-20)	ND(AH1327//1-7)	125	200	300	500	—

KM# 14 10 PIASTRES

Silver **Countermark:** "Hejaz" **Note:** Countermark on Turkey 10 Kurush, KM#772. Accession date: 1327.

CM Date	Host Date	Good	VG	F	VF	XF
(1916-20)	ND(AH1327//7-10)	125	200	300	500	—

KM# 15 10 PIASTRES

Silver **Countermark:** "Hejaz" **Note:** Countermark on Egypt 10 Qirsh, KM#309. Accession date: 1327.

CM Date	Host Date	Good	VG	F	VF	XF
(1916-20)	ND(AH1327// 2H-4H, 6H)	125	200	300	500	—

KM# 16 20 PIASTRES

Silver **Countermark:** "Hejaz" **Note:** Countermark on Egypt 20 Qirsh, KM#310. Accession date: 1327.

CM Date	Host Date	Good	VG	F	VF	XF
(1916-20)	ND(AH1327// 2H-4H, 6H)	125	200	300	500	—

KM# 17 20 PIASTRES

Silver **Countermark:** "Hejaz" **Note:** Countermark on Turkey 20 Kurush, KM#780. Accession date: 1327.

CM Date	Host Date	Good	VG	F	VF	XF
(1916-20)	ND(AH1327//8-10)	125	200	300	500	—

KM# 18 20 PIASTRES

Silver **Countermark:** "Hejaz" **Note:** Countermark on Austria Maria Theresa Thaler, KM#T1. Accession date: 1327.

CM Date	Host Date	Good	VG	F	VF	XF
ND(1916-20)	1780	100	150	250	400	—

REGULAR COINAGE

All the regular coins of Hejaz bear the accessional date AH1334 of Al-Husain Ibn Ali, plus the regnal year. Many of the bronze coins occur with a light silver wash mostly on thicker specimens. A variety of planchet thicknesses exist.

KM# 21 1/8 PIASTRE

Bronze, 12-13 mm. **Note:** Reeded and plain edge varieties exist. Size varies.

Date	Mintage	Good	VG	F	VF	XF
AH1334//5	—	—	125	200	300	600

KM# 22 1/4 PIASTRE

1.1400 g., Bronze, 16 mm. **Note:** Reeded and plain edge varieties exist.

Date	Mintage	Good	VG	F	VF	XF
AH1334//5	—	—	8.00	15.00	35.00	65.00
AH1334//6/5	—	—	75.00	300	600	1,200
AH1334//6	—	—	400	750	1,500	2,500

KM# 25 1/4 PIASTRE

Bronze, 17 mm. **Edge:** Plain

Date	Mintage	Good	VG	F	VF	XF
AH1334//8	—	—	10.00	20.00	40.00	75.00

KM# 23 1/2 PIASTRE

Bronze, 18-19 mm. **Note:** Reeded and plain edge varieties exist. Size varies.

Date	Mintage	Good	VG	F	VF	XF
AH1334//5	—	—	10.00	20.00	35.00	75.00

KM# 26 1/2 PIASTRE

3.1400 g., Bronze, 19 mm. **Note:** Similar to 1/4 Piastre, KM#25. Most known specimens were overstruck as "Hejaz & Nejd" KM#1.

Date	Mintage	Good	VG	F	VF	XF
AH1334//8 Rare	—	—	—	—	—	—

KM# 24 PIASTRE

Bronze, 21-22 mm. **Edge:** Reeded **Note:** Size varies.

Date	Mintage	Good	VG	F	VF	XF
AH1334//5	—	—	10.00	20.00	40.00	75.00
AH1334//6/5	—	—	100	200	400	750

KM# 27 PIASTRE

Bronze, 21 mm. **Edge:** Plain

Date	Mintage	Good	VG	F	VF	XF
AH1334//8	—	—	60.00	125	200	325

KM# 28 5 PIASTRES

6.1000 g., 0.9170 Silver 0.1798 oz. ASW, 24 mm.

Date	Mintage	Good	VG	F	VF	XF
AH1334//8	—	—	50.00	90.00	175	300

KM# 29 10 PIASTRES

12.0500 g., 0.9170 Silver 0.3552 oz. ASW, 28 mm.

Date	Mintage	Good	VG	F	VF	XF
AH1334//8	—	—	250	400	750	1,200

KM# 30 20 PIASTRES (1 Riyal)

24.1000 g., 0.9170 Silver 0.7105 oz. ASW, 37 mm.

Date	Mintage	Good	VG	F	VF	XF
AH1334//8	—	—	40.00	75.00	125	200
AH1334//9	—	—	125	200	300	500

KM# 31 DINAR HASHIMI

Gold

Date	Mintage	VG	F	VF	XF	Unc
AH1334-8	—	—	250	400	600	1,000

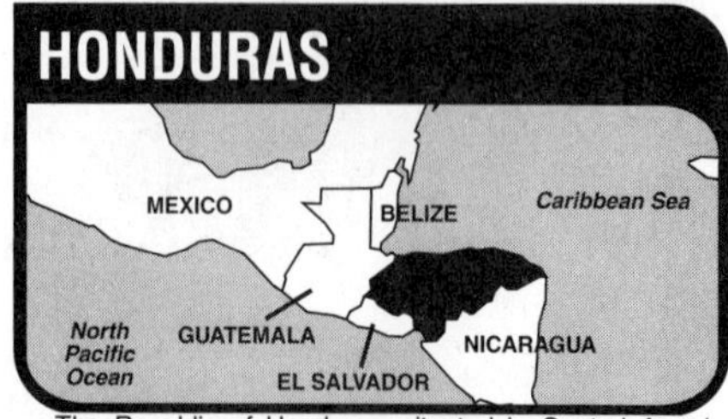

The Republic of Honduras, situated in Central America alongside El Salvador, between Nicaragua and Guatemala, has an area of 43,277sq. mi. (112,090 sq. km.) and a population of 5.6 million. Capital: Tegucigalpa. Agriculture, mining (gold and silver), and logging are the major economic activities, with increasing tourism and emerging petroleum resource discoveries. Precious metals, bananas, timber and coffee are exported.

The eastern part of Honduras was part of the ancient Mayan Empire; however, the largest Indian community in Honduras was the not too well known Lencas. Columbus claimed Honduras for Spain in 1502, during his last voyage to the Americas. Cristobal de Olid established the first settlement under orders from Hernando Cortes, then in Mexico. The area, regarded as one of the most promising sources of gold and silver in the New World, was a part of the Captaincy General of Guatemala throughout the colonial period. After declaring its independence from Spain on September 15, 1821, Honduras fell under the Mexican empire of Augustin de Iturbide, and then joined the Central American Republic (1823-39). Upon the effective dissolution of that federation (ca. 1840), Honduras reclaimed its independence as a self-standing republic. Honduras forces played a major part in permanently ending the threat of William Walker to establish a slave holding empire in Central America based on his self engineered elections to the Presidency of Nicaragua. Thrice expelled from Central America, Walker was shot by a Honduran firing squad in 1860. 1876 to 1933 saw a period of instability and for some months U.S. Marine Corp military occupation. From 1933 to 1940 General Tiburcio Carias Andino was dictator president of the Republic. Since 1990 democratic practices have become more consistent.

RULERS

Spanish, until 1821
Augustin Iturbide (Emperor of Mexico), 1822-1823

MINT MARKS

A - Paris, 1869-1871
P-Y - Provincia Yoro (?)
T - Tegucigalpa, 1825-1862
T.G. - Yoro
T.L. – Comayagua

NOTE: Extensive die varieties exist for coins struck in Honduras with almost endless date and overdate varieties. Federation style coinage continued to be struck until 1861. (See Central American Republic listings.)

MONETARY SYSTEM

16 Reales = 1 Escudo
100 Centavos = 1 Peso

REPUBLIC

DECIMAL COINAGE

100 Centavos = 1 Peso

KM# 46 CENTAVO

4.5000 g., Bronze **Obv:** Arms within circle **Rev:** Value, date within wreath **Edge:** Plain, reeded, and plain and reeded **Note:** Varieties exist.

Date	Mintage	VG	F	VF	XF	Unc
1901/0	98,000	6.50	20.00	42.50	60.00	—
1901	Inc. above	6.50	20.00	42.50	60.00	—
1902 large 0	—	5.00	15.00	27.50	50.00	125
1902 small 0	—	5.00	15.00	27.50	50.00	125
1903/2/0	—	6.00	16.50	32.50	55.00	—
1903/2/1/0	—	40.00	80.00	145	—	—
Note: 5 known						
1904	—	4.50	13.50	30.00	52.50	—
1907	Inc. above	6.50	16.50	30.00	55.00	—
1907/4	234,000	8.00	20.00	35.00	60.00	—

KM# 59 CENTAVO

4.5000 g., Bronze **Obv:** Arms within circle **Rev:** Value within circle, date below **Note:** Varieties exist.

Date	Mintage	VG	F	VF	XF	Unc
1907 large UN	—	0.50	2.00	4.00	10.00	25.00
Note: Mintage included in KM#46						
1907 small UN	—	0.50	2.00	4.00	10.00	25.00
Note: Mintage included in KM#46						
1908/7	263,000	9.00	16.50	35.00	80.00	—
1908	—	9.00	16.50	35.00	80.00	—

KM# 61 CENTAVO

4.5000 g., Bronze **Obv:** Arms within circle and wreath **Rev:** Value within circle **Note:** The 1890, 1891 and 1908 dates are found with a die-cutting error or broken die that reads REPLBLICA. Other differences exist.

Date	Mintage	VG	F	VF	XF	Unc
1908	—	6.50	14.50	28.00	55.00	—

KM# 65 CENTAVO

2.1200 g., Bronze **Obv:** Towers front pyramid within circle **Rev:** Denomination and date within wreath **Note:** Varieties exist.

Date	Mintage	VG	F	VF	XF	Unc
1910/1884	—	12.50	25.00	40.00	70.00	—
1910/5	410,000	10.00	22.00	35.00	60.00	—
1910 large 0	410,000	8.50	20.00	32.50	50.00	—
1911/811	62,000	6.00	18.00	28.00	45.00	—
Note: Struck over 1/2 centavo KM45 or simply the re-use of a recut 1/2 Centavo die						
1911/885	Inc. above	6.00	18.00	28.00	45.00	—
Note: Struck over 1/2 centavo KM45 or simply the re-use of a recut 1/2 Centavo die						
1911/886	Inc. above	6.00	18.00	28.00	45.00	—
Note: Struck over 1/2 centavo KM45 or simply the re-use of a recut 1/2 Centavo die						
1911 CENTAVO	Inc. above	6.00	15.00	25.00	40.00	—
1911 CENTAVOS	Inc. above	150	—	—	—	—

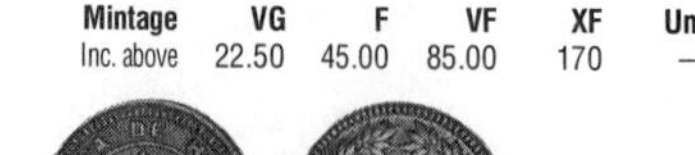

KM# 66 CENTAVO

2.1200 g., Bronze **Obv:** Towers front pyramid within circle **Rev:** Altered KM#45

Date	Mintage	VG	F	VF	XF	Unc
1910	Inc. above	9.00	25.00	45.00	90.00	—
1610 error, inverted 9	Inc. above	65.00	125	225	350	—
1910 error, second 1 inverted	Inc. above	12.00	27.50	50.00	100	—

KM# 67 CENTAVO

2.1200 g., Bronze **Obv:** Towers front pyramid within inner circle, wreath surrounds outer circle **Rev:** Denomination within wreath

Date	Mintage	VG	F	VF	XF	Unc
1910	Inc. above	4.00	8.00	17.00	40.00	—

KM# 68 CENTAVO

2.1200 g., Bronze **Obv:** Towers front pyramid within inner circle **Rev:** Denomination within wreath

Date	Mintage	VG	F	VF	XF	Unc
1910	Inc. above	22.50	45.00	85.00	170	—

KM# 70 CENTAVO

2.1200 g., Bronze **Obv:** Towers front pyramid within circle **Rev:** Denomination and date within wreath, CENTAVO omitted

Date	Mintage	VG	F	VF	XF	Unc
1919	168,000	1.50	3.00	6.50	25.00	—
1920	30,000	3.00	6.50	15.00	37.50	—

KM# 64 2 CENTAVOS

4.2500 g., Bronze **Obv:** Towers front pyramid within circle **Rev:** Denomination within thick circle

Date	Mintage	VG	F	VF	XF	Unc
1907 Rare	Inc. below	—	—	—	—	—
1908/7	Inc. below	50.00	100	200	400	—
1908	Inc. below	40.00	80.00	150	300	—

KM# 69 2 CENTAVOS

Bronze **Obv:** Towers front pyramid within circle **Rev:** Denomination and date within wreath **Note:** Reverse dies often very crudely recut, especially 1910 and 1911. Some coins of 1910 appear to be struck over earlier 1 or 2 Centavos, probably 1907 or 1908.

Date	Mintage	VG	F	VF	XF	Unc
1910	435,000	1.25	4.00	10.00	20.00	45.00
1911	68,000	6.50	18.50	40.00	85.00	—
1912 CENTAVOS	88,000	1.00	4.50	15.00	35.00	—
1912 CENTAVO	Inc. above	3.00	6.00	14.50	35.00	—
1913	258,000	1.00	2.50	6.00	18.50	—

KM# 71 2 CENTAVOS

4.2500 g., Bronze **Obv:** Towers front pyramid within circle **Rev:** Denomination and date within wreath, CENTAVOS omitted **Note:** Varieties exist.

Date	Mintage	VG	F	VF	XF	Unc
1919	117,000	2.50	9.00	18.00	55.00	—
1920 Dot divides date	Inc. above	5.00	10.00	20.00	60.00	—
1920	283,000	0.65	3.00	15.00	50.00	—

KM# 48 5 CENTAVOS

1.2500 g., 0.8350 Silver 0.0336 oz. ASW **Obv:** Arms within circle and wreath **Rev:** Value within wreath

Date	Mintage	VG	F	VF	XF	Unc
1902	—	35.00	75.00	125	200	—

KM# 50a 25 CENTAVOS

6.2500 g., 0.8350 Silver 0.1678 oz. ASW **Obv:** Flags sourround arms within circle **Rev:** Standing Liberty **Note:** Varieties exist.

Date	Mintage	VG	F	VF	XF	Unc
1901/801	54,000	4.00	8.00	15.00	45.00	—
1901/11	Inc. above	6.00	12.50	30.00	60.00	—
1901/0	—	7.00	15.00	35.00	65.00	—
1901 Large first 1	Inc. above	3.00	5.00	9.00	20.00	—
1902/801	—	10.00	17.50	25.00	50.00	—
1902/802	—	10.00	17.50	25.00	50.00	—
1902/812	—	10.00	17.50	25.00	50.00	—
1902/891	—	10.00	17.50	25.00	50.00	—
1902/1 F	—	3.75	6.00	10.00	20.00	125
1902 F	—	4.00	7.50	13.50	25.00	—
1904	—	20.00	40.00	65.00	125	—
1907/4	14,000	7.00	15.00	35.00	60.00	—
1907	Inc. above	7.50	17.50	37.50	65.00	—
1912 .835/.900	7,168	12.50	22.50	45.00	95.00	—
1913/0	52,000	25.00	50.00	100	200	—
1913/2	Inc. above	—	—	—	—	—
1913	Inc. above	10.00	18.50	30.00	55.00	—

KM# 51a 50 CENTAVOS

12.5000 g., Silver **Obv:** Towers front pyramid within inner circle, crowned and flagged decorative mantle behind **Rev:** Seated Liberty figure with flag and tablet, Neptunes symbols flank **Note:** Fineness can be .835 or .900.

Date	Mintage	VG	F	VF	XF	Unc
1908/897	447	35.00	65.00	165	275	—
1908	Inc. above	30.00	55.00	115	225	—

KM# 51 50 CENTAVOS

12.5000 g., 0.9000 Silver 0.3617 oz. ASW **Obv:** Flags sourround arms within circle **Rev:** Standing Liberty

Date	Mintage	VG	F	VF	XF	Unc
1910	602	500	900	—	—	—

KM# 56 PESO

1.6120 g., 0.9000 Gold 0.0466 oz. AGW **Obv:** Arms within circle, bouquets flanking, banner and stars above **Rev:** Liberty head left

Date	Mintage	F	VF	XF	Unc	BU
1901	—	150	300	600	1,150	—
1902	—	140	300	500	1,000	—
1907	—	140	250	450	900	—
1914/882	—	275	450	650	1,200	—
1914/03	—	275	450	600	1,150	—
1919	—	150	300	550	1,100	—
1920	—	150	300	550	1,100	—
1922	—	140	250	450	900	—
ND(ca.1922-25)	—	—	—	—	—	—

KM# 52 PESO

25.0000 g., 0.9000 Silver 0.7234 oz. ASW **Obv:** Flags sourround arms within circle **Rev:** Standing Liberty **Note:** Overdates and recut dies are prevalent.

Date	Mintage	VG	F	VF	XF	Unc
1902	—	27.50	50.00	80.00	135	—
1903 flat-top 3	—	27.50	45.00	70.00	125	—
1903 round-top 3	—	30.00	55.00	90.00	165	—
1904	20,000	30.00	55.00	90.00	165	—
1914	—	200	500	900	1,500	—

KM# 53 5 PESOS

8.0645 g., 0.9000 Gold 0.2333 oz. AGW **Obv:** Arms within inner circle, bouquets flank outer circle **Rev:** Liberty head left

Date	Mintage	F	VF	XF	Unc	BU
1902	—	450	650	1,000	2,500	—
1908/888	—	450	650	1,000	2,500	—
1913	1,200	450	650	1,000	2,500	—

REFORM COINAGE

KM# 77.1 CENTAVO

2.0000 g., Bronze, 15 mm. **Obv:** National arms **Rev:** Denomination within circle, wreath surrounds **Note:** Thick planchet.

Date	Mintage	F	VF	XF	Unc	BU
1935(P)	2,000,000	0.25	1.00	5.00	15.00	—
1939(P)	2,000,000	0.25	0.75	3.00	10.00	—
1949(P)	4,000,000	0.10	0.50	2.00	4.00	—

KM# 77.2 CENTAVO

1.5000 g., Bronze, 15 mm. **Obv:** National arms **Rev:** Denomination within circle, wreath surrounds **Note:** Thin planchet.

Date	Mintage	F	VF	XF	Unc	BU
1954	3,500,000	0.10	0.15	1.00	3.00	—
1956	2,000,000	0.10	0.15	0.75	2.00	—
1957/6	28,000,000	—	—	—	—	—
1957	Inc. above	—	0.10	0.15	0.30	—

KM# 77a CENTAVO

1.3700 g., Copper Clad Steel, 15 mm. **Obv:** National arms, without clouds behind pyramids **Rev:** Denomination within circle, wreath surrounds

Date	Mintage	F	VF	XF	Unc	BU
1974	—	—	0.10	0.15	0.25	—
1985	—	—	0.10	0.15	0.25	—
1992	—	—	0.10	0.15	0.25	—
1994	—	—	0.10	0.15	0.25	—
1998	—	—	0.10	0.15	0.25	—

KM# 77b CENTAVO

Copper Plated Steel, 15 mm. **Obv:** National arms, clouds behind pyramids **Rev:** Denomination within circle, wreath surrounds

Date	Mintage	F	VF	XF	Unc	BU
1988	50,000,000	—	0.10	0.15	0.25	—

KM# 78 2 CENTAVOS

3.0000 g., Bronze, 21 mm. **Obv:** National arms **Rev:** Denomination within circle, wreath surrounds

Date	Mintage	F	VF	XF	Unc	BU
1939(P)	2,000,000	0.25	1.00	3.00	9.00	—
1949(P)	3,000,000	0.10	0.50	2.00	6.00	—
1954	2,000,000	0.10	0.25	1.00	3.00	—
1956	20,000,000	—	0.10	0.25	1.00	—

KM# 78a 2 CENTAVOS

2.7000 g., Bronze Clad Steel, 21 mm. **Obv:** National arms **Rev:** Denomination within circle, wreath surrounds

Date	Mintage	F	VF	XF	Unc	BU
1974	—	—	0.10	0.15	0.25	—

KM# 72.1 5 CENTAVOS

5.0000 g., Copper-Nickel, 21 mm. **Obv:** National arms **Rev:** Denomination within circle, wreath surrounds **Note:** Dentilated border.

Date	Mintage	F	VF	XF	Unc	BU
1931(P)	2,000,000	0.50	2.00	7.00	20.00	—
1932(P)	1,000,000	0.35	0.75	4.00	14.00	—
1949(P)	2,000,000	0.20	0.50	3.00	9.00	—
1956(P)	10,070,000	—	0.15	0.25	0.60	—
1972	5,000,000	—	0.10	0.15	0.35	—

KM# 72.2 5 CENTAVOS

5.0000 g., Copper-Nickel, 21 mm. **Obv:** National arms **Rev:** Denomination within circle, wreath surrounds **Note:** Beaded border.

Date	Mintage	F	VF	XF	Unc	BU
1954	1,400,000	0.15	0.25	1.00	3.00	—
1980	20,000,000	—	0.10	0.50	1.00	—

KM# 72.2a 5 CENTAVOS

Brass, 21 mm. **Obv:** National arms, without clouds behind pyramids **Rev:** Denomination within circle, wreath surrounds

Date	Mintage	F	VF	XF	Unc	BU
1975	20,000,000	—	0.10	0.15	0.35	—
1989	—	—	0.10	0.15	0.35	—

KM# 72.3 5 CENTAVOS

Brass, 21 mm. **Obv:** National arms, with clouds behind pyramids **Rev:** Denomination within circle, wreath surrounds

Date	Mintage	F	VF	XF	Unc	BU
1993	—	—	0.10	0.15	0.35	—
1994	—	—	0.10	0.15	0.35	—

KM# 72.4 5 CENTAVOS

3.2500 g., Brass, 19.21 mm. **Obv:** National arms, without clouds behind pyramids **Rev:** Denomination within circle, wreath surrounds **Edge:** Plain

Date	Mintage	F	VF	XF	Unc	BU
1995	—	—	0.10	0.15	0.35	—
1998	—	—	0.10	0.15	0.35	—
1999	—	—	0.10	0.15	0.35	—
2003	—	—	0.10	0.15	0.35	—

KM# 76.1 10 CENTAVOS

7.0000 g., Copper-Nickel, 26 mm. **Obv:** National arms **Rev:** Denomination within circle, wreath surrounds **Note:** Dentilated border.

Date	Mintage	F	VF	XF	Unc	BU
1932(P)	1,500,000	1.00	2.50	10.00	35.00	—
1951(P)	1,000,000	0.50	1.00	4.00	12.00	—
1956(P)	7,560,000	0.10	0.25	0.50	1.00	—

KM# 76.2 10 CENTAVOS

7.0000 g., Copper-Nickel, 26 mm. **Obv:** National arms **Rev:** Denomination within circle, wreath surrounds **Note:** Beaded border.

Date	Mintage	F	VF	XF	Unc	BU
1954	1,200,000	0.10	0.25	1.00	7.00	—
1967	—	0.10	0.25	0.50	2.00	—
1980	15,000,000	0.10	0.25	0.50	2.00	—
1993	—	0.10	0.25	0.50	2.00	—

KM# 76.1a 10 CENTAVOS

Brass, 26 mm. **Obv:** Large letters and national arms **Rev:** Denomination within circle, wreath surrounds **Note:** Dentilated border.

Date	Mintage	F	VF	XF	Unc	BU
1976	—	0.10	0.15	0.25	0.60	—
1989	—	0.10	0.15	0.25	0.60	—

KM# 76.2a 10 CENTAVOS

6.0300 g., Brass, 26 mm. **Obv:** Small letters and national arms, with clouds behind pyramids **Rev:** Denomination within circle, wreath surrounds **Edge:** Plain **Note:** Beaded border.

Date	Mintage	F	VF	XF	Unc	BU
1993	—	—	0.10	0.20	0.45	—
1994	—	—	0.10	0.20	0.45	—
1995 Small date	—	—	0.10	0.20	0.45	—
1995	—	—	0.10	0.20	0.45	—

KM# 76.3 10 CENTAVOS
5.9700 g., Brass, 26 mm. **Obv:** National arms, without clouds behind pyramid **Rev:** Denomination within circle, wreath surrounds

Date	Mintage	F	VF	XF	Unc	BU
1995	—	—	0.10	0.20	0.45	—
1998	—	—	0.10	0.20	0.45	—
1999 Small date	—	—	0.10	0.20	0.45	—
2002	—	—	0.10	0.20	0.45	—

KM# 73 20 CENTAVOS
2.5000 g., 0.9000 Silver 0.0723 oz. ASW, 18 mm. **Obv:** National arms **Rev:** Chief Lempira left within circle

Date	Mintage	F	VF	XF	Unc	BU
1931(P)	1,000,000	1.25	3.50	9.00	30.00	—
1932(P)	750,000	1.25	3.50	8.00	22.50	—
1951(P)	1,500,000	BV	1.25	3.00	8.00	—
1952	2,500,000	BV	1.25	2.50	7.00	—
1958	2,000,000	BV	1.25	2.00	6.00	—

KM# 79 20 CENTAVOS
2.2000 g., Copper-Nickel, 18 mm. **Obv:** National arms **Rev:** Chief Lempira left within circle

Date	Mintage	F	VF	XF	Unc	BU
1967	12,000,000	—	0.10	0.35	1.00	1.50

KM# 81 20 CENTAVOS
2.2000 g., Copper-Nickel, 18 mm. **Obv:** National arms, date below **Rev:** Chief Lempira left within circle **Note:** Different style lettering.

Date	Mintage	F	VF	XF	Unc	BU
1973	15,000,000	—	0.10	0.20	0.60	1.00

KM# 83.1 20 CENTAVOS
2.2000 g., Copper-Nickel, 18 mm. **Obv:** National arms **Rev:** Head left within circle

Date	Mintage	F	VF	XF	Unc	BU
1978	30,000,000	—	0.10	0.20	0.60	1.00
1990	—	—	0.10	0.20	0.60	1.00

KM# 83.1a 20 CENTAVOS
2.0000 g., Nickel Plated Steel, 17.93 mm. **Obv:** Small arms and legend, with clouds behind pyramid **Rev:** Head left within circle **Edge:** Reeded

Date	Mintage	F	VF	XF	Unc	BU
1991	—	—	0.10	0.20	0.60	1.00
1993	—	—	0.10	0.20	0.60	1.00
1994	—	—	0.10	0.20	0.60	1.00

KM# 83.2a 20 CENTAVOS
2.0000 g., Nickel Plated Steel, 18 mm. **Obv:** National arms, without clouds **Rev:** Head left within circle

Date	Mintage	F	VF	XF	Unc	BU
1995	—	—	0.10	0.20	0.60	1.00
1996	—	—	0.10	0.20	0.60	1.00
1999	—	—	0.10	0.20	0.60	1.00

KM# 74 50 CENTAVOS
6.2500 g., 0.9000 Silver 0.1808 oz. ASW, 23.8 mm. **Obv:** National arms **Rev:** Chiefs head left within circle

Date	Mintage	F	VF	XF	Unc	BU
1931(P)	500,000	3.25	7.00	15.00	40.00	—
1932(P)	1,100,000	2.75	5.00	10.00	35.00	—
1937(P)	1,000,000	2.75	5.00	10.00	35.00	—
1951(P)	500,000	2.75	4.00	9.00	30.00	—

KM# 80 50 CENTAVOS
5.7000 g., Copper-Nickel, 24 mm. **Obv:** National arms **Rev:** Chief Lempira left within circle

Date	Mintage	F	VF	XF	Unc	BU
1967	4,800,000	—	0.25	0.35	1.25	2.00

KM# 82 50 CENTAVOS
5.7000 g., Copper-Nickel, 24 mm. **Series:** F.A.O. **Obv:** National arms **Rev:** Chief Lempira left within circle

Date	Mintage	F	VF	XF	Unc	BU
1973	4,400,000	—	0.25	0.35	1.25	2.00

KM# 84 50 CENTAVOS
5.7000 g., Copper-Nickel, 24 mm. **Obv:** National arms, with clouds behind pyramid **Rev:** Head left within circle

Date	Mintage	F	VF	XF	Unc	BU
1978	12,000,000	—	0.25	0.35	1.00	1.50
1990	—	—	0.25	0.35	1.00	1.50

KM# 84.a1 50 CENTAVOS
Nickel Plated Steel, 24 mm. **Obv:** National arms **Rev:** Head left within circle

Date	Mintage	F	VF	XF	Unc	BU
1991	—	—	0.25	0.35	1.00	1.50
1994	—	—	0.25	0.35	1.00	1.50

KM# 84.a2 50 CENTAVOS
5.0500 g., Nickel Plated Steel, 24 mm. **Obv:** National arms, no clouds behind pyramid **Rev:** Head left within circle

Date	Mintage	F	VF	XF	Unc	BU
1995	—	—	0.25	0.35	1.00	1.50
1996	—	—	0.25	0.35	1.00	1.50

KM# 88 50 CENTAVOS
Nickel Plated Steel, 24 mm. **Subject:** 50th Anniversary F.A.O. **Obv:** National arms **Rev:** Head left within circle, logo below

Date	Mintage	F	VF	XF	Unc	BU
1994	2,000,000	—	—	—	1.50	2.00

KM# 75 LEMPIRA
12.5000 g., 0.9000 Silver 0.3617 oz. ASW, 31 mm. **Obv:** National arms **Rev:** Chiefs head left within circle

Date	Mintage	F	VF	XF	Unc	BU
1931(P)	550,000	6.00	9.00	20.00	75.00	—
1932(P)	1,000,000	5.00	7.50	16.00	65.00	—
1933(P)	400,000	BV	6.50	10.00	45.00	—
1934(P)	600,000	BV	6.00	9.00	40.00	—
1935(P)	1,000,000	—	BV	9.00	40.00	—
1937(P)	4,000,000	—	BV	7.00	25.00	—

HONG KONG

Hong Kong, a former British colony, reverted to control of the People's Republic of China on July 1, 1997 as a Special Administrative Region. It is situated at the mouth of the Canton or Pearl River 90 miles (145 km.) southeast of Canton, has an area of 403 sq. mi. (1,040 sq. km.) and an estimated population of 6.3 million. Capital: Victoria. The free port of Hong Kong, the commercial center of the Far East, is a trans-shipment point for goods destined for China and the countries of the Pacific Rim. Light manufacturing and tourism are important components of the economy.

Long a haven for fishermen-pirates and opium smugglers, the island of Hong Kong was ceded to Britain at the conclusion of the first Opium War, 1839-1842. The acquisition of a 'barren rock' was ridiculed by London and English merchants operating in the Far East. The Kowloon Peninsula and Stonecutter's Island were ceded in 1860, and the so-called New Territories, comprising most of the mainland of the colony, were leased to Britain for 99 years in 1898.

The legends on Hong Kong coinage are bilingual: English and Chinese. The rare 1941 cent was dispatched to Hong Kong in several shipments. One fell into Japanese hands, while another was melted down by the British and a third was sunk during enemy action.

RULER
British 1842-1997

MINT MARKS
H - Heaton
KN - King's Norton

MONETARY SYSTEM
10 Mils (Wen, Ch'ien) = 1 Cent (Hsien)
10 Cents = 1 Chiao
100 Cents = 10 Chiao = 1 Dollar (Yuan)

BRITISH COLONY

DECIMAL COINAGE

KM# 4.3 CENT

Bronze, 27.6 mm. **Ruler:** Victoria **Obv:** Crowned bust left **Rev:** Chinese value within beaded circle

Date	Mintage	F	VF	XF	Unc	BU
1901	5,000,000	2.50	5.50	16.00	80.00	—
1901H	10,000,000	2.50	5.50	16.00	70.00	—

KM# 11 CENT

7.1700 g., Bronze, 27.6 mm. **Ruler:** Edward VII **Obv:** Crowned bust right **Rev:** English around central Chinese legend

Date	Mintage	F	VF	XF	Unc	BU
1902	5,000,000	2.50	4.50	10.00	80.00	—
1903	5,000,000	2.50	4.50	10.00	80.00	—
1904H	10,000,000	1.75	3.50	10.00	60.00	—
1905H	12,500,000	2.50	4.50	10.00	60.00	—
1905	2,500,000	3.75	7.50	15.00	125	—

KM# 16 CENT

Bronze, 27.6 mm. **Ruler:** George V **Obv:** Crowned bust left **Rev:** English around central Chinese legend

Date	Mintage	F	VF	XF	Unc	BU
1919H	2,500,000	2.00	4.00	10.00	50.00	—
1923	2,500,000	1.50	3.00	7.50	40.00	—
1924	5,000,000	1.25	2.50	4.50	20.00	—
1925	2,500,000	1.25	2.50	4.50	20.00	—
1926	2,500,000	1.25	2.50	4.50	20.00	—
1926 Proof	—	Value: 350				

KM# 17 CENT

3.9400 g., Bronze, 22 mm. **Ruler:** George V **Obv:** Crowned bust left **Rev:** English around central Chinese legend

Date	Mintage	F	VF	XF	Unc	BU
1931	5,000,000	0.75	1.00	2.00	5.50	—
1931 Proof	—	Value: 250				
1933	6,500,000	0.75	1.00	2.00	5.50	—
1933 Proof	—	Value: 250				
1934	5,000,000	0.75	1.00	2.00	5.50	—
1934 Proof	—	Value: 250				

KM# 24 CENT

Bronze **Ruler:** George VI **Obv:** Crowned head left **Rev:** English around central Chinese legend

Date	Mintage	F	VF	XF	Unc	BU
1941	5,000,000	1,500	2,500	5,000	8,500	—
1941 Proof	—	Value: 10,000				

KM# 5 5 CENTS

1.3577 g., 0.8000 Silver 0.0349 oz. ASW, 15.53 mm. **Ruler:** Victoria **Obv:** Crowned head left **Rev:** Chinese value within beaded circle **Note:** Coins dated 1866-1868 struck at the Hong Kong Mint; coins without mintmarks dated 1872-1901, were struck at the British Royal Mint.

Date	Mintage	F	VF	XF	Unc	BU
1901	10,000,000	1.25	2.50	5.00	20.00	—

KM# 12 5 CENTS

1.3577 g., 0.8000 Silver 0.0349 oz. ASW **Ruler:** Edward VII **Obv:** Crowned bust right **Rev:** English around central Chinese legend

Date	Mintage	F	VF	XF	Unc	BU
1903	6,000,000	1.00	2.00	4.00	20.00	—
1903 Proof	—	Value: 225				
1904	8,000,000	1.00	2.00	4.00	20.00	—
1904 Proof	—	Value: 200				
1905	1,000,000	1.25	3.00	6.50	30.00	—
1905H	7,000,000	1.00	2.00	4.00	20.00	—

KM# 18 5 CENTS

1.3577 g., 0.8000 Silver 0.0349 oz. ASW **Ruler:** George V **Obv:** Crowned bust left **Rev:** English around central Chinese legend

Date	Mintage	F	VF	XF	Unc	BU
1932	3,000,000	1.00	1.50	4.00	10.00	—
1932 Proof	—	Value: 165				
1933	2,000,000	1.00	1.50	3.25	10.00	—
1933 Proof	—	Value: 165				

KM# 18a 5 CENTS

Copper-Nickel **Ruler:** George V **Obv:** Crowned bust left **Rev:** English around central Chinese legend

Date	Mintage	F	VF	XF	Unc	BU
1935	1,000,000	1.00	2.00	4.50	16.50	—
1935 Proof	—	Value: 115				

KM# 20 5 CENTS

Nickel **Ruler:** George VI **Obv:** Crowned head left **Rev:** English around central Chinese legend **Edge:** Reeded with security

Date	Mintage	F	VF	XF	Unc	BU
1937	3,000,000	0.75	1.25	2.25	7.50	—
1937 Proof	—	Value: 85.00				

KM# 22 5 CENTS

Nickel, 16.5 mm. **Ruler:** George VI **Obv:** Crowned head left **Rev:** English around central Chinese legend **Edge:** Reeded with security

Date	Mintage	F	VF	XF	Unc	BU
1938	3,000,000	0.50	1.00	2.00	6.50	—
1938 Proof	—	Value: 125				
1939H	3,090,000	0.50	1.00	2.00	6.50	—
1939H Proof	—	Value: 125				
1939KN	4,710,000	0.50	1.00	2.00	6.50	—
1941H	777,000	350	750	1,400	3,150	—
1941KN	1,075,000	150	300	600	1,200	—

KM# 26 5 CENTS

Nickel-Brass, 16.5 mm. **Ruler:** George VI **Obv:** Crowned head left **Rev:** English around central Chinese legend

Date	Mintage	F	VF	XF	Unc	BU
1949	15,000,000	0.25	0.50	1.25	7.50	—
1949 Proof	—	Value: 125				
1950	20,400,000	0.25	0.50	1.25	7.50	—
1950 Proof	—	Value: 125				

KM# 29.1 5 CENTS

Nickel-Brass, 16.5 mm. **Ruler:** Elizabeth II **Obv:** Crowned head right **Rev:** English around central Chinese legend **Edge:** Reeded and security

Date	Mintage	F	VF	XF	Unc	BU
1958H	5,000,000	—	0.25	0.75	4.50	—
1960	5,000,000	—	0.15	0.50	3.50	—
1960 Proof	—	Value: 65.00				
1963	7,000,000	—	0.15	0.50	3.50	—
1963 Proof	—	Value: 65.00				
1964H	—	50.00	85.00	150	550	—
1965	18,000,000	—	0.10	0.40	2.00	—
1967	10,000,000	—	0.10	0.40	2.00	—

KM# 29.2 5 CENTS

Nickel-Brass, 16.5 mm. **Ruler:** Elizabeth II **Obv:** Crowned head right **Rev:** English around central Chinese legend **Edge:** Reeded **Note:** Error.

Date	Mintage	F	VF	XF	Unc	BU
1958H	Inc. above	2.50	5.00	9.00	20.00	—
1960	Inc. above	2.50	5.00	9.00	20.00	—

KM# 29.3 5 CENTS

2.6000 g., Nickel-Brass, 16.5 mm. **Ruler:** Elizabeth II **Obv:** Crowned head right **Rev:** English around central Chinese legend **Edge:** Reeded

Date	Mintage	F	VF	XF	Unc	BU
1971KN	14,000,000	—	—	0.25	0.50	—
1971H	6,000,000	—	—	0.25	0.50	—
1972H	14,000,000	—	—	0.25	0.50	—
1977	6,000,000	—	—	0.25	0.50	—
1978	10,000,000	—	—	0.25	0.50	—
1979	4,000,000	—	—	0.25	0.50	—
1980 Not issued	50,000,000	—	—	—	—	—

KM# 61 5 CENTS

2.6000 g., Nickel-Brass, 16.5 mm. **Ruler:** Elizabeth II **Obv:** Crowned head right **Rev:** English around central Chinese legend

Date	Mintage	F	VF	XF	Unc	BU
1988	50,000	—	—	—	4.00	—
1988 Proof	25,000	Value: 5.00				

KM# 6.3 10 CENTS

2.7154 g., 0.8000 Silver 0.0698 oz. ASW, 17.84 mm. **Ruler:** Victoria **Obv:** Crowned bust left **Rev:** Chinese value within beaded circle **Note:** Coins dated 1866-1868 struck at the Hong Kong Mint; coins without mintmarks dated 1869-1901, struck at the British Royal Mint.

Date	Mintage	F	VF	XF	Unc	BU
1901	25,000,000	1.25	2.25	4.50	18.50	—

KM# 13 10 CENTS

2.7154 g., 0.8000 Silver 0.0698 oz. ASW **Ruler:** Edward VII **Obv:** Crowned bust right **Rev:** English around central Chinese legend

Date	Mintage	F	VF	XF	Unc	BU
1902	18,000,000	1.25	2.25	4.50	30.00	—
1902 Proof	—	Value: 200				
1903	25,000,000	1.25	2.25	4.50	30.00	—
1903 Proof	—	Value: 200				

Date	Mintage	F	VF	XF	Unc	BU
1904	30,000,000	1.25	2.25	4.50	30.00	—
1904 Proof	—	Value: 165				
1905	33,487,000	225	400	650	2,100	—
1905 Proof	—	Value: 2,500				

KM# 19 10 CENTS

Copper-Nickel, 20.5 mm. **Ruler:** George V **Obv:** Crowned bust left **Rev:** English around central Chinese legend

Date	Mintage	F	VF	XF	Unc	BU
1935	10,000,000	0.50	1.00	3.50	15.00	—
1935 Proof	—	Value: 75.00				
1936	5,000,000	0.50	1.00	3.50	15.00	—
1936 Proof	—	Value: 75.00				

KM# 21 10 CENTS

Nickel, 20.5 mm. **Ruler:** George VI **Obv:** Crowned head left **Rev:** English around central Chinese legend **Edge:** Reeded with security

Date	Mintage	F	VF	XF	Unc	BU
1937	17,500,000	0.50	0.80	1.50	6.50	—
1937 Proof	—	Value: 85.00				

KM# 23 10 CENTS

Nickel, 20.5 mm. **Ruler:** George VI **Obv:** Crowned head left **Rev:** English around central Chinese legend **Edge:** Reeded with security

Date	Mintage	F	VF	XF	Unc	BU
1938	7,500,000	0.65	1.00	2.25	7.50	—
1938 Proof	—	Value: 85.00				
1939H	5,000,000	0.65	1.00	2.25	7.50	—
1939KN	5,000,000	0.65	1.00	2.25	7.50	—
1939KN Proof	—	Value: 85.00				

KM# 25 10 CENTS

Nickel-Brass, 20.5 mm. **Ruler:** George VI **Obv:** Crowned head left **Rev:** English around central Chinese legend **Edge:** Reeded and security

Date	Mintage	F	VF	XF	Unc	BU
1948	30,000,000	0.25	0.50	1.25	6.50	—
1948 Proof	—	Value: 65.00				
1949	35,000,000	0.25	0.50	1.25	6.50	—
1949 Proof	—	Value: 65.00				
1950	20,000,000	0.25	0.50	1.25	6.50	—
1950 Proof	—	Value: 65.00				
1951	5,000,000	0.50	1.00	3.00	22.50	—
1951 Proof	—	Value: 85.00				

KM# 25a 10 CENTS

Nickel-Brass, 20.5 mm. **Ruler:** George VI **Obv:** Crowned head left **Rev:** English around central Chinese legend **Edge:** Reeded **Note:** Error.

Date	Mintage	F	VF	XF	Unc	BU
1950	Inc. above	3.50	6.50	12.50	25.00	—

KM# 28.1 10 CENTS

4.4600 g., Nickel-Brass, 20.5 mm. **Ruler:** Elizabeth II **Obv:** Crowned head right **Rev:** English around central Chinese legend **Edge:** Reeded with security

Date	Mintage	F	VF	XF	Unc	BU
1955	10,000,000	0.15	0.25	0.50	5.50	—
1955 Proof	—	Value: 50.00				
1956	3,110,000	0.25	0.50	1.25	15.00	—
1956 Proof	—	Value: 50.00				

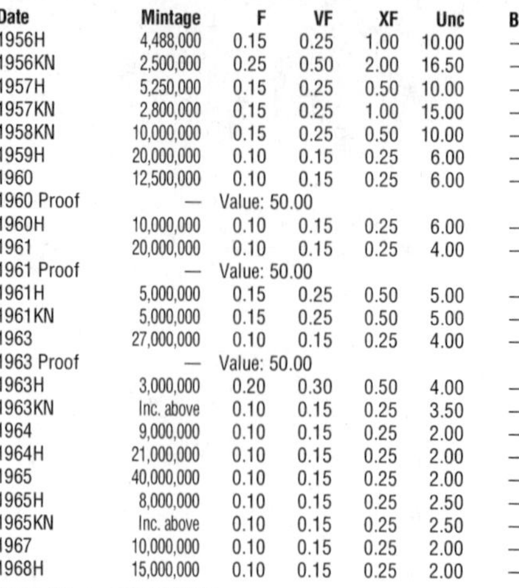

Date	Mintage	F	VF	XF	Unc	BU
1956H	4,488,000	0.15	0.25	1.00	10.00	—
1956KN	2,500,000	0.25	0.50	2.00	16.50	—
1957H	5,250,000	0.15	0.25	0.50	10.00	—
1957KN	2,800,000	0.15	0.25	1.00	15.00	—
1958KN	10,000,000	0.15	0.25	0.50	10.00	—
1959H	20,000,000	0.10	0.15	0.25	6.00	—
1960	12,500,000	0.10	0.15	0.25	6.00	—
1960 Proof	—	Value: 50.00				
1960H	10,000,000	0.10	0.15	0.25	6.00	—
1961	20,000,000	0.10	0.15	0.25	4.00	—
1961 Proof	—	Value: 50.00				
1961H	5,000,000	0.15	0.25	0.50	5.00	—
1961KN	5,000,000	0.15	0.25	0.50	5.00	—
1963	27,000,000	0.10	0.15	0.25	4.00	—
1963 Proof	—	Value: 50.00				
1963H	3,000,000	0.20	0.30	0.50	4.00	—
1963KN	Inc. above	0.10	0.15	0.25	3.50	—
1964	9,000,000	0.10	0.15	0.25	2.00	—
1964H	21,000,000	0.10	0.15	0.25	2.00	—
1965	40,000,000	0.10	0.15	0.25	2.00	—
1965H	8,000,000	0.10	0.15	0.25	2.50	—
1965KN	Inc. above	0.10	0.15	0.25	2.50	—
1967	10,000,000	0.10	0.15	0.25	2.00	—
1968H	15,000,000	0.10	0.15	0.25	2.00	—

KM# 28.2 10 CENTS

Nickel-Brass, 20.5 mm. **Ruler:** Elizabeth II **Obv:** Crowned head right **Rev:** English around central Chinese legend **Edge:** Reeded **Note:** Error.

Date	Mintage	F	VF	XF	Unc	BU
1956	Inc. above	2.25	4.50	8.50	25.00	—
1963	—	2.25	4.50	8.50	25.00	—

KM# 28.3 10 CENTS

Nickel-Brass, 20.5 mm. **Ruler:** Elizabeth II **Obv:** Crowned head right **Rev:** English around central Chinese legend **Edge:** Reeded

Date	Mintage	F	VF	XF	Unc	BU
1971H	22,000,000	—	0.10	0.15	0.65	—
1972KN	20,000,000	—	0.10	0.15	0.65	—
1973	2,250,000	0.15	0.25	0.65	3.50	—
1974	4,600,000	—	0.10	0.15	0.65	—
1975	44,840,000	—	0.10	0.15	0.65	—
1978	57,500,000	—	0.10	0.15	0.65	—
1979	101,500,000	—	0.10	0.15	0.65	—
1980	24,000,000	—	7.00	15.00	35.00	—

Note: Few pieces were released for circulation in 1980, but large numbers have found their way onto the market in subsequent years. About 3,500 are known to exist.

KM# 49 10 CENTS

2.0000 g., Nickel-Brass, 17.55 mm. **Ruler:** Elizabeth II **Obv:** Young bust right **Rev:** Denomination

Date	Mintage	F	VF	XF	Unc	BU
1982	—	—	0.10	0.15	0.25	—
1983	110,016,000	—	0.10	0.15	0.25	—
1984	30,016,000	—	0.10	0.15	0.25	—

KM# 55 10 CENTS

Nickel-Brass, 17.55 mm. **Ruler:** Elizabeth II **Obv:** Crowned head right **Rev:** Denomination

Date	Mintage	F	VF	XF	Unc	BU
1985	34,016,000	—	0.10	0.15	0.25	—
1986	40,000,000	—	0.10	0.15	0.25	—
1987	—	—	0.10	0.15	0.25	—
1988	30,000,000	—	0.10	0.15	0.25	—
1988 Proof	20,000	Value: 5.00				
1989	40,000,000	—	0.10	0.15	0.25	—
1990	—	—	0.10	0.15	0.25	—
1991	—	—	0.10	0.15	0.25	—
1992	24,000,000	—	0.10	0.15	0.25	—

KM# 66 10 CENTS

1.8400 g., Brass Plated Steel, 16.54 mm. **Ruler:** Elizabeth II **Obv:** Bauhinia flower **Rev:** Denomination **Edge:** Plain

Date	Mintage	F	VF	XF	Unc	BU
1993	—	—	0.10	0.15	0.30	—
1993 Proof	—	Value: 2.50				
1994	—	—	0.10	0.15	0.30	—
1995	—	—	0.10	0.15	0.30	—
1996	—	—	0.10	0.15	0.30	—
1997	—	—	0.10	0.15	0.30	—
1998	—	—	0.10	0.15	0.30	—

KM# 14 20 CENTS

5.4308 g., 0.8000 Silver 0.1397 oz. ASW **Ruler:** Edward VII **Obv:** Crowned bust right **Rev:** English around central Chinese legend

Date	Mintage	F	VF	XF	Unc	BU
1902	250,000	20.00	40.00	100	600	—
1902 Proof	—	Value: 1,200				
1904	250,000	20.00	40.00	110	650	—
1905	750,000	300	600	1,200	4,000	—
1905 Proof	—	Value: 7,000				

KM# 36 20 CENTS

2.6000 g., Nickel-Brass, 19 mm. **Ruler:** Elizabeth II **Obv:** Young bust right **Rev:** English around central Chinese legend **Shape:** Scalloped

Date	Mintage	F	VF	XF	Unc	BU
1975	71,000,000	—	0.10	0.20	0.35	—
1976	42,000,000	—	0.10	0.20	0.35	—
1977	Inc. above	—	0.10	0.20	0.35	—
1978	86,000,000	—	0.10	0.20	0.35	—
1979	94,500,000	—	0.10	0.20	0.35	—
1980	65,000,000	—	0.10	0.20	0.35	—
1982	30,000,000	—	0.10	0.20	0.35	—
1983	15,000,000	—	0.10	0.20	0.35	—

KM# 59 20 CENTS

2.6000 g., Brass, 19 mm. **Ruler:** Elizabeth II **Obv:** Crowned head right **Rev:** English around central Chinese legend **Shape:** Scalloped

Date	Mintage	F	VF	XF	Unc	BU
1985	10,000,000	—	0.10	0.20	0.35	—
1988	Est. 40,000	—	0.10	0.20	0.35	—
1988 Proof	Est. 20,000	Value: 5.00				
1989	17,000,000	—	0.10	0.20	0.35	—
1990	—	—	0.10	0.20	0.35	—
1991	131,000,000	—	0.10	0.20	0.35	—

KM# 67 20 CENTS

2.6200 g., Nickel-Brass, 18.95 mm. **Ruler:** Elizabeth II **Obv:** Bauhinia flower **Rev:** Denomination **Edge:** Scalloped **Shape:** Scalloped

Date	Mintage	F	VF	XF	Unc	BU
1993	—	—	0.10	0.20	0.40	—
1993 Proof	—	Value: 2.50				
1994	—	—	0.10	0.20	0.40	—
1995	—	—	0.10	0.20	0.40	—
1997	—	—	0.10	0.20	0.40	—
1998	—	—	0.10	0.20	0.40	—

KM# 15 50 CENTS

13.5769 g., 0.8000 Silver 0.3492 oz. ASW **Ruler:** Edward VII **Obv:** Crowned bust right **Rev:** English and Chinese legend, denomination at center

Date	Mintage	F	VF	XF	Unc	BU
1902	100,000	25.00	35.00	55.00	300	—
1902 Proof	—	Value: 650				
1904	100,000	25.00	35.00	60.00	350	—

Date	Mintage	F	VF	XF	Unc	BU
1904 Proof	—	Value: 650				
1905	300,000	20.00	25.00	50.00	200	—
1905 Proof	—	Value: 650				

KM# 27.1 50 CENTS

Copper-Nickel, 23.5 mm. **Ruler:** George VI **Obv:** Crowned head left **Rev:** English around central Chinese legend **Edge:** Reeded and security

Date	Mintage	F	VF	XF	Unc	BU
1951	15,000,000	1.00	2.00	3.50	12.00	—
1951 Proof	—	Value: 250				

KM# 27.2 50 CENTS

Copper-Nickel, 23.5 mm. **Ruler:** George VI **Obv:** Crowned head left **Rev:** English around central Chinese legend **Edge:** Reeded **Note:** Error.

Date	Mintage	F	VF	XF	Unc	BU
1951	Inc. above	3.00	5.00	10.00	22.00	—

KM# 30.1 50 CENTS

5.8500 g., Copper-Nickel, 23.5 mm. **Ruler:** Elizabeth II **Obv:** Crowned head right **Rev:** English around central Chinese legend **Edge:** Reeded and security

Date	Mintage	F	VF	XF	Unc	BU
1958H	4,000,000	—	0.50	1.25	4.50	—
1960	4,000,000	—	0.40	1.00	4.00	—
1960 Proof	—	Value: 100				
1961	6,000,000	—	0.40	1.00	3.50	—
1961 Proof	—	Value: 100				
1963H	10,000,000	—	0.40	1.00	3.50	—
1964	5,000,000	—	0.40	1.00	3.50	—
1965KN	8,000,000	—	0.40	1.00	3.00	—
1966	5,000,000	—	0.40	1.00	3.50	—
1967	12,000,000	—	0.40	1.00	3.00	—
1968H	12,000,000	—	0.40	1.00	3.00	—
1970H	4,600,000	—	0.40	1.00	3.00	—

KM# 30.2 50 CENTS

Copper-Nickel, 23.5 mm. **Ruler:** Elizabeth II **Obv:** Crowned head right **Rev:** English around central Chinese legend **Edge:** Reeded **Note:** Error.

Date	Mintage	F	VF	XF	Unc	BU
1958H	Inc. above	2.00	4.00	8.00	20.00	—

KM# 34 50 CENTS

Copper-Nickel, 23.5 mm. **Ruler:** Victoria **Obv:** Crowned head right **Rev:** English around central Chinese legend **Edge:** Reeded

Date	Mintage	F	VF	XF	Unc	BU
1971KN	—	—	0.20	0.40	1.50	—
1972	30,000,000	—	0.20	0.40	1.50	—
1973	36,800,000	—	0.20	0.40	1.50	—
1974	6,000,000	—	0.20	0.40	1.50	—
1975	8,000,000	—	0.20	0.40	1.50	—

KM# 41 50 CENTS

4.9000 g., Nickel-Brass, 22.5 mm. **Ruler:** Elizabeth II **Obv:** Young bust right **Rev:** English around central Chinese legend

Date	Mintage	F	VF	XF	Unc	BU
1977	60,001,000	—	0.20	0.30	0.80	—
1978	70,000,000	—	0.20	0.30	0.80	—
1979	60,640,000	—	0.20	0.30	0.80	—
1980	120,000,000	—	0.20	0.30	0.80	—

KM# 62 50 CENTS

4.9000 g., Nickel-Brass, 22.5 mm. **Ruler:** Elizabeth II **Obv:** Crowned head right **Rev:** English around central Chinese legend

Date	Mintage	F	VF	XF	Unc	BU
1988	50,000	—	—	—	8.00	—
1988 Proof	25,000	Value: 10.00				
1990	27,000	—	0.20	0.30	0.80	—

KM# 68 50 CENTS

Brass Plated Steel, 22.5 mm. **Ruler:** Elizabeth II **Obv:** Bauhinia flower **Rev:** Denomination

Date	Mintage	F	VF	XF	Unc	BU
1993	—	—	0.20	0.30	0.80	—
1993 Proof	—	Value: 5.50				
1994	—	—	0.20	0.30	0.80	—
1995	—	—	0.20	0.30	0.80	—
1997	—	—	0.20	0.30	0.80	—
1998	—	—	0.20	0.30	0.80	—

KM# 31.1 DOLLAR

Copper-Nickel, 29.8 mm. **Ruler:** Elizabeth II **Obv:** Crowned head right **Rev:** Upright crowned 3/4 lion with orb left **Edge:** Security **Note:** Mint mark is below "LL" of "DOLLAR".

Date	Mintage	F	VF	XF	Unc	BU
1960H	40,000,000	—	0.60	1.75	5.50	—
1960H Proof	—	Value: 3,350				
1960KN	40,000,000	—	0.60	1.75	5.50	—
1970H	15,000,000	—	0.60	1.25	4.50	—

KM# 31.2 DOLLAR

Copper-Nickel, 29.8 mm. **Ruler:** Elizabeth II **Obv:** Crowned head right **Rev:** Upright crowned 3/4 lion with orb left **Edge:** Reeded **Note:** Error. Mint mark is below "LL" of "DOLLAR"

Date	Mintage	F	VF	XF	Unc	BU
1960H	Inc. above	4.00	7.00	15.00	30.00	—

KM# 35 DOLLAR

Copper-Nickel, 29.8 mm. **Ruler:** Elizabeth II **Obv:** Crowned head right **Rev:** Upright crowned 3/4 lion with orb left **Edge:** Reeded

Date	Mintage	F	VF	XF	Unc	BU
1971H	8,000,000	—	0.60	1.25	4.50	—
1972	20,000,000	—	0.60	1.25	3.50	—
1973	8,125,000	—	0.60	1.25	4.50	—
1974	26,000,000	—	0.60	1.25	3.50	—
1975	22,500,000	—	0.60	1.25	3.50	—

KM# 43 DOLLAR

7.1000 g., Copper-Nickel, 25.5 mm. **Ruler:** Elizabeth II **Obv:** Young bust right **Rev:** Upright crowned 3/4 lion with orb left

Date	Mintage	F	VF	XF	Unc	BU
1978	120,000,000	—	0.40	0.70	1.50	—
1979	104,908,000	—	0.40	0.70	1.50	—
1980	100,000,000	—	0.40	0.70	1.50	—

KM# 63 DOLLAR

7.1000 g., Copper-Nickel, 25.5 mm. **Ruler:** Elizabeth II **Obv:** Crowned head right **Rev:** Upright crowned 3/4 lion with orb left

Date	Mintage	F	VF	XF	Unc	BU
1987	—	—	0.30	0.50	1.00	—
1988	20,000,000	—	0.30	0.50	1.00	—
1988 Proof	20,000	Value: 20.00				
1989	20,000,000	—	0.30	0.50	1.00	—
1990	—	—	0.30	0.50	1.00	—
1991	—	—	0.30	0.50	1.00	—
1992	25,000,000	—	0.30	0.50	1.00	—

KM# 69 DOLLAR

7.1000 g., Nickel Plated Steel, 25.5 mm. **Ruler:** Elizabeth II **Obv:** Bauhinia flower **Rev:** Denomination, large numeral

Date	Mintage	F	VF	XF	Unc	BU
1993	—	—	0.30	0.50	1.00	—
1993 Proof	—	Value: 10.00				

KM# 69a DOLLAR

7.1000 g., Copper-Nickel, 25.5 mm. **Ruler:** Elizabeth II **Obv:** Bauhinia flower **Rev:** Denomination, large numeral

Date	Mintage	F	VF	XF	Unc	BU
1994	—	—	0.30	0.50	1.00	—
1995	—	—	0.30	0.50	1.00	—
1996	—	—	0.30	0.50	1.00	—
1997	—	—	0.30	0.50	1.00	—
1998	—	—	0.30	0.50	1.00	—

KM# 37 2 DOLLARS

8.4000 g., Copper-Nickel, 28 mm. **Ruler:** Elizabeth II **Obv:** Young bust right **Rev:** Upright crowned 3/4 lion with orb left **Shape:** Scalloped

Date	Mintage	F	VF	XF	Unc	BU
1975	60,000,000	—	0.45	0.85	1.75	—
1978	504,000	—	0.45	1.00	10.00	—
1979	9,032,000	—	0.45	0.85	1.75	—
1980	30,000,000	—	0.45	0.85	1.75	—
1981	30,000,000	—	0.45	0.85	1.75	—
1982	30,000,000	—	0.45	0.85	1.75	—
1983	7,002,000	—	0.45	0.85	1.75	—
1984	22,002,000	—	0.45	0.85	1.75	—

KM# 60 2 DOLLARS

8.4000 g., Copper-Nickel, 28 mm. **Ruler:** Elizabeth II **Obv:** Crowned head right **Rev:** Upright crowned 3/4 lion with orb left **Shape:** Scalloped

Date	Mintage	F	VF	XF	Unc	BU
1985	10,002,000	—	0.45	0.65	1.25	—
1986	15,000,000	—	0.45	0.65	1.25	—

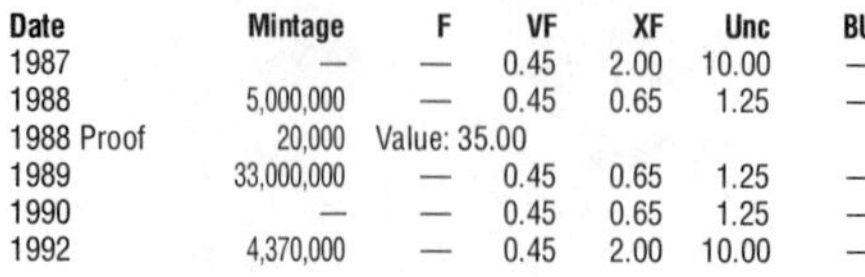

Date	Mintage	F	VF	XF	Unc	BU
1987	—	—	0.45	2.00	10.00	—
1988	5,000,000	—	0.45	0.65	1.25	—
1988 Proof	20,000	Value: 35.00				
1989	33,000,000	—	0.45	0.65	1.25	—
1990	—	—	0.45	0.65	1.25	—
1992	4,370,000	—	0.45	2.00	10.00	—

KM# 64 2 DOLLARS

8.4000 g., Copper-Nickel, 28 mm. **Ruler:** Elizabeth II **Obv:** Bauhinia flower **Rev:** Denomination, large numeral **Shazpe:** Scalloped

Date	Mintage	F	VF	XF	Unc	BU
1993	—	—	0.45	0.65	1.25	—
1993 Proof	—	Value: 12.50				
1994	—	—	0.45	0.65	1.25	—
1995	—	—	0.45	0.65	1.25	—
1997	—	—	0.45	0.65	1.25	—
1998	—	—	0.45	0.65	1.25	—

KM# 39 5 DOLLARS

10.8500 g., Copper-Nickel, 30.8 mm. **Ruler:** Elizabeth II **Obv:** Young bust right **Rev:** Upright crowned 3/4 lion with orb left **Shape:** 10-sided

Date	Mintage	F	VF	XF	Unc	BU
1976	30,000,000	—	1.00	3.00	10.00	—
1978	10,000,000	—	1.00	3.00	15.00	—
1979	12,000,000	—	1.00	3.00	12.00	—

KM# 46 5 DOLLARS

13.4000 g., Copper-Nickel, 27 mm. **Ruler:** Elizabeth II **Obv:** Young bust right **Rev:** Denomination, large numeral

Date	Mintage	F	VF	XF	Unc	BU
1980	40,000,000	—	1.00	1.50	6.00	—
1981	20,000,000	—	1.00	1.50	6.00	—
1982	10,000,000	—	1.00	1.50	6.00	—
1983	4,000,000	—	1.00	1.50	10.00	—
1984	4,500,000	—	1.00	1.50	10.00	—

KM# 56 5 DOLLARS

13.4000 g., Copper-Nickel, 27 mm. **Ruler:** Elizabeth II **Obv:** Crowned head right **Rev:** Denomination, large numeral

Date	Mintage	F	VF	XF	Unc	BU
1985	6,000,000	—	0.75	1.25	6.00	—
1986	8,000,000	—	0.75	1.25	6.00	—
1987	—	—	0.75	1.25	6.00	—
1908	16,000,000	—	0.75	1.25	6.00	—
1988 Proof	25,000	Value: 45.00				
1989	37,000,000	—	0.75	1.25	6.00	—

KM# 65 5 DOLLARS

13.4000 g., Copper-Nickel, 27 mm. **Ruler:** Elizabeth II **Obv:** Bauhinia flower **Rev:** Denomination, large numeral **Edge Lettering:** in Chinese: HONG KONG FIVE DOLLARS

Date	Mintage	F	VF	XF	Unc	BU
1993	—	—	0.75	1.25	2.25	—
1993 Proof	—	Value: 20.00				
1995	—	—	0.75	1.25	2.25	—
1997	—	—	0.75	1.25	2.25	—
1998	—	—	0.75	1.25	2.25	—

KM# 70 10 DOLLARS

Bi-Metallic Nickel-Brass center in Copper-Nickel ring, 24 mm. **Ruler:** Elizabeth II **Obv:** Bauhinia flower **Rev:** Numerals 10 and denomination in Chinese and English

Date	Mintage	F	VF	XF	Unc	BU
1993	—	—	2.50	4.50	10.00	—
1993 Proof	Est. 30,000	Value: 20.00				
1994	—	—	1.50	2.50	5.00	—
1995	—	—	1.50	2.50	5.00	—

SPECIAL ADMINISTRATION REGION (S.A.R.)

DECIMAL COINAGE

KM# 72 10 CENTS

Brass Plated Steel, 17.55 mm. **Obv:** Bauhinia flower **Rev:** Sailing junk

Date	Mintage	F	VF	XF	Unc	BU
1997	—	—	0.10	0.15	0.30	0.45
1997 Proof	Est. 97,000	Value: 1.50				

KM# 73 20 CENTS

Nickel-Brass, 19 mm. **Obv:** Bauhinia flower **Rev:** Butterfly kites

Date	Mintage	F	VF	XF	Unc	BU
1997	—	—	0.10	0.20	0.40	0.60
1997 Proof	—	Value: 1.50				

KM# 74 50 CENTS

Brass Plated Steel, 22.5 mm. **Obv:** Bauhinia flower **Rev:** Ox left divides date

Date	Mintage	F	VF	XF	Unc	BU
1997	—	—	0.20	0.30	0.80	1.25
1997 Proof	Est. 97,000	Value: 2.50				

KM# 75 DOLLAR

7.1000 g., Copper-Nickel, 25.5 mm. **Obv:** Bauhinia flower **Rev:** Chinese unicorn divides date

Date	Mintage	F	VF	XF	Unc	BU
1997	—	—	0.30	0.50	1.00	1.25
1997 Proof	—	Value: 5.50				

KM# 76 2 DOLLARS

8.4000 g., Copper-Nickel, 28 mm. **Obv:** Bauhinia flower **Rev:** Ho Ho brothers divide date **Shape:** Scalloped

Date	Mintage	F	VF	XF	Unc	BU
1997	—	—	0.45	0.65	1.25	1.50
1997 Proof	Est. 97,000	Value: 8.00				

KM# 77 5 DOLLARS

13.4000 g., Copper-Nickel, 27 mm. **Obv:** Bauhinia flower **Rev:** Shou character divides date **Edge Lettering:** in Chinese: HONG KONG FIVE DOLLARS

Date	Mintage	F	VF	XF	Unc	BU
1997	—	—	0.75	1.25	2.25	2.50
1997 Proof	Est. 97,000	Value: 12.50				

KM# 78 10 DOLLARS

Bi-Metallic Nickel-Brass center in Copper-Nickel ring, 24 mm. **Obv:** Bauhinia flower **Rev:** Suspension bridge

Date	Mintage	F	VF	XF	Unc	BU
1997	—	—	1.75	3.50	6.50	7.00
1997 Proof	Est. 97,000	Value: 13.50				

KM# 83 50 DOLLARS

35.3400 g., 0.9250 Silver Gold plated center 1.0509 oz. ASW, 40 mm. **Series:** Five Blessings **Obv:** Bauhinia flower **Rev:** Peony flower

Date	Mintage	F	VF	XF	Unc	BU
2002 Proof	60,000	Value: 60.00				

KM# 84 50 DOLLARS

35.1400 g., 0.9250 Silver Gold plated center 1.0450 oz. ASW, 40 mm. **Series:** Five Blessings **Obv:** Bauhinia flower **Rev:** Windmills

Date	Mintage	F	VF	XF	Unc	BU
2002 Proof	60,000	Value: 60.00				

The Republic of Hungary, located in central Europe, has an area of 35,929 sq. mi. (93,030 sq. km.) and a population of 10.7 million. Capital: Budapest. The economy is based on agriculture, bauxite and a rapidly expanding industrial sector. Machinery, chemicals, iron and steel, and fruits and vegetables are exported.

The ancient kingdom of Hungary, founded by the Magyars in the 9th century, achieved its greatest extension in the mid-14th century when its dominions touched the Baltic, Black and Mediterranean Seas. After suffering repeated Turkish invasions, Hungary accepted Habsburg rule to escape Turkish occupation, regaining independence in 1867 with the Emperor of Austria as king of a dual Austro-Hungarian monarchy.

After World War I, Hungary lost 2/3 of its territory and 1/2 of its population and underwent a period of drastic political revision. The short-lived republic of 1918 was followed by a chaotic interval of communist rule, 1919, and the restoration of the monarchy in 1920 with Admiral Horthy as regent of the kingdom. Although a German ally in World War II, Hungary was occupied by German troops who imposed a pro-Nazi dictatorship, 1944. Soviet armies drove out the Germans in 1945 and assisted the communist minority in seizing power. A revised constitution published on Aug. 20, 1949, established Hungary as a People's Republic' of the Soviet type. On October 23, 1989, Hungary was pro-claimed the Republic of Hungary.

RULERS

Franz Joseph I, 1848-1916
Karl I, 1916-1918

MINT MARKS

B, K, KB - Kremnitz (Kormoczbanya)
BP - Budapest

MONETARY SYSTEM

1892-1925
100 Filler = 1 Korona

1926-1945
100 Filler = 1 Pengo

Commencing 1946
100 Filler = 1 Forint

NOTE: Many coins of Hungary through 1948, especially 1925-1945, have been restruck in recent times. These may be identified by a rosette in the vicinity of the mintmark. Restrike mintages for KM#440-449, 451-458, 468-469, 475-477, 480-483, 494, 496-498 are usually about 1000 pieces, later date mintages are not known.

KINGDOM

REFORM COINAGE

100 Filler = 1 Korona

KM# 480 FILLER

Bronze **Ruler:** Franz Joseph I **Obv:** Crown above date **Rev:** Value within wreath

Date	Mintage	F	VF	XF	Unc	BU
1901KB	5,994,000	4.00	8.00	17.00	32.50	—
1902KB	16,299,000	0.20	0.50	1.25	4.00	—
1903KB	2,291,000	12.00	25.00	65.00	110	—
1906KB	61,000	65.00	160	350	600	—
1914KB Proof	—	Value: 350				
1914KB	—	65.00	130	280	380	—

KM# 481 2 FILLER

3.2800 g., Bronze **Ruler:** Franz Joseph I **Obv:** Crown above date **Rev:** Value within wreath

Date	Mintage	F	VF	XF	Unc	BU
1901KB	25,805,000	0.50	1.00	2.50	5.00	—
1902KB	6,937,000	5.50	8.50	13.50	20.00	—
1903KB	4,052,000	12.00	20.00	65.00	130	—
1904KB	4,203,000	6.00	12.00	25.00	70.00	—
1905KB	9,335,000	0.70	1.75	3.00	6.00	—
1906KB	3,140,000	1.75	2.50	5.00	7.50	—
1907KB	9,943,000	5.50	9.00	12.00	17.50	—
1908KB	16,486,000	0.50	1.00	2.50	5.00	—
1909KB	19,075,000	0.50	1.00	2.50	5.00	—
1910KB	5,338,000	4.50	7.50	10.00	15.00	—
1910KB Proof, restrike with rosette	—	Value: 10.00				
1914KB	4,106,000	0.50	1.00	2.50	5.00	—
1915KB	1,294,000	1.50	2.00	4.00	7.00	—

KM# 497 2 FILLER

Iron **Ruler:** Karl I **Obv:** Crown of St. Stephen **Rev:** Denomination above sprays **Note:** Varieties in planchet thickness exist for 1917.

Date	Mintage	F	VF	XF	Unc	BU
1916	—	6.00	10.00	15.00	25.00	—
1917	—	1.00	2.50	6.00	12.00	—
1918	—	2.00	4.50	9.00	15.00	—

KM# 482 10 FILLER

Nickel **Ruler:** Franz Joseph I **Obv:** Crown above date **Rev:** Value within wreath **Note:** Edge varieties exist.

Date	Mintage	F	VF	XF	Unc	BU
1906KB	56,000	75.00	175	250	325	—
1908KB	6,819,000	0.25	0.50	1.50	4.00	—
1909KB	17,204,000	0.30	0.60	2.00	4.00	—
1914KB	—	—	175	275	550	900

KM# 494 10 FILLER

Copper-Nickel-Zinc **Ruler:** Franz Joseph I **Obv:** Crown of St. Stephen **Rev:** Denomination above sprays **Note:** Varieties exist.

Date	Mintage	F	VF	XF	Unc	BU
1914	4,400,000	—	200	300	500	900
1915	Inc. above	0.30	0.60	1.50	4.00	—
1915 Proof	Inc. above	Value: 4.00				
Note: Restrike with rosette						
1916	Inc. above	0.50	1.25	2.50	5.00	—

KM# 496 10 FILLER

Iron **Ruler:** Karl I **Obv:** Crown of St. Stephen **Rev:** Denomination above sprays **Note:** Varieties exist.

Date	Mintage	F	VF	XF	Unc	BU
1915	11,500,000	9.00	20.00	80.00	140	—
1916 Rare	Inc. above	—	—	—	—	—
1918	Inc. above	15.00	30.00	55.00	85.00	—
1918 Proof, restrike	—	Value: 18.00				
1920	3,275,000	4.50	19.00	50.00	85.00	—
1920 Proof, restrike	—	Value: 18.00				

KM# 483 20 FILLER

Nickel **Ruler:** Franz Joseph I **Obv:** Crown above date **Rev:** Value within wreath **Note:** Edge varieties exist.

Date	Mintage	F	VF	XF	Unc	BU
1906KB	67,000	275	400	600	1,250	—
1907KB	1,248,000	3.00	6.00	12.00	24.00	—
1908KB	10,770,000	0.75	1.75	3.75	7.50	—
1914KB	5,387,000	3.75	6.50	10.00	15.00	—
1914KB Restrike; proof	—	Value: 12.50				

KM# 498 20 FILLER

Iron **Obv:** Crown of St. Stephen **Rev:** Denomination within wreath **Note:** Edge varieties exist.

Date	Mintage	F	VF	XF	Unc	BU
1914	18,826,000	18.00	32.50	45.00	70.00	—
1916	Inc. above	0.50	1.25	2.50	7.00	—
1917	Inc. above	0.75	1.75	3.50	8.00	—
1918	Inc. above	0.75	1.75	3.50	8.00	—
1918 Proof, restrike	—	Value: 6.00				
1920	12,000,000	2.50	5.00	9.00	18.00	—
1921	Inc. above	18.00	32.50	45.00	70.00	—
1921 Proof, restrike	—	Value: 12.00				
1922 Rare	—	—	—	—	—	—
1922 Proof, restrike	—	Value: 12.00				

KM# 498a 20 FILLER

Brass **Obv:** Crown of St. Stephen **Rev:** Denomination above sprays

Date	Mintage	F	VF	XF	Unc	BU
1922	400	—	—	—	—	—
1922 Proof, restrike	—	Value: 30.00				

KM# 484 KORONA

5.0000 g., 0.8350 Silver 0.1342 oz. ASW **Ruler:** Franz Joseph I **Obv:** Laureate head, right **Rev:** Crown, value within wreath **Note:** Obverse varieties exist.

Date	Mintage	F	VF	XF	Unc	BU
1906KB	24,000	150	200	300	425	—

KM# 492 KORONA

5.0000 g., 0.8350 Silver 0.1342 oz. ASW **Ruler:** Franz Joseph I **Obv:** Laureate head right **Obv. Legend:** Crown of St. Stephen within wreath

Date	Mintage	F	VF	XF	Unc	BU
1912	4,004,000	2.50	5.00	10.00	15.00	—
1913	5,214	50.00	80.00	140	200	—
1914	5,886,000	BV	3.75	6.50	10.00	—

Date	Mintage	F	VF	XF	Unc	BU
1915	3,934,000	BV	3.00	4.50	6.00	—
1916	—	BV	3.50	6.00	8.00	—

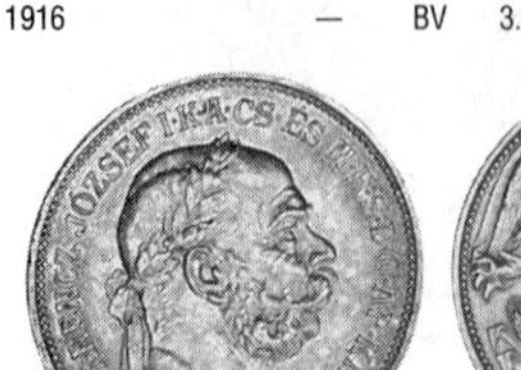

KM# 493 2 KORONA

10.0000 g., 0.8350 Silver 0.2684 oz. ASW **Ruler:** Franz Joseph I **Obv:** Laureate head right **Rev:** Crown of St. Stephen supported by two angels, spray below

Date	Mintage	F	VF	XF	Unc	BU
1912KB	4,000,000	BV	4.50	6.50	13.50	—
1913KB	3,000,000	BV	4.50	6.50	13.50	—
1914KB	500,000	20.00	30.00	50.00	80.00	—

KM# 488 5 KORONA

24.0000 g., 0.9000 Silver 0.6944 oz. ASW **Ruler:** Franz Joseph I **Obv:** Laureate head, right **Rev:** Angels holding crown above value and date within sprigs

Date	Mintage	F	VF	XF	Unc	BU
1906KB	1,263	1,000	1,500	2,000	2,500	—
1907KB	500,000	14.00	20.00	40.00	85.00	—
1908KB	1,742,000	12.00	18.00	40.00	75.00	—
1909KB	1,299,000	12.00	18.00	40.00	90.00	—
1909KB U.P. Proof, restrike	—	Value: 35.00				

KM# 489 5 KORONA

24.0000 g., 0.9000 Silver 0.6944 oz. ASW, 36 mm. **Ruler:** Franz Joseph I **Subject:** 40th Anniversary - Coronation of Franz Josef **Obv:** Laureate head right **Rev:** Coronation scene **Edge Lettering:** BIZALMAM AZ OSI ERÈNYBEN **Designer:** Karoly Gerl

Date	Mintage	F	VF	XF	Unc	BU
1907	300,000	15.00	22.00	35.00	55.00	—
1907 Proof, restrike	—	Value: 30.00				
1907 U.P. Proof, restrike	—	Value: 30.00				

KM# 485 10 KORONA

3.3875 g., 0.9000 Gold 0.0980 oz. AGW **Ruler:** Franz Joseph I **Obv:** Emperor standing **Rev:** Crowned shield with angel supporters

Date	Mintage	F	VF	XF	Unc	BU
1901KB	230,000	—	BV	BV	95.00	—
1902KB	243,000	—	BV	BV	95.00	—
1903KB	228,000	—	BV	BV	95.00	—
1904KB	1,531,000	—	BV	BV	95.00	—
1905KB	869,000	—	BV	BV	95.00	—
1906KB	748,000	—	BV	BV	95.00	—
1907KB	752,000	—	BV	BV	95.00	—
1908KB	509,000	—	BV	BV	95.00	—
1909KB	574,000	—	BV	BV	95.00	—
1910KB	1,362,000	—	BV	BV	95.00	—
1911KB	1,828,000	—	BV	BV	95.00	—
1912KB	739,000	BV	95.00	130	220	—
1913KB	137,000	BV	100	220	300	—

Date	Mintage	F	VF	XF	Unc	BU
1914KB	115,000	BV	200	450	500	—
1915KB	54,000	1,000	2,000	3,000	4,000	—

KM# 486 20 KORONA

6.7750 g., 0.9000 Gold 0.1960 oz. AGW **Ruler:** Franz Joseph I **Obv:** Emperor standing **Rev:** Crowned shield with angel supporters

Date	Mintage	F	VF	XF	Unc	BU
1901KB	510,000	—	BV	BV	190	—
1901KB	510,000	—	BV	BV	190	—
1902KB	523,000	—	BV	BV	190	—
1903KB	505,000	—	BV	BV	190	—
1904KB	572,000	—	BV	BV	190	—
1905KB	526,000	—	BV	BV	190	—
1906KB	353,000	—	BV	BV	190	—
1907KB	194,000	—	BV	BV	200	—
1908KB	138,000	—	BV	BV	190	—
1909KB	459,000	—	BV	BV	190	—
1910KB	85,000	—	BV	250	300	—
1911KB	63,000	—	BV	BV	190	—
1912KB	211,000	—	BV	BV	190	—
1913KB	320,000	—	BV	190	200	—
1914KB	176,000	—	BV	BV	190	—
1915KB	690,000	—	BV	190	200	—

KM# 495 20 KORONA

6.7750 g., 0.9000 Gold 0.1960 oz. AGW **Ruler:** Franz Joseph I **Obv:** Emperor standing **Rev:** Crowned shield (Bosnian arms added) with angel supporters

Date	Mintage	F	VF	XF	Unc	BU
1914	—	—	BV	BV	190	—
1915	—	—	—	—	—	—
1916	—	—	BV	275	400	—

KM# 500 20 KORONA

6.7750 g., 0.9000 Gold 0.1960 oz. AGW **Ruler:** Karl I **Obv. Legend:** KAROLY...

Date	Mintage	F	VF	XF	Unc	BU
1918 Rare	—	—	—	—	—	—

KM# 490 100 KORONA

33.8753 g., 0.9000 Gold 0.9802 oz. AGW, 36 mm. **Ruler:** Franz Joseph I **Subject:** 40th Anniversary - Coronation of Franz Josef **Obv:** Laureate head right **Rev:** Coronation scene **Edge Lettering:** BIZALMAM AZ ÖSI ERÈNYBEN **Designer:** Karoly Gerl

Date	Mintage	F	VF	XF	Unc	BU
1907KB	11,000	—	BV	950	1,350	—
1907KB U.P. Restrike	—	—	—	—	925	—

REGENCY COINAGE

1926 - 1945

KM# 505 FILLER

1.6800 g., Bronze **Obv:** Crown of St. Stephen **Rev:** Denomination

Date	Mintage	F	VF	XF	Unc	BU
1926BP	6,471,000	0.50	1.00	2.00	4.00	—
1927BP	16,529,000	0.10	0.20	0.50	3.00	—
1928BP	7,000,000	0.25	0.50	1.00	3.75	—
1929BP	418,000	5.00	10.00	20.00	35.00	—
1930BP	3,734,000	0.30	0.60	1.50	5.00	—
1931BP	10,849,000	0.10	0.20	0.60	3.00	—
1932BP	5,000,000	0.25	0.50	1.00	4.00	—
1932BP Proof, restrike	—	Value: 3.75				
1933BP	5,000,000	0.25	0.50	1.00	4.00	—

Date	Mintage	F	VF	XF	Unc	BU
1934BP	3,111,000	0.30	0.60	1.20	4.50	—
1935BP	6,889,000	0.25	0.50	1.00	4.00	—
1936BP	10,000,000	0.10	0.20	0.60	2.50	—
1938BP	10,575,000	0.10	0.20	0.60	2.50	—
1939BP	10,425,000	0.10	0.20	0.60	2.50	—

KM# 506 2 FILLER

3.2300 g., Bronze **Obv:** Crown of St. Stephen **Rev:** Denomination

Date	Mintage	F	VF	XF	Unc	BU
1926BP	17,777,000	0.10	0.20	0.40	2.00	—
1927BP	44,836,000	0.10	0.20	0.40	2.00	—
1928BP	11,448,000	0.10	0.20	0.40	2.00	—
1929BP	8,995,000	0.10	0.25	0.50	2.50	—
1930BP	6,943,000	0.10	0.25	0.50	2.50	—
1931BP	826,000	0.40	0.90	2.50	6.50	—
1932BP	4,174,000	4.00	8.00	15.00	25.00	—
1933BP	501,000	3.00	6.00	10.00	18.00	—
1934BP	9,499,000	0.10	0.20	0.40	2.00	—
1935BP	10,000,000	0.10	0.20	0.40	2.00	—
1936BP	2,049,000	0.15	0.30	0.75	4.00	—
1937BP	7,951,000	0.10	0.25	0.50	2.00	—
1938BP	14,125,000	0.10	0.20	0.40	1.50	—
1939BP	16,875,000	0.10	0.20	0.40	1.50	—
1940BP	7,000,000	0.10	0.25	0.50	1.50	—

KM# 518.1 2 FILLER

Steel **Obv:** Crown of St. Stephen **Rev:** Denomination

Date	Mintage	F	VF	XF	Unc	BU
1940	64,500,000	1.00	2.00	5.00	10.00	—

KM# 518.2 2 FILLER

3.3000 g., Steel **Obv:** Crown of St. Stephen **Rev:** Denomination

Date	Mintage	F	VF	XF	Unc	BU
1940	78,000,000	0.50	1.00	2.00	4.50	—
1941	12,000,000	30.00	65.00	125	200	—
1942	13,000,000	0.50	1.00	2.00	4.50	—
1942 Proof, restrike	—	Value: 6.50				

KM# 519 2 FILLER

Zinc, 17 mm. **Obv:** Crown of St. Stephen **Rev:** Denomination **Note:** Variations in planchets exist.

Date	Mintage	F	VF	XF	Unc	BU
1943	37,000,000	0.10	0.20	0.70	3.00	—
1943 Proof, restrike	—	Value: 6.50				
1944	55,159,000	0.10	0.20	0.70	2.50	—

KM# 507 10 FILLER

Copper-Nickel **Obv:** Crown of St. Stephen within small circle on radiant background **Rev:** Denomination

Date	Mintage	F	VF	XF	Unc	BU
1926BP	20,001,000	0.50	1.50	3.00	10.00	—
1927BP	12,255,000	0.50	1.50	3.00	7.00	—
1935BP	4,740,000	0.50	1.50	3.00	4.50	—
1936BP	3,005,000	0.50	1.50	3.00	4.50	—
1938BP	6,700,000	0.50	1.50	3.00	4.50	—
1939BP	4,460,000	3.00	5.00	10.00	20.00	—
1940BP	960,000	15.00	30.00	50.00	75.00	—

KM# 507a 10 FILLER

3.0800 g., Steel **Obv:** Crown of St. Stephen within small circle on radiant background **Rev:** Denomination

Date	Mintage	F	VF	XF	Unc	BU
1940	45,927,000	0.10	0.20	0.80	3.50	—
1941	24,963,000	0.10	0.20	0.80	3.50	—
1942	44,110,000	0.10	0.20	0.80	3.50	—

KM# 508 20 FILLER

Copper-Nickel **Obv:** Crown of St. Stephen within small circle on radiant background **Rev:** Denomination

Date	Mintage	F	VF	XF	Unc	BU
1926BP	25,000,000	1.50	3.50	10.00	15.00	—
1927BP	830,000	10.00	30.00	60.00	100	—
1938BP	20,150,000	0.10	0.25	1.00	2.50	—
1939BP	2,020,000	6.50	10.00	20.00	35.00	—
1940BP	2,470,000	4.00	7.50	18.00	30.00	—

KM# 520 20 FILLER

3.5600 g., Steel, 21 mm. **Obv:** Crown of St. Stephen above center hole **Rev:** Center hole divides denomination

Date	Mintage	F	VF	XF	Unc	BU
1941	75,007,000	0.10	0.20	0.90	4.00	—
1943	7,500,000	0.10	0.20	0.90	4.00	—
1944	25,000,000	0.10	0.20	0.90	4.00	—
1944 Proof, restrike	—	Value: 7.00				

KM# 509 50 FILLER

Copper-Nickel **Obv:** Crown of St. Stephen **Rev:** Denomination

Date	Mintage	F	VF	XF	Unc	BU
1926BP	14,921,000	0.75	2.00	3.50	6.00	—
1938BP	20,079,000	0.20	0.40	1.00	3.00	—
1939BP Proof, restrike	—	Value: 20.00				
1939BP	2,770,000	6.50	15.00	30.00	50.00	—
1940BP	6,230,000	4.00	7.50	18.00	30.00	—

KM# 510 PENGO

5.0000 g., 0.6400 Silver 0.1029 oz. ASW, 22.88 mm. **Obv:** Crowned shield within branches **Rev:** Denomination within wreath

Date	Mintage	F	VF	XF	Unc	BU
1926BP	15,000,000	BV	2.50	6.50	20.00	—
1927BP	18,000,000	BV	175	4.50	12.00	—
1937BP	4,000,000	BV	1.65	2.50	6.00	—
1938BP	5,000,000	BV	1.65	2.50	6.00	—
1939BP	13,000,000	—	BV	2.00	5.00	—

KM# 521 PENGO

1.5000 g., Aluminum **Obv:** Crowned shield **Rev:** Denomination and date divide wreath

Date	Mintage	F	VF	XF	Unc	BU
1941	80,000,000	0.10	0.20	0.50	1.00	—
1942	19,000,000	0.10	0.20	0.50	1.00	—
1943	2,000,000	1.00	4.00	8.00	15.00	—
1944	16,000,000	0.10	0.20	0.50	1.00	—

KM# 511 2 PENGO

10.0000 g., 0.6400 Silver 0.2058 oz. ASW, 27 mm. **Obv:** Angels flank crowned shield above spray **Rev:** Hungarian Madonna

Date	Mintage	F	VF	XF	Unc	BU
1929BP	5,000,000	BV	3.50	6.50	12.50	—
1931BP	110,000	10.00	25.00	45.00	90.00	—
1932BP	602,000	BV	4.00	8.00	15.00	—
1933BP	1,051,000	BV	3.50	6.00	12.50	—
1935BP	50,000	25.00	65.00	120	250	—
1936BP	711,000	BV	5.00	10.00	20.00	—
1937BP	1,500,000	BV	3.25	—	8.50	—
1938BP	6,417,000	BV	3.25	4.75	8.50	—
1939BP	2,103,000	BV	3.25	4.75	8.50	—

KM# 513 2 PENGO

10.0000 g., 0.6400 Silver 0.2058 oz. ASW, 27 mm. **Subject:** Tercentenary - Founding of Pazmany University **Obv:** Crowned, ornate shield **Rev:** Cardinal Peter Pazmany with two others **Designer:** Lajos Beran

Date	Mintage	F	VF	XF	Unc	BU
1935	50,000	3.50	6.50	10.00	20.00	—
1935 Proof	—	Value: 22.50				

Note: Restrike not marked

KM# 514 2 PENGO

10.0000 g., 0.6400 Silver 0.2058 oz. ASW, 27 mm. **Subject:** Bicentennial - Death of Rakoczi, Prince of Hungary and Transylvania **Obv:** Ornaments surround crowned shield **Rev:** Bust right **Designer:** Lajos Beran

Date	Mintage	F	VF	XF	Unc	BU
1935	100,000	3.00	4.50	6.50	10.00	—
1935 Proof	—	Value: 22.50				

Note: Restrike not marked

KM# 515 2 PENGO

10.0000 g., 0.6400 Silver 0.2058 oz. ASW, 27 mm. **Subject:** 50th Anniversary - Death of Franz von Liszt **Obv:** Crowned shield within wreath **Rev:** Head right **Designer:** Lajos Beran

Date	Mintage	F	VF	XF	Unc	BU
1936	200,000	BV	3.00	4.50	8.00	—
1936 Proof	—	Value: 18.00				

Note: Restrike not marked

KM# 522.1 2 PENGO

2.8000 g., Aluminum, 27 mm. **Obv:** Crowned shield within circle **Rev:** Denomination within circle, wreath surrounds

Date	Mintage	F	VF	XF	Unc	BU
1941	24,000,000	0.15	0.30	0.50	0.80	—
1942	8,000,000	0.15	0.30	0.50	0.80	—
1943	10,000,000	0.15	0.30	0.50	0.80	—

KM# 522.2 2 PENGO

Aluminum, 27 mm. **Obv:** Crowned shield within circle **Rev:** Denomination within circle, wreath surrounds, base of 2 is wavy

Date	Mintage	F	VF	XF	Unc	BU
1941	40,000	10.00	20.00	35.00	65.00	—
1941 Restrike, rose	—	—	—	—	—	—

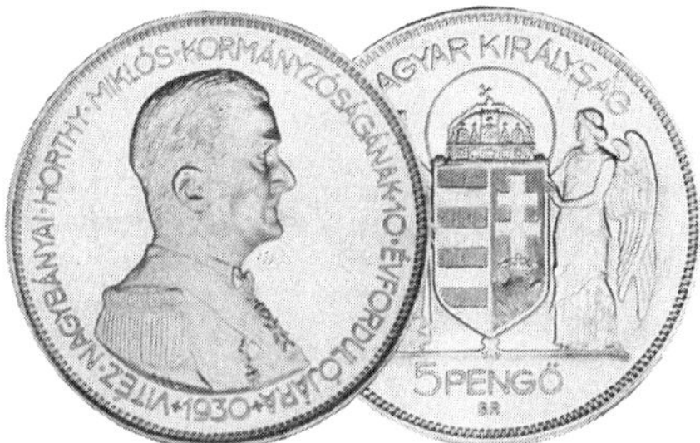

KM# 512.1 5 PENGO

25.0000 g., 0.6400 Silver 0.5144 oz. ASW, 36 mm. **Subject:** 10th Anniversary - Regency of Admiral Horthy **Obv:** Bust right **Rev:** Crowned shield with standing angel supporters **Edge:** Raised, sharp reeding **Designer:** Lojos Beran

Date	Mintage	F	VF	XF	Unc	BU
1930BP	3,650,000	7.50	9.00	12.00	17.50	—

KM# 512.2 5 PENGO

25.3300 g., 0.6400 Silver 0.5212 oz. ASW, 36 mm. **Subject:** 10th Anniversary - Regency of Admiral Horthy **Obv:** Bust right **Rev:** Crowned shield with standing angel supporters

Date	Mintage	F	VF	XF	Unc	BU
1930 Proof, restrike	—	Value: 18.50				

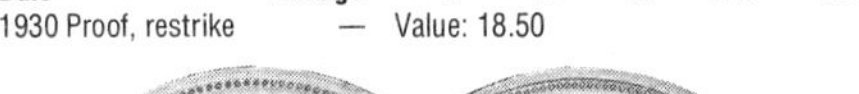

KM# 516 5 PENGO

25.0000 g., 0.6400 Silver 0.5144 oz. ASW, 36 mm. **Subject:** 900th Anniversary - Death of St. Stephan **Obv:** Sword and scepter between crown and shield **Rev:** Crowned bust right **Designer:** Lojos Beran

Date	Mintage	F	VF	XF	Unc	BU
1938	600,000	7.50	9.00	12.50	25.00	—
1938 Proof, restrike not marked	—	Value: 28.50				

KM# 517 5 PENGO
25.0000 g., 0.6400 Silver 0.5144 oz. ASW, 36 mm. **Subject:** Admiral Miklos Horthy **Obv:** Uniformed bust left **Rev:** Crowned shield with standing angel supporters **Edge:** Smooth, ornamented **Designer:** Lojos Beran

Date	Mintage	F	VF	XF	Unc	BU
1938	60	—	—	—	800	—
1939	408,000	7.50	9.00	12.50	25.00	—

KM# 523 5 PENGO
Aluminum, 36 mm. **Subject:** 75th Birthday of Admiral Horthy **Obv:** Uniformed bust left **Rev:** Crowned shield with standing angel supporters **Designer:** Lojos Beran

Date	Mintage	F	VF	XF	Unc	BU
1943	2,000,000	0.50	1.00	2.00	4.00	—
1943 Proof, restrike	—	Value: 6.00				

PROVISIONAL GOVERNMENT
1944-1946

DECIMAL COINAGE

KM# 525 5 PENGO
Aluminum **Obv:** Parliament Building **Rev:** Crowned shield flanked by grain, fruit and leaves

Date	Mintage	F	VF	XF	Unc	BU
1945BP	5,002,000	0.50	1.00	3.00	6.50	—
1945BP PROBAVERET Proof, restrike	—	Value: 17.50				

FIRST REPUBLIC
1946-1949

DECIMAL COINAGE

KM# 529 2 FILLER
3.0000 g., Bronze **Obv:** Arms of the Republic **Rev:** Grain stalk divides denomination

Date	Mintage	F	VF	XF	Unc	BU
1946BP	13,665,000	0.25	0.50	1.00	2.00	—
1947BP	23,865,000	0.25	0.50	1.00	2.50	—
1947BP Proof, restrike	—	Value: 6.50				

KM# 535 5 FILLER
6.0000 g., Aluminum **Obv:** Head left **Rev:** Denomination within wreath

Date	Mintage	F	VF	XF	Unc	BU
1948BP	24,000,000	0.40	1.00	2.00	5.00	—
1951BP	15,000,000	0.40	0.75	1.75	5.00	—

KM# 530 10 FILLER
3.0000 g., Aluminum-Bronze **Obv:** Dove with branch **Rev:** Denomination

Date	Mintage	F	VF	XF	Unc	BU
1946BP	23,565,000	0.15	0.30	0.70	2.00	—
1947BP	29,580,000	0.15	0.30	0.70	2.00	—
1947BP Proof, restrike	—	Value: 7.50				
1948BP	4,885,000	2.00	3.00	4.00	8.00	—
1950BP	8,000,000	1.00	2.00	3.50	7.50	—

KM# 530a 10 FILLER
1.0000 g., Aluminum **Obv:** Dove with branch **Rev:** Denomination

Date	Mintage	F	VF	XF	Unc	BU
1950	—	20.00	30.00	40.00	60.00	—

KM# 531 20 FILLER
4.0000 g., Aluminum-Bronze **Obv:** Three wheat ears divide date **Rev:** Denomination

Date	Mintage	F	VF	XF	Unc	BU
1946BP	16,560,000	0.40	0.80	1.50	3.00	—
1946BP Proof, restrike	—	Value: 8.00				
1947BP	18,260,000	0.50	1.00	2.00	4.00	—
1948BP	5,180,000	2.00	4.00	8.00	12.00	—
1950BP	6,000,000	1.00	2.00	4.00	10.00	—

KM# 536 50 FILLER
1.4000 g., Aluminum **Obv:** Blacksmith sitting on anvil **Rev:** Denomination within wreath

Date	Mintage	F	VF	XF	Unc	BU
1948BP	15,000,000	50.00	70.00	120	—	—
1948BP Proof, restrike	—	—	—	—	—	—

KM# 532 FORINT
1.5000 g., Aluminum **Obv:** Arms of the Republic **Rev:** Denomination flanked by leaves

Date	Mintage	F	VF	XF	Unc	BU
1946BP	38,900,000	1.00	2.00	4.00	10.00	—
1947BP	2,600,000	4.00	8.00	15.00	25.00	—
1949BP	17,000,000	2.50	5.00	10.00	20.00	—

KM# 533 2 FORINT
2.8000 g., Aluminum **Obv:** Shield within wreath, star at top **Rev:** Denomination, large numeral

Date	Mintage	F	VF	XF	Unc	BU
1946BP	10,000,000	2.00	5.00	10.00	20.00	—
1947BP	3,500,000	3.00	7.50	15.00	30.00	—

KM# 534 5 FORINT
20.0000 g., 0.8350 Silver 0.5369 oz. ASW **Subject:** Lajos Kossuth **Obv:** Arms of the Republic **Rev:** Head right **Edge Lettering:** MUNKA A NEMZETI **Note:** Thick planchet.

Date	Mintage	F	VF	XF	Unc	BU
1946BP	39,802	7.50	10.00	15.00	30.00	—

KM# 534a 5 FORINT
12.0000 g., 0.5000 Silver 0.1929 oz. ASW, 32 mm. **Subject:** Lajos Kossuth **Obv:** Arms of the Republic **Rev:** Head right **Note:** 1.7mm thin planchet.

Date	Mintage	F	VF	XF	Unc	BU
1947	10,004,252	—	BV	3.00	5.00	—
1947 Proof, restrike	—	Value: 12.00				

KM# 537 5 FORINT
12.0000 g., 0.5000 Silver 0.1929 oz. ASW, 32 mm. **Subject:** Centenary of 1848 Revolution - Sandor Petofi **Obv:** Denomination above date **Rev:** Head left **Designer:** József Remenyi

Date	Mintage	F	VF	XF	Unc	BU
1948	100,000	BV	3.00	6.00	10.00	—
1948 Proof, restrike	—	Value: 15.00				

KM# 538 10 FORINT
20.0000 g., 0.5000 Silver 0.3215 oz. ASW, 36 mm. **Subject:** Centenary of 1848 Revolution **Obv:** Denomination **Rev:** Istvan Szechenyi **Designer:** Jozsef Remenyi

Date	Mintage	F	VF	XF	Unc	BU
1948BP	100,000	BV	5.00	7.50	15.00	—
1948BP Proof, restrike	—	Value: 22.50				

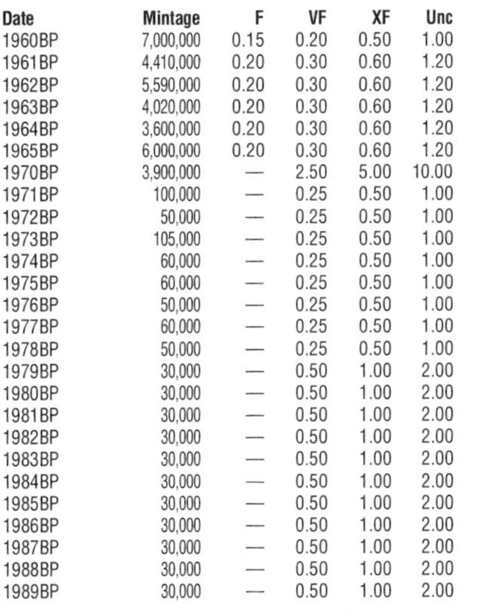

KM# 539 20 FORINT

28.0000 g., 0.5000 Silver 0.4501 oz. ASW, 40 mm. **Subject:** Centenary of 1848 Revolution **Obv:** Arms of the Republic **Rev:** Mihaly Tancsics **Designer:** Istvan Ivan

Date	Mintage	F	VF	XF	Unc	BU
1948BP	50,000	6.50	9.50	17.50	30.00	—
1948BP Proof, restrike	—	Value: 40.00				

PEOPLES REPUBLIC

1949-1989

DECIMAL COINAGE

KM# 546 2 FILLER

0.6900 g., Aluminum, 17.88 mm. **Obv:** Legend and wreath surround center hole **Rev:** Center hole divides denomination within wreath **Edge:** Plain

Date	Mintage	F	VF	XF	Unc	BU
1950BP	24,990,000	—	0.10	0.20	0.50	—
1952BP	5,600,000	—	0.10	0.30	1.00	—
1953BP	9,400,000	—	0.10	0.20	0.50	—
1954BP	10,000,000	—	0.10	0.20	0.50	—
1955BP	6,029,000	—	0.10	0.25	0.75	—
1956BP	4,000,000	—	0.15	0.30	1.00	—
1957BP	5,000,000	—	0.10	0.25	0.50	—
1960BP	3,000,000	0.10	0.15	0.30	0.60	—
1961BP	2,000,000	0.20	0.40	0.60	1.00	—
1962BP	3,000,000	0.10	0.15	0.30	0.60	—
1963BP	2,082,000	0.10	0.20	0.35	0.70	—
1965BP	540,000	—	4.00	8.00	16.00	—
1971BP	1,041,000	0.10	0.15	0.30	0.60	—
1972BP	1,000,000	0.10	0.15	0.30	0.60	—
1973BP	2,820,000	0.10	0.15	0.30	0.60	—
1974BP	50,000	—	0.40	0.80	1.50	—
1975BP	50,000	—	0.40	0.80	1.50	—
1976BP	50,000	—	0.40	0.80	1.50	—
1977BP	60,000	—	0.40	0.80	1.50	—
1978BP	50,000	—	0.40	0.80	1.50	—
1979BP	30,000	—	0.75	1.25	2.50	—
1980BP	30,000	—	0.75	1.25	2.50	—
1981BP	30,000	—	0.75	1.25	2.50	—
1982BP	30,000	—	0.75	1.25	2.50	—
1983BP	30,000	—	0.75	1.25	2.50	—
1984BP	30,000	—	0.75	1.25	2.50	—
1985BP	30,000	—	0.75	1.25	2.50	—
1986BP	30,000	—	0.75	1.25	2.50	—
1987BP	30,000	—	0.75	1.25	2.50	—
1988BP	30,000	—	0.75	1.25	2.50	—
1989BP	30,000	—	0.75	1.25	2.50	—

KM# 549 5 FILLER

0.6000 g., Aluminum, 17 mm. **Obv:** Head left **Rev:** Denomination within wreath

Date	Mintage	F	VF	XF	Unc	BU
1953BP	10,000,000	0.10	0.15	0.30	0.50	—
1955BP	6,005,000	0.15	0.20	0.50	1.00	—
1956BP	6,012,000	0.15	0.20	0.50	1.00	—
1957BP	5,000,000	0.20	0.30	0.60	1.20	—
1959BP	8,000,000	0.15	0.20	0.50	1.00	—
1960BP	7,000,000	0.15	0.20	0.50	1.00	—
1961BP	4,410,000	0.20	0.30	0.60	1.20	—
1962BP	5,590,000	0.20	0.30	0.60	1.20	—
1963BP	4,020,000	0.20	0.30	0.60	1.20	—
1964BP	3,600,000	0.20	0.30	0.60	1.20	—
1965BP	6,000,000	0.20	0.30	0.60	1.20	—
1970BP	3,900,000	—	2.50	5.00	10.00	—
1971BP	100,000	—	0.25	0.50	1.00	—
1972BP	50,000	—	0.25	0.50	1.00	—
1973BP	105,000	—	0.25	0.50	1.00	—
1974BP	60,000	—	0.25	0.50	1.00	—
1975BP	60,000	—	0.25	0.50	1.00	—
1976BP	50,000	—	0.25	0.50	1.00	—
1977BP	60,000	—	0.25	0.50	1.00	—
1978BP	50,000	—	0.25	0.50	1.00	—
1979BP	30,000	—	0.50	1.00	2.00	—
1980BP	30,000	—	0.50	1.00	2.00	—
1981BP	30,000	—	0.50	1.00	2.00	—
1982BP	30,000	—	0.50	1.00	2.00	—
1983BP	30,000	—	0.50	1.00	2.00	—
1984BP	30,000	—	0.50	1.00	2.00	—
1985BP	30,000	—	0.50	1.00	2.00	—
1986BP	30,000	—	0.50	1.00	2.00	—
1987BP	30,000	—	0.50	1.00	2.00	—
1988BP	30,000	—	0.50	1.00	2.00	—
1989BP	30,000	—	0.50	1.00	2.00	—

KM# 547 10 FILLER

0.8600 g., Aluminum **Obv:** Dove with branch **Rev:** Denomination

Date	Mintage	F	VF	XF	Unc	BU
1950BP	5,040,000	10.00	20.00	30.00	50.00	—
1951BP	80,950,000	1.50	3.00	5.00	10.00	—
1955BP	10,019,000	2.00	4.00	7.00	15.00	—
1957BP	13,000,000	2.00	4.00	7.00	15.00	—
1958BP	12,015,000	2.00	4.00	7.00	15.00	—
1959BP	15,000,000	2.00	4.00	7.00	15.00	—
1960BP	5,000,000	2.50	5.00	8.00	17.00	—
1961BP	13,000,000	2.00	4.00	7.00	15.00	—
1962BP	4,000,000	2.50	5.00	9.00	18.00	—
1963BP	8,000,000	2.50	5.00	8.00	17.00	—
1964BP	17,008,000	2.00	4.00	7.00	15.00	—
1965BP	21,880,000	2.00	4.00	7.00	15.00	—
1966BP	8,120,000	2.50	5.00	8.00	17.00	—

KM# 572 10 FILLER

0.6000 g., Aluminum, 18.5 mm. **Obv:** Dove with branch **Rev:** Denomination **Note:** Reduced size.

Date	Mintage	F	VF	XF	Unc	BU
1967	5,000	5.00	10.00	20.00	45.00	—
1968	16,000,000	0.50	1.00	2.50	5.00	—
1969	50,760,000	0.50	1.00	2.50	5.00	—
1970	28,470,000	0.50	1.00	2.50	5.00	—
1971	28,800,000	—	0.50	1.25	2.50	—
1972	17,220,000	—	0.50	1.25	2.50	—
1973	33,720,000	—	0.50	1.25	2.50	—
1974	24,930,000	—	0.50	1.25	2.50	—
1975	30,000,000	—	0.50	1.25	2.50	—
1976	20,025,000	—	0.50	1.25	2.50	—
1977	30,075,000	—	0.50	1.25	2.50	—
1978	36,005,000	—	0.40	1.00	2.00	—
1979	36,060,000	—	0.40	1.00	2.00	—
1980	36,010,000	—	0.40	1.00	2.00	—
1981	36,000,000	—	0.40	1.00	2.00	—
1982	45,015,000	—	0.30	0.75	1.50	—
1983	45,030,000	—	0.30	0.75	1.50	—
1984	42,075,000	—	0.30	0.75	1.50	—
1985	40,035,000	—	0.30	0.75	1.50	—
1986	48,075,000	—	0.30	0.75	1.50	—
1987	45,000,000	—	0.30	0.75	1.50	—
1988	48,015,000	—	0.30	0.75	1.50	—
1989	55,515,000	—	0.25	0.65	1.50	—

KM# 550 20 FILLER

1.2000 g., Aluminum, 21 mm. **Obv:** Three wheat ears divide date **Rev:** Lines divide denomination

Date	Mintage	F	VF	XF	Unc	BU
1953BP	45,000,000	1.00	2.00	4.00	8.00	—
1955BP	10,023,000	1.25	2.50	5.00	10.00	—
1957BP	5,000,000	1.75	3.50	7.00	15.00	—
1958BP	10,000,000	1.25	2.50	5.00	10.00	—
1959BP	13,000,000	1.25	2.50	5.00	10.00	—
1961BP	9,000,000	1.25	2.50	5.00	10.00	—
1963BP	7,000,000	1.50	3.00	6.00	12.00	—
1964BP	10,400,000	1.25	2.50	5.00	10.00	—
1965BP	15,000,000	1.25	2.50	5.00	10.00	—
1966BP	5,000,000	1.50	3.00	6.50	12.50	—

KM# 573 20 FILLER

0.9000 g., Aluminum, 20.4 mm. **Obv:** Three wheat ears divide date **Rev:** Lines divide denomination **Note:** Reduced size.

Date	Mintage	F	VF	XF	Unc	BU
1967	10,000,000	0.25	0.75	2.50	6.00	—
1968	56,500,000	0.10	0.40	1.25	3.00	—
1969	28,550,000	0.15	0.45	1.50	4.00	—
1970	19,960,000	0.20	0.60	2.00	5.00	—
1971	31,090,000	0.10	0.20	0.75	2.00	—
7971 Error	11,000	3.50	7.50	15.00	30.00	—
1972	21,070,000	0.15	0.30	0.75	1.50	—
1973	22,970,000	0.15	0.30	0.75	1.50	—
1974	35,010,000	0.15	0.30	0.75	1.50	—
1975	30,010,000	0.15	0.30	0.75	1.50	—
1976	30,010,000	0.15	0.30	0.75	1.50	—
1977	30,050,000	0.15	0.30	0.75	1.50	—
1978	30,140,000	0.15	0.30	0.75	1.50	—
1979	32,010,000	0.15	0.30	0.75	1.50	—
1980	45,010,000	0.10	0.20	0.50	1.00	—
1981	34,030,000	0.10	0.20	0.50	1.00	—
1982	35,010,000	0.10	0.20	0.50	1.00	—
1983	43,210,000	0.10	0.20	0.50	1.00	—
1984	42,270,000	0.10	0.20	0.50	1.00	—
1985	40,440,000	0.10	0.20	0.50	1.00	—
1986	48,000,000	0.10	0.20	0.50	1.00	—
1987	55,000,000	0.10	0.20	0.50	1.00	—
1988	48,010,000	0.10	0.20	0.50	1.00	—
1989	64,660,000	—	—	0.10	0.50	—

KM# 627 20 FILLER

0.9000 g., Aluminum, 20.4 mm. **Series:** F.A.O. **Obv:** Three wheat ears above banner **Rev:** Lines divide denomination

Date	Mintage	F	VF	XF	Unc	BU
1983	50,000	—	0.50	1.00	2.50	—

KM# 551 50 FILLER

1.4000 g., Aluminum **Obv:** Blacksmith seated on anvil **Rev:** Denomination within wreath

Date	Mintage	F	VF	XF	Unc	BU
1953BP	10,017,000	1.50	3.00	6.00	12.00	—
1965BP	3,005,000	1.25	2.50	5.00	10.00	—
1966BP	1,500,000	1.75	3.50	7.00	15.00	—

KM# 574 50 FILLER

1.2000 g., Aluminum, 21.5 mm. **Subject:** Elizabeth Bridge in Budapest **Obv:** Bridge **Rev:** Denomination above date

Date	Mintage	F	VF	XF	Unc	BU
1967	20,000,000	0.50	1.00	2.00	4.00	—
1968	13,861,000	0.60	1.25	2.50	5.00	—
1969	10,085,000	0.60	1.25	2.50	5.00	—
1971	50,000	0.30	0.60	1.25	2.50	—
1972	470,000	0.20	0.50	1.00	2.00	—
1973	7,600,000	0.20	0.50	1.00	2.00	—
1974	5,000,000	0.20	0.50	1.00	2.00	—
1975	10,160,000	0.10	0.30	0.75	1.50	—
1976	15,130,000	0.10	0.30	0.75	1.50	—
1977	10,050,000	0.10	0.30	0.75	1.50	—

Date	Mintage	F	VF	XF	Unc	BU
1978	10,110,000	0.10	0.30	0.75	1.50	—
1979	10,070,000	0.10	0.30	0.75	1.50	—
1980	15,000,000	0.10	0.30	0.75	1.50	—
1981	10,030,000	0.10	0.30	0.75	1.50	—
1982	10,000,000	0.10	0.30	0.75	1.50	—
1983	10,070,000	0.10	0.30	0.75	1.50	—
1984	14,060,000	0.10	0.30	0.75	1.50	—
1985	12,020,000	0.10	0.30	0.75	1.50	—
1986	17,140,000	0.10	0.30	0.75	1.50	—
1987	23,000,000	—	0.10	0.50	1.00	—
1988	18,050,000	—	0.10	0.50	1.00	—
1989	18,200,000	—	0.10	0.50	1.00	—

KM# 545 FORINT
1.4600 g., Aluminum **Obv:** Wreath surrounds wheat ear and hammer on radiant background below star **Rev:** Leaves flank denomination

Date	Mintage	F	VF	XF	Unc	BU
1949BP	19,440,000	1.50	3.00	6.00	12.00	—
1950BP	39,060,000	2.25	4.50	9.00	18.00	—
1952BP	63,018,000	2.00	4.00	8.00	16.00	—

KM# 555 FORINT
1.5000 g., Aluminum, 22.8 mm. **Obv:** Star above shield within wreath **Rev:** Leaves flank denomination

Date	Mintage	F	VF	XF	Unc	BU
1957	7,500,000	2.00	4.00	8.00	16.00	—
1958	5,070,000	1.50	3.00	6.00	12.00	—
1960	5,000,000	1.25	2.50	5.00	10.00	—
1961	5,000,000	1.25	2.50	5.00	10.00	—
1963	3,000,000	1.50	3.00	6.50	12.50	—
1964	6,080,000	1.00	2.00	4.00	8.00	—
1965	9,810,000	1.00	2.00	4.00	8.00	—
1966	5,680,000	1.75	3.50	7.50	15.00	—

KM# 575 FORINT
1.4000 g., Aluminum, 22.8 mm. **Obv:** Star above shield within wreath **Rev:** Leaves flank denomination

Date	Mintage	F	VF	XF	Unc	BU
1967	60,000,000	0.65	1.25	2.50	5.00	—
1968	53,230,000	0.65	1.25	2.50	6.00	—
1969	27,664,000	1.00	2.00	4.00	8.00	—
1970	11,290,000	1.00	2.00	4.00	10.00	—
1971	100,000	0.10	0.20	0.50	1.00	—
1972	110,000	0.25	0.50	1.00	2.00	—
1973	1,990,000	0.10	0.20	0.50	1.00	—
1974	4,990,000	0.10	0.20	0.50	1.00	—
1975	10,000,000	0.10	0.20	0.40	0.80	—
1976	15,000,000	0.10	0.20	0.40	0.80	—
1977	10,050,000	0.10	0.20	0.40	0.80	—
1978	50,000	0.20	0.40	0.85	1.75	—
1979	10,070,000	0.10	0.20	0.35	0.70	—
1980	20,040,000	0.10	0.20	0.35	0.70	—
1981	25,040,000	0.10	0.20	0.35	0.70	—
1982	10,000,000	0.10	0.20	0.35	0.70	—
1983	20,140,000	0.10	0.20	0.35	0.70	—
1984	6,010,000	0.15	0.30	0.60	1.20	—
1985	30,000	0.25	0.50	1.00	2.00	—
1986	30,000	0.25	0.50	1.00	2.00	—
1987	13,000,000	0.10	0.20	0.50	1.00	—
1988	20,080,000	0.10	0.20	0.35	0.75	—
1989	115,920,000	—	0.15	0.30	0.60	—

KM# 548 2 FORINT
Copper-Nickel **Obv:** Wreath surrounds hammer and wheat ear on radiant background with star above **Rev:** Denomination within 3/4 wreath

Date	Mintage	F	VF	XF	Unc	BU
1950BP	18,500,000	1.75	3.50	7.00	15.00	—
1951BP	4,000,000	2.00	4.00	8.00	16.00	—
1952BP	4,530,000	2.00	4.00	8.00	16.00	—

KM# 556 2 FORINT
4.9500 g., Copper-Nickel, 25 mm. **Obv:** Star above shield within wreath **Rev:** Denomination within 3/4 wreath **Edge:** Flora vines

Date	Mintage	F	VF	XF	Unc	BU
1957	5,000,000	1.50	3.00	6.00	12.50	—
1958	1,033,000	1.75	3.50	7.00	15.00	—
1960	4,000,000	1.50	3.00	6.00	12.50	—
1961	690,000	2.00	4.00	8.00	16.00	—
1962	1,190,000	1.50	3.00	6.00	12.50	—

KM# 556a 2 FORINT
5.1200 g., Copper-Nickel-Zinc **Obv:** Star above shield within wreath **Rev:** Denomination within 3/4 wreath

Date	Mintage	F	VF	XF	Unc	BU
1962	1,210,000	1.25	2.50	5.00	10.00	—
1963	3,100,000	1.25	2.50	5.00	10.00	—
1964	3,250,000	1.25	2.50	5.00	10.00	—
1965	4,395,000	1.25	2.50	5.00	10.00	—
1966	6,630,000	1.25	2.50	5.00	10.00	—

KM# 591 2 FORINT
4.4400 g., Brass, 22.4 mm. **Rev:** Denomination divides date

Date	Mintage	F	VF	XF	Unc	BU
1970	49,195,000	0.50	1.00	2.00	4.00	—
1971	10,830,000	0.10	0.50	1.00	2.00	—
1972	10,015,000	0.10	0.50	1.00	2.00	—
1973	820,000	1.00	2.00	4.00	8.00	—
1974	10,000,000	0.25	0.75	1.50	3.00	—
1975	20,030,000	0.25	0.75	1.50	3.00	—
1976	15,000,000	0.25	0.75	1.50	3.00	—
1977	10,115,000	0.25	0.75	1.50	3.00	—
1978	12,000,000	0.25	0.75	1.50	3.00	—
1979	10,127,000	0.25	0.75	1.50	3.00	—
1980	12,005,000	0.25	0.75	1.50	3.00	—
1981	10,010,000	0.25	0.75	1.50	3.00	—
1982	10,005,000	0.25	0.75	1.50	3.00	—
1983	20,160,000	0.25	0.75	1.50	3.00	—
1984	5,000,000	0.75	1.50	3.00	6.00	—
1985	10,675,000	0.25	0.75	1.50	3.00	—
1986	30,000	1.50	3.00	6.00	12.00	—
1987	5,030,000	0.50	1.00	2.00	4.00	—
1988	5,035,000	0.50	1.00	2.00	4.00	—
1989	79,223,000	0.10	0.25	0.50	1.00	—

KM# 576 5 FORINT
7.2100 g., Copper-Nickel, 27 mm. **Subject:** Lajos Kossuth **Obv:** Star above shield within wreath **Rev:** Head right

Date	Mintage	F	VF	XF	Unc	BU
1967BP	20,000,000	0.50	1.00	2.50	5.00	—
1968BP	29,000	5.00	10.00	20.00	35.00	—

KM# 594 5 FORINT
5.7300 g., Nickel, 24.3 mm. **Obv:** Head right **Rev:** Small shield above denomination

Date	Mintage	F	VF	XF	Unc	BU
1971	20,004,000	0.20	0.35	0.75	1.50	—
1972	5,000,000	0.25	0.50	1.00	2.00	—
1973	100,000	0.35	0.75	1.50	3.00	—
1974	50,000	0.35	0.75	1.50	3.00	—
1975	50,000	0.35	0.75	1.50	3.00	—
1976	5,090,000	0.25	0.50	1.00	2.00	—
1977	50,000	0.35	0.75	1.50	3.00	—
1978	6,000,000	0.25	0.50	1.00	2.00	—
1979	10,000,000	0.25	0.50	1.00	2.00	—
1980	6,002,000	0.25	0.50	1.00	2.00	—
1981	5,002,000	0.25	0.50	1.00	2.00	—
1982	936,000	0.30	0.60	1.25	2.50	—

KM# 628 5 FORINT
Nickel **Series:** F.A.O. **Obv:** Flower holds logo within circle **Rev:** Small shield above denomination **Designer:** György Bognar

Date	Mintage	F	VF	XF	Unc	BU
1983	50,000	—	1.00	2.00	3.50	—

KM# 635 5 FORINT
Copper-Nickel **Subject:** Lajos Kossuth **Obv:** Head right **Rev:** Small shield above denomination

Date	Mintage	F	VF	XF	Unc	BU
1983	15,240,000	0.15	0.25	0.50	1.00	—
1984	25,018,000	0.15	0.25	0.50	1.00	—
1985	25,286,000	0.15	0.25	0.50	1.00	—
1986	1,030,000	0.20	0.35	0.75	1.50	—
1987	30,000	0.30	0.60	1.25	2.50	—
1988	4,050,000	0.20	0.35	0.75	1.50	—
1989	39,014,000	0.15	0.25	0.50	1.00	—

KM# 552 10 FORINT
12.5000 g., 0.8000 Silver 0.3215 oz. ASW, 30 mm. **Subject:** 10th Anniversary of Forint **Obv:** National Museum in Budapest **Rev:** Leaves back of denomination, small shield above **Designer:** Ivan Istvan

Date	Mintage	F	VF	XF	Unc	BU
1956BP	22,000	BV	5.50	8.00	16.00	—

KM# 595 10 FORINT
8.8300 g., Nickel, 28 mm. **Obv:** Strobl Monument **Rev:** Small shield below denomination

Date	Mintage	F	VF	XF	Unc	BU
1971	24,998,000	0.35	0.75	1.50	3.00	4.50
1972	25,078,000	0.35	0.75	1.50	3.00	4.50
1973	78,000	0.60	1.25	2.50	5.00	7.50
1974	50,000	0.60	1.25	2.50	5.00	7.50
1975	50,000	0.60	1.25	2.50	5.00	7.50
1976	3,568,000	0.50	1.00	2.00	4.00	5.50
1977	4,618,000	0.50	1.00	2.00	4.00	5.50
1978	50,000	0.60	1.25	2.50	5.00	7.50
1979	5,000,000	0.50	1.00	2.00	4.00	5.50
1980	2,550,000	0.50	1.00	2.00	4.00	5.50
1982	30,000	0.60	1.25	2.50	5.00	7.50

KM# 620 10 FORINT
8.8300 g., Nickel, 28 mm. **Series:** F.A.O. **Obv:** Strobl Monument **Rev:** Small shield below denomination

Date	Mintage	F	VF	XF	Unc	BU
1981	60,000	—	—	2.50	5.00	7.50

KM# 629 10 FORINT
8.8300 g., Nickel, 28 mm. **Series:** F.A.O. **Obv:** Logo at right of figure with large jar and bowl **Rev:** Small shield below denomination **Designer:** Gyorgi Bognar

Date	Mintage	F	VF	XF	Unc	BU
1983	50,000	—	—	2.50	5.00	—

KM# 636 10 FORINT
6.0100 g., Aluminum-Bronze, 28 mm. **Obv:** Strobl Monument **Rev:** Small shield below denomination **Note:** Circulation coinage.

Date	Mintage	F	VF	XF	Unc	BU
1983	11,004,000	0.25	0.50	1.00	2.00	3.00
1984	7,578,000	0.25	0.50	1.00	2.00	3.00
1985	27,648,000	0.25	0.50	1.00	2.00	3.00
1986	15,006,000	0.25	0.50	1.00	2.00	3.00
1987	10,000,000	0.25	0.50	1.00	2.00	3.00
1988	5,000,000	0.25	0.50	1.00	2.00	3.00
1989	37,094,000	0.25	0.50	1.00	2.00	3.00

KM# 553 20 FORINT
17.5000 g., 0.8000 Silver 0.4501 oz. ASW, 32 mm. **Subject:** 10th Anniversary of Forint **Obv:** Szechenyi suspension bridge in Budapest **Rev:** Shield on ornamental background **Designer:** Ivan Istvan

Date	Mintage	F	VF	XF	Unc	BU
1956BP	22,000	6.50	8.00	12.00	20.00	—

KM# 630 20 FORINT
Copper-Nickel, 26.5 mm. **Subject:** György Dózsa **Obv:** Head looking left **Rev:** Small shield above denomination

Date	Mintage	F	VF	XF	Unc	BU
1982	13,404,000	0.25	0.50	0.80	1.60	—
1983	18,006,000	0.25	0.50	0.80	1.60	—
1984	31,016,000	0.25	0.50	0.80	1.60	—
1985	20,122,000	0.25	0.50	0.80	1.60	—
1986	6,000,000	0.35	0.65	1.25	2.25	—
1987	30,000	0.40	0.75	1.50	3.00	—
1988	30,000	0.40	0.75	1.50	3.00	—
1989	31,890,000	0.25	0.50	0.80	1.60	—

KM# 637 20 FORINT
Copper-Nickel **Subject:** Forestry for Development **Obv:** Leaf within globe above denomination **Rev:** Stylized tree within patterned archway

Date	Mintage	F	VF	XF	Unc	BU
1984	15,000	—	—	—	3.00	—
1984 Proof	5,000	Value: 7.00				

KM# 653 20 FORINT
Copper-Nickel **Series:** F.A.O. **Obv:** Logos with dates within box above stylized denomination **Rev:** Wheat ear divides fish and leaf, lined background

Date	Mintage	F	VF	XF	Unc	BU
1985	25,000	—	—	—	4.00	—

TRANSITIONAL COINAGE

KM# 736 FORINT
Aluminum **Obv:** Star above shield within wreath **Rev:** Leaves flank denomination **Note:** Communist design type with New Republic legends

Date	Mintage	F	VF	XF	Unc	BU
1990	10,000	—	—	—	10.00	12.00

KM# 737 2 FORINT
Brass **Obv:** Star above shield within wreath **Rev:** Large denomination divides date **Note:** Communist design type with New Republic legends

Date	Mintage	F	VF	XF	Unc	BU
1990	10,000	—	—	—	15.00	17.00

KM# 738 5 FORINT
Copper-Nickel **Subject:** Lajos Kossuth **Obv. Inscription:** Head right **Rev:** Small shield divides date above denomination **Note:** Communist design with New Republic legends

Date	Mintage	F	VF	XF	Unc	BU
1990	10,000	—	—	—	20.00	22.00

KM# 739 10 FORINT
Aluminum-Bronze **Obv:** Strobl Monument **Rev:** Small shield below denomination

Date	Mintage	F	VF	XF	Unc	BU
1990	10,000	—	—	—	25.00	30.00

KM# 740 20 FORINT
Copper-Nickel **Subject:** György Dózsa **Obv:** Head looking left **Rev:** Grain sprigs flank denomination, small shield above

Date	Mintage	F	VF	XF	Unc	BU
1990	10,000	—	—	—	30.00	35.00

SECOND REPUBLIC
1989-present
DECIMAL COINAGE

KM# 673 2 FILLER
6.5000 g., Aluminum **Obv:** Wreath surrounds center hole **Rev:** Center hole divides denomination within wreath

Date	Mintage	F	VF	XF	Unc	BU
1990BP	10,000	—	—	—	2.00	—
1991BP	10,000	—	—	—	3.00	—
1992BP	30,000	—	—	—	3.00	—

KM# 674 5 FILLER
6.0000 g., Aluminum **Obv:** Head left **Rev:** Denomination within wreath

Date	Mintage	F	VF	XF	Unc	BU
1990BP	10,000	—	—	—	2.00	—
1991BP	10,000	—	—	—	3.00	—
1992BP	30,000	—	—	—	3.00	—

KM# 675 10 FILLER
6.0000 g., Aluminum **Obv:** Dove with branch **Rev:** Denomination

Date	Mintage	F	VF	XF	Unc	BU
1990BP	46,515,000	0.10	0.15	0.20	0.50	—
1991BP	2,370,000	0.25	0.40	0.55	0.50	—
1992BP	15,828,000	0.15	0.25	0.35	0.50	—
1993BP	30,000	—	—	—	0.50	—
1994BP	30,000	—	—	—	0.50	—
1995BP	30,000	—	—	—	0.50	—
1996BP	20,000	—	—	—	0.50	—

KM# 676 20 FILLER
1.0000 g., Aluminum, 20.21 mm. **Obv:** Three wheat ears divide date **Rev:** Lines divide denomination **Edge:** Reeded

Date	Mintage	F	VF	XF	Unc	BU
1990BP	59,360,000	0.10	0.15	0.20	0.35	—
1991BP	20,210,000	0.20	0.35	0.50	0.75	—
1992BP	30,000	—	—	—	1.00	—
1993BP	30,000	—	—	—	1.00	—
1994BP	30,000	—	—	—	1.00	—
1995BP	30,000	—	—	—	1.00	—
1996BP	20,000	—	—	—	1.25	—

KM# 677 50 FILLER
1.2700 g., Aluminum, 19.78 mm. **Obv:** Erzsebet Bridge **Rev:** Denomination **Edge:** Plain

Date	Mintage	F	VF	XF	Unc	BU
1990BP	20,550,000	—	0.10	0.20	0.30	—
1991BP	31,250,000	—	—	0.10	0.25	—
1992BP	440,000	—	—	—	0.85	—
1993BP	30,000	—	—	—	1.20	—
1994BP	30,000	—	—	—	1.20	—
1995BP	30,000	—	—	—	1.20	—
1996BP	20,000	—	—	—	1.60	—
1997BP	10,000	—	—	—	2.50	—
1998BP	10,000	—	—	—	2.50	—
1999BP	10,000	—	—	—	2.50	—

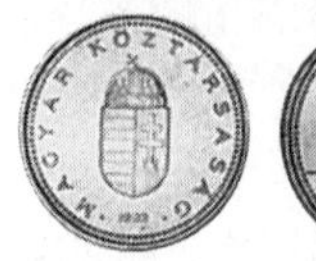

KM# 692 FORINT
2.0500 g., Brass, 16.5 mm. **Obv:** Crowned shield **Rev:** Denomination

Date	Mintage	F	VF	XF	Unc	BU
1992BP	23,890,100	—	0.10	0.25	0.35	—
1992BP Proof	1,000	Value: 6.00				
1993BP	75,100,000	—	—	0.10	0.25	—
1993BP Proof	30,000	Value: 1.00				
1994BP	66,605,005	—	—	0.10	0.25	—
1994BP Proof	15,000	Value: 1.20				
1995BP	50,535,000	—	—	0.10	0.25	—
1995BP Proof	15,000	Value: 1.20				
1996BP	67,000,010	—	—	0.10	0.25	—
1996BP Proof	10,000	Value: 1.40				
1997BP	—	—	—	0.10	0.25	—
1997BP Proof	3,000	Value: 3.75				
1998BP	—	—	—	0.10	0.25	—
1998BP Proof	3,000	Value: 3.75				
1999BP	—	—	—	0.10	0.25	—
1999BP Proof	3,000	Value: 3.75				
2000BP	—	—	—	0.10	0.25	—
2000BP Proof	3,000	Value: 3.75				
2001BP	—	—	—	—	0.10	0.25
2001BP Proof	3,000	Value: 3.75				
2002BP	—	—	—	—	0.10	0.25
2002BP Proof	3,000	Value: 3.75				
2003BP	—	—	—	—	0.10	0.25
2003BP Proof	7,000	Value: 3.50				
2004BP	—	—	—	—	0.10	0.25
2004BP Proof	7,000	Value: 3.50				
2005BP	—	—	—	—	0.10	0.25
2005BP Proof	—	Value: 3.50				
2006BP	—	—	—	—	0.10	0.25
2006BP Proof	—	Value: 3.50				

KM# 693 2 FORINT
3.1000 g., Copper-Nickel, 19 mm. **Obv:** Native flower: Colchicum Hungaricum **Rev:** Denomination

Date	Mintage	F	VF	XF	Unc	BU
1992BP	10,380,100	0.10	0.25	0.35	0.50	—
1992BP Proof	1,000	Value: 6.00				
1993BP	82,915,000	—	0.10	0.25	0.35	—
1993BP Proof	30,000	Value: 1.50				
1994BP	68,370,005	—	0.10	0.25	0.35	—
1994BP Proof	15,000	Value: 1.75				
1995BP	60,945,000	—	0.10	0.25	0.35	—
1995BP Proof	15,000	Value: 1.75				
1996BP	50,010,000	—	0.10	0.25	0.35	—
1996BP Proof	10,000	Value: 1.95				
1997BP	70,007,000	—	0.10	0.20	0.35	—
1997BP Proof	3,000	Value: 4.25				
1998BP	20,007,000	—	—	—	0.35	—
1998BP Proof	3,000	Value: 4.25				
1999BP	50,007,000	—	—	—	0.35	—
1999BP Proof	3,000	Value: 4.25				
2000BP	55,007,000	—	—	—	0.20	0.35
2000BP Proof	3,000	Value: 4.25				
2001BP	—	—	—	—	0.20	0.35
2001BP Proof	3,000	Value: 4.25				
2002BP	—	—	—	—	0.20	0.35
2002BP Proof	3,000	Value: 4.25				
2003BP	—	—	—	—	0.20	0.35
2003BP Proof	7,000	Value: 4.00				
2004BP	—	—	—	—	0.20	0.35
2004BP Proof	7,000	Value: 4.00				
2005BP	—	—	—	—	0.20	0.35
2005BP Proof	—	Value: 4.00				
2006BP	—	—	—	—	0.20	0.35
2006BP Proof	—	Value: 4.00				

KM# 694 5 FORINT
4.2000 g., Brass, 21.5 mm. **Obv:** Great White Egret **Rev:** Denomination

Date	Mintage	F	VF	XF	Unc	BU
1992BP	1,145,300	0.15	0.30	0.60	1.00	1.50
1992BP Proof	1,000	Value: 7.00				
1993BP	37,180,000	0.10	0.25	0.45	1.00	1.50
1993BP Proof	30,000	Value: 2.00				
1994BP	53,615,000	0.10	0.20	0.30	1.00	1.50
1994BP Proof	15,000	Value: 2.50				
1995BP	24,670,000	0.15	0.30	0.40	1.00	1.50
1995BP Proof	15,000	Value: 2.50				
1996BP	6,010,000	0.25	0.50	0.65	1.00	1.50
1996BP Proof	10,000	Value: 3.00				
1997BP	20,007,000	0.15	0.30	0.40	1.00	1.50
1997BP Proof	3,000	Value: 5.00				
1998BP	7,000	0.15	0.30	0.40	1.00	1.50
1998BP Proof	3,000	Value: 5.00				
1999BP	25,007,000	0.15	0.30	0.40	1.00	1.00
1999BP Proof	3,000	Value: 5.00				
2000BP	30,007,000	0.10	0.25	0.35	1.00	1.50
2000BP Proof	3,000	Value: 5.00				
2001BP	—	—	—	—	1.00	1.50
2001BP Proof	3,000	Value: 5.00				
2002BP	—	—	—	—	1.00	1.50
2002BP Proof	3,000	Value: 5.00				
2003BP	—	—	—	—	1.00	1.50
2003BP Proof	7,000	Value: 4.50				
2004BP	—	—	—	—	1.00	1.50
2004BP Proof	7,000	Value: 4.50				
2005BP	—	—	—	—	1.00	1.50
2005BP Proof	—	Value: 4.50				
2006BP	—	—	—	—	1.00	1.50
2006BP Proof	—	Value: 4.50				

KM# 695 10 FORINT
6.1000 g., Copper-Nickel Clad Brass, 25 mm. **Obv:** Crowned shield **Rev:** Denomination

Date	Mintage	F	VF	XF	Unc	BU
1992BP	2,000	—	—	—	6.00	—
1992BP Proof	1,000	Value: 8.00				
1993BP	35,565,000	0.10	0.25	0.45	1.00	2.00
1993BP Proof	30,000	Value: 2.50				
1994BP	69,078,000	—	0.15	0.35	0.85	2.00
1994BP Proof	15,000	Value: 3.00				
1995BP	40,910,000	0.10	0.25	0.45	1.00	2.00
1995BP Proof	15,000	Value: 3.00				
1996BP	13,010,000	0.15	0.30	0.50	1.00	2.00
1996BP Proof	10,000	Value: 3.50				
1997BP	8,007,000	0.20	0.35	0.55	1.00	2.00
1997BP Proof	3,000	Value: 5.50				
1998BP	7,000	—	—	—	1.00	2.50
1998BP Proof	3,000	Value: 5.50				
1999BP	7,000	—	—	—	1.00	2.50
1999BP Proof	3,000	Value: 5.50				
2000BP	7,000	—	—	—	1.00	2.50
2000BP Proof	3,000	Value: 5.50				
2001BP	—	—	—	—	1.00	2.50
2001BP Proof	3,000	Value: 5.50				
2002BP	—	—	—	—	1.00	2.50
2002BP Proof	3,000	Value: 5.50				
2003BP	—	—	—	—	1.00	2.50
2003BP Proof	7,000	Value: 5.00				
2004BP	—	—	—	—	1.00	2.50
2004BP Proof	7,000	Value: 5.00				
2005BP	—	—	—	—	1.00	2.50
2005BP Proof	—	Value: 5.00				
2006BP	—	—	—	—	1.00	2.50
2006BP Proof	—	Value: 5.00				

KM# 779 10 FORINT
6.1000 g., Copper-Nickel, 24.8 mm. **Obv:** Jozsef Attila **Rev:** Value **Edge:** Segmented reeding

Date	Mintage	F	VF	XF	Unc	BU
2005BP	20,000	—	—	—	2.50	3.00
2005BP Proof	7,000	Value: 3.50				

KM# 696 20 FORINT
6.9000 g., Nickel-Brass, 26.3 mm. **Obv:** Hungarian Iris **Rev:** Denomination

Date	Mintage	F	VF	XF	Unc	BU
1992BP	2,000	—	—	—	7.00	—
1992BP Proof	1,000	Value: 9.00				
1993BP	42,965,000	0.20	0.30	0.60	1.50	2.00
1993BP Proof	30,000	Value: 3.50				
1994BP	68,965,005	0.15	0.25	0.50	1.25	1.75
1994BP Proof	15,000	Value: 4.00				
1995BP	53,395,000	0.15	0.25	0.50	1.25	1.75
1995BP Proof	15,000	Value: 4.00				
1996BP	6,010,000	0.20	0.35	0.70	1.50	2.00
1996BP Proof	10,000	Value: 4.00				
1997BP	7,000	—	—	—	5.00	6.00
1997BP Proof	3,000	Value: 6.00				
1998BP	7,000	—	—	—	3.50	4.00
1998BP Proof	3,000	Value: 6.00				
1999BP	7,000	—	—	—	3.50	4.00
1999BP Proof	3,000	Value: 6.00				
2000BP	7,000	—	—	—	3.50	4.00
2000BP Proof	3,000	Value: 6.00				
2001BP	—	—	—	—	1.50	2.00
2001BP Proof	3,000	Value: 4.50				
2002BP	—	—	—	—	1.50	2.00
2002BP Proof	3,000	Value: 4.50				
2003BP	—	—	—	—	1.50	2.00
2003BP Proof	7,000	Value: 4.00				
2004BP	—	—	—	—	1.50	2.00
2004BP Proof	7,000	Value: 4.00				
2005BP	—	—	—	—	1.50	2.00
2005BP Proof	—	Value: 4.00				
2006BP	—	—	—	—	1.50	2.00
2006BP Proof	—	Value: 4.00				

KM# 768 20 FORINT
6.9400 g., Nickel-Brass, 26.4 mm. **Obv:** Deak Ferenc **Rev:** Denomination **Edge:** Reeded

Date	Mintage	F	VF	XF	Unc	BU
2003BP	993,000	—	—	—	1.50	2.00
2003BP Proof	7,000	Value: 4.00				

KM# 697 50 FORINT
7.7000 g., Copper-Nickel Clad Brass, 27.5 mm. **Obv:** Saker falcon **Rev:** Denomination

Date	Mintage	F	VF	XF	Unc	BU
1992BP	2,000	—	—	—	10.00	—
1992BP Proof	1,000	Value: 12.00				
1993BP	860,500	0.50	0.65	1.25	3.00	3.50
1993BP Proof	30,000	Value: 5.00				
1994BP	8,397,005	0.25	0.45	0.85	3.00	3.50
1994BP Proof	15,000	Value: 5.00				
1995BP	36,985,000	—	0.25	0.50	2.50	3.00
1995BP Proof	15,000	Value: 5.00				
1996BP	7,010,000	0.30	0.50	1.00	3.00	3.50
1996BP Proof	10,000	Value: 5.00				
1997BP	12,007,000	—	—	—	3.00	3.50
1997BP Proof	3,000	Value: 6.50				
1998BP	7,000	—	—	—	5.50	6.50
1998BP Proof	3,000	Value: 6.50				
1999BP	7,000	—	—	—	5.50	6.50
1999BP Proof	3,000	Value: 6.50				
2000BP	7,000	—	—	—	5.50	6.50
2000BP Proof	3,000	Value: 6.50				
2001BP	—	—	—	—	3.00	4.00
2001BP Proof	3,000	Value: 6.00				
2002BP	—	—	—	—	3.00	3.50
2002BP Proof	3,000	Value: 5.50				
2003BP	—	—	—	—	3.00	3.50
2003BP Proof	7,000	Value: 5.00				

Date	Mintage	F	VF	XF	Unc	BU
2004BP	—	—	—	—	3.00	3.50
2004BP Proof	7,000	Value: 5.00				
2005BP	—	—	—	—	3.00	3.50
2005BP Proof	—	Value: 5.00				
2006BP	—	—	—	—	3.00	3.50
2006BP Proof	—	Value: 5.00				

KM# 773 50 FORINT
7.7000 g., Copper-Nickel Clad Brass, 27.5 mm. **Obv:** National arms above Euro Union star circle **Rev:** Denomination **Edge:** Plain

Date	Mintage	F	VF	XF	Unc	BU
2004BP	993,000	—	—	—	3.00	3.50
2004BP Proof	7,000	Value: 6.00				

KM# 780 50 FORINT
7.7000 g., Copper-Nickel, 27.4 mm. **Subject:** International Childrens Safety Service **Obv:** Stylized crying child **Rev:** Denomination **Edge:** Plain

Date	Mintage	F	VF	XF	Unc	BU
2005BP	2,000,000	—	—	—	3.00	3.50

KM# 788 50 FORINT
7.7000 g., Copper-Nickel, 27.4 mm. **Obv:** Hungarian Red Cross 125th Anniversary seal above date and country name **Rev:** Value **Edge:** Plain

Date	Mintage	F	VF	XF	Unc	BU
2006BP	2,000,000	—	—	—	—	3.50

KM# 789 50 FORINT
7.7000 g., Copper-Nickel, 27.4 mm. **Subject:** 1956 Revolution **Obv:** Holed flag with Parliament building in background **Rev:** Value **Edge:** Plain

Date	Mintage	F	VF	XF	Unc	BU
2006BP	2,000,000	—	—	—	—	3.50

KM# 760 100 FORINT
8.0000 g., Bi-Metallic Stainless Steel center in Brass plated Steel ring, 23.7 mm. **Subject:** Lajos Kossuth **Obv:** Head right within circle **Rev:** Denomination within circle **Edge:** Reeded

Date	Mintage	F	VF	XF	Unc	BU
2002BP	997,000	—	—	—	2.00	2.50
2002BP Proof	3,000	Value: 5.00				

KM# 698 100 FORINT (Szaz)
9.4000 g., Brass **Obv:** Crowned shield **Rev:** Denomination

Date	Mintage	F	VF	XF	Unc	BU
1992BP	2,000	—	—	—	12.00	—
1992BP Proof	1,000	Value: 15.00				
1993BP	924,500	—	—	—	3.00	—
1993BP Proof	30,000	Value: 6.00				
1994BP	7,861,005	—	—	—	2.50	—
1994BP Proof	15,000	Value: 6.00				
1995BP	27,485,000	—	—	—	2.50	—
1995BP Proof	15,000	Value: 6.00				
1996BP	6,210,000	—	—	—	2.50	—
1996BP Proof	10,000	Value: 6.00				
1997BP	7,000	—	—	—	6.00	—
1997BP Proof	3,000	Value: 8.00				
1998BP	7,000	—	—	—	6.00	—
1998BP Proof	3,000	Value: 8.00				

KM# 721 100 FORINT (Szaz)
Bi-Metallic Brass plated Steel center in Stainless Steel ring, 23.6 mm. **Obv:** Crowned shield **Rev:** Denomination

Date	Mintage	F	VF	XF	Unc	BU
1996BP	35,001,000	—	—	—	3.00	4.50
1996BP Proof	1,000	Value: 12.00				
1997BP	60,007,000	—	—	—	3.00	4.50
1997BP Proof	3,000	Value: 8.00				
1998BP	60,007,000	—	—	—	3.00	4.50
1998BP Proof	3,000	Value: 8.00				
1999BP	7,000	—	—	—	3.00	4.50
1999BP Proof	3,000	Value: 8.00				
2000BP	7,000	—	—	—	4.00	6.50
2000BP Proof	3,000	Value: 8.00				
2001BP	—	—	—	—	3.50	5.00
2001BP Proof	3,000	Value: 8.00				
2002BP	—	—	—	—	3.50	5.00
2002BP Proof	3,000	Value: 8.00				
2003BP	—	—	—	—	3.50	5.00
2003BP Proof	7,000	Value: 7.50				
2004BP	—	—	—	—	3.50	5.00
2004BP Proof	7,000	Value: 7.50				
2005BP	—	—	—	—	3.50	5.00
2005BP Proof	—	Value: 7.50				
2006BP	—	—	—	—	3.50	5.00
2006BP Proof	—	Value: 7.50				

ICELAND

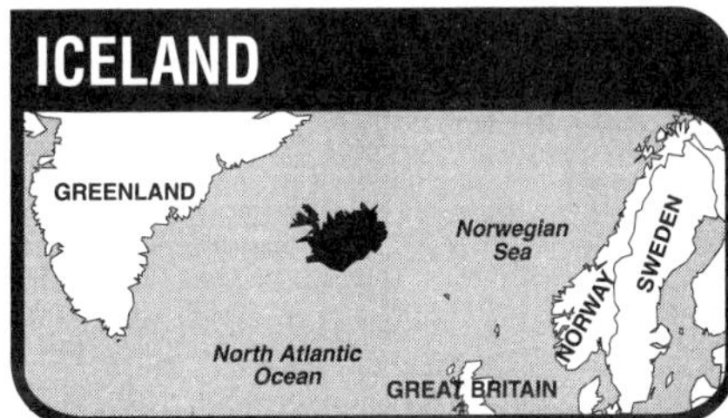

The Republic of Iceland, an island of recent volcanic origin in the North Atlantic east of Greenland and immediately south of the Arctic Circle, has an area of 39,768sq. mi. (103,000 sq. km.) and a population of just over 300,000. Capital: Reykjavik. Fishing is the chief industry and accounts for a little less than 60 percent of the exports.

Iceland was settled by Norwegians in the 9th century and established as an independent republic in 930. The Icelandic assembly called the Althingi', also established in 930, is the oldest parliament in the world. Iceland came under Norwegian sovereignty in 1262, and passed to Denmark when Norway and Denmark were united under the Danish crown in 1380. In 1918 it was established as a virtually independent kingdom in union with Denmark. On June 17, 1944, while Denmark was still under occupation by troops of the Third Reich, Iceland was established by plebiscite as an independent republic.

RULER
Christian X, 1912-1944

MINT MARK
Heart (h) - Copenhagen

MINTMASTERS' INITIALS
HCN - Hans Christian Nielsen, 1919-1927
(for Iceland, 1922-1926)
N - Niels Peter Nielsen, 1927-1955
(for Iceland, 1929-1940)

MONEYERS' INITIALS
GJ - Knud Gunnar Jensen, 1901-1933

MONETARY SYSTEM
100 Aurar = 1 Krona

KINGDOM

DECIMAL COINAGE

KM# 5.1 EYRIR
Bronze **Ruler:** Christian X **Obv:** Crown divides date above monogram **Rev:** Large denomination

Date	Mintage	F	VF	XF	Unc	BU
1926(h) HCN-GJ	405,000	1.50	3.00	7.50	32.00	—
1931(h) N-GJ	462,000	1.00	2.50	6.00	30.00	—
1937(h) N-GJ Wide date	211,000	2.00	4.00	8.00	36.50	—
1937(h) N-GJ Narrow date	Inc. above	2.00	4.00	8.00	36.50	—
1938(h) N-GJ	279,000	1.00	2.00	4.00	14.00	—
1939(h) N-GJ Large 3	305,000	1.00	2.00	3.50	12.50	—
1939(h) N-GJ Small 3	Inc. above	1.00	2.00	3.50	12.50	—

KM# 5.2 EYRIR
1.5700 g., Bronze, 15 mm. **Ruler:** Christian X **Obv:** Crown divides date above monogram **Rev:** Large denomination, ornaments flank

Date	Mintage	F	VF	XF	Unc	BU
1940	1,000,000	0.25	0.50	1.00	2.50	—
1940 Proof	—	Value: 250				
1942	2,000,000	0.25	0.40	0.75	2.00	—

KM# 6.1 2 AURAR
Bronze **Ruler:** Christian X **Obv:** Crown divides date above monogram **Rev:** Large denomination, ornaments flank **Note:** Varieties exist in the appearance of the numeral 8 in 1938 dated coins. As the die slowly deteriorated, "globs" were added to the upper loop and later to the lower loop.

Date	Mintage	F	VF	XF	Unc	BU
1926(h) HCN-GJ	498,000	1.50	3.00	8.00	42.00	—
1931(h) N-GJ	446,000	1.00	2.50	7.00	32.00	—
1938(h) N-GJ	206,000	6.00	12.00	17.50	57.50	—
1940(h) N-GJ	257,000	5.00	10.00	15.00	38.50	—

KM# 6.2 2 AURAR
3.0100 g., Bronze **Ruler:** Christian X **Obv:** Crown divides date above monogram **Rev:** Large denomination, ornaments flank

Date	Mintage	F	VF	XF	Unc	BU
1940	1,000,000	0.40	0.75	1.50	3.00	—
1940 Proof	—	Value: 280				
1942	2,000,000	0.20	0.50	1.00	2.00	—

KM# 7.1 5 AURAR
Bronze **Ruler:** Christian X **Obv:** Crown divides date above monogram **Rev:** Large denomination, ornaments flank

Date	Mintage	F	VF	XF	Unc	BU
1926(h) HCN-GJ	355,000	5.00	10.00	25.00	90.00	—
1931(h) N-GJ	311,000	5.00	10.00	25.00	90.00	—

KM# 7.2 5 AURAR

6.0200 g., Bronze **Ruler:** Christian X **Obv:** Crown divides date above monogram **Rev:** Large denomination, ornaments flank

Date	Mintage	F	VF	XF	Unc	BU
1940	1,000,000	0.60	1.25	2.50	5.00	—
1940 Proof	—	Value: 300				
1942	2,000,000	0.35	0.85	1.50	3.00	—

KM# 1.1 10 AURAR

Copper-Nickel **Ruler:** Christian X **Obv:** Ornaments flank denomination **Rev:** Crowned arms divide monogram

Date	Mintage	F	VF	XF	Unc	BU
1922(h) HCN GJ	300,000	2.00	3.50	7.00	40.00	—
1923(h) HCN GJ	302,000	3.00	4.50	9.00	48.00	—
1925(h) HCN GJ	321,000	15.00	25.00	40.00	115	—
1929(h) N-GJ	176,000	15.00	25.00	45.00	125	—
1933(h) N-GJ	157,000	10.00	20.00	30.00	90.00	—
1936(h) N-GJ	213,000	3.00	6.00	10.00	36.00	—
1939/6(h) N-GJ	208,000	5.00	10.00	15.00	44.00	—
1939(h) N-GJ	Inc. above	4.00	8.00	12.00	32.50	—

KM# 1.2 10 AURAR

1.4800 g., Copper-Nickel **Ruler:** Christian X **Obv:** Ornaments flank denomination **Rev:** Crowned arms divide monogram

Date	Mintage	F	VF	XF	Unc	BU
1940	1,500,000	0.35	0.75	1.50	4.50	—
1940 Proof	—	Value: 250				

KM# 1a 10 AURAR

1.2800 g., Zinc **Ruler:** Christian X **Obv:** Ornaments flank denomination **Rev:** Crowned arms divide monogram

Date	Mintage	F	VF	XF	Unc	BU
1942	2,000,000	1.50	3.00	6.00	31.50	—
1942 Prooflike	—	—	—	—	—	—

KM# 2.1 25 AURAR

Copper-Nickel **Ruler:** Christian X **Obv:** Ornaments flank denomination **Rev:** Crowned arms divide monogram

Date	Mintage	F	VF	XF	Unc	BU
1922(h) HCN GJ	300,000	1.00	2.50	4.00	37.00	—
1923(h) HCN GJ	304,000	1.00	2.50	4.00	37.00	—
1925(h) HCN GJ	207,000	2.50	4.50	10.00	55.00	—
1933(h) N-GJ	104,000	10.00	15.00	25.00	105	—
1937(h) N-GJ Near 7	201,000	3.00	5.00	9.00	42.50	—
1937(h) N-GJ Far 7	Inc. above	3.00	5.00	9.00	40.00	—

KM# 2.2 25 AURAR

2.4000 g., Copper-Nickel **Ruler:** Christian X **Obv:** Ornaments flank denomination **Rev:** Crowned arms divide monogram

Date	Mintage	F	VF	XF	Unc	BU
1940	1,500,000	0.25	0.50	1.00	2.50	—
1940 Proof	—	Value: 270				

KM# 2a 25 AURAR

2.0000 g., Zinc **Ruler:** Christian X **Obv:** Ornaments flank denomination **Rev:** Crowned arms divide monogram

Date	Mintage	F	VF	XF	Unc	BU
1942	2,000,000	1.00	2.50	5.00	28.50	—
1942 Prooflike	—	—	—	—	—	—

KM# 3.1 KRONA

Aluminum-Bronze **Ruler:** Christian X **Obv:** Ornaments flank denomination **Rev:** Crowned arms divide monogram

Date	Mintage	F	VF	XF	Unc	BU
1925(h) HCN GJ	252,000	3.00	6.00	25.00	190	—
1929(h) N-GJ	154,000	5.00	10.00	32.00	225	—
1940(h) N-GJ	209,000	1.50	2.50	5.00	15.00	—

KM# 3.2 KRONA

4.7400 g., Aluminum-Bronze **Ruler:** Christian X **Obv:** Ornaments flank denomination **Rev:** Crowned arms divide monogram

Date	Mintage	F	VF	XF	Unc	BU
1940	715,000	1.00	2.00	4.00	10.00	—
1940 Proof; rare	—	—	—	—	—	—

KM# 4.1 2 KRONUR

Aluminum-Bronze **Ruler:** Christian X **Obv:** Ornaments flank denomination **Rev:** Crowned arms divide monogram

Date	Mintage	F	VF	XF	Unc	BU
1925(h) HCN GJ	126,000	7.50	12.50	41.50	245	—
1929(h) N-GJ	77,000	10.00	20.00	67.50	360	—

KM# 4.2 2 KRONUR

Aluminum-Bronze **Ruler:** Christian X **Obv:** Ornaments flank denomination **Rev:** Crowned arms divide monogram

Date	Mintage	F	VF	XF	Unc	BU
1940	546,000	0.75	1.50	3.50	10.00	—
1940 Proof; rare	—	—	—	—	—	—

REPUBLIC

DECIMAL COINAGE

KM# 8 EYRIR

1.6200 g., Bronze, 15.10 mm. **Obv:** Leaves flank denomination **Rev:** Arms within wreath **Note:** Values for the 1953-59 proof issues are for impaired proofs. Brilliant proofs may bring 3 to 4 times these figures.

Date	Mintage	F	VF	XF	Unc	BU
1946	4,000,000	0.10	0.15	0.50	1.00	—
1946 Proof	—	Value: 280				
1953	4,000,000	0.10	0.15	0.40	0.75	—
1953 Proof	—	Value: 75.00				
1956	2,000,000	0.10	0.15	0.40	0.75	—
1956 Proof	—	Value: 75.00				
1957	2,000,000	0.10	0.15	0.40	0.75	—
1957 Proof	—	Value: 75.00				
1958	2,000,000	0.10	0.15	0.40	0.75	—
1958 Proof	—	Value: 75.00				
1959	1,600,000	0.10	0.15	0.40	0.75	—
1959 Proof	—	Value: 75.00				
1966	1,000,000	0.10	0.15	0.40	0.75	—
1966 Proof	15,000	Value: 3.25				

KM# 9 5 AURAR

6.0600 g., Bronze **Obv:** Leaves flank denomination **Rev:** Arms within wreath **Note:** Values for the 1958-63 proof issues are for impaired proofs. Brilliant proofs may bring 3 to 4 times these figures.

Date	Mintage	F	VF	XF	Unc	BU
1946	4,000,000	0.10	0.25	0.50	1.25	—
1946 Proof	—	Value: 435				
1958	400,000	0.50	2.00	3.50	5.00	—
1958 Proof	—	Value: 105				
1959	600,000	0.50	2.00	3.00	4.50	—
1959 Proof	—	Value: 105				
1960	1,200,000	0.15	0.40	1.00	1.75	—
1960 Proof	—	Value: 105				
1961	1,200,000	0.15	0.40	1.00	1.75	—
1961 Proof	—	Value: 105				
1963	1,200,000	0.10	0.30	0.75	1.50	—
1963 Proof	—	Value: 105				
1965	800,000	0.10	0.20	0.50	1.00	—
1966	1,000,000	0.10	0.20	0.50	1.00	—
1966 Proof	15,000	Value: 3.25				

KM# 10 10 AURAR

1.5200 g., Copper-Nickel, 14.98 mm. **Obv:** Leaves flank denomination **Rev:** Arms within wreath **Edge:** Plain **Note:** Values for the 1953-63 proof issues are for impaired proofs. Brilliant proofs may bring 3 to 4 times these figures.

Date	Mintage	F	VF	XF	Unc	BU
1946	4,000,000	—	0.10	0.20	0.60	—
1946 Proof	—	Value: 430				
1953	4,000,000	—	0.10	0.20	0.50	—
1953 Proof	—	Value: 70.00				
1957	1,200,000	0.25	0.75	2.00	5.00	—
1957 Proof	—	Value: 70.00				
1958	500,000	0.20	0.50	1.00	2.00	—
1958 Proof	—	Value: 70.00				
1959	3,000,000	0.20	0.50	1.50	4.00	—
1959 Proof	—	Value: 70.00				
1960	1,000,000	0.10	0.20	0.40	1.00	—
1960 Proof	—	Value: 70.00				
1961	2,000,000	—	—	0.10	0.30	—
1961 Proof	—	Value: 70.00				
1962	3,000,000	—	—	0.10	0.20	—
1962 Proof	—	Value: 70.00				
1963	4,000,000	—	—	0.10	0.20	—
1963 Proof	—	Value: 70.00				
1965	2,000,000	—	—	0.10	0.20	—
1966	4,000,000	—	—	0.10	0.20	—
1967	2,000,000	—	—	0.10	0.20	—
1969	3,200,000	—	—	0.10	0.20	—
Note: Coarse edge reeding						
1969	Inc. above	—	—	0.10	0.20	—
Note: Fine edge reeding						

KM# 10a 10 AURAR

0.4800 g., Aluminum, 14.64 mm. **Obv:** Leaves flank denomination **Rev:** Arms within wreath **Edge:** Reeded

Date	Mintage	F	VF	XF	Unc	BU
1970	4,800,000	—	—	0.10	0.20	—
1971	11,200,000	—	—	0.10	0.20	—
1973	4,800,000	—	—	0.10	0.20	—
1974	4,800,000	—	—	0.10	0.20	—
1974 Proof	15,000	Value: 3.25				

KM# 11 25 AURAR

2.4400 g., Copper-Nickel, 16.06 mm. **Obv:** Leaves flank denomination **Rev:** Arms within wreath **Edge:** Reeded **Note:** Values for the 1951-63 proof issues are for impaired proofs. Brilliant proofs may bring 3 to 4 times these figures.

Date	Mintage	F	VF	XF	Unc	BU
1946	2,000,000	0.10	0.15	0.35	1.25	—
1946 Proof	—	Value: 440				
1951	2,000,000	0.10	0.15	0.35	0.75	—

Date	Mintage	F	VF	XF	Unc	BU
1951 Proof	—	Value: 80.00				
1954	2,000,000	0.10	0.15	0.35	0.75	—
1954 Proof	—	Value: 80.00				
1957	1,000,000	0.20	0.50	1.50	3.50	—
1957 Proof	—	Value: 80.00				
1958	500,000	0.20	0.40	0.60	1.00	—
1958 Proof	—	Value: 80.00				
1959	2,000,000	0.20	0.50	1.50	3.00	—
1959 Proof	—	Value: 80.00				
1960	1,000,000	—	—	0.10	0.30	—
1960 Proof	—	Value: 80.00				
1961	1,200,000	—	—	0.10	0.30	—
1961 Proof	—	Value: 80.00				
1962	2,000,000	—	—	0.10	0.25	—
1962 Proof	—	Value: 80.00				
1963	3,000,000	—	—	0.10	0.25	—
1963 Proof	—	Value: 80.00				
1965	4,000,000	—	—	0.10	0.25	—
1966	2,000,000	—	—	0.10	0.25	—
1967	3,000,000	—	—	0.10	0.25	—
1967 Proof	15,000	Value: 3.25				

KM# 17 50 AURAR

2.4000 g., Nickel-Brass, 19.04 mm. **Obv:** Leaves flank denomination **Rev:** Arms within wreath **Edge:** Reeded

Date	Mintage	F	VF	XF	Unc	BU
1969	2,000,000	—	—	0.10	0.30	—
1970	2,000,000	—	—	0.10	0.30	—
1971	2,000,000	—	—	0.10	0.30	—
1973	1,000,000	—	—	0.10	0.30	—
1974	2,000,000	—	—	0.10	0.30	—
1974 Proof	15,000	Value: 3.25				

KM# 12 KRONA

4.7800 g., Aluminum-Bronze **Obv:** Leaves flank denomination **Rev:** Arms with supporters

Date	Mintage	F	VF	XF	Unc	BU
1946	2,175,000	—	0.10	0.40	1.50	—
1946 Proof	—	Value: 435				

KM# 12a KRONA

4.8000 g., Nickel-Brass, 22.3 mm. **Obv:** Denomination, leaves flank **Rev:** Shield with supporters, date below **Note:** Values for the 1957-63 proof issues are for impaired proofs. Brilliant proofs may bring 3 to 4 times these figures.

Date	Mintage	F	VF	XF	Unc	BU
1957	1,000,000	0.10	0.15	0.40	1.50	—
1957 Proof	—	Value: 95.00				
1959	500,000	0.10	0.20	0.75	2.00	—
1959 Proof	—	Value: 95.00				
1961	500,000	0.10	0.20	0.75	2.00	—
1961 Proof	—	Value: 95.00				
1962	1,000,000	0.10	0.15	0.20	0.60	—
1962 Proof	—	Value: 95.00				
1963	1,500,000	—	0.10	0.15	0.50	—
1963 Proof	—	Value: 95.00				
1965	2,000,000	—	—	0.10	0.50	—
1966	2,000,000	—	—	0.10	0.50	—
1969	2,000,000	—	—	0.10	0.25	—
1970	3,000,000	—	—	0.10	0.25	—
1971	2,500,000	—	—	0.10	0.25	—
1973 Large round-knob 3	2,500,000	—	—	0.10	0.50	—
1973 Thin, sharp-end 3	3,500,000	—	—	0.10	0.25	—
1974	5,000,000	—	—	0.10	0.25	—
1975	10,500,000	—	—	0.10	0.25	—
1975 Proof	15,000	Value: 3.25				

KM# 23 KRONA

0.5650 g., Aluminum, 16.01 mm. **Obv:** Leaves flank denomination **Rev:** Arms with supporters **Edge:** Reeded

Date	Mintage	F	VF	XF	Unc	BU
1976	10,000,000	—	—	0.10	0.20	—
1977	10,000,000	—	—	0.10	0.20	—
1978	13,000,000	—	—	0.10	0.20	—
1980	7,225,000	—	—	0.10	0.20	—
1980 Proof	15,000	Value: 3.25				

KM# 13 2 KRONUR

Aluminum-Bronze **Obv:** Leaves flank denomination **Rev:** Arms with supporters

Date	Mintage	F	VF	XF	Unc	BU
1946	1,086,000	0.20	0.40	0.80	3.50	—
1946 Proof	—	Value: 485				

KM# 13a.1 2 KRONUR

9.5000 g., Nickel-Brass, 28 mm. **Obv:** Leaves flank denomination **Rev:** Arms with supporters **Note:** Values for the 1958-63 proof issues are for impaired proofs. Brilliant proofs may bring 3 to 4 times these figures.

Date	Mintage	F	VF	XF	Unc	BU
1958	500,000	0.20	0.50	1.00	3.00	—
1958 Proof	—	Value: 125				
1962	500,000	0.20	0.50	1.00	3.00	—
1962 Proof	—	Value: 125				
1963	750,000	0.15	0.30	0.60	2.00	—
1963 Proof	—	Value: 125				
1966	1,000,000	0.10	0.20	0.40	1.50	—
1966 Proof	15,000	Value: 3.25				

KM# 13a.2 2 KRONUR

11.5000 g., Nickel-Brass **Obv:** Leaves flank denomination **Rev:** Arms with supporters **Note:** Thick planchet.

Date	Mintage	F	VF	XF	Unc	BU
1966	300	—	—	375	500	—

KM# 18 5 KRONUR

4.0000 g., Copper-Nickel **Obv:** Leaves flank denomination **Rev:** Arms with supporters

Date	Mintage	F	VF	XF	Unc	BU
1969	2,000,000	—	0.15	0.25	0.50	—
1970	1,000,000	—	0.15	0.25	0.50	—
1971	500,000	0.10	0.20	0.50	1.00	—
1973	1,100,000	—	0.10	0.20	0.40	—
1974	1,200,000	—	0.10	0.15	0.25	—
1975	1,500,000	—	0.10	0.15	0.25	—
1976	500,000	—	0.10	0.20	0.40	—
1977	1,000,000	—	0.10	0.15	0.25	—
1978	4,672,000	—	0.10	0.15	0.25	—
1980	2,400,000	—	0.10	0.15	0.25	—
1980 Proof	15,000	Value: 3.25				

KM# 15 10 KRONUR

6.5200 g., Copper-Nickel, 25 mm. **Obv:** Leaves flank denomination **Rev:** Arms with supporters

Date	Mintage	F	VF	XF	Unc	BU
1967	1,000,000	0.15	0.25	0.50	1.50	—
1969	500,000	0.15	0.30	0.75	2.00	—
1970	1,500,000	—	0.15	0.30	0.75	—
1971	1,500,000	—	0.15	0.30	0.75	—
1973	1,500,000	—	0.15	0.30	0.75	—
1974	2,000,000	—	0.10	0.25	0.60	—
1975	2,500,000	—	0.10	0.25	0.60	—
1976	2,500,000	—	0.10	0.25	0.60	—
1977	2,000,000	—	0.10	0.25	0.60	—
1978	10,500,000	—	0.10	0.25	0.60	—
1980	4,600,000	—	0.10	0.25	0.60	—
1980 Proof	15,000	Value: 3.25				

KM# 16 50 KRONUR

Nickel **Subject:** 50th Anniversary of Sovereignty **Obv:** Denomination **Rev:** Parliament Building in Reikjavik **Designer:** Magnusson Sigurdsson

Date	Mintage	F	VF	XF	Unc	BU
1968	100,000	1.50	2.50	4.00	7.00	—

KM# 19 50 KRONUR

12.3800 g., Copper-Nickel, 30 mm. **Obv:** Denomination **Rev:** Parliament Building in Reykjavic **Designer:** Magnusson Sigurdsson

Date	Mintage	F	VF	XF	Unc	BU
1970	800,000	0.25	0.50	1.00	2.00	—
1971	500,000	0.25	0.50	1.00	2.50	—
1973	50,000	1.00	1.50	2.50	4.00	—
1974	200,000	0.25	0.50	1.00	2.00	—
1975	500,000	0.20	0.35	0.75	1.50	—
1976	500,000	0.20	0.35	0.75	1.50	—
1977	200,000	0.20	0.35	0.75	1.50	—
1978	2,040,000	0.20	0.35	0.50	1.00	—
1980	1,500,000	0.20	0.35	0.50	1.00	—
1980 Proof	15,000	Value: 3.25				

REFORM COINAGE

100 Old Kronur = 1 New Krona

KM# 24 5 AURAR

1.5000 g., Bronze, 14.58 mm. **Obv:** Eagle with upraised wing **Rev:** Denomination on Skate **Edge:** Plain

Date	Mintage	F	VF	XF	Unc	BU
1981	15,000,000	—	—	—	0.35	1.00
1981 Proof	15,000	Value: 3.50				

KM# 25 10 AURAR

2.0000 g., Bronze, 16.95 mm. **Obv:** Bulls head facing **Rev:** Flying squid **Edge:** Plain

Date	Mintage	F	VF	XF	Unc	BU
1981	50,000,000	—	—	—	0.45	1.00
1981 Proof	15,000	Value: 5.00				

KM# 26 50 AURAR

Bronze, 20 mm. **Obv:** Dragons head right **Rev:** Northern shrimp

Date	Mintage	F	VF	XF	Unc	BU
1981	10,000,000	—	—	0.10	0.50	1.00
1981 Proof	15,000	Value: 6.00				

KM# 26a 50 AURAR
2.6600 g., Bronze Coated Steel, 20 mm. **Obv:** Dragons head right **Rev:** Northern shrimp

Date	Mintage	F	VF	XF	Unc	BU
1986	2,144,000	—	—	—	0.50	1.00

KM# 27 KRONA
4.5000 g., Copper-Nickel, 21.5 mm. **Obv:** Giant facing **Rev:** Cod **Edge:** Reeded

Date	Mintage	F	VF	XF	Unc	BU
1981	18,000,000	—	—	0.15	0.75	1.50
1981 Proof	15,000	Value: 8.00				
1984	7,000,000	—	—	0.15	0.75	1.50
1987	7,500,000	—	—	0.15	0.75	1.50

KM# 27a KRONA
4.0000 g., Nickel Plated Steel, 19.79 mm. **Obv:** Giant facing **Rev:** Cod **Edge:** Reeded

Date	Mintage	F	VF	XF	Unc	BU
1989	5,000,000	—	—	—	0.75	1.50
1991	5,180,000	—	—	—	0.75	1.50
1992	5,000,000	—	—	—	0.75	1.50
1994	5,000,000	—	—	—	0.75	1.50
1996	6,000,000	—	—	—	0.75	1.50
1999	10,000,000	—	—	—	0.75	1.50
2000	10,000	—	—	—	1.50	2.00
2003	5,144,000	—	—	—	0.75	1.50
2005	5,000,000	—	—	—	0.75	1.50
2006	10,000,000	—	—	—	0.75	1.50

KM# 28 5 KRONUR
6.5000 g., Copper-Nickel, 24.5 mm. **Obv:** Quartered design of Eagle, dragon, bull and giant **Rev:** Two dolphins leaping left **Edge:** Reeded

Date	Mintage	F	VF	XF	Unc	BU
1981	4,350,000	—	—	0.25	1.50	2.50
1981 Proof	15,000	Value: 10.00				
1984	1,000,000	—	—	0.25	1.50	2.50
1987	3,000,000	—	—	0.25	1.50	2.50
1992	2,000,000	—	—	0.25	1.50	2.50

KM# 28a 5 KRONUR
5.6000 g., Nickel Clad Steel, 24.5 mm. **Obv:** Quartered design of Eagle, dragon, bull and giant **Rev:** Two dolphins leaping left **Edge:** Reeded

Date	Mintage	F	VF	XF	Unc	BU
1996	1,500,000	—	—	—	1.50	2.00
1999	2,000,000	—	—	—	1.50	2.00
2000	10,000	—	—	—	2.00	3.00
2005	2,000,000	—	—	—	2.00	3.00

KM# 29.1 10 KRONUR
Copper-Nickel, 27.5 mm. **Obv:** Quartered design of Eagle, dragon, bull and giant **Rev:** Four capelins left **Edge:** Reeded

Date	Mintage	F	VF	XF	Unc	BU
1984	10,000,000	—	—	0.35	1.75	3.00
1987	7,500,000	—	—	0.35	1.75	3.00
1994	2,500,000	—	—	0.35	1.75	3.00

KM# 29.2 10 KRONUR
8.0000 g., Copper-Nickel, 24.5 mm. **Obv:** Quartered design of Eagle, dragon, bull and giant **Rev:** Four capelins left **Edge:** Reeded **Note:** Struck on flan of Indian Rupee in error.

Date	Mintage	F	VF	XF	Unc	BU
1984	Inc. above	—	—	135	185	—

KM# 29.1a 10 KRONUR
8.0000 g., Nickel Clad Steel, 27.5 mm. **Obv:** Quartered design of Eagle, dragon, bull and giant **Rev:** Four capelins left **Edge:** Reeded

Date	Mintage	F	VF	XF	Unc	BU
1996	4,000,000	—	—	—	1.75	2.50
2000	10,000	—	—	—	2.50	3.50
2004	2,000,000	—	—	—	1.75	2.50
2005	4,505,000	—	—	—	1.75	2.50
2006	6,000,000	—	—	—	1.75	2.50

KM# 31 50 KRONUR
8.2500 g., Nickel-Brass, 23 mm. **Obv:** Quartered design of eagle, dragon, bull and giant **Rev:** Crab **Edge:** Reeded

Date	Mintage	F	VF	XF	Unc	BU
1987	4,000,000	—	—	—	4.00	6.00
1992	2,000,000	—	—	—	4.00	6.00
2000	10,000	—	—	—	5.00	7.00
2001	2,000,000	—	—	—	4.00	5.00
2005	2,000,000	—	—	—	4.00	5.00

KM# 35 100 KRONUR
8.5000 g., Nickel-Brass, 25.5 mm. **Obv:** Quartered design of Eagle, dragon, bull and giant **Rev:** Lumpfish left **Edge:** Reeded

Date	Mintage	F	VF	XF	Unc	BU
1995	6,000,000	—	—	—	6.00	12.00
2000	10,000	—	—	—	7.00	12.00
2001	2,140,000	—	—	—	6.00	7.00
2004	2,400,000	—	—	—	6.00	7.00
2006	2,000,000	—	—	—	6.00	7.00

SENDING SCANNED IMAGES BY EMAIL

We have been receiving an ever-increasing flow of scanned images from sources worldwide. Unfortunately, many of these scans could not be used due to the type of scan, or simple incompatability with our systems. We appreciate the efforts it takes to produce these images and accuracy they add to the catalog listings.

Here are a few simple instructions to follow when producing these scans. We encourage you to continue sending new images or upgrades to those currently illustrated and please do not hesitate to ask questions about this process.

- Scan all images at 300 dpi
- Size setting should be at 100%
- Scan in true 4-color
- Save images as 'jpeg' or 'tif' and name in such a way, which clearly identifies the country of origin, KM# if known and diameter size of coin in millimeters (mm)
- Please email with a request to comfirm receipt of the attachment
- Please send images to Randy.Thern@fwpubs.com

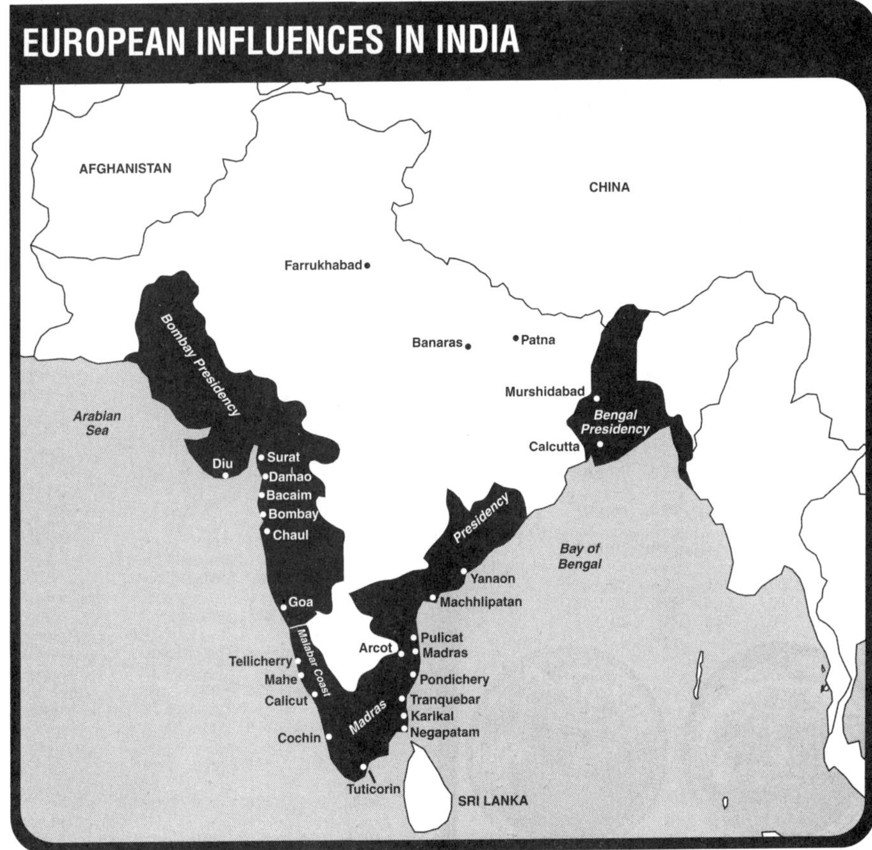

Vasco da Gama, the Portuguese explorer, first visited India in 1498. Portugal seized control of a number of islands and small enclaves on the west coast of India, and for the next hundred years enjoyed a monopoly on trade. With the arrival of powerful Dutch and English fleets in the first half of the 17th century, Portuguese power in the area declined until virtually all of India that remained under Portuguese control were the west coast enclaves of Goa, Damao and Diu. They were forcibly annexed by India in 1962.

RULER

Portuguese, until 1961

DENOMINATION

The denomination of most copper coins appears in numerals on the reverse, though 30 Reis is often given as "1/2 T," and 60 Reis as "T" (T = Tanga). The silver coins have the denomination in words, usually on the obverse until 1850, then on the reverse.

MONETARY SYSTEM

960 Reis = 16 Tanga = 1 Rupia

PORTUGUESE ADMINISTRATION

Kingdom of Portugal

MILLED COINAGE

KM# 13 1/12 TANGA

Bronze **Obv:** Head of Carlos I right **Rev:** Crowned shield **Note:** Roman numeral dating.

Date	Mintage	F	VF	XF	Unc	BU
1901	960,000	6.00	12.00	28.00	55.00	—
1901 Prooflike	—	—	—	—	—	—
1903	960,000	6.00	12.00	28.00	55.00	—

KM# 14 1/8 TANGA

Bronze **Obv:** Head of Carlos I right **Rev:** Crowned shield **Note:** Roman numeral dating

Date	Mintage	F	VF	XF	Unc	BU
1901	960,000	7.00	15.00	32.00	70.00	—
1901 Prooflike	—	—	—	—	—	—
1903	960,000	7.00	15.00	32.00	70.00	—

KM# 15 1/4 TANGA (15 Reis)

Bronze **Obv:** Head of Carlos I right **Rev:** Crowned shield **Note:** Roman numeral dating.

Date	Mintage	F	VF	XF	Unc	BU
1901	800,000	7.50	16.00	35.00	75.00	—
1901 Prooflike	—	—	—	—	200	—
1903	800,000	7.50	16.00	35.00	75.00	—

KM# 16 1/2 TANGA (30 Reis)

Bronze **Obv:** Head of Carlos I right **Note:** Roman numeral dating.

Date	Mintage	F	VF	XF	Unc	BU
1901	800,000	8.00	17.50	37.50	80.00	—
1901 Prooflike	—	—	—	—	225	—
1903	800,000	8.00	17.50	37.50	80.00	—

KM# 17 RUPIA

11.6600 g., 0.9170 Silver 0.3437 oz. ASW **Obv:** Head of Carlos I right **Rev:** Crowned shield within wreath

Date	Mintage	F	VF	XF	Unc	BU
1903	200,000	8.00	16.00	32.00	65.00	—
1904	100,000	9.00	18.00	35.00	70.00	—

PORTUGUESE ADMINISTRATION

Republic of Portugal

MILLED COINAGE

KM# 19 TANGA (60 Reis)

Bronze **Obv:** Divided shield **Rev:** Five shields on shield

Date	Mintage	F	VF	XF	Unc	BU
1934	100,000	25.00	70.00	245	500	—

KM# 24 TANGA (60 Reis)

Bronze, 25 mm. **Obv:** Denomination **Rev:** Tiny towers and shields above divided shield on lined circle

Date	Mintage	F	VF	XF	Unc	BU
1947	1,000,000	2.00	7.00	15.00	30.00	—

KM# 28 TANGA (60 Reis)

Bronze, 20 mm. **Obv:** Denomination **Rev:** Tiny towers and shields above divided shield on lined circle

Date	Mintage	F	VF	XF	Unc	BU
1952	9,600,000	1.00	4.00	9.00	20.00	—

KM# 20 2 TANGAS

Copper-Nickel

Date	Mintage	F	VF	XF	Unc	BU
1934	150,000	10.00	20.00	185	400	—

KM# 21 4 TANGAS

Copper-Nickel **Obv:** Divided shield **Rev:** Five shields on shield

Date	Mintage	F	VF	XF	Unc	BU
1934	100,000	20.00	60.00	210	450	—

KM# 25 1/4 RUPIA

Copper-Nickel **Obv:** Denomination **Rev:** Tiny towers and shields above divided shield on lined circle

Date	Mintage	F	VF	XF	Unc	BU
1947	800,000	5.00	10.00	20.00	40.00	—
1952	4,000,000	2.00	4.00	12.00	25.00	—

KM# 23 1/2 RUPIA

6.0000 g., 0.8350 Silver 0.1611 oz. ASW **Obv:** Shield on lined circle at center of Maltese Cross **Rev:** Divided shield

Date	Mintage	F	VF	XF	Unc	BU
1936	100,000	16.00	28.00	45.00	90.00	—

KM# 26 1/2 RUPIA
Copper-Nickel **Obv:** Denomination **Rev:** Tiny towers and shields above divided shield on lined circle

Date	Mintage	F	VF	XF	Unc	BU
1947	600,000	7.00	15.00	30.00	60.00	—
1952	2,000,000	2.00	5.00	12.00	25.00	—

KM# 18 RUPIA
11.6600 g., 0.9170 Silver 0.3437 oz. ASW **Obv:** Liberty head left **Rev:** Denomination within wreath

Date	Mintage	F	VF	XF	Unc	BU
1912/1	300,000	75.00	150	285	500	—
1912/1 Proof	—	Value: 1,250				
1912	Inc. above	35.00	75.00	150	285	—

KM# 22 RUPIA
12.0000 g., 0.9170 Silver 0.3538 oz. ASW **Obv:** Shield on lined circle at center of Maltese Cross **Rev:** Divided shield

Date	Mintage	F	VF	XF	Unc	BU
1935	300,000	7.50	15.00	30.00	55.00	—

KM# 27 RUPIA
12.0000 g., 0.5000 Silver 0.1929 oz. ASW **Obv:** Shield on lined circle at center of Maltese Cross **Rev:** Tiny towers and shields above divided shield on lined circle

Date	Mintage	F	VF	XF	Unc	BU
1947	900,000	7.50	15.00	30.00	60.00	—

KM# 29 RUPIA
Copper-Nickel **Obv:** Shield on lined circle at center of Maltese cross **Rev:** Tiny towers and shields above divided shield on lined circle

Date	Mintage	F	VF	XF	Unc	BU
1952	1,000,000	7.50	15.00	30.00	60.00	—

DECIMAL COINAGE

100 Centavos = 1 Escudo

KM# 30 10 CENTAVOS
2.0000 g., Bronze, 18 mm. **Obv:** Denomination **Rev:** Tiny towers and shields above divided shield on lined circle

Date	Mintage	F	VF	XF	Unc	BU
1958	5,000,000	1.00	3.00	7.00	16.00	—
1959	Inc. above	1.00	3.00	7.00	16.00	—
1961	1,000,000	0.50	1.00	1.50	3.00	—

KM# 31 30 CENTAVOS
Bronze **Obv:** Denomination **Rev:** Tiny towers and shields above divided shield on lined circle

Date	Mintage	F	VF	XF	Unc	BU
1958	5,000,000	0.75	2.50	7.00	16.00	—
1959	Inc. above	2.50	7.00	15.00	30.00	—

KM# 32 60 CENTAVOS
Copper-Nickel **Obv:** Shield on lined circle at center of Maltese Cross **Rev:** Tiny towers and shields above divided shield on lined circle

Date	Mintage	F	VF	XF	Unc	BU
1958	5,000,000	2.00	4.00	10.00	20.00	—
1959	Inc. above	1.25	2.50	6.50	13.50	—

KM# 33 ESCUDO
Copper-Nickel **Obv:** Shield on lined circle at center of Maltese Cross **Rev:** Tiny towers and shields above divided shield on lined circle

Date	Mintage	F	VF	XF	Unc	BU
1958	6,000,000	1.25	2.50	7.50	16.00	—
1959	Inc. above	1.25	2.50	6.50	13.50	—

KM# 34 3 ESCUDOS
Copper-Nickel **Obv:** Shield on lined circle at center of Maltese Cross **Rev:** Tiny towers and shields above divided shield on lined circle

Date	Mintage	F	VF	XF	Unc	BU
1958	5,000,000	2.50	5.00	12.00	22.00	—
1959	Inc. above	2.50	4.50	9.00	18.00	—

KM# 35 6 ESCUDOS
Copper-Nickel **Obv:** Shield on lined circle at center of Maltese Cross **Rev:** Tiny towers and shields above divided shield on lined circle

Date	Mintage	F	VF	XF	Unc	BU
1959	4,000,000	2.50	4.50	9.00	20.00	—

INDIA - BRITISH

The civilization of India, which began about 2500 B.C., flourished under a succession of empires - notably those of the Mauryas, the Kushans, the Guptas, the Delhi Sultans and the Mughals – until undermined in the 18th and 19th centuries by European colonial powers.

KING GEORGE VI: First and Second Heads

While King George VI's First Head is engraved in somewhat higher relief than his second head on all denominations from the 1/12 Anna to the Rupee, an easier way of distinguishing between the two types is that on the First Head the two *fleurs de lis* on the royal crown are larger and extend upward to touch the beaded crest at the top of the crown, while the two *fleurs de lis* on the crown of the Second Head are smaller and extend upward to touch only the line on the crown below the beaded crest.

ENGRAVER INITIALS

The following initials appear on the obverse on the truncation:
S incuse (Type I).
WW raised or incuse (Type II).
WWS or SWW (Type II).
WWB raised (Type II).

Proof and Prooflike restrikes

Original proofs are similar to early English Specimen strikes with wire edges and matte finish busts, arms, etc. Restrikes of most of the coins minted from the period 1835 were regularly supplied until this practice was discontinued on July 1, 1970.

Early proof restrikes are found with slight hairlines from polishing of the old dies. Bust, field, arms, etc. are of even smoothness.

Modern proof-like (P/L) restrikes usually have many hairlines from excessive polishing of the old dies and have a glassy, varnished or proof-like appearance. Many are common while some are quite scarce including some unusual mulings. These listings are indicated by **P/L-R** after the date and mint mark, for example; "1907(s) P/L R".

DISTINGUISHING FEATURES

Pice

NOTE: There are three types of the crown, which is on the obverse at the top. These are shown below and are designated as (RC) Round Crown, (HC) High Crown, and (FC) Flat Crown. Calcutta Mint issues have no mint mark. The issues from the other mints have the mint mark below the date as following: Lahore, raised "L"; Pretoria, small round dot; Mumbai (Bombay), diamond dot or "large" round dot. On the Mumbai (Bombay) issues dated 1944 the mint mark appears to be a large dot over a diamond.

Round Crown (RC)

High Crown (HC)

Flat Crown (FC)

½ Anna

The Calcutta Mint continued to issue this denomination with the dot before and after INDIA in 1946 and 1947. Mumbai (Bombay) also struck in 1946 and 1947, the 1946 issue denoted by a small dot in the center of the dashes before and after the date on the reverse (as well as a dot before and after INDIA, like Calcutta); the characteristics of the 1947 Bombay issue have not been determined but are thought also to resemble the 1946 issue. This denomination is also reported to have been struck in a quantity of 50,829,000 pieces in 1946 at the new Lahore Mint but no way of distinguishing this issue has been found. The proof issue in 1946 was struck by Mumbai (Bombay), not Calcutta. Source: Pridmore.

¼ Rupee

BUST A - Front of dress has 4 panels. The bottom panel has 3 leaves at left and a small flower at upper right.

BUST B - Front of dress has 3-1/2 panels. The bottom incomplete panel has only 3 leaf tops.

REVERSE I - Large top flower; 2 large petals above the base of the top flower are long and curved downward.

REVERSE II - Small top flower; 2 large petals above the base of the top flower are short and horizontal.

First Head
Small head, high relief, small denticles

Second Head
Small head, low relief, large denticles

Second Head
Large head, low relief, small denticles

From 1942 to 1945 the reverse designs of the silver coins change slightly every year. However, a distinct reverse variety occurs on Rupees and 1/4 Rupees dated 1943-44 and on the half Rupee dated 1944, all struck at Mumbai (Bombay). This variety may be distinguished from the other coins by the design of the center bottom flower as illustrated, and is designated as Reverse B.

On the normal common varieties dated 1943-44 the three "scalloped circles" are not connected to each other and the bead in the center is not attached to the nearest circle.

Obv: First head, reeded edge

Calcutta Mint issues have no mint mark. Mumbai (Bombay) coins have a small bead below the lotus flower at the bottom on the reverse, except those dated 1943-1944 with reverse B which has a diamond. Lahore Mint issues have a small "L" in the same position. The nickel coins have a diamond below the date on the reverse.

Rupee
Obverse Dies

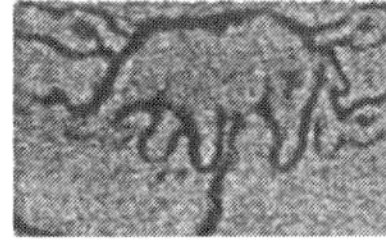

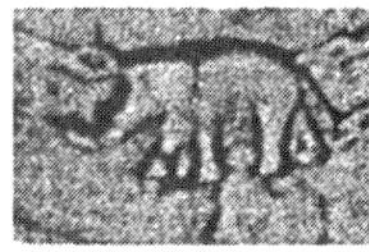

Type I **Type II**

Type I - Obv. die w/elephant with pig-like feet and short tail. Nicknamed "pig rupee".

Type II - Obv. die w/redesigned elephant with outlined ear, heavy feet and long tail.

The Rupees, dated 1911, were rejected by the public because the elephant, on the Order of the Indian Empire shown on the King's robe, was thought to resemble a pig, an animal considered unclean by most Indians. Out of a total of 9.4 million pieces struck at both mints, only 700,000 were issued, and many of these were withdrawn and melted with un-issued pieces. The issues dated 1912 and later have a re-designed elephant.

COLONY

MILLED COINAGE

Regal Style

KM# 483 1/12 ANNA (1 Pie)

2.0700 g., Copper, 17.5 mm. **Ruler:** Victoria **Obv:** Crowned bust left **Obv. Legend:** VICTORIA EMPRESS **Rev:** Value and date within beaded circle and wreath

Date	Mintage	F	VF	XF	Unc	BU
1901(c)	21,345,000	0.35	0.75	1.75	4.00	—
1901(c) Proof	—	Value: 175				
1901(c) P/L; Restrike	—	—	—	—	90.00	—

KM# 497 1/12 ANNA (1 Pie)

Copper, 17.5 mm. **Ruler:** Edward VII **Obv:** Head right **Obv. Legend:** EDWARD VII KING & EMPEROR **Rev:** Date and denomination within circle, wreath surrounds **Note:** Thick planchet.

Date	Mintage	F	VF	XF	Unc	BU
1903(c)	7,883,000	0.35	1.25	6.00	15.00	—
1903(c) Proof	—	Value: 180				
1903(c) P/L; Restrike	—	—	—	—	80.00	—
1904(c)	16,506,000	0.25	1.00	4.00	12.00	—
1904(c) Proof	—	Value: 180				
1904(c) P/L; Restrike	—	—	—	—	80.00	—
1905(c)	13,060,000	0.25	1.00	4.00	12.00	—
1905(c) P/L; Restrike	—	—	—	—	80.00	—
1906(c)	9,072,000	0.25	1.00	4.00	12.00	—
1906(c) Proof	—	Value: 180				
1906(c) P/L; Restrike	—	—	—	—	80.00	—

KM# 498 1/12 ANNA (1 Pie)

Bronze, 17.5 mm. **Ruler:** Edward VII **Obv:** Head right **Obv. Legend:** EDWARD VII KING & EMPEROR **Rev:** Date and denomination within circle, wreath surrounds **Note:** Thin planchet.

Date	Mintage	F	VF	XF	Unc	BU
1906(c)	2,184,000	0.35	0.75	5.00	15.00	—
1906(c) Proof	—	Value: 150				
1907(c)	20,985,000	0.25	0.50	3.00	9.00	—
1907(c) Proof	—	Value: 150				
1907(c) P/L; Restrike	—	—	—	—	80.00	—
1908(c)	22,036,000	0.25	0.50	3.00	9.00	—
1908(c) Proof	—	Value: 150				
1908(c) P/L; Restrike	—	—	—	—	80.00	—
1909(c)	12,316,000	0.25	0.50	3.00	9.00	—
1909(c) P/L; Restrike	—	—	—	—	80.00	—
1910(c)	23,520,000	0.25	0.50	3.00	9.00	—
1910(c) P/L; Restrike	—	—	—	—	80.00	—

KM# 509 1/12 ANNA (1 Pie)

1.6400 g., Bronze, 17.5 mm. **Ruler:** George V **Obv:** Crowned bust left **Obv. Legend:** GEORGE V KING EMPEROR **Rev:** Date and denomination within circle, wreath surrounds

Date	Mintage	F	VF	XF	Unc	BU
1912(c)	25,938,000	0.50	0.75	1.50	4.50	—
1912(c) Proof	—	Value: 150				
1912(c) P/L; Restrike	—	—	—	—	80.00	—
1913(c)	16,149,000	0.25	0.50	1.00	3.00	—
1913(c) Proof	—	Value: 120				
1913(c) P/L; Restrike	—	—	—	—	80.00	—
1914(c)	19,814,000	0.25	0.50	0.75	2.00	—
1914(c) Proof	—	Value: 120				
1914(c) P/L; Restrike	—	—	—	—	80.00	—
1915(c)	20,563,000	0.25	0.50	0.75	2.00	—
1915(c) Proof	—	Value: 120				
1915(c) P/L; Restrike	—	—	—	—	80.00	—
1916(c)	14,438,000	0.25	0.50	0.75	2.00	—
1916(c) Proof	—	Value: 120				
1916(c) P/L; Restrike	—	—	—	—	80.00	—
1917(c)	35,174,000	0.25	0.50	0.75	2.00	—
1917(c) Proof	—	Value: 120				
1917(c) P/L; Restrike	—	—	—	—	80.00	—
1918(c)	24,192,000	0.25	0.50	0.75	2.00	—
1918(c) Proof	—	Value: 120				
1918(c) P/L; Restrike	—	—	—	—	80.00	—
1919(c)	17,472,000	0.25	0.50	0.75	2.00	—
1919(c) Proof	—	Value: 120				
1919(c) P/L; Restrike	—	—	—	—	80.00	—
1920(c)	39,878,000	0.25	0.50	0.75	2.00	—
1920(c) Proof	—	Value: 120				
1920(c) P/L; Restrike	—	—	—	—	80.00	—
1921(c)	19,334,000	0.25	0.50	0.75	2.00	—
1921(c) P/L; Restrike	—	—	—	—	80.00	—
1921(c) Proof	—	Value: 120				
1923(c)	8,429,000	0.25	0.50	0.75	2.00	—
1923(c) Proof	—	Value: 120				
1923(b)	8,717,000	0.25	0.50	0.75	2.00	—
1923(b) Proof	—	Value: 120				
1923(b) P/L; Restrike	—	—	—	—	80.00	—
1924(c)	7,200,000	0.50	0.75	1.50	4.50	—
1924(c) Proof	—	Value: 120				
1924(b)	9,869,000	0.25	0.50	0.75	2.00	—
1924(b) Proof	—	Value: 120				
1924(b) P/L; Restrike	—	—	—	—	80.00	—
1925(c)	5,818,000	0.50	0.75	1.50	4.50	—
1925(c) Proof	—	Value: 120				
1925(b)	6,415,000	0.50	0.75	1.50	4.50	—
1925(b) Proof	—	Value: 120				
1925(b) P/L; Restrike	—	—	—	—	80.00	—
1926(c)	4,147,000	0.50	0.75	1.50	4.50	—
1926(c) Proof	—	Value: 120				
1926(b)	15,464,000	0.25	0.50	0.75	2.00	—
1926(b) Proof	—	Value: 120				
1926(b) P/L; Restrike	—	—	—	—	80.00	—
1927(c)	6,662,000	0.50	0.75	1.50	4.50	—
1927(c) Proof	—	Value: 120				
1927(b)	6,788,000	0.50	0.75	1.50	4.50	—
1927(b) Proof	—	Value: 120				
1927(b) P/L; Restrike	—	—	—	—	80.00	—
1928(c)	8,064,000	0.25	0.50	0.75	2.00	—
1928(c) Proof	—	Value: 120				
1928(b)	6,135,000	0.50	0.75	1.50	4.50	—
1928(b) Proof	—	Value: 120				
1928(b) P/L; Restrike	—	—	—	—	80.00	—
1929(c)	15,130,000	0.25	0.50	0.75	2.00	—
1929(c) Proof	—	Value: 120				
1929(c) P/L; Restrike	—	—	—	—	80.00	—
1930(c)	13,498,000	0.25	0.50	0.75	2.00	—
1930(c) Proof	—	Value: 120				
1930(c) P/L; Restrike	—	—	—	—	80.00	—
1931(c)	18,278,000	0.25	0.50	0.75	2.00	—
1931(c) Proof	—	Value: 120				
1931(c) P/L; Restrike	—	—	—	—	80.00	—
1932(c)	23,213,000	0.25	0.50	0.75	2.00	—
1932(c) Proof	—	Value: 120				
1932(c) P/L; Restrike	—	—	—	—	80.00	—
1933(c)	16,896,000	0.25	0.50	0.75	2.00	—
1933(c) Proof	—	Value: 120				
1933(c) P/L; Restrike	—	—	—	—	80.00	—
1934(c)	17,146,000	0.25	0.50	0.75	2.00	—
1934(c) Proof	—	Value: 120				
1934(c) P/L; Restrike	—	—	—	—	80.00	—
1935(c)	19,142,000	0.25	0.50	0.75	2.00	—
1935(c) Proof	—	Value: 120				
1935(c) P/L; Restrike	—	—	—	—	80.00	—
1936(c)	23,213,000	0.25	0.50	0.75	2.00	—
1936(b)	12,887,000	0.25	0.50	0.75	2.00	—
1936(b) P/L; Restrike	—	—	—	—	80.00	—

KM# 526 1/12 ANNA (1 Pie)

Bronze, 17.5 mm. **Ruler:** George VI **Obv:** Crowned head left **Obv. Legend:** GEORGE VI KING EMPEROR **Rev:** Date and denomination within circle, wreath surrounds **Note:** First head.

Date	Mintage	F	VF	XF	Unc	BU
1938(c) Proof	—	Value: 120				
1939(c)	3,571,000	0.50	0.75	1.50	4.50	—
1939(b)	17,407,000	0.25	0.50	1.00	2.50	—

KM# 527 1/12 ANNA (1 Pie)

Bronze, 17.5 mm. **Ruler:** George VI **Obv:** Crowned head left **Obv. Legend:** GEORGE VI KING EMPEROR **Rev:** Date and denomination within circle, wreath surrounds **Note:** Second head.

Date	Mintage	F	VF	XF	Unc	BU
1938(c) P/L; Restrike	—	—	—	—	80.00	—
1939(c)	5,245,000	0.25	0.50	1.00	2.50	—
1939(c) Proof	—	Value: 120				
1939(b)	31,306,000	0.25	0.50	0.75	2.00	—
1939(b) Proof	—	Value: 120				
1939(b) P/L; Restrike	—	—	—	—	80.00	—
1941(b)	6,137,000	0.25	0.50	0.75	2.00	—
1942(b)	6,124,000	0.50	0.75	1.50	4.50	—
1942(b) Proof	—	Value: 120				
1942(b) P/L; Restrike	—	—	—	—	80.00	—

KM# 484 1/2 PICE

Copper **Ruler:** Victoria **Obv:** Crowned bust left **Obv. Legend:** VICTORIA EMPRESS **Rev:** Value and date within beaded circle and wreath

Date	Mintage	F	VF	XF	Unc	BU
1901(c)	16,057,000	1.00	1.75	3.50	8.50	—
1901(c) Proof	—	Value: 175				
1901(c) P/L; Restrike	—	—	—	—	90.00	—

KM# 499 1/2 PICE

Copper **Ruler:** Edward VII **Obv:** Head right **Obv. Legend:** EDWARD VII KING & EMPEROR **Rev:** Date and denomination within circle, wreath surrounds

Date	Mintage	F	VF	XF	Unc	BU
1903(c)	5,376,000	0.75	1.50	5.00	15.00	—
1903(c) Proof	—	Value: 135				
1903(c) P/L; Restrike	—	—	—	—	80.00	—
1904(c)	8,464,000	0.75	1.50	5.00	15.00	—
1904(c) Proof	—	Value: 135				
1904(c) P/L; Restrike	—	—	—	—	80.00	—
1905(c)	8,922,000	0.75	1.50	5.00	15.00	—
1905(c) P/L; Restrike	—	—	—	—	80.00	—
1906(c)	6,346,000	0.75	1.50	5.00	15.00	—
1906(c) Proof	—	Value: 135				
1906(c) P/L; Restrike	—	—	—	—	80.00	—

KM# 500 1/2 PICE

Bronze **Ruler:** Edward VII **Obv. Legend:** EDWARD VII KING & EMPEROR **Note:** Thinner planchets.

Date	Mintage	F	VF	XF	Unc	BU
1904(c) Proof	—	Value: 135				
1906(c)	5,860,000	0.75	1.50	4.50	12.50	—
1906(c) Proof	—	Value: 135				
1907(c)	8,060,000	0.75	1.50	4.50	12.50	—
1907(c) Proof	—	Value: 135				
1907(c) P/L; Restrike	—	—	—	—	80.00	—
1908(c)	10,035,000	0.75	1.50	4.50	12.50	—
1908(c) Proof	—	Value: 135				
1908(c) P/L; Restrike	—	—	—	—	80.00	—
1909(c)	8,493,000	0.75	1.50	4.50	12.50	—
1909(c) P/L; Restrike	—	—	—	—	80.00	—
1910(c)	17,408,000	0.75	1.50	4.50	12.50	—

KM# 510 1/2 PICE

Bronze **Ruler:** George V **Obv:** Crowned bust left **Obv. Legend:** GEORGE V KING EMPEROR **Rev:** Date and denomination within circle, wreath surrounds

Date	Mintage	F	VF	XF	Unc	BU
1912(c)	12,911,000	0.25	0.50	0.75	3.00	—
1912(c) Proof	—	Value: 120				
1912(c) P/L; Restrike	—	—	—	—	80.00	—
1913(c)	10,897,000	0.25	0.50	0.75	3.00	—
1913(c) Proof	—	Value: 120				
1913(c) P/L; Restrike	—	—	—	—	80.00	—
1914(c)	4,877,000	0.15	0.30	0.50	2.50	—
1914(c) Proof	—	Value: 120				
1914(c) P/L; Restrike	—	—	—	—	80.00	—
1915(c)	9,830,000	0.15	0.30	0.50	2.50	—
1915(c) Proof	—	Value: 120				
1915(c) P/L; Restrike	—	—	—	—	80.00	—
1916(c)	5,734,000	0.15	0.30	0.50	2.50	—
1916(c) Proof	—	Value: 120				
1916(c) P/L; Restrike	—	—	—	—	80.00	—
1917(c)	15,296,000	0.15	0.30	0.50	2.50	—
1917(c) Proof	—	Value: 120				
1917(c) P/L; Restrike	—	—	—	—	80.00	—
1918(c)	6,244,000	0.15	0.30	0.50	2.50	—
1918(c) Proof	—	Value: 120				
1918(c) P/L; Restrike	—	—	—	—	80.00	—
1919(c)	11,162,000	0.15	0.30	0.50	2.50	—
1919(c) Proof	—	Value: 120				
1919(c) P/L; Restrike	—	—	—	—	80.00	—
1920(c)	4,493,000	0.15	0.30	0.50	2.50	—
1920(c) Proof	—	Value: 120				
1920(c) P/L; Restrike	—	—	—	—	80.00	—
1921(c)	6,234,000	0.15	0.30	0.50	2.50	—
1921(c) Proof	—	Value: 120				
1921(c) P/L; Restrike	—	—	—	—	80.00	—
1922(c)	6,336,000	0.15	0.30	0.50	2.50	—
1922(c) Proof	—	Value: 120				
1922(c) P/L; Restrike	—	—	—	—	80.00	—
1923(c)	7,411,000	0.15	0.30	0.50	2.50	—
1923(c) Proof	—	Value: 120				
1923(c) P/L; Restrike	—	—	—	—	80.00	—
1924(c)	9,523,000	0.15	0.30	0.50	2.50	—
1924(c) Proof	—	Value: 120				
1924(c) P/L; Restrike	—	—	—	—	80.00	—
1925(c)	3,981,000	0.50	0.75	1.50	4.50	—
1925(c) Proof	—	Value: 120				
1925(c) P/L; Restrike	—	—	—	—	80.00	—
1926(c)	7,885,000	0.15	0.30	0.50	2.50	—
1926(c) Proof	—	Value: 120				
1926(c) P/L; Restrike	—	—	—	—	80.00	—
1927(c)	5,888,000	0.15	0.30	0.50	2.50	—
1927(c) Proof	—	Value: 120				
1927(c) P/L; Restrike	—	—	—	—	80.00	—
1928(c)	5,456,000	0.15	0.30	0.50	2.50	—
1928(c) Proof	—	Value: 120				
1928(c) P/L; Restrike	—	—	—	—	80.00	—
1929(c)	7,654,000	0.15	0.30	0.50	2.50	—
1929(c) Proof	—	Value: 120				
1929(c) P/L; Restrike	—	—	—	—	80.00	—
1930(c)	7,181,000	0.15	0.30	0.50	2.50	—
1930(c) Proof	—	Value: 120				
1930(c) P/L; Restrike	—	—	—	—	80.00	—
1931(c)	8,794,000	0.15	0.30	0.50	2.50	—
1931(c) Proof	—	Value: 120				
1931(c) P/L; Restrike	—	—	—	—	80.00	—
1932(c)	5,440,000	0.15	0.30	0.50	2.50	—
1932(c) Proof	—	Value: 120				
1932(c) P/L; Restrike	—	—	—	—	80.00	—
1933(c)	9,242,000	0.15	0.30	0.50	2.50	—
1933(c) Proof	—	Value: 120				
1933(c) P/L; Restrike	—	—	—	—	80.00	—
1934(c)	8,947,000	0.15	0.30	0.50	2.50	—
1934(c) Proof	—	Value: 120				
1934(c) P/L; Restrike	—	—	—	—	80.00	—
1935(c)	15,501,000	0.15	0.30	0.50	2.50	—
1935(c) Proof	—	Value: 120				
1935(c) P/L; Restrike	—	—	—	—	80.00	—
1936(c)	26,726,000	0.10	0.25	0.40	1.25	—
1936(c) P/L; Restrike	—	—	—	—	80.00	—

KM# 528 1/2 PICE

Bronze **Ruler:** George VI **Obv:** First head; high relief **Obv. Legend:** GEORGE VI KING EMPEROR **Rev:** Date and denomination within circle, wreath surrounds **Note:** Calcutta Mint issues have no mint mark. Mumbai (Bombay) Mint issues have a small dot below the date.

Date	Mintage	F	VF	XF	Unc	BU
1938(c) Proof	—	Value: 100				
1938(c) P/L; Restrike	—	—	—	—	80.00	—
Note: Calcutta Mint reported 11,161,000 mintage for 1938 but only proof and modern prooflike restrikes are known						
1939(c)	17,357,000	0.15	0.40	0.60	1.75	—
1939(c) Proof	—	Value: 100				
1939(b)	9,343,000	0.20	0.45	0.85	3.50	—
1939(b) Proof	—	Value: 100				
1939(b) P/L; Restrike	—	—	—	—	80.00	—
1940(c)	23,770,000	0.15	0.40	0.65	1.75	—
1940(c) Proof	—	Value: 100				
1940(c) P/L; Restrike	—	—	—	—	80.00	—

KM# 529 1/2 PICE

Bronze **Ruler:** George VI **Obv:** Second head; low relief **Obv. Legend:** GEORGE VI KING EMPEROR **Rev:** Date and denomination within circle, wreath surrounds

Date	Mintage	F	VF	XF	Unc	BU
1942(b) Proof	—	Value: 150				
1942(b) P/L; Restrike	—	—	—	—	100	—

KM# 532 PICE

Bronze **Ruler:** George VI **Obv:** Small date, small legends

Date	Mintage	F	VF	XF	Unc	BU
1943(b) (RC) diamond	164,659	0.30	0.50	1.00	3.50	—

KM# 533 PICE

2.0000 g., Bronze, 21.32 mm. **Ruler:** George VI **Obv:** Center hole, large date, large legends **Rev:** Wreath surrounds center hole

Date	Mintage	F	VF	XF	Unc	BU
1943(b) (HC) large dot	—	0.15	0.35	0.65	1.25	—
1943(p) (HC) small dot	98,997,000	0.15	0.35	0.65	1.25	—
1944(c) (HC)	—	0.15	0.35	0.65	1.25	—
1944(c) (HC) Proof	—	Value: 100				
1944(b) (HC) large dot	195,354,000	0.15	0.35	0.65	1.25	—
1944(b) (HC) diamond	—	0.20	0.40	0.75	2.00	—
1944(b) (FC) large dot	—	0.20	0.40	0.75	2.00	—
1944(b) P/L; Restrike	—	—	—	—	80.00	—
1944(p) (HC) small dot	141,003,000	0.20	0.40	0.75	2.00	—
1944L (HC)	29,802,000	0.20	0.40	0.80	3.50	—
1945(c) (FC)	156,322,000	0.15	0.35	0.65	1.25	—
1945(b) (FC) diamond	237,197,000	0.15	0.35	0.65	1.25	—
1945(b) (FC) large dot	Inc. above	0.15	0.35	0.65	1.25	—
1945(b) P/L; Restrike	—	—	—	—	80.00	—
1945L (FC)	238,825,000	0.15	0.35	0.65	1.25	—
1947(c) (HC)	153,702,000	0.15	0.35	0.65	1.25	—
1947(b) (HC) diamond	43,654,000	0.20	0.40	0.80	3.50	—
1947(b) Proof	—	Value: 100				
1947 P/L; Restrike	—	—	—	—	80.00	—

KM# 486 1/4 ANNA

6.4000 g., Copper **Ruler:** Victoria **Obv:** Crowned bust left **Obv. Legend:** VICTORIA EMPRESS **Rev:** Value and date within beaded circle and wreath

Date	Mintage	F	VF	XF	Unc	BU
1901(c)	136,091,000	0.35	0.75	1.50	4.50	—
1901(c) Proof	—	Value: 250				
1901(c) P/L; Restrike	—	—	—	—	125	—

KM# 501 1/4 ANNA

6.4800 g., Copper **Ruler:** Edward VII **Obv. Legend:** EDWARD VII KING & EMPEROR

Date	Mintage	F	VF	XF	Unc	BU
1903(c)	105,974,000	0.35	1.75	7.50	35.00	—
1903(c) Proof	—	Value: 150				
1903(c) P/L; Restrike	—	—	—	—	85.00	—
1904(c)	104,595,000	0.35	1.75	7.50	35.00	—
1904(c) Proof	—	Value: 150				
1904(c) P/L; Restrike	—	—	—	—	85.00	—
1905(c)	130,058,000	0.35	1.75	7.50	35.00	—
1905(c) Proof	—	Value: 150				
1905(c) P/L; Restrike	—	—	—	—	85.00	—

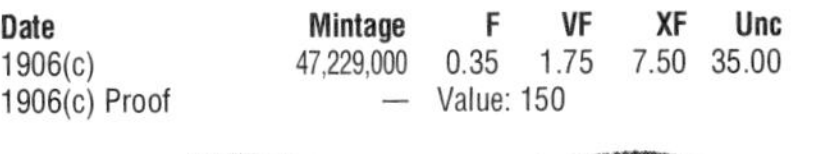

Date	Mintage	F	VF	XF	Unc	BU
1906(c)	47,229,000	0.35	1.75	7.50	35.00	—
1906(c) Proof	—	Value: 150				

KM# 502 1/4 ANNA

Bronze, 25.5 mm. **Ruler:** Edward VII **Obv:** Head right **Obv. Legend:** EDWARD VII KING & EMPEROR **Rev:** Date and denomination within circle, wreath surrounds **Note:** Thinner planchet.

Date	Mintage	F	VF	XF	Unc	BU
1906(c)	115,786,000	0.35	1.25	6.50	30.00	—
1906(c) Proof	—	Value: 120				
1907(c)	234,682,000	0.35	1.25	6.50	30.00	—
1907(c) Proof	—	Value: 120				
1907(c) P/L; Restrike	—	—	—	—	80.00	—
1908(c)	58,066,000	0.35	1.25	6.50	30.00	—
1908(c) Proof	—	Value: 120				
1908(c) P/L; Restrike	—	—	—	—	80.00	—
1909(c)	29,966,000	0.35	1.25	6.50	30.00	—
1909(c) Proof	—	Value: 120				
1909(c) P/L; Restrike	—	—	—	—	80.00	—
1910(c)	47,265,000	0.35	1.25	6.50	30.00	—
1910(c) P/L; Restrike	—	—	—	—	80.00	—

KM# 511 1/4 ANNA

Bronze **Ruler:** George V **Obv:** Type I **Obv. Legend:** GEORGE V KING EMPEROR **Note:** Calcutta Mint issues have no mint mark. Mumbai (Bombay) Mint issues have a small dot below the date. The pieces dated 1911, like the other coins with that date, show the "Pig" elephant.

Date	Mintage	F	VF	XF	Unc	BU
1911(c)	55,918,000	0.75	2.00	5.00	20.00	—
1911(c) Proof	—	Value: 175				
1911(c) P/L; Restrike	—	—	—	—	80.00	—

KM# 512 1/4 ANNA

4.8600 g., Bronze **Ruler:** George V **Obv:** Crowned bust left, type II **Obv. Legend:** GEORGE V KING EMPEROR **Rev:** Date and denomination within circle, wreath surrounds

Date	Mintage	F	VF	XF	Unc	BU
1912(c)	107,456,000	0.20	0.40	1.00	4.00	—
1912(c) Proof	—	Value: 120				
1912(c) P/L; Restrike	—	—	—	—	80.00	—
1913(c)	82,061,000	0.25	0.50	1.25	4.50	—
1913(c) Proof	—	Value: 120				
1913(c) P/L; Restrike	—	—	—	—	80.00	—
1914(c)	40,576,000	0.50	0.75	1.50	3.50	—
1914(c) Proof	—	Value: 120				
1914(c) P/L; Restrike	—	—	—	—	80.00	—
1916(c)	1,632,000	3.50	7.00	12.00	25.00	—
1916(c) Proof	—	Value: 150				
1917(c)	69,370,000	0.20	0.40	0.80	3.50	—
1917(c) Proof	—	Value: 120				
1917(c) P/L; Restrike	—	—	—	—	80.00	—
1918(c)	84,045,000	0.20	0.40	0.80	3.50	—
1918(c) Proof	—	Value: 120				
1918(c) P/L; Restrike	—	—	—	—	80.00	—
1919(c)	212,467,000	0.20	0.40	0.80	3.50	—
1919(c) Proof	—	Value: 120				
1919(c) P/L; Restrike	—	—	—	—	80.00	—
1920(c)	96,019,000	0.20	0.40	0.80	3.50	—
1920(c) Proof	—	Value: 120				
1920(c) P/L; Restrike	—	—	—	—	80.00	—
1921(c) Proof	—	Value: 120				
1924(b)	16,322,000	0.20	0.40	0.80	3.50	—
1924(b) Proof	—	Value: 120				
1925(c)	14,598,000	0.20	0.40	0.80	3.50	—
1925(b)	14,588,000	0.20	0.40	0.80	3.50	—
1925(b) Proof	—	Value: 120				
1926(c)	17,389,000	0.20	0.40	0.80	3.50	—
1926(c) Proof	—	Value: 120				
1926(b)	16,073,000	0.20	0.40	0.80	3.50	—
1926(b) Proof	—	Value: 120				
1926(b) P/L; Restrike	—	—	—	—	80.00	—
1927(c)	6,925,000	0.50	0.75	1.50	4.50	—
1927(c) Proof	—	Value: 120				
1927(b)	12,440,000	0.20	0.40	0.80	3.50	—
1927(b) Proof	—	Value: 120				
1927(b) P/L; Restrike	—	—	—	—	80.00	—
1928(c)	257,779,000	0.20	0.40	0.80	3.50	—
1928(c) Proof	—	Value: 120				
1928(b)	10,057,000	0.20	0.40	0.80	3.50	—
1928(b) Proof	—	Value: 120				
1928(b) P/L; Restrike	—	—	—	—	80.00	—
1929(c)	61,542,000	0.20	0.40	0.80	3.50	—
1929(c) Proof	—	Value: 120				
1929(c) P/L; Restrike	—	—	—	—	80.00	—
1930(c)	40,698,000	0.20	0.40	0.80	3.50	—
1930(c) Proof	—	Value: 120				
1930(b)	9,646,000	0.50	0.75	1.50	4.50	—
1930(b) Proof	—	Value: 120				
1930(b) P/L; Restrike	—	—	—	—	80.00	—
1931(c)	6,835,000	0.50	0.75	1.50	4.50	—
1931(c) Proof	—	Value: 120				
1931(c) P/L; Restrike	—	—	—	—	80.00	—
1933(c)	40,230,000	0.20	0.40	0.80	3.50	—
1933(c) Proof	—	Value: 120				
1933(c) P/L; Restrike	—	—	—	—	80.00	—
1934(c)	80,506,000	0.20	0.40	0.80	3.50	—
1934(c) Proof	—	Value: 120				
1934(c) P/L; Restrike	—	—	—	—	80.00	—
1935(c)	92,595,000	0.20	0.40	0.80	3.50	—
1935(c) Proof	—	Value: 120				
1935(c) P/L; Restrike	—	—	—	—	80.00	—
1936(c)	227,501,000	0.20	0.40	0.80	3.50	—
1936(b)	61,926,000	0.20	0.40	0.80	3.50	—
1936(b) Proof	—	Value: 120				
1936(b) P/L; Restrike	—	—	—	—	80.00	—

KM# 530 1/4 ANNA

4.8600 g., Bronze **Ruler:** George VI **Obv:** First head; high relief **Obv. Legend:** GEORGE VI KING EMPEROR **Rev:** Date and denomination within circle, wreath surrounds

Date	Mintage	F	VF	XF	Unc	BU
1938(c)	33,792,000	0.25	0.40	0.75	2.00	—
1938(c) Proof	—	Value: 120				
1938(b)	16,796,000	0.50	0.75	1.50	4.50	—
1938(b) P/L; Restrike	—	—	—	—	100	—
1939(c)	78,279,000	0.30	0.50	1.00	2.50	—
1939(c) Proof	—	Value: 120				
1939(b)	60,171,000	0.30	0.50	1.00	3.50	—
1939(b) Proof	—	Value: 120				
1939(b) P/L; Restrike	—	—	—	—	100	—
1940(b)	116,721,000	0.35	0.75	1.50	3.50	—

KM# 531 1/4 ANNA

4.6000 g., Bronze, 25.33 mm. **Ruler:** George VI **Obv:** Second head; low relief **Obv. Legend:** GEORGE VI KING EMPEROR **Rev:** Denomination and date within wreath

Date	Mintage	F	VF	XF	Unc	BU
1940(c)	140,410,000	0.30	0.50	1.00	3.50	—
1940(c) Proof	—	Value: 120				
1940(b)	—	0.30	0.50	1.00	3.50	—
Note: Mintage included in KM#530						
1940(b) P/L; Restrike	—	—	—	—	100	—
1941(c)	121,107,000	0.30	0.50	1.00	3.50	—
1941(c) P/L; Restrike	—	—	—	—	100	—
1941(b)	1,446,000	0.40	0.90	2.00	6.00	—
1942(c)	34,298,000	0.30	0.50	1.00	3.50	—
1942(b)	8,768,000	0.30	0.50	1.00	3.50	—
1942(b) P/L; Restrike	—	—	—	—	100	—

KM# 534b.2 1/2 ANNA

2.8700 g., Nickel-Brass, 17.3 mm. **Ruler:** George VI **Obv:** Crowned head left **Rev:** Denomination and date within decorative outline **Rev. Legend:** • INDIA •

Date	Mintage	F	VF	XF	Unc	BU
1942(c)	159,000,000	0.10	0.25	0.50	2.00	—
1942(c) Proof	—	Value: 100				
1943(c)	437,760,000	0.10	0.25	0.50	2.00	—
1943(c) Proof	—	Value: 120				
1944(c)	514,800,000	0.10	0.25	0.50	2.00	—
1944(c) Proof	—	Value: 120				
1945(c)	215,732,000	0.10	0.25	0.50	2.00	—
1945(c) Proof	—	Value: 120				

KM# 534b.1 1/2 ANNA

2.9200 g., Nickel-Brass **Ruler:** George VI **Obv:** Crowned head left, second head **Obv. Legend:** GEORGE VI KING EMPEROR **Rev:** Denomination and date within decorative outline **Rev. Legend:** INDIA (without dots) **Note:** Bombay Mint issues dated 1942-1945 are without a dot before and after India.

Date	Mintage	F	VF	XF	Unc	BU
1942(b)	7,945,000	0.30	0.50	1.00	3.50	—
1942(b) P/L; Restrike	—	—	—	—	120	—
1943(b) P/L; Restrike	—	—	—	—	120	—
1944(b) P/L; Restrike	—	—	—	—	120	—
1945(b) P/L; Restrike	—	—	—	—	100	—

The Calcutta Mint continued to issue this denomination with the dot before and after INDIA in 1946 and 1947. Bombay also struck in 1946 and 1947, the 1946 issue denoted by a small dot in the center of the dashes before and after the date on the reverse (as well as a dot before and after INDIA, like Calcutta); the characteristics of the 1947 Bombay issue have not been determined but are thought also to resemble the 1946 issue. This denomination is also reported to have been struck in a quantity of 50,829,000 pieces in 1946 at the new Lahore Mint but no way of distinguishing this issue has been found. The proof issue in 1946 was struck by Bombay, not Calcutta. Source: Pridmore.

KM# 535.1 1/2 ANNA

2.8700 g., Copper-Nickel **Ruler:** George VI **Obv:** Crowned head left **Rev:** Denomination and date within decorative outline **Shape:** 4-sided

Date	Mintage	F	VF	XF	Unc	BU
1946(b)	48,744,000	0.10	0.25	0.50	2.00	—
1946(b) Proof	—	Value: 120				
1946(b) P/L; Restrike	—	—	—	—	100	—
1947(b) P/L; Restrike	—	—	—	—	150	—

KM# 535.2 1/2 ANNA

2.9000 g., Copper-Nickel **Ruler:** George VI **Obv:** Crowned head left **Rev:** Denomination and date within decorative outline **Shape:** 4-sided

Date	Mintage	F	VF	XF	Unc	BU
1946(c)	75,159,000	0.15	0.30	0.50	2.50	—
1947(c)	126,392,000	0.10	0.20	0.45	1.25	—
1947(c) Proof	—	Value: 120				
1947(c) P/L; Restrike	—	—	—	—	100	—

KM# 504 ANNA

Copper-Nickel **Ruler:** Edward VII **Obv:** Crowned bust right **Obv. Legend:** EDWARD VII KING & EMPEROR **Rev:** Denomination and date within decorative outline **Shape:** Scalloped **Note:** Struck only at the Mumbai (Bombay) Mint. Small incuse "B" mint mark in the space below the cross pattee of the crown on the obverse.

Date	Mintage	F	VF	XF	Unc	BU
1906B	200,000	20.00	50.00	125	300	—
1907B	37,256,000	0.50	1.25	2.00	5.00	—
1907B Proof	—	Value: 60.00				
1908B	22,536,000	0.50	1.25	2.00	5.00	—
1908B Proof	—	Value: 60.00				
1909B	24,800,000	0.50	1.25	2.00	5.00	—
1909B Proof	—	Value: 60.00				
1910B	40,200,000	0.50	1.25	2.00	5.00	—
1910B Proof	—	Value: 60.00				

KM# 513 ANNA

3.8100 g., Copper-Nickel **Ruler:** George VI **Obv:** Crowned bust left **Obv. Legend:** GEORGE VI KING EMPEROR **Rev:** Denomination and date within decorative outline **Shape:** Scalloped **Note:** Until 1920, all were struck at the Mumbai (Bombay) Mint without mint mark. From 1923 on, the Mumbai (Bombay) Mint issues have a small, raised bead or dot below the date. Calcutta Mint issues have no mint mark.

Date	Mintage	F	VF	XF	Unc	BU
1912(b)	39,400,000	0.40	1.00	2.50	6.00	—
1912 Proof	—	Value: 150				
1913(b)	39,776,000	0.40	1.00	2.50	6.00	—
1913 Proof	—	Value: 150				
1914(b)	48,000,000	0.25	0.50	1.75	4.00	—
1914 Proof	—	Value: 150				
1915(b)	7,670,000	0.40	1.00	2.50	6.00	—
1915 Proof	—	Value: 150				
1916(b)	39,087,000	0.25	0.50	1.75	4.00	—
1917(b)	58,067,000	0.25	0.50	1.75	4.00	—
1917 Proof	—	Value: 150				
1918(b)	80,692,000	0.25	0.50	1.75	4.00	—
1918(b) Proof	—	Value: 150				
1919(b)	122,795,000	0.25	0.50	1.75	4.00	—
1919(b) Proof	—	Value: 150				
1919(c) Proof	—	Value: 150				
1920(b)	9,264,000	0.25	0.50	1.75	4.50	—
1920(b) Proof	—	Value: 150				
1923(b)	7,125,000	0.25	0.50	1.75	4.50	—
1923(b) Proof	—	Value: 150				
1924(c)	16,640,000	0.25	0.50	1.75	4.00	—
1924(c) Proof	—	Value: 150				
1924(b)	17,285,000	0.25	0.50	2.00	5.00	—
1924(b) Proof	—	Value: 150				
1924(b) P/L; Restrike	—	—	—	—	80.00	—
1925(c)	22,388,000	0.25	0.50	2.00	5.00	—
1925(c) Proof	—	Value: 150				
1925(b)	11,763,000	0.25	0.50	2.00	5.00	—
1925(b) Proof	—	Value: 150				
1925(b) P/L; Restrike	—	—	—	—	80.00	—
1926(c)	13,440,000	0.25	0.50	2.00	5.00	—
1926(c) Proof	—	Value: 150				
1926(b)	8,088,000	0.25	0.50	2.00	5.00	—
1926(b) Proof	—	Value: 150				
1926(b) P/L; Restrike	—	—	—	—	80.00	—
1927(c)	6,296,000	0.40	1.00	2.50	6.00	—
1927(c) Proof	—	Value: 150				
1927(b)	12,953,000	0.25	0.50	2.00	5.00	—
1927(b) Proof	—	Value: 150				
1927(b) P/L; Restrike	—	—	—	—	80.00	—
1928(c)	29,568,000	1.00	1.75	3.50	8.50	—
1928(c) Proof	—	Value: 150				
1928(b)	4,832,000	0.25	0.50	2.00	5.00	—
1928(b) Proof	—	Value: 150				
1928(b) P/L; Restrike	—	—	—	—	80.00	—
1929(c)	42,200,000	0.25	0.50	2.00	5.00	—
1929(c) Proof	—	Value: 150				
1929(c) P/L; Restrike	—	—	—	—	80.00	—
1930(c)	22,816,000	0.25	0.50	2.00	5.00	—
1930(c) Proof	—	Value: 150				
1930(c) P/L; Restrike	—	—	—	—	80.00	—
1933(c)	17,432,000	0.25	0.50	2.00	5.00	—
1933(c) Proof	—	Value: 150				
1933(c) P/L; Restrike	—	—	—	—	80.00	—
1934(c)	34,216,000	0.25	0.40	1.50	4.00	—
1934(c) Proof	—	Value: 150				
1934(c) P/L; Restrike	—	—	—	—	80.00	—
1935(c)	12,952,000	0.25	0.40	1.50	4.00	—
1935(c) Proof	—	Value: 150				
1935(b)	41,112,000	0.25	0.40	1.50	4.00	—
1935(b) Proof	—	Value: 150				
1935(b) P/L; Restrike	—	—	—	—	80.00	—
1936(c)	21,592,000	0.25	0.40	1.50	4.00	—
1936(b)	107,136,000	0.20	0.35	1.25	3.00	—
1936(b) Proof	—	Value: 150				

KM# 536 ANNA

3.7000 g., Copper-Nickel **Ruler:** George VI **Obv:** First head, high relief **Obv. Legend:** GEORGE VI KING EMPEROR **Rev:** Denomination and date within decorative outline **Shape:** Scalloped **Note:** Calcutta Mint issues have no mint mark. Bombay Mint issues have a small dot below the date.

Date	Mintage	VG	F	VF	XF	Unc
1938(c)	7,128,000	—	0.30	0.75	1.50	5.00
1938(c) Proof	—	Value: 120				
1938(b)	3,126,000	—	0.40	1.00	2.00	5.00
1938(b) P/L; Restrike	—	—	—	—	—	80.00
1939(c)	18,192,000	—	0.30	0.75	1.50	3.00
1939(b)	36,157,000	—	0.30	0.75	1.50	3.00
1939(b) P/L; Restrike	—	—	—	—	—	80.00
1940(c)	60,945,000	—	0.30	0.75	1.50	3.00
1940(c) P/L; Restrike	—	—	—	—	—	80.00
1940(b)	—	—	1.00	2.00	4.00	10.00

KM# 537 ANNA

Copper-Nickel **Ruler:** George VI **Obv:** Second head, low relief, large crown **Obv. Legend:** GEORGE VI KING EMPEROR **Rev:** Large denomination and date within decorative outline **Shape:** Scalloped

Date	Mintage	VG	F	VF	XF	Unc
1940(c)	76,392,000	—	0.10	0.25	0.50	2.00
1940(c) P/L; Restrike	—	—	—	—	—	100
1940(b)	144,712,000	—	0.10	0.25	0.50	2.00
1940(b) P/L; Restrike	—	—	—	—	—	80.00
1941(c)	62,480,000	—	0.10	0.25	0.50	2.00
1941(b)	40,170,000	—	0.15	0.40	1.00	1.50
1941(b) P/L; Restrike	—	—	—	—	—	100

KM# 537a ANNA

3.8900 g., Nickel-Brass, 20.50 mm. **Ruler:** George VI **Obv:** Second head, low relief, large crown **Obv. Legend:** GEORGE VI KING EMPEROR **Rev:** Large denomination and date within decorative outline **Shape:** Scalloped

Date	Mintage	VG	F	VF	XF	Unc
1942(c)	194,056,000	—	0.10	0.25	0.50	2.00
1942(c) Proof	—	Value: 120				
1942(b)	103,240,000	—	0.15	0.40	1.00	2.50
1942(b) P/L; Restrike	—	—	—	—	—	80.00
1943(c)	352,256,000	—	0.10	0.25	0.50	2.00
1943(c) Proof	—	Value: 120				
1943(b)	134,500,000	—	0.10	0.25	0.50	2.00
1943(b) P/L; Restrike	—	—	—	—	—	80.00
1944(c)	457,608,000	—	0.10	0.25	0.50	2.00
1944(c) Proof	—	Value: 120				
1944(b)	175,208,000	—	0.10	0.25	0.50	2.00
1944(b) P/L; Restrike	—	—	—	—	—	80.00
1945(c)	278,360,000	—	0.10	0.25	0.50	2.00
1945(b)	61,228,000	—	0.20	0.40	0.80	3.50

KM# 539 ANNA

Nickel-Brass, 21 mm. **Ruler:** George VI **Obv:** Second head, low relief, small crown **Obv. Legend:** GEORGE VI KING EMPEROR **Rev:** Denomination and date within decorative outline **Shape:** Scalloped

Date	Mintage	VG	F	VF	XF	Unc
1945(c)	278,360,000	—	0.10	0.25	0.75	2.00
1945(c) Proof	—	Value: 120				
1945(b)	61,228,000	—	0.10	0.25	0.75	2.00
1945(b) P/L; Restrike	—	—	—	—	—	100

KM# 538 ANNA

3.8700 g., Copper-Nickel **Ruler:** George VI **Obv:** Second head, low relief, small crown **Obv. Legend:** GEORGE VI KING EMPEROR **Rev:** Denomination and date within decorative outline **Shape:** Scalloped

Date	Mintage	F	VF	XF	Unc	BU
1946(c)	100,820,000	0.10	0.15	0.35	1.50	—
1946(b)	82,052,000	0.10	0.15	0.35	1.50	—
1946(b) Proof	—	Value: 120				
1946(b) P/L; Restrike	—	—	—	—	100	—
1947(c)	148,656,000	0.10	0.25	0.35	1.50	—
1947(c) Proof	—	Value: 120				
1947(b)	50,096,000	0.10	0.25	0.50	2.00	—
1947(b) Proof	—	Value: 120				

KM# 488 2 ANNAS

1.4600 g., 0.9170 Silver 0.0430 oz. ASW **Ruler:** Victoria **Obv:** Crowned bust left **Obv. Legend:** VICTORIA EMPRESS **Rev:** Value and date within wreath

Date	Mintage	F	VF	XF	Unc	BU
1901C Incuse	8,944,000	1.25	2.50	5.00	10.00	—
Note: Type B Bust, Type II Reverse						
1901C Proof	Inc. above	Value: 35.00				
1901B Incuse	—	2.50	5.00	10.00	20.00	—
Note: Type B Bust, Type I Reverse						
1901B Incuse	1,706,000	1.25	2.50	5.00	10.00	—
Note: Type B Bust, Type II Reverse						
1901B Proof	—	Value: 125				
1901B P/L; Restrike	—	—	—	—	30.00	—
1901B Raised	—	2.50	5.00	10.00	20.00	—
Note: Type B Bust, Type I Reverse						
1901B Raised	Inc. above	1.25	2.50	5.00	10.00	—
Note: Type B Bust, Type II Reverse						

KM# 505 2 ANNAS

1.4600 g., 0.9170 Silver 0.0430 oz. ASW **Ruler:** Edward VII **Obv:** Head right **Obv. Legend:** EDWARD VII KING AND EMPEROR **Rev:** Crown above denomination, sprays flank **Note:** Mule.

Date	Mintage	F	VF	XF	Unc	BU
1903(c)	4,434,000	1.75	3.50	7.00	14.00	—
1903(c) Proof	—	Value: 200				
1903(c) P/L; Restrike	—	—	—	—	100	—
1904(c)	14,632,000	1.50	3.00	6.00	12.00	—
1904(c) Proof	—	Value: 200				
1904(c) P/L; Restrike	—	—	—	—	100	—
1905(c)	19,303,000	1.50	3.00	6.00	12.00	—
1905(c) P/L; Restrike	—	—	—	—	100	—
1906(c)	13,031,000	1.50	3.00	6.00	12.00	—
1906(c) P/L; Restrike	—	—	—	—	100	—
1907(c)	22,145,000	1.50	3.00	6.00	12.00	—
1907(c) Proof	—	Value: 200				
1908(c)	21,600,000	1.50	3.00	6.00	12.00	—
1908(c) Proof	—	Value: 200				
1908(c) P/L; Restrike	—	—	—	—	100	—
1909(c)	6,769,000	1.75	3.50	7.00	14.00	—
1909(c) Proof	—	Value: 200				
1909(c) P/L; Restrike	—	—	—	—	100	—
1910(c)	1,604,000	1.75	3.50	7.00	14.00	—
1910(c) Proof	—	Value: 200				
1910(c) P/L; Restrike	—	—	—	—	100	—

KM# 514 2 ANNAS

1.4600 g., 0.9170 Silver 0.0430 oz. ASW **Ruler:** George V **Obv:** Crowned bust left, type I **Obv. Legend:** GEORGE V KING EMPEROR **Rev:** Denomination within wreath

Date	Mintage	F	VF	XF	Unc	BU
1911(c)	16,760,000	1.50	3.00	6.00	12.00	—
1911(c) Proof	—	Value: 200				
1911(c) P/L; Restrike	—	—	—	—	150	—

KM# 515 2 ANNAS

1.4600 g., 0.9170 Silver 0.0430 oz. ASW **Ruler:** George V **Obv:** Crowned bust left, type II **Obv. Legend:** GEORGE V KING EMPEROR **Rev:** Denomination within wreath

Date	Mintage	F	VF	XF	Unc	BU
1912(c)	7,724,000	1.25	2.50	5.00	10.00	—
1912(c) Proof	—	Value: 150				
1912(b)	2,462,000	1.50	3.00	6.00	12.00	—
1912(b) Proof	—	Value: 150				
1912(b) P/L; Restrike	—	—	—	—	100	—
1913(c)	13,959,000	1.25	2.50	5.00	10.00	—
1913(c) Proof	—	Value: 150				
1913(b)	5,461,000	1.25	2.50	5.00	10.00	—
1913(b) Proof	—	Value: 150				
1913(b) P/L; Restrike	—	—	—	—	100	—
1914(c)	13,622,000	1.25	2.50	5.00	10.00	—
1914(c) Proof	—	Value: 150				
1914(b)	8,579,000	1.25	2.50	5.00	10.00	—
1914(b) P/L; Restrike	—	—	—	—	100	—
1915(c)	5,892,000	1.25	2.50	5.00	10.00	—

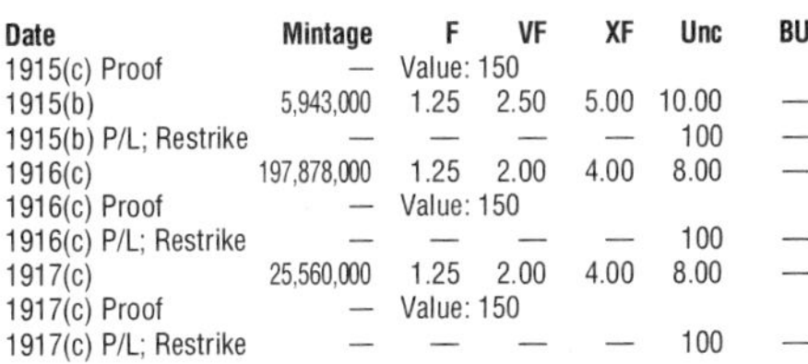

Date	Mintage	F	VF	XF	Unc	BU
1915(c) Proof	—	Value: 150				
1915(b)	5,943,000	1.25	2.50	5.00	10.00	—
1915(b) P/L; Restrike	—	—	—	—	100	—
1916(c)	197,878,000	1.25	2.00	4.00	8.00	—
1916(c) Proof	—	Value: 150				
1916(c) P/L; Restrike	—	—	—	—	100	—
1917(c)	25,560,000	1.25	2.00	4.00	8.00	—
1917(c) Proof	—	Value: 150				
1917(c) P/L; Restrike	—	—	—	—	100	—

KM# 516 2 ANNAS

5.6200 g., Copper-Nickel **Ruler:** George V **Obv:** Crowned bust left within circle **Obv. Legend:** GEORGE V KING EMPEROR **Rev:** Large denomination within square **Shape:** 4-sided **Note:** Calcutta Mint issues have no mint mark. Bombay Mint issues have a small raised dot on the reverse at the bottom near the rim.

Date	Mintage	F	VF	XF	Unc	BU
1918(c)	53,412,000	1.25	1.75	4.00	10.00	—
1918(c) Proof	—	Value: 250				
1918(b)	9,191,000	1.25	1.75	4.00	10.00	—
1918(b) Proof	—	Value: 250				
1918(b) P/L; Restrike	—	—	—	—	150	—
1919(c)	89,040,000	1.25	1.75	4.00	10.00	—
1919(c) Proof	—	Value: 250				
1919(c) P/L; Restrike	—	—	—	—	150	—
1920(b) Proof	—	Value: 350				
1920(c)	13,520,000	1.25	1.75	4.00	10.00	—
1920(c) Proof	—	Value: 250				
1921(c) P/L; Restrike	—	1.25	1.75	4.00	10.00	—
1923(c)	7,656,000	1.25	1.75	4.00	10.00	—
1923(c) Proof	—	Value: 250				
1923(b)	6,431,000	1.25	1.75	4.00	10.00	—
1923(b) Proof	—	Value: 250				
1923(b) P/L; Restrike	—	—	—	—	150	—
1924(c)	8,384,000	1.25	1.75	4.00	10.00	—
1924(c) Proof	—	Value: 250				
1924(b)	4,818,000	1.50	3.00	6.00	12.00	—
1924(b) Proof	—	Value: 250				
1924(b) P/L; Restrike	—	—	—	—	150	—
1925(c)	10,848,000	1.25	1.75	4.00	10.00	—
1925(c) Proof	—	Value: 250				
1925(b)	8,348,000	1.25	1.75	4.00	10.00	—
1925(b) Proof	—	Value: 250				
1925(b) P/L; Restrike	—	—	—	—	150	—
1926(c)	8,352,000	1.25	1.75	4.00	10.00	—
1926(c) Proof	—	Value: 250				
1926(b)	2,927,000	1.75	3.50	7.00	14.00	—
1926(b) Proof	—	Value: 250				
1926(b) P/L; Restrike	—	—	—	—	150	—
1927(c) Proof	—	Value: 250				
1927(c)	6,424,000	1.25	1,375	4.00	10.00	—
1927(b)	4,835,000	1.50	3.00	6.00	12.00	—
1927(b) Proof	—	Value: 250				
1927(b) P/L; Restrike	—	—	—	—	150	—
1928(c)	7,352,000	1.25	1.75	4.00	10.00	—
1928(c) Proof	—	Value: 250				
1928(b)	4,876,000	1.50	3.00	6.00	12.00	—
1928(b) Proof	—	Value: 250				
1928(b) P/L; Restrike	—	—	—	—	150	—
1929(c)	13,408,000	1.25	1.75	4.00	10.00	—
1929(c) Proof	—	Value: 250				
1929(c) P/L; Restrike	—	—	—	—	150	—
1930(c)	8,888,000	1.25	1.75	4.00	10.00	—
1930(c) Proof	—	Value: 250				
1930(c) P/L; Restrike	—	—	—	—	150	—
1930(b)	—	1.25	1.75	4.00	10.00	—
1933(c)	4,300,000	1.50	3.00	6.00	12.00	—
1933(c) Proof	—	Value: 250				
1933(c) P/L; Restrike	—	—	—	—	150	—
1934(c)	7,016,000	1.25	1.75	4.00	10.00	—
1934(c) Proof	—	Value: 250				
1934(c) P/L; Restrike	—	—	—	—	150	—
1935(c)	12,344,000	1.25	1.75	4.00	10.00	—
1935(b)	21,017,000	1.00	1.50	3.00	8.00	—
1935(b) Proof	—	Value: 250				
1935(b) P/L; Restrike	—	—	—	—	150	—
1936(b)	36,295,000	1.00	1.50	3.00	8.00	—
1936(b) Proof	—	Value: 250				

KM# 540 2 ANNAS

Copper-Nickel, 25 mm. **Ruler:** George VI **Obv:** First head, high relief **Obv. Legend:** GEORGE VI KING EMPEROR **Rev:** Denomination and date within decorative outlines **Shape:** Square **Note:** Calcutta Mint issues have no mint mark. Mumbai (Bombay) Mint issues have a small dot before and after the date.

Date	Mintage	F	VF	XF	Unc	BU
1939(c)	4,148,000	1.25	3.00	6.00	15.00	—
1939(b)	3,392,000	2.00	5.00	10.00	25.00	—

KM# 541 2 ANNAS

5.8400 g., Copper-Nickel, 25 mm. **Ruler:** George VI **Obv:** Second head, low relief, large crown **Obv. Legend:** GEORGE VI KING EMPEROR **Rev:** Denomination and date within decorative outlines **Shape:** 4-sided

Date	Mintage	F	VF	XF	Unc	BU
1939(c)	Inc. above	1.25	2.00	2.50	4.00	—
1939(c) Proof	—	Value: 185				
1939(b)	Inc. above	0.20	0.30	0.50	1.50	—
1939(b) Proof	—	Value: 185				
1939(b) P/L; Restrike	—	—	—	—	125	—
1940(c)	37,636,000	0.20	0.30	0.50	2.00	—
1940(c) Proof	—	Value: 185				
1940(b)	50,599,000	0.20	0.30	0.50	2.00	—
1940(b) P/L; Restrike	—	—	—	—	125	—
1941(c)	63,456,000	0.20	0.30	0.50	1.50	—
1941(b)	10,760,000	1.25	2.00	2.50	4.00	—
1941(b) Proof	—	Value: 185				
1941(b) P/L; Restrike	—	—	—	—	125	—

KM# 541a 2 ANNAS

5.7400 g., Nickel-Brass, 25 mm. **Ruler:** George VI **Obv:** Second head, low relief, large crown **Obv. Legend:** GEORGE VI KING EMPEROR **Rev:** Denomination and date within decorative outlines **Shape:** 4-sided

Date	Mintage	F	VF	XF	Unc	BU
1942(b) Small 4	133,000,000	0.25	0.35	0.50	2.25	—
1942(b) Large 4	Inc. above	0.20	0.35	0.50	2.25	—
1943(b)	343,680,000	0.25	0.35	0.50	2.25	—
1944L	6,352,000	0.50	1.25	2.00	5.00	—
Note: On 1944 Lahore issues, a tiny L replaces the decorative stroke in the four quatrefoil angles.						
1944(b) Small 4	219,700,000	0.25	0.35	0.50	2.25	—
1944(b) Large 4	Inc. above	0.25	0.35	0.50	2.25	—

KM# 543 2 ANNAS

Nickel-Brass **Ruler:** George VI **Obv:** Second head, low relief, large crown **Obv. Legend:** GEORGE VI KING EMPEROR **Rev:** Small "2" **Shape:** Square

Date	Mintage	F	VF	XF	Unc	BU
1945(c)	24,260,000	0.25	0.75	1.25	2.75	—
1945(c) Proof	—	Value: 185				
1945(b)	136,688,000	0.25	0.35	0.50	1.50	—
1945(b) P/L; Restrike	—	—	—	—	125	—

KM# 542 2 ANNAS

5.9000 g., Copper-Nickel **Ruler:** George VI **Obv:** Second head, low relief, small crown **Obv. Legend:** GEORGE VI KING EMPEROR **Rev:** Denomination and date within decorative outlines **Shape:** Square

Date	Mintage	F	VF	XF	Unc	BU
1946(c)	67,267,000	0.20	0.30	0.50	2.25	—
1946(b)	52,500,000	0.20	0.30	0.50	2.25	—
1946(b) Proof	—	Value: 185				
1946(b) P/L; Restrike	—	—	—	—	125	—
1946(l)	25,480,000	0.20	0.30	0.50	2.25	—
Note: Without "L" mintmark but with small diamond-shaped mark left of "I" on reverse						
1947(c)	57,428,000	0.20	0.30	0.50	2.25	—
1947(b)	38,908,000	0.20	0.30	0.50	2.25	—
1947(b) Proof	—	Value: 185				
1947(b) P/L; Restrike	—	—	—	—	125	—

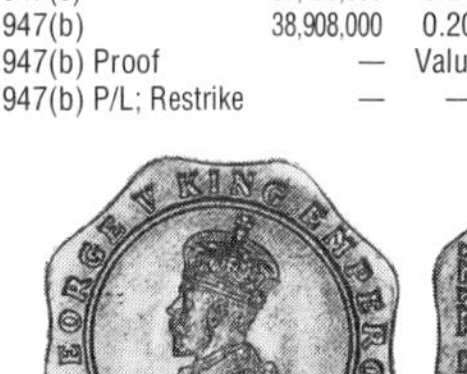

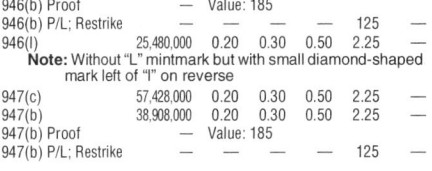

KM# 519 4 ANNAS

6.5000 g., Copper-Nickel **Ruler:** George V **Obv:** Crowned bust left within circle **Obv. Legend:** GEORGE V KING EMPEROR • INDIA • **Rev:** Denomination within square **Shape:** Scalloped **Note:** Calcutta Mint issues have no mint mark. Bombay Mint issues have a small raised dot on the reverse at the bottom near the rim.

Date	Mintage	F	VF	XF	Unc	BU
1919(c)	18,632,000	2.50	5.00	10.00	20.00	—
1919(c) Proof	—	Value: 550				
1919(b)	7,672,000	3.25	6.50	12.50	25.00	—
1919 P/L; Restrike	—	—	—	—	125	—
1920(c)	18,191,000	2.50	5.00	10.00	20.00	—
1920(c) Proof	—	Value: 550				
1920(b)	1,666,000	3.25	6.50	12.50	25.00	—
1920(b) Proof	—	Value: 550				
1920(b) P/L; Restrike	—	—	—	—	125	—
1921(c) Proof	—	Value: 550				
1921(c) P/L; Restrike	—	—	—	—	125	—
1921(b)	1,219,000	3.75	7.50	15.00	30.00	—
1921(b) Proof	—	Value: 550				

KM# 520 8 ANNAS

Copper-Nickel **Ruler:** George V **Obv:** Crowned bust left **Obv. Legend:** GEORGE V KING EMPEROR **Rev:** Denomination and date within scallop, square surrounds **Note:** Calcutta Mint issues have no mint mark. Mumbai (Bombay) Mint issues have a small raised dot on the reverse at the bottom near the rim.

Date	Mintage	F	VF	XF	Unc	BU
1919(c)	2,980,000	3.75	7.50	15.00	30.00	—
1919(c) Proof	—	Value: 550				
1919(b)	1,400,000	4.00	8.50	17.50	35.00	—
1919(b) P/L; Restrike	—	—	—	—	150	—
1920(c) Proof	—	Value: 550				
1920(c) P/L; Restrike	—	—	—	—	350	—
1920(b)	1,000,000	12.50	25.00	50.00	100	—
1920(b) Proof	—	Value: 550				
1920(b) P/L; Restrike	—	—	—	—	150	—

KM# 490 1/4 RUPEE

2.9200 g., 0.9170 Silver 0.0861 oz. ASW **Ruler:** Victoria **Obv:** Crowned bust left **Obv. Legend:** VICTORIA EMPRESS **Rev:** Value and date within wreath **Note:** Mule.

Date	Mintage	F	VF	XF	Unc	BU
1901C Incuse	4,476,000	2.00	3.00	6.00	15.00	—
Note: Type C Bust, Type II Reverse						
1901C Proof	—	Value: 600				
1901C P/L; Restrike	—	—	—	—	175	—

KM# 506 1/4 RUPEE

2.9200 g., 0.9170 Silver 0.0861 oz. ASW **Ruler:** Edward VII **Obv:** Head right **Obv. Legend:** EDWARD VII KING AND EMPEROR **Rev:** Crown above denomination, sprays flank

Date	Mintage	F	VF	XF	Unc	BU
1903(c)	7,060,000	1.75	3.50	8.00	20.00	—
1903(r) Proof	—	Value: 400				

Date	Mintage	F	VF	XF	Unc	BU
1903(c) P/L; Restrike	—	—	—	—	150	—
1904(c)	10,026,000	1.75	3.50	8.00	20.00	—
1904(c) Proof	—	Value: 400				
1904(c) P/L; Restrike	—	—	—	—	150	—
1905(c)	6,300,000	1.75	3.50	8.00	20.00	—
1905(c) Proof	—	Value: 400				
1905(c) P/L; Restrike	—	—	—	—	150	—
1906(c)	10,672,000	1.75	3.50	8.00	20.00	—
1906(c) P/L; Restrike	—	—	—	—	150	—
1907(c)	11,464,000	1.75	3.50	8.00	20.00	—
1907(c) Proof	—	Value: 400				
1907(c) P/L; Restrike	—	—	—	—	150	—
1908(c)	7,084,000	1.75	3.50	8.00	20.00	—
1908(c) Proof	—	Value: 400				
1908(c) P/L; Restrike	—	—	—	—	150	—
1909(c) Proof	—	Value: 500				
1909(c) P/L; Restrike	—	—	—	—	150	—
1910(c)	8,024,000	1.75	3.50	8.00	20.00	—
1910(c) Proof	—	Value: 400				
1910(c) P/L; Restrike	—	—	—	—	150	—

KM# 517 1/4 RUPEE

2.9200 g., 0.9170 Silver 0.0861 oz. ASW **Ruler:** George V **Obv:** Type I **Obv. Legend:** GEORGE V KING EMPEROR

Date	Mintage	F	VF	XF	Unc	BU
1911(c)	2,245,000	2.00	4.00	8.00	8.00	—
1911(c) Proof	—	Value: 350				
1911(c) P/L; Restrike	—	—	—	—	300	—

KM# 518 1/4 RUPEE

2.9200 g., 0.9170 Silver 0.0861 oz. ASW **Ruler:** George V **Obv:** Crowned bust left, type II **Obv. Legend:** GEORGE V KING EMPEROR **Rev:** Denomination and date within circle, wreath surrounds

Date	Mintage	F	VF	XF	Unc	BU
1912(c)	9,587,000	2.00	3.00	5.00	12.00	—
1912(c) Proof	—	Value: 250				
1912(b)	2,200,000	2.00	3.00	5.00	12.00	—
1912(b) Proof	—	Value: 250				
1912(b) P/L; Restrike	—	—	—	—	120	—
1913(c)	12,686,000	2.00	3.00	5.00	12.00	—
1913(c) Proof	—	Value: 250				
1913(b)	2,276,000	2.00	3.00	5.00	12.00	—
1913(b) Proof	—	Value: 250				
1913(b) P/L; Restrike	—	—	—	—	120	—
1914(c)	1,423,000	2.00	3.00	5.00	12.00	—
1914(c) Proof	—	Value: 250				
1914(b)	7,949,000	2.00	3.00	5.00	10.00	—
1914(b) P/L; Restrike	—	—	—	—	120	—
1915(c)	851,000	2.25	4.00	10.00	35.00	—
1915(c) Proof	—	Value: 250				
1915(b)	2,096,000	2.00	3.00	5.00	12.00	—
1915(c) P/L; Restrike	—	—	—	—	—	—
1915(b) P/L; Restrike	—	—	—	—	120	—
1916(c)	13,178,000	2.00	3.00	5.00	12.00	—
1916(c) Proof	—	Value: 250				
1916(c) P/L; Restrike	—	—	—	—	120	—
1917(c)	21,072,000	2.00	3.00	5.00	12.00	—
1917(c) Proof	—	Value: 250				
1917(c) P/L; Restrike	—	—	—	—	120	—
1918(c)	50,575,000	2.00	3.00	5.00	12.00	—
1918(c) Proof	—	Value: 250				
1919(b)	—	3.50	7.50	15.00	30.00	—
1919(c)	26,135,000	2.00	3.00	5.00	12.00	—
1919(c) Proof	—	Value: 250				
1920(b)	—	3.25	6.50	12.50	25.00	—
1925(b)	4,007,000	2.00	3.00	5.00	12.00	—
1925(b) Proof	—	Value: 250				
1925(b) P/L; Restrike	—	—	—	—	120	—
1926(c)	8,169,000	2.00	3.00	5.00	12.00	—
1926(c) Proof	—	Value: 250				
1926(c) P/L; Restrike	—	—	—	—	120	—
1928(b)	4,023,000	2.00	3.00	5.00	12.00	—
1928(b) Proof	—	Value: 250				
1929(c)	4,013,000	2.00	3.00	5.00	12.00	—
1929(c) Proof	—	Value: 250				
1929(c) P/L; Restrike	—	—	—	—	120	—
1930(c)	3,222,000	2.00	3.00	5.00	12.00	—
1930(c) Proof	—	Value: 250				
1930(c) P/L; Restrike	—	—	—	—	120	—
1934(c)	3,946,000	2.00	3.00	5.00	10.00	—
1936(c)	25,744,000	1.50	2.50	4.00	8.00	—
1936(b)	9,864,000	1.50	2.50	4.00	8.00	—
1936(b) P/L; Restrike	—	—	—	—	120	—

KM# 544 1/4 RUPEE

2.9200 g., 0.9170 Silver 0.0861 oz. ASW **Ruler:** George VI **Obv:** Crowned head left **Obv. Legend:** GEORGE VI KING EMPEROR **Rev:** Denomination and date within circle, wreath surrounds

Date	Mintage	F	VF	XF	Unc	BU
1938(c) Proof	—	Value: 250				
1938(c) P/L; Restrike	—	—	—	—	125	—
1939(c)	3,072,000	2.00	3.50	6.00	12.00	—
1939(c) Proof	—	Value: 250				
1939(b)	6,770,000	2.00	3.50	5.00	10.00	—
1939(b) P/L; Restrike	—	—	—	—	125	—

KM# 544a 1/4 RUPEE

2.9200 g., 0.5000 Silver 0.0469 oz. ASW **Ruler:** George VI **Obv:** Crowned head left **Obv. Legend:** GEORGE VI KING EMPEROR **Rev:** Denomination and date within circle, wreath surrounds

Date	Mintage	F	VF	XF	Unc	BU
1940(b)	24,635,000	2.00	3.50	5.00	10.00	—

KM# 545 1/4 RUPEE

2.9200 g., 0.5000 Silver 0.0469 oz. ASW **Ruler:** George VI **Obv:** Large second head, small rim decoration **Obv. Legend:** GEORGE VI KING EMPEROR **Rev:** Denomination and date within circle, wreath surrounds **Edge:** Reeded

Date	Mintage	VG	F	VF	XF	Unc
1940(c)	68,675,000	—	BV	1.50	2.50	6.00
1940(c) Proof	—	Value: 250				
1940(b)	28,947,000	—	BV	1.50	2.50	6.00

KM# 546 1/4 RUPEE

2.9200 g., 0.5000 Silver 0.0469 oz. ASW **Ruler:** George VI **Obv:** Small second head, large rim decoration **Obv. Legend:** GEORGE VI KING EMPEROR **Rev:** Denomination and date within circle, wreath surrounds **Edge:** Reeded

Date	Mintage	F	VF	XF	Unc	BU
1942(c)	88,096,000	BV	1.50	2.25	4.50	—
1943(c)	90,994,000	BV	1.50	2.25	4.50	—

KM# 547 1/4 RUPEE

2.9200 g., 0.5000 Silver 0.0469 oz. ASW **Ruler:** George VI **Obv:** Small second head, large rim decoration **Obv. Legend:** GEORGE VI KING EMPEROR **Rev:** Denomination and date within circle, wreath surrounds **Edge:** Security

Date	Mintage	F	VF	XF	Unc	BU
1943B	95,200,000	BV	1.50	2.25	4.50	—
1943B Proof	—	Value: 250				
1943B Reverse B	Inc. above	BV	1.50	2.25	4.50	—
1943L	23,700,000	BV	1.50	2.25	4.50	—
1944B	170,504,000	BV	1.50	2.25	4.50	—
1944B Reverse B	Inc. above	BV	1.50	2.25	4.50	—
1944L	86,400,000	BV	1.50	2.25	4.50	—
1945(b) Small 5	181,648,000	BV	1.50	2.25	4.50	—
1945(b) Large 5	Inc. above	10.00	15.00	25.00	40.00	—
1945L Small 5	29,751,000	BV	1.50	2.25	4.50	—
1945L Large 5	Inc. above	BV	1.00	2.00	5.00	—

KM# 548 1/4 RUPEE

2.9000 g., Nickel **Ruler:** George VI **Obv:** Crowned head left **Obv. Legend:** GEORGE VI KING EMPEROR **Rev:** Indian tiger (panthera tigris) **Edge:** Reeded

Date	Mintage	F	VF	XF	Unc	BU
1946(b)	83,600,000	0.40	0.75	2.50	7.50	12.00
1947(b)	109,948,000	0.40	0.75	2.50	7.50	12.00
1947(b) Proof	—	Value: 200				

KM# 507 1/2 RUPEE

5.8300 g., 0.9170 Silver 0.1719 oz. ASW **Ruler:** Edward VII **Obv:** Head right **Obv. Legend:** EDWARD VII KING AND EMPEROR **Rev:** Crown above denomination, sprays flank **Note:** Calcutta Mint issues have no mint mark. Mumbai (Bombay) Mint issues have a small incuse "B" in the space below the cross pattee of the crown on the reverse.

Date	Mintage	F	VF	XF	Unc	BU
1904(c) Proof	—	Value: 500				
1904(c) P/L; Restrike	—	—	—	—	175	—
1905(c)	823,000	3.50	10.00	25.00	50.00	—
1905(c) P/L; Restrike	—	—	—	—	175	—
1906(c)	3,036,000	3.50	10.00	25.00	50.00	—
1906B	400,000	3.75	12.50	30.00	60.00	—
1906B P/L; Restrike	—	—	—	—	175	—
1907(c)	2,786,000	3.50	10.00	25.00	50.00	—
1907(c) Proof	—	Value: 450				
1907B	1,856,000	3.50	10.00	25.00	50.00	—
1907B Proof	—	Value: 450				
1907B P/L; Restrike	—	—	—	—	175	—
1908(c)	1,577,000	3.50	10.00	25.00	50.00	—
1908(c) Proof	—	Value: 450				
1908(c) P/L; Restrike	—	—	—	—	175	—
1909(c)	1,569,000	3.50	10.00	25.00	50.00	—
1909(c) P/L; Restrike	—	—	—	—	175	—
1909(c) Proof	—	Value: 450				
1909B Proof	—	Value: 750				
1909B P/L; Restrike	—	—	—	—	350	—
1910(c)	3,413,000	3.50	10.00	25.00	50.00	—
1910(c) Proof	—	Value: 450				
1910B	809,000	3.50	10.00	25.00	50.00	—
1910B "B" raised	—	10.00	15.00	30.00	55.00	—
1910B Proof	—	Value: 450				
1910B P/L; Restrike	—	—	—	—	175	—

KM# 521 1/2 RUPEE

5.8300 g., 0.9170 Silver 0.1719 oz. ASW **Ruler:** George V **Obv:** Crowned bust left, type I **Obv. Legend:** GEORGE V KING EMPEROR **Rev:** Denomination and date within circle, wreath surrounds **Note:** Calcutta Mint issues have no mint mark. Mumbai (Bombay) Mint issues have a small raised bead or dot in the space below the lotus flower at the bottom of the reverse. The half Rupee dated 1911 like the Rupee and all the other issues of that year has the "Pig" elephant. It was struck only at the Calcutta Mint.

Date	Mintage	F	VF	XF	Unc	BU
1911(c)	2,293,000	2.75	6.00	12.50	30.00	—
1911(c) Proof	—	Value: 500				
1911(c) P/L; Restrike	—	—	—	—	250	—

KM# 522 1/2 RUPEE

5.8300 g., 0.9170 Silver 0.1719 oz. ASW **Ruler:** George V **Obv:** Crowned bust left, type II **Obv. Legend:** GEORGE V KING EMPEROR **Rev:** Denomination and date within circle, wreath surrounds

Date	Mintage	F	VF	XF	Unc	BU
1912(c)	3,390,000	2.75	6.00	12.00	28.00	—
1912(c) Proof	—	Value: 500				
1912(b)	1,505,000	2.75	6.00	12.00	28.00	—
1912(b) Proof	—	Value: 500				
1912(b) P/L; Restrike	—	—	—	—	150	—
1913(c)	2,723,000	2.75	6.00	12.00	28.00	—
1913(c) Proof	—	Value: 500				
1913(b)	1,825,000	2.75	6.00	12.00	28.00	—
1913(b) Proof	—	Value: 500				
1913(b) P/L; Restrike	—	—	—	—	150	—
1914(c)	1,400,000	2.75	6.00	12.00	28.00	—
1914(c) Proof	—	Value: 500				
1914(b)	903,000	2.75	6.00	12.50	30.00	—
1914(b) P/L; Restrike	—	—	—	—	150	—
1915(c)	2,804,000	2.75	6.00	12.00	28.00	—
1915(c) Proof	—	Value: 500				
1915(c) P/L; Restrike	—	2.75	6.00	12.00	28.00	—
1916(c)	3,644,000	2.75	6.00	12.00	28.00	—
1916(c) Proof	—	Value: 500				
1916(b)	5,880,000	2.75	6.00	12.00	28.00	—
1917(c) Proof	—	Value: 500				
1917(b)	8,822,000	2.75	6.00	12.00	28.00	—
1917(b) Proof	—	Value: 500				
1918(b) P/L; Restrike	—	—	—	—	150	—
1918(c) P/L; Restrike	—	—	—	—	150	—
1918(b)	10,325,000	2.75	6.00	12.00	28.00	—
1919(b)	8,958,000	2.75	6.00	12.00	28.00	—
1919(b) Proof	—	Value: 500				
1919(b) P/L; Restrike	—	—	—	—	150	—
1919(c) P/L; Restrike	—	—	—	—	150	—
1921(c)	5,804,000	2.75	6.00	12.00	28.00	—
1921(c) Proof	—	Value: 500				
1921(c) P/L; Restrike	—	—	—	—	150	—
1922(c)	5,551,000	2.75	6.00	12.00	28.00	—
1922(c) Proof	—	Value: 500				
1922(b)	1,037,000	2.75	6.00	12.00	28.00	—
1922(b) Proof	—	Value: 500				
1922(b) P/L; Restrike	—	—	—	—	150	—
1923(c)	3,925,000	2.75	6.00	12.00	28.00	—
1923(c) P/L; Restrike	—	—	—	—	150	—
1923(b)	2,076,000	2.75	6.00	12.00	28.00	—
1923(b) Proof	—	Value: 500				
1923(b) P/L; Restrike	—	—	—	—	150	—
1924(c)	4,007,000	2.75	6.00	12.00	28.00	—
1924(c) Proof	—	Value: 500				
1924(b)	2,664,000	2.75	6.00	12.00	28.00	—
1924(b) Proof	—	Value: 500				
1924(b) P/L; Restrike	—	—	—	—	150	—
1925(c)	4,119,000	2.75	6.00	12.00	28.00	—
1925(c) Proof	—	Value: 500				
1925(b)	1,627,000	2.75	6.00	12.00	28.00	—
1925(b) Proof	—	Value: 500				
1925(b) P/L; Restrike	—	—	—	—	150	—
1926(c)	4,027,000	2.75	6.00	12.00	28.00	—
1926(c) Proof	—	Value: 500				
1926(b)	2,011,000	2.75	6.00	12.00	28.00	—
1926(b) Proof	—	Value: 500				
1926(b) P/L; Restrike	—	—	—	—	150	—
1927(c)	2,032,000	2.75	6.00	12.00	28.00	—
1927(c) Proof	—	Value: 500				
1927(c) P/L; Restrike	—	—	—	—	150	—
1928(b)	2,466,000	2.75	6.00	12.00	28.00	—
1928(b) Proof	—	Value: 500				
1929(c)	4,050,000	2.75	6.00	12.00	28.00	—
1929(c) Proof	—	Value: 500				
1929(c) P/L; Restrike	—	—	—	—	150	—
1930(c)	2,036,000	2.75	6.00	12.00	28.00	—
1930(c) Proof	—	Value: 500				
1930(c) P/L; Restrike	—	—	—	—	150	—
1933/2(c)	4,056,000	5.00	10.00	25.00	50.00	—
1933(c)	Inc. above	2.75	6.00	12.00	28.00	—
1933(c) Proof	—	Value: 300				
1933(c) P/L; Restrike	—	—	—	—	150	—
1934(c)	4,056,000	2.75	6.00	12.00	28.00	—
1934(c) Proof	—	Value: 500				
1934(c) P/L; Restrike	—	—	—	—	150	—
1936(c)	16,919,000	2.75	6.00	12.00	28.00	—
1936(b)	6,693,000	2.75	6.00	12.00	28.00	—
1936(b) P/L; Restrike	—	—	—	—	150	—

KM# 549 1/2 RUPEE

5.8300 g., 0.9170 Silver 0.1719 oz. ASW **Ruler:** George VI **Obv:** Crowned head left, first head **Obv. Legend:** GEORGE VI KING EMPEROR **Rev:** Denomination and date within circle, wreath surrounds **Edge:** Reeded

Date	Mintage	F	VF	XF	Unc	BU
1938(c) Proof	—	Value: 400				
1938(b)	2,200,000	BV	3.00	7.50	15.00	—
1938(b) P/L; Restrike	—	—	—	—	150	—
1939(c)	3,300,000	BV	3.00	7.50	15.00	—
1939(c) Proof	—	Value: 300				
1939(b)	10,096,000	BV	3.00	7.50	15.00	—
1939(b) Proof	—	Value: 300				
1939(b) P/L; Restrike	—	—	—	—	150	—

KM# A553 1/2 RUPEE

Copper-Nickel **Ruler:** George VI **Obv:** Crowned head left **Obv. Legend:** GEORGE VI KING EMPEROR **Rev:** Denomination and date within circle, wreath surrounds **Note:** Mule.

Date	Mintage	F	VF	XF	Unc	BU
1938(c) P/L; Restrike	—	—	—	—	—	—

KM# 550 1/2 RUPEE

5.8300 g., 0.9170 Silver 0.1719 oz. ASW **Ruler:** George VI **Obv:** Large second head, small rim decoration **Obv. Legend:** GEORGE VI KING EMPEROR **Rev:** Denomination and date within circle, wreath surrounds **Edge:** Reeded

Date	Mintage	VG	F	VF	XF	Unc
1939(c)	Inc. above	—	BV	3.00	6.50	15.00
1939(b)	Inc. above	—	BV	3.00	6.50	13.50

KM# 550a 1/2 RUPEE

5.8300 g., 0.5000 Silver 0.0937 oz. ASW **Ruler:** George VI **Obv:** Large second head, small rim decoration **Obv. Legend:** GEORGE VI KING EMPEROR **Rev:** Denomination and date within circle, wreath surrounds

Date	Mintage	F	VF	XF	Unc	BU
1940(c)	32,898,000	BV	3.00	6.00	12.00	—
1940(c) Proof	—	Value: 300				
1940(b)	17,811,000	BV	3.00	6.50	13.50	—
1940(b) P/L; Restrike	—	—	—	—	150	—

NOTE: Example of large 5 in date 1945.

KM# 552 1/2 RUPEE

5.8300 g., 0.5000 Silver 0.0937 oz. ASW **Ruler:** George VI **Obv:** Small second head, large rim decoration **Obv. Legend:** GEORGE VI KING EMPEROR **Rev:** Denomination and inner circle smaller **Edge:** Security

Date	Mintage	F	VF	XF	Unc	BU
1942(b)	Inc. above	BV	2.00	4.50	9.00	—
1943(b) Dot	90,400,000	BV	2.00	4.50	9.00	—
1943(b) Proof	—	Value: 300				
1943(b) Diamond	—	BV	2.00	4.50	9.00	—
1943L	9,000,000	BV	2.00	4.50	9.00	—
1943L Proof	—	Value: 300				
1944(b) Dot	46,200,000	BV	2.00	4.50	9.00	—
1944(b) Diamond	Inc. above	BV	2.00	4.50	9.00	—
1944L	79,100,000	BV	2.00	4.50	9.00	—
1944L Proof	—	Value: 300				
1945(b) Small 5	32,722,000	BV	2.00	4.50	9.00	—
1945(b) Large 5	—	20.00	25.00	35.00	50.00	—
1945L Small dot	79,192,000	BV	2.00	4.50	9.00	—
1945L Proof	—	Value: 300				
1945L Large dot	Inc. above	2.50	5.00	10.00	20.00	—

KM# 553 1/2 RUPEE

5.8000 g., Nickel **Ruler:** George VI **Obv:** Crowned head left **Obv. Legend:** GEORGE VI KING EMPEROR **Rev:** Indian tiger (panthera tigris) **Edge:** Reeded

Date	Mintage	F	VF	XF	Unc	BU
1946(b)	47,500,000	0.50	1.00	2.50	7.50	15.00
1947(b)	62,724,000	0.50	1.00	2.50	7.50	15.00
1947(b) Proof	—	Value: 275				

KM# 492 RUPEE

11.6600 g., 0.9170 Silver 0.3437 oz. ASW **Ruler:** Victoria **Obv:** Crowned bust left **Obv. Legend:** VICTORIA EMPRESS **Rev:** Value and date within wreath

Date	Mintage	F	VF	XF	Unc	BU
1901C C/I, "C" incuse	72,017,000	6.00	8.00	12.00	25.00	—
1901C Proof	Inc. above	Value: 725				
1901B A/I, "B" incuse	130,258,000	6.00	8.00	12.00	25.00	—
1901B Proof	—	Value: 725				
1901B P/L; Restrike	—	—	—	—	250	—
1901B C/I, "B" incuse	Inc. above	6.00	8.00	12.00	25.00	—

KM# 508 RUPEE

11.6600 g., 0.9170 Silver 0.3437 oz. ASW **Ruler:** Edward VII **Obv:** Head right **Obv. Legend:** EDWARD VII KING & EMPEROR **Rev:** Crown above denomination, sprays flank **Note:** Calcutta Mint issues have no mint mark. Mumbai (Bombay) Mint issues have a small incuse "B" in the space below the cross pattee of the crown on the reverse.

Date	Mintage	F	VF	XF	Unc	BU
1903(c)	49,403,000	6.00	9.00	13.50	28.00	—
1903(c) Proof	—	Value: 700				
1903B In relief	52,969	6.00	9.00	13.50	28.00	—
1903B Proof	—	Value: 700				
1903B Incuse	Inc. above	6.00	9.00	13.50	28.00	—
1903B P/L; Restrike	—	—	—	—	200	—
1904(c)	58,339,000	6.00	9.00	13.50	28.00	—
1904(c) Proof	—	Value: 700				
1904B	101,949,000	6.00	9.00	13.50	28.00	—
1904B Proof	—	Value: 700				
1904B P/L; Restrike	—	—	—	—	200	—
1905(c)	51,258,000	6.00	9.00	13.50	28.00	—
1905(c) Proof	—	Value: 700				
1905B	76,202,000	6.00	9.00	13.50	28.00	—
1905B Proof	—	Value: 700				
1905B P/L; Restrike	—	—	—	—	200	—
1906(c)	104,797,000	6.00	9.00	15.00	30.00	—
1906B	158,953,000	6.00	9.00	15.00	30.00	—
1906B Proof	—	Value: 700				
1906B P/L; Restrike	—	—	—	—	200	—
1907(c)	81,338,000	6.00	9.00	15.00	30.00	—
1907(c) Proof	—	Value: 700				
1907B	170,912,000	6.00	9.00	15.00	30.00	—
1907B Proof	—	Value: 700				
1907B P/L; Restrike	—	—	—	—	200	—
1908(c)	20,218,000	6.00	9.00	15.00	30.00	—
1908(c) Proof	—	Value: 700				

Date	Mintage	F	VF	XF	Unc	BU
1908B	10,715,000	8.50	15.00	30.00	60.00	—
1908B Proof	—	Value: 700				
1908B P/L; Restrike	—	—	—	—	200	—
1909(c)	12,759,000	6.00	9.00	15.00	30.00	—
1909(c) Proof	—	Value: 700				
1909B	9,539,000	8.50	15.00	30.00	60.00	—
1909B Proof	—	Value: 700				
1909B P/L; Restrike	—	—	—	—	200	—
1910(c)	12,627,000	6.00	9.00	15.00	30.00	—
1910(c) Proof	—	Value: 700				
1910B	10,885,000	6.00	9.00	15.00	30.00	—
1910B Proof	—	Value: 700				
1910B P/L; Restrike	—	—	—	—	200	—

KM# 523 RUPEE
11.6600 g., 0.9170 Silver 0.3437 oz. ASW **Ruler:** George V **Obv:** Type I **Obv. Legend:** GEORGE V KING EMPEROR

Date	Mintage	F	VF	XF	Unc	BU
1911(c)	4,300,000	10.00	20.00	40.00	100	—
1911(c) Proof	—	Value: 1,200				
1911(b)	5,143,000	10.00	20.00	40.00	100	—
1911(b) P/L; Restrike	—	—	—	—	350	—

KM# 524 RUPEE
11.6600 g., 0.9170 Silver 0.3437 oz. ASW **Ruler:** George V **Obv:** Crowned bust left, type II **Obv. Legend:** GEORGE V KING EMPEROR **Rev:** Denomination and date within circle, wreath surrounds

Date	Mintage	F	VF	XF	Unc	BU
1912(c)	45,122,000	6.00	9.50	15.00	35.00	—
1912(c) Proof	—	Value: 1,000				
1912(b)	79,067,000	5.50	8.00	12.50	25.00	—
1912(b) Proof	—	Value: 1,000				
1912B P/L; Restrike	—	—	—	—	225	—
1913(c)	75,800,000	5.50	8.00	12.50	25.00	—
1913(c) Proof	—	Value: 1,000				
1913(b)	87,466,000	5.50	8.00	12.50	25.00	—
1913(b) Proof	—	Value: 1,000				
1913(b) P/L; Restrike	—	—	—	—	225	—
1914(c)	33,100,000	5.50	8.00	12.50	25.00	—
1914(c) Proof	—	Value: 1,000				
1914(b)	15,270,000	5.50	8.00	12.50	25.00	—
1914(b) Proof	—	Value: 1,000				
1914(b) P/L; Restrike	—	—	—	—	225	—
1915(c)	9,900,000	8.50	15.00	30.00	60.00	—
1915(c) Proof	—	Value: 1,000				
1915(b)	5,372,000	10.00	20.00	40.00	80.00	—
1915(b) Proof	—	Value: 1,000				
1915(b) P/L; Restrike	—	—	—	—	225	—
1916(c)	115,000,000	5.50	8.00	12.50	20.00	—
1916(c) Proof	—	Value: 1,000				
1916(b)	97,900,000	5.50	8.00	12.50	20.00	—
1916(b) Proof	—	—	—	—	—	—
1916(b) P/L; Restrike	—	—	—	—	225	—
1917(c)	114,974,000	5.50	8.00	12.50	20.00	—
1917(c) Proof	—	Value: 1,000				
1917(b)	151,583,000	5.50	8.00	12.50	20.00	—
1917(b) Proof	—	Value: 1,000				
1917(b) P/L; Restrike	—	—	—	—	225	—
1918(c)	205,420,000	5.50	8.00	12.50	20.00	—
1918(c) Proof	—	Value: 1,000				
1918(b)	210,550,000	5.50	8.00	12.50	20.00	—
1918(b) Proof	—	Value: 1,000				
1918(b) P/L; Restrike	—	—	—	—	225	—
1919(c)	211,206,000	5.50	8.00	12.50	20.00	—
1919(c) Proof	—	Value: 1,000				
1919(b)	226,706,000	5.50	8.00	12.50	20.00	—
1919(b) Proof	—	Value: 1,000				
1919(b) P/L; Restrike	—	—	—	—	225	—
1920(c)	50,500,000	5.50	8.00	12.50	20.00	—
1920(c) Proof	—	Value: 1,000				
1920(b)	55,937,000	5.50	8.00	12.50	20.00	—
1920(b) Proof	—	Value: 1,000				
1921(b)	5,115,000	10.00	20.00	40.00	85.00	—
1921(b) Proof	—	Value: 1,000				
1922(b)	2,051,000	10.00	20.00	40.00	85.00	—
1922(b) Proof	—	Value: 1,000				
1935(c) Proof	—	Value: 1,000				
1935(c) P/L; Restrike	—	—	—	—	225	—
1936(c) Proof	—	Value: 1,000				

KM# 554 RUPEE
11.6600 g., 0.9170 Silver 0.3437 oz. ASW **Ruler:** George VI **Obv:** Crowned head left, first head **Obv. Legend:** GEORGE VI KING EMPEROR **Rev:** Denomination and date within circle, wreath surrounds **Edge:** Reeded

Date	Mintage	F	VF	XF	Unc	BU
1938(c) Proof	—	Value: 550				
1939(c) Proof	—	Value: 700				

KM# 555 RUPEE
11.6600 g., 0.9170 Silver 0.3437 oz. ASW **Ruler:** George VI **Obv:** Second head, small rim decoration **Obv. Legend:** GEORGE VI KING EMPEROR **Rev:** Denomination and date within circle, wreath surrounds **Edge:** Reeded

Date	Mintage	F	VF	XF	Unc	BU
1938(b) Without dot	7,352,000	7.50	11.50	16.50	27.50	—
1938(b) Dot	Inc. above	7.50	11.50	16.50	27.50	—
1938(b) P/L; Restrike	—	—	—	—	375	—
1939(b) Dot	2,450,000	150	300	600	1,200	—

KM# A556 RUPEE
Copper-Nickel **Ruler:** George VI **Obv:** Small second head, large rim decoration **Obv. Legend:** GEORGE VI KING EMPEROR **Rev:** Denomination and date within circle, wreath surrounds **Note:** Mule.

Date	Mintage	F	VF	XF	Unc	BU
1938(c) P/L; Restrike	—	—	—	—	150	—

KM# 556 RUPEE
11.6600 g., 0.5000 Silver 0.1874 oz. ASW **Ruler:** George VI **Obv:** Crowned head left **Obv. Legend:** GEORGE VI KING EMPEROR **Rev:** Denomination and date within circle, wreath surrounds **Edge:** Security

Date	Mintage	F	VF	XF	Unc	BU
1939(b)	—	200	400	800	1,500	—
1940(b)	153,120,000	BV	6.00	10.00	20.00	—
1941(b)	111,480,000	BV	6.00	10.00	20.00	—
1943(b)	—	BV	6.00	10.00	20.00	—

Note: 1943(b) mintage included with KM#557.1.

KM# 557.1 RUPEE
11.6600 g., 0.5000 Silver 0.1874 oz. ASW, 30.5 mm. **Ruler:** George VI **Obv:** Small second head, large rim decoration **Obv. Legend:** GEORGE VI KING EMPEROR **Rev:** Denomination and date within circle, wreath surrounds **Edge:** Security

Date	Mintage	F	VF	XF	Unc	BU
1942(b) Without dot	7,352,000	BV	4.50	10.00	20.00	—
1943(b)	65,995,000	BV	4.50	10.00	20.00	—
1943(b) Reverse B	Inc. above	BV	4.50	10.00	20.00	—
1944(b) Reverse B	146,206,000	BV	4.50	10.00	20.00	—
1944(b)	Inc. above	BV	4.50	10.00	20.00	—
1944L Small L	91,400,000	BV	4.50	10.00	20.00	—
1944L Large L	Inc. above	BV	4.50	10.00	20.00	—
1945(b) Small 5	142,666,000	BV	3.50	6.00	12.50	—
1945(b) Large 5	Inc. above	30.00	35.00	45.00	60.00	—
1945(b) Proof	—	—	—	—	—	—
1945L	118,126,000	BV	3.50	6.00	12.50	—

KM# 557a RUPEE
Copper-Nickel, 30.5 mm. **Ruler:** George VI **Obv:** Crowned head left **Obv. Legend:** GEORGE VI KING EMPEROR **Rev:** Denomination and date within circle, wreath surrounds

Date	Mintage	F	VF	XF	Unc	BU
1943(b) P/L; Restrike	—	—	—	—	650	—

KM# 559 RUPEE
Nickel **Ruler:** George VI **Obv:** Crowned head left **Rev:** Indian tiger (panthera tigris) **Edge:** Security

Date	Mintage	F	VF	XF	Unc	BU
1947(b)	118,028,000	1.50	2.50	5.00	12.00	17.50
1947B Proof	—	Value: 375				
Note: Mumbai (Bombay) issue has diamond mark below date						
1947(l)	41,911,000	1.50	3.00	6.00	15.00	20.00
Note: Lahore issue without privy mark						

KM# 525 15 RUPEES
7.9881 g., 0.9170 Gold 0.2355 oz. AGW **Ruler:** George V **Obv:** Crowned bust left **Obv. Legend:** GEORGE V KING EMPEROR **Rev:** Denomination and date within circle, wreath surrounds **Note:** This issue is equal in weight and fineness to the British sovereign.

Date	Mintage	F	VF	XF	Unc	BU
1918(b)	2,110,000	275	350	500	750	—
1918(b) Proof	12	Value: 7,000				
1918(b) P/L; Restrike	—	—	—	—	800	—

TRADE COINAGE

The Mansfield Commission of 1868 allowed for the admission of British and Australian sovereigns (see Australian section; sovereigns with shield reverse were struck for export to India) as payment for sums due.

The fifth branch of the Royal Mint was established in a section of the Mumbai (Bombay) Mint as of December 21, 1917. This was a war-time measure, its purpose being to strike into sovereigns the gold blanks supplied by the Mumbai and other Indian mints. The Mumbai sovereigns bear the mint mark 'I' and were struck from August 15, 1918, to April 22, 1919. The branch mint was closed in May 1919.

KM# 525A SOVEREIGN
7.9881 g., 0.9170 Gold 0.2355 oz. AGW **Ruler:** George V **Obv:** Head left **Rev:** St. George slaying the dragon **Note:** Mint mark "I".

Date	Mintage	F	VF	XF	Unc	BU
1918	1,295,000	—	BV	210	240	—
1918 Proof	—	—	—	—	—	—
1918 P/L; Restrike	—	—	—	—	850	—

INDIA

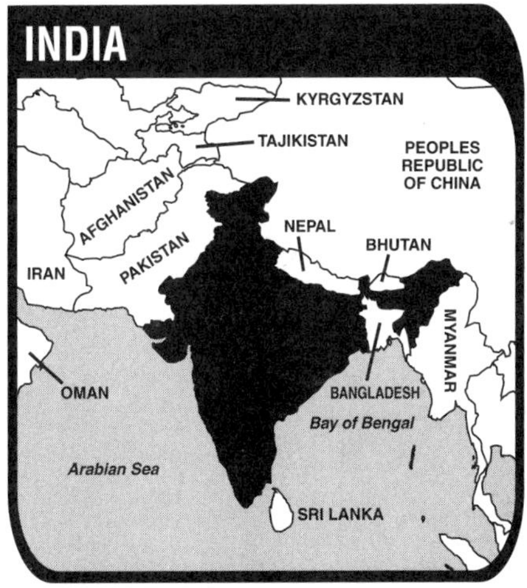

The Republic of India, a subcontinent jutting southward from the mainland of Asia, has an area of 1,269,346 sq. mi. (3,287,590 sq. km.) and a population of over 1.1 billion, second only to that of the People's Republic of China. Capital: New Delhi. India's economy is based on agriculture and industrial activity. Engineering goods, cotton apparel and fabrics, handicrafts, tea, iron and steel are exported.

The Indian Mutiny (called the first War of Independence by Indian Nationalists) of 1857-58, begun by Indian troops in the service of the British East India Company, revealed the intensity of the growing resentment against British domination. The widespread rebellion against British rule was unsuccessful, but resulted in the transfer of government from the company to the British crown, and was a source of inspiration, to later Indian nationalists. Agitation for representation in the government continued.

Following World War I, in which India sent six million troops to fight at the side of the Allies, Indian nationalism intensified under the banner of the Indian National Congress and the leadership of Mohandas Karamchand Gandhi, who called for non-violent revolt against British authority. The Government of India Act of 1935 proposed a federal status linking the British Indian provinces with the many princely states; in addition, provincial legislatures were to be created. The federal status was never implemented, but the legislatures were created after the election of 1937, with the National Congress winning majorities in most of the provinces.

When Britain declared war on Germany in Sept. 1939, the Viceroy declared India also to be at war with a common enemy. The Congress, however, demanded independence as a condition for cooperation; Britain refused. But as the Japanese advanced into Asia, Britain offered to transfer to Indians power over all but military affairs during the war, and set forth a plan for postwar independence. Congress was willing to accept the wartime transfer of power, but both Congress and the Muslim League rejected Britain's plan for independence; Congress because it did not sufficiently safeguard Indian unity, the Muslims (who wanted a separate Muslim state) because of fears of what would happen to Muslims within a united India.

Early in 1947, Prime Minister Clement Attlee announced that Britain would leave India "by a date not later than June 1948," even though the Hindus and Muslims could not agree among themselves on a plan for self-government. The National Congress, aware that the Muslim League would revolt rather than accept an all-India government, reluctantly agreed to the formation of a separate Muslim state. The Muslim-majority provinces of the North West Frontier, Sindh and West Punjab in the west, and East Bengal in the east were separated from India to form the Muslim state of Pakistan, which became independent on Aug. 14, 1947. India became independent on the following day. Because British India coins dated 1947 were struck until 1950, they can be considered the first coins of Independent India. India became a republic on Jan. 26, 1950.

The Republic of India is a member of the Commonwealth of Nations. The president is the Chief of State. The prime minister is the Head of Government.

MINT MARKS

(Mint marks usually appear directly below the date.)

B - Mumbai (Bombay), proof issues only (1969 until 1995)
(B) - Mumbai (Bombay), diamond
C – Ottawa (1985 25 Paise; 1988 10, 25 & 50 Paise)
(C) – Kolkata (Calcutta) no mint mark
H - Birmingham (1985 Rupee only)
(H) - Hyderabad, star (1963)
(Hd) - Hyderabad, diamond split vertically (1953-1960)
(Hy) - Hyderabad, incuse dot in diamond (1960-1968)
(K) - Kremnica, Slovakia, MK in circle
(L) – British Royal Mint, Llantrisant (1985 rupee only), diamond below first date digit
(Ld) – British Royal Mint Llantrisant, tower, looks like a bridge
M - Mumbai (Bombay), proof only starting 1996
(M) - Mexico City, M beneath O
(N) - Noida, dot
(P) - Pretoria, M in oval
(R) – Moscow, MMD in oval
(T) - Taegu (Korea), star below first or last date (1997 and 98 2 Rupees only)

From 1950 through 1964 the Republic of India proof coins carry the regular diamond mint mark and can be distinguished from circulation issues only by their proof-like finish. From 1969 proofs carry the capital "B" mint mark. Some Bombay issues after 1969 have a "proof-like" appearance although bearing the diamond mint mark of circulation issues. Beginning in 1972 proofs of the larger denominations - 10, 20 and 100 rupees -were partly frosted on their main features, including numerals. From 1975 all proofs were similarly frosted, from the 1 paisa to 100 rupees. Proof-like issues are often erroneously offered as proofs.

MONETARY SYSTEM

(Until 1957)

4 Pice = 1 Anna
16 Annas = 1 Rupee

In addition to the denomination, the value as fraction of the Rupee is added in words above the denomination numeral for educational purposes on all 1, 2,5, 10, 25, and 50 Naya Paisa on the first 1, 2, 5, 10, 25, and 50 Paisa types (i.e. Naya Paisa – 1/100 Rupee).

REPUBLIC

STANDARD COINAGE

KM# 1.1 PICE

Bronze **Obv:** Asoka lion pedestal **Rev:** Horse (equus caballus equidae) **Note:** 1.6mm thick, 0.3mm edge rim.

Date	Mintage	F	VF	XF	Unc	BU
1950(B)	32,080,000	—	1.00	2.00	3.00	5.00

KM# 1.2 PICE

Bronze **Obv:** Asoka lion pedestal **Rev:** Horse left **Note:** 1.6mm thick, 1.0mm edge rim.

Date	Mintage	F	VF	XF	Unc	BU
1950(B)	Inc. above	—	0.40	0.80	1.50	2.00
1950(B) Proof	—	Value: 2.50				
1950C	14,000,000	—	0.50	1.00	1.75	2.25

KM# 1.3 PICE

Bronze **Obv:** Asoka lion pedestal **Rev:** Horse left **Note:** 1.2mm thick, 0.8mm edge rim.

Date	Mintage	F	VF	XF	Unc	BU
1951(B)	104,626,000	—	0.20	0.40	0.75	1.50
1951(C)	127,300,000	—	0.20	0.40	0.75	1.50

KM# 1.4 PICE

2.9500 g., Bronze, 21 mm. **Obv:** Asoka lion pedestal **Rev:** Horse left **Note:** Larger date, 2mm thick, 0.8mm edge rim.

Date	Mintage	F	VF	XF	Unc	BU
1952(B)	213,830,000	—	0.25	0.40	0.80	1.50
1953(B)	242,358,000	—	0.25	0.50	1.00	1.50
1953(C)	111,000,000	—	—	—	—	—
1953(Hd)	Inc. above	—	15.00	20.00	—	—
1954(B)	136,758,000	—	0.25	0.50	1.00	1.50
1954(C)	52,600,000	—	0.35	0.70	1.25	2.00
1954(Hd)	Inc. above	—	10.00	15.00	—	—
1954(B) Proof	Inc. above	Value: 5.00				
1955(B)	24,423,000	—	0.50	1.25	2.00	2.50
1955(Hd)	Inc. above	—	15.00	20.00	—	—

KM# 2.1 1/2 ANNA

2.8900 g., Copper-Nickel **Obv:** Asoka lion pedestal **Rev:** Zebu **Shape:** 4-sided

Date	Mintage	F	VF	XF	Unc	BU
1950(B)	26,076,000	—	0.20	0.40	1.00	—
1950(B) Proof	—	Value: 3.00				
1950(C)	3,100,000	—	1.25	2.00	3.25	—

KM# 2.2 1/2 ANNA

2.8500 g., Copper-Nickel **Obv:** Asoka lion pedestal **Rev:** Zebu, larger date **Shape:** Square

Date	Mintage	F	VF	XF	Unc	BU
1954(B)	14,000,000	—	0.40	0.65	1.25	—
1954(B) Proof	—	Value: 5.00				
1954(C)	20,800,000	—	0.30	0.50	1.00	—
1955(B)	22,488,000	—	0.40	0.65	1.25	—

KM# 3.1 ANNA

Copper-Nickel **Obv:** Asoka lion pedestal **Rev:** Zebu **Shape:** Scalloped **Note:** A similar shaped Independence commemorative token issued in 1947, bearing a map of India, circulated to some degree as an Anna coin.

Date	Mintage	F	VF	XF	Unc	BU
1950(B)	9,944,000	—	0.45	0.75	1.50	—
1950(B) Proof	—	Value: 4.00				

KM# 3.2 ANNA

Copper-Nickel **Obv:** Asoka lion pedestal **Rev:** Zebu, larger date, first Hindi letter varieties **Shape:** Scalloped

Date	Mintage	F	VF	XF	Unc	BU
1954(B)	20,388,000	—	0.35	0.60	1.25	—
1954(B) Proof	—	Value: 6.50				
1955(B)	—	—	15.00	20.00	30.00	—

KM# 4.1 2 ANNAS

5.7800 g., Copper-Nickel **Obv:** Asoka lion pedestal **Rev:** Zebu **Note:** A similar shaped Independence commemorative token issued in 1947, bearing a map of India, circulated to some degree as a 2 Anna coin. (Refer to 5th edition of Unusual World Coins, X#104.)

Date	Mintage	F	VF	XF	Unc	BU
1950(B)	7,536,000	—	0.75	1.50	2.50	—
1950(B) Proof	—	Value: 5.00				

KM# 4.2 2 ANNAS

Copper-Nickel **Obv:** Asoka lion pedestal **Rev:** Zebu **Note:** Larger date.

Date	Mintage	F	VF	XF	Unc	BU
1954(B)	10,548,000	—	0.75	1.50	2.50	—
1954(B) Proof	—	Value: 8.00				
1955(B)	—	—	15.00	20.00	30.00	—

KM# 5.1 1/4 RUPEE

2.8600 g., Nickel **Obv:** Asoka lion pedestal **Rev:** Grain sprigs flank denomination **Note:** Large lion.

Date	Mintage	F	VF	XF	Unc	BU
1950(B) Proof	—	Value: 5.00				
1950(B)	7,650,000	—	0.60	1.50	2.50	—
1950(C)	7,800,000	—	0.60	1.50	2.50	—
1951(B)	41,439,000	—	0.45	1.00	2.00	—
1951(C)	13,500,000	—	0.55	1.00	2.00	—

KM# 5.2 1/4 RUPEE

Nickel **Obv:** Asoka lion pedestal **Rev:** Grain sprigs flank denomination **Note:** Larger date, large lion.

Date	Mintage	F	VF	XF	Unc	BU
1954(C)	58,300,000	—	0.65	1.50	2.50	—
1954(B) Proof	Inc. above	Value: 6.00				
1955(B)	57,936,000	—	2.00	4.00	6.00	—

KM# 5.3 1/4 RUPEE

2.7300 g., Nickel **Obv:** Asoka lion pedestal **Rev:** Grain sprigs flank denomination **Note:** Small lion.

Date	Mintage	F	VF	XF	Unc	BU
1954(C)	Inc. above	—	0.40	1.00	1.75	—
1955(C)	28,900,000	—	0.40	1.00	1.75	—
1956(C)	22,000,000	—	0.70	1.25	2.00	—

KM# 6.1 1/2 RUPEE

Nickel **Obv:** Asoka lion pedestal **Rev:** Grain sprigs flank denomination **Note:** Large lion.

Date	Mintage	F	VF	XF	Unc	BU
1950(B)	12,352,000	—	0.75	1.25	2.50	—
1950(B) Proof	—	Value: 5.50				
1950(C)	1,100,000	—	1.25	2.00	5.00	—
1951(B)	9,239,000	—	1.00	1.50	3.50	—

KM# 6.2 1/2 RUPEE

5.7800 g., Nickel **Obv:** Asoka lion pedestal **Rev:** Grain sprigs flank denomination **Note:** Larger date, large lion.

Date	Mintage	F	VF	XF	Unc	BU
1954(C)	36,300,000	—	0.50	1.00	2.50	—
1954(B) Proof	—	Value: 8.00				
1955(B)	18,977,000	—	0.75	1.50	4.50	—

KM# 6.3 1/2 RUPEE

Nickel **Obv:** Asoka lion pedestal within circle, dots missing between words **Rev:** Grain sprigs flank denomination

Date	Mintage	F	VF	XF	Unc	BU
1956(C)	24,900,000	—	0.50	1.00	2.50	—

KM# 7.1 RUPEE

Nickel **Obv:** Asoka lion pedestal **Rev:** Grain sprigs flank denomination, thick numeral

Date	Mintage	F	VF	XF	Unc	BU
1950(B)	19,412,000	—	1.50	2.50	4.50	—
1950(B) Proof	—	Value: 7.00				

KM# 7.2 RUPEE

Nickel **Obv:** Asoka lion pedestal **Rev:** Thick numeral, first Hindi letter varieties, larger date

Date	Mintage	F	VF	XF	Unc	BU
1954(B)	Inc. above	—	2.00	3.00	5.50	—
1954(B) Proof	—	Value: 10.00				

DECIMAL COINAGE

100 Naye Paise = 1 Rupee (1957-63);
100 Paise = 1 Rupee (1964-)

NOTE: The Paisa was at first called Naya Paisa (= New Paisa), so that people would distinguish from the old non-decimal Paisa (or Pice, equal to 1/64 Rupee).

After 7 years, the word new was dropped, and the coin was simply called a Paisa.

NOTE: Many of the Paisa standard types come with three obverse varieties.

1957-1989

TYPE 1: Side lions toothless with 2 to 3 fur rows, short squat D in INDIA.

1967-1994

TYPE 2: Asoka lion pedestal more imposing. Side lions with 3 or 4 fur rows, more elegant D in INDIA. The shape of the D in INDIA is the easiest way to distinguish this obverse.

1979-

TYPE 3: Similar to Type I but 2 teeth, 4 to 5 fur rows, smaller lion head.

NOTE: Paisa standard pieces with mint mark B, 1969 to date, were struck only in proof.

NOTE: Indian mintage figures are not divided by mint, and often include dates other than the year in which struck. They should be regarded with reserve.

KM# 8 NAYA PAISA

1.5000 g., Bronze, 16.04 mm. **Obv:** Asoka lion pedestal **Rev:** Denomination and date

Date	Mintage	F	VF	XF	Unc	BU
1957(B)	618,630,000	—	0.30	0.50	0.85	—
1957(C)	Inc. above	—	0.30	0.50	0.85	—
1957(Hd)	Inc. above	—	0.30	0.50	0.85	—
1958(B)	468,630,000	—	0.45	0.75	1.50	—
1958(Hd)	Inc. above	—	0.45	0.75	1.50	—
1959(B)	351,120,000	—	0.30	0.50	0.85	—
1959(C)	Inc. above	—	0.30	0.50	0.85	—
1959(Hd)	Inc. above	—	0.30	0.50	0.85	—
1960(B)	357,940,000	—	0.30	0.50	0.85	—
1960(B) Proof	—	Value: 2.00				
1960(C)	Inc. above	—	2.25	3.50	5.00	—
1960(Hd)	Inc. above	—	3.25	4.00	5.00	—
1961(B)	573,170,000	—	0.30	0.50	0.85	—
1961(B) Proof	—	Value: 2.00				
1961(C)	Inc. above	—	0.30	0.50	0.85	—
1961(Hy)	Inc. above	—	0.50	0.75	1.25	—
1962(B)	—	—	—	—	—	—

Note: 1962(B) has only been found in some of the 1962 uncirculated mint sets; varieties of the split diamond have been reported.

KM# 8a NAYA PAISA

1.5100 g., Nickel-Brass, 16 mm. **Obv:** Asoka lion pedestal **Rev:** Denomination and date

Date	Mintage	F	VF	XF	Unc	BU
1962(B)	235,103,000	—	0.20	0.35	0.70	—
1962(B) Proof	—	Value: 1.50				
1962(C)	Inc. above	—	0.20	0.35	0.70	—
1962(Hy)	Inc. above	—	0.50	0.75	1.25	—
1963(B)	343,313,000	—	0.20	0.35	0.70	—
1963(B) Proof	—	Value: 1.50				
1963(C)	Inc. above	—	0.25	0.50	1.00	—
1963(H)	Inc. above	—	0.25	0.40	0.80	—

KM# 9 PAISA

1.4800 g., Nickel-Brass **Obv:** Asoka lion pedestal **Rev:** Denomination and date **Note:** Type I.

Date	Mintage	F	VF	XF	Unc	BU
1964(B)	539,068,000	—	0.20	0.45	1.00	—
1964(C)	Inc. above	—	0.20	0.45	1.00	—
1964(H)	Inc. above	—	0.20	0.45	1.00	—

KM# 9a PAISA

Nickel-Brass **Obv:** Asoka lion pedestal **Rev:** Denomination and date **Note:** Included in mintage of KM#9. Type 1.

Date	Mintage	F	VF	XF	Unc	BU
1964(H)	Inc. above	—	0.20	0.45	1.00	—

KM# 10.1 PAISA

0.7500 g., Aluminum **Obv:** Asoka lion pedestal **Rev:** Denomination and date **Edge:** Plain **Shape:** Square **Note:** Type 1. 14.67mm x 14.67mm.

Date	Mintage	F	VF	XF	Unc	BU
1965(B)	223,480,000	—	0.40	0.65	1.00	—
1965(Hy)	Inc. above	—	0.40	0.65	1.00	—
1966(B)	404,200,000	—	0.20	0.30	0.50	—
1966(C)	Inc. above	—	0.30	0.50	1.00	—
1966(Hy)	Inc. above	—	0.20	0.30	0.50	—
1967(B)	450,433,000	—	0.20	0.30	0.50	—
1967(C)	Inc. above	—	0.20	0.30	0.50	—
1967(Hy)	Inc. above	—	0.20	0.30	0.50	—
1968(B)	302,720,000	—	0.20	0.30	0.50	—
1968(C)	Inc. above	—	0.20	0.30	0.50	—
1968(Hy)	Inc. above	—	0.20	0.30	0.50	—
1969(B)	125,930,000	—	1.50	2.25	3.00	—
1969B Proof	9,147	Value: 1.50				
1969(H)	Inc. above	—	3.00	4.00	5.00	—
1970(B)	15,800,000	—	2.00	2.50	5.00	—

Note: 1970(B) is found only in the uncirculated sets of that year. It has a mirror-like surface.

Date	Mintage	F	VF	XF	Unc	BU
1970B Proof	3,046	Value: 1.00				
1971B Proof	4,375	Value: 1.00				
1971(H)	112,100,000	—	0.20	0.30	0.50	—
1972(B)	62,090,000	—	0.20	0.30	0.50	—
1972B Proof	7,895	Value: 1.00				
1972(H)	Inc. above	—	0.20	0.30	0.50	—
1973B Proof	7,562	Value: 1.00				
1974B Proof	—	Value: 1.00				
1975B Proof	—	Value: 1.00				
1976B Proof	—	Value: 1.00				
1977B Proof	—	Value: 1.00				
1978B Proof	—	Value: 1.00				
1979B Proof	—	Value: 1.00				
1980B Proof	—	Value: 1.00				
1981B Proof	—	Value: 1.00				

KM# 10.2 PAISA

Aluminum **Obv:** Asoka lion pedestal **Rev:** Denomination and date **Shape:** 4-sided **Note:** Type 2.

Date	Mintage	F	VF	XF	Unc	BU
1969(C)	Inc. above	—	2.50	3.00	4.00	—
1970(C)	Inc. above	—	0.40	0.65	1.00	—

KM# 11 2 NAYE PAISE

2.9500 g., Copper-Nickel **Obv:** Asoka lion pedestal **Rev:** Denomination and date **Shape:** Scalloped

Date	Mintage	F	VF	XF	Unc	BU
1957(B)	406,230,000	—	0.15	0.40	0.80	—
1957(C)	Inc. above	—	0.15	0.40	0.80	—
1958(B)	245,660,000	—	0.15	0.40	0.80	—
1958(C)	Inc. above	—	0.15	0.40	0.80	—
1959(B)	171,445,000	—	0.15	0.40	0.80	—
1959(C)	Inc. above	—	0.15	0.40	0.80	—
1960(B)	121,820,000	—	0.15	0.40	0.80	—
1960(B) Proof	—	Value: 2.00				
1960(C)	Inc. above	—	0.20	0.40	0.80	—
1961(B)	190,610,000	—	0.20	0.40	0.80	—
1961(B) Proof	—	Value: 2.00				
1961(C)	Inc. above	—	0.20	0.40	0.80	—
1962(B)	318,181,000	—	0.20	0.40	0.80	—
1962(B) Proof	—	Value: 1.50				
1962(C)	Inc. above	—	0.20	0.40	0.80	—
1963(B)	372,380,000	—	0.20	0.40	0.80	—
1963(B) Proof	—	Value: 1.50				
1963(C)	Inc. above	—	0.20	0.40	0.80	—

KM# 12 2 PAISE

Copper-Nickel **Obv:** Asoka lion pedestal **Rev:** Denomination and date **Shape:** Scalloped **Note:** Type 1.

Date	Mintage	F	VF	XF	Unc	BU
1964(B)	323,504,000	—	0.20	0.40	0.80	—
1964(C)	Inc. above	—	0.20	0.40	0.80	—

KM# 13.1 2 PAISE

1.0200 g., Aluminum **Obv:** Asoka lion pedestal **Rev:** Denomination and date, 10mm "2" **Shape:** Scalloped **Note:** Type 1.

Date	Mintage	F	VF	XF	Unc	BU
1965(B)	175,770,000	—	0.20	0.40	0.80	—
1965(C)	Inc. above	—	0.40	0.65	1.00	—
1966(B)	386,795,000	—	0.20	0.30	0.50	—
1966(C)	Inc. above	—	0.20	0.30	0.50	—
1967(B)	454,593,000	—	0.20	0.30	0.50	—

KM# 13.2 2 PAISE

Aluminum **Obv:** Asoka lion pedestal **Rev:** Denomination and date, 10-1/2mm "2" **Note:** Type 1.

Date	Mintage	F	VF	XF	Unc	BU
1967(C)	Inc. above	—	0.40	0.65	1.25	—

KM# 13.3 2 PAISE

Aluminum **Obv:** Asoka lion pedestal **Rev:** Denomination and date, 10mm "2" **Note:** Type 2.

Date	Mintage	F	VF	XF	Unc	BU
1967(B)	—	—	3.00	5.00	8.00	—

KM# 13.4 2 PAISE

Aluminum **Obv:** Asoka lion pedestal **Rev:** Denomination and date, 11mm "2" **Note:** Type 1.

Date	Mintage	F	VF	XF	Unc	BU
1968(C)	—	—	6.00	8.00	10.00	—
1977(B)	—	—	0.60	1.00	1.50	—
1978(B)	—	—	0.40	0.65	1.00	—

KM# 13.5 2 PAISE

1.0000 g., Aluminum **Obv:** Asoka lion pedestal **Rev:** Denomination and date, 11mm "2" **Shape:** Scalloped **Note:** Type 2.

Date	Mintage	F	VF	XF	Unc	BU
1968(C)	Inc. above	—	0.20	0.30	0.50	—
1968(B)	305,205,000	—	0.10	0.25	0.50	—
1969(B)	5,335,000	—	2.00	3.00	5.00	—
1969B Proof	9,147	Value: 1.00				
1970(B)	—	—	—	—	5.00	—

Note: 1970(B) is found only in the uncirculated sets of that year; It has a mirror-like surface.

Date	Mintage	F	VF	XF	Unc	BU
1970B Proof	3,046	Value: 1.00				
1970(C)	79,100,000	—	0.20	0.30	0.50	—
1971B Proof	4,375	Value: 1.00				
1971(C)	207,900,000	—	0.20	0.30	0.50	—

KM# 13.6 2 PAISE

Aluminum, 19.84 mm. **Obv:** Asoka lion pedestal **Rev:** Denomination and small date **Edge:** Plain scalloped **Note:** Varieties of date size exist. Type 2.

Date	Mintage	F	VF	XF	Unc	BU
1972B Proof	7,895	Value: 1.00				
1972(C)	261,270,000	—	0.20	0.30	0.50	—
1972(H)	Inc. above	—	0.20	0.30	0.50	—
1973B Proof	7,562	Value: 1.00				
1973(C)	—	—	0.15	0.25	0.50	—
1973(H)	—	—	0.15	0.25	0.50	—
1974B Proof	—	Value: 1.00				
1974(C)	—	—	0.15	0.25	0.50	—
1974(H)	—	—	0.15	0.25	0.50	—
1975B Proof	—	Value: 1.00				
1975(C)	184,500,000	—	0.40	0.65	1.00	—
1975(H)	Inc. above	—	0.15	0.25	0.50	—
1976(B)	68,140,000	—	0.15	0.25	0.50	—
1976B Proof	—	Value: 1.00				
1976(H)	—	—	1.50	2.25	3.00	—
1977(B)	251,955,000	—	0.25	0.40	0.70	—
1977B Proof	—	Value: 1.00				
1977(H)	Inc. above	—	0.15	0.25	0.50	—
1978B Proof	—	Value: 1.00				
1978(H)	144,010,000	—	0.15	0.25	0.50	—
1979B Proof	—	Value: 1.00				
1979(H)	—	—	0.65	1.00	1.50	—
1980B Proof	—	Value: 1.00				
1981B Proof	—	Value: 1.00				

KM# 14.1 3 PAISE

1.2100 g., Aluminum **Obv:** Asoka lion pedestal **Rev:** Denomination and date **Shape:** 6-sided **Note:** Type 1.

Date	Mintage	F	VF	XF	Unc	BU
1964(B)	138,890,000	—	0.20	0.40	0.70	—
1964(C)	Inc. above	—	0.20	0.40	0.70	—
1965(B)	459,825,000	—	0.20	0.30	0.60	—
1965(C)	Inc. above	—	0.20	0.30	0.60	—
1966(B)	390,440,000	—	0.20	0.30	0.60	—
1966(C)	Inc. above	—	0.20	0.30	0.60	—
1966(Hy)	Inc. above	—	0.20	0.30	0.60	—
1967(B)	167,018,000	—	0.20	0.30	0.60	—
1967(C)	Inc. above	—	0.20	0.30	0.60	—
1967(H)	Inc. above	—	0.75	1.25	2.00	—
1968(B)	—	—	3.00	4.00	6.00	—
1968(H)	—	—	5.00	15.00	30.00	—

KM# 14.2 3 PAISE

1.2300 g., Aluminum **Obv:** Asoka lion pedestal **Rev:** Denomination and date **Shape:** 6-sided **Note:** Type 2.

Date	Mintage	F	VF	XF	Unc	BU
1967(C)	—	—	4.00	6.00	8.00	—
1967(H)	Inc. above	—	4.00	6.00	8.00	—
1968(B)	246,390,000	—	—	0.25	0.50	—
1968(C)	Inc. above	—	0.10	0.25	0.50	—
1968(H)	Inc. above	—	0.20	0.35	0.60	—
1969(B)	—	—	0.10	0.25	0.50	—
1969B Proof	9,147	Value: 1.00				
1969(C)	7,025,000	—	0.20	0.30	0.50	—
1969(H)	Inc. above	—	1.75	2.50	4.00	—
1970(B)	—	—	—	—	5.00	—

Note: 1970(B) is found only in the uncirculated sets of that year; It has a mirror-like surface.

Date	Mintage	F	VF	XF	Unc	BU
1970B Proof	3,046	Value: 1.00				
1970(C)	15,300,000	—	0.10	0.25	0.50	—
1971B Proof	4,375	Value: 1.00				
1971(C)	203,100,000	—	—	0.25	0.50	—
1971(H)	Inc. above	—	—	0.25	0.50	—

KM# 16 5 NAYE PAISE

4.0500 g., Copper-Nickel, 22 mm. **Obv:** Asoka lion pedestal **Rev:** Denomination and date **Shape:** Rounded square

Date	Mintage	F	VF	XF	Unc	BU
1957(B)	227,210,000	—	0.25	0.45	1.00	—
1957(C)	Inc. above	—	0.25	0.45	1.00	—
1958(B)	214,320,000	—	0.25	0.45	1.00	—
1958(C)	Inc. above	—	0.25	0.45	1.00	—
1959(B)	137,105,000	—	0.25	0.45	1.00	—
1959(C)	Inc. above	—	2.50	4.00	7.00	—
1960(B)	93,345,000	—	0.25	0.45	1.00	—
1960(B) Proof	—	Value: 2.00				
1960(C)	Inc. above	—	0.25	0.45	1.00	—
1960(Hy)	Inc. above	—	6.00	10.00	—	—
1961(B)	197,620,000	—	0.25	0.45	1.00	—
1961(B) Proof	—	Value: 2.00				
1961(C)	Inc. above	—	0.35	0.60	1.00	—
1961(Hy)	Inc. above	—	6.00	10.00	—	—
1962(B)	224,277,000	—	0.25	0.45	1.00	—
1962(B) Proof	—	Value: 1.50				
1962(C)	Inc. above	—	0.25	0.45	1.00	—
1962(Hy)	Inc. above	—	2.00	3.25	7.00	—
1963(B)	332,600,000	—	0.20	0.35	0.80	—
1963(B) Proof	—	Value: 1.50				
1963(C)	Inc. above	—	2.00	3.00	6.00	—
1963(H)	Inc. above	—	2.00	3.25	7.00	—

KM# 17 5 PAISE

4.0500 g., Copper-Nickel **Obv:** Asoka lion pedestal **Rev:** Denomination and date **Shape:** Rounded square **Note:** Type 1.

Date	Mintage	F	VF	XF	Unc	BU
1964(B)	156,000,000	—	0.40	0.60	1.00	—
1964(C)	Inc. above	—	0.40	0.60	1.00	—
1964(H)	Inc. above	—	6.00	10.00	—	—
1965(B)	203,855,000	—	0.25	0.45	0.75	—
1965(C)	Inc. above	—	0.40	0.60	1.00	—
1965(H)	Inc. above	—	6.00	10.00	—	—
1966(B)	101,395,000	—	0.75	1.25	2.00	—
1966(C)	Inc. above	—	0.40	0.60	1.00	—

KM# 18.1 5 PAISE

Aluminum **Obv:** Asoka lion pedestal **Rev:** Denomination and date, 6mm "5" **Shape:** 4-sided **Note:** Type 1.

Date	Mintage	F	VF	XF	Unc	BU
1967(C)	—	—	0.35	0.60	1.00	—
1967(B)	608,533,000	—	0.35	0.60	1.00	—

KM# 18.2 5 PAISE

Aluminum **Obv:** Asoka lion pedestal **Rev:** Denomination and date, 7mm "5". **Note:** Type 1.

Date	Mintage	F	VF	XF	Unc	BU
1967(B)	Inc. above	—	0.15	0.25	0.50	—
1967(H)	Inc. above	—	0.15	0.25	0.50	—
1967(C)	Inc. above	—	0.15	0.25	0.50	—
1968(B)	—	—	3.50	5.00	8.50	—
1968(C)	—	—	3.50	5.00	8.50	—
1968(H)	666,750,000	—	0.75	1.25	2.00	—
1971(H)	499,200,000	—	0.10	0.25	0.50	—

KM# 18.3 5 PAISE

1.5000 g., Aluminum **Obv:** Asoka lion pedestal **Rev:** Denomination and date, 7mm "5" **Note:** Type 2.

Date	Mintage	F	VF	XF	Unc	BU
1967(H)	—	—	4.50	7.00	10.00	—
1968(B)	—	—	0.15	0.25	0.50	—

Note: Mintage included in KM18.2

Date	Mintage	F	VF	XF	Unc	BU
1968(C)	—	—	0.15	0.25	0.50	—

Note: Mintage included in KM18.2

Date	Mintage	F	VF	XF	Unc	BU
1968(H)	—	—	0.40	0.60	1.00	—

Note: Mintage included in KM18.2

Date	Mintage	F	VF	XF	Unc	BU
1969(B)	3,740,000	—	2.00	3.50	5.00	—
1969B Proof	9,147	Value: 1.00				
1970(B)	39,900,000	—	1.25	2.00	3.50	—
1970B Proof	3,046	Value: 1.00				
1970(C)	Inc. above	—	0.25	0.35	0.60	—
1970(H)	Inc. above	—	0.25	0.40	0.75	—
1971(B)	—	—	0.10	0.15	0.50	—

Note: Included with 1971(H) of KM18.2

Date	Mintage	F	VF	XF	Unc	BU
1971B Proof	4,375	Value: 1.00				
1971(C)	Inc. above	—	0.10	0.15	0.50	—
1971(H)	—	—	0.25	0.45	0.75	—

KM# 18.4 5 PAISE

Aluminum **Obv:** Asoka lion pedestal **Rev:** Larger 11mm "5", date **Note:** Type 1.

Date	Mintage	F	VF	XF	Unc	BU
1972(H)	512,430,000	—	0.35	0.60	1.00	—

KM# 18.5 5 PAISE

Aluminum **Obv:** Asoka lion pedestal **Rev:** Larger 11mm "5", date **Note:** Type 1. Varieties in Hindi style exist.

Date	Mintage	F	VF	XF	Unc	BU
1973(H)	—	—	2.50	3.50	5.50	—
1977(B)	—	—	2.00	3.00	5.00	—
1978(B)	—	—	0.75	1.25	2.00	—

KM# 18.6 5 PAISE

1.5300 g., Aluminum **Obv:** Asoka lion pedestal **Rev:** Denomination and date **Shape:** Rounded-off square **Note:** Type 2.

Date	Mintage	F	VF	XF	Unc	BU
1972(B)	—	—	0.10	0.15	0.50	—
Note: Mintage included in KM18.4						
1972B Proof	7,895	Value: 1.00				
1972(C)	—	—	0.10	0.15	0.50	—
Note: Mintage included in KM18.4						
1972(H)	—	—	3.50	5.00	7.00	—
1973(B)	—	—	0.10	0.15	0.50	—
1973B Proof	7,562	Value: 1.00				
1973(C)	—	—	0.20	0.30	0.60	—
1973(H)	—	—	0.10	0.15	0.50	—
1974B Proof	—	Value: 1.00				
1974(B)	—	—	0.10	0.15	0.50	—
1974(C)	—	—	0.10	0.15	0.50	—
1974(H)	—	—	0.10	0.15	0.50	—
1975(B)	—	—	0.10	0.15	0.50	—
1975B Proof	—	Value: 1.00				
1975(C)	289,080,000	—	0.20	0.30	0.60	—
1975(H)	Inc. above	—	0.10	0.15	0.50	—
1976(B)	53,205,000	—	0.10	0.15	0.50	—
1976(C)	—	—	—	0.10	0.20	—
1976(H)	—	—	0.10	0.15	0.50	—
1977(B)	257,899,999	—	0.10	0.15	0.50	—
1977(C)	Inc. above	—	0.10	0.15	0.50	—
1977(H)	Inc. above	—	0.10	0.15	0.50	—
1978(C)	—	—	0.10	0.15	0.50	—
1978(H)	—	—	0.10	0.15	0.50	—
1979(B)	—	—	0.10	0.15	0.50	—
1979(C)	—	—	0.20	0.35	0.80	—
1979(H)	—	—	0.10	0.15	0.50	—
1980(B)	21,440,000	—	0.10	0.15	0.50	—
1980B Proof	—	Value: 1.00				
1980(C)	Inc. above	—	0.20	0.30	0.60	—
1980(H)	Inc. above	—	0.10	0.15	0.50	—
1981B Proof	—	Value: 1.00				
1981(C)	4,365,000	—	0.10	0.15	0.50	—
1981(H)	Inc. above	—	0.10	0.15	0.50	—
Note: Due to faulty dies, 1981(H) often resembles the non-existent 1981(B).						
1982B Proof	3,499,000	Value: 1.00				
1982(C)	Inc. above	—	0.10	0.15	0.50	—
1982(H)	Inc. above	—	0.10	0.15	0.50	—
1983(C)	3,110,000	—	0.25	0.50	1.00	—
1983(H)	Inc. above	—	0.10	0.15	0.50	—
1984(C)	—	—	0.25	0.50	1.00	—
1984(H)	Inc. above	—	0.10	0.15	0.50	—

KM# 19 5 PAISE

1.5100 g., Aluminum, 22 mm. **Series:** F.A.O. **Subject:** Food and Work For All **Obv:** Asoka lion pedestal **Rev:** Figure on tractor, utility pole and buildings in background **Edge:** Plain **Shape:** Square **Note:** 18.95mm x 18.95mm.

Date	Mintage	F	VF	XF	Unc	BU
1976(B)	34,680,000	—	0.35	0.50	1.00	—
1976B Proof	—	Value: 1.00				
1976(C)	60,040,000	—	0.35	0.50	1.00	—
1976(H)	60,290,000	—	0.35	1.00	2.00	—

KM# 20 5 PAISE

1.5000 g., Aluminum **Series:** F.A.O. **Subject:** Save For Development **Obv:** Asoka lion pedestal **Rev:** Symbols and date **Shape:** Square

Date	Mintage	F	VF	XF	Unc	BU
1977(B)	20,100,000	—	0.30	0.50	1.00	—
1977B Proof	2,224	Value: 1.25				
1977(C)	40,470,000	—	0.30	0.50	1.00	—
1977(H)	20,380,000	—	2.25	3.50	5.00	—

KM# 21 5 PAISE

Aluminum **Series:** F.A.O. **Subject:** Food and Shelter For All **Obv:** Asoka lion pedestal **Rev:** Building, grain sprig and road within circle **Shape:** Square

Date	Mintage	F	VF	XF	Unc	BU
1978(B)	28,440,000	—	0.35	0.50	1.00	—
1978B Proof	—	Value: 1.25				
1978(C)	30,870,000	—	0.50	1.00	2.00	—
1978(H)	21,100,000	—	1.00	1.50	2.25	—

KM# 22 5 PAISE

1.5200 g., Aluminum **Series:** International Year of the Child **Obv:** Asoka lion pedestal **Rev:** Logo within circle, wreath surrounds **Shape:** Square

Date	Mintage	F	VF	XF	Unc	BU
1979(B)	39,860,000	—	0.35	0.50	1.00	—
1979B Proof	—	Value: 1.25				
1979(C)	80,370,000	—	0.35	0.50	1.00	—
1979(H)	1,100,000	—	1.50	2.00	2.50	—

KM# 23 5 PAISE

1.0300 g., Aluminum **Obv:** Asoka lion pedestal **Rev:** Denomination and date **Edge:** Plain **Shape:** Square **Note:** Weight reduced. 19mm x 19mm.

Date	Mintage	F	VF	XF	Unc	BU
1984(C)	—	—	6.00	8.00	10.00	—
1985(B)	54,860,000	—	6.00	8.00	10.00	—
1985(C)	Inc. above	—	10.00	15.00	20.00	—
1985(H)	Inc. above	—	0.50	0.75	1.00	—
1986(C)	—	—	0.50	0.75	1.00	—
1986(H)	—	—	0.50	0.75	1.00	—
1987(C)	—	—	0.50	0.75	1.00	—
1987(H)	—	—	0.75	1.00	2.00	—
1988(C)	—	—	0.25	0.50	1.00	—
1988(H)	—	—	0.50	1.00	2.00	—
1989(C)	—	—	0.50	1.00	2.00	—
1989(H)	—	—	0.50	1.00	2.00	—
1990(B)	—	—	2.00	4.00	6.00	—
1990(C)	—	—	1.00	1.50	2.50	—
1990(H)	—	—	1.00	1.50	2.50	—
1991(C)	—	—	0.50	0.75	1.25	—
1991(H)	—	—	0.25	0.50	1.00	—
1992(B)	—	—	1.00	1.50	2.50	—
1992(H)	—	—	0.25	0.50	1.00	—
1993(C)	—	—	1.00	1.50	2.50	—
1993(H)	—	—	0.25	0.50	1.00	—
1994(H)	—	—	0.25	0.50	1.00	—

KM# 24.1 10 NAYE PAISE

4.8500 g., Copper-Nickel, 23 mm. **Obv:** Asoka lion pedestal **Rev:** Denomination and date, 6.5mm "10" **Shape:** Scalloped

Date	Mintage	F	VF	XF	Unc	BU
1957(B)	139,655,000	—	0.25	0.50	1.00	—
1957(C)	Inc. above	—	0.25	0.50	1.00	—

KM# 24.2 10 NAYE PAISE

5.0000 g., Copper-Nickel, 23 mm. **Obv:** Asoka lion pedestal **Rev:** Denomination and date, 7mm "10"

Date	Mintage	F	VF	XF	Unc	BU
1958(B)	123,160,000	—	0.25	0.50	1.00	—
1958(C)	Inc. above	—	0.25	0.50	1.00	—
1959(B)	148,570,000	—	0.25	0.50	1.00	—
1959(C)	Inc. above	—	0.25	0.50	1.00	—
1960(B) Proof	—	Value: 2.00				
1960(B)	52,335,000	—	0.35	0.75	2.00	—
1961(B)	172,545,000	—	0.25	0.50	1.00	—
1961(C)	Inc. above	—	0.25	0.50	1.00	—
1961(Hy)	Inc. above	—	3.50	6.50	11.50	—
1961(B) Proof	—	Value: 2.00				
1962(B)	172,777,000	—	0.25	0.50	1.00	—
1962(C)	Inc. above	—	0.25	0.50	1.00	—
1962(Hy)	Inc. above	—	3.25	5.00	9.00	—
1962(B) Proof	—	Value: 1.50				
1963(C)	Inc. above	—	0.25	0.50	1.00	—
1963(B) Proof	—	Value: 1.50				
1963(B)	182,834,000	—	0.25	0.50	1.00	—
1963(H)	Inc. above	—	1.00	2.50	5.00	—

KM# 25 10 PAISE

Copper-Nickel, 23 mm. **Obv:** Asoka lion pedestal **Rev:** Denomination, date, 6.5mm "10" **Shape:** Scalloped **Note:** Type 1.

Date	Mintage	F	VF	XF	Unc	BU
1964(B) Open 4	84,112,000	—	0.20	0.50	1.00	—
1964(B) Closed 4	Inc. above	—	5.00	7.00	10.00	—
1964(C)	Inc. above	—	0.20	0.50	1.00	—
1964(H)	Inc. above	—	3.00	5.00	7.00	—
1965(B)	253,430,000	—	0.20	0.50	1.00	—
1965(C)	Inc. above	—	0.20	0.50	1.00	—
1965(Hy)	Inc. above	—	4.00	6.00	8.00	—
1965(H)	Inc. above	—	3.00	5.00	7.00	—
1966(B)	326,990,000	—	0.20	0.50	1.00	—
1966(C)	Inc. above	—	0.20	1.00	1.00	—
1966(Hy)	Inc. above	—	0.40	0.75	1.25	—
1967(B)	59,443,000	—	0.40	0.75	1.25	—
1967(C)	Inc. above	—	0.40	0.75	1.25	—
1967(H)	Inc. above	—	3.00	5.00	7.00	—

KM# 26.1 10 PAISE

Nickel-Brass, 23 mm. **Obv:** Asoka lion pedestal **Rev:** Denomination and date **Note:** Type 1.

Date	Mintage	F	VF	XF	Unc	BU
1968(H)	55,940,000	—	30.00	50.00	80.00	—

KM# 26.2 10 PAISE

4.2400 g., Nickel-Brass, 23 mm. **Obv:** Asoka lion pedestal **Rev:** 6.5mm "10", date **Shape:** Scalloped **Note:** Type 2. Mintage included in KM26.1. Some, not all, have die damage in 9 of 1968.

Date	Mintage	F	VF	XF	Unc	BU
1968(B)	—	—	0.20	0.50	1.00	—
1968(C)	—	—	0.20	0.50	1.00	—
1968(H)	—	—	0.20	0.50	1.00	—

KM# 26.3 10 PAISE

4.1800 g., Nickel-Brass, 23 mm. **Obv:** Asoka lion pedestal **Rev:** Denomination and date, 7mm "10" **Shape:** Scalloped **Note:** Type 2.

Date	Mintage	F	VF	XF	Unc	BU
1969(B)	65,405,000	—	0.20	0.50	1.00	—
1969B Proof	9,147	Value: 1.50				
1969(C)	Inc. above	—	0.20	0.50	1.00	—
1969(H)	Inc. above	—	0.20	0.50	1.00	—
1970(B)	48,400,000	—	0.20	0.50	1.00	—
1970B Proof	3,046	Value: 1.50				
1970(C)	Inc. above	—	0.20	0.50	1.00	—
1971(B)	88,800,000	—	0.20	0.50	1.00	—
1971B Proof	4,375	Value: 1.30				

KM# 27.1 10 PAISE

2.3000 g., Aluminum, 26 mm. **Obv:** Asoka lion pedestal within beaded circle, wreath surrounds **Rev:** Denomination and date within beaded circle, wreath surrounds, 9mm "10" **Shape:** Scalloped **Note:** Type 2.

Date	Mintage	F	VF	XF	Unc	BU
1971(B)	146,100,000	—	0.20	0.50	1.00	—
1971(C)	Inc. above	—	0.20	0.50	1.00	—
1971(H)	Inc. above	—	0.50	1.00	2.00	—
1972(B)	735,090,000	—	0.20	0.35	1.00	—
1972B Proof	7,895	Value: 1.30				
1972(C)	Inc. above	—	0.20	0.50	1.00	—
1973(B)	—	—	0.20	0.50	1.00	—
1973B Proof	7,567	Value: 1.30				
1973(C)	—	—	0.20	0.50	1.00	—
1973(H)	—	—	0.20	0.50	1.00	—
1974(B)	—	—	0.20	0.50	1.00	—
1974(C)	—	—	0.20	0.50	1.00	—
1974(H)	—	—	2.00	3.00	5.00	—
1975(B)	—	—	1.00	2.00	3.00	—
1975(C)	298,830,000	—	1.00	2.00	3.00	—
1976(C)	Inc. above	—	2.00	3.00	5.00	—
1977(B)	25,288,000	—	1.00	2.00	3.00	—
1977(C)	Inc. above	—	0.25	0.50	1.00	—
1978(B)	48,215,000	—	0.15	0.30	1.00	—
1978(C)	Inc. above	—	0.15	0.30	1.00	—
1978(H)	Inc. above	—	0.15	0.30	1.00	—

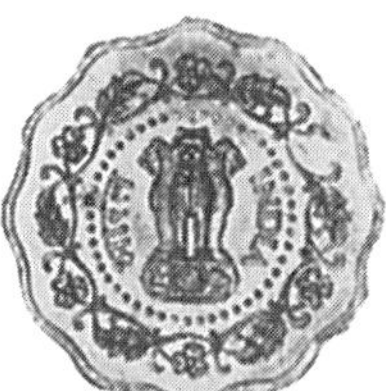

KM# 27.2 10 PAISE

Aluminum, 26 mm. **Obv:** Asoka lion pedestal within beaded circle, wreath surrounds **Rev:** Denomination and date within beaded circle, wreath surrounds, 8mm "10" **Shape:** Scalloped **Note:** Type 2.

Date	Mintage	F	VF	XF	Unc	BU
1979(B)	—	—	0.50	1.00	2.00	—
1979(C)	—	—	0.50	1.50	3.00	—
1979(H)	—	—	0.50	1.00	2.00	—
1980(C)	—	—	10.00	12.00	15.00	—

KM# 27.3 10 PAISE

2.3100 g., Aluminum, 26 mm. **Obv:** Asoka lion pedestal within beaded circle, wreath surrounds **Rev:** Denomination and date within beaded circle, wreath surrounds **Note:** Type 3.

Date	Mintage	F	VF	XF	Unc	BU
1980(B)	—	—	0.20	0.50	1.00	—
1980(C)	—	—	0.20	0.50	1.00	—
1980(H)	—	—	0.20	0.50	1.00	—
1981(B)	—	—	0.20	0.50	1.00	—
1981(C)	—	—	0.20	0.50	1.00	—
1982(C)	—	—	0.20	0.50	1.00	—
1982(H)	—	—	0.20	0.50	1.00	—

KM# 28 10 PAISE

Aluminum, 26 mm. **Series:** F.A.O. **Obv:** Asoka lion pedestal **Rev:** Family above date within triangle, grain sprigs flank **Shape:** Scalloped

Date	Mintage	F	VF	XF	Unc	BU
1974(B)	146,070,000	—	0.30	0.50	1.00	—
1974B Proof	—	Value: 1.00				

Date	Mintage	F	VF	XF	Unc	BU
1974(C)	168,500,000	—	0.50	1.00	2.00	—
1974(H)	10,010,000	—	3.00	4.00	6.00	—

KM# 29 10 PAISE

2.2800 g., Aluminum, 26 mm. **Series:** F.A.O. **Subject:** Women's Year **Obv:** Asoka lion pedestal **Rev:** Bust at left looking right, grain sprig at right **Shape:** Scalloped **Designer:** N. B. Sabannavar **Note:** Mint mark is below wheat stalk.

Date	Mintage	F	VF	XF	Unc	BU
1975(B)	69,160,000	—	0.30	0.50	1.00	—
1975B Proof	—	Value: 1.00				
1975(C)	84,820,000	—	0.30	0.60	1.00	—
1975(H)	—	—	0.30	0.60	1.00	—

KM# 30 10 PAISE

Aluminum, 26 mm. **Series:** F.A.O. **Subject:** Food and Work For All **Obv:** Asoka lion pedestal **Rev:** Figure on tractor, utility pole and buildings in background **Shape:** Scalloped

Date	Mintage	F	VF	XF	Unc	BU
1976(B)	36,040,000	—	1.00	1.50	2.00	—
1976B Proof	—	Value: 3.00				
1976(C)	26,180,000	—	2.00	3.00	5.00	—

KM# 31 10 PAISE

Aluminum, 26 mm. **Series:** F.A.O. **Subject:** Save For Development **Obv:** Asoka lion pedestal **Rev:** Symbols and date **Shape:** Scalloped

Date	Mintage	F	VF	XF	Unc	BU
1977(B)	17,040,000	—	0.25	0.50	1.00	—
1977B Proof	2,224	Value: 1.00				
1977(C)	8,020,000	—	2.00	3.00	5.00	—

KM# 32 10 PAISE

Aluminum, 26 mm. **Series:** F.A.O. **Subject:** Food and Shelter For All **Obv:** Asoka lion pedestal **Rev:** Building, grain sprig and road within circle **Shape:** Scalloped

Date	Mintage	F	VF	XF	Unc	BU
1978(B)	24,470,000	—	0.25	0.50	1.00	—
1978B Proof	—	Value: 1.00				
1978(C)	26,160,000	—	1.00	1.50	2.00	—
1978(H)	12,100,000	—	1.00	1.50	2.00	—

KM# 33 10 PAISE

2.2900 g., Aluminum, 26 mm. **Series:** International Year of the Child **Obv:** Asoka lion pedestal **Rev:** Logo on square within circle, wreath surrounds **Shape:** Scalloped

Date	Mintage	F	VF	XF	Unc	BU
1979(B)	39,270,000	—	0.25	0.50	1.00	—
1979B Proof	—	Value: 1.00				

Date	Mintage	F	VF	XF	Unc	BU
1979(C)	61,700,000	—	0.50	1.00	2.50	—
1979(H)	2,250,000	—	0.60	1.00	2.50	—

KM# 34 10 PAISE

Aluminum, 26 mm. **Obv:** Asoka lion pedestal, denomination below **Rev:** Emblem on square, within circle, wreath surrounds, date below **Note:** Mule.

Date	Mintage	F	VF	XF	Unc	BU
1979(B)	—	—	5.00	7.50	10.00	—

KM# 35 10 PAISE

Aluminum, 26 mm. **Subject:** Rural Women's Advancement **Obv:** Asoka lion pedestal **Rev:** Woman grinding wheat within circle **Shape:** Scalloped

Date	Mintage	F	VF	XF	Unc	BU
1980(B)	38,080,000	—	0.25	0.40	1.00	—
1980B Proof	—	Value: 1.00				
1980(C)	42,830,000	—	0.25	0.50	1.00	—
1980(H)	11,070,000	—	0.50	1.00	1.50	—

KM# 36 10 PAISE

2.3000 g., Aluminum, 26 mm. **Subject:** World Food Day **Obv:** Asoka lion pedestal **Rev:** Man and woman, man carrying sheaf **Shape:** Scalloped

Date	Mintage	F	VF	XF	Unc	BU
1981(B)	83,280,000	—	0.25	0.40	1.00	—
1981B Proof	—	Value: 1.00				
1981(C)	33,930,000	—	0.25	0.50	1.00	—

KM# 37 10 PAISE

2.3000 g., Aluminum, 26 mm. **Subject:** IX Asian Games **Obv:** Asoka lion pedestal **Rev:** Sun above symbol **Shape:** Scalloped

Date	Mintage	F	VF	XF	Unc	BU
1982(B)	—	—	0.25	0.45	0.75	—
1982B Proof	—	Value: 1.00				
1982(C)	30,560,000	—	0.25	0.45	0.75	—
1982(H)	17,080,000	—	0.25	0.50	1.00	—

KM# 38 10 PAISE

2.3000 g., Aluminum, 26 mm. **Subject:** World Food Day **Obv:** Asoka lion pedestal **Rev:** Grain sprig within stylized sun design **Shape:** Scalloped

Date	Mintage	F	VF	XF	Unc	BU
1982(B)	—	—	—	—	—	—
1982(C)	2,970,000	—	2.50	3.50	5.00	—
1982(H)	11,690,000	—	0.50	1.00	2.00	—

KM# 39 10 PAISE

2.3000 g., Aluminum, 26 mm. **Obv:** Asoka lion pedestal **Rev:** Denomination and date **Shape:** Scalloped

Date	Mintage	F	VF	XF	Unc	BU
1983(B)	—	—	0.10	0.25	0.50	—
1983(C)	—	—	0.10	0.25	0.50	—

Date	Mintage	F	VF	XF	Unc	BU
1983(H)	—	—	0.10	0.25	0.50	—
1984(B)	112,050,000	—	0.10	0.25	0.50	—
1984(C)	Inc. above	—	0.25	0.50	1.00	—
1984(H)	Inc. above	—	0.10	0.25	0.50	—
1985(B)	184,655,000	—	0.20	0.30	0.50	—
1985(C)	Inc. above	—	0.20	0.30	0.50	—
1985(H)	Inc. above	—	0.20	0.30	0.50	—
1986(B)	298,525,000	—	0.10	0.15	0.30	—
1986(C)	Inc. above	—	0.20	0.30	0.50	—
1986(H)	Inc. above	—	0.50	1.00	1.50	—
1987(C)	299,460,000	—	0.15	0.25	0.45	—
1987(H)	Inc. above	—	0.15	0.25	0.45	—
1988(B)	264,510,000	—	0.10	0.15	0.30	—
1988(C)	Inc. above	—	0.10	0.15	0.30	—
1988(H)	Inc. above	—	1.00	1.50	2.00	—
1989(B)	—	—	0.15	0.25	0.45	—
1989(C)	—	—	0.15	0.25	0.45	—
1989(H)	—	—	0.15	0.25	0.45	—
1990(B)	—	—	0.50	0.75	1.25	—
1991(B)	—	—	0.15	0.25	0.45	—
1991(C)	—	—	0.15	0.25	0.45	—
1991(H)	—	—	0.15	0.25	0.45	—
1993(C)	—	—	0.15	0.30	0.60	—
1993(H)	—	—	0.30	0.50	0.75	—

KM# 40.1 10 PAISE

2.0000 g., Stainless Steel, 16 mm. **Obv:** Asoka lion pedestal **Obv. Legend:** BHARAT **Rev:** Denomination and date

Date	Mintage	F	VF	XF	Unc	BU
1988C	183,040,000	—	0.10	0.15	0.25	—
1988(B)	4,040,000	—	0.25	0.40	0.75	—
1988(C)	—	—	5.00	7.00	10.00	—
1988(H)	Inc. above	—	3.00	5.00	8.00	—
1988	—	—	0.15	0.25	0.40	—
1989(B)	—	—	0.60	1.00	1.50	—
1989(C)	—	—	0.40	0.70	1.00	—
1989(H)	—	—	0.20	0.30	0.50	—
1989	—	—	0.25	0.40	0.75	—
1990(B)	—	—	0.15	0.30	0.50	—
1990(C)	—	—	0.40	0.70	1.00	—
1990(H)	—	—	0.20	0.30	0.50	—
1990 Small mm	—	—	0.15	0.30	0.50	—
1990 Large mm	—	—	1.25	1.75	2.50	—
1991(C)	—	—	0.15	0.30	0.50	—
1991(H)	—	—	0.15	0.30	0.50	—
1991	—	—	0.15	0.30	0.50	—
1992(B)	—	—	1.00	1.50	2.50	—
1992	—	—	0.30	0.60	1.00	—
1993(H)	—	—	0.15	0.30	0.50	—
1996(B)	—	—	1.50	2.50	5.00	—
1996(C)	—	—	0.15	0.30	0.50	—
1996	—	—	0.15	0.30	0.50	—
1997(B)	—	—	1.50	2.50	5.00	—
1997(C)	—	—	0.15	0.30	0.50	—
1997(H)	—	—	0.20	0.30	0.50	—
1998(B)	—	—	0.25	0.40	0.70	—
1998(C)	—	—	0.25	0.40	0.70	—

KM# 40.2 10 PAISE

2.0300 g., Stainless Steel, 15.95 mm. **Obv:** Error: MARAT for BHARAT **Rev:** Denomination and date **Edge:** Plain

Date	Mintage	F	VF	XF	Unc	BU
1988C	—	—	1.25	2.00	3.00	—
1989C	—	—	7.00	10.00	15.00	—

KM# 41 20 PAISE

Nickel-Brass **Obv:** Asoka lion pedestal **Rev:** Lotus blossom **Note:** Varieties of high and low date exist.

Date	Mintage	F	VF	XF	Unc	BU
1968(B)	10,585,000	—	0.50	1.00	1.50	—
1968(C)	Inc. above	—	0.50	1.00	1.50	—
1969(B)	197,940,000	—	0.40	0.85	1.50	—
1969(C)	—	—	0.40	0.85	1.50	—
1970(B)	Inc. above	—	0.30	0.60	1.00	—
1970(C)	Inc. above	—	0.30	0.60	1.00	—
1970(H)	Inc. above	—	0.30	0.60	1.00	—
1971(B)	124,200,000	—	0.30	0.60	1.00	—

KM# 42.1 20 PAISE

4.4500 g., Aluminum-Bronze **Subject:** Centennial - Birth of Mahatma Gandhi **Obv:** Asoka lion pedestal **Obv. Legend:** .7-.9 from rims **Rev:** Head left

Date	Mintage	F	VF	XF	Unc	BU
ND(1969)(B)	45,010	—	0.40	0.65	1.00	—
ND(1969)B Proof	9,147	Value: 2.00				
ND(1969)(C)	45,070,000	—	0.50	0.80	1.50	—
ND(1969)(H)	3,000,000	—	0.75	1.50	2.50	—

KM# 42.2 20 PAISE

Aluminum-Bronze **Obv:** Asoka lion pedestal **Obv. Legend:** 1.2mm from rim **Rev:** Head left

Date	Mintage	F	VF	XF	Unc	BU
ND(1969)(B)	—	—	2.00	3.00	5.00	—
ND(1969)(C)	—	—	3.00	5.00	8.00	—

KM# 42.3 20 PAISE

Aluminum-Bronze **Obv:** Asoka lion pedestal **Rev:** Head left **Note:** Eyes, mustache recut, legends 1.2mm from rim.

Date	Mintage	F	VF	XF	Unc	BU
ND(1969)(B)	—	—	0.60	1.00	1.50	—

Note: The KM 42 subtypes were struck during 1969 and 1970

KM# 43.1 20 PAISE

Aluminum-Bronze **Series:** F.A.O. **Subject:** Food For All **Obv:** Asoka lion pedestal **Rev:** Sun above floating lotus **Note:** Wide rims.

Date	Mintage	F	VF	XF	Unc	BU
1970(B)	5,160,000	—	0.75	1.25	2.00	—
1970B Proof	3,046	Value: 2.00				
1970(C)	5,010,000	—	0.75	1.25	2.00	—

KM# 43.2 20 PAISE

Aluminum-Bronze **Obv:** Asoka lion pedestal **Rev:** Sun above floating lotus **Note:** Narrow rims.

Date	Mintage	F	VF	XF	Unc	BU
1971(B)	60,000	—	0.70	0.90	1.25	—
1971B Proof	4,375	Value: 2.00				

KM# 44 20 PAISE

2.1500 g., Aluminum, 26 mm. **Obv:** Asoka lion pedestal **Rev:** Denomination and date within decorative wreath **Shape:** 6-sided

Date	Mintage	F	VF	XF	Unc	BU
1982(B)	—	—	0.25	0.40	1.00	—
1982(H)	—	—	0.25	0.40	1.00	—
1982(H) Without mm	—	—	0.25	0.40	1.00	—
1983(C)	28,505,000	—	0.25	0.40	1.00	—
1983(H)	Inc. above	—	0.25	0.40	1.00	—
1984(B)	—	—	0.25	0.40	1.00	—
1984(C)	Inc. above	—	0.25	0.40	1.00	—
1984(H)	Inc. above	—	0.25	0.40	1.00	—
1985(B)	84,495,000	—	0.25	0.40	1.00	—
1985(C)	Inc. above	—	0.25	0.40	1.00	—
1985(H)	Inc. above	—	0.25	0.40	1.00	—
1986(B)	155,610,000	—	0.25	0.40	0.75	—
1986(C)	Inc. above	—	0.15	0.30	0.75	—
1986(H)	Inc. above	—	0.15	0.30	0.75	—
1987(C)	—	—	0.15	0.30	0.75	—
1987(H)	153,073,000	—	0.15	0.30	0.75	—
1988(B)	125,048,000	—	0.15	0.30	0.75	—
1988(C)	Inc. above	—	0.15	0.30	0.75	—
1988(H)	Inc. above	—	0.35	0.60	1.00	—
1989(C)	—	—	0.35	0.60	1.00	—
1989(H)	—	—	0.15	0.25	0.75	—
1990(C)	—	—	0.35	0.60	1.00	—
1990(H)	—	—	0.15	0.25	0.75	—
1991(C)	—	—	0.15	0.25	0.75	—
1991(H)	—	—	0.15	0.25	0.75	—
1992(H)	—	—	0.15	0.25	0.75	—
1994(H)	—	—	0.15	0.25	0.75	—
1996(H)	—	—	1.00	2.00	4.00	—
1997(H)	—	—	3.00	5.00	10.00	—

KM# 45 20 PAISE

Aluminum **Series:** F.A.O. **Obv:** Asoka lion pedestal **Rev:** Grain sprig within stylized sun design **Shape:** 6-sided

Date	Mintage	F	VF	XF	Unc	BU
1982(C)	—	—	2.00	3.25	5.00	—
1982(H)	—	—	1.00	1.50	2.50	—

KM# 46 20 PAISE

2.1500 g., Aluminum, 26 mm. **Series:** F.A.O. **Subject:** Fisheries **Obv:** Asoka lion pedestal **Rev:** People with fishing nets **Shape:** 6-sided

Date	Mintage	F	VF	XF	Unc	BU
1983(C)	—	—	1.00	1.50	2.50	—
Note: Mintage included in KM44						
1983(H)	—	—	1.00	1.50	2.50	—
Note: Mintage included in KM44						

KM# 47.1 25 NAYE PAISE

2.4200 g., Nickel **Obv:** Asoka lion pedestal **Rev:** Denomination and date

Date	Mintage	F	VF	XF	Unc	BU
1957(B)	5,640,000	—	0.75	1.25	2.00	—
1957(C)	Inc. above	—	0.75	1.25	2.00	—
1959(B)	43,080,000	—	0.45	0.75	1.25	—
1959(C)	Inc. above	—	0.45	0.75	1.25	—
1960(B)	115,320,000	—	0.30	0.60	1.00	—
1960(B) Proof	—	Value: 2.00				
1960(C)	Inc. above	—	0.30	0.60	1.00	—

KM# 47.2 25 NAYE PAISE

2.5000 g., Nickel, 19 mm. **Obv:** Asoka lion pedestal **Rev:** Denomination and date, large 25

Date	Mintage	F	VF	XF	Unc	BU
1961(B)	109,008,000	—	0.30	0.60	1.00	—
1961(B) Proof	—	Value: 2.00				
1961(C)	Inc. above	—	0.30	0.60	1.00	—
1962(B)	79,242,000	—	0.30	0.60	1.00	—
1962(B) Proof	—	Value: 2.00				
1962(C)	Inc. above	—	0.30	0.60	1.00	—
1963(B)	101,565,000	—	0.30	0.60	1.00	—
1963(B) Proof	—	Value: 2.00				
1963(C)	Inc. above	—	0.30	0.60	1.00	—

KM# 48.1 25 PAISE

Nickel, 19 mm. **Obv:** Asoka lion pedestal **Rev:** Denomination and date **Note:** Type 1.

Date	Mintage	F	VF	XF	Unc	BU
1964(B)	85,321,000	—	0.30	0.60	1.25	—
1964(C)	Inc. above	—	0.30	0.60	1.25	—

KM# 48.2 25 PAISE

2.5500 g., Nickel, 19 mm. **Obv:** Asoka lion pedestal **Rev:** Smaller date and denomination **Note:** Type 1.

Date	Mintage	F	VF	XF	Unc	BU
1965(B)	143,662,000	—	0.30	0.60	1.00	—
1965(C)	Inc. above	—	0.30	0.60	1.00	—
1966(B)	59,040,000	—	0.30	0.60	1.00	—
1966(C)	Inc. above	—	0.30	0.60	1.00	—
1967(B)	30,027,000	—	4.50	6.00	8.00	—

KM# 48.3 25 PAISE

Nickel, 19 mm. **Obv:** Asoka lion pedestal **Rev:** Denomination and date **Note:** Type 2. Mintage included in KM48.2.

Date	Mintage	F	VF	XF	Unc	BU
1967(C)	—	—	0.30	0.70	1.50	—
1968(C)	—	—	1.50	2.25	3.50	—

KM# 48.4 25 PAISE

Nickel, 19 mm. **Obv:** Asoka lion pedestal **Rev:** Denomination and date **Note:** Type 1, lion without whiskers. Mule = Obv. of KM#48.2; Rev. of KM#49.1. Prev. KM#49.7.

Date	Mintage	F	VF	XF	Unc	BU
1972(B)	—	—	8.00	14.00	20.00	—

KM# 49.1 25 PAISE

2.5000 g., Copper-Nickel, 19 mm. **Obv:** Asoka lion pedestal **Rev:** Denomination and date **Note:** Type 1, but with lion with whiskers and faces and wheel redesigned. 1984-86 have edges rounded (local blanks) or flat (Korean blanks).

Date	Mintage	F	VF	XF	Unc	BU
1972B Proof	7,895	Value: 1.00				
1972(B)	367,640,000	—	0.20	0.40	0.70	—
1972(H)	Inc. above	—	0.45	1.00	2.00	—
1973(B)	—	—	0.20	0.40	0.70	—
1973B Proof	7,567	Value: 1.00				
1973(H)	—	—	0.35	0.60	1.00	—
1974(B)	—	—	0.20	0.40	0.70	—
1974B Proof	—	Value: 1.00				
1974(H)	—	—	0.45	0.75	1.25	—
1975(B)	559,980,000	—	0.20	0.40	0.70	—
1975B Proof	—	Value: 1.00				
1975(H)	Inc. above	—	3.00	4.00	5.00	—
1976(B)	30,016,000	—	0.60	1.00	1.50	—
1976B Proof	Inc. above	Value: 1.00				
1976(H)	Inc. above	—	0.60	1.00	1.50	—
1977(B)	270,520,000	—	0.20	0.40	0.70	—
1977(C)	Inc. above	—	0.35	0.60	1.00	—
1977(H)	Inc. above	—	0.35	0.60	1.00	—
1978B Proof	—	Value: 1.00				
1978(C)	131,632,000	—	0.25	0.40	0.70	—
1978(H)	—	—	0.25	0.40	0.70	—
1979(C)	—	—	0.50	1.00	1.50	—
1979(H)	—	—	0.50	1.00	1.50	—
1980(C)	6,175,000	—	0.25	0.40	0.70	—
1980(H)	Inc. above	—	0.25	0.40	0.70	—
1981(B)	11,048,000	—	0.25	0.40	0.70	—
1981(C)	Inc. above	—	1.50	2.00	2.50	—
1981(H)	Inc. above	—	0.45	0.75	1.25	—
1982(C)	38,288,000	—	0.45	0.75	1.25	—
1983(C)	137,488,000	—	0.45	0.75	1.25	—
1984(B)	98,740,000	—	0.45	0.75	1.25	—
1984(C)	Inc. above	—	0.45	0.75	1.25	—
1985(B)	113,872,000	—	0.45	0.75	1.25	—
1985C	Inc. above	—	0.15	0.25	0.50	—
1985(C)	Inc. above	—	0.45	0.75	1.25	—
1985(H)	Inc. above	—	0.45	0.75	1.25	—
1986(B)	362,624,000	—	0.60	0.90	1.50	—
1986(C)	Inc. above	—	0.60	0.90	1.50	—
1986(H)	Inc. above	—	0.60	0.90	1.50	—
1987(C)	341,160,000	—	0.60	0.90	1.50	—
1987(H)	Inc. above	—	0.60	0.90	1.50	—
1988(H)	303,252,000	—	0.60	0.90	1.50	—

KM# 49.2 25 PAISE

Copper-Nickel, 19 mm. **Obv:** Asoka lion pedestal **Rev:** Denomination and date **Note:** Type 2, 9mm between lions' nose tips, 15mm across field.

Date	Mintage	F	VF	XF	Unc	BU
1972(C)	—	—	0.35	0.60	1.00	—
1977(B)	—	—	0.35	0.60	1.00	—

Note: Mintage included in KM49.1

Date	Mintage	F	VF	XF	Unc	BU
1977B Proof	—	Value: 1.50				

Note: Mintage included in KM49.1

Date	Mintage	F	VF	XF	Unc	BU
1978(B)	—	—	3.25	5.00	7.00	—

Note: Mintage included in KM49.1

Date	Mintage	F	VF	XF	Unc	BU
1979B Proof	—	Value: 1.50				

KM# 49.3 25 PAISE

2.4000 g., Copper-Nickel, 19 mm. **Obv:** Asoka lion pedestal **Rev:** Denomination and date **Note:** Type 2, 10mm between lion nosetips, 16-16.3mm across field. Bull has three legs.

Date	Mintage	F	VF	XF	Unc	BU
1972(C)	—	—	2.50	3.50	5.00	—

Note: Mintage included in KM49.1

Date	Mintage	F	VF	XF	Unc	BU
1973(C)	—	—	0.85	1.25	2.00	—
1974(C)	—	—	0.85	1.25	2.00	—

KM# 49.4 25 PAISE

Copper-Nickel, 19 mm. **Obv:** Asoka lion pedestal **Rev:** Denomination and date **Note:** Type 1, central lion with bull and horse re-engraved.

Date	Mintage	F	VF	XF	Unc	BU
1974(B)	—	—	2.00	5.00	6.50	—
1975(B)	—	—	5.00	7.00	12.00	—
1975(H)	—	—	1.00	3.00	5.00	—
1976(H)	—	—	6.00	8.00	15.00	—
1977(B)	—	—	2.00	4.00	8.00	—
1978(B)	—	—	2.00	3.00	5.00	—
1979(B)	—	—	2.50	5.00	7.00	—
1981(B)	—	—	4.00	6.00	8.00	—

KM# 49.5 25 PAISE

2.5000 g., Copper-Nickel, 19 mm. **Obv:** Asoka lion pedestal **Rev:** Denomination and date **Note:** Type 3.

Date	Mintage	F	VF	XF	Unc	BU
1986(B)	—	—	0.15	0.30	1.00	—
1986(C)	—	—	0.45	0.75	1.25	—
1986(H)	—	—	0.45	0.75	1.25	—
1987(B)	—	—	0.15	0.30	1.00	—
1987(C)	—	—	0.25	0.40	1.50	—
1987(C) Long 7	—	—	0.25	0.40	1.50	—
1988(B)	—	—	0.20	0.35	1.25	—
1988(C) 8's 1.3mm tall	—	—	0.45	0.75	2.00	—
1988(C) 8's 1.8mm tall	—	—	0.45	0.75	2.00	—
1988(H)	—	—	0.45	1.00	1.75	—
1989(B)	—	—	0.45	1.00	1.75	—
1989(C)	—	—	2.00	2.50	3.00	—
1990(C)	—	—	2.00	3.50	7.00	—
1990(B)	—	—	2.00	3.50	7.00	—

KM# 49.6 25 PAISE

2.6100 g., Copper-Nickel, 19 mm. **Obv:** Asoka lion pedestal **Rev:** Denomination and date **Note:** 9-1/2mm between lions' nose tips. Bull has four legs. Type 2.

Date	Mintage	F	VF	XF	Unc	BU
1974(C)	—	—	0.85	1.25	2.00	—
1975(C)	—	—	0.85	1.25	2.00	—
1976(C)	—	—	2.00	3.50	5.00	—

KM# 49.7 25 PAISE

Nickel **Obv:** KM#48.2. **Rev:** KM#49.1. **Note:** Mule. Type 1, lion without whiskers.

Date	Mintage	F	VF	XF	Unc	BU
1972(B)	—	—	8.00	12.00	18.00	—

KM# 50 25 PAISE

Copper-Nickel, 19 mm. **Subject:** Rural Women's Advancement **Obv:** Asoka lion pedestal **Rev:** Woman grinding wheat

Date	Mintage	F	VF	XF	Unc	BU
1980(B)	15,050,000	—	0.30	0.50	1.00	—
1980B Proof	—	Value: 1.00				
1980(C)	8,520,000	—	0.50	1.00	1.50	—
1980(H)	10,380,000	—	1.00	1.50	2.00	—

KM# 51 25 PAISE

Copper-Nickel, 19 mm. **Subject:** World Food Day **Obv:** Asoka lion pedestal **Rev:** Man and woman, man carrying sheaf

Date	Mintage	F	VF	XF	Unc	BU
1981(B)	2,170,000	—	1.00	1.50	2.00	—
1981B Proof	—	Value: 2.00				
1981(C)	4,500,000	—	1.00	1.50	2.00	—
1981(H)	9,340,000	—	1.50	2.00	3.00	—

KM# 52 25 PAISE

Copper-Nickel, 19 mm. **Subject:** IX Asian Games **Obv:** Asoka lion pedestal **Rev:** Sun above symbol

Date	Mintage	F	VF	XF	Unc	BU
1982(B)	12,000,000	—	0.30	0.50	1.00	—
1982B Proof	—	Value: 1.00				
1982(C)	12,000,000	—	0.30	0.50	1.00	—
1982(H)	330,000	—	2.50	3.50	5.00	—

KM# 53 25 PAISE

2.5000 g., Copper-Nickel, 19 mm. **Subject:** Forestry **Obv:** Asoka lion pedestal **Rev:** Central tree divides squatting figure and stag **Edge:** Rounded

Date	Mintage	F	VF	XF	Unc	BU
1985(B)	—	—	1.50	2.00	2.75	—

Note: Mintage included in KM49.1. 1985 (B) have rounded or flat edge

Date	Mintage	F	VF	XF	Unc	BU
1985(C)	—	—	3.00	5.00	7.00	—
1985(H)	—	—	5.00	7.00	10.00	—

Note: Mintage included in KM49.1

KM# 54 25 PAISE

2.8200 g., Stainless Steel, 19 mm. **Obv:** Small Asoka lion pedestal **Rev:** Rhinoceros left **Edge:** Plain **Note:** Varieties of date size exist.

Date	Mintage	F	VF	XF	Unc	BU
1988C	305,280,000	—	0.10	0.20	1.00	—
1988(B)	—	—	0.45	0.75	1.25	—
1988(C)	18,920,000	—	3.50	5.00	8.00	—
1988(H)	—	—	6.00	8.00	10.00	—
1988	Inc. above	—	0.45	0.75	1.25	—
1989(B)	—	—	0.65	1.00	1.50	—
1989(C) fine grass below rhino	—	—	0.65	1.00	1.50	—
1989(C) bold grass below rhino	—	—	0.65	1.00	1.50	—
1989(H)	—	—	1.00	2.00	3.00	—
1989	—	—	0.15	0.30	1.00	—
1990(B)	—	—	0.25	0.50	1.00	—
1990(C)	—	—	0.25	0.50	1.00	—
1990(H)	—	—	0.25	0.40	1.00	—
1990 Small mm	—	—	0.40	0.65	1.00	—
1991(B)	—	—	0.25	0.40	1.00	—
1991(C)	—	—	0.25	0.40	1.00	—
1991(H)	—	—	0.25	0.40	1.00	—
1991	—	—	0.25	0.40	1.00	—
1992(B)	—	—	0.25	0.40	1.00	—
1992(C)	—	—	1.00	2.00	3.00	—
1992(H)	—	—	1.00	2.00	3.00	—
1992	—	—	0.50	1.00	2.00	—
1993(B)	—	—	0.50	1.00	2.00	—
1993(C)	—	—	0.50	1.00	2.00	—
1993(H)	—	—	2.00	3.00	5.00	—
1993	—	—	0.50	0.70	1.00	—
1994(B)	—	—	0.15	0.30	1.00	—
1994(C)	—	—	0.10	0.20	1.00	—
1994(H)	—	—	0.10	0.20	1.00	—
1994	—	—	0.10	0.20	1.00	—
1995(B)	—	—	0.10	0.20	1.00	—
1995(C)	—	—	0.25	0.50	1.00	—
1995(H)	—	—	0.10	0.20	1.00	—
1995	—	—	0.10	0.20	1.00	—
1996(B)	—	—	0.10	0.20	1.00	—
1996(C)	—	—	0.10	0.20	1.00	—
1996(H)	—	—	0.10	0.20	1.00	—
1996	—	—	0.10	0.20	1.00	—
1997(B)	—	—	0.10	0.20	1.00	—
1997(C)	—	—	0.10	0.20	1.00	—
1997(H)	—	—	0.50	1.00	2.00	—
1997	—	—	0.10	0.20	1.00	—
1998(B)	—	—	0.10	0.20	1.00	—
1998(C)	—	—	0.10	0.20	1.00	—
1998(H)	—	—	0.10	0.20	1.00	—
1998	—	—	0.10	0.20	1.00	—
1999(B)	—	—	0.10	0.20	1.00	—
1999(C)	—	—	0.10	0.20	1.00	—
1999(H)	—	—	0.10	0.20	1.00	—
1999	—	—	0.10	0.20	1.00	—
2000(B)	—	—	0.10	0.20	1.00	—
2000(C)	—	—	0.10	0.20	1.00	—
2000(H)	—	—	0.10	0.20	1.00	—
2000	—	—	0.10	0.20	1.00	—
2001(B)	—	—	0.10	0.20	1.00	—
2001(C)	—	—	0.10	0.20	1.00	—
2001(H)	—	—	0.15	0.25	1.00	—
2002(B)	—	—	0.15	0.25	1.00	—
2002(C)	—	—	0.15	0.25	1.00	—
2002(H)	—	—	0.25	0.40	1.00	—

KM# 55 50 NAYE PAISE

5.0000 g., Nickel, 24 mm. **Obv:** Asoka lion pedestal **Rev:** Denomination and date

Date	Mintage	F	VF	XF	Unc	BU
1960(B)	11,224,000	—	1.00	1.50	2.50	—
1960(B) Proof	—	Value: 3.00				
1960(C)	Inc. above	—	0.50	1.25	2.00	—
1961(B)	45,992,000	—	0.25	0.60	1.25	—
1961(B) Proof	—	Value: 3.00				
1961(C)	Inc. above	—	0.25	0.60	1.25	—
1962(B)	64,227,999	—	0.25	0.60	1.25	—
1962(B) Proof	—	Value: 3.00				
1962(C)	Inc. above	—	0.25	0.60	1.25	—
1963(B)	58,168,000	—	0.25	0.60	1.25	—
1963(B) Proof	—	Value: 3.00				
1963(C)	Inc. above	—	1.00	1.50	2.50	—

KM# 56 50 PAISE

Nickel **Subject:** Death of Jawaharlal Nehru **Obv:** Asoka lion pedestal **Rev:** Head left **Rev. Legend:** English **Note:** Struck from 1964 until 1967.

Date	Mintage	F	VF	XF	Unc	BU
ND(1964)(B)	21,900,000	—	0.40	0.65	1.00	—
ND(1964)B Proof	—	Value: 2.50				
ND(1964)(C)	7,160,000	—	0.75	1.50	2.75	—

KM# 57 50 PAISE

Nickel **Subject:** Death of Jawaharlal Nehru **Obv:** Asoka lion pedestal **Rev:** Head left **Rev. Legend:** Hindi **Note:** Struck from 1964 until 1967.

Date	Mintage	F	VF	XF	Unc	BU
ND(1964)(B)	36,190,000	—	0.40	0.65	1.00	—
ND(1964)(C)	28,350,000	—	0.40	0.65	1.00	—

KM# 58.1 50 PAISE

Nickel **Obv:** Asoka lion pedestal **Rev:** 7mm "50", date **Note:** Type 1.

Date	Mintage	F	VF	XF	Unc	BU
1964(C)	23,361,000	—	0.50	1.00	1.75	—
1967(B)	19,267,000	—	0.50	1.00	1.75	—

Note: Varieties of 1967(B) reverse edges exist, half teeth and the scarce full teeth

KM# 58.2 50 PAISE

5.0500 g., Nickel, 24.03 mm. **Obv:** Asoka lion pedestal **Rev:** 6.5mm "50", date **Note:** Type 2.

Date	Mintage	F	VF	XF	Unc	BU
1967(C)	—	—	0.60	1.00	1.50	—
1968(B)	28,076,000	—	0.25	0.60	1.00	—

Note: A scarce 1968(B) variety exists with crude obverse, no whiskers, thick horsetail

Date	Mintage	F	VF	XF	Unc	BU
1968(C)	Inc. above	—	0.25	0.60	1.00	—
1969(B)	59,388,000	—	0.25	0.60	1.00	—
1969(C)	Inc. above	—	0.35	0.75	1.25	—
1970(B)	Inc. above	—	0.35	0.75	1.25	—
1970(C)	Inc. above	—	0.25	0.60	1.00	—
1971(C)	57,900,000	—	0.25	0.50	0.85	—

KM# 58.3 50 PAISE

Nickel **Obv:** Asoka lion pedestal **Rev:** 6.5mm "50", date **Note:** Type 1.

Date	Mintage	F	VF	XF	Unc	BU
1970(B)	—	—	1.00	2.00	3.00	—

Note: Mintage included with 1969

Date	Mintage	F	VF	XF	Unc	BU
1970B Proof	3,046	Value: 2.00				
1971B Proof	4,375	Value: 2.00				

KM# 59 50 PAISE

5.0300 g., Nickel, 24 mm. **Subject:** Centennial - Birth of Mahatma Gandhi **Obv:** Asoka lion pedestal **Rev:** Head left **Note:** Struck during 1969 and 1970.

Date	Mintage	F	VF	XF	Unc	BU
ND(1969)(B)	10,260,000	—	0.25	0.50	1.00	—
ND(1969)B Proof	9,147	Value: 2.00				
ND(1969)(C)	12,100,000	—	0.25	0.50	1.00	—

KM# 61 50 PAISE

4.9500 g., Copper-Nickel, 24 mm. **Obv:** Asoka lion pedestal **Rev:** Denomination above date, lettering spaced out **Note:** Type 2. Wide and narrow security edge varieties exist.

Date	Mintage	F	VF	XF	Unc	BU
1972(C)	—	—	0.35	0.60	1.00	—
1972(B)	—	—	0.35	0.60	1.00	—
1973(B)	—	—	0.35	0.60	1.00	—
1973(C)	—	—	2.00	3.50	6.00	—

KM# 60 50 PAISE

Copper-Nickel, 24 mm. **Subject:** 25th Anniversary of Independence **Obv:** Asoka lion pedestal **Rev:** Figures with flag, building in background **Designer:** P. B. Chitnis

Date	Mintage	F	VF	XF	Unc	BU
ND(1972)(B)	43,800,000	—	0.30	0.50	1.00	—
ND(1972)B Proof	7,895	Value: 2.00				
ND(1972)(C)	40,080,000	—	0.45	0.75	1.50	—

KM# 62 50 PAISE

Copper-Nickel, 24 mm. **Series:** F.A.O. **Subject:** Grow More Food **Obv:** Asoka lion pedestal **Rev:** Inscription on shield within grain sprigs

Date	Mintage	F	VF	XF	Unc	BU
1973(B)	28,720,000	—	0.30	0.50	1.00	—
1973B Proof	11,000	Value: 2.00				
1973(C)	40,100,000	—	0.30	0.50	1.00	—

KM# 63 50 PAISE

4.9700 g., Copper-Nickel, 24 mm. **Obv:** Asoka lion pedestal **Rev:** Denomination above date, lettering close **Note:** Type 2.

Date	Mintage	F	VF	XF	Unc	BU
1974(B)	—	—	0.25	0.50	1.00	—
1974B Proof	—	Value: 2.00				
1974(C)	—	—	0.35	0.75	1.50	—
1975(B)	225,880,000	—	0.25	0.50	1.00	—
1975B Proof	—	Value: 2.00				
1975(C)	Inc. above	—	0.25	0.50	1.00	—
1975(H)	—	—	0.75	1.25	2.00	—
1976(B)	99,564,000	—	0.25	0.50	1.00	—
1976B Proof	Inc. above	Value: 2.00				
1976(C)	Inc. above	—	0.35	0.75	1.50	—
1976(H)	Inc. above	—	0.75	1.25	2.00	—
1977(B)	97,272,000	—	0.25	0.50	1.00	—
1977B Proof	Inc. above	Value: 2.00				
1977(C)	Inc. above	—	0.40	0.75	1.50	—
1977(H)	Inc. above	—	0.40	0.75	1.50	—
1978B Proof	25,648,000	Value: 2.00				
1978(C)	—	—	0.25	0.50	1.00	—
1979B Proof	—	Value: 2.00				
1980(B)	—	—	0.25	0.50	1.00	—
1980B Proof	—	Value: 2.00				
1980(C)	—	—	5.00	8.00	12.00	—
1981B Proof	—	Value: 2.00				
1983(C)	62,634,000	—	5.00	8.00	12.00	—

KM# 64 50 PAISE

Copper-Nickel, 24 mm. **Subject:** National Integration **Obv:** Asoka lion pedestal **Rev:** Flag on map

Date	Mintage	F	VF	XF	Unc	BU
1982(B)	9,804,000	—	0.40	0.75	1.25	—
1982B Proof	—	Value: 3.00				
1982(C)	Inc. above	—	10.00	15.00	20.00	—

KM# 65 50 PAISE

5.0900 g., Copper-Nickel, 24 mm. **Obv:** Asoka lion pedestal, ornaments surround **Rev:** Denomination and date, ornaments surround **Note:** Type 3.

Date	Mintage	F	VF	XF	Unc	BU
1984(B)	61,548,000	—	0.25	0.50	0.85	—
1984(C)	Inc. above	—	1.00	1.50	2.50	—
1984(H)	—	—	2.00	3.00	5.00	—
1985(B)	210,964,000	—	0.25	0.50	0.85	—
1985(C)	Inc. above	—	0.25	0.50	0.85	—
1985(H)	Inc. above	—	1.00	1.50	3.00	—
1985(T)	Inc. above	—	0.20	0.30	0.65	—
1986(C)	117,576,000	—	0.50	1.00	2.00	—
1987(B)	—	—	0.25	0.50	0.85	—
1987(C)	145,140,000	—	0.25	0.50	0.85	—
1987(H)	Inc. above	—	0.40	0.75	1.50	—
1988(B)	149,092,000	—	0.25	0.50	0.85	—
1988(C)	Inc. above	—	1.00	1.50	3.00	—
1988(H)	Inc. above	—	1.00	1.50	2.50	—
1989(B)	—	—	0.50	1.00	2.00	—
1989(C)	—	—	0.50	1.00	2.00	—
1990(B)	—	—	2.00	4.00	7.00	—

KM# 66 50 PAISE

Copper-Nickel, 24 mm. **Subject:** Golden Jubilee of Reserve Bank of India **Obv:** Asoka lion pedestal **Rev:** Lion beneath trees

Date	Mintage	F	VF	XF	Unc	BU
ND(1985)(B)	—	—	0.50	1.00	4.50	—

Note: Mintage included in KM65

Date	Mintage	F	VF	XF	Unc	BU
ND(1985)B Proof	—	Value: 15.00				

Note: Mintage included in KM#65

Date	Mintage	F	VF	XF	Unc	BU
ND(1985)(C)	—	—	2.00	3.00	6.00	—
ND(1985)(H)	—	—	0.75	1.25	4.00	—

Note: Mintage included in KM65

KM# 67.1 50 PAISE

Copper-Nickel, 24 mm. **Subject:** Death of Indira Gandhi - statesperson, 1917-1984 **Obv:** Asoka lion pedestal **Rev:** Head right

Date	Mintage	F	VF	XF	Unc	BU
ND(1985)(B)	—	—	0.20	0.40	1.00	—

Note: Mintage included in KM65

Date	Mintage	F	VF	XF	Unc	BU
ND(1985)B Proof	—	Value: 17.50				

Note: Mintage included in KM65

Date	Mintage	F	VF	XF	Unc	BU
ND(1985)(C)	—	—	0.20	0.40	1.00	—

Note: Mintage included in KM65

Date	Mintage	F	VF	XF	Unc	BU
ND(1985)(H)	—	—	0.65	1.00	1.50	—

Note: Mintage included in KM65

KM# 67.2 50 PAISE

Copper-Nickel, 24 mm. **Subject:** Death of Indira Gandhi, 1917-1984 statesperson **Obv:** Asoka lion pedestal **Rev:** Head right **Note:** Mule.

Date	Mintage	F	VF	XF	Unc	BU
ND(1985)(C)	—	—	35.00	50.00	80.00	—

KM# 68.1 50 PAISE

4.9700 g., Copper-Nickel, 24 mm. **Series:** F.A.O. **Subject:** Fisheries **Obv:** Asoka lion pedestal **Rev:** People with fishing nets

Date	Mintage	F	VF	XF	Unc	BU
1986B Proof	—	Value: 15.00				

Note: Mintage included in KM65

Date	Mintage	F	VF	XF	Unc	BU
1986(B)	—	—	0.30	0.50	1.00	—

Note: Mintage included in KM65

Date	Mintage	F	VF	XF	Unc	BU
1986(C)	—	—	2.00	3.00	5.00	—
1986(H)	—	—	2.00	3.00	5.00	—

Note: Mintage included in KM65

KM# 68.2 50 PAISE

Copper-Nickel, 24 mm. **Obv:** Asoka lion pedestal **Rev:** People with fishing nets **Note:** Mule.

Date	Mintage	F	VF	XF	Unc	BU
1986(C)	—	—	50.00	70.00	100	—

KM# 69 50 PAISE

3.8000 g., Stainless Steel, 22 mm. **Subject:** Parliament Building in New Delhi **Obv:** Denomination **Rev:** Building

Date	Mintage	F	VF	XF	Unc	BU
1988C	272,160,000	—	0.20	0.30	0.50	—
1988(B)	—	—	0.20	0.40	0.75	—
1988(C)	2,195,000	—	6.00	9.00	14.00	—
1988(H)	Inc. above	—	6.00	9.00	14.00	—
1988	—	—	0.20	0.40	0.75	—
1989(B)	—	—	0.20	0.40	0.75	—
1989(C)	—	—	1.50	3.00	5.00	—
1989(H)	—	—	0.50	1.00	2.00	—
1989	—	—	0.15	0.50	1.00	—
1990(B)	—	—	0.15	0.50	1.00	—
1990(C)	—	—	0.50	1.00	2.00	—
1990(H)	—	—	0.15	0.50	1.00	—
1990 Small mm	—	—	0.15	0.50	1.00	—
1990 Large mm	—	—	0.15	0.50	1.00	—
1991	—	—	0.10	0.35	0.60	—
1991(B)	—	—	0.15	0.50	1.00	—
1991(C)	—	—	0.15	0.50	1.00	—
1991(H)	—	—	0.15	0.25	0.50	—
1992(B)	—	—	0.10	0.35	0.60	—
1992(C)	—	—	0.50	1.00	2.00	—
1992(H)	—	—	0.10	0.35	0.60	—
1992	—	—	0.10	0.35	0.60	—
1993(C)	—	—	0.50	1.00	2.00	—
1993	—	—	0.10	0.35	0.60	—
1994(B)	—	—	0.10	0.35	0.60	—
1994(C)	—	—	0.50	1.00	2.00	—
1994(H)	—	—	0.10	0.35	0.60	—
1994	—	—	0.10	0.35	0.60	—
1995(B)	—	—	0.10	0.20	0.35	—
1995(C)	—	—	0.50	1.00	2.00	—
1995(H)	—	—	0.20	0.30	0.50	—
1995	—	—	0.10	0.20	0.35	—
1996(B)	—	—	0.10	0.20	0.35	—
1996(C)	—	—	0.10	0.20	0.35	—
1996(H)	—	—	0.10	0.20	0.35	—
1996	—	—	0.10	0.20	0.35	—
1997(B)	—	—	0.10	0.20	0.35	—
1997(C)	—	—	0.10	0.20	0.35	—
1997(H)	—	—	2.00	3.00	5.00	—
1997	—	—	0.10	0.20	0.35	—
1998(B)	—	—	0.10	0.20	0.35	—
1998(C)	—	—	0.10	0.20	0.35	—
1998(H)	—	—	1.00	1.50	3.00	—
1998	—	—	0.10	0.20	0.35	—
1999(B)	—	—	0.15	0.25	0.50	—
1999(C)	—	—	0.15	0.25	0.50	—
1999(H)	—	—	0.15	0.25	0.50	—
2000(B)	—	—	0.15	0.25	0.50	—
2000(C)	—	—	0.15	0.25	0.50	—
2000(H)	—	—	0.15	0.25	0.50	—
2001(B)	—	—	0.15	0.25	0.50	—
2001(C)	—	—	0.15	0.25	0.50	—
2001(H)	—	—	0.20	0.40	0.75	—
2001(N)	—	—	0.15	0.25	0.50	—
2002(B)	—	—	0.15	0.25	0.50	—
2002(C)	—	—	0.15	0.25	0.50	—
2002(H)	—	—	0.15	0.25	0.50	—
2002(N)	—	—	0.15	0.25	0.50	—
2003(B)	—	—	0.15	0.25	0.50	—
2003(N)	—	—	0.15	0.25	0.50	—
2003(C)	—	—	0.15	0.25	0.50	—

KM# 70 50 PAISE

Stainless Steel **Subject:** 50th Anniversary of Independence **Obv:** Small Asoka lion pedestal above denomination **Rev:** Line of people

Date	Mintage	F	VF	XF	Unc	BU
1997(B)	—	—	0.25	0.40	0.75	—
1997(C)	—	—	0.25	0.40	0.75	—
1997(H)	—	—	0.25	0.40	0.75	—
1997(M) Proof	—	Value: 15.00				
1997	—	—	0.25	0.40	0.75	—

KM# 75.1 RUPEE

10.0000 g., Nickel, 28 mm. **Obv:** Asoka lion pedestal **Rev:** Denomination and date, grain ears flank **Note:** Type 1.

Date	Mintage	F	VF	XF	Unc	BU
1962(B) Proof	—	—	—	—	—	—
1962(C)	3,689,000	—	1.00	2.00	3.00	—

KM# 75.2 RUPEE

10.0000 g., Nickel, 28 mm. **Obv:** Asoka lion pedestal **Rev:** Smaller date and denomination **Note:** Type 1.

Date	Mintage	F	VF	XF	Unc	BU
1970(B)	Inc. above	—	3.50	5.00	7.00	—
1970B Proof	3,046	Value: 3.00				
1971B Proof	4,375	Value: 3.00				
1972B Proof	7,895,000	Value: 2.50				
1973B Proof	7,567	Value: 2.50				
1974B Proof	—	Value: 2.50				

KM# 76 RUPEE

9.9300 g., Nickel, 27 mm. **Subject:** Death of Jawaharlal Nehru **Obv:** Small Asoka lion pedestal **Rev:** Head left **Note:** Type II. Struck from 1964 until 1967.

Date	Mintage	F	VF	XF	Unc	BU
ND(1964)(B)	10,010,000	—	0.65	1.00	2.00	—
ND(1964)B Proof	—	Value: 5.00				
ND(1964)(C)	10,020,000	—	0.65	1.00	2.00	—

KM# 77 RUPEE

10.0000 g., Nickel, 28 mm. **Subject:** Centennial - Birth of Mahatma Gandhi **Obv:** Asoka lion pedestal **Rev:** Head left **Note:** Struck during 1969 and 1970.

Date	Mintage	F	VF	XF	Unc	BU
ND(1969)(B)	5,180,000	—	0.70	1.25	2.00	—
ND(1969)B Proof	9,147	Value: 3.00				
ND(1969)(C)	6,690,000	—	1.00	1.50	2.50	—

KM# 78.1 RUPEE

8.0000 g., Copper-Nickel, 28 mm. **Obv:** Asoka lion pedestal **Rev:** Denomination and date, grain ears flank **Note:** Type 1.

Date	Mintage	F	VF	XF	Unc	BU
1975(B)	98,850,000	—	0.40	0.85	1.50	—
1975B Proof	—	Value: 2.50				
1975(C)	—	—	6.50	8.00	10.00	—
1976(B)	161,895,000	—	0.35	0.75	1.50	—
1976B Proof	Inc. above	Value: 2.50				
1977(B)	177,105,000	—	0.35	0.75	1.50	—
1977B Proof	Inc. above	Value: 2.50				
1978(B)	127,348,000	—	0.40	0.80	1.50	—
1978B Proof	Inc. above	Value: 2.50				
1978(C)	Inc. above	—	0.50	1.00	1.75	—
1979(B)	—	—	8.00	11.00	15.00	—
1979(C)	—	—	8.00	11.00	15.00	—

KM# 78.2 RUPEE

8.0000 g., Copper-Nickel, 28 mm. **Obv:** Asoka lion pedestal **Rev:** Denomination and date, grain ears flank **Note:** Type 2.

Date	Mintage	F	VF	XF	Unc	BU
1975(C)	—	—	0.40	0.85	1.50	—

Note: Mintage included in KM78.1

Date	Mintage	F	VF	XF	Unc	BU
1976(C)	—	—	0.50	1.25	2.25	—

Note: Mintage included in KM78.1

KM# 78.3 RUPEE

8.0000 g., Copper-Nickel, 28 mm. **Obv:** Asoka lion pedestal **Rev:** Denomination and date, grain ears flank **Note:** Type 3. Border varieties of long vs. short teeth on 1981 reverse and 1982 obverse. Wide and narrow security edge varieties exist.

Date	Mintage	F	VF	XF	Unc	BU
1979(B)	—	—	0.35	0.60	1.00	—
1979B Proof	—	Value: 2.50				
1979(C)	—	—	0.40	0.75	1.50	—
1980(B)	84,768,000	—	0.35	0.60	1.00	—
1980B Proof	—	Value: 2.50				
1980(C)	Inc. above	—	0.40	0.75	1.25	—
1981(B)	82,458,000	—	0.35	0.60	1.00	—
1981B Proof	—	Value: 2.50				
1981(C)	Inc. above	—	0.40	0.75	1.25	—
1982(B)	116,811,000	—	0.40	0.75	1.25	—

KM# 79.1 RUPEE
6.0000 g., Copper-Nickel, 26 mm. **Obv:** Asoka lion pedestal within seven sided beaded outline **Rev:** Denomination and date, grain ears flank, seven-sided outline surrounds **Edge:** Security **Note:** Type 3. Lions' hair and ears on 1984(B)-1989(B) issues vary from others.

Date	Mintage	F	VF	XF	Unc	BU
1983(B)	32,490,000	—	0.30	0.50	1.00	—
1983(C)	Inc. above	—	0.30	0.50	1.00	—
1984(B)	152,378,000	—	0.25	0.40	0.75	—
1984(C)	Inc. above	—	0.25	0.40	0.75	—
1984(H)	Inc. above	—	1.50	2.25	3.00	—
1985(B)	444,516,000	—	0.25	0.40	0.75	—
1985(C)	Inc. above	—	0.25	0.40	0.75	—
1985H	Inc. above	—	0.25	0.40	0.75	—
1985(L)	Inc. above	—	0.25	0.40	0.75	—
1986(B)	1,396,074,000	—	0.25	0.40	0.75	—
1986(C)	Inc. above	—	0.25	0.40	0.75	—
1986(H)	Inc. above	—	1.50	2.25	3.00	—
1987(B)	685,502,000	—	0.25	0.40	0.75	—
1987(C)	Inc. above	—	0.25	0.40	0.75	—
1987(H)	Inc. above	—	0.25	0.40	0.75	—
1988(B)	240,447,000	—	0.75	1.25	2.00	—
1988(C)	Inc. above	—	0.25	0.40	0.75	—
1988(H)	Inc. above	—	0.40	0.75	1.25	—
1989(B)	—	—	1.50	2.25	3.00	—
1989(C)	—	—	0.25	0.45	0.75	—
1989(H)	—	—	0.25	0.45	0.75	—
1990(H)	—	—	0.25	0.45	0.75	—
1990(C)	—	—	1.50	2.25	3.00	—

KM# 79.2 RUPEE
6.0000 g., Copper-Nickel, 26 mm. **Obv:** Horse on pedestal different, more detailed, 7-sided beaded outline surrounds **Rev:** Denomination and date, grain ears flank, within 7-sided beaded outline **Note:** Type 3.

Date	Mintage	F	VF	XF	Unc	BU
1988(B)	—	—	1.00	1.50	2.50	—
1989	—	—	1.00	1.50	2.50	—
1990	—	—	1.00	1.50	2.50	—

KM# 79.3 RUPEE
6.0000 g., Copper-Nickel, 26 mm. **Obv:** Lions' chest hairs restyled, 7-sided beaded outline surrounds **Rev:** Denomination and date, grain ears flank, 7-sided beaded outline surrounds **Note:** Type 3.

Date	Mintage	F	VF	XF	Unc	BU
1988(B)	—	—	0.25	0.50	1.00	—
1989(B)	—	—	0.25	0.50	1.00	—
1990(B)	—	—	0.25	0.50	1.00	—

KM# 79.4 RUPEE
6.0000 g., Copper-Nickel, 26 mm. **Obv:** Asoka lion pedestal, within 7-sided beaded outline, similar to 79.1 **Rev:** Denomination and date, grain ears flank, 7-sided beaded outline surrounds **Edge:** Milled **Note:** Traces of security edge and/or mostly smooth edges are encountered, especially for 1989. 1989-1991(C) is a variety with bulging eyes on side lions and irregular straight hair on central lion.

Date	Mintage	F	VF	XF	Unc	BU
1988(C)	—	—	5.00	7.00	11.00	—
1989(B)	—	—	10.00	15.00	20.00	—
1989(C)	—	—	5.00	7.00	11.00	—
1989(H)	—	—	10.00	15.00	20.00	—
1990(C)	—	—	0.35	0.50	1.00	—
1990(H)	—	—	0.50	0.75	1.50	—
1991(C)	—	—	0.35	0.50	1.00	—

KM# 79.5 RUPEE
6.0000 g., Copper-Nickel, 26 mm. **Obv:** Lions' chest hairs restyled, 7-sided beaded outline surrounds **Rev:** Denomination and date, grain ears flank, 7-sided beaded outline surrounds **Note:** Type 3.

Date	Mintage	F	VF	XF	Unc	BU
1990(C)	—	—	0.50	1.00	2.00	—
1990(B)	—	—	0.35	0.60	1.00	—
1991(B)	—	—	0.20	0.35	0.85	—
1991(H)	—	—	0.35	0.60	1.00	—

KM# 80 RUPEE
6.0000 g., Copper-Nickel, 26 mm. **Subject:** Youth Year **Obv:** Small asoka lion pedestal above denomination **Rev:** Three outlined profiles between dove and laurel branch **Edge:** Security

Date	Mintage	F	VF	XF	Unc	BU
1985(B)	—	—	0.35	0.60	1.25	—
Note: Mintage included in KM79.1						
1985(C)	—	—	0.50	1.00	2.00	—
Note: Mintage included in KM79.1						
1985(C) Proof	—	Value: 10.00				
Note: Mintage included in KM79.1						
1985(H)	—	—	2.00	3.00	5.00	—

KM# 81 RUPEE
6.0000 g., Copper-Nickel, 26 mm. **Series:** F.A.O. **Obv:** Asoka lion pedestal **Rev:** Two figures working in field

Date	Mintage	F	VF	XF	Unc	BU
1987(B)	234,223,000	—	0.35	0.60	1.25	—
1987B Proof	—	Value: 5.00				
1987(C)	Inc. above	—	0.50	1.00	2.00	—
1987(H)	191,120,000	—	1.50	3.00	4.00	—

KM# 82 RUPEE
6.0000 g., Copper-Nickel, 26 mm. **Series:** F.A.O. **Subject:** Rainfed farming **Obv:** Asoka lion pedestal **Rev:** Figure with flowers, rain cloud in background

Date	Mintage	F	VF	XF	Unc	BU
1988(B)	—	—	1.00	1.50	3.00	—
Note: Mintage included in KM79.1						
1988(C)	—	—	1.00	2.00	4.00	—
1988(H)	—	—	3.00	5.00	8.00	—

KM# 84 RUPEE
6.0000 g., Copper-Nickel, 26 mm. **Series:** F.A.O. **Subject:** Food and Environment **Obv:** Asoka lion pedestal **Rev:** Sun above wheat stalks

Date	Mintage	F	VF	XF	Unc	BU
1989	—	—	1.00	2.00	3.50	—
1989(H)	—	—	5.00	8.00	10.00	—
1989(B)	—	—	1.00	2.00	3.50	—

KM# 83.1 RUPEE
6.0000 g., Copper-Nickel, 26 mm. **Subject:** 100th Anniversary of Nehru's Birth **Obv:** Asoka lion pedestal **Rev:** Head right

Date	Mintage	F	VF	XF	Unc	BU
1989B Proof	—	Value: 5.00				
1989(C)	—	—	1.00	2.00	3.00	—
1989(H)	—	—	1.00	2.00	3.00	—
1989(B)	—	—	0.25	0.50	1.00	—

KM# 83.2 RUPEE
Copper-Nickel, 26 mm. **Obv:** Asoka lion pedestal, similar to KM#90. **Rev:** Head right

Date	Mintage	F	VF	XF	Unc	BU
1989(B)	—	—	20.00	50.00	80.00	—

KM# 87.1 RUPEE
6.0000 g., Copper-Nickel, 26 mm. **Subject:** SAARC Year - Care for the Girl Child **Obv:** Asoka lion pedestal **Rev:** Girl cutout below sun, symbol at left **Edge:** Security

Date	Mintage	F	VF	XF	Unc	BU
1990(B)	—	—	0.40	0.80	2.00	—

KM# 87.2 RUPEE
6.0000 g., Copper-Nickel, 26 mm. **Subject:** SAARC Year - Care for the Girl Child **Obv:** Asoka lion pedestal, denomination below **Rev:** Girl cutout below sun, symbol at left **Edge:** Milled **Note:** Edge varieties exist.

Date	Mintage	F	VF	XF	Unc	BU
1990(B)	—	—	0.50	1.25	3.00	—
1990(H)	—	—	0.50	1.25	3.00	—

KM# 85 RUPEE
6.0000 g., Copper-Nickel, 26 mm. **Subject:** Dr. Ambedkar **Obv:** Asoka lion pedestal, denomination below **Rev:** Bust looking right

Date	Mintage	F	VF	XF	Unc	BU
1990(B)	—	—	0.20	0.75	1.50	—
1990(H)	—	—	0.40	1.25	2.50	—

KM# 86 RUPEE
6.0000 g., Copper-Nickel, 26 mm. **Subject:** 15th Anniversary of I.C.D.S. **Obv:** Asoka lion pedestal, denomination below **Rev:** Seated figure holding child, radiant design surrounds **Edge:** Narrow and wide reeded **Note:** Varieties exist.

Date	Mintage	F	VF	XF	Unc	BU
ND(1990)(B)	—	—	0.20	0.75	1.50	—
ND(1990)(H)	—	—	0.40	1.25	2.50	—

KM# 88.1 RUPEE

6.0000 g., Copper-Nickel, 26 mm. **Series:** F.A.O. **Obv:** Asoka lion pedestal, denomination below **Rev:** Farming scene **Edge:** Reeded

Date	Mintage	F	VF	XF	Unc	BU
1990(C)	—	—	3.00	5.00	8.00	—
Note: 1990(C) is seldom well struck						
1990(H)	—	—	5.00	7.00	10.00	—

KM# 88.2 RUPEE

6.0000 g., Copper-Nickel, 26 mm. **Series:** F.A.O. **Obv:** Asoka lion pedestal **Rev:** Farming scene **Edge:** Plain

Date	Mintage	F	VF	XF	Unc	BU
1990(H)	—	—	5.00	12.00	15 .00	—

KM# 89 RUPEE

6.0000 g., Copper-Nickel, 26 mm. **Subject:** Rajiv Gandhi **Obv:** Asoka lion pedestal, denomination below **Rev:** Head looking left **Note:** Edge varieties exist.

Date	Mintage	F	VF	XF	Unc	BU
ND(1991)(B)	—	—	0.35	0.75	1.50	—
Note: The Mumbai (Bombay) mint mark occasionally resembles the Noida mintmark						
ND(1991)(H)	—	—	0.40	1.00	2.00	—

KM# 90 RUPEE

6.0000 g., Copper-Nickel, 26 mm. **Subject:** Commonwealth Parliamentary Conference **Obv:** Asoka lion pedestal, denomination below **Rev:** Building **Note:** Variety of breast with flat details exist (worn dies).

Date	Mintage	F	VF	XF	Unc	BU
1991(B)	—	—	0.35	0.75	1.50	—
1991(B) Prooflike	—	—	—	—	3.00	—
1991B Proof	—	Value: 5.00				

KM# 91 RUPEE

6.0000 g., Copper-Nickel, 26 mm. **Subject:** Tourism Year **Obv:** Asoka lion pedestal above denomination **Rev:** Stylized peacock

Date	Mintage	F	VF	XF	Unc	BU
1991(B)	—	—	0.35	0.75	1.50	—
1991(H)	—	—	0.60	1.25	2.50	—
1991(B) Prooflike	—	—	—	—	3.00	—
1991B Proof	—	Value: 5.00				

KM# 92.1 RUPEE

4.8500 g., Stainless Steel, 25 mm. **Obv:** Asoka lion pedestal **Rev:** Denomination and date, grain ears flank **Edge:** Milled **Note:** Edge sometimes faint, mintmark varieties exist.

Date	Mintage	F	VF	XF	Unc	BU
1992(H)	—	—	0.20	0.30	0.60	—
1992(B)	—	—	0.20	0.30	0.60	—
1993(B)	—	—	0.20	0.30	0.60	—
Note: Two mintmark shapes exist						
1993(C)	—	—	0.20	0.30	0.60	—
1993(H)	—	—	0.20	0.30	0.60	—
1993	—	—	0.20	0.30	0.60	—
1994(B)	—	—	0.15	0.25	0.50	—
Note: Two mintmark shapes exist						
1994(C)	—	—	0.15	0.25	0.50	—
1994(H)	—	—	0.15	0.25	0.50	—
1994	—	—	0.15	0.25	0.50	—
1995(B)	—	—	0.15	0.25	0.50	—
1995(C)	—	—	0.15	0.25	0.50	—
1995(H)	—	—	0.15	0.25	0.50	—
1995	—	—	0.15	0.25	0.50	—
1996(H)	—	—	1.00	1.50	2.50	—

KM# 92.2 RUPEE

4.8500 g., Stainless Steel, 25 mm. **Obv:** Asoka lion pedestal **Rev:** Denomination and date, grain ears flank **Edge:** Plain **Note:** Mintmark varieties exist.

Date	Mintage	F	VF	XF	Unc	BU
1995(B)	—	—	1.00	1.50	2.50	—
1995(H)	—	—	1.00	1.50	2.50	—
1995	—	—	1.00	1.50	2.50	—
1996(B)	—	—	0.15	0.35	0.60	—
1996(C)	—	—	0.15	0.35	0.60	—
1996(H)	—	—	0.15	0.35	0.60	—
1996	—	—	0.15	0.35	0.60	—
1997(B)	—	—	0.15	0.35	0.60	—
1997(C)	—	—	0.15	0.35	0.60	—
1997(H)	—	—	1.50	2.00	3.00	—
1997(M)	—	—	0.15	0.35	0.50	—
1997	—	—	0.15	0.35	0.50	—
1998(P)	—	—	0.15	0.30	0.45	—
1998(B)	—	—	0.15	0.35	0.50	—
1998(C)	—	—	0.15	0.35	0.50	—
1998(H)	—	—	0.15	0.35	0.50	—
1998(K)	—	—	0.15	0.35	0.50	—
1998	—	—	0.15	0.35	0.50	—
1999(K)	—	—	0.15	0.30	0.45	—
1999(P)	—	—	0.15	0.30	0.45	—
1999(B)	—	—	0.15	0.35	0.50	—
1999	—	—	0.15	0.30	0.45	—
1999(C)	—	—	0.15	0.35	0.50	—
1999(H)	—	—	0.15	0.35	0.50	—
2000(K)	—	—	0.15	0.30	0.45	—
2000(B)	—	—	0.15	0.30	0.45	—
2000(C)	—	—	0.15	0.30	0.45	—
2000(H)	—	—	0.15	0.30	0.45	—
2000	—	—	0.15	0.30	0.45	—
2001(H)	—	—	0.15	0.30	0.45	—
Note: Small and large mint mark exist, doubled left or right of wheat stalks						
2001(B)	—	—	0.15	0.30	0.45	—
2001(C)	—	—	0.15	0.30	0.45	—
2001(K)	—	—	0.15	0.30	0.45	—
2002(B)	—	—	0.15	0.30	0.45	—
2002(C)	—	—	0.15	0.30	0.45	—
2002(H)	—	—	0.15	0.30	0.45	—
2003(B)	—	—	0.15	0.30	0.45	—
2003(C)	—	—	0.15	0.30	0.45	—
2003(H)	—	—	0.15	0.30	0.45	—
2004(B)	—	—	0.15	0.30	0.45	—
2004(C)	—	—	0.15	0.30	0.45	—

KM# 93 RUPEE

Copper-Nickel **Subject:** Quit India **Obv:** Asoka lion pedestal, denomination below **Rev:** Monument **Edge:** Milled

Date	Mintage	F	VF	XF	Unc	BU
ND(1992)(C)	—	—	1.00	3.00	6.00	—
ND(1992)(H)	—	—	2.00	3.50	8.00	—
ND(1992)(B)	—	—	0.50	1.00	2.00	—

KM# 94 RUPEE

Copper-Nickel **Series:** World Food Day **Obv:** Asoka lion pedestal, denomination below **Rev:** Food items left of grain stalks **Edge:** Milled

Date	Mintage	F	VF	XF	Unc	BU
1992(C)	—	—	1.50	2.50	4.50	—

KM# 95 RUPEE

Copper-Nickel **Subject:** Inter Parliamentary Union Conference **Obv:** Asoka lion pedestal, denomination below **Rev:** Small building and date within wreath below curved building

Date	Mintage	F	VF	XF	Unc	BU
1993(B)	—	—	0.50	1.25	3.00	—

KM# 96.1 RUPEE

Stainless Steel **Subject:** International Year of the Family **Obv:** Asoka lion pedestal, denomination below **Rev:** Family group forms circular design at center **Edge:** Reeded

Date	Mintage	F	VF	XF	Unc	BU
1994(B)	—	—	0.40	0.75	2.00	—
1994	—	—	1.00	1.50	2.50	—

KM# 96.2 RUPEE

Stainless Steel **Subject:** International Year of the Family **Obv:** Arms **Rev:** Family inside inner circle **Edge:** Plain

Date	Mintage	F	VF	XF	Unc	BU
1994(B)	—	—	5.00	12.00	15.00	—

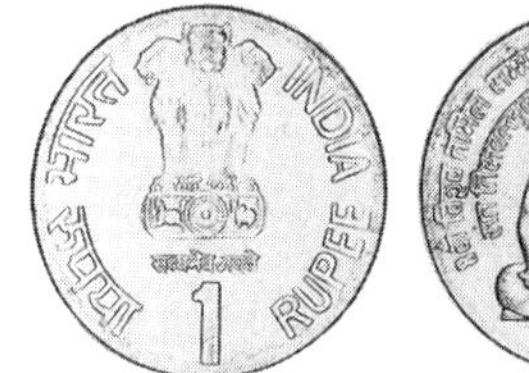

KM# 97.1 RUPEE

Stainless Steel **Subject:** Eighth World Tamil Conference **Obv:** Asoka lion pedestal, denomination below **Rev:** St. Thiruvalluvar **Edge:** Milled

Date	Mintage	F	VF	XF	Unc	BU
1995(B)	—	—	0.50	1.00	1.50	—
1995(H)	—	—	0.70	1.25	2.00	—
1995	—	—	0.50	1.00	1.75	—

KM# 97.2 RUPEE

Stainless Steel **Subject:** Eighth World Tamil Conference **Obv:** Asoka lion pedestal, denomination below **Rev:** St. Thiruvalluvar **Edge:** Plain

Date	Mintage	F	VF	XF	Unc	BU
1995(H)	—	—	4.00	7.00	10.00	—
1995	—	—	4.00	7.00	10.00	—

KM# 98 RUPEE

Stainless Steel **Obv:** Asoka lion pedestal, denomination below **Rev:** Cellular jail, Port Blair **Note:** Varieties exist.

Date	Mintage	F	VF	XF	Unc	BU
1997(B)	—	—	0.30	0.50	0.80	—
1997(C)	—	—	0.30	0.50	0.80	—
1997(H)	—	—	0.30	0.50	0.80	—
1997	—	—	0.40	0.60	1.00	—

KM# 295.1 RUPEE

4.8500 g., Stainless Steel **Subject:** St. Dnyaneshwar **Obv:** Asoka lion pedestal, denomination below **Rev:** Seated figure **Note:** Asoka column 13.2mm tall.

Date	Mintage	F	VF	XF	Unc	BU
1999(B)	—	—	1.75	3.00	5.00	—
1999(C)	—	—	0.60	0.90	1.50	—
1999(C) Proof	—	Value: 5.00				

KM# 295.2 RUPEE

4.8500 g., Stainless Steel **Subject:** St. Dnyaneshwar **Obv:** Asoka lion pedestal, denomination below **Rev:** Seated figure **Note:** Asoka column 13.8mm tall.

Date	Mintage	F	VF	XF	Unc	BU
1999(B)	—	—	0.40	0.60	1.00	—

KM# 295.3 RUPEE

4.8500 g., Stainless Steel **Subject:** St. Dnyaneshwar **Obv:** Asoka lion pedestal, denominaton below **Rev:** Seated figure **Note:** Asoka column 14.5mm tall.

Date	Mintage	F	VF	XF	Unc	BU
1999	—	—	1.50	2.50	4.00	—

KM# 313 RUPEE

4.9500 g., Stainless Steel, 25 mm. **Subject:** 100th Anniversary Birth of Jaya Prakash Narayan **Obv:** Asoka column **Rev:** Bust of Jaya Prakash Narayan slightly left **Edge:** Plain

Date	Mintage	F	VF	XF	Unc	BU
2002(B)	—	—	0.45	0.75	1.00	—
2002(B)	—	—	—	—	—	3.00
Note: In sets only						
2002(H)	—	—	0.45	0.75	1.00	—

KM# 314 RUPEE

4.9500 g., Stainless Steel, 25 mm. **Subject:** Maharana Pratap **Edge:** Plain

Date	Mintage	F	VF	XF	Unc	BU
2003(B)	—	—	0.45	0.75	1.00	—
2003(B)	—	—	—	—	—	2.50
Note: In sets only						
2003(H)	—	—	0.45	0.75	1.00	—

KM# 316 RUPEE

4.8500 g., Stainless Steel, 25 mm. **Obv:** Asoka lions **Rev:** 3/4 length military figure Veer Durgadass with spear left **Edge:** Plain

Date	Mintage	F	VF	XF	Unc	BU
2003(B)	—	—	0.50	0.80	1.25	—
2003(B)	—	—	—	—	—	2.50
Note: In sets only						
2003(H)	—	—	0.50	0.80	1.25	—

KM# 321 RUPEE

5.0000 g., Stainless Steel, 24.9 mm. **Subject:** 150th Anniversary of the Indian Postal Service **Obv:** Asoka lions above value **Rev:** Partial postage stamp design **Edge:** Grooved

Date	Mintage	F	VF	XF	Unc	BU
2004	—	—	—	—	2.00	—
2004	—	—	—	—	—	3.50
Note: In sets only						

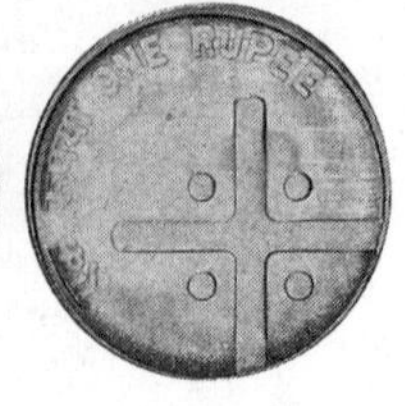

KM# 322 RUPEE

4.9500 g., Stainless Steel, 24.8 mm. **Obv:** Asoka lions and value **Rev:** Cross dividing four dots **Edge:** Plain

Date	Mintage	F	VF	XF	Unc	BU
2005(C)	—	—	—	—	2.00	—
2007(H)	—	—	—	—	2.00	—

KM# 331 RUPEE

4.9300 g., Stainless Steel, 24.98 mm. **Subject:** Bharata Natyam Dance Expressions **Obv:** Asoka lion pedestal **Rev:** Jesture of hand with thumb up **Edge:** Plain

Date	Mintage	F	VF	XF	Unc	BU
2007(N)	—	—	—	—	2.00	—

2 RUPEES

2 Rupee Obverses

Type A. Asoka column 15mm tall. 5 fur rows on right lion. No lion whiskers.

Type B. Asoka column 14mm tall. 3 fur rows on right lion. 5 lion whiskers.

Type C. Asoka column 13mm tall. 4 fur rows on right lion.

Type D. Asoka column 13mm tall. 4 fur rows. Recut chest on central lion.

Type E. Asoka column 13mm tall. No fur rows on right lion. 2 whiskers on central lion

NOTE: Obverses C and D include both 4.5 x 5mm and 5 x 5.5mm numeral 2 varieties.

KM# 120 2 RUPEES

Copper-Nickel, 28 mm. **Subject:** IX Asian Games **Obv:** Asoka lion pedestal, denomination below **Rev:** Sun above logo **Note:** Incomplete security edge known.

Date	Mintage	F	VF	XF	Unc	BU
1982(B)	12,720,000	—	0.35	0.50	1.25	—
1982B Proof	Inc. above	Value: 2.50				
1982(C)	Inc. above	—	0.35	0.50	1.25	—

KM# 121.1 2 RUPEES

7.9500 g., Copper-Nickel, 28 mm. **Subject:** National Integration **Rev:** Flag on map **Note:** Security edge, small date.

Date	Mintage	F	VF	XF	Unc	BU
1982B Proof	—	Value: 3.50				
1982(C)	—	—	0.30	1.00	2.25	—
Note: Mintage included in KM120						
1982(B)	—	—	0.30	1.00	1.75	—
Note: Mintage included in KM120						

KM# 121.2 2 RUPEES

8.0200 g., Copper-Nickel, 28 mm. **Subject:** National Integration **Rev:** Flag on map **Note:** Incomplete security edges known, lg. date.

Date	Mintage	F	VF	XF	Unc	BU
1990(C) Plain edge	—	—	10.00	30.00	50.00	—
1990(H) Reeded edge	—	—	20.00	40.00	80.00	—
1990(C)	—	—	0.40	1.00	2.25	—
1990(H)	—	—	0.80	3.00	5.00	—
1990(B)	—	—	0.40	1.00	2.25	—

KM# 121.3 2 RUPEES

6.0000 g., Copper-Nickel, 26 mm. **Subject:** National Integration **Obv:** Type A **Rev:** Flag on map **Edge:** Plain **Shape:** 11-sided **Note:** Reduced size, non magnetic.

Date	Mintage	F	VF	XF	Unc	BU
1992(B)	—	—	2.50	4.00	7.00	—
1992(C)	—	—	0.30	0.50	1.00	—
1992(H)	—	—	0.40	1.00	1.50	—
1993(C)	—	—	0.40	1.25	2.00	—
1993(H)	—	—	0.35	0.60	1.25	—
1994(C)	—	—	0.40	1.25	2.00	—
1994(H)	—	—	0.35	0.80	1.50	—
1995(B)	—	—	2.50	4.00	7.00	—
1995(C)	—	—	0.30	0.50	1.00	—
1995(H)	—	—	0.30	0.50	1.00	—
1996(C)	—	—	0.30	0.50	1.00	—
1996(H)	—	—	0.30	0.50	1.00	—
1997(C)	—	—	0.30	0.50	1.00	—
1997(H)	—	—	0.30	0.50	1.00	—
1998(C)	—	—	0.30	0.50	1.00	—
1999(C)	—	—	0.30	0.50	1.00	—
2000(C)	—	—	0.30	0.50	1.00	—
2000(R)	—	—	0.30	0.50	1.00	—
2001(B)	—	—	0.30	0.50	1.00	—
2001(C)	—	—	0.30	0.50	1.00	—
2002(C)	—	—	0.30	0.50	1.00	—
2003(C)	—	—	0.30	0.50	1.00	—

KM# 121.3a 2 RUPEES

Nickel magnetic **Obv:** Type A **Edge:** Plain **Shape:** 11-sided

Date	Mintage	F	VF	XF	Unc	BU
1998(C)	—	—	30.00	60.00	100	—

KM# 121.4 2 RUPEES

5.0000 g., Copper-Nickel, 26 mm. **Subject:** National Integration **Obv:** Type B **Rev:** Flag on map **Edge:** Plain

Date	Mintage	F	VF	XF	Unc	BU
1992(B)	—	—	0.30	0.50	1.00	—
1993(B)	—	—	0.30	0.50	1.00	—
1994(B)	—	—	0.30	0.50	1.00	—
1994(C)	—	—	0.30	0.50	1.00	—
1994(H)	—	—	2.75	5.00	6.50	—
1994	—	—	2.75	5.00	6.50	—
1995(B)	—	—	0.30	0.50	1.00	—
1995(H)	—	—	3.00	5.50	8.00	—
1995	—	—	0.30	0.50	1.00	—
1996(B)	—	—	2.50	4.00	6.00	—
1996(B-H)	—	—	5.00	10.00	15.00	—
1996	—	—	0.30	0.50	1.00	—
1997(B)	—	—	0.30	0.50	1.00	—
1998	—	—	0.30	0.50	1.00	—
1999(N)	—	—	0.30	0.50	1.00	—

KM# 121.5 2 RUPEES
6.0600 g., Copper-Nickel, 26 mm. **Subject:** National Integration **Obv:** Type C **Rev:** Flag on map **Edge:** Plain **Note:** 11-sided

Date	Mintage	F	VF	XF	Unc	BU
1995(B)	—	—	2.50	4.00	6.00	—
1996(B)	—	—	0.30	0.50	1.00	—
1996(H)	—	—	0.30	0.50	1.00	—
1997(B)	—	—	0.30	0.50	1.00	—
1997(H)	—	—	0.30	0.50	1.00	—
1997(T)	—	—	0.30	0.50	1.00	—
1998(B)	—	—	0.30	0.50	1.00	—
1998(H)	—	—	0.30	0.50	1.00	—
1998(P)	—	—	0.30	0.50	1.00	—
1998(T)	—	—	0.30	0.50	1.00	—
1999(B)	—	—	0.30	0.50	1.00	—
1999(H)	—	—	0.30	0.50	1.00	—
1999(Ld)	—	—	0.30	0.50	1.00	—
1999	—	—	0.30	0.50	1.00	—
1999(C)	—	—	0.30	0.50	1.00	—
2000(B)	—	—	0.30	0.50	1.00	—
2000(C)	—	—	0.30	0.50	1.00	—
2000(H)	—	—	0.30	0.50	1.00	—
2000(R)	—	—	0.30	0.50	1.00	—
2001(B)	—	—	0.30	0.50	1.00	—
2001(C)	—	—	0.30	0.50	1.00	—
2001(H)	—	—	0.30	0.50	1.00	—
2002(B)	—	—	0.30	0.50	1.00	—
2002(C)	—	—	0.30	0.50	1.00	—
2002(H)	—	—	0.30	0.50	1.00	—
2002(N)	—	—	0.30	0.50	1.00	—
2003(B)	—	—	0.30	0.50	1.00	—
2003(C)	—	—	0.30	0.50	1.00	—
2003(H)	—	—	0.30	0.50	1.00	—

KM# 121.6 2 RUPEES
Copper-Nickel, 26 mm. **Subject:** National Integration **Obv:** Type D **Rev:** Flag on map **Edge:** Plain **Shape:** 11-sided

Date	Mintage	F	VF	XF	Unc	BU
1998(B)	—	—	0.30	0.50	1.00	—
1998(H)	—	—	0.30	0.50	1.00	—
1999(B)	—	—	0.75	1.00	1.50	—
2000(B)	—	—	0.75	1.00	1.50	—

KM# A128 2 RUPEES
Copper-Nickel **Subject:** National Land Conservation Week

Date	Mintage	F	VF	XF	Unc	BU
1992(C)	—	—	—	—	—	—

Note: Not released for general circulation

KM# 323 2 RUPEES
5.7500 g., Copper-Nickel, 26.4 mm. **Subject:** National Land Conservation **Obv:** Asoka lion pedestal above denomination **Rev:** Tree above wavy lines **Edge:** Plain **Shape:** Eleven sided

Date	Mintage	F	VF	XF	Unc	BU
1992 (1993)	—	—	—	—	—	—

KM# 124.1 2 RUPEES
Copper-Nickel **Subject:** Small Family Happy Family **Obv:** Type B **Rev:** Family scene

Date	Mintage	F	VF	XF	Unc	BU
1993(B)	—	—	0.50	0.90	1.50	—

KM# 124.2 2 RUPEES
Copper-Nickel **Subject:** Small Family Happy Family **Obv:** Type A **Rev:** Family scene

Date	Mintage	F	VF	XF	Unc	BU
1993(H)	—	—	2.00	3.00	5.00	—

KM# 125.1 2 RUPEES
Copper-Nickel **Series:** World Food Day **Subject:** Bio Diversity **Obv:** Type B **Rev:** Mountains, trees and fish

Date	Mintage	F	VF	XF	Unc	BU
1993(B)	—	—	0.50	0.90	1.50	—

KM# 125.2 2 RUPEES
Copper-Nickel **Subject:** Bio Diversity **Obv:** Type A **Rev:** Mountains, trees and fish

Date	Mintage	F	VF	XF	Unc	BU
1993(H)	—	—	2.00	3.00	5.00	—

KM# 126.1 2 RUPEES
Copper-Nickel **Series:** F.A.O. **Subject:** Water For Life **Obv:** Type A **Rev:** Large teardrop above water

Date	Mintage	F	VF	XF	Unc	BU
1994(B)	—	—	0.60	1.10	2.00	—
1994(C)	—	—	1.00	2.00	4.00	—
1994(H)	—	—	2.00	4.50	11.00	—

KM# 126.2 2 RUPEES
Copper-Nickel **Subject:** Water for Life **Obv:** Type B **Rev:** Large teardrop above water

Date	Mintage	F	VF	XF	Unc	BU
1994(B)	—	20.00	35.00	50.00	75.00	—

KM# 127.1 2 RUPEES
Copper-Nickel **Subject:** Globalizing Indian Agriculture - Agriexpo 95 **Obv:** Type A **Rev:** Steer head within wreath of two stalks of wheat

Date	Mintage	F	VF	XF	Unc	BU
1995(B)	—	—	0.60	1.25	2.00	—
1995(C)	—	—	1.00	3.00	6.00	—

KM# 127.2 2 RUPEES
Copper-Nickel **Subject:** Globalizing Indian Agriculture - Agriexpo 55 **Obv:** Type B **Rev:** Steer head within wreath of two stalks of wheat

Date	Mintage	F	VF	XF	Unc	BU
1995(B)	—	20.00	30.00	50.00	75.00	—

KM# 127.3 2 RUPEES
Copper-Nickel **Obv:** Type C **Rev:** Steer head within wreath of two stalks of wheat

Date	Mintage	F	VF	XF	Unc	BU
1995(B)	—	30.00	50.00	75.00	100	—

KM# 128.1 2 RUPEES
Copper-Nickel **Subject:** Eighth World Tamil Conference **Obv:** Type C, Asoka column 13mm tall **Rev:** St. Thiruvalluvar

Date	Mintage	F	VF	XF	Unc	BU
1995(B)	—	—	0.60	1.00	1.75	—

KM# 128.2 2 RUPEES
Copper-Nickel **Subject:** 8th World Tamil Conference **Obv:** Type B **Rev:** St. Thiruvalluvar

Date	Mintage	F	VF	XF	Unc	BU
1995(B)	—	—	1.00	2.00	3.00	—

KM# 129.1 2 RUPEES
Copper-Nickel **Subject:** Sardar Vallabhbhai Patel **Obv:** Type A **Rev:** Bust right

Date	Mintage	F	VF	XF	Unc	BU
1996(C)	—	—	2.50	4.00	7.00	—

KM# 129.2 2 RUPEES
Copper-Nickel **Subject:** Sardar Vallabhbhai Patel **Obv:** Type B **Rev:** Bust right

Date	Mintage	F	VF	XF	Unc	BU
1996	—	—	1.00	1.50	3.00	—

KM# 129.3 2 RUPEES
Copper-Nickel **Subject:** Sardar Vallabhbhai Patel **Obv:** Type C **Rev:** Bust right

Date	Mintage	F	VF	XF	Unc	BU
1996(B)	—	—	2.00	3.00	5.00	—
1996(H)	—	—	0.40	0.70	1.25	—
1996M Proof	—	Value: 8.00				

KM# 129.4 2 RUPEES
Copper-Nickel **Subject:** Sardar Vallabhbhai Patel **Obv:** Type D **Rev:** Bust right

Date	Mintage	F	VF	XF	Unc	BU
1996(B)	—	—	0.40	0.70	1.25	—
1996(C)	—	—	0.30	0.60	1.00	—

KM# 129.5 2 RUPEES
Copper-Nickel **Subject:** Sardar Vallabhbhai Patel **Obv:** Type E **Rev:** Bust right

Date	Mintage	F	VF	XF	Unc	BU
1996(B)	—	30.00	40.00	55.00	80.00	—
1996(H)	—	30.00	40.00	55.00	80.00	—

KM# 130.1 2 RUPEES
6.0000 g., Copper-Nickel **Subject:** Subhas Chandra Bose **Obv:** Type C **Rev:** Bust left

Date	Mintage	F	VF	XF	Unc	BU
1996(C)	—	—	10.00	12.00	15.00	—
1997(B)	—	—	0.60	0.90	1.25	—
1997(C)	—	—	0.60	0.90	1.25	—
1997(H)	—	—	1.50	2.50	4.00	—
1997(C) Proof	—	Value: 3.25				

KM# 130.2 2 RUPEES
6.0000 g., Copper-Nickel **Subject:** Subhas Chandra Bose **Obv:** Type B **Rev:** Bust left

Date	Mintage	F	VF	XF	Unc	BU
1997	—	—	1.00	2.00	3.50	—
1997(H)	—	—	0.60	0.90	1.25	—

KM# 131.1 2 RUPEES
6.0000 g., Copper-Nickel **Subject:** Sri Aurobindo **Obv:** Type C **Rev:** Head 3/4 facing

Date	Mintage	F	VF	XF	Unc	BU
1998(B)	—	—	0.60	0.90	1.50	—
1998	—	—	1.00	1.50	3.00	—
1998(C)	—	—	1.00	1.50	3.00	—
1998M Proof	—	Value: 3.50				

KM# 131.2 2 RUPEES
Copper-Nickel **Subject:** Sri Aurobindo **Obv:** Type D **Rev:** Head 3/4 facing

Date	Mintage	F	VF	XF	Unc	BU
1998(B)	—	—	3.00	5.00	8.00	—

KM# 131.3 2 RUPEES
Copper-Nickel **Subject:** Sri Aurobindo **Obv:** Type A **Rev:** Bust facing

Date	Mintage	F	VF	XF	Unc	BU
1998	—	—	—	—	—	5.00

KM# 296.1 2 RUPEES
6.0000 g., Copper-Nickel **Subject:** Deshbandhu Chittaranjan Das **Obv:** Type A **Rev:** Head facing

Date	Mintage	F	VF	XF	Unc	BU
1998(C)	—	—	10.00	15.00	25.00	—

KM# 296.2 2 RUPEES

Copper-Nickel **Subject:** Deshbandhu Chittaranjan Das **Obv:** Type B **Rev:** Head facing

Date	Mintage	F	VF	XF	Unc	BU
1998	—	—	3.00	4.00	6.00	—

KM# 296.3 2 RUPEES

Copper-Nickel **Subject:** Deshbandhu Chittaranjan Das **Obv:** Type C **Rev:** Head facing **Note:** 7mm, edge flat.

Date	Mintage	F	VF	XF	Unc	BU
1998(C)	—	—	4.00	6.00	8.00	—
1998(C) Proof	—	—	—	—	—	—

KM# 296.4 2 RUPEES

6.0000 g., Copper-Nickel **Subject:** Deshbandhu Chittaranjan Das **Obv:** Type C **Rev:** Head facing **Note:** 5-6mm, edge flat.

Date	Mintage	F	VF	XF	Unc	BU
1998(C)	—	—	6.00	8.00	12.00	—

KM# 296.5 2 RUPEES

6.0000 g., Copper-Nickel **Subject:** Deshbandhu Chittaranjan Das **Obv:** Type C **Rev:** Head facing **Note:** 3-5mm, edge flat.

Date	Mintage	F	VF	XF	Unc	BU
1998	—	—	2.00	3.00	5.00	—
1998(C)	—	—	3.00	4.00	6.00	—

KM# 296.6 2 RUPEES

Copper-Nickel **Subject:** Deshbandhu Chittaranjan Das **Obv:** Type D **Rev:** Head facing **Note:** 3-5mm, edge flat.

Date	Mintage	F	VF	XF	Unc	BU
1998(C)	—	—	0.75	1.25	2.00	—

KM# 290 2 RUPEES

6.0000 g., Copper-Nickel **Subject:** Chhatrapati Shivaji **Obv:** Type C **Rev:** Turbaned bust right

Date	Mintage	F	VF	XF	Unc	BU
1999M Proof	—	Value: 3.50				
1999(B)	—	—	0.75	1.25	2.00	—
1999	—	—	0.75	1.25	2.00	—
1999(C)	—	—	0.75	1.25	2.00	—
1999(H)	—	—	1.00	1.75	3.00	—

KM# 291 2 RUPEES

6.0000 g., Copper-Nickel **Subject:** Supreme Court: 50 Years **Obv:** Type C **Rev:** Wheel above asoka lion pedestal **Edge:** Plain

Date	Mintage	F	VF	XF	Unc	BU
2000(B)	—	—	0.75	1.25	2.00	—
2000(C)	—	—	0.75	1.25	2.00	—

KM# 303 2 RUPEES

6.2400 g., Copper-Nickel, 25.7 mm. **Subject:** 100th Anniversary Birth of Dr. Syama P. Mookerjee **Obv:** Asoka lion pedestal above denomination, type B **Rev:** Bust of Dr. Mookerjeeright **Edge:** Plain

Date	Mintage	F	VF	XF	Unc	BU
2001(C)	—	—	1.25	2.00	3.00	—
2001(C) Proof	—	Value: 7.50				

KM# 305 2 RUPEES

6.1000 g., Copper-Nickel, 25.7 mm. **Subject:** St. Tukaram **Obv:** Asoka column above value **Rev:** Seated musician **Shape:** 11-sided

Date	Mintage	F	VF	XF	Unc	BU
2002(B)	—	—	0.75	1.25	2.00	—
2002(C)	—	—	0.75	1.25	2.00	—

KM# 346 2 RUPEES

6.0000 g., Copper-Nickel, 26 mm. **Subject:** Sant Tukaram (film about poet) **Obv:** Asoka column **Edge:** Plain **Shape:** 11-sided

Date	Mintage	F	VF	XF	Unc	BU
2002(C)	—	—	—	2.00	3.00	—
2002(C)	—	Value: 5.00				

KM# 307 2 RUPEES

6.0500 g., Copper-Nickel **Subject:** 150th Anniversary - Indian Railways **Obv:** Asoka column above value **Rev:** Cartoon elephant holding railroad lantern **Edge:** Plain **Shape:** 11-sided

Date	Mintage	F	VF	XF	Unc	BU
2003(B)	—	—	0.75	1.25	2.00	—
2003(C)	—	—	0.75	1.25	2.00	—
2003(C) Proof	—	Value: 5.00				

KM# 334 2 RUPEES

6.0000 g., Copper-Nickel, 26 mm. **Subject:** 150th Anniversary Telecommunications **Obv:** Asoka lions **Rev:** Cartoon bird standing holding cell phone **Edge:** Plain **Shape:** 11-sided

Date	Mintage	F	VF	XF	Unc	BU
2004(B)	—	—	—	—	2.00	—
2004(B) Proof	—	—	—	—	—	5.00

KM# 326 2 RUPEES

5.8000 g., Stainless Steel **Obv:** Asoka Pillar and value in center **Rev:** Cross with U-shaped arms and dots **Edge:** Plain **Note:** Size varies 26.75 - 27.07 mm

Date	Mintage	F	VF	XF	Unc	BU
2005(B)	—	—	—	0.50	1.35	—
2005(C)	—	—	—	0.50	1.35	—
2006(B) small date	—	—	—	0.40	1.00	—
2006(B) large date	—	—	—	0.40	1.00	—
2006(H)	—	—	—	0.40	1.00	—
2006(N)	—	—	—	0.40	1.00	—
2007(B)	—	—	—	0.40	1.00	—
2007(H)	—	—	—	0.40	1.00	—

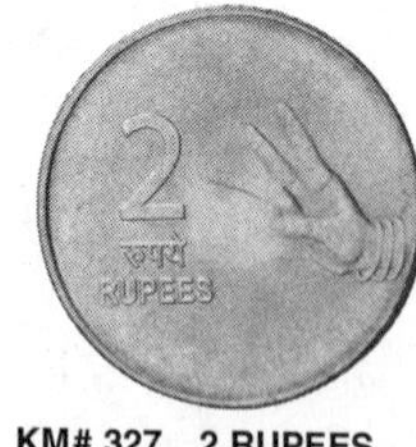

KM# 327 2 RUPEES

5.8000 g., Stainless Steel, 26.97 mm. **Obv:** Asoka Pillar at center **Obv. Inscription:** INDIA in Hindi and English **Rev:** Hasta Mudra - hand gesture from the dance Bharata Natyam **Edge:** Plain

Date	Mintage	F	VF	XF	Unc	BU
2007(B)	—	—	—	0.40	1.00	—
2007(C)	—	—	—	0.40	1.00	—

KM# 350 2 RUPEES

6.0000 g., Copper-Nickel, 26 mm. **Subject:** 75th Anniversary Indian Air Force **Obv:** Asoka column **Edge:** Plain **Shape:** 11-sided

Date	Mintage	F	VF	XF	Unc	BU
2007(C)	—	—	—	—	3.00	1.25
2007(C) Proof	—	Value: 5.00				

KM# 150 5 RUPEES

Copper-Nickel **Subject:** Death of Indira Gandi - statesperson, 1917-1984 **Obv:** Asoka lion pedestal, denomination below **Rev:** Bust right

Date	Mintage	F	VF	XF	Unc	BU
ND(1985)(B)	59,288,000	—	0.75	1.50	3.00	—
ND(1985)B Proof	Inc. above	Value: 27.50				
ND(1985)(H)	Inc. above	—	3.50	6.00	15.00	—

KM# 151 5 RUPEES

Copper-Nickel **Subject:** 100th Anniversary - Nehru's Birth **Obv:** Asoka lion pedestal, denomination below **Rev:** Head right

Date	Mintage	F	VF	XF	Unc	BU
1989(B)	—	—	1.00	2.00	3.00	—
Note: Short rim teeth.						
1989(B)	—	—	2.00	3.00	4.50	—
Note: Long rim teeth.						
1989B Proof	—	Value: 25.00				
1989(H)	—	—	3.50	6.00	15.00	—

KM# 154.1 5 RUPEES

9.0000 g., Copper-Nickel, 35 mm. **Obv:** Asoka lion pedestal **Rev:** Denomination flanked by flowers **Note:** (C) - Calcutta mint has issued 2 distinctly different security edge varieties every year 1992-2003 with large dots and thick center line, w/small dots and narrow center line.

Date	Mintage	F	VF	XF	Unc	BU
1992(B)	—	—	0.20	0.75	1.50	—
1992(C)	—	—	0.20	0.75	1.50	—
1992(H)	—	—	0.20	0.75	1.50	—
1993(B)	—	—	0.20	0.75	1.50	—
1993(C)	—	—	0.20	0.75	1.50	—
1994(B)	—	—	0.20	0.75	1.50	—
1994(C)	—	—	0.20	0.75	1.50	—
1994(H)	—	—	0.20	0.75	1.50	—
1995(B)	—	—	0.20	0.75	1.50	—
1995(C)	—	—	0.20	0.75	1.50	—
1995(H)	—	—	0.20	0.75	1.50	—
1995	—	—	0.20	0.75	1.50	—
1996(B)	—	—	0.20	0.50	1.00	—
1996(C)	—	—	0.20	0.50	1.00	—
1996(H)	—	—	0.20	0.50	1.00	—
1996	—	—	0.20	0.50	1.00	—
1997(B)	—	—	0.20	0.50	1.00	—
1997(C)	—	—	0.20	0.50	1.00	—
1997(H)	—	—	0.20	0.50	1.00	—
1997	—	—	0.20	0.50	1.00	—
1998(B)	—	—	0.20	0.50	1.00	—
1998(C)	—	—	0.20	0.50	1.00	—
1998(H)	—	—	0.25	0.50	1.00	—
1998	—	—	0.25	0.50	1.00	—
1999(B)	—	—	0.50	0.25	1.00	—
1999M	—	—	0.25	0.50	1.00	—
1999(C)	—	—	0.25	0.50	1.00	—
1999(H)	—	—	0.25	0.50	1.00	—
1999	—	—	0.25	0.50	1.00	—
1999(R)	—	—	0.25	0.50	1.00	—
2000(B)	—	—	0.50	0.25	1.00	—
2000(C)	—	—	0.25	0.50	1.00	—
2000(H)	—	—	0.50	1.00	2.00	—
2000(R)	—	—	0.25	0.50	1.00	—
2000	—	—	0.25	0.50	1.00	—
2001(B)	—	—	0.25	0.50	1.00	—
2001(C) Plain 1	—	—	0.25	0.50	1.00	—
2001(C) Serif 1	—	—	1.00	2.00	3.00	—
2001(H)	—	—	0.35	0.60	1.50	—

Date	Mintage	F	VF	XF	Unc	BU
2002(C)	—	—	0.25	0.50	1.00	—
2002(N)	—	—	0.25	0.50	1.00	—
2003(C)	—	—	0.25	0.50	1.00	—

KM# 154.2 5 RUPEES

8.9100 g., Copper-Nickel, 23 mm. **Obv:** Asoka lion pedestal **Rev:** Denomination flanked by flowers **Edge:** Milled

Date	Mintage	F	VF	XF	Unc	BU
1992(C)	—	—	8.00	10.00	15.00	—
1992(C) Milled edge	—	—	8.00	10.00	15.00	—
1992(H)	—	—	8.00	10.00	15.00	—
1993(B)	—	—	8.00	10.00	15.00	—
1993(C)	—	—	8.00	10.00	15.00	—
1994(B)	—	—	8.00	10.00	15.00	—
1994(C)	—	—	8.00	10.00	15.00	—
1994(H)	—	—	8.00	10.00	15.00	—
1995(B)	—	—	8.00	10.00	15.00	—
1995(C)	—	—	8.00	10.00	15.00	—
1995(H)	—	—	8.00	10.00	15.00	—
1996(B)	—	—	8.00	10.00	15.00	—
1996(C)	—	—	8.00	10.00	15.00	—
1996(H)	—	—	8.00	10.00	15.00	—
1997(B)	—	—	8.00	10.00	15.00	—
1997(C)	—	—	8.00	10.00	15.00	—
1998(C)	—	—	8.00	10.00	15.00	—
1998(B)	—	—	8.00	10.00	15.00	—
1998(H)	—	—	8.00	10.00	15.00	—
1999(B)	—	—	8.00	10.00	15.00	—
1999(C)	—	—	8.00	10.00	15.00	—
1999(H)	—	—	8.00	10.00	15.00	—
2000(C)	—	—	8.00	10.00	15.00	—
2000(B)	—	—	8.00	10.00	15.00	—
2000(H)	—	—	8.00	10.00	15.00	—
2001(C)	—	—	8.00	10.00	15.00	—
2002(C)	—	—	8.00	10.00	15.00	—
2003(C)	—	—	8.00	10.00	15.00	—

KM# 154.3 5 RUPEES

Copper-Nickel, 23 mm. **Obv:** Asoka lion pedestal **Rev:** Denomination flanked by flowers **Edge:** Plain

Date	Mintage	F	VF	XF	Unc	BU
1998(H)	—	—	5.00	10.00	15.00	—
1999(H)	—	—	5.00	10.00	15.00	—

KM# 154.4 5 RUPEES

Copper-Nickel, 23 mm. **Obv:** Asoka lion pedestal as seen on 2 Rupees, KM#121.5 **Rev:** Denomination flanked by flowers

Date	Mintage	F	VF	XF	Unc	BU
1998(B)	—	—	0.25	0.50	1.00	—
1999(B)	—	—	0.25	0.50	1.00	—
2000(B)	—	—	0.25	0.50	1.00	—
2001(B)	—	—	0.25	0.50	1.00	—
2002(B)	—	—	0.25	0.50	1.00	—
2003(B)	—	—	0.25	0.50	1.00	—
2004(B)	—	—	0.25	0.50	1.00	—

KM# 155.1 5 RUPEES

Copper-Nickel, 23 mm. **Subject:** World of Work **Obv:** Asoka lion pedestal, denomination below **Rev:** Denomination within broken dentil circle, wreath surrounds **Edge:** Security

Date	Mintage	F	VF	XF	Unc	BU
ND(1994)(B)	—	—	0.75	1.00	1.75	—
ND(1994)B Proof	—	Value: 5.00				
ND(1994)(H)	—	—	1.50	2.25	4.00	—
ND(1994)	—	—	1.00	1.50	3.00	—

KM# 155.2 5 RUPEES

Copper-Nickel, 23 mm. **Subject:** World of Work **Obv:** Asoka lion pedestal, denomination below **Rev:** Denomination within broken dentil circle, wreath surrounds **Edge:** Milled

Date	Mintage	F	VF	XF	Unc	BU
1994(B)	—	—	8.00	10.00	15.00	—
1994(H)	—	—	8.00	10.00	15.00	—

KM# 157 5 RUPEES

Copper-Nickel, 23 mm. **Series:** 50th Anniversary - F.A.O. **Obv:** Asoka lion pedestal, denomination below **Rev:** Hand clutching stalks of wheat **Edge:** Milled or security

Date	Mintage	F	VF	XF	Unc	BU
1995(B)	—	—	0.75	1.00	1.75	—
1995(H)	—	—	1.50	3.00	5.00	—
1995	—	—	1.00	1.50	3.00	—

KM# 158 5 RUPEES

Copper-Nickel, 23 mm. **Subject:** Eighth World Tamil Conference **Obv:** Asoka lion pedestal, denomination below **Rev:** St. Thiruvalluvar **Edge:** Milled or security

Date	Mintage	F	VF	XF	Unc	BU
1995(B)	—	—	0.75	1.00	1.75	—

KM# 156.1 5 RUPEES

Copper-Nickel, 23 mm. **Series:** 50 Years - United Nations **Obv:** Asoka lion pedestal, denomination below **Rev:** Date above UN logo **Edge:** Security or plain **Note:** Tall and short letters

Date	Mintage	F	VF	XF	Unc	BU
1995(B)	—	—	0.75	1.00	1.75	—
1995	—	—	1.00	1.50	3.00	—

KM# 156.2 5 RUPEES

Copper-Nickel, 23 mm. **Subject:** 50 Years United Nations **Obv:** Asoka lion pedestal similar to 2 Rupees, KM#121.3 **Rev:** Date above UN logo

Date	Mintage	F	VF	XF	Unc	BU
1995(B)	—	—	10.00	—	—	—

KM# 160 5 RUPEES

Copper-Nickel, 23 mm. **Subject:** 2nd International Crop Science Conference **Obv:** Asoka lion pedestal, denomination below **Rev:** Plants on globe, spray below, braid above **Edge:** Security **Note:** This conference was never held.

Date	Mintage	F	VF	XF	Unc	BU
1996(C)	11,000	—	20.00	30.00	40.00	—

KM# 159 5 RUPEES

Copper-Nickel, 23 mm. **Subject:** Mother's Health is Child's Health **Edge:** Milled or security

Date	Mintage	F	VF	XF	Unc	BU
1996(B)	—	—	0.75	1.00	1.50	—
1996(H)	—	—	0.75	1.00	1.50	—
1996	—	—	1.00	1.50	2.25	—

KM# 304 5 RUPEES

9.0700 g., Copper-Nickel, 23.19 mm. **Subject:** 2600th Anniversary Birth of Bhagwan Mahavir **Obv:** Asoka column above denomination **Rev:** Swastika above hand in irregular frame **Edge:** Security

Date	Mintage	F	VF	XF	Unc	BU
2001(B)	—	—	1.00	2.00	3.00	5.00
2001(B) Proof	—	Value: 6.50				
2001(N)	—	—	1.00	2.00	3.00	5.00

KM# 308 5 RUPEES

8.9200 g., Copper-Nickel, 23.1 mm. **Subject:** Dadabhai Naroji **Obv:** Asoka column above value **Rev:** Bust of Dadabhai Naroji 3/4 right **Edge:** Security

Date	Mintage	F	VF	XF	Unc	BU
ND(2003)(B)	—	—	1.00	1.75	3.00	5.00

KM# 317.1 5 RUPEES

8.8000 g., Copper-Nickel, 23.1 mm. **Obv:** Asoka lions **Rev:** K. Kamaraj above life dates **Edge:** Security

Date	Mintage	F	VF	XF	Unc	BU
ND(2003)(B)	—	—	1.00	1.75	3.00	5.00
ND(2003)(H)	—	—	1.25	2.00	3.50	5.50
ND(2003)(C)	—	—	1.00	1.75	3.00	5.00

KM# 317.2 5 RUPEES

8.8000 g., Copper-Nickel, 23.1 mm. **Obv:** Asoka lion pedestal **Rev:** K. Kamaraj above life dates **Edge:** Reeded

Date	Mintage	F	VF	XF	Unc	BU
ND (2003)(H)	—	—	5.00	7.00	11.00	—

KM# 329 5 RUPEES

9.0700 g., Bi-Metallic Brass center in Copper-Nickel ring, 23.25 mm. **Obv:** Asoka column, value below **Rev:** Bust of Shastri 3/4 left **Rev. Legend:** LALBAHADUR SHASTRI BIRTH CENTENARY **Edge:** Security

Date	Mintage	F	VF	XF	Unc	BU
ND(2004)	—	—	—	—	3.50	5.00

KM# 336 5 RUPEES

9.0000 g., Copper-Nickel, 23 mm. **Subject:** 100th Anniversary Birth of Lal Bahadur Shastri **Obv:** Asoka lions **Rev:** Bust of Lal Bahadur Shastri 3/4 right **Edge:** Security

Date	Mintage	F	VF	XF	Unc	BU
ND(2004)(C)	—	—	—	—	3.50	—
ND(2004)(C) Proof	—	Value: 8.00				

KM# 325 5 RUPEES

8.8500 g., Copper-Nickel, 23 mm. **Subject:** 75th Anniversary Dandi March **Obv:** Asoka column **Rev:** Ghandi leading marchers **Edge:** Security type

Date	Mintage	F	VF	XF	Unc	BU
ND (2005)(B)	—	—	—	—	3.00	—
ND(2005)(B)	—	—	—	—	—	5.00

Note: In sets only

KM# 324 5 RUPEES

8.8500 g., Copper-Nickel, 23 mm. **Obv:** Asoka column **Rev:** Bust of Mahatma Basaveshwara slightly left **Edge:** Security

Date	Mintage	F	VF	XF	Unc	BU
ND(2006)(B)	—	—	0.40	1.00	3.00	5.00
ND(2006)(B)	—	Value: 6.00				

KM# 328 5 RUPEES

9.5000 g., Copper-Nickel, 23.10 mm. **Subject:** 150th Anniversary Birth of L. B. G. Tilak **Obv:** Asoka Lion pedestal **Rev:** Bust of Tilak facing slightly right **Edge:** Security

Date	Mintage	F	VF	XF	Unc	BU
2007(B)	—	—	—	—	3.50	5.00

KM# 330 5 RUPEES
6.0300 g., Stainless Steel, 22.88 mm. **Obv:** Asoka column **Rev:** Waves **Edge:** Security

Date	Mintage	F	VF	XF	Unc	BU
2007(B)	—	—	—	—	4.00	5.00
2007(H)	—	—	—	—	4.00	5.00

KM# 185 10 RUPEES
15.0000 g., 0.8000 Silver 0.3858 oz. ASW **Subject:** Centennial - Mahatma Gandhi's Birth **Obv:** Asoka lion pedestal, denomination below **Rev:** Head left **Note:** Struck during 1969 and 1970.

Date	Mintage	F	VF	XF	Unc	BU
ND(1969)(B)	3,160,000	—	—	6.00	9.00	—
ND(1969)B Proof	9,147	Value: 10.00				
ND(1969)(C)	100,000	—	—	7.00	10.00	—

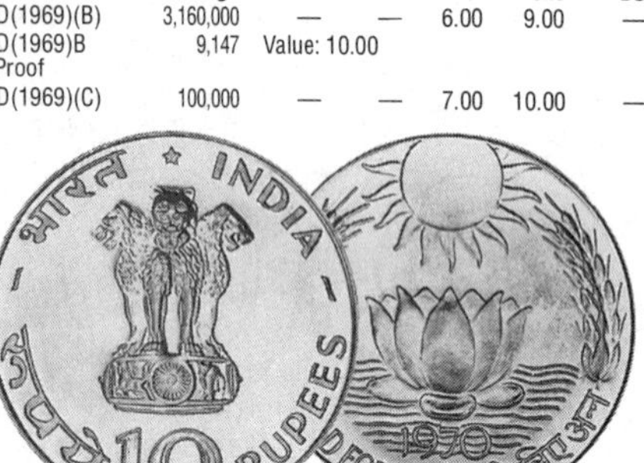

KM# 186 10 RUPEES
15.0000 g., 0.8000 Silver 0.3858 oz. ASW **Series:** F.A.O. **Obv:** Asoka lion pedestal **Rev:** Floating lotus flower below sun

Date	Mintage	F	VF	XF	Unc	BU
1970(B)	300,000	—	—	6.00	9.00	—
1970B Proof	3,046	Value: 9.00				
1970(C)	100,000	—	—	7.00	10.00	—
1971(B)	—	—	—	7.00	10.00	—
1971B Proof	1,594	Value: 10.00				

KM# 344 10 RUPEES
12.5000 g., Copper-Nickel, 31 mm. **Subject:** 100th Anniversary Birth of Jaya Prakash Narayan **Obv:** Asoka column **Rev:** Bust of Jaya Prakash Narayan slightly left **Edge:** Reeded

Date	Mintage	F	VF	XF	Unc	BU
2002(B)	—	—	—	—	9.00	—
2002(B) Proof	—	Value: 15.00				

KM# 347 10 RUPEES
12.5000 g., Copper-Nickel, 31 mm. **Subject:** Sant Tukaram (film about poet) **Obv:** Asoka column **Edge:** Reeded

Date	Mintage	F	VF	XF	Unc	BU
2002(C)	—	—	—	—	9.00	—
2002(C) Proof	—	Value: 15.00				

KM# 332 10 RUPEES
12.5000 g., Copper-Nickel, 31 mm. **Obv:** Asoka lions **Rev:** 3/4 length military figure Veer Durgadass with spear left **Edge:** Reeded

Date	Mintage	F	VF	XF	Unc	BU
2003(B)	—	—	—	—	9.00	—
2003(B) Proof	—	Value: 15.00				

KM# 335 100 RUPEES
35.0000 g., 0.5000 Silver 0.5626 oz. ASW, 44 mm. **Subject:** 150th Anniversary Telecommunications **Obv:** Asoka lions **Rev:** Cartoon bird standing holding cell phone **Edge:** Reeded

Date	Mintage	F	VF	XF	Unc	BU
2004(B)	—	—	—	—	40.00	—
2004(B) Proof	—	Value: 70.00				

INDONESIA

The Republic of Indonesia, the world's largest archipelago, extends for more than 3,000 miles (4,827 km.) along the equator from the mainland of southeast Asia to Australia. The 17,508 islands comprising the archipelago have a combined area of 788,425 sq. mi. (1,919,440 sq.km.) and a population of 205 million, including East Timor. On August 30, 1999, the Timorese majority voted for independence. The Inter FET (International Forces for East Timor) is now in charge of controlling the chaotic situation. Capitol: Jakarta. Petroleum, timber, rubber, and coffee are exported.

Had Columbus succeeded in reaching the fabled Spice Islands, he would have found advanced civilizations a millennium old, and temples still ranking among the finest examples of ancient art. During the opening centuries of the Christian era, the islands were influenced by Hindu priests and traders who spread their culture and religion. Moslem invasions began in the 13th century, fragmenting the island kingdoms into small states which were unable to resist Western colonial infiltration. Portuguese traders established posts in the 16th century, but they were soon outnumbered by the Dutch who arrived in 1596 and gradually asserted control over the islands comprising present-day Indonesia. Dutch dominance, interrupted by British incursions during the Napoleonic Wars, established the Netherlands East Indies as one of the richest colonial possessions in the world.

The Indonesian independence movement, which began between the two world wars, was encouraged by the Japanese during their 3 1/2-year occupation during World War II. Indonesia proclaimed its independence on Aug. 17,1945, three days after the surrender of Japan and full sovereignty. On Dec. 27, 1949, after four years of guerilla warfare including two large-scale campaigns by the Dutch in an effort to reassert control, complete independence was established. Rebellions in Bandung and on the Molluccan Islands occurred in 1950. During the reign of President Mohammad Achmad Sukarno (1950-67) the new Republic not only held together but started to develop. West Irian, formerly Netherlands New Guinea, came under the administration of Indonesia on May 1, 1963. In 1965, the army staged an anti-communist coup in which thousands perished.

On November 28, 1975, the Portuguese Province of Timor, an overseas province occupying the eastern half of the East Indian island of Timor, attained independence as the People's Democratic Republic of East Timor. On December 5, 1975, the government of the People's Democratic Republic was seized by a guerrilla faction sympathetic to the Indonesian territorial claim to East Timor which ousted the constitutional government and replaced it with the Provisional Government of East Timor. On July 17, 1976, the Provisional Government enacted a law that dissolved the free republic and made East Timor the 27th province of Indonesia.

The VOC (United East India Company) struck coins and emergency issues for the Indonesian Archipelago and for the islands at various mints in the Netherlands and the islands. In 1798 the VOC was subsumed by the Dutch government, which issued VOC type transitional and regal types during the Batavian Republic and the Kingdom of the Netherlands until independence. The British issued a coinage during the various occupations by the British East Indian Company, 1811-24. Modern coinage issued by the Republic of Indonesia includes separate series for West Irian and for the Riau Archipelago, an area of small islands between Singapore and Sumatra.

MONETARY SYSTEM
100 Sen = 1 Rupiah

REPUBLIC

STANDARD COINAGE

100 Sen = 1 Rupiah

KM# 7 SEN
0.7500 g., Aluminum **Obv:** Rice stalk surrounds center hole **Rev:** Text around center hole

Date	Mintage	F	VF	XF	Unc	BU
1952(u)	100,000	—	0.20	0.40	0.75	1.50

KM# 5 5 SEN
1.3000 g., Aluminum, 22 mm. **Obv:** Rice stalk surrounds center hole **Rev:** Text around center hole

Date	Mintage	F	VF	XF	Unc	BU
1951(u)	—	—	0.10	0.25	0.50	1.00
1954	—	—	0.10	0.25	0.50	1.00

KM# 6 10 SEN
1.7200 g., Aluminum **Obv:** Denomination within scalloped design, ornaments flank date below **Rev:** National emblem

Date	Mintage	F	VF	XF	Unc	BU
1951(u)	—	—	0.10	0.20	0.35	0.65
1954	50,000,000	—	0.10	0.20	0.35	0.75

KM# 12 10 SEN
Aluminum **Obv:** Denomination within scalloped design, ornaments flank date below **Rev:** National emblem

Date	Mintage	F	VF	XF	Unc	BU
1957	50,224,000	—	0.20	0.40	0.75	1.25

KM# 8 25 SEN
2.2000 g., Aluminum, 27.7 mm. **Obv:** Denomination within scalloped design, ornaments flank date below **Rev:** National emblem

Date	Mintage	F	VF	XF	Unc	BU
1952(u)	200,000,000	—	0.10	0.20	0.25	0.45

KM# 11 25 SEN
Aluminum **Obv:** Denomination within scalloped design, ornaments flank date below **Rev:** National emblem

Date	Mintage	F	VF	XF	Unc	BU
1955	25,767,000	—	0.10	0.20	0.35	0.65
1957	99,752,926	—	0.10	0.20	0.35	0.50

KM# 9 50 SEN
Copper-Nickel **Obv:** Denomination within scalloped design, ornaments flank date below **Rev:** Turbaned head left

Date	Mintage	F	VF	XF	Unc	BU
1952(u)	100,000,000	—	0.10	0.20	0.35	0.50

KM# 10.1 50 SEN
3.2400 g., Copper-Nickel **Obv:** Denomination within scalloped design, ornaments flank date below **Rev:** Turbaned head left

Date	Mintage	F	VF	XF	Unc	BU
1954	1,290,000	—	1.00	2.25	4.50	—
1955	15,000,000	—	0.10	0.20	0.35	0.75

KM# 10.2 50 SEN
Copper-Nickel **Obv:** Denomination within scalloped design, ornaments flank date below **Rev:** Different head, larger lettering

Date	Mintage	F	VF	XF	Unc	BU
1957	26,267,313	—	0.10	0.20	0.35	0.65

KM# 13 50 SEN
Aluminum **Obv:** Denomination within inner circle, ornaments flank date below **Rev:** National emblem

Date	Mintage	F	VF	XF	Unc	BU
1958	33,740,000	—	0.10	0.20	0.40	0.75

KM# 14 50 SEN
3.0200 g., Aluminum, 29 mm. **Obv:** Denomination within inner circle, ornaments flank date below **Rev:** National emblem, modified eagle

Date	Mintage	F	VF	XF	Unc	BU
1959	100,009,000	—	0.10	0.20	0.40	0.65
1961	150,000,000	—	0.10	0.20	0.40	0.65

KM# 20 RUPIAH
1.4400 g., Aluminum, 20.36 mm. **Rev:** Fantail flycatcher **Edge:** Plain

Date	Mintage	F	VF	XF	Unc	BU
1970	136,010,000	—	—	0.15	0.50	0.75

KM# 21 2 RUPIAH
2.3000 g., Aluminum, 26 mm. **Obv:** Stars flank date below denomination **Rev:** Rice and cotton stalks

Date	Mintage	F	VF	XF	Unc	BU
1970	139,230,000	—	—	0.15	0.25	0.40

KM# 22 5 RUPIAH
Aluminum **Obv:** Stars flank date below denomination **Rev:** Black drongo

Date	Mintage	F	VF	XF	Unc	BU
1970	448,000,000	—	0.15	0.30	0.75	1.00

KM# 37 5 RUPIAH
Aluminum, 28.6 mm. **Subject:** Family Planning Program **Obv:** Stars flank date below denomination **Rev:** The ideal family within rice and cotton stalk wreath

Date	Mintage	F	VF	XF	Unc	BU
1974	447,910,000	—	0.10	0.15	0.25	0.35

KM# 43 5 RUPIAH
1.4000 g., Aluminum, 23 mm. **Subject:** Family Planning Program **Obv:** Stars flank date below denomination, inner circle surrounds **Rev:** The ideal family within rice and cotton stalk wreath, inner circle surrounds

Date	Mintage	F	VF	XF	Unc	BU
1979	413,200,000	—	0.10	0.15	0.25	0.35
1995	6,420,000	—	0.20	0.30	0.60	1.00
1996	—	—	0.20	0.30	0.60	1.00

KM# 33 10 RUPIAH
1.7700 g., Copper-Nickel, 15.6 mm. **Series:** F.A.O. **Rev:** Rice and cotton stalks

Date	Mintage	F	VF	XF	Unc	BU
1971	286,360,000	—	0.10	0.25	0.50	0.75

KM# 38 10 RUPIAH
Brass-Clad Steel, 22 mm. **Subject:** National Saving Program **Obv:** Stars flank date below denomination **Rev:** Rice and cotton stalks form wreath around teapot design

Date	Mintage	F	VF	XF	Unc	BU
1974	222,910,000	—	0.10	0.25	0.75	1.25

KM# 44 10 RUPIAH
1.9000 g., Aluminum, 25 mm. **Series:** F.A.O. **Obv:** Stars flank date below denomination **Rev:** Rice and cotton stalks form wreath around teapot design

Date	Mintage	F	VF	XF	Unc	BU
1979	285,670,000	—	0.10	0.20	0.40	0.65

KM# 34 25 RUPIAH
3.5000 g., Copper-Nickel, 28 mm. **Obv:** Stars flank date below denomination **Rev:** Victoria crowned pigeon

Date	Mintage	F	VF	XF	Unc	BU
1971	1,221,610,000	—	0.10	0.20	0.40	0.75

KM# 55 25 RUPIAH
1.2500 g., Aluminum, 18.01 mm. **Obv:** National emblem **Rev:** Nutmeg plant **Edge:** Plain

Date	Mintage	F	VF	XF	Unc	BU
1991	30,000,000	—	—	0.40	0.75	1.25
1992	64,000,000	—	—	0.40	0.75	1.25
1993	20,000,000	—	—	0.40	0.75	1.25
1994	250,000,000	—	—	0.25	0.50	0.75
1995	184,480,000	—	—	0.25	0.50	0.75
1996	—	—	—	0.25	0.50	0.75

KM# 35 50 RUPIAH
6.0000 g., Copper-Nickel, 24 mm. **Obv:** Stars flank date below denomination **Rev:** Greater Bird of Paradise

Date	Mintage	F	VF	XF	Unc	BU
1971	1,035,435,000	—	0.15	0.30	0.65	1.00

KM# 52 50 RUPIAH
3.2000 g., Aluminum-Bronze, 19.94 mm. **Obv:** National emblem **Rev:** Komodo dragon lizard **Edge:** Reeded

Date	Mintage	F	VF	XF	Unc	BU
1991	67,000,000	—	0.10	0.20	0.50	1.25
1992	70,000,000	—	0.10	0.20	0.50	1.25
1993	120,000,000	—	0.10	0.20	0.50	1.25
1994	300,000,000	—	0.10	0.20	0.50	1.25
1995	591,880,000	—	0.10	0.20	0.50	1.25
1996	—	—	0.10	0.25	0.60	1.25
1997	150,000	—	0.10	0.25	0.60	1.25
1998	150,000	—	0.10	0.25	0.60	1.25

KM# 60 50 RUPIAH
1.3600 g., Aluminum, 19.95 mm. **Obv:** National emblem **Rev:** Black-naped Oriole **Edge:** Plain

Date	Mintage	F	VF	XF	Unc	BU
1999	—	—	—	—	0.40	0.75
2001	—	—	—	—	0.30	1.00
2002	—	—	—	—	0.30	1.00

KM# 36 100 RUPIAH

Copper-Nickel **Obv:** Stars flank date below denomination **Rev:** Minangkabu house

Date	Mintage	F	VF	XF	Unc	BU
1973	252,868,000	—	0.35	0.75	1.50	3.00

KM# 42 100 RUPIAH

7.0000 g., Copper-Nickel, 28.5 mm. **Subject:** Forestry for prosperity **Obv:** Minangkabu house **Rev:** Legendary tree of life

Date	Mintage	F	VF	XF	Unc	BU
1978	907,773,000	—	0.25	0.50	1.50	3.00

KM# 53 100 RUPIAH

4.0600 g., Aluminum-Bronze, 22 mm. **Subject:** Buffalo racing **Obv:** National emblem **Rev:** Buffalo racers **Edge:** Reeded

Date	Mintage	F	VF	XF	Unc	BU
1991	94,000,000	—	0.15	0.30	0.60	1.00
1992	120,000,000	—	0.15	0.30	0.60	1.00
1993	300,000,000	—	0.15	0.30	0.60	1.00
1994	550,000,000	—	0.15	0.30	0.60	1.00
1995	798,100,000	—	0.15	0.30	0.60	1.00
1996	41,000,000	—	0.15	0.30	0.65	1.00
1997	150,000,000	—	0.15	0.30	0.65	1.00
1998	59,000,000	—	0.15	0.30	0.65	1.00

KM# 61 100 RUPIAH

1.7900 g., Aluminum, 23 mm. **Obv:** National emblem **Rev:** Palm Cockatoo **Edge:** Plain

Date	Mintage	F	VF	XF	Unc	BU
1999	—	—	—	—	0.75	1.50
2000	—	—	—	—	0.75	1.50
2001	—	—	—	—	0.75	1.25
2002	—	—	—	—	0.75	1.25
2003	—	—	—	—	0.75	1.25
2004	—	—	—	—	0.75	1.25

KM# 66 200 RUPIAH

2.4000 g., Aluminum, 25 mm. **Obv:** National arms **Rev:** Balinese starling bird above value **Edge:** Plain

Date	Mintage	F	VF	XF	Unc	BU
2003	—	—	—	—	1.00	1.50

KM# 54 500 RUPIAH

Aluminum-Bronze, 24 mm. **Obv:** National emblem **Rev:** Jasmine **Edge:** Plain

Date	Mintage	F	VF	XF	Unc	BU
1991	71,000,000	—	—	1.25	2.50	3.00
1992	100,000,000	—	—	1.25	2.50	3.00
1993	—	—	—	1.25	2.50	3.00
1994	—	—	—	1.25	2.50	3.00

KM# 59 500 RUPIAH

5.3200 g., Aluminum-Bronze, 24 mm. **Obv:** National emblem **Rev:** Denomination

Date	Mintage	F	VF	XF	Unc	BU
1997	—	—	—	—	2.00	2.50
1999	—	—	—	—	2.00	2.50
2000	—	—	—	—	2.00	2.50
2001	—	—	—	—	2.00	2.50
2002	—	—	—	—	2.00	2.50
2003	—	—	—	—	2.00	2.50

KM# 67 500 RUPIAH

3.1100 g., Aluminum, 27.2 mm. **Obv:** National arms **Rev:** Jasmine flower above value **Edge:** Segmented reeding

Date	Mintage	F	VF	XF	Unc	BU
2003	—	—	—	—	2.00	2.50

IRIAN BARAT

(West Irian, Irian Jaya,
Netherlands New Guinea)

A province of Indonesia comprising the western half of the island of New Guinea. A special set of coins dated 1962 were issued in 1964, were recalled December 31, 1971, and are no longer legal tender.

INDONESIAN PROVINCE

STANDARD COINAGE

No inscription on edge

KM# 5 SEN

Aluminum **Subject:** Mohammed Ahmad Sukarno **Obv:** Head left **Rev:** Denomination within wreath of cotton and rice stalks **Edge:** Plain

Date	Mintage	F	VF	XF	Unc	BU
1962	—	0.25	0.50	1.00	2.00	—

KM# 6 5 SEN

Aluminum **Subject:** Mohammed Ahmad Sukarno **Obv:** Head left **Rev:** Denomination within wreath of cotton and rice stalks **Edge:** Plain

Date	Mintage	F	VF	XF	Unc	BU
1962	—	0.25	0.50	1.25	2.00	—

KM# 7 10 SEN

Aluminum **Subject:** Mohammed Ahmad Sukarno **Obv:** Head left **Rev:** Denomination within rice and cotton stalks **Edge:** Plain

Date	Mintage	F	VF	XF	Unc	BU
1962	—	0.25	0.50	1.25	2.50	—

KM# 8.1 25 SEN

Aluminum **Subject:** Mohammed Ahmad Sukarno **Obv:** Head left **Rev:** Denomination within wreath of cotton and rice stalks **Edge:** Reeded

Date	Mintage	F	VF	XF	Unc	BU
1962	—	—	—	—	—	—

KM# 8.2 25 SEN

Aluminum **Obv:** Head left **Rev:** Denomination within wreath of cotton and rice stalks

Date	Mintage	F	VF	XF	Unc	BU
1962	—	0.75	1.50	2.50	4.00	—

KM# 9 50 SEN

Aluminum **Subject:** Mohammed Ahmad Sukarno **Obv:** Head left **Rev:** Denomination within wreath of cotton and rice stalks **Edge:** Reeded

Date	Mintage	F	VF	XF	Unc	BU
1962	—	0.85	1.60	3.00	5.00	—

RIAU ARCHIPELAGO

A group of 3,214 islands off the tip of the Malay Peninsula. Coins were issued near the end of 1963 (although dated 1962) and recalled as worthless on Sept. 30, 1964. They were legal tender from Oct. 15, 1963 to July 1, 1964.

INSCRIPTION ON EDGE
KEPULAUAN RIAU

INDONESIAN PROVINCE

STANDARD COINAGE

Inscription on edge: "Kepulauan Riau"

KM# 5 SEN

Aluminum **Obv:** Head left **Rev:** Denomination within wreath of cotton and rice stalks

Date	Mintage	F	VF	XF	Unc	BU
1962	—	0.35	0.75	1.25	2.00	—

KM# 6 5 SEN
Aluminum **Obv:** Head left **Rev:** Denomination within wreath of cotton and rice stalks

Date	Mintage	F	VF	XF	Unc	BU
1962	—	0.30	0.60	1.50	2.00	—

KM# 7 10 SEN
Aluminum **Subject:** Mohammed Ahmad Sukarno **Obv:** Head left **Rev:** Denomination within wreath of cotton and rice stalks

Date	Mintage	F	VF	XF	Unc	BU
1962	—	0.35	0.70	1.75	2.75	—

KM# 8.1 25 SEN
Aluminum **Obv:** Head left **Rev:** Denomination within wreath of cotton and rice stalks

Date	Mintage	F	VF	XF	Unc	BU
1962	—	—	—	—	—	—

KM# 8.2 25 SEN
Aluminum **Subject:** Mohammed Ahmad Sukarno **Obv:** Head left **Rev:** Denomination within wreath of cotton and rice stalks

Date	Mintage	F	VF	XF	Unc	BU
1962	—	0.85	1.60	2.75	4.50	—

KM# 9 50 SEN
Aluminum **Subject:** Mohammed Ahmad Sukarno **Obv:** Bust left **Rev:** Denomination within wreath of cotton and rice stalks

Date	Mintage	F	VF	XF	Unc	BU
1962	—	1.00	2.00	3.50	5.50	—

IRAN

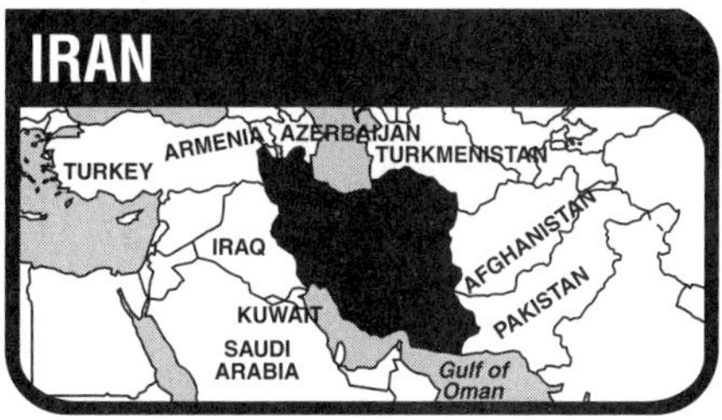

The Islamic Republic of Iran, located between the Caspian Sea and the Persian Gulf in southwestern Asia, has an area of 636,296 sq. mi. (1,648,000 sq. km.) and a population of 40 million. Capital: Tehran. Although predominantly an agricultural state, Iran depends heavily on oil for foreign exchange. Crude oil, carpets and agricultural products are exported.

Iran (historically known as Persia until 1931AD) is one of the world's most ancient and resilient nations. Strategically astride the lower land gate to Asia, it has been conqueror and conquered, sovereign nation and vassal state, ever emerging from its periods of glory or travail with its culture and political individuality intact. Iran (Persia) was a powerful empire under Cyrus the Great (600-529 B.C.), its borders extending from the Indus to the Nile. It has also been conquered by the predatory empires of antique and recent times - Assyrian, Medean, Macedonian, Seljuq, Turk, Mongol - and more recently been coveted by Russia, the Third Reich and Great Britain. Revolts against the absolute power of the Persian shahs resulted in the establishment of a constitutional monarchy in1906.

With 4,000 troops, Reza Khan marched on the capital arriving in Tehran in the early morning of Feb. 22,1921. The government was taken over with hardly a shot and Zia ad-Din was set up as premier, but the real power was with Reza Khan, although he was officially only the minister of war. In 1923, Reza Khan appointed himself prime minister and summoned the "majlis." Who eventually gave him military powers and he became independent of the shah's authority. In 1925 Reza Khan Pahlavi was elected Shah of Persia. A few weeks later his eldest son, Shahpur Mohammed Reza was appointed Crown Prince and was crowned on April 25, 1926.

In 1931 the Kingdom of Persia became known as the Kingdom of Iran. In 1979 the monarchy was toppled and an Islamic Republic proclaimed.

RULERS

Qajar Dynasty

مظفر الدين

Muzaffar al-Din Shah, AH1313-1324/1896-1907AD

محمد علی

Muhammad Ali Shah, AH1324-1327/1907-1909AD

سلطان احمد

Sultan Ahmad Shah, AH1327-1344/1909-1925AD

Pahlavi Dynasty

رضا

Reza Shah, as prime minister, SH1302-1304/1923-1925AD
as Shah, SH1304-1320/1925-1941AD

محمد رضا

Mohammad Reza Pahlavi, Shah SH1320-1358/1941-1979AD

جمهوری اسلامی ایران

Islamic Republic, SH1358-/1979-AD

MINT NAMES

طهران

Tehran

MINT MARKS

H - Heaton (Birmingham)
L - Leningrad (St. Petersburg)

COIN DATING

Iranian coins were dated according to the Moslem lunar calendar until March 21, 1925 (AD), when dating was switched to a new calendar based on the solar year, indicated by the notation SH. The monarchial calendar system was adopted in 1976 = MS2535 and was abandoned in 1978 = MS2537. The previously used solar year calendar was restored at that time.

MONETARY SYSTEM

1825-1931
(AH1241-1344, SH1304-09)
50 Dinars = 1 Shahi
20 Shahis = 1 Kran (Qiran)
10 Krans = 1 Toman

1932-Date (SH1310-Date)
5 Dinars = 1 Shahi
20 Shahis = 1 Rial (100 Dinars)
10 Rials = 1 Toman

NOTE: The Toman ceased to be an official unit in 1932, but continues to be applied in popular usage. Thus, 135 Rials' is always expressed as 13 Toman, 5 Rials'. The term Rial' is often used in conversation, as well as either Kran' or Ezar' (short for Hazar = 1000) is used.

NOTE: The Law of 18 March 1930 fixed the gold Pahlavi at 20 Rials. No gold coins were struck. The Law of 13 March1932 divided the Pahlavi into 100 Rials, instead of 20. The Rial's weight was reduced from 0.3661 grams of pure gold to 0.0732. Since 1937 gold has been allowed to float and the Pahlavi is quoted daily in Rials in the marketplaces.

KINGDOM

SILVER AND GOLD COINAGE

The precious metal monetary system of Qajar Persia prior to the reforms of 1878 was the direct descendant of the Mongol system introduced by Ghazan Mahmud in 1297AD, and was the last example of a medieval islamic coinage. It is not a modern system, and cannot be understood as such. It is not possible to list types, dates, and mints as for other countries, both because of the nature of the coinage, and because very little research has been done on the series. The following comments should help elucidate its nature.

STANDARDS: The weight of the primary silver and gold coins was set by law and was expressed in terms of the Mesqal (about 4.61 g) and the Nokhod (24 Nokhod = 1 Mesqal). The primary silver coin was the Rupee from AH1211-1212, the Riyal from AH1212-1241, and the Gheran from AH1241-1344. The standard gold coin was the Toman. Currently the price of gold is quoted in Mesqals.

DENOMINATIONS: In addition to the primary denominations, noted in the last paragraph, fractional pieces were coined, valued at one-eighth, one-fourth, and one-half the primary denomination, usually in much smaller quantities. These were ordinarily struck from the same dies as the larger pieces, sometimes on broad, thin flans, sometimes on thick, dumpy flans. On the smaller coins, the denomination can best be determined only by weighing the coin. The denomination is almost never expressed on the coin!

DEVALUATIONS: From time to time, the standard for silver and gold was reduced, and the old coin recalled and replaced with lighter coin, the difference going to the government coffers. The effect was that of a devaluation of the primary silver and gold coins, or inversely regarded, an increase in the price of silver and gold. The durations of each standard varied from about 2 to 20 years. The standards are given for each ruler, as the denomination can only be determined when the standard is known.

LIGHTWEIGHT AND ALLOYED PIECES: Most of the smaller denomination coins were issued at lighter weights than those prescribed by law, with the difference going to the pockets of the mintmasters. Other mints, notably Hamadan, added excessive amounts of alloy to the coins, and some mintmasters lost their heads as a result. Discrepancies in weight of as much as 15 percent and more are observed, with the result that it is often quite impossible to determine the denomination of a coin!

OVERSIZE COINS: Occasionally, multiples of the primary denominations were produced, usually on special occasions for presentation by the Shah to his favorites. These 'coins' did not circulate (except as bullion), and were usually worn as ornaments. They were the 'NCLT's' of their day.

MINTS & EPITHETS: Qajar coinage was struck at 34 mints (plus at least a dozen others striking only copper Falus), which are listed previously, with drawings of the mintnames in Persian, as they appear on the coins. However, the Persian script admits of infinite variation and stylistic whimsy, so the forms given are only guides, and not absolute. Only a knowledge of the script will assure correct reading. In addition to the city name, most mintnames were given identifying epithets, which occasionally appear in lieu of the mintname, particularly at Iravan and Mashhad.

ARRANGEMENT

The following listings are arranged first by ruler, with various standards explained. Then, the coins are listed by denomination within each reign. For each denomination, one or more pieces, when available, are illustrated, with the mint and date noted beneath each photo. For each type, a date range is given, but this range indicates the years during which the particular type was current, and does not imply that every year of the interval is known on actual coins. Because dates were carelessly engraved, and old dies were used until they wore out or broke, we occasionally find coins of a particular type dated before or after the indicated interval. Such coins command no premium. No attempt has been made to determine which mints actually exist for which types.

KRAN STANDARD
AH1293-1344, SH1304-1309,
1876-1931AD
50 Dinars = 1 Shahi
1000 Dinars = 20 Shahis = 1 Kran (Qiron)
10 Krans = 1 Toman

Special Gold Issue
AH1337/1918-1919AD
1 Ashrafi (= 1 Toman)
SH1305-1309/1927-1931AD

Toman replaced by Pahlavi (light standard). Relationship of Pahlavi to Kran not known.

NOTE: Dated reverse dies lacking the ruler's name were not discarded at the end of a reign (especially from Nasir al-Din to Muzaffar al-Din), but remained in use until broken or worn out. Sometimes the old date was scratched out or changed, but often the die was used with the old date unaltered. Some dies with date below wreath retained the old date but had the new date engraved among the lion's legs.

SHAHI SEFID
(White Shahi)

Called the White (i.e. silver) Shahi to distinguish it from the Black or Copper Shahi, the Shahi Sefid was actually worth 3 Shahis (150 Dinars) or 3 1/8 Shahis (156 ¼ Dinars). It was used primarily for distribution on New Year's Day (now RUZ) as good-luck gifts. Since 1926 special privately struck tokens, having no monetary value, have been used instead of coins. The Shahi Sefid was broader, but much thinner than the ¼ Kran (Rob'l), worth 250 Dinars.

Milled Gold Coinage:

Modern imitations exist of many types, particularly the small 1/5, 1/2, and 1 Toman coins. These are usually underweight (or rarely overweight), and are sold in the bazaars at a small premium over bullion. They are usually crude and probably not intended to deceive collectors, but some are sold for jewelry and some are dated outside the reign of the ruler whose name or portrait they bear. A few deceptive counterfeits are known of the large 10 Toman pieces.

KINGDOM

Muzaffar al-Din Shah
AH1313-1324 / 1896-1907AD

MILLED COINAGE

KM# 961 50 DINARS
Copper-Nickel **Obv:** Legend within beaded circle with crown on top **Rev:** Radiant lion holding sword within wreath **Mint:** Tehran

Date	Mintage	F	VF	XF	Unc	BU
AH1319	12,000,000	1.00	3.50	7.00	10.00	—
AH1321	10,000,000	0.75	1.50	4.00	8.00	—
AH1326	8,000,000	4.00	10.00	20.00	30.00	—
AH1332	6,000,000	1.00	2.00	5.00	12.50	—
AH1337	7,000,000	1.50	4.00	8.00	12.00	—

KM# 965 SHAHI SEFID (White Shahi)
0.8000 g., 0.9000 Silver 0.0231 oz. ASW **Obv:** Legend and value within circle and wreath **Obv. Legend:** "Muzaffar al-Din Shah" **Rev:** Crown above lion and sun within wreath **Mint:** Tehran

Date	Mintage	F	VF	XF	Unc	BU
AH1319	—	15.00	30.00	60.00	120	—
AH1039	—	25.00	50.00	100	200	—
Note: Error for 1319						
AH1320	150,000	15.00	30.00	60.00	120	—

KM# 966 SHAHI SEFID (White Shahi)
0.8000 g., 0.9000 Silver 0.0231 oz. ASW **Obv:** Legend within circle and wreath **Rev:** Radiant lion holding sword within crowned wreath **Mint:** Tehran

Date	Mintage	F	VF	XF	Unc	BU
ND (1901)	—	50.00	80.00	165	300	—
AH1319 (1901) Rare	—	—	—	—	—	—

Note: A number of varieties and mulings of KM#965 and KM#966 with other denominations, especially 1/4 Krans and 500 Dinar pieces, are reported; these command a premium over others of the same types; a total of 58,000 pieces were reported struck in AH1322, 1323 and 1324, but none are known with those dates; the specimens were either struck from old dies or were undated types.

KM# 967 SHAHI SEFID (White Shahi)
0.8000 g., 0.9000 Silver 0.0231 oz. ASW **Obv:** Legend within center circle of wreath **Obv. Legend:** "Muzaffar al-Din Shah" **Rev:** Legend within center circle of wreath **Rev. Legend:** "Sahib al-Zaman" **Mint:** Tehran **Note:** Thick and thin lettering varieties exist.

Date	Mintage	F	VF	XF	Unc	BU
ND (1903)	—	50.00	85.00	165	300	—

KM# 962 100 DINARS (2 Shahi)
4.4000 g., Copper-Nickel **Obv:** Legend within beaded circle and crowned wreath **Rev:** Radiant lion holding sword within crowned wreath

Date	Mintage	F	VF	XF	Unc	BU
AH1319	9,000,000	2.50	5.00	10.00	20.00	—
AH1321/19	5,000,000	6.00	12.00	30.00	50.00	—
AH1321	Inc. above	0.75	1.50	4.00	8.00	—
AH1326	6,000,000	1.50	2.50	6.00	15.00	—
AH1332	5,000,000	1.00	2.00	5.00	12.50	—
AH1337	6,500,000	2.00	5.00	10.00	15.00	—

KM# 968 1/4 KRAN (Robi = 5 Shahis)
1.1513 g., 0.9000 Silver 0.0333 oz. ASW **Obv:** Legend and value within circle and wreath **Obv. Legend:** "Muzaffar al-din Shah" **Rev:** Crown above lion and sun within wreath **Mint:** Tehran **Note:** 300 specimens reportedly struck in AH1322, but none known to exist.

Date	Mintage	F	VF	XF	Unc	BU
AH1319	—	20.00	35.00	65.00	130	—

KM# 969 500 DINARS (10 Shahis = 1/2 Kran)
2.3025 g., 0.9000 Silver 0.0666 oz. ASW **Obv:** Legend and value within circle and wreath **Obv. Legend:** "Muzaffar al-din", 500 Dinars **Rev:** Crown above lion and sun within wreath **Mint:** Tehran **Note:** Some reverse dies were previously used under Nasir al-Din and show traces of old date beneath wreath on reverse.

Date	Mintage	F	VF	XF	Unc	BU
AH1319	—	20.00	40.00	100	200	—
AH1322	—	20.00	30.00	50.00	100	—

KM# 977 500 DINARS (10 Shahis = 1/2 Kran)
2.3025 g., 0.9000 Silver 0.0666 oz. ASW **Obv:** Uniformed bust 1/4 right **Rev:** Radiant lion holding sword within crowned wreath **Mint:** Tehran

Date	Mintage	F	VF	XF	Unc	BU
AH1323 (1905)	130,000	20.00	35.00	80.00	160	—

1000 DINARS: 

1 KRAN: 

KM# 972 1000 DINARS (Kran, Qiran)
4.6050 g., 0.9000 Silver 0.1332 oz. ASW **Obv:** Legend and value within circle and wreath **Rev:** Crown above lion and sun within wreath **Mint:** Tehran

Date	Mintage	F	VF	XF	Unc	BU
AH1319	—	150	225	350	500	—
AH1322	—	100	175	250	350	—

KM# 978 1000 DINARS (Kran, Qiran)
4.6050 g., 0.9000 Silver 0.1332 oz. ASW **Obv:** Uniformed bust 1/4 right **Rev:** Radiant lion holding sword within crowned wreath **Mint:** Tehran

Date	Mintage	F	VF	XF	Unc	BU
AH1323 (1905)	125,000	20.00	30.00	65.00	125	—

KM# 974 2000 DINARS (2 Kran)
9.2100 g., 0.9000 Silver 0.2665 oz. ASW **Obv:** Legend and value within wreath, star above **Rev:** Crown above lion and sun within wreath **Mint:** Tehran **Note:** Blundered dates exist.

Date	Mintage	F	VF	XF	Unc	BU
AH1319	—	10.00	20.00	35.00	90.00	—
AH1320	13,959,000	10.00	20.00	35.00	75.00	—

KM# 975 2000 DINARS (2 Kran)
9.2100 g., 0.9000 Silver 0.2665 oz. ASW **Obv:** Legend within circle and wreath **Rev:** Radiant lion holding sword within crowned wreath **Rev. Legend:** 2 Krans **Mint:** Tehran

Date	Mintage	F	VF	XF	Unc	BU
AH1320 (1902)	Inc. above	12.50	20.00	40.00	100	—
AH1321 (1903)	18,108,000	15.00	22.50	45.00	100	—
Note: In blundered form as 13201						
AH1322 (1904)	8,640,000	8.00	15.00	30.00	80.00	—

KM# 979 2000 DINARS (2 Kran)
9.2100 g., 0.9000 Silver 0.2665 oz. ASW **Obv:** Uniformed bust 1/4 right within wreath **Rev:** Radiant lion holding sword within crowned wreath **Mint:** Tehran

Date	Mintage	F	VF	XF	Unc	BU
AH1323 (1905)	—	15.00	30.00	60.00	120	—
Note: Mintage inluded in AH1323 above						
AH'13' (1905)	—	60.00	100	200	400	—
Note: 23 of 1323 filled in or never punched						
AH13233 (1905)	—	45.00	85.00	190	380	—
Note: Error						

KM# 976 5000 DINARS (5 Kran)
23.0251 g., 0.9000 Silver 0.6662 oz. ASW **Obv:** Legend within crowned wreath **Obv. Legend:** "Muzaffar al-din Shah" **Rev:** Radiant lion holding sword within crowned wreath **Note:** Dav.#288.

Date	Mintage	F	VF	XF	Unc	BU
AH1320 (1902)	250,000	12.00	16.00	32.00	60.00	—
Note: Actual mintage must be considerably greater						

KM# 980 5000 DINARS (5 Kran)
23.0251 g., 0.9000 Silver 0.6662 oz. ASW, 36 mm. **Subject:** Royal Birthday **Obv:** Uniformed bust 1/4 right within wreath **Rev:** Radiant lion holding sword within crowned wreath **Note:** Dav.#287.

Date	Mintage	F	VF	XF	Unc	BU
AH1322 (1904)	—	400	550	800	1,200	—

KM# 981 5000 DINARS (5 Kran)
23.0251 g., 0.9000 Silver 0.6662 oz. ASW, 36 mm. **Obv:** Uniformed bust 1/4 right within wreath **Rev:** Radiant lion holding sword within crowned wreath **Note:** Dav.#289. Without additional inscription flanking head

Date	Mintage	F	VF	XF	Unc	BU
AH1324 (1906)	3,040	1,000	2,000	3,000	4,000	—

KM# 991 2000 DINARS (1/5 Toman)
0.5749 g., 0.9000 Gold 0.0166 oz. AGW **Obv:** Uniformed bust left **Rev:** Legend and value within circle and wreath

Date	Mintage	F	VF	XF	Unc	BU
AH1319 (1901)	—	200	300	400	500	—

KM# 992 2000 DINARS (1/5 Toman)
0.5749 g., 0.9000 Gold 0.0166 oz. AGW **Obv:** Date and denomination added

Date	Mintage	F	VF	XF	Unc	BU
AH1319 (1901)	—	50.00	100	150	250	—
AH1322 (1904)	—	50.00	100	150	250	—
AH1323 (1905)	—	100	200	300	400	—
AH1324 (1906)	—	100	200	300	400	—

KM# 994.1 5000 DINARS (1/2 Toman)
1.4372 g., 0.9000 Gold 0.0416 oz. AGW **Obv:** Uniformed bust 3/4 right **Rev:** Legend and value within cirlce and wreath **Note:** Prev. KM#994.

Date	Mintage	F	VF	XF	Unc	BU
AH1319	—	100	200	300	400	—
AH1320	—	35.00	60.00	100	200	—
AH1321	—	35.00	60.00	100	200	—
AH1322	—	35.00	60.00	100	200	—
AH1324	—	100	200	300	400	—

KM# 994.2 5000 DINARS (1/2 Toman)
1.4372 g., 0.9000 Gold 0.0416 oz. AGW **Obv:** Bust with headdress 3/4 right divides date **Rev:** Legend within cirlce and wreath

Date	Mintage	F	VF	XF	Unc	BU
AH1323	—	100	200	300	400	—

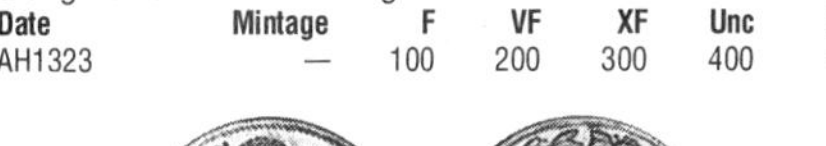

KM# 995 TOMAN
2.8744 g., 0.9000 Gold 0.0832 oz. AGW, 19 mm. **Obv:** Uniformed bust 3/4 right, accession date, AH1314 above left **Rev:** Legend and value within circle and wreath

Date	Mintage	F	VF	XF	Unc	BU
AH1319	—	60.00	100	160	250	—
AH1321	—	100	200	300	400	—

Muhammad Ali Shah
AH1324-1327 / 1907-1909AD

MILLED COINAGE

KM# 1006 SHAHI SEFID (White Shahi)
0.0691 g., 0.9000 Silver 0.0020 oz. ASW, 17 mm. **Obv:** Legend within circle and wreath **Obv. Legend:** "Muhammad Ali Shah" **Rev:** Radiant lion holding sword within crowned wreath **Mint:** Tehran

Date	Mintage	F	VF	XF	Unc	BU
AH1325 (1907)	—	30.00	60.00	110	200	—
AH1326 (1908)	—	25.00	40.00	90.00	180	—
AH1327 (1909)	—	20.00	40.00	80.00	160	—

KM# 1007 SHAHI SEFID (White Shahi)
0.0691 g., 0.9000 Silver 0.0020 oz. ASW **Obv:** Legend within circle and wreath **Obv. Legend:** "Sahib al-Zaman" **Rev:** Radiant lion holding sword within crowned wreath **Mint:** Tehran

Date	Mintage	F	VF	XF	Unc	BU
AH1326 (1908)	—	60.00	125	175	325	—

KM# 1008 SHAHI SEFID (White Shahi)
0.0691 g., 0.9000 Silver 0.0020 oz. ASW **Obv:** Legend within circle and wreath **Rev:** Radiant lion holding sword within crowned wreath **Mint:** Tehran

Date	Mintage	F	VF	XF	Unc	BU
ND (1909)	—	50.00	80.00	150	300	—

KM# 1009 1/4 KRAN (Robi = 5 Shahis)
1.1513 g., 0.9000 Silver 0.0333 oz. ASW, 15 mm. **Obv:** Legend within circle and wreath **Obv. Legend:** "Muhammad Ali Shah" **Rev:** Radiant lion holding sword within crowned wreath **Mint:** Tehran

Date	Mintage	F	VF	XF	Unc	BU
AH1325 (1907)	—	30.00	50.00	100	200	—
AH1326 (1908)	—	15.00	27.50	40.00	80.00	—
AH1327 (1909)	—	10.00	20.00	35.00	70.00	—

KM# 1010 500 DINARS (10 Shahis = 1/2 Kran)
2.3025 g., 0.9000 Silver 0.0666 oz. ASW, 18 mm. **Obv:** Legend within circle and wreath **Obv. Legend:** "Muhammad Ali Shah" **Rev:** Radiant lion holding sword within crowned wreath **Mint:** Tehran

Date	Mintage	F	VF	XF	Unc	BU
AH1325 (1907)	218,000	40.00	75.00	160	300	—
AH1326 (1908)	218,000	25.00	50.00	110	225	—
AH1336 (1908) Error for 1326	Inc. above	35.00	60.00	125	250	—

KM# 1014 500 DINARS (10 Shahis = 1/2 Kran)
2.3025 g., 0.9000 Silver 0.0666 oz. ASW **Obv:** Uniformed bust 3/4 left within wreath, date **Rev:** Crown above lion and sun within wreath, date **Mint:** Tehran

Date	Mintage	F	VF	XF	Unc	BU
AH1325 (1907)	—	125	175	320	500	—
AH1326 (1908)	—	100	150	240	400	—

KM# 1013 500 DINARS (10 Shahis = 1/2 Kran)
2.3025 g., 0.9000 Silver 0.0666 oz. ASW **Obv:** Uniformed bust 1/4 left within sprigs **Rev:** Radiant lion holding sword within crowned wreath **Mint:** Tehran

Date	Mintage	F	VF	XF	Unc	BU
AH1326 (1908)	—	40.00	85.00	150	300	—
Note: Mintage included in KM#1010						
AH1327 (1909)	—	40.00	85.00	150	300	—

KM# 1011 1000 DINARS (Kran, Qiran)
4.6050 g., 0.9000 Silver 0.1332 oz. ASW, 23 mm. **Obv:** Legend within circle and crowned wreath **Obv. Legend:** "Muhammad Ali Shah" **Rev:** Radiant lion holding sword within crowned wreath **Mint:** Tehran

Date	Mintage	F	VF	XF	Unc	BU
AH1325 (1907)	289,000	150	300	600	800	—
AH1326 (1908)	289,000	150	300	600	800	—

KM# 1015 1000 DINARS (Kran, Qiran)
4.6050 g., 0.9000 Silver 0.1332 oz. ASW **Obv:** Uniformed bust 3/4 left within wreath, date below **Rev:** Radiant lion holding sword within crowned wreath **Mint:** Tehran

Date	Mintage	F	VF	XF	Unc	BU
AH1326 (1908)	—	45.00	70.00	150	375	—
Note: Mintage included in KM#1011						
AH1327/6 (1909)	—	40.00	60.00	125	350	—
AH1327 (1909)	—	40.00	60.00	125	350	—

KM# 1016 1000 DINARS (Kran, Qiran)
4.6050 g., 0.9000 Silver 0.1332 oz. ASW **Obv:** Uniformed bust 3/4 left within wreath, date **Rev:** Radiant lion holding sword within crowned wreath, date **Mint:** Tehran

Date	Mintage	F	VF	XF	Unc	BU
AH1326 (1908)	—	125	200	350	500	—
Note: Mintage included in KM#1011						

KM# 1012 2000 DINARS (2 Kran)
9.2100 g., 0.9000 Silver 0.2665 oz. ASW, 28 mm. **Obv:** Legend within circle and crowned wreath **Obv. Legend:** "Muhammad Ali Shah" **Rev:** Radiant lion holding sword within crowned wreath **Mint:** Tehran

Date	Mintage	F	VF	XF	Unc	BU
AH1325 (1907)	3,076,000	15.00	25.00	50.00	100	—
AH1326 (1908)	3,069,000	7.50	11.50	20.00	50.00	—
AH1327 (1909)	—	7.50	11.50	20.00	50.00	—

KM# 1017 2000 DINARS (2 Kran)
9.2100 g., 0.9000 Silver 0.2665 oz. ASW **Obv:** Uniformed bust 3/4 left within wreath, date below **Rev:** Radiant lion holding sword within crowned wreath **Mint:** Tehran

Date	Mintage	F	VF	XF	Unc	BU
AH1326 (1908)	—	500	1,000	1,500	2,500	—
Note: Mintage included in KM#1012						

KM# 1018 5000 DINARS (5 Kran)
23.0251 g., 0.9000 Silver 0.6662 oz. ASW **Obv:** Uniformed bust 3/4 left within wreath **Rev:** Crown above lion and sun within wreath **Note:** Dav.#290.

Date	Mintage	F	VF	XF	Unc	BU
AH1327 (1909)	—	250	500	1,000	1,500	—

Note: Obverse always weakly struck with little detail in head and face

KM# 1024 2000 DINARS (1/5 Toman)
0.5749 g., 0.9000 Gold 0.0166 oz. AGW **Obv:** Uniformed bust 3/4 left within wreath **Rev:** Legend in wreath

Date	Mintage	F	VF	XF	Unc	BU
AH1326 (1908)	—	75.00	100	150	275	—
AH1327 (1909)	—	75.00	100	150	275	—

KM# 1021 5000 DINARS (1/2 Toman)
1.4372 g., 0.9000 Gold 0.0416 oz. AGW, 17 mm. **Obv:** Legend within circle and wreath **Obv. Legend:** Muhammad Ali Shah **Rev:** Radiant lion holding sword within crowned wreath

Date	Mintage	F	VF	XF	Unc	BU
AH1324 (1906)	—	75.00	100	150	275	—
AH1325 (1907)	—	75.00	100	150	275	—

KM# 1025 5000 DINARS (1/2 Toman)
1.4372 g., 0.9000 Gold 0.0416 oz. AGW, 17 mm. **Obv:** Uniformed bust 3/4 left divides date **Rev:** Legend within circle and wreath **Rev. Legend:** "Muhammad Ali Shah"

Date	Mintage	F	VF	XF	Unc	BU
AH1326 (1908)	—	75.00	100	150	275	—
AH1362 (1908) Error for 1326	—	75.00	100	150	275	—
AH1327 (1909)	—	75.00	100	150	275	—

KM# 1022 TOMAN
2.8744 g., 0.9000 Gold 0.0832 oz. AGW, 19 mm. **Obv:** Legend within circle and wreath **Obv. Legend:** "Muhammad Ali Shah" **Rev:** Radiant lion holding sword within crowned wreath

Date	Mintage	F	VF	XF	Unc	BU
AH1324 (1906)	—	90.00	150	300	500	—

KM# 1026 TOMAN
2.8744 g., 0.9000 Gold 0.0832 oz. AGW **Obv:** Uniformed bust 3/4 left divides date **Rev:** Legend within circle and closed wreath **Rev. Legend:** "Muhammad Ali Shah"

Date	Mintage	F	VF	XF	Unc	BU
AH1327 (1909)	—	90.00	150	300	500	—

MILLED COINAGE

Silver Kran Standard

KM# 891 SHAHI SEFID (White Shahi)
Copper-Nickel Clad Brass **Obv. Legend:** "Nasir al-Din" (KM#889) **Rev. Legend:** "Shahib al-zaman" (obverse of KM#1007) **Mint:** Tehran **Note:** Mule using old obverse die.

Date	Mintage	F	VF	XF	Unc	BU
ND	—	50.00	75.00	125	250	—

Sultan Ahmad Shah

AH1327-1344 / 1909-1925AD

MILLED COINAGE

KM# 1031 SHAHI SEFID (White Shahi)
0.0691 g., 0.9000 Silver 0.0020 oz. ASW **Obv:** Legend within circle and wreath **Obv. Legend:** "Ahmad Shah" **Rev:** Radiant lion holding sword within crowned wreath **Mint:** Tehran

Date	Mintage	F	VF	XF	Unc	BU
AH1328 (1910)	—	5.00	10.00	20.00	40.00	—
AH1329 (1911)	—	6.00	12.00	25.00	50.00	—
AH1330 (1911)	189,000	4.00	10.00	20.00	40.00	—

KM# 1032 SHAHI SEFID (White Shahi)
0.0691 g., 0.9000 Silver 0.0020 oz. ASW **Obv:** Legend within circle and wreath **Rev:** Radiant lion holding sword within crowned wreath **Mint:** Tehran

Date	Mintage	F	VF	XF	Unc	BU
AH1332 (1913)	10,000	30.00	50.00	85.00	150	—

KM# 1033 SHAHI SEFID (White Shahi)
0.0691 g., 0.9000 Silver 0.0020 oz. ASW **Obv:** Legend within circle and wreath **Obv. Legend:** "Ahmad Shah" **Rev:** Legend within circle and wreath **Rev. Legend:** "Sahib-al-Zaman" **Mint:** Tehran

Date	Mintage	F	VF	XF	Unc	BU
ND (1913)	—	60.00	125	200	400	—

KM# 1049 SHAHI SEFID (White Shahi)
0.0691 g., 0.9000 Silver 0.0020 oz. ASW **Obv:** Legend within circle and wreath **Rev:** Radiant lion holding sword within crowned wreath **Rev. Legend:** "Sahib-al-Zaman" **Mint:** Tehran

Date	Mintage	F	VF	XF	Unc	BU
ND (1913)	—	10.00	20.00	40.00	75.00	—
AH1332 (1913)	—	10.00	18.00	35.00	80.00	—
Note: Included in KM#1032						
AH1333 (1914)	—	10.00	20.00	40.00	80.00	—
Note: Included in KM#1047						
AH1337 (1918)	—	10.00	20.00	40.00	80.00	—
Note: Included in KM#1047						
AH1341 (1922)	3,000	15.00	25.00	50.00	100	—
AH1342 (1923)	—	15.00	25.00	50.00	100	—
Note: Included in KM#1047						

KM# 1047 SHAHI SEFID (White Shahi)
0.0691 g., 0.9000 Silver 0.0020 oz. ASW **Obv:** Legend within circle and wreath, date below **Rev:** Radiant lion holding sword within crowned wreath **Mint:** Tehran **Note:** Varieties exist.

Date	Mintage	F	VF	XF	Unc	BU
AH1333 (1914)	78,000	5.00	10.00	20.00	40.00	—
AH1334 (1915)	6,000	12.00	20.00	40.00	80.00	—
AH1335 (1916)	73,000	8.00	15.00	30.00	60.00	—
AH1335//1337 (1918)	Inc. above	40.00	80.00	165	250	—
AH1337 (1918)	76,000	8.00	15.00	30.00	60.00	—
AH1337//1337 (1918)	—	40.00	75.00	150	280	—
AH1339 (1920)	10,000	12.00	20.00	40.00	80.00	—
AH1342 (1923)	20,000	12.00	20.00	40.00	80.00	—

KM# 1048 SHAHI SEFID (White Shahi)
0.0691 g., 0.9000 Silver 0.0020 oz. ASW **Obv:** Legend within circle and wreath **Rev:** Legend within circle and wreath, date below **Rev. Legend:** "Sahib-al-Zaman" **Mint:** Tehran

Date	Mintage	F	VF	XF	Unc	BU
AH1335 (1916)	—	50.00	80.00	150	300	—

Note: Mintage included in KM#1047 of AH1335

KM# 1050 SHAHI SEFID (White Shahi)
0.6908 g., 0.9000 Silver 0.0200 oz. ASW **Obv:** Legend within circle and wreath, dated AH1339 **Rev:** Radiant lion with sword within crowned wreath with AH1341 between lion's legs, AH1327 below wreath **Mint:** Tehran

Date	Mintage	F	VF	XF	Unc	BU
AH1339//1341 & 1327 (1922)	—	50.00	80.00	150	300	—

Note: Numerous silver Nouruz tokens, some with dates SH1328-1346, are available in Tehran for a fraction of the price of true Shahis

KM# 1035 1/4 KRAN (Robi = 5 Shahis)
1.1513 g., 0.9000 Silver 0.0333 oz. ASW, 15 mm. **Obv:** Legend within circle and wreath **Obv. Legend:** "Ahmad Shah" **Rev:** Radiant lion holding sword within crowned wreath **Mint:** Tehran

Date	Mintage	F	VF	XF	Unc	BU
AH1327 (1909)	—	5.00	10.00	20.00	40.00	—
AH1328 (1910)	—	4.00	7.50	15.00	30.00	—
AH1329 (1911)	130,000	12.50	20.00	40.00	80.00	—
AH1330 (1911)	156,000	4.00	7.50	15.00	30.00	—
AH1331 (1912)	30,000	—	—	—	—	—
Note: Reported, not confirmed.						
AH1313 (1912) Error for 1331	Inc. above	—	—	—	—	—
Note: Reported, not confirmed.						

KM# 1052 1/4 KRAN (Robi = 5 Shahis)
1.1513 g., 0.9000 Silver 0.0333 oz. ASW **Obv:** Legend within circle and wreath, date below **Obv. Legend:** "Ahmad Shah" **Rev:** Radiant lion holding sword within crowned wreath **Mint:** Tehran **Note:** Mule.

Date	Mintage	F	VF	XF	Unc	BU
ND (1909)	—	45.00	65.00	125	200	—
AH1327 (1909)	—	65.00	135	185	300	—

KM# 1051 1/4 KRAN (Robi = 5 Shahis)
1.1513 g., 0.9000 Silver 0.0333 oz. ASW **Obv:** Legend within circle and wreath **Obv. Legend:** "Ahmad Shah" **Rev:** Radiant lion holding sword within crowned wreath **Mint:** Tehran

Date	Mintage	F	VF	XF	Unc	BU
AH1332 (1913)	252,000	5.00	10.00	20.00	40.00	—
AH1333 (1914)	Inc. above	6.00	12.00	25.00	50.00	—
AH1334 (1915)	70,000	10.00	20.00	50.00	100	—
AH1335 (1916)	260,000	4.00	8.00	15.00	30.00	—
AH1336 (1917)	160,000	4.00	8.00	15.00	30.00	—
AH1337 (1918)	80,000	6.00	12.00	25.00	50.00	—
AH1339 (1920)	28,000	9.00	15.00	30.00	60.00	—
AH1341 (1922)	22,000	12.00	20.00	40.00	80.00	—
AH1342 (1923)	110,000	6.00	12.00	25.00	50.00	—
AH1343 (1924)	186,000	4.00	8.00	15.00	30.00	—

KM# 1053 1/4 KRAN (Robi = 5 Shahis)
1.1513 g., 0.9000 Silver 0.0333 oz. ASW **Obv:** Legend within circle and wreath **Rev:** Radiant lion holding sword within crowned wreath **Mint:** Tehran

Date	Mintage	F	VF	XF	Unc	BU
AH1334 (1915)	—	35.00	75.00	150	250	—

Note: Mintage included with KM#1051

KM# 1036 500 DINARS (10 Shahis = 1/2 Kran)
2.3025 g., 0.9000 Silver 0.0666 oz. ASW, 18 mm. **Obv:** Legend within circle and wreath **Obv. Legend:** "Ahmad Shah" **Rev:** Radiant lion holding sword within crowned wreath **Mint:** Tehran

Date	Mintage	F	VF	XF	Unc	BU
AH1327 (1909)	—	8.00	15.00	30.00	50.00	—
AH1328 (1910)	—	5.00	12.50	20.00	40.00	—
AH1329 (1911)	44,000	10.00	20.00	40.00	80.00	—
AH1330 (1911)	627,000	8.00	15.00	30.00	50.00	—

KM# 1054 500 DINARS (10 Shahis = 1/2 Kran)
2.3025 g., 0.9000 Silver 0.0666 oz. ASW **Obv:** Uniformed bust 1/4 left within wreath, date below **Rev:** Radiant lion holding sword within crowned wreath **Mint:** Tehran

Date	Mintage	F	VF	XF	Unc	BU
AH1331 (1912)	—	8.00	15.00	30.00	50.00	—
Note: Mintage included in AH1330 above						
AH1332 (1913)	560,000	8.00	15.00	30.00	50.00	—
AH1333 (1914)	292,000	5.00	10.00	15.00	30.00	—
AH1334 (1915)	65,000	5.00	10.00	15.00	30.00	—
AH1335 (1916)	150,000	8.00	15.00	30.00	60.00	—
AH1336 (1917)	240,000	4.00	8.00	20.00	40.00	—
AH1339 (1920)	—	17.50	25.00	40.00	80.00	—
AH1343 (1924)	160,000	6.00	10.00	25.00	50.00	—

Note: 10,000 reported struck in AH1337 probably dated AH1336

KM# 1055 500 DINARS (10 Shahis = 1/2 Kran)
2.3025 g., 0.9000 Silver 0.0666 oz. ASW **Obv:** Uniformed bust 1/4 left within wreath, date below **Rev:** Radiant lion holding sword within crowned wreath **Mint:** Tehran

Date	Mintage	F	VF	XF	Unc	BU
AH1332 (1913)	—	30.00	50.00	90.00	200	—

Note: Mintage included in KM#1054

KM# 1038 1000 DINARS (Kran, Qiran)
4.6050 g., 0.9000 Silver 0.1332 oz. ASW, 23 mm. **Obv:** Legend within circle and wreath **Obv. Legend:** "Sultan Ahmad Shah" **Rev:** Radiant lion holding sword within crowned wreath **Mint:** Tehran

Date	Mintage	F	VF	XF	Unc	BU
AH1327 (1909)	—	7.50	15.00	30.00	60.00	—
AH1328 (1910)	—	6.50	12.50	25.00	50.00	—
AH1329 (1911)	3,000,000	6.50	12.50	25.00	50.00	—
AH1330 (1911)	—	6.50	12.50	25.00	50.00	—

KM# 1037 1000 DINARS (Kran, Qiran)
4.6050 g., 0.9000 Silver 0.1332 oz. ASW **Obv:** Legend within circle and wreath **Rev:** Radiant lion holding sword within crowned wreath **Mint:** Tehran **Note:** Mule.

Date	Mintage	F	VF	XF	Unc	BU
AH1336 (1909)	—	—	—	100	200	—

KM# 1056 1000 DINARS (Kran, Qiran)
4.6050 g., 0.9000 Silver 0.1332 oz. ASW **Obv:** Uniformed bust 1/4 left within wreath, date below **Rev:** Radiant lion holding sword within crowned wreath **Mint:** Tehran

Date	Mintage	F	VF	XF	Unc	BU
AH1331 (1912)	1,310,000	5.00	8.00	25.00	40.00	—
AH1332 (1913)	1,891,000	3.00	5.00	12.50	30.00	—
AH1333 (1914)	2,179,000	7.50	12.00	25.00	40.00	—
AH1334 (1915)	1,273,000	3.00	5.00	12.50	25.00	—
AH1335 (1916)	2,162,000	3.00	5.00	12.50	25.00	—
AH1336 (1917)	1,412,000	3.50	6.00	15.00	30.00	—
AH1337 (1918)	3,330,000	3.00	5.00	12.50	25.00	—
AH1339 (1920)	35,000	12.50	25.00	55.00	90.00	—
AH1330 (1921) Error for 1340	—	30.00	65.00	125	175	—
AH1340 (1921)	28,000	15.00	30.00	60.00	100	—
AH1341 (1922)	170,000	8.00	15.00	35.00	60.00	—
AH1342 (1923)	255,000	3.00	6.00	20.00	30.00	—
AH1343 (1924)	1,345,000	3.00	6.00	20.00	30.00	—
AH1344 (1925)	2,978,000	4.00	6.00	20.00	35.00	—

KM# 1059 1000 DINARS (Kran, Qiran)
4.6050 g., 0.9000 Silver 0.1332 oz. ASW, 23 mm. **Subject:** 10th Year of Reign **Obv:** Uniformed bust 1/4 left within wreath, date below **Rev:** Radiant lion holding sword within crowned wreath **Mint:** Tehran

Date	Mintage	F	VF	XF	Unc	BU
AH1337 (1918)	975,000	35.00	75.00	125	250	—

KM# 1040 2000 DINARS (2 Kran)
9.2100 g., 0.9000 Silver 0.2665 oz. ASW, 28 mm. **Obv:** Legend within circle and crowned wreath **Obv. Legend:** "Ahmad Shah" **Rev:** Radiant lion holding sword within crowned wreath **Mint:** Tehran

Date	Mintage	F	VF	XF	Unc	BU
AH1327 (1909)	—	7.50	15.00	30.00	50.00	—
Note: Mintage included in KM#1328						
AH1328 (1910)	30,000,000	5.00	10.00	20.00	40.00	—
AH1329 (1911)	29,250,000	5.00	10.00	20.00	40.00	—

KM# 1041 2000 DINARS (2 Kran)
9.2100 g., 0.9000 Silver 0.2665 oz. ASW **Obv:** Legend within circle and crowned wreath **Rev:** Radiant lion holding sword within crowned wreath **Mint:** Tehran

Date	Mintage	F	VF	XF	Unc	BU
AH1330 (1911)	2,901,000	7.50	15.00	30.00	60.00	—

KM# 1043 2000 DINARS (2 Kran)
9.2100 g., 0.9000 Silver 0.2665 oz. ASW **Obv:** Legend within circle and crowned wreath **Obv. Legend:** "Ahmad Shah" **Rev:** Radiant lion holding sword within crowned wreath **Mint:** Tehran

Date	Mintage	F	VF	XF	Unc	BU
AH1330 (1911)	—	7.50	15.00	30.00	60.00	—
Note: Mintage included in KM#1041						
AH1331 (1912)	13,412,000	7.50	15.00	30.00	60.00	—

KM# 1057 2000 DINARS (2 Kran)
9.2100 g., 0.9000 Silver 0.2665 oz. ASW **Obv:** Uniformed bust 1/4 left within wreath, date below **Rev:** Radiant lion holding sword within crowned wreath **Mint:** Tehran

Date	Mintage	F	VF	XF	Unc	BU
AH1331 (1912)	—	6.00	12.50	25.00	50.00	—
Note: Mintage included in KM#1043						
AH1332 (1913)	12,926,000	5.00	7.50	15.00	30.00	—
AH1333 (1914)	Inc. above	5.00	7.50	15.00	30.00	—
AH1334 (1915)	4,299,000	5.00	7.50	15.00	30.00	—
AH1335 (1916)	9,777,000	5.00	7.50	15.00	30.00	—
AH1336 (1917)	5,401,000	5.00	7.50	15.00	30.00	—
AH1337 (1918)	2,951,000	5.00	7.50	15.00	30.00	—
AH1339 (1920)	1,085,000	6.00	12.50	25.00	50.00	—
AH1330 (1921) Error for 1340	—	50.00	100	150	250	—
Note: Mintage included in KM#1043						
AH1340 (1921)	254,000	9.00	15.00	30.00	65.00	—
AH1341 (1922)	4,460,000	5.00	7.50	15.00	30.00	—
AH1342 (1923)	2,245,000	5.00	8.00	20.00	35.00	—
AH1343 (1924)	5,205,000	5.00	8.00	20.00	35.00	—
AH1344/34 (1925)	12,354	7.00	12.00	25.00	55.00	—
AH1344 (1925)	Inc. above	6.00	10.00	20.00	40.00	—

KM# 1060 2000 DINARS (2 Kran)
9.2100 g., 0.9000 Silver 0.2665 oz. ASW, 28 mm. **Subject:** 10th Anniversary of Reign **Obv:** Uniformed bust 1/4 left within wreath **Rev:** Radiant lion with sword within crowned wreath **Mint:** Tehran

Date	Mintage	F	VF	XF	Unc	BU
AH1337 (1918)	3,503,000	60.00	100	150	300	—

KM# 1058 5000 DINARS (5 Kran)
23.0251 g., 0.9000 Silver 0.6662 oz. ASW **Obv:** Uniformed bust 1/4 left within wreath, date below **Rev:** Radiant lion holding sword within crowned wreath **Note:** Dav.#291.

Date	Mintage	F	VF	XF	Unc	BU
AH1331 (1912)	—	60.00	150	250	500	—
AH1332 (1913)	3,000,000	10.00	14.00	30.00	85.00	—
AH1333 (1914)	667,000	12.00	16.00	35.00	90.00	—
AH1334 (1915)	443,000	12.00	16.00	35.00	90.00	—
AH1335 (1916)	1,884,000	12.00	16.00	35.00	90.00	—
AH1337 (1918)	165,000	14.00	25.00	55.00	110	—
AH1339 (1920)	90,000	20.00	30.00	65.00	125	—
AH1340 (1921)	303,000	14.00	25.00	55.00	110	—
AH1341 (1922)	757,000	12.00	16.00	35.00	90.00	—
AH1342/32 (1923)	546,000	12.00	16.00	35.00	90.00	—
AH1342 (1923)	Inc. above	12.00	16.00	35.00	90.00	—
AH1343 (1924)	935,000	12.00	16.00	35.00	90.00	—
AH1344/34 (1925)	2,284,000	12.00	16.00	30.00	85.00	—
AH1344 (1925)	Inc. above	15.00	20.00	40.00	95.00	—

Note: Beware of altered date AH1331 specimens. 9,000 reported minted in AH1336, probably dated earlier

KM# 1066 2000 DINARS (1/5 Toman)

0.5749 g., 0.9000 Gold 0.0166 oz. AGW, 14 mm. **Obv:** Legend within circle and wreath **Obv. Legend:** "Ahmad Shah" **Rev:** Radiant lion holding sword within crowned wreath

Date	Mintage	F	VF	XF	Unc	BU
AH1328 (1910)	—	100	175	250	500	—
AH1329 (1911)	—	250	550	750	900	—
AH1330 (1911)	—	100	175	250	500	—

KM# 1070 2000 DINARS (1/5 Toman)

0.5749 g., 0.9000 Gold 0.0166 oz. AGW, 14 mm. **Obv:** Uniformed bust 1/4 left divides date **Rev:** Legend within circle and wreath **Rev. Legend:** "Ahmad Shah"

Date	Mintage	F	VF	XF	Unc	BU
AH1332 (1913)	—	22.50	40.00	60.00	130	—
AH1333 (1914)	—	18.50	35.00	60.00	125	—
AH1334 (1915)	—	25.00	50.00	100	200	—
AH1335 (1916)	—	16.50	30.00	40.00	60.00	—
AH1337 (1918)	—	16.50	30.00	40.00	100	—
AH1339 (1920)	—	18.50	35.00	50.00	100	—
AH1340 (1921)	—	18.50	40.00	60.00	120	—
AH1341 (1922)	—	18.50	35.00	50.00	100	—
AH1342 (1923)	—	18.50	35.00	50.00	100	—
AH1343/33 (1924)	—	50.00	100	200	400	—
AH1343 (1924)	—	25.00	50.00	100	200	—

KM# 1067 5000 DINARS (1/2 Toman)

1.4372 g., 0.9000 Gold 0.0416 oz. AGW **Obv:** Legend within circle and wreath **Obv. Legend:** "Ahmad Shah" **Rev:** Radiant lion holding sword within crowned wreath

Date	Mintage	F	VF	XF	Unc	BU
AH1328 (1910)	—	60.00	125	200	275	—
AH1329 (1911)	—	175	400	600	750	—
AH1330 (1911)	—	175	400	600	750	—

KM# 1071 5000 DINARS (1/2 Toman)

1.4372 g., 0.9000 Gold 0.0416 oz. AGW, 17 mm. **Obv:** Uniformed bust 1/4 left divides date **Rev:** Legend within circle and wreath **Rev. Legend:** "Ahmad Shah"

Date	Mintage	F	VF	XF	Unc	BU
AH1331 (1912)	—	50.00	100	150	300	—
AH1332 (1913)	—	40.00	60.00	100	150	—
AH1333 (1914)	—	50.00	100	200	300	—
AH1334 (1915)	—	50.00	100	200	300	—
AH1335 (1916)	—	50.00	100	200	300	—
AH1336 (1917)	—	40.00	45.00	60.00	90.00	—
AH1337 (1918)	—	50.00	100	200	300	—
AH1339 (1920)	—	60.00	125	250	350	—
AH1340 (1921)	—	40.00	45.00	60.00	110	—
AH1341 (1922)	—	40.00	45.00	60.00	90.00	—
AH1342 (1923)	—	40.00	45.00	60.00	90.00	—
AH1343/33 (1924)	—	100	200	400	600	—
AH1343 (1924)	—	50.00	100	200	300	—

KM# 1072 5000 DINARS (1/2 Toman)

1.4372 g., 0.9000 Gold 0.0416 oz. AGW **Obv:** Bust with headdress 1/4 left within sprigs **Rev. Legend:** "Sahib al-Zaman"

Date	Mintage	F	VF	XF	Unc	BU
AH1339 (1920)	—	100	150	250	600	—
AH1340 (1921)	—	100	150	250	600	—

KM# 1068 TOMAN

2.8744 g., 0.9000 Gold 0.0832 oz. AGW, 19 mm. **Obv. Legend:** "Ahmad Shah", AH1328-1332 **Rev:** Lion and sun

Date	Mintage	F	VF	XF	Unc	BU
AH1329 (1911) Rare	—	—	—	—	—	—

Note: Only two examples are known

KM# 1074 TOMAN

2.8744 g., 0.9000 Gold 0.0832 oz. AGW, 19 mm. **Obv:** Uniformed bust 1/4 left divides date **Rev:** Legend within circle and wreath **Rev. Legend:** "Ahmad Shah"

Date	Mintage	F	VF	XF	Unc	BU
AH1332 (1913)	—	80.00	150	250	500	—
AH1333 (1914)	—	500	750	1,000	1,250	—
AH1334 (1915)	—	80.00	125	175	300	—
AH1335 (1916)	—	80.00	125	175	300	—
AH1337 (1918)	—	BV	80.00	100	175	—
AH1339 (1920)	—	BV	80.00	100	175	—
AH1340 (1921)	—	100	200	300	400	—
AH1341 (1922)	—	BV	80.00	100	150	—
AH1342 (1923)	—	BV	80.00	100	150	—
AH1343 (1924)	—	BV	80.00	100	150	—

KM# 1073 TOMAN

2.8744 g., 0.9000 Gold 0.0832 oz. AGW, 19 mm. **Obv:** Bust with headdress 1/4 left **Rev:** Ahmad Shah Pattern 2 Toman **Note:** The reverse die used was of an unadopted pattern.

Date	Mintage	F	VF	XF	Unc	BU
AH1332 (1913)	—	300	600	900	1,500	—
AH1333 (1914)	—	350	650	1,000	1,750	—

CLANDESTINE COINAGE

KM# 1039 1000 DINARS (Kran, Qiran)

Silver **Obv:** Legend within beaded circle and wreath **Rev:** Radiant lion holding sword within crowned wreath **Mint:** Tehran

Date	Mintage	F	VF	XF	Unc	BU
AH1330 (sic) (1915)	—	12.00	25.00	50.00	75.00	—
AH1330 (sic) (1915) Proof, rare	—	—	—	—	—	—

Note: KM#1039 differs from KM#1038 in that it is about 1 millimeter broader and has a much thicker rim and more clearly defined denticles. Struck in Germany, without Iranian authorization, for circulation in western Iran during World War I. Also, the lion lacks the triangular face and fierce expression of KM#1038 and the point of the Talwar (scimitar) does not touch the sunburst as it does on Tehran issues.

KM# 1042 2000 DINARS (2 Kran)

Silver **Rev:** Lion's face has friendly expression **Mint:** Tehran

Date	Mintage	F	VF	XF	Unc	BU
AH1330 (sic) (1915)	—	12.00	25.00	50.00	75.00	—

Note: See general note for KM#1039

Reza Shah

AH1344-1360 / 1925-1941AD

MILLED COINAGE

KM# 1091 50 DINARS

Copper-Nickel **Obv:** Legend within circle and crowned wreath **Rev:** Radiant lion holding sword within crowned wreath **Mint:** Tehran

Date	Mintage	F	VF	XF	Unc	BU
SH1305 (1926)	11,000,000	2.50	5.00	10.00	20.00	—
SH1307 (1928)	2,500,000	2.50	5.00	10.00	20.00	—

KM# 1092 100 DINARS (2 Shahi)

Copper-Nickel **Obv:** Legend within circle and crowned wreath **Rev:** Radiant lion holding sword within crowned wreath

Date	Mintage	F	VF	XF	Unc	BU
SH1305 (1926)	4,500,000	2.50	5.00	10.00	20.00	—
SH1307 (1928)	3,750,000	2.50	5.00	10.00	20.00	—

KM# 1093 1/4 KRAN (Robi = 5 Shahis)

1.1513 g., 0.9000 Silver 0.0333 oz. ASW **Obv:** Legend within circle and wreath **Rev:** Crown above lion and sun within wreath **Mint:** Tehran **Note:** 8,000 reported struck in SH1305, but that year not yet found and presumed not to exist.

Date	Mintage	F	VF	XF	Unc	BU
SH1304 (1925)	Est. 24,000	20.00	50.00	85.00	160	—

Note: For similar looking coins dated SH1315, see 1/4 Rial, KM#1127.

KM# 1094 500 DINARS (10 Shahis = 1/2 Kran)

2.3025 g., 0.9000 Silver 0.0666 oz. ASW **Obv:** Legend within circle and wreath **Rev:** Radiant lion holding sword within crowned wreath **Mint:** Tehran

Date	Mintage	F	VF	XF	Unc	BU
SH1304 (1925) Rare	—	—	—	—	—	—

KM# 1098 500 DINARS (10 Shahis = 1/2 Kran)

2.3025 g., 0.9000 Silver 0.0666 oz. ASW **Obv:** Legend within wreath **Obv. Legend:** "Reza Shah" **Rev:** Lion and sun within wreath **Mint:** Tehran

Date	Mintage	F	VF	XF	Unc	BU
SH1305 (1926)	10,000	150	250	500	750	—

KM# 1102 500 DINARS (10 Shahis = 1/2 Kran)

2.3025 g., 0.9000 Silver 0.0666 oz. ASW **Obv:** Uniformed bust 3/4 right within wreath divides date **Rev:** Radiant lion holding sword within crowned wreath **Mint:** Tehran

Date	Mintage	F	VF	XF	Unc	BU
SH1306 (1927)	5,000	50.00	100	150	250	—
SH1307 (1928)	46,000	10.00	15.00	30.00	60.00	—
SH1308 (1929)	464,000	10.00	15.00	30.00	60.00	—

Note: Some of the coins reported in SH1308 were dated 1307

KM# 1095 1000 DINARS (Kran, Qiran)

4.6050 g., 0.9000 Silver 0.1332 oz. ASW **Obv:** Legend within circle and wreath **Rev:** Radiant lion holding sword within crowned wreath **Mint:** Tehran

Date	Mintage	F	VF	XF	Unc	BU
SH1304 (1925)	2,573,000	10.00	20.00	30.00	50.00	—
SH1305 (1926)	2,265,000	10.00	20.00	30.00	50.00	—

KM# 1099 1000 DINARS (Kran, Qiran)

4.6050 g., 0.9000 Silver 0.1332 oz. ASW **Obv:** Legend within circle and wreath **Obv. Legend:** "Reza Shah" **Rev:** Radiant lion holding sword within crowned wreath **Mint:** Tehran

Date	Mintage	F	VF	XF	Unc	BU
SH1305 (1926)	—	10.00	20.00	30.00	50.00	—
Note: Mintage included in KM#1095						
SH1306/5 (1927)	3,130,000	5.00	8.00	15.00	25.00	—
SH1306 (1927)	Inc. above	10.00	20.00	30.00	50.00	—

KM# 1103 1000 DINARS (Kran, Qiran)

4.6050 g., 0.9000 Silver 0.1332 oz. ASW **Obv:** Uniformed bust 3/4 right within wreath divides date of Ascession in SH1304 **Rev:** Lion and sun within crowned wreath **Mint:** Tehran

Date	Mintage	F	VF	XF	Unc	BU
SH1306 (1927)	—	10.00	20.00	30.00	60.00	—
Note: Mintage included in KM#1099						
SH1307 (1928)	4,300,000	10.00	20.00	30.00	50.00	—
SH1308 (1929)	603,000	10.00	20.00	30.00	50.00	—

KM# 1096 2000 DINARS (2 Kran)

9.2100 g., 0.9000 Silver 0.2665 oz. ASW **Obv:** Legend within circle and wreath **Rev:** Date below lion **Mint:** Tehran

Date	Mintage	F	VF	XF	Unc	BU
SH1304 (1925)	11,920,000	15.00	30.00	50.00	75.00	—
SH1305 (1926)	9,785,000	15.00	30.00	50.00	75.00	—

KM# 1100 2000 DINARS (2 Kran)
9.2100 g., 0.9000 Silver 0.2665 oz. ASW **Obv:** Legend within circle and wreath **Obv. Legend:** "Reza Shah" **Rev:** Radiant lion holding sword within crowned wreath **Mint:** Tehran

Date	Mintage	F	VF	XF	Unc	BU
SH1305 (1926)	—	15.00	30.00	50.00	75.00	—
SH1306 (1927)	9,380,000	4.50	7.50	12.50	25.00	—

KM# 1104 2000 DINARS (2 Kran)
9.2100 g., 0.9000 Silver 0.2665 oz. ASW **Obv:** Uniformed bust 3/4 right within wreath divides date of Ascession in SH1304 **Rev:** Radiant lion holding sword within crowned wreath

Date	Mintage	F	VF	XF	Unc	BU
SH1306 (1927)	—	5.00	10.00	25.00	50.00	—
Note: Mintage included in KM#1100						
SH1306 (1927) H	11,714,000	5.00	10.00	25.00	50.00	—
SH1306 (1927) L	7,500,000	5.00	10.00	25.00	50.00	—
SH1306 (1927) H Proof	—	Value: 375				
SH1307 (1928)	11,146,000	5.00	10.00	25.00	50.00	—
SH1308 (1929)	1,611,000	5.00	10.00	25.00	50.00	—

KM# 1105 2000 DINARS (2 Kran)
9.2100 g., 0.9000 Silver 0.2665 oz. ASW **Obv:** Uniformed bust 3/4 right within wreath **Rev:** Crown above lion and sun within wreath **Mint:** Tehran **Note:** Mule.

Date	Mintage	F	VF	XF	Unc	BU
SH1306 (1927)	—	—	—	50.00	100	—

KM# 1097 5000 DINARS (5 Kran)
23.0251 g., 0.9000 Silver 0.6662 oz. ASW **Obv:** Legend within crowned wreath **Rev:** Radiant lion holding sword within wreath **Note:** Dav.#292.

Date	Mintage	F	VF	XF	Unc	BU
SH1304 (1925)	500,000	16.00	40.00	75.00	150	—
SH1305 (1926)	1,363,000	16.00	40.00	75.00	150	—

KM# 1101 5000 DINARS (5 Kran)
23.0251 g., 0.9000 Silver 0.6662 oz. ASW **Obv:** Legend within crowned wreath **Obv. Legend:** "Reza Shah" **Rev:** Radiant lion holding sword within wreath **Note:** Dav.#293.

Date	Mintage	F	VF	XF	Unc	BU
SH1305 (1926)	—	35.00	70.00	100	150	—
Note: Mintage included in KM#1097						
SH1306 (1927)	3,186,000	35.00	70.00	100	150	—

KM# 1106 5000 DINARS (5 Kran)
23.0251 g., 0.9000 Silver 0.6662 oz. ASW **Obv:** Uniformed bust 3/4 right within divides date of Ascession in SH1304 **Rev:** Crown above lion and sun within wreath **Note:** Dav.#294. Mint marks located as on 2000 Dinars, KM#1104.

Date	Mintage	F	VF	XF	Unc	BU
SH1306 (1927)	—	12.00	25.00	50.00	100	—
Note: Mintage including in KM#1101						
SH1306 (1927) Proof	—	Value: 400				
SH1306 (1927) H	4,711,000	12.00	25.00	50.00	100	—
SH1306 (1927) L	3,000,000	12.00	25.00	50.00	100	—
SH1307 (1928)	3,928,000	15.00	35.00	75.00	150	—
SH1308 (1929)	584,000	15.00	35.00	75.00	150	—

KM# 1107 5000 DINARS (5 Kran)
23.0251 g., 0.9000 Silver 0.6662 oz. ASW **Obv:** Uniformed bust 3/4 right within wreath **Rev:** Crown above lion and sun within wreath **Note:** Mule.

Date	Mintage	F	VF	XF	Unc	BU
SH1306 (1927)	—	—	—	75.00	150	—

REFORM COINAGE

KM# 1126.1 2-1/2 ABBASI (10 Shahi)
Copper, 24.5 mm. **Obv:** Radiant lion holding sword within crowned wreath **Rev:** Legend within beaded heart-shaped circle within designed crowned wreath **Edge:** Reeded

Date	Mintage	F	VF	XF	Unc	BU
SH1314 (1935) Large date	Inc. above	3.00	4.00	12.50	30.00	—
SH1314 (1935) Small date	15,714,000	3.00	4.00	12.50	30.00	—

KM# 1126.2 2-1/2 ABBASI (10 Shahi)
Copper, 24.5 mm. **Obv:** Radiant lion holding sword within crowned wreath **Rev:** Legend within beaded heart shaped circle within designed crowned wreath **Edge:** Plain

Date	Mintage	F	VF	XF	Unc	BU
SH1314 (1935)	Inc. above	5.00	7.00	15.00	40.00	—

KM# 1121 DINAR
Bronze **Obv:** Radiant lion holding sword within crowned wreath **Rev:** Value within large flowered wreath

Date	Mintage	F	VF	XF	Unc	BU
SH1310 (1931)	10,000,000	30.00	50.00	75.00	175	—

KM# 1122 2 DINARS
Bronze **Obv:** Radiant lion holding sword within crowned wreath **Rev:** Value within large flowered wreath

Date	Mintage	F	VF	XF	Unc	BU
SH1310 (1931)	5,000,000	30.00	50.00	75.00	175	—

KM# 1123 5 DINARS
Copper-Nickel, 18.5 mm. **Obv:** Radiant lion holding sword within crowned wreath **Rev:** Value within beaded circle and designed crowned wreath

Date	Mintage	F	VF	XF	Unc	BU
SH1310 (1931)	3,750,000	20.00	40.00	100	275	—

KM# 1123a 5 DINARS
Copper **Obv:** Radiant lion holding sword within crowned wreath **Rev:** Value within beaded circle and crowned designed wreath

Date	Mintage	F	VF	XF	Unc	BU
SH1314	480,000	200	400	750	—	—

KM# 1138 5 DINARS
Aluminum-Bronze, 16 mm. **Obv:** Radiant lion holding sword within crowned wreath **Rev:** Value within large flowered wreath

Date	Mintage	F	VF	XF	Unc	BU
SH1315 (1936)	5,665,000	2.50	4.00	10.00	20.00	—
SH1316 (1937)	Inc. above	0.40	0.75	1.50	5.00	—
SH1317 (1938)	13,025,000	0.40	0.75	1.50	5.00	—
SH1318 (1939)	—	0.40	0.75	1.50	5.00	—
SH1319 (1940)	—	0.40	0.75	1.50	5.00	—
SH1320 (1941)	—	0.40	0.75	1.50	4.00	—
SH1321 (1942)	—	0.40	0.75	1.50	5.00	—

KM# 1124 10 DINARS
4.0000 g., Copper-Nickel, 21 mm. **Obv:** Radiant lion holding sword within crowned wreath **Rev:** Value within beaded circle and crowned designed wreath **Note:** Struck at Berlin.

Date	Mintage	F	VF	XF	Unc	BU
SH1310 (1931)	3,750,000	15.00	40.00	100	350	—

KM# 1124a 10 DINARS
3.2000 g., Copper **Obv:** Radiant lion holding sword within crowned wreath **Rev:** Value within beaded circle and crowned designed wreath **Mint:** Tehran **Note:** Struck at Tehran.

Date	Mintage	F	VF	XF	Unc	BU
SH1314 (1935)	11,350,000	11.50	20.00	45.00	125	—

KM# 1139 10 DINARS
2.6500 g., Aluminum-Bronze, 18 mm. **Obv:** Radiant lion holding sword within crowned wreath **Rev:** Value within wreath

Date	Mintage	F	VF	XF	Unc	BU
SH1315 (1936)	6,195,000	2.00	5.00	15.00	25.00	—
SH1316 (1937)	Inc. above	0.80	1.50	4.00	10.00	—
SH1317 (1938)	17,120,000	0.40	0.80	2.00	6.00	—
SH1318 (1939)	—	0.40	0.80	2.00	6.00	—
SH1319 (1940)	—	0.40	0.80	2.00	6.00	—
SH1320 (1941)	—	0.40	0.80	2.00	6.00	—
SH1321 (1942)	—	0.45	1.00	2.50	6.00	—

KM# 1125 25 DINARS
Copper-Nickel, 24 mm. **Obv:** Radiant lion holding sword within crowned wreath **Rev:** Value within beaded circle and crowned designed wreath

Date	Mintage	F	VF	XF	Unc	BU
SH1310 (1931)	750,000	25.00	60.00	150	300	—

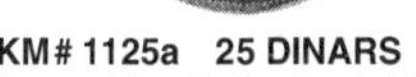

KM# 1125a 25 DINARS
Copper **Obv:** Radiant lion holding sword within crowned wreath **Rev:** Value within beaded circle and crowned designed wreath

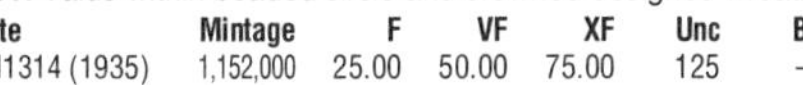

Date	Mintage	F	VF	XF	Unc	BU
SH1314 (1935)	1,152,000	25.00	50.00	75.00	125	—

KM# 1142 50 DINARS

3.4700 g., Aluminum-Bronze, 20 mm. **Obv:** Radiant lion holding sword within crowned wreath **Rev:** Value within wreath

Date	Mintage	F	VF	XF	Unc	BU
SH1315 (1936)	15,968,000	3.00	4.50	10.00	35.00	—
SH1316 (1937)	34,200,000	1.25	2.50	6.00	20.00	—
SH1317 (1938)	17,314,000	0.60	1.50	4.00	15.00	—
SH1318 (1939)	—	0.60	1.50	4.00	15.00	—
SH1319 (1940)	—	1.50	2.50	6.00	20.00	—
SH1320 (1941)	—	0.75	1.50	3.00	10.00	—
SH1321/0 (1942)	—	0.75	1.50	3.00	15.00	—
SH1322/10 (1943)	—	0.75	1.50	3.00	15.00	—
SH1322/12 (1943)	—	0.75	1.50	3.00	10.00	—
SH1322/0 (1943)	—	0.75	1.50	3.00	10.00	—
SH1322/1 (1943)	—	0.75	1.50	3.00	10.00	—
SH1331 (1952)	8,162,000	3.50	4.50	10.00	25.00	—
SH1332 (1953)	22,892,000	2.00	3.00	5.00	10.00	—

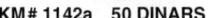

KM# 1142a 50 DINARS

Copper **Obv:** Radiant lion holding sword within crowned wreath **Rev:** Value within wreath

Date	Mintage	F	VF	XF	Unc	BU
SH1322 (1943)	—	2.00	4.00	7.00	12.00	—
SH1322/0 (1943)	—	2.00	6.00	9.00	15.00	—

KM# 1127 1/4 RIAL

1.2500 g., 0.8280 Silver 0.0333 oz. ASW **Obv:** Value within circle and wreath **Rev:** Radiant lion holding sword within crowned wreath

Date	Mintage	F	VF	XF	Unc	BU
SH1315	600,000	1.50	2.50	5.00	10.00	—

Note: The second "1" is often short, so that the date looks like 1305

KM# 1128 1/2 RIAL

2.5000 g., 0.8280 Silver 0.0665 oz. ASW, 18 mm. **Obv:** Value within crowned wreath **Obv. Legend:** "Reza Shah" **Rev:** Radiant lion holding sword within crowned wreath **Note:** All 1/2 Rials dated SH1311-1315 are recut dies, usually from SH1310.

Date	Mintage	F	VF	XF	Unc	BU
SH1310 (1931)	2,000,000	2.50	5.00	10.00	20.00	—
SH1311 (1932)	—	50.00	100	150	200	—
SH1312 (1933)	—	2.50	5.00	10.00	20.00	—
SH1313 (1934)	1,945,000	2.50	5.00	10.00	20.00	—
SH1314 (1935)	100,000	2.50	5.00	10.00	20.00	—
SH1315 (1936)	800,000	5.00	10.00	20.00	30.00	—

KM# 1130 2 RIALS

10.0000 g., 0.8280 Silver 0.2662 oz. ASW, 26 mm. **Obv:** Value within crowned wreath **Obv. Legend:** "Reza Shah" **Rev:** Radiant lion holding sword within crowned wreath **Note:** All coins dated SH1311-13 cut or punched over SH1310.

Date	Mintage	F	VF	XF	Unc	BU
SH1310 (1931)	6,145,000	10.00	20.00	25.00	35.00	—
SH1311 (1932)	8,838,000	20.00	30.00	50.00	75.00	—
SH1312 (1933)	19,175,000	10.00	15.00	25.00	35.00	—
SH1313 (1934)	4,015,000	20.00	30.00	50.00	75.00	—

KM# 1131 5 RIALS

25.0000 g., 0.8280 Silver 0.6655 oz. ASW, 37 mm. **Obv:** Value within crowned wreath **Obv. Legend:** "Reza Shah" **Rev:** Radiant lion holding sword within crowned wreath **Note:** Most coins dated SH1311-13 are cut or punched over SH1310.

Date	Mintage	F	VF	XF	Unc	BU
SH1310 (1931)	5,471,000	12.00	18.00	25.00	50.00	—
SH1311 (1932)	4,527,000	12.00	18.00	25.00	50.00	—
SH1312/0 (1933)	5,502,000	15.00	20.00	30.00	60.00	—
SH1312 (1933)	Inc. above	12.00	18.00	25.00	50.00	—
SH1313 (1934)	1,208,000	15.00	20.00	30.00	60.00	—

KM# 1132 1/2 PAHLAVI

4.0680 g., 0.9000 Gold 0.1177 oz. AGW **Obv:** Uniformed bust left **Rev:** Radiant lion holding sword within crowned wreath

Date	Mintage	F	VF	XF	Unc	BU
SH1310 (1931)	696	BV	150	275	375	—
SH1311 (1932)	286	BV	175	300	400	—
SH1312 (1933)	892	BV	150	250	350	—
SH1313 (1934)	531	BV	175	300	400	—
SH1314 (1935)	—	BV	175	300	400	—
SH1315 (1936)	1,042	BV	175	275	375	—

KM# 1133 PAHLAVI

8.1360 g., 0.9000 Gold 0.2354 oz. AGW **Obv:** Uniformed bust left **Rev:** Radiant lion holding sword within crowned wreath

Date	Mintage	F	VF	XF	Unc	BU
SH1310 (1931)	304	1,500	3,000	4,000	5,000	—

Muhammad Reza Pahlavi Shah

SH1320-1358 / 1941-1979AD

REFORM COINAGE

KM# 1140 25 DINARS

Aluminum-Bronze, 19 mm. **Obv:** Radiant lion holding sword within crowned wreath **Rev:** Value within wreath

Date	Mintage	F	VF	XF	Unc	BU
SH1326 (1947)	—	20.00	30.00	60.00	125	—
SH1327 (1948)	—	25.00	50.00	100	150	—
SH1329 (1950)	—	25.00	50.00	100	150	—

KM# 1141 25 DINARS

Aluminum-Bronze **Obv:** Value within wreath **Rev:** Radiant lion holding sword within crowned wreath **Note:** Mule

Date	Mintage	F	VF	XF	Unc	BU
SH1329 (1950)	—	500	750	1,000	1,500	—

KM# 1156 50 DINARS

2.9100 g., Aluminum-Bronze **Obv:** Radiant lion holding sword within crowned wreath **Rev:** Value within wreath **Note:** Reduced thickness = 1mm; wide and narrow rim varieties exist for some dates.

Date	Mintage	F	VF	XF	Unc	BU
SH1332 (1953)	—	25.00	30.00	40.00	50.00	—
SH1333 (1954)	4,036,000	0.75	1.50	2.50	8.00	—
SH1334 (1955)	1,370,000	0.75	1.50	4.00	10.00	—
SH1335 (1956)	926,000	0.75	1.50	2.50	8.00	—
SH1336 (1957)	—	1.00	1.25	2.00	8.00	—

Note: Mint reports record 126,500 in SH1337 and 20,000 in SH1338; these were probably dated SH1336

Date	Mintage	F	VF	XF	Unc	BU
SH1342 (1963)	800,000	0.60	1.00	1.75	6.00	—
SH1343 (1964)	1,400,000	0.60	1.00	1.75	6.00	—
SH1344 (1965)	1,600,000	0.35	0.65	1.25	5.00	—
SH1345 (1966)	1,690,000	0.35	0.65	1.25	5.00	—
SH1346 (1967)	—	0.20	0.25	0.50	2.00	—

Note: Mintage report seems excessive for this and all SH1346 coinage

Date	Mintage	F	VF	XF	Unc	BU
SH1347 (1968)	2,000,000	0.20	0.25	0.50	2.00	—
SH1348 (1969)	1,500,000	0.20	0.25	0.50	2.00	—
SH1349 (1970)	360,000	2.00	3.00	4.50	12.50	—
SH1350 (1971)	—	0.30	0.50	0.75	2.00	—
SH1351 (1972)	—	0.30	0.50	0.75	2.00	—
SH1353 (1974)	60,000	0.30	0.50	0.75	2.00	—
SH1354 (1975)	16,000	0.75	1.25	2.00	5.00	—

KM# 1156a 50 DINARS

Brass-Coated Steel **Obv:** Radiant lion holding sword within crowned wreath **Rev:** Value within wreath

Date	Mintage	F	VF	XF	Unc	BU
MS2535 (1976)	27,000	5.00	10.00	20.00	30.00	—
MS2536 (1977)	—	5.00	10.00	20.00	30.00	—
MS2537 (1978)	—	5.00	10.00	20.00	30.00	—
SH1357 (1978)	—	5.00	10.00	20.00	30.00	—
SH1358 (1979)	—	—	—	—	—	—

Note: Reported, not confirmed

KM# 1143 RIAL

1.6000 g., 0.6000 Silver 0.0309 oz. ASW, 18 mm. **Obv:** Value within crowned wreath **Obv. Legend:** "Muhammad Reza Shah Pahlavi" **Rev:** Radiant lion holding sword within crowned wreath

Date	Mintage	F	VF	XF	Unc	BU
SH1322 (1943)	—	0.60	1.00	2.00	5.00	—
SH1323/3 (1944)	—	—	—	—	—	—
SH1323 (1944)	—	0.60	1.00	2.00	5.00	—
SH1324/3 (1945)	—	—	—	—	—	—
SH1324 (1945)	—	0.60	1.00	2.00	5.00	—
SH1424 (1945) Error for 1324	—	—	—	—	—	—
SH1325 (1946)	—	0.75	1.50	2.00	5.00	—
SH1326 (1947)	567,000	35.00	40.00	50.00	100	—
SH1327 (1948)	5,795,000	1.50	2.50	4.00	8.00	—
SH1328 (1949)	1,565,000	1.50	2.50	4.00	8.00	—
SH1329 (1950)	144,000	50.00	100	150	200	—
SH1330 (1951)	—	2.00	3.00	5.00	15.00	—

KM# 1157 RIAL

Copper-Nickel, 18.5 mm. **Obv:** Value within wreath **Obv. Legend:** "Muhammad Reza Shah Pahlavi" **Rev:** Radiant lion holding sword within crowned wreath

Date	Mintage	F	VF	XF	Unc	BU
SH(13)31 (1952)	4,735,000	1.00	2.00	5.00	15.00	—
SH(13)32 (1953)	3	4.00	8.00	15.00	30.00	—
SH(13)33 (1954)	16,405,000	0.60	1.00	2.00	5.00	—
SH(13)34 (1955)	8,980,000	0.60	1.00	2.00	5.00	—
SH(13)35 (1956)	8,910,000	0.50	1.00	1.00	5.00	—
SH(13)36 (1957)	4,450,000	1.00	2.00	8.00	20.00	—

KM# 1171 RIAL

2.0000 g., Copper-Nickel **Obv:** Value within crowned wreath **Obv. Legend:** "Muhammad Reza Pahlavi" **Rev:** Radiant lion holding sword within crowned wreath

Date	Mintage	F	VF	XF	Unc	BU
SH1337 (1958)	8,005,000	0.50	1.00	2.00	5.00	—

KM# 1171a RIAL

1.7500 g., Copper-Nickel, 18.3 mm. **Obv:** Value within crowned wreath **Rev:** Radiant lion holding sword within crowned wreath **Note:** Date varieties exist.

Date	Mintage	F	VF	XF	Unc	BU
SH1338 (1959)	14,940,000	0.10	0.20	0.40	3.00	—
SH1339 (1960)	8,400,000	0.25	0.50	1.00	4.00	—
SH1340 (1961)	8,490,000	0.25	0.50	1.00	4.00	—
SH1341 (1962)	8,680,000	0.25	0.50	1.00	4.00	—
SH1342 (1963)	13,332,000	0.10	0.20	0.40	3.00	—
SH1343 (1964)	14,746,000	0.10	0.15	0.25	2.00	—
SH1344 (1965)	12,050,000	0.10	0.20	0.50	3.50	—
SH1345 (1966)	13,786,000	0.10	0.15	0.20	2.00	—
SH1346 (1967)	155,321,000	0.10	0.15	0.20	2.00	—
SH1347 (1968)	20,664,000	0.10	0.15	0.25	3.00	—
SH1348 (1969)	22,960,000	0.10	0.15	0.20	2.00	—
SH1349 (1970)	19,918,000	0.10	0.15	0.20	2.00	—
SH1350 (1971)	24,248,000	0.10	0.20	0.65	2.00	—
SH1351/0 (1972)	21,825,000	0.10	0.25	0.40	3.00	—
SH1351 (1972)	Inc. above	0.10	0.15	0.20	2.00	—
SH1352 (1973)	31,449,000	0.10	0.15	0.20	2.00	—
SH1353 (1974) Large date	33,700,000	0.10	0.20	0.25	3.00	—
SH1353 (1974) Small date	Inc. above	0.10	0.15	0.20	2.00	—
SH1354 (1975)	—	3.00	6.00	8.00	10.00	—
MS2536 (1977)	—	3.00	6.00	8.00	10.00	—

KM# 1183 RIAL

1.7600 g., Copper-Nickel, 18.5 mm. **Series:** F.A.O. **Obv:** Head left divides date **Obv. Legend:** "Muhammad Reza Shah Pahlavi" **Rev:** Crown above lion and sun within wreath

Date	Mintage	F	VF	XF	Unc	BU
SH1350 (1971)	2,770,000	3.00	6.00	8.00	10.00	—
SH1351 (1972)	8,605,000	3.00	6.00	8.00	10.00	—
SH1353 (1974)	2,000,000	3.00	6.00	8.00	10.00	—
SH1354 (1975)	1,000,000	3.00	6.00	8.00	10.00	—

KM# 1205 RIAL

Copper-Nickel, 18.3 mm. **Subject:** 50th Anniversary of Pahlavi Rule **Obv:** Value within crowned wreath **Rev:** Radiant lion holding sword within crowned wreath

Date	Mintage	F	VF	XF	Unc	BU
MS2535 (1976)	61,945,000	3.00	6.00	8.00	10.00	—

KM# 1172 RIAL

1.7500 g., Copper-Nickel **Obv:** Value within crowned wreath, "Aryamehr" added to legend **Rev:** Radiant lion holding sword within crowned wreath

Date	Mintage	F	VF	XF	Unc	BU
MS2536 (1977)	71,150,000	3.00	6.00	8.00	10.00	—
MS2537 (1978)	—	3.00	6.00	8.00	10.00	—
MS2537/6537 (1978) Error 2/6	—	—	—	—	6.00	—
SH1357/6 (1978)	—	3.00	6.00	8.00	10.00	—
SH1357 (1978)	—	2.50	5.00	10.00	15.00	—

KM# 1144 2 RIALS

3.2000 g., 0.6000 Silver 0.0617 oz. ASW, 22 mm. **Obv:** Value within crowned wreath **Obv. Legend:** "Muhammad Reza Shah Pahlavi" **Rev:** Radiant lion holding sword within crowned wreath

Date	Mintage	F	VF	XF	Unc	BU
SH1322 (1943)	—	1.00	1.50	3.50	7.00	—
SH1323/2 (1944)	—	10.00	20.00	30.00	50.00	—
SH1323 (1944)	—	1.00	1.50	3.00	6.00	—
SH1324 (1945)	—	2.50	5.00	10.00	15.00	—
SH1325 (1946)	—	5.00	10.00	15.00	25.00	—
SH1326 (1947)	187,000	5.00	10.00	25.00	50.00	—
SH1327 (1948)	3,140,000	1.50	3.00	5.00	12.50	—
SH1328 (1949)	1,198,000	2.50	4.50	7.50	16.00	—
SH1329 (1950)	—	100	200	300	400	—
SH1330 (1951)	—	5.00	8.00	12.50	30.00	—

KM# 1158 2 RIALS

Copper-Nickel, 22.5 mm. **Obv:** Value above sprigs **Obv. Legend:** "Muhammad Reza Shah Pahlavi" **Rev:** Crown above radiant lion holding sword within wreath

Date	Mintage	F	VF	XF	Unc	BU
SH1331 (1952)	5,335,000	1.25	3.00	7.00	20.00	—
SH1332 (1953)	6,870,000	1.00	2.00	4.00	8.00	—
SH1333 (1954)	13,668,000	0.15	0.75	2.00	7.00	—
SH1334 (1955)	7,185,000	0.15	0.75	2.00	7.00	—
SH1335 (1956)	2,400,000	0.15	0.75	3.00	12.50	—
SH1336 (1957)	325,000	25.00	50.00	75.00	100	—

KM# 1173 2 RIALS

3.0000 g., Copper-Nickel **Obv:** Value within crowned wreath **Obv. Legend:** "Muhammad Reza Pahlavi" **Rev:** Radiant lion holding sword within crowned wreath

Date	Mintage	F	VF	XF	Unc	BU
SH1338 (1959)	17,610,000	0.10	0.25	0.75	4.00	—
SH1339 (1960)	8,575,000	0.10	0.25	0.50	4.00	—
SH1340 (1961)	5,668,000	0.10	0.25	0.50	4.00	—
SH1341 (1962)	5,820,000	0.10	0.25	0.75	4.00	—
SH1342 (1963)	8,570,000	0.10	0.25	0.50	4.00	—
SH1343 (1964)	11,250,000	0.10	0.25	0.50	3.00	—
SH1344 (1965)	5,155,000	0.10	0.25	0.50	4.00	—
SH1345 (1966)	2,267,000	0.15	0.30	1.00	5.00	—
SH1346 (1967)	92,792,000	—	0.10	0.20	4.00	—
SH1347 (1968)	10,300,000	—	0.10	1.00	6.00	—
SH1348 (1969)	9,319,000	0.20	0.45	1.10	4.00	—
SH1349 (1970)	9,895,000	0.20	0.40	1.00	4.00	—
SH1350 (1971)	9,545,000	0.15	0.35	1.00	4.00	—
SH1351 (1972)	13,305,000	0.15	0.35	1.00	3.00	—
SH1352 (1973)	15,910,000	—	0.10	0.20	3.00	—
SH1353 (1974)	28,477,000	—	0.10	0.20	3.00	—
SH1354/3 (1975)	—	0.20	0.40	1.00	5.00	—
SH1354 (1975)	41,700,000	—	0.10	0.20	3.00	—
MS2536 (1977)	54,725,000	—	0.10	0.20	3.00	—

KM# 1206 2 RIALS

Copper-Nickel **Subject:** 50th Anniversary of Pahlavi Rule **Obv:** Value within crowned wreath **Rev:** Radiant lion holding sword within crowned wreath

Date	Mintage	F	VF	XF	Unc	BU
MS2535 (1976)	59,568,000	2.50	5.00	10.00	15.00	—

KM# 1174 2 RIALS

3.0400 g., Copper-Nickel **Obv:** Value within crowned wreath **Obv. Legend:** "Muhammad Reza Pahlavi","Aryamehr" added **Rev:** Radiant lion holding sword within crowned wreath

Date	Mintage	F	VF	XF	Unc	BU
MS2536 (1977)	Inc. above	0.50	1.00	2.50	5.00	—
MS2537 (1978)	—	0.50	1.00	2.50	5.00	—
SH1357 (1978)	—	2.50	5.00	10.00	20.00	—

KM# 1145 5 RIALS

8.0000 g., 0.6000 Silver 0.1543 oz. ASW, 26 mm. **Obv:** Value within crowned wreath **Obv. Legend:** "Muhammad Reza Shah Pahlavi" **Rev:** Radiant lion holding sword within crowned wreath

Date	Mintage	F	VF	XF	Unc	BU
SH1322 (1943)	—	BV	2.50	3.50	6.00	—
SH1323 (1944)	—	BV	2.50	3.50	6.00	—
SH1324 (1945)	—	BV	2.75	4.50	10.00	—
SH1325 (1946)	—	BV	2.50	3.50	6.00	—
SH1326 (1947)	61,000	5.00	10.00	25.00	50.00	—
SH1327 (1948)	836,000	2.50	5.00	7.50	20.00	—
SH1328 (1949)	282,000	3.50	10.00	20.00	40.00	—
SH1329 (1950)	—	85.00	125	200	350	—

KM# 1159 5 RIALS

Copper-Nickel, 26 mm. **Obv:** Value above sprigs, date below **Obv. Legend:** "Muhammad Reza Shah Pahlavi" **Rev:** Crown above radiant lion holding sword within wreath

Date	Mintage	F	VF	XF	Unc	BU
SH1331 (1952)	3,660,000	2.50	5.00	10.00	20.00	—
SH1332 (1953)	16,350,000	1.00	2.50	5.00	10.00	—
SH1333 (1954)	6,582,000	1.00	2.50	5.00	10.00	—
SH1334 (1955)	300,000	15.00	25.00	50.00	75.00	—
SH1336 (1957)	1,410,000	15.00	25.00	50.00	75.00	—

KM# 1175 5 RIALS

7.0000 g., Copper-Nickel, 25.5 mm. **Obv:** Value within crowned wreath **Obv. Legend:** "Muhammad Reza Shah Pahlavi" **Rev:** Radiant lion holding sword within crowned wreath

Date	Mintage	F	VF	XF	Unc	BU
SH1337 (1958)	3,660,000	1.00	2.50	7.50	22.50	—
SH1338 (1959)	10,467,000	0.50	2.50	8.00	20.00	—

KM# 1175a 5 RIALS

5.0000 g., Copper-Nickel, 25.6 mm. **Obv:** Value within crowned wreath **Rev:** Radiant lion holding sword within crowned wreath

Date	Mintage	F	VF	XF	Unc	BU
SH1338 (1959)	Inc. above	0.25	0.40	1.50	5.00	—
SH1339 (1960)	3,980,000	0.25	0.40	1.50	5.00	—
SH1340 (1961)	3,814,000	0.25	0.40	1.50	5.00	—
SH1341 (1962)	2,332,000	0.25	0.40	1.50	5.00	—
SH1342 (1963)	7,838,000	0.25	0.40	1.00	4.00	—
SH1343 (1964)	9,484,000	0.25	0.40	1.00	4.00	—
SH1344 (1965)	3,468,000	0.25	0.40	1.00	4.00	—
SH1345 (1966)	6,092,000	0.25	0.40	1.00	4.00	—
SH1346/36 (1967)	74,781,000	0.25	0.40	1.50	5.00	—
SH1346 (1967)	Inc. above	0.25	0.40	1.00	4.00	—

KM# 1176 5 RIALS
4.6000 g., Copper-Nickel **Obv:** Value and legend within crowned wreath, "Aryamehr" added to legend **Rev:** Radiant lion holding sword within crowned wreath

Date	Mintage	F	VF	XF	Unc	BU
SH1347 (1968)	7,745,000	0.50	0.85	1.50	4.00	—
SH1348 (1969)	9,193,000	0.50	0.75	1.25	4.00	—
SH1349 (1970)	7,300,000	0.50	0.75	1.25	4.00	—
SH1350 (1971)	10,160,000	0.35	0.75	1.25	3.50	—
SH1351 (1972)	20,582,000	0.25	0.75	1.25	3.50	—
SH1352 (1973)	23,590,000	0.25	0.75	1.25	3.50	—
SH1353 (1974)	28,367,000	0.25	0.75	1.25	3.50	—
SH1353 (1974) Large date	Inc. above	0.25	0.75	1.25	3.50	—
SH1354 (1975)	27,294,000	0.25	0.75	1.25	3.50	—
MS2536 (1977)	47,906,000	0.20	0.50	1.25	3.50	—
MS2537 (1978)	—	0.35	0.65	1.25	3.50	—
SH1357 (1978)	—	2.50	5.00	10.00	20.00	—

KM# 1207 5 RIALS
Copper-Nickel **Subject:** 50th Anniversary of Pahlavi Rule

Date	Mintage	F	VF	XF	Unc	BU
MS2535 (1976)	37,144,000	1.00	2.50	5.00	10.00	—

KM# 1146 10 RIALS
16.0000 g., 0.6000 Silver 0.3086 oz. ASW, 32 mm. **Obv:** Value and legend within crowned wreath **Obv. Legend:** "Muhammad Reza Shah Pahlavi" **Rev:** Radiant lion holding sword within crowned wreath **Note:** Counterfeits are known dated SH1322.

Date	Mintage	F	VF	XF	Unc	BU
SH1323/2 (1944)	—	—	4.50	7.50	20.00	—
SH1323 (1944)	—	—	BV	5.00	12.00	—
SH1324 (1945)	—	—	BV	5.50	15.00	—
SH1325 (1946)	—	—	BV	6.00	17.50	—
SH1326 (1947)	—	5.50	15.00	35.00	75.00	—

KM# 1177 10 RIALS
12.0000 g., Copper-Nickel **Obv:** Crown above value and legend within wreath **Obv. Legend:** "Muhammad Reza Shah Pahlavi" **Rev:** Crown above lion and sun within wreath

Date	Mintage	F	VF	XF	Unc	BU
SH1333 (1954)	—	—	—	—	—	—
SH1335 (1956)	6,225,000	0.50	2.00	4.00	9.00	—
SH1336 (1957)	4,415,000	5.00	10.00	15.00	25.00	—
SH1337 (1958)	715,000	3.00	6.00	9.00	20.00	—
SH1338 (1959)	1,210,000	0.50	2.00	6.00	14.00	—
SH1339 (1960)	2,775,000	0.50	2.00	4.00	9.00	—
SH1340 (1961)	3,660,000	0.50	2.00	4.00	9.00	—
SH1341 (1962)	744,000	20.00	35.00	50.00	75.00	—
SH1343 (1963)	6,874,000	0.50	2.00	4.00	9.00	—

KM# 1177a 10 RIALS
9.0000 g., Copper-Nickel **Obv:** Crown above value and legend wtihin wreath **Rev:** Crown above radiant lion holding sword within wreath **Note:** Thin flan.

Date	Mintage	F	VF	XF	Unc	BU
SH1341 (1962)	—	0.35	1.00	2.50	5.00	—
Note: Mintage included in KM#1177						
SH1342 (1963)	3,763,000	0.35	1.00	2.00	4.00	—
SH1343 (1964)	—	0.35	0.75	1.50	2.50	—
Note: Mintage included in KM#1177						
SH1344 (1965)	1,627,000	0.35	0.75	1.50	2.50	—

KM# 1178 10 RIALS
6.8000 g., Copper-Nickel, 28 mm. **Obv:** Head left, legend above, date below **Obv. Legend:** "Muhammad Reza Shah Pahlavi" **Rev:** Crown above radiant lion holding sword within wreath

Date	Mintage	F	VF	XF	Unc	BU
SH1345 (1966)	1,699,000	0.50	0.60	2.00	5.00	—
SH1346 (1967)	38,897,000	0.40	0.50	1.00	4.00	—
SH1347 (1968)	8,220,000	0.40	0.65	1.50	8.00	—
SH1348 (1969)	7,156,000	0.40	0.50	1.00	4.00	—
SH1349 (1970)	7,397,000	0.40	0.50	1.00	4.00	—
SH1350 (1971)	8,972,000	0.40	0.50	1.00	4.00	—
SH1351 (1972)	9,912,000	0.40	0.50	1.00	4.00	—
SH1352 (1973)	28,776,000	0.50	2.00	4.50	7.00	—

KM# 1182 10 RIALS
Copper-Nickel **Series:** F.A.O. **Obv:** Head left, legend above **Rev:** Crown above radiant lion holding sword within wreath, dates and F.A.O

Date	Mintage	F	VF	XF	Unc	BU
SH1348 (1969)	150,000	1.00	2.50	5.00	10.00	—

KM# 1179 10 RIALS
Copper-Nickel **Obv:** Head left, legend above, date below **Rev:** Crown above lion, sun and numeral value within wreath

Date	Mintage	F	VF	XF	Unc	BU
SH1352 (1973)	Inc. above	0.30	0.60	1.00	4.00	—
SH1353 (1974)	22,234,000	0.30	0.60	1.00	3.00	—
SH1354 (1975)	23,482,000	0.30	0.60	1.00	4.00	—
MS2536 (1977)	24,324,000	0.30	0.60	1.00	3.00	—
MS2537 (1978)	—	0.30	0.60	1.00	4.00	—
SH1357 (1978)	—	10.00	15.00	20.00	25.00	—

KM# 1208 10 RIALS
Copper-Nickel **Subject:** 50th Anniversary of Pahlavi Rule **Obv:** Head left, legend above, date below **Rev:** Crown above lion, sun and numeral value within wreath

Date	Mintage	F	VF	XF	Unc	BU
MS2535 (1976)	29,859,000	0.50	1.00	2.50	5.00	—

KM# 1180 20 RIALS
Copper-Nickel **Obv:** Head left, legend above, date below **Obv. Legend:** "Muhammad Reza Shah Pahlavi" **Rev:** Crown above lion, sun and written value within wreath

Date	Mintage	F	VF	XF	Unc	BU
SH1350 (1971)	2,349,000	0.25	1.00	3.00	6.00	—
SH1351 (1972)	11,416,000	0.25	0.85	1.00	3.00	—
SH1352 (1973)	7,172,000	0.25	0.85	1.25	5.00	—

KM# 1181 20 RIALS
Copper-Nickel, 30 mm. **Obv:** Head left, legend above, date below **Rev:** Crown above lion, sun and numeral value within wreath **Note:** Varieties exist in date size.

Date	Mintage	F	VF	XF	Unc	BU
SH1352 (1973)	—	0.25	0.75	1.00	3.50	—
Note: Mintage included in KM#1180						
SH1353 (1974)	12,601,000	0.25	0.75	1.00	3.75	—
SH1354 (1975)	16,246,000	0.25	0.75	1.00	4.00	—
MS2536 (1977)	—	0.40	0.75	1.00	4.00	—
MS2537 (1978)	—	0.50	0.75	1.00	4.00	—
SH1357 (1978)	—	5.00	10.00	15.00	25.00	—

KM# 1196 20 RIALS
Copper-Nickel **Subject:** 7th Asian Games **Obv:** Head left, legend above **Rev:** Star design within entwined circles and written words

Date	Mintage	F	VF	XF	Unc	BU
SH1353 (1974)	Inc. above	5.00	10.00	15.00	25.00	—

KM# 1209 20 RIALS
Copper-Nickel **Subject:** 50th Anniversary of Pahlavi Rule **Obv:** Head left, legend above, date below **Rev:** Crown above lion, sun and numeral value within wreath

Date	Mintage	F	VF	XF	Unc	BU
MS2535 (1976)	—	3.00	7.50	12.00	15.00	—

KM# 1211 20 RIALS
Copper-Nickel **Series:** F.A.O. **Obv:** Head left, legend above **Rev:** Crown above lion, sun and numeral value within wreath

Date	Mintage	F	VF	XF	Unc	BU
MS2535-1976	10,000,000	3.00	7.50	12.00	15.00	—
MS2536-1977	23,370,000	3.00	7.50	12.00	15.00	—

KM# 1215 20 RIALS
Copper-Nickel **Series:** F.A.O. **Obv:** Head left, legend above **Rev:** Crown above lion, sun, numeral value, dates and F.A.O. within wreath

Date	Mintage	F	VF	XF	Unc	BU
SH1357-1978	5,000,000	3.00	7.50	12.00	15.00	—

KM# 1214 20 RIALS
Copper-Nickel **Subject:** 50th Anniversary of Bank Melli **Obv:** Head left, legend above and below **Rev:** Head left, legend above and below

Date	Mintage	F	VF	XF	Unc	BU
SH1357 (1978)	—	5.00	10.00	20.00	30.00	—

KM# 1184 25 RIALS
7.5000 g., 0.9990 Silver 0.2409 oz. ASW **Subject:** 2500th Anniversary of Persian Empire **Obv:** Small crown over lion and sun above value within circle of crowns **Rev:** Conjoined column heads **Note:** Column head from Artaxerxes' Palace in Susa.

With "1 AR" and 1000 assayer's marks

Date	Mintage	F	VF	XF	Unc	BU
SH1350-1971 Proof	18,000	Value: 12.00				

KM# 1186 75 RIALS
22.5000 g., 0.9990 Silver 0.7226 oz. ASW **Subject:** 2500th Anniversary of Persian Empire **Obv:** Small crown above radiant lion holding sword above value and dates within circle of crowns **Rev:** Arms above Stone of Cyrus II and inscription, wreath of crowns surrounds **Note:** With "1 AR" and 1000 assayer's marks

Date	Mintage	F	VF	XF	Unc	BU
SH1350-1971 Proof	18,000	Value: 18.50				

KM# 1160 1/4 PAHLAVI
2.0340 g., 0.9000 Gold 0.0589 oz. AGW, 14 mm. **Obv:** Head left, legend above, date below **Rev:** Crown over lion and sun above value within wreath

Date	Mintage	F	VF	XF	Unc	BU
SH1332 (1953)	41,000	BV	60.00	100	125	—
SH1333 (1954)	7,000	60.00	70.00	125	175	—
SH1334 (1955)	—	—	BV	60.00	70.00	—
SH1335 (1956)	41,000	BV	60.00	100	125	—
SH1336 (1957)	—	BV	60.00	100	175	—

KM# 1160a 1/4 PAHLAVI
2.0340 g., 0.9000 Gold 0.0589 oz. AGW, 16 mm. **Obv:** Head left, legend above, date below **Rev:** Crown above lion holding sword within wreath **Note:** Thinner and broader.

Date	Mintage	F	VF	XF	Unc	BU
SH1336 (1957)	7,000	—	60.00	75.00	125	—
SH1337 (1958)	33,000	—	—	BV	60.00	—
SH1338 (1959)	136,000	—	—	BV	60.00	—
SH1339 (1960)	156,000	—	—	BV	60.00	—
SH1340 (1961)	60,000	—	—	BV	60.00	—
SH1342 (1963)	80,000	—	—	BV	60.00	—
SH1344 (1965)	30,000	—	60.00	90.00	125	—
SH1345 (1966)	40,000	—	—	BV	60.00	—
SH1346 (1967)	30,000	—	—	BV	60.00	—
SH1347 (1968)	60,000	—	—	BV	60.00	—
SH1348 (1969)	60,000	—	—	BV	60.00	—
SH1349 (1970)	80,000	—	—	BV	60.00	—
SH1350 (1971)	80,000	—	—	BV	60.00	—
SH1351 (1972)	103,000	—	—	BV	60.00	—
SH1353 (1974)	—	—	—	BV	60.00	—

KM# 1198 1/4 PAHLAVI
2.0340 g., 0.9000 Gold 0.0589 oz. AGW **Obv:** Head left, legend above, date below, "Aryamehr" added to legend **Rev:** Crown above lion and sun within wreath

Date	Mintage	F	VF	XF	Unc	BU
SH1354 (1975)	106,000	—	—	BV	60.00	—
SH1355 (1976)	186,000	—	—	BV	60.00	—
MS2536 (1977)	—	—	—	BV	60.00	—
MS2537 (1978)	—	—	—	BV	60.00	—
SH1358 (1979)	—	200	300	400	500	—

KM# 1147 1/2 PAHLAVI
4.0680 g., 0.9000 Gold 0.1177 oz. AGW **Obv:** Legend **Obv. Legend:** "Muhammad Reza Shah" **Rev:** Crown above radiant lion holding sword within wreath

Date	Mintage	F	VF	XF	Unc	BU
SH1320 (1941)	—	1,000	2,000	2,500	3,000	—
SH1321 (1942)	—	—	115	200	300	—
SH1322 (1943)	—	—	—	BV	115	—
SH1323 (1944)	76,000	—	—	BV	115	—

KM# 1149 1/2 PAHLAVI
4.0680 g., 0.9000 Gold 0.1177 oz. AGW **Obv:** High relief head left, legend above and date below **Rev:** Crown above radiant lion holding sword within wreath

Date	Mintage	F	VF	XF	Unc	BU
SH1324 (1945)	—	—	—	BV	115	—
SH1325 (1946)	—	—	—	BV	115	—
SH1326 (1947)	36,000	—	BV	115	125	—
SH1327 (1948)	36,000	—	BV	115	125	—
SH1328 (1949)	—	—	BV	115	130	—
SH1329 (1950)	75	—	275	475	750	—
SH1330 (1951)	98,000	—	175	300	500	—

KM# 1161 1/2 PAHLAVI
4.0680 g., 0.9000 Gold 0.1177 oz. AGW **Obv:** Low relief head left, legend above with date below **Rev:** Crown above radiant lion holding sword within wreath

Date	Mintage	F	VF	XF	Unc	BU
SH1330 (1951)	—	—	—	BV	115	—
Note: Mintage included in KM#1149						
SH1332 (1952)	—	—	1,250	2,000	2,500	—
SH1333 (1954)	—	BV	200	250	300	—
SH1334 (1955)	—	BV	200	250	300	—
SH1335 (1956)	—	—	—	BV	115	—
SH1336 (1957)	132,000	—	—	BV	115	—
SH1337 (1958)	102,000	—	—	BV	115	—
SH1338 (1959)	140,000	—	—	BV	115	—
SH1339 (1960)	142,000	—	—	BV	115	—
SH1340 (1961)	439,000	—	—	BV	115	—
SH1342 (1963)	40,000	—	—	BV	115	—
SH1344 (1965)	30,000	BV	200	250	300	—
SH1345 (1966)	40,000	—	—	BV	115	—
SH1346 (1967)	40,000	—	—	BV	115	—
SH1347 (1968)	50,000	—	—	BV	115	—
SH1348 (1969)	40,000	—	—	BV	115	—
SH1349 (1970)	80,000	—	—	BV	115	—
SH1350 (1971)	80,000	—	—	BV	115	—
SH1351 (1972)	103,000	—	—	BV	115	—
SH1352 (1973)	67,000	—	—	BV	115	—
SH1353 (1974)	—	—	—	BV	115	—

KM# 1199 1/2 PAHLAVI
4.0680 g., 0.9000 Gold 0.1177 oz. AGW **Obv:** Head left, legend above and date below, "Aryamehr" added to legend **Rev:** Crown above radiant lion holding sword within wreath

Date	Mintage	F	VF	XF	Unc	BU
SH1354 (1975)	37,000	—	—	BV	115	—
SH1355 (1976)	153,000	—	—	BV	115	—
MS2536 (1977)	—	—	—	BV	115	—
MS2537 (1978)	—	—	—	BV	115	—
SH1358 (1979)	—	—	700	1,000	1,500	—

KM# 1148 PAHLAVI
8.1360 g., 0.9000 Gold 0.2354 oz. AGW **Obv:** Legend and date **Obv. Legend:** "Muhammad Reza Shah" **Rev:** Crown above radiant lion holding sword within wreath

Date	Mintage	F	VF	XF	Unc	BU
SH1320 (1941)	—	—	—	3,000	4,000	—
Note: Possibly a pattern						
SH1321 (1942)	—	—	—	3,000	4,000	—
Note: Possibly a pattern						
SH1322 (1943)	—	—	—	BV	210	—
SH1323 (1944)	311,000	—	—	BV	210	—
SH1324 (1945)	—	—	—	BV	210	—

KM# 1150 PAHLAVI
8.1360 g., 0.9000 Gold 0.2354 oz. AGW **Obv:** High relief head left, legend above and date below **Rev:** Crown above radiant lion holding sword within wreath

Date	Mintage	F	VF	XF	Unc	BU
SH1324 (1945)	—	—	—	BV	215	—
SH1325 (1946)	—	—	—	BV	215	—
SH1326 (1947)	151,000	—	—	BV	215	—
SH1327 (1948)	20,000	—	—	BV	215	—
SH1328 (1949)	4,000	—	BV	215	260	—
SH1329 (1950)	4,000	—	300	500	750	—
SH1330 (1951)	48,000	—	215	300	400	—

KM# 1162 PAHLAVI
8.1360 g., 0.9000 Gold 0.2354 oz. AGW **Obv:** Low relief head left, legend above and date below **Rev:** Crown above radiant lion holding sword within wreath

Date	Mintage	F	VF	XF	Unc	BU
SH1330 (1951)	—	—	—	BV	215	—
SH1331 (1952)	—	2,000	3,000	3,500	3,750	—
SH1332 (1953)	—	2,000	3,000	3,500	3,750	—
SH1333 (1954)	—	BV	215	250	350	—
SH1334 (1955)	—	BV	215	250	350	—
SH1335 (1956)	—	—	—	BV	215	—
SH1336 (1957)	453,000	—	—	BV	215	—
SH1337 (1958)	665,000	—	—	BV	215	—

Date	Mintage	F	VF	XF	Unc	BU
SH1338 (1959)	776,000	—	—	BV	215	—
SH1339 (1960)	847,000	—	—	BV	215	—
SH1340 (1961)	528,000	—	—	BV	215	—
SH1342 (1963)	20,000	—	—	BV	215	—
SH1344 (1965)	—	BV	215	250	350	—
SH1345 (1966)	20,000	—	—	BV	215	—
SH1346 (1967)	30,000	—	—	BV	215	—
SH1347 (1968)	40,000	—	—	BV	215	—
SH1348 (1969)	70,000	—	—	BV	215	—
SH1349 (1970)	70,000	—	—	BV	215	—
SH1350 (1971)	60,000	—	—	BV	215	—
SH1351 (1972)	100,000	—	—	BV	215	—
SH1352 (1973)	320,000	—	—	BV	215	—
SH1353 (1974)	—	—	—	BV	215	—

KM# 1200 PAHLAVI

8.1360 g., 0.9000 Gold 0.2354 oz. AGW **Obv:** Head left, legend above, date below, "Aryamehr" added to legend **Rev:** Crown above radiant lion holding sword within wreath

Date	Mintage	F	VF	XF	Unc	BU
SH1354 (1975)	21,000	—	—	BV	165	—
SH1355 (1976)	203,000	—	—	BV	165	—
MS2536 (1977)	—	—	—	BV	165	—
MS2537 (1978)	—	—	—	BV	165	—
SH1358 (1979)	—	—	700	1,000	1,500	—

KM# A1163 2-1/2 PAHLAVI

20.3400 g., 0.9000 Gold 0.5885 oz. AGW **Obv:** Head left, legend above **Rev:** Inscription and date

Date	Mintage	F	VF	XF	Unc	BU
SH1338 (1959)	—	—	BV	540	575	—

KM# 1163 2-1/2 PAHLAVI

20.3400 g., 0.9000 Gold 0.5885 oz. AGW **Obv:** Head left, legend above **Rev:** Crown above lion, sun and value within wreath

Date	Mintage	F	VF	XF	Unc	BU
SH1339 (1960)	1,682	—	—	BV	550	—
SH1340 (1961)	2,788	—	—	BV	550	—
SH1342 (1963)	30	—	—	—	—	—
SH1348 (1969)	3,000	—	—	BV	550	—
SH1350 (1971)	2,000	—	—	BV	550	—
SH1351 (1972)	2,500	—	—	BV	550	—
SH1352 (1973)	3,000	—	—	BV	550	—
SH1353 (1974)	—	—	—	BV	550	—

KM# 1201 2-1/2 PAHLAVI

20.3400 g., 0.9000 Gold 0.5885 oz. AGW, 30 mm. **Obv:** Head left, legend above, date below, "Aryamehr" added to legend **Rev:** Crown above radiant lion holding sword within wreath **Edge:** Reeded

Date	Mintage	F	VF	XF	Unc	BU
SH1354 (1975)	18,000	—	—	BV	550	—
SH1355 (1976)	16,000	—	—	BV	550	—
MS2536 (1977)	—	—	—	BV	550	—
MS2537 (1978)	—	—	—	BV	550	—
SH1358 (1979) Rare	—	—	—	—	—	—

KM# 1164 5 PAHLAVI

40.6799 g., 0.9000 Gold 1.1771 oz. AGW **Obv:** Head left, legend above **Rev:** Crown above lion and sun within wreath

Date	Mintage	F	VF	XF	Unc	BU
SH1339 (1960)	2,225	—	—	BV	1,100	—
SH1340 (1961)	2,430	—	—	BV	1,100	—
SH1342 (1963)	20	—	—	2,500	4,000	—
SH1348 (1969)	2,000	—	—	BV	1,100	—
SH1350 (1971)	2,000	—	—	BV	1,100	—
SH1351 (1972)	2,500	—	—	BV	1,100	—
SH1352 (1973)	2,100	—	—	BV	1,100	—
SH1353 (1974)	—	—	—	BV	1,100	—

KM# 1202 5 PAHLAVI

40.6799 g., 0.9000 Gold 1.1771 oz. AGW **Obv:** Head left, legend above, date below, "Aryamehr" added to legend **Rev:** Crown above radiant lion holding sword within wreath

Date	Mintage	F	VF	XF	Unc	BU
SH1354 (1975)	10,000	—	—	BV	1,100	—
SH1355 (1976)	17,000	—	—	BV	1,100	—
MS2536 (1977)	—	—	—	BV	1,100	—
MS2537 (1978)	—	—	—	BV	1,100	—
SH1358 (1979)	—	—	1,250	1,500	1,750	—

ISLAMIC REPUBLIC

MILLED COINAGE

KM# 1231 50 DINARS

Brass Clad Steel **Obv:** Radiant lion holding sword within wreath **Rev:** Value within flowered wreath

Date	Mintage	F	VF	XF	Unc	BU
SH1358 (1979)	—	10.00	20.00	30.00	40.00	—

KM# 1232 RIAL

1.8000 g., Copper-Nickel **Obv:** Inscription within wreath **Rev:** Value and date within wreath

Date	Mintage	F	VF	XF	Unc	BU
SH1358 (1979)	—	—	0.25	0.75	1.75	—
SH1359 (1980)	—	—	0.25	0.75	1.75	—
SH1360 (1981)	—	—	0.25	0.75	1.75	—
SH1361 (1982)	—	—	0.25	0.75	1.75	—
SH1362 (1983)	—	—	0.25	0.75	1.75	—
SH1363 (1984)	—	—	0.25	0.75	1.75	—
SH1364 (1985)	—	—	0.25	0.75	1.75	—
SH1365 (1986)	—	—	0.15	0.65	1.25	—
SH1366 (1987)	—	—	0.15	0.65	1.25	—
SH1367 (1988)	—	—	0.15	0.65	1.25	—

KM# 1245 RIAL

Brass Clad Steel, 20 mm. **Subject:** World Jerusalem Day **Obv:** Value flanked by tulips **Rev:** Mosque above date

Date	Mintage	F	VF	XF	Unc	BU
SH1359 (1980)	—	—	1.00	2.50	5.00	—

KM# 1263 RIAL

Brass **Obv:** Value and date divides inscription and flower sprig within beaded circle **Rev:** Mountain within beaded circle

Date	Mintage	F	VF	XF	Unc	BU
SH1371 (1992)	—	—	10.00	20.00	30.00	—
SH1372 (1993)	—	—	10.00	10.00	15.00	—
SH1373 (1994)	—	—	10.00	20.00	30.00	—
SH1374 (1995)	—	—	10.00	20.00	30.00	—

KM# 1233 2 RIALS

3.0100 g., Copper-Nickel **Obv:** Inscription within tulip wreath **Rev:** Value and date within wreath

Date	Mintage	F	VF	XF	Unc	BU
SH1358 (1979)	—	—	0.60	1.25	3.50	—
SH1359 (1980)	—	—	0.50	1.25	3.50	—
SH1360 (1981)	—	—	0.50	1.25	3.50	—
SH1361 (1982)	—	—	0.50	1.00	3.00	—
SH1362 (1983)	—	—	0.35	0.75	2.75	—
SH1363 (1984)	—	—	0.50	1.00	3.00	—
SH1364 (1985)	—	—	0.35	0.75	2.75	—
SH1365 (1986)	—	—	0.25	0.75	2.50	—
SH1366 (1987)	—	—	0.25	0.75	2.50	—
SH1367 (1988)	—	—	0.25	0.75	2.50	—

KM# 1234 5 RIALS

5.0000 g., Copper-Nickel, 25 mm. **Obv:** Inscription within tulip wreath **Rev:** Value and date within wreath **Note:** Date varieties exist.

Date	Mintage	F	VF	XF	Unc	BU
SH1358 (1979)	—	—	0.75	1.25	3.50	—
SH1359 (1980)	—	—	0.75	1.25	3.50	—
SH1360 (1981)	—	—	0.75	1.25	3.50	—
SH1361 (1982)	—	—	0.75	1.25	3.50	—
SH1362 (1983)	—	—	0.75	1.25	3.50	—
SH1363 (1984)	—	—	0.75	1.25	3.50	—
SH1364 (1985)	—	—	0.75	1.25	3.50	—
SH1365 (1986)	—	—	0.75	1.25	3.50	—
SH1366 (1987)	—	—	0.75	1.25	3.50	—
SH1367 (1988)	—	—	0.75	1.25	3.50	—
SH1368 (1989)	—	—	0.75	1.25	3.50	—

KM# 1258 5 RIALS

Brass, 19.5 mm. **Obv:** Value and date divides inscription and flower sprig within beaded circle **Rev:** Tomb within beaded circle

Date	Mintage	F	VF	XF	Unc	BU
SH1371 (1992)	—	—	0.50	1.25	3.00	—
SH1372 (1993)	—	—	0.50	1.25	3.00	—
SH1373 (1994)	—	—	0.50	1.25	3.00	—
SH1375 (1996)	—	—	0.50	1.25	3.00	—
SH1376 (1997)	—	—	0.50	1.25	3.00	—
SH1378 (1999)	—	—	—	2.00	5.00	—

KM# 1235.1 10 RIALS

Copper-Nickel, 28 mm. **Obv:** Inscription and value within tulip wreath **Rev:** Value and date within wreath

Date	Mintage	F	VF	XF	Unc	BU
SH1358 (1979)	—	—	1.00	2.50	4.50	—
SH1358 (1979) Large date	—	—	1.00	2.50	4.50	—
SH1359 (1980)	—	—	1.00	2.50	4.50	—
SH1360 (1981)	—	—	1.00	2.50	4.50	—
SH1361 (1982)	—	—	1.00	2.00	4.00	—

KM# 1235.2 10 RIALS

Copper-Nickel, 28 mm. **Obv:** Inscription and value within tulip wreath **Rev:** Value and date within wreath **Note:** Date varieties exist.

Date	Mintage	F	VF	XF	Unc	BU
SH1361 (1982)	—	—	1.00	2.00	4.00	—
SH1362 (1983)	—	—	1.00	2.00	4.00	—
SH1363 (1984)	—	—	1.00	2.00	4.00	—
SH1364 (1985)	—	—	0.90	1.50	4.00	—
SH1365 (1986)	—	—	0.90	1.50	4.00	—
SH1366 (1987)	—	—	0.90	1.50	4.00	—
SH1366 (1987) Small date	—	—	0.90	1.50	4.00	—
SH1367 (1988)	—	—	0.65	1.50	3.00	—

KM# 1243 10 RIALS

Copper-Nickel, 28 mm. **Subject:** 1st Anniversary of Revolution **Obv:** Value and inscription within wreath **Rev:** Tulips in center of inscription, dates and value

Date	Mintage	F	VF	XF	Unc	BU
SH1358 (1979)	—	—	5.00	10.00	15.00	—

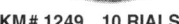

KM# 1249 10 RIALS

6.9700 g., Copper-Nickel, 28 mm. **Subject:** Moslem Unity **Obv:** Capitol building flanked by dates **Rev:** Kaaba at Mecca, date with value below **Edge:** Reeded

Date	Mintage	F	VF	XF	Unc	BU
SH1361-AH1402 (1982)	—	—	5.00	10.00	15.00	—

KM# 1253.1 10 RIALS

3.0200 g., Copper-Nickel, 21.2 mm. **Subject:** World Jerusalem Day **Obv:** Capitol building divides date **Rev:** Kaaba at Mecca divides date with value below **Edge:** Plain

Date	Mintage	F	VF	XF	Unc	BU
SH1368 (1989)	—	—	1.50	3.00	6.00	—

KM# 1253.2 10 RIALS

3.0200 g., Copper-Nickel, 21.2 mm. **Obv:** Capitol building divides dates **Rev:** Kaaba at Mecca divides dates with value below

Date	Mintage	F	VF	XF	Unc	BU
SH1368 (1989)	—	—	1.50	3.00	6.00	—

KM# 1259 10 RIALS

Aluminum-Bronze, 21 mm. **Subject:** Tomb of Ferdousi **Obv:** Value and date divides inscription and flower sprig within beaded circle **Rev:** Tomb within beaded circle

Date	Mintage	F	VF	XF	Unc	BU
SH1371 (1992)	—	—	1.00	2.00	3.75	—
SH1372 (1993)	—	—	1.00	2.00	3.75	—
SH1373 (1994)	—	—	1.00	2.00	3.75	—
SH1374 (1995)	—	—	1.00	2.00	3.75	—
SH1375 (1996)	—	—	1.00	2.00	3.75	—
SH1376 (1997)	—	—	1.00	2.00	3.75	—

KM# 1244 20 RIALS

Copper-Nickel, 31 mm. **Subject:** 1400th Anniversary of Mohammed's Flight **Obv:** Value and inscription within wreath **Rev:** Inscription within banner on top of world globe under radiant sun

Date	Mintage	F	VF	XF	Unc	BU
SH1358-AH1400 (1979)	—	—	5.00	10.00	15.00	—

KM# 1236 20 RIALS

Copper-Nickel, 31 mm. **Obv:** Inscription within tulip wreath **Rev:** Value and date within wreath **Note:** Date varieties exist.

Date	Mintage	F	VF	XF	Unc	BU
SH1358 (1979)	—	—	1.00	1.75	4.50	—
SH1359 (1980)	—	—	1.00	1.75	4.50	—
SH1360 (1981)	—	—	1.00	1.75	4.50	—
SH1361 (1982)	—	—	1.00	1.75	4.50	—
SH1362 (1983)	—	—	1.00	1.75	4.50	—
SH1363 (1984)	—	—	1.00	1.75	4.50	—
SH1364 (1985)	—	—	1.00	1.75	4.50	—
SH1365 (1986)	—	—	1.00	1.75	4.50	—
SH1366 (1987)	—	—	1.00	1.75	4.50	—
SH1367 (1988)	—	—	1.00	1.75	4.50	—

KM# 1246 20 RIALS

Copper-Nickel, 31 mm. **Subject:** 2nd Anniversary of Islamic Revolution **Obv:** Value flanked by tulips and inscription with date below **Rev:** Legend

Date	Mintage	F	VF	XF	Unc	BU
SH1359 (1980)	—	—	5.00	10.00	15.00	—

KM# 1247 20 RIALS

Copper-Nickel, 31 mm. **Subject:** 3rd Anniversary of Islamic Revolution **Obv:** Artistic tulip design within circle **Rev:** Inscription within artistic design

Date	Mintage	F	VF	XF	Unc	BU
SH1360 (1981)	—	—	5.00	10.00	15.00	—

KM# 1251 20 RIALS

Copper-Nickel, 31 mm. **Subject:** Islamic Banking Week **Obv:** Inscription within tulip wreath **Rev:** Building within 1/2 wreath and gear design

Date	Mintage	F	VF	XF	Unc	BU
SH1367 (1988)	—	—	5.00	10.00	15.00	—

KM# 1254.1 20 RIALS

Copper-Nickel, 24 mm. **Subject:** 8 Years of Sacred Defense **Obv:** Value and date within circle of 22 small ornaments **Rev:** Shield divides dates and inscription within wreath **Note:** 1.48 mm thick.

Date	Mintage	F	VF	XF	Unc	BU
SH1368 (1989)	—	—	3.00	5.00	10.00	—

KM# 1254.2 20 RIALS

4.6400 g., Copper-Nickel, 24 mm. **Obv:** Value, date and inscription within circle of 20 small ornaments **Rev:** Shield divides inscription and dates within wreath **Note:** 1.46 mm thick.

Date	Mintage	F	VF	XF	Unc	BU
SH1368 (1989)	—	—	3.00	5.00	10.00	—

KM# 1254.3 20 RIALS

Copper-Nickel, 24 mm. **Obv:** Inscription, value and date within circle of 20 small ornaments **Rev:** Shield divides inscription and dates within wreath

Date	Mintage	F	VF	XF	Unc	BU
SH1368 (1989)	—	—	3.00	5.00	10.00	—

KM# 1237.1 50 RIALS
Aluminum-Bronze, 26 mm. **Subject:** Oil and Agriculture **Obv:** Value at upper left of towers within 1/2 gear and oat sprigs **Rev:** Map in relief **Edge:** Lettered in Arabic **Note:** Two varieties of edge lettering exist.

Date	Mintage	F	VF	XF	Unc	BU
SH1359 (1980)	—	—	2.00	3.50	8.00	—
SH1360 (1981)	—	—	2.00	3.50	8.00	—
SH1361 (1982)	—	—	2.00	3.50	8.00	—
SH1362 (1983)	—	—	2.00	3.50	8.00	—
SH1364 (1985)	—	—	2.00	3.50	8.00	—
SH1365 (1986)	—	—	2.00	3.50	8.00	—

KM# 1237.2 50 RIALS
Aluminum-Bronze, 26 mm. **Obv:** Value at upper left of towers within 1/2 gear and oat sprigs **Rev:** Map incuse **Edge:** Lettered in Arabic

Date	Mintage	F	VF	XF	Unc	BU
SH1366 (1987)	—	—	4.00	6.00	9.00	—
SH1367 (1988)	—	—	—	4.50	7.00	—
SH1368 (1989)	—	—	—	4.50	7.00	—

KM# 1252 50 RIALS
Copper-Nickel **Subject:** 10th Anniversary of Revolution **Obv:** Value at upper left of towers within 1/2 gear and oat sprigs **Rev:** Flower-like design above inscription and date within designed border

Date	Mintage	F	VF	XF	Unc	BU
SH1367 (1988)	—	—	5.00	10.00	15.00	—

KM# 1237.1a 50 RIALS
Copper-Nickel **Obv:** Value at upper left of towers within 1/2 gear and oat sprigs **Rev:** Map in relief **Edge:** Lettered in Arabic

Date	Mintage	F	VF	XF	Unc	BU
SH1368 (1989)	—	—	2.00	3.50	7.50	—
SH1369 (1990)	—	—	2.00	3.50	7.50	—
SH1370 (1991)	—	—	2.00	3.50	7.50	—

KM# 1260 50 RIALS
Copper-Nickel, 26 mm. **Subject:** Shrine of Hazrat Masumah **Obv:** Value and date **Rev:** Shrine within beaded circle **Edge:** Reeded

Date	Mintage	F	VF	XF	Unc	BU
SH1371 (1992)	—	—	2.50	3.50	5.00	—
SH1372 (1993)	—	—	2.50	3.50	5.00	—
SH1373 (1994)	—	—	2.50	3.50	5.00	—
SH1374 (1995)	—	—	2.50	3.50	5.00	—
SH1375 (1996)	—	—	2.50	3.50	5.00	—
SH1376 (1997)	—	—	2.50	3.50	5.00	—
SH1377 (1998)	—	—	2.50	3.50	5.00	—
SH1378 (1999)	—	—	2.50	3.50	5.00	—
SH1379 (2000)	—	—	2.50	3.50	5.00	—
SH1380 (2001)	—	—	2.50	3.50	5.00	—
SH1382 (2003)	—	—	2.50	3.50	5.00	—

KM# 1266 50 RIALS
3.5100 g., Aluminum-Bronze, 20.1 mm. **Obv:** Value and date **Rev:** Hazrat Masumah Shrine **Edge:** Reeded **Mint:** Tehran

Date	Mintage	F	VF	XF	Unc	BU
SH1382(2003)	—	—	—	—	50.00	—
SH1383(2004)	—	—	—	—	2.50	—
SH1384(2005)	—	—	—	—	2.50	—
SH1385(2006)	—	—	—	—	2.50	—

KM# 1261.1 100 RIALS
8.7800 g., Copper-Nickel **Subject:** Shrine of Imam Reza **Obv:** Value and date divides inscription and flower sprig within beaded border **Rev:** Shrine within designed border **Note:** Thin denomination and numerals

Date	Mintage	F	VF	XF	Unc	BU
SH1371 (1992)	—	—	—	—	6.50	—

KM# 1261.2 100 RIALS
Copper-Nickel, 29 mm. **Obv:** Value and date **Rev:** Shrine within designed border **Note:** Thick denomination and numerals

Date	Mintage	F	VF	XF	Unc	BU
SH1372 (1993)	—	—	—	—	6.50	—
SH1373 (1994)	—	—	—	—	6.50	—
SH1375 (1996)	—	—	—	—	6.50	—
SH1376 (1997)	—	—	—	—	6.50	—
SH1377 (1998)	—	—	—	—	6.50	—
SH1378 (1999)	—	—	—	—	6.50	—
SH1379 (2000)	—	—	—	—	6.50	—
SH1380 (2001)	—	—	—	—	6.50	—
SH1382 (2003)	—	—	—	—	6.50	—

KM# 1267 100 RIALS
4.6200 g., Aluminum-Bronze, 22.9 mm. **Obv:** Value, date divides wreath below **Rev:** Imam Reza Shrine **Edge:** Reeded **Mint:** Tehran

Date	Mintage	F	VF	XF	Unc	BU
SH1382(2003)	—	—	—	—	50.00	—
SH1383(2004)	—	—	—	—	3.50	—
SH1384(2005)	—	—	—	—	3.50	—
SH1385(2006)	—	—	—	—	3.50	—

KM# 1262 250 RIALS
Bi-Metallic Copper-Nickel center in Brass ring, 28 mm. **Obv:** Value within circle, inscription and date divide wreath **Rev:** Stylized flower within circle and wreath

Date	Mintage	F	VF	XF	Unc	BU
SH1372 (1993)	—	—	—	—	7.50	—
SH1373 (1994)	—	—	—	—	7.50	—
SH1374 (1995)	—	—	—	—	7.50	—
SH1375 (1996)	—	—	—	—	7.50	—
SH1376 (1997)	—	—	—	—	7.50	—
SH1377 (1998)	—	—	—	—	7.50	—
SH1378 (1999)	—	—	—	—	7.50	—
SH1379 (2000)	—	—	—	—	7.50	—
SH1381 (2002)	—	—	—	—	7.50	—
SH1382 (2003)	—	—	—	—	7.50	—

KM# 1268 250 RIALS
5.5000 g., Copper-Nickel, 24.6 mm. **Obv:** Value, date below divides sprays **Rev:** Stylized flower within sprays **Edge:** Plain **Mint:** Tehran

Date	Mintage	F	VF	XF	Unc	BU
SH1382(2003)	—	—	—	—	50.00	—
SH1383(2004)	—	—	—	—	4.50	—
SH1384(2005)	—	—	—	—	4.50	—
SH1385(2006)	—	—	—	—	4.50	—

KM# 1268a 250 RIALS
Aluminum-Bronze **Obv:** Value, date below divides sprays **Rev:** Stylized flower within sprays **Mint:** Tehran

Date	Mintage	F	VF	XF	Unc	BU
SH1386(2007)	—	—	—	—	4.50	—

KM# 1269 500 RIALS
8.9100 g., Bi-Metallic Aluminum-Bronze center in Copper-Nickel ring, 27.1 mm. **Obv:** Value **Rev:** Bird and flowers **Edge:** Reeded **Mint:** Tehran

Date	Mintage	F	VF	XF	Unc	BU
SH1382(2003)	—	—	—	—	50.00	—
SH1383(2004)	—	—	—	—	6.00	—
SH1384(2005)	—	—	—	—	6.00	—
SH1385(2006)	—	—	—	—	6.00	—

KM# 1269a 500 RIALS
Aluminum-Bronze **Obv:** Value in ornamental circle **Rev:** Bird and flowers **Mint:** Tehran

Date	Mintage	F	VF	XF	Unc	BU
SH1386(2007)	—	—	—	—	6.00	—

IRAQ

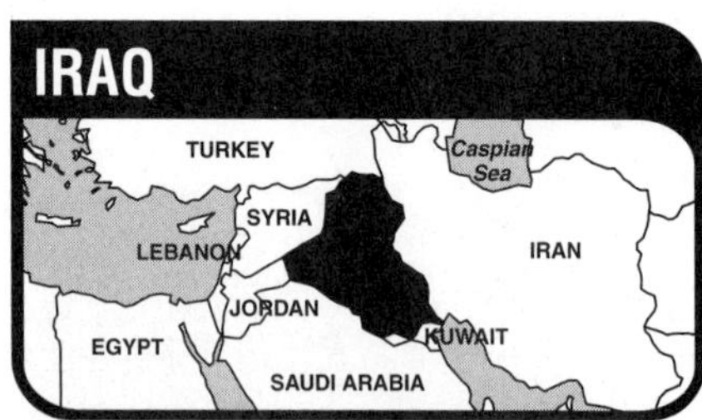

The Republic of Iraq, historically known as Mesopotamia, is located in the Near East and is bordered by Kuwait, Iran, Turkey, Syria, Jordan and Saudi Arabia. It has area of 167,925 sq. mi. (434,920 sq. km.) and a population of 14 million. Capital: Baghdad. The economy of Iraq is based on agriculture and petroleum. Crude oil accounted for 94 percent of the exports before the war with Iran began in 1980.

Mesopotamia was the site of a number of flourishing civilizations of antiquity - Sumeria, Assyria, Babylonia, Parthia, Persia and the Biblical cities of Ur, Ninevehand and Babylon. Desired because of its favored location, which embraced the fertile alluvial plains of the Tigris and Euphrates Rivers, Mesopotamia - 'land between the rivers'- was conquered by Cyrus the Great of Persia, Alexander of Macedonia and by Arabs who made the legendary city of Baghdad the capital of the ruling caliphate. Suleiman the Magnificent conquered Mesopotamia for Turkey in1534, and it formed part of the Ottoman Empire until 1623, and from 1638 to 1917. Great Britain, given a League of Nations mandate over the territory in 1920, recognized Iraq as a kingdom in 1922. Iraq became an independent constitutional monarchy presided over by the Hashemite family, direct descendants of the prophet Mohammed, in 1932. In 1958, the army-led revolution of July 14 overthrew the monarchy and proclaimed a republic.

NOTE: The 'I' mintmark on 1938 and 1943 issues appears on the obverse near the point of the bust. Some of the issues of 1938 have a dot to denote a composition change from nickel to copper-nickel.

RULERS

Ottoman, until 1917
British, 1921-1922
Faisal I, 1921-1933
Ghazi I, 1933-1939
Faisal II, Regency, 1939-1953
As King, 1953-1958

MINT MARK

I – Bombay

MONETARY SYSTEM

Falus, Fulus — Fals, Fils — Falsan

50 Fils = 1 Dirham
200 Fils = 1 Riyal
1000 Fils = 1 Dinar (Pound)

TITLES

العراق

Al-Iraq

المملكة العراقية

SAl-Mamlaka(t) al-Iraqiya(t)

الجمهورية العرقية

Al-Jumhuriya(t) al-Iraqiya(t)

KINGDOM OF IRAQ

Faisal I
1921-1933AD

DECIMAL COINAGE

KM# 95 FILS

2.5000 g., Bronze, 19.5 mm. **Obv:** Head right **Rev:** Value in center circle flanked by dates

Date	Mintage	F	VF	XF	Unc	BU
1931	4,000,000	1.00	3.00	10.00	25.00	—
1931 Proof	—	—	—	—	—	—
1933	6,000,000	1.00	3.00	10.00	25.00	—
1933 Proof	—	—	—	—	—	—

KM# 96 2 FILS

5.0000 g., Bronze, 24 mm. **Obv:** Head right **Rev:** Value in center circle flanked by dates

Date	Mintage	F	VF	XF	Unc	BU
1931	2,500,000	1.25	3.50	10.00	25.00	—
1931 Proof	—	—	—	—	—	—
1933	1,000,000	1.50	4.00	15.00	35.00	—
1933 Proof	—	—	—	—	—	—

KM# 97 4 FILS

4.0000 g., Nickel, 21 mm. **Obv:** Head right **Rev:** Value in center circle flanked by dates **Shape:** Scalloped

Date	Mintage	F	VF	XF	Unc	BU
1931	4,500,000	1.50	4.00	15.00	50.00	—
1931 Proof	—	—	—	—	—	—
1933	6,500,000	1.50	4.00	15.00	50.00	—
1933 Proof	—	—	—	—	—	—

KM# 98 10 FILS

6.7500 g., Nickel, 25 mm. **Obv:** Head right **Rev:** Value within center circle flanked by dates **Shape:** Scalloped

Date	Mintage	F	VF	XF	Unc	BU
1931	2,400,000	2.00	5.00	16.50	50.00	—
1931 Proof	—	—	—	—	—	—
1933	2,200,000	2.00	5.00	16.50	50.00	—
1933 Proof	—	—	—	—	—	—

KM# 99 20 FILS

3.6000 g., 0.5000 Silver 0.0579 oz. ASW, 20.5 mm. **Obv:** Head right **Rev:** Value in center circle flanked by dates

Date	Mintage	F	VF	XF	Unc	BU
1931	1,500,000	2.50	9.00	25.00	75.00	—
1931 Proof	—	—	—	—	—	—
1933	1,100,000	2.50	9.00	25.00	75.00	—
1933 Proof	—	—	—	—	—	—
1933 (error) 1252	Inc. above	20.00	60.00	100	200	—

KM# 100 50 FILS

9.0000 g., 0.5000 Silver 0.1447 oz. ASW, 26.5 mm. **Obv:** Head right **Rev:** Value in center circle flanked by dates

Date	Mintage	F	VF	XF	Unc	BU
1931	8,800,000	3.50	10.00	28.00	80.00	—
1931 Proof	—	—	—	—	—	—
1933	800,000	6.00	15.00	35.00	100	—
1933 Proof	—	—	—	—	—	—

KM# 101 RIYAL (200 Fils)

20.0000 g., 0.5000 Silver 0.3215 oz. ASW, 34 mm. **Obv:** Head right **Rev:** Value in center circle flanked by dates **Note:** Dav. #255.

Date	Mintage	F	VF	XF	Unc	BU
1932	500,000	7.50	15.00	35.00	350	—
1932 Proof	Est. 20	Value: 1,600				

Ghazi I
1933-1939AD

DECIMAL COINAGE

KM# 102 FILS

2.5000 g., Bronze, 19.5 mm. **Obv:** Head left **Rev:** Value in center circle flanked by dates **Note:** Struck at Royal and Bombay Mint.

Date	Mintage	F	VF	XF	Unc	BU
1936	3,000,000	1.25	4.00	10.00	25.00	—
1936 Proof	—	—	—	—	—	—
1938	36,000,000	0.25	0.50	1.00	3.00	—
1938 Proof	—	—	—	—	—	—
1938 -I	3,000,000	0.50	2.00	5.00	15.00	—

KM# 105 4 FILS

4.0000 g., Nickel, 21 mm. **Obv:** Head left **Rev:** Value within center circle flanked by dates **Shape:** Scalloped

Date	Mintage	F	VF	XF	Unc	BU
1938	1,000,000	1.00	2.00	6.00	15.00	—
1938 Proof	—	—	—	—	—	—
1939	1,000,000	1.25	2.50	10.00	30.00	—
1939 Proof	—	—	—	—	—	—

KM# 105a 4 FILS

21.0000 g., Copper-Nickel, 21 mm. **Obv:** Head left **Rev:** Value within center circle flanked by dates **Shape:** Scalloped **Note:** Struck at Royal and Bombay Mint.

Date	Mintage	F	VF	XF	Unc	BU
1938	2,750,000	0.75	1.00	2.00	6.00	—
1938 Proof	—	—	—	—	—	—
1938 -I	2,500,000	1.00	2.00	7.50	15.00	—

KM# 105b 4 FILS

4.0000 g., Bronze, 21 mm. **Obv:** Head left **Rev:** Value in center circle flanked by dates **Shape:** Scalloped

Date	Mintage	F	VF	XF	Unc	BU
1938	8,000,000	0.50	1.00	2.00	6.00	—
1938 Proof	—	—	—	—	—	—

KM# 103 10 FILS

6.7500 g., Nickel, 25 mm. **Obv:** Head left **Rev:** Value in center circle flanked by dates **Shape:** Scalloped

Date	Mintage	F	VF	XF	Unc	BU
1937	400,000	3.00	5.00	16.50	50.00	—
1937 Proof	—	—	—	—	—	—
1938	600,000	2.50	4.00	10.00	35.00	—
1938 Proof	—	—	—	—	—	—

KM# 103a 10 FILS

6.7500 g., Copper-Nickel, 25 mm. **Obv:** Head left **Rev:** Value within center circle flanked by dates **Shape:** Scalloped **Note:** Struck at Royal and Bombay Mint.

Date	Mintage	F	VF	XF	Unc	BU
1938	1,100,000	1.00	2.00	4.00	10.00	—
1938 Proof	—	—	—	—	—	—
1938 -I	1,500,000	1.50	2.50	6.00	15.00	—

KM# 103b 10 FILS

6.7500 g., Bronze, 25 mm. **Obv:** Head left **Rev:** Value within center circle flanked by dates **Shape:** Scalloped

Date	Mintage	F	VF	XF	Unc	BU
1938	8,250,000	0.50	1.00	2.50	6.50	—
1938 Proof	—	—	—	—	—	—

KM# 106 20 FILS

3.6000 g., 0.5000 Silver 0.0579 oz. ASW, 20.5 mm. **Obv:** Head left **Rev:** Value in center circle flanked by dates

Date	Mintage	F	VF	XF	Unc	BU
1938	1,200,000	2.00	3.50	8.00	22.00	—
1938 -I	1,350,000	2.00	4.00	9.00	26.00	—

KM# 104 50 FILS
9.0000 g., 0.5000 Silver 0.1447 oz. ASW, 26.5 mm. **Obv:** Head left **Rev:** Value in center circle flanked by dates **Note:** Struck at Royal and Bombay Mint.

Date	Mintage	F	VF	XF	Unc	BU
1937	1,200,000	3.00	7.00	10.00	30.00	—
1937 Proof	—	—	—	—	—	—
1938	5,300,000	2.50	4.00	8.00	25.00	—
1938 Proof	—	—	—	—	—	—
1938 -I	7,500,000	2.50	4.00	8.00	25.00	—

Faisal II - Regency
1939-1953AD
DECIMAL COINAGE

KM# 107 4 FILS
4.0000 g., Bronze, 21 mm. **Obv:** Head right **Rev:** Value in center circle flanked by dates **Shape:** Scalloped

Date	Mintage	F	VF	XF	Unc	BU
1943 -I	1,500,000	2.00	3.00	7.00	15.00	—

KM# 108 10 FILS
6.7500 g., Bronze, 25 mm. **Obv:** Head right **Rev:** Value in center circle flanked by dates **Shape:** Scalloped

Date	Mintage	F	VF	XF	Unc	BU
1943 -I	1,500,000	3.00	7.00	20.00	50.00	—

Faisal II - King
1953-1958AD
DECIMAL COINAGE

KM# 109 FILS
Bronze **Obv:** Head right **Rev:** Value in center circle flanked by dates

Date	Mintage	F	VF	XF	Unc	BU
1953	41,000,000	0.25	0.40	0.60	1.00	—
1953 Proof	200	Value: 75.00				

KM# 110 2 FILS
Bronze **Obv:** Head right **Rev:** Value in center circle flanked by dates

Date	Mintage	F	VF	XF	Unc	BU
1953	500,000	0.50	1.00	3.00	12.50	—
1953 Proof	200	Value: 100				

KM# 111 4 FILS
4.0000 g., Copper-Nickel, 21 mm. **Obv:** Head right **Rev:** Value in center circle flanked by dates **Shape:** Scalloped

Date	Mintage	F	VF	XF	Unc	BU
1953	20,750,000	0.50	0.75	1.00	2.50	—
1953 Proof	200	Value: 75.00				

KM# 112 10 FILS
6.7500 g., Copper-Nickel, 25 mm. **Obv:** Head right **Rev:** Value in center circle flanked by dates **Shape:** Scalloped

Date	Mintage	F	VF	XF	Unc	BU
1953	11,400,000	0.50	0.75	1.00	2.50	—
1953 Proof	200	Value: 75.00				

KM# 113 20 FILS
3.6000 g., 0.5000 Silver 0.0579 oz. ASW, 20.5 mm. **Obv:** Head right **Rev:** Value in center circle flanked by dates

Date	Mintage	F	VF	XF	Unc	BU
1953	250,000	25.00	45.00	70.00	140	—
1953 Proof	200	Value: 300				

KM# 116 20 FILS
2.8000 g., 0.5000 Silver 0.0450 oz. ASW, 19 mm. **Obv:** Head right **Rev:** Value in center circle, date above sprigs, legend above

Date	Mintage	F	VF	XF	Unc	BU
1955 Proof	—	Value: 80.00				
1955	4,000,000	1.50	3.00	5.00	10.00	—

KM# 114 50 FILS
9.0000 g., 0.5000 Silver 0.1447 oz. ASW, 26.5 mm. **Obv:** Head right **Rev:** Value in center circle flanked by dates

Date	Mintage	F	VF	XF	Unc	BU
1953	560,000	50.00	100	150	250	—
1953 Proof	200	Value: 450				

KM# 117 50 FILS
7.0000 g., 0.5000 Silver 0.1125 oz. ASW, 26 mm. **Obv:** Head right **Rev:** Value in center circle, date above sprigs, legend above

Date	Mintage	F	VF	XF	Unc	BU
1955	12,000,000	2.50	4.00	6.00	11.50	—
1955 Proof	—	Value: 80.00				

KM# 115 100 FILS
10.0000 g., 0.9000 Silver 0.2893 oz. ASW, 29 mm. **Obv:** Head right **Rev:** Value in center circle flanked by dates

Date	Mintage	F	VF	XF	Unc	BU
1953	1,200,000	5.00	7.50	20.00	50.00	—
1953 Proof	200	Value: 250				

KM# 118 100 FILS
10.0000 g., 0.5000 Silver 0.1607 oz. ASW, 29 mm. **Obv:** Head right **Rev:** Value in center circle flanked by dates

Date	Mintage	F	VF	XF	Unc	BU
1955	1,000,000	—	700	1,000	1,500	—
1955 Proof	—	Value: 300				

REPUBLIC
DECIMAL COINAGE

KM# 119 FILS
2.5000 g., Bronze, 19 mm. **Obv:** Value in center circle, dates above sprig, legend above **Rev:** Oat sprig within center circle of star design **Shape:** 10-sided

Date	Mintage	F	VF	XF	Unc	BU
1959	72,000,000	0.15	0.25	0.50	1.00	—
1959 Proof	400	Value: 30.00				

KM# 120 5 FILS
5.0000 g., Copper-Nickel, 22 mm. **Obv:** Value in center circle above dates and sprigs, legend above **Rev:** Oat sprig within center circle of star design **Shape:** Scalloped

Date	Mintage	F	VF	XF	Unc	BU
1959	30,000,000	0.15	0.25	0.50	1.00	—
1959 Proof	400	Value: 30.00				

KM# 125 5 FILS
Copper-Nickel **Obv:** Value in center circle above oat sprigs, legend above **Rev:** Palm trees divide dates **Shape:** Scalloped

Date	Mintage	F	VF	XF	Unc	BU
1967	17,000,000	0.15	0.25	0.35	0.50	—
1971	15,000,000	0.15	0.25	0.35	0.50	—

KM# 125a 5 FILS
3.9000 g., Stainless Steel, 22 mm. **Obv:** Value in center circle above oat sprigs, legend above **Rev:** Palm trees divide dates

Date	Mintage	F	VF	XF	Unc	BU
1971	2,000,000	0.20	0.30	0.50	0.75	—
1974	15,000,000	0.10	0.15	0.25	0.35	—
1975	94,800,000	0.10	0.15	0.25	0.35	—
1980	20,160,000	0.10	0.15	0.25	0.35	—
1981	29,840,000	0.10	0.15	0.25	0.35	—

Note: Non-magnetic

KM# 141 5 FILS
Stainless Steel **Series:** F.A.O. **Obv:** Value in center circle divides legend **Rev:** Palm trees divide date **Shape:** Scalloped

Date	Mintage	F	VF	XF	Unc	BU
1975	2,000,000	0.10	0.15	0.25	0.50	—

KM# 159 5 FILS
Stainless Steel **Subject:** Babylon-Ruins **Obv:** Value in center circle divides legend **Rev:** Dates above ruins **Shape:** Scalloped

Date	Mintage	F	VF	XF	Unc	BU
1982	—	0.10	0.15	0.25	0.50	—

KM# 121 10 FILS
6.7500 g., Copper-Nickel, 26 mm. **Obv:** Value in center circle above dates and sprigs, legend above **Rev:** Oat sprig within center circle of star-like design **Shape:** Scalloped

Date	Mintage	F	VF	XF	Unc	BU
1959	24,000,000	0.25	0.35	0.65	1.50	—
1959 Proof	400	Value: 30.00				

KM# 126 10 FILS
6.8100 g., Copper-Nickel, 26 mm. **Obv:** Value in center circle above oat sprigs, legend above **Rev:** Palm trees divide dates **Shape:** Scalloped

Date	Mintage	F	VF	XF	Unc	BU
1967	13,400,000	0.20	0.30	0.60	1.25	—
1971	12,000,000	0.20	0.30	0.60	1.25	—

KM# 126a 10 FILS
5.6400 g., Stainless Steel, 27 mm. **Obv:** Value in center circle above sprigs, legend above **Rev:** Palm trees divide dates

Date	Mintage	F	VF	XF	Unc	BU
1971	1,550,000	0.25	0.35	0.65	1.50	—
1974	12,000,000	0.20	0.30	0.50	1.00	—
1975	52,456,000	0.20	0.30	0.50	1.00	—
1979	13,800,000	0.20	0.30	0.50	1.00	—
1980	11,264,000	0.20	0.30	0.50	1.00	—
1981	63,736,000	0.20	0.30	0.50	1.00	—

Note: Non-magnetic

KM# 142 10 FILS
Stainless Steel, 26 mm. **Series:** F.A.O. **Obv:** Value within circle divides legend **Rev:** Palm trees divide dates **Shape:** Scalloped

Date	Mintage	F	VF	XF	Unc	BU
1975	1,000,000	0.15	0.25	0.50	0.75	—

KM# 160 10 FILS
Stainless Steel, 26 mm. **Obv:** Value within circle divides legends **Rev:** Dates above ruins **Rev. Legend:** Babylon - Ishtar Gate **Shape:** Scalloped

Date	Mintage	F	VF	XF	Unc	BU
1982	—	—	—	—	0.75	—

KM# 160a 10 FILS
Copper-Nickel **Obv:** Value within circle divides legends **Rev:** Dates above ruins **Rev. Legend:** Babylon - Ishtar Gate **Shape:** Scalloped

Date	Mintage	F	VF	XF	Unc	BU
1982 Proof	—	Value: 3.00				

KM# 122 25 FILS
2.5000 g., 0.5000 Silver 0.0402 oz. ASW, 20 mm. **Obv:** Value within circle above dates and sprigs, legend above **Rev:** Oat sprig within center circle of star-like design

Date	Mintage	F	VF	XF	Unc	BU
1959 Proof	400	Value: 40.00				
1959	12,000,000	0.65	0.85	1.50	3.00	—

KM# 127 25 FILS
2.7900 g., Copper-Nickel, 20 mm. **Obv:** Value in center circle above sprigs, legend above **Rev:** Palm trees divide dates

Date	Mintage	F	VF	XF	Unc	BU
1969	6,000,000	0.20	0.30	0.50	1.00	—
1970	6,000,000	0.20	0.30	0.50	1.00	—
1972	12,000,000	0.20	0.30	0.50	1.00	—
1975	48,000,000	0.20	0.30	0.50	1.00	—
1981	60,000,000	0.20	0.30	0.50	1.00	—

KM# 161 25 FILS
Copper-Nickel, 20 mm. **Obv:** Value in center circle divides legend **Rev:** Dates above lion

Date	Mintage	F	VF	XF	Unc	BU
1982 Proof	—	Value: 4.00				
1982	—	—	—	—	1.25	—

KM# 123 50 FILS
5.0000 g., 0.5000 Silver 0.0804 oz. ASW, 23 mm. **Obv:** Value in center circle above dates and sprigs, legend above **Rev:** Oat sprig within center circle of star-like design

Date	Mintage	F	VF	XF	Unc	BU
1959	24,000,000	1.25	1.50	2.50	5.00	—
1959 Proof	400	Value: 80.00				

KM# 128 50 FILS
5.5400 g., Copper-Nickel, 23 mm. **Obv:** Value within circle above sprigs, legend above **Rev:** Palm trees divide dates

Date	Mintage	F	VF	XF	Unc	BU
1969	12,000,000	0.25	0.35	0.65	1.25	—
1970	12,000,000	0.25	0.35	0.65	1.25	—
1972	12,000,000	0.25	0.35	0.65	1.25	—
1975	36,000,000	0.25	0.35	0.65	1.25	—
1979	1,500,000	0.25	0.35	0.65	1.75	—
1980	23,520,000	0.25	0.35	0.65	1.25	—
1981	138,995,000	0.25	0.35	0.65	1.00	—
1990	—	0.25	0.35	0.65	1.00	—

KM# 162 50 FILS
Copper-Nickel, 23 mm. **Obv:** Value in center circle divides legend **Rev:** Horse right

Date	Mintage	F	VF	XF	Unc	BU
1982	—	0.25	0.50	0.75	2.50	—
1982 Proof	—	Value: 6.00				

KM# 124 100 FILS
10.0000 g., 0.5000 Silver 0.1607 oz. ASW, 29 mm. **Obv:** Value within circle above dates and sprigs, legend above **Rev:** Oat sprig within center circle of star-like design

Date	Mintage	F	VF	XF	Unc	BU
1959	6,000,000	2.75	3.75	6.00	10.00	—
1959 Proof	400	Value: 150				

KM# 129 100 FILS
10.8300 g., Copper-Nickel **Obv:** Value within circle above sprigs, legend above **Rev:** Palm trees divide dates

Date	Mintage	F	VF	XF	Unc	BU
1970	6,000,000	0.35	0.50	0.75	1.50	—
1972	6,000,000	0.35	0.50	0.75	1.50	—
1975	12,000,000	0.35	0.50	0.75	1.50	—
1979	1,000,000	0.35	0.75	1.50	3.00	—

KM# 130 250 FILS
Nickel **Series:** F.A.O. **Subject:** Agrarian Reform Day **Obv:** Value within circle above sprigs, legend above **Rev:** Palm trees divide dates

Date	Mintage	F	VF	XF	Unc	BU
1970	500,000	—	1.50	3.00	6.00	—
1970 Proof	1,000	Value: 14.50				

Note: Varieties with edge inscription w/FAO-250-repeated three times in relief have been reported

KM# 131 250 FILS
Nickel **Subject:** 1st Anniversary Peace with Kurds **Obv:** Value within circle above dates and sprigs, legend above **Rev:** Value, design and dove within circle, outer circle consists of 1/2 gear and 1/2 sprigs

Date	Mintage	F	VF	XF	Unc	BU
1971 Proof	1,000	Value: 14.50				
1971	500,000	—	1.50	3.00	6.00	—

KM# 135 250 FILS
Nickel **Subject:** Silver Jublilee of Al Baath Party **Obv:** Value within circle above dates, legend above and below **Rev:** Palm trees divide dates

Date	Mintage	F	VF	XF	Unc	BU
1972	250,000	—	1.50	3.00	6.00	—

KM# 136 250 FILS
Nickel **Subject:** 25th Anniversary of Central Bank **Obv:** Value within circle above dates, legend above and below **Rev:** Palm trees divide dates

Date	Mintage	F	VF	XF	Unc	BU
1972	250,000	—	1.50	3.00	6.00	—

KM# 138 250 FILS
Nickel **Subject:** Oil Nationalization **Obv:** Value within circle above dates, legend above and below **Rev:** Torch divides oil rig tower and pump, flanked by dates

Date	Mintage	F	VF	XF	Unc	BU
1973 Proof	5,000	Value: 12.00				
1973	260,000	—	1.50	3.00	6.50	—

KM# 144 250 FILS
Nickel **Subject:** International Year of the Child **Obv:** Value within circle divides legends and emblems **Rev:** Child's laureate head right within circle

Date	Mintage	F	VF	XF	Unc	BU
1979 Proof	10,000	Value: 8.00				

KM# 146 250 FILS
Copper-Nickel **Subject:** 1st Anniversary of Hussein as President **Obv:** Value within center circle flanked by dates,legend above and below **Rev:** Bust 1/4 left

Date	Mintage	F	VF	XF	Unc	BU
1980	—	—	3.00	6.00	12.00	30.00

KM# 147 250 FILS
10.4000 g., Copper-Nickel, 29.8 mm. **Obv:** Value within circle above sprigs, legend above **Rev:** Palm trees divide dates **Shape:** Octagon

Date	Mintage	F	VF	XF	Unc	BU
1980	—	—	1.00	2.00	5.00	—
1981	25,568,000	—	1.00	2.00	5.00	—
1990	—	—	1.00	2.00	5.00	—

KM# 152 250 FILS
Copper-Nickel **Subject:** World Food Day **Obv:** F.A.O logo below value flanked by designs, legend above and below **Rev:** Design within circle divides dates **Shape:** Octagon

Date	Mintage	F	VF	XF	Unc	BU
1981	46,432,000	—	1.00	2.00	4.00	—

KM# 155 250 FILS
Copper-Nickel **Subject:** Nonaligned Nations Baghdad Conference **Obv:** Value within circle, legend above and below **Rev:** Stylized tree divides dates above legend **Shape:** Octagon

Date	Mintage	F	VF	XF	Unc	BU
1982	—	—	1.00	2.00	5.00	—

KM# 163 250 FILS
Copper-Nickel **Obv:** Value within circle, legend above and below **Rev:** Monument flanked by dates **Shape:** Octagon

Date	Mintage	F	VF	XF	Unc	BU
1982	—	—	1.00	2.00	4.50	—
1982 Proof	—	Value: 8.00				

KM# 132 500 FILS
Nickel **Subject:** 50th Anniversary of Iraqi Army **Obv:** Value in circle flanked by designs , legend above and below **Rev:** Conjoined armored busts divide dates

Date	Mintage	F	VF	XF	Unc	BU
1971	100,000	—	2.50	4.50	10.00	12.50
1971 Proof	5,000	Value: 15.00				

KM# 139 500 FILS
Nickel **Subject:** Oil Nationalization **Obv:** Value within circle, date below, legend above and below **Rev:** Oil rig divides dates

Date	Mintage	F	VF	XF	Unc	BU
1973	260,000	—	2.50	4.50	10.00	—
1973 Proof	5,000	Value: 17.50				

KM# 165 500 FILS
9.0800 g., Nickel, 30.1 mm. **Obv:** Value within circle above sprigs, "500 Fals" **Rev:** Palm trees divide dates **Shape:** Square

Date	Mintage	F	VF	XF	Unc	BU
1982	—	—	2.50	4.00	7.00	—

KM# 165a 500 FILS
8.9800 g., Nickel, 30.1 mm. **Obv:** Value within circle above sprigs, "500 Falsan" **Rev:** Palm trees divide dates **Shape:** Square **Note:** Reduced weight.

Date	Mintage	F	VF	XF	Unc	BU
1982	—	—	20.00	35.00	85.00	—

KM# 168 500 FILS
9.0800 g., Nickel **Obv:** Value within circle divides legend, "500 Fals" **Rev:** Lion of Babylon flanked by dates **Shape:** Square

Date	Mintage	F	VF	XF	Unc	BU
1982	—	—	2.00	3.50	8.00	—
1982 Proof	—	Value: 12.50				

KM# 168a 500 FILS
9.0800 g., Nickel **Obv:** Value within circle divides legend, "500 Falsan" **Rev:** Lion of Babylon flanked by dates **Shape:** Square

Date	Mintage	F	VF	XF	Unc	BU
1982	—	—	15.00	25.00	75.00	—

KM# 133 DINAR

31.0000 g., 0.9000 Silver 0.8970 oz. ASW **Subject:** 50th Anniversary of Iraqi Army **Obv:** Value within circle flanked by designs, legend above and below **Rev:** Conjoined armored busts divide dates

Date	Mintage	F	VF	XF	Unc	BU
1971	14,500	—	—	—	22.50	30.00
1971 Proof	5,500	Value: 40.00				

KM# 137 DINAR

31.0000 g., 0.5000 Silver 0.4983 oz. ASW **Subject:** 25th Anniversary of Central Bank **Obv:** Value within circle flanked by designs, legend above and below **Rev:** Palm trees divide dates

Date	Mintage	F	VF	XF	Unc	BU
1972	50,000	—	—	—	20.00	—
1972 Proof	—	Value: 35.00				

KM# 140 DINAR

31.0000 g., 0.5000 Silver 0.4983 oz. ASW **Subject:** Oil Nationalization **Obv:** Value within circle flanked by designs, legend above and below **Rev:** Half radiant sun divides dates above long ship

Date	Mintage	F	VF	XF	Unc	BU
1973	60,000	—	—	—	20.00	25.00
1973 Proof	5,000	Value: 37.50				

KM# 149 DINAR

Nickel **Subject:** Battle of Qadissyiat **Obv:** Value within circle flanked by dates, legends and map **Rev:** Bust 1/4 left in front of battle scene **Shape:** 10-sided

Date	Mintage	F	VF	XF	Unc	BU
1980	—	—	—	7.50	15.00	35.00
1980 Proof	—	Value: 35.00				

KM# 153 DINAR

Nickel **Subject:** 50th Anniversary of Iraq Air Force **Obv:** Value within circle with legend above and dates and legend below **Rev:** Bust left divides dates, planes above with banner, sprigs below **Shape:** 10-sided

Date	Mintage	F	VF	XF	Unc	BU
1981	—	—	—	10.00	20.00	40.00

KM# 170 DINAR

Nickel **Subject:** Circulation Coinage **Obv:** Value within circle above sprigs, legend above **Rev:** Palm trees divide dates **Shape:** 10-sided

Date	Mintage	F	VF	XF	Unc	BU
1981	—	—	—	—	6.50	—

KM# 156 DINAR

Nickel **Subject:** Nonaligned Nations Baghdad Conference **Obv:** Value within circle with legend above and below **Rev:** Stylized tree divides dates within legend **Shape:** 10-sided

Date	Mintage	F	VF	XF	Unc	BU
1982	—	—	—	3.50	8.00	—

KM# 164 DINAR

Nickel **Obv:** Value within circle divides legend **Rev:** Tower of Babylon flanked by dates **Shape:** 10-sided

Date	Mintage	F	VF	XF	Unc	BU
1982	—	—	—	3.50	8.00	—
1982 Proof	—	Value: 12.50				

KM# 171 5 DINARS

Bronze, 28 mm. **Obv:** Denomination and legend **Rev:** Two swords arched above palm tree

Date	Mintage	F	VF	XF	Unc	BU
1990	—	—	—	—	5.00	—

Note: Not released to circulation

KM# 172 10 DINARS

Bronze **Obv:** Denomination and legend **Rev:** Two swords arched above palm tree

Date	Mintage	F	VF	XF	Unc	BU
1990	—	—	—	—	10.00	—

Note: Not released to circulation

IRELAND REPUBLIC

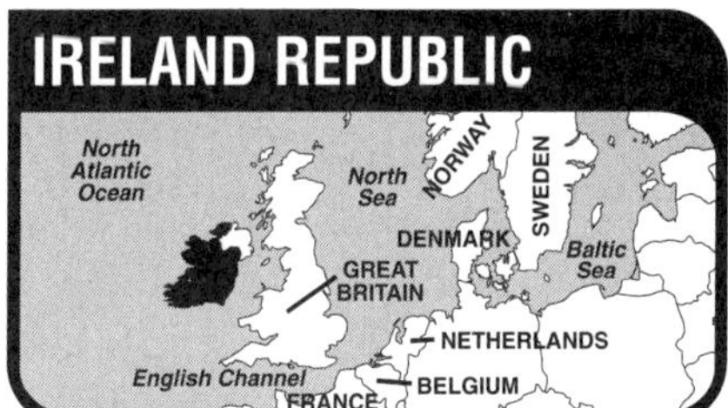

The Republic of Ireland, which occupies five-sixths of the island of Ireland located in the Atlantic Ocean west of Great Britain, has an area of 27,136 sq. mi. (70,280 sq. km.) and a population of 4.3 million. Capital: Dublin. Agriculture and dairy farming are the principal industries. Meat, livestock, dairy products and textiles are exported.

A race of tall, red-haired Celts from Gaul arrived in Ireland about 400 B.C., assimilated the native Erainn and Picts, and established a Gaelic civilization. After the arrival of St. Patrick in 432AD, Ireland evolved into a center of Latin learning, which sent missionaries to Europe and possibly North America. In 1154, Pope Adrian IV gave all of Ireland to English King Henry II to administer as a Papal fief. Because of the enactment of anti-Catholic laws and the awarding of vast tracts of Irish land to Protestant absentee landowners, English control did not become reasonably absolute until 1800 when England and Ireland became the 'United Kingdom of Great Britain and Ireland'. Religious freedom was restored to the Irish in 1829, but agitation for political autonomy continued until the Irish Free State was established as a dominion on Dec. 6, 1921 until 1937 when it became Éire. Ireland proclaimed itself a republic on April 18, 1949. The government, however, does not use the term 'Republic of Ireland,' which tacitly acknowledges the partitioning of the island into Ireland and Northern Ireland, but refers to the country simply as 'Ireland.'

RULER

British, until 1921

MONETARY SYSTEM

(1928-1971)

4 Farthings = 1 Penny
12 Pence = 1 Shilling
2 Shillings = 1 Florin
20 Shillings = 1 Pound

NOTE: This section has been renumbered to segregate the coinage of the Irish Free State from the earlier crown coinage of Ireland.

REPUBLIC

STERLING COINAGE

KM# 1 FARTHING

2.8300 g., Bronze, 20.3 mm. **Obv:** Irish harp divides date **Obv. Legend:** SAORSTAT EIREANN (Irish Free State) **Rev:** Woodcock below value **Edge:** Plain **Designer:** Percy Metcalfe

Date	Mintage	F	VF	XF	Unc	BU
1928	300,000	0.50	1.50	4.50	10.00	—
1928 Proof	6,001	Value: 15.00				
1930	288,000	0.75	1.50	4.50	16.50	—
1930 Proof; Rare	—	—	—	—	—	—
1931	192,000	4.50	8.00	15.00	35.00	—

Date	Mintage	F	VF	XF	Unc	BU
1931 Proof	—	—	—	—	—	—
1932	192,000	5.00	10.00	18.00	45.00	—
1932 Proof; Rare	—	—	—	—	—	—
1933	480,000	0.75	1.50	4.00	16.50	—
1933 Proof; Rare	—	—	—	—	—	—
1935	192,000	5.00	8.00	15.00	35.00	—
1935 Proof; Rare	—	—	—	—	—	—
1936	192,000	5.00	8.00	16.50	37.50	—
1936 Proof; Rare	—	—	—	—	—	—
1937	480,000	0.50	1.50	3.00	14.50	—
1937 Proof; Rare	—	—	—	—	—	—

KM# 9 FARTHING

2.8300 g., Bronze, 20.3 mm. **Obv:** Irish harp divides date **Obv. Legend:** EIRE (Ireland) **Rev:** Woodcock below value **Edge:** Plain **Designer:** Percy Metcalfe

Date	Mintage	F	VF	XF	Unc	BU
1939	786,000	0.50	1.00	2.00	7.50	—
1939 Proof	—	Value: 815				
1940	192,000	2.00	4.00	8.00	20.00	—
1940 Proof; Rare	—	—	—	—	—	—
1941	480,000	0.50	0.75	2.00	6.50	—
1941 Proof; Rare	—	—	—	—	—	—
1943	480,000	0.50	0.75	2.00	6.50	15.00
1944	480,000	0.75	1.25	3.00	10.00	—
1946	480,000	0.50	0.75	2.00	6.00	12.50
1946 Proof	—	—	—	—	—	—
1949	192,000	0.75	3.00	6.00	18.00	—
1949 Proof	—	Value: 300				
1953	192,000	0.25	0.50	1.25	3.00	7.50
1953 Proof	—	Value: 300				
1959	192,000	0.25	0.50	1.25	3.00	—
1959 Proof; Rare	—	—	—	—	—	—
1966	96,000	0.35	0.75	1.50	3.50	8.00

KM# 2 1/2 PENNY

5.6700 g., Bronze, 25.5 mm. **Obv:** Irish harp divides date **Obv. Legend:** SAORSTAT EIREANN (Irish Free State) **Rev:** Sow with piglets below value **Edge:** Plain **Designer:** Percy Metcalfe

Date	Mintage	F	VF	XF	Unc	BU
1928	2,880,000	0.75	2.00	5.00	14.00	—
1928 Proof	6,001	Value: 15.00				
1933	720,000	5.00	15.00	80.00	450	—
1933 Proof; Rare	—	—	—	—	—	—
1935	960,000	2.00	6.00	50.00	275	—
1935 Proof; Rare	—	—	—	—	—	—
1937	960,000	1.00	3.00	15.00	35.00	—

KM# 10 1/2 PENNY

5.6700 g., Bronze, 25.5 mm. **Obv:** Irish harp **Obv. Legend:** EIRE (Ireland) **Rev:** Sow with piglets below value **Edge:** Plain **Designer:** Percy Metcalfe

Date	Mintage	F	VF	XF	Unc	BU
1939	240,000	10.00	17.50	60.00	200	—
1939 Proof	—	Value: 1,000				
1940	1,680,000	1.00	4.50	40.00	150	—
1940 Proof; Rare	—	—	—	—	—	—
1941	2,400,000	0.20	0.50	2.50	20.00	—
1941 Proof; Rare	—	—	—	—	—	—
1942	6,931,000	0.10	0.25	1.50	8.00	—
1943	2,669,000	0.20	0.50	3.00	22.00	35.00
1946	720,000	1.00	2.50	15.00	60.00	—
1946 Proof; Rare	—	—	—	—	—	—
1949	1,344,000	0.10	0.25	1.50	12.50	—
1949 Proof; Rare	—	—	—	—	—	—
1953	2,400,000	0.10	0.15	0.25	1.50	5.00
1953 Proof	—	Value: 400				
1964	2,160,000	0.10	0.15	0.25	1.50	2.50
1964 Proof; Rare	—	—	—	—	—	—
1965	1,440,000	0.10	0.15	0.75	2.50	3.50
1966	1,680,000	0.10	0.15	0.25	1.50	2.50
1967	1,200,000	0.10	0.15	0.25	1.50	5.00

KM# 3 PENNY

9.4500 g., Bronze, 30.9 mm. **Obv:** Irish harp divides date **Obv. Legend:** SAORSTAT EIREANN (Irish Free State) **Rev:** Hen with chicks **Edge:** Plain **Designer:** Percy Metcalfe

Date	Mintage	F	VF	XF	Unc	BU
1928	9,000,000	0.50	1.00	4.00	20.00	—
1928 Proof	6,001	Value: 18.50				
1931 Proof	—	Value: 1,500				
1931	2,400,000	1.00	2.00	12.00	50.00	—
1933	1,680,000	1.00	2.50	20.00	125	—
1933 Proof; Rare	—	—	—	—	—	—
1935	5,472,000	0.50	1.00	8.00	32.00	—
1935 Proof; Rare	—	—	—	—	—	—
1937	5,400,000	0.50	1.00	15.00	70.00	—
1937 Proof	—	Value: 1,250				

KM# 11 PENNY

9.4500 g., Bronze, 30.9 mm. **Obv:** Irish harp **Obv. Legend:** EIRE (Ireland) **Rev:** Hen with chicks **Edge:** Plain **Designer:** Percy Metcalfe **Note:** Varieties exist.

Date	Mintage	F	VF	XF	Unc	BU
1940	312,000	3.00	10.00	65.00	325	—
1940 Proof; Rare	—	—	—	—	—	—
1941	4,680,000	0.25	0.50	8.00	50.00	—
1941 Proof; Rare	—	—	—	—	—	—
1942	17,520,000	0.25	0.50	2.00	11.50	—
1942 Proof; Rare	—	—	—	—	—	—
1943	3,360,000	0.75	1.50	7.50	45.00	—
1946	4,800,000	0.25	0.50	3.00	20.00	30.00
1946 Proof; Rare	—	—	—	—	—	—
1948	4,800,000	0.25	0.50	3.00	8.00	—
1948 Proof; Rare	—	—	—	—	—	—
1949	4,080,000	0.25	0.50	3.00	8.00	—
1949 Proof	—	Value: 600				
1950 Proof	—	Value: 600				
1950	2,400,000	0.25	0.50	3.50	12.50	—
1952	2,400,000	0.25	0.50	2.00	6.00	—
1952 Proof; Rare	—	—	—	—	—	—
1962	1,200,000	0.75	2.50	3.50	12.50	—
1962 Proof	—	Value: 175				
1963 Proof	—	Value: 175				
1963	9,600,000	0.20	0.40	0.75	2.00	—
1964	6,000,000	0.20	0.40	0.75	1.50	3.00
1964 Proof	—	—	—	—	—	—
1965	11,160,000	0.20	0.40	0.75	1.50	3.00
1966	6,000,000	0.20	0.40	0.75	1.50	3.00
1967	2,400,000	0.20	0.40	0.75	1.50	3.00
1968	21,000,000	0.20	0.40	0.75	1.50	3.00
1968 Proof	—	Value: 350				

KM# 4 3 PENCE

3.2400 g., Nickel, 17.6 mm. **Obv:** Irish harp divides date **Obv. Legend:** SAORSTAT EIREANN (Irish Free State) **Rev:** Hare **Edge:** Plain **Designer:** Percy Metcalfe

Date	Mintage	F	VF	XF	Unc	BU
1928	1,500,000	0.50	1.00	3.50	10.00	—
1928 Proof	6,001	Value: 20.00				
1933	320,000	3.00	10.00	75.00	350	—
1933 Proof; Rare	—	—	—	—	—	—
1934	800,000	1.00	2.00	12.50	70.00	—
1934 Proof; Rare	—	—	—	—	—	—
1935	240,000	3.00	8.00	35.00	225	—
1935 Proof; Rare	—	—	—	—	—	—

KM# 12 3 PENCE

3.2400 g., Nickel, 17.6 mm. **Obv:** Irish harp **Obv. Legend:** EIRE (Ireland) **Rev:** Hare **Edge:** Plain **Designer:** Percy Metcalfe

Date	Mintage	F	VF	XF	Unc	BU
1939	64,000	10.00	20.00	70.00	525	—
1939 Proof	—	Value: 1,500				
1940	720,000	1.50	3.00	12.50	50.00	—
1940 Proof; Rare	—	—	—	—	—	—

KM# 12a 3 PENCE

3.2400 g., Copper-Nickel, 18 mm. **Obv:** Irish harp **Obv. Legend:** EIRE (Ireland) **Rev:** Hare **Edge:** Plain **Designer:** Percy Metcalfe

Date	Mintage	F	VF	XF	Unc	BU
1942 Proof	—	Value: 350				
1942	4,000,000	0.25	0.75	6.00	30.00	—
1943 Proof	—	—	—	—	—	—
1943	1,360,000	0.50	2.00	15.00	80.00	—
1946	800,000	1.00	2.00	10.00	45.00	—
1946 Proof	—	Value: 200				
1948	1,600,000	1.00	2.00	35.00	125	—
1948 Proof; Rare	—	—	—	—	—	—
1949	1,200,000	0.25	0.50	3.00	25.00	—
1949 Proof	—	Value: 200				
1950 Proof	—	Value: 400				
1950	1,600,000	0.25	0.50	3.00	20.00	—
1953	1,600,000	0.25	0.50	2.00	10.00	—
1953 Proof; Rare	—	—	—	—	—	—
1956	1,200,000	0.25	0.50	2.00	8.00	15.00
1956 Proof; Rare	—	—	—	—	—	—
1961	2,400,000	0.15	0.25	0.50	6.00	—
1961 Proof; Rare	—	—	—	—	—	—
1962	3,200,000	0.15	0.25	0.50	8.00	—
1962 Proof; Rare	—	—	—	—	—	—
1963	4,000,000	0.15	0.25	0.50	2.50	—
1963 Proof; Rare	—	—	—	—	—	—
1964	4,000,000	0.10	0.15	0.50	1.50	3.00
1965	3,600,000	0.10	0.15	0.50	1.50	3.00
1966	4,000,000	0.10	0.15	0.50	1.50	3.00
1967	2,400,000	0.10	0.15	0.50	1.50	3.00
1968	4,000,000	0.10	0.15	0.50	1.50	3.00
1968 Proof	—	—	—	—	—	—

KM# 5 6 PENCE

4.5400 g., Nickel, 20.8 mm. **Obv:** Irish harp divides date **Obv. Legend:** SAORSTAT EIREANN (Irish Free State) **Rev:** Irish Wolfhound **Edge:** Plain **Designer:** Percy Metcalfe

Date	Mintage	F	VF	XF	Unc	BU
1928	3,201,000	0.50	1.00	5.00	17.50	—
1928 Proof	6,001	Value: 25.00				
1933 Proof; Rare	—	—	—	—	—	—
1934	600,000	1.00	2.00	18.00	120	—
1934 Proof; Rare	—	—	—	—	—	—
1935	520,000	1.00	3.00	30.00	320	—
1935 Proof; Rare	—	—	—	—	—	—

KM# 13 6 PENCE

4.5400 g., Nickel, 20.8 mm. **Obv:** Irish harp **Obv. Legend:** EIRE (Ireland) **Rev:** Irish Wolfhound **Edge:** Plain **Designer:** Percy Metcalfe

Date	Mintage	F	VF	XF	Unc	BU
1939 Proof	—	Value: 1,150				
1939	876,000	0.75	2.00	8.00	55.00	—
1940	1,120,000	0.75	2.00	6.00	45.00	—
1940 Proof; Rare	—	—	—	—	—	—

KM# 13a 6 PENCE
4.5400 g., Copper-Nickel, 20.8 mm. **Obv:** Irish harp **Obv. Legend:** EIRE (Ireland) **Rev:** Irish Wolfhound **Edge:** Plain **Designer:** Percy Metcalfe

Date	Mintage	F	VF	XF	Unc	BU
1942	1,320,000	0.50	1.00	5.00	40.00	—
1942 Proof; Rare	—	—	—	—	—	—
1945	400,000	2.00	8.00	50.00	160	—
1945 Proof; Rare	—	—	—	—	—	—
1946	720,000	2.00	10.00	75.00	350	—
1946 Proof; Rare	—	—	—	—	—	—
1947	800,000	1.00	12.00	30.00	70.00	—
1947 Proof; Rare	—	—	—	—	—	—
1948	800,000	1.00	1.50	10.00	55.00	—
1948 Proof; Rare	—	—	—	—	—	—
1949	600,000	1.50	3.50	15.00	65.00	—
1949 Proof; Rare	—	—	—	—	—	—
1950	800,000	1.00	3.00	12.00	60.00	—
1950 Proof; Rare	—	—	—	—	—	—
1952	800,000	0.50	1.00	5.00	20.00	—
1952 Proof	—	Value: 175				
1953	800,000	0.50	1.00	5.00	18.00	—
1953 Proof; Rare	—	—	—	—	—	—
1955	600,000	1.00	2.50	8.00	20.00	—
1955 Proof; Rare	—	—	—	—	—	—
1956	600,000	0.75	2.00	4.00	15.00	—
1956 Proof; Rare	—	—	—	—	—	—
1958	600,000	1.00	2.50	6.00	65.00	—
1958	—	Value: 350				
1959	2,000,000	0.25	0.50	3.00	15.00	—
1959 Proof; Rare	—	—	—	—	—	—
1960	2,020,000	0.25	0.50	2.00	12.00	—
1960 Proof; Rare	—	—	—	—	—	—
1961	3,000,000	0.25	0.25	1.00	6.50	—
1961 Proof; Rare	—	—	—	—	—	—
1962	4,000,000	0.25	0.75	4.00	60.00	—
1962 Proof; Rare	—	—	—	—	—	—
1963	4,000,000	0.15	0.25	0.50	3.00	—
1963 Proof; Rare	—	—	—	—	—	—
1964	6,000,000	0.15	0.25	0.50	3.00	—
1966	2,000,000	0.15	0.25	0.50	3.00	—
1967	4,000,000	0.15	0.25	0.50	3.00	—
1968	8,000,000	0.15	0.25	0.50	3.00	—
1969	2,000,000	0.15	0.25	0.50	3.00	—

KM# 6 SHILLING
5.6552 g., 0.7500 Silver 0.1364 oz. ASW, 23.6 mm. **Obv:** Irish harp divides date **Obv. Legend:** SAORSTAT EIREANN (Irish Free State) **Rev:** Bull **Edge:** Reeded **Designer:** Percy Metcalfe

Date	Mintage	F	VF	XF	Unc	BU
1928	2,700,000	2.00	5.00	10.00	30.00	—
1928 Proof	6,001	Value: 27.50				
1930	460,000	6.00	25.00	100	450	—
1930 Proof	—	Value: 1,200				
1931	400,000	4.50	18.00	90.00	275	—
1931 Proof; Rare	—	—	—	—	—	—
1933	300,000	5.00	20.00	100	325	—
1933 Proof; Rare	—	—	—	—	—	—
1935	400,000	3.00	7.00	25.00	85.00	—
1935 Proof; Rare	—	—	—	—	—	—
1937	100,000	12.00	65.00	500	2,000	—
1937 Proof; Rare	—	—	—	—	—	—

KM# 14 SHILLING
5.6552 g., 0.7500 Silver 0.1364 oz. ASW, 23.6 mm. **Obv:** Irish harp **Obv. Legend:** EIRE (Ireland) **Rev:** Bull **Edge:** Reeded **Designer:** Percy Metcalfe

Date	Mintage	F	VF	XF	Unc	BU
1939 Proof	—	Value: 775				
1939	1,140,000	2.50	4.50	12.50	40.00	—
1940	580,000	3.00	5.00	15.00	45.00	—
1940 Proof; Rare	—	—	—	—	—	—
1941	300,000	4.00	12.00	22.50	50.00	—
1941 Proof; Rare	—	—	—	—	—	—

Date	Mintage	F	VF	XF	Unc	BU
1942	286,000	4.00	7.50	15.00	40.00	60.00
1942 Proof; Rare	—	—	—	—	—	—

KM# 14a SHILLING
5.6600 g., Copper-Nickel, 23.6 mm. **Obv:** Irish harp **Obv. Legend:** EIRE (Ireland) **Rev:** Bull **Edge:** Reeded **Designer:** Percy Metcalfe

Date	Mintage	F	VF	XF	Unc	BU
1951	2,000,000	0.25	0.50	2.50	15.00	—
1951 Proof	—	Value: 500				
1954	3,000,000	0.25	0.50	2.50	11.50	—
1954 Proof	—	—	—	—	—	—
1955	1,000,000	1.00	2.00	5.00	15.00	—
1955 Proof	—	—	—	—	—	—
1959	2,000,000	0.25	0.50	4.00	35.00	—
1959 Proof; Rare	—	—	—	—	—	—
1962	4,000,000	0.25	0.50	1.00	7.00	—
1962 Proof; Rare	—	—	—	—	—	—
1963	4,000,000	0.25	0.50	1.00	3.00	7.50
1963 Proof; Rare	—	—	—	—	—	—
1964	4,000,000	0.25	0.50	1.00	2.50	3.00
1966	3,000,000	0.25	0.50	1.00	2.50	5.00
1968	4,000,000	0.25	0.50	1.00	2.50	3.00

KM# 7 FLORIN
11.3104 g., 0.7500 Silver 0.2727 oz. ASW, 28.5 mm. **Obv:** Irish harp divides date **Obv. Legend:** SAORSTAT EIREANN (Irish Free State) **Rev:** Salmon **Edge:** Reeded **Designer:** Percy Metcalfe

Date	Mintage	F	VF	XF	Unc	BU
1928	2,025,000	4.00	7.00	15.00	40.00	—
1928 Proof	6,001	Value: 42.50				
1930	330,000	6.50	25.00	135	400	—
1930 Proof; Rare	—	—	—	—	—	—
1931	200,000	8.00	35.00	175	500	—
1931 Proof; Rare	—	—	—	—	—	—
1933	300,000	6.50	27.50	195	575	—
1933 Proof; Rare	—	—	—	—	—	—
1934	150,000	10.00	60.00	250	750	—
1934 Proof	—	Value: 2,750				
1935	390,000	5.00	17.50	65.00	185	—
1935 Proof; Rare	—	—	—	—	—	—
1937	150,000	10.00	35.00	210	750	—
1937 Proof; Rare	—	—	—	—	—	—

KM# 15 FLORIN
11.3104 g., 0.7500 Silver 0.2727 oz. ASW, 28.5 mm. **Obv:** Irish harp **Obv. Legend:** EIRE (Ireland) **Rev:** Salmon **Edge:** Reeded **Designer:** Percy Metcalfe

Date	Mintage	F	VF	XF	Unc	BU
1939 Proof	—	Value: 800				
1939	1,080,000	4.00	7.00	18.00	45.00	—
1940	670,000	4.00	7.50	20.00	50.00	—
1940 Proof; Rare	—	—	—	—	—	—
1941 Proof	—	Value: 800				
1941	400,000	4.00	8.50	22.50	60.00	—
1942	109,000	5.00	15.00	25.00	55.00	—
1943	—	1,200	2,000	4,000	8,000	—

Note: Approximately 35 known

KM# 15a FLORIN
11.3100 g., Copper-Nickel, 28.5 mm. **Obv:** Irish harp **Obv. Legend:** EIRE (Ireland) **Rev:** Salmon **Edge:** Reeded **Designer:** Percy Metcalfe

Date	Mintage	F	VF	XF	Unc	BU
1951	1,000,000	1.00	2.00	6.00	16.00	—
1951 Proof	—	Value: 600				
1954	1,000,000	1.00	2.00	6.00	18.00	—
1954 Proof	—	Value: 450				
1955	1,000,000	1.00	2.00	5.00	15.00	—
1955 Proof	—	Value: 450				
1959	2,000,000	0.50	1.00	2.50	10.00	—
1959 Proof; Rare	—	—	—	—	—	—
1961	2,000,000	0.50	1.00	7.00	22.00	—
1961 Proof; Rare	—	—	—	—	—	—
1962	2,400,000	0.50	1.00	2.00	10.00	—
1962 Proof; Rare	—	—	—	—	—	—
1963	3,000,000	0.25	0.50	0.75	4.00	15.00
1963 Proof; Rare	—	—	—	—	—	—
1964	4,000,000	0.25	0.50	0.75	2.00	8.00
1965	2,000,000	0.25	0.50	0.75	2.00	—
1966	3,625,000	0.25	0.50	0.75	2.00	4.00
1968	1,000,000	0.25	0.35	1.00	4.50	5.00
1969	—	0.25	0.35	1.00	4.50	5.00

KM# 8 1/2 CROWN
14.1380 g., 0.7500 Silver 0.3409 oz. ASW, 32.3 mm. **Obv:** Irish harp divides date **Obv. Legend:** SAORSTAT EIREANN (Irish Free State) **Rev:** Horse **Rev. Designer:** Percy Metcalfe **Edge:** Reeded **Note:** Close O and I in COROIN. 8 tufts in horse's tail, with 156 beads.

Date	Mintage	F	VF	XF	Unc	BU
1928	2,160,000	5.00	10.00	20.00	50.00	—
1928 Proof	6,001	Value: 55.00				
1930	352,000	7.00	20.00	125	400	—
1930 Proof; Rare	—	—	—	—	—	—
1931	160,000	10.00	30.00	250	650	—
1931 Proof; Rare	—	—	—	—	—	—
1933	336,000	7.00	20.00	125	400	—
1933 Proof; Rare	—	—	—	—	—	—
1934	480,000	6.00	15.00	40.00	175	—
1934 Proof; Rare	—	—	—	—	—	—
1937	40,000	65.00	150	750	1,750	—
1937 Proof; Rare	—	—	—	—	—	—

KM# 16 1/2 CROWN
14.1380 g., 0.7500 Silver 0.3409 oz. ASW, 32.3 mm. **Obv:** Irish harp **Obv. Legend:** EIRE (Ireland) **Rev:** Horse **Edge:** Reeded **Designer:** Percy Metcalfe **Note:** Normal spacing between O and I in COROIN, 7 tufts in horse's tail, with 151 beads in border.

Date	Mintage	F	VF	XF	Unc	BU
1939	888,000	5.00	9.50	17.50	55.00	—
1939 Proof	—	Value: 800				
1940	752,000	5.00	9.00	15.00	50.00	—
1940 Proof; Rare	—	—	—	—	—	—
1941	320,000	5.50	12.50	30.00	75.00	—
1941 Proof; Rare	—	—	—	—	—	—
1942	286,000	5.50	12.50	25.00	50.00	—
1943	Est. 1,000	250	500	1,350	2,500	—

Note: Approximately 500 known

KM# 16a 1/2 CROWN

14.1400 g., Copper-Nickel, 32.3 mm. **Obv:** Irish harp **Obv. Legend:** EIRE (Ireland) **Rev:** Horse **Edge:** Reeded **Designer:** Percy Metcalfe **Note:** Normal spacing between O and I on "COROIN", 7 tufts in horse's tail, with 151 beads in border.

Date	Mintage	F	VF	XF	Unc	BU
1951	800,000	1.50	3.00	10.00	35.00	—
1951 Proof	—	Value: 600				
1954	400,000	2.00	4.00	15.00	50.00	—
1954 Proof	—	Value: 500				
1955	1,080,000	1.00	2.00	6.00	25.00	—
1955 Proof	—	Value: 200				
1959	1,600,000	1.00	1.75	3.00	12.50	—
1959 Proof; Rare	—	—	—	—	—	—
1961	1,600,000	1.00	1.75	3.50	20.00	—
1961 Proof	—	—	—	—	—	—
1962	3,200,000	0.50	1.00	2.50	12.50	—
1962 Proof	—	—	—	—	—	—
1963	2,400,000	0.50	1.00	2.00	8.00	12.00
1963 Proof; Rare	—	—	—	—	—	—
1964	3,200,000	0.50	1.00	2.00	8.00	12.00
1966	700,000	0.75	1.50	3.00	8.00	12.00
1967	2,000,000	0.50	1.00	2.00	8.00	12.00

Note: 1967 exists struck with a polished reverse die; Estimated value is $15.00 in Uncirculated

KM# 17 1/2 CROWN

Copper-Nickel **Obv:** Irish harp **Rev:** Horse **Note:** Mule. Distinguishing characteristics: 2s6d the d is open, PM the P is not under the hoof.

Date	Mintage	VG	F	VF	XF	Unc
1961	Inc. above	—	8.00	25.00	200	—

KM# 18 10 SHILLING

18.1400 g., 0.8333 Silver 0.4860 oz. ASW, 30.5 mm. **Subject:** 50th Anniversary - Irish Uprising of Easter, 1916 **Obv:** Bust right **Rev:** Monument **Rev. Designer:** Cuchulainn modified by T.H. Paget **Edge Lettering:** EIRI AMAC NA CASCA 1916

Date	Mintage	F	VF	XF	Unc	BU
1966	Est. 2,000,000	—	—	15.00	30.00	35.00

Note: Approximately 1,270,000 melted down

Date	Mintage	F	VF	XF	Unc	BU
1966 Proof	20,000	Value: 45.00				

DECIMAL COINAGE

100 Pence = 1 Pound (Punt)

KM# 19 1/2 PENNY

1.7800 g., Bronze, 17.1 mm. **Subject:** Stylized bird adapted from an illumination in a celtic manuscript from Cologne Cathedral **Obv:** Irish harp **Rev:** Stylized bird and value **Rev. Designer:** G. Hayes **Edge:** Plain **Note:** This mintage figure represents a surplus of coins minted for Polished Standard Specimen Sets (proof sets) later released into circulation. The entire surplus was presumably remelted due to demonitization of this denomination Jan. 1, 1987

Date	Mintage	F	VF	XF	Unc	BU
1971	100,500,000	—	—	0.10	0.30	0.50
1971 Proof	50,000	Value: 1.00				
1975	10,500,000	—	—	0.10	0.30	0.50
1976	5,464,000	—	—	0.10	0.30	0.50
1978	20,302,000	—	—	—	0.25	0.50
1980	20,616,000	—	—	—	0.25	0.50
1982	9,660,000	—	—	—	0.30	0.50
1985	2,784,000	—	—	—	—	—
1986 Proof	6,750	Value: 12.50				
1986	Est. 12,250	—	—	—	—	—

Note: This mintage figure represents a surplus of coins minted for Polished Standard Specimen Sets (Proof Sets) later released into circulation. The entire surplus was presumably remelted due to demonitization of this denomination Jan. 1, 1987.

KM# 20 PENNY

3.5600 g., Bronze, 20.3 mm. **Obv:** Irish harp **Rev:** Stylized bird **Rev. Designer:** G. Hayes **Edge:** Plain **Note:** Stylized bird adapted form an ornamental detail in the book of Kells

Date	Mintage	F	VF	XF	Unc	BU
1971	100,500,000	—	—	0.10	0.30	0.75
1971 Proof	50,000	Value: 1.25				
1974	10,000,000	—	—	0.10	0.35	0.75
1975	10,000,000	—	—	0.10	0.35	0.75
1976	38,164,000	—	—	0.10	0.30	0.75
1978	25,746,000	—	—	0.10	0.30	0.75
1979	21,766,000	—	—	0.10	0.30	0.75
1980	86,712,000	—	—	0.10	0.30	0.75
1982	54,189,000	—	—	0.10	0.30	0.75
1985	19,242,000	—	—	0.10	0.30	0.75
1986	36,584,000	—	—	0.10	0.30	0.75
1986 Proof	6,750	Value: 1.25				
1988	56,772,000	—	—	0.10	0.30	0.75

KM# 20a PENNY

3.5600 g., Copper Plated Steel, 20.3 mm. **Subject:** Stylized bird adapted from an ornamental detail in the book of Kells **Obv:** Irish harp **Rev:** Stylized bird **Edge:** Plain

Date	Mintage	F	VF	XF	Unc	BU
1988	Inc. above	—	—	—	—	—
1990	65,099,000	—	—	0.10	0.15	0.50
1992	25,643,000	—	—	0.10	0.15	0.50
1993	10,000,000	—	—	0.10	0.15	0.50
1994	45,800,000	—	—	0.10	0.15	0.50
1995	70,836,000	—	—	0.10	0.15	0.50
1996	190,092,000	—	—	0.10	0.15	0.50
1998	40,744,000	—	—	0.10	0.15	0.50
2000	133,760,000	—	—	0.10	0.15	0.50

KM# 21 2 PENCE

7.1200 g., Bronze, 25.9 mm. **Subject:** Stylized bird detail from the Second Bible of Charles the Bald **Obv:** Irish harp **Rev:** Stylized bird **Rev. Designer:** G. Hayes **Edge:** Plain

Date	Mintage	F	VF	XF	Unc	BU
1971	75,500,000	—	—	0.10	1.00	1.20
1971 Proof	50,000	Value: 1.50				
1975	20,010,000	—	—	0.10	0.50	0.75
1976	5,414,000	—	—	0.10	0.60	0.85
1978	12,000,000	—	—	0.10	0.50	0.75
1979	32,373,000	—	—	0.10	0.50	0.75
1980	59,828,000	—	—	0.10	0.50	0.75
1982	30,435,000	—	—	0.10	0.50	0.75
1985	14,469,000	—	—	0.10	0.50	0.75
1986	23,865,000	—	—	0.10	0.50	0.75
1986 Proof	6,750	Value: 1.50				
1988	35,868,000	—	—	0.10	0.50	0.75

KM# 21a 2 PENCE

7.1200 g., Copper Plated Steel, 25.9 mm. **Subject:** Stylized bird detail from the Second Bible of Charles the Bald **Obv:** Irish harp **Rev:** Stylized bird **Edge:** Plain

Date	Mintage	F	VF	XF	Unc	BU
1988	Inc. above	—	—	—	—	—
1990	34,284,000	—	—	0.10	0.25	0.50
1992	10,215,000	—	—	0.10	0.25	0.50
1995	55,459,000	—	—	0.10	0.25	0.50
1996	69,342,000	—	—	0.10	0.25	0.50
1998	33,688,000	—	—	0.10	0.25	0.50
2000	66,960,000	—	—	0.10	0.25	0.50

KM# 22 5 PENCE

5.6600 g., Copper-Nickel, 23.6 mm. **Obv:** Irish harp **Rev:** Bull right **Edge:** Reeded **Designer:** Percy Metcalfe

Date	Mintage	F	VF	XF	Unc	BU
1969	5,000,000	—	0.10	0.15	1.00	1.25
1970	10,000,000	—	—	0.10	0.75	1.20
1971 Proof	50,000	Value: 2.00				
1971	8,000,000	—	—	0.10	0.75	1.25
1974	7,000,000	—	—	0.10	0.75	1.25
1975	10,000,000	—	—	0.10	0.75	1.25
1976	20,616,000	—	—	0.10	0.75	1.25
1978	28,536,000	—	—	0.10	0.75	1.25
1980	22,190,000	—	—	0.10	0.75	1.25
1982	24,404,000	—	—	0.10	0.75	1.20
1985	4,202,000	—	—	0.10	0.75	1.20
1986 Proof	6,750	Value: 2.00				
1986	15,298,000	—	0.10	0.15	1.00	1.25
1990	7,547,000	—	—	0.10	0.75	1.20

KM# 28 5 PENCE

3.2500 g., Copper-Nickel, 18.5 mm. **Obv:** Irish harp **Rev:** Bull left **Edge:** Reeded **Designer:** Percy Metcalfe **Note:** Reduced size: 18.5mm. Varieties exist.

Date	Mintage	F	VF	XF	Unc	BU
1992	74,526,000	—	—	0.10	0.50	0.75
1993	89,109,000	—	—	0.10	0.50	0.75
1994	31,058,000	—	—	0.10	0.50	0.75
1995	14,667,000	—	—	0.10	0.50	0.75
1996	158,546,000	—	—	0.10	0.50	0.75
1998	63,247,000	—	—	0.10	0.50	0.75
2000	58,000,000	—	—	0.10	0.50	0.75

KM# 23 10 PENCE

11.3200 g., Copper-Nickel, 28.5 mm. **Obv:** Irish harp **Rev:** Salmon **Edge:** Reeded **Designer:** Percy Metcalfe

Date	Mintage	F	VF	XF	Unc	BU
1969	27,000,000	—	—	0.40	1.25	2.00
1971	4,000,000	—	—	0.40	1.25	2.00
1971 Proof	50,000	Value: 2.50				
1973	2,500,000	—	—	0.40	1.50	2.25
1974	7,500,000	—	—	0.35	1.25	2.00
1975	15,000,000	—	—	0.35	1.25	2.00
1976	9,433,000	—	—	0.35	1.25	2.00
1978	30,905,000	—	—	0.25	1.00	1.75
1980	44,605,000	—	—	0.25	1.00	1.75
1982	7,374,000	—	—	0.25	1.00	1.75
1985	4,099,999	—	—	0.25	1.25	2.00
1986 Proof	6,750	Value: 16.50				
1986	Est. 4,250	—	2.00	5.00	16.50	—

Note: This mintage figure represents a surplus of coins minted for Polished Standard Specimen Sets (Proof Sets), later released into circulation.

KM# 29 10 PENCE

5.4500 g., Copper-Nickel, 22 mm. **Obv:** Irish harp **Rev:** Salmon **Edge:** Reeded **Designer:** Percy Metcalfe **Note:** Reduced size.

Date	Mintage	F	VF	XF	Unc	BU
1993	80,061,000	—	—	—	0.75	1.25
1994	58,510,000	—	—	—	0.75	1.25
1995	15,781,000	—	—	—	0.75	1.25
1996	18,402,000	—	—	—	0.75	1.25
1997	10,033,000	—	—	—	0.75	1.25
1998	10,000,000	—	—	—	0.75	1.25

Date	Mintage	F	VF	XF	Unc	BU
1999	24,500,000	—	—	—	0.75	1.25
2000	45,679,000	—	—	—	0.75	1.25

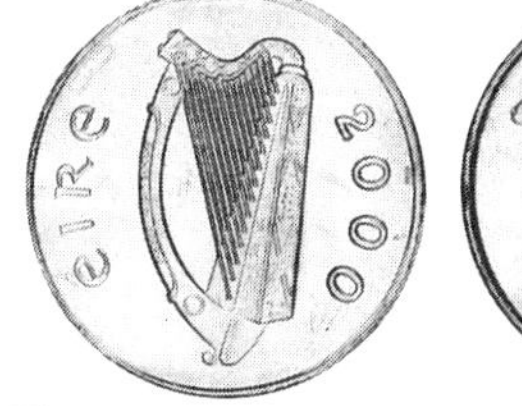

KM# 25 20 PENCE

8.4700 g., Nickel-Bronze, 27.1 mm. **Obv:** Irish harp **Rev:** Horse **Edge:** Alternating plain and reeded **Designer:** Percy Metcalfe

Date	Mintage	F	VF	XF	Unc	BU
1986 Proof	6,750	Value: 3.50				
1986	50,430,000	—	—	0.50	2.00	4.00
1988	20,661,000	—	—	0.50	2.00	4.00
1992	14,761,000	—	—	0.50	2.00	4.00
1994	11,086,000	—	—	0.50	2.00	4.00
1995	18,160,000	—	—	0.50	2.00	4.00
1996	29,291,000	—	—	0.50	2.00	4.00
1998	25,024,000	—	—	0.50	2.00	4.00
1999	11,000,000	—	—	0.50	2.00	4.00
2000	28,500,000	—	—	0.50	2.00	4.00

KM# 24 50 PENCE

13.3000 g., Copper-Nickel, 30 mm. **Obv:** Harp **Rev:** Woodcock **Edge:** Plain **Shape:** 7 curved sides **Designer:** Percy Metcalfe

Date	Mintage	F	VF	XF	Unc	BU
1970	9,000,000	—	—	1.50	4.00	5.00
1971	600,000	—	1.00	2.00	6.00	8.00
1971 Proof	50,000	Value: 3.50				
1974	1,000,000	—	1.00	2.00	7.00	9.00
1975	2,000,000	—	—	1.50	4.00	5.00
1976	3,000,000	—	—	1.25	3.00	4.00
1977	4,800,000	—	—	1.25	3.00	4.00
1978	4,500,000	—	—	1.25	3.00	4.00
1979	4,000,000	—	—	1.25	3.00	4.00
1981	6,000,000	—	—	1.00	2.00	3.50
1982	2,000,000	—	—	1.25	3.00	4.00
1983	7,000,000	—	—	1.00	2.00	3.50
1984	—	—	—	—	—	—
1986	3,250	—	3.00	6.00	18.50	—

Note: This circulation mintage figure represents a surplus of coins minted for Polished Standard Specimen Sets (Proof Sets), later released into circulation

Date	Mintage	F	VF	XF	Unc	BU
1986 Proof	6,750	Value: 18.50				
1988	Est. 7,000,500	—	—	1.00	2.00	3.50
1996	6,000,000	—	—	1.00	2.00	3.50
1997	6,000,000	—	—	1.00	2.00	3.50
1998	13,825,000	—	—	1.00	2.00	3.50
1999	7,000,000	—	—	1.00	2.00	3.50
2000	15,600,000	—	—	1.00	2.00	3.50

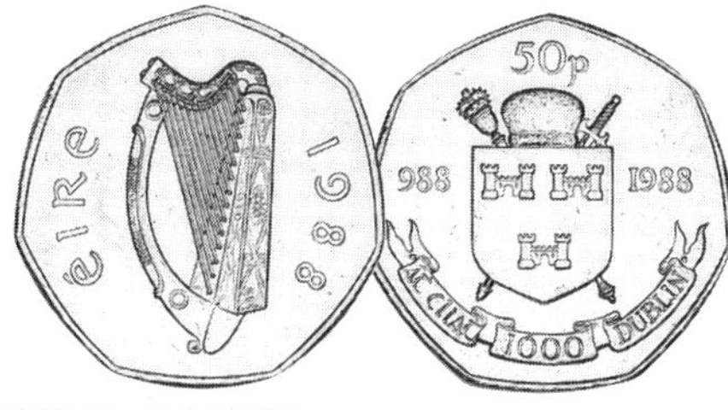

KM# 26 50 PENCE

13.5000 g., Copper-Nickel, 30 mm. **Subject:** Dublin Millennium **Obv:** Irish harp **Rev:** Sheild above banner with value above **Rev. Designer:** Thomas Ryan

Date	Mintage	F	VF	XF	Unc	BU
1988 Proof	50,000	Value: 15.00				
1988	5,000,000	—	—	—	2.50	3.50

KM# 27 PUNT (Pound)

10.0000 g., Copper-Nickel, 31.1 mm. **Obv:** Irish harp **Rev:** Irish Red Deer left **Rev. Designer:** Thomas Ryan **Note:** The normal KM27 was struck with an milled and engrailed edge. Examples with plain edge, or partial engrailing command a premium of approximately four times the values listed here.

Date	Mintage	F	VF	XF	Unc	BU
1990	62,292,000	2.00	3.00	5.50	7.00	8.00
1990 Proof	42,000	Value: 27.50				
1994	14,925,000	2.00	3.00	5.50	7.50	8.50
1995	10,215,000	2.00	3.00	5.50	7.50	8.50
1996	9,230,000	2.00	3.00	5.50	7.50	8.50
1998	22,955,000	2.00	3.00	5.50	7.50	8.50
1999	10,000,000	2.00	3.00	5.50	7.50	8.50
2000	31,913,000	2.00	3.00	5.50	7.50	8.50

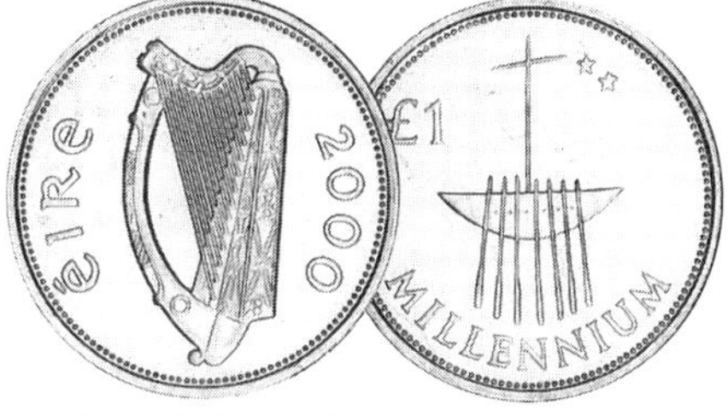

KM# 31 PUNT (Pound)

10.0000 g., Copper-Nickel **Subject:** Millennium **Obv:** Irish harp **Rev:** Cross within stylized ancient ship **Edge:** Milled and engrailed **Designer:** Alan Ardiff and Garret Stokes **Note:** Struck at Sandyford.

Date	Mintage	F	VF	XF	Unc	BU
2000	5,000,000	—	—	—	7.50	8.50

EURO COINAGE

European Union Issues

KM# 32 EURO CENT

2.2700 g., Copper Plated Steel, 16.25 mm. **Obv:** Harp **Obv. Designer:** Jarlath Hayes **Rev:** Denomination and globe **Rev. Designer:** Luc Luycx **Edge:** Plain

Date	Mintage	VG	F	VF	XF	Unc
2002	404,339,788	—	—	—	—	0.35
2003	67,902,182	—	—	—	—	0.35
2004	174,833,634	—	—	—	—	0.35
2005	127,019	—	—	—	—	0.35
2006	—	—	—	—	—	0.35
2007	—	—	—	—	—	0.35

KM# 33 2 EURO CENT

3.0000 g., Copper Plated Steel, 18.75 mm. **Obv:** Harp **Obv. Designer:** Jarlath Hayes **Rev:** Denomination and globe **Rev. Designer:** Luc Luycx **Edge:** Plain with groove

Date	Mintage	VG	F	VF	XF	Unc
2002	354,643,386	—	—	—	—	0.50
2003	177,290,034	—	—	—	—	0.50
2004	143,004,694	—	—	—	—	0.50
2005	72,600	—	—	—	—	0.50
2006	—	—	—	—	—	0.50
2007	—	—	—	—	—	0.50

KM# 34 5 EURO CENT

4.0000 g., Copper-Plated-Steel, 19.60 mm. **Obv:** Harp **Obv. Designer:** Jarlath Hayes **Rev:** Denomination and globe **Rev. Designer:** Luc Luycx **Edge:** Plain

Date	Mintage	VG	F	VF	XF	Unc
2002	456,270,848	—	—	—	—	0.75
2003	48,352,370	—	—	—	—	0.75
2004	80,354,322	—	—	—	—	0.75
2005	42,224	—	—	—	—	0.75
2006	—	—	—	—	—	0.75
2007	—	—	—	—	—	0.75

KM# 35 10 EURO CENT

4.0700 g., Aluminum-Bronze, 19.75 mm. **Obv:** Harp **Obv. Designer:** Jarlath Hayes **Rev:** Denomination and map **Rev. Designer:** Luc Luycx **Edge:** Reeded

Date	Mintage	VG	F	VF	XF	Unc
2002	275,913,000	—	—	—	—	1.00
2003	133,815,907	—	—	—	—	1.00
2004	16,922,898	—	—	—	—	1.00
2005	4,707	—	—	—	—	1.00
2006	—	—	—	—	—	1.00

KM# 47 10 EURO CENT

4.0700 g., Aluminum-Bronze, 19.75 mm. **Obv:** Harp **Obv. Designer:** Jarlath Hayes **Rev:** Relief map of Western Europe, stars, lines and value **Rev. Designer:** Luc Luycz **Edge:** Reeded

Date	Mintage	VG	F	VF	XF	Unc
2007	—	—	—	—	—	1.00

KM# 36 20 EURO CENT

5.7300 g., Aluminum-Bronze, 22.25 mm. **Obv:** Harp **Obv. Designer:** Jarlath Hayes **Rev:** Denomination and map **Rev. Designer:** Luc Luycx **Edge:** Notched

Date	Mintage	VG	F	VF	XF	Unc
2002	234,575,562	—	—	—	—	1.25
2003	57,142,221	—	—	—	—	1.25
2004	32,421,447	—	—	—	—	1.25
2005	30,675	—	—	—	—	1.25
2006	—	—	—	—	—	1.25

KM# 48 20 EURO CENT

5.7300 g., Aluminum-Bronze, 22.25 mm. **Obv:** Harp **Obv. Designer:** Jarlath Hayes **Rev:** Relief map of Western Europe, stars, lines and value **Rev. Designer:** Luc Luycz **Edge:** Notched

Date	Mintage	F	VF	XF	Unc	BU
2007	—	—	—	—	1.25	—

KM# 37 50 EURO CENT

7.8100 g., Aluminum-Bronze, 24.25 mm. **Obv:** Harp **Obv. Designer:** Jarlath Hayes **Rev. Designer:** Denomination and map **Edge:** Reeded

Date	Mintage	VG	F	VF	XF	Unc
2002	144,144,592	—	—	—	—	1.50
2003	11,811,926	—	—	—	—	1.50
2004	6,748,912	—	—	—	—	1.50
2005	7,529	—	—	—	—	1.50
2006	—	—	—	—	—	1.50

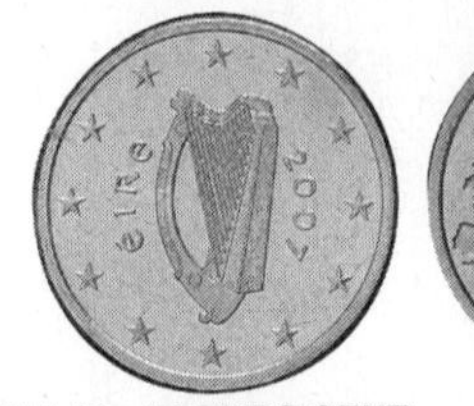

KM# 49 50 EURO CENT

7.8100 g., Aluminum-Bronze, 24.25 mm. **Obv:** Harp **Obv. Designer:** Jarlath Hayes **Rev:** Relief map of Western Europe, stars, lines and value **Rev. Designer:** Luc Luycx **Edge:** Reeded

Date	Mintage	F	VF	XF	Unc	BU
2007	—	—	—	—	1.50	—

KM# 38 EURO

7.5000 g., Bi-Metallic Copper-Nickel center in Brass ring, 23.25 mm. **Obv:** Harp **Obv. Designer:** Jarlath Hayes **Rev:** Denomination and map **Rev. Designer:** Luc Luycx **Edge:** Reeded and plain sections

Date	Mintage	VG	F	VF	XF	Unc
2002	135,139,737	—	—	—	—	2.75
2003	2,520,000	—	—	—	—	2.75
2004	1,632,990	—	—	—	—	2.75
2005	6,024	—	—	—	—	2.75
2006	—	—	—	—	—	2.75

KM# 50 EURO

7.5000 g., Bi-Metallic, 23.25 mm. **Obv:** Harp **Obv. Designer:** Jarlath Hayes **Rev:** Relief map of Western Europe, stars, lines and value **Rev. Designer:** Luc Luycz **Edge:** Reeded and plain sections

Date	Mintage	VG	F	VF	XF	Unc
2007	—	—	—	—	—	2.75

KM# 39 2 EURO

8.5200 g., Bi-Metallic Brass center in Copper-Nickel ring, 25.7 mm. **Obv:** Harp **Obv. Designer:** Jarlath Hayes **Rev:** Denomination and map **Rev. Designer:** Luc Luycx **Edge:** Reeded with 2's and stars

Date	Mintage	VG	F	VF	XF	Unc
2002	90,548,166	—	—	—	—	4.00
2003	2,631,076	—	—	—	—	4.00
2004	3,738,186	—	—	—	—	4.00
2005	11,714	—	—	—	—	4.00
2006	—	—	—	—	—	4.00

KM# 51 2 EURO

8.5200 g., Bi-Metallic, 25.7 mm. **Obv:** Harp **Obv. Designer:** Jarlath Hayes **Rev:** Relief map of Western Europe, stars, lines and value **Rev. Designer:** Luc Luycx **Edge:** Reeded with 2's and stars

Date	Mintage	VG	F	VF	XF	Unc
2007	—	—	—	—	—	4.00

KM# 53 2 EURO

8.4500 g., Bi-Metallic **Ring Composition:** Copper Nickel **Center Composition:** Brass, 25.72 mm. **Subject:** 50th Anniversary Treaty of Rome **Obv:** Open treaty book **Rev:** Large value at left, modified outline of Europe at right **Edge:** Reeded with stars and 2's

Date	Mintage	F	VF	XF	Unc	BU
2007	—	—	—	—	—	9.00

ISLE OF MAN

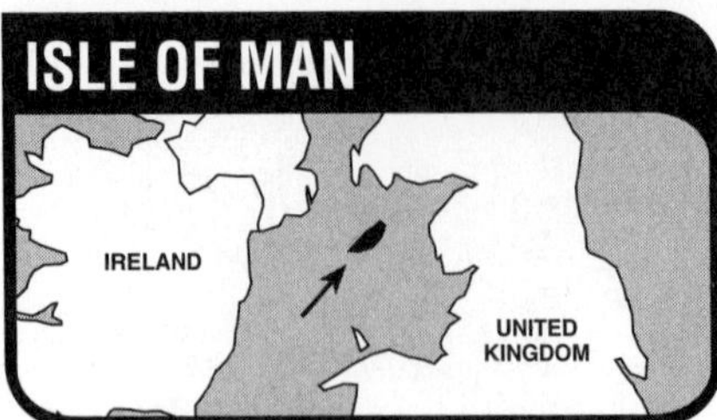

The Isle of Man, a dependency of the British Crown located in the Irish Sea equidistant from Ireland, Scotland and England, has an area of 227 sq. mi. (588 sq. km.) and a population of 68,000. Capital: Douglas. Agriculture, dairy farming, fishing and tourism are the chief industries.

The prevalence of prehistoric artifacts and monuments on the island give evidence that its' mild, almost sub-tropical climate was enjoyed by mankind before the dawn of history. Vikings came to the Isle of Man during the 9th century and remained until ejected by the Scottish in 1266. The island came under the protection of the British Crown in 1288, and in 1406 was granted, in perpetuity, to the earls of Derby, from whom it was inherited, 1736, by the Duke of Atholl. The British Crown purchased the rights and title in 1765; the remaining privileges of the Atholl family were transferred to the crown in 1829. The Isle of Man is ruled by its own legislative council and the House of Keys, the oldest, continuous legislative assembly in the world. Acts of Parliament passed in London do not affect the island unless it is specifically mentioned.

RULERS

James Murray, Duke of Atholl, 1736-1765
British Commencing 1765

MINT MARK

PM - Pobjoy Mint

PRIVY MARKS

(a) - Big Apple - 1988
(at) - Angel Blowing Trumpet – 1997

(b) - Baby Crib - 1982
(ba) - Basel Bugle - 1990
(bb) - Big Ben - 1987-1988
(br) - Brooklyn Bridge - 1989
(bs) - Teddy Bear in Stocking - 1996
(c) - Chicago Water Tower CICF - 1990-1991
(cc) - Christmas cracker - 1991
(d) - St. Paul's Cathedral - 1989
(f) - FUN logo - 1988
(fl) - Fleur de Lis - 1990
(fr) - Frauenkirche - Munich Numismata - 1990-1991
(fw) - Fairy w/magic wand - 1999
(h) - Horse - Hong Kong Int. - 1990
(l) - Statue of Liberty - 1987
(lc) - Lion crowned - 1989
(m) - Queen mother's portrait - 1980
(ma) - Maple leaf - CNA - 1990
(mt) - Mistletoe - Christmas - 1987, 1989
(ns) - North Star - 1994
(p) - Carrier Pigeon - Basel - 1988-1989
(pi) - Pine tree - 1986
(pt) - Partridge in a pear tree - 1988
(py) - Poppy - 1995
(s) - Bridge - SINPEX - 1987
(sb) - Soccer ball - 1982
(sc) - Santa Claus - 1995
(sg) - Sleigh - Christmas - 1990
(SL) - St. Louis Arch - 1987
(ss) - Sailing Ship - Sydney - 1988
(t) - Stylized triskelion - 1979
(tb) - Tower Bridge - 1990
(ti) - TICC logo - Tokyo - 1990
(v) - Viking ship - 1980
(vw) - Viking ship in wreath - 1986
(w) - Stylized triskelion - 1985
(x) - Snowman - 1998

PRIVY LETTERS

A - ANA - 1985-1992
C - Coinex, London - 1985-1989
D.M.I.H.E. - Ideal Home Exhibit, London, 1980
D.M.I.H.E.N. - Ideal Home Exhibit, Manchester, 1980
F - FUN - 1987
H - Hong Kong Expo - 1985
L - Long Beach - 1985-1987
T - Torex, Toronto - 1986
U - Uncirculated - 1988, 1990, 1994, 1995
X - Ameripex - 1986

BRITISH DEPENDENCY

DECIMAL COINAGE

100 Pence = 1 Pound

KM# 19 1/2 NEW PENNY

1.7700 g., Bronze, 17.14 mm. **Ruler:** Elizabeth II **Obv:** Young bust right **Obv. Designer:** Arnold Machin **Rev:** Flowered weed **Rev. Designer:** Christopher Ironside

Date	Mintage	F	VF	XF	Unc	BU
1971	495,000	—	—	0.15	0.35	0.75
1971 Proof	10,000	Value: 1.50				
1972	1,000	—	—	—	18.00	20.00
1973	1,000	—	—	—	18.00	20.00
1974	1,000	—	—	—	18.00	20.00
1975	825,000	—	—	0.15	0.25	0.65

KM# 32 1/2 PENNY

Bronze, 17.14 mm. **Ruler:** Elizabeth II **Obv:** Young bust right **Obv. Designer:** Arnold Machin **Rev:** Atlantic herring

Date	Mintage	F	VF	XF	Unc	BU
1976	600,000	—	—	0.20	0.45	1.00
1978	—	—	—	0.20	0.45	1.00
1978 Proof	—	Value: 1.25				
1979(t) AA	—	—	—	0.20	0.45	1.00
1979(t) AB	—	—	—	0.20	0.45	1.00

KM# 40 1/2 PENNY

1.7600 g., Bronze, 17.14 mm. **Ruler:** Elizabeth II **Series:** F.A.O. **Obv:** Young bust right **Obv. Designer:** Arnold Machin **Rev:** Atlantic herring

Date	Mintage	F	VF	XF	Unc	BU
1977	700,000	—	—	0.20	0.45	1.00
Note: "1977 PM" on both sides						
1977	Inc. above	—	—	—	5.00	6.00
Note: "1977 PM" on obverse only						

KM# 58 1/2 PENNY

1.7700 g., Bronze, 17.14 mm. **Ruler:** Elizabeth II **Obv:** Young bust right **Obv. Designer:** Arnold Machin **Rev:** Atlantic herring within net **Rev. Designer:** Leslie Lindsay

Date	Mintage	F	VF	XF	Unc	BU
1980 AA	—	—	—	0.15	0.35	0.75
1980 AB	—	—	—	0.15	0.35	0.75
1980PM DD Proof	—	Value: 1.00				
1981 AA	—	—	—	0.15	0.35	0.75
1981 DD Proof	—	Value: 1.00				
1982 AA	—	—	—	0.15	0.35	0.75
1982 (b)	—	—	—	0.15	0.35	0.75
1982 (b) Proof	25,000	Value: 1.00				
1983 AA	—	—	—	0.15	0.35	0.75

KM# 72.1 1/2 PENNY

Bronze, 17.14 mm. **Ruler:** Elizabeth II **Series:** F.A.O. **Obv:** Young bust right **Obv. Designer:** Arnold Machin **Rev:** Atlantic herring

Date	Mintage	F	VF	XF	Unc	BU
1981	—	—	—	—	0.50	1.00

KM# 72.2 1/2 PENNY

Bronze, 17.14 mm. **Ruler:** Elizabeth II **Obv:** Young bust right **Obv. Designer:** Arnold Machin **Rev:** Atlantic herring

Date	Mintage	F	VF	XF	Unc	BU
1981	10,000	—	2.00	5.00	10.00	12.50

KM# 111 1/2 PENNY

Bronze, 17.14 mm. **Ruler:** Elizabeth II **Subject:** Quincentenary of the College of Arms **Obv:** Young bust right **Obv. Designer:**

Arnold Machin **Rev:** Fuchsia blossom on garnished and scrolled shield **Rev. Designer:** Leslie Lindsay

Date	Mintage	F	VF	XF	Unc	BU
1984 AA	—	—	—	—	0.15	0.25

KM# 142 1/2 PENNY

Bronze, 17.14 mm. **Ruler:** Elizabeth II **Obv:** Crowned head right **Obv. Designer:** Raphael Maklouf **Rev:** Fuchsia blossom on garnished and scrolled shield **Rev. Designer:** Leslie Lindsay

Date	Mintage	F	VF	XF	Unc	BU
1985(w) AA	—	—	—	—	0.15	0.25
1985 Proof	50,000	Value: 2.00				

KM# 20 NEW PENNY

3.5500 g., Bronze, 20.32 mm. **Ruler:** Elizabeth II **Obv:** Young bust right **Obv. Designer:** Arnold Machin **Rev:** Celtic cross **Rev. Designer:** Christopher Ironside

Date	Mintage	F	VF	XF	Unc	BU
1971	100,000	—	—	0.10	0.35	0.65
1971 Proof	10,000	Value: 2.00				
1972	1,000	—	—	—	18.00	20.00
1973	1,000	—	—	—	18.00	20.00
1974	1,000	—	—	—	18.00	20.00
1975	855,000	—	—	0.10	0.20	0.40

KM# 33 PENNY

3.5600 g., Bronze, 20.32 mm. **Ruler:** Elizabeth II **Obv:** Young bust right **Obv. Designer:** Arnold Machin **Rev:** Loaghtyn sheep

Date	Mintage	F	VF	XF	Unc	BU
1976	900,000	—	—	0.25	0.75	1.25
1977	1,000,000	—	—	0.25	0.75	1.25
1978	—	—	—	0.25	0.75	1.25
1978 Proof	—	Value: 1.50				
1979 AA(t)	—	—	—	0.25	0.75	1.25
1979 AB(t)	—	—	—	0.25	0.75	1.25
1979 AC(t)	—	—	—	0.25	0.75	1.25
1979 AD(t)	—	—	—	0.25	0.75	1.25
1979 AE(t)	—	—	—	0.25	0.75	1.25

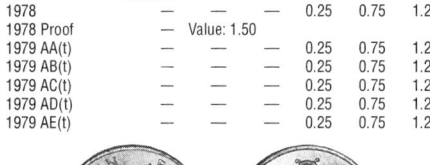

KM# 59 PENNY

3.5600 g., Bronze, 20.32 mm. **Ruler:** Elizabeth II **Obv:** Young bust right **Obv. Designer:** Arnold Machin **Rev:** Manx cat **Rev. Designer:** Leslie Lindsay

Date	Mintage	F	VF	XF	Unc	BU
1980 AA	—	—	—	0.25	1.50	3.00
1980 AB	—	—	—	0.25	1.50	3.00
1980 AC	—	—	—	0.25	1.50	3.00
1980PM DD Proof	—	Value: 2.75				
1981 AA	—	—	—	0.25	1.50	3.00
1981 DD Proof	—	Value: 2.75				
1982 AA	—	—	—	0.25	1.50	3.00
1982 (b)	—	—	—	0.25	1.50	3.00
1982 (b) Proof	25,000	Value: 2.75				
1983 AA	—	—	—	0.25	1.50	3.00
1983 AC	—	—	—	0.25	1.50	3.00
1983 AB	—	—	—	0.25	1.50	3.00

KM# 112 PENNY

3.5600 g., Bronze, 20.32 mm. **Ruler:** Elizabeth II **Subject:** Quincentenary of the College of Arms **Obv:** Young bust right **Obv. Designer:** Arnold Machin **Rev:** Shag bird on tilting shield **Rev. Designer:** Leslie Lindsay

Date	Mintage	F	VF	XF	Unc	BU
1984 AA	—	—	—	0.25	0.50	1.50

KM# 143 PENNY

3.5600 g., Bronze, 20.32 mm. **Ruler:** Elizabeth II **Obv:** Crowned head right **Obv. Designer:** Raphael Maklouf **Rev:** Shag bird on tilting shield **Rev. Designer:** Leslie Lindsay

Date	Mintage	F	VF	XF	Unc	BU
1985 AA(w)	—	—	—	0.10	0.50	1.50
1985 Proof	50,000	Value: 2.00				
1986 AA	—	—	—	0.10	0.50	1.50
1987 AA	—	—	—	0.10	0.50	1.50
1987 AB	—	—	—	0.10	0.50	1.50
1987 AC	—	—	—	0.10	0.50	1.50

KM# 207 PENNY

3.5600 g., Bronze, 20.32 mm. **Ruler:** Elizabeth II **Obv:** Crowned head right **Obv. Designer:** Raphael Maklouf **Rev:** Precision lathe superimposed on a cog wheel

Date	Mintage	F	VF	XF	Unc	BU
1988 AA	—	—	—	—	0.20	0.35
1988 AB	—	—	—	0.10	0.30	0.50
1988 AC	—	—	—	0.10	0.30	0.50
1988 AD	—	—	—	0.10	0.30	0.50
1989 AA	—	—	—	—	0.20	0.35
1989 AB	—	—	—	0.10	0.30	0.50
1989 AC	—	—	—	0.10	0.30	0.50
1989 AD	—	—	—	0.10	0.30	0.50
1989 AE	—	—	—	0.10	0.30	0.50
1990 AA	—	—	—	—	0.20	0.35
1991 AA	—	—	—	—	0.20	0.35
1991 AB	—	—	—	—	0.20	0.35
1991 AC	—	—	—	—	0.20	0.35
1991 AD	—	—	—	—	0.20	0.35
1991 AE	—	—	—	—	0.20	0.35
1992 AA	—	—	—	—	0.20	0.35
1993 AA	—	—	—	—	0.20	0.35
1994 AA	—	—	—	—	0.20	0.35
1995 AA	—	—	—	—	0.20	0.35

KM# 588 PENNY

Bronze-Plated Steel, 20.32 mm. **Ruler:** Elizabeth II **Subject:** Sports **Obv:** Crowned head right **Obv. Designer:** Raphael Maklouf **Rev:** Rugby ball within 3/4 square and wreath

Date	Mintage	F	VF	XF	Unc	BU
1996 AA	—	—	—	—	0.20	0.35
1997 AA	—	—	—	—	0.20	0.35
1998 AA	—	—	—	—	0.20	0.35

KM# 823.1 PENNY

Bronze-Plated Steel, 20.32 mm. **Ruler:** Elizabeth II **Obv:** Head with tiara right **Obv. Designer:** Ian Rank-Broadley **Rev:** Rugby ball within 3/4 square and wreath

Date	Mintage	F	VF	XF	Unc	BU
1998PM AA	—	—	—	—	0.20	0.35

KM# 823.2 PENNY

Bronze-Plated Steel, 20.32 mm. **Ruler:** Elizabeth II **Obv:** Head with tiara right with small triskeles dividing legend **Obv. Designer:** Ian Rank-Broadley **Rev:** Rugby ball within 3/4 square and wreath

Date	Mintage	F	VF	XF	Unc	BU
1998PM AA	—	—	—	—	0.20	0.35
1999PM AA	—	—	—	—	0.20	0.35
1999PM AB	—	—	—	—	0.20	0.35

KM# 1036 PENNY

3.5600 g., Bronze-Plated Steel, 20.32 mm. **Ruler:** Elizabeth II **Obv:** Head with tiara right with small triskeles dividing legend **Obv. Designer:** Ian Rank-Broadley **Rev:** Ruins **Edge:** Plain

Date	Mintage	F	VF	XF	Unc	BU
2000PMM AA	—	—	—	—	0.25	0.45
2001PM AA	—	—	—	—	0.25	0.45
2001PM AC	—	—	—	—	0.25	0.45
2002PM AA	—	—	—	—	0.25	0.45
2002PM AE	—	—	—	—	0.25	0.45
2003PM AA	—	—	—	—	0.25	0.45
2003PM AE	—	—	—	—	0.25	0.45

KM# 1253 PENNY

3.5600 g., Copper-Plated-Steel, 20.3 mm. **Ruler:** Elizabeth II **Obv:** Head with tiara right **Rev:** Stanton War Memorial **Edge:** Reeded

Date	Mintage	F	VF	XF	Unc	BU
2004PM AA	—	—	—	—	0.25	0.45
2004PM AB	—	—	—	—	0.25	0.45
2005PM AA	—	—	—	—	0.25	0.45
2005PM AB	—	—	—	—	0.25	0.45
2006PM AA	—	—	—	—	0.25	0.45
2006PM AB	—	—	—	—	0.25	0.45
2007PM AA	—	—	—	—	0.25	0.45
2007PM AB	—	—	—	—	0.25	0.45

KM# 21 2 NEW PENCE

7.0000 g., Bronze, 25.91 mm. **Ruler:** Elizabeth II **Obv:** Young bust right **Obv. Designer:** Arnold Machin **Rev:** Falcons

Date	Mintage	F	VF	XF	Unc	BU
1971	100,000	—	—	0.25	1.00	2.00
1971 Proof	10,000	Value: 2.50				
1972	1,000	—	—	—	18.00	20.00
1973	1,000	—	—	—	18.00	20.00
1974	1,000	—	—	—	18.00	20.00
1975	725,000	—	—	0.25	1.00	1.50

KM# 34 2 PENCE

7.1200 g., Bronze, 25.91 mm. **Ruler:** Elizabeth II **Obv:** Young bust right **Obv. Designer:** Arnold Machin **Rev:** Bird in flight over map

Date	Mintage	F	VF	XF	Unc	BU
1976	800,000	—	—	0.20	0.50	1.00
1977	1,000,000	—	—	0.20	0.50	1.00
1978	—	—	—	—	0.50	1.00
1978 Proof	—	Value: 1.25				
1979 AA(t)	10,000	—	—	0.20	0.50	1.00
1979 AB(t)	—	—	—	0.20	0.50	1.00
1979 AC(t)	—	—	—	0.20	0.50	1.00
1979 AD(t)	—	—	—	0.20	0.50	1.00
1979 AE(t)	—	—	—	0.20	0.50	1.00
1979 AF(t)	—	—	—	0.20	0.50	1.00
1979 AG(t)	—	—	—	0.20	0.50	1.00
1979 AH(t)	—	—	—	0.20	0.50	1.00

KM# 60 2 PENCE

7.1200 g., Bronze, 25.91 mm. **Ruler:** Elizabeth II **Obv:** Young bust right **Obv. Designer:** Arnold Machin **Rev:** Bird in center of design **Rev. Designer:** Leslie Lindsay

Date	Mintage	F	VF	XF	Unc	BU
1980 AA	—	—	—	0.25	0.60	1.50
1980 AB	—	—	—	0.25	0.60	1.50
1980 AC	—	—	—	0.25	0.60	1.50
1980 AD	—	—	—	0.25	0.60	1.50
1980PM DD Proof	—	Value: 1.75				
1981 AA	—	—	—	0.25	0.60	1.50
1981 AB	—	—	—	0.25	0.60	1.50
1981 DD Proof	—	Value: 1.75				
1982 AA	—	—	—	0.25	0.60	1.50
1982 (b)	—	—	—	0.25	0.60	1.50
1982 (b) Proof	25,000	Value: 1.75				
1983 AA	—	—	—	0.25	0.60	1.50

Date	Mintage	F	VF	XF	Unc	BU
1983 AB	—	—	—	0.25	0.60	1.50
1983 AC	—	—	—	0.25	0.60	1.50
1983 AD	—	—	—	0.25	0.60	1.50
1983 AE	—	—	—	0.25	0.60	1.50

KM# 113 2 PENCE

7.1200 g., Bronze, 25.91 mm. **Ruler:** Elizabeth II **Subject:** Quincentenary of the College of Arms **Obv:** Young bust right **Obv. Designer:** Arnold Machin **Rev:** Falcon on ornamented shield **Rev. Designer:** Leslie Lindsay

Date	Mintage	F	VF	XF	Unc	BU
1984 AA	—	—	—	0.20	1.00	3.00

KM# 144 2 PENCE

7.1200 g., Bronze, 25.91 mm. **Ruler:** Elizabeth II **Obv:** Crowned head right **Obv. Designer:** Raphael Maklouf **Rev:** Falcon on ornamented shield **Rev. Designer:** Leslie Lindsay

Date	Mintage	F	VF	XF	Unc	BU
1985(w) AA	—	—	—	0.20	1.25	3.00
1985(w) AB	—	—	—	0.20	1.25	3.00
1985 Proof	50,000	Value: 3.00				
1986 AA	—	—	—	0.20	1.25	3.00
1986 AB	—	—	—	0.20	1.25	3.00
1986 AC	—	—	—	0.20	1.25	3.00
1986 AD	—	—	—	0.20	1.25	3.00
1987 AA	—	—	—	0.20	1.25	3.00
1987 AB	—	—	—	0.20	1.25	3.00
1987 AC	—	—	—	0.20	1.25	3.00
1987 AD	—	—	—	0.20	1.25	3.00

KM# 208 2 PENCE

7.1200 g., Bronze, 25.91 mm. **Ruler:** Elizabeth II **Obv:** Crowned head right **Obv. Designer:** Raphael Maklouf **Rev:** Assorted designs within celtic cross within circle

Date	Mintage	F	VF	XF	Unc	BU
1988 AA	—	—	—	—	0.30	0.50
1988 AB	—	—	—	0.10	0.30	0.50
1988 AC	—	—	—	0.10	0.30	0.50
1988 AD	—	—	—	0.10	0.30	0.50
1989 AA	—	—	—	—	0.30	0.50
1989 AB	—	—	—	0.10	0.30	0.50
1989 AC	—	—	—	0.10	0.30	0.50
1989 AD	—	—	—	0.10	0.30	0.50
1989 AE	—	—	—	0.10	0.30	0.50
1990 AA	—	—	—	—	0.30	0.50
1991 AA	—	—	—	—	0.30	0.50
1992 AA	—	—	—	—	0.30	0.50
1993 AA	—	—	—	—	0.30	0.50
1994 AA	—	—	—	—	0.30	0.50
1995 AA	—	—	—	—	0.30	0.50

KM# 589 2 PENCE

Bronze Clad Steel, 25.91 mm. **Ruler:** Elizabeth II **Subject:** Sports **Obv:** Crowned head right **Obv. Designer:** Raphael Maklouf **Rev:** Bicyclists within sprigs

Date	Mintage	F	VF	XF	Unc	BU
1996 AA	—	—	—	—	0.20	0.40
1997 AA	—	—	—	—	0.20	0.40

KM# 901.1 2 PENCE

Bronze Clad Steel, 25.91 mm. **Ruler:** Elizabeth II **Obv:** Head with tiara right **Obv. Designer:** Ian Rank-Broadley **Rev:** Two bicyclists within sprigs

Date	Mintage	F	VF	XF	Unc	BU
1998PM AA	—	—	—	—	0.20	0.40

KM# 901.2 2 PENCE

Bronze Plated Steel, 25.91 mm. **Ruler:** Elizabeth II **Obv:** Head with tiara right with small triskeles dividing legend **Obv. Designer:** Ian Rank-Broadley **Rev:** Two bicyclists within sprigs

Date	Mintage	F	VF	XF	Unc	BU
1998PM AA	—	—	—	—	0.20	0.40
1999PM AA	—	—	—	—	0.20	0.40

KM# 1037 2 PENCE

7.1650 g., Brass Plated Steel, 25.86 mm. **Ruler:** Elizabeth II **Obv:** Head with tiara right **Obv. Designer:** Ian Rank-Broadley **Rev:** Sailboat **Edge:** Plain

Date	Mintage	F	VF	XF	Unc	BU
2000PM AA	—	—	—	—	0.40	0.60
2001PM AA	—	—	—	—	0.40	0.60
2001PM AB	—	—	—	—	0.40	0.60
2002PM AA	—	—	—	—	0.40	0.60
2002PM AB	—	—	—	—	0.40	0.60
2002PM AC	—	—	—	—	0.40	0.60
2002PM AF	—	—	—	—	0.40	0.60
2003PM AA	—	—	—	—	0.40	0.60
2003PM AF	—	—	—	—	0.40	0.60

KM# 1254 2 PENCE

7.1200 g., Copper-Plated-Steel, 25.9 mm. **Ruler:** Elizabeth II **Obv:** Head with tiara right **Obv. Designer:** Ian Rank-Broadley **Rev:** Albert Tower **Edge:** Reeded

Date	Mintage	F	VF	XF	Unc	BU
2004PM AA	—	—	—	—	0.40	0.60
2004PM AB	—	—	—	—	0.40	0.60
2005PM AA	—	—	—	—	0.40	0.60
2005PM AB	—	—	—	—	0.40	0.60
2006PM AA	—	—	—	—	0.40	0.60
2006PM AB	—	—	—	—	0.40	0.60
2007PM AA	—	—	—	—	0.40	0.60
2007PM AB	—	—	—	—	0.40	0.60

KM# 22 5 NEW PENCE

5.6500 g., Copper-Nickel, 23.59 mm. **Ruler:** Elizabeth II **Obv:** Young bust right **Obv. Designer:** Arnold Machin **Rev:** Towers on hill **Rev. Designer:** Christopher Ironside

Date	Mintage	F	VF	XF	Unc	BU
1971	100,000	—	—	0.10	0.50	1.00
1971 Proof	10,000	Value: 2.50				
1972	1,000	—	—	—	20.00	22.50
1973	1,000	—	—	—	20.00	22.50
1974	1,000	—	—	—	20.00	22.50
1975	1,400,000	—	—	0.10	0.25	0.50

KM# 902.1 5 PENCE

Copper-Nickel, 18 mm. **Ruler:** Elizabeth II **Obv:** Head with tiara right **Obv. Designer:** Ian Rank-Broadley **Rev:** Golfer within sprigs

Date	Mintage	F	VF	XF	Unc	BU
1998 AA	—	—	—	—	0.50	0.75

KM# 902.2 5 NEW PENCE

Copper Nickel, 18 mm. **Ruler:** Elizabeth II **Obv:** Head with tiara right with small triskeles dividing legend **Obv. Designer:** Ian Rank-Broadley **Rev:** Golpher within sprigs

Date	Mintage	F	VF	XF	Unc	BU
1998PM AA	—	—	—	—	0.50	0.75
1999PM AA	—	—	—	—	0.50	0.75
1999PM AB	—	—	—	—	0.50	0.75

KM# 35.1 5 PENCE

5.6500 g., Copper-Nickel, 23.59 mm. **Ruler:** Elizabeth II **Obv:** Young bust right **Obv. Designer:** Arnold Machin **Rev:** Laxey wheel **Note:** Lady Isabella; Mint mark: PM on obverse and reverse.

Date	Mintage	F	VF	XF	Unc	BU
1976	800,000	—	—	0.10	0.60	0.85
1977	—	—	—	0.10	0.60	0.85
1978	—	—	—	0.10	0.60	0.85
1978 Proof	—	Value: 1.50				
1979(t) AA	—	—	—	0.10	0.60	0.85
1979(t) AB	—	—	—	0.10	0.60	0.85

KM# 35.2 5 PENCE

5.6500 g., Copper-Nickel, 23.59 mm. **Ruler:** Elizabeth II **Obv:** Young bust right **Obv. Designer:** Arnold Machin **Rev:** Laxey wheel **Note:** Mint mark: PM on obverse only.

Date	Mintage	F	VF	XF	Unc	BU
1976	Inc. above	—	—	0.15	0.75	1.00

KM# 61 5 PENCE

5.6500 g., Copper-Nickel, 23.59 mm. **Ruler:** Elizabeth II **Obv:** Young bust right **Obv. Designer:** Arnold Machin **Rev:** Stylized Loagthyn sheep **Rev. Designer:** Leslie Lindsay

Date	Mintage	F	VF	XF	Unc	BU
1980 AA	—	—	—	0.15	0.75	1.25
1980 AB	—	—	—	0.15	0.75	1.25
1980 AC	—	—	—	0.15	0.75	1.25
1980PM DD Proof	—	Value: 1.50				
1981 AA	—	—	—	0.15	0.75	1.25
1981 DD Proof	—	Value: 1.50				
1982 (b)	—	—	—	0.15	0.75	1.25
1982 AA	—	—	—	0.15	0.75	1.00
1982 (b) Proof	25,000	Value: 1.50				
1983 AA	—	—	—	0.15	0.75	1.25

KM# 114 5 PENCE

5.6500 g., Copper-Nickel, 23.59 mm. **Ruler:** Elizabeth II **Subject:** Quincentenary of the College of Arms **Obv:** Young bust right **Obv. Designer:** Arnold Machin **Rev:** Cushag within design **Rev. Designer:** Leslie Lindsay

Date	Mintage	F	VF	XF	Unc	BU
1984 AA	—	—	—	0.10	0.50	0.75

KM# 145 5 PENCE

5.6500 g., Copper-Nickel, 23.59 mm. **Ruler:** Elizabeth II **Obv:** Crowned head right **Obv. Designer:** Raphael Maklouf **Rev:** Cushag within design **Rev. Designer:** Leslie Lindsay

Date	Mintage	F	VF	XF	Unc	BU
1985(w) AA	—	—	—	0.10	0.50	0.75
1985 Proof	50,000	Value: 3.00				
1986 AA	—	—	—	0.10	0.50	0.75
1986 AB	—	—	—	0.10	0.50	0.75
1986 AC	—	—	—	0.10	0.50	0.75
1986 AD	—	—	—	0.10	0.50	0.75
1987 AA	—	—	—	0.10	0.50	0.75

KM# 209.1 5 PENCE
5.6500 g., Copper-Nickel, 23.59 mm. **Ruler:** Elizabeth II **Obv:** Crowned head right **Obv. Designer:** Raphael Maklouf **Rev:** Windsurfing

Date	Mintage	F	VF	XF	Unc	BU
1988 AA	—	—	—	—	0.50	0.75
1989 AA	—	—	—	—	0.50	0.75
1990	—	—	—	—	0.50	0.75

KM# 209.2 5 PENCE
Copper-Nickel, 18 mm. **Ruler:** Elizabeth II **Obv:** Crowned head right **Obv. Designer:** Raphael Maklouf **Rev:** Windsurfing **Note:** Reduced size.

Date	Mintage	F	VF	XF	Unc	BU
1990 AA	—	—	—	—	0.50	0.75
1991 AA	—	—	—	—	0.50	0.75
1991 AB	—	—	—	—	0.50	0.75
1992 AA	—	—	—	—	0.50	0.75
1993 AA	—	—	—	—	0.50	0.75

KM# 392 5 PENCE
Copper-Nickel, 18 mm. **Ruler:** Elizabeth II **Obv:** Crowned head right **Obv. Designer:** Raphael Maklouf **Rev:** Golf clubs and ball

Date	Mintage	F	VF	XF	Unc	BU
1994 AA	—	—	—	—	0.50	0.75
1995 AA	—	—	—	—	0.50	0.75

KM# 590 5 PENCE
Copper-Nickel, 18 mm. **Ruler:** Elizabeth II **Subject:** Sports **Obv:** Crowned head right **Obv. Designer:** Raphael Maklouf **Rev:** Golfer within sprigs

Date	Mintage	F	VF	XF	Unc	BU
1996 AA	—	—	—	—	0.50	0.75
1997 AA	—	—	—	—	0.50	0.75

KM# 1038 5 PENCE
3.2500 g., Copper-Nickel, 18 mm. **Ruler:** Elizabeth II **Obv:** Head with tiara right **Obv. Designer:** Ian Rank-Broadley **Rev:** Gaut's Cross **Edge:** Reeded

Date	Mintage	F	VF	XF	Unc	BU
2000 AA	—	—	—	—	0.75	1.00
2000PMM AA	—	—	—	—	—	—
2000 AB	—	—	—	—	0.75	1.00
2000PMM AC	—	—	—	—	0.75	1.00
2001PM AA	—	—	—	—	0.75	1.00
2002PM AA	—	—	—	—	0.75	1.00
2002PM AC	—	—	—	—	0.75	1.00
2003PM AA	—	—	—	—	0.75	1.00
2003PM AD	—	—	—	—	0.75	1.00

KM# 1255 5 PENCE
3.2500 g., Copper-Nickel, 18 mm. **Ruler:** Elizabeth II **Obv:** Head with tiara right **Obv. Designer:** Ian Rank-Broadley **Rev:** Tower of Refuge **Edge:** Reeded

Date	Mintage	F	VF	XF	Unc	BU
2004PM AA	—	—	—	—	0.75	1.00
2004PM AB	—	—	—	—	0.75	1.00
2005PM AA	—	—	—	—	0.75	1.00
2005PM AB	—	—	—	—	0.75	1.00
2006PM AA	—	—	—	—	0.75	1.00
2006PM AB	—	—	—	—	0.75	1.00
2007PM AA	—	—	—	—	0.75	1.00
2007PM AB	—	—	—	—	0.75	1.00

KM# 23 10 NEW PENCE
11.5000 g., Copper-Nickel, 28.5 mm. **Ruler:** Elizabeth II **Obv:** Young bust right **Obv. Designer:** Arnold Machin **Rev:** Triskeles **Rev. Designer:** Christopher Ironside

Date	Mintage	F	VF	XF	Unc	BU
1971	100,000	—	—	0.20	0.50	1.00
1971 Proof	10,000	Value: 3.50				
1972	1,000	—	—	—	20.00	22.50
1973	1,000	—	—	—	20.00	22.50
1974	1,000	—	—	—	20.00	22.50
1975	1,500,000	—	—	0.20	0.40	0.75

KM# 36.1 10 PENCE
11.5000 g., Copper-Nickel, 28.5 mm. **Ruler:** Elizabeth II **Obv:** Young bust right **Obv. Designer:** Arnold Machin **Rev:** Triskeles on map **Rev. Designer:** Christopher Ironside **Note:** Mintmark: PM on obverse and reverse.

Date	Mintage	F	VF	XF	Unc	BU
1976	2,800,000	—	—	0.20	0.80	1.00
1977	—	—	—	0.20	0.80	1.00
1978	—	—	—	0.20	0.80	1.00
1978 Proof	—	Value: 2.00				
1979(t) AA	—	—	—	0.20	0.80	1.00
1979(t) AB	—	—	—	0.20	0.80	1.00

KM# 36.2 10 PENCE
Copper-Nickel, 28.5 mm. **Ruler:** Elizabeth II **Obv:** Young bust right **Obv. Designer:** Arnold Machin **Rev:** Triskeles on map **Rev. Designer:** Christopher Ironside **Note:** Mintmark: PM on obverse only.

Date	Mintage	F	VF	XF	Unc	BU
1976	Inc. above	—	—	0.20	1.00	1.25
1977	—	—	—	0.20	1.00	1.25

KM# 62 10 PENCE
11.5000 g., Copper-Nickel, 28.5 mm. **Ruler:** Elizabeth II **Obv:** Young bust right **Obv. Designer:** Arnold Machin **Rev:** Falcon within design **Rev. Designer:** Leslie Lindsay

Date	Mintage	F	VF	XF	Unc	BU
1980 AA	—	—	—	0.25	1.00	2.00
1980 AB	—	—	—	0.25	1.00	2.00
1980PM DD Proof	—	Value: 2.50				
1981 AA	—	—	—	0.25	1.00	2.00
1981 DD Proof	—	Value: 2.50				
1982 AA	—	—	—	0.25	1.00	2.00
1982 AB	—	—	—	0.25	1.00	2.00
1982 AB(b)	—	—	—	0.25	1.00	2.00
1982 AC	—	—	—	0.25	1.00	2.00
1982 AD	—	—	—	0.25	1.00	2.00
1982 (b) Proof	25,000	Value: 2.50				
1983 AA	—	—	—	0.25	1.00	2.00
1983 AB	—	—	—	0.25	1.00	2.00
1983 AC	—	—	—	0.25	1.00	2.00
1983 AD	—	—	—	0.25	1.00	2.00

KM# 115 10 PENCE
11.5000 g., Copper-Nickel, 28.5 mm. **Ruler:** Elizabeth II **Subject:** Quincentenary of the College of Arms **Obv:** Young bust right **Obv. Designer:** Arnold Machin **Rev:** Loagthyn ram within shield **Rev. Designer:** Leslie Lindsay

Date	Mintage	F	VF	XF	Unc	BU
1984 AA	—	—	—	0.25	1.00	1.25
1984 AB	—	—	—	0.25	1.00	1.25
1984 AC	—	—	—	0.25	1.00	1.25
1984 AD	—	—	—	0.25	1.00	1.25
1984 AE	—	—	—	0.25	1.00	1.25
1984 AF	—	—	—	0.25	1.00	1.25
1984 AG	—	—	—	0.25	1.00	1.25

KM# 146 10 PENCE
11.5000 g., Copper-Nickel, 28.5 mm. **Ruler:** Elizabeth II **Obv:** Crowned head right **Obv. Designer:** Raphael Maklouf **Rev:** Loagthyn ram within designed shield **Rev. Designer:** Leslie Lindsay

Date	Mintage	F	VF	XF	Unc	BU
1985(w) AA	—	—	—	0.20	0.80	1.00
1985(w) AB	—	—	—	0.20	0.80	1.00
1985 Proof	50,000	Value: 3.00				
1986 AA	—	—	—	0.20	0.80	1.00
1987 AA	—	—	—	0.20	0.80	1.00

KM# 210 10 PENCE
11.5000 g., Copper-Nickel, 28.5 mm. **Ruler:** Elizabeth II **Obv:** Crowned head right **Obv. Designer:** Raphael Maklouf **Rev:** Island and portcullis on globe

Date	Mintage	F	VF	XF	Unc	BU
1988 AA	—	—	—	—	0.75	1.00
1989 AA	—	—	—	—	0.75	1.00
1990 AA	—	—	—	—	0.75	1.00
1991 AA	—	—	—	—	0.75	1.00
1991 AB	—	—	—	—	0.75	1.00
1991 AC	—	—	—	—	0.75	1.00
1992 AA	—	—	—	—	0.75	1.00

KM# 337 10 PENCE
6.5000 g., Copper-Nickel, 24.5 mm. **Ruler:** Elizabeth II **Obv:** Crowned head right **Obv. Designer:** Raphael Maklouf **Rev:** Triskeles and value **Note:** Varieties exist.

Date	Mintage	F	VF	XF	Unc	BU
1992PM AA	—	—	—	—	0.75	1.00
1992PM AB	—	—	—	—	0.75	1.00
1992PM AC	—	—	—	—	0.75	1.00
1992PM AD	—	—	—	—	0.75	1.00
1992PM AE	—	—	—	—	1.00	1.25
1993PM AA	—	—	—	—	0.75	1.00
1994PM AA	—	—	—	—	0.75	1.00
1995PM AA	—	—	—	—	0.75	1.00

KM# 591 10 PENCE

6.5000 g., Copper-Nickel, 24.5 mm. **Ruler:** Elizabeth II **Subject:** Sports **Obv:** Crowned head right **Obv. Designer:** Raphael Maklouf **Rev:** Sailboat divides wreath

Date	Mintage	F	VF	XF	Unc	BU
1996 AA	—	—	—	—	1.00	1.50
1997 AA	—	—	—	—	1.00	1.50

KM# 903.1 10 PENCE

6.5000 g., Copper-Nickel, 24.5 mm. **Ruler:** Elizabeth II **Obv:** Head with tiara right **Obv. Designer:** Ian Rank-Broadley **Rev:** Sailboat divides wreath

Date	Mintage	F	VF	XF	Unc	BU
1998PM AA	—	—	—	—	1.00	1.50

KM# 903.2 10 PENCE

6.5000 g., Copper-Nickel, 24.5 mm. **Ruler:** Elizabeth II **Obv:** Head with tiara right with small triskeles dividing legend **Obv. Designer:** Ian Rank-Broadley **Rev:** Sailboat divides wreath

Date	Mintage	F	VF	XF	Unc	BU
1998PM AA	—	—	—	—	1.00	1.50
1999PM AA	—	—	—	—	1.00	1.50

KM# 1039 10 PENCE

6.5000 g., Copper-Nickel, 24.5 mm. **Ruler:** Elizabeth II **Obv:** Head with tiara right **Obv. Designer:** Ian Rank-Broadley **Rev:** Cathedral **Edge:** Reeded

Date	Mintage	F	VF	XF	Unc	BU
2000PM AA	—	—	—	—	1.00	1.50
2001PM AA	—	—	—	—	1.00	1.50
2002PM AA	—	—	—	—	1.00	1.50
2003PM AA	—	—	—	—	1.00	1.50

KM# 1256 10 PENCE

6.5000 g., Copper-Nickel, 24.5 mm. **Ruler:** Elizabeth II **Obv:** Head with tiara right **Obv. Designer:** Ian Rank-Broadley **Rev:** Chicken Rock Lighthouse **Edge:** Reeded

Date	Mintage	F	VF	XF	Unc	BU
2004PM AA	—	—	—	—	1.00	1.50
2004PM AB	—	—	—	—	1.00	1.50
2005PM AA	—	—	—	—	1.00	1.50
2005PM AB	—	—	—	—	1.00	1.50
2006PM AA	—	—	—	—	1.00	1.50
2006PM AB	—	—	—	—	1.00	1.50
2007PM AA	—	—	—	—	1.00	1.50
2007PM AB	—	—	—	—	1.00	1.50

KM# 90 20 PENCE

5.0000 g., Copper-Nickel, 21.4 mm. **Ruler:** Elizabeth II **Subject:** Medieval Norse History **Obv:** Young bust right **Obv. Designer:** Arnold Machin **Rev:** Ship within small circle within artistic design with viking helmet above **Rev. Designer:** Leslie Lindsay **Shape:** 7-sided

Date	Mintage	F	VF	XF	Unc	BU
1982 AA	30,000	—	—	0.35	1.00	1.50
1982 AB	—	—	—	0.35	1.00	1.50
1982 AB(b)	—	—	0.50	1.00	5.00	—
1982 AC	—	—	—	0.35	1.00	1.50
1982 AD	—	—	—	0.35	1.00	1.50
1982 (b) Proof	25,000	Value: 6.00				
1982 BB Proof	—	Value: 1.50				
1982 BC Proof	—	Value: 1.50				
1983 AA	—	—	—	0.35	1.00	1.50

KM# 116 20 PENCE

5.0000 g., Copper-Nickel, 21.4 mm. **Ruler:** Elizabeth II **Subject:** Quincentenary of the College of Arms **Obv:** Young bust right **Obv. Designer:** Arnold Machin **Rev:** Atlantic herring within designed shield **Rev. Designer:** Leslie Lindsay **Shape:** 7-sided

Date	Mintage	F	VF	XF	Unc	BU
1984 AA	—	—	—	0.35	1.00	1.50

KM# 147 20 PENCE

5.0000 g., Copper-Nickel, 21.4 mm. **Ruler:** Elizabeth II **Obv:** Crowned head right **Obv. Designer:** Raphael Maklouf **Rev:** Atlantic herring within designed shield **Rev. Designer:** Leslie Lindsay **Shape:** 7-sided

Date	Mintage	F	VF	XF	Unc	BU
1985(w) AA	—	—	—	0.35	1.00	1.50
1985 Proof	50,000	Value: 3.00				
1986 AA	—	—	—	0.35	1.00	1.50
1986 AB	—	—	—	0.35	1.00	1.50
1986 AC	—	—	—	0.35	1.00	1.50
1987 AA	—	—	—	0.35	1.00	1.50

KM# 211 20 PENCE

5.0000 g., Copper-Nickel, 21.4 mm. **Ruler:** Elizabeth II **Obv:** Crowned head right **Obv. Designer:** Raphael Maklouf **Rev:** Combine within sprigs **Shape:** 7-sided

Date	Mintage	F	VF	XF	Unc	BU
1988 AA	—	—	—	—	1.00	1.50
1989 AA	—	—	—	—	1.00	1.50
1990 AA	—	—	—	—	1.00	1.50
1991 AA	—	—	—	—	1.00	1.50
1992 AA	—	—	—	—	1.00	1.50

KM# 391 20 PENCE

5.0000 g., Copper-Nickel, 21.4 mm. **Ruler:** Elizabeth II **Obv:** Crowned head right **Obv. Designer:** Raphael Maklouf **Rev:** Combine within sprigs **Shape:** 7-sided **Note:** Obverse and reverse design revised with border.

Date	Mintage	F	VF	XF	Unc	BU
1993 AA	—	—	—	—	1.00	1.50
1994 AA	—	—	—	—	1.00	1.50
1995 AA	—	—	—	—	1.00	1.50

KM# 592 20 PENCE

5.0000 g., Copper-Nickel, 21.4 mm. **Ruler:** Elizabeth II **Subject:** Sports **Obv:** Crowned head right **Obv. Designer:** Raphael Maklouf **Rev:** Race cars within sprigs **Shape:** 7-sided

Date	Mintage	F	VF	XF	Unc	BU
1996 AA	—	—	—	—	1.25	1.75
1997 AA	—	—	—	—	1.25	1.75

KM# 904.1 20 PENCE

5.0000 g., Copper-Nickel, 21.4 mm. **Ruler:** Elizabeth II **Obv:** Head with tiara right with small triskeles dividing legend **Obv. Legend:** "ELIZABETH II" **Obv. Designer:** Ian Rank-Broadley **Rev:** Rally cars above sprigs **Shape:** 7-sided **Note:** Prev. KM#904.

Date	Mintage	F	VF	XF	Unc	BU
1998PM AA	—	—	—	—	1.25	1.75

KM# 904.2 20 PENCE

5.0000 g., Copper Nickel, 21.4 mm. **Ruler:** Elizabeth II **Obv:** Head with tiara right with small triskeles dividing legend **Obv. Legend:** ISLE OF MAN **Obv. Designer:** Ian Rank-Broadley **Rev:** Rally cars above sprigs

Date	Mintage	F	VF	XF	Unc	BU
1999PM AA	—	—	—	—	1.25	1.75

KM# 1040 20 PENCE

5.0000 g., Copper-Nickel, 21.4 mm. **Ruler:** Elizabeth II **Subject:** Rushen Abbey **Obv:** Head with tiara right **Obv. Designer:** Ian Rank-Broadley **Rev:** Monk writing **Edge:** Plain **Shape:** 7-sided

Date	Mintage	F	VF	XF	Unc	BU
2000 AA	—	—	—	—	1.50	2.00
2001PM AA	—	—	—	—	1.50	2.00
2002PM AA	—	—	—	—	1.50	2.00
2002PM AB	—	—	—	—	1.50	2.00
2003PM AA	—	—	—	—	1.50	2.00
2003PM BA	—	—	—	—	1.50	2.00

KM# 1257 20 PENCE

5.0000 g., Copper-Nickel, 21.5 mm. **Ruler:** Elizabeth II **Obv:** Head with tiara right **Obv. Designer:** Ian Rank-Broadley **Rev:** Castle Rushen Clock **Edge:** Plain **Shape:** 7-sided

Date	Mintage	F	VF	XF	Unc	BU
2004PM AA	—	—	—	—	1.50	2.00
2004PM AB	—	—	—	—	1.50	2.00
2005PM AA	—	—	—	—	1.50	2.00
2005PM AB	—	—	—	—	1.50	2.00
2006PM AA	—	—	—	—	1.50	2.00
2006PM AB	—	—	—	—	1.50	2.00
2007PM AA	—	—	—	—	1.50	2.00
2007PM AB	—	—	—	—	1.50	2.00

KM# 24 50 NEW PENCE

13.5000 g., Copper-Nickel, 30 mm. **Ruler:** Elizabeth II **Obv:** Young bust right **Obv. Designer:** Arnold Machin **Rev:** Sailing Viking ship **Rev. Designer:** Christopher Ironside **Shape:** 7-sided

Date	Mintage	F	VF	XF	Unc	BU
1971	100,000	—	—	1.00	5.00	7.50
1971 Proof	10,000	Value: 8.00				
1972	1,000	—	—	—	27.50	32.50
1973	1,000	—	—	—	27.50	32.50
1974	1,000	—	—	—	27.50	32.50
1975	227,000	—	—	1.00	5.00	7.50

KM# 39 50 PENCE

13.5000 g., Copper-Nickel, 30 mm. **Ruler:** Elizabeth II **Obv:** Young bust right **Obv. Designer:** Arnold Machin **Rev:** Sailing Viking ship **Shape:** 7-sided

Date	Mintage	F	VF	XF	Unc	BU
1976	250,000	—	—	0.75	2.00	3.00
1977	50,000	—	—	0.75	2.50	3.50
1978	25,000	—	—	0.75	2.50	3.50
1978 Proof	—	Value: 4.50				
1979 (t)AA	—	—	—	0.75	3.00	4.00

KM# 51.1 50 PENCE
13.5000 g., Copper-Nickel, 30 mm. **Ruler:** Elizabeth II **Subject:** Manx Day of Tynwald, July 5 **Obv:** Young bust right **Obv. Designer:** Arnold Machin **Rev:** Viking ship **Edge:** Upright with obverse on top **Edge Lettering:** H.M Q.E-II ROYAL VISIT I.O.M. JULY 1979 **Shape:** 7-sided

Date	Mintage	F	VF	XF	Unc	BU
1979 AA	50,000	—	—	—	4.50	5.00
1979 AB	—	—	—	—	4.50	5.00

KM# 51.2 50 PENCE
13.5000 g., Copper-Nickel, 30 mm. **Ruler:** Elizabeth II **Obv:** Young bust right **Obv. Designer:** Arnold Machin **Rev:** Viking ship **Edge:** Lettering upright with reverse on top **Shape:** 7-sided

Date	Mintage	F	VF	XF	Unc	BU
1979 AA	—	—	—	—	4.50	5.00
1979 AB	—	—	—	—	4.50	5.00

KM# 51.3 50 PENCE
13.5000 g., Copper-Nickel, 30 mm. **Ruler:** Elizabeth II **Obv:** Young bust right **Obv. Designer:** Arnold Machin **Rev:** Viking ship **Note:** Inscription not centered in flat sections.

Date	Mintage	F	VF	XF	Unc	BU
1979 AA	—	—	—	—	4.50	5.00
1979 AB	—	—	—	—	4.50	5.00

KM# 53 50 PENCE
13.5000 g., Copper-Nickel, 30 mm. **Ruler:** Elizabeth II **Obv:** Young bust right **Obv. Designer:** Arnold Machin **Rev:** Odin's Raven, Point of Ayre lighthouse **Note:** Same as KM#51.1 with no edge lettering.

Date	Mintage	F	VF	XF	Unc	BU
1979 AA	—	—	—	—	3.00	4.00
1979 AB	—	—	—	—	3.00	4.00

KM# 69 50 PENCE
13.5000 g., Copper-Nickel, 30 mm. **Ruler:** Elizabeth II **Obv:** Young bust right **Obv. Legend:** ELIZABETH THE SECOND **Obv. Designer:** Arnold Machin **Edge Lettering:** ODINS RAVEN VIKING EXHIBN NEW YORK 1980 **Note:** Same as KM#51.1, different edge lettering.

Date	Mintage	F	VF	XF	Unc	BU
1980 AA Prooflike	20,000	—	—	—	4.00	5.00
1980PM AB Prooflike	Inc. above	—	—	—	4.00	5.00
1980PM AC Prooflike	Inc. above	—	—	—	4.00	5.00

KM# 70.1 50 PENCE
13.5000 g., Copper-Nickel, 30 mm. **Ruler:** Elizabeth II **Obv:** Young bust right **Obv. Designer:** Arnold Machin **Rev:** Viking longship within design **Rev. Designer:** Leslie Lindsay **Shape:** 7-sided

Date	Mintage	F	VF	XF	Unc	BU
1980 AA	10,000	—	—	1.00	5.00	7.50
1980 AB	—	—	—	1.00	5.00	7.50
1980PM DD Proof	—	Value: 8.00				

KM# 70.2 50 PENCE
13.5000 g., Copper-Nickel **Ruler:** Elizabeth II **Obv:** Young bust right **Obv. Designer:** Arnold Machin **Rev:** Viking longship within design **Rev. Designer:** Leslie Lindsay **Shape:** 7-sided

Date	Mintage	F	VF	XF	Unc	BU
1981 AA	—	—	—	1.00	5.00	7.50
1982 (b)	—	—	—	1.00	5.00	7.50
1982 (b) Proof	Est. 25,000	Value: 8.00				
1982 AC	—	—	—	1.00	5.00	7.50
1983 AA	—	—	—	1.00	5.00	7.50
1983 AB	—	—	—	1.00	5.00	7.50
1984 AA	—	—	—	1.00	5.00	7.50

KM# 125 50 PENCE
13.5000 g., Copper-Nickel, 30 mm. **Ruler:** Elizabeth II **Subject:** Quincentenary of the College of Arms **Obv:** Young bust right **Obv. Designer:** Arnold Machin **Rev:** Viking longship on shield **Shape:** 7-sided

Date	Mintage	F	VF	XF	Unc	BU
1984 AA	—	—	—	—	5.00	6.00
1984 AB	—	—	—	—	5.00	6.00

KM# 148 50 PENCE
13.5000 g., Copper-Nickel, 30 mm. **Ruler:** Elizabeth II **Obv:** Crowned head right **Obv. Designer:** Raphael Maklouf **Rev:** Viking longship on shield **Shape:** 7-sided

Date	Mintage	F	VF	XF	Unc	BU
1985(w) AA	—	—	—	—	5.00	6.00
1985(w) AB	—	—	—	—	5.00	6.00
1985 (w) Proof	50,000	Value: 8.00				
1986 AA	—	—	—	—	5.00	6.00
1986 AB	—	—	—	—	5.00	6.00
1987 AA	—	—	—	—	5.00	6.00

KM# 212 50 PENCE
13.5000 g., Copper-Nickel, 30 mm. **Ruler:** Elizabeth II **Obv:** Crowned head right **Obv. Designer:** Raphael Maklouf **Rev:** Computer **Shape:** 7-sided

Date	Mintage	F	VF	XF	Unc	BU
1988 AA	—	—	—	—	5.00	6.00
1989 AA	—	—	—	—	5.00	6.00
1990 AA	—	—	—	—	5.00	6.00
1991 AA	—	—	—	—	5.00	6.00
1992 AA	—	—	—	—	5.00	6.00
1993 AA	—	—	—	—	5.00	6.00
1994 AA	—	—	—	—	5.00	6.00
1995 AA	—	—	—	—	5.00	6.00
1997 AA	—	—	—	—	5.00	6.00

KM# 806 50 PENCE
8.0000 g., Copper Nickel, 27.3 mm. **Ruler:** Elizabeth II **Obv:** Crowned head right **Obv. Designer:** Raphael Maklouf **Rev:** Two motorcycle racers **Edge:** Plain **Shape:** 7-sided

Date	Mintage	F	VF	XF	Unc	BU
1997PM AA	—	—	—	—	3.00	4.00

KM# 1258 50 PENCE
8.0000 g., Copper-Nickel, 21.5 mm. **Ruler:** Elizabeth II **Obv:** Head with tiara right **Obv. Designer:** Ian Rank-Broadley **Rev:** Milner's Tower **Edge:** Plain **Shape:** 7-sided

Date	Mintage	F	VF	XF	Unc	BU
2004PM AA	—	—	—	—	2.25	2.75
2004PM AB	—	—	—	—	2.25	2.75
2005PM AA	—	—	—	—	2.25	2.75
2005PM AB	—	—	—	—	2.25	2.75
2006PM AA	—	—	—	—	2.25	2.75
2006PM AB	—	—	—	—	2.25	2.75
2007PM AA	—	—	—	—	2.25	2.75
2007PM AB	—	—	—	—	2.25	2.75

KM# 1262 50 PENCE
8.0000 g., Copper-Nickel, 27.3 mm. **Ruler:** Elizabeth II **Subject:** Christmas **Obv:** Head with tiara right **Obv. Designer:** Ian Rank-Broadley **Rev:** Laxey Wheel **Edge:** Plain **Shape:** 7-sided

Date	Mintage	F	VF	XF	Unc	BU
2004PM AA	—	—	—	—	6.00	7.00
2004PM BA	30,000	—	—	—	6.00	7.00

KM# 1321.1 50 PENCE
8.0000 g., Copper-Nickel, 27.3 mm. **Ruler:** Elizabeth II **Series:** 12 Days of Christmas **Obv:** Head with tiara right **Obv. Legend:** ISLE OF MAN - ELIZABETH II **Obv. Designer:** Ian Rank-Broadley **Rev:** Two Turtle Doves, multicolor **Rev. Legend:** CHRISTMAS **Edge:** Plain **Shape:** 7-sided

Date	Mintage	F	VF	XF	Unc	BU
2006PM	—	—	—	—	6.00	7.00

KM# 1321.2 50 PENCE
8.0000 g., Copper-Nickel, 27.3 mm. **Ruler:** Elizabeth II **Series:** 12 Days of Christmas **Obv:** Head with tiara right **Obv. Legend:** ISLE OF MAN - ELIZABETH II **Obv. Designer:** Ian Rank-Broadley **Rev:** Two Turtle Doves **Rev. Legend:** CHRISTMAS **Edge:** Plain **Shape:** 7-sided

Date	Mintage	F	VF	XF	Unc	BU
2006PM	—	—	—	—	8.00	10.00

KM# 1322.1 50 PENCE
8.0000 g., Copper-Nickel, 27.3 mm. **Ruler:** Elizabeth II **Series:** 12 Days of Christmas **Obv:** Head with tiara right **Obv. Legend:** ISLE OF MAN - ELIZABETH II **Obv. Designer:** Ian Rank-Broadley **Rev:** Three French Hens **Rev. Legend:** CHRISTMAS **Edge:** Plain **Shape:** 7-sided

Date	Mintage	F	VF	XF	Unc	BU
2007PM	—	—	—	—	6.00	7.00

KM# 1322.2 50 PENCE
8.0000 g., Copper-Nickel, 27.3 mm. **Ruler:** Elizabeth II **Series:** 12 Days of Christmas **Obv:** Head with tiara right **Obv. Legend:** ISLE OF MAN - ELIZABETH II **Obv. Designer:** Ian Rank-Broadley **Rev:** Three French Hens, multicolor **Rev. Legend:** CHRISTMAS **Edge:** Plain **Shape:** 7-sided

Date	Mintage	F	VF	XF	Unc	BU
2007PM	—	—	—	—	8.00	10.00

KM# 44 SOVEREIGN (Pound)
Virenium **Ruler:** Elizabeth II **Obv:** Young bust right **Obv. Designer:** Arnold Machin **Rev:** Triskeles flanked by designs

Date	Mintage	F	VF	XF	Unc	BU
1978 AA	—	—	—	—	3.00	3.50
1978 AB	—	—	—	—	3.00	3.50
1978 AC	—	—	—	—	2.50	3.00
1978 AD	3,780	—	—	—	7.50	8.50
1978 BB Proof	150,000	—	—	—	—	—
1978 BC Proof	Inc. above	Value: 3.50				
1979 AA(t)	—	—	—	—	2.50	3.00
1979 AB(t)	—	—	—	—	2.50	3.00
1979 AC(t)	—	—	—	—	2.50	3.00
1979 BB(t) Proof	—	Value: 3.50				
1979 (t) Crossed oars	—	—	—	—	2.50	3.00
1980 AA DMIHE	30,000	—	—	—	2.50	3.00
1980 AA DMIHEN	—	—	—	—	2.50	3.00
1980 AA TT	—	—	—	—	2.50	3.00
1980 AB DMIHE	—	—	—	—	2.50	3.00
1980 AB DHIHEN	—	—	—	—	2.50	3.00
1980 AB TT	—	—	—	—	5.50	6.50
1980 AC DMIHE	100,000	—	—	—	2.50	3.00
1980PM BB Proof	5,000	Value: 10.00				
1980 AA	—	—	—	—	2.50	3.00
1980 AB	—	—	—	—	2.50	3.00
1980 AC	—	—	—	—	2.50	3.00
1981PM BB Proof	26,000	Value: 10.00				
1981 AA	—	—	—	—	2.50	3.00
1982PM (b) Proof	—	—	—	—	—	—

KM# 109 SOVEREIGN (Pound)
9.5000 g., Nickel-Brass, 22.5 mm. **Ruler:** Elizabeth II **Obv:** Young bust right **Obv. Designer:** Arnold Machin **Rev:** City view with ships within circle **Rev. Designer:** Leslie Lindsay

Date	Mintage	F	VF	XF	Unc	BU
1983 AA	—	—	—	—	3.50	4.00
1983 AB	—	—	—	—	3.50	4.00

KM# 128 SOVEREIGN (Pound)
9.5000 g., Nickel-Brass, 22.5 mm. **Ruler:** Elizabeth II **Obv:** Young bust right **Obv. Designer:** Arnold Machin **Rev:** Crown flanked by designs above city view within shield **Rev. Designer:** Leslie Lindsay **Edge:** Reeded, smooth alternating edge

Date	Mintage	F	VF	XF	Unc	BU
1984 D	—	—	—	—	4.00	4.50
1984 AA	—	—	—	—	4.00	4.50

KM# 151 SOVEREIGN (Pound)
9.5000 g., Nickel-Brass, 22.5 mm. **Ruler:** Elizabeth II **Obv:** Crowned head right **Obv. Designer:** Raphael Maklouf **Rev:** Shield **Rev. Designer:** Leslie Lindsay **Edge:** Smooth, reeded alternating edge

Date	Mintage	F	VF	XF	Unc	BU
1985 AA	—	—	—	—	3.50	4.00
1985 AA Proof	25,000	Value: 6.00				
1985(w) AA	—	—	—	—	3.50	4.00
1985 AA Proof	25,000	Value: 6.00				

KM# 175 SOVEREIGN (Pound)

9.5000 g., Nickel-Brass, 22.5 mm. **Ruler:** Elizabeth II **Obv:** Crowned head right **Obv. Designer:** Raphael Maklouf **Rev:** Shield **Rev. Designer:** Leslie Lindsay

Date	Mintage	F	VF	XF	Unc	BU
1986	—	—	—	—	3.50	4.00
1986 Proof	25,000	Value: 6.00				

KM# 182 SOVEREIGN (Pound)

9.5000 g., Nickel-Brass, 22.5 mm. **Ruler:** Elizabeth II **Obv:** Crowned head right **Obv. Designer:** Raphael Maklouf **Rev:** Rearing armored equestrian within circle **Edge:** Reeded, smooth alternating edge

Date	Mintage	F	VF	XF	Unc	BU
1987 AA	—	—	—	—	3.50	4.00

KM# 213 SOVEREIGN (Pound)

9.5000 g., Nickel-Brass, 22.5 mm. **Ruler:** Elizabeth II **Obv:** Crowned head right **Obv. Designer:** Raphael Maklouf **Rev:** Cordless phone divides satellite and receiving station **Edge:** Reeded, smooth alternating edge

Date	Mintage	F	VF	XF	Unc	BU
1988 AA	—	—	—	—	2.50	3.00
1988 BB	—	—	—	—	2.50	3.00
1988 D	—	—	—	—	2.50	3.00
1989 AA	—	—	—	—	2.50	3.00
1990 AA	—	—	—	—	2.50	3.00
1991 AA	—	—	—	—	2.50	3.00
1992 AB	—	—	—	—	2.50	3.00
1993 AA	—	—	—	—	2.50	3.00
1994 AA	—	—	—	—	2.50	3.00
1995 AA	—	—	—	—	2.50	3.00

KM# 594 SOVEREIGN (Pound)

9.5000 g., Nickel-Brass, 22.5 mm. **Ruler:** Elizabeth II **Subject:** Sports **Obv:** Crowned head right **Obv. Designer:** Raphael Maklouf **Rev:** Cricket equipment

Date	Mintage	F	VF	XF	Unc	BU
1996 AA	—	—	—	—	4.00	4.50
1997 AA	—	—	—	—	4.00	4.50

KM# 655 SOVEREIGN (Pound)

9.5000 g., Nickel-Brass, 22.5 mm. **Ruler:** Elizabeth II **Subject:** Douglas Centenary **Obv:** Crowned head right **Obv. Designer:** Raphael Maklouf **Rev:** City arms **Rev. Designer:** Leslie Lindsay

Date	Mintage	F	VF	XF	Unc	BU
1996 AA	—	—	—	—	4.00	4.50

KM# 906.1 SOVEREIGN (Pound)

9.5000 g., Nickel-Brass, 22.5 mm. **Ruler:** Elizabeth II **Obv:** Head with tiara right **Obv. Designer:** Ian Rank-Broadley **Rev:** Cricket equipment flanked by sprigs

Date	Mintage	F	VF	XF	Unc	BU
1998 AA	—	—	—	—	4.00	4.50

KM# 906.2 POUND

9.5000 g., Nickel-Brass, 22.5 mm. **Ruler:** Elizabeth II **Obv:** Head with tiara right with small triskeles dividing legend **Obv. Designer:** Ian Rank-Broadley **Rev:** Cricket equipment

Date	Mintage	F	VF	XF	Unc	BU
1998PM AA	—	—	—	—	4.00	4.50
1999PM AA	—	—	—	—	4.00	4.50

KM# 1042 POUND

9.5000 g., Brass, 22.5 mm. **Ruler:** Elizabeth II **Subject:** Millennium Bells **Obv:** Head with tiara right **Obv. Designer:** Ian Rank-Broadley **Rev:** Triskeles and three bells **Edge:** Reeded and plain sections

Date	Mintage	F	VF	XF	Unc	BU
2000PM AA	—	—	—	—	4.00	5.00
2001PM AA	—	—	—	—	4.00	5.00
2002PM AA	—	—	—	—	4.00	5.00
2003PM AA	—	—	—	—	4.00	5.00

KM# 1259 POUND

9.5000 g., Nickel-Brass, 22.5 mm. **Ruler:** Elizabeth II **Obv:** Head with tiara right **Obv. Designer:** Ian Rank-Broadley **Rev:** St. John's Chapel **Edge:** Reeded and Plain Sections

Date	Mintage	F	VF	XF	Unc	BU
2004PM AA	—	—	—	—	4.00	5.00
2004PM AB	—	—	—	—	4.00	5.00
2004PM AC	—	—	—	—	4.00	5.00
2005PM AA	—	—	—	—	4.00	5.00
2005PM AB	—	—	—	—	4.00	5.00
2006PM AA	—	—	—	—	4.00	5.00
2006PM AB	—	—	—	—	4.00	5.00
2007PM AA	—	—	—	—	4.00	5.00
2007PM AB	—	—	—	—	4.00	5.00

KM# 167 2 POUNDS

Virenium **Ruler:** Elizabeth II **Obv:** Crowned head right **Obv. Designer:** Raphael Maklouf **Rev:** Bird above towered building

Date	Mintage	F	VF	XF	Unc	BU
1986 (vw)	—	—	—	—	7.50	8.50
1986 Proof	—	Value: 10.00				
1987 AA	—	—	—	—	7.50	8.50

KM# 214 2 POUNDS

Virenium **Ruler:** Elizabeth II **Obv:** Crowned head right **Obv. Designer:** Raphael Maklouf **Rev:** BAC 146-100 jet

Date	Mintage	F	VF	XF	Unc	BU
1988 AA	—	—	—	—	7.50	8.50
1988 D	—	—	—	—	7.50	8.50
1989	—	—	—	—	7.50	8.50
1990 AA	—	—	—	—	7.50	8.50
1991 AA	—	—	—	—	7.50	8.50
1992 AA	—	—	—	—	7.50	8.50
1993 AA	—	—	—	—	7.50	8.50

KM# 257 2 POUNDS

Virenium **Ruler:** Elizabeth II **Obv:** Crowned head right **Obv. Designer:** Raphael Maklouf **Rev:** Blimp

Date	Mintage	F	VF	XF	Unc	BU
1989 AA Rare	—	—	—	—	—	—

Note: Most recalled by government; Few actually issued

KM# 1043 2 POUNDS

12.0000 g., Bi-Metallic Copper-Nickel center in Brass ring, 28.4 mm. **Ruler:** Elizabeth II **Subject:** Thorwald's Cross **Obv:** Head with tiara right within beaded circle **Obv. Designer:** Ian Rank-Broadley **Rev:** Ancient drawing within circle **Edge:** Reeded

Date	Mintage	F	VF	XF	Unc	BU
2000PM AA	—	—	—	—	6.50	7.50
2001PM AA	—	—	—	—	6.50	7.50
2002PM AA	—	—	—	—	6.50	7.50
2003PM AA	—	—	—	—	6.50	7.50

KM# 1260 2 POUNDS

12.0000 g., Bi-Metallic Copper-Nickel center in Brass ring, 28.4 mm. **Ruler:** Elizabeth II **Obv:** Head with tiara right **Obv. Designer:** Ian Rank-Broadley **Rev:** Round Tower of Peel Castle **Edge:** Reeded

Date	Mintage	F	VF	XF	Unc	BU
2004PM AA	—	—	—	—	6.50	7.50
2005PM AA	—	—	—	—	6.50	7.50
2006PM AA	—	—	—	—	6.50	7.50
2007PM AA	—	—	—	—	6.50	7.50
2007PM AB	—	—	—	—	6.50	7.50

ISRAEL

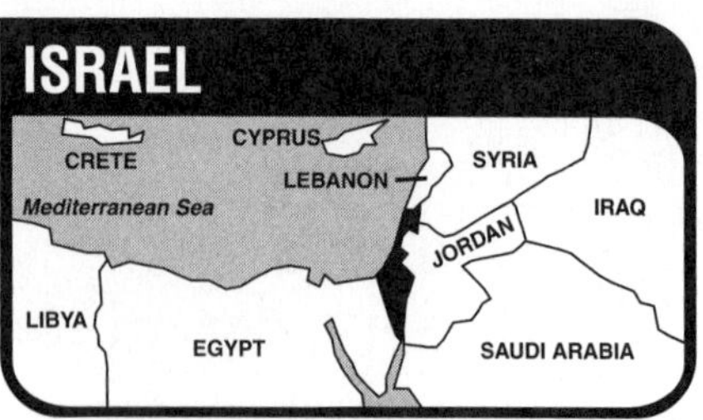

The state of Israel, a Middle Eastern republic at the eastern end of the Mediterranean Sea, bounded by Lebanon on the north, Syria on the northeast, Jordan on the east, and Egypt on the southwest, has an area of 9,000sq. mi. (20,770 sq. km.) and a population of 6 million. Capital: Jerusalem. Finished diamonds, chemicals, citrus, textiles, minerals, electronic and transportation equipment are exported.

HEBREW COIN DATING

Modern Israel's coins carry Hebrew dating formed from a combination of the 22 consonant letters of the Hebrew alphabet and read from right to left. The Jewish calendar dates back more than 5700 years; but five millenniums are assumed in the dating of coins (until 1981). Thus, the year 5735 (1975AD) appears as 735, with the first two characters from the right indicating the number of years in hundreds; tav (400), plus shin (300). The next is lamedh (30), followed by a separation mark which has the appearance of double quotation marks, then heh (5).

The separation mark - generally similar to a single quotation mark through 5718 (1958 AD), and like a double quotation mark thereafter - serves the purpose of indicating that the letters form a number, not a word, and on some issues can be confused with the character yodh (10), which in a stylized rendering can appear similar, although slightly larger and thicker. The separation mark does not appear in either form on a few commemorative issues.

The Jewish New Year falls in September or October by Christian calendar reckoning. Where dual dating is encountered, with but a few exceptions the Hebrew dating on the coins of modern Israel is 3760 years greater than the Christian dating; 5735 is equivalent to 1975AD, with the 5000 assumed until 1981, when full dates appear on the coins. These exceptions are most of the Hanukka coins, (Feast of Lights), the Bank of Israel gold 50 Pound commemorative of 5725 (1964AD) and others. In such special instances the differential from Christian dating is 3761 years, except in the instance of the 5720 Chanuka Pound, which is dated 1960AD, as is the issue of 5721, an arrangement reflecting the fact that the events fall early in the Jewish year and late in the Christian.

The Star of David is not a mintmark. It appears only on some coins sold by the Israel Government Coins and Medals Corporation Ltd., which is owned by the Israel government, and is a division of the Prime Minister's office and sole distributor to collectors. The Star of David was first used in 1971 on the science coin to signify that it was minted in Jerusalem, but was later used by different mint facilities.

AD Date		Jewish Era
1948	תש״ח	5708
1949	תש״ט	5709
1952	תשי״ב	5712
1954	תשי״ד	5714
1955	תשט״ו	5715
1957	תשי״ז	5717
1958	תשי״ח	5718
1959	תשי״ט	5719
1960	תש״ך	5720
1960	תשך	5720
1961	תשכ״א	5721
1962	תשכ״ב	5722
1963	תשכ״ג	5723
1964	תשכ״ד	5724
1965	תשכ״ה	5725

1966	תשכ״ו	5726
1967	תשכ״ז	5727
1968	תשכ״ח	5728
1969	תשכ״ט	5729
1970	תש״ל	5730
1971	תשל״א	5731
1972	תשל״ב	5732
1973	תשל״ג	5733
1974	תשל״ד	5734
1975	תשל״ה	5735
1976	תשל״ו	5736
1977	תשל״ז	5737
1978	תשל״ח	5738
1979	תשל״ט	5739
1980	תש״ם	5740
1981	תשמ״א	5741
1981	התשמ״א	5741
1982	התשמ״ב	5742
1983	התשמ״ג	5743
1984	התשמ״ד	5744
1985	התשמ״ה	5745
1986	התשמ״ו	5746
1987	התשמ״ז	5747
1988	התשמ״ח	5748
1989	התשמ״ט	5749
1990	התש״ן	5750
1991	התשנ״א	5751
1992	התשנ״ב	5752
1993	התשנ״ג	5753
1994	התשנ״ד	5754
1995	התשנ״ה	5755
1996	התשנ״ו	5756
1997	התשנ״ז	5757
1998	התשנ״ח	5758
1999	התשנ״ט	5759
2000	התש״ס	5760
2001	התשס״א	5761
2002	התשס״ב	5762
2003	התשס״ג	5763
2004	התשס״ד	5764
2005	התשס״ה	5765
2006	התשס״ו	5766
2007	התשס״ז	5767
2008	התשס״ח	5768
2009	התשס״ט	5769
2010	התש״ע	5770

MINT MARKS
(o) - Ottawa
(s) - San Francisco
None – Jerusalem

(M) MATTE - Normal circulation strike or a dull finish produced by sandblasting special uncirculated (polish finish) or proof quality dies.

(U) SPECIAL UNCIRCULATED - Polished or prooflike in appearance without any frosted features.

(P) PROOF - The highest quality obtainable having mirror-like fields and frosted features.

MONETARY SYSTEM
1000 Mils = 1 Pound

REPUBLIC

MIL COINAGE

KM# 8 25 MILS
Aluminum, 30 mm. **Obv:** Grape cluster **Rev:** Value within wreath **Note:** Released April 6, 1949.

Date	Mintage	F	VF	XF	Unc	BU
JE5708 (1948)(hn)	43,000	35.00	75.00	200	800	1,000
JE5709 (1949) closed link	—	5.00	10.00	15.00	50.00	—
JE5709 (1949) open link	650,000	15.00	25.00	70.00	150	—

REFORM COINAGE

1000 Pruta (Prutot) = 1 Lira

NOTE: The 1949 Pruta coins, except for the 100 and 500 Pruta values, occur with and without a small pearl under the bar connecting the wreath on the reverse. Only the 50 and 100 Pruta coins were issued in 5709. All later coins were struck with frozen dates.

KM# 9 PRUTA
Aluminum, 21 mm. **Obv:** Anchor **Rev:** Value within wreath

Date	Mintage	F	VF	XF	Unc	BU
JE5709 (1949)(i) With pearl	2,685,000	—	0.50	1.00	2.00	—
JE5709(1949)(j) With pearl, Proof like	Inc. above	—	—	—	5.00	—
JE5709 (1949)(ht) Without pearl	2,500,000	1.00	2.00	5.00	20.00	—
JE5709 (1949)(i) Proof	20,000	Value: 500				

KM# 10 5 PRUTOT
3.1800 g., Bronze, 20 mm. **Obv:** 4-stringed lyre

Date	Mintage	F	VF	XF	Unc	BU
JE5709 (1949)(i) With pearl	5,045,000	—	0.50	1.00	2.50	—
JE5709 (1949)(i) Proof	25,000	Value: 500				
JE5709(1949)(ht) Without pearl	5,000,000	1.00	3.50	8.00	20.00	—

KM# 11 10 PRUTOT
6.1000 g., Bronze, 27 mm. **Obv:** Amphora **Rev:** Value within wreath

Date	Mintage	F	VF	XF	Unc	BU
JE5709 (1949)(i) With pearl	7,448,000	—	0.75	5.00	20.00	—
JE5709 (1949)(i) Proof	20,000	Value: 500				
JE5709 (1949)(ht) Without pearl	7,500,000	—	0.50	1.00	3.00	—

KM# 17 10 PRUTOT
1.5900 g., Aluminum, 24.5 mm. **Obv:** Ceremonial pitcher flanked by sprigs **Rev:** Value within wreath **Shape:** Scalloped

Date	Mintage	F	VF	XF	Unc	BU
JE5712 (1952)(i)	26,042,000	—	0.35	0.75	2.00	—

KM# 20 10 PRUTOT
1.6000 g., Aluminum, 24.5 mm. **Obv:** Ceremonial pitcher flanked by sprigs **Rev:** Value within wreath

Date	Mintage	F	VF	XF	Unc	BU
JE5717 (1957)(t)	1,000,000	—	0.35	0.75	2.50	—

KM# 20a 10 PRUTOT
Copper Electroplated Aluminum, 24.5 mm. **Obv:** Ceremonial pitcher flanked by sprigs **Rev:** Value within wreath

Date	Mintage	F	VF	XF	Unc	BU
JE5717 (1957)(t)	1,088,000	—	0.35	0.75	2.00	—

KM# 12 25 PRUTA
Copper-Nickel, 19.5 mm. **Obv:** Grape cluster **Rev:** Value within wreath

Date	Mintage	F	VF	XF	Unc	BU
JE5709 (1949)(i) With pearl	10,520,000	—	0.50	0.75	2.00	—
JE5709 (1949)(ht) Without pearl	2,500,000	—	5.00	10.00	30.00	—
JE5709 (1949)(i) Proof	20,000	Value: 500				

KM# 12a 25 PRUTA
Nickel-Clad Steel, 19.5 mm. **Obv:** Grape cluster **Rev:** Value within wreath

Date	Mintage	F	VF	XF	Unc	BU
JE5714 (1954)(t)	3,697,000	—	0.50	1.00	2.50	—

KM# 13.1 50 PRUTA
5.6200 g., Copper-Nickel, 23.5 mm. **Obv:** Grape leaves **Rev:** Value within wreath **Edge:** Reeded

Date	Mintage	F	VF	XF	Unc	BU
JE5709 (1949)(i)	6,040,000	—	5.00	10.00	25.00	—
JE5709 (1949)(i) Proof	20,000	Value: 500				
JE5709 (1949) Without pearl	Inc. above	—	0.75	1.50	3.00	—
JE5714 (1954)(t)	250,000	—	5.00	15.00	32.00	—

KM# 13.2 50 PRUTA
Copper-Nickel, 23.5 mm. **Obv:** Grape leaves **Rev:** Value within wreath **Edge:** Plain

Date	Mintage	F	VF	XF	Unc	BU
JE5714 (1954)(t)	4,500,000	—	0.50	1.00	2.00	—

KM# 13.2a 50 PRUTA
5.0100 g., Nickel-Clad Steel, 23.6 mm. **Obv:** Grape leaves **Rev:** Value within wreath **Edge:** Plain

Date	Mintage	F	VF	XF	Unc	BU
JE5714 (1954)(t)	17,774,000	—	0.50	1.00	2.00	—

KM# 14 100 PRUTA
Copper-Nickel, 28.5 mm. **Obv:** Date palm **Rev:** Value within wreath

Date	Mintage	F	VF	XF	Unc	BU
JE5709 (1949)	6,062,000	—	0.75	1.25	2.50	—

Note: 3,062,000 minted at (j) and 3,000,000 minted at (ht).

Date	Mintage	F	VF	XF	Unc	BU
JE5709 (1949)(i) Proof	20,000	Value: 500				
JE5715 (1955)(t)	5,868,000	—	1.00	1.50	2.50	—

KM# 19 100 PRUTA
Nickel-Coated Steel, 25.6 mm. **Obv:** Date palm **Rev:** Value within wreath **Note:** Reduced size, greater space between wreath and rim.

Date	Mintage	F	VF	XF	Unc	BU
JE5714 (1954)(u)	20,000	75.00	150	300	1,000	—

KM# 18 100 PRUTA
Nickel-Clad Steel, 25.6 mm. **Obv:** Date palm **Rev:** Value within wreath **Note:** Reduced size.

Date	Mintage	F	VF	XF	Unc	BU
JE5714 (1954)(b)	700,000	—	1.00	1.50	3.00	—

KM# 15 250 PRUTA
Copper-Nickel, 32.2 mm. **Obv:** Oat sprigs **Rev:** Value within wreath

Date	Mintage	F	VF	XF	Unc	BU
JE5709 (1949)(i) With pearl	1,496,000	—	2.50	10.00	20.00	—
JE5709 (1949)(ht) Without pearl	524,000	—	1.00	2.00	5.00	—

KM# 16 500 PRUTA
25.5000 g., 0.5000 Silver 0.4099 oz. ASW, 38 mm. **Obv:** Pomegranates **Rev:** Value within wreath **Note:** Dav. #257.

Date	Mintage	F	VF	XF	Unc	BU
JE5709 (1949)(ht)	34,000	—	8.50	12.50	35.00	50.00

Note: Not placed into circulation

REFORM COINAGE

100 Agorot = 1 Lira

Commencing January 1, 1960-1980

KM# 24.1 AGORA
1.0000 g., Aluminum, 20 mm. **Obv:** Text to left and below oat sprigs **Rev:** Value **Shape:** Scalloped

Date	Mintage	F	VF	XF	Unc	BU
JE5720 (1960)	12,768,000	—	4.00	8.00	20.00	—
Note: Letter "Lamed" in Israel with serif						
JE5720 (1960)	Inc. above	—	10.00	20.00	100	—
Note: Letter "Lamed" in Israel without lower serif						
JE5720 (1960)	300	—	150	300	750	—
Note: Large date						
JE5721 (1961)	19,262,000	—	0.50	2.00	5.00	—
JE5721 (1961)	Inc. above	—	5.00	15.00	100	—
Note: Thick date						
JE5721 (1961)	Inc. above	—	5.00	15.00	100	—
Note: Wide date						
JE5722 (1962)	14,500,000	—	0.10	0.40	0.75	—
Note: Large date						
JE5722 (1962)	Inc. above	—	5.00	10.00	20.00	—
Note: Small date, small serifs						
JE5723 (1963)	14,804,000	—	0.10	0.40	0.75	—
Note: Medal alignment						
JE5723 (1963)	10,000	—	2.50	4.50	10.00	20.00
Note: Coin alignment						
JE5724 (1964)	27,552,000	—	—	—	0.75	—
JE5725 (1965)	20,708,000	—	—	—	0.25	—
JE5726 (1966)	10,165,000	—	—	—	0.25	—
JE5727 (1967)	6,781,000	—	—	—	0.25	—
JE5728 (1968)	20,899,000	—	—	—	0.25	—
JE5729 (1969)	22,120,000	—	—	—	0.25	—
JE5730 (1970)	17,748,000	—	—	—	0.25	—
JE5731 (1971)	10,290,000	—	—	—	0.25	—
JE5732 (1972)	24,512,000	—	—	—	0.25	—
JE5733 (1973)	20,496,000	—	—	—	0.25	—
JE5734 (1974)(j) Matte	8,080,000	—	—	—	0.75	—
JE5734 (1974)(o) Prooflike	34,000,000	—	—	—	0.25	—
JE5735 (1975)	1,574,000	—	—	—	0.25	—
JE5736 (1976)	4,512,000	—	—	—	0.25	—
JE5737 (1977)	9,680,000	—	—	—	0.25	—
JE5738 (1978)	8,864,000	—	—	—	0.25	—
JE5739 (1979)	4,048,000	—	—	—	0.25	—
JE5740 (1980)	2,600,000	—	—	—	1.00	—

KM# 24.2 AGORA
1.0000 g., Aluminum, 20 mm. **Obv:** Text to left and below oat sprigs, star of David in field **Rev:** Value **Edge:** Plain **Shape:** Scalloped

Date	Mintage	F	VF	XF	Unc	BU
JE5731 (1971)(j)	125,921	—	—	—	0.75	—
JE5732 (1972)(j)	68,513	—	—	—	0.75	—
JE5734 (1974)(j)	92,868	—	—	—	0.75	—
JE5735 (1975)(j)	61,686	—	—	—	1.00	—
JE5736 (1976)(j)	64,654	—	—	—	0.75	—
JE5737 (1977)(j)	37,208	—	—	—	1.00	—
JE5738 (1978)(j)	57,072	—	—	—	0.75	—
JE5739 (1979)(j)	31,590	—	—	—	1.00	—

KM# 96 AGORA
Nickel, 20 mm. **Subject:** 25th Anniversary - Bank of Israel **Obv:** Text to left and below oat sprigs **Rev:** Value **Shape:** Scalloped **Note:** Struck for sets only

Date	Mintage	F	VF	XF	Unc	BU
JE5740 (1980)(b)	35,000	—	—	—	2.00	—

KM# 25 5 AGOROT
2.3600 g., Aluminum-Bronze, 16.53 mm. **Obv:** Pomegranates **Rev:** Value **Edge:** Plain

Date	Mintage	F	VF	XF	Unc	BU
JE5720 (1960)	8,019,000	—	5.00	10.00	25.00	—
JE5721 (1961)	15,090,000	—	0.25	0.50	1.50	—
Note: Sharp, flat date						
JE5721 (1961)	5,000,000	—	10.00	20.00	60.00	—
Note: I.C.I. issue; high date with serifs						
JE5722 (1962) Large date	11,198,000	—	0.25	0.50	1.00	—
JE5722 (1962) Small date	Inc. above	—	5.00	10.00	25.00	—
JE5723 (1963)	1,429,000	—	0.25	0.50	1.25	—
JE5724 (1964)	21,000	—	12.00	120	400	500
JE5725 (1965)	201,000	—	—	0.10	0.25	—
JE5726 (1966)	291,000	—	—	0.10	0.25	—
JE5727 (1967)	2,195,000	—	—	0.10	0.25	—
JE5728 (1968)	4,019,999	—	—	0.10	0.25	—
JE5729 (1969)	2,200,000	—	—	0.10	0.25	—
JE5730 (1970)	4,003,999	—	—	0.10	0.25	—
JE5731 (1971)	14,010,000	—	—	0.10	0.25	—
JE5732 (1972)	9,005,000	—	—	0.10	0.25	—
JE5733 (1973)	25,720,000	—	—	0.10	0.25	—
JE5734 (1974)	10,470,000	—	—	0.10	0.25	—
JE5735 (1975)	10,232,000	—	—	0.10	0.25	—
JE5736 (1976)	—	—	—	0.10	0.25	—
JE5737 (1977)	—	—	—	0.10	0.25	—

KM# 25a 5 AGOROT
2.3000 g., Aluminum-Bronze, 17.5 mm. **Obv:** Pomegranates, Star of David in field **Rev:** Value

Date	Mintage	F	VF	XF	Unc	BU
JE5731 (1971)(j)	125,921	—	—	—	0.75	—
JE5732 (1972)(j)	68,513	—	—	—	0.75	—

KM# 25b 5 AGOROT
0.7700 g., Aluminum, 17.5 mm. **Obv:** Pomegranates **Rev:** Value

Date	Mintage	F	VF	XF	Unc	BU
JE5736 (1976)	13,156,000	—	—	0.10	0.50	—
JE5737 (1977)(j) Matte	16,800,000	—	—	0.10	0.50	—
JE5737 (1977)(o) Prooflike	15,000,000	—	—	0.10	0.50	—
JE5738 (1978)(j) Matte	21,480,000	—	—	0.10	0.50	—
JE5738 (1978)(o) Prooflike	38,760,000	—	—	0.10	0.50	—
JE5739 (1979)	12,836,000	—	—	0.10	0.50	—

KM# 25c 5 AGOROT
Copper-Nickel, 17.5 mm. **Rev:** Value

Date	Mintage	F	VF	XF	Unc	BU
JE5735 (1974)(j)	92,868	—	—	—	0.75	—
JE5735 (1975)(j)	61,686	—	—	—	1.00	—
JE5736 (1976)(j)	64,654	—	—	—	0.75	—
JE5737 (1977)(j)	37,208	—	—	—	1.00	—
JE5738 (1978)(j)	57,072	—	—	—	0.75	—
JE5739 (1979)(j)	31,590	—	—	—	1.00	—

KM# 97 5 AGOROT
Nickel, 17.5 mm. **Subject:** 25th Anniversary - Bank of Israel **Obv:** Pomegranates **Rev:** Value **Note:** Struck for sets only.

Date	Mintage	F	VF	XF	Unc	BU
JE5740 (1980)(b)	35,000	—	—	—	2.00	—

KM# 26 10 AGOROT
5.0000 g., Aluminum-Bronze, 21.5 mm. **Obv:** Date palm **Rev:** Value

Date	Mintage	F	VF	XF	Unc	BU
JE5720 (1960)	14,397,000	—	0.50	1.00	10.00	—
JE5721 (1961)	12,821,000	—	0.50	1.00	6.00	—
JE5721 (1961)	Inc. above	—	25.00	60.00	325	—
Note: "Fatha" in Arabic, legend: "Israel"						
JE5722 (1962) Large date, thick letters	8,845,000	—	0.25	0.50	1.00	—
JE5722 (1962) Small date, thin letters	Inc. above	—	5.00	10.00	20.00	—
JE5723 (1963)	3,931,000	—	0.25	0.50	1.00	—
JE5724 (1964) Large date	3,612,000	—	0.25	0.50	1.00	—
JE5724 (1964) Small date	Inc. above	—	8.00	15.00	50.00	—
JE5725 (1965)	201,000	—	—	0.20	0.25	—
JE5726 (1966)	7,276,000	—	—	0.10	0.25	—
JE5727 (1967)	6,426,000	—	—	0.10	0.25	—
JE5728 (1968)	4,825,000	—	—	0.10	0.25	—
JE5729 (1969)	6,810,000	—	—	0.10	0.25	—
JE5730 (1970)	6,131,000	—	—	0.10	0.25	—
JE5731 (1971)	6,810,000	—	—	0.10	0.25	—
JE5732 (1972)	19,653,000	—	—	0.10	0.25	—

Date	Mintage	F	VF	XF	Unc	BU
JE5733 (1973)	16,205,000	—	—	0.10	0.25	—
JE5734 (1974)	22,040,000	—	—	0.10	0.25	—
JE5735 (1975)	25,135,000	—	—	0.10	0.25	—
JE5736 (1976)	54,870,000	—	—	0.10	0.25	—
JE5737 (1977)	27,886,000	—	—	0.10	0.25	—

KM# 26a 10 AGOROT

5.0000 g., Aluminum-Bronze, 21.5 mm. **Obv:** Date palm with star of David in field **Rev:** Value

Date	Mintage	F	VF	XF	Unc	BU
JE5731 (1971)(j)	125,921	—	—	—	0.75	—
JE5732 (1972)(j)	68,513	—	—	—	0.75	—

KM# 26b 10 AGOROT

1.6100 g., Aluminum, 21.5 mm. **Obv:** Date palm **Rev:** Value

Date	Mintage	F	VF	XF	Unc	BU
JE5737 (1977)(o) Prooflike	30,100,000	—	—	0.10	0.25	—
JE5738 (1978)(j) Matte	24,050,000	—	—	0.10	0.25	—
JE5738 (1978)(o) Prooflike	104,336,000	—	—	0.10	0.25	—
JE5739 (1979)	22,201,000	—	—	0.10	0.25	—
JE5740 (1980)	4,752,000	—	—	0.10	0.25	—

Note: Most of the 5740 dated coins were melted down before being issued.

KM# 65 10 AGOROT

Copper-Nickel, 21.5 mm. **Subject:** 25th Anniversary of Independence **Obv:** Date palm **Rev:** Value **Note:** In sets only.

Date	Mintage	F	VF	XF	Unc	BU
JE5733 (1973)(j)	98,107	—	—	—	0.75	—

KM# 98 10 AGOROT

Nickel, 21.5 mm. **Subject:** 25th Anniversary - Bank of Israel **Obv:** Date palm **Rev:** Value **Note:** Struck for sets only.

Date	Mintage	F	VF	XF	Unc	BU
JE5740 (1980)(b)	35,000	—	—	—	2.00	—

KM# 27 25 AGOROT

6.5000 g., Aluminum-Bronze, 25.5 mm. **Obv:** Three-string lyre **Rev:** Value

Date	Mintage	F	VF	XF	Unc	BU
JE5720 (1960)	4,391,000	—	0.25	0.50	3.00	—
JE5721 (1961)	5,009,000	—	0.10	0.20	1.00	—
JE5722 (1962)	882,000	—	0.15	0.30	1.00	—
JE5723 (1963)	194,000	—	0.50	1.00	5.00	—
JE5724 (1964)	—	—	—	—	—	—

Note: Five trial pieces only

Date	Mintage	F	VF	XF	Unc	BU
JE5725 (1965)	187,000	—	0.10	0.20	0.50	—
JE5726 (1966)	320,000	—	—	0.10	0.40	—
JE5727 (1967)	325,000	—	—	0.10	0.40	—
JE5728 (1968)	445,000	—	—	0.10	0.40	—
JE5729 (1969)	432,000	—	—	0.10	0.40	—
JE5730 (1970)	417,000	—	—	0.10	0.40	—
JE5731 (1971)	500,000	—	—	0.10	0.40	—
JE5732 (1972)	1,883,000	—	—	0.10	0.40	—
JE5733 (1973)	3,370,000	—	—	0.10	0.40	—
JE5734 (1974)	2,320,000	—	—	0.10	0.40	—
JE5735 (1975)	3,968,000	—	—	0.10	0.40	—
JE5736 (1976)	3,901,000	—	—	0.10	0.40	—
JE5737 (1977)	1,832,000	—	—	0.10	0.40	—
JE5738 (1978)	12,200,000	—	—	0.10	0.40	—
JE5739 (1979)	10,842,000	—	—	0.10	0.40	—

KM# 27a 25 AGOROT

6.5000 g., Aluminum-Bronze, 25.5 mm. **Obv:** Three stringed lyre with star of David in field **Rev:** Value

Date	Mintage	F	VF	XF	Unc	BU
JE5731 (1971)(j)	125,921	—	—	—	0.75	—
JE5732 (1972)(j)	68,513	—	—	—	0.75	—

KM# 27b 25 AGOROT

Copper-Nickel, 25.5 mm. **Obv:** Three stringed lyre with star of David in field **Rev:** Value **Note:** Struck for sets only.

Date	Mintage	F	VF	XF	Unc	BU
JE5734 (1974)(j)	92,868	—	—	—	0.75	—
JE5735 (1975)(j)	61,686	—	—	—	1.00	—
JE5736 (1976)(j)	64,654	—	—	—	0.75	—
JE5737 (1977)(j)	37,208	—	—	—	1.00	—
JE5738 (1978)(j)	57,072	—	—	—	0.75	—
JE5739 (1979)(j)	31,590	—	—	—	1.00	—

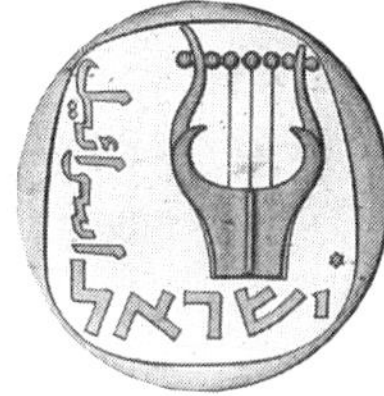

KM# 99 25 AGOROT

Nickel, 25.5 mm. **Subject:** 25th Anniversary - Bank of Israel **Obv:** Three-string lyre **Rev:** Value **Note:** Struck for sets only.

Date	Mintage	F	VF	XF	Unc	BU
JE5740 (1980)(b)	35,000	—	—	—	2.00	—

KM# 36.1 1/2 LIRA

6.8000 g., Copper-Nickel, 24.5 mm. **Obv:** Menorah flanked by sprigs **Rev:** Value

Date	Mintage	F	VF	XF	Unc	BU
JE5723 (1963) Large animals	5,593,000	—	0.50	2.00	5.00	—
JE5723 (1963) Small animals	14,000	—	3.00	15.00	30.00	—
JE5724 (1964)	3,762,000	—	0.10	0.75	2.00	—
JE5725 (1965)	1,551,000	—	0.10	0.15	1.00	—
JE5726 (1966)	2,139,000	—	0.10	0.15	0.50	—
JE5727 (1967)	1,942,000	—	0.10	0.15	0.50	—
JE5728 (1968)	1,183,000	—	0.10	0.15	0.50	—
JE5729 (1969)	450,000	—	0.10	0.20	0.60	—
JE5730 (1970)	1,000,999	—	0.10	0.20	0.60	—
JE5731 (1971)	500,000	—	0.10	0.20	0.60	—
JE5732 (1972)	421,000	—	0.10	0.20	0.60	—
JE5733 (1973)	3,225,000	—	0.10	0.15	0.50	—
JE5734 (1974)	4,275,000	—	0.10	0.15	0.50	—
JE5735 (1975)	11,066,000	—	0.10	0.15	0.50	—
JE5736 (1976)	4,959,000	—	0.10	0.15	0.50	—
JE5737 (1977)	4,983,000	—	0.10	0.15	0.50	—
JE5738 (1978)	14,325,000	—	0.10	0.15	0.50	—
JE5739 (1979)	21,391,000	—	0.10	0.15	0.50	—

KM# 100 1/2 LIRA

Nickel, 24.5 mm. **Subject:** 25th Anniversary - Bank of Israel **Obv:** Menorah flanked by sprigs **Rev:** Value **Edge:** Reeded **Note:** Struck for sets only.

Date	Mintage	F	VF	XF	Unc	BU
JE5740 (1980)(b)	35,000	—	—	—	3.00	—

KM# 37 LIRA

Copper-Nickel, 27.5 mm. **Obv:** Menorah flanked by sprigs **Rev:** Value

Date	Mintage	F	VF	XF	Unc	BU
JE5723 (1963) Large animals	4,212,000	—	0.50	1.50	3.00	—
JE5723 (1963) Small animals	Inc. above	—	1.00	10.00	20.00	—
JE5724 (1964)	—	—	—	—	—	—

Note: Only ten trial pieces struck

Date	Mintage	F	VF	XF	Unc	BU
JE5725 (1965)	166,000	—	0.25	0.50	1.25	—
JE5726 (1966)	290,000	—	0.25	0.50	1.25	—
JE5727 (1967)	180,000	—	0.25	0.50	1.25	—

KM# 47.1 LIRA

9.0000 g., Copper-Nickel, 27.5 mm. **Obv:** Pomegranates **Rev:** Value flanked by stars above text **Edge:** Reeded, smooth alternating edge

Date	Mintage	F	VF	XF	Unc	BU
JE5727 (1967)	3,830,000	—	0.10	0.25	1.00	—
JE5728 (1968)	3,932,000	—	0.10	0.25	1.00	—
JE5729 (1969)	12,484,000	—	0.10	0.25	0.75	—
JE5730 (1970)	4,794,000	—	0.10	0.25	0.75	—
JE5731 (1971)	2,993,000	—	0.10	0.25	0.75	—
JE5732 (1972)	2,489,000	—	0.10	0.25	0.75	—
JE5733 (1973)	10,265,000	—	0.10	0.25	0.75	—
JE5734 (1974)	6,287,000	—	0.10	0.25	0.75	—
JE5735 (1975)	13,225,000	—	0.10	0.25	0.75	—
JE5736 (1976)	4,268,000	—	0.10	0.25	0.75	—
JE5737 (1977)	11,129,000	—	0.10	0.25	0.75	—
JE5738 (1978)	61,752,000	—	0.10	0.25	0.75	—
JE5739 (1979)	34,815,000	—	0.10	0.25	0.75	—
JE5740 (1980)	10,840,000	—	0.10	0.25	0.75	—

Note: Most of the 5740 dated coins were melted down before being issued.

KM# 101 LIRA

9.0000 g., Nickel, 27.5 mm. **Subject:** 25th Anniversary - Bank of Israel **Obv:** Pomegranates with star of David in field **Rev:** Value flanked by stars above text **Edge:** Reeded, smooth alternating edge **Note:** Struck for sets only.

Date	Mintage	F	VF	XF	Unc	BU
JE5740 (1980)(b)	35,000	—	—	—	4.00	—

KM# 90 5 LIROT

Copper-Nickel, 30 mm. **Obv:** Roaring lion left with menorah above **Rev:** Value flanked by stars **Edge:** Smooth

Date	Mintage	F	VF	XF	Unc	BU
JE5738 (1978)	8,350,000	—	0.40	1.00	3.50	7.50
JE5739 (1979)	37,646,000	—	0.40	1.00	3.00	7.50

KM# 102 5 LIROT
Nickel, 30 mm. **Subject:** 25th Anniversary - Bank of Israel **Obv:** Roaring lion left with menorah above **Rev:** Value flanked by stars **Edge:** Smooth **Note:** Struck for sets only.

Date	Mintage	F	VF	XF	Unc	BU
JE5740 (1980)(b)	35,000	—	—	3.00	7.00	—

REFORM COINAGE

10 (old) Agorot = 1 New Agora; 100 New Agorot = 1 Sheqel

Commencing February 24, 1980-1985

KM# 106 NEW AGORA
0.6000 g., Aluminum, 15 mm. **Obv:** Date palm **Rev:** Value **Edge:** Plain

Date	Mintage	F	VF	XF	Unc	BU
JE5740 (1980)(o)	200,000,000	—	—	—	0.20	—

Note: 110 million coins were reportedly melted down

Date	Mintage	F	VF	XF	Unc	BU
JE5741 (1981)(o)	1,000,000	—	—	0.20	1.00	—
JE5742 (1982)(f)	1,000,000	—	—	0.20	1.00	—

KM# 107 5 NEW AGOROT
0.9000 g., Aluminum, 18.5 mm. **Obv:** Menorah flanked by sprigs **Rev:** Value **Edge:** Reeded

Date	Mintage	F	VF	XF	Unc	BU
JE5740 (1980)(o)	69,532,000	—	—	—	0.25	—
JE5741 (1981)(o)	1,000,000	—	—	0.20	1.00	—
JE5742 (1982)(f)	5,000,000	—	—	—	0.25	—

KM# 108 10 NEW AGOROT
2.1100 g., Bronze, 15.96 mm. **Obv:** Pomegranate **Rev:** Value **Edge:** Reeded

Date	Mintage	F	VF	XF	Unc	BU
JE5740 (1980)(o)	167,932,000	—	—	—	0.20	—

Note: 70,200 million coins were reportedly melted down

Date	Mintage	F	VF	XF	Unc	BU
JE5741 (1981)	241,100,000	—	—	—	0.20	—

Note: 123,000,000 were minted at (f); 90,000,000 at (p) and 28,160,000 at (j).

Date	Mintage	F	VF	XF	Unc	BU
JE5742 (1982)(f)	23,000,000	—	—	—	0.20	—
JE5743 (1983)(j)	2,500,000	—	—	0.15	0.50	—
JE5744 (1984)(j)	500,000	—	—	0.20	1.00	—

KM# 109 1/2 SHEQEL
3.0300 g., Copper-Nickel, 19.96 mm. **Obv:** Roaring lion left **Rev:** Value flanked by stars **Edge:** Reeded

Date	Mintage	F	VF	XF	Unc	BU
JE5740 (1980)(b)	52,308,000	—	—	0.50	1.00	1.25
JE5741 (1981)	53,272,000	—	—	0.50	1.00	1.25

Note: 37,976,000 minted at (j) and 15,296,000 minted at (p).

Date	Mintage	F	VF	XF	Unc	BU
JE5742 (1982)(j)	18,808,484	—	—	0.50	1.00	1.25
JE5743 (1983)(j)	250,000	—	—	0.50	1.00	1.25
JE5744 (1984)(j)	250,000	—	—	0.50	1.00	1.25

KM# 111 SHEQEL
5.0000 g., Copper-Nickel, 22.54 mm. **Obv:** Value **Rev:** Chalice **Edge:** Reeded and plain segments

Date	Mintage	F	VF	XF	Unc	BU
JE5741 (1981)	154,540,000	—	—	0.30	0.50	—

Note: 99,000,000 minted at (p); 389,970,000 minted at (j) and 15,570,000 minted at (b).

Date	Mintage	F	VF	XF	Unc	BU
JE5742 (1982)(p)	15,850,000	—	—	0.30	0.50	—
JE5743 (1983)(j)	26,360,000	—	—	0.30	0.50	—
JE5744 (1984)	32,205,000	—	—	0.30	0.50	—

Note: 30,000,000 minted at (o); 2,205,000 minted at (j).

Date	Mintage	F	VF	XF	Unc	BU
JE5745 (1985)(j)	500,000	—	—	1.00	2.00	—

KM# 118 5 SHEQALIM
6.2000 g., Aluminum-Bronze, 24 mm. **Obv:** Cornucopia **Rev:** Value flanked by stars

Date	Mintage	F	VF	XF	Unc	BU
JE5742 (1982)	30,000,000	—	—	0.50	0.75	—

Note: 18,000,000 minted at (o); 12,000,000 minted at (p).

Date	Mintage	F	VF	XF	Unc	BU
JE5743 (1983)(j)	994,000	—	—	1.00	2.00	—
JE5744 (1984)	17,389,000	—	—	0.50	0.75	—

Note: 9,000,000 minted at (o); 8,389,400 minted at (j).

Date	Mintage	F	VF	XF	Unc	BU
JE5745 (1985)(j)	250,005	—	—	1.00	2.50	—

KM# 119 10 SHEQALIM
8.0000 g., Copper-Nickel, 26 mm. **Obv:** Ancient Galley **Rev:** Value flanked by stars

Date	Mintage	F	VF	XF	Unc	BU
JE5742 (1982)	36,084,000	—	—	0.75	1.25	—

Note: 18,000,000 minted by (f) and 18,084,123 by (j).

Date	Mintage	F	VF	XF	Unc	BU
JE5743 (1983)	17,850,750	—	—	0.75	1.25	—
JE5744 (1984)	31,950,200	—	—	0.75	1.25	—
JE5745 (1985)	25,864,000	—	—	0.50	0.75	—

Note: 15,864,436 struck by (j) and 10,000,000 by (f).

KM# 134 10 SHEQALIM
8.0000 g., Copper-Nickel, 26 mm. **Subject:** Hanukkah **Obv:** Ancient Galley **Rev:** Value flanked by stars

Date	Mintage	F	VF	XF	Unc	BU
JE5744 (1984)	2,000,000	—	—	1.00	1.50	—

KM# 137 10 SHEQALIM
Copper-Nickel, 26 mm. **Obv:** Head of Theodore Herzl left **Rev:** Value flanked by stars

Date	Mintage	F	VF	XF	Unc	BU
JE5744 (1984)(b)	2,002,500	—	—	1.00	1.50	—

KM# 139 50 SHEQALIM
Aluminum-Bronze, 28 mm. **Obv:** Ancient coin **Rev:** Value flanked by stars

Date	Mintage	F	VF	XF	Unc	BU
JE5744 (1984)	13,993,658	—	—	0.50	1.00	—
JE5745 (1985)	1,000,100	—	—	1.00	2.00	—

KM# 147 50 SHEQALIM
Aluminum-Bronze, 28 mm. **Obv:** Head left **Obv. Designer:** Gabi Neuman **Rev:** Value flanked by stars

Date	Mintage	F	VF	XF	Unc	BU
JE5745 (1985)	1,000,000	—	—	1.00	2.00	—

KM# 143 100 SHEQALIM
10.8200 g., Copper-Nickel, 29 mm. **Obv:** Menorah **Rev:** Value

Date	Mintage	F	VF	XF	Unc	BU
JE5744 (1984)	30,028,000	—	—	0.75	1.50	—
JE5745 (1985)	19,638,000	—	—	0.75	1.50	—

KM# 146 100 SHEQALIM
Copper-Nickel, 29 mm. **Subject:** Hanukkah **Obv:** Menorah **Rev:** Value

Date	Mintage	F	VF	XF	Unc	BU
JE5745 (1985)	2,000,000	—	—	1.25	2.25	—

KM# 151 100 SHEQALIM
Copper-Nickel, 29 mm. **Obv:** Head 1/4 left of Ze'ev Jabotinsky **Obv. Designer:** Gabi Neuman **Rev:** Value

Date	Mintage	F	VF	XF	Unc	BU
JE5745 (1985)(p)	2,000,000	—	—	1.25	2.25	—

REFORM COINAGE

100 Agorot = 1 New Sheqel

September 4, 1985

KM# 156 AGORA
2.0400 g., Aluminum-Bronze, 17 mm. **Obv:** Ancient ship **Rev:** Value within lined square

Date	Mintage	F	VF	XF	Unc	BU
JE5745 (1985)	58,144,000	—	—	—	0.50	—

Note: 40,000,000 struck by (p) and 18,144,000 by (f).

Date	Mintage	F	VF	XF	Unc	BU
JE5746 (1986)	95,272,000	—	—	—	0.50	—

Note: 50,112,000 struck by (p); 30,856,000 by (f) and 14,304,000 by (j).

Date	Mintage	F	VF	XF	Unc	BU
JE5747 (1987)	1,080,000	—	—	—	0.50	—
JE5748 (1988)	15,768,000	—	—	—	0.50	—
JE5749 (1989)	10,801,000	—	—	—	0.50	—
JE5750 (1990)	4,968,000	—	—	—	0.50	—
JE5751 (1991)(j)	12,000	—	—	—	2.00	—

Note: In sets only, probably 5,254 melted.

KM# 171 AGORA

Aluminum-Bronze **Subject:** Hanukkah **Obv:** Ancient ship **Rev:** Value within lined square

Date	Mintage	F	VF	XF	Unc	BU
JE5747 (1987)	1,004,000	—	—	0.15	0.75	—
JE5748 (1988)	540,000	—	—	0.20	0.75	—
JE5749 (1989)	504,000	—	—	0.20	0.75	—
JE5750 (1990)	2,160,000	—	—	0.15	0.75	—
JE5751 (1991)(j)	432,000	—	—	0.20	0.75	—

KM# 193 AGORA

Aluminum-Bronze **Subject:** 40th Anniversary of Independence **Obv:** Ancient ship **Rev:** Value within lined square

Date	Mintage	F	VF	XF	Unc	BU
JE5748 (1988)	504,000	—	—	0.20	0.75	—

KM# 157 5 AGOROT

2.9500 g., Aluminum-Bronze, 19.45 mm. **Obv:** Ancient coin **Rev:** Value within lined square **Edge:** Plain

Date	Mintage	F	VF	XF	Unc	BU
JE5745 (1985)(p)	25,000,000	—	—	0.10	0.15	—
JE5745 (1985)(s)	9,504,000	—	—	0.10	0.15	—
JE5746 (1986)(j)	6,912,050	—	—	0.10	0.15	—
JE5746 (1986)(f)	5,472,000	—	—	0.10	0.15	—
JE5747 (1987)(j)	14,257,298	—	—	0.10	0.15	—
JE5748 (1988)(j)	9,360,000	—	—	0.10	0.15	—
JE5749 (1989)(j)	4,896,000	—	—	0.10	0.15	—
JE5750 (1990)(j)	576,000	—	—	0.15	0.25	—
JE5751 (1991)(j)	4,464,000	—	—	0.10	0.15	—
JE5752 (1992)(j)	7,664,000	—	—	0.10	0.15	—
JE5752 (1992)(so)	18,432,000	—	—	0.10	0.15	—
Note: A coin-alignment error exists. Value $200.						
JE5754 (1994)(a)	5,952,000	—	—	0.10	0.15	—
JE5754 (1994)(h)	6,144,000	—	—	0.10	0.15	—
JE5755 (1995)(so)	6,144,000	—	—	0.10	0.15	—
JE5756 (1996)(sg)	6,144,000	—	—	0.10	0.15	—
JE5757 (1997)(so)	6,144,000	—	—	0.10	0.15	—
JE5758 (1998)(so)	12,288,000	—	—	0.10	0.15	—
Note: A coin-alignment error exists. Value $200.						
JE5759 (1999)(so)	6,144,000	—	—	0.10	0.15	—
JE5760 (2000)(so)	12,288,000	—	—	0.10	0.15	—
Note: A coin-alignment error exists. Value $200.						
JE5761 (2001)(sl)	6,144,000	—	—	—	0.15	—
JE5762 (2002)(sl)	6,144,000	—	—	—	0.15	—
JE5764 (2004)	—	—	—	—	0.15	—
JE5765 (2005)	—	—	—	—	0.15	—
JE5766 (2006)	—	—	—	—	0.15	—
JE5767 (2007)	—	—	—	—	0.15	—

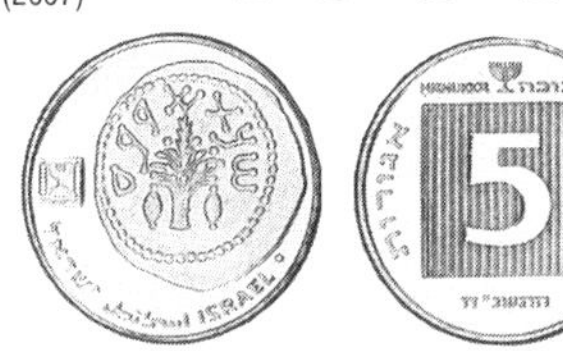

KM# 172 5 AGOROT

Aluminum-Bronze, 20.5 mm. **Subject:** Hanukkah **Obv:** Ancient coin **Rev:** Value within lined square **Note:** JE5754-5767 coins contain the Star of David mint mark; the JE5747-5753 coins do not.

Date	Mintage	F	VF	XF	Unc	BU
JE5747 (1987)(p)	1,004,000	—	—	0.10	0.30	—
JE5748 (1988)(j)	536,000	—	—	0.20	0.50	—
JE5749 (1989)(j)	504,000	—	—	0.20	0.50	—
JE5750 (1990)(j)	2,016,000	—	—	0.10	0.30	—
JE5751 (1991)(j)	1,488,000	—	—	0.10	0.30	—
JE5752 (1992)(j)	960,000	—	—	0.10	0.30	—
JE5753 (1993)(j)	960,000	—	—	0.10	0.30	—
JE5754 (1994)(u)	12,000	—	—	—	2.00	—
Note: In sets only						
JE5755 (1995)(u)	10,000	—	—	—	2.00	—
Note: In sets only						
JE5756 (1996)(u)	7,500	—	—	—	2.00	—
Note: In sets only						
JE5757 (1997)(u)	7,500	—	—	—	2.00	—
Note: In sets only						
JE5758 (1998)(u)	10,000	—	—	—	2.00	—
Note: In sets only						
JE5759 (1999)(u)	6,000	—	—	—	2.50	—
Note: In sets only						
JE5760 (2000)(u)	5,000	—	—	—	2.50	—
Note: In sets only						
JE5761 (2001)(u)	4,000	—	—	—	2.50	—
Note: In sets only						
JE5762 (2002)(u)	4,000	—	—	—	2.50	—
Note: In sets only						
JE5763 (2003)(u)	3,000	—	—	—	2.50	—
Note: In sets only						
JE5764 (2004)(u)	3,000	—	—	—	2.50	—
Note: In sets only						
JE5765 (2005)(u)	2,500	—	—	—	2.50	—
Note: In sets only						
JE5766 (2006)(u)	3,000	—	—	—	2.50	—
Note: In sets only						
JE5767 (2007)(u)	3,000	—	—	—	2.50	—
Note: In sets only						
JE5768 (2008)(u)	3,000	—	—	—	2.50	—
Note: In sets only						

KM# 194 5 AGOROT

Aluminum-Bronze **Subject:** 40th Anniversary of Independence **Obv:** Ancient coin **Rev:** Value within lined square

Date	Mintage	F	VF	XF	Unc	BU
JE5748 (1988)(j)	504,000	—	—	0.20	0.50	—

KM# 158 10 AGOROT

4.0000 g., Aluminum-Bronze, 22 mm. **Obv:** Menorah **Rev:** Value within lined square **Edge:** Plain

Date	Mintage	F	VF	XF	Unc	BU
JE5745 (1985)(f)	45,000,000	—	—	0.10	0.20	—
JE5746 (1986)(j)	20,934,048	—	—	0.10	0.20	—
JE5746 (1986)(b)	71,820,000	—	—	0.10	0.20	—
JE5747 (1987)(j)	19,351,000	—	—	0.10	0.20	—
JE5748 (1988)(j)	8,640,000	—	—	0.10	0.20	—
JE5749 (1989)(j)	420,000	—	—	0.20	0.50	—
JE5750 (1990)(j)	2,376,000	—	—	0.10	0.20	—
JE5751 (1991)(j)	11,905,000	—	—	0.10	0.20	—
Note: Exist with 6mm or 7mm long date; thick or thin letters; and 7mm or 7.5mm value 10						
JE5751 (1991)(so)	30,240,000	—	—	0.10	0.20	—
JE5751 (1991)(f)	17,280,000	—	—	0.10	0.20	—
JE5752 (1992)(j)	1,728,000	—	—	0.10	0.20	—
JE5753 (1993)(so)	25,920,000	—	—	0.10	0.20	—
JE5754 (1994)(u)	30,096,000	—	—	0.10	0.20	—
JE5754 (1994)(f)	21,600,000	—	—	0.10	0.20	—
JE5755 (1995)(h)	17,280,000	—	—	0.10	0.20	—
JE5756 (1996)(so)	43,200,000	—	—	0.10	0.20	—
JE5757 (1997)(h)	21,600,000	—	—	0.10	0.20	—
Note: The Hebrew letter "heh" in the date (first letter) is open.						
JE5757 (1997)(u)	21,600,000	—	—	0.10	0.20	—
Note: The Hebrew letter "heh" in the date (first letter) is closed.						
JE5758 (1998)(so)	60,450,000	—	—	0.10	0.20	—
Note: A coin-alignment error exists. Value $250.						
JE5759 (1999)(a)	21,600,000	—	—	0.10	0.20	—
JE5759 (1999)(sl)	4,601,000	—	—	0.10	0.20	—
JE5759 (1999)(w)	2,000	—	—	0.10	0.20	—
JE5760 (2000)(so)	82,944,000	—	—	0.10	0.20	—
JE5761 (2001)(sl)	46,140,000	—	—	—	0.20	—
Note: Sides of central part of zero are rounded.						
JE5761 (2001)(so)	32,256,000	—	—	—	0.20	—
Note: Sides of central part of zero are straight.						
JE5762 (2002)(w)	4,608,000	—	—	—	0.20	—
JE5763 (2003)(sl)	22,980,000	—	—	—	0.20	—
JE5764 (2004)	—	—	—	—	0.20	—
JE5765 (2005)	—	—	—	—	0.20	—
JE5766 (2006)	—	—	—	—	0.20	—
JE5767 (2007)	—	—	—	—	0.20	—

KM# 173 10 AGOROT

4.0700 g., Aluminum-Bronze, 22 mm. **Subject:** Hanukkah **Obv:** Menorah **Rev:** Value within lined square **Note:** JE5754-5768 have the Star of David mint mark, JE5747-5753 coins do not.

Date	Mintage	F	VF	XF	Unc	BU
JE5747 (1987)(p)	1,004,000	—	—	0.10	0.40	—
JE5748 (1988)(j)	834,000	—	—	0.10	0.40	—
JE5749 (1989)(j)	798,000	—	—	0.10	0.40	—
JE5750 (1990)(j)	2,052,000	—	—	0.10	0.40	—
JE5751 (1991)(j)	1,488,000	—	—	0.10	0.40	—
JE5752 (1992)(j)	1,404,000	—	—	0.10	0.40	—
JE5753 (1993)(j)	1,404,000	—	—	0.10	0.40	—
JE5754 (1994)(u)	12,000	—	—	—	2.00	—
Note: In sets only						
JE5755 (1995)(u)	10,000	—	—	—	2.00	—
Note: In sets only						
JE5756 (1996)(u)	7,500	—	—	—	2.00	—
Note: In sets only						
JE5757 (1997)(u)	7,500	—	—	—	2.00	—
Note: In sets only						
JE5758 (1998)(u)	10,000	—	—	—	2.00	—
Note: In sets only						
JE5759 (1999)(u)	6,000	—	—	—	2.50	—
Note: In sets only						
JE5760 (2000)(u)	5,000	—	—	—	3.00	—
Note: In sets only						
JE5761 (2001)(u)	4,000	—	—	—	2.50	—
Note: In sets only						
JE5762 (2002)(u)	4,000	—	—	—	2.50	—
Note: In sets only						
JE5763 (2003)(u)	3,000	—	—	—	2.50	—
Note: In sets only						
JE5764 (2004)(u)	3,000	—	—	—	2.50	—
Note: In sets only						
JE5765 (2005)(u)	2,500	—	—	—	2.50	—
Note: In sets only						
JE5766 (2006)(u)	3,000	—	—	—	2.50	—
Note: In sets only						
JE5767 (2007)(u)	3,000	—	—	—	2.50	—
Note: In sets only						
JE5768 (2009)(u)	3,000	—	—	—	2.50	—
Note: In sets only						

KM# 195 10 AGOROT

Aluminum-Bronze **Subject:** 40th Anniversary of Independence **Obv:** Menorah **Rev:** Value within lined square

Date	Mintage	F	VF	XF	Unc	BU
JE5748 (1988)(j)	504,000	—	—	0.20	0.50	—

KM# 159 1/2 NEW SHEQEL

6.5200 g., Aluminum-Bronze, 25.95 mm. **Obv:** Value **Rev:** Lyre **Edge:** Plain

Date	Mintage	F	VF	XF	Unc	BU
JE5745 (1985)(f)	4,032,000	—	—	0.35	0.75	—
Note: Exist with thick E and trimmed thin E						
JE5745 (1985)(j)	1,296,000	—	—	0.35	0.75	—
Note: Exist with thick E and trimmed thin E						
JE5745 (1985)(p)	15,000,000	—	—	0.35	0.75	—
Note: Exist with thick E and trimmed thin E						
JE5746 (1986)(j)	4,392,000	—	—	0.35	0.75	—
JE5747 (1987)(j)	144,000	—	—	1.00	2.00	—
JE5748 (1988)(j)	20,000	—	—	—	3.00	—
Note: In sets only						
JE5749 (1989)(j)	756,000	—	—	0.40	1.00	—
JE5750 (1990)(j)	648,000	—	—	0.40	1.00	—
JE5751 (1991)(j)	288,000	—	—	0.75	1.50	—
JE5752 (1992)(f)	2,688,000	—	—	0.35	0.75	—
JE5752 (1992)(j)	828,000	—	—	0.35	0.75	—
JE5752 (1992)(so)	10,752,000	—	—	0.35	0.75	—
JE5753 (1993)(c)	2,496,000	—	—	0.35	0.75	—
JE5753 (1993)(f)	2,688,000	—	—	0.35	0.75	—
JE5755 (1995)(a)	5,376,000	—	—	0.35	0.75	—
JE5755 (1995)(so)	5,376,000	—	—	0.35	0.75	—
JE5757 (1997)(so)	5,376,000	—	—	0.35	0.75	—
JE5758 (1998)(u)	5,376,000	—	—	0.35	0.75	—
JE5759 (1999)(so)	8,064,000	—	—	0.35	0.75	—
Note: A coin-alignment error exists. Value $250.						
JE5760 (2000)(so)	2,880,000	—	—	—	—	—
Note: Reported in the 2000 Annual review, a correction in the 2002 Annual review, stated that it was in error.						
JE5762 (2002)(so)	2,880,000	—	—	—	0.75	—
JE5762 (2002)(v)	5,760,000	—	—	—	0.75	—
Note: Length of fraction line is 4 or 4.5 mm. But which mint is which is not known.						

Date	Mintage	F	VF	XF	Unc	BU
JE5763 (2003)	—	—	—	—	0.75	—
JE5764 (2004)(so)	2,640,000	—	—	—	0.75	—
JE5765 (2005)	—	—	—	—	0.75	—
JE5766 (2006)	—	—	—	—	0.75	—
JE5767 (2007)	—	—	—	—	0.75	—

KM# 167 1/2 NEW SHEQEL

Aluminum-Bronze, 26 mm. **Obv:** Value **Rev:** Bust facing within names of settlements funded

Date	Mintage	F	VF	XF	Unc	BU
JE5746 (1986)(u)	2,000,000	—	—	1.00	3.00	—

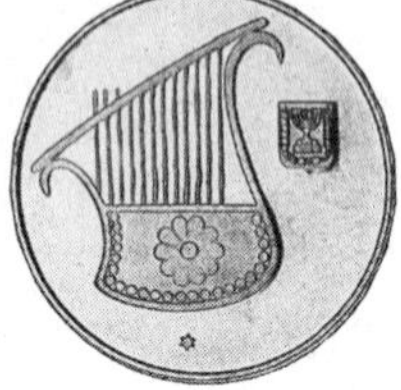

KM# 174 1/2 NEW SHEQEL

6.5000 g., Aluminum-Bronze, 26 mm. **Subject:** Hanukka **Obv:** Value **Rev:** Lyre **Note:** Coins dated JE5754-5768 have the Star of David mint mark; the coins dated JE5747-5753 do not.

Date	Mintage	F	VF	XF	Unc	BU
JE5747 (1987)(p)	1,004,000	—	—	0.35	0.85	—
JE5748 (1988)(j)	532,000	—	—	0.40	1.00	—
JE5749 (1989)(j)	504,000	—	—	0.40	1.00	—
JE5750 (1990)(j)	2,016,000	—	—	0.35	0.85	—
JE5751 (1991)(j)	960,000	—	—	0.35	0.85	—
JE5752 (1992)(j)	288,000	—	—	0.75	1.50	—
JE5753 (1993)(j)	304,000	—	—	0.75	1.50	—
JE5754 (1994)(u)	12,000	—	—	—	2.00	—
Note: In sets only						
JE5755 (1995)(u)	10,000	—	—	—	2.00	—
Note: In sets only						
JE5756 (1996)(u)	7,500	—	—	—	2.00	—
Note: In sets only						
JE5757 (1997)(u)	7,500	—	—	—	2.00	—
Note: In sets only						
JE5758 (1998)(u)	10,000	—	—	—	2.00	—
Note: In sets only						
JE5759 (1999)(u)	6,000	—	—	—	2.50	—
Note: In sets only						
JE5760 (2000)(u)	5,000	—	—	—	3.00	—
Note: In sets only						
JE5761 (2001)(u)	4,000	—	—	—	2.50	—
Note: In sets only						
JE5762 (2002)(u)	4,000	—	—	—	2.50	—
Note: In sets only						
JE5763 (2003)(u)	3,000	—	—	—	2.50	—
Note: In sets only						
JE5764 (2004)(u)	3,000	—	—	—	2.50	—
Note: In sets only						
JE5765 (2005)(u)	2,500	—	—	—	2.50	—
Note: In sets only						
JE5766 (2006)(u)	3,000	—	—	—	2.50	—
Note: In sets only						
JE5767 (2007)(u)	3,000	—	—	—	2.50	—
Note: In sets only						
JE5768 (2008)(u)	3,000	—	—	—	2.50	—
Note: In sets only						

KM# 196 1/2 NEW SHEQEL

Aluminum-Bronze, 26 mm. **Subject:** 40th Anniversary of Independence **Obv:** Value **Rev:** Lyre

Date	Mintage	F	VF	XF	Unc	BU
JE5748 (1988)(j)	500,000	—	—	0.40	1.00	—

KM# 160 NEW SHEQEL

4.0000 g., Copper-Nickel, 18 mm. **Obv:** Value **Rev:** Lilly, state emblem and ancient Hebrew inscription

Date	Mintage	F	VF	XF	Unc	BU
JE5745 (1985)(b)	29,088,000	—	—	0.65	1.50	—
JE5746 (1986)(f)	8,000,000	—	—	0.65	1.50	—
JE5746 (1986)(j)	12,960,055	—	—	0.65	1.50	—
JE5747 (1987)(j)	216,000	—	—	1.00	3.00	—
JE5748 (1988)(j)	6,372,000	—	—	0.65	1.50	—
JE5748 (1988)(u)	14,004,000	—	—	0.65	1.50	—
JE5749 (1989)(j)	8,706,000	—	—	0.65	1.50	—
JE5750 (1990)(j)	756,000	—	—	0.75	2.00	—
JE5751 (1991)(j)	1,152,000	—	—	0.65	1.50	—
JE5752 (1992)(f)	8,640,000	—	—	0.65	1.50	—
JE5752 (1992)(j)	1,512,000	—	—	0.65	1.50	—
JE5752 (1992)(o)	17,280,000	—	—	0.65	1.50	—
JE5753 (1993)(f)	8,640,000	—	—	0.65	1.50	—

KM# 160a NEW SHEQEL

3.4500 g., Nickel-Clad Steel, 17.97 mm. **Obv:** Value **Rev:** Lilly, state emblem and ancient Hebrew inscription **Edge:** Plain

Date	Mintage	F	VF	XF	Unc	BU
JE5754 (1994)(f)	8,496,000	—	—	—	1.00	—
JE5754 (1994)(u)	12,960,000	—	—	—	1.00	—
Note: Coin alignment error exists. Value: $200.						
JE5755 (1995)(u)	25,920,000	—	—	—	1.00	—
JE5756 (1996)(u)	8,640,000	—	—	—	1.00	—
JE5757 (1997)(u)	30,240,000	—	—	—	1.00	—
JE5758 (1998)(sa)	4,295,500	—	—	—	1.00	—
JE5758(1998)(o)	—	—	—	—	1.00	—
JE5759 (1999)(u)	17,280,000	—	—	—	1.00	—
JE5760 (2000)(o)	20,738,000	—	—	—	1.00	—
JE5761 (2001)(h)	9,648,000	—	—	—	1.00	—
JE5762 (2002)(h)	18,816,000	—	—	—	1.00	—
JE5763 (2003)(v)	10,198,500	—	—	—	1.00	—
JE5765 (2005)	—	—	—	—	1.00	—
JE5766 (2006)	—	—	—	—	1.00	—
Note: Coin alignment error exists. Value: $200.						
JE5767 (2007)	—	—	—	—	1.00	—

KM# 163 NEW SHEQEL

4.0500 g., Copper-Nickel, 18 mm. **Subject:** Hanukka **Obv:** Value **Rev:** Lilly **Note:** Coins dated JE5754-5768 have the Star of David mint mark; the JE5746-5753 coins do not.

Date	Mintage	F	VF	XF	Unc	BU
JE5746 (1986)(b)	1,056,000	—	—	0.65	1.50	—
JE5747 (1987)(p)	1,004,000	—	—	0.65	1.50	—
JE5748 (1988)(j)	534,000	—	—	0.75	2.00	—
JE5749 (1989)(j)	504,000	—	—	0.75	2.00	—
JE5750 (1990)(j)	2,052,000	—	—	0.65	1.50	—
JE5751 (1991)(f)	1,080,000	—	—	0.65	1.50	—
JE5751 (1991)(j)	24,000	—	—	0.65	1.50	—
JE5752 (1992)(j)	1,044,000	—	—	0.65	1.50	—
JE5753 (1993)(j)	922,000	—	—	0.65	1.50	—
JE5754 (1994)(u)	12,000	—	—	—	2.50	—
Note: In sets only						
JE5755 (1995)(u)	10,000	—	—	—	2.50	—
Note: In sets only						
JE5756 (1996)(u)	7,500	—	—	—	2.50	—
Note: In sets only						
JE5757 (1997)(u)	7,500	—	—	—	2.50	—
Note: In sets only						
JE5758 (1998)(u)	10,000	—	—	—	2.50	—
Note: In sets only						
JE5759 (1999)(u)	6,000	—	—	—	3.00	—
Note: In sets only						
JE5760 (2000)(u)	5,000	—	—	—	3.50	—
Note: In sets only						
JE5761 (2001)(u)	4,000	—	—	—	2.50	—
Note: In sets only						
JE5762 (2002)(u)	4,000	—	—	—	2.50	—
Note: In sets only						
JE5763 (2003)(u)	3,000	—	—	—	2.50	—
Note: In sets only						
JE5764 (2004)(u)	3,000	—	—	—	2.50	—
Note: In sets only						
JE5765 (2005)(u)	2,500	—	—	—	2.50	—
Note: In sets only						
JE5766 (2006)(u)	3,000	—	—	—	2.50	—
Note: In sets only						
JE5767 (2007)(u)	3,000	—	—	—	2.50	—
Note: In sets only						
JE5768 (2008)	3,000	—	—	—	2.50	—
Note: In sets only.						

KM# 197 NEW SHEQEL

Copper-Nickel, 18 mm. **Subject:** 40th Anniversary of Independence **Obv:** Value **Rev:** English lamp

Date	Mintage	F	VF	XF	Unc	BU
JE5748 (1988)(j)	504,000	—	—	—	1.75	—

KM# 198 NEW SHEQEL

Copper-Nickel, 18 mm. **Obv:** Value **Rev:** Bust of Maimonides facing

Date	Mintage	F	VF	XF	Unc	BU
JE5748 (1988)(d)	1,000,000	—	—	—	1.75	—

KM# 435 2 NEW SHEQALIM

5.6000 g., Nickel Plated Steel, 21.48 mm. **Obv:** Large value **Rev:** Small national arms above stylized double cornucopiae **Edge:** Segmented reeding

Date	Mintage	F	VF	XF	Unc	BU
JE5765(2005)	—	—	—	—	1.50	—

KM# 207 5 NEW SHEQALIM

8.1800 g., Copper-Nickel, 24 mm. **Obv:** Value **Rev:** Ancient column capitol **Edge:** Plain **Shape:** 12-sided

Date	Mintage	F	VF	XF	Unc	BU
JE5750 (1990)(f)	15,000,000	—	—	—	3.75	—
JE5751 (1991)(j)	324,000	—	—	3.00	5.00	—
JE5752 (1992)(j)	413,000	—	—	3.00	5.00	—
JE5754 (1994)(v)	2,016,000	—	—	—	3.75	—
JE5755 (1995)(v)	2,160,000	—	—	—	3.75	—
JE5757 (1997)(u)	2,160,000	—	—	—	3.75	—
JE5757 (1997)(v)	2,160,000	—	—	—	3.75	—
JE5758 (1998)(h)	2,160,000	—	—	—	3.75	—
JE5759 (1999)(h)	2,160,000	—	—	—	3.75	—
JE5759 (1999)(u)	2,160,000	—	—	—	3.75	—
JE5760 (2000)(v)	4,464,000	—	—	—	3.75	—
JE5762 (2002)(o)	4,464,000	—	—	—	3.75	—
Note: The JE5762 coins are practically round.						
JE5765 (2005)	—	—	—	—	3.00	—
JE5766 (2006)	—	—	—	—	3.00	—

KM# 208 5 NEW SHEQALIM

Copper-Nickel, 24 mm. **Obv:** Value **Rev:** Bust of Levi Eshlol facing

Date	Mintage	F	VF	XF	Unc	BU
JE5750 (1990)(f)	1,500,000	—	—	2.50	5.00	—

KM# 217 5 NEW SHEQALIM

Copper-Nickel, 24 mm. **Obv:** Value **Rev:** Ancient column capitol **Note:** Coins dated JE5754-5768 have the Star of David mint mark; the JE5751-5753 coins do not.

Date	Mintage	F	VF	XF	Unc	BU
JE5751 (1991)(j)	500,000	—	—	2.00	4.00	—
JE5751 (1991)	—	—	—	—	3.75	—
JE5752 (1992)(j)	486,000	—	—	2.00	4.00	—
JE5753 (1993)(j)	500,000	—	—	2.00	4.00	—
JE5754 (1994)(u)	12,000	—	—	—	4.00	—
Note: In sets only						
JE5755 (1995)(u)	10,000	—	—	—	4.00	—
Note: In sets only						
JE5756 (1996)(u)	7,500	—	—	—	4.00	—
Note: In sets only						
JE5757 (1997)(u)	7,500	—	—	—	4.00	—
Note: In sets only						
JE5758 (1998)(u)	10,000	—	—	—	4.00	—

Date	Mintage	F	VF	XF	Unc	BU
Note: In sets only						
JE5759 (1999)(u)	6,000	—	—	—	5.00	—
Note: In sets only						
JE5760 (2000)(u)	5,000	—	—	—	5.00	—
Note: In sets only						
JE5761 (2001)(u)	4,000	—	—	—	3.75	—
Note: In sets only						
JE5762 (2002)(u)	4,000	—	—	—	3.75	—
Note: In sets only						
JE5763 (2003)(u)	3,000	—	—	—	3.75	—
Note: In sets only						
JE5764 (2004)(u)	3,000	—	—	—	3.75	—
Note: In sets only						
JE5765 (2005)(u)	2,500	—	—	—	3.75	—
Note: In sets only						
JE5766 (2006)(u)	3,000	—	—	—	3.75	—
Note: In sets only						
JE5767 (2007)(u)	3,000	—	—	—	3.75	—
Note: In sets only						
JE5768 (2008)	3,000	—	—	—	3.75	—
Note: In sets only						

KM# 237 5 NEW SHEQALIM

Copper-Nickel **Obv:** Value **Rev:** Bust of Chiam Weizmann facing

Date	Mintage	F	VF	XF	Unc	BU
JE5753 (1993)(j)	1,500,000	—	—	—	5.00	—

KM# 270 10 NEW SHEQALIM

7.0000 g., Bi-Metallic Aureate bonded Bronze center in Nickel bonded Steel ring, 22.95 mm. **Obv:** Value, vertical lines and text within circle **Rev:** Palm tree and baskets within half beaded circle **Edge:** Reeded

Date	Mintage	F	VF	XF	Unc	BU
JE5755 (1995)(u)	28,224,000	—	—	—	5.00	—
JE5762 (2002)(h)	4,749,000	—	—	—	5.00	—
JE5765 (2005)	—	—	—	—	5.00	—
Note: Coin alignment error exists. Value: $500.						
JE5766 (2006)	—	—	—	—	5.00	—

KM# 273 10 NEW SHEQALIM

Bi-Metallic Aureate bonded Bronze center in Nickel bonded Steel ring, 22.5 mm. **Obv:** Value, text and vertical lines within circle **Rev:** Bust of Golda Meir facing at right within vertical lines and circle

Date	Mintage	F	VF	XF	Unc	BU
JE5755 (1995)(u)	1,584,000	—	—	—	10.00	—

ITALIAN SOMALILAND

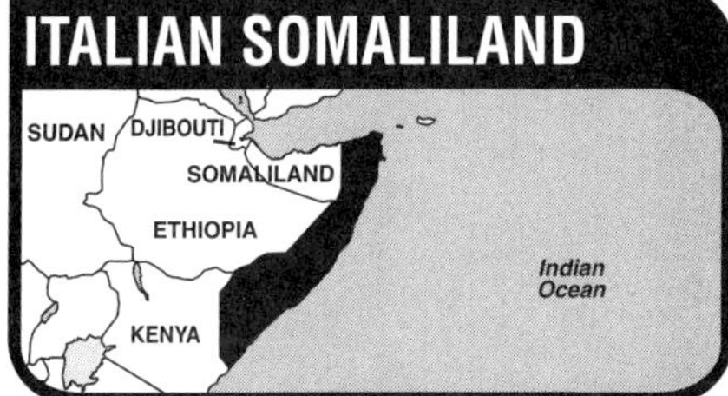

Italian Somaliland, a former Italian Colony in East Africa, extended south from Ras Asir to Kenya. Area: 178,218 sq. miles (461,585 sq. km). Capital: Mogadisho. In 1885, Italy obtained commercial concessions in the area of the sultan of Zanzibar, and in 1905 purchased the coast from Warshek to Brava. The Italians then extended their occupation inward. Cession of the Jubaland Province by Britain in 1924, and seizure of the sultanates of Obbia and Mejertein in 1925-27 brought direct Italian administration over the whole territory. Italian dominance continued until WW II. British troops occupied Italian Somaliland in 1941. Britain administered the colony until 1950 when it became a UN trust territory administered by Italy. On July 1, 1960. Italian Somaliland united with British Somaliland to form the Independent Somali Democratic Republic.

TITLE

الصومال الايطليانية

Al-Somal Al-Italiyaniya(t)

MONETARY SYSTEM

100 Bese = 1 Rupia

COLONY

STANDARD COINAGE

KM# 1 BESA

Bronze **Ruler:** Vittorio Emanuele III **Obv:** Uniformed bust left **Rev:** Value and date within circle

Date	Mintage	F	VF	XF	Unc	BU
1909R	2,000,000	15.00	30.00	70.00	300	—
1910R	500,000	15.00	30.00	90.00	350	—
1913R	200,000	22.50	45.00	150	700	—
1921R	500,000	18.50	35.00	100	400	—

KM# 2 2 BESE

Bronze **Ruler:** Vittorio Emanuele III **Obv:** Uniformed bust left **Rev:** Value and date within circle

Date	Mintage	F	VF	XF	Unc	BU
1909R	500,000	18.50	37.50	140	550	—
1910R	250,000	18.50	37.50	160	600	—
1913R	300,000	22.50	45.00	225	900	—
1921R	600,000	18.50	37.50	140	550	—
1923R	1,500,000	18.50	35.00	130	500	—
1924R	Inc. above	18.50	30.00	110	450	—

KM# 3 4 BESE

Bronze **Ruler:** Vittorio Emanuele III **Obv:** Uniformed bust left **Rev:** Value and date within circle

Date	Mintage	F	VF	XF	Unc	BU
1909R	250,000	27.50	55.00	180	900	—
1910R	250,000	27.50	55.00	200	1,000	—
1913R	50,000	50.00	125	500	1,500	—
1921R	200,000	30.00	60.00	200	1,000	—
1923R	1,000,000	30.00	60.00	200	1,000	—
1924R	Inc. above	30.00	75.00	225	1,100	—

KM# 4 1/4 RUPIA

2.9160 g., 0.9170 Silver 0.0860 oz. ASW **Ruler:** Vittorio Emanuele III **Obv:** Head right **Rev:** Crown above value and date flanked by sprigs

Date	Mintage	F	VF	XF	Unc	BU
1910R	400,000	20.00	40.00	150	400	—
1913R	100,000	50.00	100	300	600	—

KM# 5 1/2 RUPIA

5.8319 g., 0.9170 Silver 0.1719 oz. ASW **Ruler:** Vittorio Emanuele III **Obv:** Head right **Rev:** Crown above value and date flanked by sprigs

Date	Mintage	F	VF	XF	Unc	BU
1910R	400,000	30.00	65.00	250	650	—
1912R	100,000	35.00	70.00	225	600	—
1913R	100,000	35.00	70.00	200	550	—
1915R	50,000	55.00	120	400	1,000	—
1919R	200,000	30.00	60.00	180	450	—

KM# 6 RUPIA

11.6638 g., 0.9170 Silver 0.3439 oz. ASW **Ruler:** Vittorio Emanuele III **Obv:** Head right **Rev:** Crown above value and date flanked by sprigs

Date	Mintage	F	VF	XF	Unc	BU
1910R	300,000	40.00	90.00	275	550	—
1912R	600,000	40.00	85.00	250	500	—
1913R	300,000	40.00	75.00	225	450	—
1914R	300,000	40.00	75.00	225	450	—
1915R	250,000	40.00	75.00	225	450	—
1919R	400,000	40.00	75.00	225	450	—
1920R	1,300,000	900	1,500	3,750	7,500	—
1921R	940,000	1,850	3,750	6,000	12,500	—

REFORM COINAGE

100 Centesimi = 1 Lira

KM# 7 5 LIRE

6.0000 g., 0.8350 Silver 0.1611 oz. ASW **Ruler:** Vittorio Emanuele III **Obv:** Crowned bust right **Rev:** Crowned shield flanked by sprigs divides value with date below **Designer:** Attilio Motti

Date	Mintage	F	VF	XF	Unc	BU
1925R	400,000	125	300	500	1,000	1,500

KM# 8 10 LIRE

12.0000 g., 0.8350 Silver 0.3221 oz. ASW **Ruler:** Vittorio Emanuele III **Obv:** Crowned bust right **Rev:** Crowned shield flanked by sprigs divides value with date below **Designer:** Attilio Motti

Date	Mintage	F	VF	XF	Unc	BU
1925R	100,000	200	500	700	1,200	2,000

The Italian Republic, a 700-mile-long peninsula extending into the heart of the Mediterranean Sea, has an area of 116,304 sq. mi. (301,230 sq. km.) and a population of 60 million. Capital: Rome. The economy centers around agriculture, manufacturing, forestry and fishing. Machinery, textiles, clothing and motor vehicles are exported.

From the fall of Rome until modern times, 'Italy' was little more than a geographical expression. Although nominally included in the Empire of Charlemagne and the Holy Roman Empire, it was in reality divided into a number of independent states and kingdoms presided over by wealthy families, soldiers of fortune or hereditary rulers. The 19th century unification movement fostered by Mazzini, Garibaldi and Cavour attained fruition in 1860-70 with the creation of the Kingdom of Italy and the installation of Victor Emmanuel, king of Sardinia, as king of Italy. Benito Mussolini came to power during the post-World War I period of economic and political unrest, and installed a Fascist dictatorship with a figurehead king as titular Head of State. Mussolini entered Italy into the German-Japanese anti-comitern pact (Tri-Partite Pact) and withdrew from the League of Nations. The war did not go well for Italy and Germany was forced to assist Italy in its failed invasion of Greece. The Allied invasion of Sicily on July 10, 1943 and bombings of Rome brought the Fascist council to a no vote of confidence on July 23, 1943. Mussolini was arrested but soon escaped and set up a government in Salo. Rome fell to the Allied forces in June, 1944 and the country was allowed the status of cobelligerent against Germany. The Germans held northern Italy for another year. Mussolini was eventually captured and executed by partisans.

Following the defeat of the Axis powers, the Italian monarchy was dissolved by plebiscite, and the Italian Republic proclaimed.

RULERS

Vittorio Emanuele III, 1900-1946
Umberto II, 1946
Republic, 1946-

MONETARY SYSTEM

100 Centesimi = 1 Lira

KINGDOM

DECIMAL COINAGE

KM# 35 CENTESIMO

Copper **Ruler:** Vittorio Emanuele III **Obv:** Head left **Rev:** Value and date within wreath with star above

Date	Mintage	F	VF	XF	Unc	BU
1902R	26,000	380	700	1,500	2,800	—
1903R	5,655,000	1.00	3.00	6.00	35.00	—
1904/0R	14,626,000	2.00	3.00	7.50	22.00	—
1904R	Inc. above	1.00	3.00	6.00	30.00	—
1905/0R	8,531,000	6.00	12.00	30.00	80.00	—
1905R	Inc. above	1.00	3.00	6.00	30.00	—
1908R	3,859,000	1.00	3.00	6.00	35.00	—

KM# 40 CENTESIMO

Copper **Ruler:** Vittorio Emanuele III **Obv:** Bust left **Rev:** Female standing on prow **Rev. Designer:** Pietro Canonia

Date	Mintage	F	VF	XF	Unc	BU
1908R	57,000	300	650	1,100	1,800	—
1909R	3,539,000	2.00	3.00	7.00	20.00	—
1910R	3,599,000	2.00	3.00	7.00	20.00	—
1911R	700,000	18.00	40.00	75.00	120	—
1912R	3,995,000	2.00	3.00	8.00	28.00	—
1913R	3,200,000	2.00	3.00	8.00	28.00	—
1914R	11,585,000	2.00	3.00	7.00	20.00	—
1915R	9,757,000	2.00	3.00	7.00	20.00	—
1916R	9,845,000	2.00	3.00	7.00	20.00	—
1917R	2,400,000	2.00	3.00	7.00	20.00	—
1918R	2,710,000	10.00	20.00	50.00	100	—

KM# 38 2 CENTESIMI

Copper **Ruler:** Vittorio Emanuele III **Obv:** Head left **Rev:** Value and date within wreath

Date	Mintage	F	VF	XF	Unc	BU
1903R	5,000,000	2.00	4.00	15.00	30.00	—
1905R	1,260,000	10.00	20.00	40.00	90.00	—
1906R	3,145,000	2.00	8.00	20.00	50.00	—
1907R	230,000	80.00	160	380	800	—
1908R	1,518,000	2.00	8.00	20.00	50.00	—

KM# 41 2 CENTESIMI

Copper **Ruler:** Vittorio Emanuele III **Obv:** Bust left **Rev:** Female standing on prow **Rev. Designer:** Pietro Canonia

Date	Mintage	F	VF	XF	Unc	BU
1908R	298,000	25.00	60.00	120	300	—
1909R	2,419,000	1.00	3.00	7.00	30.00	—
1910R	590,000	15.00	45.00	100	200	—
1911R	2,777,000	1.00	3.00	7.00	30.00	—
1912R	840,000	12.00	30.00	60.00	120	—
1914R	1,648,000	2.00	5.00	15.00	40.00	—
1915R	4,860,000	1.00	3.00	5.00	25.00	—
1916R	1,540,000	1.00	4.00	8.00	30.00	—
1917R	3,638,000	1.00	3.00	7.00	30.00	—

KM# 42 5 CENTESIMI

Copper, 25.5 mm. **Ruler:** Vittorio Emanuele III **Obv:** Bust left **Rev:** Female standing on prow **Rev. Designer:** Pietro Canonia

Date	Mintage	F	VF	XF	Unc	BU
1908R	824,000	25.00	40.00	90.00	190	—
1909R	1,734,000	3.00	10.00	40.00	100	—
1912R	743,000	4.00	15.00	60.00	150	—
1913R Dot after D	1,964,000	5.00	25.00	50.00	100	—
1913R Without dot after D	Inc. above	60.00	180	450	900	—
1915R	1,038,000	3.00	10.00	60.00	100	—
1918R	4,242,000	2.00	7.00	20.00	60.00	—

KM# 59 5 CENTESIMI

3.2600 g., Copper, 19.8 mm. **Ruler:** Vittorio Emanuele III **Obv:** Head left **Rev:** Wheat ear divides value

Date	Mintage	F	VF	XF	Unc	BU
1919R	13,208,000	3.00	8.00	25.00	100	—
1920R	33,372,000	0.10	0.60	3.00	15.00	—
1921R	80,111,000	0.10	0.60	3.00	15.00	—
1922R	42,914,000	0.10	0.60	3.00	15.00	—
1923R	29,614,000	0.10	0.60	3.00	15.00	—
1924R	20,352,000	0.10	0.60	3.00	15.00	—
1925R	40,460,000	0.10	0.60	3.00	15.00	—
1926R	21,158,000	0.10	0.60	3.00	15.00	—
1927R	15,800,000	0.10	0.60	3.00	15.00	—
1928R	16,090,000	0.10	0.60	3.00	15.00	—
1929R	29,000,000	0.10	0.60	3.00	15.00	—
1930R	22,694,000	0.10	0.60	3.00	15.00	—
1931R	20,000,000	0.10	0.60	3.00	15.00	—
1932R	11,456,000	0.10	0.60	3.00	15.00	—
1933R	20,720,000	0.10	0.60	3.00	15.00	—
1934R	16,000,000	0.10	0.60	3.00	15.00	—
1935R	11,000,000	0.10	0.60	3.00	15.00	—
1936R	9,462,000	0.30	2.00	10.00	25.00	—
1937R	972,000	20.00	45.00	80.00	180	—

KM# 73 5 CENTESIMI

3.2000 g., Copper **Ruler:** Vittorio Emanuele III **Obv:** Head right **Rev:** Eagle with wings spread

Date	Mintage	F	VF	XF	Unc	BU
1936R Yr. XIV	4,998,000	4.00	10.00	20.00	40.00	—
1937R Yr. XV	7,207,000	1.00	2.00	6.00	15.00	—
1938R Yr. XVI	24,000,000	0.10	0.50	2.50	5.00	—
1939R Yr. XVII	22,000,000	0.10	0.50	2.50	5.00	—

KM# 73a 5 CENTESIMI

3.0000 g., Aluminum-Bronze **Ruler:** Vittorio Emanuele III **Obv:** Head right **Rev:** Eagle with wings spread

Date	Mintage	F	VF	XF	Unc	BU
1939R Yr. XVII	10,000,000	0.20	0.50	2.00	6.00	—
1940R Yr. XVIII	16,340,000	0.20	0.50	2.00	6.00	—
1941R Yr. XIX	25,200,000	0.20	0.50	2.00	6.00	—
1942R Yr. XX	13,922,000	0.20	0.50	2.00	6.00	—
1943R Yr. XXI	372,000	3.00	6.00	15.00	30.00	—

KM# 43 10 CENTESIMI

Copper **Ruler:** Vittorio Emanuele III **Obv:** Bust left **Rev:** Female standing on prow

Date	Mintage	F	VF	XF	Unc	BU
1908R Unique	—	—	—	—	—	—

KM# 51 10 CENTESIMI

Copper, 30 mm. **Ruler:** Vittorio Emanuele III **Subject:** 50th Anniversary of the Kingdom **Obv:** Head left **Rev:** Two classical figures standing **Designer:** Trentacoste

Date	Mintage	F	VF	XF	Unc	BU
1911R	2,000,000	3.00	10.00	45.00	90.00	—

KM# 60 10 CENTESIMI

5.3400 g., Copper, 23 mm. **Ruler:** Vittorio Emanuele III **Obv:** Head left **Rev:** Honey Bee

Date	Mintage	F	VF	XF	Unc	BU
1919R	986,000	20.00	50.00	250	500	—
1920R	37,995,000	0.10	0.75	4.00	15.00	—
1921R	66,510,000	0.10	0.75	4.00	15.00	—
1922R	45,217,000	0.10	0.75	4.00	15.00	—
1923R	31,529,000	0.10	0.75	4.00	15.00	—
1924R	35,312,000	0.10	0.75	4.00	15.00	—
1925R	22,370,000	0.10	0.75	4.00	15.00	—
1926R	25,190,000	0.10	0.75	4.00	15.00	—
1927R	22,673,000	0.10	0.75	4.00	15.00	—
1928R	15,680,000	0.20	5.00	20.00	60.00	—
1929R	15,593,000	0.30	0.75	4.00	15.00	—
1930R	17,115,000	0.30	0.75	4.00	15.00	—
1931R	10,750,000	0.30	0.75	4.00	15.00	—
1932R	5,678,000	1.00	3.00	20.00	90.00	—
1933R	10,250,000	0.30	0.75	4.00	15.00	—
1934R	18,300,000	0.30	0.75	4.00	15.00	—
1935R	10,500,000	0.30	0.75	4.00	15.00	—
1936R	8,770,000	1.00	2.50	8.00	40.00	—
1937R	5,500,000	1.00	2.50	8.00	40.00	—

KM# 74 10 CENTESIMI

Copper **Ruler:** Vittorio Emanuele III **Obv:** Head left **Rev:** Savoy arms on fasces with wheat ear and oak leaf flanking

Date	Mintage	F	VF	XF	Unc	BU
1936R Yr. XIV	8,195,000	2.50	5.00	15.00	45.00	—
1937R Yr. XV	7,212,000	1.00	2.00	5.00	20.00	—

Date	Mintage	F	VF	XF	Unc	BU
1938R Yr. XVI	18,750,000	0.30	1.00	2.00	7.00	—
1939R Yr. XVII	24,750,000	0.50	1.00	2.00	7.00	—

KM# 74a 10 CENTESIMI

4.8000 g., Aluminum-Bronze, 23 mm. **Ruler:** Vittorio Emanuele III **Obv:** Head right **Rev:** Savoy arms on fasces with wheat ear and oak leaf flanking

Date	Mintage	F	VF	XF	Unc	BU
1939R Yr. XVII	26,105,000	0.10	0.50	1.00	4.50	—
1940R Yr. XVIII	23,355,000	0.10	0.50	1.00	4.50	—
1941R Yr. XIX	27,050,000	0.10	0.50	1.00	4.50	—
1942R Yr. XX	18,100,000	0.10	0.50	1.00	4.50	—
1943R Yr. XXI	25,400,000	0.10	0.50	1.00	4.50	—

KM# 44 20 CENTESIMI

Nickel, 21.5 mm. **Ruler:** Vittorio Emanuele III **Obv:** Head left admiring wheat ear **Rev:** Victory in flight with Savoy arms below **Rev. Designer:** Leonardo Bistolfi

Date	Mintage	F	VF	XF	Unc	BU
1908R	14,315,000	0.50	2.00	6.00	40.00	—
1909R	19,280,000	0.50	2.00	6.00	40.00	—
1910R	21,887,000	0.50	2.00	6.00	60.00	—
1911R	13,671,000	0.50	2.00	6.00	60.00	—
1912R	21,040,000	0.50	2.00	6.00	40.00	—
1913R	20,729,000	0.50	2.00	6.00	40.00	—
1914R	14,308,000	0.50	2.00	6.00	60.00	—
1919R	3,475,000	3.00	7.00	40.00	120	—
1920R	27,284,000	0.50	2.00	6.00	40.00	—
1921R	50,372,000	0.50	2.00	6.00	40.00	—
1922R	17,134,000	0.50	2.00	6.00	40.00	—
1926R	500	—	—	—	550	—
1927R	100	—	—	—	650	—
1928R	50	—	—	—	750	—
1929R	50	—	—	—	750	—
1930R	50	—	—	—	750	—
1931R	50	—	—	—	750	—
1932R	50	—	—	—	750	—
1933R	50	—	—	—	750	—
1934R	50	—	—	—	750	—
1935R	50	—	—	—	750	—

KM# 58 20 CENTESIMI

Copper-Nickel, 21.5 mm. **Ruler:** Vittorio Emanuele III **Obv:** Crowned Savoy shield flanked by oak and laurel sprigs **Rev:** Value and date within hexagon box **Edge:** Plain and reeded **Note:** Overstruck on KM#28.

Date	Mintage	F	VF	XF	Unc	BU
1918R	43,097,000	0.50	2.00	10.00	60.00	—
1919R	33,432,000	0.50	2.00	10.00	60.00	—
1920R	923,000	5.00	15.00	60.00	150	—

KM# 75 20 CENTESIMI

Nickel, 21.5 mm. **Ruler:** Vittorio Emanuele III **Obv:** Head left **Rev:** Savoy shield within head right

Date	Mintage	F	VF	XF	Unc	BU
1936R Yr. XIV	117,000	40.00	80.00	210	450	—
1937R Yr. XV	50	—	—	—	1,500	—
1938R Yr. XVII	20	—	—	—	2,000	—

KM# 75a 20 CENTESIMI

Stainless Steel, 22.5 mm. **Ruler:** Vittorio Emanuele III **Obv:** Head left **Rev:** Savoy shield within head right **Edge:** Plain **Note:** Magnetic.

Date	Mintage	F	VF	XF	Unc	BU
1939R Yr. XVII	10,462,000	0.20	1.00	10.00	45.00	—
1940R Yr. XVIII	35,350,000	0.20	1.00	10.00	45.00	—
1942R Yr. XX	48,500,000	0.20	1.00	10.00	55.00	—

KM# 75b 20 CENTESIMI

4.0400 g., Stainless Steel, 21.8 mm. **Ruler:** Vittorio Emanuele III **Obv:** Head left **Rev:** Savoy shield within head right **Edge:** Reeded **Note:** Magnetic.

Date	Mintage	F	VF	XF	Unc	BU
1939R Yr. XVII	10,462,000	0.50	3.00	10.00	20.00	—
1939R Yr. XVIII	Inc. above	0.10	0.40	1.00	3.00	—
1940R Yr. XVIII	Inc. above	0.10	0.40	1.00	3.00	—
1941R Yr. XIX	97,300,000	0.10	0.40	1.00	3.00	—
1942R Yr. XX	Inc. above	0.10	0.40	1.00	3.00	—
1943R Yr. XXI	18,453,000	0.10	0.40	1.00	3.00	—

KM# 75c 20 CENTESIMI

Stainless Steel, 22.5 mm. **Ruler:** Vittorio Emanuele III **Obv:** Head left **Rev:** Savoy shield within head right **Edge:** Plain **Note:** Non-magnetic.

Date	Mintage	F	VF	XF	Unc	BU
1939R Yr. XVII	Inc. above	2.00	6.00	14.00	38.00	—

KM# 75d 20 CENTESIMI

4.0300 g., Stainless Steel, 21.8 mm. **Ruler:** Vittorio Emanuele III **Obv:** Head left **Rev:** Savoy shield within head right **Edge:** Reeded **Note:** Non-magnetic.

Date	Mintage	F	VF	XF	Unc	BU
1939R Yr. XVII	Inc. above	0.50	1.00	3.00	5.00	—
1939R Yr. XVIII	25,300,000	0.50	1.00	3.50	5.00	—
1940R Yr. XVIII	Inc. above	0.10	0.40	1.00	3.00	—

KM# 36 25 CENTESIMI

Nickel **Ruler:** Vittorio Emanuele III **Obv:** Crowned eagle with Savoy shield on chest **Rev:** Value above sprigs

Date	Mintage	F	VF	XF	Unc	BU
1902R	7,773,000	35.00	80.00	150	400	—
1903R	5,895,000	35.00	80.00	150	400	—

KM# 61.1 50 CENTESIMI

6.1000 g., Nickel, 24 mm. **Ruler:** Vittorio Emanuele III **Obv:** Head left **Rev:** Four lions pulling cart with seated Aequitas **Edge:** Plain

Date	Mintage	F	VF	XF	Unc	BU
1919R	3,700,000	7.00	15.00	80.00	180	—
1920R	29,450,000	1.00	2.00	6.00	30.00	—
1921R	16,849,000	1.00	3.00	12.00	40.00	—
1924R	599,000	200	400	700	2,000	—
1925R	24,884,000	1.00	3.00	12.00	40.00	—
1926R	500	—	—	—	550	—
1927R	100	—	—	—	750	—
1928R	50	—	—	—	950	—

KM# 61.2 50 CENTESIMI

6.0000 g., Nickel, 24 mm. **Ruler:** Vittorio Emanuele III **Obv:** Head left **Rev:** Four lions pulling cart with seated Aequitas **Edge:** Reeded

Date	Mintage	F	VF	XF	Unc	BU
1919R	Inc. above	20.00	50.00	350	1,000	—
1920R	Inc. above	2.00	14.00	180	400	—
1921R	Inc. above	2.00	14.00	200	150	—
1924R	Inc. above	60.00	120	400	1,000	—
1925R	Inc. above	2.00	14.00	120	1,000	—
1929R	50	—	—	—	800	—
1930R	50	—	—	—	800	—
1931R	50	—	—	—	800	—
1932R	50	—	—	—	800	—
1933R	50	—	—	—	800	—
1934R	50	—	—	—	800	—
1935R	50	—	—	—	800	—

KM# 76 50 CENTESIMI

Nickel, 24 mm. **Ruler:** Vittorio Emanuele III **Obv:** Head right **Obv. Designer:** Giuseppe Romagnoli **Rev:** Eagle standing right on fasces

Date	Mintage	F	VF	XF	Unc	BU
1936R Yr. XIV	118,000	30.00	90.00	180	350	—
1937R Yr. XV	50	—	—	—	1,200	—
1938R Yr. XVII	20	—	—	—	2,200	—

KM# 76a 50 CENTESIMI

6.1300 g., Stainless Steel, 24 mm. **Ruler:** Vittorio Emanuele III **Obv:** Head right **Obv. Designer:** Giuseppe Romagnoli **Rev:** Eagle standing right on fasces **Edge:** Reeded **Note:** Non-magnetic.

Date	Mintage	F	VF	XF	Unc	BU
1939R Yr. XVII	9,373,000	0.10	0.50	2.00	12.00	—
1939R Yr. XVIII	10,005,000	0.10	0.50	3.00	16.00	—
1940R Yr. XVIII	19,005,000	0.10	0.50	1.50	7.00	—

KM# 76b 50 CENTESIMI

6.0000 g., Stainless Steel, 24 mm. **Ruler:** Vittorio Emanuele III **Obv:** Head right **Rev:** Eagle standing right on fasces **Edge:** Reeded **Note:** Magnetic.

Date	Mintage	F	VF	XF	Unc	BU
1939R Yr. XVII	9,373,000	0.10	0.50	5.00	15.00	—
1939R Yr. XVIII	Inc. above	0.10	0.50	5.00	15.00	—
1940R Yr. XVIII	19,005,000	0.10	0.40	4.00	12.00	—
1941R Yr. XIX	58,100,000	0.10	0.20	1.50	5.00	—
1942R Yr. XX	26,450,000	0.10	0.20	1.50	5.00	—
1943R Yr. XXI	3,681,000	40.00	80.00	150	280	—

KM# 32 LIRA

5.0000 g., 0.8350 Silver 0.1342 oz. ASW **Ruler:** Vittorio Emanuele III **Obv:** Head right **Rev:** Crowned eagle with savoy shield

Date	Mintage	F	VF	XF	Unc	BU
1901R	2,590,000	10.00	20.00	90.00	400	—
1902R	4,084,000	8.00	16.00	75.00	280	—
1905R	700,000	150	300	1,000	2,500	—
1906R	4,665,000	8.00	16.00	75.00	300	—
1907R	8,472,000	8.00	16.00	60.00	250	—

KM# 45 LIRA

5.0000 g., 0.8350 Silver 0.1342 oz. ASW **Ruler:** Vittorio Emanuele III **Obv:** Bust right **Rev:** Quadriga with standing female figure **Rev. Designer:** Davide Calandra

Date	Mintage	F	VF	XF	Unc	BU
1908R	2,212,000	30.00	75.00	325	700	—
1909R	3,475,000	15.00	50.00	280	600	—
1910R	5,525,000	10.00	25.00	75.00	250	—
1912R	5,865,000	5.00	15.00	40.00	180	—
1913R	16,177,000	5.00	10.00	30.00	90.00	—

KM# 57 LIRA

5.0000 g., 0.8350 Silver 0.1342 oz. ASW **Ruler:** Vittorio Emanuele III **Obv:** Bust right **Rev:** Quadriga with standing female figure

Date	Mintage	F	VF	XF	Unc	BU
1915R	5,229,000	5.00	30.00	60.00	120	—
1916R	1,835,000	15.00	60.00	175	450	—
1917R	9,744,000	4.00	15.00	30.00	90.00	—

KM# 62 LIRA

Nickel, 27 mm. **Ruler:** Vittorio Emanuele III **Obv:** Female seated left **Rev:** Crowned Savoy shield and value within wreath

Date	Mintage	F	VF	XF	Unc	BU
1922R	82,267,000	0.60	2.00	15.00	70.00	—
1923R	20,175,000	1.00	5.00	45.00	130	—
1924R Closed 2	29,288,000	1.00	5.00	40.00	120	—
1926R	500	—	—	—	500	—
1927R	100	—	—	—	600	—
1928R	19,996,000	4.00	10.00	70.00	180	—
1929R	50	—	—	—	1,000	—
1930R	50	—	—	—	1,000	—
1931R	50	—	—	—	1,000	—
1932R	50	—	—	—	1,000	—
1933R	50	—	—	—	1,000	—
1934R	50	—	—	—	1,000	—
1935R	50	—	—	—	1,000	—

KM# 77 LIRA

Nickel, 27 mm. **Ruler:** Vittorio Emanuele III **Obv:** Head left **Rev:** Eagle with wings open

Date	Mintage	F	VF	XF	Unc	BU
1936R Yr. XIV	119,000	30.00	110	220	450	—
1937R Yr. XV	50	—	—	—	1,150	—
1938R XVII	20	—	—	—	1,650	—

KM# 77a LIRA

8.1000 g., Stainless Steel, 27 mm. **Ruler:** Vittorio Emanuele III **Obv:** Head left **Rev:** Eagle with wings open **Edge:** Reeded **Note:** Non-magnetic.

Date	Mintage	F	VF	XF	Unc	BU
1939R Yr. XVII	10,034,000	0.40	1.00	4.00	20.00	—
1939R Yr. XVIII	15,977,000	0.20	0.60	3.00	10.00	—
1940R Yr. XVIII	25,997,000	0.20	0.50	2.00	6.00	—

KM# 77b LIRA

7.9000 g., Stainless Steel, 27 mm. **Ruler:** Vittorio Emanuele III **Obv:** Head left **Rev:** Eagle with wings open **Edge:** Reeded **Note:** Magnetic.

Date	Mintage	F	VF	XF	Unc	BU
1939R Yr. XVII	Inc. above	0.40	1.50	4.00	12.00	—
1939R Yr. XVIII	Inc. above	0.20	0.60	3.00	12.00	—
1940R Yr. XVIII	Inc. above	0.20	0.50	2.00	6.00	—
1941R Yr. XIX	8,550,000	1.00	5.00	10.00	20.00	—
1942R Yr. XX	5,700,000	0.20	1.00	5.00	12.00	—
1943R Yr. XXI	11,500,000	15.00	40.00	90.00	120	—

KM# 33 2 LIRE

10.0000 g., 0.8350 Silver 0.2684 oz. ASW **Ruler:** Vittorio Emanuele III **Obv:** Head right **Rev:** Crowned eagle with Savoy shield on chest

Date	Mintage	F	VF	XF	Unc	BU
1901R	72,000	600	1,300	3,900	7,500	—
1902R	549,000	100	350	1,100	2,200	—
1903R	54,000	1,800	3,000	7,500	16,000	—
1904R	157,000	500	1,100	2,800	6,000	—
1905R	1,643,000	100	180	400	1,100	—
1906R	970,000	110	200	500	1,200	—
1907R	1,245,000	90.00	180	480	1,100	—

KM# 46 2 LIRE

10.0000 g., 0.8350 Silver 0.2684 oz. ASW **Ruler:** Vittorio Emanuele III **Obv:** Bust right **Rev:** Quadriga with standing female **Rev. Designer:** Davide Calandra

Date	Mintage	F	VF	XF	Unc	BU
1908R	2,283,000	30.00	70.00	200	550	—
1910R	719,000	100	210	600	1,700	—
1911R	535,000	200	800	1,200	2,800	—
1912R	2,166,000	30.00	70.00	200	850	—

KM# 52 2 LIRE

10.0000 g., 0.8350 Silver 0.2684 oz. ASW, 27 mm. **Ruler:** Vittorio Emanuele III **Subject:** 50th Anniversary of the Kingdom **Obv:** Head left **Rev:** Two classical figures standing **Designer:** Dominico Trentacoste

Date	Mintage	F	VF	XF	Unc	BU
1911R	1,000,000	50.00	80.00	175	400	—

KM# 55 2 LIRE

10.0000 g., 0.8350 Silver 0.2684 oz. ASW **Ruler:** Vittorio Emanuele III **Obv:** Bust right **Rev:** Quadriga with standing female

Date	Mintage	F	VF	XF	Unc	BU
1914R	10,390,000	10.00	20.00	40.00	90.00	—
1915R	7,948,000	10.00	20.00	40.00	100	—
1916R	10,923,000	10.00	20.00	40.00	90.00	—
1917R	6,123,000	30.00	55.00	100	190	—

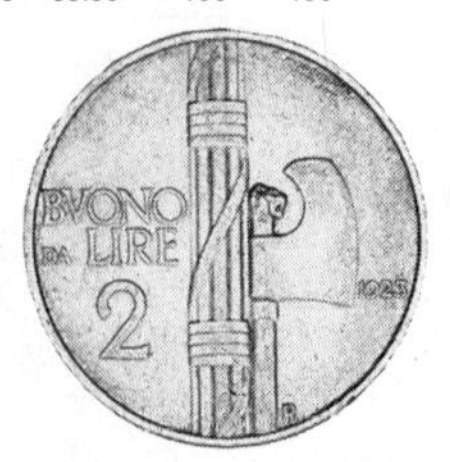

KM# 63 2 LIRE

Nickel **Ruler:** Vittorio Emanuele III **Obv:** Bust right **Rev:** Axe head within fasces with value at left

Date	Mintage	F	VF	XF	Unc	BU
1923R	32,260,000	1.00	5.00	30.00	100	—
1924R	45,051,000	1.00	5.00	30.00	100	—
1925R	14,628,000	2.00	20.00	80.00	190	—
1926R	5,101,000	22.00	90.00	400	1,000	—
1927R	1,632,000	100	250	1,000	2,500	—
1928R	50	—	—	—	1,100	—
1929R	50	—	—	—	1,100	—
1930R	50	—	—	—	1,100	—
1931R	50	—	—	—	1,100	—
1932R	50	—	—	—	1,100	—
1933R	50	—	—	—	1,100	—
1934R	50	—	—	—	1,100	—
1935R	50	—	—	—	1,100	—

KM# 78 2 LIRE

Nickel **Ruler:** Vittorio Emanuele III **Obv:** Head right **Rev:** Eagle with open wings standing on fasces within wreath **Edge:** Plain

Date	Mintage	F	VF	XF	Unc	BU
1936R Yr. XIV	120,000	70.00	120	240	600	—
1937R Yr. XV	50	—	—	—	1,000	—
1939R Yr. XVII	20	—	—	—	2,500	—

KM# 78a 2 LIRE

Stainless Steel, 29 mm. **Ruler:** Vittorio Emanuele III **Obv:** Head right **Rev:** Eagle with open wings standing on fasces within wreath **Edge:** Reeded **Note:** Non-magnetic.

Date	Mintage	F	VF	XF	Unc	BU
1939R Yr. XVII	2,900,000	0.60	2.00	5.00	40.00	—
1939R Yr. XVIII	4,873,000	0.40	1.00	4.00	10.00	—
1940R Yr. XVIII	5,742,000	0.40	1.00	4.00	10.00	—

KM# 78b 2 LIRE

Stainless Steel, 29 mm. **Ruler:** Vittorio Emanuele III **Obv:** Head right **Rev:** Eagle with open wings standing on fasces within wreath **Edge:** Reeded **Note:** Magnetic.

Date	Mintage	F	VF	XF	Unc	BU
1939R Yr. XVII	Inc. above	1.00	2.00	6.00	24.00	—
1939R Yr. XVIII	Inc. above	1.00	2.00	5.00	24.00	—
1940R Yr. XVIII	Inc. above	0.40	0.90	2.00	5.50	—
1941R Yr. XIX	1,865,000	0.50	1.50	3.00	8.00	—
1942R Yr. XX	2,450,000	80.00	150	300	700	—
1943R Yr. XXI	600,000	70.00	160	300	580	—

KM# 34 5 LIRE

25.0000 g., 0.9000 Silver 0.7234 oz. ASW **Ruler:** Vittorio Emanuele III **Obv:** Head right **Obv. Designer:** Filippo Speranza **Rev:** Crowned eagle with Savoy shield on chest

Date	Mintage	F	VF	XF	Unc	BU
1901R	114	10,000	20,000	40,000	50,000	—

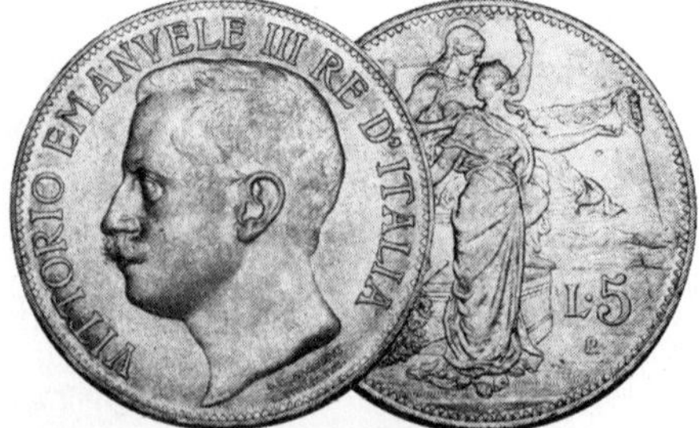

KM# 53 5 LIRE

25.0000 g., 0.9000 Silver 0.7234 oz. ASW, 37 mm. **Ruler:** Vittorio Emanuele III **Subject:** 50th Anniversary of the Kingdom **Obv:** Head left **Rev:** Two classical figures standing **Designer:** Dominico Trentacoste

Date	Mintage	F	VF	XF	Unc	BU
1911R	60,000	1,100	1,500	2,200	3,800	—

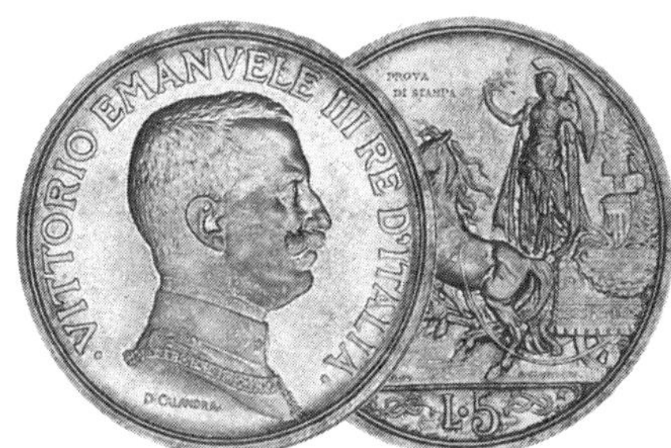

KM# 56 5 LIRE
25.0000 g., 0.9000 Silver 0.7234 oz. ASW **Ruler:** Vittorio Emanuele III **Obv:** Head right **Rev:** Quadriga with standing female **Rev. Designer:** Davide Calandra

Date	Mintage	F	VF	XF	Unc	BU
1914R	273,000	5,000	8,000	10,000	15,000	—

KM# 67.1 5 LIRE
5.0000 g., 0.8350 Silver 0.1342 oz. ASW, 23 mm. **Ruler:** Vittorio Emanuele III **Obv:** Head left **Rev:** Eagle with open wings standing on fascis **Edge Lettering:** *FERT*

Date	Mintage	F	VF	XF	Unc	BU
1926R	5,405,000	5.00	15.00	50.00	120	—
1927R	92,887,000	2.00	5.00	12.00	40.00	—
1928R	9,908,000	4.00	15.00	50.00	120	—
1929R	33,803,000	2.00	5.00	10.00	35.00	—
1930R	19,525,000	2.00	5.00	10.00	30.00	—
1931R	50	—	—	—	1,000	—
1932R	50	—	—	—	1,000	—
1933R	50	—	—	—	1,000	—
1934R	50	—	—	—	1,000	—
1935R	50	—	—	—	1,000	—

KM# 67.2 5 LIRE
5.0000 g., 0.8350 Silver 0.1342 oz. ASW, 23 mm. **Ruler:** Vittorio Emanuele III **Obv:** Head left **Rev:** Eagle with wings open standing on fascis **Edge Lettering:** ** FERT **

Date	Mintage	F	VF	XF	Unc	BU
1927R	Inc. above	2.00	5.00	12.00	40.00	—
1928R	Inc. above	8.00	20.00	80.00	120	—
1929R	Inc. above	2.00	5.00	12.00	40.00	—

KM# 79 5 LIRE
5.0000 g., 0.8350 Silver 0.1342 oz. ASW **Ruler:** Vittorio Emanuele III **Obv:** Head left **Rev:** Mother seated with three children

Date	Mintage	F	VF	XF	Unc	BU
1936R Yr. XIV	1,016,000	30.00	60.00	80.00	150	—
1937R Yr. XV	100,000	60.00	90.00	130	220	—
1938R Yr. XVIII	20	—	—	—	1,700	—
1939R Yr. XVIII	20	—	—	—	1,700	—
1940R Yr. XIX	20	—	—	—	1,700	—
1941R Yr. XX	20	—	—	—	1,700	—

KM# 47 10 LIRE
3.2258 g., 0.9000 Gold 0.0933 oz. AGW, 18 mm. **Ruler:** Vittorio Emanuele III **Rev. Designer:** Egidio Boninsegna

Date	Mintage	F	VF	XF	Unc	BU
1910R Rare	—	—	—	—	—	—
Note: All but one piece melted						
1912R	6,796	3,000	4,000	7,000	10,000	—
1926R	40	—	—	10,000	18,000	—
1927R	30	—	—	14,000	20,000	—

KM# 68.1 10 LIRE
10.0000 g., 0.8350 Silver 0.2684 oz. ASW **Ruler:** Vittorio Emanuele III **Obv:** Head left **Obv. Designer:** Giuseppe Romagnoli **Rev:** Biga with female **Edge Lettering:** *FERT*

Date	Mintage	F	VF	XF	Unc	BU
1926R	1,748,000	140	280	400	800	—
1927R	44,801,000	10.00	30.00	100	200	—
1928R	6,652,000	50.00	80.00	180	350	—
1929R	6,800,000	80.00	150	300	700	—
1930R	3,668,000	140	280	400	800	—
1931R	50	—	—	—	1,500	—
1932R	50	—	—	—	1,500	—
1933R	50	—	—	—	1,500	—
1934R	50	—	—	—	1,500	—

KM# 68.2 10 LIRE
10.0000 g., 0.8350 Silver 0.2684 oz. ASW **Ruler:** Vittorio Emanuele III **Obv:** Head left **Obv. Designer:** Giuseppe Romagnoli **Rev:** Biga with female **Edge Lettering:** **FERT**

Date	Mintage	F	VF	XF	Unc	BU
1927R	Inc. above	10.00	30.00	90.00	200	—
1928R	Inc. above	150	400	900	1,500	—
1929R	Inc. above	50.00	80.00	180	350	—

KM# 80 10 LIRE
10.0000 g., 0.8350 Silver 0.2684 oz. ASW **Ruler:** Vittorio Emanuele III **Obv:** Head right **Rev:** Female standing on prow **Designer:** Giuseppe Romagnoli

Date	Mintage	F	VF	XF	Unc	BU
1936R Yr. XIV	619,000	40.00	50.00	110	220	—
1937R Yr. XV	50	—	—	—	1,800	—
1938R Yr. XVII	20	—	—	—	3,000	—
1939R Yr. XVIII	20	—	—	—	3,000	—
1940R Yr. XIX	20	—	—	—	3,000	—
1941R Yr. XX	20	—	—	—	3,000	—

KM# 37.1 20 LIRE
6.4516 g., 0.9000 Gold 0.1867 oz. AGW **Ruler:** Vittorio Emanuele III **Obv:** Head left **Rev:** Crowned eagle with Savoy shield on chest

Date	Mintage	F	VF	XF	Unc	BU
1902R	181	8,000	15,000	25,000	36,000	—
1903R	1,800	1,200	2,000	2,500	4,000	—
1905R	8,715	1,000	1,400	1,800	3,000	—
1908R Rare	—	—	—	—	—	—

KM# 37.2 20 LIRE
6.4516 g., 0.9000 Gold 0.1867 oz. AGW **Ruler:** Vittorio Emanuele III **Obv:** Head left **Rev:** Crowned eagle with Savoy shield on chest **Note:** A small anchor below the neck indicates that the gold in the coin is from Eritrea.

Date	Mintage	F	VF	XF	Unc	BU
1902R	115	8,000	15,000	28,000	52,000	—

KM# 48 20 LIRE
6.4516 g., 0.9000 Gold 0.1867 oz. AGW **Ruler:** Vittorio Emanuele III **Obv:** Uniformed bust left **Rev:** Female standing on prow **Designer:** Egidio Boninsegna

Date	Mintage	F	VF	XF	Unc	BU
1910R	Est. 33,000	—	—	—	70,000	—
Note: Six pieces currently known to exist						
1912R	59,000	800	1,200	1,600	2,300	—
1926R	40	—	—	10,500	17,500	—
1927R	30	—	—	12,000	20,000	—

KM# 64 20 LIRE
6.4516 g., 0.9000 Gold 0.1867 oz. AGW, 21 mm. **Ruler:** Vittorio Emanuele III **Subject:** 1st Anniversary of Fascist Government **Obv:** Head left **Rev:** Axe head within fasces with value at left **Designer:** Attilio Motti

Date	Mintage	F	VF	XF	Unc	BU
1923R	20,000	700	1,000	1,500	2,300	2,500

KM# 69 20 LIRE
15.0000 g., 0.8000 Silver 0.3858 oz. ASW **Ruler:** Vittorio Emanuele III **Obv:** Head right **Rev:** Standing male with fasces approaching seated Italia **Designer:** Giuseppe Romagnoli

Date	Mintage	F	VF	XF	Unc	BU
1927R Yr. V	100	—	8,000	18,000	85,000	—
1927R Yr. VI	3,518,000	100	250	400	900	—
1928R Yr. VI	2,487,000	120	280	500	1,000	—
1929R Yr. VII	50	—	—	—	4,000	—
1930R Yr. VIII	50	—	—	—	4,000	—
1931R Yr. IX	50	—	—	—	4,000	—
1932R Yr. X	50	—	—	—	4,000	—
1933R Yr. XI	50	—	—	—	4,000	—
1934R Yr. XII	50	—	—	—	4,000	—

KM# 70 20 LIRE
20.0000 g., 0.6000 Silver 0.3858 oz. ASW, 35 mm. **Ruler:** Vittorio Emanuele III **Subject:** 10th Anniversary - End of World War I **Obv:** Helmeted head left **Rev:** Fasces, lion's head and axe head **Designer:** Giuseppe Romagnoli **Note:** Similar 20 and 100 Lire pieces were struck in gold. Silver and silvered brass items are modern fantasies.

Date	Mintage	F	VF	XF	Unc	BU
1928R Yr. VI	3,536,250	150	300	650	1,200	—

KM# 81 20 LIRE
20.0000 g., 0.8000 Silver 0.5144 oz. ASW **Ruler:** Vittorio Emanuele III **Obv:** Head left **Rev:** Quadriga and seated female **Designer:** Giuseppe Romagnoli

Date	Mintage	F	VF	XF	Unc	BU
1936R Yr. XIV	10,000	—	—	3,000	4,500	—
1937R Yr. XV	50	—	—	—	7,500	—
1938R Yr. XVII	20	—	—	—	10,000	—
1939R Yr. XVIII	20	—	—	—	10,000	—
1940R Yr. XIX	20	—	—	—	10,000	—
1941R Yr. XX	20	—	—	—	10,000	—

KM# 49 50 LIRE
16.1290 g., 0.9000 Gold 0.4667 oz. AGW **Ruler:** Vittorio Emanuele III **Obv:** Bust left **Rev:** Female with plow **Designer:** Egidio Boninsegna

Date	Mintage	F	VF	XF	Unc	BU
1910R Rare	2,096	—	—	—	—	—
1912R	11,000	1,200	1,600	2,200	3,500	4,500
1926R	40	—	—	—	28,000	—
1927R	30	—	—	—	30,000	—

KM# 54 50 LIRE

16.1290 g., 0.9000 Gold 0.4667 oz. AGW, 28 mm. **Ruler:** Vittorio Emanuele III **Subject:** 50th Anniversary of the Kingdom **Obv:** Head left **Rev:** Standing classical couple **Designer:** Domenico Trentacoste

Date	Mintage	F	VF	XF	Unc	BU
ND(1911)R	20,000	800	1,200	1,800	2,400	3,000

KM# 71 50 LIRE

4.3995 g., 0.9000 Gold 0.1273 oz. AGW **Ruler:** Vittorio Emanuele III **Obv:** Head left **Rev:** Man striding right

Date	Mintage	F	VF	XF	Unc	BU
1931R Yr. IX	19,750	300	400	500	620	—
1931R Yr. X	12,630	400	500	650	850	—
1932R Yr. X	12,000	300	400	550	700	—
1933R Yr. XI	6,463	800	1,000	1,300	2,000	—

KM# 82 50 LIRE

4.3995 g., 0.9000 Gold 0.1273 oz. AGW **Ruler:** Vittorio Emanuele III **Obv:** Head left **Rev:** Eagle with wings spread above Savoy shield

Date	Mintage	F	VF	XF	Unc	BU
1936R Yr. XIV	790	3,000	6,000	8,000	11,000	15,000

REPUBLIC

DECIMAL COINAGE

KM# 87 LIRA

Aluminum **Obv:** Wheat sprigs within head left **Rev:** Orange sprig

Date	Mintage	F	VF	XF	Unc	BU
1946R	104,000	25.00	50.00	120	250	—
1947R	12,000	200	500	900	1,500	—
1948R	9,000,000	0.50	4.00	7.00	30.00	—
1949R	13,200,000	0.50	4.00	7.00	30.00	—
1950R	1,942,000	1.00	3.00	10.00	40.00	—

KM# 91 LIRA

0.6200 g., Aluminum, 17 mm. **Obv:** Balance scales **Rev:** Cornucopia, value and date **Designer:** Giuseppe Romagnoli **Note:** The 1968-1969 and 1982-2001 dates were issued in sets only.

Date	Mintage	F	VF	XF	Unc	BU
1951R	3,680,000	0.10	0.50	3.00	10.00	—
1952R	2,720,000	0.10	0.50	3.00	10.00	—
1953R	2,800,000	0.10	0.50	3.00	10.00	—
1954R	41,040,000	0.10	0.25	0.50	2.00	—
1955R	32,640,000	0.10	0.25	0.50	2.00	—
1956R	1,840,000	4.00	8.00	25.00	60.00	—
1957R	7,440,000	0.10	0.25	0.50	2.00	—
1958R	5,280,000	0.10	0.25	0.50	2.00	—
1959R	1,680,000	0.10	0.25	0.50	2.00	—
1968R	100,000	—	—	—	25.00	—
1969R	310,000	—	—	—	4.00	—
1970R	1,011,000	—	—	—	2.00	—
1980R	1,500,000	—	—	—	4.00	—
1981R	500,000	—	—	—	4.00	—

Date	Mintage	F	VF	XF	Unc	BU
1982R	85,000	—	—	—	4.00	—
1983R	76,000	—	—	—	25.00	—
1984R	77,000	—	—	—	20.00	—
1985R	73,000	—	—	—	10.00	—
1985R Proof	20,000	Value: 10.00				
1986R	13,200	—	—	—	8.00	—
1986R Proof	17,500	Value: 12.00				
1987R	177,000	—	—	—	20.00	—
1987R Proof	—	Value: 25.00				
1988R	51,000	—	—	—	30.00	—
1988R Proof	9,000	Value: 25.00				
1989R	51,200	—	—	—	20.00	—
1989R Proof	9,260	Value: 20.00				
1990R	52,300	—	—	—	20.00	—
1990R Proof	9,600	Value: 20.00				
1991R	56,000	—	—	—	8.00	—
1991R Proof	11,000	Value: 20.00				
1992R	52,000	—	—	—	20.00	—
1992R Proof	9,500	Value: 20.00				
1993R	50,200	—	—	—	20.00	—
1993R Proof	8,500	Value: 20.00				
1994R	44,500	—	—	—	30.00	—
1994R Proof	8,500	Value: 30.00				
1995R	44,600	—	—	—	30.00	—
1995R Proof	7,960	Value: 30.00				
1996R	45,000	—	—	—	20.00	—
1996R Proof	8,000	Value: 20.00				
1997R	43,600	—	—	—	30.00	—
1997R Proof	8,440	Value: 35.00				
1998R	55,200	—	—	—	10.00	—
1998R Proof	9,000	Value: 15.00				
1999R	51,800	—	—	—	10.00	—
1999R Proof	8,000	Value: 15.00				
2000R	61,400	—	—	—	20.00	—
2000R Proof	9,000	Value: 30.00				
2001R Proof	10,000	Value: 40.00				
2001R	100,000	—	—	—	30.00	—

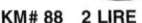

KM# 88 2 LIRE

1.7400 g., Aluminum **Obv:** Ploughman **Rev:** Wheat ear divides value **Designer:** Giuseppe Romagnoli

Date	Mintage	F	VF	XF	Unc	BU
1946R	123,000	50.00	90.00	170	320	—
1947R	12,000	200	400	900	1,600	—
1948R	7,200,000	0.50	2.00	10.00	30.00	—
1949R	1,350,000	3.00	20.00	40.00	110	—
1950R	2,640,000	0.60	2.50	10.00	35.00	—

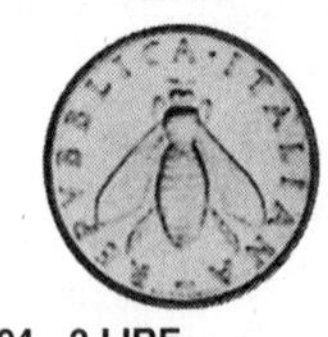

KM# 94 2 LIRE

0.8000 g., Aluminum **Obv:** Honey bee **Rev:** Olive branch and value **Note:** The 1968-1969 and 1982-2001 dates were issued in sets only.

Date	Mintage	F	VF	XF	Unc	BU
1953R	4,125,000	0.20	0.50	2.00	5.00	—
1954R	22,500,000	0.20	0.50	2.00	5.00	—
1955R	2,750,000	0.20	0.50	2.00	5.00	—
1956R	1,500,000	2.00	4.00	8.00	20.00	—
1957R	6,313,000	0.20	0.50	2.00	5.00	—
1958R	125,000	25.00	90.00	140	250	—
1959R	2,000,000	0.20	0.50	2.00	5.00	—
1968R	100,000	—	—	—	20.00	—
1969R	310,000	—	—	—	3.00	—
1970R	1,140,000	—	—	—	2.50	—
1980R	500,000	—	—	—	2.00	—
1981R	500,000	—	—	—	2.00	—
1982R	85,000	—	—	—	2.00	—
1983R	76,000	6.00	15.00	20.00	40.00	—
1984R	77,000	—	—	8.00	15.00	—
1985R	91,220	—	—	—	10.00	—
1985R Proof	20,000	Value: 12.00				
1986R	73,200	—	—	—	10.00	—
1986R Proof	17,500	Value: 15.00				
1987R	57,500	—	—	—	18.00	—
1987R Proof	10,000	Value: 30.00				
1988R	51,050	—	—	—	25.00	—
1988R Proof	9,000	Value: 30.00				
1989R	51,200	—	—	—	25.00	—
1989R Proof	9,260	Value: 18.00				
1990R	53,300	—	—	—	25.00	—
1990R Proof	9,600	Value: 20.00				
1991R	54,000	—	—	—	25.00	—
1991R Proof	11,000	Value: 25.00				
1992R	52,000	—	—	—	8.00	—
1992R Proof	9,500	Value: 20.00				

Date	Mintage	F	VF	XF	Unc	BU
1993R	50,200	—	—	—	25.00	—
1993R Proof	8,500	Value: 20.00				
1994R	44,500	—	—	—	25.00	—
1994R Proof	8,500	Value: 25.00				
1995R	44,588	—	—	—	40.00	—
1995R Proof	7,960	Value: 45.00				
1996R	65,000	—	—	—	20.00	—
1996R Proof	8,000	Value: 22.00				
1997R	43,600	—	—	—	40.00	—
1997R Proof	8,660	Value: 40.00				
1998R	55,200	—	—	—	10.00	—
1998R Proof	9,000	Value: 15.00				
1999R	51,800	—	—	—	15.00	—
1999R Proof	8,500	Value: 18.00				
2000R	61,500	—	—	—	18.00	—
2000R Proof	9,000	Value: 20.00				
2001R Proof	10,000	Value: 40.00				
2001R	100,000	—	—	—	18.00	—

KM# 89 5 LIRE

Aluminum **Obv:** Female head holding torch facing right **Rev:** Grape cluster

Date	Mintage	F	VF	XF	Unc	BU
1946R	81,000	200	400	800	1,200	—
1947R	17,000	300	600	1,000	1,500	—
1948R	25,125,000	0.50	3.00	10.00	50.00	—
1949R	71,100,000	0.30	3.00	5.00	25.00	—
1950R	114,790,000	0.30	3.00	10.00	35.00	—

KM# 92 5 LIRE

1.0350 g., Aluminum, 20.12 mm. **Obv:** Rudder **Rev:** Dolphin and value **Edge:** Plain **Designer:** Giuseppe Romagnoli

Date	Mintage	F	VF	XF	Unc	BU
1951R	40,260,000	0.10	0.25	1.00	6.00	—
1952R	57,400,000	0.10	0.25	1.00	6.00	—
1953R	196,200,000	0.10	0.25	0.50	3.00	—
1954R	436,400,000	0.10	0.25	0.50	3.00	—
1955R	159,000,000	0.10	0.25	0.50	2.00	—
1956R	400,000	30.00	70.00	400	1,200	—
1966R	1,200,000	0.25	0.50	2.00	6.00	—
1967R	10,600,000	0.10	0.25	0.50	1.00	—
1968R	7,500,000	—	—	0.10	0.75	—
1969R	7,910,000	—	—	0.10	0.75	—
1969R Inverted 1 (die break at base of 1)	969,000	3.00	6.00	18.00	65.00	—
1970R	4,200,000	—	—	0.10	0.75	—
1971R	8,600,000	—	—	0.10	0.75	—
1972R	16,400,000	—	—	0.10	0.50	—
1973R	28,800,000	—	—	0.10	0.50	—
1974R	6,600,000	—	—	0.10	0.50	—
1975R	7,000,000	—	—	0.10	0.50	—
1976R	8,800,000	—	—	0.10	0.50	—
1977R	6,700,000	—	—	0.10	0.50	—
1978R	3,600,000	—	—	0.10	0.50	—
1979R	5,000,000	—	—	0.10	0.50	—
1980R	5,000,000	—	—	0.10	0.50	—
1981R	5,000,000	—	—	0.10	0.50	—
1982R	8,700,000	—	—	0.10	0.50	—
1983R	5,000,000	—	—	0.10	1.00	—
1984R	2,100,000	—	—	0.10	1.00	—
1985R	3,000,000	—	—	0.10	1.00	—
1985R Proof	20,000	Value: 10.00				
1986R	5,000,000	—	—	0.10	0.50	—
1986R Proof	17,500	Value: 10.00				
1987R	7,000,000	—	—	0.10	0.50	—
1987R Proof	10,000	Value: 10.00				
1988R	5,000,000	—	—	0.10	0.50	—
1988R Proof	9,000	Value: 10.00				
1989R	2,500,000	—	—	0.10	0.50	—
Note: Coin rotation						
1989R	—	1.00	4.00	7.00	18.00	—
Note: Medal rotation						
1989R Proof	9,260	Value: 10.00				
1990R	2,500,000	—	—	0.10	0.50	—
1990R Proof	9,400	Value: 10.00				
1991R	2,000,000	—	—	0.10	0.50	—
1991R Proof	11,000	Value: 10.00				
1992R	1,000,000	—	—	0.10	0.50	—
1992R Proof	9,500	Value: 10.00				
1993R	1,000,000	—	—	0.10	0.50	—
1993R Proof	9,500	Value: 14.00				

Date	Mintage	F	VF	XF	Unc	BU
1994R	1,000,000	—	—	0.10	0.50	—
1994R Proof	8,500	Value: 14.00				
1995R	3,000,000	—	—	0.10	0.50	—
1995R Proof	7,960	Value: 15.00				
1996R	2,500,000	—	—	0.10	0.50	—
1996R Proof	8,000	Value: 15.00				
1997R	1,000,000	—	—	0.10	0.50	—
1997R Proof	8,660	Value: 15.00				
1998R	1,500,000	—	—	0.10	0.50	—
1998R Proof	9,000	Value: 10.00				
1999R	51,800	—	—	—	25.00	—
1999R Proof	8,500	Value: 15.00				
2000R	61,400	—	—	—	20.00	—
2000R Proof	10,000	Value: 20.00				
2001R	100,000	—	—	—	12.00	—
2001R Proof	10,000	Value: 20.00				

KM# 90 10 LIRE

Aluminum, 29 mm. **Obv:** Pegasus **Rev:** Olive branch divides value **Designer:** Giuseppe Romagnoli

Date	Mintage	F	VF	XF	Unc	BU
1946R	101,000	60.00	180	360	750	—
1947R	12,000	375	1,000	2,000	3,500	—
1948R	14,400,000	1.00	10.00	40.00	100	—
1949R	49,500,000	0.50	1.00	5.00	30.00	—
1950R	53,311,000	0.50	1.00	5.00	30.00	—

KM# 93 10 LIRE

1.6000 g., Aluminum, 23.25 mm. **Obv:** Plow **Rev:** Value within wheat ears **Edge:** Plain **Designer:** Giuseppe Romagnoli

Date	Mintage	F	VF	XF	Unc	BU
1951R	96,600,000	0.10	0.50	3.00	30.00	—
1952R	105,150,000	0.10	0.50	3.00	30.00	—
1953R	151,500,000	0.10	0.50	3.00	30.00	—
1954R	95,250,000	0.50	1.00	5.00	40.00	—
1955R	274,950,000	0.10	0.15	2.00	5.00	—
1956R	76,650,000	0.10	1.00	5.00	20.00	—
1965R	1,050,000	0.25	1.00	5.00	35.00	—
1966R	16,500,000	0.10	0.25	1.00	3.00	—
1967R	29,450,000	0.10	0.25	1.00	3.00	—
1968R	32,200,000	—	—	0.10	0.75	—
1969R	23,710,000	—	—	0.10	0.75	—
1970R	14,100,000	—	—	0.10	0.75	—
1971R	23,550,000	—	—	0.10	0.75	—
1972R	61,300,000	—	—	0.10	0.50	—
1973R	145,800,000	—	—	0.10	0.50	—
1974R	85,000,000	—	—	0.10	0.50	—
1975R	76,800,000	—	—	0.10	0.50	—
1976R	82,000,000	—	—	0.10	0.50	—
1977R	80,750,000	—	—	0.10	0.50	—
1978R	43,800,000	—	—	0.10	0.50	—
1979R	98,000,000	—	—	0.10	0.50	—
1980R	89,000,000	—	—	0.10	0.50	—
1981R	91,750,000	—	—	0.10	0.50	—
1982R	44,500,000	—	—	0.10	0.50	—
1983R	15,110,000	—	—	0.50	1.00	—
1984R	11,122,000	—	—	0.50	1.00	—
1985R	15,000,000	—	—	0.10	0.50	—
1985R Proof	20,000	Value: 10.00				
1986R	16,000,000	—	—	0.10	0.50	—
1986R Proof	17,500	Value: 8.00				
1987R	13,000,000	—	—	0.10	0.50	—
1987R Proof	10,000	Value: 8.00				
1988R	13,000,000	—	—	0.10	0.50	—
1988R Proof	9,000	Value: 10.00				
1989R	16,000,000	—	—	0.10	0.50	—
1989R Proof	9,260	Value: 10.00				
1990R	14,000,000	—	—	0.10	1.00	—
1990R Proof	9,400	Value: 10.00				
1991R	5,000,000	—	—	0.10	1.00	—
1991R Proof	11,000	Value: 10.00				
1992R	1,000,000	—	—	0.10	1.00	—
1992R Proof	9,500	Value: 10.00				
1993R	1,000,000	—	—	0.10	1.00	—
1993R Proof	8,500	Value: 10.00				
1994R	1,000,000	—	—	0.10	1.00	—
1994R Proof	8,500	Value: 10.00				
1995R	2,500,000	—	—	0.10	1.00	—
1995R Proof	7,960	Value: 15.00				
1996R	3,500,000	—	—	0.10	1.00	—

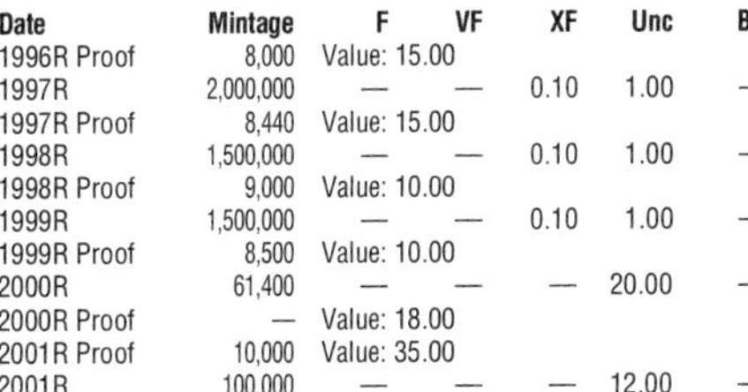

Date	Mintage	F	VF	XF	Unc	BU
1996R Proof	8,000	Value: 15.00				
1997R	2,000,000	—	—	0.10	1.00	—
1997R Proof	8,440	Value: 15.00				
1998R	1,500,000	—	—	0.10	1.00	—
1998R Proof	9,000	Value: 10.00				
1999R	1,500,000	—	—	0.10	1.00	—
1999R Proof	8,500	Value: 10.00				
2000R	61,400	—	—	—	20.00	—
2000R Proof	—	Value: 18.00				
2001R Proof	10,000	Value: 35.00				
2001R	100,000	—	—	—	12.00	—

KM# 97.1 20 LIRE

3.6000 g., Aluminum-Bronze, 21.25 mm. **Obv:** Wheat sprigs within head left **Rev:** Oak leaves divide value and date **Designer:** Pietro Giampaoli

Date	Mintage	F	VF	XF	Unc	BU
1957R Serifed 7	Est. 60,075,000	0.20	0.40	2.00	10.00	—
1957R Plain 7	Inc. above	0.20	0.40	2.00	10.00	—
1958R	80,550,000	0.10	0.40	3.00	12.00	—
1959R	4,005,000	0.50	2.00	10.00	60.00	—

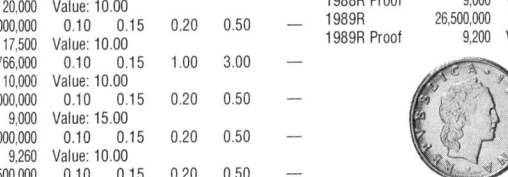

KM# 97.2 20 LIRE

3.6000 g., Aluminum-Bronze, 19.63 mm. **Obv:** Wheat sprigs within head left **Rev:** Oak leaves divide value and date **Edge:** Plain **Designer:** Pietro Giampaoli

Date	Mintage	F	VF	XF	Unc	BU
1968R	100,000	3.00	6.00	25.00	60.00	—
1969R	16,735,000	0.10	0.15	0.25	1.00	—
1970R	31,500,000	0.10	0.15	0.25	0.65	—
1971R	12,375,000	0.10	0.15	0.25	1.00	—
1972R	34,400,000	0.10	0.15	0.25	0.65	—
1973R	20,000,000	0.10	0.15	0.25	0.65	—
1974R	17,000,000	0.10	0.15	0.20	0.65	—
1975R	25,000,000	0.10	0.15	0.20	0.65	—
1976R	17,325,000	0.10	0.15	0.20	0.65	—
1977R	10,000,000	0.10	0.15	0.20	0.65	—
1978R	13,521,000	0.10	0.15	0.20	0.65	—
1979R	40,465,000	0.10	0.15	0.20	0.50	—
1980R	61,795,000	0.10	0.15	0.20	0.50	—
1981R	81,510,000	0.10	0.15	0.20	0.50	—
1982R	34,500,000	0.10	0.15	0.20	0.50	—
1983R	15,110,000	0.10	0.15	0.20	0.50	—
1984R	5,122,000	0.10	0.15	1.00	3.00	—
1985R	15,000,000	0.10	0.15	0.20	0.50	—
1985R Proof	20,000	Value: 10.00				
1986R	13,000,000	0.10	0.15	0.20	0.50	—
1986R Proof	17,500	Value: 10.00				
1987R	2,766,000	0.10	0.15	1.00	3.00	—
1987R Proof	10,000	Value: 10.00				
1988R	13,000,000	0.10	0.15	0.20	0.50	—
1988R Proof	9,000	Value: 15.00				
1989R	16,000,000	0.10	0.15	0.20	0.50	—
1989R Proof	9,260	Value: 10.00				
1990R	15,500,000	0.10	0.15	0.20	0.50	—
1990R Proof	9,400	Value: 10.00				
1991R	13,000,000	0.10	0.15	0.20	0.50	—
1991R Proof	11,000	Value: 10.00				
1992R	2,500,000	0.10	0.15	1.00	3.00	—
1992R Proof	9,500	Value: 10.00				
1993R	1,000,000	0.10	0.15	0.50	1.00	—
1993R Proof	8,500	Value: 10.00				
1994R	1,000,000	0.10	0.15	0.20	0.50	—
1994R Proof	8,500	Value: 10.00				
1995R	1,000,000	0.10	0.15	0.50	1.00	—
1995R Proof	7,950	Value: 15.00				
1996R	1,000,000	0.10	0.15	0.50	1.00	—
1996R Proof	8,000	Value: 10.00				
1997R	1,000,000	0.10	0.15	0.50	1.00	—
1997R Proof	8,440	Value: 20.00				
1998R	1,000,000	0.10	0.15	0.50	1.00	—
1998R Proof	9,000	Value: 10.00				
1999R	500,000	0.10	0.15	1.00	3.00	—
1999R Proof	8,500	Value: 10.00				
2000R	61,400	—	—	—	20.00	—
2000R Proof	8,960	Value: 15.00				
2001R Proof	10,000	Value: 35.00				
2001R	100,000	—	—	—	12.00	—

KM# 95.1 50 LIRE

6.2500 g., Stainless Steel, 24.8 mm. **Obv:** Head right **Rev:** Vulcan standing at anvil facing left divides date and value **Designer:** Giuseppe Romagnoli

Date	Mintage	F	VF	XF	Unc	BU
1954R	17,600,000	1.00	5.00	25.00	100	—
1955R	70,500,000	0.50	1.50	10.00	40.00	—
1956R	69,400,000	0.50	1.50	10.00	40.00	—
1957R	8,925,000	2.00	8.00	30.00	120	—
1958R	825,000	5.00	15.00	60.00	200	—
1959R	8,800,000	4.00	7.00	12.00	40.00	—
1960R	2,025,000	5.00	10.00	40.00	100	—
1961R	11,100,000	0.50	1.50	10.00	40.00	—
1962R	17,700,000	0.50	1.50	5.00	30.00	—
1963R	31,600,000	0.20	0.75	2.50	20.00	—
1964R	37,900,000	0.20	0.75	2.50	18.00	—
1965R	25,300,000	0.20	0.50	1.50	12.00	—
1966R	27,400,000	0.20	0.40	0.80	8.00	—
1967R	28,000,000	0.20	0.40	0.80	6.00	—
1968R	17,800,000	0.20	0.30	0.50	1.50	—
1969R	23,010,000	0.20	0.30	0.50	1.50	—
1970R	21,411,000	0.10	0.20	0.50	1.50	—
1971R	33,410,000	0.10	0.20	0.50	1.50	—
1972R	39,000,000	0.10	0.20	0.50	1.50	—
1973R	48,700,000	0.10	0.20	0.50	1.50	—
1974R	63,000,000	0.10	0.20	0.35	1.00	—
1975R	87,000,000	0.10	0.15	0.25	0.75	—
1976R	180,600,000	0.10	0.15	0.25	0.75	—
1977R	293,800,000	0.10	0.15	0.25	0.75	—
1978R	416,808,000	0.10	0.15	0.25	0.75	—
1979R	321,086,000	0.10	0.15	0.25	0.75	—
1980R	94,819,000	0.10	0.15	0.25	0.75	—
1981R	139,080,000	0.10	0.15	0.25	0.75	—
1982R	54,500,000	0.10	0.15	0.25	0.75	—
1983R	20,000,000	0.10	0.15	0.25	0.75	—
1984R	10,000,000	0.10	0.15	0.25	0.75	—
1985R	10,000,000	0.10	0.15	0.25	0.75	—
1985R Proof	20,000	Value: 10.00				
1986R	15,000,000	0.10	0.15	0.25	0.75	—
1986R Proof	17,500	Value: 10.00				
1987R	14,682,000	0.10	0.15	0.25	0.75	—
1987R Proof	10,000	Value: 10.00				
1988R	20,000,000	0.10	0.15	0.25	0.75	—
1988R Proof	9,000	Value: 20.00				
1989R	26,500,000	0.10	0.15	0.25	0.75	—
1989R Proof	9,200	Value: 12.00				

KM# 95.2 50 LIRE

2.7300 g., Stainless Steel, 17 mm. **Obv:** Head right **Rev:** Vulcan standing at anvil facing left divides date and value **Edge:** Plain **Designer:** Giuseppe Romagnoli **Note:** Reduced size.

Date	Mintage	F	VF	XF	Unc	BU
1990R	45,500,000	—	0.10	0.20	0.50	—
1990R Proof	—	Value: 10.00				
1991R	60,000,000	—	0.10	0.20	0.50	—
1991R Proof	11,000	Value: 10.00				
1992R	90,000,000	—	0.10	0.20	0.50	—
1992R Proof	9,500	Value: 10.00				
1993R	160,000,000	—	0.10	0.20	0.50	—
1993R Proof	8,500	Value: 10.00				
1994R	95,255,000	—	0.10	0.20	0.50	—
1994R Proof	8,500	Value: 10.00				
1995R	82,000,000	—	0.10	0.20	0.50	—
1995R Proof	7,960	Value: 12.00				

KM# 183 50 LIRE

Copper-Nickel, 19 mm. **Obv:** Turreted head left **Rev:** Large value within wreath of produce **Designer:** L. Cretara

Date	Mintage	F	VF	XF	Unc	BU
1996R	110,000,000	—	0.10	0.20	0.50	—
1996R Proof	8,000	Value: 15.00				
1997R	10,000,000	—	0.10	0.20	1.00	—
1997R Proof	8,440	Value: 20.00				
1998R	10,000,000	—	0.10	0.20	1.00	—
1998R Proof	9,000	Value: 15.00				
1999R	55,000,000	—	0.10	0.20	1.00	—
1999R Proof	8,500	Value: 18.00				

Date	Mintage	F	VF	XF	Unc	BU
2000R	61,400	—	—	—	12.00	—
2000R Proof	8,960	Value: 18.00				
2001R Proof	10,000	Value: 35.00				
2001R	100,000	—	—	—	12.00	—

KM# 96.1 100 LIRE

8.0000 g., Stainless Steel, 27.8 mm. **Obv:** Laureate head left **Rev:** Standing figure holding olive tree

Date	Mintage	F	VF	XF	Unc	BU
1955R	8,600,000	1.00	4.00	50.00	185	—
1956R	99,800,000	0.25	1.00	4.00	50.00	—
1957R	90,600,000	0.25	1.50	4.00	50.00	—
1958R	25,640,000	0.25	1.50	10.00	120	—
1959R	19,500,000	0.25	1.50	10.00	120	—
1960R	20,700,000	0.25	1.50	10.00	100	—
1961R	11,860,000	0.25	1.50	10.00	100	—
1962R	21,700,000	0.20	0.50	3.00	40.00	—
1963R	33,100,000	0.20	0.50	2.00	30.00	—
1964R	31,300,000	0.20	0.50	1.50	20.00	—
1965R	37,000,000	0.20	0.50	1.50	20.00	—
1966R	52,500,000	0.15	0.25	1.00	15.00	—
1967R	23,700,000	0.15	0.25	1.00	15.00	—
1968R	34,200,000	0.15	0.25	0.50	2.00	—
1969R	27,710,000	0.15	0.25	0.50	2.00	—
1970R	25,011,000	0.15	0.25	0.50	2.00	—
1971R	24,700,000	0.15	0.25	0.50	2.00	—
1972R	31,170,000	0.15	0.25	0.50	3.00	—
1973R	30,780,000	0.15	0.25	0.50	3.00	—
1974R	61,000,000	0.15	0.25	0.35	0.85	—
1975R	106,650,000	0.15	0.25	0.35	0.85	—
1976R	160,020,000	0.15	0.25	0.35	0.85	—
1977R	253,980,000	0.15	0.25	0.35	0.85	—
1978R	343,626,000	0.15	0.25	0.35	0.85	—
1979R	351,583,600	0.15	0.25	0.35	0.85	—
1980R	69,938,500	0.15	0.25	0.35	0.85	—
1981R	122,381,700	0.15	0.25	0.35	0.85	—
1982R	39,500,000	0.15	0.25	0.35	0.85	—
1983R	25,000,000	0.15	0.25	1.00	3.00	—
1984R	10,000,000	0.15	0.25	1.00	3.00	—
1985R	10,000,000	0.15	0.25	1.00	3.00	—
1985R Proof	20,000	Value: 10.00				
1986R	18,000,000	0.15	0.25	0.50	1.00	—
1986R Proof	17,500	Value: 10.00				
1987R	25,000,000	0.15	0.25	0.50	1.00	—
1987R Proof	10,000	Value: 10.00				
1988R	23,000,000	0.15	0.25	0.85	1.00	—
1988R Proof	9,000	Value: 15.00				
1989R	34,000,000	0.15	0.25	0.85	1.00	—
1989R Proof	9,260	Value: 15.00				

KM# 96.2 100 LIRE

Stainless Steel **Obv:** Laureate head left **Rev:** Standing figure holding olive tree **Note:** Reduced size. Prev. KM#96a.

Date	Mintage	F	VF	XF	Unc	BU
1990R Proof	9,600	Value: 10.00				
1990R	60,000,000	—	—	—	1.00	—
1991R	100,000,000	—	—	—	1.00	—
1991R Proof	11,000	Value: 12.00				
1992R	166,000,000	—	—	—	1.00	—
1992R Proof	9,500	Value: 12.00				

KM# 102 100 LIRE

8.0000 g., Stainless Steel, 27.8 mm. **Subject:** 100th Anniversary - Birth of Guglielmo Marconi, Physicist **Obv:** Head facing **Rev:** Early radio-wave receiver flanked by date and value **Designer:** Guerrino M. Monassi

Date	Mintage	F	VF	XF	Unc	BU
ND(1974)R	50,000,000	0.15	0.25	0.35	1.50	—

KM# 106 100 LIRE

8.0000 g., Stainless Steel, 27.8 mm. , Young head left **Series:** F.A.O. **Rev:** Cow nursing calf, value and date **Designer:** Giandomenico

Date	Mintage	F	VF	XF	Unc	BU
1979R	78,340,000	0.15	0.25	0.50	2.00	—

KM# 108 100 LIRE

8.0000 g., Stainless Steel, 27.8 mm. **Subject:** Centennial of Livorno Naval Academy **Obv:** Anchor and ship's wheel **Rev:** Building divides dates with flag and value below **Designer:** M. Vallucci

Date	Mintage	F	VF	XF	Unc	BU
ND(1981)R	39,500,000	0.15	0.25	0.35	1.50	—

KM# 159 100 LIRE

Copper-Nickel, 22 mm. **Obv:** Turreted head left **Rev:** Large value within circle flanked by sprigs **Designer:** Laura Cretara

Date	Mintage	F	VF	XF	Unc	BU
1993R	211,501,200	0.15	0.25	0.35	0.75	—
1993R Proof	8,500	Value: 15.00				
1994R	180,000,000	0.15	0.25	0.35	0.75	—
1994R Proof	8,500	Value: 15.00				
1996R	210,000,000	0.15	0.25	0.35	0.75	—
1996R Proof	8,000	Value: 20.00				
1997R	70,000,000	0.15	0.25	0.35	0.75	—
1997R Proof	8,440	Value: 35.00				
1998R	120,000,000	0.15	0.25	0.35	0.75	—
1998R Proof	9,000	Value: 15.00				
1999R	120,000,000	0.15	0.25	0.35	0.75	—
1999R Proof	8,500	Value: 15.00				
2000R	61,400	0.15	0.25	0.35	15.00	—
2000R Proof	10,000	Value: 20.00				
2001R	100,000	—	—	—	12.00	—
2001R Proof	10,000	Value: 35.00				

KM# 180 100 LIRE

4.5300 g., Copper-Nickel, 22 mm. **Series:** F.A.O. **Obv:** Turreted head left **Rev:** Logo and value within globe design **Designer:** Laura Cretara

Date	Mintage	F	VF	XF	Unc	BU
ND(1995)R	100,000,000	0.15	0.25	0.35	0.75	—
ND(1995)R Proof	7,960	Value: 25.00				

KM# 105 200 LIRE

5.0000 g., Aluminum-Bronze, 24 mm. **Obv:** Head right **Rev:** Value within gear **Designer:** M. Vallucci

Date	Mintage	F	VF	XF	Unc	BU
1977R	15,900,000	0.20	0.25	0.35	1.25	—
1978R	461,034,000	0.20	0.25	0.35	1.25	—
1979R	487,325,000	0.20	0.25	0.35	1.25	—
1980R	105,690,000	0.20	0.25	0.45	2.00	—
1981R	72,500,000	0.20	0.25	0.45	2.00	—
1982R	9,500,000	0.20	0.25	1.00	4.00	—
1983R	20,000,000	0.20	0.25	0.75	3.00	—
1984R	10,000,000	0.20	0.25	0.75	3.00	—
1985R	15,000,000	0.20	0.25	0.75	3.00	—
1985R Proof	20,000	Value: 10.00				
1986R	15,000,000	0.20	0.25	0.75	3.00	—
1986R Proof	17,500	Value: 10.00				
1987R	26,180,000	0.20	0.25	0.35	1.25	—
1987R Proof	10,000	Value: 10.00				
1988R	37,000,000	0.20	0.25	0.35	1.25	—
1988R Proof	9,000	Value: 20.00				
1991R	70,000,000	0.20	0.25	0.35	1.25	—
1991R Proof	11,000	Value: 15.00				
1995R	170,000,000	0.20	0.25	0.35	1.25	—
1995R Proof	7,960	Value: 35.00				
1998R	120,000,000	0.20	0.25	0.35	1.25	—
1998R Proof	9,000	Value: 10.00				
2000R	61,400	—	—	—	15.00	—
2000R Proof	8,960	Value: 20.00				
2001R Proof	10,000	Value: 35.00				
2001R	100,000	—	—	—	18.00	—

KM# 107 200 LIRE

5.0000 g., Aluminum-Bronze, 24 mm. **Series:** F.A.O. **Subject:** International Women's Year **Obv:** Bust facing **Rev:** Seated woman with knee bent and child standing at her back facing right **Designer:** Giondomenico

Date	Mintage	F	VF	XF	Unc	BU
1980R	48,500,000	0.20	0.25	0.35	2.00	—

KM# 109 200 LIRE

5.0000 g., Aluminum-Bronze, 24 mm. **Subject:** World Food Day **Obv:** Villa Lubin façade **Rev:** Female advancing left holding cornucopia **Designer:** Guido Veroi

Date	Mintage	F	VF	XF	Unc	BU
1981R	45,207,600	0.20	0.25	0.35	2.00	—

KM# 130 200 LIRE

5.0000 g., Bronzital, 24 mm. **Subject:** Taranto Naval Yards **Obv:** Head right **Rev:** Ships and dates **Designer:** M. Vallucci

Date	Mintage	F	VF	XF	Unc	BU
ND(1989)R	48,000,000	—	—	—	2.00	—
ND(1989)R Proof	9,260	Value: 10.00				

KM# 135 200 LIRE

5.0000 g., Bronzital, 24 mm. **Obv:** Head right **Obv. Designer:** M. Vallucci **Rev:** State Council building divides dates and value **Rev. Designer:** Driutti

Date	Mintage	F	VF	XF	Unc	BU
ND(1990)R	64,500,000	—	—	—	2.00	—
ND(1990)R Proof	9,600	Value: 10.00				

KM# 151 200 LIRE

5.0000 g., Aluminum-Bronze, 24 mm. **Subject:** Genoa Stamp Exposition **Obv:** Head right **Rev:** Stylized sailing ship **Designer:** M. Vallucci

Date	Mintage	F	VF	XF	Unc	BU
1992R	110,000,000	—	—	—	2.50	—
1992R Proof	9,500	Value: 12.00				

KM# 155 200 LIRE

5.0000 g., Aluminum-Bronze, 24 mm. **Subject:** 70th Anniversary of Military Aviation **Obv:** Head right **Obv. Designer:** M. Vallucci **Rev:** Quartered arms within circle **Rev. Designer:** Zanelli

Date	Mintage	F	VF	XF	Unc	BU
1993R	170,000,000	—	—	—	2.50	—
1993R Proof	8,500	Value: 10.00				

KM# 164 200 LIRE

5.0000 g., Aluminum-Bronze, 24 mm. **Subject:** 180th Anniversary - Carabinieri **Obv:** Head right **Obv. Designer:** M. Vallucci **Rev:** Flaming bomb above banner and value **Rev. Designer:** Zanelli

Date	Mintage	F	VF	XF	Unc	BU
ND(1994)R	200,000,000	—	—	—	2.00	—
ND(1994)R Proof	8,500	Value: 12.00				

KM# 184 200 LIRE

5.0000 g., Brass, 24 mm. **Subject:** Centennial - Customs Service Academy **Obv:** Old and new buildings **Rev:** Shield above value, hat and sword **Designer:** Eugnio Driutti

Date	Mintage	F	VF	XF	Unc	BU
ND(1996)R	200,000,000	—	—	—	1.50	—
ND(1996)R Proof	8,000	Value: 12.00				

KM# 186 200 LIRE

5.0000 g., Brass, 24 mm. **Subject:** Centennial - Italian Naval League **Obv:** Head right **Obv. Designer:** M. Vallucci **Rev:** Naval League seal divides dates and value **Rev. Designer:** G. C. Frapiccini **Edge:** Reeded

Date	Mintage	F	VF	XF	Unc	BU
ND(1997)R	40,000,000	—	—	—	1.25	1.75
ND(1997)R Proof	8,440	Value: 15.00				

KM# 218 200 LIRE

5.0000 g., Aluminum-Bronze, 24 mm. **Subject:** The Carabinieri, Protectors of Art Heritage **Obv. Designer:** M. Vallucci **Rev:** Flaming bomb and David statue **Rev. Designer:** C. Frapiccini **Edge:** Reeded

Date	Mintage	F	VF	XF	Unc	BU
ND(1999)R	105,000,000	—	—	—	1.50	—
ND(1999)R Proof	8,500	Value: 10.00				

KM# 98 500 LIRE

11.0000 g., 0.8350 Silver 0.2953 oz. ASW, 29.3 mm. **Obv:** Columbus' ships **Obv. Designer:** Guido Veroi **Rev:** Bust left within wreath **Rev. Designer:** Pietro Giampaoli **Edge:** Dates in raised lettering

Date	Mintage	F	VF	XF	Unc	BU
1958R	24,240,000	—	2.00	4.50	10.00	—
1958R Proof	Inc. above	Value: 36.00				
1959R	19,360,000	—	2.00	4.50	10.00	—
1959R Proof	Inc. above	Value: 36.00				
1960R	24,080,000	—	2.00	4.50	9.00	—
1960R Proof	Inc. above	Value: 36.00				
1961R	6,560,000	—	5.00	10.00	20.00	—
1961R Proof	Inc. above	Value: 50.00				
1964R	4,880,000	—	2.00	7.50	18.00	—
1964R Proof	Inc. above	Value: 30.00				
1965R	3,120,000	—	2.00	8.00	20.00	—
1965R Proof	Inc. above	Value: 30.00				
1966R	13,120,000	—	2.00	4.50	10.00	—
Note: Varieties exist						
1966R Proof	Inc. above	Value: 25.00				
1967R	2,480,000	—	2.00	4.50	10.00	—
1967R Proof	Inc. above	Value: 25.00				
1968R	100,000	—	—	—	70.00	—
1968R Proof	Inc. above	Value: 100				
1969R	310,000	—	—	—	40.00	—
1969R Proof	Inc. above	Value: 30.00				
1970R	1,140,000	—	—	—	20.00	—
1970R Proof	Inc. above	Value: 25.00				
1980R	257,270	—	—	—	15.00	—
1980R Proof	Inc. above	Value: 25.00				
1981R	162,794	—	—	—	16.50	—
1981R Proof	Inc. above	Value: 30.00				
1982R	115,000	—	—	—	16.50	—
1982R Proof	Inc. above	—	—	—	30.00	—
1983R	76,000	—	—	—	100	—
1984R	77,000	—	—	—	80.00	—
1985R	74,600	—	—	—	30.00	—
1985R Proof	15,000	Value: 40.00				
1986R	73,200	—	—	—	30.00	—
1986R Proof	Inc. above	Value: 40.00				
1987R	57,500	—	—	—	50.00	—
1987R Proof	10,000	Value: 65.00				
1988R	51,050	—	—	—	100	—
1988R Proof	10,000	Value: 90.00				
1989R	51,200	—	—	—	50.00	—
1989R Proof	10,000	Value: 75.00				
1990R	52,300	—	—	—	40.00	—
1990R Proof	10,000	Value: 50.00				
1991R	54,000	—	—	—	40.00	—
1991R Proof	11,000	Value: 60.00				
1992R	52,000	—	—	—	35.00	—
1992R Proof	9,500	Value: 60.00				
1993R	50,200	—	—	—	35.00	—
1993R Proof	8,500	Value: 60.00				
1994R	44,500	—	—	—	80.00	—
1994R Proof	8,500	Value: 95.00				
1995R	44,558	—	—	—	100	—
1995R Proof	7,960	Value: 150				
1996R	45,000	—	—	—	40.00	—
1996R Proof	8,000	Value: 90.00				
1997R	43,600	—	—	—	90.00	—
1997R Proof	8,440	Value: 150				
1998R	55,100	—	—	—	30.00	—
1998R Proof	9,000	Value: 60.00				
1999R	51,800	—	—	—	50.00	—
1999R Proof	8,500	Value: 70.00				
2000R	61,400	—	—	—	95.00	—
2000R Proof	8,960	Value: 55.00				
2001R	100,000	—	—	—	40.00	—
2001R Proof	10,000	Value: 200				

KM# 99 500 LIRE

11.0000 g., 0.8350 Silver 0.2953 oz. ASW, 29.3 mm. **Subject:** Italian Unification Centennial **Obv:** Female seated left **Rev:** Quadriga **Designer:** Guido Veroi

Date	Mintage	F	VF	XF	Unc	BU
ND(1961)R	27,120,000	—	BV	4.50	7.00	—
ND(1961)R Prooflike	Inc. above	—	—	—	20.00	—

KM# 100 500 LIRE

11.0000 g., 0.8350 Silver 0.2953 oz. ASW, 29.3 mm. **Subject:** 700th Anniversary - Birth of Dante Alighieri, Poet **Obv:** Head left **Rev:** Radiant sun above flame, value and date

Date	Mintage	F	VF	XF	Unc	BU
1965R	4,272,000	—	BV	5.00	10.00	—
1965R Proof	Inc. above	Value: 15.00				

KM# 111 500 LIRE

6.8000 g., Bi-Metallic Bronzital center in Acmonital ring, 25.8 mm. **Obv:** Head left within circle **Rev:** Plaza within circle flanked by sprigs **Designer:** Cretara

Date	Mintage	F	VF	XF	Unc	BU
1982R	162,000	—	0.40	0.60	2.00	—
Note: Obverse portrait varieties exist						
1983R	137,974,000	—	0.40	0.60	2.00	—
1984R	162,000,000	—	0.40	0.60	2.00	—
1985R	162,000,000	—	0.40	0.60	2.00	—
1985R Proof	20,000	Value: 10.00				
1986R	165,000,000	—	0.40	0.60	2.00	—
1986R Proof	17,500	Value: 10.00				
1987R	200,000,000	—	0.40	0.60	2.00	—
1987R Proof	10,000	Value: 10.00				
1988R	142,000,000	—	0.40	0.60	2.00	—
1988R Proof	9,000	Value: 25.00				
1989R	155,000,000	—	0.40	0.60	2.00	—
1989R Proof	9,250	Value: 10.00				
1990R	130,000,000	—	0.40	0.60	2.00	—
1990R Proof	9,400	Value: 12.00				
1991R	140,000,000	—	0.40	0.60	2.00	—
1991R Proof	11,400	Value: 18.00				
1992R	150,000,000	—	0.40	0.60	2.00	—
Note: Obverse portrait varieties exist						
1992R Proof	9,500	Value: 18.00				
1995R	110,000,000	—	—	0.60	2.00	—
1995R Proof	7,960	Value: 35.00				
2000R	61,400	—	—	—	15.00	—
2000R Proof	10,000	Value: 30.00				
2001R	100,000	—	—	—	12.00	—
2001R Proof	10,000	Value: 35.00				

KM# 111a 500 LIRE

14.0000 g., Bi-Metallic .750 Gold center in .900 Gold ring, 25.8 mm. **Obv:** Head left within circle **Rev:** Plaza within circle flanked by sprigs **Edge:** Segmented reeding **Note:** Official Restrike

Date	Mintage	F	VF	XF	Unc	BU
1982 (2006)R Proof	1,999	Value: 270				

KM# 160 500 LIRE

6.8000 g., Bi-Metallic Bronzital center in Acmonital ring, 25.8 mm. **Subject:** Centennial - Bank of Italy **Obv:** Head left within circle **Obv. Designer:** Laura Cretara **Rev:** Monogram within design divides dates within circle **Rev. Designer:** G. Rossi **Note:** Large and small designer's name, G ROSSI, exist.

Date	Mintage	F	VF	XF	Unc	BU
ND(1993)R	Est. 90,000,000	—	—	—	2.50	—
ND(1993)R Proof	8,500	Value: 10.00				

KM# 167 500 LIRE

6.8000 g., Bi-Metallic Bronzital center in Acmonital ring, 25.8 mm. **Subject:** 500th Anniversary - Publication of Mathematical Work by Luca Pacioli **Obv:** Head left within circle **Obv. Designer:** Laura Cretara **Rev:** Bust facing within circle

Date	Mintage	F	VF	XF	Unc	BU
ND(1994)R	50,000,000	—	—	—	2.00	—
ND(1994)R Proof	8,500	Value: 15.00				

KM# 181 500 LIRE

6.8000 g., Bi-Metallic Bronzital center in Acmonital ring, 25.8 mm. **Subject:** Istituto Nazionale di Statistica **Obv:** Head left within circle **Rev:** Institute building within circle **Rev. Designer:** C. Momoni

Date	Mintage	F	VF	XF	Unc	BU
ND(1996)R	96,755,000	—	—	—	2.00	—
ND(1996)R Proof	8,000	Value: 15.00				

KM# 187 500 LIRE

6.8000 g., Bi-Metallic Bronzital center in Acmonital ring, 25.8 mm. **Subject:** 50th Anniversary - National Police Code **Obv:** Head left within circle **Obv. Designer:** Laura Cretara **Rev:** Mythological figure above crowned shield within wreath and circle **Rev. Designer:** Carmela Colaneri

Date	Mintage	F	VF	XF	Unc	BU
ND(1997)R	40,000,000	—	—	—	2.00	—
ND(1997)R Proof	8,440	Value: 25.00				

KM# 193 500 LIRE

6.8000 g., Bi-Metallic Bronzital center in Acmonital ring, 25.8 mm. **Series:** F.A.O. **Subject:** 20 years - IFAD **Obv:** Allegorical portrait **Obv. Designer:** Laura Cretara **Rev:** Hand and grains **Rev. Designer:** L. Desimoni

Date	Mintage	F	VF	XF	Unc	BU
ND(1998)R	100,000,000	—	—	—	2.00	—
ND(1998)R Proof	9,000	Value: 15.00				

KM# 203 500 LIRE

6.8200 g., Bi-Metallic Bronzital center in Acmonital ring, 25.9 mm. **Subject:** European Parliamentary Elections **Obv:** Allegorical portrait **Obv. Designer:** Laura Cretara **Rev:** Ballot box **Edge:** Reeded and plain sections

Date	Mintage	F	VF	XF	Unc	BU
ND(1999)R	50,000,000	—	—	—	2.00	—
ND(1999)R Proof	8,500	Value: 15.00				

KM# 194 1000 LIRE

Bi-Metallic Copper-Nickel center in Aluminum-Bronze ring, 27 mm. **Subject:** European Union **Obv:** Head left within circle **Obv. Designer:** Laura Cretara **Rev:** Corrected map with United Germany within globe design **Rev. Designer:** Pernazza

Date	Mintage	F	VF	XF	Unc	BU
1997R	80,000,000	—	—	—	3.00	—
1997R Proof	8,440	Value: 25.00				
1998R	180,000,000	—	—	—	3.00	—
1998R Proof	9,000	Value: 25.00				
1999R	51,800	—	—	—	15.00	—
1999R Proof	8,500	Value: 25.00				
2000R	61,400	—	—	—	20.00	—
2000R Proof	8,960	Value: 25.00				
2001R	100,000	—	—	—	10.00	—
2001R Proof	10,000	Value: 35.00				

KM# 190 1000 LIRE

Bi-Metallic Copper-Nickel center in Aluminum-Bronze ring, 27 mm. **Subject:** European Union **Obv:** Allegorical portrait **Obv. Designer:** L. Cretara **Rev:** Pernazza

Date	Mintage	F	VF	XF	Unc	BU
1997R	100,000,000	—	—	—	3.50	—

EURO COINAGE

European Union Issues

KM# 210 EURO CENT

2.3000 g., Copper Plated Steel, 16.2 mm. **Obv:** Castle del Monte **Obv. Designer:** Eugenio Drutti **Rev:** Value and globe **Rev. Designer:** Luc Luycx **Edge:** Plain

Date	Mintage	F	VF	XF	Unc	BU
2002R	1,348,899,500	—	—	—	0.25	—
2003R	9,629,000	—	—	—	0.35	—
2003R Proof	12,000	Value: 10.00				
2004R	100,000,000	—	—	—	0.25	—
2004R Proof	—	Value: 7.00				
2005R	180,000,000	—	—	—	0.35	—
2005R Proof	12,000	Value: 5.00				
2006R	159,000,000	—	—	—	0.25	—
2006R Proof	—	Value: 5.00				
2007R	140,000,000	—	—	—	0.25	—
2007R Proof	—	Value: 5.00				
2008R	—	—	—	—	0.25	—
2008R Proof	—	Value: 5.00				

KM# 211 2 EURO CENT

3.0300 g., Copper Plated Steel, 18.7 mm. **Obv:** Observation tower in Turin **Obv. Designer:** Luciana de Simoni **Rev:** Value and globe **Rev. Designer:** Luc Luycx **Edge:** Plain

Date	Mintage	F	VF	XF	Unc	BU
2002R	1,099,166,250	—	—	—	0.25	—
2003R	21,817,000	—	—	—	0.25	—
2003R Proof	12,000	Value: 10.00				
2004R	120,000,000	—	—	—	0.25	—
2004R Proof	—	Value: 7.00				
2005R	120,000,000	—	—	—	0.25	—
2005R Proof	12,000	Value: 5.00				
2006R	196,000,000	—	—	—	0.25	—
2006R Proof	—	Value: 5.00				
2007R	140,000,000	—	—	—	0.25	—
2007R Proof	—	Value: 5.00				
2008R	—	—	—	—	0.25	—
2008R Proof	—	Value: 5.00				

KM# 212 5 EURO CENT

3.9500 g., Copper Plated Steel, 19.64 mm. **Obv:** Colosseum **Obv. Designer:** Lorenzo Frapiccini **Rev:** Value and globe **Rev. Designer:** Luc Luycx **Edge:** Plain

Date	Mintage	F	VF	XF	Unc	BU
2002R	1,341,742,204	—	—	—	0.25	—
2003R	1,960,000	—	—	—	0.50	—
2003R Proof	12,000	Value: 12.00				
2004R	10,000,000	—	—	—	0.50	—
2004R Proof	—	Value: 8.00				
2005R	70,000,000	—	—	—	0.50	—
2005R Proof	12,000	Value: 6.00				
2006R	119,000,000	—	—	—	0.50	—
2006R Proof	—	Value: 6.00				
2007R	85,000,000	—	—	—	0.50	—
2007R Proof	—	Value: 6.00				
2008R	—	—	—	—	0.50	—
2008R Proof	—	Value: 6.00				

KM# 213 10 EURO CENT

4.0700 g., Brass, 19.7 mm. **Obv:** Venus by Botticelli **Obv. Designer:** Claudia Momoni **Rev:** Value and map **Rev. Designer:** Luc Luycx **Edge:** Reeded

Date	Mintage	F	VF	XF	Unc	BU
2002R	1,142,383,000	—	—	—	0.25	—
2003R	29,976,000	—	—	—	0.50	—
2003R Proof	12,000	Value: 15.00				
2004R	5,000,000	—	—	—	0.50	—
2004R Proof	—	Value: 12.00				
2005R	100,000,000	—	—	—	0.50	—
2005R Proof	12,000	Value: 7.00				
2006R	180,000,000	—	—	—	0.50	—
2006R Proof	—	Value: 7.00				
2007R	105,000,000	—	—	—	0.50	—
2007R Proof	—	Value: 7.00				

KM# 247 10 EURO CENT

4.0700 g., Brass, 19.7 mm. **Obv:** Venus by Botticelli **Obv. Designer:** Claudia Momoni **Rev:** Relief Map of Western Europe, stars, lines and value **Rev. Designer:** Luc Luycx **Edge:** Reeded

Date	Mintage	F	VF	XF	Unc	BU
2008R	—	—	—	—	0.25	—

KM# 214 20 EURO CENT

5.7300 g., Brass, 22.1 mm. **Obv:** Futuristic sculpture **Obv. Designer:** Maria Cassol **Rev:** Value and map **Rev. Designer:** Luc Luycx **Edge:** Notched

Date	Mintage	F	VF	XF	Unc	BU
2002R	1,411,836,000	—	—	—	0.30	—
2003R	26,155,000	—	—	—	0.50	—
2003R Proof	12,000	Value: 16.00				
2004R	5,000,000	—	—	—	0.50	—
2004R Proof	—	Value: 14.00				
2005R	5,000,000	—	—	—	0.50	—
2005R Proof	12,000	Value: 8.00				
2006R	5,000,000	—	—	—	0.50	—
2006R Proof	—	Value: 8.00				
2007R	5,000,000	—	—	—	0.50	—
2007R Proof	—	Value: 8.00				

KM# 248 20 EURO CENT

5.7300 g., Brass, 22.1 mm. **Obv:** Futuristic sculpture **Obv. Designer:** Maria Cassoll **Rev:** Relief map of Western Europe, stars, lines and value **Rev. Designer:** Luc Luycx **Edge:** Reeded

Date	Mintage	F	VF	XF	Unc	BU
2008R	—	—	—	—	1.00	—

KM# 215 50 EURO CENT

7.8100 g., Brass, 24.2 mm. **Obv:** Sculpture of Marcus Aurelius on horseback **Obv. Designer:** Roberto Mauri **Rev:** Value and map **Rev. Designer:** Luc Luycx **Edge:** Reeded

Date	Mintage	F	VF	XF	Unc	BU
2002R	1,136,718,000	—	—	—	0.80	—
2003R	44,825,000	—	—	—	1.00	—
2003R Proof	12,000	Value: 18.00				
2004R	5,000,000	—	—	—	1.00	—
2004R Proof	—	Value: 16.00				
2005R	5,000,000	—	—	—	1.00	—
2005R Proof	12,000	Value: 10.00				
2006R	5,000,000	—	—	—	1.00	—
2006R Proof	—	Value: 10.00				
2007R	5,000,000	—	—	—	1.00	—
2007R Proof	—	Value: 10.00				

KM# 249 50 EURO CENT

7.8100 g., Brass, 24.2 mm. **Obv:** Sculpture of Marcus Aurelius on horseback **Obv. Designer:** Roberto Mauri **Rev:** Relief map of Western Europe, stars, lines and value **Rev. Designer:** Luc Luycx **Edge:** Reeded

Date	Mintage	F	VF	XF	Unc	BU
2008R	—	—	—	—	1.25	—

KM# 216 EURO

7.5000 g., Bi-Metallic Copper-Nickel center in Brass ring, 23.2 mm. **Obv:** Male figure drawing by Leonardo da Vinci within circle of stars **Obv. Designer:** Laura Cretara **Rev:** Value and map within circle **Rev. Designer:** Luc Luycx **Edge:** Reeded and plain sections

Date	Mintage	F	VF	XF	Unc	BU
2002R	966,025,300	—	—	—	1.60	—
2003R	66,474,000	—	—	—	2.00	—
2003R Proof	12,000	Value: 20.00				
2004R	5,000,000	—	—	—	2.00	—
2004R Proof	—	Value: 18.00				
2005R	5,000,000	—	—	—	2.00	—
2005R Proof	12,000	Value: 15.00				
2006R	108,000,000	—	—	—	2.00	—
2006R Proof	—	Value: 15.00				
2007R	135,000,000	—	—	—	2.00	—
2007R Proof	—	Value: 15.00				

KM# 250 EURO

7.5000 g., Bi-Metallic Copper-Nickel center in Brass ring, 23.2 mm. **Obv:** Male figure drawing by Leonardo da Vinci **Obv. Designer:** Laura Cretara **Rev:** Relief map of Western Europe, stars, lines and value **Rev. Designer:** Luc Luycx **Edge:** Reeded and plain sections

Date	Mintage	F	VF	XF	Unc	BU
2008R	—	—	—	—	2.50	—

KM# 217 2 EURO

8.5200 g., Bi-Metallic Brass center in Copper-Nickel ring, 25.7 mm. **Obv:** Head left within circle **Obv. Designer:** Maria Colanieri **Rev:** Value and map within circle **Rev. Designer:** Luc Luycx **Edge:** Reeded **Edge Lettering:** 2's and stars

Date	Mintage	F	VF	XF	Unc	BU
2002R	463,702,000	—	—	—	3.00	—
2003R	36,160,000	—	—	—	3.00	—
2003R Proof	12,000	Value: 25.00				
2004R	2,000,000	—	—	—	3.00	—
2004R Proof	—	Value: 22.00				
2005R	80,000,000	—	—	—	3.00	—
2005R Proof	12,000	Value: 20.00				
2006R	50,000,000	—	—	—	3.00	—
2006R Proof	—	Value: 20.00				
2007R	5,000,000	—	—	—	3.00	—
2007R Proof	—	Value: 20.00				

KM# 237 2 EURO

8.5300 g., Bi-Metallic Aluminum-Bronze center in Copper-Nickel ring, 25.7 mm. **Obv:** World Food Program globe within circle **Rev:** Value and map within circle **Edge:** Reeded and lettered **Edge Lettering:** 2's and stars

Date	Mintage	F	VF	XF	Unc	BU
2004R	160,000,000	—	—	—	3.50	—

KM# 245 2 EURO

8.5200 g., Bi-Metallic Brass center in Copper-Nickel ring, 25.6 mm. **Subject:** European Constitution **Obv:** Europa holding an open book while sitting on a bull within circle **Rev:** Value and map within circle **Edge:** Reeding over stars and 2's

Date	Mintage	F	VF	XF	Unc	BU
2005R	—	—	—	—	4.50	—

KM# 246 2 EURO

8.5100 g., Bi-Metallic Brass center in Copper-Nickel ring, 25.7 mm. **Subject:** Torino Winter Olympics **Obv:** Skier and other designs within circle **Rev:** Value and map within circle **Edge:** Reeded with stars and 2's

Date	Mintage	F	VF	XF	Unc	BU
2006R	—	—	—	—	6.00	—

KM# 251 2 EURO

8.5200 g., Bi-Metallic Brass center in Copper-Nickel ring, 25.7 mm. **Obv:** Bust of Dante Aligheri **Obv. Designer:** Maria Colanieri **Rev:** Relief map of Western Europe, stars, lines and value **Rev. Designer:** Luc Luycx **Edge:** Reeded **Edge Lettering:** 2's and stars

Date	Mintage	F	VF	XF	Unc	BU
2008R	—	—	—	—	3.75	—

JAMAICA

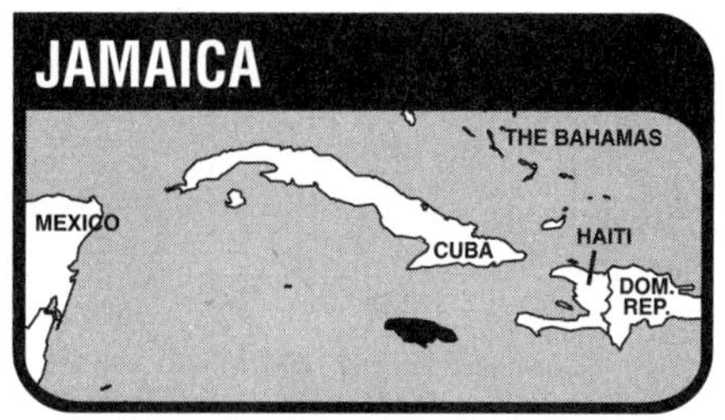

Jamaica is situated in the Caribbean Sea 90 miles south of Cuba, has an area of 4,244 sq. mi. (10,990 sq. km.) and a population of 2.1 million. Capital: Kingston. The economy is founded chiefly on mining, tourism and agriculture. Aluminum, bauxite, sugar, rum and molasses are exported.

Jamaica was discovered by Columbus on May 3, 1494, and settled by Spain in 1509. The island was captured in 1655 by a British naval force under the command of Admiral William Penn, sent by Oliver Cromwell and ceded to Britain by the Treaty of Madrid, 1670. For more than 150 years, the Jamaican economy of sugar, slaves and piracy was one of the most prosperous in the new world. Dissension between the property-oriented island legislature and the home government prompted parliament to establish a crown colony government for Jamaica in 1866. From 1958 to 1961 Jamaica was a member of the West Indies Federation, withdrawing when Jamaican voters rejected the association. The colony attained independence on Aug. 6, 1962. Jamaica is a member of the Commonwealth of Nations. Elizabeth II is the Head of State, as Queen of Jamaica.

In 1758, the Jamaican Assembly authorized stamping a certain amount of Spanish milled coinage. Token coinage by merchants aided the island's monetary supply in the early19th century. Sterling coinage was introduced in Jamaica in 1825, with the additional silver three halfpence under William IV and Victoria. Certain issues of three pence of William IV and Victoria were intended for colonial use, including Jamaica, as were the last dates of three pence for George VI.

There was an extensive token and work tally coinage for Jamaica in the late 19th and early 20th centuries.

A decimal standard currency system was adopted on Sept. 8, 1969.

RULER

British, until 1962

MINT MARKS

C - Royal Canadian Mint, Ottawa
H - Heaton
FM - Franklin Mint, U.S.A.**
(fm) - Franklin Mint, U.S.A.*
no mint mark - Royal Mint, London

***NOTE:** During 1970 the Franklin Mint produced matte and proof coins (1 cent-1 dollar) using dies similar to/or Royal Mint without the FM mint mark.

NOTE: From 1975-1985 the Franklin Mint produced coinage in up to 3 different qualities. Qualities of issue are designated in ( ) after each date and are defined as follows:

(M) MATTE - Normal circulation strike or a dull finish produced by sandblasting special uncirculated (polish finish) or proof quality dies.

(U) SPECIAL UNCIRCULATED - Polished or proof-like in appearance without any frosted features.

(P) PROOF - The highest quality obtainable having mirror-like fields and frosted features.

MONETARY SYSTEM

4 Farthings = 1 Penny
12 Pence = 1 Shilling
8 Reales = 6 Shillings, 8 Pence
(Commencing 1969)
100 Cents = 1 Dollar

COMMONWEALTH

REGULAR COINAGE

KM# 18 FARTHING

Copper-Nickel **Ruler:** Edward VII **Obv:** Crowned bust right within beaded circle **Rev:** Arms with horizontal shading within beaded circle **Designer:** G. W. DeSaulles

Date	Mintage	F	VF	XF	Unc	BU
1902	144,000	5.00	10.00	20.00	45.00	50.00
1903	144,000	5.00	10.00	20.00	45.00	50.00

KM# 21 FARTHING

Copper-Nickel **Ruler:** Edward VII **Obv:** Crowned bust right within beaded circle **Rev:** Arms with vertical shading within beaded circle **Designer:** G. W. DeSaulles

Date	Mintage	F	VF	XF	Unc	BU
1904	192,000	2.00	5.00	12.00	35.00	42.50
1904 Proof	—	Value: 250				
1905	192,000	2.00	5.00	12.00	35.00	42.50
1906	528,000	2.00	3.00	9.00	28.00	35.00
1907	192,000	2.00	5.00	12.00	35.00	42.50
1909	144,000	2.00	6.00	20.00	45.00	50.00
1910	48,000	5.00	15.00	30.00	50.00	60.00

KM# 24 FARTHING

Copper-Nickel **Ruler:** George V **Obv:** Crowned bust left within beaded circle **Obv. Designer:** E. B. MacKennal **Rev:** Arms within beaded circle **Rev. Designer:** G. W. DeSaulles

Date	Mintage	F	VF	XF	Unc	BU
1914	192,000	2.00	5.00	12.00	35.00	42.50
1916H	480,000	0.75	2.00	6.00	20.00	27.50
1916H Proof	—	Value: 250				
1918C	208,000	1.00	2.00	8.00	25.00	30.00
1918C Proof	—	Value: 225				
1919C	401,000	0.75	2.00	6.00	20.00	27.50
1926	240,000	1.00	2.00	8.00	25.00	30.00
1928	480,000	0.75	2.00	6.00	20.00	25.00
1928 Proof	—	Value: 225				
1932	480,000	0.75	2.00	6.00	20.00	27.50
1932 Proof	—	—	—	—	—	—
1934	480,000	0.75	2.00	6.00	20.00	27.50
1934 Proof	—	—	—	—	—	—

KM# 27 FARTHING

Nickel-Brass **Ruler:** George VI **Obv:** Crowned head left **Rev:** Arms divide date **Designer:** Percy Metcalfe

Date	Mintage	F	VF	XF	Unc	BU
1937	480,000	0.50	1.50	5.00	15.00	20.00
1937 Proof	—	Value: 175				

KM# 30 FARTHING

Nickel-Brass **Ruler:** George VI **Obv:** Crowned head left **Rev:** Arms divide date **Designer:** Percy Metcalfe

Date	Mintage	F	VF	XF	Unc	BU
1938	480,000	0.50	1.50	5.00	15.00	20.00
1938 Proof	—	—	—	—	—	—
1942	480,000	0.50	1.50	5.00	15.00	20.00
1945	480,000	0.50	1.50	5.00	15.00	20.00
1945 Proof	—	Value: 120				
1947	192,000	1.00	3.00	7.50	20.00	27.50
1947 Proof	—	Value: 120				

KM# 33 FARTHING

Nickel-Brass **Ruler:** George VI **Obv:** Crowned head left **Obv. Legend:** Without AND EMPEROR OF INDIA in legend **Rev:** Arms divide date **Designer:** Percy Metcalfe

Date	Mintage	F	VF	XF	Unc	BU
1950	288,000	0.10	0.25	0.80	3.25	15.00
1950 Proof	—	Value: 175				
1952	288,000	0.10	0.25	0.80	3.50	17.50
1952 Proof	—	Value: 175				

KM# 19 1/2 PENNY

Copper-Nickel **Ruler:** Edward VII **Obv:** Crowned bust right within beaded circle **Rev:** Arms with horizontal shading within beaded circle **Designer:** G. W. DeSaulles

Date	Mintage	F	VF	XF	Unc	BU
1902	48,000	5.00	10.00	20.00	50.00	60.00
1903	48,000	5.00	10.00	20.00	60.00	70.00

KM# 22 1/2 PENNY

Copper-Nickel, 25.3 mm. **Ruler:** Edward VII **Obv:** Crowned bust right within beaded circle **Rev:** Arms with vertical shading within beaded circle **Designer:** G. W. DeSaulles

Date	Mintage	F	VF	XF	Unc	BU
1904	48,000	1.50	5.00	25.00	70.00	80.00
1905	48,000	1.50	5.00	25.00	70.00	80.00
1906	432,000	1.00	3.00	7.50	25.00	32.50
1907	504,000	1.00	3.00	7.50	25.00	32.50
1909	144,000	3.00	5.00	10.00	40.00	45.00
1910	144,000	0.75	2.00	10.00	40.00	45.00

KM# 25 1/2 PENNY

Copper-Nickel **Ruler:** George V **Obv:** Crowned bust left within beaded circle **Obv. Designer:** E. B. MacKennal **Rev:** Arms within beaded circle **Rev. Designer:** G. W. DeSaulles

Date	Mintage	F	VF	XF	Unc	BU
1914	96,000	3.00	6.00	25.00	75.00	90.00
1916H	192,000	0.35	1.50	6.00	20.00	27.50
1918C	251,000	0.35	1.50	6.00	20.00	27.50
1918C Proof	—	Value: 200				
1919C	312,000	0.35	1.50	7.50	20.00	27.50
1920	480,000	0.35	1.50	7.50	20.00	27.50
1926	240,000	0.35	1.50	7.50	30.00	35.00
1928	120,000	0.35	3.00	10.00	35.00	40.00
1928 Proof	—	Value: 200				

KM# 28 1/2 PENNY

Nickel-Brass **Ruler:** George VI **Obv:** Crowned head left **Rev:** Arms divide date **Designer:** Percy Metcalfe

Date	Mintage	F	VF	XF	Unc	BU
1937	960,000	0.50	1.00	3.50	12.00	15.00
1937 Proof	—	Value: 175				

KM# 34 1/2 PENNY

4.3800 g., Nickel-Brass **Ruler:** George VI **Obv:** Crowned head left **Rev:** Arms divide date **Designer:** Percy Metcalfe

Date	Mintage	F	VF	XF	Unc	BU
1950	1,440,000	0.10	0.20	0.30	3.25	5.00
1950 Proof	—	Value: 175				
1952	1,200,000	0.10	0.20	0.30	3.25	5.00
1952 Proof	—	Value: 175				

KM# 36 1/2 PENNY

4.3400 g., Nickel-Brass **Ruler:** Elizabeth II **Obv:** Crowned bust right **Rev:** Arms divide date **Rev. Designer:** Percy Metcalfe

Date	Mintage	F	VF	XF	Unc	BU
1955	1,440,000	0.10	0.15	0.40	2.00	3.00
1955 Proof	—	Value: 150				
1957	600,000	1.00	2.00	4.00	6.00	9.00
1957 Proof	—	—	—	—	—	—
1958	960,000	0.10	0.20	0.50	2.00	3.00
1958 Proof	—	Value: 150				
1959	960,000	0.10	0.20	0.50	2.00	3.00
1959 Proof	—	—	—	—	—	—
1961	480,000	0.20	0.40	1.00	4.00	5.00
1961 Proof	—	—	—	—	—	—
1962	960,000	0.10	0.15	0.30	1.75	2.50
1962 Proof	—	Value: 150				
1963	960,000	0.10	0.15	0.30	1.75	2.50
1963 Proof	—	Value: 150				

KM# 38 1/2 PENNY

4.5000 g., Nickel-Brass **Ruler:** Elizabeth II **Obv:** Crowned bust right **Rev:** Arms with supporters

Date	Mintage	F	VF	XF	Unc	BU
1964	1,440,000	0.10	0.15	0.20	0.80	1.00
1965	1,200,000	0.10	0.15	0.20	0.80	1.00
1966	1,680,000	0.10	0.15	0.20	0.80	1.00

KM# 41 1/2 PENNY

Copper-Nickel-Zinc **Ruler:** Elizabeth II **Subject:** Jamaican Coinage Centennial **Obv:** Crowned bust right **Rev:** Arms with supporters

Date	Mintage	F	VF	XF	Unc	BU
1969	30,000	0.10	0.15	0.25	0.75	1.00
1969 Proof	5,000	Value: 2.50				

KM# 20 PENNY

Copper-Nickel **Ruler:** Edward VII **Obv:** Crowned bust right within beaded circle **Rev:** Arms with horizontal shading within beaded circle **Designer:** G. W. DeSaulles

Date	Mintage	F	VF	XF	Unc	BU
1902	60,000	2.25	6.00	25.00	70.00	85.00
1903	60,000	2.25	6.00	25.00	70.00	85.00

KM# 23 PENNY

8.1000 g., Copper-Nickel **Ruler:** Edward VII **Obv:** Crowned bust right within beaded circle **Rev:** Arms with vertical shading within beaded circle **Designer:** G. W. DeSaulles

Date	Mintage	F	VF	XF	Unc	BU
1904	24,000	10.00	20.00	50.00	125	150
1904 Proof	—	Value: 250				
1905	48,000	2.00	6.50	35.00	70.00	85.00
1906	156,000	1.25	2.50	12.00	45.00	60.00
1907	108,000	1.25	2.50	12.00	45.00	60.00
1909	144,000	1.25	2.50	12.00	45.00	60.00
1910	144,000	1.25	2.50	12.00	45.00	60.00

KM# 26 PENNY

Copper-Nickel **Ruler:** George V **Obv:** Crowned bust left within beaded circle **Obv. Designer:** E. B. MacKennal **Rev:** Arms within beaded circle **Rev. Designer:** G. W. DeSaulles

Date	Mintage	F	VF	XF	Unc	BU
1914	24,000	10.00	20.00	65.00	175	200
1916H	24,000	10.00	20.00	60.00	175	200
1918C	187,000	2.00	5.00	15.00	60.00	75.00
1918C Proof	—	Value: 200				
1919C	251,000	1.25	4.75	12.00	50.00	65.00
1920	360,000	0.75	2.50	9.50	32.50	40.00
1926	240,000	0.75	2.50	9.50	35.00	40.00
1928	360,000	0.75	2.50	9.50	35.00	40.00
1928 Proof	—	Value: 200				

KM# 29 PENNY

Nickel-Brass **Ruler:** George VI **Obv:** Crowned head left **Rev:** Arms divide date **Designer:** Percy Metcalfe

Date	Mintage	F	VF	XF	Unc	BU
1937	1,200,000	1.00	1.75	3.25	12.00	15.00
1937 Proof	—	Value: 200				

KM# 32 PENNY

Nickel-Brass **Ruler:** George VI **Obv:** Crowned head left **Rev:** Arms divide date **Designer:** Percy Metcalfe

Date	Mintage	F	VF	XF	Unc	BU
1938	1,200,000	0.35	0.65	3.25	12.00	15.00
1938 Proof	—	Value: 200				
1940	1,200,000	0.35	0.65	3.25	12.00	15.00
1940 Proof	—	Value: 200				
1942	1,200,000	0.35	0.65	3.25	12.00	15.00
1942 Proof	—	Value: 200				
1945	1,200,000	0.35	0.65	3.25	12.00	15.00
1945 Proof	—	Value: 200				
1947	480,000	3.00	7.50	10.00	25.00	32.50
1947 Proof	—	Value: 200				

KM# 35 PENNY

Nickel-Brass **Ruler:** George VI **Obv:** Crowned head left **Obv. Legend:** Without AND EMPEROR OF INDIA in legend **Rev:** Arms divide date **Designer:** Percy Metcalfe

Date	Mintage	F	VF	XF	Unc	BU
1950	600,000	0.20	0.35	2.00	10.00	14.00
1950 Proof	—	Value: 200				
1952	725,000	0.20	0.35	2.00	10.00	14.00
1952 Proof	—	Value: 200				

KM# 37 PENNY

7.4800 g., Nickel-Brass **Ruler:** Elizabeth II **Obv:** Crowned bust right **Rev:** Arms divide date **Rev. Designer:** Percy Metcalfe

Date	Mintage	F	VF	XF	Unc	BU
1953	1,200,000	0.10	0.20	0.50	1.50	2.00
1953 Proof	—	Value: 115				
1955	960,000	0.10	0.25	1.00	4.00	5.00
1955 Proof	—	Value: 115				
1957	600,000	0.10	0.25	1.00	4.00	5.00
1957 Proof	—	—	—	—	—	—
1958	1,080,000	0.10	0.20	0.30	3.00	4.50
1958 Proof	—	Value: 100				
1959	1,368,000	0.10	0.20	0.30	2.50	3.00
1959 Proof	—	—	—	—	—	—
1960	1,368,000	0.10	0.20	0.30	2.50	3.00
1960 Proof	—	—	—	—	—	—
1961	1,368,000	0.10	0.20	0.30	2.50	3.00
1961 Proof	—	—	—	—	—	—
1962	1,920,000	0.10	0.20	0.30	2.50	3.00
1962 Proof	—	Value: 100				
1963	720,000	2.00	4.00	10.00	50.00	65.00
1963 Proof	—	Value: 100				

KM# 39 PENNY

7.4700 g., Nickel-Brass **Ruler:** Elizabeth II **Obv:** Crowned bust right **Rev:** Arms with supporters

Date	Mintage	F	VF	XF	Unc	BU
1964	480,000	0.10	0.15	0.50	1.00	1.50
1965	1,200,000	0.10	0.15	0.20	0.35	1.00
1966	1,200,000	0.10	0.15	0.20	0.35	1.00
1967	2,760,000	0.10	0.15	0.20	0.35	1.00

KM# 42 PENNY

Copper-Nickel-Zinc **Ruler:** Elizabeth II **Subject:** Jamaican Coinage Centennial **Obv:** Crowned bust right **Rev:** Arms with supporters

Date	Mintage	F	VF	XF	Unc	BU
1969	30,000	0.10	0.15	0.30	0.75	1.25
1969 Proof	5,000	Value: 2.50				

DECIMAL COINAGE

The Franklin Mint and Royal Mint have both been striking the 1 Cent through 1 Dollar coinage. The 1970 issues were all struck with dies similar to/or Royal Mint without the FM mint mark. The Royal Mint issues have the name JAMAICA extending beyond the native headdress feathers. Those struck after 1970 by the Franklin Mint have the name JAMAICA within the headdress feathers.

KM# 45 CENT

Bronze **Ruler:** Elizabeth II **Obv:** Arms with supporters **Rev:** Ackee fruit above value **Designer:** Christopher Ironside

Date	Mintage	F	VF	XF	Unc	BU
1969	30,200,000	—	—	0.10	0.25	0.50
1969 Proof	19,000	Value: 0.50				
1970 (RM) Small date	10,000,000	—	—	0.10	0.25	0.50
1970(fm) (M); Large date	5,000	—	—	0.10	0.25	0.50

Date	Mintage	F	VF	XF	Unc	BU
1970(fm) (P)	12,000	Value: 0.50				
1971 (RM)	5,625,000	—	—	0.10	0.25	0.50

KM# 51 CENT

Bronze **Ruler:** Elizabeth II **Obv:** Arms with supporters **Rev:** Ackee fruit above value **Designer:** Christopher Ironside

Date	Mintage	F	VF	XF	Unc	BU
1971FM (M)	4,834	—	—	0.10	0.25	0.50
1971FM (P)	14,000	Value: 0.50				
1972FM (M)	7,982	—	—	0.10	0.25	0.50
1972FM (P)	17,000	Value: 0.50				
1973FM (M)	29,000	—	—	0.10	0.25	0.50
1973FM (P)	28,000	Value: 0.50				
1974FM (M)	28,000	—	—	0.10	0.25	0.50
1974FM (P)	22,000	Value: 0.50				
1975FM (M)	36,000	—	—	0.10	0.25	0.50
1975FM (U)	4,683	—	—	—	0.25	0.50
1975FM (P)	16,000	Value: 0.50				

KM# 52 CENT

4.2000 g., Bronze **Ruler:** Elizabeth II **Series:** F.A.O. **Obv:** Arms with supporters **Rev:** Ackee fruit above value **Designer:** Christopher Ironside

Date	Mintage	F	VF	XF	Unc	BU
1971	20,000	—	—	0.50	1.00	1.50
1972	5,000,000	—	—	0.10	0.30	1.00
1973	5,500,000	—	—	0.10	0.30	1.00
1974	3,000,000	—	—	0.10	0.30	1.00

KM# 64 CENT

1.2000 g., Aluminum, 20.05 mm. **Ruler:** Elizabeth II **Series:** F.A.O. **Obv:** National arms **Obv. Legend:** JAMAICA **Rev:** Ackee fruit above value **Edge:** Plain **Shape:** 12-sided **Designer:** Christopher Ironside

Date	Mintage	F	VF	XF	Unc	BU
1975	15,000,000	—	—	0.10	0.20	0.50
1976	16,000,000	—	—	0.10	0.20	0.50
1977	—	—	—	0.10	0.20	0.50
1978	8,400,000	—	—	0.10	0.20	0.50
1980	10,000,000	—	—	0.10	0.20	0.50
1981	8,000,000	—	—	0.10	0.20	0.50
1982	10,000,000	—	—	0.10	0.20	0.50
1983	1,342,000	—	—	—	0.15	0.50
1984	8,704,000	—	—	—	0.15	0.50
1985	5,112,000	—	—	—	0.15	0.50
1985 Proof	—	Value: 0.50				
1986	17,534,000	—	—	—	0.15	0.50
1987	9,968,000	—	—	—	0.15	0.50
1987 Proof	—	Value: 0.50				
1988 Proof	—	Value: 0.50				
1989 Proof	—	Value: 0.50				
1990	—	—	—	—	0.15	0.50
1990 Proof	—	Value: 0.50				
1991	—	—	—	—	0.15	0.50
1991 Proof	—	Value: 0.50				
1992 Proof	—	Value: 0.50				
1993 Proof	—	Value: 0.50				
1995 Proof	—	Value: 0.50				
1996	—	—	—	—	0.15	0.50
2000	—	—	—	—	—	—
2000 Proof	—	Value: 1.00				
2002	—	—	—	0.25	0.50	0.75
2002 Proof	500	Value: 1.00				

KM# 68 CENT

1.2000 g., Aluminum, 21.05 mm. **Ruler:** Elizabeth II **Obv:** Arms with supporters **Rev:** Ackee fruit above value **Shape:** 12-sided **Designer:** Christopher Ironside

Date	Mintage	F	VF	XF	Unc	BU
1976FM (M)	28,000	—	—	—	0.15	0.50
1976FM (U)	1,802	—	—	—	0.25	0.50
1976FM (P)	24,000	Value: 0.50				
1977FM (M)	28,000	—	—	—	0.15	0.30
1977FM (U)	597	—	—	—	1.50	2.00
1977FM (P)	10,000	Value: 0.50				
1978FM (M)	28,000	—	—	—	0.15	0.30
1978FM (U)	1,282	—	—	—	0.40	0.75
1978FM (P)	6,058	Value: 0.60				
1979FM (M)	28,000	—	—	—	0.15	0.50
1979FM (U)	2,608	—	—	—	0.40	0.75
1979FM (P)	4,049	Value: 0.60				
1980FM (M)	28,000	—	—	—	0.15	0.50
1980FM (U)	3,668	—	—	—	0.35	0.70
1980FM (P)	2,688	Value: 0.75				
1981FM (U)	482	—	—	—	1.50	2.00
1981FM (P)	1,577	Value: 0.75				
1982FM (U)	—	—	—	—	0.35	0.70
1982FM (P)	—	Value: 0.75				
1984FM (U)	—	—	—	—	0.35	0.70
1984FM (P)	—	Value: 0.75				

KM# 136 CENT

1.2000 g., Aluminum, 21.05 mm. **Ruler:** Elizabeth II **Note:** Mule. Two obverses of KM#64.

Date	Mintage	F	VF	XF	Unc	BU
1982FM	—	—	—	220	250	275

KM# 137 CENT

1.2000 g., Aluminum, 21.05 mm. **Ruler:** Elizabeth II **Note:** Mule. Two reverses of KM#64.

Date	Mintage	F	VF	XF	Unc	BU
1982FM	—	—	—	250	300	325

KM# 101 CENT

1.2000 g., Aluminum, 21.05 mm. **Ruler:** Elizabeth II **Subject:** 21st Anniversary of Independence **Obv:** Arms with supporters **Rev:** Ackee plant (blighia sapida) **Designer:** Christopher Ironside

Date	Mintage	F	VF	XF	Unc	BU
ND(1983)M (U)	—	—	—	—	0.35	0.75
ND(1983)FM (P)	—	Value: 0.75				

KM# 46 5 CENTS

2.8000 g., Copper-Nickel, 19.4 mm. **Ruler:** Elizabeth II **Obv:** Arms with supporters **Rev:** American crocodile above value **Designer:** Christopher Ironside

Date	Mintage	F	VF	XF	Unc	BU
1969	12,008,000	—	—	0.10	0.50	1.00
1969 Proof	30,000	Value: 0.65				
1970(fm) (M)	5,000	—	—	0.10	0.50	1.00
1970(fm) (P)	12,000	Value: 0.65				
1972	6,000,000	—	—	0.10	0.50	0.75
1975	6,010,000	—	—	0.10	0.50	0.75
1977	2,400,000	—	—	0.10	0.50	0.75
1978	2,000,000	—	—	0.10	0.50	0.75
1980	2,272,000	—	—	0.10	0.50	0.75
1981	2,001,000	—	—	0.10	0.50	0.75
1982	2,000,000	—	—	0.10	0.50	0.75
1983	992,000	—	—	0.75	1.00	1.50
1984	3,508,000	—	—	0.10	0.50	0.75
1985	4,760,000	—	—	0.10	0.50	0.75
1985 Proof	—	Value: 0.65				
1986	14,504,000	—	—	0.10	0.50	0.75
1987	13,166,000	—	—	0.10	0.50	0.75
1987 Proof	—	Value: 0.65				
1988	9,780,000	—	—	0.10	0.50	0.75
1988 Proof	—	Value: 0.65				
1989	—	—	—	0.10	0.50	0.75
1989 Proof	—	Value: 0.65				

KM# 46a 5 CENTS

2.8000 g., Nickel Plated Steel, 19.4 mm. **Ruler:** Elizabeth II **Obv:** Arms with supporters **Rev:** American crocodile above value **Designer:** Christopher Ironside

Date	Mintage	F	VF	XF	Unc	BU
1990	—	—	—	0.10	0.50	0.75
1990 Proof	—	Value: 0.65				
1991	—	—	—	0.10	0.50	0.75
1991 Proof	—	Value: 0.65				
1992	—	—	—	0.10	0.50	0.75
1992 Proof	—	Value: 0.65				
1993	—	—	—	0.10	0.50	0.75
1993 Proof	—	Value: 0.65				

KM# 53 5 CENTS

2.8000 g., Copper-Nickel, 19.4 mm. **Ruler:** Elizabeth II **Obv:** Arms with supporters **Rev:** American crocodile above value **Designer:** Christopher Ironside

Date	Mintage	F	VF	XF	Unc	BU
1971FM (M)	4,834	—	—	0.10	0.75	1.00
1971FM (P)	14,000	Value: 0.50				
1972FM (M)	7,982	—	—	0.10	0.75	1.00
1972FM (P)	17,000	Value: 0.50				
1973FM (M)	17,000	—	—	0.10	0.75	1.00
1973FM (P)	28,000	Value: 0.50				
1974FM (M)	16,000	—	—	0.10	0.75	1.00
1974FM (P)	22,000	Value: 0.50				
1975FM (M)	6,240	—	—	0.10	0.75	1.00
1975FM (U)	4,683	—	—	—	0.75	1.00
1975FM (P)	16,000	Value: 0.50				
1976FM (M)	5,560	—	—	0.10	0.75	1.00
1976FM (U)	1,802	—	—	—	0.75	1.00
1976FM (P)	24,000	Value: 0.50				
1977FM (M)	5,560	—	—	0.10	0.75	1.00
1977FM (U)	597	—	—	—	1.50	2.00
1977FM (P)	10,000	Value: 0.50				
1978FM (M)	5,560	—	—	0.10	0.75	1.00
1978FM (U)	1,282	—	—	—	0.85	1.50
1978FM (P)	6,058	Value: 0.85				
1979FM (M)	5,560	—	—	0.10	0.75	1.50
1979FM (U)	2,608	—	—	—	0.80	1.60
1979FM (P)	4,049	Value: 0.85				
1980FM (M)	5,560	—	—	0.10	0.75	1.50
1980FM (U)	3,668	—	—	—	0.80	1.60
1980FM (P)	2,688	Value: 1.00				
1981FM (U)	482	—	—	—	1.50	2.00
1981FM (P)	1,577	Value: 1.00				
1982FM (U)	—	—	—	—	0.80	1.60
1982FM (P)	—	Value: 1.00				
1984FM (U)	—	—	—	—	0.80	1.60
1984FM (P)	—	Value: 1.00				

KM# 102 5 CENTS

2.8000 g., Copper-Nickel, 19.4 mm. **Ruler:** Elizabeth II **Subject:** 21st Anniversary of Independence **Obv:** Arms with supporters **Rev:** American crocodile above value **Designer:** Christopher Ironside

Date	Mintage	F	VF	XF	Unc	BU
ND(1983)FM (U)	—	—	—	—	1.25	1.75
ND(1983)FM (P)	—	Value: 1.75				

KM# 47 10 CENTS

5.7500 g., Copper-Nickel, 23.6 mm. **Ruler:** Elizabeth II **Obv:** Arms with supporters **Rev:** Butterfly within leafy sprigs above value **Designer:** Christopher Ironside

Date	Mintage	F	VF	XF	Unc	BU
1969	19,508,000	—	—	0.10	0.50	0.75
1969 Proof	30,000	Value: 0.75				
1970(fm) (M)	5,000	—	—	0.10	0.50	0.75
1970(fm) (P)	12,000	Value: 0.75				
1972	6,000,000	—	—	0.10	0.50	0.75
1975	10,010,000	—	—	0.10	0.40	0.65
1977	8,000,000	—	—	0.10	0.40	0.65
1981	8,000,000	—	—	0.10	0.30	0.60
1982	8,000,000	—	—	0.10	0.30	0.60
1983	2,000,000	—	—	0.10	0.30	0.60
1984	5,000,000	—	—	0.10	0.30	0.60
1985	8,310,000	—	—	0.10	0.30	0.60
1985 Proof	—	Value: 0.75				
1986	21,677,000	—	—	0.10	0.30	0.60
1987	29,089,000	—	—	0.10	0.30	0.60
1987 Proof	—	Value: 0.75				
1988	15,660,000	—	—	0.10	0.30	0.60
1988 Proof	—	Value: 0.75				
1989	—	—	—	0.10	0.30	0.60
1989 Proof	—	Value: 0.75				

KM# 47a 10 CENTS

5.7500 g., Nickel Plated Steel, 23.6 mm. **Ruler:** Elizabeth II **Obv:** Arms with supporters **Rev:** Butterfly within leafy sprigs above value **Designer:** Christopher Ironside

Date	Mintage	F	VF	XF	Unc	BU
1990	—	—	—	0.10	0.30	0.60
1990 Proof	—	Value: 0.75				

KM# 54 10 CENTS

5.7500 g., Copper-Nickel, 23.6 mm. **Ruler:** Elizabeth II **Obv:** Arms with supporters **Rev:** Butterfly within leafy sprigs above value **Designer:** Christopher Ironside

Date	Mintage	F	VF	XF	Unc	BU
1971FM (M)	4,834	—	—	0.10	0.35	0.70
1971FM (P)	14,000	Value: 0.75				
1972FM (M)	7,982	—	—	0.10	0.35	0.70
1972FM (P)	17,000	Value: 0.75				
1973FM (M)	15,000	—	—	0.10	0.35	0.70
1973FM (P)	28,000	Value: 0.75				
1974FM (M)	14,000	—	—	0.10	0.35	0.70
1974FM (P)	22,000	Value: 0.75				
1975FM (M)	3,120	—	—	0.10	0.35	0.75
1975FM (U)	4,683	—	—	—	0.35	0.75
1975FM (P)	16,000	Value: 0.75				
1976FM (M)	2,780	—	—	0.10	0.35	0.75
1976FM (U)	1,802	—	—	—	0.35	0.75
1976FM (P)	24,000	Value: 0.75				
1977FM (M)	2,780	—	—	0.10	0.50	0.80
1977FM (U)	597	—	—	—	1.50	2.50
1977FM (P)	10,000	Value: 0.75				
1978FM (M)	2,780	—	—	0.10	0.50	0.80
1978FM (U)	4,062	—	—	—	0.60	0.85
1978FM (P)	6,058	Value: 1.00				
1979FM (M)	2,780	—	—	0.10	0.50	0.80
1979FM (U)	2,608	—	—	—	0.60	0.85
1979FM (P)	4,049	Value: 1.00				
1980FM (M)	2,780	—	—	0.10	0.50	0.80
1980FM (U)	3,668	—	—	—	0.50	0.80
1980FM (P)	2,688	Value: 1.50				
1981FM (U)	482	—	—	—	1.50	2.00
1981FM (P)	1,577	Value: 1.50				
1982FM (U)	—	—	—	—	0.50	0.80
1982FM (P)	—	Value: 1.50				
1984FM (U)	—	—	—	—	0.50	0.80
1984FM (P)	—	Value: 1.50				

KM# 103 10 CENTS

5.7500 g., Copper-Nickel, 23.6 mm. **Ruler:** Elizabeth II **Subject:** 21st Anniversary of Independence **Obv:** Arms with supporters **Rev:** Butterfly within leafy sprigs above value **Designer:** Christopher Ironside

Date	Mintage	F	VF	XF	Unc	BU
ND(1983)FM (U)	—	—	—	—	0.50	0.80
ND(1983)FM (P)	—	Value: 1.50				

KM# 146.1 10 CENTS

5.6800 g., Nickel Plated Steel **Ruler:** Elizabeth II **Subject:** Paul Bogle **Obv:** Arms with supporters **Rev:** Bust facing

Date	Mintage	F	VF	XF	Unc	BU
1991	—	—	—	—	0.50	0.80
1991 Proof	—	Value: 1.50				
1992	—	—	—	—	0.50	0.80
1992 Proof	—	Value: 1.50				
1993	—	—	—	—	0.50	0.80
1993 Proof	—	Value: 1.50				
1994	—	—	—	—	0.50	0.80
1994 Proof	—	Value: 1.50				

KM# 146.2 10 CENTS

2.4500 g., Copper Plated Steel, 17 mm. **Ruler:** Elizabeth II **Series:** National Heroes **Subject:** Paul Bogle **Obv:** National arms **Obv. Legend:** JAMAICA **Rev:** Bust facing **Edge:** Plain **Note:** Reduced size.

Date	Mintage	F	VF	XF	Unc	BU
1995	—	—	—	—	0.25	0.50
1995 Proof	—	Value: 2.00				
1996	—	—	—	—	0.25	0.50
2000	—	—	—	—	0.25	0.50
2000 Proof	—	Value: 2.00				
2002	—	—	—	0.25	0.50	0.75
2002 Proof	500	Value: 2.00				
2003	—	—	—	0.25	0.50	0.75

KM# 48 20 CENTS

11.3000 g., Copper-Nickel, 28.5 mm. **Ruler:** Elizabeth II **Obv:** Arms with supporters **Rev:** Mahoe trees above value **Designer:** Christopher Ironside

Date	Mintage	F	VF	XF	Unc	BU
1969	3,758,000	—	—	0.20	0.75	1.00
1969 Proof	30,000	Value: 1.00				
1970(fm) (M)	5,000	—	—	0.20	0.75	1.00
1970(fm) (P)	12,000	Value: 1.00				
1975	10,000	—	—	0.80	2.50	3.00
1982	1,000,000	—	—	0.20	0.65	1.00
1984	2,000,000	—	—	0.20	0.65	1.00
1986	2,530,000	—	—	0.20	0.65	1.00
1987	5,545,000	—	—	0.20	0.65	1.00
1987 Proof	—	Value: 1.00				
1988	5,016,000	—	—	0.20	0.65	1.00
1988 Proof	—	Value: 1.00				
1989	—	—	—	0.20	0.65	1.00
1989 Proof	—	Value: 1.00				
1990 Proof	—	Value: 1.00				

KM# 55 20 CENTS

11.3000 g., Copper-Nickel, 28.5 mm. **Ruler:** Elizabeth II **Obv:** Arms with supporters **Rev:** Mahoe trees above value **Designer:** Christopher Ironside

Date	Mintage	F	VF	XF	Unc	BU
1971FM (M)	4,834	—	—	0.20	0.50	1.00
1971FM (P)	14,000	Value: 1.00				
1972FM (M)	7,982	—	—	0.20	0.50	1.00
1972FM (P)	17,000	Value: 1.00				
1973FM (M)	13,000	—	—	0.20	0.50	1.00
1973FM (P)	28,000	Value: 1.00				
1974FM (M)	12,000	—	—	0.20	0.50	1.00
1974FM (P)	22,000	Value: 1.00				
1975FM (M)	1,560	—	—	0.20	0.50	1.00
1975FM (U)	4,683	—	—	—	0.50	1.00
1975FM (P)	16,000	Value: 1.00				
1976FM (M)	1,390	—	—	0.20	0.50	1.00
1976FM (U)	1,802	—	—	—	0.50	1.00
1976FM (P)	24,000	Value: 1.00				

KM# 69 20 CENTS

11.3000 g., Copper-Nickel, 28.5 mm. **Ruler:** Elizabeth II **Series:** F.A.O. **Obv:** Arms with supporters **Rev:** Mahoe trees above value **Designer:** Christopher Ironside

Date	Mintage	F	VF	XF	Unc	BU
1976	3,000,000	—	—	0.20	1.00	1.50
1981	—	—	—	0.20	1.00	1.50
1982	—	—	—	0.20	1.00	1.50
Note: Mintage included with KM#48						
1984	—	—	—	0.20	1.00	1.50
1987	—	—	—	0.20	1.00	1.50

KM# 73 20 CENTS

11.3000 g., Copper-Nickel, 28.5 mm. **Ruler:** Elizabeth II **Obv:** Arms with supporters **Rev:** Mahoe trees above value **Designer:** Christopher Ironside

Date	Mintage	F	VF	XF	Unc	BU
1977FM (M)	1,390	—	—	0.20	0.75	1.25
1977FM (U)	597	—	—	—	2.00	2.50
1977FM (P)	10,000	Value: 1.00				
1978FM (M)	1,390	—	—	0.20	0.75	1.25
1978FM (U)	1,282	—	—	—	0.75	1.25
1978FM (P)	6,058	Value: 1.50				
1979FM (M)	1,390	—	—	0.20	0.75	1.25
1979FM (U)	2,608	—	—	—	0.75	1.25
1979FM (P)	4,049	Value: 1.50				
1980FM (M)	1,390	—	—	0.20	0.60	1.00
1980FM (U)	3,668	—	—	—	0.60	1.00
1980FM (P)	2,688	Value: 2.00				
1981FM (U)	482	—	—	—	2.00	2.50
1981FM (P)	1,577	Value: 2.00				
1982FM (U)	—	—	—	—	0.60	1.00
1982FM (P)	—	Value: 2.00				
1984FM (U)	—	—	—	—	0.60	1.00
1984FM (P)	—	Value: 2.00				

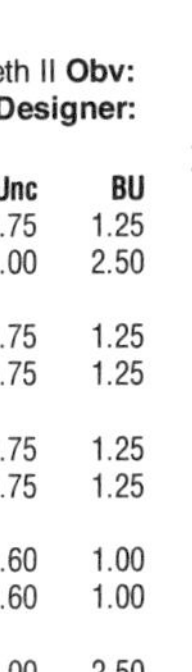

KM# 90 20 CENTS

11.3000 g., Copper-Nickel, 28.5 mm. **Ruler:** Elizabeth II **Subject:** World Food Day **Obv:** Arms with supporters **Rev:** Figs within leaves above value

Date	Mintage	F	VF	XF	Unc	BU
1981FM (M)	—	—	—	—	1.50	2.00

KM# 120 20 CENTS

11.3000 g., Copper-Nickel, 28.5 mm. **Ruler:** Elizabeth II **Obv:** Arms with supporters **Rev:** Figs within leaves above value

Date	Mintage	F	VF	XF	Unc	BU
1981	—	—	—	—	0.60	1.00
1984	2,000,000	—	—	—	0.60	1.00
1985	2,988,000	—	—	—	0.60	1.00
1985 Proof	—	Value: 2.00				
1986	2,530,000	—	—	—	0.60	1.00
1988	—	—	—	—	0.60	1.00

KM# 104 20 CENTS

11.3000 g., Copper-Nickel, 28.5 mm. **Ruler:** Elizabeth II **Subject:** 21st Anniversary of Independence **Obv:** Arms with supporters **Rev:** Mahoe trees above value **Designer:** Christopher Ironside

Date	Mintage	F	VF	XF	Unc	BU
ND(1983)FM (U)	—	—	—	—	0.60	1.00
ND(1983)FM (P)	—	Value: 2.00				

KM# 49 25 CENTS

14.5500 g., Copper-Nickel, 32.3 mm. **Ruler:** Elizabeth II **Obv:** Arms with supporters **Rev:** Streamer-tailed hummingbird above value **Designer:** Christopher Ironside

Date	Mintage	F	VF	XF	Unc	BU
1969	758,000	—	—	0.60	1.50	2.50
1969 Proof	30,000	Value: 3.00				
1970(fm) (M)	5,000	—	—	0.60	1.50	2.50
1970(fm) (P)	12,000	Value: 3.00				
1973	160,000	—	—	0.60	1.50	2.50
1975	3,110,000	—	—	0.60	1.50	2.50
1982	1,000,000	—	—	0.60	1.50	2.50
1984	2,002,000	—	—	0.60	1.50	2.50
1985	1,999,000	—	—	0.60	1.50	2.50
1985 Proof	—	Value: 3.00				
1986	2,635,000	—	—	0.60	1.50	2.50
1987	6,006,000	—	—	0.60	1.50	2.50
1987 Proof	—	Value: 3.00				
1988	3,034,000	—	—	0.60	1.50	2.50
1988 Proof	—	Value: 3.00				
1989	—	—	—	0.60	1.50	2.50
1989 Proof	—	Value: 3.00				
1990 Proof	—	Value: 3.00				

KM# 56 25 CENTS

14.5500 g., Copper-Nickel, 32.3 mm. **Ruler:** Elizabeth II **Obv:** Arms with supporters **Rev:** Streamer-tailed hummingbird above value **Designer:** Christopher Ironside

Date	Mintage	F	VF	XF	Unc	BU
1971FM (M)	4,834	—	—	0.75	1.50	2.50
1971FM (P)	14,000	Value: 3.00				
1972FM (M)	8,382	—	—	0.75	1.50	2.50
1972FM (P)	17,000	Value: 3.00				
1973FM (M)	13,000	—	—	0.75	1.50	2.50
1973FM (P)	28,000	Value: 3.00				
1974FM (M)	12,000	—	—	0.75	1.50	2.50
1974FM (P)	22,000	Value: 3.00				
1975FM (M)	1,503	—	—	0.75	1.50	2.50
1975FM (U)	4,683	—	—	—	1.50	2.50
1975FM (P)	16,000	Value: 3.00				
1976FM (M)	1,112	—	—	0.75	1.50	2.50
1976FM (U)	1,802	—	—	—	1.50	2.50
1976FM (P)	24,000	Value: 3.00				
1977FM (M)	1,112	—	—	0.75	1.50	2.50
1977FM (U)	597	—	—	—	3.00	4.50
1977FM (P)	10,000	Value: 3.00				
1978FM (M)	1,112	—	—	0.75	1.50	2.50
1978FM (U)	1,282	—	—	0.75	1.50	2.50
1978FM (P)	6,058	Value: 3.00				
1979FM (M)	1,112	—	—	0.75	1.50	2.50
1979FM (U)	2,608	—	—	0.75	1.50	2.50
1979FM (P)	4,049	Value: 3.00				
1980FM (M)	1,112	—	—	0.75	1.50	2.50
1980FM (U)	3,668	—	—	0.75	1.50	2.50
1980FM (P)	2,688	Value: 3.50				
1981FM (U)	482	—	—	—	3.00	4.50
1981FM (P)	1,577	Value: 3.50				
1982FM (U)	—	—	—	0.75	1.50	2.50
1982FM (P)	—	Value: 3.50				
1984FM (U)	—	—	—	0.75	1.50	2.50
1984FM (P)	—	Value: 3.50				

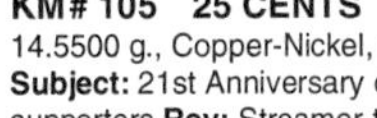

KM# 105 25 CENTS

14.5500 g., Copper-Nickel, 32.3 mm. **Ruler:** Elizabeth II **Subject:** 21st Anniversary of Independence **Obv:** Arms with supporters **Rev:** Streamer-tailed hummingbird above value **Designer:** Christopher Ironside

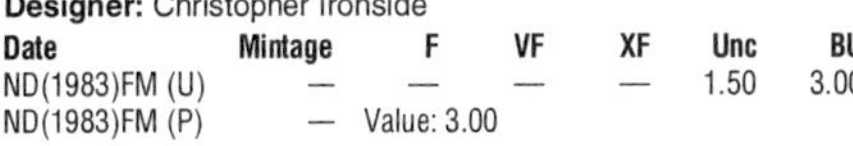

Date	Mintage	F	VF	XF	Unc	BU
ND(1983)FM (U)	—	—	—	—	1.50	3.00
ND(1983)FM (P)	—	Value: 3.00				

KM# 154 25 CENTS

14.5500 g., Copper-Nickel, 32.3 mm. **Ruler:** Elizabeth II **Subject:** 25th Anniversary - Bank of Jamaica **Obv:** Arms with supporters **Rev:** Streamer-tailed hummingbird above value **Designer:** Christopher Ironside

Date	Mintage	F	VF	XF	Unc	BU
1985	—	—	—	0.75	3.50	6.00

KM# 147 25 CENTS

6.0000 g., Nickel Plated Steel **Ruler:** Elizabeth II **Subject:** Marcus Garvey **Obv:** Arms with supporters **Rev:** Head 1/4 right **Shape:** 7-sided

Date	Mintage	F	VF	XF	Unc	BU
1991	—	—	—	—	1.00	1.50
1991 Proof	—	Value: 3.00				
1992	—	—	—	—	1.00	1.50
1992 Proof	—	Value: 3.00				
1993	—	—	—	—	1.00	1.50
1993 Proof	—	Value: 3.00				
1994	—	—	—	—	1.00	1.50

KM# 167 25 CENTS

3.6100 g., Copper Plated Steel, 20 mm. **Ruler:** Elizabeth II **Series:** National Heroes **Subject:** Marcus Garvey **Obv:** National arms **Obv. Legend:** JAMAICA **Rev:** Head 1/4 right **Edge:** Plain

Date	Mintage	F	VF	XF	Unc	BU
1995	—	—	—	—	0.50	0.75
1995 Proof	—	Value: 3.00				
1996	—	—	—	—	0.50	0.75
2000	—	—	—	—	0.50	0.75
2000 Proof	—	Value: 3.00				
2002	—	—	—	0.25	0.50	0.75
2002 Proof	500	Value: 3.00				
2003	—	—	—	0.25	0.50	0.75

KM# 65 50 CENTS
12.4500 g., Copper-Nickel, 30 mm. **Ruler:** Elizabeth II **Subject:** Marcus Garvey **Obv:** Arms with supporters **Rev:** Head 1/4 right **Shape:** 10-sided

Date	Mintage	F	VF	XF	Unc	BU
1975	12,010,000	—	0.15	0.50	1.50	2.00
1984	2,000,000	—	0.15	0.50	1.50	2.00
1985	2,119,000	—	0.15	0.50	1.50	2.00
1985 Proof	—	Value: 3.00				
1986	3,404,000	—	0.15	0.50	1.50	2.00
1987	5,545,000	—	0.15	0.50	1.50	2.00
1988	10,505,000	—	0.15	0.50	1.50	2.00
1988 Proof	—	Value: 3.00				
1989	—	—	0.15	0.50	1.50	2.00
1989 Proof	—	Value: 3.00				
1990 Proof	—	Value: 3.00				

KM# 70 50 CENTS
12.4500 g., Copper-Nickel, 30 mm. **Ruler:** Elizabeth II **Subject:** Marcus Garvey **Obv:** Arms with supporters **Rev:** Head 1/4 right **Shape:** 10-sided

Date	Mintage	F	VF	XF	Unc	BU
1976FM (M)	1,112	—	—	0.25	1.50	2.00
1976FM (U)	1,802	—	—	—	1.50	2.00
1976FM (P)	24,000	Value: 1.50				
1977FM (M)	556	—	—	0.50	3.50	5.00
1977FM (U)	597	—	—	—	3.50	5.00
1977FM (P)	10,000	Value: 1.50				
1978FM (M)	556	—	—	0.50	3.50	5.00
1978FM (U)	1,838	—	—	—	2.00	3.00
1978FM (P)	6,058	Value: 2.50				
1979FM (M)	556	—	—	0.50	3.50	5.00
1979FM (U)	1,282	—	—	—	2.50	3.50
1979FM (P)	4,049	Value: 3.00				
1980FM (M)	556	—	—	0.50	3.50	5.00
1980FM (U)	3,668	—	—	—	2.00	3.00
1980FM (P)	2,688	Value: 3.00				
1981FM (U)	482	—	—	—	3.50	5.00
1981FM (P)	1,577	Value: 3.00				
1982FM (U)	—	—	—	—	2.00	3.00
1982FM (P)	—	Value: 3.00				
1984FM (U)	—	—	—	—	2.00	3.00
1984FM (P)	—	Value: 3.00				

KM# 106 50 CENTS
12.4500 g., Copper-Nickel, 30 mm. **Ruler:** Elizabeth II **Subject:** 21st Anniversary of Independence - Marcus Garvey **Obv:** Arms with supporters **Rev:** Head 1/4 right **Shape:** 10-sided

Date	Mintage	F	VF	XF	Unc	BU
ND(1983)FM (U)	—	—	—	—	2.00	3.00
ND(1983)FM (P)	—	Value: 4.00				

KM# 50 DOLLAR
Copper-Nickel **Ruler:** Elizabeth II **Obv:** Arms with supporters **Rev:** Bust right

Date	Mintage	F	VF	XF	Unc	BU
1969	47,000	—	—	1.00	3.00	4.00
1969 Proof	30,000	Value: 4.50				
1970(fm) (M)	5,000	—	—	0.30	3.50	4.75
1970(fm) (P)	14,000	Value: 5.00				

KM# 57 DOLLAR
Copper-Nickel **Ruler:** Elizabeth II **Obv:** Arms with supporters **Rev:** Bust right

Date	Mintage	F	VF	XF	Unc	BU
1971FM	5,024	—	—	0.30	3.00	4.00
1971FM (P)	15,000	Value: 4.00				
1972FM (M)	7,982	—	—	0.30	2.00	3.00
1972FM (P)	17,000	Value: 3.00				
1973FM	10,000	—	—	0.30	2.00	3.00
1973FM (P)	28,000	Value: 3.00				
1974FM (M)	8,961	—	—	0.30	2.00	3.00
1974FM (P)	22,000	Value: 3.00				
1975FM (M)	5,312	—	—	0.30	2.50	3.50
1975FM (U)	4,683	—	—	—	2.50	3.50
1975FM (P)	16,000	Value: 3.00				
1976FM (M)	284	—	—	—	17.50	20.00
1976FM (U)	1,802	—	—	—	4.00	5.00
1976FM (P)	24,000	Value: 2.50				
1977FM (M)	287	—	—	—	17.50	20.00
1977FM (U)	597	—	—	—	8.00	10.00
1977FM (P)	10,000	Value: 4.00				
1978FM (U)	1,566	—	—	—	4.00	5.00
1978FM (P)	6,058	Value: 5.00				
1979FM (M)	284	—	—	—	17.50	20.00
1979FM (U)	2,608	—	—	—	4.00	5.00
1979FM (P)	4,049	Value: 5.00				

KM# 84.1 DOLLAR
Copper-Nickel **Ruler:** Elizabeth II **Obv:** Arms with supporters **Rev:** Bust right

Date	Mintage	F	VF	XF	Unc	BU
1980FM (M)	284	—	—	—	20.00	22.50
1980FM (U)	3,668	—	—	—	5.00	6.00
1980FM (P)	2,688	Value: 15.00				
1981FM (U)	482	—	—	—	10.00	12.50
1981FM (P)	1,577	Value: 17.50				
1982FM (U)	—	—	—	—	7.00	10.00
1982FM (P)	—	Value: 17.50				

KM# 84.2 DOLLAR
Copper-Nickel **Ruler:** Elizabeth II **Obv:** Arms with supporters **Rev:** Bust right **Edge:** Reeded

Date	Mintage	F	VF	XF	Unc	BU
1985	—	—	—	—	3.00	4.00
1985 Proof	—	Value: 7.50				
1987 Proof	—	Value: 7.50				
1988 Proof	—	Value: 7.50				

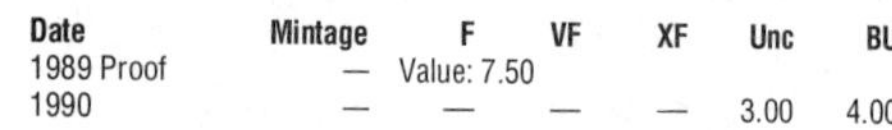

Date	Mintage	F	VF	XF	Unc	BU
1989 Proof	—	Value: 7.50				
1990	—	—	—	—	3.00	4.00

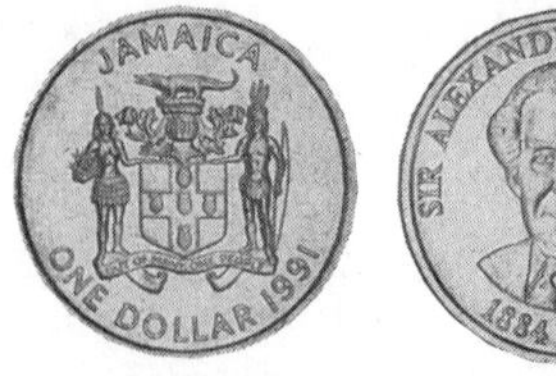

KM# 145 DOLLAR
9.0000 g., Nickel-Brass, 23.8 mm. **Ruler:** Elizabeth II **Subject:** Sir Alexander Bustamante **Obv:** Arms with supporters **Rev:** Bust facing **Edge:** BANK OF JAMAICA

Date	Mintage	F	VF	XF	Unc	BU
1990	—	—	—	—	2.25	3.00
1990 Proof	—	Value: 5.00				
1991	—	—	—	—	2.25	3.00
1991 Proof	—	Value: 5.00				
1992	—	—	—	—	2.25	3.00
1992 Proof	—	Value: 10.00				
1993	—	—	—	—	2.25	3.00
1993 Proof	—	Value: 5.00				

KM# 145a DOLLAR
Brass Plated Steel, 23.8 mm. **Ruler:** Elizabeth II **Subject:** Sir Alexander Bustamante **Obv:** Arms with supporters **Rev:** Bust facing **Edge:** Reeded

Date	Mintage	F	VF	XF	Unc	BU
1993	—	—	—	—	2.25	3.00
1993 Proof	500	Value: 15.00				
1994	—	—	—	—	2.25	3.00

KM# 164 DOLLAR
2.9100 g., Nickel Clad Steel, 18.5 mm. **Ruler:** Elizabeth II **Series:** National Heroes **Subject:** Sir Alexander Bustamante **Obv:** National arms **Obv. Legend:** JAMAICA **Rev:** Bust facing **Edge:** Plain **Shape:** 7-sided

Date	Mintage	F	VF	XF	Unc	BU
1994	—	—	—	0.40	1.00	1.50
1995	—	—	—	0.40	1.00	1.50
1995 Proof	—	Value: 4.00				
1996	—	—	—	0.40	1.00	1.50
1999	—	—	—	0.40	1.00	1.50
2000	—	—	—	0.40	1.00	1.50
2000 Proof	—	Value: 4.00				
2002	—	—	—	0.40	1.00	1.50
2002 Proof	500	Value: 4.00				
2003	—	—	—	0.40	1.00	1.50
2005	—	—	—	0.40	1.00	1.50
2006	—	—	—	0.40	1.00	1.50

KM# 163 5 DOLLARS
Steel, 21.5 mm. **Ruler:** Elizabeth II **Series:** National Heroes **Subject:** Norman Manley **Obv:** National arms **Obv. Legend:** JAMAICA **Rev:** Head left

Date	Mintage	F	VF	XF	Unc	BU
1994	—	—	—	—	2.50	3.50
1995	—	—	—	—	2.50	3.50
1995 Proof	—	Value: 5.00				
1996	—	—	—	—	2.50	3.50
2000	—	—	—	—	2.50	3.50
2000 Proof	—	Value: 5.00				
2002	—	—	—	1.50	2.50	3.50
2002 Proof	500	Value: 5.00				

KM# 181 10 DOLLARS
5.9400 g., Stainless Steel **Ruler:** Elizabeth II **Series:** National Heroes **Subject:** George William Gordon **Obv:** National arms **Obv. Legend:** JAMAICA **Rev:** Bust facing **Edge:** Plain **Shape:** Scalloped **Note:** Diameter varies: 24-24.6.

Date	Mintage	F	VF	XF	Unc	BU
1999	—	—	—	—	3.00	4.00
2000	—	—	—	—	3.00	4.00

Date	Mintage	F	VF	XF	Unc	BU
2000 Proof	—	Value: 9.00				
2002	—	—	—	1.50	3.00	4.00
2002 Proof	500	Value: 9.00				
2005	—	—	—	1.50	3.00	4.00

KM# 182 20 DOLLARS

Center Weight: 7.8000 g. **Center Composition:** Bi-Metallic Copper-Nickel center in Brass ring, 23 mm. **Ruler:** Elizabeth II **Series:** National Heroes **Subject:** Marcus Garvey **Obv:** Value above national arms within circle **Obv. Legend:** JAMAICA **Rev:** Head 1/4 right within circle **Edge:** Alternate reeding and plain

Date	Mintage	F	VF	XF	Unc	BU
2000	—	—	—	—	3.00	4.00
2000 Proof	—	Value: 15.00				
2001	—	—	—	1.50	3.00	4.00
2002	—	—	—	1.50	3.00	4.00
2002 Proof	500	Value: 15.00				

JAPAN

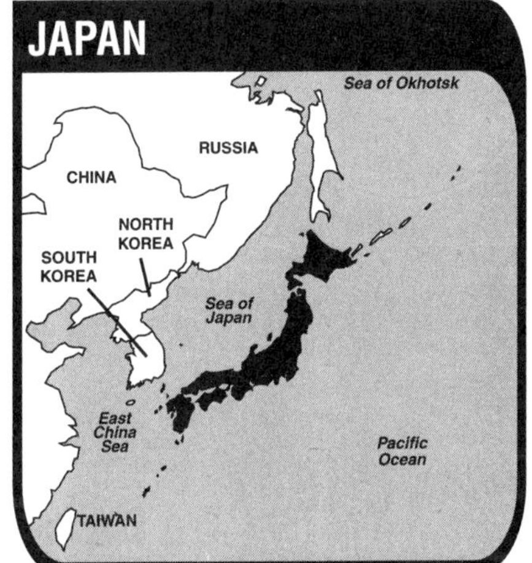

Japan, a constitutional monarchy situated off the east coast of Asia, has an area of 145,809 sq. mi. (377,835 sq. km.) and a population of 123.2 million. Capital: Tokyo. Japan, one of the major industrial nations of the world, exports machinery, motor vehicles, electronics and chemicals.

Japan, founded (so legend holds) in 660 B.C. by a direct descendant of the Sun Goddess, was first brought into contact with the west by a storm-blown Portuguese ship in 1542. European traders and missionaries proceeded to enlarge the contact until the Shogunate, sensing a military threat in the foreign presence, expelled all foreigners and restricted relations with the outside world in the 17th century. After Commodore Perry's U.S. flotilla visited in 1854, Japan rapidly industrialized, abolished the Shogunate and established a parliamentary form of government, and by the end of the 19th century achieved the status of a modern economic and military power. A series of wars with China and Russia, and participation with the allies in World War I, enlarged Japan territorially but brought its interests into conflict with the Far Eastern interests of the United States, Britain and the Netherlands, causing it to align with the Axis Powers for the pursuit of World War II. After its defeat in World War II, General Douglas MacArthur forced Japan to renounce military aggression as a political instrument, and he instituted constitutional democratic self-government. Japan quickly gained a position as an economic world power.

Japanese coinage of concern to this catalog includes those issued for the Ryukyu Islands (also called Liuchu), a chain of islands extending southwest from Japan toward Taiwan (Formosa), before the Japanese government converted the islands into a prefecture under the name Okinawa. Many of the provinces of Japan issued their own definitive coinage under the Shogunate.

RULERS

Emperors

Mutsuhito (Meiji), 1867-1912

Years 1-45 明治 or 治明

Yoshihito (Taisho), 1912-1926

Years 1-15 大正 or 正大

Hirohito (Showa), 1926-1989

Years 1-64 昭和 or 和昭

Akihito (Heisei), 1989-

Years 1- 平成

NOTE: The personal name of the emperor is followed by the name that he chose for his regnal era.

MONETARY SYSTEM

Commencing 1870

10 Rin = 1 Sen
100 Sen = 1 Yen

MONETARY UNITS

Rin 厘

Sen 銭

Yen 円 or 圓 or 圓

DATING

EMPIRE

DECIMAL COINAGE

Y# 41 5 RIN

2.1000 g., Bronze, 12.8 mm. **Ruler:** Yoshihito (Taisho) **Obv:** Large paulownia crest in center flanked by cherry blossoms **Rev:** Value within circle of flowered wreath

Date	Mintage	F	VF	XF	Unc	BU
Yr.5(1916)	8,000,000	0.50	1.50	2.75	10.00	22.00
Yr.6(1917)	5,287,584	0.50	1.50	2.75	10.00	26.00
Yr.7(1918)	11,661,877	0.25	0.75	2.00	7.50	18.50
Yr.8(1919)	17,130,539	0.25	0.75	2.00	7.50	11.50

Y# 20 SEN

7.1300 g., Bronze, 27.8 mm. **Ruler:** Mutsuhito (Meiji) **Obv:** Sunburst within beaded circle with legend separated by dots around border **Rev:** Value within center of rice wreath

Date	Mintage	F	VF	XF	Unc	BU
Yr.34(1901)	5,555,155	2.00	4.50	16.00	65.00	175
Yr.35(1902)	4,444,845	5.00	10.00	25.00	145	200
Yr.39(1906)	—	—	—	—	—	—

Note: None struck for circulation

Date	Mintage	F	VF	XF	Unc	BU
Yr.42(1909)	—	—	—	—	—	—

Note: None struck for circulation

Y# 35 SEN

7.1300 g., Bronze, 27.8 mm. **Ruler:** Yoshihito (Taisho) **Obv:** Sunburst within beaded circle with legend separated by dots around border **Rev:** Value within center of rice wreath

Date	Mintage	F	VF	XF	Unc	BU
Yr.2(1913)	15,000,000	1.50	2.25	4.00	32.00	100
Yr.3(1914)	10,000,000	1.50	2.25	4.00	32.00	75.00
Yr.4(1915)	13,000,000	1.50	2.25	4.00	32.00	75.00

Y# 42 SEN

3.7500 g., Bronze, 23 mm. **Ruler:** Yoshihito (Taisho) **Obv:** Paulownia crest flanked by cherry blossoms **Rev:** Value within circle of flowered wreath

Date	Mintage	F	VF	XF	Unc	BU
Yr.5(1916)	19,193,946	0.45	0.75	1.25	30.00	100
Yr.6(1917)	27,183,078	0.25	0.45	0.75	25.00	75.00
Yr.7(1918)	121,794,756	0.25	0.45	0.75	9.50	22.00
Yr.8(1919)	209,959,359	0.15	0.25	0.50	4.50	14.50
Yr.9(1920)	118,829,256	0.15	0.25	0.50	4.50	14.50
Yr.10(1921)	252,440,000	0.15	0.25	0.50	4.50	14.50
Yr.11(1922)	253,210,000	0.15	0.25	0.50	4.50	14.50
Yr.12(1923)	155,500,000	0.15	0.25	0.50	5.50	20.00
Yr.13(1924)	106,250,000	0.15	0.25	0.50	4.50	14.50

Y# 47 SEN

3.7500 g., Bronze, 23 mm. **Ruler:** Hirohito (Showa) **Obv:** Paulownia crest flanked by cherry blossoms with authority on top and date below **Rev:** Value within circle of flowered wreath

Date	Mintage	F	VF	XF	Unc	BU
Yr.2(1927)	26,500,000	1.25	2.00	2.75	32.00	75.00
Yr.4(1929)	3,000,000	2.75	5.50	12.50	45.00	100
Yr.5(1930)	5,000,000	2.00	3.50	6.00	70.00	250
Yr.6(1931)	25,001,222	0.25	0.45	1.25	12.50	35.00
Yr.7(1932)	35,066,715	0.25	0.45	1.25	9.00	29.00
Yr.8(1933)	38,936,907	0.15	0.25	0.50	2.50	12.50
Yr.9(1934)	100,004,950	0.15	0.25	0.50	2.50	12.50
Yr.10(1935)	200,009,912	0.15	0.25	0.50	1.50	6.50
Yr.11(1936)	109,170,428	0.15	0.25	0.50	1.50	6.50
Yr.12(1937)	133,196,568	0.15	0.25	0.50	1.50	6.50
Yr.13(1938)	87,649,338	0.15	0.25	0.50	1.50	6.50

Y# 55 SEN

3.7500 g., Bronze, 23 mm. **Ruler:** Hirohito (Showa) **Obv:** Bird within clouds flanked by cherry blossoms **Rev:** Value in center of sacred mirror within wave-like wreath

Date	Mintage	F	VF	XF	Unc	BU
Yr.13(1938)	113,600,000	0.15	0.25	0.50	1.50	3.50

Y# 56 SEN

0.9000 g., Aluminum, 17.6 mm. **Ruler:** Hirohito (Showa) **Obv:** Bird within clouds flanked by cherry blossoms **Rev:** Value in center of sacred mirror within wave-like wreath

Date	Mintage	F	VF	XF	Unc	BU
Yr.13(1938)	45,502,266	—	0.50	1.50	8.50	17.00
Yr.14(1939) Type A	444,602,146	—	1.25	2.25	12.00	24.00
Yr.14(1939) Type B	Inc. above	—	0.25	0.45	1.50	2.00
Yr.15(1940)	601,110,015	—	0.25	0.45	1.50	2.00

Y# 59 SEN

0.6500 g., Aluminum, 16 mm. **Ruler:** Hirohito (Showa) **Obv:** Value in center with authority above and date below **Rev:** Chrysanthemum above Mount Fuji with value below

Date	Mintage	F	VF	XF	Unc	BU
Yr.16(1941)	1,016,620,734	—	0.15	0.25	0.50	1.00
Yr.17(1942)	119,709,832	—	0.15	0.25	0.75	1.00
Yr.18(1943)	1,163,949,434	—	0.15	0.25	0.50	1.00

Y# 59a SEN

0.5500 g., Aluminum, 16 mm. **Ruler:** Hirohito (Showa) **Obv:** Value in center with authority above and date below **Rev:** Chrysanthemum above Mt. Fuji with value below **Note:** Thinner

Date	Mintage	F	VF	XF	Unc	BU
Yr.18(1943)	627,191,000	—	0.15	0.50	1.00	1.50

Y# 62 SEN

1.3000 g., Tin-Zinc, 15 mm. **Ruler:** Hirohito (Showa) **Obv:** Chrysanthemum flanked by sprigs with value above and date below **Rev:** Authority inscribed vertically in center with date below

Date	Mintage	F	VF	XF	Unc	BU
Yr.19(1944)	1,629,580,000	—	0.15	0.25	0.50	1.00
Yr.20(1945)	Inc. above	—	0.25	0.50	0.75	1.50

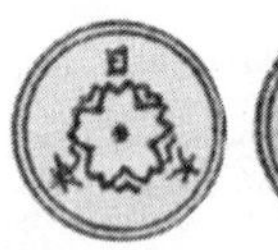

KM# 110 SEN

0.8000 g., Reddish Brown Baked Clay, 15 mm. **Ruler:** Hirohito (Showa) **Obv:** Stylized cherry blossom in center flanked by paulownia buds below value **Rev:** Mountain with symbol at upper left

Date	Mintage	F	VF	XF	Unc	BU
ND(1945)	—	13.00	18.00	22.50	30.00	40.00

Note: Circulated unofficially for a few days before the end of WWII in Central Japan; varieties of color exist

Y# 21 5 SEN

4.6700 g., Copper-Nickel **Ruler:** Mutsuhito (Meiji) **Obv:** Sunburst within circle, 3 legends separated by dots around border **Rev:** Value within rice wreath

Date	Mintage	F	VF	XF	Unc	BU
Yr.34(1901)	7,124,824	6.00	12.00	18.50	125	225
Yr.35(1902)	2,448,544	9.00	18.50	30.00	285	350
Yr.36(1903)	372,000	120	200	300	2,500	3,000
Yr.37(1904)	1,628,000	15.00	27.50	60.00	400	900
Yr.38(1905)	6,000,000	4.00	8.00	13.50	115	225
Yr.39(1906)	—	—	—	—	—	—

Note: None struck for circulation; Spink-Taisei Hong Kong sale 9-91 BU realized $10,000

Y# 43 5 SEN

4.2800 g., Copper-Nickel, 20.6 mm. **Ruler:** Yoshihito (Taisho) **Obv:** Flower-like form of sacred mirror around hole in center flanked by dots **Rev:** Chrysanthemum flanked by value with hole in center and paulownia foliage on bottom 1/2

Date	Mintage	F	VF	XF	Unc	BU
Yr.6(1917)	6,781,830	6.00	12.00	18.50	50.00	95.00
Yr.7(1918)	9,131,201	4.00	8.00	15.00	35.00	75.00
Yr.8(1919)	44,980,633	2.50	4.50	9.00	20.00	35.00
Yr.9(1920)	21,906,326	2.50	4.50	9.00	20.00	35.00

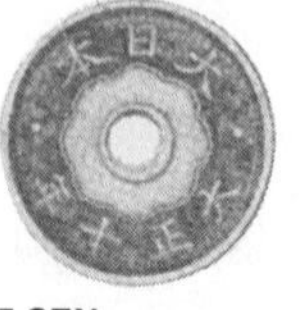

Y# 44 5 SEN

2.6300 g., Copper-Nickel, 19.1 mm. **Ruler:** Yoshihito (Taisho) **Obv:** Flower-like form of sacred mirror around hole in center flanked by dots **Rev:** Chrysanthemum flanked by value with hole in center and paulownia foliage on bottom 1/2

Date	Mintage	F	VF	XF	Unc	BU
Yr.9(1920)	100,455,537	0.35	0.65	1.50	15.00	65.00
Yr.10(1921)	133,020,000	0.25	0.45	1.20	5.00	13.50
Yr.11(1922)	163,980,000	0.25	0.45	1.20	5.00	13.50
Yr.12(1923)	8,000,394	0.25	0.45	1.20	5.00	13.50

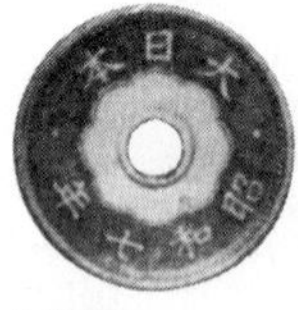
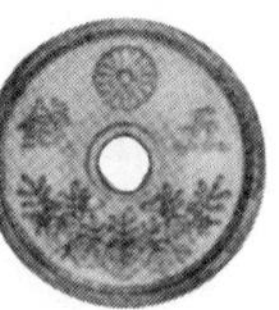

Y# 48 5 SEN

2.6300 g., Copper-Nickel, 19.1 mm. **Ruler:** Hirohito (Showa) **Obv:** Flower-like form of sacred mirror around hole in center flanked by dots **Rev:** Chrysanthemum flanked by value with hole in center and paulownia foliage on bottom 1/2

Date	Mintage	F	VF	XF	Unc	BU
Yr.7(1932)	8,000,394	0.25	0.45	1.50	7.00	40.00

Y# 53 5 SEN

2.8000 g., Nickel, 19 mm. **Ruler:** Hirohito (Showa) **Obv:** Rings around center hole flanked by cherry blossoms with authority above and date below **Rev:** Bird with wings spread below hole in center with rays of sun on upper 1/2 of border with chrysanthemum flanked by value

Date	Mintage	F	VF	XF	Unc	BU
Yr.8(1933)	16,150,808	0.45	1.25	2.25	5.50	15.00
Yr.9(1934)	33,851,607	0.45	0.75	1.50	4.50	13.00
Yr.10(1935)	13,680,677	0.75	1.50	2.75	7.50	15.00
Yr.11(1936)	36,321,796	0.45	0.75	1.50	4.50	1.00
Yr.12(1937)	44,402,201	0.45	0.75	1.50	5.50	15.00
Yr.13(1938) 4 known	10,000,000	—	—	—	—	—

Note: Almost entire mintage remelted

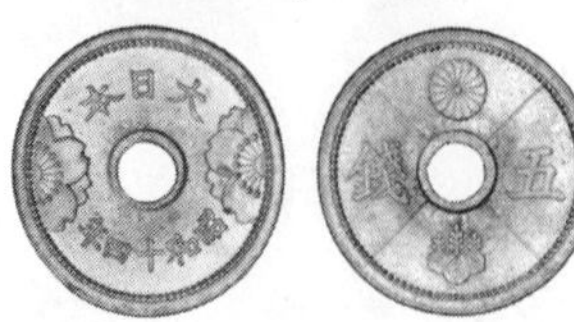

Y# 57 5 SEN

Aluminum-Bronze **Ruler:** Hirohito (Showa) **Obv:** Hole in center flanked by 1/2 cherry blossoms with authority above and date below **Rev:** Hole in center divides quarters, upper and lower quarter in relief, value at either side

Date	Mintage	F	VF	XF	Unc	BU
Yr.13(1938)	90,001,977	0.45	0.75	1.25	4.00	10.00
Yr.14(1939)	97,903,873	0.45	0.75	1.25	4.00	10.00
Yr.15(1940)	34,501,216	0.45	0.75	1.25	5.00	11.00

Y# 60 5 SEN

1.2000 g., Aluminum, 19 mm. **Ruler:** Hirohito (Showa) **Obv:** Bird with wings spread with authority on top and date below **Rev:** Chrysanthemum within clouds with value above and below **Note:** Variety I

Date	Mintage	F	VF	XF	Unc	BU
Yr.15(1940)	167,638,000	—	0.25	0.75	3.00	6.00
Yr.16(1941)	242,361,000	—	0.25	0.50	2.25	4.50

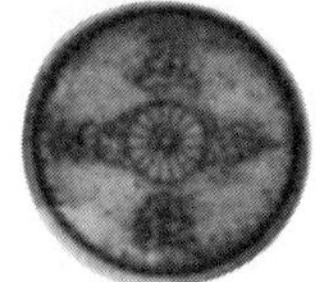

Y# 60a 5 SEN

1.0000 g., Aluminum, 19 mm. **Ruler:** Hirohito (Showa) **Obv:** Bird with wings spread with authority on top and date below **Rev:** Chrysanthemum among clouds with value above and below **Note:** Variety 2

Date	Mintage	F	VF	XF	Unc	BU
Yr.16(1941)	478,023,877	1.25	2.75	6.00	37.50	55.00
Yr.17(1942)	Inc. above	—	0.25	0.65	1.50	2.00

Y# 60b 5 SEN

0.8000 g., Aluminum, 19 mm. **Ruler:** Hirohito (Showa) **Obv:** Bird with wings spread with authority on top and date below **Rev:** Chrysanthemum within clouds with value above and below **Note:** Variety 3

Date	Mintage	F	VF	XF	Unc	BU
Yr.18(1943)	276,493,742	—	0.25	0.75	2.00	4.00

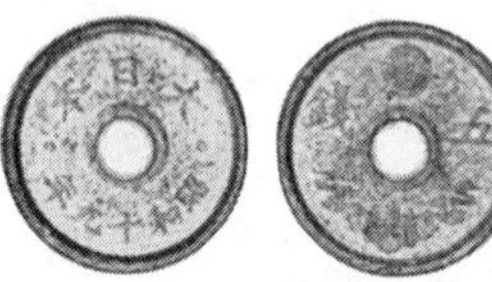

Y# 63 5 SEN

1.9500 g., Tin-Zinc, 17 mm. **Ruler:** Hirohito (Showa) **Obv:** Hole in center flanked by dots with authority on top and date below **Rev:** Chrysanthemum on top flanked by value above hole in center with paulownia crest within cloud-like swirls below

Date	Mintage	F	VF	XF	Unc	BU
Yr.19(1944)	70,000,000	—	0.25	0.75	2.50	3.00

Y# 65 5 SEN

2.0000 g., Tin-Zinc, 17 mm. **Ruler:** Hirohito (Showa) **Obv:** Large value in center flanked by paulownia crests with authority above and date below **Rev:** Bird with wings spread flanked by value with chrysanthemum above

Date	Mintage	F	VF	XF	Unc	BU
Yr.20(1945)	180,000,000	—	0.45	1.00	3.50	6.00
Yr.21(1946)	Inc. above	—	0.45	1.00	3.50	4.50

KM# 111 5 SEN

1.3000 g., Reddish Brown Baked Clay, 18 mm. **Ruler:** Hirohito (Showa) **Obv:** Heart shapes around symbol in center with authority on top and value below **Rev:** Chrysanthemum above text

Date	Mintage	F	VF	XF	Unc	BU
Yr.20(1945)	—	250	350	450	650	750

Note: Not issued for circulation; varieties of color exist

Y# 23 10 SEN

2.6957 g., 0.8000 Silver 0.0693 oz. ASW **Ruler:** Mutsuhito (Meiji) **Obv:** Dragon within beaded circle, 3 legends separated by dots around border **Rev:** Value within center of flowered wreath, chrysanthemum above

Date	Mintage	F	VF	XF	Unc	BU
Yr.34(1901)	797,561	95.00	135	185	800	1,700
Yr.35(1902)	1,204,439	75.00	120	150	775	2,000
Yr.37(1904)	11,106,638	3.50	5.50	7.50	35.00	100
Yr.38(1905)	34,182,194	3.50	5.50	7.50	35.00	100
Yr.39(1906)	4,710,168	3.50	5.50	7.50	35.00	100

Y# 29 10 SEN

2.2500 g., 0.7200 Silver 0.0521 oz. ASW **Ruler:** Mutsuhito (Meiji) **Obv:** Sunburst within cherry blossom circle with 3 legends separated by dots around border **Rev:** Value within center of flowered wreath with chrysanthemum above

Date	Mintage	F	VF	XF	Unc	BU
Yr.40(1907)	12,000,000	2.00	3.75	7.50	65.00	350
Yr.41(1908)	12,273,239	2.00	3.75	7.50	60.00	250
Yr.42(1909)	20,279,846	1.00	2.50	3.75	27.50	90.00
Yr.43(1910)	20,339,816	1.00	2.50	3.75	25.00	85.00
Yr.44(1911)	38,729,680	1.00	2.50	3.75	27.50	85.00
Yr.45(1912)	10,755,009	1.00	2.50	3.75	30.00	100

Y# 36.1 10 SEN

2.2500 g., 0.7200 Silver 0.0521 oz. ASW **Ruler:** Yoshihito (Taisho) **Obv:** Sunburst within cherry blossom circle with 3 legends separated by dots around border **Rev:** Value within flowered wreath with chrysanthemum on top

Date	Mintage	F	VF	XF	Unc	BU
Yr.1(1912)	10,344,307	2.00	3.75	7.50	60.00	200

Y# 36.2 10 SEN

2.2500 g., 0.7200 Silver 0.0521 oz. ASW **Ruler:** Yoshihito (Taisho) **Obv:** Sunburst within cherry blossom circle with 3 legends separated by dots around border **Rev:** Value within flowered wreath with chrysanthemum on top

Date	Mintage	F	VF	XF	Unc	BU
Yr.2(1913)	13,321,466	1.00	2.00	3.75	12.00	35.00
Yr.3(1914)	10,325,327	1.00	2.00	3.75	12.00	35.00
Yr.4(1915)	16,836,225	1.00	2.00	3.75	12.00	35.00
Yr.5(1916)	10,324,128	1.00	2.00	3.00	12.00	35.00
Yr.6(1917)	35,170,906	0.85	1.50	2.25	10.00	22.00

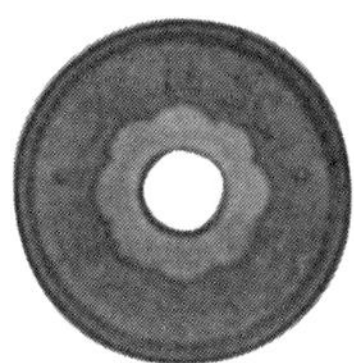

Y# 45 10 SEN

3.7500 g., Copper-Nickel, 22 mm. **Ruler:** Yoshihito (Taisho) **Obv:** Flower-like form of sacred mirror around hole in center flanked by dots with authority on top and date below **Rev:** Chrysanthemum flanked by value above hole in center with paulownia foliage on bottom 1/2

Date	Mintage	F	VF	XF	Unc	BU
Yr.9(1920)	4,894,420	0.45	0.75	2.50	25.00	75.00
Yr.10(1921)	61,870,000	0.25	0.50	1.25	5.00	13.00
Yr.11(1922)	159,770,000	0.25	0.50	1.25	5.00	13.00
Yr.12(1923)	190,010,000	0.25	0.50	1.25	4.50	13.00
Yr.14(1925)	54,475,000	0.25	0.50	1.25	5.00	13.00
Yr.15(1926)	58,675,000	0.25	0.50	1.25	5.00	13.00

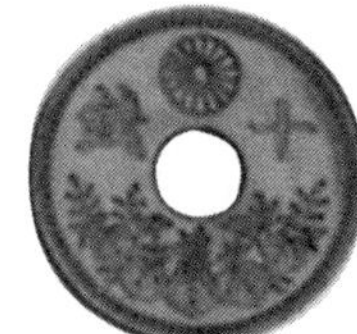

Y# 49 10 SEN

3.7500 g., Copper-Nickel **Ruler:** Hirohito (Showa) **Obv:** Flower-like form of sacred mirror around hole in center flanked by dots with authority on top and date below **Rev:** Chrysanthemum flanked by value above hole in center with paulownia foliage on bottom 1/2

Date	Mintage	F	VF	XF	Unc	BU
Yr.2(1927)	36,050,000	0.25	0.45	1.25	5.00	17.00
Yr.3(1928)	41,450,000	0.25	0.45	1.25	5.00	13.00
Yr.4(1929)	10,050,000	0.45	0.75	1.50	25.00	150
Yr.6(1931)	1,850,087	0.60	1.25	2.00	9.00	30.00
Yr.7(1932)	23,151,177	0.25	0.45	1.25	5.00	15.00

Y# 54 10 SEN

4.0200 g., Nickel **Ruler:** Hirohito (Showa) **Obv:** Center hole within 1/3 vertical portion recessed flanked by wave-like pattern with cherry blossoms **Rev:** Hole in center flanked by value and denomination, karakusa sprays are vertical in rectangular display, chrysanthemum on top, paulownia on bottom

Date	Mintage	F	VF	XF	Unc	BU
Yr.8(1933)	14,570,714	0.45	0.75	1.50	5.50	20.00
Yr.9(1934)	37,351,832	0.25	0.50	1.25	4.75	11.00
Yr.10(1935)	35,586,755	0.30	0.75	1.50	5.25	11.00
Yr.11(1936)	77,948,804	0.25	0.50	1.25	4.75	11.00
Yr.12(1937)	40,001,969	0.30	0.75	1.50	5.50	15.00

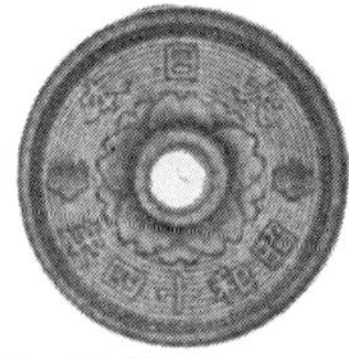
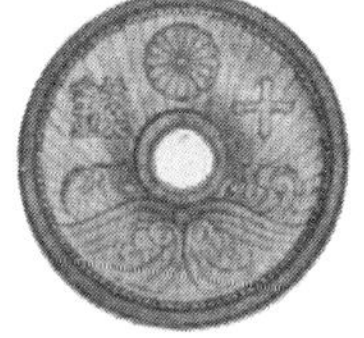

Y# 58 10 SEN

4.0000 g., Aluminum-Bronze **Ruler:** Hirohito (Showa) **Obv:** Double petal cherry blossom around center hole flanked by paulownia crest with authority on top and date below **Rev:** Chrysanthemum flanked by value with sun rays on upper 1/2 above hole in center with rolling waves below

Date	Mintage	F	VF	XF	Unc	BU
Yr.13(1938)	47,077,320	0.35	0.65	1.25	4.75	11.00
Yr.14(1939)	121,796,011	0.25	0.45	1.00	4.50	11.00
Yr.15(1940)	16,135,794	0.65	1.25	2.25	12.00	26.00

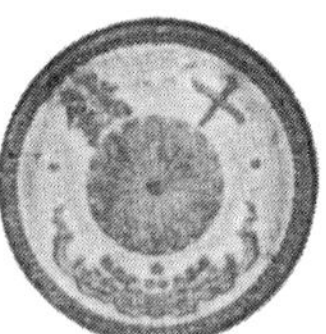

Y# 61 10 SEN

1.5000 g., Aluminum, 22 mm. **Ruler:** Hirohito (Showa) **Obv:** Double petal cherry blossom flanked by dots with authority on top and date below **Rev:** Chrysanthemum flanked by dots with value above and paulownia foliage below

Date	Mintage	F	VF	XF	Unc	BU
Yr.15(1940)	575,600,000	—	0.20	0.35	1.50	3.00
Yr.16(1941)	Inc. above	—	0.20	0.35	1.50	3.00

Y# 61a 10 SEN

1.2000 g., Aluminum, 22 mm. **Ruler:** Hirohito (Showa) **Obv:** Double petal cherry blossom flanked by dots with authority on top and date below **Rev:** Chrysanthemum flanked by dots with value above and paulownia foliage below

Date	Mintage	F	VF	XF	Unc	BU
Yr.16(1941)	944,900,000	0.10	0.35	0.50	2.00	4.00
Yr.17(1942)	Inc. above	—	0.20	0.35	1.50	2.00
Yr.18(1943)	Inc. above	0.75	2.25	3.75	30.00	60.00

Y# 61b 10 SEN

1.0000 g., Aluminum, 22 mm. **Ruler:** Hirohito (Showa) **Obv:** Double petal cherry blossom flanked by dots with authority on top and date below **Rev:** Chrysanthemum flanked by dots with value above and paulownia foliage below

Date	Mintage	F	VF	XF	Unc	BU
Yr.18(1943)	756,000,000	—	0.20	0.35	1.25	2.50

Y# 64 10 SEN

2.4000 g., Tin-Zinc, 19 mm. **Ruler:** Hirohito (Showa) **Obv:** Hole in center flanked by dots, authority on top, date on bottom **Rev:** Chrysanthemum on top flanked by value with paulownia crest within cloud-like swirls below

Date	Mintage	F	VF	XF	Unc	BU
Yr.19(1944)	450,000,000	—	0.20	0.35	1.25	1.75

KM# 112 10 SEN

2.0000 g., Reddish Brown Baked Clay, 21.9 mm. **Ruler:** Hirohito (Showa) **Obv:** Paulownia crest flanked by cherry blossoms with authority on top and date below **Rev:** Chrysandthemum in center with value above and below flanked by sprigs

Date	Mintage	F	VF	XF	Unc	BU
Yr.20(1945)	—	300	500	750	1,000	1,350

Note: Not issued for circulation; varieties of color exist

Y# 68 10 SEN

1.0000 g., Aluminum **Ruler:** Hirohito (Showa) **Obv:** Large numeral 10 overlaps double petal cherry blossom in center, authority on top, date on bottom **Rev:** Two rice stalks drooping downward, value and denomination at lower left, chrysanthemum at top

Date	Mintage	F	VF	XF	Unc	BU
Yr.20(1945)	237,590,000	—	0.20	0.35	1.00	1.50
Yr.21(1946)	Inc. above	—	0.20	0.35	1.00	1.50

Y# 24 20 SEN

5.3900 g., 0.8000 Silver 0.1386 oz. ASW, 23 mm. **Ruler:** Mutsuhito (Meiji) **Obv:** Dragon within beaded circle **Rev:** Chrysanthemum divides wreath, value within

Date	Mintage	F	VF	XF	Unc	BU
Yr.34(1901)	500,000	120	175	275	2,250	3,000
Yr.37(1904)	5,250,000	4.00	8.00	15.00	70.00	150
Yr.38(1905)	8,444,930	4.00	8.00	15.00	60.00	150

Y# 30 20 SEN

4.0500 g., 0.8000 Silver 0.1042 oz. ASW **Ruler:** Mutsuhito (Meiji) **Obv:** Sunburst within cherry blossom circle with 3 legends separated by dots around border **Rev:** Value and denomination within flowered wreath, chrysanthemum on top

Date	Mintage	F	VF	XF	Unc	BU
Yr.39(1906)	6,555,070	5.00	10.00	18.50	200	500
Yr.40(1907)	20,000,000	2.00	4.00	12.00	75.00	150
Yr.41(1908)	15,000,000	2.00	4.00	12.00	75.00	150
Yr.42(1909)	8,824,702	2.00	4.00	12.00	75.00	150
Yr.43(1910)	21,175,298	2.00	4.00	12.00	75.00	150
Yr.44(1911)	500,000	45.00	90.00	200	1,150	2,800

Y# 25 50 SEN

13.4800 g., 0.8000 Silver 0.3467 oz. ASW **Ruler:** Mutsuhito (Meiji) **Obv:** Dragon within beaded circle with 3 legends separated by dots around border **Rev:** Value within wreath, chrysanthemum above

Date	Mintage	F	VF	XF	Unc	BU
Yr.34(1901)	1,790,000	18.50	35.00	60.00	375	1,200
Yr.35(1902)	1,023,200	37.50	65.00	120	625	1,800
Yr.36(1903)	1,503,068	22.50	37.50	70.00	425	1,300
Yr.37(1904)	5,373,652	6.00	10.00	18.50	125	350
Yr.38(1905)	9,566,100	6.00	10.00	18.50	125	350

Y# 31 50 SEN

10.1000 g., 0.8000 Silver 0.2598 oz. ASW **Ruler:** Mutsuhito (Meiji) **Obv:** Sunburst within cherry blossom circle with 3 legends separated by dots around border **Rev:** Value and denomination within flowered wreath, chrysanthemum on top

Date	Mintage	F	VF	XF	Unc	BU
Yr.39(1906)	12,478,264	4.00	7.50	20.00	225	600
Yr.40(1907)	24,062,952	3.75	6.50	13.50	75.00	225
Yr.41(1908)	25,470,321	3.75	6.50	13.50	75.00	225
Yr.42(1909)	21,998,600	3.75	6.50	13.50	75.00	225
Yr.43(1910)	15,323,276	3.75	6.50	13.50	75.00	225
Yr.44(1911)	9,900,437	3.75	6.50	13.50	75.00	225
Yr.45(1912)	3,677,704	6.50	12.50	17.50	100	300

Y# 37.1 50 SEN

10.1300 g., 0.8000 Silver 0.2605 oz. ASW **Ruler:** Yoshihito (Taisho) **Obv:** Sunburst within cherry blossom circle, 3 legends separated by dots around border **Rev:** Value and denomination within flowered wreath, chrysanthemum on top

Date	Mintage	F	VF	XF	Unc	BU
Yr.1(1912)	1,928,649	12.50	20.00	40.00	160	450

Y# 37.2 50 SEN

10.1300 g., 0.8000 Silver 0.2605 oz. ASW **Ruler:** Yoshihito (Taisho) **Obv:** Sunburst within cherry blossom circle, 3 legends separated by dots around border **Rev:** Value and denomination within flowered wreath, chrysanthemum on top

Date	Mintage	F	VF	XF	Unc	BU
Yr.2(1913)	5,910,063	4.50	9.00	20.00	60.00	250
Yr.3(1914)	1,872,331	20.00	35.00	55.00	200	600
Yr.4(1915)	2,011,253	17.50	30.00	50.00	160	450
Yr.5(1916)	8,736,768	4.00	7.50	15.00	35.00	125
Yr.6(1917)	9,963,232	4.00	7.50	15.00	35.00	125

Y# 46 50 SEN

4.9500 g., 0.7200 Silver 0.1146 oz. ASW, 23.8 mm. **Ruler:** Yoshihito (Taisho) **Obv:** Sunburst in center flanked by cherry blossoms, authority on top, date on bottom, all within sacred mirror **Rev:** Vertical value and denomination flanked by phoenix, paulownia crest flanked by karakusa sprigs, chrysanthemum on top

Date	Mintage	F	VF	XF	Unc	BU
Yr.11(1922)	76,320,000	BV	2.00	4.00	25.00	75.00
Yr.12(1923)	185,180,000	BV	1.75	2.50	18.00	25.00
Yr.13(1924)	78,520,000	BV	1.75	2.50	18.00	25.00
Yr.14(1925)	47,808,000	BV	1.75	2.50	20.00	45.00
Yr.15(1926)	32,572,000	BV	1.75	2.50	22.00	50.00

Y# 50 50 SEN

4.9500 g., 0.7200 Silver 0.1146 oz. ASW **Ruler:** Hirohito (Showa) **Obv:** Sunburst in center flanked by cherry blossoms, authority on top, date on bottom, all within sacred mirror **Rev:** Vertical value and denomination flanked by phoenix, paulownia crest flanked by karakusa sprigs, chrysanthemum on top

Date	Mintage	F	VF	XF	Unc	BU
Yr.3(1928)	38,592,000	—	BV	2.00	10.00	30.00
Yr.4(1929)	12,568,000	BV	2.00	5.00	30.00	100
Yr.5(1930)	10,200,000	BV	2.25	5.50	20.00	65.00
Yr.6(1931)	27,677,501	—	BV	2.00	9.00	18.00
Yr.7(1932)	24,132,795	—	BV	2.00	9.00	18.00
Yr.8(1933)	10,001,973	BV	2.25	7.00	22.00	65.00
Yr.9(1934)	20,003,995	—	BV	2.00	9.00	18.00
Yr.10(1935)	11,738,334	—	BV	2.00	9.00	22.00
Yr.11(1936)	44,272,796	—	BV	2.00	7.00	15.00
Yr.12(1937)	48,000,533	—	BV	2.00	7.00	15.00
Yr.13(1938)	3,600,717	50.00	75.00	125	250	350

Y# 67 50 SEN

4.5000 g., Brass **Ruler:** Hirohito (Showa) **Obv:** Stalks of wheat and rice flanked by fish, crossed pick and hoe within stalks, authority on top, date on bottom **Rev:** Phoenix among clouds, chrysanthemum on top, value and denomination on bottom **Note:** Varieties exist.

Date	Mintage	F	VF	XF	Unc	BU
Yr.21(1946)	268,161,000	0.25	0.50	1.00	2.50	3.50
Yr.22(1947)	Inc. above	—	600	900	1,700	2,250

Note: Not released to circulation

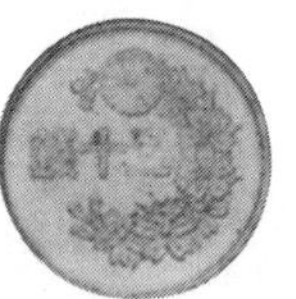

Y# 69 50 SEN

2.8000 g., Brass **Ruler:** Hirohito (Showa) **Obv:** Numeral 50 within center circle flanked by dots, authority on top, date on bottom **Rev:** Value and denomination at left of 1/2 cherry blossom wreath, chrysanthemum on top

Date	Mintage	F	VF	XF	Unc	BU
Yr.22(1947)	849,234,445	0.10	0.20	0.40	0.90	1.25
Yr.23(1948)	Inc. above	0.10	0.20	0.40	0.90	1.25

Y# A25.3 YEN

26.9600 g., 0.9000 Silver 0.7801 oz. ASW, 38.1 mm. **Ruler:** Mutsuhito (Meiji) **Obv:** Dragon within beaded circle, legends above, written value below **Rev:** Value within wreath, chrysanthemum above **Note:** Reduced size.

Date	Mintage	F	VF	XF	Unc	BU
Yr.34(1901)	1,256,252	25.00	50.00	95.00	225	250
Yr.35(1902)	668,782	40.00	85.00	150	300	400
Yr.36(1903)	5,131,096	22.00	40.00	70.00	140	200
Yr.37(1904)	6,970,843	22.00	40.00	70.00	200	200
Yr.38(1905)	5,031,096	22.00	40.00	70.00	200	200
Yr.39(1906)	3,471,297	25.00	50.00	95.00	450	550
Yr.41(1908)	334,705	85.00	175	300	1,000	1,000
Yr.45(1912)	5,000,000	20.00	40.00	60.00	175	175

Y# 38 YEN

26.9600 g., 0.9000 Silver 0.7801 oz. ASW **Ruler:** Yoshihito (Taisho) **Obv:** Dragon within beaded circle, 3 legends separated by dots around border **Rev:** Value and denomination within flowered wreath, chrysanthemum on top

Date	Mintage	F	VF	XF	Unc	BU
Yr.3(1914)	11,500,000	18.00	35.00	55.00	150	225

Y# 32 5 YEN

4.1666 g., 0.9000 Gold 0.1206 oz. AGW **Ruler:** Mutsuhito (Meiji) **Obv:** Sunburst superimposed on sacred mirror, legends around border, value separated by paulownia crests **Rev:** Value within wreath, chrysanthemum above

Date	Mintage	F	VF	XF	Unc	BU
Yr.36(1903)	21,956	800	950	1,250	2,250	2,750
Yr.44(1911)	59,880	750	900	1,200	2,150	2,500
Yr.45(1912)	59,880	600	750	1,000	1,750	2,000

Y# 39 5 YEN

4.1666 g., 0.9000 Gold 0.1206 oz. AGW **Ruler:** Yoshihito (Taisho) **Obv:** Sunburst within mirror, 3 legends around border, value on bottom **Rev:** Value and denomination within flowered wreath, chrysanthemum on top

Date	Mintage	F	VF	XF	Unc	BU
Yr.2(1913)	89,820	700	900	1,150	1,850	2,250
Yr.13(1924)	76,037	600	750	950	1,650	2,000

Y# 51 5 YEN

4.1666 g., 0.9000 Gold 0.1206 oz. AGW **Ruler:** Hirohito (Showa)

Date	Mintage	F	VF	XF	Unc	BU
Yr.5(1930)	852,563	20,000	35,000	50,000	65,000	75,000

Y# 33 10 YEN

8.3333 g., 0.9000 Gold 0.2411 oz. AGW **Ruler:** Mutsuhito (Meiji) **Obv:** Sunburst superimposed on sacred mirror, legends around border, value separated by paulownia crests **Rev:** Value within wreath, chrysanthemum above

Date	Mintage	VG	F	VF	XF	BU
Yr.34(1901)	1,654,682	—	400	550	750	1,250
Yr.35(1902)	3,023,940	—	400	550	750	1,350
Yr.36(1903)	2,902,184	—	400	550	750	1,350
Yr.37(1904)	724,548	—	750	1,500	2,000	4,000
Yr.40(1907)	157,684	—	450	700	1,250	2,350
Yr.41(1908)	1,160,674	—	400	550	750	1,250
Yr.42(1909)	2,165,660	—	350	550	750	1,200
Yr.43(1910)	8,982	—	7,500	10,000	15,000	25,000

Y# 34 20 YEN

16.6666 g., 0.9000 Gold 0.4822 oz. AGW **Ruler:** Mutsuhito (Meiji) **Obv:** Sunburst superimposed on sacred mirror, legends around border, authority above, date below **Rev:** Value within wreath, chrysanthemum above

Date	Mintage	VG	F	VF	XF	BU
Yr.36(1903) Rare	—	—	—	—	—	—
Yr.37(1904)	2,759,470	—	550	1,250	1,750	2,400
Yr.38(1905)	1,045,904	—	550	1,250	1,750	2,400
Yr.39(1906)	1,331,332	—	550	1,250	1,750	2,400
Yr.40(1907)	817,363	—	1,000	2,000	2,500	4,500
Yr.41(1908)	458,082	—	1,250	2,500	3,500	5,500
Yr.42(1909)	557,882	—	1,500	3,000	4,000	6,500
Yr.43(1910)	2,163,644	—	500	1,000	1,600	2,200
Yr.44(1911)	1,470,057	—	500	1,000	1,600	2,200
Yr.45(1912)	1,272,450	—	525	1,100	1,700	2,300

Y# 40.1 20 YEN

16.6666 g., 0.9000 Gold 0.4822 oz. AGW **Ruler:** Yoshihito (Taisho) **Obv:** Japanese character "first" used in date **Rev:** Value and denomination within wreath, chrysanthemum on top

Date	Mintage	VG	F	VF	XF	BU
Yr.1(1912)	177,644	—	700	1,400	2,200	3,000

Y# 40.2 20 YEN

16.6666 g., 0.9000 Gold 0.4822 oz. AGW **Ruler:** Yoshihito (Taisho) **Obv:** Sunburst within mirror, 3 legends separated by cherry blossoms, date on bottom **Rev:** Value and denomination within wreath, chrysanthemum on top

Date	Mintage	VG	F	VF	XF	BU
Yr.2(1913)	869,248	—	500	1,000	1,700	2,300
Yr.3(1914)	1,042,890	—	500	1,000	1,700	2,300
Yr.4(1915)	1,509,960	—	500	1,000	1,700	2,300
Yr.5(1916)	2,376,641	—	460	900	1,600	2,200
Yr.6(1917)	6,208,885	—	460	850	1,550	2,150
Yr.7(1918)	3,118,647	—	460	900	1,600	2,200
Yr.8(1919)	1,531,217	—	460	900	1,600	2,200
Yr.9(1920)	370,366	—	550	1,150	1,800	2,650

Y# 52 20 YEN

16.6666 g., 0.9000 Gold 0.4822 oz. AGW **Ruler:** Hirohito (Showa) **Obv:** Sunburst within mirror, legends separated by cherry blossoms around border **Rev:** Value and denomination within wreath, chrysanthemum on top

Date	Mintage	VG	F	VF	XF	BU
Yr.5(1930)	11,055,500	—	15,000	25,000	35,000	45,000
Yr.6(1931)	7,526,476	—	17,500	27,500	37,500	47,500
Yr.7(1932) Rare	—	—	—	—	—	—

REFORM COINAGE

Y# 70 YEN

3.2000 g., Brass, 19.5 mm. **Ruler:** Hirohito (Showa) **Obv:** Numeral 1 within circle, flanked by dots, authority on top, date on bottom **Rev:** Value and denomination above 3/4 orange blossom wreath

Date	Mintage	F	VF	XF	Unc	BU
Yr.23(1948)	451,170,000	—	0.25	0.50	2.00	—
Yr.24(1949)	Inc. above	—	0.15	0.35	1.25	—
Yr.25(1950)	Inc. above	—	0.15	0.35	1.25	—

Y# 74 YEN

1.0000 g., Aluminum, 20 mm. **Ruler:** Hirohito (Showa) **Obv:** Sprouting branch in center, authority on top, value and denomination on bottom **Rev:** Numeral 1 within 2 inner circles, date on bottom

Date	Mintage	VG	F	VF	XF	BU
Yr.30(1955)	381,700,000	—	—	—	—	15.00
Yr.31(1956)	500,900,000	—	—	—	—	7.50
Yr.32(1957)	492,000,000	—	—	—	—	7.50
Yr.33(1958)	374,900,000	—	—	—	—	7.50
Yr.34(1959)	208,600,000	—	—	—	—	9.00
Yr.35(1960)	300,000,000	—	—	—	—	5.00
Yr.36(1961)	432,400,000	—	—	—	—	3.00
Yr.37(1962)	572,000,000	—	—	—	—	2.00
Yr.38(1963)	788,700,000	—	—	—	—	2.00
Yr.39(1964)	1,665,100,000	—	—	—	—	2.00
Yr.40(1965)	1,743,256,000	—	—	—	—	1.50
Yr.41(1966)	807,344,000	—	—	—	—	1.50
Yr.42(1967)	220,600,000	—	—	—	—	1.50
Yr.44(1969)	184,700,000	—	—	—	—	1.50
Yr.45(1970)	556,400,000	—	—	—	—	1.00
Yr.46(1971)	904,950,000	—	—	—	—	1.00
Yr.47(1972)	1,274,950,000	—	—	—	—	0.75
Yr.48(1973)	1,470,000,000	—	—	—	—	0.75
Yr.49(1974)	1,750,000,000	—	—	—	—	0.75
Yr.50(1975)	1,656,150,000	—	—	—	—	0.75
Yr.51(1976)	928,800,000	—	—	—	—	0.75
Yr.52(1977)	895,000,000	—	—	—	—	0.50
Yr.53(1978)	864,000,000	—	—	—	—	0.50
Yr.54(1979)	1,015,000,000	—	—	—	—	0.50
Yr.55(1980)	1,145,000,000	—	—	—	—	0.50
Yr.56(1981)	1,206,000,000	—	—	—	—	0.50
Yr.57(1982)	1,017,000,000	—	—	—	—	0.50
Yr.58(1983)	1,086,000,000	—	—	—	—	0.50
Yr.59(1984)	981,850,000	—	—	—	—	0.50
Yr.60(1985)	837,150,000	—	—	—	—	0.50
Yr.61(1986)	417,960,000	—	—	—	—	0.25
Yr.62(1987)	958,520,000	—	—	—	—	0.25
Yr.62(1987) Proof	230,000	Value: 1.50				
Yr.63(1988)	1,268,842,000	—	—	—	—	0.25
Yr.63(1988) Proof	200,000	Value: 1.50				
Yr.64(1989)	116,100,000	—	—	—	—	0.25

Y# 95.1 YEN

1.0000 g., Aluminum, 20 mm. **Ruler:** Akihito (Heisei) **Obv:** Sprouting branch in center, authority on top, value and denomination on bottom **Rev:** Numeral 1 within two circles, date on bottom

Date	Mintage	VG	F	VF	XF	BU
Yr.1(1989)	2,366,770,000	—	—	—	—	0.15
Yr.1(1989) Proof	200,000	Value: 1.50				

Y# 95.2 YEN

1.0000 g., Aluminum, 20 mm. **Ruler:** Akihito (Heisei) **Obv:** Sprouting branch divides authority and value **Rev:** Value within circles above date **Edge:** Plain

Date	Mintage	F	VF	XF	Unc	BU
Yr.2(1990)	2,768,753,000	—	—	—	—	0.15
Yr.2(1990) Proof	200,000	Value: 1.50				
Yr.3(1991)	2,300,900,000	—	—	—	—	0.15
Yr.3(1991) Proof	220,000	Value: 1.50				
Yr.4(1992)	1,298,880,000	—	—	—	—	0.15
Yr.4(1992) Proof	250,000	Value: 1.50				
Yr.5(1993)	1,260,990,000	—	—	—	—	0.15
Yr.5(1993) Proof	250,000	Value: 1.50				
Yr.6(1994)	1,040,540,000	—	—	—	—	0.15
Yr.6(1994) Proof	227,000	Value: 1.50				
Yr.7(1995)	1,041,674,000	—	—	—	—	0.15
Yr.7(1995) Proof	200,000	Value: 1.50				
Yr.8(1996)	942,024,000	—	—	—	—	0.15
Yr.8(1996) Proof	189,000	Value: 1.50				
Yr.9(1997)	782,874,000	—	—	—	—	0.15
Yr.9(1997) Proof	212,000	Value: 1.50				
Yr.10(1998)	452,412,000	—	—	—	—	0.15
Yr.10(1998) Proof	200,000	Value: 1.50				
Yr.11(1999)	66,850,000	—	—	—	—	0.15
Yr.11(1999) Proof	280,000	Value: 1.50				
Yr.12(2000)	11,800,000	—	—	—	—	0.50
Yr.12(2000) Proof	226,000	Value: 5.00				
Yr,13(2001)	7,786,000	—	—	0.70	—	1.50
Yr.13(2001) Proof	8,024,000	Value: 3.00				
Yr.14(2002)	9,425,000	—	—	—	—	0.50
Yr.14(2002) Proof	242,000	Value: 3.00				
Yr.15(2003)	117,131,000	—	—	—	—	0.50
Yr.15(2003) Proof	275,000	Value: 3.00				
Yr.16(2004)	52,623,000	—	—	—	—	0.50
Yr.16(2004) Proof	280,000	Value: 3.00				
Yr.17(2005)	29,761,000	—	—	—	—	0.50
Yr.17(2005) Proof	258,000	Value: 3.00				
Yr.18(2006)	—	—	—	—	—	0.50
Yr.18(2006) Proof	246,000	Value: 3.00				
Yr.19(2007)	—	—	—	—	—	0.50
Yr.19(2007) Proof	—	Value: 3.00				

Y# 71 5 YEN

4.0000 g., Brass **Ruler:** Hirohito (Showa) **Obv:** Pigeon within circle with authority on top, date below **Rev:** Building within circle flanked by value and denomination, all within wreath

Date	Mintage	VG	F	VF	XF	BU
Yr.23(1948)	74,520,000	—	—	0.50	0.75	12.50
Yr.24(1949)	179,692,000	—	—	0.15	0.40	8.00

Y# 72 5 YEN

3.7500 g., Brass, 22 mm. **Ruler:** Hirohito (Showa) **Obv:** Hole in center flanked by seed leaf, authority on top and date below **Rev:** Gear design around center hole with horizontal lines below, large bending stalk of rice above **Note:** Old script.

Date	Mintage	VG	F	VF	XF	BU
Yr.24(1949)	111,896,000	—	—	0.15	0.25	9.00
Yr.25(1950)	181,824,000	—	—	0.15	0.25	6.50
Yr.26(1951)	197,980,000	—	—	0.15	0.25	6.50
Yr.27(1952)	55,000,000	—	—	0.30	0.60	100
Yr.28(1953)	45,000,000	—	—	0.30	0.60	6.50
Yr.32(1957)	10,000,000	—	—	4.00	8.00	40.00
Yr.33(1958)	50,000,000	—	—	0.25	0.50	3.50

Y# 72a 5 YEN

3.7500 g., Brass, 22 mm. **Ruler:** Hirohito (Showa) **Obv:** Hole in center flanked by a seed leaf with authority on top and date below **Rev:** Gear design around center hole with horizontal lines below, large bending stalk of rice above **Note:** New script.

Date	Mintage	VG	F	VF	XF	BU
Yr.34(1959)	33,000,000	—	—	0.25	0.50	5.00
Yr.35(1960)	34,800,000	—	—	0.20	0.40	5.00
Yr.36(1961)	61,000,000	—	—	0.15	0.35	4.00
Yr.37(1962)	126,700,000	—	—	0.10	0.30	3.00
Yr.38(1963)	171,800,000	—	—	0.10	0.30	2.50
Yr.39(1964)	379,700,000	—	—	0.10	0.30	2.50
Yr.40(1965)	384,200,000	—	—	0.10	0.30	2.00
Yr.41(1966)	163,100,000	—	—	0.10	0.30	2.00
Yr.42(1967)	26,000,000	—	—	0.25	0.50	2.50
Yr.43(1968)	114,000,000	—	—	—	0.10	1.50
Yr.44(1969)	240,000,000	—	—	—	0.10	1.50
Yr.45(1970)	340,000,000	—	—	—	0.10	1.50
Yr.46(1971)	362,050,000	—	—	—	0.10	1.50
Yr.47(1972)	562,950,000	—	—	—	0.10	0.75
Yr.48(1973)	745,000,000	—	—	—	0.10	0.75
Yr.49(1974)	950,000,000	—	—	—	0.10	0.75
Yr.50(1975)	970,000,000	—	—	—	0.10	0.75
Yr.51(1976)	200,000,000	—	—	—	0.10	0.75
Yr.52(1977)	340,000,000	—	—	—	0.10	0.75
Yr.53(1978)	318,000,000	—	—	—	0.10	0.75
Yr.54(1979)	317,000,000	—	—	—	0.10	0.75
Yr.55(1980)	385,000,000	—	—	—	0.10	0.75
Yr.56(1981)	95,000,000	—	—	—	0.10	1.50
Yr.57(1982)	455,000,000	—	—	—	0.10	0.75
Yr.58(1983)	410,000,000	—	—	—	0.10	0.75
Yr.59(1984)	202,850,000	—	—	—	0.10	0.75
Yr.60(1985)	153,150,000	—	—	—	0.10	1.00
Yr.61(1986)	113,960,000	—	—	—	0.10	1.50
Yr.62(1987)	631,545,000	—	—	—	0.10	0.25
Yr.62(1987) Proof	230,000	Value: 1.75				
Yr.63(1988)	368,920,000	—	—	—	—	0.25
Yr.63(1988) Proof	200,000	Value: 1.75				
Yr.64(1989)	67,332,000	—	—	—	—	0.50

Y# 96.1 5 YEN

3.7500 g., Brass, 22 mm. **Ruler:** Akihito (Heisei) **Obv:** Hole in center flanked by a seed leaf with authority on top and date below **Rev:** Gear around center hole with bending rice stalk above value

Date	Mintage	VG	F	VF	XF	BU
Yr.1(1989)	960,460,000	—	—	—	—	0.35
Yr.1(1989) Proof	200,000	Value: 1.75				

Y# 96.2 5 YEN

3.7500 g., Brass, 22 mm. **Ruler:** Akihito (Heisei) **Obv:** Hole in center flanked by a seed leaf with authority on top and date below **Rev:** Gear design around center hole with bending rice stalk above value in horizontal lines below

Date	Mintage	F	VF	XF	Unc	BU
Yr.2(1990)	520,753,000	—	—	—	—	0.35
Yr.2(1990) Proof	200,000	Value: 1.75				
Yr.3(1991)	516,900,000	—	—	—	—	0.35
Yr.3(1991) Proof	220,000	Value: 1.75				
Yr.4(1992)	300,880,000	—	—	—	—	0.35
Yr.4(1992) Proof	250,000	Value: 1.75				
Yr.5(1993)	412,990,000	—	—	—	—	0.35
Yr.5(1993) Proof	250,000	Value: 1.75				
Yr.6(1994)	197,540,000	—	—	—	—	0.35
Yr.6(1994) Proof	227,000	Value: 1.75				
Yr.7(1995)	351,674,000	—	—	—	—	0.35
Yr.7(1995) Proof	200,000	Value: 1.75				
Yr.8(1996)	207,024,000	—	—	—	—	0.35
Yr.8(1996) Proof	189,000	Value: 1.75				
Yr.9(1997)	238,874,000	—	—	—	—	0.35
Yr.9(1997) Proof	212,000	Value: 1.75				
Yr.10(1998)	172,412,000	—	—	—	—	0.35
Yr.10(1998) Proof	200,000	Value: 1.75				
Yr.11(1999)	59,850,000	—	—	—	—	0.35
Yr.11(1999) Proof	280,000	Value: 1.75				
Yr.12(2000)	8,804,000	—	—	—	—	2.50
Yr.12(2000) Proof	226,000	Value: 5.00				
Yr.13(2001)	78,025,000	—	—	—	—	0.35
Yr.13(2001) Proof	238,000	Value: 1.75				
Yr.14(2002)	143,423,000	—	—	—	—	0.35
Yr.14(2002) Proof	242,000	Value: 1.75				
Yr.15(2003)	102,406,000	—	—	—	—	0.35
Yr.15(2003) Proof	275,000	Value: 1.75				
Yr.16(2004)	70,623,000	—	—	—	—	0.35
Yr.16(2004) Proof	280,000	Value: 1.75				
Yr.17(2005)	15,761,000	—	—	—	—	0.35
Yr.17(2005) Proof	258,000	Value: 1.75				
Yr.18(2006)	—	—	—	—	—	0.35
Yr.18(2006) Proof	246,000	Value: 1.75				
Yr.19(2007)	—	—	—	—	—	0.35
Yr.19(2007) Proof	—	Value: 1.75				

Y# 73 10 YEN

4.5000 g., Bronze, 23.5 mm. **Ruler:** Hirohito (Showa) **Obv:** Temple in center with authority on top and value below **Rev:** Value and denomination within wreath **Edge:** Reeded

Date	Mintage	VG	F	VF	XF	BU
Yr.26(1951)	101,068,000	—	—	0.20	0.35	150
Yr.27(1952)	486,632,000	—	—	0.20	0.35	40.00
Yr.28(1953)	466,300,000	—	—	0.20	0.35	40.00
Yr.29(1954)	520,900,000	—	—	0.20	0.35	50.00
Yr.30(1955)	123,100,000	—	—	0.20	0.35	50.00
Yr.32(1957)	50,000,000	—	—	0.25	0.65	100
Yr.33(1958)	25,000,000	—	—	0.40	1.00	115

Y# 73a 10 YEN

4.5000 g., Bronze, 23.5 mm. **Ruler:** Hirohito (Showa) **Obv:** Temple in center with authority on top and value below **Rev:** Value and denomination within wreath **Edge:** Plain

Date	Mintage	VG	F	VF	XF	BU
Yr.34(1959)	62,400,000	—	—	—	0.20	60.00
Yr.35(1960)	225,900,000	—	—	—	0.20	45.00
Yr.36(1961)	229,900,000	—	—	—	0.20	40.00
Yr.37(1962)	284,200,000	—	—	—	0.20	5.00
Yr.38(1963)	411,300,000	—	—	—	0.20	5.00
Yr.39(1964)	479,200,000	—	—	—	0.20	3.50
Yr.40(1965)	387,600,000	—	—	—	0.20	2.50
Yr.41(1966)	395,900,000	—	—	—	0.20	2.50
Yr.42(1967)	158,900,000	—	—	—	0.20	10.00
Yr.43(1968)	363,600,000	—	—	—	0.20	2.50
Yr.44(1969)	414,800,000	—	—	—	0.20	1.50
Yr.45(1970)	382,700,000	—	—	—	0.20	2.50
Yr.46(1971)	610,050,000	—	—	—	0.20	2.00
Yr.47(1972)	634,950,000	—	—	—	0.20	1.50
Yr.48(1973)	1,345,000,000	—	—	—	0.20	1.00
Yr.49(1974)	1,780,000,000	—	—	—	0.20	1.00
Yr.50(1975)	1,280,260,000	—	—	—	0.20	1.00
Yr.51(1976)	1,369,740,000	—	—	—	0.20	1.00
Yr.52(1977)	1,467,000,000	—	—	—	0.20	1.00
Yr.53(1978)	1,435,000,000	—	—	—	0.20	1.00
Yr.54(1979)	1,207,000,000	—	—	—	0.20	1.00
Yr.55(1980)	1,127,000,000	—	—	—	0.20	0.75
Yr.56(1981)	1,369,000,000	—	—	—	0.20	0.75
Yr.57(1982)	890,000,000	—	—	—	0.20	0.75
Yr.58(1983)	870,000,000	—	—	—	0.20	0.75
Yr.59(1984)	533,850,000	—	—	—	0.20	0.75
Yr.60(1985)	335,150,000	—	—	—	0.20	0.75
Yr.61(1986)	68,960,000	—	—	—	0.25	1.50
Yr.62(1987)	165,545,000	—	—	—	0.20	0.50
Yr.62(1987) Proof	230,000	Value: 1.75				
Yr.63(1988)	617,912,000	—	—	—	0.20	0.50
Yr.63(1988) Proof	200,000	Value: 1.75				
Yr.64(1989)	74,692,000	—	—	—	0.25	0.75

Y# 97.1 10 YEN

4.5000 g., Bronze, 23.5 mm. **Ruler:** Akihito (Heisei) **Obv:** Temple divides authority and value **Rev:** Japanese character "first" in date

Date	Mintage	VG	F	VF	XF	BU
Yr.1(1989)	666,108,000	—	—	—	—	0.45
Yr.1(1989) Proof	200,000	Value: 1.75				

Y# 97.2 10 YEN

4.5000 g., Bronze, 23.5 mm. **Ruler:** Akihito (Heisei) **Obv:** Temple divides authority and value **Rev:** Value within wreath

Date	Mintage	F	VF	XF	Unc	BU
Yr.2(1990)	754,753,000	—	—	—	—	0.45
Yr.2(1990) Proof	200,000	Value: 1.75				
Yr.3(1991)	631,900,000	—	—	—	—	0.45
Yr.3(1991) Proof	220,000	Value: 1.75				
Yr.4(1992)	537,880,000	—	—	—	—	0.45
Yr.4(1992) Proof	250,000	Value: 1.75				
Yr.5(1993)	248,990,000	—	—	—	—	0.45
Yr.5(1993) Proof	250,000	Value: 1.75				
Yr.6(1994)	190,540,000	—	—	—	—	0.45
Yr.6(1994) Proof	227,000	Value: 1.75				
Yr.7(1995)	248,674,000	—	—	—	—	0.45
Yr.7(1995) Proof	200,000	Value: 1.75				
Yr.8(1996)	546,024,000	—	—	—	—	0.45
Yr.8(1996) Proof	189,000	Value: 1.75				
Yr.9(1997)	490,874,000	—	—	—	—	0.45
Yr.9(1997) Proof	212,000	Value: 1.75				
Yr.10(1998)	410,412,000	—	—	—	—	0.45
Yr.10(1998) Proof	200,000	Value: 1.75				
Yr.11(1999)	356,250,000	—	—	—	—	0.45
Yr.11(1999) Proof	280,000	Value: 1.75				
Yr.12(2000)	314,800,000	—	—	—	—	0.45
Yr.12(2000) Proof	226,000	Value: 1.75				
Yr.13(2001)	542,024,000	—	—	—	—	0.45
Yr.13(2001) Proof	238,000	Value: 1.75				
Yr.14(2002)	455,667,000	—	—	—	—	0.45
Yr.14(2002) Proof	242,000	Value: 1.75				
Yr.15(2003)	551,406,000	—	—	—	—	0.45
Yr.15(2003) Proof	275,000	Value: 1.75				
Yr.16(2004)	592,623,000	—	—	—	—	0.45
Yr.16(2004) Proof	280,000	Value: 1.75				
Yr.17(2005)	503,761,000	—	—	—	—	0.45
Yr.17(2005) Proof	258,000	Value: 1.75				
Yr.18(2006)	—	—	—	—	—	0.45
Yr.18(2006) Proof	246,000	Value: 1.75				
Yr.19(2007)	—	—	—	—	—	0.45
Yr.19(2007) Proof	—	Value: 1.75				

Y# 75 50 YEN

5.5000 g., Nickel, 24 mm. **Ruler:** Hirohito (Showa) **Obv:** Chrysanthemum blossom, authority on top, value at bottom **Rev:** Numeral 50 within center design, regnal era on top, date on bottom

Date	Mintage	VG	F	VF	XF	BU
Yr.30(1955)	63,700,000	—	—	0.75	1.50	15.00
Yr.31(1956)	91,300,000	—	—	0.75	1.00	15.00
Yr.32(1957)	39,000,000	—	—	0.75	1.50	15.00
Yr.33(1958)	18,000,000	—	—	1.00	2.50	25.00

Y# 76 50 YEN

5.0000 g., Nickel, 25 mm. **Ruler:** Hirohito (Showa) **Rev:** Value above hole in center

Date	Mintage	VG	F	VF	XF	BU
Yr.34(1959)	23,900,000	—	—	1.00	2.50	12.50
Yr.35(1960)	6,000,000	—	—	12.50	22.50	50.00
Yr.36(1961)	16,000,000	—	—	2.00	4.00	15.00
Yr.37(1962)	50,300,000	—	—	0.75	1.25	5.00
Yr.38(1963)	55,000,000	—	—	0.75	1.25	5.00
Yr.39(1964)	69,200,000	—	—	0.75	1.25	5.00
Yr.40(1965)	189,300,000	—	—	0.75	1.00	2.00
Yr.41(1966)	171,500,000	—	—	0.75	1.25	2.50

Y# 81 50 YEN

4.0000 g., Copper-Nickel, 21 mm. **Ruler:** Hirohito (Showa) **Obv:** Center hole flanked by chrysanthemums, authority on top and value below **Rev:** Numeral 50 above center hole with date below

Date	Mintage	VG	F	VF	XF	BU
Yr.42(1967)	238,400,000	—	—	—	0.75	7.50
Yr.43(1968)	200,000,000	—	—	—	0.75	5.00
Yr.44(1969)	210,000,000	—	—	—	0.75	5.00
Yr.45(1970)	269,800,000	—	—	—	0.75	5.00
Yr.46(1971)	80,950,000	—	—	—	0.75	5.00
Yr.47(1972)	138,980,000	—	—	—	0.75	4.00
Yr.48(1973)	200,970,000	—	—	—	0.75	4.00
Yr.49(1974)	470,000,000	—	—	—	0.75	2.00
Yr.50(1975)	238,120,000	—	—	—	0.75	1.50
Yr.51(1976)	241,880,000	—	—	—	0.75	1.50
Yr.52(1977)	176,000,000	—	—	—	0.75	4.00
Yr.53(1978)	234,000,000	—	—	—	0.75	1.50
Yr.54(1979)	110,000,000	—	—	—	0.75	2.00
Yr.55(1980)	51,000,000	—	—	—	0.75	2.00
Yr.56(1981)	179,000,000	—	—	—	0.75	1.00
Yr.57(1982)	30,000,000	—	—	—	0.75	2.00
Yr.58(1983)	30,000,000	—	—	—	0.75	2.00
Yr.59(1984)	29,850,000	—	—	—	0.75	2.50
Yr.60(1985)	10,150,000	—	—	—	0.75	4.00
Yr.61(1986)	9,960,000	—	—	—	0.75	2.50
Yr.62(1987)	545,000	—	—	40.00	60.00	85.00
Yr.62(1987) Proof	230,000	Value: 100				

Date	Mintage	VG	F	VF	XF	BU
Yr.63(1988)	108,912,000	—	—	—	—	1.50
Yr.63(1988) Proof	200,000	Value: 2.00				

Y# 101.1 50 YEN

4.0000 g., Copper-Nickel, 21 mm. **Ruler:** Akihito (Heisei) **Obv:** Center hole flanked by chrysanthemums, authority at top and value below **Rev:** Numeral 50 above center hole with date below

Date	Mintage	VG	F	VF	XF	BU
Yr.1(1989)	244,800,000	—	—	—	—	1.00
Yr.1(1989) Proof	200,000	Value: 2.00				

Y# 101.2 50 YEN

4.0000 g., Copper-Nickel, 21 mm. **Ruler:** Akihito (Heisei) **Obv:** Center hole flanked by chrysanthemums, authority at top and value below **Rev:** Value above hole in center

Date	Mintage	F	VF	XF	Unc	BU
Yr.2(1990)	274,753,000	—	—	—	—	1.00
Yr.2(1990) Proof	200,000	Value: 2.00				
Yr.3(1991)	208,900,000	—	—	—	—	1.00
Yr.3(1991) Proof	220,000	Value: 2.00				
Yr.4(1992)	48,880,000	—	—	—	—	1.00
Yr.4(1992) Proof	250,000	Value: 2.00				
Yr.5(1993)	50,990,000	—	—	—	—	1.00
Yr.5(1993) Proof	250,000	Value: 2.00				
Yr.6(1994)	65,540,000	—	—	—	—	1.00
Yr.6(1994) Proof	227,000	Value: 2.00				
Yr.7(1995)	111,674,000	—	—	—	—	1.00
Yr.7(1995) Proof	200,000	Value: 2.00				
Yr.8(1996)	82,024,000	—	—	—	—	1.00
Yr.8(1996) Proof	189,000	Value: 2.00				
Yr.9(1997)	149,876,000	—	—	—	—	1.00
Yr.9(1997) Proof	212,000	Value: 2.00				
Yr.10(1998)	100,412,000	—	—	—	—	1.00
Yr.10(1998) Proof	200,000	Value: 2.00				
Yr.11(1999)	58,850,000	—	—	—	—	1.00
Yr.11(1999) Proof	280,000	Value: 2.00				
Yr.12(2000)	6,800,000	—	—	—	—	7.50
Yr.12(2000) Proof	226,000	Value: 8.00				
Yr.13(2001)	8,024,000	—	—	—	—	3.00
Yr.13(2001) Proof	238,000	Value: 4.00				
Yr.14(2002)	11,667,000	—	—	—	—	5.00
Yr.14(2002) Proof	242,000	Value: 7.00				
Yr.15(2003)	10,406,000	—	—	—	—	5.00
Yr.15(2003) Proof	275,000	Value: 7.00				
Yr.16(2004)	9,623,000	—	—	—	—	5.00
Yr.16(2004) Proof	280,000	Value: 7.00				
Yr.17(2005)	9,761,000	—	—	—	—	5.00
Yr.17(2005) Proof	258,000	Value: 7.00				
Yr.18(2006)	—	—	—	—	—	5.00
Yr.18(2006) Proof	246,000	Value: 7.00				
Yr.19(2007)	—	—	—	—	—	5.00
Yr.19(2007) Proof	—	Value: 7.00				

Y# 77 100 YEN

4.8000 g., 0.6000 Silver 0.0926 oz. ASW, 22.5 mm. **Ruler:** Hirohito (Showa) **Obv:** Phoenix

Date	Mintage	F	VF	XF	Unc	BU
Yr.32(1957)	30,000,000	—	1.50	2.50	7.00	9.00
Yr.33(1958)	70,000,000	—	1.50	2.50	5.00	6.00

Y# 78 100 YEN

4.8000 g., 0.6000 Silver 0.0926 oz. ASW, 22.5 mm. **Ruler:** Hirohito (Showa) **Obv:** Sheaf of rice in center with authority on top and value below **Rev:** Numeral 100 within circle flanked by 1/4 lined wreath with era on top and year below

Date	Mintage	VG	F	VF	XF	BU
Yr.34(1959)	110,000,000	—	—	1.50	2.50	7.00
Yr.35(1960)	50,000,000	—	—	1.50	2.50	9.00
Yr.36(1961)	15,000,000	—	—	1.50	2.50	9.00
Yr.38(1963)	45,000,000	—	—	1.50	2.50	9.00
Yr.39(1964)	10,000,000	—	—	1.75	3.50	9.00
Yr.40(1965)	62,500,000	—	—	1.50	2.50	4.00
Yr.41(1966)	97,500,000	—	—	1.50	2.50	4.00

Y# 79 100 YEN

4.8000 g., 0.6000 Silver 0.0926 oz. ASW, 22.5 mm. **Ruler:** Hirohito (Showa) **Subject:** 1964 Olympic Games **Obv:** Olympic circles on base of flaming torch flanked by authority above and value below **Rev:** Numeral 100 within center circle

Date	Mintage	VG	F	VF	XF	BU
Yr.39/1964	80,000,000	—	—	1.50	2.50	4.00

Y# 82 100 YEN

4.2000 g., Copper-Nickel, 22.5 mm. **Ruler:** Hirohito (Showa) **Obv:** Cherry blossoms **Rev:** Large numeral 100 in center

Date	Mintage	VG	F	VF	XF	BU
Yr.42(1967)	432,200,000	—	—	—	1.50	7.50
Note: Varieties exist						
Yr.43(1968)	471,000,000	—	—	—	1.50	5.00
Yr.44(1969)	323,700,000	—	—	—	1.50	7.50
Yr.45(1970)	237,100,000	—	—	—	1.50	5.00
Yr.46(1971)	481,050,000	—	—	—	1.50	2.50
Yr.47(1972)	468,950,000	—	—	—	1.50	2.00
Yr.48(1973)	680,000,000	—	—	—	1.50	2.00
Yr.49(1974)	660,000,000	—	—	—	1.50	2.00
Yr.50(1975)	437,160,000	—	—	—	1.50	2.00
Yr.51(1976)	322,840,000	—	—	—	1.50	2.00
Yr.52(1977)	440,000,000	—	—	—	1.50	2.00
Yr.53(1978)	292,000,000	—	—	—	1.50	2.00
Yr.54(1979)	382,000,000	—	—	—	1.50	2.00
Yr.55(1980)	588,000,000	—	—	—	1.50	2.00
Yr.56(1981)	348,000,000	—	—	—	1.50	2.00
Yr.57(1982)	110,000,000	—	—	—	1.50	3.00
Yr.58(1983)	50,000,000	—	—	—	1.50	5.00
Yr.59(1984)	41,850,000	—	—	—	1.50	5.00
Yr.60(1985)	58,150,000	—	—	—	1.50	5.00
Yr.61(1986)	99,960,000	—	—	—	1.50	2.00
Yr.62(1987)	193,545,000	—	—	—	1.50	2.00
Yr.62(1987) Proof	230,000	Value: 5.00				
Yr.63(1988)	362,912,000	—	—	—	1.50	2.00
Yr.63(1988) Proof	200,000	Value: 5.00				

Y# 83 100 YEN

9.0000 g., Copper-Nickel, 28 mm. **Ruler:** Hirohito (Showa) **Subject:** Osaka Expo '70 **Obv:** Mt. Fuji **Rev:** Circles within world globe with value above

Date	Mintage	VG	F	VF	XF	BU
Yr.45(1970)	40,000,000	—	—	2.50	3.50	6.00

Y# 84 100 YEN

12.0000 g., Copper-Nickel, 30 mm. **Ruler:** Hirohito (Showa) **Subject:** 1972 Winter Olympic Games - Sapporo **Obv:** Olympic torch with flame flanked by authority and city name **Rev:** Large numeral 100 above olympic circles flanked by flower designs

Date	Mintage	VG	F	VF	XF	BU
Yr.47/1972	30,000,000	—	—	3.00	4.50	7.50

Y# 85 100 YEN

9.8000 g., Copper-Nickel, 22.5 mm. **Ruler:** Hirohito (Showa) **Subject:** Okinawa Expo '75 **Obv:** Gate of Shurei **Rev:** Value in center flanked by dolphins with legend above and below

Date	Mintage	VG	F	VF	XF	BU
Yr.50(1975)	120,000,000	—	—	1.75	2.50	3.50

Y# 86 100 YEN

12.0000 g., Copper-Nickel, 30 mm. **Ruler:** Hirohito (Showa) **Subject:** 50th Anniversary of Reign **Obv:** Imperial Palace and Niju Bridge **Rev:** Chrysanthemum in center flanked by phoenix with inscription above and below

Date	Mintage	VG	F	VF	XF	BU
Yr.51(1976)	70,000,000	—	—	2.50	3.50	6.00

Y# 98.1 100 YEN

9.8000 g., Copper-Nickel, 22.5 mm. **Ruler:** Akihito (Heisei) **Obv:** Cherry blossoms **Rev:** Japanese character "first" in date

Date	Mintage	VG	F	VF	XF	BU
Yr.1(1989)	368,800,000	—	—	—	—	2.00
Yr.1(1989) Proof	200,000	Value: 5.00				

Y# 98.2 100 YEN

9.8000 g., Copper-Nickel, 22.6 mm. **Ruler:** Akihito (Heisei) **Obv:** Cherry blossoms **Rev:** Large numeral 100

Date	Mintage	F	VF	XF	Unc	BU
Yr.2(1990)	444,753,000	—	—	—	—	2.00
Yr.2(1990) Proof	200,000	Value: 5.00				
Yr.3(1991)	374,900,000	—	—	—	—	2.00
Yr.3(1991) Proof	220,000	Value: 5.00				
Yr.4(1992)	211,050,000	—	—	—	—	2.00
Yr.4(1992) Proof	250,000	Value: 5.00				
Yr.5(1993)	81,990,000	—	—	—	—	2.00
Yr.5(1993) Proof	250,000	Value: 5.00				
Yr.6(1994)	81,540,000	—	—	—	—	2.00
Yr.6(1994) Proof	227,000	Value: 5.00				
Yr.7(1995)	92,674,000	—	—	—	—	2.00
Yr.7(1995) Proof	200,000	Value: 5.00				
Yr.8(1996)	237,024,000	—	—	—	—	2.00
Yr.8(1996) Proof	189,000	Value: 5.00				
Yr.9(1997)	271,876,000	—	—	—	—	2.00
Yr.9(1997) Proof	212,000	Value: 5.00				
Yr.10(1998)	252,412,000	—	—	—	—	2.00
Yr.10(1998) Proof	200,000	Value: 5.00				
Yr.11(1999)	178,850,000	—	—	—	—	2.00
Yr.11(1999) Proof	280,000	Value: 5.00				
Yr.12(2000)	171,800,000	—	—	—	—	2.00
Yr.12(2000) Proof	226,000	Value: 5.00				
Yr.13(2001)	8,024,000	—	—	—	—	7.50
Yr.13(2001) Proof	238,000	Value: 10.00				
Yr.14(2002)	10,667,000	—	—	—	—	5.00
Yr.14(2002) Proof	242,000	Value: 8.00				
Yr.15(2003)	98,406,000	—	—	—	—	2.00
Yr.15(2003) Proof	275,000	Value: 5.00				
Yr.16(2004)	204,623,000	—	—	—	—	2.00
Yr.16(2004) Proof	280,000	Value: 5.00				
Yr.17(2005)	299,761,000	—	—	—	—	2.00
Yr.17(2005) Proof	258,000	Value: 5.00				
Yr.18(2006)	—	—	—	—	—	2.00
Yr.18(2006) Proof	246,000	Value: 5.00				
Yr.19(2007)	—	—	—	—	—	2.00
Yr.19(2007) Proof	—	Value: 5.00				

Y# 87 500 YEN
7.2000 g., Copper-Nickel, 26.5 mm. **Ruler:** Hirohito (Showa) **Obv:** Pawlownia flower **Rev:** Numeral 500 in center flanked by cherry blossoms **Edge Lettering:** NIPPON 500

Date	Mintage	VG	F	VF	XF	BU
Yr.57(1982)	300,000,000	—	—	—	7.00	9.00
Yr.58(1983)	240,000,000	—	—	—	7.00	9.00
Yr.59(1984)	342,850,000	—	—	—	7.00	9.00
Yr.60(1985)	97,150,000	—	—	—	7.00	9.00
Yr.61(1986)	49,960,000	—	—	—	7.00	9.00
Yr.62(1987)	2,545,000	—	—	7.00	9.00	15.00
Yr.62(1987) Proof	230,000	Value: 25.00				
Yr.63(1988)	148,018,000	—	—	—	7.00	9.00
Yr.63(1988) Proof	200,000	Value: 15.00				
Yr.64(1989)	16,042,000	—	—	—	7.00	12.00

Y# 88 500 YEN
13.0000 g., Copper-Nickel, 30 mm. **Ruler:** Hirohito (Showa) **Subject:** 1985 Tsukuba Expo **Obv:** Mt. Tsukuba above cherry blossoms **Rev:** Circles within triangular design above value flanked by cherry blossom **Edge Lettering:** TSUKUBA EXPO '85

Date	Mintage	VG	F	VF	XF	BU
Yr.60(1985)	70,000,000	—	—	—	7.50	10.00

Y# 89 500 YEN
13.0000 g., Copper-Nickel, 30 mm. **Ruler:** Hirohito (Showa) **Subject:** 100th Anniversary - Governmental Cabinet System **Obv:** Prime Minister's official residence **Rev:** Large numeral 500 within center square **Edge Lettering:** NAIKAKU 100 NEN

Date	Mintage	VG	F	VF	XF	BU
Yr.60(1985)	70,000,000	—	—	—	7.50	10.00

Y# 90 500 YEN
13.0000 g., Copper-Nickel, 30 mm. **Ruler:** Hirohito (Showa) **Subject:** 60 Years of Reign of Hirohito **Obv:** Large chrysanthemum with legends around border **Rev:** Shishinden Palace **Designer:** Ikuo Hirayama

Date	Mintage	VG	F	VF	XF	BU
Yr.61(1986)	50,000,000	—	—	—	8.00	12.00

Y# 93 500 YEN
13.0000 g., Copper-Nickel, 30 mm. **Ruler:** Hirohito (Showa) **Subject:** Opening of Seikan Tunnel **Obv:** Seikan tunnel flanked by sea gulls **Rev:** Map within ribbon above value

Date	Mintage	VG	F	VF	XF	BU
Yr.63(1988)	20,000,000	—	—	—	8.50	12.50

Y# 94 500 YEN
13.0000 g., Copper-Nickel, 30 mm. **Ruler:** Hirohito (Showa) **Subject:** Opening of Seto Bridge **Obv:** Seto Bridge **Rev:** Map within ribbon above value

Date	Mintage	VG	F	VF	XF	BU
Yr.63(1988)	20,000,000	—	—	—	8.50	12.50

Y# 99.1 500 YEN
7.2000 g., Copper-Nickel, 26.5 mm. **Ruler:** Akihito (Heisei) **Obv:** Pawlownia flower **Rev:** Value flanked by cherry blossoms

Date	Mintage	VG	F	VF	XF	BU
Yr.1(1989)	192,652,000	—	—	—	7.00	9.00
Yr.1(1989) Proof	200,000	Value: 15.00				

Y# 99.2 500 YEN
7.2000 g., Copper-Nickel, 26.5 mm. **Ruler:** Akihito (Heisei) **Obv:** Pawlownia flower **Rev:** Value flanked by cherry blossoms

Date	Mintage	VG	F	VF	XF	BU
Yr.2(1990)	159,753,000	—	—	—	7.00	9.00
Yr.2(1990) Proof	200,000	Value: 15.00				
Yr.3(1991)	169,900,000	—	—	—	7.00	9.00
Yr.3(1991) Proof	220,000	Value: 15.00				
Yr.4(1992)	87,880,000	—	—	—	7.00	9.00
Yr.4(1992) Proof	250,000	Value: 15.00				
Yr.5(1993)	131,990,000	—	—	—	7.00	9.00
Yr.5(1993) Proof	250,000	Value: 15.00				
Yr.6(1994)	105,545,000	—	—	—	7.00	9.00
Yr.6(1994) Proof	227,000	Value: 15.00				
Yr.7(1995)	182,669,000	—	—	—	—	9.00
Yr.7(1995) Proof	200,000	Value: 15.00				
Yr.8(1996)	99,024,000	—	—	—	—	9.00
Yr.8(1996) Proof	189,000	Value: 15.00				
Yr.9(1997)	172,878,000	—	—	—	—	9.00
Yr.9(1997) Proof	212,000	Value: 15.00				
Yr.10(1998)	214,408,000	—	—	—	—	9.00
Yr.10(1998) Proof	200,000	Value: 15.00				
Yr.11(1999)	164,840,000	—	—	—	—	9.00
Yr.11(1999) Proof	280,000	Value: 15.00				

Y# 102 500 YEN
13.0000 g., Copper-Nickel, 30 mm. **Ruler:** Akihito (Heisei) **Subject:** Enthronement of Emperor Akihito **Obv:** Carriage **Rev:** Chrysanthemum crest among leaves above value

Date	Mintage	VG	F	VF	XF	BU
Yr.2(1990)	30,000,000	—	—	—	—	13.50

Y# 106 500 YEN
13.0000 g., Copper-Nickel, 30 mm. **Ruler:** Akihito (Heisei) **Subject:** 20th Anniversary - Reversion of Okinawa **Obv:** Building **Rev:** Value and denomination flanked by upright dragons

Date	Mintage	VG	F	VF	XF	BU
Yr.4(1992)	19,953,000	—	—	—	—	14.50
Yr.4(1992) Proof	47,000	Value: 27.50				

Y# 107 500 YEN
7.2000 g., Copper-Nickel, 26.5 mm. **Ruler:** Akihito (Heisei) **Subject:** Royal wedding of Crown Prince **Obv:** Chrysanthemum flanked by cherry blossom sprigs with legend around border **Rev:** Pair of flying herons

Date	Mintage	VG	F	VF	XF	BU
Yr.5(1993)	29,800,000	—	—	—	—	16.00
Yr.5(1993) Proof	200,000	Value: 22.50				

Y# 110 500 YEN
7.2000 g., Copper-Nickel, 26.5 mm. **Ruler:** Akihito (Heisei) **Subject:** Opening of Kansai International Airport **Obv:** Flying jet **Rev:** Design within ribbon

Date	Mintage	VG	F	VF	XF	BU
Yr.6(1994)	19,900,000	—	—	—	—	14.50
Yr.6(1994) Proof	100,000	Value: 42.50				

Y# 111 500 YEN
7.2000 g., Copper-Nickel, 26.5 mm. **Ruler:** Akihito (Heisei) **Subject:** 12th Asian Games **Obv:** Stylized runners **Rev:** Artistic design above value

Date	Mintage	VG	F	VF	XF	BU
Yr.6(1994)	9,900,000	—	—	—	—	13.50
Yr.6(1994) Proof	100,000	Value: 32.50				

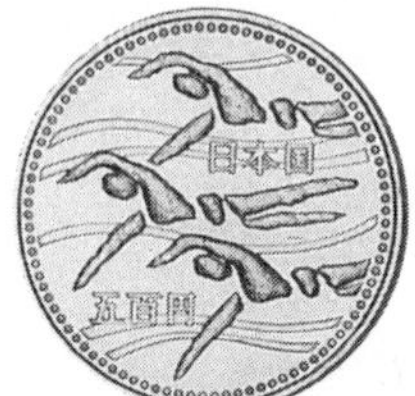

Y# 112 500 YEN
7.2000 g., Copper-Nickel, 26.5 mm. **Ruler:** Akihito (Heisei) **Subject:** 12th Asian Games **Obv:** Stylized swimmers **Rev:** Artistic design above value

Date	Mintage	VG	F	VF	XF	BU
Yr.6(1994)	9,900,000	—	—	—	—	13.50
Yr.6(1994) Proof	100,000	Value: 32.50				

Y# 113 500 YEN
7.2000 g., Copper-Nickel, 26.5 mm. **Ruler:** Akihito (Heisei) **Subject:** 12th Asian Games **Obv:** Stylized jumper **Rev:** Artistic design above value

Date	Mintage	VG	F	VF	XF	BU
Yr.6(1994)	9,900,000	—	—	—	—	13.50
Yr.6(1994) Proof	100,000	Value: 32.50				

Y# 114 500 YEN
7.2000 g., Copper-Nickel, 26.5 mm. **Ruler:** Akihito (Heisei) **Series:** 1998 Nagano Winter Olympics **Obv:** Snowboarder **Rev:** Bird, value and dates

Date	Mintage	VG	F	VF	XF	BU
Yr.9(1997)	19,867,000	—	—	—	—	14.50
Yr.9(1997) Proof	133,000	Value: 35.00				

Y# 117 500 YEN
7.2000 g., Copper-Nickel, 26.5 mm. **Ruler:** Akihito (Heisei) **Series:** 1998 Nagano Winter Olympics **Obv:** Bobsledding **Rev:** Bird, value and dates

Date	Mintage	VG	F	VF	XF	BU
Yr.9(1997)	19,867,000	—	—	—	—	14.50
Yr.9(1997) Proof	133,000	Value: 35.00				

Y# 118 500 YEN
7.2000 g., Copper-Nickel, 26.5 mm. **Ruler:** Akihito (Heisei) **Series:** 1998 Nagano Winter Olympics **Obv:** Acrobat skier **Rev:** Bird, value and dates

Date	Mintage	VG	F	VF	XF	BU
Yr.10(1998)	19,867,000	—	—	—	—	14.50
Yr.10(1998) Proof	133,000	Value: 35.00				

Y# 123 500 YEN
7.2000 g., Copper-Nickel, 26.5 mm. **Ruler:** Akihito (Heisei) **Subject:** 10th Anniversary of Enthronement **Obv:** Mt. Fuji and chrysanthemums **Rev:** Chrysanthemum within wreath

Date	Mintage	VG	F	VF	XF	BU
Yr.11(1999)	14,900,000	—	—	—	—	11.50
Yr.11(1999) Proof	100,000	Value: 32.00				

Y# 125 500 YEN
7.0000 g., Nickel-Brass, 26.5 mm. **Ruler:** Akihito (Heisei) **Obv:** Pawlownia flower and highlighted legends **Rev:** Value with latent zeros **Edge:** Slanted reeding

Date	Mintage	F	VF	XF	Unc	BU
Yr.12(2000)	595,746,000	—	—	—	—	9.00
Yr.12(2000) Proof	226,000	Value: 15.00				
Yr.13(2001)	607,813,000	—	—	—	—	9.00
Yr.13(2001) Proof	238,000	Value: 15.00				
Yr.14(2002)	504,419,000	—	—	—	—	9.00
Yr.14(2002) Proof	242,000	Value: 15.00				
Yr.15(2003)	438,130,000	—	—	—	—	9.00
Yr.15(2003) Proof	275,000	Value: 15.00				
Yr.16(2004)	356,623,000	—	—	—	—	9.00
Yr.16(2004) Proof	280,000	Value: 15.00				
Yr.17(2005)	334,762,000	—	—	—	—	9.00
Yr.17(2005) Proof	258,000	Value: 15.00				
Yr.18(2006)	—	—	—	—	—	9.00
Yr.18(2006) Proof	246,000	Value: 15.00				
Yr.19(2007)	—	—	—	—	—	9.00
Yr.19(2007) Proof	—	Value: 15.00				

Y# 126 500 YEN
7.0000 g., Copper-Zinc-Nickel, 26.5 mm. **Ruler:** Akihito (Heisei) **Subject:** World Cup Soccer - Europe & Africa **Obv:** Four players and map background **Rev:** Games logo within shooting star wreath **Edge:** Reeded

Date	Mintage	VG	F	VF	XF	BU
Yr.14(2002)	10,000,000	—	—	—	—	10.00

Y# 127 500 YEN
7.0000 g., Copper-Zinc-Nickel, 26.5 mm. **Ruler:** Akihito (Heisei) **Subject:** World Cup Soccer - Asia & Oceania **Obv:** Three players and map background **Rev:** Games logo within shooting star wreath **Edge:** Reeded

Date	Mintage	VG	F	VF	XF	BU
Yr. 14(2002)	10,000,000	—	—	—	—	10.00

Y# 128 500 YEN
7.0000 g., Copper-Zinc-Nickel, 26.5 mm. **Ruler:** Akihito (Heisei) **Subject:** World Cup Soccer - North & South America **Obv:** Four players and map background **Rev:** Games logo **Edge:** Reeded

Date	Mintage	VG	F	VF	XF	BU
Yr. 14 (2002)	10,000,000	—	—	—	—	10.00

Y# 133 500 YEN
7.0000 g., Copper-Zinc-Nickel, 26.5 mm. **Ruler:** Akihito (Heisei) **Subject:** Expo 2005 - Aichi, Japan **Obv:** Pacific map **Rev:** Expo logo

Date	Mintage	VG	F	VF	XF	BU
Yr. 17(2005)	8,241,000	—	—	—	—	10.00

Y# 137 500 YEN
7.0000 g., Copper-Zinc-Nickel, 26.5 mm. **Ruler:** Akihito (Heisei) **Subject:** 50th Anniversary of Japanese Antarctic Research **Obv:** Ship and two dogs **Rev:** Map of Antarctica

Date	Mintage	F	VF	XF	Unc	BU
Yr.19(2007)	6,600,000	—	—	—	—	10.00

Y# 80 1000 YEN
20.0000 g., 0.9250 Silver 0.5948 oz. ASW **Ruler:** Hirohito (Showa) **Series:** 1964 Olympic Games **Obv:** Mt. Fuji within sprigs of cherry blossoms **Rev:** Value and olympic circles flanked by cherry blossoms **Note:** Dav. #276

Date	Mintage	VG	F	VF	XF	BU
Yr.39(1964)	15,000,000	—	—	—	20.00	35.00

OCCUPATION COINAGE

The following issues were struck at the Osaka Mint for use in the Netherlands East Indies. The only inscription found on them is Dai Nippon: Great Japan. The war situation had worsened to the point that shipping the coins became virtually impossible. Consequently, none of these coins were issued in the East Indies and almost the entire issue was lost or were remelted at the mint. Y numbers are for the Netherlands Indies and dates are from the Japanese Shinto dynastic calendar.

Y# A66 SEN
Aluminum **Obv:** Stylized fish **Note:** Prev. NEI Y#22.

Date	Mintage	F	VF	XF	Unc	BU
NE2603 (1943)	233,190,000	250	300	350	400	500
NE2604 (1944)	66,810,000	175	200	250	350	450

Y# 66 10 SEN
Tin Alloy **Rev:** Stylized native figure standing **Note:** Prev. NEI Y#24.

Date	Mintage	F	VF	XF	Unc	BU
NE2603 (1943)	69,490,000	125	150	175	225	350
NE2604 (1944)	110,510,000	90.00	100	150	225	350

JERSEY

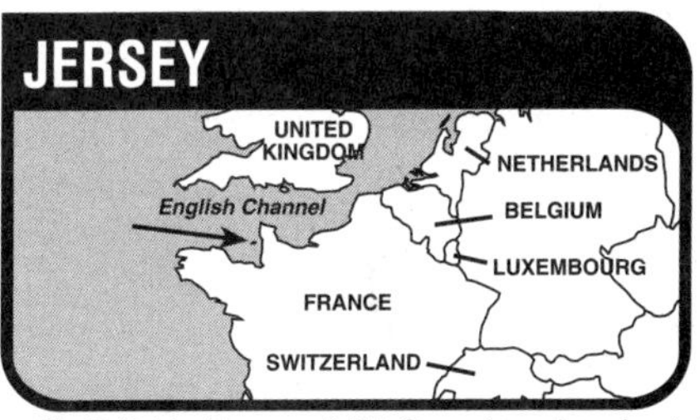

The Bailiwick of Jersey, a British Crown dependency located in the English Channel 12 miles (19 km.) west of Normandy, France, has an area of 45 sq. mi. (117 sq. km.) and a population of 74,000. Capital: St. Helier. The economy is based on agriculture and cattle breeding – the importation of cattle is prohibited to protect the purity of the island's world-famous strain of milch cows.

Jersey was occupied by Neanderthal man by 100,000 B.C., and by Iberians of 2000 B.C. who left their chamber tombs in the island's granite cliffs. Roman legions almost certainly visited the island although they left no evidence of settlement. The country folk of Jersey still speak an archaic form of Norman-French, lingering evidence of the Norman annexation of the island in 933 A.D. Jersey was annexed to England in 1206, 140 years after the Norman Conquest. The dependency is administered by its own laws and customs; laws enacted by the British Parliament do not apply to Jersey unless it is specifically mentioned. During World War II, German troops occupied the island from July1, 1940 until May 9, 1945.

Coins of pre-Roman Gaul and of Rome have been found in abundance on Jersey.

RULER
British

MINT MARK
H - Heaton, Birmingham

MONETARY SYSTEM
Commencing 1877
12 Pence = 1 Shilling
5 Shillings = 1 Crown
20 Shillings = 1 Pound
100 New Pence = 1 Pound

BRITISH DEPENDENCY

STANDARD COINAGE

KM# 9 1/24 SHILLING
Bronze **Obv:** Crowned bust right **Obv. Designer:** G. W. DeSaulles **Rev:** Pointed shield divides date

Date	Mintage	F	VF	XF	Unc	BU
1909	120,000	1.00	2.50	11.50	40.00	—

KM# 11 1/24 SHILLING

Bronze **Obv:** Crowned bust left **Obv. Designer:** E. B. MacKennal **Rev:** Pointed shield divides date

Date	Mintage	F	VF	XF	Unc	BU
1911	72,000	1.00	2.50	11.50	40.00	—
1913	72,000	1.00	2.50	11.50	28.00	—
1923	72,000	1.00	2.50	11.50	28.00	—

KM# 13 1/24 SHILLING

Bronze **Obv:** Crowned bust left **Obv. Designer:** E. B. MacKennal **Rev:** Shield divides date

Date	Mintage	F	VF	XF	Unc	BU
1923	72,000	0.75	3.00	5.50	22.50	—
1923 Proof	—	Value: 550				
1926	120,000	0.75	2.50	4.50	20.00	—
1926 Proof	—	Value: 550				

KM# 15 1/24 SHILLING

Bronze **Obv:** Crowned bust left **Obv. Designer:** E. B. MacKennal **Rev:** Shield divides date **Rev. Designer:** Kruger-Gray

Date	Mintage	F	VF	XF	Unc	BU
1931	72,000	0.50	1.00	3.00	15.00	—
1931 Proof	—	Value: 165				
1933	72,000	0.50	1.00	3.00	15.00	—
1933 Proof	—	Value: 165				
1935	72,000	0.50	1.00	3.00	15.00	—
1935 Proof	—	Value: 165				

KM# 17 1/24 SHILLING

Bronze **Obv:** Crowned head left **Obv. Designer:** Percy Metcalfe **Rev:** Shield divides date **Rev. Designer:** Kruger-Gray

Date	Mintage	F	VF	XF	Unc	BU
1937	72,000	0.50	1.00	3.00	15.00	—
1937 Proof	—	Value: 125				
1946	72,000	0.50	1.00	3.00	15.00	—
1946 Proof	—	Value: 125				
1947	72,000	0.50	1.00	3.00	15.00	—
1947 Proof	—	Value: 125				

KM# 10 1/12 SHILLING

Bronze **Obv:** Crowned bust right **Obv. Designer:** G. W. DeSaulles **Rev:** Pointed shield divides date

Date	Mintage	F	VF	XF	Unc	BU
1909	180,000	0.75	3.50	12.50	60.00	—

KM# 12 1/12 SHILLING

9.4500 g., Bronze **Obv:** Crowned bust left **Obv. Designer:** E. B. MacKennal **Rev:** Pointed shield divides date

Date	Mintage	F	VF	XF	Unc	BU
1911	204,000	0.50	1.50	5.00	35.00	—
1913	204,000	0.50	1.50	5.00	35.00	—
1923	204,000	0.50	1.50	5.00	35.00	—

KM# 14 1/12 SHILLING

Bronze **Obv:** Crowned bust left **Obv. Designer:** E. B. MacKennal **Rev:** Shield divides date **Rev. Designer:** Kruger-Gray

Date	Mintage	F	VF	XF	Unc	BU
1923	301,000	0.75	2.50	8.00	30.00	—
1926	83,000	0.75	2.50	10.00	40.00	—

KM# 16 1/12 SHILLING

9.5000 g., Bronze **Obv:** Crowned bust left **Obv. Designer:** E. B. MacKennal **Rev:** Shield divides date **Rev. Designer:** Kruger-Gray

Date	Mintage	F	VF	XF	Unc	BU
1931	204,000	0.50	1.25	3.00	19.00	—
1931 Proof	—	Value: 125				
1933	204,000	0.50	1.25	3.00	19.00	—
1933 Proof	—	Value: 125				
1935	204,000	0.50	1.25	3.00	19.00	—
1935 Proof	—	Value: 125				

KM# 18 1/12 SHILLING

Bronze **Obv:** Crowned head left **Obv. Designer:** Percy Metcalfe **Rev:** Shield divides date **Rev. Designer:** Kruger-Gray

Date	Mintage	F	VF	XF	Unc	BU
1937	204,000	0.50	1.00	2.50	10.00	—
1937 Proof	—	Value: 125				
1946	204,000	0.50	1.00	2.50	10.00	—
1946 Proof	—	Value: 125				
1947	444,000	0.25	0.50	1.50	7.50	—
1947 Proof	—	Value: 125				

KM# 19 1/12 SHILLING

9.5900 g., Bronze, 21.1 mm. **Subject:** Liberation Commemorative **Obv:** Crowned head left **Obv. Designer:** Percy Metcalfe **Rev:** Shield above written value **Rev. Designer:** Kruger-Gray

Date	Mintage	F	VF	XF	Unc	BU
1945	1,000,000	0.25	0.50	1.00	5.00	—
1945 Proof	—	Value: 100				

Note: Struck between 1949-52

KM# 20 1/12 SHILLING

9.4000 g., Bronze **Ruler:** Elizabeth II **Obv:** Crowned head right **Rev:** Shield above written value

Date	Mintage	F	VF	XF	Unc	BU
(1954)	720,000	0.25	0.50	1.00	3.50	—
(1954) Proof	—	Value: 100				

KM# 21 1/12 SHILLING

Bronze **Ruler:** Elizabeth II **Obv:** Crowned head right **Rev:** Shield above written value

Date	Mintage	F	VF	XF	Unc	BU
1957	720,000	0.25	0.45	0.75	2.00	—
1957 Proof	2,100	Value: 7.50				
1964	1,200,000	0.25	0.45	0.75	1.50	—
1964 Proof	20,000	Value: 2.00				

KM# 23 1/12 SHILLING

Bronze **Ruler:** Elizabeth II **Subject:** 300th Anniversary - Accession of King Charles II **Obv:** Crowned head right **Rev:** Shield above dates and written value

Date	Mintage	F	VF	XF	Unc	BU
ND (1960)	1,200,000	0.25	0.45	0.75	1.50	—
ND (1960) Proof	4,200	Value: 4.00				

KM# 26 1/12 SHILLING

Bronze **Ruler:** Elizabeth II **Subject:** Norman Conquest **Obv:** Crowned head right **Rev:** Shield divides dates

Date	Mintage	F	VF	XF	Unc	BU
ND (1966)	1,200,000	0.25	0.45	0.75	1.50	—
ND (1966) Proof	30,000	Value: 2.00				

KM# 22 1/4 SHILLING (3 Pence)
Nickel-Brass **Ruler:** Elizabeth II **Obv:** Crowned head right

Date	Mintage	F	VF	XF	Unc	BU
1957	2,000,000	0.10	0.15	0.50	3.00	—
1957 Proof	6,300	Value: 7.50				
1960 Proof	4,200	Value: 8.50				

KM# 25 1/4 SHILLING (3 Pence)
Nickel-Brass **Ruler:** Elizabeth II **Obv:** Crowned head right **Rev:** Shield divides date **Shape:** 12-sided

Date	Mintage	F	VF	XF	Unc	BU
1964	1,200,000	0.10	0.15	0.20	0.75	—
1964 Proof	20,000	Value: 2.00				

KM# 27 1/4 SHILLING (3 Pence)
Nickel-Brass **Ruler:** Elizabeth II **Subject:** Norman Conquest **Obv:** Crowned head right **Rev:** Shield divides dates **Shape:** 12-sided

Date	Mintage	F	VF	XF	Unc	BU
ND (1966)	1,200,000	0.10	0.15	0.35	1.25	—
ND (1966) Proof	30,000	Value: 2.00				

KM# 28 5 SHILLING
Copper-Nickel **Ruler:** Elizabeth II **Subject:** Norman Conquest **Obv:** Crowned head right **Rev:** Shield divides dates

Date	Mintage	F	VF	XF	Unc	BU
ND (1966)	300,000	—	1.00	2.00	3.50	—
ND (1966) Proof	30,000	Value: 6.00				

DECIMAL COINAGE

100 New Pence = 1 Pound

Many of the following coins are also struck in silver, gold, and platinum for collectors

KM# 29 1/2 NEW PENNY
Bronze, 17.14 mm. **Ruler:** Elizabeth II **Obv:** Young bust right **Rev:** Shield above written value and date

Date	Mintage	F	VF	XF	Unc	BU
1971	3,000,000	—	—	0.10	0.20	—
1980	200,000	—	—	0.10	0.20	—
1980 Proof	10,000	Value: 1.35				

KM# 45 1/2 PENNY
Bronze, 17.14 mm. **Ruler:** Elizabeth II **Obv:** Young bust right **Rev:** Shield divides date

Date	Mintage	F	VF	XF	Unc	BU
1981	50,000	—	—	—	0.10	—
1981 Proof	15,000	Value: 0.90				

KM# 30 NEW PENNY
3.5500 g., Bronze, 20.32 mm. **Ruler:** Elizabeth II **Obv:** Young bust right **Rev:** Shield above written value

Date	Mintage	F	VF	XF	Unc	BU
1971	4,500,000	—	—	0.10	0.20	—
1980	3,000,000	—	—	0.10	0.20	—
1980 Proof	10,000	Value: 1.80				

KM# 46 PENNY
3.5500 g., Bronze, 20.32 mm. **Ruler:** Elizabeth II **Obv:** Young bust right **Rev:** Shield divides date

Date	Mintage	F	VF	XF	Unc	BU
1981	50,000	—	—	0.10	0.15	—
1981 Proof	15,000	Value: 1.10				

KM# 54 PENNY
3.6400 g., Bronze, 20.23 mm. **Ruler:** Elizabeth II **Obv:** Young bust right **Rev:** Le Hocq Watch Tower, St. Clement **Edge:** Plain

Date	Mintage	F	VF	XF	Unc	BU
1983	500,000	—	—	0.10	0.25	—
1984	1,000,000	—	—	0.10	0.25	—
1985	1,000,000	—	—	0.10	0.25	—
1986	2,000,000	—	—	0.10	0.25	—
1987	1,500,000	—	—	0.10	0.25	—
1988	1,000,000	—	—	0.10	0.25	—
1989	1,500,000	—	—	0.10	0.25	—
1990	2,000,000	—	—	0.10	0.25	—
1992	—	—	—	—	0.50	—

Note: In sets only

KM# 54b PENNY
Copper Plated Steel, 20.32 mm. **Ruler:** Elizabeth II **Obv:** Young bust right **Rev:** Le Hocq Watch Tower, St. Clement

Date	Mintage	F	VF	XF	Unc	BU
1994	2,000,000	—	—	0.10	0.50	—
1997	320,000	—	—	0.10	0.50	—

KM# 103 PENNY
3.5500 g., Copper Plated Steel, 20.27 mm. **Ruler:** Elizabeth II **Obv:** Crowned head right **Obv. Designer:** Ian Rank-Broadley **Rev:** Le Hoeq Watch Tower, St. Clement **Edge:** Plain

Date	Mintage	F	VF	XF	Unc	BU
1998	9,300,000	—	—	0.10	0.50	—
2002	1,500,000	—	—	0.10	0.50	—
2003	1,485,000	—	—	0.10	0.50	—
2005	—	—	—	0.10	0.50	—
2006	—	—	—	0.10	0.50	—

KM# 31 2 NEW PENCE
7.1000 g., Bronze, 25.91 mm. **Ruler:** Elizabeth II **Obv:** Young bust right **Rev:** Shield above written value

Date	Mintage	F	VF	XF	Unc	BU
1971	2,225,000	—	—	0.15	0.30	—
1975	750,000	—	—	0.15	0.40	—
1980	2,000,000	—	—	0.15	0.30	—
1980 Proof	10,000	Value: 2.25				

KM# 47 2 PENCE
7.1000 g., Bronze, 25.91 mm. **Ruler:** Elizabeth II **Obv:** Young bust right **Rev:** Shield divides date

Date	Mintage	F	VF	XF	Unc	BU
1981	50,000	—	—	0.15	0.25	—
1981 Proof	15,000	Value: 1.35				

KM# 55 2 PENCE
7.1000 g., Bronze, 25.91 mm. **Ruler:** Elizabeth II **Obv:** Young bust right **Rev:** L'Hermitage, St. Helier

Date	Mintage	F	VF	XF	Unc	BU
1983	800,000	—	—	0.15	0.25	—
1984	750,000	—	—	0.15	0.25	—
1985	250,000	—	—	0.15	0.25	—
1986	1,000,000	—	—	0.15	0.25	—
1987	2,000,000	—	—	0.15	0.25	—
1988	750,000	—	—	0.15	0.25	—
1989	1,000,000	—	—	0.15	0.25	—
1990	2,600,000	—	—	0.15	0.25	—

KM# 55b 2 PENCE
Copper Plated Steel, 25.91 mm. **Ruler:** Elizabeth II **Obv:** Young bust right **Rev:** L'Hermitage, St. Helier **Note:** Released into circulation in 1998.

Date	Mintage	F	VF	XF	Unc	BU
1992	—	—	—	0.15	0.50	—
1997 In sets only	—	—	—	0.15	0.50	—

KM# 104 2 PENCE
7.1000 g., Copper Plated Steel, 25.91 mm. **Ruler:** Elizabeth II **Obv:** Head with tiara right **Obv. Designer:** Ian Rank-Broadley **Rev:** L'Hermitage, St. Helier **Edge:** Plain

Date	Mintage	F	VF	XF	Unc	BU
1998	50,000	—	—	0.15	0.50	—
2002	1,250,000	—	—	0.15	0.50	—
2003	10,000	—	—	0.15	0.50	—
2005	—	—	—	0.15	0.50	—
2006	—	—	—	0.15	0.50	—

KM# 32 5 NEW PENCE
5.6500 g., Copper-Nickel, 23.59 mm. **Ruler:** Elizabeth II **Obv:** Young bust right **Rev:** Shield above written value

Date	Mintage	F	VF	XF	Unc	BU
1968	3,600,000	—	0.15	0.25	1.00	—
1980	800,000	—	0.15	0.25	1.00	—
1980 Proof	10,000	Value: 2.75				

KM# 48 5 PENCE
5.6500 g., Copper-Nickel, 23.59 mm. **Ruler:** Elizabeth II **Obv:** Young bust right **Rev:** Shield divides date

Date	Mintage	F	VF	XF	Unc	BU
1981	50,000	—	0.15	0.25	1.00	—
1981 Proof	15,000	Value: 1.80				

KM# 56.1 5 PENCE

5.6500 g., Copper-Nickel, 23.59 mm. **Ruler:** Elizabeth II **Obv:** Young bust right **Rev:** Seymour Tower, Grouville, L'Avathison

Date	Mintage	F	VF	XF	Unc	BU
1983	400,000	—	0.10	0.20	1.00	—
1984	300,000	—	0.10	0.20	1.00	—
1985	600,000	—	0.10	0.20	1.00	—
1986	200,000	—	0.10	0.20	1.00	—
1987	—	—	—	—	0.50	—
Note: In sets only						
1988	400,000	—	0.10	0.20	1.00	—

KM# 56.2 5 PENCE

Copper-Nickel, 18 mm. **Ruler:** Elizabeth II **Obv:** Young bust right **Rev:** Seymour Tower, Grouville, L'Avathison **Note:** Reduced size.

Date	Mintage	F	VF	XF	Unc	BU
1990	4,000,000	—	—	0.15	0.35	—
1991	2,000,000	—	—	0.15	0.35	—
1992	1,000,000	—	—	0.15	0.50	—
1993	2,000,000	—	—	0.15	0.50	—
1997	5,500	—	—	—	1.00	—
Note: In sets only						

KM# 105 5 PENCE

3.2900 g., Copper-Nickel, 18 mm. **Ruler:** Elizabeth II **Obv:** Head with tiara right **Obv. Designer:** Ian Rank-Broadley **Rev:** Seymour Tower, Grouville, L'Avathigon

Date	Mintage	F	VF	XF	Unc	BU
1998	50,000	—	—	0.15	0.50	—
2002	1,200,000	—	—	0.15	0.50	—
2003	1,002,000	—	—	0.15	0.50	—
2005	—	—	—	0.15	0.50	—

KM# 33 10 NEW PENCE

11.3000 g., Copper-Nickel, 28.5 mm. **Ruler:** Elizabeth II **Obv:** Young bust right **Rev:** Shield above written value

Date	Mintage	F	VF	XF	Unc	BU
1968	1,500,000	—	0.20	0.35	1.00	—
1975	1,022,000	—	0.20	0.30	0.90	—
1980	1,000,000	—	0.20	0.30	0.75	—
1980 Proof	10,000	Value: 5.50				

KM# 49 10 PENCE

11.3000 g., Copper-Nickel, 28.5 mm. **Ruler:** Elizabeth II **Obv:** Young bust right **Rev:** Shield divides date

Date	Mintage	F	VF	XF	Unc	BU
1981	50,000	—	—	0.30	1.00	—
1981 Proof	15,000	Value: 2.25				

KM# 57.1 10 PENCE

11.3000 g., Copper-Nickel, 28.5 mm. **Ruler:** Elizabeth II **Obv:** Young bust right **Rev:** La Houque Bie, Faldouet, St. Martin

Date	Mintage	F	VF	XF	Unc	BU
1983	30,000	—	—	0.30	1.00	—
1984	100,000	—	—	0.30	1.00	—
1985	100,000	—	—	0.30	1.00	—
1986	400,000	—	—	0.30	0.75	—
1987	800,000	—	—	0.30	0.75	—
1988	650,000	—	—	0.30	0.75	—
1989	700,000	—	—	0.30	0.75	—
1990	850,000	—	—	0.30	0.75	—

KM# 57.2 10 PENCE

Copper-Nickel, 24.5 mm. **Ruler:** Elizabeth II **Obv:** Young bust right **Rev:** La Houque Bie, Faldouet, St. Martin **Note:** Reduced size.

Date	Mintage	F	VF	XF	Unc	BU
1992	7,000,000	—	—	0.30	0.50	—
1997	5,500	—	—	—	1.00	—
Note: In sets only						
2002	—	—	—	—	1.00	—

KM# 106 10 PENCE

Copper-Nickel, 24.5 mm. **Ruler:** Elizabeth II **Obv:** Head with tiara right **Obv. Designer:** Ian Rank-Broadley **Rev:** La Hougne Bie, Faldouet, St. Martin

Date	Mintage	F	VF	XF	Unc	BU
1998	—	—	—	—	1.00	—
Note: In sets only						
2002	500,000	—	—	—	1.00	—
2003	10,000	—	—	—	1.00	—
2005	—	—	—	—	1.00	—

KM# 53 20 PENCE

5.0000 g., Copper-Nickel, 21.4 mm. **Ruler:** Elizabeth II **Subject:** 100th Anniversary of Lighthouse at Corbiere **Obv:** Young bust right **Rev:** Date below lighthouse **Rev. Designer:** Robert Lowe **Shape:** 7-sided

Date	Mintage	F	VF	XF	Unc	BU
1982	200,000	—	—	0.50	1.50	—

KM# 66 20 PENCE

5.0000 g., Copper-Nickel, 21.4 mm. **Ruler:** Elizabeth II **Subject:** 100th Anniversary of Lighthouse at Corbiere **Obv:** Young bust right **Rev:** Written value below lighthouse **Rev. Designer:** Robert Lowe **Shape:** 7-sided

Date	Mintage	F	VF	XF	Unc	BU
1983	400,000	—	—	0.50	1.00	—
1984	250,000	—	—	0.50	1.00	—
1986	100,000	—	—	0.50	1.00	—
1987	100,000	—	—	0.50	1.00	—
1989	100,000	—	—	0.50	1.00	—
1990	150,000	—	—	0.50	1.00	—
1992	—	—	—	—	2.00	—
Note: In sets only						
1994	200,000	—	—	0.50	1.00	—
1996	250,000	—	—	0.50	1.00	—
1997	600,000	—	—	0.50	1.00	—
1998	—	—	—	0.50	1.00	—
2002	—	—	—	0.50	1.00	—

KM# 107 20 PENCE

Copper-Nickel, 21.4 mm. **Ruler:** Elizabeth II **Obv:** Head with tiara right **Obv. Designer:** Ian Rank-Broadley

Date	Mintage	F	VF	XF	Unc	BU
1998	90,000	—	—	0.50	1.00	—
2002	515,000	—	—	—	1.00	—
2003	10,000	—	—	—	1.00	—
2005	—	—	—	—	1.00	—

KM# 44 25 PENCE

Copper-Nickel **Ruler:** Elizabeth II **Subject:** Queen's Silver Jublilee **Obv:** Young bust right **Rev:** Mont Orgueil Castle and Gorey Harbour **Rev. Designer:** Bernard Sindall

Date	Mintage	F	VF	XF	Unc	BU
ND(1977)	262,000	—	0.75	1.25	3.75	—

KM# 34 50 PENCE

13.5000 g., Copper-Nickel, 30 mm. **Ruler:** Elizabeth II **Obv:** Young bust right **Rev:** Shield above written value **Shape:** 7-sided

Date	Mintage	F	VF	XF	Unc	BU
1969	480,000	—	—	0.90	1.50	—
1980	100,000	—	—	0.90	1.50	—
1980 Proof	10,000	Value: 9.00				

KM# 50 50 PENCE

13.5000 g., Copper-Nickel, 30 mm. **Ruler:** Elizabeth II **Obv:** Young bust right **Rev:** Shield divides date **Shape:** 7-sided

Date	Mintage	F	VF	XF	Unc	BU
1981	50,000	—	—	1.00	1.75	—
1981 Proof	15,000	Value: 3.00				

KM# 58.1 50 PENCE

13.5000 g., Copper-Nickel, 30 mm. **Ruler:** Elizabeth II **Obv:** Young bust right **Rev:** Grosnez Castle **Shape:** 7-sided

Date	Mintage	F	VF	XF	Unc	BU
1983	50,000	—	—	1.00	1.75	—
1984	50,000	—	—	1.00	1.75	—
1986	30,000	—	—	1.00	1.75	—
1987	150,000	—	—	1.00	1.75	—
1988	130,000	—	—	1.00	1.75	—
1989	180,000	—	—	1.00	1.75	—
1990	370,000	—	—	1.00	1.75	—
1992	—	—	—	—	2.50	—
Note: In sets only						
1994	200,000	—	—	1.00	1.75	—
1997	5,500	—	—	—	2.50	—
Note: In sets only						

KM# 58.2 50 PENCE

Copper-Nickel, 27.3 mm. **Ruler:** Elizabeth II **Obv:** Young bust right **Rev:** Grosnez Castle **Shape:** 7-sided **Note:** Small size.

Date	Mintage	F	VF	XF	Unc	BU
1997	1,500,000	—	—	—	2.50	—

KM# 63 50 PENCE

13.5000 g., Copper-Nickel, 30 mm. **Ruler:** Elizabeth II **Subject:** 40th Anniversary - Liberation of 1945 **Obv:** Crowned bust right **Rev:** Crossed flags divides dates above chain links with value below **Shape:** 7-sided

Date	Mintage	F	VF	XF	Unc	BU
1985	65,000	—	—	1.25	2.00	—

KM# 108 50 PENCE

Copper-Nickel, 27.3 mm. **Ruler:** Elizabeth II **Obv:** Crowned bust right **Obv. Designer:** Ian Rank-Broadley

Date	Mintage	F	VF	XF	Unc	BU
1998	25,000	—	—	1.00	2.50	—
2003	—	—	—	1.00	2.50	—
2005	—	—	—	1.00	2.50	—
2006	—	—	—	1.00	2.50	—

KM# 123 50 PENCE

8.0000 g., Copper-Nickel, 27.3 mm. **Ruler:** Elizabeth II **Subject:** Golden Coronation Anniversary **Obv:** Crowned head right **Rev:** Coronation scene **Edge:** Plain **Shape:** 7-sided

Date	Mintage	F	VF	XF	Unc	BU
2003	10,000	—	—	—	2.50	—

KM# 51 POUND

9.0000 g., Copper-Nickel **Ruler:** Elizabeth II **Subject:** Bicentennial - Battle of Jersey **Obv:** Young bust right **Rev:** Badge of the Royal Jersey Militia **Shape:** 4-sided

Date	Mintage	F	VF	XF	Unc	BU
ND(1981)	200,000	—	—	2.00	3.25	—
ND(1981) Proof	15,000	Value: 8.00				

KM# 59 POUND

9.5000 g., Nickel-Brass, 22.5 mm. **Ruler:** Elizabeth II **Obv:** Young bust right **Rev:** Shield above written value **Edge Lettering:** CAESAREA INSULA

Date	Mintage	F	VF	XF	Unc	BU
1983	100,000	—	—	2.00	3.25	—

KM# 60 POUND

9.5000 g., Nickel-Brass, 22.5 mm. **Ruler:** Elizabeth II **Obv:** Young bust right **Rev:** Shield above written value **Edge Lettering:** CAESAREA INSULA

Date	Mintage	F	VF	XF	Unc	BU
1984	20,000	—	—	2.00	3.25	—

KM# 61 POUND

9.5000 g., Nickel-Brass, 22.5 mm. **Ruler:** Elizabeth II **Obv:** Young bust right **Rev:** Shield above written value **Edge Lettering:** CAESAREA INSULA

Date	Mintage	F	VF	XF	Unc	BU
1984	20,000	—	—	2.00	3.25	—

KM# 62 POUND

9.5000 g., Nickel-Brass, 22.5 mm. **Ruler:** Elizabeth II **Obv:** Young bust right **Rev:** Shield above written value **Edge Lettering:** CAESAREA INSULA

Date	Mintage	F	VF	XF	Unc	BU
1985	25,000	—	—	2.00	3.25	—

KM# 65 POUND

9.5000 g., Nickel-Brass, 22.5 mm. **Ruler:** Elizabeth II **Obv:** Young bust right **Rev:** Shield above written value **Edge Lettering:** CAESAREA INSULA

Date	Mintage	F	VF	XF	Unc	BU
1985	10,000	—	—	2.00	3.50	—

KM# 68 POUND

9.5000 g., Nickel-Brass, 22.5 mm. **Ruler:** Elizabeth II **Obv:** Young bust right **Rev:** Shield above written value **Edge Lettering:** CAESAREA INSULA

Date	Mintage	F	VF	XF	Unc	BU
1986	10,000	—	—	2.00	3.25	—

KM# 69 POUND

9.5000 g., Nickel-Brass, 22.5 mm. **Ruler:** Elizabeth II **Obv:** Young bust right **Rev:** Shield above written value **Edge Lettering:** CAESAREA INSULA

Date	Mintage	F	VF	XF	Unc	BU
1986	10,000	—	—	2.00	3.25	—

KM# 71 POUND

9.5000 g., Nickel-Brass, 22.5 mm. **Ruler:** Elizabeth II **Obv:** Young bust right **Rev:** Shield above written value **Edge Lettering:** CAESAREA INSULA

Date	Mintage	F	VF	XF	Unc	BU
1987	10,000	—	—	2.00	3.50	—

KM# 72 POUND

9.5000 g., Nickel-Brass, 22.5 mm. **Ruler:** Elizabeth II **Obv:** Young bust right **Rev:** Shield above written value **Edge Lettering:** CAESAREA INSULA

Date	Mintage	F	VF	XF	Unc	BU
1987	10,000	—	—	2.00	3.25	—

KM# 73 POUND

9.5000 g., Nickel-Brass, 22.5 mm. **Ruler:** Elizabeth II **Obv:** Young bust right **Rev:** Shield above written value **Edge Lettering:** CAESAREA INSULA

Date	Mintage	F	VF	XF	Unc	BU
1988	10,000	—	—	2.00	4.00	—

KM# 74 POUND

9.5000 g., Nickel-Brass, 22.5 mm. **Ruler:** Elizabeth II **Obv:** Young bust right **Rev:** Shield above written value **Edge Lettering:** CAESAREA INSULA

Date	Mintage	F	VF	XF	Unc	BU
1988	10,000	—	—	2.00	3.25	—

KM# 75 POUND

9.5000 g., Nickel-Brass, 22.5 mm. **Ruler:** Elizabeth II **Obv:** Young bust right **Rev:** Shield above written value **Edge Lettering:** CAESAREA INSULA

Date	Mintage	F	VF	XF	Unc	BU
1989	25,000	—	—	2.00	3.25	—

KM# 84 POUND

9.5000 g., Nickel-Brass, 22.5 mm. **Ruler:** Elizabeth II **Obv:** Young bust right **Rev:** Schooner, The Tickler **Rev. Designer:** Robert Evans **Edge Lettering:** CAESAREA INSULA

Date	Mintage	F	VF	XF	Unc	BU
1991	15,000	—	—	—	3.25	—

KM# 85 POUND

9.5000 g., Nickel-Brass, 22.5 mm. **Ruler:** Elizabeth II **Obv:** Young bust right **Rev:** Sailing ship, Percy Douglas **Rev. Designer:** Robert Evans **Edge Lettering:** CAESAREA INSULA

Date	Mintage	F	VF	XF	Unc	BU
1991	20,000	—	—	—	3.25	—

KM# 86 POUND

9.5000 g., Nickel-Brass, 22.5 mm. **Ruler:** Elizabeth II **Obv:** Young bust right **Rev:** Brig, Hebe **Rev. Designer:** Robert Evans

Date	Mintage	F	VF	XF	Unc	BU
1992	2,000	—	—	—	3.25	—

KM# 87 POUND
9.5000 g., Nickel-Brass, 22.5 mm. **Ruler:** Elizabeth II **Obv:** Young bust right **Rev:** Bailiwick seal **Rev. Designer:** Robert Evans

Date	Mintage	F	VF	XF	Unc	BU
1992	20,000	—	—	—	3.50	—

KM# 88 POUND
9.5000 g., Nickel-Brass, 22.5 mm. **Ruler:** Elizabeth II **Obv:** Young bust right **Rev:** Barque, Gemini **Rev. Designer:** Robert Evans

Date	Mintage	F	VF	XF	Unc	BU
1993	—	—	—	—	3.25	—

KM# 90 POUND
9.5000 g., Nickel-Brass, 22.5 mm. **Ruler:** Elizabeth II **Obv:** Young bust right **Rev:** Brigantine, Century **Rev. Designer:** Robert Evans

Date	Mintage	F	VF	XF	Unc	BU
1993	—	—	—	—	3.25	—

KM# 91 POUND
9.5000 g., Nickel-Brass, 22.5 mm. **Ruler:** Elizabeth II **Obv:** Young bust right **Rev:** Topsail Schooner, Resolute **Rev. Designer:** Robert Evans

Date	Mintage	F	VF	XF	Unc	BU
1994	60,000	—	—	—	3.25	—
1997	101,000	—	—	—	3.25	—

KM# 101 POUND
9.5000 g., Nickel-Brass, 22.5 mm. **Ruler:** Elizabeth II **Obv:** Head with tiara right **Obv. Designer:** Ian Rank-Broadley **Rev:** Schooner, Resolute **Rev. Designer:** Robert Evans **Edge Lettering:** CAESAREA INSULA

Date	Mintage	F	VF	XF	Unc	BU
1998	174,000	—	—	—	3.25	—
2003	10,000	—	—	—	4.00	—
2005	—	—	—	—	4.00	—

KM# 102 2 POUNDS
12.0000 g., Bi-Metallic Copper-Nickel center in Nickel-Brass ring, 28.35 mm. **Ruler:** Elizabeth II **Obv:** Head with tiara right **Obv. Designer:** Ian Rank-Broadley **Rev:** Latent image value within circle of assorted shields **Rev. Designer:** Alan Copp **Edge Lettering:** CAESAREA INSULA

Date	Mintage	F	VF	XF	Unc	BU
1998	800,000	—	—	—	8.50	—
2003	10,000	—	—	—	10.00	—

JORDAN

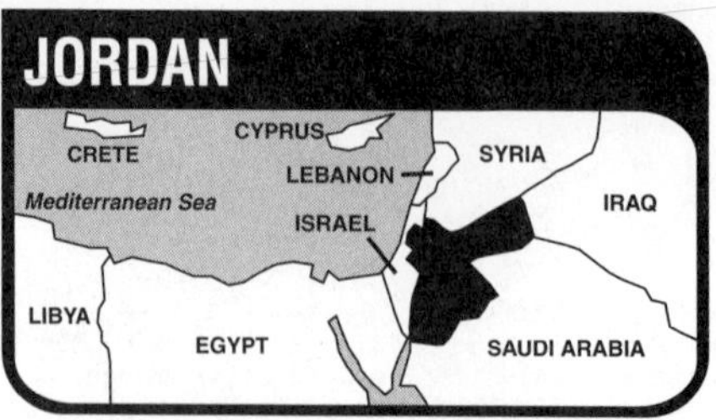

The Hashemite Kingdom of Jordan, a constitutional monarchy in southwest Asia, has an area of 37,738 sq. mi.(91,880 sq. km.) and a population of 3.5 million. Capital: Amman. Agriculture and tourism comprise Jordan's economic base. Chief exports are phosphates, tomatoe sand oranges.

Jordan is the Edom and Moab of the time of Moses. It became part of the Roman province of Arabia in 106 A.D., was conquered by the Arabs in 633-36, and was part of the Ottoman Empire from the 16th century until World War I. At that time, the regions presently known as Jordan and Israel were mandated to Great Britain by the League of Nations as Transjordan and Palestine. In 1922 Transjordan was established as the semi-autonomous Emirate of Transjordan, ruled by the Hashemite Prince Abdullah but still nominally a part of the British mandate. The mandate over Transjordan was terminated in 1946, the country becoming the independent Hashemite Kingdom of Transjordan. The kingdom was renamed the Hashemite Kingdom of Jordan in 1950.

Several 1964 and 1965 issues were limited to respective quantities of 3,000 and 5,000 examples struck to make up sets for sale to collectors.

TITLE

المملكة الاردنية الهاشمية

el-Mamlaka(t)el-Urduniya(t)el-Hashemiya(t)

RULERS
Abdullah Ibn Al-Hussein, 1946-1951
Talal Ibn Abdullah, 1951-1952
Hussein Ibn Talal, 1952-1999
Abdullah Ibn Al-Hussein, 1999-

MONETARY SYSTEM
100 Fils = 1 Dirham
1000 Fils = 10 Dirhams = 1 Dinar
Commencing 1992
100 Piastres = 1 Dinar

KINGDOM

DECIMAL COINAGE

KM# 1 FIL
3.0000 g., Bronze, 18 mm. **Ruler:** Abdullah Ibn Al-Hussein **Obv:** Value and date within crowned circle within sprigs **Rev:** Value within circle above date **Edge:** Plain

Date	Mintage	F	VF	XF	Unc	BU
AH1368//1949	350,000	—	1.00	1.50	3.50	—
AH1368//1949 Proof	25	Value: 50.00				

Note: "FIL" is an error for "FILS," the correct Arabic singular

KM# 2 FILS
3.0000 g., Bronze, 18 mm. **Ruler:** Abdullah Ibn Al-Hussein **Obv:** Value and date within crowned circle within sprigs **Rev:** Value within circle above date **Edge:** Plain

Date	Mintage	F	VF	XF	Unc	BU
AH1368//1949	Inc. above	—	0.50	0.90	2.25	—
AH1368//1949 Proof	25	Value: 50.00				

KM# 8 FILS
3.0000 g., Bronze, 18 mm. **Ruler:** Hussein Ibn Talal **Obv:** Value and date within crowned circle within sprigs **Rev:** Value within circle above date **Edge:** Plain

Date	Mintage	F	VF	XF	Unc	BU
AH1374//1955	200,000	—	0.35	0.50	1.00	—
AH1374//1955 Proof	—	Value: 50.00				
AH1379//1960	150,000	—	0.40	0.60	1.25	—
AH1379//1960 Proof	—	Value: 50.00				
AH1382//1963	200,000	—	0.25	0.50	1.00	—
AH1382//1963 Proof	—	Value: 50.00				

Date	Mintage	F	VF	XF	Unc	BU
AH1383//1964	3,000	—	1.50	3.00	5.00	—
Note: In sets only						
AH1385//1965	5,000	—	1.00	2.00	3.00	—
Note: In sets only						
AH1385//1965 Proof	10,000	Value: 3.00				

KM# 14 FILS
3.0000 g., Bronze, 18 mm. **Ruler:** Hussein Ibn Talal **Obv:** Head right **Rev:** Value and date within circle flanked by sprigs **Edge:** Plain

Date	Mintage	F	VF	XF	Unc	BU
AH1387-1968	60,000	—	0.15	0.25	0.75	—

KM# 35 FILS
3.0000 g., Bronze, 18 mm. **Ruler:** Hussein Ibn Talal **Obv:** Head right **Rev:** Value and date within circle flanked by sprigs **Edge:** Plain

Date	Mintage	F	VF	XF	Unc	BU
AH1398-1978 Proof	20,000	Value: 0.75				
AH1404-1984	100,000	—	0.10	0.20	0.50	—
AH1406-1985	—	—	—	1.50	2.00	—
Note: In sets only						
AH1406-1985 Proof	5,000	Value: 2.00				

KM# 3 5 FILS (1/2 Qirsh)
4.5000 g., Bronze, 21 mm. **Ruler:** Abdullah Ibn Al-Hussein **Obv:** Value and date within crowned circle within sprigs **Rev:** Value within circle above date **Edge:** Plain

Date	Mintage	F	VF	XF	Unc	BU
AH1368//1949	3,300,000	—	0.40	0.75	1.50	—
AH1368//1949 Proof	25	Value: 60.00				

KM# 9 5 FILS (1/2 Qirsh)
4.5000 g., Bronze, 21 mm. **Ruler:** Hussein Ibn Talal **Obv:** Value and date within crowned circle within sprigs **Rev:** Value within circle above date **Edge:** Plain

Date	Mintage	F	VF	XF	Unc	BU
AH1374-1955	3,500,000	—	0.35	0.50	0.75	—
AH1374-1955 Proof	—	Value: 50.00				
AH1379-1960	540,000	—	0.50	0.70	1.25	—
AH1379-1960 Proof	—	Value: 50.00				
AH1382-1962	250,000	—	0.45	0.70	1.25	—
AH1382-1962 Proof	—	Value: 50.00				
AH1383-1964	3,000	—	—	2.75	3.50	—
Note: In sets only						
AH1384-1964	2,500,000	—	0.30	0.50	1.00	—
AH1385-1965	5,000	—	1.25	2.50	3.00	—
Note: In sets only						
AH1385-1965 Proof	10,000	Value: 5.00				
AH1387-1967	2,000,000	—	0.10	0.20	0.40	—

KM# 15 5 FILS (1/2 Qirsh)
4.5000 g., Bronze, 21 mm. **Ruler:** Hussein Ibn Talal **Obv:** Head right **Rev:** Value and date within circle flanked by sprigs **Edge:** Plain

Date	Mintage	F	VF	XF	Unc	BU
AH1387//1968	800,000	—	0.20	0.50	0.75	—
AH1390//1970	1,400,000	—	0.10	0.25	0.50	—
AH1392//1972	400,000	—	0.10	0.25	0.65	—
AH1394//1974	2,000,000	—	0.10	0.20	0.40	—
AH1395//1975	9,000,000	—	0.10	0.15	0.30	—

KM# 36 5 FILS (1/2 Qirsh)
4.5000 g., Bronze, 21 mm. **Ruler:** Hussein Ibn Talal **Obv:** Head right **Rev:** Value and date within circle flanked by sprigs **Edge:** Plain

Date	Mintage	F	VF	XF	Unc	BU
AH1398-1978	60,200,000	—	0.10	0.15	0.30	—
AH1398-1978 Proof	20,000	Value: 1.25				
AH1406-1985	—	—	—	1.50	2.00	—

Note: In sets only

Date	Mintage	F	VF	XF	Unc	BU
AH1406-1985 Proof	5,000	Value: 2.50				

KM# 60 1/2 QIRSH (1/2 Piastre)
Copper Plated Steel **Ruler:** Hussein Ibn Talal **Obv:** Bust left **Rev:** Value at left within lines with date above and written value at lower right **Edge:** Plain

Date	Mintage	F	VF	XF	Unc	BU
AH1416-1996	—	—	—	0.35	0.65	1.00
AH1416-1996 Proof	—	Value: 5.00				

KM# 4 10 FILS (Qirsh, Piastre)
5.9000 g., Bronze, 25 mm. **Ruler:** Abdullah Ibn Al-Hussein **Obv:** Value and date within crowned circle within sprigs **Rev:** Value within circle above date and star **Edge:** Plain

Date	Mintage	F	VF	XF	Unc	BU
AH1368//1949	2,700,000	—	0.75	1.25	2.00	—
AH1368//1949 Proof	25	Value: 75.00				

KM# 10 10 FILS (Qirsh, Piastre)
5.9000 g., Bronze, 25 mm. **Ruler:** Hussein Ibn Talal **Obv:** Value and date within crowned circle within sprigs **Rev:** Value within circle above date and star **Edge:** Plain

Date	Mintage	F	VF	XF	Unc	BU
AH1374//1955	1,500,000	—	0.60	1.00	2.00	—
AH1374//1955 Proof	—	Value: 50.00				
AH1379//1960	60,000	—	1.25	2.00	3.50	—
AH1379//1960 Proof	—	Value: 50.00				
AH1382//1962	2,300,000	—	0.30	0.50	1.00	—
AH1382//1962 Proof	—	Value: 50.00				
AH1383//1964	1,253,000	—	0.30	0.50	1.00	—
AH1385//1965	1,003,000	—	0.20	0.40	1.00	—
AH1385//1965 Proof	10,000	Value: 5.00				
AH1387//1967	1,000,000	—	0.20	0.35	1.00	—

KM# 16 10 FILS (Qirsh, Piastre)
5.9000 g., Bronze, 25 mm. **Ruler:** Hussein Ibn Talal **Obv:** Head right **Rev:** Value and date within circle flanked by sprigs

Date	Mintage	F	VF	XF	Unc	BU
AH1387-1968	500,000	—	0.20	0.50	0.90	—
AH1390-1970	1,000,000	—	0.20	0.35	0.60	—
AH1392-1972	600,000	—	0.20	0.40	0.75	—
AH1394-1974	1,000,000	—	0.20	0.40	0.65	—
AH1395-1975	5,000,000	—	0.20	0.35	0.50	—

KM# 37 10 FILS (Qirsh, Piastre)
5.9000 g., Bronze, 25 mm. **Ruler:** Hussein Ibn Talal **Obv:** Head right **Rev:** Value and date within circle flanked by sprigs **Edge:** Plain

Date	Mintage	F	VF	XF	Unc	BU
AH1398-1978	30,000,000	—	0.10	0.15	0.40	—
AH1398-1978 Proof	20,000	Value: 2.00				
AH1404-1984	10,000,000	—	0.10	0.15	0.40	—
AH1406-1985	—	—	—	1.25	1.75	—

Note: In sets only

Date	Mintage	F	VF	XF	Unc	BU
AH1406-1985 Proof	5,000	Value: 3.00				
AH1409-1989	8,000,000	—	0.25	2.00	2.50	—

KM# 5 20 FILS
Copper-Nickel **Ruler:** Abdullah Ibn Al-Hussein **Obv:** Value and date within crowned circle within sprigs **Rev:** Value within circle above date and star **Edge:** Milled

Date	Mintage	F	VF	XF	Unc	BU
AH1368//1949	1,570,000	—	0.50	1.00	1.75	—
AH1368//1949 Proof	25	Value: 90.00				

KM# 13 20 FILS
Copper-Nickel, 19.8 mm. **Ruler:** Hussein Ibn Talal **Obv:** Value and date within crowned circle within sprigs **Rev:** Value within circle above date and star **Edge:** Milled

Date	Mintage	F	VF	XF	Unc	BU
AH1383//1964	3,000	—	—	3.00	5.00	—

Note: In sets only

Date	Mintage	F	VF	XF	Unc	BU
AH1385//1965	5,000	—	—	3.00	5.00	—

Note: In sets only

Date	Mintage	F	VF	XF	Unc	BU
AH1385//1965 Proof	10,000	Value: 5.00				

KM# 17 25 FILS (1/4 Dirham)
4.7500 g., Copper-Nickel, 22 mm. **Ruler:** Hussein Ibn Talal **Obv:** Head right **Rev:** Value and date within circle flanked by sprigs **Edge:** Milled

Date	Mintage	F	VF	XF	Unc	BU
AH1387-1968	200,000	—	0.30	0.50	1.00	—
AH1390-1970	240,000	—	0.15	0.35	0.75	—
AH1394-1974	800,000	—	0.15	0.35	0.75	—
AH1395-1975	2,000,000	—	0.15	0.35	0.75	—
AH1397-1977	1,600,000	—	0.15	0.35	0.75	—

KM# 38 25 FILS (1/4 Dirham)
4.7500 g., Copper-Nickel, 22 mm. **Ruler:** Hussein Ibn Talal **Obv:** Head right **Rev:** Value and date within circle flanked by sprigs **Edge:** Milled

Date	Mintage	F	VF	XF	Unc	BU
AH1398-1978 Proof	20,000	Value: 3.00				
AH1401-1981	2,000,000	—	0.20	0.30	0.75	—
AH1404-1984	4,000,000	—	0.20	0.30	0.75	—
AH1406-1985	—	—	—	2.50	3.00	—

Note: In sets only

Date	Mintage	F	VF	XF	Unc	BU
AH1406-1985 Proof	5,000	Value: 4.00				
AH1411-1991	5,000,000	—	0.20	0.30	0.75	—

KM# 6 50 FILS (1/2 Dirham)
7.5000 g., Copper-Nickel, 26 mm. **Ruler:** Abdullah Ibn Al-Hussein **Obv:** Value and date within crowned circle within sprigs **Rev:** Value within circle above date and star **Edge:** Milled

Date	Mintage	F	VF	XF	Unc	BU
AH1368//1949	2,500,000	—	0.75	2.00	3.50	—
AH1368//1949 Proof	25	Value: 100				

KM# 11 50 FILS (1/2 Dirham)
7.5000 g., Copper-Nickel, 26 mm. **Ruler:** Hussein Ibn Talal **Obv:** Value and date within crowned circle within sprigs **Rev:** Value within circle above date and star **Edge:** Milled

Date	Mintage	F	VF	XF	Unc	BU
AH1374//1955	2,500,000	—	0.75	1.50	3.50	—
AH1374//1955 Proof	—	Value: 50.00				
AH1382//1962	750,000	—	0.85	1.00	1.50	—
AH1382//1962 Proof	—	Value: 50.00				
AH1383//1964	1,003,000	—	0.40	0.60	1.00	—
AH1385//1965	1,505,000	—	0.40	0.60	1.00	—
AH1385//1965 Proof	10,000	Value: 4.50				

KM# 18 50 FILS (1/2 Dirham)
7.5000 g., Copper-Nickel, 26 mm. **Ruler:** Hussein Ibn Talal **Obv:** Head right **Rev:** Value and date within circle flanked by sprigs **Edge:** Milled

Date	Mintage	F	VF	XF	Unc	BU
AH1387-1968	400,000	—	0.75	1.00	2.75	—
AH1390-1970	1,000,000	—	0.40	0.60	1.25	—
AH1394-1974	1,000,000	—	0.40	0.60	1.25	—
AH1395-1975	2,000,000	—	0.40	0.60	1.25	—
AH1397-1977	6,000,000	—	0.40	0.60	1.25	—

KM# 39 50 FILS (1/2 Dirham)
7.5000 g., Copper-Nickel, 26 mm. **Ruler:** Hussein Ibn Talal **Edge:** Milled

Date	Mintage	F	VF	XF	Unc	BU
AH1398-1978	6,168,000	—	0.25	0.50	1.25	—
AH1398-1978 Proof	20,000	Value: 2.50				
AH1401-1981	5,000,000	—	0.25	0.50	1.25	—
AH1404-1984	10,000,000	—	0.25	0.50	1.25	—
AH1406-1985	—	—	—	2.75	3.25	—

Note: In sets only

Date	Mintage	F	VF	XF	Unc	BU
AH1406-1985 Proof	5,000	Value: 3.50				
AH1409-1989	6,000,000	—	0.25	0.50	1.25	—
AH1411-1991	10,000,000	—	0.25	0.50	1.25	—

KM# 7 100 FILS (Dirham)
12.0000 g., Copper-Nickel, 30 mm. **Ruler:** Abdullah Ibn Al-Hussein **Obv:** Value and date within crowned circle within sprigs **Rev:** Value within circle above date and star **Edge:** Milled

Date	Mintage	F	VF	XF	Unc	BU
AH1368//1949	2,000,000	—	2.00	3.00	5.00	—
AH1368//1949 Proof	25	Value: 120				

KM# 12 100 FILS (Dirham)
12.0000 g., Copper-Nickel, 30 mm. **Ruler:** Hussein Ibn Talal **Obv:** Value and date within crowned circle within sprigs **Rev:** Value within circle above date and star **Edge:** Milled

Date	Mintage	F	VF	XF	Unc	BU
AH1374//1955	500,000	—	2.00	2.50	4.00	—
AH1374//1955 Proof	—	Value: 50.00				
AH1382//1962	600,000	—	1.00	1.50	3.00	—
AH1382//1962 Proof	—	Value: 50.00				
AH1383//1964 In sets only	3,000	—	1.50	3.00	5.00	—
AH1385//1965	405,000	—	1.00	1.25	2.25	—
AH1385//1965 Proof	10,000	Value: 5.00				

KM# 19 100 FILS (Dirham)
12.0000 g., Copper-Nickel, 30 mm. **Ruler:** Hussein Ibn Talal **Obv:** Head right **Rev:** Value and date within circle flanked by sprigs **Edge:** Milled

Date	Mintage	F	VF	XF	Unc	BU
AH1387-1968	175,000	—	1.00	1.50	2.50	—
AH1395-1975	2,500,000	—	0.40	1.00	2.00	—
AH1397-1977	2,000,000	—	0.40	1.00	2.00	—

KM# 40 100 FILS (Dirham)
12.0000 g., Copper-Nickel, 30 mm. **Ruler:** Hussein Ibn Talal **Obv:** Head right **Rev:** Value and date within circle flanked by sprigs **Edge:** Milled

Date	Mintage	F	VF	XF	Unc	BU
AH1398-1978	3,000,000	—	0.40	1.00	2.00	—
AH1398-1978 Proof	20,000	Value: 3.50				
AH1401-1981	4,000,000	—	0.40	1.00	2.00	—
AH1404-1984	5,000,000	—	0.40	1.00	1.50	—
AH1406-1985	—	—	—	2.50	3.50	—
Note: In sets only						
AH1406-1985 Proof	5,000	Value: 4.50				
AH1409-1989	4,000,000	—	0.40	1.00	1.50	—
AH1411-1991	6,000,000	—	0.40	1.00	1.50	—

KM# 20 1/4 DINAR
17.0000 g., Copper-Nickel, 34 mm. **Ruler:** Hussein Ibn Talal **Series:** F.A.O. **Obv:** Head right **Rev:** Date below olive tree within circled wreath with F.A.O. logo below **Edge:** Milled

Date	Mintage	F	VF	XF	Unc	BU
AH1389-1969	60,000	—	2.00	3.00	5.50	—

KM# 28 1/4 DINAR
17.0000 g., Copper-Nickel, 34 mm. **Ruler:** Hussein Ibn Talal **Obv:** Head right **Rev:** Date below olive tree within circled wreath **Edge:** Milled

Date	Mintage	F	VF	XF	Unc	BU
AH1390-1970	500,000	—	1.00	1.50	4.00	—
AH1394-1974	400,000	—	1.00	1.50	4.00	—
AH1395-1975	100,000	—	1.00	1.50	4.00	—

KM# 30 1/4 DINAR
17.0000 g., Copper-Nickel, 34 mm. **Ruler:** Hussein Ibn Talal **Subject:** 25th Anniversary of Reign **Obv:** Head facing 1/4 right within small circle flanked by sprigs, all within design with crown on top and date below **Rev:** Castle above dates **Edge:** Milled

Date	Mintage	F	VF	XF	Unc	BU
AH1397-1977	200,000	—	1.00	2.00	4.50	—

KM# 41 1/4 DINAR
17.0000 g., Copper-Nickel, 34 mm. **Ruler:** Hussein Ibn Talal **Obv:** Head right **Rev:** Date below olive tree within circled wreath **Designer:** Milled

Date	Mintage	F	VF	XF	Unc	BU
AH1398-1978	200,000	—	1.00	2.00	4.50	—
AH1398-1978 Proof	20,000	Value: 5.00				
AH1401-1981	800,000	—	0.75	1.50	4.00	—
AH1406-1985	—	—	—	3.00	4.00	—
Note: In sets only						
AH1406-1985 Proof	5,000	Value: 6.50				

KM# 42 1/2 DINAR
Copper-Nickel **Ruler:** Hussein Ibn Talal **Subject:** 1400th Anniversary of Hijra (Mohammed's Pilgrimage) **Obv:** Bust facing 1/4 right **Rev:** Capitol building and sun within circle at right, sprig to left within larger circle **Edge:** Plain **Shape:** 7-sided

Date	Mintage	F	VF	XF	Unc	BU
AH1400-1980	2,006,000	—	1.50	2.50	5.00	—

KM# 47 DINAR
14.0000 g., Nickel-Bronze, 29 mm. **Ruler:** Hussein Ibn Talal **Subject:** King Hussein's 50th Birthday **Obv:** Head right within beaded circle **Rev:** Crowned sun within 3/4 wreath flanked by dates **Edge:** Milled

Date	Mintage	F	VF	XF	Unc	BU
AH1406-1985	—	—	—	—	7.50	—
AH1406-1985 Proof	5,000	Value: 10.00				

REFORM COINAGE

1992

KM# 56 QIRSH (Piastre)
5.5000 g., Bronze Plated Steel, 25 mm. **Ruler:** Hussein Ibn Talal **Obv:** Head left **Rev:** Value to left within lines below date with written value at lower right **Edge:** Plain

Date	Mintage	F	VF	XF	Unc	BU
AH1414-1994	—	—	—	0.50	1.25	1.50
AH1416-1996	—	—	—	0.50	1.25	1.50
AH1416-1996 Proof	—	Value: 5.00				

KM# 78.1 QIRSH (Piastre)
5.4700 g., Copper Plated Steel, 25 mm. **Ruler:** Abdullah Ibn Al-Hussein **Obv:** King Abdullah II **Rev:** Christian date left, Islamic date right **Edge:** Plain

Date	Mintage	F	VF	XF	Unc	BU
AH1421-2000	—	—	—	—	1.00	1.50
2000-AH1421 dates flipped	—	—	—	—	1.00	1.25

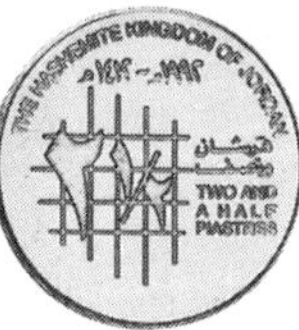

KM# 53 2-1/2 PIASTRES
Stainless Steel **Ruler:** Hussein Ibn Talal **Obv:** Bust left **Rev:** Value at left within lines below date with written value to lower right **Edge:** Milled

Date	Mintage	F	VF	XF	Unc	BU
AH1412-1992	—	—	—	0.75	1.50	1.75
AH1416-1996	—	—	—	0.75	1.50	1.75
AH1416-1996 Proof	—	Value: 5.00				

KM# 54 5 PIASTRES
Nickel Plated Steel **Ruler:** Hussein Ibn Talal **Obv:** Bust left **Rev:** Value at left within lines below date with written value at lower right **Edge:** Milled

Date	Mintage	F	VF	XF	Unc	BU
AH1412-1992	—	—	—	1.00	2.00	2.50
AH1414-1993	—	—	—	1.00	2.00	2.50
AH1416-1996	—	—	—	1.00	2.00	2.50
AH1416-1996 Proof	—	Value: 5.00				
AH1418-1998	—	—	—	1.00	2.00	2.50

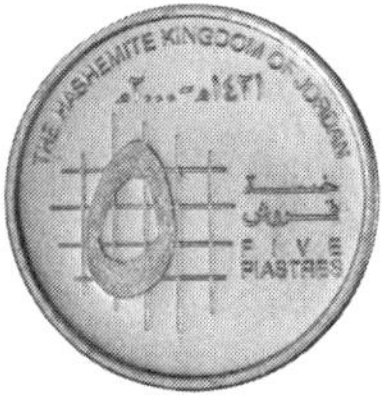

KM# 73 5 PIASTRES
5.0000 g., Nickel-Clad Steel, 25.8 mm. **Ruler:** Abdullah Ibn Al-Hussein **Obv:** Bust right **Rev:** Value to left within lines below date with written value at lower right **Edge:** Milled

Date	Mintage	F	VF	XF	Unc	BU
AH1421-2000	—	—	—	—	2.00	2.50
AH1427-2006	—	—	—	—	2.00	2.50

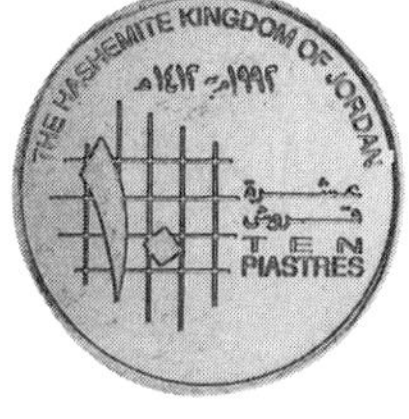

KM# 55 10 PIASTRES
Nickel Plated Steel **Ruler:** Hussein Ibn Talal **Obv:** Bust left **Rev:** Value at left within lines below date with written value at lower right **Edge:** Milled

Date	Mintage	F	VF	XF	Unc	BU
AH1412-1992	—	—	—	1.25	2.25	2.75
AH1414-1993	—	—	—	1.25	2.25	2.75
AH1416-1996	—	—	—	1.25	2.25	2.75
AH1416-1996 Proof	—	Value: 5.00				

KM# 74 10 PIASTRES
8.0000 g., Nickel Clad Steel, 27.9 mm. **Ruler:** Abdullah Ibn Al-Hussein **Obv:** Bust right **Rev:** Value at left within lines below date with written value at lower right **Edge:** Milled

Date	Mintage	F	VF	XF	Unc	BU
AH1421-2000	—	—	—	—	4.00	5.00
AH1425-2004	—	—	—	—	4.00	5.00

KM# 61 1/4 DINAR
7.4000 g., Nickel-Brass **Ruler:** Hussein Ibn Talal **Obv:** Bust left **Rev:** Value in circle within artistic design **Edge:** Plain **Shape:** 7-sided

Date	Mintage	F	VF	XF	Unc	BU
AH1416-1996	—	—	—	—	3.00	4.00
AH1416-1996 Proof	—	Value: 7.50				
AH1417-1997	—	—	—	—	3.00	4.00

KM# 83 1/4 DINAR
7.4000 g., Nickel-Brass **Ruler:** Abdullah Ibn Al-Hussein **Obv:** Bust right **Edge:** Plain

Date	Mintage	F	VF	XF	Unc	BU
AH1425-2004	—	—	—	—	3.00	4.00

KM# 58 1/2 DINAR
9.6800 g., Brass **Ruler:** Hussein Ibn Talal **Obv:** Bust left **Rev:** Value in circle within artistic design **Edge:** Plain

Date	Mintage	F	VF	XF	Unc	BU
AH1416-1996	—	—	—	—	4.00	5.00
AH1416-1996 Proof	—	Value: 8.50				

KM# 63 1/2 DINAR
Bi-Metallic Copper-Nickel center in Aluminum-Bronze ring **Ruler:** Hussein Ibn Talal **Obv:** Bust left within circle **Rev:** Value in center of circled wreath **Edge:** Plain **Shape:** 7-sided

Date	Mintage	F	VF	XF	Unc	BU
AH1417-1997	—	—	—	—	8.00	10.00

KM# 79 1/2 DINAR
9.6700 g., Bi-Metallic Copper-Nickel center in Brass ring, 29 mm. **Ruler:** Abdullah Ibn Al-Hussein **Obv:** Bust right within circle **Rev:** Value in center of circled wreath **Edge:** Plain **Shape:** 7-sided

Date	Mintage	F	VF	XF	Unc	BU
AH1421-2000	—	—	—	—	6.00	8.00

KM# 62 DINAR
Brass **Ruler:** Hussein Ibn Talal **Subject:** 50th Anniversary - F.A.O. **Obv:** Bust left **Rev:** F.A.O. logo within artistic design **Edge:** Plain **Shape:** 7-sided

Date	Mintage	F	VF	XF	Unc	BU
AH1415-1995	—	—	—	—	10.00	12.00

KM# 59 DINAR
Brass **Ruler:** Hussein Ibn Talal **Obv:** Bust left **Rev:** Value within center of artistic design **Edge:** Plain **Shape:** 7-sided

Date	Mintage	F	VF	XF	Unc	BU
AH1416-1996	—	—	—	—	8.00	10.00
AH1416-1996 Proof	—	Value: 11.50				
AH1417-1997	—	—	—	—	7.00	9.00

KM# 64 DINAR
Brass **Ruler:** Hussein Ibn Talal **Obv:** Bust left **Rev:** Value within ornamented circle **Edge:** Milled

Date	Mintage	F	VF	XF	Unc	BU
AH1419-1998	—	—	—	—	5.50	6.50

KM# 65 DINAR
Brass **Ruler:** Hussein Ibn Talal **Subject:** Human Rights **Obv:** Bust left **Rev:** Commemorative legend with value within ornamented circle **Edge:** Milled

Date	Mintage	F	VF	XF	Unc	BU
AH1419-1998	—	—	—	—	7.00	8.00

KATANGA

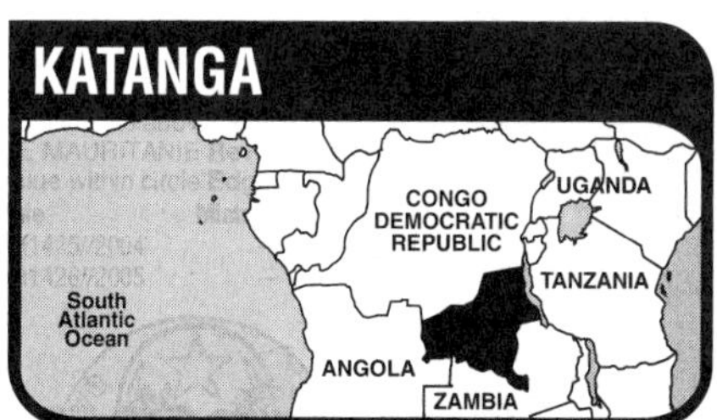

Katanga, the southern province of the former Belgian Congo, had an area of 191,873 sq. mi. (496,951 sq. km.) and was noted for its mineral wealth.

MONETARY SYSTEM
100 Centimes = 1 Franc

PROVINCE

DECIMAL COINAGE

KM# 1 FRANC
4.7000 g., Bronze **Obv:** Bananas (musax paradisiaca-Musaceae) within circle **Rev:** Cross, value and date within circle

Date	Mintage	F	VF	XF	Unc	BU
1961	—	—	1.25	2.00	4.00	—

KM# 2 5 FRANCS
6.5400 g., Bronze, 26.3 mm. **Obv:** Bananas (musax paradisiaca-Musaceae) within circle **Rev:** Cross, value and date within circle

Date	Mintage	F	VF	XF	Unc	BU
1961	—	—	2.50	4.00	8.00	—

The Republic of Kazakhstan (formerly Kazakhstan S.S.R.) is bordered to the west by the Caspian Sea and Russia, to the north by Russia, in the east by the Peoples Republic of China and in the south by Uzbekistan and Kirghizia. It has an area of 1,049,155 sq. mi. (2,717,300 sq. km.) and a population of 16.7 million. Capital: Astana. Rich in mineral resources including coal, tungsten, copper, lead, zinc and manganese with huge oil and natural gas reserves. Agriculture is very important, (it previously represented 20 percent of the total arable acreage of the combined U.S.S.R.) Non-ferrous metallurgy, heavy engineering and chemical industries are leaders in its economy.

The Kazakhs are a branch of the Turkic peoples which led the nomadic life of herdsmen until WW I. In the 13th century they came under Genghis Khan's eldest son Jujiand. Later they became a part of the Golden Horde, a western Mongol empire. Around the beginning of the 16th century they were divided into 3 confederacies, known as *zhuz* or hordes, in the steppes of Turkestan. At the end of the 17th century an incursion by the Kalmucks, a remnant of the Oirat Mongol confederacy, resulted in heavy losses on both sides which facilitated Russian penetration. Resistance to Russian settlements varied throughout the 1800's, but by 1900 over 100 million acres were declared Czarist state property and used for a planned peasant colonization. After a revolution in 1905 Kazakh deputies were elected. In 1916 the tsarist government ordered mobilization of all males, between 19 and 43, for auxiliary service. The Kazakhs rose in defiance which led the governor general of Turkestan to send troops against the rebels. Shortly after the Russian revolution, Kazakh Nationalists asked for full autonomy. The Communist *coup d'etat* of Nov. 1917 led to civil war. In 1919-20 the Red army defeated the "White" Russian forces and occupied Kazakhstan and fought against the Nationalist government formed on Nov. 17, 1917 by Ali Khan Bukey Khan. The Kazakh Autonomous Soviet Socialist Republic was proclaimed on Aug. 26, 1920 within the R.S.F.S.R. Russian and Ukrainian colonization continued while 2 purges in 1927 and 1935 quelled any Kazakh feelings of priority in the matters of their country. On Dec. 5, 1936 Kazakhstan qualified for full status as an S.S.R. and held its first congress in 1937. Independence was declared on Dec. 16, 1991 and Kazakhstan joined the C.I.S.

MONETARY SYSTEM

100 Tyin = 1 Tenge

REPUBLIC

DECIMAL COINAGE

KM# 1 2 TYIN

1.9000 g., Yellow Brass, 17.2 mm. **Obv:** National emblem **Rev:** Star design divides date with value within

Date	Mintage	F	VF	XF	Unc	BU
1993	—	—	—	—	0.45	0.75

KM# 1a 2 TYIN

2.2000 g., Copper Clad Brass, 17.2 mm. **Obv:** National emblem **Rev:** Star design divides date with value within **Edge:** Plain

Date	Mintage	F	VF	XF	Unc	BU
1993	—	—	—	—	0.45	0.75

KM# 2 5 TYIN

1.9000 g., Yellow Brass, 17.2 mm. **Obv:** National emblem **Rev:** Star design divides date with value within

Date	Mintage	F	VF	XF	Unc	BU
1993	—	—	—	—	0.60	1.00

KM# 2a 5 TYIN

2.2400 g., Copper Clad Brass, 17.2 mm. **Obv:** National emblem **Rev:** Star design divides date with value within **Edge:** Plain

Date	Mintage	F	VF	XF	Unc	BU
1993	—	—	—	—	0.60	1.00

KM# 3 10 TYIN

3.3000 g., Yellow Brass, 19.95 mm. **Obv:** National emblem **Rev:** Star design divides date with value within **Edge:** Plain

Date	Mintage	F	VF	XF	Unc	BU
1993	—	—	—	—	0.80	1.50

KM# 3a 10 TYIN

3.1000 g., Copper Clad Brass, 19.6 mm. **Obv:** National emblem **Rev:** Star design divides date with value within

Date	Mintage	F	VF	XF	Unc	BU
1993	—	—	—	—	0.80	1.50

KM# 4 20 TYIN

4.5200 g., Brass Plated Zinc, 22 mm. **Obv:** National emblem **Rev:** Star design divides date with value within

Date	Mintage	F	VF	XF	Unc	BU
1993	—	—	—	—	1.25	2.00

KM# 5 50 TYIN

6.8000 g., Brass Plated Zinc, 25.1 mm. **Obv:** National emblem **Rev:** Star design divides date with value within

Date	Mintage	F	VF	XF	Unc	BU
1993	—	—	—	—	1.50	2.50

KM# 6 TENGE

Copper-Nickel, 17.3 mm. **Obv:** Mythical animal **Rev:** Star design with value and date within

Date	Mintage	F	VF	XF	Unc	BU
1992	—	—	—	—	1.00	1.75
1993	—	—	—	—	0.50	0.85

KM# 23 TENGE

1.6000 g., Brass, 14.60 mm. **Obv:** National emblem **Rev:** Value flanked by designs **Edge:** Plain

Date	Mintage	F	VF	XF	Unc	BU
1997	—	—	—	—	0.50	0.85
2000	—	—	—	—	0.50	0.85
2002	—	—	—	—	0.50	0.85
2004	—	—	—	—	0.50	0.85
2005	—	—	—	—	0.50	0.85

KM# 64 2 TENGE

1.8200 g., Brass, 16 mm. **Obv:** National emblem **Rev:** Value flanked by designs **Edge:** Plain

Date	Mintage	F	VF	XF	Unc	BU
2005	—	—	—	—	0.65	1.20

KM# 8 3 TENGE

Copper-Nickel **Obv:** Mythical animal within circle **Rev:** Star design with value and date within

Date	Mintage	F	VF	XF	Unc	BU
1993	—	—	—	—	0.75	1.25
2005	—	—	—	—	0.75	1.25

KM# 9 5 TENGE

Copper-Nickel **Obv:** Mythical animal within circle **Rev:** Star design with date and value within

Date	Mintage	F	VF	XF	Unc	BU
1993	—	—	—	—	1.25	2.00

KM# 24 5 TENGE

Brass **Obv:** National emblem **Rev:** Value flanked by designs

Date	Mintage	F	VF	XF	Unc	BU
1997	—	—	—	—	0.50	0.85
2000	—	—	—	—	0.50	0.85
2002	—	—	—	—	0.50	0.85
2004	—	—	—	—	0.50	0.85
2005	—	—	—	—	0.50	0.85

KM# 10 10 TENGE

Copper-Nickel **Obv:** National emblem above value **Rev:** Stylized double headed eagle within circle above date

Date	Mintage	F	VF	XF	Unc	BU
1993	—	—	—	—	2.00	3.50

KM# 25 10 TENGE

Brass **Obv:** National emblem **Rev:** Value above design

Date	Mintage	F	VF	XF	Unc	BU
1997	—	—	—	—	0.75	1.25
2000	—	—	—	—	0.75	1.25
2002	—	—	—	—	0.75	1.25
2004	—	—	—	—	0.75	1.25
2005	—	—	—	—	0.75	1.25

KM# 11 20 TENGE

Copper-Nickel **Obv:** National emblem above value **Rev:** Turbaned head 1/4 right within circle

Date	Mintage	F	VF	XF	Unc	BU
1993	—	—	—	—	3.00	5.00

KM# 12 20 TENGE

Copper-Nickel **Subject:** 50th Anniversary - United Nations **Obv:** National emblem above value **Rev:** UN logo and anniversary dates within circle

Date	Mintage	F	VF	XF	Unc	BU
1995	—	—	—	—	3.50	5.50

KM# 18 20 TENGE

Copper-Nickel **Subject:** 150th Anniversary - Jambyl **Obv:** National emblem above value **Rev:** Man with stringed instrument

Date	Mintage	F	VF	XF	Unc	BU
1996	—	—	—	—	3.50	5.50

KM# 19 20 TENGE

Copper-Nickel **Subject:** 5th Anniversary - Independence **Obv:** National emblem above value **Rev:** Monument and buildings

Date	Mintage	F	VF	XF	Unc	BU
1996	—	—	—	—	3.50	5.50

KM# 20 20 TENGE

Copper-Nickel **Subject:** Centennial - Birth of Muchtar Auezov **Obv:** National emblem above value **Rev:** Head facing divides dates

Date	Mintage	F	VF	XF	Unc	BU
ND(1997)	—	—	—	—	3.50	5.50

KM# 26 20 TENGE

2.8600 g., Copper-Nickel, 18.3 mm. **Obv:** National emblem **Rev:** Value above design **Edge:** Segmented reeding **Edge Lettering:** * СТО TENGE * Y 3 TENGE

Date	Mintage	F	VF	XF	Unc	BU
1997	—	—	—	—	1.00	1.75
2000	—	—	—	—	1.00	1.75
2002	—	—	—	—	1.00	1.75
2004	—	—	—	—	1.00	1.75
2006	—	—	—	—	1.00	1.75

KM# 21 20 TENGE

Copper-Nickel **Subject:** Year of Peace and Harmony **Obv:** National emblem above value **Rev:** Stylized dove

Date	Mintage	F	VF	XF	Unc	BU
1997	—	—	—	—	3.50	5.50

KM# 22 20 TENGE

Copper-Nickel **Subject:** New Capital - Astana **Obv:** National emblem above value **Rev:** Flower-like design

Date	Mintage	F	VF	XF	Unc	BU
1998	—	—	—	—	3.50	5.50

KM# 28 20 TENGE

Copper-Nickel **Subject:** 100th Birthday - K.I. Satbaev **Obv:** National emblem above value **Rev:** Head facing

Date	Mintage	F	VF	XF	Unc	BU
1999	—	—	—	—	3.85	6.50

KM# 27 50 TENGE

Copper-Nickel **Obv:** National emblem **Rev:** Value above design

Date	Mintage	F	VF	XF	Unc	BU
1997	—	—	—	—	2.00	3.50
2000	—	—	—	—	2.00	3.50
2002	—	—	—	—	2.00	3.50

KM# 30 50 TENGE

Copper-Nickel **Subject:** Millennium **Obv:** National emblem above value **Rev:** Rising sun above three blocks

Date	Mintage	F	VF	XF	Unc	BU
1999	—	—	—	—	3.50	5.50

KM# 31 50 TENGE

10.7000 g., Copper-Nickel, 31 mm. **Subject:** Victorious conclusion of World War II **Obv:** National emblem above value **Rev:** Soldiers celebrating **Edge:** Reeded and plain sections

Date	Mintage	F	VF	XF	Unc	BU
ND(2000)	—	—	—	—	4.00	6.50

KM# 48 50 TENGE

11.0600 g., Copper-Nickel, 31 mm. **Subject:** 1500th Anniversary of Akhmet Yasaui Kesenesi Mosque **Obv:** National emblem above value **Rev:** Mosque **Edge:** Reeded and plain sections

Date	Mintage	F	VF	XF	Unc	BU
2000	—	—	—	—	3.00	5.00

KM# 33 50 TENGE

11.5000 g., Copper-Nickel **Obv:** National emblem above value **Rev:** Bust 1/4 left **Edge:** Reeded and plain sections

Date	Mintage	F	VF	XF	Unc	BU
2000	—	—	—	—	4.00	6.50

KM# 41 50 TENGE

11.2000 g., Copper Nickel, 31.1 mm. **Subject:** Gabiden Mustafin **Obv:** National emblem above value **Rev:** Bust 1/4 left **Edge:** Segmented reeding

Date	Mintage	F	VF	XF	Unc	BU
ND(2002)	—	—	—	—	4.00	6.50

KM# 65 50 TENGE

11.5000 g., Copper-Nickel, 31.1 mm. **Subject:** Alken Margulan **Obv:** National emblem above value **Rev:** Bust facing **Edge:** Segmented reeding

Date	Mintage	F	VF	XF	Unc	BU
2004	—	—	—	—	4.00	6.50

KM# 73 50 TENGE

11.3700 g., Copper-Nickel, 31 mm. **Obv:** Human figure and solar system **Rev:** Astronaut and solar system **Edge:** Segmented reeding

Date	Mintage	F	VF	XF	Unc	BU
2006	50,000	—	—	—	4.00	6.00

KM# 74 50 TENGE

11.3700 g., Copper-Nickel, 31 mm. **Obv:** National arms on tapestry **Rev:** Woman with baby in cradle **Edge:** Segmented reeding

Date	Mintage	F	VF	XF	Unc	BU
2006	—	—	—	—	4.00	6.00

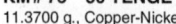

KM# 75 50 TENGE

11.3700 g., Copper-Nickel, 31 mm. **Obv:** National arms **Rev:** Tetraogallus Altaicus birds **Edge:** Segmented reeding

Date	Mintage	F	VF	XF	Unc	BU
2006	50,000	—	—	—	4.00	6.00

KM# 76 50 TENGE

11.3700 g., Copper-Nickel, 31 mm. **Obv:** National arms **Rev:** Altyn Kyran Order Grand Collar and Badge **Edge:** Segmented reeding

Date	Mintage	F	VF	XF	Unc	BU
2006	50,000	—	—	—	4.00	6.00

KM# 77 50 TENGE

11.3700 g., Copper-Nickel, 31 mm. **Obv:** National arms **Rev:** Altyn Kyran Order Breast Star **Edge:** Segmented reeding

Date	Mintage	F	VF	XF	Unc	BU
2006	50,000	—	—	—	4.00	6.00

KM# 78 50 TENGE

11.3700 g., Copper-Nickel, 31 mm. **Obv:** National arms **Rev:** Zhubanov bust and music score **Edge:** Segmented reeding

Date	Mintage	F	VF	XF	Unc	BU
2006	50,000	—	—	—	4.00	6.00

KM# 79 50 TENGE

11.2200 g., Copper-Nickel, 31 mm. **Subject:** 20th Anniversary **Obv:** National arms above value **Rev:** Happy woman **Edge:** Segmented reeding

Date	Mintage	F	VF	XF	Unc	BU
ND (2006)	—	—	—	—	4.00	6.50

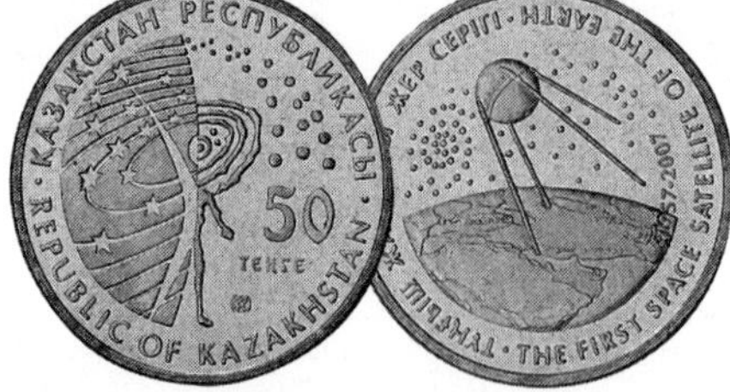

KM# 80 50 TENGE

10.8900 g., Copper-Nickel, 31.10 mm. **Subject:** 50th Anniversary Launch of Sputnik I **Obv:** Stylized view of solar system **Obv. Legend:** REPUBLIC OF KAZAKHSTAN **Rev:** Sputnik I in space, earth in background **Rev. Legend:** THE FIRST SPACE SATELLITE OF THE EARTH **Edge:** Segmented reeding

Date	Mintage	F	VF	XF	Unc	BU
ND(2007)	—	—	—	—	4.00	6.00

KM# 81 50 TENGE

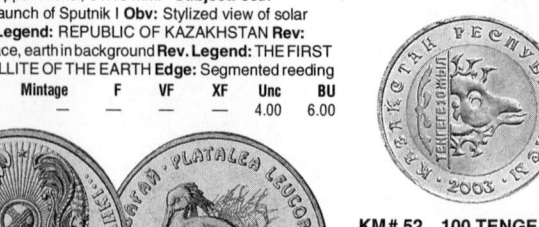

11.1100 g., Copper-Nickel, 31 mm. **Obv:** National arms, value below **Obv. Legend:** КАЗАКСТАН.... **Rev:** Ibise - Pure White Crested Spoonbill standing left **Rev. Legend:** ... • PLATALEA LEUCORODIA **Edge:** Segmented reeding

Date	Mintage	F	VF	XF	Unc	BU
2007	—	—	—	—	4.00	6.00

KM# 39 100 TENGE

6.2300 g., Bi-Metallic Copper-Nickel center in Brass ring, 24.4 mm. **Obv:** National emblem **Rev:** Value within lined circle flanked by designs **Edge:** Reeding over incuse value

Date	Mintage	F	VF	XF	Unc	BU
2002	—	—	—	—	3.50	5.50
2004	—	—	—	—	3.50	5.50
2006	—	—	—	—	3.50	5.50
2007	—	—	—	—	3.50	5.50

KM# 49 100 TENGE

6.4000 g., Bi-Metallic Copper-Nickel center in Brass ring, 24.5 mm. **Obv:** Stylized chicken **Rev:** Value within lined circle flanked by designs **Edge:** Reeded and lettered

Date	Mintage	F	VF	XF	Unc	BU
2003	100,000	—	—	—	4.00	6.50

KM# 50 100 TENGE

6.4000 g., Bi-Metallic Copper-Nickel center in Brass ring, 24.5 mm. **Obv:** Stylized panther **Rev:** Value within lined circle flanked by designs **Edge:** Reeded and lettered

Date	Mintage	F	VF	XF	Unc	BU
2003	100,000	—	—	—	4.00	6.50

KM# 51 100 TENGE

6.4000 g., Bi-Metallic Copper-Nickel center in Brass ring, 24.5 mm. **Obv:** Stylized wolf's head **Rev:** Value within lined circle flanked by designs **Edge:** Reeded and lettered

Date	Mintage	F	VF	XF	Unc	BU
2003	100,000	—	—	—	4.00	6.50

KM# 52 100 TENGE

6.4000 g., Bi-Metallic Copper-Nickel center in Brass ring, 24.5 mm. **Obv:** Stylized sheep's head **Rev:** Value within lined circle flanked by designs **Edge:** Reeded and lettered

Date	Mintage	F	VF	XF	Unc	BU
2003	100,000	—	—	—	4.00	6.50

KM# 57 100 TENGE
6.4000 g., Bi-Metallic Copper-Nickel center in Brass ring, 24.5 mm. **Subject:** 60th Anniversary of the UN **Obv:** UN logo as part of the number 60 **Rev:** Value within lined circle flanked by designs **Edge:** Reeded and lettered

Date	Mintage	F	VF	XF	Unc	BU
2005	—	—	—	—	5.00	7.50

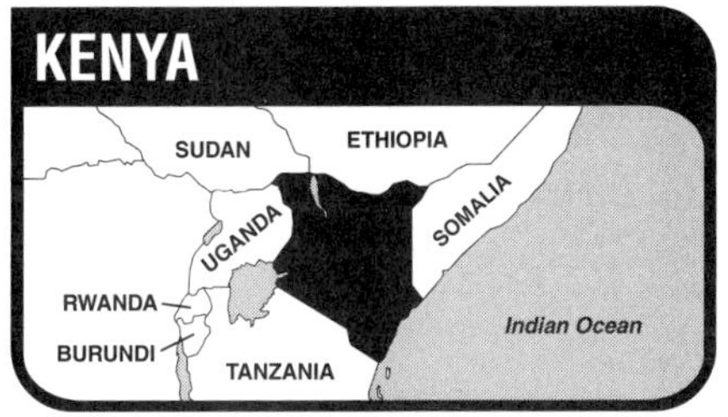

The Republic of Kenya, located on the east coast of Central Africa, has an area of 224,961 sq. mi. (582,650 sq. km.) and a population of 20.1 million. Capital: Nairobi. The predominantly agricultural country exports coffee, tea and petroleum products.

The Arabs came to the coast of Kenya in the 8th century and established posts to conduct an ivory and slave trade. The Portuguese followed in the 16th century. After a lengthy and bitter struggle with the sultans of Zanzibar who controlled much of the southeastern coast of Africa, the Portuguese were driven away (late 17th century) and for many years Kenya was simply a port of call on the route to India. German and British interests in the 19th century produced agreements defining their respective spheres of influence. The British sphere was administrated by the Imperial East Africa Co. until 1895, when the British government purchased the company's rights in the East Africa Protectorate which, in 1920, was designated as Kenya Colony and protectorate - the latter being a 10-mile-wide coastal strip together with Mombasa, Lamuand other small islands nominally retained by the Sultan of Zanzibar. Kenya achieved self-government in June of 1963 as a consequence of the 1952-60 Mau Mau terrorist campaign to secure land reforms and political rights for Africans. Independence was attained on Dec. 12, 1963. Kenya became a republic in 1964. It is a member of the Commonwealth of Nations. The president is Chief of State and Head of Government.

RULER
British, until 1964

MONETARY SYSTEM
100 Cents = 1 Shilling

REPUBLIC

STANDARD COINAGE

KM# 1 5 CENTS
Nickel-Brass **Obv:** Arms with supporters above value **Rev:** Bust left **Rev. Designer:** Norman Sillman

Date	Mintage	F	VF	XF	Unc	BU
1966	28,000,000	—	0.25	0.50	1.00	2.00
1966 Proof	27	Value: 80.00				
1967	9,600,000	—	0.25	0.50	1.00	2.00
1968	12,000,000	—	0.25	0.50	1.00	2.00

KM# 10 5 CENTS
Nickel-Brass **Obv:** Arms with supporters divide date above value **Rev:** Bust left **Rev. Designer:** Norman Sillman

Date	Mintage	F	VF	XF	Unc	BU
1969	800,000	—	0.50	1.00	2.25	4.00
1969 Proof	15	Value: 110				
1970	10,000,000	—	0.15	0.25	1.00	—
1971	29,680,000	—	0.15	0.25	1.00	—
1973 Proof	500	Value: 25.00				
1974	5,599,000	—	0.15	0.25	1.00	—
1975	28,000,000	—	0.15	0.25	1.00	—
1978	23,168,000	—	0.15	0.25	1.00	—

KM# 17 5 CENTS
5.6000 g., Nickel-Brass, 25.5 mm. **Obv:** Arms with supporters divide date above value **Rev:** Bust right

Date	Mintage	F	VF	XF	Unc	BU
1978	—	—	—	—	1.00	—
1978 Proof	—	Value: 10.00				
1980	—	—	0.15	0.25	1.00	—
1984	—	—	0.15	0.25	1.00	—
1986	—	—	0.15	0.25	1.00	—
1987	—	—	0.15	0.25	1.00	—
1989	—	—	0.15	0.25	0.75	—
1990	—	—	0.15	0.25	0.75	—
1991	—	—	0.15	0.25	0.75	—

KM# 2 10 CENTS
Nickel-Brass, 30.8 mm. **Obv:** Arms with supporters divide date above value **Rev:** Bust left **Rev. Designer:** Norman Sillman

Date	Mintage	F	VF	XF	Unc	BU
1966	26,000,000	0.20	0.65	1.25	2.50	—
1966 Proof	27	Value: 80.00				
1967	7,300,000	0.20	0.65	1.25	2.50	—
1968	12,000,000	0.20	0.65	1.25	2.50	—

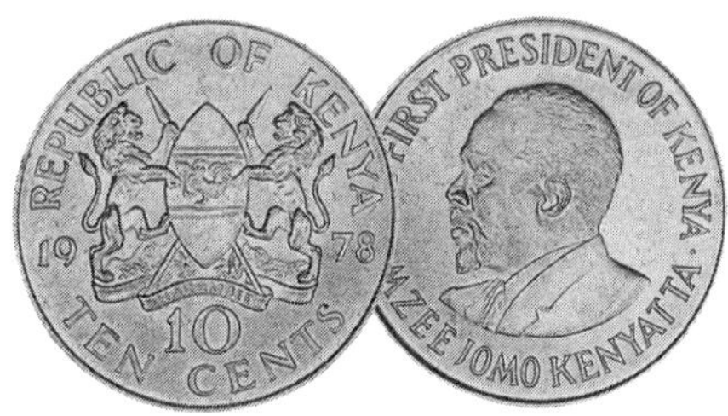

KM# 11 10 CENTS
5.6000 g., Nickel-Brass, 30.8 mm. **Obv:** Arms with supporters divide date above value **Rev:** Bust left

Date	Mintage	F	VF	XF	Unc	BU
1969	3,900,000	—	0.15	0.25	1.00	—
1969 Proof	15	Value: 110				
1970	7,200,000	—	0.15	0.25	1.00	—
1971	32,400,000	—	0.15	0.25	0.75	—
1973	3,000,000	—	0.15	0.25	1.00	—
1973 Proof	500	Value: 25.00				
1974	3,000,000	—	0.15	0.25	1.00	—
1975	3,000,000	—	0.15	0.25	1.00	—
1977	45,600,000	—	0.15	0.25	0.75	—
1978	22,600,000	—	0.15	0.25	0.75	—

KM# 18 10 CENTS
Nickel-Brass, 30.8 mm. **Obv:** Arms with supporters divide date above value **Rev:** Bust right

Date	Mintage	F	VF	XF	Unc	BU
1978	—	—	—	—	1.00	—
1978 Proof	—	Value: 15.00				
1980	—	—	0.15	0.25	1.00	—
1984	—	—	0.15	0.25	1.25	—
1986	—	—	0.15	0.25	1.25	—
1987	—	—	0.15	0.25	1.25	—
1989	—	—	0.15	0.25	1.00	—
1990	—	—	0.15	0.25	1.00	—
1991	—	—	0.15	0.25	0.75	—

KM# 18a 10 CENTS
9.3000 g., Brass Plated Steel, 30.8 mm. **Obv:** Arms with supporters divide date above value **Rev:** Bust right

Date	Mintage	F	VF	XF	Unc	BU
1994	—	—	0.20	0.30	1.00	—

KM# 31 10 CENTS
2.1700 g., Brass Plated Steel **Obv:** Arms with supporters divide date below value **Rev:** Bust right

Date	Mintage	F	VF	XF	Unc	BU
1995	—	—	0.10	0.20	0.40	—

KM# 3 25 CENTS
Copper-Nickel **Obv:** Arms with supporters divide date above value **Rev:** Bust left **Rev. Designer:** Norman Sillman

Date	Mintage	F	VF	XF	Unc	BU
1966	4,000,000	0.30	1.00	2.00	3.50	—
1966 Proof	27	Value: 100				
1967	4,000,000	0.30	1.00	2.00	3.50	—

KM# 12 25 CENTS
Copper-Nickel **Obv:** Arms with supporters divide date above value **Rev:** Bust left **Rev. Designer:** Norman Sillman

Date	Mintage	F	VF	XF	Unc	BU
1969	200,000	0.50	1.00	2.50	10.00	—
1969 Proof	15	Value: 125				
1973 Proof	500	Value: 35.00				

KM# 4 50 CENTS
3.8200 g., Copper-Nickel, 21 mm. **Obv:** Arms with supporters divide date above value **Rev:** Bust left **Rev. Designer:** Norman Sillman

Date	Mintage	F	VF	XF	Unc	BU
1966	4,000,000	0.20	0.40	1.00	2.75	—
1966 Proof	27	Value: 100				
1967	5,120,000	0.20	0.40	0.85	2.25	—
1968	6,000,000	0.20	0.40	0.85	2.00	—

KM# 13 50 CENTS
Copper-Nickel, 21 mm. **Obv:** Arms with supporters divide date above value **Rev:** Bust left **Rev. Designer:** Norman Sillman

Date	Mintage	F	VF	XF	Unc	BU
1969	400,000	0.40	0.80	1.50	3.00	—
1969 Proof	15	Value: 125				
1971	9,600,000	—	0.20	0.40	1.00	—
1973	3,360,000	0.20	0.40	0.80	1.75	—
1973 Proof	500	Value: 25.00				
1974	12,640,000	—	0.20	0.40	1.00	—
1975	8,000,000	—	0.20	0.40	1.00	—
1977	16,000,000	—	0.20	0.40	1.00	—
1978	20,480,000	—	0.20	0.40	1.00	—

KM# 19 50 CENTS
Copper-Nickel, 21 mm. **Obv:** Arms with supporters divide date above value **Rev:** Bust right

Date	Mintage	F	VF	XF	Unc	BU
1978	—	—	—	—	1.00	—
1978 Proof	—	Value: 20.00				
1980	—	—	0.15	0.25	0.75	—
1989	—	—	0.15	0.25	0.75	—

KM# 19a 50 CENTS
Nickel-Plated Steel, 21 mm. **Obv:** Arms with supporters divide date above value **Rev:** Bust right

Date	Mintage	F	VF	XF	Unc	BU
1994	—	—	0.25	0.35	1.00	—

KM# 28 50 CENTS
3.1000 g., Brass Plated Steel, 17.9 mm. **Obv:** Arms with supporters divide date below value **Rev:** Bust right

Date	Mintage	F	VF	XF	Unc	BU
1995	—	—	0.15	0.25	0.50	—
1997	—	—	0.15	0.25	0.50	—

KM# 5 SHILLING
Copper-Nickel, 27.8 mm. **Obv:** Arms with supporters divide date above value **Rev:** Bust left **Rev. Designer:** Norman Sillman

Date	Mintage	F	VF	XF	Unc	BU
1966	20,000,000	0.25	0.50	1.00	3.00	—
1966 Proof	27	Value: 100				
1967	4,000,000	0.25	0.50	1.00	2.75	—
1968	8,000,000	0.20	0.40	0.80	2.25	—

KM# 14 SHILLING
7.9000 g., Copper-Nickel, 27.8 mm. **Obv:** Arms with supporters divide date above value **Rev:** Bust left **Rev. Designer:** Norman Sillman

Date	Mintage	F	VF	XF	Unc	BU
1969	4,000,000	0.15	0.30	0.75	2.25	—
1969 Proof	15	Value: 125				
1971	24,000,000	0.10	0.30	0.65	2.00	—
1973	2,480,000	0.20	0.40	0.80	2.75	—
1973 Proof	500	Value: 30.00				
1974	13,520,000	0.10	0.30	0.65	2.00	—
1975	40,856,000	0.10	0.30	0.65	2.00	—
1978	20,000,000	0.10	0.30	0.65	2.00	—

KM# 20 SHILLING
Copper-Nickel, 27.8 mm. **Obv:** Arms with supporters divide date above value **Rev:** Bust right

Date	Mintage	F	VF	XF	Unc	BU
1978	—	—	—	—	1.50	—
1978 Proof	—	Value: 30.00				
1980	—	0.15	0.25	0.50	1.50	—
1989	—	0.15	0.25	0.50	1.50	—

KM# 20a SHILLING
8.0000 g., Nickel-Plated Steel, 27.8 mm. **Obv:** Arms with supporters divide date above value **Rev:** Bust right

Date	Mintage	F	VF	XF	Unc	BU
1994	—	0.25	0.35	0.65	1.75	—

KM# 29 SHILLING
4.3500 g., Brass Plated Steel, 22 mm. **Obv:** Arms with supporters divide date below value **Rev:** Bust right

Date	Mintage	F	VF	XF	Unc	BU
1995	—	0.10	0.20	0.40	0.75	—
1997	—	0.10	0.20	0.40	0.75	—
1998	—	0.10	0.20	0.40	0.75	—

KM# 34 SHILLING
5.4600 g., Nickel Clad Steel, 23.9 mm. **Obv:** Value and national arms **Rev:** Jomo Kenyata **Edge:** Reeded and plain sections

Date	Mintage	F	VF	XF	Unc	BU
2005	—	—	—	—	—	1.00

KM# 6 2 SHILLINGS
Copper-Nickel **Obv:** Arms with supporters divide date above value **Rev:** Bust left **Rev. Designer:** Norman Sillman **Note:** Similar to KM#2.

Date	Mintage	F	VF	XF	Unc	BU
1966	3,000,000	1.00	2.00	3.00	7.00	—
1966 Proof	27	Value: 120				
1968	1,100,000	1.00	2.75	4.50	10.00	—

KM# 15 2 SHILLINGS
Copper-Nickel **Obv:** Arms with supporters divide date above value **Rev:** Bust left **Rev. Designer:** Norman Sillman **Note:** Similar to KM#11.

Date	Mintage	F	VF	XF	Unc	BU
1969	100,000	2.00	4.00	8.00	12.50	—
1969 Proof	15	Value: 150				
1971	1,920,000	0.60	1.25	3.50	7.50	—
1973 Proof	500	Value: 35.00				

KM# 16 5 SHILLINGS
Brass **Subject:** 10th Anniversary of Independence **Obv:** Arms with supporters divide date above value **Rev:** Bust left **Shape:** 9-sided

Date	Mintage	F	VF	XF	Unc	BU
1973	100,000	4.50	10.00	17.50	30.00	—
1973 Proof	1,500	Value: 45.00				

KM# 23 5 SHILLINGS
Copper-Nickel, 30 mm. **Obv:** Arms with supporters divide date above value **Rev:** Bust right **Shape:** 7-sided

Date	Mintage	F	VF	XF	Unc	BU
1985	—	0.35	0.75	1.50	3.00	—

KM# 23a 5 SHILLINGS
Nickel-Plated Steel **Obv:** Arms with supporters divide date above value **Rev:** Bust right **Shape:** 7-sided

Date	Mintage	F	VF	XF	Unc	BU
1994	—	0.50	1.00	2.25	4.50	—

KM# 30 5 SHILLINGS
Ring Composition: Copper-Nickel **Center Weight:** 3.4000 g. **Center Composition:** Brass, 20 mm. **Obv:** President Arap Moi bust right within circle **Rev:** Arms with supporters below value within circle

Date	Mintage	F	VF	XF	Unc	BU
1995	—	—	—	—	4.00	6.00
1997	—	—	—	—	4.00	6.00

KM# 27 10 SHILLINGS
Ring Composition: Brass **Center Weight:** 5.0000 g. **Center Composition:** Copper-Nickel, 22.9 mm. **Obv:** Arms with supporters below value within circle **Rev:** Bust right within circle

Date	Mintage	F	VF	XF	Unc	BU
1994	—	—	—	—	5.00	8.00
1995	—	—	—	—	5.00	8.00
1997	—	—	—	—	5.00	8.00

KM# 35 10 SHILLINGS
5.0300 g., Bi-Metallic **Ring Composition:** Brass **Center Composition:** Copper-Nickel, 22.95 mm. **Subject:** First President **Obv:** Value above national arms **Obv. Legend:** REPUBLIC OF KENYA **Rev:** Bust of Mzee Jomo Kenyatta left **Edge:** Reeded

Date	Mintage	F	VF	XF	Unc	BU
2005	—	—	—	—	—	4.00

KM# 32 20 SHILLINGS
Ring Composition: Copper-Nickel **Center Composition:** Brass, 25.5 mm. **Obv:** Arms with supporters below value within circle **Rev:** Bust right within circle

Date	Mintage	F	VF	XF	Unc	BU
1998	—	—	—	—	8.00	10.00

KM# 36 20 SHILLINGS
9.0200 g., Bi-Metallic **Ring Composition:** Copper-Nickel **Center Composition:** Brass, 25.97 mm. **Subject:** First President **Obv:** Large value above national arms **Obv. Legend:** REPUBLIC OF KENYA **Rev:** Bust of Mzee Jomo Kenyatta left **Edge:** Segmented reeding

Date	Mintage	F	VF	XF	Unc	BU
2005	—	—	—	—	—	5.00

KM# 33 40 SHILLINGS
11.1000 g., Bi-Metallic Copper-Nickel center in Brass ring, 27.4 mm. **Obv:** Bust facing within circle **Rev:** Arms with supporters and value within circle **Edge:** Reeding over lettering **Edge Lettering:** "40 YEARS OF INDEPENDENCE" **Note:** Issued December 11, 2003.

Date	Mintage	F	VF	XF	Unc	BU
ND(2003)	—	—	—	—	6.00	7.50

KIAU CHAU

Kiau Chau (Kiao Chau, Kiaochow, Kiautscho, now Jiaozhou), a former German trading enclave, including the port of Tsingtao (Qingdao), was located on the Shantung (Shandong) Peninsula of eastern China. Following the murder of two missionaries in Shantung in 1897, Germany occupied Kiaochow Bay, and during subsequent negotiations with the Chinese government obtained a 99-year lease on 177 sq. mi. of land. The enclave was established as a free port in 1899, and a customs house set up to collect tariffs on goods moving to and from the Chinese interior. The Japanese took siege to the port on Aug. 27, 1914, as their first action in World War I to deprive German sea marauders of their east Asian supply and refitting base. Aided by the British forces, the siege ended Nov. 7. Japan retained possession until 1922, when it was restored to China by the Washington Conference on China and naval armaments. It fell again to Japan in 1938, but not before the Chinese had destroyed its manufacturing facilities. It is presently a part of the Peoples Republic of China. The major city is Tsingtao (Qingdao) and is noted for its beer.

RULERS

Wilhelm II, 1897-1914
Japan, 1914-1922, 1938-1945

MONETARY SYSTEM

100 Cents = 1 Dollar

GERMAN OCCUPATION

STANDARD COINAGE

Y# 1 5 CENTS

Copper-Nickel **Ruler:** Wilhelm II **Obv:** German Imperial Eagle **Obv. Legend:** DEUTSCH.KIAUTSHAU GEBIET **Rev:** Inscription within beaded circle **Rev. Inscription:** Kuang-hsü Yüan-pao

Date	Mintage	F	VF	XF	Unc	BU
1909	610,000	50.00	75.00	115	185	—
1909 Proof	—	Value: 450				

Y# 2 10 CENTS

Copper-Nickel **Ruler:** Wilhelm II **Obv:** German Imperial Eagle **Obv. Legend:** DEUTSCH.KIAUTSHAU GEBIET **Rev:** Inscription within beaded circle **Rev. Inscription:** Kuang-hsü Yüan-pao

Date	Mintage	F	VF	XF	Unc	BU
1909	670,000	30.00	50.00	90.00	160	—
1909 Proof	—	Value: 500				

KIRIBATI

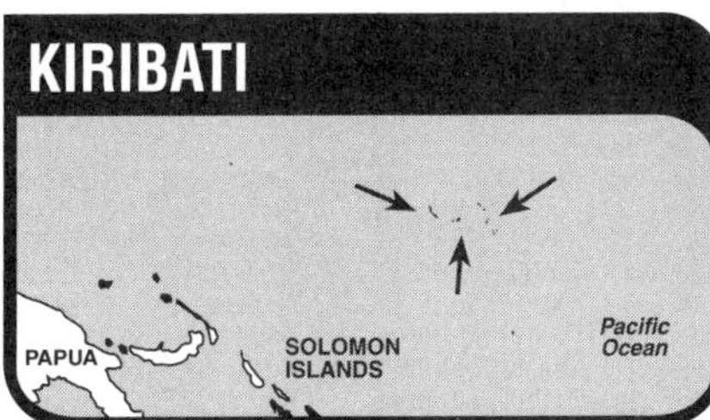

The Republic of Kiribati (formerly the Gilbert Islands), consists of 30 coral atolls and islands spread over more than one million sq. mi. (2,590,000 sq. km.) of the southwest Pacific Ocean, has an area of 332 sq. mi. (717 sq. km.) and a population of 64,200. Capital: Bairiki, on Tarawa. In addition to the Gilbert Islands proper, Kiribati includes Ocean Island, the Central and Southern Line Islands, and the Phoenix Islands, though possession of Canton and Enderbury of the Phoenix Islands is disputed with the United States. Most families engage in subsistence fishing. Copra and phosphates are exported, mostly to Australia and New Zealand.

The Gilbert Islands and the group formerly called the Ellice Islands (now Tuvalu) comprised a single British crown colony, the Gilbert and Ellice Islands.

Spanish mutineers first sighted the islands in 1537, succeeding visits were made by the English navigators John Byron (1764), James Cook (1777), and Thomas Gilbert and John Marshall (1788). An American, Edward Fanning, arrived in 1798. Britain declared a protectorate over the Gilbert and Ellice Islands, and in 1915 began the formation of a colony which was completed when the Phoenix Islands were added to the group in 1937. The Central and Southern Line Islands were administratively attached to the Gilbert and Ellice Islands colony in 1972, and remained attached to the Gilberts when Tuvalu was created in 1975. The colony became self-governing in 1971. Kiribati attained independence on July 12, 1979.

RULER

British, until 1979

MONETARY SYSTEM

100 Cents = 1 Dollar

REPUBLIC

DECIMAL COINAGE

KM# 1 CENT

2.6000 g., Bronze, 17.5 mm. **Subject:** Christmas Island Frigate Bird **Obv:** National arms **Rev:** Frigate bird on branch **Designer:** Mike Hibbert

Date	Mintage	F	VF	XF	Unc	BU
1979	90,000	—	—	0.15	0.50	1.00
1979 Proof	10,000	Value: 1.00				
1992	—	—	—	0.15	0.50	1.00

KM# 1a CENT

2.6000 g., Bronze-Plated Steel, 17.5 mm. **Obv:** National arms **Rev:** Frigate bird on branch **Designer:** Mike Hibbert

Date	Mintage	F	VF	XF	Unc	BU
1992	—	—	—	—	0.50	1.00

KM# 2 2 CENTS

5.2000 g., Bronze, 21.6 mm. **Subject:** B'abal plant **Obv:** National arms **Rev:** B'abal plant below value **Designer:** Mike Hibbert

Date	Mintage	F	VF	XF	Unc	BU
1979	25,000	—	—	0.15	0.35	0.60
1979 Proof	10,000	Value: 1.25				
1992	—	—	—	0.15	0.35	0.60

KM# 3 5 CENTS

2.7300 g., Copper-Nickel, 19.3 mm. **Subject:** Tokai lizard **Obv:** National arms **Rev:** Lizard below value **Edge:** Reeded **Designer:** Mike Hibbert

Date	Mintage	F	VF	XF	Unc	BU
1979	20,000	—	0.15	0.30	1.50	2.50
1979 Proof	10,000	Value: 2.75				

KM# 3a 5 CENTS

Copper-Nickel-Plated Steel, 19.3 mm. **Obv:** National arms **Rev:** Lizard below value **Designer:** Mike Hibbert

Date	Mintage	F	VF	XF	Unc	BU
1992	—	—	—	—	1.50	2.00

KM# 40 5 CENTS

4.2400 g., Brass, 22.9 mm. **Obv:** National arms **Rev:** Gorilla **Edge:** Reeded

Date	Mintage	F	VF	XF	Unc	BU
2003	—	—	—	—	1.00	1.50

KM# 4 10 CENTS

5.7000 g., Copper-Nickel, 23.6 mm. **Subject:** Bread fruit **Obv:** National arms **Rev:** Bread fruit above value **Designer:** Mike Hibbert

Date	Mintage	F	VF	XF	Unc	BU
1979	20,000	—	0.15	0.25	1.25	1.50
1979 Proof	10,000	Value: 3.00				

KM# 5 20 CENTS

11.1500 g., Copper-Nickel, 28.45 mm. **Subject:** Dolphins **Obv:** National arms **Rev:** Dolphins above value **Designer:** Mike Hibbert

Date	Mintage	F	VF	XF	Unc	BU
1979	20,000	—	0.60	1.50	6.00	8.00
1979 Proof	10,000	Value: 9.00				

KM# 6 50 CENTS

15.4000 g., Copper-Nickel, 31.65 mm. **Subject:** Panda nut **Obv:** National arms **Rev:** Panda nut above value **Designer:** Mike Hibbert

Date	Mintage	F	VF	XF	Unc	BU
1979	20,000	—	0.50	1.00	3.00	4.50
1979 Proof	10,000	Value: 6.50				

KM# 7 DOLLAR

11.7000 g., Copper-Nickel, 30 mm. **Subject:** Outrigger sailboat **Obv:** National arms **Rev:** Outrigger sailboat above written value **Shape:** 12-sided **Designer:** Mike Hibbert

Date	Mintage	F	VF	XF	Unc	BU
1979	20,000	—	0.85	1.25	4.00	5.00
1979 Proof	10,000	Value: 8.00				

KM# 14 2 DOLLARS
Nickel-Brass **Subject:** 10th Anniversary of Independence **Obv:** National arms above message within ribbon **Rev:** Meeting house with shell at lower left **Designer:** Mike Hibbert

Date	Mintage	F	VF	XF	Unc	BU
1989	—	—	—	—	5.00	6.50

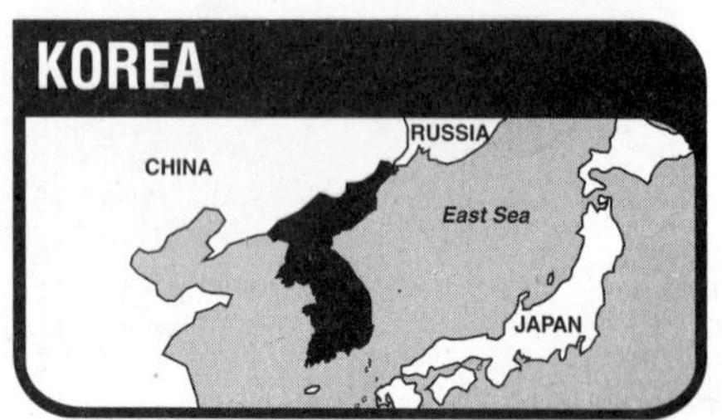

Korea, 'Land of the Morning Calm', occupies a mountainous peninsula in northeast Asia bounded by Manchuria, the Yellow Sea and the Sea of Japan.

According to legend, the first Korean dynasty, that of the House of Tangun, ruled from 2333 B.C. to 1122 B.C. It was followed by the dynasty of Kija, a Chinese scholar, which continued until 193 B.C. and brought a high civilization to Korea. The first recorded period in the history of Korea, the period of the Three Kingdoms, lasted from 57 B.C. to 935 A.D. and achieved the first political unification of the peninsula. The Kingdom of Koryo, from which Korea derived its name, was founded in 935 and continued until 1392, when it was superseded by the Yi Dynasty of King Yi. Sung Kye was to last until the Japanese annexation in 1910.

At the end of the 16th century Korea was invaded and occupied for 7 years by Japan, and from 1627 until the late 19th century it was a semi-independent tributary of China. Japan replaced China as the predominant foreign influence at the end of the Sino-Japanese War (1894-95), only to find her position threatened by Russian influence from 1896 to 1904. The Russian threat was eliminated by the Russo-Japanese War (1904-05) and in 1905 Japan established a direct protectorate over Korea. On Aug. 22,1910, the last Korean ruler signed the treaty that annexed Korea to Japan as a government generalcy in the Japanese Empire. Japanese suzerainty was maintained until the end of World War II.

From 1633 to 1891 the monetary system of Korea employed cast coins with a square center hole. Fifty-two agencies were authorized to procure these coins from a lesser number of coin foundries. They exist in thousands of varieties. Seed, or mother coins, were used to make the impressions in the molds in which the regular cash coins were cast. Czarist-Russian Korea experimented with Korean coins when Alexiev of Russia, Korea's Financial Advisor, founded the First Asian Branch of the Russo-Korean Bank on March 1, 1898, and authorized the issuing of a set of new Korean coins with a crowned Russian-style quasi-eagle. British-Japanese opposition and the Russo-Japanese War operated to end the Russian coinage experiment in 1904.

RULERS

Yi Hyong (Kojong), 1864-1897
as Emperor Kuang Mu, 1897-1907
Japanese Puppet
Yung Hi (Sunjong), 1907-1910

DATING

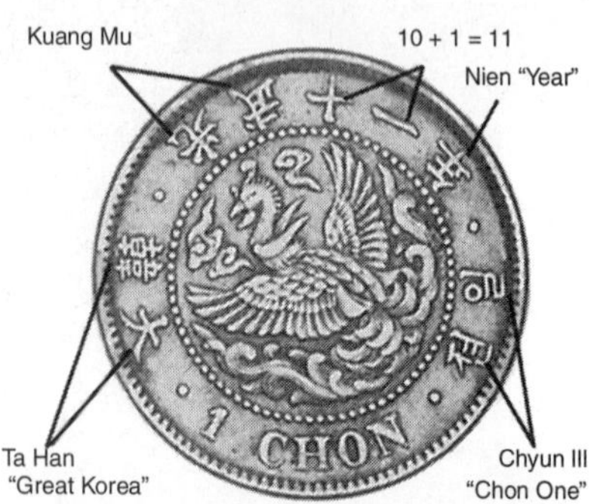

JAPANESE PROTECTORATE

MILLED COINAGE

Coinage Reform of 1902

KM# 1124 1/2 CHON
3.5600 g., Bronze, 22 mm. **Ruler:** Kuang Mu **Obv:** Imperial eagle left within beaded circle **Rev:** Value within wreath below flower

Date	Mintage	F	VF	XF	Unc	BU
10 (1906)	24,000,000	5.00	15.00	50.00	150	—

KM# 1145 1/2 CHON
2.1000 g., Bronze **Ruler:** Kuang Mu

Date	Mintage	F	VF	XF	Unc	BU
11 (1907) Rare	Est. 800,000	—	—	—	—	—

KM# 1136 1/2 CHON
2.1000 g., Bronze, 19 mm. **Ruler:** Yung Hi (Sunjong) **Obv:** Imperial eagle facing left within beaded circle **Rev:** Value within wreath below flower

Date	Mintage	F	VF	XF	Unc	BU
1 (1907)	Inc. above	175	300	600	1,000	—
Note: Mintage for year 1 is included in the mintage for Year 11 of KM#1124						
2 (1908)	21,000,000	10.00	30.00	65.00	250	—
3 (1909)	8,200,000	10.00	30.00	65.00	250	—
4 (1910)	5,070,000	100	300	700	1,000	—

KM# 1125 CHON
7.1300 g., Bronze, 28 mm. **Ruler:** Kuang Mu **Obv:** Imperial eagle facing left within beaded circle **Rev:** Value within wreath below flower

Date	Mintage	F	VF	XF	Unc	BU
9 (1905)	11,800,000	12.50	25.00	50.00	200	—
10 (1906)	Inc. above	10.00	20.00	50.00	200	—

KM# 1132 CHON
4.2000 g., Bronze, 23.5 mm. **Ruler:** Kuang Mu **Obv:** Imperial eagle facing left within beaded circle **Rev:** Value within wreath below flower

Date	Mintage	F	VF	XF	Unc	BU
11 (1907)	11,200,000	6.00	12.00	30.00	150	—

KM# 1137 CHON
4.2000 g., Bronze, 24 mm. **Ruler:** Yung Hi (Sunjong) **Obv:** Imperial eagle facing left within beaded circle **Rev:** Value within wreath below flower

Date	Mintage	F	VF	XF	Unc	BU
1 (1907)	Inc. above	8.00	20.00	50.00	180	—
2 (1908)	6,800,000	6.00	15.00	35.00	140	—
3 (1909)	9,200,000	6.00	15.00	30.00	140	—
4 (1910)	3,500,000	8.00	18.00	45.00	180	—

KM# 1126 5 CHON
4.5000 g., Copper-Nickel, 21 mm. **Ruler:** Kuang Mu **Obv:** Imperial eagle facing left within beaded circle **Rev:** Value within wreath below flower

Date	Mintage	F	VF	XF	Unc	BU
9 (1905)	20,000,000	12.50	30.00	60.00	150	—
9 (1905) Proof	—	Value: 1,500				
11 (1907)	160,000,000	15.00	35.00	75.00	200	—

KM# 1138 5 CHON
4.5000 g., Copper-Nickel, 21 mm. **Ruler:** Yung Hi (Sunjong)

Date	Mintage	F	VF	XF	Unc	BU
3 (1909)	—	1,200	2,300	4,000	5,000	—

KM# 1127 10 CHON
2.7000 g., 0.8000 Silver 0.0694 oz. ASW, 18 mm. **Ruler:** Kuang Mu **Obv:** Dragon within beaded circle **Rev:** Value within wreath below flower **Note:** 1.5 millimeters thick

Date	Mintage	F	VF	XF	Unc	BU
10 (1906)	2,000,000	24.00	45.00	80.00	200	—

KM# 1133 10 CHON
2.0250 g., 0.8000 Silver 0.0521 oz. ASW, 18 mm. **Ruler:** Kuang Mu **Obv:** Dragon within beaded circle **Rev:** Value within wreath below flower **Note:** 1.0 millimeters thick

Date	Mintage	F	VF	XF	Unc	BU
11 (1907)	2,400,000	28.00	50.00	125	300	—

KM# 1139 10 CHON
2.2500 g., 0.8000 Silver 0.0579 oz. ASW **Ruler:** Yung Hi (Sunjong) **Obv:** Dragon within beaded circle **Rev:** Value within wreath below flower

Date	Mintage	F	VF	XF	Unc	BU
2 (1908)	6,300,000	20.00	40.00	65.00	200	—
3 (1909) Rare	—	—	—	—	—	—
4 (1910)	9,500,000	20.00	35.00	60.00	150	—

KM# 1128 20 CHON
5.3900 g., 0.8000 Silver 0.1386 oz. ASW, 22 mm. **Ruler:** Kuang Mu **Obv:** Dragon within beaded circle **Rev:** Value within wreath below flower

Date	Mintage	F	VF	XF	Unc	BU
9 (1905)	1,000,000	50.00	100	200	400	—
9 (1905) Proof	—	Value: 2,250				
10 (1906)	2,500,000	45.00	65.00	175	350	—
10 (1906) Proof	—	Value: 1,275				

KM# 1134 20 CHON
4.0500 g., 0.8000 Silver 0.1042 oz. ASW, 20 mm. **Ruler:** Kuang Mu **Obv:** Dragon within beaded circle **Rev:** Value within wreath below flower

Date	Mintage	F	VF	XF	Unc	BU
11 (1907)	1,500,000	30.00	60.00	125	300	—

KM# 1140 20 CHON
4.0500 g., 0.8000 Silver 0.1042 oz. ASW, 20 mm. **Ruler:** Yung Hi (Sunjong) **Obv:** Dragon within beaded circle **Rev:** Value within wreath below flower

Date	Mintage	F	VF	XF	Unc	BU
2 (1908)	3,000,000	27.00	50.00	100	250	—
3 (1909)	2,000,000	27.00	50.00	100	250	—
4 (1910)	2,000,000	27.00	50.00	100	250	—

KM# 1129 1/2 WON
13.4800 g., 0.8000 Silver 0.3467 oz. ASW, 31 mm. **Ruler:** Kuang Mu **Obv:** Dragon within beaded circle **Rev:** Value within wreath below flower

Date	Mintage	F	VF	XF	Unc	BU
9 (1905)	600,000	100	200	300	600	—
9 (1905) Proof	—	Value: 1,850				
10 (1906)	1,200,000	100	200	300	600	—

KM# 1135 1/2 WON
10.1300 g., 0.8000 Silver 0.2605 oz. ASW, 26.5 mm. **Ruler:** Kuang Mu **Obv:** Dragon within beaded circle **Rev:** Value within wreath below flower

Date	Mintage	F	VF	XF	Unc	BU
11 (1907)	1,000,000	100	200	350	800	—

KM# 1141 1/2 WON
10.1300 g., 0.8000 Silver 0.2605 oz. ASW, 26 mm. **Ruler:** Yung Hi (Sunjong) **Obv:** Dragon within beaded circle **Rev:** Value within wreath below flower

Date	Mintage	F	VF	XF	Unc	BU
2 (1908)	1,400,000	100	200	350	700	—

KINGDOM

MILLED COINAGE

Coinage Reform of 1902

KM# 1116 5 FUN
17.2000 g., Copper **Ruler:** Kuang Mu **Obv:** Encircled dragons within circle **Rev:** Value within wreath below flower

Date	Mintage	F	VF	XF	Unc	BU
6 (1902)	—	10.00	25.00	50.00	150	—

KM# 1117 1/4 YANG
Copper-Nickel **Ruler:** Kuang Mu **Obv:** Dragon within beaded circle **Rev:** Value within wreath below flower

Date	Mintage	F	VF	XF	Unc	BU
5 (1901)	—	200	350	600	1,350	—

RUSSIAN DOMINATION

MILLED COINAGE

Coinage Reform of 1902

KM# 1121 CHON
6.8000 g., Bronze **Ruler:** Kuang Mu **Obv:** Crowned imperial eagle within beaded circle **Rev:** Value within wreath below flower

Date	Mintage	F	VF	XF	Unc	BU
6 (1902)	3,001,000	2,000	4,000	6,750	11,000	—

KM# 1122 5 CHON
4.3000 g., Copper-Nickel **Ruler:** Kuang Mu **Obv:** Crowned imperial eagle within beaded circle **Rev:** Value within wreath below flower

Date	Mintage	F	VF	XF	Unc	BU
6 (1902)	2,800,000	1,500	2,850	4,850	7,500	—

KM# 1123 1/2 WON
13.5000 g., 0.8000 Silver 0.3472 oz. ASW **Ruler:** Kuang Mu **Obv:** Crowned imperial eagle within beaded circle **Rev:** Value within wreath below flower

Date	Mintage	F	VF	XF	Unc	BU
5 (1901)	1,831,000	3,000	7,000	12,500	17,500	—

Note: Ponterio & Assoc. Witte Museum sale 8-89 choice BU realized $12,500; Heritage Piedmont sale 6-2000 choice BU realized $18,400

KOREA-NORTH

The Democratic Peoples Republic of Korea, situated in northeastern Asia on the northern half of the Korean peninsula between the Peoples Republic of China and the Republic of Korea, has an area of 46,540 sq. mi. (120,540 sq. km.) and a population of 20 million. Capital: Pyongyang. The economy is based on heavy industry and agriculture. Metals, minerals and farm produce are exported.

Japan replaced China as the predominant foreign influence in Korea in 1895 and annexed the peninsular country in 1910. Defeat in World War II brought an end to Japanese rule. U.S. troops entered Korea from the south and Soviet forces entered from the north. The Cairo conference (1943) had established that Korea should be *free and independent.* The Potsdam conference (1945) set the 38th parallel as the line dividing the occupation forces of the United States and Russia. When Russia refused to permit a U.N. commission designated to supervise reunification elections to enter North Korea, an election was held in South Korea which established the Republic of Korea on Aug. 15,1948. North Korea held an unsupervised election on Aug. 25, 1948, and on Sept. 9, 1948, proclaimed the establishment of the Democratic Peoples Republic of Korea.

NOTE: For earlier coinage see Korea.

MONETARY SYSTEM
100 Chon = 1 Won

MINT:
Pyongyang

CIRCULATION RESTRICTIONS
W/o star: KM#1-4 - General circulation
1 star: KM#5-8 - Issued to visitors from Communist countries.
2 stars: KM#9-12 - Issued to visitors from hard currency countries.

PEOPLES REPUBLIC

DECIMAL COINAGE

KM# 183 1/2 CHON
2.1600 g., Aluminum, 27.02 mm. **Obv:** State arms **Rev:** Horse **Edge:** Plain

Date	Mintage	F	VF	XF	Unc	BU
2002	—	—	—	—	1.25	1.50

KM# 184 1/2 CHON
2.1600 g., Aluminum, 27.02 mm. **Obv:** State arms **Rev:** Orangutan **Edge:** Plain

Date	Mintage	F	VF	XF	Unc	BU
2002	—	—	—	—	1.25	1.50

KM# 185 1/2 CHON
2.1600 g., Aluminum, 27.02 mm. **Obv:** State arms **Rev:** Leopard **Edge:** Plain

Date	Mintage	F	VF	XF	Unc	BU
2002	—	—	—	—	1.25	1.50

KM# 186 1/2 CHON
2.1600 g., Aluminum, 27.02 mm. **Obv:** State arms **Rev:** Two giraffes **Edge:** Plain

Date	Mintage	F	VF	XF	Unc	BU
2002	—	—	—	—	1.25	1.50

KM# 187 1/2 CHON

2.1600 g., Aluminum, 27.02 mm. **Obv:** State arms **Rev:** Helmeted guineafowl **Edge:** Plain

Date	Mintage	F	VF	XF	Unc	BU
2002	—	—	—	—	1.25	1.50

KM# 188 1/2 CHON

2.1600 g., Aluminum, 27.02 mm. **Obv:** State arms **Rev:** Mamushi pit viper **Edge:** Plain

Date	Mintage	F	VF	XF	Unc	BU
2002	—	—	—	—	1.25	1.50

KM# 189 1/2 CHON

2.1600 g., Aluminum, 27.02 mm. **Obv:** State arms **Rev:** Bighorn sheep **Edge:** Plain

Date	Mintage	F	VF	XF	Unc	BU
2002	—	—	—	—	1.25	1.50

KM# 190 1/2 CHON

2.1600 g., Aluminum, 27.02 mm. **Obv:** State arms **Rev:** Hippopotamus **Edge:** Plain

Date	Mintage	F	VF	XF	Unc	BU
2002	—	—	—	—	1.25	1.50

KM# 191 1/2 CHON

2.1600 g., Aluminum, 27.02 mm. **Subject:** FAO **Obv:** State arms **Rev:** Ancient ship **Edge:** Plain

Date	Mintage	F	VF	XF	Unc	BU
2002	—	—	—	—	1.25	1.50

KM# 192 1/2 CHON

2.1600 g., Aluminum, 27.02 mm. **Subject:** FAO **Obv:** State arms **Rev:** Archaic ship **Edge:** Plain

Date	Mintage	F	VF	XF	Unc	BU
2002	—	—	—	—	1.25	1.50

KM# 193 1/2 CHON

2.1600 g., Aluminum, 27.02 mm. **Subject:** FAO **Obv:** State arms **Rev:** Modern train **Edge:** Plain

Date	Mintage	F	VF	XF	Unc	BU
2002	—	—	—	—	1.25	1.50

KM# 194 1/2 CHON

2.1600 g., Aluminum, 27.02 mm. **Subject:** FAO **Obv:** State arms **Rev:** Jet airliner **Edge:** Plain

Date	Mintage	F	VF	XF	Unc	BU
2002	—	—	—	—	1.25	1.50

KM# 1 CHON

0.6400 g., Aluminum, 16 mm. **Obv:** National arms **Rev:** Value

Date	Mintage	F	VF	XF	Unc	BU
1959	—	0.15	0.25	0.50	1.00	—
1970	—	0.20	0.35	0.75	1.50	—

KM# 5 CHON

0.6200 g., Aluminum, 16 mm. **Obv:** National arms within circle **Rev:** Value flanked by stars

Date	Mintage	F	VF	XF	Unc	BU
1959	—	—	—	0.50	1.00	—

KM# 9 CHON

Aluminum, 16 mm. **Obv:** National arms within circle **Rev:** Star to left of value

Date	Mintage	F	VF	XF	Unc	BU
1959	—	—	—	0.50	1.00	—

KM# 195 CHON

4.6300 g., Brass, 21.7 mm. **Subject:** FAO **Obv:** State arms **Rev:** Antique steam locomotive **Edge:** Plain

Date	Mintage	F	VF	XF	Unc	BU
2002	—	—	—	—	1.50	1.75

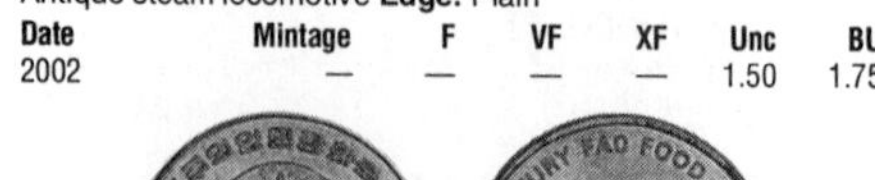

KM# 196 CHON

4.6300 g., Brass, 21.7 mm. **Subject:** FAO **Obv:** State arms **Rev:** Antique automobile **Edge:** Plain

Date	Mintage	F	VF	XF	Unc	BU
2002	—	—	—	—	1.50	1.75

KM# 197 2 CHON

6.0400 g., Copper Nickel, 24.2 mm. **Subject:** FAO **Obv:** State arms **Rev:** Antique touring car **Edge:** Plain

Date	Mintage	F	VF	XF	Unc	BU
2002	—	—	—	—	2.00	2.50

KM# 2 5 CHON

0.8100 g., Aluminum, 18 mm. **Obv:** National arms within circle **Rev:** Value

Date	Mintage	F	VF	XF	Unc	BU
1959	—	0.50	0.75	1.00	2.00	—
1974	—	0.25	0.50	1.00	2.00	—

KM# 6 5 CHON

Aluminum, 18 mm. **Obv:** National arms within circle **Rev:** Value flanked by stars

Date	Mintage	F	VF	XF	Unc	BU
1974	—	—	—	1.00	2.00	—

KM# 10 5 CHON

Aluminum, 18 mm. **Obv:** National arms within circle **Rev:** Star to left of value

Date	Mintage	F	VF	XF	Unc	BU
1974	—	—	—	1.00	2.00	—

KM# 3 10 CHON

0.9500 g., Aluminum, 20 mm. **Obv:** National arms within circle **Rev:** Value

Date	Mintage	F	VF	XF	Unc	BU
1959	—	0.50	0.75	1.00	2.00	—

KM# 7 10 CHON

Aluminum, 20 mm. **Obv:** National arms within circle **Rev:** Value flanked by stars

Date	Mintage	F	VF	XF	Unc	BU
1959	—	—	—	1.00	2.00	—

KM# 11 10 CHON

Aluminum, 20 mm. **Obv:** National arms within circle **Rev:** Star to left of value

Date	Mintage	F	VF	XF	Unc	BU
1959	—	—	—	1.00	2.00	—

KM# 4 50 CHON

2.0100 g., Aluminum, 25 mm. **Obv:** National arms within circle above value **Rev:** Leaping equestrian within radiant sun

Date	Mintage	F	VF	XF	Unc	BU
1978	—	0.75	1.00	1.75	3.00	—

KM# 8 50 CHON

Aluminum, 25 mm. **Obv:** National arms within circle above value **Rev:** Leaping equestrian divides stars within radiant sun

Date	Mintage	F	VF	XF	Unc	BU
1978	—	—	—	1.75	3.00	—

KM# 12 50 CHON

Aluminum, 25 mm. **Obv:** National arms within circle above value **Rev:** Star to left of leaping equestrian within radiant sun

Date	Mintage	F	VF	XF	Unc	BU
1978	—	—	—	1.75	3.00	—

KM# 13 WON

Copper-Nickel **Obv:** National arms above date **Rev:** Kim Il Sung's birthplace among radiant sun

Date	Mintage	F	VF	XF	Unc	BU
1987	—	—	—	—	4.00	—
1987 Proof	—	Value: 5.00				

KM# 18 WON

2.3200 g., Aluminum, 27 mm. **Obv:** National arms above date **Rev:** Palace

Date	Mintage	F	VF	XF	Unc	BU
1987	—	—	—	—	3.50	—

KM# 14 WON

Copper-Nickel **Obv:** National arms above value divides date **Rev:** Kim Il Sung's Arch of Triumph within beaded circle

Date	Mintage	F	VF	XF	Unc	BU
1987	—	—	—	—	4.00	—
1987 Proof	—	Value: 5.00				

KM# 15 WON

Copper-Nickel **Obv:** National arms above value **Rev:** Kim Il Sung's Tower of Juche within beaded circle

Date	Mintage	F	VF	XF	Unc	BU
1987	—	—	—	—	4.00	—
1987 Proof	—	Value: 5.00				

KM# 425 10 WON

1.6700 g., Aluminum, 23 mm. **Obv:** State arms **Rev:** Value

Date	Mintage	F	VF	XF	Unc	BU
JU94(2005)	—	—	—	—	1.00	1.25

KM# 426 50 WON

2.0100 g., Aluminum, 25 mm. **Obv:** State arms **Rev:** Value

Date	Mintage	F	VF	XF	Unc	BU
JU94(2005)	—	—	—	—	1.20	1.50

KM# 427 100 WON

2.2700 g., Aluminum, 27 mm. **Obv:** State arms **Rev:** Value

Date	Mintage	F	VF	XF	Unc	BU
JU94(2005)	—	—	—	—	1.35	1.75

KOREA-SOUTH

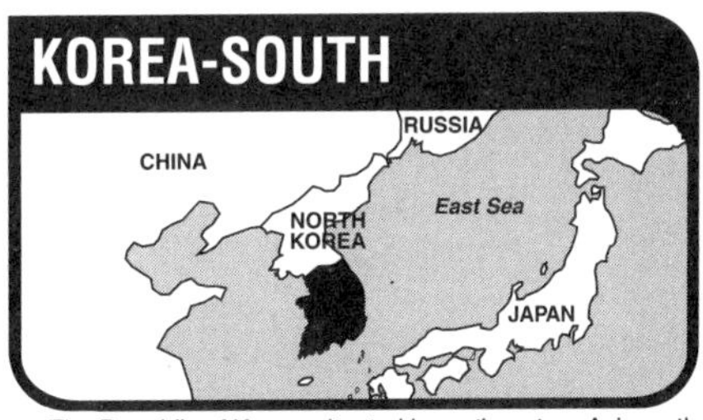

The Republic of Korea, situated in northeastern Asia on the southern half of the Korean peninsula between North Korea and the Korean Strait, has an area of 38,025 sq. mi. (98,480 sq. km.) and a population of 42.5 million. Capital: Seoul. The economy is based on agriculture and light and medium industry. Some of the world's largest oil tankers are built here. Automobiles, plywood, electronics, and textile products are exported.

Japan replaced China as the predominant foreign influence in Korea in 1895 and annexed the peninsular country in 1910. Defeat in World War II brought an end to Japanese rule. U.S. troops entered Korea from the south and Soviet forces entered from the north. The Cairo conference (1943) had established that Korea should be *free and independent*. The Potsdam conference (1945) set the 38th parallel as the line dividing the occupation forces of the United States and Russia. When Russia refused to permit a U.N. commission designated to supervise reunification elections to enter North Korea, an election was held in South Korea on May 10, 1948. By its determination, the Republic of Korea was inaugurated on Aug. 15,1948.

NOTE: For earlier coinage see Korea.

MONETARY SYSTEM

100 Chon = 1 Hwan

REPUBLIC

DECIMAL COINAGE

KM# 1 10 HWAN

2.4600 g., Bronze, 19.1 mm. **Obv:** Value **Rev:** Rose of Sharon

Date	Mintage	F	VF	XF	Unc	BU
KE4292(1959)	100,000,000	2.00	4.00	15.00	25.00	75.00
Note: Issued 10-20-59						
KE4294(1961)	100,000,000	0.30	0.70	1.00	2.50	3.00

KM# 2 50 HWAN

3.6900 g., Nickel-Brass, 22.86 mm. **Obv:** Value **Rev:** Iron-clad turtle boat

Date	Mintage	F	VF	XF	Unc	BU
KE4292(1959)	24,640,000	0.60	1.00	2.00	3.00	5.00
Note: Issued 10-20-59						
KE4294(1961)	20,000,000	0.60	1.00	2.00	3.00	5.00

KM# 3 100 HWAN

6.7400 g., Copper-Nickel, 26 mm. **Obv:** Value flanked by phoenix **Rev:** Bust left

Date	Mintage	F	VF	XF	Unc	BU
KE4292(1959)	—	2.00	3.00	4.00	10.00	15.00

Note: Issued 10-30-59. Quantities of KM#1-3 dated 4292 in uncirculated condition were countermarked "SAMPLE" in Korean for distribution to government and banking agencies. See bank samples section at end of listing. KM#3 was withdrawn from circulation June 10, 1962, and melted; KM#1 and KM#2 continued to circulate as 1 Won and 5 Won coins for 13 years, respectively, until demonetized and withdrawn from circulation March 22, 1975.

REFORM COINAGE

10 Hwan = 1 Won

KM# 4 WON

1.7000 g., Brass, 17.2 mm. **Obv:** Rose of Sharon **Rev:** Inscription, value and date

Date	Mintage	F	VF	XF	Unc	BU
1966	7,000,000	0.25	0.50	1.00	9.00	20.00
Note: Issued 8-16-66						
1967	48,500,000	0.10	0.25	0.50	1.50	2.50

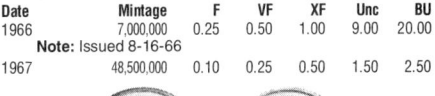

KM# 4a WON

0.7290 g., Aluminum, 17.2 mm. **Obv:** Rose of Sharon **Rev:** Inscription, value and date

Date	Mintage	F	VF	XF	Unc	BU
1968	66,500,000	—	0.25	0.50	1.00	1.50
Note: Issued 8-26-68						
1969	85,000,000	—	0.10	0.15	0.25	0.50
1970	45,000,000	—	0.10	0.15	0.25	0.50
1974	12,000,000	—	0.25	0.50	2.00	3.00
1975	10,000,000	—	0.10	0.20	0.50	1.00
1976	20,000,000	—	—	—	0.30	0.60
1977	30,000,000	—	—	—	0.30	0.60
1978	30,000,000	—	—	—	0.15	0.25
1979	30,000,000	—	—	—	0.15	0.25
1980	20,000,000	—	—	—	0.15	0.25
1981	20,000,000	—	—	—	0.15	0.25
1982	30,000,000	—	—	—	0.15	0.25
1982 Proof	2,000	—	—	—	—	—

KM# 31 WON

0.7290 g., Aluminum, 17.2 mm. **Obv:** Rose of Sharon **Rev:** Value and date

Date	Mintage	F	VF	XF	Unc	BU
1983	40,000,000	—	—	—	0.15	0.25
Note: Issued 1-15-83						
1984	20,000,000	—	—	—	0.15	0.25
1985	10,000,000	—	—	—	0.15	0.25
1987	10,000,000	—	—	—	0.15	0.25
1988	6,500,000	—	—	—	0.15	0.25
1989	10,000,000	—	—	—	0.15	0.25
1990	6,000,000	—	—	—	0.15	0.25
1991	5,000,000	—	—	—	0.15	0.25
1995	15,000	—	—	—	0.15	0.25
1996	15,000	—	—	—	0.15	0.25
1997	15,000	—	—	—	0.15	0.25

Date	Mintage	F	VF	XF	Unc	BU
1998	—	—	—	—	0.15	0.25
1999	—	—	—	—	0.15	0.25
2000	—	—	—	—	0.15	0.25
2001	—	—	—	—	0.15	0.25
2002	—	—	—	—	0.15	0.25
2003	—	—	—	—	0.15	0.25
2004	—	—	—	—	0.15	0.25
2005	—	—	—	—	0.15	0.25
2006	—	—	—	—	0.15	0.25

KM# 5 5 WON
2.9500 g., Bronze, 20.4 mm. **Obv:** Iron-clad turtle boat **Rev:** Value, inscription and date

Date	Mintage	F	VF	XF	Unc	BU
1966	4,500,000	0.15	0.25	1.50	22.50	50.00
Note: Issued 8-16-66						
1967	18,000,000	0.15	0.25	1.00	17.50	50.00
1968	20,000,000	0.15	0.25	1.00	17.50	50.00
1969	25,000,000	—	0.10	0.25	3.25	7.00
1970	50,000,000	—	0.10	0.25	3.00	5.00

KM# 5a 5 WON
2.9500 g., Brass, 20 mm. **Obv:** Iron-clad turtle boat **Rev:** Value, inscription and date

Date	Mintage	F	VF	XF	Unc	BU
1970	Inc. above	—	—	0.10	0.50	1.00
Note: Issued 7-16-70						
1971	64,038,000	—	—	—	0.10	0.20
1972	60,084,000	—	—	—	0.10	0.20
1977	1,000,000	—	—	0.10	0.65	1.00
1978	1,000,000	—	—	0.10	0.65	1.00
1979	1,000,000	—	—	0.10	0.65	1.00
1980	200,000	—	0.25	0.50	2.25	3.00
1981	200,000	—	0.25	0.50	1.50	2.00
1982	200,000	—	0.25	0.50	1.50	2.00
1982 Proof	2,000	—	—	—	—	—

KM# 32 5 WON
2.9500 g., Brass, 20.4 mm. **Obv:** Iron-clad turtle boat **Rev:** Value and date

Date	Mintage	F	VF	XF	Unc	BU
1983	6,000,000	—	—	0.10	0.20	0.30
Note: Issued 1-15-83						
1987	1,000,000	—	—	0.10	0.20	0.30
1988	500,000	—	—	0.10	0.20	0.30
1989	600,000	—	—	0.10	0.20	0.30
1990	600,000	—	—	0.10	0.20	0.30
1991	500,000	—	—	0.10	0.20	0.30
1995	15,000	—	—	0.10	0.20	0.30
1996	15,000	—	—	0.10	0.20	0.30
1997	15,000	—	—	0.10	0.20	0.30
1998	—	—	—	0.10	0.20	0.30
1999	—	—	—	0.10	0.20	0.30
2000	—	—	—	0.10	0.20	0.30
2001	—	—	—	0.10	0.20	0.30
2002	—	—	—	0.10	0.20	0.30
2003	—	—	—	0.10	0.20	0.30
2004	—	—	—	0.10	0.20	0.30
2005	—	—	—	0.10	0.20	0.30
2006	—	—	—	0.10	0.20	0.30

KM# 6 10 WON
4.0600 g., Bronze, 22.86 mm. **Obv:** Pagoda at Pul Guk Temple **Rev:** Value, inscription and date

Date	Mintage	F	VF	XF	Unc	BU
1966	10,600,000	0.15	0.25	1.50	25.00	60.00
Note: Issued 8-16-66						
1967	22,500,000	0.15	0.25	1.50	25.00	60.00
1968	35,000,000	0.15	0.25	1.50	18.50	50.00
1969	46,500,000	0.15	0.25	1.50	18.50	90.00
1970	157,000,000	0.15	0.25	1.50	16.50	130

KM# 6a 10 WON
4.0600 g., Brass, 22.86 mm. **Obv:** Pagoda at Pul Guk Temple **Rev:** Value, inscription and date

Date	Mintage	F	VF	XF	Unc	BU
1970	Inc. above	—	0.35	1.25	13.50	30.00
Note: Issued 7-16-70						
1971	220,000,000	—	—	0.15	1.75	3.00
1972	270,000,000	—	—	0.15	1.75	3.00
1973	30,000,000	—	0.10	0.35	6.50	15.00
1974	15,000,000	—	0.10	0.35	6.50	15.00
1975	20,000,000	—	0.10	0.50	11.50	30.00
1977	1,000,000	—	0.10	0.35	3.50	8.00
1978	80,000,000	—	0.10	0.15	1.25	2.00
1979	200,000,000	—	—	0.10	0.55	1.00
1980	150,000,000	—	—	0.10	0.55	1.00
1981	100,000	—	0.25	0.75	4.00	10.00
1982	20,000,000	—	—	0.10	0.60	1.10
1982 Proof	2,000	—	—	—	—	—

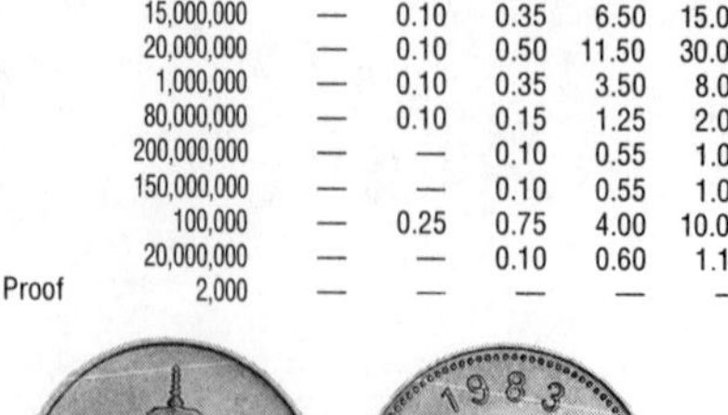

KM# 33.1 10 WON
4.0600 g., Brass, 22.86 mm. **Obv:** Pagoda at Pul Guk Temple **Rev:** Value below date

Date	Mintage	F	VF	XF	Unc	BU
1983	25,000,000	—	—	0.10	0.35	0.50
Note: Issued 1-15-83						
1985	35,000,000	—	—	0.10	0.35	0.50
1986	195,000,000	—	—	0.10	0.35	0.50
1987	155,000,000	—	—	0.10	0.35	0.50
1988	189,000,000	—	—	0.10	0.35	0.50
1989	310,000,000	—	—	0.10	0.35	0.50
1990	395,000,000	—	—	0.10	0.35	0.50
1991	300,000,000	—	—	0.10	0.35	0.50
1992	150,000,000	—	—	0.10	0.35	0.50
1993	110,000,000	—	—	0.10	0.35	0.50
1994	300,000,000	—	—	0.10	0.35	0.50
1995	380,000,000	—	—	0.10	0.35	0.50
1996	290,000,000	—	—	0.10	0.35	0.50
1997	177,000,000	—	—	0.10	0.35	0.50
1999	—	—	—	0.10	0.35	0.50
2000	—	—	—	0.10	0.35	0.50

KM# 33.2 10 WON
4.0600 g., Brass **Obv:** Pagoda at Pul Guk Temple **Rev:** Thicker value below date

Date	Mintage	F	VF	XF	Unc	BU
1991	—	—	—	0.10	0.35	0.50
1997	—	—	—	0.10	0.35	0.50
1998	—	—	—	0.10	0.35	0.50
1999	—	—	—	0.10	0.35	0.50
2000	—	—	—	0.10	0.35	0.50
2001	345,000,000	—	—	0.10	0.35	0.50
2002	100,000,000	—	—	0.10	0.35	0.50
2003	128,000,000	—	—	0.10	0.35	0.50
2004	135,000,000	—	—	0.10	0.35	0.50
2005	250,000,000	—	—	0.10	0.35	0.50

KM# 33.2a 10 WON
1.2200 g., Aluminum-Bronze, 18 mm. **Obv:** Pagoda at Pul Guk Temple **Rev:** Value below date

Date	Mintage	F	VF	XF	Unc	BU
2006	109,200,000	—	—	—	0.10	0.35
2007	—	—	—	—	0.10	0.35
2008	—	—	—	—	0.10	0.35

KM# 106 10 WON
1.3500 g., Copper Plated Aluminum, 18 mm. **Obv:** Pagoda at Pul Guk Temple **Rev:** Value below date **Edge:** Plain **Mint:** KOMSCO

Date	Mintage	F	VF	XF	Unc	BU
2006	40,800,000	—	—	0.10	0.20	0.25
2007	—	—	—	0.10	0.20	0.25

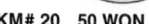

KM# 20 50 WON
4.0000 g., Copper-Nickel **Series:** F.A.O. **Obv:** Text within sagging oat sprig **Rev:** Value below date

Date	Mintage	F	VF	XF	Unc	BU
1972	6,000,000	0.20	0.40	1.00	16.50	40.00
Note: Issued 12-1-72						
1973	40,000,000	—	0.15	0.25	3.50	8.00
1974	25,000,000	—	0.15	0.25	1.50	3.00
1977	1,000,000	—	0.15	0.25	2.00	3.50
1978	15,000,000	—	0.15	0.25	1.25	2.50
1979	20,000,000	—	0.10	0.20	1.25	2.00
1980	10,000,000	—	0.10	0.20	1.25	2.00
1981	25,000,000	—	0.10	0.20	1.25	2.00
1982	40,000,000	—	0.10	0.20	0.75	1.50
1982 Proof	2,000	—	—	—	—	—

KM# 34 50 WON
4.1600 g., Copper-Nickel, 21.16 mm. **Series:** F.A.O. **Obv:** Text below sagging oat sprig **Rev:** Value and date **Note:** Die varieties exist.

Date	Mintage	F	VF	XF	Unc	BU
1983	50,000,000	—	—	0.10	0.45	1.00
Note: Issued 1-15-83						
1984	40,000,000	—	—	0.10	0.45	1.00
1985	4,000,000	—	—	0.10	0.45	1.00
1987	32,000,000	—	—	0.10	0.45	1.00
1988	53,000,000	—	—	0.10	0.45	1.00
1989	70,000,000	—	—	0.10	0.45	0.60
1990	85,000,000	—	—	0.10	0.35	0.60
1991	80,000,000	—	—	0.10	0.35	0.60
1992	50,000,000	—	—	0.10	0.35	0.60
1993	5,000,000	—	—	0.10	0.35	0.50
1994	102,000,000	—	—	0.10	0.35	0.50
1995	98,000,000	—	—	0.10	0.35	0.50
1996	52,000,000	—	—	0.10	0.35	0.50
1997	129,000,000	—	—	0.10	0.35	0.50
1998	—	—	—	0.10	0.35	0.50
1999	—	—	—	0.10	0.35	0.50
2000	—	—	—	0.10	0.35	0.50
2001	102,000,000	—	—	0.10	0.35	0.50
2002	10,000,000	—	—	0.10	0.35	0.50
2003	169,000,000	—	—	0.10	0.35	0.50
2004	100,000,000	—	—	0.10	0.45	1.00
2005	90,000,000	—	—	0.10	0.35	0.50
2006	120,000,000	—	—	0.10	0.35	0.50
2007	50,000,000	—	—	0.10	0.35	0.50
2008	—	—	—	0.10	0.35	0.50

KM# 9 100 WON
5.4200 g., Copper-Nickel, 24 mm. **Obv:** Bust with hat facing **Rev:** Value and date within designed wreath

Date	Mintage	F	VF	XF	Unc	BU
1970	1,500,000	0.50	0.75	1.50	18.50	50.00
Note: Issued 11-30-70						
1971	13,000,000	0.15	0.25	0.50	13.50	45.00
1972	20,000,000	—	0.20	0.40	11.50	40.00
1973	80,000,000	—	0.15	0.30	3.00	5.00
1974	50,000,000	—	0.15	0.35	4.50	10.00
Note: Die varieties exist						
1975	75,000,000	—	0.15	0.35	6.00	15.00
Note: Die varieties exist						
1977	30,000,000	—	0.15	0.35	2.25	5.00
1978	50,000,000	—	0.15	0.25	1.50	3.00
1979	130,000,000	—	0.15	0.25	1.50	3.00
1980	60,000,000	—	0.15	0.25	1.50	3.00
1981	100,000	—	0.25	0.50	4.00	6.50
1982	70,000,000	—	0.15	0.25	1.25	2.00
1982 Proof	2,000	—	—	—	—	—

KM# 21 100 WON
12.0000 g., Copper-Nickel, 30 mm. **Subject:** 30th Anniversary of Liberation **Obv:** Gate of Liberty **Rev:** Standing figures and value

Date	Mintage	F	VF	XF	Unc	BU
ND(1975)	4,998,000	0.30	0.60	0.90	2.25	—
Note: Issued 8-15-75						
ND(1975) Proof	2,000	Value: 170				

KM# 24 100 WON
12.0000 g., Copper-Nickel, 30 mm. **Subject:** 1st Anniversary of the 5th Republic **Obv:** Yin-yang symbol within rectangle above value flanked by flames **Rev:** Cluster of flowers

Date	Mintage	F	VF	XF	Unc	BU
1981	4,980,000	0.20	0.35	0.65	2.00	—
Note: Issued 8-81						
1981 Unfrosted, Proof	18,000	Value: 25.00				
1981 Proof	2,000	Value: 165				

KM# 35.1 100 WON
5.4200 g., Copper-Nickel, 24 mm. **Obv:** Bust with hat facing **Rev:** Value and date

Date	Mintage	F	VF	XF	Unc	BU
1983	8,000,000	—	0.15	0.25	0.60	1.00
Note: Issued 1-15-83						

KM# 35.2 100 WON
5.4200 g., Copper-Nickel, 24 mm. **Obv:** Bust with hat facing **Rev:** Value and date

Date	Mintage	F	VF	XF	Unc	BU
1984	40,000,000	—	0.15	0.25	0.60	1.00
Note: Issued 1-15-83						
1985	25,000,000	—	0.15	0.30	1.25	3.00
1986	131,000,000	—	0.15	0.25	0.60	1.00
1987	170,000,000	—	0.15	0.25	0.55	0.75
1988	298,000,000	—	0.15	0.25	0.55	0.75
1989	250,000,000	—	0.15	0.25	0.55	0.75
1990	185,000,000	—	0.15	0.25	0.55	0.75
1991	400,000,000	—	0.15	0.25	0.55	0.75
1992	425,000,000	—	0.15	0.25	0.55	0.75
1993	185,000,000	—	0.15	0.25	0.55	0.75
1994	401,000,000	—	0.15	0.25	0.55	0.75
1995	228,000,000	—	0.15	0.25	0.55	0.75
1996	447,000,000	—	0.15	0.25	0.55	0.75
1997	147,000,000	—	0.15	0.25	0.55	0.75
1999	—	—	0.15	0.25	0.55	0.75
2000	—	—	0.15	0.25	0.55	0.75
2001	470,000,000	—	0.15	0.25	0.55	0.75
2002	490,000,000	—	0.15	0.25	0.55	0.75
2003	415,000,000	—	0.15	0.25	0.55	0.75
2004	250,000,000	—	0.15	0.25	0.55	0.75
2005	205,000,000	—	0.15	0.25	0.55	0.75
2006	310,000,000	—	0.15	0.25	0.55	0.75
2007	240,000,000	—	0.15	0.25	0.55	0.75
2008	—	—	0.15	0.25	0.55	0.75

KM# 27 500 WON
7.7000 g., Copper-Nickel, 26.5 mm. **Obv:** Manchurian crane **Rev:** Value and date

Date	Mintage	F	VF	XF	Unc	BU
1982	15,000,000	—	—	1.00	3.75	8.00
Note: Issued 6-12-82						
1982 Proof	2,000	—	—	—	—	—
1983	64,000,000	—	—	1.00	2.50	5.00
1984	70,000,000	—	—	1.00	2.50	5.00
1987	1,000,000	—	—	1.00	2.50	5.00
1988	27,000,000	—	—	1.00	2.50	5.00

Date	Mintage	F	VF	XF	Unc	BU
1989	25,000,000	—	—	1.00	2.50	5.00
1990	60,000,000	—	—	1.00	2.50	5.00
1991	90,000,000	—	—	1.00	2.50	5.00
1992	105,000,000	—	—	1.00	2.50	5.00
1993	32,000,000	—	—	1.00	2.50	5.00
1994	50,600,000	—	—	1.00	2.50	5.00
1995	87,000,000	—	—	1.00	2.50	5.00
1996	122,000,000	—	—	1.00	2.50	5.00
1997	62,000,000	—	—	1.00	2.50	5.00
1998	—	—	—	1.00	2.50	5.00
1999	—	—	—	1.00	2.50	5.00
2000	—	—	—	1.00	2.50	5.00
2001	113,000,000	—	—	1.00	2.50	5.00
2002	110,000,000	—	—	1.00	2.50	5.00
2003	122,000,000	—	—	1.00	2.50	5.00
2004	45,000,000	—	—	1.00	2.50	5.00
2005	105,000,000	—	—	1.00	2.50	5.00
2006	170,000,000	—	—	1.00	2.50	5.00
2007	70,000,000	—	—	1.00	2.50	5.00
2008	—	—	—	1.00	2.50	5.00

KM# 88 2000 WON
10.7000 g., Bi-Metallic Copper-Aluminum-Nickel center in Copper-Nickel ring, 28 mm. **Subject:** New Millennium **Obv:** Astronomical observation instrument **Rev:** Stylized design **Edge:** Reeded **Mint:** KOMSCO **Note:** Korea Minting and Security Printing Corp.

Date	Mintage	F	VF	XF	Unc	BU
2000	—	—	—	—	9.00	10.00

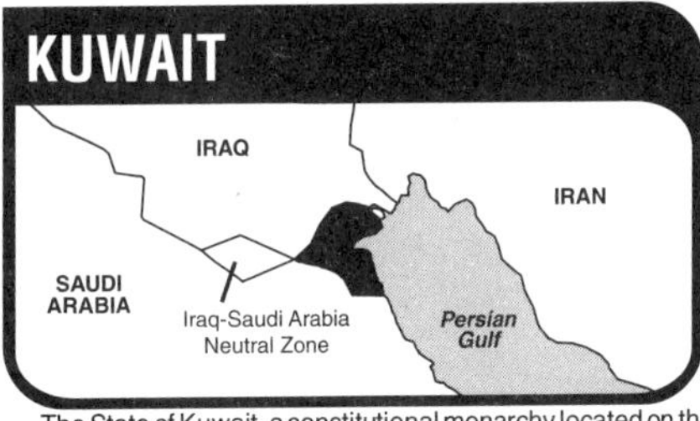

The State of Kuwait, a constitutional monarchy located on the Arabian Peninsula at the northwestern corner of the Persian Gulf, has an area of 6,880 sq. mi. (17,820 sq. km.) and a population of 1.7 million. Capital: Kuwait. Petroleum, the basis of the economy, provides 95 percent of the exports.

The modern history of Kuwait began with the founding of the city of Kuwait, 1740, by tribesmen who wandered northward from the region of the Qatar Peninsula of eastern Arabia. Fearing that the Turks would take over the sheikhdom, Sheikh Mubarak entered into an agreement with Great Britain, 1899, placing Kuwait under the protection of Britain and empowering Britain to conduct its foreign affairs. Britain terminated the protectorate on June19, 1961, giving Kuwait its independence (by a simple exchange of notes) but agreeing to furnish military aid on request.

Kuwait was invaded and occupied by an army from neighboring Iraq Aug. 2, 1990. Soon thereafter Iraq declared that the country would become a province of Iraq. An international coalition of military forces primarily based in Saudi Arabia led by the United States under terms set by the United Nations, attacked Iraqi military installations to liberate Kuwait. This occurred Jan. 17, 1991. Kuwait City was liberated Feb.27, and a cease-fire was declared Feb. 28. New paper currency was introduced March 24, 1991 to replace earlier notes.

TITLE

al-Kuwait

RULER
British Protectorate, until 1961

LOCAL
Al Sabah Dynasty
Mubarak Ibn Sabah, 1896-1915
Jabir Ibn Mubarak, 1915-1917
Salim Ibn Mubarak, 1917-1921
Ahmad Ibn Jabir, 1921-1950
Abdullah Ibn Salim, 1950-1965
Sabah Ibn Salim, 1965-1977
Jabir Ibn Ahmad, 1977-

MONETARY SYSTEM
1000 Fils = 1 Dinar

SOVEREIGN EMIRATE

MODERN COINAGE

KM# 2 FILS
2.0000 g., Nickel-Brass, 17 mm. **Ruler:** Abdullah Ibn Salim **Obv:** Value within circle **Rev:** Ship with sails

Date	Mintage	F	VF	XF	Unc	BU
AH1380-1961	2,000,000	—	0.50	1.00	1.50	—
AH1380-1961 Proof	60	Value: 30.00				

KM# 9 FILS
2.0000 g., Nickel-Brass, 17 mm. **Ruler:** Jabir Ibn Ahmad **Obv:** Value within circle **Rev:** Ship with sails

Date	Mintage	F	VF	XF	Unc	BU
AH1382-1962	500,000	—	0.10	0.15	0.35	—
AH1382-1962 Proof	60	Value: 30.00				
AH1384-1964	600,000	—	0.25	0.75	1.50	—
AH1385-1966	500,000	—	0.25	0.75	1.50	—
AH1386-1967	1,875,000	—	0.25	0.75	1.50	—
AH1389-1970	375,000	—	0.35	1.00	2.50	—
AH1390-1971	500,000	—	0.25	0.75	1.50	—
AH1391-1971	500,000	—	0.25	0.75	1.50	—
AH1392-1972	500,000	—	0.25	0.75	1.50	—
AH1393-1973	375,000	—	0.35	1.00	2.50	—
AH1395-1975	500,000	—	0.25	0.75	1.50	—
AH1396-1976	2,500,000	—	0.15	0.25	0.50	—
AH1397-1977	2,500,000	—	0.15	0.25	0.50	—
AH1399-1979	1,500,000	—	0.15	0.25	0.50	—
AH1400-1980	—	—	0.15	0.25	0.50	—
AH1403-1983	—	—	0.15	0.25	0.50	—
AH1407-1987	—	—	0.15	0.25	0.50	—
AH1408-1988	500,000	—	0.15	0.25	0.50	—

KM# 3 5 FILS
2.5000 g., Nickel-Brass, 19.5 mm. **Ruler:** Abdullah Ibn Salim **Obv:** Value within circle **Rev:** Ship with sails

Date	Mintage	F	VF	XF	Unc	BU
AH1380-1961 (1961)	2,400,000	—	0.60	1.25	2.00	—
AH1380-1961 (1961) Proof	60	Value: 35.00				

KM# 10 5 FILS
2.5000 g., Nickel-Brass, 19.5 mm. **Ruler:** Jabir Ibn Ahmad **Obv:** Value within circle **Rev:** Dhow, dates below

Date	Mintage	F	VF	XF	Unc	BU
AH1382-1962	1,800,000	—	0.10	0.20	0.45	—
AH1382-1962 Proof	60	Value: 35.00				
AH1382-1962 Proof	60	Value: 35.00				
AH1384-1964	600,000	—	0.30	0.75	2.00	—
AH1386-1967	1,600,000	—	0.20	0.35	1.00	—
AH1388-1968	800,000	—	0.30	0.75	2.25	—
AH1389-1969	—	—	0.30	0.75	2.25	—
AH1389-1970	600,000	—	0.30	0.75	2.25	—
AH1390-1971	600,000	—	0.30	0.75	2.25	—
AH1391-1971	600,000	—	0.30	0.75	2.25	—
AH1392-1972	800,000	—	0.25	0.65	1.75	—
AH1393-1973	800,000	—	0.25	0.65	1.75	—
AH1394-1974	1,200,000	—	0.10	0.20	1.00	—
AH1395-1975	5,020,000	—	0.10	0.20	0.50	—
AH1396-1976	180,000	—	0.35	1.00	3.00	—
AH1397-1977	4,000,000	—	0.10	0.20	0.40	—
AH1399-1979	6,700,000	—	0.10	0.20	0.40	—
AH1400-1980	—	—	0.10	0.20	0.40	—
AH1401-1981	7,000,000	—	0.10	0.20	0.40	—
AH1403-1983	—	—	0.10	0.20	0.40	—
AH1405-1985	—	—	0.10	0.20	0.40	—
AH1407-1987	—	—	0.10	0.20	0.40	—

Date	Mintage	F	VF	XF	Unc	BU
AH1408-1988	3,000,000	—	0.10	0.20	0.40	—
AH1410-1990	—	—	0.10	0.20	0.40	—
AH1414-1993	—	—	0.10	0.20	0.40	—
AH1415 1994	—	—	0.10	0.20	0.40	—
Note: Varieties exist						
AH1415-1995	—	—	0.10	0.20	0.40	—
AH1417-1997	—	—	0.10	0.20	0.40	—
AH1422-2001	—	—	0.10	0.20	0.40	—
AH1424-2003	—	—	0.10	0.20	0.40	—
AH1426-2005	—	—	0.10	0.20	0.40	—

KM# 4 10 FILS

3.7500 g., Nickel-Brass, 21 mm. **Ruler:** Abdullah Ibn Salim **Obv:** Value within circle **Rev:** Ship with sails

Date	Mintage	F	VF	XF	Unc	BU
AH1380-1961	2,600,000	—	0.65	1.25	2.00	—
AH1380-1961 Proof	60	Value: 40.00				

KM# 11 10 FILS

3.7500 g., Nickel-Brass, 21 mm. **Ruler:** Jabir Ibn Ahmad **Obv:** Value within circle **Rev:** Dhow, dates below

Date	Mintage	F	VF	XF	Unc	BU
AH1382-1962	1,360,000	—	0.15	0.25	0.65	—
AH1382-1962 Proof	60	Value: 40.00				
AH1384-1964	800,000	—	0.35	0.85	2.50	—
AH1386-1967	1,360,000	—	0.30	0.75	1.75	—
AH1388-1968	672,000	—	0.35	0.85	2.50	—
AH1389-1969	480,000	—	0.50	1.00	2.75	—
AH1389-1970	640,000	—	0.35	0.85	2.50	—
AH1390-1971	480,000	—	0.50	1.00	2.75	—
AH1391-1971	800,000	—	0.35	0.85	2.50	—
AH1392-1972	1,120,000	—	0.15	0.40	2.00	—
AH1393-1973	1,440,000	—	0.15	0.40	2.00	—
AH1394-1974	1,280,000	—	0.15	0.40	2.00	—
AH1395-1975	5,280,000	—	0.15	0.25	0.75	—
AH1396-1976	2,400,000	—	0.15	0.25	0.75	—
AH1397-1977	—	—	0.15	0.25	0.75	—
AH1399-1979	6,160,000	—	0.15	0.25	0.75	—
AH1400-1980	—	—	0.15	0.25	0.75	—
AH1401-1981	8,320,000	—	0.15	0.25	0.75	—
AH1403-1983	—	—	0.15	0.25	0.75	—
AH1405-1985	—	—	0.15	0.25	0.75	—
AH1407-1987	—	—	0.15	0.25	0.75	—
AH1408-1988	5,000,000	—	0.15	0.25	0.75	—
AH1410-1990	—	—	0.15	0.25	0.75	—
Note: Varieties exist						
AH1415-1995	—	—	0.15	0.25	0.75	—
AH1418-1998	—	—	0.15	0.25	0.75	—
AH1422-2001	—	—	0.15	0.25	0.75	—
AH1424-2003	—	—	0.15	0.25	0.75	—
AH1426-2005	—	—	0.15	0.25	0.75	—

KM# 5 20 FILS

3.0000 g., Copper-Nickel, 20 mm. **Ruler:** Abdullah Ibn Salim **Obv:** Value within circle **Rev:** Ship with sails

Date	Mintage	F	VF	XF	Unc	BU
AH1380-1961	2,000,000	—	0.75	1.50	2.50	—
AH1380-1961 Proof	60	Value: 45.00				

KM# 12 20 FILS

3.0000 g., Copper-Nickel, 20 mm. **Ruler:** Jabir Ibn Ahmad **Obv:** Value within circle **Rev:** Dhow, dates below **Note:** Varieties exist.

Date	Mintage	F	VF	XF	Unc	BU
AH1382-1962	1,200,000	—	0.25	0.35	0.75	—
AH1382-1962 Proof	60	Value: 45.00				
AH1384-1964	480,000	—	0.50	1.00	3.00	—
AH1386-1967	1,280,000	—	0.35	0.85	2.00	—
AH1388-1968	672,000	—	0.35	0.85	2.50	—
AH1389-1969	800,000	—	0.35	0.85	2.50	—
AH1389-1970	480,000	—	0.50	1.00	3.00	—
AH1390-1971	480,000	—	0.50	1.00	3.00	—
AH1391-1971	960,000	—	0.35	0.85	2.00	—
AH1392-1972	1,440,000	—	0.20	0.45	2.00	—
AH1393-1973	1,280,000	—	0.20	0.45	2.00	—
AH1394-1974	1,600,000	—	0.20	0.45	1.50	—
AH1395-1975	2,400,000	—	0.20	0.30	1.25	—
AH1396-1976	3,200,000	—	0.20	0.30	1.25	—
AH1397-1977	3,400,000	—	0.20	0.30	1.25	—
AH1399-1979	5,520,000	—	0.20	0.30	1.25	—
AH1400-1980	—	—	0.20	0.30	1.00	—
AH1401-1981	8,960,000	—	0.20	0.30	1.00	—
AH1403-1983	—	—	0.20	0.30	1.00	—
AH1405-1985	—	—	0.20	0.30	1.00	—
AH1407-1987	—	—	0.20	0.30	1.00	—
AH1408-1988	5,000,000	—	0.20	0.30	1.00	—
AH1410-1990	—	—	0.20	0.30	1.00	—
AH1415-1995	—	—	0.20	0.30	1.00	—
AH1417-1997	—	—	0.20	0.45	2.00	—
AH1424-2003	—	—	0.20	0.45	2.00	—
AH1426-2005	—	—	0.20	0.45	2.00	—

KM# 12c 20 FILS

Stainless Steel, 20 mm. **Ruler:** Jabir Ibn Ahmad **Obv:** Value **Rev:** Dhow, dates below

Date	Mintage	F	VF	XF	Unc	BU
AH1422-2001	—	—	—	—	1.00	—
AH1424-2003	—	—	—	—	1.00	—
AH1426-2005	—	—	—	—	1.00	—

KM# 6 50 FILS

4.5000 g., Copper-Nickel, 23 mm. **Ruler:** Sabah Ibn Salim **Obv:** Value within circle **Rev:** Ship with sails

Date	Mintage	F	VF	XF	Unc	BU
AH1380-1961	1,720,000	—	0.85	1.75	2.75	—
AH1380-1961 Proof	60	Value: 60.00				

KM# 13 50 FILS

4.5000 g., Copper-Nickel, 23 mm. **Ruler:** Jabir Ibn Ahmad **Obv:** Value within circle **Rev:** Dhow, dates below

Date	Mintage	F	VF	XF	Unc	BU
AH1382-1962	900,000	—	0.50	0.75	1.25	—
AH1382-1962 Proof	60	Value: 60.00				
AH1384-1964	300,000	—	0.75	1.50	4.00	—
AH1386-1966	800,000	—	0.40	0.85	2.50	—
AH1388-1968	200,000	—	1.00	2.00	6.00	—
AH1389-1969	500,000	—	0.50	1.00	3.00	—
AH1390-1970	300,000	—	0.75	1.50	4.00	—
AH1391-1971	500,000	—	0.50	1.00	3.00	—
AH1392-1972	900,000	—	0.50	0.85	2.50	—
AH1393-1973	800,000	—	0.50	0.85	2.50	—
AH1394-1974	1,000,000	—	0.35	0.50	2.00	—
AH1395-1975	1,950,000	—	0.35	0.50	2.00	—
AH1396-1976	2,250,000	—	0.25	0.35	2.00	—
AH1397-1977	6,000,000	—	0.25	0.35	1.35	—
AH1399-1979	6,050,000	—	0.25	0.35	1.35	—
AH1400-1980	—	—	0.25	0.35	1.35	—
AH1401-1981	3,000,000	—	0.25	0.35	1.35	—
AH1403-1983	—	—	0.25	0.35	1.35	—
AH1405-1985	—	—	0.25	0.35	1.35	—
AH1407-1987	2,000,000	—	0.25	0.35	1.35	—
AH1408-1988	3,000,000	—	0.25	0.35	1.35	—
AH1410-1990	—	—	0.25	0.35	1.35	—
AH1414-1993	—	—	0.25	0.35	1.35	—
AH1415-1995	—	—	0.20	0.35	1.35	—
AH1417-1997	—	—	0.25	0.35	1.35	—
AH1420-1999	—	—	0.25	0.35	1.25	—
AH1424-2003	—	—	0.25	0.35	1.00	—
AH1426-2005	—	—	0.25	0.35	1.00	—
AH1427-2006	—	—	0.25	0.35	1.00	—

KM# 7 100 FILS

6.5000 g., Copper-Nickel, 26 mm. **Ruler:** Abdullah Ibn Salim **Obv:** Value within circle **Rev:** Ship with sails

Date	Mintage	F	VF	XF	Unc	BU
AH1380-1961	1,260,000	—	1.00	2.00	3.25	—
AH1380-1961 Proof	60	Value: 90.00				

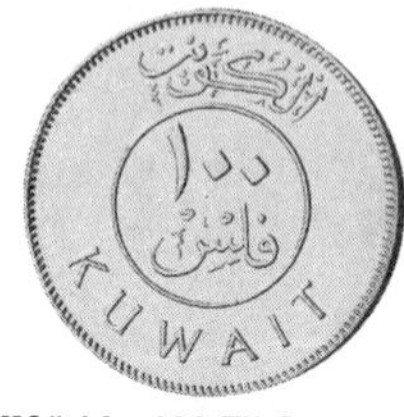

KM# 14 100 FILS

6.5000 g., Copper-Nickel, 26 mm. **Ruler:** Jabir Ibn Ahmad **Obv:** Value within circle **Rev:** Dhow, dates below

Date	Mintage	F	VF	XF	Unc	BU
AH1382-1962	640,000	—	0.50	0.65	1.50	—
AH1382-1962 Proof	60	Value: 90.00				
AH1384-1964	160,000	—	1.75	3.00	6.00	—
AH1386-1967	640,000	—	1.00	1.50	3.00	—
AH1388-1968	160,000	—	1.75	3.00	6.00	—
AH1389-1969	320,000	—	1.00	2.00	4.00	—
AH1391-1971	240,000	—	1.25	2.00	4.00	—
AH1392-1972	400,000	—	1.00	1.50	3.00	—
AH1393-1973	480,000	—	1.00	1.50	3.00	—
AH1394-1974	480,000	—	1.00	1.50	3.00	—
AH1395-1975	3,040,000	—	0.50	0.75	1.75	—
AH1396-1976	—	—	0.50	0.75	1.75	—
AH1397-1977	1,600,000	—	0.50	0.75	1.75	—
AH1399-1979	3,040,000	—	0.50	0.75	1.75	—
AH1400-1980	—	—	0.50	0.75	1.75	—
AH1401-1981	2,960,000	—	0.50	0.75	1.75	—
AH1403-1983	—	—	0.50	0.75	1.75	—
AH1405-1985	—	—	0.50	0.75	1.75	—
AH1407-1987	2,000,000	—	0.50	0.75	1.75	—
AH1408-1988	2,000,000	—	0.50	0.75	1.75	—
AH1410-1990	—	—	0.50	0.75	1.75	—
AH1415-1995	—	—	0.50	0.75	1.75	—
Note: Varieties exist						
AH1418-1998	—	—	0.50	0.75	1.75	—
AH1424-2003	—	—	0.50	0.75	1.50	—
AH1426-2005	—	—	0.50	0.75	1.50	—

KYRGYZSTAN

The Republic of Kyrgyzstan, (formerly Kirghiz S.S.R., a Union Republic of the U.S.S.R.), is an independent state since Aug. 31, 1991, a member of the United Nations and of the C.I.S. It was the last state of the Union Republics to declare its sovereignty. Capital: Bishkek (formerly Frunze).

Originally part of the autonomous Turkestan S.S.R. founded on May 1, 1918, the Kyrgyz ethnic area was established on October 14, 1924, as the Kara-Kirghiz Autonomous Region within the R.S.F.S.R. Then on May 25, 1925, the name Kara (black) was dropped. It became an A.S.S.R. on Feb. 1, 1926, and a Union Republic of the U.S.S.R. in 1936. On Dec. 12, 1990, the name was then changed to the Republic of Kyrgyzstan.

MONETARY SYSTEM

100 Tiyin = 1 Som

REPUBLIC

STANDARD COINAGE

KM# 8 TIYIN

0.9700 g., Aluminum-Bronze, 13.98 mm. **Obv:** National arms **Rev:** Flower at left of value **Edge:** Reeded

Date	Mintage	F	VF	XF	Unc	BU
2008	—	—	—	—	—	0.25

KM# 9 10 TIYIN

1.3300 g., Brass Plated Steel, 14.94 mm. **Obv:** National arms **Rev:** Flower at left of value **Edge:** Plain

Date	Mintage	F	VF	XF	Unc	BU
2008	—	—	—	—	—	0.50

KM# 10 50 TIYIN

1.8600 g., Brass Plated Steel, 16.94 mm. **Obv:** National arms **Rev:** Flower at left of value **Edge:** Plain

Date	Mintage	F	VF	XF	Unc	BU
2008	—	—	—	—	—	0.75

KM# 11 SOM

2.5700 g., Nickel Plated Steel, 18.96 mm. **Obv:** National arms **Rev:** Symbol at left of denomination **Edge:** Reeded

Date	Mintage	F	VF	XF	Unc	BU
2008	—	—	—	—	1.00	—

KM# 13 5 SOM

4.2800 g., Nickel Plated Steel, 22.95 mm. **Obv:** National arms **Rev:** Symbol at right of value **Edge:** Reeded

Date	Mintage	F	VF	XF	Unc	BU
2008	—	—	—	—	1.50	—

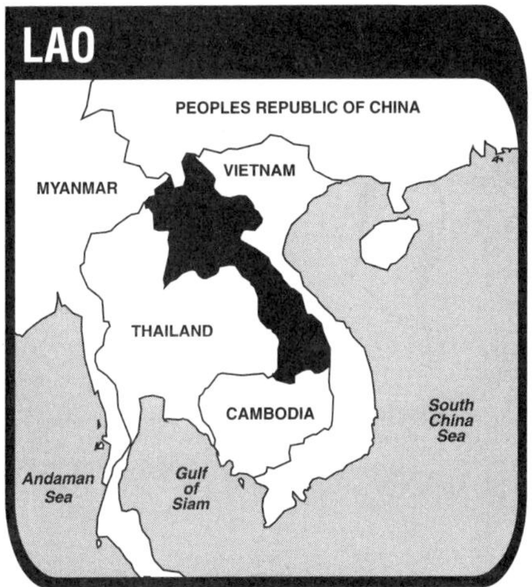

The Lao Peoples Democratic Republic, located on the Indo-Chinese Peninsula between the Socialist Republic of Vietnam and the Kingdom of Thailand, has an area of 91,428 sq. mi. (236,800 km.) and a population of 3.6 million. Capital: Vientiane. Agriculture employs 95 percent of the people. Tin, lumber and coffee are exported.

The first United Kingdom of Lan Xang (Million Elephants) was established in the mid-14th century by King Fa Ngum who ruled an area including present Laos, northeastern Thailand, and the southern part of China's Yunnan province from his capital at Luang Prabang. Thailand and Vietnam obtained control over much of the present Lao territory in the 18th century and remained dominant until France established a protectorate over the area in 1893 and incorporated it into the Union of Indo-China. The Independence of Laos was proclaimed in March of 1945, during the last days of the Japanese occupation of World War II. France reoccupied Laos in 1946, and established it as a constitutional monarchy within the French Union in 1949. In 1953 war erupted between the government and the Pathet Lao, a Communist movement supported by the Vietnamese Communist forces. Peace was declared in 1954 with Laos becoming fully independent in 1955 and the Pathet Lao being permitted to occupy two northern provinces. Civil war broke out again in 1960 with the United States supporting the government of the Kingdom of Laos and the North Vietnamese helping the Communist Pathet Lao, and continued, with intervals of truce and political compromise, until the formation of the Lao Peoples Democratic Republic on Dec. 2, 1975.

NOTE: For earlier coinage, see French Indo-China.

RULERS

Sisavang Vong, 1904-1959
Savang Vatthana, 1959-1975

MONETARY SYSTEM

100 Cents = 1 Piastre

Commencing 1955

100 Att = 1 Kip

MINT MARKS

(a) - Paris, privy marks only
Key - Havana
None - Berlin

NOTE: Private bullion issues previously listed here are now listed in *Unusual World Coins,* 4th Edition, Krause Publications, Inc., 2005.

KINGDOM

STANDARD COINAGE

KM# 4 10 CENTS

1.3200 g., Aluminum, 23 mm. **Ruler:** Sisavang Vong **Obv:** Center hole in head right **Rev:** Center hole in flower design above date

Date	Mintage	F	VF	XF	Unc	BU
1952(a)	2,000,000	—	0.25	0.60	1.25	2.50

KM# 5 20 CENTS

2.2300 g., Aluminum, 27 mm. **Ruler:** Sisavang Vong **Obv:** Center hole within conjoined elephants above date **Rev:** Center hole within flower design above date

Date	Mintage	F	VF	XF	Unc	BU
1952(a)	3,000,000	—	0.35	0.75	2.00	4.00

KM# 6 50 CENTS

3.8400 g., Aluminum, 31 mm. **Ruler:** Sisavang Vong **Obv:** Center hole within pedestal holding book divides radiant sun and date **Rev:** Center hole within flower design above date

Date	Mintage	F	VF	XF	Unc	BU
1952(a)	1,400,000	—	0.75	1.25	2.50	5.00

PEOPLES DEMOCRATIC REPUBLIC

STANDARD COINAGE

100 Att = 1 Kip

KM# 22 10 ATT

1.2000 g., Aluminum, 21 mm. **Obv:** National arms **Rev:** Half length figure facing holding wheat stalks divides sprigs with value above

Date	Mintage	F	VF	XF	Unc	BU
1980	—	—	0.20	0.40	0.85	—

KM# 23 20 ATT

1.5500 g., Aluminum, 23 mm. **Obv:** National arms **Rev:** Value flanked by designs above ox, man and plow

Date	Mintage	F	VF	XF	Unc	BU
1980	—	—	0.20	0.40	0.85	—

KM# 24 50 ATT

2.5000 g., Aluminum, 26 mm. **Obv:** National arms **Rev:** Value above fish and date flanked by palm trees

Date	Mintage	F	VF	XF	Unc	BU
1980	—	—	0.45	0.90	2.00	—

KM# 37 KIP

Copper-Nickel **Subject:** 10th Anniversary of People's Democratic Republic **Obv:** National arms **Rev:** Value flanked by designs above date

Date	Mintage	F	VF	XF	Unc	BU
1985	—	—	0.50	1.00	2.50	—

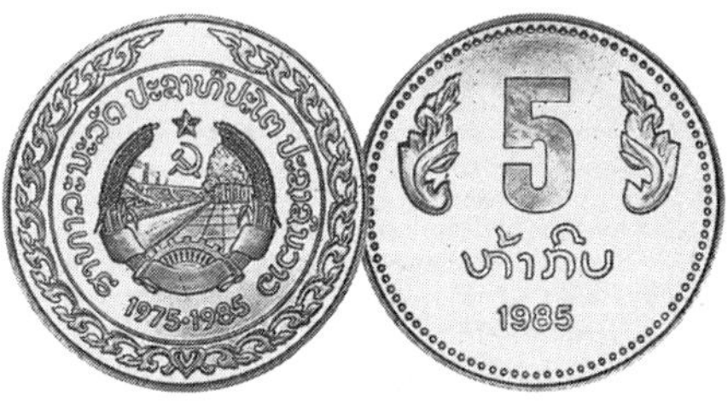

KM# 38 5 KIP

Copper-Nickel **Subject:** 10th Anniversary of People's Democratic Republic **Obv:** National arms **Rev:** Value flanked by designs above date

Date	Mintage	F	VF	XF	Unc	BU
1985	—	—	0.75	1.50	4.00	—

KM# 39 10 KIP

Copper-Nickel **Subject:** 10th Anniversary of People's Democratic Republic **Obv:** National arms **Rev:** Value flanked by designs above date

Date	Mintage	F	VF	XF	Unc	BU
1985	—	—	1.25	2.50	6.50	—

KM# 40 20 KIP

Copper-Nickel **Subject:** 10th Anniversary of People's Democratic Republic **Obv:** National arms within circle and wreath **Rev:** Value flanked by designs above date

Date	Mintage	F	VF	XF	Unc	BU
1985	—	—	1.50	2.50	7.00	—

KM# 41 50 KIP
Copper-Nickel **Subject:** 10th Anniversary of People's Democratic Republic **Obv:** National arms within circle and wreath **Rev:** Value flanked by designs above date

Date	Mintage	F	VF	XF	Unc	BU
1985	—	—	2.00	3.50	8.50	—

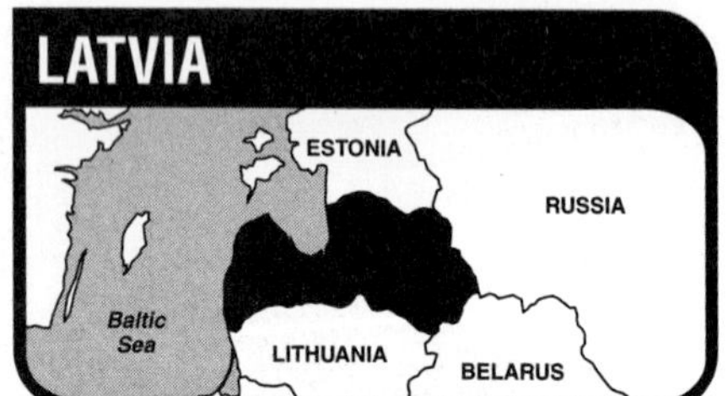

The Republic of Latvia, the central Baltic state in east Europe, has an area of 24,749 sq. mi. (43,601 sq. km.) and a population of 2.6 million. Capital: Riga. Livestock raising and manufacturing are the chief industries. Butter, bacon, fertilizers and telephone equipment are exported.

The Latvians, of Aryan descent primarily from the German Order of Livonian Knights, were nomadic tribesmen who settled along the Baltic prior to the 13th century. Ideally situated as a trade route and lacking a central government, conquered in 1561 by Poland and Sweden. Following the third partition of Poland by Austria, Prussia and Russia in 1795, Latvia came under Russian domination and did not experience autonomy until the Russian Revolution of 1917 provided an opportunity for freedom. The Latvian Republic was established on Nov. 18, 1918. The republic was occupied by Soviet troops and annexed to the Soviet Union in 1940. Following the German occupation of 1941-44, it was retaken by Russia and reestablished as a member republic of the Soviet Union. Western countries, including the United States, did not recognize Latvia's incorporation into the Soviet Union.

The coinage issued during the early 20th Century Republic is now obsolete.

Latvia declared their independence from the U.S.S.R. on August 22, 1991.

MONETARY SYSTEM
100 Santimu = 1 Lats

FIRST REPUBLIC
1918-1939

STANDARD COINAGE
100 Santimu = 1 Lats

KM# 1 SANTIMS
1.6500 g., Bronze, 17 mm. **Obv:** National arms above ribbon **Rev:** Value and date **Edge:** Plain **Note:** Struck at Huguenin Freres, Le Locle, Switzerland.

Date	Mintage	F	VF	XF	Unc	BU
1922	5,000,000	2.00	3.00	5.00	10.00	—
1923	10	—	—	—	1,500	—
1924	4,990,000	2.00	3.00	6.00	10.00	—
1926	5,000,000	2.00	3.00	6.00	10.00	—
1928	5,000,000	2.00	3.00	6.00	10.00	—

Note: Mint name below ribbon

Date	Mintage	F	VF	XF	Unc	BU
1928	Inc. above	5.00	10.00	20.00	40.00	—

Note: Without mint name below ribbon

Date	Mintage	F	VF	XF	Unc	BU
1932	5,000,000	2.00	3.00	5.00	10.00	—
1932 Proof	—	—	—	—	—	—
1935	5,000,000	2.00	3.00	5.00	10.00	—

KM# 10 SANTIMS
1.8000 g., Bronze, 17 mm. **Obv:** National arms above sprigs **Rev:** Value divides sprigs above date **Edge:** Plain

Date	Mintage	F	VF	XF	Unc	BU
1937	2,700,000	2.00	3.00	6.00	12.00	—
1938	1,900,000	3.00	4.00	8.00	16.00	—
1939	3,400,000	1.00	2.00	3.00	5.00	—

Note: Most were never placed into circulation

KM# 2 2 SANTIMI
2.0000 g., Bronze, 19.5 mm. **Obv:** National arms above ribbon **Rev:** Value and date **Edge:** Plain

Date	Mintage	F	VF	XF	Unc	BU
1922	10,000,000	2.00	3.00	7.00	14.00	—

Note: Mint name below ribbon

Date	Mintage	F	VF	XF	Unc	BU
1922	Inc. above	5.00	10.00	20.00	40.00	—

Note: Without mint name below ribbon

Date	Mintage	F	VF	XF	Unc	BU
1923	2	—	—	—	2,000	—
1926	5,000,000	2.00	3.00	7.00	14.00	—
1928	5,000,000	2.00	3.00	7.00	14.00	—
1932	5,000,000	2.00	3.00	7.00	14.00	—
1932 Proof	—	—	—	—	—	—

KM# 11.1 2 SANTIMI
2.0000 g., Bronze, 19 mm. **Obv:** National arms above sprigs **Rev:** Value flanked by sprigs above date **Edge:** Plain

Date	Mintage	F	VF	XF	Unc	BU
1937	45,000	15.00	25.00	40.00	80.00	—

KM# 11.2 2 SANTIMI
2.0000 g., Bronze, 19.5 mm. **Obv:** National arms above sprigs **Rev:** Value flanked by sprigs above date **Edge:** Plain

Date	Mintage	F	VF	XF	Unc	BU
1939	5,000,000	3.00	4.00	6.00	12.00	—

Note: Most were never placed in circulation

KM# 3 5 SANTIMI
3.0000 g., Bronze, 22 mm. **Obv:** National arms above ribbon **Rev:** Value and date

Date	Mintage	F	VF	XF	Unc	BU
1922	15,000,000	2.00	3.00	6.00	12.00	—

Note: Mint name below ribbon

Date	Mintage	F	VF	XF	Unc	BU
1922	Inc. above	4.00	8.00	15.00	30.00	—

Note: Without name below ribbon

Date	Mintage	F	VF	XF	Unc	BU
1923	2	—	—	—	2,250	—

KM# 4 10 SANTIMU
3.0000 g., Nickel, 19 mm. **Obv:** National arms above ribbon divides date **Rev:** Value above oat sprig **Edge:** Plain **Note:** Struck at Huguenin.

Date	Mintage	F	VF	XF	Unc	BU
1922	15,000,000	2.00	3.00	6.00	9.00	—

KM# 5 20 SANTIMU
6.0000 g., Nickel, 21 mm. **Obv:** National arms above ribbon divides date **Rev:** Value above oat sprig **Edge:** Plain **Note:** Struck at Huguenin.

Date	Mintage	F	VF	XF	Unc	BU
1922	15,000,000	2.00	4.00	7.00	12.00	—

KM# 6 50 SANTIMU
6.5000 g., Nickel, 25 mm. **Obv:** National arms above ribbon divides date **Rev:** Value to right of standing figure **Edge:** Plain **Note:** Struck at Huguenin.

Date	Mintage	F	VF	XF	Unc	BU
1922	9,000,000	3.00	6.00	8.00	16.00	—

KM# 7 LATS
5.0000 g., 0.8350 Silver 0.1342 oz. ASW, 23 mm. **Obv:** Arms with supporters **Rev:** Value and date within wreath **Edge:** Milled

Date	Mintage	F	VF	XF	Unc	BU
1923	—	—	—	900	—	—
1924	10,000,000	5.00	8.00	15.00	35.00	—

KM# 8 2 LATI
10.0000 g., 0.8350 Silver 0.2684 oz. ASW, 27 mm. **Obv:** Arms with supporters **Rev:** Value and date within wreath **Edge:** Milled

Date	Mintage	F	VF	XF	Unc	BU
1925	6,386,000	5.00	10.00	20.00	40.00	—
1926	1,114,000	5.00	10.00	20.00	45.00	—

KM# 9 5 LATI
25.0000 g., 0.8350 Silver 0.6711 oz. ASW, 37 mm. **Obv:** Crowned head right **Rev:** Arms with supporters above value **Edge:** Plain with DIEVS *** SVETI *** LATVOJU ***

Date	Mintage	F	VF	XF	Unc	BU
1929	1,000,000	15.00	20.00	30.00	60.00	—
1929 Proof	—	—	—	—	—	—
1931	2,000,000	15.00	20.00	30.00	55.00	—
1931 Proof	—	—	—	—	—	—
1932	600,000	18.00	25.00	35.00	70.00	—
1932 Proof	—	—	—	—	—	—

MODERN REPUBLIC

1991-present

STANDARD COINAGE

100 Santimu = 1 Lats

KM# 15 SANTIMS

1.6200 g., Copper-Clad Steel, 15.67 mm. **Obv:** National arms **Rev:** Value flanked by diamonds below lined arch **Edge:** Plain

Date	Mintage	F	VF	XF	Unc	BU
1992	—	—	—	—	0.30	0.50
1997	—	—	—	—	0.30	0.50
2003	—	—	—	—	0.30	0.50
2005	—	—	—	—	0.30	0.50
2007	—	—	—	—	0.30	0.50

KM# 21 2 SANTIMI

Bronze-Plated Steel, 17 mm. **Obv:** National arms **Rev:** Lined arch above value flanked by diamonds

Date	Mintage	F	VF	XF	Unc	BU
1992	—	—	—	—	0.50	1.00
2000	—	—	—	—	0.50	1.00
2003	—	—	—	—	0.50	1.00
2006	—	—	—	—	0.50	1.00

KM# 16 5 SANTIMI

2.5200 g., Brass, 18.5 mm. **Obv:** National arms **Obv. Legend:** LATVIJAS REPUBLIKA **Rev:** Lined arch above value flanked by diamonds **Edge:** Plain

Date	Mintage	F	VF	XF	Unc	BU
1992	—	—	—	—	1.00	2.00
2006	—	—	—	—	1.00	2.00

KM# 17 10 SANTIMU

Brass, 20 mm. **Obv:** National arms **Rev:** Lined arch above value flanked by diamonds

Date	Mintage	F	VF	XF	Unc	BU
1992	—	—	—	—	2.00	3.00

KM# 22 20 SANTIMU

Brass **Obv:** National arms **Rev:** Lined arch above value flanked by diamonds

Date	Mintage	F	VF	XF	Unc	BU
1992	—	—	—	—	2.00	2.50

KM# 13 50 SANTIMU

Copper-Nickel **Obv:** National arms **Rev:** Triple sprig above value

Date	Mintage	F	VF	XF	Unc	BU
1992	—	—	—	—	3.00	4.00

KM# 12 LATS

Copper-Nickel **Obv:** Arms with supporters **Rev:** Fish above value

Date	Mintage	F	VF	XF	Unc	BU
1992	—	—	—	—	4.00	5.00

KM# 58 LATS

4.8000 g., Copper Nickel, 21.75 mm. **Obv:** Arms with supporters **Rev:** Ant above value **Edge:** Lettered **Edge Lettering:** LATVIJAS BANKA

Date	Mintage	F	VF	XF	Unc	BU
2003	254,000	—	—	—	5.00	7.50

KM# 61 LATS

4.8000 g., Copper-Nickel, 21.75 mm. **Obv:** Arms with supporters **Rev:** Child with shovel above value **Edge:** Lettered **Edge Lettering:** "LATVIJAS BANKA" twice

Date	Mintage	F	VF	XF	Unc	BU
2004	500,000	—	—	—	5.50	6.00

KM# 67 LATS

4.8000 g., Copper-Nickel, 21.75 mm. **Obv:** National arms **Obv. Legend:** LATVIJAS REPUBLIKA **Rev:** Mushroom above value **Edge Lettering:** "LATVIJAS BANKA" repeated twice and inverted

Date	Mintage	F	VF	XF	Unc	BU
2004	500,000	—	—	—	4.00	5.00

KM# 65 LATS

4.8000 g., Copper-Nickel, 21.75 mm. **Obv:** Arms with supporters **Rev:** Chicken above value **Edge:** Lettered **Edge Lettering:** :LATVIJAS BANKA" twice

Date	Mintage	F	VF	XF	Unc	BU
2005	500,000	—	—	—	6.00	7.00

KM# 66 LATS

4.8000 g., Copper-Nickel, 21.7 mm. **Obv:** Arms with supporters **Rev:** Pretzel above value **Edge Lettering:** "LATVIJAS BANKA"

Date	Mintage	F	VF	XF	Unc	BU
2005	500,000	—	—	—	5.00	6.00

KM# 74 LATS

4.8200 g., Copper-Nickel, 21.75 mm. **Obv:** National arms **Rev:** Pine cone above value **Edge Lettering:** "LATVIJAS BANKA" twice

Date	Mintage	F	VF	XF	Unc	BU
2006	—	—	—	—	5.00	6.00

KM# 73 LATS

4.8100 g., Copper-Nickel, 21.8 mm. **Subject:** Summer Solstice **Obv:** National arms **Rev:** Head wearing leaves above value **Edge Lettering:** "LATVIJAS BANKA"

Date	Mintage	F	VF	XF	Unc	BU
2006	—	—	—	—	5.00	6.00

KM# 14 2 LATI

Copper-Nickel **Obv:** Arms with supporters **Rev:** Cow grazing above value

Date	Mintage	F	VF	XF	Unc	BU
1992	—	—	—	—	8.00	9.00

KM# 18 2 LATI

Copper-Nickel **Subject:** 75th Anniversary - Declaration of Independence **Obv:** Arms with supporters **Rev:** Artistic lined art above value and dates

Date	Mintage	F	VF	XF	Unc	BU
ND(1993)	4,000,000	—	—	—	10.00	12.00
ND(1993) Proof	200,000	Value: 15.00				

KM# 38 2 LATI

Ring Composition: Copper-Nickel **Center Composition:** Brass **Obv:** Arms with supporters within circle **Rev:** Cow above value within circle

Date	Mintage	F	VF	XF	Unc	BU
1999	—	—	—	—	10.00	12.00

LEBANON

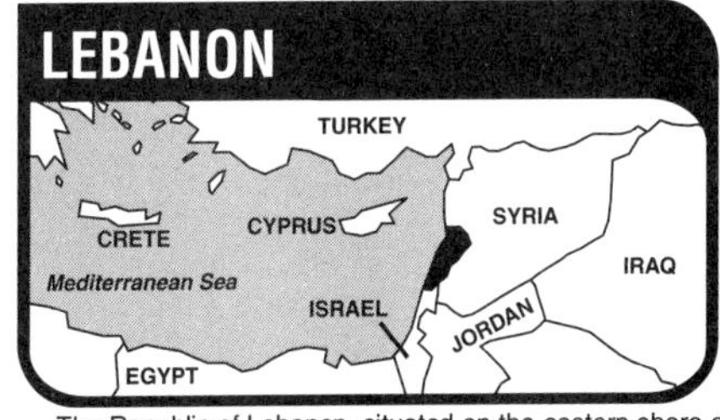

The Republic of Lebanon, situated on the eastern shore of the Mediterranean Sea between Syria and Israel, has an area of 4,015 sq. mi. (10,400 sq. km.) and a population of 3.5 million. Capital: Beirut. The economy is based on agriculture, trade and tourism. Fruit, other foodstuffs and textiles are exported.

Almost at the beginning of recorded history, Lebanon appeared as the well-wooded hinterland of the Phoenicians who exploited its famous forests of cedar. The mountains were a Christian refuge and a Crusader stronghold. Lebanon, the history of which is essentially the same as that of Syria, came under control of the Ottoman Turks early in the 16th century. Following the collapse of the Ottoman Empire after World War I, Lebanon, along with Syria, became a French mandate. The French drew a border around the predominantly Christian Lebanon *Sanjak* or administrative subdivision and on Sept. 1, 1920 proclaimed the area the State of Grand Lebanon (*Etat du Grand Liban*) a republic under French control. France announced the independence of Lebanon on Nov. 26, 1941, but the last British and French troops didn't leave until the end of August 1946.

TITLE

الجمهورية اللبنانية

al-Jomhuriya(t) al-Lubnaniya(t)

MINT MARKS

(a) - Paris, privy marks only

(u) - Utrecht, privy marks only

MONETARY SYSTEM

100 Piastres = 1 Livre (Pound)

FRENCH PROTECTORATE

STANDARD COINAGE

KM# 9 1/2 PIASTRE

4.0000 g., Copper-Nickel, 21 mm. **Obv:** Value within sprigs above date **Rev:** Value within roped wreath flanked by oat sprigs above date

Date	Mintage	F	VF	XF	Unc	BU
1934(a)	200,000	2.00	5.00	12.50	40.00	—
1936(a)	1,200,000	1.25	3.00	7.50	25.00	—

KM# 9a 1/2 PIASTRE

Zinc **Obv:** Value within sprigs above date **Rev:** Value within roped wreath flanked by oat sprigs above date

Date	Mintage	F	VF	XF	Unc	BU
1941(a)	1,000,000	0.50	1.00	4.00	10.00	—

KM# 3 PIASTRE

5.0000 g., Copper-Nickel **Obv:** Hole in center of wreath **Rev:** Hole in center flanked by lion heads with value and dates below

Date	Mintage	F	VF	XF	Unc	BU
1925(a)	1,500,000	0.50	2.00	7.50	25.00	—
1931(a)	300,000	1.00	4.00	12.50	45.00	—
1933(a)	500,000	1.00	4.00	10.00	45.00	—
1936(a)	2,200,000	0.50	1.00	6.50	20.00	—

KM# 3a PIASTRE

Zinc **Obv:** Hole in center of wreath **Rev:** Hole in center flanked by lion heads with value and date below

Date	Mintage	F	VF	XF	Unc	BU
1940(a)	2,000,000	0.75	1.50	4.00	10.00	—

KM# 1 2 PIASTRES

2.0000 g., Aluminum-Bronze **Obv:** Cedar tree within circle above date **Rev:** Value flanked by stars

Date	Mintage	F	VF	XF	Unc	BU
1924(a)	1,800,000	1.25	3.00	12.50	50.00	—

KM# 4 2 PIASTRES

2.0000 g., Aluminum-Bronze **Obv:** Cedar tree **Rev:** Ancient ship

Date	Mintage	F	VF	XF	Unc	BU
1925(a)	1,000,000	3.00	8.00	20.00	80.00	—

KM# 10 2-1/2 PIASTRES

Aluminum-Bronze **Obv:** Hole in center of wreath **Rev:** Hole in center of flowered wreath

Date	Mintage	F	VF	XF	Unc	BU
1940(a)	1,000,000	1.00	2.00	3.50	12.00	—

KM# 2 5 PIASTRES

Aluminum-Bronze **Obv:** Cedar tree within circle **Rev:** Value flanked by stars

Date	Mintage	F	VF	XF	Unc	BU
1924(a)	1,000,000	1.25	3.00	10.00	45.00	—

KM# 5.1 5 PIASTRES

Aluminum-Bronze **Obv:** Cedar tree **Rev:** Ancient ship above value and dates

Date	Mintage	F	VF	XF	Unc	BU
1925(a)	1,500,000	1.00	2.00	8.00	30.00	—

KM# 5.2 5 PIASTRES

4.1000 g., Aluminum-Bronze **Obv:** Cedar tree **Rev:** Privy marks to left and right of "5 Piastres"

Date	Mintage	F	VF	XF	Unc	BU
1925(a)	Inc. above	1.00	2.00	7.50	30.00	—
1931(a)	400,000	1.50	4.00	12.50	40.00	—
1933(a)	500,000	1.50	4.00	12.50	40.00	—
1936(a)	900,000	1.00	2.00	7.50	25.00	—
1940(a)	1,000,000	0.75	1.50	5.00	15.00	—

KM# 6 10 PIASTRES

2.0000 g., 0.6800 Silver 0.0437 oz. ASW **Obv:** Cedar tree on rectangular box **Rev:** Crossed cornucopia above value

Date	Mintage	F	VF	XF	Unc	BU
1929	880,000	3.00	7.00	25.00	70.00	—

KM# 7 25 PIASTRES

5.0000 g., 0.6800 Silver 0.1093 oz. ASW **Obv:** Cedar tree on rectangular box **Rev:** Crossed cornucopia above value

Date	Mintage	F	VF	XF	Unc	BU
1929	600,000	3.00	7.00	25.00	75.00	—
1933(a)	200,000	4.50	15.00	40.00	125	—
1936(a)	400,000	3.50	10.00	27.50	85.00	—

KM# 8 50 PIASTRES

10.0000 g., 0.6800 Silver 0.2186 oz. ASW **Obv:** Cedar tree on rectangular box **Rev:** Crossed cornucopia with value above and below

Date	Mintage	F	VF	XF	Unc	BU
1929	500,000	5.00	10.00	40.00	125	—
1933(a)	100,000	7.00	20.00	65.00	190	—
1936(a)	100,000	7.00	17.50	50.00	140	—

WORLD WAR II COINAGE

KM# 11 1/2 PIASTRE

2.1700 g., Brass **Obv:** Hole in center flanked by english value **Rev:** Hole in center flanked by value **Note:** Three varieties known. Usually crudely struck, off-center, etc. Perfectly struck, centered uncirculated specimens command a considerable premium. Finely struck coins appear with medal rotation while crude examples have coin rotation. Size of letters also vary.

Date	Mintage	F	VF	XF	Unc	BU
ND(1941)	—	1.00	2.50	5.00	12.00	—

KM# 12 PIASTRE

Brass **Obv:** English value **Rev:** Value **Note:** Two varieties known. Usually crudely struck, off-center, etc. Perfectly struck, centered unc. specimens command a considerable premium.

Date	Mintage	F	VF	XF	Unc	BU
ND(1941)	—	1.00	3.00	7.50	18.00	—

KM# 12a PIASTRE

Aluminum **Obv:** English value **Rev:** Value

Date	Mintage	F	VF	XF	Unc	BU
ND(1941)	—	—	—	—	—	—

KM# 13 2-1/2 PIASTRES

Aluminum **Obv:** English value **Rev:** Value **Designer:** Gilroy Roberts **Note:** Seven varieties known. Usually crudely struck, off-center, etc. Perfectly struck, centered unc. specimens command a considerable premium.

Date	Mintage	F	VF	XF	Unc	BU
ND(1941)	—	1.50	3.50	8.00	20.00	—

KM# 13a 2-1/2 PIASTRES

Aluminum-Bronze **Obv:** English value **Rev:** Value

Date	Mintage	F	VF	XF	Unc	BU
ND(1941)	—	—	650	850	—	—

KM# A14 5 PIASTRES

Aluminum **Obv:** English value **Rev:** Value **Note:** Did not enter circulation in significant numbers.

Date	Mintage	F	VF	XF	Unc	BU
ND(1941)	—	—	—	2,000	3,000	—

REPUBLIC

STANDARD COINAGE

KM# 19 PIASTRE

2.0400 g., Aluminum-Bronze, 18 mm.

Date	Mintage	F	VF	XF	Unc	BU
1955(a)	4,000,000	—	0.20	0.50	1.50	3.00

KM# 20 2-1/2 PIASTRES
2.7000 g., Aluminum-Bronze, 20 mm. **Obv:** Hole in center of wreath flanked by value above **Rev:** Hole in center of wreath

Date	Mintage	F	VF	XF	Unc	BU
1955(a)	5,000,000	—	0.10	0.25	0.50	1.00

KM# 14 5 PIASTRES
Aluminum **Obv:** Cedar tree divides date **Rev:** Value below boat **Designer:** Gilroy Roberts

Date	Mintage	F	VF	XF	Unc	BU
1952(a)	3,600,000	0.75	1.50	3.00	6.00	10.00

KM# 18 5 PIASTRES
Aluminum **Obv:** Cedar tree **Rev:** Wreath with value above and below

Date	Mintage	F	VF	XF	Unc	BU
1954	4,440,000	0.25	0.50	1.00	2.50	5.00

KM# 21 5 PIASTRES
2.8500 g., Aluminum-Bronze **Obv:** Cedar tree **Rev:** Lion head and value

Date	Mintage	F	VF	XF	Unc	BU
1955(a)	3,000,000	0.20	0.50	1.00	2.00	3.50
1961(a)	—	0.20	0.40	0.75	1.50	3.00

KM# 25.1 5 PIASTRES
Nickel-Brass, 18 mm. **Obv:** Cedar tree above date **Rev:** Value within wreath

Date	Mintage	F	VF	XF	Unc	BU
1968	2,000,000	—	0.10	0.15	0.20	0.45
1969	4,000,000	—	0.10	0.15	0.20	0.45
1970	—	—	0.10	0.15	0.25	0.50

KM# 25.2 5 PIASTRES
Nickel-Brass, 18 mm. **Obv:** Cedar tree above dates **Rev:** Value within wreath

Date	Mintage	F	VF	XF	Unc	BU
1972(a)	12,000,000	—	—	0.10	0.15	0.35
1975(a)	—	—	—	0.10	0.15	0.35
1980	—	—	—	0.10	0.15	0.35

KM# 15 10 PIASTRES
1.2700 g., Aluminum, 21.8 mm. **Obv:** Cedar tree above dates **Rev:** Lion head flanked by value

Date	Mintage	F	VF	XF	Unc	BU
1952(a)	3,600,000	0.75	1.50	5.00	15.00	25.00

KM# 22 10 PIASTRES
Aluminum-Bronze, 21.8 mm. **Obv:** Boat with sail above date **Rev:** Cedar tree above value

Date	Mintage	F	VF	XF	Unc	BU
1955	2,175,000	0.50	1.00	3.50	12.50	18.50

KM# 23 10 PIASTRES
Aluminum-Bronze, 21.8 mm. **Obv:** Boat with sail above date with value at upper left **Rev:** Cedar tree above date

Date	Mintage	F	VF	XF	Unc	BU
1955(a)	6,000,000	0.20	0.40	1.00	2.00	4.00

KM# 24 10 PIASTRES
Copper-Nickel, 21.8 mm. **Obv:** Boat with sail above date with value at upper left **Rev:** Cedar tree above date

Date	Mintage	F	VF	XF	Unc	BU
1961	7,000,000	—	0.15	0.35	1.00	2.00
1961 Proof	—	—	—	—	—	—

KM# 26 10 PIASTRES
Nickel-Brass, 21.8 mm. **Obv:** Cedar tree above dates **Rev:** Value within wreath

Date	Mintage	F	VF	XF	Unc	BU
1968(a)	2,000,000	—	0.10	0.15	0.25	0.50
1969(a)	5,000,000	—	—	0.10	0.20	0.45
1970(a)	8,000,000	—	—	0.10	0.20	0.45
1972(a)	12,000,000	—	—	0.10	0.20	0.45
1975(a)	—	—	—	0.10	0.20	0.45

KM# 16.1 25 PIASTRES
Aluminum-Bronze, 23.3 mm. **Obv:** Cedar tree **Rev:** Value within rectangular box divides wreath and dates

Date	Mintage	F	VF	XF	Unc	BU
1952(u)	7,200,000	0.10	0.40	0.60	1.00	2.00

KM# 16.2 25 PIASTRES
Aluminum-Bronze, 23.3 mm. **Obv:** Cedar tree **Rev:** Value within rectangular box divides wreath and dates **Note:** Different style of inscription and larger date.

Date	Mintage	F	VF	XF	Unc	BU
1961(u)	5,000,000	0.10	0.40	0.50	0.75	1.50

KM# 27.1 25 PIASTRES
Nickel-Brass, 23.3 mm. **Obv:** Cedar tree above dates **Rev:** Value within wreath

Date	Mintage	F	VF	XF	Unc	BU
1968	1,500,000	0.10	0.15	0.25	0.50	1.00
1969	2,500,000	0.10	0.15	0.20	0.40	0.85
1970	—	0.10	0.15	0.20	0.40	0.85
1972	8,000,000	0.10	0.15	0.20	0.30	0.65
1975	—	0.10	0.15	0.20	0.30	0.65

KM# 27.2 25 PIASTRES
Nickel-Brass, 23.3 mm. **Obv:** Cedar tree above dates **Rev:** Value within wreath

Date	Mintage	F	VF	XF	Unc	BU
1980	—	0.10	0.15	0.20	0.30	0.65

KM# 17 50 PIASTRES
4.9710 g., 0.6000 Silver 0.0959 oz. ASW **Obv:** Cedar tree above dates **Rev:** Value within wreath

Date	Mintage	F	VF	XF	Unc	BU
1952(u)	7,200,000	—	BV	2.50	4.50	7.00

KM# 28.1 50 PIASTRES
Nickel **Obv:** Cedar tree above dates **Rev:** Value within wreath

Date	Mintage	F	VF	XF	Unc	BU
1968	2,000,000	0.20	0.40	0.60	1.00	2.00
1969	3,488,000	0.10	0.25	0.40	0.75	1.50
1970	2,000,000	0.10	0.25	0.40	0.50	1.00
1971	2,000,000	0.10	0.25	0.40	0.50	1.00
1975	—	0.10	0.25	0.40	0.50	1.00
1978	22,400,000	0.10	0.25	0.40	0.50	1.00

KM# 28.2 50 PIASTRES
Nickel **Obv:** Cedar tree above dates **Rev:** Value within wreath

Date	Mintage	F	VF	XF	Unc	BU
1980	—	0.10	0.25	0.40	0.50	1.00

KM# 29 LIVRE
Nickel **Series:** F.A.O. **Obv:** Cedar tree above dates **Rev:** Cluster of fruit above value **Rev. Designer:** Paul Koroleff

Date	Mintage	F	VF	XF	Unc	BU
1968	300,000	0.35	0.75	1.50	3.50	6.00

KM# 30 LIVRE
7.2000 g., Nickel, 27.3 mm. **Obv:** Cedar tree above dates **Rev:** Value within wreath **Note:** Varieties exist.

Date	Mintage	F	VF	XF	Unc	BU
1975	—	0.20	0.40	0.60	1.00	2.00
1975 Proof	—	—	—	—	—	—
1977	8,000,000	0.20	0.40	0.60	1.00	2.00
1980	12,000,000	0.20	0.40	0.60	1.00	2.00
1981	—	0.20	0.40	0.60	1.00	2.00

KM# 30a LIVRE
Nickel Clad Steel, 27.3 mm. **Obv:** Cedar tree above dates **Rev:** Value within wreath **Note:** Varieties exist.

Date	Mintage	F	VF	XF	Unc	BU
1986	—	0.20	0.40	0.60	1.00	2.00

KM# 31 5 LIVRES

Nickel **Series:** F.A.O. **Obv:** Cedar tree above dates **Rev:** Cluster of fruit below radiant sun and value

Date	Mintage	F	VF	XF	Unc	BU
1978	1,000,000	—	—	—	3.00	5.00

KM# 35 10 LIVRES

Copper-Nickel **Series:** World Food Day **Obv:** Cedar tree above dates **Rev:** Man, oxen, radiant sun and value

Date	Mintage	F	VF	XF	Unc	BU
1981	15,000	—	—	—	8.50	11.50

KM# 40 25 LIVRES

2.8200 g., Nickel Plated Steel, 20.5 mm. **Obv:** Value on tree **Rev:** Value within square design **Edge:** Plain

Date	Mintage	F	VF	XF	Unc	BU
2002	—	—	—	—	1.00	2.00

KM# 37 50 LIVRES

Stainless Steel **Obv:** Arabic legend above value and cedar tree within circle **Rev:** French legend below value within circle **Shape:** 8-sided

Date	Mintage	F	VF	XF	Unc	BU
1996	—	—	—	0.45	1.00	2.00

KM# 38 100 LIVRES

4.0000 g., Copper-Zinc **Obv:** Arabic legend above value within cedar tree **Rev:** French legend and date below value

Date	Mintage	F	VF	XF	Unc	BU
1995	—	—	—	0.65	1.50	2.00
1995 Proof	—	Value: 4.00				
1996	—	—	—	0.65	1.50	2.00
2000	—	—	—	0.65	1.50	2.00

KM# 38a 100 LIVRES

4.0500 g., Stainless Steel, 22.5 mm. **Obv:** Value on tree **Rev:** Value above date **Edge:** Plain

Date	Mintage	F	VF	XF	Unc	BU
2003	—	—	—	—	1.50	2.50

KM# 38b 100 LIVRES

4.0700 g., Copper Plated Steel, 22.49 mm. **Obv:** Value on tree **Rev:** Value above date **Rev. Legend:** BANQUE DU LIBAN **Edge:** Plain

Date	Mintage	F	VF	XF	Unc	BU
2006	—	—	—	—	1.50	2.50

KM# 36 250 LIVRES

5.0100 g., Brass, 23.5 mm. **Obv:** Arabic legend above value within tree **Rev:** French legend within beaded circle and value

Date	Mintage	F	VF	XF	Unc	BU
1995	—	—	—	0.75	2.00	2.50
1995 Proof	—	Value: 5.00				
1996	—	—	—	0.75	2.00	2.50
2000	—	—	—	0.75	2.00	2.50
2003	—	—	—	0.75	2.00	2.50

KM# 39 500 LIVRES

5.9700 g., Stainless Steel, 24.5 mm. **Obv:** Arabic legend above value within tree **Rev:** French legend below value and dates within circle

Date	Mintage	F	VF	XF	Unc	BU
1995	—	—	—	1.00	2.50	3.00
1995 Proof	—	Value: 6.00				
1996	—	—	—	1.00	2.50	3.00
2000	—	—	—	1.00	2.50	3.00

LESOTHO

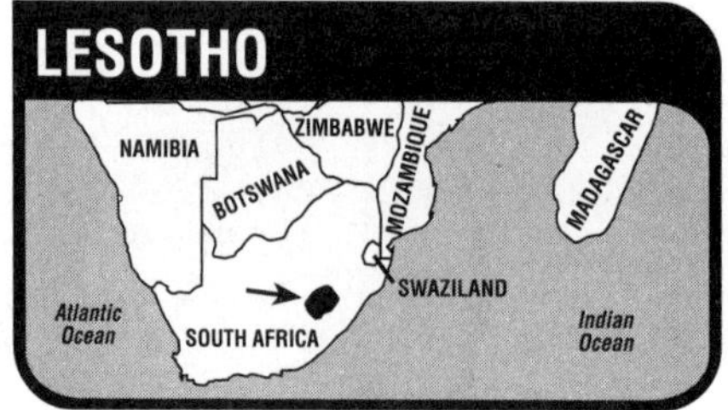

The Kingdom of Lesotho, a constitutional monarchy located within the east-central part of the Republic of South Africa, has an area of 11,720 sq. mi. (30,350 sq. km.) and a population of 1.5 million. Capital: Maseru. The economy is based on subsistence agriculture and livestock raising. Wool, mohair, and cattle are exported.

Lesotho (formerly Basutoland) was sparsely populated until the end of the 16th century. Between the 16th and 19th centuries an influx of refugees from tribal wars led to the development of a distinct Basotho group. During the reign of tribal chief Mashoeshoe I (1823-70), a series of wars with the Orange Free State resulted in the loss of large areas of territory to South Africa. Mashoeshoe appealed to the British for help, and Basutoland was constituted a native state under British protection. In 1871 it was annexed to Cape Colony, but was restored to direct control by the Crown in 1884. From 1884 to 1959 legislative and executive authority was vested in a British High Commissioner. The constitution of 1959 recognized the expressed wish of the people for independence, which was attained on Oct.4, 1966.

Lesotho is a member of the Commonwealth of Nations. The king is Head of State.

RULERS

Moshoeshoe II, 1966-1990
Letsie III, 1990-1995
Moshoeshoe II, 1995-

MONETARY SYSTEM

100 Licente/Lisente = 1 Maloti/Loti

KINGDOM

STANDARD COINAGE

100 Licente/Lisente = 1 Maloti/Loti

KM# 16 SENTE

1.5000 g., Nickel-Brass, 16.5 mm. **Ruler:** Moshoeshoe II **Obv:** Uniformed bust 1/4 left **Rev:** Basotho hat and value

Date	Mintage	F	VF	XF	Unc	BU
1979	4,500,000	—	—	0.15	0.40	0.60
1979 Proof	10,000	Value: 0.65				
1980	—	—	—	0.15	0.40	0.60
1980 Proof	10,000	Value: 0.65				
1981 Proof	2,500	Value: 0.65				
1983	—	—	—	0.15	0.40	0.60
1985	—	—	—	0.15	0.40	0.60
1989	—	—	—	0.15	0.40	0.60

KM# 54 SENTE

Brass, 16.5 mm. **Ruler:** Letsie III **Obv:** Arms with supporters **Rev:** Basotho hat and value

Date	Mintage	F	VF	XF	Unc	BU
1992	—	—	—	0.15	0.75	1.00

KM# 17 2 LISENTE

2.5000 g., Nickel-Brass, 19.5 mm. **Ruler:** Moshoeshoe II **Obv:** Uniformed bust 1/4 left **Rev:** Steer and value

Date	Mintage	F	VF	XF	Unc	BU
1979	3,000,000	—	—	0.20	0.50	0.75
1979 Proof	10,000	Value: 1.00				
1980	—	—	—	0.20	0.50	0.75
1980 Proof	10,000	Value: 1.00				
1981 Proof	2,500	Value: 2.00				
1985	—	—	—	0.20	0.50	0.75
1989	—	—	—	0.20	0.50	0.75

KM# 55 2 LISENTE

Brass, 19.5 mm. **Ruler:** Letsie III **Obv:** Arms with supporters **Rev:** Bull and value

Date	Mintage	F	VF	XF	Unc	BU
1992	—	—	—	0.20	0.75	1.00

KM# 55a 2 LISENTE

2.2500 g., Brass Plated Steel, 19.5 mm. **Ruler:** Letsie III **Obv:** Arms with supporters **Rev:** Bull and value **Edge:** Plain

Date	Mintage	F	VF	XF	Unc	BU
1992	—	—	—	0.20	0.75	1.00

KM# 18 5 LICENTE (Lisente)

4.0000 g., Nickel-Brass, 23.25 mm. **Ruler:** Moshoeshoe II **Obv:** Uniformed bust 1/4 left **Rev:** Single pine tree among hills, grass and value

Date	Mintage	F	VF	XF	Unc	BU
1979	2,700,000	—	—	0.25	0.60	0.85
1979 Proof	10,000	Value: 1.25				
1980	—	—	—	0.25	0.60	0.85

Date	Mintage	F	VF	XF	Unc	BU
1980 Proof	10,000	Value: 1.25				
1981	—	—	—	0.25	0.60	0.85
1981 Proof	2,500	Value: 2.50				
1989	—	—	—	0.25	0.60	0.85

KM# 56 5 LICENTE (Lisente)
Brass, 23.25 mm. **Ruler:** Letsie III **Obv:** Arms with supporters **Rev:** Single pine tree among grass, hills and value

Date	Mintage	F	VF	XF	Unc	BU
1994	—	—	—	0.25	0.60	0.85

KM# 62 5 LICENTE (Lisente)
1.6400 g., Brass Plated Steel, 15 mm. **Ruler:** Letsie III **Obv:** Arms with supporters **Rev:** Single pine tree among grass, hills and value

Date	Mintage	F	VF	XF	Unc	BU
1998	—	—	—	0.25	0.60	0.85

KM# 19 10 LICENTE (Lisente)
2.0000 g., Copper-Nickel, 18.35 mm. **Ruler:** Moshoeshoe II **Obv:** Uniformed bust 1/4 left **Rev:** Angora goat

Date	Mintage	F	VF	XF	Unc	BU
1979	2,000,000	—	0.15	0.30	1.00	1.50
1979 Proof	10,000	Value: 1.75				
1980	—	—	0.15	0.30	1.00	1.50
1980 Proof	10,000	Value: 1.75				
1981 Proof	2,500	Value: 3.00				
1983	—	—	0.15	0.30	1.00	1.50
1989	—	—	0.15	0.30	1.00	1.50

KM# 61 10 LICENTE (Lisente)
2.0000 g., Copper-Nickel, 18.35 mm. **Ruler:** Letsie III **Obv:** Arms with supporters **Rev:** Angora goat

Date	Mintage	F	VF	XF	Unc	BU
1992	—	—	—	—	1.00	1.50

KM# 63 10 LICENTE (Lisente)
1.9600 g., Brass Plated Steel, 16 mm. **Ruler:** Moshoeshoe II **Obv:** Arms with supporters **Rev:** Angora goat

Date	Mintage	F	VF	XF	Unc	BU
1998	—	—	—	—	1.00	1.50

KM# 64 20 LICENTE
2.6700 g., Brass Plated Steel, 18 mm. **Ruler:** Moshoeshoe II **Obv:** Arms with supporters **Rev:** Flora

Date	Mintage	F	VF	XF	Unc	BU
1998	—	—	—	—	0.75	1.00

KM# 20 25 LISENTE
3.5000 g., Copper-Nickel, 21.7 mm. **Ruler:** Moshoeshoe II **Obv:** Uniformed bust 1/4 left **Rev:** Woman in native costume weaving baskets

Date	Mintage	F	VF	XF	Unc	BU
1979	1,200,000	—	0.10	0.20	1.00	1.25
1979 Proof	10,000	Value: 2.00				
1980	—	—	0.10	0.20	1.00	1.25
1980 Proof	10,000	Value: 2.00				
1981 Proof	2,500	Value: 3.50				
1985	—	—	0.10	0.20	1.00	1.25
1989	—	—	0.10	0.20	1.00	1.25

KM# 4.1 50 LICENTE (Lisente)
28.1000 g., 0.9000 Silver 0.8131 oz. ASW, 35 mm. **Ruler:** Moshoeshoe II **Subject:** Independence Attained **Obv:** Native bust right **Rev:** 900/1000 to right of date

Date	Mintage	F	VF	XF	Unc	BU
1966	17,500	—	—	—	12.00	14.00
1966 Proof	Inc. above	Value: 22.00				

KM# 4.2 50 LICENTE (Lisente)
28.1000 g., 0.9000 Silver 0.8131 oz. ASW **Ruler:** Moshoeshoe II **Subject:** Independence Attained **Obv:** Native bust right **Rev:** Large 900/1000 to right of date

Date	Mintage	F	VF	XF	Unc	BU
1966	—	—	—	—	12.00	14.00
1966 Proof	5,000	Value: 22.00				

KM# 4.3 50 LICENTE (Lisente)
28.1000 g., 0.9000 Silver 0.8131 oz. ASW **Ruler:** Moshoeshoe II **Subject:** Independence Attained **Obv:** Native bust right **Rev:** Mint mark and fineness below date

Date	Mintage	F	VF	XF	Unc	BU
1966	—	—	—	—	12.00	14.00
1966 Proof	—	Value: 22.00				

KM# 21 50 LICENTE (Lisente)
5.5000 g., Copper-Nickel, 25.5 mm. **Ruler:** Moshoeshoe II **Obv:** Uniformed bust 1/4 left **Rev:** Equestrian and value

Date	Mintage	F	VF	XF	Unc	BU
1979	480,000	—	0.35	0.50	1.25	1.50
1979 Proof	10,000	Value: 2.50				
1980	—	—	0.35	0.50	1.25	1.50
1980 Proof	10,000	Value: 2.50				
1981 Proof	2,500	Value: 4.00				
1983	—	—	0.35	0.50	1.25	1.50
1989	—	—	0.35	0.50	1.25	1.50

KM# 65 50 LICENTE (Lisente)
3.4000 g., Brass Plated Steel, 20 mm. **Ruler:** Moshoeshoe II

Date	Mintage	F	VF	XF	Unc	BU
1998	—	—	—	—	1.00	1.25

KM# 22 LOTI
11.3000 g., Copper-Nickel, 28.5 mm. **Ruler:** Moshoeshoe II **Obv:** Uniformed bust 1/4 left **Rev:** Value at left of arms with supporters

Date	Mintage	F	VF	XF	Unc	BU
1979	1,275,000	—	0.65	1.25	3.00	3.50
1979 Proof	10,000	Value: 5.00				
1980	—	—	0.75	1.50	4.00	4.50
1980 Proof	10,000	Value: 5.00				
1981 Proof	2,500	Value: 7.00				
1989	—	—	0.75	1.50	4.00	4.50

KM# 66 LOTI
3.8800 g., Nickel-Plated Steel, 21 mm. **Ruler:** Letsie III **Obv:** Native seated right **Rev:** Value at left of arms with supporters

Date	Mintage	F	VF	XF	Unc	BU
1998	—	—	—	—	1.50	2.00

KM# 58 2 MALOTI
4.4900 g., Nickel-Clad Steel, 22 mm. **Ruler:** Moshoeshoe II **Obv:** Arms with supporters **Rev:** Maize plants

Date	Mintage	F	VF	XF	Unc	BU
1996	—	—	—	—	2.50	3.00
1998	—	—	—	—	2.00	2.50

KM# 59 5 MALOTI
6.3700 g., Nickel-Clad Steel, 25 mm. **Ruler:** Moshoeshoe II **Obv:** Arms with supporters **Rev:** Wheat sprigs and value

Date	Mintage	F	VF	XF	Unc	BU
1996	—	—	—	—	5.50	6.00
1998	—	—	—	—	4.50	5.00

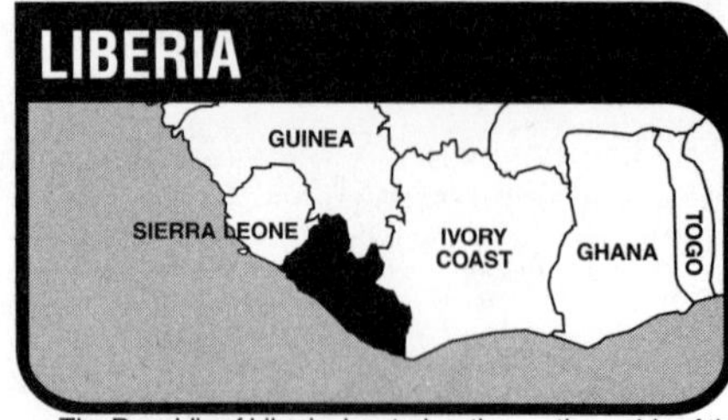

The Republic of Liberia, located on the southern side of the West African bulge between Sierra Leone and Ivory Coast, has an area of 38,250 sq. mi. (111,370 sq. km) and a population of 2.2 million. Capital: Monrovia. The major industries are agriculture, mining and lumbering. Iron ore, diamonds, rubber, coffee and coca are exported.

The Liberian coast was explored and charted by Portuguese navigator Pedro de Cintra in 1461. For the three centuries following Portuguese traders visited the area regularly to trade for gold, slaves and pepper. The modern country of Liberia, Africa's first republic, was settled in1822 by the American Colonization Society as a homeland for American freed slaves, with the U.S. government furnishing funds and assisting in negotiations for procurement of land from the native chiefs. The various settlements united in 1839 to form the Commonwealth of Liberia, and in 1847 established the country as a republic with a constitution modeled after that of the United States.

U.S. money was declared legal tender in Liberia in 1943, replacing British West African currency.

Most of the Liberian pattern series, particularly of the 1888-90 period, are acknowledged to have been "unofficial" privately sponsored issues, but many collectors of Liberian coins nonetheless, avidly collect them. The "K" number designations on these pieces refer to a listing of Liberian patterns compiled and published by Ernst Kraus.

MINT MARKS

B - Bern, Switzerland
H - Heaton, Birmingham
(l) – London
(d) – Denver, U.S.A.
(s) - San Francisco, U.S.
FM - Franklin Mint, U.S.A.*
PM - Pobjoy Mint

***NOTE:** From 1975-1985 the Franklin Mint produced coinage in up to 3 different qualities. Qualities of issue are designated in ( ) after each date and are defined as follows:

(M) MATTE - Normal circulation strike or a dull finish produced by sandblasting special uncirculated (polish finish) or proof quality dies.

(U) SPECIAL UNCIRCULATED - Polished or prooflike in appearance without any frosted features.

(P) PROOF - The highest quality obtainable having mirror-like fields and frosted features.

MONETARY SYSTEM

100 Cents = 1 Dollar

REPUBLIC

STANDARD COINAGE

100 Cents = 1 Dollar

KM# 10 1/2 CENT

2.4200 g., Brass, 18 mm. **Obv:** Laureate head left with star below **Rev:** Palm tree (Elaeis guineensis-Palmae) within circle flanked by stars

Date	Mintage	F	VF	XF	Unc	BU
1937	1,000,000	0.10	0.25	0.40	1.00	2.50

KM# 10a 1/2 CENT

Copper-Nickel **Obv:** Head laureate left with star below **Rev:** Palm tree within circle flanked by stars

Date	Mintage	F	VF	XF	Unc	BU
1941	250,000	0.15	0.35	0.55	1.50	2.50

KM# 5 CENT

Bronze **Obv:** Head laureate left above star **Obv. Legend:** REPUBLIC OF LIBERIA **Rev:** Palm tree divides ship and radiant sun within circle, 2 stars, date and value around border

Date	Mintage	F	VF	XF	Unc	BU
1906H	180,000	4.50	10.00	30.00	65.00	—
1906H Proof	—	Value: 130				

KM# 11 CENT

5.1900 g., Brass, 25.45 mm. **Obv:** Elephant within circle above star **Rev:** Palm tree within circle above date

Date	Mintage	F	VF	XF	Unc	BU
1937	1,000,000	0.20	0.50	1.50	6.00	12.00

KM# 11a CENT

Copper-Nickel **Obv:** Elephant within circle above star **Rev:** Palm tree within circle above date

Date	Mintage	F	VF	XF	Unc	BU
1941	250,000	1.00	7.00	18.00	40.00	—

KM# 13 CENT

2.6000 g., Bronze, 18 mm. **Obv:** Elephant within circle above star **Rev:** Ship and bird to right of palm tree within 3/4 circle above date

Date	Mintage	F	VF	XF	Unc	BU
1960	500,000	—	—	0.10	0.75	2.00
1961	7,000,000	—	—	0.10	0.75	2.00
1968(l)	3,000,000	—	—	0.10	0.75	2.00
1968(s) Proof	14,000	Value: 1.25				
1969 Proof	5,056	Value: 1.25				
1970 Proof	3,464	Value: 1.25				
1971 Proof	3,032	Value: 1.25				
1972(d)	10,000,000	—	—	0.10	0.75	2.00
1972(s) Proof	4,866	Value: 1.25				
1973 Proof	11,000	Value: 1.25				
1974 Proof	9,362	Value: 1.25				
1975	5,000,000	—	—	0.10	0.75	2.00
1975 Proof	4,056	Value: 1.25				
1976 Proof	2,131	Value: 1.25				
1977	2,500,000	—	—	0.10	0.75	2.00
1977 Proof	920	Value: 1.25				
1978FM Proof	7,311	Value: 1.25				
1983FM	2,500,000	—	—	0.10	0.75	2.00
1984	2,500,000	—	—	0.10	0.75	2.00

KM# 6 2 CENTS

Bronze **Obv:** Laureate head left above star **Obv. Legend:** REPUBLIC OF LIBERIA **Rev:** Palm tree divides ship and radiant sun within circle, 2 stars, date and value around border

Date	Mintage	F	VF	XF	Unc	BU
1906H	108,000	5.00	12.00	30.00	75.00	—
1906H Proof	—	Value: 160				

KM# 12 2 CENTS

Brass **Obv:** Elephant within circle above star **Rev:** Palm tree divides ship and sun within circle flanked by stars above date

Date	Mintage	F	VF	XF	Unc	BU
1937	1,000,000	0.15	0.35	1.00	6.00	9.00

KM# 12a 2 CENTS

Copper-Nickel **Obv:** Elephant within circle above star **Rev:** Palm tree divides sun and ship within circle flanked by stars above date

Date	Mintage	F	VF	XF	Unc	BU
1941	810,000	0.10	0.25	0.50	2.50	3.00
1978FM Proof	7,311	Value: 2.00				

KM# 14 5 CENTS

4.1000 g., Copper-Nickel, 20 mm. **Obv:** Elephant within circle above star **Rev:** Ship and bird to right of palm tree within 3/4 circle above date

Date	Mintage	F	VF	XF	Unc	BU
1960	1,000,000	—	0.10	0.15	0.50	1.50
1961	3,200,000	—	0.10	0.15	0.50	1.50
1968 Proof	15,000	Value: 1.00				
1969 Proof	5,056	Value: 1.00				
1970 Proof	3,464	Value: 1.25				
1971 Proof	3,032	Value: 1.25				
1972(d)	3,000,000	—	0.10	0.15	0.40	1.50
1972(s) Proof	4,866	Value: 1.00				
1973 Proof	11,000	Value: 1.00				
1974 Proof	9,362	Value: 1.00				
1975	3,000,000	—	0.10	0.15	0.40	1.50
1975 Proof	4,056	Value: 1.00				
1976 Proof	2,131	Value: 1.00				
1977	—	—	0.10	0.15	0.50	1.50
1977 Proof	920	Value: 1.00				
1978FM Proof	7,311	Value: 1.00				
1983FM	1,000,000	—	0.10	0.15	0.40	1.50
1984	1,000,000	—	0.10	0.15	0.40	1.50

KM# 474 5 CENTS

2.2500 g., Aluminum, 26.9 mm. **Obv:** National arms **Rev:** Dragon above value **Edge:** Plain

Date	Mintage	F	VF	XF	Unc	BU
2000	—	—	—	—	1.00	1.50

KM# 618 5 CENTS

5.0200 g., Copper-Nickel, 23.8 mm. **Obv:** National arms **Rev:** Chimpanzee family **Edge:** Plain

Date	Mintage	F	VF	XF	Unc	BU
2003	—	—	—	—	1.50	2.00

KM# 7 10 CENTS

2.3200 g., 0.9250 Silver 0.0690 oz. ASW **Obv:** Laureate head left above star **Obv. Legend:** REPUBLIC OF LIBERIA **Rev:** Value and date within wreath

Date	Mintage	F	VF	XF	Unc	BU
1906H	35,000	5.00	25.00	65.00	150	—
1906H Proof	—	Value: 250				

KM# 15 10 CENTS

2.0700 g., 0.9000 Silver 0.0599 oz. ASW, 17 mm. **Obv:** Head with headdress left above star **Rev:** Value and date within wreath

Date	Mintage	F	VF	XF	Unc	BU
1960	1,000,000	BV	1.00	1.50	3.00	5.00
1961	1,200,000	BV	1.00	1.50	3.00	5.00

KM# 15a.1 10 CENTS

2.1000 g., Copper-Nickel **Obv:** Head with headdress left above star **Rev:** Value and date within wreath

Date	Mintage	F	VF	XF	Unc	BU
1966	2,000,000	—	0.15	0.25	0.50	0.75

KM# 15a.2 10 CENTS

1.8000 g., Copper-Nickel **Obv:** Head with headdress left above star **Rev:** Value and date within wreath

Date	Mintage	F	VF	XF	Unc	BU
1968 Proof	14,000	Value: 1.25				
1969 Proof	5,056	Value: 1.25				
1970(d)	2,500,000	—	0.15	0.25	0.50	0.75
1970(s) Proof	3,464	Value: 1.50				
1971 Proof	3,032	Value: 1.50				
1972 Proof	4,866	Value: 1.25				
1973 Proof	11,000	Value: 1.00				
1974 Proof	9,362	Value: 1.00				
1975	4,500	—	0.15	0.20	0.35	0.75
1975 Proof	4,056	Value: 1.00				
1976 Proof	2,131	Value: 1.00				
1977	—	—	0.15	0.25	0.75	1.25
1977 Proof	920	Value: 4.00				
1978FM Proof	7,311	Value: 1.00				
1983FM	500,000	—	0.15	0.25	0.75	1.25
1984FM	500,000	—	0.15	0.25	0.75	1.25
1987	10,000,000	—	0.15	0.25	0.75	1.25

KM# 8 25 CENTS

5.8000 g., 0.9250 Silver 0.1725 oz. ASW **Obv:** Head laureate left above star **Obv. Legend:** REPUBLIC OF LIBERIA **Rev:** Value and date within wreath

Date	Mintage	F	VF	XF	Unc	BU
1906H	34,000	10.00	40.00	125	250	—
1906H Proof	—	Value: 375				

KM# 16 25 CENTS

5.1800 g., 0.9000 Silver 0.1499 oz. ASW **Obv:** Head with headdress left above star **Rev:** Value and date within wreath

Date	Mintage	F	VF	XF	Unc	BU
1960	900,000	BV	2.25	2.75	5.00	7.00
1961	1,200,000	BV	2.25	2.75	5.00	7.00

KM# 16a.1 25 CENTS

5.2000 g., Copper-Nickel **Obv:** Head with headdress left above star **Rev:** Value and date within wreath

Date	Mintage	F	VF	XF	Unc	BU
1966	800,000	—	0.25	0.65	1.25	2.00

KM# 16a.2 25 CENTS

4.8000 g., Copper-Nickel, 23 mm. **Obv:** Head with headdress left above star **Rev:** Value and date within wreath **Note:** 1 and 1.15mm rim varieties exist.

Date	Mintage	F	VF	XF	Unc	BU
1968(d)	1,600,000	—	0.25	0.50	1.00	1.50
1968(s) Proof	14,000	Value: 1.50				
1969 Proof	5,056	Value: 1.50				
1970 Proof	3,464	Value: 1.75				
1971 Proof	3,032	Value: 1.75				

Date	Mintage	F	VF	XF	Unc	BU
1972 Proof	4,866	Value: 1.50				
1973	2,000,000	—	0.25	0.50	1.00	1.50
1973 Proof	11,000	Value: 1.25				
1974 Proof	9,362	Value: 1.25				
1975	1,600,000	—	0.25	0.50	1.00	1.50
1975 Proof	4,056	Value: 1.25				

KM# 16a.3 25 CENTS

5.2000 g., Copper-Nickel **Obv:** Head with headdress left above star **Rev:** Value and date within wreath **Rev. Legend:** Large letters, higher inscription **Note:** Struck in 1988.

Date	Mintage	F	VF	XF	Unc	BU
1968 Restrike	2,400,000	—	0.25	0.50	1.00	1.50

KM# 30 25 CENTS

5.2000 g., Copper-Nickel **Series:** F.A.O. **Obv:** Head 1/4 right flanked by stars **Rev:** Woman with basket of leaves on head divides date and value within circle

Date	Mintage	F	VF	XF	Unc	BU
1976	800,000	—	0.25	0.75	1.75	3.00
1976 Proof	2,131	Value: 4.00				
1977 Proof	920	Value: 5.00				
1978FM Proof	7,311	Value: 2.50				

KM# 9 50 CENTS

11.6000 g., 0.9250 Silver 0.3450 oz. ASW **Obv:** Laureate head left above star **Obv. Legend:** REPUBLIC OF LIBERIA **Rev:** Value and date within wreath

Date	Mintage	F	VF	XF	Unc	BU
1906H	24,000	15.00	35.00	90.00	450	—
1906H Proof	—	Value: 600				

KM# 17 50 CENTS

10.3700 g., 0.9000 Silver 0.3001 oz. ASW **Obv:** Head with headdress left above star **Rev:** Value and date within wreath

Date	Mintage	F	VF	XF	Unc	BU
1960	1,100,000	BV	4.50	5.00	9.00	12.50
1961	800,000	BV	4.50	5.00	9.00	12.50

KM# 17a.2 50 CENTS

8.9000 g., Copper-Nickel, 29 mm. **Obv:** Head with headdress left above star **Rev:** Value and date within wreath

Date	Mintage	F	VF	XF	Unc	BU
1968(l)	1,000,000	—	0.60	0.80	1.50	2.50
1968(s) Proof	14,000	Value: 1.50				
1969 Proof	5,056	Value: 1.50				
1970 Proof	3,464	Value: 2.50				
1971 Proof	3,032	Value: 2.50				
1972 Proof	4,866	Value: 1.50				
1973	1,000,000	—	0.60	0.75	1.25	2.00
1973 Proof	11,000	Value: 1.50				
1974 Proof	9,362	Value: 1.50				
1975	800,000	—	0.60	0.75	1.25	2.00
1975 Proof	4,056	Value: 1.50				

KM# 17a.1 50 CENTS

10.4000 g., Copper-Nickel **Obv:** Head with headdress left above star **Rev:** Value and date within wreath

Date	Mintage	F	VF	XF	Unc	BU
1966	200,000	—	0.75	1.00	1.50	2.50

KM# 17b.2 50 CENTS

9.0000 g., Nickel-Clad Steel, 28 mm. **Obv:** Head with headdress left above star **Rev:** Value and date within wreath **Edge:** Reeded

Date	Mintage	F	VF	XF	Unc	BU
2000	—	—	—	—	3.50	—

KM# 31 50 CENTS

8.9000 g., Copper-Nickel **Obv:** Head 1/4 right flanked by stars **Rev:** National arms

Date	Mintage	F	VF	XF	Unc	BU
1976	1,000,000	—	0.60	1.00	2.50	4.00
1976 Proof	2,131	Value: 5.50				
1977 Proof	920	Value: 6.50				
1978FM Proof	7,311	Value: 4.00				
1987	1,800,000	—	0.60	1.00	2.50	4.00

KM# 18 DOLLAR

20.7400 g., 0.9000 Silver 0.6001 oz. ASW **Obv:** Head with headdress left above star **Rev:** Value and date within wreath

Date	Mintage	F	VF	XF	Unc	BU
1961	200,000	BV	9.00	10.00	12.50	16.50
1962	1,000,000	BV	8.50	9.50	11.00	14.50

KM# 18a.1 DOLLAR

20.7000 g., Copper-Nickel, 34 mm. **Obv:** Head with headdress left above star **Rev:** Value and date within wreath

Date	Mintage	F	VF	XF	Unc	BU
1966	1,000,000	—	1.00	1.50	2.25	3.50

KM# 18a.2 DOLLAR

18.0000 g., Copper-Nickel, 34 mm. **Obv:** Head with headdress left above star **Rev:** Value and date within wreath

Date	Mintage	F	VF	XF	Unc	BU
1968(l)	1,000,000	—	1.00	1.50	2.25	3.50
1968(s) Proof	14,000	Value: 2.00				
1969 Proof	5,056	Value: 2.00				
1970(d)	2,000,000	—	1.00	1.50	3.00	4.50
1970(s) Proof	3,464	Value: 6.00				
1971 Proof	3,032	Value: 4.50				
1972 Proof	4,866	Value: 4.50				
1973 Proof	11,000	Value: 3.00				
1974 Proof	9,362	Value: 3.00				
1975	400,000	—	1.25	1.75	3.00	4.50
1975 Proof	4,056	Value: 3.00				

KM# 32 DOLLAR

18.0000 g., Copper-Nickel, 34 mm. **Obv:** Head 1/4 right flanked by stars **Rev:** Liberia, map and date within circle flanked by stars

Date	Mintage	F	VF	XF	Unc	BU
1976	2,000,000	—	2.50	4.50	8.00	12.00
1976 Proof	2,131	Value: 12.00				
1977 Proof	920	Value: 13.50				
1978FM Proof	7,311	Value: 11.00				
1987	1,500,000	—	1.50	3.00	6.00	10.00

KM# 44 5 DOLLARS

Copper-Nickel **Subject:** Military Memorial **Obv:** National arms above date **Rev:** Memorial statue and value flanked by shrubs **Shape:** 7-sided

Date	Mintage	F	VF	XF	Unc	BU
1982	4,000,000	—	5.00	6.50	9.00	—
1985	2,000,000	—	5.00	6.50	9.00	—

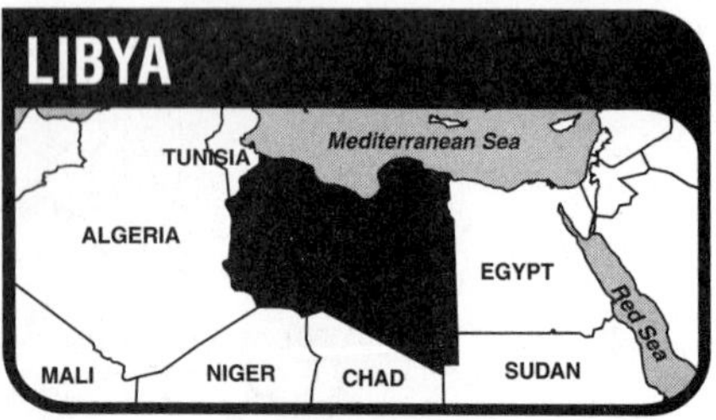

The Socialist People's Libyan Arab Jamahariya, located on the north-central coast of Africa between Tunisia and Egypt, has an area of 679,358 sq. mi. (1,759,540 sq. km.) and a population of 3.9 million. Capital: Tripoli. Crude oil, which accounts for 90 per cent of the export earnings, is the mainstay of the economy.

Libya has been subjected to foreign rule throughout most of its history, various parts of it having been ruled by the Phoenicians, Carthaginians, Vandals, Byzantines, Greeks, Romans, Egyptians, and in the following centuries the Arabs' language, culture and religion were adopted by the indigenous population. Libya was conquered by the Ottoman Turks in 1553, and remained under Turkish domination, becoming a Turkish vilayet in 1835, until it was conquered by Italy and made into a colony in 1911. The name 'Libya', the ancient Greek name for North Africa exclusive of Egypt, was given to the colony by Italy in1934. Libya came under Allied administration after the fall of Tripoli on Jan. 23, 1943, divided into zones of British and French control. On Dec. 24, 1951, in accordance with a United Nations resolution, Libya proclaimed its independence as a constitutional monarchy, thereby becoming the first country to achieve independence through the United Nations. The monarchy was overthrown by a *coup d'etat* on Sept. 1, 1969, and Libya was established as a republic.

TITLES

المملكة الليبية

al-Mamlaka(t) al-Libiya(t)

al-Jomhuriya(t) al-Arabiya(t) al-Libiya(t)

RULERS

Idris I, 1951-1969

MONETARY SYSTEM

10 Milliemes = 1 Piastre
100 Piastres = 1 Pound

MONARCHY

STANDARD COINAGE

10 Milliemes = 1 Piastre; 100 Piastres = 1 Pound

KM# 1 MILLIEME

3.0000 g., Bronze, 18 mm. **Ruler:** Idris I **Obv:** Bust right **Rev:** Crown divides wreath with value and date within **Note:** Date in Arabic.

Date	Mintage	F	VF	XF	Unc	BU
1952	7,750,000	—	0.15	0.25	0.75	1.50
1952 Proof	32	Value: 75.00				

KM# 6 MILLIEME

1.7500 g., Nickel-Brass, 16.03 mm. **Ruler:** Idris I **Obv:** Crowned national arms above dates **Rev:** Value within wreath

Date	Mintage	F	VF	XF	Unc	BU
AH1385-1965	11,000,000	—	0.10	0.20	0.40	0.85

KM# 2 2 MILLIEMES

6.0000 g., Bronze, 24 mm. **Ruler:** Idris I **Obv:** Bust right **Rev:** Crown divides wreath with value and date within **Note:** Date in Arabic.

Date	Mintage	F	VF	XF	Unc	BU
1952	6,650,000	—	0.15	0.35	1.00	2.00
1952 Proof	32	Value: 75.00				

KM# 3 5 MILLIEMES

Bronze **Ruler:** Idris I **Obv:** Bust right **Rev:** Crown divides wreath with value and date within **Note:** Date in Arabic.

Date	Mintage	F	VF	XF	Unc	BU
1952	7,680,000	—	0.25	0.50	1.50	3.00
1952 Proof	32	Value: 75.00				

KM# 7 5 MILLIEMES

Nickel-Brass **Ruler:** Idris I **Obv:** Crowned national arms above dates **Rev:** Value within 3/4 wreath

Date	Mintage	F	VF	XF	Unc	BU
AH1385-1965	8,500,000	—	0.15	0.25	0.50	1.00

KM# 4 PIASTRE

Copper-Nickel **Ruler:** Idris I **Obv:** Bust right **Rev:** Crown divides wreath with value and date within **Note:** Date in Arabic.

Date	Mintage	F	VF	XF	Unc	BU
1952	10,200,000	—	0.35	0.60	1.25	2.50
1952 Proof	32	Value: 100				

KM# 5 2 PIASTRES

7.5300 g., Copper-Nickel, 26 mm. **Ruler:** Idris I **Obv:** Bust right **Rev:** Crown divides wreath with value and dates within **Note:** Date in Arabic.

Date	Mintage	F	VF	XF	Unc	BU
1952	6,075,000	—	0.35	0.75	1.75	3.50
1952 Proof	32	Value: 125				

KM# 8 10 MILLIEMES

Copper-Nickel **Ruler:** Idris I **Obv:** Crowned national arms above dates **Rev:** Value within wreath

Date	Mintage	F	VF	XF	Unc	BU
AH1385-1965	17,000,000	—	0.15	0.25	0.50	1.00

KM# 9 20 MILLIEMES

Copper-Nickel **Ruler:** Idris I **Obv:** Crowned national arms above dates **Rev:** Value within wreath

Date	Mintage	F	VF	XF	Unc	BU
AH1385-1965	8,750,000	—	0.20	0.50	2.00	3.50

KM# 10 50 MILLIEMES

Copper-Nickel, 26 mm. **Ruler:** Idris I **Obv:** Crowned national arms above dates **Rev:** Value within wreath **Shape:** Scalloped

Date	Mintage	F	VF	XF	Unc	BU
AH1385-1965	8,000,000	—	0.35	0.75	3.00	5.00

KM# 11 100 MILLIEMES

Copper-Nickel **Ruler:** Idris I **Obv:** Crowned national arms above dates **Rev:** Value within wreath

Date	Mintage	F	VF	XF	Unc	BU
AH1385 (1965)	8,000,000	—	0.75	1.50	4.00	—

SOCIALIST PEOPLE'S REPUBLIC

STANDARD COINAGE

1000 Dirhams = 1 Dinar

KM# 12 DIRHAM

Brass Clad Steel **Obv:** Eagle flanked by dates **Rev:** Value within wreath

Date	Mintage	F	VF	XF	Unc	BU
AH1395-1975	20,000,000	—	0.25	0.50	1.50	—

KM# 18 DIRHAM

Brass Clad Steel **Obv:** Armored equestrian **Rev:** Value within wreath

Date	Mintage	F	VF	XF	Unc	BU
AH1399-1979	1,000,000	—	0.50	1.00	3.00	—

KM# 13 5 DIRHAM

Brass Clad Steel **Obv:** Eagle flanked by dates **Rev:** Value above oat sprigs within wreath

Date	Mintage	F	VF	XF	Unc	BU
AH1395-1975	23,000,000	—	0.25	0.60	2.00	—

KM# 19 5 DIRHAM
Brass Clad Steel **Obv:** Armored equestrian **Rev:** Value above oat sprigs within wreath

Date	Mintage	F	VF	XF	Unc	BU
AH1399-1979	2,000,000	—	0.75	2.00	4.00	—

KM# 14 10 DIRHAMS
Copper-Nickel Clad Steel **Obv:** Eagle flanked by dates **Rev:** Value above oat sprigs within wreath

Date	Mintage	F	VF	XF	Unc	BU
AH1395-1975	52,750,000	—	0.25	0.65	2.25	—

KM# 20 10 DIRHAMS
Copper-Nickel Clad Steel, 20 mm. **Obv:** Armored equestrian **Rev:** Value above oat sprigs within wreath

Date	Mintage	F	VF	XF	Unc	BU
AH1399-1979	4,000,000	—	0.75	2.00	4.00	—

KM# 15 20 DIRHAMS
5.6600 g., Copper-Nickel Clad Steel, 24 mm. **Obv:** Eagle flanked by dates **Rev:** Value above oat sprigs within wreath

Date	Mintage	F	VF	XF	Unc	BU
AH1395-1975	25,500,000	—	0.50	1.75	3.00	—

KM# 21 20 DIRHAMS
Copper-Nickel Clad Steel **Obv:** Armored equestrian **Rev:** Value above oat sprigs within wreath

Date	Mintage	F	VF	XF	Unc	BU
AH1399-1979	6,000,000	—	1.00	3.00	5.00	—

KM# 16 50 DIRHAMS
6.2500 g., Copper-Nickel, 25 mm. **Obv:** Eagle flanked by dates **Rev:** Value above oat sprigs within wreath

Date	Mintage	F	VF	XF	Unc	BU
AH1395-1975	25,640,000	—	1.00	2.50	6.00	—

KM# 22 50 DIRHAMS
Copper-Nickel **Obv:** Armored equestrian **Rev:** Value above oat sprigs within wreath

Date	Mintage	F	VF	XF	Unc	BU
AH1399-1979	9,120,000	—	1.50	3.50	7.00	—

KM# 17 100 DIRHAMS
Copper-Nickel **Obv:** Eagle flanked by dates **Rev. Inscription:** Value above oat sprigs within wreath

Date	Mintage	F	VF	XF	Unc	BU
AH1395-1975	15,433,000	—	1.50	3.50	8.00	—

KM# 23 100 DIRHAMS
Copper-Nickel **Obv:** Armored equestrian **Rev:** Value above oat sprigs within wreath

Date	Mintage	F	VF	XF	Unc	BU
AH1399-1979	15,000,000	—	2.00	4.50	9.00	—

KM# 26 1/4 DINAR
11.1500 g., Nickel-Brass, 28 mm. **Obv:** Man on horse with gun 1/2 left, ornamental legend with date **Rev:** Value in Arabic script above wheat ears in ornamented frame **Edge:** Ten alternating reeded and plain flat sections **Shape:** 10-sided

Date	Mintage	F	VF	XF	Unc	BU
AH1369	—	—	—	6.00	10.00	15.00

Note: Restruck in 2001-2002

KM# 27 1/2 DINAR
11.5000 g., Bi-Metallic, 30 mm. **Obv:** Man on horse with gun 1/2 left, ornamental legend with date **Rev:** Value in Arabic script above wheat ears in ornamented frame **Edge:** Reeded

Date	Mintage	F	VF	XF	Unc	BU
ND(2004)(AH1372)	—	—	—	—	—	15.00

Note: Restruck in 2004-2005.

The Principality of Liechtenstein, located in central Europe on the east bank of the Rhine between Austria and Switzerland, has an area of 62 sq. mi. (160 sq. km.) and a population of 27,200. Capital: Vaduz. The economy is based on agriculture and light manufacturing. Canned goods, textiles, ceramics and precision instruments are exported.

The lordships of Schellenburg and Vaduz were merged into the principality of Liechtenstein. It was a member of the Rhine Confederation from 1806 to 1815, and of the German Confederation from 1815 to 1866 when it became independent. Liechtenstein's long and close association with Austria was terminated by World War I. In 1921 it adopted the coinage of Switzerland, and two years later entered into a customs union with the Swiss, who also operated its postal and telegraph systems and represented it in international affairs. The tiny principality abolished its army in 1868 and has avoided involvement in all European wars since that time.

RULERS

Prince John II, 1858-1929
Prince Franz I, 1929-1938
Prince Franz Josef II, 1938-1990
Prince Hans Adam II, 1990-

MINT MARKS

A - Vienna
B - Bern
M - Munich (restrikes)

MONETARY SYSTEM

100 Heller = 1 Krone

PRINCIPALITY

REFORM COINAGE
100 Heller = 1 Krone

Y# 2 KRONE
5.0000 g., 0.8350 Silver 0.1342 oz. ASW **Ruler:** Prince John II **Obv:** Head left **Obv. Legend:** JOHANN II.FURST... **Rev:** Crowned shield within wreath divides value, date below

Date	Mintage	F	VF	XF	Unc	BU
1904	75,000	10.00	15.00	20.00	45.00	—
1910	50,000	10.00	15.00	20.00	45.00	—
1915	75,000	10.00	15.00	20.00	45.00	—

Y# 3 2 KRONEN
10.0000 g., 0.8350 Silver 0.2684 oz. ASW **Ruler:** Prince John II **Obv:** Head left **Rev:** Crowned shield within wreath flanked by value and letters

Date	Mintage	F	VF	XF	Unc	BU
1912	50,000	10.00	15.00	25.00	40.00	75.00
1915	37,500	12.00	20.00	35.00	60.00	85.00

Y# 4 5 KRONEN
24.0000 g., 0.9000 Silver 0.6944 oz. ASW **Ruler:** Prince John II **Obv:** Head left **Obv. Legend:** JOHANN II. FURST... **Rev:** Crowned shield within wreath divides value above date

Date	Mintage	F	VF	XF	Unc	BU
1904	15,000	40.00	70.00	100	185	275
1910	10,000	50.00	85.00	140	220	335
1915	10,000	45.00	75.00	120	190	275

REFORM COINAGE
100 Rappen = 1 Frank

Y# 7 1/2 FRANK
2.5000 g., 0.8350 Silver 0.0671 oz. ASW **Ruler:** Prince John II **Obv:** Head left **Rev:** Crowned shield within wreath flanked by value and letters **Note:** 15,745 were melted.

Date	Mintage	F	VF	XF	Unc	BU
1924	30,000	40.00	75.00	115	200	265

Y# 8 FRANK
5.0000 g., 0.8350 Silver 0.1342 oz. ASW **Ruler:** Prince John II **Obv:** Head left **Rev:** Crowned shield within wreath flanked by value and letters **Note:** 45,355 were melted.

Date	Mintage	F	VF	XF	Unc	BU
1924	60,000	20.00	35.00	70.00	100	175

Y# 9 2 FRANKEN

10.0000 g., 0.8350 Silver 0.2684 oz. ASW **Ruler:** Prince John II **Obv:** Head left **Rev:** Crowned shield within wreath flanked by value and letters **Note:** 41,707 were melted.

Date	Mintage	F	VF	XF	Unc	BU
1924	50,000	25.00	50.00	90.00	170	250

Y# 10 5 FRANKEN

25.0000 g., 0.9000 Silver 0.7234 oz. ASW **Ruler:** Prince John II **Obv:** Head left **Rev:** Crowned shield within wreath flanked by value and letters **Note:** 11,260 were melted.

Date	Mintage	F	VF	XF	Unc	BU
1924	15,000	100	200	350	650	975

LITHUANIA

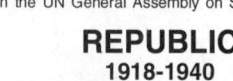

The Republic of Lithuania, southernmost of the Baltic states in east Europe, has an area of 25,174 sq. mi.(65,201 sq. km.) and a population of *3.6 million. Capital: Vilnius. The economy is based on livestock raising and manufacturing. Hogs, cattle, hides and electric motors are exported.

Lithuania emerged as a grand duchy in the 14th century. In the 15th century it was a major power of central Europe, stretching from the Baltic to the Black Sea. It was joined with Poland in 1569, but lost Smolensk, Chernihiv, and the right bank of the river Dnepr Ukraina in 1667, while the left bank remained under Polish – Lithuania rule until 1793. Following the third partition of Poland by Austria, Prussia and Russia, 1795, Lithuania came under Russian domination and did not regain its independence until shortly before the end of World War I when it declared itself a sovereign republic on Feb. 16, 1918. In fall of 1920, Poland captured Vilna (Vilnius). The republic was occupied by Soviet troops and annexed to the U.S.S.R. in 1940. Following the German occupation of 1941-44, it was retaken by Russia and reestablished as a member republic of the Soviet Union. Western countries, including the United States, did not recognize Lithuania's incorporation into the Soviet Union.

Lithuania declared its independence March 11, 1990 and it was recognized by the United States on Sept. 2, 1991, followed by the Soviet government in Moscow on Sept. 6. They were seated in the UN General Assembly on Sept. 17, 1991.

REPUBLIC
1918-1940

STANDARD COINAGE

100 Centas = 1 Litas

KM# 71 CENTAS

1.6000 g., Aluminum-Bronze, 16 mm. **Obv:** National arms **Rev:** Value within circle divides stem of flowers **Edge:** Plain **Designer:** Juozas Zikaras **Note:** Struck at King's Norton.

Date	Mintage	F	VF	XF	Unc	BU
1925	5,000,000	5.00	10.00	20.00	40.00	—

KM# 79 CENTAS

Bronze, 16.6 mm. **Obv:** National arms **Rev:** Large value with oat sprig at right **Edge:** Plain **Designer:** Juozas Zikaras

Date	Mintage	F	VF	XF	Unc	BU
1936	9,995,000	4.00	7.00	15.00	35.00	—

KM# 80 2 CENTAI

2.3000 g., Bronze, 18.5 mm. **Obv:** National arms **Rev:** Large value divides date within wreath **Edge:** Plain **Designer:** Juozas Zikaras

Date	Mintage	F	VF	XF	Unc	BU
1936	4,951,000	5.00	10.00	20.00	40.00	—

KM# 72 5 CENTAI

Aluminum-Bronze **Obv:** National arms **Rev:** Value within circle divides stem of flowers **Designer:** Juozas Zikaras

Date	Mintage	F	VF	XF	Unc	BU
1925	12,000,000	5.00	10.00	20.00	40.00	—

KM# 81 5 CENTAI

2.5000 g., Bronze, 20 mm. **Obv:** National arms **Rev:** Large value within wreath, date on top **Edge:** Plain **Designer:** Juozas Zikaras

Date	Mintage	F	VF	XF	Unc	BU
1936	4,800,000	5.00	10.00	15.00	40.00	—

KM# 73 10 CENTU

3.0000 g., Aluminum-Bronze, 21 mm. **Obv:** National arms **Rev:** Value to right of sagging grain ears **Edge:** Plain **Designer:** Juozas Zikaras

Date	Mintage	F	VF	XF	Unc	BU
1925	12,000,000	5.00	10.00	15.00	40.00	—

KM# 74 20 CENTU

4.0000 g., Aluminum-Bronze, 23 mm. **Obv:** National arms **Rev:** Value to right of sagging grain ears **Edge:** Plain **Designer:** Juozas Zikaras

Date	Mintage	F	VF	XF	Unc	BU
1925	8,000,000	5.00	10.00	20.00	40.00	—

KM# 75 50 CENTU

5.0000 g., Aluminum-Bronze, 25 mm. **Obv:** National arms **Rev:** Value to right of sagging grain ears **Edge:** Plain **Designer:** Juozas Zikaras

Date	Mintage	F	VF	XF	Unc	BU
1925	5,000,000	10.00	15.00	25.00	50.00	—
1925 Proof	2	Value: 1,000				

KM# 76 LITAS

2.7000 g., 0.5000 Silver 0.0434 oz. ASW, 19 mm. **Obv:** National arms **Rev:** Value above oak leaves **Edge:** Milled **Designer:** Juozas Zikaras **Note:** Struck at Royal Mint, London.

Date	Mintage	F	VF	XF	Unc	BU
1925	5,985,000	4.00	8.00	15.00	30.00	—
1925 Proof	—	Value: 800				

Note: Struck as proof record specimens by the Royal Mint, less than 12 were issued

KM# 77 2 LITU

5.4000 g., 0.5000 Silver 0.0868 oz. ASW, 22.9 mm. **Rev:** Denomination within wreath **Edge:** Milled **Designer:** Juozas Zikaras

Date	Mintage	F	VF	XF	Unc	BU
1925	3,000,000	4.00	8.00	15.00	35.00	—
1925 Proof	—	Value: 800				

Note: Struck as proof record specimens by the Royal Mint, less than 12 were issued

KM# 78 5 LITAI

13.5000 g., 0.5000 Silver 0.2170 oz. ASW, 29.5 mm. **Obv:** National arms **Rev:** Value within flowered wreath **Edge:** Milled **Designer:** Juozas Zikaras

Date	Mintage	F	VF	XF	Unc	BU
1925	1,000,000	10.00	15.00	30.00	65.00	—
1925 Proof	—	Value: 800				

Note: Struck as proof record specimens by the Royal Mint, less than 12 were issued

KM# 82 5 LITAI

9.0000 g., 0.7500 Silver 0.2170 oz. ASW, 27 mm. **Obv:** National arms **Rev:** Head left **Edge Lettering:** TAUTOS GEROVE TAVO GEROVE **Designer:** Juozas Zikaras **Note:** Designer's initials below bust.

Date	Mintage	F	VF	XF	Unc	BU
1936	2,612,000	6.00	10.00	15.00	30.00	—

KM# 83 10 LITU

18.0000 g., 0.7500 Silver 0.4340 oz. ASW, 32 mm. **Obv:** National arms **Rev:** Head left **Edge Lettering:** VIENYBEJE TAUTOS JEGA **Designer:** Juozas Zikaras

Date	Mintage	F	VF	XF	Unc	BU
1936	720,000	12.00	15.00	25.00	40.00	70.00

KM# 84 10 LITU

18.0000 g., 0.7500 Silver 0.4340 oz. ASW, 32 mm. **Subject:** 20th Anniversary of Republic **Obv:** Columns of Gediminas above LIETUVA and dates 1918-1938 **Rev:** Head left **Edge Lettering:** VIENYBEJE TAUTOS JEGA **Designer:** Juozas Zikaras

Date	Mintage	F	VF	XF	Unc	BU
ND(1938)	170,000	25.00	35.00	45.00	70.00	100

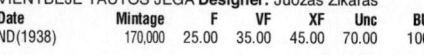

MODERN REPUBLIC

1991-present

REFORM COINAGE

100 Centas = 1 Litas

KM# 85 CENTAS

0.6200 g., Aluminum, 18.73 mm. **Obv:** National arms **Rev:** Large value to right of design

Date	Mintage	F	VF	XF	Unc	BU
1991	—	—	—	—	0.20	—

KM# 86 2 CENTAI

0.9300 g., Aluminum, 21.75 mm. **Obv:** National arms **Rev:** Large value to right of design

Date	Mintage	F	VF	XF	Unc	BU
1991	—	—	—	—	0.25	—

KM# 87 5 CENTAI

1.2400 g., Aluminum, 24.4 mm. **Obv:** National arms **Rev:** Large value to right of artistic design on pole flanked by men blowing horns

Date	Mintage	F	VF	XF	Unc	BU
1991	—	—	—	—	0.30	—

KM# 88 10 CENTU

1.2400 g., Bronze, 15.64 mm. **Obv:** National arms **Rev:** Value

Date	Mintage	F	VF	XF	Unc	BU
1991	—	—	0.50	1.00	2.00	—

KM# 106 10 CENTU

2.6700 g., Brass, 17 mm. **Obv:** National arms **Rev:** Value **Edge:** Reeded

Date	Mintage	F	VF	XF	Unc	BU
1997	—	—	—	—	0.40	—
1998	—	—	—	—	0.40	—
1999	—	—	—	—	0.40	—
2000	—	—	—	—	0.40	—
2000 Proof	5,000	Value: 1.00				
2003 Proof	10,000	Value: 0.75				
2003	—	—	—	—	0.40	—
2006 Proof	2,000	Value: 45.00				
2006	—	—	—	—	0.40	—
2007	—	—	—	—	0.40	—

KM# 89 20 CENTU

1.8700 g., Bronze, 17.38 mm. **Obv:** National arms **Rev:** Value

Date	Mintage	F	VF	XF	Unc	BU
1991	—	0.50	1.00	2.00	4.00	—

KM# 107 20 CENTU

4.7700 g., Brass, 20.43 mm. **Obv:** National arms **Rev:** Value **Edge:** Reeded

Date	Mintage	F	VF	XF	Unc	BU
1997	—	—	—	—	0.75	—
1998	—	—	—	—	0.75	—
1999	—	—	—	—	0.75	—
2000	—	—	—	—	0.75	—
2000 Proof	5,000	Value: 1.25				
2003 Proof	10,000	Value: 1.00				
2003	—	—	—	—	0.75	—
2007	—	—	—	—	0.75	—

KM# 90 50 CENTU

2.7900 g., Bronze, 21.02 mm. **Obv:** National arms **Rev:** Value

Date	Mintage	F	VF	XF	Unc	BU
1991	—	1.00	2.00	4.00	8.00	—

KM# 108 50 CENTU

6.0000 g., Brass **Obv:** National arms **Rev:** Value within designed circle

Date	Mintage	F	VF	XF	Unc	BU
1997	—	—	—	—	1.00	—
1998	—	—	—	—	1.00	—
1999	—	—	—	—	1.00	—
2000	—	—	—	—	1.00	—
2000 Proof	5,000	Value: 2.00				
2003	—	—	—	—	1.00	—
2003 Proof	10,000	Value: 1.50				

KM# 91 LITAS

Copper-Nickel, 22.3 mm. **Obv:** National arms **Rev:** Value with lines above

Date	Mintage	F	VF	XF	Unc	BU
1991	—	2.00	3.00	5.00	10.00	—

KM# 109 LITAS

Copper-Nickel, 22.3 mm. **Subject:** 75th Anniversary - Bank of Lithuania **Obv:** National arms above value **Rev:** Bust 1/4 right

Date	Mintage	F	VF	XF	Unc	BU
1997	200,000	1.00	2.00	4.00	10.00	—

KM# 111 LITAS

6.1800 g., Copper-Nickel, 22.3 mm. **Obv:** National arms **Rev:** Value within circle above lined designs **Edge:** Reeded

Date	Mintage	F	VF	XF	Unc	BU
1998	—	—	—	—	1.50	—
1999	—	—	—	—	1.50	—
2000	—	—	—	—	1.50	—
2000 Proof	5,000	Value: 3.00				
2001	—	—	—	—	1.50	—
2002	—	—	—	—	1.50	—
2003 Proof	10,000	Value: 2.00				
2003	—	—	—	—	1.50	—

KM# 117 LITAS

Copper-Nickel, 22.3 mm. **Subject:** The Baltic Highway **Obv:** National arms on shield within shaded circle divides date **Rev:** Six clasped hands within artistic design **Edge:** Reeded and plain sections

Date	Mintage	F	VF	XF	Unc	BU
1999	1,000,000	1.00	2.00	3.00	5.00	—

KM# 137 LITAS

6.1500 g., Copper-Nickel, 22.2 mm. **Subject:** 425th Anniversary - University of Vilnius **Obv:** Knight on horse within rope wreath **Rev:** Building within court yard **Edge:** Segmented reeding

Date	Mintage	F	VF	XF	Unc	BU
2004	200,000	1.00	2.00	3.00	5.00	—

KM# 142 LITAS

6.4100 g., Copper-Nickel, 22.35 mm. **Obv:** Knight on horse within circle **Rev:** Palace **Edge:** Segmented reeding

Date	Mintage	F	VF	XF	Unc	BU
2005	1,000,000	—	—	2.00	4.00	—

KM# 92 2 LITAI

Copper-Nickel **Obv:** National arms **Rev:** Value within design

Date	Mintage	F	VF	XF	Unc	BU
1991	—	2.00	3.00	6.00	12.00	—

KM# 112 2 LITAI

7.5000 g., Bi-Metallic Copper-Nickel ring in Brass center, 25 mm. **Obv:** National arms within circle **Rev:** Value within circle **Edge:** Segmented reeding

Date	Mintage	F	VF	XF	Unc	BU
1998	—	—	—	—	3.00	—
1999	—	—	—	—	3.00	—
2000	—	—	—	—	3.00	—
2000 Proof	5,000	Value: 4.00				
2001	—	—	—	—	3.00	—
2002	—	—	—	—	3.00	—
2003	—	—	—	—	3.00	—
2003 Proof	10,000	Value: 3.50				

KM# 93 5 LITAI

Copper-Nickel **Obv:** National arms **Rev:** Value within design

Date	Mintage	F	VF	XF	Unc	BU
1991	—	3.00	5.00	10.00	18.00	—

KM# 113 5 LITAI

10.2600 g., Bi-Metallic Copper-Nickel ring in Brass center, 22.5 mm. **Obv:** National arms within circle **Rev:** Value within circle **Edge Lettering:** PENKI LITAI

Date	Mintage	F	VF	XF	Unc	BU
1998	—	—	—	—	7.50	8.50
1999	—	—	—	—	7.50	8.50

Date	Mintage	F	VF	XF	Unc	BU
2000	—	—	—	—	7.50	8.50
2000 Proof	5,000	Value: 10.00				
2003	—	—	—	—	6.00	7.50
2003 Proof	10,000	Value: 9.00				

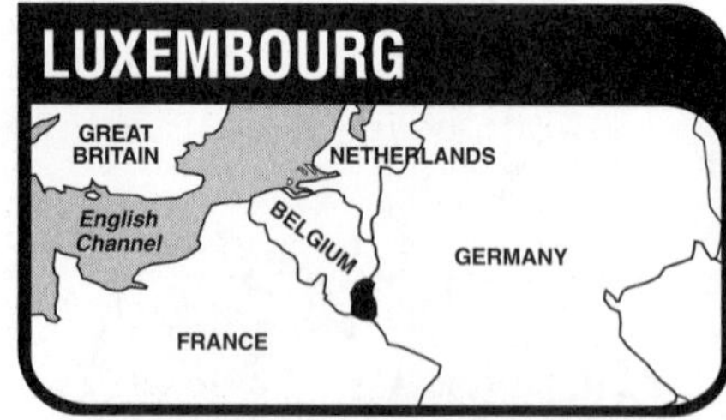

The Grand Duchy of Luxembourg is located in western Europe between Belgium, Germany and France, has an area of 1,103 sq. mi. (2,586 sq. km.) and a population of 377,100. Capital: Luxembourg. The economy is based on steel.

Founded about 963, Luxembourg was a prominent country of the Holy Roman Empire; one of its sovereigns became Holy Roman Emperor as Henry VII, 1308. After being made a duchy by Emperor Charles IV, 1354, Luxembourg passed under the domination of Burgundy, Spain, Austria and France, 1443-1815, regaining autonomy under the Treaty of Vienna, 1815, as a grand duchy in union with the Netherlands, though ostensibly a member of the German Confederation. When Belgium seceded from the Kingdom of the Netherlands, 1830, Luxembourg was forced to cede its greater western section to Belgium. The tiny duchy left the German Confederation in 1867 when the Treaty of London recognized it as an independent state and guaranteed its perpetual neutrality. Luxembourg was occupied by Germany and liberated by American troops in both World Wars.

RULERS

Adolphe, 1890-1905
William IV, 1905-1912
Marie Adelaide, 1912-1919
Charlotte, 1919-1964
Jean, 1964-2000
Henri, 2000-

MINT MARKS

A - Paris
(b) - Brussels, privy marks only
H – Gunzburg
(n) – lion - Namur
(u) - Utrecht, privy marks only

PRIVY MARKS

Angel's head, two headed eagle - Brussels
Sword, Caduceus - Utrecht (1846-74 although struck at Brussels until 1909)

NOTE: Beginning in 1994 the letters "qp" for quality proof appear on Proof coins.

MONETARY SYSTEM

100 Centimes = 1 Franc

GRAND DUCHY

STANDARD COINAGE RESUMED

100 Centimes = 1 Franc

KM# 21 2-1/2 CENTIMES

Bronze **Ruler:** William III Netherlands **Obv:** Crowned ornate shield within rope wreath **Obv. Legend:** GRAND-DUCHE DE LUXEMBOURG **Rev:** Value and date within wreath

Date	Mintage	F	VF	XF	Unc	BU
1901(u)	800,000	0.50	1.50	7.50	40.00	—
Note: BARTH on reverse						
1901(u)	Inc. above	0.50	1.50	8.50	42.00	—
Note: BAPTH on reverse						
1908(u)	400,000	0.50	1.50	9.50	45.00	—

KM# 24 5 CENTIMES

1.9500 g., Copper-Nickel, 17 mm. **Ruler:** Adolphe **Obv:** Head right **Rev:** Value within wreath **Designer:** A. Michaux

Date	Mintage	F	VF	XF	Unc	BU
1901	2,000,000	0.25	0.75	4.50	17.50	—

KM# 26 5 CENTIMES

Copper-Nickel **Ruler:** William IV **Obv:** Head right **Rev:** Value within wreath

Date	Mintage	F	VF	XF	Unc	BU
1908	1,500,000	0.35	1.00	6.50	20.00	—

KM# 27 5 CENTIMES

Zinc **Ruler:** Marie Adelaide **Obv:** Plain and beaded circle around hole in center with date below **Rev:** Value above hole in center with 1/2 wreath below

Date	Mintage	F	VF	XF	Unc	BU
1915	1,200,000	1.00	6.00	15.00	30.00	—

KM# 30 5 CENTIMES

Iron **Ruler:** Charlotte **Obv:** National arms **Rev:** Value within wreath

Date	Mintage	F	VF	XF	Unc	BU
1918	1,200,000	1.00	4.00	8.00	30.00	—
1921	600,000	10.00	20.00	40.00	80.00	—
1922	400,000	15.00	30.00	80.00	120	—

KM# 33 5 CENTIMES

Copper-Nickel **Ruler:** Charlotte **Obv:** Crowned monogram **Rev:** Value within wreath

Date	Mintage	F	VF	XF	Unc	BU
1924	3,000,000	0.20	0.40	3.00	10.00	—

KM# 40 5 CENTIMES

Bronze **Ruler:** Charlotte **Obv:** Head left **Rev:** Value

Date	Mintage	F	VF	XF	Unc	BU
1930	5,000,000	0.10	0.25	2.00	4.00	—

KM# 25 10 CENTIMES

Copper-Nickel, 20 mm. **Ruler:** Adolphe **Obv:** Head right **Rev:** Value within wreath **Designer:** A. Michaux

Date	Mintage	F	VF	XF	Unc	BU
1901	4,000,000	0.25	0.75	6.00	14.00	—

KM# 28 10 CENTIMES

Zinc **Ruler:** Marie Adelaide **Obv:** Beaded circle around hole in center with date below **Rev:** Large value above hole in center with 1/2 wreath below

Date	Mintage	F	VF	XF	Unc	BU
1915	1,400,000	1.25	4.00	8.00	20.00	—

KM# 31 10 CENTIMES

Iron **Ruler:** Charlotte **Obv:** National arms **Rev:** Value within wreath

Date	Mintage	F	VF	XF	Unc	BU
1918	1,603,000	1.50	3.50	10.00	25.00	—
1921	626,000	2.00	10.00	20.00	40.00	—
1923	350,000	12.00	30.00	60.00	125	—

KM# 34 10 CENTIMES

Copper-Nickel **Ruler:** Charlotte **Obv:** Crowned monogram **Rev:** Value within wreath

Date	Mintage	F	VF	XF	Unc	BU
1924	3,500,000	0.25	0.50	2.00	8.00	—

KM# 41 10 CENTIMES

Bronze **Ruler:** Charlotte **Obv:** Head left **Rev:** Value flanked by sprigs with star above

Date	Mintage	F	VF	XF	Unc	BU
1930	5,000,000	0.10	0.25	2.00	4.50	—

KM# 29 25 CENTIMES

Zinc **Ruler:** Charlotte **Obv:** Beaded circle around hole in center with date below **Rev:** Large value above hole in center with wreath below

Date	Mintage	F	VF	XF	Unc	BU
1916	800,000	1.50	6.00	12.00	25.00	—
1920	—	200	400	600	1,000	—

KM# 32 25 CENTIMES

Iron **Ruler:** Charlotte **Obv:** National arms **Rev:** Value within wreath

Date	Mintage	F	VF	XF	Unc	BU
1919	804,000	2.75	6.50	12.50	35.00	—
1920	800,000	2.75	8.00	14.00	35.00	—
1922	600,000	2.75	8.50	16.00	40.00	—

KM# 37 25 CENTIMES

Copper-Nickel **Ruler:** Charlotte **Obv:** Crowned national arms flanked by stars **Rev:** Value and date to right of sprig

Date	Mintage	F	VF	XF	Unc	BU
1927	2,500,000	0.35	0.65	5.00	25.00	—

KM# 42 25 CENTIMES

Bronze **Ruler:** Charlotte **Obv:** Crowned national arms flanked by stars **Rev:** Value and date to right of sprig **Designer:** Everaerts

Date	Mintage	F	VF	XF	Unc	BU
1930	1,000,000	0.35	1.00	8.00	30.00	—

KM# 42a.1 25 CENTIMES

Copper-Nickel, 25 mm. **Ruler:** Charlotte **Obv:** Crowned national arms flanked by stars **Rev:** Value and date to right of sprig **Note:** Coin alignment.

Date	Mintage	F	VF	XF	Unc	BU
1938	2,000,000	0.35	1.00	3.00	10.00	—

KM# 42a.2 25 CENTIMES

Copper-Nickel, 25 mm. **Ruler:** Charlotte **Obv:** Crowned national arms flanked by stars **Rev:** Value and date to right of sprig **Note:** Medal alignment.

Date	Mintage	F	VF	XF	Unc	BU
1938	Inc. above	50.00	75.00	100	200	—

KM# 45 25 CENTIMES

Bronze, 19 mm. **Ruler:** Charlotte **Obv:** Crowned national arms flanked by diamonds **Rev:** Value and date to right of sprig

Date	Mintage	F	VF	XF	Unc	BU
1946	1,000,000	—	0.15	0.25	0.75	—
1947	1,000,000	—	0.15	0.25	0.75	—

KM# 45a.1 25 CENTIMES

Aluminum, 18.5 mm. **Ruler:** Jean **Obv:** Crowned national arms flanked by diamonds **Rev:** Value and date to right of sprig **Note:** Coin alignment.

Date	Mintage	F	VF	XF	Unc	BU
1954	7,000,000	—	—	—	0.10	0.20
1957	3,020,000	—	—	—	0.10	0.20
1960	3,020,000	—	—	—	0.10	0.20
1963	4,000,000	—	—	—	0.10	0.20
1965	2,000,000	—	—	—	0.10	0.20
1967	3,000,000	—	—	—	0.10	0.20
1968	600,000	0.10	0.25	0.50	1.00	2.00
1970	4,000,000	—	—	—	0.10	0.20
1972	4,000,000	—	—	—	0.10	0.20

KM# 43 50 CENTIMES

Nickel **Ruler:** Charlotte **Obv:** Man working field with date below **Rev:** Value divides wheat sprays

Date	Mintage	F	VF	XF	Unc	BU
1930	2,000,000	0.25	1.00	10.00	20.00	—

KM# 35 FRANC

5.1000 g., Nickel, 22.8 mm. **Ruler:** Charlotte **Obv:** Crowned monogram **Rev:** Man working field with date below

Date	Mintage	F	VF	XF	Unc	BU
1924	1,000,000	0.25	1.50	10.00	20.00	—
1928	2,000,000	0.20	1.50	10.00	20.00	—
1935	1,000,000	0.25	2.00	14.00	30.00	—

KM# 44 FRANC

Copper-Nickel, 24 mm. **Ruler:** Charlotte **Obv:** Crowned monogram flanked by flower blossoms at top **Rev:** Woman figure divides date and value

Date	Mintage	F	VF	XF	Unc	BU
1939	5,000,000	0.25	0.75	1.50	5.00	—

KM# 46.1 FRANC

Copper-Nickel, 23 mm. **Ruler:** Charlotte **Obv:** Man working field **Rev:** Crowned monogram divides value

Date	Mintage	F	VF	XF	Unc	BU
1946	4,000,000	0.15	0.35	0.50	1.50	—
1947	2,000,000	0.20	0.40	1.00	3.00	—

KM# 46.2 FRANC

Copper-Nickel, 21 mm. **Ruler:** Charlotte **Obv:** Man working field **Rev:** Crowned monogram divides value

Date	Mintage	F	VF	XF	Unc	BU
1952	5,000,000	0.10	0.25	0.50	2.00	—
1953	2,000,000	0.10	0.25	0.50	1.50	—
1955	1,000,000	0.10	0.25	0.50	1.50	—
1957	2,000,000	—	0.10	0.25	1.00	—
1960	2,000,000	—	0.10	0.25	1.00	—
1962	2,000,000	—	0.10	0.25	1.00	—
1964	2,000,000	—	0.10	0.25	1.00	—

KM# 55 FRANC

3.8900 g., Copper-Nickel, 21 mm. **Ruler:** Jean **Obv:** Head left **Rev:** Crown above value within wreath **Designer:** J. N. Lefevre

Date	Mintage	F	VF	XF	Unc	BU
1965	3,000,000	—	—	0.10	0.20	0.40
1966	1,000,000	—	—	0.10	0.20	0.40
1968	3,000,000	—	—	0.10	0.20	0.40
1970	3,000,000	—	—	0.10	0.20	0.40
1972	3,000,000	—	—	0.10	0.20	0.40
1973	3,000,000	—	—	0.10	0.20	0.40
1976	3,000,000	—	—	0.10	0.20	0.40
1977	1,000,000	—	—	0.10	0.20	0.40
1978	3,000,000	—	—	0.10	0.20	0.40
1979	2,000,000	—	—	0.10	0.20	0.40
1980	4,000,000	—	—	0.10	0.20	0.40
1981	5,000,000	—	—	0.10	0.20	0.40
1982	3,000,000	—	—	0.10	0.20	0.40
1983	3,000,000	—	—	0.10	0.20	0.40
1984	3,000,000	—	—	0.10	0.20	0.40

KM# 59 FRANC

Copper-Nickel, 21 mm. **Ruler:** Jean **Obv:** Head left **Rev:** IML added **Designer:** J. N. Lefevre

Date	Mintage	F	VF	XF	Unc	BU
1986	3,000,000	—	—	0.10	0.20	0.40
1987	3,000,000	—	—	0.10	0.20	0.40

KM# 63 FRANC

Nickel-Steel **Ruler:** Jean **Obv:** Head left **Rev:** Crown divides date above value **Designer:** J. N. Lefevre

Date	Mintage	F	VF	XF	Unc	BU
1988	10,000,000	—	—	—	0.40	0.60
1989	3,000,000	—	—	—	0.40	0.60
1990	25,010,000	—	—	—	0.40	0.60
1991	10,010,000	—	—	—	0.40	0.60
1992 In sets only	10,000	—	—	—	0.60	1.00
1993 In sets only	10,000	—	—	—	0.60	1.00
1994 In sets only	10,000	—	—	—	0.60	1.00
1995 In sets only	10,000	—	—	—	0.60	1.00

KM# 36 2 FRANCS

Nickel **Ruler:** Charlotte **Obv:** Crowned monogram above sprig **Rev:** Man working field

Date	Mintage	F	VF	XF	Unc	BU
1924	1,000,000	1.00	4.00	20.00	40.00	—

KM# 38 5 FRANCS

8.0000 g., 0.6250 Silver 0.1607 oz. ASW, 27.8 mm. **Ruler:** Charlotte **Rev:** Wing above national arms on shield divides value

Date	Mintage	F	VF	XF	Unc	BU
1929	2,000,000	BV	3.50	12.50	25.00	—

KM# 50 5 FRANCS

Copper-Nickel **Ruler:** Charlotte **Obv:** Head left **Rev:** Value flanked by flowers below crown and ribbon

Date	Mintage	F	VF	XF	Unc	BU
1949	2,000,000	0.30	0.60	1.00	3.50	—

KM# 51 5 FRANCS

Copper-Nickel **Ruler:** Charlotte **Obv:** Head right **Rev:** Crowned arms divide value

Date	Mintage	F	VF	XF	Unc	BU
1962	2,000,000	0.10	0.25	0.40	1.00	—

KM# 56 5 FRANCS

Copper-Nickel **Ruler:** Jean **Obv:** Head left **Rev:** Crown above value and date within sprigs **Designer:** J. N. Lefevre

Date	Mintage	F	VF	XF	Unc	BU
1971	1,000,000	—	—	0.20	0.50	0.80
1976	1,000,000	—	—	0.20	0.50	0.80
1979	1,000,000	—	—	0.20	0.50	0.80
1981	1,000,000	—	—	0.20	0.50	0.80

KM# 60.1 5 FRANCS

Brass **Ruler:** Jean **Obv:** Head left **Rev:** Crown divides date above value within sprigs with IML added **Designer:** J. N. Lefevre

Date	Mintage	F	VF	XF	Unc	BU
1986	9,000,000	—	—	0.15	0.40	0.65
1987	7,000,000	—	—	0.15	0.40	0.65
1988	2,000,000	—	—	0.15	0.40	0.65

KM# 60.2 5 FRANCS

Brass **Ruler:** Jean **Obv:** Head left **Rev:** Larger crown divides date above value within sprigs **Designer:** J. N. Lefevre

Date	Mintage	F	VF	XF	Unc	BU
1986	—	—	—	0.15	0.40	0.65
1987	—	—	—	0.15	0.40	0.65

KM# 65 5 FRANCS

Brass **Ruler:** Jean **Obv:** Head left **Rev:** Crown divides date above value **Designer:** J. N. Lefevre

Date	Mintage	F	VF	XF	Unc	BU
1989	2,000,000	—	—	—	0.60	1.00
1990	4,010,000	—	—	—	0.60	1.00
1991 In sets only	10,000	—	—	—	0.75	1.25
1992 In sets only	20,000	—	—	—	0.75	1.25
1993 In sets only	17,500	—	—	—	0.75	1.25
1994 In sets only	10,000	—	—	—	0.75	1.25
1995 In sets only	10,000	—	—	—	0.75	1.25

KM# 39 10 FRANCS

13.5000 g., 0.7500 Silver 0.3255 oz. ASW **Ruler:** Charlotte **Obv:** Head left **Rev:** Helmeted shield **Edge:** Reeded

Date	Mintage	F	VF	XF	Unc	BU
1929	1,000,000	BV	6.00	12.00	32.50	—

KM# 57 10 FRANCS

Nickel, 27 mm. **Ruler:** Jean **Obv:** Head left **Rev:** Crown above value and date flanked by leaves **Designer:** J. N. Lefevre

Date	Mintage	F	VF	XF	Unc	BU
1971	3,000,000	—	—	0.30	0.60	1.00
1972	3,000,000	—	—	0.30	0.60	1.00
1974	3,000,000	—	—	0.30	0.60	1.00
1976	3,000,000	—	—	0.30	0.60	1.00
1977	1,000,000	—	—	0.30	0.60	1.00
1978	1,000,000	—	—	0.30	0.60	1.00
1979	1,000,000	—	—	0.30	0.60	1.00
1980	1,000,000	—	—	0.30	0.60	1.00

KM# 47 20 FRANCS

8.5000 g., 0.8350 Silver 0.2282 oz. ASW, 27 mm. **Ruler:** Charlotte **Subject:** 600th Anniversary - John the Blind **Obv:** Head left flanked by shields **Rev:** Armored Knight on horse above dates **Designer:** Armand Bonnetain

Date	Mintage	F	VF	XF	Unc	BU
ND(1946)	100,000	BV	5.00	12.00	18.00	—
ND(1946) Proof	100	Value: 200				

KM# 58 20 FRANCS

Bronze, 25.5 mm. **Ruler:** Jean **Obv:** Head left **Rev:** Crown above value flanked by sprigs **Edge:** Dashes all around **Designer:** J. N. Lefevre

Date	Mintage	F	VF	XF	Unc	BU
1980	3,000,000	—	—	0.60	1.00	1.50
1981	3,000,000	—	—	0.60	1.00	1.50
1982	3,000,000	—	—	0.60	1.00	1.50
1983	2,000,000	—	—	0.60	1.00	1.50

KM# 67 20 FRANCS

Bronze, 25.5 mm. **Ruler:** Jean **Obv:** Head left **Rev:** Crown divides date above value **Designer:** J. N. Lefevre

Date	Mintage	F	VF	XF	Unc	BU
1990	1,110,000	—	—	—	2.00	3.00
1991 In sets only	10,000	—	—	—	2.50	3.50
1992 In sets only	10,000	—	—	—	2.50	3.50
1993 In sets only	10,000	—	—	—	2.50	3.50
1994 In sets only	10,000	—	—	—	2.50	3.50
1995 In sets only	10,000	—	—	—	2.50	3.50

KM# 48 50 FRANCS

12.5000 g., 0.8350 Silver 0.3356 oz. ASW, 30 mm. **Ruler:** Charlotte **Subject:** 600th Anniversary - John the Blind **Designer:** Armand Bonnetain

Date	Mintage	F	VF	XF	Unc	BU
ND(1946)	100,000	—	10.00	15.00	35.00	—
ND(1946) Proof	100	Value: 225				

KM# 62 50 FRANCS

Nickel, 22.5 mm. **Ruler:** Jean **Obv:** Head left **Rev:** Crown divides date above value **Designer:** J. N. Lefevre

Date	Mintage	F	VF	XF	Unc	BU
1987	3,000,000	—	—	1.50	3.50	5.00
1988	1,000,000	—	—	1.50	3.50	5.00
1989	1,200,000	—	—	1.50	3.50	5.00

KM# 66 50 FRANCS

7.0200 g., Nickel, 22.5 mm. **Ruler:** Jean **Designer:** J. N. Lefevre **Note:** Similar to 5 Francs, KM#65.

Date	Mintage	F	VF	XF	Unc	BU
1989	2,000,000	—	—	—	3.50	5.00
1990	2,010,000	—	—	—	3.50	5.00
1991 In sets only	10,000	—	—	—	4.00	6.00
1992 In sets only	10,000	—	—	—	4.00	6.00
1993 In sets only	10,000	—	—	—	4.00	6.00
1994 In sets only	10,000	—	—	—	4.00	6.00
1995 In sets only	10,000	—	—	—	4.00	6.00

KM# 49 100 FRANCS

25.0000 g., 0.8350 Silver 0.6711 oz. ASW, 37 mm. **Ruler:** Charlotte **Subject:** 600th Anniversary - John the Blind **Obv:** Head left flanked by crowned shields **Rev:** Armored Knight on horse above dates **Designer:** Armand Bonnetain

Date	Mintage	F	VF	XF	Unc	BU
ND(1946)	98,000	—	20.00	40.00	50.00	—
ND(1946) Proof	100	Value: 250				
ND(1946) Restrike	2,000	—	—	—	100	—

Note: Without designer's name

KM# 52 100 FRANCS

18.0000 g., 0.8350 Silver 0.4832 oz. ASW **Ruler:** Charlotte **Obv:** Head right **Rev:** Crowned arms with supporters above value

Date	Mintage	F	VF	XF	Unc	BU
1963	50,000	—	—	10.00	15.00	—

KM# 54 100 FRANCS

18.0000 g., 0.8350 Silver 0.4832 oz. ASW **Ruler:** Charlotte **Rev:** Crowned mantled arms with supporters **Designer:** J. N. Lefevre

Date	Mintage	F	VF	XF	Unc	BU
1964	50,000	—	—	9.00	14.00	—

EURO COINAGE

European Economic Community Issues

KM# 75 EURO CENT

2.2700 g., Copper Plated Steel, 16.2 mm. **Ruler:** Henri **Obv:** Head right **Obv. Designer:** Yvette Gastauer-Claire **Rev:** Value and globe **Rev. Designer:** Luc Luycx **Edge:** Plain

Date	Mintage	F	VF	XF	Unc	BU
2002(u)	34,517,500	—	—	—	0.35	—
2002(u) Proof	1,500	—	—	—	—	—
2003(u)	1,500,000	—	—	—	0.50	—
2003(u) Proof	1,500	—	—	—	—	—
2004(u)	21,001,000	—	—	—	0.35	—
2004(u) Proof	1,500	—	—	—	—	—
2005(u)	7,000,000	—	—	—	0.35	—
2006(u)	4,000,000	—	—	—	0.35	—
2007(a)	—	—	—	—	0.35	—

KM# 76 2 EURO CENT

3.0300 g., Copper Plated Steel, 18.7 mm. **Ruler:** Henri **Obv:** Head right **Obv. Designer:** Yvette Gastauer-Claire **Rev:** Value and globe **Rev. Designer:** Luc Luycx **Edge:** Grooved

Date	Mintage	F	VF	XF	Unc	BU
2002(u)	35,917,500	—	—	—	0.50	—
2002(u) Proof	1,500	—	—	—	—	—
2003(u)	1,500,000	—	—	—	0.65	—
2003(u) Proof	1,500	—	—	—	—	—
2004(u)	20,001,000	—	—	—	0.50	—
2004(u) Proof	1,500	—	—	—	—	—
2005(u)	13,000,000	—	—	—	0.50	—
2006(u)	4,000,000	—	—	—	0.50	—
2007(a)	—	—	—	—	0.50	—

KM# 77 5 EURO CENT

3.8600 g., Copper Plated Steel, 21.2 mm. **Ruler:** Henri **Obv:** Head right **Obv. Designer:** Yvette Gastauer-Claire **Rev:** Value and globe **Rev. Designer:** Luc Luycx **Edge:** Plain

Date	Mintage	F	VF	XF	Unc	BU
2002(u)	28,917,500	—	—	—	0.75	—
2002(u) Proof	1,500	—	—	—	—	—

Date	Mintage	F	VF	XF	Unc	BU
2003(u)	4,500,000	—	—	—	1.00	—
2003(u) Proof	1,500	—	—	—	—	—
2004(u)	16,001,000	—	—	—	0.75	—
2004(u) Proof	1,500	—	—	—	—	—
2005(u)	6,000,000	—	—	—	0.75	—
2006(u)	5,000,000	—	—	—	0.75	—
2007(a)	—	—	—	—	0.75	—

KM# 78 10 EURO CENT

4.0700 g., Brass, 19.7 mm. **Ruler:** Henri **Obv:** Grand Duke's portrait **Obv. Designer:** Yvette Gastauer-Claire **Rev:** Value and map **Rev. Designer:** Luc Luycx **Edge:** Reeded

Date	Mintage	F	VF	XF	Unc	BU
2002(u)	25,117,500	—	—	—	0.75	—
2002(u) Proof	1,500	—	—	—	—	—
2003(u)	1,500,000	—	—	—	1.00	—
2003(u) Proof	1,500	—	—	—	—	—
2004(u)	12,001,000	—	—	—	0.75	—
2004(u) Proof	1,500	—	—	—	—	—
2005(u)	2,000,000	—	—	—	0.75	—
2006(u)	4,000,000	—	—	—	0.75	—

KM# 89 10 EURO CENT

4.0700 g., Brass, 19.7 mm. **Ruler:** Henri **Obv:** Prince's portrait **Obv. Designer:** Yvette Gastauer-Claire **Rev:** Relief map of Western Europe, stars, lines and value **Rev. Designer:** Luc Luycx **Edge:** Reeded

Date	Mintage	F	VF	XF	Unc	BU
2007(a)	—	—	—	—	0.75	—

KM# 79 20 EURO CENT

5.7300 g., Brass, 22.1 mm. **Ruler:** Henri **Obv:** Grand Duke's portrait **Obv. Designer:** Yvette Gastauer-Claire **Rev:** Value and map **Rev. Designer:** Luc Luycx **Edge:** Notched

Date	Mintage	F	VF	XF	Unc	BU
2002(u)	25,717,500	—	—	—	1.00	—
2002(u) Proof	1,500	—	—	—	—	—
2003(u)	1,500,000	—	—	—	1.25	—
2003(u) Proof	1,500	—	—	—	—	—
2004(u)	14,001,000	—	—	—	1.00	—
2004(u) Proof	1,500	—	—	—	—	—
2005(u)	6,000,000	—	—	—	1.00	—
2006(u)	7,000,000	—	—	—	1.00	—

KM# 90 20 EURO CENT

5.7300 g., Brass, 22.1 mm. **Ruler:** Henri **Obv:** Prince's portrait **Obv. Designer:** Yvette Gastauer-Claire **Rev:** Relief map of Western Europe, stars, lines and value **Rev. Designer:** Luc Luycx **Edge:** Notched

Date	Mintage	F	VF	XF	Unc	BU
2007(a)	—	—	—	—	1.00	1.25

KM# 80 50 EURO CENT

7.8100 g., Brass, 24.1 mm. **Ruler:** Henri **Obv:** Grand Duke's portrait **Obv. Designer:** Yvette Gastauer-Claire **Rev:** Value and map **Rev. Designer:** Luc Luycx **Edge:** Reeded

Date	Mintage	F	VF	XF	Unc	BU
2002(u)	21,917,500	—	—	—	1.25	—
2002(u) Proof	1,500	—	—	—	—	—
2003(u)	2,500,000	—	—	—	1.50	—
2003(u) Proof	1,500	—	—	—	—	—
2004(u)	10,001,000	—	—	—	1.25	—
2004(u) Proof	1,500	—	—	—	—	—
2005(u)	3,000,000	—	—	—	1.25	—
2006(u)	3,000,000	—	—	—	1.25	—

KM# 91 50 EURO CENT

7.8100 g., Brass, 24.1 mm. **Ruler:** Henri **Obv:** Prince's portrait **Obv. Designer:** Yvette Gastauer-Claire **Rev:** Relief map of Western Europe, stars, lines and value **Rev. Designer:** Luc Luycx **Edge:** Reeded

Date	Mintage	F	VF	XF	Unc	BU
2007(a)	—	—	—	—	1.25	1.50

KM# 81 EURO

7.5000 g., Bi-Metallic Copper-Nickel center in Brass ring, 23.2 mm. **Ruler:** Henri **Obv:** Grand Duke's portrait **Obv. Designer:** Yvette Gastauer-Claire **Rev:** Value and map within divided circle **Rev. Designer:** Luc Luycx **Edge:** Reeded and plain sections

Date	Mintage	F	VF	XF	Unc	BU
2002(u)	21,318,525	—	—	—	2.50	—
2002(u) Proof	1,500	—	—	—	—	—
2003(u)	1,500,000	—	—	—	2.75	—
2003(u) Proof	1,500	—	—	—	—	—
2004(u)	9,001,000	—	—	—	2.50	—

Date	Mintage	F	VF	XF	Unc	BU
2004(u) Proof	1,500	—	—	—	—	—
2005(u)	2,000,000	—	—	—	2.50	—
2006(u)	1,000,000	—	—	—	2.50	—

KM# 92 EURO

7.5000 g., Bi-Metallic Copper-Nickel center in Brass ring, 23.2 mm. **Ruler:** Henri **Obv:** Prince's portrait **Obv. Designer:** Yvette Gastauer-Claire **Rev:** Relief map of Western Europe, stars, lines and value **Rev. Designer:** Luc Luycx **Edge:** Segmented reeding

Date	Mintage	F	VF	XF	Unc	BU
2007(a)	—	—	—	—	2.25	2.75

KM# 82 2 EURO

8.5200 g., Bi-Metallic Brass center in Copper-Nickel ring, 25.7 mm. **Ruler:** Henri **Obv:** Grand Duke's portrait **Obv. Designer:** Yvette Gastauer-Claire **Rev:** Value and map within divided circle **Rev. Designer:** Luc Luycx **Edge:** Reeded with 2's and stars

Date	Mintage	F	VF	XF	Unc	BU
2002(u)	18,517,500	—	—	—	3.75	—
2002(u) Proof	1,500	—	—	—	—	—
2003(u)	3,500,000	—	—	—	4.50	—
2003(u) Proof	1,500	—	—	—	—	—
2004(u)	7,553,200	—	—	—	4.00	—
2004(u) Proof	1,500	—	—	—	—	—
2005(u)	3,500,000	—	—	—	4.00	—
2006(u)	2,000,000	—	—	—	4.00	—

KM# 85 2 EURO

8.5200 g., Bi-Metallic Brass center in Copper-Nickel ring, 25.7 mm. **Ruler:** Henri **Obv:** Head right and crowned monogram within 1/2 star circle **Rev:** Value and map within divided circle

Date	Mintage	F	VF	XF	Unc	BU
2004(u)	2,447,800	—	—	—	5.50	—
2004(u) Proof	1,500	—	—	—	—	—

KM# 87 2 EURO

8.5200 g., Bi-Metallic Brass center in Copper-Nickel ring, 25.7 mm. **Ruler:** Henri **Obv:** Conjoined heads right within circle **Rev:** Value and map within divided circle **Edge:** Reeding over stars and 2's

Date	Mintage	F	VF	XF	Unc	BU
2005(u)	2,720,000	—	—	—	5.00	—

KM# 88 2 EURO

8.5000 g., Bi-Metallic, 25.7 mm. **Ruler:** Henri **Obv:** Conjoined heads right within circle and star border **Rev:** Value and map within divided circle **Edge:** Reeding over 2's and stars

Date	Mintage	F	VF	XF	Unc	BU
2006(u)	1,000,000	—	—	—	5.00	—

KM# 93 2 EURO

8.5200 g., Bi-Metallic Brass center in Copper-Nickel ring, 25.7 mm. **Ruler:** Henri **Obv:** Prince's portrait **Obv. Designer:** Yvette Gastauer-Claire **Rev:** Relief map of Western Europe, stars, lines and value **Rev. Designer:** Luc Luycx **Edge:** Reeded with 2's and stars

Date	Mintage	F	VF	XF	Unc	BU
2007(a)	1,000,000	—	—	—	4.00	5.00

KM# 94 2 EURO

Bi-Metallic Brass center in Copper-Nickel ring, 25.71 mm. **Ruler:** Henri **Subject:** 50th Anniversary Treaty of Rome **Obv:** Open treaty book with latent image on left hand page **Obv. Legend:** LËTZEBUERG **Rev:** Large value at left, modified outline of Europe at right **Edge:** Reeded with 2's and stars

Date	Mintage	F	VF	XF	Unc	BU
2007(a)	—	—	—	—	—	9.00

KM# 95 2 EURO

8.5400 g., Bi-Metallic Brass center in Copper-Nickel ring, 25.71 mm. **Ruler:** Henri **Obv:** Palace in background at left, head 3/4 left at right **Obv. Legend:** LËTZEBUERG **Rev:** Large value at left, modified outline of Europe at right **Edge:** Reeded with 2's and stars

Date	Mintage	F	VF	XF	Unc	BU
2007(a)	—	—	—	—	—	9.00

KM# 96 2 EURO

8.5200 g., Bi-Metallic Brass center in Copper-Nickel ring., 25.71 mm. **Ruler:** Henri **Obv:** Head at left, Chateau de Berg at right **Obv. Legend:** LËTZEBUERG **Rev:** Large value at left, modified outline of Europe at right **Edge:** Reeded with 2's and stars

Date	Mintage	F	VF	XF	Unc	BU
2008(a)	—	—	—	4.00	5.00	6.25

MACAO

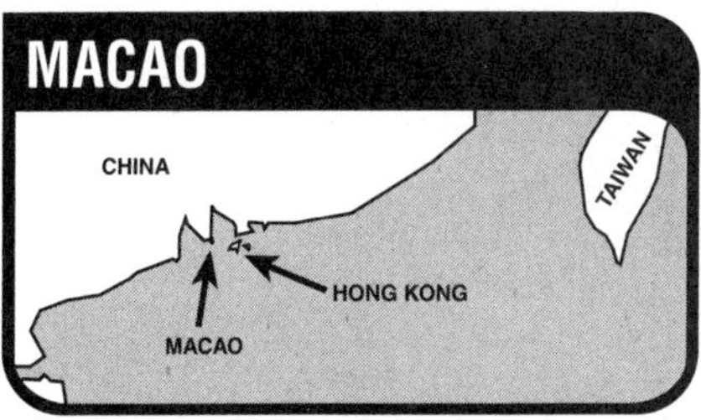

The Province of Macao, a Portuguese overseas province located in the South China Sea 40 miles southwest of Hong Kong, consists of the peninsula of Macao and the islands of Taipa and Coloane. It has an area of 6.2 sq. mi.(16 sq. km.) and a population of 500,000. Capital: Macao. Macao's economy is based on light industry, commerce, tourism, fishing, and gold trading - Macao is one of the entirely free markets for gold in the world. Cement, textiles, fireworks, vegetable oils, and metal products are exported.

Established by the Portuguese in 1557, Macao is the oldest European settlement in the Far East. The Chinese, while agreeing to Portuguese settlement, did not recognize Portuguese sovereign rights and the Portuguese remained largely under control of the Chinese until 1849, when the Portuguese abolished the Chinese customhouse and declared the independence of the port. The Manchu government formally recognized the Portuguese right to *perpetual occupation* of Macao in 1887.

In 1987, Portugal and China agreed that Macao would become a Chinese Territory in 1999. In December of 1999, Macao became a special administrative zone of China.

RULER

Portuguese 1887-1999

MINT MARKS

(p) - Pobjoy Mint
(s) - Singapore Mint

Pobjoy Mint

Singapore Mint

MONETARY SYSTEM

100 Avos = 1 Pataca

PORTUGUESE COLONY

STANDARD COINAGE

100 Avos = 1 Pataca

KM# 1 5 AVOS

Bronze **Obv:** Value flanked by upper and lower dots within circle **Rev:** Shield within crowned globe flanked by stars below

Date	Mintage	F	VF	XF	Unc	BU
1952	500,000	—	3.50	15.00	30.00	50.00

KM# 1a 5 AVOS

2.6000 g., Nickel-Brass **Obv:** Value flanked by upper and lower dots within circle **Rev:** Shield within crowned globe flanked by stars below

Date	Mintage	F	VF	XF	Unc	BU
1967	5,000,000	—	0.50	1.00	2.50	—

KM# 2 10 AVOS

4.0200 g., Bronze, 20.3 mm. **Obv:** Value flanked by upper and lower dots within circle **Rev:** Shield within crowned globe flanked by stars below

Date	Mintage	F	VF	XF	Unc	BU
1952	12,500,000	—	0.30	0.80	6.00	—

KM# 2a 10 AVOS

3.9000 g., Nickel-Brass **Obv:** Value flanked by upper and lower dots within circle **Rev:** Shield within crowned globe flanked by stars below

Date	Mintage	F	VF	XF	Unc	BU
1967	5,525,000	—	0.50	1.00	2.00	—
1968	6,975,000	—	0.25	1.00	2.00	—
1975	20,000,000	—	0.10	0.50	1.50	—
1976	Inc. above	—	0.10	0.50	1.50	—

KM# 20 10 AVOS

3.3000 g., Brass, 19.1 mm. **Obv:** Portuguese shield flanked by stars below **Rev:** Value above building

Date	Mintage	F	VF	XF	Unc	BU
1982	24,580,000	—	0.10	0.50	1.50	—
1983	—	—	0.10	0.50	1.50	—
1984	—	—	0.25	0.75	2.50	—
1985	—	—	0.10	0.50	1.50	—
1988	—	—	0.10	0.50	1.50	—

KM# 70 10 AVOS

1.3800 g., Brass, 17 mm. **Obv:** MACAU written at center with date below **Rev:** Crowned design above value flanked by mint marks

Date	Mintage	F	VF	XF	Unc	BU
1993	—	—	—	—	0.75	1.25
1998	—	—	—	—	0.75	1.25
2005	—	—	—	—	0.75	1.25

KM# 21 20 AVOS

4.7000 g., Brass, 21.1 mm. **Obv:** Portuguese shield flanked by stars below **Rev:** Value above block letter design within vertical rectangle

Date	Mintage	F	VF	XF	Unc	BU
1982	9,960,000	—	0.10	0.50	1.50	—
1983	—	—	0.10	0.50	1.50	—
1984	—	—	0.25	0.75	2.50	—
1985	—	—	0.10	0.50	1.50	—

KM# 71 20 AVOS

Brass, 20 mm. **Obv:** MACAU written over inner circle with date below **Rev:** Man standing above his crew on ancient ship flanked by mint marks with value above **Shape:** 12-sided

Date	Mintage	F	VF	XF	Unc	BU
1993	—	—	—	—	1.00	1.75
1998	—	—	—	—	1.00	1.75

KM# 3 50 AVOS

Copper-Nickel, 20 mm. **Obv:** Portuguese shield within globe and cross **Rev:** Macau shield within crowned globe

Date	Mintage	F	VF	XF	Unc	BU
1952	2,560,000	—	0.75	3.50	9.00	—

KM# 7 50 AVOS

5.8000 g., Copper-Nickel, 23 mm. **Obv:** Portuguese shield within globe and cross **Rev:** Macau shield within crowned globe

Date	Mintage	F	VF	XF	Unc	BU
1972	1,600,000	—	0.50	1.50	4.00	—
1973	4,840,000	—	0.50	1.00	3.00	—

KM# 9 50 AVOS

Copper-Nickel, 23 mm. **Obv:** Value and denomination flanked by upper and lower flower buds within circle **Rev:** Macau shield within crowned globe flanked by stars and mint marks

Date	Mintage	F	VF	XF	Unc	BU
1978	3,000,000	—	0.50	1.50	4.00	—

KM# 22 50 AVOS

5.1000 g., Brass, 23 mm. **Obv:** Portuguese shield flanked by stars below above date **Rev:** Value above fallen block letters within vertical rectangle

Date	Mintage	F	VF	XF	Unc	BU
1982	16,952,000	—	0.50	1.00	3.00	—
1983	—	—	0.75	4.00	9.00	—
1984	—	—	0.75	3.50	7.00	—
1985	—	—	0.50	2.00	5.00	—

KM# 72 50 AVOS

4.5900 g., Brass, 23 mm. **Obv:** MACAU written across center of globe with date below **Rev:** Figure in ceremonial dragon costume being led by a man

Date	Mintage	F	VF	XF	Unc	BU
1993	—	—	—	—	1.50	2.50
2003	—	—	—	—	1.50	2.50
2005	—	—	—	—	1.50	2.50

KM# 4 PATACA

3.0000 g., 0.7200 Silver 0.0694 oz. ASW **Obv:** Portuguese shield within globe and long cross **Rev:** Macau shield within crowned globe

Date	Mintage	F	VF	XF	Unc	BU
1952	4,500,000	5.00	10.00	20.00	40.00	—

KM# 6 PATACA

10.6000 g., Nickel **Obv:** Portuguese shield within globe and long cross **Rev:** Macau shield within crowned globe

Date	Mintage	F	VF	XF	Unc	BU
1968	5,000,000	—	1.00	3.00	6.50	—
1975	6,000,000	—	0.75	2.00	5.00	—

KM# 6a PATACA

Copper-Nickel **Obv:** Portuguese shield within globe and long cross **Rev:** Macau shield within crowned globe

Date	Mintage	F	VF	XF	Unc	BU
1980	—	—	3.50	12.00	25.00	—

KM# 23.1 PATACA

9.2000 g., Copper-Nickel, 26 mm. **Obv:** Portuguese shield flanked by stars below above date (high stars) **Rev:** Artistic design flanked by upright fish

Date	Mintage	F	VF	XF	Unc	BU
1982(s)	6,427,000	—	1.00	2.00	6.00	—
1983(s)	—	—	1.50	3.50	8.00	—
1984(s)	—	—	2.00	4.50	10.00	—
1985(s)	—	—	1.50	3.50	8.00	—

KM# 23.2 PATACA

9.0000 g., Copper-Nickel, 26 mm. **Obv:** Portuguese shield flanked by stars below above date (low stars) **Rev:** Artistic design flanked by upright fish

Date	Mintage	F	VF	XF	Unc	BU
1982(p)	—	—	1.00	2.00	6.00	—
1983(p)	—	—	1.50	3.50	8.00	—

KM# 57 PATACA

9.1800 g., Copper-Nickel, 25.98 mm. **Obv:** MACAU written across center of globe with date below **Rev:** Lighthouse above value **Edge:** Reeded

Date	Mintage	F	VF	XF	Unc	BU
1992	—	—	—	—	2.50	4.00
1998	—	—	—	—	2.50	4.00
2003	—	—	—	—	2.50	4.00
2005	—	—	—	—	2.50	4.00

KM# 97 2 PATACAS

Nickel-Brass, 27.5 mm. **Obv:** MACAU written accross center of globe above date **Rev:** Church and Chinese arch **Edge:** Plain **Shape:** Octagonal

Date	Mintage	F	VF	XF	Unc	BU
1998	—	—	—	—	3.50	5.50

KM# 5 5 PATACAS

15.0000 g., 0.7200 Silver 0.3472 oz. ASW **Obv:** Portuguese shield within globe and long cross **Rev:** Macau shield within crowned globe

Date	Mintage	F	VF	XF	Unc	BU
1952	900,000	6.00	8.00	12.00	25.00	—

KM# 5a 5 PATACAS
10.0000 g., 0.6500 Silver 0.2090 oz. ASW **Obv:** Portuguese shield within globe and long cross **Rev:** Macau shield within crowned globe

Date	Mintage	F	VF	XF	Unc	BU
1971	500,000	5.00	7.50	12.00	20.00	—

KM# 24.1 5 PATACAS
10.7000 g., Copper-Nickel, 29 mm. **Obv:** Portuguese shield flanked by stars below above date (high stars) **Rev:** Large stylized dragon above value

Date	Mintage	F	VF	XF	Unc	BU
1982(s)	1,102,000	—	1.00	2.00	6.00	—
1983(s)	—	—	3.50	7.00	20.00	—
1984(s)	—	—	5.00	10.00	60.00	—
1985(s)	—	—	3.50	7.00	45.00	—
1988(s)	—	—	1.00	2.00	6.00	—

KM# 24.2 5 PATACAS
10.7000 g., Copper-Nickel, 29 mm. **Obv:** Portuguese shield flanked by stars below above date (low stars) **Rev:** Small stylized dragon above value

Date	Mintage	F	VF	XF	Unc	BU
1982(p)	—	—	1.00	2.00	6.00	—
1983(p)	—	—	1.00	2.00	6.00	—

KM# 56 5 PATACAS
10.1000 g., Copper-Nickel **Obv:** MACAU written across center of globe with date below **Rev:** Sailing ship and building scene **Edge:** Plain **Shape:** 12-sided

Date	Mintage	F	VF	XF	Unc	BU
1992	—	—	—	—	6.50	10.00
2003	—	—	—	—	6.50	10.00

KM# 83 10 PATACAS
Bi-Metallic Copper-Nickel center in Brass ring, 28 mm. **Obv:** MACAU written across center of globe within circle above date **Rev:** Cathedral within circle above value

Date	Mintage	F	VF	XF	Unc	BU
1997	—	—	—	—	8.50	12.50

SPECIAL ADMINISTRATIVE REGION (S.A.R.)

STANDARD COINAGE

100 Avos = 1 Pataca

KM# 111 10 AVOS
2.5000 g., Brass, 17 mm. **Subject:** Macao's Return to China **Obv:** City arms **Rev:** Sun Yat Sen Memorial above clasped hands with building in background

Date	Mintage	F	VF	XF	Unc	BU
1999	288,888	—	—	—	8.00	12.00

KM# 112 20 AVOS
3.2600 g., Brass, 19.5 mm. **Subject:** Macao's Return to China **Obv:** City arms **Rev:** Monetary and Foreign Exchange Authority Building

Date	Mintage	F	VF	XF	Unc	BU
1999	288,888	—	—	—	9.00	14.00

KM# 113 50 AVOS
4.5400 g., Brass, 23 mm. **Subject:** Macao's Return to China **Obv:** City arms **Rev:** Jet above bridge and ship

Date	Mintage	F	VF	XF	Unc	BU
1999	288,888	—	—	—	10.00	15.00

KM# 114 PATACA
6.0500 g., Copper-Nickel, 25.9 mm. **Subject:** Macao's Return to China **Obv:** City arms **Rev:** Cultural and recreational center building

Date	Mintage	F	VF	XF	Unc	BU
1999	288,888	—	—	—	12.00	17.00

KM# 115 2 PATACAS
5.5800 g., Copper-Nickel, 25 mm. **Subject:** Macao's Return to China **Obv:** City arms **Rev:** Cathedral and race car

Date	Mintage	F	VF	XF	Unc	BU
1999	288,888	—	—	—	15.00	20.00

KM# 116 5 PATACAS
6.6800 g., Copper-Nickel, 27 mm. **Subject:** Macao's Return to China **Obv:** City arms **Rev:** Racing dogs with Lisboa Hotel in background **Shape:** 12-sided

Date	Mintage	F	VF	XF	Unc	BU
1999	288,888	—	—	—	18.00	22.00

KM# 117 10 PATACAS
7.2000 g., Bi-Metallic Copper-Nickel center in Brass ring, 27.8 mm. **Subject:** Macao's Return to China **Obv:** City arms **Rev:** Government House Building **Edge:** Segmented reeding

Date	Mintage	F	VF	XF	Unc	BU
1999	288,888	—	—	—	20.00	25.00

MACEDONIA

The Republic of Macedonia is land-locked, and is bordered in the north by Yugoslavia, to the east by Bulgaria, in the south by Greece and to the west by Albania and has an area of 9,781 sq. mi. (25,713 sq. km.) and a population at the 1991 census was 2,038,847, of which the predominating ethnic groups were Macedonians. The capital is Skopje.

The Slavs settled in Macedonia since the 6th century, who had been Christianized by Byzantium, were conquered by the non-Slav Bulgars in the 7th century and in the 9th century formed a Macedo-Bulgarian empire, the western part of which survived until Byzantine conquest in 1014. In the 14th century, it fell to Serbia, and in1355 to the Ottomans. After the Balkan Wars of 1912-13 Turkey was ousted, and Serbia received the greater part of the territory, the balance going to Bulgaria and Greece. In 1918, Yugoslav Macedonia was incorporated into Serbia as "South Serbia", becoming a republic in the S.F.R. of Yugoslavia. Claims to the historical Macedonian territory have long been a source of contention between Bulgaria and Greece.

On Nov. 20, 1991, parliament promulgated a new constitution, and declared its independence on Nov.20, 1992, but failed to secure EC and US recognition owing to Greek objections to the use of the name *Macedonia.* On Dec. 11, 1992, the UN Security Council authorized the expedition of a small peacekeeping force to prevent hostilities spreading into Macedonia.

There is a 120-member single-chamber National Assembly.

REPUBLIC

STANDARD COINAGE

KM# 1 50 DENI
4.0500 g., Brass, 21.5 mm. **Obv:** Seagull flying offshore **Rev:** Radiant value

Date	Mintage	F	VF	XF	Unc	BU
1993	11,051,000	—	0.10	0.30	0.60	1.50

KM# 2 DENAR
5.1500 g., Brass, 23.7 mm. **Obv:** Sheepdog **Obv. Legend:** РЕПУБЛИКА МАКЕДОНИЈА **Rev:** Radiant value **Edge:** Plain

Date	Mintage	F	VF	XF	Unc	BU
1993	21,040,000	—	0.20	0.35	1.50	4.00
1997	11,200,000	—	0.20	0.35	1.50	4.00
2001	12,874,000	—	0.20	0.35	1.50	4.00
2006	—	—	—	—	1.25	3.75

KM# 5 DENAR

5.1500 g., Brass, 23.7 mm. **Series:** F.A.O. **Obv:** Sheep dog **Rev:** Value below F.A.O logo

Date	Mintage	F	VF	XF	Unc	BU
1995	2,314,000	—	—	—	2.00	4.00

KM# 5a DENAR

Copper-Nickel-Zinc, 23.7 mm. **Series:** F.A.O. **Obv:** Sheep dog **Rev:** F.A.O. logo above value

Date	Mintage	F	VF	XF	Unc	BU
1995	1,001,000	—	—	—	2.50	4.50

KM# 27 DENAR

5.1000 g., Bronze, 23.8 mm. **Obv:** Byzantine copper folis coin design **Rev:** Radiant rising sun behind value **Edge:** Plain

Date	Mintage	F	VF	XF	Unc	BU
2000	—	—	—	—	13.00	17.00

Note: Mule of KM-9 obverse and KM-2 reverse?

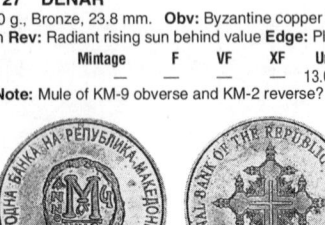

KM# 9 DENAR

5.1000 g., Bronze, 23.8 mm. **Subject:** 2000 Years of Christianity **Obv:** Byzantine copper folis coin **Rev:** Ornamented cross **Edge:** Plain

Date	Mintage	F	VF	XF	Unc	BU
2000	2,000	—	—	—	12.00	15.00

KM# 3 2 DENARI

5.1500 g., Brass, 23.7 mm. **Obv:** Trout above water **Obv. Legend:** РЕПУБЛИКА МАКЕДОНИЈА **Rev:** Radiant value **Edge:** Plain

Date	Mintage	F	VF	XF	Unc	BU
1993	8,998,000	—	0.25	0.50	1.25	3.00
2001	11,672,000	—	0.25	0.50	1.25	3.00
2006	—	—	0.25	0.50	1.00	2.50

KM# 6 2 DENARI

6.2500 g., Brass, 25.5 mm. **Series:** F.A.O. **Obv:** Trout above water **Rev:** Value below F.A.O logo

Date	Mintage	F	VF	XF	Unc	BU
1995	2,637,500	—	—	—	2.00	3.50

KM# 6a 2 DENARI

Copper-Nickel-Zinc, 25.5 mm. **Series:** F.A.O. **Obv:** Trout above water **Rev:** Value below F.A.O. logo

Date	Mintage	F	VF	XF	Unc	BU
1995	1,000,000	—	—	—	2.50	4.50

KM# 4 5 DENARI

7.2500 g., Brass, 27.5 mm. **Obv:** European lynx **Obv. Legend:** РЕПУБЛИКА МАКЕДОНИЈА **Rev:** Radiant value **Edge:** Plain

Date	Mintage	F	VF	XF	Unc	BU
1993	12,330,000	—	0.35	0.75	1.75	3.50
2001	6,921,000	—	0.35	0.75	1.75	3.50
2006	—	—	—	—	1.50	3.00

KM# 7 5 DENARI

7.2500 g., Brass, 27.5 mm. **Series:** F.A.O. **Obv:** European lynx **Rev:** Value below F.A.O logo

Date	Mintage	F	VF	XF	Unc	BU
1995	3,123,000	—	—	—	2.00	3.50

KM# 7a 5 DENARI

Copper-Nickel-Zinc, 27.5 mm. **Series:** F.A.O. **Obv:** European lynx **Rev:** Value below F.A.O. logo

Date	Mintage	F	VF	XF	Unc	BU
1995	1,000,000	—	—	—	2.50	4.50

MADAGASCAR

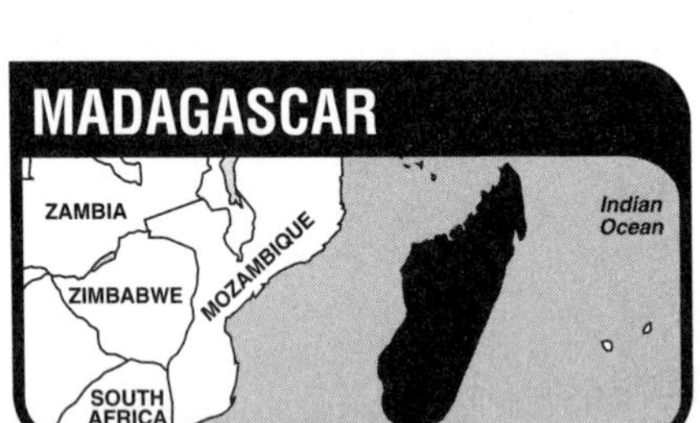

The Democratic Republic of Madagascar, an independent member of the French Community, located in the Indian Ocean 250 miles (402 km.) off the southeast coast of Africa, has an area of 226,656 sq. mi. (587,040 sq. km.) and a population of 10 million. Capital: Antananarivo. The economy is primarily agricultural; large bauxite deposits are being developed. Coffee, vanilla, graphite, and rice are exported.

Successive waves of immigrants from southeast Asia, Africa, Arabia and India populated Madagascar beginning about 2,000 years ago. Diago Diaz, a Portuguese navigator, sighted the island of Madagascar on Aug. 10, 1500, when his ship became separated from an India-bound fleet. Attempts at settlement by the British during the reign of Charles I and by the French during the 17th and 18th centuries were of no avail, and the island became a refuge and supply base for Indian Ocean pirates. Despite considerable influence on the island, the British accepted the imposition of a French protectorate in 1886 in return for French recognition of Britain's sphere of influence in Zanzibar. Madagascar was made a French colony in 1896 after absolute control had been established by military force. Britain occupied the island after the fall of France, 1942, to prevent its seizure by the Japanese, returning it to the Free French in 1943. On Oct. 14, 1958, following a decade of intermittent but bitter warfare, Madagascar, as the Malagasy Republic, became an autonomous state within the French Community. On June 27, 1960, it became a sovereign, independent nation, though remaining nominally within the French Community. The Malagasy Republic was renamed the Democratic Republic of Madagascar in 1975.

MONETARY SYSTEM

100 Centimes = 1 Franc

MINT MARKS

(a) - Paris, privy marks only
SA - Pretoria

FRENCH COLONY

STANDARD COINAGE

KM# 1 50 CENTIMES

Bronze **Obv:** Rooster **Rev:** Cross of Lorraine

Date	Mintage	F	VF	XF	Unc	BU
1943SA	2,000,000	1.50	2.50	10.00	20.00	40.00

KM# 2 FRANC

Bronze **Obv:** Rooster **Rev:** Cross of Lorraine

Date	Mintage	F	VF	XF	Unc	BU
1943SA	5,000,000	3.00	6.00	22.00	65.00	100

KM# 3 FRANC

1.3000 g., Aluminum, 23 mm. **Obv:** Liberty bust left **Rev:** Conjoined ox heads flanked by sprigs, value within horns **Designer:** G.B.L. Bazor

Date	Mintage	F	VF	XF	Unc	BU
1948(a)	7,400,000	0.25	0.35	0.75	2.75	3.50
1958(a)	2,600,000	0.25	0.35	0.75	2.75	3.50

KM# 4 2 FRANCS

Aluminum **Obv:** Liberty bust left **Rev:** Conjoined ox heads flanked by sprigs, value within horns **Designer:** G.B.L. Bazor

Date	Mintage	F	VF	XF	Unc	BU
1948(a)	10,000,000	0.25	0.45	0.85	2.50	3.50

KM# 5 5 FRANCS

Aluminum **Obv:** Liberty bust left **Rev:** Conjoined ox heads flanked by sprigs, value within horns **Designer:** G.B.L. Bazor

Date	Mintage	F	VF	XF	Unc	BU
1953(a)	30,012,000	0.25	0.55	1.00	3.00	5.00

KM# 6 10 FRANCS

Aluminum-Bronze, 20 mm. **Obv:** Liberty bust left **Rev:** Value within horns flanked by cluster of sprigs with shaded area above value **Designer:** G.B.L. Bazor

Date	Mintage	F	VF	XF	Unc	BU
1953(a)	25,000,000	0.35	0.65	1.25	3.50	6.00

KM# 7 20 FRANCS

4.0000 g., Aluminum-Bronze **Obv:** Liberty bust left **Rev:** Value within horns flanked by cluster of sprigs with shaded area above value **Designer:** G.B.L. Bazor

Date	Mintage	F	VF	XF	Unc	BU
1953(a)	15,000,000	0.75	1.50	3.00	6.50	9.00

MALAGASY REPUBLIC

STANDARD COINAGE

KM# 8 FRANC

2.4000 g., Stainless Steel **Obv:** Poinsettia **Rev:** Value within horns of ox head above sprigs

Date	Mintage	F	VF	XF	Unc	BU
1965(a)	1,170,000	0.10	0.15	0.30	1.25	—
1966(a)	—	0.10	0.15	0.30	1.25	—
1970(a)	—	0.10	0.15	0.30	1.25	—
1974(a)	1,250,000	0.10	0.15	0.30	1.25	—
1975(a)	7,355,000	0.10	0.15	0.30	1.25	—
1976(a)	—	0.10	0.15	0.30	1.25	—
1977(a)	—	0.10	0.15	0.30	1.25	—
1979(a)	—	0.10	0.15	0.30	1.25	—
1980(a)	—	0.15	0.20	0.40	1.45	—
1981(a)	—	0.15	0.20	0.40	1.45	—
1982(a)	—	0.15	0.20	0.40	1.45	—
1983(a)	—	0.15	0.20	0.40	1.45	—
1986(a)	—	0.15	0.20	0.40	1.45	—
1987(a)	—	0.15	0.20	0.40	1.45	—
1988(a)	—	0.15	0.20	0.40	1.45	—
1989(a)	—	0.15	0.20	0.40	1.45	—
1991(a)	—	0.15	0.20	0.40	1.45	—
1993(a)	—	0.15	0.20	0.40	1.45	—
2002(a)	—	0.15	0.20	0.40	1.45	—

KM# 9 2 FRANCS

3.4000 g., Stainless Steel **Obv:** Poinsettia **Rev:** Value within horns of ox head above sprigs

Date	Mintage	F	VF	XF	Unc	BU
1965(a)	760,000	0.15	0.25	0.50	1.50	—
1970(a)	—	0.15	0.25	0.45	1.25	—
1974(a)	1,250,000	0.15	0.25	0.45	1.25	—
1975(a)	8,250,000	0.15	0.25	0.45	1.25	—
1976(a)	—	0.15	0.25	0.45	1.25	—
1977(a)	—	0.15	0.25	0.45	1.25	—
1979(a)	—	0.15	0.25	0.45	1.25	—
1980(a)	—	0.15	0.25	0.45	1.25	—
1981(a)	—	0.15	0.25	0.45	1.25	—
1982(a)	—	0.15	0.25	0.45	1.25	—
1983(a)	—	0.15	0.25	0.45	1.25	—
1984(a)	—	0.15	0.25	0.45	1.25	—
1986(a)	—	0.15	0.25	0.45	1.25	—
1987(a)	—	0.15	0.25	0.45	1.25	—
1988(a)	—	0.15	0.25	0.45	1.25	—
1989(a)	—	0.15	0.25	0.45	1.25	—

KM# 10 5 FRANCS (Ariary)

5.0000 g., Stainless Steel **Obv:** Poinsettia **Rev:** Value within horns of ox head above sprigs

Date	Mintage	F	VF	XF	Unc	BU
1966(a)	—	0.15	0.25	0.60	1.75	—
1967(a)	—	0.15	0.25	0.60	1.75	—
1968(a)	7,500,000	0.15	0.25	0.60	1.75	—
1970(a)	—	0.15	0.25	0.60	1.75	—
1972(a)	19,100,000	0.15	0.25	0.60	1.75	—
1976(a)	—	0.15	0.25	0.60	1.75	—
1977(a)	—	0.15	0.25	0.60	1.75	—
1979(a)	—	0.15	0.25	0.60	1.75	—
1980(a)	—	0.20	0.30	0.65	1.85	—
1981(a)	—	0.20	0.30	0.65	1.85	—
1982(a)	—	0.20	0.30	0.65	1.85	—
1983(a)	—	0.20	0.30	0.65	1.85	—
1984(a)	—	0.20	0.30	0.65	1.85	—
1986(a)	—	0.20	0.30	0.65	1.85	—
1987(a)	—	0.20	0.30	0.65	1.85	—
1988(a)	—	0.20	0.30	0.65	1.85	—
1989(a)	—	0.20	0.30	0.65	1.85	—

KM# 11 10 FRANCS (2 Ariary)

3.5000 g., Aluminum-Bronze **Series:** F.A.O. **Obv:** Vanilla plant **Rev:** Value within horns of ox head flanked by sprigs and marks

Date	Mintage	F	VF	XF	Unc	BU
1970(a)	7,000,000	0.20	0.30	0.70	2.00	—
1971(a)	10,000,000	0.20	0.30	0.70	2.00	—
1972(a)	5,050,000	0.20	0.30	0.70	2.00	—
1973(a)	3,000,000	0.20	0.30	0.70	2.00	—
1974(a)	—	0.20	0.30	0.70	2.00	—
1975(a)	—	0.20	0.30	0.70	2.00	—
1976(a)	9,500,000	0.20	0.30	0.70	2.00	—
1977(a)	—	0.20	0.30	0.70	2.00	—
1978(a)	—	0.20	0.30	0.70	2.00	—
1979(a)	—	0.20	0.30	0.70	2.00	—
1980(a)	—	0.25	0.35	0.80	2.25	—
1981(a)	—	0.25	0.35	0.80	2.25	—
1982(a)	—	0.25	0.35	0.80	2.25	—
1983(a)	—	0.25	0.35	0.80	2.25	—
1984(a)	—	0.25	0.35	0.80	2.25	—
1986(a)	—	0.25	0.35	0.80	2.25	—
1987(a)	3,200,000	0.25	0.35	0.80	2.25	—
1988(a)	—	0.25	0.35	0.80	2.25	—
1989(a)	—	0.25	0.35	0.80	2.25	—

Note: Struck by Royal Canadian Mint.

KM# 11a 10 FRANCS (2 Ariary)

Copper Plated Steel **Series:** F.A.O. **Obv:** Vanilla plant **Rev:** Value within horns of ox head flanked by sprigs (without other marks)

Date	Mintage	F	VF	XF	Unc	BU
1991	—	0.25	0.45	1.50	3.50	—

KM# 12 20 FRANCS (4 Ariary)

6.0000 g., Aluminum-Bronze **Series:** F.A.O. **Obv:** Cotton plant **Rev:** Value within horns of ox head above sprigs and marks

Date	Mintage	F	VF	XF	Unc	BU
1970(a)	4,000,000	0.25	0.35	0.75	2.50	—
1971(a)	2,000,000	0.25	0.35	0.75	2.50	—
1972(a)	2,000,000	0.30	0.40	0.80	2.75	—
1973(a)	3,000,000	0.30	0.40	0.80	2.75	—
1974(a)	—	0.30	0.40	0.80	2.75	—
1975(a)	—	0.30	0.40	0.80	2.75	—
1976(a)	2,700,000	0.30	0.40	0.80	2.75	—
1977(a)	—	0.30	0.40	0.80	2.75	—
1978(a)	—	0.30	0.40	0.80	2.75	—
1979(a)	—	0.30	0.40	0.80	2.75	—
1980(a)	—	0.35	0.45	0.85	3.00	—
1981(a)	—	0.35	0.45	0.85	3.00	—
1982(a)	—	0.35	0.45	0.85	3.00	—
1983(a)	—	0.35	0.45	0.85	3.00	—
1984(a)	—	0.35	0.45	0.85	3.00	—
1986(a)	—	0.35	0.45	0.85	3.00	—
1987(a)	5,200,000	0.35	0.45	0.85	3.00	—
1988(a)	—	0.35	0.45	0.85	3.00	—
1989(a)	—	0.35	0.45	0.85	3.00	—

Note: Struck by the Royal Canadian Mint

DEMOCRATIC REPUBLIC

NOTE: Reverse legends found on Malagasy Democratic Republic coinages.

A. - *Tanindrazana – Tolom – Piavotana – Fahafahana*; Fatherland – Revolution – Liberty

B. - *Tanindrazana – Fahafahana – Fahamarinana*; Fatherland – Liberty – Justice

C. - *Tanindrazana – Fahafahana – Fandrosoana*; Fatherland – Liberty - Progress

MONETARY SYSTEM

5 Francs = 1 Ariary

1 Ariary = 100 Iraimbilanja

STANDARD COINAGE

KM# 17 5 ARIARY

4.5000 g., Copper Plated Steel **Obv:** Star above value within 3/4 wreath **Rev:** Rice plant within circle **Rev. Legend:** Motto A

Date	Mintage	F	VF	XF	Unc	BU
1992	—	0.65	1.25	2.25	4.00	—

KM# 13 10 ARIARY

Nickel **Series:** F.A.O. **Obv:** Star above value within 3/4 wreath **Rev:** Man cutting peat within circle **Rev. Legend:** Motto A

Date	Mintage	F	VF	XF	Unc	BU
1978	8,001,000	1.50	2.75	5.00	10.00	—

KM# 13b 10 ARIARY

Copper-Nickel **Obv:** Star above value within 3/4 wreath **Rev:** Man cutting peat within circle **Rev. Legend:** Motto A

Date	Mintage	F	VF	XF	Unc	BU
1983	—	2.00	4.00	8.00	15.00	—

KM# 18 10 ARIARY

6.4700 g., Stainless Steel, 23.5 mm. **Obv:** Star above value within 3/4 wreath **Rev:** Man cutting peat within circle **Rev. Legend:** Motto A **Shape:** 7-sided

Date	Mintage	F	VF	XF	Unc	BU
1992	—	0.75	1.50	2.75	5.00	—

KM# 14 20 ARIARY

Nickel **Series:** F.A.O. **Obv:** Star above value within 3/4 wreath **Rev:** Farmer on tractor disking field **Rev. Legend:** Motto A

Date	Mintage	F	VF	XF	Unc	BU
1978	8,001,000	2.00	4.00	8.00	16.50	—

KM# 14b 20 ARIARY

12.0000 g., Copper-Nickel **Obv:** Star above value within 3/4 wreath **Rev:** Man on tractor disking field **Rev. Legend:** Motto A

Date	Mintage	F	VF	XF	Unc	BU
1983	—	2.50	4.50	9.00	17.50	—

KM# 19 20 ARIARY

Stainless Steel **Obv:** Star above value within 3/4 wreath **Rev:** Farmer on tractor disking field **Rev. Legend:** Motto A

Date	Mintage	F	VF	XF	Unc	BU
1992	—	1.25	2.50	4.50	10.00	—

KM# 20 50 ARIARY
Stainless Steel **Obv:** Star above value within 3/4 wreath **Rev:** Avenue of Baobabs **Rev. Legend:** Motto A

Date	Mintage	F	VF	XF	Unc	BU
1992	—	2.00	3.50	6.00	12.50	—

REPUBLIC

Madagasikara Republic

STANDARD COINAGE

KM# 21 5 FRANCS (Ariary)
5.0000 g., Stainless Steel, 22 mm. **Obv:** Poinsettia **Rev:** Value within horns of ox head flanked by sprigs

Date	Mintage	F	VF	XF	Unc	BU
1996(a)	—	—	—	—	2.50	4.00

KM# 22 10 FRANCS (2 Ariary)
Copper Plated Steel, 21 mm. **Obv:** Vanilla plant **Rev:** Value within horns of ox head flanked by sprigs

Date	Mintage	F	VF	XF	Unc	BU
1996	—	—	—	—	3.00	5.00

KM# 23 5 ARIARY
4.7000 g., Copper Plated Steel, 24 mm. **Obv:** Star above value within 3/4 wreath **Rev:** Rice plant within circle **Rev. Legend:** Motto B

Date	Mintage	F	VF	XF	Unc	BU
1994	—	—	—	—	2.50	4.00
1996	—	—	—	—	2.50	4.00

KM# 24.1 20 ARIARY
Nickel Clad Steel, 28 mm. **Issuer:** F.A.O. **Obv:** Star above value within 3/4 wreath **Rev:** Farmer on tractor disking field **Rev. Legend:** Motto B

Date	Mintage	F	VF	XF	Unc	BU
1994	—	—	—	—	6.50	9.00

KM# 24.2 20 ARIARY
Nickel Clad Steel, 28 mm. **Obv:** Star above value within 3/4 wreath **Rev:** Man on tractor disking field **Rev. Legend:** Motto C

Date	Mintage	F	VF	XF	Unc	BU
1999	—	—	—	—	6.50	9.00

KM# 25.1 50 ARIARY
Stainless Steel, 30.5 mm. **Obv:** Star above value within 3/4 wreath **Rev:** Avenue of Baobabs **Rev. Legend:** Motto B **Shape:** 11-sided

Date	Mintage	F	VF	XF	Unc	BU
1994	—	—	—	—	8.00	12.00
1996	—	—	—	—	8.00	12.00

STANDARD COINAGE

KM# 28 10 FRANCS (2 Ariary)
4.3400 g., Bronze (Red To Yellow), 21.9 mm. **Obv:** Monkey **Rev:** Value within steer horns flanked by sprigs **Edge:** Plain

Date	Mintage	F	VF	XF	Unc	BU
2003	—	—	—	—	2.50	3.50

KM# 29 ARIARY
4.9300 g., Stainless Steel, 22 mm. **Obv:** Flower **Rev:** Value within steer horns above sprigs **Edge:** Plain

Date	Mintage	F	VF	XF	Unc	BU
2004(a)	—	—	—	—	2.00	3.00

KM# 30 2 ARIARY
3.2300 g., Copper Plated Steel, 21 mm. **Obv:** Plant **Rev:** Value within steer horns flanked by sprigs **Edge:** Reeded

Date	Mintage	F	VF	XF	Unc	BU
2003	—	—	—	—	2.00	3.00

MADEIRA ISLANDS

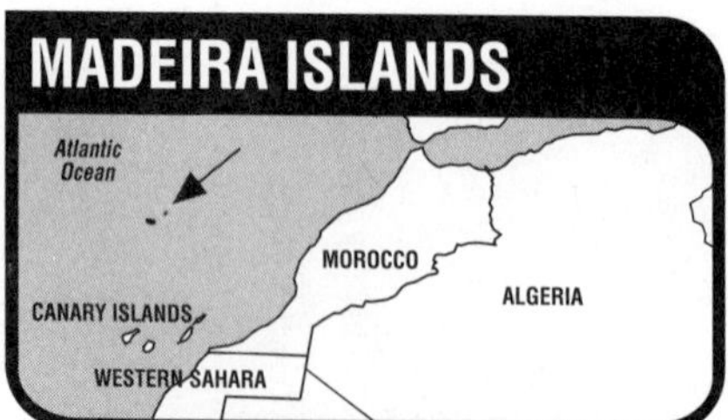

The Madeira Islands, which belong to Portugal, are located 360 miles (492 km.) off the northwest coast of Africa. They have an area of 307 sq. mi. (795 sq. km.). The group consists of two inhabited islands named Madeira and Porto Santo and two groups of uninhabited rocks named Desertas and Selvagens. Capital: Funchal. The two staple products are wine and sugar. Bananas and pineapples are also produced for export.

Although the evidence is insufficient, it is thought that the Phoenicians visited Madeira at an early period. It is also probable that the entire archipelago was explored by Genoese adventurers; an Italian map dated 1351 shows the Madeira Islands quite clearly. The Portuguese navigator Goncalvez Zarco first sighted Porto Santo in 1418, having been driven there by a storm while he was exploring the coast of West Africa. Madeira itself was discovered in 1420. The islands were uninhabited when visited by Zarco, but soon after 1418 Madeira was quickly colonized by Prince Henry the Navigator, aided by the knights of the Order of Christ. British troops occupied the islands in 1801, and again in 1807-14.

RULER
Portuguese

PORTUGUESE COLONY

MODERN COINAGE

KM# 4 25 ESCUDOS
11.0000 g., Copper-Nickel, 28.5 mm. **Subject:** Autonomy of Madeira **Obv:** Shields above value **Rev:** Head facing

Date	Mintage	F	VF	XF	Unc	BU
1981	750,000	—	—	—	6.00	8.00

KM# 5 100 ESCUDOS
Copper-Nickel, 33.8 mm. **Subject:** Autonomy of Madeira **Obv:** Shields above value **Rev:** Head facing

Date	Mintage	F	VF	XF	Unc	BU
1981	250,000	—	—	—	12.00	15.00

MALAWI

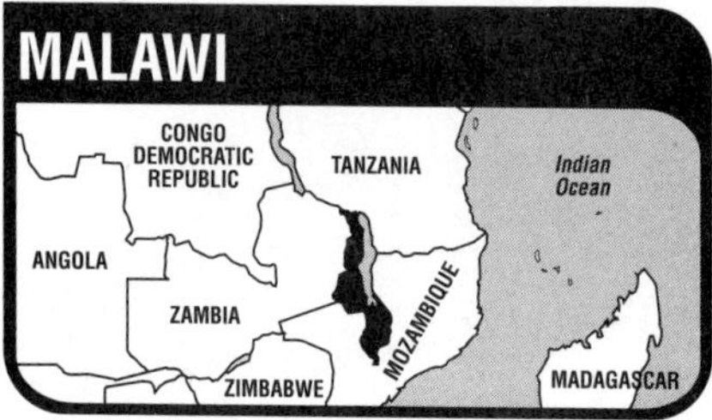

The Republic of Malawi (formerly Nyasaland), located in southeastern Africa to the west of Lake Malawi (Nyasa), has an area of 45,745 sq. mi. (118,480 sq. km.) and a population of 7 million. Capital: Lilongwe. The economy is predominantly agricultural. Tobacco, tea, peanuts and cotton are exported.

Although the Portuguese were the first Europeans to reach the Malawi area, the first meaningful contact was made by missionary-explorer Dr. David Livingstone. He arrived at Lake Malawi on Sept. 16, 1859, and remained to make extensive explorations in the 1860's. Subsequent clashes between settlements of Scottish missionaries and Arab slave traders, and the procurement of development rights by Cecil Rhodes, 1884, stimulated British interest and brought about the establishment of the Nyasaland protectorate in 1891. In 1953 Nyasaland reluctantly joined the Federation of Rhodesia and Nyasaland and, after prolonged protest, was granted self-government within the federation. Nyasaland became the independent nation of Malawi on July 6, 1964, and became a republic two years later. Malawi is a member of the Commonwealth of Nations. The president is the Chief of State and Head of Government.

NOTE: For earlier coinage see Rhodesia and Nyasaland.

MONETARY SYSTEM
12 Pence = 1 Shilling
2 Shillings = 1 Florin
5 Shillings = 1 Crown
20 Shillings = 1 Pound

REPUBLIC

STERLING COINAGE

KM# 6 PENNY
Bronze **Obv:** Malawi written above date and value **Rev:** Written and numeral value above designs

Date	Mintage	F	VF	XF	Unc	BU
1967	6,000,000	0.35	0.65	1.25	2.50	—
1968	3,600,000	3.00	6.00	12.00	25.00	—

KM# 1 6 PENCE
2.7900 g., Copper-Nickel-Zinc **Obv:** Head right **Rev:** Rooster **Designer:** Paul Vinze

Date	Mintage	F	VF	XF	Unc	BU
1964	14,800,000	0.25	0.50	1.00	2.50	4.00
1964 Proof	10,000	Value: 1.50				
1967	6,000,000	0.50	1.00	2.50	5.00	6.50

KM# 2 SHILLING
5.3700 g., Copper-Nickel-Zinc, 23.5 mm. **Obv:** Head right **Rev:** Bundled corncobs **Designer:** Paul Vinze

Date	Mintage	F	VF	XF	Unc	BU
1964	11,900,000	0.35	0.65	1.25	2.50	3.50
1964 Proof	10,000	Value: 1.50				
1968	3,000,000	0.75	1.50	3.00	5.50	7.00

KM# 3 FLORIN
11.3100 g., Copper-Nickel-Zinc, 28 mm. **Obv:** Head right **Rev:** Elephants **Designer:** Paul Vinze

Date	Mintage	F	VF	XF	Unc	BU
1964	6,500,000	0.75	1.50	3.00	6.00	7.00
1964 Proof	10,000	Value: 4.50				

KM# 4 1/2 CROWN
Copper-Nickel-Zinc **Obv:** Head right **Rev:** Arms with supporters **Designer:** Paul Vinze

Date	Mintage	F	VF	XF	Unc	BU
1964	6,400,000	1.00	2.00	4.00	6.00	—
1964 Proof	10,000	Value: 4.50				

DECIMAL COINAGE

100 Tambala = 1 Kwacha

KM# 7.1 TAMBALA
1.7600 g., Bronze, 17 mm. **Obv:** Head right **Rev:** Rooster **Designer:** Paul Vinze

Date	Mintage	F	VF	XF	Unc	BU
1971	15,000,000	0.15	0.20	0.40	0.75	1.50
1971 Proof	4,000	Value: 1.00				
1973	5,000,000	0.15	0.20	0.40	0.75	1.50
1974	12,500,000	0.15	0.20	0.40	0.75	1.50

KM# 7.2 TAMBALA
1.7800 g., Bronze, 17 mm. **Obv:** Head right with accent mark above "W" in MALAWI **Rev:** Rooster

Date	Mintage	F	VF	XF	Unc	BU
1975	10,000,000	0.15	0.20	0.40	0.75	1.50
1977	10,000,000	0.15	0.20	0.40	0.75	1.50
1979	15,000,000	0.15	0.20	0.40	0.75	1.50
1982	15,000,000	0.15	0.20	0.40	0.75	1.50

KM# 7.2a TAMBALA
1.8000 g., Copper Plated Steel **Obv:** Head right **Rev:** Rooster divides value and date

Date	Mintage	F	VF	XF	Unc	BU
1984	201,000	0.20	0.30	0.50	0.80	1.50
1985 Proof	10,000	Value: 3.00				
1987	—	0.20	0.30	0.50	0.80	1.50
1989	—	0.20	0.30	0.50	0.80	1.50
1991	—	0.20	0.30	0.50	0.80	1.50
1994	—	0.20	0.30	0.50	0.80	1.50

KM# 24 TAMBALA
1.8000 g., Copper Plated Steel, 17.2 mm. **Obv:** Bust right **Rev:** Two Talapia fish

Date	Mintage	F	VF	XF	Unc	BU
1995	—	—	—	—	1.00	1.50

KM# 33 TAMBALA
1.6800 g., Bronze, 17.3 mm. **Obv:** Arms with supporters **Rev:** Two Talapia fish **Edge:** Plain

Date	Mintage	F	VF	XF	Unc	BU
1995	—	—	—	—	1.00	1.50

KM# 33a TAMBALA
Copper-Plated-Steel, 17.3 mm. **Obv:** Arms with supporters **Rev:** 2 Talapia fish **Edge:** Plain

Date	Mintage	F	VF	XF	Unc	BU
2003	—	—	—	—	1.00	1.50

KM# 8.1 2 TAMBALA
Bronze **Obv:** Head right **Rev:** Paradise whydah bird divides date and value **Designer:** Paul Vinze

Date	Mintage	F	VF	XF	Unc	BU
1971	10,000,000	0.25	0.40	0.75	1.50	2.00
1971 Proof	4,000	Value: 1.75				
1973	5,000,000	0.25	0.40	0.75	1.50	2.00
1974	5,000,000	0.25	0.40	0.75	1.50	2.00

KM# 8.2 2 TAMBALA
3.6000 g., Bronze **Obv:** Head right with accent mark above "W" in MALAWI **Rev:** Paradise whydah bird divides date and value

Date	Mintage	F	VF	XF	Unc	BU
1975	5,000,000	0.25	0.40	0.75	1.50	2.00
1977	5,000,000	0.25	0.40	0.75	1.50	2.00
1979	7,637,000	0.25	0.40	0.75	1.50	2.00
1982	15,000,000	0.25	0.40	0.75	1.50	2.00

KM# 8.2a 2 TAMBALA
3.4600 g., Copper Plated Steel **Obv:** Head right **Rev:** Paradise whydah bird divides date and value

Date	Mintage	F	VF	XF	Unc	BU
1984	150,000	0.30	0.50	0.85	2.00	—
1985 Proof	10,000	Value: 4.00				
1987	—	0.30	0.50	0.85	2.00	—
1989	—	0.30	0.50	0.85	2.00	—
1991	—	0.30	0.50	0.85	1.75	—
1994	—	0.30	0.50	0.85	1.75	—

KM# 25 2 TAMBALA
3.5000 g., Copper Plated Steel, 20.3 mm. **Obv:** Bust right **Rev:** Paradise whydah bird divides date and value

Date	Mintage	F	VF	XF	Unc	BU
1995	—	—	—	—	1.00	1.50

KM# 34 2 TAMBALA
3.5000 g., Bronze, 20.3 mm. **Obv:** Arms with supporters **Rev:** Paradise whydah bird divides date and value **Edge:** Plain

Date	Mintage	F	VF	XF	Unc	BU
1995	—	—	—	—	1.00	1.50

KM# 34a 2 TAMBALA
Copper-Plated-Steel, 20.3 mm. **Obv:** Arms with supporters **Rev:** Paradise whydah bird divides date and value, designer's initials "P.V." **Edge:** Plain

Date	Mintage	F	VF	XF	Unc	BU
2003	—	—	—	—	1.00	1.50

KM# 9.1 5 TAMBALA
2.8600 g., Copper-Nickel **Obv:** Head right **Rev:** Purple heron and value **Designer:** Paul Vinze

Date	Mintage	F	VF	XF	Unc	BU
1971	7,000,000	0.25	0.45	0.85	1.75	2.00
1971 Proof	4,000	Value: 2.00				

KM# 9.2 5 TAMBALA
Copper-Nickel **Obv:** Head right with accent mark above "W" in MALAWI **Rev:** Purple heron and value

Date	Mintage	F	VF	XF	Unc	BU
1985 Proof	10,000	Value: 5.00				

KM# 9.2a 5 TAMBALA
2.8000 g., Nickel Clad Steel, 19.35 mm. **Obv:** Head right **Rev:** Purple heron and value

Date	Mintage	F	VF	XF	Unc	BU
1989	—	0.30	0.50	0.85	2.00	3.00
1994	—	0.30	0.50	0.85	2.00	3.00

KM# 26 5 TAMBALA
2.8300 g., Nickel Plated Steel, 19.35 mm. **Obv:** Bust right **Rev:** Purple heron and value

Date	Mintage	F	VF	XF	Unc	BU
1995	—	—	—	—	1.50	3.00

KM# 32.1 5 TAMBALA
Nickel Plated Steel, 19.35 mm. **Obv:** Arms with supporters **Rev:** Purple heron and value

Date	Mintage	F	VF	XF	Unc	BU
1995	—	—	—	—	2.50	3.00

KM# 32.2 5 TAMBALA
Nickel-Plated Steel, 19.35 mm. **Obv:** Arms with supporters **Rev:** Purple heron, value, designer's initials "P.V."

Date	Mintage	F	VF	XF	Unc	BU
2003	—	—	—	—	2.50	3.00

KM# 10.1 10 TAMBALA
Copper-Nickel, 23.6 mm. **Obv:** Head right **Rev:** Bundled corncob divides date and value

Date	Mintage	F	VF	XF	Unc	BU
1971	4,000,000	0.30	0.50	1.00	2.25	3.00
1971 Proof	4,000	Value: 2.50				

KM# 10.2 10 TAMBALA
Copper-Nickel, 23.6 mm. **Obv:** Head right **Rev:** Bundled corncobs divide date and value

Date	Mintage	F	VF	XF	Unc	BU
1985 Proof	10,000	Value: 6.00				
1989	—	0.40	0.80	1.50	2.75	3.50

KM# 10.2a 10 TAMBALA
Nickel Clad Steel, 23.6 mm. **Obv:** Head right **Rev:** Bundled cobs of corn divide value and date

Date	Mintage	F	VF	XF	Unc	BU
1989	—	0.40	0.80	1.50	2.75	—

KM# 27 10 TAMBALA
5.6200 g., Nickel Plated Steel, 23.6 mm. **Obv:** Bust right **Rev:** Bundled corncobs divide date and value

Date	Mintage	F	VF	XF	Unc	BU
1995	—	—	—	—	2.25	3.00
2003	—	—	—	—	2.25	3.00

KM# 11.1 20 TAMBALA
10.9700 g., Copper-Nickel, 26.5 mm. **Obv:** Head right **Rev:** Elephants **Designer:** Paul Vinze

Date	Mintage	F	VF	XF	Unc	BU
1971	3,000,000	0.75	1.50	2.50	4.00	—
1971 Proof	4,000	Value: 5.00				

KM# 11.2 20 TAMBALA
Copper-Nickel, 26.5 mm. **Obv:** Head right with accent mark above "W" in MALAWI **Rev:** Elephants

Date	Mintage	F	VF	XF	Unc	BU
1985 Proof	10,000	Value: 7.00				

KM# 11.2a 20 TAMBALA
11.3300 g., Nickel Clad Steel, 26.5 mm. **Obv:** Head right **Rev:** Elephants

Date	Mintage	F	VF	XF	Unc	BU
1989	—	0.60	1.20	2.25	4.00	—
1994	—	0.60	1.20	2.25	4.00	—

KM# 29 20 TAMBALA
7.5200 g., Nickel Clad Steel, 26.5 mm. **Obv:** Bust right **Rev:** Elephants

Date	Mintage	F	VF	XF	Unc	BU
1996	—	—	—	—	3.75	4.50

KM# 19 50 TAMBALA
11.3500 g., Copper-Nickel-Zinc, 30 mm. **Obv:** Head right **Rev:** Arms with supporters **Designer:** Paul Vinze **Note:** The 1989 date for this coin does not exist.

Date	Mintage	F	VF	XF	Unc	BU
1986	—	2.00	3.00	5.00	10.00	—
1994	—	2.00	3.00	5.00	10.00	—

KM# 30 50 TAMBALA
4.4000 g., Brass Plated Steel, 22 mm. **Obv:** Bust right **Rev:** Arms with supporters **Shape:** 7-sided

Date	Mintage	F	VF	XF	Unc	BU
1996	—	—	—	—	4.50	5.00
2003	—	—	—	—	4.50	5.00

KM# 66 50 TAMBALA
4.4000 g., Brass Plated Steel, 22 mm. **Obv:** State arms and supporters with country name below **Rev:** Zebras with date above and value below **Shape:** 7-sided

Date	Mintage	F	VF	XF	Unc	BU
2004	—	—	—	—	4.50	5.00

KM# 12 KWACHA
Copper-Nickel **Subject:** Decimalization of coinage **Obv:** Head right **Rev:** Arms with supporters **Edge Lettering:** DECIMAL CURRENCY INTRODUCED FEBRUARY 15TH, 1971 **Designer:** Paul Vinze

Date	Mintage	F	VF	XF	Unc	BU
1971	20,000	1.00	2.00	3.50	6.00	—
1971 Proof	4,000	Value: 6.50				

KM# 20 KWACHA
8.8000 g., Nickel-Brass, 26 mm. **Obv:** Head right **Rev:** Rooster

Date	Mintage	F	VF	XF	Unc	BU
1992	—	1.00	2.00	3.00	5.50	8.00

KM# 28 KWACHA
9.0000 g., Brass Plated Steel, 26 mm. **Obv:** Bust right **Rev:** Fish eagle

Date	Mintage	F	VF	XF	Unc	BU
1996	—	—	—	—	7.00	10.00
2003	—	—	—	—	7.00	10.00

KM# 65 KWACHA
Brass Plated Steel, 26 mm. **Obv:** State arms, country name **Rev:** Fish eagle, date

Date	Mintage	F	VF	XF	Unc	BU
2004	—	—	—	—	2.50	3.50

KM# 57 5 KWACHA
10.2500 g., Bi-Metallic Copper-Nickel ring and Nickel-Brass center, 27.05 mm. **Subject:** Fishing **Obv:** State arms and supporters with country name below **Obv. Legend:** MALAWI **Rev:** Fisherman at work with date above and value below **Edge:** Reeded

Date	Mintage	F	VF	XF	Unc	BU
2006	—	—	—	—	—	6.00

KM# 58 10 KWACHA
15.1000 g., Bi-Metallic Copper-Nickel center with Nickel-Brass ring, 28.04 mm. **Obv:** State arms and supporters with country name below **Obv. Legend:** MALAWI **Rev:** Farm worker harvesting **Edge:** Coarse reeding

Date	Mintage	F	VF	XF	Unc	BU
2006	—	—	—	—	—	7.00

MALAYA

Malaya, a former member of the British Commonwealth located in the southern part of the Malay peninsula, consisted of 11 states: the un-federated Malay states of Johore, Kelantan, Kedah, Perlis and Trengganu; the federated Malay states of Negri-Sembilan, Pahang, Perakand Selangor; former members of the Straits Settlements Penang and Malacca. Malaya was occupied by the Japanese during the years 1942-1945. The only local opposition to the Japanese had come mainly from the Chinese Communists who then continued their guerilla operations after the war, finally being defeated in 1956. Malaya was granted full independence on Aug. 31, 1957, and became part of Malaysia in 1963.

RULER
British

MINT MARKS
I - Calcutta Mint (1941)
I - Bombay Mint (1945)
No Mint mark - Royal Mint

MONETARY SYSTEM
100 Cents = 1 Dollar

BRITISH COLONY

STANDARD COINAGE

100 Cents = 1 Dollar

KM# 1 1/2 CENT

Bronze **Obv:** Crowned head of King George VI left **Obv. Designer:** Percy Metcalfe **Rev:** Value within beaded circle **Shape:** 4-sided **Note:** 18 mm x 18 mm.

Date	Mintage	F	VF	XF	Unc	BU
1940	6,000,000	2.00	6.00	10.00	20.00	—
1940 Proof	—	Value: 720				

KM# 2 CENT

5.8200 g., Bronze, 21 mm. **Obv:** Crowned head of King George VI left **Obv. Designer:** Percy Metcalfe **Rev:** Value within beaded circle **Shape:** Square

Date	Mintage	F	VF	XF	Unc	BU
1939	20,000,000	0.25	0.40	0.60	2.00	—
1939 Proof	—	Value: 720				
1940	23,600,000	0.25	0.40	0.60	2.00	—
1940 Proof	—	Value: 720				
1941 I	33,620,000	0.75	1.50	10.00	28.00	—

KM# 6 CENT

4.3000 g., Bronze, 20 mm. **Obv:** Crowned head of King George VI left **Obv. Designer:** Percy Metcalfe **Rev:** Value within beaded circle **Shape:** 4-sided **Note:** Reduced size.

Date	Mintage	F	VF	XF	Unc	BU
1943	50,000,000	0.10	0.20	0.45	1.50	—
1943 Proof	—	Value: 500				
1945	40,033,000	0.10	0.20	0.45	1.50	—
1945 Proof	—	Value: 500				

KM# 3 5 CENTS

1.3600 g., 0.7500 Silver 0.0328 oz. ASW **Obv:** Crowned head of King George VI left **Obv. Designer:** Percy Metcalfe **Rev:** Value within beaded circle

Date	Mintage	F	VF	XF	Unc	BU
1939	2,000,000	0.60	1.00	2.25	5.00	—
1939 Proof	—	Value: 660				
1941	4,000,000	0.50	0.65	1.20	2.50	—
1941 Proof	—	Value: 660				
1941 I	Inc. above	0.50	0.65	1.20	2.50	—

KM# 3a 5 CENTS

1.3600 g., 0.5000 Silver 0.0219 oz. ASW **Obv:** Crowned head of King George VI left **Obv. Designer:** Percy Metcalf **Rev:** Value within beaded circle

Date	Mintage	F	VF	XF	Unc	BU
1943	10,000,000	0.35	0.45	0.65	2.00	—
1943 Proof	—	Value: 660				
1945	8,800,000	0.35	0.45	0.65	2.00	—
1945 I	4,600,000	0.50	0.75	1.25	3.50	—

KM# 7 5 CENTS

1.3900 g., Copper-Nickel **Obv:** Crowned head of King George VI left **Obv. Designer:** Percy Metcalfe **Rev:** Value within beaded circle

Date	Mintage	F	VF	XF	Unc	BU
1948	30,000,000	0.10	0.25	1.25	3.00	—
1948 Proof	—	Value: 660				
1950	40,000,000	0.10	0.25	1.25	3.00	—

KM# 4 10 CENTS

2.7100 g., 0.7500 Silver 0.0653 oz. ASW, 18 mm. **Obv:** Crowned head of King George VI left **Obv. Designer:** Percy Metcalfe **Rev:** Value within beaded circle

Date	Mintage	F	VF	XF	Unc	BU
1939	10,000,000	1.00	1.25	1.50	3.00	—
1939 Proof	—	Value: 660				
1941	17,000,000	1.00	1.25	1.50	3.00	—
1941 Proof	—	Value: 660				
1941 I	—	—	—	2,500	3,200	—

KM# 4a 10 CENTS

2.7100 g., 0.5000 Silver 0.0436 oz. ASW **Obv:** Crowned head of King George VI left **Obv. Designer:** Percy Metcalf **Rev:** Value within beaded circle

Date	Mintage	F	VF	XF	Unc	BU
1943	5,000,000	0.85	1.20	1.50	3.00	—
1943 Proof	—	Value: 660				
1945	3,152,000	0.85	2.00	4.00	8.50	—
1945 I	—	—	—	2,500	3,200	—

KM# 8 10 CENTS

2.8500 g., Copper-Nickel, 19.5 mm. **Obv:** Crowned head of George VI left **Obv. Designer:** Percy Metcalfe **Rev:** Value within beaded circle

Date	Mintage	F	VF	XF	Unc	BU
1948	23,885,000	0.15	0.30	1.40	4.50	—
1948 Proof	—	Value: 660				
1949	26,115,000	0.25	0.50	1.75	6.25	—
1950	65,000,000	0.15	0.30	1.25	4.50	—
1950 Proof	—	Value: 660				

KM# 5 20 CENTS

5.4300 g., 0.7500 Silver 0.1309 oz. ASW **Obv:** Crowned head of King George VI left **Obv. Designer:** Percy Metcalfe **Rev:** Value within beaded circle

Date	Mintage	F	VF	XF	Unc	BU
1939	8,000,000	2.00	2.50	3.50	6.00	—
1939 Proof	—	Value: 660				

KM# 5a 20 CENTS

5.4300 g., 0.5000 Silver 0.0873 oz. ASW **Obv:** Crowned head of King George VI left **Obv. Designer:** Percy Metcalf **Rev:** Value within beaded circle

Date	Mintage	F	VF	XF	Unc	BU
1943	5,000,000	1.45	1.75	2.75	5.50	—
1943 Proof	—	Value: 660				
1945	10,000,000	2.00	7.00	13.00	22.00	—
1945 I	—	—	—	2,500	3,200	—

KM# 9 20 CENTS

5.6900 g., Copper-Nickel, 23.4 mm. **Obv:** Crowned head of King George VI left **Obv. Designer:** Percy Metcalfe **Rev:** Value within beaded circle

Date	Mintage	F	VF	XF	Unc	BU
1948	40,000,000	0.35	0.75	1.75	6.00	—
1948 Proof	—	Value: 660				
1950	20,000,000	0.35	0.75	1.75	6.00	—
1950 Proof	—	Value: 660				

MALAYA & BRITISH BORNEO

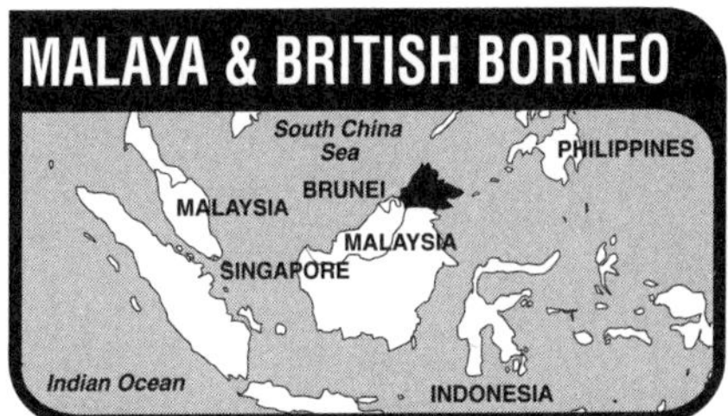

Malaya & British Borneo, a Currency Commission named the Board of Commissioners of Currency, Malaya and British Borneo, was initiated on Jan. 1, 1952, for the purpose of providing a common currency for use in Johore, Kelantan, Kedah, Perlis, Trengganu, Negri Sembilan, Pahang, Perak, Selangor, Penang, Malacca, Singapore, North Borneo, Sarawak and Brunei.

RULER

British

MINT MARKS

KN - King's Norton, Birmingham
H - Heaton, Birmingham
No Mint mark - Royal Mint

MONETARY SYSTEM

100 Cents = 1 Dollar

BRITISH COLONY

STANDARD COINAGE

100 Cents = 1 Dollar

KM# 5 CENT

4.2700 g., Bronze **Obv:** Crowned bust of Queen Elizabeth II right **Obv. Designer:** Cecil Thomas **Rev:** Value within beaded circle **Shape:** 4-sided

Date	Mintage	F	VF	XF	Unc	BU
1956	6,250,000	—	0.10	0.45	2.00	—
1956 Proof	—	Value: 700				
1957	12,500,000	—	0.10	0.45	2.00	—
1958	5,000,000	—	0.10	0.45	2.00	—
1958 Proof	—	Value: 700				
1961	10,000,000	—	0.10	0.45	2.00	—
1961 Proof	—	Value: 700				

KM# 6 CENT

1.9600 g., Bronze, 18 mm. **Obv:** Value **Rev:** Crossed encased swords

Date	Mintage	F	VF	XF	Unc	BU
1962	45,000,000	—	—	0.35	1.00	—
1962 Proof	Est. 25	Value: 300				

KM# 1 5 CENTS

1.4200 g., Copper-Nickel, 16 mm. **Obv:** Crowned bust of Queen Elizabeth II right **Obv. Designer:** Cecil Thomas **Rev:** Value within beaded circle

Date	Mintage	F	VF	XF	Unc	BU
1953	20,000,000	—	0.75	1.50	7.00	—
1953 Proof	—	Value: 700				
1957	10,000,000	—	0.75	1.75	10.00	—
1957H	10,000,000	—	0.75	1.75	10.00	—
1957H Proof	—	Value: 700				
1957KN	Inc. above	—	2.00	5.00	15.00	—
1958	10,000,000	—	1.00	2.25	7.00	—
1958 Proof	—	Value: 700				
1958H	10,000,000	—	1.25	2.00	6.50	—
1961	90,000,000	—	BV	1.35	3.00	—
1961 Proof	—	Value: 700				
1961H	5,000,000	—	2.00	7.00	22.00	—
1961KN	Inc. above	—	1.50	4.00	10.00	—

KM# 2 10 CENTS
2.9000 g., Copper-Nickel, 19.5 mm. **Obv:** Crowned bust of Queen Elizabeth II right **Obv. Designer:** Cecil Thomas **Rev:** Value within beaded circle

Date	Mintage	F	VF	XF	Unc	BU
1953	20,000,000	—	0.75	1.50	4.50	—
1953 Proof	—	Value: 700				
1956	10,000,000	—	0.75	1.50	4.50	—
1956 Proof	—	Value: 700				
1957H	10,000,000	—	0.75	1.50	5.00	—
1957H Proof	—	Value: 700				
1957KN	10,000,000	—	1.00	2.50	5.25	—
1958	10,000,000	—	1.00	2.50	5.25	—
1960	10,000,000	—	0.75	1.50	5.00	—
1960 Proof	—	Value: 700				
1961	60,784,000	—	0.40	0.80	2.50	—
1961 Proof	—	Value: 700				
1961H	69,220,000	—	0.40	0.80	2.50	—
1961KN	Inc. above	—	1.00	2.50	5.00	—

KM# 3 20 CENTS
5.6800 g., Copper-Nickel, 23.51 mm. **Obv:** Crowned bust of Queen Elizabeth II right **Obv. Designer:** Cecil Thomas **Rev:** Value within beaded circle

Date	Mintage	F	VF	XF	Unc	BU
1954	10,000,000	—	1.25	3.00	6.00	—
1954 Proof	—	Value: 700				
1956	5,000,000	—	1.00	3.00	6.00	—
1956 Proof	—	Value: 700				
1957H	2,500,000	—	1.50	4.00	8.00	—
1957H Proof	—	Value: 700				
1957KN	2,500,000	—	1.50	4.00	8.00	—
1961	32,000,000	—	0.75	1.50	5.00	—
1961 Proof	—	Value: 700				
1961H	23,000,000	—	0.75	1.50	5.00	—

KM# 4.1 50 CENTS
9.3800 g., Copper-Nickel **Obv:** Crowned bust of Queen Elizabeth II right **Obv. Designer:** Cecil Thomas **Rev:** Value within beaded circle **Edge:** Security

Date	Mintage	F	VF	XF	Unc	BU
1954	8,000,000	—	2.00	4.00	13.00	—
1954 Proof	—	Value: 820				
1955H	4,000,000	—	2.00	4.50	14.00	—
1956	3,440,000	—	2.00	4.50	14.00	—
1956 Proof	—	Value: 820				
1957H	2,000,000	—	2.50	4.75	13.50	—
1957H Proof	—	Value: 820				
1957KN	2,000,000	—	3.00	6.00	14.00	—
1958H	4,000,000	—	1.50	3.00	12.00	—
1961	17,000,000	—	1.50	3.00	12.00	—
1961 Proof	—	Value: 820				
1961H	4,000,000	—	2.00	5.00	14.00	—
1961H Proof	—	Value: 820				

KM# 4.2 50 CENTS
Copper-Nickel **Obv:** Crowned bust of Queen Elizabeth II right **Obv. Designer:** Cecil Thomas **Rev:** Value within beaded circle **Note:** Error, without security edge.

Date	Mintage	F	VF	XF	Unc	BU
1954	Inc. above	—	160	300	660	—
1957KN	Inc. above	—	160	300	660	—
1958H	Inc. above	—	160	300	660	—
1961	Inc. above	—	160	300	660	—
1961H	Inc. above	—	160	300	660	—

KELANTAN

A state in northern Malaysia, colonized by the Javanese in 1300's. It was subject to Thailand from 1780 to 1909.

TITLE

Khalifa(t) Al-Mu'minin

MINT

كلنتن

Kelantan

SULTAN
Muhammed IV, 1902-1919

SULTANATE

STANDARD COINAGE

KM# 12 PITIS
Tin, 24-29 mm. **Ruler:** Muhammed IV **Obv:** Arabic legend **Obv. Legend:** Belanjaan Negri Kelantan Adama Mulkahu **Rev:** Arabic legend **Rev. Legend:** Duriba Fi Dhul Hijja Sanat 1321

Date	Mintage	VG	F	VF	XF	Unc
AH1321 (1903)	—	8.00	12.00	20.00	30.00	—

KM# 15 PITIS
Tin **Ruler:** Muhammed IV **Obv:** Arabic legend **Obv. Legend:** Belanjaan Kerajaan Kelan Tan **Rev:** Arabic legend **Rev. Legend:** Duriba Fi Dhul Hijja Sanat 1321

Date	Mintage	VG	F	VF	XF	Unc
AH1321 (1903)	—	2.00	3.00	5.00	9.00	—

KM# 18 KEPING
Tin **Ruler:** Muhammed IV **Obv:** Arabic legend **Obv. Legend:** Negri Kelantan Satu Keping **Rev:** Uninscribed, but obverse legend shows through in negative form

Date	Mintage	VG	F	VF	XF	Unc
AH1323 (1905)	—	15.00	25.00	40.00	60.00	—

KM# 20 10 KEPINGS
Tin **Ruler:** Muhammed IV **Obv:** Arabic legend **Obv. Legend:** Belanjaan Kerajaan Kelantin Sepuloh Keping **Rev:** Border of diamonds around Arabic legend **Rev. Legend:** Sunia Fi Dhul Hijja Sanat 1321

Date	Mintage	VG	F	VF	XF	Unc
AH1321 (1903)	—	6.00	12.00	25.00	40.00	—

TRENGGANU

A state in eastern Malaysia on the shore of the south China Sea. Area of dispute between Malacca and Thailand with the latter emerging with possession. Trengganu became a British dependency in 1909.

TITLE

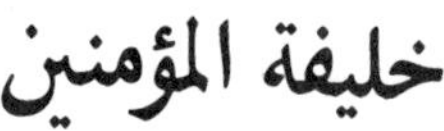

Khalifa(t) al-Mu'minin

MINT

Trengganu

SULTANS
Zainal Abidin III, 1881-1918
Muhammed, 1918-1920
Sulaiman, 1920-1942

SULTANATE

STANDARD COINAGE

KM# 16 1/2 CENT
Tin, 22 mm. **Ruler:** Zainal Abidin III **Obv:** Legend within circle **Rev:** Value within circle and wreath **Note:** Recast.

Date	Mintage	VG	F	VF	XF	Unc
AH1322 (1904)	—	3.00	6.00	10.00	20.00	—

KM# 18 1/2 CENT
Tin, 22 mm. **Ruler:** Zainal Abidin III **Obv:** Legend within circle flanked by stars **Rev:** Value within circle and wreath **Note:** Recast. Originals are rare.

Date	Mintage	VG	F	VF	XF	Unc
AH1325 (1907)	—	3.00	6.00	10.00	20.00	—

KM# 19 CENT
Tin, 29 mm. **Ruler:** Zainal Abidin III **Obv:** Legend within beaded circle flanked by stars **Rev:** Value within beaded circle and wreath

Date	Mintage	VG	F	VF	XF	Unc
AH1325 (1907)	—	5.00	9.00	16.00	35.00	—

KM# 20 CENT

Tin, 29 mm. **Ruler:** Zainal Abidin III **Obv:** Legend within beaded circle flanked by stars **Rev:** Value flanked by stars within diamond shape within beaded circle and wreath **Note:** Although dated AH1325 (1907), this coin was actually struck in 1920 under Sultan Sulaiman. Authorized mintage was 1 million. Beware of thin lead counterfeits.

Date	Mintage	VG	F	VF	XF	Unc
AH1325 (1907)	—	5.00	9.00	16.00	35.00	—

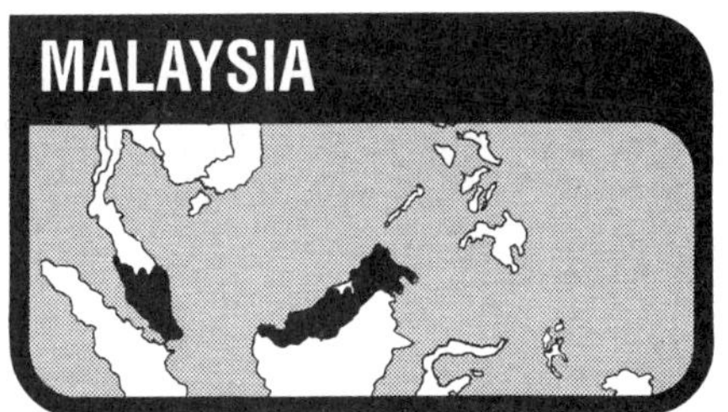

The independent limited constitutional monarchy of Malaysia, which occupies the southern part of the Malay Peninsula in Southeast Asia and the northern part of the island of Borneo, has an area of 127,316 sq. mi. (329,750 sq. km.) and a population of 15.4 million. Capital: Kuala Lumpur. The economy is based on agriculture, mining and forestry. Rubber, tin, timber and palm oil are exported.

Malaysia came into being on Sept. 16, 1963, as a federation of Malaya (Johore, Kelantan, Kedah, Perlis, Trengganu, Negri Sembilan, Pahang, Selangor, Penang, Malacca), Singapore, Sabah (British North Borneo) and Sarawak. Following two serious racial riots involving Malays and Chinese, Singapore withdrew from the federation on Aug. 9, 1965. Malaysia is a member of the Commonwealth of Nations.

MINT MARK

FM - Franklin Mint, U.S.A.

***NOTE:** From 1975-1985 the Franklin Mint produced coinage in up to 3 different qualities. Qualities of issue are designated in ( ) after each date and are defined as follows:

(M) MATTE - Normal circulation strike or a dull finish produced by sandblasting special uncirculated (polish finish) or proof quality dies.

(U) SPECIAL UNCIRCULATED - Polished or prooflike in appearance without any frosted features.

(P) PROOF - The highest quality obtainable having mirror-like fields and frosted features.

MONETARY SYSTEM

100 Sen = 1 Ringgit (Dollar)

CONSTITUTIONAL MONARCHY

STANDARD COINAGE

100 Sen = 1 Ringgit (Dollar)

KM# 1 SEN

1.9500 g., Bronze **Obv:** Value **Obv. Designer:** Geoffrey Colley **Rev:** Parliament house **Note:** Varieties exist.

Date	Mintage	F	VF	XF	Unc	BU
1967	45,000,000	—	—	0.50	2.00	3.00
1967 Proof	500	Value: 15.00				
1968	10,500,000	—	—	2.00	5.00	6.00
1970	2,535,000	—	—	2.00	10.00	15.00
1971	47,862,000	—	—	0.45	1.50	2.00
1973	21,400,000	—	—	0.25	0.60	1.00
1976	100	—	40.00	100	200	280
1980FM (P)	5,000	Value: 1.50				
1981FM (P)	6,628	Value: 1.50				

KM# 1a SEN

1.7200 g., Copper-Clad Steel, 17.69 mm. **Obv:** Value **Obv. Designer:** Geoffrey Colley **Rev:** Parliament house

Date	Mintage	F	VF	XF	Unc	BU
1973	Inc. above	—	—	0.65	1.50	2.00
1976	27,406,000	—	—	0.25	0.80	1.30

Date	Mintage	F	VF	XF	Unc	BU
1977	21,751,000	—	—	0.25	0.50	0.65
1978	30,844,000	—	—	0.25	0.50	0.65
1979	15,714,000	—	—	0.25	0.50	0.65
1980	16,152,000	—	—	0.25	0.50	0.65
1981	24,633,000	—	—	0.25	0.50	0.65
1982	37,295,000	—	—	0.25	0.50	0.65
1983	19,333,000	—	—	0.45	0.75	0.90
1984	26,267,000	—	—	0.45	0.75	0.90
1985	52,402,000	—	—	0.25	0.50	0.65
1986	48,920,000	—	—	0.25	0.50	0.65
1987	35,284,000	—	—	0.25	0.50	0.65
1988	56,749,000	—	—	0.25	0.50	0.65

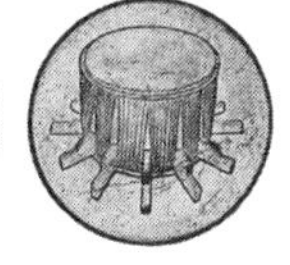

KM# 49 SEN

1.8000 g., Bronze Clad Steel, 17.66 mm. **Obv:** Value divides date below flower blossom **Obv. Legend:** BANK NEGARA MALAYSIA **Rev:** Drum **Edge:** Plain

Date	Mintage	F	VF	XF	Unc	BU
1989	28,429,000	—	—	—	0.25	0.35
1990	102,539,000	—	—	—	0.15	0.25
1991	100,314,734	—	—	—	0.15	0.25
1992	122,824,000	—	—	—	0.15	0.25
1993	153,805,875	—	—	—	0.15	0.25
1994	185,085,000	—	—	—	0.15	0.25
1995	208,611,295	—	—	—	0.15	0.25
1996	183,272,598	—	—	—	0.15	0.25
1997	172,215,681	—	—	—	0.15	0.25
1998	1,917,633,834	—	—	—	0.15	0.25
1999	265,502,565	—	—	—	0.15	0.25
2000	268,762,170	—	—	—	0.15	0.25
2001	213,645,000	—	—	—	0.15	0.25
2002	185,220,000	—	—	—	0.15	0.25
2003	235,350,000	—	—	—	0.15	0.25
2004	227,700,000	—	—	—	0.15	0.25
2005	437,400,000	—	—	—	0.15	0.25
2006	328,050,000	—	—	—	0.15	0.25

KM# 2 5 SEN

1.4200 g., Copper-Nickel **Obv:** Value **Obv. Designer:** Geoffrey Colley **Rev:** Parliament house **Note:** Varieties exist.

Date	Mintage	F	VF	XF	Unc	BU
1967	75,464,000	—	—	0.25	0.50	1.00
1967 Proof	500	Value: 25.00				
1968	74,536,000	—	—	0.25	0.50	1.00
1971	16,658,000	—	—	0.45	0.75	1.20
1973	102,942,000	—	—	0.25	0.50	1.00
1976	65,659,000	—	—	0.25	0.50	1.00
1977	10,609,000	—	—	0.30	0.60	1.20
1978	50,044,000	—	—	0.25	0.50	1.00
1979	38,824,000	—	—	0.25	0.50	1.00
1980	33,893,000	—	—	0.25	0.50	1.00
1980FM (P)	6,628	Value: 2.00				
1981	51,490,000	—	—	0.25	0.50	1.00
1981FM (P)	—	Value: 3.00				
1982	118,594,000	—	—	0.25	0.50	1.00
1985	15,553,000	—	—	0.25	0.50	0.65
1987	17,723,000	—	—	0.25	0.50	0.65
1988	26,788,000	—	—	0.25	0.50	0.65

KM# 50 5 SEN

1.4000 g., Copper-Nickel, 16.28 mm. **Obv:** Value divides date below flower blossom **Obv. Legend:** BANK NEGARA MALAYSIA **Rev:** Top with string **Edge:** Reeded

Date	Mintage	F	VF	XF	Unc	BU
1989	20,484,000	—	—	—	0.20	0.30
1990	58,909,000	—	—	—	0.20	0.30
1991	46,092,000	—	—	—	0.20	0.30
1992	67,844,000	—	—	—	0.20	0.30
1993	70,703,000	—	—	—	0.20	0.30
1994	83,026,000	—	—	—	0.20	0.30
1995	53,069,000	—	—	—	0.15	0.25
1996	51,812,529	—	—	—	0.15	0.25
1997	7,703,850	—	—	—	0.15	0.25
1998	1,293,910,233	—	—	—	0.15	0.25
1999	79,224,000	—	—	—	0.15	0.25
2000	61,198,528	—	—	—	0.15	0.25
2001	94,617,472	—	—	—	0.15	0.25
2002	85,316,000	—	—	—	0.15	0.25
2003	75,690,000	—	—	—	0.15	0.25
2004	11,520,000	—	—	—	0.15	0.25
2005	119,520,000	—	—	—	0.15	0.25
2006	87,120,000	—	—	—	0.15	0.25

KM# 3 10 SEN

2.8200 g., Copper-Nickel, 19.3 mm. **Obv:** Value **Obv. Designer:** Geoffrey Colley **Rev:** Parliament house **Note:** Varieties exist.

Date	Mintage	F	VF	XF	Unc	BU
1967	106,708,000	—	0.25	0.45	1.30	1.80
1967 Proof	500	Value: 35.00				
1968	128,292,000	—	0.25	0.45	1.10	1.50
1971	42,000	—	20.00	30.00	50.00	70.00
1973	214,832,000	—	0.10	0.30	1.00	1.30
1976	148,841,000	—	0.10	0.30	1.00	1.30
1977	52,720,000	—	0.10	0.30	1.00	1.30
1978	21,162,000	—	0.10	0.30	0.75	1.10
1979	50,633,000	—	0.10	0.25	0.60	1.10
1980	51,797,000	—	0.10	0.25	0.60	1.10
1980FM (P)	6,628	Value: 3.00				
1981	236,639,000	—	0.10	0.25	0.60	1.00
1981FM (P)	—	Value: 4.00				
1982	145,639,000	—	—	0.25	0.60	1.00
1983	30,832,000	—	—	0.25	0.60	1.00
1988	17,852,000	—	—	0.25	0.60	1.00

KM# 51 10 SEN

2.8200 g., Copper-Nickel, 19.43 mm. **Obv:** Value divides date below flower blossom **Obv. Legend:** BANK NEGARA MALAYSIA **Rev:** Ceremonial table **Edge:** Reeded

Date	Mintage	F	VF	XF	Unc	BU
1989	32,392,000	—	—	—	0.25	0.40
1990	132,982,000	—	—	—	0.25	0.40
1991	133,293,000	—	—	—	0.25	0.40
1992	89,919,000	—	—	—	0.25	0.40
1993	44,224,000	—	—	—	0.25	0.40
1994	7,122,000	—	—	—	0.30	0.50
1995	82,217,000	—	—	—	0.25	0.40
1996	77,347,125	—	—	—	0.25	0.40
1997	78,955,862	—	—	—	0.25	0.40
1998	1,966,056,746	—	—	—	0.25	0.40
1999	163,080,000	—	—	—	0.25	0.40
2000	162,940,000	—	—	—	0.25	0.40
2001	313,422,000	—	—	—	0.25	0.40
2002	290,451,948	—	—	—	0.25	0.40
2003	8,640,000	—	—	—	0.25	0.40
2004	170,640,000	—	—	—	0.25	0.40
2005	316,800,000	—	—	—	0.25	0.40
2006	304,560,000	—	—	—	0.25	0.40
2007	—	—	—	—	0.25	0.40

KM# 4 20 SEN

Copper-Nickel, 23.4 mm. **Obv:** Value **Obv. Designer:** Geoffrey Colley **Rev:** Parliament house **Note:** Varieties exist.

Date	Mintage	F	VF	XF	Unc	BU
1967	49,560,000	—	0.25	0.50	1.50	2.20
1967 Proof	500	Value: 45.00				
1968	40,440,000	—	0.25	0.50	1.50	2.20
1969	15,000,000	—	0.25	0.50	1.50	2.20
1970	1,054,000	—	0.60	1.20	3.00	7.00
1971	9,958,000	—	0.25	0.50	1.50	3.00
1973	116,075,000	—	0.25	0.50	1.00	2.00
1976	47,396,000	—	0.25	0.50	1.00	2.00
1977	66,139,000	—	0.25	0.50	1.00	2.00
1978	6,847,000	—	0.25	0.50	1.00	2.00
1979	17,346,000	—	0.25	0.50	1.00	2.00
1980	32,837,000	—	0.15	0.30	0.65	1.20
1980FM (P)	6,628	Value: 4.00				
1981	144,128,000	—	0.15	0.30	0.65	1.20
1981FM (P)	—	Value: 5.00				
1982	97,905,000	—	—	0.25	0.60	1.20
1983	8,105,000	—	—	0.25	0.60	1.00
1987	26,225,000	—	—	0.25	0.60	1.00
1988	67,218,000	—	—	0.25	0.60	1.00

KM# 52 20 SEN

5.6900 g., Copper-Nickel, 23.57 mm. **Obv:** Value divides date below flower blossom **Obv. Legend:** BANK NEGARA MALAYSIA **Rev:** Basket with food and utensils **Edge:** Reeded

Date	Mintage	F	VF	XF	Unc	BU
1989	28,945,000	—	—	—	0.35	0.50
1990	56,249,000	—	—	—	0.35	0.50
1991	82,774,000	—	—	—	0.35	0.50
1992	48,975,000	—	—	—	0.35	0.50
1993	55,753,000	—	—	—	0.35	0.50
1994	2,680,000	—	—	—	0.35	0.50
1997	78,479,804	—	—	—	0.35	0.50
1998	1,161,791,361	—	—	—	0.35	0.50
2000	63,908,000	—	—	—	0.35	0.50
2001	278,802,000	—	—	—	0.35	0.50
2002	131,279,881	—	—	—	0.35	0.50
2003	—	—	—	—	0.35	0.50
2004	96,840,000	—	—	—	0.35	0.50
2005	209,700,000	—	—	—	0.35	0.50
2006	155,880,000	—	—	—	0.35	0.50
2007	—	—	—	—	0.35	0.50

KM# 5.1 50 SEN

Copper-Nickel, 27.8 mm. **Obv:** Value **Rev:** Parliament house

Date	Mintage	F	VF	XF	Unc	BU
1967	15,000,000	—	0.35	0.75	3.00	6.00
1967 Proof	500	Value: 55.00				
1968	12,000,000	—	0.35	0.75	3.00	6.00
1969	2,000,000	—	0.75	7.00	22.00	40.00

KM# 5.2 50 SEN

Copper-Nickel, 27.8 mm. **Obv:** Value **Rev:** Parliament house **Note:** Error, no security edge.

Date	Mintage	F	VF	XF	Unc	BU
1967	Inc. above	—	80.00	160	260	380
1968	Inc. above	—	80.00	160	260	380
1969	Inc. above	—	390	500	750	900

KM# 5.3 50 SEN

9.3000 g., Copper-Nickel, 27.8 mm. **Obv:** Value **Rev:** Parliament house **Edge Lettering:** MALAYSIA BANK NEGARA (repeated)

Date	Mintage	F	VF	XF	Unc	BU
1971	8,404,000	—	0.30	1.00	3.00	5.00
1973	50,135,000	—	0.25	1.00	3.00	5.00
1977	17,720,000	—	0.25	0.60	2.00	5.00
1978	11,033,000	—	0.25	0.60	2.00	5.00
1979	5,361,000	—	0.25	0.60	2.00	5.00
1980	15,911,000	—	0.25	0.50	1.00	3.00
1980FM Proof	6,628	Value: 4.50				
1981	22,969,000	—	—	0.35	1.00	3.00
1982	20,585,000	—	—	0.35	1.00	3.00
1983	11,560,000	—	—	0.35	1.00	3.00
1984	10,139,000	—	—	0.35	1.00	3.00
1985	7,115,000	—	—	0.35	1.00	3.00
1986	8,193,000	—	—	0.35	1.00	3.00
1987	7,696,000	—	—	0.35	1.00	3.00
1988	26,788,000	—	—	0.35	1.00	3.00

KM# 53 50 SEN

9.2800 g., Copper-Nickel, 27.78 mm. **Obv:** Value divides date below flower blossom **Obv. Legend:** BANK NEGARA MALAYSIA **Rev:** Ceremonial kite **Edge:** Lettered **Edge Lettering:** BANK NEGARA MALAYSIA (twice)

Date	Mintage	F	VF	XF	Unc	BU
1989	6,639,057	—	—	—	0.65	0.85
1990	26,276,464	—	—	—	0.65	0.85
1991	20,720,531	—	—	—	0.65	0.85
1992	15,134,992	—	—	—	0.65	0.85
1993	7,657,991	—	—	—	0.65	0.85
1994	6,565,914	—	—	—	0.65	0.85
1995	1,650,423	—	—	—	0.65	0.85
1996	7,475,790	—	—	—	0.65	0.85
1997	16,143,327	—	—	—	0.65	0.85
1998	401,622,135	—	—	—	0.65	0.85
1999	12,085,000	—	—	—	0.65	0.85
2000	48,206,000	—	—	—	0.65	0.85
2001	67,371,000	—	—	—	0.65	0.85
2002	61,928,000	—	—	—	0.65	0.85
2003	32,580,000	—	—	—	0.65	0.85
2004	37,890,000	—	—	—	0.65	0.85
2005	691,680,006	—	—	—	0.65	0.85
2006	19,480,006	—	—	—	0.65	0.85

KM# 7 RINGGIT

Copper-Nickel, 33.5 mm. **Subject:** 10th Anniversary - Bank Negara **Obv:** Artistic value and dollar sign within 3/4 flower wreath **Rev:** Bust with headdress left

Date	Mintage	F	VF	XF	Unc	BU
ND(1969)	1,000,000	—	1.20	1.80	4.00	6.00

KM# 9.1 RINGGIT

Copper-Nickel, 33.5 mm. **Obv:** Artistic value and dollar sign above date **Rev:** Parliament house within cresent **Edge Lettering:** BANK NEGARA MALAYSIA

Date	Mintage	F	VF	XF	Unc	BU
1971	2,000,000	—	0.50	0.75	1.50	—
1971 Proof	500	Value: 850				
1980	472,000	—	0.60	0.85	1.65	—
1980FM (P)	6,628	Value: 8.00				
1981	765,000	—	0.60	0.85	1.65	—
1982	202,000	—	0.60	0.85	1.65	—
1984	355,000	—	0.60	0.85	1.65	—
1985	302,000	—	0.60	0.85	1.65	—
1986	253,000	—	0.60	0.85	1.65	—

KM# 12 RINGGIT

Copper-Nickel, 33.5 mm. **Subject:** Kuala Lumpur Anniversary **Obv:** Artistic value and dollar sign above date **Rev:** Artistic design **Edge Lettering:** MALAYSIA BANK NEGARA **Note:** Issued in 1973.

Date	Mintage	F	VF	XF	Unc	BU
1972	500,000	—	0.60	0.85	4.00	—
1972 Proof	500	Value: 410				

KM# 13 RINGGIT

Copper-Nickel, 33.5 mm. **Subject:** 25th Anniversary - Employee Provident Fund **Obv:** Value **Rev:** Two upper circles among assorted heads

Date	Mintage	F	VF	XF	Unc	BU
1976FM (U)	500,000	—	0.60	1.00	5.00	—
1976FM (P)	7,810	Value: 28.00				

KM# 16 RINGGIT

Copper-Nickel, 33 mm. **Subject:** 3rd Malaysian 5-Year Plan **Obv:** Arms with supporters **Rev:** Head with headdress facing within circle and block-like artistic design **Shape:** 14-sided

Date	Mintage	F	VF	XF	Unc	BU
ND(1976)	1,000,000	—	0.60	0.75	4.00	—
ND(1976)FM (P)	17,000	Value: 15.00				

KM# 22 RINGGIT

Copper-Nickel, 33.5 mm. **Subject:** 9th Southeast Asian Games **Obv:** Arms with supporters **Rev:** Kite flyer **Edge Lettering:** MALAYSIA BANK NEGARA

Date	Mintage	F	VF	XF	Unc	BU
1977	1,000,000	—	0.60	0.75	4.00	—
1977FM (P)	11,000	Value: 25.00				

KM# 25 RINGGIT

Copper-Nickel, 33.5 mm. **Subject:** 20th Anniversary of Independence **Obv:** Head facing **Rev:** Arms with supporters

Date	Mintage	F	VF	XF	Unc	BU
ND(1977)	500,000	—	0.75	1.00	5.00	—
ND(1977)FM (P)	3,100	Value: 50.00				

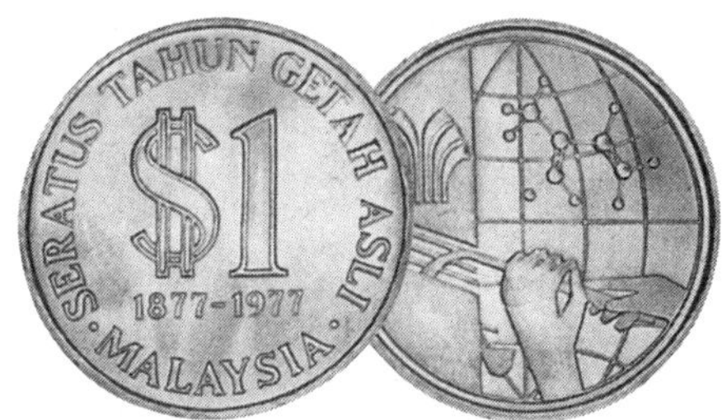

KM# 26 RINGGIT
Copper-Nickel, 33.5 mm. **Subject:** 100th Anniversary of Natural Rubber Production **Obv:** Value and dollar sign above dates **Rev:** Artistic design with a pair of hands **Edge Lettering:** MALAYSIA BANK NEGARA

Date	Mintage	F	VF	XF	Unc	BU
ND(1977)	500,000	—	0.60	0.75	4.00	—

KM# 27 RINGGIT
Copper-Nickel, 33.5 mm. **Subject:** 20th Anniversary of Bank Negara **Obv:** Value **Rev:** Building above dates

Date	Mintage	F	VF	XF	Unc	BU
ND(1979)	300,000	—	0.60	0.75	4.00	—

KM# 28 RINGGIT
Copper-Nickel, 33.5 mm. **Subject:** 15th Century of Hejira **Obv:** Value, date **Rev:** Design within spider web **Edge Lettering:** MALAYSIA BANK NEGARA

Date	Mintage	F	VF	XF	Unc	BU
AH1401(1981)	500,000	—	0.60	0.75	4.00	—

KM# 29 RINGGIT
Copper-Nickel, 33.5 mm. **Subject:** 4th Malaysian Plan **Obv:** Arms with supporters **Rev:** Bust with headdress facing 1/4 right **Edge Lettering:** MALAYSIA BANK NEGARA **Note:** Tun Hussein Onn

Date	Mintage	F	VF	XF	Unc	BU
ND(1981)	1,000,000	—	0.50	0.65	4.00	—
ND(1981) Proof	10,000	Value: 20.00				

KM# 32 RINGGIT
Copper-Nickel, 33.5 mm. **Subject:** 25th Anniversary of Independence **Obv:** Star design and bust with headdress with left arm raised facing right **Rev:** Arms with supporters

Date	Mintage	F	VF	XF	Unc	BU
ND(1982)	1,500,000	—	0.50	0.65	4.00	—
ND(1982) Proof	15,000	Value: 20.00				

KM# 36 RINGGIT
Copper-Nickel **Subject:** 5th Malaysian 5-Year Plan **Obv:** Arms with supporters with value and dollar sign below **Rev:** Tractor tire, plants, scale and sun within circle

Date	Mintage	F	VF	XF	Unc	BU
ND(1986)	1,000,000	—	0.50	0.65	4.00	—
ND(1986) Proof	8,000	Value: 12.00				

KM# 39 RINGGIT
Copper-Nickel **Subject:** 35th Annual PATA Conference **Obv:** Value **Rev:** Standing turtle

Date	Mintage	F	VF	XF	Unc	BU
ND(1986)	500,000	—	0.50	1.50	5.00	15.00

KM# 43 RINGGIT
Copper-Zinc, 24 mm. **Subject:** 30th Anniversary of Independence **Obv:** Arms with supporters above value and dollar sign **Rev:** Numeral 30 divides dates below with flyin doves and sun above

Date	Mintage	F	VF	XF	Unc	BU
ND(1987)	1,000,000	—	—	0.60	3.50	—
ND(1987) Proof	20,000	Value: 14.00				

KM# 54 RINGGIT
Aluminum-Bronze, 24 mm. **Obv:** Value and dollar sign divide date with flower blossom above **Rev:** Native dagger and scabbard within designs **Note:** Varying degrees of filled die variations exist.

Date	Mintage	F	VF	XF	Unc	BU
1989	20,410,000	—	—	—	1.75	2.25
1990	80,102,000	—	—	—	1.75	2.25
1991	169,001,000	—	—	—	1.75	2.00
1992	139,042,000	—	—	—	1.75	2.00
1993	178,894,000	—	—	—	1.75	2.00

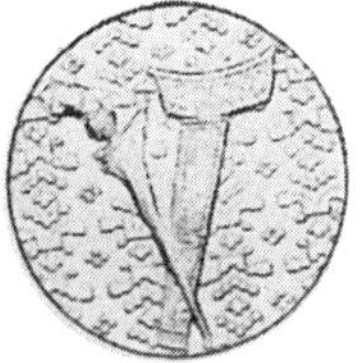

KM# 64 RINGGIT
9.3500 g., Aluminum-Bronze, 24 mm. **Obv:** Value divides date below flower blossom **Rev:** Native dagger and scabbard within designs

Date	Mintage	F	VF	XF	Unc	BU
1993	Inc. above	—	—	—	2.00	2.25
1994	36,899,000	—	—	—	1.75	2.00
1995	132,173,000	—	—	—	1.75	2.00
1996	59,460,000	—	—	—	1.75	2.00
1997	41,842,514	—	—	—	—	—
Note: Full mintage withdrawn						
1998	607,756,026	—	—	—	—	—
Note: Full mintage withdrawn						

KM# 65 RINGGIT
8.1500 g., Bi-Metallic Copper-Nickel center in Nickel-Brass ring, 26.5 mm. **Subject:** Thomas-Uber Cup **Obv:** City view within circle **Rev:** Two-handled cup on radiant background **Edge:** Reeded

Date	Mintage	F	VF	XF	Unc	BU
2000	2,000,000	—	—	—	4.00	5.00

KM# 165 RINGGIT
Copper Plated Zinc **Subject:** 10th Men's Hockey World Cup **Obv:** Logo **Obv. Legend:** BANK NEGARA MALAYSIA **Rev:** 2 stylized players **Rev. Legend:** KEJOHANAN HOKI LELAKI PIALA DUNIA **Edge:** Reeded

Date	Mintage	F	VF	XF	Unc	BU
2002	100,000	—	—	—	—	6.00

MALDIVE ISLANDS

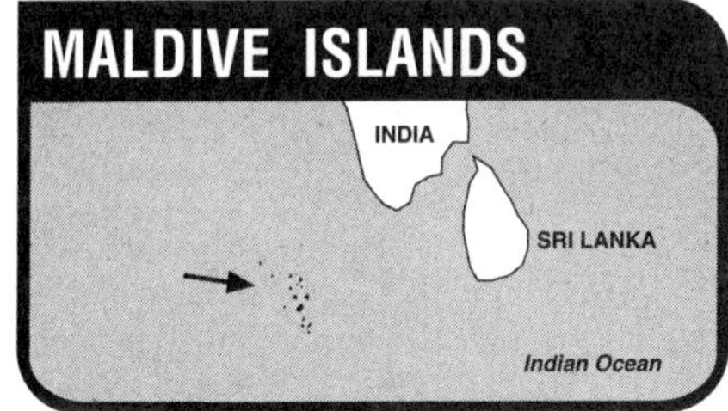

The Republic of Maldives, an archipelago of 2,000 coral islets in the northern Indian Ocean 417 miles (671 km.) west of Ceylon, has an area of 116 sq. mi. (298 sq. km.)and a population of 189,000. Capital: Male. Fishing employs 95 % of the male work force. Dried fish, copra and coir yarn are exported.

The Maldive Islands were visited by Arab traders and converted to Islam in 1153. After being harassed in the16th and 17th centuries by Mopla pirates of the Malabar coast and Portuguese raiders, the Maldivians voluntarily placed themselves under the suzeraintv of Ceylon. In 1887 the islands became an internally self-governing British protectorate and a nominal dependency of Ceylon. Traditionally a sultanate, the Maldives became a republic in 1953 but restored the sultanate in 1954. The Sultanate of the Maldive Islands attained complete internal and external autonomy on July 26, 1965, and on Nov. 11,1968, again became a republic. The Maldives is a member of the Commonwealth of Nations.

RULERS

Muhammad Imad al-Din V, AH1318-1322/1900-1904AD
Muhammad Shams al-Din III, AH1322-1353/1904-1935AD
Hasan Nur al-Din II, AH1353-1364/1935-1945AD
Abdul-Majid Didi, AH1364-1371/1945-1953AD
First Republic, AH1371-1372/1953-1954AD
Muhammad Farid Didi, AH1372-1388/1954-1968AD
Second Republic, AH1388 to date/1968AD to date*

MINT NAME

Mahle (Male)

MONETARY SYSTEM

100 Lari = 1 Rupee (Rufiyaa)

SULTANATE

STANDARD COINAGE

KM# 41 LARIN

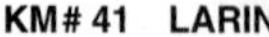

0.9000 g., Bronze, 13 mm. **Ruler:** Muhammad Shams al-Din III AH 1322-53 / 1904-35 AD **Obv:** Legend **Rev:** Legend **Note:** Struck at Birmingham, England. Rare mint proof strikes in silver and gold exist.

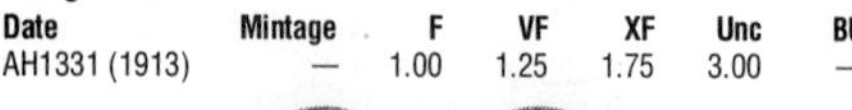

Date	Mintage	F	VF	XF	Unc	BU
AH1331 (1913)	—	1.00	1.25	1.75	3.00	—

KM# 39 2 LARIAT

Copper-Brass, 13 mm. **Ruler:** Muhammad Imad al-Din V AH 1318-22 / 1900-04 AD **Obv:** Legend **Rev:** Legend **Note:** 1.4-2.2 grams. Previously listed date AH1311 is merely poor die cutting of AH1319. Many die varieties exist.

Date	Mintage	F	VF	XF	Unc	BU
AH1319 (1901)	—	1.50	3.50	5.00	7.50	—

KM# 40.1 4 LARIAT

Copper-Brass **Ruler:** Muhammad Imad al-Din V AH 1318-22 / 1900-04 AD **Obv:** Legend **Rev:** Legend **Edge:** Plain or reeded **Note:** 2.5-4.5 grams. Many die varieties exist; size varies 17 - 18mm.

Date	Mintage	F	VF	XF	Unc	BU
AH1320 (1902)	—	1.50	2.50	4.50	8.00	—

KM# 40.2 4 LARIAT

Copper-Brass **Ruler:** Muhammad Imad al-Din V AH 1318-22 / 1900-04 AD **Obv:** Legend **Rev:** Legend with Arabic "Sana(t)" below date **Note:** Silver strikes are most likely presentation pieces; size varies 16.8-18mm.

Date	Mintage	F	VF	XF	Unc	BU
AH1320 (1902)	—	3.50	8.00	12.00	16.00	—

KM# 42 4 LARIAT

3.3000 g., Bronze, 19 mm. **Ruler:** Muhammad Shams al-Din III AH 1322-53 / 1904-35 AD **Obv:** Legend **Rev:** Legend **Note:** Struck at Birmingham, England. Rare mint proof strikes in silver and gold exist.

Date	Mintage	F	VF	XF	Unc	BU
AH1331 (1913)	—	1.00	1.50	2.75	6.00	—

2ND SULTANATE

STANDARD COINAGE

KM# 43 LAARI

1.5000 g., Bronze, 15 mm. **Ruler:** Muhammad Farid Didi AH 1372-88 / 1954-68 AD **Obv:** National emblem divides dates above **Rev:** Value **Note:** Similar to Laari, KM#49.

Date	Mintage	F	VF	XF	Unc	BU
AH1379-1960	300,000	—	0.15	0.25	0.50	—
AH1379-1960 Proof	1,270	Value: 3.00				

KM# 44 2 LAARI

3.1500 g., Bronze, 18.2 mm. **Ruler:** Muhammad Farid Didi AH 1372-88 / 1954-68 AD **Obv:** National emblem divides dates above **Rev:** Value **Shape:** 4-sided

Date	Mintage	F	VF	XF	Unc	BU
AH1379-1960	600,000	—	0.20	0.35	0.75	—
AH1379-1960 Proof	1,270	Value: 3.50				

KM# 45 5 LAARI

2.6000 g., Nickel-Brass, 20.4 mm. **Ruler:** Muhammad Farid Didi AH 1372-88 / 1954-68 AD **Obv:** National emblem divides dates above **Rev:** Value **Shape:** Scalloped

Date	Mintage	F	VF	XF	Unc	BU
AH1379-1960	300,000	—	0.25	0.40	0.75	—
AH1379-1960 Proof	1,270	Value: 4.00				

KM# 45a 5 LAARI

Bronze **Ruler:** Muhammad Farid Didi AH 1372-88 / 1954-68 AD **Obv:** National emblem divides dates above **Rev:** Value

Date	Mintage	F	VF	XF	Unc	BU
AH1379-1960	—	—	0.25	0.40	0.75	—

KM# 46 10 LAARI

5.2000 g., Nickel-Brass, 23 mm. **Ruler:** Muhammad Farid Didi AH 1372-88 / 1954-68 AD **Obv:** National emblem divides dates above **Rev:** Value **Shape:** Scalloped

Date	Mintage	F	VF	XF	Unc	BU
AH1379-1960	600,000	—	0.50	0.75	1.50	—
AH1379-1960 Proof	1,270	Value: 5.00				

KM# 47.1 25 LAARI

4.1000 g., Nickel-Brass, 20.4 mm. **Ruler:** Muhammad Farid Didi AH 1372-88 / 1954-68 AD **Obv:** National emblem divides dates above **Rev:** Value **Edge:** Security

Date	Mintage	F	VF	XF	Unc	BU
AH1379-1960	300,000	—	0.60	1.00	1.50	—
AH1379-1960 Proof	1,270	Value: 6.00				

KM# 47.2 25 LAARI

4.1000 g., Nickel-Brass, 20.4 mm. **Ruler:** Muhammad Farid Didi AH 1372-88 / 1954-68 AD **Obv:** National emblem divides dates above **Rev:** Value **Edge:** Reeded

Date	Mintage	F	VF	XF	Unc	BU
AH1379-1960	—	—	2.00	3.50	6.00	—

KM# 48.1 50 LAARI

5.6000 g., Nickel-Brass, 23.5 mm. **Ruler:** Muhammad Farid Didi AH 1372-88 / 1954-68 AD **Obv:** National emblem divides dates above **Rev:** Value **Edge:** Security

Date	Mintage	F	VF	XF	Unc	BU
AH1379-1960	300,000	—	1.00	1.75	2.50	—
AH1379-1960 Proof	1,270	Value: 8.00				

KM# 48.2 50 LAARI

Nickel-Brass, 23.5 mm. **Ruler:** Muhammad Farid Didi AH 1372-88 / 1954-68 AD **Obv:** National emblem divides dates above **Rev:** Value **Edge:** Reeded

Date	Mintage	F	VF	XF	Unc	BU
AH1379-1960	—	—	3.00	5.00	8.00	—

2ND REPUBLIC

STANDARD COINAGE

KM# 45b 5 LAARI

Nickel-Brass, 20.4 mm. **Ruler:** Muhammad Farid Didi AH 1372-88 / 1954-68 AD **Obv:** National emblem divides dates above **Shape:** Scalloped **Note:** Similar to 5 Laari, KM#45.

Date	Mintage	F	VF	XF	Unc	BU
AH1389-1970	300,000	—	0.20	0.30	0.40	—
AH1389-1970 Proof	—	Value: 3.50				
AH1399-1979	—	—	—	0.10	0.20	—
AH1399-1979 Proof	—	Value: 2.50				

STANDARD COINAGE

100 Laari = 1 Rufiyaa

KM# 49 LAARI

0.4500 g., Aluminum, 15 mm. **Obv:** National emblem divides dates above **Rev:** Value

Date	Mintage	F	VF	XF	Unc	BU
AH1389-1970	500,000	—	0.10	0.20	0.40	—
AH1399-1979	—	—	0.10	0.20	0.40	—
AH1399-1979 Proof	100,000	Value: 1.25				

KM# 68 LAARI

0.4700 g., Aluminum, 18.2 mm. **Obv:** Value **Rev:** Palm tree within circle

Date	Mintage	F	VF	XF	Unc	BU
AH1404-1984	—	—	—	0.10	0.15	—
AH1404-1984 Proof	2,500	Value: 2.50				

KM# 50 2 LAARI

Aluminum, 18.2 mm.

Date	Mintage	F	VF	XF	Unc	BU
AH1389-1970	500,000	—	0.15	0.25	0.50	—
AH1389-1970 Proof	—	—	—	—	—	—
AH1399-1979	—	—	0.15	0.25	0.50	—
AH1399-1979 Proof	100,000	Value: 1.25				

KM# 69 5 LAARI

1.0000 g., Aluminum, 20.4 mm. **Obv:** Value **Rev:** Two Bonito fish swimming upward left **Shape:** Scalloped

Date	Mintage	F	VF	XF	Unc	BU
AH1404-1984	—	—	—	0.10	0.35	0.75
AH1404-1984 Proof	2,500	Value: 3.00				
AH1411-1990	—	—	—	0.10	0.35	0.75

KM# 46a 10 LAARI

Aluminum, 23 mm. **Ruler:** Muhammad Farid Didi AH 1372-88 / 1954-68 AD **Obv:** National emblem divides dates above **Shape:** Scalloped **Note:** Similar to 10 Laari, KM#46.

Date	Mintage	F	VF	XF	Unc	BU
AH1399-1979	—	—	—	0.10	0.25	—
AH1399-1979 Proof	—	Value: 2.50				

KM# 70 10 LAARI

1.9500 g., Aluminum, 23 mm. **Obv:** Value **Rev:** Maldivian sailing ship - Odi **Shape:** Scalloped

Date	Mintage	F	VF	XF	Unc	BU
AH1404-1984	—	—	—	0.10	0.20	—
AH1404-1984 Proof	2,500	Value: 3.50				

KM# 47.3 25 LAARI

Nickel-Brass, 20.4 mm. **Obv:** National emblem divides dates above **Rev:** Palm tree **Note:** Similar to 25 Laari, KM#47.2.

Date	Mintage	F	VF	XF	Unc	BU
AH1399-1979	—	—	—	0.10	0.25	—
AH1399-1979 Proof	100,000	Value: 3.50				

KM# 71 25 LAARI

4.1500 g., Nickel-Brass, 20.4 mm. **Obv:** Value **Rev:** Mosque and minaret at Male

Date	Mintage	F	VF	XF	Unc	BU
AH1404-1984	—	—	—	0.15	0.45	—
AH1404-1984 Proof	—	Value: 4.00				
AH1411-1990	—	—	—	0.15	0.45	—
AH1416-1996	—	—	—	0.15	0.45	—

KM# 48.3 50 LAARI

Nickel-Brass, 23.5 mm. **Obv:** National emblem divides dates above **Rev:** Palm tree **Note:** Similar to 50 Laari, KM#48.2.

Date	Mintage	F	VF	XF	Unc	BU
AH1399-1979	—	—	0.10	0.20	0.40	—
AH1399-1979 Proof	100,000	Value: 6.50				

KM# 72 50 LAARI

5.6500 g., Nickel-Brass, 23.6 mm. **Obv:** Value **Rev:** Loggerhead sea turtle

Date	Mintage	F	VF	XF	Unc	BU
AH1404-1984	—	—	0.15	0.35	1.50	2.50
AH1404-1984 Proof	—	Value: 6.00				
AH1411-1990	—	—	0.15	0.35	1.50	2.50
AH1415-1995	—	—	0.15	0.35	1.50	2.50

KM# 73 RUFIYAA

Copper-Nickel Clad Steel, 25.9 mm. **Obv:** Value **Rev:** National emblem divides dates above

Date	Mintage	F	VF	XF	Unc	BU
AH1402-1982	—	—	0.20	0.50	2.00	—

KM# 73a RUFIYAA

6.3800 g., Copper-Nickel, 25.9 mm. **Obv:** Value **Rev:** National emblem divides dates above

Date	Mintage	F	VF	XF	Unc	BU
AH1404-1984	—	—	0.20	0.50	2.00	—
AH1404-1984 Proof	—	Value: 9.00				
AH1411-1990	—	—	0.20	0.50	2.00	—
AH1416-1996	—	—	0.20	0.50	2.00	—

KM# 88 2 RUFIYAA

Brass **Obv:** Value **Rev:** Pacific triton sea shell **Edge:** Lettering over reeding **Edge Lettering:** REPUBLIC OF MALDIVES

Date	Mintage	F	VF	XF	Unc	BU
AH1415-1995	—	—	—	—	6.50	7.50

MALI

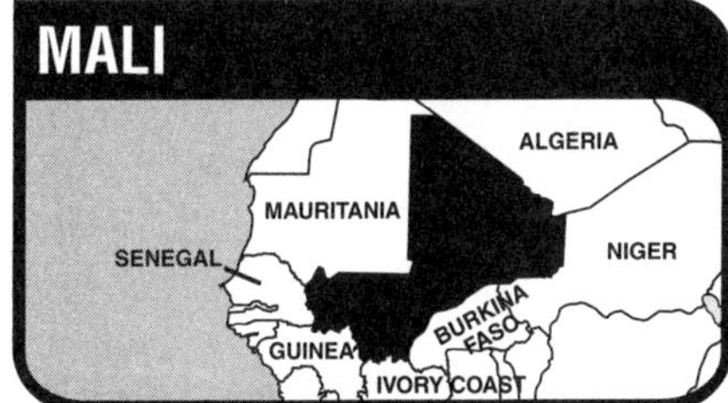

The Republic of Mali, a landlocked country in the interior of West Africa southwest of Algeria, has an area of 482,077 sq. mi. (1,240,000 sq. km.) and a population of 8.1 million. Capital: Bamako. Livestock, fish, cotton and peanuts are exported.

Malians are descendants of the ancient Malinke Kingdom of Mali that controlled the middle Niger from the 11th to the 17th centuries. The French penetrated the Sudan (now Mali) about 1880, and established their rule in 1898 after subduing fierce native resistance. In 1904 the area became the colony of Upper Senegal-Niger (changed to French Sudan in 1920), and became part of the French Union in 1946. In 1958 French Sudan became the Sudanese Republic with complete internal autonomy. Senegal joined with the Sudanese Republic in 1959 to form the Mali Federation which, in 1960, became a fully independent member of the French Community. Upon Senegal's subsequent withdrawal from the Federation, the Sudanese, on Sept. 22, 1960, proclaimed their nation the fully independent Republic of Mali and severed all ties with France.

MINT MARK

(a) - Paris, privy marks only

REPUBLIC

STANDARD COINAGE

KM# 2 5 FRANCS

1.0000 g., Aluminum, 20 mm. **Obv:** Hippo facing **Rev:** Value above crossed leaves

Date	Mintage	F	VF	XF	Unc	BU
1961	—	0.15	0.25	0.50	2.00	6.00

KM# 3 10 FRANCS

1.5500 g., Aluminum, 23.5 mm. **Obv:** Horse head left **Rev:** Value within leaf wreath

Date	Mintage	F	VF	XF	Unc	BU
1961	—	0.50	1.00	2.00	5.00	7.00

KM# 11 10 FRANCS

1.5500 g., Aluminum, 23.5 mm. **Obv:** Value flanked by triangles with date below **Rev:** Rice plants

Date	Mintage	F	VF	XF	Unc	BU
1976(a)	10,000,000	1.25	2.50	4.50	12.50	15.00

KM# 4 25 FRANCS

2.5000 g., Aluminum, 27 mm. **Obv:** Lion's head facing **Rev:** Value within leaf wreath

Date	Mintage	F	VF	XF	Unc	BU
1961	—	0.35	0.65	1.75	4.50	10.00

KM# 12 25 FRANCS

2.5000 g., Aluminum, 27 mm. **Obv:** Value flanked by triangles with date below **Rev:** Rice plants

Date	Mintage	F	VF	XF	Unc	BU
1976(a)	10,000,000	2.50	4.00	8.00	18.00	22.00

KM# 9 50 FRANCS

4.0000 g., Nickel-Brass, 23.5 mm. **Series:** F.A.O. **Obv:** Value flanked by triangles with date below **Rev:** Millet plant

Date	Mintage	F	VF	XF	Unc	BU
1975(a)	10,000,000	0.25	0.50	1.50	3.75	5.50
1977(a)	10,000,000	0.25	0.50	1.50	3.75	5.50

KM# 10 100 FRANCS

8.0000 g., Nickel-Brass, 27.8 mm. **Series:** F.A.O. **Obv:** Value flanked by triangles with date below **Rev:** 3 Ears of corn

Date	Mintage	F	VF	XF	Unc	BU
1975(a)	23,000,000	0.65	1.25	2.50	5.00	9.00

MALTA

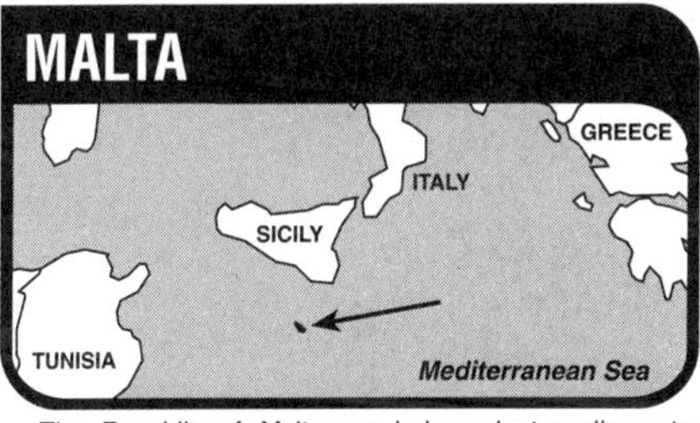

The Republic of Malta, an independent parliamentary democracy, is situated in the Mediterranean Sea between Sicily and North Africa. With the islands of Gozo and Comino, Malta has an area of 124 sq. mi. (320 sq. km.) and a population of 386,000. Capital: Valletta. Malta has no proven mineral resources, an agriculture insufficient to its needs, and a small, but expanding, manufacturing facility. Clothing, textile yarns and fabrics, and knitted wear are exported.

For more than 3,500 years Malta was ruled, in succession by Phoenicians, Carthaginians, Romans, Arabs, Normans, the Knights of Malta, France and Britain. Napoleon seized Malta by treachery in 1798. The French were ousted by a Maltese insurrection assisted by Britain, and in 1814 Malta, of its own free will, became a part of the British Empire. Malta obtained full independence in Sept., 1964; electing to remain within the Commonwealth with the British monarch as the nominal head of state.

Malta became a republic on Dec. 13, 1974, but remained a member of the Commonwealth of Nations. The president is Chief of State. The prime minister is the Head of Government.

RULER

British, until 1964

MONETARY SYSTEM

10 Mils = 1 Cent
100 Cents = 1 Pound

REPUBLIC

DECIMAL COINAGE

10 Mils = 1 Cent; 100 Cents = 1 Pound

KM# 54 2 MILS

0.9500 g., Aluminum, 20.3 mm. **Subject:** 10th Anniversary of Decimalization **Obv:** Maltese cross **Rev:** Value within 3/4 wreath **Shape:** Scalloped

Date	Mintage	F	VF	XF	Unc	BU
1982FM (U)	850	—	—	—	15.00	—
1982FM (P)	1,793	Value: 15.00				

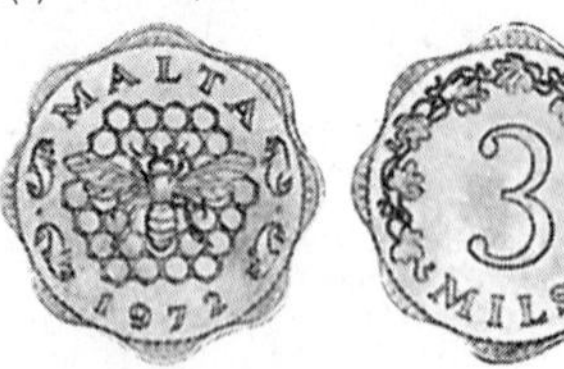

KM# 6 3 MILS

1.4500 g., Aluminum, 23.25 mm. **Obv:** Bee and honeycomb **Rev:** Value within 3/4 wreath **Shape:** Scalloped

Date	Mintage	F	VF	XF	Unc	BU
1972	—	—	1.00	2.00	3.00	—
1972 Proof	8,000	Value: 5.00				
1976FM (M)	5,000	—	—	—	3.00	—
1976FM (P)	26,000	Value: 5.00				
1977FM (U)	5,252	—	—	—	3.00	—
1977FM (P)	6,884	Value: 5.00				
1978FM (U)	5,252	—	—	—	3.00	—
1978FM (P)	3,244	Value: 5.00				
1979FM (U)	537	—	—	—	5.00	—
1979FM (P)	6,577	Value: 5.00				
1980FM (U)	385	—	—	—	5.00	—
1980FM (P)	3,451	Value: 5.00				
1981FM (U)	449	—	—	—	5.00	—
1981FM (P)	1,453	Value: 5.00				

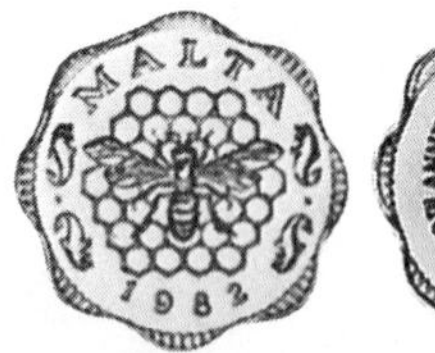

KM# 55 3 MILS

1.4500 g., Aluminum, 23.25 mm. **Subject:** 10th Anniversary of Decimalization **Obv:** Bee and honeycomb **Rev:** Value **Shape:** Scalloped

Date	Mintage	F	VF	XF	Unc	BU
1982FM (U)	850	—	—	—	4.00	—
1982FM (P)	1,793	Value: 2.00				

KM# 7 5 MILS

2.1000 g., Aluminum, 26 mm. **Obv:** Earthen lampstand **Rev:** Value within 3/4 wreath **Shape:** Scalloped

Date	Mintage	F	VF	XF	Unc	BU
1972	4,320,000	—	1.00	2.00	3.00	—
1972 Proof	13,000	Value: 5.00				
1976FM (M)	5,000	—	—	—	3.00	—
1976FM (P)	26,000	Value: 5.00				
1977FM (U)	5,252	—	—	—	3.00	—
1977FM (P)	6,884	Value: 5.00				
1978FM (U)	5,252	—	—	—	3.00	—
1978FM (P)	3,244	Value: 5.00				
1979FM (U)	537	—	—	—	7.00	—
1979FM (P)	6,577	Value: 5.00				
1980FM (U)	385	—	—	—	7.00	—
1980FM (P)	3,451	Value: 5.00				
1981FM (U)	449	—	—	—	7.00	—
1981FM (P)	1,453	Value: 5.00				

KM# 56 5 MILS

2.1000 g., Aluminum, 26 mm. **Subject:** 10th Anniversary of Decimalization **Obv:** Earthen lampstand **Rev:** Value **Shape:** Scalloped

Date	Mintage	F	VF	XF	Unc	BU
1982FM (U)	850	—	—	—	15.00	—
1982FM (P)	1,793	Value: 15.00				

KM# 8 CENT

7.1500 g., Bronze, 25.9 mm. **Obv:** The George Cross **Rev:** Value within 3/4 wreath

Date	Mintage	F	VF	XF	Unc	BU
1972	5,650,000	—	0.25	0.50	1.00	—
1972 Proof	13,000	Value: 5.00				
1975	1,500,000	—	0.25	0.50	1.00	—
1976FM (M)	5,000	—	—	—	5.00	—
1976FM (P)	26,000	Value: 5.00				
1977	2,793,000	—	0.25	0.50	1.00	—
1977FM (U)	5,252	—	—	—	5.00	—
1977FM (P)	6,884	Value: 5.00				
1978FM (U)	5,252	—	—	—	5.00	—
1978FM (P)	3,244	Value: 5.00				
1979FM (U)	537	—	—	—	9.00	—
1979FM (P)	6,577	Value: 5.00				
1980FM (U)	385	—	—	—	9.00	—
1980FM (P)	3,451	Value: 5.00				
1981FM (U)	449	—	—	—	9.00	—
1981FM (P)	1,453	Value: 15.00				
1982	—	—	5.00	5.00	10.00	—

KM# 57 CENT

7.1500 g., Bronze, 25.9 mm. **Subject:** 10th Anniversary of Decimalization **Obv:** The George cross **Rev:** Value

Date	Mintage	F	VF	XF	Unc	BU
1982FM (U)	850	—	—	—	15.00	—
1982FM (P)	1,793	Value: 15.00				

KM# 9 2 CENTS

2.2500 g., Copper-Zinc, 17.75 mm. **Subject:** Penthesilea, Queen of the Amazons **Obv:** Helmeted bust right **Rev:** Value within 3/4 wreath

Date	Mintage	F	VF	XF	Unc	BU
1972	5,640,000	—	0.10	0.50	1.00	—
1972 Proof	13,000	Value: 5.00				
1976	1,000,000	—	1.50	2.00	2.50	—
1976FM (M)	2,500	—	—	—	4.50	—
1976FM (P)	26,000	Value: 5.00				
1977	6,105,000	—	1.50	2.00	2.50	—
1977FM (U)	2,752	—	—	—	4.50	—
1977FM (P)	6,884	Value: 5.00				
1978FM (U)	2,752	—	—	—	4.50	—
1978FM (P)	3,244	Value: 5.00				
1979FM (U)	537	—	—	—	12.00	—
1979FM (P)	6,577	Value: 5.00				
1980FM (U)	385	—	—	—	12.00	—
1980FM (P)	3,451	Value: 5.00				
1981FM (U)	449	—	—	—	12.00	—
1981FM (P)	1,453	Value: 5.00				
1982	—	—	0.10	0.15	0.30	—

KM# 58 2 CENTS

2.2500 g., Copper-Zinc, 17.75 mm. **Subject:** 10th Anniversary of Decimalization **Obv:** Helmeted bust right **Rev:** Value

Date	Mintage	F	VF	XF	Unc	BU
1982FM (U)	850	—	—	—	10.00	—
1982FM (P)	1,793	Value: 15.00				

KM# 10 5 CENTS

5.6500 g., Copper-Nickel, 23.6 mm. **Obv:** Ritual altar in the Temple of Hagar Qim **Rev:** Value within 3/4 wreath

Date	Mintage	F	VF	XF	Unc	BU
1972	4,180,000	—	3.00	4.00	5.00	—
1972 Proof	13,000	Value: 7.00				
1976	1,009,000	—	1.00	2.00	3.00	—
1976FM (M)	2,500	—	—	—	5.00	—
1976FM (P)	26,000	Value: 2.00				
1977	—	—	1.00	2.00	3.00	—
1977FM (U)	2,752	—	—	—	5.00	—
1977FM (P)	6,884	Value: 3.00				
1978FM (U)	2,752	—	—	—	5.00	—
1978FM (P)	3,244	Value: 3.00				
1979FM (U)	537	—	—	—	15.00	—
1979FM (P)	6,577	Value: 3.00				
1980FM (U)	385	—	—	—	15.00	—
1980FM (P)	3,451	Value: 3.00				
1981FM (U)	449	—	—	—	15.00	—
1981FM (P)	1,453	Value: 3.00				

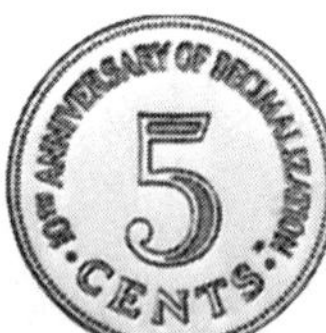

KM# 59 5 CENTS

5.6500 g., Copper-Nickel, 23.6 mm. **Subject:** 10th Anniversary of Decimalization **Obv:** Floral altar in the Temple of Hagar Qim **Rev:** Value

Date	Mintage	F	VF	XF	Unc	BU
1982FM (U)	850	—	—	—	15.00	—
1982FM (P)	1,793	Value: 3.00				

KM# 11 10 CENTS

11.3000 g., Copper-Nickel, 28.5 mm. **Obv:** Barge of the grand master **Rev:** Value within 3/4 wreath

Date	Mintage	F	VF	XF	Unc	BU
1972	10,680,000	—	4.00	6.00	8.00	—
1972 Proof	13,000	Value: 2.25				
1976FM (M)	1,000	—	—	—	8.00	—
1976FM (P)	26,000	Value: 2.50				
1977FM (U)	1,252	—	—	—	8.00	—
1977FM (P)	6,884	Value: 3.50				
1978FM (U)	1,252	—	—	—	8.00	—
1978FM (P)	3,244	Value: 3.50				
1979FM (U)	537	—	—	—	20.00	—
1979FM (P)	6,577	Value: 3.50				
1980FM (U)	385	—	—	—	20.00	—
1980FM (P)	3,451	Value: 3.50				
1981FM (U)	449	—	—	—	20.00	—
1981FM (P)	1,453	Value: 3.50				

KM# 60 10 CENTS

11.3000 g., Copper-Nickel, 28.5 mm. **Subject:** 10th Anniversary of Decimalization **Obv:** Barge of the grand master **Rev:** Value

Date	Mintage	F	VF	XF	Unc	BU
1982FM (U)	850	—	—	—	25.00	—
1982FM (P)	1,793	Value: 30.00				

KM# 29 25 CENTS

10.5500 g., Brass, 30 mm. **Subject:** 1st Anniversary - Republic of Malta **Obv:** Republic emblem within circle **Rev:** Value within 3/4 wreath **Shape:** 8-sided

Date	Mintage	F	VF	XF	Unc	BU
1975	4,750,000	—	8.00	9.00	10.00	—
1975 Matte proof	—	—	—	—	200	—

KM# 29b 25 CENTS

Copper-Nickel, 30 mm. **Obv:** Republic emblem within circle **Rev:** Value within 3/4 wreath

Date	Mintage	F	VF	XF	Unc	BU
1976FM (M)	300	—	—	—	40.00	—
1976FM (P)	26,000	Value: 3.00				
1977FM (U)	552	—	—	—	20.00	—
1977FM (P)	6,884	Value: 4.50				
1978FM (U)	552	—	—	—	20.00	—
1978FM (P)	3,244	Value: 4.50				
1979FM (U)	537	—	—	—	20.00	—
1979FM (P)	6,577	Value: 4.50				
1980FM (U)	385	—	—	—	20.00	—
1980FM (P)	3,451	Value: 4.50				
1981FM (U)	449	—	—	—	20.00	—
1981FM (P)	1,453	Value: 4.50				

KM# 61 25 CENTS

Copper-Nickel, 30 mm. **Subject:** 10th Anniversary of Decimalization **Obv:** Republic emblem within circle **Rev:** Value **Shape:** Octagon

Date	Mintage	F	VF	XF	Unc	BU
1982FM (U)	850	—	—	—	35.00	—
1982FM (P)	1,793	Value: 40.00				

KM# 12 50 CENTS

13.6000 g., Copper-Nickel, 32.95 mm. **Obv:** Great Siege Monument **Rev:** Value within 3/4 wreath **Shape:** 10-sided

Date	Mintage	F	VF	XF	Unc	BU
1972	5,500,000	—	9.00	12.00	15.00	—
1972 Proof	13,000	Value: 4.50				
1976FM (M)	150	—	—	—	90.00	—
1976FM (P)	26,000	Value: 5.00				
1977FM (U)	402	—	—	—	25.00	—
1977FM (P)	6,884	Value: 6.00				
1978FM (U)	402	—	—	—	25.00	—
1978FM (P)	3,244	Value: 6.00				
1979FM (U)	537	—	—	—	25.00	—
1979FM (P)	6,577	Value: 6.00				
1980FM (U)	385	—	—	—	25.00	—
1980FM (P)	3,451	Value: 6.00				
1981FM (U)	449	—	—	—	25.00	—
1981FM (P)	1,453	Value: 6.00				

KM# 62 50 CENTS

13.6000 g., Copper-Nickel, 32.95 mm. **Subject:** 10th Anniversary of Decimalization **Obv:** Great Siege Monument **Rev:** Value **Shape:** 10-sided

Date	Mintage	F	VF	XF	Unc	BU
1982FM (U)	850	—	—	—	40.00	—
1982FM (P)	1,793	Value: 40.00				

KM# 13 POUND

10.0000 g., 0.9870 Silver 0.3173 oz. ASW **Obv:** Crowned arms with supporters **Rev:** Bust left

Date	Mintage	F	VF	XF	Unc	BU
1972	55,000	—	—	16.00	17.00	18.00

Note: Appears to be proof, but officially issued as "BU"

KM# 19 POUND

10.0000 g., 0.9870 Silver 0.3173 oz. ASW **Obv:** Crowned arms with supporters **Rev:** Bust left

Date	Mintage	F	VF	XF	Unc	BU
1973	30,000	—	—	16.00	17.00	18.00

KM# 45 POUND

5.6600 g., 0.9250 Silver 0.1683 oz. ASW **Obv:** Republic emblem within circle **Rev:** Dog

Date	Mintage	F	VF	XF	Unc	BU
1977	66,000	—	—	30.00	35.00	45.00
1977 Proof	2,500	Value: 75.00				

KM# 51 POUND

5.6600 g., 0.9250 Silver 0.1683 oz. ASW **Subject:** Departure of foreign forces **Obv:** Republic emblem within circle **Rev:** Flames within helping hands divide date and value

Date	Mintage	F	VF	XF	Unc	BU
1979FM (U)	49,526	—	—	25.00	30.00	—
1979FM (P)	7,871	Value: 55.00				

REFORM COINAGE

1982 - Present

10 Mils = 1 Cent; 100 Cents = 1 Lira = (Pound)

KM# 5 2 MILS

0.9500 g., Aluminum, 20.3 mm. **Obv:** Maltese cross **Rev:** Value within 3/4 wreath **Shape:** Scalloped

Date	Mintage	F	VF	XF	Unc	BU
1972	30,000	—	1.00	2.00	3.00	—
1972 Proof	13,000	Value: 5.00				
1976FM (M)	5,000	—	—	—	2.00	—
1976FM (P)	26,000	Value: 5.00				
1977FM (U)	5,252	—	—	—	1.00	—
1977FM (P)	6,884	Value: 5.00				
1978FM (U)	5,252	—	—	—	1.00	—
1978FM (P)	3,244	Value: 5.00				
1979FM (U)	537	—	—	—	3.00	—
1979FM (P)	6,577	Value: 5.00				
1980FM (U)	385	—	—	—	3.00	—
1980FM (P)	3,451	Value: 5.00				
1981FM (U)	444	—	—	—	3.00	—
1981FM (P)	1,453	Value: 5.00				
2005	—	—	—	—	4.00	—
Note: In sets only, not issued for circulation						
2006	—	—	—	—	4.00	—
2007	—	—	—	—	4.00	—

KM# 78 CENT

Copper-Zinc, 18 mm. **Obv:** Republic emblem within circle **Rev:** Common weasel

Date	Mintage	F	VF	XF	Unc	BU
1986	21,526,000	—	0.40	0.50	1.00	—
1986 Proof	10,000	Value: 75.00				

KM# 93 CENT

2.8000 g., Copper-Zinc, 18.53 mm. **Obv:** Crowned shield within sprigs **Obv. Designer:** Galea Bason **Rev:** Common Weasel below value

Date	Mintage	F	VF	XF	Unc	BU
1991	—	—	0.40	0.50	1.00	—
1995	—	—	0.40	0.50	1.00	—
1998	—	—	0.40	0.50	1.00	—
2001	—	—	0.40	0.50	1.00	—
2002	—	—	0.40	0.50	1.00	—
Note: In sets only, not issued for circulation						
2004	—	—	0.40	0.50	0.75	—
2005	—	—	—	—	0.75	—
Note: In sets only, not issued for circulation						
2006	—	—	—	—	0.75	—
Note: In sets only, not issued for circulation						
2007	—	—	—	—	0.75	—

KM# 79 2 CENTS

Copper-Zinc **Obv:** Republic emblem within circle **Rev:** Olive branch **Designer:** Noel Galea

Date	Mintage	F	VF	XF	Unc	BU
1986	280,000	—	1.25	1.50	2.00	—
1986 Proof	10,000	Value: 6.00				

KM# 94 2 CENTS

2.2400 g., Copper-Zinc, 17.8 mm. **Obv:** Crowned shield within sprigs **Obv. Designer:** Galea Bason **Rev:** Olive branch and value

Date	Mintage	F	VF	XF	Unc	BU
1991	—	—	0.75	1.00	1.25	—
1992	—	—	0.75	1.00	1.25	—
1993	—	—	0.75	1.00	1.25	—
1995	—	—	0.75	1.00	1.25	—
1998	—	—	0.75	1.00	1.25	—

Date	Mintage	F	VF	XF	Unc	BU
2002	—	—	0.75	1.00	1.25	—
2004	—	—	0.75	1.00	1.25	—
2005	—	—	—	—	1.25	—
2006	—	—	—	—	1.25	—
Note: Not in circulation						
2007	—	—	—	—	1.25	—
Note: Not in circulation						

KM# 77 5 CENTS

Copper-Nickel, 20 mm. **Obv:** Republic emblem within circle **Rev:** Freshwater crab **Designer:** Noel Galea

Date	Mintage	F	VF	XF	Unc	BU
1986	150,000	—	0.75	1.00	1.25	2.00
1986 Proof	10,000	Value: 7.00				

KM# 95 5 CENTS

3.5100 g., Copper-Nickel, 20 mm. **Obv:** Crowned shield within sprigs **Obv. Designer:** Galea Bason **Rev:** Crab and value

Date	Mintage	F	VF	XF	Unc	BU
1991	—	—	0.75	1.00	1.25	2.00
1995	—	—	0.75	1.00	1.25	2.00
1998	—	—	0.75	1.00	1.25	2.00
2001	—	—	0.75	1.00	1.25	2.00
2005	—	—	—	—	1.25	2.00
Note: In sets only, not issued for circulation						
2006	—	—	—	—	1.25	2.00
Note: In sets only, not issued for circulation						
2007	—	—	—	—	1.25	2.00
Note: In sets only, not issued for circulation						

KM# 76 10 CENTS

5.0400 g., Copper-Nickel, 22 mm. **Obv:** Republic emblem within circle **Rev:** Dolphin fish **Designer:** Noel Galea

Date	Mintage	F	VF	XF	Unc	BU
1986	4,188,000	—	1.25	1.50	2.00	—
1986 Proof	10,000	Value: 8.00				

KM# 96 10 CENTS

5.0000 g., Copper-Nickel, 22 mm. **Obv:** Crowned shield within sprigs **Obv. Designer:** Galea Bason **Rev:** Dolphin fish and value

Date	Mintage	F	VF	XF	Unc	BU
1991	—	—	1.25	1.50	2.00	—
1992	—	—	1.25	1.50	2.00	—
1995	—	—	1.25	1.50	2.00	—
1998	—	—	1.25	1.50	2.00	—
2005	—	—	1.25	1.50	2.00	—
2006	—	—	—	—	2.00	—
Note: In sets only, not issued for circulation						
2007	—	—	—	—	2.00	—
Note: In sets only, not issued for circulation						

KM# 80 25 CENTS

Copper-Nickel, 25 mm. **Rev:** Ghirlanda flower **Designer:** Noel Galea

Date	Mintage	F	VF	XF	Unc	BU
1986	3,090,000	—	2.25	2.50	3.00	—
1986 Proof	10,000	Value: 10.00				

KM# 97 25 CENTS

6.2300 g., Copper-Nickel, 25 mm. **Obv:** Crowned shield within sprigs **Obv. Designer:** Galea Bason **Rev:** Ghirlanda flower and value

Date	Mintage	F	VF	XF	Unc	BU
1991	—	—	2.25	2.50	3.00	—
1993	—	—	2.25	2.50	3.00	—
1995	—	—	2.25	2.50	3.00	—
1998	—	—	2.25	2.50	3.00	—
2005	—	—	2.25	2.50	3.00	—
2006	—	—	—	—	3.00	—
Note: In sets only						
2007	—	—	—	—	3.00	—
Note: Not in circulation						

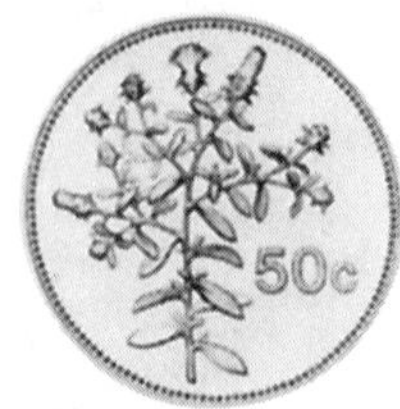

KM# 81 50 CENTS

Copper-Nickel **Obv:** Republic emblem within circle **Rev:** Tulliera plant **Designer:** Noel Galea

Date	Mintage	F	VF	XF	Unc	BU
1986	2,086,000	—	5.00	6.00	7.00	—
1986 Proof	10,000	Value: 15.00				

KM# 98 50 CENTS

7.9500 g., Copper-Nickel, 26.9 mm. **Obv:** Crowned shield within sprigs **Obv. Designer:** Galea Bason **Rev:** Tulliera plant and value

Date	Mintage	F	VF	XF	Unc	BU
1991	—	—	2.50	4.50	6.00	—
1992	—	—	2.50	4.50	6.00	—
1995	—	—	2.50	5.00	10.00	—
1998	—	—	2.50	5.00	10.00	—
2001	—	—	2.50	5.00	10.00	—
2005	—	—	—	—	10.00	—
Note: In sets only, not issued for circulation						
2006	—	—	—	—	10.00	—
Note: In sets only, not issued for circulation						
2007	—	—	—	—	10.00	—
Note: In sets only, not issued for circulation						

KM# 82 LIRA

Nickel, 30 mm. **Obv:** Republic emblem within circle **Rev:** Merill bird **Edge Lettering:** BANK CENTRALITA MALTA **Designer:** Noel Galea

Date	Mintage	F	VF	XF	Unc	BU
1986	2,272,000	—	—	4.00	8.00	12.00
1986 Proof	10,000	Value: 20.00				

KM# 99 LIRA

Nickel **Obv:** Crowned shield within sprigs **Obv. Designer:** Galea Bason **Rev:** Merill bird and value **Rev. Designer:** Noel Galea

Date	Mintage	F	VF	XF	Unc	BU
1991	—	—	—	4.00	6.00	10.00
1992	—	—	—	4.00	6.00	10.00
1994	—	—	—	4.00	6.00	10.00
1995	—	—	—	4.50	6.50	12.00
2000	—	—	—	4.50	6.50	12.00
2005	—	—	—	4.50	6.50	12.00
2006	—	—	—	—	—	12.00

Date	Mintage	F	VF	XF	Unc	BU
Note: In sets only						
2007	—	—	—	—	—	12.00

EURO COINAGE

KM# 125 EURO CENT

Copper Plated Steel **Obv:** Doorway **Rev:** Denomination and globe

Date	Mintage	F	VF	XF	Unc	BU
2008	—	—	—	—	—	0.35

KM# 126 2 EURO CENT

Copper Plated Steel **Obv:** Doorway **Rev:** Denomination and globe

Date	Mintage	F	VF	XF	Unc	BU
2008	—	—	—	—	—	0.50

KM# 127 5 EURO CENT

Copper Plated Steel **Obv:** Doorway **Rev:** Denomination and globe

Date	Mintage	F	VF	XF	Unc	BU
2008	—	—	—	—	—	0.75

KM# 128 10 EURO CENT

Aluminum-Bronze **Obv:** Crowned shield within wreath

Date	Mintage	F	VF	XF	Unc	BU
2008	—	—	—	—	—	1.00

KM# 129 20 EURO CENT

Aluminum-Brass **Obv:** Crowned shield within wreath **Rev:** Denomination and Map of Western Europe

Date	Mintage	F	VF	XF	Unc	BU
2008	—	—	—	—	—	1.25

KM# 130 50 EURO CENT

Aluminum-Brass **Obv:** Crowned shield within wreath **Rev:** Relief map of Western Europe

Date	Mintage	F	VF	XF	Unc	BU
2008	—	—	—	—	—	1.50

KM# 131 EURO
Bi-Metallic Copper-Nickel center in Brass ring **Obv:** Maltese Cross **Rev:** Value and relief map of Europe

Date	Mintage	F	VF	XF	Unc	BU
2008	—	—	—	—	—	2.75

KM# 132 2 EURO
Bi-Metallic Brass center in Copper-Nickel ring **Obv:** Maltese Cross **Rev:** Value and Relief Map of Western Europe

Date	Mintage	F	VF	XF	Unc	BU
2008	—	—	—	—	—	4.00

MARTINIQUE

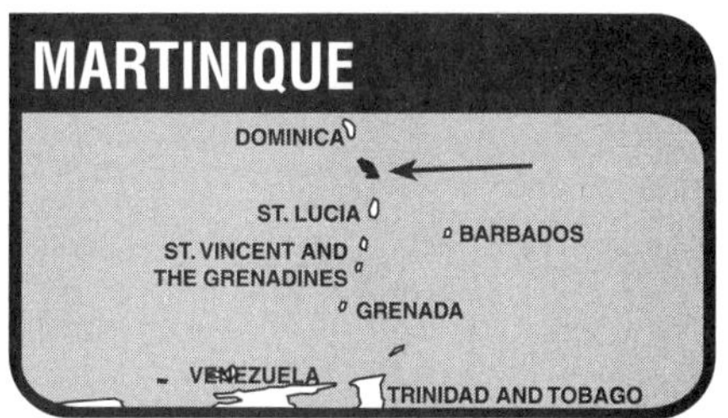

The French Overseas Department of Martinique, located in the Lesser Antilles of the West Indies between Dominica and Saint Lucia, has an area of 425 sq. mi.(1,100 sq. km.) and a population of 290,000. Capital: Fort-de-France. Agriculture and tourism are the major sources of income. Bananas, sugar, and rum are exported.

Christopher Columbus discovered Martinique, probably on June 15, 1502. France took possession on June 25, 1635, and has maintained possession since that time except for three short periods of British occupation during the Napoleonic Wars. A French department since 1946, Martinique voted a reaffirmation of that status in 1958, remaining within the new French Community. Martinique was the birthplace of Napoleon's Empress Josephine, and the site of the eruption of Mt. Pelee in 1902 that claimed 40,000 lives.

The official currency of Martinique is the French franc. The 1897-1922 coinage of the Colony of Martinique is now obsolete.

MONETARY SYSTEM
15 Sols = 1 Escalin
20 Sols = 1 Livre
66 Livres = 4 Escudos = 6400 Reis

FRENCH COLONY

DECIMAL COINAGE

KM# 40 50 CENTIMES
Copper-Nickel **Obv:** Bust left within circle with star above **Rev:** Value and date within wreath

Date	Mintage	VG	F	VF	XF	Unc
1922	500,000	12.00	22.00	50.00	200	450

KM# 41 FRANC
Copper-Nickel **Obv:** Bust left within circle with star above **Rev:** Value and date within wreath

Date	Mintage	VG	F	VF	XF	Unc
1922	350,000	15.00	25.00	60.00	225	500

MAURITANIA

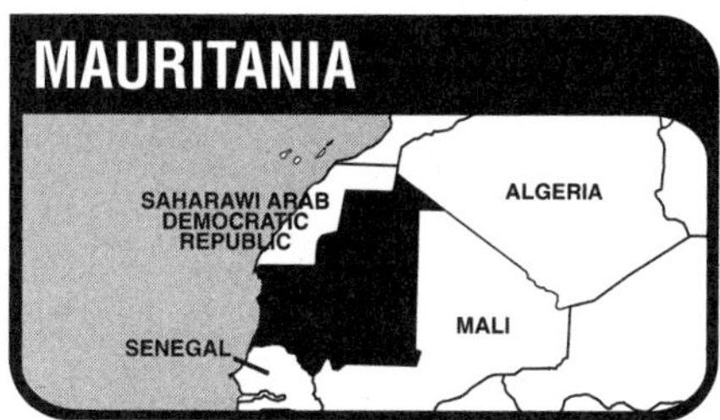

The Islamic Republic of Mauritania, located in northwest Africa bounded by Western Sahara, Mali, Algeria, Senegal and the Atlantic Ocean, has an area of 397,955 sq. mi.(1,030,700 sq. km.) and a population of 1.9 million. Capital: Nouakchott. The economy centers on herding, agriculture, fishing and mining. Iron ore, copper concentrates and fish products are exported.

The indigenous Negroid inhabitants were driven out of Mauritania by Berber invaders of the Islamic faith in the 11th century. The Berbers in turn were conquered by Arab invaders, the Beni Hassan, in the 16th century. Arab traders carried on a gainful trade in gum arabic, gold and slaves with Portuguese, Dutch, English and French traders until late in the 19th century when France took control of the area and made it a part of French West Africa, in 1920.Mauritania became a part of the French Union in 1946 and was made an autonomous republic within the new French Community in 1958, when the Islamic Republic of Mauritania was proclaimed. The republic became independent on November 28, 1960, and withdrew from the French Community in 1966.

On June 28, 1973, in a move designed to emphasize its non-alignment with France, Mauritania converted its currency from the old French-supported C.F.A. franc unit to a new unit called the Ouguiya.

MONETARY SYSTEM
5 Khoums = 1 Ouguiya

REPUBLIC

STANDARD COINAGE

KM# 1 1/5 OUGUIYA (Khoums)
Aluminum **Obv:** National emblem divides date above value **Obv. Legend:** BANQUE CENTRALE DE MAURITANIE **Rev:** Star and crescent divide sprigs within circle with legend around border

Date	Mintage	VG	F	VF	XF	Unc
AH1393//1973	1,000,000	—	0.35	0.75	1.50	3.00

KM# 2 OUGUIYA
Copper-Nickel-Aluminum **Obv:** National emblem divides date above value **Obv. Legend:** BANQUE CENTRALE DE MAURITANIE **Rev:** Star and crescent divide sprigs below value within circle, legend around border

Date	Mintage	VG	F	VF	XF	Unc
AH1393//1973	—	—	7.00	20.00	37.50	85.00

KM# 6 OUGUIYA
3.6000 g., Copper-Nickel-Aluminum, 21 mm. **Obv:** National emblem divides date above value **Obv. Legend:** BANQUE CENTRALE DE MAURITANIE **Rev:** Star and crescent divide sprigs with legend below value, all within circle **Edge:** Reeded

Date	Mintage	F	VF	XF	Unc	BU
AH1394//1974	—	2.50	5.50	10.00	18.50	—
AH1401//1981	—	1.50	3.00	4.50	7.50	—
AH1403//1983	—	1.00	2.00	3.50	6.50	—
AH1406//1986	—	0.75	1.50	2.50	4.50	—
AH1407//1987	—	0.50	1.00	2.00	4.00	—
AH1410//1990	—	0.50	1.00	2.00	4.00	—
AH1414//1993	—	0.50	1.00	2.00	4.00	—
AH1416//1995	—	0.50	1.00	2.00	4.00	—
AH1423//2003	—	—	—	0.50	1.25	2.00

KM# 3 5 OUGUIYA
5.8800 g., Copper-Nickel-Aluminum, 25 mm. **Obv:** National emblem divides date above value **Obv. Legend:** BANQUE CENTRALE DE MAURITANIE **Rev:** Star and crescent divide sprigs below value within circle **Edge:** Plain

Date	Mintage	F	VF	XF	Unc	BU
AH1393//1973	—	2.50	5.50	10.00	15.00	—
AH1394//1974	—	2.50	5.50	10.00	17.50	—
AH1401//1981	—	2.00	4.00	6.00	12.50	—
AH1404//1984	—	1.50	2.50	4.50	10.00	—
AH1407//1987	—	0.75	1.50	2.50	5.00	—
AH1410//1990	—	0.50	1.00	2.00	4.00	—
AH1414//1993	—	0.50	1.00	2.00	4.00	—
AH1416//1995	—	0.50	1.00	2.00	4.00	—
AH1418//1997	—	0.50	1.00	2.00	4.00	—
AH1420//1999	—	0.50	1.00	2.00	4.00	—
AH1423//2003	—	—	—	1.75	3.50	5.00

KM# 3a 5 OUGUIYA
6.0000 g., Copper Plated Steel, 25 mm. **Obv:** National emblem divides date above value **Obv. Legend:** BANQUE CENTRALE DE MAURITANIE **Rev:** Star and crescent divides sprigs below value within circle **Edge:** Plain

Date	Mintage	F	VF	XF	Unc	BU
AH1425//2004	—	—	0.50	1.00	2.00	3.00
AH1426//2005	—	—	0.50	1.00	2.00	3.00

KM# 4 10 OUGUIYA
6.0000 g., Copper-Nickel, 25 mm. **Obv:** National emblem divides date above value **Obv. Legend:** BANQUE CENTRALE DE MAURITANIE **Rev:** Crescent and star divide sprigs below value within circle **Edge:** Reeded

Date	Mintage	F	VF	XF	Unc	BU
AH1393//1973	—	2.50	5.50	10.00	17.50	—
AH1394//1974	—	2.50	5.50	10.00	17.50	—
AH1401//1981	—	2.00	5.00	7.50	15.00	—
AH1403//1983	—	1.25	2.50	4.00	8.00	—
AH1407//1987	—	1.25	2.50	4.00	8.00	—
AH1410//1990	—	0.75	1.50	2.50	4.50	—
AH1411//1991	—	0.75	1.50	2.50	4.50	—
AH1414//1993	—	0.75	1.50	2.50	4.50	—
AH1416//1995	—	0.75	1.50	2.50	4.50	—
AH1418//1997	—	0.75	1.50	2.50	4.50	—
AH1420//1999	—	0.75	1.50	2.50	4.50	—
AH1423//2003	—	—	—	2.00	4.00	5.50

KM# 4a 10 OUGUIYA
5.8000 g., Nickel Plated Steel, 25 mm. **Obv:** National emblem divides date above value **Obv. Legend:** BANQUE CENTRALE DE MAURITANIE **Rev:** Crescent and star divides sprigs below value within circle **Edge:** Reeded

Date	Mintage	F	VF	XF	Unc	BU
AH1425//2004	—	—	—	1.25	3.00	4.50
AH1426//2005	—	—	—	1.25	3.00	4.50

KM# 5 20 OUGUIYA
8.0000 g., Copper-Nickel, 28 mm. **Obv:** National emblem divides date above value **Obv. Legend:** BANQUE CENTRALE DE MAURITANIE **Rev:** Star and crescent divide sprigs below value within circle **Edge:** Reeded

Date	Mintage	F	VF	XF	Unc	BU
AH1393//1973	—	2.00	5.00	10.00	18.00	—
AH1394//1974	—	2.00	5.00	10.00	18.00	—

Date	Mintage	F	VF	XF	Unc	BU
AH1403//1983	—	1.25	2.50	4.00	8.00	—
AH1407//1987	—	1.25	2.50	4.00	8.00	—
AH1410//1990	—	1.25	2.50	4.00	8.00	—
AH1414//1993	—	1.25	2.50	4.00	8.00	—
AH1416//1995	—	1.25	2.50	4.00	8.00	—
AH1418//1997	—	1.25	2.50	4.00	8.00	—
AH1420//1999	—	1.25	2.50	4.00	8.00	—
AH1423//2003	—	—	—	3.00	6.00	8.00

KM# 5a 20 OUGUIYA

7.8000 g., Nickel Plated Steel, 28.05 mm. **Obv:** National emblem divides date above value **Obv. Legend:** BANQUE CENTRALE DE MAURITANIE **Rev:** Star and crescent divide sprigs below value within circle **Edge:** Reeded

Date	Mintage	F	VF	XF	Unc	BU
AH1425//2004	—	—	—	2.00	4.00	6.00
AH1426//2005	—	—	—	2.00	4.00	6.00

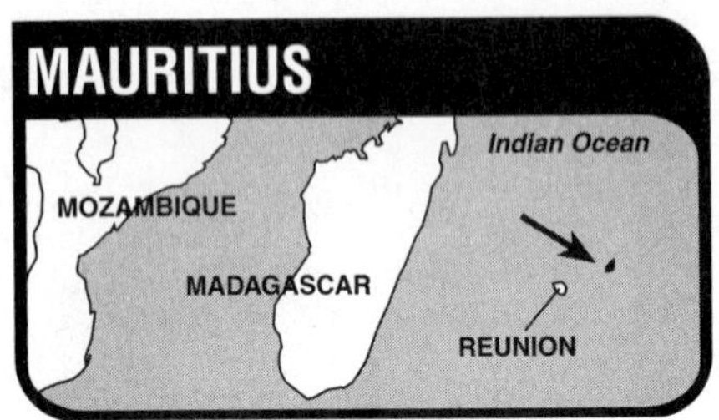

The Republic of Mauritius, is located in the Indian Ocean 500 miles (805 km.) east of Madagascar, has an area of 790 sq. mi. (1,860 sq. km.) and a population of 1 million. Capital: Port Louis. Sugar provides 90 percent of the export revenue.

Mauritius became independent on March 12, 1968. It is a member of the Commonwealth of Nations.

RULER
British, until 1968

MINT MARKS
H - Heaton, Birmingham
SA - Pretoria Mint

MONETARY SYSTEM
100 Cents = 1 Rupee

CROWN COLONY

STANDARD COINAGE

100 Cents = 1 Rupee

KM# 12 CENT

Bronze **Ruler:** George V **Obv:** Crowned bust left **Obv. Designer:** E.B. MacKennal **Rev:** Value within beaded circle

Date	Mintage	F	VF	XF	Unc	BU
1911	1,000,000	1.00	6.00	22.00	40.00	90.00
1912	500,000	1.25	6.50	28.50	55.00	100
1917	500,000	1.00	6.00	22.00	35.00	70.00
1920	500,000	1.50	8.00	32.50	60.00	120
1921	500,000	2.00	8.00	32.50	60.00	120
1922	1,800,000	0.75	1.50	9.00	25.00	50.00
1923	200,000	3.00	17.00	45.00	75.00	150
1924	200,000	3.00	17.00	45.00	75.00	150

KM# 21 CENT

Bronze **Ruler:** George VI **Obv:** Crowned head left **Obv. Designer:** Percy Metcalfe **Rev:** Value within beaded circle

Date	Mintage	F	VF	XF	Unc	BU
1943SA	520,000	0.50	1.25	4.00	10.00	22.00
1944SA	500,000	0.50	1.25	4.00	10.00	22.00
1945SA	500,000	0.50	1.25	4.00	10.00	22.00
1946SA	500,000	0.50	1.25	4.00	10.00	22.00
1947SA	500,000	0.50	1.25	4.00	10.00	22.00

KM# 25 CENT

Bronze **Ruler:** George VI **Obv:** Crowned head left **Obv. Designer:** Percy Metcalfe **Rev:** Value within beaded circle

Date	Mintage	F	VF	XF	Unc	BU
1949	500,000	0.75	1.25	2.50	7.50	15.00
1949 Proof	—	Value: 100				
1952	500,000	0.75	1.25	2.50	7.50	15.00
1952 Proof	—	Value: 100				

KM# 31 CENT

1.9500 g., Bronze, 17.8 mm. **Ruler:** Elizabeth II **Obv:** Crowned head right **Obv. Designer:** Cecil Thomas **Rev:** Value within beaded circle

Date	Mintage	F	VF	XF	Unc	BU
1953	500,000	0.10	0.25	0.50	1.50	—
1953 Proof	—	Value: 75.00				
1955	501,000	0.10	0.25	0.50	2.50	—
1955 Proof	—	Value: 75.00				
1956	500,000	0.10	0.20	0.50	2.50	—
1956 Proof	—	Value: 75.00				
1957	501,000	0.10	0.20	0.50	2.50	—
1959	501,000	0.10	0.20	0.50	2.50	—
1959 Proof	—	Value: 75.00				
1960	500,000	0.10	0.20	0.50	2.50	—
1960 Proof	—	Value: 75.00				
1961	500,000	0.10	0.20	0.50	2.50	—
1961 Proof	—	Value: 75.00				
1962	500,000	0.10	0.20	0.50	1.50	—
1962 Proof	—	Value: 50.00				
1963	500,000	0.10	0.20	0.50	1.50	—
1963 Proof	—	Value: 50.00				
1964	1,500,000	—	0.10	0.20	0.50	—
1964 Proof	—	Value: 50.00				
1965	1,500,000	—	0.10	0.20	0.50	—
1969	500,000	—	0.10	0.15	0.30	—
1970	1,500,000	—	—	0.10	0.20	—
1971	1,000,000	—	—	0.10	0.20	—
1971 Proof	750	Value: 17.50				
1975	400,000	—	—	0.10	0.20	—
1978	—	—	—	0.10	0.20	—

KM# 13 2 CENTS

Bronze **Ruler:** George V **Obv:** Crowned bust left **Obv. Designer:** E.B. MacKennal **Rev:** Value within beaded circle

Date	Mintage	F	VF	XF	Unc	BU
1911	500,000	2.00	12.00	25.00	40.00	85.00
1911 Proof	—	Value: 300				
1912	250,000	3.00	15.00	40.00	70.00	140
1917	250,000	1.25	14.50	22.00	50.00	80.00
1920	250,000	1.50	14.00	28.00	55.00	90.00
1921	250,000	1.50	10.00	28.00	55.00	90.00
1922	900,000	0.50	4.00	15.00	30.00	60.00
1923	400,000	1.25	5.50	28.50	55.00	95.00
1924	400,000	1.25	5.50	28.50	50.00	90.00

KM# 22 2 CENTS

3.8500 g., Bronze **Ruler:** George VI **Obv:** Crowned head left **Obv. Designer:** Percy Metcalfe **Rev:** Value within beaded circle

Date	Mintage	F	VF	XF	Unc	BU
1943SA	290,000	0.75	2.00	4.00	10.00	22.00
1944SA	500,000	0.75	2.00	4.00	10.00	22.00
1945SA	250,000	0.75	2.00	4.00	10.00	22.00
1946SA	400,000	0.75	2.00	4.00	10.00	22.00
1947SA	250,000	0.75	2.00	4.00	10.00	22.00

KM# 26 2 CENTS

3.8500 g., Bronze, 23.2 mm. **Ruler:** George VI **Obv:** Crowned head left **Obv. Designer:** Percy Metcalfe **Rev:** Value within beaded circle

Date	Mintage	F	VF	XF	Unc	BU
1949	250,000	0.75	1.25	2.50	6.50	12.50
1949 Proof	—	Value: 120				
1952	250,000	0.75	1.25	2.50	6.50	12.50
1952 Proof	—	Value: 120				

KM# 32 2 CENTS

3.8500 g., Bronze, 23.2 mm. **Ruler:** Elizabeth II **Obv:** Crowned head right **Obv. Designer:** Cecil Thomas **Rev:** Value within beaded circle

Date	Mintage	F	VF	XF	Unc	BU
1953	250,000	0.10	0.25	0.50	2.50	—
1953 Proof	—	Value: 100				
1954 Proof	—	Value: 300				
1955	501,000	0.10	0.25	0.50	2.50	—
1955 Proof	—	Value: 100				
1956	250,000	0.10	0.25	0.50	3.50	—
1956 Proof	—	Value: 100				
1957	501,000	0.10	0.25	0.50	3.50	—
1959	503,000	0.10	0.25	0.50	3.50	—
1959 Proof	—	Value: 100				
1960	250,000	0.10	0.25	0.50	3.50	—
1960 Proof	—	Value: 100				
1961	500,000	0.10	0.25	0.50	3.50	—
1961 Proof	—	Value: 100				
1962	500,000	0.10	0.25	0.50	1.50	—
1962 Proof	—	Value: 75.00				
1963	500,000	0.10	0.25	0.50	1.50	—
1963 Proof	—	Value: 75.00				
1964	1,000,000	—	0.10	0.25	0.50	—
1964 Proof	—	Value: 50.00				
1965	750,000	0.10	0.20	0.40	0.60	—
1966	500,000	0.10	0.20	0.40	0.50	—
1967	250,000	0.10	0.20	0.40	0.50	—
1969	500,000	0.10	0.20	0.40	0.50	—
1971	1,000,000	—	0.10	0.20	0.40	—
1971 Proof	750	Value: 17.50				
1975	5,200,000	—	—	0.10	0.35	—
1978	—	—	—	0.10	0.35	—
1978 Proof	9,268	Value: 1.50				

KM# 14 5 CENTS

9.7000 g., Bronze, 28.4 mm. **Ruler:** George V **Obv:** Crowned bust left **Obv. Designer:** E.B. MacKennal **Rev:** Value within beaded circle

Date	Mintage	F	VF	XF	Unc	BU
1917	600,000	2.00	24.50	57.50	80.00	160
1920	200,000	2.00	24.50	60.00	100	200
1921	100,000	3.00	26.50	65.00	120	250
1922	360,000	2.00	14.50	42.50	100	200
1923	400,000	3.00	16.50	45.00	120	250
1924	400,000	2.00	14.50	42.50	100	200

KM# 20 5 CENTS

9.7000 g., Bronze, 28.4 mm. **Ruler:** George VI **Obv:** Crowned head left **Obv. Designer:** Percy Metcalfe **Rev:** Value within beaded circle

Date	Mintage	F	VF	XF	Unc	BU
1942SA	940,000	1.50	2.50	6.50	15.00	35.00
1944SA	1,000,000	1.25	1.75	4.00	10.00	22.00
1945SA	500,000	1.25	1.75	4.00	12.00	30.00

KM# 34 5 CENTS

9.7000 g., Bronze, 28.4 mm. **Ruler:** Elizabeth II **Obv:** Crowned head right **Obv. Designer:** Cecil Thomas **Rev:** Value within beaded circle

Date	Mintage	F	VF	XF	Unc	BU
1956	201,000	0.25	0.50	0.75	5.00	—
1956 Proof	—	Value: 100				
1957	203,000	0.25	0.50	2.00	8.00	—
1957 Proof	—	Value: 100				
1959	801,000	0.25	0.50	1.00	4.00	—
1959 Proof	—	Value: 75.00				
1960	400,000	0.25	0.50	1.00	4.00	—
1960 Proof	—	Value: 75.00				
1963	200,000	0.25	0.50	1.00	2.00	—
1963 Proof	—	Value: 70.00				
1964	600,000	0.25	0.50	1.00	2.00	—
1964 Proof	—	Value: 70.00				
1965	200,000	0.25	0.50	0.75	2.00	—
1966	200,000	0.25	0.50	0.75	1.50	—
1967	200,000	0.25	0.50	0.75	2.00	—
1969	500,000	0.10	0.15	0.25	0.50	—
1970	800,000	0.10	0.15	0.25	0.50	—
1971	500,000	0.10	0.15	0.25	0.50	—
1971 Proof	750	Value: 17.50				
1975	3,700,000	0.10	0.15	0.25	0.50	—
1978	8,000,000	—	0.10	0.20	0.50	—
1978 Proof	9,268	Value: 2.00				

KM# 24 10 CENTS

5.1500 g., Copper-Nickel, 23.5 mm. **Ruler:** George VI **Obv:** Crowned head left **Obv. Designer:** Percy Metcalfe **Rev:** Value **Shape:** Scalloped

Date	Mintage	F	VF	XF	Unc	BU
1947	500,000	1.50	4.50	18.00	45.00	—
1947 Proof	—	Value: 200				

KM# 30 10 CENTS

5.1500 g., Copper-Nickel, 23.5 mm. **Ruler:** George VI **Obv:** Crowned head left **Obv. Designer:** Percy Metcalfe **Rev:** Value **Shape:** Scalloped

Date	Mintage	F	VF	XF	Unc	BU
1952	250,000	0.50	1.00	3.50	9.50	17.50
1952 Proof	—	Value: 150				

KM# 33 10 CENTS

5.1500 g., Copper-Nickel, 23.5 mm. **Ruler:** Elizabeth II **Obv:** Crowned head right **Obv. Designer:** Cecil Thomas **Rev:** Value **Shape:** Scalloped

Date	Mintage	F	VF	XF	Unc	BU
1954	252,000	0.20	0.35	0.75	2.50	—
1954 Proof	—	Value: 150				
1957	250,000	0.20	0.35	0.75	2.50	—
1959	253,000	0.20	0.35	0.75	2.50	—
1959 Proof	—	Value: 175				
1960	50,000	0.20	0.35	0.75	2.00	—
1960 Proof	—	Value: 175				
1963	200,000	0.15	0.30	0.60	1.50	—
1963 Proof	—	Value: 175				
1964	200,000	0.15	0.30	0.60	1.00	—
1965	200,000	0.15	0.30	0.60	1.00	—
1966	200,000	0.10	0.25	0.50	0.75	—
1969	200,000	0.10	0.25	0.50	0.75	—
1970	500,000	0.10	0.25	0.50	0.75	—
1971	300,000	0.10	0.25	0.50	0.75	—
1971 Proof	750	Value: 17.50				
1975	6,675,000	0.10	0.25	0.50	0.75	—
1978	13,000,000	0.10	0.25	0.50	0.75	—
1978 Proof	9,268	Value: 2.50				

KM# 15 1/4 RUPEE

2.9200 g., 0.9160 Silver 0.0860 oz. ASW, 19 mm. **Ruler:** George V **Obv:** Crowned bust left **Obv. Designer:** E.B. MacKennal **Rev:** Crown above 3 emblems **Rev. Designer:** G. E. Kruger-Gray

Date	Mintage	F	VF	XF	Unc	BU
1934	400,000	2.50	10.00	30.00	60.00	—
1934 Proof	—	Value: 600				
1935	400,000	2.50	10.00	30.00	60.00	—
1935 Proof	—	Value: 750				
1936	400,000	2.50	10.00	30.00	55.00	—
1936 Proof	—	Value: 650				

KM# 18 1/4 RUPEE

2.9200 g., 0.9160 Silver 0.0860 oz. ASW, 19 mm. **Ruler:** George VI **Obv:** Crowned bust left **Obv. Designer:** Percy Metcalfe **Rev. Designer:** G. E. Kruger-Gray

Date	Mintage	F	VF	XF	Unc	BU
1938	2,000,000	3.50	15.00	40.00	80.00	—
1938 Proof	—	Value: 375				

KM# 18a 1/4 RUPEE

2.9200 g., 0.5000 Silver 0.0469 oz. ASW, 19 mm. **Ruler:** George VI **Obv:** Crowned bust left

Date	Mintage	F	VF	XF	Unc	BU
1946	2,000,000	7.50	30.00	60.00	100	—
1946 Proof	—	Value: 400				

KM# 27 1/4 RUPEE

2.9500 g., Copper-Nickel, 19 mm. **Ruler:** George VI **Obv:** Crowned head left **Obv. Designer:** Percy Metcalfe **Rev:** Crown above 3 emblems **Rev. Designer:** G. E. Kruger-Gray

Date	Mintage	F	VF	XF	Unc	BU
1950	2,000,000	0.50	1.00	2.00	9.50	18.00
1950 Proof	—	Value: 175				
1951	1,000,000	0.50	1.00	2.00	9.50	18.00
1951 Proof	—	Value: 175				

KM# 36 1/4 RUPEE

2.9500 g., Copper-Nickel, 19 mm. **Ruler:** Elizabeth II **Obv:** Crowned head right **Obv. Designer:** Cecil Thomas **Rev:** Crown above 3 emblems **Rev. Designer:** G. E. Kruger-Gray

Date	Mintage	F	VF	XF	Unc	BU
1960	1,000,000	0.35	0.75	1.00	2.00	—
1960 Proof	—	Value: 100				
1964	400,000	0.25	0.50	0.75	1.50	—
1964 Proof	—	Value: 100				
1965	400,000	0.25	0.50	0.75	1.25	—

Date	Mintage	F	VF	XF	Unc	BU
1970	400,000	0.20	0.35	0.65	1.25	—
1971	540,000	0.25	0.50	0.75	1.25	—
1971 Proof	750	Value: 17.50				
1975	8,940,000	0.15	0.30	0.60	1.00	—
1978	8,800,000	0.15	0.30	0.60	1.00	—

Note: Variety exists with lower hole in 8 filled

Date	Mintage	F	VF	XF	Unc	BU
1978 Proof	9,268	Value: 3.50				

KM# 16 1/2 RUPEE

5.8300 g., 0.9160 Silver 0.1717 oz. ASW, 23.65 mm. **Ruler:** George V **Obv:** Crowned bust left **Obv. Designer:** E.B. MacKennal **Rev:** Stag left **Rev. Designer:** G. E. Kruger-Gray **Edge:** Reeded with security

Date	Mintage	F	VF	XF	Unc	BU
1934	1,000,000	3.25	6.50	18.00	60.00	—
1934 Proof	—	Value: 450				

KM# 23 1/2 RUPEE

5.8300 g., 0.5000 Silver 0.0937 oz. ASW, 23.65 mm. **Ruler:** George VI **Obv:** Crowned head left **Obv. Designer:** Percy Metcalfe **Rev:** Stag left **Rev. Designer:** G. E. Kruger-Gray

Date	Mintage	F	VF	XF	Unc	BU
1946	1,000,000	10.00	25.00	125	200	—
1946 Proof	—	Value: 700				

KM# 28 1/2 RUPEE

5.8500 g., Copper-Nickel, 23.65 mm. **Ruler:** George VI **Obv:** Crowned head left **Obv. Designer:** Percy Metcalfe **Rev:** Stag left **Rev. Designer:** G. E. Kruger-Gray

Date	Mintage	F	VF	XF	Unc	BU
1950	1,000,000	0.50	1.00	1.75	12.00	—
1950 Proof	—	Value: 175				
1951	570,000	0.75	1.25	2.00	12.00	—
1951 Proof	—	Value: 225				

KM# 37.1 1/2 RUPEE

5.8500 g., Copper-Nickel, 23.65 mm. **Ruler:** Elizabeth II **Obv:** Crowned head right **Obv. Designer:** Cecil Thomas **Rev:** Stag left **Rev. Designer:** G. E. Kruger-Gray

Date	Mintage	F	VF	XF	Unc	BU
1965	200,000	0.50	1.00	2.00	9.00	—
1971	400,000	0.25	0.50	0.75	8.00	—
1971 Proof	750	Value: 22.50				
1975	4,160,000	0.25	0.50	0.75	8.00	—
1978	400,000	0.25	0.50	0.75	8.00	—
1978 Proof	9,268	Value: 6.00				

KM# 37.2 1/2 RUPEE

5.8500 g., Copper-Nickel, 23.65 mm. **Ruler:** Elizabeth II **Obv:** Crowned head right **Obv. Designer:** Cecil Thomas **Rev:** Stag left **Edge:** Without security feature **Note:** Error.

Date	Mintage	F	VF	XF	Unc	BU
1971	Inc. above	—	—	—	—	—

KM# 17 RUPEE
11.6600 g., 0.9160 Silver 0.3434 oz. ASW **Ruler:** George V **Obv:** Crowned bust left **Obv. Designer:** E.B. MacKennal **Rev:** National arms divide date above value **Rev. Designer:** G. E. Kruger-Gray **Edge:** Reeded with security

Date	Mintage	F	VF	XF	Unc	BU
1934	1,500,000	6.00	10.00	25.00	65.00	85.00
1934 Proof	—	Value: 600				

KM# 19 RUPEE
11.6600 g., 0.9160 Silver 0.3434 oz. ASW **Ruler:** George VI **Obv:** Crowned head left **Obv. Designer:** Percy Metcalfe **Rev:** National arms divide date above value **Rev. Designer:** G. E. Kruger-Gray

Date	Mintage	F	VF	XF	Unc	BU
1938	200,000	10.00	20.00	60.00	175	—
1938 Proof	—	Value: 550				

KM# 29.1 RUPEE
11.7000 g., Copper-Nickel, 29.6 mm. **Ruler:** George VI **Obv:** Crowned head left **Obv. Designer:** Percy Metcalfe **Rev:** National arms divide date above value **Rev. Designer:** G. E. Kruger-Gray

Date	Mintage	F	VF	XF	Unc	BU
1950	1,500,000	0.75	1.50	3.00	16.00	—
1950 Proof	—	Value: 200				
1951	1,000,000	0.50	1.25	2.00	12.00	—
1951 Proof	—	Value: 300				

KM# 29.2 RUPEE
11.7000 g., Copper-Nickel, 29.6 mm. **Ruler:** George VI **Obv:** Crowned head left **Obv. Designer:** Percy Metcalfe **Rev:** National arms divide date above value **Rev. Designer:** G. E. Kruger-Gray **Edge:** Without security feature **Note:** Error.

Date	Mintage	F	VF	XF	Unc	BU
1951	Inc. above	—	—	—	—	—

KM# 35.1 RUPEE
11.7000 g., Copper-Nickel, 29.6 mm. **Ruler:** Elizabeth II **Obv:** Crowned head right **Obv. Designer:** Cecil Thomas **Rev:** National arms divide date above value **Rev. Designer:** G. E. Kruger-Gray

Date	Mintage	F	VF	XF	Unc	BU
1956	1,000,000	0.25	0.75	1.50	7.50	—
1956 Proof	—	Value: 200				
1964	200,000	0.50	1.00	3.00	5.00	—
1971	600,000	0.25	0.60	1.00	2.00	—
1971 Proof	750	Value: 45.00				
1975	4,525,000	0.25	0.60	1.00	2.00	—
1978	2,000,000	0.25	0.60	1.00	2.00	—
1978 Proof	9,268	Value: 5.00				

KM# 35.2 RUPEE
11.7000 g., Copper-Nickel, 29.6 mm. **Ruler:** Elizabeth II **Obv:** Crowned head right **Obv. Designer:** Cecil Thomas **Rev:** National arms divide date above value **Edge:** Without security feature **Note:** Error.

Date	Mintage	F	VF	XF	Unc	BU
1971	Inc. above	0.25	0.75	1.25	2.50	—

COMMONWEALTH

STANDARD COINAGE

100 Cents = 1 Rupee

KM# 38 10 RUPEES
Copper-Nickel, 35 mm. **Ruler:** Elizabeth II **Subject:** Independence **Obv:** Crowned head right **Obv. Designer:** Cecil Thomas **Rev:** Dodo bird

Date	Mintage	F	VF	XF	Unc	BU
1971	50,000	—	1.50	4.00	8.00	14.00

REPUBLIC

STANDARD COINAGE

100 Cents = 1 Rupee

KM# 51 CENT
Copper Plated Steel **Obv:** Value within beaded circle **Rev:** Bust of Sir Seewoosagur Ramgoolam 3/4 right

Date	Mintage	F	VF	XF	Unc	BU
1987	—	—	—	—	0.20	0.40
1987 Proof	Est. 2,500	Value: 1.00				

KM# 52 5 CENTS
3.0000 g., Copper Plated Steel **Obv:** Value within beaded circle **Rev:** Bust of Sir Seewoosagur Ramgoolam 3/4 right

Date	Mintage	F	VF	XF	Unc	BU
1987	—	—	—	—	0.30	0.50
1987 Proof	Est. 2,500	Value: 2.00				
1990	—	—	—	—	0.30	0.50
1991	—	—	—	—	0.30	0.50
1993	—	—	—	—	0.30	0.50
1994	—	—	—	—	0.30	0.50
1995	—	—	—	—	0.30	0.50
1996	—	—	—	—	0.30	0.50
1999	—	—	—	—	0.30	0.50
2003	—	—	—	—	0.30	0.50
2004	—	—	—	—	0.30	0.50

KM# 53 20 CENTS
3.0000 g., Nickel Plated Steel **Obv:** Value within beaded circle **Rev:** Bust of Sir Seewoosagur Ramgoolam 3/4 right

Date	Mintage	F	VF	XF	Unc	BU
1987	—	—	—	—	0.50	0.75
1987 Proof	Est. 2,500	Value: 3.00				
1990	—	—	—	—	0.50	0.75
1991	—	—	—	—	0.50	0.75
1993	—	—	—	—	0.50	0.75
1994	—	—	—	—	0.50	0.75
1995	—	—	—	—	0.50	0.75
1996	—	—	—	—	0.50	0.75
1999	—	—	—	—	0.50	0.75
2001	—	—	—	—	0.50	0.75
2003	—	—	—	—	0.50	0.75

KM# 54 1/2 RUPEE
6.0000 g., Nickel Plated Steel **Obv:** Stag left **Rev:** Bust of Sir Seewoosagur Ramgoolam 3/4 right **Rev. Designer:** G.E. Kruger-Gray

Date	Mintage	F	VF	XF	Unc	BU
1987	—	—	—	—	1.50	2.50
1987 Proof	Est. 2,500	Value: 5.00				
1990	—	—	—	—	1.50	2.50
1991	—	—	—	—	1.50	2.50
1997	—	—	—	—	1.50	2.50
1999	—	—	—	—	1.50	2.50
2002	—	—	—	—	1.50	3.00
2003	—	—	—	—	1.50	3.00

KM# 55 RUPEE
Copper-Nickel **Obv:** Shield divides date above value **Rev:** Bust of Sir Seewoosagur Ramgoolam 3/4 right **Rev. Designer:** G.E. Kruger-Gray

Date	Mintage	F	VF	XF	Unc	BU
1987	—	—	—	—	1.65	2.75
1987 Proof	Est. 2,500	Value: 10.00				
1990	—	—	—	—	1.65	2.75
1991	—	—	—	—	1.65	2.75
1993	—	—	—	—	1.65	2.75
1994	—	—	—	—	1.65	2.75
1997	—	—	—	—	1.65	2.75
2002	—	—	—	—	1.65	2.75
2004	—	—	—	—	1.65	2.75
2005	—	—	—	—	1.65	2.75

KM# 56 5 RUPEES
Copper-Nickel **Obv:** Value within palm trees **Rev:** Bust of Sir Seewoosagur Ramgoolam 3/4 right

Date	Mintage	F	VF	XF	Unc	BU
1987	—	—	—	—	3.00	5.00
1987 Proof	Est. 2,500	Value: 16.00				
1991	—	—	—	—	3.00	5.00
1992	—	—	—	—	3.00	5.00

KM# 61 10 RUPEES
Copper-Nickel **Obv:** Sugar cane harvesting **Rev:** Bust of Sir Seewoosagur Ramgoolam 3/4 right **Shape:** 7-sided

Date	Mintage	F	VF	XF	Unc	BU
1997	—	—	—	—	4.00	6.50
2000	—	—	—	—	4.00	6.50

MEXICO

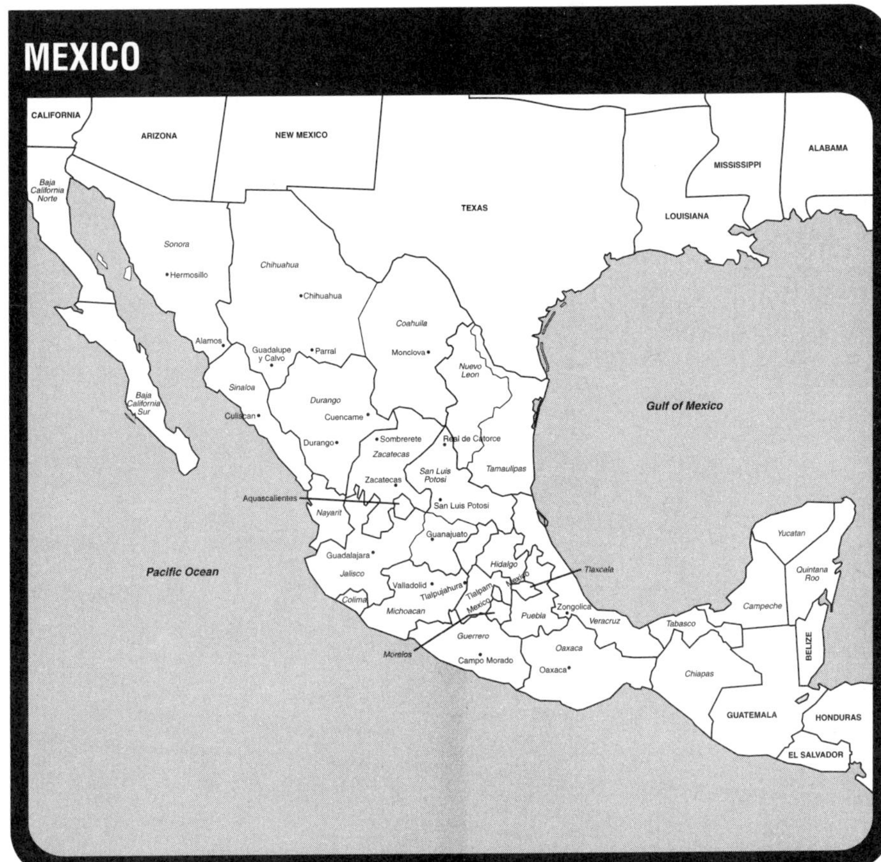

The United States of Mexico, located immediately south of the United States has an area of 759,529 sq. mi. (1,967,183 sq. km.) and an estimated population of 100 million. Capital: Mexico City. The economy is based on agriculture, manufacturing and mining. Oil, cotton, silver, coffee, and shrimp are exported.

Mexico was the site of highly advanced Indian civilizations 1,500 years before conquistador Hernando Cortes conquered the wealthy Aztec empire of Montezuma, 1519-21, and founded a Spanish colony, which lasted for nearly 300 years. During the Spanish period, Mexico, then called New Spain, stretched from Guatemala to the present states of Wyoming and California, its present northern boundary having been established by the secession of Texas during 1836 and the war of 1846-48 with the United States.

Independence from Spain was declared by Father Miguel Hidalgo on Sept. 16, 1810, (Mexican Independence Day) and was achieved by General Agustin de Iturbide in1821. Iturbide became emperor in 1822 but was deposed when a republic was established a year later. For more than fifty years following the birth of the republic, the political scene of Mexico was characterized by turmoil, which saw two emperors (including the unfortunate Maximilian), several dictators and an average of one new government every nine months passing swiftly from obscurity to oblivion. The land, social, economic and labor reforms promulgated by the Reform Constitution of Feb. 5, 1917 established the basis for sustained economic development and participative democracy that have made Mexico one of the most politically stable countries of modern Latin America.

REPUBLIC

Second

DECIMAL COINAGE

100 Centavos = 1 Peso

KM# 394 CENTAVO

Copper **Obv:** National arms **Rev:** Value below date within wreath **Note:** Reduced size. Varieties exist.

Date	Mintage	F	VF	XF	Unc	BU
1901C	220,000	15.00	22.50	35.00	65.00	—
1902C	320,000	15.00	22.50	50.00	90.00	—
1903C	536,000	7.50	12.50	20.00	50.00	—
1904/3C	148,000	35.00	50.00	75.00	125	—
1905C	110,000	100	150	300	600	—

KM# 394.1 CENTAVO

2.6100 g., Copper **Obv:** Facing eagle, snake in beak **Obv. Legend:** REPUBLICA MEXICANA **Rev:** Value below date within wreath **Note:** Reduced size. Varieties exist.

Date	Mintage	F	VF	XF	Unc	BU
1901M	1,494,000	3.00	8.00	17.50	50.00	—
1902/899M	2,090,000	30.00	60.00	125	225	—
1902M	Inc. above	2.25	4.00	10.00	40.00	—
1903M	8,400,000	1.50	3.00	7.00	20.00	—
1904/3M	10,250,000	1.50	10.00	20.00	55.00	—
1904M	Inc. above	1.50	3.00	8.00	25.00	—
1905M	3,643,000	2.25	4.00	10.00	40.00	—

KM# 400 5 CENTAVOS

1.3530 g., 0.9027 Silver 0.0393 oz. ASW, 14 mm. **Obv:** Facing eagle, snake in beak **Obv. Legend:** REPUBLICA MEXICANA **Rev:** Value within 1/2 wreath **Note:** Varieties exist.

Date	Mintage	F	VF	XF	Unc	BU
1901Cn Q	148,000	1.75	2.50	4.50	15.00	—
1902Cn Q	262,000	1.75	3.00	6.00	16.50	—
Note: Narrow C, heavy serifs						
1902Cn Q	Inc. above	1.75	3.00	6.00	16.50	—
Note: Wide C, light serifs						
1903/1Cn Q	331,000	2.00	3.00	6.00	16.50	20.00
1903Cn Q	Inc. above	1.75	2.50	4.50	15.00	18.00
1903/1898Cn V	Inc. above	3.50	4.50	9.00	22.50	—
1903Cn V	Inc. above	1.75	2.50	4.50	15.00	—
1904Cn H	352,000	1.75	2.25	5.00	16.50	—
1904Cn H/C	—	1.75	2.50	5.00	16.50	—
1904Cn H 0/9	—	1.75	2.50	5.00	16.50	—

KM# 400.2 5 CENTAVOS

1.3530 g., 0.9027 Silver 0.0393 oz. ASW **Obv:** Facing eagle, snake in beak **Rev:** Value within 1/2 wreath

Date	Mintage	F	VF	XF	Unc	BU
1901Mo M	100,000	1.75	2.50	4.50	15.00	—
1902Mo M	144,000	1.25	2.00	3.75	12.00	—
1902/1Mo MoM	—	1.75	3.00	7.00	16.50	—
1903Mo M	500,000	1.25	2.00	3.75	12.00	—
1904/804Mo M	1,090,000	1.75	3.50	8.50	16.50	18.50
1904/94Mo M	Inc. above	1.75	3.75	9.00	16.50	18.50
1904Mo M	Inc. above	1.75	3.00	6.00	15.00	—
1905Mo M	344,000	1.75	3.00	7.00	16.50	—

KM# 400.3 5 CENTAVOS

1.3530 g., 0.9027 Silver 0.0393 oz. ASW **Obv:** Facing eagle, snake in beak **Rev:** Value within 1/2 wreath

Date	Mintage	F	VF	XF	Unc	BU
1901Zs Z	40,000	1.75	2.50	5.00	16.50	—
1902/1Zs Z	34,000	2.00	4.50	9.00	22.50	—
1902Zs Z	Inc. above	1.75	3.75	7.50	18.50	—
1903Zs Z	217,000	1.25	2.00	5.00	12.50	—
1904Zs Z	191,000	1.75	2.50	5.00	12.50	—
1904Zs M	Inc. above	1.75	2.50	6.00	16.50	—
1905Zs M	46,000	2.00	4.50	9.00	22.50	—
1905Zs M Repullica - Rare	Inc. above	—	—	—	—	—

KM# 404 10 CENTAVOS

2.7070 g., 0.9030 Silver 0.0786 oz. ASW **Obv:** Facing eagle, snake in beak **Obv. Legend:** REPUBLICA MEXICANA **Rev:** Value within 1/2 wreath **Note:** Varieties exist.

Date	Mintage	F	VF	XF	Unc	BU
1901Cn Q	235,000	1.50	2.50	5.00	18.00	20.00
1902Cn Q	186,000	1.50	2.50	5.00	20.00	—
1903Cn V	Inc. above	1.50	2.50	5.00	15.00	—
1903Cn Q	256,000	1.50	2.50	6.00	20.00	—
1904Cn H	307,000	1.50	2.50	5.00	15.00	—

KM# 404.2 10 CENTAVOS

2.7070 g., 0.9030 Silver 0.0786 oz. ASW **Obv:** Facing eagle, snake in beak **Obv. Legend:** REPUBLICA MEXICANA **Rev:** Value within 1/2 wreath

Date	Mintage	F	VF	XF	Unc	BU
1901Mo M	80,000	2.50	3.50	7.00	22.50	—
1902Mo M	181,000	1.50	2.50	6.00	20.00	—
1903Mo M	581,000	1.50	2.50	6.00	20.00	—
1904Mo M	1,266,000	1.25	2.00	4.50	18.00	—
1904Mo MM (Error)	Inc. above	2.50	5.00	10.00	25.00	—
1905Mo M	266,000	2.00	3.75	7.50	20.00	—

KM# 404.3 10 CENTAVOS

2.7070 g., 0.9020 Silver 0.0785 oz. ASW **Obv:** Facing eagle, snake in beak **Rev:** Value within 1/2 wreath

Date	Mintage	F	VF	XF	Unc	BU
1901Zs Z	70,000	2.50	5.00	10.00	25.00	—
1902Zs Z	120,000	2.50	5.00	10.00	25.00	—
1903Zs Z	228,000	1.50	3.00	9.00	18.00	20.00
1904Zs Z	368,000	1.50	3.00	9.00	18.00	20.00
1904Zs M	Inc. above	1.50	3.00	9.00	22.00	25.00
1905Zs M	66,000	7.50	20.00	50.00	200	—

KM# 405 20 CENTAVOS

5.4150 g., 0.9030 Silver 0.1572 oz. ASW **Obv:** Facing eagle, snake in beak **Rev:** Value within 1/2 wreath

Date	Mintage	F	VF	XF	Unc	BU
1901Cn Q	185,000	5.00	10.00	30.00	120	—
1902/802Cn Q	98,000	6.00	10.00	30.00	120	—
1902Cn Q	Inc. above	4.00	9.00	30.00	120	—
1903Cn Q	93,000	4.00	9.00	30.00	120	—
1904/3Cn H	258,000	—	—	—	—	—
1904Cn H	Inc. above	5.00	10.00	30.00	120	—

KM# 405.2 20 CENTAVOS

5.4150 g., 0.9030 Silver 0.1572 oz. ASW **Obv:** Facing eagle, snake in beak **Rev:** Value within 1/2 wreath **Note:** Varieties exist.

Date	Mintage	F	VF	XF	Unc	BU
1901Mo M	110,000	4.00	8.00	20.00	90.00	—
1902Mo M	120,000	4.00	8.00	20.00	90.00	—
1903Mo M	213,000	4.00	8.00	20.00	90.00	—
1904Mo M	276,000	4.00	8.00	20.00	90.00	—
1905Mo M	117,000	6.50	20.00	50.00	150	—

KM# 405.3 20 CENTAVOS

5.4150 g., 0.9027 Silver 0.1572 oz. ASW **Obv:** Facing eagle, snake in beak **Obv. Legend:** REPUBLICA MEXICANA **Rev:** Value within 1/2 wreath

Date	Mintage	F	VF	XF	Unc	BU
1901Zs Z	Inc. above	5.00	10.00	20.00	100	—
1901/0Zs Z	130,000	25.00	50.00	100	250	—
1902Zs Z	105,000	5.00	10.00	20.00	100	—
1903Zs Z	143,000	5.00	10.00	20.00	100	—
1904Zs Z	246,000	5.00	10.00	20.00	100	—
1904Zs M	Inc. above	5.00	10.00	50.00	300	—
1905Zs M	59,000	10.00	70.00	50.00	400	—

KM# 409 PESO
27.0730 g., 0.9030 Silver 0.7860 oz. ASW **Obv:** Facing eagle, snake in beak **Rev:** Radiant cap

Date	Mintage	F	VF	XF	Unc	BU
1901Cn JQ	1,473,000	12.00	15.00	25.00	75.00	—
1902Cn JQ	1,194,000	12.00	15.00	45.00	125	—
1903Cn JQ	1,514,000	12.00	15.00	30.00	85.00	—
1903Cn FV	Inc. above	25.00	50.00	100	225	—
1904Cn MH	1,554,000	12.00	15.00	25.00	75.00	—
1904Cn RP	Inc. above	50.00	100	150	350	—
1905Cn RP	598,000	25.00	50.00	100	250	—

KM# 410.2 PESO
1.6920 g., 0.8750 Gold 0.0476 oz. AGW **Obv:** Facing eagle, snake in beak **Obv. Legend:** REPUBLICA MEXICANA **Rev:** Value within 1/2 wreath

Date	Mintage	F	VF	XF	Unc	BU
1901Cn Q	Inc. above	65.00	100	150	225	—
1901/0Cn Q	2,350	65.00	100	150	225	—
1902Cn Q	2,480	65.00	100	150	225	—
1902Cn/MoQ/C	Inc. above	65.00	100	150	225	—
1904Cn H	3,614	65.00	100	150	225	—
1904Cn/Mo/ H	Inc. above	65.00	100	150	250	—
1905Cn P	1,000	—	—	—	—	—

Note: Reported, not confirmed

KM# 410.5 PESO
1.6920 g., 0.8750 Gold 0.0476 oz. AGW **Obv:** Facing eagle, snake in beak **Obv. Legend:** REPUBLICA MEXICANA **Rev:** Value within 1/2 wreath

Date	Mintage	F	VF	XF	Unc	BU
1901Mo M Small date	Inc. above	45.00	65.00	95.00	185	—
1901/801Mo M Large date	8,293	45.00	65.00	95.00	185	—
1902Mo M Large date	11,000	45.00	65.00	95.00	185	—
1902Mo M Small date	Inc. above	45.00	65.00	95.00	185	—
1903Mo M Large date	10,000	45.00	65.00	95.00	185	—
1903Mo M Small date	Inc. above	55.00	85.00	125	200	—
1904Mo M	9,845	45.00	65.00	95.00	185	—
1905Mo M	3,429	45.00	65.00	95.00	185	—

KM# 409.3 PESO
27.0730 g., 0.9030 Silver 0.7860 oz. ASW **Obv:** Facing eagle, snake in beak **Rev:** Radiant cap **Note:** Mint mark Zs. Varieties exist.

Date	Mintage	F	VF	XF	Unc	BU
1901Zs FZ	Inc. above	11.50	13.50	20.00	55.00	—
1901Zs AZ	5,706,000	4,000	6,500	10,000	—	—
1902Zs FZ	7,134,000	11.50	13.50	20.00	55.00	—
1903/2Zs FZ	3,080,000	12.50	15.00	50.00	125	—
1903Zs FZ	Inc. above	11.50	13.50	20.00	65.00	—
1904Zs FZ	2,423,000	12.00	15.00	25.00	85.00	—
1904Zs FM	Inc. above	12.00	15.00	25.00	75.00	—
1905Zs FM	995,000	20.00	40.00	60.00	150	—

KM# 409.2 PESO
27.0730 g., 0.9027 Silver 0.7857 oz. ASW **Obv:** Facing eagle, snake in beak **Obv. Legend:** REPUBLICA MEXICANA **Rev:** Radiant cap **Note:** Varieties exist.

Date	Mintage	F	VF	XF	Unc	BU
1901Mo AM	14,505,000	11.50	13.50	20.00	70.00	—
1902/1Mo AM	16,224,000	150	300	500	950	—
1902Mo AM	Inc. above	11.50	13.50	20.00	70.00	—
1903Mo AM	22,396,000	11.50	13.50	20.00	70.00	—
1903Mo MA (Error)	Inc. above	1,500	2,500	3,500	7,500	—
1904Mo AM	14,935,000	11.50	13.50	20.00	70.00	—
1905Mo AM	3,557,000	15.00	25.00	55.00	125	—
1908Mo AM	7,575,000	11.50	13.50	20.00	60.00	—
1908Mo GV	Inc. above	11.50	13.50	18.50	40.00	—
1909Mo GV	2,924,000	11.50	13.50	18.50	40.00	—

KM# 412.6 5 PESOS
8.4600 g., 0.8750 Gold 0.2380 oz. AGW **Obv:** Facing eagle, snake in beak **Obv. Legend:** REPUBLICA MEXICANA **Rev:** Radiant cap above scales

Date	Mintage	F	VF	XF	Unc	BU
1901Mo M	1,071	230	300	400	650	—
1902Mo M	1,478	230	300	400	650	—
1903Mo M	1,162	230	300	400	650	—
1904Mo M	1,415	230	300	400	650	—
1905Mo M	563	230	400	550	1,500	—

KM# 412.2 5 PESOS
8.4600 g., 0.8750 Gold 0.2380 oz. AGW **Obv:** Facing eagle, snake in beak **Obv. Legend:** REPUBLICA MEXICANA **Rev:** Radiant cap above scales

Date	Mintage	F	VF	XF	Unc	BU
1903Cn Q	1,000	230	300	400	750	—

KM# 413.7 10 PESOS
16.9200 g., 0.8750 Gold 0.4760 oz. AGW **Obv:** Facing eagle, snake in beak **Obv. Legend:** REPUBLICA MEXICANA **Rev:** Radiant cap above scales

Date	Mintage	F	VF	XF	Unc	BU
1901Mo M	562	450	500	800	1,250	—
1902Mo M	719	450	500	800	1,250	—
1903Mo M	713	450	500	800	1,250	—
1904Mo M	694	450	500	800	1,250	—
1905Mo M	401	450	600	950	1,500	—

KM# 413.2 10 PESOS
16.9200 g., 0.8750 Gold 0.4760 oz. AGW **Obv:** Facing eagle, snake in beak **Obv. Legend:** REPUBLICA MEXICANA **Rev:** Radiant cap above scales

Date	Mintage	F	VF	XF	Unc	BU
1903Cn Q	774	450	600	1,000	1,750	—

KM# 414.2 20 PESOS
33.8400 g., 0.8750 Gold 0.9519 oz. AGW **Obv:** Facing eagle, snake in beak **Obv. Legend:** REPUBLICA MEXICANA **Rev:** Radiant cap above scales

Date	Mintage	F	VF	XF	Unc	BU
1901Cn Q	Inc. above	BV	685	950	2,000	—
1901/0Cn Q	1,496	—	—	—	—	—
1902Cn Q	1,059	BV	685	950	2,000	—
1903Cn Q	1,121	BV	685	950	2,000	—
1904Cn H	4,646	BV	685	950	2,000	—
1905Cn P	1,738	BV	900	1,200	2,250	—

KM# 414.6 20 PESOS
33.8400 g., 0.8750 Gold 0.9519 oz. AGW **Obv:** Facing eagle, snake in beak **Obv. Legend:** REPUBLICA MEXICANA **Rev:** Radiant cap above scales

Date	Mintage	F	VF	XF	Unc	BU
1901Mo M	29,000	BV	BV	900	1,500	—
1902Mo M	38,000	BV	BV	900	1,500	—

Date	Mintage	F	VF	XF	Unc	BU
1903/2Mo M	31,000	BV	BV	900	1,500	—
1903Mo M	Inc. above	BV	BV	900	1,500	—
1904Mo M	52,000	BV	BV	900	1,500	—
1905Mo M	9,757	BV	BV	900	1,500	—

UNITED STATES

DECIMAL COINAGE

100 Centavos = 1 Peso

KM# 415 CENTAVO

3.0000 g., Bronze, 20 mm. **Obv:** National arms **Rev:** Value below date within wreath **Note:** Mint mark Mo.

Date	Mintage	F	VF	XF	Unc	BU
1905 Narrow date	6,040,000	4.00	6.50	14.00	90.00	—
1905 Wide date	—	4.00	6.50	14.00	90.00	—
1906 Narrow date	Est. 67,505,000	0.50	0.75	1.25	14.00	—
Note: 50,000,000 pcs. were struck at the Birmingham Mint						
1906 Wide date	Inc. above	0.75	1.50	2.50	20.00	—
1910 Narrow date	8,700,000	2.00	3.00	6.50	85.00	—
1910 Wide date	—	2.00	3.00	6.50	85.00	—
1911 Narrow date	16,450,000	0.60	1.00	2.75	22.50	—
1911 Wide date	Inc. above	0.75	1.00	4.00	32.00	—
1912	12,650,000	1.00	1.35	3.25	32.00	—
1913	12,850,000	0.75	1.25	3.00	35.00	—
1914 Narrow date	17,350,000	0.75	1.00	3.00	13.50	18.00
1914 Wide date	Inc. above	0.75	1.00	3.00	13.50	18.00
1915	2,277,000	11.00	25.00	67.50	250	—
1916	500,000	45.00	80.00	170	1,200	—
1920	1,433,000	22.00	50.00	110	400	—
1921	3,470,000	5.50	15.50	47.00	275	—
1922	1,880,000	9.00	17.00	50.00	250	—
1923	4,800,000	0.75	1.25	1.75	13.50	—
1924/3	2,000,000	65.00	170	285	525	—
1924	Inc. above	4.50	11.00	22.00	235	275
1925	1,550,000	4.50	10.00	25.00	220	—
1926	5,000,000	1.00	2.00	4.00	26.00	30.00
1927/6	6,000,000	30.00	45.00	70.00	150	—
1927	Inc. above	0.75	1.25	4.50	36.00	—
1928	5,000,000	0.75	1.00	3.25	16.50	25.00
1929	4,500,000	0.75	1.00	1.75	17.00	25.00
1930	7,000,000	0.75	1.00	2.50	19.00	—
1933	10,000,000	0.25	0.35	1.75	16.50	—
1934	7,500,000	0.25	0.95	3.25	30.00	—
1935	12,400,000	0.15	0.25	0.40	11.50	—
1936	20,100,000	0.15	0.20	0.30	8.00	—
1937	20,000,000	0.15	0.25	0.35	3.25	5.00
1938	10,000,000	0.10	0.15	0.30	2.00	2.75
1939	30,000,000	0.10	0.20	0.30	1.00	1.50
1940	10,000,000	0.20	0.30	0.60	5.50	7.50
1941	15,800,000	0.15	0.25	0.35	2.00	3.00
1942	30,400,000	0.15	0.20	0.30	1.25	2.00
1943	4,310,000	0.30	0.50	0.75	8.00	10.00
1944	5,645,000	0.15	0.25	0.50	6.00	7.50
1945	26,375,000	0.10	0.15	0.25	1.00	1.25
1946	42,135,000	—	0.15	0.20	0.60	1.00
1947	13,445,000	—	0.10	0.15	0.80	1.25
1948	20,040,000	0.10	0.15	0.30	1.10	2.00
1949	6,235,000	0.10	0.15	0.30	1.25	2.00

Note: Varieties exist.

KM# 416 CENTAVO

Bronze, 16 mm. **Obv:** National arms **Rev:** Value below date within wreath **Note:** Zapata issue. Struck at Mexico City Mint, mint mark Mo. Reduced size. Weight varies 1.39-1.5g.

Date	Mintage	F	VF	XF	Unc	BU
1915	179,000	18.00	30.00	50.00	75.00	—

KM# 417 CENTAVO

2.0000 g., Brass, 16 mm. **Obv:** National arms, eagle left **Rev:** Oat sprigs **Note:** Mint mark Mo.

Date	Mintage	F	VF	XF	Unc	BU
1950	12,815,000	—	0.15	0.35	1.65	2.00
1951	25,740,000	—	0.15	0.35	0.65	1.00
1952	24,610,000	—	0.10	0.25	0.40	0.75
1953	21,160,000	—	0.10	0.25	0.40	0.85
1954	25,675,000	—	0.10	0.15	0.85	1.20
1955	9,820,000	—	0.15	0.25	0.85	1.50
1956	11,285,000	—	0.15	0.25	0.80	1.25
1957	9,805,000	—	0.15	0.25	0.85	1.35
1958	12,155,000	—	0.10	0.25	0.45	0.75
1959	11,875,000	—	0.10	0.25	0.75	1.25
1960	10,360,000	—	0.10	0.15	0.40	0.65
1961	6,385,000	—	0.10	0.15	0.45	0.85
1962	4,850,000	—	0.10	0.15	0.55	0.90
1963	7,775,000	—	0.10	0.15	0.25	0.45
1964	4,280,000	—	0.10	0.15	0.20	0.30
1965	2,255,000	—	0.10	0.15	0.25	0.40
1966	1,760,000	—	0.10	0.25	0.60	0.75
1967	1,290,000	—	0.10	0.15	0.40	0.60
1968	1,000,000	—	0.10	0.20	0.85	1.25
1969	1,000,000	—	0.10	0.15	0.65	0.85

KM# 418 CENTAVO

1.5000 g., Brass, 13 mm. **Obv:** National arms, eagle left **Rev:** Oat sprigs **Note:** Reduced size.

Date	Mintage	F	VF	XF	Unc	BU
1970	1,000,000	—	0.20	0.40	1.45	1.75
1972	1,000,000	—	0.20	0.45	2.50	3.25
1972/2	—	—	0.50	1.25	3.50	5.00
1973	1,000,000	—	1.65	2.75	8.50	12.00

KM# 419 2 CENTAVOS

6.0000 g., Bronze, 25 mm. **Obv:** National arms **Rev:** Value below date within wreath **Note:** Mint mark Mo.

Date	Mintage	F	VF	XF	Unc	BU
1905	50,000	150	300	500	1,200	1,350
1906 Inverted 6	9,998,000	30.00	55.00	120	375	—
1906 Wide date	Inc. above	5.00	11.00	23.00	80.00	—
1906 Narrow date	Inc. above	6.50	14.00	28.00	85.00	—
Note: 5,000,000 pieces were struck at the Birmingham Mint						
1920	1,325,000	6.50	17.50	35.00	350	—
1921	4,275,000	2.50	4.75	10.00	90.00	—
1922	—	225	550	1,350	4,000	—
1924	750,000	8.50	22.50	55.00	450	—
1925	3,650,000	2.50	3.50	7.50	38.00	—
1926	4,750,000	1.00	2.25	5.50	35.00	—
1927	7,250,000	0.60	1.00	4.50	22.00	—
1928	3,250,000	0.75	1.50	4.75	30.00	—
1929	250,000	65.00	180	500	1,000	—
1935	1,250,000	4.25	9.25	22.50	200	—
1939	5,000,000	0.60	0.90	2.25	20.00	22.00
1941	3,550,000	0.45	0.60	1.25	18.00	20.00

KM# 420 2 CENTAVOS

Bronze, 20 mm. **Obv:** National arms **Rev:** Value below date within wreath **Note:** Zapata issue. Mint mark Mo. Reduced size. Weight varies 3-3.03g.

Date	Mintage	F	VF	XF	Unc	BU
1915	487,000	7.50	9.00	17.50	75.00	—

KM# 421 5 CENTAVOS

5.0000 g., Nickel, 20 mm. **Obv:** National arms **Rev:** Value and date within beaded circle **Note:** Mint mark Mo. Varieties exist.

Date	Mintage	F	VF	XF	Unc	BU
1905	1,420,000	7.00	10.00	25.00	300	375
1906/5	10,615,000	13.00	30.00	70.00	375	—
1906	Inc. above	0.75	1.35	3.25	55.00	75.00
1907	4,000,000	1.25	4.00	12.00	350	—
1909	2,052,000	3.25	10.00	48.00	360	—
1910	6,181,000	1.30	3.50	6.00	78.00	115
1911 Narrow date	4,487,000	1.00	3.00	5.00	85.00	125
1911 Wide date	Inc. above	2.50	5.00	9.00	110	160
1912 Small mint mark	420,000	90.00	100	230	725	—
1912 Large mint mark	Inc. above	70.00	95.00	175	575	—
1913	2,035,000	1.75	4.25	9.00	100	150
Note: Wide and narrow dates exist for 1913						
1914	2,000,000	1.00	2.00	3.50	70.00	95.00
Note: 5,000,000 pieces appear to have been struck at the Birmingham Mint in 1914 and all of 1909-1911. The Mexican Mint report does not mention receiving the 1914 dated coins						

Large and small date varieties

KM# 422 5 CENTAVOS

9.0000 g., Bronze, 28 mm. **Obv:** National arms **Rev:** Value below date within wreath

Date	Mintage	F	VF	XF	Unc	BU
1914Mo	2,500,000	10.00	23.00	50.00	240	—
1915Mo	11,424,000	3.00	5.00	20.00	145	—
1916Mo	2,860,000	15.00	35.00	150	645	—
1917Mo	800,000	75.00	195	375	825	—
1918Mo	1,332,000	35.00	90.00	200	625	—
1919Mo	400,000	115	225	360	925	—
1920Mo	5,920,000	3.00	8.00	40.00	265	—
1921Mo	2,080,000	10.00	24.00	75.00	275	—
1924Mo	780,000	40.00	95.00	260	625	—
1925Mo	4,040,000	5.50	11.00	47.50	200	—
1926Mo	3,160,000	5.50	11.00	48.00	300	—
1927Mo	3,600,000	4.00	7.00	30.00	215	250
1928Mo Large date	1,740,000	11.00	18.00	65.00	250	—
1928Mo Small date	Inc. above	30.00	45.00	95.00	385	—
1929Mo	2,400,000	5.50	11.00	48.00	195	—
1930Mo	2,600,000	5.00	8.00	27.50	210	—
Note: Large oval O in date						
1930Mo	Inc. above	60.00	125	250	565	—
Note: Small square O in date						
1931Mo	—	475	750	1,150	3,000	—
1933Mo	8,000,000	1.50	2.25	3.50	27.50	35.00
1934Mo	10,000,000	1.25	1.75	2.75	25.00	40.00
1935Mo	21,980,000	0.75	1.20	2.50	22.50	30.00

KM# 423 5 CENTAVOS

4.0000 g., Copper-Nickel, 20.5 mm. **Obv:** National arms, eagle left **Rev:** Value and date within circle

Date	Mintage	F	VF	XF	Unc	BU
1936M	46,700,000	—	0.65	1.25	6.50	7.50
1937M	49,060,000	—	0.50	1.00	6.00	7.00
1938M	3,340,000	—	4.00	10.00	75.00	250
1940M	22,800,000	—	0.75	1.25	8.00	10.00
1942M	7,100,000	—	1.50	3.00	35.00	45.00

KM# 424 5 CENTAVOS

6.5000 g., Bronze, 25.5 mm. **Obv:** National arms, eagle left **Rev:** Head left

Date	Mintage	F	VF	XF	Unc	BU
1942Mo	900,000	—	25.00	75.00	375	550
1943Mo	54,660,000	—	0.50	0.75	2.50	3.50
1944Mo	53,463,000	—	0.25	0.35	0.75	1.00
1945Mo	44,262,000	—	0.25	0.35	0.75	1.25
1946Mo	49,054,000	—	0.50	1.00	2.00	3.00
1951Mo	50,758,000	—	0.75	0.90	3.00	5.00
1952Mo	17,674,000	—	1.50	2.50	9.50	11.50
1953Mo	31,568,000	—	1.25	2.00	6.00	9.00

Date	Mintage	F	VF	XF	Unc	BU
1954Mo	58,680,000	—	0.40	1.00	2.75	4.00
1955Mo	31,114,000	—	2.00	3.00	11.00	14.00

KM# 425 5 CENTAVOS

4.0000 g., Copper-Nickel, 20.5 mm. **Obv:** National arms, eagle left **Rev:** Bust right flanked by date and value

Date	Mintage	F	VF	XF	Unc	BU
1950Mo	5,700,000	—	0.75	1.50	6.00	7.00

Note: 5,600,000 pieces struck at Connecticut melted

KM# 426 5 CENTAVOS

4.0000 g., Brass, 20.5 mm. **Obv:** National arms, eagle left **Rev:** Bust right

Date	Mintage	F	VF	XF	Unc	BU
1954Mo Dot	—	—	10.00	45.00	300	375
1954Mo Without dot	—	—	15.00	30.00	250	290
1955Mo	12,136,000	—	0.75	1.50	9.00	12.50
1956Mo	60,216,000	—	0.20	0.30	0.75	1.25
1957Mo	55,288,000	—	0.15	0.20	0.90	1.50
1958Mo	104,624,000	—	0.15	0.20	0.60	1.00
1959Mo	106,000,000	—	0.15	0.25	0.75	1.25
1960Mo	99,144,000	—	0.10	0.15	0.50	0.75
1961Mo	61,136,000	—	0.10	0.15	0.50	0.75
1962Mo	47,232,000	—	0.10	0.15	0.25	0.35
1963Mo	156,680,000	—	—	0.15	0.25	0.40
1964Mo	71,168,000	—	—	0.15	0.20	0.40
1965Mo	155,720,000	—	—	0.15	0.25	0.35
1966Mo	124,944,000	—	—	0.15	0.40	0.65
1967Mo	118,816,000	—	—	0.15	0.25	0.40
1968Mo	189,588,000	—	—	0.15	0.50	0.75
1969Mo	210,492,000	—	—	0.15	0.55	0.80

KM# 426a 5 CENTAVOS

Copper-Nickel, 20.5 mm. **Obv:** National arms, eagle left **Rev:** Bust right

Date	Mintage	F	VF	XF	Unc	BU
1960Mo	—	—	250	300	350	—
1962Mo	19	—	250	300	350	—
1965Mo	—	—	250	300	350	—

KM# 427 5 CENTAVOS

2.7500 g., Brass, 18 mm. **Obv:** National arms, eagle left **Rev:** Bust right **Note:** Due to some minor alloy variations this type is often encountered with a bronze-color toning. Reduced size.

Date	Mintage	F	VF	XF	Unc	BU
1970	163,368,000	—	0.10	0.15	0.35	0.45
1971	198,844,000	—	0.10	0.15	0.25	0.30
1972	225,000,000	—	0.10	0.15	0.25	0.30
1973 Flat top 3	595,070,000	—	0.10	0.15	0.25	0.40
1973 Round top 3	Inc. above	—	0.10	0.15	0.20	0.30
1974	401,584,000	—	0.10	0.15	0.30	0.40
1975	342,308,000	—	0.10	0.15	0.25	0.35
1976	367,524,000	—	0.10	0.15	0.40	0.60

KM# 428 10 CENTAVOS

2.5000 g., 0.8000 Silver 0.0643 oz. ASW, 18 mm. **Obv:** National arms **Rev:** Value and date within 3/4 wreath with Liberty cap above **Note:** Mint mark Mo.

Date	Mintage	F	VF	XF	Unc	BU
1905	3,920,000	—	6.00	8.00	40.00	50.00
1906	8,410,000	—	5.50	7.50	27.00	35.00
1907/6	5,950,000	—	50.00	135	275	350
1907	Inc. above	—	5.50	6.25	35.00	42.50
1909	2,620,000	—	8.50	13.00	70.00	85.00
1910/00	3,450,000	—	10.00	40.00	75.00	85.00
1910	Inc. above	—	7.00	15.00	25.00	30.00
1911 Narrow date	2,550,000	—	11.00	17.00	88.00	125
1911 Wide date	Inc. above	—	7.50	10.00	42.00	60.00
1912	1,350,000	—	10.00	18.00	130	160

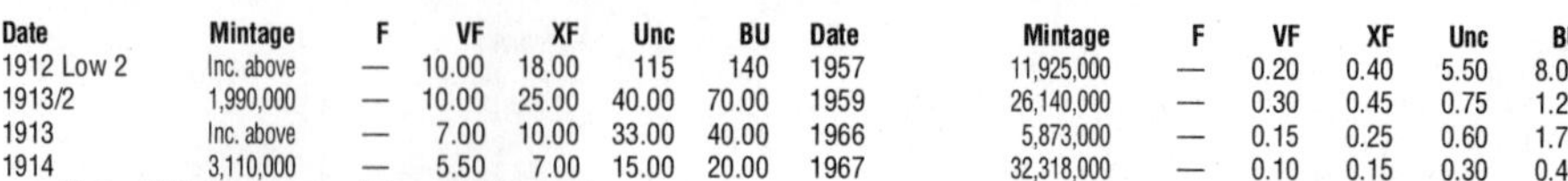

Date	Mintage	F	VF	XF	Unc	BU
1912 Low 2	Inc. above	—	10.00	18.00	115	140
1913/2	1,990,000	—	10.00	25.00	40.00	70.00
1913	Inc. above	—	7.00	10.00	33.00	40.00
1914	3,110,000	—	5.50	7.00	15.00	20.00

Note: Wide and narrow dates exist for 1914

KM# 429 10 CENTAVOS

1.8125 g., 0.8000 Silver 0.0466 oz. ASW, 15 mm. **Obv:** National arms **Rev:** Value and date within 3/4 wreath with Liberty cap above **Note:** Mint mark Mo. Reduced size.

Date	Mintage	F	VF	XF	Unc	BU
1919	8,360,000	—	10.00	15.00	85.00	110

KM# 430 10 CENTAVOS

12.0000 g., Bronze, 30.5 mm. **Obv:** National arms **Rev:** Value below date within wreath **Note:** Mint mark Mo.

Date	Mintage	F	VF	XF	Unc	BU
1919	1,232,000	—	25.00	70.00	450	525
1920	6,612,000	—	15.00	50.00	400	475
1921	2,255,000	—	35.00	80.00	650	800
1935	5,970,000	—	14.00	30.00	120	175

KM# 431 10 CENTAVOS

1.6600 g., 0.7200 Silver 0.0384 oz. ASW, 15 mm. **Obv:** National arms **Rev:** Value and date within wreath with Liberty cap above **Note:** Mint mark Mo.

Date	Mintage	F	VF	XF	Unc	BU
1925/15	5,350,000	—	30.00	75.00	125	175
1925/3	Inc. above	—	20.00	40.00	125	150
1925	Inc. above	—	2.00	5.00	40.00	45.00
1926/16	2,650,000	—	30.00	75.00	125	175
1926	Inc. above	—	3.50	7.50	65.00	85.00
1927	2,810,000	—	2.25	3.00	17.50	22.50
1928	5,270,000	—	2.00	2.75	13.50	16.50
1930	2,000,000	—	3.75	5.00	18.75	25.00
1933	5,000,000	—	1.50	3.00	10.00	11.50
1934	8,000,000	—	1.75	2.50	8.00	10.00
1935	3,500,000	—	2.75	5.00	11.00	12.50

KM# 432 10 CENTAVOS

5.5000 g., Copper-Nickel, 23.5 mm. **Obv:** National arms, eagle left **Rev:** Value and date within circle **Note:** Mint mark Mo.

Date	Mintage	F	VF	XF	Unc	BU
1936	33,030,000	—	0.75	2.50	9.00	10.00
1937	3,000,000	—	8.00	45.00	215	250
1938	3,650,000	1.25	2.00	7.00	60.00	75.00
1939	6,920,000	—	1.00	3.50	27.50	30.00
1940	12,300,000	—	0.40	1.25	5.00	6.00
1942	14,380,000	—	0.60	1.50	7.00	9.00
1945	9,558,000	—	0.40	0.70	3.50	4.00
1946	46,230,000	—	0.40	0.60	2.50	3.00

KM# 433 10 CENTAVOS

5.5000 g., Bronze, 23.5 mm. **Obv:** National arms, eagle left **Rev:** Bust left **Note:** Mint mark Mo.

Date	Mintage	F	VF	XF	Unc	BU
1955	1,818,000	—	0.75	3.25	23.00	30.00
1956	5,255,000	—	0.75	3.25	23.00	28.00

Date	Mintage	F	VF	XF	Unc	BU
1957	11,925,000	—	0.20	0.40	5.50	8.00
1959	26,140,000	—	0.30	0.45	0.75	1.25
1966	5,873,000	—	0.15	0.25	0.60	1.75
1967	32,318,000	—	0.10	0.15	0.30	0.40

  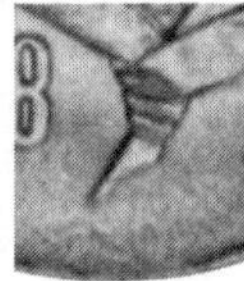

Sharp stem

KM# 434.1 10 CENTAVOS

1.5200 g., Copper-Nickel **Obv:** National arms, eagle left **Rev:** Upright ear of corn **Note:** Variety I- Sharp stem and wide date

Date	Mintage	F	VF	XF	Unc	BU
1974	6,000,000	—	—	0.35	0.75	1.00
1975	5,550,000	—	0.10	0.35	0.75	1.00
1976	7,680,000	—	0.10	0.20	0.30	0.40
1977	144,650,000	—	1.25	2.25	3.00	3.50
1978	271,870,000	—	—	1.00	1.50	2.25
1979	375,660,000	—	—	0.50	1.00	1.75
1980/79	21,290,000	—	2.45	3.75	6.00	7.00
1980	Inc. above	—	1.50	2.00	4.50	5.50

  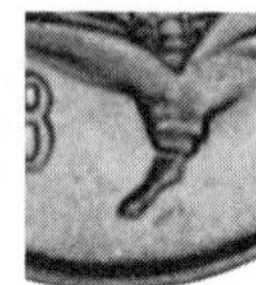

Blunt stem

KM# 434.2 10 CENTAVOS

1.5600 g., Copper-Nickel **Obv:** National arms, eagle left **Rev:** Upright ear of corn **Note:** Variety II- Blunt stem and narrow date

Date	Mintage	F	VF	XF	Unc	BU
1974	Inc. above	—	—	0.10	0.20	0.30
1977	Inc. above	—	0.15	0.50	1.25	2.25
1978	Inc. above	—	—	0.10	0.30	0.40
1979	Inc. above	—	0.15	0.35	0.85	1.50
1980	Inc. above	—	—	0.10	0.20	0.30

KM# 434.4 10 CENTAVOS

Copper-Nickel **Obv:** National arms, eagle left **Rev:** Upright ear of corn **Note:** Variety IV- Sharp stem and narrow date

Date	Mintage	F	VF	XF	Unc	BU
1974	—	—	—	—	1.50	2.50
1979	—	—	—	—	1.50	2.50

KM# 434.3 10 CENTAVOS

Copper-Nickel **Obv:** National arms, eagle left **Rev:** Upright ear of corn **Note:** Variety III- Blunt stem and wide date

Date	Mintage	F	VF	XF	Unc	BU
1980/79	—	—	—	—	5.00	6.00

KM# 435 20 CENTAVOS

5.0000 g., 0.8000 Silver 0.1286 oz. ASW, 22 mm. **Obv:** National arms **Rev:** Value and date within wreath with Liberty cap above **Note:** Mint mark Mo.

Date	Mintage	F	VF	XF	Unc	BU
1905	2,565,000	—	12.00	20.00	145	175
1906	6,860,000	—	9.00	16.50	60.00	80.00
1907 Straight 7	4,000,000	—	11.50	20.00	70.00	100
1907 Curved 7	5,435,000	—	7.50	13.50	65.00	90.00
1908	350,000	50.00	90.00	225	1,500	—
1910	1,135,000	—	11.00	16.00	80.00	95.00
1911	1,150,000	12.00	15.00	35.00	125	150
1912	625,000	20.00	40.00	70.00	335	375
1913	1,000,000	—	14.50	30.00	95.00	115
1914	1,500,000	—	10.00	21.50	62.50	75.00

KM# 436 20 CENTAVOS

3.6250 g., 0.8000 Silver 0.0932 oz. ASW, 19 mm. **Obv:** National arms **Rev:** Value and date within wreath with Liberty cap above **Note:** Mint mark Mo. Reduced size.

Date	Mintage	F	VF	XF	Unc	BU
1919	4,155,000	—	30.00	55.00	190	225

KM# 437 20 CENTAVOS

15.0000 g., Bronze, 32.5 mm. **Obv:** National arms **Rev:** Value below date within wreath **Note:** Mint mark Mo.

Date	Mintage	F	VF	XF	Unc	BU
1920	4,835,000	—	45.00	140	650	750
1935	20,000,000	—	6.00	10.00	80.00	125

KM# 438 20 CENTAVOS

3.3333 g., 0.7200 Silver 0.0772 oz. ASW, 19 mm. **Obv:** National arms **Rev:** Value and date within wreath with Liberty cap above **Note:** Mint mark Mo.

Date	Mintage	F	VF	XF	Unc	BU
1920	3,710,000	—	6.00	17.50	165	200
1921	6,160,000	—	6.00	14.00	100	145
1925	1,450,000	—	12.00	20.00	125	150
1926/5	1,465,000	—	20.00	65.00	325	375
1926	Inc. above	—	3.25	7.50	80.00	110
1927	1,405,000	—	3.50	8.00	85.00	115
1928	3,630,000	—	4.00	5.25	14.50	19.50
1930	1,000,000	—	5.00	8.00	25.00	35.00
1933	2,500,000	—	2.25	3.00	10.00	11.50
1934	2,500,000	—	2.25	4.00	11.00	12.50
1935	2,460,000	—	2.25	4.00	11.00	12.50
1937	10,000,000	—	1.75	2.25	4.00	5.00
1939	8,800,000	—	1.75	2.25	4.00	5.00
1940	3,000,000	—	1.75	2.25	3.50	5.00
1941	5,740,000	—	1.50	2.25	3.00	4.00
1942	12,460,000	—	1.50	2.25	3.25	3.75
1943	3,955,000	—	2.00	2.50	3.50	4.25

KM# 439 20 CENTAVOS

Bronze, 28.5 mm. **Obv:** National arms, eagle left **Rev:** Liberty cap divides value above Pyramid of the Sun at Teotihuacán, volcanos Ixtaccihuatl and Popocatepet in background **Edge:** Plain **Note:** Mint mark Mo.

Date	Mintage	F	VF	XF	Unc	BU
1943	46,350,000	—	1.25	3.00	18.00	25.00
1944	83,650,000	—	0.40	0.65	8.00	10.00
1945	26,801,000	—	1.25	3.50	9.50	12.00
1946	25,695,000	—	1.10	2.25	6.00	8.25
1951	11,385,000	—	3.00	8.75	90.00	110
1952	6,560,000	—	3.00	5.00	25.00	32.00
1953	26,948,000	—	0.35	0.80	8.25	12.00
1954	40,108,000	—	0.35	0.80	8.00	11.50
1955	16,950,000	—	2.75	7.00	60.00	75.00

KM# 440 20 CENTAVOS

Bronze, 28.5 mm. **Obv:** National arms, eagle left **Rev:** Liberty cap divides value above Pyramid of the Sun at Teotihuacán, volcanos Ixtaccihuatl and Popocatepet in background **Edge:** Plain **Note:** Mint mark Mo.

Date	Mintage	F	VF	XF	Unc	BU
1955 Inc. KM#439	Inc. above	—	0.75	1.75	17.00	22.00
1956	22,431,000	—	0.30	0.35	3.00	4.00
1957	13,455,000	—	0.45	1.25	9.00	12.00
1959	6,017,000	—	4.50	9.00	75.00	100
1960	39,756,000	—	0.15	0.25	0.75	1.00
1963	14,869,000	—	0.25	0.35	0.80	1.00
1964	28,654,000	—	0.25	0.40	0.90	1.25
1965	74,162,000	—	0.20	0.35	0.80	1.00
1966	43,745,000	—	0.15	0.25	0.75	1.00
1967	46,487,000	—	0.20	0.50	1.00	1.25
1968	15,477,000	—	0.30	0.55	1.35	1.65
1969	63,647,000	—	0.20	0.35	0.80	1.00

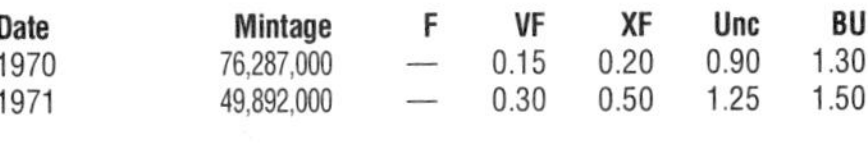

Date	Mintage	F	VF	XF	Unc	BU
1970	76,287,000	—	0.15	0.20	0.90	1.30
1971	49,892,000	—	0.30	0.50	1.25	1.50

KM# 441 20 CENTAVOS

Bronze, 28.5 mm. **Obv:** National arms, eagle left **Rev:** Liberty cap divides value above Pyramid of the Sun at Teotihuacán, volcanos Ixtaccihuatl and Popocatepet in background **Edge:** Plain

Date	Mintage	F	VF	XF	Unc	BU
1971 Inc. KM#440	Inc. above	—	0.20	0.35	1.85	2.35
1973	78,398,000	—	0.25	0.35	0.95	1.50
1974	34,200,000	—	0.20	0.35	1.25	1.75

KM# 442 20 CENTAVOS

3.0600 g., Copper-Nickel, 20 mm. **Obv:** National arms, eagle left **Rev:** Bust 3/4 facing flanked by value and date

Date	Mintage	F	VF	XF	Unc	BU
1974	112,000,000	—	0.10	0.15	0.25	0.30
1975	611,000,000	—	0.10	0.15	0.30	0.35
1976	394,000,000	—	0.10	0.15	0.35	0.45
1977	394,350,000	—	0.10	0.15	0.40	0.45
1978	527,950,000	—	0.10	0.15	0.25	0.30
1979	524,615,000	—	0.10	0.15	0.25	0.30
1979	—	—	1.25	2.00	4.00	8.00
Note: Doubled die obv. small letters						
1979	—	—	1.25	2.00	4.00	8.00
Note: Doubled die obv. large letters						
1980	326,500,000	—	0.15	0.20	0.30	0.40
1981 Open 8	106,205,000	—	0.30	0.50	1.00	2.00
1981 Closed 8, high date	248,500,000	—	0.30	0.50	1.00	2.00
1981 Closed 8, low date	—	—	1.00	1.50	3.50	4.25
1981/1982	—	—	40.00	75.00	175	195
Note: The 1981/1982 overdate is often mistaken as 1982/1981						
1982	286,855,000	—	0.40	0.60	0.90	1.10
1983 Round top 3	100,930,000	—	0.25	0.40	1.75	2.25
1983 Flat top 3	Inc. above	—	0.25	0.50	1.25	1.75
1983 Proof	998	Value: 15.00				

KM# 491 20 CENTAVOS

3.0000 g., Bronze, 20 mm. **Subject:** Olmec Culture **Obv:** National arms, eagle left **Rev:** Mask 3/4 right with value below

Date	Mintage	F	VF	XF	Unc	BU
1983	260,000,000	—	0.20	0.25	1.25	1.75
1983 Proof	53	Value: 185				
1984	180,320,000	—	0.20	0.35	1.85	2.25

KM# 443 25 CENTAVOS

3.3330 g., 0.3000 Silver 0.0321 oz. ASW, 21.5 mm. **Obv:** National arms, eagle left **Rev:** Scale below Liberty cap **Note:** Mint mark Mo.

Date	Mintage	F	VF	XF	Unc	BU
1950	77,060,000	—	0.60	0.80	1.60	2.00
1951	41,172,000	—	0.60	0.80	1.60	2.00
1952	29,264,000	—	0.75	1.10	1.75	2.25
1953	38,144,000	—	0.65	0.85	1.60	2.00

KM# 444 25 CENTAVOS

5.5000 g., Copper-Nickel, 23 mm. **Obv:** National arms, eagle left **Rev:** Bust 3/4 facing

Date	Mintage	F	VF	XF	Unc	BU
1964	20,686,000	—	—	0.15	0.20	0.30
1966 Closed beak	180,000	—	0.65	1.00	2.25	2.50
1966 Open beak	Inc. above	—	1.75	3.50	10.00	13.50

KM# 445 50 CENTAVOS

12.5000 g., 0.8000 Silver 0.3215 oz. ASW, 30 mm. **Obv:** National arms **Rev:** Value and date within 3/4 wreath with Liberty cap above **Note:** Mint mark Mo.

Date	Mintage	F	VF	XF	Unc	BU
1905	2,446,000	12.50	20.00	30.00	150	225
1906 Open 9	16,966,000	—	6.00	10.00	40.00	60.00
1906 Closed 9	Inc. above	—	5.00	9.00	35.00	50.00
1907 Straight 7	18,920,000	—	5.00	9.00	25.00	28.50
1907 Curved 7	14,841,000	—	5.25	9.00	25.00	32.00
1908	488,000	—	80.00	190	545	650
1912	3,736,000	—	11.00	14.00	45.00	60.00
1913/07	10,510,000	—	40.00	90.00	240	275
1913/2	Inc. above	—	20.00	27.50	65.00	85.00
1913	Inc. above	—	5.50	8.50	27.50	35.00
1914	7,710,000	—	6.75	13.50	32.00	45.00
1916 Narrow date	480,000	—	60.00	85.00	200	290
1916 Wide date	Inc. above	—	60.00	85.00	200	290
1917	37,112,000	—	6.00	9.50	20.00	22.50
1918	1,320,000	—	70.00	135	250	335

KM# 446 50 CENTAVOS

9.0625 g., 0.8000 Silver 0.2331 oz. ASW, 27 mm. **Obv:** National arms **Rev:** Value and date within 3/4 wreath with Liberty cap above **Note:** Mint mark Mo. Reduced size.

Date	Mintage	F	VF	XF	Unc	BU
1918/7	2,760,000	—	525	675	1,250	—
1918	Inc. above	—	17.50	55.00	300	385
1919	29,670,000	—	9.50	22.50	95.00	125

KM# 447 50 CENTAVOS

8.3333 g., 0.7200 Silver 0.1929 oz. ASW, 27 mm. **Obv:** National arms **Rev:** Value and date within 3/4 wreath with Liberty cap above **Note:** Mint mark Mo.

Date	Mintage	F	VF	XF	Unc	BU
1919	10,200,000	—	10.00	20.00	90.00	110
1920	27,166,000	—	8.00	14.00	70.00	80.00
1921	21,864,000	—	8.00	14.00	85.00	100
1925	3,280,000	—	17.50	30.00	125	160
1937	20,000,000	—	4.25	5.50	7.50	8.50
1938	100,000	—	50.00	85.00	225	300
1939	10,440,000	—	6.00	8.00	15.00	18.50
1942	800,000	—	6.00	9.00	16.00	20.00
1943	41,512,000	—	3.25	4.25	5.50	6.50
1944	55,806,000	—	3.25	4.25	5.50	6.50
1945	56,766,000	—	3.25	4.25	5.50	6.50

KM# 448 50 CENTAVOS

7.9730 g., 0.4200 Silver 0.1077 oz. ASW, 27 mm. **Obv:** National arms **Rev:** Value and date within 3/4 wreath with Liberty cap above **Note:** Mint mark Mo.

Date	Mintage	F	VF	XF	Unc	BU
1935	70,800,000	—	2.50	3.25	5.50	7.00

KM# 449 50 CENTAVOS

6.6600 g., 0.3000 Silver 0.0642 oz. ASW, 26 mm. **Obv:** National arms, eagle left **Rev:** Head with head covering right **Note:** Mint mark Mo.

Date	Mintage	F	VF	XF	Unc	BU
1950	13,570,000	—	1.50	1.85	3.00	4.50
1951	3,650,000	—	2.00	2.50	3.75	5.75

KM# 450 50 CENTAVOS

14.0000 g., Bronze, 33 mm. **Obv:** National arms, eagle left **Rev:** Head with headdress left **Note:** Mint mark Mo.

Date	Mintage	F	VF	XF	Unc	BU
1955	3,502,000	—	1.50	3.00	29.00	35.00
1956	34,643,000	—	0.75	1.50	3.75	4.50
1957	9,675,000	—	1.00	2.00	6.50	7.50
1959	4,540,000	—	0.50	0.75	2.00	2.75

KM# 451 50 CENTAVOS

6.5000 g., Copper-Nickel, 25 mm. **Obv:** National arms, eagle left **Rev:** Head with headdress left

Date	Mintage	F	VF	XF	Unc	BU
1964	43,806,000	—	0.15	0.20	0.40	0.60
1965	14,326,000	—	0.20	0.25	0.45	0.65
1966	1,726,000	—	0.20	0.40	1.30	1.75
1967	55,144,000	—	0.20	0.30	0.65	1.00
1968	80,438,000	—	0.15	0.30	0.65	0.90
1969	87,640,000	—	0.20	0.35	0.80	1.00

KM# 452 50 CENTAVOS

6.5000 g., Copper-Nickel, 25 mm. **Obv:** National arms, eagle left **Rev:** Head with headdress left **Note:** Coins dated 1975 and 1976 exist with and without dots in centers of three circles on plumage on reverse. Edge varieties exist.

Date	Mintage	F	VF	XF	Unc	BU
1970	76,236,000	—	0.15	0.20	0.80	1.00
1971	125,288,000	—	0.15	0.20	0.90	1.30
1972	16,000,000	—	1.25	2.00	3.00	4.75
1975 Dots	177,958,000	—	0.60	1.25	3.50	6.00
1975 No dots	Inc. above	—	0.15	0.20	0.75	1.00
1976 Dots	37,480,000	—	0.75	1.25	5.00	6.00
1976 No dots	Inc. above	—	0.15	0.20	0.50	0.75
1977	12,410,000	—	6.50	10.00	32.50	42.50
1978	85,400,000	—	0.15	0.25	0.50	0.75
1979 Round 2nd 9 in date	229,000,000	—	0.15	0.25	0.50	0.65
1979 Square 9's in date	Inc. above	—	0.20	0.40	1.60	2.00
1980 Narrow date, square 9	89,978,000	—	0.45	0.75	1.75	2.50
1980 Wide date, round 9	178,188,000	—	0.20	0.25	1.00	1.15
1981 Rectangular 9, narrow date	142,212,000	—	0.50	0.75	1.75	2.50
1981 Round 9, wide date	Inc. above	—	0.30	0.50	1.25	1.75
1982	45,474,000	—	0.20	0.40	1.00	1.25
1983	90,318,000	—	0.50	0.75	2.00	2.50
1983 Proof	998	Value: 35.00				

KM# 492 50 CENTAVOS

Stainless Steel, 22 mm. **Subject:** Palenque Culture **Obv:** National arms, eagle left **Rev:** Head with headdress 3/4 left

Date	Mintage	F	VF	XF	Unc	BU
1983	99,540,000	—	—	0.30	1.50	2.50
1983 Proof	53	Value: 195				

KM# 453 PESO

27.0700 g., 0.9030 Silver 0.7859 oz. ASW, 39 mm. **Subject:** Caballito **Obv:** National arms **Rev:** Horse and rider facing left among sun rays **Designer:** Charles Pillet **Note:** Mint mark Mo.

Date	Mintage	F	VF	XF	Unc	BU
1910	3,814,000	—	45.00	50.00	160	250
1911	1,227,000	—	45.00	75.00	200	275
Note: Long lower left ray on reverse						
1911	Inc. above	—	145	210	650	800
Note: Short lower left ray on reverse						
1912	322,000	—	100	210	365	500
1913/2	2,880,000	—	45.00	75.00	270	400
1913	Inc. above	—	45.00	70.00	175	250
Note: 1913 coins exist with even and unevenly spaced date						
1914	120,000	—	600	950	2,800	—

KM# 454 PESO

18.1300 g., 0.8000 Silver 0.4663 oz. ASW, 34 mm. **Obv:** National arms **Rev:** Value and date within 3/4 wreath with Liberty cap above **Note:** Mint mark Mo.

Date	Mintage	F	VF	XF	Unc	BU
1918	3,050,000	—	35.00	125	1,350	2,100
1919	6,151,000	—	20.00	50.00	900	1,600

KM# 455 PESO

16.6600 g., 0.7200 Silver 0.3856 oz. ASW, 34 mm. **Obv:** National arms **Rev:** Value and date within 3/4 wreath with Liberty cap above **Note:** Mint mark Mo.

Date	Mintage	F	VF	XF	Unc	BU
1920/10	8,830,000	—	50.00	90.00	325	—
1920	Inc. above	—	8.00	25.00	185	300
1921	5,480,000	—	8.00	25.00	155	200
1922	33,620,000	—	BV	6.00	20.00	26.00
1923	35,280,000	—	BV	6.00	20.00	28.00
1924	33,060,000	—	BV	6.00	20.00	26.00
1925	9,160,000	—	4.50	10.00	60.00	75.00
1926	28,840,000	—	BV	6.00	20.00	25.00
1927	5,060,000	—	7.00	10.00	70.00	85.00
1932 Open 9	50,770,000	—	—	BV	6.00	7.50
1932 Closed 9	Inc. above	—	—	BV	6.00	7.50
1933/2	43,920,000	—	15.00	25.00	85.00	—
1933	Inc. above	—	—	BV	6.50	8.50
1934	22,070,000	—	—	BV	8.00	10.00
1935	8,050,000	—	BV	6.00	11.50	13.50
1938	30,000,000	—	—	BV	6.00	7.50
1940	20,000,000	—	—	BV	6.50	8.00
1943	47,662,000	—	—	BV	5.75	6.50
1944	39,522,000	—	—	BV	6.00	7.00
1945	37,300,000	—	—	BV	6.00	7.00

KM# 456 PESO

14.0000 g., 0.5000 Silver 0.2250 oz. ASW, 32 mm. **Obv:** National arms, eagle left **Rev:** Head with headcovering right **Note:** Mint mark Mo.

Date	Mintage	F	VF	XF	Unc	BU
1947	61,460,000	—	BV	3.50	4.50	5.50
1948	22,915,000	—	3.50	4.50	5.50	6.50
1949	4,000,000	—	—	1,200	1,600	2,500
Note: Not released for circulation						
1949 Proof	—	Value: 4,000				

KM# 457 PESO

13.3300 g., 0.3000 Silver 0.1286 oz. ASW, 32 mm. **Obv:** National arms, eagle left **Rev:** Armored bust 3/4 left **Note:** Mint mark Mo.

Date	Mintage	F	VF	XF	Unc	BU
1950	3,287,000	—	2.50	4.00	7.00	8.50

KM# 458 PESO

16.0000 g., 0.1000 Silver 0.0514 oz. ASW, 34.5 mm. **Subject:** 100th Anniversary of Constitution **Obv:** National arms, eagle left within wreath **Obv. Designer:** Manuel L. Negrete **Rev:** Head left **Edge Lettering:** INDEPENDENCIA Y LIBERTAD **Note:** Mint mark Mo.

Date	Mintage	F	VF	XF	Unc	BU
1957	500,000	—	3.50	5.00	12.50	15.00

KM# 459 PESO

16.0000 g., 0.1000 Silver 0.0514 oz. ASW, 34.5 mm. **Obv:** National arms, eagle left within wreath **Rev:** Armored bust right within wreath **Edge Lettering:** INDEPENDENCIA Y LIBERTAD **Note:** Mint mark Mo.

Date	Mintage	F	VF	XF	Unc	BU
1957	28,273,000	—	0.75	1.00	2.50	10.00
1958	41,899,000	—	BV	0.80	1.65	2.00
1959	27,369,000	—	1.25	2.00	5.50	8.00
1960	26,259,000	—	0.75	1.10	3.25	4.50
1961	52,601,000	—	BV	0.90	2.25	3.00
1962	61,094,000	—	BV	0.80	1.75	2.25
1963	26,394,000	—	BV	0.80	1.75	2.00
1964	15,615,000	—	BV	0.80	2.00	2.40
1965	5,004,000	—	—	0.80	1.85	2.00
1966	30,998,000	—	—	0.75	1.35	1.85
1967	9,308,000	—	—	0.85	2.75	3.50

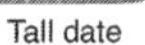

Tall date

Short date

KM# 460 PESO

9.0000 g., Copper-Nickel, 29 mm. **Obv:** National arms, eagle left **Rev:** Head left

Date	Mintage	F	VF	XF	Unc	BU
1970 Narrow date	102,715,000	—	0.25	0.35	0.65	0.80
1970 Wide date	Inc. above	—	1.25	2.50	7.50	9.00
1971	426,222,000	—	0.20	0.25	0.55	0.75
1972	120,000,000	—	0.20	0.25	0.40	0.65
1974	63,700,000	—	0.20	0.25	0.65	0.90
1975 Tall narrow date	205,979,000	—	0.25	0.45	1.00	1.35
1975 Short wide date	Inc. above	—	0.30	0.40	0.75	1.00
1976	94,489,000	—	0.15	0.20	0.50	0.75
1977 Thick date close to rim	94,364,000	—	0.25	0.45	1.00	1.25
1977 Thin date, space between sideburns and collar	Inc. above	—	1.00	2.00	6.50	13.50
1978 Closed 8	208,300,000	—	0.20	0.30	1.00	1.50
1978 Open 8	55,140,000	—	0.75	1.75	12.00	15.00
1979 Thin date	117,884,000	—	0.20	0.30	1.15	1.50
1979 Thick date	Inc. above	—	0.20	0.30	1.25	1.75
1980 Closed 8	318,800,000	—	0.25	0.35	1.00	1.25
1980 Open 8	23,865,000	—	0.75	1.50	8.00	12.00
1981 Closed 8	413,349,000	—	0.20	0.30	0.75	0.90
1981 Open 8	58,616,000	—	0.50	1.25	6.50	8.00
1982 Closed 8	235,000,000	—	0.25	0.75	2.25	2.50
1982 Open 8	—	—	0.75	1.50	8.00	12.00
1983 Wide date	100,000,000	—	0.30	0.45	3.00	3.50
1983 Narrow date	Inc. above	—	0.30	0.45	3.00	3.50
1983 Proof	1,051,000	Value: 38.00				

KM# 496 PESO

Stainless Steel, 24.5 mm. **Obv:** National arms, eagle left **Rev:** Armored bust right

Date	Mintage	F	VF	XF	Unc	BU
1984	722,802,000	—	0.10	0.25	0.65	1.00
1985	985,000,000	—	0.10	0.25	0.50	0.75
1986	740,000,000	—	0.10	0.25	0.50	0.75
1987	250,000,000	—	—	0.25	0.50	0.80
1987 Proof; 2 known	—	Value: 1,000				

KM# 461 2 PESOS

1.6666 g., 0.9000 Gold 0.0482 oz. AGW, 13 mm. **Obv:** National arms **Rev:** Date above value within wreath **Note:** Mint mark Mo.

Date	Mintage	F	VF	XF	Unc	BU
1919	1,670,000	—	BV	47.50	65.00	—
1920/10	—	BV	47.50	55.00	100	—
1920	4,282,000	—	BV	47.50	50.00	—
1944	10,000	BV	47.50	50.00	70.00	—
1945	Est. 140,000	—	—	—	BV+20%	—
1946	168,000	BV	47.50	50.00	100	—
1947	25,000	BV	47.50	50.00	75.00	—
1948 No specimens known	45,000	—	—	—	—	—

Note: During 1951-1972 a total of 4,590,493 pieces were restruck, most likely dated 1945. In 1996 matte restrikes were produced

KM# 462 2 PESOS

26.6667 g., 0.9000 Silver 0.7716 oz. ASW, 39 mm. **Subject:** Centennial of Independence **Obv:** National arms, eagle left within wreath **Rev:** Winged Victory **Designer:** Emilio del Moral **Note:** Mint mark Mo.

Date	Mintage	F	VF	XF	Unc	BU
1921	1,278,000	—	40.00	55.00	325	450

KM# 463 2-1/2 PESOS

2.0833 g., 0.9000 Gold 0.0603 oz. AGW, 15.5 mm. **Obv:** National arms **Rev:** Miguel Hidalgo y Costilla **Note:** Mint mark Mo.

Date	Mintage	F	VF	XF	Unc	BU
1918	1,704,000	—	BV	60.00	80.00	—
1919	984,000	—	BV	60.00	80.00	—
1920/10	607,000	—	BV	60.00	130	—
1920	Inc. above	—	BV	60.00	65.00	—
1944	20,000	—	BV	60.00	65.00	—
1945	Est. 180,000	—	—	—	BV+18%	—
1946	163,000	—	BV	60.00	65.00	—
1947	24,000	200	265	325	500	—
1948	63,000	—	BV	60.00	70.00	—

Note: During 1951-1972 a total of 5,025,087 pieces were restruck, most likely dated 1945. In 1996 matte restrikes were produced

KM# 464 5 PESOS

4.1666 g., 0.9000 Gold 0.1206 oz. AGW, 19 mm. **Obv:** National arms **Rev:** Miguel Hidalgo y Costilla **Note:** Mint mark Mo.

Date	Mintage	F	VF	XF	Unc	BU
1905	18,000	120	175	245	600	—
1906	4,638,000	—	—	BV	115	—
1907/6	—	—	—	—	—	—
1907	1,088,000	—	—	BV	115	—
1910	100,000	—	—	BV	150	—
1918/7	609,000	—	—	BV	200	—
1918	Inc. above	—	—	BV	115	—
1919	506,000	—	—	BV	115	—
1920	2,385,000	—	—	BV	115	—
1955	Est. 48,000	—	—	—	BV+12%	—

Note: During 1955-1972 a total of 1,767,645 pieces were restruck, most likely dated 1955. In 1996 matte restrikes were produced

KM# 465 5 PESOS

30.0000 g., 0.9000 Silver 0.8680 oz. ASW, 40 mm. **Obv:** National arms, eagle left **Rev:** Head with headdress left **Note:** Mint mark Mo.

Date	Mintage	F	VF	XF	Unc	BU
1947	5,110,000	—	—	BV	12.75	14.50
1948	26,740,000	—	—	BV	12.50	13.50

KM# 466 5 PESOS

27.7800 g., 0.7200 Silver 0.6430 oz. ASW, 40 mm. **Subject:** Opening of Southern Railroad **Obv:** National arms, eagle left **Rev:** Radiant sun flanked by palm trees above train **Edge Lettering:** COMERCIO - AGRICULTURA - INDUSTRIA **Designer:** Manuel L. Negrete **Note:** Mint mark Mo.

Date	Mintage	F	VF	XF	Unc	BU
1950	200,000	—	22.50	40.00	50.00	55.00

Note: It is recorded that 100,000 pieces were melted to be used for the 1968 Mexican Olympic 25 Pesos

KM# 467 5 PESOS

27.7800 g., 0.7200 Silver 0.6430 oz. ASW, 40 mm. **Obv:** National arms, eagle left **Rev:** Head left within wreath **Edge Lettering:** COMERCIO - AGRICULTURA - INDUSTRIA **Note:** Mint mark Mo.

Date	Mintage	F	VF	XF	Unc	BU
1951	4,958,000	—	—	BV	10.00	12.00
1952	9,595,000	—	—	BV	9.50	11.00
1953	20,376,000	—	—	BV	9.50	11.00
1954	30,000	—	30.00	60.00	70.00	85.00

KM# 468 5 PESOS

27.7800 g., 0.7200 Silver 0.6430 oz. ASW, 40 mm. **Subject:** Bicentennial of Hidalgo's Birth **Obv:** National arms, eagle left **Rev:** Half-length figure facing to right of building and dates **Edge Lettering:** COMERCIO - AGRICULTURA - INDUSTRIA **Designer:** Manuel L. Negrete **Note:** Mint mark Mo.

Date	Mintage	F	VF	XF	Unc	BU
1953	1,000,000	—	BV	9.50	11.00	13.50

KM# 469 5 PESOS

18.0500 g., 0.7200 Silver 0.4178 oz. ASW, 36 mm. **Obv:** National arms, eagle left **Rev:** Head left **Note:** Mint mark Mo.

Date	Mintage	F	VF	XF	Unc	BU
1955	4,271,000	—	BV	6.25	7.00	8.50
1956	4,596,000	—	BV	6.25	7.00	8.50
1957	3,464,000	—	BV	6.25	7.00	8.50

KM# 470 5 PESOS

18.0500 g., 0.7200 Silver 0.4178 oz. ASW, 36 mm. **Subject:** 100th Anniversary of Constitution **Obv:** National arms, eagle left **Rev:** Head left **Edge Lettering:** INDEPENDENCIA Y LIBERTAD **Designer:** Manuel L. Negrete **Note:** Mint mark Mo.

Date	Mintage	F	VF	XF	Unc	BU
1957	200,000	—	6.50	7.50	13.50	15.50

KM# 471 5 PESOS

18.0500 g., 0.7200 Silver 0.4178 oz. ASW, 36 mm. **Subject:** Centennial of Carranza's Birth **Obv:** National arms, eagle left **Rev:** Head left **Edge:** Plain **Designer:** Manuel L. Negrete **Note:** Mint mark Mo.

Date	Mintage	F	VF	XF	Unc	BU
1959	1,000,000	—	—	BV	7.00	9.00

Small date   Large date

KM# 472 5 PESOS

14.0000 g., Copper-Nickel, 33 mm. **Obv:** National arms, eagle left **Rev:** Armored bust right **Edge Lettering:** INDEPENDENCIA Y LIBERTAD **Note:** Small date, large date varieties.

Date	Mintage	F	VF	XF	Unc	BU
1971	28,457,000	—	0.50	0.95	2.50	3.25
1972	75,000,000	—	0.60	1.25	2.00	2.50
1973	19,405,000	—	1.25	2.00	4.50	5.50
1974	34,500,000	—	0.50	0.80	1.75	2.25
1976 Small date	26,121,000	—	0.75	1.45	3.25	4.00
1976 Large date	121,550,000	—	0.35	0.50	1.50	1.75
1977	102,000,000	—	0.35	0.50	1.50	1.75
1978	25,700,000	—	1.00	1.50	4.50	6.25

KM# 485 5 PESOS

Copper-Nickel, 27 mm. **Subject:** Quetzalcoatl **Obv:** National arms, eagle left **Rev:** Native sculpture to lower right of value and dollar sign **Edge Lettering:** LIBERTAD Y INDEPENDENCIA **Note:** Inverted and normal edge legend varieties exist for the 1980 and 1981 dates.

Date	Mintage	F	VF	XF	Unc	BU
1980	266,899,999	—	0.25	0.50	1.75	2.25
1981	30,500,000	—	0.45	0.65	2.75	3.25
1982	20,000,000	—	1.50	2.35	4.25	5.25
1982 Proof	1,051	Value: 18.00				
1983 Proof; 7 known	—	Value: 1,200				
1984	16,300,000	—	1.25	2.00	4.75	6.00
1985	76,900,000	—	2.00	3.25	4.25	5.00

KM# 502 5 PESOS

Brass, 17 mm. **Subject:** Quetzalcoatl **Obv:** National arms, eagle left **Rev:** Date and value **Note:** Circulation coinage.

Date	Mintage	F	VF	XF	Unc	BU
1985	30,000,000	—	—	0.15	0.35	0.50
1987	81,900,000	—	8.00	9.50	12.50	15.00
1988	76,600,000	—	—	0.10	0.25	0.35
1988 Proof; 2 known	—	Value: 600				

KM# 473 10 PESOS

8.3333 g., 0.9000 Gold 0.2411 oz. AGW, 22.5 mm. **Obv:** National arms **Rev:** Miguel Hidalgo y Costilla **Note:** Mint mark Mo.

Date	Mintage	F	VF	XF	Unc	BU
1905	39,000	—	BV	170	225	—
1906	2,949,000	—	BV	165	185	—
1907	1,589,000	—	BV	165	185	—
1908	890,000	—	BV	165	185	—
1910	451,000	—	BV	165	185	—
1916	26,000	—	BV	175	350	—
1917	1,967,000	—	BV	165	185	—
1919	266,000	—	BV	165	200	—
1920	12,000	—	BV	425	700	—
1959	Est. 50,000	—	—	—	BV+7%	—

Note: *During 1961-1972 a total of 954,983 pieces were restruck, most likely dated 1959. In 1996 matte re-strikes were produced

KM# 474 10 PESOS

28.8800 g., 0.9000 Silver 0.8356 oz. ASW, 40 mm. **Obv:** National arms **Rev:** Head left **Note:** Mint mark Mo.

Date	Mintage	F	VF	XF	Unc	BU
1955	585,000	—	—	BV	12.50	14.50
1956	3,535,000	—	—	BV	12.25	13.50

KM# 475 10 PESOS
28.8800 g., 0.9000 Silver 0.8356 oz. ASW, 40 mm. **Subject:** 100th Anniversary of Constitution **Obv:** National arms, eagle left **Rev:** Head left **Edge Lettering:** INDEPENDENCIA Y LIBERTAD **Designer:** Manuel L. Negrete **Note:** Mint mark Mo.

Date	Mintage	F	VF	XF	Unc	BU
1957	100,000	—	13.50	27.50	45.00	50.00

KM# 476 10 PESOS
28.8800 g., 0.9000 Silver 0.8356 oz. ASW, 40 mm. **Subject:** 150th Anniversary - War of Independence **Obv:** National arms, eagle left **Rev:** Conjoined busts facing flanked by dates **Designer:** Manuel L. Negrete **Note:** Mint mark Mo.

Date	Mintage	F	VF	XF	Unc	BU
1960	1,000,000	—	—	BV	12.50	15.00

KM# 477.1 10 PESOS
Copper-Nickel, 30.5 mm. **Obv:** National arms, eagle left **Rev:** Miguel Hidalgo y Costilla **Shape:** 7-sided **Note:** Thin flan - 1.6mm

Date	Mintage	F	VF	XF	Unc	BU
1974	3,900,000	—	0.50	1.00	3.00	4.00
1974 Proof	—	Value: 625				
1975	1,000,000	—	2.25	3.25	7.50	8.50
1976	74,500,000	—	0.25	0.75	1.75	2.25
1977	79,620,000	—	0.50	1.00	2.00	3.00

KM# 477.2 10 PESOS
Copper-Nickel, 30.5 mm. **Obv:** National arms, eagle left **Rev:** Head left **Shape:** 7-sided **Note:** Thick flan - 2.3mm

Date	Mintage	F	VF	XF	Unc	BU
1978	124,850,000	—	0.50	0.75	2.50	2.75
1979	57,200,000	—	0.50	0.75	2.25	2.50
1980	55,200,000	—	0.50	0.75	2.50	3.75
1981	222,768,000	—	0.40	0.60	2.25	2.65
1982	151,770,000	—	0.50	0.80	2.50	3.50
1982 Proof	1,051	Value: 40.00				
1983 Proof; 3 known	—	Value: 1,800				
1985	58,000,000	—	1.25	1.75	5.75	7.50

KM# 512 10 PESOS
3.8400 g., Stainless Steel, 19 mm. **Obv:** National arms, eagle left **Rev:** Head facing with diagonal value at left **Note:** Date varieties exist.

Date	Mintage	F	VF	XF	Unc	BU
1985	257,000,000	—	—	0.15	0.50	0.75
1986	392,000,000	—	—	0.15	0.50	1.50
1987	305,000,000	—	—	0.15	0.35	0.50
1988	500,300,000	—	—	0.15	0.25	0.35
1989	—	—	0.20	0.25	0.75	1.50
1990	—	—	—	0.25	0.75	1.25
1990 Proof; 2 known	—	Value: 550				

KM# 478 20 PESOS
16.6666 g., 0.9000 Gold 0.4822 oz. AGW, 27.5 mm. **Obv:** National arms, eagle left **Rev:** Aztec Sunstone with denomination below **Edge:** Lettered **Edge Lettering:** INDEPEDENCIA Y LIBERTAD **Note:** Mint mark Mo.

Date	Mintage	F	VF	XF	Unc	BU
1917	852,000	—	—	BV	450	—
1918	2,831,000	—	—	BV	450	—
1919	1,094,000	—	—	BV	450	—
1920/10	462,000	—	—	BV	450	—
1920	Inc. above	—	—	BV	450	—
1921/11	922,000	—	—	BV	450	—
1921/10	—	—	—	—	—	—
1921	Inc. above	—	—	BV	450	—
1959	Est. 13,000	—	—	—	—	—

Note: During 1960-1971 a total of 1,158,414 pieces were restruck, most likely dated 1959. In 1996 matte re-strikes were produced

KM# 486 20 PESOS
Copper-Nickel, 32 mm. **Obv:** National arms, eagle left **Rev:** Figure with headdress facing left within circle

Date	Mintage	F	VF	XF	Unc	BU
1980	84,900,000	—	0.50	0.85	2.25	3.00
1981	250,573,000	—	0.60	0.80	2.25	3.25
1982	236,892,000	—	1.00	1.75	2.50	3.50
1982 Proof	1,051	Value: 45.00				
1983 Proof; 3 known	—	Value: 575				
1984	55,000,000	—	1.00	1.50	2.50	4.75

KM# 508 20 PESOS
6.0000 g., Brass, 21 mm. **Obv:** National arms, eagle left **Rev:** Bust facing with diagonal value at left

Date	Mintage	F	VF	XF	Unc	BU
1985 Wide date	25,000,000	—	0.10	0.20	1.00	1.25
1985 Narrow date	Inc. above	—	0.10	0.25	1.50	2.00
1986	10,000,000	—	1.00	1.75	5.00	5.50
1988	355,200,000	—	0.10	0.20	0.45	0.75
1989	—	—	0.15	0.30	1.50	2.00
1990	—	—	0.15	0.30	1.50	2.50
1990 Proof; 3 known	—	Value: 575				

Snake's tongue straight

KM# 479.1 25 PESOS
22.5000 g., 0.7200 Silver 0.5208 oz. ASW, 38 mm. **Obv:** National arms, eagle left **Rev:** Olympic rings below dancing native left, numeral design in background **Designer:** Lorenzo Rafael **Note:** Type I, Rings aligned.

Date	Mintage	F	VF	XF	Unc	BU
1968	27,182,000	—	—	BV	7.50	8.00

KM# 479.2 25 PESOS
22.5000 g., 0.7200 Silver 0.5208 oz. ASW, 38 mm. **Subject:** Summer Olympics - Mexico City **Obv:** National arms, eagle left **Rev:** Olympic rings below dancing native left, numeral design in background **Note:** Type II, center ring low.

Date	Mintage	F	VF	XF	Unc	BU
1968	Inc. above	—	BV	7.50	8.50	10.00

Snake's tongue curved

KM# 479.3 25 PESOS
22.5000 g., 0.7200 Silver 0.5208 oz. ASW, 38 mm. **Subject:** Summer Olympics - Mexico City **Obv:** National arms, eagle left **Rev:** Olympic rings below dancing native left, numeral design in background **Note:** Snake with long curved or normal tongue. Type III, center rings low.

Date	Mintage	F	VF	XF	Unc	BU
1968	Inc. above	—	BV	7.50	9.50	11.00

KM# 480 25 PESOS
22.5000 g., 0.7200 Silver 0.5208 oz. ASW, 38 mm. **Obv:** National arms, eagle left **Rev:** Bust facing

Date	Mintage	F	VF	XF	Unc	BU
1972	2,000,000	—	—	BV	7.50	8.50

KM# 481 50 PESOS
41.6666 g., 0.9000 Gold 1.2056 oz. AGW, 37 mm. **Subject:** Centennial of Independence **Obv:** National arms **Rev:** Winged Victory **Edge:** Reeded **Designer:** Emilio del Moral **Note:** During 1949-1972 a total of 3,975,654 pieces were restruck, most likely dated 1947. In 1996 matte restrikes were produced. Mint mark Mo.

Date	Mintage	F	VF	XF	Unc	BU
1921	180,000	—	—	BV	1,075	1,125
1922	463,000	—	—	BV	1,075	1,125
1923	432,000	—	—	BV	1,075	1,125
1924	439,000	—	—	BV	1,075	1,125
1925	716,000	—	—	BV	1,075	1,125
1926	600,000	—	—	BV	1,075	1,125
1927	606,000	—	—	BV	1,075	1,125
1928	538,000	—	—	BV	1,075	1,125
1929	458,000	—	—	BV	1,075	1,125
1930	372,000	—	—	BV	1,075	1,125
1931	137,000	—	—	BV	1,075	1,125
1944	593,000	—	—	BV	1,075	1,125
1945	1,012,000	—	—	BV	1,075	1,125
1946	1,588,000	—	—	BV	1,075	1,125
1947	309,000	—	—	—	BV+3%	—
1947 Specimen	—	—	—	—	—	—

Note: Value, $6,500

KM# 490 50 PESOS
19.8400 g., Copper-Nickel, 35 mm. **Subject:** Coyolxauhqui **Obv:** National arms, eagle left **Rev:** Value to right of artistic designs **Edge:** Reeded **Note:** Doubled die examples of 1982 and 1983 dates exist.

Date	Mintage	F	VF	XF	Unc	BU
1982	222,890,000	—	1.00	2.50	5.00	6.00
1983	45,000,000	—	1.50	3.00	6.00	6.50
1983 Proof	1,051	Value: 40.00				
1984	73,537,000	—	1.00	1.35	3.50	4.00
1984 Proof; 4 known	—	Value: 750				

KM# 495 50 PESOS
Copper-Nickel, 23.5 mm. **Subject:** Benito Juarez **Obv:** National arms, eagle left **Rev:** Bust 1/4 left with diagonal value at left **Edge:** Reeded

Date	Mintage	F	VF	XF	Unc	BU
1984	94,216,000	—	0.65	1.25	2.70	3.00
1985	296,000,000	—	0.25	0.45	1.25	2.00
1986	50,000,000	—	6.00	10.00	12.00	14.00
1987	210,000,000	—	0.25	0.45	1.00	1.25
1988	80,200,000	—	6.25	9.00	13.50	15.50

KM# 495a 50 PESOS
Stainless Steel, 23.5 mm. **Subject:** Benito Juarez **Obv:** National arms, eagle left **Rev:** Bust 1/4 left with diagonal value at left **Edge:** Plain

Date	Mintage	F	VF	XF	Unc	BU
1988	353,300,000	—	—	0.20	1.25	1.75
1990	—	—	—	0.30	1.00	2.00
1992	—	—	—	0.25	1.00	2.75

Low 7's

KM# 483.1 100 PESOS
27.7700 g., 0.7200 Silver 0.6428 oz. ASW, 39 mm. **Obv:** National arms, eagle left **Rev:** Bust facing, sloping right shoulder, round left shoulder with no clothing folds **Edge:** Reeded

Date	Mintage	F	VF	XF	Unc	BU
1977 Low 7's	5,225,000	—	—	BV	9.50	11.50
1977 High 7's	Inc. above	—	—	BV	9.50	12.00

High 7's

KM# 483.2 100 PESOS
27.7700 g., 0.7200 Silver 0.6428 oz. ASW, 39 mm. **Obv:** National arms, eagle left **Rev:** Bust facing, higher right shoulder, left shoulder with clothing folds. **Note:** Mintage inc. KM#483.1

Date	Mintage	F	VF	XF	Unc	BU
1977 Date in line	—	—	—	BV	9.25	10.00
1978	9,879,000	—	—	BV	9.50	11.50
1979	784,000	—	—	BV	9.50	11.50
1979 Proof	—	Value: 650				

KM# 493 100 PESOS
Aluminum-Bronze, 26.5 mm. **Obv:** National arms, eagle left **Rev:** Head 1/4 right with diagonal value at right

Date	Mintage	F	VF	XF	Unc	BU
1984	227,809,000	—	0.45	0.60	2.50	4.00
1985	377,423,000	—	0.30	0.50	2.00	3.00
1986	43,000,000	—	1.00	2.50	4.75	7.50
1987	165,000,000	—	0.60	1.25	2.25	3.00
1988	433,100,000	—	0.30	0.50	2.00	2.75
1989	—	—	0.35	0.65	2.00	2.75
1990	—	—	0.15	0.40	1.50	2.50
1990 Proof; 1 known	—	Value: 650				
1991	—	—	0.15	0.25	1.00	2.50
1992	—	—	0.30	0.75	1.75	3.00

KM# 509 200 PESOS
Copper-Nickel, 29.5 mm. **Subject:** 175th Anniversary of Independence **Obv:** National arms, eagle left **Rev:** Conjoined busts left

Date	Mintage	F	VF	XF	Unc	BU
1985	75,000,000	—	—	0.25	3.00	4.00

KM# 510 200 PESOS

Copper-Nickel, 29.5 mm. **Subject:** 75th Anniversary of 1910 Revolution **Obv:** National arms, eagle left **Rev:** Conjoined heads left below building

Date	Mintage	F	VF	XF	Unc	BU
1985	98,590,000	—	—	0.25	3.25	4.50

KM# 525 200 PESOS

Copper-Nickel, 29.5 mm. **Subject:** 1986 World Cup Soccer Games **Obv:** National arms, eagle left **Rev:** Soccer players **Edge:** Reeded

Date	Mintage	F	VF	XF	Unc	BU
1986	50,000,000	—	—	1.00	3.50	4.50

KM# 529 500 PESOS

Copper-Nickel, 28.5 mm. **Obv:** National arms, eagle left **Rev:** Head 1/4 right

Date	Mintage	F	VF	XF	Unc	BU
1986	20,000,000	—	—	1.00	3.25	3.50
1987	180,000,000	—	—	0.75	2.25	2.50
1988	230,000,000	—	—	0.50	2.25	2.50
1988 Proof; 2 known	—	Value: 650				
1989	—	—	—	0.75	2.25	3.00
1992	—	—	—	1.00	2.25	3.50

KM# 536 1000 PESOS

15.0000 g., Aluminum-Bronze, 30.5 mm. **Obv:** National arms, eagle left **Rev:** Bust 1/4 left with diagonal value at left **Note:** Juana de Asbaje

Date	Mintage	F	VF	XF	Unc	BU
1988	229,300,000	—	0.85	2.00	4.25	5.75
1989	—	—	0.85	2.00	4.25	5.75
1990	—	—	0.85	2.00	4.00	5.50
1990 Proof; 2 known	—	Value: 550				
1991	—	—	1.00	2.00	3.00	7.00
1992	—	—	1.00	2.00	3.00	7.00

KM# 643 1000 PESOS

Aluminum-Bronze, 22 mm. **Obv:** National arms, eagle left **Rev:** Stylized boat and "ATLAN" above denomination **Note:** Unissued type due to currency reform.

Date	Mintage	F	VF	XF	Unc	BU
1991Mo	—	—	—	—	15.00	—

REFORM COINAGE

1 New Peso = 1000 Old Pesos

KM# 546 5 CENTAVOS

1.5900 g., Stainless Steel, 15.58 mm. **Obv:** National arms **Rev:** Large value **Edge:** Plain

Date	Mintage	F	VF	XF	Unc	BU
1992	136,800,000	—	—	0.15	0.20	0.25
1993	234,000,000	—	—	0.15	0.20	0.25
1994	125,000,000	—	—	0.15	0.20	0.25
1995	195,000,000	—	—	0.15	0.20	0.25
1995 Proof	6,981	Value: 0.50				
1996	104,831,000	—	—	0.15	0.20	0.25
1997	153,675,000	—	—	0.15	0.20	0.25
1998	64,417,000	—	—	0.15	0.20	0.25
1999	9,949,000	—	—	0.15	0.20	0.25
2000Mo	10,871,000	—	—	0.15	0.20	0.25
2001Mo	34,811,000	—	—	0.15	0.20	0.25
2002Mo	14,901,000	—	—	0.15	0.20	0.25

KM# 547 10 CENTAVOS

2.0300 g., Stainless Steel, 17 mm. **Obv:** National arms, eagle left **Rev:** Value

Date	Mintage	F	VF	XF	Unc	BU
1992	121,250,000	—	—	0.20	0.30	0.35
1993	755,000,000	—	—	0.20	0.25	0.30
1994	557,000,000	—	—	0.20	0.25	0.30
1995	560,000,000	—	—	0.20	0.25	0.30
1995 Proof	6,981	Value: 0.50				
1996	594,216,000	—	—	0.20	0.25	0.30
1997	581,622,000	—	—	0.20	0.25	0.30
1998	602,667,000	—	—	0.20	0.25	0.30
1999	488,346,000	—	—	0.20	0.25	0.30
2000	577,546,000	—	—	0.20	0.30	0.35
2001	618,061,000	—	—	0.20	0.25	0.30
2002	463,968,000	—	—	0.20	0.25	0.30
2003Mo	378,938,000	—	—	0.20	0.25	0.30
2004	393,705,000	—	—	0.20	0.25	0.30
2005	488,773,000	—	—	0.20	0.25	0.30
2006	473,104,000	—	—	0.20	0.25	0.30

KM# 548 20 CENTAVOS

Aluminum-Bronze, 19 mm. **Obv:** National arms, eagle left **Rev:** Value and date within 3/4 wreath **Shape:** 12-sided

Date	Mintage	F	VF	XF	Unc	BU
1992	95,000,000	—	—	0.25	0.35	0.40
1993	95,000,000	—	—	0.25	0.35	0.40
1994	105,000,000	—	—	0.25	0.35	0.40
1995	180,000,000	—	—	0.25	0.35	0.40
1995 Proof	6,981	Value: 0.75				
1996	54,896,000	—	—	0.25	0.35	0.40
1997	178,807,000	—	—	0.25	0.35	0.40
1998	223,847,000	—	—	0.25	0.35	0.40
1999	233,753,000	—	—	0.25	0.35	0.40
2000	223,973,000	—	—	0.25	0.35	0.40
2001	234,360,000	—	—	0.25	0.35	0.40
2002Mo	229,256,000	—	—	0.25	0.35	0.40
2003Mo	149,518,000	—	—	0.25	0.35	0.40
2004	174,351,000	—	—	0.25	0.35	0.40
2005	204,444,000	—	—	0.25	0.35	0.40
2006	233,989,000	—	—	0.25	0.35	0.40

KM# 549 50 CENTAVOS

Aluminum-Bronze, 22 mm. **Obv:** National arms, eagle left **Rev:** Value and date within 1/2 designed wreath **Shape:** 12-sided

Date	Mintage	F	VF	XF	Unc	BU
1992	120,150,000	—	—	0.45	0.85	1.00
1993	330,000,000	—	—	0.45	0.75	1.00
1994	100,000,000	—	—	0.45	0.75	1.00
1995	60,000,000	—	—	0.45	0.75	1.00
1995 Proof	6,981	Value: 0.90				
1996	69,956,000	—	—	0.45	0.75	1.00
1997	129,029,000	—	—	0.45	0.75	1.00
1998	223,605,000	—	—	0.45	0.75	1.00
1999	89,516,000	—	—	0.45	0.75	1.00
2000	135,112,000	—	—	0.45	0.75	1.00
2001	199,006,000	—	—	0.45	0.75	1.00
2002	94,552,000	—	—	0.45	0.75	1.00
2003Mo	124,522,000	—	—	0.45	0.75	1.00
2004	154,434,000	—	—	0.45	0.75	1.00
2005	179,304,000	—	—	0.45	0.75	1.00
2006	233,786,000	—	—	0.45	0.75	1.00

KM# 550 NUEVO PESO

3.9400 g., Bi-Metallic Aluminum-Bronze center in Stainless Steel ring, 22 mm. **Obv:** National arms, eagle left **Rev:** Value

Date	Mintage	F	VF	XF	Unc	BU
1992	144,000,000	—	—	0.60	1.50	2.25
1993	329,860,000	—	—	0.60	1.50	2.25
1994	221,000,000	—	—	0.60	1.50	2.25
1995 Small date	125,000,000	—	—	0.60	1.50	2.25
1995 Large date	Inc. above	—	—	0.60	1.50	2.25
1995 Proof	6,981	Value: 2.75				

KM# 603 PESO

3.9500 g., Bi-Metallic Stainless-steel ring in Aluminum Bronze center, 21 mm. **Obv:** National arms, eagle left within circle **Rev:** Value and date within circle **Note:** Similar to KM#550 but without N.

Date	Mintage	F	VF	XF	Unc	BU
1996Mo	169,510,000	—	—	—	1.25	2.25
1997Mo	222,870,000	—	—	—	1.25	2.25
1998Mo	261,942,000	—	—	—	1.25	2.25
1999Mo	99,168,000	—	—	—	1.25	2.25
2000Mo	158,379,000	—	—	—	1.25	2.25
2001Mo	208,576,000	—	—	—	1.25	2.25
2002Mo	119,541,000	—	—	—	1.25	2.25
2003Mo	169,320,000	—	—	—	1.25	2.25
2004	208,611,000	—	—	—	1.25	2.25
2005	253,924,000	—	—	—	1.25	2.25
2006	289,717,000	—	—	—	1.25	2.25

KM# 604 2 PESOS

5.2100 g., Bi-Metallic Aluminum-Bronze center in Stainless Steel ring, 23 mm. **Obv:** National arms, eagle left within circle **Rev:** Value and date within center circle of assorted emblems **Note:** Similar to KM#551, but denomination without N.

Date	Mintage	F	VF	XF	Unc	BU
1996Mo	24,902,000	—	—	—	2.35	2.50
1997Mo	34,560,000	—	—	—	2.35	2.50
1998Mo	104,138,000	—	—	—	2.35	2.50
1999Mo	34,713,000	—	—	—	2.35	2.50
2000Mo	69,322,000	—	—	—	2.35	2.50
2001Mo	74,563,000	—	—	—	2.35	2.50
2002Mo	74,547,000	—	—	—	2.35	2.50
2003Mo	39,814,000	—	—	—	2.35	2.50
2004	89,496,000	—	—	—	2.35	2.50
2005	94,532,000	—	—	—	2.35	2.50
2006	143,919,000	—	—	—	2.35	2.50

KM# 552 5 NUEVO PESOS

Bi-Metallic Aluminum-Bronze center in Stainless Steel ring, 25.5 mm. **Obv:** National arms, eagle left within circle **Rev:** Value and date within circle with bow below

Date	Mintage	F	VF	XF	Unc	BU
1992	70,000,000	—	—	2.00	4.00	4.50
1993	168,240,000	—	—	2.00	4.00	4.50
1994	58,000,000	—	—	2.00	4.00	4.50
1995 Proof	6,981	Value: 25.00				

KM# 605 5 PESOS

Bi-Metallic Aluminum-Bronze center in Stainless Steel ring, 25.5 mm. **Obv:** National arms, eagle left within circle **Rev:** Value within circle **Note:** Similar to KM#552 but denomination without N.

Date	Mintage	F	VF	XF	Unc	BU
1997Mo	39,468,000	—	—	3.00	4.00	5.00
1998Mo	103,729,000	—	—	3.00	4.00	5.00
1999Mo	59,427,000	—	—	3.00	4.00	5.00
2000Mo	20,869,000	—	—	3.00	4.00	5.00
2001Mo	79,169,000	—	—	3.00	4.00	5.00
2002Mo	34,754,000	—	—	3.00	4.00	5.00
2003Mo	54,676,000	—	—	3.00	4.00	5.00
2004	89,518,000	—	—	3.00	4.00	5.00
2005	94,482,000	—	—	3.00	4.00	5.00
2006	89,189,000	—	—	3.00	4.00	5.00

KM# 553 10 NUEVO PESOS

11.1300 g., Bi-Metallic 0.925 Silver center, .1667 oz. ASW within Aluminum-Bronze ring, 27.95 mm. **Obv:** National arms **Obv. Legend:** Estados Unidos Mexicanos **Rev:** Assorted shields within circle **Edge:** Reeded

Date	Mintage	F	VF	XF	Unc	BU
1992	20,000,000	—	—	—	7.50	8.50
1993	47,981,000	—	—	—	7.50	8.50
1994	15,000,000	—	—	—	7.50	8.50
1995	15,000,000	—	—	—	7.50	8.50
1995 Proof	6,981	Value: 15.00				

KM# 616 10 PESOS

10.3500 g., Bi-Metallic Copper-Nickel-Brass center within Brass ring, 27.95 mm. **Obv:** National arms **Obv. Legend:** ESTADOS UNIDOS MEXICANOS **Rev:** Aztec design

Date	Mintage	F	VF	XF	Unc	BU
1997Mo	44,837,000	—	—	—	5.00	6.50
1998Mo	203,735,000	—	—	—	5.00	6.50
1999Mo	29,842,000	—	—	—	5.00	6.50

KM# 636 10 PESOS

10.3500 g., Bi-Metallic Copper-Nickel center in Brass ring, 28 mm. **Series:** Millennium **Obv:** National arms **Obv. Legend:** ESTADOS UNIDOS MEXICANOS **Rev:** Aztec carving **Edge:** Lettered **Edge Lettering:** ANO and date repeated 3 times

Date	Mintage	F	VF	XF	Unc	BU
2000Mo	24,839,000	—	—	—	5.00	6.50
2001Mo	44,768,000	—	—	—	5.00	6.50
2002Mo	44,721,000	—	—	—	5.00	6.50
2004Mo	74,739,000	—	—	—	5.00	6.50
2005Mo	64,635,000	—	—	—	5.00	6.50
2006Mo	84,480,000	—	—	—	5.00	6.50

KM# 561 20 NUEVO PESOS

16.9200 g., Bi-Metallic 0.925 Silver 16.9g, (.2500 oz. ASW) center within Aluminum-Bronze ring, 31.86 mm. **Obv:** National arms **Obv. Legend:** ESTADOS UNIDOS MEXICANOS **Rev:** Head of Hidalgo left within wreath **Edge:** Reeded

Date	Mintage	F	VF	XF	Unc	BU
1993Mo	25,000,000	—	—	—	12.00	15.00
1994Mo	5,000,000	—	—	—	12.00	15.00
1995Mo	5,000,000	—	—	—	12.00	15.00

KM# 571 50 NUEVO PESOS

34.1100 g., Bi-Metallic 0.925 Silver .5000 ASW center within Brass ring, 38.87 mm. **Subject:** Nino Heroes **Obv:** National arms **Obv. Legend:** ESTADOS UNIDOS MEXICANOS **Rev:** Six heads facing with date at upper right, all within circle and 1/2 wreath **Edge:** Reeded

Date	Mintage	F	VF	XF	Unc	BU
1993Mo	2,000,000	—	—	—	25.00	28.00
1994Mo	1,500,000	—	—	—	25.00	28.00
1995Mo	1,500,000	—	—	—	25.00	28.00

KM# 705 100 PESOS

33.7400 g., Bi-Metallic .925 Silver center in Aluminum-Bronze ring, 39 mm. **Subject:** 400th Anniversary of Don Quijote de la Manchia **Obv:** National arms **Obv. Legend:** ESTADOS UNIDOS MEXICANOS **Rev:** Sekeletal figure Horseback with spear galloping right **Edge:** Segmented reeding

Date	Mintage	F	VF	XF	Unc	BU
2005Mo Proof	3,761	Value: 75.00				
2005Mo	726,833	—	—	—	35.00	45.00

KM# 730 100 PESOS

33.8250 g., Bi-Metallic .925 Silver 20.1753g center in Aluminum-Bronze ring, 39.9 mm. **Subject:** Monetary Reform Centennial **Obv:** National arms **Rev:** Radiant Liberty Cap divides date above value within circle **Edge:** Segmented reeding

Date	Mintage	F	VF	XF	Unc	BU
2005Mo	49,716	—	—	—	35.00	45.00

KM# 731 100 PESOS

33.8250 g., Bi-Metallic .925 Silver 20.1753g center in Aluminum-Bronze ring, 39.9 mm. **Subject:** Mexico City Mint's 470th Anniversary **Obv:** National arms **Rev:** Screw press, value and date within circle **Edge:** Segmented reeding

Date	Mintage	F	VF	XF	Unc	BU
2005Mo	49,895	—	—	—	35.00	45.00

KM# 732 100 PESOS

33.8250 g., Bi-Metallic .925 Silver 20.1753g center in Aluminum-Bronze ring, 39.9 mm. **Subject:** Bank of Mexico's 80th

Anniversary **Obv:** National arms **Rev:** Back design of the 1925 hundred peso note **Edge:** Segmented reeding

Date	Mintage	F	VF	XF	Unc	BU
2005Mo	49,712	—	—	—	35.00	45.00

KM# 764 100 PESOS

33.7000 g., Bi-Metallic .925 Silver 20.1753g center in Aluminum-Bronze ring **Subject:** 200th Anniversary Birth of Benito Juarez Garcia **Obv:** National arms **Rev:** Bust 1/4 left within circle

Date	Mintage	F	VF	XF	Unc	BU
2006Mo	49,913	—	—	—	35.00	45.00

REFORM COINAGE

State Commemoratives

KM# 688 100 PESOS

33.9400 g., Bi-Metallic .925 Silver 20.1753g center in Aluminum-Bronze ring, 39.04 mm. **Series:** First **Subject:** 180th Anniversary of Federation **Obv:** National arms **Obv. Legend:** ESTADOS UNIDOS MEXICANOS **Rev:** State arms **Rev. Legend:** ESTADO DE ZACATECAS **Edge:** Segmented reeding

Date	Mintage	F	VF	XF	Unc	BU
2003Mo	244,900	—	—	—	35.00	45.00

KM# 689 100 PESOS

33.9400 g., Bi-Metallic .925 Silver 20.1753g center in Aluminum-Bronze ring, 39.04 mm. **Series:** First **Subject:** 180th Anniversary of Federation **Obv:** National arms **Obv. Legend:** ESTADOS UNIDOS MEXICANOS **Rev:** State arms **Rev. Legend:** ESTADO DE YUCATÁN **Edge:** Segmented reeding

Date	Mintage	F	VF	XF	Unc	BU
2003Mo	235,763	—	—	—	35.00	45.00

KM# 690 100 PESOS

33.9400 g., Bi-Metallic .925 Silver 20.1753g center in Aluminum-Bronze ring, 39.04 mm. **Series:** First **Subject:** 180th Anniversary of Federation **Obv:** National arms **Obv. Legend:** ESTADOS UNIDOS MEXICANOS **Rev:** State arms **Rev. Legend:** ESTADO DE VERACRUZ-LLAVE **Edge:** Segmented reeding

Date	Mintage	F	VF	XF	Unc	BU
2003Mo	248,810	—	—	—	35.00	45.00

KM# 691 100 PESOS

33.9400 g., Bi-Metallic .925 Silver 20.1753g center in Aluminum-Bronze ring, 39.9 mm. **Series:** First **Subject:** 180th Anniversary of Federation **Obv:** National arms **Obv. Legend:** ESTADOS UNIDOS MEXICANOS **Rev:** State arms **Rev. Legend:** ESTADO DE TLAXCALA **Edge:** Segmented reeding

Date	Mintage	F	VF	XF	Unc	BU
2003Mo	248,976	—	—	—	35.00	45.00

KM# 692 100 PESOS

33.9400 g., Bi-Metallic .925 Silver 20.1753g center in Aluminum-Bronze ring, 39.04 mm. **Series:** First **Subject:** 180th Anniversay of Federation **Obv:** National arms **Obv. Legend:** ESTADOS UNIDOS MEXICANOS **Rev:** State arms **Rev. Legend:** ESTADO DE TAMAULIPAS **Edge:** Segmented reeding

Date	Mintage	F	VF	XF	Unc	BU
2004Mo	249,398	—	—	—	35.00	45.00

KM# 693 100 PESOS
33.9400 g., Bi-Metallic .925 Silver 20.1753g center in Aluminum-Bronze ring, 39.04 mm. **Series:** First **Subject:** 180th Anniversary of Federation **Obv:** National arms **Obv. Legend:** ESTADOS UNIDOS MEXICANOS **Rev:** State arms **Rev. Legend:** ESTADO DE TABASCO **Edge:** Segmented reeding

Date	Mintage	F	VF	XF	Unc	BU
2004Mo	249,318	—	—	—	35.00	45.00

KM# 694 100 PESOS
33.9400 g., Bi-Metallic .925 Silver 20.1753g center in Aluminum-Bronze ring, 39.04 mm. **Series:** First **Subject:** 180th Anniversary of Federation **Obv:** National arms **Obv. Legend:** ESTADOS UNIDOS MEXICANOS **Rev:** State arms **Rev. Legend:** ESTADO DE SONORA **Edge:** Segmented reeding

Date	Mintage	F	VF	XF	Unc	BU
2004Mo	249,300	—	—	—	—	30.00

KM# 695 100 PESOS
33.9400 g., Bi-Metallic .925 Silver 20.1753g center in Aluminum-Bronze ring, 39.04 mm. **Series:** First **Subject:** 180th Anniversary of Federation **Obv:** National arms **Obv. Legend:** ESTADOS UNIDOS MEXICANOS **Rev:** State arms **Rev. Legend:** ESTADO DE SINALOA **Edge:** Segmented reeding

Date	Mintage	F	VF	XF	Unc	BU
2004Mo	244,722	—	—	—	35.00	45.00

KM# 803 100 PESOS
33.9400 g., Bi-Metallic .925 Silver 20.1753g center in Aluminum-Bronze ring, 39.04 mm. **Series:** First **Subject:** 180th Anniversary of Federation **Obv:** National arms **Obv. Legend:** ESTADOS UNIDOS MEXICANOS **Rev:** State arms **Rev. Legend:** ESTADO DE SAN LUIS POTOSÍ **Edge:** Segmented reeding

Date	Mintage	F	VF	XF	Unc	BU
2004Mo	249,662	—	—	—	35.00	45.00

KM# 736 100 PESOS
33.9400 g., Bi-Metallic .925 Silver 20.1753g center in Aluminum-Bronze ring, 39.04 mm. **Series:** First **Subject:** 180th Anniversary of Federation **Obv:** National arms **Obv. Legend:** ESTADOS UNIDOS MEXICANOS **Rev:** State arms **Rev. Legend:** ESTADO DE QUINTANA ROO **Edge:** Segmented reeding

Date	Mintage	F	VF	XF	Unc	BU
2004Mo	249,134	—	—	—	35.00	45.00

KM# 734 100 PESOS
33.9400 g., Bi-Metallic .925 Silver 20.1753g center in Aluminum-Bronze ring, 39.04 mm. **Series:** First **Subject:** 180th Anniversary of Federation **Obv:** National arms **Obv. Legend:** ESTADOS UNIDOS MEXICANOS **Rev:** State arms **Rev. Legend:** ESTADO DE QUERÉTARO ARTEAGA **Edge:** Segmented reeding

Date	Mintage	F	VF	XF	Unc	BU
2004Mo	249,263	—	—	—	35.00	45.00

KM# 738 100 PESOS
33.9400 g., Bi-Metallic .925 Silver 20.1753g center in Aluminum-Bronze ring, 39.04 mm. **Series:** First **Subject:** 180th Anniversary of Federation **Obv:** National arms **Obv. Legend:** ESTADOS UNIDOS MEXICANOS **Rev:** State arms **Rev. Legend:** ESTADO DE PUEBLA **Edge:** Segmented reeding

Date	Mintage	F	VF	XF	Unc	BU
2004Mo	248,850	—	—	—	35.00	45.00

KM# 740 100 PESOS
33.9400 g., Bi-Metallic .925 Silver 20.1753g center in Aluminum-Bronze ring, 39.04 mm. **Series:** First **Subject:** 180th

Anniversary of Federation **Obv:** National arms **Obv. Legend:** ESTADOS UNIDOS MEXICANOS **Rev:** State arms **Rev. Legend:** ESTADO DE OAXACA **Edge:** Segmented reeding

Date	Mintage	F	VF	XF	Unc	BU
2004Mo	249,589	—	—	—	35.00	45.00

KM# 742 100 PESOS

33.9400 g., Bi-Metallic .925 Silver 20.1753g center in Aluminum-Bronze ring, 39.04 mm. **Series:** First **Subject:** 180th Anniversary of Federation **Obv:** National arms **Obv. Legend:** ESTADOS UNIDOS MEXICANOS **Rev:** State arms **Rev. Legend:** ESTADO DE NUEVO LEÓN **Edge:** Segmented reeding

Date	Mintage	F	VF	XF	Unc	BU
2004Mo	249,199	—	—	—	35.00	45.00

KM# 744 100 PESOS

33.9400 g., Bi-Metallic .925 Silver 20.1753g center in Aluminum-Bronze ring, 39.04 mm. **Series:** First **Subject:** 180th Anniversary of Federation **Obv:** National arms **Obv. Legend:** ESTADOS UNIDOS MEXICANOS **Rev:** State arms **Rev. Legend:** ESTADO DE NAYARIT **Edge:** Segmented reeding

Date	Mintage	F	VF	XF	Unc	BU
2004Mo	248,305	—	—	—	35.00	45.00

KM# 746 100 PESOS

33.9400 g., Bi-Metallic .925 Silver 20.1753g center in Aluminum-Bronze ring, 39.04 mm. **Series:** First **Subject:** 180th Anniversary of Federation **Obv:** National arms **Obv. Legend:** ESTADOS UNIDOS MEXICANOS **Rev:** State arms **Rev. Legend:** ESTADO DE MORELOS **Edge:** Segmented reeding

Date	Mintage	F	VF	XF	Unc	BU
2004Mo	249,260	—	—	—	35.00	45.00

KM# 804 100 PESOS

33.9400 g., Bi-Metallic o.925 Silver 20.1763g center in Aluminum-Bronze ring, 39.04 mm. **Series:** First **Subject:** 180th Anniversary of Federation **Obv:** National arms **Obv. Legend:** ESTADOS UNIDOS MEXICANOS **Rev:** State arms **Rev. Legend:** ESTADO DE MICHOACÁN DE OCAMPO **Edge:** Segmented reeding

Date	Mintage	F	VF	XF	Unc	BU
2004Mo	249,492	—	—	—	35.00	45.00

KM# 748 100 PESOS

33.9400 g., Bi-Metallic .925 Silver 20.1753g center in Aluminum-Bronze ring, 39.04 mm. **Series:** First **Subject:** 180th

Anniversary of Federation **Obv:** National arms **Obv. Legend:** ESTADOS UNIDOS MEXICANOS **Rev:** State arms **Rev. Legend:** ESTADO DE MÉXICO **Edge:** Segmented reeding

Date	Mintage	F	VF	XF	Unc	BU
2004Mo	249,800	—	—	—	35.00	45.00

KM# 750 100 PESOS

33.9400 g., Bi-Metallic .925 Silver 20.1753g center in Aluminum-Bronze ring, 39.04 mm. **Series:** First **Subject:** 180th Anniversary of Federation **Obv:** National arms **Obv. Legend:** ESTADOS UNIDOS MEXICANOS **Rev:** State arms **Rev. Legend:** ESTADO DE JALISCO **Edge:** Segmented reeding

Date	Mintage	F	VF	XF	Unc	BU
2004Mo	249,115	—	—	—	35.00	45.00

KM# 717 100 PESOS

33.9400 g., Bi-Metallic .925 Silver center in Brass ring, 39.04 mm. **Series:** First **Subject:** 180th Anniversary of Federation **Obv:** National arms **Obv. Legend:** ESTADOS UNIDOS MEXICANOS **Rev:** State arms **Rev. Legend:** ESTADO DE HIDALGO **Edge:** Segmented reeding

Date	Mintage	F	VF	XF	Unc	BU
2005Mo	249,820	—	—	—	35.00	45.00

KM# 716 100 PESOS
33.9400 g., Bi-Metallic .925 Silver center in Brass ring, 39.04 mm. **Series:** First **Subject:** 180th Anniversary of Federation **Obv:** National arms **Obv. Legend:** ESTADOS UNIDOS MEXICANOS **Rev:** State arms **Rev. Legend:** ESTADO DE GUERRERO **Edge:** Segmented reeding

Date	Mintage	F	VF	XF	Unc	BU
2005Mo	248,850	—	—	—	35.00	45.00

KM# 715 100 PESOS
33.9400 g., Bi-Metallic .925 Silver center in Brass ring, 39.04 mm. **Series:** First **Subject:** 180th Anniversary of Federation **Obv:** National arms **Obv. Legend:** ESTADOS UNIDOS MEXICANOS **Rev:** State arms **Rev. Legend:** ESTADO DE GUANAJUATO **Edge:** Segmented reeding

Date	Mintage	F	VF	XF	Unc	BU
2005Mo	249,489	—	—	—	35.00	45.00

KM# 714 100 PESOS
33.9400 g., Bi-Metallic .925 Silver center in Brass ring, 39.04 mm. **Series:** First **Subject:** 180th Anniversary of Federation **Obv:** National arms **Obv. Legend:** ESTADOS UNIDOS MEXICANOS **Rev:** State arms **Rev. Legend:** ESTADO DE DURANGO **Edge:** Segmented reeding

Date	Mintage	F	VF	XF	Unc	BU
2005Mo	249,774	—	—	—	35.00	45.00

KM# 713 100 PESOS
33.9400 g., Bi-Metallic .925 Silver 20.1753g center in Brass ring, 39.04 mm. **Series:** First **Subject:** 180th Anniversary of Federation **Obv:** National arms **Obv. Legend:** ESTADOS UNIDOS MEXICANOS **Rev:** Federal District arms **Rev. Legend:** DISTRITO FEDERAL **Edge:** Segmented reeding

Date	Mintage	F	VF	XF	Unc	BU
2005Mo	249,461	—	—	—	35.00	45.00

KM# 754 100 PESOS
33.9400 g., Bi-Metallic .925 Silver 20.1753g center in Aluminum-Bronze ring, 39.04 mm. **Series:** First **Subject:** 180th Anniversary of Federation **Obv:** National arms **Obv. Legend:** ESTADOS UNIDOS MEXICANOS **Rev:** State arms **Rev. Legend:** ESTADO DE CHIHUAHUA **Edge:** Segmented reeding

Date	Mintage	F	VF	XF	Unc	BU
2005Mo	249,102	—	—	—	35.00	45.00

KM# 712 100 PESOS
33.9400 g., Bi-Metallic .925 Silver 20.1753g center in Brass ring, 39.04 mm. **Series:** First **Subject:** 180th Anniversary of Federation **Obv:** National arms **Obv. Legend:** ESTADOS UNIDOS MEXICANOS **Rev:** State arms **Rev. Legend:** ESTADO DE CHIAPAS **Edge:** Segmented reeding

Date	Mintage	F	VF	XF	Unc	BU
2005Mo	249,417	—	—	—	35.00	45.00

KM# 729 100 PESOS
33.8250 g., Bi-Metallic .925 Silver 20.1753g center in Aluminum-Bronze ring, 39.04 mm. **Series:** First **Subject:** 180th Anniversary of Federation **Obv:** National arms **Obv. Legend:** ESTADOS UNIDOS MEXICANOS **Rev:** State arms **Rev. Legend:** ESTADO DE COLIMA **Edge:** Segmented reeding

Date	Mintage	F	VF	XF	Unc	BU
2005Mo	248,850	—	—	—	35.00	45.00

KM# 752 100 PESOS
33.9400 g., Bi-Metallic .925 Silver 20.1753g center in Aluminum-Bronze ring, 39.04 mm. **Series:** First **Subject:** 180th Anniversary of Federation **Obv:** National arms **Obv. Legend:** ESTADOS UNIDOS MEXICANOS **Rev:** State arms **Rev. Legend:** ESTADO DE COAHUILA DE ZARAGOZA **Edge:** Segmented reeding

Date	Mintage	F	VF	XF	Unc	BU
2005Mo	247,991	—	—	—	35.00	45.00

KM# 727 100 PESOS

33.9400 g., Bi-Metallic .925 Silver 20.1753g center in Aluminum-Bronze ring, 39.04 mm. **Series:** First **Subject:** 180th Anniversary of Federation **Obv:** National arms **Obv. Legend:** ESTADOS UNIDOS MEXICANOS **Rev:** State arms **Rev. Legend:** ESTADO DE CAMPECHE **Edge:** Segmented reeding

Date	Mintage	F	VF	XF	Unc	BU
2005Mo	249,040	—	—	—	35.00	45.00

KM# 723 100 PESOS

33.9400 g., Bi-Metallic .925 Silver 20.1753g center in Aluminum-Bronze ring, 39.04 mm. **Series:** First **Subject:** 180th Anniversary of Federation **Obv:** National arms **Obv. Legend:** ESTADOS UNIDOS MEXICANOS **Rev:** State arms **Rev. Legend:** ESTADO DE BAJA CALIFORNIA **Edge:** Segmented reeding

Date	Mintage	F	VF	XF	Unc	BU
2005Mo	249,263	—	—	—	35.00	45.00

KM# 719 100 PESOS

33.8250 g., Bi-Metallic .925 Silver 20.1753g center in Aluminum-Bronze ring, 39.04 mm. **Series:** Second **Obv:** National arms **Obv. Legend:** ESTADOS UNIDOS MEXICANOS **Rev:** Facade of the San Marcos garden above sculpture of national emblem at left, San Antonio Temple at right **Rev. Legend:** AGUASCALIENTES **Edge:** Segmented reeding

Date	Mintage	F	VF	XF	Unc	BU
2005Mo	149,705	—	—	—	35.00	45.00

KM# 725 100 PESOS

33.9400 g., Bi-Metallic .925 Silver 20.1753g center in Aluminum-Bronze ring, 39.04 mm. **Series:** First **Subject:** 180th Anniversary of Federation **Obv:** National arms **Obv. Legend:** ESTADOS UNIDOS MEXICANOS **Rev:** State arms **Rev. Legend:** ESTADO DE BAJA CALIFORNIA SUR **Edge:** Segmented reeding

Date	Mintage	F	VF	XF	Unc	BU
2005Mo	249,585	—	—	—	35.00	45.00

KM# 721 100 PESOS

33.9400 g., Bi-Metallic .925 Silver 20.1753g center in Aluminum-Bronze ring, 39.04 mm. **Series:** First **Subject:** 180th Anniversary of Federation **Obv:** National arms **Obv. Legend:** ESTADOS UNIDOS MEXICANOS **Rev:** Estados de Aguascalientes state arms **Rev. Legend:** ESTADO DE AGUASCALIENTES **Edge:** Segmented reeding

Date	Mintage	F	VF	XF	Unc	BU
2005Mo	248,410	—	—	—	35.00	45.00

KM# 758 100 PESOS

33.9400 g., Bi-Metallic .925 Silver 20.1753g center in Aluminum-Bronze ring, 39.04 mm. **Series:** Second **Obv:** National arms **Obv. Legend:** ESTADOS UNIDOS MEXICANOS **Rev:** Ram's head and value within circle **Rev. Legend:** BAJA CALIFORNIA - GOBIERNO DEL ESTADO **Edge:** Segmented reeding

Date	Mintage	F	VF	XF	Unc	BU
2005Mo	—	—	—	—	25.00	30.00

KM# 762 100 PESOS

33.9400 g., Bi-Metallic .925 Silver 20.175g center in Aluminum-Bronze ring, 39.04 mm. **Series:** Second **Obv:** National arms **Obv. Legend:** ESTADOS UNIDOS MEXICANOS **Rev:** Outlined map of peninsula at center, cave painting of deer behind, cactus at right **Rev. Legend:** ESTADO DE BAJA CALIFORNIA SUR **Edge:** Segmented reeding

Date	Mintage	F	VF	XF	Unc	BU
2005Mo	149,152	—	—	—	—	25.00

KM# 760 100 PESOS

33.9400 g., Bi-Metallic .925 Silver 20.1753g center in Aluminum-Bronze ring, 39.04 mm. **Series:** Second **Subject:** Estado de Campeche **Obv:** National arms **Obv. Legend:** ESTADOS UNIDOS MEXICANOS **Rev:** Jade mask - Calakmul, Campeche **Rev. Legend:** ESTADO DE CAMPECHE **Edge:** Segmented reeding

Date	Mintage	F	VF	XF	Unc	BU
2006Mo	—	—	—	—	—	25.00

KM# 781 100 PESOS

33.7000 g., Bi-Metallic .925 Silver 20.1753g center in Aluminum-Bronze ring, 39.04 mm. **Series:** Second **Obv:** National arms **Obv. Legend:** ESTADOS UNIDOS MEXICANOS **Rev:** Outlined map with turtle, mine cart above grapes at center, Friendship Dam above Christ of the Nodas at left, chimneys above crucibles and bell tower of Santiago's cathedral at right **Rev. Legend:** COAHUILA DE ZARAGOZA **Edge:** Segmented reeding

Date	Mintage	F	VF	XF	Unc	BU
2006Mo	—	—	—	—	35.00	45.00

KM# 777 100 PESOS

33.9400 g., Bi-Metallic .925 Silver 20.1753g center in Aluminum-Bronze ring, 39.04 mm. **Series:** Second **Obv:** National arms **Obv. Legend:** ESTADOS UNIDOS MEXICANOS **Rev:** State arms at lower center, Nevado de Colima and Volcan de Fuego volcanos in background **Rev. Legend:** *Colima* **Rev. Inscription:** GENEROSO **Edge:** Segmented reeding

Date	Mintage	F	VF	XF	Unc	BU
2006Mo	149,041	—	—	—	35.00	45.00

KM# 773 100 PESOS

33.9400 g., Bi-Metallic .925 Silver 20.1753g center in Aluminum-Bronze ring, 39.04 mm. **Series:** Second **Obv:** National arms **Obv. Legend:** ESTADOS UNIDOS MEXICANOS **Rev:** Head of Pakal, ancient Mayan king, Palenque **Rev. Legend:** ESTADO DE CHIAPAS - CABEZA MAYA DEL REY PAKAL, PALENQUE **Edge:** Segmented reeding

Date	Mintage	F	VF	XF	Unc	BU
2006Mo	149,491	—	—	—	35.00	45.00

KM# 775 100 PESOS

33.9400 g., Bi-Metallic .925 Silver 20.1753g center in Aluminum-Bronze ring, 39.04 mm. **Series:** Second **Obv:** National arms **Obv. Legend:** ESTADOS UNIDOS MEXICANOS **Rev:** Angel of Liberty **Rev. Legend:** MÉXICO - ANGEL DE LA LIBERTAD, CHIHUAHUA **Edge:** Segmented reeding

Date	Mintage	F	VF	XF	Unc	BU
2006Mo	149,557	—	—	—	35.00	45.00

KM# 779 100 PESOS

33.9400 g., Bi-Metallic .925 Silver 20.1753g center in Aluminum-Bronze ring, 39.04 mm. **Series:** Second **Obv:** National arms **Obv. Legend:** ESTADOS UNIDOS MEXICANOS **Rev:** National Palace **Rev. Legend:** DISTRITO FEDERAL - ANTIGUO AYUNTAMIENTO **Edge:** Segmented reeding

Date	Mintage	F	VF	XF	Unc	BU
2006Mo	149,525	—	—	—	35.00	45.00

KM# 787 100 PESOS

33.9400 g., Bi-Metallic .925 Silver 20.1753g center in Brass ring, 39.04 mm. **Series:** Second **Obv:** National arms **Obv. Legend:** ESTADOS UNIDOS MEXICANOS **Rev:** Tree **Rev. Legend:** PRIMERA RESERVA NACIONAL FORESTAL - DURANGO **Edge:** Segmented reeding

Date	Mintage	F	VF	XF	Unc	BU
2006Mo	149,034	—	—	—	35.00	45.00

KM# 789 100 PESOS

33.9400 g., Bi-Metallic .925 Silver 20.1753g center in Brass ring, 39.04 mm. **Series:** Second **Obv:** National arms **Obv. Legend:**

ESTADOS UNIDOS MEXICANOS **Rev:** State arms at center, statue of Miguel Hidalgo at left, monument to Pipla at lower right **Rev. Inscription:** *Guanajuato* **Edge:** Segmented reeding

Date	Mintage	F	VF	XF	Unc	BU
2006Mo	149,921	—	—	—	—	25.00

KM# 791 100 PESOS
33.9400 g., Bi-Metallic .925 Silver 20.1753g center in Brass ring, 39.04 mm. **Series:** Second **Obv:** National arms **Obv. Legend:** ESTADOS UNIDOS MEXICANOS **Rev:** Stylized portrait of Vicente Guerrero at left, church of Taxco at upper center, Acapulco's la Quebrada with diver above Christmas Eve flower and mask **Rev. Legend:** GUERRERO **Edge:** Segmented reeding

Date	Mintage	F	VF	XF	Unc	BU
2006Mo	149,675	—	—	—	35.00	45.00

KM# 793 100 PESOS
33.9400 g., Bi-Metallic .925 Silver 20.1753g center in Aluminum-Bronze ring, 39.04 mm. **Series:** Second **Obv:** National arms **Obv. Legend:** ESTADOS UNIDOS MEXICANOS **Rev:** Monument of Pachuca Hidalgo **Rev. Inscription:** *RELOJ / MONUMENTAL / DE / PACHUCA / HIDALGO - La / Bella / Airosa* **Edge:** Segmented reeding

Date	Mintage	F	VF	XF	Unc	BU
2006Mo	149,273	—	—	—	35.00	45.00

KM# 795 100 PESOS
33.9400 g., Bi-Metallic .925 Silver 20.1753g center in Brass ring, 39.04 mm. **Series:** Second **Obv:** National arms **Obv. Legend:** ESTADOS UNIDOS MEXICANOS **Rev:** Hospicio Cabañas orphanage **Rev. Legend:** ESTADO DE JALISCO **Edge:** Segmented reeding

Date	Mintage	F	VF	XF	Unc	BU
2006Mo	149,750	—	—	—	—	25.00

KM# 802 100 PESOS
33.9400 g., Bi-Metallic .925 Silver 20.1753g center in Aluminum-Bronze ring, 33.7, 39.04 mm. **Series:** Second **Obv:** National arms **Obv. Legend:** ESTADOS UNIDOS MEXICANOS **Rev:** Pyramid de la Loona (moon) **Rev. Legend:** ESTADO DE MÉXICO **Edge:** Segmented reeding

Date	Mintage	F	VF	XF	Unc	BU
2006Mo	149,377	—	—	—	—	25.00

KM# 785 100 PESOS
33.9400 g., Bi-Metallic .925 Silver 20.1753g center in Aluminum-Bronze ring, 33.7, 39.04 mm. **Series:** Second **Obv:** National arms **Obv. Legend:** ESTADOS UNIDOS MEXICANOS **Rev:** Four Monarch butterflies **Rev. Legend:** ESTADO DE MICHOACÁN **Edge:** Segmented reeding

Date	Mintage	F	VF	XF	Unc	BU
2006Mo	149,730	—	—	—	—	25.00

KM# 800 100 PESOS
33.9400 g., Bi-Metallic .925 Silver 20.1753g center in Aluminum-Bronze ring, 33.7, 39.04 mm. **Series:** Second **Obv:** National arms **Obv. Legend:** ESTADOS UNIDOS MEXICANOS **Rev:** 1/2 length figure of Chinelo (local dancer) at right, Palacio de Cortes in background **Rev. Inscription:** ESTADO DE / MORELOS **Edge:** Segmented reeding

Date	Mintage	F	VF	XF	Unc	BU
2006Mo	149,648	—	—	—	—	25.00

KM# 798 100 PESOS
33.9400 g., 33.8250 Bi-Metallic 0.925 Silver 20.1753g center in Aluminum-Bronze ring 36.908 oz., 39.04 mm. **Series:** Second **Obv:** National arms **Obv. Legend:** ESTADOS UNIDOS MEXICANOS **Rev:** Isle de Mexcaltitlán **Rev. Legend:** ESTADO DE NAYARIT **Edge:** Segmented reeding

Date	Mintage	F	VF	XF	Unc	BU
2007Mo	149,560	—	—	—	—	25.00

KM# 848 100 PESOS
33.9400 g., Bi-Metallic .925 Silver 20.1753 center in Aluminum-Bronze ring, 39.04 mm. **Series:** Second **Obv:** National arms

Obv. Legend: ESTADOS UNIDOS MEXICANOE **Rev:** Old foundry in Parque Fundidora (public park) at right, Cerro de la Silla (Saddle Hill) in background **Rev. Legend:** ESTADO DE NUEVO LÉON **Edge:** Segmented reeding

Date	Mintage	F	VF	XF	Unc	BU
2007Mo	—	—	—	—	—	25.00

KM# 849 100 PESOS

33.9400 g., Bi-Metallic .925 Silver 20.1753g center in Aluminum-Bronze ring, 39.04 mm. **Series:** Second **Obv:** National arms **Obv. Legend:** ESTADOS UNIDOS MEXICANOS **Rev:** Teatro Macedonio Alcala (theater) **Rev. Legend:** OAXACA **Edge:** Segmented reeding

Date	Mintage	F	VF	XF	Unc	BU
2007Mo	—	—	—	—	—	25.00

KM# 850 100 PESOS

33.9400 g., Bi-Metallic .925 Silver 20.1753g center in Aluminum-Bronze ring, 39.04 mm. **Series:** Second **Obv:** National arms **Obv. Legend:** ESTADOS UNIDOS MEXICANOS **Rev:** Talavera porcelain dish **Rev. Legend:** ESTADO DE PUEBLA **Edge:** Segmented reeding

Date	Mintage	F	VF	XF	Unc	BU
2007Mo	—	—	—	—	—	25.00

KM# 851 100 PESOS

33.9400 g., Bi-Metallic .925 Silver 20.1753g center in Aluminum-Bronze ring, 39.04 mm. **Series:** Second **Obv:** National arms **Obv. Legend:** ESTADOS UNIDOS MEXICANOS **Rev:** Mask at left, rays above state arms at center, Mayan ruins at right **Rev. Legend:** QUINTANA ROO **Edge:** Segmented reeding

Date	Mintage	F	VF	XF	Unc	BU
2007Mo	—	—	—	—	—	25.00

KM# 852 100 PESOS

33.9400 g., Bi-Metallic .925 Silver 20.1753 center in Aluminum-Bronze ring, 39.04 mm. **Series:** Second **Obv:** National arms **Obv. Legend:** ESTADOS UNIDOS MEXICANOS **Rev:** Acueduct of Querétaro at left, church of Santa Rosa de Viterbo at right **Rev. Legend:** ESTADO DE QUERÉTARO ARTEAGA **Edge:** Segmented reeding

Date	Mintage	F	VF	XF	Unc	BU
2007Mo	—	—	—	—	—	25.00

KM# 853 100 PESOS

33.9400 g., Bi-Metallic .925 Silver 20.1753g center in Aluminum-Bronze ring, 39.04 mm. **Series:** Second **Obv:** National arms **Obv. Legend:** ESRADOS UNIDOS MEXICANOS **Rev:** Facade of Caja Real **Rev. Legend:** • SAN LUIS POTOSÍ • **Edge:** Segmented reeding

Date	Mintage	F	VF	XF	Unc	BU
2007Mo	—	—	—	—	—	25.00

KM# 854 100 PESOS

33.9400 g., Bi-Metallic .925 Silver 20.1753g center in Aluminum-Bronze ring, 39.04 mm. **Series:** Second **Obv:** National arms **Obv. Legend:** ESTADOS UNIDOS MEXICANOS **Rev:** Shield on pile of cactus fruits **Rev. Legend:** ESTADO DE SINALOA - LUGAR DE PITAHAYAS **Edge:** Segmented reeding

Date	Mintage	F	VF	XF	Unc	BU
2007Mo	—	—	—	—	—	25.00

KM# 855 100 PESOS

33.9400 g., Bi-Metallic .925 Silver 20.1753g center in Aluminum-Bronze ring, 39.04 mm. **Series:** Second **Obv:** National arms **Obv. Legend:** ESTADOS UNIDOS MEXICANOS **Rev:** Local in Dance of the Deer at left, cactus at right, mountains in background **Rev. Legend:** ESTADO DE SONORA **Edge:** Segmented reeding

Date	Mintage	F	VF	XF	Unc	BU
2007Mo	—	—	—	—	—	25.00

KM# 856 100 PESOS

33.9400 g., Bi-Metallic .925 Silver 20.1753 center in Aluminum-Bronze ring, 39.04 mm. **Series:** Second **Obv:** National arms **Obv.**

Legend: ESTADOS UNIDOS MEXICANOS **Rev:** Fuente de los Pescadores (fisherman fountain) at lower left, giant head from the Olmec-pre-Hispanic culture at right, Planetario Tabasco in background **Rev. Legend:** TABASCO **Edge:** Segmented reeding

Date	Mintage	F	VF	XF	Unc	BU
2007Mo	—	—	—	—	—	25.00

KM# 858 100 PESOS

33.9400 g., Bi-Metallic .925 Silver 20.1753g center in Aluminum-Bronze ring, 39.04 mm. **Series:** Second **Obv:** National arms **Obv. Legend:** ESTADOS UNIDOS MEXICANOS **Rev:** Basilica de Ocotlán at left, state arms above Capilla Abierta, Plaza de Toros Ranchero Aguilar below, Exconvento de San Francisco at right **Rev. Legend:** ESTADO DE TLAXCALA **Edge:** Segmented reeding

Date	Mintage	F	VF	XF	Unc	BU
2007Mo	—	—	—	—	—	25.00

KM# 859 100 PESOS

33.9400 g., Bi-Metallic .912 Silver 20.1753g center in Aluminum-Bronze ring, 39.04 mm. **Series:** Second **Obv:** National arms **Obv. Legend:** ESTADOS UNIDOS MEXICANOS **Rev:** Pyramid of El Tajín **Rev. Legend:** • VERACRUZ • - • DE IGNACIO DE LA LLAVE • **Edge:** Segmented reeding

Date	Mintage	F	VF	XF	Unc	BU
2007Mo	—	—	—	—	—	25.00

KM# 860 100 PESOS

33.9400 g., Bi-Metallic .925 Silver 20.1753 center in Aluminum-Bronze ring, 39.04 mm. **Series:** Second **Obv:** National arms **Obv. Legend:** ESTADOS UNIDOS MEXICANOS **Rev:** Stylized pryamid of Chichén Itzá **Rev. Legend:** Castillo de Chichén Itzá **Edge:** Segmented reeding

Date	Mintage	F	VF	XF	Unc	BU
2007Mo	—	—	—	—	—	25.00

KM# 861 100 PESOS

33.9400 g., Bi-Metallic .925 Silver 20.1753g center in Aluminum-Bronze ring, 39.04 mm. **Series:** Second **Obv:** National arms **Obv. Legend:** ESTADOS UNIDOS MEXICANOS **Rev:** Cable car above Monumento al Minero at left, Catedral de Zacatecas at center right **Rev. Legend:** ZACATEXAS **Edge:** Segmented reeding

Date	Mintage	F	VF	XF	Unc	BU
2007Mo	—	—	—	—	—	25.00

The Republic of Moldova (formerly the Moldavian S.S.R.) is bordered in the north, east and south by the Ukraine and on the west by Romania. It has an area of 13,000 sq. mi. (33,700 sq. km.) and a population of 4.4 million. The capital is Chisinau. Agricultural products are mainly cereals, grapes, tobacco, sugar beets and fruits. Food processing, clothing, building materials and agricultural machinery manufacturing dominate the industry.

The historical Romanian principality of Moldova was established in the 14th century. It fell under Turkish suzerainty in the 16th century. From 1812 to 1918 Russians occupied the eastern portion of Moldova, which they named Bessarabia. In March 1918 the Bessarabian legislature voted in favor of reunification with Romania. At the Paris Peace Conference in 1920 United States, France, U.K., and Italy a.s.o officially recognized the union. The new Soviet government did not accept the union. In 1924, due to Soviet pressure against Romania a Moldavian Autonomous Soviet Socialist Republic (A.S.S.R.) was established within the USSR on the border strip that extends east of Nistru River (today it is Transdniestra or Transdniester).

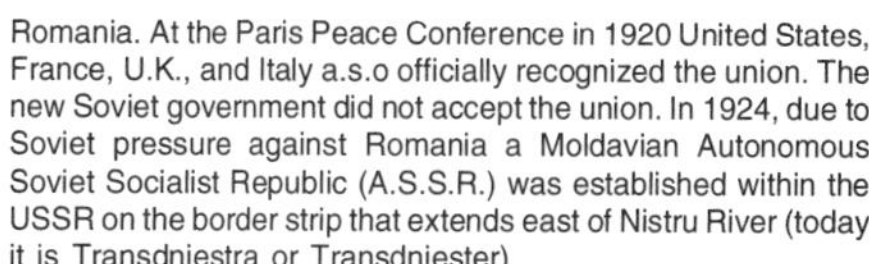

Following the Molotov-Ribbentrop Pact (1939), the Soviet - German agreement, which divided Eastern Europe, the Soviet forces, reoccupied the region in June 1940 and the Moldavian S.S.R. was proclaimed. The Transdniestra region was transferred to the new republic, while Ukrainian S.S.R. obtained possession of southern part of Bessarabia. Romanian forces liberated the region in 1941. The Soviets reconquered the territory (in 1944).

A declaration of republican sovereignty was adopted in June 1990 and in Aug. 1991 the area was renamed Moldova, an independent republic. In Dec. 1991 Moldova became a member of the C.I.S. In 1992, as a result of Russian involvement, Transdniestra seceded from Moldova. In May 1992 fighting began between Moldavian separatists (Romanians) and rebels aided by contingents of Cossacks and the Russian14th Army. The Moldavian government made several futile requests for United Nations intervention. On July 3, 1992, Russian and Moldavian presidents agreed upon a neutral demarcation line with the withdrawal of Russian forces from Transdniestra. This status will remain until a more feasible constitution is proclaimed.

RULER

Romanian, until 1940

MONETARY SYSTEM

100 Bani = 1 Leu

REPUBLIC

DECIMAL COINAGE

KM# 1 BAN

0.6800 g., Aluminum, 14.5 mm. **Obv:** National arms **Rev:** Value divides date above monogram **Edge:** Plain

Date	Mintage	F	VF	XF	Unc	BU
1993	—	—	—	—	0.20	0.40
1995	—	—	—	—	0.20	0.40
1996	—	—	—	—	0.25	0.50
2000	—	—	—	—	0.25	0.50
2004	—	—	—	—	0.25	0.50

KM# 2 5 BANI

0.8000 g., Aluminum, 16 mm. **Obv:** National arms **Rev:** Monogram divides sprigs below value and date **Edge:** Plain

Date	Mintage	F	VF	XF	Unc	BU
1993	—	—	—	—	0.30	0.50
1995	—	—	—	—	0.30	0.50
1996	—	—	—	—	0.30	0.50
1999	—	—	—	—	0.30	0.50
2000	—	—	—	—	0.30	0.50
2001	—	—	—	—	0.30	0.50
2002	—	—	—	—	0.30	0.50
2003	—	—	—	—	0.30	0.50
2005	—	—	—	—	0.30	0.50

KM# 7 10 BANI

0.8400 g., Aluminum, 16.6 mm. **Obv:** National arms **Rev:** Value, date and monogram **Edge:** Plain

Date	Mintage	F	VF	XF	Unc	BU
1995	—	—	—	—	0.40	0.60
1996	—	—	—	—	0.40	0.60
1997	—	—	—	—	0.40	0.60
1998	—	—	—	—	0.40	0.60
2000	—	—	—	—	0.40	0.60
2001	—	—	—	—	0.40	0.60
2002	—	—	—	—	0.40	0.60
2003	—	—	—	—	0.40	0.60
2005	—	—	—	—	0.40	0.60

KM# 3 25 BANI

0.9200 g., Aluminum, 17.5 mm. **Obv:** National arms **Rev:** Monogram divides sprigs below value and date **Edge:** Plain

Date	Mintage	F	VF	XF	Unc	BU
1993	—	—	—	—	0.50	0.75
1995	—	—	—	—	0.50	0.75
1999	—	—	—	—	0.50	0.75
2000	—	—	—	—	0.50	0.75
2001	—	—	—	—	0.50	0.75
2002	—	—	—	—	0.50	0.75
2003	—	—	—	—	0.50	0.75
2004	—	—	—	—	0.50	0.75

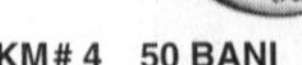

KM# 4 50 BANI

1.0700 g., Aluminum, 19 mm. **Obv:** National arms **Rev:** Monogram divides sprigs below date and value

Date	Mintage	F	VF	XF	Unc	BU
1993	—	—	—	—	0.75	1.00

KM# 10 50 BANI

3.1000 g., Brass-Clad Steel, 19 mm. **Obv:** National arms **Rev:** Value and date within grapevine **Edge:** Reeded

Date	Mintage	F	VF	XF	Unc	BU
1997	—	—	—	—	1.50	2.00
2003	—	—	—	—	1.50	2.00
2005	—	—	—	—	1.50	2.00

KM# 5 LEU

Nickel Clad Steel **Obv:** National arms **Rev:** Value divides date with monogram above

Date	Mintage	F	VF	XF	Unc	BU
1992	—	—	—	—	1.50	2.00

KM# 6 5 LEI

Nickel Clad Steel **Obv:** National arms **Rev:** Value flanked by monogram and date

Date	Mintage	F	VF	XF	Unc	BU
1993	—	—	—	—	3.50	4.00

MONACO

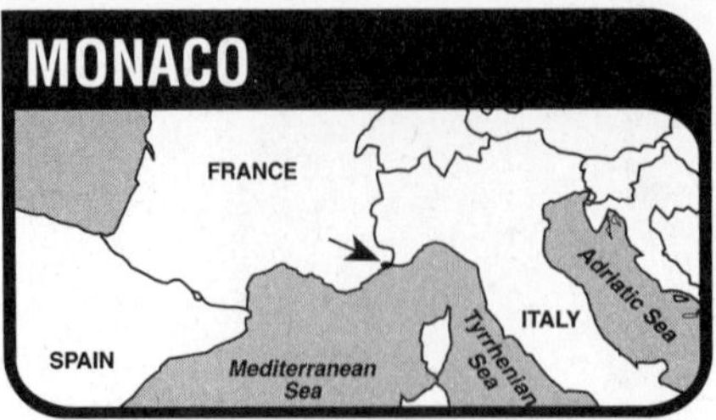

The Principality of Monaco, located on the Mediterranean coast nine miles from Nice, has an area of 0.58 sq. mi. (1.9 sq. km.) and a population of 26,000. Capital: Monaco-Ville. The economy is based on tourism and the manufacture of cosmetics, gourmet foods and highly specialized electronics. Monaco also derives its revenue from a tobacco monopoly and the sale of postage stamps for philatelic purpose. Gambling in Monte Carlo accounts for only a small fraction of the country's revenue.

Monaco derives its name from Monoikos', the Greek surname for Hercules, the mythological strong man who, according to legend, formed the Monacan headland during one of his twelve labors. Monaco has been ruled by the Grimaldi dynasty since 1297 - Prince Albert II, the present and 32nd monarch of Monaco, is still of that line - except for a period during the French Revolution until Napoleon's downfall when the Principality was annexed to France. Since 1865, Monaco has maintained a customs union with France which guarantees its privileged position as long as the royal line remains intact. Under the new constitution proclaimed on December 17, 1962, the Prince shares his power with an 18-member unicameral National Council.

RULERS

Albert I, 1889-1922
Louis II, 1922-1949
Rainier III, 1949-2005

MINT MARKS

M - Monaco
A – Paris

MINT PRIVY MARKS

(a) - Paris (privy marks only)
(p) - Thunderbolt - Poissy

MONETARY SYSTEM

10 Centimes = 1 Decime
10 Decimes = 1 Franc

PRINCIPALITY

DECIMAL COINAGE

10 Centimes = 1 Decime; 10 Decimes = 1 Franc

KM# 110 50 CENTIMES

Aluminum-Bronze **Ruler:** Louis II **Obv:** Hercules shooting bow to right **Rev:** Shield below value within circle

Date	Mintage	F	VF	XF	Unc	BU
1924 (p)	150,000	3.50	8.00	18.00	40.00	70.00

KM# 113 50 CENTIMES

Aluminum-Bronze **Ruler:** Louis II **Obv:** Hercules shooting bow to right **Rev:** Shield below value within circle

Date	Mintage	F	VF	XF	Unc	BU
1926 (p)	100,000	4.00	9.00	20.00	45.00	75.00

KM# 111 FRANC

Aluminum-Bronze **Ruler:** Louis II **Obv:** Hercules shooting bow to right **Rev:** Shield below value within circle

Date	Mintage	F	VF	XF	Unc	BU
1924 (p)	150,000	3.00	7.00	14.00	30.00	60.00

KM# 114 FRANC

Aluminum-Bronze **Ruler:** Louis II **Obv:** Hercules shooting bow to right **Rev:** Shield below value within circle

Date	Mintage	F	VF	XF	Unc	BU
1926 (p)	100,000	4.00	9.00	16.00	35.00	65.00

KM# 120 FRANC

Aluminum, 22.9 mm. **Ruler:** Louis II **Obv:** Head left **Obv. Designer:** L. Maubert **Rev:** Crowned mantled arms flanked by value below

Date	Mintage	F	VF	XF	Unc	BU
ND(1943) (a)	2,500,000	0.50	1.00	2.00	4.50	7.00

KM# 120a FRANC

Aluminum-Bronze, 22.9 mm. **Ruler:** Louis II **Obv:** Head left **Obv. Designer:** L. Maubert **Rev:** Crowned mantled arms flanked by value below

Date	Mintage	F	VF	XF	Unc	BU
ND(1945) (a)	1,509,000	0.50	1.00	2.00	5.00	8.00

KM# 112 2 FRANCS

Aluminum-Bronze **Ruler:** Louis II **Obv:** Hercules shooting bow to right **Rev:** Shield below value within circle

Date	Mintage	F	VF	XF	Unc	BU
1924 (p)	75,000	8.00	14.00	30.00	75.00	100

KM# 115 2 FRANCS

Aluminum-Bronze **Ruler:** Louis II **Obv:** Hercules shooting bow to right **Rev:** Shield below value within circle

Date	Mintage	F	VF	XF	Unc	BU
1926 (p)	75,000	7.00	12.00	25.00	70.00	90.00

KM# 121 2 FRANCS

Aluminum **Ruler:** Louis II **Obv:** Head left **Rev:** Crowned mantled arms flanked by value below

Date	Mintage	F	VF	XF	Unc	BU
ND(1943) (a)	1,250,000	0.75	1.50	5.00	10.00	15.00

KM# 121a 2 FRANCS

Aluminum-Bronze **Ruler:** Louis II **Obv:** Head left **Rev:** Crowned mantles arms flanked by value below

Date	Mintage	F	VF	XF	Unc	BU
ND(1945) (a)	1,080,000	0.50	1.00	2.50	6.00	10.00

KM# 122 5 FRANCS
Aluminum **Ruler:** Louis II **Obv:** Head left **Rev:** Crowned mantled arms flanked by value below

Date	Mintage	F	VF	XF	Unc	BU
1945 (a)	1,000,000	1.50	3.00	7.00	15.00	20.00

KM# 123 10 FRANCS
Copper-Nickel, 26 mm. **Ruler:** Louis II **Obv:** Bust left **Rev:** Crowned mantled arms above value flanked by sprigs

Date	Mintage	F	VF	XF	Unc	BU
1946 (a)	1,000,000	1.50	3.00	6.00	12.50	20.00

KM# 130 10 FRANCS
Aluminum-Bronze **Ruler:** Rainier III **Obv:** Head left within circle **Rev:** Crowned shield flanked by value

Date	Mintage	F	VF	XF	Unc	BU
1950 (a)	500,000	0.50	1.00	2.00	4.00	6.00
1951 (a)	500,000	0.50	1.00	2.00	4.00	6.00

KM# 124 20 FRANCS (Vingt)
Copper-Nickel **Ruler:** Louis II **Obv:** Bust left **Rev:** Crowned mantled arms above value flanked by sprigs

Date	Mintage	F	VF	XF	Unc	BU
1947 (a)	1,000,000	2.00	4.00	8.00	20.00	30.00

KM# 131 20 FRANCS (Vingt)
Aluminum-Bronze **Ruler:** Rainier III **Obv:** Head left divides circle **Rev:** Crowned shield flanked by value

Date	Mintage	F	VF	XF	Unc	BU
1950 (a)	500,000	0.65	1.25	2.50	6.00	8.00
1951 (a)	500,000	0.65	1.25	2.50	6.00	8.00

KM# 132 50 FRANCS (Cinquante)
Aluminum-Bronze **Ruler:** Rainier III **Obv:** Head left divides circle **Rev:** Armored equestrian divides circle above value

Date	Mintage	F	VF	XF	Unc	BU
1950 (a)	500,000	1.50	3.00	5.00	12.00	15.00

KM# 105 100 FRANCS (Cent)
32.2580 g., 0.9000 Gold 0.9334 oz. AGW **Ruler:** Albert I **Obv:** Head left **Obv. Legend:** ALBERT I PRINCE.... **Rev:** Crowned oval arms within wreath with ribbon above

Date	Mintage	F	VF	XF	Unc	BU
1901A	15,000	—	BV	BV	875	950
1904A	10,000	—	BV	BV	875	950

KM# 133 100 FRANCS (Cent)
Copper-Nickel **Ruler:** Rainier III **Obv:** Head left divides circle **Rev:** Armored equestrian divides circle above value

Date	Mintage	F	VF	XF	Unc	BU
1950 (a)	500,000	2.00	4.00	8.00	18.00	30.00

KM# 134 100 FRANCS (Cent)
Copper-Nickel **Ruler:** Rainier III **Obv:** Head left **Rev:** Value below crowned shield

Date	Mintage	F	VF	XF	Unc	BU
1956 (a)	500,000	1.50	2.50	5.50	15.00	25.00

REFORM COINAGE

100 Old Francs = 1 New Franc

KM# 155 CENTIME
1.6500 g., Stainless Steel **Ruler:** Rainier III **Obv:** Crowned shield **Rev:** Sprig divides value and date

Date	Mintage	F	VF	XF	Unc	BU
1976 (a)	25,000	—	0.15	0.30	4.00	—
1977 (a)	25,000	—	0.15	0.30	4.00	—
1978 (a)	50,000	—	0.15	0.30	4.00	—
1979 (a)	50,000	—	0.15	0.30	4.00	—
1982 (a)	10,000	—	0.15	0.30	4.00	—
1995 (a)	—	—	0.15	0.30	4.00	—

KM# 156 5 CENTIMES
2.0000 g., Copper-Aluminum-Nickel **Ruler:** Rainier III **Obv:** Head right **Rev:** Figure with hand on shield divides crown and value **Designer:** G. Simon

Date	Mintage	F	VF	XF	Unc	BU
1976 (a)	25,000	—	0.20	0.40	4.50	—
1977 (a)	25,000	—	0.20	0.40	4.50	—
1978 (a)	75,000	—	0.20	0.40	4.50	—
1979 (a)	75,000	—	0.20	0.40	4.50	—
1982 (a)	10,000	—	0.20	0.40	4.50	—
1995 (a)	—	—	0.20	0.40	4.50	—

KM# 142 10 CENTIMES
Aluminum-Bronze **Ruler:** Rainier III **Obv:** Head right **Obv. Designer:** G. Simon **Rev:** Figure with hand on shield divides crown and value

Date	Mintage	F	VF	XF	Unc	BU
1962 (a)	750,000	—	0.15	0.30	1.50	—
1974 (a)	172,000	—	0.15	0.30	2.25	—
1975 (a)	172,000	—	0.15	0.30	2.25	—
1976 (a)	172,000	—	0.15	0.30	2.25	—
1977 (a)	172,000	—	0.15	0.30	2.25	—
1978 (a)	300,000	—	0.15	0.30	2.50	—
1979 (a)	300,000	—	0.15	0.30	2.50	—
1982 (a)	100,000	—	0.15	0.30	2.50	—
1995 (a)	—	—	0.15	0.30	2.50	—

KM# 143 20 CENTIMES
3.9600 g., Aluminum-Bronze, 23.5 mm. **Ruler:** Rainier III **Obv:** Head right **Obv. Designer:** G. Simon **Rev:** Figure with hand on shield divides crown and value

Date	Mintage	F	VF	XF	Unc	BU
1962 (a)	750,000	—	0.25	0.50	1.75	—
1974 (a)	104,000	—	0.25	0.50	2.75	—
1975 (a)	97,000	—	0.25	0.50	2.75	—
1976 (a)	103,000	—	0.25	0.50	2.75	—
1977 (a)	97,000	—	0.25	0.50	2.75	—
1978 (a)	25,000	—	0.25	0.50	2.75	—
1979 (a)	25,000	—	0.25	0.50	2.75	—
1982 (a)	100,000	—	0.25	0.50	2.75	—
1995 (a)	30,000	—	0.25	0.50	2.75	—

KM# 144 50 CENTIMES
Aluminum-Bronze **Ruler:** Rainier III **Obv:** Head right **Obv. Designer:** G. Simon **Rev:** Figure with hand on shield divides crown and value

Date	Mintage	F	VF	XF	Unc	BU
1962 (a)	375,000	—	1.25	2.50	4.50	—

KM# 145 1/2 FRANC
4.5500 g., Nickel, 20.5 mm. **Ruler:** Rainier III **Obv:** Head right **Obv. Designer:** R. Cochet **Rev:** Crown overlapping shield, value at lower left

Date	Mintage	F	VF	XF	Unc	BU
1965 (a)	375,000	0.30	0.60	1.25	2.50	—
1968 (a)	125,000	0.30	0.60	1.25	2.50	—
1974 (a)	62,500	0.35	0.70	1.50	3.50	—
1975 (a)	62,500	0.35	0.70	1.50	3.50	—
1976 (a)	62,500	0.35	0.70	1.50	3.50	—
1977 (a)	62,500	0.35	0.70	1.50	3.50	—
1978 (a)	230,000	0.30	0.60	1.25	2.75	—
1979 (a)	230,000	0.30	0.60	1.25	2.75	—
1982 (a)	460,000	0.30	0.60	1.25	2.75	—
1989 (a)	10,000	0.30	0.60	1.25	2.75	—
1995 (a)	30,000	0.30	0.60	1.25	2.75	—

KM# 140 FRANC
Nickel **Ruler:** Rainier III **Obv:** Head right **Obv. Designer:** R. Cochet **Rev:** Crown overlapping shield, value at lower left

Date	Mintage	F	VF	XF	Unc	BU
1960 (a)	500,000	0.35	0.70	1.50	3.25	—
1966 (a)	175,000	0.40	0.80	1.75	4.00	—
1968 (a)	250,000	0.40	0.80	1.75	4.00	—
1974 (a)	194,000	0.40	0.80	1.75	4.00	—
1975 (a)	195,000	0.40	0.80	1.75	4.00	—
1976 (a)	193,000	0.40	0.80	1.75	4.00	—
1977 (a)	188,000	0.40	0.80	1.75	4.00	—
1978 (a)	280,000	0.40	0.80	1.75	3.50	—
1979 (a)	280,000	0.40	0.80	1.75	3.50	—
1982 (a)	525,000	0.40	0.80	1.75	3.50	—
1986 (a)	50,000	0.35	0.70	1.50	3.00	—
1989 (a)	50,000	0.35	0.70	1.50	2.75	—
1995 (a)	30,000	0.35	0.70	1.50	2.75	—

KM# 157 2 FRANCS
Nickel, 26.5 mm. **Ruler:** Rainier III **Obv:** Head right **Obv. Designer:** G. Simon **Rev:** Monogram within crowned shield

Date	Mintage	F	VF	XF	Unc	BU
1979 (a)	162,000	0.60	0.85	1.75	4.00	—
1981 (a)	275,000	0.60	0.85	1.75	4.00	—
1982 (a)	446,000	0.60	0.85	1.75	4.00	—
1995 (a)	—	0.60	0.85	1.75	4.00	—

Note: May not exist in this date

KM# 166 2 FRANCS
Nickel, 26.5 mm. **Ruler:** Rainier III **Obv:** Head left

Date	Mintage	F	VF	XF	Unc	BU
1995 (a)	—	0.60	0.85	1.75	4.00	—

KM# 141 5 FRANCS
12.0000 g., 0.8350 Silver 0.3221 oz. ASW **Ruler:** Rainier III **Obv:** Head left **Rev:** Crowned arms with supporters flanked by value

Date	Mintage	F	VF	XF	Unc	BU
1960 (a)	125,000	—	—	7.50	10.00	—
1966 (a)	125,000	—	—	7.50	10.00	—

KM# 150 5 FRANCS
Nickel Clad Copper-Nickel **Ruler:** Rainier III **Obv:** Head right **Obv. Designer:** Raymond Joly **Rev:** Value below monogram and crown, all flanked by lined designs

Date	Mintage	F	VF	XF	Unc	BU
1971 (a)	250,000	—	1.50	2.50	4.50	—
1974 (a)	250,000	—	1.50	2.50	4.50	—
1975 (a)	14,000	—	2.50	6.00	12.50	—
1976 (a)	14,000	—	2.50	6.00	12.50	—
1977 (a)	14,500	—	2.00	5.00	10.00	—
1978 (a)	10,000	—	2.00	5.00	10.00	—
1979 (a)	10,000	—	2.00	5.00	10.00	—
1982 (a)	152,000	—	2.00	5.00	10.00	—
1989	35,000	—	2.00	5.00	10.00	—
1995 (a)	30,000	—	2.00	5.00	10.00	—

KM# 146 10 FRANCS
25.0000 g., 0.9000 Silver 0.7234 oz. ASW **Ruler:** Rainier III **Subject:** 100th Anniversary - Accession of Charles III **Obv:** Head right **Rev:** Crowned shield **Rev. Designer:** Delannoy

Date	Mintage	F	VF	XF	Unc	BU
1966 (a)	62,500	—	—	—	25.00	40.00

KM# 151 10 FRANCS
10.2000 g., Copper-Nickel-Aluminum **Ruler:** Rainier III **Subject:** 25th Anniversary of Reign **Obv:** Head left **Obv. Designer:** G. Simon **Rev:** Monogram within crowned arms with supporters

Date	Mintage	F	VF	XF	Unc	BU
ND(1974) (a)	25,000	—	2.50	4.50	8.00	—

KM# 154 10 FRANCS
Copper-Nickel-Aluminum **Ruler:** Rainier III **Obv:** Head left **Rev:** Monogram within crowned arms with supporters

Date	Mintage	F	VF	XF	Unc	BU
1975 (a)	16,000	—	2.25	3.75	8.00	—
1976 (a)	16,000	—	2.50	4.00	9.00	—
1977 (a)	18,000	—	2.25	3.25	5.50	—
1978 (a)	190,000	—	2.25	3.25	5.50	—
1979 (a)	190,000	—	2.25	3.25	5.50	—
1981 (a)	230,000	—	2.25	3.25	5.50	—
1982 (a)	230,000	—	2.25	3.25	5.50	—

KM# 160 10 FRANCS
Copper-Nickel-Aluminum **Ruler:** Rainier III **Obv:** Head of Princess Grace left **Rev:** Single rose divides value

Date	Mintage	F	VF	XF	Unc	BU
1982 (a)	30,000	—	—	—	12.50	—

KM# 162 10 FRANCS
10.0000 g., Nickel-Aluminum-Bronze **Ruler:** Rainier III **Subject:** Prince Pierre Foundation **Obv:** Bust right and single sprig on paper to left of dates **Rev:** Small doubled wreath divides date on top of shield flanked by symbols

Date	Mintage	F	VF	XF	Unc	BU
1989 (a)	100,000	—	—	—	6.50	—

KM# 163 10 FRANCS
Bi-Metallic Nickel center in Aluminum-Bronze ring **Ruler:** Rainier III **Obv:** Value and monogram within circle **Rev:** Armored knight right within circle

Date	Mintage	F	VF	XF	Unc	BU
1989 (a)	100,000	—	—	—	9.00	10.00
1991 (a)	250,000	—	—	—	14.00	15.00
1992 (a)	250,000	—	—	—	12.50	13.50
1993 (a)	250,000	—	—	—	14.00	15.00
1994 (a)	250,000	—	—	—	14.00	15.00
1995 (a)	250,000	—	—	—	9.00	10.00
1996 (a)	250,000	—	—	—	9.00	10.00
1997 (a)	250,000	—	—	—	9.00	10.00
1998 (a)	250,000	—	—	—	9.00	10.00
2000 (a)	240,000	—	—	—	9.00	10.00

KM# 165 20 FRANCS
Tri-Metallic Copper-Aluminum-Nickel center; Nickel ring; Copper-Aluminum-Nickel outer ring, 26.8 mm. **Ruler:** Rainier III **Obv:** Value and monogram within circle **Rev:** Prince's palace within circle with crown above **Designer:** R. B. Baron

Date	Mintage	F	VF	XF	Unc	BU
1992 (a)	100,000	—	—	—	15.00	16.50
1995 (a)	—	—	—	—	15.00	16.50
1997 (a)	120,000	—	—	—	15.00	16.50

EURO COINAGE

KM# 167 EURO CENT
2.2700 g., Copper Plated Steel, 16.2 mm. **Ruler:** Rainier III **Obv:** Crowned arms **Obv. Designer:** Robert Cochet **Rev:** Value and globe **Rev. Designer:** Luc Luycx **Edge:** Plain

Date	Mintage	F	VF	XF	Unc	BU
2001 (a)	347	—	—	—	20.00	30.00
2001 (a) Proof	3,500	Value: 75.00				
2002 (a)	Est. 40,000	—	—	—	—	65.00
Note: Initially available only in sets						
2003 (a)	—	—	—	—	—	—
2004 (a) Proof	14,999	Value: 25.00				
2005 (a) Proof	35,000	Value: 50.00				

KM# 168 2 EURO CENT
3.0300 g., Copper Plated Steel, 18.7 mm. **Ruler:** Rainier III **Obv:** Crowned arms **Obv. Designer:** Robert Cochet **Rev:** Value and globe **Rev. Designer:** Luc Luycx **Edge:** Grooved **Note:** Initially available only in sets

Date	Mintage	F	VF	XF	Unc	BU
2001 (a)	393,400	—	—	—	15.00	25.00
2001 (a) Proof	3,500	Value: 85.00				
2002 (a)	Est. 40,000	—	—	—	—	65.00
Note: Initially available only in sets						
2003 (a)	—	—	—	—	—	—
2004 (a) Proof	14,999	Value: 35.00				
2005 (a) Proof	35,000	Value: 50.00				

KM# 169 5 EURO CENT
3.8600 g., Copper-Nickel Plated Steel, 21.2 mm. **Ruler:** Rainier III **Obv:** Crowned arms **Obv. Designer:** Robert Cochet **Rev:** Value and globe **Rev. Designer:** Luc Luycx **Edge:** Plain **Note:** Initially available only in sets

Date	Mintage	F	VF	XF	Unc	BU
2001 (a)	320,000	—	—	—	20.00	30.00
2001 (a) Proof	3,500	Value: 95.00				
2002 (a)	Est. 40,000	—	—	—	—	70.00
Note: Initially available only in sets						
2003 (a)	—	—	—	—	—	—
2004 (a) Proof	14,999	Value: 45.00				
2005 (a) Proof	35,000	Value: 55.00				

KM# 170 10 EURO CENT
4.0700 g., Brass, 19.7 mm. **Ruler:** Rainier III **Obv:** Knight on horse **Obv. Designer:** R. Baron **Rev:** Value and map **Rev. Designer:** Luc Luycx **Edge:** Reeded

Date	Mintage	F	VF	XF	Unc	BU
2001 (a)	320,000	—	—	—	15.00	20.00
2001 (a) Proof	3,500	Value: 110				
2002 (a)	407,200	—	—	—	8.00	12.00
2003 (a)	100,800	—	—	—	12.00	16.00
2004 (a) Proof	14,999	Value: 50.00				

KM# 181 10 EURO CENT
4.0700 g., Brass, 19.7 mm. **Ruler:** Albert II **Obv:** Charging knight **Obv. Designer:** R. Baron **Rev:** Relief map of Western Europe, stars, lines and value **Rev. Designer:** Luc Luyckx **Edge:** Reeded

Date	Mintage	F	VF	XF	Unc	BU
2007 (a)	—	—	—	—	12.00	16.00

KM# 171 20 EURO CENT
5.7300 g., Brass, 22.1 mm. **Ruler:** Rainier III **Obv:** Knight on horse **Rev:** Value and map **Edge:** Notched **Designer:** R. Baron

Date	Mintage	F	VF	XF	Unc	BU
2001 (a)	386,400	—	—	—	15.00	20.00
2001 (a) Proof	3,500	Value: 120				
2002 (a)	376,000	—	—	—	12.00	16.00
2003 (a)	100,000	—	—	—	12.00	16.00
2004 (a) Proof	14,999	Value: 60.00				

KM# 182 20 EURO CENT
5.7300 g., Brass, 22.1 mm. **Ruler:** Albert II **Obv:** Charging knight **Rev:** Relief map of Western Europe, stars, lines and value **Edge:** Notched **Designer:** R. Baron

Date	Mintage	F	VF	XF	Unc	BU
2007 (a)	—	—	—	—	12.00	16.00

KM# 172 50 EURO CENT
7.8100 g., Brass **Ruler:** Rainier III **Obv:** Knight on horse **Obv. Designer:** R. Baron **Rev:** Value and map **Rev. Designer:** Luc Luyckx **Edge:** Reeded

Date	Mintage	F	VF	XF	Unc	BU
2001 (a)	320,000	—	—	—	15.00	20.00
2001 (a) Proof	3,500	Value: 130				
2002 (a)	364,000	—	—	—	8.00	12.00
2003 (a)	100,000	—	—	—	12.00	16.00
2004 (a) Proof	14,999	Value: 65.00				

KM# 183 50 EURO CENT
7.8100 g., Brass **Ruler:** Albert II **Obv:** Charging knight **Obv. Designer:** R. Baron **Rev:** Relief map of Western Europe, stars, lines and value **Rev. Designer:** Luc Luyckx **Edge:** Reeded

Date	Mintage	F	VF	XF	Unc	BU
2007 (a)	—	—	—	—	12.00	16.00

KM# 173 EURO
7.5000 g., Bi-Metallic Copper- Nickel center in Brass ring, 23.2 mm. **Ruler:** Rainier III **Obv:** Conjoined heads of Prince Ranier and Crown Prince Albert right within circle **Obv. Designer:** Pierre Rodier **Rev:** Value and map **Rev. Designer:** Luc Luyckx **Edge:** Reeded and plain sections

Date	Mintage	F	VF	XF	Unc	BU
2001 (a)	991,100	—	—	—	10.00	12.00
2001 (a) Proof	3,500	Value: 145				
2002 (a)	512,500	—	—	—	11.00	14.00
2003 (a)	135,000	—	—	—	13.50	18.50
2004 (a) Proof	14,999	Value: 75.00				

KM# 184 EURO
7.5000 g., Bi-Metallic Copper-Nickel center in Brass ring, 23.2 mm. **Ruler:** Albert II **Obv:** Conjoined heads of Prince Rainier and Crown Prince Albert right **Obv. Designer:** Pierre Rodier **Rev:** Relief map of Western Europe, stars, lines and value **Rev. Designer:** Luc Luyckx **Edge:** Reeded and plain sections

Date	Mintage	F	VF	XF	Unc	BU
2007 (a)	—	—	—	—	13.50	18.50

KM# 174 2 EURO
8.5200 g., Bi-Metallic Brass center in Copper-Nickel ring, 25.7 mm. **Ruler:** Rainier III **Obv:** Head right within circle flanked by stars **Obv. Designer:** Pierre Rodier **Rev:** Value and map **Rev. Designer:** Luc Luyckx **Edge:** Reeding over "2's" and stars

Date	Mintage	F	VF	XF	Unc	BU
2001 (a)	919,800	—	—	—	14.00	16.00
2001 (a) Proof	3,500	Value: 165				
2002 (a)	496,000	—	—	—	15.00	18.00
2003 (a)	228,000	—	—	—	17.50	22.50
2004 (a) Proof	14,999	Value: 95.00				

KM# 185 2 EURO
8.5200 g., Bi-Metallic Brass center in Copper-Nickel ring, 25.7 mm. **Ruler:** Albert II **Obv:** Prince Rainer's portrait right **Obv. Designer:** Pierre Rodier **Rev:** Relief map of Western Europe, stars, lines and value **Rev. Designer:** Luc Luyckx **Edge:** Reeding over 2's and stars

Date	Mintage	F	VF	XF	Unc	BU
2007 (a)	—	—	—	—	17.50	22.50

KM# 186 2 EURO
8.5200 g., Bi-Metallic Copper-Nickel center with brass ring, 25.75 mm. **Ruler:** Albert II **Subject:** 25th Anniversary Death of Princess Grace **Obv:** Head of Princess Grace left **Rev:** Relief map of Western Europe, stars, lines and value **Edge:** Reeded

Date	Mintage	F	VF	XF	Unc	BU
2007 (a)	20,000	—	—	—	—	—

The State of Mongolia, (formerly the Mongolian People's Republic) a landlocked country in central Asia between Russia and the People's Republic of China, has an area of 604,250 sq. mi. (1,565,000 sq. km.) and a population of 2.26 million. Capital: Ulaan Baator. Animal herds and flocks are the chief economic asset. Wool, cattle, butter, meat and hides are exported.

Mongolia (often referred to as Outer Mongolia), one of the world's oldest countries, attained its greatest power in the 13th century when Genghis Khan and his successors conquered all of China and extended their influence westward as far as Hungary and Poland. The empire dissolved in later centuries and in 1691 was brought under suzerainty of the Manchus, who had conquered China in 1644. Afterward the Chinese republican movement led by Sun Yat-sen overthrew the Manchus and set up the Chinese Republic in 1911. Mongolia, with the support of Russia, proclaimed their independence from China and, on March 13, 1921 a Provisional People's Government was established and later, on Nov. 26, 1924 the government proclaimed the Mongolian People's Republic.

Although nominally a dependency of China, Outer Mongolia voted at a plebiscite Oct. 20, 1945 to sever all ties with China and become an independent nation. Opposition to the communist party developed in late 1989 and after demonstrations and hunger strikes, the Politburo resigned on March 12, 1990 and the new State of Mongolia was organized.

On Feb. 12, 1992 it became the first to discard communism as the national political system by adopting a new constitution.

For earlier issues see Russia - Tannu Tuva.

MONETARY SYSTEM
100 Mongo = 1 Tugrik

PEOPLE'S REPUBLIC

DECIMAL COINAGE

KM# 1 MONGO
Copper, 21 mm. **Obv:** Soembo arms, text **Rev:** Value within 1/2 wreath

Date	Mintage	F	VF	XF	Unc	BU
AH15 (1925)	—	5.00	8.00	12.00	22.00	—

KM# 9 MONGO
Aluminum-Bronze **Obv:** Soembo arms, text **Rev:** Value within 1/2 wreath

Date	Mintage	F	VF	XF	Unc	BU
AH27 (1937)	—	2.50	3.50	7.50	16.50	—

KM# 15 MONGO
Aluminum-Bronze **Obv:** National arms within circle **Rev:** Value within 1/2 wreath

Date	Mintage	F	VF	XF	Unc	BU
AH35 (1945)	—	2.00	3.00	5.50	12.50	—

KM# 21 MONGO
Aluminum **Obv:** Wreath around center hole with inscription around border **Rev:** Value above hole in center and 3/4 wreath

Date	Mintage	F	VF	XF	Unc	BU
1959	9,000,000	0.25	0.60	1.00	2.00	—

KM# 27 MONGO
0.7500 g., Aluminum, 17.5 mm. **Obv:** National arms **Rev:** Value above 1/2 wreath

Date	Mintage	F	VF	XF	Unc	BU
1970	—	0.25	0.60	0.85	1.50	—
1977	—	0.25	0.60	0.85	1.50	—
1980	—	0.25	0.60	0.85	1.50	—
1981	—	0.25	0.60	0.85	1.50	—

KM# 2 2 MONGO
Copper, 24 mm. **Obv:** Soembo arms, text **Rev:** Value within 1/2 wreath

Date	Mintage	F	VF	XF	Unc	BU
AH15 (1925)	—	3.50	6.50	12.00	22.00	—

KM# 10 2 MONGO
Aluminum-Bronze, 22 mm. **Obv:** Soembo, text **Rev:** Value within 1/2 wreath

Date	Mintage	F	VF	XF	Unc	BU
AH27 (1937)	—	2.50	3.50	6.00	14.00	—

KM# 16 2 MONGO
Aluminum-Bronze **Obv:** National arms within circle **Rev:** Value within 1/2 wreath

Date	Mintage	F	VF	XF	Unc	BU
AH35 (1945)	—	1.00	2.00	4.00	9.00	—

KM# 22 2 MONGO
Aluminum **Obv:** Wreath around center hole with inscription around border **Rev:** Value above center hole and 3/4 wreath

Date	Mintage	F	VF	XF	Unc	BU
1959	4,000,000	0.25	0.65	1.50	3.50	—

KM# 28 2 MONGO

1.0500 g., Aluminum, 20 mm. **Obv:** National arms above date **Rev:** Value within 1/2 wreath **Edge:** Plain

Date	Mintage	F	VF	XF	Unc	BU
1970	—	0.25	0.65	1.20	2.50	—
1977	—	0.25	0.65	1.20	2.50	—
1980	—	0.25	0.65	1.20	2.50	—
1981	—	0.25	0.65	1.20	2.50	—

KM# 3.1 5 MONGO

Copper, 32 mm. **Obv:** Soembo arms, text **Rev:** Value within 1/2 wreath

Date	Mintage	F	VF	XF	Unc	BU
AH15 (1925)	—	5.00	10.00	20.00	38.00	—

Note: Variety in obverse legend exists

KM# 3.2 5 MONGO

Copper, 32 mm. **Note:** Error: letter "m" looking like a horse's tail omitted in nayramdax (Vertically written word lower left of Soyombo)

Date	Mintage	F	VF	XF	Unc	BU
1925	—	—	—	—	40.00	—

KM# 11 5 MONGO

Aluminum-Bronze, 28 mm. **Obv:** Soembo arms, text **Rev:** Value within 1/2 wreath

Date	Mintage	F	VF	XF	Unc	BU
AH27 (1937)	—	2.75	3.50	6.00	14.00	—

KM# 17 5 MONGO

Aluminum-Bronze **Obv:** National arms within circle **Rev:** Value within 1/2 wreath

Date	Mintage	F	VF	XF	Unc	BU
AH35 (1945)	—	1.75	2.50	5.00	12.00	—

KM# 23 5 MONGO

Aluminum **Obv:** Wreath around hole in center with inscription around border **Rev:** Value above hole in center and 1/2 wreath

Date	Mintage	F	VF	XF	Unc	BU
1959	2,400,000	0.25	1.00	2.00	4.00	—

KM# 29 5 MONGO

1.6000 g., Aluminum, 23 mm. **Obv:** Date below national arms **Rev:** Value within 1/2 wreath

Date	Mintage	F	VF	XF	Unc	BU
1970	—	0.25	0.85	1.75	3.50	—
1977	—	0.25	0.85	1.75	3.50	—
1980	—	0.25	0.85	1.75	3.50	—
1981	—	0.25	0.85	1.75	3.50	—

KM# 4 10 MONGO

1.7996 g., 0.5000 Silver 0.0289 oz. ASW, 17 mm. **Obv:** Soembo arms, text **Rev:** Value within 1/2 wreath

Date	Mintage	VG	F	VF	XF	Unc
AH15 (1925)	1,500,000	—	3.00	5.00	9.00	20.00

KM# 12 10 MONGO

Copper-Nickel **Obv:** Soembo arms, text **Rev:** Value within 1/2 wreath

Date	Mintage	F	VF	XF	Unc	BU
AH27 (1937)	—	2.00	3.50	7.00	16.00	—

KM# 18 10 MONGO

Copper-Nickel **Obv:** National arms within circle **Rev:** Value within 1/2 wreath

Date	Mintage	F	VF	XF	Unc	BU
AH35 (1945)	—	1.50	3.00	5.00	12.00	—

KM# 24 10 MONGO

Aluminum **Obv:** National arms within circle **Rev:** Value within 3/4 wreath

Date	Mintage	F	VF	XF	Unc	BU
1959	3,000,000	0.75	1.50	3.00	6.00	—

KM# 30 10 MONGO

2.3000 g., Copper-Nickel, 18.5 mm. **Obv:** Date below national arms **Rev:** Value within 1/2 wreath

Date	Mintage	F	VF	XF	Unc	BU
1970	—	0.35	0.85	1.75	3.50	—
1977	—	0.35	0.85	1.75	3.50	—
1980	—	0.35	0.85	1.75	3.50	—
1981	—	0.35	0.85	1.75	3.50	—

KM# 5 15 MONGO

2.6994 g., 0.5000 Silver 0.0434 oz. ASW, 19 mm. **Obv:** Soembo arms, text **Rev:** Value within 1/2 wreath

Date	Mintage	VG	F	VF	XF	Unc
AH15 (1925)	417,000	—	3.50	6.00	12.00	22.00

KM# 13 15 MONGO

Copper-Nickel **Obv:** Soembo arms, text **Rev:** Value within 1/2 wreath

Date	Mintage	F	VF	XF	Unc	BU
AH27 (1937)	—	2.00	3.00	6.00	14.00	—

KM# 19 15 MONGO

Copper-Nickel **Obv:** National arms within circle **Rev:** Value within 3/4 wreath

Date	Mintage	F	VF	XF	Unc	BU
AH35 (1945)	—	1.50	2.25	4.00	9.00	—

KM# 25 15 MONGO

Aluminum **Obv:** National arms within circle **Rev:** Value within 3/4 wreath

Date	Mintage	F	VF	XF	Unc	BU
1959	4,600,000	0.35	0.85	1.75	4.00	—

KM# 31 15 MONGO

4.0500 g., Copper-Nickel, 22 mm. **Obv:** Date below national arms **Rev:** Value within 1/2 wreath

Date	Mintage	F	VF	XF	Unc	BU
1970	—	0.25	0.65	1.25	2.75	—
1977	—	0.25	0.65	1.25	2.75	—
1980	—	0.25	0.65	1.25	2.75	—
1981	—	0.25	0.65	1.25	2.75	—

KM# 6 20 MONGO

3.5992 g., 0.5000 Silver 0.0579 oz. ASW, 22 mm. **Obv:** Soembo arms, text **Rev:** Value within 1/2 wreath

Date	Mintage	VG	F	VF	XF	Unc
AH15 (1925)	1,625,000	—	4.00	7.50	14.00	28.00

KM# 14 20 MONGO

Copper-Nickel **Obv:** Soembo arms, text **Rev:** Value within 1/2 wreath

Date	Mintage	F	VF	XF	Unc	BU
AH27 (1937)	—	2.50	4.50	10.00	20.00	—

KM# 20 20 MONGO
Copper-Nickel **Obv:** National arms within circle **Rev:** Value within 3/4 wreath

Date	Mintage	F	VF	XF	Unc	BU
AH35 (1945)	—	1.50	2.50	5.00	12.00	—

KM# 26 20 MONGO
Aluminum **Obv:** National arms within circle **Rev:** Value within 3/4 wreath

Date	Mintage	F	VF	XF	Unc	BU
1959	3,600,000	0.60	1.25	2.25	4.50	—

KM# 32 20 MONGO
5.9000 g., Copper-Nickel, 25 mm. **Obv:** Date below national arms **Rev:** Value within 1/2 wreath

Date	Mintage	F	VF	XF	Unc	BU
1970	—	0.40	0.80	1.50	3.50	—
1977	—	0.40	0.80	1.50	3.50	—
1980	—	0.40	0.80	1.50	3.50	—
1981	—	0.40	0.80	1.50	3.50	—

KM# 7 50 MONGO
9.9979 g., 0.9000 Silver 0.2893 oz. ASW, 27 mm. **Obv:** Soembo arms, text **Rev:** Value within 1/2 wreath

Date	Mintage	VG	F	VF	XF	Unc
AH15 (1925)	920,000	—	7.50	12.00	18.50	32.00

KM# 33 50 MONGO
8.6000 g., Copper-Nickel, 27.5 mm. **Obv:** Date below national arms **Rev:** Value within 1/2 wreath

Date	Mintage	F	VF	XF	Unc	BU
1970	—	0.50	1.00	1.75	3.75	—
1977	—	0.50	1.00	1.75	3.75	—
1980	—	0.50	1.00	1.75	3.75	—
1981	—	0.50	1.00	1.75	3.75	—

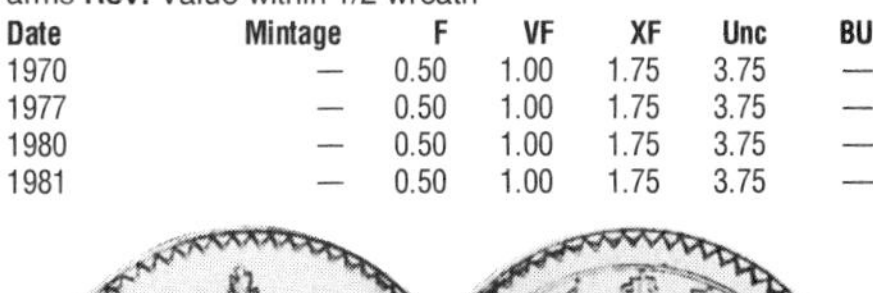
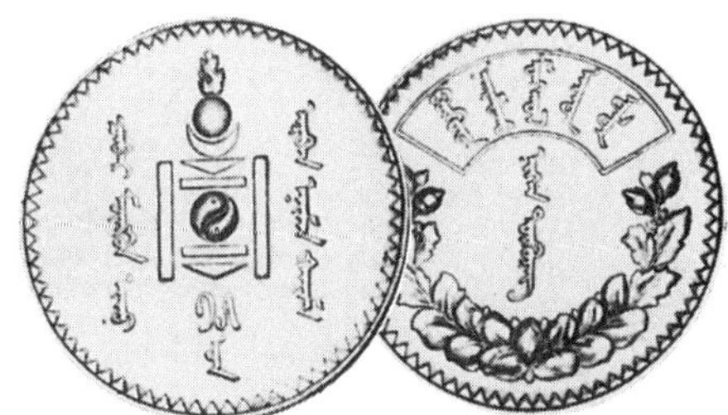

KM# 8 TUGRIK
19.9957 g., 0.9000 Silver 0.5786 oz. ASW, 34 mm. **Obv:** Soembo arms, text **Rev:** Value within 1/2 wreath

Date	Mintage	VG	F	VF	XF	Unc
AH15 (1925)	400,000	—	12.00	16.00	22.00	40.00

KM# 34 TUGRIK
14.9000 g., Aluminum-Bronze, 32 mm. **Subject:** 50th Anniversary of the Revolution **Obv:** National arms **Rev:** Man on horse left within beaded circle **Edge Lettering:** ONE TUGRIK 1921 - 1971 **Note:** Date on edge.

Date	Mintage	F	VF	XF	Unc	BU
ND(1971)	—	—	4.00	6.00	10.00	—

KM# 34a TUGRIK
Copper-Nickel, 32 mm. **Obv:** National arms **Rev:** Man on horse left within beaded circle

Date	Mintage	F	VF	XF	Unc	BU
ND(1971)	—	6.00	8.00	12.00	18.00	—

KM# 41 TUGRIK
14.9000 g., Aluminum-Bronze, 32 mm. **Subject:** 60th Anniversary of the Revolution **Obv:** National arms **Rev:** Man on horse left within beaded circle **Edge:** Lettered

Date	Mintage	F	VF	XF	Unc	BU
1981	—	—	—	4.00	7.50	9.00

KM# 42 TUGRIK
14.9000 g., Aluminum-Bronze, 32 mm. **Subject:** Soviet - Mongolian Space Flight **Obv:** National arms **Rev:** Conjoined helmeted heads left with stars at upper left and date at lower right **Edge:** Smooth

Date	Mintage	F	VF	XF	Unc	BU
1981	—	—	—	3.00	6.00	—

KM# 43 TUGRIK
14.9000 g., Aluminum-Bronze, 32 mm. **Subject:** 60th Anniversary of the State Bank **Obv:** National arms **Rev:** Value within design with date within 1/2 wreath **Edge:** Lettered

Date	Mintage	F	VF	XF	Unc	BU
1984	—	—	—	3.00	6.00	—

Note: Edge varieties exist

KM# 44 TUGRIK
14.9000 g., Aluminum-Bronze, 32 mm. **Subject:** 60th Anniversary of the People's Republic **Obv:** National arms **Rev:** Soembo arms and value within 1/2 wreath **Edge:** Lettered

Date	Mintage	F	VF	XF	Unc	BU
1984	—	—	—	3.00	5.50	—

KM# 48 TUGRIK
14.9000 g., Aluminum-Bronze, 32 mm. **Subject:** Year of Peace **Obv:** National arms **Rev:** Dove above hands and 3/4 wreath **Edge:** Lettered

Date	Mintage	F	VF	XF	Unc	BU
1986	—	—	—	3.50	7.50	—

KM# 49 TUGRIK
14.9000 g., Aluminum-Bronze, 32 mm. **Subject:** 65th Anniversary of the Revolution **Obv:** National arms **Rev:** Bust left **Edge:** Lettered

Date	Mintage	F	VF	XF	Unc	BU
1986	—	—	—	3.00	5.50	—

KM# 52 TUGRIK
14.9000 g., Aluminum-Bronze, 32 mm. **Subject:** 170th Anniversary - Birth of Karl Marx **Obv:** National arms **Rev:** Head facing flanked by dates

Date	Mintage	F	VF	XF	Unc	BU
ND(1988)	—	—	—	4.00	12.50	—

KM# 35 10 TUGRIK
Copper-Nickel **Subject:** 50th Anniversary of State Bank **Obv:** National arms **Rev:** State bank

Date	Mintage	F	VF	XF	Unc	BU
ND(1974)	—	—	—	—	9.00	—
ND(1974)	—	—	—	—	9.00	—

STATE

DECIMAL COINAGE

KM# 122 20 TUGRIK

Aluminum **Obv:** Soembo arms, text **Rev:** Value

Date	Mintage	F	VF	XF	Unc	BU
1994	—	—	—	—	1.50	1.75

KM# 123 50 TUGRIK

Aluminum **Obv:** Soembo arms, text **Rev:** Value within design

Date	Mintage	F	VF	XF	Unc	BU
1994	—	—	—	—	1.75	2.00

KM# 124 100 TUGRIK

Copper-Nickel **Obv:** Soembo arms, text **Rev:** Value below building

Date	Mintage	F	VF	XF	Unc	BU
1994	—	—	—	—	2.50	3.00

KM# 125 200 TUGRIK

Copper-Nickel **Obv:** Soembo arms, text **Rev:** Value below building

Date	Mintage	F	VF	XF	Unc	BU
1994	—	—	—	—	3.00	4.00

KM# 184 500 TUGRIK

25.0000 g., 0.9250 Bi-Metallic Goldine center in Silver ring 0.7435 oz. **Subject:** Genius of the Millennium - Edison **Obv:** National emblem **Rev:** Light bulb, telephone, record player **Note:** Goldine center is square.

Date	Mintage	F	VF	XF	Unc	BU
1999 Proof	2,500	Value: 43.50				

Note: KM#90, previously listed here, has been reported as never released.

KM# 195 500 TUGRIK

Copper-Nickel, 22.1 mm. **Subject:** Sukhe-Bataar **Obv:** National emblem and value **Rev:** Crowned head facing **Edge:** Plain

Date	Mintage	F	VF	XF	Unc	BU
2001	—	—	—	—	2.50	3.00

MONTENEGRO

The former independent kingdom of Montenegro, now one of the nominally autonomous federated units of Yugoslavia, was located in southeastern Europe north of Albania. As a kingdom, it had an area of 5,333 sq. mi. (13,812 sq. km.) and a population of about 250,000. Capital: Podgorica.

Montenegro became an independent state in 1355 following the break-up of the Serb empire. During the Turkish invasion of Albania and Herzegovina in the 15th century, the Montenegrins moved their capital to the remote mountain village of Cetinje where they maintained their independence through two centuries of intermittent attack, emerging as the only one of the Balkan states not subjugated by the Turks. When World War I began, Montenegro joined with Serbia and was subsequently invaded and occupied by the Austrians. Austria withdrew upon the defeat of the Central Powers, permitting the Serbians to move in and maintain the occupation. Montenegro then joined the kingdom of the Serbs, Croats and Slovenes, which later became Yugoslavia.

The coinage, issued under the autocratic rule of Prince Nicholas, is obsolete.

RULER

Nicholas I, as Prince, 1860-1910 as King, 1910-1918

MINT MARK

(a) - Paris, privy marks only

MONETARY SYSTEM

100 Para, ПАРА = 1 Perper, ПЕРПЕР

KINGDOM

STANDARD COINAGE

KM# 1 PARA

Bronze **Ruler:** Nicholas I **Obv:** Crowned arms **Rev:** Value

Date	Mintage	F	VF	XF	Unc	BU
1906	200,000	10.00	20.00	40.00	100	—

KM# 16 PARA

Bronze **Ruler:** Nicholas I **Obv:** Crowned arms **Rev:** Value

Date	Mintage	F	VF	XF	Unc	BU
1913	100,000	13.00	30.00	70.00	150	—
1914	200,000	7.00	15.00	30.00	100	—

KM# 2 2 PARE

Bronze **Ruler:** Nicholas I **Obv:** Crowned arms **Rev:** Value

Date	Mintage	F	VF	XF	Unc	BU
1906	600,125	5.00	10.00	20.00	50.00	—
1908	250,000	9.00	20.00	35.00	90.00	—

KM# 17 2 PARE

Bronze **Ruler:** Nicholas I **Obv:** Crowned arms **Rev:** Value

Date	Mintage	F	VF	XF	Unc	BU
1913	500,000	5.00	8.00	17.00	35.00	—
1914	400,000	6.00	10.00	20.00	48.00	—

KM# 3 10 PARA

Nickel **Ruler:** Nicholas I **Obv:** Crowned arms **Rev:** Value

Date	Mintage	F	VF	XF	Unc	BU
1906	750,156	2.50	5.00	12.00	26.00	—
1908	250,000	3.00	6.50	16.00	36.00	—

KM# 18 10 PARA

Nickel **Ruler:** Nicholas I

Date	Mintage	F	VF	XF	Unc	BU
1913	200,000	3.50	8.00	18.00	42.00	—
1914	800,000	2.50	5.00	12.00	25.00	—

KM# 4 20 PARA

Nickel **Ruler:** Nicholas I **Obv:** Crowned arms **Rev:** Value

Date	Mintage	F	VF	XF	Unc	BU
1906	600,156	3.00	6.00	12.00	26.00	—
1908	400,000	3.00	7.00	15.00	35.00	—

KM# 19 20 PARA

Nickel **Ruler:** Nicholas I **Obv:** Crowned arms **Rev:** Value

Date	Mintage	F	VF	XF	Unc	BU
1913	200,000	4.00	8.00	18.00	45.00	—
1914	800,000	3.00	6.00	12.00	25.00	—

KM# 5 PERPER

5.0000 g., 0.8350 Silver 0.1342 oz. ASW **Ruler:** Nicholas I **Obv:** Head right **Rev:** Crowned mantled arms within sprigs above date and value **Note:** Approximately 30 percent melted.

Date	Mintage	F	VF	XF	Unc	BU
1909(a)	500,018	12.00	22.00	42.00	95.00	—

KM# 14 PERPER

5.0000 g., 0.8350 Silver 0.1342 oz. ASW **Ruler:** Nicholas I **Obv:** Head right **Rev:** Crowned mantled arms within sprigs above value and date

Date	Mintage	F	VF	XF	Unc	BU
1912	520,008	8.00	14.00	30.00	85.00	—
1914	500,000	9.00	18.00	35.00	90.00	—

KM# 7 2 PERPERA
10.0000 g., 0.8350 Silver 0.2684 oz. ASW **Ruler:** Nicholas I **Obv:** Head right **Rev:** Crowned mantled arms within sprigs above date and value

Date	Mintage	F	VF	XF	Unc	BU
1910	300,006	15.00	35.00	70.00	180	—

KM# 20 2 PERPERA
10.0000 g., 0.8350 Silver 0.2684 oz. ASW **Ruler:** Nicholas I **Obv:** Head right **Rev:** Crowned mantled arms within sprigs above date and value

Date	Mintage	F	VF	XF	Unc	BU
1914	200,008	15.00	35.00	75.00	185	—

KM# 6 5 PERPERA
24.0000 g., 0.9000 Silver 0.6944 oz. ASW **Ruler:** Nicholas I **Obv:** Head right **Rev:** Crowned and mantled arms **Note:** Approximately 50 percent melted.

Date	Mintage	F	VF	XF	Unc	BU
1909(a)	60,010	70.00	140	330	800	—

KM# 15 5 PERPERA
24.0000 g., 0.9000 Silver 0.6944 oz. ASW **Ruler:** Nicholas I **Obv:** Head right **Rev:** Crowned mantled arms within sprigs above date and value

Date	Mintage	F	VF	XF	Unc	BU
1912	40,002	80.00	160	300	850	—
1914	20,002	85.00	160	330	970	1,000

MOROCCO

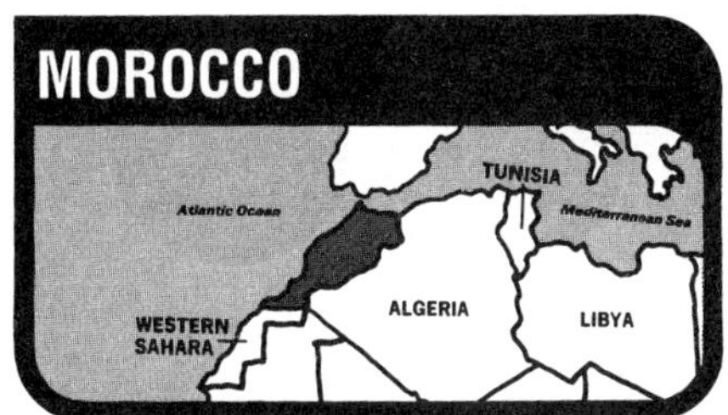

The Kingdom of Morocco, situated on the northwest corner of Africa, has an area of 275,117 sq. mi. (446,550 sq. km.) and a population of 28.5 million. Capital: Rabat. The economy is essentially agricultural. Phosphates, fresh and preserved vegetables, canned fish, and raw materials are exported.

Morocco's strategic position at the gateway to Western Europe has been the principal determinant of its violent, frequently unfortunate history. Time and again the fertile plain between the rugged Atlas Mountains and the sea has echoed the battle's trumpet as Phoenicians, Romans, Vandals, Visigoths, Byzantine Greeks and Islamic Arabs successively conquered and occupied the land. Modern Morocco is a remnant of an early empire formed by the Arabs at the close of the 7th century, which encompassed all of northwest Africa, and most of the Iberian Peninsula. During the 17th and 18th centuries, while under the control of native dynasties, it was the headquarters of the famous Sale pirates. Morocco's strategic position involved it in the competition of 19th century European powers for political influence in Africa, and resulted in the division of Morocco into French and Spanish spheres of interest, which were established as protectorates in 1912. Morocco became independent on March 2, 1956, after France agreed to end its protectorate. Spain signed similar agreements on April 7 of the same year.

TITLES

المعربية

Al-Maghribiya(t)

المملكة المغربية

Al-Mamlaka(t) al-Maghribiya(t)

المحمدية الشريفة

Al-Mohammediya(t) esh-Sherifiya(t)

RULERS

Abd al-Aziz, AH1311-1326/1894-1908AD
Abd al-Hafiz, AH1326-1330/1908-1912AD

French Protectorate, AH1330/1912AD
Yusuf, AH1330-1346/1912-1927AD
Mohammed V, AH1346-1375/1927-1955AD

Kingdom
Mohammed V, AH1376-1381/1956-1962AD
Al-Hasan II, AH1381-1420/1962-1999AD
Mohammed VI, AH1420- /1999- AD

MINTS

(a) - Paris privy marks only

Silver Coins — Bronze Coins

Bi - England (Birmingham)

بانكلند

Ln = bi-England (London)

بباريز

Pa = bi-Bariz (Paris)

فاس

Fs = Fes (Fas, Fez)

Py - Poissy Inscribed "Paris" but with thunderbolt privy mark.

NOTE: Some of the above forms of the mint names are shown as they appear on the coins, not in regular Arabic script.

NOTES: On the silver coins the denominations are written in words and each series has its own characteristic names:
Y#9-13 (1313-1319) Denomination in 'Preferred" Dirhams.
Y#18-22 (1320-1323) Denomination in fractions of a Rial, but on the 3 larger sizes, the equivalent is given in "Urti parts", 1 Rial 20 = Urti parts.
Y#23-25 (1329) Denomination in Dirhams and in fraction of a Rial.
Y#30-33 (1331-1336) Denomination in Yusuti or "Treasury" Dirhams.

On most of the larger denominations, the denomination is given in the form of a rhymed couplet.

NOTE: Various copper and silver coins dated AH1297-1311 are believed to be patterns. Copper coins similar to Y#14-17, but without denomination on reverse, are patterns.

NOTE: 1, 2, 5 and 10 Mazunas of AH1320 Fes exist in medal alignment and coin alignment (rare). AH1321-1323 Fes strikes are medal alignment only.

KINGDOM

Filali Sharifs - Alawi Dynasty

Abd al-Aziz

AH1311-1326/1894-1908AD

MILLED COINAGE

Y# 9.2 1/2 DIRHAM
1.4558 g., 0.8350 Silver 0.0391 oz. ASW **Obv:** Star of David within inner circle flanked by arrow heads facing inwards **Rev:** Star of David within inner circle flanked by arrow heads facing inwards

Date	Mintage	F	VF	XF	Unc	BU
AH1319Pa	572,000	15.00	40.00	120	280	—

REFORM COINAGE

AH1320 / 1902AD

Y# 14.1 MUZUNA
1.0000 g., Bronze **Obv:** Date within circle **Rev:** Value within circle

Date	Mintage	F	VF	XF	Unc	BU
AH1320Bi	3,000,000	4.50	9.00	20.00	40.00	—
AH1321Bi	900,000	8.00	20.00	50.00	120	—

Y# 14.2 MUZUNA
1.0000 g., Bronze **Obv:** Date within circle **Rev:** Value within circle **Note:** Varieties exist.

Date	Mintage	F	VF	XF	Unc	BU
AH1320Fs	—	80.00	200	400	—	—

Y# 15.1 2 MAZUNAS
2.0000 g., Bronze **Obv:** Date within circle **Rev:** Value within circle

Date	Mintage	F	VF	XF	Unc	BU
AH1320Bi	1,500,000	8.50	18.50	35.00	75.00	—
AH1321Bi	450,000	15.00	35.00	60.00	120	—

Y# 15.2 2 MAZUNAS
2.0000 g., Bronze **Note:** Normal rim design; varieties exist.

Date	Mintage	F	VF	XF	Unc	BU
AH1320Fs	—	30.00	100	250	—	—
AH1322Fs	—	100	250	500	—	—
AH1323Fs	—	50.00	150	350	—	—

Y# 15.3 2 MAZUNAS
2.0000 g., Bronze **Obv:** Date within circle **Rev:** Value within circle, rim design reversed

Date	Mintage	F	VF	XF	Unc	BU
AH1320Fs Rare	—	—	—	—	—	—

Y# 15.4 2 MAZUNAS
2.0000 g., Bronze, 20.1 mm. **Note:** Normal rim design.

Date	Mintage	F	VF	XF	Unc	BU
AH1321Pa	6,500,000	2.00	6.00	12.00	30.00	—

Y# 16.1 5 MAZUNAS
5.0000 g., Bronze **Obv:** Date within circle **Rev:** Value within circle

Date	Mintage	F	VF	XF	Unc	BU
AH1320Bi	2,400,000	2.00	5.00	10.00	30.00	—
AH1321Bi	720,000	4.00	10.00	20.00	50.00	—

Y# 16.2 5 MAZUNAS
5.0000 g., Bronze **Obv:** Date within circle **Rev:** Value within circle **Note:** Varieties exist.

Date	Mintage	F	VF	XF	Unc	BU
AH1320Fs	—	25.00	50.00	130	—	—
AH1322Fs	—	40.00	90.00	240	—	—

Y# 16.3 5 MAZUNAS
5.0000 g., Bronze **Obv:** Date within circle **Rev:** Value within circle

Date	Mintage	F	VF	XF	Unc	BU
AH1321Pa	7,950,000	2.00	5.00	10.00	30.00	—

Y# 17.1 10 MAZUNAS
10.0000 g., Bronze

Date	Mintage	F	VF	XF	Unc	BU
AH1320Be	2,400,000	2.00	5.00	15.00	40.00	—
AH1321Be	2,600,000	2.00	5.00	15.00	40.00	—

Y# 17.2 10 MAZUNAS
10.0000 g., Bronze **Obv:** Date within circle **Rev:** Value within circle

Date	Mintage	F	VF	XF	Unc	BU
AH1320Bi	1,200,000	3.00	6.00	18.00	50.00	—
AH1321Bi	360,000	4.00	12.00	35.00	100	—

Y# 17.3 10 MAZUNAS
10.0000 g., Bronze **Obv:** Date within circle **Rev:** Value within circle **Note:** Varieties exist.

Date	Mintage	F	VF	XF	Unc	BU
AH1320Fs Small letters	—	200	350	600	1,000	—
AH1320Fs Large letters	—	20.00	60.00	150	300	—
AH1321Fs	—	18.00	50.00	150	300	—
AH1323Fs Large 10	—	75.00	150	300	600	—
AH1323Fs Small 10	—	85.00	175	375	700	—

Y# 18.1 1/20 RIAL (1/2 Dirham)
1.2500 g., 0.8350 Silver 0.0336 oz. ASW **Obv:** Inscription **Rev:** Value and date

Date	Mintage	F	VF	XF	Unc	BU
AH1320Ln	3,920,000	2.00	6.00	20.00	50.00	—
AH1321Ln	2,105,000	3.00	8.00	25.00	55.00	—

Y# 18.2 1/20 RIAL (1/2 Dirham)
1.2500 g., 0.8350 Silver 0.0336 oz. ASW

Date	Mintage	F	VF	XF	Unc	BU
AH1320Pa	2,400,000	3.00	8.00	25.00	55.00	—

Y# 19 1/10 RIAL (Dirham)
2.5000 g., 0.8350 Silver 0.0671 oz. ASW

Date	Mintage	F	VF	XF	Unc	BU
AH1320Ln	2,940,000	3.00	8.00	25.00	55.00	—
AH1321Ln	770,000	6.00	18.00	40.00	100	—

Y# 20.1 1/4 RIAL (2-1/2 Dirhams)
6.2500 g., 0.8350 Silver 0.1678 oz. ASW, 25 mm. **Obv:** Inscription within inner circle, legend around border **Rev:** Inscription and date within the Star of David, legend flanked by star points

Date	Mintage	F	VF	XF	Unc	BU
AH1320Be	1,380,000	4.00	12.50	45.00	120	—
AH1321Be	4,450,000	3.00	8.00	30.00	80.00	—
AH1321Be Proof; Rare	5	—	—	—	—	—

Y# 20.2 1/4 RIAL (2-1/2 Dirhams)
6.2500 g., 0.8350 Silver 0.1678 oz. ASW, 25 mm.

Date	Mintage	F	VF	XF	Unc	BU
AH1320Ln	3,056,000	4.00	12.50	35.00	90.00	—
AH1321Ln	1,889,000	5.00	15.00	45.00	100	—

Y# 20.3 1/4 RIAL (2-1/2 Dirhams)
6.2500 g., 0.8350 Silver 0.1678 oz. ASW, 25 mm.

Date	Mintage	F	VF	XF	Unc	BU
AH1320Pa	480,000	12.00	30.00	125	250	—
AH1321Pa	160,000	40.00	80.00	250	450	—

Y# 21.1 1/2 RIAL (5 Dirhams)
12.5000 g., 0.8350 Silver 0.3356 oz. ASW, 32 mm.

Date	Mintage	F	VF	XF	Unc	BU
AH1320Be	2,510,000	10.00	25.00	80.00	180	—

Y# 21.2 1/2 RIAL (5 Dirhams)
12.5000 g., 0.8350 Silver 0.3356 oz. ASW, 32 mm.

Date	Mintage	F	VF	XF	Unc	BU
AH1320Ln	900,000	12.00	30.00	90.00	200	—
AH1321Ln	1,041,000	10.00	25.00	80.00	180	—

Y# 21.3 1/2 RIAL (5 Dirhams)
12.5000 g., 0.8350 Silver 0.3356 oz. ASW, 32 mm.

Date	Mintage	F	VF	XF	Unc	BU
AH1321Pa	1,800,000	8.00	20.00	70.00	160	—
AH1322Pa	540,000	15.00	40.00	110	240	—
AH1323Pa	1,090,000	12.00	30.00	90.00	200	—

Y# 22.1 RIAL (10 Dirhams)
25.0000 g., 0.9000 Silver 0.7234 oz. ASW, 37 mm.

Date	Mintage	F	VF	XF	Unc	BU
AH1320Ln	330,000	25.00	70.00	160	300	—

Y# 22.2 RIAL (10 Dirhams)
25.0000 g., 0.9000 Silver 0.7234 oz. ASW, 37 mm. **Obv:** Inscription within circle, legend around border **Rev:** Inscription and date within the Star of David, legend flanked by star points

Date	Mintage	F	VF	XF	Unc	BU
AH1321Pa	300,000	25.00	70.00	160	300	—

Abd al-Hafiz
AH1326-1330/1908-1912AD

REFORM COINAGE
AH1320 / 1902AD

Y# 23 1/4 RIAL (2-1/2 Dirhams)
6.2500 g., 0.8350 Silver 0.1678 oz. ASW **Obv:** Inscription below star within sprays **Rev:** Mint, name and date within doubled tri-lobe star

Date	Mintage	F	VF	XF	Unc	BU
AH1329Pa	3,900,000	12.00	25.00	60.00	130	—

Y# 24 1/2 RIAL (5 Dirhams)
12.5000 g., 0.8350 Silver 0.3356 oz. ASW **Obv:** Star above inscription within sprays **Rev:** Mint, name and date within doubled tri-lobe star

Date	Mintage	F	VF	XF	Unc	BU
AH1329Pa	6,200,000	10.00	22.00	55.00	120	—

Y# 25 RIAL (10 Dirhams)
25.0000 g., 0.9000 Silver 0.7234 oz. ASW **Obv:** Star above inscription within sprays **Rev:** Mint, name and date within doubled tri-lobe star

Date	Mintage	F	VF	XF	Unc	BU
AH1329Pa	10,100,000	12.00	25.00	55.00	120	—

Yusuf
AH1330-1346/1912-1927AD

REFORM COINAGE
AH1320 / 1902AD

Y# 26 MUZUNA
Bronze **Obv:** Value within star **Rev:** Mint name and date within doubled tri-lobe star

Date	Mintage	F	VF	XF	Unc	BU
AH1330Pa	1,850,000	2.00	7.00	20.00	40.00	—

Y# 27 2 MAZUNAS
Bronze **Obv:** Value within star **Rev:** Mint name and date within doubled tri-lobe star

Date	Mintage	F	VF	XF	Unc	BU
AH1330Pa	2,790,000	2.00	5.00	20.00	45.00	—

Note: Coins reportedly dated 1331Pa probably bore date AH1330

Y# 28.1 5 MAZUNAS
Bronze **Obv:** Value within star **Rev:** Mint name and date within doubled tri-lobe star

Date	Mintage	F	VF	XF	Unc	BU
AH1330Pa	2,983,000	2.00	5.00	20.00	50.00	—
AH1340Pa	2,000,000	2.00	5.00	20.00	50.00	—

Y# 28.2 5 MAZUNAS
Bronze **Obv:** Value within star **Rev:** Mint name and date within doubled tri-lobe star

Date	Mintage	F	VF	XF	Unc	BU
AH1340Py	2,010,000	2.00	5.00	20.00	50.00	—

Y# 29.1 10 MAZUNAS
Bronze **Obv:** Value within star **Rev:** Mint name and date within doubled tri-lobe star

Date	Mintage	F	VF	XF	Unc	BU
AH1330Pa	1,500,000	2.00	6.00	22.00	55.00	—
AH1340Pa	1,000,000	2.00	6.00	22.00	55.00	—

Y# 29.2 10 MAZUNAS
Bronze **Obv:** Value within star **Rev:** Mint name and date within doubled tri-lobe star, privy marks

Date	Mintage	F	VF	XF	Unc	BU
AH1340Py	1,000,000	2.00	6.00	22.00	55.00	—

Y# 30 1/10 RIAL (Dirham)
2.5000 g., 0.8350 Silver 0.0671 oz. ASW **Obv:** Inscription **Rev:** Mint name and date

Date	Mintage	F	VF	XF	Unc	BU
AH1331Pa	500,000	30.00	45.00	75.00	200	—
AH1331Pa Proof	—	Value: 800				

Y# 31 1/4 RIAL (2-1/2 Dirhams)
6.2500 g., 0.8350 Silver 0.1678 oz. ASW **Obv:** Inscription and date within the Star of David, legend flanked by star points **Rev:** Mint name and date within circle

Date	Mintage	F	VF	XF	Unc	BU
AH1331Pa	1,700,000	30.00	45.00	90.00	225	—

Y# 32 1/2 RIAL (5 Dirhams)
0.8350 Silver **Obv:** Inscription and date within the Star of David, legend flanked by star points **Rev:** Mint name and date within circle

Date	Mintage	F	VF	XF	Unc	BU
AH1331Pa	4,300,000	10.00	20.00	40.00	125	—
AH1336Pa	7,200,000	6.00	11.00	25.00	60.00	—

Y# 33 RIAL (10 Dirhams)
25.0000 g., 0.9000 Silver 0.7234 oz. ASW **Obv:** Inscription and date within the Star of David, legend flanked by star points **Rev:** Mint name and date within circle

Date	Mintage	F	VF	XF	Unc	BU
AH1331Pa	4,200,000	12.00	20.00	60.00	120	—
AH1336Pa	2,500,000	13.00	22.00	70.00	130	—

FRENCH PROTECTORATE

Yusuf
AH1330-1346/1912-1927AD

STANDARD COINAGE
100 Centimes = 1 Franc

Y# 34.1 25 CENTIMES
Copper-Nickel, 24 mm. **Obv:** Hole in center of the star of David within circle, without privy marks **Rev:** Hole in center flanked by value within circle, without privy marks

Date	Mintage	F	VF	XF	Unc	BU
ND(1921)Pa	8,000,000	1.00	3.00	8.00	30.00	—

Y# 34.2 25 CENTIMES
Copper-Nickel, 24 mm. **Obv:** Hole in center of the star of David within circle **Rev:** Hole in center flanked by value within circle

Date	Mintage	F	VF	XF	Unc	BU
ND(1924)Py	2,037,000	2.00	4.00	15.00	45.00	—

Y# 34.3 25 CENTIMES
Copper-Nickel, 24 mm. **Rev:** Thunderbolt and torch at left and right of CENTIMES

Date	Mintage	F	VF	XF	Unc	BU
ND(1924)Py	Inc. above	2.00	4.00	15.00	45.00	—

Y# 35.1 50 CENTIMES
Nickel **Obv:** Star within circle ,without privy marks **Rev:** Value within artistic designed star, without privy marks

Date	Mintage	F	VF	XF	Unc	BU
ND(1921)Pa	7,976,000	0.50	1.00	6.50	25.00	—

Y# 35.2 50 CENTIMES
Nickel **Obv:** Star within circle **Rev:** Value within artistic designed star, thunderbolt at bottom

Date	Mintage	F	VF	XF	Unc	BU
ND(1924)Py	3,000,000	1.00	2.00	8.00	30.00	—

Y# 36.1 FRANC
Nickel, 27 mm. **Obv:** Star within circle, without privy marks **Rev:** Value within artistic designed star, without privy marks

Date	Mintage	F	VF	XF	Unc	BU
ND(1921)Pa	8,325,000	0.50	1.00	6.50	25.00	—

Y# 36.2 FRANC
Nickel, 27 mm. **Obv:** Star within circle **Rev:** Value within artistic designed star, thunderbolt below 1

Date	Mintage	F	VF	XF	Unc	BU
ND(1924)Py	4,796,000	1.25	2.50	10.00	35.00	—

Mohammed V
AH1346-1381/1927-1962AD

STANDARD COINAGE
100 Centimes = 1 Franc

Y# 40 50 CENTIMES
Aluminum-Bronze **Obv:** Star **Rev:** Value flanked by dates

Date	Mintage	F	VF	XF	Unc	BU
AH1364-1945(a)	24,000,000	—	0.50	2.00	6.00	—

Y# 41 FRANC

Aluminum-Bronze **Obv:** Legend around star **Rev:** Value flanked by dates

Date	Mintage	F	VF	XF	Unc	BU
AH1364-1945(a)	24,000,000	—	0.50	2.00	6.00	—

Y# 46 FRANC

Aluminum, 19.5 mm. **Obv:** Legend around star **Rev:** Value flanked by dates

Date	Mintage	F	VF	XF	Unc	BU
AH1370-1951(a)	33,000,000	—	0.25	1.00	3.00	—

Note: Note: Y#46-51 were struck for more than 20 years without change of date, until a new currency was introduced in 1974

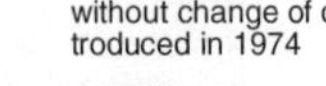

Y# 42 2 FRANCS

Aluminum-Bronze **Obv:** Legend around star **Rev:** Value flanked by dates

Date	Mintage	F	VF	XF	Unc	BU
AH1364-1945(a)	12,000,000	—	1.00	5.00	12.00	—

Y# 47 2 FRANCS

Aluminum, 22 mm. **Obv:** Legend around star **Rev:** Value flanked by dates

Date	Mintage	F	VF	XF	Unc	BU
AH1370-1951(a)	20,000,000	—	0.25	1.00	3.00	—

Y# 37 5 FRANCS

5.0000 g., 0.6800 Silver 0.1093 oz. ASW **Obv:** Date within small circle of doubled tri-lobe star, all within circle **Rev:** Value within doubled square within circle

Date	Mintage	F	VF	XF	Unc	BU
AH1347(a)	4,000,000	—	3.00	15.00	35.00	—
AH1352(a)	5,000,000	—	2.00	12.00	28.00	—

Y# 43 5 FRANCS

Aluminum-Bronze **Obv:** Date within small circle of doubled tri-lobe star, all within circle **Rev:** Value in doubled square within circle

Date	Mintage	F	VF	XF	Unc	BU
AH1365(a)	20,000,000	0.25	0.50	3.00	10.00	—

Y# 48 5 FRANCS

Aluminum, 25 mm. **Obv:** Date within small circle of doubled tri-lobe star, all within circle **Rev:** Value flanked by marks in doubled square within circle

Date	Mintage	F	VF	XF	Unc	BU
AH1370(a)	23,000,000	0.15	0.30	1.00	5.00	—

Y# 38 10 FRANCS

10.0000 g., 0.6800 Silver 0.2186 oz. ASW **Obv:** Date in small circle of doubled tri-lobe star, all within circle **Rev:** Date in doubled square within circle

Date	Mintage	F	VF	XF	Unc	BU
AH1347(a)	1,600,000	4.50	10.00	22.00	50.00	—
AH1352(a)	2,900,000	3.00	5.00	15.00	40.00	—

Y# 44 10 FRANCS

Copper-Nickel **Obv:** Date in small circle of doubled tri-lobe star, all within circle **Rev:** Value in doubled square within circle

Date	Mintage	F	VF	XF	Unc	BU
AH1366(a)	20,000,000	0.50	1.00	2.00	6.00	—

Y# 49 10 FRANCS

Aluminum-Bronze, 20 mm. **Obv:** Star flanked by designs, date on bottom **Rev:** Value flanked by designs

Date	Mintage	F	VF	XF	Unc	BU
AH1371(a)	40,000,000	0.15	0.50	2.00	6.00	—

Y# 39 20 FRANCS

20.0000 g., 0.6800 Silver 0.4372 oz. ASW **Obv:** Date in inner circle of doubled tri-lobe star, all within circle **Rev:** Value in doubled square within circle

Date	Mintage	F	VF	XF	Unc	BU
AH1347(a)	177,000	7.50	22.00	60.00	120	—
AH1352(a)	2,000,000	4.00	8.00	30.00	60.00	—

Y# 45 20 FRANCS

Copper-Nickel **Obv:** Date in inner circle of doubled tri-lobe star, all within circle **Rev:** Value in doubled square within circle

Date	Mintage	F	VF	XF	Unc	BU
AH1366(a)	6,000,000	0.35	0.65	2.00	6.00	—
AH1366(a) Proof	—	Value: 50.00				

Y# 50 20 FRANCS

Aluminum-Bronze, 23.8 mm. **Obv:** Star flanked by designs, date on bottom **Rev:** Value flanked by designs

Date	Mintage	F	VF	XF	Unc	BU
AH1371(a)	20,000,000	0.25	0.50	1.00	4.00	—

Y# 51 50 FRANCS

Aluminum-Bronze, 27 mm. **Obv:** Date in inner circle of doubled tri-lobe star, all within circle **Rev:** Value in doubled square within circle

Date	Mintage	F	VF	XF	Unc	BU
AH1371(a)	20,600,000	0.35	0.65	2.00	8.00	—

Y# 51a 50 FRANCS

Gold **Obv:** Date in inner circle of doubled tri-lobe star, all within circle **Rev:** Value within doubled square within circle

Date	Mintage	F	VF	XF	Unc	BU
AH1371(a) Rare	—	—	—	—	—	—

Y# A54 100 FRANCS

2.5000 g., 0.7200 Silver 0.0579 oz. ASW **Obv:** Star flanked by designs, date on bottom **Rev:** Value flanked by designs

Date	Mintage	F	VF	XF	Unc	BU
AH1370(a)	10,000,000	—	—	—	500	—

Note: Nearly all specimens were melted, only 100 known

Y# 52 100 FRANCS

4.0000 g., 0.7200 Silver 0.0926 oz. ASW **Obv:** Star within small circle in center of larger star with designs in points **Rev:** Value within beaded circle, legend around border

Date	Mintage	F	VF	XF	Unc	BU
AH1372-1953(a)	20,000,000	—	2.00	10.00	20.00	—

Y# 53 200 FRANCS
8.0000 g., 0.7200 Silver 0.1852 oz. ASW **Obv:** Star within small circle in center of larger star with designs in points **Rev:** Value and date within beaded circle

Date	Mintage	F	VF	XF	Unc	BU
AH1372-1953 (1953) (a)	10,176,000	—	3.00	12.00	25.00	—

Y# 54 500 FRANCS
22.5000 g., 0.9000 Silver 0.6510 oz. ASW **Obv:** Bust left within circle **Rev:** Crown in center of star flanked by dates and value

Date	Mintage	F	VF	XF	Unc	BU
AH1376-1956(a)	2,000,000	—	5.00	18.00	40.00	—

KINGDOM
1956-

Mohammed V
AH1346-1381/1927-1962AD

REFORM COINAGE
100 Francs = 1 Dirham

Y# 55 DIRHAM
6.0000 g., 0.6000 Silver 0.1157 oz. ASW **Obv:** Head left **Rev:** Crowned arms with supporters flanked by dates above and value below

Date	Mintage	F	VF	XF	Unc	BU
AH1380-1960(a)	33,000,000	—	1.00	3.00	8.00	—

al-Hassan II
AH1381-1420/1962-1999AD

REFORM COINAGE
100 Francs = 1 Dirham

Y# 56 DIRHAM
Nickel, 23.6 mm. **Obv:** Head left **Rev:** Crowned arms with supporters

Date	Mintage	F	VF	XF	Unc	BU
AH1384-1965(a)	30,000,000	—	0.50	0.75	2.00	—
AH1388-1968(a)	5,000,000	1.00	2.00	4.00	10.00	—
AH1389-1969(a)	17,200,000	—	0.50	0.75	2.00	—

Y# 57 5 DIRHAMS
11.7500 g., 0.7200 Silver 0.2720 oz. ASW **Obv:** Head left **Rev:** Crowned arms with supporters

Date	Mintage	F	VF	XF	Unc	BU
AH1384-1965(a)	2,000,000	—	5.00	12.00	30.00	—
AH1384-1965(a) Proof	200	Value: 60.00				

REFORM COINAGE
100 Santimat = 1 Dirham

Y# 87 1/2 DIRHAM
Copper-Nickel **Obv:** Head left **Obv. Designer:** David Wynne **Rev:** Crowned arms with supporters

Date	Mintage	F	VF	XF	Unc	BU
AH1407-1987	—	—	—	—	1.50	—

Y# 63 DIRHAM
6.0000 g., Copper-Nickel, 24 mm. **Obv:** Head left **Obv. Designer:** David Wynne **Rev:** Crowned arms with supporters

Date	Mintage	F	VF	XF	Unc	BU
AH1394-1974	32,850,000	—	0.30	0.50	1.00	—

Y# 88 DIRHAM
Copper-Nickel **Obv:** Head left **Obv. Designer:** David Wynne **Rev:** Crowned arms with supporters

Date	Mintage	F	VF	XF	Unc	BU
AH1407-1987	—	—	—	—	2.75	—

Y# 58 SANTIM
0.7000 g., Aluminum, 17 mm. **Obv:** Crowned arms with supporters **Rev:** Value flanked by designs

Date	Mintage	F	VF	XF	Unc	BU
AH1394-1974	10,240,000	—	—	0.50	2.00	—

Y# 93 SANTIM
0.7000 g., Aluminum, 17 mm. **Obv:** Crowned arms with supporters **Rev:** Fish above value

Date	Mintage	F	VF	XF	Unc	BU
AH1407-1987	—	—	—	6.00	12.00	—

Note: Most were melted

Y# 59 5 SANTIMAT
2.0000 g., Brass, 17.5 mm. **Series:** F.A.O. **Obv:** Crowned arms with supporters **Rev:** Value at lower right of captains wheel

Date	Mintage	F	VF	XF	Unc	BU
AH1394-1974	54,820,000	—	—	0.15	1.00	—

Y# 83 5 SANTIMAT
2.0000 g., Brass, 17.5 mm. **Series:** F.A.O. **Obv:** Crowned arms with supporters **Rev:** Value to upper left of center design **Edge:** Plain

Date	Mintage	F	VF	XF	Unc	BU
AH1407-1987	—	—	—	—	1.00	—

Y# 60 10 SANTIMAT
3.0000 g., Brass, 20 mm. **Series:** F.A.O. **Obv:** Crowned arms with supporters **Rev:** Value at lower left of designs

Date	Mintage	F	VF	XF	Unc	BU
AH1394-1974	67,950,000	—	—	0.15	1.00	—

Y# 84 10 SANTIMAT
3.4000 g., Brass, 20 mm. **Series:** F.A.O. **Obv:** Crowned arms with supporters **Rev:** Single ear of corn to left of value **Edge:** Reeded

Date	Mintage	F	VF	XF	Unc	BU
AH1407-1987	—	—	—	—	1.00	—

Y# 61 20 SANTIMAT
4.0000 g., Brass, 23 mm. **Obv:** Head left **Obv. Designer:** David Wynne **Rev:** Crowned arms with supporters

Date	Mintage	F	VF	XF	Unc	BU
AH1394-1974	59,840,000	—	0.30	0.40	1.00	—

Y# 85 20 SANTIMAT
4.0000 g., Brass, 23 mm. **Series:** F.A.O. **Obv:** Crowned arms with supporters **Rev:** Value to right of designs

Date	Mintage	F	VF	XF	Unc	BU
AH1407-1987	—	—	—	—	1.00	—

Y# 62 50 SANTIMAT
4.0000 g., Copper-Nickel, 21 mm. **Obv:** Head left **Obv. Designer:** David Wynne **Rev:** Crowned arms with supporters

Date	Mintage	F	VF	XF	Unc	BU
AH1394-1974	40,380,000	—	0.20	0.40	1.00	—

Y# 64 5 DIRHAMS
Copper-Nickel **Series:** World Food Conference **Obv:** Head left **Obv. Designer:** David Wynne **Rev:** Small value within center of designs

Date	Mintage	F	VF	XF	Unc	BU
AH1395-1975	500,000	—	—	4.00	12.00	—
AH1395-1975 Proof	500	Value: 80.00				

Y# 72 5 DIRHAMS
12.0000 g., Copper-Nickel, 29 mm. **Obv:** Head left **Obv. Designer:** David Wynne **Rev:** Crowned arms with supporters

Date	Mintage	F	VF	XF	Unc	BU
AH1400-1980	10,000,000	—	1.50	4.00	10.00	—

Y# 82 5 DIRHAMS
6.8000 g., Bi-Metallic Aluminum-Bronze center in Stainless Steel ring, 26.2 mm. **Obv:** Head left within circle **Obv. Designer:** David Wynne **Rev:** Crowned arms with supporters and value within circle

Date	Mintage	F	VF	XF	Unc	BU
AH1407-1987	—	—	2.00	4.50	7.50	—

Y# 92 10 DIRHAMS
12.0000 g., Bi-Metallic Copper-Nickel center in Brass ring, 28 mm. **Obv:** Hooded head left within circle with star below **Rev:** Crowned arms with supporters and value within circle with star above

Date	Mintage	F	VF	XF	Unc	BU
AH1415-1995	—	—	—	—	8.00	—

MOZAMBIQUE

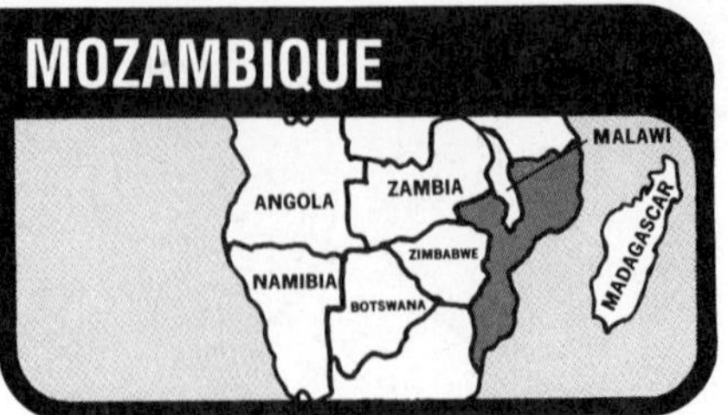

The Republic of Mozambique, a former overseas province of Portugal, stretches for 1,430 miles (2,301 km.) along the southeast coast of Africa, has an area of 302,330 sq. mi. (801,590 sq. km.) and a population of 14.1 million, 99 % of whom are native Africans of the Bantu tribes. Capital: Maputo. Agriculture is the chief industry. Cashew nuts, cotton, sugar, copra and tea are exported.

Vasco de Gama explored all the coast of Mozambique in 1498 and found Arab trading posts already established along the coast. Portuguese settlement dates from the establishment of the trading post of Mozambique in 1505. Within five years Portugal absorbed all the former Arab sultanates along the east African coast. The area was organized as a colony in 1907 and became an overseas province in 1952. In Sept. of 1974, after more than a decade of guerrilla warfare with the forces of the Mozambique Liberation Front, Portugal agreed to the independence of Mozambique, effective June 25, 1975. The Socialist party, led by President Joaquim Chissano was in power until the 2nd of November, 1990 when they became a republic.

Mozambique became a member of the Commonwealth of Nations in November 1995. The President is Head of State; the Prime Minister is Head of Government.

RULER
Portuguese, until 1975

MONETARY SYSTEM
100 Centavos = 1 Escudo

PORTUGUESE COLONY

DECIMAL COINAGE

100 Centavos = 1 Escudo

KM# 63 10 CENTAVOS
Bronze **Obv:** Value **Rev:** Arms

Date	Mintage	F	VF	XF	Unc	BU
1936	2,000,000	2.00	10.00	35.00	50.00	—

KM# 72 10 CENTAVOS
3.9400 g., Bronze, 22.57 mm. **Obv:** Value **Rev:** Arms within crowned globe **Edge:** Plain

Date	Mintage	F	VF	XF	Unc	BU
1942	2,000,000	1.00	2.50	12.50	20.00	—

KM# 83 10 CENTAVOS
1.7000 g., Bronze, 16 mm. **Obv:** Value **Rev:** Arms within crowned globe

Date	Mintage	F	VF	XF	Unc	BU
1960	3,750,000	—	0.50	1.25	3.00	—
1961	10,300,000	—	0.25	1.00	2.50	—

KM# 64 20 CENTAVOS
Bronze **Obv:** Value **Rev:** Arms

Date	Mintage	F	VF	XF	Unc	BU
1936	2,500,000	2.00	14.50	50.00	90.00	—

KM# 71 20 CENTAVOS
Bronze **Obv:** Value **Rev:** Arms within crowned globe

Date	Mintage	F	VF	XF	Unc	BU
1941	2,000,000	1.75	14.50	50.00	90.00	—

KM# 75 20 CENTAVOS
Bronze, 20.3 mm. **Obv:** Value **Rev:** Arms within crowned globe

Date	Mintage	F	VF	XF	Unc	BU
1949	8,000,000	0.75	1.50	4.00	10.00	—
1950	12,500,000	0.75	1.50	3.00	8.50	—

KM# 85 20 CENTAVOS
2.5300 g., Bronze, 18 mm. **Obv:** Value **Rev:** Arms within crowned globe

Date	Mintage	F	VF	XF	Unc	BU
1961	12,500,000	—	0.25	1.00	2.50	—

KM# 88 20 CENTAVOS
1.8000 g., Bronze, 16 mm. **Obv:** Value **Rev:** Arms within crowned globe **Edge:** Plain **Note:** Reduced size.

Date	Mintage	F	VF	XF	Unc	BU
1973	1,798,000	1.00	2.00	3.00	7.50	—
1974	13,044,000	1.00	2.50	3.75	9.00	—

KM# 65 50 CENTAVOS
Copper-Nickel **Obv:** Value **Rev:** Arms

Date	Mintage	F	VF	XF	Unc	BU
1936	2,500,000	5.00	45.00	125	225	—

KM# 73 50 CENTAVOS
4.0000 g., Bronze **Obv:** Value **Rev:** Arms within crowned globe

Date	Mintage	F	VF	XF	Unc	BU
1945	2,500,000	1.50	3.50	25.00	50.00	80.00

KM# 76 50 CENTAVOS
Nickel-Bronze **Obv:** Value **Rev:** Arms within crowned globe

Date	Mintage	F	VF	XF	Unc	BU
1950	20,000,000	1.00	3.00	12.00	22.00	32.00
1951	16,000,000	1.00	3.00	10.00	20.00	30.00

KM# 81 50 CENTAVOS
Bronze **Obv:** Value **Rev:** Arms within crowned globe

Date	Mintage	F	VF	XF	Unc	BU
1953	5,010,000	0.50	1.50	4.00	10.00	—
1957	24,990,000	—	0.50	1.25	4.50	8.00

KM# 89 50 CENTAVOS
4.5300 g., Bronze, 22.49 mm. **Obv:** Value **Rev:** Arms within crowned globe

Date	Mintage	F	VF	XF	Unc	BU
1973	6,841,000	—	0.50	1.00	3.00	—
1974	23,810,000	—	0.50	1.00	4.00	—

KM# 66 ESCUDO
8.0000 g., Copper-Nickel **Obv:** Value **Rev:** Arms

Date	Mintage	F	VF	XF	Unc	BU
1936	2,000,000	4.00	25.00	150	210	—

KM# 74 ESCUDO
Bronze **Obv:** Value **Rev:** Arms within crowned globe

Date	Mintage	F	VF	XF	Unc	BU
1945	2,000,000	2.00	15.00	45.00	110	200

KM# 77 ESCUDO
Nickel-Bronze, 27 mm. **Obv:** Value **Rev:** Arms within crowned globe

Date	Mintage	F	VF	XF	Unc	BU
1950	10,000,000	2.00	15.00	45.00	90.00	—
1951	10,000,000	1.50	3.00	12.50	30.00	—

KM# 82 ESCUDO
8.0000 g., Bronze, 26 mm. **Obv:** Value **Rev:** Arms within crowned globe

Date	Mintage	F	VF	XF	Unc	BU
1953	2,013,000	0.75	1.50	15.00	25.00	35.00
1957	2,987,000	0.75	1.50	17.50	35.00	45.00
1962	600,000	0.50	1.25	15.00	22.50	30.00
1963	3,258,000	0.50	0.75	4.00	12.50	18.00
1965	5,000,000	—	0.25	1.50	3.50	6.00
1968	4,500,000	—	0.25	1.50	3.50	6.00
1969	1,642,000	—	0.50	1.75	4.00	7.00

Date	Mintage	F	VF	XF	Unc	BU
1973	501,000	0.20	0.50	2.00	6.50	9.00
1974	25,281,000	—	0.25	1.50	3.00	5.00

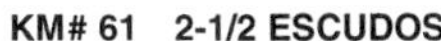

KM# 61 2-1/2 ESCUDOS
3.5000 g., 0.6500 Silver 0.0731 oz. ASW **Obv:** Shield within globe and maltese cross **Rev:** Arms

Date	Mintage	F	VF	XF	Unc	BU
1935	1,200,000	4.50	12.50	40.00	100	—

KM# 68 2-1/2 ESCUDOS
3.5000 g., 0.6500 Silver 0.0731 oz. ASW **Obv:** Shield within globe and maltese cross **Rev:** Arms within crowned globe

Date	Mintage	F	VF	XF	Unc	BU
1938	1,000,000	3.50	10.00	35.00	65.00	—
1942	1,200,000	2.50	7.50	30.00	55.00	—
1950	4,000,000	1.50	2.50	7.50	20.00	—
1951	4,000,000	2.00	6.50	25.00	50.00	—

KM# 78 2-1/2 ESCUDOS
3.5000 g., Copper-Nickel **Obv:** Shield within globe and maltese cross **Rev:** Arms within crowned globe

Date	Mintage	F	VF	XF	Unc	BU
1952	4,000,000	0.50	8.00	50.00	80.00	—
1953	4,000,000	0.30	5.00	25.00	45.00	—
1954	4,000,000	0.25	3.00	12.00	22.00	40.00
1955	4,000,000	0.30	1.50	13.50	42.50	—
1965	8,000,000	0.10	0.25	1.00	4.00	—
1973	1,767,000	0.25	0.65	2.50	6.50	15.00

KM# 62 5 ESCUDOS
7.0000 g., 0.6500 Silver 0.1463 oz. ASW **Obv:** Shield within globe and maltese cross **Rev:** Arms

Date	Mintage	F	VF	XF	Unc	BU
1935	1,000,000	5.50	22.50	65.00	120	—

KM# 69 5 ESCUDOS
7.0000 g., 0.6500 Silver 0.1463 oz. ASW **Obv:** Shield within globe and maltese cross **Rev:** Arms within crowned globe

Date	Mintage	F	VF	XF	Unc	BU
1938	800,000	7.50	20.00	80.00	130	—
1949	8,000,000	2.75	5.50	25.00	45.00	—

KM# 84 5 ESCUDOS
4.0000 g., 0.6500 Silver 0.0836 oz. ASW **Obv:** Shield within globe and maltese cross **Rev:** Arms within crowned globe

Date	Mintage	F	VF	XF	Unc	BU
1960	8,000,000	1.50	2.25	3.50	7.00	10.00

KM# 86 5 ESCUDOS
Copper-Nickel **Obv:** Shield within globe and maltese cross **Rev:** Arms within crowned globe

Date	Mintage	F	VF	XF	Unc	BU
1971	8,000,000	0.20	0.50	1.00	3.00	6.00
1973	3,352,000	0.20	0.50	1.75	4.50	7.00

KM# 67 10 ESCUDOS
12.5000 g., 0.8350 Silver 0.3356 oz. ASW **Obv:** Shield within globe and maltese cross **Rev:** Arms

Date	Mintage	F	VF	XF	Unc	BU
1936	497,000	10.00	20.00	67.50	130	—

KM# 70 10 ESCUDOS
12.5000 g., 0.8350 Silver 0.3356 oz. ASW **Obv:** Shield within globe and maltese cross **Rev:** Arms within crowned globe

Date	Mintage	F	VF	XF	Unc	BU
1938	530,000	20.00	35.00	75.00	165	225

KM# 79 10 ESCUDOS
5.0000 g., 0.7200 Silver 0.1157 oz. ASW **Obv:** Shield within globe and maltese cross **Rev:** Arms within crowned globe

Date	Mintage	VG	F	VF	XF	Unc
1952	1,503,000	—	2.00	4.50	15.00	35.00
1954	1,335,000	—	2.00	4.50	20.00	50.00
1955	1,162,000	—	2.00	4.50	15.00	35.00
1960	2,000,000	—	2.00	3.00	6.00	12.00

KM# 79a 10 ESCUDOS
5.0000 g., 0.6800 Silver 0.1093 oz. ASW **Obv:** Shield within globe and maltese cross **Rev:** Arms within crowned globe

Date	Mintage	F	VF	XF	Unc	BU
1966	500,000	1.75	2.75	5.50	12.50	—

KM# 79b 10 ESCUDOS
Copper-Nickel **Obv:** Shield within globe and maltese cross **Rev:** Arms within crowned globe

Date	Mintage	F	VF	XF	Unc	BU
1968	5,000,000	0.30	0.70	2.50	5.00	—
1970	4,000,000	0.30	0.70	2.50	5.00	—
1974	3,366,000	0.40	1.00	3.00	6.50	—

KM# 80 20 ESCUDOS

10.0000 g., 0.7200 Silver 0.2315 oz. ASW **Obv:** Shield within globe and maltese cross **Rev:** Arms within crowned globe

Date	Mintage	F	VF	XF	Unc	BU
1952	1,004,000	3.75	4.50	10.00	25.00	—
1955	996,000	3.75	5.00	12.50	30.00	—
1960	2,000,000	3.75	4.25	6.50	12.50	—

KM# 80a 20 ESCUDOS

10.0000 g., 0.6800 Silver 0.2186 oz. ASW **Obv:** Shield within globe and maltese cross **Rev:** Arms within crowned globe

Date	Mintage	F	VF	XF	Unc	BU
1966	250,000	3.75	5.50	9.50	18.00	—

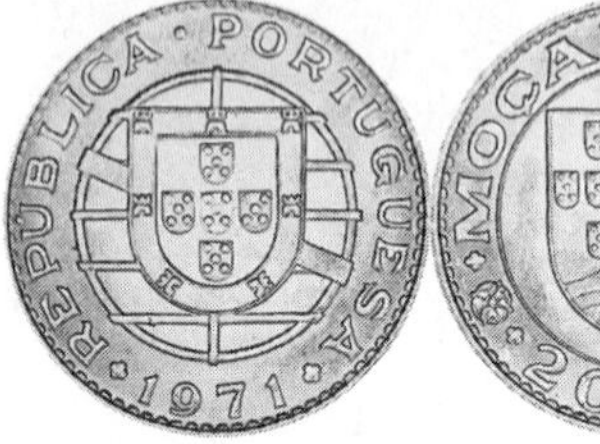

KM# 87 20 ESCUDOS

Nickel **Obv:** Shield within globe **Rev:** Arms within circle

Date	Mintage	F	VF	XF	Unc	BU
1971	2,000,000	0.35	0.75	1.75	5.00	—
1972	1,158,000	0.50	1.00	2.50	6.00	—

REPUBLIC

DECIMAL COINAGE

100 Centimos = 1 Metica

KM# 90 CENTIMO

Aluminum **Obv:** Head right **Obv. Designer:** Samora Machel **Rev:** Value and flower sprig

Date	Mintage	F	VF	XF	Unc	BU
1975	15,050,000	—	—	60.00	120	200

KM# 91 2 CENTIMOS

Copper-Zinc **Obv:** Head right **Obv. Designer:** Samora Machel **Rev:** Value and flower sprig

Date	Mintage	F	VF	XF	Unc	BU
1975	8,242,000	—	—	70.00	125	—

KM# 92 5 CENTIMOS

Copper-Zinc **Obv:** Head right **Obv. Designer:** Samora Machel **Rev:** Value and flower sprig

Date	Mintage	F	VF	XF	Unc	BU
1975	14,898,000	—	—	60.00	110	—

KM# 93 10 CENTIMOS

Copper-Zinc **Obv:** Head right **Obv. Designer:** Samora Machel **Rev:** Value and 3 flower sprigs

Date	Mintage	F	VF	XF	Unc	BU
1975	18,000,000	—	—	50.00	90.00	—

KM# 94 20 CENTIMOS

Copper-Nickel **Obv:** Head right **Obv. Designer:** Samora Machel **Rev:** Value and flower sprig

Date	Mintage	F	VF	XF	Unc	BU
1975	8,050,000	—	—	120	200	—

KM# 95 50 CENTIMOS

Copper-Nickel **Obv:** Head right **Obv. Designer:** Samora Machel **Rev:** Value and 2 1/2 seeds

Date	Mintage	F	VF	XF	Unc	BU
1975	3,050,000	—	—	145	265	—

KM# 96 METICA

Copper-Nickel **Obv:** Head right **Obv. Designer:** Samora Machel **Rev:** Plant in vase

Date	Mintage	F	VF	XF	Unc	BU
1975	2,550,000	—	—	50.00	85.00	—

KM# 97 2-1/2 METICAIS

Copper-Nickel **Obv:** Head right **Obv. Designer:** Samora Machel **Rev:** Leafy plant **Shape:** 7-sided

Date	Mintage	F	VF	XF	Unc	BU
1975	1,500,000	—	—	145	225	—

REFORM COINAGE

100 Centavos = 1 Metical; 1980

KM# 98 50 CENTAVOS

1.4000 g., Aluminum, 20 mm. **Obv:** Emblem **Rev:** Value above xylophone

Date	Mintage	F	VF	XF	Unc	BU
1980	5,160,000	0.15	0.30	0.60	1.25	2.00
1981	—	—	—	—	—	—
1982	—	0.15	0.30	0.60	1.25	2.00

KM# 99 METICAL

8.0000 g., Brass, 26 mm. **Obv:** Emblem **Rev:** Female student and value

Date	Mintage	F	VF	XF	Unc	BU
1980	32,000	1.50	3.00	5.00	10.00	20.00
1981	—	—	—	—	—	—
1982	—	1.50	3.00	5.00	10.00	20.00

KM# 99a METICAL

Aluminum **Obv:** Emblem **Rev:** Female student and value

Date	Mintage	F	VF	XF	Unc	BU
1986	—	0.20	0.40	0.60	1.00	—

KM# 100 2-1/2 METICAIS

Aluminum, 22.6 mm. **Obv:** Emblem **Rev:** Ship and crane in harbor **Note:** 1.80-2.00 grams.

Date	Mintage	F	VF	XF	Unc	BU
1980	1,088,000	0.25	0.50	1.00	1.75	—
1981	—	—	—	—	—	—
1982	—	0.25	0.50	1.00	1.75	—
1986	—	0.25	0.50	1.00	1.75	—

Note: Edge varieties exist

KM# 101 5 METICAIS

2.6000 g., Aluminum, 24.5 mm. **Obv:** Emblem **Rev:** Tractor and value

Date	Mintage	F	VF	XF	Unc	BU
1980	7,736,000	0.35	0.75	1.25	2.00	—
1981	—	—	—	—	—	—
1982	—	0.35	0.75	1.25	2.00	—
1986	—	0.35	0.75	1.25	2.00	—

KM# 102 10 METICAIS

9.1000 g., Copper-Nickel, 28 mm. **Obv:** Emblem **Rev:** Industrial skyline

Date	Mintage	F	VF	XF	Unc	BU
1980	152,000	0.75	1.50	2.50	6.00	—
1981	—	0.75	1.50	2.50	6.00	—

KM# 102a 10 METICAIS

Aluminum, 28 mm. **Obv:** Emblem **Rev:** Industrial skyline

Date	Mintage	F	VF	XF	Unc	BU
1986	—	0.25	0.45	1.00	2.00	—

KM# 103 20 METICAIS

12.0000 g., Copper-Nickel, 30 mm. **Obv:** Emblem **Rev:** Panzer tank

Date	Mintage	F	VF	XF	Unc	BU
1980	78,000	1.00	2.00	4.00	9.00	—

KM# 103a 20 METICAIS
Aluminum, 30 mm. **Obv:** Emblem **Rev:** Panzer tank

Date	Mintage	F	VF	XF	Unc	BU
1986	—	0.40	0.80	1.50	3.00	—

KM# 106 50 METICAIS
Copper-Nickel, 35 mm. **Subject:** World Fisheries Conference **Obv:** Emblem above value and date **Rev:** Traditional fishing raft **Rev. Designer:** Stuart Devlin

Date	Mintage	F	VF	XF	Unc	BU
1983	130,000	2.50	5.00	8.00	12.50	—

KM# 112 50 METICAIS
Aluminum **Obv:** Emblem **Rev:** Woman and soldier with provisions

Date	Mintage	F	VF	XF	Unc	BU
1986	—	0.75	1.50	2.50	5.50	—

REFORM COINAGE

100 Centavos = 1 Metical; 1994

KM# 115 METICAL
Brass Clad Steel, 17 mm. **Obv:** Emblem **Rev:** Female student

Date	Mintage	F	VF	XF	Unc	BU
1994	—	—	—	—	0.50	1.00

KM# 116 5 METICAIS
Brass Clad Steel **Obv:** Emblem **Rev:** Kingfisher

Date	Mintage	F	VF	XF	Unc	BU
1994	—	—	—	—	1.50	2.50

KM# 117 10 METICAIS
Brass Clad Steel, 23 mm. **Obv:** Emblem **Rev:** Cotton plant

Date	Mintage	F	VF	XF	Unc	BU
1994	—	—	—	—	1.25	2.00

KM# 118 20 METICAIS
Brass Clad Steel, 26 mm. **Obv:** Emblem **Rev:** Pepper plant

Date	Mintage	F	VF	XF	Unc	BU
1994	—	—	—	—	1.50	—

KM# 119 50 METICAIS
Nickel Clad Steel **Obv:** Emblem **Rev:** Leopard's head

Date	Mintage	F	VF	XF	Unc	BU
1994	—	—	—	—	3.00	5.00

KM# 120 100 METICAIS
Nickel Clad Steel, 27 mm. **Obv:** Emblem **Rev:** Lobster

Date	Mintage	F	VF	XF	Unc	BU
1994	—	—	—	—	3.50	5.00

KM# 121 500 METICAIS
Nickel Clad Steel, 30 mm. **Obv:** Emblem **Rev:** Building

Date	Mintage	F	VF	XF	Unc	BU
1994	—	—	—	—	4.50	5.50

KM# 131 10000 METICAIS
8.0400 g., Bi-Metallic Stainless Steel center in Brass ring, 26.6 mm. **Obv:** National arms within circle **Rev:** Rhino within circle **Edge:** Segmented reeding

Date	Mintage	F	VF	XF	Unc	BU
2003	—	—	3.50	5.00	7.50	12.00

REFORM COINAGE

(New) Metical = 1,000 Meticals; 2005

KM# 132 CENTAVO
2.0000 g., Copper-Plated-Steel, 15 mm. **Obv:** Bank logo, date **Obv. Legend:** BANCO DE MOÇAMBIQUE **Rev:** Rhinoceros standing left, value **Edge:** Reeded

Date	Mintage	F	VF	XF	Unc	BU
2006	—	—	—	—	0.15	0.25

KM# 133 5 CENTAVOS
2.3000 g., Copper-Plated-Steel, 19 mm. **Obv:** Bank logo, date **Obv. Legend:** BANCO DE MOÇAMBIQUE **Rev:** Cheetah standing left, value **Edge:** Reeded

Date	Mintage	F	VF	XF	Unc	BU
2006	—	—	—	0.10	0.25	0.35

KM# 134 10 CENTAVOS
3.0600 g., Brass Plated Steel, 17 mm. **Obv:** Bank logo, date **Obv. Legend:** BANCO DE MOÇAMBIQUE **Rev:** Farmer cultivating with tractor, value **Edge:** Reeded

Date	Mintage	F	VF	XF	Unc	BU
2006	—	—	—	0.15	0.35	0.50

KM# 135 20 CENTAVOS
4.1000 g., Brass Plated Steel, 20 mm. **Obv:** Bank logo, date **Obv. Legend:** BANCO DE MOÇAMBIQUE **Rev:** Cotton plant, value **Edge:** Reeded

Date	Mintage	F	VF	XF	Unc	BU
2006	—	—	—	0.20	0.50	0.75

KM# 136 50 CENTAVOS
5.7400 g., Brass Plated Steel, 23 mm. **Obv:** Bank logo, date **Obv. Legend:** BANCO DE MOÇAMBIQUE **Rev:** Woodpecker perched on branch, value **Edge:** Reeded

Date	Mintage	F	VF	XF	Unc	BU
2006	—	—	—	0.30	0.75	1.00

KM# 137 METICAL
5.3000 g., Nickel-Plated Steel, 21 mm. **Obv:** Bank logo, date **Obv. Legend:** BANCO DE MOÇAMBIQUE **Rev:** Young woman seated left writing, value **Edge:** Plain **Shape:** 7-sided

Date	Mintage	F	VF	XF	Unc	BU
2006	—	—	—	0.45	1.10	1.50

KM# 138 2 METICAIS
6.0000 g., Nickel-Plated Steel, 24 mm. **Obv:** Bank logo, date **Obv. Legend:** BANCO DE MOÇAMBIQUE **Rev:** Coelacanth fish, value **Edge:** Segmented reeding

Date	Mintage	F	VF	XF	Unc	BU
2006	—	—	—	0.75	1.80	2.50

KM# 139 5 METICAIS
6.5000 g., Nickel-Plated Steel, 27 mm. **Obv:** Bank logo, date **Obv. Legend:** BANCO DE MOÇAMBIQUE **Rev:** Timbila (similar to a xylophone), value **Edge:** Reeded

Date	Mintage	F	VF	XF	Unc	BU
2006	—	—	—	1.20	3.00	4.00

KM# 140 10 METICAIS
7.5100 g., Bi-Metallic **Ring Composition:** Brass **Center Composition:** Nickel Clad Steel, 24.92 mm. **Obv:** Bank logo **Obv. Legend:** BANCO • DE • MOCAMBIQUE **Rev:** Modern bank building, value below **Edge:** Reeded

Date	Mintage	F	VF	XF	Unc	BU
2006	—	—	—	1.50	3.75	5.00

MUSCAT & OMAN

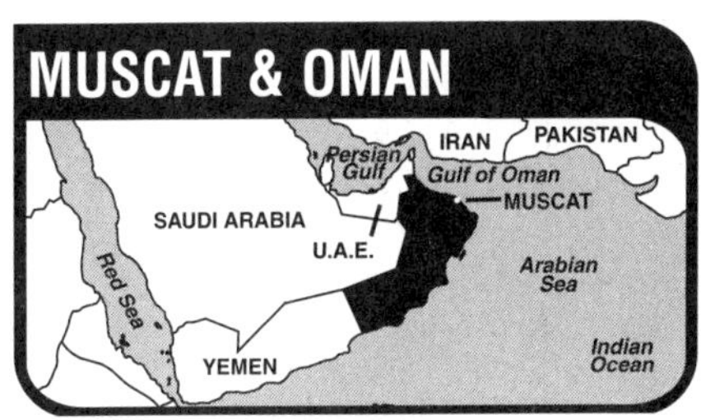

RULERS

al-Bu Sa'id Dynasty
Faisal bin Turkee, AH1306-1332/1888-1913AD
Taimur bin Faisal, AH1332-1351/1913-1932AD
Sa'id bin Taimur, AH1351-1390/1932-1970AD
Qabus bin Sa'id, AH1390-/1970-AD

MONETARY SYSTEM

Until 1970

4 Baiza = 1 Anna
64 Baiza = 1 Rupee
200 Baiza = 1 Saidi (Dasin Dog)/Dhofari Rial

1970-1972

1000 (new) Baisa = 1 Saidi Rial

Commencing 1972

1000 Baisa = 1 Omani Rial

NOTE: For later coin issues, please refer to Oman.

SULTANATE

REFORM COINAGE

1000 (new) Baisa = 1 Saidi Rial

KM# 25 2 BAISA (Baiza)
Copper-Nickel **Ruler:** Sa'id bin Taimur **Obv:** Arms flanked by marks **Rev:** Arabic legend and inscription **Shape:** 4-sided

Date	Mintage	F	VF	XF	Unc	BU
AH1365	1,500,000	0.50	0.75	1.00	2.00	—
AH1365 Proof	—	Value: 4.00				

Note: Coins of AH1365 have the monetary unit spelled "Baiza", on all other coins it is spelled "Baisa". Most of the proof issues of the AH1359 and 1365 dated coins of Muscat and Oman now on the market are probably later restrikes produced by the Bombay Mint

KM# 36 2 BAISA (Baiza)
1.7500 g., Bronze, 16 mm. **Ruler:** Sa'id bin Taimur **Obv:** Arms **Rev:** Value flanked by marks

Date	Mintage	F	VF	XF	Unc	BU
AH1390	4,000,000	0.15	0.20	0.30	0.50	—
AH1390 Proof	—	Value: 2.50				

KM# 30 3 BAISA
Bronze, 20 mm. **Ruler:** Sa'id bin Taimur **Obv:** Arms **Rev:** Value flanked by marks

Date	Mintage	F	VF	XF	Unc	BU
AH1378	8,000,000	0.75	1.00	1.50	2.50	—
AH1378 Proof	—	—	—	—	—	—

Note: Struck for use in Dhofar Province

KM# 32 3 BAISA
Bronze, 18 mm. **Ruler:** Sa'id bin Taimur **Obv:** Arms **Rev:** Value flanked by marks

Date	Mintage	F	VF	XF	Unc	BU
AH1380	10,000,000	0.35	0.50	0.60	1.25	—
AH1380 Proof	Inc. above	—	—	—	—	—

Note: Struck for use in Muscat Province

KM# 26 5 BAISA (Baiza)
Copper-Nickel, 21 mm. **Ruler:** Sa'id bin Taimur **Obv:** Arms **Rev:** Arabic legend and inscription **Shape:** Scalloped

Date	Mintage	F	VF	XF	Unc	BU
AH1365	3,849,000	1.00	1.25	1.50	2.50	—
AH1365 Proof	—	Value: 5.00				

Note: Coins of AH1365 have the monetary unit spelled "Baiza", on all other coins it is spelled "Baisa"

KM# 33 5 BAISA (Baiza)
Copper-Nickel **Ruler:** Sa'id bin Taimur **Obv:** Arms **Rev:** Sailing ship within circle

Date	Mintage	F	VF	XF	Unc	BU
AH1381	5,000,000	0.40	0.60	1.00	2.00	—
AH1381 Proof	Inc. above	—	—	—	—	—

Note: Struck for use in Muscat Province

KM# 37 5 BAISA (Baiza)
3.1000 g., Bronze, 19 mm. **Ruler:** Sa'id bin Taimur **Obv:** Arms **Rev:** Value flanked by marks

Date	Mintage	F	VF	XF	Unc	BU
AH1390	3,400,000	0.15	0.20	0.30	0.50	—
AH1390 Proof	—	Value: 2.00				

KM# 22 10 BAISA
Copper-Nickel **Ruler:** Sa'id bin Taimur **Obv:** Arms **Rev:** Inscription

Date	Mintage	F	VF	XF	Unc	BU
AH1359	572,000	2.50	3.25	4.00	6.00	—
AH1359 Proof	—	Value: 8.50				

Note: Struck for use in Dhofar Province

KM# 38 10 BAISA
4.7000 g., Bronze, 22.5 mm. **Ruler:** Sa'id bin Taimur **Obv:** Arms **Rev:** Value flanked by marks

Date	Mintage	F	VF	XF	Unc	BU
AH1390	4,500,000	0.15	0.20	0.35	0.75	—
AH1390 Proof	—	Value: 2.50				

KM# 23 20 BAISA (Baiza)
Copper-Nickel **Ruler:** Sa'id bin Taimur **Obv:** Arms **Rev:** Inscription **Shape:** Square

Date	Mintage	F	VF	XF	Unc	BU
AH1359	35,000	3.00	5.00	7.50	11.50	—
AH1359 Proof	—	Value: 14.50				

Note: Struck for use in Dhofar Province

KM# 27 20 BAISA (Baiza)
Copper-Nickel **Ruler:** Sa'id bin Taimur **Obv:** Arms **Rev:** Arabic legend and inscription **Shape:** Square

Date	Mintage	F	VF	XF	Unc	BU
AH1365	1,135,000	1.00	2.00	2.75	4.50	—
AH1365 Proof	—	Value: 7.00				

KM# 28 20 BAISA (Baiza)
Copper-Nickel **Ruler:** Sa'id bin Taimur **Obv:** Arms **Rev:** Inscription **Note:** Mule.

Date	Mintage	F	VF	XF	Unc	BU
AH1359/1365 Restrike	—	—	—	—	17.50	—

KM# 39 25 BAISA
2.9000 g., Copper-Nickel, 18 mm. **Ruler:** Sa'id bin Taimur **Obv:** Arms **Rev:** Value flanked by marks

Date	Mintage	F	VF	XF	Unc	BU
AH1390	2,000,000	0.20	0.30	0.45	1.00	—
AH1390 Proof	—	Value: 2.75				

KM# 24 50 BAISA
Copper-Nickel **Ruler:** Sa'id bin Taimur **Obv:** Arms **Rev:** Inscription **Shape:** Octagon

Date	Mintage	F	VF	XF	Unc	BU
AH1359	65,000	2.00	6.50	8.50	12.50	—
AH1359 Proof	—	Value: 16.50				

Note: Struck for use in Dhofar Province

KM# 40 50 BAISA
6.4000 g., Copper-Nickel, 24 mm. **Ruler:** Sa'id bin Taimur **Obv:** Arms **Rev:** Value flanked by marks

Date	Mintage	F	VF	XF	Unc	BU
AH1390	1,600,000	0.25	0.45	0.75	1.50	—
AH1390 Proof	—	Value: 3.50				

KM# 41 100 BAISA
Copper-Nickel **Ruler:** Sa'id bin Taimur **Obv:** Arms **Rev:** Value flanked by marks

Date	Mintage	F	VF	XF	Unc	BU
AH1390	1,000,000	0.35	0.50	0.85	1.75	—
AH1390 Proof	—	Value: 5.00				

KM# 29 1/2 DHOFARI RIAL
14.0300 g., 0.5000 Silver 0.2255 oz. ASW **Ruler:** Sa'id bin Taimur **Obv:** Arms above sprig **Rev:** Inscription within circle and wreath

Date	Mintage	F	VF	XF	Unc	BU
AH1367	200,000	12.00	14.00	18.00	28.00	—
AH1367 Proof	—	Value: 45.00				

Note: Struck for use in Dhofar Province

KM# 34 1/2 SAIDI RIAL
14.0300 g., 0.5000 Silver 0.2255 oz. ASW **Ruler:** Sa'id bin Taimur **Obv:** Arms **Rev:** Value

Date	Mintage	F	VF	XF	Unc	BU
AH1380	300,000	3.75	4.50	6.00	9.00	—
AH1380 Proof	—	Value: 75.00				
AH1381	850,000	3.75	4.50	6.00	9.00	—

KM# 31 SAIDI RIAL

28.0700 g., 0.8330 Silver 0.7517 oz. ASW **Ruler:** Sa'id bin Taimur **Obv:** Arms within circle, designs around border **Rev:** Value and date

Date	Mintage	F	VF	XF	Unc	BU
AH1378	1,000,000	—	12.50	16.00	20.00	—
AH1378 Proof	100	Value: 650				

KM# 31a SAIDI RIAL

28.0700 g., 0.5000 Silver 0.4512 oz. ASW **Ruler:** Sa'id bin Taimur **Obv:** Arms within circle, designs around border **Rev:** Value and date

Date	Mintage	F	VF	XF	Unc	BU
AH1378	400,000	—	10.00	12.50	15.00	—

MYANMAR

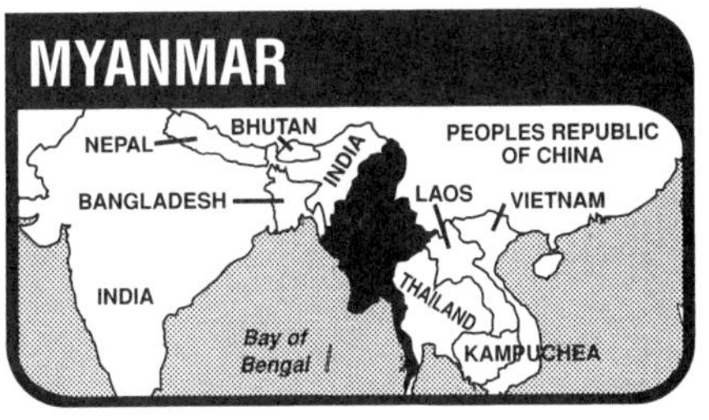

(BURMA)

The Union of Myanmar, formerly Burma, a country of Southeast Asia fronting on the Bay of Bengal and the Andaman Sea, has an area of 261,218 sq. mi. (678,500 sq. km.) and a population of 38.8 million. Capital: Yangon (Rangoon) until 2005; followed thereafter by Naypyidaw. Myanmar is an agricultural country heavily dependent on its leading product (rice), which occupies two-thirds of the cultivated area and accounts for 40 % of the value of exports. Mineral resources are extensive, but production is low. Petroleum, lead, tin, silver, zinc, nickel cobalt, and precious stones are exported.

The British East India Company, while unsuccessful in its 1612 effort to establish posts along the Bay of Bengal, was enabled by the Anglo-Burmese Wars of 1824-86 to expand to the whole of Burma and to secure its annexation to British India. In 1937, Burma was separated from India, becoming a separate British colony with limited self-government. Burma became an independent nation outside the British Commonwealth on Jan. 4, 1948, the constitution of 1948 providing for a parliamentary democracy and the nationalization of certain industries. However, political and economic problems persisted, and on March 2, 1962, Gen. Ne Win took over the government, suspended the constitution, installed himself as chief of state, and pursued a socialistic program with nationalization of nearly all industry and trade. On Jan. 4, 1974, a new constitution adopted by referendum established Burma as a socialist republic under one-party rule. The country name was changed to Myanmar in 1989.

Burmese coins are frequently known by the equivalent Indian denominations, although their values are inscribed in Burmese units. Upper Burma was annexed in 1885 and the Burmese coinage remained in circulation until 1889, when Indian coins became current throughout Burma. Coins were again issued in the old Burmese denominations after independence in 1948, but decimal issues replaced these in 1952. The Chula-Sakarat (CS) dating is sometimes referred to as BE-Burmese Era and began in 638AD.

RULER

British, 1886-1948

MONETARY SYSTEM

(Until 1952)

4 Pyas = 1 Pe
2 Pe = 1 Mu
2 Mu = 1 Mat
5 Mat = 1 Kyat

NOTE: Originally 10 light Mu = 1 Kyat, eventually 8 heavy Mu = 1 Kyat.

Indian Equivalents

1 Silver Kyat = 1 Rupee = 16 Annas
1 Gold Kyat = 1 Mohur = 16 Rupees

UNION OF BURMA

STANDARD COINAGE

KM# 27 2 PYAS

Copper-Nickel **Obv:** Chinze **Rev:** Value and date flanked by sprays **Shape:** 4-sided

Date	Mintage	F	VF	XF	Unc	BU
1949	7,000,000	0.25	0.50	1.00	3.00	—
1949 Proof	100	Value: 100				

KM# 28 PE

Copper-Nickel **Obv:** Chinze **Rev:** Value and date flanked by sprays **Shape:** Scalloped

Date	Mintage	F	VF	XF	Unc	BU
1949	8,000,000	0.35	0.75	1.75	4.00	—
1949 Proof	100	Value: 100				
1950	9,500,000	0.35	0.75	1.75	4.00	—
1950 Proof	—	—	—	—	—	—
1951	6,500,000	0.50	1.00	2.00	5.00	—
1951 Proof	—	—	—	—	—	—

KM# 29 2 PE

Copper-Nickel **Obv:** Chinze **Rev:** Value and date flanked by sprays **Shape:** 4-sided

Date	Mintage	F	VF	XF	Unc	BU
1949	7,100,000	0.50	1.00	2.00	5.00	—
1949 Proof	100	Value: 100				
1950	8,500,000	0.50	1.00	2.00	5.00	—
1950 Proof	—	—	—	—	—	—
1951	7,480,000	0.50	1.00	2.00	5.00	—
1951 Proof	—	—	—	—	—	—

KM# 30 4 PE

Nickel **Obv:** Chinze **Rev:** Value and date flanked by sprays

Date	Mintage	F	VF	XF	Unc	BU
1949	6,500,000	1.25	2.50	5.00	15.00	—
1949 Proof	100	Value: 100				
1950	6,120,000	1.00	2.00	4.00	12.00	—

KM# 31 8 PE

Nickel **Obv:** Chinze **Rev:** Value and date flanked by sprays

Date	Mintage	F	VF	XF	Unc	BU
1949	3,270,000	1.50	3.00	6.00	25.00	—
1949 Proof	100	Value: 100				
1950	3,900,000	1.25	2.50	5.00	20.00	—
1950 Proof	—	—	—	—	—	—

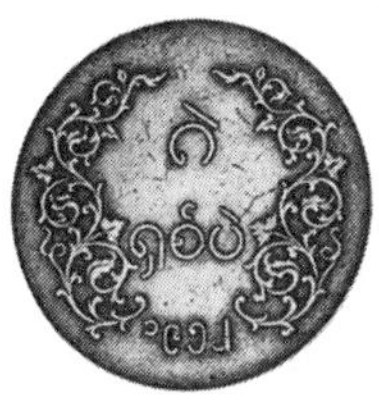

KM# 31a 8 PE

Copper-Nickel **Obv:** Chinze flanked by stars **Rev:** Value and date flanked by sprays

Date	Mintage	VG	F	VF	XF	Unc
CS1314-1952	1,642,000	—	50.00	100	150	200
CS1314-1952 Proof	—	Value: 400				

DECIMAL COINAGE

100 Pyas = 1 Kyat

KM# 32 PYA

2.2000 g., Bronze, 18 mm. **Obv:** Chinze **Rev:** Value and date flanked by sprays

Date	Mintage	VG	F	VF	XF	Unc
1952	500,000	—	0.10	0.15	0.20	0.35
1952 Proof	100	Value: 60.00				
1953	14,000,000	—	0.10	0.15	0.20	0.35
1953 Proof	—	—	—	—	—	—
1955	30,000,000	—	0.10	0.15	0.20	0.35
1955 Proof	—	—	—	—	—	—
1956 Proof	100	Value: 60.00				
1962 Proof	100	Value: 60.00				
1965	15,000,000	—	0.10	0.15	0.20	0.35
1965 Proof	—	—	—	—	—	—

KM# 38 PYA

0.6000 g., Aluminum, 17 mm. **Subject:** Aung San **Obv:** Head 1/4 right flanked by stars below **Rev:** Value and date flanked by sprays

Date	Mintage	VG	F	VF	XF	Unc
1966	8,000,000	—	0.10	0.15	0.25	0.65

KM# 33 5 PYAS

3.1700 g., Copper-Nickel **Obv:** Chinze **Rev:** Value and date flanked by sprays **Shape:** Scalloped

Date	Mintage	VG	F	VF	XF	Unc
1952	20,000,000	—	0.10	0.15	0.35	0.75
1952 Proof	100	Value: 65.00				
1953	59,700,000	—	0.10	0.15	0.35	0.75
1953 Proof	—	—	—	—	—	—
1955	40,272,000	—	0.10	0.15	0.35	0.75
1955 Proof	—	—	—	—	—	—
1956	20,000,000	—	0.10	0.15	0.35	0.75
1956 Proof	100	Value: 65.00				
1961	12,000,000	—	0.10	0.15	0.35	0.75
1961 Proof	—	—	—	—	—	—
1962	10,000,000	—	0.10	0.15	0.35	0.75
1962 Proof	100	Value: 65.00				
1963	40,400,000	—	0.10	0.15	0.25	0.60
1963 Proof	—	—	—	—	—	—
1965	43,600,000	—	0.10	0.15	0.20	0.40
1965 Proof	—	—	—	—	—	—
1966	20,000,000	—	0.10	0.15	0.20	0.40
1966 Proof	—	—	—	—	—	—

KM# 39 5 PYAS

0.9000 g., Aluminum, 18.4 mm. **Subject:** Aung San **Obv:** Head 1/4 right flanked by stars below **Rev:** Value and date flanked by sprays **Shape:** Scalloped

Date	Mintage	VG	F	VF	XF	Unc
1966	—	—	0.10	0.20	0.35	0.75

KM# 51 5 PYAS
Aluminum-Bronze **Series:** F.A.O. **Obv:** Rice plant **Rev:** Value and date within square

Date	Mintage	VG	F	VF	XF	Unc
1987	—	—	0.10	0.20	0.40	1.00

KM# 34 10 PYAS
4.4600 g., Copper-Nickel **Obv:** Chinze **Rev:** Value and date flanked by sprays **Shape:** 4-sided

Date	Mintage	VG	F	VF	XF	Unc
1952	20,000,000	—	0.10	0.20	0.40	1.00
1952 Proof	100	Value: 70.00				
1953	37,250,000	—	0.10	0.20	0.40	1.00
1953 Proof	—	—	—	—	—	—
1955	22,750,000	—	0.10	0.20	0.40	1.00
1955 Proof	—	—	—	—	—	—
1956	35,000,000	—	0.10	0.15	0.40	1.00
1956 Proof	100	Value: 70.00				
1962	6,000,000	—	0.10	0.20	0.40	1.00
1962 Proof	100	Value: 70.00				
1963	10,750,000	—	0.10	0.20	0.40	1.00
1963 Proof	10,750,000	—	—	—	—	—
1965	32,619,999	—	0.10	0.20	0.40	1.00
1965 Proof	—	—	—	—	—	—

KM# 40 10 PYAS
1.0000 g., Aluminum **Subject:** Aung San **Obv:** Head 1/4 right flanked by stars below **Rev:** Value and date flanked by sprays **Shape:** Square

Date	Mintage	VG	F	VF	XF	Unc
1966	—	—	0.15	0.30	0.60	1.25

KM# 49 10 PYAS
3.0000 g., Brass, 20.45 mm. **Series:** F.A.O. **Obv:** Rice plant **Rev:** Value within square

Date	Mintage	VG	F	VF	XF	Unc
1983	—	—	0.15	0.30	0.60	1.00

KM# 35 25 PYAS
Copper-Nickel **Obv:** Chinze flanked by stars **Rev:** Value and date flanked by sprays **Shape:** Scalloped

Date	Mintage	VG	F	VF	XF	Unc
1952	13,540,000	—	0.10	0.20	0.50	1.25
1952 Proof	100	Value: 75.00				
1954	18,000,000	—	0.10	0.20	0.50	1.25
1954 Proof	—	—	—	—	—	—
1955 Proof	—	Value: 75.00				
1956	14,000,000	—	0.10	0.20	0.50	1.25
1956 Proof	100	Value: 75.00				
1959	6,000,000	—	0.10	0.20	0.50	1.25
1959 Proof	—	—	—	—	—	—
1961	4,000,000	—	0.10	0.20	0.50	1.25
1961 Proof	—	—	—	—	—	—
1962	3,200,000	—	0.10	0.20	0.50	1.25
1962 Proof	100	Value: 75.00				
1963	16,000,000	—	0.10	0.15	0.30	0.75
1963 Proof	—	—	—	—	—	—
1965	26,000,000	—	0.10	0.15	0.30	0.75
1965 Proof	—	—	—	—	—	—

KM# 41 25 PYAS
1.8000 g., Aluminum **Subject:** Aung San **Obv:** Head 1/4 right flanked by stars below **Rev:** Value and date flanked by sprays **Shape:** Scalloped

Date	Mintage	VG	F	VF	XF	Unc
1966	—	—	0.15	0.30	0.60	1.25

KM# 48 25 PYAS
4.3000 g., Bronze, 22.35 mm. **Series:** F.A.O. **Obv:** Rice plant **Rev:** Value and date within square

Date	Mintage	VG	F	VF	XF	Unc
1980	—	—	0.15	0.30	0.60	1.00

KM# 50 25 PYAS
Bronze **Series:** F.A.O. **Obv:** Rice plant **Rev:** Large value **Shape:** 6-sided

Date	Mintage	VG	F	VF	XF	Unc
1986	—	—	0.10	0.20	0.35	0.60

KM# 36 50 PYAS
7.8000 g., Copper-Nickel **Obv:** Chinze flanked by stars **Rev:** Value and date flanked by vine sprigs

Date	Mintage	VG	F	VF	XF	Unc
1952	2,500,000	—	0.20	0.50	0.75	1.75
1952 Proof	100	Value: 80.00				
1954	12,000,000	—	0.20	0.50	0.75	1.75
1954 Proof	—	—	—	—	—	—
1956	8,000,000	—	0.20	0.50	0.75	1.75
1956 Proof	100	Value: 80.00				
1961	2,000,000	—	0.15	0.40	0.75	1.75
1961 Proof	—	—	—	—	—	—
1962	600,000	—	0.25	0.75	1.25	2.25
1962 Proof	100	Value: 80.00				
1963	4,800,000	—	0.15	0.25	0.65	1.25
1963 Proof	—	—	—	—	—	—
1965	2,800,000	—	0.15	0.40	0.75	1.75
1965 Proof	—	—	—	—	—	—
1966	3,400,000	—	0.10	0.30	0.75	1.75
1966 Proof	—	—	—	—	—	—

KM# 42 50 PYAS
2.0000 g., Aluminum **Subject:** Aung San **Obv:** Head 1/4 right flanked by stars below **Rev:** Value and date flanked by sprays

Date	Mintage	VG	F	VF	XF	Unc
1966	—	—	0.15	0.40	1.00	2.25

KM# 46 50 PYAS
5.7000 g., Brass, 24.6 mm. **Series:** F.A.O. **Obv:** Rice plant **Rev:** Value within square

Date	Mintage	VG	F	VF	XF	Unc
1975	—	—	0.15	0.35	0.70	1.25
1976	—	—	0.15	0.35	0.70	1.25

KM# 37 KYAT
11.6500 g., Copper-Nickel, 30.5 mm. **Obv:** Chinze flanked by stars **Rev:** Value and date flanked by sprays

Date	Mintage	VG	F	VF	XF	Unc
1952	2,500,000	—	0.35	0.75	1.50	3.00
1952 Proof	100	Value: 85.00				
1953	7,500,000	—	0.25	0.50	1.00	2.00
1953 Proof	—	—	—	—	—	—
1956	3,500,000	—	0.35	0.75	1.50	3.00
1956 Proof	100	Value: 85.00				
1962 Proof	100	Value: 85.00				
1965	1,000,000	—	0.35	0.75	1.50	3.00
1965 Proof	—	—	—	—	—	—

KM# 47 KYAT
7.2000 g., Copper-Nickel, 26.45 mm. **Series:** F.A.O. **Obv:** Rice plant **Rev:** Value within square

Date	Mintage	VG	F	VF	XF	Unc
1975	20,000,000	—	0.25	0.50	1.00	2.00

UNION OF MYANMAR

DECIMAL COINAGE

100 Pyas = 1 Kyat

KM# 60 KYAT
2.9500 g., Bronze, 19.03 mm. **Obv:** Chinze flanked by stars **Rev:** Value **Edge:** Plain

Date	Mintage	F	VF	XF	Unc	BU
1999	—	—	—	—	0.25	0.40

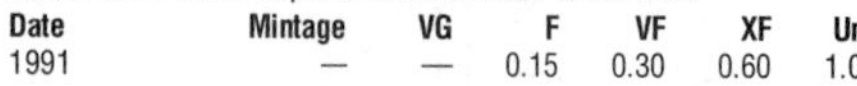

KM# 57 10 PYAS
Brass **Obv:** Rice plant **Obv. Legend:** Myanmar Central Bank **Rev:** Value within square **Note:** Similar to KM#49.

Date	Mintage	VG	F	VF	XF	Unc
1991	—	—	0.15	0.30	0.60	1.00

KM# 58 25 PYAS

5.0000 g., Copper Plated Steel **Obv:** Rice plant **Obv. Legend:** Myanmar Central Bank **Rev:** Large value **Shape:** Hexagon

Date	Mintage	VG	F	VF	XF	Unc
1991	—	—	0.15	0.30	0.60	1.00

KM# 59 50 PYAS

Brass, 24.6 mm. **Obv:** Rice plant **Obv. Legend:** Myanmar Central Bank **Rev:** Value within square **Edge:** Reeded

Date	Mintage	VG	F	VF	XF	Unc
1991	—	—	0.15	0.35	0.70	1.25

KM# 61 5 KYATS

2.7300 g., Brass, 20 mm. **Obv:** Chinze flanked by stars **Rev:** Value **Edge:** Plain

Date	Mintage	F	VF	XF	Unc	BU
1999	—	—	—	—	0.50	0.75

KM# 62 10 KYATS

4.4500 g., Brass **Obv:** Chinze flanked by stars **Rev:** Value

Date	Mintage	F	VF	XF	Unc	BU
1999	—	—	—	—	0.75	1.00

KM# 63 50 KYATS

5.0600 g., Copper-Nickel, 23.85 mm. **Obv:** Chinze flanked by stars **Rev:** Value **Edge:** Reeded

Date	Mintage	F	VF	XF	Unc	BU
1999	—	—	—	—	1.75	2.00

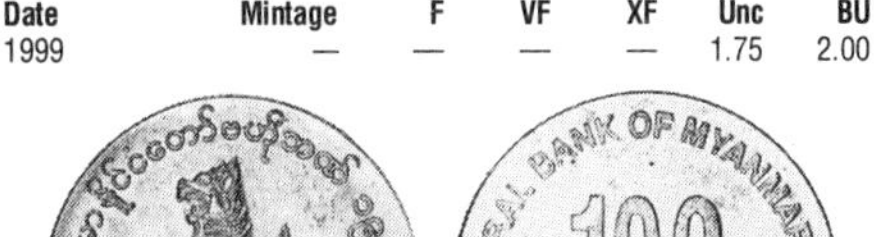

KM# 64 100 KYATS

7.5200 g., Copper-Nickel, 26.8 mm. **Obv:** Chinze flanked by stars **Rev:** Value **Edge:** Reeded

Date	Mintage	F	VF	XF	Unc	BU
1999	—	—	—	—	3.00	3.50

NAGORNO-KARABAKH

Nagorno-Karabakh, an ethnically Armenian enclave inside Azerbaijan (pop., 1991 est.: 193,000), SW region. It occupies an area of 1,700 sq mi (4,400 square km) on the NE flank of the Karabakh Mountain Range, with the capital city of Stepanakert.

Russia annexed the area from Persia in 1813, and in 1923 it was established as an autonomous province of the Azerbaijan S.S.R. In 1988 the region's ethnic Armenian majority demonstrated against Azerbaijani rule, and in 1991, after the breakup of the U.S.S.R. brought independence to Armenia and Azerbaijan, war broke out between the two ethnic groups. On January 8, 1992 the leaders of Nagorno-Karabakh declared independence as the Republic of Mountainous Karabakh (RMK). Since 1994, following a cease-fire, ethnic Armenians have held Karabakh, though officially it remains part of Azerbaijan. Karabakh remains sovereign, but the political and military condition is volatile and tensions frequently flare into skirmishes.

Its marvelous nature and geographic situation, have all facilitated Karabakh to be a center of science, poetry and, especially, of the musical culture of Azerbaijan.

REPUBLIC

STANDARD COINAGE

KM# 6 50 LUMA

0.9500 g., Aluminum, 19.8 mm. **Obv:** National arms **Rev:** Horse cantering left **Edge:** Plain

Date	Mintage	F	VF	XF	Unc	BU
2004	—	—	—	—	1.00	1.25

KM# 7 50 LUMA

0.9500 g., Aluminum, 19.8 mm. **Obv:** National arms **Rev:** Gazelle **Edge:** Plain

Date	Mintage	F	VF	XF	Unc	BU
2004	—	—	—	—	1.00	1.25

KM# 8 DRAM

1.1300 g., Aluminum, 21.7 mm. **Obv:** National arms **Rev:** Pheasant **Edge:** Plain

Date	Mintage	F	VF	XF	Unc	BU
2004	—	—	—	—	1.00	1.25

KM# 9 DRAM

1.1200 g., Aluminum, 21.7 mm. **Obv:** National arms **Rev:** 1/2-length Saint facing **Edge:** Plain

Date	Mintage	F	VF	XF	Unc	BU
2004	—	—	—	—	1.00	1.25

KM# 10 DRAM

1.1300 g., Aluminum, 21.7 mm. **Obv:** National arms **Rev:** Cheetah facing **Edge:** Plain

Date	Mintage	F	VF	XF	Unc	BU
2004	—	—	—	—	1.00	1.25

KM# 11 5 DRAMS

4.4000 g., Brass, 21.8 mm. **Obv:** National arms **Rev:** Church **Edge:** Plain

Date	Mintage	F	VF	XF	Unc	BU
2004	—	—	—	—	1.00	1.50

KM# 12 5 DRAMS

4.5000 g., Brass, 21.8 mm. **Obv:** National arms **Rev:** Monument faces **Edge:** Plain

Date	Mintage	F	VF	XF	Unc	BU
2004	—	—	—	—	1.00	1.50

NAMIBIA

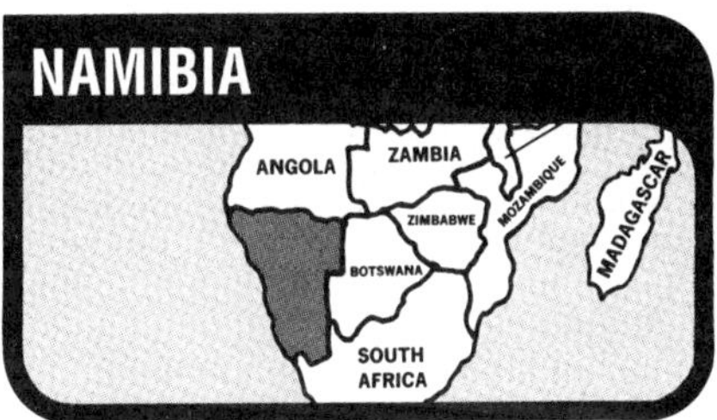

The Republic of Namibia, once the German colonial territory of German Southwest Africa, and later Southwest Africa, is situated on the Atlantic coast of southern Africa, bounded on the north by Angola, on the east by Botswana, and on the south by South Africa. It has an area of 318,261 sq. mi. (824,290 sq. km.) and a population of *1.4 million. Capital: Windhoek. Diamonds, copper, lead, zinc, and cattle are exported.

South Africa undertook the administration of Southwest Africa under the terms of a League of Nations mandate on Dec. 17, 1920. When the League of Nations was dissolved in 1946, its supervisory authority for Southwest Africa was inherited by the United Nations. In 1946 the UN denied South Africa's request to annex Southwest Africa. South Africa responded by refusing to place the territory under a UN trusteeship. In 1950 the International Court of Justice ruled that South Africa could not unilaterally modify the international status of Southwest Africa. A 1966 UN resolution declaring the mandate terminated was rejected by South Africa, and the status of the area remained in dispute. In June 1968 the UN General Assembly voted to rename the territory Namibia. In 1971 the International Court of Justice ruled that South Africa's presence in Namibia was illegal. In Dec. 1973 the UN appointed a UN Commissioner and a multi-racial Advisory Council was appointed. An interim government was formed in 1977 and independence was to be declared by Dec. 31, 1978. This resolution was rejected by major UN powers. In April 1978 South Africa accepted a plan for UN-supervised elections, which led to a political abstention by the Southwest Africa People's Organization (SWAPO) party leading to dissolving of the Minister's Council and National Assembly in Jan. 1983. A Multi-Party Conference (MPC) was formed in May 1984, which held talks with SWAPO. The MPC petitioned South Africa for self-government and on June 17, 1985 the Transitional Government of National Unity was installed. Negotiations were held in 1988 between Angola, Cuba, and South Africa reaching a peaceful settlement on Aug. 5, 1988. By April 1989 Cuban troops were to withdraw from Angola and South African troops from Namibia. The Transitional Government resigned on Feb. 28, 1988 for the upcoming elections of the constituent assembly in Nov. 1989. Independence was finally achieved on March 12, 1990 within the Commonwealth of Nations. The President is the Head of State; the Prime Minister is Head of Government.

MONETARY SYSTEM
100 Cents = 1 Namibia Dollar
1 Namibia Dollar = 1 South African Rand

REPUBLIC
1990 - present
DECIMAL COINAGE

KM# 1 5 CENTS
2.2000 g., Nickel Plated Steel, 16.9 mm. **Obv:** National arms **Rev:** Value left, aloe plant within 3/4 sun design

Date	Mintage	F	VF	XF	Unc	BU
1993	—	—	—	0.20	0.50	0.75
2002	—	—	—	0.20	0.50	0.75
2007	—	—	—	0.20	0.50	0.75

KM# 16 5 CENTS
3.1000 g., Stainless Steel, 20.03 mm. **Series:** F.A.O **Obv:** Arms with supporters **Rev:** Fish below value **Edge:** Plain

Date	Mintage	F	VF	XF	Unc	BU
1999	—	—	—	—	1.00	1.50
2000	—	—	—	—	1.00	1.50

KM# 2 10 CENTS
3.3900 g., Nickel Plated Steel, 21.5 mm. **Obv:** National arms **Rev:** Camelthorn tree right, partial sun design left, value below

Date	Mintage	F	VF	XF	Unc	BU
1993	—	—	—	0.35	1.00	1.25
1996	—	—	—	0.35	1.00	1.25
1998	—	—	—	0.35	1.00	1.25
2002	—	—	—	0.35	1.00	1.25

KM# 3 50 CENTS
4.4300 g., Nickel Plated Steel, 24 mm. **Obv:** National arms **Rev:** Quiver tree right, partial sun design upper left, value below

Date	Mintage	F	VF	XF	Unc	BU
1993	—	—	—	0.75	1.75	2.00
1996	—	—	—	0.75	1.75	2.00

KM# 4 DOLLAR
4.9600 g., Brass, 22.3 mm. **Obv:** National arms **Rev:** Value divides Bateleur eagle at right, partial sun design at left

Date	Mintage	F	VF	XF	Unc	BU
1993	—	—	—	1.25	3.50	6.00
1996	—	—	—	1.25	3.50	6.00
Note: Edge varieties exist for 1996						
1998	—	—	—	1.25	3.50	6.00
2002	—	—	—	1.25	3.50	6.00
2006	—	—	—	1.25	3.50	6.00

KM# 5 5 DOLLARS
6.2200 g., Brass, 24.9 mm. **Obv:** National arms **Rev:** Partial sun design at top, value at center, African fish eagle below

Date	Mintage	F	VF	XF	Unc	BU
1993	—	—	—	4.00	7.50	10.00

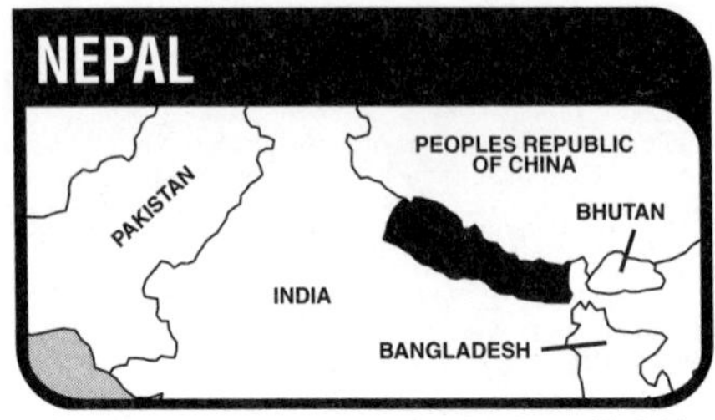

The Kingdom of Nepal, the world's only surviving Hindu kingdom, is a landlocked country occupying the southern slopes of the Himalayas. It has an area of 56,136 sq. mi. (140,800 sq. km.) and a population of 18 million. Capital: Kathmandu. Nepal has deposits of coal, copper, iron and cobalt, but they are largely unexploited. Agriculture is the principal economic activity. Rice, timber and jute are exported, with tourism being the other major foreign exchange earner.

After Prithvi Narayan's death a period of political instability ensued which lasted until the 1840's when the Rana family reduced the monarch to a figurehead and established the post of hereditary Prime Minister. A popular revolution in 1950 toppled the Rana family and reconstituted power in the throne. In 1959 King Mahendra declared Nepal a constitutional monarchy, and in 1962 a new constitution set up a system of *panchayat* (village council) democracy. In 1990, following political unrest, the king's powers were reduced. The country then adopted a system of parliamentary democracy.

On June 2, 2001 tragedy struck the royal family when Crown Prince Dipendra used an assault rifle to kill his father, mother and other members of the royal family as the result of a dispute over his current lady friend. He died 48 hours later, as King, from self inflicted gunshot wounds. Gyanendra began his second reign as King (his first was a short time as a toddler, 1950-51).

DATING

Bikram Samvat Era (VS)

From 1888AD most copper coins were dated in the Bikram Samvat (VS) era. To convert take VS date - 57 =AD date. Coins with this era have VS before the year in the listing. With the exception of a few gold coins struck in 1890 & 1892, silver and gold coins only changed to the VS era in 1911AD, but now this era is used for all coins struck in Nepal.

RULERS

SHAH DYNASTY

पृथ्वी वीर विक्रम
Prithvi Bir Bikram
SE1803-1833/1881-1911AD, VS1938-1968/

लक्ष्मी दिव्येश्वरी
Queen of Prithvi Bir Bikram: Lakshmi Divyeswari

त्रिभुवनवीर विक्रम
Tribhuvana Bir Bikram
VS1968-2007, 2007-2011/1911-1950, 1951-1955AD (first reign)
VS2058- / 2001- AD (second reign)

ज्ञानेन्द्रवीर विक्रम
Gyanendra Bir Bikram
VS2007/1950-1951AD

महेन्द्रवीर विक्रम
Mahendra Bir Bikram
VS2012-2028/1955-1971AD

रत्न राज लक्ष्मी
Queen of Mahendra Bir Bikram: Ratna Rajya Lakshmi

वीरेन्द्र वीर विक्रम
Birendra Bir Bikram
VS2028-2058 /1971-2001AD

ऐश्वर्य राज्य लक्ष्मी देवी
Queen of Birendra Bir Bikram: Aishvarya Rajya Lakshmi
VS2028-2058 /1971-2001AD

Dipendra Bir Bikram
VS2058 / 2001AD (reign of 48 hours)

Gyanendra Bir Bikram
VS2058-/2001-AD

MONETARY SYSTEM

Many of the mohars circulated in Tibet as well as in Nepal, and on a number of occasions coins were struck from bullion supplied by the Tibetan authorities. The smaller denominations never circulated in Tibet, but some of the mohars were cut for use as small change in Tibet.

In these listings only major changes in design have been noted. There are numerous minor varieties of ornamentation or spelling.

With a few exceptions, most all coins were struck at Kathmandu.

COPPER

Initially the copper paisa was not fixed in value relative to the silver coins, and generally fluctuated in value from 1/32 mohar in 1865AD to around 1/50 mohar after 1880AD, and was fixed at that value in 1903AD.
4 Dam = 1 Paisa
2 Paisa = 1 Dyak, Adhani

COPPER and SILVER
Decimal Series
100 Paisa = 1 Rupee

Although the value of the copper paisa was fixed at 100 paisa to the rupee in 1903, it was not until 1932 that silver coins were struck in the decimal system.

GOLD COINAGE

Nepalese gold coinage, until recently, did not carry any denominations and was traded for silver, etc. at the local bullion exchange rate. The three basic weight standards used in the following listing are distinguished for convenience, although all were known as Asarphi (gold coin) locally as follows:

GOLD MOHAR
5.60 g multiples and fractions

TOLA
12.48 g multiples and fractions

GOLD RUPEE or ASHRPHI/ASARFI
11.66 g multiples and fractions
(Reduced to 10.00 g in 1966)

NOTE: In some instances the gold and silver issues were struck from the same dies.

NUMERALS

Nepal has used more variations of numerals on their coins than any other nation. The most common are illustrated in the numeral chart in the introduction. The chart below illustrates some variations encompassing the last four centuries.

1	2	3	4	5	6	7	8	9	0
१	२	३	४	५	६	७	८	९	०

NUMERICS

आधा
Half

One	एक
Two	दुइ
Four	चार
Five	पाच
Ten	दसा
Twenty	विसा
Twenty-five	पचीसा
Fifty	पचासा
Hundred	सय

DENOMINATIONS

Paisa	पैसा
Dam	दाम
Mohar	मोरु
Rupee	रुपैयाँ
Ashrapi	असार्फी
Asarphi (Asarfi)	अश्रफी

KINGDOM

Shah Dynasty

Prithvi Bir Bikram

VS1938-1968 / 1881-1911AD

COPPER COINAGE

KM# 620.2 DAM

Copper **Rev. Inscription:** "Sarkar"

Date	Mintage	F	VF	XF	Unc	BU
VS(19)64(1907)	—	7.50	12.00	15.00	20.00	—

KM# 621 DAM

Copper

Date	Mintage	F	VF	XF	Unc	BU
VS(19)68(1911)	—	4.50	7.50	10.00	17.50	—
VS(19)68(1911) Proof	—	Value: 60.00				

KM# 622 1/2 PAISA

Copper, 19 mm.

Date	Mintage	F	VF	XF	Unc	BU
VS(19)64(1907)	—	4.50	7.50	10.00	17.50	—
VS(19)68(1911)	—	4.50	7.50	10.00	17.50	—
VS(19)68(1911) Proof	—	Value: 60.00				

KM# 629 PAISA

Copper **Obv:** Legend within squares **Rev:** Legend within squares

Date	Mintage	Good	VG	F	VF	XF
VS1959 (1902)	—	1.00	1.50	2.50	4.00	—
VS1962 (1905)	—	1.00	1.50	2.50	4.00	—
VS1963 (1906)	—	1.00	1.50	2.50	4.00	—
VS1964 (1907)	—	1.00	1.50	2.50	4.00	—
VS1965 (1908)	—	1.00	1.50	2.50	4.00	—
VS1966 (1909)	—	1.00	1.50	2.50	4.00	—
VS1967 (1910)	—	1.00	1.50	2.50	4.00	—
VS1968 (1911)	—	1.00	1.50	2.50	4.00	—

KM# 630 PAISA

Copper-Iron Alloy **Obv:** Legend within square **Rev:** Legend within circle **Note:** Magnetic and non-magnetic alloy.

Date	Mintage	Good	VG	F	VF	XF
VS1959 (1902)	—	7.50	12.50	20.00	33.50	—

KM# 628 PAISA

Copper **Obv:** Legend within sprays **Rev:** Legend within sprays **Note:** Varieties in sprays exist. Coin and medal alignment varieties exist. Also struck between VS1343-1357.

Date	Mintage	Good	VG	F	VF	XF
VS1959 (1902)	—	1.00	1.50	3.00	5.00	—
VS1960 (1903)	—	1.00	1.50	3.00	5.00	—
VS1961 (1904)	—	1.00	1.50	3.00	5.00	—
VS1962 (1905)	—	1.00	1.50	3.00	5.00	—
VS(19)62 (1905)	—	—	—	—	—	—
VS1963 (1906)	—	1.00	1.50	3.00	5.00	—
VS1964 (1907)	—	1.00	1.50	3.00	5.00	—
VS(19)64 (1907)	—	—	—	—	—	—

KM# 631 PAISA

Copper, 23 mm. **Note:** Also Tribhuvaua Bir Bikram struck a Paisa VS1968, see KM#685.1.

Date	Mintage	F	VF	XF	Unc	BU
VS1964 (1907)	—	5.50	9.00	15.00	22.50	—
VS1968 (1911)	—	8.50	13.50	20.00	30.00	—
VS1968 (1911) Proof	—	Value: 90.00				

KM# 633 2 PAISA (Dak)

Copper-Iron Alloy **Obv:** Legend within square **Rev:** Legend within circle **Note:** Magnetic and non-magnetic alloy. Similar to KM#630.

Date	Mintage	Good	VG	F	VF	XF
VS1959 (1902)	—	12.50	17.50	25.00	50.00	—

KM# 634 2 PAISA (Dak)

Copper, 26.5 mm.

Date	Mintage	F	VF	XF	Unc	BU
VS1964 (1907)	—	8.50	13.50	20.00	30.00	—
VS1968 (1911)	—	9.00	15.00	22.50	35.00	—
VS1968 (1911) Proof	—	Value: 110				

SILVER COINAGE

KM# 643 1/4 MOHAR

1.4000 g., Silver **Rev:** Moon and dot for sun **Note:** Machine struck. Also struck between SE1804-1817.

Date	Mintage	VG	F	VF	XF	Unc
SE1827 (1905)	—	1.75	3.00	5.00	7.00	—

KM# 644 1/4 MOHAR

1.4000 g., Silver, 15.5 mm. **Note:** Machine struck.

Date	Mintage	VG	F	VF	XF	Unc
SE1833 (1911)	—	1.75	3.00	5.00	7.00	—
SE1833 (1911) Proof	—	Value: 25.00				

KM# 647 1/2 MOHAR

2.7700 g., Silver, 21 mm. **Edge:** Plain **Note:** Machine struck. Varieties exist. Also struck between SE1803-1817.

Date	Mintage	F	VF	XF	Unc	BU
SE1824 (1902)	—	20.00	25.00	30.00	35.00	—

KM# 648 1/2 MOHAR

2.7700 g., Silver, 21 mm. **Note:** Machine struck.

Date	Mintage	F	VF	XF	Unc	BU
SE1826 (1904)	—	3.00	5.00	7.00	10.00	—
SE1827 (1905)	—	3.00	5.00	7.00	10.00	—
SE1829 (1907)	—	3.50	5.50	8.50	11.50	—

KM# 649 1/2 MOHAR

2.7700 g., Silver, 19 mm. **Edge:** Milled **Note:** Machine struck.

Date	Mintage	F	VF	XF	Unc	BU
SE1832 (1910)	—	20.00	25.00	30.00	35.00	—
SE1833 (1911)	—	2.25	3.50	5.00	7.00	—
SE1833 (1911) Proof	—	Value: 35.00				

KM# 651.1 MOHAR

5.6000 g., Silver, 26 mm. **Edge:** Plain **Note:** Machine struck. Also struck between SE1807-1822.

Date	Mintage	F	VF	XF	Unc	BU
SE1823 (1901)	—	4.50	6.50	8.00	10.00	—
SE1824 (1902)	—	4.50	6.50	8.00	10.00	—
SE1825 (1903)	—	4.50	6.50	8.00	10.00	—
SE1826 (1904)	—	4.50	6.50	8.00	10.00	—
SE1827 (1905)	—	4.50	6.50	8.00	10.00	—

KM# 651.2 MOHAR

5.6000 g., Silver, 26 mm. **Edge:** Milled **Note:** Machine struck.

Date	Mintage	F	VF	XF	Unc	BU
SE1826 (1904)	—	4.50	6.50	8.00	10.00	—
SE1827 (1905)	—	4.50	6.50	8.00	10.00	—
SE1828 (1906)	—	4.50	6.50	8.00	10.00	—
SE1829 (1907)	—	4.50	6.50	8.00	10.00	—
SE1830 (1908)	—	4.50	6.50	8.00	10.00	—
SE1831 (1909)	—	4.50	6.50	8.00	10.00	—
SE1832 (1910)	—	4.50	6.50	8.00	10.00	—
SE1833 (1911)	—	—	25.00	35.00	50.00	—

Note: The date SE1833 was only issued in presentation sets

KM# 652 MOHAR

5.6000 g., Silver, 26 mm. **Rev:** Gold die, in error

Date	Mintage	F	VF	XF	Unc	BU
SE1825 (1903)	—	10.00	15.00	25.00	32.50	—

KM# 655 2 MOHARS

11.2000 g., Silver, 27 mm. **Edge:** Milled **Note:** Machine struck.

Date	Mintage	F	VF	XF	Unc	BU
SE1829 (1907)	—	15.00	27.50	40.00	60.00	—
SE1831 (1909)	—	6.50	9.00	12.50	20.00	—

KM# 656 2 MOHARS

Silver, 29 mm. **Note:** Machine struck.

Date	Mintage	F	VF	XF	Unc	BU
SE1832 (1910)	—	7.00	9.00	11.50	18.50	—
SE1833 (1911)	—	6.50	8.00	10.00	16.50	—
SE1833 (1911) Proof	—	Value: 75.00				

KM# 658 4 MOHARS

22.4000 g., Silver, 29 mm. **Edge:** Milled

Date	Mintage	F	VF	XF	Unc	BU
SE1833 (1911)	—	60.00	100	140	200	—
SE1833 (1911) Proof	—	Value: 450				

GOLD COINAGE

KM# 668 1/16 MOHAR

0.3500 g., Gold

Date	Mintage	F	VF	XF	Unc	BU
SE(18)33 (1911)	—	15.00	30.00	75.00	100	—
SE(18)33 (1911) Proof	—	—	—	—	—	—

KM# 671.1 1/4 MOHAR

1.4000 g., Gold

Date	Mintage	F	VF	XF	Unc	BU
SE1823 (1901)	—	45.00	60.00	80.00	100	—
SE1829 (1907)	—	40.00	50.00	60.00	80.00	—

KM# 671.2 1/4 MOHAR

1.4000 g., Gold

Date	Mintage	F	VF	XF	Unc	BU
SE1833 (1911)	—	40.00	50.00	60.00	80.00	—
SE1833 (1911) Proof	—	—	—	—	—	—

KM# 672.3 1/2 MOHAR

2.8000 g., Gold

Date	Mintage	F	VF	XF	Unc	BU
SE1823 (1901)	—	75.00	85.00	100	125	—

KM# 672.4 1/2 MOHAR

2.8000 g., Gold

Date	Mintage	F	VF	XF	Unc	BU
SE1829 (1907)	—	70.00	80.00	90.00	110	—

KM# 672.5 1/2 MOHAR

2.8000 g., Gold

Date	Mintage	F	VF	XF	Unc	BU
SE1833 (1911)	—	70.00	80.00	90.00	110	—
SE1833 (1911) Proof	—	—	—	—	—	—

KM# 673.1 MOHAR

5.6000 g., Gold

Date	Mintage	F	VF	XF	Unc	BU
SE1823 (1901)	—	140	150	165	200	350
SE1825 (1903)	—	140	150	165	200	350
SE1826 (1904)	—	140	150	165	200	350
SE1827 (1905)	—	140	150	165	200	350

KM# 673.2 MOHAR

5.6000 g., Gold **Edge:** Milled

Date	Mintage	F	VF	XF	Unc	BU
SE1828 (1906)	—	140	150	165	200	350
SE1829 (1907)	—	140	150	165	200	350
SE1831 (1909)	—	140	150	165	200	350
SE1833 (1911)	—	140	150	165	200	350
SE1833 (1911) Proof	—	—	—	—	—	—

KM# 674.3 TOLA

12.4800 g., Gold **Edge:** Plain

Date	Mintage	F	VF	XF	Unc	BU
SE1823 (1901)	—	300	310	320	345	—
SE1824 (1902)	—	300	310	320	345	—
SE1825 (1903)	—	300	310	320	345	—
SE1826 (1904)	—	300	310	320	345	—

KM# 675.1 TOLA

12.4800 g., Gold **Edge:** Vertical milling

Date	Mintage	F	VF	XF	Unc	BU
SE1828 (1906)	—	300	310	320	345	—
SE1829 (1907)	—	300	310	320	345	—
SE1831 (1909)	—	300	310	320	345	—
SE1832 (1910)	—	300	310	320	345	—
SE1833 (1911)	—	300	310	320	345	—
SE1833 (1911) Proof	—	—	—	—	—	—

KM# 678 DUITOLA ASARPHI

23.3200 g., Gold **Edge:** Plain

Date	Mintage	F	VF	XF	Unc	BU
SE1825 (1902)	—	625	725	850	1,000	—

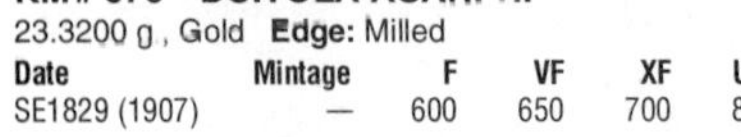

KM# 679 DUITOLA ASARPHI

23.3200 g., Gold **Edge:** Milled

Date	Mintage	F	VF	XF	Unc	BU
SE1829 (1907)	—	600	650	700	800	—

KM# 680 DUITOLA ASARPHI

23.3200 g., Gold **Edge:** Milled

Date	Mintage	F	VF	XF	Unc	BU
SE1833 (1911)	—	600	650	700	800	—
SE1833 (1911) Proof	—	—	—	—	—	—

Tribhuvana Bir Bikram

VS1968-2007 / 1911-1950AD

COPPER COINAGE

KM# 684 1/2 PAISA

Copper **Note:** Struck only for presentation sets.

Date	Mintage	F	VF	XF	Unc	BU
VS1978 (1921)	—	—	—	50.00	75.00	—
VS1985 (1928)	—	—	—	50.00	75.00	—

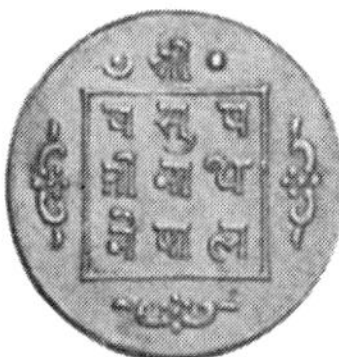

KM# 685.1 PAISA

Copper **Note:** Machine struck. Also Prithvi Bir Bikram struck a Paisa VS1968, see KM#631.

Date	Mintage	Good	VG	F	VF	XF
VS1968 (1911)	—	10.00	20.00	50.00	75.00	—

KM# 685.2 PAISA

Copper **Note:** Hand struck. Many varieties exist.

Date	Mintage	Good	VG	F	VF	XF
VS1969 (1912)	—	1.00	1.50	2.25	3.50	—
VS1970 (1913)	—	1.00	1.50	2.25	3.50	—
VS1971 (1914)	—	1.00	1.50	2.25	3.50	—
VS1972 (1915)	—	1.00	1.50	2.25	3.50	—
VS1973 (1916)	—	1.00	1.50	2.25	3.50	—
VS1974 (1917)	—	1.00	1.50	2.25	3.50	—
VS1975 (1918)	—	1.00	1.50	2.25	3.50	—
VS1976 (1919)	—	1.00	1.50	2.25	3.50	—
VS1977 (1920)	—	1.00	1.50	2.25	3.50	—

KM# 686.1 PAISA

5.2000 g., Copper, 23.5 mm. **Rev:** Without "Nepal" below

Date	Mintage	F	VF	XF	Unc	BU
VS1975 (1918)	—	—	—	37.50	50.00	—

KM# 686.2 PAISA

3.7000 g., Copper, 21.5 mm. **Rev:** Without "Nepal" below

Date	Mintage	Good	VG	F	VF	XF
VS1975 (1918)	—	—	—	60.00	90.00	—

Note: The above issues are believed to be patterns

KM# 687.1 PAISA

Copper, 21.5 mm. **Obv:** Outlined Khukris **Note:** Machine struck. Fine style. Weight varies: 3.50-3.80 g.

Date	Mintage	F	VF	XF	Unc	BU
VS1977 (1920)	—	1.25	1.75	3.00	6.00	—
VS1977 (1920) **Note:** Inverted date	—	1.25	1.75	3.00	6.00	—
VS1978	—	1.25	1.75	3.00	6.00	—

KM# 687.2 PAISA

Copper, 22 mm. **Obv:** Outlined Khukris always right over left **Note:** Machine struck. Weight varies: 2.6-3.1 grams. Prev. KM#688.

Date	Mintage	F	VF	XF	Unc	BU
VS1978 (1921)	—	1.25	1.75	3.00	6.00	—
VS1979 (1922)	—	1.25	1.75	3.00	6.00	—
VS1980 (1923)	—	1.50	3.00	5.00	10.00	—
VS1981 (1924)	—	1.50	3.00	5.00	10.00	—
VS1982 (1925)	—	1.25	1.75	3.00	6.00	—
VS1984 (1927)	—	1.25	1.75	3.00	6.00	—
VS1985 (1928)	—	1.25	1.75	3.00	6.00	—
VS1986 (1929)	—	1.25	1.75	3.00	6.00	—
VS1987 (1930)	—	1.25	1.75	3.00	6.00	—

KM# 687.3 PAISA

3.7500 g., Copper, 21 mm. **Obv:** Outlined Khukris left over right and right over left **Note:** Crude, hand struck. Varieties of the Khukris exist

Date	Mintage	Good	VG	F	VF	XF
VS1978 (1921)	—	2.00	3.00	4.50	7.50	—
VS1979 (1922)	—	2.00	3.00	4.50	7.50	—
VS1980 (1923)	—	4.00	5.00	7.50	12.50	—
VS1981 (1924)	—	4.00	5.00	7.50	12.50	—
VS1982 (1925)	—	4.00	5.00	7.50	12.50	—
VS1983 (1926)	—	4.00	5.00	7.50	12.50	—

KM# 689.1 2 PAISA

Copper, 26 mm. **Obv:** Outlined Khukris **Note:** Machine struck. Varieties of the Khukris exist. Weight varies: 6.9-7.5 grams.

Date	Mintage	VG	F	VF	XF	Unc
VS1976 (1919)	—	1.00	2.00	3.00	5.00	—
VS1977 (1920)	—	1.00	2.00	3.00	5.00	—
VS1977 (1920) Inverted date	—	3.50	5.00	8.50	13.50	—

KM# 689.2 2 PAISA

Copper **Obv:** Outlined Khukris left over right and right over left **Note:** Crude struck. Varieties of the Khukris exist. Weight varies: 4.6-5.5 grams.

Date	Mintage	Good	VG	F	VF	XF
VS1978 (1921)	—	1.00	2.00	3.50	6.50	—
VS1979 (1922)	—	1.00	2.00	3.50	6.50	—
VS1980 (1923)	—	1.00	2.00	3.50	6.50	—
VS1981 (1924)	—	1.00	2.00	3.50	6.50	—
VS1982 (1925)	—	1.00	2.00	3.50	6.50	—
VS1983 (1926)	—	1.00	2.00	3.50	6.50	—
VS1984 (1927)	—	1.00	2.00	3.50	6.50	—
VS1985 (1928)	—	1.00	2.00	3.50	6.50	—
VS1986 (1929)	—	1.50	2.50	4.00	7.50	—
VS1987 (1930)	—	1.50	2.50	4.00	7.50	—
VS1988 (1931)	—	2.00	3.00	5.00	9.00	—

KM# 689.3 2 PAISA

5.0000 g., Copper **Obv:** Outlined Khukris always right over left **Note:** Machine struck. Weight varies: 5.00-5.700 grams.

Date	Mintage	VG	F	VF	XF	Unc
VS1978 (1921)	—	1.00	2.00	3.00	4.50	—
VS1979 (1922)	—	1.00	2.00	3.00	4.50	—
VS1980 (1923)	—	1.00	2.00	3.00	4.50	—
VS1981 (1924)	—	1.00	2.00	3.00	4.50	—
VS1982 (1925)	—	1.00	2.00	3.00	4.50	—
VS1983 (1926)	—	1.00	2.00	3.00	4.50	—
VS1984 (1927)	—	1.00	2.00	3.00	4.50	—
VS1991 (1934)	—	1.50	2.50	4.00	6.00	—

KM# 690.1 5 PAISA

Copper, 29.5 mm. **Obv:** Outlined Khukris **Note:** Weight varies: 18.1-18.8 g.

Date	Mintage	F	VF	XF	Unc	BU
VS1976 (1919) **Note:** Fine style	—	6.00	10.00	14.00	20.00	—
VS1977 (1920)	—	1.25	2.25	3.50	6.00	—
VS1977 (1920) Inverted date	—	3.00	5.00	8.50	12.50	—

KM# 690.2 5 PAISA

Copper **Obv:** Outlined Khukris, left over right and right over left **Note:** Crude hand struck. Weight varies: 11.0-13.2 g. Size varies: 29.0-32.5mm.

Date	Mintage	F	VF	XF	Unc	BU
VS1978 (1921)	—	1.75	3.00	5.00	8.00	—
VS1979 (1922)	—	1.75	3.00	5.00	8.00	—
VS1980 (1923)	—	1.75	3.00	5.00	8.00	—
VS1981 (1924)	—	1.75	3.00	5.00	8.00	—
VS1982 (1925)	—	1.75	3.00	5.00	8.00	—
VS1983 (1926)	—	1.75	3.00	5.00	8.00	—
VS1984 (1927)	—	1.75	3.00	5.00	8.00	—
VS1985 (1928)	—	1.75	3.00	5.00	8.00	—
VS1986 (1929)	—	1.75	3.00	5.00	8.00	—
VS1987 (1930)	—	1.75	3.00	5.00	8.00	—
VS1988 (1931)	—	6.00	10.00	14.00	20.00	—
VS1989 (1932)	—	1.75	3.00	5.00	8.00	—

KM# 690.3 5 PAISA

14.0000 g., Copper **Obv:** Outlined Khukris always right over left **Note:** Machine struck. Weight varies: 13.5-14.0 g. Varieties exist. Size varies: 29.0-30.0mm.

Date	Mintage	F	VF	XF	Unc	BU
VS1978 (1921)	—	1.25	2.25	3.50	5.00	—
VS1979 (1922)	—	1.25	2.25	3.50	5.00	—
VS1979 (1922) Backwards date	—	1.25	2.25	3.50	5.00	—
VS1980 (1923)	—	1.25	2.25	3.50	5.00	—
VS1981 (1924)	—	1.25	2.25	3.50	5.00	—
VS1982 (1925)	—	1.25	2.25	3.50	5.00	—
VS1983 (1926)	—	1.25	2.25	3.50	5.00	—
VS1984 (1927)	—	1.25	2.25	3.50	5.00	—
VS1991 (1934)	—	15.00	20.00	25.00	30.00	—

SILVER COINAGE

KM# 691 DAM

0.0400 g., Silver **Note:** Uniface.

Date	Mintage	F	VF	XF	Unc	BU
ND (1911)	—	15.00	25.00	30.00	50.00	—

KM# 692 1/4 MOHAR

1.4000 g., Silver, 16 mm.

Date	Mintage	VG	F	VF	XF	Unc
VS1969 (1912)	—	1.75	3.00	5.00	7.00	—
VS1970 (1913)	—	1.75	3.00	5.00	7.00	—

KM# 693 1/2 MOHAR
2.8000 g., Silver

Date	Mintage	F	VF	XF	Unc	BU
VS1968 (1911)	—	2.25	3.50	5.00	7.00	—
VS1970 (1913)	—	2.25	3.50	5.00	7.00	—
VS1971 (1914)	—	2.25	3.50	5.00	7.00	—

KM# 681 1/2 MOHAR
2.7700 g., Silver **Note:** In the name of "Queen Lakshmi Divyeswari" - Regent for Tribhuvana Bir Bikram.

Date	Mintage	F	VF	XF	Unc	BU
VS1971 (1914)	—	4.00	6.00	9.00	11.50	—

KM# 694 MOHAR
5.6000 g., Silver

Date	Mintage	F	VF	XF	Unc	BU
VS1968 (1911)	—	4.50	6.50	8.00	10.00	—
VS1969 (1912)	—	4.50	6.50	8.00	10.00	—
VS1971 (1914)	—	4.50	6.50	8.00	10.00	—

KM# 682 MOHAR
5.6000 g., Silver **Note:** In the name of "Queen Lakshmi Divyeswari" - Regent for Tribhuvana Bir Bikram.

Date	Mintage	F	VF	XF	Unc	BU
VS1971 (1914)	—	4.50	6.50	9.00	11.50	—

KM# 695 2 MOHARS
11.2000 g., Silver, 29 mm. **Note:** Varieties exist for this type.

Date	Mintage	F	VF	XF	Unc	BU
VS1968 (1911)	—	BV	7.50	10.00	16.50	—
VS1969 (1912)	—	BV	7.50	10.00	16.50	—
VS1970 (1913)	—	BV	7.50	10.00	16.50	—
VS1971 (1914)	—	BV	7.50	10.00	16.50	—
VS1972 (1915)	—	BV	7.50	10.00	16.50	—
VS1973 (1916)	—	BV	7.50	10.00	16.50	—
VS1974 (1917)	—	BV	7.50	10.00	16.50	—
VS1975 (1918)	—	BV	7.50	10.00	16.50	—
VS1976 (1919)	—	BV	7.50	10.00	16.50	—
VS1977 (1920)	—	BV	7.50	10.00	16.50	—
VS1978 (1921)	—	BV	7.50	10.00	16.50	—
VS1979 (1922)	—	BV	7.50	10.00	16.50	—
VS1980 (1923)	—	BV	7.50	10.00	16.50	—
VS1982 (1925)	—	BV	7.50	10.00	16.50	—
VS1983 (1926)	—	BV	7.50	10.00	16.50	—
VS1984 (1927)	—	BV	7.50	10.00	16.50	—
VS1985 (1928)	—	BV	7.50	10.00	16.50	—
VS1986 (1929)	—	BV	7.50	10.00	16.50	—
VS1987 (1930)	—	BV	7.50	10.00	16.50	—
VS1988 (1931)	—	BV	7.50	10.00	16.50	—
VS1989 (1932)	—	BV	7.50	10.00	16.50	—

KM# 696 4 MOHARS
22.4000 g., Silver

Date	Mintage	F	VF	XF	Unc	BU
VS1971 (1914)	—	40.00	75.00	125	175	—

GOLD COINAGE

KM# 697 DAM
0.0400 g., Gold **Note:** Uniface.

Date	Mintage	F	VF	XF	Unc	BU
ND (1911)	—	28.00	40.00	75.00	100	—

KM# 698 1/32 MOHAR
0.1800 g., Gold **Note:** Uniface.

Date	Mintage	F	VF	XF	Unc	BU
ND (1911)	—	38.00	60.00	90.00	125	—

KM# 699 1/16 MOHAR
0.3500 g., Gold

Date	Mintage	F	VF	XF	Unc	BU
VS(19)77 (1920)	—	50.00	90.00	120	150	—

KM# 700 1/8 MOHAR
0.7000 g., Gold

Date	Mintage	F	VF	XF	Unc	BU
VS(19)76 (1919)	—	75.00	120	150	200	—

KM# 701 1/2 MOHAR
2.8000 g., Gold

Date	Mintage	F	VF	XF	Unc	BU
VS1969 (1912)	—	—	—	—	—	—

KM# 717 1/2 MOHAR
2.8000 g., Gold

Date	Mintage	F	VF	XF	Unc	BU
VS1995 (1938)	—	—	—	—	—	—

KM# 702 MOHAR
5.6000 g., Gold

Date	Mintage	F	VF	XF	Unc	BU
VS1969 (1912)	—	135	140	150	200	300
VS1975 (1918)	—	135	140	150	200	300
VS1978 (1921)	—	135	140	150	200	300
VS1979 (1922)	—	135	140	150	200	300
VS1981 (1924)	—	135	140	150	200	300
VS1983 (1926)	—	135	140	150	200	300
VS1985 (1928)	—	135	140	150	200	300
VS1986 (1929)	—	135	140	150	200	300
VS1987 (1930)	—	135	140	150	200	300
VS1989 (1932)	—	135	140	150	200	300
VS1990 (1933)	—	135	140	150	200	300
VS1991 (1934)	—	135	140	150	200	300
VS1998 (1941)	—	135	140	150	200	300
VS1999 (1942)	—	135	140	150	200	300
VS2000 (1943)	—	135	140	150	200	300
VS2003 (1946)	—	135	140	150	200	300
VS2005 (1948)	—	135	140	150	200	300

KM# 683 MOHAR
5.6000 g., Gold **Note:** In the name of "Queen Lakshmi Divyeswari" - Regent for Tribhuvana Bir Bikram.

Date	Mintage	F	VF	XF	Unc	BU
VS1971 (1914)	—	135	140	150	185	—

KM# 722 MOHAR
5.6000 g., Gold

Date	Mintage	F	VF	XF	Unc	BU
VS1993 (1936)	376,000	—	—	—	—	—
VS1994 (1937)	283,000	—	—	—	—	—

KM# 703.1 ASHRAPHI (Tola)
Gold **Rev:** Moon and sun in center **Rev. Legend:** SRI 3 BHAVANI

Date	Mintage	F	VF	XF	Unc	BU
VS1969 (1912)	—	285	300	310	335	—
VS1974 (1917)	—	285	300	310	335	—
VS1975 (1918)	—	285	300	310	335	—
VS1976 (1919)	—	285	300	310	335	—
VS1977 (1920)	—	285	300	310	335	—
VS1978 (1921)	—	285	300	310	335	—
VS1979 (1922)	—	285	300	310	335	—
VS1980 (1923)	—	285	300	310	335	—
VS1981 (1924)	—	285	300	310	335	—
VS1982 (1925)	—	285	300	310	335	—
VS1983 (1926)	—	285	300	310	335	—
VS1984 (1927)	—	285	300	310	335	—
VS1985 (1928)	—	285	300	310	335	—
VS1986 (1929)	—	285	300	310	335	—
VS1987 (1930)	—	285	300	310	335	—
VS1988 (1931)	—	285	300	310	335	—
VS1989 (1932)	—	285	300	310	335	—
VS1990 (1933)	—	285	300	310	335	—
VS1991 (1934)	—	285	300	310	335	—
VS1998 (1941)	—	285	300	310	335	—
VS1999 (1942)	—	285	300	310	335	—
VS2000 (1943)	—	285	300	310	335	—
VS2003 (1946)	—	285	300	310	335	—

KM# 703.2 ASHRAPHI (Tola)
Gold

Date	Mintage	F	VF	XF	Unc	BU
VS2005 (1948)	—	285	300	310	335	—

KM# 727 ASHRAPHI (Tola)
Gold **Obv:** Trident between moon and sun above crossed Khukris in center

Date	Mintage	F	VF	XF	Unc	BU
VS1992 (1935)	—	300	310	320	350	400

KM# 728 DUITOLA ASARPHI
Gold **Note:** Similar to 1 Tola, KM#703.

Date	Mintage	F	VF	XF	Unc	BU
VS2005 (1948)	—	550	575	600	700	—

DECIMAL COINAGE
100 Paisa = 1 Rupee

KM# 704 1/4 PAISA
Copper, 14 mm. **Obv:** Footprints above crossed daggers within circle **Rev:** Crescent moon and star flank center dagger

Date	Mintage	F	VF	XF	Unc	BU
VS2000 (1943)	—	15.00	25.00	30.00	40.00	—
VS2004 (1947)	—	15.00	25.00	30.00	40.00	—

KM# 705 1/2 PAISA
Copper, 16 mm. **Obv:** Footprints above crossed daggers within circle **Rev:** Crescent moon and star flank dagger at center

Date	Mintage	F	VF	XF	Unc	BU
VS2004 (1947)	—	—	25.00	30.00	40.00	—

KM# 706.1 PAISA

Copper, 23 mm. **Obv:** Footprints above crossed daggers within circle **Rev:** Right wreath with sharp end **Note:** Prev. KM#706.

Date	Mintage	F	VF	XF	Unc	BU
VS1990 (1933)	—	0.75	1.50	3.00	5.00	—
VS1991 (1934)	—	0.75	1.50	3.00	5.00	—
VS1992 (1935)	—	0.75	1.50	3.00	5.00	—

KM# 706.2 PAISA

Copper, 23 mm. **Obv:** Footprints above crossed daggers within circle **Rev:** Right wreath with round end

Date	Mintage	VG	F	VF	XF	Unc
VS1993	—	—	0.75	1.50	3.00	5.00
VS1994	456,000	—	0.75	1.50	3.00	5.00
VS1995	—	—	0.75	1.50	3.00	5.00
VS1996	—	—	0.75	1.50	3.00	5.00

KM# 707a PAISA

Brass, 20 mm. **Obv:** Footprints above crossed daggers within circle **Rev:** Crescent moon and star flank dagger at center

Date	Mintage	F	VF	XF	Unc	BU
VS2003 (1946)	—	0.30	0.50	0.75	1.00	—
VS2004 (1947)	—	3.00	5.00	7.00	10.00	—
VS2005 (1948)	—	0.30	0.50	0.75	1.00	—
VS2001 (1948)	—	0.30	0.50	0.75	1.00	—
VS2006 (1949)	—	0.60	1.00	1.25	1.75	—

KM# 707 PAISA

Copper, 20 mm.

Date	Mintage	F	VF	XF	Unc	BU
VS2005 (1948)	—	0.75	1.25	1.75	2.50	—

KM# 709.1 2 PAISA

Copper, 27 mm. **Obv:** Footprints above crossed daggers within circle **Rev:** Crescent moon and star flank dagger ant center **Note:** 2mm wide rim.

Date	Mintage	F	VF	XF	Unc	BU
VS1992 (1935)	—	1.00	2.00	3.00	5.00	—
VS1993 (1936)	473,000	1.00	2.00	3.00	5.00	—
VS1994 (1937)	1,133,000	1.00	2.00	3.00	5.00	—
VS1995 (1938)	—	1.00	2.00	3.00	5.00	—
VS1996 (1939)	—	1.00	2.00	3.00	5.00	—
VS1997 (1940)	—	1.00	2.00	3.00	5.00	—

KM# 709.2 2 PAISA

Copper, 25 mm. **Obv:** Footprints above crossed daggers within circle **Rev:** Crescent moon and star flank dagger at center **Note:** Rim is 1mm wide or less.

Date	Mintage	F	VF	XF	Unc	BU
VS1992 (1935)	—	0.60	1.00	1.75	3.00	—
VS1993 (1936)	—	0.60	1.00	1.75	3.00	—
VS1994 (1937)	—	0.50	0.75	1.50	2.50	—
VS1995 (1938)	—	2.00	3.50	5.00	7.50	—
VS1996 (1939)	—	0.30	0.50	1.00	1.50	—
VS1997 (1940)	—	0.50	0.75	1.50	2.50	—
VS1998 (1941)	—	0.50	0.75	1.50	2.50	—
VS1999 (1942)	—	0.50	0.75	1.50	2.50	—

KM# 708 2 PAISA

Copper, 27 mm. **Obv:** Footprints above crossed daggers within circle **Rev:** Crescent moon and star flank trident at center

Date	Mintage	VG	F	VF	XF	Unc
VS1992 (1935)	—	3.00	5.00	8.50	13.50	—

KM# 710 2 PAISA

Copper, 23 mm. **Obv:** Footprints above crossed daggers within circle **Rev:** Crescent moon and star flank dagger at center

Date	Mintage	F	VF	XF	Unc	BU
VS1999 (1942)	—	0.30	0.50	1.00	2.00	—
VS2000 (1943)	—	0.30	0.50	1.00	2.00	—
VS2003 (1946)	—	0.30	0.50	1.00	2.00	—
VS2005 (1948)	—	3.00	5.00	7.00	10.00	—

KM# 710a 2 PAISA

Brass **Obv:** Footprints above crossed daggers within circle **Rev:** Crescent moon and star flank dagger at center

Date	Mintage	F	VF	XF	Unc	BU
VS1999 (1942)	—	0.30	0.50	1.00	2.00	—
VS2000 (1943)	—	0.30	0.50	1.00	2.00	—
VS2001 (1944)	—	0.30	0.50	1.00	2.00	—
VS2005 (1948)	—	1.75	3.00	5.00	7.50	—
VS2008 (1951)	—	0.30	0.50	1.00	2.00	—
VS2009 (1952)	—	0.30	0.50	1.00	2.00	—
VS2010 (1953)	—	0.30	0.50	1.00	2.00	—

KM# 711 5 PAISA

Copper, 30 mm. **Obv:** Footprints above crossed daggers within circle **Rev:** Crescent moon and star flank trident at center

Date	Mintage	F	VF	XF	Unc	BU
VS1992 (1935)	—	1.50	3.00	4.50	6.50	—
VS1993 (1936)	878,000	1.50	3.00	4.50	6.50	—
VS1994 (1937)	403,000	1.50	3.00	4.50	6.50	—
VS1995 (1938)	—	1.00	2.00	3.00	5.00	—
VS1996 (1939)	—	1.50	3.00	4.50	6.50	—
VS1997 (1940)	—	1.50	3.00	4.50	6.50	—
VS1998 (1941)	—	—	—	—	—	—

KM# 712 5 PAISA

Copper-Nickel-Zinc **Obv:** Lamp within center circle **Rev:** Crescent moon and star flank trident above inscription

Date	Mintage	F	VF	XF	Unc	BU
VS2000 (1943)	—	0.65	1.00	1.50	2.50	—
VS2009 (1952)	—	1.75	3.00	5.00	8.50	—
VS2010 (1953)	—	1.25	2.00	3.00	5.00	—

KM# 712a 5 PAISA

Copper-Nickel **Obv:** Lamp within center circle **Rev. Inscription:** Crescent moon and star flank trident above inscription

Date	Mintage	F	VF	XF	Unc	BU
VS2010 (1953) Restrike	—	0.65	1.00	1.50	2.50	—

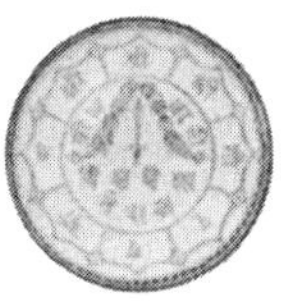

KM# 714 20 PAISA

2.2161 g., 0.3330 Silver 0.0237 oz. ASW **Obv:** Trident **Rev:** Dagger flanked by garlands from above

Date	Mintage	F	VF	XF	Unc	BU
VS1989 (1932)	—	2.25	4.00	5.00	6.50	—
VS1991 (1934)	—	1.75	3.50	4.50	6.00	—
VS1992 (1935)	—	1.75	3.50	4.50	6.00	—
VS1993 (1936)	—	1.75	3.50	4.50	6.00	—
VS1994 (1937)	—	3.75	6.50	10.00	15.00	—
VS1995 (1938)	—	1.75	3.50	4.50	6.00	—
VS1996 (1939)	—	1.75	3.50	4.50	6.00	—
VS1997 (1940)	—	1.75	3.50	4.50	6.00	—
VS1998 (1941)	—	1.75	3.50	4.50	6.00	—
VS1999 (1942)	—	1.75	3.50	4.50	6.00	—
VS2000 (1943)	—	1.75	3.50	4.50	6.00	—
VS2001 (1944)	—	1.75	3.50	4.50	6.00	—
VS2003 (1946)	—	1.75	3.50	4.50	6.00	—
VS2004 (1947)	—	1.75	3.50	4.50	6.00	—

KM# 715 20 PAISA

2.2161 g., 0.3330 Silver 0.0237 oz. ASW

Date	Mintage	F	VF	XF	Unc	BU
VS1989 (1932)	—	2.25	4.00	6.00	8.50	—

Note: The date VS1989 is given in different style characters. Refer to 50 Paisa KM#719 and 1 Rupee, KM#724 for style

KM# 716 20 PAISA

2.2161 g., 0.3330 Silver 0.0237 oz. ASW

Date	Mintage	F	VF	XF	Unc	BU
VS2006 (1949)	—	0.75	1.00	1.25	1.75	—
VS2007 (1950)	—	—	—	—	—	—
VS2009 (1952)	—	0.75	1.00	1.50	2.50	—
VS2010 (1953)	—	0.75	1.00	1.50	2.50	—

KM# 718 50 PAISA

5.5403 g., 0.8000 Silver 0.1425 oz. ASW **Obv:** Trident within small center circle **Rev:** Dagger flanked by garlands from above

Date	Mintage	F	VF	XF	Unc	BU
VS1989 (1932)	—	5.50	6.50	8.00	10.00	—
VS1991 (1934)	—	2.75	4.50	7.00	10.00	—
VS1992 (1935)	—	2.75	4.50	7.00	10.00	—
VS1993 (1936)	—	2.75	4.50	7.00	10.00	—
VS1994 (1937)	—	2.75	4.50	7.00	10.00	—
VS1995 (1938)	—	2.75	4.50	7.00	10.00	—
VS1996 (1939)	—	2.75	4.50	7.00	10.00	—
VS1997 (1940)	—	2.75	4.50	7.00	10.00	—
VS1998 (1941)	—	2.75	4.50	7.00	10.00	—
VS1999 (1942)	—	2.75	4.50	7.00	10.00	—
VS2000 (1943)	—	2.75	4.50	7.00	10.00	—
VS2001 (1944)	—	2.75	4.50	7.00	10.00	—
VS2003 (1946)	—	2.75	4.50	7.00	10.00	—
VS2004 (1947)	—	2.75	4.50	7.00	10.00	—
VS2005 (1948)	—	2.75	4.50	7.00	10.00	—

KM# 719 50 PAISA

5.5403 g., 0.8000 Silver 0.1425 oz. ASW **Obv:** Trident within small center circle **Rev:** Dagger flanked by garlands from above

Date	Mintage	F	VF	XF	Unc	BU
VS1989 (1932)	—	2.50	4.50	7.00	9.00	—

Note: The date is given in different style characters

KM# 720 50 PAISA

5.5403 g., 0.3330 Silver 0.0593 oz. ASW **Obv:** Four dots around trident **Rev:** Dagger flanked by garlands from above

Date	Mintage	F	VF	XF	Unc	BU
VS2005 (1948)	—	45.00	65.00	90.00	125	—

KM# 721 50 PAISA
5.5403 g., 0.3330 Silver 0.0593 oz. ASW **Obv:** Without dots around trident **Rev:** Dagger flanked by garlands from above

Date	Mintage	F	VF	XF	Unc	BU
VS2006 (1949)	—	1.50	2.00	2.75	4.50	—
VS2007 (1950)	—	1.50	2.00	2.75	4.50	—
VS2009/7 (1952)	—	1.50	2.25	3.00	5.00	—
VS2009 (1952)	—	1.50	2.00	2.75	4.50	—
VS2010 (1953)	—	1.50	2.00	2.75	4.50	—

KM# 713 1/16 RUPEE
Silver **Obv:** Inscription **Rev:** Inscription

Date	Mintage	F	VF	XF	Unc	BU
VS(19)96(1939)	—	12.50	20.00	32.50	50.00	—

KM# 723 RUPEE
11.0806 g., 0.8000 Silver 0.2850 oz. ASW **Obv:** Trident within small center circle **Rev:** Dagger flanked by garlands from above

Date	Mintage	F	VF	XF	Unc	BU
VS1989 (1932)	—	4.50	6.00	8.00	20.00	—
VS1991 (1934)	—	4.50	6.00	8.00	16.50	—
VS1992 (1935)	—	4.50	6.00	8.00	16.50	—
VS1993 (1936)	1,717,000	4.50	6.00	8.00	16.50	—
VS1994 (1937)	2,097,000	4.50	6.00	8.00	16.50	—
VS1995 (1938)	—	4.50	6.00	8.00	16.50	—
VS1996 (1939)	—	4.50	6.00	8.00	16.50	—
VS1997 (1940)	—	4.50	6.00	8.00	16.50	—
VS1998 (1941)	—	4.50	6.00	8.00	16.50	—
VS1999 (1942)	—	4.50	6.00	8.00	16.50	—
VS2000 (1943)	—	4.50	6.00	8.00	16.50	—
VS2001 (1944)	—	4.50	6.00	8.00	16.50	—
VS2003 (1946)	—	4.50	6.00	8.00	16.50	—
VS2005 (1948)	—	4.50	6.00	8.00	16.50	—

KM# 724 RUPEE
11.0806 g., 0.8000 Silver 0.2850 oz. ASW **Obv:** Trident within small center circle **Rev:** Dagger flanked by garlands from above

Date	Mintage	F	VF	XF	Unc	BU
VS1989 (1932)	—	7.50	10.00	12.50	15.00	—

Note: The date is given in different style characters

KM# 725 RUPEE
11.0806 g., 0.3330 Silver 0.1186 oz. ASW **Obv:** Four dots around trident **Rev:** Dagger flanked by garlands from above

Date	Mintage	F	VF	XF	Unc	BU
VS2005 (1948)	—	5.00	7.50	10.00	13.50	—

KM# 726 RUPEE
11.0806 g., 0.3330 Silver 0.1186 oz. ASW **Obv:** Without dots around trident **Rev:** Dagger flanked by garlands from above

Date	Mintage	F	VF	XF	Unc	BU
VS2006 (1949)	—	2.50	3.50	5.00	7.50	—
VS2007 (1950)	—	2.50	3.50	5.00	7.50	—
VS2008 (1951)	—	2.50	3.50	5.00	7.50	—
VS2009 (1951)	—	2.50	3.50	5.00	7.50	—
VS2010 (1952)	—	2.50	3.50	5.00	7.50	—

ASARFI GOLD COINAGE

(Asarphi)

Fractional designations are approximate for this series. Actual Gold Weight (AGW) is used to identify each type.

KM# 741 1/2 ASARPHI
5.8000 g., Gold **Obv:** Head of Tribhuvan Bir Bikram right on 5-pointed star **Note:** Portrait type.

Date	Mintage	F	VF	XF	Unc	BU
VS2010 (1953)	—	—	145	165	185	—

Note: KM#741 is normally found as a restrike ca. 1968

ANONYMOUS COINAGE

KM# 733 PAISA
Brass, 18 mm. **Obv:** Sun rising above three hills within grain sprigs **Rev:** Dagger in front of hills within circle

Date	Mintage	F	VF	XF	Unc	BU
VS2010 (1953)	—	8.00	15.00	20.00	25.00	—
VS2011 (1954)	—	17.50	25.00	35.00	40.00	—
VS2012 (1955) Restrike	—	—	1.00	1.50	2.00	—

KM# 734 PAISA
Brass, 17.5 mm.

Date	Mintage	F	VF	XF	Unc	BU
VS2012 (1955)	—	1.25	2.00	2.50	3.50	—

KM# 735 2 PAISA
Brass, 21 mm. **Obv:** Sun rising above three hills within grain sprigs **Rev:** Dagger in front of hills within circle

Date	Mintage	F	VF	XF	Unc	BU
VS2010 (1953)	—	12.50	20.00	37.50	60.00	—
VS2011 (1954)	—	30.00	40.00	50.00	75.00	—
VS2011 (1954) Restrike	—	—	—	1.50	2.50	—

KM# 749 2 PAISA
Brass, 19.5 mm. **Obv:** Sun rising above three hills within grain sprigs **Rev:** Dagger in front of hills within circle

Date	Mintage	F	VF	XF	Unc	BU
VS2012 (1955)	—	0.30	0.50	0.75	1.50	—
VS2013 (1956)	—	0.30	0.50	0.75	1.50	—
VS2014 (1957)	—	0.30	0.50	0.75	1.50	—

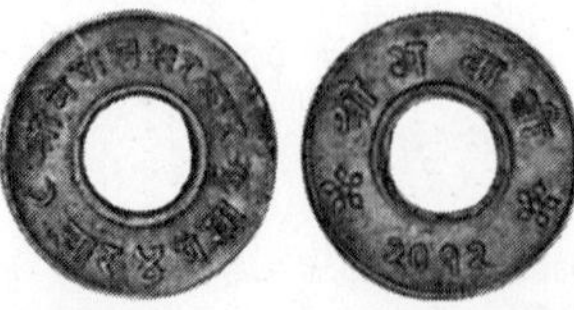

KM# 754 4 PAISA
Brass **Obv:** Legend around center circle **Rev:** Date below center circle

Date	Mintage	F	VF	XF	Unc	BU
VS2012 (1955)	—	1.00	1.75	3.00	5.00	—

KM# 736 5 PAISA
3.8900 g., Bronze **Obv:** Sun rising above three hills within grain sprigs **Rev:** Hand divides date within decorative outline

Date	Mintage	F	VF	XF	Unc	BU
VS2010 (1953)	—	2.75	4.50	7.00	10.00	—
VS2011 (1954)	—	0.65	1.00	2.75	5.00	—
VS2012 (1955)	—	0.30	0.50	0.75	1.25	—
VS2013 (1956)	—	0.30	0.50	0.75	1.25	—
VS2014 (1957)	—	0.30	0.50	0.75	1.25	—

KM# 736a 5 PAISA
4.0400 g., Copper-Nickel **Obv:** Sun rising above three hills within grain sprigs **Rev:** Hand divides date within decorative outline

Date	Mintage	F	VF	XF	Unc	BU
VS2014 (1957)	—	—	—	—	—	—

KM# 737 10 PAISA
Bronze **Obv:** Sun rising above three hills within grain sprigs **Rev:** Dagger in front of three hills within circle

Date	Mintage	F	VF	XF	Unc	BU
VS2010 (1953)	—	2.75	4.50	7.00	10.00	—
VS2011 (1954)	—	0.15	0.25	0.50	1.00	—
VS2011 (1954) Restrike	—	—	—	0.15	0.25	—
VS2012 (1955)	—	0.15	0.25	0.50	1.00	—

KM# 738 20 PAISA
Copper-Nickel, 18 mm. **Obv:** Sun rising above three hills within grain sprigs **Rev:** Dagger in front of three hills within circle

Date	Mintage	F	VF	XF	Unc	BU
VS2010 (1953)	—	12.50	20.00	30.00	40.00	—
VS2010 (1953) Restrike	—	—	—	2.50	3.00	—
VS2011 (1954)	—	32.50	40.00	50.00	60.00	—

KM# 739 25 PAISA
Copper-Nickel, 19 mm. **Obv:** Sun rising above three hills within grain sprigs **Rev:** Dagger in front of three hills within circle

Date	Mintage	F	VF	XF	Unc	BU
VS2010 (1953)	—	2.00	3.50	4.50	6.00	—
VS2011 (1954)	—	2.00	3.50	4.50	6.00	—
VS2012 (1955)	—	1.25	2.00	2.50	3.50	—
VS2014 (1957)	—	1.25	2.00	2.50	3.50	—

KM# 768 1/5 ASARPHI
2.3300 g., Gold

Date	Mintage	F	VF	XF	Unc	BU
VS2010 (1953)	—	—	65.00	75.00	100	—

Note: Coins dated VS2010 are normally found as restrikes ca. 1968

Date	Mintage	F	VF	XF	Unc	BU
VS2012 (1955)	—	—	—	—	—	—

KM# 774 1/4 ASARPHI
2.9000 g., Gold

Date	Mintage	F	VF	XF	Unc	BU
VS2010 (1953)	—	75.00	85.00	95.00	125	—

Note: Coins dated VS2010 are normally found as restrikes ca. 1968

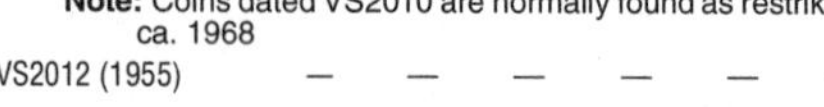

Date	Mintage	F	VF	XF	Unc	BU
VS2012 (1955)	—	—	—	—	—	—

Gyanendra Bir Bikram
VS2007 / 1950-51AD (first reign)

DECIMAL COINAGE
100 Paisa = 1 Rupee

KM# 729 50 PAISA
5.5403 g., 0.3330 Silver 0.0593 oz. ASW **Obv:** Trident within small center circle **Rev:** Dagger flanked by garlands from above

Date	Mintage	F	VF	XF	Unc	BU
VS2007 (1950)	26	—	175	275	350	—

KM# 731 MOHAR
Gold

Date	Mintage	F	VF	XF	Unc	BU
VS2007 (1950) Rare	—	—	—	—	—	—

KM# 730 RUPEE
11.0806 g., 0.3330 Silver 0.1186 oz. ASW **Obv:** Trident within small center circle **Rev:** Dagger flanked by garlands from above

Date	Mintage	F	VF	XF	Unc	BU
VS2007 (1950)	—	4.50	6.50	9.00	12.50	—

Trivhuvan Bir Bikram
VS2007-2011 / 1951-1955AD (second reign)

DECIMAL COINAGE
100 Paisa = 1 Rupee

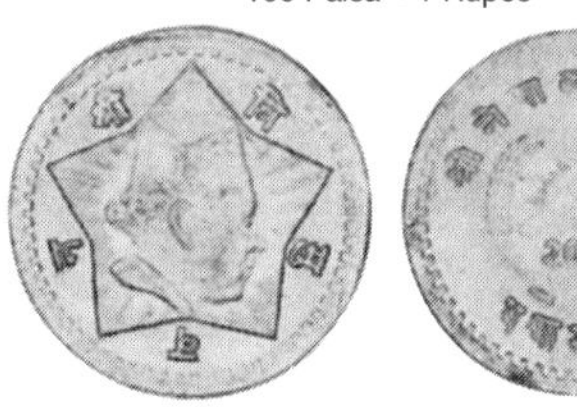

KM# 740 50 PAISA
Copper-Nickel, 25 mm. **Obv:** Head of Tribhuvan Bir Bikram right on 5-pointed star **Rev:** Sun rising back of hills, grain sprigs flank

Date	Mintage	F	VF	XF	Unc	BU
VS2010 (1953)	—	0.50	1.00	2.00	4.00	—
VS2011 (1954)	—	0.35	0.75	1.50	3.00	—

KM# 742 RUPEE
Copper-Nickel **Obv:** Head of Tribhuvan Bir Bikram right on 5-pointed star **Note:** Equal denticles at rim.

Date	Mintage	F	VF	XF	Unc	BU
VS2010 (1953)	—	0.75	1.25	2.25	4.50	—
VS2011 (1954)	—	0.75	1.25	2.25	4.50	—

KM# 743 RUPEE
Copper-Nickel **Obv:** Head of Tribhuvan Bir Bikram right on 5-pointed star **Rev:** Sun rising back of hills, grain sprigs flank **Note:** Unequal denticles at rim.

Date	Mintage	F	VF	XF	Unc	BU
VS2011 (1954)	—	0.75	1.25	2.25	4.50	—

ASARFI GOLD COINAGE
(Asarphi)

Fractional designations are approximate for this series. Actual Gold Weight (AGW) is used to identify each type.

KM# 744 ASARPHI
11.6600 g., Gold **Obv:** Head of Tribhuvan Bir Bikram right on 5-pointed star

Date	Mintage	F	VF	XF	Unc	BU
VS2010 (1953)	—	—	300	325	350	—

Note: KM#744 normally found as a restrike ca. 1968

Mahendra Bir Bikram
VS2012-2028 / 1955-1971AD

DECIMAL COINAGE
100 Paisa = 1 Rupee

KM# 745.1 PAISA
Brass, 18 mm. **Subject:** Mahendra Coronation **Obv:** Crown **Rev:** Numeral at center, sprigs at sides **Note:** Prev. KM#745.

Date	Mintage	F	VF	XF	Unc	BU
VS2013 (1956) Narrow rim	—	0.30	0.50	0.75	1.00	—

KM# 745.2 PAISA
Brass **Subject:** Mahendra coronation

Date	Mintage	F	VF	XF	Unc	BU
VS2013 (1958) Wide rim	—	0.30	0.50	0.75	1.00	—

KM# 746 PAISA
Brass, 16 mm. **Obv:** Crescent and star flank trident at center **Rev:** Numerals with shading

Date	Mintage	F	VF	XF	Unc	BU
VS2014 (1957)	—	0.10	0.15	0.25	0.40	—
VS2015 (1958)	—	0.10	0.15	0.25	0.40	—
VS2018 (1961)	—	0.10	0.15	0.25	0.40	—
VS2019 (1962)	—	0.10	0.15	0.25	0.40	—
VS2020 (1963)	—	0.10	0.15	0.25	0.40	—

KM# 747 PAISA
1.4500 g., Brass, 16.5 mm. **Obv:** Crescent moon and star flank trident at center **Rev:** Numerals without shading

Date	Mintage	F	VF	XF	Unc	BU
VS2021 (1964)	—	0.10	0.15	0.20	0.30	—
VS2022 (1965)	—	0.10	0.15	0.25	0.40	—

KM# 748 PAISA
0.6100 g., Aluminum, 16.6 mm. **Obv:** Flower above hills **Rev:** National flower

Date	Mintage	F	VF	XF	Unc	BU
VS2023 (1966)	—	—	0.10	0.15	0.25	—
VS2025 (1968)	—	—	0.10	0.15	0.25	—
VS2026 (1969)	—	—	0.10	0.15	0.25	—

Date	Mintage	F	VF	XF	Unc	BU
VS2027 (1970) Proof	2,187	Value: 1.25				
VS2028 (1971)	—	—	0.10	0.15	0.25	—
VS2028 (1971) Proof	2,380	Value: 1.25				

KM# 750.1 2 PAISA
Brass, 20.5 mm. **Subject:** Mahendra Coronation **Obv:** Crown **Rev:** Numeral at center **Note:** Narrow rim.

Date	Mintage	F	VF	XF	Unc	BU
VS2013 (1956)	—	0.30	0.50	0.75	1.00	—

KM# 750.2 2 PAISA
Brass **Subject:** Mahendra coronation **Obv:** Crown **Rev:** Numeral at center **Note:** Wide rim.

Date	Mintage	F	VF	XF	Unc	BU
VS2013 (1956)	—	0.30	0.50	0.75	1.00	—

KM# 751 2 PAISA
2.1600 g., Brass, 19.1 mm. **Obv:** Crescent moon and sun flank trident **Rev:** Numerals with shading

Date	Mintage	F	VF	XF	Unc	BU
VS2014 (1957)	—	0.10	0.15	0.25	0.40	—
VS2015 (1958)	—	0.10	0.15	0.25	0.40	—
VS2016 (1959)	—	0.10	0.15	0.25	0.40	—
VS2018 (1961)	—	0.10	0.15	0.25	0.40	—
VS2019 (1962)	—	0.10	0.15	0.25	0.40	—
VS2020 (1963)	—	0.10	0.15	0.25	0.40	—

KM# 752 2 PAISA
Brass **Obv:** Crescent moon and sun flank trident at center **Rev:** Numerals wtihout shading

Date	Mintage	F	VF	XF	Unc	BU
VS2021 (1964)	—	0.10	0.15	0.20	0.35	—
VS2022 (1965)	—	0.10	0.15	0.25	0.50	—
VS2023 (1966)	—	0.10	0.15	0.25	0.50	—

KM# 753 2 PAISA
0.9100 g., Aluminum, 18.6 mm. **Obv:** Trident with sun and moon flanking above hills **Rev:** Himalayan Monal pheasant

Date	Mintage	F	VF	XF	Unc	BU
VS2023 (1966)	—	—	0.10	0.15	0.75	—
VS2024 (1967)	—	—	0.10	0.15	0.75	—
VS2025 (1968)	—	—	0.10	0.15	0.75	—
VS2026 (1969)	—	—	0.10	0.15	0.75	—
VS2027 (1970)	—	—	0.10	0.15	0.75	—
VS2027 (1970) Proof	2,187	Value: 1.50				
VS2028 (1971)	—	—	0.10	0.15	0.75	—
VS2028 (1971) Proof	2,380	Value: 1.50				

KM# 756.1 5 PAISA
Bronze, 22 mm. **Subject:** Mahendra Coronation **Obv:** Crown **Rev:** Numeral within floral outline **Note:** Wide rim with accent mark.

Date	Mintage	F	VF	XF	Unc	BU
VS2013 (1955)	—	10.00	20.00	30.00	40.00	—

KM# 756.2 5 PAISA

Bronze, 22 mm. **Subject:** Mahendra coronation **Obv:** Crown **Rev:** Numeral within floral outline **Note:** Narrow rim.

Date	Mintage	F	VF	XF	Unc	BU
VS2013 (1955) Restrike	—	0.35	0.60	1.00	1.50	—

KM# 756.3 5 PAISA

Bronze, 22 mm. **Subject:** Mahendra coronation **Obv:** Crown **Rev:** Numeral within floral outline **Note:** Without accent mark.

Date	Mintage	F	VF	XF	Unc	BU
VS2013 (1955)	—	1.00	2.00	3.00	5.00	—

KM# 757 5 PAISA

3.8500 g., Bronze, 22.5 mm. **Obv:** Trident at center **Rev:** Numerals with shading

Date	Mintage	F	VF	XF	Unc	BU
VS2014 (1957)	—	0.10	0.20	0.30	0.75	—
VS2015 (1958)	—	0.10	0.20	0.30	0.75	—
VS2016 (1959)	—	0.10	0.30	0.50	1.00	—
VS2017 (1960)	—	0.10	0.20	0.30	0.75	—
VS2018 (1961)	—	0.10	0.20	0.30	0.75	—
VS2019 (1962)	—	0.10	0.20	0.30	0.75	—
VS2020 (1963)	—	0.10	0.20	0.30	0.75	—

KM# 758 5 PAISA

Aluminum-Bronze, 22.5 mm. **Obv:** Crescent moon and sun flank trident at center **Rev:** Numerals without shading

Date	Mintage	F	VF	XF	Unc	BU
VS2021 (1964)	—	0.50	1.00	1.50	2.50	—

KM# 758a 5 PAISA

3.0800 g., Bronze, 21 mm. **Obv:** Crescent moon and sun flank trident at center **Rev:** Numeral within shaded floral outline

Date	Mintage	F	VF	XF	Unc	BU
VS2021 (1964)	—	0.10	0.15	0.25	0.50	—
VS2022 (1965)	—	0.10	0.15	0.30	0.60	—
VS2023 (1966)	—	0.10	0.15	0.30	0.60	—

KM# 759 5 PAISA

Aluminum, 21 mm. **Obv:** Trident with sun and moon flanking above hills **Rev:** Ox left

Date	Mintage	F	VF	XF	Unc	BU
VS2023 (1966)	—	—	0.15	0.25	1.00	—
VS2024 (1967)	—	—	0.10	0.20	1.00	—
VS2025 (1968)	—	—	0.10	0.20	1.00	—
VS2026 (1969)	—	—	0.10	0.20	1.00	—
VS2027 (1970)	—	—	0.10	0.20	1.00	—
VS2027 (1970) Proof	2,187	Value: 1.75				

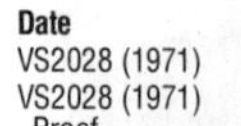

Date	Mintage	F	VF	XF	Unc	BU
VS2028 (1971)	—	—	0.10	0.20	1.00	—
VS2028 (1971) Proof	2,038	Value: 1.75				

KM# 761 10 PAISA

Bronze, 24.5 mm. **Subject:** Mahendra Coronation **Obv:** Crown **Rev:** Shaded numeral

Date	Mintage	F	VF	XF	Unc	BU
VS2013 (1956)	—	0.25	0.50	0.75	1.50	—

KM# 762 10 PAISA

6.3000 g., Bronze, 25 mm. **Obv:** Crescent moon and sun flank trident **Rev:** Numerals with shading

Date	Mintage	F	VF	XF	Unc	BU
VS2014 (1957)	—	2.75	4.50	7.00	10.00	—
VS2015 (1958)	—	0.15	0.25	0.50	0.75	—
VS2016 (1959)	—	3.00	5.00	7.00	10.00	—
VS2018 (1961)	—	0.15	0.25	0.50	0.75	—
VS2019 (1962)	—	0.15	0.25	0.50	0.75	—
VS2020 (1963)	—	0.15	0.25	0.50	0.75	—

KM# 763 10 PAISA

Aluminum-Bronze **Obv:** Crescent moon and sun flank trident at center **Rev:** Numerals without shading

Date	Mintage	F	VF	XF	Unc	BU
VS2021 (1964)	—	0.75	1.25	2.00	3.00	—

KM# 764 10 PAISA

4.9300 g., Bronze, 25 mm. **Note:** Modified design.

Date	Mintage	F	VF	XF	Unc	BU
VS2021 (1964)	—	0.10	0.15	0.25	0.50	—
VS2022 (1965)	—	0.10	0.15	0.25	0.50	—
VS2023 (1966)	—	0.10	0.15	0.25	0.50	—

KM# 765 10 PAISA

Brass **Obv:** Trident with sun and moon flanking above hills **Rev:** Ox left

Date	Mintage	F	VF	XF	Unc	BU
VS2023 (1966)	—	—	0.15	0.25	1.00	—
VS2024 (1967)	—	—	0.15	0.25	1.00	—
VS2025 (1968)	—	—	15.00	17.50	20.00	—
VS2026 (1969)	—	—	0.10	0.20	1.00	—
VS2027 (1970)	—	—	0.10	0.20	1.00	—
VS2027 (1970) Proof	2,187	Value: 2.00				
VS2028 (1971)	—	—	0.10	0.20	1.00	—
VS2028 (1971) Proof	2,380	Value: 2.00				

Note: Birendra Bir Bikram also struck a 10 Paisa VS2028, see KM#806

KM# 766 10 PAISA

4.0600 g., Brass, 21 mm. **Series:** F.A.O. **Obv:** Grain sprig at center **Rev:** Ox left

Date	Mintage	F	VF	XF	Unc	BU
VS2028 (1971)	1,500,000	—	0.10	0.20	1.00	—

KM# 770 25 PAISA

Copper-Nickel **Subject:** Mahendra Coronation

Date	Mintage	F	VF	XF	Unc	BU
VS2013 (1956)	—	0.30	0.50	0.70	1.00	—

KM# 771 25 PAISA

Copper-Nickel, 19 mm. **Obv:** Four characters in line above trident **Rev:** Small character at bottom (outer circle)

Date	Mintage	F	VF	XF	Unc	BU
VS2015 (1958)	—	1.50	2.50	4.00	6.00	—
VS2018 (1961)	—	0.25	0.40	0.60	0.80	—
VS2020 (1963)	—	0.25	0.40	0.60	0.80	—
VS2021 (1964)	—	0.30	0.50	0.75	1.00	—
VS2022 (1965)	—	2.00	3.50	6.00	9.00	—

KM# 771a 25 PAISA

2.9900 g., 840.0000 Silver 80.746 oz. ASW **Obv:** Trident within small center circle **Rev:** Dagger flanked by garlands from above

Date	Mintage	F	VF	XF	Unc	BU
VS2017/6/5 (1960)	—	—	—	—	100	—

KM# 772 25 PAISA

3.0500 g., Copper-Nickel, 19 mm. **Obv:** Trident within small center circle **Rev:** Large different character at bottom

Date	Mintage	F	VF	XF	Unc	BU
VS2021 (1964)	—	0.30	0.50	0.70	1.00	—
VS2022 (1965)	—	0.30	0.50	0.70	1.00	—
VS2023 (1966)	—	0.30	0.50	0.70	1.00	—

KM# 773 25 PAISA

Copper-Nickel **Obv:** Five characters in line above trident **Rev:** Dagger flanked by garlands from above

Date	Mintage	F	VF	XF	Unc	BU
VS2024 (1967)	—	—	0.35	0.50	0.75	—
VS2025 (1968)	—	—	15.00	20.00	25.00	—
VS2026 (1969)	—	—	0.35	0.50	0.75	—
VS2027 (1970)	—	—	0.35	0.50	0.75	—
VS2027 (1970) Proof	2,187	Value: 2.50				
VS2028 (1971)	—	—	0.35	0.50	0.75	—
VS2028 (1971) Proof	2,380	Value: 2.50				
VS2030 (1973)	—	—	0.35	0.50	0.75	—

KM# 777 50 PAISA

Copper-Nickel, 25 mm. **Obv:** Trident within small center circle **Rev:** Small character at bottom

Date	Mintage	F	VF	XF	Unc	BU
VS2011 (1954)	—	0.50	1.00	1.50	3.00	—
VS2012 (1955)	—	0.25	0.50	0.75	1.00	—
VS2013 (1956)	—	0.25	0.50	1.00	2.00	—
VS2014 (1957)	—	0.25	0.50	1.00	2.00	—
VS2015 (1958)	—	0.25	0.50	1.00	2.00	—
VS2016 (1959)	—	0.25	0.50	1.00	2.00	—
VS2017 (1960)	—	0.25	0.30	0.75	1.25	—
VS2018 (1961)	—	0.25	0.50	1.00	2.00	—
VS2020 (1963)	—	0.25	0.30	0.75	1.50	—

KM# 795 50 PAISA
Copper-Nickel **Obv:** Trident within small center circle **Rev:** Dagger flanked by garlands from above **Note:** In the name of "Queen Ratna Rajya Lakshmi".

Date	Mintage	F	VF	XF	Unc	BU
VS2012 (1955)	—	3,000	100	125	150	—

KM# 776 50 PAISA
Copper-Nickel **Subject:** Mahendra Coronation **Obv:** Crown **Rev:** Dagger flanked by garlands from above

Date	Mintage	F	VF	XF	Unc	BU
VS2013 (1956)	—	0.35	0.75	1.00	1.50	—

KM# 778 50 PAISA
Copper-Nickel, 25 mm. **Obv:** Trident within small center circle **Rev:** Large different character at bottom

Date	Mintage	F	VF	XF	Unc	BU
VS2021 (1964)	—	0.25	0.35	0.50	0.75	—
VS2022 (1965)	—	0.25	0.50	0.75	1.50	—
VS2023 (1966)	—	0.25	0.50	0.75	1.00	—

KM# 779 50 PAISA
Copper-Nickel **Obv:** Four characters in line above trident **Rev:** Dagger flanked by garlands from above **Note:** Reduced size, 23.5mm.

Date	Mintage	F	VF	XF	Unc	BU
VS2023 (1966)	—	0.25	0.50	0.75	1.50	—

KM# 780 50 PAISA
Copper-Nickel **Obv:** Five characters in line above trident **Rev:** Dagger flanked by garlands from above

Date	Mintage	F	VF	XF	Unc	BU
VS2025 (1968)	—	—	0.30	0.50	1.00	—
VS2026 (1969)	—	—	0.30	0.50	0.85	—
VS2027 (1970) Proof	2,187	Value: 3.00				
VS2028 (1971) Proof	2,380	Value: 3.00				
VS2030 (1973)	—	—	0.30	0.50	0.85	—

KM# 784 RUPEE
Copper-Nickel, 30 mm.

Date	Mintage	F	VF	XF	Unc	BU
VS2011 (1954)	—	1.25	2.25	3.50	5.00	—
VS2012 (1955)	—	1.00	1.75	2.50	4.00	—

KM# 797 RUPEE
Copper-Nickel **Obv:** Trident within small center circle **Rev:** Dagger flanked by garlands from above **Note:** In the name of "Queen Ratna Rajya Lakshmi".

Date	Mintage	F	VF	XF	Unc	BU
VS2012 (1955)	2,000	—	100	150	175	—

KM# 785 RUPEE
Copper-Nickel, 28.5 mm. **Obv:** Trident within small center circle **Rev:** Small character at bottom **Note:** Reduced size.

Date	Mintage	F	VF	XF	Unc	BU
VS2012 (1955)	—	0.50	0.85	1.25	1.75	—
VS2013 (1956)	—	0.50	0.85	1.25	1.75	—
VS2014 (1957)	—	0.50	0.85	1.25	1.75	—
VS2015 (1958)	—	0.50	0.85	1.25	1.75	—
VS2016 (1959)	—	0.50	0.85	1.25	1.75	—
VS2018 (1961)	—	0.50	0.85	1.25	1.75	—
VS2020 (1963)	—	0.50	0.85	1.25	1.75	—

KM# 790 RUPEE
Copper-Nickel **Subject:** Mahendra Coronation **Obv:** Crown **Rev:** Dagger flanked by garlands from above

Date	Mintage	F	VF	XF	Unc	BU
VS2013 (1956)	—	—	1.25	1.75	2.50	—

KM# 786 RUPEE
Copper-Nickel **Obv:** Trident within small center circle **Rev:** Large character at bottom **Note:** Illustration reduced.

Date	Mintage	F	VF	XF	Unc	BU
VS2021 (1964)	—	0.50	0.75	1.00	1.50	—
VS2022 (1965)	—	0.50	1.00	1.50	2.50	—
VS2023 (1966)	—	4.50	7.50	10.00	15.00	—

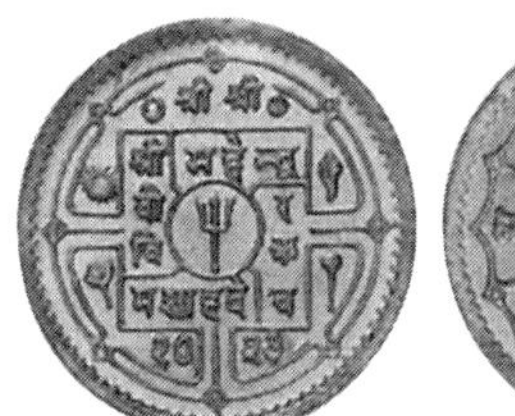

KM# 787 RUPEE
Copper-Nickel, 27 mm. **Obv:** Four characters in line above trident **Rev:** Dagger flanked by garlands from above **Note:** Reduced size, 27.5mm.

Date	Mintage	F	VF	XF	Unc	BU
VS2023 (1966)	—	0.75	1.00	1.35	2.00	—

KM# 788 RUPEE
Copper-Nickel **Obv:** Five characters in line above trident **Rev:** Dagger flanked by garlands from above

Date	Mintage	F	VF	XF	Unc	BU
VS2025 (1968)	—	—	1.00	1.50	2.00	—
VS2026 (1969)	—	—	1.00	1.40	2.00	—
VS2027 (1970) Proof	2,187	Value: 4.50				
VS2028 (1971) Proof	2,380	Value: 4.50				

KM# 794 10 RUPEE
15.6000 g., 0.6000 Silver 0.3009 oz. ASW **Series:** F.A.O. **Obv:** Bust of Mahendra Bir Bikram left **Rev:** Trident and 1/2 cogwheel above grain sprig

Date	Mintage	F	VF	XF	Unc	BU
VS2025 (1968)	1,000,000	—	5.00	6.00	9.00	—

ASARFI GOLD COINAGE

(Asarphi)

Fractional designations are approximate for this series. Actual Gold Weight (AGW) is used to identify each type.

KM# 767 1/6 ASARPHI
1.9000 g., Gold **Subject:** Mahendra Coronation

Date	Mintage	F	VF	XF	Unc	BU
VS2013 (1956)	—	—	50.00	60.00	100	—

KM# 775 1/4 ASARPHI
2.5000 g., Gold **Obv:** Trident within small circle at center **Rev:** Dagger flanked by garlands from above **Note:** Reduced weight.

Date	Mintage	F	VF	XF	Unc	BU
VS2026 (1969)	—	—	—	75.00	110	—

KM# 782 1/2 ASARPHI
5.8000 g., Gold **Obv:** Trident within small circle at center **Rev:** Dagger flanked by garlands from above

Date	Mintage	F	VF	XF	Unc	BU
VS2012 (1955)	—	—	145	160	180	—
VS2019 (1962)	—	—	145	160	180	—

KM# 796 1/2 ASARPHI
Gold **Note:** In the name of "Queen Ratna Rajya Lakshmi".

Date	Mintage	F	VF	XF	Unc	BU
VS2012 (1955)	—	—	—	—	—	—

KM# 781 1/2 ASARPHI
5.8000 g., Gold **Subject:** Mahendra Coronation

Date	Mintage	F	VF	XF	Unc	BU
VS2013 (1956)	—	—	145	160	180	—

KM# 783 1/2 ASARPHI
5.0000 g., Gold **Subject:** Birendra Marriage

Date	Mintage	F	VF	XF	Unc	BU
VS2026 (1969)	—	—	—	150	180	—

KM# 789 ASARPHI

Gold **Obv:** Trident within small center circle **Rev:** Dagger flanked by garlands from above

Date	Mintage	F	VF	XF	Unc	BU
VS2012 (1955)	—	—	300	335	365	—
VS2019 (1962)	—	—	300	335	365	—

KM# 798 ASARPHI

11.6600 g., Gold **Note:** In the name of "Queen Ratna Rajya Lakshmi".

Date	Mintage	F	VF	XF	Unc	BU
VS2012 (1955)	—	—	300	335	365	—
VS2018 (1960)	—	—	300	335	365	—

KM# 791 ASARPHI

Gold **Subject:** Mahendra Coronation

Date	Mintage	F	VF	XF	Unc	BU
VS2013 (1956)	—	—	300	335	365	—

KM# 792 ASARPHI

10.0000 g., Gold **Obv:** Trident within small center circle **Rev:** Dagger flanked by garlands from above

Date	Mintage	F	VF	XF	Unc	BU
VS2026 (1969)	—	—	300	325	350	—

KM# 793 2 ASARFI

Gold

Date	Mintage	F	VF	XF	Unc	BU
VS2012 (1955)	—	—	550	600	650	—

Birendra Bir Bikram
VS2028-2058 / 1971-2001 AD

DECIMAL COINAGE

100 Paisa = 1 Rupee

KM# 799 PAISA

Aluminum **Obv:** Trident with sun and moon flanking above hills **Rev:** National flower

Date	Mintage	F	VF	XF	Unc	BU
VS2028 (1971)	10,000	—	0.20	0.30	0.40	—
VS2029 (1972)	3,036,000	—	0.10	0.15	0.25	—
VS2029 (1972) Proof	3,943	Value: 0.60				
VS2030 (1973)	1,279,000	—	0.10	0.15	0.25	—
VS2030 (1973) Proof	8,891	Value: 0.40				
VS2031 (1974)	430,000	—	0.10	0.15	0.25	—
VS2031 (1974) Proof	11,000	Value: 0.40				
VS2032 (1975)	324,000	—	0.10	0.15	0.25	—
VS2033 (1976)	217,000	—	—	0.10	0.25	—
VS2034 (1977)	1,040,000	—	0.10	0.15	0.25	—
VS2035 (1978)	394,000	—	0.10	0.15	0.25	—
VS2036 (1979)	—	—	0.10	0.15	0.25	—

KM# 800 PAISA

Aluminum **Subject:** Birendra Coronation **Obv:** Crown

Date	Mintage	F	VF	XF	Unc	BU
VS2031 (1974)	75,000	—	0.10	0.15	0.25	—

KM# 1012 PAISA

Aluminum **Obv:** Crown **Rev:** Value

Date	Mintage	F	VF	XF	Unc	BU
VS2039 (1982)	—	—	4.00	6.00	8.00	—
VS2040 (1983)	42,000	—	—	—	—	—

KM# 801 2 PAISA

Aluminum, 20 mm. **Obv:** Flower above hills with sun and moon flanking **Rev:** Himalayan Monal pheasant

Date	Mintage	F	VF	XF	Unc	BU
VS2028 (1971)	8,319	—	0.20	0.30	0.75	—
VS2029 (1972)	5,206,000	—	0.10	0.15	0.75	—
VS2029 (1972) Proof	3,943	Value: 1.00				
VS2030 (1973)	2,563,000	—	0.10	0.15	0.75	—
VS2030 (1973) Proof	8,891	Value: 0.75				
VS2031 (1974) Proof	11,000	Value: 0.75				
VS2033 (1976)	72,000	—	0.10	0.15	0.75	—
VS2035 (1978)	26,000	—	0.10	0.15	0.75	—

KM# 802 5 PAISA

1.1400 g., Aluminum, 20.5 mm. **Obv:** Trident with sun and moon flanking above hills **Rev:** Ox left

Date	Mintage	F	VF	XF	Unc	BU
VS2028 (1971)	3,700,000	—	0.10	0.20	0.75	—
VS2029 (1972)	23,578,000	—	0.10	0.20	0.75	—
VS2029 (1972) Proof	3,943	Value: 1.00				
VS2030 (1973)	12,320,000	—	0.10	0.20	0.75	—
VS2030 (1973) Proof	8,891	Value: 1.00				
VS2031 (1974)	15,730,000	—	0.10	0.20	0.75	—
VS2031 (1974) Proof	11,000	Value: 1.00				
VS2032 (1975)	19,747,000	—	0.10	0.20	0.75	—
VS2033 (1976)	29,619,000	—	0.10	0.20	0.75	—
VS2034 (1977)	27,222,000	—	0.10	0.20	0.75	—
VS2035 (1978)	27,613,000	—	0.10	0.20	0.75	—
VS2036 (1979)	—	—	0.10	0.20	0.75	—
VS2037 (1980)	13,235,000	—	0.10	0.20	0.75	—
VS2038 (1981)	15,137,000	—	0.10	0.20	0.75	—
VS2039 (1982)	8,971,000	—	0.10	0.20	0.75	—

KM# 803 5 PAISA

1.2300 g., Aluminum, 21.0 mm. **Series:** F.A.O. **Obv:** Value **Designer:** Gopal Bahadur Shrestha

Date	Mintage	F	VF	XF	Unc	BU
VS2031 (1974)	4,584,000	—	0.10	0.15	0.25	—

KM# 804 5 PAISA

Aluminum **Subject:** Birendra Coronation **Obv:** Crown **Rev:** Dagger flanked by garlands from above

Date	Mintage	F	VF	XF	Unc	BU
VS2031 (1974)	2,869,000	—	0.10	0.25	0.50	—

KM# 1013 5 PAISA

0.8500 g., Aluminum, 18 mm. **Obv:** Crown **Rev:** Value

Date	Mintage	F	VF	XF	Unc	BU
VS2039 (1982)	8,971,000	—	7.00	10.00	15.00	—
VS2040 (1983)	6,430,000	—	—	0.10	0.25	—
VS2041 (1984)	9,634,000	—	—	0.10	0.25	—
VS2042 (1985)	58,000	—	—	0.10	0.25	—
VS2043 (1986)	2,937,000	—	—	0.10	0.25	—
VS2044 (1987)	3,126,000	—	—	0.10	0.25	—
VS2045 (1988)	1,030,000	—	—	0.10	0.25	—
VS2046 (1989)	—	—	—	0.10	0.25	—
VS2047 (1990)	—	—	—	0.10	0.25	—

KM# 806 10 PAISA

Brass **Obv:** Trident with sun and moon flanking above hills **Rev:** Ox left

Date	Mintage	F	VF	XF	Unc	BU
VS2028 (1971) In sets only	5,035	—	0.25	0.40	1.50	—

Note: Mahendra Bir Bikram also struck a 10 Paisa VS2028, see KM#765

KM# 807 10 PAISA

4.1400 g., Brass, 21 mm. **Obv:** Trident with sun and moon flanking above hills **Rev:** Value with grain sprigs at sides of coin

Date	Mintage	F	VF	XF	Unc	BU
VS2029 (1972)	3,297,000	—	0.15	0.25	0.40	—
VS2029 (1972) Proof	3,943	Value: 1.00				
VS2030 (1973)	5,670,000	—	0.15	0.25	0.40	—
VS2030 (1973) Proof	8,891	Value: 0.70				
VS2031 (1974) Proof	11,000	Value: 0.70				

KM# 808 10 PAISA

Aluminum **Subject:** Birendra Coronation **Obv:** Crown **Rev:** Dagger flanked by garlands from above

Date	Mintage	F	VF	XF	Unc	BU
VS2031 (1974)	192,000	—	0.10	0.20	0.35	—

KM# 809 10 PAISA

Brass **Series:** F.A.O. International Women's Year **Obv:** Busts left **Rev:** Value within grain sprigs

Date	Mintage	F	VF	XF	Unc	BU
VS2032 (1975)	2,500,000	—	0.10	0.15	0.25	—

KM# 810 10 PAISA

Brass **Subject:** Agricultural Developement **Obv:** Crown **Rev:** Value

Date	Mintage	F	VF	XF	Unc	BU
VS2033 (1976)	10,000,000	—	0.10	0.15	0.25	—

KM# 811 10 PAISA

Aluminum **Series:** International Year of the Child **Obv:** Trident within small circle at center **Rev:** Symbol at center, rising sun above

Date	Mintage	F	VF	XF	Unc	BU
VS2036 (1979)	213,000	—	0.10	0.15	0.25	—

KM# 812 10 PAISA

Aluminum **Subject:** Education for Village Women **Obv:** Trident within small circle at center **Rev:** Open book

Date	Mintage	F	VF	XF	Unc	BU
VS2036 (1979)	Inc. above	—	0.10	0.15	0.50	—

KM# 1014.1 10 PAISA

1.3000 g., Aluminum, 21.5 mm. **Obv:** Crown **Rev:** Large ears of grain

Date	Mintage	F	VF	XF	Unc	BU
VS2039 (1982)	796	—	7.00	10.00	15.00	—
VS2040 (1983)	—	—	—	0.10	0.30	—
VS2041 (1984)	7,834,000	—	—	0.10	0.30	—
VS2042 (1985)	99,000	—	—	0.10	0.30	—

KM# 1014.2 10 PAISA

1.3000 g., Aluminum, 21.5 mm. **Obv:** Crown **Rev:** Small ears of grain

Date	Mintage	F	VF	XF	Unc	BU
VS2041 (1984)	—	—	—	0.10	0.30	—
VS2042 (1985)	Inc. above	—	—	0.10	0.30	—
VS2043 (1986)	10,000	—	—	0.10	0.30	—
VS2044 (1987)	30,172,000	—	—	0.10	0.30	—
VS2045 (1988)	4,140,000	—	—	0.10	0.30	—
VS2046 (1989)	—	—	—	0.10	0.30	—
VS2047 (1990)	—	—	—	0.10	0.30	—
VS2048 (1991)	—	—	—	0.10	0.30	—
VS2049 (1992)	—	—	—	0.10	0.30	—

KM# 1014.3 10 PAISA

0.7200 g., Aluminum, 17 mm. **Obv:** Crown **Rev:** Value, grain ears flank **Edge:** Plain **Note:** Reduced size.

Date	Mintage	F	VF	XF	Unc	BU
VS2051 (1994)	—	—	—	0.10	0.30	—
VS2052 (1995)	—	—	—	0.10	0.30	—
VS2053 (1996)	—	—	—	0.10	0.30	—
VS2054 (1997)	—	—	—	0.10	0.30	—
VS2055 (1998)	—	—	—	0.10	0.30	—
VS2056 (1999)	—	—	—	0.10	0.30	—
VS2057 (2000)	—	—	—	0.10	0.30	—

KM# 813 20 PAISA

Brass **Series:** F.A.O. **Obv:** Trident within small circle at center

Date	Mintage	F	VF	XF	Unc	BU
VS2035 (1978)	234,000	—	0.35	0.75	1.00	—

KM# 814 20 PAISA

Brass **Series:** International Year of the Child **Obv:** Trident within small center circle **Rev:** Emblem below rising sun

Date	Mintage	F	VF	XF	Unc	BU
VS2036 (1979)	30,000	—	0.35	0.75	1.00	—

KM# 815 25 PAISA

3.0000 g., Copper-Nickel **Obv:** Trident within small center circle **Rev:** Dagger flanked by garlands from above **Note:** Varieties exist.

Date	Mintage	F	VF	XF	Unc	BU
VS2028 (1971)	5,691	—	0.40	0.60	0.80	—
VS2029 (1972) Proof	3,943	Value: 1.25				
VS2030 (1973)	8,676,000	—	0.30	0.40	0.50	—
VS2030 (1973) Proof	8,891	Value: 0.80				
VS2031 (1974)	1,172,000	—	0.35	0.50	0.75	—
VS2031 (1974) Proof	11,000	Value: 0.80				
VS2032 (1975)	4,584,000	—	0.30	0.40	0.50	—
VS2033 (1976)	1,837,000	—	0.30	0.40	0.50	—
VS2034 (1977)	3,808,000	—	0.30	0.40	0.50	—
VS2035 (1978)	5,964,000	—	0.30	0.40	0.50	—
VS2036 (1979)	—	—	0.30	0.40	0.50	—
VS2037 (1980)	2,047,000	—	0.30	0.40	0.50	—
VS2038 (1981)	1,580,000	—	0.30	0.40	0.50	—
VS2039 (1982)	7,185,000	—	0.30	0.40	0.50	—

KM# 816.1 25 PAISA

2.9300 g., Copper-Nickel, 18.8 mm. **Subject:** Birendra Coronation **Obv:** Crown **Rev:** Dagger flanked by garlands from above

Date	Mintage	F	VF	XF	Unc	BU
VS2031 (1974)	431,000	—	0.35	0.50	0.75	—

KM# 817 25 PAISA

Brass **Series:** World Food Day **Obv:** Trident within small center circle **Rev:** Corn ear at left, logo at right

Date	Mintage	F	VF	XF	Unc	BU
VS2038 (1981)	2,000,000	—	—	0.10	0.30	—

KM# 818 25 PAISA

Brass **Series:** International Year of Disabled Persons **Obv:** Trident within small center circle **Rev:** Emblem at center

Date	Mintage	F	VF	XF	Unc	BU
VS2038 (1981)	Inc. above	—	0.10	0.25	0.50	—

KM# 1015.1 25 PAISA

1.8000 g., Aluminum, 24.5 mm. **Obv:** Crown **Rev:** Value flanked by grain ears

Date	Mintage	F	VF	XF	Unc	BU
VS2039 (1982)	—	—	4.00	6.00	8.00	—
VS2040 (1983)	7,603,000	—	0.10	0.25	0.50	—
VS2041 (1984)	15,534,000	—	0.10	0.25	0.50	—
VS2042 (1985)	12,586,000	—	0.10	0.25	0.50	—
VS2043 (1986)	54,000	—	0.10	0.25	0.50	—
VS2044 (1987)	13,633,000	—	0.10	0.25	0.50	—
VS2045 (1988)	13,046,000	—	0.10	0.25	0.50	—
VS2046 (1989)	—	—	0.10	0.25	0.50	—
VS2047 (1990)	—	—	0.10	0.25	0.50	—
VS2048 (1991)	—	—	0.10	0.25	0.50	—
VS2049 (1992)	—	—	0.10	0.25	0.50	—
VS2050 (1993)	—	—	0.10	0.25	0.50	—

KM# 1015.2 25 PAISA

1.5000 g., Aluminum, 20 mm. **Obv:** Crown **Rev:** Value flanked by grain ears **Edge:** Plain **Note:** Reduced size.

Date	Mintage	F	VF	XF	Unc	BU
VS2051 (1994)	—	—	0.10	0.25	0.50	—
VS2052 (1995)	—	—	0.10	0.25	0.50	—
VS2053 (1996)	—	—	0.10	0.25	0.50	—
VS2054 (1997)	—	—	0.10	0.25	0.50	—
VS2055 (1998)	—	—	0.10	0.25	0.50	—
VS2056 (1999)	—	—	0.10	0.25	0.50	—
VS2057 (2000)	—	—	0.10	0.25	0.50	—

KM# 821 50 PAISA

5.0000 g., Copper-Nickel, 23.5 mm. **Obv:** Trident within small center circle **Rev:** Dagger flanked by garlands from above

Date	Mintage	F	VF	XF	Unc	BU
VS2028 (1971)	5,343	—	0.35	0.50	1.00	—
VS2029 (1972)	347,000	—	0.35	0.50	0.90	—
VS2029 (1972) Proof	3,943	Value: 1.50				
VS2030 (1973)	998,000	—	0.35	0.50	0.90	—
VS2030 (1973) Proof	8,891	Value: 1.00				
VS2031 (1974)	16,000	—	0.35	0.50	1.00	—
VS2031 (1974) Proof	11,000	Value: 1.00				
VS2032 (1975)	227,000	—	0.35	0.50	0.90	—
Note: Dot in moon on reverse						
VS2033 (1976)	3,446,000	—	0.35	0.50	0.75	—
VS2034 (1977)	6,016,000	—	0.35	0.50	0.75	—
VS2035 (1978)	2,355,000	—	0.35	0.50	0.75	—
VS2036 (1979)	—	—	0.35	0.50	0.75	—
VS2037 (1980)	4,861,000	—	0.35	0.50	0.75	—
VS2038 (1981)	929,000	—	0.35	0.50	0.75	—
VS2039 (1982)	2,954,000	—	0.35	0.50	0.75	—

KM# 821a 50 PAISA

5.0900 g., Copper-Nickel, 20 mm. **Obv:** Trident within small center circle **Rev:** Dagger flanked by garlands from above

Date	Mintage	F	VF	XF	Unc	BU
VS2039 (1971)	Inc. above	—	0.10	0.25	0.50	—
VS2040 (1983)	72,000	—	0.10	0.25	0.50	—
VS2041 (1984)	5,917,000	—	0.10	0.25	0.50	—

KM# 822.1 50 PAISA

Copper-Nickel **Subject:** Birendra Coronation **Obv:** Crown **Rev:** Dagger flanked by garlands from above **Note:** 1mm thick.

Date	Mintage	F	VF	XF	Unc	BU
VS2031 (1974)	136,000	—	0.50	0.75	1.25	—

KM# 823 50 PAISA

Copper-Nickel **Series:** World Food Day **Obv:** Trident within small center circle **Rev:** Corn ear at left, logo at right

Date	Mintage	F	VF	XF	Unc	BU
VS2038 (1981)	2,000,000	—	0.10	0.30	0.60	—

KM# 824 50 PAISA
Copper-Nickel **Series:** International Year of Disabled Persons **Obv:** Trident within small center circle **Rev:** Emblem at center

Date	Mintage	F	VF	XF	Unc	BU
VS2038 (1981)	Inc. above	—	0.50	0.75	1.25	—

KM# 1016 50 PAISA
3.0000 g., Copper-Nickel, 20 mm. **Subject:** Family Planning **Obv:** Logo above inscription **Rev:** Value

Date	Mintage	F	VF	XF	Unc	BU
VS2041 (1984)	—	—	0.10	0.25	0.50	—

KM# 1018.1 50 PAISA
Stainless Steel, 23.5 mm. **Obv:** Small trident in center **Rev:** Dagger flanked by garlands from above

Date	Mintage	F	VF	XF	Unc	BU
VS2044 (1987)	6,341,000	—	0.10	0.25	0.50	—
VS2045 (1988)	7,350,000	—	0.10	0.25	0.50	—
Note: Varieties with small and large Nepalese "5" exist						
VS2046 (1989)	—	—	0.10	0.25	0.50	—

KM# 1018.2 50 PAISA
Stainless Steel, 23.5 mm. **Obv:** Larger trident in center of traditional design **Rev:** Dagger flanked by garlands from above

Date	Mintage	F	VF	XF	Unc	BU
VS2047 (1990)	—	—	0.10	0.25	0.50	—
VS2048 (1991)	—	—	0.10	0.25	0.50	—
VS2049 (1992)	—	—	0.10	0.25	0.50	—

KM# 1072 50 PAISA
1.4100 g., Aluminum, 22.5 mm. **Obv:** Royal crown **Rev:** Crown **Edge:** Plain **Note:** Coins dated VS2051 exist in two minor varieties being struck at Kathmandu (round edge) and Singapore (sharp edge).

Date	Mintage	F	VF	XF	Unc	BU
VS2051 (1994)	—	—	0.10	0.20	0.40	—
VS2052 (1995)	—	—	0.10	0.20	0.40	—
VS2053 (1996)	—	—	0.10	0.20	0.40	—
VS2054 (1997)	—	—	0.10	0.20	0.40	—
VS2055 (1998)	—	—	0.10	0.20	0.40	—
VS2056 (1999)	—	—	0.10	0.20	0.40	—
VS2057 (2000)	—	—	0.10	0.20	0.40	—

KM# 828.1 RUPEE
10.2000 g., Copper-Nickel **Obv:** Trident within small center circle **Rev:** Dagger flanked by garlands from above

Date	Mintage	F	VF	XF	Unc	BU
VS2028 (1971)	5,030	—	0.50	1.00	2.00	—
VS2029 (1972)	22,000	—	0.50	1.00	1.50	—
VS2029 (1972) Proof	3,943	Value: 2.50				
VS2030 (1973)	5,667	—	0.50	1.00	2.00	—
VS2030 (1973) Proof	8,891	Value: 2.00				
VS2031 (1974) Proof	11,000	Value: 1.50				

KM# 828a RUPEE
7.5000 g., Copper-Nickel, 27.5 mm. **Note:** Reduced weight. Coins dated VS2036 were struck at the Canberra Mint and have a very shiny surface. High quality examples of VS2034 were struck at Canberra Mint while dull surfaced examples were probably struck at Kathmandu Mint.

Date	Mintage	F	VF	XF	Unc	BU
VS2033 (1976)	58,000	—	0.50	1.00	1.50	—
VS2034 (1977)	30,000,000	—	0.25	0.50	1.00	—
VS2035 (1978)	—	—	0.25	0.50	1.00	—
VS2036 (1979)	30,000,000	—	0.25	0.50	1.00	—

KM# 828.2 RUPEE
Copper-Nickel **Note:** Reduced size: 23mm. Like 821a.

Date	Mintage	F	VF	XF	Unc	BU
VS2039 (1982)	—	—	1.50	3.00	—	—

KM# 829.1 RUPEE
Copper-Nickel **Subject:** Birendra Coronation **Obv:** Crown at center of ornamental frame **Rev:** Dagger flanked by garlands from above **Note:** 2 millimeters thick.

Date	Mintage	F	VF	XF	Unc	BU
VS2031 (1973)	—	—	0.75	1.25	1.75	—

KM# 829.2 RUPEE
Copper-Nickel **Subject:** Birendra Coronation **Obv:** Crown at center of ornamental frame **Rev:** Dagger flanked by garlands from above **Edge:** Reeded **Note:** 2.5 millimeters thick.

Date	Mintage	F	VF	XF	Unc	BU
VS2031 (1973) Proof	1,000	Value: 6.00				

KM# 831 RUPEE
Copper-Nickel **Series:** F.A.O. International Women's Year **Obv:** Busts left **Rev:** Value above logo, grain ears flank

Date	Mintage	F	VF	XF	Unc	BU
VS2032 (1975)	1,500,000	—	0.25	0.50	1.25	—

KM# 1019 RUPEE
Copper-Nickel **Subject:** Family Planning **Obv:** Logo at center within design **Rev:** Value

Date	Mintage	F	VF	XF	Unc	BU
VS2041 (1984)	21,000	—	—	—	0.75	—

KM# 1061 RUPEE
6.7500 g., Stainless Steel **Obv:** Small trident in center **Rev:** Dagger flanked by garlands from above

Date	Mintage	F	VF	XF	Unc	BU
VS2045 (1988) Prooflike	—	—	0.25	0.50	1.00	—
VS2048 (1991) Prooflike	—	—	0.25	0.50	1.00	—
Note: Varieties exist						
VS2049 (1992) Prooflike	—	—	0.25	0.50	1.25	—

KM# 1073 RUPEE
3.5000 g., Brass Plated Steel, 22 mm. **Obv:** Small trident at center **Rev:** Large legends **Edge:** Plain **Note:** Sharp and round edge varieties.

Date	Mintage	F	VF	XF	Unc	BU
VS2051 (1994)	—	—	0.25	0.50	1.00	—
VS2052 (1995)	—	—	0.25	0.50	1.00	—

KM# 1073a RUPEE
4.0800 g., Brass, 20 mm. **Obv:** Traditional design **Rev:** Small legends

Date	Mintage	F	VF	XF	Unc	BU
VS2052 (1995)	—	—	—	—	1.00	—
VS2053 (1996)	—	—	—	—	1.00	—
VS2054 (1997)	—	—	—	—	1.00	—
VS2055 (1998)	—	—	—	—	1.00	—
VS2056 (1999)	—	—	—	—	1.00	—
VS2057 (2000)	—	—	—	—	1.00	—

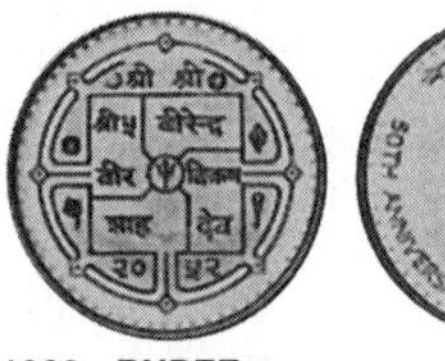

KM# 1092 RUPEE
Brass Plated Steel, 22 mm. **Series:** U.N. 50th Anniversary **Obv:** Traditional design **Rev:** UN logo and dates

Date	Mintage	F	VF	XF	Unc	BU
VS2052 (1995)	—	—	—	—	1.75	—

KM# 1152 RUPEE
28.1600 g., 0.9990 Copper-Nickel 0.9044 oz., 38.5 mm. **Subject:** UN 50th Anniversary **Obv:** Traditional design **Rev:** UN 50 logo **Edge:** Reeded

Date	Mintage	F	VF	XF	Unc	BU
VS2052 (1995)	—	—	—	—	—	8.00

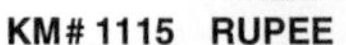

KM# 1115 RUPEE
Brass, 20 mm. **Subject:** Visit Nepal '98 **Obv:** Traditional design **Rev:** Moon and sun flanking mountaintop

Date	Mintage	F	VF	XF	Unc	BU
VS2054 (1997)	—	—	—	—	1.00	—

KM# 832 2 RUPEES
Copper-Nickel **Series:** World Food Day **Obv:** Trident within small circle at center **Rev:** Corn ear at left, logo at right

Date	Mintage	F	VF	XF	Unc	BU
VS2038 (1981)	1,000,000	—	0.50	0.75	1.50	—

KM# 1025 2 RUPEES
Copper-Nickel **Series:** F.A.O. **Obv:** Traditional design **Note:** Size of obverse square varies. With or without dot in reverse sun.

Date	Mintage	F	VF	XF	Unc	BU
VS2039 (1982)	366,000	—	0.50	0.75	1.50	—

KM# 1020 2 RUPEES
Copper-Nickel **Subject:** Family Planning **Obv:** Emblem within decorative outlines **Rev:** Value

Date	Mintage	F	VF	XF	Unc	BU
VS2041 (1984)	11,000	—	0.50	0.75	1.50	—

KM# 1074.1 2 RUPEES
4.9600 g., Brass Plated Steel, 24.4 mm. **Obv:** Small trident at center **Rev:** Building above value **Edge:** Plain **Note:** Sharp and round edge varieties exist.

Date	Mintage	F	VF	XF	Unc	BU
VS2051 (1994)	—	—	0.35	0.60	1.25	—
VS2052 (1995)	—	—	0.35	0.60	1.25	—

KM# 1074.2 2 RUPEES
Brass, 25 mm.

Date	Mintage	F	VF	XF	Unc	BU
VS2053 (1996)	—	—	0.35	0.60	1.25	—
VS2055 (1998)	—	—	0.35	0.60	1.25	—
VS2056 (1999)	—	—	0.35	0.60	1.25	—
VS2057 (2000)	—	—	0.35	0.60	1.25	—

KM# 1116 2 RUPEES
Brass, 25 mm. **Subject:** Visit Nepal '98 **Obv:** Traditional design **Rev:** Moon and sun flanking mountaintop

Date	Mintage	F	VF	XF	Unc	BU
VS2053 (1996)	—	—	—	—	1.25	—
VS2054 (1997)	—	—	—	—	1.25	—

KM# 833 5 RUPEE
Copper-Nickel **Subject:** Rural Women's Advancement **Obv:** Trident within small circle at center

Date	Mintage	F	VF	XF	Unc	BU
VS2037 (1980)	50,000	—	0.75	1.50	3.00	—

KM# 834 5 RUPEE
Copper-Nickel, 28.7-30.0 mm. **Subject:** National Bank Silver Jubilee **Obv:** Trident within small circle at center **Rev:** Small figurine of native god at center **Note:** Size varies.

Date	Mintage	F	VF	XF	Unc	BU
VS2038 (1981)	64,000	—	0.75	1.50	3.00	—

KM# 1009 5 RUPEE
Copper-Nickel **Obv:** Traditional design **Rev:** Dagger flanked by garlands from above **Note:** Circulation coinage

Date	Mintage	F	VF	XF	Unc	BU
VS2039 (1982)	Inc. above	—	0.50	1.00	2.00	—
VS2040 (1983)	478,000	—	0.30	0.50	1.00	—

KM# 1017 5 RUPEE
Copper-Nickel **Subject:** Family Planning **Obv:** Value **Rev:** Logo above inscription

Date	Mintage	F	VF	XF	Unc	BU
VS2041 (1984)	458,000	—	0.50	1.00	2.00	—

KM# 1023 5 RUPEE
Copper-Nickel **Subject:** Year of Youth **Obv:** Value **Rev:** Emblem below hills

Date	Mintage	F	VF	XF	Unc	BU
VS2042 (1985)	1,124,000	—	—	—	2.50	—

KM# 1047 5 RUPEE
Copper-Nickel **Subject:** Social Services **Obv:** Value **Rev:** Ox left within small center circle

Date	Mintage	F	VF	XF	Unc	BU
VS2042 (1985)	Inc. above	—	—	—	3.50	—

KM# 1028 5 RUPEE
Copper-Nickel **Series:** World Food Day **Obv:** Traditional design **Rev:** Fish left below logo

Date	Mintage	F	VF	XF	Unc	BU
VS2043 (1986)	99,000	—	—	—	3.50	—

KM# 1042 5 RUPEE
Copper-Nickel **Subject:** 15th World Buddhist Conference **Obv:** Value **Rev:** Figure at center of globe within ornamented circle **Note:** Two different obverse dies exist.

Date	Mintage	F	VF	XF	Unc	BU
VS2043//1986	135,000	—	—	—	3.50	—

KM# 1030 5 RUPEE
Copper-Nickel **Subject:** 10th Year of National Social Security Administration **Obv:** Traditional design **Rev:** Emblem at center

Date	Mintage	F	VF	XF	Unc	BU
VS2044 (1987)	104,000	—	—	—	3.50	—
VS2045 (1988)	—	—	—	—	3.50	—

KM# 1053 5 RUPEE
Copper-Nickel **Series:** World Food Day **Obv:** Traditional design **Rev:** Emblem above symbols

Date	Mintage	F	VF	XF	Unc	BU
VS2047 (1990)	—	—	—	—	4.00	—

KM# 1063 5 RUPEE
Copper-Nickel **Subject:** New Constitution **Obv:** Traditional design **Rev:** Flags above open book

Date	Mintage	F	VF	XF	Unc	BU
VS2047 (1990)	—	—	—	—	3.25	—

KM# 1062 5 RUPEE
Copper-Nickel **Subject:** Parliament Session **Obv:** Traditional design **Rev:** Outlined drawings symbolizing figures of parliament

Date	Mintage	F	VF	XF	Unc	BU
VS2048 (1991)	—	—	—	—	3.00	—

KM# 1075.1 5 RUPEE
6.5200 g., Brass Plated Steel, 27 mm. **Obv:** Traditional design **Rev:** Temple **Edge:** Plain

Date	Mintage	F	VF	XF	Unc	BU
VS2051 (1994)	—	—	—	—	1.50	—

KM# 1075.2 5 RUPEE
Brass, 25 mm. **Edge:** Reeded

Date	Mintage	F	VF	XF	Unc	BU
VS2053 (1996)	—	—	—	—	1.50	—

KM# 1117 5 RUPEE
Copper, 25 mm. **Subject:** Visit Nepal '98 **Obv:** Traditional design **Rev:** Sun and moon flanking mountaintop **Edge:** Reeded

Date	Mintage	F	VF	XF	Unc	BU
VS2054 (1997)	—	—	—	—	1.50	—

KM# 1076 10 RUPEE
8.0000 g., Brass Plated Steel, 29 mm. **Obv:** Traditional design **Rev:** Closed book

Date	Mintage	F	VF	XF	Unc	BU
VS2051 (1994)	—	—	—	—	2.50	—

KM# 1083 10 RUPEE
Copper-Nickel **Subject:** 75th Anniversary - International Labor Organization **Obv:** Traditional design **Rev:** Logo above legend

Date	Mintage	F	VF	XF	Unc	BU
VS2051 (1994)	—	—	—	—	4.50	—

KM# 1089 10 RUPEE
Copper-Nickel **Subject:** 50th Anniversary - F.A.O. Logo **Obv:** Traditional design **Rev:** Logo with grain ears flanking

Date	Mintage	F	VF	XF	Unc	BU
VS2052 (1995)	—	—	—	—	4.00	—

KM# 1118 10 RUPEE
Copper-Nickel, 25 mm. **Subject:** Visit Nepal '98 **Obv:** Traditional design **Rev:** Moon and sun flanking mountaintop **Edge:** Reeded

Date	Mintage	F	VF	XF	Unc	BU
VS2054 (1997)	—	—	—	—	3.00	—

NETHERLANDS

The Kingdom of the Netherlands, a country of western Europe fronting on the North Sea and bordered by Belgium and Germany, has an area of 15,770 sq. mi. (41,500 sq. km.) and a population of 16.1 million. Capital: Amsterdam, but the seat of government is at The Hague. The economy is based on dairy farming and a variety of industrial activities. Chemicals, yarns and fabrics, and meat products are exported.

After being a part of Charlemagne's empire in the 8th and 9th centuries, the Netherlands came under control of Burgundy and the Austrian Hapsburgs, and finally was subjected to Spanish dominion in the 16th century. Led by William of Orange, the Dutch revolted against Spain in 1568. The seven northern provinces formed the Union of Utrecht and declared their independence in 1581, becoming the Republic of the United Netherlands. In the following century, the *Golden Age* of Dutch history, the Netherlands became a great sea and colonial power, a patron of the arts and a refuge for the persecuted. The United Dutch Republic ended in 1795 when the French formed the Batavian Republic. Napoleon made his brother Louis, the King of Holland in 1806, however he abdicated in 1810 when Napoleon annexed Holland. The French were expelled in 1813, and all the provinces of Holland and Belgium were merged into the Kingdom of the United Netherlands under William I, in 1814. The Belgians withdrew in 1830 to form their own kingdom, the last substantial change in the configuration of European Netherlands. German forces invaded in 1940 as the royal family fled to England where a government-in-exile was formed.

WORLD WAR II COINAGE

U.S. mints in the name of the government in exile and its remaining Curacao and Suriname Colonies during the years 1941-45 minted coinage of the Netherlands Homeland Types - KM #152, 153, 163, 164, 161.1 and 161.2 -. The Curacao and Suriname strikes, distinguished by the presence of a palm tree in combination with a mint mark (P-Philadelphia; D-Denver; S-San Francisco) flanking the date, are incorporated under those titles in this volume. Pieces of this period struck in the name of the homeland bear an acorn and mint mark and are incorporated in the following tabulation.

NOTE: Excepting the World War II issues struck at U.S. mints, all of the modern coins were struck at the Utrecht Mint and bear the caduceus mint mark of that facility. They also bear the mintmasters' marks.

RULERS

KINGDOM OF THE NETHERLANDS
Wilhelmina I, 1890-1948
Juliana, 1948-1980
Beatrix, 1980—

MINT MARKS

D - Denver, 1943-1945
P - Philadelphia, 1941-1945
S - San Francisco, 1944-1945

MINT PRIVY MARKS

Utrecht

Date	Privy Mark
1806-present	Caduceus

MINTMASTERS' PRIVY MARKS

U. S. Mints

Date	Privy Mark
1941-45	Palm tree

Utrecht Mint

Date	Privy Mark
1888-1909	Halberd
1909	Halberd and star
1909-1933	Seahorse
1933-42	Grapes
1943-1945	No privy mark
1945-69	Fish
1969-79	Cock
1980	Cock and star (temporal)
1980-88	Anvil with hammer
1989-99	Bow and arrow
2000-	Bow, arrow and star

NOTE: A star adjoining the privy mark indicates that the piece was struck at the beginning of the term of office of a successor. (The star was used only if the successor had not chosen his own mark yet.)

NOTE: Since October, 1999, the Dutch Mint has taken the title of Royal Dutch Mint.

MONETARY SYSTEM

Until January 29, 2002
100 Cents = 1 Gulden

KINGDOM

DECIMAL COINAGE

KM# 109 1/2 CENT
1.2500 g., Bronze, 14 mm. **Ruler:** Wilhelmina I **Obv:** Crowned rampant lion left within beaded circle, date below **Obv. Legend:** KONINGRIJK DER NEDERLANDEN **Rev:** Value within wreath **Edge:** Reeded **Designer:** J.P.M. Menger

Date	Mintage	F	VF	XF	Unc	BU
1901	6,000,000	1.50	3.00	6.00	25.00	45.00

KM# 133 1/2 CENT
1.2500 g., Bronze, 14 mm. **Ruler:** Wilhelmina I **Obv:** Crowned arms with 17 small shields within beaded circle **Obv. Legend:** KONINGRIJK DER NEDERLANDEN **Rev:** Value within wreath **Edge:** Reeded **Designer:** J.P.M. Menger

Date	Mintage	F	VF	XF	Unc	BU
1903	10,000,000	1.00	2.00	3.00	10.00	20.00
1906	10,000,000	1.00	2.00	3.00	10.00	20.00

KM# 138 1/2 CENT
1.2500 g., Bronze, 14 mm. **Ruler:** Wilhelmina I **Obv:** Crowned arms with 15 large shields within beaded circle, date and legend **Rev:** Value within wreath **Edge:** Reeded **Designer:** J.P.M. Menger

Date	Mintage	F	VF	XF	Unc	BU
1909	5,000,000	1.00	2.00	3.00	10.00	17.50
1911	5,000,000	1.00	2.00	3.00	10.00	17.50
1912	5,000,000	1.00	2.00	3.00	10.00	17.50
1914	5,000,000	1.00	2.00	3.00	10.00	17.50

Date	Mintage	F	VF	XF	Unc	BU
1915	2,500,000	5.00	10.00	15.00	25.00	50.00
1916	4,000,000	2.00	4.00	7.00	15.00	25.00
1917	5,000,000	1.00	2.00	4.00	10.00	15.00
1921	1,500,000	5.00	10.00	15.00	25.00	45.00
1922/1	—	200	450	800	1,200	1,750
1922	2,500,000	5.00	10.00	15.00	25.00	45.00
1928	4,000,000	1.00	2.00	3.00	8.00	15.00
1930	6,000,000	1.00	1.50	2.50	6.00	10.00
1934	5,000,000	0.75	1.75	2.50	5.00	8.00
1936	5,000,000	0.75	1.75	2.50	5.00	8.00
1937	1,600,000	1.00	2.50	4.00	8.00	12.50
1938	8,400,000	0.75	1.50	2.00	3.00	5.00
1940	6,000,000	0.75	1.50	2.00	3.00	5.00

KM# 130 CENT

2.5000 g., Bronze, 19 mm. **Ruler:** Wilhelmina I **Obv:** Crowned arms with 15 large shields within beaded circle **Obv. Legend:** KONINKRIJK DER NEDERLANDEN **Rev:** Value within wreath **Edge:** Reeded **Designer:** J.P.M. Menger

Date	Mintage	F	VF	XF	Unc	BU
1901	10,000,000	1.00	2.50	5.00	20.00	50.00

KM# 131 CENT

2.5000 g., Bronze, 19 mm. **Ruler:** Wilhelmina I **Obv:** Crowned arms with 10 large shields within beaded circle **Obv. Legend:** KONINGRIJK DER NEDERLANDEN **Rev:** Value within wreath **Edge:** Reeded **Designer:** J.P.M. Menger

Date	Mintage	F	VF	XF	Unc	BU
1901	10,000,000	1.00	2.50	5.00	20.00	50.00

KM# 132.1 CENT

2.5000 g., Bronze, 19 mm. **Ruler:** Wilhelmina I **Obv:** Crowned arms with 15 medium shields within beaded circle **Obv. Legend:** KONINGRIJK DER NEDERLANDEN **Rev:** Value within wreath **Edge:** Reeded **Designer:** J.P.M. Menger

Date	Mintage	F	VF	XF	Unc	BU
1902	10,000,000	1.00	2.00	3.00	15.00	30.00
1904	15,000,000	1.00	2.00	3.00	15.00	30.00
1905	10,000,000	1.00	2.00	3.00	15.00	30.00
1906	9,000,000	1.00	2.00	3.00	15.00	30.00
1907	6,000,000	6.00	12.00	30.00	60.00	120

KM# 152 CENT

2.5000 g., Bronze, 19 mm. **Ruler:** Wilhelmina I **Obv:** Crowned arms with 17 small shields within beaded circle **Rev:** Value within wreath

Date	Mintage	F	VF	XF	Unc	BU
1913	5,000,000	2.50	6.00	12.00	28.00	50.00
1914	9,000,000	1.00	2.00	3.00	15.00	25.00
1915	10,800,000	1.00	2.00	3.00	12.00	18.00
1916	21,700,000	0.75	1.00	2.00	10.00	15.00
1916 Proof	—	Value: 110				
1917	20,000,000	0.75	1.00	2.00	10.00	15.00
1918	10,000,000	1.00	2.00	4.00	12.00	20.00
1919	6,000,000	2.75	5.00	10.00	20.00	30.00
1920	11,400,000	0.75	1.50	2.00	10.00	15.00
1921	12,600,000	0.75	1.50	2.00	10.00	15.00
1922	20,000,000	0.75	1.50	2.00	10.00	15.00
1924	1,400,000	15.00	30.00	55.00	110	160
1925	18,600,000	0.75	1.50	2.00	10.00	15.00
1926	10,000,000	0.75	1.50	2.00	10.00	15.00
1927	10,000,000	0.75	1.50	2.00	10.00	15.00
1928	10,000,000	0.75	1.50	2.00	10.00	15.00
1929	20,000,000	0.75	1.50	2.00	8.00	12.00
1930	10,000,000	0.75	1.50	2.00	8.00	12.00
1931	3,400,000	3.50	7.50	12.50	35.00	50.00
1937	10,000,000	0.50	1.00	1.50	5.00	8.00
1938	16,600,000	0.50	1.00	1.50	5.00	8.00
1939	22,000,000	0.50	1.00	1.50	5.00	7.00
1940	24,600,000	0.50	1.00	1.50	5.00	7.00

Date	Mintage	F	VF	XF	Unc	BU
1941	66,600,000	0.25	0.60	1.00	2.50	4.00

Note: For similar coins dated 1942P see Curacao; 1943P, 1957-1960 see Suriname

KM# 170 CENT

2.0000 g., Zinc, 17 mm. **Ruler:** Wilhelmina I **Obv:** Circled cross with banner below **Rev:** Value, waves, date and sprig **Edge:** Reeded **Designer:** N. de Haas

Date	Mintage	F	VF	XF	Unc	BU
1941	31,800,000	1.00	2.00	4.00	15.00	25.00
1942	241,000,000	0.25	0.50	1.00	3.00	8.00
1943	71,000,000	0.50	1.00	2.00	5.00	15.00
1944	29,600,000	1.00	2.00	4.00	15.00	25.00

KM# 175 CENT

2.0000 g., Bronze, 14 mm. **Ruler:** Wilhelmina I **Obv:** Head left **Rev:** Value divides date **Edge:** Plain **Designer:** L.O. Wenckebach

Date	Mintage	F	VF	XF	Unc	BU
1948	175,000,000	0.10	0.25	0.50	3.50	9.00
1948 Proof	—	Value: 80.00				

KM# 180 CENT

2.0000 g., Bronze, 14 mm. **Ruler:** Juliana **Obv:** Head right **Rev:** Value divides date **Designer:** L.O. Wenckeback

Date	Mintage	F	VF	XF	Unc	BU
1950	46,400,000	0.10	0.20	2.00	6.00	10.00
1950 Proof	—	Value: 50.00				
1951	45,800,000	0.10	0.20	2.00	6.00	10.00
1951 Proof	—	Value: 45.00				
1952	68,000,000	0.10	0.20	2.00	6.00	10.00
1952 Proof	—	Value: 45.00				
1953	54,000,000	0.10	0.20	2.00	6.00	10.00
1953 Proof	—	Value: 45.00				
1954	54,000,000	0.10	0.20	2.00	6.00	10.00
1954 Proof	—	Value: 45.00				
1955	52,000,000	0.10	0.20	2.00	6.00	10.00
1955 Proof	—	Value: 45.00				
1956	34,800,000	0.10	0.20	2.00	6.00	10.00
1956 Proof	—	Value: 45.00				
1957	48,000,000	0.10	0.20	0.25	6.00	10.00
1957 Proof	—	Value: 45.00				
1958	34,000,000	0.10	0.20	0.25	6.00	10.00
1958 Proof	—	Value: 40.00				
1959	36,000,000	0.10	0.20	1.00	6.00	10.00
1959 Proof	—	Value: 35.00				
1960	40,000,000	0.10	0.20	1.00	2.00	6.00
1960 Proof	—	Value: 35.00				
1961	52,000,000	0.10	0.20	1.00	1.50	3.00
1961 Proof	—	Value: 35.00				
1962	57,000,000	0.10	0.20	1.00	1.50	3.00
1962 Proof	—	Value: 35.00				
1963	70,000,000	0.10	0.20	1.00	1.50	3.00
1963 Proof	—	Value: 35.00				
1964	73,000,000	0.10	0.20	1.00	1.50	3.00
1964 Proof	—	Value: 35.00				
1965	91,000,000	0.10	0.20	1.00	1.50	3.00
1965 Proof	—	Value: 35.00				
1966 large date	104,000,000	0.10	0.20	1.00	1.50	3.00
1966 Proof, large date	—	Value: 35.00				
1966 small date	Inc. above	0.10	0.20	1.00	1.50	3.00
1966 Proof, small date	—	Value: 20.00				
1967	140,000,000	0.10	0.20	1.00	1.50	3.00
1967 Proof	—	Value: 25.00				
1968	28,000,000	0.10	0.20	1.00	1.50	3.00
1968 Proof	—	Value: 20.00				
1969 fish privy mark	50,000,000	0.10	0.20	0.30	0.75	1.25
1969 Proof, fish privy mark	—	Value: 20.00				
1969 cock privy mark	50,000,000	0.10	0.20	0.30	0.75	1.25
1969 Proof, cock privy mark	—	Value: 20.00				
1970	100,000,000	0.10	0.20	0.30	0.75	1.25
1970 Proof	—	Value: 20.00				
1971	70,000,000	—	—	—	0.75	1.25
1972	40,000,000	—	—	—	0.75	1.25
1973	34,000,000	—	—	—	0.75	1.25
1974	46,000,000	—	—	—	0.75	1.25
1975	25,000,000	—	—	—	0.75	1.25
1976	15,000,000	—	—	—	0.75	1.25
1977	15,000,000	—	—	—	0.75	1.25
1978	15,000,000	—	—	—	0.75	1.25
1979	15,000,000	—	—	—	0.75	1.25
1980 cock and star privy mark	15,300,000	—	—	0.10	0.20	0.50

KM# 134 2-1/2 CENT

4.0000 g., Bronze, 23.5 mm. **Ruler:** Wilhelmina I **Obv:** Crowned arms with 15 large shields within beaded circle **Obv. Legend:** KONINGRIJK DER NEDERLANDEN **Rev:** Value within wreath **Edge:** Reeded **Designer:** J.P.M. Menger

Date	Mintage	F	VF	XF	Unc	BU
1903	4,000,000	2.00	3.50	6.50	20.00	40.00
1904	4,000,000	2.00	3.50	6.50	20.00	40.00
1905	4,000,000	2.00	3.50	6.50	20.00	40.00
1906	8,000,000	2.00	3.50	6.50	20.00	35.00

KM# 150 2-1/2 CENT

4.0000 g., Bronze, 23 mm. **Ruler:** Wilhelmina I **Obv:** Crowned arms with 15 large shields within beaded circle **Obv. Legend:** KONINGRIJK. **Rev:** Value within wreath **Designer:** J.P.M. Menger

Date	Mintage	F	VF	XF	Unc	BU
1912	2,000,000	4.00	8.00	16.50	50.00	100
1913	4,000,000	2.50	4.50	8.00	15.00	35.00
1914	2,000,000	4.00	8.00	16.50	50.00	100
1915	3,000,000	3.00	6.00	12.00	25.00	55.00
1916	8,000,000	2.00	3.50	6.00	15.00	25.00
1918	4,000,000	2.50	4.00	8.00	22.50	45.00
1919	2,000,000	3.00	6.00	12.00	25.00	50.00
1929	8,000,000	2.00	3.50	6.00	10.00	15.00
1941	19,800,000	1.25	2.00	3.00	6.00	9.00

KM# 171 2-1/2 CENT

2.0000 g., Zinc, 20 mm. **Ruler:** Wilhelmina I **Obv:** Two swans on roof **Rev:** Value with four waves **Designer:** N. de Haas

Date	Mintage	F	VF	XF	Unc	BU
1941	27,600,000	1.00	3.00	5.00	15.00	3,500
1942	Est. 200,000	750	3,500	5,500	8,500	12,000

Note: Almost entire issue melted, about 30 pieces known

KM# 137 5 CENTS

4.5000 g., Copper-Nickel, 12 mm. **Ruler:** Wilhelmina I **Obv:** Crown flanked by sprigs **Rev:** Value within wreath **Designer:** J.C. Wienecke

Date	Mintage	F	VF	XF	Unc	BU
1907	6,000,000	3.00	6.00	10.00	20.00	35.00
1908	5,430,000	4.00	8.00	12.50	22.50	40.00
1909	2,570,000	20.00	30.00	40.00	80.00	130

KM# 153 5 CENTS

4.5000 g., Copper-Nickel, 21.3 mm. **Ruler:** Wilhelmina I **Obv:** Orange branch within circle **Rev:** Value within shells and beaded circle **Shape:** 4-sided **Designer:** J.C. Wienecke

Date	Mintage	F	VF	XF	Unc	BU
1913	6,000,000	1.50	3.00	5.00	15.00	30.00
1914	7,400,000	1.50	3.00	5.00	15.00	30.00

Date	Mintage	F	VF	XF	Unc	BU
1923	10,000,000	1.50	3.00	5.00	15.00	30.00
1929	8,000,000	1.50	3.00	5.00	15.00	30.00
1932	2,000,000	5.50	12.00	20.00	35.00	65.00
1933	1,400,000	20.00	30.00	50.00	70.00	140
1934	2,600,000	4.00	6.00	10.00	20.00	40.00
1936	2,600,000	4.00	6.00	10.00	20.00	40.00
1938	4,200,000	2.00	3.50	4.50	10.00	20.00
1939	4,600,000	2.00	3.50	4.50	10.00	20.00
1940	7,200,000	2.00	3.00	4.00	9.00	15.00

Note: For a similar coin dated 1943, see Curacao

KM# 172 5 CENTS

2.6000 g., Zinc, 18 mm. **Ruler:** Wilhelmina I **Obv:** Two crossed horse heads and sun within square **Rev:** Value within circle flanked by nine waves and sprig **Shape:** 4-sided **Designer:** N. de Haas

Date	Mintage	F	VF	XF	Unc	BU
1941	32,200,000	1.00	2.50	6.00	18.00	35.00
1942	11,800,000	2.00	3.50	9.00	22.00	40.00
1943	7,000,000	5.00	8.00	16.50	42.50	75.00

KM# 176 5 CENTS

2.5000 g., Bronze, 21 mm. **Ruler:** Wilhelmina I **Obv:** Head left **Rev:** Value divides date and orange branch **Designer:** L.O. Wencheback

Date	Mintage	F	VF	XF	Unc	BU
1948	23,600,000	—	0.50	0.75	7.00	16.50
1948 Proof	—	Value: 100				

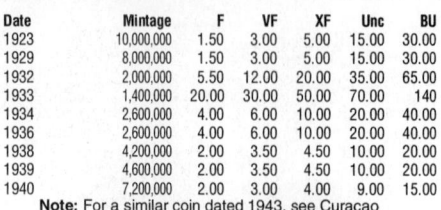

KM# 181 5 CENTS

3.5000 g., Bronze, 21 mm. **Ruler:** Juliana **Obv:** Head right **Rev:** Value divides date and orange branch **Designer:** L.O. Wenckeback

Date	Mintage	F	VF	XF	Unc	BU
1950	20,000,000	—	0.10	0.25	7.50	15.00
1950 Proof	—	Value: 70.00				
1951	16,200,000	—	0.10	0.25	7.50	15.00
1951 Proof	—	Value: 70.00				
1952	14,400,000	—	0.10	0.25	7.50	15.00
1952 Proof	—	Value: 70.00				
1953	12,000,000	—	0.10	0.25	7.50	15.00
1953 Proof	—	Value: 70.00				
1954	14,000,000	—	0.10	0.25	7.50	15.00
1954 Proof	—	Value: 70.00				
1955	11,400,000	—	0.10	0.25	7.50	15.00
1955 Proof	—	Value: 70.00				
1956	7,400,000	—	0.15	0.35	8.50	20.00
1956 Proof	—	Value: 70.00				
1957	16,000,000	—	0.10	0.25	6.50	15.00
1957 Proof	—	Value: 70.00				
1958	9,000,000	—	0.10	0.25	8.50	15.00
1958 Proof	—	Value: 70.00				
1960	11,000,000	—	0.10	0.25	3.50	10.00
1960 Proof	—	Value: 40.00				
1961	12,000,000	—	0.10	0.25	3.50	10.00
1961 Proof	—	Value: 40.00				
1962	15,000,000	—	0.10	0.25	2.00	6.50
1962 Proof	—	Value: 40.00				
1963	18,000,000	—	0.10	0.25	2.00	6.50
1963 Proof	—	Value: 40.00				
1964	21,000,000	—	0.10	0.25	2.00	6.50
1964 Proof	—	Value: 40.00				
1965	28,000,000	—	0.10	0.25	1.50	6.00
1965 Proof	—	Value: 40.00				
1966	22,000,000	—	0.10	0.25	2.00	6.50
1966 Proof	—	Value: 40.00				
1967 leaves far from rim	32,000,000	—	—	0.20	1.50	6.50
1967 Proof, leaves far from rim	—	Value: 50.00				
1967 leaves touching rim	Inc. above	—	0.15	0.50	1.50	6.50
1967 Proof, leaves touching rim	—	Value: 40.00				
1969 fish privy mark	5,000,000	—	0.15	0.50	3.50	15.00
1969 Proof, fish privy mark	—	Value: 40.00				
1969 cock privy mark	11,000,000	—	—	0.10	1.00	4.00
1969 Proof, cock privy mark	—	Value: 40.00				
1970	22,000,000	—	—	0.10	0.75	3.00
1970 Proof	—	Value: 40.00				
1970 date close to rim	Inc. above	—	—	0.10	0.75	3.00
1970 Proof, date close to rim	—	Value: 40.00				
1971	25,000,000	—	—	0.10	0.50	2.00
1972	25,000,000	—	—	0.10	0.50	2.00
1973	22,000,000	—	—	0.10	0.50	2.00
1974	20,000,000	—	—	—	0.50	2.00
1975	46,000,000	—	—	—	0.25	1.50
1976	50,000,000	—	—	—	0.25	1.50
1977	50,000,000	—	—	—	0.25	1.50
1978	60,000,000	—	—	—	0.25	1.50
1979	80,000,000	—	—	—	0.25	1.50
1980 cock and star privy mark	252,500,000	—	—	—	0.10	0.35

KM# 202 5 CENTS

3.5000 g., Bronze, 21 mm. **Ruler:** Beatrix **Obv:** Head left with vertical inscription **Rev:** Value within vertical lines **Edge:** Plain **Designer:** Bruno Ninaber von Eyben

Date	Mintage	F	VF	XF	Unc	BU
1982	47,100,000	—	—	—	0.10	0.40
1982 Proof	10,000	Value: 10.00				
1983	60,200,000	—	—	—	0.10	0.40
1983 Proof	15,000	Value: 7.50				
1984	70,700,000	—	—	—	0.10	0.40
1984 Proof	20,000	Value: 4.00				
1985	36,100,000	—	—	—	0.10	0.40
1985 Proof	17,000	Value: 4.00				
1986	7,700,000	—	—	—	0.50	1.50
1986 Proof	20,000	Value: 4.00				
1987	33,299,999	—	—	—	—	0.40
1987 Proof	18,000	Value: 4.00				
1988	22,600,000	—	—	—	—	0.40
1988 Proof	20,000	Value: 4.00				
1989	27,100,000	—	—	—	—	0.40
1989 Proof	15,000	Value: 4.00				
1990	39,300,000	—	—	—	—	0.40
1990 Proof	15,000	Value: 4.00				
1991	73,100,000	—	—	—	—	0.40
1991 Proof	14,000	Value: 4.00				
1992	52,700,000	—	—	—	—	0.40
1992 Proof	13,000	Value: 4.00				
1993	40,000,000	—	—	—	—	0.40
1993 Proof	12,000	Value: 4.00				
1994	14,000,000	—	—	—	—	1.50
1994 Proof	13,000	Value: 4.00				
1995	6,000,000	—	—	—	0.75	3.00
1995 Proof	12,000	Value: 4.00				
1996	40,000,000	—	—	—	—	0.40
1996 Proof	14,000	Value: 4.00				
1997	36,000,000	—	—	—	—	0.40
1997 Proof	12,000	Value: 4.00				
1998	65,099,999	—	—	—	—	0.40
1998 Proof	12,000	Value: 4.00				
1999	16,480,000	—	—	—	—	0.40
1999 Proof	15,000	Value: 4.00				
2000	30,076,000	—	—	—	—	0.40
2000 Proof	15,000	Value: 4.00				
2001 Proof	17,000	Value: 4.00				
2001	16,060,000	—	—	—	—	0.40

KM# 119 10 CENTS

1.4000 g., 0.6400 Silver 0.0288 oz. ASW, 15 mm. **Ruler:** Wilhelmina I **Obv:** Small crowned head left divides legend **Obv. Legend:** WILHELMINA... **Rev:** Value and date within wreath **Edge:** Reeded **Designer:** P. Pander

Date	Mintage	F	VF	XF	Unc	BU
1901	2,000,000	10.00	25.00	70.00	150	250

KM# 135 10 CENTS

1.4000 g., 0.6400 Silver 0.0288 oz. ASW, 15 mm. **Ruler:** Wilhelmina I **Obv:** Head left **Rev:** Value in wreath **Designer:** P. Pander

Date	Mintage	F	VF	XF	Unc	BU
1903	6,000,000	4.00	12.00	30.00	50.00	75.00

KM# 136 10 CENTS

1.4000 g., 0.6400 Silver 0.0288 oz. ASW, 15 mm. **Ruler:** Wilhelmina I **Obv:** Small head left with continous legend **Rev:** Value in wreath **Designer:** P. Pander

Date	Mintage	F	VF	XF	Unc	BU
1904	3,000,000	6.00	16.50	30.00	70.00	130
1905	2,000,000	8.00	25.00	50.00	100	200
1906	4,000,000	4.00	14.50	25.00	55.00	110

KM# 145 10 CENTS

1.4000 g., 0.6400 Silver 0.0288 oz. ASW, 15 mm. **Ruler:** Wilhelmina I **Obv:** Small head left with continuous legend **Rev:** Value within wreath **Edge:** Reeded **Designer:** J.C. Wienecke

Date	Mintage	F	VF	XF	Unc	BU
1910	2,250,000	10.00	25.00	45.00	100	200
1911	4,000,000	4.00	9.00	22.00	45.00	85.00
1912	4,000,000	4.00	9.00	22.00	45.00	85.00
1913	5,000,000	3.00	7.00	15.00	40.00	75.00
1914	9,000,000	1.50	4.00	10.00	25.00	45.00
1915	5,000,000	1.75	5.00	12.00	30.00	60.00
1916	5,000,000	1.75	5.00	12.00	30.00	60.00
1917	10,000,000	1.50	3.50	8.00	16.00	30.00
1918	20,000,000	1.00	2.50	5.00	13.50	30.00
1919	10,000,000	1.50	3.50	8.00	16.00	30.00
1921	5,000,000	2.00	6.00	10.00	22.00	55.00
1925	5,000,000	2.00	6.00	10.00	22.00	55.00

KM# 163 10 CENTS

1.4000 g., 0.6400 Silver 0.0288 oz. ASW, 15 mm. **Ruler:** Wilhelmina I **Obv:** Small head left with continuous legend **Rev:** Value within wreath **Edge:** Reeded **Designer:** J.C. Wienecke

Date	Mintage	F	VF	XF	Unc	BU
1926	2,700,000	2.50	6.00	15.00	55.00	100
1927	2,300,000	2.50	6.00	15.00	60.00	110
1928	10,000,000	0.75	2.00	5.00	16.00	35.00
1930	5,000,000	1.00	3.50	7.50	22.00	40.00
1934	2,000,000	2.50	6.00	15.00	60.00	100
1935	8,000,000	0.75	1.50	3.50	10.00	20.00
1936	15,000,000	0.50	0.75	2.00	5.00	10.00
1937	18,600,000	0.50	0.75	2.00	3.50	5.00
1938	21,400,000	0.50	0.75	2.00	3.50	5.00
1939	20,000,000	0.50	0.75	2.00	3.50	5.00
1941	43,000,000	0.50	0.50	1.50	2.25	3.00
1943P Acorn privy mark	—	0.75	1.00	2.00	10.00	20.00
1944P	120,000,000	0.50	0.75	1.25	2.00	3.00
1944D	25,400,000	1,200	3,000	6,000	10,000	12,000
Note: Almost entire issue melted						
1944S	64,040,000	1.00	2.00	4.50	15.00	25.00
1945P	90,560,000	120	300	550	900	1,200

Note: For similar coins dated 1941P-1943P with palm tree privy mark, see Curacao and Suriname

KM# 173 10 CENTS

3.3000 g., Zinc, 22 mm. **Ruler:** Wilhelmina I **Obv:** Three tulips flanked by dots within circle **Rev:** Value flanked by sprigs **Edge:** Reeded **Designer:** N. de Haas

Date	Mintage	F	VF	XF	Unc	BU
1941	29,800,000	0.75	1.50	3.50	10.00	20.00
1942	95,600,000	0.25	0.50	2.00	5.00	10.00
1943	29,000,000	0.75	1.50	3.50	10.00	20.00

KM# 177 10 CENTS

1.5000 g., Nickel, 15 mm. **Ruler:** Wilhelmina I **Obv:** Head left **Rev:** Crowned value divides date **Edge:** Reeded **Designer:** L.O. Wencheback

Date	Mintage	F	VF	XF	Unc	BU
1948	69,200,000	—	0.25	0.50	3.00	8.50
1948 Proof	—	Value: 100				

KM# 182 10 CENTS

1.5000 g., Nickel, 15 mm. **Ruler:** Juliana **Obv:** Head right **Rev:** Crowned value divides date **Edge:** Reeded **Designer:** L.O. Wenchaback

Date	Mintage	F	VF	XF	Unc	BU
1950	56,600,000	—	0.10	0.35	0.75	3.50
1950 Proof	—	Value: 80.00				
1951	54,200,000	—	0.10	0.35	0.75	3.50
1951 Proof	—	Value: 60.00				
1954	8,200,000	—	0.20	0.50	1.00	7.50
1954 Proof	—	Value: 60.00				
1955	18,200,000	—	0.10	0.35	0.75	4.00
1955 Proof	—	Value: 60.00				
1956	12,000,000	—	0.10	0.35	0.75	4.00
1956 Proof	—	Value: 60.00				
1957	18,600,000	—	0.10	0.35	0.75	4.00
1957 Proof	—	Value: 60.00				
1958	34,000,000	—	0.10	0.35	0.75	3.00
1958 Proof	—	Value: 60.00				
1959	44,000,000	—	0.10	0.35	0.75	3.00
1959 Proof	—	Value: 50.00				
1960	12,000,000	—	0.10	0.35	0.75	6.00
1960 Proof	—	Value: 50.00				
1961	25,000,000	—	—	0.10	0.25	2.50
1961 Proof	—	Value: 50.00				
1962	30,000,000	—	—	0.10	0.25	1.50
1962 Proof	—	Value: 50.00				
1963	35,000,000	—	—	0.10	0.25	1.50
1963 Proof	—	Value: 60.00				
1964	41,000,000	—	—	0.10	0.25	1.50
1964 Proof	—	Value: 60.00				
1965	59,000,000	—	—	0.10	0.25	1.50
1965 Proof	—	Value: 60.00				
1966	44,000,000	—	—	—	0.10	1.00
1966 Proof	—	Value: 50.00				
1967	39,000,000	—	—	—	0.10	1.00
1967 Proof	—	Value: 50.00				
1968	42,000,000	—	—	—	0.10	1.00
1968 Proof	—	Value: 40.00				
1969 fish privy mark	29,100,000	—	—	—	0.10	1.50
1969 Proof, fish privy mark	—	Value: 40.00				
1969 cock privy mark	24,000,000	—	—	—	0.10	1.50
1969 Proof, cock privy mark	—	Value: 40.00				
1970	50,000,000	—	—	—	0.10	1.00
1970 Proof	—	Value: 40.00				
1971	55,000,000	—	—	—	0.10	1.00
1972	60,000,000	—	—	—	0.10	1.00
1973	90,000,000	—	—	—	0.10	1.00
1974	75,000,000	—	—	—	0.20	1.50
1975	110,000,000	—	—	—	0.10	0.50
1976	85,000,000	—	—	—	0.10	0.50
1977	100,000,000	—	—	—	0.10	0.50
1978	110,000,000	—	—	—	0.10	0.50
1979	120,000,000	—	—	—	0.10	0.50
1980 cock and star privy mark	195,300,000	—	—	—	0.10	0.50

KM# 203 10 CENTS

1.5000 g., Nickel, 15 mm. **Ruler:** Beatrix **Obv:** Head left with vertical inscription **Rev:** Value and vertical lines **Edge:** Reeded **Designer:** Bruno Ninaber von Eyben

Date	Mintage	F	VF	XF	Unc	BU
1982	10,300,000	—	—	—	0.10	0.50
1982 Proof	10,000	Value: 10.00				
1983	38,200,000	—	—	—	—	0.50
1983 Proof	15,000	Value: 8.00				
1984	42,200,000	—	—	—	0.10	0.50
1984 Proof	20,000	Value: 4.00				
1985	29,100,000	—	—	—	0.10	0.50
1985 Proof	17,000	Value: 4.00				
1986	23,100,000	—	—	—	0.10	0.50
1986 Proof	20,000	Value: 4.00				
1987	21,700,000	—	—	—	0.10	0.50
1987 Proof	18,000	Value: 4.00				
1988	2,200,000	—	—	—	0.25	2.00
1988 Proof	20,000	Value: 6.00				
1989	5,300,000	—	—	—	—	1.50
1989 Proof	15,000	Value: 5.00				
1990	13,300,000	—	—	—	—	0.50
1990 Proof	15,000	Value: 4.00				
1991	41,100,000	—	—	—	—	0.50
1991 Proof	14,000	Value: 4.00				
1992	41,300,000	—	—	—	—	0.50
1992 Proof	13,000	Value: 4.00				
1993	30,100,000	—	—	—	—	0.50
1993 Proof	12,000	Value: 4.00				
1994	25,685,000	—	—	—	—	0.50
1994 Proof	13,000	Value: 4.00				
1995	35,100,000	—	—	—	—	0.50
1995 Proof	12,000	Value: 4.00				
1996	34,900,000	—	—	—	—	0.50
1996 Proof	14,000	Value: 4.00				
1997	20,100,000	—	—	—	—	0.50
1997 Proof	12,000	Value: 4.00				
1998	24,540,000	—	—	—	—	0.50
1998 Proof	12,000	Value: 4.00				
1999	50,040,000	—	—	—	—	0.50
1999 Proof	15,000	Value: 4.00				
2000	75,476,000	—	—	—	—	0.50
2000 Proof	15,000	Value: 4.00				
2001	26,140,000	—	—	—	—	0.50
2001 Proof	17,000	Value: 4.00				

KM# 120.1 25 CENTS

3.5750 g., 0.6400 Silver 0.0736 oz. ASW, 19 mm. **Ruler:** Wilhelmina I **Obv:** Bust with wide truncation **Rev:** Value within wreath **Edge:** Reeded **Designer:** P. Pander

Date	Mintage	F	VF	XF	Unc	BU
1901	1,600,000	40.00	100	275	550	950

KM# 120.2 25 CENTS

3.5750 g., 0.6400 Silver 0.0736 oz. ASW, 19 mm. **Ruler:** Wilhelmina I **Obv:** Head left **Rev:** Value within wreath **Edge:** Reeded **Designer:** P. Pander

Date	Mintage	F	VF	XF	Unc	BU
1901	Inc. above	8.00	22.00	45.00	110	170
1901 Proof	3	Value: 1,500				
1902	1,200,000	8.00	25.00	50.00	120	180
1903	1,200,000	8.00	25.00	50.00	120	180
1904	1,600,000	7.00	20.00	40.00	100	150
1905	1,200,000	8.00	25.00	50.00	120	180
1906	2,000,000	6.00	18.00	35.00	85.00	140

KM# 146 25 CENTS

3.5750 g., 0.6400 Silver 0.0736 oz. ASW, 19 mm. **Ruler:** Wilhelmina I **Obv:** Bust left, legend **Rev:** Value within wreath **Edge:** Reeded **Designer:** J.C. Wienecke

Date	Mintage	F	VF	XF	Unc	BU
1910	880,000	18.00	35.00	75.00	175	350
1910 Proof	—	Value: 600				
1911	1,600,000	8.00	20.00	40.00	135	220
1912	1,600,000	8.00	20.00	40.00	135	220
1913	1,200,000	20.00	40.00	75.00	175	300
1914	5,600,000	3.50	8.00	20.00	50.00	85.00
1915	2,000,000	4.50	12.00	25.00	90.00	170
1916	2,000,000	4.50	12.00	25.00	90.00	170
1917	4,000,000	3.50	8.00	20.00	50.00	75.00
1918	6,000,000	2.00	6.00	12.00	32.00	50.00
1919	4,000,000	3.50	8.00	20.00	50.00	75.00
1925	2,000,000	4.50	12.00	20.00	55.00	100

KM# 164 25 CENTS

3.5750 g., 0.6400 Silver 0.0736 oz. ASW, 19 mm. **Ruler:** Wilhelmina I **Obv:** Small head left **Rev:** Value within wreath **Edge:** Reeded **Designer:** J.C. Wienecke

Date	Mintage	F	VF	XF	Unc	BU
1926	2,000,000	6.00	12.00	30.00	90.00	170
1928	8,000,000	BV	1.75	5.00	18.00	30.00
1939	4,000,000	BV	1.25	2.00	5.00	8.00
1940	9,000,000	BV	1.25	2.00	5.00	8.00
1941	40,000,000	—	BV	1.50	2.50	4.50
1943P acorn privy mark	—	BV	1.50	3.50	12.50	20.00
1944P acorn privy mark	40,000,000	—	BV	1.50	2.50	5.50
1945 acorn privy mark	92,000,000	40.00	110	200	300	400

Note: For similar coins dated 1941P and 1943P with palm tree privy mark, see Curacao

KM# 174 25 CENTS

5.0000 g., Zinc, 26 mm. **Ruler:** Wilhelmina I **Obv:** Sailing boat **Rev:** Value flanked by sprigs **Designer:** N. de Haas

Date	Mintage	F	VF	XF	Unc	BU
1941	34,600,000	0.75	1.50	3.50	12.00	25.00
1942	27,800,000	0.75	1.50	3.50	12.00	25.00
1943	13,600,000	2.50	6.00	12.00	35.00	60.00

KM# 178 25 CENTS

3.0000 g., Nickel, 19 mm. **Ruler:** Wilhelmina I **Obv:** Head left **Rev:** Crowned value divides date **Edge:** Reeded **Designer:** L.O. Wencheback

Date	Mintage	F	VF	XF	Unc	BU
1948	27,400,000	—	0.25	0.50	4.00	12.00
1948 Proof	—	Value: 150				

KM# 183 25 CENTS

3.0000 g., Nickel, 19 mm. **Ruler:** Juliana **Obv:** Head right **Rev:** Crowned value divides date **Edge:** Reeded **Designer:** L.O. Wenchebach

Date	Mintage	F	VF	XF	Unc	BU
1950	43,000,000	—	0.20	0.30	1.50	6.50
1950 Proof	—	Value: 75.00				
1951	33,200,000	—	0.20	0.30	1.50	6.50
1951 Proof	—	Value: 65.00				
1954	6,400,000	—	0.50	1.50	2.00	12.00
1954 Proof	—	Value: 65.00				
1955	10,000,000	—	0.20	0.30	1.50	4.00
1955 Proof	—	Value: 65.00				
1956	8,000,000	—	0.20	0.30	1.50	4.00
1956 Proof	—	Value: 65.00				
1957	8,000,000	—	0.20	0.30	1.50	4.00
1957 Proof	—	Value: 65.00				
1958	15,000,000	—	0.20	0.30	1.00	3.00
1958 Proof	—	Value: 65.00				
1960	9,000,000	—	0.20	0.30	1.50	4.00
1960 Proof	—	Value: 60.00				
1961	6,000,000	—	0.40	1.25	1.50	5.00
1961 Proof	—	Value: 50.00				
1962	12,000,000	—	0.20	0.30	1.00	3.00
1962 Proof	—	Value: 50.00				
1963	18,000,000	—	0.20	0.30	1.00	3.00
1963 Proof	—	Value: 50.00				
1964	25,000,000	—	0.20	0.30	1.00	3.00
1964 Proof	—	Value: 50.00				
1965	18,000,000	—	0.20	0.30	1.00	1.50
1965 Proof	—	Value: 50.00				
1966	25,000,000	—	—	0.20	0.75	1.50
1966 Proof	—	Value: 50.00				
1967	18,000,000	—	—	0.20	0.75	1.50
1967 Proof	—	Value: 60.00				
1968	26,000,000	—	—	0.20	0.75	1.00
1968 Proof	—	Value: 60.00				
1969 fish privy mark	14,000,000	—	—	0.20	0.30	1.00
1969 Proof, fish privy mark	—	Value: 60.00				
1969 cock privy mark	21,000,000	—	—	0.20	0.75	1.00
1969 Proof, cock privy mark	—	Value: 60.00				
1970	39,000,000	—	—	0.20	0.30	1.00
1970 Proof	—	Value: 60.00				
1971	40,000,000	—	—	0.20	0.30	1.00
1972	50,000,000	—	—	0.20	0.30	1.00
1973	45,000,000	—	—	0.20	0.30	1.00
1974	10,000,000	—	—	0.20	0.50	1.50
1975	25,000,000	—	—	0.20	0.30	1.00
1976	64,000,000	—	—	0.20	0.30	1.00
1977	55,000,000	—	—	0.20	0.30	1.00
1978	35,000,000	—	—	0.20	0.30	1.00
1979	45,000,000	—	—	0.20	0.30	1.00
1980 cock and star privy mark	159,300,000	—	—	—	0.20	0.50

KM# 183a 25 CENTS
Aluminum **Ruler:** Juliana **Obv:** Head right **Rev:** Crowned value divides date **Note:** Thought by many sources to be a pattern.

Date	Mintage	F	VF	XF	Unc	BU
1980	15	—	—	—	—	500

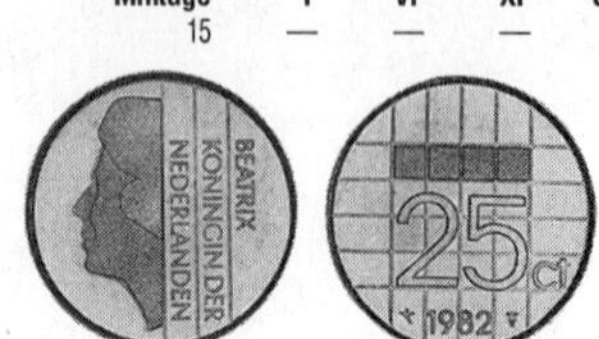

KM# 204 25 CENTS
3.0000 g., Nickel, 19 mm. **Ruler:** Beatrix **Obv:** Head left with vertical inscription **Obv. Inscription:** Beatrix/Konincin Der/Nederlanden **Rev:** Value within vertical and horizontal lines **Edge:** Reeded **Designer:** Bruno Ninaber van Eyben

Date	Mintage	F	VF	XF	Unc	BU
1982	18,300,000	—	—	—	0.20	0.60
1982 Proof	10,000	Value: 15.00				
1983	18,200,000	—	—	—	0.20	0.60
1983 Proof	15,000	Value: 12.00				
1984	19,200,000	—	—	—	0.20	0.60
1984 Proof	20,000	Value: 6.00				
1985	29,100,000	—	—	—	0.20	0.60
1985 Proof	17,000	Value: 6.00				
1986	20,300,000	—	—	—	0.20	0.60
1986 Proof	20,000	Value: 6.00				
1987	30,100,000	—	—	—	0.20	0.60
1987 Proof	18,000	Value: 6.00				
1988	17,400,000	—	—	—	0.20	0.60
1988 Proof	20,000	Value: 6.00				
1989	30,500,000	—	—	—	0.20	0.60
1989 Proof	15,000	Value: 6.00				
1990	23,100,000	—	—	—	0.20	0.60
1990 Proof	15,000	Value: 6.00				
1991	25,100,000	—	—	—	0.20	0.60
1991 Proof	14,000	Value: 6.00				
1992	41,600,000	—	—	—	0.20	0.60
1992 Proof	13,000	Value: 6.00				
1993	15,100,000	—	—	—	0.25	1.00
1993 Proof	12,000	Value: 6.00				
1994	1,700,000	—	—	—	1.00	5.00
1994 Proof	13,000	Value: 10.00				
1995	30,300,000	—	—	—	0.20	0.60
1995 Proof	12,000	Value: 8.00				
1996	24,900,000	—	—	—	0.20	0.60
1996 Proof	14,000	Value: 6.00				
1997	29,900,000	—	—	—	0.20	0.60
1997 Proof	12,000	Value: 6.00				
1998	69,660,000	—	—	—	0.20	0.60
1998 Proof	12,000	Value: 6.00				
1999	10,720,074	—	—	—	0.20	0.80
1999 Proof	15,000	Value: 6.00				
2000	31,176,000	—	—	—	0.20	0.60
2000 Proof	15,000	Value: 6.00				
2001 Proof	17,000	Value: 6.00				
2001	11,800,000	—	—	—	0.20	0.60

KM# 121.2 1/2 GULDEN
5.0000 g., 0.9450 Silver 0.1519 oz. ASW, 22 mm. **Ruler:** Wilhelmina I **Obv:** Head left **Rev:** Crowned Arms without 50 C. below shield **Edge:** Reeded **Designer:** P. Pander

Date	Mintage	F	VF	XF	Unc	BU
1904	1,000,000	25.00	60.00	150	275	400
1905	4,000,000	7.00	15.00	35.00	90.00	150
1906	1,000,000	30.00	70.00	200	300	450
1907	3,300,000	7.00	15.00	35.00	90.00	150
1907 Proof	—	Value: 400				
1908	4,000,000	7.00	15.00	35.00	90.00	150
1909	3,000,000	7.00	15.00	35.00	90.00	150

KM# 147 1/2 GULDEN
5.0000 g., 0.9450 Silver 0.1519 oz. ASW, 22 mm. **Ruler:** Wilhelmina I **Obv:** Head left **Rev:** Crowned Arms **Edge:** Reeded **Designer:** J.C. Wienecke

Date	Mintage	F	VF	XF	Unc	BU
1910	4,000,000	7.00	16.50	50.00	100	160
1912	4,000,000	7.00	16.50	50.00	100	160
1913	8,000,000	6.00	10.00	30.00	65.00	100
1919	8,000,000	6.00	10.00	30.00	65.00	100

KM# 160 1/2 GULDEN
5.0000 g., 0.7200 Silver 0.1157 oz. ASW, 22 mm. **Ruler:** Wilhelmina I **Obv:** Head left **Rev:** Crowned Arms **Edge:** Reeded **Designer:** J.C. Wienecke

Date	Mintage	F	VF	XF	Unc	BU
1921	5,000,000	BV	2.75	5.00	22.00	40.00
1921 Proof	—	Value: 250				
1922	11,240,000	BV	2.50	3.50	15.00	22.00
1928	5,000,000	BV	2.75	5.00	22.00	30.00
1929	9,500,000	—	BV	3.00	12.00	18.00
Note: Pearls contact the edge						
1929	Inc. above	BV	5.00	25.00	50.00	100
Note: Pearls from the edge						
1930	18,500,000	—	BV	2.75	9.00	15.00

KM# 122.1 GULDEN
10.0000 g., 0.9450 Silver 0.3038 oz. ASW, 28 mm. **Ruler:** Wilhelmina I **Obv:** Crowned head left **Obv. Legend:** WILHELMINA... **Rev:** Crowned arms divide value **Rev. Legend:** DER NEDERLANDEN... **Edge Lettering:** GOD * ZIJ * MET * ONS * **Designer:** P. Pander

Date	Mintage	F	VF	XF	Unc	BU
1901	2,000,000	25.00	65.00	150	300	400
1901 Proof	—	Value: 950				

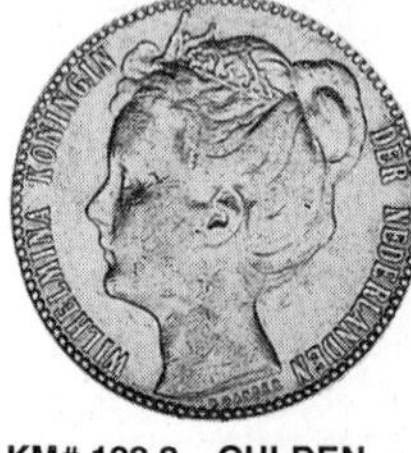

KM# 122.2 GULDEN
10.0000 g., 0.9450 Silver 0.3038 oz. ASW **Ruler:** Wilhelmina I **Obv:** Head left **Rev:** Crowned arms without 100 C. below shield **Edge Lettering:** GOD*ZY*MET*ONS*

Date	Mintage	F	VF	XF	Unc	BU
1904	2,000,000	12.00	35.00	75.00	175	275
1905	1,000,000	25.00	65.00	150	300	400
1905 Proof	—	Value: 1,000				
1906	500,000	150	300	900	1,250	1,750
1906 Proof	—	Value: 2,500				
1907	5,100,000	8.00	20.00	45.00	100	150
1908	4,700,000	8.00	20.00	45.00	100	150
1908 Proof	—	Value: 500				
1909	2,000,000	20.00	35.00	90.00	175	300

KM# 148 GULDEN
10.0000 g., 0.9450 Silver 0.3038 oz. ASW, 28 mm. **Ruler:** Wilhelmina I **Obv:** Head left **Obv. Legend:** Crowned arms **Edge Lettering:** GOD * ZIJ * MET * ONS * **Designer:** J.C. Wienecke

Date	Mintage	F	VF	XF	Unc	BU
1910	1,000,000	50.00	200	500	800	1,300
1910 Proof	—	Value: 2,000				
1911	2,000,000	20.00	45.00	150	300	500
1912	3,000,000	10.00	35.00	75.00	200	275
1913	8,000,000	7.00	20.00	65.00	100	150
1914	15,785,000	6.00	15.00	32.50	75.00	130
1915	14,215,000	6.00	16.50	35.00	75.00	130
1916	5,000,000	16.00	50.00	85.00	175	225
1917	2,300,000	20.00	65.00	100	200	250

KM# 161.1 GULDEN
10.0000 g., 0.7200 Silver 0.2315 oz. ASW, 28 mm. **Ruler:** Wilhelmina I **Obv:** Head left **Obv. Legend:** Ends below truncation **Rev:** Crowned arms **Edge Lettering:** GOD * ZIJ * MET * ONS * **Designer:** J.C. Wienecke

Date	Mintage	F	VF	XF	Unc	BU
1922	9,550,000	BV	3.75	15.00	40.00	65.00
1922 Proof	—	Value: 450				
1923	8,050,000	BV	3.75	20.00	40.00	65.00
1924	8,000,000	BV	4.50	20.00	40.00	65.00
1928	6,150,000	BV	3.75	15.00	50.00	100
1929	32,350,000	—	BV	4.00	10.00	18.00
1930	13,500,000	—	BV	5.00	12.00	35.00
1931	38,100,000	—	BV	4.00	10.00	15.00
1938	5,000,000	BV	4.25	7.00	18.00	25.00
1939	14,200,000	—	BV	3.75	7.00	15.00
1940	21,300,000	—	BV	3.75	7.00	15.00
1940 Proof	—	Value: 200				
1944P acorn privy mark	105,125,000	80.00	250	450	525	600

KM# 161.2 GULDEN
10.0000 g., 0.7200 Silver 0.2315 oz. ASW, 28 mm. **Ruler:** Wilhelmina I **Obv:** Head left **Obv. Legend:** Ends at right of truncation **Rev:** Crowned arms **Edge Lettering:** GOD * ZIJ * MET * ONS * **Note:** For similar coins dated 1943D with palm tree privy mark, see Netherlands East Indies

Date	Mintage	F	VF	XF	Unc	BU
1944P acorn privy mark	Inc. above	7.50	20.00	35.00	55.00	80.00
1945P acorn privy mark	25,375,000	225	600	1,200	1,750	2,250
Note: Only a small number placed into circulation						

KM# 184 GULDEN
6.5000 g., 0.7200 Silver 0.1505 oz. ASW, 25 mm. **Ruler:** Juliana **Obv:** Head right **Rev:** Crowned arms divide date **Edge Lettering:** GOD * ZIJ * MET * ONS * **Designer:** L.O. Wenckebach

Date	Mintage	F	VF	XF	Unc	BU
1954	6,600,000	—	—	BV	4.00	6.00
1954 Proof	—	Value: 65.00				
1955	37,500,000	—	—	BV	3.00	5.00
1955 Proof	—	Value: 65.00				
1956	38,900,000	—	—	BV	3.00	5.00
1956 Proof	—	Value: 65.00				
1957	27,000,000	—	—	BV	3.00	5.00
1957 Proof	—	Value: 65.00				
1958	30,000,000	—	—	BV	4.50	5.00
1958 Proof	—	Value: 65.00				
1963	5,000,000	—	—	BV	4.50	7.50
1963 Proof	—	Value: 80.00				
1964	9,000,000	—	—	BV	3.00	5.00
1964 Proof	—	Value: 80.00				
1965	21,000,000	—	—	BV	3.00	4.00
1965 Proof	—	Value: 80.00				
1966	5,000,000	—	—	BV	3.00	5.00
1966 Proof	—	Value: 80.00				
1967	7,000,000	—	—	BV	4.50	6.00
1967 Proof	—	Value: 110				

KM# 184a GULDEN
6.0000 g., Nickel, 25 mm. **Ruler:** Juliana **Obv:** Head right **Rev:** Crowned arms divide date

Date	Mintage	F	VF	XF	Unc	BU
1967	31,000,000	—	—	0.75	2.00	5.00
1967 Proof	—	Value: 55.00				
1968	61,000,000	—	—	0.75	2.00	5.00
1969 fish	27,500,000	—	—	—	2.50	6.00
1969 Proof, fish	—	Value: 50.00				
1969 cock	15,500,000	—	—	—	2.50	6.00

Date	Mintage	F	VF	XF	Unc	BU
1969 Proof, cock	—	Value: 50.00				
1970	18,000,000	—	—	0.75	2.00	5.00
1970 Proof	—	Value: 50.00				
1971	50,000,000	—	—	—	0.75	2.00
1972	60,000,000	—	—	—	0.75	2.00
1973	27,000,000	—	—	—	0.75	3.00
1975	9,000,000	—	—	—	2.00	5.00
1976	32,000,000	—	—	—	0.75	2.00
1977	38,000,000	—	—	—	0.75	2.00
1978	30,000,000	—	—	—	0.75	2.00
1979	25,000,000	—	—	—	0.75	2.00
1980 cock and star privy mark	118,300,000	—	—	—	0.65	1.00

KM# 200 GULDEN

6.0000 g., Nickel, 25 mm. **Ruler:** Beatrix **Subject:** Investiture of New Queen **Obv:** Conjoined heads left **Rev:** Crowned arms divide date **Edge Lettering:** GOD * ZIJ * MET * ONS * **Designer:** C.E. Bruyn-van Rood

Date	Mintage	F	VF	XF	Unc	BU
1980	30,500,000	—	—	—	0.65	1.00

KM# 205 GULDEN

6.0000 g., Nickel, 25 mm. **Ruler:** Beatrix **Obv:** Head left with vertical inscription **Rev:** Value within vertical and horizontal lines **Edge Lettering:** GOD * ZIJ * MET * ONS * **Designer:** Bruno Ninaber von Eyben

Date	Mintage	F	VF	XF	Unc	BU
1982	31,300,000	—	—	—	—	1.25
1982 Proof	10,000	Value: 20.00				
1983	5,200,000	—	—	—	—	1.50
1983 Proof	15,000	Value: 15.00				
1984	4,200,000	—	—	—	—	1.50
1984 Proof	20,000	Value: 7.50				
1985	3,100,000	—	—	—	—	2.50
1985 Proof	17,000	Value: 7.50				
1986	12,100,000	—	—	—	—	1.75
1986 Proof	18,000	Value: 7.50				
1987	20,100,000	—	—	—	—	1.75
1987 Proof	20,000	Value: 7.50				
1988	13,600,000	—	—	—	—	1.75
1988 Proof	20,000	Value: 7.50				
1989	1,100,000	—	—	—	—	3.50
1989 Proof	15,000	Value: 7.50				
1990	1,100,000	—	—	—	—	3.50
1990 Proof	15,000	Value: 7.50				
1991	500,000	—	—	—	—	4.00
1991 Proof	14,000	Value: 7.50				
1992	10,100,000	—	—	—	—	1.50
1992 Proof	13,000	Value: 7.50				
1993	15,100,000	—	—	—	—	1.50
1993 Proof	12,000	Value: 7.50				
1994	16,600,000	—	—	—	—	1.50
1994 Proof	13,000	Value: 7.50				
1995	12,600,000	—	—	—	—	1.50
1995 Proof	12,000	Value: 7.50				
1996	6,660,000	—	—	—	—	1.50
1996 Proof	14,000	Value: 7.50				
1997	12,800,000	—	—	—	—	1.50
1997 Proof	12,000	Value: 7.50				
1998	15,100,000	—	—	—	—	1.75
1998 Proof	12,000	Value: 7.50				
1999	8,900,000	—	—	—	—	1.25
1999 Proof	15,000	Value: 7.50				
2000	37,680,000	—	—	—	—	1.25
2000 Proof	15,000	Value: 7.50				
2001 Proof	17,000	Value: 7.50				
2001	6,650,000	—	—	—	—	1.25

KM# 233 GULDEN

6.0400 g., Nickel, 25 mm. **Ruler:** Beatrix **Obv:** Head left within inscription **Obv. Designer:** Geerten Verheus and Michael Raedecker **Rev:** Child art design **Rev. Designer:** Tim van Melis **Edge Lettering:** GOD ZIJ MET ONS

Date	Mintage	F	VF	XF	Unc	BU
2001	16,045,000	—	—	—	—	4.00
2001 Prooflike	32,000	—	—	—	—	6.00

KM# 165 2-1/2 GULDEN

25.0000 g., 0.7200 Silver 0.5787 oz. ASW, 38 mm. **Ruler:** Wilhelmina I **Obv:** Head left **Rev:** Crowned arms divide value **Edge Lettering:** GOD * ZIJ * MET * ONS * **Designer:** J.C. Wienecke

Date	Mintage	F	VF	XF	Unc	BU
1929	4,400,000	BV	10.00	25.00	75.00	100
1930	11,600,000	BV	9.00	12.00	20.00	30.00
1931	4,400,000	BV	9.00	12.00	20.00	30.00
1932	6,320,000	BV	9.00	12.00	20.00	30.00
1932 Deep hair lines	Inc. above	70.00	125	250	350	500
1933	3,560,000	BV	9.50	15.00	25.00	50.00
1937	4,000,000	—	BV	10.00	20.00	30.00
1938	2,000,000	BV	10.00	18.00	30.00	45.00
1938 Deep hair lines	Inc. above	45.00	100	235	325	450
1939	3,760,000	—	BV	10.00	20.00	30.00
1940	4,640,000	12.00	20.00	30.00	50.00	100

Note: For similar coins dated 1943D with palm tree privy mark, see Netherlands East Indies

KM# 185 2-1/2 GULDEN

15.0000 g., 0.7200 Silver 0.3472 oz. ASW, 33 mm. **Ruler:** Juliana **Obv:** Head right **Rev:** Crowned arms divide value **Edge Lettering:** GOD * ZIJ * MET * ONS * **Designer:** L.O. Wenchebach

Date	Mintage	F	VF	XF	Unc	BU
1959	7,200,000	—	—	BV	5.50	9.00
1959 Proof	—	Value: 175				
1960	12,800,000	—	—	BV	5.50	9.00
1960 Proof	—	Value: 175				
1961	10,000,000	—	—	BV	5.50	9.00
1961 Proof	—	Value: 175				
1962	5,000,000	—	—	BV	5.50	10.00
1962 Proof	—	Value: 175				
1963	4,000,000	—	BV	5.50	9.00	14.00
1963 Proof	—	Value: 175				
1964	2,800,000	—	BV	6.00	10.00	15.00
1964 Proof	—	Value: 175				
1966	5,000,000	—	—	BV	5.50	9.00
1966 Proof	—	Value: 175				

KM# 191 2-1/2 GULDEN

10.0000 g., Nickel, 29 mm. **Ruler:** Juliana **Obv:** Head right **Rev:** Crowned arms divide value **Edge Lettering:** GOD * ZIJ * MET * ONS * **Designer:** L.O. Wenckebach

Date	Mintage	F	VF	XF	Unc	BU
1969	1,200,000	—	—	1.00	3.00	8.00
Note: Fish privy mark						
1969 Proof	—	Value: 120				
Note: Fish privy mark with front hair lock						
1969 Proof; rare	—	—	—	—	—	—
Note: Fish privy mark without front hair lock						
1969	15,600,000	—	—	—	3.00	5.00
Note: Cock privy mark						
1969 Proof	—	Value: 90.00				
Note: Cock privy mark						
1970	22,000,000	—	—	—	2.50	4.00
1970 Proof	—	Value: 90.00				
1971	8,000,000	—	—	—	2.50	4.00
1972	20,000,000	—	—	—	2.50	4.00
1978	5,000,000	—	—	—	3.00	6.00
1980	37,300,000	—	—	—	2.50	4.00

Note: Cock and star privy mark

KM# 197 2-1/2 GULDEN

10.0000 g., Nickel, 29 mm. **Ruler:** Juliana **Subject:** 400th Anniversary - The Union of Utrecht **Obv:** Head right **Obv. Designer:** L.O. Wenchkebach **Rev:** Text, value and date **Rev. Designer:** G. Noordzij **Edge Lettering:** GOD * ZIJ * MET * ONS *

Date	Mintage	F	VF	XF	Unc	BU
1979	25,000,000	—	—	—	1.50	2.00

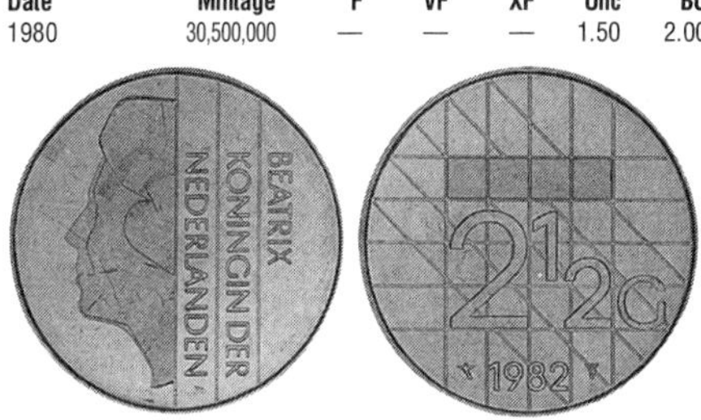

KM# 201 2-1/2 GULDEN

10.0000 g., Nickel, 29 mm. **Ruler:** Beatrix **Subject:** Investiture of New Queen **Obv:** Conjoined heads left **Rev:** Crowned arms divide date **Edge Lettering:** GOD * ZIJ * MET * ONS * **Designer:** L. E. Bruijn-van Rood

Date	Mintage	F	VF	XF	Unc	BU
1980	30,500,000	—	—	—	1.50	2.00

KM# 206 2-1/2 GULDEN

10.0000 g., Nickel, 29 mm. **Ruler:** Beatrix **Obv:** Head left with vertical inscription **Rev:** Value within horizontal, vertical and diagonal lines **Edge Lettering:** GOD * ZIJ * MET * ONS * **Designer:** Bruno Ninaber van Eyben

Date	Mintage	F	VF	XF	Unc	BU
1982	14,300,000	—	—	—	—	2.00
1982 Proof	10,000	Value: 35.00				
1983	3,800,000	—	—	—	—	2.50
1983 Proof	15,000	Value: 27.50				
1984	5,200,000	—	—	—	—	2.50
1984 Proof	20,000	—	—	—	—	—
1985	3,100,000	—	—	—	—	4.50
1985 Proof	17,000	Value: 16.00				
1986	5,800,000	—	—	—	—	4.50
1986 Proof	20,000	Value: 16.00				
1987	2,500,000	—	—	—	—	8.50
1987 Proof	18,000	Value: 16.00				
1988	6,200,000	—	—	—	—	4.50
1988 Proof	20,000	Value: 16.00				
1989	4,099,999	—	—	—	—	4.00
1989 Proof	15,000	Value: 16.00				
1990	1,100,000	—	—	—	—	3.00
1990 Proof	15,000	Value: 16.00				
1991	500,000	—	—	—	—	10.00
1991 Proof	14,000	Value: 16.00				
1992	500,000	—	—	—	—	10.00
1992 Proof	13,000	Value: 16.00				
1993	500,000	—	—	—	—	10.00
1993 Proof	12,000	Value: 16.00				
1994	500,000	—	—	—	—	10.00
1994 Proof	13,000	Value: 16.00				
1995	240,000	—	—	—	—	12.00
1995 Proof	12,000	Value: 16.00				
1996	240,000	—	—	—	—	12.00
1996 Proof	14,000	Value: 16.00				
1997	300,000	—	—	—	—	12.00
1997 Proof	12,000	Value: 16.00				
1998	300,000	—	—	—	—	12.00
1998 Proof	12,000	Value: 16.00				
1999	400,000	—	—	—	—	12.00
1999 Proof	15,000	Value: 16.00				

Date	Mintage	F	VF	XF	Unc	BU
2000	500,000	—	—	—	—	12.00
2000 Proof	15,000	Value: 16.00				
2001	560,000	—	—	—	—	12.00
2001 Proof	17,000	Value: 16.00				

KM# 151 5 GULDEN

3.3600 g., 0.9000 Gold 0.0972 oz. AGW, 18 mm. **Ruler:** Wilhelmina I **Obv:** Bust right **Rev:** Crowned arms divide value **Edge:** Reeded **Designer:** J. C. Wienecke **Note:** Counterfeits are prevalent.

Date	Mintage	F	VF	XF	Unc	BU
1912	1,000,000	90.00	100	120	165	200
1912 Matte Proof	120	Value: 800				

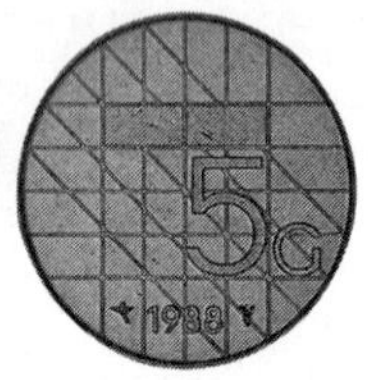

KM# 210 5 GULDEN

9.2500 g., Bronze Clad Nickel, 23.5 mm. **Ruler:** Beatrix **Obv:** Head left with vertical inscription **Rev:** Value within horizontal, vertical and diagonal lines **Edge:** GOD * ZIJ * MET * ONS * **Designer:** Bruno Ninaber van Eyben

Date	Mintage	F	VF	XF	Unc	BU
1987 Proof	2	—	—	—	—	—
1988	73,700,000	—	—	—	—	8.00
1988 Proof	20,000	Value: 12.50				
1989	69,100,000	—	—	—	—	8.00
1989 Proof	15,000	Value: 12.50				
1990	47,300,000	—	—	—	—	8.00
1990 Proof	15,000	Value: 15.00				
1991	17,100,000	—	—	—	—	8.00
1991 Proof	14,000	Value: 15.00				
1992	500,000	—	—	—	—	8.00
1992 Proof	13,000	Value: 15.00				
1993	5,500,000	—	—	—	—	5.00
1993 Proof	12,000	Value: 15.00				
1994	488,000	—	—	—	—	12.00
1994 Proof	13,000	Value: 17.50				
1995	488,000	—	—	—	—	12.00
1995 Proof	12,000	Value: 17.50				
1996	240,000	—	—	—	—	12.00
1996 Proof	14,000	Value: 17.50				
1997	278,000	—	—	—	—	12.00
1997 Proof	12,000	Value: 17.50				
1998	204,000	—	—	—	—	12.00
1998 Proof	12,000	Value: 16.00				
1999	280,000	—	—	—	—	12.00
1999 Proof	15,000	Value: 16.00				
2000	385,000	—	—	—	—	10.00
2000 Proof	15,000	Value: 16.00				
2001 Proof	17,000	Value: 15.50				
2001	360,000	—	—	—	—	10.00

KM# 231 5 GULDEN

9.2500 g., Brass Plated Nickel, 23.5 mm. **Ruler:** Beatrix **Subject:** Soccer **Obv:** Head left **Rev:** Value within soccerball **Edge:** Reeded **Edge Lettering:** GOD * ZIJ * MET * ONS * **Designer:** G. Verheus and M. Raedecker **Note:** A joint issue proof set exists containing the Netherlands KM#231, Belgium KM#213-214 plus a medal.

Date	Mintage	F	VF	XF	Unc	BU
2000 Proof	Est. 1,000	Value: 175				
Note: Small mintmarks						
2000	2,500,000	—	—	—	4.00	8.50
2000 Proof	19,000	Value: 12.50				
Note: Large mintmarks						

KM# 149 10 GULDEN

6.7290 g., 0.9000 Gold 0.1947 oz. AGW, 22.5 mm. **Ruler:** Wilhelmina I **Obv:** Head right **Rev:** Crowned arms divide value **Edge:** Reeded **Designer:** J. C. Wienecke

Date	Mintage	F	VF	XF	Unc	BU
1911	774,544	—	—	—	BV	200
1911 Proof	8	Value: 1,750				
1912	3,000,000	—	—	—	BV	195
1912 Proof	20	Value: 1,500				
1913	1,133,476	—	—	—	BV	195
1917	4,000,000	—	—	—	BV	195

KM# 162 10 GULDEN

6.7290 g., 0.9000 Gold 0.1947 oz. AGW, 22.5 mm. **Ruler:** Wilhelmina I **Obv:** Head right **Rev:** Crowned arms divide value **Edge:** Reeded **Designer:** J. C. Wienecke

Date	Mintage	F	VF	XF	Unc	BU
1925	2,000,000	—	—	—	BV	195
1925 Proof	12	Value: 1,500				
1926	2,500,000	—	—	—	BV	195
1926 Proof	—	Value: 1,300				
1927	1,000,000	—	—	—	BV	195
1932	4,323,954	—	—	—	BV	195
1933	2,462,101	—	—	—	BV	195

EURO COINAGE

European Union Issues

KM# 234 EURO CENT

2.3000 g., Copper Plated Steel, 16.2 mm. **Ruler:** Beatrix **Obv:** Head left among stars **Obv. Designer:** Bruno Ninaber van Eyben **Rev:** Value and globe **Rev. Designer:** Luc Luycx **Edge:** Plain

Date	Mintage	F	VF	XF	Unc	BU
1999	47,800,000	—	—	—	0.50	0.75
1999 Proof	16,500	—	—	—	—	—
2000	276,800,000	—	—	—	0.35	0.50
2000 Proof	16,500	—	—	—	—	—
2001	179,300,000	—	—	—	0.35	0.50
2001 Proof	16,500	—	—	—	—	—
2002	800,000	—	—	—	1.00	1.25
2002 Proof	16,500	—	—	—	—	—
2003	58,100,000	—	—	—	0.50	0.75
2003 Proof	13,000	—	—	—	—	—
2004	113,900,000	—	—	—	0.50	0.75
2004 Proof	5,000	—	—	—	—	—
2005	413,000	—	—	—	1.50	2.00
2005 Proof	5,000	—	—	—	—	—
2006	200,000	—	—	—	1.50	2.00
2006 Proof	3,500	—	—	—	—	—
2007	225,000	—	—	—	1.50	2.00
2007 Proof	10,000	—	—	—	—	—
2008	—	—	—	—	1.50	2.00
2008 Proof	—	—	—	—	—	—

KM# 235 2 EURO CENT

3.0000 g., Copper Plated Steel, 18.7 mm. **Ruler:** Beatrix **Obv:** Head left among stars **Obv. Designer:** Bruno Ninaber van Eyben **Rev:** Value and globe **Rev. Designer:** Luc Luycx **Edge:** Grooved

Date	Mintage	F	VF	XF	Unc	BU
1999	109,000,000	—	—	—	0.50	0.75
1999 Proof	16,500	—	—	—	—	—
2000	122,000,000	—	—	—	0.50	0.75
2000 Proof	16,500	—	—	—	—	—
2001	145,800,000	—	—	—	0.50	0.75
2001 Proof	16,500	—	—	—	—	—
2002	53,100,000	—	—	—	0.75	1.00
2002 Proof	16,500	—	—	—	—	—
2003	151,200,000	—	—	—	0.50	0.75
2003 Proof	13,000	—	—	—	—	—
2004	115,622,000	—	—	—	0.50	0.75
2004 Proof	5,000	—	—	—	—	—
2005	413,000	—	—	—	1.50	2.00
2005 Proof	5,000	—	—	—	—	—
2006	200,000	—	—	—	1.50	2.00
2006 Proof	3,500	—	—	—	—	—
2007	225,000	—	—	—	1.50	2.00
2007 Proof	10,000	—	—	—	—	—

Date	Mintage	F	VF	XF	Unc	BU
2008	—	—	—	—	1.50	2.00
2008	—	—	—	—	—	—

KM# 236 5 EURO CENT

3.9000 g., Copper Plated Steel, 21.25 mm. **Ruler:** Beatrix **Obv:** Head left among stars **Obv. Designer:** Bruno Ninaber van Eyben **Rev:** Value and globe **Rev. Designer:** Luc Luycx **Edge:** Plain

Date	Mintage	F	VF	XF	Unc	BU
1999	213,000,000	—	—	—	0.50	0.75
1999 Proof	16,500	—	—	—	—	—
2000	184,200,000	—	—	—	0.50	0.75
2000 Proof	16,500	—	—	—	—	—
2001	205,900,000	—	—	—	0.50	0.75
2001 Proof	16,500	—	—	—	—	—
2002	900,000	—	—	—	1.75	2.25
2002 Proof	16,500	—	—	—	—	—
2003	1,400,000	—	—	—	1.50	2.00
2003 Proof	13,000	—	—	—	—	—
2004	306,000	—	—	—	2.00	2.50
2004 Proof	5,000	—	—	—	—	—
2005	80,413,000	—	—	—	1.00	1.25
2005 Proof	5,000	—	—	—	—	—
2006	60,100,000	—	—	—	1.00	1.25
2006 Proof	3,500	—	—	—	—	—
2007	50,225,000	—	—	—	1.00	1.25
2007 Proof	10,000	—	—	—	—	—
2008	—	—	—	—	1.00	1.25
2008	—	—	—	—	—	—

KM# 237 10 EURO CENT

4.1000 g., Brass, 19.7 mm. **Ruler:** Beatrix **Obv:** Head left among stars **Obv. Designer:** Bruno Ninaber van Eyben **Rev:** Value and map **Rev. Designer:** Luc Luycx

Date	Mintage	F	VF	XF	Unc	BU
1999	149,700,000	—	—	—	0.75	1.00
1999 Proof	16,500	—	—	—	—	—
2000	156,700,000	—	—	—	0.75	1.00
2000 Proof	16,500	—	—	—	—	—
2001	193,500,000	—	—	—	0.75	1.00
2001 Proof	16,500	—	—	—	—	—
2002	800,000	—	—	—	1.50	2.00
2002 Proof	16,500	—	—	—	—	—
2003	1,200,000	—	—	—	1.50	2.00
2003 Proof	13,000	—	—	—	—	—
2004	262,000	—	—	—	2.00	2.50
2004 Proof	5,000	—	—	—	—	—
2005	363,000	—	—	—	1.75	2.25
2005 Proof	5,000	—	—	—	—	—
2006	150,000	—	—	—	1.75	2.25
2006 Proof	3,500	—	—	—	—	—

KM# 268 10 EURO CENT

4.1000 g., Brass, 19.7 mm. **Ruler:** Beatrix **Obv:** Head of Queen Beatrix left **Obv. Designer:** Bruno Ninaber van Eybew **Rev:** Relief map of Western Europe, stars, lines and value **Rev. Designer:** Luc Luycx

Date	Mintage	F	VF	XF	Unc	BU
2007	180,000	—	—	—	1.75	2.50
2007 Proof	10,000	—	—	—	—	—
2008	—	—	—	—	1.75	2.50
2008 Proof	—	—	—	—	—	—

KM# 238 20 EURO CENT

5.7000 g., Brass, 22.2 mm. **Ruler:** Beatrix **Obv:** Head left among stars **Obv. Designer:** Bruno Ninaber van Eyben **Rev:** Value and map **Rev. Designer:** Luc Luycx **Edge:** Notched

Date	Mintage	F	VF	XF	Unc	BU
1999	86,500,000	—	—	—	1.00	1.25
1999 Proof	16,500	—	—	—	—	—
2000	67,500,000	—	—	—	1.00	1.25
2000 Proof	16,500	—	—	—	—	—
2001	97,600,000	—	—	—	1.00	1.25
2001 Proof	16,500	—	—	—	—	—
2002	51,200,000	—	—	—	1.75	2.25
2002 Proof	16,500	—	—	—	—	—
2003	58,200,000	—	—	—	1.75	2.25
2003 Proof	13,000	—	—	—	—	—
2004	20,430,000	—	—	—	2.00	2.50
2004 Proof	5,000	—	—	—	—	—
2005	363,000	—	—	—	2.50	3.00
2005 Proof	5,000	—	—	—	—	—
2006	150,000	—	—	—	2.50	3.00
2006 Proof	3,500	—	—	—	—	—

KM# 269 20 EURO CENT

5.7000 g., Brass, 22.2 mm. **Ruler:** Beatrix **Obv:** Head of Queen Beatrix left **Obv. Designer:** Bruno Ninaber van Eybew **Rev:** Relief map of Western Europe, stars, lines and value **Rev. Designer:** Luc Luycx **Edge:** Notched

Date	Mintage	F	VF	XF	Unc	BU
2007	180,000	—	—	—	2.50	3.00
2007 Proof	10,000	—	—	—	—	—
2008	—	—	—	—	2.50	3.00
2008 Proof	—	—	—	—	—	—

KM# 239 50 EURO CENT

7.8000 g., Brass, 24.2 mm. **Ruler:** Beatrix **Obv:** Head left among stars **Obv. Designer:** Bruno Ninaber van Eyben **Rev:** Value and map **Rev. Designer:** Luc Luycx **Edge:** Notched

Date	Mintage	F	VF	XF	Unc	BU
1999	99,600,000	—	—	—	1.25	1.50
1999 Proof	16,500	—	—	—	—	—
2000	87,000,000	—	—	—	1.25	1.50
2000 Proof	16,500	—	—	—	—	—
2001	94,500,000	—	—	—	1.25	1.50
2001 Proof	16,500	—	—	—	—	—

Date	Mintage	F	VF	XF	Unc	BU
2002	80,900,000	—	—	—	1.25	1.50
2002 Proof	16,500	—	—	—	—	—
2003	1,200,000	—	—	—	2.00	2.50
2003 Proof	13,000	—	—	—	—	—
2004	269,000	—	—	—	2.25	2.75
2004 Proof	5,000	—	—	—	—	—
2005	363,000	—	—	—	2.00	2.50
2005 Proof	5,964	—	—	—	—	—
2006	150,000	—	—	—	2.00	2.50
2006 Proof	3,500	—	—	—	—	—

KM# 270 50 EURO CENT

7.8000 g., Brass, 24.2 mm. **Ruler:** Beatrix **Obv:** Head of Quen Beatrix left **Obv. Designer:** Bruno Ninaber van Eybew **Rev:** Relief map of Western Europe, stars, lines and value **Rev. Designer:** Luc Luyck **Edge:** Notched

Date	Mintage	F	VF	XF	Unc	BU
2007	180,000	—	—	—	2.00	2.75
2007 Proof	10,000	—	—	—	—	—
2008	—	—	—	—	2.00	2.75
2008 Proof	—	—	—	—	—	—

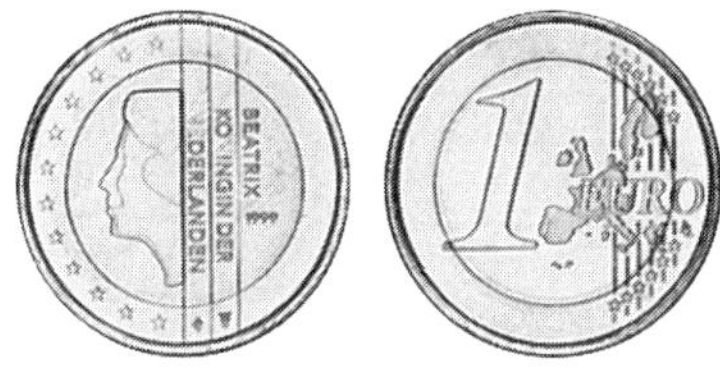

KM# 240 EURO

7.5000 g., Bi-Metallic Copper-Nickel center in Brass ring, 23.2 mm. **Ruler:** Beatrix **Obv:** Half head left within 1/2 circle and star border, name within vertical lines **Obv. Designer:** Bruno Ninaber van Eyben **Rev:** Value and map within circle **Rev. Designer:** Luc Luycx **Edge:** Plain and reeded sections

Date	Mintage	F	VF	XF	Unc	BU
1999	63,500,000	—	—	—	2.50	3.00
1999 Proof	16,500	—	—	—	—	—
2000	62,800,000	—	—	—	2.50	3.00
2000 Proof	16,500	—	—	—	—	—
2001	67,900,000	—	—	—	2.50	3.00
2001 Proof	16,500	—	—	—	—	—
2002	20,100,000	—	—	—	3.25	3.75
2002 Proof	16,500	—	—	—	—	—
2003	1,400,000	—	—	—	3.50	4.00
2003 Proof	13,000	—	—	—	—	—
2004	235,000	—	—	—	5.00	6.00
2004 Proof	5,000	—	—	—	—	—
2005	288,000	—	—	—	4.00	5.00
2005 Proof	5,964	—	—	—	—	—
2006	100,000	—	—	—	4.00	5.00
2006 Proof	3,500	—	—	—	—	—

KM# 271 EURO

7.5000 g., Bi-Metallic Copper-Nickel center in Brass ring, 23.2 mm. **Ruler:** Beatrix **Obv:** Queen's profile left **Obv. Designer:** Bruno Ninaber van Eybew **Rev:** Relief map of Western Europe, stars, lines and value **Edge:** Plain and reeded sections

Date	Mintage	F	VF	XF	Unc	BU
2007	112,500	—	—	—	4.00	5.00
2007 Proof	10,000	—	—	—	—	—

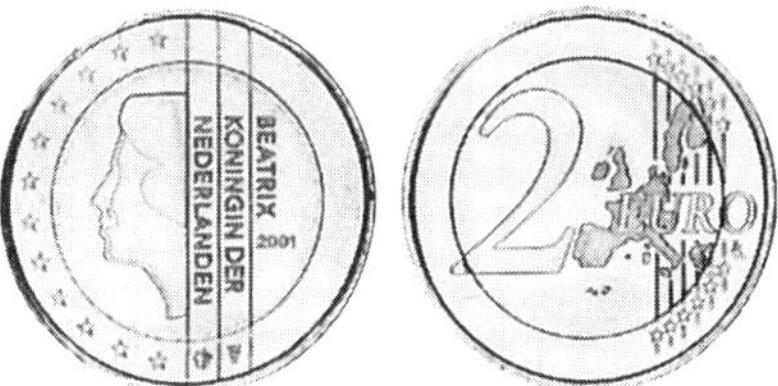

KM# 241 2 EURO

8.5000 g., Bi-Metallic Brass center in Copper-Nickel ring, 25.7 mm. **Ruler:** Beatrix **Obv:** Profile left within 1/2 circle and star border, name within vertical lines **Obv. Designer:** Bruno Ninaber van Eyben **Rev:** Value and map within circle **Rev. Designer:** Luc Luycx **Edge:** Reeded **Edge Lettering:** "GOD*ZIJ*MET*ONS*"

Date	Mintage	F	VF	XF	Unc	BU
1999	9,900,000	—	—	—	6.00	8.00
1999 Proof	16,500	—	—	—	—	—
2000	24,400,000	—	—	—	5.00	6.00
2000 Proof	16,500	—	—	—	—	—
2001	140,500,000	—	—	—	4.00	5.00
2001 Proof	16,500	—	—	—	—	—
2002	37,200,000	—	—	—	4.50	5.50
2002 Proof	16,500	—	—	—	—	—
2003	1,200,000	—	—	—	5.50	6.50
2003 Proof	13,000	—	—	—	—	—
2004	245,000	—	—	—	7.00	9.00
2004 Proof	5,000	—	—	—	—	—
2005	288,000	—	—	—	6.00	8.00
2005 Proof	5,964	—	—	—	—	—
2006	100,000	—	—	—	6.00	8.00
2006 Proof	3,500	—	—	—	—	—

KM# 273 2 EURO

8.5100 g., Bi-Metallic Brass center in Copper-Nickel ring, 25.69 mm. **Ruler:** Beatrix **Subject:** 50th Anniversary Treaty of Rome **Obv:** Open treaty book **Rev:** Large value at left, modified outline of Europe at right **Edge:** Reeded and lettered **Edge Lettering:** GOD ZU MET ONS

Date	Mintage	F	VF	XF	Unc	BU
2007	112,500	—	—	—	6.00	9.00
2007 Proof	10,000	—	—	—	—	—

KM# 272 2 EURO

8.5000 g., Bi-Metallic Brass center in Copper-Nickel ring, 25.7 mm. **Ruler:** Beatrix **Obv:** Queen's profile left **Obv. Designer:** Bruno Ninaber van Eybew **Rev:** Relief map of Western Europe, stars, lines and value **Rev. Designer:** Luc Luycx **Edge:** Reeded **Edge Lettering:** "GOD*ZIJ*MET*ONS*"

Date	Mintage	F	VF	XF	Unc	BU
2008	—	—	—	—	6.00	8.00
2008 Proof	—	—	—	—	—	—

TRADE COINAGE

KM# 83.1 DUCAT

3.4940 g., 0.9830 Gold 0.1104 oz. AGW, 21 mm. **Obv:** Standing knight divides date **Rev:** Inscription within ornamented square **Edge:** Slant-reeded

Date	Mintage	F	VF	XF	Unc	BU
1901	29,284	400	1,000	1,500	2,400	2,900
1903/1	91,000	400	1,000	1,850	2,400	2,900
1903	Inc. above	250	700	1,000	1,600	2,200
1905	87,995	175	450	700	1,000	1,500
1906	29,379	400	1,000	1,500	2,400	2,900
1908	91,006	175	450	700	1,000	1,500
1909	106,021	300	600	1,000	1,600	2,000
Note: Halberd with star privy mark						
1909	30,182	400	1,000	2,000	3,000	4,000
Note: Sea horse privy mark						
1910	421,447	125	375	525	900	1,100
1910 Proof	—	Value: 1,200				
1912	147,860	125	375	525	900	1,100
1912 Proof	—	Value: 1,200				
1913	205,464	125	375	525	900	1,100
1914	246,560	125	375	525	900	1,100
1916	116,997	125	375	525	900	1,100
1916 Proof	—	Value: 1,250				
1917	216,892	—	BV	110	125	155
1920	293,389	—	BV	110	125	155
1920 Proof	—	Value: 800				
1921	409,001	—	BV	110	120	135
1922	49,837	120	350	500	900	1,100
1923	106,674	BV	110	250	350	450
1924	84,206	BV	110	250	350	450
1925	573,071	—	BV	110	120	135
1925 Proof	Inc. above	Value: 450				
1926	191,311	—	BV	110	125	155
1927	654,424	—	—	—	BV	110
1928	571,801	—	—	—	BV	110
1932	88,268	200	500	900	1,700	2,300
1937	116,660	BV	110	115	120	145

NETHERLANDS ANTILLES

Caribbean Sea
COLOMBIA
VENEZUELA

The Netherlands Antilles, comprises two groups of islands in the West Indies: Aruba (until 1986), Bonaire and Curacao and their dependencies near the Venezuelan coast and St. Eustatius, Saba, and the southern part of St. Martin (*St. Maarten*) southeast of Puerto Rico. The island group has an area of 371 sq. mi. (960 sq. km.) and a population of 225,000. Capital: Willemstad. Chief industries are the refining of crude oil and tourism. Petroleum products and phosphates are exported.

On Dec. 15, 1954, the Netherlands Antilles were given complete domestic autonomy and granted equality within the Kingdom with Surinam and the Netherlands. On Jan. I, 1986, Aruba achieved *status aparte* as the fourth part of the Dutch realm that was a step towards total independence.

RULERS

Juliana, 1948-1980
Beatrix, 1980-

MINT MARKS

Y - York Mint

Utrecht Mint
(privy marks only)

Date	Privy Mark
1945-1969	Fish
1969	Fish with star
1970-1979	Cock
1980	Cock with star
1982-1988	Anvil with hammer
1988-1999	Bow and arrow
2000	Bow and arrow with star
2001	Wine tendril with grapes
2002	Wine tendril with grapes and star
2003	Sails of a clipper

FM - Franklin Mint, U.S.A.

NOTE: See Kingdom of the Netherlands for more details.

NOTE: From 1975-1985 the Franklin Mint produced coinage in up to 3 different qualities. Qualities of issue are designated in ( ) after each date and are defined as follows:

(M) MATTE - Normal circulation strike or a dull finish produced by sandblasting special uncirculated (polish finish) or proof quality dies.

(U) SPECIAL UNCIRCULATED - Polished or prooflike in appearance without any frosted features.

(P) PROOF - The highest quality obtainable having mirror-like fields and frosted features.

MONETARY SYSTEM

100 Cents = 1 Gulden

DUTCH ADMINISTRATION

DECIMAL COINAGE

KM# 1 CENT

2.5000 g., Bronze, 19 mm. **Ruler:** Juliana **Obv:** Rampant lion left **Rev:** Value within wreath **Edge:** Reeded

Date	Mintage	F	VF	XF	Unc	BU
1952	1,000,000	1.50	2.50	5.00	12.50	14.00
1952 Proof	100	Value: 40.00				
1954	1,000,000	1.50	2.50	5.00	12.50	14.00
1954 Proof	200	Value: 45.00				
1957	1,000,000	0.50	1.00	2.50	6.00	14.00
1957 Proof	250	Value: 35.00				
1959	1,000,000	0.50	1.00	2.50	5.00	10.00
1959 Proof	250	Value: 30.00				
1960 Proof	300	Value: 30.00				
1961	1,000,000	0.35	0.60	1.25	2.50	4.50
1961 Proof	—	Value: 25.00				
1963	1,000,000	0.35	0.60	1.25	2.50	4.50
1963 Proof	—	Value: 20.00				
1964 Proof	—	Value: 20.00				
1965	1,200,000	0.35	0.60	1.25	2.50	4.00
1965 Proof	—	Value: 20.00				
1967	850,000	0.35	0.60	1.25	2.50	4.50
1967 Proof	—	Value: 20.00				
1968 fish	900,000	0.35	0.60	1.25	2.50	4.50
1968 star and fish	700,000	0.75	1.00	2.00	4.00	9.00
Note: Struck in 1969						
1970	200,000	0.75	1.00	2.00	4.00	9.00
1970 Proof	—	Value: 25.00				

KM# 8 CENT

2.5000 g., Bronze, 19 mm. **Ruler:** Juliana **Obv:** Crowned shield above date and ribbon **Rev:** Value flanked by stars **Edge:** Plain

Date	Mintage	F	VF	XF	Unc	BU
1970	1,200,000	0.10	0.40	0.75	1.50	2.50
1970 Proof	—	Value: 17.50				
1971	3,000,000	0.10	0.40	0.75	1.50	2.50
1971 Proof	—	Value: 17.50				
1972	1,000,000	0.10	0.40	0.75	1.50	2.50
1973	3,000,000	0.10	0.20	0.40	0.80	2.00
1973 Proof	—	Value: 17.50				
1974	3,000,000	0.10	0.20	0.40	0.80	2.00
1974 Proof	—	Value: 17.50				
1975	2,000,000	0.10	0.20	0.40	0.80	2.00
1975 Proof	—	Value: 17.50				
1976	3,000,000	—	0.20	0.40	0.80	2.00
1977	4,000,000	—	0.20	0.40	0.80	2.00
1978	2,000,000	—	0.20	0.40	0.80	2.00

Note: 1969 date is now listed in the Patterns section

KM# 8a CENT

0.8000 g., Aluminum, 19 mm. **Ruler:** Juliana **Obv:** Crowned shield above date and ribbon **Rev:** Value flanked by stars **Edge:** Plain

Date	Mintage	F	VF	XF	Unc	BU
1979	7,512,000	—	0.10	0.25	0.50	0.75
1979 Proof	—	Value: 7.50				
1980	2,518,000	—	0.10	0.25	0.50	1.25
1981	2,423,000	—	0.10	0.25	0.50	0.75
1982	2,410,000	—	0.10	0.25	0.50	0.75
1983	2,925,000	—	0.10	0.25	0.50	0.75
1984	3,626,000	—	0.10	0.25	0.50	0.75
1985	3,024,000	—	0.10	0.25	0.50	0.75

KM# 32 CENT

0.7000 g., Aluminum, 14 mm. **Ruler:** Beatrix **Obv:** Orange blossom within circle **Rev:** Value within circle of geometric designed border **Edge:** Reeded

Date	Mintage	F	VF	XF	Unc	BU
1989	1,365,000	—	—	—	0.20	0.50
1990	2,711,000	—	—	—	0.20	0.50
1991	4,016,000	—	—	—	0.20	0.50
1992	3,049,000	—	—	—	0.20	0.50
1993	3,997,000	—	—	—	0.20	0.50
1994	1,997,000	—	—	—	0.20	0.50
1995	997,000	—	—	—	0.20	0.50
1996	3,595,000	—	—	—	0.20	0.50
1997	4,107,000	—	—	—	0.20	0.50
1998	5,757,000	—	—	—	0.20	0.50
1999	15,876,000	—	—	—	0.20	0.50
2000	6,607,500	—	—	—	0.20	0.50
2001(u)	12,806,500	—	—	0.10	0.20	0.50
2002(u)	6,000	—	—	0.50	1.00	1.25
Note: In sets only						
2003(u)	19,604,000	—	—	0.10	0.20	0.50
2004(u)	7,100	—	—	0.10	0.20	0.50
2005(u)	—	—	—	0.10	0.20	0.50
2006(u)	—	—	—	0.10	0.20	0.50
2007(u)	—	—	—	0.10	0.20	0.50

KM# 5 2-1/2 CENTS

4.0000 g., Bronze, 23.5 mm. **Ruler:** Juliana **Obv:** Rampant lion left **Rev:** Value within orange wreath **Edge:** Reeded

Date	Mintage	F	VF	XF	Unc	BU
1956	400,000	0.50	1.25	2.50	5.00	8.00
1956 Proof	500	Value: 25.00				
1959	1,000,000	0.50	1.00	2.00	4.00	5.00
1959 Proof	250	Value: 25.00				
1965 fish	500,000	0.50	1.00	2.00	4.00	6.00
1965 Proof	—	Value: 25.00				
1965 fish and star	150,000	1.00	2.00	4.00	7.50	17.50
Note: Struck in 1969						

KM# 9 2-1/2 CENTS

4.0000 g., Bronze, 23.5 mm. **Ruler:** Juliana **Obv:** Crowned shield above date and ribbon **Rev:** Value flanked by stars **Edge:** Plain

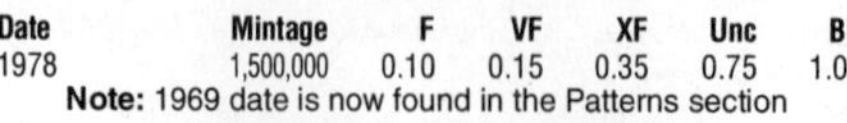

Date	Mintage	F	VF	XF	Unc	BU
1970	500,000	0.40	0.75	1.50	3.00	2.75
1970 Proof	—	Value: 20.00				
1971	3,000,000	0.10	0.25	0.50	1.00	1.50
1971 Proof	—	Value: 20.00				
1973	1,000,000	0.10	0.15	0.35	0.75	1.00
1973 Proof	—	Value: 20.00				
1974	1,000,000	0.10	0.15	0.35	0.75	1.00
1974 Proof	—	Value: 20.00				
1975	1,000,000	0.10	0.15	0.35	0.75	1.00
1976	1,000,000	0.10	0.15	0.35	0.75	1.00
1977	1,000,000	0.10	0.15	0.35	0.75	1.00
1978	1,500,000	0.10	0.15	0.35	0.75	1.00

Note: 1969 date is now found in the Patterns section

KM# 9a 2-1/2 CENTS

1.2000 g., Aluminum, 23.5 mm. **Ruler:** Juliana **Obv:** Crowned shield above date and ribbon **Rev:** Value flanked by stars **Edge:** Plain

Date	Mintage	F	VF	XF	Unc	BU
1979	2,012,000	—	0.10	0.25	0.50	0.75
1979 Proof	—	Value: 10.00				
1980	2,018,000	—	0.10	0.25	0.50	0.75
1981	1,023,000	—	0.10	0.25	0.50	0.75
1982	1,010,000	—	0.10	0.25	0.50	0.75
1983	1,025,000	—	0.10	0.25	0.50	0.75
1984	1,026,000	—	0.10	0.25	0.50	0.75
1985	1,024,000	—	0.10	0.25	0.50	0.75

KM# 6 5 CENTS

4.5000 g., Copper-Nickel, 21.3 mm. **Ruler:** Juliana **Obv:** Orange blossom within circle **Rev:** Value within circle, pearls and shells around border **Edge:** Plain **Shape:** Square

Date	Mintage	F	VF	XF	Unc	BU
1957	500,000	0.35	0.75	1.50	3.00	6.00
1957 Proof	250	Value: 40.00				
1962	250,000	1.25	2.50	5.00	10.00	12.00
1962 Proof	200	Value: 30.00				
1963	400,000	0.35	0.75	1.50	3.00	6.00
1963 Proof	—	Value: 30.00				
1965	500,000	0.35	0.75	1.50	3.00	6.00
1965 Proof	—	Value: 30.00				
1967	600,000	0.35	0.75	1.50	3.00	6.00
1967 Proof	—	Value: 30.00				
1970	450,000	0.35	0.75	1.50	3.00	6.00
1970 Proof	—	Value: 30.00				

Note: KM#A13, previously listed here, is now under Patterns

KM# 13 5 CENTS

4.5000 g., Copper-Nickel, 21.3 mm. **Ruler:** Juliana **Obv:** Crowned shield **Rev:** Value flanked by stars **Edge:** Plain **Shape:** 4-sided

Date	Mintage	F	VF	XF	Unc	BU
1971	2,000,000	0.10	0.15	0.30	0.60	0.95
1971 Proof	—	Value: 22.50				
1974	500,000	0.30	0.60	1.25	2.50	2.75
1974 Proof	—	Value: 22.50				
1975	2,000,000	0.10	0.15	0.30	0.60	0.95
1975 Proof	—	Value: 22.50				
1976	1,500,000	0.10	0.15	0.30	0.60	0.95
1977	1,000,000	0.10	0.15	0.30	0.60	0.95
1978	1,500,000	0.10	0.15	0.30	0.60	0.95
1979	1,512,000	0.10	0.15	0.30	0.60	0.95
1980	1,518,000	—	0.15	0.30	0.60	0.95
1981	1,022,999	—	0.15	0.30	0.60	0.95
1982	1,010,000	—	0.15	0.30	0.60	0.95
1983	1,024,999	—	0.15	0.30	0.60	0.95
1984	1,526,000	—	0.15	0.30	0.60	0.95
1985	1,524,000	—	0.15	0.30	0.60	0.95

KM# 33 5 CENTS

1.1600 g., Aluminum, 16 mm. **Ruler:** Beatrix **Obv:** Orange blossom within circle **Rev:** Value within circle, geometric designed border **Edge:** Reeded

Date	Mintage	F	VF	XF	Unc	BU
1989	915,000	—	—	0.25	0.60	0.75
1990	1,811,000	—	—	0.25	0.60	0.75
1991	2,513,000	—	—	—	0.60	0.75
1992	1,599,000	—	—	—	0.60	0.75
1993	2,497,000	—	—	—	0.60	0.75
1994	1,497,000	—	—	—	0.60	0.75
1995	997,000	—	—	—	0.60	0.75
1996	796,000	—	—	—	0.60	0.75
1997	2,207,000	—	—	—	0.60	0.75
1998	2,507,000	—	—	—	0.60	0.75
1999	2,501,000	—	—	—	0.60	0.75
2000	1,007,500	—	—	—	0.60	0.75
2001	2,006,500	—	—	0.20	0.60	0.75
2002	6,000	—	—	0.20	2.00	2.50
Note: In sets only						
2003	3,104,000	—	—	0.30	0.60	0.75
2004	2,402,100	—	—	0.30	0.50	0.75
2005	—	—	—	0.30	0.50	0.75
2006	—	—	—	0.30	0.50	0.75
2007	—	—	—	0.30	0.50	0.75

KM# 3 1/10 GULDEN

1.4000 g., 0.6400 Silver 0.0288 oz. ASW, 15 mm. **Ruler:** Juliana **Obv:** Head right **Rev:** Value **Edge:** Reeded

Date	Mintage	F	VF	XF	Unc	BU
1954	200,000	1.50	3.00	8.00	15.00	30.00
1954 Proof	200	Value: 40.00				
1956	250,000	1.00	2.00	4.00	8.00	12.00
1956 Proof	500	Value: 40.00				
1957	250,000	1.00	2.00	4.00	8.00	12.00
1957 Proof	250	Value: 35.00				
1959	250,000	1.00	2.00	4.00	8.00	12.00
1959 Proof	250	Value: 40.00				
1960	400,000	0.50	1.00	2.00	4.00	5.00
1960 Proof	300	Value: 40.00				
1962	400,000	0.50	1.00	2.00	4.00	5.00
1962 Proof	200	Value: 35.00				
1963	900,000	0.50	1.00	2.00	4.00	5.00
1963 Proof	—	Value: 35.00				
1966 fish	1,000,000	0.50	1.00	2.00	4.00	5.00
1966 fish and star	200,000	1.00	2.00	3.75	7.50	12.00
Note: Struck in 1969						
1970	300,000	0.50	0.75	1.50	3.00	5.00
1970 Proof	—	Value: 35.00				

KM# 10 10 CENTS

2.0000 g., Nickel, 15 mm. **Ruler:** Juliana **Obv:** Crowned shield above date and ribbon **Rev:** Value flanked by stars **Edge:** Reeded

Date	Mintage	F	VF	XF	Unc	BU
1970	1,000,000	—	0.30	0.60	1.25	1.50
1970 Proof	—	Value: 25.00				
1971	3,000,000	—	0.10	0.25	0.50	0.60
1971 Proof	—	Value: 25.00				
1974	1,000,000	—	0.30	0.60	1.25	1.50
1974 Proof	—	Value: 25.00				
1975	1,500,000	—	0.10	0.25	0.50	0.60
1975 Proof	—	Value: 25.00				
1976	2,000,000	—	0.10	0.35	0.50	0.60
1977	1,000,000	—	0.10	0.35	0.50	0.60
1978	1,500,000	—	0.10	0.35	0.50	0.60
1979	1,512,000	—	0.10	0.35	0.50	0.60
1979 Proof	—	Value: 12.50				
1980	1,518,000	—	0.10	0.35	0.50	0.60
1981	1,022,999	—	0.10	0.35	0.50	0.60
1982	1,010,000	—	0.10	0.35	0.50	0.60
1983	1,024,999	—	0.10	0.35	0.50	0.60
1984	1,026,000	—	0.10	0.35	0.50	0.60
1985	1,024,000	—	0.10	0.35	0.50	0.60

Note: 1969 date of this variety is now in the Patterns section

KM# 34 10 CENTS

3.0000 g., Nickel Bonded Steel, 18 mm. **Ruler:** Beatrix **Obv:** Orange blossom within circle **Rev:** Value within circle, geometric designed border **Edge:** Reeded

Date	Mintage	F	VF	XF	Unc	BU
1989	915,000	—	—	—	0.45	0.75
1990	1,811,000	—	—	—	0.45	0.65
1991	2,513,000	—	—	—	0.45	0.65
1992	898,000	—	—	—	0.45	0.65
1993	1,996,000	—	—	—	0.45	0.65
1994	997,000	—	—	—	0.45	0.65
1995	97,000	—	—	0.50	1.25	2.00
1996	895,000	—	—	—	0.45	0.65
1997	1,607,000	—	—	—	0.45	0.65
1998	2,007,000	—	—	—	0.45	0.65
1999	1,501,000	—	—	—	0.45	0.65

Date	Mintage	F	VF	XF	Unc	BU
2000	12,500	—	—	—	2.00	3.00
2001	11,500	—	—	0.50	1.25	2.00
2002	6,000	—	—	0.50	2.00	3.00
Note: In sets only						
2003	2,104,000	—	—	0.50	1.00	1.75
2004	2,202,100	—	—	0.50	1.00	1.75
2005	—	—	—	0.50	1.00	1.75
2006	—	—	—	0.50	1.00	1.75
2007	—	—	—	0.50	1.00	1.75

KM# 4 1/4 GULDEN

3.5750 g., 0.6400 Silver 0.0736 oz. ASW, 19 mm. **Ruler:** Juliana **Obv:** Head right **Rev:** Value **Edge:** Reeded

Date	Mintage	F	VF	XF	Unc	BU
1954	200,000	1.75	7.75	7.50	15.00	30.00
1954 Proof	200	Value: 45.00				
1956	200,000	1.50	2.50	5.00	10.00	20.00
1956 Proof	500	Value: 45.00				
1957	200,000	1.50	2.50	5.00	10.00	20.00
1957 Proof	250	Value: 45.00				
1960	240,000	BV	1.50	2.50	5.00	10.00
1960 Proof	300	Value: 40.00				
1962	240,000	BV	1.50	2.50	5.00	10.00
1962 Proof	200	Value: 45.00				
1963	300,000	BV	1.50	2.50	5.00	10.00
1963 Proof	—	Value: 45.00				
1965	500,000	BV	1.50	2.50	5.00	10.00
1965 Proof	—	Value: 45.00				
1967 fish	310,000	BV	1.50	2.50	5.00	10.00
1967 Proof, fish	—	Value: 45.00				
1967 fish and star	200,000	BV	1.50	2.50	5.00	10.00
1970	150,000	BV	1.50	2.50	5.00	10.00
1970 Proof	—	Value: 35.00				

KM# 11 25 CENTS

3.5000 g., Nickel, 19 mm. **Ruler:** Beatrix **Obv:** Crowned shield above date and value **Rev:** Value flanked by stars **Edge:** Reeded

Date	Mintage	F	VF	XF	Unc	BU
1970	750,000	0.25	0.50	1.00	2.00	3.00
1970 Proof	—	Value: 30.00				
1971	3,000,000	—	0.15	0.30	0.60	2.00
1971 Proof	—	Value: 30.00				
1975	1,000,000	—	0.15	0.30	0.60	2.00
1975 Proof	—	Value: 30.00				
1976	1,000,000	—	0.15	0.30	0.60	1.00
1977	1,000,000	—	0.15	0.30	0.60	1.00
1978	1,000,000	—	0.15	0.30	0.60	1.00
1979	1,012,000	—	0.15	0.30	0.60	1.00
1979 Proof	—	Value: 17.50				
1980 cock and star	1,018,000	—	0.15	0.30	0.60	1.00
1981	1,022,999	—	0.15	0.30	0.60	1.00
1982	1,010,000	—	0.15	0.30	0.60	1.00
1983	1,024,999	—	0.15	0.30	0.60	1.00
1984	1,026,000	—	0.15	0.30	0.60	1.00
1985	774,000	—	0.15	0.30	0.60	1.00

KM# 35 25 CENTS

3.5000 g., Nickel Bonded Steel, 20.2 mm. **Ruler:** Beatrix **Obv:** Orange blossom within circle **Rev:** Value within circle, geometric designed border **Edge:** Reeded

Date	Mintage	F	VF	XF	Unc	BU
1989	915,000	—	—	—	0.50	1.00
1990	1,811,000	—	—	—	0.50	1.00
1991	2,013,000	—	—	—	0.50	1.00
1992	898,000	—	—	—	0.50	1.00
1993	997,000	—	—	—	0.50	1.00
1994	997,000	—	—	—	0.50	1.00
1995	297,000	—	—	—	0.50	1.00
1996	420,000	—	—	—	0.50	1.00
1997	1,297,000	—	—	—	0.50	1.00
1998	2,007,000	—	—	—	0.50	1.00
1999	1,501,000	—	—	—	0.50	1.00
2000	12,500	—	—	—	1.25	1.50
2001	11,500	—	—	0.50	1.25	1.50
2002	6,000	—	—	0.50	2.00	3.00

Date	Mintage	F	VF	XF	Unc	BU
Note: In sets only						
2003	1,404,000	—	—	0.50	1.25	1.50
2004	1,502,100	—	—	0.50	1.25	1.50
2005	—	—	—	0.50	1.25	1.50
2006	—	—	—	0.50	1.25	1.50
2007	—	—	—	0.50	1.25	1.50

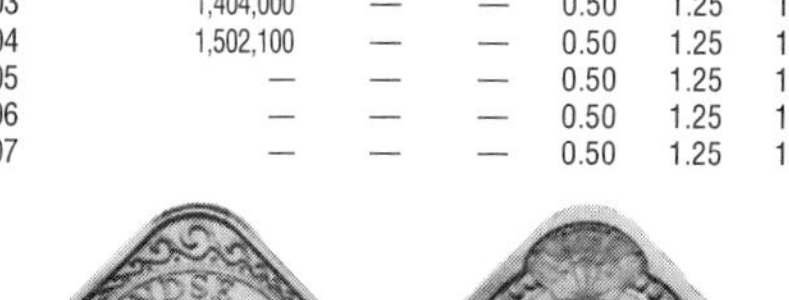

KM# 36 50 CENTS

5.0000 g., Aureate Steel, 24 mm. **Ruler:** Beatrix **Obv:** Orange blossom within circle, designed border **Rev:** Value within circle of pearls and shell border **Edge:** Plain **Shape:** 4-sided

Date	Mintage	F	VF	XF	Unc	BU
1989	315,000	—	—	—	1.00	2.00
1990	611,000	—	—	—	1.00	2.00
1991	513,000	—	—	—	1.00	2.00
1992	48,000	—	—	—	1.00	2.00
1993	8,560	—	—	—	2.00	3.00
Note: In sets only						
1994	9,000	—	—	—	1.50	2.25
Note: In sets only						
1995	9,000	—	—	—	1.50	2.25
Note: In sets only						
1996	7,500	—	—	—	1.50	2.25
Note: In sets only						
1997	9,000	—	—	—	1.00	2.00
1998	18,900	—	—	—	1.00	2.00
1999	11,000	—	—	—	1.00	2.00
2000	12,500	—	—	—	3.00	4.00
2001	11,500	—	—	0.75	3.00	4.00
2002	6,000	—	—	0.75	4.50	6.00
Note: In sets only						
2003	9,000	—	—	0.75	3.00	4.00
2004	7,100	—	—	0.75	3.00	4.00
2005	—	—	—	0.75	3.00	4.00
2006	—	—	—	0.75	3.00	4.00
2007	—	—	—	0.75	3.00	4.00

KM# 2 GULDEN

10.0000 g., 0.7200 Silver 0.2315 oz. ASW, 28 mm. **Ruler:** Juliana **Obv:** Head right **Rev:** Crowned arms **Edge Lettering:** GOD * ZIJ * MET * ONS *

Date	Mintage	F	VF	XF	Unc	BU
1952	1,000,000	BV	2.25	4.00	8.00	14.00
1952 Proof	100	Value: 125				
1963	100,000	2.00	4.00	8.00	16.00	25.00
1963 Proof	—	Value: 100				
1964 fish	300,000	BV	2.25	4.00	8.00	14.00
1964 Proof	—	Value: 100				
1964 fish and star	200,000	1.75	3.00	6.00	12.50	15.00
Note: Struck in 1969						
1970	50,000	1.75	3.00	6.00	12.50	20.00
1970 Proof	—	Value: 100				

KM# 12 GULDEN

9.0000 g., Nickel, 28 mm. **Ruler:** Juliana **Obv:** Head right **Rev:** Crowned shield above date and ribbon **Edge Lettering:** GOD * ZIJ * MET * ONS *

Date	Mintage	F	VF	XF	Unc	BU
1970	500,000	0.30	0.60	1.25	2.50	4.00
1970 Proof	—	Value: 50.00				
1971	3,000,000	0.30	0.60	1.25	2.50	3.50
1971 Proof	—	Value: 50.00				
1978	500,000	—	0.50	1.00	2.00	4.00
1979	512,000	—	0.50	1.00	2.00	4.00
1979 Proof	—	Value: 25.00				
1980 cock and star	518,000	—	0.40	0.75	1.50	2.50

Note: 1969 date is now listed in the Patterns section

KM# 24 GULDEN

9.0000 g., Nickel, 28 mm. **Ruler:** Beatrix **Obv:** Head left **Rev:** Crowned shield above date and ribbon **Edge Lettering:** GOD * ZIJ * MET * ONS *

Date	Mintage	F	VF	XF	Unc	BU
1980 anvil	223,000	—	0.50	1.00	2.00	2.50
1981	223,000	—	0.50	1.00	2.00	2.50
1982	510,000	—	0.25	0.50	1.00	2.00
1983	525,000	—	0.25	0.50	1.00	2.00
1984	526,000	—	0.25	0.50	1.00	2.00
1985	424,000	—	0.25	0.50	1.00	2.00

KM# 37 GULDEN

6.0000 g., Aureate Steel **Ruler:** Beatrix **Obv:** Head left **Rev:** Crowned shield divides value above date and ribbon **Edge Lettering:** GOD * ZIJ * MET * ONS *

Date	Mintage	F	VF	XF	Unc	BU
1989	715,000	—	—	0.50	1.00	1.00
1990	1,411,000	—	—	0.50	1.00	1.00
1991	2,013,000	—	—	0.50	1.00	1.00
1992	1,198,000	—	—	0.50	1.00	1.00
1993	1,986,000	—	—	0.50	1.00	1.00
1994	997,000	—	—	0.50	1.00	1.00
1995	9,000	—	—	—	2.00	3.00
Note: In sets only						
1996	7,500	—	—	—	2.00	3.00
Note: In sets only						
1997	9,500	—	—	0.40	3.00	1.00
1998	18,500	—	—	0.40	3.00	1.00
1999	12,000	—	—	—	3.00	4.00
2000	12,500	—	—	—	3.00	4.00
2001	11,500	—	—	0.75	3.00	4.00
2002	6,000	—	—	0.75	5.00	6.00
Note: In sets only						
2003	504,000	—	—	0.75	3.00	4.00
2004	7,100	—	—	0.75	5.00	6.00
2005	—	—	—	0.75	3.00	4.00
2006	—	—	—	0.75	3.00	4.00
2007	—	—	—	0.75	3.00	4.00

KM# 7 2-1/2 GULDEN

25.0000 g., 0.7200 Silver 0.5787 oz. ASW, 37 mm. **Ruler:** Juliana **Obv:** Head right **Rev:** Crowned arms **Edge Lettering:** GOD * ZIJ * MET * ONS *

Date	Mintage	F	VF	XF	Unc	BU
1964	162,400	—	—	BV	11.50	13.50
1964 Proof	—	Value: 200				

KM# 19 2-1/2 GULDEN

14.0000 g., Nickel, 32 mm. **Ruler:** Juliana **Obv:** Head right **Rev:** Crowned shield above date and ribbon **Edge Lettering:** GOD * ZIJ * MET * ONS *

Date	Mintage	F	VF	XF	Unc	BU
1978	100,000	—	—	2.50	5.00	6.00
1979	110,000	—	—	2.50	5.00	6.00
1979 Proof	—	Value: 35.00				
1980 cock and star	84,000	—	—	2.50	5.00	6.00

KM# 25 2-1/2 GULDEN

14.0000 g., Nickel, 32 mm. **Ruler:** Beatrix **Obv:** Head left **Rev:** Crowned shield above date and ribbon **Edge Lettering:** GOD * ZIJ * MET * ONS *

Date	Mintage	F	VF	XF	Unc	BU
1980 anvil	80,000	—	—	2.00	4.00	6.00
1981	30,000	—	—	2.00	4.00	6.00
1982	44,000	—	—	2.00	4.00	6.00
1984	12,500	—	—	3.00	6.00	7.00
1985	12,500	—	—	3.00	6.00	7.00

KM# 38 2-1/2 GULDEN

9.0000 g., Aureate Steel, 28 mm. **Ruler:** Beatrix **Obv:** Head left **Rev:** Crowned shield divides value above date and ribbon **Edge Lettering:** GOD * ZIJ * MET * ONS *

Date	Mintage	F	VF	XF	Unc	BU
1989	35,000	—	—	—	3.00	4.00
1990	60,000	—	—	—	3.00	4.00
1991	63,000	—	—	—	3.00	4.00
1992	23,000	—	—	—	3.00	4.00
1993	8,560	—	—	—	4.25	6.00
Note: In sets only						
1994	9,000	—	—	—	3.50	5.00
Note: In sets only						
1995	9,000	—	—	—	3.50	5.00
Note: In sets only						
1996	7,500	—	—	—	3.50	5.00
Note: In sets only						
1997	9,500	—	—	—	5.00	4.00
1998	20,000	—	—	—	3.00	4.00
1999	11,000	—	—	—	3.00	4.00
2000	12,500	—	—	—	3.00	6.00
2001	11,500	—	—	1.00	5.00	6.00
2002	6,000	—	—	1.00	7.00	8.00
Note: In sets only						
2003	9,000	—	—	1.00	5.00	6.00
2004	7,100	—	—	1.00	5.00	6.00
2005	—	—	—	1.00	5.00	6.00
2006	—	—	—	1.00	5.00	6.00
2007	—	—	—	1.00	5.00	6.00

KM# 43 5 GULDEN

11.0000 g., Brass Plated Steel, 26 mm. **Ruler:** Beatrix **Obv:** Head left **Rev:** Crowned shield divides value above date and ribbon **Edge Lettering:** GOD * ZIJ * MET * ONS *

Date	Mintage	F	VF	XF	Unc	BU
1998	607,000	—	—	—	4.50	4.00
1999	999,000	—	—	—	4.50	4.00
2000	9,000	—	—	—	7.50	5.00
2001	9,500	—	—	1.00	4.00	5.00
2002	6,000	—	—	1.00	5.00	6.00
Note: In sets only						
2003	7,000	—	—	1.00	4.00	5.00
2004	102,100	—	—	1.00	4.00	5.00
2005	—	—	—	1.00	4.00	5.00
2006	—	—	—	1.00	4.00	5.00
2007	—	—	—	1.00	4.00	5.00

Netherlands East Indies, (Kingdom of the Netherlands) is the world's largest archipelago extending for more than 3,000 mi. along the equator from the mainland of southeast Asia to Australia. At present time, since the late 1940's, it is known as Indonesia. The Dutch were in control until 1942 when the Japanese invaded. At the end of World War II, with Japanese encouragement, Indonesia declared its independence.

World War II Coinage

Netherlands and Netherlands East Indies coins of the 1941-45 period were struck at U.S. Mints (P - Philadelphia, D – Denver, S – San Francisco) and bear the mint mark and a palm tree (acorn on Homeland issues) flanking the date. The following issues, KM#330 and KM#331, are of the usual Netherlands type, being distinguished from similar 1944-45 issues produced in the name of the Homeland by the presence of the palm tree, but were produced for release in the colony. See other related issues under Curacao and Suriname.

RULER

Dutch, 1816-1942

MINT MARKS

Utrecht

Privy Marks

(a) – Halberd
(b) – Halberd and star
(c) – Sea horse
(d) - Grapes

KINGDOM OF NETHERLANDS

Dutch Administration 1817-1949

DECIMAL COINAGE

KM# 306 1/2 CENT

2.3000 g., Copper, 17 mm. **Ruler:** Wilhelmina I **Obv:** Crowned arms divide date within circle **Obv. Legend:** NEDERLANDSCH INDIE **Rev:** Value and inscription within circle **Edge:** Plain

Date	Mintage	F	VF	XF	Unc	BU
1902(u)	20,000,000	1.00	3.00	8.00	15.00	25.00
1902(u) Proof	—	Value: 75.00				
1908(u)	10,600,000	3.00	6.25	12.50	25.00	60.00
1908(u) Proof	—	Value: 85.00				
1909(u)	4,400,000	6.00	12.50	25.00	45.00	75.00

KM# 314.1 1/2 CENT

2.3000 g., Bronze, 17 mm. **Ruler:** Wilhelmina I **Obv:** Crowned arms divide date within circle **Obv. Legend:** NEDERLANDSCH INDIE **Rev:** Value and inscription within circle **Edge:** Plain **Note:** Mintmaster's mark: Sea horse.

Date	Mintage	F	VF	XF	Unc	BU
1914(u)	50,000,000	0.75	1.50	3.00	6.00	8.00
1916(u)	10,000,000	1.50	3.00	6.00	12.00	15.00
1921(u)	4,000,000	5.00	10.00	20.00	35.00	55.00
1932(u)	10,000,000	1.50	3.00	6.00	12.00	15.00
1933(u)	20,000,000	1.50	3.00	6.00	12.00	15.00

KM# 314.2 1/2 CENT

2.3000 g., Bronze, 17 mm. **Ruler:** Wilhelmina I **Obv:** Crowned arms divide date within circle **Obv. Legend:** NEDERLANDSCH INDIE **Rev:** Inscription and value within circle **Edge:** Plain **Note:** Mintmaster's mark: Grapes.

Date	Mintage	F	VF	XF	Unc	BU
1933(u)	Inc. above	25.00	50.00	100	200	300
1934(u)	30,000,000	0.75	1.50	3.00	6.00	8.00
1935(u)	14,000,000	1.50	2.50	5.00	10.00	12.00
1936(u)	12,000,000	1.50	2.50	5.00	10.00	12.00
1936(u) Proof	—	Value: 35.00				
1937(u)	8,400,000	1.50	2.50	5.00	10.00	25.00
1937(u) Proof	—	Value: 35.00				
1938(u)	3,600,000	3.00	6.00	12.50	25.00	35.00
1939(u)	2,000,000	6.00	12.50	25.00	45.00	60.00
1945P	400,000,000	0.15	0.25	0.50	1.00	1.25

KM# 307.2 CENT

4.8000 g., Copper, 23 mm. **Ruler:** William III **Obv:** Crowned Dutch arms, legend begins and ends beside date **Obv. Legend:** NEDERLANDSCH INDIE **Rev:** Value in Javanese and Malayan text **Edge:** Plain

Date	Mintage	F	VF	XF	Unc	BU
1901(u)	15,000,000	4.00	8.00	15.00	35.00	85.00
1901(u) Proof	—	Value: 175				
1902(u)	10,000,000	4.00	8.00	15.00	30.00	60.00
1907(u)	7,500,000	4.00	8.00	15.00	30.00	55.00
1907(u) Proof	—	Value: 175				
1908(u)	12,500,000	4.00	8.00	15.00	30.00	55.00
1908(u) Proof	—	Value: 165				
1909(u)	7,500,000	4.00	8.00	15.00	30.00	65.00
1909(u) Proof	—	Value: 175				
1912(u)	25,000,000	1.50	3.00	6.00	12.00	25.00

KM# 315 CENT

4.6500 g., Bronze **Ruler:** Wilhelmina I **Obv:** Crowned arms divide date within circle **Obv. Legend:** NEDERLANDSCH INDIE **Rev:** Inscription and value within circle

Date	Mintage	F	VF	XF	Unc	BU
1914(u)	85,000,000	1.00	2.25	4.50	9.00	15.00
1914(u) Proof	—	Value: 45.00				
1916(u)	16,440,000	2.00	4.00	8.00	16.00	25.00
1919(u)	20,000,000	2.00	4.00	8.00	16.00	25.00
1919(u) Proof	—	Value: 65.00				
1920(u)	120,000,000	1.00	2.25	4.50	9.00	8.00
1926(u)	10,000,000	2.00	4.00	8.00	16.00	30.00
1929(u)	50,000,000	1.00	2.50	5.00	10.00	15.00
1929(u) Proof	—	Value: 100				

KM# 317 CENT

4.8000 g., Bronze, 23 mm. **Ruler:** Wilhelmina I **Obv:** 3/4 spray around hole in center with value below **Obv. Legend:** NEDERLANDSCH INDIE **Rev:** Inscription and flowers around hole in center **Edge:** Plain

Date	Mintage	F	VF	XF	Unc	BU
1936(u)	52,000,000	0.50	1.00	1.75	3.50	6.00
1937(u)	120,400,000	0.50	1.00	1.75	3.50	4.50
1937(u) Proof	—	Value: 40.00				
1938(u)	150,000,000	0.50	1.00	1.75	3.50	4.50
1939(u)	81,400,000	0.50	1.00	1.75	3.50	5.00
1942P	100,000,000	0.10	0.25	0.50	1.25	2.00
1945P	335,000,000	—	0.10	0.25	0.50	1.50
1945D	133,800,000	0.10	0.25	0.50	1.25	2.00
1945S	102,568,000	0.10	0.25	0.50	1.25	2.00

KM# 308 2-1/2 CENTS
12.5000 g., Copper, 31 mm. **Ruler:** Wilhelmina I **Obv:** Crowned Dutch arms divide date **Obv. Legend:** NEDERLANDSCH INDIE **Rev:** Value in Javanese and Malayan text **Edge:** Plain

Date	Mintage	F	VF	XF	Unc	BU
1902	6,000,000	5.00	10.00	20.00	40.00	70.00
1907	3,000,000	5.00	10.00	20.00	40.00	75.00
1908	5,940,000	5.00	10.00	20.00	40.00	70.00
1908 Proof	—	Value: 160				
1909	3,060,000	8.00	15.00	30.00	60.00	95.00
1913	4,000,000	8.00	15.00	30.00	60.00	95.00
1913 Proof	—	Value: 160				

KM# 316 2-1/2 CENTS
12.5000 g., Bronze, 31 mm. **Ruler:** Wilhelmina I **Obv:** Crowned Dutch arms divide date **Obv. Legend:** NEDERLANDSCH INDIE **Rev:** Inscription and value within beaded circle **Edge:** Plain

Date	Mintage	F	VF	XF	Unc	BU
1914(u)	22,000,000	1.50	3.00	6.00	12.00	25.00
1914(u)	—	Value: 165				
1915(u)	6,000,000	5.00	10.00	20.00	40.00	70.00
1920(u)	48,000,000	1.50	3.00	6.00	12.00	22.00
1920(u)	—	Value: 165				
1945P	200,000,000	0.25	0.50	1.00	2.00	2.00

KM# 313 5 CENTS
5.0000 g., Copper-Nickel, 21 mm. **Ruler:** Wilhelmina I **Obv:** Crown above hole in center flanked by value and rice stalks **Obv. Legend:** NEDERLANDSCH INDIE **Rev:** Inscription around hole in center flanked by designs **Edge:** Plain

Date	Mintage	F	VF	XF	Unc	BU
1913(u)	60,000,000	1.00	2.00	3.75	7.50	20.00
1913(u) Proof	—	Value: 100				
1921(u)	40,000,000	1.50	3.00	6.00	12.50	28.00
1921(u) Proof	—	Value: 220				
1922(u)	20,000,000	2.50	5.00	10.00	20.00	35.00

KM# 304 1/10 GULDEN
1.2500 g., 0.7200 Silver 0.0289 oz. ASW, 15 mm. **Ruler:** Wilhelmina I **Obv:** Crowned Dutch arms **Obv. Legend:** NEDERL INDIE **Rev:** Inscription and value within circle **Edge:** Reeded

Date	Mintage	F	VF	XF	Unc	BU
1901(u)	5,000,000	2.50	5.00	10.00	20.00	30.00
1901(u) Proof	—	Value: 100				

KM# 309 1/10 GULDEN
1.2500 g., 0.7200 Silver 0.0289 oz. ASW, 15 mm. **Ruler:** Wilhelmina I **Obv:** Crowned arms divide value **Obv. Legend:** NEDERL INDIE **Rev:** Inscription within circle **Edge:** Reeded

Date	Mintage	F	VF	XF	Unc	BU
1903(u)	5,000,000	2.50	5.00	8.00	16.00	22.00
1903(u) Proof	—	Value: 110				
1904(u)	5,000,000	2.50	5.00	8.00	16.00	22.00
1904(u) Proof	—	Value: 100				
1905(u)	5,000,000	2.50	5.00	8.00	16.00	22.00
1906(u)	7,500,000	1.00	2.50	5.00	10.00	15.00
1907(u)	14,000,000	1.00	2.50	5.00	10.00	15.00
1907(u) Proof	—	Value: 60.00				
1908(u)	3,000,000	2.50	5.00	10.00	20.00	30.00
1909(u)	10,000,000	1.00	2.50	5.00	10.00	15.00
1909(u) Proof	—	Value: 110				

KM# 311 1/10 GULDEN
1.2500 g., 0.7200 Silver 0.0289 oz. ASW, 15 mm. **Ruler:** Wilhelmina I **Obv:** Crowned arms divide value **Obv. Legend:** NEDERL INDIE **Rev:** Inscription within circle **Edge:** Reeded **Note:** Wide rims.

Date	Mintage	F	VF	XF	Unc	BU
1910(u)	15,000,000	1.25	2.50	5.00	10.00	20.00
1910(u) Proof	—	Value: 140				
1911(u)	10,000,000	2.50	4.00	8.00	15.00	25.00
1912(u)	25,000,000	0.60	1.50	3.00	7.00	10.00
1913(u)	15,000,000	0.75	1.50	3.00	7.00	12.00
1914(u)	25,000,000	0.60	1.50	3.00	7.00	10.00
1915(u)	15,000,000	0.65	1.50	3.00	7.00	12.00
1918(u)	30,000,000	0.60	1.50	3.00	7.00	12.00
1919(u)	20,000,000	0.60	1.50	3.00	7.00	12.00
1920(u)	8,500,000	1.00	2.00	4.00	8.00	15.00
1928(u)	30,000,000	0.60	1.00	2.00	4.00	10.00
1930(u)	15,000,000	0.60	1.00	2.00	4.00	10.00

KM# 318 1/10 GULDEN
1.2500 g., 0.7200 Silver 0.0289 oz. ASW, 15 mm. **Ruler:** Wilhelmina I **Obv:** Crowned arms divide value **Obv. Legend:** NEDERL INDIE **Rev:** Inscription within circle **Edge:** Reeded **Note:** Narrow rims.

Date	Mintage	F	VF	XF	Unc	BU
1937(u)	20,000,000	0.45	0.75	1.50	2.50	4.00
1937(u) Proof	—	Value: 130				
1938(u)	30,000,000	0.45	0.75	1.50	2.50	4.00
1939(u)	5,500,000	0.75	1.50	3.00	6.00	12.00
1939(u) Proof	—	Value: 130				
1940(u)	10,000,000	0.45	0.75	1.25	2.50	5.00
1941P	41,850,000	BV	0.50	1.00	2.00	3.00
1941S	58,150,000	BV	0.50	1.00	2.00	3.00
1942S	75,000,000	BV	0.50	1.00	2.00	3.00
1945P	100,720,000	BV	0.50	1.00	2.00	3.00
Note: Mint mark horizontal						
1945P	Inc. above	3.00	10.00	15.00	25.00	35.00
Note: Mint mark slanted with three variations						
1945S	19,280,000	BV	0.50	1.00	2.00	3.00

KM# 305 1/4 GULDEN
3.1800 g., 0.7200 Silver 0.0736 oz. ASW, 18.5 mm. **Ruler:** Wilhelmina I **Obv:** Crowned arms **Obv. Legend:** NEDERL INDIE **Rev:** Value in Javanese and Malayan text **Edge:** Reeded

Date	Mintage	F	VF	XF	Unc	BU
1901(u)	2,000,000	10.00	20.00	35.00	70.00	90.00
1901(u) Proof	—	Value: 120				

KM# 310 1/4 GULDEN
3.1800 g., 0.7200 Silver 0.0736 oz. ASW, 15 mm. **Ruler:** Wilhelmina I **Obv:** Crowned arms divide value **Obv. Legend:** NEDERL INDIE **Rev:** Inscription within sun design flanked by small legends at points **Edge:** Reeded **Note:** Like KM#305 but with smaller privy mark and mint mark.

Date	Mintage	F	VF	XF	Unc	BU
1903(u)	2,000,000	3.75	7.50	15.00	30.00	50.00
1903(u) Proof	—	Value: 115				
1904(u)	2,000,000	2.75	7.50	15.00	30.00	45.00
1904(u) Proof	—	Value: 100				
1905(u)	2,000,000	3.75	7.50	15.00	30.00	45.00
1905(u) Proof	—	Value: 170				
1906(u)	4,000,000	2.50	5.00	10.00	20.00	35.00
1907(u)	4,400,000	2.50	5.00	10.00	20.00	35.00
1907(u) Proof	—	Value: 110				
1908(u)	2,000,000	3.75	7.50	15.00	30.00	45.00
1909(u)	4,000,000	2.50	5.00	10.00	20.00	35.00
1909(u) Proof	—	Value: 110				

KM# 312 1/4 GULDEN
3.1800 g., 0.7200 Silver 0.0736 oz. ASW, 15 mm. **Ruler:** Wilhelmina I **Obv:** Crowned arms divide value **Obv. Legend:** NEDERL INDIE **Rev:** Inscription within sun design flanked by small legends at points **Edge:** Reeded

Date	Mintage	F	VF	XF	Unc	BU
1910(u)	6,000,000	2.50	5.00	10.00	20.00	50.00
1910(u) Proof	—	Value: 100				
1911(u)	4,000,000	2.50	5.00	10.00	20.00	50.00
1911(u) Proof	—	Value: 110				
1912(u)	10,000,000	2.50	5.00	10.00	20.00	35.00
1912(u) Proof	—	Value: 400				
1913(u)	6,000,000	2.50	5.00	10.00	20.00	35.00
1914(u)	10,000,000	2.50	5.00	10.00	20.00	35.00
1915(u)	6,000,000	2.50	5.00	10.00	20.00	35.00
1917(u)	12,000,000	2.00	3.75	7.50	15.00	20.00
1919(u)	6,000,000	2.50	5.00	10.00	20.00	35.00
1920(u)	20,000,000	1.35	2.00	4.00	8.00	12.00
1921(u)	24,000,000	1.35	2.00	4.00	8.00	12.00
1929(u)	5,000,000	2.00	3.75	7.50	15.00	20.00
1930(u)	7,000,000	2.00	3.75	7.50	15.00	20.00
1930(u) Proof	—	Value: 160				

KM# 319 1/4 GULDEN
3.1800 g., 0.7200 Silver 0.0736 oz. ASW, 18.8 mm. **Ruler:** Wilhelmina I **Obv:** Crowned arms divide value **Obv. Legend:** NEDERL INDIE **Rev:** Inscription within sun design flanked by small legends at points **Edge:** Reeded **Note:** Narrow rims.

Date	Mintage	F	VF	XF	Unc	BU
1937(u)	8,000,000	BV	1.50	2.50	5.00	8.00
1938(u)	12,000,000	BV	1.50	2.50	5.00	8.00
1939(u)	10,400,000	BV	1.50	2.50	5.00	8.00
1939(u) Proof	—	Value: 80.00				
1941P	34,947,000	BV	BV	1.25	2.50	3.50
1941S	5,053,000	BV	1.50	2.50	5.00	10.00
1942S	32,000,000	—	BV	1.50	2.50	3.50
1945S	56,000,000	—	BV	1.50	2.50	3.50

KM# 330 GULDEN
10.0000 g., 0.7200 Silver 0.2315 oz. ASW, 28 mm. **Ruler:** Wilhelmina I **Obv:** Head left **Obv. Legend:** WILHELMINA KONINGIN DER NEDERLANDEN **Rev:** Crowned arms divide value **Rev. Legend:** MUNT VAN HET KONINGRIJK DER NEDERLANDEN **Edge Lettering:** GOD * ZIJ * MET * ONS *

Date	Mintage	F	VF	XF	Unc	BU
1943D	20,000,000	BV	4.50	7.50	15.00	20.00

KM# 331 2-1/2 GULDEN
25.0000 g., 0.7200 Silver 0.5787 oz. ASW, 38 mm. **Ruler:** Wilhelmina I **Obv:** Head left **Obv. Legend:** WILHELMINA KONINGIN DER NEDERLANDEN **Rev:** Crowned arms divide value **Rev. Legend:** MUNT VAN HET KONINGRIJK DER NEDERLANDEN **Edge Lettering:** GOD * ZIJ * MET * ONS *

Date	Mintage	F	VF	XF	Unc	BU
1943D	2,000,000	—	BV	11.50	18.50	25.00

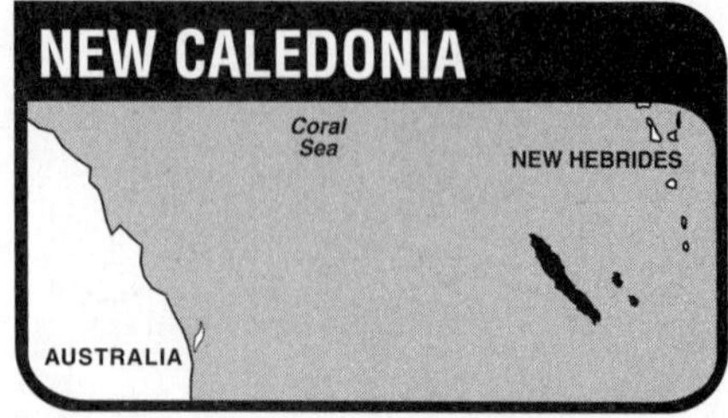

The French Overseas Territory of New Caledonia, is a group of about 25 islands in the South Pacific. They are situated about 750 miles (1,207 km.) east of Australia. The territory, which includes the dependencies of Isle des Pins, Loyalty Islands, Isle Huon, Isles Belep, Isles Chesterfield, Isle Walpole, Wallis and Futuna Islands and has a total land area of 7,358 sq. mi.(19,060 sq. km.) and a population of *156,000. Capital: Noumea. The islands are rich in minerals; New Caledonia has some of the world's largest known deposit of nickel. Nickel, nickel castings, coffee and copra are exported.

The first European to sight New Caledonia was the British navigator Capt. James Cook in 1774. The French took possession in 1853, and established a penal colony on the island in 1864. The European population of the colony remained disproportionately convict until 1897. New Caledonia became an overseas territory within the French Community in 1946, and in 1958 and 1972 chose to remain affiliated with France. Its status changed to that of a French Associated State after 1998.

MINT MARK

Paris, privy marks only

MONETARY SYSTEM

100 Centimes = 1 Franc

FRENCH OVERSEAS TERRITORY

1958-1998

DECIMAL COINAGE

KM# 1 50 CENTIMES

Aluminum, 18 mm. **Obv:** Seated figure holding torch **Rev:** Kagu bird within sprigs below value **Designer:** G.B.L. Bazor

Date	Mintage	F	VF	XF	Unc	BU
1949(a)	1,000,000	—	0.50	1.00	3.50	7.50

KM# 2 FRANC

1.3000 g., Aluminum, 23 mm. **Obv:** Seated figure holding torch **Rev:** Kagu bird within sprigs below value **Designer:** G.B.L. Bazor

Date	Mintage	F	VF	XF	Unc	BU
1949(a)	4,000,000	—	0.25	0.75	2.00	5.00

KM# 8 FRANC

1.3000 g., Aluminum, 23 mm. **Obv:** Seated figure holding torch **Rev:** Kagu bird within sprigs below value **Designer:** G.B.L. Bazor

Date	Mintage	F	VF	XF	Unc	BU
1971(a)	1,000,000	—	0.25	0.75	1.75	4.50

KM# 10 FRANC

1.3000 g., Aluminum, 23 mm. **Obv:** Seated figure holding torch, legend added **Obv. Legend:** I. E. O. M. **Rev:** Kagu bird within sprigs below value **Designer:** G.B.L. Bazor

Date	Mintage	F	VF	XF	Unc	BU
1972(a)	600,000	—	0.25	0.75	1.75	4.00
1973(a)	1,000,000	—	0.10	0.25	1.00	2.00
1977(a)	1,500,000	—	0.10	0.25	1.00	2.00
1981(a)	1,000,000	—	0.10	0.20	0.75	1.50
1982(a)	1,000,000	—	0.10	0.20	0.75	1.50
1983(a)	2,000,000	—	0.10	0.20	0.75	1.50
1984(a)	—	—	0.10	0.20	0.75	1.50
1985(a)	2,000,000	—	0.10	0.20	0.75	1.50
1988(a)	2,000,000	—	0.10	0.20	0.75	1.50
1989(a)	1,000,000	—	0.10	0.20	0.75	1.50
1990(a)	1,500,000	—	0.10	0.20	0.75	1.50
1991(a)	1,600,000	—	0.10	0.20	0.75	1.50
1994(a)	2,000,000	—	0.10	0.20	0.70	1.25
1996(a)	1,900,000	—	0.10	0.20	0.70	1.25
1997(a)	1,200,000	—	0.10	0.20	0.70	1.25
1998(a)	400,000	—	0.10	0.25	0.75	1.50
1999(a)	1,200,000	—	0.10	0.20	0.70	1.25
2000(a)	1,300,000	—	—	0.15	0.50	1.00
2001(a)	100,000	—	—	0.15	0.50	1.25
2002(a)	1,200,000	—	—	0.15	0.50	1.25
2003(a)	2,000,000	—	—	0.15	0.50	1.25
2004(a)	1,200,000	—	—	0.15	0.50	1.25
2005(a)	700,000	—	—	0.15	0.50	1.25

KM# 3 2 FRANCS

2.2600 g., Aluminum, 27 mm. **Obv:** Seated figure holding torch **Rev:** Kagu bird within sprigs below value **Designer:** G.B.L. Bazor

Date	Mintage	F	VF	XF	Unc	BU
1949(a)	3,000,000	—	0.35	1.00	2.50	5.50

KM# 9 2 FRANCS

2.2000 g., Aluminum, 27 mm. **Obv:** Seated figure holding torch **Rev:** Kagu bird within sprigs below value **Designer:** G.B.L. Bazor

Date	Mintage	F	VF	XF	Unc	BU
1971(a)	1,000,000	—	0.35	1.25	2.25	3.50

KM# 14 2 FRANCS

2.2000 g., Aluminum, 27 mm. **Obv:** Seated figure holding torch, legend added **Obv. Legend:** I. E. O. M. **Rev:** Kagu bird and value within sprigs

Date	Mintage	F	VF	XF	Unc	BU
1973(a)	400,000	—	0.20	0.75	2.00	3.00
1977(a)	1,500,000	—	0.20	0.50	1.50	2.50
1982(a)	1,000,000	—	0.20	0.35	1.00	2.25
1983(a)	2,000,000	—	0.20	0.35	0.75	2.00
1987(a)	2,000,000	—	0.20	0.35	0.75	2.00
1989(a)	1,200,000	—	0.20	0.35	0.75	2.00
1990(a)	1,500,000	—	0.20	0.35	0.75	2.00
1991(a)	1,500,000	—	0.20	0.35	0.75	2.00
1995(a)	400,000	—	0.20	0.35	0.75	2.00
1996(a)	900,000	—	0.20	0.35	0.75	2.00
1997(a)	400,000	—	0.20	0.35	0.75	2.00
1998(a)	400,000	—	0.20	0.35	0.85	2.25
1999(a)	800,000	—	0.20	0.35	0.85	2.25
2000(a)	700,000	—	—	0.25	0.75	2.00
2001(a)	800,000	—	—	0.25	0.75	1.50
2002(a)	1,200,000	—	—	0.25	0.75	1.50
2003(a)	2,400,000	—	—	0.20	0.65	1.50
2004(a)	200,000	—	—	0.20	0.65	1.50
2005(a)	530,000	—	—	0.20	0.65	1.50

KM# 4 5 FRANCS

3.7500 g., Aluminum, 31 mm. **Obv:** Seated figure holding torch **Rev:** Kagu bird and value within sprigs **Designer:** G.B.L. Bazor

Date	Mintage	F	VF	XF	Unc	BU
1952(a)	4,000,000	—	0.50	1.50	3.50	6.00

KM# 16 5 FRANCS

3.7500 g., Aluminum, 31 mm. **Obv:** Seated figure holding torch, legend added **Obv. Legend:** I. E. O. M. **Rev:** Kagu bird and value within sprigs **Designer:** G.B.L. Bazor

Date	Mintage	F	VF	XF	Unc	BU
1983(a)	500,000	—	0.45	0.75	2.50	4.50
1986(a)	1,000,000	—	0.45	0.75	2.50	3.50
1989(a)	500,000	—	0.45	0.75	2.50	3.50
1990(a)	500,000	—	0.45	0.75	2.25	3.50
1991(a)	480,000	—	0.45	0.75	2.25	3.50
1992(a)	480,000	—	0.45	0.75	2.00	3.00
1994(a)	1,200,000	—	0.45	0.75	2.00	3.00
1997(a)	240,000	—	0.35	0.65	1.75	3.00
1998(a)	120,000	—	0.35	0.65	1.75	3.00
1999(a)	480,000	—	0.35	0.50	1.50	3.00
2000(a)	400,000	—	0.35	0.50	1.50	3.00
2001(a)	600,000	—	—	0.50	1.00	2.00
2002(a)	480,000	—	—	0.50	1.00	2.00
2003(a)	700,000	—	—	0.40	1.00	2.00
2004(a)	1,000,000	—	—	0.40	1.00	2.00
2005(a)	360,000	—	—	0.40	1.00	2.00

KM# 5 10 FRANCS

6.0000 g., Nickel, 24 mm. **Obv:** Liberty head left **Rev:** Sailboat above value **Designer:** R. Joly

Date	Mintage	F	VF	XF	Unc	BU
1967(a)	400,000	—	1.00	2.00	4.00	7.00
1970(a)	1,000,000	—	0.50	1.00	2.50	5.00

KM# 11 10 FRANCS

6.0000 g., Nickel, 24 mm. **Obv:** Liberty head left **Obv. Legend:** I. E. O. M. **Rev:** Sailboat above value **Designer:** R. Joly

Date	Mintage	F	VF	XF	Unc	BU
1972(a)	600,000	—	0.70	1.50	2.00	5.25
1973(a)	400,000	—	0.70	1.00	2.00	4.25
1977(a)	1,000,000	—	0.70	1.00	1.50	4.00
1983(a)	800,000	—	0.60	0.85	1.50	4.00
1986(a)	1,000,000	—	0.60	0.85	1.50	4.00
1989(a)	500,000	—	0.60	0.85	1.50	4.00
1990(a)	500,000	—	0.60	0.85	1.25	3.75
1991(a)	500,000	—	0.50	0.75	1.25	3.75
1992(a)	500,000	—	0.50	0.75	1.25	3.75
1995(a)	200,000	—	0.50	0.75	1.25	3.50
1996(a)	300,000	—	0.50	0.75	1.25	3.50
1997(a)	300,000	—	0.50	0.75	1.25	3.50
1998(a)	300,000	—	0.50	0.75	1.25	3.50
1999(a)	500,000	—	0.50	0.75	1.25	3.50
2000(a)	350,000	—	—	0.65	1.25	2.75
2001(a)	100,000	—	—	0.65	1.25	2.75
2002(a)	200,000	—	—	0.65	1.25	2.75
2003(a)	800,000	—	—	0.65	1.25	2.75

Date	Mintage	F	VF	XF	Unc	BU
2004(a)	600,000	—	—	0.65	1.25	2.75
2005(a)	64,000	—	—	0.65	1.25	2.75

KM# 6 20 FRANCS

10.0000 g., Nickel, 28.5 mm. **Rev:** Three zebu heads left **Designer:** R. Joly

Date	Mintage	F	VF	XF	Unc	BU
1967(a)	300,000	—	1.25	2.50	5.00	8.50
1970(a)	1,200,000	—	0.60	1.00	3.00	5.50

KM# 12 20 FRANCS

10.0000 g., Nickel, 28.5 mm. **Obv:** Liberty head left **Obv. Legend:** I. O. E. M. **Rev:** Three ox heads above value **Designer:** R. Joly

Date	Mintage	F	VF	XF	Unc	BU
1972(a)	700,000	—	0.85	2.00	3.00	5.00
1977(a)	350,000	—	0.85	2.50	4.00	6.50
1983(a)	600,000	—	0.75	1.75	3.00	5.00
1986(a)	800,000	—	0.75	1.50	2.00	4.50
1990(a)	500,000	—	0.75	1.50	2.00	4.50
1991(a)	500,000	—	0.75	1.50	2.00	4.50
1992(a)	500,000	—	0.75	1.50	2.00	4.50
1996(a)	150,000	—	0.75	1.50	2.00	4.50
1997(a)	—	—	0.75	1.00	1.75	3.25
1999(a)	300,000	—	0.75	15.00	2.00	4.50
2000(a)	250,000	—	0.75	1.50	200	4.50
2001(a)	150,000	—	—	1.00	1.75	3.25
2002(a)	250,000	—	—	1.00	1.75	3.25
2003(a)	250,000	—	—	1.00	1.75	3.25
2004(a)	500,000	—	—	1.00	1.75	3.25
2005(a)	300,000	—	—	1.00	1.75	3.25

KM# 7 50 FRANCS

15.0000 g., Nickel, 33 mm. **Obv:** Liberty head left **Rev:** Small hut within pines and palm, value at bottom **Designer:** R. Joly

Date	Mintage	F	VF	XF	Unc	BU
1967(a)	700,000	—	1.50	3.00	6.50	10.00

KM# 13 50 FRANCS

15.0000 g., Nickel, 33 mm. **Obv:** Liberty head left **Obv. Legend:** I. E. O. M. **Rev:** Hut above value in center of palm and pine trees **Designer:** R. Joly

Date	Mintage	F	VF	XF	Unc	BU
1972(a)	300,000	—	1.25	2.00	5.00	7.00
1983(a)	300,000	—	1.25	2.00	4.50	6.50
1987(a)	300,000	—	1.00	2.00	4.50	6.50
1991(a)	450,000	—	1.00	1.85	3.00	4.25
1992(a)	450,000	—	1.00	1.85	3.00	4.25
1996(a)	—	—	1.00	1.75	3.00	4.25
1997(a)	150,000	—	1.00	1.75	3.00	4.25
2000(a)	1,000,000	—	1.00	1.75	3.00	4.25
2001(a)	100,000	—	—	1.25	2.00	4.00
2002(a)	—	—	—	1.25	2.00	4.00
2003(a)	75,000	—	—	1.25	2.00	4.00
2004(a)	150,000	—	—	1.25	2.00	4.00
2005(a)	54,000	—	—	1.25	2.00	4.00

KM# 15 100 FRANCS

10.0000 g., Nickel-Bronze, 30 mm. **Obv:** Liberty head left **Rev:** Hut above value in center of palm and pine trees **Designer:** R. Joly

Date	Mintage	F	VF	XF	Unc	BU
1976(a)	2,000,000	—	1.50	2.50	6.00	9.00
1984(a)	600,000	—	1.50	2.50	6.00	8.50
1987(a)	800,000	—	1.50	2.50	5.50	7.00
1988(a)	—	—	1.50	2.50	5.50	7.00
1991(a)	500,000	—	1.35	2.25	4.00	6.00
1992(a)	500,000	—	1.35	2.25	4.00	6.00
1994(a)	250,000	—	1.35	2.25	4.00	6.00
1995(a)	—	—	1.35	2.00	3.50	5.50
1996(a)	250,000	—	1.35	2.25	4.00	6.00
1997(a)	190,000	—	1.35	2.00	3.50	5.50
1998(a)	310,000	—	1.25	2.00	3.50	5.50
1999(a)	400,000	—	1.25	2.00	3.50	5.50
2000(a)	300,000	—	1.25	2.00	3.50	5.50
2001(a)	100,000	—	—	1.50	3.00	5.00
2002(a)	620,000	—	—	1.50	3.00	6.00
2003(a)	500,000	—	—	1.50	3.00	5.00
2004(a)	500,000	—	—	1.50	3.00	5.00
2005(a)	180,000	—	—	1.50	3.00	5.00

NEW GUINEA

Spanish navigator Jorge de Menezes, who landed on the northwest shore in 1527, discovered New Guinea, the world's largest island after Greenland. European interests, attracted by exaggerated estimates of the resources of the area, resulted in the island being claimed in part by Spain, the Netherlands, Great Britain and Germany.

RULER

British, 1910-1952

MONETARY SYSTEM

12 Pence = 1 Shilling
20 Shillings = 1 Pound

AUSTRALIAN TERRITORY

STANDARD COINAGE

12 Pence = 1 Shilling; 20 Shillings = 1 Pound

KM# 1 1/2 PENNY

Copper-Nickel **Obv:** Hole in center flanked by scepters with crown above and value below **Rev:** Hole in center flanked by designs **Designer:** G.E. Kruger-Gray **Note:** Entire mintage returned to Melbourne Mint which later sold 400 pcs. in sets with KM#2. The balance of mintage was destroyed.

Date	Mintage	F	VF	XF	Unc	BU
1929	25,000	—	—	275	495	650
1929 Proof	—	Value: 450				

KM# 2 PENNY

Copper-Nickel **Obv:** Hole in center flanked by scepters with crown above and value below **Rev:** Hole in center flanked by designs **Designer:** G.E. Kruger-Gray **Note:** Entire mintage returned to Melbourne Mint which later sold 400 pcs. in sets with KM#1. The balance of mintage was destroyed.

Date	Mintage	F	VF	XF	Unc	BU
1929	63,000	—	—	275	495	650
1929 Proof	—	Value: 800				

KM# 6 PENNY

Bronze **Obv:** Hole in center flanked by swimming birds with crown above and monogram below **Rev:** Artistic design around hole in center **Designer:** G.E. Kruger-Gray

Date	Mintage	F	VF	XF	Unc	BU
1936	360,000	1.20	1.50	2.50	5.00	10.00
1936 Proof	—	Value: 300				

KM# 7 PENNY

Bronze **Obv:** Hole in center flanked by swimming birds with crown above and monogram below **Rev:** Artistic design around hole in center **Designer:** G.E. Kruger-Gray

Date	Mintage	F	VF	XF	Unc	BU
1938	360,000	2.50	5.00	9.50	15.00	20.00
1944	240,000	1.50	3.00	6.00	10.00	15.00

KM# 3 3 PENCE

Copper-Nickel **Obv:** Hole in center divides date with crown above and monogram below **Rev:** Square-star design around hole in center **Designer:** G.E. Kruger-Gray

Date	Mintage	F	VF	XF	Unc	BU
1935	1,200,000	2.50	5.00	10.00	20.00	30.00
1935 Proof	—	Value: 250				

KM# 10 3 PENCE

Copper-Nickel **Obv:** Hole in center divides date with crown above and monogram below **Rev:** Square-star design around hole in center **Designer:** G.E. Kruger-Gray

Date	Mintage	F	VF	XF	Unc	BU
1944	500,000	2.00	4.00	8.50	20.00	30.00

KM# 4 6 PENCE

Copper-Nickel **Obv:** Hole in center divides date with crown above and monogram below **Rev:** Star design around hole in center **Designer:** G.E. Kruger-Gray

Date	Mintage	F	VF	XF	Unc	BU
1935	2,000,000	2.00	4.00	8.00	22.50	32.50
1935 Proof	—	Value: 250				

KM# 9 6 PENCE

Copper-Nickel **Obv:** Hole in center divides date with crown above and monogram below **Rev:** Star design around hole in center **Designer:** G.E. Kruger-Gray

Date	Mintage	F	VF	XF	Unc	BU
1943	130,000	3.50	6.00	15.00	40.00	55.00

KM# 5 SHILLING

5.3800 g., 0.9250 Silver 0.1600 oz. ASW, 23.5 mm. **Obv:** Hole in center flanked by crossed scepters with crown above and star below **Rev:** Hole in center flanked by artistic designs **Designer:** G.E. Kruger-Gray

Date	Mintage	F	VF	XF	Unc	BU
1935	2,100,000	BV	2.50	3.50	6.00	7.50
1936	1,360,000	BV	2.50	3.50	6.00	7.50

KM# 8 SHILLING

5.3800 g., 0.9250 Silver 0.1600 oz. ASW, 23.5 mm. **Obv:** Hole in center flanked by crossed scepters with crown above and star below **Rev:** Hole in center flanked by artistic designs **Designer:** G.E. Kruger-Gray

Date	Mintage	F	VF	XF	Unc	BU
1938	3,400,000	BV	2.50	3.50	6.00	7.50
1945	2,000,000	BV	2.50	3.50	6.00	7.50

NEW HEBRIDES

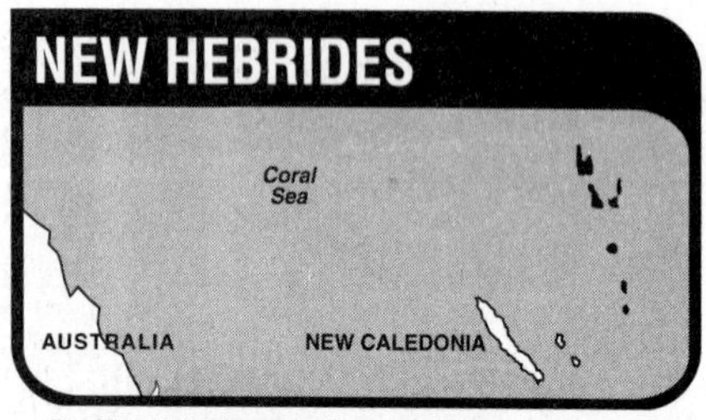

The New Hebrides were discovered by Portuguese navigator Pedro de Quiros in 1606, visited by French explorer Bougainville in 1768, and named by British navigator Capt. James Cook in 1774. Ships of all nations converged on the islands to trade for sandalwood, prompting France and Britain to relinquish their individual claims and declare the islands a neutral zone in 1878. The New Hebrides were placed under the control of a mixed Anglo-French commission of naval officers during the native uprisings of 1887, until achieving independence as Vanuatu, within the Commonwealth of nations on September 30, 1980.

MINT MARK

(a) - Paris, privy marks only

MONETARY SYSTEM

100 Centimes = 1 Franc

FRENCH/BRITISH CONDOMINIUM
(Jointly Governed Territory)

STANDARD COINAGE

KM# 4.1 FRANC

Nickel-Brass **Obv:** Liberty head left, date below **Obv. Legend:** REPVBLIQVE FRANCAISE **Rev:** Frigate bird above value **Designer:** R. Joly

Date	Mintage	F	VF	XF	Unc	BU
1970(a)	435,000	—	0.25	0.50	0.85	1.75

KM# 4.2 FRANC

Nickel-Brass **Obv:** I.E.O.M. below head **Obv. Legend:** REPVBLIQVE FRANCAISE **Rev:** Frigate bird above value **Designer:** R. Joly

Date	Mintage	F	VF	XF	Unc	BU
1975(a)	350,000	—	0.20	0.40	0.75	—
1978(a)	200,000	—	0.20	0.40	0.75	—
1979(a)	350,000	—	0.20	0.40	0.75	—
1982(a)	—	—	0.20	0.40	0.75	—

KM# 5.1 2 FRANCS

3.0000 g., Nickel-Brass **Obv:** Liberty head left, date below **Obv. Legend:** REPVBLIQVE FRANCAISE **Rev:** Frigate bird above value **Designer:** R. Joly

Date	Mintage	F	VF	XF	Unc	BU
1970(a)	264,000	—	0.50	0.75	1.50	2.50

KM# 5.2 2 FRANCS

Nickel-Brass **Obv:** Liberty head left, I.E.O.M. and date below head **Obv. Legend:** REPVBLIQVE FRANCAISE **Rev:** Frigate bird above value **Designer:** R. Joly

Date	Mintage	F	VF	XF	Unc	BU
1973(a)	200,000	—	0.20	0.50	1.00	—
1975(a)	300,000	—	0.20	0.50	1.00	—
1978(a)	150,000	—	0.20	0.50	1.00	—
1979(a)	250,000	—	0.20	0.50	1.00	—

KM# 6.1 5 FRANCS

Nickel-Brass **Obv:** Liberty head left, date below **Obv. Legend:** REPVBLIQVE FRANCAISE **Rev:** Frigate bird above value **Designer:** R. Joly

Date	Mintage	F	VF	XF	Unc	BU
1970(a)	375,000	—	0.50	0.75	1.65	2.75

KM# 6.2 5 FRANCS

Nickel-Brass **Obv:** Liberty head left, I.E.O.M. and date below head **Obv. Legend:** REPVBLIQVE FRANCAISE **Rev:** Frigate bird above value **Designer:** R. Joly

Date	Mintage	F	VF	XF	Unc	BU
1975(a)	350,000	—	0.30	0.75	1.25	—
1979(a)	250,000	—	0.30	0.75	1.25	—

KM# 2.1 10 FRANCS

Nickel **Obv:** Liberty head left, date below **Obv. Legend:** REPVBLIQVE FRANCAISE **Rev:** Mask left flanked by designs with value below **Designer:** R. Joly

Date	Mintage	F	VF	XF	Unc	BU
1967(a)	200,000	—	0.30	1.00	1.85	3.00
1970(a)	400,000	—	0.30	1.00	1.85	3.00

KM# 2.2 10 FRANCS

6.0000 g., Nickel **Obv:** Liberty head left, I.E.O.M. and date below head **Obv. Legend:** REPVBLIQVE FRANCAISE **Rev:** Mask left flanked by designs with value below **Designer:** R. Joly

Date	Mintage	F	VF	XF	Unc	BU
1973(a)	200,000	—	0.30	1.15	1.85	2.75
1975(a)	300,000	—	0.30	1.15	1.85	2.75
1977(a)	200,000	—	0.30	1.15	1.85	2.75
1979(a)	400,000	—	0.30	1.15	1.85	2.75

KM# 3.1 20 FRANCS

Nickel **Obv:** Liberty head left, date below **Obv. Legend:** REPVBLEQVE FRANCAISE **Rev:** Mask left flanked by designs with value below **Designer:** R. Joly

Date	Mintage	F	VF	XF	Unc	BU
1967(a)	250,000	—	0.60	1.25	2.25	4.00
1970(a)	300,000	—	0.60	1.25	2.25	4.00

KM# 3.2 20 FRANCS

Nickel **Obv:** Liberty head left, I.E.O.M. and date below head **Obv. Legend:** REPVBLIQVE FRANCAISE **Rev:** Mask left flanked by designs, value at bottom **Designer:** R. Joly

Date	Mintage	F	VF	XF	Unc	BU
1973(a)	300,000	—	0.60	1.25	2.25	3.25
1975(a)	150,000	—	0.60	1.25	2.25	3.25
1977(a)	150,000	—	0.60	1.25	2.25	3.25
1979(a)	300,000	—	0.60	1.25	2.25	3.25

KM# 7 50 FRANCS

Nickel **Obv:** Liberty head left, I.E.O.M. and date below head **Obv. Legend:** REPVBLIQVE FRANCAISE **Rev:** Scepter above value **Designer:** R. Joly

Date	Mintage	F	VF	XF	Unc	BU
1972(a)	200,000	—	1.00	2.00	3.00	5.00

KM# 1 100 FRANCS

25.0000 g., 0.8350 Silver 0.6711 oz. ASW **Obv:** Liberty head left, date below **Obv. Legend:** REPVBLIQVE FRANCAISE **Rev:** Scepter above value **Designer:** R. Joly

Date	Mintage	F	VF	XF	Unc	BU
1966(a)	200,000	—	—	—	12.00	20.00

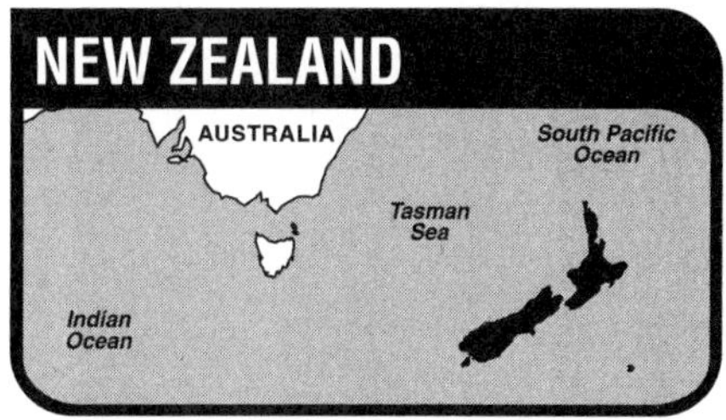

New Zealand, a parliamentary state located in the Southwest Pacific 1,250 miles (2,011 km.) east of Australia, has an area of 103,883 sq. mi. (268,680 sq. km.) and a population of *3.4 million. Capital: Wellington. Wool, meat, dairy products and some manufactured items are exported.

The first European to sight New Zealand was the Dutch navigator Abel Tasman in 1642. The islands were explored by British navigator Capt. James Cook who surveyed it in 1769 and annexed the land to Great Britain. The British government disavowed the annexation and for the next 70 years the only white settlers to arrive were adventurers attracted by the prospects of lumbering, sealing and whaling. Great Britain annexed the land in 1840 by treaty with the native chiefs and made it a dependency of New South Wales. The colony was granted self-government in1852, a ministerial form of government in 1856, and full dominion status on Sept. 26, 1907. Full internal and external autonomy, which New Zealand had in effect possessed for many years, was formally extended in 1947.New Zealand is a member of the Commonwealth of Nations. Elizabeth II is Head of State as Queen of New Zealand.

Prior to 1933 British coins were the official legal tender but Australian coins were accepted in small transactions. Currency fluctuations caused a distinctive New Zealand coinage to be introduced in 1933. The 1935 Waitangi crown and proof set were originally intended to mark the introduction but delays caused their date to be changed to 1935. The 1940 half crown marked the centennial of British rule, the 1949 and 1953 crowns commemorated Royal visits and the 1953 proof set marked the coronation of Queen Elizabeth.

Decimal Currency was introduced in 1967 with special sets commemorating the last issued of pound sterling (1965) and the first of the decimal issues. Since then dollars and set of coins have been issued nearly every year.

RULER

British

MINTS

(l) – British Royal Mint (Llantrisant)
(c) – Royal Australian Mint (Canberra)
(o) – Royal Canadian Mint
(n) – Norwegian Mint
(p) – South African Mint (Pretoria)

MONETARY SYSTEM

4 Farthings = 1 Penny
12 Pence = 1 Shilling
20 Shillings = 1 Pound

STATE

1907 - present

POUND STERLING COINAGE

KM# 12 1/2 PENNY

5.8000 g., Bronze, 25.3 mm. **Ruler:** George VI **Obv:** Head left **Rev:** Hei Tiki **Designer:** L.C. Mitchell

Date	Mintage	F	VF	XF	Unc	BU
1940	3,432,000	0.20	0.50	8.00	20.00	40.00
1940 Proof; 5 known	—	Value: 1,000				
1941	960,000	0.10	0.25	8.00	50.00	70.00
1941 Proof	—	Value: 275				
1942	1,920,000	1.00	2.50	30.00	100	230
1944	2,035,000	0.10	0.25	7.00	15.00	35.00
1945	1,516,000	0.10	0.25	7.00	15.00	35.00
1945 Proof	—	Value: 210				
1946	3,120,000	0.10	0.25	5.00	12.50	28.00
1946 Proof	—	Value: 210				
1947	2,726,400	0.10	0.25	5.00	12.50	22.00
1947 Proof	—	Value: 180				

KM# 20 1/2 PENNY

Bronze, 25.4 mm. **Ruler:** George VI **Obv:** Head left **Rev:** Hei Tiki **Designer:** L.C. Mitchell

Date	Mintage	F	VF	XF	Unc	BU
1949	1,766,400	0.10	0.25	5.00	12.50	22.00
1949 Proof	—	Value: 180				
1950	1,425,600	0.10	0.25	6.00	15.00	35.00
1950 Proof	—	Value: 210				
1951	2,342,400	0.10	0.25	4.00	8.00	12.00
1951 Proof	—	Value: 180				
1952	2,400,000	0.10	0.20	3.00	5.00	8.00
1952 Proof	—	Value: 180				

KM# 23.1 1/2 PENNY

Bronze, 25.4 mm. **Ruler:** Elizabeth II **Obv:** Laureate bust right without shoulder strap **Obv. Designer:** Mary Gillick **Rev:** Hei Tiki

Date	Mintage	F	VF	XF	Unc	BU
1953	720,000	0.20	0.50	5.00	12.50	20.00
1953 Proof	7,000	Value: 5.00				
1953 Matte proof	—	Value: 110				
1954	240,000	3.00	6.00	40.00	85.00	125
1954 Proof	—	Value: 170				
1955	240,000	3.00	6.00	40.00	85.00	125
1955	—	Value: 170				

KM# 23.2 1/2 PENNY

5.6000 g., Bronze, 25.4 mm. **Ruler:** Elizabeth II **Obv:** Laureate bust right with shoulder strap **Rev:** Hei Tiki **Designer:** L.C. Mitchell

Date	Mintage	F	VF	XF	Unc	BU
1956	1,200,000	0.10	0.25	4.00	10.00	18.00
1956 Proof	—	Value: 150				
1957	1,440,000	0.10	0.25	4.00	10.00	18.00
1957 Proof	—	Value: 150				
1958	1,920,000	0.10	0.25	4.00	10.00	18.00
1958 Proof	—	Value: 150				
1959	1,920,000	0.10	0.20	3.00	8.00	17.00
1959 Proof	—	Value: 150				
1960	2,400,000	0.10	0.20	2.00	4.00	8.00
1960 Proof	—	Value: 150				
1961	2,880,000	0.10	0.15	4.00	7.00	3.00
1961 Proof	—	Value: 150				
1962	2,880,000	0.10	0.15	6.00	7.00	3.00
1962 Proof	—	Value: 150				
1963	1,680,000	0.10	0.15	0.30	1.00	2.00
1963 Proof	—	Value: 150				
1964	2,885,000	0.10	0.15	0.20	0.75	2.50
1964 Proof	—	Value: 100				
1965	5,200,000	0.10	0.15	0.20	0.50	2.50
1965 Prooflike	25,000	—	—	—	—	1.00
1965 Proof	10	—	—	—	—	—

KM# 13 PENNY

9.5600 g., Bronze, 31 mm. **Ruler:** George VI **Obv:** Head left **Obv. Designer:** T.H. Paget **Rev:** Tui bird sitting on branch **Rev. Designer:** L.C. Mitchell

Date	Mintage	F	VF	XF	Unc	BU
1940	5,424,000	0.20	0.50	8.00	25.00	45.00
1940 Proof	—	Value: 1,200				
Note: 5 known						
1941	1,200,000	0.20	0.50	30.00	100	175
1942	3,120,000	1.00	5.00	35.00	110	195
1942 Proof	—	Value: 350				
1943	8,400,000	0.20	0.40	8.00	25.00	45.00
1943 Proof	—	Value: 300				
1944	3,696,000	0.20	0.40	8.00	25.00	45.00
1944 Proof	—	Value: 300				
1945	4,764,000	0.20	0.40	8.00	25.00	45.00
1945 Proof	—	Value: 300				
1946	6,720,000	0.20	0.40	6.00	15.00	25.00
1946 Proof	—	Value: 300				
1947	5,880,000	0.20	0.40	5.00	12.50	22.00
1947 Proof	—	Value: 300				

KM# 13a PENNY

Bronze, 31 mm. **Ruler:** George VI **Obv:** Head left **Obv. Designer:** T.H. Paget **Rev:** Tui bird sitting on branch **Note:** Burnished

Date	Mintage	F	VF	XF	Unc	BU
1945	—	—	—	100	180	250

Note: Struck in error by the Royal Mint on Great Britain blanks

KM# 21 PENNY

Bronze, 31 mm. **Ruler:** George VI **Obv:** Head left **Obv. Designer:** T.H. Paget **Rev:** Tui bird sitting on branch **Rev. Designer:** L.C. Mitchell

Date	Mintage	F	VF	XF	Unc	BU
1949	2,016,000	0.20	0.40	5.00	12.50	25.00
1949 Proof	—	Value: 300				
1950	5,784,000	0.20	0.40	5.00	12.50	20.00
1950 Proof	—	Value: 210				
1951	6,888,000	0.20	0.40	5.00	10.00	20.00
1951 Proof	—	Value: 210				
1952	10,800,000	0.20	0.40	5.00	10.00	20.00
1952 Proof	—	Value: 190				

KM# 24.1 PENNY

9.4000 g., Bronze, 31 mm. **Ruler:** Elizabeth II **Obv:** Laureate bust right without shoulder strap **Obv. Designer:** Mary Gillick **Rev:** Tui bird sitting on branch **Rev. Designer:** L.C. Mitchell

Date	Mintage	F	VF	XF	Unc	BU
1953	2,400,000	0.20	0.40	5.00	10.00	20.00
1953 Proof	7,000	Value: 10.00				
1953 Matte proof	—	Value: 110				
1954	1,080,000	1.00	3.00	25.00	50.00	120
1954 Proof	—	Value: 210				
1955	3,720,000	0.20	0.30	3.00	10.00	20.00
1955 Proof	—	Value: 190				
1956	Inc. below	25.00	45.00	350	700	1,100

KM# 24.2 PENNY

9.5000 g., Bronze, 31 mm. **Ruler:** Elizabeth II **Obv:** Laureate bust right with shoulder strap **Obv. Designer:** Mary Gillick **Rev:** Tui bird sitting on branch **Rev. Designer:** L.C. Mitchell

Date	Mintage	F	VF	XF	Unc	BU
1956	3,600,000	0.20	0.30	3.00	8.00	16.00
1956 Proof	—	Value: 190				
1957	2,400,000	0.20	0.30	3.00	8.00	16.00
1957 Proof	—	Value: 150				
1958	10,800,000	0.20	0.30	3.00	8.00	16.00
1958 Proof	—	Value: 190				
1959	8,400,000	0.20	0.30	3.00	8.00	16.00

Date	Mintage	F	VF	XF	Unc	BU
1959 Proof	—	Value: 190				
1960	7,200,000	0.20	0.30	2.00	4.00	6.50
1960 Proof	—	Value: 170				
1961	7,200,000	0.20	0.30	1.00	2.00	4.00
1961 Proof	—	Value: 170				
1962	6,000,000	—	0.20	1.00	2.00	4.00
1962 Proof	—	Value: 170				
1963	2,400,000	—	0.20	0.50	1.00	2.50
1963 Proof	—	Value: 170				
1964	18,000,000	—	0.20	0.25	0.50	1.00
1964 Proof	—	Value: 170				
1965	200,000	—	—	—	5.00	6.00
1965 Prooflike	25,000	—	—	—	—	5.00
1965 Proof	10	—	—	—	—	—

KM# 1 3 PENCE

0.5000 Silver, 16.3 mm. **Ruler:** George V **Subject:** Crossed Patu **Obv:** Crowned bust left **Obv. Designer:** Percy Metcalfe **Rev:** Crossed patu flanked by value and date **Rev. Designer:** G.E. Kruger-Gray

Date	Mintage	F	VF	XF	Unc	BU
1933	6,000,000	1.00	3.00	10.00	20.00	40.00
1933 Proof	Est. 20	Value: 600				
1934	6,000,000	1.00	3.00	10.00	20.00	40.00
1934 Proof	Est. 20	Value: 1,700				
1935	40,000	100	220	500	900	1,250
1935 Proof	364	Value: 1,400				
1936	2,760,000	1.00	3.00	12.00	22.50	50.00
1936 Proof	—	Value: 600				

KM# 7 3 PENCE

1.4000 g., 0.5000 Silver 0.0225 oz. ASW, 16.3 mm. **Ruler:** George VI **Subject:** Crossed Patu **Obv:** Head left **Obv. Designer:** T.H. Paget **Rev:** Crossed patu flanked by value and date **Rev. Designer:** G.E. Kruger-Gray

Date	Mintage	F	VF	XF	Unc	BU
1937	2,880,000	1.00	3.00	10.00	20.00	45.00
1937 Proof	Est. 200	Value: 400				
1939	3,000,000	1.00	3.00	10.00	20.00	45.00
1939 Proof	—	Value: 550				
1940	2,000,000	1.00	3.00	12.00	25.00	50.00
1940 Proof	—	Value: 550				
1941	1,760,000	2.00	20.00	70.00	200	400
1941 Proof	—	Value: 500				
1942	3,120,000	1.00	3.00	10.00	20.00	40.00
1942 With 1 dot	Est. 250,000	4.00	60.00	200	400	600
1943	4,400,000	1.00	2.00	6.00	15.00	35.00
1944	2,840,000	1.00	2.50	6.00	15.00	35.00
1944 Proof	—	Value: 500				
1945	2,520,000	1.00	2.00	6.00	15.00	27.50
1945 Proof	—	Value: 500				
1946	6,080,000	1.00	2.00	6.00	15.00	25.00
1946 Proof	—	Value: 450				

KM# 7a 3 PENCE

Copper-Nickel, 16.3 mm. **Ruler:** George VI **Obv:** Head left **Obv. Designer:** T.H. Paget **Rev:** Crossed patu flanked by value and date **Rev. Designer:** G.E. Kruger-Gray

Date	Mintage	F	VF	XF	Unc	BU
1947	6,400,000	0.10	1.00	6.00	15.00	30.00
1947 Proof	Est. 20	Value: 400				

KM# 15 3 PENCE

1.4000 g., Copper-Nickel, 16.3 mm. **Ruler:** George VI **Obv:** Head left **Obv. Designer:** T.H. Paget **Rev:** Crossed patu flanked by value and date **Rev. Designer:** G.E. Kruger-Gray

Date	Mintage	F	VF	XF	Unc	BU
1948	4,000,000	0.10	1.00	6.00	15.00	30.00
1948 Proof	—	Value: 250				
1950	800,000	1.00	7.50	50.00	100	200
1950 Proof	—	Value: 300				
1951	3,600,000	0.10	0.75	3.00	6.00	12.00
1951 Proof	—	Value: 225				

Date	Mintage	F	VF	XF	Unc	BU
1952	8,000,000	0.10	0.75	3.00	6.00	10.00
1952 Proof	—	Value: 225				

KM# 25.1 3 PENCE

1.4000 g., Copper-Nickel, 16.3 mm. **Ruler:** Elizabeth II **Obv:** Laureate bust right without shoulder strap **Obv. Designer:** Mary Gillick **Rev:** Crossed patu flanked by value and date **Rev. Designer:** G.E. Kruger-Gray

Date	Mintage	F	VF	XF	Unc	BU
1953	4,000,000	0.10	0.75	3.00	6.00	12.00
1953 Proof	7,000	Value: 7.00				
1953 Matte proof	—	Value: 130				
1954	4,000,000	0.10	2.00	3.00	6.00	10.00
1954 Proof	—	Value: 225				
1955	4,000,000	0.10	0.75	3.00	6.00	10.00
1955 Proof	—	Value: 225				
1956	Inc. below	2.50	6.00	125	220	400
1956 Proof	—	Value: 300				

KM# 25.2 3 PENCE

1.4000 g., Copper-Nickel, 16.3 mm. **Ruler:** Elizabeth II **Obv:** Laureate bust right with shoulder strap **Obv. Designer:** Mary Gillick **Rev:** Crossed patu flanked by value and date **Rev. Designer:** G.E. Kruger-Gray

Date	Mintage	F	VF	XF	Unc	BU
1956	4,800,000	0.10	0.15	1.00	4.00	8.00
1956 Proof	—	Value: 225				
1957	8,000,000	0.10	0.15	0.50	2.00	4.00
1957 Proof	—	Value: 225				
1958	4,800,000	0.10	0.15	1.00	4.00	8.00
1958 Proof	—	Value: 225				
1959	4,000,000	0.10	0.15	1.00	4.00	8.00
1959 Proof	—	Value: 225				
1960	4,000,000	0.10	0.15	0.50	1.00	2.00
1960 Proof	—	Value: 225				
1961	4,800,000	0.10	0.15	0.50	2.00	4.00
1961 Proof	—	Value: 225				
1962	6,000,000	0.10	0.15	0.20	0.75	1.25
1962 Proof	—	Value: 225				
1963	4,000,000	0.10	0.15	0.20	0.75	1.25
1963 Proof	—	Value: 225				
1964	6,400,000	0.10	0.15	0.20	0.40	0.75
1964 Proof	—	Value: 175				
1965	4,200,000	—	0.10	0.20	0.40	0.75
1965 Prooflike	25,000	—	—	—	—	1.00
1965 Proof	10	—	—	—	—	—

KM# 2 6 PENCE

2.8300 g., 0.5000 Silver 0.0455 oz. ASW, 19.3 mm. **Ruler:** George V **Obv:** Crowned bust left **Obv. Designer:** Percy Metcalfe **Rev:** Huia bird sitting on branch **Rev. Designer:** G.E. Kruger-Gray

Date	Mintage	F	VF	XF	Unc	BU
1933	3,000,000	1.00	8.00	25.00	60.00	100
1933 Proof	20	Value: 750				
1934	3,600,000	1.00	8.00	25.00	60.00	100
1934 Proof	20	Value: 1,750				
1935	560,000	2.00	15.00	75.00	175	325
1935 Proof	364	Value: 500				
1936	1,480,000	1.00	12.00	35.00	70.00	125
1936 Proof	—	—	—	—	—	—

KM# 8 6 PENCE

2.8300 g., 0.5000 Silver 0.0455 oz. ASW, 19.3 mm. **Ruler:** George VI **Obv:** Head left **Obv. Designer:** T.H. Paget **Rev:** Huia bird sitting on branch **Rev. Designer:** G.E. Kruger-Gray

Date	Mintage	F	VF	XF	Unc	BU
1937	1,280,000	1.00	8.00	30.00	65.00	125
1937 Proof	Est. 200	Value: 350				
1939	700,000	1.50	12.00	35.00	70.00	150
1939 Proof	—	Value: 350				

Date	Mintage	F	VF	XF	Unc	BU
1940	800,000	1.50	8.00	35.00	70.00	150
1940 Proof	—	Value: 350				
1941	440,000	2.00	35.00	120	250	475
1941 Proof	—	Value: 550				
1942	360,000	2.00	35.00	120	250	475
1943	1,800,000	1.00	7.00	20.00	45.00	100
1944	1,160,000	1.50	7.00	20.00	45.00	100
1944 Proof	—	Value: 300				
1945	940,000	1.50	7.00	20.00	45.00	100
1945 Proof	—	Value: 300				
1946	—	Value: 300				
1946	2,120,000	1.00	8.00	20.00	45.00	60.00

KM# 8a 6 PENCE

Copper-Nickel, 19.3 mm. **Ruler:** George VI **Obv:** Head left **Obv. Designer:** T.H. Paget **Rev:** Huia bird sitting on branch **Rev. Designer:** G.E. Kruger-Gray

Date	Mintage	F	VF	XF	Unc	BU
1947	3,200,000	0.20	5.00	20.00	40.00	80.00
1947 Proof	Est. 20	Value: 300				

KM# 16 6 PENCE

Copper-Nickel, 19.3 mm. **Ruler:** George VI **Obv:** Head left **Obv. Designer:** T.H. Paget **Rev:** Huia bird sitting on branch **Rev. Designer:** G.E. Kruger-Gray

Date	Mintage	F	VF	XF	Unc	BU
1948	2,000,000	0.20	5.00	20.00	45.00	85.00
1948 Proof	—	Value: 275				
1950	800,000	2.00	15.00	60.00	125	220
1950 Proof	—	Value: 275				
1951	1,800,000	0.20	1.00	2.50	4.00	6.00
1951 Proof	—	Value: 275				
1952	3,200,000	0.20	6.00	15.00	30.00	50.00
1952 Proof	—	Value: 225				

KM# 26.1 6 PENCE

Copper-Nickel, 19.3 mm. **Ruler:** Elizabeth II **Obv:** Laureate bust right without shoulder strap **Obv. Designer:** Mary Gillick **Rev:** Huia bird sitting on branch **Rev. Designer:** G.E. Kruger-Gray

Date	Mintage	F	VF	XF	Unc	BU
1953	1,200,000	0.20	3.00	8.00	15.00	22.50
1953 Proof	7,000	Value: 7.00				
1953 Matte proof	—	—	—	—	125	—
1954	1,200,000	0.20	3.00	8.00	20.00	35.00
1954 Proof	—	Value: 175				
1955	1,600,000	0.20	3.00	8.00	20.00	35.00
1955 Proof	—	Value: 200				
1957	Inc. below	5.00	17.50	150	400	650
1957 Proof	—	Value: 600				

KM# 26.2 6 PENCE

2.8000 g., Copper-Nickel, 19.3 mm. **Ruler:** Elizabeth II **Obv:** Laureate bust right with shoulder strap **Obv. Designer:** Mary Gillick **Rev:** Huia bird sitting on branch **Rev. Designer:** G.E. Kruger-Gray

Date	Mintage	F	VF	XF	Unc	BU
1956	2,000,000	0.20	2.00	5.00	10.00	22.50
1956 Proof	—	Value: 200				
1957	2,400,000	0.10	0.20	3.00	5.00	10.00
1957 Proof	—	Value: 200				
1958	3,000,000	0.10	0.20	3.00	5.00	10.00
1958 Proof	—	Value: 200				
1959	2,000,000	0.10	0.15	1.00	5.00	10.00
1959 Proof	—	Value: 200				
1960	1,600,000	0.10	0.15	1.00	2.00	4.00
1960 Proof	—	Value: 200				
1961	800,000	0.10	0.15	1.00	2.00	4.00
1961 Proof	—	Value: 200				

Date	Mintage	F	VF	XF	Unc	BU
1962	1,200,000	0.10	0.15	1.00	2.50	6.00
1962 Proof	—	Value: 200				
1963	800,000	0.10	0.15	0.75	2.00	4.00
1963 Proof	—	Value: 200				
1964	3,800,000	—	0.10	0.15	0.50	6.00
1964 Proof	—	Value: 175				
1965	8,600,000	—	—	0.10	0.50	1.00
1965 Broken wing	Inc. above	3.50	7.00	12.00	30.00	40.00
1965 Prooflike	25,000	—	—	—	—	1.00
1965 Proof	10	—	—	—	—	—

KM# 3 SHILLING

5.6500 g., 0.5000 Silver 0.0908 oz. ASW, 23.62 mm. **Ruler:** George V **Obv:** Crowned bust left **Obv. Designer:** Percy Metcalfe **Rev:** Crouched Maori warrior left **Rev. Designer:** G.E. Kruger-Gray

Date	Mintage	F	VF	XF	Unc	BU
1933	2,000,000	1.50	10.00	25.00	110	225
1933 Proof	Est. 20	Value: 1,500				
1934	3,400,000	1.50	10.00	25.00	110	225
1934 Proof	Est. 20	Value: 2,500				
1935	1,680,000	2.00	20.00	60.00	200	400
1935 Proof	364	Value: 500				

KM# 9 SHILLING

5.6500 g., 0.5000 Silver 0.0908 oz. ASW, 23.62 mm. **Ruler:** George VI **Obv:** Head left **Obv. Designer:** T.H. Paget **Rev:** Crouched Maori warrior left **Rev. Designer:** G.E. Kruger-Gray

Date	Mintage	F	VF	XF	Unc	BU
1937	890,000	2.00	10.00	25.00	70.00	125
1937 Proof	Est. 200	Value: 550				
1940	500,000	2.50	12.00	30.00	90.00	200
1940 Proof	—	Value: 550				
1941	360,000	4.00	40.00	125	250	500
1941 Proof	—	Value: 550				
1942	240,000	4.00	40.00	125	250	500
1942 Broken back	Est. 80,000	8.00	95.00	350	650	—
1943	900,000	2.00	10.00	25.00	50.00	100
1944	480,000	2.50	12.00	30.00	60.00	150
1944 Proof	—	Value: 550				
1945	1,030,000	2.00	9.00	20.00	40.00	75.00
1945 Proof	—	Value: 550				
1946	1,060,000	2.00	9.00	20.00	37.50	72.00
1946 Proof	—	Value: 550				

KM# 9a SHILLING

5.5000 g., Copper-Nickel, 23.62 mm. **Ruler:** George VI **Obv:** Head left **Obv. Designer:** T.H. Paget **Rev:** Crouched Maori warrior left **Rev. Designer:** G.E. Kruger-Gray

Date	Mintage	F	VF	XF	Unc	BU
1947	2,800,000	1.00	8.00	35.00	80.00	230
1947 Proof	Est. 20	Value: 350				

KM# 17 SHILLING

Copper-Nickel, 23.62 mm. **Ruler:** George VI **Obv:** Head left **Obv. Designer:** T.H. Paget **Rev:** Crouched Maori warrior left **Rev. Designer:** G.E. Kruger-Gray

Date	Mintage	F	VF	XF	Unc	BU
1948	1,000,000	1.00	8.00	35.00	80.00	180
1948 Proof	—	Value: 350				
1950	600,000	1.00	8.00	35.00	80.00	200
1950 Proof	—	Value: 350				
1951	1,200,000	1.00	8.00	35.00	70.00	150
1951 Proof	—	Value: 350				
1952	600,000	2.00	10.00	35.00	80.00	160
1952 Proof	—	Value: 350				

KM# 27.1 SHILLING

Copper-Nickel, 23.62 mm. **Ruler:** Elizabeth II **Obv:** Laureate bust right without shoulder strap **Obv. Designer:** Mary Gillick **Rev:** Crouched Maori warrior left **Rev. Designer:** G.E. Kruger-Gray

Date	Mintage	F	VF	XF	Unc	BU
1953	200,000	1.50	5.00	12.00	25.00	45.00
1953 Proof	14,000	Value: 8.00				
1953 Matte proof	—	Value: 125				
1954 Proof	—	—	—	—	—	—
1955	200,000	2.00	15.00	60.00	120	220
1955 Proof	—	Value: 350				

KM# 27.2 SHILLING

5.6400 g., Copper-Nickel, 23.62 mm. **Ruler:** Elizabeth II **Obv:** Laureate bust right with shoulder strap **Obv. Designer:** Mary Gillick **Rev:** Crouched Maori warrior left **Rev. Designer:** G.E. Kruger-Gray

Date	Mintage	F	VF	XF	Unc	BU
1956	800,000	0.20	1.00	8.00	15.00	27.50
1956 Proof	—	Value: 350				
1957	800,000	0.20	1.00	8.00	15.00	27.50
1957 Proof	—	Value: 350				
1958	1,000,000	0.20	1.00	8.00	15.00	25.00
1958 Proof	—	Value: 350				
1958 Broken back	—	8.00	20.00	40.00	120	220
1959	600,000	0.20	1.00	5.00	12.50	25.50
1959 Proof	—	Value: 350				
1960	600,000	0.20	1.00	5.00	12.50	22.50
1960 Proof	—	Value: 350				
1961	400,000	0.20	0.50	5.00	12.00	20.00
1961 Proof	—	Value: 350				
1962	1,000,000	0.20	0.30	1.00	2.50	5.00
1962 Proof	—	Value: 350				
1962 No Horizon	—	10.00	20.00	30.00	70.00	110
1963	600,000	0.15	0.25	0.75	2.50	7.50
1963 Proof	—	Value: 350				
1964	3,400,000	0.10	0.15	0.30	1.00	2.00
1964 Proof	—	Value: 350				
1965	3,500,000	0.10	0.15	0.30	1.00	2.00
1965 Prooflike	25,000	—	—	—	—	1.25
1965 Proof	10	—	—	—	—	—

KM# 4 FLORIN

11.3100 g., 0.5000 Silver 0.1818 oz. ASW, 28.58 mm. **Ruler:** George V **Obv:** Crowned bust left **Obv. Designer:** Percy Metcalfe **Rev:** Kiwi bird **Rev. Designer:** G.E. Kruger-Gray

Date	Mintage	F	VF	XF	Unc	BU
1933	2,100,000	2.50	17.50	35.00	110	250
1933 Proof	Est. 20	Value: 600				
1934	2,850,000	2.50	17.50	35.00	110	225
1934 Proof	Est. 20	Value: 2,000				
1935	755,000	2.50	30.00	60.00	190	500
1935 Proof	364	Value: 600				
1936	150,000	6.00	80.00	400	1,500	4,000
1936 Proof	—	Value: 1,250				

KM# 10.1 FLORIN

11.3100 g., 0.5000 Silver 0.1818 oz. ASW, 28.58 mm. **Ruler:** George VI **Obv:** Head left **Obv. Designer:** T.H. Paget **Rev:** Kiwi bird **Rev. Designer:** G.E. Kruger-Gray

Date	Mintage	F	VF	XF	Unc	BU
1937	1,190,000	2.50	17.50	40.00	110	170
1937 Proof	Est. 200	Value: 600				
1940	500,000	3.00	35.00	150	500	1,000
1940 Proof	—	Value: 800				
1941	820,000	2.50	15.00	30.00	70.00	150
1941 Proof	—	Value: 600				
1942	150,000	2.50	20.00	40.00	100	190
1943	1,400,000	2.50	15.00	30.00	70.00	170
1944	140,000	6.00	35.00	120	220	500
1944 Proof	—	Value: 800				
1945	515,000	3.00	15.00	35.00	70.00	180
1945 Proof	—	Value: 650				
1946	1,200,000	2.50	12.00	30.00	60.00	125
1946 Proof	—	Value: 650				

KM# 10.2 FLORIN

11.3100 g., 0.5000 Silver 0.1818 oz. ASW, 28.58 mm. **Ruler:** George VI **Obv:** Head left **Obv. Designer:** T.H. Paget **Rev:** Flat back on Kiwi **Rev. Designer:** G.E. Kruger-Gray

Date	Mintage	F	VF	XF	Unc	BU
1946	Est. 300,000	4.00	40.00	200	500	800

KM# 10.2a FLORIN

Copper-Nickel, 28.58 mm. **Ruler:** George VI **Obv:** Head left **Obv. Designer:** T.H. Paget **Rev:** Kiwi bird **Rev. Designer:** G.E. Kruger-Gray

Date	Mintage	F	VF	XF	Unc	BU
1947	2,500,000	1.00	10.00	30.00	70.00	175
1947 Proof	Est. 20	Value: 450				

KM# 18 FLORIN

Copper-Nickel, 28.58 mm. **Ruler:** George VI **Obv:** Head left **Obv. Designer:** T.H. Paget **Rev:** Kiwi bird **Rev. Designer:** G.E. Kruger-Gray

Date	Mintage	F	VF	XF	Unc	BU
1948	1,750,000	1.00	10.00	30.00	70.00	175
1948 Proof	—	Value: 400				
1949	3,500,000	1.00	10.00	30.00	70.00	175
1949 Proof	—	Value: 400				
1950	3,500,000	0.75	4.00	8.00	20.00	35.00
1950 Proof	—	Value: 400				
1951	2,000,000	0.75	4.00	8.00	20.00	35.00
1951 Proof	—	Value: 400				

KM# 28.1 FLORIN

Copper-Nickel, 28.58 mm. **Ruler:** Elizabeth II **Obv:** Laureate bust right without shoulder strap **Obv. Designer:** Mary Gillick **Rev:** Kiwi bird **Rev. Designer:** G.E. Kruger-Gray

Date	Mintage	F	VF	XF	Unc	BU
1953	250,000	2.00	4.00	12.00	25.00	45.00
1953 Proof	7,000	Value: 12.50				

Date	Mintage	F	VF	XF	Unc	BU
1953 Matte proof	—	Value: 180				
1954 Proof	—	—	—	—	—	—

KM# 28.2 FLORIN

Copper-Nickel, 28.58 mm. **Ruler:** Elizabeth II **Obv:** Laureate bust right with shoulder strap **Obv. Designer:** Mary Gillick **Rev:** Kiwi bird **Rev. Designer:** G.E. Kruger-Gray

Date	Mintage	F	VF	XF	Unc	BU
1961	1,500,000	0.75	1.50	4.00	10.00	20.00
1961 Proof	—	Value: 375				
1962	1,500,000	0.75	1.50	3.50	8.00	15.00
1962 Proof	—	Value: 375				
1963	100,000	2.00	3.50	6.00	10.00	20.00
1963 Proof	—	Value: 375				
1964	7,000,000	0.20	0.50	1.00	3.00	6.00
1964 Proof	—	Value: 375				
1965	9,450,000	0.20	0.50	0.75	1.00	1.50
1965 Prooflike	25,000	—	—	—	—	2.50
1965 Proof	10	—	—	—	—	—

KM# 5 1/2 CROWN

14.1400 g., 0.5000 Silver 0.2273 oz. ASW, 32 mm. **Ruler:** George V **Obv:** Crowned bust left **Obv. Designer:** Percy Metcalfe **Rev:** Crowned shield within ornamental design **Rev. Designer:** G.E. Kruger-Gray

Date	Mintage	F	VF	XF	Unc	BU
1933	2,000,000	3.00	20.00	45.00	200	300
1933 Proof	Est. 20	Value: 650				
1934	2,720,000	3.00	20.00	45.00	200	350
1934 Proof	Est. 20	Value: 2,250				
1935	612,000	4.00	40.00	110	350	650
1935 Proof	364	Value: 700				

KM# 11 1/2 CROWN

14.1400 g., 0.5000 Silver 0.2273 oz. ASW, 32 mm. **Ruler:** George VI **Obv:** Head left **Obv. Designer:** T.H. Paget **Rev:** Crowned shield within ornamental design **Rev. Designer:** G.E. Kruger-Gray

Date	Mintage	F	VF	XF	Unc	BU
1937	672,000	4.00	22.50	60.00	200	300
1937 Proof	200	Value: 700				
1941	776,000	4.00	22.50	40.00	100	220
1941 Proof	—	Value: 700				
1942	240,000	4.00	25.00	50.00	120	250
1943	1,120,000	3.50	15.00	37.50	80.00	180
1944	180,000	6.00	45.00	180	375	750
1944 Proof	—	Value: 700				
1945	420,000	4.00	15.00	45.00	120	225
1945 Proof	—	Value: 700				
1946	960,000	3.50	15.00	45.00	115	175
1946 Proof	—	Value: 700				

KM# 14 1/2 CROWN

14.1400 g., 0.5000 Silver 0.2273 oz. ASW, 32 mm. **Ruler:** George VI **Subject:** New Zealand Centennial **Obv:** Head left **Obv. Designer:** T.H. Paget **Rev:** Radiant sun above city, standing figure in foreground **Rev. Designer:** L.C. Mitchell

Date	Mintage	F	VF	XF	Unc	BU
1940	100,800	10.00	13.00	20.00	35.00	60.00
1940 Proof	—	Value: 5,000				

KM# 11a 1/2 CROWN

Copper-Nickel, 32 mm. **Ruler:** George VI **Obv:** Head left **Obv. Designer:** T.H. Paget **Rev:** Crowned shield within ornamental design **Rev. Designer:** G.E. Kruger-Gray

Date	Mintage	F	VF	XF	Unc	BU
1947	1,600,000	1.25	5.00	30.00	120	200
1947 Proof	Est. 20	Value: 550				

KM# 19 1/2 CROWN

Copper-Nickel, 32 mm. **Ruler:** George VI **Obv:** Head left **Obv. Designer:** T.H. Paget **Rev:** Crowned shield within ornamental design **Rev. Designer:** G.E. Kruger-Gray

Date	Mintage	F	VF	XF	Unc	BU
1948	1,400,000	1.25	5.00	30.00	120	200
1948 Proof	—	Value: 500				
1949	2,800,000	1.25	5.00	30.00	120	200
1949 Proof	—	Value: 500				
1950	3,600,000	1.25	2.50	15.00	25.00	45.00
Note: K. G. close to dots						
1950 Proof	—	Value: 500				
1950	Inc. above	2.00	8.00	25.00	60.00	100
Note: K. G. close to rim						
1950 Proof	—	Value: 500				
1951	1,200,000	1.25	2.50	12.00	25.00	40.00
1951 Proof	—	Value: 500				

KM# 29.1 1/2 CROWN

Copper-Nickel, 32 mm. **Ruler:** Elizabeth II **Obv:** Laureate bust right without shoulder strap **Obv. Designer:** Mary Gillick **Rev:** Crowned shield within ornamental design **Rev. Designer:** G.E. Kruger-Gray

Date	Mintage	F	VF	XF	Unc	BU
1953	120,000	3.50	6.00	20.00	25.00	55.00
1953 Proof	7,000	Value: 20.00				
1953 Matte proof	—	Value: 245				

KM# 29.2 1/2 CROWN

Copper-Nickel, 32 mm. **Ruler:** Elizabeth II **Obv:** Laureate bust right with shoulder strap **Obv. Designer:** Mary Gillick **Rev:** Crowned shield within ornamental design **Rev. Designer:** G.E. Kruger-Gray

Date	Mintage	F	VF	XF	Unc	BU
1961	80,000	4.00	8.00	15.00	30.00	60.00
1961 Proof	—	Value: 450				
1962	600,000	1.25	2.00	3.00	4.00	8.00
1962 Proof	—	Value: 450				
1963	400,000	1.25	2.50	3.50	6.00	8.00
1963 Proof	—	Value: 450				
1965	200,000	1.25	2.50	3.50	4.00	5.00
1965 Prooflike	25,000	—	—	—	—	5.00
1965 Proof	10	—	—	—	—	—

KM# 6 CROWN

28.2800 g., 0.5000 Silver 0.4546 oz. ASW, 38.8 mm. **Ruler:** George V **Subject:** Treaty of Waitangi in 1840. **Obv:** Crowned bust left **Rev:** Crown above standing figures shaking hands **Designer:** James Berry **Note:** 364 Proofs issued in sets, 104 issued loose.

Date	Mintage	F	VF	XF	Unc	BU
1935	660	1,500	2,500	3,500	4,500	5,500
1935 Proof	468	Value: 6,500				

KM# 22 CROWN

28.2800 g., 0.5000 Silver 0.4546 oz. ASW, 38.8 mm. **Ruler:** George VI **Subject:** Proposed Royal Visit **Obv:** Head left **Obv. Designer:** T.H. Paget **Rev:** Silver fern leaf flanked by stars **Rev. Designer:** James Berry

Date	Mintage	F	VF	XF	Unc	BU
1949	200,000	BV	10.00	15.00	25.00	40.00
1949 Proof	Est. 3	Value: 12,000				

KM# 30 CROWN

Copper-Nickel, 38.8 mm. **Ruler:** Elizabeth II **Subject:** Queen Elizabeth II Coronation **Obv:** Laureate bust right **Obv. Designer:** Mary Gillick **Rev:** Crowned monogram flanked by stars above design **Rev. Designer:** R.M. Conly

Date	Mintage	F	VF	XF	Unc	BU
1953	250,000	—	5.00	6.50	10.00	12.50
1953 Proof	7,000	Value: 80.00				
1953 Matte proof	—	Value: 345				
Note: Mintage: 4-10.						

DECIMAL COINAGE

100 Cents = 1 Dollar

(c) Royal Australian Mint, Canberra

(l) Royal Mint, Llantrisant

(o) Royal Canadian Mint, Ottawa

(m) B.H. Mayer, Germany

(n) Norwegian Mint, Kongsberg

(p) South African Mint, Pretoria

(v) Valcambi SA, Switzerland

(w) Perth Mint, Western Australia

KM# 31.1 CENT

2.0500 g., Bronze, 17.5 mm. **Ruler:** Elizabeth II **Obv:** Young bust right **Obv. Designer:** Arnold Machin **Rev:** Value within silver fern leaf **Rev. Designer:** James Berry **Note:** Rounded, high relief portrait.

Date	Mintage	F	VF	XF	Unc	BU
1967(l)	120,000,000	—	—	0.10	0.15	0.25
1967(l) Prooflike	50,000	—	—	—	—	0.80
1967 Proof	10	—	—	—	—	—
1968	35,000	—	—	—	2.00	—
Note: In sets only						
1968 Prooflike	40,000	—	—	—	—	2.00
1969	50,000	—	—	—	2.00	—
Note: In sets only						
1969 Prooflike	50,000	—	—	—	—	2.00
1970(c)	10,060,000	—	—	0.10	0.50	1.00
1970 Prooflike	20,010	—	—	—	—	1.00
1971(c)	10,000,000	—	—	0.10	6.00	8.00
Note: Serifs on date numerals						
1971(l)	15,000	—	—	0.10	3.00	5.00
Note: Without serifs						
1971(l) Proof	5,000	Value: 12.50				
1972(c)	10,055,000	—	0.20	1.00	5.00	7.00
1972(c) Proof	8,045	Value: 5.00				
1973(c)	15,055,000	—	—	0.10	5.00	7.00
1973(c) Proof	8,000	Value: 5.00				
1974(c)	35,035,000	—	—	0.10	0.50	1.00
1974(c) Proof	8,000	Value: 4.00				
1975(l)	60,015,000	—	—	0.10	0.50	1.00
1975(l) Proof	10,000	Value: 4.00				
1976(l)	20,016,000	—	—	0.10	0.50	1.00
1976(l) Proof	11,000	Value: 4.00				
1977 In sets only	20,000	—	—	—	4.00	6.00
1977 Proof	12,000	Value: 6.00				
1978(o)	15,023,000	—	—	0.10	0.50	1.00
1978(o) Proof	15,000	Value: 2.00				
1979(o)	35,025,000	—	—	0.10	0.50	1.00
1979(o) Proof	16,000	Value: 2.00				
1980(l)	27,000	—	—	—	0.50	1.00
Note: Round 0 in date. In sets only.						
1980(l) Proof	17,000	Value: 2.00				
1980(o)	40,000,000	—	—	0.10	0.50	1.00
Note: Oval O in date						
1981(o)	10,000,000	—	—	0.10	0.50	1.00
Note: Oval hole in 8						
1981(l)	25,000	—	—	—	0.50	1.00
Note: Round hole in 8. In sets only.						
1981(l) Proof	18,000	Value: 2.00				
Note: Round hole in 8						
1982(o)	10,000,000	—	—	0.10	0.50	1.00
Note: Blunt-tipped 2						
1982(l)	25,000	—	—	—	0.50	1.00
Note: Round-tipped 2						
1982(l) Proof	18,000	Value: 2.00				
Note: Round-tipped 2						
1983(o)	40,000,000	—	—	0.10	0.50	1.00
Note: Round-top 3						
1983(l)	25,000	—	—	0.10	0.50	1.00
Note: Flat-top 3. In sets only.						
1983(l) Proof	18,000	Value: 2.00				
Note: Flat-top 3						
1984(l)	25,000	—	—	0.10	0.50	1.00
Note: In sets only.						
1984(l) Proof	15,000	Value: 2.00				
1985(c)	20,000	—	—	0.10	0.50	1.00
Note: In sets only.						
1985(c) Proof	12,000	Value: 2.00				

KM# 31.2 CENT

2.0500 g., Bronze, 17.5 mm. **Obv:** Crowned bust right **Obv. Designer:** Arnold Machin **Rev:** Value within silver fern leaf **Rev. Designer:** James Berry **Note:** Die recut, low relief portrait.

Date	Mintage	F	VF	XF	Unc	BU
1984(o)	30,000,000	—	—	0.10	0.50	1.00
1985(o)	40,000,000	—	—	0.10	0.50	1.00

KM# 58 CENT

2.0500 g., Bronze, 17.5 mm. **Ruler:** Elizabeth II **Obv:** Crowned head right **Obv. Designer:** R.D. Maklouf **Rev:** Value within silver fern leaf **Rev. Designer:** James Berry **Edge:** Plain

Date	Mintage	F	VF	XF	Unc	BU
1986(o)	25,000,000	—	—	0.10	0.50	1.00
1986(l)	18,000	—	—	—	1.00	—
Note: In sets only.						
1986(l) Proof	10,000	Value: 1.00				
1987(o)	27,500,000	—	—	0.10	0.50	1.00
1987(l)	18,000	—	—	—	1.00	—
Note: In sets only.						
1987(l) Proof	10,000	Value: 1.00				
1988(l)	15,000	—	—	—	5.00	7.50
Note: In sets only						
1988(l) Proof	9,000	Value: 2.00				
Note: 1988 cent was struck for sets only						

KM# 33 2 CENTS

4.1500 g., Bronze, 21.1 mm. **Ruler:** Elizabeth II **Obv:** Young bust right **Obv. Designer:** Arnold Machin **Rev:** Value within kowhai leaves **Note:** Mule with Bahamas KM#3.

Date	Mintage	F	VF	XF	Unc	BU
ND(1967)	Est. 50,000	—	8.00	15.00	22.50	30.00

KM# 32.1 2 CENTS

4.1500 g., Bronze, 21.1 mm. **Ruler:** Elizabeth II **Obv:** Young bust right **Obv. Designer:** Arnold Machin **Rev:** Value within kowhai leaves **Rev. Designer:** James Berry **Note:** Rounded, high relief portrait.

Date	Mintage	F	VF	XF	Unc	BU
1967(l)	75,000,000	—	—	0.10	0.15	0.25
1967(l) Prooflike	50,000	—	—	—	—	0.75
1967(l) Proof	10	—	—	—	—	—
1968	35,000	—	—	—	2.00	3.00
Note: In sets only						
1968 Prooflike	40,000	—	—	—	—	1.25
1969(c)	20,510,000	—	—	0.15	0.25	0.50
1969 Prooflike	50,000	—	—	—	—	1.25
1970(c)	30,000	—	—	—	2.00	3.00
Note: In sets only						
1970 Prooflike	20,010	—	—	—	—	1.25
1971(c)	15,050,000	—	0.10	1.00	5.00	6.00
Note: Serifs on date numerals						
1971(l)	15,000	—	—	2.00	4.00	5.00
Note: Without serifs						
1971(l) Proof	5,000	Value: 12.50				
1972(c)	17,525,000	—	0.10	1.00	5.00	6.00
1972(c) Proof	8,045	Value: 5.00				
1973(c)	38,565,000	—	0.10	1.00	5.00	6.00
1973(c) Proof	8,000	Value: 5.25				
1974(c)	50,015,000	—	0.10	0.50	1.00	2.00
1974(c) Proof	8,000	Value: 3.00				
1975(l)	20,015,000	—	—	0.10	1.00	1.50
1975(l) Proof	10,000	Value: 3.00				
1976(l)	15,016,000	—	—	0.10	1.00	1.50
1976(l) Proof	11,000	Value: 3.00				
1977(l)	20,000,000	—	—	0.10	1.00	1.50
1977(l) Proof	12,000	Value: 3.00				
1978(o)	23,000	—	—	—	5.00	6.00
Note: In sets only						
1978(o) Proof	15,000	Value: 3.00				
1979(o)	25,000	—	—	—	5.00	6.00
Note: In sets only						
1979(o) Proof	16,000	Value: 3.00				
1980(l)	27,000	—	—	—	1.00	1.25
Note: Round 0 in date. In sets only.						
1980(l) Proof	17,000	Value: 3.00				
1980(o)	10,000,000	—	—	0.10	1.00	1.25
Note: Oval 0 in date						
1981(o)	25,000,000	—	—	0.10	1.00	1.25
Note: Oval hole in 8						
1981(l)	25,000	—	—	—	1.00	1.25
Note: Round hole in 8. In sets only.						
1981(l) Proof	18,000	Value: 3.00				
1982(o)	50,000,000	—	—	0.10	1.00	1.25
Note: Blunt open 2						
1982(l)	25,000	—	—	—	1.00	1.25
Note: Pointed tight 2. In sets only.						
1982(l) Proof	18,000	Value: 3.00				
1983(o)	15,000,000	—	—	0.10	1.00	1.25
Note: Round-topped 3						
1983(l)	25,000	—	—	—	1.00	1.25
Note: Flat-topped 3. In sets only.						
1983(l) Proof	18,000	Value: 3.00				
1984(l)	25,000	—	—	—	1.00	1.25
Note: Smooth shoulder folds. In sets only.						
1984(l) Proof	15,000	Value: 2.00				
1985(c)	20,000	—	—	—	2.00	2.50
Note: In sets only.						
1985(c) Proof	12,000	Value: 2.00				

KM# 32.2 2 CENTS

Bronze, 21.1 mm. **Obv:** Crowned bust right **Obv. Designer:** Arnold Machin **Rev:** Value within kowhai leaves **Rev. Designer:** James Berry **Note:** Die recut, low relief portrait.

Date	Mintage	F	VF	XF	Unc	BU
1984(o)	10,000,000	—	—	0.10	1.00	1.50
1985(o)	22,500,000	—	—	0.10	1.00	1.50

KM# 59 2 CENTS

4.1500 g., Bronze, 21.1 mm. **Ruler:** Elizabeth II **Obv:** Crowned head right **Obv. Designer:** R.D. Maklouf **Rev:** Kowhai **Rev. Designer:** James Berry

Date	Mintage	F	VF	XF	Unc	BU
1986(l)	18,000	—	—	—	8.00	9.50
Note: In sets only						
1986(l) Proof	10,000	Value: 8.00				
1987(o)	36,250,000	—	—	—	1.00	1.25
1987(l)	18,000	—	—	—	2.00	2.50
Note: In sets only.						
1987(l) Proof	10,000	Value: 2.00				
1988(l)	15,000	—	—	—	5.00	7.50
Note: In sets only						
1988(l) Proof	9,000	Value: 1.25				

KM# 34.1 5 CENTS

2.8300 g., Copper-Nickel, 19.43 mm. **Ruler:** Elizabeth II **Subject:** Tuatara **Obv:** Young bust right **Obv. Designer:** Arnold Machin **Rev:** Value below tuatara **Rev. Designer:** James Berry **Note:** Rounded, high relief portrait. Many recalled and melted in 2006.

Date	Mintage	F	VF	XF	Unc	BU
1967(l)	26,000,000	—	—	0.10	0.20	0.50
1967(l)	Inc. above	3.00	5.00	15.00	30.00	50.00
Note: Without sea line at right of Tuatara						
1967(l)	Inc. above	3.00	5.00	15.00	30.00	50.00
Note: No tail triangle under chin						
1967(l) Prooflike	50,000	—	—	—	—	1.00
1967(l) Proof	10	—	—	—	—	—
1968	35,000	—	—	—	1.00	2.00
Note: In sets only						
1968 Prooflike	40,000	—	—	—	—	2.00
1969(c)	10,260,000	—	—	0.10	0.50	1.00

Date	Mintage	F	VF	XF	Unc	BU
1969 Prooflike	50,000	—	—	—	—	2.00
1970(c)	11,202,000	—	—	0.10	0.50	1.00
1970 Prooflike	20,010	—	—	—	—	2.00
1971(c)	11,152,000	—	0.10	0.50	5.00	10.00
Note: Serifs on date numerals						
1971(l)	15,000	—	—	0.50	3.00	6.00
Note: Without serifs						
1971(l) Proof	5,000	Value: 5.00				
1972(c)	20,015,000	—	—	0.10	1.00	2.00
1972(c) Proof	8,000	Value: 5.00				
1973(c)	4,038,999	—	—	0.10	1.00	2.00
1973(c) Proof	8,000	Value: 4.50				
1974(c)	18,015,000	—	—	0.10	1.50	3.00
1974(c) Proof	8,000	Value: 4.00				
1975(c)	32,015,000	—	—	0.10	0.50	1.00
1975(c) Proof	10,000	Value: 4.50				
1976	16,000	—	—	—	5.00	6.00
Note: In sets only						
1976 Proof	11,000	Value: 2.00				
1977	20,000	—	—	—	5.00	6.00
Note: In sets only						
1977 Proof	12,000	Value: 3.00				
1978(o)	20,023,000	—	—	0.10	0.40	1.00
1978(o) Proof	15,000	Value: 3.00				
1979(o)	25,000	—	—	—	4.00	6.00
Note: In sets only						
1979(o) Proof	16,000	Value: 3.00				
1980(l)	27,000	—	—	—	0.50	1.00
Note: Round O in date. In sets only.						
1980(l) Proof	17,000	Value: 2.00				
1980(o)	12,000,000	—	—	0.10	0.50	1.00
Note: Oval O in date						
1981(o)	20,000,000	—	—	0.10	0.50	1.00
Note: Oval hole in 8						
1981(l)	25,000	—	—	0.50	0.50	1.00
Note: Round hole in 8. In sets only.						
1981(l) Proof	18,000	Value: 2.00				
1982(o)	50,000,000	—	—	0.10	0.50	1.00
Note: Blunt 2						
1982(l)	25,000	—	—	0.50	1.00	2.00
Note: Pointed 2. In sets only.						
1982(l) Proof	18,000	Value: 2.00				
1983(l)	25,000	—	—	—	3.00	4.00
Note: In sets only						
1983(l) Proof	18,000	Value: 3.00				
1984(l)	25,000	—	—	—	3.00	4.00
Note: In sets only						
1984(l) Proof	15,000	Value: 3.00				
1985(c)	20,000	—	—	0.50	1.00	2.00
Note: In sets only.						
1985(c) Proof	12,000	Value: 2.00				

KM# 34.2 5 CENTS

2.8300 g., Copper-Nickel, 19.43 mm. **Subject:** Tuatara **Obv:** Crowned bust right **Obv. Designer:** Arnold Machin **Rev:** James Berry **Note:** Die recut, low relief.

Date	Mintage	F	VF	XF	Unc	BU
1985(o)	14,000,000	—	—	0.10	0.50	1.00

KM# 64 5 CENTS

Copper-Nickel **Ruler:** Elizabeth II **Obv:** Young bust right **Rev:** Small ship **Note:** Mule with Canada KM#77.

Date	Mintage	F	VF	XF	Unc	BU
1981(o) Rare; Serif on 1	—	—	—	—	—	—

KM# 60 5 CENTS

2.8300 g., Copper-Nickel, 19.43 mm. **Ruler:** Elizabeth II **Obv:** Crowned head right **Obv. Designer:** R.D. Maklouf **Rev:** Value below tuatara **Rev. Designer:** James Berry **Note:** Many recalled and melted in 2006.

Date	Mintage	F	VF	XF	Unc	BU
1986(o)	18,000,000	—	—	0.10	0.50	1.00
1986(l)	18,000	—	—	—	1.00	2.00
Note: In sets only.						
1986(l) Proof	10,000	Value: 3.00				
1987(o)	40,000,000	—	—	0.10	0.50	1.00
1987(l)	18,000	—	—	—	2.00	3.00
Note: In sets only.						
1987(l) Proof	10,000	Value: 3.00				
1988(c)	16,000,000	—	—	0.10	0.50	1.00
Note: Round-topped numerals						
1988(l)	15,000	—	—	—	2.00	2.50
Note: Flat-topped numerals. In sets only.						
1988(l) Proof	9,000	Value: 3.00				
1989(o)	36,000,000	—	—	0.10	0.50	1.00
1989(c)	15,000	—	—	—	1.00	1.50
Note: In sets only.						
1989(c) Proof	8,500	Value: 3.00				
1990(c)	18,000	—	—	—	3.00	4.00
Note: In sets only						
1990(c) Proof	10,000	Value: 3.00				
1991(c)	20,000	—	—	—	3.00	4.00
Note: In sets only						
1991(c) Proof	9,000	Value: 4.00				
1992(l)	15,000	—	—	—	3.00	4.00
Note: In sets only						
1992(l) Proof	9,000	Value: 4.00				
1993(l)	15,000	—	—	—	3.00	4.00
Note: In sets only						
1993(l) Proof	10,000	Value: 4.00				
1994(l)	20,026,000	—	—	0.10	0.50	1.00
1994(l) Proof	10,000	Value: 3.00				
1995(l)	40,010,000	—	—	0.10	0.50	1.00
1995(l) Proof	4,000	Value: 3.00				
1996(n)	19,008,000	—	—	0.10	0.50	1.00
1996(l) Proof	4,000	Value: 3.00				
1997(n)	14,000,000	—	—	0.10	0.50	1.00
1997(l) Proof	2,500	Value: 5.00				
1998(p)	8,000,000	—	—	0.10	0.50	1.00
1998(l) Proof	2,000	Value: 3.00				

KM# 72 5 CENTS

2.8300 g., Copper-Nickel, 19.43 mm. **Ruler:** Elizabeth II **Subject:** 1990 Anniversary Celebrations **Obv:** Crowned head right **Rev:** Stylized kotuku bird

Date	Mintage	F	VF	XF	Unc	BU
1990	10,000	—	—	—	6.00	8.00
Note: In sets only.						

KM# 116 5 CENTS

2.8300 g., Copper-Nickel, 19.43 mm. **Ruler:** Elizabeth II **Obv:** Head with tiara right **Obv. Designer:** Ian Rank-Broadley **Rev:** Value below tuatara **Rev. Designer:** James Berry **Edge:** Reeded **Note:** Many recalled and melted in 2006.

Date	Mintage	F	VF	XF	Unc	BU
1999(p)	25,040,000	—	—	0.10	0.50	1.00
1999(p) Wart on nose	—	—	—	—	6.00	8.00
Note: Die crack error						
1999(l)	3,199	—	—	—	5.00	6.00
Note: In sets only.						
1999(l) Proof	1,800	Value: 3.00				
2000(o)	26,000,000	—	—	0.10	0.50	1.00
2000(c)	3,000	—	—	—	12.00	15.00
Note: In sets only.						
2000(c) Proof	1,500	Value: 15.00				
2001(l)	20,000,000	—	—	0.10	0.50	1.00
2001(c)	Est. 52,910,000	—	—	—	4.00	5.00
Note: In sets only						
2001(c) Proof	Est. 1,364	Value: 3.00				
2002(l)	40,500,000	—	—	0.10	0.50	1.00
2002(c)	3,000	—	—	—	5.00	6.00
Note: In sets only						
2002(c) Proof	1,500	Value: 3.00				
2003(l)	30,000,000	—	—	—	0.50	1.00
2003(c)	1,496	—	—	—	5.00	6.00
Note: In sets only						
2003 Proof	3,000	Value: 3.00				
2004(l)	15,000,000	—	—	—	25.00	50.00
Note: All but 48,000 melted						
2004(c)	2,800	—	—	—	20.00	30.00
Note: In sets only						
2004(c) Proof	1,750	Value: 3.00				
2005(c)	3,000	—	—	—	8.00	12.00
Note: In sets only						
2005(c) Proof	2,250	Value: 3.00				

KM# 35 10 CENTS

5.6500 g., Copper-Nickel, 23.62 mm. **Ruler:** Elizabeth II **Obv:** Young bust right **Obv. Designer:** Arnold Machin **Rev:** Value above Maori mask, koruru **Rev. Designer:** James Berry **Note:** Many recalled and melted in 2006.

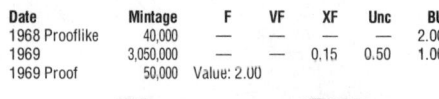

Date	Mintage	F	VF	XF	Unc	BU
1967(l)	17,000,000	—	—	0.10	0.25	0.50
1967(l) Prooflike	50,000	—	—	—	—	1.00
1967(l) Proof	10	—	—	—	—	—
1968	35,000	—	—	1.00	2.00	3.00
Note: In sets only						
1968 Prooflike	40,000	—	—	—	—	2.00
1969	3,050,000	—	—	0.15	0.50	1.00
1969 Proof	50,000	Value: 2.00				

KM# 41.1 10 CENTS

5.6500 g., Copper-Nickel, 23.62 mm. **Ruler:** Elizabeth II **Obv:** Young bust right **Obv. Designer:** Arnold Machin **Rev:** Value above Maori mask, koruru **Rev. Designer:** James Berry **Note:** Rounded, high relief portrait. Many recalled and melted in 2006.

Date	Mintage	F	VF	XF	Unc	BU
1970	2,046,000	—	—	0.15	0.50	1.00
1970 Prooflike	20,010	—	—	—	—	1.50
1971(c)	2,800,000	—	0.10	5.00	30.00	40.00
Note: Serifs on date numerals						
1971(l)	15,000	—	—	1.00	2.00	3.00
Note: Without serifs						
1971(l) Proof	5,000	Value: 5.00				
1972(c)	2,039,000	—	—	0.15	1.00	2.00
1972(c) Proof	8,000	Value: 5.00				
1973(c)	3,525,000	—	—	0.10	1.00	2.00
1973(c) Proof	8,000	Value: 3.00				
1974(c)	4,619,000	—	—	0.10	1.00	2.00
1974(c) Proof	8,000	Value: 3.00				
1975(l)	7,015,000	—	—	0.10	1.00	2.00
1975(l) Proof	10,000	Value: 3.00				
1976(l)	5,016,000	—	—	0.10	1.00	2.00
1976(l) Proof	11,000	Value: 3.00				
1977(l)	5,000,000	—	—	0.10	1.00	2.00
1977(o) Proof	12,000	Value: 3.00				
1978(o)	16,023,000	—	—	0.10	1.00	2.00
1978(o) Proof	15,000	Value: 3.00				
1979(o)	6,000,000	—	—	0.10	0.50	1.00
1979(o) Proof	16,000	Value: 3.00				
1980(l)	27,000	—	—	—	0.50	1.00
Note: Round O in date. In sets only.						
1980(l) Proof	17,000	Value: 3.00				
1980(o)	28,000,000	—	—	0.10	0.50	1.00
Note: Oval O in date						
1981(o)	5,000,000	—	—	0.10	0.50	1.00
Note: Oval holes in 8						
1981(l)	25,000	—	—	0.10	0.50	1.00
Note: Round holes in 8. In sets only.						
1981(l) Proof	18,000	Value: 3.00				
1982(o)	18,000,000	—	—	0.10	0.50	1.00
Note: Blunt open 2						
1982(l)	25,000	—	—	—	1.00	2.00
Note: Point-tipped 2. In sets only.						
1982(l) Proof	18,000	Value: 3.00				
1983(l)	25,000	—	—	—	3.00	4.00
Note: In sets only						
1983(l) Proof	18,000	Value: 3.00				
1984(l)	25,000	—	—	—	3.00	4.00
Note: In sets only						
1984(l) Proof	15,000	Value: 4.00				
1985(c)	20,000	—	—	—	3.00	4.00
Note: In sets only.						
1985(c) Proof	12,000	Value: 4.00				

KM# 41.2 10 CENTS

5.6500 g., Copper-Nickel, 23.62 mm. **Obv:** Crowned bust right **Rev. Designer:** James Berry **Note:** Recut due, low relief.

Date	Mintage	F	VF	XF	Unc	BU
1985(o)	8,000,000	—	—	0.50	3.00	4.00
Note: Wiry hair, bushy eyebrow						

KM# 61 10 CENTS

5.6500 g., Copper-Nickel, 23.62 mm. **Ruler:** Elizabeth II **Obv:** Crowned head right **Obv. Designer:** R.D. Maklouf **Rev:** Value above Maori mask, koruru **Rev. Designer:** James Berry **Note:** Many recalled and melted in 2006.

Date	Mintage	F	VF	XF	Unc	BU
1986(l)	18,000	—	—	—	3.00	4.00
Note: In sets only						
1986(l) Proof	10,000	Value: 4.00				
1987(o)	21,000,000	—	—	0.10	0.50	1.00
1987(l)	18,000	—	—	—	1.00	2.00
Note: In sets only.						
1987(l) Proof	10,000	Value: 3.00				
1988(c)	26,702,000	—	—	0.10	0.50	1.00
1988(l)	15,000	—	—	—	1.00	2.00
Note: In sets only.						
1988(l) Proof	9,000	Value: 3.00				

Date	Mintage	F	VF	XF	Unc	BU
1989(o)	9,000,000	—	—	—	0.50	1.00
1989(c)	14,600	—	—	—	2.50	3.50
Note: In sets only.						
1989(c) Proof	8,500	Value: 3.00				
1990(c)	18,000	—	—	—	2.00	3.00
Note: In sets only						
1990(c) Proof	10,000	Value: 3.00				
1991(c)	20,000	—	—	—	2.00	3.00
Note: In sets only						
1991(c) Proof	15,000	Value: 3.00				
1992	15,000	—	—	—	2.00	3.00
Note: In sets only						
1992 Proof	9,000	Value: 3.00				
1993	15,000	—	—	—	2.00	3.00
Note: In sets only						
1993 Proof	10,000	Value: 3.00				
1994	7,000	—	—	—	2.00	3.00
Note: In sets only						
1994 Proof	4,600	Value: 3.00				
1995	6,000	—	—	—	1.00	2.00
Note: In sets only						
1995 Proof	3,560	Value: 3.00				
1996(n)	12,960,000	—	—	—	0.50	1.00
1996(l) Proof	2,569	Value: 3.00				
1997(n)	8,000,000	—	—	—	0.50	1.00
1997(l) Proof	2,132	Value: 3.00				
1998	4,000	—	—	—	8.00	10.00
Note: In sets only						
1998(l) Proof	2,000	Value: 3.00				

KM# 73 10 CENTS

5.6500 g., Copper-Nickel, 23.62 mm. **Ruler:** Elizabeth II **Subject:** 1990 Anniversary Celebrations **Obv:** Crowned head right **Rev:** Value above sailboats within rainbow design

Date	Mintage	F	VF	XF	Unc	BU
1990	10,000	—	—	—	7.00	9.00

KM# 117 10 CENTS

5.6600 g., Copper-Nickel, 23.62 mm. **Ruler:** Elizabeth II **Obv:** Head with tiara right **Obv. Designer:** Ian Rank-Broadley **Rev:** Value above koruru **Rev. Designer:** James Berry **Note:** Many recalled and melted in 2006.

Date	Mintage	F	VF	XF	Unc	BU
1999(l)	3,199	—	—	—	10.00	12.00
Note: In sets only						
1999(l) Proof	1,800	Value: 10.00				
2000(o)	11,000,000	—	—	0.10	0.30	0.50
2000(l)	4,500	—	—	—	12.00	15.00
Note: In sets only.						
2000(l) Proof	1,500	Value: 15.00				
2001(l)	10,000,000	—	—	0.10	0.30	0.50
2001(c)	2,910	—	—	—	6.00	8.00
Note: In sets only						
2001(c) Proof	1,364	Value: 4.00				
2002(l)	10,000,000	—	—	0.10	0.30	0.50
2002(c) Proof	1,500	Value: 4.00				
2002(c)	3,000	—	—	—	3.00	5.00
Note: In sets only						
2003(l)	13,000,000	—	—	0.10	0.30	0.50
2003(c)	3,000	—	—	—	5.00	8.00
Note: In sets only						
2003(l) Proof	1,496	Value: 4.00				
2004(l)	6,500,000	—	—	—	0.30	0.50
2004(c)	—	—	—	—	5.00	8.00
Note: In sets only						
2004(c) Proof	1,750	Value: 4.00				
2005	2,000,000	—	—	—	30.00	40.00
Note: All but 28,000 melted						
2005(c)	3,000	—	—	—	20.00	30.00
Note: In sets only						
2005(c) Proof	2,250	Value: 4.00				
2006(c)	3,000	—	—	—	10.00	15.00
Note: In sets only						
2006(c) Proof	2,100	Value: 4.00				

KM# 117a 10 CENTS

Copper Plated Steel, 20.5 mm. **Ruler:** Elizabeth II **Obv:** Head with tiara right **Obv. Designer:** Ian Rank-Broadley **Rev:** Value above koruru

Date	Mintage	F	VF	XF	Unc	BU
2006(o)	140,200,000	—	—	—	0.20	0.40
2007(c) Proof	4,000	Value: 4.00				
2007(c)	5,000	—	—	—	3.00	5.00
Note: In sets only						

KM# 36.1 20 CENTS

11.3100 g., Copper-Nickel, 28.58 mm. **Ruler:** Elizabeth II **Obv:** Young bust right **Obv. Designer:** Arnold Machin **Rev:** Value below Kiwi bird with sprigs above **Rev. Designer:** James Berry **Note:** Rounded, high relief portrait. Prev. KM#36. Many recalled and melted in 2006.

Date	Mintage	F	VF	XF	Unc	BU
1967(l)	13,000,000	—	—	0.20	0.50	1.00
1967(l) Prooflike	50,000	—	—	—	—	1.00
1967(l) Proof	10	—	—	—	—	—
1968	35,000	—	—	—	2.00	3.00
Note: In sets only						
1968 Prooflike	40,000	—	—	—	—	2.00
1969	2,500,000	—	—	0.20	1.00	1.50
1969 Prooflike	50,000	—	—	—	—	2.00
1970	30,000	—	—	—	2.00	3.00
Note: In sets only						
1970 Prooflike	20,010	—	—	—	—	3.00
1971(c)	1,600,000	—	1.00	5.00	30.00	40.00
Note: Serifs on date numerals						
1971(l)	15,000	—	—	1.00	2.50	4.00
Note: Without serifs						
1971(l) Proof	5,000	Value: 10.00				
1972(c)	1,531,000	—	—	0.20	2.00	—
1972(c) Proof	8,000	Value: 12.50				
1973(c)	3,043,000	—	—	0.20	2.00	—
1973(c) Proof	8,000	Value: 7.00				
1974(c)	4,527,000	—	—	0.20	5.00	—
1974(c) Proof	8,000	Value: 8.00				
1975(l)	5,015,000	—	—	0.20	2.00	—
1975(l) Proof	12,000	Value: 6.50				
1976(l)	7,516,000	—	—	0.20	2.00	—
1976(l) Proof	11,000	Value: 6.00				
1977(l)	7,500,000	—	—	0.20	2.00	—
1977(l) Proof	12,000	Value: 6.50				
1978(o)	2,523,000	—	—	0.20	2.00	—
1978(o) Proof	15,000	Value: 5.00				
1979(o)	8,025,000	—	—	0.20	2.00	—
1979(o) Proof	16,000	Value: 5.00				
1980(l)	27,000	—	—	0.15	1.00	—
Note: Round O in date. In sets only.						
1980(l) Proof	17,000	Value: 5.00				
1980(o)	9,000,000	—	—	0.15	2.00	—
Note: Oval O in date						
1981(o)	7,500,000	—	—	0.15	1.00	—
Note: Oval holes in 8						
1981(l)	25,000	—	—	—	2.00	—
Note: Round holes in 8. In sets only.						
1981(l) Proof	18,000	Value: 4.00				
1982(o)	17,500,000	—	—	0.15	2.00	—
Note: Blunt 2						
1982(l)	25,000	—	—	—	1.00	—
Note: Pointed 2. In sets only.						
1982(l) Proof	18,000	Value: 5.00				
1983(o)	2,500,000	—	—	0.15	3.00	—
Note: Round topped 3						
1983(l)	25,000	—	—	—	1.00	—
Note: Flat topped 3. In sets only.						
1983(l) Proof	18,000	Value: 4.00				
1984(l)	25,000	—	—	—	1.00	—
Note: In sets only.						
1984(l) Proof	18,000	Value: 4.00				
1985(c)	20,000	—	—	—	1.00	—
Note: Round tip 5. In sets only.						
1985(c) Proof	12,000	Value: 4.00				

KM# 36.2 20 CENTS

11.3100 g., Copper-Nickel, 28.58 mm. **Obv:** Crowned bust right **Obv. Designer:** Arnold Machin **Rev. Designer:** James Berry **Note:** Die recut, low relief. Many recalled and melted in 2006.

Date	Mintage	F	VF	XF	Unc	BU
1984(o)	1,500,000	—	—	0.15	2.00	—
1985(o)	6,000,000	—	—	0.15	2.00	—

KM# 62 20 CENTS

11.3100 g., Copper-Nickel, 28.58 mm. **Ruler:** Elizabeth II **Obv:** Crowned head right **Obv. Designer:** R.D. Maklouf **Rev:** Kiwi **Rev. Designer:** James Berry

Date	Mintage	F	VF	XF	Unc	BU
1986(o)	12,500,000	—	—	0.15	1.00	—
1986(l)	18,000	—	—	—	2.00	—
Note: In sets only.						
1986(l) Proof	10,000	Value: 4.00				
1987(o)	14,000,000	—	—	0.15	1.00	—
1987(l)	18,000	—	—	—	2.00	—
Note: In sets only.						
1987(l) Proof	10,000	Value: 4.00				
1988(c)	12,500,000	—	—	0.15	1.00	—
1988(l)	15,000	—	—	—	2.00	—
Note: In sets only.						
1988(l) Proof	9,000	Value: 4.00				
1989(o)	5,000,000	—	—	0.15	1.00	—
1989(c) Proof	8,500	Value: 4.00				
1989(c)	15,000	—	—	—	2.00	—
Note: In sets only.						

KM# 74 20 CENTS

11.3100 g., Copper-Nickel, 28.58 mm. **Ruler:** Elizabeth II **Subject:** 1990 Anniversary Celebrations **Obv:** Crowned head right **Rev:** Ship, H.M.S. Tory

Date	Mintage	F	VF	XF	Unc	BU
1990(c)	10,000	—	—	—	10.00	—
Note: In sets only.						

KM# 81 20 CENTS

11.3100 g., Copper-Nickel, 28.58 mm. **Ruler:** Elizabeth II **Obv:** Crowned head right **Rev:** Value below Hei Tiki **Rev. Designer:** Pukaki **Note:** Many recalled and melted in 2006.

Date	Mintage	F	VF	XF	Unc	BU
1990(l)	5,000,000	—	—	0.20	1.00	—
1990(c)	18,000	—	—	—	2.00	—
Note: In sets only.						
1990(c) Proof	10,000	Value: 4.00				
1991(c)	20,000	—	—	—	3.00	—
Note: In sets only						
1991(c) Proof	15,000	Value: 4.00				
1992(l)	15,000	—	—	—	4.00	—
Note: In sets only						
1992(l) Proof	9,000	Value: 4.00				
1993(l)	15,000	—	—	—	4.00	—
Note: In sets only						
1993(l) Proof	10,000	Value: 4.00				
1994(l)	7,000	—	—	—	4.00	—
Note: In sets only						
1994(l) Proof	4,600	Value: 5.00				
1995(l)	6,000	—	—	—	4.00	—
Note: In sets only						
1995(l) Proof	3,560	Value: 10.00				
1996(l)	5,150	—	—	—	5.00	—
Note: In sets only						
1996(l) Proof	2,569	Value: 5.00				
1997(l)	4,150	—	—	—	5.00	—
Note: In sets only						
1997(l) Proof	2,132	Value: 10.00				
1998(l)	4,000	—	—	—	5.00	—
Note: In sets only						
1998(l) Proof	2,000	Value: 10.00				

KM# 118 20 CENTS

11.3100 g., Copper-Nickel, 28.58 mm. **Ruler:** Elizabeth II **Obv:** Head with tiara right **Obv. Designer:** Ian Rank-Broadley **Rev:** Value below Hei Tiki **Note:** Many recalled and melted in 2006.

Date	Mintage	F	VF	XF	Unc	BU
1999(I)	3,199	—	—	—	—	5.00
Note: In sets only						
1999(I) Proof	1,800	Value: 10.00				
2000(I)	3,000	—	—	—	—	5.00
Note: In sets only						
2000(I) Proof	1,500	Value: 10.00				
2001(c) Proof	1,364	Value: 10.00				
2001(c)	2,910	—	—	—	—	4.00
Note: In sets only						
2002(I)	7,000,000	—	—	—	0.50	—
2002(c)	3,000	—	—	—	—	5.00
Note: In sets only						
2002(c) Proof	1,500	Value: 10.00				
2003(c)	3,000	—	—	—	—	4.00
Note: In sets only						
2003(c) Proof	3,000	Value: 10.00				
2004(I)	8,500,000	—	—	—	0.50	—
2004(c)	2,800	—	—	—	—	5.00
Note: In sets only						
2004(c) Proof	1,750	Value: 10.00				
2005(I)	4,000,000	—	—	—	—	15.00
Note: All but 178,000 melted						
2005(c)	3,000	—	—	—	—	5.00
Note: In sets only						
2005(c) Proof	2,250	Value: 10.00				
2006(c)	3,000	—	—	—	—	5.00
Note: In sets only						
2006(c) Proof	2,100	Value: 10.00				

KM# 118a 20 CENTS

4.0000 g., Nickel Plated Steel, 21.75 mm. **Ruler:** Elizabeth II **Obv:** Head with tiara right **Obv. Designer:** Ian Rank-Broadley **Rev:** Value below Hei Tiki

Date	Mintage	F	VF	XF	Unc	BU
2006(o)	116,600,000	—	—	—	0.40	0.65
2007(c) Proof	4,000	Value: 8.00				
2007(c)	5,000	—	—	—	5.00	7.00
Note: In sets only						

KM# 37.1 50 CENTS

13.6100 g., Copper-Nickel, 31.75 mm. **Ruler:** Elizabeth II **Obv:** Young bust right **Obv. Designer:** Arnold Machin **Rev:** Ship, H.M.S. Endeavour **Rev. Designer:** James Berry **Note:** Rounded, high relief portrait. Many recalled and melted in 2006.

Date	Mintage	F	VF	XF	Unc	BU
1967(I)	10,000,000	—	—	0.30	1.00	—
1967(I)	Est. 750,000	—	5.00	20.00	100	—
Note: Dot above 1						
1967(I) Prooflike	50,000	—	—	—	—	2.00
1967(I)	10	—	—	—	—	—
1968	35,000	—	—	—	2.00	—
Note: In sets only						
1968 Prooflike	40,000	—	—	—	—	3.00
1970	30,000	—	—	—	2.00	—
Note: In sets only						
1970 Prooflike	20,010	—	—	—	—	3.00
1971(c)	1,123,000	0.15	1.00	5.00	40.00	—
Note: Serifs on date numerals						
1971(I)	15,000	—	—	0.50	5.00	—
Note: Without serifs						
1971(I) Proof	5,000	Value: 40.00				
1972(c)	1,423,000	—	—	0.50	5.00	—
1972(c) Proof	8,045	Value: 15.00				
1973(c)	2,523,000	—	—	0.50	5.00	—
1973(c) Proof	8,000	Value: 10.00				
1974(c)	1,215,000	—	—	0.50	5.00	—
1974(c) Proof	8,000	Value: 10.00				
1975(I)	3,815,000	—	—	0.50	4.00	—
1975(I) Proof	10,000	Value: 7.50				
1976(I)	2,016,000	—	—	0.50	3.00	—
1976(I) Proof	11,000	Value: 7.50				
1977(I)	2,000,000	—	—	0.50	3.00	—
1977(I) Proof	12,000	Value: 7.50				
1978(o)	2,023,000	—	—	0.50	3.00	—
1978(o) Proof	15,000	Value: 6.00				
1979(o)	2,425,000	—	—	0.50	3.00	—
1979(o) Proof	16,000	Value: 6.00				
1980(I)	27,000	—	—	0.50	2.00	—
Note: Thick 8 in date. In sets only.						
1980(I) Proof	17,000	Value: 6.00				
1980(o)	8,000,000	—	0.30	0.50	3.00	—
Note: Thin 8 in date						
1981(o)	4,000,000	—	0.30	0.50	3.00	—
Note: Blunt end on 9, oval holes in 8						
1981(I)	25,000	—	—	0.50	2.00	—
Note: Pointed end on 9, round holes in 8. In sets only.						
1981(I) Proof	18,000	Value: 6.00				
1982(o)	6,000,000	—	—	0.50	3.00	—
Note: Blunt end on 2						
1982(I)	25,000	—	—	0.50	3.00	—
Note: Pointed end on 2. In sets only.						
1982(I) Proof	18,000	Value: 6.00				
1983(I)	25,000	—	—	—	3.00	—
Note: In sets only						
1983(I) Proof	18,000	Value: 6.00				
1984(I)	25,000	—	—	0.50	3.00	—
Note: In sets only.						
1984(I) Proof	15,000	Value: 5.00				
1985(c)	20,000	—	—	0.50	3.00	—
Note: In sets only.						
1985(c) Proof	12,000	Value: 5.00				

KM# 39 50 CENTS

13.6100 g., Copper-Nickel, 31.75 mm. **Ruler:** Elizabeth II **Subject:** 200th Anniversary - Captain Cook's Voyage **Obv:** Young bust right **Obv. Designer:** Arnold Machin **Rev:** Ship, H.M.S. Endeavour **Edge Lettering:** Cook Bi-Centenary 1769-1969 **Note:** Similar to KM#37.

Date	Mintage	F	VF	XF	Unc	BU
1969	50,000	—	—	1.00	3.00	—
1969 Prooflike	50,000	—	—	—	—	3.00

KM# 37.2 50 CENTS

13.6100 g., Copper-Nickel, 31.75 mm. **Obv:** Crowned bust right **Rev:** Value in upper left **Note:** Recut die, low relief. Many recalled and melted in 2006.

Date	Mintage	F	VF	XF	Unc	BU
1984(o)	2,000,000	—	—	—	3.00	—
1985(o)	2,000,000	—	—	0.50	4.00	—

KM# 95 50 CENTS

Nickel **Ruler:** Elizabeth II **Obv:** Young bust right **Obv. Designer:** Arnold Machin **Rev:** Voyageur, date and value below **Note:** Mule with Canada Dollar, KM#120..

Date	Mintage	F	VF	XF	Unc	BU
1985 6 known	—	—	1,200	1,900	—	—

KM# 63 50 CENTS

13.6100 g., Copper-Nickel, 31.75 mm. **Ruler:** Elizabeth II **Obv:** Crowned head right **Obv. Designer:** R.D. Maklouf **Rev:** Ship, H.M.S. Endeavour **Rev. Designer:** James Berry **Note:** Many recalled and melted in 2006.

Date	Mintage	F	VF	XF	Unc	BU
1986(o)	5,200,000	—	—	0.50	2.00	—
1986(I)	18,000	—	—	1.00	2.00	—
Note: In sets only.						
1986(I) Proof	10,000	Value: 5.00				
1987(o)	3,600,000	—	—	0.50	2.00	—
1987(I)	18,000	—	—	1.00	2.00	—
Note: In sets only.						
1987(I) Proof	10,000	Value: 5.00				
1988(c)	8,800,000	—	—	0.50	2.00	—
1988(I)	15,000	—	—	1.00	2.00	—
Note: In sets only.						
1988(I) Proof	9,000	Value: 5.00				
1989(c)	15,000	—	—	—	3.00	—
Note: In sets only						
1989(c) Proof	8,500	Value: 5.00				
1990(c)	18,000	—	—	—	5.00	—
Note: In sets only						
1990(c) Proof	10,000	Value: 5.00				
1991(c)	20,000	—	—	—	3.00	—
Note: In sets only						
1991(c) Proof	15,000	Value: 5.00				
1992(I)	15,000	—	—	—	4.00	—
Note: In sets only						
1992(I) Proof	9,000	Value: 5.00				
1993(I)	15,000	—	—	—	4.00	—
Note: In sets only						
1993(I) Proof	10,000	Value: 5.00				
1995(I)	10,000	—	—	—	4.00	—
Note: In sets only						
1995(I) Proof	4,000	Value: 5.00				
1996(I)	5,150	—	—	—	4.00	—
Note: In sets only						
1996(I) Proof	2,569	Value: 5.00				
1997(I)	4,150	—	—	—	5.00	—
Note: In sets only						
1997(I) Proof	2,132	Value: 5.00				
1998(I)	4,000	—	—	—	4.00	—
Note: In sets only						
1998(I) Proof	2,000	Value: 5.00				

KM# 75 50 CENTS

13.6100 g., Copper-Nickel, 31.75 mm. **Ruler:** Elizabeth II **Subject:** 1990 Anniversary Celebrations **Obv:** Crowned head right **Rev:** Child with shovel sitting beside tree, value slanted at right

Date	Mintage	F	VF	XF	Unc	BU
1990(c)	10,000	—	—	—	8.00	—
Note: In sets only.						

KM# 90 50 CENTS

Bi-Metallic Aluminum-Bronze center in Copper-Nickel ring, 32 mm. **Ruler:** Elizabeth II **Subject:** H.M.S. Endeavour **Obv:** Crowned head right within circle **Rev:** Sailing ship within circle **Rev. Designer:** James Berry

Date	Mintage	F	VF	XF	Unc	BU
1994	52,500	—	—	—	15.00	—

KM# 119 50 CENTS

13.6100 g., Copper-Nickel, 31.75 mm. **Ruler:** Elizabeth II **Obv:** Head with tiara right **Obv. Designer:** Ian Rank-Broadley **Rev:** Ship, H.M.S. Endeavour **Rev. Designer:** James Berry **Note:** Many recalled and melted in 2006.

Date	Mintage	F	VF	XF	Unc	BU
1999	3,199	—	—	—	4.00	—
Note: In sets only						
1999 Proof	1,800	Value: 5.00				
2000	3,000	—	—	—	4.00	—

Date	Mintage	F	VF	XF	Unc	BU
Note: In sets only						
2000 Proof	1,500	Value: 5.00				
2001(l)	5,000,000	—	—	—	1.00	—
2001(c)	2,910	—	—	—	—	4.00
Note: In sets only						
2001(c) Proof	1,364	Value: 5.00				
2002(l)	3,000,000	—	—	0.50	1.00	—
2002(c)	3,000	—	—	—	—	4.00
Note: In sets only						
2002(c) Proof	1,500	Value: 5.00				
2003(l)	2,500,000	—	—	0.50	1.00	—
2003(c)	3,000	—	—	—	—	4.00
Note: In sets only						
2003(c) Proof	1,496	Value: 5.00				
2004(l)	2,000,000	—	—	—	1.00	—
2004(c)	2,800	—	—	—	—	4.00
Note: In sets only						
2004(c) Proof	1,750	Value: 5.00				
2005(l)	1,000,000	—	—	—	7.50	—
Note: All but 503,800 melted						
2005(c)	3,000	—	—	—	—	4.00
Note: In sets only						
2005(c) Proof	2,250	Value: 5.00				
2006(c)	3,000	—	—	—	—	4.00
Note: In sets only.						
2006(c) Proof	2,100	Value: 5.00				

KM# 119a 50 CENTS

5.0000 g., Nickel Plated Steel, 24.75 mm. **Ruler:** Elizabeth II **Obv:** Head with tiara right **Rev:** Ship, H.M.S. Endeavour **Rev. Designer:** James Berry

Date	Mintage	F	VF	XF	Unc	BU
2006(o)	70,200,000	—	—	—	0.75	1.00
2007(c)	5,000	Value: 8.00				
Note: In sets only						

KM# 38.1 DOLLAR

Copper-Nickel, 38.8 mm. **Ruler:** Elizabeth II **Subject:** Decimalization Commemorative **Obv:** Young bust right **Obv. Designer:** Arnold Machin **Rev:** Crowned shield within silver fern leaves **Rev. Designer:** William Gardner **Edge:** DECIMAL CURRENCY INTRODUCED JULY 10 1967

Date	Mintage	F	VF	XF	Unc	BU
1967(l)	250,000	—	—	0.75	1.00	—
1967 Prooflike	50,000	—	—	—	—	2.00
1967 Proof	10	—	—	—	—	—

KM# 38.2 DOLLAR

Copper-Nickel, 38.8 mm. **Ruler:** Elizabeth II **Obv:** Young bust right **Obv. Designer:** Arnold Machin **Rev:** Crowned shield within silver fern leaves **Rev. Designer:** William Gardner **Edge:** Reeded **Note:** Regular issue.

Date	Mintage	F	VF	XF	Unc	BU
1971(l)	45,000	—	—	2.00	3.00	—
1971 Proof	5,000	Value: 25.00				
1972(c)	42,000	—	—	2.00	3.00	—
1972(c) Proof	8,045	Value: 10.00				
1972(c) RAM case; Proof	3,000	Value: 30.00				
1973(c)	37,000	—	—	2.00	3.00	—
1973 Proof	16,000	Value: 5.00				
1975(l)	30,000	—	—	2.00	3.00	—
1975 Proof	20,000	Value: 5.00				
1976(l)	36,000	—	—	2.00	4.00	—
1976 Proof	22,000	Value: 5.00				

KM# 40.1 DOLLAR

Copper-Nickel, 38.8 mm. **Ruler:** Elizabeth II **Subject:** 200th Anniversary - Captain Cook's Voyage **Obv:** Young bust right **Obv. Designer:** Arnold Machin **Rev:** Map flanked by bust at left and ship at right **Rev. Designer:** James Berry **Edge:** COMMEMORATING COOK BI-CENTENERY 1769-1969

Date	Mintage	F	VF	XF	Unc	BU
1969(c)	450,000	—	—	1.00	2.00	—
1969 Prooflike	50,000	—	—	—	—	3.00

KM# 40.2 DOLLAR

Copper-Nickel, 38.8 mm. **Ruler:** Elizabeth II **Obv:** Young bust right **Obv. Designer:** Arnold Machin **Rev:** Map flanked by bust at left and ship at right **Rev. Designer:** James Berry **Edge:** No hyphen in edge inscription

Date	Mintage	F	VF	XF	Unc	BU
1969(c)	Inc. above	—	—	—	4.00	—

KM# 40.3 DOLLAR

Copper Nickel, 38.8 mm. **Ruler:** Elizabeth II **Obv:** Young bust right **Obv. Designer:** Arnold Machin **Rev:** Map flanked by bust at left and ship at right **Rev. Designer:** James Berry **Edge Lettering:** No I in BI-CENTENARY

Date	Mintage	F	VF	XF	Unc	BU
1969(c)	Inc. above	—	—	—	—	—

KM# 78 DOLLAR

8.0000 g., Aluminum-Bronze, 23 mm. **Ruler:** Elizabeth II **Obv:** Crowned head right **Obv. Designer:** R.D. Maklouf **Rev:** Kiwi Bird **Note:** Regular circulation issue.

Date	Mintage	F	VF	XF	Unc	BU
1990(l)	40,000,000	—	—	1.00	3.00	5.00
1990(c)	10,000	—	—	—	4.00	5.00
Note: In sets only.						
1991(l)	10,000,000	—	—	1.00	3.00	5.00
1991(c)	20,000	—	—	—	3.00	5.00
Note: In sets only.						
1991(c) Proof	15,000	Value: 20.00				
1992(l)	15,000	—	—	—	15.00	—
Note: In sets only						
1992(l) Proof	9,000	Value: 20.00				
1993(l)	15,000	—	—	—	10.00	—
Note: In sets only						
1993(l) Proof	10,000	Value: 20.00				
1994(l)	16,000	—	—	—	20.00	—
Note: In sets only						
1994(l) Proof	4,600	Value: 25.00				
1995(l)	6,000	—	—	—	20.00	—
Note: In sets only						
1995(l) Proof	3,560	Value: 25.00				
1996(l)	5,150	—	—	—	20.00	—
Note: In sets only						
1996(l) Proof	4,000	Value: 25.00				
1997(l)	4,150	—	—	—	20.00	—
Note: In sets only						
1997(l) Proof	2,132	Value: 25.00				
1998(l)	4,000	—	—	—	20.00	—
Note: In sets only						
1998(l) Proof	2,000	Value: 25.00				

KM# 120 DOLLAR

8.0000 g., Aluminum-Bronze **Ruler:** Elizabeth II **Obv:** Head with tiara right **Obv. Designer:** Ian Rank-Broadley **Rev:** Kiwi bird within sprigs **Rev. Designer:** R. Maurice Conly

Date	Mintage	F	VF	XF	Unc	BU
1999	3,199	—	—	—	—	20.00
Note: In sets only						
1999 Proof	1,800	Value: 20.00				
2000(o)	5,000,000	—	—	—	1.00	3.00
2000 Proof	1,500	Value: 5.00				
2001(c) Proof	1,364	Value: 5.00				
2001(c)	2,910	—	—	—	1.00	2.50
Note: In sets only						
2002(l)	8,000,000	—	—	—	1.00	2.50
2002(c)	4,000	—	—	—	—	4.00
Note: In sets only						
2002(c) Proof	1,500	Value: 5.00				
2003(l)	4,000,000	—	—	—	1.00	2.50
2003(c)	5,000	—	—	—	—	4.00
Note: In sets only						
2003(c) Proof	1,750	Value: 5.00				
2004(l)	2,700,000	—	—	—	1.00	2.50
2004(c)	3,500	—	—	—	—	4.00
Note: In sets only						
2004(c) Proof	2,250	Value: 5.00				
2005(l)	2,000,000	—	—	—	1.00	2.50
2005(c)	4,000	—	—	—	—	4.00
Note: In sets only						
2005(c) Proof	2,250	Value: 5.00				
2006(c)	3,000	—	—	—	—	4.00
Note: In sets only.						
2006(c) Proof	2,100	Value: 5.00				
2007(c)	—	—	—	—	—	4.00
2007(c) Proof	—	Value: 5.00				

KM# 79 2 DOLLARS

10.0000 g., Aluminum-Bronze, 26.5 mm. **Ruler:** Elizabeth II **Obv:** Crowned head right **Obv. Designer:** R.D. Maklouf **Rev:** Kotuku, white heron **Rev. Designer:** R. Maurice Conly

Date	Mintage	F	VF	XF	Unc	BU
1990(c)	18,000	—	—	—	3.00	5.00
1990(l)	30,000,000	—	—	2.00	3.00	5.00
1991(l)	10,000,000	—	—	2.00	3.00	5.00
1991(c)	20,000	—	—	—	3.00	5.00
1991(c) Proof	15,000	Value: 6.00				
1992(l)	15,000	—	—	—	6.00	—
Note: In sets only						
1992(l) Proof	9,000	Value: 6.00				
1994(l)	7,000	—	—	—	6.00	—

Date	Mintage	F	VF	XF	Unc	BU
Note: In sets only						
1994(l) Proof	4,600	Value: 6.00				
1995(l)	6,000	—	—	—	6.00	—
Note: In sets only						
1995(l) Proof	3,560	Value: 20.00				
1996(l)	5,150	—	—	—	20.00	—
Note: In sets only						
1996(l) Proof	2,569	Value: 20.00				
1997(l)	4,150	—	—	—	—	—
Note: In sets only.						
1997(l) Proof	2,132	—	—	—	—	—
1997(p)	1,000,000	—	—	—	3.00	5.00
Note: Entire mintage recalled, but many left in circulation						
1998(p)	6,000,000	—	—	—	3.00	5.00
1998(p) Proof	2,000	Value: 6.00				

KM# 121 2 DOLLARS

10.0000 g., Aluminum-Bronze, 26.5 mm. **Ruler:** Elizabeth II **Obv:** Head with tiara right **Obv. Designer:** Ian Rank-Broadley **Rev:** Heron above value **Rev. Designer:** R. Maurice Conley

Date	Mintage	F	VF	XF	Unc	BU
1999(p)	5,050,000	—	—	—	3.00	5.00
1999(l) Proof	2,000	Value: 25.00				
2000	3,000	—	—	—	2.50	50.00
Note: In sets only						
2000(l) Proof	1,500	Value: 25.00				
2001(l)	3,000,000	—	—	—	2.50	5.00
2001(c)	2,910	—	—	—	—	6.00
Note: In sets only						
2001(c) Proof	2,000	Value: 7.50				
2002(l)	6,000,000	—	—	—	2.50	5.00
2002(c)	3,000	—	—	—	—	6.00
Note: In sets only						
2002(c) Proof	2,000	Value: 7.50				
2003(l)	6,000,000	—	—	—	2.50	5.00
2003(c)	3,000	—	—	—	—	6.00
Note: In sets only						
2003(c) Proof	3,000	Value: 7.50				
2004 Proof	3,500	Value: 7.50				
2004(c)	2,800	—	—	—	2.50	5.00
Note: In sets only						
2005(l)	5,000,000	—	—	—	2.50	5.00
2005(c)	3,000	—	—	—	—	6.00
Note: In sets only						
2005(c) Proof	3,000	Value: 7.50				
2006(c)	3,000	—	—	—	—	6.00
Note: In sets only.						
2006(c) Proof	2,100	Value: 7.50				
2007(c) Proof	4,000	Value: 7.50				
2007(c)	—	—	—	—	—	6.00

NICARAGUA

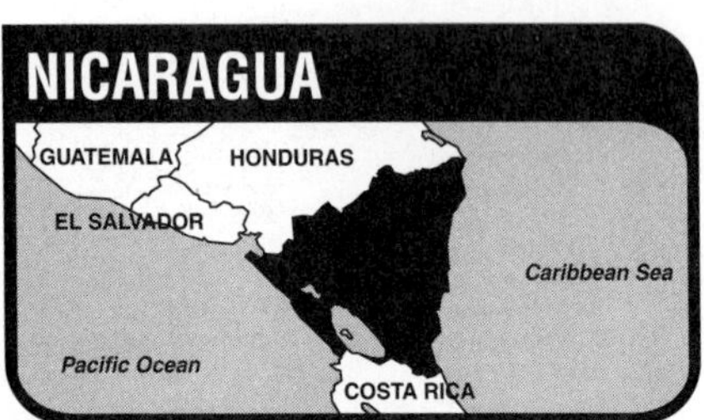

The Republic of Nicaragua, situated in Central America between Honduras and Costa Rica, has an area of 50,193 sq. mi. (129,494 sq. km.).

Columbus sighted the coast of Nicaragua on Sept. 12,1502 during the course of his last voyage of discovery. It was first visited in 1522 by conquistadors from Panama, under the command of Gil Gonzalez. Francisco Hernandez de Cordoba established the first settlements in 1524 at Granada and Leon. Nicaragua was incorporated, for administrative purpose, in the Captaincy General of Guatemala, which included every Central American state but Panama. On September 15, 1821 the Captaincy General of Guatemala declared itself and all the Central American provinces independent of Spain. The next year Nicaragua united with the Mexican Empire of Augustin de Iturbide, only to join in 1823 the federation of the Central American Republic. Within Nicaragua rival cities or juntas such as Leon, Granada and El Viejo vied for power, wealth and influence, often attacking each other at will. To further prove their legitimacy as well as provide an acceptable circulating coinage in those turbulent times (1821-1825), provisional mints functioned intermittently at Granada, Leon and El Viejo. The early coinage reflected traditional but crude Spanish colonial cob-style designs. Nicaragua's first governor was Pedro Arias Davila, appointed on June 1, 1827. When the federation was dissolved, Nicaragua declared itself an independent republic on April 30, 1838.

Dissension between the Liberals and Conservatives of the contending cities kept Nicaragua in turmoil, which made it possible for William Walker to make himself President in 1855. The two major political parties finally united to drive him out and in 1857 he was expelled. A relative peace followed, but by 1912, Nicaragua had requested the U.S. Marines to restore order, which began a U.S. involvement that lasted until the Good Neighbor Policy was adopted in 1933.

MINT MARKS

H - Heaton, Birmingham

HF - Huguenin Freres, Le Locle, Switzerland

Mo - Mexico City

MONETARY SYSTEM

100 Centavos = 1 Peso

NOTE: Former listing for 1823 IL 1/2 Real of Leon has been identified by recognized authorities as a Honduras issue 1823 TL 1/2 Real cataloged there as KM#9.

REPUBLIC

DECIMAL COINAGE

KM# 10 1/2 CENTAVO

Bronze **Obv:** National emblem **Rev:** Value within sprigs

Date	Mintage	F	VF	XF	Unc	BU
1912H	900,000	1.00	2.50	15.00	40.00	—
1912H Proof	—	Value: 275				
1915H	320,000	1.50	4.00	30.00	100	—
1916H	720,000	1.50	4.00	30.00	100	—
1917	720,000	1.50	4.00	20.00	65.00	—
1922	400,000	2.00	5.00	20.00	80.00	—
1924	400,000	1.00	3.00	12.00	70.00	—
1934	500,000	1.00	3.00	10.00	45.00	—
1936	600,000	0.50	0.75	5.00	35.00	—
1937	1,000,000	0.40	0.60	4.00	20.00	—

KM# 11 CENTAVO

Bronze **Obv:** National emblem **Rev:** Value within sprigs

Date	Mintage	F	VF	XF	Unc	BU
1912H	450,000	1.00	3.00	10.00	45.00	—
1912H Proof	—	Value: 275				
1914H	300,000	5.00	10.00	30.00	85.00	—
1915H	500,000	5.00	10.00	35.00	100	—
1916H	450,000	5.00	10.00	35.00	100	—
1917	450,000	3.00	7.00	28.00	75.00	—
1919	750,000	2.00	6.00	18.00	50.00	—
1920	700,000	1.00	4.50	14.50	45.00	—
1922	500,000	1.00	4.50	14.50	45.00	—
1924	300,000	2.00	6.00	22.00	65.00	—
1927	250,000	3.50	8.50	28.00	75.00	—
1928	500,000	2.00	6.00	18.00	45.00	—
1929	500,000	2.00	5.00	13.50	35.00	—
1930	250,000	3.00	8.00	25.00	70.00	—
1934	500,000	1.50	4.00	12.00	35.00	—
1935	500,000	1.00	4.00	12.00	35.00	—
1936	500,000	1.00	3.00	8.00	25.00	—
1937	1,000,000	0.75	2.00	7.00	20.00	—
1938	2,000,000	0.75	1.50	5.00	15.00	—
1940	2,000,000	0.75	1.50	5.00	15.00	—

KM# 20 CENTAVO

Brass **Obv:** National emblem **Rev:** Value within sprigs

Date	Mintage	F	VF	XF	Unc	BU
1943	1,000,000	0.50	1.50	4.50	18.00	—

KM# 12 5 CENTAVOS

5.0000 g., Copper-Nickel **Obv:** National emblem **Rev:** Value within sprigs

Date	Mintage	F	VF	XF	Unc	BU
1912H	460,000	4.00	10.00	25.00	75.00	—
1912H Proof	—	Value: 300				
1914H	300,000	4.00	10.00	30.00	85.00	—
1915H	160,000	8.00	20.00	50.00	225	—
1919	100,000	4.00	10.00	30.00	110	—
1920	150,000	4.00	10.00	30.00	100	—
1927	100,000	4.00	10.00	30.00	100	—
1928	100,000	4.00	10.00	30.00	100	—
1929	100,000	5.00	12.00	35.00	120	—
1930	100,000	4.00	10.00	30.00	100	—
1934	200,000	3.00	10.00	25.00	90.00	—
1935	200,000	2.00	5.00	20.00	85.00	—
1936	300,000	1.50	3.00	15.00	65.00	—
1937	300,000	1.50	3.00	10.00	40.00	—
1938	800,000	1.00	2.00	8.00	30.00	—
1940	800,000	1.00	2.00	6.00	20.00	—

KM# 21 5 CENTAVOS

Brass **Obv:** Bust facing within circle **Rev:** Radiant sun and hills within circle **Edge:** Plain

Date	Mintage	F	VF	XF	Unc	BU
1943	2,000,000	0.75	2.50	10.00	60.00	—

KM# 24.1 5 CENTAVOS

3.0000 g., Copper-Nickel **Obv:** Bust facing within circle **Rev:** Radiant sun and hills within circle **Edge Lettering:** B. N. N **Note:** Reduced size. Medal rotation.

Date	Mintage	F	VF	XF	Unc	BU
1946	4,000,000	0.10	0.25	2.50	18.00	—
1946 Proof	—	Value: 200				
1950	—	0.10	0.25	2.50	18.00	—
1952	4,000,000	0.10	0.25	3.50	25.00	—
1952 Proof	—	Value: 250				
1954	4,000,000	0.10	0.15	0.25	5.00	—
1954 Proof	—	Value: 250				
1956	5,000,000	0.10	0.15	0.50	5.00	—
1956 Proof	—	Value: 250				

KM# 24.2 5 CENTAVOS

Copper-Nickel **Obv:** Bust facing within circle **Rev:** Radiant sun and hills within circle **Edge Lettering:** B. C. N. **Note:** Medal rotation.

Date	Mintage	F	VF	XF	Unc	BU
1962	3,000,000	—	0.10	0.15	2.00	—
1962 Proof	—	Value: 200				
1964	4,000,000	—	0.10	0.15	2.00	—
1965	10,000,000	—	0.10	0.15	2.00	—

KM# 24.3 5 CENTAVOS

3.0000 g., Copper-Nickel **Obv:** Bust facing within circle **Rev:** Radiant sun and hills within circle **Edge:** Reeded **Note:** Coin rotation.

Date	Mintage	F	VF	XF	Unc	BU
1972 Proof	20,000	Value: 2.50				

KM# 27 5 CENTAVOS

Aluminum, 21.5 mm. **Obv:** National emblem within circle **Rev:** Value within circle **Note:** Medal rotation.

Date	Mintage	F	VF	XF	Unc	BU
1974	18,000,000	—	—	0.10	0.50	—

KM# 28 5 CENTAVOS
1.4600 g., Aluminum, 21.5 mm. **Series:** F.A.O. **Obv:** National emblem within circle **Rev:** Value within circle **Note:** Medal rotation.

Date	Mintage	F	VF	XF	Unc	BU
1974	2,000,000	—	—	0.40	2.00	—

KM# 49 5 CENTAVOS
1.0400 g., Aluminum, 16.8 mm. **Obv:** Head with hat facing **Rev:** Value **Note:** Coin rotation.

Date	Mintage	F	VF	XF	Unc	BU
1981	5,000,000	—	—	0.40	1.50	—

KM# 55 5 CENTAVOS
0.7500 g., Aluminum, 15 mm. **Obv:** Hat above date and sprigs **Rev:** Value **Note:** Medal rotation.

Date	Mintage	F	VF	XF	Unc	BU
1987	38,000,000	—	—	0.40	1.00	—

KM# 80 5 CENTAVOS
2.1100 g., Chromium Plated Steel, 14.97 mm. **Obv:** National emblem **Rev:** Bird flying over map **Edge:** Plain **Note:** Coin rotation.

Date	Mintage	F	VF	XF	Unc	BU
1994	20,000,000	—	—	—	0.50	0.75

KM# 97 5 CENTAVOS
3.0000 g., Copper Plated Steel, 18.5 mm. **Obv:** National arms **Rev:** Value within circle **Edge:** Plain

Date	Mintage	F	VF	XF	Unc	BU
2002	—	—	—	—	0.25	0.50

KM# 13 10 CENTAVOS
2.5000 g., 0.8000 Silver 0.0643 oz. ASW **Obv:** Bust facing within circle **Rev:** Radiant sun and hills within circle **Note:** All dates struck with medal rotation except 1935, which appears only in coin rotation.

Date	Mintage	F	VF	XF	Unc	BU
1912H	230,000	2.50	7.00	25.00	100	—
1912H Proof	—	Value: 300				
1914H	220,000	3.00	10.00	35.00	115	—
1914H Proof	—	Value: 375				
1927	500,000	2.00	4.00	20.00	85.00	—
1928	1,000,000	1.25	3.00	15.00	65.00	—
1930	150,000	1.50	4.00	30.00	95.00	—
1935	250,000	1.25	3.00	12.50	45.00	—
1936	250,000	1.25	3.00	10.00	30.00	—

KM# 17.1 10 CENTAVOS
4.0000 g., Copper-Nickel **Obv:** Bust facing within circle **Rev:** Radiant sun and hills within circle **Edge Lettering:** B.N.N **Note:** Medal rotation.

Date	Mintage	F	VF	XF	Unc	BU
1939	2,500,000	1.25	3.00	10.00	30.00	—
1939 Proof	—	Value: 250				
1946	2,000,000	1.25	3.00	10.00	30.00	—
1946 Proof	—	Value: 200				
1950	2,000,000	0.25	0.50	3.00	20.00	—
1950 Proof	—	Value: 200				
1952	1,500,000	0.25	0.50	3.00	25.00	—
1952 Proof	—	Value: 200				
1954	3,000,000	0.10	0.25	1.50	10.00	—
1954 Proof	—	Value: 200				
1956	5,000,000	0.10	0.20	1.00	6.00	—
1956 Proof	—	Value: 200				

KM# 17.2 10 CENTAVOS
3.9100 g., Copper-Nickel **Obv:** Bust facing within circle **Rev:** Radiant sun and hills within circle **Edge Lettering:** B.C.N **Note:** Medal rotation.

Date	Mintage	F	VF	XF	Unc	BU
1962	4,000,000	—	0.10	0.15	5.00	—
1962 Proof	—	Value: 225				
1964	4,000,000	—	0.10	0.15	5.00	—
1965	12,000,000	—	0.10	0.15	1.00	—

KM# 22 10 CENTAVOS
Brass **Obv:** Bust facing within circle **Rev:** Radiant sun and hills within circle **Edge:** Reeded **Note:** Coin rotation.

Date	Mintage	F	VF	XF	Unc	BU
1943	2,000,000	0.50	1.00	5.00	50.00	—

KM# 17.3 10 CENTAVOS
Copper-Nickel, 17 mm. **Issuer:** Banco Central De Nicaragua **Obv:** Bust facing within circle - Francisco Hernandez de Cordoba **Obv. Legend:** Republica de Nicaragua **Rev:** Radiant sun and hills within circle, Seal of the Central America Federation **Rev. Legend:** In God We Trust (En DIos Confiamos) **Edge:** Reeded **Note:** Coin rotation.

Date	Mintage	F	VF	XF	Unc	BU
1972 Proof	20,000	Value: 2.50				

Note: In sets only

KM# 30 10 CENTAVOS
Aluminum **Obv:** Map within circle **Rev:** Value within circle

Date	Mintage	F	VF	XF	Unc	BU
1974	18,000,000	—	—	0.10	0.20	—

KM# 29 10 CENTAVOS
Aluminum **Series:** F.A.O. **Obv:** Map within circle **Rev:** Value within circle **Note:** Medal rotation.

Date	Mintage	F	VF	XF	Unc	BU
1974	2,000,000	—	—	0.10	1.00	—

KM# 31 10 CENTAVOS
Copper-Nickel

Date	Mintage	F	VF	XF	Unc	BU
1978	20,000,000	—	—	0.40	2.00	—

KM# 50 10 CENTAVOS
Aluminum **Obv:** Head with hat facing **Rev:** Value **Note:** Coin rotation.

Date	Mintage	F	VF	XF	Unc	BU
1981	10,000,000	—	—	0.15	1.00	—

KM# 56 10 CENTAVOS
0.9000 g., Aluminum, 17 mm. **Obv:** Hat above date and sprigs **Rev:** Value **Note:** Medal rotation.

Date	Mintage	F	VF	XF	Unc	BU
1987	16,000,000	—	—	0.15	0.40	—

KM# 81 10 CENTAVOS
Chromium Plated Steel **Obv:** National emblem **Rev:** Bird flying above map **Note:** Coin rotation.

Date	Mintage	F	VF	XF	Unc	BU
1994	6,439,000	—	—	—	0.75	1.00

KM# 98 10 CENTAVOS
4.0000 g., Brass Plated Steel, 20.5 mm. **Obv:** National arms **Rev:** Value within circle **Edge:** Reeded and plain sections

Date	Mintage	F	VF	XF	Unc	BU
2002	—	—	—	—	0.45	0.85

KM# 14 25 CENTAVOS
6.2500 g., 0.8000 Silver 0.1607 oz. ASW **Obv:** Bust facing within circle **Rev:** Radiant sun and hills within circle **Note:** Medal rotation.

Date	Mintage	F	VF	XF	Unc	BU
1912H	320,000	3.00	10.00	35.00	90.00	—
1912H Proof	—	Value: 350				
1914H	100,000	5.00	15.00	50.00	170	—
1928	200,000	3.00	10.00	30.00	90.00	—
1929	20,000	8.00	35.00	90.00	275	—
1930	20,000	8.00	35.00	90.00	250	—
1936	100,000	2.75	8.00	20.00	65.00	—

KM# 23 25 CENTAVOS
Brass, 26.8 mm. **Obv:** Bust facing within circle **Rev:** Radiant sun and hills within circle **Edge:** Reeded **Note:** Coin rotation.

Date	Mintage	F	VF	XF	Unc	BU
1943	1,000,000	0.50	1.50	8.50	50.00	—

KM# 18.1 25 CENTAVOS
5.0000 g., Copper-Nickel, 23 mm. **Obv:** Bust facing within circle **Rev:** Radiant sun and hills within circle **Edge Lettering:** B N N (repeated)

Date	Mintage	F	VF	XF	Unc	BU
1939	1,000,000	2.00	6.00	15.00	50.00	—
1939 Proof	—	Value: 300				
1946	1,000,000	1.50	4.00	12.00	40.00	—
1946 Proof	—	Value: 280				
1950	1,000,000	0.25	0.50	1.50	20.00	—
1950 Proof	—	Value: 300				
1952	1,000,000	0.25	0.50	1.50	15.00	—

Date	Mintage	F	VF	XF	Unc	BU
1952 Proof	—	Value: 280				
1954	2,000,000	0.10	0.20	0.50	6.00	—
1954 Proof	—	Value: 280				
1956	3,000,000	0.10	0.20	0.50	5.00	—
1956 Proof	—	Value: 280				

KM# 18.2 25 CENTAVOS

5.1000 g., Copper-Nickel, 23 mm. **Obv:** Bust facing within circle **Rev:** Radiant sun and hills within circle **Edge Lettering:** B. C. N. **Note:** Medal rotation.

Date	Mintage	F	VF	XF	Unc	BU
1964	3,000,000	0.10	0.20	0.40	4.00	—
1965	4,400,000	0.10	0.20	0.30	4.00	—

KM# 18.3 25 CENTAVOS

Copper-Nickel **Obv:** Bust facing within circle **Rev:** Radiant sun and hills within circle **Edge:** Reeded

Date	Mintage	F	VF	XF	Unc	BU
1972	4,000,000	—	0.10	0.15	2.00	—
1972 Proof	20,000	Value: 2.50				
Note: Coin rotation						
1974	6,000,000	—	0.10	0.15	2.00	—
Note: Medal rotation						

KM# 51 25 CENTAVOS

3.4000 g., Nickel Clad Steel **Obv:** Head with hat facing **Rev:** Value **Note:** Coin rotation

Date	Mintage	F	VF	XF	Unc	BU
1981	10,000,000	—	—	0.25	1.50	—
1985	8,000,000	5.00	10.00	20.00	30.00	—

KM# 57 25 CENTAVOS

1.3500 g., Aluminum, 19 mm. **Obv:** Hat above date and sprigs **Rev:** Value **Note:** Medal rotation.

Date	Mintage	F	VF	XF	Unc	BU
1987	—	—	—	0.25	2.00	—

KM# 82 25 CENTAVOS

Chromium Plated Steel **Obv:** National emblem **Rev:** Bird flying above map **Note:** Coin rotation.

Date	Mintage	F	VF	XF	Unc	BU
1994	2,500,000	—	—	—	1.00	1.50

KM# 99 25 CENTAVOS

5.0000 g., Brass Plated Steel, 23.25 mm. **Obv:** National arms **Rev:** Value within circle **Edge:** Reeded and plain sections

Date	Mintage	F	VF	XF	Unc	BU
2002	—	—	—	—	0.65	1.25

KM# 15 50 CENTAVOS

12.5000 g., 0.8000 Silver 0.3215 oz. ASW **Obv:** Bust facing within circle **Rev:** Radiant sun and hills within circle **Note:** Medal rotation.

Date	Mintage	F	VF	XF	Unc	BU
1912H	260,000	5.50	15.00	75.00	200	—
1912H Proof	—	Value: 500				
1929	20,000	6.50	20.00	90.00	275	—

KM# 19.1 50 CENTAVOS

7.9200 g., Copper-Nickel **Obv:** Bust facing within circle **Rev:** Radiant sun and hills within circle **Edge Lettering:** B. N. N **Note:** Medal rotation.

Date	Mintage	F	VF	XF	Unc	BU
1939	1,000,000	3.00	8.00	20.00	65.00	—
1939 Proof	—	Value: 300				
1946	500,000	2.00	5.00	12.50	50.00	—
1946 Proof	—	Value: 300				
1950	500,000	1.00	2.00	10.00	50.00	—
1950 Proof	—	Value: 300				
1952	1,000,000	0.75	1.50	5.00	30.00	—
1952 Proof	—	Value: 300				
1954	2,000,000	0.50	1.00	4.00	15.00	—
1954 Proof	—	Value: 300				
1956	2,000,000	0.50	1.00	4.00	15.00	—
1956 Proof	—	Value: 300				

KM# 19.2 50 CENTAVOS

Copper-Nickel **Obv:** Bust facing within circle **Rev:** Radiant sun and hills within circle **Edge Lettering:** B. C. N

Date	Mintage	F	VF	XF	Unc	BU
1965	600,000	0.50	1.25	4.50	15.00	—
1965 Proof	—	Value: 150				

KM# 19.3 50 CENTAVOS

Copper-Nickel **Obv:** Bust facing within circle **Rev:** Radiant sun and hills within circle **Edge:** Reeded

Date	Mintage	F	VF	XF	Unc	BU
1972	—	—	—	—	—	—
1972 Proof	20,000	Value: 2.50				
Note: Coin rotation						
1974	2,000,000	0.10	0.25	0.50	3.50	—
Note: Medal rotation						

KM# 42 50 CENTAVOS

7.0000 g., Copper-Nickel **Obv:** Head with hat facing **Rev:** Value **Note:** Coin rotation.

Date	Mintage	F	VF	XF	Unc	BU
1980Mo	15,000,000	0.10	0.25	0.50	1.75	—

KM# 42a 50 CENTAVOS

6.1600 g., Nickel Clad Steel, 25.9 mm. **Obv:** Head with hat facing **Rev:** Value **Note:** Coin rotation.

Date	Mintage	F	VF	XF	Unc	BU
1983	10,000,000	—	—	0.40	2.50	—
1985	10,000,000	3.50	7.50	15.00	25.00	—

KM# 58 50 CENTAVOS

4.8500 g., Aluminum-Bronze, 22 mm. **Obv:** Hat above date and sprigs **Rev:** Value **Note:** Medal rotation.

Date	Mintage	F	VF	XF	Unc	BU
1987	12,000,000	—	—	0.40	2.50	—

KM# 83 50 CENTAVOS

4.6800 g., Chromium Plated Steel, 22 mm. **Obv:** National emblem **Rev:** Bird flying above map **Note:** Coin rotation.

Date	Mintage	F	VF	XF	Unc	BU
1994	12,000,000	—	—	—	1.25	1.75

KM# 88 50 CENTAVOS

4.8000 g., Nickel Clad Steel, 22 mm. **Obv:** National emblem **Rev:** Value above sprigs within circle, date flanked by stars

Date	Mintage	F	VF	XF	Unc	BU
1997	24,000,000	—	—	—	1.25	1.75

KM# 16 CORDOBA

25.0000 g., 0.9000 Silver 0.7234 oz. ASW **Obv:** Bust facing within circle **Rev:** Radiant sun and hills within circle **Note:** Medal rotation.

Date	Mintage	F	VF	XF	Unc	BU
1912H	35,000	30.00	75.00	285	1,900	—
1912H Proof	—	Value: 2,850				

KM# 26 CORDOBA

9.4500 g., Copper-Nickel, 28.9 mm. **Obv:** Bust facing within circle **Rev:** Radiant sun and hills within circle **Edge:** Reeded

Date	Mintage	F	VF	XF	Unc	BU
1972	20,000,000	0.10	0.20	2.00	4.00	—
Note: Medal rotation						
1972 Proof	40,000	Value: 10.00				
Note: Coin rotation						

KM# 43 CORDOBA

8.8400 g., Copper-Nickel **Obv:** Head with hat facing **Rev:** Value **Note:** Coin rotation.

Date	Mintage	F	VF	XF	Unc	BU
1980Mo	10,000,000	0.10	0.20	0.50	2.00	—
1983Mo	10,000,000	0.10	0.20	0.50	2.00	—

KM# 43a CORDOBA

Nickel Clad Steel **Obv:** Head with hat facing **Rev:** Value **Note:** Coin rotation.

Date	Mintage	F	VF	XF	Unc	BU
1984	10,000,000	—	0.10	0.50	2.00	—
1985	10,000,000	1.00	2.00	7.00	35.00	—

KM# 59 CORDOBA

6.1500 g., Aluminum-Bronze, 24 mm. **Obv:** Hat above date and sprigs **Rev:** Value **Note:** Medal rotation.

Date	Mintage	F	VF	XF	Unc	BU
1987	23,000,000	—	0.75	1.00	3.75	—

KM# 89 CORDOBA

6.2500 g., Nickel Clad Steel, 25 mm. **Obv:** National emblem **Rev:** Value above sprigs within circle

Date	Mintage	F	VF	XF	Unc	BU
1997	39,000,000	—	—	—	2.50	3.00
2000	35,000,000	—	—	—	2.50	3.00
2002	—	—	—	—	2.50	3.00

KM# 44 5 CORDOBAS

Copper-Nickel, 27 mm. **Obv:** Value **Rev:** Head with hat facing **Shape:** 7-sided **Note:** Medal rotation.

Date	Mintage	F	VF	XF	Unc	BU
1980	10,000,000	0.15	0.25	1.00	3.00	—

KM# 44a 5 CORDOBAS

Nickel Clad Steel **Obv:** Value **Rev:** Head with hat facing **Shape:** 7-sided **Note:** Medal rotation.

Date	Mintage	F	VF	XF	Unc	BU
1984	8,000,000	—	0.25	1.00	3.50	—

KM# 60 5 CORDOBAS

7.5000 g., Aluminum-Bronze, 25.9 mm. **Obv:** Hat above date and sprigs **Rev:** Value

Date	Mintage	F	VF	XF	Unc	BU
1987	23,000,000	—	1.00	2.50	4.00	—

KM# 63 500 CORDOBAS

Aluminum **Obv:** Hat above date and sprigs **Rev:** Value

Date	Mintage	F	VF	XF	Unc	BU
1987	—	—	—	2.50	6.50	—

NIGERIA

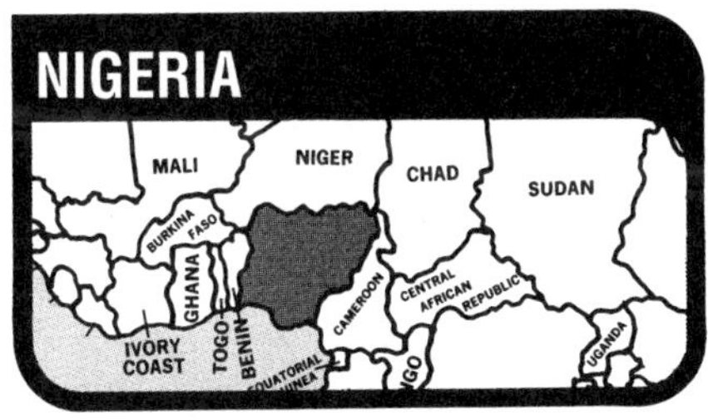

Nigeria, situated on the Atlantic coast of West Africa has an area of 356,669 sq. mi. (923,770 sq. km.).

Following the Napoleonic Wars, the British expanded their trade with the interior of Nigeria. The Berlin Conference of 1885 recognized British claims to a sphere of influence in that area, and in the following year the Royal Niger Company was chartered. Direct British control of the territory was initiated in 1900, and in 1914 the amalgamation of Northern and Southern Nigeria into the Colony and Protectorate of Nigeria was effected. In 1960, following a number of territorial and constitutional changes, Nigeria was granted independence within the British Commonwealth as a federation of the Northern, Western and Eastern regions. Nigeria altered its political relationship with Great Britain on Oct. 1, 1963, by proclaiming itself a republic. It did, however, elect to remain a member of the Commonwealth of Nations.

On May 30, 1967, the Eastern Region of the republic an area occupied principally by the proud and resourceful Ibo tribe – seceded from Nigeria and proclaimed itself the independent Republic of Biafra with Odumegwu Ojukwu as Chief of State. Civil war erupted and raged for 31 months. Casualties, including civilian, were about two million, the majority succumbing to malnutrition and disease. Biafra surrendered to the federal government on January 15, 1970.

For earlier coinage refer to British West Africa.

Arms Mottos

Short: Unity and faith

Long: Unity and Faith, Peace and Progress

BRITISH PROTECTORATE OF NIGERIA

POUND STERLING COINAGE

KM# 1 1/2 PENNY

Bronze **Ruler:** Elizabeth II **Obv:** Crown above center hole flanked by curved sprig **Rev:** Star design around center hole

Date	Mintage	F	VF	XF	Unc	BU
1959	52,800,000	—	0.15	0.25	1.00	—
1959 Proof	6,031	Value: 2.50				

KM# 2 PENNY

7.5000 g., Bronze, 28 mm. **Ruler:** Elizabeth II **Obv:** Crown above center hole flanked by curved sprig **Rev:** Star design around center hole

Date	Mintage	F	VF	XF	Unc	BU
1959	93,368,000	—	0.15	0.25	2.00	—
1959 Proof	6,031	Value: 2.50				

KM# 3 3 PENCE

Nickel-Brass **Ruler:** Elizabeth II **Obv:** Crowned head right **Obv. Designer:** Cecil Thomas **Rev:** Cotton plant

Date	Mintage	F	VF	XF	Unc	BU
1959	52,000,000	—	0.20	0.40	2.00	—
1959 Proof	6,031	Value: 3.50				

KM# 4 6 PENCE

2.5000 g., Copper-Nickel, 17.8 mm. **Ruler:** Elizabeth II **Obv:** Crowned head right **Obv. Designer:** Cecil Thomas **Rev:** Cocoa beans **Rev. Designer:** T.H. Paget

Date	Mintage	F	VF	XF	Unc	BU
1959	35,000,000	—	0.40	0.80	2.50	—
1959 Proof	6,031	Value: 5.00				

KM# 5 SHILLING

5.0000 g., Copper-Nickel, 22.8 mm. **Ruler:** Elizabeth II **Obv:** Crowned head right **Obv. Designer:** Cecil Thomas **Rev:** Palm divides date

Date	Mintage	F	VF	XF	Unc	BU
1959	18,000,000	—	0.65	1.45	3.50	—
1959 Proof	6,031	Value: 6.50				
1961	48,584,000	—	0.65	1.45	3.50	—
1962	39,416,000	—	0.65	1.45	3.50	—

KM# 6 2 SHILLING

Copper-Nickel, 27 mm. **Ruler:** Elizabeth II **Obv:** Crowned head right **Obv. Designer:** Cecil Thomas **Rev:** Flowers **Edge:** Security

Date	Mintage	F	VF	XF	Unc	BU
1959	15,000,000	—	1.25	2.50	6.00	—
1959 Proof	6,031	Value: 9.00				

FEDERAL REPUBLIC

DECIMAL COINAGE

100 Kobo = 1 Naira

KM# 7 1/2 KOBO

3.5300 g., Bronze **Ruler:** Elizabeth II **Obv:** Arms with supporters **Rev:** Value flanked by flowers

Date	Mintage	F	VF	XF	Unc	BU
1973	166,618,000	—	0.45	1.00	3.50	—
1973 Proof	10,000	Value: 3.50				

KM# 8.1 KOBO

Bronze **Ruler:** Elizabeth II **Obv:** Arms with supporters and short motto **Rev:** Value flanked by oil derricks

Date	Mintage	F	VF	XF	Unc	BU
1973	586,944,000	—	0.25	0.50	2.00	—
1973 Proof	10,000	Value: 3.50				
1974	14,500,000	—	0.25	0.50	3.00	—

KM# 8.2 KOBO

Bronze **Ruler:** Elizabeth II **Obv:** Arms with supporters and long motto **Rev:** Value flanked by oil derricks

Date	Mintage	F	VF	XF	Unc	BU
1987	—	—	0.50	1.50	6.00	—
1988	—	—	0.50	1.50	6.00	—

KM# 8.2a KOBO

2.5700 g., Copper Plated Steel, 17 mm. **Ruler:** Elizabeth II **Obv:** Arms with supporters and long motto **Rev:** Value flanked by oil derricks

Date	Mintage	F	VF	XF	Unc	BU
1991	—	—	—	—	0.25	0.45

KM# 17 KOBO

4.6700 g., Brass, 23.2 mm. **Obv:** Arms with supporters **Rev:** Monkey musicians below value **Edge:** Reeded

Date	Mintage	F	VF	XF	Unc	BU
2003	—	—	—	—	1.50	2.00

KM# 9.1 5 KOBO
Copper-Nickel **Ruler:** Elizabeth II **Obv:** Arms with supporters and short motto **Rev:** Cocoa beans

Date	Mintage	F	VF	XF	Unc	BU
1973	96,920,000	—	0.35	0.75	2.75	—
1973 Proof	10,000	Value: 4.00				
1974	—	—	0.45	0.85	3.00	—
1976	9,800,000	—	0.45	0.85	3.00	—
1986	—	—	0.45	0.85	3.00	—

KM# 9.2 5 KOBO
Copper-Nickel **Ruler:** Elizabeth II **Obv:** Arms with supporters and long motto **Rev:** Cocoa beans

Date	Mintage	F	VF	XF	Unc	BU
1987	—	—	1.00	2.50	7.00	—
1988	—	—	1.00	2.50	7.00	—
1989	—	—	1.00	2.50	7.00	—

KM# 10.1 10 KOBO
Copper-Nickel, 22.8 mm. **Ruler:** Elizabeth II **Obv:** Arms with supporters and short motto **Rev:** Value at left of oil palms

Date	Mintage	F	VF	XF	Unc	BU
1973	340,870,000	—	0.50	1.00	3.50	—
1973 Proof	10,000	Value: 5.00				
1974	—	—	0.60	1.20	3.75	—
1976	7,000,000	—	0.60	1.20	3.75	—

KM# 10.2 10 KOBO
4.0000 g., Copper-Nickel, 22.8 mm. **Ruler:** Elizabeth II **Obv:** Arms with supporters and long motto **Rev:** Value to left of oil palms

Date	Mintage	F	VF	XF	Unc	BU
1987	—	—	1.25	3.50	9.00	—
1988	—	—	1.25	3.50	9.00	—
1989	—	—	1.25	3.50	9.00	—
1990	—	—	1.25	3.50	9.00	—

KM# 12 10 KOBO
3.4800 g., Copper Plated Steel, 19.9 mm. **Ruler:** Elizabeth II **Obv:** Arms with supporters and long motto **Rev:** Value to left of oil palms **Shape:** 12-sided

Date	Mintage	F	VF	XF	Unc	BU
1991	—	—	—	—	0.45	0.75

KM# 11 25 KOBO
Copper-Nickel **Ruler:** Elizabeth II **Obv:** Arms with supporters and short motto **Rev:** Groundnuts **Edge:** Security

Date	Mintage	F	VF	XF	Unc	BU
1973	4,616,000	—	1.00	2.50	7.50	—
1973 Proof	10,000	Value: 8.50				
1975	—	—	1.00	2.50	7.50	—

KM# 11a 25 KOBO
4.4900 g., Copper Plated Steel, 22.45 mm. **Ruler:** Elizabeth II **Obv:** Arms with supporters and long motto **Rev:** Groundnuts **Edge:** Reeded

Date	Mintage	F	VF	XF	Unc	BU
1991	—	—	—	—	0.65	1.00

KM# 13.1 50 KOBO
5.5300 g., Nickel Plated Steel, 24.72 mm. **Ruler:** Elizabeth II **Obv:** Arms with supporters with long motto **Rev:** Corn and value **Shape:** 12 rounded sides

Date	Mintage	F	VF	XF	Unc	BU
1991	—	—	—	—	1.25	1.50

KM# 13.2 50 KOBO
5.5300 g., Nickel Clad Steel, 24.72 mm. **Obv:** Arms with supporters with long motto **Rev:** Corn with value **Shape:** Round with a multi-sided inner rim

Date	Mintage	F	VF	XF	Unc	BU
1993	—	—	—	—	1.25	1.50

KM# 13.3 50 KOBO
3.5000 g., Nickel Clad Steel, 19.44 mm. **Obv:** Arms with supporters **Obv. Legend:** FEDERAL REPUBLIC of NIGERIA **Rev:** Value at left, corn cob and stalk at right **Edge:** Plain **Note:** Reduced size.

Date	Mintage	F	VF	XF	Unc	BU
2006	—	—	—	—	1.00	1.35

KM# 14 NAIRA
12.1500 g., Nickel Plated Steel, 27.5 mm. **Ruler:** Elizabeth II **Obv:** Arms with supporters and long motto **Rev:** Head 1/4 right

Date	Mintage	F	VF	XF	Unc	BU
1991	—	—	—	—	1.75	2.00
1993	—	—	—	—	1.75	2.00

KM# 18 NAIRA
5.4300 g., Bi-Metallic Brass center in Stainless Steel ring, 21.48 mm. **Obv:** National arms **Obv. Legend:** FEDERAL REPUBLIC OF NIGERIA **Rev:** Small bust of Herbert Macaulay above value **Edge:** Plain

Date	Mintage	F	VF	XF	Unc	BU
2006	—	—	—	—	—	4.00

KM# 19 2 NAIRA
7.4800 g., Bi-Metallic Stainless Steel center in Copper-Brass ring, 25.99 mm. **Obv:** National arms **Obv. Legend:** FEDERAL REPUBLIC OF NIGERIA **Rev:** Large value, National Assembly in background **Edge:** Coarse reeding

Date	Mintage	F	VF	XF	Unc	BU
2006	—	—	—	—	—	5.00

NORWAY

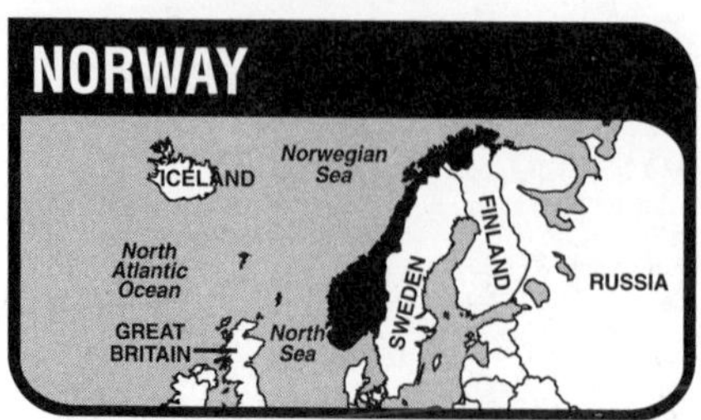

The Kingdom of Norway (*Norge, Noreg*), a constitutional monarchy located in northwestern Europe, has an area of 150,000sq. mi. (324,220 sq. km.), including the island territories of Spitzbergen (Svalbard) and Jan Mayen, and a population of *4.2 million. Capital: Oslo (Christiania). The diversified economic base of Norway includes shipping, fishing, forestry, agriculture, and manufacturing. Nonferrous metals, paper and paperboard, paper pulp, iron, steel and oil are exported.

A united Norwegian kingdom was established in the 9th century, the era of the indomitable Norse Vikings who ranged far and wide, visiting the coasts of northwestern Europe, the Mediterranean, Greenland and North America. In the 13th century the Norse kingdom was united briefly with Sweden, then passed through inheritance in 1380 to the rule of Denmark which was maintained until 1814. In 1814 Norway fell again under the rule of Sweden. The union lasted until 1905 when the Norwegian Parliament arranged a peaceful separation and invited a Danish prince (King Haakon VII) to ascend the throne of an independent Kingdom of Norway.

RULERS
Swedish, 1814-1905
Haakon VII, 1905-1957
Olav V, 1957-1991
Harald V, 1991-

MINT MARK
(h) - Crossed hammers – Kongsberg

MINT OFFICIALS' INITIALS

Letter	Date	Name
AB, B	1961-1980	Arne Jon Bakken
AB*	1980	Ole R. Kolberg
I, IT	1880-1918	Ivar Trondsen, engraver
IAR	-	Angrid Austlid Rise, engraver
K	1981	Ole R. Kolberg
OH	1959	Oivind Hansen, engraver

MONETARY SYSTEM
100 Ore = 1 Krone (30 Skilling)

KINGDOM

DECIMAL COINAGE

KM# 352 ORE
2.0000 g., Bronze **Obv:** Crowned arms divide monograms **Rev:** Value within wreath, crossed hammers divide date below **Note:** Varieties exist.

Date	Mintage	VG	F	VF	XF	BU
1902	4,500,000	—	2.00	5.00	15.00	45.00

KM# 361 ORE
2.0000 g., Bronze **Ruler:** Haakon VII **Obv:** Crowned shield divides monogram **Rev:** Value within sprigs

Date	Mintage	VG	F	VF	XF	BU
1906	3,000,000	—	2.00	3.00	10.00	25.00
1907	2,550,000	—	2.00	3.00	12.00	27.50

KM# 367 ORE
2.0000 g., Bronze **Ruler:** Haakon VII **Obv:** Crowned monogram within circle **Rev:** Value

Date	Mintage	VG	F	VF	XF	BU
1908	1,450,000	—	10.00	20.00	45.00	165
1910	2,480,000	—	1.00	2.50	12.00	40.00
1911	3,270,000	—	1.00	2.50	15.00	70.00
1912	2,850,000	—	3.00	10.00	35.00	225
1913	2,840,000	—	1.00	2.50	7.50	35.00
1914	5,020,000	—	1.00	2.50	10.00	40.00
1915	1,540,000	—	10.00	25.00	75.00	325
1921	3,805,000	—	25.00	45.00	95.00	275
1922	Inc. above	—	0.50	2.00	15.00	55.00
1923	770,000	—	6.00	17.50	35.00	175
1925	3,000,000	—	0.50	1.50	15.00	60.00
1926	2,200,000	—	0.50	1.50	15.00	60.00
1927	800,000	—	4.00	10.00	30.00	165
1928	3,000,000	—	0.25	0.75	4.50	25.00
1929	4,990,000	—	0.25	0.75	4.50	20.00
1930 large date	2,009,999	—	0.50	1.00	6.00	27.50
1930 small date	Inc. above	—	0.50	1.00	6.00	27.50
1931	2,000,000	—	0.50	1.00	6.00	25.00
1932	2,500,000	—	0.50	1.00	6.00	25.00
1933	2,000,000	—	0.50	1.00	6.00	20.00
1934	2,000,000	—	0.50	1.00	6.00	25.00
1935	5,495,000	—	0.25	0.75	2.50	12.50
1936	6,855,000	—	0.25	0.75	2.50	12.50
1937	6,020,000	—	0.20	0.50	1.50	10.00
1938	4,920,000	—	0.20	0.50	1.50	10.00
1939	2,500,000	—	0.20	0.50	1.50	12.50
1940	5,010,000	—	0.20	0.50	1.50	10.00
1941	12,260,000	—	0.10	0.25	1.50	5.00
1946	2,200,000	—	0.10	0.25	1.50	12.00
1947	4,870,000	—	0.10	0.25	0.90	6.00
1948	9,405,000	—	0.10	0.25	0.90	5.00
1949	2,785,000	—	0.10	0.25	0.90	8.00
1950	5,730,000	—	0.10	0.25	0.90	5.00

Date	Mintage	VG	F	VF	XF	BU
1951	16,670,000	—	0.10	0.25	0.90	5.00
1952	Inc. above	—	0.10	0.25	0.90	4.00

KM# 367a ORE

1.7400 g., Iron **Ruler:** Haakon VII **Obv:** Crowned monogram **Rev:** Value

Date	Mintage	VG	F	VF	XF	BU
1918	6,000,000	—	5.00	10.00	20.00	65.00
1919	12,930,000	—	1.50	3.50	12.00	30.00
1920	4,445,000	—	6.00	12.50	35.00	165
1921	2,270,000	—	30.00	40.00	75.00	210

KM# 387 ORE

1.7400 g., Iron **Ruler:** Haakon VII **Subject:** World War II German Occupation **Obv:** Shield **Rev:** Value

Date	Mintage	VG	F	VF	XF	BU
1941	13,410,000	—	0.15	0.50	1.75	12.50
1942	37,710,000	—	0.15	0.50	1.75	6.00
1943	33,030,000	—	0.15	0.50	1.75	6.00
1944	8,820,000	—	0.25	0.75	2.25	6.50
1945	1,740,000	—	4.00	8.00	15.00	35.00

KM# 398 ORE

2.0000 g., Bronze, 11 mm. **Ruler:** Haakon VII **Obv:** Crowned monogram divides date **Rev:** Value

Date	Mintage	VG	F	VF	XF	BU
1952	—	—	—	0.10	1.00	6.50
Note: Mintage included with KM#367						
1953	7,440,000	—	—	0.10	0.75	4.50
1954	7,650,000	—	—	0.10	0.75	4.50
1955	8,635,000	—	—	0.10	0.75	4.50
1956	11,705,000	—	—	0.10	0.75	4.50
1957	15,750,000	—	—	0.10	0.50	3.25

KM# 403 ORE

2.0000 g., Bronze, 11 mm. **Ruler:** Olav V **Obv:** Crowned monogram **Rev:** Squirrel and value **Note:** Varieties exist.

Date	Mintage	VG	F	VF	XF	BU
1958	2,820,000	—	0.25	0.50	2.25	8.00
1959	9,120,000	—	0.10	0.20	0.85	7.00
1960	7,890,000	—	—	0.10	0.30	3.00
1961	5,670,600	—	—	0.10	0.30	3.00
1962	12,180,000	—	—	0.10	0.25	2.00
1963	8,010,000	—	—	0.10	0.30	2.50
1964	11,020,000	—	—	—	0.10	0.75
1965	8,081,000	—	—	—	0.15	2.00
1966	12,431,000	—	—	—	0.15	1.25
1967	13,026,000	—	—	—	0.10	0.75
1968	125,500	—	0.50	1.00	2.25	8.50
1969	6,290,500	—	—	—	0.10	0.50
1970	6,607,500	—	—	—	0.10	0.50
1971	18,966,000	—	—	—	0.10	0.45
1972	21,102,984	—	—	—	0.10	0.45

KM# 353 2 ORE

4.0000 g., Bronze, 21 mm. **Obv:** Crowned arms divide monograms **Rev:** Value within wreath, crossed hammers divide date below

Date	Mintage	VG	F	VF	XF	BU
1902	1,005,000	—	1.50	4.00	15.00	150

KM# 362 2 ORE

4.0000 g., Bronze, 21 mm. **Ruler:** Haakon VII **Obv:** Crowned shield **Rev:** Value within sprigs

Date	Mintage	VG	F	VF	XF	BU
1906	500,000	—	5.00	15.00	50.00	300
1907	980,000	—	3.00	5.00	25.00	145

KM# 371 2 ORE

4.0000 g., Bronze, 21 mm. **Ruler:** Haakon VII **Obv:** Crowned momogram within circle **Rev:** Value

Date	Mintage	VG	F	VF	XF	BU
1909	520,000	—	6.00	20.00	60.00	250
1910	500,000	—	6.00	20.00	100	500
1911	195,000	—	6.00	17.50	70.00	375
1912	805,000	—	6.00	17.50	70.00	400
1913	2,010,000	—	0.75	2.00	12.00	115
1914	2,990,000	—	0.75	2.00	12.00	115
1915	Inc. above	—	5.00	20.00	85.00	475
1921	2,028,000	—	0.50	1.00	17.00	90.00
1922	2,288,000	—	0.50	1.00	17.00	75.00
1923	745,000	—	1.00	2.00	30.00	145
1928	2,250,000	—	0.50	1.00	12.50	70.00
1929	750,000	—	1.00	2.00	20.00	110
1931	1,570,000	—	0.50	1.00	15.00	75.00
1932	630,000	—	3.50	7.50	45.00	210
1933	750,000	—	0.50	1.50	10.00	75.00
1934	500,000	—	0.50	1.50	10.00	75.00
1935	2,223,000	—	0.25	1.00	7.50	45.00
1936	4,533,000	—	0.25	1.00	7.50	45.00
1937	3,790,000	—	0.20	0.50	2.75	20.00
1938	3,765,000	—	0.20	0.50	2.75	20.00
1939	4,420,000	—	0.20	0.50	2.75	20.00
1940	2,655,000	—	0.20	0.50	2.75	20.00
1946	1,575,000	—	0.20	0.50	3.50	20.00
1947	4,679,000	—	0.10	0.25	1.25	10.00
1948	1,002,999	—	1.00	3.00	5.00	12.50
1949	1,455,000	—	0.10	0.25	1.00	9.00
1950	5,790,000	—	0.10	0.25	1.00	6.00
1951	10,540,000	—	0.10	0.25	1.00	5.00
1952	Inc. above	—	0.10	0.25	1.00	5.00

KM# 371a 2 ORE

3.4800 g., Iron, 21 mm. **Ruler:** Haakon VII **Obv:** Crowned monogram **Rev:** Value

Date	Mintage	VG	F	VF	XF	BU
1917	720,000	—	80.00	145	250	475
1918	1,280,000	—	35.00	50.00	110	250
1919	3,365,000	—	10.00	15.00	55.00	265
1920	2,635,000	—	10.00	15.00	55.00	275

KM# 394 2 ORE

3.4700 g., Iron, 21 mm. **Ruler:** Haakon VII **Obv:** Shield **Rev:** Value **Note:** World War II German occupation issue.

Date	Mintage	VG	F	VF	XF	BU
1943	6,575,000	—	0.50	0.75	1.75	9.00
1944	9,805,000	—	0.50	0.75	1.75	9.00
1945	2,520,000	—	1.50	3.00	6.00	20.00

KM# 399 2 ORE

4.0000 g., Bronze, 21 mm. **Ruler:** Haakon VII **Obv:** Crowned monogram divides date **Rev:** Value

Date	Mintage	VG	F	VF	XF	BU
1952	Inc. above	—	—	0.10	0.85	8.50
1953	6,705,000	—	—	0.10	0.85	7.00
1954	2,805,000	—	—	0.10	0.85	10.00
1955	3,600,000	—	—	0.10	0.85	10.00
1956	6,780,000	—	—	0.10	0.85	7.00
1957	6,090,000	—	—	0.10	0.85	7.00

KM# 404 2 ORE

4.0000 g., Bronze, 21 mm. **Ruler:** Olav V **Obv:** Crowned monogram **Rev:** Moor hen and value, small lettering

Date	Mintage	VG	F	VF	XF	BU
1958	2,700,000	—	0.20	0.50	1.75	10.00

KM# 410 2 ORE

4.0000 g., Bronze, 21 mm. **Ruler:** Olav V **Obv:** Crowned monogram **Rev:** Moor hen and value, large lettering

Date	Mintage	VG	F	VF	XF	BU
1959	4,125,000	—	0.10	0.20	1.25	8.00
1960	3,735,000	—	—	0.10	0.85	16.50
1961	4,477,000	—	—	0.10	0.35	2.00
1962	6,205,000	—	—	0.10	0.35	2.00
1963	4,840,000	—	—	0.10	0.35	2.00
1964	7,250,000	—	—	0.10	0.20	1.50
1965	6,241,000	—	—	0.10	0.30	3.00
1966	10,485,000	—	—	—	0.15	2.50
1967	11,993,000	—	—	—	0.15	1.50
1968	3,467	—	—	—	—	950
Note: In mint sets only						
1969	315,600	—	0.50	1.00	1.75	6.00
1970	6,794,000	—	—	—	0.10	1.25
1971	15,462,000	—	—	—	0.10	1.00
1972	15,897,984	—	—	—	0.10	1.00

KM# 349 5 ORE

8.0000 g., Bronze, 27 mm. **Obv:** Crowned arms divide monograms **Rev:** Value within wreath, crossed hammers divide date below

Date	Mintage	VG	F	VF	XF	BU
1902	705,000	—	2.50	6.00	55.00	400

KM# 364 5 ORE

8.0000 g., Bronze, 27 mm. **Ruler:** Haakon VII **Obv:** Crowned shield divides monogram **Rev:** Value within sprigs

Date	Mintage	VG	F	VF	XF	BU
1907	200,000	—	3.50	12.50	70.00	285

KM# 368 5 ORE

8.0000 g., Bronze, 27 mm. **Ruler:** Haakon VII **Obv:** Crowned monogram within circle **Rev:** Numeral and written value

Date	Mintage	VG	F	VF	XF	BU
1908	600,000	—	25.00	45.00	130	565
1911	480,000	—	2.00	15.00	65.00	340
1912	520,000	—	6.00	25.00	135	825
1913	1,000,000	—	1.25	5.00	30.00	190
1914	1,000,000	—	1.25	5.00	30.00	190
1915	Inc. above	—	10.00	35.00	145	850
1916	300,000	—	6.00	15.00	60.00	315

Date	Mintage	VG	F	VF	XF	BU
1921	683,000	—	1.50	7.50	60.00	280
1922	2,296,000	—	1.25	5.00	30.00	150
1923	456,000	—	2.50	10.00	60.00	260
1928	848,000	—	0.60	3.00	25.00	110
1929	452,000	—	3.00	10.00	60.00	300
1930	1,292,000	—	0.60	2.50	30.00	150
1931	808,000	—	0.60	2.50	30.00	120
1932	500,000	—	3.00	15.00	45.00	225
1933	300,000	—	3.00	12.00	65.00	325
1935	496,000	—	1.50	5.00	25.00	160
1936	760,000	—	1.00	2.50	20.00	115
1937	1,552,000	—	0.50	1.50	12.00	50.00
1938	1,332,000	—	0.50	1.50	12.00	50.00
1939	1,370,000	—	0.50	1.50	9.00	50.00
1940	2,554,000	—	0.30	1.00	7.00	32.50
1941	3,576,000	—	0.30	1.00	6.00	32.50
1951	8,128,000	—	0.25	0.50	2.25	20.00
1952	Inc. above	—	1.50	3.50	9.00	50.00

KM# 368a 5 ORE

6.6900 g., Iron, 27 mm. **Ruler:** Haakon VII **Obv:** Crowned monogram within circle **Rev:** Numeral and written value

Date	Mintage	VG	F	VF	XF	BU
1917	1,700,000	—	25.00	40.00	70.00	125
1918/7	432,000	—	135	225	—	850
1918	Inc. above	—	135	225	425	900
1919	3,464,000	—	12.00	30.00	70.00	250
1920	1,629,000	—	25.00	55.00	120	500

KM# 388 5 ORE

6.9400 g., Iron, 27 mm. **Ruler:** Haakon VII **Note:** World War II German occupation issue.

Date	Mintage	VG	F	VF	XF	BU
1941	6,608,000	—	0.50	1.50	5.50	40.00
1942	10,312,000	—	0.50	1.50	5.00	20.00
1943	6,184,000	—	0.75	2.00	7.00	32.50
1944	4,256,000	—	1.25	3.00	9.00	32.50
1945	408,000	—	145	165	270	600

KM# 400 5 ORE

8.0000 g., Bronze, 27 mm. **Ruler:** Haakon VII **Obv:** Crowned monogram divides date **Rev:** Value

Date	Mintage	VG	F	VF	XF	BU
1952	—	—	0.10	0.50	2.50	35.00
	Note: Mintage included with KM#368					
1953	6,216,000	—	0.10	0.35	2.25	20.00
1954	4,536,000	—	0.10	0.35	2.25	20.00
1955	6,570,000	—	0.10	0.35	2.25	20.00
1956	2,959,000	—	0.10	0.35	2.25	30.00
1957	5,624,000	—	0.10	0.35	2.25	12.50

KM# 405 5 ORE

8.0000 g., Bronze, 27 mm. **Ruler:** Olav V **Obv:** Head left **Rev:** Moose

Date	Mintage	VG	F	VF	XF	BU
1958	2,205,000	—	1.00	2.00	6.00	60.00
1959	3,208,000	—	0.10	0.50	2.25	25.00
1960	5,519,000	—	0.10	0.20	1.25	17.00
1961	4,554,000	—	0.10	0.20	1.25	15.00
1962	7,764,000	—	0.10	0.15	0.75	9.00
1963	3,204,000	—	0.10	0.15	0.75	9.00
1964	6,108,000	—	—	0.10	0.50	3.00
1965	6,841,000	—	—	0.10	0.50	7.00
1966	8,415,000	—	—	0.10	0.50	3.00
1967	9,071,000	—	—	0.10	0.45	3.00
1968	4,286,000	—	—	0.10	0.85	8.00
1969	4,328,000	—	—	0.10	0.35	1.25
1970	7,350,600	—	—	0.10	0.35	1.25
1971	13,450,100	—	—	0.10	0.35	1.25

Date	Mintage	VG	F	VF	XF	BU
1972	19,001,784	—	—	—	0.15	1.00
1973	9,584,175	—	—	—	0.15	1.00

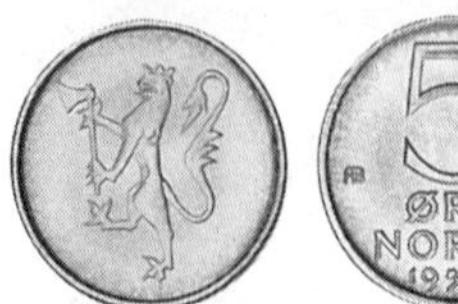

KM# 415 5 ORE

3.0000 g., Bronze, 19 mm. **Ruler:** Olav V **Obv:** Arms **Rev:** Value **Designer:** Oivind Hansen **Note:** Varieties exist.

Date	Mintage	VG	F	VF	XF	BU
1973	52,886,175	—	—	—	0.10	0.45
1974	37,150,223	—	—	—	0.10	0.45
1975	32,478,744	—	—	—	0.10	0.45
1976	24,232,824	—	—	—	0.10	0.25
1977	29,646,000	—	—	—	0.10	0.25
1978	13,838,000	—	—	—	0.10	0.25
1979	25,255,000	—	—	—	0.10	0.25
1980	12,315,000	—	—	—	0.10	0.25
1980 Without star	27,515,000	—	—	—	0.10	0.25
1981	24,529,000	—	—	—	0.10	0.25
1982	21,900,650	—	—	—	0.10	0.25

KM# 350 10 ORE

1.5000 g., 0.4000 Silver 0.0193 oz. ASW, 15 mm. **Obv:** Crowned monogram **Obv. Legend:** BRODERFOLKENES VEL **Rev:** Crowned arms divide date

Date	Mintage	VG	F	VF	XF	BU
1901	2,021,100	—	10.00	22.00	30.00	50.00
1903	1,500,700	—	12.00	24.00	40.00	50.00

KM# 372 10 ORE

1.4500 g., 0.4000 Silver 0.0186 oz. ASW, 15 mm. **Ruler:** Haakon VII **Obv:** Crowned monogram **Rev:** Value

Date	Mintage	VG	F	VF	XF	BU
1909	2,000,000	—	6.50	13.00	30.00	100
1911	1,650,000	—	9.00	22.00	60.00	200
1912	2,350,000	—	6.00	12.00	30.00	85.00
1913	2,000,000	—	6.00	11.00	28.00	70.00
1914	1,180,000	—	11.00	25.00	50.00	150
1915	2,820,000	—	3.00	5.00	13.00	100
1916	1,500,000	—	10.00	17.00	45.00	130
1917	5,950,000	—	1.50	3.00	5.00	20.00
1918	Inc. above	—	3.00	5.00	13.00	50.00
1918/7	1,650,000	—	15.00	35.00	75.00	—
1919	Inc. above	—	1.50	3.00	5.00	20.00
1919/7	7,800,000	—	15.00	35.00	75.00	—

KM# 378 10 ORE

1.5000 g., Copper-Nickel, 15 mm. **Ruler:** Haakon VII **Obv:** Crowned monogram **Rev:** Value flanked by designs

Date	Mintage	VG	F	VF	XF	BU
1920	2,535,000	—	10.00	20.00	30.00	60.00
1921	6,465,000	—	7.00	15.00	25.00	55.00
1922	3,965,000	—	7.00	15.00	20.00	50.00
1923	7,135,000	—	15.00	25.00	30.00	55.00

KM# 383 10 ORE

1.5000 g., Copper-Nickel, 15 mm. **Ruler:** Haakon VII **Obv:** Crown above center hole **Rev:** Value above center hole

Date	Mintage	VG	F	VF	XF	BU
1924	12,079,100	—	0.30	0.75	9.00	40.00
1925	7,050,700	—	0.30	0.75	9.00	60.00
1926	11,764,200	—	0.30	0.75	9.00	40.00
1927	526,000	5.00	10.00	20.00	120	600
1937	5,000,000	—	0.30	0.75	5.00	35.00
1938	3,412,600	—	0.30	0.75	5.00	35.00
1939	1,538,400	—	1.00	2.50	9.50	65.00
1940	4,800,000	—	0.30	0.75	1.75	17.50
1941	10,150,000	—	0.30	0.75	1.75	10.00
1945	1,718,000	—	0.10	0.25	1.75	15.00

Date	Mintage	VG	F	VF	XF	BU
1946	3,723,200	—	0.10	0.25	1.75	9.00
1947	7,256,700	—	0.10	0.25	1.75	6.50
1948	3,104,500	—	0.10	0.25	2.00	7.00
1949	11,545,500	—	0.10	0.25	1.75	7.00
1951	5,150,000	—	0.10	0.25	1.75	7.00

KM# 389 10 ORE

1.2500 g., Zinc, 15 mm. **Ruler:** Haakon VII **Obv:** Shield flanked by designs **Rev:** Value flanked by designs **Note:** World War II German occupation issue.

Date	Mintage	F	VF	XF	Unc	BU
1941	15,309,900	0.75	2.00	6.00	—	32.50
1942	50,387,600	0.35	1.00	3.50	—	12.50
1943	13,377,700	0.75	2.00	5.50	—	35.00
1944	3,549,400	7.50	12.50	30.00	—	135
1945	5,645,500	4.00	8.00	18.00	—	50.00

KM# 391 10 ORE

1.1500 g., Nickel-Brass, 15 mm. **Ruler:** Haakon VII **Obv:** Crown above center hole **Rev:** Value above center hole **Note:** World War II government in exile issue.

Date	Mintage	VG	F	VF	XF	BU
1942	6,000,000	—	—	—	120	225
	Note: All except 9,667 were melted					

KM# 396 10 ORE

1.5000 g., Copper-Nickel, 15 mm. **Ruler:** Haakon VII **Obv:** Crowned monogram divides date **Rev:** Value flanked by designs

Date	Mintage	VG	F	VF	XF	BU
1951	17,400,000	—	0.10	0.30	2.50	60.00
1952	Inc. above	—	0.10	0.20	1.50	20.00
1953	7,700,000	—	0.10	0.20	1.50	20.00
1954	10,105,000	—	0.10	0.20	1.50	20.00
1955	9,829,500	—	0.10	0.20	1.50	50.00
1956	10,066,000	—	0.10	0.20	1.50	20.00
1957	22,900,000	—	0.10	0.20	1.50	12.00

KM# 406 10 ORE

1.5000 g., Copper-Nickel, 15 mm. **Ruler:** Olav V **Obv:** Crowned monogram **Rev:** Honey bee and value, small lettering

Date	Mintage	VG	F	VF	XF	BU
1958	1,425,000	—	0.50	1.50	3.00	30.00

KM# 411 10 ORE

1.5000 g., Copper-Nickel, 15 mm. **Ruler:** Olav V **Obv:** Crowned monogram **Rev:** Honey bee and value, large lettering

Date	Mintage	VG	F	VF	XF	BU
1959	2,500,000	—	—	0.75	3.00	20.00
1960	12,490,200	—	—	0.10	0.60	7.00
1961	10,385,000	—	—	0.10	0.60	20.00
1962	16,210,000	—	—	0.10	0.60	5.00
1963	17,560,000	—	—	0.10	0.60	5.00
1964	9,781,000	—	—	0.10	0.35	1.35
1965	10,561,000	—	—	0.10	0.60	14.00
1966	16,610,000	—	—	0.10	0.50	3.00
1967	18,243,000	—	—	0.10	0.35	5.00
1968	24,998,300	—	—	0.10	0.35	7.00
1969	27,157,200	—	—	0.10	0.25	2.25
1970	639,300	—	0.50	1.00	2.25	5.00
1971	8,903,800	—	—	0.10	0.25	1.35
1972	24,834,484	—	—	—	0.25	1.00
1973	22,300,925	—	—	—	0.25	1.00

KM# 416 10 ORE

1.2500 g., Copper-Nickel, 15 mm. **Ruler:** Olav V **Obv:** Crowned monogram divides date **Rev:** Value **Designer:** Oivind Hansen **Note:** Varieties exist in monogram.

Date	Mintage	VG	F	VF	XF	BU
1974	30,995,223	—	—	—	0.10	0.60
1975	21,845,496	—	—	—	0.10	0.60
1976	42,403,074	—	—	—	0.10	0.40

Date	Mintage	VG	F	VF	XF	BU
1977	43,304,000	—	—	—	0.10	0.40
1978	37,395,000	—	—	—	0.10	0.40
1979	25,808,000	—	—	—	0.10	0.40
1980	28,620,000	—	—	—	0.10	0.40
1980 Without star	14,050,000	—	—	—	0.10	0.40
1981	43,083,400	—	—	—	0.10	0.40
1982	40,974,256	—	—	—	0.10	0.40
1983	45,637,300	—	—	—	0.10	0.40
1984	100,066,000	—	—	—	0.10	0.35
1985	103,108,000	—	—	—	0.10	0.35
1986	146,392,000	—	—	—	0.10	0.35
1987	166,040,000	—	—	—	0.10	0.35
1988	94,677,000	—	—	—	0.10	0.35
1989	97,273,500	—	—	—	0.10	0.35
1990	150,290,000	—	—	—	0.10	0.35
1991	79,597,000	—	—	—	0.10	0.35

KM# 360 25 ORE

2.4200 g., 0.6000 Silver 0.0467 oz. ASW **Obv:** Crowned arms within wreath **Obv. Legend:** BRODERFOLKENES VEL **Rev:** Value within wreath, crossed hammers divide date below

Date	Mintage	VG	F	VF	XF	BU
1901	606,900	9.00	21.00	40.00	60.00	130
1902	611,700	9.00	21.00	40.00	60.00	130
1904	600,000	9.00	21.00	40.00	60.00	130

KM# 373 25 ORE

2.4200 g., 0.6000 Silver 0.0467 oz. ASW **Ruler:** Haakon VII **Obv:** Arms flanked by designs **Rev:** Crowned cross with monogram

Date	Mintage	VG	F	VF	XF	BU
1909	600,000	8.00	16.00	30.00	55.00	110
1911	400,000	15.00	30.00	45.00	80.00	200
1912	200,000	50.00	100	150	270	650
1913	400,000	12.00	20.00	35.00	70.00	165
1914	399,600	12.00	18.00	50.00	100	200
1915	1,032,300	4.50	10.00	15.00	40.00	110
1916	368,000	17.00	35.00	50.00	80.00	225
1917	400,000	15.00	30.00	45.00	70.00	200
1918/6	800,000	6.00	12.00	20.00	40.00	65.00
1918	Inc. above	5.00	12.00	20.00	40.00	95.00
1919	1,600,000	3.50	6.00	12.00	25.00	80.00

KM# 381 25 ORE

4.4000 g., Copper-Nickel, 17 mm. **Ruler:** Haakon VII **Obv:** Crowned monogram **Rev:** Arms flanked by designs

Date	Mintage	VG	F	VF	XF	BU
1921	4,800,000	4.00	10.00	15.00	20.00	40.00
1922	14,200,000	4.00	10.00	15.00	20.00	40.00
1923	5,200,000	8.00	16.50	25.00	35.00	60.00

KM# 382 25 ORE

2.4000 g., Copper-Nickel, 17 mm. **Ruler:** Haakon VII **Obv:** Crowned monogram, hole in center **Rev:** Arms flanked by designs, hole in center

Date	Mintage	VG	F	VF	XF	BU
1921	—	1.50	3.00	5.00	75.00	625
1922	—	1.50	3.00	4.00	45.00	375
1923	—	1.00	1.50	3.00	25.00	190

Note: Respective mintages included with KM#381

KM# 384 25 ORE

2.4000 g., Copper-Nickel, 17 mm. **Ruler:** Haakon VII **Obv:** Crowned cross with monogram, hole in center **Rev:** Center hole flanked by designs, crown above

Date	Mintage	VG	F	VF	XF	BU
1924	4,000,000	—	0.50	2.00	7.00	65.00
1927	6,200,000	—	0.50	1.50	7.00	65.00
1929	800,000	—	1.50	6.00	42.00	250
1939	1,220,000	—	0.25	0.75	3.50	70.00
1940	1,160,000	—	0.25	0.75	3.50	50.00
1946	1,850,000	—	0.20	0.50	1.75	20.00
1947	2,592,000	—	0.20	0.50	1.75	15.00
1949	2,602,000	—	0.20	0.50	1.75	15.00
1950	2,800,000	—	0.20	0.50	1.75	15.00

KM# 392 25 ORE

2.4000 g., Nickel-Brass, 17 mm. **Ruler:** Haakon VII **Obv:** Crowned monograms form cross, hole at center **Rev:** Crown on top divides date, hole in center flanked by designs, value on bottom **Note:** World War II government in exile issue.

Date	Mintage	VG	F	VF	XF	BU
1942	2,400,000	—	—	—	120	225

Note: All but 10,300 were melted

KM# 395 25 ORE

2.0000 g., Zinc, 17 mm. **Ruler:** Haakon VII **Obv:** Shield flanked by designs **Rev:** Value flanked by designs **Note:** World War II German occupation.

Date	Mintage	VG	F	VF	XF	BU
1943	14,104,800	—	1.00	1.50	4.00	25.00
1944	3,030,500	2.00	4.00	7.50	20.00	50.00
1945	3,010,000	3.00	6.00	10.00	22.00	60.00

KM# 401 25 ORE

2.4000 g., Copper-Nickel, 17 mm. **Ruler:** Haakon VII **Obv:** Crowned monogram divides date **Rev:** Value flanked by designs **Note:** Mint marks exist with mint mark on square or without square.

Date	Mintage	VG	F	VF	XF	BU
1952	4,060,000	—	0.10	0.25	1.20	30.00
1953	3,320,000	—	0.10	0.25	1.20	35.00
1954	3,140,000	—	0.10	0.25	1.20	30.00
1955	2,000,000	—	0.10	0.25	1.20	75.00
1956	3,980,000	—	0.10	0.25	1.20	30.00
1957	7,660,000	—	0.10	0.25	1.20	20.00

KM# 407 25 ORE

2.4000 g., Copper-Nickel, 17 mm. **Ruler:** Olav V **Obv:** Head left **Rev:** Bird above value

Date	Mintage	VG	F	VF	XF	BU
1958	1,316,000	—	0.50	1.00	3.00	40.00
1959	1,184,000	—	0.50	1.00	3.00	35.00
1960	3,964,200	—	—	0.10	1.25	20.00
1961	4,656,000	—	—	0.10	1.00	7.50
1962	6,304,000	—	—	0.10	1.00	7.50
1963	3,640,000	—	—	0.10	1.00	7.50
1964	4,953,000	—	—	0.10	0.50	2.75
1965	2,798,000	—	—	0.10	0.65	30.00
1966	6,075,000	—	—	0.10	0.65	3.00
1967	6,641,000	—	—	0.10	0.65	3.00
1968	4,963,400	—	—	0.10	0.50	5.00
1969	12,426,500	—	—	0.10	0.15	2.00
1970	1,545,400	—	—	0.15	0.75	6.50
1971	5,247,200	—	—	—	0.10	1.25
1972	7,928,584	—	—	—	0.10	1.25
1973	8,516,175	—	—	—	0.10	1.25

KM# 417 25 ORE

2.0000 g., Copper-Nickel, 17 mm. **Ruler:** Olav V **Obv:** Crowned monograms in cross formation **Rev:** Value **Designer:** Oivind Hansen

Date	Mintage	VG	F	VF	XF	BU
1974	8,048,223	—	—	—	0.10	0.65
1975	15,594,696	—	—	—	0.10	0.65
1976	24,721,074	—	—	—	0.10	0.50
1977	20,150,000	—	—	—	0.10	0.50
1978	11,259,000	—	—	—	0.10	0.50
1979	16,666,000	—	—	—	0.10	0.50
1980	6,289,000	—	—	—	0.10	0.50
1980 Without star	8,176,000	—	—	—	0.10	0.50
1981	17,971,000	—	—	—	0.10	0.50
1982	16,862,650	—	—	—	0.10	0.50

KM# 356 50 ORE

5.0000 g., 0.6000 Silver 0.0964 oz. ASW **Obv:** Head left **Obv. Legend:** OSCAR II NORGES... **Rev:** Crowned shield within wreath, crossed hammers divide date below

Date	Mintage	VG	F	VF	XF	BU
1901	404,000	7.00	14.00	35.00	70.00	200
1902	301,200	7.00	14.00	35.00	70.00	200
1904	100,500	35.00	70.00	165	260	550

KM# 374 50 ORE

5.0000 g., 0.6000 Silver 0.0964 oz. ASW **Ruler:** Haakon VII **Obv:** Head right **Rev:** Crowned shield flanked by designs

Date	Mintage	VG	F	VF	XF	BU
1909	200,000	14.00	27.00	35.00	65.00	175
1911	200,000	14.00	40.00	60.00	90.00	250
1912	200,000	30.00	60.00	90.00	150	325
1913	200,000	14.00	40.00	60.00	90.00	250
1914	800,000	3.50	8.00	15.00	25.00	120
1915	300,000	12.00	23.00	40.00	60.00	150
1916	700,000	4.50	9.00	19.00	45.00	150
1918	3,090,000	2.50	5.00	8.00	12.00	100
1919	1,219,000	3.00	6.00	9.00	18.00	60.00

KM# 379 50 ORE

4.8000 g., Copper-Nickel, 22 mm. **Ruler:** Haakon VII **Obv:** Crowned monograms form cross **Rev:** Crowned shield flanked by designs

Date	Mintage	VG	F	VF	XF	BU
1920	1,236,000	15.00	25.00	35.00	60.00	125
1921	7,345,000	4.00	8.00	12.00	25.00	50.00
1922	3,000,000	4.00	8.00	12.00	25.00	50.00
1923	4,540,000	25.00	60.00	85.00	115	185

KM# 380 50 ORE

4.8000 g., Copper-Nickel, 22 mm. **Ruler:** Haakon VII **Obv:** Crowned monograms form cross with hole in center **Rev:** Crowned shield flanked by designs, hole in center **Note:** Respective mintages are included with KM#379.

Date	Mintage	VG	F	VF	XF	BU
1920	—	—	30.00	90.00	300	1,000
1921	—	—	3.00	15.00	135	700

Date	Mintage	VG	F	VF	XF	BU
1922	—	—	2.50	10.00	85.00	500
1923	—	—	2.50	6.00	70.00	350

KM# 386 50 ORE

4.8000 g., Copper-Nickel, 22 mm. **Ruler:** Haakon VII **Obv:** Crowned monograms form cross with hole in center **Rev:** Center hole flanked by designs, crown above, value below

Date	Mintage	VG	F	VF	XF	BU
1926	2,000,000	—	0.35	1.50	17.50	95.00
1927	2,502,100	—	0.35	1.50	12.00	75.00
1928/7	1,458,200	—	0.50	2.50	20.00	110
1928	Inc. above	—	0.35	1.50	20.00	110
1929	600,000	—	1.50	6.00	70.00	520
1939	900,000	—	0.25	0.60	5.00	150
1940	2,193,000	—	0.20	0.50	3.50	40.00
1941	2,373,000	—	0.20	0.50	3.50	25.00
1945	1,354,000	—	0.20	0.50	2.50	32.50
1946	1,532,500	—	0.20	0.50	3.50	20.00
1947	2,465,300	—	0.20	0.50	3.50	12.50
1948	5,911,400	—	0.20	0.40	1.75	12.50
1949	1,029,600	—	0.25	1.00	5.00	25.00

KM# 390 50 ORE

Zinc, 22 mm. **Ruler:** Haakon VII **Obv:** Shield flanked by designs **Rev:** Value flanked by designs **Note:** World War II German occupation issue.

Date	Mintage	VG	F	VF	XF	BU
1941	7,760,800	—	1.25	3.00	15.00	80.00
1942	7,605,550	—	1.00	2.50	7.00	50.00
1943	3,348,500	7.00	15.00	25.00	60.00	200
1944	1,542,400	5.00	10.00	15.00	35.00	65.00
1945	226,000	90.00	180	285	425	675

KM# 393 50 ORE

4.8000 g., Nickel-Brass, 22 mm. **Ruler:** Haakon VII **Obv:** Crowned monograms form cross with hole in center **Rev:** Center hole flanked by designs, crown above, value below **Note:** World War II government in exile issue.

Date	Mintage	VG	F	VF	XF	BU
1942	1,600,000	—	—	—	125	250

Note: All but 9,238 were melted

KM# 402 50 ORE

4.8000 g., Copper-Nickel, 22 mm. **Ruler:** Haakon VII **Obv:** Crowned monogram **Rev:** Crowned shield divides date

Date	Mintage	VG	F	VF	XF	BU
1953	2,370,000	—	0.20	0.60	1.75	35.00
1954	230,000	1.25	5.00	15.00	85.00	550
1955	1,930,000	—	0.10	0.40	2.25	65.00
1956	1,630,000	—	0.10	0.40	2.25	65.00
1957	1,800,000	—	0.10	0.40	2.25	32.50

KM# 408 50 ORE

4.8000 g., Copper-Nickel, 22 mm. **Ruler:** Olav V **Obv:** Head left **Rev:** Dog right divides date and value

Date	Mintage	VG	F	VF	XF	BU
1958	1,560,000	—	0.25	0.75	3.00	75.00
1959	340,000	—	1.00	2.00	12.00	75.00
1960	1,584,200	—	—	0.10	1.75	20.00
1961	2,424,600	—	—	0.10	0.85	12.50
1962	3,064,000	—	—	0.10	0.85	12.50
1963	2,168,000	—	—	0.10	0.85	12.50
1964	2,692,000	—	—	0.10	0.60	8.00
1965	1,248,000	—	0.25	0.75	3.00	55.00
1966	4,262,000	—	—	0.10	0.50	8.00
1967	4,001,000	—	—	0.10	0.50	6.50
1968	5,430,800	—	—	0.10	0.50	12.50
1969	7,591,000	—	—	0.10	0.50	3.00
1970	481,000	—	0.25	0.75	2.25	6.50
1971	2,489,300	—	—	0.10	0.50	3.00
1972	4,452,784	—	—	0.10	0.50	3.00
1973	3,317,175	—	—	0.10	0.50	3.00

KM# 418 50 ORE

4.8000 g., Copper-Nickel, 22 mm. **Ruler:** Olav V **Obv:** Crowned shield divides date **Rev:** Value **Designer:** Oivind Hansen **Note:** Varieties in shield exist.

Date	Mintage	VG	F	VF	XF	BU
1974	8,494,223	—	—	0.10	0.15	0.75
1975	10,123,496	—	—	0.10	0.15	0.75
1976	15,177,324	—	—	0.10	0.15	0.65
1977	19,411,750	—	—	0.10	0.15	0.50
1978	15,305,000	—	—	0.10	0.15	0.50
1979	10,152,000	—	—	0.10	0.15	0.50
1980	7,082,000	—	—	0.10	0.15	0.50
1980 Without star	7,066,000	—	—	0.10	0.15	0.50
1981	3,402,000	—	—	0.10	0.15	0.50
1982	11,156,650	—	—	0.10	0.15	0.40
1983	15,762,300	—	—	0.10	0.15	0.40
1984	8,615,000	—	—	0.10	0.15	0.40
1985	4,444,000	—	—	0.10	0.15	0.40
1986	4,178,000	—	—	0.10	0.15	0.40
1987	5,167,000	—	—	0.10	0.15	0.40
1988	9,610,000	—	—	0.10	0.15	0.35
1989	5,785,000	—	—	0.10	0.15	0.35
1990	1,729,000	—	—	0.10	0.15	0.50
1991	2,924,008	—	—	0.10	0.15	0.35
1992	6,802,027	—	—	0.10	0.15	0.35
1992 Proof	20,000	Value: 10.00				
1993	8,056,000	—	—	0.10	0.15	0.35
1994	7,173,000	—	—	0.10	0.15	0.35
1994 Proof	12,000	Value: 10.00				
1995	6,835,000	—	—	—	—	0.35
1995 Proof	—	Value: 10.00				
1996	4,500,000	—	—	—	—	0.40
1996 Proof	—	Value: 10.00				

KM# 460 50 ORE

3.6000 g., Bronze, 18.49 mm. **Ruler:** Harald V **Obv:** Crown **Rev:** Stylized animal and value **Edge:** Plain **Designer:** Grazyna Jolanta Linday

Date	Mintage	VG	F	VF	XF	BU
1996	81,956,200	—	—	—	—	0.50
1997	24,089,873	—	—	—	—	0.40
1997 Proof	—	Value: 10.00				
1998	30,913,000	—	—	—	—	0.40
1998 Proof	—	Value: 10.00				
1999	25,314,273	—	—	—	—	0.40
1999 Proof	—	Value: 10.00				
2000	18,979,552	—	—	—	—	0.40
2000 Proof	—	Value: 10.00				
2001 with star	13,291,750	—	—	—	—	0.40
2001 without star	16,848,250	—	—	—	—	0.40
2001 Proof	—	Value: 10.00				
2002 Proof	—	Value: 10.00				
2002	—	—	—	—	—	0.40
2003 Proof	—	Value: 10.00				
2003	—	—	—	—	—	0.40
2004 Proof	—	Value: 10.00				
2004	—	—	—	—	—	0.40
2005	—	—	—	—	—	0.40
2005 Proof	—	Value: 10.00				
2006	—	—	—	—	—	0.40

KM# 357 KRONE

7.5000 g., 0.8000 Silver 0.1929 oz. ASW **Obv:** Head left **Obv. Legend:** OSCAR II NORGES... **Rev:** Crowned arms within wreath, crossed hammers divide date below **Note:** Without 30 SK

Date	Mintage	VG	F	VF	XF	BU
1901	151,800	17.00	30.00	60.00	175	550
1904	100,100	35.00	70.00	125	230	625

KM# 369 KRONE

7.5000 g., 0.8000 Silver 0.1929 oz. ASW **Ruler:** Haakon VII **Obv:** Head right **Rev:** Order of St. Olaf

Date	Mintage	VG	F	VF	XF	BU
1908	180,000	26.00	50.00	80.00	120	265
Note: Crossed hammers on shield						
1908	170,000	21.00	40.00	60.00	100	200
Note: Crossed hammers without shield						
1910	100,000	50.00	100	150	235	550
1912	200,000	30.00	45.00	100	160	325
1913	230,000	22.00	40.00	90.00	125	285
1914	602,000	11.00	19.00	35.00	50.00	125
1915	498,000	12.00	22.00	40.00	90.00	125
1916	400,000	12.00	25.00	40.00	100	265
1917	600,000	11.00	19.00	30.00	55.00	95.00

KM# 385 KRONE

7.0000 g., Copper-Nickel, 25 mm. **Ruler:** Haakon VII **Obv:** Crowned monograms form cross with hole in center **Rev:** Crowned order chain with hole in center

Date	Mintage	VG	F	VF	XF	BU
1925	8,686,000	—	0.30	3.00	25.00	140
1926	1,984,000	—	0.50	4.00	35.00	240
1927	1,000,000	—	1.00	5.00	65.00	500
1936	700,000	—	1.25	5.50	65.00	475
1937	1,000,000	—	1.00	4.00	45.00	325
1938	926,000	—	0.60	2.50	20.00	150
1939	2,253,000	—	0.60	1.50	10.00	85.00
1940	3,890,000	—	0.30	1.00	6.00	75.00
1946	5,499,000	—	0.25	0.50	3.00	20.00
1947	802,000	—	1.00	2.00	12.00	65.00
1949	7,846,000	—	0.20	0.50	3.00	15.00
1950	9,942,000	—	0.20	0.50	3.00	15.00
1951	4,761,000	—	0.20	0.50	3.00	15.00

KM# 397.1 KRONE

7.0000 g., Copper-Nickel, 25 mm. **Ruler:** Haakon VII **Obv:** Crowned monogram **Rev:** Crowned shield divides date **Note:** Thin border dentilations

Date	Mintage	F	VF	XF	Unc	BU
1951	3,819,000	0.20	0.50	2.50	32.50	—

KM# 397.2 KRONE

7.0000 g., Copper-Nickel, 25 mm. **Ruler:** Haakon VII **Obv:** Crowned monogram **Rev:** Crowned shield divides date **Note:** Thick border dentilations.

Date	Mintage	VG	F	VF	XF	BU
1953	1,465,000	—	0.20	0.50	2.50	70.00
1954	3,045,000	—	0.20	0.50	2.50	70.00
1955	1,970,000	—	0.20	0.50	2.50	100
1956	4,300,000	—	0.20	0.50	2.50	60.00
1957	7,630,000	—	0.20	0.50	2.50	40.00

KM# 409 KRONE
7.0000 g., Copper-Nickel, 25 mm. **Ruler:** Olav V **Obv:** Head left **Rev:** Horse

Date	Mintage	VG	F	VF	XF	BU
1958	540,000	—	3.00	10.00	50.00	325
1959	4,450,000	—	—	0.20	2.50	35.00
1960	1,790,200	—	—	0.20	2.50	30.00
1961	3,933,600	—	—	0.20	0.85	15.00
1962	6,015,000	—	—	0.20	0.85	15.00
1963	4,677,000	—	—	0.20	0.85	15.00
1964	3,469,000	—	—	0.20	0.60	7.50
1965	3,222,000	—	—	0.20	1.20	70.00
1966	3,084,000	—	—	0.20	0.85	30.00
1967	6,680,000	—	—	0.20	0.85	15.00
1968	6,149,200	—	—	0.20	0.85	60.00
1969	5,185,500	—	—	0.20	0.40	5.00
1970	8,637,900	—	—	0.20	0.50	15.00
1971	10,257,800	—	—	0.20	0.40	5.00
1972	13,179,394	—	—	0.20	0.40	4.75
1973	9,140,175	—	—	0.20	0.40	4.75

KM# 419 KRONE
7.0000 g., Copper-Nickel, 25 mm. **Ruler:** Olav V **Obv:** Head left **Rev:** Value and date below crown **Designer:** Oivind Hansen **Note:** Varieties with and without star mint mark exist.

Date	Mintage	VG	F	VF	XF	BU
1974	16,537,223	—	—	0.20	0.35	1.25
1975	26,043,966	—	—	0.20	0.35	1.25
1976	35,926,574	—	—	0.20	0.35	0.85
1977	26,263,500	—	—	0.20	0.35	0.85
1978	23,360,000	—	—	0.20	0.35	0.85
1979	15,896,500	—	—	0.20	0.35	0.85
1980	5,918,000	—	—	0.20	0.35	2.50
1981	16,308,150	—	—	0.20	0.35	0.75
1982	29,187,000	—	—	0.20	0.35	0.75
1983	24,293,300	—	—	0.20	0.35	0.75
1984	3,677,000	—	—	0.20	0.35	1.50
1985	10,985,000	—	—	0.20	0.35	0.75
1986	5,612,500	—	—	0.20	0.35	0.75
1987	11,015,500	—	—	0.20	0.35	0.75
1988	14,880,000	—	—	0.20	0.35	0.75
1989	5,605,000	—	—	0.20	0.35	0.65
1990	8,804,000	—	—	0.20	0.35	0.65
1990 Proof	15,110	Value: 85.00				
1991	21,064,500	—	—	0.20	0.35	0.65

KM# 436 KRONE
7.0000 g., Copper-Nickel, 25 mm. **Ruler:** Harald V **Obv:** Head right **Rev:** Value and date below crown **Designer:** Ingrid Austlid Rase

Date	Mintage	VG	F	VF	XF	BU
1992	7,425,500	—	—	0.20	0.35	0.65
1992 Proof	20,000	Value: 10.00				
1993	12,295,000	—	—	0.20	0.35	0.65
1994	25,951,000	—	—	0.20	0.35	0.65
1994 Proof	12,000	Value: 10.00				
1995	12,883,000	—	—	0.20	0.35	0.65
1995 Proof	—	Value: 10.00				
1996	20,844,000	—	—	0.20	0.35	0.65
1996 Proof	—	Value: 10.00				

KM# 462 KRONE
4.3000 g., Copper-Nickel, 21 mm. **Ruler:** Harald V **Obv:** Crowned monograms form cross within circle with center hole **Rev:** Bird on vine above center hole date and value below

Date	Mintage	VG	F	VF	XF	BU
1997	141,099,873	—	—	—	—	0.65
1997 Proof	—	Value: 10.00				
1998	139,493,000	—	—	—	—	0.65
1998 Proof	—	Value: 10.00				
1999	74,454,273	—	—	—	—	0.65
1999 Proof	—	Value: 10.00				
2000	42,689,277	—	—	—	—	0.65
2000 Proof	—	Value: 10.00				
2001 with star	7,355,350	—	—	—	—	0.75
2001 without star	43,128,650	—	—	—	—	0.65
2001 Proof	—	Value: 10.00				
2002 Proof	—	Value: 10.00				
2002	—	—	—	—	—	0.65
2003	—	—	—	—	—	0.65
2003 Proof	—	Value: 10.00				
2004 Proof	—	Value: 10.00				
2004	—	—	—	—	—	0.65
2005	—	—	—	—	—	0.65
2005 Proof	—	Value: 10.00				
2006	—	—	—	—	—	0.65

KM# 359 2 KRONER
15.0000 g., 0.8000 Silver 0.3858 oz. ASW, 31 mm. **Obv:** Head left **Obv. Legend:** OSCAR II NORGES... **Rev:** Crowned arms within wreath, crossed hammers divide date below **Note:** Restrikes are made by the Royal Mint, Norway, in gold, silver and bronze.

Date	Mintage	VG	F	VF	XF	BU
1902	153,100	50.00	85.00	125	225	500
1904	75,600	50.00	100	150	250	525

KM# 363 2 KRONER
15.0000 g., 0.8000 Silver 0.3858 oz. ASW, 31 mm. **Ruler:** Haakon VII **Subject:** Norway Independence **Obv:** Crowned mantled shield **Rev:** Inscription and date within tree, wreath of grasped hands surround **Designer:** Gerhard Munthe and Ivar Thorndsen

Date	Mintage	VG	F	VF	XF	BU
1906	100,000	23.00	35.00	60.00	100	175

KM# 365 2 KRONER
15.0000 g., 0.8000 Silver 0.3858 oz. ASW, 31 mm. **Ruler:** Haakon VII **Obv:** Crowned mantled shield **Rev:** Inscription and date within tree, wreath of grasped hands surround **Designer:** Herhard Munthe and Ivar Thorndsen

Date	Mintage	VG	F	VF	XF	BU
1907	54,600	30.00	55.00	100	175	275

KM# 366 2 KRONER
15.0000 g., 0.8000 Silver 0.3858 oz. ASW, 31 mm. **Ruler:** Haakon VII **Subject:** Border watch **Obv:** Crowned and mantled arms **Rev:** Inscription and date within tree, wreath of grasped hands surround **Designer:** Gerhard Munthe and Ivar Thorndsen

Date	Mintage	VG	F	VF	XF	BU
1907	27,500	100	200	350	550	900

KM# 370 2 KRONER
15.0000 g., 0.8000 Silver 0.3858 oz. ASW, 31 mm. **Ruler:** Haakon VII **Obv:** Head right **Rev:** Crowned shield within designed circle, various emblems around border

Date	Mintage	VG	F	VF	XF	BU
1908	200,000	—	50.00	85.00	125	250
1910	150,000	—	80.00	125	175	425
1912	150,000	—	65.00	100	150	400
1913	270,000	—	45.00	65.00	90.00	175
1914	255,000	—	45.00	70.00	95.00	215
1915	225,000	—	40.00	65.00	95.00	215
1916	250,000	—	60.00	85.00	125	265
1917	377,500	—	30.00	40.00	60.00	165

KM# 377 2 KRONER
15.0000 g., 0.8000 Silver 0.3858 oz. ASW, 31 mm. **Ruler:** Haakon VII **Subject:** Constitution centennial **Obv:** Crowned shield **Rev:** Standing figure facing right **Designer:** Gunner Utsand

Date	Mintage	VG	F	VF	XF	BU
1914	225,600	10.00	17.00	30.00	60.00	135

KM# 412 5 KRONER
11.5000 g., Copper-Nickel, 29.5 mm. **Ruler:** Olav V **Obv:** Head left **Rev:** Crowned shield divides value

Date	Mintage	VG	F	VF	XF	BU
1963	7,074,000	—	—	1.00	3.50	30.00
1964	7,346,000	—	—	1.00	2.25	15.00
1965	2,233,000	—	—	1.00	3.00	90.00
1966	2,502,000	—	—	1.00	3.00	65.00
1967	583,000	—	1.00	1.75	6.50	60.00
1968	1,813,400	—	—	1.00	2.25	45.00
1969	2,403,700	—	—	1.00	2.25	12.00
1970	202,300	—	1.50	2.50	6.50	22.50
1971	177,900	—	1.50	2.50	7.00	27.50
1972	2,208,704	—	—	—	1.25	3.50
1973	2,778,055	—	—	—	1.25	7.50

KM# 420 5 KRONER

11.5000 g., Copper-Nickel, 29.5 mm. **Ruler:** Olav V **Obv:** Head left **Rev:** Crowned shield divides date **Designer:** Oivind Hansen **Note:** Varieties exist with large and small shields.

Date	Mintage	VG	F	VF	XF	BU
1974	1,983,423	—	—	—	1.00	7.50
1975	2,946,442	—	—	—	1.00	4.50
1976	9,055,574	—	—	—	1.00	2.25
1977	4,629,600	—	—	—	1.00	1.50
1978	5,853,000	—	—	—	1.00	1.50
1979	6,818,000	—	—	—	1.00	1.50
1980	1,578,400	—	—	—	1.00	2.50
1981	1,104,800	—	—	—	1.00	2.25
1982	3,919,890	—	—	—	1.00	1.50
1983	2,932,260	—	—	—	1.00	1.50
1984	1,233,000	—	—	—	1.00	2.25
1985	1,399,600	—	—	—	1.00	1.50
1987	900,200	—	—	—	1.00	2.50
1988	865,200	—	—	—	1.00	2.50

KM# 421 5 KRONER

11.5000 g., Copper-Nickel, 29.5 mm. **Ruler:** Olav V **Subject:** 100th Anniversary of Krone System **Obv:** Crowned shield divides value **Rev:** Balance scale and miner **Designer:** Oivind Hansen

Date	Mintage	VG	F	VF	XF	BU
ND(1975)	1,191,813	—	—	1.00	1.50	3.50

KM# 422 5 KRONER

11.5000 g., Copper-Nickel, 29.5 mm. **Ruler:** Olav V **Subject:** 150th Anniversary - Immigration to America **Obv:** Value below arms **Rev:** Sailing ship, The "Restaurasjonen"(Restoration)

Date	Mintage	VG	F	VF	XF	BU
ND(1975)	1,222,827	—	—	1.00	1.50	3.50

KM# 423 5 KRONER

11.5000 g., Copper-Nickel, 29.5 mm. **Ruler:** Olav V **Subject:** 350th Anniversary of Norwegian Army **Obv:** Value below arms **Rev:** Sword divides crowned monograms

Date	Mintage	VG	F	VF	XF	BU
ND(1978)	2,989,768	—	—	1.00	1.50	3.00

KM# 428 5 KRONER

11.5000 g., Copper-Nickel, 29.5 mm. **Ruler:** Olav V **Subject:** 300th Anniversary of the Mint **Obv:** Crossed mining tools below crown, circle surrounds **Rev:** Conjoined heads left and right within circle **Designer:** Oivind Hansen

Date	Mintage	VG	F	VF	XF	BU
1986	2,345,500	—	—	1.00	1.50	3.00
1986 Prooflike	5,000	—	—	—	—	—

KM# 430 5 KRONER

11.5000 g., Copper-Nickel, 29.5 mm. **Ruler:** Olav V **Subject:** 175th Anniversary of the National Bank **Obv:** Arms **Rev:** Stein above date and inscription

Date	Mintage	VG	F	VF	XF	BU
1991	512,000	—	—	—	—	7.00

KM# 437 5 KRONER

11.5000 g., Copper-Nickel, 29.5 mm. **Ruler:** Harald V **Obv:** Crowned shield divides date **Designer:** Ingrid Austlid Rise

Date	Mintage	VG	F	VF	XF	BU
1992	549,600	—	—	—	—	2.25
Note: 100,000 are in mint sets						
1992 Proof	20,000	Value: 10.00				
1993	509,600	—	—	—	—	2.50
1994	2,111,800	—	—	—	—	2.00
1994 Proof	12,000	Value: 10.00				

KM# 456 5 KRONER

11.5000 g., Copper-Nickel, 29.5 mm. **Ruler:** Harald V **Obv:** Head right **Rev:** Old coin design divides value above legend and date **Designer:** Ingrid Austlid Rise **Note:** 1,000 years of Norwegian coinage

Date	Mintage	VG	F	VF	XF	BU
1995	500,000	—	—	—	—	3.50
1995 Proof	12,000	Value: 22.50				

KM# 458 5 KRONER

11.5000 g., Copper-Nickel, 29.5 mm. **Ruler:** Harald V **Subject:** 50th Anniversary - United Nations **Obv:** Head right **Rev:** Standing figure with arms outstretched, children holding hands by tree **Designer:** Ingrid Austlid Rise

Date	Mintage	VG	F	VF	XF	BU
ND(1995)	500,000	—	—	—	—	3.50

KM# 459 5 KRONER

11.5000 g., Copper-Nickel, 29.5 mm. **Ruler:** Harald V **Subject:** Centennial - Nansen's Return From the Arctic **Obv:** Head right **Rev:** Sailing ship facing **Designer:** Ingrid Austlid Rise

Date	Mintage	VG	F	VF	XF	BU
1996	1,381,909	—	—	—	—	3.00
1996 Proof	12,000	Value: 22.50				

KM# 461 5 KRONER

11.5000 g., Copper-Nickel, 29.5 mm. **Ruler:** Harald V **Subject:** 350th Anniversary - Norwegian Postal Service **Obv:** Arms **Rev:** Horse and rider left

Date	Mintage	VG	F	VF	XF	BU
ND(1997)	1,742,073	—	—	—	—	3.00
ND(1997) Proof	12,000	Value: 10.00				

KM# 463 5 KRONER

7.8500 g., Copper-Nickel **Ruler:** Harald V **Subject:** Order of St. Olaf **Obv:** Hole at center of order chain **Rev:** Center hole divides sprigs, value above and date below

Date	Mintage	VG	F	VF	XF	BU
1998	47,701,000	—	—	—	—	1.50
1998 Proof	10,000	Value: 12.50				
1999	21,754,273	—	—	—	—	1.50
1999 Proof	10,000	Value: 12.50				
2000	9,691,387	—	—	—	—	1.50
2000 Proof	10,000	Value: 12.50				
2001	460,000	—	—	—	—	2.00
2001 Proof	—	Value: 12.50				
2002 Proof	—	Value: 12.50				
2002	—	—	—	—	—	1.50
2003 Proof	—	Value: 12.50				
2003	—	—	—	—	—	1.50
2004 Proof	—	Value: 12.50				
2004	—	—	—	—	—	1.50
2005	—	—	—	—	—	1.50
2005 Proof	—	Value: 12.50				
2006	—	—	—	—	—	1.50

KM# 358 10 KRONER

4.4803 g., 0.9000 Gold 0.1296 oz. AGW **Obv:** Head right **Obv. Legend:** OSCAR II NORGES... **Rev:** Crowned arms within wreath

Date	Mintage	VG	F	VF	XF	Unc
1902	24,100	BV	120	200	375	600

KM# 375 10 KRONER
4.4803 g., 0.9000 Gold 0.1296 oz. AGW **Ruler:** Haakon VII **Obv:** Crowned head right **Rev:** King Olaf Haraldson, the Saint

Date	Mintage	F	VF	XF	Unc	BU
1910	52,600	BV	175	275	450	—

KM# 413 10 KRONER
20.0000 g., 0.9000 Silver 0.5787 oz. ASW, 35 mm. **Ruler:** Haakon VII **Subject:** Constitution sesquicentennial **Obv:** Crowned shield **Rev:** Eidsval Mansion **Edge Lettering:** ENIGE OG TRO TIL DOVRE FALLER **Note:** Edge lettering varieties exist.

Date	Mintage	VG	F	VF	XF	BU
ND(1964)	1,408,000	—	—	—	9.00	11.50

KM# 427 10 KRONER
9.0000 g., Copper-Zinc-Nickel **Ruler:** Olav V **Obv:** Head left within circle **Rev:** Value within small circle at center of order chain

Date	Mintage	VG	F	VF	XF	BU
1983	20,193,060	—	—	—	2.00	5.50
1984	11,073,500	—	—	—	1.75	3.25
1985	22,457,550	—	—	—	1.75	3.00
1986	29,060,950	—	—	—	1.75	3.00
1987	8,809,750	—	—	—	1.75	3.25
1988	2,630,500	—	—	—	1.75	3.25
1989	3,259,000	—	—	—	1.75	3.25
1990	3,004,000	—	—	—	1.75	3.25
1991	20,287,150	—	—	—	1.75	2.75

KM# 457 10 KRONER
6.8000 g., Copper-Zinc-Nickel **Ruler:** Harald V **Obv:** Head right **Rev:** Stylized church rooftop, value and date **Designer:** Ingrid Austlid Rise

Date	Mintage	VG	F	VF	XF	BU
1995	60,740,000	—	—	—	—	3.50
1995 Proof	—	Value: 10.00				
1996	36,372,000	—	—	—	—	3.50
1996 Proof	—	Value: 10.00				
1997	1,229,873	—	—	—	—	3.50
1997 Proof	—	Value: 10.00				
1998	1,058,000	—	—	—	—	3.50
1998 Proof	—	Value: 10.00				
1999	1,059,273	—	—	—	—	3.50
1999 Proof	—	Value: 10.00				
2000	1,096,727	—	—	—	—	3.50
2000 Proof	—	Value: 10.00				
2001 without star	9,837,500	—	—	—	—	3.50
2001 with star	10,000	—	—	—	—	7.50
2001 Proof	—	Value: 10.00				
2002 Proof	—	Value: 10.00				
2002	—	—	—	—	—	3.50
2003 Proof	—	Value: 10.00				
2003	—	—	—	—	—	3.50
2004 Proof	—	Value: 10.00				
2004	—	—	—	—	—	3.50
2005	—	—	—	—	—	3.50
2005 Proof	—	Value: 10.00				
2006	—	—	—	—	—	3.50

KM# 478 20 KRONER (5 Speciedaler)
9.9000 g., Copper-Zinc-Nickel, 27.5 mm. **Ruler:** Harald V **Subject:** First Norwegian Railroad **Obv:** Head right **Rev:** Switch track and value **Edge:** Plain

Date	Mintage	F	VF	XF	Unc	BU
2004	10,000	—	—	—	17.50	20.00
2004 Proof	—	Value: 25.00				

KM# 355 20 KRONER
8.9600 g., 0.9000 Gold 0.2593 oz. AGW **Obv:** Head right **Obv. Legend:** OSCAR II NORGES... **Rev:** Crowned arms within wreath

Date	Mintage	VG	F	VF	XF	Unc
1902	50,400	—	—	BV	250	350

KM# 376 20 KRONER
8.9600 g., 0.9000 Gold 0.2593 oz. AGW **Ruler:** Haakon VII **Obv:** Crowned head right **Rev:** King Olaf II, the Saint

Date	Mintage	F	VF	XF	Unc	BU
1910	250,000	BV	235	300	450	—

KM# 453 20 KRONER
8.7000 g., Copper-Zinc-Nickel **Ruler:** Harald V **Obv:** Head right **Rev:** Value above 1/2 ancient boat **Designer:** Ingrid Austlid Rise

Date	Mintage	VG	F	VF	XF	BU
1994	18,598,000	—	—	—	—	6.50
1994 Proof	12,000	Value: 25.00				
1995	21,760,000	—	—	—	—	6.50
1995 Proof	—	Value: 25.00				
1996	1,519,500	—	—	—	—	6.50
1996 Proof	—	Value: 25.00				
1997	1,049,873	—	—	—	—	6.50
1997 Proof	—	Value: 25.00				
1998	5,007,000	—	—	—	—	6.50
1998 Proof	—	Value: 25.00				
1999	6,171,000	—	—	—	—	6.50
1999 Proof	—	Value: 25.00				
2000	11,113,370	—	—	—	—	6.50
2000 Proof	10,000	Value: 25.00				
2001	4,178,010	—	—	—	—	6.50
2001 Proof	—	Value: 25.00				
2002 Proof	—	Value: 25.00				
2002	—	—	—	—	—	6.50
2003 Proof	—	Value: 25.00				
2003	—	—	—	—	—	6.50
2004	—	—	—	—	—	6.50
2004 Proof	—	Value: 25.00				
2005	—	—	—	—	—	6.50
2005 Proof	—	Value: 25.00				

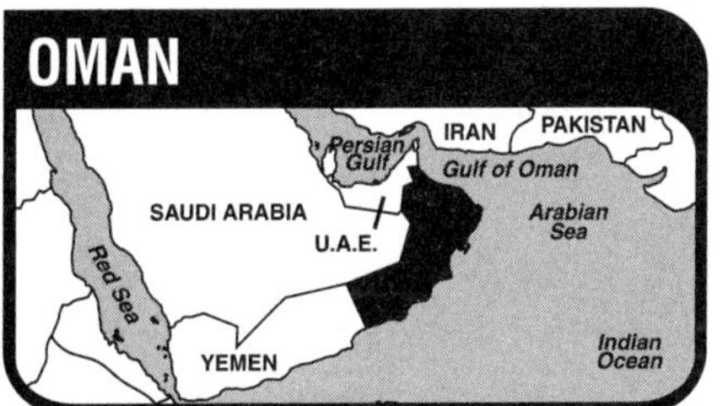

The Sultanate of Oman (formerly Muscat and Oman), an independent monarchy located in the southeastern part of the Arabian Peninsula, has an area of 82,030 sq. mi. (212,460 sq. km.) and a population of *1.3 million. Capital: Muscat. The economy is based on agriculture, herding and petroleum. Petroleum products, dates, fish and hides are exported.

The Portuguese who captured Muscat, the capital and chief port, in 1508, made the first European contact with Muscat and Oman. They occupied the city, utilizing it as a naval base and factory and holding it against land and sea attacks by Arabs and Persians until finally ejected by local Arabs in 1650. It was next occupied by the Persians who maintained control until 1741,when it was taken by Ahmed ibn Sa'id of the present ruling family. Muscat and Oman was the most powerful state in Arabia during the first half of the 19th century, until weakened by the persistent attack of interior nomadic tribes. British influence, initiated by the signing of a treaty of friendship with the Sultanate in 1798,remains a dominant fact of the civil and military phases of the government, although Britain recognizes the Sultanate as a sovereign state.

Sultan Sa'id bin Taimur was overthrown by his son, Qabus bin Sa'id, on July 23, 1970. The new sultan changed the nation's name to Sultanate of Oman.

TITLES

Muscat مسقط

Oman عمان

SULTANATE

REFORM COINAGE

1000 Baisa = 1 Omani Rial

KM# 50 5 BAISA
3.1000 g., Bronze, 19 mm. **Ruler:** Qabus bin Sa'id AH1390-/1970AD- **Obv:** National arms **Rev:** Value and date

Date	Mintage	F	VF	XF	Unc	BU
AH1395 (1975)	6,000,000	—	0.10	0.20	0.45	—
AH1400 (1979)	3,000,000	—	0.10	0.20	0.45	—
AH1406 (1985)	2,000,000	—	0.10	0.20	0.45	—
AH1410 (1989)	5,000,000	—	0.10	0.20	0.45	—

KM# 50a 5 BAISA
2.6400 g., Bronze-Plated Steel, 18.98 mm. **Ruler:** Qabus bin Sa'id AH1390-/1970AD- **Obv:** National arms **Rev:** Large value, dates below **Edge:** Plain

Date	Mintage	F	VF	XF	Unc	BU
AH1420-1999	—	—	0.10	0.20	0.40	0.50

KM# 150 5 BAISA
2.6500 g., Bronze Clad Steel, 19.1 mm. **Ruler:** Qabus bin Sa'id AH1390-/1970AD-

Date	Mintage	F	VF	XF	Unc	BU
AH1420-1999	—	—	—	0.25	0.50	0.75

KM# 51 10 BAISA
4.7000 g., Bronze, 22.5 mm. **Ruler:** Qabus bin Sa'id AH1390-/1970AD- **Series:** F.A.O. **Obv:** Date palms **Rev:** Value and date

Date	Mintage	F	VF	XF	Unc	BU
AH1395 (1975)	1,000,000	—	0.15	0.30	0.65	—

KM# 52 10 BAISA
4.7000 g., Bronze, 22.5 mm. **Ruler:** Qabus bin Sa'id AH1390-/1970AD- **Series:** F.A.O. **Obv:** National arms **Rev:** Value and date

Date	Mintage	F	VF	XF	Unc	BU
AH1395 (1975)	6,000,000	—	0.15	0.30	0.65	—
AH1400 (1979)	5,250,000	—	0.15	0.30	0.65	—
AH1406 (1985)	3,000,000	—	0.15	0.30	0.65	—
AH1410 (1989)	6,000,000	—	0.15	0.30	0.65	—
AH1418 (1997)	—	—	0.15	0.30	0.65	—

KM# 77 10 BAISA
Bronze Clad Steel **Ruler:** Qabus bin Sa'id AH1390-/1970AD- **Subject:** 20th National Day - Central Bank of Oman **Obv:** National emblem **Rev:** Central Bank building

Date	Mintage	F	VF	XF	Unc	BU
AH1411 (1990) Proof	3,200	Value: 5.00				

KM# 94 10 BAISA
Bronze Clad Steel, 22.5 mm. **Ruler:** Qabus bin Sa'id AH1390-/1970AD- **Series:** F.A.O. **Subject:** 50 Years **Obv:** National arms **Rev:** FAO symbol and dates

Date	Mintage	F	VF	XF	Unc	BU
ND	—	—	—	—	1.25	—
ND(1995)	224	—	—	—	1.25	—

KM# 151 10 BAISA
Bronze Clad Steel, 22.5 mm. **Ruler:** Qabus bin Sa'id AH1390-/1970AD-

Date	Mintage	F	VF	XF	Unc	BU
AH1420-1999	—	—	—	0.35	0.75	1.00

KM# 45a 25 BAISA
3.0300 g., Copper-Nickel, 18 mm. **Ruler:** Qabus bin Sa'id AH1390-/1970AD- **Obv:** National arms **Rev:** Value and date

Date	Mintage	F	VF	XF	Unc	BU
AH1395 (1975)	4,500,000	—	0.20	0.40	0.85	—
AH1400 (1979)	5,250,000	—	0.20	0.40	0.85	—
AH1406 (1985)	4,000,000	—	0.20	0.40	0.85	—
AH1410 (1989)	7,000,000	—	0.20	0.40	0.85	—
AH1418 (1997)	—	—	0.20	0.40	0.85	—

KM# 152 25 BAISA
3.0300 g., Copper-Nickel, 18 mm. **Ruler:** Qabus bin Sa'id AH1390-/1970AD-

Date	Mintage	F	VF	XF	Unc	BU
AH1420-1999	—	—	—	0.50	1.00	1.25

KM# 46a 50 BAISA
6.4000 g., Copper-Nickel, 24 mm. **Ruler:** Qabus bin Sa'id AH1390-/1970AD- **Obv:** National arms **Rev:** Value and date

Date	Mintage	F	VF	XF	Unc	BU
AH1395 (1975)	2,500,000	—	0.30	0.60	1.50	—
AH1400 (1979)	2,750,000	—	0.30	0.60	1.50	—
AH1406 (1985)	4,000,000	—	0.30	0.60	1.50	—
AH1410 (1989)	4,000,000	—	0.30	0.60	1.50	—
AH1418 (1997)	—	—	0.30	0.60	1.50	—

KM# 95 50 BAISA
6.4000 g., Copper-Nickel, 24 mm. **Ruler:** Qabus bin Sa'id AH1390-/1970AD- **Subject:** U.N. - 50 Years **Obv:** National arms **Rev:** UN symbol and anniversary dates

Date	Mintage	F	VF	XF	Unc	BU
ND (1995)	—	—	—	—	3.00	—

KM# 153 50 BAISA
6.4000 g., Copper-Nickel, 24 mm. **Ruler:** Qabus bin Sa'id AH1390-/1970AD-

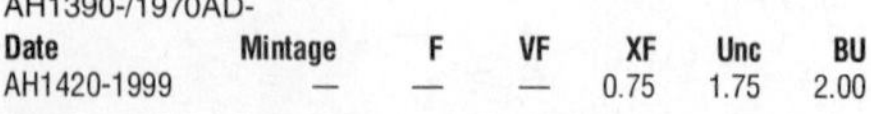

Date	Mintage	F	VF	XF	Unc	BU
AH1420-1999	—	—	—	0.75	1.75	2.00

KM# 68 100 BAISA
4.2000 g., Copper-Nickel, 21.5 mm. **Ruler:** Qabus bin Sa'id AH1390-/1970AD- **Obv:** National arms **Rev:** Arms and date

Date	Mintage	VG	F	VF	XF	Unc
AH1404-1983	4,000,000	—	—	0.40	0.80	2.25

KM# 82 100 BAISA
Bi-Metallic Aluminumn-Bronze center in Copper-Nickel ring, 25 mm. **Ruler:** Qabus bin Sa'id AH1390-/1970AD- **Subject:** 100 Years of Coinage **Obv:** Arms within circle **Rev:** Fortress within circle

Date	Mintage	F	VF	XF	Unc	BU
AH1411-1991	—	—	—	—	5.00	7.00
AH1411-1991 Proof	1,000	Value: 20.00				

KM# 66 1/4 OMANI RIAL
6.5000 g., Aluminum-Bronze, 26 mm. **Ruler:** Qabus bin Sa'id AH1390-/1970AD- **Obv:** National arms and dates **Rev:** Value

Date	Mintage	VG	F	VF	XF	Unc
AH1400-1980	4,000,000	—	—	0.75	1.00	2.00

KM# 64 1/2 OMANI RIAL
Copper-Nickel **Ruler:** Qabus bin Sa'id AH1390-/1970AD- **Series:** F.A.O. **Obv:** National arms flanked by dates **Rev:** Fruit above value **Shape:** 7-sided

Date	Mintage	VG	F	VF	XF	Unc
AH1398-1978	15,000	—	—	2.75	3.50	5.00

KM# 67 1/2 OMANI RIAL
10.0000 g., Aluminum-Bronze, 30 mm. **Ruler:** Qabus bin Sa'id AH1390-/1970AD- **Obv:** National arms and dates **Rev:** Value

Date	Mintage	VG	F	VF	XF	Unc
AH1400-1980	2,000,000	—	—	2.75	3.50	5.00

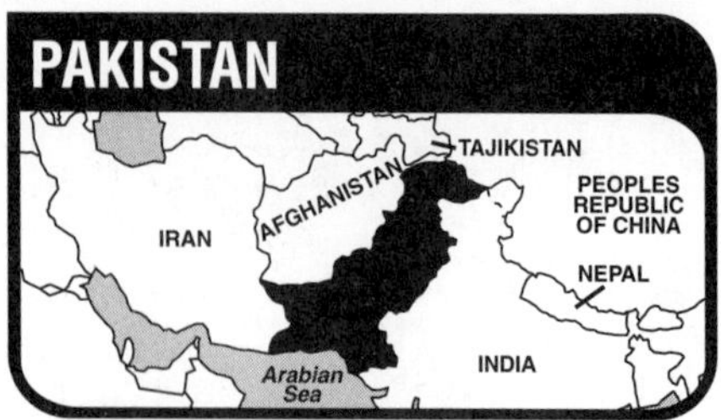

The Islamic Republic of Pakistan, located on the Indian subcontinent between India and Afghanistan, has an area of 310,404 sq. mi. (803,940 sq. km.) and a population of130 million. Capital: Islamabad. Pakistan is mainly an agricultural land although the industrial base is expanding rapidly. Yarn, textiles, cotton, rice, medical instruments, sports equipment and leather are exported.

Afghan and Turkish intrusions into northern India between the 11th and 18th centuries resulted in large numbers of Indians being converted to Islam. The idea of a separate Moslem state independent of Hindu India developed in the 1930's and was agreed to by Britain in1946. The Islamic majority areas of India, consisting of the separate geographic entities known as East and West Pakistan, achieved self-government as Pakistan, with dominion status in the British Commonwealth, when the British withdrew from India on Aug. 14, 1947. Pakistan became a republic in 1956. When a basic constitutional crisis initiated by the election of Dec. 1, 1970 - the first direct general election in Pakistani history - could not be resolved by the leaders of East and West Pakistan, the East Pakistanis seceded from the Islamic Republic of Pakistan (March 26, 1971) and formed the independent People's Republic of Bangladesh. After many years of vacillation between civilian and military regimes, the people of Pakistan held a free national election in November, 1988 and installed the first of a series of democratic governments under a parliamentary system.

TITLE

Pakistan

MONETARY SYSTEM
100 Paisa = 1 Rupee

ISLAMIC REPUBLIC

STANDARD COINAGE

3 Pies = 1 Pice; 4 Pice = 1 Anna; 16 Annas = 1 Rupee

KM# 11 PIE
1.2500 g., Bronze, 15.87 mm. **Obv:** Crescent and star above tughra **Rev:** Value and date flanked by stars within wreath **Edge:** Plain

Date	Mintage	F	VF	XF	Unc	BU
1951	2,950,000	0.25	0.50	1.00	2.50	—
1951 Proof	—	Value: 4.00				
1953	110,000	3.00	5.00	7.00	10.00	—
1953 Proof	—	Value: 5.00				
1955	211,000	0.25	0.75	1.50	3.00	—
1955 Proof	—	Value: 15.00				
1956	3,390,000	0.25	0.50	1.00	2.50	—
1957	—	0.25	0.50	1.00	2.50	—

KM# 1 PICE
1.5500 g., Bronze, 21.3 mm. **Obv:** Legend around center hole **Rev:** Crescent and star divides value around the top, center hole divides date **Note:** Varieties exist.

Date	Mintage	F	VF	XF	Unc	BU
1948	101,070,000	0.20	0.40	0.75	1.50	—
1948 Proof	—	Value: 2.00				
1949	25,740,000	0.20	0.40	0.75	1.50	—
1949 Proof	—	Value: 2.00				
1951	14,050,000	0.20	0.45	0.85	1.75	—
1952	41,680,000	0.20	0.40	0.75	1.50	—

KM# 12 PICE

2.3000 g., Nickel-Brass, 20.59 mm. **Obv:** Crescent and star above tughra **Rev:** Value flanked by oat sprigs **Edge:** Plain

Date	Mintage	F	VF	XF	Unc	BU
1953	47,540,000	0.15	0.30	0.50	1.00	—
1953 Proof	—	Value: 1.50				
1955	31,280,000	0.15	0.30	0.50	1.00	—
1956	9,710,000	0.50	0.70	1.00	1.50	—
1957	57,790,000	0.15	0.30	0.50	1.00	—
1958	52,470,000	0.15	0.30	0.50	1.00	—
1959	41,620,000	0.15	0.30	0.50	1.00	—

KM# 2 1/2 ANNA

2.9000 g., Copper-Nickel, 19.8 mm. **Obv:** Tughra and date flanked by stars within sprigs, circle surrounds **Rev:** Crescent, stars and value above sprigs within circle **Shape:** 4-sided

Date	Mintage	F	VF	XF	Unc	BU
1948	73,920,000	0.15	0.30	0.50	1.00	—
1948 Proof	—	Value: 1.50				
1949 Dot after date	16,940,000	0.50	0.75	1.00	1.50	—
1951	75,360,000	0.15	0.30	0.50	1.00	—

KM# 13 1/2 ANNA

2.5000 g., Nickel-Brass, 19.8 mm. **Obv:** Crescent and star above tughra **Rev:** Date divides wreath, value in center **Shape:** 4-sided

Date	Mintage	F	VF	XF	Unc	BU
1953	8,350,000	0.20	0.35	0.60	1.15	—
1953 Proof	—	Value: 1.50				
1955	17,310,000	0.15	0.30	0.50	1.00	—
1958	38,250,000	0.15	0.30	0.50	1.00	—

KM# 3 ANNA

3.7500 g., Copper-Nickel, 21.0 mm. **Obv:** Tughra and date flanked by stars above sprigs within circle **Rev:** Crescent and star above sprigs within circle **Shape:** Scalloped

Date	Mintage	F	VF	XF	Unc	BU
1948	73,460,000	0.15	0.30	0.50	1.00	—
1948 Proof	—	Value: 1.50				
1949	11,140,000	0.20	0.35	0.60	1.15	—
1949 Dot after date	—	0.50	0.75	1.00	1.50	—

Note: Mintage included with KM#8.

Date	Mintage	F	VF	XF	Unc	BU
1951	40,800,000	0.15	0.30	0.50	1.00	—
1952	15,430,000	0.20	0.35	0.60	1.15	—

KM# 8 ANNA

3.7500 g., Copper-Nickel, 21.0 mm. **Obv:** Tughra and date flanked by stars above sprigs within circle **Rev:** Crescent, stars and value above sprigs within circle **Shape:** Scalloped

Date	Mintage	F	VF	XF	Unc	BU
1950	94,830,000	3.00	4.50	6.50	10.00	—
1950 Proof	—	Value: 15.00				

KM# 14 ANNA

2.9000 g., Copper-Nickel, 19.5 mm. **Obv:** Crescent and star above tughra **Rev:** Date divides wreath, value in center **Shape:** Scalloped

Date	Mintage	F	VF	XF	Unc	BU
1953	9,350,000	0.15	0.30	0.50	1.00	—
1953 Proof	—	Value: 1.50				
1954	35,360,000	0.15	0.30	0.50	1.00	—
1955	6,230,000	0.20	0.35	0.60	1.15	—
1956	4,580,000	0.20	0.35	0.60	1.15	—
1957	12,500,000	0.15	0.30	0.50	1.00	—
1958	44,320,000	0.15	0.30	0.50	1.00	—

KM# 4 2 ANNAS

5.8000 g., Copper-Nickel, 25.4 mm. **Obv:** Tughra and date flanked by stars above sprigs within circle **Rev:** Crescent, stars and value above sprigs within circle **Shape:** 4-sided

Date	Mintage	F	VF	XF	Unc	BU
1948	55,930,000	0.15	0.30	0.50	1.00	—
1948 Proof	—	Value: 1.50				
1949	19,720,000	0.20	0.35	0.60	1.15	—
1949 Dot after date	—	0.50	0.75	1.00	1.50	—

Note: Mintage included with KM#9.

Date	Mintage	F	VF	XF	Unc	BU
1951	33,130,000	0.15	0.30	0.50	1.00	—

KM# 9 2 ANNAS

5.8000 g., Copper-Nickel, 25.4 mm. **Obv:** Tughra and date flanked by stars above sprigs within circle **Rev:** Crescent, stars and value above sprigs within circle **Shape:** 4-sided

Date	Mintage	F	VF	XF	Unc	BU
1950	21,190,000	3.50	5.00	7.50	12.50	—
1950 Proof	—	Value: 20.00				

KM# 15 2 ANNAS

5.8000 g., Copper-Nickel, 25.4 mm. **Obv:** Crescent and star above tughra **Rev:** Date divides wreath, value in center **Shape:** 4-sided

Date	Mintage	F	VF	XF	Unc	BU
1953	7,910,000	0.15	0.30	0.50	1.00	—
1953 Proof	—	Value: 1.50				
1954	5,740,000	0.15	0.30	0.50	1.00	—
1955	6,230,000	0.15	0.30	0.50	1.00	—
1956	1,370,000	0.20	0.35	0.60	1.15	—
1957	2,570,000	0.20	0.35	0.60	1.15	—
1958	6,200,000	0.15	0.30	0.50	1.00	—
1959	8,010,000	0.15	0.30	0.50	1.00	—

KM# 5 1/4 RUPEE

2.7500 g., Nickel, 19 mm. **Obv:** Tughra and date flanked by stars above sprigs **Rev:** Crescent, stars and value above sprigs **Edge:** Reeded

Date	Mintage	F	VF	XF	Unc	BU
1948	52,680,000	0.20	0.30	0.50	1.00	—
1948 Proof	—	Value: 2.25				
1949	46,000,000	0.20	0.30	0.50	1.00	—
1951	19,120,000	0.20	0.35	0.60	1.15	—

KM# 10 1/4 RUPEE

2.7500 g., Nickel, 19 mm. **Obv:** Tughra and date flanked by stars above sprigs **Rev:** Crescent, stars and value above sprigs **Edge:** Reeded

Date	Mintage	F	VF	XF	Unc	BU
1950	19,400,000	5.00	7.50	12.00	20.00	—
1950 Proof	—	Value: 25.00				

KM# 6 1/2 RUPEE

6.0000 g., Nickel, 24 mm. **Obv:** Tughra and date flanked by stars above sprigs **Rev:** Crescent, stars and value above sprigs **Edge:** Reeded

Date	Mintage	F	VF	XF	Unc	BU
1948	33,260,000	0.40	0.60	0.75	1.50	—
1948 Proof	—	Value: 2.00				
1949	20,300,000	0.40	0.60	0.75	1.50	—
1951	11,430,000	0.40	0.65	0.90	1.75	—

KM# 7 RUPEE

11.5000 g., Nickel, 28 mm. **Obv:** Tughra and date flanked by stars above sprigs **Rev:** Crescent, stars and value above sprigs **Edge:** Reeded **Note:** Varieties exist.

Date	Mintage	F	VF	XF	Unc	BU
1948	46,200,000	0.75	1.25	2.00	3.50	—
1948 Proof	—	Value: 5.00				
1949	37,100,000	0.75	1.25	2.00	3.50	—

DECIMAL COINAGE

100 Paisa = 1 Rupee

KM# 16 PICE

1.4000 g., Bronze, 16 mm. **Obv:** Crescent and star above tughra **Rev:** Date and value flanked by oat sprigs

Date	Mintage	F	VF	XF	Unc	BU
1961	74,910,000	0.15	0.30	0.50	1.00	—

KM# 17 PAISA

1.4000 g., Bronze, 16 mm. **Obv:** Crescent and star above tughra **Rev:** Value and date flanked by oat sprigs

Date	Mintage	F	VF	XF	Unc	BU
1961	134,650,000	0.15	0.25	0.40	0.80	—
1961 Proof	—	Value: 1.50				
1962	149,380,000	0.15	0.25	0.40	0.80	—
1963	127,810,000	0.15	0.25	0.40	0.80	—

KM# 24 PAISA

1.5000 g., Bronze, 17 mm. **Obv:** Crescent and star above tughra **Rev:** Value flanked by oat sprigs

Date	Mintage	F	VF	XF	Unc	BU
1964	39,890,000	0.20	0.35	0.50	1.00	—
1964 Proof	—	Value: 1.50				
1965	69,660,000	0.20	0.35	0.50	1.00	—

KM# 24a PAISA

1.5000 g., Nickel-Brass, 17 mm. **Obv:** Crescent and star above tughra **Rev:** Value flanked by oat sprigs

Date	Mintage	F	VF	XF	Unc	BU
1965	32,950,000	0.20	0.35	0.50	1.00	—
1966	179,370,000	0.15	0.25	0.40	0.80	—

KM# 29 PAISA

0.6000 g., Aluminum, 17 mm. **Obv:** Crescent and star above tughra **Rev:** Value flanked by oat sprigs

Date	Mintage	F	VF	XF	Unc	BU
1967	170,070,000	—	0.20	0.40	0.75	—
1968	—	—	0.20	0.40	0.75	—
1969	—	—	0.20	0.40	0.75	—
1970	204,606,000	—	0.20	0.40	0.75	—
1971	191,880,000	—	0.20	0.40	0.75	—
1972	108,510,000	—	0.20	0.40	0.75	—
1973	Inc. above	—	0.20	0.40	0.75	—

KM# 33 PAISA

0.7500 g., Aluminum, 17 mm. **Series:** F.A.O. **Obv:** Crescent within monument with star at upper left **Rev:** Value flanked by abstract cotton plant **Edge:** Plain

Date	Mintage	F	VF	XF	Unc	BU
1974	14,230,000	—	0.20	0.40	0.75	—
1975	43,000,000	—	0.20	0.40	0.75	—
1976	49,180,000	—	0.20	0.40	0.75	—
1977	62,750,000	—	0.20	0.40	0.75	—
1978	20,380,000	—	0.20	0.40	0.75	—
1978/7	—	—	4.00	6.00	8.00	—
1979	5,630,000	—	2.00	3.00	4.00	—

KM# 25 2 PAISA

2.2500 g., Bronze, 18.0 mm. **Obv:** Crescent and star above tughra **Rev:** Value within sprigs **Shape:** Scalloped

Date	Mintage	F	VF	XF	Unc	BU
1964	67,660,000	0.15	0.35	0.50	1.00	—
1964 Proof	—	Value: 1.50				
1965	27,880,000	0.15	0.35	0.50	1.00	—
1966	50,590,000	0.15	0.35	0.50	1.00	—

KM# 28 2 PAISA

0.7500 g., Aluminum, 18 mm. **Obv:** Crescent and star above tughra **Rev:** Value within sprigs

Date	Mintage	F	VF	XF	Unc	BU
1966	11,940,000	—	0.35	0.50	1.00	—
1967	73,970,000	—	0.35	0.50	1.00	—
1968	—	—	0.35	0.50	1.00	—

KM# 25a 2 PAISA

0.7500 g., Aluminum, 18.0 mm. **Obv:** Crescent and star above tughra **Rev:** Value within sprigs **Shape:** Scalloped

Date	Mintage	F	VF	XF	Unc	BU
1968	—	—	0.35	0.50	1.00	—
1969	—	—	0.35	0.50	1.00	—
1970	24,401,000	—	0.35	0.50	1.00	—
1971	10,140,000	—	0.35	0.50	1.00	—
1972	4,040,000	—	0.65	1.00	2.00	—

KM# 34 2 PAISA

1.0000 g., Aluminum, 19.0 mm. **Series:** F.A.O. **Obv:** Crescent within monument with star at upper left **Rev:** Value flanked by rice plant **Shape:** Scalloped

Date	Mintage	F	VF	XF	Unc	BU
1974	3,600,000	—	0.35	0.50	1.00	—
1975	4,020,000	—	0.35	0.50	1.00	—
1976	5,750,000	—	0.50	0.75	1.50	—

KM# 18 5 PICE

2.7500 g., Nickel-Brass, 24.0 mm. **Obv:** Crescent and star above tughra **Rev:** Sailboat with value on sails **Shape:** 4-sided

Date	Mintage	F	VF	XF	Unc	BU
1961	40,050,000	0.20	0.35	0.50	1.00	—

KM# 19 5 PAISA

2.7500 g., Nickel-Brass, 21.0 mm. **Obv:** Crescent and star above tughra **Rev:** Sailboat with value on sails **Shape:** 4-sided

Date	Mintage	F	VF	XF	Unc	BU
1961	40,790,000	0.20	0.35	0.50	1.00	—
1961 Proof	—	Value: 1.50				
1962	48,200,000	0.20	0.35	0.50	1.00	—
1963	45,020,000	0.20	0.35	0.50	1.00	—

KM# 26 5 PAISA

2.7500 g., Nickel-Brass, 21.0 mm. **Obv:** Crescent and star above tughra **Rev:** Sailboat with value on the sails **Shape:** 4-sided

Date	Mintage	F	VF	XF	Unc	BU
1964	82,730,000	0.20	0.35	0.50	1.00	—
1965	72,570,000	0.20	0.35	0.50	1.00	—
1966	32,900,000	0.20	0.35	0.50	1.00	—
1967	24,470,000	0.20	0.35	0.50	1.00	—
1968	—	0.20	0.35	0.50	1.00	—
1969	5,690,000	0.20	0.35	0.50	1.00	—
1970	24,655,000	0.20	0.35	0.50	1.00	—
1971	23,860,000	0.20	0.35	0.50	1.00	—
1972	40,345,000	0.20	0.35	0.50	1.00	—
1973	Inc. above	0.20	0.35	0.50	1.00	—
1974	7,695,000	0.65	1.00	2.00	3.00	—

KM# 35 5 PAISA

1.0000 g., Aluminum, 21.0 mm. **Series:** F.A.O. **Obv:** Crescent within monument with star at upper left **Rev:** Value within sugar cane **Shape:** 4-sided

Date	Mintage	F	VF	XF	Unc	BU
1974	23,395,000	—	0.35	0.50	1.00	—
1975	50,030,000	—	0.35	0.50	1.00	—
1976	58,255,000	—	0.35	0.50	1.00	—
1977	32,840,000	—	0.35	0.50	1.00	—
1978	61,940,000	—	0.35	0.50	1.00	—
1979	65,485,000	—	0.35	0.50	1.00	—
1980	55,940,000	—	0.35	0.50	1.00	—
1981	18,290,000	—	0.35	0.50	1.00	—

KM# 52 5 PAISA

1.0000 g., Aluminum, 19.12 mm. **Obv:** Crescent, star and date above sprigs **Rev:** Value within sugar cane flanked by stars **Edge:** Plain **Shape:** 4-sided

Date	Mintage	F	VF	XF	Unc	BU
1981	16,730,000	—	0.35	0.50	1.00	—
1982	51,210,000	—	0.35	0.50	1.00	—
1983	42,915,000	—	0.35	0.50	1.00	—
1984	45,105,000	—	0.35	0.50	1.00	—
1985	46,555,000	—	0.35	0.50	1.00	—
1986	20,065,000	—	0.35	0.50	1.00	—
1987	37,710,000	—	0.35	0.50	1.00	—
1988	40,150,000	—	0.35	0.50	1.00	—
1989	—	—	0.35	0.50	1.00	—
1990	—	—	0.35	0.50	1.00	—
1991	—	—	0.35	0.50	1.00	—
1992	—	—	0.35	0.50	1.00	—

KM# 20 10 PICE

4.7500 g., Copper-Nickel, 23.0 mm. **Obv:** Crescent and star above tughra **Rev:** Date divides wreath, value in center **Shape:** Scalloped

Date	Mintage	F	VF	XF	Unc	BU
1961	22,230,000	0.20	0.35	0.50	1.00	—

KM# 21 10 PAISA

4.7500 g., Copper-Nickel, 23.0 mm. **Obv:** Crescent and star above tughra **Rev:** Date divides wreath, value in center **Shape:** Scalloped

Date	Mintage	F	VF	XF	Unc	BU
1961	31,090,000	0.20	0.35	0.50	1.00	—
1961 Proof	—	Value: 2.00				
1962	29,440,000	0.20	0.35	0.50	1.00	—
1963	19,760,000	0.20	0.35	0.50	1.00	—

KM# 27 10 PAISA

4.7500 g., Copper-Nickel, 23.0 mm. **Obv:** Crescent and star above tughra **Rev:** Value within wreath **Shape:** Scalloped

Date	Mintage	F	VF	XF	Unc	BU
1964	52,580,000	0.20	0.35	0.50	1.00	—
1965	51,540,000	0.20	0.35	0.50	1.00	—
1966	—	0.20	0.35	0.50	1.00	—
1967	16,430,000	0.20	0.35	0.50	1.00	—
1968	—	0.20	0.35	0.50	1.00	—

KM# 31 10 PAISA

4.0000 g., Copper-Nickel, 22.0 mm. **Obv:** Crescent and star above tughra **Rev:** Value within wreath **Shape:** Scalloped **Note:** Reduced size.

Date	Mintage	F	VF	XF	Unc	BU
1969	—	0.20	0.35	0.50	1.00	—
1970	30,250,000	0.20	0.35	0.50	1.00	—
1971	26,270,000	0.20	0.35	0.50	1.00	—
1972	24,845,000	0.20	0.35	0.50	1.00	—
1973	Inc. above	0.20	0.35	0.50	1.00	—
1974	4,780,000	0.20	0.35	0.50	1.00	—

KM# 36 10 PAISA

1.2500 g., Aluminum, 22.0 mm. **Series:** F.A.O. **Obv:** Crescent within monument with star at upper left **Rev:** Value within wheat ears **Shape:** Scalloped

Date	Mintage	F	VF	XF	Unc	BU
1974	18,640,000	—	0.35	0.50	1.00	—
1975	28,875,000	—	0.35	0.50	1.00	—
1976	43,755,000	—	0.35	0.50	1.00	—
1977	29,045,000	—	0.35	0.50	1.00	—
1978	55,185,000	—	0.35	0.50	1.00	—
1979	56,100,000	—	0.35	0.50	1.00	—
1980	40,985,000	—	0.35	0.50	1.00	—
1981	15,500,000	—	0.35	0.50	1.00	—

KM# 53 10 PAISA

1.1900 g., Aluminum, 22 mm. **Obv:** Crescent, star and date above sprigs **Rev:** Value within square **Edge:** Plain **Shape:** Scalloped

Date	Mintage	F	VF	XF	Unc	BU
1981	7,995,000	—	0.35	0.50	1.00	—
1982	39,770,000	—	0.35	0.50	1.00	—
1983	44,705,000	—	0.35	0.50	1.00	—
1984	35,255,000	—	0.35	0.50	1.00	—
1985	41,545,000	—	0.35	0.50	1.00	—
1986	43,280,000	—	0.35	0.50	1.00	—
1987	39,090,000	—	0.35	0.50	1.00	—
1988	42,510,000	—	0.35	0.50	1.00	—
1989	—	—	0.35	0.50	1.00	—
1990	—	—	0.35	0.50	1.00	—
1991	—	—	0.35	0.50	1.00	—
1992	—	—	0.35	0.50	1.00	—
1993	—	—	0.35	0.50	1.00	—

KM# 22 25 PAISA

2.9000 g., Nickel, 19 mm. **Obv:** Crescent and star above tughra **Rev:** Value flanked by flower sprigs **Edge:** Reeded

Date	Mintage	F	VF	XF	Unc	BU
1963	16,900,000	0.20	0.35	0.50	1.00	—
1964	7,990,000	0.20	0.35	0.50	1.00	—
1965	9,290,000	0.20	0.35	0.50	1.00	—
1966	6,650,000	0.20	0.35	0.50	1.00	—
1967	3,740,000	0.20	0.35	0.50	1.00	—

KM# 30 25 PAISA

4.0000 g., Copper-Nickel, 20 mm. **Obv:** Crescent and star above tughra **Rev:** Value below flowers **Edge:** Reeded

Date	Mintage	F	VF	XF	Unc	BU
1967	5,500,000	0.20	0.35	0.50	1.00	—
Note: Mintage unconfirmed						
1968	5,500,000	0.20	0.35	0.50	1.00	—
Note: Mintage unconfirmed						
1969	—	0.20	0.35	0.50	1.00	—
1970	30,392,000	0.20	0.35	0.50	1.00	—
1971	12,664,000	0.20	0.35	0.50	1.00	—
1972	10,824,000	0.20	0.35	0.50	1.00	—
1973	—	0.20	0.35	0.50	1.00	—
1974	9,756,000	0.20	0.35	0.50	1.00	—

KM# 37 25 PAISA

4.0000 g., Copper-Nickel, 20 mm. **Obv:** Crescent within monument with star at upper left **Rev:** Value within flowers **Edge:** Reeded

Date	Mintage	F	VF	XF	Unc	BU
1975	14,264,000	0.20	0.35	0.50	1.00	—
1976	20,440,000	0.20	0.35	0.50	1.00	—
1977	22,092,000	0.20	0.35	0.50	1.00	—
1978	33,544,000	0.20	0.35	0.50	1.00	—
1979	29,648,000	0.20	0.35	0.50	1.00	—
1980	49,556,000	0.20	0.35	0.50	1.00	—
1981	33,952,000	0.20	0.35	0.50	1.00	—

KM# 58 25 PAISA

2.5000 g., Copper-Nickel, 18 mm. **Obv:** Crescent, star and date above sprigs **Rev:** Value within artistic designed wreath **Edge:** Reeded **Note:** Varieties in date and crescent size exist.

Date	Mintage	F	VF	XF	Unc	BU
1981	5,648,000	0.20	0.35	0.50	1.00	—
1982	28,940,000	0.20	0.35	0.50	1.00	—
1983	40,844,000	0.20	0.35	0.50	1.00	—
1984	50,988,000	0.20	0.35	0.50	1.00	—
1985	53,748,000	0.20	0.35	0.50	1.00	—
1986	75,764,000	0.20	0.35	0.50	1.00	—
1987	53,560,000	0.20	0.35	0.50	1.00	—
1988	58,900,000	0.20	0.35	0.50	1.00	—
1989	—	0.20	0.35	0.50	1.00	—
1990	—	0.20	0.35	0.50	1.00	—
1991	—	0.20	0.35	0.50	1.00	—
1992	—	0.20	0.35	0.50	1.00	—
1993	—	0.20	0.35	0.50	1.00	—
1994	—	0.20	0.35	0.50	1.00	—
1995	—	0.20	0.35	0.50	1.00	—
1996	—	0.20	0.35	0.50	1.00	—

KM# 23 50 PAISA

5.8000 g., Nickel, 24 mm. **Obv:** Crescent and star above tughra **Rev:** Value flanked by flowers **Edge:** Reeded

Date	Mintage	F	VF	XF	Unc	BU
1963	8,110,000	0.20	0.35	0.50	1.00	—
1964	4,580,000	0.20	0.35	0.50	1.00	—
1965	8,980,000	0.20	0.35	0.50	1.00	—
1966	2,860,000	0.20	0.35	0.50	1.00	—
1968	—	0.20	0.35	0.50	1.00	—
1969	—	0.20	0.35	0.50	1.00	—

KM# 32 50 PAISA

5.0000 g., Copper-Nickel, 22 mm. **Obv:** Crescent and star above tughra **Rev:** Value below flowers **Edge:** Reeded

Date	Mintage	F	VF	XF	Unc	BU
1969	9,240,000	0.20	0.35	0.50	1.00	—
1970	Inc. above	0.20	0.35	0.50	1.00	—
1971	4,670,000	0.20	0.35	0.50	1.00	—
1972	4,900,000	0.20	0.35	0.50	1.00	—
1974	1,128,000	0.50	0.75	1.00	2.00	—

KM# 38 50 PAISA

5.0000 g., Copper-Nickel, 23 mm. **Obv:** Crescent within monument with star at upper left **Rev:** Value within circle and designed wreath **Edge:** Reeded **Note:** Varieties in date size exist.

Date	Mintage	F	VF	XF	Unc	BU
1975	9,180,000	0.20	0.35	0.50	1.00	—
1976	—	0.20	0.35	0.50	1.00	—
1977	5,548,000	0.20	0.35	0.50	1.00	—
1978	18,252,000	0.20	0.35	0.50	1.00	—
1979	14,596,000	0.20	0.35	0.50	1.00	—
1980	22,332,000	0.20	0.35	0.50	1.00	—
1981	13,552,000	0.20	0.35	0.50	1.00	—

KM# 39 50 PAISA

5.8300 g., Copper-Nickel, 24 mm. **Subject:** 100th Anniversary - Birth of Mohammad Ali Jinnah **Obv:** Value within circle and designed wreath **Rev:** Bust facing flanked by dates **Edge:** Reeded

Date	Mintage	F	VF	XF	Unc	BU
1976	5,600,000	0.35	0.50	1.00	1.50	2.00

KM# 54 50 PAISA

4.0000 g., Copper-Nickel, 21 mm. **Obv:** Crescent, star and date above sprigs **Rev:** Value within circle and leaf wreath **Edge:** Reeded

Date	Mintage	F	VF	XF	Unc	BU
1981	4,612,000	0.20	0.35	0.50	1.00	—
1982	15,844,000	0.20	0.35	0.50	1.00	—
1983	9,608,000	0.20	0.35	0.50	1.00	—
1984	17,520,000	0.20	0.35	0.50	1.00	—
1985	20,144,000	0.20	0.35	0.50	1.00	—
1986	14,116,000	0.20	0.35	0.50	1.00	—
1987	23,044,000	0.20	0.35	0.50	1.00	—
1988	37,140,000	0.20	0.35	0.50	1.00	—
1989	—	0.20	0.35	0.50	1.00	—
1990	—	0.20	0.35	0.50	1.00	—
1991	—	0.20	0.35	0.50	1.00	—
1992	—	0.20	0.35	0.50	1.00	—
1993	—	0.20	0.35	0.50	1.00	—
1994	—	0.20	0.35	0.50	1.00	—
1995	—	0.20	0.35	0.50	1.00	—
1996	—	0.20	0.35	0.50	1.00	—

KM# 51 50 PAISA

5.0000 g., Copper-Nickel, 23 mm. **Subject:** 1,400th Hejira Anniversary **Obv:** Crescent and star above design **Rev:** Value within wreath **Edge:** Reeded

Date	Mintage	F	VF	XF	Unc	BU
AH1401 (1981)	—	0.50	0.75	1.00	2.00	2.50

KM# 45 RUPEE

7.5000 g., Copper-Nickel, 27.5 mm. **Subject:** Islamic Summit Conference **Obv:** Islamic summit minar flanked by designs **Rev:** Design within inner circle **Edge:** Reeded

Date	Mintage	F	VF	XF	Unc	BU
1977	5,074,000	0.50	0.75	1.00	2.00	2.50

KM# 46 RUPEE
7.5000 g., Copper-Nickel, 27.5 mm. **Subject:** 100th Anniversary - Birth of Allama Mohammad Iqbal **Obv:** Value and date above sprigs **Rev:** Head leaning on arm facing 1/4 left **Edge:** Reeded

Date	Mintage	F	VF	XF	Unc	BU
1977	5,000,000	0.50	0.75	1.00	2.00	2.50

KM# 57.1 RUPEE
6.5000 g., Copper-Nickel, 26.5 mm. **Obv:** Crescent, star and date above sprigs **Rev:** Value within sprigs **Edge:** Reeded

Date	Mintage	F	VF	XF	Unc	BU
1979	—	0.30	0.40	0.55	1.15	—
1980	14,522,000	0.30	0.40	0.55	1.15	—
1981	12,038,000	0.30	0.40	0.55	1.15	—

KM# 57.2 RUPEE
6.0000 g., Copper-Nickel, 25 mm. **Obv:** Crescent, star and date above sprigs **Rev:** Value within sprigs **Edge:** Reeded

Date	Mintage	F	VF	XF	Unc	BU
1981	4,084,000	0.25	0.40	0.60	1.20	—
1982	27,878,000	0.20	0.35	0.50	1.00	—
1983	18,746,000	0.20	0.35	0.50	1.00	—
1984	14,562,000	0.20	0.35	0.50	1.00	—
1985	4,934,000	0.25	0.40	0.60	1.20	—
1986	11,840,000	0.20	0.35	0.50	1.00	—
1987	50,416,000	0.20	0.35	0.50	1.00	—
1988	10,644,000	0.20	0.35	0.50	1.00	—
1990	—	0.20	0.35	0.50	1.00	—
1991	—	0.20	0.35	0.50	1.00	—

KM# 55 RUPEE
6.5000 g., Copper-Nickel, 26.5 mm. **Subject:** 1,400th Hejira Anniversary **Obv:** Crescent and star above design **Rev:** Value within wreath **Edge:** Reeded

Date	Mintage	F	VF	XF	Unc	BU
AH1401 (1981)	45,000	0.50	0.75	1.25	2.50	3.00

KM# 56 RUPEE
6.0000 g., Copper-Nickel, 25 mm. **Series:** World Food Day **Obv:** Crescent, star and date above sprigs **Rev:** F.A.O. logo within circle **Edge:** Reeded

Date	Mintage	F	VF	XF	Unc	BU
1981	45,000	0.35	0.75	1.50	3.00	3.50

KM# 62 RUPEE
4.0000 g., Bronze, 20 mm. **Obv:** Head left **Rev:** Mosque above value **Edge:** Reeded

Date	Mintage	F	VF	XF	Unc	BU
1998	—	0.20	0.25	0.35	0.65	0.75
1999	—	0.20	0.25	0.35	0.65	0.75
2000	—	0.20	0.25	0.35	0.65	0.75
2001	—	0.20	0.25	0.35	0.65	0.75
2002	—	0.20	0.25	0.35	0.65	0.75
2003	—	0.20	0.25	0.35	0.65	0.75
2004	—	0.20	0.25	0.35	0.65	0.75
2005	—	0.20	0.25	0.35	0.65	0.75
2006	—	0.20	0.25	0.35	0.65	0.75

KM# 63 2 RUPEES
4.0000 g., Nickel-Brass, 22.5 mm. **Obv:** Crescent, star and date above sprigs **Rev:** Mosque **Edge:** Reeded

Date	Mintage	F	VF	XF	Unc	BU
1998	—	0.20	0.30	0.45	0.85	1.00
1999	—	0.25	0.45	0.75	1.25	1.50

KM# 64 2 RUPEES
5.0000 g., Nickel-Brass, 22.5 mm. **Obv:** Crescent, star and date above sprigs **Rev:** Value below mosque and clouds **Edge:** Reeded

Date	Mintage	F	VF	XF	Unc	BU
1999	—	0.20	0.30	0.45	0.85	1.00
2000	—	0.20	0.30	0.45	0.85	1.00
2001	—	0.20	0.30	0.45	0.85	1.00
2002	—	0.20	0.30	0.45	0.85	1.00
2003	—	0.20	0.30	0.45	0.85	1.00
2004	—	0.20	0.30	0.45	0.85	1.00
2005	—	0.20	0.30	0.45	0.85	1.00
2006	—	0.20	0.30	0.45	0.85	1.00

KM# 65 5 RUPEES
6.5000 g., Copper-Nickel, 24 mm. **Obv:** Cresent, star and date above sprays **Rev:** Value within star design and sprigs **Edge:** Reeded

Date	Mintage	F	VF	XF	Unc	BU
2002	—	0.50	1.00	1.50	3.00	3.25
2003	—	0.50	1.00	1.50	3.00	3.25
2004	—	0.50	1.00	1.50	3.00	3.25
2005	—	0.50	1.00	1.50	3.00	3.25

KM# 61 10 RUPEES
10.0000 g., Copper-Nickel, 26 mm. **Subject:** 25th Anniversary - Pakistan's Senate **Obv:** Crescent, star and date above sprigs **Rev:** Shield within sprigs above banner and dates to left of numeral 25 **Edge:** Reeded

Date	Mintage	F	VF	XF	Unc	BU
1998	100,000	—	—	4.00	6.50	7.50

KM# 66 10 RUPEES
7.5000 g., Copper-Nickel, 27.5 mm. **Obv:** Cresent, star and date above sprays **Rev:** Flowers and inscription **Rev. Inscription:** Year of Fatima Jinnah **Edge:** Reeded

Date	Mintage	F	VF	XF	Unc	BU
2003	200,000	—	—	4.00	6.50	7.50

PALESTINE

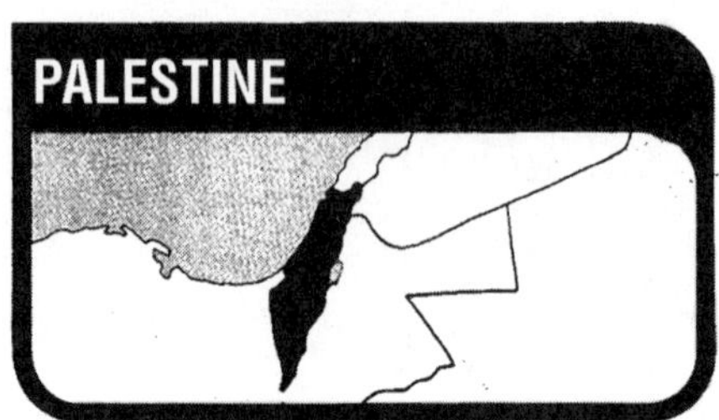

Palestine, which corresponds to Canaan of the Bible, was settled by the Philistines about the 12th century B.C. and shortly thereafter was settled by the Jews who established the kingdoms of Israel and Judah. Because of its position as part of the land bridge connecting Asia and Africa, Palestine was invaded and conquered by nearly all of the historic empires of ancient Europe and Asia. In the16th century it became a part of the Ottoman Empire. After falling to the British in World War I, it, together with Transjordan, was mandated to Great Britain by the League of Nations, 1922.

For more than half a century prior to the termination of the British mandate over Palestine, 1948, Zionist leaders had sought to create a Jewish homeland for Jews who were dispersed throughout the world. For almost as long, Jews fleeing persecution had immigrated to Palestine. The Nazi persecutions of the 1930s and 1940s increased the Jewish movement to Palestine and generated international support for the creation of a Jewish state, first promulgated by the Balfour Declaration of 1917, which asserted British support for the endeavor. The state of Israel was proclaimed as the Jewish state in the territory that was Palestine. The remainder of that territory was occupied by Jordanian and Egyptian armies. Israel demonetized the coins of Palestine on Sept. 15, 1948, the Jordan government declared Palestine currency no longer legal tender on June 30, 1951, and Egypt declared it no longer legal tender in Gaza on June 9, 1951.

TITLES

فلسطين

Filastin

פלשתינה (א"י).

Paleshtina (E.I.)

MONETARY SYSTEM
1000 Mils = 1 Pound
1000 Mils = 1 Pound

BRITISH ADMINISTRATION

MIL COINAGE

KM# 1 MIL
3.2000 g., Bronze **Obv:** Inscription **Obv. Inscription:** PALESTINE 1927 (IN ENGLISH AND ARABIC) **Rev:** Value, plant

Date	Mintage	F	VF	XF	Unc	BU
1927	10,000,000	0.50	2.00	4.00	12.00	18.00
1927 Proof	66	Value: 650				
1935	704,000	2.00	3.00	5.00	25.00	40.00
1937	1,200,000	1.50	2.00	10.00	150	250
1939	3,700,000	1.00	2.00	10.00	30.00	40.00
1939 Proof	—	Value: 400				
1940	396,000	6.50	12.50	50.00	150	—
1941	1,920,000	1.00	2.00	5.00	20.00	30.00
1942	4,480,000	1.00	2.00	5.00	25.00	40.00

Date	Mintage	F	VF	XF	Unc	BU
1943	2,800,000	0.75	2.00	5.00	35.00	45.00
1944	1,400,000	0.75	2.00	5.00	18.00	25.00
1946	1,632,000	2.00	4.00	8.00	35.00	50.00
1946 Proof	—	Value: 500				
1947	2,880,000	—	—	—	10,000	—

Note: Only 5 known; The entire issue was to be melted down

KM# 2 2 MILS

8.0000 g., Bronze **Obv:** Inscription **Obv. Inscription:** PALESTINE, 1927 (In English and Arabic) **Rev:** Value, plant

Date	Mintage	F	VF	XF	Unc	BU
1927	5,000,000	2.00	3.00	10.00	20.00	—
1927 Proof	66	Value: 700				
1941	1,600,000	1.00	2.00	6.00	40.00	—
1941 Proof	—	Value: 400				
1942	2,400,000	1.00	2.50	10.00	25.00	40.00
1945	960,000	2.00	5.00	20.00	150	—
1946	960,000	4.00	10.00	30.00	175	—
1947	480,000	—	—	—	—	—

Note: The entire issue was melted down

KM# 3 5 MILS

Copper-Nickel, 20 mm. **Obv:** Wreath around center hole **Rev:** Value above center hole

Date	Mintage	F	VF	XF	Unc	BU
		—	—	—	—	—
1927	10,000,000	0.75	2.00	5.00	25.00	35.00
1927 Proof	66	Value: 550				
1934	500,000	6.50	12.50	50.00	175	—
1935	2,700,000	0.75	2.00	7.00	40.00	60.00
1939	2,000,000	0.75	2.00	5.00	30.00	45.00
1939 Proof	—	Value: 425				
1941	400,000	10.00	20.00	35.00	125	175
1941 Proof	—	Value: 375				
1946	1,000,000	2.00	4.00	8.00	30.00	45.00
1946 Proof	—	Value: 450				
1947	1,000,000	—	—	—	—	25,000

Note: Almost the entire issue was melted down, with only 3 remaining pieces known to exist

KM# 3a 5 MILS

Bronze **Obv:** Wreath around center hole **Rev:** Value above center hole

Date	Mintage	F	VF	XF	Unc	BU
1942	2,700,000	1.50	2.00	8.00	45.00	60.00
1944	1,000,000	2.00	5.00	10.00	45.00	60.00

KM# 4 10 MILS

Copper-Nickel **Obv:** Date above and below center hole **Rev:** Wreath around center hole with value above and below

Date	Mintage	F	VF	XF	Unc	BU
1927	5,000,000	2.00	6.00	10.00	45.00	60.00
1927 Proof	66	Value: 575				
1933	500,000	4.00	8.00	75.00	400	—
1933 Proof	—	Value: 350				
1934	500,000	5.00	12.00	50.00	300	—
1934 Proof	—	Value: 375				
1935	1,150,000	1.00	10.00	35.00	250	—
1935 Proof	—	Value: 425				
1937	750,000	2.00	5.00	15.00	175	—
1937 Proof	—	Value: 425				
1939	1,000,000	1.00	5.00	15.00	100	—
1939 Proof	—	Value: 350				
1940	1,500,000	1.00	5.00	15.00	100	—
1940 Proof	—	Value: 100				
1941	400,000	6.00	15.00	50.00	125	200
1941 Proof	—	Value: 350				
1942	600,000	4.00	10.00	25.00	175	—
1946	1,000,000	2.00	15.00	25.00	75.00	—
1946 Proof	—	Value: 300				
1947	1,000,000	—	—	—	—	—

KM# 4a 10 MILS

Bronze **Obv:** Date above and below center hole **Rev:** Wreath around center hole with value above and below

Date	Mintage	F	VF	XF	Unc	BU
1942	1,000,000	4.00	5.00	15.00	125	—
1943	1,000,000	7.00	10.00	20.00	175	—

KM# 5 20 MILS

Copper-Nickel **Obv:** Wreath around center hole with dates below **Rev:** Value above and below center hole

Date	Mintage	F	VF	XF	Unc	BU
1927	1,500,000	7.00	12.00	35.00	100	—
1927 Proof	66	Value: 800				
1933	250,000	10.00	20.00	50.00	400	—
1934	125,000	40.00	70.00	175	750	—
1934 Proof	—	—	—	—	—	—
1935	575,000	5.00	15.00	50.00	300	—
1940	200,000	10.00	15.00	50.00	350	—
1940 Proof	—	Value: 500				
1941	100,000	50.00	75.00	150	1,000	—
1941 Proof	—	Value: 1,200				

KM# 5a 20 MILS

Bronze **Obv:** Wreath around center hole with dates below **Rev:** Value above and below center hole

Date	Mintage	F	VF	XF	Unc	BU
		—	—	—	—	—
1942	1,100,000	10.00	12.00	30.00	175	—
1944	1,000,000	25.00	60.00	200	600	—

KM# 6 50 MILS

5.8319 g., 0.7200 Silver 0.1350 oz. ASW **Obv:** Plant flanked by dates within circle **Rev:** Written and numeric value

Date	Mintage	F	VF	XF	Unc	BU
1927	8,000,000	8.00	10.00	25.00	75.00	—
1927 Proof	66	Value: 775				
1931	500,000	25.00	45.00	150	500	—
1933	1,000,000	20.00	25.00	50.00	125	—
1934	399,000	25.00	40.00	60.00	150	—
1935	5,600,000	6.00	8.00	12.00	50.00	—
1939	3,000,000	6.00	8.00	12.00	40.00	—
1939 Proof	—	Value: 275				
1940	2,000,000	8.00	20.00	30.00	75.00	—
1940 Proof	—	Value: 150				
1942	5,000,000	6.00	8.00	12.00	40.00	—

PANAMA

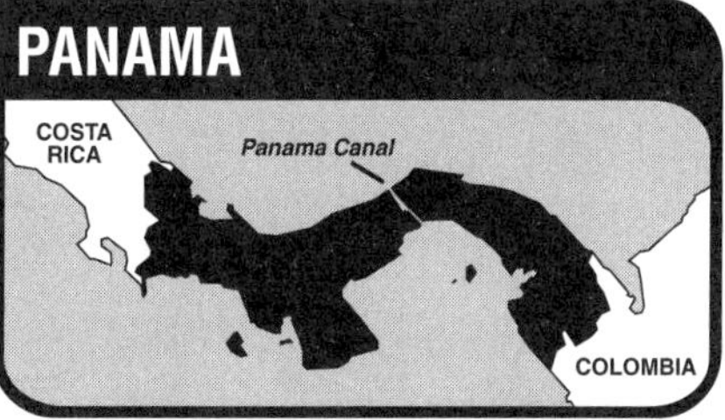

The Republic of Panama, a Central American Country situated between Costa Rica and Colombia, has an area of 29,762 sq. mi. (78,200 sq. km.) and a population of *2.4 million. Capital: Panama City. The Panama Canal is the country's biggest asset; servicing world related transit trade and international commerce. Bananas, refined petroleum, sugar and shrimp are exported.

Discovered in 1501 by the Spanish conquistador Rodrigo Galvan de Bastidas, the land of Panama was soon explored and after a few attempts at settlement was successfully colonized by the Spanish. It was in Panama in 1513 that Vasco Nunez de Balboa became the first European to see the Pacific Ocean. The first Pacific-coast settlement, founded in 1519 on the site of a village the natives called Panama, was named *Nuestra Senora de la Asuncion de Panama* (Our Lady of the Assumption of Panama). The settlement soon became a city and eventually, albeit briefly, an Audiencia (judicial tribunal).

In 1578 the city of Panama, being a primary transshipment center for treasure and supplies to and from Spain's South Pacific-coast colonies, was chosen for a new mint, and minting had begun there by 1580. By late 1582 or 1583 production was halted, possibly due to the fact that there were no nearby silver mines to sustain it. In it's brief operation, the Panama Mint must not have made many coins, as the corpus of surviving specimens known today from this colonial mint is less than 40.

The city of Panama, known today as the Old City of Panama, was sacked and burned in 1671 by the famous Henry Morgan in one of the greatest pirate victories against the Spanish Main.

Panama declared its independence in 1821 and joined the Confederation of Greater Colombia. In 1903, after Colombia rejected a treaty enabling the United States to build a canal across the Isthmus, Panama with the support of the United States proclaimed its independence from Colombia and became a sovereign republic.

The 1904 2-1/2 centesimos known as the 'Panama Pill' or 'Panama Pearl' is one of the world's smaller silver coins and a favorite with collectors.

MINT MARKS

FM - Franklin Mint, U.S.A.*

CHI in circle - Valcambi Mint, Balerna, Switzerland

RCM – Royal Canadian Mint

***NOTE:** From 1975-1985 the Franklin Mint produced coinage in up to 3 different qualities. Qualities of issue are designated in ( ) after each date and are defined as follows:

(M) MATTE - Normal circulation strike or a dull finish produced by sandblasting special uncirculated (polish finish) or proof quality dies.

(U) SPECIAL UNCIRCULATED - Polished or proof-like in appearance without any frosted features.

(P) PROOF - The highest quality obtainable having mirror-like fields and frosted features.

MONETARY SYSTEM

100 Centesimos = 1 Balboa

REPUBLIC

DECIMAL COINAGE

KM# 6 1/2 CENTESIMO

Copper-Nickel, 16 mm. **Obv:** Bust of Balboa left **Rev:** Written value **Note:** Previously listed re-engraved overdates were struck from very common doubled dies. The plain date in unc. is scarcer.

Date	Mintage	F	VF	XF	Unc	BU
1907	1,000,000	1.50	2.50	3.50	10.00	15.00
1907 Proof	—	Value: 200				

KM# 14 CENTESIMO

Bronze, 19.05 mm. **Subject:** Uracca **Obv:** Written value above sprigs **Rev:** Bust with headcovering left

Date	Mintage	F	VF	XF	Unc	BU
1935	200,000	4.00	6.00	15.00	35.00	80.00
1937	200,000	3.00	5.00	12.50	25.00	60.00

KM# 17 CENTESIMO

Bronze, 19.05 mm. **Subject:** 50th Anniversary of the Republic **Obv:** Written value above sprigs **Rev:** Bust of Uracca with headcovering left

Date	Mintage	F	VF	XF	Unc	BU
1953	1,500,000	0.10	0.50	1.00	4.00	7.00

KM# 22 CENTESIMO

3.1000 g., Bronze, 19.05 mm. **Obv:** Written value above sprigs with stars above **Obv. Legend:** Bust with headcovering left **Note:** Varieties exist.

Date	Mintage	F	VF	XF	Unc	BU
1961	2,500,000	—	0.25	0.50	2.50	5.00
1962	2,000,000	—	0.25	0.50	2.00	5.00
1962 Proof	Est. 50	Value: 200				
1966	3,000,000	—	0.25	0.50	2.00	3.00
1966 Proof	13,000	Value: 1.00				
1967	7,600,000	—	0.25	0.50	2.00	3.00
1967 Proof	20,000	Value: 1.00				

Date	Mintage	F	VF	XF	Unc	BU
1968	25,000,000	—	0.25	0.50	2.00	3.00
1968 Proof	23,000	Value: 3.00				
1969 Proof	14,000	Value: 3.00				
1970 Proof	9,528	Value: 3.00				
1971 Proof	11,000	Value: 3.00				
1972 Proof	13,000	Value: 3.00				
1973 Proof	17,000	Value: 3.00				
1974	Est. 10,000,000	—	0.10	0.30	2.00	3.00

Note: The 1974 circulation coins were stuck at West Point, NY.

Date	Mintage	F	VF	XF	Unc	BU
1974 Proof	Est. 18,000	Value: 3.00				

Note: The 1974 proof coins were struck at San Francisco

Date	Mintage	F	VF	XF	Unc	BU
1975	10,000,000	—	0.15	0.35	2.00	2.00
1977	10,000,000	—	0.15	0.35	2.00	3.00
1978	10,000,000	—	0.15	0.35	2.00	3.00
1979	10,000,000	—	0.15	0.35	2.00	2.00
1980	20,500,000	—	0.15	0.35	2.00	3.00
1982	20,000,000	—	0.25	0.50	2.00	3.00
1983	5,000,000	—	0.25	0.50	2.00	5.00
1983FM (P)	—	Value: 3.00				
1984FM (P)	—	Value: 3.00				
1985FM (P)	—	Value: 3.00				

Note: Unauthorized striking

Date	Mintage	F	VF	XF	Unc	BU
1986	20,000,000	—	0.25	0.50	2.00	4.00
1987	20,000,000	—	0.25	0.50	2.00	4.00

KM# 22a CENTESIMO

2.5000 g., Copper Coated Zinc, 19.05 mm. **Obv:** Value above sprigs with stars above **Rev:** Covered head left

Date	Mintage	F	VF	XF	Unc	BU
1983	45,000,000	—	0.25	1.00	2.00	4.00

KM# 33.1 CENTESIMO

2.5000 g., Copper Coated Zinc, 19.05 mm. **Obv:** National arms **Rev:** Covered head 1/4 left **Note:** Medal rotation.

Date	Mintage	F	VF	XF	Unc	BU
1975FM (U)	1,410	—	—	—	3.00	5.00
1975 (RCM)	500,000	—	0.10	0.20	1.00	3.00
1975FM (M)	125,000	—	0.10	0.25	1.00	3.00
1975FM (P)	41,000	Value: 3.00				
1976 (RCM)	50,000	—	0.15	0.50	1.50	2.00
1976FM (M)	63,000	—	0.15	0.50	1.50	2.00
1976FM (P)	12,000	Value: 3.00				
1977FM (U)	63,000	—	0.15	0.50	1.50	2.00
1977FM (P)	9,548	Value: 3.00				
1979FM (U)	20,000	—	0.50	1.00	2.00	3.00
1979FM (P)	5,949	Value: 3.00				
1980FM (U)	40,000	—	0.25	0.50	1.50	3.00
1981FM (P)	1,973	Value: 3.00				
1982FM (U)	5,000	—	0.75	1.50	3.50	5.00
1982FM (P)	1,480	Value: 3.00				

KM# 45 CENTESIMO

2.5000 g., Copper Coated Zinc, 19.05 mm. **Subject:** 75th Anniversary of Independence **Obv:** National coat of arms **Rev:** Covered head 1/4 left **Note:** Medal rotation.

Date	Mintage	F	VF	XF	Unc	BU
1978FM (U)	50,000	—	0.10	0.25	1.00	3.00
1978FM (P)	11,000	Value: 3.00				

KM# 124 CENTESIMO

2.5000 g., Copper Plated Zinc, 19.05 mm. **Obv:** Written value **Rev:** Covered head 1/4 left **Edge:** Plain

Date	Mintage	F	VF	XF	Unc	BU
1991	—	—	—	—	1.00	2.00
1993	30,000,000	—	—	—	1.00	2.00

KM# 125 CENTESIMO

2.4400 g., Copper Plated Zinc, 18.96 mm. **Obv:** Written value **Obv. Legend:** REPUBLICA DE PANAMA **Rev:** Native Urraca bust left **Edge:** Plain

Date	Mintage	F	VF	XF	Unc	BU
1996 (RCM)	180,000,000	—	—	—	0.50	1.00
2001 (RCM)	160,000,000	—	—	—	0.50	1.00

KM# 15 1-1/4 CENTESIMOS

3.1000 g., Bronze **Obv:** Written value **Rev:** Uniformed bust left

Date	Mintage	F	VF	XF	Unc	BU
1940	1,600,000	0.45	1.25	2.50	10.00	15.00

KM# 1 2-1/2 CENTESIMOS

1.2500 g., 0.9000 Silver 0.0362 oz. ASW **Obv:** Uniformed bust left **Rev:** National arms **Note:** This coin is popularly referred to as the "Panama Pill."

Date	Mintage	F	VF	XF	Unc	BU
1904	400,000	9.00	15.00	20.00	27.50	35.00

KM# 7.1 2-1/2 CENTESIMOS

Copper-Nickel **Obv:** National coat of arms **Rev:** Value above stars **Rev. Legend:** DOS Y MEDIOS

Date	Mintage	F	VF	XF	Unc	BU
1907	800,000	1.25	4.00	18.00	50.00	75.00

KM# 7.2 2-1/2 CENTESIMOS

Copper-Nickel **Obv:** National coat of arms **Rev:** Value above stars **Rev. Legend:** DOS Y MEDIO

Date	Mintage	F	VF	XF	Unc	BU
1916	800,000	2.50	6.00	35.00	90.00	125
1918 7 Known	—	—	1,800	3,000	—	—

Note: Unauthorized issue, 1 million pieces were struck and nearly all were melted in June 1918.

KM# 8 2-1/2 CENTESIMOS

3.2700 g., Copper-Nickel **Obv:** Uniformed bust left **Rev:** Written value

Date	Mintage	F	VF	XF	Unc	BU
1929	1,000,000	2.00	3.50	40.00	120	200
1929 Proof	—	—	—	—	—	—

KM# 16 2-1/2 CENTESIMOS

Copper-Nickel **Obv:** Uniformed bust left **Rev:** Written value

Date	Mintage	F	VF	XF	Unc	BU
1940	1,200,000	1.00	1.25	2.50	15.00	25.00

KM# 32 2-1/2 CENTESIMOS

1.6500 g., Copper-Nickel Clad Copper, 15 mm. **Series:** F.A.O. **Obv:** National coat of arms **Rev:** Hand holding leafy plant flanked by stars below **Designer:** Frank Gasparro

Date	Mintage	F	VF	XF	Unc	BU
1973	2,000,000	—	0.10	0.15	0.25	0.50
1975	1,000,000	—	0.25	0.50	1.00	2.00

KM# 34.1 2-1/2 CENTESIMOS

Copper-Nickel Clad Copper, 10 mm. **Subject:** Victoriano Lorenzo **Obv:** National coat of arms **Rev:** Head facing **Note:** Medal rotation.

Date	Mintage	F	VF	XF	Unc	BU
1975FM (U)	1,410	—	1.50	2.50	3.50	4.00
1975 (RCM)	40,000	—	0.75	1.00	2.00	3.00
1975FM (M)	50,000	—	0.75	1.00	2.00	3.00
1975FM (P)	41,000	Value: 3.00				
1976 (RCM)	20,000	—	0.75	1.00	2.25	3.00
1976FM (M)	25,000	—	0.75	1.00	3.00	5.00
1976FM (P)	24,000	Value: 3.00				
1977FM (U)	25,000	—	0.75	1.00	2.50	3.00
1977FM (P)	9,548	Value: 3.00				
1979FM (U)	12,000	—	0.75	1.00	2.50	3.00
1979FM (P)	5,949	Value: 3.00				
1980FM (U)	40,000	—	0.75	1.00	2.00	3.00
1981FM (P)	1,973	Value: 3.00				
1982FM (U)	2,000	—	1.50	2.50	5.00	7.00
1982FM (P)	1,480	Value: 5.00				

KM# 46 2-1/2 CENTESIMOS

Copper-Nickel Clad Copper, 10 mm. **Subject:** 75th Anniversary of Independence **Obv:** National coat of arms **Rev:** Head facing **Note:** Medal rotation.

Date	Mintage	F	VF	XF	Unc	BU
1978FM (U)	40,000	—	0.50	1.00	2.50	3.00
1978FM (P)	11,000	Value: 3.00				

KM# 85 2-1/2 CENTESIMOS

Copper-Nickel Clad Copper, 10 mm. **Subject:** Victoriano Lorenzo **Obv:** National coat of arms **Rev:** Head facing

Date	Mintage	F	VF	XF	Unc	BU
1983FM (P)	—	Value: 5.00				
1984FM (P)	—	Value: 5.00				
1985FM (P)	—	Value: 5.00				

Note: Unauthorized striking

KM# 2 5 CENTESIMOS

2.5000 g., 0.9000 Silver 0.0723 oz. ASW **Obv:** Uniformed bust left **Rev:** National coat of arms

Date	Mintage	F	VF	XF	Unc	BU
1904	1,500,000	4.00	6.00	12.00	35.00	60.00
1904 Proof	12	Value: 1,500				
1916	100,000	85.00	125	195	300	425

KM# 9 5 CENTESIMOS

5.0000 g., Copper-Nickel, 21.2 mm. **Obv:** National coat of arms **Rev:** Numeric value

Date	Mintage	F	VF	XF	Unc	BU
1929	500,000	2.50	6.00	15.00	75.00	100
1932	332,000	3.00	7.00	20.00	100	120

KM# 23.1 5 CENTESIMOS
5.0000 g., Copper-Nickel, 21.2 mm. **Obv:** National coat of arms **Rev:** Numeric value

Date	Mintage	F	VF	XF	Unc	BU
1961	1,000,000	—	0.50	1.00	2.50	5.00

KM# 23.2 5 CENTESIMOS
5.0000 g., Copper-Nickel, 21.2 mm. **Obv:** National coat of arms **Rev:** Numeric value **Note:** The 1962 & 1966 Royal Mint strikes are normally sharper in detail. The stars on the reverse above the eagle are flat while previous dates are raised. Varieties exist.

Date	Mintage	F	VF	XF	Unc	BU
1962	2,600,000	—	0.25	0.50	2.00	5.00
1962 Proof	Est. 25	Value: 350				
1966	4,900,000	—	0.15	0.35	2.00	3.00
1966 Proof	13,000	Value: 2.00				
1967	2,600,000	—	0.25	0.50	2.25	3.00
1967 Proof	20,000	Value: 1.00				
1968	6,000,000	—	0.10	0.20	2.00	3.00
1968 Proof	23,000	Value: 2.00				
1969 Proof	14,000	Value: 2.00				
1970	5,000,000	—	0.10	0.20	2.00	3.00
1970 Proof	9,528	Value: 2.00				
1971 Proof	11,000	Value: 2.00				
1972 Proof	13,000	Value: 2.00				
1973	5,000,000	—	0.10	0.20	2.00	5.00
1973 Proof	17,000	Value: 2.00				
1974 Proof	19,000	Value: 2.00				
1975	5,000,000	—	0.10	0.35	2.50	5.00
1982	8,000,000	—	0.10	0.35	2.50	5.00
1983	7,500,000	—	0.10	0.35	2.50	5.00
1993	6,000,000	—	0.10	0.25	2.00	5.00
1993 Proof	—	Value: 250				

Note: The 1993 proof strike was not authorized by the Panamanian government

KM# 35.1 5 CENTESIMOS
5.0000 g., Copper-Nickel Clad Copper, 21.2 mm. **Subject:** Carlos J. Finlay **Obv:** National coat of arms **Rev:** Head 1/4 left **Note:** Medal rotation.

Date	Mintage	F	VF	XF	Unc	BU
1975 (RCM)	80,000	—	0.15	0.40	1.00	3.00
1975FM (M)	15,000	—	0.25	0.75	2.00	5.00
1975FM (U)	1,410	—	—	—	2.50	6.00
1975FM (P)	41,000	Value: 2.00				
1976 (RCM)	20,000	—	0.25	0.75	2.00	5.00
1976FM (M)	13,000	—	0.25	0.75	2.00	5.00
1976FM (P)	12,000	Value: 2.00				
1977FM (U)	13,000	—	0.25	0.75	2.00	5.00
1977FM (P)	9,548	Value: 2.00				
1979FM (U)	12,000	—	0.25	0.75	2.00	5.00
1979FM (P)	5,949	Value: 2.00				
1980FM (U)	43,000	—	0.25	0.50	1.50	5.00
1981FM (P)	1,973	Value: 5.00				
1982FM (U)	3,000	—	10.00	15.00	20.00	25.00
1982FM (P)	1,480	Value: 5.00				

KM# 47 5 CENTESIMOS
5.0000 g., Copper-Nickel Clad Copper, 21.2 mm. **Subject:** 75th Anniversary of Independence **Obv:** National coat of arms **Rev:** Head 1/4 left **Note:** Medal rotation.

Date	Mintage	F	VF	XF	Unc	BU
1978FM (U)	30,000	—	0.25	0.50	1.00	4.00
1978FM (P)	11,000	Value: 2.00				

KM# 126 5 CENTESIMOS
5.0400 g., Copper-Nickel, 21.2 mm. **Obv:** National coat of arms **Rev. Legend:** Numeric value **Edge:** Plain

Date	Mintage	F	VF	XF	Unc	BU
1996	4,000,000	—	—	—	0.40	1.00

KM# 133 5 CENTESIMOS
5.0000 g., Copper Nickel, 21.15 mm. **Subject:** Sara Sotillo **Obv:** National coat of arms **Obv. Legend:** REPUBLICA DE PANAMA **Rev:** Head of Sotillo 3/4 right **Edge:** Plain

Date	Mintage	F	VF	XF	Unc	BU
2001 (RCM)	8,000,000	—	—	—	0.25	0.30

KM# 3 10 CENTESIMOS
5.0000 g., 0.9000 Silver 0.1447 oz. ASW **Obv:** Armored bust left **Rev:** National coat of arms

Date	Mintage	F	VF	XF	Unc	BU
1904	1,100,000	4.00	12.00	35.00	100	150
1904 Proof	12	Value: 1,500				

KM# 36.1 10 CENTESIMOS
2.2500 g., Copper-Nickel Clad Copper, 17.9 mm. **Subject:** Manuel E. Amador **Obv:** National coat of arms **Rev:** Head 1/4 right **Note:** Medal rotation.

Date	Mintage	F	VF	XF	Unc	BU
1975 (RCM)	50,000	—	0.25	0.50	1.00	3.00
1975FM (M)	13,000	—	0.25	0.50	1.50	5.00
1975FM (U)	1,410	—	—	—	2.50	6.00
1975FM (P)	41,000	Value: 2.00				
1976 (RCM)	20,000	—	0.25	1.00	1.50	3.00
1976FM (M)	6,250	—	1.00	1.50	3.00	6.00
1976FM (P)	12,000	Value: 3.00				
1977FM (U)	6,250	—	1.00	1.50	5.00	8.00
1977FM (P)	9,548	Value: 3.00				
1979FM (U)	10,000	—	0.75	1.25	3.50	7.00
1979FM (P)	5,949	Value: 3.00				
1980FM (U)	40,000	—	0.50	1.00	2.00	7.00
1981FM (P)	1,973	Value: 5.00				
1982FM (U)	2,500	—	1.00	2.00	5.00	8.00
1982FM (P)	1,480	Value: 5.00				

KM# 48 10 CENTESIMOS
2.2500 g., Copper-Nickel Clad Copper, 17.9 mm. **Subject:** 75th Anniversary of Independence **Obv:** National coat of arms **Rev:** Bust 1/4 right **Note:** Medal rotation.

Date	Mintage	F	VF	XF	Unc	BU
1978 FM (U)	20,000	—	0.25	0.50	1.50	4.00
1978 FM (P)	11,000	Value: 3.00				

KM# 10.1 1/10 BALBOA
2.5000 g., 0.9000 Silver 0.0723 oz. ASW, 17.9 mm. **Obv:** National coat of arms **Rev:** Armored bust left **Note:** High relief.

Date	Mintage	F	VF	XF	Unc	BU
1930	500,000	2.00	4.00	8.00	35.00	60.00
1930 Matte proof	20	—	—	—	1,000	—
1931	200,000	5.00	8.00	25.00	100	125
1932	150,000	6.00	10.00	25.00	100	150
1933	100,000	12.00	30.00	75.00	200	350
1934	75,000	15.00	35.00	75.00	250	400
1947	1,000,000	1.25	4.00	7.00	25.00	40.00

KM# 18 1/10 BALBOA
2.5000 g., 0.9000 Silver 0.0723 oz. ASW, 17.9 mm. **Subject:** 50th Anniversary of the Republic **Obv:** National coat of arms **Rev:** Armored bust left

Date	Mintage	F	VF	XF	Unc	BU
1953	3,300,000	—	BV	1.50	6.00	10.00

KM# 24 1/10 BALBOA
2.5000 g., 0.9000 Silver 0.0723 oz. ASW, 17.9 mm. **Obv:** National coat of arms **Rev:** Armored bust left

Date	Mintage	F	VF	XF	Unc	BU
1961	2,500,000	—	BV	1.50	3.50	5.00

KM# 10.2 1/10 BALBOA
2.5000 g., 0.9000 Silver 0.0723 oz. ASW, 17.9 mm. **Obv:** National coat of arms **Rev:** Armored bust left **Note:** Low relief.

Date	Mintage	F	VF	XF	Unc	BU
1962	5,000,000	—	BV	1.25	3.00	5.00
1962 Proof	Est. 25	Value: 500				

KM# 10a 1/10 BALBOA
2.2500 g., Copper-Nickel Clad Copper, 17.9 mm. **Obv:** National coat of arms **Rev:** Armored bust left

Date	Mintage	F	VF	XF	Unc	BU
1966 Type 1	6,955,000	—	0.75	1.00	3.00	3.50
Note: The Type I is similar to the 1962 strike on a thick flan (London) with diamonds on both sides of DE						
1966 Type 2	1,000,000	—	1.25	3.50	10.00	15.00
Note: The Type II strike similar to the 1947 strikes on a thin flan (U.S.) with elongated diamonds on both sides of DE						
1966 Proof	13,000	Value: 2.00				
Note: Thick and thin planchets						
1967 Proof	20,000	Value: 2.00				
1968	5,000,000	—	0.20	0.30	2.50	3.00
1968 Proof	23,000	Value: 2.00				
1969 Proof	14,000	Value: 2.00				
1970	7,500,000	—	0.15	0.25	2.00	22.50
1970 Proof	9,528	Value: 2.00				
1971 Proof	11,000	Value: 2.00				
1972 Proof	13,000	Value: 2.00				
1973	10,000,000	—	0.15	0.20	2.00	3.00
1973 Proof	17,000	Value: 2.00				
1974 Proof	18,000	Value: 2.00				
1975	500,000	—	0.25	0.50	2.50	3.50
1980	5,000,000	—	0.20	0.50	3.00	4.00
1982	7,740,000	—	0.25	0.50	2.75	3.75
1983 (RCM)	7,750,000	—	0.15	0.25	2.75	3.75
1986 (RCM)	1,000,000	—	0.15	0.25	2.50	3.75
1993	7,000,000	—	0.15	0.25	1.00	2.25
1993 Proof	—	Value: 300				

Note: Unauthorized striking

KM# 127 1/10 BALBOA
2.2800 g., Copper-Nickel Clad Copper, 17.9 mm. **Obv:** National coat of arms **Obv. Legend:** REPUBLICA DE PANAMA **Rev:** Armored bust of Balboa left **Edge:** Reeded

Date	Mintage	F	VF	XF	Unc	BU
1996	21,000,000	—	—	—	0.25	0.50
2001 (RCM)	15,000,000	—	—	—	0.25	0.50

KM# 4 25 CENTESIMOS
12.5000 g., 0.9000 Silver 0.3617 oz. ASW **Obv:** Armored bust left **Rev:** National coat of arms

Date	Mintage	F	VF	XF	Unc	BU
1904	16,000,000	8.00	15.00	20.00	120	150
1904 Proof	12	Value: 2,500				

KM# 37.1 25 CENTESIMOS
5.6500 g., Copper-Nickel Clad Copper, 24.25 mm. **Obv:** National coat of arms **Rev:** Head 1/4 left **Note:** Medal rotation.

Date	Mintage	F	VF	XF	Unc	BU
1975FM (M)	5,000	—	1.00	2.00	4.00	5.00
1975 (RCM)	40,000	—	0.35	0.50	1.00	2.00
1975FM (U)	1,410	—	—	—	4.00	5.00
1975FM (P)	41,000	Value: 3.00				
1976 (RCM)	12,000	—	0.45	0.60	1.50	3.00
1976FM (M)	2,500	—	0.75	1.50	3.50	5.00
1976FM (P)	12,000	Value: 3.00				
1977FM (U)	2,500	—	0.75	1.50	3.50	7.50
1977FM (P)	9,548	Value: 3.00				
1979FM (U)	4,000	—	1.00	2.00	5.00	8.00
1979FM (P)	5,949	Value: 3.00				
1980FM (U)	4,000	—	1.00	2.00	4.00	7.50
1981FM (P)	1,973	Value: 3.00				
1982FM (U)	2,000	—	1.50	2.50	5.00	7.50
1982FM (P)	1,480	Value: 3.00				

KM# 49 25 CENTESIMOS
5.6500 g., Copper-Nickel Clad Copper, 24.25 mm. **Subject:** 75th Anniversary of Independence **Obv:** National coat of arms **Rev:** Head 1/4 left **Note:** Medal rotation.

Date	Mintage	F	VF	XF	Unc	BU
1978 FM (U)	8,000	—	0.75	1.25	2.50	5.00
1978 FM (P)	11,000	Value: 3.00				

KM# 135 25 CENTESIMOS
5.5600 g., Copper-Nickel Clad Copper, 24.2 mm. **Obv:** National coat of arms **Rev:** Tower and Spanish ruins **Edge:** Reeded **Note:** Released in 2004

Date	Mintage	F	VF	XF	Unc	BU
2003 (RCM) Proof	2,000	Value: 15.00				
2003 (RCM)	6,000,000	—	—	—	0.75	1.50

KM# 11.1 1/4 BALBOA
6.2500 g., 0.9000 Silver 0.1808 oz. ASW, 24.25 mm. **Obv:** National coat of arms **Rev:** Armored bust left

Date	Mintage	F	VF	XF	Unc	BU
1930	400,000	BV	3.00	25.00	50.00	85.00
1930 Matte proof	20	—	—	—	2,000	—
1931	48,000	15.00	70.00	350	1,100	2,000
1932	126,000	3.50	7.00	75.00	400	750
1933	120,000	3.00	6.00	40.00	275	400
1934	90,000	3.00	6.00	27.50	180	350
1947	700,000	BV	3.00	6.00	35.00	70.00

KM# 11.2 1/4 BALBOA
6.2500 g., 0.9000 Silver 0.1808 oz. ASW, 24.25 mm. **Obv:** National coat of arms **Rev:** Armored bust left **Note:** Low relief.

Date	Mintage	F	VF	XF	Unc	BU
1962	4,000,000	—	BV	3.00	4.00	6.00
1962 Proof	25	Value: 500				

KM# 19 1/4 BALBOA
6.2500 g., 0.9000 Silver 0.1808 oz. ASW, 24.25 mm. **Obv:** National coat of arms **Rev:** Armored bust left

Date	Mintage	F	VF	XF	Unc	BU
1953	1,200,000	BV	3.00	4.00	15.00	30.00
1953 Proof	Est. 5	Value: 1,350				

KM# 25 1/4 BALBOA
6.2500 g., 0.9000 Silver 0.1808 oz. ASW, 24.25 mm. **Obv:** National coat of arms **Rev:** Armored bust left

Date	Mintage	F	VF	XF	Unc	BU
1961	2,000,000	—	BV	3.00	5.00	7.00

KM# 11a 1/4 BALBOA
5.6500 g., Copper-Nickel Clad Copper, 24.25 mm. **Obv:** National coat of arms **Rev:** Armored bust left **Note:** Varieties exist.

Date	Mintage	F	VF	XF	Unc	BU
1966 (RCM)	7,400,000	—	0.35	0.50	1.50	3.00
1966 (RCM) Proof	13,000	Value: 3.00				
1967 Proof	20,000	Value: 3.00				
1968	1,200,000	—	0.35	0.60	2.00	3.00
1968 Proof	23,000	Value: 3.00				
1969 Proof	14,000	Value: 3.00				
1970	2,000,000	—	0.35	0.60	1.25	3.00
1970 Proof	9,528	Value: 3.00				
1971 Proof	11,000	Value: 3.00				
1972 Proof	13,000	Value: 3.00				
1973	800,000	—	0.40	1.00	2.00	3.00
1973 Proof	17,000	Value: 3.00				
1974 Proof	18,000	Value: 3.00				
1975	1,500,000	—	0.35	0.50	3.00	7.00
1979	2,000,000	—	0.25	0.50	3.00	6.00
1980	2,000,000	—	0.25	0.50	2.75	6.00
1982	3,000,000	—	0.25	0.50	2.75	5.50
1983 (RCM)	6,000,000	—	0.25	0.50	2.75	5.00
1986 (RCM)	3,000,000	—	0.25	0.50	2.75	5.50
1993	4,000,000	—	0.25	0.50	2.00	5.00
1993 Proof	—	Value: 350				

Note: The 1993 Proof strikes were not authorized by the Panamanian government

KM# 128 1/4 BALBOA
5.6500 g., Copper-Nickel Clad Copper, 24.25 mm. **Obv:** National coat of arms **Rev:** Armored bust left **Edge:** Reeded

Date	Mintage	F	VF	XF	Unc	BU
1996	7,200,000	—	—	—	0.75	2.25
2001 (RCM)	12,000,000	—	—	—	0.50	1.00

KM# 5 50 CENTESIMOS
25.0000 g., 0.9000 Silver 0.7234 oz. ASW **Obv:** Armored bust left **Rev:** National coat of arms

Date	Mintage	F	VF	XF	Unc	BU
1904	1,800,000	35.00	75.00	150	250	300
1904 Proof	12	Value: 5,000				
1905	1,000,000	50.00	90.00	275	500	750

Note: 1,000,000 of both 1904 and 1905 dates were melted in 1931 for the metal to issue 1 Balboa coin at San Francisco Mint

KM# 38.1 50 CENTESIMOS
11.3000 g., Copper-Nickel Clad Copper, 30.6 mm. **Subject:** Fernando de Lesseps **Obv:** National coat of arms **Rev:** Head 1/4 right **Note:** Medal rotation.

Date	Mintage	F	VF	XF	Unc	BU
1975 (RCM)	20,000	—	1.00	1.50	2.75	5.00
1975FM (M)	2,000	—	1.50	3.00	5.00	8.00
1975FM (U)	1,410	—	—	—	7.00	10.00
1975FM (P)	41,000	Value: 2.00				
1976 (RCM)	12,000	—	1.25	2.00	5.00	7.00
1976FM (M)	1,250	—	3.00	6.00	13.00	18.00
1976FM (P)	12,000	Value: 3.00				
1977FM (U)	1,250	—	3.00	6.00	13.00	18.00
1977FM (P)	9,548	Value: 3.00				
1979FM (U)	2,000	—	4.00	6.00	12.00	18.00
1979FM (P)	5,949	Value: 5.00				
1980FM (U)	2,000	—	4.00	6.00	12.00	18.00
1981FM (P)	1,973	Value: 7.00				
1982FM (U)	1,000	—	7.00	10.00	18.00	25.00
1982FM (P)	1,480	Value: 7.50				

Note: (Error) Without edge lettering

KM# 50 50 CENTESIMOS
11.3000 g., Copper-Nickel Clad Copper, 30.6 mm. **Subject:** 75th Anniversary of Independence **Obv:** National coat of arms **Rev:** Bust 1/4 right **Note:** Medal rotation.

Date	Mintage	F	VF	XF	Unc	BU
1978FM (U)	8,000	—	1.50	3.00	5.00	10.00
1978FM (P)	11,000	Value: 6.00				

KM# 12.1 1/2 BALBOA
12.5000 g., 0.9000 Silver 0.3617 oz. ASW, 30.6 mm. **Obv:** National coat of arms **Rev:** Armored bust left **Rev. Designer:** William Clark Noble **Note:** High relief.

Date	Mintage	F	VF	XF	Unc	BU
1930	300,000	BV	9.00	40.00	100	125
1930 Matte proof	20	Value: 2,200				
1932	63,000	6.50	18.00	150	480	850
1933	120,000	5.50	12.00	75.00	350	600
1934	90,000	5.50	8.00	50.00	325	480
1947	450,000	BV	6.00	12.00	45.00	95.00

KM# 12.2 1/2 BALBOA
12.5000 g., 0.9000 Silver 0.3617 oz. ASW, 30.6 mm. **Obv:** National coat of arms **Rev:** Armored bust left **Note:** Low relief.

Date	Mintage	F	VF	XF	Unc	BU
1962	700,000	—	BV	5.50	7.50	12.00
1962 Proof	25	Value: 750				

KM# 20 1/2 BALBOA
12.5000 g., 0.9000 Silver 0.3617 oz. ASW, 30.6 mm. **Obv:** National coat of arms **Rev:** Armored bust left

Date	Mintage	F	VF	XF	Unc	BU
1953	600,000	—	BV	6.50	12.00	20.00
1953 Proof	Est. 5	Value: 1,850				

KM# 26 1/2 BALBOA
12.5000 g., 0.9000 Silver 0.3617 oz. ASW, 30.6 mm. **Obv:** National coat of arms **Rev:** Armored bust left

Date	Mintage	F	VF	XF	Unc	BU
1961	350,000	—	BV	6.00	12.00	15.00

KM# 12a.1 1/2 BALBOA
12.5000 g., 0.4000 Silver Clad 0.1607 oz. ASW, 30.6 mm. **Obv:** National coat of arms **Rev:** Normal helmet **Note:** Varieties exist.

Date	Mintage	F	VF	XF	Unc	BU
1966 (RCM)	1,000,000	BV	2.50	3.50	6.50	8.00
1966 (RCM) Proof	13,000	Value: 6.00				
1967	300,000	BV	2.50	3.50	9.00	12.00
1967 Proof	20,000	Value: 5.00				
1968	1,000,000	BV	2.50	3.50	6.50	8.50
1968 Proof	23,000	Value: 5.00				
1969 Proof	14,000	Value: 5.00				
1970	610,000	BV	2.50	3.50	8.50	10.00
1970 Proof	9,528	Value: 6.00				
1971 Proof	11,000	Value: 6.00				
1972 Proof	13,000	Value: 6.00				
1993 Proof	—	Value: 450				

Note: The 1993 Proof strike was not authorized by the Panamanian government

KM# 12a.2 1/2 BALBOA
12.5000 g., 0.4000 Silver Clad 0.1607 oz. ASW, 30.6 mm. **Obv:** National coat of arms **Rev:** Error: Type II helmet rim incomplete.

Date	Mintage	F	VF	XF	Unc	BU
1966	Inc. above	2.50	3.50	7.50	15.00	25.00

KM# 12b 1/2 BALBOA
11.3000 g., Copper-Nickel Clad Copper, 30.6 mm. **Obv:** National coat of arms **Rev:** Armored bust left **Note:** Varieties exist.

Date	Mintage	F	VF	XF	Unc	BU
1973	1,000,000	—	1.00	1.50	3.00	6.00
1973 Proof	17,000	Value: 3.00				
1974 Proof	18,000	Value: 3.00				
1975	1,200,000	—	0.75	1.50	3.00	6.00
1979	1,000,000	—	—	1.00	3.00	6.00
1980	400,000	—	—	1.75	3.50	6.50
1982	400,000	—	—	1.75	3.50	6.50
1983 (RCM)	1,850,000	—	—	1.00	3.00	6.00
1986 (RCM)	200,000	—	2.00	3.00	7.50	10.00
1993	600,000	—	0.75	1.25	3.00	—

KM# 129 1/2 BALBOA
11.3000 g., Copper-Nickel Clad Copper, 30.54 mm. **Obv:** National coat of arms **Obv. Legend:** REPUBLICA DE PANAMA **Rev:** Armored bust of Balboa left **Edge:** Reeded

Date	Mintage	F	VF	XF	Unc	BU
1996	200,000	—	1.00	2.00	4.00	7.50
2001 (RCM)	600,000	—	—	1.00	2.00	3.50

KM# 13 BALBOA
26.7300 g., 0.9000 Silver 0.7734 oz. ASW, 38.1 mm. **Subject:** Vasco Nunez de Balboa **Obv:** Standing figure with arm on shield **Obv. Designer:** Roberto Lewis **Rev:** Armored bust left **Rev. Designer:** William Clark Noble

Date	Mintage	F	VF	XF	Unc	BU
1931	200,000	BV	12.00	20.00	75.00	100
1931 Proof	20	Value: 3,000				
1934	225,000	BV	12.00	20.00	60.00	90.00
1947	500,000	—	BV	12.00	18.00	25.00

KM# 21 BALBOA
26.7300 g., 0.9000 Silver 0.7734 oz. ASW, 38.1 mm. **Subject:** 50th Anniversary of the Republic **Obv:** Standing figure with hand on shield **Rev:** Armored bust left

Date	Mintage	F	VF	XF	Unc	BU
1953	50,000	BV	13.50	20.00	35.00	50.00

PAPUA NEW GUINEA

Papua New Guinea occupies the eastern half of the island of New Guinea. It lies north of Australia near the equator and borders on West Irian. The country, which includes nearby Bismark archipelago, Buka and Bougainville, has an area of 178,260 sq. mi. (461,690 sq. km.).and a population of 3.7 million that is divided into more than 1,000 separate tribes speaking more than 700 mutually unintelligible languages. Capital: Port Moresby. The economy is agricultural, and exports copra, rubber, cocoa, coffee, tea, gold and copper

In 1884 Germany annexed the area known as German New Guinea (also Neu Guinea or Kaiser Wilhelmsland) comprising the northern section of eastern New Guinea, and granted its administration and development to the Neu-Guinea Compagnie. Administration reverted to Germany in 1889 following the failure of the company to exercise adequate administration. While a German protectorate, German New Guinea had an area of 92,159 sq. mi. (238,692 sq. km.) and a population of about 250,000. Capital: Herbertshohe, 1 of 4 capitals of German New Guinea. The seat of government was transferred to Rabaul in 1910. Copra was the chief crop.

Australian troops occupied German New Guinea in Aug. 1914, shortly after Great Britain declared war on Germany. It was mandated to Australia by the League of Nations in 1920, known as the Territory of New Guinea. The territory was invaded and most of it was occupied by Japan in 1942. Following the Japanese surrender, it came under U.N. trusteeship, Dec. 13, 1946, with Australia as the administering power.

The Papua and New Guinea act, 1949, provided for the government of Papua and New Guinea as one administrative unit. On Dec. 1, 1973, Papua New Guinea became self-governing with Australia retaining responsibility for defense and foreign affairs. Full independence was achieved on Sept. 16, 1975. Papua New Guinea is a member of the Commonwealth of Nations. Elizabeth II is Head of State.

MINT MARK

FM - Franklin Mint, U.S.A.

NOTE: From 1975-1985 the Franklin Mint produced coinage in up to 3 different qualities. Qualities of issue are designated in ( ) after each date and are defined as follows:

(M) MATTE - Normal circulation strike or a dull finish produced by sandblasting special uncirculated (polish finish) or proof quality dies.

(U) SPECIAL UNCIRCULATED - Polished or prooflike in appearance without any frosted features.

(P) PROOF - The highest quality obtainable having mirror-like fields and frosted features.

MONETARY SYSTEM

100 Toea = 1 Kina

CONSTITUTIONAL MONARCHY

Commonwealth of Nations

STANDARD COINAGE

100 Toea = 1 Kina

KM# 1 TOEA

2.0000 g., Bronze, 17.65 mm. **Obv:** National emblem **Rev:** Butterfly and value

Date	Mintage	F	VF	XF	Unc	BU
1975	14,400,000	—	—	0.15	0.35	1.00
1975FM (M)	83,000	—	—	—	0.45	1.00
1975FM (U)	4,134	—	—	—	1.00	1.50
1975FM (P)	67,000	Value: 1.00				
1976	25,175,000	—	—	—	0.35	1.00
1976FM (M)	84,000	—	—	—	0.35	1.00
1976FM (U)	976	—	—	—	1.00	1.50
1976FM (P)	16,000	Value: 1.00				
1977FM (M)	84,000	—	—	—	0.35	1.00
1977FM (U)	603	—	—	—	1.50	2.50
1977FM (P)	7,721	Value: 1.25				
1978	—	—	—	—	0.35	1.00
1978FM (M)	83,000	—	—	—	0.35	1.00
1978FM (U)	777	—	—	—	1.00	1.50
1978FM (P)	5,540	Value: 1.50				
1979FM (M)	84,000	—	—	—	0.35	1.00
1979FM (U)	1,366	—	—	—	1.00	1.50
1979FM (P)	2,728	Value: 1.50				
1980FM (U)	1,160	—	—	—	1.00	1.50
1980FM (P)	2,125	Value: 1.50				
1981	—	—	—	—	1.00	1.50
1981FM (P)	10,000	Value: 1.25				
1981FM (M)	—	—	—	—	0.35	1.00
1982FM (M)	—	—	—	—	1.00	1.50
1982FM (P)	—	Value: 2.25				
1983	—	—	—	—	0.45	1.25
1983FM (U)	360	—	—	—	1.00	1.50
1983FM (P)	—	Value: 2.25				
1984	—	—	—	—	0.45	1.25
1984FM (P)	—	Value: 2.25				
1987	—	—	—	—	0.45	1.25
1990	—	—	—	—	0.45	1.25
1995	—	—	—	—	0.45	1.25
1996	—	—	—	—	0.45	1.25
2001	—	—	—	—	1.00	1.25
2002	—	—	—	—	1.00	1.25

KM# 2 2 TOEA

4.0000 g., Bronze, 21.72 mm. **Obv:** National emblem **Rev:** Lion fish

Date	Mintage	F	VF	XF	Unc	BU
1975	11,400,000	—	—	0.10	0.60	1.00
1975FM (M)	42,000	—	—	—	0.65	1.00
1975FM (U)	4,134	—	—	—	1.00	1.50
1975FM (P)	67,000	Value: 1.50				
1976	15,175,000	—	—	0.10	0.50	1.00
1976FM (M)	42,000	—	—	—	0.50	1.00
1976FM (U)	976	—	—	—	1.00	1.50
1976FM (P)	16,000	Value: 1.50				
1977FM (M)	42,000	—	—	—	0.50	1.00
1977FM (U)	603	—	—	—	1.50	2.50
1977FM (P)	7,721	Value: 1.75				
1978	—	—	—	—	0.50	1.00
1978FM (M)	42,000	—	—	—	0.50	1.00
1978FM (U)	777	—	—	—	1.00	1.50
1978FM (P)	5,540	Value: 1.75				
1979FM (M)	42,000	—	—	—	0.50	1.00
1979FM (U)	1,366	—	—	—	1.00	1.50
1979FM (P)	2,728	Value: 1.75				
1980FM (U)	1,160	—	—	—	1.00	1.50
1980FM (P)	2,125	Value: 1.75				
1981	—	—	—	—	0.50	1.25
1981FM (P)	10,000	Value: 1.50				
1982FM (M)	—	—	—	—	1.00	1.50
1982FM (P)	—	Value: 2.50				
1983	—	—	—	—	0.50	1.25
1983FM (U)	360	—	—	—	1.50	2.50
1983FM (P)	—	Value: 2.50				
1984	—	—	—	—	0.50	1.25
1984 Proof	—	Value: 2.50				
1987	—	—	—	—	0.50	1.25
1990	—	—	—	—	0.50	1.25
1995	—	—	—	—	0.50	1.25
1996	—	—	—	—	0.50	1.25
2001	—	—	—	—	0.50	1.25
2002	—	—	—	—	0.50	1.25
2004	—	—	—	—	0.50	1.25

KM# 3 5 TOEA

3.0000 g., Copper-Nickel, 19.53 mm. **Obv:** National emblem **Rev:** Plateless turtle

Date	Mintage	F	VF	XF	Unc	BU
1975	11,000,000	—	0.15	0.25	0.75	2.00
1975FM (M)	17,000	—	—	—	0.75	2.00
1975FM (U)	4,134	—	—	—	1.25	3.00
1975FM (P)	67,000	Value: 2.00				
1976	24,000,000	—	0.15	0.25	0.75	2.00
1976FM (M)	17,000	—	—	—	0.75	3.00
1976FM (U)	976	—	—	—	1.25	3.00
1976FM (P)	16,000	Value: 2.00				
1977FM (M)	17,000	—	—	—	0.75	2.00
1977FM (U)	603	—	—	—	1.75	3.00
1977FM (P)	7,721	Value: 2.25				
1978	2,000	—	—	—	2.50	3.00
1978FM (M)	17,000	—	—	—	0.75	2.00
1978FM (U)	777	—	—	—	1.25	3.00
1978FM (P)	5,540	Value: 2.25				
1979	—	—	—	—	0.75	2.00
1979FM (M)	17,000	—	—	—	0.75	2.00
1979FM (U)	1,366	—	—	—	1.25	2.00
1979FM (P)	2,728	Value: 2.25				
1980FM (U)	1,160	—	—	—	1.25	2.00
1980FM (P)	2,125	Value: 2.25				
1981FM (P)	10,000	Value: 2.00				
1982	—	—	—	—	0.75	2.00
1982FM (M)	—	—	—	—	1.25	2.00
1982FM (P)	—	Value: 3.00				
1983FM (U)	360	—	—	—	2.25	5.00
1983FM (P)	—	Value: 3.00				
1984	—	—	—	—	0.75	2.00
1984FM (P)	—	Value: 3.00				
1987	—	—	—	—	0.75	2.00
1990	—	—	—	—	0.75	2.00
1995	—	—	—	—	0.75	2.00
1996	—	—	—	—	0.75	2.00
1998	—	—	—	—	0.75	2.00
1999	—	—	—	—	0.75	2.00

KM# 3a 5 TOEA

Nickel Plated Steel, 19.53 mm. **Obv:** National emblem **Rev:** Plateless turtle

Date	Mintage	F	VF	XF	Unc	BU
2002	—	—	—	—	0.75	1.50

KM# 4 10 TOEA

5.6700 g., Copper-Nickel, 23.72 mm. **Obv:** National emblem **Rev:** Cuscus and value

Date	Mintage	F	VF	XF	Unc	BU
1975	8,600,000	—	0.20	0.35	0.65	1.50
1975FM (M)	8,300	—	—	—	1.00	1.75
1975FM (U)	4,134	—	—	—	1.50	2.00
1975FM (P)	67,000	Value: 2.00				
1976	—	—	0.20	0.35	0.65	1.50
1976FM (M)	8,300	—	—	—	1.00	1.75
1976FM (U)	976	—	—	—	1.50	2.00
1976FM (P)	16,000	Value: 2.00				
1977FM (M)	8,300	—	—	—	1.00	1.75
1977FM (U)	603	—	—	—	2.25	2.75
1977FM (P)	7,721	Value: 2.50				
1978FM (M)	8,300	—	—	—	1.00	1.75
1978FM (U)	777	—	—	—	1.50	2.00
1978FM (P)	5,540	Value: 2.75				
1979FM (M)	8,300	—	—	—	1.00	1.75
1979FM (U)	1,366	—	—	—	1.50	2.00
1979FM (P)	2,728	Value: 2.75				
1980FM (U)	1,160	—	—	—	1.50	2.00
1980FM (P)	2,125	Value: 2.75				
1981FM (P)	10,000	Value: 2.75				
1982FM (M)	—	—	—	—	1.50	2.00
1982FM (P)	—	Value: 3.50				
1983FM (U)	360	—	—	—	2.50	3.00
1983FM (P)	—	Value: 3.50				
1984FM (P)	—	Value: 3.50				
1995	—	—	—	—	1.50	2.00
1996	—	—	—	—	1.50	2.00
1999	—	—	—	—	1.50	2.00
2001	—	—	—	—	1.50	2.00

KM# 4a 10 TOEA

Nickel Plated Steel, 23.72 mm. **Obv:** National emblem **Rev:** Cuscus and value

Date	Mintage	F	VF	XF	Unc	BU
2002	—	—	—	—	1.50	2.00
2004	—	—	—	—	1.50	2.00

KM# 5 20 TOEA

11.3000 g., Copper-Nickel, 28.65 mm. **Obv:** National emblem **Rev:** Bennett's Cassowary and value

Date	Mintage	F	VF	XF	Unc	BU
1975	15,500,000	—	0.30	0.65	1.25	1.75
1975FM (M)	4,150	—	—	—	1.50	2.00
1975FM (U)	4,134	—	—	—	1.50	2.00
1975FM (P)	67,000	Value: 2.50				
1976FM (M)	4,150	—	—	—	1.50	2.00
1976FM (U)	976	—	—	—	1.75	2.25
1976FM (P)	16,000	Value: 2.50				
1977FM (M)	4,150	—	—	—	1.75	2.25
1977FM (U)	603	—	—	—	2.25	2.75
1977FM (P)	7,721	Value: 3.00				
1978	2,500,000	—	0.35	0.70	1.25	1.75
1978FM (M)	4,150	—	—	—	1.50	2.00
1978FM (U)	777	—	—	—	1.75	2.25
1978FM (P)	5,540	Value: 3.00				
1979FM (M)	4,150	—	—	—	1.50	2.00
1979FM (U)	1,366	—	—	—	1.75	2.25
1979FM (P)	2,728	Value: 3.00				
1980FM (U)	1,160	—	—	—	1.75	2.25
1980FM (P)	2,125	Value: 3.00				
1981	—	—	0.25	0.50	1.25	1.50
1981FM (P)	10,000	Value: 2.50				
1982FM (M)	—	—	—	—	2.00	2.25
1982FM (P)	—	Value: 4.00				
1983FM (U)	360	—	—	—	3.00	3.50
1983FM (P)	—	Value: 4.00				
1984	—	—	0.25	0.50	1.25	1.50
1984FM (P)	—	Value: 4.00				
1987	—	—	0.25	0.50	1.25	1.50
1990	—	—	0.25	0.50	1.25	1.50
1995	—	—	0.25	0.50	1.25	1.50
1998	—	—	0.25	0.50	1.25	1.50
1999	—	—	0.25	0.50	1.25	1.50

KM# 5a 20 TOEA

Nickel Plated Steel, 28.65 mm. **Obv:** National emblem **Rev:** Bennett's Cassowary and value

Date	Mintage	F	VF	XF	Unc	BU
2004	—	—	0.25	0.50	1.25	1.50

KM# 15 50 TOEA

Copper-Nickel **Subject:** South Pacific Festival of Arts **Obv:** National emblem **Rev:** Design divides circles **Shape:** 7-sided

Date	Mintage	F	VF	XF	Unc	BU
1980	—	—	0.75	1.25	2.50	—
1980FM (U)	1,160	—	—	—	10.00	—
1980FM (P)	2,125	Value: 6.50				

KM# 31 50 TOEA

Copper-Nickel **Subject:** 9th South Pacific Games **Obv:** National emblem **Rev:** Games emblem **Shape:** 7-sided

Date	Mintage	F	VF	XF	Unc	BU
1991	25,000	—	—	—	4.00	—

KM# 41 50 TOEA

13.6300 g., Copper Nickel, 30 mm. **Subject:** Silver Jubilee of Bank **Obv:** National emblem **Rev:** Symbolic design **Edge:** Reeded **Shape:** 7-sided

Date	Mintage	F	VF	XF	Unc	BU
1998	—	—	—	—	4.50	—

KM# 6 KINA

Copper-Nickel, 33 mm. **Obv:** Symbolic design around center hole **Rev:** Crocodiles flank center hole

Date	Mintage	F	VF	XF	Unc	BU
1975	2,000,000	—	1.35	2.00	3.50	7.50
1975FM (U)	4,134	—	—	—	3.50	7.50
1975FM (M)	829	—	—	—	8.50	9.50
1975FM (P)	67,000	Value: 5.00				
1976FM (M)	829	—	—	—	8.50	9.50
1976FM (U)	976	—	—	—	3.50	7.50
1976FM (P)	16,000	Value: 5.00				
1977FM (M)	829	—	—	—	8.50	9.50
1977FM (U)	603	—	—	—	12.50	13.50
1977FM (P)	7,721	Value: 6.00				
1978FM (M)	829	—	—	—	8.50	9.50
1978FM (U)	777	—	—	—	3.50	6.00
1978FM (P)	5,540	Value: 5.00				
1979FM (M)	829	—	—	—	8.50	9.50
1979FM (U)	1,366	—	—	—	3.50	6.50
1979FM (P)	2,728	Value: 6.00				
1980FM (U)	1,160	—	—	—	3.50	6.50
1980FM (P)	2,125	Value: 5.00				
1981FM (P)	10,000	Value: 5.00				
1982FM (M)	—	—	—	—	3.50	6.50
1982FM (P)	—	Value: 7.50				
1983FM (U)	360	—	—	—	14.50	15.50
1983FM (P)	—	Value: 7.00				
1984FM (P)	—	Value: 7.00				
1995	—	—	—	—	3.50	6.00
1996	—	—	—	—	3.50	6.00
1998	—	—	—	—	3.50	6.00
1999	—	—	—	—	3.50	6.00

KM# 6a KINA

Nickel Plated Steel, 33 mm. **Obv:** Symbolic design around center hole **Rev:** Crocidiles flank center hole

Date	Mintage	F	VF	XF	Unc	BU
2002	—	—	—	—	3.50	6.00
2004	—	—	—	—	3.50	6.00

KM# 6.1 KINA

11.1300 g., Nickel Plated Steel, 30 mm. **Obv:** Native design **Rev:** Two Salt Water Crocodiles **Edge:** Reeded

Date	Mintage	F	VF	XF	Unc	BU
2005	—	—	—	—	5.00	7.00

PARAGUAY

The Republic of Paraguay, a landlocked country in the heart of South America surrounded by Argentina, Bolivia and Brazil, has an area of 157,048 sq. mi. (406,750 sq. km.) and a population of *4.5 million, 95 percent of whom are of mixed Spanish and Indian descent. Capital: Asuncion. The country is predominantly agrarian, with no important mineral deposits or oil reserves. Meat, timber, hides, oilseeds, tobacco and cotton account for 70 percent of Paraguay's export revenue.

Paraguay was first visited by a ship-wrecked Spaniard named Alejo Garcia, in 1524. The interior was explored by Sebastian Cabot in 1527 and 1528, when he sailed up the Parana and Paraguay rivers. Asuncion, which would become the center of a Spanish colonial province embracing much of southern South America, was established by the Spanish explorer Juan de Salazar on Aug. 15,1537. For 150 years the history of Paraguay was largely the history of the agricultural colonies established by the Jesuits in the south and east to Christianize the Indians. In 1811, following the outbreak of the South American wars of independence, Paraguayan patriots over-threw the local Spanish authorities and proclaimed their country's independence.

During the Triple Alliance War (1864-1870) in which Paraguay faced Argentina, Brazil and Uruguay, Asuncion's ladies gathered in an Assembly on Feb. 24, 1867 and decided to give up their jewelry in order to help the national defense. The President of the Republic, Francisco Solano Lopez accepted the offering and ordered one twentieth of it be used to mint the first Paraguayan gold coins according to the Decree of the 11th of Sept.,1867.

Two dies were made, one by Bouvet, and another by an American, Leonard Charles, while only the die made by Bouvet was eventually used.

MONETARY SYSTEM

100 Centavos (Centesimos) = 1 Peso

MINT MARK

HF – LeLocle (Swiss)

REPUBLIC

DECIMAL COINAGE

100 Centavos (Centesimos) = Peso

KM# 6 5 CENTAVOS

Copper-Nickel **Obv:** Seated lion with liberty cap on pole, date below **Obv. Legend:** REPUBLICA DEL PARAGUAY **Rev:** Value within wreath

Date	Mintage	F	VF	XF	Unc	BU
1903	600,000	2.00	8.00	25.00	75.00	—

KM# 9 5 CENTAVOS

Copper-Nickel **Obv:** Radiant star within wreath **Rev:** Value within flower chain

Date	Mintage	F	VF	XF	Unc	BU
1908	400,000	2.50	8.00	30.00	75.00	—

KM# 7 10 CENTAVOS

Copper-Nickel **Obv:** Seated lion with liberty cap on pole, date below **Obv. Legend:** REPUBLICA DEL PARAGUAY **Rev:** Value within wreath

Date	Mintage	F	VF	XF	Unc	BU
1903	1,200,000	1.50	4.00	15.00	35.00	—

KM# 10 10 CENTAVOS

Copper-Nickel **Obv:** Radiant star within wreath **Rev:** Value within flower chain

Date	Mintage	F	VF	XF	Unc	BU
1908	800,000	2.50	6.50	25.00	75.00	—

KM# 8 20 CENTAVOS

Copper-Nickel **Obv:** Seated lion with liberty cap on pole, date below **Obv. Legend:** REPUBLICA DEL PARAGUAY **Rev:** Value within wreath

Date	Mintage	F	VF	XF	Unc	BU
1903	750,000	1.50	4.00	20.00	65.00	—

KM# 11 20 CENTAVOS

Copper-Nickel **Obv:** Radiant star within wreath **Rev:** Value

Date	Mintage	F	VF	XF	Unc	BU
1908	1,000,000	2.50	7.00	35.00	80.00	—

KM# 12 50 CENTAVOS

2.0000 g., Copper-Nickel **Obv:** Radiant star within wreath **Rev:** Value

Date	Mintage	F	VF	XF	Unc	BU
1925	4,000,000	0.50	1.50	5.00	15.00	—

KM# 15 50 CENTAVOS

Aluminum **Obv:** Radiant star within wreath **Rev:** Value

Date	Mintage	F	VF	XF	Unc	BU
1938	400,000	0.50	1.00	3.50	10.00	—

KM# 13 PESO
2.9300 g., Copper-Nickel **Obv:** Radiant star within wreath **Rev:** Value

Date	Mintage	F	VF	XF	Unc	BU
1925	3,500,000	0.50	1.00	5.00	10.00	—

KM# 16 PESO
Aluminum **Obv:** Radiant star within wreath **Rev:** Value

Date	Mintage	F	VF	XF	Unc	BU
1938	—	0.50	1.50	3.00	8.00	—

KM# 14 2 PESOS
Copper-Nickel **Obv:** Radiant star within wreath **Rev:** Value

Date	Mintage	F	VF	XF	Unc	BU
1925	2,500,000	0.50	1.00	6.00	12.00	—

KM# 17 2 PESOS
1.7600 g., Aluminum **Obv:** Radiant star within wreath **Rev:** Value

Date	Mintage	F	VF	XF	Unc	BU
1938	—	0.50	1.50	3.00	10.00	—

KM# 18 5 PESOS
Copper-Nickel **Obv:** Radiant star within wreath **Rev:** Value

Date	Mintage	F	VF	XF	Unc	BU
1939	4,000,000	1.00	3.50	10.00	20.00	—

KM# 19 10 PESOS
Copper-Nickel **Obv:** Radiant star within wreath **Rev:** Value

Date	Mintage	F	VF	XF	Unc	BU
1939	4,000,000	1.00	2.00	7.00	18.00	—

REFORM COINAGE

100 Centimos = 1 Guarani

KM# 20 CENTIMO
2.0000 g., Aluminum-Bronze **Obv:** Flower within circle **Rev:** Value within wreath

Date	Mintage	F	VF	XF	Unc	BU
1944	3,500,000	0.10	0.50	1.00	5.00	—
1948HF	2,000,000	0.10	0.50	1.00	4.00	—
1950HF	1,096,000	0.10	0.25	0.75	3.00	—

KM# 21 5 CENTIMOS
Aluminum-Bronze **Obv:** Passion flower within circle **Rev:** Value within wreath

Date	Mintage	F	VF	XF	Unc	BU
1944	2,195,000	0.10	0.50	1.00	4.00	—
1947HF	13,111,000	0.10	0.20	0.50	2.00	—

KM# 22 10 CENTIMOS
Aluminum-Bronze **Obv:** Orchid within circle **Rev:** Value within wreath

Date	Mintage	F	VF	XF	Unc	BU
1944	975,000	0.25	0.75	3.00	6.00	—
1947	6,656,000	0.10	0.25	1.00	3.00	—
1947HF	—	0.20	0.50	2.00	5.00	—

KM# 25 10 CENTIMOS
Aluminum-Bronze **Obv:** Seated lion with liberty cap on pole within circle **Rev:** Value within wreath **Shape:** Scalloped

Date	Mintage	F	VF	XF	Unc	BU
1953	5,000,000	0.10	0.15	0.50	1.00	—
1953 Proof; 1 known	—	Value: 375				

Note: Medal die rotation

KM# 26 15 CENTIMOS
Aluminum-Bronze **Obv:** Seated lion with liberty cap on pole within circle **Rev:** Value within wreath **Shape:** Scalloped

Date	Mintage	F	VF	XF	Unc	BU
1953	5,000,000	0.10	0.20	0.35	1.00	—
1953 Proof; 1 known	—	Value: 375				

Note: Medal die rotation

KM# 23 25 CENTIMOS
Aluminum-Bronze **Obv:** Orchid within circle **Rev:** Value within wreath

Date	Mintage	F	VF	XF	Unc	BU
1944	700,000	0.25	1.00	3.00	12.00	—
1948HF	600,000	0.25	0.75	2.50	9.00	—
1951HF	1,000,000	0.25	0.75	1.50	5.00	—

KM# 27 25 CENTIMOS
Aluminum-Bronze **Obv:** Seated lion with liberty cap on pole within circle **Rev:** Value within wreath **Shape:** Scalloped

Date	Mintage	F	VF	XF	Unc	BU
1953	2,000,000	0.10	0.15	0.30	1.00	2.00
1953 Proof; 1 known	—	Value: 450				

Note: Medal die rotation

KM# 24 50 CENTIMOS
Aluminum-Bronze **Obv:** Seated lion with liberty cap on pole within circle **Rev:** Value within wreath

Date	Mintage	F	VF	XF	Unc	BU
1944	2,485,000	0.25	1.00	2.00	7.00	—
1951	2,893,000	0.25	0.50	1.25	3.00	4.00

KM# 28 50 CENTIMOS
Aluminum-Bronze **Obv:** Seated lion with liberty cap on pole within circle **Rev:** Value within wreath **Shape:** Scalloped

Date	Mintage	F	VF	XF	Unc	BU
1953	2,000,000	0.10	0.15	0.30	1.00	2.50
1953 Proof; 1 known	—	Value: 450				

Note: Medal die rotation

KM# 151 GUARANI
2.9000 g., Stainless Steel **Obv:** Soldier 3/4 facing **Rev:** Tobacco plant and value

Date	Mintage	F	VF	XF	Unc	BU
1975	10,000,000	—	—	0.15	0.50	0.75
1975 Proof	1,000	Value: 6.00				
1976	12,000,000	—	—	0.10	0.40	0.65
1976 Proof	1,000	Value: 8.00				

KM# 165 GUARANI
2.6000 g., Stainless Steel **Series:** F.A.O. **Obv:** Standing 3/4 figure facing **Rev:** Plant and value **Note:** Varieties exist.

Date	Mintage	F	VF	XF	Unc	BU
1978	15,000,000	—	—	0.15	0.50	0.75
1980	13,000,000	—	—	0.15	0.50	0.75
1980 Proof	1,000	Value: 6.00				
1984	15,000,000	—	—	0.10	0.30	0.50
1986	15,000,000	—	—	0.10	0.30	0.50
1988	15,000,000	—	—	0.10	0.30	0.50

KM# 152 5 GUARANIES
3.8000 g., Stainless Steel, 20 mm. **Obv:** Half-length figure with jug looking right **Rev:** Cotton plant and value

Date	Mintage	F	VF	XF	Unc	BU
1975	7,500,000	—	—	0.15	0.50	0.75
1975 Proof	1,000	Value: 6.00				

KM# 166 5 GUARANIES
3.8000 g., Stainless Steel, 20 mm. **Series:** F.A.O. **Obv:** Half-length figure with jug looking right **Rev:** Cotton plant and value **Note:** Varieties exist.

Date	Mintage	F	VF	XF	Unc	BU
1978	10,000,000	—	—	0.15	0.60	0.85
1980	12,000,000	—	—	0.15	0.60	0.85
1980 Proof	1,000	Value: 6.00				

Date	Mintage	F	VF	XF	Unc	BU
1984	15,000,000	—	—	0.10	0.40	0.60
1986	15,000,000	—	—	0.10	0.40	0.60

KM# 166a 5 GUARANIES

1.9500 g., Nickel-Bronze, 16.97 mm. **Series:** F.A.O. **Obv:** Half-length figure with jug looking right **Rev:** Cotton plant and value **Edge:** Reeded

Date	Mintage	F	VF	XF	Unc	BU
1992	15,000,000	—	—	0.10	0.30	0.50

KM# 153 10 GUARANIES

4.5000 g., Stainless Steel, 22 mm. **Obv:** Bust 1/4 left **Rev:** Cow head left and value

Date	Mintage	F	VF	XF	Unc	BU
1975	10,000,000	—	0.10	0.20	0.75	1.00
1975 Proof	1,000	Value: 8.00				
1976	10,000,000	—	0.10	0.20	0.75	1.00
1976 Proof	1,000	Value: 10.00				

KM# 167 10 GUARANIES

4.5000 g., Stainless Steel, 22 mm. **Series:** F.A.O. **Obv:** Bust 1/4 left **Rev:** Cow head left and value **Note:** Varieties exist.

Date	Mintage	F	VF	XF	Unc	BU
1978	15,000,000	—	0.10	0.20	0.75	1.00
1980	15,000,000	—	0.10	0.20	0.75	1.00
1980 Proof	1,000	Value: 8.00				
1984	20,000,000	—	0.10	0.15	0.50	0.75
1986	35,000,000	—	0.10	0.15	0.50	0.75
1988	40,000,000	—	0.10	0.15	0.50	0.75

KM# 178 10 GUARANIES

2.6900 g., Nickel-Bronze, 19.34 mm. **Series:** F.A.O. **Obv:** Bust 1/4 left **Rev:** Cow head left and value **Edge:** Reeded

Date	Mintage	F	VF	XF	Unc	BU
1990	40,000,000	—	—	0.10	0.40	0.60

KM# 178a 10 GUARANIES

Brass Plated Steel **Series:** F.A.O. **Obv:** Bust of Garay 1/4 left **Rev:** Cow's head left at left of value **Note:** Magnetic.

Date	Mintage	F	VF	XF	Unc	BU
1996	20,000,000	—	—	0.10	0.40	0.60

KM# 154 50 GUARANIES

7.4000 g., Stainless Steel, 26.1 mm. **Obv:** Uniformed bust facing **Rev:** Value above dam on the Acaray River

Date	Mintage	F	VF	XF	Unc	BU
1975	9,500,000	0.20	0.40	0.60	1.25	1.50
1975 Proof	1,000	Value: 10.00				

KM# 169 50 GUARANIES

7.4000 g., Stainless Steel, 26.1 mm. **Obv:** Bust of General Estigarribia facing **Obv. Legend:** REPUBLICA DEL PARAGUAY **Rev:** Acaray River Dam **Note:** Examples of each date differ slightly.

Date	Mintage	F	VF	XF	Unc	BU
1980	10,700,000	0.20	0.40	0.60	1.25	1.50
1980 Proof	1,000	Value: 10.00				
1986	15,000,000	0.20	0.40	0.60	1.25	1.50
1988	25,000,000	0.20	0.30	0.50	1.00	1.25

KM# 191a 50 GUARANIES

Brass Plated Steel **Obv:** Uniformed bust facing **Rev:** Value above river dam **Note:** Magnetic

Date	Mintage	F	VF	XF	Unc	BU
1995	25,000,000	—	—	—	0.75	1.00
1998	22,000,000	—	—	—	0.75	1.00
2005	—	—	—	—	0.75	1.00

KM# 191b 50 GUARANIES

1.0100 g., Aluminum, 18.98 mm. **Obv:** Bust of Major General J.F. Estigarribia facing **Obv. Legend:** REPUBLICA DEL PARAGUAY **Rev:** Acaray River Dam **Rev. Inscription:** REPRESA ACARAY **Edge:** Plain **Note:** Reduced size

Date	Mintage	F	VF	XF	Unc	BU
2006	25,000,000	—	—	—	1.00	2.00

KM# 177 100 GUARANIES

10.4500 g., Copper-Zinc-Nickel **Obv:** Bust of General Jose E. Dias facing **Obv. Legend:** REPUBLICA DEL PARAGUAY **Rev:** Ruins of Humaita **Rev. Inscription:** RUINAS DE HUMAITA 1865/70

Date	Mintage	F	VF	XF	Unc	BU
1990	35,000,000	—	—	—	2.25	2.75

KM# 177a 100 GUARANIES

5.4500 g., Brass Plated Steel **Obv:** Bust of General Jose E. Dias facing **Obv. Legend:** REPUBLICA DEL PARAGUAY **Rev:** Ruins of Humaita **Rev. Inscription:** RUINAS DE HUMAITA 1865/70 **Note:** Reduced weight and thickness.

Date	Mintage	F	VF	XF	Unc	BU
1993	35,000,000	—	—	—	1.50	2.00
1995	10,000,000	—	—	—	1.50	2.00
1996	30,000,000	—	—	—	1.50	2.00
2004	15,000,000	—	—	—	1.50	2.00
2005	10,000,000	—	—	—	1.50	2.00

KM# 177b 100 GUARANIES

3.7200 g., Nickel-Steel, 20.94 mm. **Obv:** Bust of General Jose E. Dias facing **Obv. Legend:** REPUBLICA DEL PARAGUAY **Rev:** Ruins of Humaita **Rev. Inscription:** RUINAS DE HUMAITA 1865/70 **Edge:** Plain

Date	Mintage	F	VF	XF	Unc	BU
2006	30,000,000	—	—	—	1.50	2.00

KM# 195 500 GUARANIES

7.8200 g., Brass Plated Steel **Obv:** Head of General Bernardino Caballero facing **Obv. Legend:** REPUBLICA DEL PARAGUAY **Rev:** Bank above value within circle **Rev. Legend:** BANCO CENTRAL DEL PARAGUAY

Date	Mintage	F	VF	XF	Unc	BU
1997	—	—	—	—	35.00	50.00
1998	15,000,000	—	—	—	2.50	3.00
2002	15,000,000	—	—	—	2.50	3.00
2005	5,000,000	—	—	—	2.50	3.00

KM# 195a 500 GUARANIES

4.8000 g., Nickel-Steel, 23 mm. **Obv:** Head of General Bernardino Caballero facing **Obv. Legend:** REPUBLICA DEL PARAGUAY **Rev:** Bank above value in circle **Rev. Legend:** BANCO CENTRAL DEL PARAGUAY **Edge:** Plain

Date	Mintage	F	VF	XF	Unc	BU
2006	12,000,000	—	—	—	2.00	2.50

KM# 198 MIL (1000) GUARANIES

6.0700 g., Nickel-Steel, 25 mm. **Obv:** Bust of Major General Francisco Solano Lopez facing **Obv. Legend:** REPUBLICA DEL PARAGUAY **Rev:** National Heroes Pantheon **Rev. Legend:** BANCO CENTRAL DEL PARAGUAY **Rev. Inscription:** PANTEON NACIONAL / DE LOS HEROES **Edge:** Plain

Date	Mintage	F	VF	XF	Unc	BU
2006	25,000,000	—	—	—	4.00	6.00

The Republic of Peru, located on the Pacific coast of South America, has an area of 496,225 sq. mi. (1,285,220sq. km.) and a population of *21.4 million. Capital: Lima. The diversified economy includes mining, fishing and agriculture. Fishmeal, copper, sugar, zinc and iron ore are exported.

MINT MARKS

AREQUIPA, AREQ = Arequipa
AYACUCHO = Ayacucho
(B) = Brussels
CUZCO (monogram), Cuzco, Co. Cuzco
L, LIMAE (monogram), Lima
(monogram), LIMA = Lima
(L) = London
PASCO (monogram), Pasco, Paz, Po= Pasco
P, (P) = Philadelphia
S = San Francisco
(W) = Waterbury, CT, USA

NOTE: The LIMAE monogram appears in three forms. The early LM monogram form looks like a dotted L with M. The later LIMAE monogram has all the letters of LIMAE more readily distinguishable. The third form appears as an M monogram during early Republican issues.

MINT ASSAYERS' INITIALS

The letter(s) following the dates of Peruvian coins are the assayer's initials appearing on the coins. They generally appear at the 11 o'clock position on the Colonial coinage and at the 5 o'clock position along the rim on the obverse or reverse on the Republican coinage.

DATING

Peruvian 5, 10 and 20 centavos, issued from 1918-1944, bear the dates written in Spanish. The following table translates those written dates into numerals:

1918 - UN MIL NOVECIENTOS DIECIOCHO
1919 - UN MIL NOVECIENTOS DIECINUEVE
1920 - UN MIL NOVECIENTOS VEINTE

1921 - UN MIL NOVECIENTOS VEINTIUNO
1923 - UN MIL NOVECIENTOS VEINTITRES
1926 - UN MIL NOVECIENTOS VEINTISEIS
1934 - UN MIL NOVECIENTOS TREINTICUATRO
1935 - UN MIL NOVECIENTOS TREINTICINCO
1937 - UN MIL NOVECIENTOS TREINTISIETE
1939 - UN MIL NOVECIENTOS TREINTINUEVE
1940 - UN MIL NOVECIENTOS CUARENTA
1941 - UN MIL NOVECIENTOS CUARENTIUNO

U.S. Mints

1942 - MIL NOVECIENTOS CUARENTA Y DOS

Lima Mint

1942 - UN MIL NOVECIENTOS CUARENTIDOS

U.S. Mints

1943 - MIL NOVECIENTOS CUARENTA Y TRES
1944 - MIL NOVECIENTOS CUARENTA Y CUATRO

Lima Mint

1944 - MIL NOVECIENTOS CUARENTICUATRO

MONETARY SYSTEM

100 Centavos (10 Dineros) = 1 Sol
10 Soles = 1 Libra

REPUBLIC

DECIMAL COINAGE

100 Centavos (10 Dineros) = 1 Sol; 10 Soles = 1 Libra

KM# 208.1 CENTAVO

Bronze **Obv:** Radiant star design around center circle with small date below and legend above **Rev:** Value within wreath, straight centavo **Note:** Thick planchet.

Date	Mintage	F	VF	XF	Unc	BU
1901	600,000	1.00	3.00	8.00	20.00	—
1904	1,000,000	8.00	15.00	30.00	60.00	—

KM# 211 CENTAVO

Bronze **Obv:** Radiant star design around center circle **Rev:** Value within wreath **Note:** Thick planchet. Engravers initial R appears below ribbon on most or all new dies, but often became weak or filled. Most coins show at least a faint trace of an R. Date varieteis also exist.

Date	Mintage	F	VF	XF	Unc	BU
1909/999 R	Inc. above	10.00	20.00	35.00	70.00	—
1909 R	Inc. above	10.00	20.00	35.00	70.00	—
1909	252,000	10.00	20.00	35.00	70.00	—
1915	250,000	3.00	6.00	10.00	30.00	—
1916	360,000	1.00	2.00	7.00	20.00	—
1916 R	Inc. above	1.00	2.00	6.00	15.00	—
1917	830,000	1.00	2.00	6.00	15.00	—
1917 R	Inc. above	1.00	2.00	6.00	15.00	—
1918	1,060,000	1.00	2.00	5.00	14.00	—
1918 R	Inc. above	1.00	2.00	5.00	14.00	—
1920	360,000	1.00	2.50	7.00	20.00	—
1920 R	Inc. above	1.00	2.50	7.00	20.00	—
1933 R Inc. KM208.2	—	1.00	2.50	7.00	20.00	—
1934 Inc. KM#208.2	—	4.50	8.00	20.00	55.00	—
1935 R Inc. KM#208.2	—	4.00	7.00	20.00	50.00	—
1936 R Inc. KM#208.2	—	1.50	3.50	7.00	20.00	—
1937	—	—	—	—	—	—
1937 R Inc. KM#208.2	—	1.50	3.50	7.00	20.00	—
1939 R Inc. KM#208.2	—	4.50	8.00	20.00	55.00	—

KM# 208.2 CENTAVO

Bronze **Obv:** Large date and legend **Rev:** Curved centavo **Note:** Thick planchet. Varieties exist.

Date	Mintage	F	VF	XF	Unc	BU
1933	275,000	1.50	3.00	8.00	20.00	—
1934	1,185,000	1.00	2.00	5.00	15.00	—
1935	1,105,000	1.00	2.00	5.00	15.00	—
1936	565,000	1.50	3.00	8.00	20.00	—
1937/6	735,000	1.00	2.00	4.00	20.00	—
1937	Inc. above	0.75	1.50	2.50	15.00	—
1938	340,000	0.75	1.50	2.50	15.00	—
1939	1,225,000	1.50	3.00	5.50	20.00	—
1940	1,250,000	1.50	3.00	5.50	20.00	—
1941	2,593,000	0.40	0.75	1.50	10.00	—

KM# 208a CENTAVO

Bronze **Obv:** Large date and legend **Rev:** Straight centavo **Note:** Thin planchet.

Date	Mintage	F	VF	XF	Unc	BU
1941 Inc. KM#208.2	—	0.40	0.75	2.00	8.00	—
1942	2,865,000	0.50	1.00	2.50	10.00	—
1944	—	10.00	20.00	35.00	70.00	—

KM# 211a CENTAVO

Bronze **Obv:** Radiant star design around center circle, large date and legend **Rev:** Value within wreath, curved centavo **Note:** Thin planchet. Many varieties exist.

Date	Mintage	F	VF	XF	Unc	BU
1941 Inc. KM#208.2	—	1.00	2.00	5.00	15.00	—
1942 Inc. KM#208a	—	0.50	1.00	3.00	10.00	—
1943	—	2.50	5.00	15.00	35.00	—
1944	2,490,000	0.15	0.40	1.00	4.00	—
1945	2,157,000	0.15	0.40	1.00	4.00	—
1946	3,198,000	0.15	0.40	1.00	4.00	—
1947	2,976,000	0.15	0.40	1.00	4.00	—
1948	3,195,000	0.15	0.40	1.00	4.00	—
1949	1,104,000	0.25	0.65	2.00	6.00	—

KM# 227 CENTAVO

1.0200 g., Zinc, 14.98 mm. **Obv:** Radiant star design around center circle **Rev:** Value within wreath, curved centavo **Edge:** Plain **Note:** Varieties exist.

Date	Mintage	F	VF	XF	Unc	BU
1950	3,196,000	0.35	0.25	1.25	5.00	—
1951	3,289,000	0.25	0.40	0.65	3.00	—
Note: Copper-plated examples of type dated 1951 are known						
1952	3,050,000	0.25	0.40	0.65	3.00	—
1953	3,260,000	0.35	0.60	1.00	4.00	—
1954	3,215,000	0.75	1.50	2.50	10.00	—
1955	3,400,000	0.25	0.40	0.65	3.00	—
1956 Pointed 6	2,500,000	0.25	0.40	0.65	3.00	—
1956 Knobbed 6	Inc. above	0.25	0.40	0.65	3.00	—
1957	4,400,000	0.40	0.85	2.00	7.00	—
1958/7	—	0.35	0.60	1.00	4.00	—
1958/8	3,200,000	0.50	1.00	2.00	7.00	—
1958	2,600,000	0.35	0.60	1.00	4.00	—
1959/8	Inc. above	0.35	0.75	1.50	5.00	—
1959	Inc. above	0.25	0.40	0.65	3.00	—
1960/50	3,060,000	0.35	0.60	1.00	4.00	—
1960	Inc. above	0.75	1.50	3.00	8.00	—
1961/51	2,600,000	0.25	0.40	1.00	3.00	—
1961	Inc. above	0.25	0.40	1.00	3.00	—
1962/52	2,600,000	0.25	0.40	1.00	3.00	—
1962	Inc. above	0.25	0.40	1.00	3.00	—
1963/53	2,400,000	0.25	0.40	1.00	3.00	—
1963	Inc. above	0.25	0.40	1.00	3.00	—
1965	360,000	0.75	1.50	3.00	10.00	—

KM# 187 CENTAVO

Bronze **Obv:** Radiant star design around center circle **Rev:** Value within wreath **Note:** Earlier dates 1875-1878 are listed as KM#187.1a in our 19th Century book.

Date	Mintage	F	VF	XF	Unc	BU
1919(P)	4,000,000	0.50	1.00	2.50	10.00	—

KM# 212.1 2 CENTAVOS

Copper Or Bronze **Obv:** Date at bottom **Rev:** Curved "CENTAVOS" **Note:** Thick planchet. Engraver's initial C appeared below ribbon on most or all new dies, but often became weak or filled. Most coins show at least a faint trace of C. Other varieties also exist.

Date	Mintage	F	VF	XF	Unc	BU
1917 C	73,000	4.00	6.50	15.00	40.00	—
1918/17	580,000	3.50	6.00	12.00	40.00	—
1918	Inc. above	3.50	6.00	15.00	40.00	—
1918/17 C	Inc. above	4.00	10.00	20.00	50.00	—
1918 C	Inc. above	3.50	6.00	15.00	40.00	—
1920/7 C	328,000	2.00	4.00	10.00	30.00	—
1920	Inc. above	1.00	2.00	5.00	15.00	—
1920 C	Inc. above	1.00	2.00	5.00	15.00	—
1933	285,000	1.00	2.00	5.00	15.00	—
1933 C	Inc. above	1.00	2.00	5.00	15.00	—
1934	973,000	0.75	1.50	4.00	15.00	—
1934 C	Inc. above	0.75	1.50	4.00	15.00	—
1935	950,000	0.75	1.50	4.00	15.00	—
1935 C	Inc. above	0.75	1.50	4.00	15.00	—
1936	763,000	0.75	1.50	4.00	15.00	—
1936/5 C	Inc. above	1.50	2.50	8.00	20.00	—
1936 C	Inc. above	0.75	1.25	3.00	12.00	—
1937	963,000	0.75	1.50	4.00	15.00	—
1937 C	Inc. above	0.75	1.50	4.00	15.00	—
1938 C	428,000	1.00	1.75	4.00	15.00	—
1939/8 C	—	—	—	—	—	—
Note: Reported, not confirmed						
1939/8	—	1.50	2.50	8.00	20.00	—
1939 C Inverted A for V in CENTAVOS	783,000	0.75	1.50	4.00	15.00	—
1940	—	1.00	2.00	4.00	15.00	—
1940 C	565,000	1.00	1.75	4.00	15.00	—
1941/0	Inc. above	1.00	2.00	4.00	15.00	—
1941/0 C	Inc. above	1.00	2.00	4.00	15.00	—
1941/22	Inc. above	1.00	2.00	4.00	15.00	—
1941	Inc. above	1.00	2.00	4.00	15.00	—
1941 C	Inc. above	2.00	5.00	12.00	20.00	—

KM# 212.2 2 CENTAVOS

5.8000 g., Copper Or Bronze, 23.93 mm. **Obv:** Radiant star design around center circle **Rev:** Value within sprays **Edge:** Plain **Note:** Thin planchet. Varieties exist.

Date	Mintage	F	VF	XF	Unc	BU
1941/32	870,000	1.00	2.00	3.50	10.00	—
1941/33 C	Inc. above	1.00	2.00	3.50	10.00	—
1941/33	Inc. above	1.00	2.00	3.50	10.00	—
1941/38	Inc. above	1.00	2.00	3.50	10.00	—
1941/38 C	Inc. above	1.00	2.00	3.50	10.00	—
1941/39 C	Inc. above	1.00	2.00	3.50	10.00	—
1941/0	Inc. above	1.00	2.00	3.50	10.00	—
1941	Inc. above	0.50	1.00	2.00	7.00	—
1942/22	4,418,000	—	0.50	1.00	5.00	—
1942/32	4,418,000	—	0.50	1.00	5.00	—
1942	Inc. above	0.25	0.50	1.00	5.00	—
1943/2	1,829,000	0.50	1.00	3.00	10.00	—
1943	Inc. above	0.50	1.00	3.00	10.00	—
1944	2,068,000	1.00	2.00	4.00	12.00	—
1945	2,288,000	1.00	2.00	4.00	12.00	—
1946	2,121,000	0.25	0.50	0.75	4.00	—
1947	1,280,000	0.25	0.50	0.75	4.00	—
1948	1,518,000	0.25	0.50	0.75	5.00	—
1949/8	938,000	0.25	0.60	4.00	7.00	—
1949	Inc. above	0.50	1.00	4.00	7.00	—

KM# 228 2 CENTAVOS

Zinc **Obv:** Radiant star design around center circle **Rev:** Value within wreath

Date	Mintage	F	VF	XF	Unc	BU
1950	1,702,000	0.35	0.75	1.25	3.00	—
1951	3,289,000	0.35	0.75	1.25	3.00	—
Note: Copper-plated examples of type dated 1951 exist						
1952	1,155,000	0.35	0.75	1.25	3.00	—
1953	1,150,000	0.40	0.85	1.50	4.00	—
1954	—	2.00	4.00	10.00	30.00	—
1955	1,185,000	0.35	0.75	1.25	3.00	—
1956	400,000	0.50	1.00	2.00	5.00	—
1957	520,000	1.50	3.00	6.00	25.00	—
1958	200,000	1.25	2.50	4.50	15.00	—

KM# A212 2 CENTAVOS

Copper Or Bronze **Obv:** Radiant star design around center circle **Rev:** Value within wreath **Note:** Sharper diework. Earlier date 1895 listed as KM#188.2 in 19th Century book.

Date	Mintage	F	VF	XF	Unc	BU
1919(P)	3,000,000	0.35	0.75	2.00	9.00	—

KM# 213.1 5 CENTAVOS

Copper-Nickel **Obv:** Date: UN MIL NOVECIENTOS DIECIOCHO **Rev:** Value to right of sprig

Date	Mintage	F	VF	XF	Unc	BU
1918	4,000,000	0.50	1.25	2.50	10.00	—
1919	10,000,000	0.40	1.00	2.00	7.00	—
1923	2,000,000	1.00	2.00	3.50	12.50	—
1926	4,000,000	1.50	3.00	6.00	20.00	—

KM# 213.2 5 CENTAVOS

3.0000 g., Copper-Nickel **Obv:** Head right **Rev:** Value to right of sprig

Date	Mintage	F	VF	XF	Unc	BU
1934	4,000,000	0.75	2.00	3.00	9.00	—
1934 Proof	—	Value: 200				
1935	4,000,000	0.50	1.25	2.00	6.00	—
1935 Proof	—	—	—	—	—	—
1937	2,000,000	0.75	2.00	3.00	9.00	—
1937 Proof	—	—	—	—	—	—
1939	2,000,000	0.50	1.25	2.00	6.00	—
1939 Proof	—	—	—	—	—	—
1940	2,000,000	0.50	1.25	2.00	6.00	—
1940 Proof	—	—	—	—	—	—
1941	2,000,000	0.50	1.25	2.00	6.00	—
1941 Proof	—	—	—	—	—	—

KM# 213.2a.1 5 CENTAVOS

Brass **Obv:** Date: MIL NOVECIENTOS CUARENTA Y DOS **Rev:** Value to right of sprig

Date	Mintage	F	VF	XF	Unc	BU
1942	4,000,000	1.00	3.00	5.00	20.00	—
1943	4,000,000	1.00	3.00	5.00	20.00	—
1944	4,000,000	1.00	2.75	4.50	20.00	—

KM# 213.2a.2 5 CENTAVOS

Brass **Obv:** Head right with date spelled out **Rev:** Value to right of sprig

Date	Mintage	F	VF	XF	Unc	BU
1942S	4,000,000	2.50	4.50	10.00	50.00	—
1943S	4,000,000	2.50	4.50	8.00	40.00	—

KM# 213.2a.3 5 CENTAVOS

Brass **Obv:** Date: MIL NOVECIENTOS CUARENTICUATRO **Rev:** Value to right of sprig

Date	Mintage	F	VF	XF	Unc	BU
1944	1,106,000	1.50	3.50	6.00	15.00	—

KM# 223.1 5 CENTAVOS

2.0000 g., Brass **Obv:** Head right with short legend **Rev:** Value to right of sprig **Note:** Thick planchet.

Date	Mintage	F	VF	XF	Unc	BU
1945	2,768,000	0.35	0.75	1.50	4.00	—
1946/5	4,270,000	1.00	2.50	5.00	14.00	—
1946	Inc. above	0.25	0.50	1.00	3.50	—

KM# 223.2 5 CENTAVOS

2.8500 g., Brass, 17 mm. **Obv:** Head right **Rev:** Value to right of sprig **Note:** Thin planchet. Varieties exist.

Date	Mintage	F	VF	XF	Unc	BU
1951	Inc. above	0.10	0.25	0.50	6.00	—
1952	7,840,000	0.10	0.25	0.50	6.00	—
1953	6,976,000	0.10	0.25	0.50	6.00	—
AFP	—	—	—	—	—	—
1954	6,244,000	0.10	0.20	0.40	1.00	—
1955	8,064,000	0.10	0.20	0.40	2.00	—
1956	16,200,000	—	0.10	0.35	1.50	—
1957 Small date	16,000,000	—	0.10	0.25	1.00	—
1957 Large date	Inc. above	—	0.10	0.25	1.00	—
1958	4,600,000	—	0.10	0.25	1.00	—
1959	8,300,000	—	0.10	0.25	1.00	—
1960/50	9,900,000	—	0.10	0.25	1.00	—
1960 Large date	Inc. above	—	0.10	0.25	1.00	—
1960 Small date	Inc. above	—	0.10	0.25	1.00	—
1961	10,200,000	—	0.10	0.20	1.00	—
1962 Curved 9	11,064,000	—	0.10	0.20	1.00	—
1962 Straight 9	Inc. above	—	0.10	0.20	1.00	—
1963	12,012,000	—	0.10	0.20	1.00	—
1964/3	12,304,000	—	0.10	0.35	1.50	—
1964	Inc. above	—	—	0.10	1.00	—
1965 Small date	12,500,000	—	—	0.10	1.00	—
1965 Large date	Inc. above	—	0.10	0.20	1.00	—
1965 Proof	—	Value: 20.00				

KM# 223.3 5 CENTAVOS

Brass **Obv:** Head right with long legend with 3mm gap above head **Rev:** Value to right of sprig **Note:** Thick planchet.

Date	Mintage	F	VF	XF	Unc	BU
1947	7,683,000	0.25	0.50	1.00	3.00	—
1948	6,711,000	0.25	0.50	1.00	3.00	—
1949	—	0.25	0.50	1.00	3.00	—
1949/8	5,550,000	1.00	2.00	4.00	10.00	—

KM# 223.4 5 CENTAVOS

Brass **Obv:** Head right **Rev:** Value to right of sprig **Note:** Thick planchet.

Date	Mintage	F	VF	XF	Unc	BU
1949	Inc. above	1.00	2.00	4.00	10.00	—
1950	7,933,000	0.25	0.50	1.00	3.00	—
195.1	8,064,000	0.25	0.50	1.00	3.00	—
1951	Inc. above	1.00	2.00	4.00	35.00	—

KM# 232 5 CENTAVOS

Brass, 17 mm. **Obv:** Head right **Rev:** Value to right of torch within chain circle **Designer:** Raymond P. Testu

Date	Mintage	F	VF	XF	Unc	BU
1954	2,080,000	1.00	2.00	4.00	8.00	—

KM# 290 5 CENTAVOS

1.4400 g., Brass **Subject:** 400th Anniversary of Lima Mint **Obv:** National arms above value **Obv. Designer:** Armando Pareja **Rev:** Pillars of Hercules within inner circle **Rev. Designer:** Alonso de Rincon

Date	Mintage	F	VF	XF	Unc	BU
1965 Proof	—	Value: 100				
1965	712,000	—	—	0.25	1.00	—

KM# 244.1 5 CENTAVOS

Brass **Obv:** National arms within circle above date **Rev:** Value to left of flower sprig

Date	Mintage	F	VF	XF	Unc	BU
1966 Proof	1,000	Value: 15.00				
1966	14,620,000	—	—	0.10	0.20	0.35
Note: PAREJA in field at lower left of arms						
1967	14,088,000	—	—	0.10	0.20	0.35
1968	17,880,000	—	—	0.10	0.20	0.35

KM# 244.1a 5 CENTAVOS

Silver Plated Brass **Obv:** National arms within circle above date **Rev:** Value to left of flower sprig

Date	Mintage	F	VF	XF	Unc	BU
1967	—	—	—	—	—	—

KM# 244.1b 5 CENTAVOS

Silver **Obv:** National arms within circle above date **Rev:** Value to left of flower sprig

Date	Mintage	F	VF	XF	Unc	BU
1967	—	—	—	—	—	—

KM# 244.2 5 CENTAVOS

1.5000 g., Brass **Obv:** National arms within circle **Rev:** Value to left of flower sprig **Edge:** Plain

Date	Mintage	F	VF	XF	Unc	BU
1969	17,880,000	—	—	—	0.10	0.20
1970	—	—	—	—	0.10	0.20
1971	24,320,000	—	—	—	0.10	0.20
1972	24,342,000	—	—	—	0.10	0.20
1973	25,074,000	—	—	—	0.10	0.20

KM# 244.3 5 CENTAVOS

1.4500 g., Brass, 14.8 mm. **Obv:** National arms within circle **Rev:** Value to left of flower sprig **Edge:** Plain

Date	Mintage	F	VF	XF	Unc	BU
1973	Inc. above	—	—	—	0.10	0.20
1974	—	—	—	—	0.10	0.20
1975	—	—	—	—	0.10	0.20

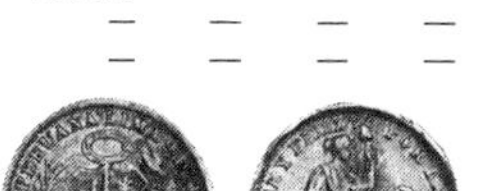

KM# 206.2 1/2 DINERO

1.2500 g., 0.9000 Silver 0.0362 oz. ASW **Obv:** National arms above date **Rev:** Seated Liberty flanked by shield and column **Note:** Most coins 1900-06 show faint to strong traces of 9/8 or 90/89 in date. Non-overdates without such traces are scarce. Most coins of 1907-17 have engraver's initial R at left of shield tip on reverse. Many other varieties exist.

Date	Mintage	F	VF	XF	Unc	BU
1901/801 JF	500,000	65.00	1.25	2.50	6.00	—
1901/801/701 JF	Inc. above	0.65	1.25	2.50	6.00	—
1901/891/791	Inc. above	0.65	1.25	2.00	5.00	—
1901/891 JF	Inc. above	0.65	1.25	2.00	5.00	—
1901 JF	Inc. above	0.75	1.50	3.50	10.00	—
1902/802 JF	616,000	0.65	1.25	2.00	5.00	—
1902/892 JF	Inc. above	0.65	1.25	2.00	5.00	—
1902/92	Inc. above	0.65	1.25	2.00	5.00	—
1902 JF	Inc. above	0.75	1.50	3.50	10.00	—
1903/803 JF	1,798,000	0.65	1.50	3.00	9.00	—
1903/893 JF	Inc. above	0.65	1.50	3.00	9.00	—
1903/897 JF	Inc. above	0.60	1.00	2.50	7.00	—
1903 JF	Inc. above	0.75	1.50	3.00	10.00	—
1904/804 JF	723,000	0.65	1.25	2.00	5.00	—
1904/804 JF FFLIZ Error	Inc. above	3.00	6.00	12.00	25.00	—
1904/884 JF	Inc. above	0.65	1.25	2.00	6.00	—
1904/891 JF	Inc. above	0.65	1.25	2.00	6.00	—
1904/893 JF	Inc. above	0.65	1.25	2.00	5.00	—
1904/894 JF	Inc. above	0.65	1.25	2.00	5.00	—
1904/894 JF FFLIZ Error	Inc. above	2.00	4.50	8.00	12.00	—
1904 JF	Inc. above	0.75	1.50	3.50	10.00	—
1904 JF FFLIZ Error	Inc. above	2.00	4.50	8.00	12.00	—
1905/805 JF	1,400,000	0.75	1.50	3.50	8.00	—
1905/891 JF	Inc. above	1.00	2.00	4.50	12.00	—
1905/893 JF	Inc. above	1.00	2.00	4.50	12.00	—
1905/894	Inc. above	1.00	2.00	4.50	12.00	—
1905/895 JF	Inc. above	0.60	1.25	2.00	5.00	—
1905/3 JF	Inc. above	1.00	2.00	4.50	12.00	—
1905 JF	Inc. above	0.75	1.50	3.50	10.00	—
1906/806 JF	900,000	0.75	1.50	3.50	8.00	—
1906/886 JF	Inc. above	0.75	1.50	3.50	8.00	—
1906/895 JF	Inc. above	0.75	1.50	3.50	8.00	—
1906/896 JF	Inc. above	0.60	1.25	2.00	5.00	—
1906 JF	Inc. above	0.75	1.50	3.00	10.00	—
1907 FG	600,000	0.75	1.50	3.00	10.00	—
1908/7 FG	200,000	1.50	3.00	6.00	15.00	—
1908 FG	Inc. above	0.75	1.50	3.50	10.00	—
1909/7 FG	—	3.00	6.00	12.50	30.00	—
1909 FG	—	0.75	1.50	3.50	8.00	—
1910 FG	640,000	0.60	1.00	2.00	5.00	—
1911 FG	460,000	0.60	1.25	2.00	5.00	—
1912 FG	120,000	0.65	1.25	2.50	6.00	—
1913 FG	480,000	0.60	1.00	2.00	5.00	—
1914/3 FG	—	0.75	1.50	3.50	10.00	—
1914/03 FG	—	1.00	2.50	5.50	15.00	—
1914/04 FG	—	1.00	2.50	5.50	15.00	—
1914 FG	—	0.60	1.00	2.00	5.00	—
1916/3 FG	860,000	0.60	1.00	2.00	5.00	—
1916/3 FG FERUANA Error	—	1.00	2.00	4.50	12.00	—
1916 FG	Inc. above	BV	0.75	1.75	4.50	—
1916/5 FG PERUANA Error	Inc. above	1.00	2.00	4.50	12.00	—
1916/5 FG FERUANA Error	Inc. above	1.00	2.00	4.50	12.00	—
1916/5 Without FERUANA	Inc. above	1.00	2.00	4.50	12.00	—
1916 FG FERUANA Error	Inc. above	1.00	2.00	4.50	15.00	—
1916 Matte	—	—	—	—	—	—
1917/87 FG	140,000	0.60	1.00	2.00	5.00	—
1917 FG	Inc. above	0.60	1.00	2.00	5.00	—

KM# 214.1 10 CENTAVOS

Copper-Nickel **Obv:** Head right **Rev:** Value to right of sprig

Date	Mintage	F	VF	XF	Unc	BU
1918	3,000,000	0.40	1.00	2.00	12.00	—
1919	2,500,000	0.40	1.00	2.00	12.00	—
1920	3,080,000	0.35	0.75	1.50	10.00	—
1921	6,920,000	0.35	0.75	1.50	10.00	—
1926	3,000,000	2.50	5.00	8.50	25.00	—

KM# 214.2 10 CENTAVOS

3.8600 g., Copper-Nickel **Obv:** Head right **Rev:** Value to right of sprig

Date	Mintage	F	VF	XF	Unc	BU
1935	1,000,000	0.75	1.50	3.00	12.00	—
1935 Proof	—	Value: 150				
1937	1,000,000	0.40	1.00	2.00	7.00	—
1937 Proof	—	—	—	—	—	—
1939	2,000,000	0.35	0.75	1.25	5.00	—
1939 Proof	—	—	—	—	—	—
1940	2,000,000	0.35	0.75	1.25	5.00	—
1940 Proof	—	Value: 175				
1941	2,000,000	0.35	0.75	1.25	5.00	—
1941 Proof	—	—	—	—	—	—

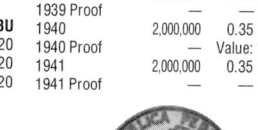

KM# 214a.1 10 CENTAVOS

Brass **Obv:** Head right, date begins MIL..., spelled out w/a "Y" **Rev:** Value to right of sprig

Date	Mintage	F	VF	XF	Unc	BU
1942	2,000,000	1.50	3.00	6.00	20.00	—
1943	2,000,000	1.50	3.00	6.00	20.00	—
1944	2,000,000	1.50	3.50	7.00	25.00	—

KM# 214a.2 10 CENTAVOS

Brass **Obv:** Head right **Rev:** Value to right of sprig **Edge:** Plain

Date	Mintage	F	VF	XF	Unc	BU
1942S	2,000,000	6.00	12.00	20.00	50.00	—
1943S	2,000,000	1.50	3.00	6.00	20.00	—

KM# 214a.3 10 CENTAVOS

Brass **Obv:** Date behins MIL..., spelled out with an "I" **Rev:** Value to right of sprig

Date	Mintage	F	VF	XF	Unc	BU
1942	—	5.00	9.00	15.00	40.00	—

KM# 214a.4 10 CENTAVOS

Brass **Obv:** Date behins MIL..., spelled out with an "I" **Rev:** Value to right of sprig **Note:** Varieties exist.

Date	Mintage	F	VF	XF	Unc	BU
1944	—	3.50	7.00	12.00	35.00	—

KM# 224.1 10 CENTAVOS

Brass **Obv:** Head right with short legend **Rev:** Value to right of sprig **Note:** Thick planchet.

Date	Mintage	F	VF	XF	Unc	BU
1945	2,810,000	0.25	0.50	1.50	4.00	—
1946/5	4,863,000	0.50	1.00	2.50	8.00	—
1946	Inc. above	0.35	0.75	2.00	7.00	—

KM# 226.1 10 CENTAVOS

3.8900 g., Brass **Obv:** Long legend with 3mm gap above head **Rev:** Value to right of sprig **Note:** Thick planchet.

Date	Mintage	F	VF	XF	Unc	BU
1947	6,806,000	0.25	0.50	1.00	3.00	—
1948	5,771,000	0.25	0.50	1.25	4.00	—
1949/8	4,730,000	0.50	1.00	1.50	7.50	—

KM# 226.2 10 CENTAVOS

Brass **Obv:** Head right **Rev:** Value to right of sprig

Date	Mintage	F	VF	XF	Unc	BU
1949	Inc. above	0.25	0.50	1.00	5.00	—
1950	5,298,000	0.20	0.40	0.80	4.00	—
1950 AFP	Inc. above	0.25	0.50	1.25	8.00	—
1951	7,324,000	6.00	10.00	15.00	40.00	—
1951/0 AFP	—	0.25	0.50	1.00	4.00	—
1951 AFP	—	0.20	0.40	0.80	3.00	—

KM# 224.2 10 CENTAVOS

2.5100 g., Brass **Obv:** Head right **Rev:** Value to right of sprig **Note:** Thin planchet - 1.3mm. Date varieties exist.

Date	Mintage	F	VF	XF	Unc	BU
1951	Inc. above	0.10	0.20	0.40	2.00	—
1951 AFP	—	0.10	0.20	0.40	2.00	—
1952	6,694,000	0.10	0.20	0.40	3.00	—
1952 AFP	—	0.10	0.20	0.40	3.00	—
1953	5,668,000	0.10	0.20	0.40	2.00	—
1953 AFP	—	0.10	0.20	0.40	2.00	—
1954	7,786,000	—	0.10	0.35	1.50	—
1954 AFP	—	—	0.10	0.35	1.50	—
1955	6,690,000	—	0.10	0.35	1.50	—
1955 AFP	—	—	0.10	0.35	1.50	—
1956/5	8,410,000	0.10	0.35	0.75	3.50	—
1956	Inc. above	—	0.10	0.25	1.00	—
1956 AFP	—	—	0.20	0.40	2.00	—
1957	8,420,000	—	0.10	0.25	1.00	—
1957 AFP	—	—	0.10	0.25	1.00	—
1958	10,380,000	—	0.10	0.25	1.00	—
1958 AFP	—	—	—	—	—	—
1959	8,300,000	—	0.10	0.25	1.00	—
1959 AFP	—	—	—	—	—	—
1960	12,600,000	—	0.10	0.25	1.00	—

Date	Mintage	F	VF	XF	Unc	BU
1961	12,700,000	—	0.10	0.15	1.00	—
1962	14,598,000	—	0.10	0.15	1.00	—
1963	16,100,000	—	0.10	0.15	1.00	—
1964	16,504,000	—	0.10	0.15	1.00	—
1965	17,808,000	—	0.10	0.15	1.00	—
1965 Proof	—	Value: 25.00				

KM# 233 10 CENTAVOS

Brass, 20 mm. **Obv:** Head right **Rev:** Value to upper right of torch, all within chain circle **Designer:** Raymond P. Testu

Date	Mintage	F	VF	XF	Unc	BU
1954	1,818,000	1.00	2.00	4.50	10.00	—

KM# 237 10 CENTAVOS

2.1000 g., Brass **Subject:** 400th Anniversary of Lima Mint **Obv:** National arms above value **Obv. Designer:** Amando Pareja **Rev:** Pillars of Hercules within inner circle **Rev. Designer:** Alonso de Rincon

Date	Mintage	F	VF	XF	Unc	BU
1965	572,000	—	—	0.35	1.00	—
1965 Proof	—	Value: 150				

KM# 245.1 10 CENTAVOS

Brass **Obv:** National arms within circle **Rev:** Value to left of flower sprig **Edge:** Reeded **Designer:** Armando Pareja **Note:** Date varieties exist.

Date	Mintage	F	VF	XF	Unc	BU
1966	14,930,000	—	—	0.10	0.75	1.25
Note: PAREJA in field at lower left of arms						
1966 Proof	1,000	Value: 15.00				
1967	19,330,000	—	—	0.10	0.75	1.25
1968	24,390,000	—	—	0.10	0.75	1.25

KM# 245.2 10 CENTAVOS

2.1700 g., Brass, 17.90 mm. **Obv:** National arms within circle **Rev:** Value to left of flower sprig **Edge:** Reeded **Designer:** Armando Pareja **Note:** Date varieties exist.

Date	Mintage	F	VF	XF	Unc	BU
1967	—	—	—	0.10	0.25	0.40
1968	—	—	—	0.10	0.20	0.35
1969	24,390,000	—	—	0.10	0.25	0.40
1970	29,110,000	—	—	0.10	0.20	0.35
1971	30,590,000	—	—	0.10	0.20	0.35
1972	34,442,000	—	—	0.10	0.20	0.35
1973	33,864,000	—	—	0.10	0.20	0.35

KM# 245.3 10 CENTAVOS

2.1800 g., Brass **Obv:** National arms within circle **Rev:** Value to left of flower sprig **Edge:** Plain

Date	Mintage	F	VF	XF	Unc	BU
1973	Inc. above	—	—	0.10	0.15	0.25
1974	—	—	—	0.10	0.15	0.25
1975	10,430,000	—	—	0.10	0.15	0.25

KM# 263 10 CENTAVOS

Brass **Obv:** National arms within circle **Rev:** Value

Date	Mintage	F	VF	XF	Unc	BU
1975	—	—	—	0.10	0.15	0.25

KM# 204.2 DINERO

2.5000 g., 0.9000 Silver 0.0723 oz. ASW **Obv:** National arms above date **Rev:** Seated Liberty flanked by shield and column **Note:** Varieties exist.

Date	Mintage	F	VF	XF	Unc	BU
1902/1 JF	375,000	1.20	2.00	3.50	15.00	—
1902/891 JF	Inc. above	1.20	2.00	3.50	15.00	—
1902/892 JF	Inc. above	1.20	2.00	3.50	15.00	—
1902/897 JF	Inc. above	1.20	2.00	3.50	15.00	—
1902 JF	Inc. above	1.20	2.00	4.00	18.00	—
1903/803 JF	887,000	1.20	2.00	3.50	15.00	—
1903/807 JF	Inc. above	1.20	2.00	3.50	15.00	—
1903/892 JF	Inc. above	1.20	2.00	3.50	12.00	—
1903/893 JF	Inc. above	1.20	2.00	3.50	12.00	—
1903/92 JF	Inc. above	1.20	2.00	3.50	12.00	—
1903 JF	Inc. above	1.20	2.00	3.50	15.00	—
1904 JF	380,000	1.20	2.50	4.00	15.00	—
1905/1 JF	700,000	1.20	2.50	4.00	15.00	—
1905/3 JF	Inc. above	1.20	2.50	4.00	15.00	—
1905 JF	Inc. above	1.20	2.00	3.50	15.00	—
1906 JF	826,000	1.20	2.00	3.50	15.00	—
1907 JF Rare	500,000	—	—	—	—	—
1907 FG/JF	Inc. above	1.25	2.50	4.50	15.00	—
1907 FG	Inc. above	1.20	1.75	3.00	12.00	—
1908/6 FG/JF	Inc. above	1.20	2.25	4.00	15.00	—
1908 FG/JF	200,000	1.20	2.25	4.00	15.00	—
1908 FG/GF	Inc. above	1.20	2.25	4.00	15.00	—
1908 FG	Inc. above	1.20	1.75	3.00	15.00	—
1909 FG	—	2.00	4.00	8.00	20.00	—
1909 FG/FO	—	2.00	4.00	8.00	20.00	—
1909 FG/FF	—	2.00	4.00	8.00	20.00	—
1910 FG	210,000	BV	1.25	3.00	15.00	—

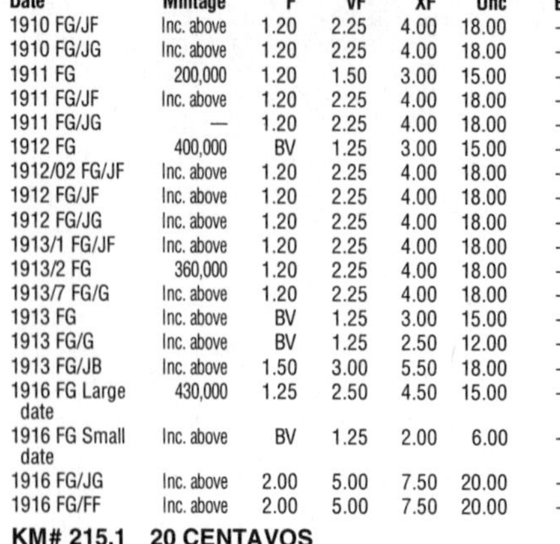

Date	Mintage	F	VF	XF	Unc	BU
1910 FG/JF	Inc. above	1.20	2.25	4.00	18.00	—
1910 FG/JG	Inc. above	1.20	2.25	4.00	18.00	—
1911 FG	200,000	1.20	1.50	3.00	15.00	—
1911 FG/JF	Inc. above	1.20	2.25	4.00	18.00	—
1911 FG/JG	—	1.20	2.25	4.00	18.00	—
1912 FG	400,000	BV	1.25	3.00	15.00	—
1912/02 FG/JF	Inc. above	1.20	2.25	4.00	18.00	—
1912 FG/JF	Inc. above	1.20	2.25	4.00	18.00	—
1912 FG/JG	Inc. above	1.20	2.25	4.00	18.00	—
1913/1 FG/JF	Inc. above	1.20	2.25	4.00	18.00	—
1913/2 FG	360,000	1.20	2.25	4.00	18.00	—
1913/7 FG/G	Inc. above	1.20	2.25	4.00	18.00	—
1913 FG	Inc. above	BV	1.25	3.00	15.00	—
1913 FG/G	Inc. above	BV	1.25	2.50	12.00	—
1913 FG/JB	Inc. above	1.50	3.00	5.50	18.00	—
1916 FG Large date	430,000	1.25	2.50	4.50	15.00	—
1916 FG Small date	Inc. above	BV	1.25	2.00	6.00	—
1916 FG/JG	Inc. above	2.00	5.00	7.50	20.00	—
1916 FG/FF	Inc. above	2.00	5.00	7.50	20.00	—

KM# 215.1 20 CENTAVOS

7.0000 g., Copper-Nickel, 24 mm. **Obv:** Date spelled: UN MIL NOVECIENTOS DIECIOCHO **Rev:** Value to right of sprig

Date	Mintage	F	VF	XF	Unc	BU
1918	2,500,000	0.40	1.00	5.00	20.00	—
1919	1,250,000	1.25	2.50	5.00	20.00	—
1920	1,464,000	1.25	2.25	4.00	25.00	—
1921	8,536,000	0.85	3.00	6.00	25.00	—
1926	2,500,000	2.50	5.00	9.00	30.00	—

KM# 215a.1 20 CENTAVOS

Brass, 24 mm. **Obv:** Date spelling: MIL NOVECIENTOS CUARENTA Y TRES **Rev:** Value to right of sprig

Date	Mintage	F	VF	XF	Unc	BU
1942	500,000	3.00	6.00	13.50	60.00	—
1943	500,000	3.00	6.00	13.50	60.00	—
1944	500,000	4.00	7.50	16.50	65.00	—

KM# 215a.2 20 CENTAVOS

Brass, 24 mm. **Obv:** Head right **Rev:** Value to right of sprig

Date	Mintage	F	VF	XF	Unc	BU
1942S	500,000	6.00	12.00	50.00	150	—
1943S	500,000	3.00	6.00	12.50	200	—

KM# 221.1 20 CENTAVOS

Brass, 24 mm. **Obv:** Head right, divided legend **Rev:** Value to right of sprig **Note:** Thick planchet.

Date	Mintage	F	VF	XF	Unc	BU
1942	300,000	1.00	2.50	5.00	12.50	—
1943	1,900,000	0.75	1.50	2.50	7.50	—
1944	2,963,000	0.60	1.25	2.00	6.00	—

KM# 221.2 20 CENTAVOS

6.8300 g., Brass, 24 mm. **Obv:** AFP on truncation, continuous legend **Rev:** Value to right of sprig

Date	Mintage	F	VF	XF	Unc	BU
1946	3,410,000	0.25	0.50	0.85	3.00	—
1947	4,307,000	0.25	0.50	0.85	3.00	—
1948	3,578,000	0.25	0.50	0.85	3.00	—
1949/8	2,709,000	0.75	1.50	2.50	6.50	—

KM# 221.3 20 CENTAVOS

Brass **Obv:** Head right, continuous legend **Rev:** Value to right of sprig

Date	Mintage	F	VF	XF	Unc	BU
1945	3,043,000	0.25	—	0.75	1.50	—
1946/5	Inc. above	0.25	0.65	1.00	2.00	—
1946	Inc. above	0.25	0.50	0.75	1.50	—

KM# 221.4 20 CENTAVOS

Brass **Obv:** Different style legend **Rev:** Value to right of sprig

Date	Mintage	F	VF	XF	Unc	BU
1949	Inc. above	0.50	1.00	1.75	4.50	—
1950	2,427,000	1.00	1.75	3.00	8.00	—
1951	2,941,000	3.00	7.50	15.00	40.00	—

KM# 221.2b 20 CENTAVOS

3.8000 g., Brass, 23 mm. **Obv:** Head right **Rev:** Value to right of sprig **Note:** Thin planchet - 1.3mm. AFP. Date varieties exist.

Date	Mintage	F	VF	XF	Unc	BU
1951	Inc. above	0.20	0.40	0.75	2.00	—
1951 Without AFP	—	—	—	—	—	—
1952	4,410,000	0.20	0.40	0.75	2.50	—
1952 Without AFP	Inc. above	—	—	—	—	—
1953	2,615,000	0.20	0.40	1.50	8.00	—
1954	1,816,000	1.50	2.50	4.00	12.00	—
1955 Large oval 9	4,050,000	0.10	0.15	0.30	1.50	—
1955 Small oval 9	Inc. above	0.20	0.40	1.50	8.00	—
1955 Round nine	Inc. above	—	—	—	—	—
1956	3,760,000	0.10	0.15	0.30	1.50	—
1957	3,680,000	0.10	0.15	0.30	1.00	—
1958	3,100,000	0.10	0.15	0.30	1.00	—
1959	5,450,000	—	0.10	0.20	1.00	—
1959 Without AFP	—	—	—	—	—	—
1960/90 With AFP	—	—	—	—	—	—
1960/90 Without AFP	—	—	—	—	—	—
1960	6,750,000	—	0.10	0.20	1.00	—
1960 Without AFP	—	0.25	0.75	1.50	4.00	—
1961	6,800,000	—	0.10	0.20	1.00	—
1961 Without AFP	—	—	—	—	—	—
1962	7,357,000	—	0.10	0.20	1.00	—
1963/2	8,843,000	0.15	0.25	0.50	2.00	—
1963	Inc. above	—	0.10	0.20	1.00	—
1964	9,550,000	—	0.10	0.20	1.00	—
1965 With inverted V for A in AFP	—	—	0.10	0.20	1.00	—
1965 Without AFP	—	0.10	0.15	0.30	1.00	—
1965 Proof	—	Value: 35.00				

KM# 234 20 CENTAVOS

Brass, 24 mm. **Subject:** President Castilla **Obv:** Head right **Rev:** Value to right of torch within chain circle **Edge:** Reeded **Designer:** Raymond P. Testu **Note:** Thin planchet - 1.3mm. AFP.

Date	Mintage	F	VF	XF	Unc	BU
1954	799,000	2.00	4.00	8.00	15.00	—

KM# 221.2c 20 CENTAVOS

Copper-Nickel **Obv:** Head right **Rev:** Value to right of sprig **Edge:** Reeded **Note:** Thin planchet - 1.3mm. AFP.

Date	Mintage	F	VF	XF	Unc	BU
1958	—	—	—	—	150	—
1963	—	8.00	15.00	25.00	—	—
1965 Proof	—	Value: 30.00				

KM# 205.2 1/5 SOL

5.0000 g., 0.9000 Silver 0.1447 oz. ASW **Obv:** National arms **Rev:** Libertad incuse **Edge:** Plain **Note:** Die varieties exist. Some coins 1911-17 have engraver's initial R left of shield on reverse.

Date	Mintage	F	VF	XF	Unc	BU
1901 JF	638,000	BV	2.50	5.50	12.00	—
1903/1 JF	702,000	2.50	4.00	7.00	17.50	—
1903/13 JF	Inc. above	BV	3.50	6.00	15.00	—
1903 JF	Inc. above	BV	3.25	5.50	12.00	—
1906 JF	660,000	BV	3.25	5.50	12.00	—
1907 JF	1,370,000	BV	2.25	4.00	10.00	—
1907 FG	Inc. above	BV	3.25	5.50	12.00	—
1908/7 FG	560,000	BV	3.50	6.00	15.00	—
1908 FG	Inc. above	BV	3.25	5.50	15.00	—
1909 FG	42,000	2.50	4.00	9.00	27.50	—
1910/00 FG	165,000	3.00	7.00	15.00	35.00	—
1910 FG	Inc. above	3.00	7.00	12.00	25.00	—
1911 FG	250,000	BV	3.25	5.50	9.00	—
1911 FG-R	Inc. above	BV	3.25	5.50	9.00	—
1912 FG	300,000	BV	2.25	4.00	8.00	—
1912 R	—	BV	2.25	4.00	8.00	—
1912/1 FG-R	—	BV	2.50	5.00	10.00	—
1912 FG-R	Inc. above	BV	3.25	5.50	15.00	—
1913 FG	223,000	BV	3.50	6.00	15.00	—
1913 FG-R	Inc. above	BV	3.50	6.00	15.00	—
1914 FG	10,000	5.00	12.00	25.00	55.00	—
1915 FG	—	25.00	40.00	75.00	125	—
1916 FG	425,000	2.50	5.00	10.00	25.00	—
1916 FG-R	Inc. above	BV	3.25	5.00	9.00	—
1917 FG-R	20,000	8.00	17.00	35.00	75.00	—

KM# 238 25 CENTAVOS

Brass **Subject:** 400th Anniversary of Lima Mint **Obv:** National arms above value **Obv. Designer:** Armando Pareja **Rev:** Pillars of Hercules within inner circle **Rev. Designer:** Alonso de Rincon

Date	Mintage	F	VF	XF	Unc	BU
ND(1965)	1,113,000	—	0.25	0.35	0.75	—
1965 Proof	—	Value: 200				

KM# 246.1 25 CENTAVOS

Brass **Obv:** PAREJA in field at lower left of arms **Rev:** Value to left of flower sprig **Edge:** Reeded

Date	Mintage	F	VF	XF	Unc	BU
1966 PAREJA in field at lower left of arms	9,300,000	—	0.15	0.25	0.50	0.75
1966 Proof	1,000	Value: 15.00				
1967	8,150,000	—	0.15	0.25	0.50	0.75
1968	7,440,000	—	0.15	0.25	0.50	0.75

KM# 246.2 25 CENTAVOS

3.2000 g., Brass, 21.03 mm. **Obv:** National arms within circle **Rev:** Value to left of flower sprig **Edge:** Reeded **Designer:** Armando Pareja

Date	Mintage	F	VF	XF	Unc	BU
1968 AP	Inc. above	—	0.15	0.25	0.50	0.75
1969 AP on reverse	7,440,000	—	0.20	0.40	1.00	1.50
1969 With inverted V for A in AP	Inc. above	—	0.20	0.40	1.00	1.50
1969 Without AP	Inc. above	—	0.15	0.25	0.50	0.75
1970	6,341,000	—	0.20	0.40	1.00	1.50
1971	3,196,000	—	0.20	0.40	1.00	1.50
1972	5,523,000	—	0.20	0.40	1.00	1.50
1973	7,492,000	—	0.15	0.25	0.50	0.75

KM# 259 25 CENTAVOS

3.1000 g., Brass **Obv:** National arms within circle **Rev:** Value to left of flower sprig **Designer:** Armando Pareja

Date	Mintage	F	VF	XF	Unc	BU
1973	Inc. above	—	0.10	0.15	0.25	0.40
1974	—	—	0.10	0.15	0.25	0.40
1975	—	—	0.10	0.15	0.25	0.40

KM# 303.4a CENTIMO

0.8300 g., Aluminum, 15.96 mm. **Obv:** National arms **Edge:** Plain **Note:** LIMA monogram is mint mark.

Date	Mintage	F	VF	XF	Unc	BU
2006	—	—	—	—	0.50	—
2007	—	—	—	—	0.50	—

KM# 304.4a 5 CENTIMOS

1.0200 g., Aluminum, 18 mm. **Obv:** National arms **Edge:** Plain **Note:** LIMA monogram is mint mark.

Date	Mintage	F	VF	XF	Unc	BU
2007	—	—	—	—	0.50	—

KM# 203 1/2 SOL

12.5000 g., 0.9000 Silver 0.3617 oz. ASW **Obv:** National arms above date **Rev:** Seated Liberty flanked by shield and column **Note:** Mint mark: LIMA. Date varieties exist. Most coins have engraver's initials JR left of shield tip on reverse.

Date	Mintage	F	VF	XF	Unc	BU
1907LIMA FG-JR	1,000,000	BV	6.00	10.00	20.00	—
1908/7LIMA FG-JR	30,000	15.00	30.00	75.00	300	—
1908LIMA FG-JR	Inc. above	12.00	25.00	65.00	175	—
1914LIMA FG-JR	173,000	BV	6.50	15.00	35.00	—
1915LIMA FG-JR	570,000	BV	5.50	7.50	15.00	—
1916LIMA FG	384,000	BV	5.50	7.50	15.00	—
1916LIMA FG-JR	—	BV	5.50	7.50	15.00	—
1917LIMA FG-JR	178,000	BV	6.00	10.00	20.00	—

KM# 216 1/2 SOL

12.5000 g., 0.5000 Silver 0.2009 oz. ASW, 30 mm. **Obv:** National arms above date **Rev:** Seated Liberty flanked by shield and column **Note:** Date varieties exist. Engraver's initials appear on stems of obverse wreath.

Date	Mintage	F	VF	XF	Unc	BU
1922LIMA LIBERTAD incuse, J.R. on reverse	465,000	BV	7.00	25.00	80.00	—
1922LIMA LIBERTAD in relief	Inc. above	BV	7.00	25.00	80.00	—
1923LIMA GM LIBER/TAD, round-top 3	2,520,000	BV	4.00	10.00	30.00	—
1923/2LIMA Flat-top 3	Inc. above	BV	3.25	5.50	20.00	—
1923LIMA Flat-top 3	Inc. above	BV	3.50	7.00	25.00	—
1924LIMA GM	238,000	BV	6.50	20.00	50.00	—
1926LIMA GM	694,000	BV	3.50	7.50	25.00	—
1927LIMA GM	2,640,000	BV	3.25	5.50	15.00	—
1928/7LIMA GM	3,028,000	—	—	—	—	—
1928LIMA GM	Inc. above	BV	3.25	5.50	15.00	—
1929LIMA GM	3,068,000	BV	3.25	5.50	15.00	—
1935LIMA AP	2,653,000	BV	3.25	5.00	14.00	—
1935LIMA	—	—	—	—	—	—

KM# 220.1 1/2 SOL

Brass **Obv:** Five palm leaves point to llama on shield **Rev:** Value and legend

Date	Mintage	F	VF	XF	Unc	BU
1935	10,000,000	0.50	1.25	2.25	7.00	—
1935 Proof	—	Value: 200				
1941	4,000,000	0.50	1.25	2.25	7.00	—

KM# 220.2 1/2 SOL

Brass **Obv:** Arms within wreath **Rev:** Value and legend

Date	Mintage	F	VF	XF	Unc	BU
1942	4,000,000	1.50	3.00	5.00	20.00	—
1943	4,000,000	3.00	6.50	12.50	35.00	—
1944	Inc. above	1.50	3.00	5.00	20.00	—

KM# 220.3 1/2 SOL

Brass **Obv:** National arms within wreath **Rev:** Value and legend **Note:** The coins struck in Philadelphia and San Francisco have a serif on the "4" of the date; the Lima and London coins do not.

Date	Mintage	F	VF	XF	Unc	BU
1942S	1,668,000	1.50	3.00	5.00	15.00	—
1943S	6,332,000	1.50	3.00	5.00	15.00	—

KM# 220.4 1/2 SOL

7.3200 g., Brass **Obv:** Three palm leaves point to llama on shield **Rev:** Value and legend **Note:** Dates 1941-44 have thick flat-top 4 without serifs. 1945 has narrow 4 like KM#220.5.

Date	Mintage	F	VF	XF	Unc	BU
1941	2,000,000	3.00	6.50	12.50	35.00	—
1942	Inc. above	1.50	3.00	5.00	15.00	—
1942 AP	—	—	—	—	—	—
1943	2,000,000	0.50	1.00	2.00	12.00	—
1944	Inc. above	0.40	0.85	1.75	7.00	—
1944/2	4,000,000	—	—	—	—	—
1944 AP	Inc. above	—	—	—	—	—
1945	4,000,000	0.75	1.50	3.00	10.00	—

KM# 220.5 1/2 SOL

7.6000 g., Brass, 27 mm. **Obv:** Three palm leaves point to llama on shield **Rev:** Value and legend **Note:** 1942, 1944 AP, and all 1945-49 have narrow 4 without serif on crossbar. 1944 without AP has flat-top 4 like KM#220.4. Engraver's initials AP appear on wreath stems of some 1944-45, all 1946 and some 1947 coins. Varieties exist, including narrow and wide dates for 1956 and 1961 issues.

Date	Mintage	F	VF	XF	Unc	BU
1942 Long-top 2	Inc. above	1.50	3.00	5.00	15.00	—
1944	Inc. above	0.75	1.50	3.00	10.00	—
1944 AP	Inc. above	0.50	1.00	2.00	7.00	—
1945	Inc. above	0.75	1.50	3.00	10.00	—
1945 AP	Inc. above	0.75	1.50	3.00	10.00	—
1946/5 AP	3,744,000	2.00	3.50	6.50	17.50	—
1946 AP	Inc. above	0.40	0.75	1.25	7.00	—
1947 AP	6,066,000	0.40	0.75	1.25	7.00	—
1947	Inc. above	0.40	0.75	1.25	7.00	—
1948	3,324,000	0.40	0.75	1.25	7.00	—
1949/8	420,000	1.00	2.00	4.00	12.00	—
1949	Inc. above	1.50	3.00	6.00	18.00	—
1950	91,000	1.25	2.25	4.50	15.00	—
1951/8	930,000	0.50	1.00	2.00	7.00	—
1951	Inc. above	0.50	1.00	2.00	7.00	—
1952	935,000	0.75	1.50	3.00	10.00	—
1953	817,000	0.50	1.00	2.00	7.00	—
1954	637,000	0.75	1.50	3.00	10.00	—
1955	1,383,000	0.15	0.35	0.75	4.00	—
1956	2,309,000	0.10	0.25	0.40	1.50	—
1957	2,700,000	0.10	0.25	0.50	2.00	—
1958	2,691,000	0.10	0.25	0.40	1.50	—
1959	3,609,000	0.10	0.25	0.40	1.50	—
1960	5,600,000	0.10	0.20	0.35	0.75	—
1961 Narrow date	4,400,000	0.10	0.20	0.35	0.75	—
1961 Wide date	Inc. above	0.10	0.20	0.35	0.75	—
1962	3,540,000	0.10	0.20	0.35	1.00	—
1963	4,345,000	0.10	0.20	0.35	0.75	—
1964	5,315,000	0.10	0.20	0.35	1.50	—
1965	7,090,000	0.10	0.20	0.35	1.75	—
1965 Proof	—	Value: 75.00				

KM# 239 1/2 SOL

Brass **Subject:** 400th Anniversary of Lima Mint **Obv:** National arms above value **Obv. Designer:** Armando Pareja **Rev:** Pillars of Hercules within inner circle **Rev. Designer:** Alonso de Rincon

Date	Mintage	F	VF	XF	Unc	BU
ND(1965)	10,971,000	—	0.10	0.20	0.50	—
ND(1965) Proof	—	Value: 400				

KM# 247 1/2 SOL

Brass, 22.5 mm. **Obv:** National arms within circle **Rev:** Value to right of llama **Designer:** Armando Pareja

Date	Mintage	F	VF	XF	Unc	BU
1966	13,720,000	—	0.10	0.20	1.00	2.50
1966 Proof	1,000	Value: 20.00				
1967	15,500,000	—	0.10	0.20	1.00	2.50
1967 PAREJA on obverse and reverse	—	—	0.10	0.20	1.00	2.50
1968	13,890,000	3.00	7.00	15.00	30.00	—
1968 JAS	—	—	0.10	0.20	1.00	2.50
1969	13,890,000	—	0.10	0.20	1.00	2.50
1970	11,901,000	—	0.10	0.20	1.00	2.50
Note: Date varieties exist						
1971	7,524,000	—	0.15	0.20	1.00	2.50
1972	19,441,000	—	0.10	0.20	1.00	2.50
1973	14,951,000	—	0.10	0.20	1.00	2.50

KM# 260 1/2 SOL

4.1600 g., Brass, 22.5 mm. **Obv:** National arms within circle **Rev:** Value to right of llama **Edge:** Reeded **Designer:** Armando Pareja

Date	Mintage	F	VF	XF	Unc	BU
1973	Inc. above	—	0.10	0.20	1.00	2.50
1974/1	—	—	0.10	0.20	1.00	2.50
1974	14,518,000	—	0.10	0.20	1.00	2.50
1975	14,039,000	—	0.10	0.20	1.00	2.50

KM# 265 1/2 SOL

2.1000 g., Brass, 17.97 mm. **Obv:** National arms within circle **Rev:** Value **Edge:** Plain **Note:** Without mint mark.

Date	Mintage	F	VF	XF	Unc	BU
1975	62,682,000	—	0.10	0.20	0.30	0.50
1976	388,771,000	—	0.10	0.20	0.30	0.50

KM# 196.26 SOL

25.0000 g., 0.9000 Silver 0.7234 oz. ASW **Obv:** National arms above date **Rev:** Libertad incuse **Note:** Type XII. Legends have smaller lettering. Varieties exist.

Date	Mintage	F	VF	XF	Unc	BU
1914 FG	620,000	—	BV	12.50	24.00	—
1915 FG	Inc. above	—	BV	12.50	22.00	—

KM# 196.28 SOL

25.0000 g., 0.9000 Silver 0.7234 oz. ASW **Obv:** National arms above date **Rev:** LIBERTAD in relief **Note:** Type III.

Date	Mintage	F	VF	XF	Unc	BU
1916 FG	Inc. above	—	BV	12.50	22.00	—

KM# 196.27 SOL

25.0000 g., 0.9000 Silver 0.7234 oz. ASW **Obv:** National arms above date **Rev:** LIBERTAD incuse

Date	Mintage	F	VF	XF	Unc	BU
1916 FG	1,927,000	—	BV	12.50	22.00	—

KM# 217.1 SOL

25.0000 g., 0.5000 Silver 0.4019 oz. ASW, 37 mm. **Obv:** National arms, fineness omitted **Rev:** LEBERTAD in relief

Date	Mintage	F	VF	XF	Unc	BU
1922 Rare	—	—	—	—	—	—
1923	3,600	15.00	30.00	70.00	275	—

KM# 217.2 SOL

25.0000 g., 0.5000 Silver 0.4019 oz. ASW, 37 mm. **Obv:** National arms above date **Rev:** LIBERTAD incuse

Date	Mintage	F	VF	XF	Unc	BU
1923	1,400	35.00	75.00	165	475	—

KM# 218.1 SOL

25.0000 g., 0.5000 Silver 0.4019 oz. ASW, 37 mm. **Obv:** National arms **Rev:** Seated Liberty flanked by shield and column **Note:** Small letters. The Philadelphia and Lima strikings may be distinguished by the fact that the letters in the legends are smaller on those pieces produced at Philadelphia. All bear the name of the Lima Mint.

Date	Mintage	F	VF	XF	Unc	BU
1923	Est. 2,369,000	BV	6.50	8.50	15.00	—
1924/823	3,113,000	6.50	10.00	20.00	40.00	—
1924/824	Inc. above	6.50	10.00	20.00	40.00	—
1924	Inc. above	BV	6.50	8.50	15.00	—
1925	1,291,000	BV	6.50	10.00	20.00	—
1926	2,157,000	BV	6.50	8.50	15.00	—

KM# 218.2 SOL

25.0000 g., 0.5000 Silver 0.4019 oz. ASW, 37 mm. **Obv:** National arms, engraver's initials GM on stems flanking date **Rev:** Seated Liberty flanked by shield and column **Note:** Large letters.

Date	Mintage	F	VF	XF	Unc	BU
1924	96,000	6.50	9.00	20.00	65.00	—
1925	1,004,999	BV	6.50	8.50	15.00	—
1930	76,000	BV	6.50	10.00	20.00	—
1931	24,000	BV	6.50	10.00	22.00	—
1933	5,000	7.00	12.00	20.00	40.00	—
1934/3	2,855,000	BV	6.50	10.00	20.00	—
1934	Inc. above	BV	6.50	7.00	12.50	—
1935	695,000	BV	6.50	10.00	20.00	—

KM# 222 SOL

14.5300 g., Brass, 33 mm. **Obv:** National arms **Rev:** Value within circle **Note:** Date varieties exist.

Date	Mintage	F	VF	XF	Unc	BU
1943	10,000,000	0.35	1.25	3.00	8.00	—
1944	Inc. above	0.35	1.25	3.00	7.00	—
1945	—	0.50	1.50	3.50	9.00	—
1946	1,752,000	0.50	1.50	3.00	8.00	—
1947	3,302,000	0.35	1.00	2.00	6.00	—
1948	1,992,000	0.35	1.00	2.00	6.00	—
1949/8	751,000	2.00	4.00	7.00	20.00	—
1949	Inc. above	3.50	7.50	12.00	25.00	—
1950	1,249,000	7.00	10.00	15.00	25.00	—
1951	Inc. above	0.25	0.50	1.50	6.00	—
1951/0	2,093,999	0.25	0.50	1.50	6.00	—
1952	2,037,000	0.25	0.50	1.50	6.00	—
1953	1,243,000	3.00	6.00	10.00	25.00	—
1954	1,220,000	0.35	0.75	1.75	6.00	—
1955	1,323,000	0.35	0.75	1.75	6.00	—
1956	3,450,000	0.15	0.35	0.75	3.00	—
1957	3,086,000	0.15	0.35	1.00	5.00	—
1958 Wide date	3,390,000	0.15	0.35	0.75	3.00	—
1958 Narrow date	Inc. above	0.15	0.35	0.75	3.00	—
1959	4,975,000	0.15	0.35	1.00	5.00	—
1960	5,800,000	0.15	0.35	0.75	1.50	—
1961	5,200,000	0.15	0.35	0.75	2.00	—
1962	5,102,000	0.15	0.35	0.75	1.50	—
1963	5,499,000	0.15	0.35	0.75	2.00	—
1964 Wide date	5,888,000	0.15	0.35	0.75	2.00	—
1964 Narrow date	Inc. above	0.15	0.35	0.75	2.00	—
1965	5,504,000	0.15	0.35	0.75	2.00	—
1965 Proof	—	Value: 75.00				

KM# 240 SOL

Brass, 28 mm. **Subject:** 400th Anniversary of the Lima Mint **Obv:** National arms above value **Obv. Designer:** Armando Pareja **Rev:** Pillars of Hercules within inner circle **Rev. Designer:** Alonso de Rincon

Date	Mintage	F	VF	XF	Unc	BU
ND(1965)	3,103,000	—	0.35	0.75	1.50	—
ND(1965) Proof	—	Value: 500				

KM# 248 SOL

9.2000 g., Brass, 28 mm. **Obv:** National arms **Rev:** Llama **Designer:** Armando Pareja

Date	Mintage	F	VF	XF	Unc	BU
1966	16,410,000	—	0.10	0.25	1.00	3.00
1966 Proof	1,000	Value: 25.00				
1967	13,920,000	—	0.10	0.25	1.00	3.00
1968	12,260,000	—	0.10	0.25	1.00	3.00
1969	12,260,000	—	0.10	0.25	1.00	3.00
1970	12,336,000	—	0.10	0.25	1.00	3.00
1971	11,927,000	—	0.10	0.25	1.00	3.00
1972	3,945,000	—	0.10	0.25	1.00	3.00
1973	12,856,000	—	0.10	0.25	1.00	3.00
1974	14,966,000	—	0.10	0.25	1.00	3.00
1975	—	—	0.10	0.25	1.00	3.00

KM# 266.1 SOL

3.2400 g., Brass, 21 mm. **Obv:** National arms within circle **Rev:** Value **Edge:** Plain

Date	Mintage	F	VF	XF	Unc	BU
1975	354,485,000	—	—	0.10	0.25	0.40
1976	114,660,000	—	—	0.10	0.25	0.40

KM# 266.2 SOL

2.0000 g., Brass **Obv:** National arms within circle **Rev:** Value **Edge:** Plain **Note:** Mint mark in monogram.

Date	Mintage	F	VF	XF	Unc	BU
1978LIMA	9,000,000	—	—	0.15	0.35	0.50
1979LIMA	4,842,000	—	—	0.15	0.35	0.50
1980LIMA	28,826,000	—	—	0.15	0.35	0.50
1981LIMA	55,785,000	—	—	0.15	0.35	0.50

KM# 235 5 SOLES

2.3404 g., 0.9000 Gold 0.0677 oz. AGW **Obv:** National arms above date **Rev:** Seated Liberty flanked by shield and column

Date	Mintage	F	VF	XF	Unc	BU
1956	4,510	—	—	BV	65.00	—
1957	2,146	—	—	BV	65.00	—
1959	1,536	—	—	BV	65.00	—
1960	8,133	—	—	BV	65.00	—
1961	1,154	—	—	BV	65.00	—
1962	1,550	—	—	BV	65.00	—
1963	3,945	—	—	BV	65.00	—
1964	2,063	—	—	BV	65.00	—
1965	14,000	—	—	BV	65.00	—
1966	4,738	—	—	BV	65.00	—
1967	3,651	—	—	BV	65.00	—
1969	127	—	—	BV	175	—

KM# 252 5 SOLES

2.3000 g., Copper-Nickel **Obv:** National arms within circle **Rev:** Value above designed Incan cup, written value around bottom half

Date	Mintage	F	VF	XF	Unc	BU
1969	10,000,000	0.20	0.40	0.60	1.50	2.00

KM# 254 5 SOLES

Copper-Nickel **Subject:** 150th Anniversary of Independence **Obv:** National arms **Obv. Designer:** Armando Parejo **Rev:** Bust of Tupac Amaru right **Note:** Mint mark in monogram.

Date	Mintage	F	VF	XF	Unc	BU
1971LIMA	3,480,000	0.20	0.40	0.80	2.00	—

KM# 257 5 SOLES

7.8800 g., Copper-Nickel, 25.57 mm. **Obv:** National arms within circle **Rev:** Bust of Tupac Amaru **Edge:** Reeded **Designer:** Armando Pareja **Note:** Mint mark in monogram.

Date	Mintage	F	VF	XF	Unc	BU
1972	2,068,000	—	0.10	0.35	1.00	—
1973	475,000	—	0.10	0.35	1.00	—
1974	—	—	0.10	0.35	1.50	—
1975	—	—	0.10	0.35	1.50	—

KM# 267 5 SOLES

4.4000 g., Copper-Nickel, 22 mm. **Obv:** National arms **Rev:** Bust of Tupac Amaru **Designer:** Armando Pareja **Note:** Mint mark in monogram.

Date	Mintage	F	VF	XF	Unc	BU
1975	—	—	0.10	0.35	1.00	1.75
1976	17,016,000	—	0.10	0.35	1.00	1.75
1977	94,272,000	—	0.10	0.35	1.00	1.75

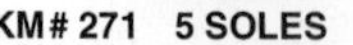

KM# 271 5 SOLES

4.2400 g., Brass, 22.49 mm. **Obv:** National arms within circle **Rev:** Value **Edge:** Plain **Note:** Mint mark in monogram.

Date	Mintage	F	VF	XF	Unc	BU
1978	38,015,000	—	0.10	0.20	0.60	1.00
1979	64,524,000	—	0.10	0.20	0.60	1.00
1980	76,964,000	—	0.10	0.20	0.60	1.00
1981	31,632,000	—	0.10	0.20	0.60	1.00

Date	Mintage	F	VF	XF	Unc	BU
1982	23,252,000	—	0.10	0.20	0.60	1.00
1983	650	20.00	30.00	40.00	60.00	—

KM# 236 10 SOLES

4.6070 g., 0.9000 Gold 0.1333 oz. AGW **Obv:** National arms above date **Rev:** Seated Liberty flanked by shield and column

Date	Mintage	F	VF	XF	Unc	BU
1956	5,410	—	—	BV	130	—
1957	1,300	—	—	BV	130	—
1959	1,103	—	—	BV	130	—
1960	7,178	—	—	BV	130	—
1961	1,634	—	—	BV	130	—
1962	1,676	—	—	BV	130	—
1963	3,372	—	—	BV	130	—
1964	1,554	—	—	BV	130	—
1965	14,000	—	—	BV	130	—
1966	2,601	—	—	BV	130	—
1967	3,002	—	—	BV	130	—
1968	100	—	BV	130	220	—
1969	100	—	BV	130	220	—

KM# 253 10 SOLES

10.0000 g., Copper-Nickel **Obv:** National arms within circle **Rev:** Stylized fish below value **Designer:** Armando Parejo

Date	Mintage	F	VF	XF	Unc	BU
1969	15,000,000	0.25	0.50	0.75	1.75	2.50

KM# 255 10 SOLES

Copper-Nickel **Subject:** 150th Anniversary of Independence **Obv:** National arms **Rev:** Bust of Tupac Amaru right **Designer:** Armando Pareja **Note:** Mint mark in monogram.

Date	Mintage	F	VF	XF	Unc	BU
1971LIMA	2,460,000	0.25	0.50	1.00	2.50	—

KM# 258 10 SOLES

11.7000 g., Copper-Nickel, 30.94 mm. **Obv:** National arms within circle **Rev:** Bust of Tupac Amaru right **Edge:** Reeded **Designer:** Armando Pareja **Note:** Mint mark in monogram.

Date	Mintage	F	VF	XF	Unc	BU
1972	2,235	—	0.10	0.40	1.25	—
1973	1,765	—	0.10	0.40	1.25	—
1974	—	—	0.10	0.40	1.25	—
1975	—	—	0.10	0.40	1.25	—

KM# 272.1 10 SOLES

Brass **Obv:** National arms, small letters: inner circle 18.1mm **Rev:** Head with hat 3/4 right **Edge:** Plain **Designer:** Armando Pareja **Note:** Mint mark in monogram.

Date	Mintage	F	VF	XF	Unc	BU
1978	46,970,000	—	0.10	0.40	0.85	1.50

KM# 272.2 10 SOLES

5.6500 g., Brass, 24.48 mm. **Subject:** Tupac Amaru **Obv:** Small arms , large letters, inner circle 17.2mm **Rev:** Head with hat 3/4 right **Rev. Legend:** TUPAC AMARU, SOLES DE ORO **Edge:** Plain **Designer:** Armando Pareja **Note:** Mint mark in monogram.

Date	Mintage	F	VF	XF	Unc	BU
1978	—	—	0.10	0.40	0.85	1.50
1979	82,220,000	—	0.10	0.40	0.85	1.50
1980	99,595,000	—	0.10	0.40	0.85	1.50
1981	25,660,000	—	0.10	0.40	0.85	1.50
1982	61,035,000	—	0.10	0.40	0.85	1.50
1983	15,820,000	—	0.10	0.40	0.85	1.50

KM# 287 10 SOLES

Brass **Subject:** 150th Anniversary - Birth of Admiral Grau **Obv:** Value within circle **Rev:** Head 1/4 right **Note:** Mint mark in monogram.

Date	Mintage	F	VF	XF	Unc	BU
1984	30,000,000	—	—	0.20	0.50	0.75

KM# 229 20 SOLES

9.3614 g., 0.9000 Gold 0.2709 oz. AGW, 22 mm. **Obv:** National arms **Rev:** Seated Liberty flanked by shield and column

Date	Mintage	F	VF	XF	Unc	BU
1950	1,800	—	—	BV	260	—
1951	9,264	—	—	BV	250	260
1952	424	—	—	BV	260	—
1953	1,435	—	—	BV	260	—
1954	1,732	—	—	BV	260	—
1955	1,971	—	—	BV	260	—
1956	1,201	—	—	BV	260	—
1957	11,000	—	—	BV	250	260
1958	11,000	—	—	BV	250	260
1959	12,000	—	—	BV	250	260
1960	7,753	—	—	BV	250	260
1961	1,825	—	—	BV	260	—
1962	2,282	—	—	BV	260	—
1963	3,892	—	—	BV	260	—
1964	1,302	—	—	BV	260	—
1965	12,000	—	—	BV	250	260
1966	4,001	—	—	BV	250	260
1967	5,003	—	—	BV	250	260
1968	640	—	—	BV	260	—
1969	640	—	—	BV	260	—

KM# 219 50 SOLES

33.4363 g., 0.9000 Gold 0.9675 oz. AGW **Obv:** Head with headdress left **Rev:** Sculpture

Date	Mintage	F	VF	XF	Unc	BU
1930	5,584	—	BV	950	1,600	—
1931	5,538	—	BV	950	1,500	—
1967	10,000	—	—	—	925	—
1968	300	—	—	—	925	—
1969	403	—	—	—	925	—

KM# 230 50 SOLES

23.4056 g., 0.9000 Gold 0.6772 oz. AGW **Obv:** National arms **Rev:** Seated Liberty flanked by shield and column **Note:** Similar to KM#229.

Date	Mintage	F	VF	XF	Unc	BU
1950	1,927	—	—	BV	650	—
1951	5,292	—	—	BV	640	650
1952	1,201	—	—	BV	650	—
1953	1,464	—	—	BV	650	—
1954	1,839	—	—	BV	650	—
1955	1,898	—	—	BV	650	—
1956	11,000	—	—	BV	640	650
1957	11,000	—	—	BV	640	650
1958	11,000	—	—	BV	640	650
1959	5,734	—	—	BV	640	650
1960	2,139	—	—	BV	650	—
1961	1,110	—	—	BV	650	—
1962	3,319	—	—	BV	650	—
1963	3,089	—	—	BV	650	—
1964/3	2,425	—	—	BV	650	—
1964	Inc. above	—	—	BV	650	—
1965	23,000	—	—	BV	640	650
1966	3,409	—	—	BV	640	650
1967	5,805	—	—	BV	640	650
1968	443	—	—	BV	650	—
1969	443	—	—	BV	650	—
1970	553	—	—	BV	650	—

KM# 273 50 SOLES

9.0000 g., Aluminum-Bronze **Obv:** National arms **Rev:** Value within circle **Note:** Mint mark in monogram.

Date	Mintage	F	VF	XF	Unc	BU
1979	1,323,000	—	0.15	0.35	1.00	—
1980	452,573,000	—	0.10	0.20	0.50	—
1981	19,923,000	—	0.10	0.20	0.50	—
1982LIMA	18,471,000	—	0.10	0.20	0.50	—
1982 Without LIMA	Inc. above	—	0.15	0.35	1.00	—
1983	8,175,000	—	0.10	0.20	0.50	—

KM# 297 50 SOLES

Brass **Subject:** 150th Anniversary - Birth of Admiral Grau **Obv:** Value within circle **Rev:** Head 1/4 right **Note:** Mint mark in monogram.

Date	Mintage	F	VF	XF	Unc	BU
1984	11,475,000	—	—	0.20	0.50	—

KM# 321 50 SOLES

Brass, 17 mm. **Subject:** Admiral Grau **Obv:** Value within circle **Rev:** Head 1/4 right **Edge:** Plain

Date	Mintage	F	VF	XF	Unc	BU
1985LIMAE	8,525,000	—	—	0.20	0.50	—

KM# 283 100 SOLES

11.6600 g., Copper-Nickel, 29.83 mm. **Obv:** National arms **Rev:** Value within circle **Edge:** Reeded **Note:** Without mint mark.

Date	Mintage	F	VF	XF	Unc	BU
1980	100,000,000	—	0.20	0.40	1.50	—
1982	—	—	0.20	0.40	1.50	—

KM# 288 100 SOLES

3.0000 g., Brass **Subject:** 150th Anniversary - Birth of Admiral Grau **Obv:** Value within circle **Rev:** Head 1/4 right **Note:** Mint mark in monogram.

Date	Mintage	F	VF	XF	Unc	BU
1984LIMA	20,000,000	—	0.15	0.35	1.00	—

KM# 262 200 SOLES

22.0000 g., 0.8000 Silver 0.5658 oz. ASW **Subject:** Aviation Heroes - Chavez and Guinones **Obv:** National arms **Rev:** Conjoined heads left within circle **Note:** No mint mark.

Date	Mintage	F	VF	XF	Unc	BU
1974	25,000	—	—	—	16.00	—
1975	90,000	—	—	—	12.00	—
1976	25,000	—	—	—	20.00	—
1977	3,000	—	—	—	30.00	—
1978	3,000	—	—	—	30.00	—

KM# 289 500 SOLES

5.2000 g., Brass **Subject:** 150th Anniversary - Birth of Admiral Grau **Obv:** Value within circle **Rev:** Head 1/4 right **Note:** Mint mark in monogram.

Date	Mintage	F	VF	XF	Unc	BU
1984LIMA	16,962,000	—	0.20	0.50	2.00	—

KM# 310 500 SOLES

5.1200 g., Brass **Subject:** Admiral Grau **Obv:** National arms **Rev:** Head 1/4 right without date **Note:** Mint mark in monogram.

Date	Mintage	F	VF	XF	Unc	BU
1985LIMA	13,038,000	—	0.20	0.50	2.50	—

REFORM COINAGE

1000 Soles de Oro = 1 Inti

KM# 291 CENTIMO

1.5000 g., Brass, 15 mm. **Subject:** General Grau **Obv:** Value within circle **Rev:** Head 1/4 right **Note:** Mint mark: LIMA (monogram)

Date	Mintage	F	VF	XF	Unc	BU
1985LIMA	4,199,999	—	—	—	0.25	0.45

KM# 292 5 CENTIMOS

2.0000 g., Brass, 17 mm. **Subject:** General Grau **Obv:** Value within circle **Rev:** Head 1/4 right **Note:** Mint mark: LIMA (monogram)

Date	Mintage	F	VF	XF	Unc	BU
1985LIMA	20,000,000	—	—	—	0.35	0.50

KM# 293 10 CENTIMOS

2.9000 g., Brass, 19 mm. **Subject:** General Grau **Obv:** Value within circle **Rev:** Head 1/4 right **Rev. Legend:** GRAN ALMIRANTE MIGUEL GRAU **Edge:** Plain **Note:** Mint mark: LIMA (monogram)

Date	Mintage	F	VF	XF	Unc	BU
1985LIMA	143,900,000	—	—	—	0.50	0.85
1986LIMA	48,730,000	—	—	—	0.65	1.00
1987LIMA	42,370,000	—	—	—	0.65	1.00

KM# 294 20 CENTIMOS

4.0600 g., Brass, 21 mm. **Subject:** General Grau **Obv:** Value within circle **Rev:** Head 1/4 right **Rev. Legend:** GRAN ALMIRANTE MIGUEL GRAU **Edge:** Plain **Note:** Mint mark: LIMA (monogram)

Date	Mintage	F	VF	XF	Unc	BU
1985LIMA	4,739,000	—	—	—	1.25	1.50
1986LIMA	96,699,000	—	—	—	1.00	1.25
1987LIMA	59,668,000	—	—	—	1.00	1.25

KM# 295 50 CENTIMOS

5.2000 g., Brass, 23 mm. **Subject:** General Grau **Obv:** Value within circle **Rev:** Head 1/4 right **Note:** Mint mark: LIMA (monogram)

Date	Mintage	F	VF	XF	Unc	BU
1985LIMA	43,320,000	—	—	—	1.25	1.50
1986LIMA	72,802,000	—	—	—	1.25	1.50
1987LIMA	63,878,000	—	—	—	1.25	1.50
1988LIMA	80,000,000	—	—	—	1.25	1.50

KM# 296 INTI

7.0000 g., Copper-Nickel, 25 mm. **Subject:** Admiral Grau **Obv:** National arms **Rev:** Head 1/4 right **Rev. Legend:** GRAN ALMIRANTE MIGUEL GRAU, value **Edge:** Reeded **Note:** Mint mark: LIMA (monogram)

Date	Mintage	F	VF	XF	Unc	BU
1985LIMA	15,760,000	—	—	—	1.75	2.00
1986LIMA	87,240,000	—	—	—	1.25	1.50
1987LIMA	120,000,000	—	—	—	1.00	1.25
1988LIMA	17,304,000	—	—	—	1.75	2.00

KM# 300 5 INTIS

8.2000 g., Copper-Nickel, 27 mm. **Subject:** Admiral Grau **Obv:** National arms **Rev:** Head 1/4 right **Rev. Legend:** GRAN ALMIRANTE MIGUEL GRAU, value **Edge:** Reeded **Note:** Mint mark: LIMA (monogram)

Date	Mintage	F	VF	XF	Unc	BU
1985LIMA	3,972	—	—	—	—	—
1986LIMA	28,000	—	—	—	3.50	5.00
1987LIMA	20,106,000	—	—	—	2.50	3.00
1988LIMA	34,084,000	—	—	—	2.50	3.00

REFORM COINAGE

1/M Intis = 1 Nuevo Sol; 100 (New) Centimos = 1 Nuevo Sol

KM# 303.1 CENTIMO

Brass **Obv:** National arms **Rev:** Value flanked by designs **Note:** LIMA monogram is mint mark.

Date	Mintage	F	VF	XF	Unc	BU
1991 CHAVEZ	—	—	—	—	0.35	0.50
1992 CHAVEZ	—	—	—	—	0.45	0.65
1993 CHAVEZ	—	—	—	—	0.35	0.50
1994 CHAVEZ	—	—	—	—	0.35	0.50

KM# 303.2 CENTIMO

Brass **Obv:** National arms **Obv. Legend:** No accent in Peru **Rev:** Large braille, no accent mark above E in centimo, no Chavez **Note:** LIMA monogram is mint mark.

Date	Mintage	F	VF	XF	Unc	BU
1997	—	—	—	—	0.35	—

KM# 303.3 CENTIMO

1.7300 g., Brass, 15.94 mm. **Obv:** National arms **Obv. Legend:** Accent mark in Peru **Rev:** Large braille, accent mark in centimo, no Chavez **Edge:** Plain **Note:** LIMA monogram is mint mark.

Date	Mintage	F	VF	XF	Unc	BU
1999	—	—	—	—	2.50	—

KM# 303.4 CENTIMO

1.8800 g., Brass, 15.9 mm. **Obv:** National arms, accent mark above "u" **Rev:** Without Braille dots, no Chavez **Edge:** Plain **Note:** LIMA monogram is mint mark.

Date	Mintage	F	VF	XF	Unc	BU
2001LIMA	—	—	—	—	0.25	0.40
2002LIMA	—	—	—	—	0.25	0.40
2004LIMA	—	—	—	—	0.25	0.40
2005LIMA	—	—	—	—	0.25	0.40
2006LIMA	—	—	—	—	0.25	0.40

KM# 303.5 CENTIMO

Aluminum **Obv:** National arms **Rev:** Value flanked by designs **Note:** LIMA monogram mint mark.

Date	Mintage	F	VF	XF	Unc	BU
2005	—	—	—	—	0.25	0.40
2006	—	—	—	—	0.25	0.40

KM# 304.1 5 CENTIMOS

2.2600 g., Brass **Obv:** National arms **Rev:** Value flanked by designs **Note:** LIMA monogram is mint mark.

Date	Mintage	F	VF	XF	Unc	BU
1991 CHAVEZ	—	—	—	—	0.45	0.65
1992 CHAVEZ	—	—	—	—	0.50	0.75
1993	—	—	—	—	0.45	0.65
1993 CHAVEZ	—	—	—	—	0.45	0.65
1994	—	—	—	—	0.45	0.65
1995	—	—	—	—	0.45	0.65
1996	—	—	—	—	0.45	0.65

KM# 304.2 5 CENTIMOS

2.7800 g., Brass, 17.92 mm. **Obv:** National arms **Rev:** Small braille with no accent mark above E in centimos, no Chavez **Edge:** Plain **Note:** LIMA monogram is mint mark.

Date	Mintage	F	VF	XF	Unc	BU
1997	—	—	—	—	0.35	0.50
1998	—	—	—	—	0.35	0.50

KM# 304.3 5 CENTIMOS

Brass **Obv:** National arms **Rev:** Small braille with accent mark above E in centimos **Note:** LIMA monogram is mint mark.

Date	Mintage	F	VF	XF	Unc	BU
2000	—	—	—	—	0.35	0.50

KM# 304.4 5 CENTIMOS

2.6900 g., Brass, 18.01 mm. **Obv:** National arms, accent above "u" **Rev:** Without Braille dots, with accent above "e" **Edge:** Plain **Note:** LIMA monogram is mint mark.

Date	Mintage	F	VF	XF	Unc	BU
2001LIMA	—	—	—	—	0.35	0.50
2002LIMA	—	—	—	—	0.35	0.50
2005LIMA	—	—	—	—	0.35	0.50
2006LIMA	—	—	—	—	0.35	0.50
2007LIMA	—	—	—	—	0.35	0.50

KM# 305.1 10 CENTIMOS

3.5000 g., Brass, 20.47 mm. **Obv:** National arms within octagon **Rev:** Value flanked by designs within octagon **Edge:** Plain **Note:** LIMA monogram is mint mark.

Date	Mintage	F	VF	XF	Unc	BU
1991	—	—	—	—	0.65	0.85
1992	—	—	—	—	0.75	1.00
1993	—	—	—	—	0.65	0.85
1993 CHAVEZ	—	—	—	—	0.65	0.85
1994	—	—	—	—	0.65	0.85
1995	—	—	—	—	0.65	0.85
1996	—	—	—	—	0.65	0.85

KM# 305.2 10 CENTIMOS

3.5000 g., Brass **Obv:** National arms within octagon **Rev:** Value flanked by designs within octagon **Note:** LIMA monogram mint mark.

Date	Mintage	F	VF	XF	Unc	BU
1997	—	—	—	—	0.65	0.85
1998LIMA	—	—	—	—	0.65	0.85

KM# 305.3 10 CENTIMOS

3.5000 g., Brass, 20.47 mm. **Obv:** National arms within octagon **Rev:** Value flanked by designs within octagon **Edge:** Plain **Note:** LIMA monogram is mint mark.

Date	Mintage	F	VF	XF	Unc	BU
1999	—	—	—	—	0.65	0.85
2000	—	—	—	—	0.65	0.85

KM# 305.4 10 CENTIMOS

3.5000 g., Brass, 20.47 mm. **Obv:** National arms, accent above "u" **Rev:** Without braille dots, accent above "e" **Edge:** Plain **Note:** LIMA monogram is mint mark.

Date	Mintage	F	VF	XF	Unc	BU
2001LIMA	—	—	—	—	0.65	0.85
2002LIMA	—	—	—	—	0.65	0.85
2003LIMA	—	—	—	—	0.65	0.85
2004LIMA	—	—	—	—	0.65	0.85

Date	Mintage	F	VF	XF	Unc	BU
2005LIMA	—	—	—	—	0.65	0.85
2006LIMA	—	—	—	—	0.65	0.85
2007LIMA	—	—	—	—	0.65	0.85

KM# 306.1 20 CENTIMOS

4.4300 g., Brass, 23 mm. **Obv:** National arms **Rev:** Value **Edge:** Plain **Note:** LIMA monogram is mint mark. Varieties exist.

Date	Mintage	F	VF	XF	Unc	BU
1991 CHAVEZ	—	—	—	—	0.85	1.20
1992 CHAVEZ	—	—	—	—	0.85	1.20
1993 CHAVEZ	—	—	—	—	0.85	1.20
1994	—	—	—	—	0.85	1.20
1996	—	—	—	—	0.85	1.20

KM# 306.2 20 CENTIMOS

4.5300 g., Brass, 23 mm. **Obv:** National arms, accent above "u" **Rev:** Small braille dots, accent above "e" **Edge:** Plain **Note:** LIMA monogram is mint mark. Prev. KM#306.3.

Date	Mintage	F	VF	XF	Unc	BU
2000LIMA	—	—	—	—	0.85	1.20

KM# 306.4 20 CENTIMOS

4.5300 g., Brass, 23 mm. **Obv:** National arms, accent above "u" **Rev:** Without braille dots, accent above "e" **Edge:** Plain **Note:** LIMA monogram is mint mark.

Date	Mintage	F	VF	XF	Unc	BU
2001LIMA	—	—	—	—	0.85	1.20
2002LIMA	—	—	—	—	0.85	1.20
2004LIMA	—	—	—	—	0.85	1.20
2006LIMA	—	—	—	—	0.85	1.20
2007LIMA	—	—	—	—	0.85	1.20

KM# 307.1 50 CENTIMOS

5.5200 g., Copper-Nickel, 22 mm. **Obv:** National arms within octagon **Rev:** Value flanked by sprig and monogram within octagon **Edge:** Reeded **Note:** LIMA monogram is mint mark. Varieties exist.

Date	Mintage	F	VF	XF	Unc	BU
1991	—	—	—	—	1.50	1.75
1992	—	—	—	—	1.75	2.00
1993	—	—	—	—	1.50	1.75
1994	—	—	—	—	1.50	1.75
1996	—	—	—	—	1.50	1.75

KM# 307.2 50 CENTIMOS

5.5200 g., Copper-Nickel, 22 mm. **Obv:** National arms within octagon **Rev:** Value flanked by sprig and monogram within octagon **Edge:** Reeded **Note:** LIMA monogram is mint mark.

Date	Mintage	F	VF	XF	Unc	BU
1997	—	—	—	—	1.50	1.75
1998	—	—	—	—	1.50	1.75

KM# 307.3 50 CENTIMOS

5.5200 g., Copper-Nickel, 22 mm. **Obv:** National arms within octagon **Rev:** Value flanked by sprig and monogram within octagon **Edge:** Reeded **Note:** LIMA monogram is mint mark.

Date	Mintage	F	VF	XF	Unc	BU
2000	—	—	—	—	1.50	1.75

KM# 307.4 50 CENTIMOS

5.5200 g., Copper-Nickel, 22 mm. **Obv:** National arms, accent above "u" **Rev:** Without braille, accent above "e" **Edge:** Reeded **Note:** LIMA monogram is mint mark.

Date	Mintage	F	VF	XF	Unc	BU
2001LIMA	—	—	—	—	1.50	1.75
2002LIMA	—	—	—	—	1.50	1.75
2003LIMA	—	—	—	—	1.50	1.75
2004LIMA	—	—	—	—	1.50	1.75
2006LIMA	—	—	—	—	1.50	1.75
2007LIMA	—	—	—	—	1.50	1.75

KM# 308.1 NUEVO SOL

7.3000 g., Copper-Nickel, 25.48 mm. **Obv:** National arms within octagon **Rev:** Written value flanked by sprig and monogram within octagon **Edge:** Reeded **Note:** LIMA monogram is mint mark.

Date	Mintage	F	VF	XF	Unc	BU
1991	—	—	—	—	5.00	5.50
1992	—	—	—	—	5.00	5.50
1993	—	—	—	—	5.00	5.50
1994	—	—	—	—	4.00	4.50
1995	—	—	—	—	4.00	4.50
1996	—	—	—	—	4.00	4.50

KM# 308.2 NUEVO SOL

7.3000 g., Copper-Nickel, 25.48 mm. **Obv:** National arms within octagon **Rev:** Written value flanked by sprig and monogram within octagon **Edge:** Reeded **Note:** LIMA monogram is mint mark.

Date	Mintage	F	VF	XF	Unc	BU
1991	—	5.00	10.00	25.00	55.00	—

KM# 308.3 NUEVO SOL

7.3000 g., Copper-Nickel, 25.48 mm. **Obv:** National arms within octagon **Rev:** Value flanked by sprig and monogram within octagon **Edge:** Reeded **Note:** LIMA monogram is mint mark.

Date	Mintage	F	VF	XF	Unc	BU
1999	—	—	—	—	4.00	4.50
2000	—	—	—	—	4.00	4.50

KM# 308.4 NUEVO SOL

7.3000 g., Copper-Nickel, 25.48 mm. **Obv:** National arms, accent above "u" **Rev:** Without braille, accent above "e" **Edge:** Reeded **Note:** LIMA monogram is mint mark.

Date	Mintage	F	VF	XF	Unc	BU
2001LIMA	—	—	—	—	4.00	4.50
2002LIMA	—	—	—	—	4.00	4.50
2003LIMA	—	—	—	—	4.00	4.50
2004LIMA	—	—	—	—	4.00	4.50
2005LIMA	—	—	—	—	4.00	4.50
2006LIMA	—	—	—	—	4.00	4.50
2007LIMA	—	—	—	—	4.00	4.50

KM# 313 2 NUEVOS SOLES

5.5800 g., Bi-Metallic Brass center in Steel ring, 22.22 mm. **Obv:** National arms within circle **Rev:** Stylized bird in flight to left of value within circle **Edge:** Plain **Note:** LIMA monogram is mint mark.

Date	Mintage	F	VF	XF	Unc	BU
1994LIMA	—	—	—	—	4.50	5.00
1995LIMA	—	—	—	—	4.50	5.00
2002LIMA	—	—	—	—	4.50	5.00
2003LIMA	—	—	—	—	4.50	5.00
2004LIMA	—	—	—	—	4.50	5.00
2005LIMA	—	—	—	—	4.50	5.00
2006LIMA	—	—	—	—	4.50	5.00

KM# 316 5 NUEVOS SOLES

6.6700 g., Bi-Metallic Brass center in Steel ring, 24.27 mm. **Obv:** National arms within circle **Rev:** Stylized bird in flight to left of value within circle **Edge:** Plain **Note:** LIMA monogram is mint mark.

Date	Mintage	F	VF	XF	Unc	BU
1994LIMA	—	—	—	—	6.50	7.00
1995LIMA	—	—	—	—	6.50	7.00
2000LIMA	—	—	—	—	6.50	7.00
2001LIMA	—	—	—	—	6.50	7.00
2002LIMA	—	—	—	—	6.50	7.00
2004LIMA	—	—	—	—	6.50	7.00
2005LIMA	—	—	—	—	6.50	7.00
2006LIMA	—	—	—	—	6.50	7.00

TRADE COINAGE

KM# 210 1/5 LIBRA (Pound)

1.5976 g., 0.9170 Gold 0.0471 oz. AGW **Obv:** Shield within sprigs with small radiant sun above **Rev:** Head with headband right **Note:** Struck at Lima.

Date	Mintage	F	VF	XF	Unc	BU
1906 GOZF	106,000	—	—	BV	45.00	—
1907 GOZF	31,000	—	—	BV	45.00	—
1907 GOZG	—	—	—	BV	45.00	—
1909 GOZG	—	—	—	BV	45.00	—
1910 GOZG	—	—	—	BV	45.00	—
1911 GOZF	62,000	—	—	BV	45.00	—
1911 GOZG	—	—	—	BV	45.00	—
1912 GOZG	—	—	—	BV	45.00	—
1912 POZG	—	—	—	BV	45.00	—
1913 POZG	60,000	—	—	BV	45.00	—
1914 POZG	25,000	—	—	BV	45.00	—
1914 PBLG	Inc. above	—	—	—	—	—
Note: Reported, not confirmed						
1915	10,000	—	—	BV	45.00	—
1916	13,000	—	—	—	—	—
Note: Reported, not confirmed						
1917	3,896	—	—	BV	45.00	—
1918	16,000	—	—	BV	45.00	—
1919	10,000	—	—	BV	45.00	—
1920	72,000	—	—	BV	45.00	—
1922	8,110	—	—	BV	45.00	—
1923	27,000	—	—	BV	45.00	—
1924	—	—	—	BV	45.00	—
1925	20,000	—	—	BV	45.00	—
1926	11,000	—	—	BV	45.00	—
1927	14,000	—	—	BV	45.00	—
1928	9,322	—	—	BV	45.00	—
1929	8,971	—	—	BV	45.00	—
1930	9,991	—	—	BV	55.00	—
1953 BBR	9,821	—	—	BV	50.00	—
1955 ZBR	10,000	—	—	BV	50.00	—
1958 ZBR	5,098	—	—	BV	45.00	—
1959 ZBR	6,308	—	—	BV	45.00	—
1960 ZBR	6,083	—	—	BV	45.00	—
1961 ZBR	12,000	—	—	BV	45.00	—
1962 ZBR	5,431	—	—	BV	45.00	—
1963 ZBR	11,000	—	—	BV	45.00	—
1964 ZBR	25,000	—	—	BV	45.00	—
1965 ZBR	19,000	—	—	BV	45.00	—
1966 ZBR	60,000	—	—	BV	45.00	—
1967 BBR	9,914	—	—	BV	45.00	—
1968 BBR	—	—	—	BV	45.00	—
1968 BBB	4,781	—	—	BV	45.00	—
1969 BBB	15,000	—	—	BV	45.00	—

KM# 209 1/2 LIBRA (Pound)

3.9940 g., 0.9170 Gold 0.1177 oz. AGW **Obv:** Shield within sprigs with radiant sun above **Rev:** Head with headband right

Date	Mintage	F	VF	XF	Unc	BU
1902 ROZF	7,800	—	BV	110	120	—
1903 ROZF	7,245	—	BV	110	120	—
1904 ROZF	8,360	—	BV	110	120	—
1905 ROZF	8,010	—	BV	110	120	—
1905 GOZF	Inc. above	—	BV	110	120	—
1906 GOZF	9,176	—	BV	110	120	—
1907 GOZG	—	—	BV	110	120	—
1908 GOZG	8,180	—	BV	110	120	—
1953 BBR	9,210	—	BV	110	120	—

Date	Mintage	F	VF	XF	Unc	BU
1955 ZBR	14,000	—	—	BV	110	—
1961 ZBR	752	—	—	BV	110	—
1962 ZBR	4,286	—	—	BV	110	—
1963 ZBR	908	—	—	BV	110	—
1964 ZBR	10,000	—	—	BV	110	—
1965 ZBR	5,490	—	—	BV	110	—
1966 ZBR	44,000	—	—	BV	110	—
1967 BBR	—	—	—	BV	110	—
1968 BBB	Inc. above	—	—	BV	110	—
1968 BBR	—	—	—	—	—	—
1969 BBB	4,400	—	—	BV	110	—

KM# 207 LIBRA (Pound)

7.9881 g., 0.9170 Gold 0.2355 oz. AGW **Obv:** Shield within sprigs with radiant sun above **Rev:** Head with headband right

Date	Mintage	VG	F	VF	XF	Unc
1901 ROZF	81,000	—	—	—	BV	225
1902 ROZF	89,000	—	—	—	BV	225
1903 ROZF	100,000	—	—	—	BV	225
1904 ROZF	33,000	—	—	—	BV	225
1905 GOZF	—	—	—	—	BV	225
1905 ROZF	141,000	—	—	—	BV	225
1906 GOZF	201,000	—	—	—	BV	225
1907 GOZG	Inc. above	—	—	—	BV	225
1908 GOZG	36,000	—	—	—	BV	225
1909 GOZG	52,000	—	—	—	BV	225
1910 GOZG	47,000	—	—	—	BV	225
1911 GOZG	42,000	—	—	—	BV	225
1912 GOZG	54,000	—	—	—	BV	225
1912 POZG	Inc. above	—	—	—	BV	225
1913 POZG	—	—	—	—	BV	225
1914 POZG	—	—	—	—	BV	225
1914 PBLG	119,000	—	—	—	BV	225
1915 PVG	91,000	—	—	—	BV	225
1915 PMGG	Inc. above	—	—	—	BV	225
1915	Inc. above	—	—	—	BV	225
1916	582,000	—	—	—	BV	225
1917	1,928,000	—	—	—	BV	225
1918	600,000	—	—	—	BV	225
1919	Inc. above	—	—	—	BV	225
1920	152,000	—	—	—	BV	225
1921	Inc. above	—	—	—	BV	225
1922	13,000	—	—	—	BV	225
1923	15,000	—	—	—	BV	225
1924	8,113	—	—	—	BV	225
1925	9,068	—	—	—	BV	225
1926	4,596	—	—	—	BV	225
1927	8,360	—	—	—	BV	225
1928	2,184	—	—	—	BV	225
1929	3,119	—	—	—	BV	225
1930	1,050	—	—	—	BV	225
1959 ZBR	605	—	—	—	BV	250
1961 ZBR	402	—	—	—	BV	250
1962 ZBR	6,203	—	—	—	BV	225
1963 ZBR	302	—	—	—	BV	260
1964 ZBR	13,000	—	—	—	BV	225
1965 ZBR	9,917	—	—	—	BV	225
1966 ZBR	39,000	—	—	—	BV	225
1967 BBR	2,002	—	—	—	BV	225
1968 BBR	7,307	—	—	—	BV	225
1969 BBR	7,307	—	—	—	BV	225

PHILIPPINES

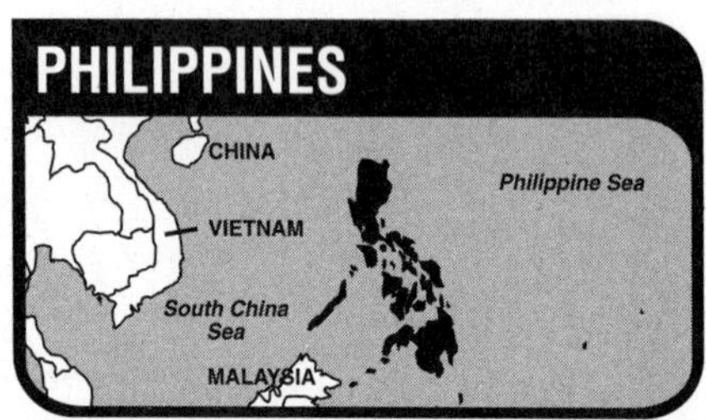

The Republic of the Philippines, an archipelago in the western Pacific 500 miles (805 km.) from the southeast coast of Asia, has an area of 115,830 sq. mi. (300,000 sq. km.) and a population of *64.9 million. Capital: Manila. The economy of the 7,000-island group is based on agriculture, forestry and fishing. Timber, coconut products, sugar and hemp are exported.

Migration to the Philippines began about 30,000 years ago when land bridges connected the islands with Borneo and Sumatra. Ferdinand Magellan claimed the islands for Spain in 1521. The first permanent settlement was established by Miguel de Legazpi at Cebu April 1565. Manila was established in 1572. A British expedition captured Manila and occupied the Spanish colony in October 1762, but returned it to Spain by the treaty of Paris, 1763. Spain held the Philippines despite growing Filipino nationalism until 1898 when they were ceded to the United States at the end of the Spanish-American War. The Philippines became a self-governing commonwealth under the United States in 1935, and attained independence as the Republic of the Philippines on July 4, 1946.

MINT MARKS

(b) Brussels, privy marks only
BSP - Bangko Sentral Pilipinas
D - Denver, 1944-1945
(Lt) - Llantrisant
M, MA - Manila
PM - Pobjoy Mint
S - San Francisco, 1903-1947
SGV - Madrid
(Sh) - Sherritt
(US) - United States
FM - Franklin Mint, U.S.A.*
(VDM) - Vereinigte Deutsche Metall Werks; Altona, Germany
Star - Manila (Spanish) = Manila

***NOTE:** From 1975-1977 the Franklin Mint produced coinage in up to 3 different qualities. Beginning in 1978only (U) and (P) were struck. Qualities of issue are designated in ( ) after each date and are defined as follows:

(M) MATTE - Normal circulation strike or a dull finish produced by sandblasting special uncirculated (polish-finish) or proof quality dies.

(U) SPECIAL UNCIRCULATED - Polished or prooflike in appearance without any frosted features.

(P) PROOF - The highest quality obtainable having mirror-like fields and frosted features.

MONETARY SYSTEM

4 Quartos = 1 Real
8 Reales = 1 Peso

UNITED STATES ADMINISTRATION

DECIMAL COINAGE

KM# 162 1/2 CENTAVO

Bronze **Obv:** Man seated beside hammer and anvil **Rev:** Eagle above stars and striped shield

Date	Mintage	F	VF	XF	Unc	BU
1903	12,084,000	0.50	1.00	1.50	10.00	20.00
1903 Proof	2,558	Value: 65.00				
1904	5,654,000	0.50	1.25	2.00	15.00	35.00
1904 Proof	1,355	Value: 85.00				
1905 Proof	471	Value: 350				
1906 Proof	500	Value: 225				
1908 Proof	500	Value: 225				

KM# 163 CENTAVO

4.7000 g., Bronze **Obv:** Man seated beside hammer and anvil **Rev:** Eagle above stars and striped shield

Date	Mintage	F	VF	XF	Unc	BU
1903	10,790,000	0.50	1.25	2.50	17.50	40.00
1903 Proof	2,558	Value: 70.00				
1904	17,040,000	0.50	1.25	3.00	20.00	40.00
1904 Proof	1,355	Value: 75.00				
1905	10,000,000	0.50	1.50	3.50	22.00	45.00
1905 Proof	471	Value: 140				
1906 Proof	500	Value: 100				
1908 Proof	500	Value: 100				
1908S	2,187,000	2.50	4.00	10.00	60.00	90.00
1909S	1,738,000	8.00	14.00	25.00	100	175
1910S	2,700,000	2.00	5.00	10.00	55.00	90.00
1911S	4,803,000	1.00	2.50	5.00	30.00	60.00
1912S	3,000,000	3.00	5.00	12.50	80.00	125
1913S	5,000,000	2.00	4.00	6.50	50.00	85.00
1914S	5,000,000	1.00	2.50	6.00	50.00	75.00
1915S	2,500,000	20.00	40.00	95.00	650	1,200
1916S	4,330,000	6.00	12.50	25.00	110	200
1917/6S	7,070,000	25.00	45.00	95.00	375	550
1917S	Inc. above	4.50	8.00	10.00	45.00	85.00
1918S	11,660,000	2.00	4.00	10.00	70.00	150
1918S Large S	Inc. above	75.00	125	300	1,300	1,900
1919S	4,540,000	0.75	2.50	6.00	60.00	125
1920S	2,500,000	4.50	9.50	22.00	150	300
1920	3,552,000	1.00	4.00	8.50	60.00	125
1921	7,283,000	0.75	3.50	7.50	50.00	100
1922	3,519,000	0.50	2.50	7.50	50.00	100
1925M	9,332,000	0.50	2.50	5.00	25.00	65.00
1926M	9,000,000	0.50	2.00	5.00	25.00	55.00
1927M	9,270,000	0.35	2.00	6.00	25.00	65.00
1928M	9,150,000	0.35	2.00	5.00	25.00	50.00
1929M	5,657,000	1.00	3.00	6.00	35.00	80.00
1930M	5,577,000	0.50	2.00	4.00	25.00	50.00
1931M	5,659,000	0.50	2.00	4.00	25.00	50.00
1932M	4,000,000	0.75	2.50	6.00	30.00	55.00
1933M	8,393,000	0.25	2.00	4.00	25.00	45.00
1934M	3,179,000	0.75	2.50	10.00	60.00	100
1936M	17,455,000	0.25	2.00	7.00	40.00	80.00

KM# 164 5 CENTAVOS

Copper-Nickel, 21.3 mm. **Obv:** Man seated beside hammer and anvil **Rev:** Eagle above stars and striped shield

Date	Mintage	F	VF	XF	Unc	BU
1903	8,910,000	0.50	1.25	3.00	25.00	40.00
1903 Proof	2,558	Value: 60.00				
1904	1,075,000	0.75	2.00	5.00	27.00	40.00
1904 Proof	1,355	Value: 75.00				
1905 Proof	471	Value: 175				
1906 Proof	500	Value: 145				
1908 Proof	500	Value: 145				
1916S	300,000	25.00	60.00	125	600	1,100
1917S	2,300,000	2.00	5.00	10.00	125	250
1918/7S	—	3.00	9.00	18.50	150	—
1918S	2,780,000	2.00	5.00	12.50	120	250
1919S	1,220,000	2.50	7.50	13.00	150	300
1920	1,421,000	3.00	10.00	15.00	150	250
1921	2,132,000	2.00	5.00	10.00	90.00	200
1925M	1,000,000	5.00	12.50	25.00	160	250
1926M	1,200,000	3.00	6.50	17.50	125	175
1927M	1,000,000	2.00	5.00	7.50	75.00	125
1928M	1,000,000	3.00	5.00	7.50	75.00	120

KM# 173 5 CENTAVOS

Copper-Nickel **Obv:** Man seated beside hammer and anvil **Rev:** Eagle above stars and striped shield **Note:** Mule.

Date	Mintage	F	VF	XF	Unc	BU
1918S	—	200	500	1,250	3,000	8,000

KM# 175 5 CENTAVOS

4.7500 g., Copper-Nickel, 19 mm. **Obv:** Man seated beside hammer and anvil **Rev:** Eagle above stars and striped shield

Date	Mintage	F	VF	XF	Unc	BU
1930M	2,905,000	1.00	2.50	4.50	35.00	60.00
1931M	3,477,000	1.00	2.50	5.00	50.00	95.00
1932M	3,956,000	1.00	1.50	4.00	35.00	70.00
1934M	2,154,000	1.00	3.50	7.50	65.00	125
1935M	2,754,000	1.00	1.50	6.50	100	200

KM# 165 10 CENTAVOS

2.6924 g., 0.9000 Silver 0.0779 oz. ASW **Obv:** Female standing beside hammer and anvil **Rev:** Eagle above stars and striped shield

Date	Mintage	F	VF	XF	Unc	BU
1903	5,103,000	1.25	3.50	5.50	35.00	65.00
1903 Proof	2,558	Value: 80.00				
1903S	1,200,000	9.00	17.50	30.00	250	700
1904	11,000	10.00	20.00	35.00	80.00	135
1904 Proof	1,355	Value: 80.00				
1904S	5,040,000	1.50	3.00	6.00	40.00	80.00
1905 Proof	471	Value: 125				
1906 Proof	500	Value: 100				

KM# 169 10 CENTAVOS

2.0000 g., 0.7500 Silver 0.0482 oz. ASW **Obv:** Female standing beside hammer and anvil **Rev:** Eagle above stars and striped shield

Date	Mintage	F	VF	XF	Unc	BU
1907	1,501,000	1.50	4.00	8.00	50.00	85.00
1907S	4,930,000	1.25	2.00	3.00	40.00	70.00
1908 Proof	500	Value: 100				
1908S	3,364,000	1.25	2.00	4.00	45.00	80.00
1909S	312,000	15.00	25.00	60.00	400	900
1910S	—	—	—	—	—	—

Note: Unknown in any collection. Counterfeits of the 1910S are commonly encountered

Date	Mintage	F	VF	XF	Unc	BU
1911S	1,101,000	3.00	4.00	10.00	125	350
1912S	1,010,000	2.25	4.50	11.00	125	300
1913S	1,361,000	1.50	5.00	12.00	110	250
1914S	1,180,000	3.00	7.50	17.50	175	300
1915S	450,000	9.50	20.00	40.00	300	650

Date	Mintage	F	VF	XF	Unc	BU
1917S	5,991,000	1.75	2.00	3.50	40.00	75.00
1918S	8,420,000	1.25	1.50	3.00	30.00	50.00
1919S	1,630,000	1.25	2.00	5.00	45.00	75.00
1920	520,000	4.50	6.50	15.00	85.00	200
1921	3,863,000	1.25	2.00	3.00	30.00	50.00
1929M	1,000,000	1.25	1.50	2.50	25.00	45.00
1935M	1,280,000	1.25	1.50	2.25	20.00	40.00

KM# 166 20 CENTAVOS

5.3849 g., 0.9000 Silver 0.1558 oz. ASW **Obv:** Female standing beside hammer and anvil **Rev:** Eagle above stars and striped shield

Date	Mintage	F	VF	XF	Unc	BU
1903	5,353,000	2.50	3.00	7.50	40.00	90.00
1903 Proof	2,558	Value: 125				
1903S	150,000	12.00	22.00	70.00	750	1,100
1904	11,000	16.00	30.00	40.00	100	175
1904 Proof	1,355	Value: 125				
1904S	2,060,000	3.00	5.00	10.00	100	175
1905 Proof	471	Value: 200				
1905S	420,000	10.00	16.00	35.00	200	700
1906 Proof	500	Value: 150				

KM# 170 20 CENTAVOS

4.0000 g., 0.7500 Silver 0.0964 oz. ASW **Obv:** Female standing beside hammer and anvil **Rev:** Eagle above stars and striped shield

Date	Mintage	F	VF	XF	Unc	BU
1907	1,251,000	2.25	4.00	12.50	150	250
1907S	3,165,000	2.25	3.00	6.00	35.00	125
1908 Proof	500	Value: 200				
1908S	1,535,000	2.25	4.00	12.50	60.00	125
1909S	450,000	7.50	25.00	50.00	375	950
1910S	500,000	7.50	22.00	80.00	400	950
1911S	505,000	6.00	20.00	45.00	275	850
1912S	750,000	4.00	12.50	30.00	200	300
1913S/S	949,000	9.00	22.00	50.00	250	400
1913S	Inc. above	3.00	7.50	15.00	150	225
1914S	795,000	3.50	8.00	20.00	200	450
1915S	655,000	10.00	15.00	40.00	425	950
1916S	1,435,000	3.00	8.50	20.00	125	225
1917S	3,151,000	2.25	3.00	5.00	50.00	95.00
1918S	5,560,000	BV	2.00	5.00	45.00	75.00
1919S	850,000	2.25	5.00	12.50	125	200
1920	1,046,000	2.50	6.00	15.00	125	175
1921	1,843,000	BV	2.00	5.00	75.00	100
1929M	1,970,000	BV	2.00	4.00	30.00	50.00

KM# 174 20 CENTAVOS

4.0000 g., 0.7500 Silver 0.0964 oz. ASW **Obv:** Female standing beside hammer and anvil **Rev:** Eagle above stars and striped shield **Note:** Mule.

Date	Mintage	F	VF	XF	Unc	BU
1928M	100,000	7.50	20.00	75.00	800	1,300

KM# 167 50 CENTAVOS

13.4784 g., 0.9000 Silver 0.3900 oz. ASW **Obv:** Female standing beside hammer and anvil **Rev:** Eagle above stars and striped shield

Date	Mintage	F	VF	XF	Unc	BU
1903	3,102,000	6.50	8.50	17.50	80.00	125
1903 Proof	2,558	Value: 145				
1903S 2 Known	—	—	—	22,000	—	—
1904	11,000	25.00	40.00	70.00	150	225
1904 Proof	1,355	Value: 175				

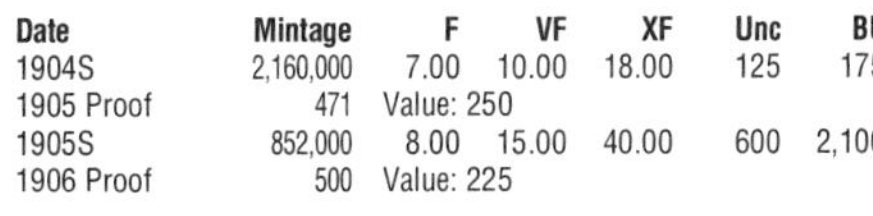

Date	Mintage	F	VF	XF	Unc	BU
1904S	2,160,000	7.00	10.00	18.00	125	175
1905 Proof	471	Value: 250				
1905S	852,000	8.00	15.00	40.00	600	2,100
1906 Proof	500	Value: 225				

KM# 171 50 CENTAVOS

10.0000 g., 0.7500 Silver 0.2411 oz. ASW **Obv:** Female standing beside hammer and anvil **Rev:** Eagle above stars and striped shield

Date	Mintage	F	VF	XF	Unc	BU
1907	1,201,000	6.00	15.00	40.00	150	550
1907S	2,112,000	4.25	7.50	20.00	125	300
1908 Proof	500	Value: 225				
1908S	1,601,000	4.50	10.00	25.00	250	2,000
1909S	528,000	6.00	17.50	50.00	300	800
1917S	674,000	5.00	10.00	20.00	150	300
1918S	2,202,000	4.00	5.00	9.50	100	150
1919S	1,200,000	4.00	6.50	12.50	125	175
1920	420,000	4.00	5.50	10.00	40.00	100
1921	2,317,000	BV	4.00	6.00	30.00	60.00

KM# 168 PESO

26.9568 g., 0.9000 Silver 0.7800 oz. ASW **Obv:** Female standing beside hammer and anvil **Rev:** Eagle above stars and striped shield

Date	Mintage	F	VF	XF	Unc	BU
1903	2,791,000	14.50	18.00	27.00	175	450
1903 Proof	2,558	Value: 250				
1903S	11,361,000	13.50	16.00	20.00	125	200
1904	11,000	65.00	75.00	110	250	400
1904 Proof	1,355	Value: 275				
1904S	6,600,000	14.00	17.00	25.00	150	225
1905S curved serif on 1	6,056,000	15.00	20.00	30.00	225	350
1905 Proof	471	Value: 750				
1905S straight serif on 1	—	30.00	45.00	60.00	400	2,400
1906 Proof	500	Value: 600				
1906S	201,000	1,000	1,800	3,000	16,000	26,000

Note: Counterfeits of the 1906S exist

KM# 172 PESO

20.0000 g., 0.8000 Silver 0.5144 oz. ASW **Obv:** Female standing beside hammer and anvil **Rev:** Eagle above stars and striped shield

Date	Mintage	F	VF	XF	Unc	BU
1907 Proof, 2 known	—	—	—	—	—	—
1907S	10,276,000	9.50	10.00	13.00	75.00	140
1908 Proof	500	Value: 650				
1908S	20,955,000	9.50	10.00	13.00	75.00	140
1909S	7,578,000	9.50	10.00	15.00	90.00	150
1910S	3,154,000	10.00	12.50	25.00	175	400
1911S	463,000	16.00	30.00	60.00	750	2,700
1912S	680,000	17.00	35.00	80.00	1,500	6,500

UNITED STATES ADMINISTRATION

Commonwealth

DECIMAL COINAGE

KM# 179 CENTAVO

5.3000 g., Bronze, 25 mm. **Obv:** Male seated beside hammer and anvil **Rev:** Eagle above shield

Date	Mintage	F	VF	XF	Unc	BU
1937M	15,790,000	0.25	2.00	3.00	20.00	35.00
1938M	10,000,000	0.25	1.50	3.00	15.00	30.00
1939M	6,500,000	0.25	2.00	4.00	30.00	40.00
1940M	4,000,000	0.25	1.25	2.25	15.00	25.00
1941M	5,000,000	0.25	2.00	3.50	20.00	30.00
1944S	58,000,000	—	0.25	0.50	1.50	2.50

KM# 180 5 CENTAVOS

4.8000 g., Copper-Nickel **Obv:** Male seated beside hammer and anvil **Rev:** Eagle with wings open above shield

Date	Mintage	F	VF	XF	Unc	BU
1937M	2,494,000	1.00	2.50	5.50	45.00	80.00
1938M	4,000,000	0.50	1.25	2.50	20.00	35.00
1941M	2,750,000	1.00	2.50	6.00	40.00	90.00

KM# 180a 5 CENTAVOS

4.9200 g., Copper-Nickel-Zinc, 19 mm. **Obv:** Male seated beside hammer and anvil **Rev:** Eagle with wings open above shield

Date	Mintage	F	VF	XF	Unc	BU
1944	21,198,000	—	0.50	1.00	2.50	4.50
1944S	14,040,000	—	0.25	0.30	1.25	2.50
1945S	72,796,000	—	0.25	0.30	1.00	2.50

KM# 181 10 CENTAVOS

2.0000 g., 0.7500 Silver 0.0482 oz. ASW, 16.7 mm. **Obv:** Female standing beside hammer and anvil **Rev:** Eagle with wings open above shield

Date	Mintage	F	VF	XF	Unc	BU
1937M	3,500,000	1.00	2.00	3.00	20.00	30.00
1938M	3,750,000	BV	1.00	2.00	12.50	18.00
1941M	2,500,000	BV	1.50	2.50	15.00	25.00
1944D	31,592,000	—	—	BV	2.00	3.00
1945D	137,208,000	—	—	BV	2.00	2.50

Note: 1937, 1938, and 1941 dated strikes have inverted W's for M's

KM# 182 20 CENTAVOS

4.0000 g., 0.7500 Silver 0.0964 oz. ASW, 21 mm. **Obv:** Female standing beside hammer and anvil **Rev:** Eagle with wings open above shield

Date	Mintage	F	VF	XF	Unc	BU
1937M	2,665,000	BV	1.75	3.00	17.50	30.00
1938M	3,000,000	BV	1.50	2.50	13.00	23.00
1941M	1,500,000	BV	1.50	2.50	13.00	27.00
1944D	28,596,000	—	—	BV	2.00	3.00
1944D/S	—	12.00	16.50	20.00	55.00	100
1945D	82,804,000	—	—	BV	2.00	3.00

KM# 176 50 CENTAVOS

10.0000 g., 0.7500 Silver 0.2411 oz. ASW, 27.5 mm. **Subject:** Establishment of the Commonwealth **Obv:** Busts facing each other **Rev:** Eagle above shield **Designer:** Ambrosia Morales

Date	Mintage	F	VF	XF	Unc	BU
1936	20,000	—	30.00	50.00	100	150

KM# 183 50 CENTAVOS

10.0000 g., 0.7500 Silver 0.2411 oz. ASW, 27.5 mm. **Obv:** Female standing beside hammer and anvil **Rev:** Eagle with wings open above shield

Date	Mintage	F	VF	XF	Unc	BU
1944S	19,187,000	—	—	BV	5.00	7.00
1945S	18,120,000	—	—	BV	5.00	7.00

KM# 177 PESO

20.0000 g., 0.9000 Silver 0.5787 oz. ASW, 35 mm. **Subject:** Establishment of the Commonwealth **Obv:** Conjoined busts left **Rev:** Eagle with wings open above shield **Designer:** Ambrosia Morales

Date	Mintage	F	VF	XF	Unc	BU
1936	10,000	—	50.00	75.00	140	235

KM# 178 PESO

20.0000 g., 0.9000 Silver 0.5787 oz. ASW, 35 mm. **Subject:** Establishment of the Commonwealth **Obv:** Conjoined busts left **Rev:** Eagle with wings open above shield **Designer:** Ambrosia Morales

Date	Mintage	F	VF	XF	Unc	BU
1936	10,000	—	50.00	75.00	140	235

REPUBLIC

DECIMAL COINAGE

KM# 186 CENTAVO

Bronze, 19 mm. **Obv:** Shield of arms **Rev:** Male seated beside hammer and anvil

Date	Mintage	F	VF	XF	Unc	BU
1958	20,000,000	—	—	0.10	0.25	0.50
1960	40,000,000	—	—	0.10	0.15	0.35
1962	30,000,000	—	—	0.10	0.15	0.35
1963	130,000,000	—	—	0.10	0.15	0.25

KM# 187 5 CENTAVOS

4.8000 g., Brass, 21 mm. **Obv:** Shield of arms **Rev:** Male seated beside hammer and anvil

Date	Mintage	F	VF	XF	Unc	BU
1958	10,000,000	—	—	0.10	0.25	0.50
1959	10,000,000	—	—	0.10	0.20	0.50
1960	40,000,000	—	—	0.10	0.15	0.40
1962	40,000,000	—	—	0.10	0.15	0.40
1963	50,000,000	—	—	0.10	0.15	0.40
1964	100,000,000	—	—	—	0.10	0.40
1966	10,000,000	—	—	0.10	0.20	0.50

KM# 188 10 CENTAVOS

2.0000 g., Copper-Zinc-Nickel, 17.8 mm. **Obv:** Shield of arms **Rev:** Female standing beside hammer and anvil

Date	Mintage	F	VF	XF	Unc	BU
1958	10,000,000	—	—	0.15	0.25	0.50
1960	70,000,000	—	—	0.15	0.20	0.40
1962	50,000,000	—	—	0.15	0.20	0.40
1963	50,000,000	—	—	0.15	0.20	0.40
1964	100,000,000	—	—	0.10	0.20	0.40
1966	110,000,000	—	—	0.10	0.20	0.45

KM# 189.1 25 CENTAVOS

5.0000 g., Copper-Zinc-Nickel **Obv:** Shield of arms **Rev:** Female standing beside hammer and anvil

Date	Mintage	F	VF	XF	Unc	BU
1958	10,000,000	—	—	0.25	0.50	0.75
1960	10,000,000	—	—	0.30	0.50	0.75
1962	40,000,000	—	—	0.25	0.50	0.75
1964	49,800,000	—	—	0.20	0.35	0.75
1966	50,000,000	—	0.25	0.50	1.00	1.25

KM# 189.2 25 CENTAVOS

Copper-Zinc-Nickel **Obv:** Shield of arms **Rev:** Female standing beside hammer and anvil

Date	Mintage	F	VF	XF	Unc	BU
1966	40,000,000	—	—	0.20	0.40	1.00
1966 Matte finish	Inc. above	—	—	—	—	—

KM# 184 50 CENTAVOS

10.0000 g., 0.7500 Silver 0.2411 oz. ASW, 27.5 mm. **Obv:** Shield of arms above date and value **Rev:** Uniformed bust right **Designer:** Laura Gardin Fraser

Date	Mintage	F	VF	XF	Unc	BU
1947S	200,000	—	BV	4.00	7.50	9.00

KM# 190 50 CENTAVOS

10.0000 g., Copper-Zinc-Nickel, 30.3 mm. **Obv:** Shield of arms **Rev:** Female standing beside hammer and anvil

Date	Mintage	F	VF	XF	Unc	BU
1958	5,000,000	—	0.30	0.45	1.00	1.50
1964	25,000,000	—	0.20	0.30	0.75	1.25

KM# 191 1/2 PESO

12.5000 g., 0.9000 Silver 0.3617 oz. ASW **Subject:** 100th Anniversary Birth of Dr. Jose Rizal **Obv:** Shield of arms **Rev:** Head left

Date	Mintage	F	VF	XF	Unc	BU
ND(1961)	100,000	—	—	3.00	4.00	5.00

KM# 185 PESO

20.0000 g., 0.9000 Silver 0.5787 oz. ASW, 35.5 mm. **Obv:** Shield of arms above date and value **Rev:** Uniformed bust right **Designer:** Laura Gardin Fraser

Date	Mintage	F	VF	XF	Unc	BU
1947S	100,000	—	BV	12.00	18.50	20.00

KM# 192 PESO

26.0000 g., 0.9000 Silver 0.7523 oz. ASW **Subject:** 100th Anniversary Birth of Dr. Jose Rizal **Obv:** Shield of arms **Rev:** Bust 1/4 right divides dates

Date	Mintage	F	VF	XF	Unc	BU
ND(1961)	100,000	—	—	BV	8.00	9.00

KM# 193 PESO

26.0000 g., 0.9000 Silver 0.7523 oz. ASW **Subject:** 100th Anniversary Birth of Andres Bonifacio **Obv:** Shield of arms **Rev:** Head 1/4 left divides dates

Date	Mintage	F	VF	XF	Unc	BU
ND(1963)	100,000	—	—	BV	7.00	8.00

KM# 194 PESO

26.0000 g., 0.9000 Silver 0.7523 oz. ASW **Subject:** 100th Anniversary Birth of Apolinario Mabini **Obv:** Shield of arms **Rev:** Head 1/4 right divides dates

Date	Mintage	F	VF	XF	Unc	BU
ND(1964)	100,000	—	—	BV	7.00	8.00

KM# 195 PESO

26.0000 g., 0.9000 Silver 0.7523 oz. ASW **Subject:** 25th Anniversary of Bataan Day **Obv:** Shield of arms **Rev:** Flaming broken sword flanked by sprigs, dates and stars

Date	Mintage	F	VF	XF	Unc	BU
ND(1967)	100,000	—	—	BV	7.00	8.00

Note: KM#195 is a prooflike issue

REFORM COINAGE

100 Sentimos = 1 Piso

KM# 270.2 10 CENTIMOS

2.4600 g., Bronze-Plated Steel, 16.9 mm. **Obv:** Value high on coin, different font, date **Rev:** Central Bank seal within circle and gear design **Edge:** Reeded

Date	Mintage	F	VF	XF	Unc	BU
2006	—	—	—	—	0.25	0.50

KM# 196 SENTIMO

Aluminum **Obv:** Shield of arms **Rev:** Head left

Date	Mintage	F	VF	XF	Unc	BU
1967	10,000,000	—	—	—	0.25	—
1968	27,940,000	—	—	—	0.10	—
1969/6	12,060,000	—	—	—	0.20	—
1970	130,000,000	—	—	—	0.10	—
1974 0	165,000,000	—	—	—	0.10	—
1974 1 Proof	10,000	Value: 3.50				

KM# 205 SENTIMO

1.2200 g., Aluminum, 19 mm. **Obv:** Head 3/4 right **Rev:** Redesigned bank seal within circle **Edge:** Plain **Shape:** Square

Date	Mintage	F	VF	XF	Unc	BU
1975FM (M)	108,000	—	—	—	0.50	—
1975FM (U)	5,875	—	—	—	2.00	—
1975FM (P)	37,000	Value: 1.50				
1975(Lt)	10,000,000	—	—	—	0.10	—
1975(US)	60,190,000	—	—	—	0.10	—
1976FM (M)	10,000	—	—	—	0.75	—
1976FM (U)	1,826	—	—	1.00	2.50	—
1976FM (P)	9,901	Value: 1.50				
1976(US)	60,000,000	—	—	—	0.10	—
1977	4,808,000	—	—	—	0.25	—
1977FM (M)	10,000	—	—	—	1.00	—
1977FM (U)	354	—	—	—	4.00	—
1977FM (P)	4,822	Value: 2.00				
1978	24,813,000	—	—	—	0.10	—
1978FM (U)	10,000	—	—	—	1.00	—
1978FM (P)	4,792	Value: 2.00				

KM# 224 SENTIMO

Aluminum **Obv:** Head 3/4 right **Rev:** Redesigned bank seal within circle **Shape:** Square **Note:** Varieties exist in date.

Date	Mintage	F	VF	XF	Unc	BU
1979BSP	—	—	—	—	0.25	—
1979FM (U)	10,000	—	—	—	1.00	—
1979FM (P)	3,645	Value: 2.00				
1980BSP	12,601,000	—	—	—	0.25	—
1980FM (U)	10,000	—	—	—	1.00	—
1980FM (P)	3,133	Value: 2.00				
1981BSP	33,391,000	—	—	—	0.20	—
1981FM (U)	—	—	—	—	1.00	—
1981FM (P)	1,795	Value: 2.00				
1982BSP	51,730,000	—	—	—	0.10	—
1982FM (P)	—	Value: 2.00				

KM# 238 SENTIMO

0.7000 g., Aluminum, 15.5 mm. **Obv:** Head left **Rev:** Sea shell and value within circle

Date	Mintage	F	VF	XF	Unc	BU
1983	62,090,000	—	—	—	0.50	—
1983 Proof	—	Value: 2.00				
1984	320,000	—	—	—	0.75	—
1985	16,000	—	—	—	1.00	—
1986	80,000	—	—	—	1.00	—
1987	13,570,000	—	—	—	0.75	—
1988	26,861,000	—	—	—	0.75	—
1989	—	—	—	—	0.75	—
1990	—	—	—	—	0.75	12.00
1991	—	—	—	—	—	20.00
1992	—	—	—	—	0.50	20.00
1993	—	—	0.35	1.50	9.00	16.00

KM# 273 SENTIMO

2.0000 g., Copper Plated Steel **Obv:** Value and date **Rev:** Central bank seal within circle and gear design, 1993 (date Cenral Bank was established) below

Date	Mintage	F	VF	XF	Unc	BU
1995	—	—	—	—	0.25	0.45
1996	—	—	—	—	0.35	0.50
1997	—	—	—	—	0.35	0.50
1998	—	—	—	—	0.35	0.50
1999	—	—	—	—	0.35	0.50
2000	—	—	—	—	0.35	0.50
2004	—	—	—	—	0.35	0.50
2005	—	—	—	—	0.35	0.50
2006	—	—	—	—	0.35	0.50

KM# 197 5 SENTIMOS

Brass, 18 mm. **Obv:** Shield above banner **Rev:** Head right

Date	Mintage	F	VF	XF	Unc	BU
1967	40,000,000	—	—	—	0.30	—
1968	50,000,000	—	—	—	0.30	—
1970	5,000,000	—	—	1.00	3.50	—
1972	71,744,000	—	—	—	0.30	—
1974	90,025,000	—	—	—	0.30	—
1974 Proof	10,000	Value: 4.00				

KM# 206 5 SENTIMOS

2.4000 g., Brass **Obv:** Head 3/4 left **Rev:** Redesigned bank seal within circle **Shape:** Scalloped

Date	Mintage	F	VF	XF	Unc	BU
1975FM (M)	104,000	—	—	—	0.50	—
1975FM (U)	5,875	—	—	—	2.50	—
1975FM (P)	37,000	Value: 2.00				
1975(US)	98,928,000	—	—	—	0.10	—
1975(Lt)	10,000,000	—	—	—	0.10	—
1976FM (M)	10,000	—	—	—	1.50	—
1976FM (U)	1,826	—	—	—	2.50	—
1976FM (P)	9,901	Value: 1.50				
1976(US)	98,000,000	—	—	—	0.20	—
1977	19,367,000	—	—	—	0.35	—
1977FM (M)	10,000	—	—	—	1.25	—
1977FM (U)	354	—	—	—	4.00	—
1977FM (P)	4,822	Value: 2.50				
1978	61,838,000	—	—	—	0.20	—
1978FM (U)	10,000	—	—	—	1.50	—
1978FM (P)	4,792	Value: 2.50				

KM# 225 5 SENTIMOS

2.5000 g., Brass **Obv:** Head 3/4 left **Rev:** Redesigned bank seal within circle **Shape:** Scalloped

Date	Mintage	F	VF	XF	Unc	BU
1979BSP	12,805,000	—	—	—	0.30	—
1979FM (U)	10,000	—	—	—	1.25	—
1979FM (P)	3,645	Value: 2.50				
1980BSP	111,339,000	—	—	—	0.10	—
1980FM (U)	—	—	—	—	1.00	—
1980FM (P)	3,133	Value: 2.50				
1981BSP	—	—	—	—	0.10	—
1981FM (U)	—	—	—	—	1.25	—
1981FM (P)	1,795	Value: 3.00				
1982BSP	—	—	—	—	0.10	—
1982FM (P)	—	Value: 3.00				

KM# 239 5 SENTIMOS

1.2000 g., Aluminum, 17 mm. **Obv:** Head right **Rev:** Orchid and value

Date	Mintage	F	VF	XF	Unc	BU
1983	100,016,000	—	—	—	0.50	—
1983 Proof	—	Value: 2.00				
1984	141,744,000	—	—	—	0.40	—
1985	50,416,000	—	—	—	0.25	—
1986	11,664,000	—	—	—	0.35	—
1987	79,008,000	—	—	—	0.10	—
1988	90,487,000	—	—	—	0.10	—
1989	—	—	—	—	0.25	—
1990	—	—	—	—	0.25	—
1991	—	—	—	—	1.00	—
1992	—	—	—	—	0.25	—

KM# 268 5 SENTIMOS

1.9000 g., Copper Plated Steel, 15.43 mm. **Obv:** Numeral value around center hole **Rev:** Hole in center with date, bank and name around border, 1993 (date Cenral Bank was established) below **Rev. Legend:** 1993 BANGKO CENTRAL NG PILIPINAS **Edge:** Plain

Date	Mintage	F	VF	XF	Unc	BU
1995	—	—	—	—	0.50	0.75
1996	—	—	—	—	0.50	0.75
1997	—	—	—	—	0.50	0.75
1998	—	—	—	—	0.50	0.75
1999	—	—	—	—	0.50	0.75
2000	—	—	—	—	0.50	0.75
2002	—	—	—	—	0.50	0.75
2005	—	—	—	—	0.50	1.00
2006	—	—	—	—	0.50	1.00

KM# 198 10 SENTIMOS

2.0000 g., Copper-Zinc-Nickel, 18 mm. **Obv:** Shield of arms **Rev:** Bust left

Date	Mintage	F	VF	XF	Unc	BU
1967	50,000,000	—	—	—	0.35	—
1968	60,000,000	—	—	—	0.35	—
1969	40,000,000	—	—	—	0.35	—
1970	50,000,000	—	—	—	0.35	—
1971	80,000,000	—	—	—	0.35	—
1972	121,390,000	—	—	—	0.35	—
1974	60,208,000	—	—	—	0.35	—
1974 Proof	10,000	Value: 4.00				

KM# 207 10 SENTIMOS
2.0000 g., Copper-Nickel **Obv:** Head 3/4 right **Rev:** Redesigned bank seal within circle

Date	Mintage	F	VF	XF	Unc	BU
1975FM (M)	104,000	—	—	—	0.50	—
1975FM (U)	5,875	—	—	—	2.50	—
1975FM (P)	37,000	Value: 2.50				
1975(VDM)	10,000,000	—	—	—	0.25	—
1975(US)	50,000,000	—	—	—	0.20	—
1976FM (M)	10,000	—	—	—	0.50	—
1976FM (U)	1,826	—	—	—	5.00	—
1976FM (P)	9,901	Value: 2.00				
1976(US)	50,000,000	—	—	—	0.20	—
1977	29,314,000	—	—	—	0.25	—
1977FM (M)	10,000	—	—	—	1.50	—
1977FM (U)	354	—	—	—	6.00	—
1977FM (P)	4,822	Value: 3.00				
1978	60,042,000	—	—	—	0.10	—
1978FM (U)	10,000	—	—	—	3.00	—
1978FM (P)	4,792	Value: 3.00				

KM# 226 10 SENTIMOS
Copper-Nickel, 18 mm. **Obv:** Head 3/4 right **Rev:** Redesigned bank seal within circle **Note:** Varieties with thick and thin legends exist for coins with BSP mint mark.

Date	Mintage	F	VF	XF	Unc	BU
1979BSP	6,446,000	—	—	—	0.50	—
1979FM (U)	10,000	—	—	—	2.00	—
1979FM (P)	3,645	Value: 3.00				
1980BSP	—	—	—	—	0.30	—
1980FM (U)	10,000	—	—	—	1.50	—
1980FM (P)	3,133	Value: 3.25				
1981BSP	—	—	—	—	0.30	—
1981FM (U)	—	—	—	—	2.00	—
1981FM (P)	1,795	Value: 3.50				
1982BSP	—	—	—	—	0.30	—
1982FM (P)	—	Value: 3.50				

KM# 240.1 10 SENTIMOS
2.4500 g., Aluminum, 18.95 mm. **Series:** F.A.O. **Subject:** World Conference on Fisheries **Obv:** Head left **Rev:** Fish and value within circle **Edge:** Plain

Date	Mintage	F	VF	XF	Unc	BU
1983	95,640,000	—	—	—	8.00	—
1983 Proof	—	Value: 8.00				
1986	—	—	—	—	1.00	—
1987	Inc. below	—	—	—	1.00	—

KM# 240.2 10 SENTIMOS
1.5000 g., Aluminum, 19 mm. **Series:** F.A.O. **Subject:** World Conference on Fisheries **Obv:** Head left **Rev:** Fish and value within circle

Date	Mintage	F	VF	XF	Unc	BU
1983	—	—	—	—	0.50	1.50
1984	235,900,000	—	—	—	0.35	1.00
1985	90,169,000	—	—	—	0.35	1.00
1986	4,270,000	—	—	—	0.50	0.65
1987	99,520,000	—	—	—	0.50	0.75
1988	117,166,000	—	—	—	0.35	0.50
1989	—	—	—	—	0.35	0.50
1990	—	—	—	—	0.35	0.50
1991	—	—	—	—	0.35	0.50
1992	—	—	—	—	0.35	0.50
1993	—	—	—	—	0.50	7.00
1994	—	—	—	—	0.50	7.00

KM# 270.1 10 SENTIMOS
2.4600 g., Bronze Plated Steel, 16.9 mm. **Obv:** Value and date **Rev:** Central Bank seal within circle and gear design, 1993 (date Cenral Bank was established) below **Edge:** Reeded

Date	Mintage	F	VF	XF	Unc	BU
1995	—	—	—	—	0.25	0.40
1996	—	—	—	—	1.00	1.50
1997	—	—	—	—	0.25	0.40
1998	—	—	—	—	0.25	0.40
1999	—	—	—	—	0.25	0.40
2002	—	—	—	—	0.25	0.40
2004	—	—	—	—	0.25	0.40
2005	—	—	—	—	0.25	0.50

KM# 199 25 SENTIMOS
4.0000 g., Copper-Zinc-Nickel, 21 mm. **Obv:** Shield of arms **Rev:** Head left

Date	Mintage	F	VF	XF	Unc	BU
1967	40,000,000	—	—	0.10	0.50	—
1968	10,000,000	—	—	0.10	0.50	—
1969	10,000,000	—	—	0.10	0.50	—
1970	40,000,000	—	—	0.10	0.40	—
1971	60,000,000	—	—	0.10	0.40	—
1972	90,000,000	—	—	0.10	0.40	—
1974	10,000,000	—	—	0.10	0.50	—
1974 Proof	10,000	Value: 12.00				

KM# 208 25 SENTIMOS
4.0000 g., Copper-Nickel, 21 mm. **Obv:** Head 3/4 left **Rev:** Redesigned bank seal within circle

Date	Mintage	F	VF	XF	Unc	BU
1975FM (M)	104,000	—	—	—	0.75	—
1975FM (U)	5,875	—	—	—	5.00	—
1975FM (P)	37,000	Value: 3.00				
1975(US)	10,000,000	—	—	0.10	0.40	—
1975(VDM)	10,000,000	—	—	0.10	0.40	—
1976FM (M)	10,000	—	—	0.10	1.00	—
1976FM (U)	1,826	—	—	—	6.50	—
1976FM (P)	9,901	Value: 3.00				
1976(US)	10,000,000	—	—	0.10	0.25	—
1977	24,654,000	—	—	0.10	0.25	—
1977FM (M)	10,000	—	—	—	1.25	—
1977FM (U)	354	—	—	—	8.00	—
1977FM (P)	4,822	Value: 4.50				
1978	40,466,000	—	—	0.10	0.25	—
1978FM (U)	10,000	—	—	—	2.50	—
1978FM (P)	4,792	Value: 4.00				

KM# 227 25 SENTIMOS
Copper-Nickel, 21 mm. **Obv:** Head 3/4 left **Rev:** Redesigned bank seal within circle

Date	Mintage	F	VF	XF	Unc	BU
1979BSP	20,725,000	—	—	0.10	0.50	—
1979FM (U)	10,000	—	—	—	2.50	—
1979FM (P)	3,645	Value: 2.00				
1980BSP	—	—	—	0.10	0.75	—
1980FM (U)	10,000	—	—	—	1.50	—
1980FM (P)	3,133	Value: 4.50				
1981BSP	—	—	—	0.10	1.00	—
1981FM (U)	—	—	—	—	3.00	—
1981FM (P)	1,795	Value: 5.00				
1982BSP	—	—	—	0.10	0.50	—
1982FM (P)	—	Value: 5.00				

KM# 241.1 25 SENTIMOS
3.9000 g., Brass, 21 mm. **Obv:** Juan Luna right **Rev:** Butterfly

Date	Mintage	F	VF	XF	Unc	BU
1983	92,944,000	—	—	0.15	1.00	2.00
1983 Proof	—	Value: 2.50				
1984	254,324,000	—	—	0.15	0.75	2.00
1985	84,922,000	—	—	0.15	0.75	2.00
1986	65,284,000	—	—	0.15	0.75	2.00
1987	1,680,000	—	—	0.50	2.00	2.75
1988	51,062,000	—	—	—	0.75	2.00
1989	—	—	—	—	0.75	2.00
1990	—	—	—	—	0.75	2.00

KM# 241.2 25 SENTIMOS
2.2400 g., Brass **Obv:** Juan Luna right **Rev:** Butterfly **Note:** Reduced size.

Date	Mintage	F	VF	XF	Unc	BU
1991	—	—	—	—	1.00	1.25
1992	—	—	—	—	1.00	1.25
1993	—	—	—	—	4.00	6.00
1994	—	—	—	—	3.50	5.00

KM# 271.1 25 SENTIMOS
3.8000 g., Brass, 20 mm. **Obv:** Value and date **Rev:** Central Bank seal within circle and gear design, 1993 (date Cenral Bank was established) below **Edge:** Plain

Date	Mintage	F	VF	XF	Unc	BU
1995	—	—	—	—	0.75	1.00
1996	—	—	—	—	1.00	1.25
1997	—	—	—	—	1.00	1.25
1998	—	—	—	—	1.00	1.25
1999	—	—	—	—	1.00	1.25
2000	—	—	—	—	1.00	1.25
2001	—	—	—	—	1.00	1.25
2002	—	—	—	—	1.00	1.25
2003	—	—	—	—	1.00	1.25
2006	—	—	—	—	1.00	1.25

KM# 271.2 25 SENTIMOS
Brass Plated Steel, 20 mm. **Obv:** Value and date **Rev:** Central Bank seal within circle and gear design **Edge:** Plain

Date	Mintage	F	VF	XF	Unc	BU
2004	—	—	—	—	1.00	1.25
2005	—	—	—	—	1.00	1.25

KM# 200 50 SENTIMOS
8.0000 g., Copper-Zinc-Nickel, 27.5 mm. **Obv:** Shield of arms **Rev:** Marcelo H. del Pilar right

Date	Mintage	F	VF	XF	Unc	BU
1967	20,000,000	—	0.10	0.25	0.75	1.25
1971	10,000,000	—	0.10	0.50	1.00	2.00
1972 Knob on 2	30,000,000	—	0.10	0.75	1.50	2.50
1972 Plain 2	20,517,000	—	0.10	0.50	1.25	2.25
1974	5,004,000	—	0.10	0.75	1.25	2.50
1974 Proof	10,000	Value: 20.00				
1975	5,714,000	—	0.10	0.20	1.00	2.00

KM# 242.1 50 SENTIMOS

6.0000 g., Copper-Nickel, 25 mm. **Obv:** Head of Marcelo H. del Pilar left **Rev:** Eagle with talons out **Note:** Eagle's name: PITHECOPHAGA

Date	Mintage	F	VF	XF	Unc	BU
1983	27,644,000	—	0.10	0.50	1.25	2.00
1983 Proof	—	Value: 4.25				
1984	121,408,000	—	0.10	0.20	1.00	1.50
1985	107,048,000	—	0.10	0.20	1.00	1.50
1986	120,000,000	—	0.10	0.20	0.75	1.25
1987	1,078,000	—	0.10	1.00	1.50	2.50
1988	24,008,000	—	0.10	0.20	1.00	1.50
1989	—	—	0.10	0.20	1.00	2.50
1990	—	—	0.10	0.20	1.00	1.50

KM# 242.2 50 SENTIMOS

6.0000 g., Copper-Nickel, 25 mm. **Obv:** Head of Marcelo H. del Pilar left **Rev:** Eagle attacking **Note:** Error eagle's name: PITHECOBHAGA

Date	Mintage	F	VF	XF	Unc	BU
1983	Inc. above	—	3.00	5.00	9.00	—

KM# 242.3 50 SENTIMOS

3.0000 g., Brass **Obv:** Head of Marcelo H. Pilar left **Rev:** Eagle with talons out **Note:** Reduced size.

Date	Mintage	F	VF	XF	Unc	BU
1991	—	—	—	0.25	1.50	2.00
1992	—	—	—	0.25	1.50	2.00
1993	—	—	—	—	5.00	7.00
1994	—	—	—	—	3.50	5.00

KM# 201 PISO

26.4500 g., 0.9000 Silver 0.7653 oz. ASW **Subject:** Centennial - Birth of Aguinaldo **Obv:** Shield of arms **Rev:** Bust facing divides dates

Date	Mintage	F	VF	XF	Unc	BU
ND(1969) Prooflike	100,000	—	—	BV	9.00	10.00

KM# 202 PISO

Nickel, 38.3 mm. **Subject:** Pope Paul VI Visit **Obv:** Bust of Ferdinand Marcos left **Rev:** Bust of Pope Paul VI right **Designer:** Frank Gasparro

Date	Mintage	F	VF	XF	Unc	BU
1970	70,000	—	—	—	2.25	2.75

KM# 202a PISO

26.4500 g., 0.9000 Silver 0.7653 oz. ASW, 38.3 mm. **Obv:** Bust of Ferdinand Marcos left **Rev:** Bust of Pope Paul VI right **Designer:** Frank Gasparro

Date	Mintage	F	VF	XF	Unc	BU
1970	30,000	—	—	—	8.50	10.00

KM# 203 PISO

Copper-Zinc-Nickel, 33 mm. **Obv:** Shield of arms **Rev:** Head of Jose Rizal left

Date	Mintage	F	VF	XF	Unc	BU
1972	121,821,000	—	0.25	0.50	1.00	2.50
1974	45,631,000	—	0.25	0.50	1.00	3.00
1974 Proof	10,000	Value: 30.00				

KM# 209.1 PISO

9.5000 g., Copper-Nickel, 29 mm. **Obv:** Head of Jose Rizal 1/4 right within octogon **Rev:** Shield of arms

Date	Mintage	F	VF	XF	Unc	BU
1975FM (M)	104,000	—	—	—	2.00	—
1975FM (U)	5,877	—	—	—	5.50	—
1975FM (P)	37,000	Value: 3.00				
1975(VDM)	10,000,000	—	0.15	0.25	1.25	—
1975(US)	30,000,000	—	0.15	0.25	0.75	1.00
1976FM (M)	10,000	—	—	—	2.00	—
1976FM (U)	1,826	—	—	—	8.00	—
1976FM (P)	9,901	Value: 3.00				
1976(US)	30,000,000	—	0.15	0.25	0.75	—
1977	14,771,000	—	0.15	0.25	0.75	—
1977FM (M)	12,000	—	—	—	3.00	—
1977FM (U)	354	—	—	—	7.00	—
1977FM (P)	4,822	Value: 3.00				
1978	19,408,000	—	0.15	0.25	1.00	—
1978FM (U)	10,000	—	—	—	4.00	—
1978FM (P)	4,792	Value: 7.50				

KM# 209.2 PISO

9.5000 g., Copper-Nickel, 29 mm. **Obv:** Head of Jose Rizal 1/4 right within octogon **Rev:** Shield of arms **Rev. Inscription:** ISANG BANSA ISANG DIWA

Date	Mintage	F	VF	XF	Unc	BU
1979BSP	321,000	—	0.15	0.25	2.00	—
1979FM (U)	10,000	—	—	—	2.50	—
1979FM (P)	3,645	Value: 3.00				
1980BSP	19,693,000	—	0.15	0.25	0.75	1.00
1980FM (U)	10,000	—	—	—	7.50	—
1980FM (P)	3,133	Value: 12.50				
1981BSP	7,944,000	—	0.15	0.25	1.00	—
1981FM (U)	—	—	—	—	4.00	—
1981FM (P)	1,795	Value: 6.00				
1982FM (P)	—	Value: 7.00				
1982BSP Large date	52,110,000	—	0.15	0.25	1.00	—
1982BSP Small date	Inc. above	—	0.15	0.25	1.00	—

KM# 243.1 PISO

9.5000 g., Copper-Nickel, 28.9 mm. **Obv:** Head of Jose Rizal right **Rev:** Tamaraw bull **Edge:** Reeded **Note:** Large legends and design elements.

Date	Mintage	F	VF	XF	Unc	BU
1983	55,869,000	—	—	0.30	1.25	2.00
1983 Proof	—	Value: 6.50				
1984	4,997,000	—	—	1.00	2.00	3.00
1985	182,592,000	—	—	0.30	1.00	1.75
1986	19,072,000	—	—	0.30	1.25	2.25
1987	1,391,000	—	—	3.00	5.00	6.25
1988	54,636,000	—	—	0.30	1.25	2.00
1989	—	—	—	—	—	7.50

KM# 243.2 PISO

4.0000 g., Stainless Steel, 21.6 mm. **Obv:** Head of Jose Rizal right **Rev:** Tamaraw bull **Edge:** Plain **Note:** Reduced size.

Date	Mintage	F	VF	XF	Unc	BU
1991	—	—	—	0.50	1.25	2.25
1992	—	—	—	0.50	1.25	2.25
1993	—	—	—	—	3.50	4.00
1994	—	—	—	—	5.00	6.50

KM# 243.3 PISO

Copper-Nickel **Obv:** Head of Jose Rizal right **Rev:** Tamaraw bull **Note:** Smaller legends and design elements.

Date	Mintage	F	VF	XF	Unc	BU
1989	—	—	—	0.30	1.00	1.25
1990	—	—	—	0.30	1.00	1.25

KM# 251 PISO

Copper-Nickel, 28.5 mm. **Subject:** Philippine Cultures Decade **Obv:** Shield of arms divides date **Rev:** Three conjoined vertical busts right

Date	Mintage	F	VF	XF	Unc	BU
1989	—	—	—	—	2.50	—

KM# 257 PISO

Copper-Nickel **Obv:** Shield of arms **Rev:** Waterfall, ship, and flower within circle

Date	Mintage	F	VF	XF	Unc	BU
ND(1991)	—	—	—	—	1.25	2.00
ND(1991) Matte	—	—	—	—	8.00	—

Note: Special striking by CB

KM# 260 PISO

Nickel Clad Steel, 21.5 mm. **Subject:** 50th Anniversary - Battle of Kagitingan **Obv:** Shield of arms **Rev:** Military head left, cross, flag and dates

Date	Mintage	F	VF	XF	Unc	BU
ND(1992)	—	—	—	—	2.50	—

KM# 269.1 PISO

Copper-Nickel, 24 mm. **Obv:** Head of Jose Rizal right, value and date **Rev:** Bank seal within circle and gear design, 1993 (date Cenral Bank was established) below

Date	Mintage	F	VF	XF	Unc	BU
1995	—	—	—	—	1.00	1.50
1996	—	—	—	—	1.25	1.75
1997	—	—	—	—	1.25	1.75
1998	—	—	—	—	1.25	1.75
1999	—	—	—	—	1.25	1.75
2000	—	—	—	—	1.25	1.75
2001	—	—	—	—	1.25	1.75
2002	—	—	—	—	1.25	1.75
2003	—	—	—	—	1.25	1.75
2004	—	—	—	—	2.50	5.00
2006	—	—	—	—	1.50	2.00

KM# 244 2 PISO

12.0000 g., Copper-Nickel, 31 mm. **Obv:** Head of Andres Bonifacio left **Rev:** Coconut palm **Shape:** 10-sided

Date	Mintage	F	VF	XF	Unc	BU
1983	15,640,000	—	—	0.35	2.50	3.50
1983 Proof	—	Value: 5.00				
1984	121,111,000	—	—	0.35	1.00	1.50
1985	115,211,000	—	—	0.35	1.25	1.50
1986	25,260,000	—	—	0.35	1.25	1.50
1987	2,196,000	—	—	5.00	8.00	10.00
1988	16,094,000	—	—	—	7.00	10.00
1989	—	—	—	—	1.25	1.50
1990	—	—	—	—	1.25	1.50

KM# 253 2 PISO

12.0000 g., Copper-Nickel, 31 mm. **Obv:** Design within beaded circle **Rev:** Head of Elpidio Quirino right **Shape:** 10-sided

Date	Mintage	F	VF	XF	Unc	BU
ND(1991)	10,000,000	—	—	—	1.25	2.00
ND(1991) Matte	—	—	—	—	10.00	—

Note: Special striking by CB

KM# 258 2 PISO

5.0100 g., Stainless Steel, 23.5 mm. **Obv:** Head of Andres Bonifacio left **Rev:** Coconut palm

Date	Mintage	F	VF	XF	Unc	BU
1991	—	—	—	—	2.50	3.50
1992	—	—	—	—	3.00	3.50
1993	—	—	—	—	3.00	3.50
1994	—	—	—	—	3.00	4.00

KM# 261 2 PISO

Nickel Clad Steel, 23.5 mm. **Obv:** Design within beaded circle **Rev:** Head of Manuel A. Roxas right

Date	Mintage	F	VF	XF	Unc	BU
ND(1992)	—	—	—	—	2.50	3.00
ND(1992) Matte	—	—	—	—	10.00	—

Note: Special striking by CB

KM# 256 2 PISO

Copper-Nickel **Obv:** Triangular design within circle **Rev:** Head of Jose Laurel right **Shape:** 10-sided

Date	Mintage	F	VF	XF	Unc	BU
ND(1992)	—	—	—	1.75	2.00	3.00
ND(1992) Matte	—	—	—	—	10.00	—

Note: Special striking by CB

KM# 269.2 2 PISO

Nickel-Plated Steel, 24 mm. **Obv:** Head of Jose Rizal right, value and date **Rev:** Bank seal within circle and gear design

Date	Mintage	F	VF	XF	Unc	BU
2004	—	—	—	—	1.25	2.00
2005	—	—	—	—	1.25	2.00

KM# 210.1 5 PISO

Nickel, 36.5 mm. **Obv:** Shield of arms above value **Rev:** Head of Ferdinand E. Marcos left

Date	Mintage	F	VF	XF	Unc	BU
1975FM (M)	3,850	—	—	—	7.50	—
1975FM (U)	7,875	—	—	—	6.00	—
1975FM (P)	39,000	Value: 5.00				
1975(Sh)	20,000,000	—	0.50	0.75	1.00	1.50
1976FM (M)	10,000	—	—	—	4.00	—
1976FM (U)	1,826	—	—	—	15.00	—
1976FM (P)	9,901	Value: 6.00				
1977FM (M)	10,000	—	—	—	4.00	—
1977FM (U)	354	—	—	—	10.00	—
1977FM (P)	4,822	Value: 6.50				
1978FM (U)	10,000	—	—	—	2.50	—
1978FM (P)	4,792	Value: 8.00				
1982	—	—	0.50	0.75	1.50	—

KM# 210.2 5 PISO

Nickel, 36.5 mm. **Obv:** Shield of arms **Obv. Inscription:** ISANG BANSA ISANG DIWA below shield **Rev:** Head of Ferdinand E. Marcos left

Date	Mintage	F	VF	XF	Unc	BU
1979FM (U)	10,000	—	—	—	4.50	—
1979FM (P)	3,645	Value: 8.00				
1980FM (U)	10,000	—	—	—	4.50	—
1980FM (P)	3,133	Value: 10.00				
1981FM (U)	11,000	—	—	—	4.00	—
1981FM (P)	1,795	Value: 10.00				
1982FM (P)	—	Value: 10.00				
1982FM (U); Prooflike	—	—	—	—	10.00	—

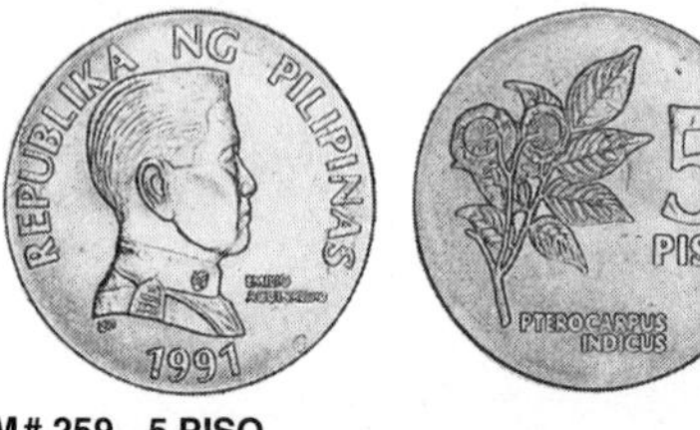

KM# 259 5 PISO

Nickel-Brass, 25.5 mm. **Obv:** Head of Emilio Aguinaldo right **Rev:** Pterocarpus Indicus Flower

Date	Mintage	F	VF	XF	Unc	BU
1991	—	—	—	—	2.00	3.00
1992	—	—	—	—	3.50	4.50
1993	—	—	—	—	9.00	12.00
1994	—	—	—	—	10.00	15.00

KM# 262 5 PISO

Nickel-Brass, 25.5 mm. **Subject:** 30th Chess Olympiad **Obv:** Shield of arms **Rev:** Stylized horse head on chess board **Note:** Varieties exist.

Date	Mintage	F	VF	XF	Unc	BU
1992	—	—	—	—	11.00	12.50

KM# 263 5 PISO

Nickel-Brass, 25.5 mm. **Subject:** Leyte Gulf Landings **Obv:** Shield of arms **Rev:** Standing figures

Date	Mintage	F	VF	XF	Unc	BU
ND(1994)	7,800	—	—	—	8.50	9.50

KM# 272 5 PISO

7.6700 g., Nickel-Brass, 25.5 mm. **Obv:** Head of Emilio Aguinaldo right, value and date within scalloped border **Rev:** Central Bank seal within circle and gear design within scalloped border, 1993 (date Cenral Bank was established) below **Edge:** Plain

Date	Mintage	F	VF	XF	Unc	BU
1995	—	—	—	—	2.50	3.00
1996	—	—	—	—	1.50	3.00
1997	—	—	—	—	1.50	2.50
Note: Struck at Royal Canadian Mint, without designer initials						
1997BSP	—	—	—	—	1.50	2.50
Note: With designer initials below shoulder						
1998	—	—	—	—	1.50	3.00
1999	—	—	—	—	1.50	3.00
2001BSP	—	—	—	—	1.50	3.00
2002	—	—	—	—	1.50	3.00
2003	—	—	—	—	1.50	3.00
2004	—	—	—	—	1.50	3.00
2005	—	—	—	—	1.75	4.00
2006	—	—	—	—	1.50	3.00

KM# 250 10 PISO

Nickel, 36 mm. **Subject:** People Power Revolution **Obv:** Shield of arms divides date **Rev:** Group of people

Date	Mintage	F	VF	XF	Unc	BU
1988	—	—	—	—	4.00	5.00

KM# 278 10 PISO

8.7000 g., Bi-Metallic Brass center in Copper-Nickel ring, 26.5 mm. **Obv:** Conjoined heads right within circle **Rev:** Bank seal within circle and gear design, 1993 (date Cenral Bank was established) below **Edge:** Plain and reeded sections

Date	Mintage	F	VF	XF	Unc	BU
2000	—	—	—	—	3.50	5.00
2001	—	—	—	—	3.00	4.50
2002	—	—	—	—	3.00	4.00
2003	—	—	—	—	3.00	4.00
2004	—	—	—	—	5.00	7.00
2005	—	—	—	—	3.00	5.00
2006	—	—	—	—	3.00	4.00

POLAND

The Republic of Poland, located in central Europe, has an area of 120,725 sq. mi. (312,680 sq. km.) and a population of *38.2 million. Capital: Warszawa (Warsaw). The economy is essentially agricultural, but industrial activity provides the products for foreign trade. Machinery, coal, coke, iron, steel and transport equipment are exported.

Poland, which began as a Slavic duchy in the 10th century and reached its peak of power between the 14th and 16th centuries, has had a turbulent history of invasion, occupation or partition by Mongols, Turkey, Transylvania, Sweden, Austria, Prussia and Russia.

The first partition took place in 1772. Prussia took Polish Pomerania, Russia took part of the eastern provinces, and Austria occupied Galicia and its capital city Lwów. The second partition occurred in 1793 when Russia took another slice of the eastern provinces and Prussia took what remained of western Poland. The third partition, 1795, literally removed Poland from the map. Russia took what was left of the eastern provinces. Prussia seized most of central Poland, including Warsaw. Austria took what was left of the south. Napoleon restored to Poland much of the territory lost to Prussia and Austria, but after his defeat another partition returned the Duchy of Warsaw to Prussia, made Kraków into a tiny republic, and declared what remained to be the Kingdom of Poland under the czar and in permanent union with Russia.

Poland re-emerged as an independent state recognized by the Treaty of Versailles on June 28, 1919, and maintained its independence until 1939 when it was invaded by, and partitioned between, Germany and Russia. Poland's present boundaries were determined by the U.S.-British-Russian agreement of Aug. 16, 1945. The Government of National Unity was replaced when the Polish Communist-Socialist faction claimed victory at the polls in 1947 and established a Peoples Democratic Republic' of the Soviet type in 1952. On December 29, 1989 Poland was proclaimed as the Republic of Poland.

MINT MARKS

MV, MW, MW-monogram - Warsaw Mint, 1965-
FF - Stuttgart Germany 1916-1917
(w) - Warsaw 1923-39 (opened officially in 1924) arrow mintmark
CHI - Valcambi, Switzerland

Other letters appearing with date denote the Mintmaster at the time the coin was struck.

GERMAN OCCUPATION

REGENCY COINAGE

100 Fenigow = 1 Marka

Y# 4 FENIG

1.9700 g., Iron, 15 mm. **Obv:** Value **Rev:** Crowned eagle with wings open

Date	Mintage	F	VF	XF	Unc	BU
1918FF	51,484,000	0.50	1.00	3.00	10.00	30.00
1918FF Proof	—	Value: 200				

Y# 5 5 FENIGOW

2.5300 g., Iron, 18 mm. **Obv:** Value **Rev:** Crowned eagle with wings open

Date	Mintage	F	VF	XF	Unc	BU
1917FF	18,700,000	0.25	0.75	1.50	3.50	—
1917FF Proof	—	Value: 100				
1918FF	22,690,000	0.25	0.75	1.50	3.50	—
1918FF Proof	—	Value: 200				

Y# 6 10 FENIGOW

3.5600 g., Iron, 21 mm. **Obv:** Value **Rev:** Crowned eagle with wings open

Date	Mintage	F	VF	XF	Unc	BU
1917FF	33,000,000	7.50	15.00	20.00	28.00	—
Note: Obverse legend touches edge						
1917FF Proof	—	Value: 100				
1917FF	Inc. above	0.25	0.75	1.25	3.50	—
Note: Obverse legend away from edge						
1918FF	14,990,000	0.50	1.00	2.00	5.00	—
Note: Obverse legend away from edge						
1918FF Proof	—	Value: 200				
Note: Obverse legend away from edge						

Y# 6a 10 FENIGOW

3.5600 g., Zinc, 21 mm. **Obv:** Value **Rev:** Crowned eagle with wings open **Note:** Error planchet.

Date	Mintage	F	VF	XF	Unc	BU
1917FF	—	25.00	45.00	85.00	150	—

Y# 7 20 FENIGOW

3.9000 g., Iron, 23 mm. **Obv:** Value **Rev:** Crowned eagle with wings open

Date	Mintage	F	VF	XF	Unc	BU
1917FF	1,900,000	2.00	4.00	6.00	11.50	—
1918FF	19,260,000	0.75	1.25	2.50	5.50	—

Y# 7a 20 FENIGOW

Zinc **Obv:** Value **Rev:** Crowned eagle with wings open **Note:** Error planchet.

Date	Mintage	F	VF	XF	Unc	BU
1917FF	—	35.00	60.00	100	200	—

REPUBLIC

STANDARD COINAGE

100 Groszy = 1 Zloty

Y# 8 GROSZ

1.5000 g., Brass, 14.7 mm. **Obv:** Crowned eagle with wings open **Rev:** Stylized value **Designer:** Wojciech Jastrebowski **Note:** Some authorities consider this strike a pattern.

Date	Mintage	F	VF	XF	Unc	BU
1923	—	—	—	—	200	—

Y# 8a GROSZ

1.5000 g., Bronze, 14.7 mm. **Obv:** Crowned eagle with wings open **Rev:** Stylized value

Date	Mintage	F	VF	XF	Unc	BU
1923	30,000,000	0.25	0.50	1.75	10.00	—
1925(w)	40,000,000	0.25	0.50	1.75	9.00	—
1927(w)	17,000,000	0.25	0.50	1.75	10.00	—
1928(w)	13,600,000	0.25	0.50	1.75	9.00	—
1930(w)	22,500,000	4.00	10.00	25.00	40.00	—
1931(w)	9,000,000	0.50	1.00	2.00	10.00	—
1932(w)	12,000,000	0.50	1.00	2.00	10.00	—
1933(w)	7,000,000	0.50	1.00	2.00	10.00	—
1934(w)	5,900,000	0.50	1.00	2.00	12.00	—
1935(w)	7,300,000	0.50	1.00	2.00	5.00	—
1936(w)	12,600,000	0.50	1.00	2.00	5.00	—
1937(w)	17,370,000	0.25	0.50	0.75	2.50	—
1938(w)	20,530,000	0.25	0.50	0.75	2.50	—
1939(w)	12,000,000	0.25	0.50	0.75	2.50	—

Y# 9 2 GROSZE

2.0000 g., Brass, 17.6 mm. **Obv:** Crowned eagle with wings open **Rev:** Stylized value **Designer:** W. Jastrzebowski

Date	Mintage	F	VF	XF	Unc	BU
1923	20,500,000	3.50	12.50	22.50	45.00	60.00

Y# 9a 2 GROSZE

2.0000 g., Bronze, 17.6 mm. **Obv:** Crowned eagle with wings open **Rev:** Stylized value **Designer:** Wojciech Jastrebowski

Date	Mintage	F	VF	XF	Unc	BU
1925(w)	39,000,000	0.50	2.00	4.50	10.00	—
1927(w)	15,300,000	0.50	2.00	4.50	10.00	—
1928(w)	13,400,000	0.50	2.00	4.50	10.00	—
1930(w)	20,000,000	0.50	2.00	4.50	10.00	—
1931(w)	9,500,000	1.75	2.50	5.50	12.75	—
1932(w)	6,500,000	2.00	4.00	6.00	15.00	—
1933(w)	7,000,000	2.00	4.00	6.00	15.00	—
1934(w)	9,350,000	1.75	3.00	7.50	17.50	—
1935(w)	5,800,000	0.20	0.75	2.00	5.00	—
1936(w)	5,800,000	0.20	0.75	2.00	5.00	—
1937(w)	17,360,000	0.20	0.40	0.60	2.50	—
1938(w)	20,530,000	0.20	0.40	0.60	2.50	—
1939(w)	12,000,000	0.20	0.40	0.60	2.50	—

Y# 10 5 GROSZY

3.0000 g., Brass, 20. mm. **Obv:** Crowned eagle with wings open **Rev:** Stylized value **Designer:** W. Jastrzebowski

Date	Mintage	F	VF	XF	Unc	BU
1923	32,000,000	0.50	2.00	5.00	10.00	—

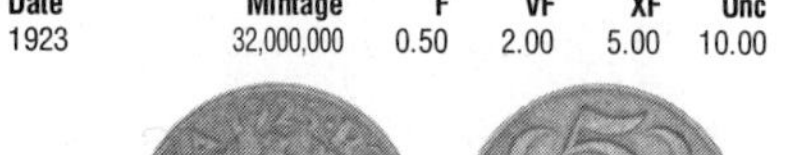

Y# 10a 5 GROSZY

3.0000 g., Bronze, 20 mm. **Obv:** Crowned eagle with wings open **Rev:** Stylized value **Designer:** Wojciech Jastrebowski

Date	Mintage	F	VF	XF	Unc	BU
1923 Proof	350	Value: 150				
1925(w)	45,500,000	0.20	0.40	4.00	8.00	—
1928(w)	8,900,000	0.20	0.40	5.00	10.00	—
1930(w)	14,200,000	0.20	0.40	5.00	12.00	—
1931(w)	1,500,000	0.50	1.00	10.00	20.00	—
1934(w)	420,000	5.00	7.50	35.00	75.00	—
1935(w)	4,660,000	0.20	0.40	0.60	5.00	—
1936(w)	4,660,000	0.20	0.40	0.60	5.00	—
1937(w)	9,050,000	0.20	0.40	0.60	2.50	—
1938(w)	17,300,000	0.20	0.40	0.60	2.50	—
1939(w)	10,000,000	0.20	0.40	0.60	2.50	—

Y# 11 10 GROSZY

2.0000 g., Nickel, 17.6 mm. **Obv:** Crowned eagle with wings open **Rev:** Value within wreath **Designer:** Wojciech Jastrebowski

Date	Mintage	F	VF	XF	Unc	BU
1923	100,000,000	0.20	0.45	0.80	1.25	—

Y# 12 20 GROSZY

3.0000 g., Nickel, 20 mm. **Obv:** Crowned eagle with wings open **Rev:** Value within wreath

Date	Mintage	F	VF	XF	Unc	BU
1923	150,000,000	0.35	0.75	1.25	2.00	—
1923 Proof	10	Value: 300				

Y# 13 50 GROSZY

5.0000 g., Nickel, 23 mm. **Obv:** Crowned eagle with wings open **Rev:** Value within wreath

Date	Mintage	F	VF	XF	Unc	BU
1923	100,000,000	0.40	0.80	1.50	3.50	—
1923 Proof	10	Value: 350				

Y# 15 ZLOTY

5.0000 g., 0.7500 Silver 0.1206 oz. ASW, 23 mm. **Obv:** Crowned eagle with wings open **Rev:** Bust left **Edge:** Reeded **Designer:** Tadeusz Breyer

Date	Mintage	F	VF	XF	Unc	BU
1924 (Paris)	16,000,000	2.50	6.00	20.00	55.00	—
Note: Torch and cornucopia flank date						
1924 (Birmingham); Proof	8	Value: 600				
1925 (London)	24,000,000	2.50	5.00	12.00	30.00	—
Note: Dot after date						

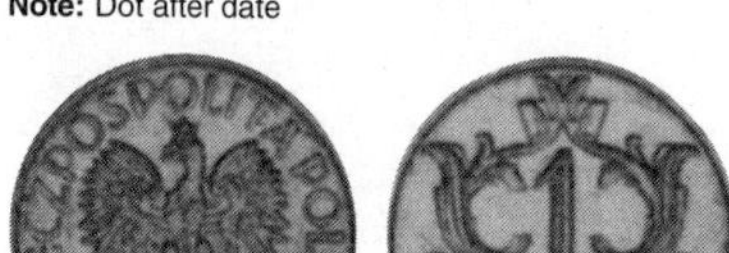

Y# 14 ZLOTY

7.0000 g., Nickel, 25 mm. **Obv:** Crowned eagle with wings open **Rev:** Value within stylized design **Designer:** T. Kotarbinski

Date	Mintage	F	VF	XF	Unc	BU
1929(w)	32,000,000	0.75	1.50	2.50	7.00	—

Y# 16 2 ZLOTE

10.0000 g., 0.7500 Silver 0.2411 oz. ASW, 27 mm. **Obv:** Crowned eagle with wings open **Rev:** Head left **Edge:** Reeded **Designer:** Tadeusz Breyer

Date	Mintage	F	VF	XF	Unc	BU
1924 (Paris)	8,200,000	5.50	10.00	20.00	85.00	—
Note: Torch and cornucopia flank date						
1924 H (Birmingham)	1,200,000	17.50	35.00	175	450	—
1924 (Birmingham); Proof	60	Value: 600				
1924 (Philadelphia)	800,000	10.00	20.00	60.00	125	—
Note: Without privy marks, coin alignment						
1925 (London)	11,000,000	5.00	9.00	17.50	47.50	—
Note: Dot after date						
1925 (Philadelphia)	5,200,000	6.50	12.00	40.00	75.00	—
Note: Without privy marks						

Y# 20 2 ZLOTE

4.4000 g., 0.7500 Silver 0.1061 oz. ASW, 22 mm. **Obv:** National arms **Obv. Legend:** RRZECZPOSPOLITA POLSKA **Rev:** Radiant head of Queen Jadwiga left **Edge:** Milled **Designer:** A. Madeyski

Date	Mintage	F	VF	XF	Unc	BU
1932(w)	15,700,000	2.25	4.00	7.00	13.50	16.50
1933(w)	9,250,000	2.25	4.00	7.00	13.50	16.50
1934(w)	250,000	4.00	7.00	12.00	27.50	—

Y# 27 2 ZLOTE

4.4000 g., 0.7500 Silver 0.1061 oz. ASW, 22 mm. **Obv:** Crowned eagle with wings open **Rev:** Head of Jozef Pilsudski left **Edge:** Reeded **Designer:** Stanislaw K. Ostrowski

Date	Mintage	F	VF	XF	Unc	BU
1934(w)	10,425,000	3.00	6.00	10.00	25.00	—
1936(w)	75,000	20.00	75.00	125	250	—

Y# 30 2 ZLOTE

4.4000 g., 0.7500 Silver 0.1061 oz. ASW, 22 mm. **Subject:** 15th Anniversary of Gdynia Seaport **Obv:** Crowned eagle with wings open **Rev:** Sailing ship **Designer:** J. Aumiller

Date	Mintage	F	VF	XF	Unc	BU
1936(w)	3,918,000	3.00	6.00	12.00	30.00	—

Y# 18 5 ZLOTYCH

18.0000 g., 0.7500 Silver 0.4340 oz. ASW, 33 mm. **Obv:** Crowned eagle with wings open **Rev:** Winged Victory right **Edge Lettering:** SALUS REIPUBLICAE SUPREMA LEX **Designer:** E. Wittig

Date	Mintage	F	VF	XF	Unc	BU
1928(w)	7,500,000	15.00	30.00	65.00	125	—
Note: Conjoined arrow and K mint mark						
1928 Error	Inc. above	40.00	75.00	100	225	—
Note: "SUPRMA" edge inscription						
1928 Without mint mark	10,000,000	13.50	25.00	65.00	125	—
Note: 4,300,000 struck in London and 5,700,000 in Belgium						
1930(w)	5,900,000	60.00	120	275	450	—
1931(w)	2,200,000	75.00	150	200	500	—
1932(w)	3,100,000	90.00	175	350	—	—

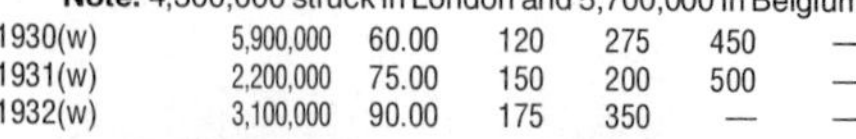

Y# 19.1 5 ZLOTYCH

18.0000 g., 0.7500 Silver 0.4340 oz. ASW, 33 mm. **Subject:** Centennial of 1830 Revolution **Obv:** Crowned eagle with wings open flanked by value **Rev:** Pole with flag and banner divides dates **Edge Lettering:** SALUS REIPUBLICAE SUPREMA LEX **Designer:** Wojciech Jastrebowski

Date	Mintage	F	VF	XF	Unc	BU
1930(w)	1,000,000	8.00	16.50	35.00	100	—

Y# 19.2 5 ZLOTYCH

18.0000 g., 0.7500 Silver 0.4340 oz. ASW **Obv:** Crowned imperial eagle **Rev:** Pole with flag and banner divides dates **Note:** High relief.

Date	Mintage	VF	XF	Unc	BU
1930(w)	200	75.00	175	375	750	—

Y# 21 5 ZLOTYCH

11.0000 g., 0.7500 Silver 0.2652 oz. ASW, 28 mm. **Obv:** National arms flanked by value **Obv. Legend:** RZECZPOSPOLITA POLSKA **Rev:** Radiant head of Queen Jadwiga left **Edge:** Reeded **Designer:** A. Madeyski

Date	Mintage	F	VF	XF	Unc	BU
1932 (Warsaw : tiny arrow in space between talons of eagle's left claw)	1,000,000	15.00	50.00	200	475	—
1932 (London); without mint mark	3,000,000	—	BV	6.50	15.00	20.00
1933(w)	11,000,000	—	BV	5.00	12.50	17.50
1933(w) Proof	100	—	—	—	—	—
1934(w)	250,000	BV	4.00	8.00	20.00	—

Y# 25 5 ZLOTYCH

11.0000 g., 0.7500 Silver 0.2652 oz. ASW, 28 mm. **Obv:** Rifle Corps symbol below eagle with wings open **Rev:** Head of Jozef Pilsudski left **Edge:** Reeded **Designer:** Stanislaw K. Ostrowski

Date	Mintage	F	VF	XF	Unc	BU
1934(w)	300,000	6.00	9.00	17.50	40.00	—

Y# 28 5 ZLOTYCH

11.0000 g., 0.7500 Silver 0.2652 oz. ASW, 28 mm. **Obv:** Radiant crowned eagle with wings open **Rev:** Head of Jozef Pilsudski left **Edge:** Reeded **Designer:** Stanislaw K. Ostrowski

Date	Mintage	F	VF	XF	Unc	BU
1934(w)	6,510,000	BV	4.50	9.00	20.00	25.00
1935(w)	1,800,000	BV	4.75	10.00	22.00	28.00
1936(w)	1,800,000	BV	4.75	10.00	22.00	28.00
1938(w)	289,000	5.00	7.50	15.00	30.00	—

Y# 31 5 ZLOTYCH

11.0000 g., 0.7500 Silver 0.2652 oz. ASW, 28 mm. **Subject:** 15th Anniversary of Gdynia Seaport **Obv:** Crowned eagle with wings open **Rev:** Sailing ship **Edge:** Reeded **Designer:** J. Aumiller

Date	Mintage	F	VF	XF	Unc	BU
1936(w)	1,000,000	7.00	12.00	25.00	50.00	—

Y# 32 10 ZLOTYCH

3.2258 g., 0.9000 Gold 0.0933 oz. AGW, 19 mm. **Obv:** Crowned eagle with wings open **Rev:** Crowned head left **Note:** Never released into circulation; similar design to Y#33.

Date	Mintage	F	VF	XF	Unc	BU
ND(1925)(w)	50,350	—	BV	90.00	165	225

Y# 22 10 ZLOTYCH

22.0000 g., 0.7500 Silver 0.5305 oz. ASW, 34 mm. **Obv:** National arms **Obv. Legend:** RZECZPOSPOLITA POLSKA **Rev:** Radiant head of Queen Jadwiga left **Edge:** Reeded **Designer:** J. Aumiller

Date	Mintage	F	VF	XF	Unc	BU
1932(w)	3,100,000	8.50	9.50	13.50	30.00	38.00
Note: Warsaw Mint : tiny arrow in space between talons of eagle's left claw						
1932	6,000,000	8.50	9.50	13.50	30.00	38.00
Note: London Mint: without mint mark						
1932(w) Proof	100	—	—	—	—	—
1933(w)	2,800,000	8.50	9.50	13.50	30.00	38.00
1933(w) Proof	100	—	—	—	—	—

Y# 23 10 ZLOTYCH

22.0000 g., 0.7500 Silver 0.5305 oz. ASW, 34 mm. **Subject:** Jan III Sobieski's Victory Over the Turks **Obv:** Crowned eagle with wings open **Rev:** Uniformed bust right **Edge:** Reeded **Designer:** Zofia Trzcinski-Kaminska

Date	Mintage	F	VF	XF	Unc	BU
ND(1933)(w)	300,000	9.00	16.00	25.00	55.00	—
ND(1933)(w) Proof	100	—	—	—	—	—

Y# 24 10 ZLOTYCH

22.0000 g., 0.7500 Silver 0.5305 oz. ASW, 34 mm. **Subject:** 70th Anniversary of 1863 Insurrection **Obv:** Crowned eagle with wings open **Rev:** Head of Romuald Traugutt 3/4 facing divides dates **Edge:** Reeded **Designer:** Z. Trzcinska-Kaminska

Date	Mintage	F	VF	XF	Unc	BU
ND(1933)(w)	300,000	12.00	20.00	40.00	65.00	—
ND(1933)(w) Proof	100	—	—	—	—	—

Y# 26 10 ZLOTYCH

22.0000 g., 0.7500 Silver 0.5305 oz. ASW, 34 mm. **Obv:** Rifle Corps symbol below eagle with wings open **Rev:** Head of Jozef Pilsudski left **Edge:** Reeded **Designer:** Stanislaw K. Ostrowski

Date	Mintage	F	VF	XF	Unc	BU
1934(w)	300,000	10.00	17.50	25.00	50.00	—

Y# 29 10 ZLOTYCH

22.0000 g., 0.7500 Silver 0.5305 oz. ASW, 34 mm. **Obv:** Eagle with wings open with no symbols below **Rev:** Head of Jozef Pilsudski left **Edge:** Reeded **Designer:** Stanislaw K. Ostrowski

Date	Mintage	F	VF	XF	Unc	BU
1934(w)	200,000	12.00	18.00	25.00	55.00	—
1935(w)	1,670,000	BV	8.50	14.00	30.00	40.00
1936(w)	2,130,000	BV	8.50	14.00	30.00	40.00
1937(w)	908,000	BV	8.50	16.00	40.00	—
1938(w)	234,000	8.50	10.00	22.00	50.00	—
1939(w)	—	BV	8.50	16.00	40.00	—

WWII GERMAN OCCUPATION

OCCUPATION COINAGE

Y# 34 GROSZ

1.1700 g., Zinc, 14.7 mm. **Obv:** Crowned eagle with wings open **Rev:** Stylized value **Designer:** W. Jastrebowski

Date	Mintage	F	VF	XF	Unc	BU
1939(w)	33,909,000	0.50	1.00	1.75	3.50	—

Y# 35 5 GROSZY

1.7200 g., Zinc, 16 mm. **Obv:** Crowned eagle with wings open, hole in center **Rev:** Stylized value, hole in center **Designer:** W. Jastrebowski

Date	Mintage	F	VF	XF	Unc	BU
1939(w)	15,324,000	0.50	1.50	2.00	5.00	—

Y# 36 10 GROSZY

2.0000 g., Zinc, 17.6 mm. **Obv:** Crowned imperial eagle **Rev:** Value **Designer:** W. Jastrzebowski

Date	Mintage	F	VF	XF	Unc	BU
1923(w)	42,175,000	0.10	0.20	0.40	2.00	—

Note: Actually struck in 1941-44

Y# 37 20 GROSZY

2.9700 g., Zinc, 20 mm. **Obv:** Crowned eagle with wings open **Rev:** Value within wreath **Designer:** W. Jastrzebowski

Date	Mintage	F	VF	XF	Unc	BU
1923(w)	40,025,000	0.15	0.25	0.50	2.00	—

Note: Actually struck in 1941-44

Y# 38 50 GROSZY

5.0000 g., Nickel Plated Iron, 23 mm. **Obv:** Crowned eagle with wings open **Rev:** Value within wreath **Designer:** W. Jastrzebowski

Date	Mintage	F	VF	XF	Unc	BU
1938(w)	32,000,000	1.00	2.00	4.00	8.50	—

Y# 38a 50 GROSZY

Iron **Obv:** Crowned eagle with wings open **Rev:** Value within wreath

Date	Mintage	F	VF	XF	Unc	BU
1938(w)	—	1.25	2.50	5.00	10.00	—

Note: Varieties exist

REPUBLIC

Post War

STANDARD COINAGE

Y# 39 GROSZ

0.5000 g., Aluminum, 14.7 mm. **Obv:** Eagle with wings open **Rev:** Value at upper right of sprig **Edge:** Reeded **Designer:** A. Peter **Note:** 116,000 were struck at Warsaw, the remainder at Budapest.

Date	Mintage	F	VF	XF	Unc	BU
1949	400,116,000	0.10	0.20	0.30	0.75	—

Y# 40 2 GROSZE

0.5800 g., Aluminum, 16 mm. **Obv:** Eagle with wings open **Rev:** Value at upper right of sprig **Edge:** Reeded **Designer:** A. Peter **Note:** 106,000 were struck at Warsaw, the remainder at Budapest.

Date	Mintage	F	VF	XF	Unc	BU
1949	300,106,000	0.10	0.25	0.50	1.00	—

Y# 41 5 GROSZY

3.0000 g., Bronze, 20 mm. **Obv:** Eagle with wings open **Rev:** Value at upper right of sprig **Designer:** A. Peter

Date	Mintage	F	VF	XF	Unc	BU
1949	300,000,000	0.10	0.25	0.50	1.00	—

Y# 41a 5 GROSZY

1.0000 g., Aluminum, 20 mm. **Obv:** Eagle with wings open **Rev:** Value at upper right of sprig **Designer:** A. Peter

Date	Mintage	F	VF	XF	Unc	BU
1949	200,000,000	0.10	0.25	0.75	1.50	—

Y# 42 10 GROSZY

2.0000 g., Copper-Nickel, 17.6 mm. **Obv:** Eagle with wings open **Rev:** Value above sprig **Designer:** A. Peter

Date	Mintage	F	VF	XF	Unc	BU
1949	200,000,000	0.20	0.40	0.60	1.50	—

Y# 42a 10 GROSZY

0.7000 g., Aluminum, 17.6 mm. **Obv:** Eagle with wings open **Rev:** Value above sprig **Designer:** A. Peter

Date	Mintage	F	VF	XF	Unc	BU
1949	31,047,000	0.10	0.25	0.75	2.50	—

Y# 43 20 GROSZY

2.8900 g., Copper-Nickel, 20 mm. **Obv:** Eagle with wings open **Rev:** Value above sprig **Designer:** A. Peter

Date	Mintage	F	VF	XF	Unc	BU
1949	133,383,000	0.25	0.45	0.75	2.00	—

Y# 43a 20 GROSZY

1.0000 g., Aluminum, 20 mm. **Obv:** Eagle with wings open **Rev:** Value above sprig **Designer:** A. Peter

Date	Mintage	F	VF	XF	Unc	BU
1949	197,472,000	0.10	0.25	0.75	2.50	—

Y# 44 50 GROSZY

5.0000 g., Copper-Nickel, 23 mm. **Obv:** Eagle with wings open **Rev:** Value above sprig **Edge:** Reeded **Designer:** A. Peter

Date	Mintage	F	VF	XF	Unc	BU
1949	109,000,000	0.35	0.65	1.00	2.50	—

Y# 44a 50 GROSZY

1.6000 g., Aluminum, 23 mm. **Obv:** Eagle with wings open **Rev:** Value above sprig **Edge:** Reeded **Designer:** A. Peter

Date	Mintage	F	VF	XF	Unc	BU
1949	59,393,000	0.10	0.25	1.50	5.00	—

Y# 45 ZLOTY

7.0000 g., Copper-Nickel, 25 mm. **Obv:** Eagle with wings open **Rev:** Value within wreath **Edge:** Reeded **Designer:** A. Ham

Date	Mintage	F	VF	XF	Unc	BU
1949	87,053,000	1.00	1.50	2.25	4.00	—

Y# 45a ZLOTY

2.1200 g., Aluminum, 25 mm. **Obv:** Eagle with wings open **Rev:** Value within wreath **Edge:** Reeded **Designer:** A. Ham

Date	Mintage	F	VF	XF	Unc	BU
1949	43,000,000	0.10	0.25	2.50	6.00	—

PEOPLES REPUBLIC

STANDARD COINAGE

Y# A46 5 GROSZY

0.6100 g., Aluminum, 16 mm. **Obv:** Eagle with wings open **Rev:** Value to upper right of sprig **Designer:** A. Peter

Date	Mintage	F	VF	XF	Unc	BU
1958	53,521,000	—	—	0.10	0.20	—
1959	28,564,000	—	—	0.10	0.15	—
1960	12,246,000	—	0.50	1.50	2.75	—
1961	29,502,000	—	—	0.10	0.20	—
1962	90,257,000	—	—	0.10	0.15	—
1963	20,878,000	—	—	0.10	0.15	—
1965MW	5,050,000	—	0.75	2.00	4.00	—
1967MW	10,056,000	—	0.75	2.00	4.00	—
1968MW	10,196,000	—	0.75	2.00	4.00	—
1970MW	20,095,000	—	—	0.10	0.20	—
1971MW	20,000,000	—	—	0.10	0.20	—
1972MW	10,000,000	—	—	0.10	0.20	—

Y# AA47 10 GROSZY

0.7000 g., Aluminum, 17.6 mm. **Obv:** Eagle with wings open **Rev:** Value above sprig **Edge:** Plain **Note:** Varieties in date size exist.

Date	Mintage	F	VF	XF	Unc	BU
1961	73,400,000	—	0.75	2.50	4.00	—
1962	25,362,000	—	1.75	5.00	20.00	—
1963	40,434,000	—	—	0.50	1.50	—
1965MW	50,521,000	—	0.25	1.00	2.00	—
1966MW	70,749,000	—	—	0.50	1.50	—
1967MW	62,059,000	—	—	0.50	1.50	—
1968MW	62,204,000	—	—	0.50	1.50	—
1969MW	71,566,000	—	—	0.50	1.00	—
1970MW	38,844,000	—	—	0.10	0.50	—
1971MW	50,000,000	—	—	0.10	0.50	—
1972MW	60,000,000	—	—	0.10	0.50	—
1973MW	80,000,000	—	—	0.10	0.25	—
1973 Rare	—	—	—	—	—	—
1974	50,000,000	—	—	0.10	0.15	—
Note: Struck at Kremnica Mint						
1975MW	50,000,000	—	—	0.10	0.15	—
1976MW	100,000,000	—	—	—	0.10	—
1977MW	100,000,000	—	—	—	0.10	—
1978MW	71,204,000	—	—	—	0.10	—
1979MW	73,191,000	—	—	—	0.10	—
1979MW Proof	5,000	Value: 1.00				
1980MW	60,623,000	—	—	—	0.10	—
1980MW Proof	5,000	Value: 1.00				
1981MW	70,000,000	—	—	—	0.10	—
1981MW Proof	5,000	Value: 1.00				
1983MW	9,600,000	—	—	—	0.10	—
1985MW	9,957,000	—	—	—	0.10	—

Y# A47 20 GROSZY

1.0000 g., Aluminum, 20 mm. **Obv:** Eagle with wings open **Rev:** Value above sprig **Edge:** Plain **Designer:** A. Peter **Note:** Date varieties exist.

Date	Mintage	F	VF	XF	Unc	BU
1957	3,940,000	—	5.00	17.00	40.00	—
1961	53,108,000	—	1.75	3.75	8.00	—
1962	19,140,000	—	2.00	5.00	12.50	—
1963	41,217,000	—	—	0.50	2.00	—
1965MW	32,022,000	—	—	0.50	2.00	—
1966MW	23,860,000	—	—	0.50	2.00	—
1967MW	29,099,000	—	—	1.00	5.00	—
1968MW	29,191,000	—	—	1.00	5.00	—
1969MW	40,227,000	—	—	0.50	1.50	—
1970MW	20,028,000	—	—	0.10	1.00	—
1971MW	20,000,000	—	—	0.10	1.00	—
1972MW	60,000,000	—	—	0.10	1.00	—
1973	50,000,000	—	—	0.10	0.50	—
Note: Struck at Kremnica Mint						
1973MW	65,000,000	—	—	0.10	0.50	—
Note: Struck at Kremnica Mint						
1975MW	50,000,000	—	—	0.10	0.50	—
1976MW Large date	100,000,000	—	—	0.10	0.50	—
1976MW Small date	Inc. above	—	—	0.10	0.50	—
1977MW	80,730,000	—	—	0.10	0.20	—
1978MW	50,730,000	—	—	0.10	0.20	—
1979MW	45,252,000	—	—	0.10	0.20	—
1979MW Proof	5,000	Value: 1.00				
1980MW	30,020,000	—	—	0.10	0.20	—
1980MW Proof	5,000	Value: 1.00				
1981MW	60,082,000	—	—	0.10	0.20	—
1981MW Proof	5,000	Value: 1.00				
1983MW	—	—	—	0.10	0.20	—
1985MW	16,227,000	—	—	0.10	0.20	—

Y# 48.1 50 GROSZY

1.6000 g., Aluminum, 23 mm. **Obv:** Eagle with wings open **Obv. Designer:** J. Koren **Rev:** Value above sprig **Rev. Designer:** A. Ham **Edge:** Reeded

Date	Mintage	F	VF	XF	Unc	BU
1957	91,316,000	—	0.75	2.00	5.00	—
1965MW	22,090,000	—	0.25	1.50	4.00	—
1967MW	2,027,000	—	1.25	4.00	15.00	—
1968MW	2,065,000	—	1.25	4.00	15.00	—
1970MW	3,273,000	—	0.15	0.30	2.00	—
1971MW	7,000,000	—	0.10	0.25	1.00	—
1972MW	10,000,000	—	0.10	0.25	0.50	—
1973MW	39,000	—	0.10	0.20	0.50	—
1974MW	33,000,000	—	0.10	0.20	0.50	—
1975	25,000,000	—	0.10	0.20	0.50	—
Note: Struck at Kremnica Mint						
1976	25,000,000	—	0.10	0.20	0.40	—
Note: Struck at Kremnica Mint						
1977MW	50,000,000	—	0.10	0.20	0.40	—
1978MW	50,020,000	—	0.10	0.20	0.40	—
1978	18,600,000	—	0.10	0.20	0.40	—
Note: Struck at Kremnica Mint						

Date	Mintage	F	VF	XF	Unc	BU
1982MW	16,067,000	—	0.10	0.20	0.40	—
1982MW Proof	5,000	Value: 3.50				
1983MW	39,667,000	—	0.10	0.20	0.40	—
1984MW	44,217,000	—	0.10	0.20	0.40	—
1985MW	49,052,000	—	0.10	0.20	0.40	—

Y# 48.2 50 GROSZY

1.6000 g., Aluminum, 23 mm. **Obv:** Eagle with wings open **Obv. Designer:** J. Koren **Rev:** Value above sprig **Rev. Designer:** A. Ham **Edge:** Reeded

Date	Mintage	F	VF	XF	Unc	BU
1986MW	45,796,000	—	0.10	0.20	0.40	—
1986MW Proof	5,000	Value: 3.50				
1987MW	21,257,000	—	0.10	0.20	0.40	—
1987MW Proof	5,000	Value: 3.50				

Y# 49.1 ZLOTY

2.1200 g., Aluminum, 25 mm. **Obv:** Eagle with wings open **Obv. Designer:** A. Peter **Rev:** Value within wreath **Rev. Designer:** J. Koren and A. Ham **Edge:** Reeded

Date	Mintage	F	VF	XF	Unc	BU
1957	58,631,000	—	1.00	3.50	20.00	—
1965MW	15,015,000	—	0.50	1.00	3.00	—
1966MW	18,185,000	—	0.75	2.00	4.00	—
1967MW	1,002,000	—	2.25	6.00	15.00	—
1968MW	1,176,000	—	2.25	6.00	15.00	—
1969MW	3,024,000	—	1.25	3.00	6.00	—
1970MW	6,016,000	—	0.15	0.50	1.50	—
1971MW	6,000,000	—	0.15	0.50	1.00	—
1972MW	7,000,000	—	0.15	0.50	1.00	—
1973MW	15,000,000	—	0.10	0.50	1.00	—
1974MW	42,000,000	—	0.10	0.15	0.50	—
1975	22,000,000	—	0.10	0.15	0.50	—
Note: Struck at Kremnica Mint						
1975MW	33,000,000	—	0.10	0.15	0.50	—
1976	22,000,000	—	0.10	0.50	1.00	—
Note: Struck at Kremnica Mint						
1977MW	65,000,000	—	0.10	0.50	1.00	—
1978	16,399,999	—	0.10	0.50	1.50	—
Note: Struck at Kremnica Mint						
1978MW	80,000,000	—	0.10	0.50	1.00	—
1980MW	100,002,000	—	0.10	0.15	0.50	—
1980MW Proof	5,000	Value: 2.50				
1981MW	4,082,000	—	0.10	0.15	1.00	—
1981MW Proof	5,000	Value: 2.50				
1982MW	59,643,000	—	0.10	0.15	0.30	—
1982MW Proof	5,000	Value: 3.50				
1983MW	49,636,000	—	0.10	0.15	0.25	—
1984MW	61,036,000	—	0.10	0.15	0.25	—
1985MW	167,939,000	—	0.10	0.15	0.25	—

Y# 49.2 ZLOTY

2.2000 g., Aluminum, 25 mm. **Obv:** Eagle with wings open **Obv. Designer:** A. Peter **Rev:** Value within wreath **Rev. Designer:** J. Koren and A. Ham **Edge:** Reeded

Date	Mintage	F	VF	XF	Unc	BU
1986MW	130,697,000	—	0.10	0.15	0.25	—
1986MW Proof	5,000	Value: 3.50				
1987MW	100,081,000	—	0.10	0.15	0.25	—
1987MW Proof	5,000	Value: 3.50				
1988MW	96,400,000	—	0.10	0.15	0.25	—
1988MW Proof	5,000	Value: 3.50				

Y# 49.3 ZLOTY

0.5700 g., Aluminum, 16 mm. **Obv:** Eagle with wings open **Obv. Designer:** A. Peter **Rev:** Value within wreath **Rev. Designer:** J. Koren and A. Ham **Edge:** Reeded

Date	Mintage	F	VF	XF	Unc	BU
1989MW	49,410,000	—	0.10	0.15	0.25	—
1989MW Proof	5,000	Value: 3.50				
1990MW	30,667,000	—	0.10	0.15	0.25	—
1990MW Proof	5,000	Value: 3.50				

Y# 46 2 ZLOTE

2.7000 g., Aluminum, 27 mm. **Obv:** Eagle with wings open **Rev:** Value above design and fruit **Edge:** Reeded **Designer:** W. Jastrzebowski

Date	Mintage	F	VF	XF	Unc	BU
1958	83,640,000	—	0.20	1.50	6.00	—
1959	7,170,000	—	0.50	4.00	20.00	—
1960	36,131,000	—	0.20	0.50	3.00	—
1970MW	2,013,999	—	0.30	1.00	4.00	—
1971MW	3,000,000	—	0.20	1.00	4.00	—
1972MW	3,000,000	—	0.20	1.00	4.00	—
1973MW	10,000,000	—	0.15	0.50	1.50	—
1974MW	46,000,000	—	0.15	0.30	1.00	—

Y# 80.1 2 ZLOTE

3.0000 g., Brass, 21 mm. **Obv:** Eagle with wings open **Rev:** Value above design **Edge:** Reeded **Designer:** W. Kowalik

Date	Mintage	F	VF	XF	Unc	BU
1975	25,000,000	—	0.15	0.25	0.50	—
Note: Struck at Leningrad Mint						
1976	60,000,000	—	0.15	0.25	0.50	—
Note: Struck at Leningrad Mint						
1977	50,000,000	—	0.15	0.25	0.50	—
Note: Struck at Leningrad Mint						
1978	2,600,000	—	0.15	0.25	1.75	—
Note: Struck at Leningrad Mint						
1978MW	2,382,000	—	0.15	0.25	1.75	—
1979MW	85,752,000	—	0.15	0.25	0.50	—
1979MW Proof	5,000	Value: 2.50				
1980MW	66,610,000	—	0.15	0.25	0.50	—
1980MW Proof	5,000	Value: 2.50				
1981MW	40,306,000	—	0.15	0.25	0.50	—
1981MW Proof	5,000	Value: 2.50				
1982MW	43,318,000	—	0.15	0.25	0.50	—
1982MW Proof	5,000	Value: 3.50				
1983MW	35,244,000	—	0.15	0.25	0.50	—
1984MW	59,999,000	—	0.15	0.25	0.50	—
1985MW	100,300,000	—	0.15	0.25	0.50	—

Y# 80.2 2 ZLOTE

3.0000 g., Brass, 21 mm. **Obv:** Eagle with wings open **Rev:** Value above design **Edge:** Reeded **Designer:** W. Kowalik

Date	Mintage	F	VF	XF	Unc	BU
1986MW	60,718,000	—	0.15	0.25	0.50	—
1986MW Proof	5,000	Value: 3.50				
1987MW	44,673,000	—	0.15	0.25	0.50	—
1987MW Proof	5,000	Value: 3.50				
1988MW	94,651,000	—	0.15	0.25	0.50	—
1988MW Proof	5,000	Value: 3.50				

Y# 80.3 2 ZLOTE

0.7100 g., Aluminum, 18 mm. **Obv:** Eagle with wings open **Rev:** Value above design **Edge:** Reeded **Designer:** W. Kowalik

Date	Mintage	F	VF	XF	Unc	BU
1989MW	91,494,000	—	0.10	0.20	0.40	—
1989MW Proof	5,000	Value: 3.50				
1990MW	40,723,000	—	0.10	0.20	0.40	—
1990MW Proof	5,000	Value: 3.50				

Y# 47 5 ZLOTYCH

3.4500 g., Aluminum, 29 mm. **Obv:** Eagle with wings open **Obv. Designer:** W. Jastrebowski **Rev:** Fisherman with net **Rev. Designer:** J. Goslawski **Edge:** Reeded

Date	Mintage	F	VF	XF	Unc	BU
1958	1,328,000	—	7.50	12.50	20.00	—
Note: Two date varieties exist for strikes dated 1958						
1959	56,811,000	—	0.75	2.50	7.00	—
1960	16,300,999	—	0.25	1.50	5.00	—
1971MW	1,000,000	—	7.50	12.50	20.00	—
1973MW	5,000,000	—	0.20	1.00	4.00	—
1974MW	46,000,000	—	0.20	0.50	2.50	—

Y# 81.1 5 ZLOTYCH

5.0000 g., Brass, 24 mm. **Obv:** Eagle with wings open **Rev:** Value **Edge:** Reeded **Designer:** J. Markiewicz **Note:** Varieties in the letter size exist.

Date	Mintage	F	VF	XF	Unc	BU
1975	25,000,000	—	0.20	0.40	0.85	—
Note: Struck at Leningrad Mint						
1976	60,000,000	—	0.20	0.40	0.85	—
Note: Struck at Leningrad Mint						
1977	50,000,000	—	0.20	0.40	0.85	—
Note: Struck at Leningrad Mint						
1978MW Rare	—	—	—	—	—	—
1979MW	5,098,000	—	0.20	0.40	1.50	—
1979MW	5,000	Value: 3.50				
1980MW	10,100,000	—	0.20	0.40	0.85	—
1980MW Proof	5,000	Value: 2.50				
1981MW	4,008,000	—	0.20	0.40	1.75	—
1981MW Proof	5,000	Value: 2.50				
1982MW	25,379,000	—	0.20	0.40	0.85	—
1982MW Proof	5,000	Value: 3.50				
1983MW	30,531,000	—	0.20	0.40	0.85	—
1984MW	85,598,000	—	0.20	0.40	0.85	—
1985MW	20,501,000	—	0.20	0.40	0.85	—

Y# 81.2 5 ZLOTYCH

5.0000 g., Brass, 24 mm. **Obv:** Eagle with wings open **Rev:** Value **Edge:** Reeded **Designer:** J. Markiewicz

Date	Mintage	F	VF	XF	Unc	BU
1986MW	57,108,000	—	0.20	0.40	0.85	—
1986MW Proof	5,000	Value: 3.50				
1987MW	58,843,000	—	0.20	0.40	0.85	—
1987MW Proof	5,000	Value: 3.50				
1988MW	18,668,000	—	0.20	0.40	0.85	—
1988MW Proof	5,000	Value: 3.50				

Y# 81.3 5 ZLOTYCH

0.8800 g., Aluminum, 20 mm. **Obv:** Eagle with wings open **Rev:** Value **Edge:** Reeded **Designer:** J. Markiewicz

Date	Mintage	F	VF	XF	Unc	BU
1989MW	30,253,000	—	0.15	0.30	0.65	—
1989MW Proof	5,000	Value: 3.50				
1990MW	38,248,000	—	0.15	0.30	0.65	—
1990MW Proof	5,000	Value: 3.50				

Y# 50 10 ZLOTYCH

12.9000 g., Copper-Nickel, 31 mm. **Obv:** Eagle with wings open **Rev:** Head of Tadeusz Kosciuszko left **Edge:** Reeded **Designer:** K. Zielinski

Date	Mintage	F	VF	XF	Unc	BU
1959	13,107,000	—	0.60	2.00	6.50	—
1960	27,551,000	—	0.60	2.00	6.50	—
1966MW	4,157,000	—	1.00	8.00	18.00	—

Y# 50a 10 ZLOTYCH

9.5000 g., Copper-Nickel, 28 mm. **Obv:** Eagle with wings open **Rev:** Head of Tadeusz Kosciuszko left **Note:** Reduced size.

Date	Mintage	F	VF	XF	Unc	BU
1969MW	5,428,000	—	0.50	1.75	5.00	—
1970MW	13,783,000	—	0.50	1.00	2.00	—
1971MW	12,000,000	—	0.50	1.00	2.00	—
1972MW	10,000,000	—	0.50	1.00	2.00	—
1973MW	3,900,000	—	0.50	2.00	8.00	—

Y# 51 10 ZLOTYCH

12.9000 g., Copper-Nickel, 31 mm. **Obv:** Eagle with wings open **Rev:** Bust of Mikolaj Kopernik facing **Edge:** Reeded **Designer:** J. Goslawski

Date	Mintage	F	VF	XF	Unc	BU
1959	12,559,000	—	0.75	1.25	2.50	—
1965MW	3,000,000	—	1.00	5.00	15.00	—

Y# 51a 10 ZLOTYCH

9.5000 g., Copper-Nickel, 28 mm. **Obv:** Eagle with wings open **Rev:** Bust of Mikolaj Kopernik facing **Designer:** J.G. Miedzionkiel **Note:** Reduced size.

Date	Mintage	F	VF	XF	Unc	BU
1967MW	2,128,000	—	0.75	2.00	7.50	—
1968MW	9,389,000	—	0.75	1.25	2.50	—
1969MW	8,612,000	—	0.75	1.25	2.75	—

Y# 52 10 ZLOTYCH

12.9000 g., Copper-Nickel, 31 mm. **Subject:** 600th Anniversary of Jagiello University **Obv:** Eagle with wings open **Rev:** Stylized crowned head left **Edge:** Reeded **Designer:** W. Kowalik **Note:** Legends raised.

Date	Mintage	F	VF	XF	Unc	BU
ND(1964)	2,610,000	—	0.50	1.50	3.50	—

Y# 52a 10 ZLOTYCH

12.9000 g., Copper-Nickel, 31 mm. **Subject:** 600th Anniversary of Jagiello University **Obv:** Eagle with wings open **Rev:** Stylized crowned head left **Edge:** Reeded **Designer:** W. Kowalik **Note:** Legends incuse.

Date	Mintage	F	VF	XF	Unc	BU
ND(1964)	2,612,000	—	0.50	1.50	3.50	—

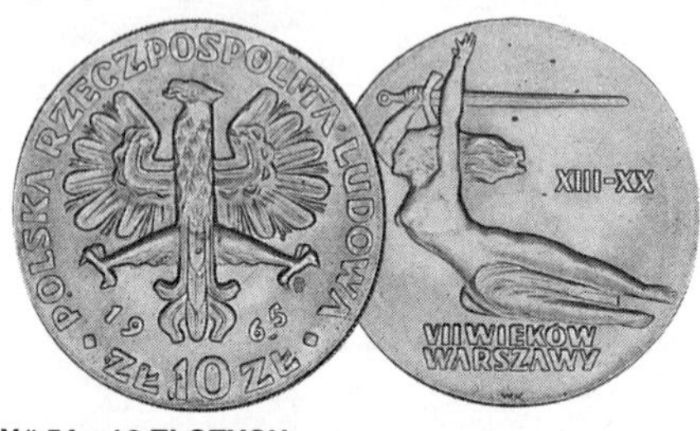

Y# 54 10 ZLOTYCH

12.9000 g., Copper-Nickel, 31 mm. **Subject:** 700th Anniversary of Warsaw **Obv:** Eagle with wings open **Rev:** Nike of Warsaw with sword **Edge:** Reeded **Designer:** Waclaw Kowalik

Date	Mintage	F	VF	XF	Unc	BU
1965MW	3,492,000	—	0.75	2.00	3.50	5.00

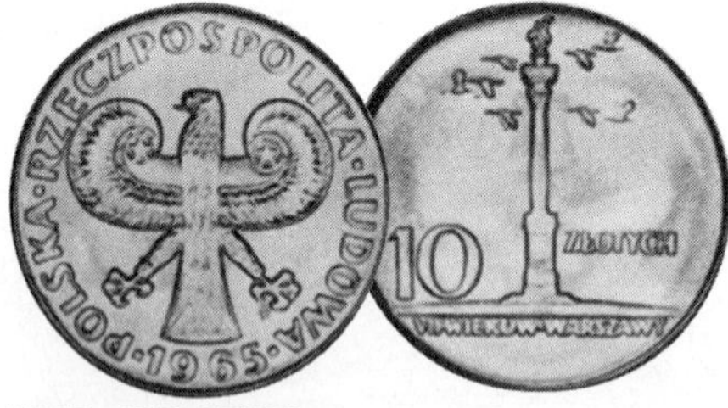

Y# 55 10 ZLOTYCH

12.9000 g., Copper-Nickel, 31 mm. **Subject:** 700th Anniversary of Warsaw **Obv:** Stylized eagle with wings open **Rev:** Sigismund Pillar **Edge:** Reeded **Designer:** Jerzy Jarnuszkiewics

Date	Mintage	F	VF	XF	Unc	BU
1965MW	2,000,000	—	0.75	2.00	3.50	5.00

Y# 56 10 ZLOTYCH

9.5000 g., Copper-Nickel, 28 mm. **Subject:** 200th Anniversary of Warsaw Mint **Obv:** Stylized eagle with wings open **Rev:** Sigismund Pillar **Edge Lettering:** W DWUSETNA ROCZNICE MENNICY WARSZAWSKIEJ **Designer:** Jerzy Jarnuszkiewicz

Date	Mintage	F	VF	XF	Unc	BU
1966MW	102,000	—	2.50	6.50	22.50	40.00

Y# 58 10 ZLOTYCH

9.5000 g., Copper-Nickel, 28 mm. **Subject:** 20th Anniversary - Death of General Swierczewski **Obv:** Eagle with wings open **Rev:** Military head left **Edge:** Reeded **Designer:** W. Kowalik

Date	Mintage	F	VF	XF	Unc	BU
1967MW	2,000,000	—	0.50	1.00	2.25	—

Y# 59 10 ZLOTYCH

9.5000 g., Copper-Nickel, 28 mm. **Subject:** Centennial - Birth of Marie Sklodowska Curie **Obv:** Eagle with wings open **Rev:** Head facing **Edge:** Reeded **Designer:** J. Markiewicz

Date	Mintage	F	VF	XF	Unc	BU
1967MW	2,000,000	—	0.50	1.00	2.25	—

Y# 60 10 ZLOTYCH

9.5000 g., Copper-Nickel, 28 mm. **Subject:** 25th Anniversary - Peoples Army **Obv:** Eagle with wings open standing on perch **Rev:** XXV and helmeted head right **Edge:** Reeded **Designer:** Jozef Markiewicz

Date	Mintage	F	VF	XF	Unc	BU
1968MW	2,000,000	—	0.50	1.00	2.25	—

Y# 61 10 ZLOTYCH

9.5000 g., Copper-Nickel, 28 mm. **Subject:** 25th Anniversary - Peoples Republic **Obv:** Eagle with wings open within circle **Obv. Designer:** J. Jarnuszkiewicz **Rev:** Radiant design within circle **Edge:** Reeded

Date	Mintage	F	VF	XF	Unc	BU
1969MW	2,000,000	—	0.50	1.00	2.25	—

Y# 62 10 ZLOTYCH

9.5000 g., Copper-Nickel, 28 mm. **Subject:** 25th Anniversary - Provincial Annexations **Obv:** Eagle with wings open, shield divides value **Rev:** Assorted shields **Edge:** Reeded **Designer:** Jerzy Jarnuszkiewicz

Date	Mintage	F	VF	XF	Unc	BU
1970MW	2,000,000	—	0.50	1.00	2.25	—

Y# 63 10 ZLOTYCH

9.5000 g., Copper-Nickel, 28 mm. **Series:** F.A.O. **Obv:** Eagle with wings open on shield **Rev:** Atlantic turbot and ear of barley **Edge:** Reeded **Designer:** Jerzy Jarnuszkiewicz

Date	Mintage	F	VF	XF	Unc	BU
1971MW	2,000,000	—	0.75	1.50	3.50	5.00

Y# 64 10 ZLOTYCH

9.5000 g., Copper-Nickel, 28 mm. **Subject:** 50th Anniversary - Battle of Upper Silesia **Obv:** Eagle with wings open divides date **Rev:** Design and emblem **Edge:** Reeded **Designer:** Waclaw Kowalik

Date	Mintage	F	VF	XF	Unc	BU
1971MW	2,000,000	—	0.50	1.00	2.25	—

Y# 65 10 ZLOTYCH

9.5000 g., Copper-Nickel, 28 mm. **Subject:** 50th Anniversary - Gdynia Seaport **Obv:** Eagle with wings open **Rev:** Map and emblem **Edge:** Reeded **Designer:** Waclaw Kowalik

Date	Mintage	F	VF	XF	Unc	BU
1972MW	2,000,000	—	0.50	1.00	2.25	—

Y# 73 10 ZLOTYCH

7.7000 g., Copper-Nickel, 25 mm. **Obv:** Eagle with wings open divides date **Rev:** Head of Boleslaw Prus left **Edge:** Reeded **Designer:** Jerzy Jarnuszkiewicz

Date	Mintage	F	VF	XF	Unc	BU
1975MW	35,000,000	—	0.25	0.65	1.25	—
1976MW	20,000,000	—	0.25	0.65	1.25	—
1977MW	25,000,000	—	0.25	0.65	1.25	—
1978MW	4,006,999	—	0.25	0.75	2.25	—
1981MW	2,655,000	—	0.25	1.00	3.75	—
1981MW Proof	5,000	Value: 5.50				
1982MW	16,341,000	—	0.25	0.65	1.25	—
1982MW Proof	5,000	Value: 6.50				
1983MW	14,248,000	—	0.25	0.65	1.25	—
1984MW	19,064,000	—	0.25	0.65	1.25	—

Y# 74 10 ZLOTYCH

7.7000 g., Copper-Nickel, 28 mm. **Obv:** Eagle with wings open **Rev:** Head of Adam Micklewicz left **Edge:** Reeded **Designer:** Jerzy Jarnuszkiewicz

Date	Mintage	F	VF	XF	Unc	BU
1975MW	35,000,000	—	0.25	0.65	1.25	—
1976MW	20,000,000	—	0.25	0.65	1.25	—

Y# 152.1 10 ZLOTYCH

7.7000 g., Copper-Nickel, 25 mm. **Obv:** Eagle with wings open **Rev:** Value **Edge:** Reeded

Date	Mintage	F	VF	XF	Unc	BU
1984MW	15,756,000	—	0.20	0.50	1.00	—
1985MW	5,282,000	—	0.20	0.50	1.00	—
1986MW	31,043,000	—	0.20	0.50	1.00	—
1986MW Proof	5,000	Value: 4.00				
1987MW	69,636,000	—	0.20	0.50	1.00	—
1987MW Proof	5,000	Value: 4.00				
1988MW	102,493,000	—	0.20	0.50	1.00	—
1988MW Proof	5,000	Value: 4.00				

Y# 152.2 10 ZLOTYCH

4.2700 g., Brass, 22 mm. **Obv:** Imperial eagle **Rev:** Value **Edge:** Reeded

Date	Mintage	F	VF	XF	Unc	BU
1989MW	80,800,000	—	0.20	0.40	0.80	—
1989MW Proof	5,000	Value: 4.00				
1990MW	106,892,000	—	0.20	0.40	0.80	—
1990MW Proof	5,000	Value: 4.00				

Y# 67 20 ZLOTYCH

10.1500 g., Copper-Nickel, 29 mm. **Obv:** Eagle with wings open within circle **Rev:** Value within designed waterfall **Edge:** Reeded **Designer:** Anna Jarnuszkiewicz

Date	Mintage	F	VF	XF	Unc	BU
1973	25,000,000	—	0.25	1.00	2.50	—
Note: Struck at Kremnica Mint						
1974	12,000,000	—	0.25	0.75	1.50	—
Note: Struck at Kremnica Mint						
1976	20,000,000	—	0.25	0.75	1.50	—
Note: Struck at Warsaw Mint						

Y# 69 20 ZLOTYCH

10.1500 g., Copper-Nickel, 29 mm. **Obv:** Eagle with wings open, value below **Rev:** Bust of Marceli Nowotko 1/4 left **Edge:** Reeded **Designer:** Stanislawa Watrobska

Date	Mintage	F	VF	XF	Unc	BU
1974MW	10,000,000	—	0.25	1.00	2.50	—
1975	10,000,000	—	0.25	1.00	2.00	—
Note: Struck at Kremnica Mint						
1976	20,000,000	—	0.25	0.75	1.50	—
Note: Struck at Kremnica Mint						
1976MW	30,000,000	—	0.25	0.75	1.50	—
1977MW	16,000,000	—	0.25	1.00	2.00	—
1983MW	152,000	—	0.25	5.00	12.50	—

Y# 70 20 ZLOTYCH

10.1500 g., Copper-Nickel, 29 mm. **Subject:** 25th Anniversary of the Comcon **Obv:** Imperial eagle above value **Rev:** Half sunflower, half cog wheel **Edge:** Reeded **Designer:** Jozef Markiewicz

Date	Mintage	F	VF	XF	Unc	BU
1974MW	2,000,000	—	0.75	1.25	2.50	—

Y# 75 20 ZLOTYCH

10.1500 g., Copper-Nickel, 29 mm. **Subject:** International Women's Year **Obv:** Imperial eagle above value **Rev:** Stylized head left **Edge:** Reeded **Designer:** Anna Jarnuszkiewicz

Date	Mintage	F	VF	XF	Unc	BU
1975MW	2,000,000	—	0.75	1.25	2.50	—

Y# 95 20 ZLOTYCH

10.1500 g., Copper-Nickel, 29 mm. **Obv:** Imperial eagle above value **Rev:** Head of Maria Konopnicka facing **Edge:** Reeded

Date	Mintage	F	VF	XF	Unc	BU
1978MW	2,010,000	—	0.75	1.25	2.75	—

Y# 97 20 ZLOTYCH

10.1500 g., Copper-Nickel, 29 mm. **Subject:** First Polish Cosmonaut **Obv:** Imperial eagle above value **Rev:** Cosmonaut head 1/4 left **Edge:** Reeded

Date	Mintage	F	VF	XF	Unc	BU
1978MW	2,009,000	—	0.75	1.25	2.75	—

Y# 99 20 ZLOTYCH

10.1500 g., Copper-Nickel, 29 mm. **Series:** International Year of the Child **Obv:** Imperial eagle above value **Rev:** Children playing **Edge:** Reeded

Date	Mintage	F	VF	XF	Unc	BU
1979MW	2,007,000	—	1.00	1.50	3.00	—
1979MW Proof	5,000	Value: 12.00				

Y# 108 20 ZLOTYCH
10.1500 g., Copper-Nickel, 29 mm. **Series:** 1980 Olympics **Obv:** Imperial eagle above value **Rev:** Runner **Edge:** Reeded

Date	Mintage	F	VF	XF	Unc	BU
1980MW	2,012,000	—	1.00	1.75	5.00	—
1980MW Proof	5,000	Value: 12.00				

Y# 112 20 ZLOTYCH
10.1500 g., Copper-Nickel, 29 mm. **Subject:** 50th Anniversary - Training Ship Daru Pomorza **Obv:** Imperial eagle above value **Rev:** Sailing ship **Edge:** Reeded

Date	Mintage	F	VF	XF	Unc	BU
1980MW	2,069,200	—	1.00	1.75	3.50	—
1980MW Proof	5,000	Value: 10.00				

Y# 153.1 20 ZLOTYCH
8.7000 g., Copper-Nickel, 26.5 mm. **Obv:** Eagle with wings open **Rev:** Value **Edge:** Reeded **Note:** Circulation coinage.

Date	Mintage	F	VF	XF	Unc	BU
1984MW	12,703,000	—	0.25	0.60	1.25	1.50
1985MW	15,514,000	—	0.25	0.60	1.25	1.50
1986MW	37,959,000	—	0.25	0.60	1.25	1.50
1986MW Proof	5,000	Value: 4.00				
1987MW	22,213,000	—	0.25	0.60	1.25	1.50
1987MW Proof	5,000	Value: 4.00				
1988MW	14,994,000	—	0.25	0.60	1.25	1.50
1988MW Proof	5,000	Value: 4.00				

Y# 153.2 20 ZLOTYCH
5.6500 g., Copper-Nickel, 24 mm. **Obv:** Eagle with wings open **Rev:** Value **Edge:** Reeded **Note:** Reduced size.

Date	Mintage	F	VF	XF	Unc	BU
1989MW	95,974,000	—	0.25	0.35	0.75	1.00
1989MW Proof	5,000	Value: 4.00				
1990MW	104,712,000	—	0.25	0.35	0.75	1.00
1990MW Proof	5,000	Value: 4.00				

Y# 100 50 ZLOTYCH
11.7000 g., Copper-Nickel, 30.5 mm. **Obv:** Imperial eagle above value **Rev:** Bust of Duke Mieszko I 3/4 left **Edge:** Reeded

Date	Mintage	F	VF	XF	Unc	BU
1979MW	2,640,000	—	1.00	2.00	5.00	—
1979MW Proof	5,000	Value: 15.00				

Y# 114 50 ZLOTYCH
11.7000 g., Copper-Nickel, 30.5 mm. **Obv:** Imperial eagle above value **Rev:** King Boleslaw I Chrobry **Edge:** Reeded

Date	Mintage	F	VF	XF	Unc	BU
1980MW	2,564,000	—	1.00	2.00	5.00	—
1980MW Proof	5,000	Value: 12.50				

Y# 117 50 ZLOTYCH
11.7000 g., Copper-Nickel, 30.5 mm. **Obv:** Imperial eagle above value **Rev:** Crowned bust of Duke Kazimierz I Odnowiciel facing **Edge:** Reeded

Date	Mintage	F	VF	XF	Unc	BU
1980MW	2,504,000	—	1.00	2.00	5.00	—
1980MW Proof	5,000	Value: 12.50				

Y# 122 50 ZLOTYCH
11.7000 g., Copper-Nickel, 30.5 mm. **Obv:** Imperial eagle above value **Rev:** General Broni Wladyslaw Sikorski left **Edge:** Reeded

Date	Mintage	F	VF	XF	Unc	BU
1981MW	2,505,000	—	1.00	2.00	5.00	—
1981MW Proof	5,000	Value: 12.50				

Y# 124 50 ZLOTYCH
11.7000 g., Copper-Nickel, 30.5 mm. **Obv:** Imperial eagle above value **Rev:** Crowned bust of King Boleslaw II Smialy 1/4 right **Edge:** Reeded

Date	Mintage	F	VF	XF	Unc	BU
1981MW	2,538,000	—	1.00	2.00	4.50	—
1981MW Proof	5,000	Value: 12.00				

Y# 128 50 ZLOTYCH
11.7000 g., Copper-Nickel, 30.5 mm. **Obv:** Imperial eagle above value **Rev:** Head of King Wladyslaw I Herman 3/4 left **Edge:** Reeded

Date	Mintage	F	VF	XF	Unc	BU
1981MW	2,500,000	—	1.00	2.00	4.50	—
1981MW Proof	5,000	Value: 12.00				

Y# 127 50 ZLOTYCH
11.7000 g., Copper-Nickel, 30.5 mm. **Series:** F.A.O. - World Food Day **Obv:** Imperial eagle above value **Rev:** F.A.O. logo within circle **Edge:** Reeded

Date	Mintage	F	VF	XF	Unc	BU
1981MW	2,524,000	—	1.00	2.00	4.50	—
1981MW Proof	5,000	Value: 12.00				

Y# 133 50 ZLOTYCH
11.7000 g., Copper-Nickel, 30.5 mm. **Obv:** Imperial eagle above value **Rev:** King Boleslaw III Krzywousty **Edge:** Reeded

Date	Mintage	F	VF	XF	Unc	BU
1982MW	2,616,000	—	1.00	2.00	4.50	—
1982MW Proof	5,000	Value: 12.50				

Y# 142 50 ZLOTYCH
11.7000 g., Copper-Nickel, 30.5 mm. **Subject:** 150th Anniversary of Great Theater **Obv:** Imperial eagle above value **Rev:** Theater building **Edge:** Reeded

Date	Mintage	F	VF	XF	Unc	BU
1983MW	615,000	—	1.00	4.00	8.00	—

Y# 145 50 ZLOTYCH
11.7000 g., Copper-Nickel, 30.5 mm. **Obv:** Imperial eagle above value **Rev:** King Jan III Sobieski facing **Edge:** Reeded **Designer:** Stanislawa Watrobska-Frindl

Date	Mintage	F	VF	XF	Unc	BU
1983MW	2,576,000	—	1.00	2.00	4.50	—

Y# 146 50 ZLOTYCH
11.7000 g., Copper-Nickel, 30.5 mm. **Obv:** Imperial eagle above value **Rev:** Bust of Ignacy Lukasiewicz right **Edge:** Reeded **Designer:** Stanislawa Watrobska-Frindl

Date	Mintage	F	VF	XF	Unc	BU
1983MW	612,000	—	1.00	4.00	8.00	—

REPUBLIC

Democratic

STANDARD COINAGE

Y# 216 50 ZLOTYCH
6.8000 g., Copper-Nickel, 26 mm. **Obv:** Crowned eagle with wings open, date below **Rev:** Value with sprig in 0

Date	Mintage	F	VF	XF	Unc	BU
1990MW	28,707,000	—	—	—	1.25	2.00
1990MW Proof	5,000	Value: 12.00				

REFORM COINAGE

100 Old Zlotych = 1 Grosz; 10,000 Old Zlotych = 1 Zloty

As far back as 1990, production was initiated for the new 1 Grosz - 1 Zlotych coins for a forthcoming monetary reform. It wasn't announced until the Act of July 7, 1994 and was enacted on January 1, 1995.

Y# 276 GROSZ
1.6400 g., Brass, 15.5 mm. **Obv:** National arms **Obv. Legend:** RZECZPOSPOLITA POLSKA **Rev:** Drooping oak leaf over value **Edge:** Reeded

Date	Mintage	F	VF	XF	Unc	BU
1990MW	29,140,000	—	—	—	0.10	0.20
1991MW	79,000,000	—	—	—	0.10	0.20
1992MW	362,000,000	—	—	—	0.10	0.20
1993MW	80,780,000	—	—	—	0.10	0.20
1995MW	102,280,109	—	—	—	0.10	0.20
1997MW	103,080,002	—	—	—	0.10	0.20
1998MW	255,830,003	—	—	—	0.10	0.20
1999MW	204,470,000	—	—	—	0.10	0.20
2000MW	211,410,000	—	—	—	0.10	0.20
2001MW	210,000,020	—	—	—	0.10	0.20
2002MW	240,000,000	—	—	—	0.10	0.20
2003MW	250,000,000	—	—	—	0.10	0.20
2004MW	300,000,000	—	—	—	0.10	0.20
2005MW	375,000,000	—	—	—	0.10	0.20
2007MW	—	—	—	—	0.10	0.20

Y# 277 2 GROSZE
2.1300 g., Brass, 17.5 mm. **Obv:** National arms **Obv. Legend:** RZECZPOSPOLITA POLSKA **Rev:** Drooping oak leaves above value

Date	Mintage	F	VF	XF	Unc	BU
1990MW	34,400,000	—	—	—	0.15	0.25
1991MW	97,410,000	—	—	—	0.15	0.25
1992MW	157,000,003	—	—	—	0.15	0.25
1997MV	92,400,002	—	—	—	0.15	0.25
1998MW	154,840,050	—	—	—	0.15	0.25
1999MW	187,900,000	—	—	—	0.15	0.25
2000MW	92,400,000	—	—	—	0.15	0.25
2001MW	86,100,000	—	—	—	0.15	0.25
2002MW	83,910,000	—	—	—	0.15	0.25
2003MV	80,000,000	—	—	—	0.15	0.25
2004MW	100,000,000	—	—	—	0.15	0.25
2005MW	163,003,250	—	—	—	0.15	0.25
2007MW	—	—	—	—	0.15	0.25

Y# 278 5 GROSZY
2.5900 g., Brass, 19.5 mm. **Obv:** National arms **Obv. Legend:** RZECZPOSPOLITA POLSKA **Rev:** Value at upper left of oak leaves **Edge:** Segmented reeding

Date	Mintage	F	VF	XF	Unc	BU
1990MW	70,240,000	—	—	—	0.25	0.45
1991MW	171,040,000	—	—	—	0.25	0.45
1992MW	103,784,000	—	—	—	0.25	0.45
1993MW	20,280,101	—	—	—	0.25	0.45
1998MW	93,472,002	—	—	—	0.25	0.45
1999MW	99,024,000	—	—	—	0.25	0.45
2000MW	75,600,000	—	—	—	0.25	0.45
2001MW	67,368,000	—	—	—	0.25	0.45
2002MW	67,200,000	—	—	—	0.25	0.45
2003MW	48,000,000	—	—	—	0.25	0.45
2004MW	62,500,000	—	—	—	0.25	0.45
2005MW	113,000,000	—	—	—	0.25	0.45
2006MW	—	—	—	—	0.25	0.45
2007MW	—	—	—	—	0.25	0.45

Y# 279 10 GROSZY
2.5100 g., Copper-Nickel, 16.5 mm. **Obv:** National arms **Obv. Legend:** RZECZPOSPOLITA POLSKA **Rev:** Value within wreath

Date	Mintage	F	VF	XF	Unc	BU
1990MW	43,055,000	—	—	—	0.40	0.60
1991MW	123,164,300	—	—	—	0.40	0.60
1992MW	210,005,000	—	—	—	0.40	0.60
1993MW	80,240,008	—	—	—	0.40	0.60
1998MW	62,695,000	—	—	—	0.40	0.60
1999MW	47,040,000	—	—	—	0.40	0.60
2000MW	104,060,000	—	—	—	0.40	0.60
2001MW	62,820,000	—	—	—	0.40	0.60
2002MW	10,500,000	—	—	—	0.40	0.60
2003MW	31,500,000	—	—	—	0.40	0.60
2004MW	70,500,000	—	—	—	0.40	0.60
2005MW	94,000,000	—	—	—	0.40	0.60
2007MW	—	—	—	—	0.40	0.60

Y# 280 20 GROSZY
3.2200 g., Copper-Nickel, 18.5 mm. **Obv:** National arms **Obv. Legend:** RZECZPOSPOLITA POLSKA **Rev:** Value within artistic design **Edge:** Reeded

Date	Mintage	F	VF	XF	Unc	BU
1990MW	25,100,000	—	—	—	0.65	0.85
1991MW	75,400,000	—	—	—	0.65	0.85
1992MW	106,100,001	—	—	—	0.65	0.85
1996MW	29,745,000	—	—	—	0.65	0.85
1997MW	59,755,000	—	—	—	0.65	0.85
1998MW	52,500,000	—	—	—	0.65	0.85
1999MW	25,985,000	—	—	—	0.65	0.85
2000MW	52,135,000	—	—	—	0.65	0.85
2001MW	41,980,001	—	—	—	0.65	0.85
2002MW	10,500,000	—	—	—	0.65	0.85
2003MW	20,400,000	—	—	—	0.65	0.85
2004MV	40,000,025	—	—	—	0.65	0.85
2005MW	37,000,000	—	—	—	0.65	0.85
2006MW	—	—	—	—	0.65	0.85

Y# 281 50 GROSZY
3.9400 g., Copper-Nickel, 20.5 mm. **Obv:** National arms **Obv. Legend:** RZECZPOSPOLITA POLSKA **Rev:** Value to right of sprig **Edge:** Reeded

Date	Mintage	F	VF	XF	Unc	BU
1990MW	29,152,000	—	—	—	1.00	1.25
1991MW	99,120,000	—	—	—	1.00	1.25
1992MW	116,000,000	—	—	—	1.00	1.25
1994MW	—	—	—	—	1.00	1.25
1995MW	101,600,113	—	—	—	1.00	1.25

Y# 282 ZLOTY
5.0300 g., Copper-Nickel, 23 mm. **Obv:** National arms **Obv. Legend:** RZECZPOSPOLITA POLSKA **Rev:** Value within wreath

Date	Mintage	F	VF	XF	Unc	BU
1990MW	20,240,000	—	—	—	1.75	2.00
1991MW	60,080,000	—	—	—	1.75	2.00
1992MW	102,240,000	—	—	—	1.75	2.00
1993MW	20,904,000	—	—	—	1.75	2.00
1994MW	69,956,000	—	—	—	1.75	2.00
1995MW	99,740,122	—	—	—	1.75	2.00

Y# 283 2 ZLOTE
5.2100 g., Bi-Metallic Copper-Nickel center in Brass ring, 21.5 mm. **Obv:** National arms within circle **Obv. Legend:** RZECZPOSPOLITA POLSKA **Rev:** Value flanked by oak leaves

Date	Mintage	F	VF	XF	Unc	BU
1994MW	79,644,000	—	—	—	4.00	4.50
1995MW	122,880,020	—	—	—	4.00	4.50
2005MW	5,000,000	—	—	—	4.00	4.50
2006MW	—	—	—	—	4.00	4.50

Y# 423 2 ZLOTE
8.1500 g., Brass, 26.8 mm. **Subject:** Jan III Sobieski **Obv:** Crowned eagle with wings open **Rev:** Bust facing **Edge Lettering:** *NBP* repeated

Date	Mintage	F	VF	XF	Unc	BU
2001	500,000	—	—	—	3.00	5.00

Y# 426 2 ZLOTE
8.1500 g., Brass, 26.8 mm. **Subject:** Henryk Wieniawski **Obv:** Crowned eagle with wings open **Rev:** Bust left and violin **Edge Lettering:** *NBP* repeated

Date	Mintage	F	VF	XF	Unc	BU
2001	600,000	—	—	—	3.00	5.00

Y# 427 2 ZLOTE
8.1000 g., Brass, 26.7 mm. **Obv:** Crowned eagle with wings open **Rev:** Turtles **Edge:** Lettered **Edge Lettering:** "NBP" repeatedly

Date	Mintage	F	VF	XF	Unc	BU
2002	750,000	—	—	—	6.00	10.00

Y# 431 2 ZLOTE
8.1500 g., Brass, 27 mm. **Subject:** Bronislaw Malinowski **Obv:** Crowned eagle with wings open **Rev:** Bust facing and Trobriand Islanders **Edge Lettering:** "NBP" eight times

Date	Mintage	F	VF	XF	Unc	BU
2002	680,000	—	—	—	3.50	5.50

Y# 433 2 ZLOTE
8.1500 g., Brass, 27 mm. **Subject:** World Cup Soccer **Obv:** National arms **Rev:** Soccer players **Edge Lettering:** "NBP" eight times

Date	Mintage	F	VF	XF	Unc	BU
2002	1,000,000	—	—	—	3.50	5.50

Y# 439 2 ZLOTE
8.1000 g., Brass, 26.8 mm. **Subject:** August II (1697-1706, 1709-1733) **Obv:** National arms **Rev:** Head facing **Edge Lettering:** NBP* repeated

Date	Mintage	F	VF	XF	Unc	BU
2002MW	620,000	—	—	—	3.00	5.00

Y# 440 2 ZLOTE
8.1300 g., Brass, 26.7 mm. **Subject:** Gen. Wladyslaw Anders **Obv:** Crowned eagle with wings open **Rev:** Uniformed bust facing and cross **Edge:** "NBP" repeated eight times

Date	Mintage	F	VF	XF	Unc	BU
2002MW	680,000	—	—	—	3.00	5.00

Y# 443 2 ZLOTE
8.1500 g., Brass, 26.8 mm. **Subject:** Zamek W. Malborku **Obv:** Crowned eagle with wings open **Rev:** Castle **Edge:** "*NBP*" repeatedly

Date	Mintage	F	VF	XF	Unc	BU
2002MW	680,000	—	—	—	3.00	5.00

Y# 444 2 ZLOTE
8.1300 g., Brass, 26.8 mm. **Subject:** Jan Matejko **Obv:** Denomination, crowned eagle and artist's palette **Rev:** Jester behind portrait **Edge:** "NBP" repeatedly

Date	Mintage	F	VF	XF	Unc	BU
2002MW	700,000	—	—	—	3.00	5.00

Y# 445 2 ZLOTE
8.1300 g., Brass, 26.8 mm. **Subject:** Eels **Obv:** Crowned eagle with wings open **Rev:** Two eels **Edge:** "NBP" repeatedly

Date	Mintage	F	VF	XF	Unc	BU
2003MW	—	—	—	—	5.00	9.00

Y# 446 2 ZLOTE
7.7500 g., Brass, 26.7 mm. **Subject:** Children **Obv:** Children and square design above crowned eagle, date and value **Rev:** Children on square design **Edge:** "NBP" repeatedly **Note:** minted with center hole

Date	Mintage	F	VF	XF	Unc	BU
2003MW	—	—	—	—	4.50	6.50

Y# 447 2 ZLOTE
8.1500 g., Brass, 26.8 mm. **Subject:** City of Poznan (Posen) **Obv:** Crowned eagle with wings open **Rev:** Clock face and tower flanked by goat heads **Edge:** NBP repeated eight times

Date	Mintage	F	VF	XF	Unc	BU
2003MW	—	—	—	—	4.50	6.50

Y# 451 2 ZLOTE
8.2100 g., Brass, 26.8 mm. **Subject:** Easter Monday Festival **Obv:** Crowned eagle with wings open **Rev:** Festival scene **Edge:** Lettered **Edge Lettering:** NBP eight times

Date	Mintage	F	VF	XF	Unc	BU
2003MW	—	—	—	—	3.00	5.00

Y# 455 2 ZLOTE
8.1400 g., Brass, 26.7 mm. **Subject:** Petroleum and Gas Industry 150th Anniversary **Obv:** Crowned eagle with wings open **Rev:** Portrait and refinery **Edge:** "NBP" repeated eight times

Date	Mintage	F	VF	XF	Unc	BU
2003MW	—	—	—	—	3.50	5.50

Y# 456 2 ZLOTE
8.1400 g., Brass, 26.7 mm. **Subject:** General B. S. Maczek **Obv:** Crowned eagle with wings open **Rev:** Military uniformed portrait **Edge:** "NBP" repeated eight times

Date	Mintage	F	VF	XF	Unc	BU
2003MW	600,000	—	—	—	3.00	5.00

Y# 465 2 ZLOTE
8.1700 g., Aluminum-Bronze, 26.7 mm. **Subject:** Pope John-Paul II **Obv:** Small national arms at lower right with cross in background **Obv. Inscription:** RZECZPOSPOLITA POLSKA **Rev:** Pope in prayer at left, cross in background **Edge:** Lettered **Edge Lettering:** "NBP" repeated 8 times

Date	Mintage	F	VF	XF	Unc	BU
2003MW	2,000,000	—	—	—	3.00	5.00

Y# 473 2 ZLOTE
8.1500 g., Brass, 27 mm. **Obv:** Crowned eagle with wings open **Rev:** Stanislaus Leszcywski **Edge:** Lettered **Edge Lettering:** "NBP" repeated eight times

Date	Mintage	F	VF	XF	Unc	BU
2003MW	600,000	—	—	—	3.50	5.50

Y# 477 2 ZLOTE
8.1500 g., Brass, 27 mm. **Obv:** Crowned eagle with wings open and artist's palette **Rev:** Self portrait of Jacek Malczewski **Edge:** Lettered **Edge Lettering:** "NBP" repeated eight times

Date	Mintage	F	VF	XF	Unc	BU
2003MW	600,000	—	—	—	3.50	5.50

Y# 479 2 ZLOTE
8.1500 g., Brass, 27 mm. **Subject:** 80th Anniversary of the Modern Zloty Currency **Obv:** Crowned eagle with wings open above value **Rev:** Bust left **Edge:** Lettered **Edge Lettering:** "NBP" eight times

Date	Mintage	F	VF	XF	Unc	BU
2004MW	800,000	—	—	—	3.00	5.00

Y# 481 2 ZLOTE
8.1500 g., Brass, 27 mm. **Subject:** Poland Joining the European Union **Obv:** Crowned eagle with wings open above value **Rev:** Map and stars **Edge:** Lettered **Edge Lettering:** "NBP" eight times

Date	Mintage	F	VF	XF	Unc	BU
2004MW	1,000,000	—	—	—	3.00	5.00

Y# 484 2 ZLOTE
8.1500 g., Brass, 27 mm. **Subject:** Dolnoslaskie (Lower Silesian) District **Obv:** Crowned eagle with wings open on map **Rev:** Silesian eagle on shield **Edge:** Lettered **Edge Lettering:** "NBP" eight times

Date	Mintage	F	VF	XF	Unc	BU
2004MW	700,000	—	—	—	3.00	5.00

Y# 485 2 ZLOTE
8.1500 g., Brass, 27 mm. **Subject:** Kujawsko-Pomorskie District **Obv:** Crowned eagle with wings open on map **Rev:** Shield with crowned half eagle and griffin **Edge:** Lettered **Edge Lettering:** "NBP" eight times

Date	Mintage	F	VF	XF	Unc	BU
2004MW	750,000	—	—	—	3.00	5.00

Y# 486 2 ZLOTE
8.1500 g., Brass, 27 mm. **Subject:** Lubuskie District **Obv:** Crowned eagle with wings open on map **Rev:** Shield with half eagle and two stars **Edge:** Lettered **Edge Lettering:** "NBP" eight times

Date	Mintage	F	VF	XF	Unc	BU
2004MW	820,000	—	—	—	3.00	5.00

Y# 487 2 ZLOTE
8.1500 g., Brass, 27 mm. **Subject:** Lodzkie District **Obv:** Crowned eagle with wings open on map **Rev:** Shield with two creatures above an eagle **Edge:** Lettered **Edge Lettering:** "NBP" eight times

Date	Mintage	F	VF	XF	Unc	BU
2004MW	920,000	—	—	—	3.00	5.00

Y# 488 2 ZLOTE
8.1500 g., Brass, 27 mm. **Subject:** Malopolskie District **Obv:** Crowned eagle with wings open on map **Rev:** Shield with crowned eagle **Edge:** Lettered **Edge Lettering:** "NBP" eight times

Date	Mintage	F	VF	XF	Unc	BU
2004MW	920,000	—	—	—	3.00	5.00

Y# 489 2 ZLOTE
8.1500 g., Brass, 27 mm. **Subject:** Mazowieckie District **Obv:** Crowned eagle with wings open on map **Rev:** Eagle on shield **Edge:** Lettered **Edge Lettering:** "NBP" eight times

Date	Mintage	F	VF	XF	Unc	BU
2004MW	920,000	—	—	—	3.00	5.00

Y# 490 2 ZLOTE
8.1500 g., Brass, 27 mm. **Subject:** Podkarpackie District **Obv:** Crowned eagle with wings open on map **Rev:** Shield with iron cross above griffin and lion **Edge:** Lettered **Edge Lettering:** "NBP" eight times

Date	Mintage	F	VF	XF	Unc	BU
2004MW	920,000	—	—	—	3.00	5.00

Y# 491 2 ZLOTE
8.1500 g., Brass, 27 mm. **Subject:** Podlaskie District **Obv:** Crowned eagle with wings open on map **Rev:** Shield with Polish eagle above Lithuanian knight **Edge:** Lettered **Edge Lettering:** "NBP" eight times

Date	Mintage	F	VF	XF	Unc	BU
2004MW	900,000	—	—	—	3.00	5.00

Y# 492 2 ZLOTE
8.1500 g., Brass, 27 mm. **Subject:** Pomorskie District **Obv:** Crowned eagle with wings open on map **Rev:** Griffin on shield **Edge:** Lettered **Edge Lettering:** "NBP" eight times

Date	Mintage	F	VF	XF	Unc	BU
2004MW	900,000	—	—	—	3.00	5.00

Y# 493 2 ZLOTE
8.1500 g., Brass, 27 mm. **Subject:** Slaskie (Silesia) District **Obv:** Crowned eagle with wings open on map **Rev:** Eagle on shield **Edge:** Lettered **Edge Lettering:** "NBP" eight times

Date	Mintage	F	VF	XF	Unc	BU
2004MW	960,000	—	—	—	3.00	5.00

Y# 496 2 ZLOTE
8.1500 g., Brass, 27 mm. **Subject:** Warsaw Uprising 60th Anniversary **Obv:** Crowned eagle with wings open **Rev:** Resistance symbol on brick wall **Edge Lettering:** "NBP" eight times

Date	Mintage	F	VF	XF	Unc	BU
2004MW	900,000	—	—	—	3.00	5.00

Y# 499 2 ZLOTE
8.1500 g., Brass, 27 mm. **Obv:** Crowned eagle with wings open **Rev:** Gen. Stanislaw F. Sosabowski **Edge:** Lettered **Edge Lettering:** "NBP" eight times

Date	Mintage	F	VF	XF	Unc	BU
2004MW	850,000	—	—	—	3.00	5.00

Y# 501 2 ZLOTE
8.1500 g., Brass, 27 mm. **Subject:** Polish Police 85th Anniversary **Obv:** Crowned eagle with wings open **Rev:** Police badge **Edge:** Lettered **Edge Lettering:** "NBP" eight times

Date	Mintage	F	VF	XF	Unc	BU
2004MW	760,000	—	—	—	3.00	5.00

Y# 503 2 ZLOTE
8.1500 g., Brass, 27 mm. **Subject:** Polish Senate **Obv:** Crowned eagle with wings open **Rev:** Senate eagle and speaker's staff **Edge:** Lettered **Edge Lettering:** "NBP" eight times

Date	Mintage	F	VF	XF	Unc	BU
2004MW	760,000	—	—	—	3.00	5.00

Y# 505 2 ZLOTE

8.1500 g., Brass, 27 mm. **Obv:** Crowned eagle with wings open **Rev:** Aleksander Czekanowski (1833-1876) **Edge:** Lettered **Edge Lettering:** "NBP" eight times

Date	Mintage	F	VF	XF	Unc	BU
2004MW	700,000	—	—	—	3.00	5.00

Y# 507 2 ZLOTE

8.1500 g., Brass, 26.83 mm. **Obv:** National arms **Obv. Legend:** RZECZPOSPOLITA POLSKA **Rev:** Harvest fest couple in folk costume at left, large group in background at right **Rev. Inscription:** DOZYNKI **Edge:** Lettered **Edge Lettering:** "NBP" eight times

Date	Mintage	F	VF	XF	Unc	BU
2004MW	850,000	—	—	—	3.00	5.00

Y# 509 2 ZLOTE

8.1500 g., Brass, 27 mm. **Subject:** Warsaw Fine Arts Academy Centennial **Obv:** Crowned eagle with wings open **Rev:** Painter's hands **Edge:** Lettered **Edge Lettering:** "NBP" eight times

Date	Mintage	F	VF	XF	Unc	BU
2004MW	850,000	—	—	—	3.00	5.00

Y# 512 2 ZLOTE

8.1500 g., Brass, 27 mm. **Obv:** Crowned eagle with wings open and artist's palette **Rev:** Stanislaw Wyspianski (1869-1907) **Edge:** Lettered **Edge Lettering:** "NBP" eight times

Date	Mintage	F	VF	XF	Unc	BU
2004MW	900,000	—	—	—	3.00	5.00

Y# 516 2 ZLOTE

8.1500 g., Brass, 27 mm. **Subject:** Olympics **Obv:** Crowned eagle with wings open **Rev:** Ancient runners **Edge:** Lettered **Edge Lettering:** "NBP" eight times

Date	Mintage	F	VF	XF	Unc	BU
2004MW	1,000,000	—	—	—	3.00	5.00

Y# 464 2 ZLOTE

8.1300 g., Brass, 26.8 mm. **Obv:** Crowned eagle with wings open **Rev:** Two dolphins **Edge:** Lettered **Edge Lettering:** "NBP" repeated

Date	Mintage	F	VF	XF	Unc	BU
2004MW	—	—	—	—	4.00	6.00

Y# 514 2 ZLOTE

8.1500 g., Brass, 27 mm. **Obv:** National arms on outlined map **Rev:** Wojewodztwo-Lubelskie arms with stag on shield **Edge Lettering:** "NBP" eight times

Date	Mintage	F	VF	XF	Unc	BU
2004MW	—	—	—	—	—	5.00

Y# 607 2 ZLOTE

8.1500 g., Brass, 26.79 mm. **Obv:** National arms on outlined map **Obv. Legend:** RZECZPOSPOLITA POLSKA **Rev:** Region arms **Rev. Legend:** WOJEWODZTWO - OPOLSKIE **Edge Lettering:** NBP repeated

Date	Mintage	F	VF	XF	Unc	BU
2004MW	—	—	—	—	3.00	5.00

Y# 608 2 ZLOTE

8.0600 g., Brass, 26.80 mm. **Subject:** 500th Anniversary Birth of Nikolaja Reja **Obv:** National arms **Obv. Legend:** RZECZPOSPOLITA POLSKA **Rev:** Bust of Reja facing 3/4 right **Edge Lettering:** NBP repeated

Date	Mintage	F	VF	XF	Unc	BU
2005	—	—	—	—	3.00	5.00

Y# 541 2 ZLOTE

8.1500 g., Brass, 27 mm. **Obv:** Eagle, value, palette and paint brushes **Rev:** Painter Tadeusz Makowski **Edge Lettering:** "NBP" repeated eight times

Date	Mintage	F	VF	XF	Unc	BU
2005MW	900,000	—	—	—	3.00	5.00

Y# 559 2 ZLOTE

Brass, 26.7 mm. **Subject:** 500th Anniversary of Mikolaja Reja **Obv:** National arms

Date	Mintage	F	VF	XF	Unc	BU
2005MW	—	—	—	—	3.00	5.00

Y# 560 2 ZLOTE

8.0600 g., Brass, 26.79 mm. **Obv:** National arms on outline map **Obv. Legend:** RZECZPOSPOLITA POLSKA **Rev:** Region arms **Rev. Legend:** WOJEWÓDZTWO SWIETOKRZYSKIE **Edge Lettering:** NBP repeated

Date	Mintage	F	VF	XF	Unc	BU
2005MW	—	—	—	—	3.00	5.00

Y# 562 2 ZLOTE

Brass, 26.7 mm. **Obv:** National arms **Rev:** Region Wielkopolskie

Date	Mintage	F	VF	XF	Unc	BU
2005	—	—	—	—	3.00	5.00

Y# 563 2 ZLOTE

8.1100 g., Brass, 26.81 mm. **Obv:** National arms on outlined map **Obv. Legend:** RZECZPOSPOLITA POLSKA **Rev:** Region arms **Rev. Legend:** WOJEWODZTWO ZACHODIOPOMORSKIE **Edge Lettering:** NBP repeated

Date	Mintage	F	VF	XF	Unc	BU
2005MW	—	—	—	—	3.00	5.00

Y# 564 2 ZLOTE

Brass, 26.7 mm. **Obv:** National arms **Rev:** City of Gniezno

Date	Mintage	F	VF	XF	Unc	BU
2005MW	—	—	—	—	3.00	5.00

Y# 565 2 ZLOTE

Brass, 26.7 mm. **Obv:** National arms **Rev:** Solidarity

Date	Mintage	F	VF	XF	Unc	BU
2005MW	—	—	—	—	3.00	5.00

Y# 520 2 ZLOTE

8.1500 g., Brass, 26.8 mm. **Obv:** Crowned eagle with wings open **Rev:** Owl on nest with chicks **Edge:** Lettered **Edge Lettering:** "NBP" repeated eight times

Date	Mintage	F	VF	XF	Unc	BU
2005MW	990,000	—	—	—	3.50	5.50

Y# 521 2 ZLOTE

8.1500 g., Brass, 26.8 mm. **Obv:** Crowned eagle with wings open **Rev:** Ship within circle **Edge:** Lettered **Edge Lettering:** "NBP" repeatedly

Date	Mintage	F	VF	XF	Unc	BU
2005MW	—	—	—	—	3.50	5.50

Y# 522 2 ZLOTE

8.1500 g., Brass, 26.8 mm. **Subject:** Japan's Aichi Expo **Obv:** Crowned eagle with wings open **Rev:** Two cranes flying over Mt. Fuji with rising sun background **Edge:** Lettered **Edge Lettering:** "NBP" repeatedly

Date	Mintage	F	VF	XF	Unc	BU
2005MW	—	—	—	—	3.50	5.50

Y# 524 2 ZLOTE

8.1300 g., Brass, 26.7 mm. **Subject:** Obrony Jasnej Gory **Obv:** Crowned eagle with wings open **Rev:** Half length figure left and bombarded city scene **Edge:** Lettered **Edge Lettering:** "NBP" repeatedly

Date	Mintage	F	VF	XF	Unc	BU
2005MW	—	—	—	—	4.00	6.00

Y# 525 2 ZLOTE

8.1300 g., Brass, 26.7 mm. **Subject:** Pope John-Paul II **Obv:** National arms **Obv. Legend:** RZECZPOSPOLITA POLSKA **Rev:** Bust right at left, outline of church steeple at center right **Edge:** Lettered **Edge Lettering:** "NBP" repeated 8 times

Date	Mintage	F	VF	XF	Unc	BU
2005MW	4,000,000	—	—	—	4.00	6.00

Y# 527 2 ZLOTE

8.2000 g., Brass, 26.7 mm. **Obv:** Crowned eagle with wings open **Rev:** Bust 1/4 left with horse head and goose at left **Edge Lettering:** "NBP" repeatedly

Date	Mintage	F	VF	XF	Unc	BU
2005MW	—	—	—	—	3.00	5.00

Y# 528 2 ZLOTE

8.2000 g., Brass, 26.7 mm. **Obv:** Crowned eagle above wall **Rev:** Kolobrzeg Lighthouse **Edge Lettering:** "NBP" repeatedly

Date	Mintage	F	VF	XF	Unc	BU
2005MW	—	—	—	—	3.00	5.00

Y# 529 2 ZLOTE

8.2000 g., Brass, 26.7 mm. **Obv:** National arms above gateway **Rev:** Wioclawek Cathedral **Edge Lettering:** "NBP" repeatedly

Date	Mintage	F	VF	XF	Unc	BU
2005MW	—	—	—	—	3.00	5.00

Y# 530 2 ZLOTE

8.2000 g., Brass, 26.7 mm. **Obv:** National arms **Rev:** Bust of King Stanislaus Poniatowski right **Edge Lettering:** "NBP" repeatedly

Date	Mintage	F	VF	XF	Unc	BU
2005MW	990,000	—	—	—	3.00	5.00

Y# 532 2 ZLOTE

8.1500 g., Copper-Aluminum-Zinc-Tin, 27 mm. **Obv:** National arms **Rev:** St. John's Night dancer **Edge Lettering:** NBP repeated

Date	Mintage	F	VF	XF	Unc	BU
2006MW	1,000,000	—	—	—	—	4.00

Y# 534 2 ZLOTE

8.1500 g., Copper-Aluminum-Zinc-Tin, 27 mm. **Obv:** National arms **Rev:** Alpine Marmot standing **Edge Lettering:** NBP repeated eight times

Date	Mintage	F	VF	XF	Unc	BU
2006MW	1,400,000	—	—	—	—	4.00

Y# 566 2 ZLOTE

Brass, 26.7 mm. **Obv:** National arms **Rev:** City of Jaroslaw

Date	Mintage	F	VF	XF	Unc	BU
2006MW	—	—	—	—	3.00	5.00

Y# 567 2 ZLOTE

Brass, 26.7 mm. **Obv:** National arms **Rev:** 2006 Olympic Games Turin

Date	Mintage	F	VF	XF	Unc	BU
2006MW	—	—	—	—	3.00	5.00

Y# 569 2 ZLOTE

Brass, 26.7 mm. **Obv:** National arms **Rev:** Castle Zagan

Date	Mintage	F	VF	XF	Unc	BU
2006MW	—	—	—	—	3.00	5.00

Y# 570 2 ZLOTE

Brass, 26.7 mm. **Obv:** National arms above gateway **Rev:** City of Nysa **Edge Lettering:** NBP repeated

Date	Mintage	F	VF	XF	Unc	BU
2006MW	—	—	—	—	5.00	3.00

Y# 543 2 ZLOTE

8.1300 g., Brass, 26.7 mm. **Obv:** Polish Eagle above castle gate **Rev:** Bochnia church **Edge Lettering:** NBP repeatedly

Date	Mintage	F	VF	XF	Unc	BU
2006MW	1,100,000	—	—	—	3.00	5.00

Y# 544 2 ZLOTE

8.1300 g., Brass, 26.7 mm. **Obv:** Polish Eagle above castle gate **Rev:** Chelm church **Edge Lettering:** NBP repeatedly

Date	Mintage	F	VF	XF	Unc	BU
2006MW	1,100,000	—	—	—	3.00	5.00

Y# 545 2 ZLOTE

8.1300 g., Brass, 26.7 mm. **Obv:** Polish Eagle above castle gate **Rev:** Chelmno Palace **Edge Lettering:** NBP repeatedly

Date	Mintage	F	VF	XF	Unc	BU
2006MW	1,100,000	—	—	—	3.00	5.00

Y# 546 2 ZLOTE

8.1300 g., Brass, 26.7 mm. **Obv:** Polish Eagle above castle gate **Rev:** Elblag tower **Edge Lettering:** NBP repeatedly

Date	Mintage	F	VF	XF	Unc	BU
2006MW	1,100,000	—	—	—	3.00	5.00

Y# 547 2 ZLOTE

8.1300 g., Brass, 26.7 mm. **Obv:** Polish Eagle above castle gate **Rev:** Kosciol W. Haczowie church **Edge Lettering:** NBP repeatedly

Date	Mintage	F	VF	XF	Unc	BU
2006MW	—	—	—	—	3.00	5.00

Y# 548 2 ZLOTE

8.1300 g., Brass, 26.7 mm. **Obv:** National arms above gateway **Rev:** Legnica tower and building **Edge Lettering:** NBP repeatedly

Date	Mintage	F	VF	XF	Unc	BU
2006MW	—	—	—	—	3.00	5.00

Y# 549 2 ZLOTE

8.1300 g., Brass, 26.7 mm. **Obv:** Polish Eagle above castle gate **Rev:** Pszczyna palace **Edge Lettering:** NBP repeatedly

Date	Mintage	F	VF	XF	Unc	BU
2006MW	1,100,000	—	—	—	3.00	5.00

Y# 550 2 ZLOTE

8.1300 g., Brass, 26.7 mm. **Obv:** Polish Eagle above castle gate **Rev:** Sandomierz palace **Edge Lettering:** NBP repeatedly

Date	Mintage	F	VF	XF	Unc	BU
2006MW	1,100,000	—	—	—	3.00	5.00

Y# 551 2 ZLOTE

8.1300 g., Brass, 26.7 mm. **Obv:** National arms above castle gate **Rev:** Soccer ball **Edge Lettering:** NBP repeatedly

Date	Mintage	F	VF	XF	Unc	BU
2006MW	—	—	—	—	3.00	5.00

Y# 576 2 ZLOTE

8.2000 g., Brass, 26.7 mm. **Obv:** National arms **Rev:** Knight on horseback **Edge Lettering:** NBP repeated

Date	Mintage	F	VF	XF	Unc	BU
2006MW	—	—	—	—	3.00	5.00

Y# 609 2 ZLOTE

8.1300 g., Brass, 26.79 mm. **Subject:** 100th Anniversary Warsaw School of Economics **Obv:** National arms **Obv. Legend:** RZECZPOSPOLITA POLSKA **Rev:** School facade **Rev. Legend:** SZKOLA CLOWNA HANDLOWA W WARSZAWIE **Rev. Inscription:** Large SGH **Edge Lettering:** NBP repeated

Date	Mintage	F	VF	XF	Unc	BU
2006MW	—	—	—	—	3.00	5.00

Y# 582 2 ZLOTE

8.1300 g., Brass, 26.8 mm. **Obv:** National arms **Obv. Legend:** RZECZPOSPOLITA POLSKA **Rev:** Old Y-20 Queen's fead left coin design from the 1930's **Edge Lettering:** "NPB" repeatedly

Date	Mintage	F	VF	XF	Unc	BU
2006MW	—	—	—	—	3.00	5.00

Y# 573 2 ZLOTE

8.1600 g., Brass, 26.7 mm. **Obv:** Polish eagle above wall **Rev:** Nowy Sacz church **Edge Lettering:** "NBP" eight times

Date	Mintage	F	VF	XF	Unc	BU
2006MW	—	—	—	—	3.00	5.00

Y# 574 2 ZLOTE

8.1600 g., Brass, 26.7 mm. **Subject:** 500th Anniversary of the Publication of the Statute by Laski **Obv:** National arms above value **Rev:** Jan Laskjego and book **Edge Lettering:** "NBP" eight times

Date	Mintage	F	VF	XF	Unc	BU
2006MW	—	—	—	—	3.00	5.00

Y# 580 2 ZLOTE

8.1600 g., Brass, 26.7 mm. **Obv:** Polish eagle above wall **Rev:** Kalisz building **Edge Lettering:** "NBP" eight times

Date	Mintage	F	VF	XF	Unc	BU
2006MW	—	—	—	—	3.00	5.00

Y# 605 2 ZLOTE

8.2000 g., Brass, 26.80 mm. **Obv:** National arms **Obv. Legend:** RZECZPOSPOLITA POLSKA **Rev:** Skier and marksman standing **Rev. Legend:** XX ZIMOWE IGAZYSKA OLIMPIJSKIE **Rev. Inscription:** TURYN **Edge:** NBP repeatedly

Date	Mintage	F	VF	XF	Unc	BU
2006MW	—	—	—	—	3.00	5.00

Y# 606 2 ZLOTE

8.3000 g., Brass, 26.81 mm. **Obv:** National arms **Obv. Legend:** RZECZPOSPOLITA POLSKA **Rev:** Large soccer ball with fancy linked date 2006 **Rev. Legend:** MISTRZOSTWA SWIATA W PItCE NOZNEJ NIEMCY - FIFA **Edge:** NBP repeatedly

Date	Mintage	F	VF	XF	Unc	BU
2006MW	—	—	—	—	3.00	5.00

Y# 577 2 ZLOTE

8.1500 g., Brass, 27 mm. **Obv:** Crowned eagle **Rev:** Kwidzyn Castle **Edge Lettering:** "NBP" eight times

Date	Mintage	F	VF	XF	Unc	BU
2007MW	1,000,000	—	—	—	3.00	5.00

Y# 578 2 ZLOTE

8.1500 g., Brass, 27 mm. **Obv:** Crowned eagle **Rev:** Grey Seal and silhouette **Edge Lettering:** "NBP" eight times

Date	Mintage	F	VF	XF	Unc	BU
2007MW	1,000,000	—	—	—	3.00	5.00

Y# 590 2 ZLOTE

8.0200 g., Brass, 26.80 mm. **Obv:** National arms **Obv. Legend:** RZECZPOSPOLITA POLSKA **Rev:** Bust of Domeyko facing **Rev. Legend:** IGNACY DOMEYKO 1802 - 1889 **Edge Lettering:** NBP repeated

Date	Mintage	F	VF	XF	Unc	BU
2007MW	—	—	—	—	3.00	5.00

Y# 592 2 ZLOTE

8.1500 g., Brass, 26.77 mm. **Subject:** History of Zloty **Obv:** Nike at left, obverse of 5 Zlotych, Y#18, national arms below **Obv. Legend:** RZECZPOLPOLITA POLSKA **Rev:** Spray at left of reverse of 5 Zlotych, Y# 18 **Edge Lettering:** NBP repeated

Date	Mintage	F	VF	XF	Unc	BU
2007MW	—	—	—	—	3.00	5.00

Y# 594 2 ZLOTE

8.0800 g., Brass, 26.78 mm. **Subject:** 750th Anniversary Municipality of Krakau **Obv:** National arms **Obv. Legend:** RZECZPOSPOLITA POLSKA **Rev:** Knight standing facing with spear and shield **Edge Lettering:** NBP repeated

Date	Mintage	F	VF	XF	Unc	BU
2007MW	—	—	—	—	3.00	5.00

Y# 610 2 ZLOTE

8.1800 g., Brass, 26.78 mm. **Subject:** Artic Explorers Antoni B. Dombrowolski and Henryk Arctowski **Obv:** National arms **Obv. Legend:** RZCEZPOSPOLITA POLSKA **Rev:** Explorer's bust facing at bottom, sailing ship in background **Edge Lettering:** NBP repeated

Date	Mintage	F	VF	XF	Unc	BU
2007MW	—	—	—	—	3.00	5.00

Y# 611 2 ZLOTE

8.1400 g., Brass, 26.77 mm. **Obv:** National arms **Obv. Legend:** RZECZPOSPOLIYA POLSKA **Rev:** Ciezkozbrojny in armor, horseback left **Rev. Legend:** RYCERZ CIEZKOZBROJNY-XV **Edge Lettering:** NBP repeated

Date	Mintage	F	VF	XF	Unc	BU
2007MW	—	—	—	—	3.00	5.00

Y# 612 2 ZLOTE

8.2400 g., Brass, 26.79 mm. **Subject:** 70th Anniversary Death of Szymanowskiego **Obv:** National arms **Obv. Legend:** RZECZPOSPOLITA POLSKA **Rev:** Bust facing 3/4 right at left, music score in background **Rev. Legend:** ROCZNICA URODZIN KAROLA SYMANOWSKIEGO **Edge Lettering:** NBP repeated

Date	Mintage	F	VF	XF	Unc	BU
2007MW	—	—	—	—	3.00	5.00

Y# 613 2 ZLOTE

8.2600 g., Brass, 26.79 mm. **Obv:** National arms above gateway **Obv. Legend:** RZECZPOSPOLITA POLSKA **Rev:** Buildings **Rev. Legend:** STARGARD - SZCZECINSKI **Edge Lettering:** NBP repeated

Date	Mintage	F	VF	XF	Unc	BU
2007MW	—	—	—	—	3.00	5.00

Y# 614 2 ZLOTE

8.1100 g., Brass, 26.78 mm. **Obv:** National arms on outlined map **Obv. Legend:** RZECZPOSPOLITA POLSKA **Rev:** Region arms **Rev. Legend:** WOJEWÓDZTWO WARMINSKO-MAZURSKIE **Edge Lettering:** NBP repeated

Date	Mintage	F	VF	XF	Unc	BU
2007MW	—	—	—	—	3.00	5.00

Y# 615 2 ZLOTE

8.2000 g., Brass, 26.80 mm. **Obv:** National arms above gateway **Obv. Legend:** RZECZPOSPOLITA POLSKA **Rev:** Building with branches at left and right **Rev. Legend:** BRZEG **Edge Lettering:** NBP repeated

Date	Mintage	F	VF	XF	Unc	BU
2007MW	—	—	—	—	3.00	5.00

Y# 616 2 ZLOTE

8.2300 g., Brass, 26.80 mm. **Obv:** National arms above gateway **Obv. Legend:** RZECZPOSPOLITA POLSKA **Rev:** Church **Rev. Legend:** LOMZA **Edge Lettering:** NBP repeated

Date	Mintage	F	VF	XF	Unc	BU
2007MW	—	—	—	—	3.00	5.00

Y# 617 2 ZLOTE

8.1900 g., Brass, 26.80 mm. **Obv:** National arms above gateway **Obv. Legend:** RZECZPOSPOLITA POLSKA **Rev:** Church **Rev. Legend:** PLOCK **Edge Lettering:** NBP repeated

Date	Mintage	F	VF	XF	Unc	BU
2007MW	—	—	—	—	3.00	5.00

Y# 618 2 ZLOTE

8.0700 g., Brass, 26.79 mm. **Obv:** National arms above gateway **Obv. Legend:** RZECZPOSPOLITA POLSKA **Rev:** Church **Rev. Legend:** PRZEMYSL **Edge Lettering:** NBP repeated

Date	Mintage	F	VF	XF	Unc	BU
2007MW	—	—	—	—	3.00	5.00

Y# 619 2 ZLOTE

8.0900 g., Brass, 26.81 mm. **Obv:** National arms above gateway **Obv. Legend:** RZECZPOSPOLITA POLSKA **Rev:** Towered gateway **Rev. Inscription:** RACIBÓRZ **Edge Lettering:** NBP repeated

Date	Mintage	F	VF	XF	Unc	BU
2007MW	—	—	—	—	3.00	5.00

Y# 620 2 ZLOTE

8.2100 g., Brass, 26.79 mm. **Obv:** National arms above gateway **Obv. Legend:** RZECZPOSPOLITA POLSKA **Rev:** Church **Rev. Legend:** SLUPSK **Edge Lettering:** NBP repeated

Date	Mintage	F	VF	XF	Unc	BU
2007MW	—	—	—	—	3.00	5.00

Y# 621 2 ZLOTE

8.0700 g., Brass, 26.78 mm. **Obv:** National arms above gateway **Obv. Legend:** RZECZPOSPOLITA POLSKA **Rev:** Church **Rev. Inscription:** SWIDNICA **Edge Lettering:** NBP repeated

Date	Mintage	F	VF	XF	Unc	BU
2007MW	—	—	—	—	3.00	5.00

Y# 622 2 ZLOTE

8.0200 g., Brass, 26.78 mm. **Obv:** National arms **Obv. Legend:** RZECZPOSPOLITA POLSKE **Rev:** Chuches **Rev. Legend:** MIASTO SREDNIOWIECZNE - W TORUNIU **Edge Lettering:** NBP repeated

Date	Mintage	F	VF	XF	Unc	BU
2007MW	—	—	—	—	3.00	5.00

Y# 623 2 ZLOTE

8.0700 g., Brass, 26.80 mm. **Obv:** National arms above gateway **Obv. Legend:** RZECZPOSPOLITA POLSKA **Rev:** Church **Rev. Legend:** GORZÓW WIELKOPOLSKI **Edge Lettering:** NBP repeated

Date	Mintage	F	VF	XF	Unc	BU
2007MW	—	—	—	—	3.00	5.00

Y# 624 2 ZLOTE

8.2000 g., Brass, 26.78 mm. **Obv:** National arms above gateway **Obv. Legend:** RZECZPOSPOLITA POLSKA **Rev:** Church at lower right, houses to left, fortress in upper background **Rev. Inscription:** KLODZKO **Edge Lettering:** NBP repeated

Date	Mintage	F	VF	XF	Unc	BU
2007MW	—	—	—	—	3.00	5.00

Y# 625 2 ZLOTE

8.2200 g., Brass, 26.77 mm. **Obv:** National arms above gateway **Obv. Legend:** RZECZPOSPOLITA POLSKE **Rev:** Church **Rev. Legend:** TARNÓW **Edge Lettering:** BNP repeated

Date	Mintage	F	VF	XF	Unc	BU
2007MW	—	—	—	—	3.00	5.00

Y# 626 2 ZLOTE

8.2200 g., Brass, 26.79 mm. **Subject:** Leon Wyczótkowski **Obv:** Artist's palette, brushes at left, national arms at right **Obv. Legend:** RZECZPOSPOLITA POLSKA **Rev:** Bust facing **Edge Lettering:** NBP repeated

Date	Mintage	F	VF	XF	Unc	BU
2007MW	—	—	—	—	3.00	5.00

Y# 627 2 ZLOTE

8.3000 g., Brass, 26.81 mm. **Obv:** National arms above flags **Obv. Legend:** RZECZPOSPOLITA POLSKA **Rev:** Peregrine Falcon perched on branch **Rev. Legend:** SOKÓI WEDROWNY - Falco peregrinus **Edge:** Lettered **Edge Lettering:** NBP repeated

Date	Mintage	F	VF	XF	Unc	BU
2008MW	—	—	—	0.90	2.25	3.00

Y# 628 2 ZLOTE

8.2000 g., Brass, 26.79 mm. **Obv:** National arms above gateway **Obv. Legend:** RZECZPOSPOLITA POLSKA **Rev:** National arms ar upper left, Piotrków Tribunal building at lower right **Rev. Legend:** PIOTRKÓW - TRYBUNALSKI **Edge:** Lettered **Edge Lettering:** BNP repeated

Date	Mintage	F	VF	XF	Unc	BU
2008MW	—	—	—	0.90	2.25	3.00

Y# 629 2 ZLOTE

8.1700 g., Brass, 26.77 mm. **Subject:** 40th Anniversary "Rocznica" March **Obv:** National arms above value **Obv. Legend:** RZECZPOSPOLITA POLSKA **Rev:** University of Warsaw coat of arms above political protest marchers **Edge:** Lettered **Edge Lettering:** NBP repeated

Date	Mintage	F	VF	XF	Unc	BU
2008MW	—	—	—	0.90	2.25	3.00

Y# 630 2 ZLOTE

8.1000 g., Brass, 26.80 mm. **Obv:** National arms above gateway **Obv. Legend:** RZECZPOSPOLITA POLSKA **Rev:** Building **Rev. Legend:** LOWICZ **Edge:** Lettered **Edge Lettering:** NBP repeated

Date	Mintage	F	VF	XF	Unc	BU
2008MW	—	—	—	0.90	2.25	3.00

Y# 631 2 ZLOTE

8.1400 g., Brass, 26.77 mm. **Obv:** National arms above gateway **Obv. Legend:** RZECZPOSPOLITA POLSKA **Rev:** Monument **Rev. Legend:** KONIN **Edge:** Lettered **Edge Lettering:** NBP repeated

Date	Mintage	F	VF	XF	Unc	BU
2008MW	—	—	—	0.90	2.25	3.00

Y# 284 5 ZLOTYCH

6.5400 g., Bi-Metallic Brass center in Copper-Nickel ring, 24 mm. **Obv:** National arms within circle **Obv. Legend:** RZECZPOSPOLITA POLSKA **Rev:** Value within circle flanked by oak leaves

Date	Mintage	F	VF	XF	Unc	BU
1994MW	112,896,033	—	—	—	7.00	8.00
1996MW	52,940,003	—	—	—	7.00	8.00

PORTUGAL

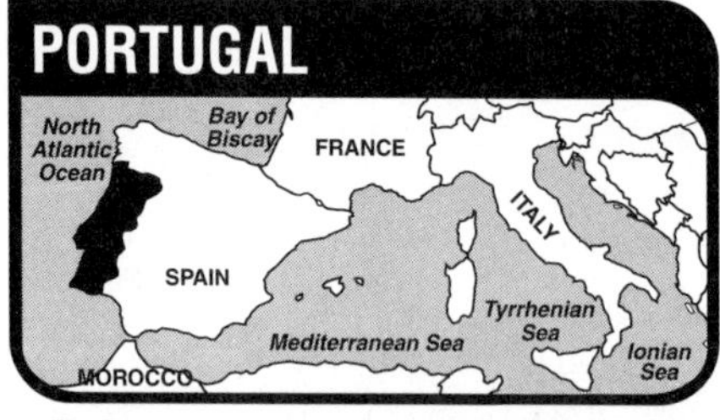

The Portuguese Republic, located in the western part of the Iberian Peninsula in southwestern Europe, has an area of 35,553 sq. mi. (92,080 sq. km.) and a population of *10.5 million. Capital: Lisbon. Portugal's economy is based on agriculture, tourism, minerals, fisheries and a rapidly expanding industrial sector. Textiles account for 33% of the exports and Portuguese wine is world famous. Portugal has become Europe's number one producer of copper and the world's largest producer of cork.

After centuries of domination by Romans, Visigoths and Moors, Portugal emerged in the 12th century as an independent kingdom financially and philosophically prepared for the great period of exploration that would soon follow. Attuned to the inspiration of Prince Henry the Navigator (1394-1460), Portugal's daring explorers of the15th and 16th centuries roamed the world's oceans from Brazil to Japan in an unprecedented burst of energy and endeavor that culminated in 1494 with Portugal laying claim to half the transoceanic world. Unfortunately for the fortunes of the tiny kingdom, the Portuguese population was too small to colonize this vast territory. Less than a century after Portugal laid claim to half the world, English, French and Dutch trading companies had seized the lion's share of the world's colonies and commerce, and Portugal's place as an imperial power was lost forever. The monarchy was overthrown in 1910 and a republic was established.

On April 25, 1974, the government of Portugal was seized by a military junta which reached agreements providing for independence for the Portuguese overseas provinces of Portuguese Guinea (*Guinea-Bissau*), Mozambique, Cape Verde Islands, Angola, and St. Thomas and Prince Islands (*Sao Tome and Principe*).

On January 1, 1986, Portugal became the eleventh member of the European Economic Community and in the first half of 1992 held its first EEC Presidency.

RULERS

Carlos I, 1889-1908
Manuel II, 1908-1910
Republic, 1910 to date

MONETARY SYSTEM

Beginning in 1836 all coins were expressed in terms of Reis and arranged in a decimal sequence (until 1910).

Commencing 1910

100 Centavos = 1 Escudo

KINGDOM

DECIMAL COINAGE

KM# 530 5 REIS

2.8000 g., Bronze **Ruler:** Carlos I **Obv:** Head right **Obv. Legend:** CARLOS I REI... **Rev:** Value within wreath

Date	Mintage	F	VF	XF	Unc	BU
1901	1,070,000	2.50	12.50	40.00	90.00	—
1904	720,000	0.75	1.75	12.50	28.00	—
1905	1,340,000	0.75	1.50	6.00	15.00	—
1906/0	1,260	0.30	1.00	2.50	8.00	—
1906/9	Inc. above	0.25	0.75	2.00	7.00	—
1906	Inc. above	0.75	2.00	4.00	10.00	—

KM# 555 5 REIS
Bronze **Ruler:** Manuel II **Obv:** Head left **Rev:** Value within wreath

Date	Mintage	F	VF	XF	Unc	BU
1910	1,000,000	0.30	1.00	2.50	7.00	—

KM# 548 100 REIS
2.5000 g., 0.8350 Silver 0.0671 oz. ASW, 20 mm. **Ruler:** Manuel II **Obv:** Bust left **Obv. Legend:** EMANVEL II PORTVG: ET ALGARB: REX

Date	Mintage	F	VF	XF	Unc	BU
1909	6,363,000	1.50	3.50	6.50	22.00	—
1910	Inc. above	1.25	2.50	4.00	10.00	—

KM# 534 200 REIS
5.0000 g., 0.9170 Silver 0.1474 oz. ASW **Ruler:** Carlos I **Obv:** Head right **Obv. Legend:** CARLOS I... **Rev:** Value within wreath

Date	Mintage	VG	F	VF	XF	Unc
1901	205,000	30.00	75.00	125	300	—
1903	200,000	12.50	35.00	65.00	115	—

KM# 549 200 REIS
5.0000 g., 0.8350 Silver 0.1342 oz. ASW **Ruler:** Manuel II **Obv:** Head left **Obv. Legend:** EMANVEL II... **Rev:** Crown above value within wreath

Date	Mintage	VG	F	VF	XF	Unc
1909	7,656,000	2.25	3.50	6.50	12.00	25.00

KM# 535 500 REIS
12.5000 g., 0.9170 Silver 0.3685 oz. ASW, 30 mm. **Ruler:** Carlos I **Obv:** Head right **Obv. Legend:** CARLOS I... **Rev:** Crowned arms within wreath

Date	Mintage	VG	F	VF	XF	Unc
1901	1,050,000	7.50	22.50	40.00	75.00	150
1903	680,000	6.50	9.00	15.00	30.00	60.00
1906	Inc. above	12.00	30.00	60.00	90.00	200
1906/3	240,000	15.00	35.00	70.00	100	250
1907	384,000	6.00	8.00	12.00	18.00	35.00
1908	1,840,000	5.50	7.50	11.50	16.00	25.00

KM# 547 500 REIS
12.5000 g., 0.9170 Silver 0.3685 oz. ASW, 30 mm. **Ruler:** Manuel II **Obv:** Head left **Obv. Legend:** EMANVEL II.. **Rev:** Crowned shield within sprigs

Date	Mintage	VG	F	VF	XF	Unc
1908	2,500,000	BV	6.00	10.00	18.00	30.00
1909	Inc. above	8.00	25.00	45.00	85.00	190
1909/8	1,513,000	8.00	25.00	45.00	85.00	195

KM# 556 500 REIS
12.5000 g., 0.9170 Silver 0.3685 oz. ASW, 30 mm. **Ruler:** Manuel II **Subject:** Peninsular War Centennial **Obv:** Head left **Obv. Legend:** EMANVEL II... **Rev:** Crowned shield **Designer:** Valancio Alves

Date	Mintage	VG	F	VF	XF	Unc
1910	200,000	12.50	35.00	55.00	90.00	175

KM# 557 500 REIS
12.5000 g., 0.9170 Silver 0.3685 oz. ASW, 30 mm. **Ruler:** Manuel II **Subject:** Marquis De Pombal **Obv:** Head left **Obv. Legend:** EMANVEL II... **Rev:** Seated Victory flanked by crowned shield and bust statue **Designer:** Venancio Alves

Date	Mintage	VG	F	VF	XF	Unc
1910	400,000	10.00	15.00	25.00	45.00	85.00
1910 Proof	—	Value: 600				

KM# 558 1000 REIS
25.0000 g., 0.9170 Silver 0.7370 oz. ASW, 37 mm. **Ruler:** Manuel II **Subject:** Peninsular War Centennial **Obv:** Head left **Obv. Legend:** EMANVEL II... **Rev:** Crowned shield **Designer:** Valancio Alves

Date	Mintage	VG	F	VF	XF	Unc
1910	200,000	20.00	45.00	75.00	125	250
1910 Proof	—	Value: 900				

REPUBLIC

DECIMAL COINAGE

KM# 565 CENTAVO
Bronze **Obv:** Value **Rev:** Shield within designed circle

Date	Mintage	F	VF	XF	Unc	BU
1917	2,250,000	0.50	1.00	2.00	4.00	6.00
1918	22,996,000	0.50	1.00	2.00	4.00	6.00
1920	12,535,000	0.50	1.00	2.50	5.00	7.00
1921	4,492,000	10.00	30.00	40.00	70.00	—
1922 Rare	Inc. above	—	—	—	—	—

KM# 567 2 CENTAVOS
Iron **Obv:** Value **Rev:** Shield within designed circle

Date	Mintage	F	VF	XF	Unc	BU
1918	170,000	65.00	150	300	700	—

KM# 568 2 CENTAVOS
Bronze

Date	Mintage	F	VF	XF	Unc	BU
1918	4,295,000	0.50	0.75	2.00	4.00	6.00
1920	10,109,000	0.50	1.50	2.50	5.00	7.00
1921	679,000	25.00	50.00	100	150	—

KM# 566 4 CENTAVOS
Copper-Nickel **Obv:** Value **Rev:** Liberty head left

Date	Mintage	F	VF	XF	Unc	BU
1917	4,961,000	0.35	0.65	1.50	4.00	7.00
1919	10,067,000	0.35	0.65	1.75	4.50	8.00

KM# 569 5 CENTAVOS
Bronze **Obv:** Value **Rev:** Shield within designed circle

Date	Mintage	F	VF	XF	Unc	BU
1920	114,000	35.00	70.00	120	200	—
1921	5,916,000	0.75	2.00	4.00	7.00	9.00
1922	Inc. above	125	250	500	750	—

KM# 572 5 CENTAVOS
Bronze **Obv:** Value **Rev:** Liberty head left

Date	Mintage	F	VF	XF	Unc	BU
1924	6,480,000	0.50	1.50	4.50	10.00	—
1925	7,260,000	3.50	7.50	22.00	40.00	—
1927	26,320,000	0.25	0.75	1.50	5.00	10.00

KM# 563 10 CENTAVOS
2.5000 g., 0.8350 Silver 0.0671 oz. ASW **Obv:** Liberty head left **Rev:** Shield within designed circle within wreath

Date	Mintage	F	VF	XF	Unc	BU
1915	3,418,000	1.25	2.50	3.50	8.00	12.00

KM# 570 10 CENTAVOS
Copper-Nickel **Obv:** Value **Rev:** Liberty head left

Date	Mintage	F	VF	XF	Unc	BU
1920	1,120,000	3.00	6.00	12.00	20.00	—
1921	1,285,000	3.00	6.00	15.00	25.00	—

KM# 573 10 CENTAVOS
4.0000 g., Bronze **Obv:** Value **Rev:** Liberty head left

Date	Mintage	F	VF	XF	Unc	BU
1924	1,210,000	3.00	12.50	45.00	100	—
1925	9,090,000	0.75	1.50	11.00	35.00	—
1926	26,250,000	0.75	2.75	14.50	40.00	—
1930	1,730,000	55.00	125	250	550	—
1938	2,000,000	5.00	20.00	40.00	100	—
1940	3,384,000	1.50	4.00	10.00	25.00	—

KM# 583 10 CENTAVOS
2.0000 g., Bronze, 17 mm. **Obv:** Circles within cross **Rev:** Value above sprig **Designer:** M. Norte

Date	Mintage	F	VF	XF	Unc	BU
1942	1,035,000	2.00	4.00	22.50	45.00	—
1943	18,765,000	2.00	5.00	10.00	40.00	—
1944	5,090,000	2.00	5.00	15.00	40.00	—
1945	6,090,000	2.00	4.50	15.00	35.00	—
1946	7,740,000	1.00	2.50	8.00	30.00	—
1947	9,283,000	1.00	2.00	7.50	15.00	—
1948	5,900,000	10.00	30.00	100	150	—
1949	15,240,000	0.25	1.00	5.00	15.00	20.00
1950	8,860,000	1.50	5.00	20.00	60.00	—
1951	5,040,000	1.50	5.00	35.00	75.00	—
1952	4,960,000	2.50	12.00	50.00	125	—
1953	7,548,000	1.50	3.00	5.00	10.00	15.00
1954	2,452,000	1.50	5.00	15.00	60.00	—
1955	10,000,000	0.10	0.50	2.50	6.00	—
1956	3,336,000	0.10	0.50	2.00	5.00	7.50
1957	6,654,000	0.10	0.25	2.00	5.00	—
1958	7,320,000	0.10	0.25	2.00	5.00	—
1959	7,140,000	0.10	0.25	2.00	4.00	5.00
1960	15,055,000	0.10	0.25	2.00	2.00	—
1961	5,020,000	—	0.10	1.50	4.00	—
1962	14,980,000	—	0.10	0.50	1.00	1.50
1963	5,393,000	—	0.10	1.25	2.50	—
1964	10,257,000	—	0.10	0.75	1.50	2.00
1965	15,550,000	—	0.10	1.00	1.75	—
1966	10,200,000	—	0.10	0.50	1.00	—
1967	18,592,000	—	0.10	0.50	1.00	1.50
1968	22,515,000	—	0.10	0.50	1.00	2.00
1969	3,871,000	0.10	0.25	1.25	2.50	—

KM# 594 10 CENTAVOS
0.5000 g., Aluminum, 15 mm. **Obv:** Circles within cross **Obv. Legend:** REPVBLICA PORTVGVESA **Rev:** Value above sprig **Designer:** M. Norte

Date	Mintage	F	VF	XF	Unc	BU
1969	—	—	500	750	1,000	—
1970 Rare	—	—	—	—	—	—
1971	25,673,000	—	—	0.50	1.00	—
1972	10,558,000	—	—	0.50	1.00	—
1973	3,149,000	—	—	1.25	3.50	—
1974	17,043,000	—	—	0.50	1.00	—
1975	22,410,000	—	—	0.50	1.00	—
1976	19,907,000	—	—	0.50	1.00	—
1977	8,431,000	—	—	0.50	1.00	—
1978	2,205,000	—	—	0.50	1.00	—
1979	9,083,000	—	—	1.00	2.50	—

KM# 562 20 CENTAVOS
5.0000 g., 0.8350 Silver 0.1342 oz. ASW **Obv:** Liberty head left **Rev:** Shield within designed circle and wreath

Date	Mintage	F	VF	XF	Unc	BU
1913	540,000	5.00	35.00	75.00	175	—
1916	706,000	3.00	30.00	40.00	100	—

KM# 571 20 CENTAVOS
Copper-Nickel **Obv:** Value and date within circle **Rev:** Liberty head left within circle

Date	Mintage	F	VF	XF	Unc	BU
1920	1,568,000	3.50	7.00	15.00	20.00	—
1921	3,030,000	4.00	8.00	14.00	22.50	—
1922	580,000	500	900	1,500	3,000	—

KM# 574 20 CENTAVOS
Bronze, 24 mm. **Obv:** Value **Rev:** Liberty head left

Date	Mintage	F	VF	XF	Unc	BU
1924	6,220,000	1.00	4.00	20.00	50.00	—
1925	10,580,000	1.00	4.00	20.00	50.00	—

KM# 584 20 CENTAVOS
3.0000 g., Bronze, 20.8 mm. **Obv:** Circles within cross **Rev:** Value above sprig **Designer:** M. Norte

Date	Mintage	F	VF	XF	Unc	BU
1942	10,170,000	1.50	3.50	25.00	60.00	—
1943	Inc. above	1.50	3.00	20.00	60.00	—
1944	7,290,000	1.50	3.00	20.00	60.00	—
1945	7,552,000	1.00	2.00	25.00	60.00	—
1948	2,750,000	2.50	12.00	35.00	135	—
1949	12,250,000	0.10	0.50	6.00	15.00	20.00
1951	3,185,000	0.50	2.00	20.00	150	—
1952	1,815,000	2.00	12.00	35.00	200	—
1953	9,426,000	—	0.75	4.00	8.00	—
1955	5,574,000	—	0.75	4.00	8.00	—
1956	6,450,000	—	0.50	2.75	5.50	7.50
1958	7,470,000	—	0.50	2.75	5.50	7.50
1959	4,780,000	—	0.50	2.75	5.50	7.50
1960	4,790,000	—	0.50	3.50	8.00	—
1961	5,180,000	—	0.50	3.50	8.00	—
1962	2,500,000	0.25	1.50	10.00	18.00	25.00
1963	7,990,000	—	0.25	2.00	3.50	4.50
1964	7,010,000	—	0.25	1.50	3.00	4.00
1965	7,365,000	—	0.25	1.00	2.50	—
1966	8,074,999	—	0.25	0.50	2.00	—
1967	9,220,000	—	0.25	0.50	2.00	—
1968	10,372,000	—	0.25	0.50	1.50	2.00
1969	8,657,000	—	0.25	1.00	3.00	—

KM# 595 20 CENTAVOS
1.7000 g., Bronze, 16 mm. **Obv:** Circles within cross **Rev:** Value above sprig **Designer:** M. Norte

Date	Mintage	F	VF	XF	Unc	BU
1969	10,891,000	—	0.25	0.75	2.50	—
1970	16,120,000	—	0.25	1.00	3.00	—
1971	1,933,000	—	1.00	2.50	7.50	—
1972	16,354,000	—	—	0.25	1.00	—
1973	4,900,000	—	—	0.25	1.00	—
1974	26,975,000	—	—	0.25	1.00	—

KM# 561 50 CENTAVOS
12.5000 g., 0.8350 Silver 0.3356 oz. ASW **Obv:** Liberty head left **Rev:** Shield within designed circle and wreath

Date	Mintage	F	VF	XF	Unc	BU
1912	1,695,000	5.50	8.00	15.00	30.00	—
1913	4,443,000	BV	6.00	10.00	20.00	—
1914	4,992,000	5.50	8.00	15.00	30.00	—
1916	5,080,000	BV	6.00	10.00	20.00	—

KM# 575 50 CENTAVOS
Aluminum-Bronze **Obv:** Seated figure **Rev:** Shield within designed circle and wreath

Date	Mintage	F	VF	XF	Unc	BU
1924	810,000	65.00	125	250	400	—
1925	—	1,000	1,500	3,500	7,000	—
1926	4,340,000	2.00	6.00	18.00	40.00	55.00

KM# 577 50 CENTAVOS
4.4500 g., Copper-Nickel, 23 mm. **Obv:** Liberty head right **Rev:** Shield within designed circle and wreath above value

Date	Mintage	F	VF	XF	Unc	BU
1927	2,330,000	2.50	12.50	30.00	125	150
1928	6,823,000	2.50	12.50	35.00	220	—
1929	9,779,000	2.50	12.50	30.00	125	150
1930	1,116,000	2.50	20.00	200	550	—
1931	7,127,000	8.00	22.00	225	550	—
1935	902,000	25.00	55.00	400	900	—
Note: For exclusive use in Azores						
1938	923,000	25.00	55.00	325	950	—
1940	2,000,000	1.00	5.00	30.00	125	—
1944	2,974,000	0.25	1.00	7.00	15.00	25.00
1945	5,700,000	0.25	1.00	5.50	20.00	30.00
1946	4,334,000	—	2.00	10.00	35.00	45.00
1947	6,998,000	0.10	1.00	9.00	20.00	30.00
1951	4,610,000	—	0.50	2.75	10.00	15.00
1952	2,421,000	0.10	1.00	4.00	20.00	30.00
1953	2,369,000	0.10	1.00	12.50	50.00	65.00
1955	3,057,000	0.10	0.50	3.00	9.00	12.00
1956	3,003,000	—	0.50	3.00	6.00	8.00
1957	3,940,000	—	0.50	3.00	6.50	9.00
1958	2,687,000	—	0.50	4.00	9.00	12.00
1959	4,027,000	—	0.50	2.00	6.00	8.00
1960	2,592,000	—	0.50	2.00	5.50	7.50
1961	3,324,000	—	0.50	2.00	4.00	6.00
1962	6,678,000	—	0.25	1.00	2.50	3.50
1963	2,346,000	—	0.25	3.00	9.00	12.00
1964	7,654,000	—	0.25	1.00	1.75	2.75
1965	3,366,000	—	0.25	1.00	2.50	3.50
1966	6,085,000	—	0.25	1.00	2.50	3.50
1967	19,391,000	—	0.25	1.00	2.50	3.50
1968	11,448,000	—	0.25	1.00	2.00	3.00

KM# 596 50 CENTAVOS
4.2500 g., Bronze, 22.5 mm. **Obv:** Circles within cross **Obv. Legend:** REPVBLICA PORTVGVESA **Rev:** Value above spears of grain

Date	Mintage	F	VF	XF	Unc	BU
1969	3,481,000	—	—	1.00	3.50	—
1970	17,280,000	—	—	1.00	3.00	—
1971	9,139,000	—	—	1.00	3.00	—
1972	24,729,000	—	—	1.00	3.00	—
1973	35,588,000	—	—	0.75	2.50	—
1974	28,719,000	—	—	0.75	2.50	—
1975	17,793,000	—	—	0.75	2.50	—
1976	23,734,000	—	—	0.75	2.50	—
1977	16,340,000	—	—	0.75	2.50	—
1978	48,348,000	—	—	0.75	2.25	—
1979	61,652,000	—	—	0.75	2.00	—

KM# 560 ESCUDO

25.0000 g., 0.8350 Silver 0.6711 oz. ASW, 37 mm. **Subject:** October 5, 1910, Birth of the Republic **Obv:** Bust holding torch facing left **Rev:** Shield within designed circle and wreath **Designer:** Domingos Rego

Date	Mintage	F	VF	XF	Unc	BU
1910	Est. 1,000	40.00	80.00	125	200	—

Note: Struck in 1914

KM# 564 ESCUDO

25.0000 g., 0.8350 Silver 0.6711 oz. ASW, 37 mm. **Obv:** Liberty head left

Date	Mintage	F	VF	XF	Unc	BU
1915	1,818,000	15.00	35.00	50.00	80.00	—
1916	1,405,000	15.00	40.00	60.00	90.00	—

KM# 576 ESCUDO

Aluminum-Bronze **Obv:** Sitting figure **Rev:** Shield within designed circle, value divides wreath

Date	Mintage	F	VF	XF	Unc	BU
1924	2,709,000	10.00	20.00	40.00	80.00	—
1926	2,346,000	85.00	175	300	700	—

KM# 578 ESCUDO

8.0000 g., Copper-Nickel, 26.5 mm. **Designer:** M. Simoes

Date	Mintage	F	VF	XF	Unc	BU
1927	1,917,000	2.00	12.00	65.00	200	—
1928	7,462,000	1.00	5.00	35.00	225	—
1929	1,617,000	1.00	15.00	110	300	—
1930	1,911,000	6.00	25.00	350	1,000	—
1931	2,039,000	7.50	25.00	300	900	—
1935	—	125	325	2,750	6,000	—
Note: For exclusive use in Azores						
1939	304,000	12.00	50.00	250	700	—
1940	1,259,000	1.00	25.00	75.00	150	—
1944	993,000	30.00	75.00	200	400	—
1945	Inc. above	0.50	1.50	22.00	65.00	—
1946	2,507,000	0.50	1.50	12.50	65.00	—
1951	2,500,000	0.50	1.00	6.00	10.00	15.00
1952	2,500,000	1.50	4.00	45.00	125	—
1957	1,656,000	0.10	0.50	4.50	10.00	20.00
1958	1,447,000	0.10	0.50	4.50	12.00	20.00
1959	1,908,000	0.10	0.50	4.50	10.00	20.00
1961	2,505,000	0.10	0.25	2.50	5.00	7.00
1962	2,757,000	0.10	0.25	2.00	4.00	6.00
1964	1,611,000	0.10	0.25	2.00	3.50	5.00
1965	1,683,000	0.10	0.25	1.50	3.00	4.00
1966	2,607,000	0.10	0.20	1.50	4.00	4.00
1968	4,099,000	0.10	0.20	1.50	3.50	5.00

KM# 597 ESCUDO

8.0000 g., Bronze, 26 mm. **Obv:** Circles within cross **Obv. Legend:** REPVBLICA PORTVGVESA **Rev:** Value above spears of grain **Edge:** Plain **Designer:** M. Norte

Date	Mintage	F	VF	XF	Unc	BU
1969	3,020,000	—	0.10	1.50	5.00	—
1970	6,009,000	—	0.10	1.50	4.00	—
1971	7,860,000	—	0.10	1.50	4.00	—
1972	3,815,000	—	0.10	1.50	4.50	—
1973	20,467,000	—	0.10	1.00	3.00	—
1974	11,444,000	—	0.10	1.00	3.00	—
1975	8,473,000	—	0.10	1.00	3.00	—
1976	7,353,000	—	0.10	0.50	2.00	—
1977	6,218,000	—	0.10	0.50	2.00	—
1978	7,061,000	—	0.10	0.50	2.00	—
1979	14,241,000	—	0.10	0.25	1.50	—

KM# 614 ESCUDO

3.0000 g., Nickel-Brass, 18 mm. **Obv:** Shield **Rev:** Value **Note:** Prev. KM#611.

Date	Mintage	F	VF	XF	Unc	BU
1981	30,165,000	—	—	0.10	1.00	—
1982	53,018,000	—	—	0.10	1.00	—
1983	53,165,000	—	—	0.10	0.50	—
1984	59,463,000	—	—	0.10	0.50	—
1985	46,832,000	—	—	0.10	0.50	—
1986	8,029,999	—	—	0.10	4.00	—

KM# 612 ESCUDO

Nickel-Brass, 18 mm. **Subject:** World Roller Hockey Championship Games **Obv:** Shield **Rev:** Hockey player

Date	Mintage	F	VF	XF	Unc	BU
ND(1983)	1,990,000	—	0.10	0.25	0.75	—

KM# 631 ESCUDO

1.6900 g., Nickel-Brass, 16 mm. **Obv:** Design above shield **Rev:** Flower design above value **Edge:** Reeded **Designer:** Helder Batista

Date	Mintage	F	VF	XF	Unc	BU
1986	14,882,000	—	—	0.10	0.35	—
1987	21,922,000	—	—	0.10	0.35	—
1988	17,168,000	—	—	0.10	0.35	—
1989	17,194,000	—	—	0.10	0.35	—
1990	19,008,000	—	—	0.10	0.35	—
1991	21,500,000	—	—	—	0.35	—
1992	22,000,000	—	—	—	0.35	—
1993	10,505,000	—	—	—	0.35	—
1994	—	—	—	—	0.35	—
1995	—	—	—	—	0.50	—
Note: In Mint sets only						
1996	—	—	—	—	0.35	—
1996 Proof	7,000	Value: 0.50				
1997	—	—	—	—	0.35	—
1997 Proof	—	Value: 0.50				
1998	—	—	—	—	0.35	—
1998 Proof	—	Value: 2.00				
1999	—	—	—	—	0.35	—
2000	—	—	—	—	0.35	—

KM# 580 2-1/2 ESCUDOS

3.5000 g., 0.6500 Silver 0.0731 oz. ASW, 20.41 mm. **Obv:** Early sailing ship **Rev:** Shield on globe **Edge:** Reeded

Date	Mintage	F	VF	XF	Unc	BU
1932	2,592,000	5.00	20.00	50.00	120	—
1933	2,457,000	15.00	40.00	100	200	—
1937	1,000,000	150	350	700	1,500	—
1940	2,763,000	3.00	10.00	25.00	70.00	—
1942	3,847,000	BV	3.00	6.50	20.00	—
1943	8,302,000	BV	1.75	2.50	10.00	15.00
1944	9,134,000	BV	1.50	2.25	7.00	10.00
1945	6,316,000	BV	3.50	10.00	20.00	30.00
1946	3,208,000	BV	3.00	7.50	15.00	25.00
1947	2,610,000	BV	3.00	7.50	15.00	25.00
1948	1,814,000	10.00	20.00	40.00	110	—
1951	4,000,000	BV	1.25	2.00	5.00	7.00

KM# 590 2-1/2 ESCUDOS

3.5000 g., Copper-Nickel, 20 mm. **Obv:** Ship **Obv. Designer:** Martins Barata **Rev:** Shield flanked by stars **Rev. Designer:** M. Norte

Date	Mintage	F	VF	XF	Unc	BU
1963	12,711,000	—	0.50	20.00	32.00	45.00
1964	17,948,000	—	0.50	20.00	32.00	45.00
1965	19,512,000	—	0.25	5.00	11.00	15.00
1966	3,828,000	—	2.00	35.00	55.00	80.00
1967	5,545,000	—	0.25	7.00	18.00	—
1968	6,087,000	—	0.25	2.00	3.50	5.00
1969	9,969,000	—	0.25	1.75	3.00	4.00
1970	2,400,000	—	0.25	2.25	4.00	5.00
1971	6,791,000	—	0.25	1.50	3.00	4.00
1972	6,713,000	—	0.25	1.75	3.00	4.00
1973	9,104,000	—	0.25	1.00	2.00	3.00
1974	22,743,000	—	0.10	0.75	2.50	3.50
1975	16,623,999	—	0.10	0.50	1.50	2.00
1976	21,516,000	—	0.10	0.50	1.50	2.00
1977	45,726,000	—	0.10	0.50	1.50	2.00
1978	27,375,000	—	0.10	0.25	0.75	1.00
1979	44,804,000	—	0.10	0.25	0.75	1.00
1980	22,319,000	—	0.10	0.25	1.00	1.25
1981	25,420,000	—	0.10	0.20	1.00	1.25
1982	45,910,000	—	0.10	0.20	0.75	1.00
1983	62,946,000	—	0.10	0.20	0.75	1.00
1984	58,210,000	—	0.10	0.20	0.75	1.00
1985	60,142,000	—	0.10	0.20	0.75	1.00

KM# 605 2-1/2 ESCUDOS

3.5000 g., Copper-Nickel, 20 mm. **Subject:** 100th Anniversary - Death of Alexandre Herculano, Poet **Obv:** Shield **Rev:** Bust facing flanked by dates

Date	Mintage	F	VF	XF	Unc	BU
ND(1977)	5,990,000	—	0.20	0.75	2.00	—
ND(1977) Proof	13,000	Value: 3.50				

KM# 613 2-1/2 ESCUDOS

3.5000 g., Copper-Nickel, 20 mm. **Subject:** World Rolller Hockey Championship Games **Obv:** Shield **Rev:** Hockey player

Date	Mintage	F	VF	XF	Unc	BU
ND(1983)	1,990,000	—	0.10	0.25	1.00	—

KM# 617 2-1/2 ESCUDOS

3.5000 g., Copper-Nickel, 20 mm. **Series:** F.A.O. **Obv:** Shield **Rev:** Ear of corn, FAO and date

Date	Mintage	F	VF	XF	Unc	BU
1983	995,000	—	0.10	0.35	1.25	—

KM# 581 5 ESCUDOS

7.0000 g., 0.6500 Silver 0.1463 oz. ASW, 25 mm. **Obv:** Ship **Rev:** Shield in front of circular design

Date	Mintage	F	VF	XF	Unc	BU
1932	800,000	10.00	35.00	200	600	—
1933	6,717,000	2.50	5.50	20.00	60.00	—
1934	1,012,000	4.00	15.00	30.00	120	—
1937	1,500,000	30.00	80.00	200	600	—
1940	1,500,000	4.00	15.00	50.00	120	—
1942	2,051,000	2.50	4.50	9.00	20.00	25.00
1943	1,354,000	6.00	20.00	60.00	140	—
1946	404,000	4.00	12.50	25.00	55.00	—
1947	2,420,000	BV	3.00	5.00	12.00	—
1948	2,017,999	BV	3.00	5.00	11.00	15.00
1951	966,000	BV	3.00	5.00	11.00	15.00

KM# 587 5 ESCUDOS
7.0000 g., 0.6500 Silver 0.1463 oz. ASW, 25 mm. **Subject:** 500th Anniversary - Death of Prince Henry the Navigator **Obv:** Shield **Rev:** Head with sombrero facing 1/4 left **Designer:** M. Norte

Date	Mintage	F	VF	XF	Unc	BU
1960	800,000	—	2.50	3.50	6.50	10.00
1960 Matte	—	—	—	—	20.00	—

Note: A small quantity of these coins were given a matte finish by the Lisbon Mint on private contract

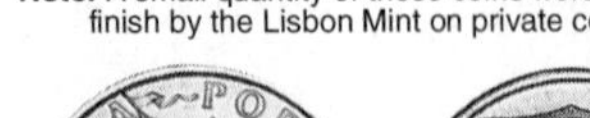

KM# 591 5 ESCUDOS
7.0000 g., Copper-Nickel, 24.5 mm. **Obv:** Ship **Rev:** Shield flanked by stars **Designer:** M. Norte

Date	Mintage	F	VF	XF	Unc	BU
1963	2,200,000	—	0.50	15.00	30.00	—
1964	4,268,000	—	0.50	12.50	25.00	35.00
1965	7,294,000	—	0.35	12.50	25.00	35.00
1966	8,119,999	—	0.35	10.00	25.00	35.00
1967	8,128,000	—	0.25	7.00	20.00	25.00
1968	5,023,000	—	0.25	3.00	5.00	10.00
1969	3,571,000	—	0.10	2.00	5.00	6.00
1970	1,200,000	—	0.10	2.50	5.50	7.00
1971	2,721,000	—	0.10	2.00	5.00	6.00
1972	1,880,000	—	0.10	2.00	6.00	—
1973	2,836,000	—	0.10	1.25	4.00	—
1974	3,984,000	—	0.10	1.00	3.50	—
1975	7,496,000	—	0.10	1.00	2.50	3.50
1976	11,379,000	—	0.10	1.00	2.50	3.50
1977	29,058,000	—	0.10	0.50	1.50	2.00
1978	672,000	—	2.00	5.00	10.00	—
1979	19,546,000	—	0.10	0.50	1.50	—
1980	46,244,000	—	0.10	0.50	1.50	2.00
1981	15,267,000	—	0.10	0.50	1.50	2.00
1982	31,318,000	—	0.10	0.50	1.50	2.00
1983	51,056,000	—	0.10	0.50	1.50	2.00
1984	46,794,000	—	0.10	0.50	1.50	2.00
1985	45,441,000	—	0.10	0.50	1.25	1.75
1986	18,753,000	—	0.10	0.50	1.50	—

KM# 606 5 ESCUDOS
7.0000 g., Copper-Nickel, 24.5 mm. **Subject:** 100th Anniversary - Death of Alexandre Herculano, Poet **Obv:** Shield **Rev:** Bust 1/4 right flanked by dates **Designer:** M. Norte

Date	Mintage	F	VF	XF	Unc	BU
ND(1977)	9,176,000	—	0.35	1.00	2.00	2.50
ND(1977) Proof	10,000	Value: 4.00				

KM# 615 5 ESCUDOS
7.0000 g., Copper-Nickel, 24.5 mm. **Subject:** World Roller Hockey Championship Games **Obv:** Shield **Rev:** Hockey player

Date	Mintage	F	VF	XF	Unc	BU
ND(1983)	1,990,000	—	0.25	0.50	1.00	1.50

KM# 618 5 ESCUDOS
7.0000 g., Copper-Nickel, 24.5 mm. **Series:** F.A.O. **Obv:** Shield **Rev:** Bull

Date	Mintage	F	VF	XF	Unc	BU
ND(1983)	995,000	—	0.30	0.75	1.50	2.50

KM# 632 5 ESCUDOS
Nickel-Brass **Obv:** Design above shield **Rev:** Star design above value **Designer:** Helder Batista

Date	Mintage	F	VF	XF	Unc	BU
1986	21,426,000	—	0.10	0.25	0.50	—
1987	40,548,000	—	0.10	0.25	0.50	—
1988	19,382,000	—	0.10	0.25	0.50	—
1989	27,641,000	—	0.10	0.25	0.50	—
1990	77,977,000	—	0.10	0.25	0.50	—
1991	32,000,000	—	—	—	0.50	—
1992	16,000,000	—	—	—	0.50	—
1993	8,300,000	—	—	—	0.50	—
1994	—	—	—	—	0.50	—
1995	—	—	—	—	0.50	—
1996	—	—	—	—	0.50	—
1996 Proof	7,000	Value: 0.75				
1997	—	—	—	—	0.50	—
1997 Proof	—	Value: 0.75				
1998	—	—	—	—	0.50	—
1998 Proof	—	Value: 0.75				
1999	—	—	—	—	0.50	—
2000	—	—	—	—	0.50	—

KM# 579 10 ESCUDOS
12.5000 g., 0.8350 Silver 0.3356 oz. ASW, 30 mm. **Subject:** Battle of Ourique **Obv:** Crowned shield flanked by value **Rev:** Armored figure on horse holding sword **Designer:** Domingos Rega

Date	Mintage	F	VF	XF	Unc	BU
1928	200,000	7.00	15.00	25.00	40.00	50.00

KM# 582 10 ESCUDOS
12.5000 g., 0.8350 Silver 0.3356 oz. ASW, 30 mm. **Obv:** Ship **Rev:** Shield in front of circular design

Date	Mintage	F	VF	XF	Unc	BU
1932	3,220,000	5.50	10.00	20.00	60.00	—
1933	1,780,000	30.00	70.00	200	500	—
1934	400,000	15.00	30.00	50.00	150	—
1937	500,000	60.00	150	400	650	—
1940	1,200,000	10.00	20.00	40.00	60.00	—
1942	186,000	200	400	700	1,200	—
1948	507,000	30.00	75.00	150	220	—

KM# 586 10 ESCUDOS
12.5000 g., 0.8350 Silver 0.3356 oz. ASW, 30 mm. **Obv:** Ship **Obv. Designer:** João da Silva **Rev:** Shield above circular design flanked by value

Date	Mintage	F	VF	XF	Unc	BU
1954	5,764,000	—	BV	5.50	8.00	10.00
1955	4,056,000	—	BV	5.50	8.00	10.00

KM# 588 10 ESCUDOS
12.5000 g., 0.6800 Silver 0.2733 oz. ASW, 30 mm. **Subject:** 500th Anniversary - Death of Prince Henry the Navigator **Obv:** Shield flanked by designs **Rev:** Head with sombrero facing 1/4 left **Designer:** M. Norte

Date	Mintage	F	VF	XF	Unc	BU
1960	200,000	—	9.00	20.00	30.00	35.00
1960 Matte	—	—	—	—	50.00	—

Note: A small quantity of these coins were given a matte finish by the Lisbon Mint on private contract

KM# 600 10 ESCUDOS
10.0000 g., Copper-Nickel Clad Nickel **Obv:** Ship **Rev:** Shield flanked by stars **Designer:** M. Norte

Date	Mintage	F	VF	XF	Unc	BU
1971	3,876,000	—	0.25	0.75	2.00	2.50
1972	2,694,000	—	0.25	1.00	2.50	3.50
1973	5,418,000	—	0.25	0.75	2.00	2.50
1974	4,043,000	—	0.25	0.75	2.00	2.50

KM# 633 10 ESCUDOS
Nickel-Brass **Obv:** Design above shield **Rev:** Artistic design above value **Designer:** Helder Batista

Date	Mintage	F	VF	XF	Unc	BU
1986	12,818,000	—	0.20	0.40	1.00	1.50
1987	32,814,999	—	0.20	0.40	1.00	1.50
1988	32,579,000	—	0.20	0.40	1.00	1.50
1989	12,788,000	—	0.20	0.40	1.00	1.50
1990	26,500,000	—	0.20	0.40	1.00	1.50
1991	9,500,000	—	—	—	1.00	1.75
1992	5,600,000	—	—	—	1.00	1.75
1993	20,000	—	—	—	10.00	—
Note: In Mint sets only						
1994	20,000	—	—	—	10.00	—
Note: In Mint sets only						
1995	—	—	—	—	10.00	—
Note: In Mint sets only						
1996	—	—	—	—	1.00	—
1996 Proof	7,000	Value: 2.50				
1997	—	—	—	—	1.00	—
1997 Proof	—	Value: 2.50				
1998	—	—	—	—	1.00	—
1998 Proof	—	Value: 3.00				
1999	—	—	—	—	1.00	—
2000	—	—	—	—	1.00	—

KM# 638 10 ESCUDOS
7.4000 g., Nickel-Brass **Subject:** Rural World **Obv:** Design above shield **Rev:** Hand holding sprig flanked by stars all around **Designer:** Helder Batista

Date	Mintage	F	VF	XF	Unc	BU
1987	2,000,000	—	0.40	0.60	1.50	—

KM# 585 20 ESCUDOS
21.0000 g., 0.8000 Silver 0.5401 oz. ASW, 34 mm. **Subject:** 25th Anniversary of Financial Reform **Obv:** Shield above globe, value at left, all within circle **Rev:** Seated figure facing left reading a book **Designer:** Joao daSilva

Date	Mintage	F	VF	XF	Unc	BU
1953	1,000,000	—	BV	8.50	9.50	11.50
1953 Matte	—	—	—	—	—	—

Note: A small quantity of these coins were given a matte finish by the Lisbon Mint on private contract

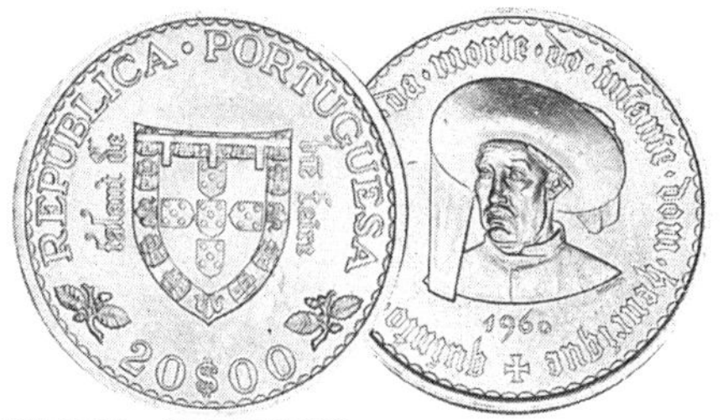

KM# 589 20 ESCUDOS
21.0000 g., 0.8000 Silver 0.5401 oz. ASW, 34 mm. **Subject:** 500th Anniversary - Death of Prince Henry the Navigator **Obv:** Shield flanked by designs **Rev:** Head with sombrero facing 1/4 left **Designer:** M. Norte

Date	Mintage	F	VF	XF	Unc	BU
1960	200,000	—	12.00	20.00	30.00	40.00
1960 Matte	—	—	—	—	55.00	—

Note: A small quantity of these coins were given a matte finish by the Lisbon Mint on private contract

KM# 592 20 ESCUDOS
10.0000 g., 0.6500 Silver 0.2090 oz. ASW **Subject:** Opening of Salazar Bridge **Obv:** Shield and value within artistic design **Rev:** Salazar bridge

Date	Mintage	F	VF	XF	Unc	BU
1966	2,000,000	—	BV	3.50	4.50	6.00
1966 Matte	200	—	—	—	35.00	—

Note: A small quantity of these coins were given a matte finish by the Lisbon Mint on private contract

KM# 634.1 20 ESCUDOS
Copper-Nickel, 26.5 mm. **Obv:** Shield divides date with value below **Rev:** Nautical windrose **Designer:** Euclides Vaz

Date	Mintage	F	VF	XF	Unc	BU
1986	45,361,000	—	0.15	0.25	1.00	1.50
1987	68,216,000	—	0.15	0.25	1.00	1.50
1988	57,482,000	—	0.15	0.25	1.00	1.50
1989	25,060,000	—	0.15	0.25	1.00	1.50
1990	50,000	—	—	—	10.00	—
Note: In Mint sets only						
1991	50,000	—	—	—	10.00	—
Note: In Mint sets only						
1992	20,000	—	—	—	10.00	—
Note: In Mint sets only						
1993	20,000	—	—	—	10.00	—
Note: In Mint sets only						
1994	20,000	—	—	—	10.00	—
Note: In Mint sets only						
1995	—	—	—	—	10.00	—
Note: In Mint sets only						
1996	—	—	—	—	10.00	—
Note: In Mint sets only						
1996 Proof	7,000	Value: 2.50				
1997	—	—	—	—	10.00	—
Note: In Mint sets only						
1997 Proof	—	Value: 2.50				

KM# 634.2 20 ESCUDOS
Copper-Nickel **Obv:** Larger shield divides date with larger value below **Obv. Designer:** Euclides Vaz **Rev:** Nautical windrose

Date	Mintage	F	VF	XF	Unc	BU
1998	—	—	—	—	1.00	—
1998 Proof	—	Value: 4.00				
1999	—	—	—	—	1.00	—
2000	—	—	—	—	1.00	—

KM# 607 25 ESCUDOS
Copper-Nickel **Obv:** Value to right of shield **Rev:** Head laureate left **Designer:** Norte d'Almeida

Date	Mintage	F	VF	XF	Unc	BU
1977	7,657,000	—	0.40	1.00	2.00	4.50
1978	12,277,000	—	0.40	1.50	3.00	5.00

KM# 608 25 ESCUDOS
Copper-Nickel, 26.5 mm. **Subject:** 100th Anniversary - Death of Alexandre Herculano, Poet **Obv:** Shield **Rev:** Bust flanked by dates facing 1/4 right **Designer:** M. Norte

Date	Mintage	F	VF	XF	Unc	BU
ND(1977)	5,990,000	—	0.50	1.00	2.50	4.75
ND(1977) Proof	13,000	Value: 7.00				

KM# 609 25 ESCUDOS
Copper-Nickel **Subject:** International Year of the Child **Obv:** Shield **Rev:** Two faces, one facing left, the other 3/4 right

Date	Mintage	F	VF	XF	Unc	BU
1979	990,000	—	0.50	1.00	2.50	—
1979 Prooflike	10,000	—	—	—	8.00	—

KM# 616 25 ESCUDOS
Copper-Nickel, 28.5 mm. **Subject:** World Roller Hockey Championship Games **Obv:** Shield **Rev:** Suited hockey player

Date	Mintage	F	VF	XF	Unc	BU
ND(1983)	1,990,000	—	0.50	1.00	2.00	2.50

KM# 619 25 ESCUDOS
Copper-Nickel, 28.5 mm. **Series:** F.A.O. **Obv:** Shield **Rev:** Fish, F.A.O. and date

Date	Mintage	F	VF	XF	Unc	BU
1983	995,000	—	0.60	1.25	2.25	3.00

KM# 623 25 ESCUDOS
Copper-Nickel, 28.5 mm. **Subject:** 10th Anniversary of Revolution **Obv:** Waves breaking over shield **Rev:** Stylized 25 **Designer:** Helder Batista

Date	Mintage	F	VF	XF	Unc	BU
ND(1984)	1,980,000	—	0.40	1.00	1.50	2.00

KM# 624 25 ESCUDOS
Copper-Nickel, 28.5 mm. **Subject:** International Year of Disabled Persons **Obv:** Shield **Rev:** Head 1/4 left with legend above **Designer:** M. Simoes

Date	Mintage	F	VF	XF	Unc	BU
ND(1984)	1,990,000	—	0.40	1.00	2.00	2.50

KM# 627 25 ESCUDOS
Copper-Nickel, 28.5 mm. **Subject:** 600th Anniversary - Battle of Aljubarrota **Obv:** Shield within circle **Rev:** Seated crowned figure flanked by shields **Designer:** C. Meneres

Date	Mintage	F	VF	XF	Unc	BU
ND(1985)	500,000	—	0.50	1.00	2.75	—

KM# 635 25 ESCUDOS
Copper-Nickel, 28.5 mm. **Subject:** Admission to European Common Market **Obv:** Shield **Rev:** Small square and lined design **Designer:** Armando Matos Simoes

Date	Mintage	F	VF	XF	Unc	BU
1986	4,990,000	—	0.40	1.00	2.00	—

KM# 593 50 ESCUDOS
18.0000 g., 0.6500 Silver 0.3761 oz. ASW **Subject:** 500th Anniversary - Birth of Pedro Alvares Cabral, Navigator, Discoverer of Brazil **Obv:** Crowned shield **Rev:** Bust with headdress right within circle **Designer:** M. Norte

Date	Mintage	F	VF	XF	Unc	BU
1968	1,000,000	—	—	—	6.50	7.50
1968 Matte	400	—	—	—	32.50	—

Note: A small quantity of these coins were given a matte finish by the Lisbon Mint on private contract

KM# 598 50 ESCUDOS
18.0000 g., 0.6500 Silver 0.3761 oz. ASW **Subject:** 500th Anniversary - Birth of Vasco daGama, Discoverer of the sea route to India **Obv:** Shield within maltese cross **Rev:** Head with headdress left **Designer:** A. Lucas

Date	Mintage	F	VF	XF	Unc	BU
ND(1969)	1,000,000	—	—	—	6.50	7.50
ND(1969) Matte	400	—	—	—	32.50	—

Note: A small quantity of these coins were given a matte finish by the Lisbon Mint on private contract

KM# 599 50 ESCUDOS
18.0000 g., 0.6500 Silver 0.3761 oz. ASW **Subject:** 100th Anniversary - Birth of Marechal Carmona, President **Obv:** Shield **Rev:** Uniformed bust 3/4 right

Date	Mintage	F	VF	XF	Unc	BU
ND(1969)	500,000	—	—	—	7.50	10.00
ND(1969) Matte	400	—	—	—	32.50	—

Note: A small quantity of these coins were given a matte finish by the Lisbon Mint on private contract

KM# 601 50 ESCUDOS
18.0000 g., 0.6500 Silver 0.3761 oz. ASW **Subject:** 125th Anniversary - Bank of Portugal **Obv:** Circles within circled cross design **Rev:** Stylized tree

Date	Mintage	F	VF	XF	Unc	BU
ND(1971)	500,000	—	—	—	8.50	11.50
ND(1971) Matte	—	—	—	—	32.50	—

Note: A small quantity of these coins were given a matte finish by the Lisbon Mint on private contract

KM# 602 50 ESCUDOS
18.0000 g., 0.6500 Silver 0.3761 oz. ASW, 34.5 mm. **Subject:** 400th Anniversary of Heroic Epic 'Os Lusiadas' **Obv:** Book appears as part of Quinas Cross, all within circle **Rev:** Victory within design flanked by dates, all within circle **Designer:** M. Norte

Date	Mintage	F	VF	XF	Unc	BU
ND(1972)	1,000,000	—	—	—	7.00	9.00
ND(1972) Matte	—	—	—	—	32.50	—

Note: A small quantity of these coins were given a matte finish by the Lisbon Mint on private contract

KM# 636 50 ESCUDOS
9.4100 g., Copper-Nickel, 31 mm. **Obv:** Shield divides date with value below **Rev:** Sailboat, water and fish **Designer:** Euclides Vaz

Date	Mintage	F	VF	XF	Unc	BU
1986	51,110,000	—	—	—	2.25	2.75
1987	28,248,000	—	—	—	2.25	2.75
1988	41,905,000	—	—	—	2.25	2.75
1989	18,327,000	—	—	—	2.25	2.75
1990	50,000	—	—	—	15.00	—
Note: In Mint sets only						
1991	2,000,000	—	—	—	3.00	—
1992	20,000	—	—	—	15.00	—
Note: In Mint sets only						
1993	20,000	—	—	—	15.00	—
Note: In Mint sets only						
1994	20,000	—	—	—	15.00	—
Note: In Mint sets only						
1995	20,000	—	—	—	15.00	—
Note: In Mint sets only						
1996	—	—	—	—	8.00	—
Note: In Mint sets only						
1996 Proof	7,000	Value: 5.00				
1997	—	—	—	—	8.00	—
Note: In Mint sets only						
1997 Proof	—	Value: 5.00				
1998	—	—	—	—	8.00	—
Note: In Mint sets only						
1998 Proof	—	Value: 6.00				
1999	—	—	—	—	3.00	—
2000	—	—	—	—	3.00	—

KM# 603 100 ESCUDOS
18.0000 g., 0.6500 Silver 0.3761 oz. ASW **Subject:** 1974 Revolution **Obv:** Small cross design within circle with numeral and written value above **Rev:** Inscription and date flanked by vertical block designs

Date	Mintage	F	VF	XF	Unc	BU
ND(1976)	950,000	—	BV	6.00	7.50	8.50
ND(1976) Proof	10,000	Value: 15.00				

KM# 625 100 ESCUDOS
Copper-Nickel, 33.5 mm. **Subject:** International Year of Disabled Persons **Obv:** Shield **Rev:** Stylized head facing 1/4 right **Designer:** M. Simoes

Date	Mintage	F	VF	XF	Unc	BU
ND(1984)	990,000	—	0.75	1.50	2.50	3.50

KM# 628 100 ESCUDOS
Copper-Nickel, 33.5 mm. **Subject:** 50th Anniversary - Death of Fernando Pessoa - Poet **Obv:** Shield above value **Rev:** Four conjoined faces facing right and flying birds within circle **Designer:** Jose Aurelio

Date	Mintage	F	VF	XF	Unc	BU
1985	480,000	—	0.75	2.00	3.50	4.50

KM# 630 100 ESCUDOS
Copper-Nickel, 33.5 mm. **Subject:** 600th Anniversary - Battle of Aljubarrota **Obv:** Shield within circle **Rev:** Standing figure facing within pillar arch **Designer:** C. Meneres

Date	Mintage	F	VF	XF	Unc	BU
ND(1985)	500,000	—	0.75	2.00	3.50	4.50

KM# 637 100 ESCUDOS
Copper-Nickel, 33.5 mm. **Subject:** World Cup Soccer - Mexico

Date	Mintage	F	VF	XF	Unc	BU
1986	500,000	—	0.75	2.00	3.50	4.50

KM# 639 100 ESCUDOS
Copper Nickel, 34 mm. **Subject:** Golden Age of Portuguese Discoveries - Gil Eanes **Obv:** Shield within circle **Rev:** Ship with flag on top of sails **Designer:** S. Machado

Date	Mintage	F	VF	XF	Unc	BU
1987	1,000,000	—	0.75	1.00	2.50	3.50

KM# 640 100 ESCUDOS

Copper-Nickel, 34 mm. **Subject:** Golden Age of Portuguese Discoveries - Nuno Tristao **Obv:** Shield flanked by crowns within circle **Rev:** Ship **Designer:** Isabel C. Branco and F. Branco

Date	Mintage	F	VF	XF	Unc	BU
1987	1,000,000	—	0.75	1.00	2.50	3.50

KM# 641 100 ESCUDOS

Copper-Nickel, 34 mm. **Subject:** Golden Age of Portuguese Discoveries - Diogo Cao **Obv:** Shield to upper right of design with value below **Rev:** Compass within center of sailboat and map **Designer:** Dega

Date	Mintage	F	VF	XF	Unc	BU
1987	1,000,000	—	0.75	1.00	2.50	3.50

KM# 644 100 ESCUDOS

Copper-Nickel, 34 mm. **Subject:** Amadeo de Souza Cardoso **Obv:** Shield and value to left of design **Rev:** Head facing flanked by dates with design at left **Designer:** Vilar

Date	Mintage	F	VF	XF	Unc	BU
1987	800,000	—	0.75	1.25	2.50	3.50

KM# 642 100 ESCUDOS

Copper-Nickel, 34 mm. **Subject:** Golden Age of Portuguese Discoveries - Bartolomeu Dias **Obv:** Shield within circle **Rev:** Stylized boat and map **Designer:** Jorge Vieira

Date	Mintage	F	VF	XF	Unc	BU
ND(1988)	1,000,000	—	0.75	1.00	2.50	3.50

KM# 645.2 100 ESCUDOS

Bi-Metallic Aluminumn-Bronze center in Copper-Nickel ring, 25.5 mm. **Rev:** Pedro Nunes **Edge:** Six reeded and six plain sections

Date	Mintage	F	VF	XF	Unc	BU
1989	Inc. above	—	1.00	1.50	3.00	5.00
1990	Inc. above	—	1.25	2.00	3.50	5.50
1991	Inc. above	—	1.00	1.50	3.00	5.00

KM# 646 100 ESCUDOS

Copper-Nickel, 34 mm. **Subject:** Discovery of the Canary Islands **Obv:** Shield with supporters above value **Rev:** Ship

Date	Mintage	F	VF	XF	Unc	BU
1989	2,000,000	—	—	1.00	2.50	4.00

KM# 647 100 ESCUDOS

Copper-Nickel,34 mm. **Subject:** Discovery of Madeira **Obv:** Cross and shield **Rev:** Ship **Designer:** Isabel C. Branco and F. Branco

Date	Mintage	F	VF	XF	Unc	BU
1989	2,000,000	—	—	1.00	2.50	4.00

KM# 648 100 ESCUDOS

Copper-Nickel, 34 mm. **Subject:** Discovery of the Azores **Obv:** Shield at right within design **Rev:** Ship and stars within design

Date	Mintage	F	VF	XF	Unc	BU
ND(1989)	2,000,000	—	—	1.00	2.50	—

KM# 645.1 100 ESCUDOS

8.3000 g., Bi-Metallic Aluminum-Bronze center in Copper-Nickel ring, 25.5 mm. **Obv:** Shield within globe above value within circle **Rev:** Armored 1/2 length figure holding globe facing left within circle **Edge:** Five reeded and five plain sections **Designer:** Jose Candido **Note:** Varieties exist with fine and bold letters.

Date	Mintage	F	VF	XF	Unc	BU
1989	20,000,000	—	—	1.00	2.50	3.00
1990	52,000,000	—	—	1.00	2.50	3.00
1991	45,500,000	—	—	1.00	2.50	3.00
1992	14,500,000	—	—	1.00	2.50	3.00
1993	20,000	—	—	—	15.00	—
Note: In Mint sets only						
1994	20,000	—	—	—	15.00	—
Note: In Mint sets only						
1996	—	—	—	—	15.00	—
Note: In Mint sets only						
1996 Proof	7,000	Value: 10.00				
1997	—	—	—	—	2.50	—
1997 Proof	—	Value: 2.50				
1998	—	—	—	—	2.50	—
1998 Proof	—	Value: 10.00				
1999	—	—	—	—	2.50	—
2000	—	—	—	—	2.50	—

KM# 649 100 ESCUDOS

Copper-Nickel, 34 mm. **Subject:** Celestial Navigation **Obv:** Value in center flanked by shield and circled star designs **Rev:** Artistic designs

Date	Mintage	F	VF	XF	Unc	BU
1990	2,000,000	—	—	1.00	2.50	—

KM# 651 100 ESCUDOS

Copper-Nickel, 33 mm. **Subject:** 350th Anniversary - Restoration of Portuguese Independence **Obv:** Shield within beaded circle **Rev:** Half length figure facing left holding sword under design **Designer:** A. Marinho

Date	Mintage	F	VF	XF	Unc	BU
ND(1990)	1,000,000	—	—	1.00	2.50	4.00

KM# 656 100 ESCUDOS

Copper-Nickel, 33 mm. **Rev:** Camilo Castelo Branco **Designer:** Vilar

Date	Mintage	F	VF	XF	Unc	BU
1990	1,000,000	—	—	1.00	2.50	3.50

KM# 664 100 ESCUDOS

26.0000 g., Copper-Nickel, 36 mm. **Subject:** Antero DeQuental **Obv:** Hand above national arms and value **Rev:** Portrait, signature, life dates and name **Edge:** Reeded

Date	Mintage	F	VF	XF	Unc	BU
1991INCM	—	—	—	—	3.00	—

KM# 678 100 ESCUDOS

Bi-Metallic Aluminumn-Bronze center in Copper-Nickel ring, 25.5 mm. **Subject:** 50th Anniversary - F.A.O. **Obv:** Shield within globe above value within circle **Obv. Designer:** Jose Candido **Rev:** F.A.O. logo within oat wreath **Rev. Designer:** J. Duarte

Date	Mintage	F	VF	XF	Unc	BU
1995	500,000	—	—	1.50	4.00	—
1995 Proof	17,000	Value: 15.00				

KM# 680 100 ESCUDOS

Copper-Nickel, 33 mm. **Subject:** 400th Anniversary - Antonio Prior de Crato **Obv:** Bird, shield, cross and designs within circle **Rev:** Bust 1/4 right within circle

Date	Mintage	F	VF	XF	Unc	BU
ND(1995)	—	—	—	1.00	2.50	4.00

KM# 693 100 ESCUDOS

Bi-Metallic Aluminumn-Bronze center in Copper-Nickel ring, 25.5 mm. **Subject:** Lisbon World Expo '98 **Obv:** Shield and flying bird above value **Rev:** Monk Seal

Date	Mintage	F	VF	XF	Unc	BU
1997	—	—	—	1.50	3.00	6.00
1997 Proof	7,000	Value: 15.00				

KM# 722.1 100 ESCUDOS

Bi-Metallic Brass center in Copper-Nickel ring, 25 mm. **Obv:** National arms, value and country name **Rev:** UNICEF logo **Edge:** Reeded and plain sections

Date	Mintage	F	VF	XF	Unc	BU
1999INCM	—	—	—	—	5.00	6.50

KM# 722.2 100 ESCUDOS

Bi-Metallic Brass center in Copper-Nickel ring, 25 mm. **Obv:** Shield within globe in center circle, numeral and written value in outer circle **Rev:** Silhouette heads of mother and baby and partial globe in center circle flanked by sprigs **Edge:** Reeded and plain sections

Date	Mintage	F	VF	XF	Unc	BU
1999INCM	—	—	—	—	6.00	7.50

KM# 655 200 ESCUDOS

Bi-Metallic Copper-Nickel center in Aluminum-Bronze ring, 28 mm. **Obv:** Shield within globe above value **Rev:** Armored 1/2 length bust right holding flower within circle **Designer:** J. Candido

Date	Mintage	F	VF	XF	Unc	BU
1991	33,000,000	—	—	1.25	3.00	4.00
1992	11,000,000	—	—	1.50	3.50	5.00
1993	20,000	—	—	—	18.00	—
Note: In Mint sets only						
1996	—	—	—	—	18.00	—
Note: In Mint sets only						
1996 Proof	7,000	Value: 20.00				
1997	—	—	—	1.50	4.00	—
1997 Proof	—	Value: 20.00				
1998	—	—	—	1.50	4.00	—
1998 Proof	—	Value: 20.00				
1999	—	—	—	1.50	4.00	—
2000	—	—	—	1.50	4.00	—

KM# 669 200 ESCUDOS

Bi-Metallic Copper-Nickel center in Aluminum-Bronze ring, 28 mm. **Subject:** Lisbon - European Cultural Capital **Obv:** Shield within globe above value **Rev:** Cultural building within circle

Date	Mintage	F	VF	XF	Unc	BU
1994	1,000,000	—	—	—	4.50	—
1994 Proof	7,000	Value: 20.00				

KM# 679 200 ESCUDOS

Bi-Metallic Copper-Nickel center in Aluminum-Bronze ring, 28 mm. **Subject:** 50th Anniversary - United Nations **Obv:** Shield within globe above value **Obv. Designer:** J. Candido **Rev:** Numeral 50 and emblem in center of puzzle pieces **Rev. Designer:** J. Duarte

Date	Mintage	F	VF	XF	Unc	BU
1995	500,000	—	—	—	5.50	—
1995 Proof	17,000	Value: 20.00				

KM# 687 200 ESCUDOS

Bi-Metallic Copper-Nickel center in Brass ring, 28 mm. **Series:** Olympics **Obv:** Shield, value and olympic circles **Rev:** High jumper **Designer:** Vitor Santos

Date	Mintage	F	VF	XF	Unc	BU
1996	—	—	—	—	5.00	—
1996 Proof	7,000	Value: 20.00				

KM# 694 200 ESCUDOS

Bi-Metallic Copper-Nickel center in Copper-Aluminum ring, 28 mm. **Subject:** Lisbon World Expo '98 **Obv:** Shield and value within circle **Rev:** Dolphins **Rev. Designer:** Jose Simão

Date	Mintage	F	VF	XF	Unc	BU
1997	—	—	—	—	6.00	—
1997 Proof	7,000	Value: 20.00				

KM# 706 200 ESCUDOS

Bi-Metallic Copper-Nickel center in Aluminum-Bronze ring, 28 mm. **Subject:** International Year of the Oceans Expo **Obv:** Small shield within sprigs above value **Rev:** Expo 98 and fish within sprigs

Date	Mintage	F	VF	XF	Unc	BU
1998	Est. 50,000	—	—	—	4.50	—
1998 Proof	Est. 20,000	Value: 12.00				

KM# 720 200 ESCUDOS

Bi-Metallic Copper-Nickel center in Brass ring, 28 mm. **Obv:** Shield within globe above value **Rev:** Stylized dove on wheels and logo **Edge:** Segmented reeding **Designer:** Meneres

Date	Mintage	F	VF	XF	Unc	BU
1999INCM	—	—	—	—	6.50	7.50

KM# 726 200 ESCUDOS

Bi-Metallic Copper-Nickel center in Nickel-Brass ring, 28 mm. **Obv:** Torch, cross design and value **Rev:** Olympic logo **Edge:** Reeded and plain sections **Designer:** Nogueira DaSilva

Date	Mintage	F	VF	XF	Unc	BU
2000INCM	10,000	—	—	—	4.00	—
2000INCM Proof	5,000	Value: 7.50				

EURO COINAGE

European Union Issues

KM# 740 EURO CENT

2.3000 g., Copper Plated Steel, 16.25 mm. **Obv:** Royal seal of 1134 with country name and cross **Obv. Designer:** Vitor Santos **Rev:** Value and globe **Rev. Designer:** Luc Luycx **Edge:** Plain

Date	Mintage	F	VF	XF	Unc	BU
2002INCM	278,106,172	—	—	—	0.35	0.50
2002INCM Proof	15,000	Value: 7.00				
2003INCM	50,000	—	—	—	0.35	0.50
2003INCM Proof	15,000	Value: 7.00				
2004INCM	75,000,000	—	—	—	0.35	0.50
2004INCM Proof	15,000	Value: 7.00				
2005INCM	40,000,000	—	—	—	0.35	0.50
2005INCM Proof	10,000	Value: 7.00				
2006INCM	30,000,000	—	—	—	0.35	0.50
2006INCM Proof	3,000	Value: 7.00				

KM# 741 2 EURO CENT

3.0300 g., Copper Plated Steel, 18.7 mm. **Obv:** Royal seal of 1134 with country name and cross **Obv. Designer:** Vitor Santos **Rev:** Value and globe **Rev. Designer:** Luc Luycx **Edge:** Grooved

Date	Mintage	F	VF	XF	Unc	BU
2002INCM	324,376,590	—	—	—	0.50	0.65
2002INCM Proof	15,000	Value: 9.00				
2003INCM	50,000	—	—	—	—	—
Note: In sets only						
2003INCM Proof	15,000	Value: 9.00				
Note: In sets only						
2004INCM	1,000,000	—	—	—	0.50	0.65
2004INCM Proof	15,000	Value: 9.00				
2005INCM	10,000,000	—	—	—	0.50	0.65
2005INCM Proof	10,000	Value: 9.00				
2006INCM	1,000,000	—	—	—	0.50	0.65
2006INCM Proof	3,000	Value: 9.00				

KM# 742 5 EURO CENT

3.8600 g., Copper Plated Steel, 21.2 mm. **Obv:** Royal seal of 1134 with country name and cross **Obv. Designer:** Vitor Santos **Rev:** Value and globe **Rev. Designer:** Luc Luycx **Edge:** Plain

Date	Mintage	F	VF	XF	Unc	BU
2002INCM	234,512,047	—	—	—	0.75	1.00
2002INCM Proof	15,000	Value: 10.00				
2003INCM	50,000	—	—	—	—	—
Note: In sets only						
2003INCM Proof	15,000	Value: 10.00				
Note: In sets only						
2004INCM	40,000,000	—	—	—	0.75	1.00
2004INCM Proof	15,000	Value: 10.00				
2005INCM	30,000,000	—	—	—	0.75	1.00
2005INCM Proof	10,000	Value: 10.00				
2006INCM	20,000,000	—	—	—	0.75	1.00
2006INCM Proof	3,000	Value: 10.00				

KM# 743 10 EURO CENT
4.0700 g., Brass, 19.7 mm. **Obv:** Royal seal of 1142, country name in circular design **Obv. Designer:** Vitor Santos **Rev:** Value and map **Rev. Designer:** Luc Luycx **Edge:** Reeded

Date	Mintage	F	VF	XF	Unc	BU
2002INCM	220,289,835	—	—	—	0.75	1.00
2002INCM Proof	15,000	Value: 12.00				
2003INCM	50,000	—	—	—	1.00	1.50
Note: In sets only						
2003INCM Proof	15,000	Value: 12.00				
Note: In sets only						
2004INCM	1,000,000	—	—	—	1.50	2.00
2004INCM Proof	15,000	Value: 12.00				
2005INCM	1,000,000	—	—	—	1.50	2.00
2005INCM Proof	10,000	Value: 12.00				
2006INCM	1,000,000	—	—	—	1.50	2.00
2006INCM Proof	3,000	Value: 12.00				
2007INCM	—	—	—	—	1.50	2.00

KM# 763 10 EURO CENT
4.0700 g., Brass, 19.7 mm. **Obv:** Royal seal of 1142, country name in circular design **Obv. Designer:** Vitor Santos **Rev:** Relief map of Western Europe, stars, lines and value **Rev. Designer:** Luc Luycx **Edge:** Reeded

Date	Mintage	F	VF	XF	Unc	BU
2008INCM	—	—	—	—	1.50	2.00

KM# 744 20 EURO CENT
5.7300 g., Brass, 22.1 mm. **Obv:** Royal seal of 1142, country name in circular design **Obv. Designer:** Vitor Santos **Rev:** Value and map **Rev. Designer:** Luc Luycx **Edge:** Notched

Date	Mintage	F	VF	XF	Unc	BU
2002INCM	147,411,038	—	—	—	1.00	1.25
2002INCM Proof	15,000	Value: 14.00				
2003INCM	50,000	—	—	—	1.25	1.50
Note: In sets only						
2003INCM Proof	15,000	Value: 14.00				
Note: In sets only						
2004INCM	1,000,000	—	—	—	1.50	2.00
2004INCM Proof	15,000	Value: 14.00				
2005INCM	25,000,000	—	—	—	1.50	2.00
2005INCM Proof	10,000	Value: 14.00				
2006INCM	20,000,000	—	—	—	1.50	2.00
2006INCM Proof	3,000	Value: 14.00				
2007INCM	—	—	—	—	1.50	2.00

KM# 764 20 EURO CENT
5.7300 g., Brass, 22.1 mm. **Obv:** Royal seal of 1142, country name in circular design **Obv. Designer:** Vitor Santos **Rev:** Relief map of Western Europe, stars, lines and value **Rev. Designer:** Luc Luycx **Edge:** Notched

Date	Mintage	F	VF	XF	Unc	BU
2008INCM	—	—	—	—	1.50	2.00

KM# 745 50 EURO CENT
7.8100 g., Brass, 24.2 mm. **Obv:** Royal seal of 1142, country name in circular design **Obv. Designer:** Vitor Santos **Rev:** Value and map **Rev. Designer:** Luc Luycx **Edge:** Reeded

Date	Mintage	F	VF	XF	Unc	BU
2002INCM	151,947,133	—	—	—	1.50	2.00
2002INCM Proof	15,000	Value: 16.00				
2003INCM	50,000	—	—	—	1.50	2.00
Note: In sets only						
2003INCM Proof	15,000	Value: 16.00				
Note: In sets only						
2004INCM	1,000,000	—	—	—	2.50	3.00
2004INCM Proof	15,000	Value: 16.00				
2005INCM	1,000,000	—	—	—	2.50	3.00
2005INCM Proof	10,000	Value: 16.00				
2006INCM	1,000,000	—	—	—	2.50	3.00
2006INCM Proof	3,000	Value: 16.00				
2007INCM	—	—	—	—	2.50	3.00

KM# 765 50 EURO CENT
7.8100 g., Brass, 24.2 mm. **Obv:** Royal seal of 1142, country name in circular design **Obv. Designer:** Vitor Santos **Rev:** Relief map of Western Europe, stars, lines and value **Rev. Designer:** Luc Luycx **Edge:** Reeded

Date	Mintage	F	VF	XF	Unc	BU
2008INCM	—	—	—	—	2.50	3.00

KM# 746 EURO
7.5000 g., Bi-Metallic Copper-Nickel center in Brass ring, 23.2 mm. **Obv:** Royal seal of 1144, country name in looped design **Obv. Designer:** Vitor Santos **Rev:** Value and map **Rev. Designer:** Luc Luycx **Edge:** Reeded and plain sections

Date	Mintage	F	VF	XF	Unc	BU
2002INCM	100,228,135	—	—	—	2.00	2.50
2002INCM Proof	15,000	Value: 18.00				
2003INCM	50,000	—	—	—	2.00	2.50
Note: In sets only						
2003INCM Proof	15,000	Value: 18.00				
Note: In sets only						
2004INCM	20,000,000	—	—	—	2.00	2.50
2004INCM Proof	15,000	Value: 18.00				
2005INCM	20,000,000	—	—	—	2.00	2.50
2005INCM Proof	10,000	Value: 18.00				
2006INCM	20,000,000	—	—	—	2.00	2.50
2006INCM Proof	3,000	Value: 18.00				
2007INCM	—	—	—	—	2.00	2.50

KM# 766 EURO
7.5000 g., Bi-Metallic Copper-Nickel center in Brass ring, 23.2 mm. **Obv:** Royal seal of 1144, country name in looped design **Obv. Designer:** Vitor Santos **Rev:** Relief map of Western Europe, stars, lines and value **Rev. Designer:** Luc Luycx **Edge:** Reeded and plain sections

Date	Mintage	F	VF	XF	Unc	BU
2008INCM	—	—	—	—	2.75	3.50

KM# 747 2 EURO
8.5200 g., Bi-Metallic Brass center in Copper-Nickel ring, 25.7 mm. **Obv:** Royal seal of 1144, country name in looped design **Obv. Designer:** Vitor Santos **Rev:** Value and map **Rev. Designer:** Luc Luycx **Edge:** Reeding over castles and shields

Date	Mintage	F	VF	XF	Unc	BU
2002INCM	61,930,775	—	—	—	3.50	4.00
2002INCM Proof	15,000	Value: 22.00				
2003INCM	50,000	—	—	—	4.25	5.00
Note: In sets only						
2003INCM Proof	15,000	Value: 22.00				
Note: In sets only						
2004INCM	1,000,000	—	—	—	5.50	6.00
2004INCM Proof	15,000	Value: 22.00				
2005INCM	1,000,000	—	—	—	5.50	6.00
2005INCM Proof	10,000	Value: 22.00				
2006INCM	1,000,000	—	—	—	5.50	6.00
2006INCM Proof	3,000	Value: 22.00				
2007INCM	—	—	—	—	5.50	6.00

KM# 771 2 EURO
8.4700 g., Bi-Metallic Brass center in Copper-Nickel ring, 25.74 mm. **Subject:** 50th Anniversary Treaty of Rome **Obv:** Open treaty book **Rev:** Large value at left, modified outline of Europe at right **Edge:** Reeded and lettered

Date	Mintage	F	VF	XF	Unc	BU
2007	—	—	—	—	—	9.00

KM# 772 2 EURO
8.4000 g., Bi-Metallic Brass center in Copper-Nickel ring, 25.73 mm. **Subject:** European Union President **Obv:** Large tree, small national arms at lower left **Obv. Inscription:** POR / TV / GAL **Rev:** Large value at left, revised map of Europe at right **Edge:** Reeded with repeated symbols

Date	Mintage	F	VF	XF	Unc	BU
2007	—	—	—	—	4.25	5.00

KM# 767 2 EURO
8.5200 g., Bi-Metallic Brass center in Copper-Nickel ring, 25.7 mm. **Obv:** Royal seal of 1144, country name in looped design **Obv. Designer:** Vitor Santos **Rev:** Relief map of Western Europe, stars, lines and value **Rev. Designer:** Luc Luycx **Edge:** Reeding over castles and shields

Date	Mintage	F	VF	XF	Unc	BU
2008INCM	—	—	—	—	5.50	6.00

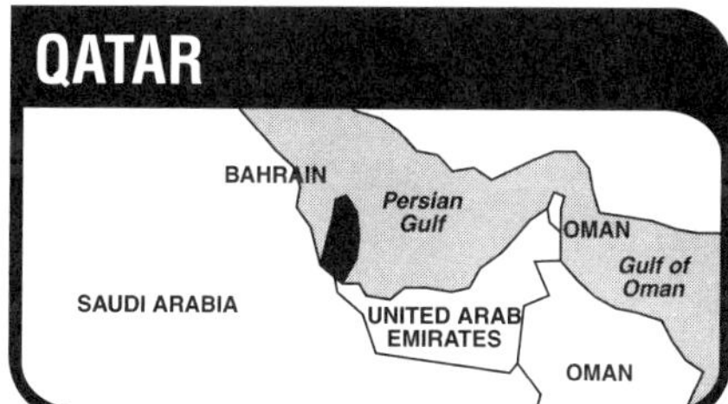

The State of Qatar, an emirate in the Persian Gulf between Bahrain and Trucial Oman, has an area of 4,247sq. mi. (11,000 sq. km.) and a population of *469,000. Capital: Doha. Oil is the chief industry and export.

Qatar was under Turkish control from 1872 until the beginning of World War I when the Ottoman Turks evacuated the Qatar Peninsula. In 1916 Sheikh Abdullah placed Qatar under the protection of Great Britain and gave Britain responsibility for its defense and foreign relations. Qatar joined with Dubai in a Monetary Union and issued coins and paper money in 1966 and 1969. When Britain announced in 1968 that it would end treaty relationships with the Persian Gulf sheikhdoms in 1971, this union was dissolved; Qatar joined Bahrain and the seven trucial sheikhdoms (called the United Arab Emirates) in an effort to form a union of Arab Emirates. However the nine sheikhdoms were unable to agree on terms of union, and Qatar declared its independence as the State of Qatar on Sept. 3, 1971.

TITLE

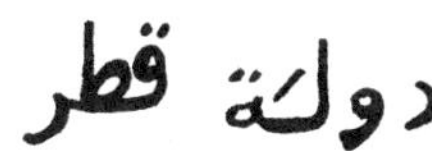

Daulat Qatar

RULERS

Al-Thani Dynasty

Qasim Bin Muhammad, 1876-1913
Abdullah Bin Qasim, 1913-1948
Ali Bin Abdullah, 1948-1960
Ahmad Bin Ali, 1960-1972
Khalifah bin Hamad, 1972-1995
Hamad bin Khalifah, 1995-

MONETARY SYSTEM
100 Dirhem = 1 Riyal

STATE

STANDARD COINAGE

KM# 2 DIRHAM
1.5000 g., Bronze, 15 mm. **Ruler:** Khalifah Bin Hamad **Obv:** Value **Rev:** Sail boat and palm trees flanked by beads

Date	Mintage	F	VF	XF	Unc	BU
AH1393 - 1973	500,000	—	0.25	0.50	1.00	2.00

KM# 3 5 DIRHAMS
3.7500 g., Bronze, 22 mm. **Ruler:** Khalifah Bin Hamad **Obv:** Value **Rev:** Sail boat and palm trees flanked by beads **Edge:** Plain

Date	Mintage	F	VF	XF	Unc	BU
AH1393 - 1973	1,000,000	—	0.15	0.30	0.75	1.50
AH1398 - 1978	1,000,000	—	0.15	0.30	0.75	1.50

KM# 12 5 DIRHAMS
3.8000 g., Bronze, 22 mm. **Ruler:** Hamad bin Khalifah **Obv:** Arms **Rev:** Value **Edge:** Plain

Date	Mintage	F	VF	XF	Unc	BU
AH1427-2006	—	—	—	—	0.75	1.25

KM# 1 10 DIRHAMS
7.5000 g., Bronze, 27 mm. **Ruler:** Khalifah Bin Hamad **Obv:** Value **Rev:** Sail boat and palm trees flanked by beads

Date	Mintage	F	VF	XF	Unc	BU
AH1392 - 1972	1,500,000	—	0.50	1.00	2.50	4.00
AH1393 - 1973	1,500,000	—	0.25	0.50	1.50	3.00

KM# 13 10 DIRHAMS
7.5000 g., Bronze, 26 mm. **Ruler:** Hamad bin Khalifah **Obv:** Arms **Rev:** Value **Edge:** Plain

Date	Mintage	F	VF	XF	Unc	BU
AH1427-2006	—	—	—	—	1.25	2.00

KM# 8 25 DIRHAMS
3.5000 g., Copper-Nickel, 19 mm. **Ruler:** Hamad bin Khalifah **Obv:** Value **Obv. Legend:** STATE OF QATAR **Rev:** Sail boat and palm trees flanked by beads **Edge:** Reeded

Date	Mintage	F	VF	XF	Unc	BU
AH1421 - 2000	—	—	—	—	1.50	2.50
AH1424-2003	—	—	0.30	0.65	1.50	2.50

KM# 14 25 DIRHAMS
3.5000 g., Copper-Nickel, 19 mm. **Ruler:** Hamad bin Khalifah **Obv:** Arms **Rev:** Value **Edge:** Reeded

Date	Mintage	F	VF	XF	Unc	BU
AH1427-2006	—	—	—	—	1.50	2.50

KM# 5 50 DIRHAMS
6.5000 g., Copper-Nickel, 25 mm. **Ruler:** Khalifah Bin Hamad **Obv:** Value **Rev:** Sail boat and palm trees flanked by beads

Date	Mintage	F	VF	XF	Unc	BU
AH1393 - 1973	1,500,000	—	0.40	0.85	2.00	3.00
AH1398 - 1978	2,000,000	—	0.40	0.85	2.25	3.25
AH1401 - 1981	—	—	0.40	0.85	2.25	3.25
AH1407 - 1987	—	—	0.40	0.85	2.25	3.25
AH1410 - 1990	—	—	0.40	0.85	2.25	3.25
AH1414 - 1993	—	—	0.40	0.85	2.25	3.25
AH1419 - 1998	—	—	0.40	0.85	2.25	3.25

KM# 9 50 DIRHAMS
6.5000 g., Copper-Nickel, 24 mm. **Ruler:** Hamad bin Khalifah **Obv:** Arms **Rev:** Value **Edge:** Reeded

Date	Mintage	F	VF	XF	Unc	BU
AH1421-2000	—	—	—	—	2.00	3.00
AH1424-2003	—	—	—	—	2.00	3.00

KM# 15 50 DIRHAMS
6.5000 g., Copper-Nickel, 24 mm. **Ruler:** Hamad bin Khalifah **Obv:** Arms **Rev:** Value **Edge:** Reeded

Date	Mintage	F	VF	XF	Unc	BU
AH1427-2006	—	—	—	—	1.75	2.75

QATAR & DUBAI

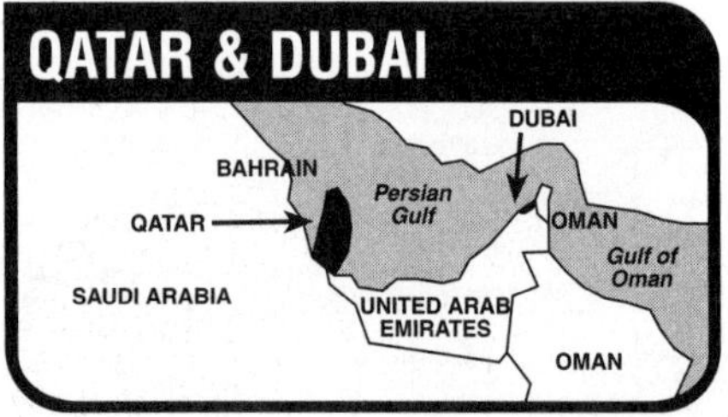

The State of Qatar, which occupies the Qatar Peninsula jutting into the Persian Gulf from eastern Saudi Arabia, has an area of 4,247 sq. mi. (11,000 sq. km.) and a population of *469,000. Capital: Doha. The traditional occupations of pearling, fishing, and herding have been replaced in economics by petroleum-related industries. Crude oil, petroleum products, and tomatoes are exported.

Dubai is one of the seven sheikhdoms comprising the United Arab Emirates (formerly Trucial States) located along the southern shore of the Persian Gulf. It has a population of about 60,000. Capital (of the United Arab Emirates): Abu Dhabi.

Qatar, which initiated protective treaty relations with Great Britain in 1916, achieved independence on Sept. 3,1971, upon withdrawal of the British military presence from the Persian Gulf, and replaced its special treaty arrangement with Britain with a treaty of general friendship. Dubai attained independence on Dec. 1, 1971, upon termination of Britain's protective treaty with the trucial Sheikhdoms, and on Dec. 2, 1971, entered into the union of the United Arab Emirates.

Despite the fact that the Emirate of Qatar and the Sheikhdom of Dubai were merged under a monetary union, the two territories were governed independently from each other. Qatar now uses its own currency while Dubai uses the United Arab Emirates currency and coins.

TITLE

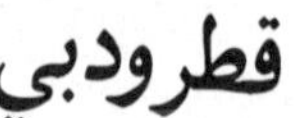

Qatar Wa Dubai

RULER
Ahmad II, 1960-1972

MONETARY SYSTEM
100 Dirhem = 1 Riyal

BRITISH PROTECTORATE

STANDARD COINAGE

KM# 1 DIRHEM
1.5000 g., Bronze, 15 mm. **Ruler:** Ahmad II **Obv:** Value **Rev:** Goitered gazelle

Date	Mintage	F	VF	XF	Unc	BU
AH1386 - 1966	1,000,000	Value: 2.00				

KM# 2 5 DIRHEMS
3.7500 g., Bronze, 22 mm. **Ruler:** Ahmad II **Obv:** Value **Rev:** Goitered gazelle

Date	Mintage	F	VF	XF	Unc	BU
AH1386 - 1966	2,000,000	—	2.50	4.50	8.00	15.00
AH1389 - 1969	2,000,000	—	2.50	4.50	8.00	15.00

KM# 3 10 DIRHEMS
7.5000 g., Bronze, 27 mm. **Ruler:** Ahmad II **Obv:** Value **Rev:** Goitered gazelle

Date	Mintage	F	VF	XF	Unc	BU
AH1386 - 1966	2,000,000	—	3.50	6.00	10.00	18.00
AH1391 - 1971	1,500	—	—	—	—	—

Note: Official mintage figure reported for Qatar by British Royal Mint.

KM# 4 25 DIRHEMS
3.5000 g., Copper-Nickel, 20 mm. **Ruler:** Ahmad II **Obv:** Value **Rev:** Goitered gazelle

Date	Mintage	F	VF	XF	Unc	BU
AH1386 - 1966	2,000,000	—	4.50	7.50	12.50	20.00
AH1389 - 1969	2,000,000	—	4.50	7.50	12.50	20.00

KM# 5 50 DIRHEMS
6.5000 g., Copper-Nickel, 25 mm. **Ruler:** Ahmad II **Obv:** Value **Rev:** Goitered gazelle

Date	Mintage	F	VF	XF	Unc	BU
AH1386 - 1966	2,000,000	—	6.00	9.00	15.00	22.00

REUNION

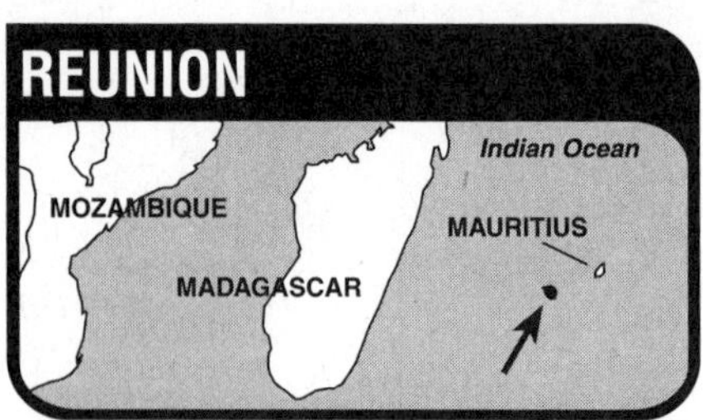

The Department of Reunion, an overseas department of France located in the Indian Ocean 400 miles (640 km.) east of Madagascar, has an area of 969 sq. mi. (2,510 sq. km.) and a population of *566,000. Capital: Saint-Denis. The island's volcanic soil is extremely fertile. Sugar, vanilla, coffee and rum are exported.

Although first visited by Portuguese navigators in the 16th century, Reunion was uninhabited when claimed for France by Capt. Goubert in 1638. The French first colonized the Isle de Bourbon in 1662 as a layover station for ships rounding the Cape of Good Hope to India. It was renamed Reunion in 1793. The island remained in French possession except for the period of 1810-15, when the British occupied it. Reunion became an overseas department of France in 1946, and in 1958 voted to continue that status within the new French Union.

During the first half of the 19th century, Reunion was officially known as Isle de Bonaparte (1801-14) and Isle de Bourbon (1814-48). Reunion coinage of those periods is so designated.

The world debut of the Euro was here on January 1, 2002.

MINT MARK
(a) – Paris, privy marks only

MONETARY SYSTEM
100 Centimes = 1 Franc

FRENCH OVERSEAS DEPARTMENT

STANDARD COINAGE

KM# 6.1 FRANC
Aluminum, 23 mm. **Obv:** Winged liberty head left **Rev:** Sugar cane plants divide value **Edge:** Plain **Designer:** G.B.L. Bazor

Date	Mintage	F	VF	XF	Unc	BU
1948(a)	3,000,000	—	0.35	0.60	2.50	3.00
1964(a)	1,000,000	—	0.35	0.60	3.00	3.50
1968(a)	450,000	—	0.60	1.25	4.50	5.50
1969(a)	500,000	—	0.60	0.85	3.50	4.00
1971(a)	800,000	—	0.60	0.85	3.00	3.50
1973(a)	500,000	—	0.60	0.85	3.50	4.00

KM# 6.2 FRANC
Aluminum **Designer:** G.B.L. Bazor **Note:** Thinner planchet.

Date	Mintage	F	VF	XF	Unc	BU
1969(a)	Inc. above	—	0.75	1.50	5.00	6.00

KM# 7 FRANC
Aluminum **Obv:** Winged liberty head left **Rev:** Sugar cane plants divide value **Designer:** G.B.L. Bazor **Note:** Mule.

Date	Mintage	F	VF	XF	Unc	BU
1948(a)	Inc. above	—	650	1,300	2,600	—

KM# 8 2 FRANCS
Aluminum **Obv:** Winged liberty head left **Rev:** Sugar cane plants divide value **Designer:** G.B.L. Bazor

Date	Mintage	F	VF	XF	Unc	BU
1948(a)	2,000,000	—	0.35	0.85	3.50	4.00
1968(a)	100,000	—	3.00	5.00	10.00	12.50
1969(a)	150,000	—	1.75	3.50	6.50	9.00

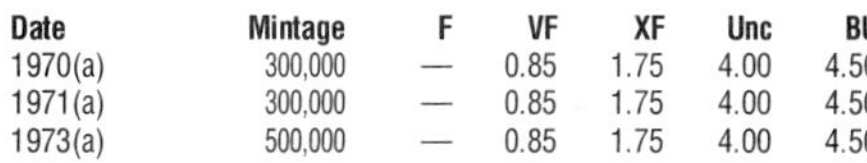

Date	Mintage	F	VF	XF	Unc	BU
1970(a)	300,000	—	0.85	1.75	4.00	4.50
1971(a)	300,000	—	0.85	1.75	4.00	4.50
1973(a)	500,000	—	0.85	1.75	4.00	4.50

KM# 9 5 FRANCS

Aluminum **Obv:** Winged liberty head left **Rev:** Sugar cane plants divides value **Designer:** G.B.L. Bazor

Date	Mintage	F	VF	XF	Unc	BU
1955(a)	3,000,000	—	0.60	1.00	3.00	3.50
1969(a)	100,000	—	2.50	5.00	9.00	11.50
1970(a)	200,000	—	1.75	3.50	6.50	9.00
1971(a)	100,000	—	1.75	3.50	6.50	9.00
1972(a)	300,000	—	0.85	1.75	3.50	4.00
1973(a)	250,000	—	0.85	1.75	3.50	4.00

KM# 10 10 FRANCS

Aluminum-Bronze **Obv:** Winged liberty head left **Rev:** Crowned shield divides value **Designer:** G.B.L. Bazor

Date	Mintage	F	VF	XF	Unc	BU
1955(a)	1,500,000	—	0.45	0.75	3.00	3.50
1962(a)	700,000	—	1.75	3.50	6.50	9.00
1964(a)	1,000,000	—	0.45	0.75	3.00	3.50

KM# 10a 10 FRANCS

Aluminum-Nickel-Bronze **Obv:** Winged Liberty head left **Rev:** Crowned shield divides value **Designer:** G.B.L. Bazor

Date	Mintage	F	VF	XF	Unc	BU
1964(a)	Inc. above	—	0.45	0.75	3.00	3.50
1969(a)	300,000	—	1.25	2.50	6.00	7.00
1970(a)	300,000	—	1.25	2.50	5.00	6.00
1971(a)	200,000	—	1.75	3.75	7.50	10.00
1972(a)	400,000	—	1.25	2.50	6.00	7.00
1973(a)	700,000	—	0.85	1.75	3.50	4.00

KM# 11 20 FRANCS

Aluminum-Bronze **Obv:** Winged liberty head left **Rev:** Crowned shield divides value **Designer:** G.B.L. Bazor

Date	Mintage	F	VF	XF	Unc	BU
1955(a)	1,250,000	—	0.75	1.50	4.00	4.50
1960(a)	100,000	—	3.00	6.00	12.00	15.00
1961(a)	300,000	—	2.50	4.75	8.00	10.00
1962(a)	190,000	—	2.75	5.50	9.00	12.00
1964(a)	750,000	—	0.75	1.50	3.50	4.00

KM# 11a 20 FRANCS

Aluminum-Nickel-Bronze **Obv:** Winged Liberty head left **Rev:** Crowned shield divides value **Designer:** G.B.L. Bazor

Date	Mintage	F	VF	XF	Unc	BU
1969(a)	200,000	—	2.75	5.50	9.00	12.00
1970(a)	200,000	—	2.75	5.50	9.00	12.00
1971(a)	200,000	—	2.75	5.50	9.00	12.00
1972(a)	300,000	—	2.00	3.50	6.50	8.50
1973(a)	550,000	—	0.75	1.50	3.50	4.50

KM# 12 50 FRANCS

Nickel **Obv:** Winged liberty head left **Rev:** Crowned shield divides value **Designer:** G.B.L. Bazor

Date	Mintage	F	VF	XF	Unc	BU
1962(a)	1,000,000	—	1.50	2.50	5.00	6.00
1964(a)	500,000	—	2.00	3.00	6.00	7.50
1969(a)	100,000	—	2.75	5.00	9.00	12.00
1970(a)	100,000	—	2.75	5.00	9.00	12.00
1973(a)	350,000	—	2.00	3.50	6.50	8.00

KM# 13 100 FRANCS

8.5400 g., Nickel, 26.5 mm. **Obv:** Winged liberty head left **Rev:** Crowned shield divides value **Designer:** G.B.L. Bazor

Date	Mintage	F	VF	XF	Unc	BU
1964(a)	2,000,000	—	1.00	2.00	4.00	5.00
1969(a)	200,000	—	2.25	4.50	7.50	9.50
1970(a)	150,000	—	2.25	5.00	9.00	12.00
1971(a)	200,000	—	2.75	6.00	12.50	15.00
1972(a)	300,000	—	2.00	3.50	6.00	7.50
1973(a)	550,000	—	2.25	4.50	7.50	9.50

RHODESIA

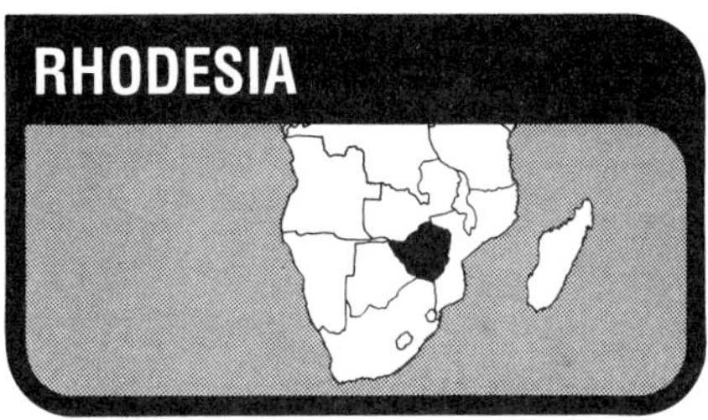

The Republic of Rhodesia or Southern Rhodesia (now known as the Republic of Zimbabwe), located in the east-central part of southern Africa, has an area of 150,804 sq. mi. (390,580sq. km.) and a population of *10.1 million. Capital: Harare (formerly Salisbury). The economy is based on agriculture and mining. Tobacco, sugar, asbestos, copper, chrome, ore and coal are exported.

The Rhodesian area contains extensive evidence of the habitat of paleolithic man and earlier civilizations, notably the world-famous ruins of Zimbabwe, a gold-trading center that flourished about the 14th or 15th century A.D. The Portuguese of the 16th century were the first Europeans to attempt to develop south-central Africa, but it remained for Cecil Rhodes and the British South Africa Co. to open the hinterlands. Rhodes obtained a concession for mineral rights from local chiefs in 1888 and administered his African empire (named Southern Rhodesia in 1895) through the British South Africa Co. until 1923, when the British government annexed the area after the white settlers voted for existence as a separate entity, rather than for incorporation into the Union of South Africa. From Sept. of 1953 through 1963 Southern Rhodesia was joined with the British Protectorates of Northern Rhodesia and Nyasaland into a multiracial federation, known as the Federation of Rhodesia and Nyasaland. When the federation was dissolved at the end of 1963, Northern Rhodesia and Nyasaland became the independent states of Zambia and Malawi.

Britain was prepared to grant independence to Southern Rhodesia but declined to do so when the politically dominant white Rhodesians refused to give assurances of representative government. On Nov. 11, 1965, following two years of unsuccessful negotiation with the British government, Prime Minister Ian Smith issued an unilateral declaration of independence. Britain responded with economic sanctions supported by the United Nations. After further futile attempts to effect an accommodation, the Rhodesian Parliament severed all ties with Britain and on March 2, 1970, established the Republic of Rhodesia.

On March 3, 1978, Prime Minister Ian Smith and three moderate black nationalist leaders signed an agreement providing for black majority rule. The name of the country was changed to Zimbabwe Rhodesia. Following a conference in London in December 1979, the opposition government conceded and it was agreed that the British Government should resume control. A British Governor soon returned to Southern Rhodesia. One of his first acts was to affirm the nullification of the purported declaration of independence. On April 18, 1980 pursuant to an act of the British Parliament, the colony of Southern Rhodesia became independent as the Republic of Zimbabwe, which remains a member of the British Commonwealth of Nations.

RULER

British, until 1966

MONETARY SYSTEM

12 Pence = 1 Shilling = 10 Cents
10 Shillings = 1 Dollar
20 Shillings = 1 Pound

BRITISH COLONY

Self-Governing

POUND COINAGE

KM# 8 3 PENCE = 2-1/2 CENTS

Copper-Nickel **Obv:** Crowned bust of Queen Elizabeth II right **Obv. Designer:** Arnold Machin **Rev:** Three spear points divides date

Date	Mintage	F	VF	XF	Unc	BU
1968	2,400,000	0.25	0.50	0.75	2.00	—
1968 Doubleshaft error	—	—	10.00	20.00	35.00	—
1968 Proof	10	Value: 1,200				

KM# 1 6 PENCE = 5 CENTS

Copper-Nickel, 19.5 mm. **Obv:** Crowned bust of Queen Elizabeth II right **Obv. Designer:** Arnold Machin **Rev:** Flame lily **Rev. Designer:** Thomas Sasseen

Date	Mintage	F	VF	XF	Unc	BU
1964	13,500,000	0.15	0.25	0.40	1.25	—
1964 Proof	2,060	Value: 15.00				

KM# 2 SHILLING = 10 CENTS

Copper-Nickel, 23.5 mm. **Obv:** Crowned bust of Queen Elizabeth II right **Obv. Designer:** Arnold Machin **Rev:** Shield **Rev. Designer:** Thomas Sasseen

Date	Mintage	F	VF	XF	Unc	BU
1964	15,500,000	0.15	0.25	0.65	1.50	—
1964 Proof	2,060	Value: 18.00				

KM# 3 2 SHILLINGS = 20 CENTS

Copper-Nickel **Obv:** Crowned bust of Queen Elizabeth II right **Obv. Designer:** Arnold Machin **Rev:** Native headdress **Rev. Designer:** Thomas Sasseen

Date	Mintage	F	VF	XF	Unc	BU
1964	10,500,000	0.25	0.50	1.25	3.00	—
1964 Proof	2,060	Value: 20.00				

KM# 4 2-1/2 SHILLINGS = 25 CENTS

14.0000 g., Copper-Nickel, 32.5 mm. **Obv:** Crowned bust of Queen Elizabeth II right **Obv. Designer:** Arnold Machin **Rev:** Sable antelope **Rev. Designer:** Thomas Sasseen

Date	Mintage	F	VF	XF	Unc	BU
1964	11,500,000	0.50	1.00	2.00	4.50	6.00
1964 Proof	2,060	Value: 25.00				

REPUBLIC

DECIMAL COINAGE

KM# 9 1/2 CENT

Bronze, 20 mm. **Obv:** Value and date to upper left of sprig **Rev:** Arms with supporters **Designer:** Thomas Sasseen

Date	Mintage	F	VF	XF	Unc	BU
1970	10,000,000	—	0.10	0.50	1.00	—
1970 Proof	12	Value: 1,000				
1971	2,000,000	—	0.10	0.50	1.25	—
1972	2,000,000	—	0.10	0.50	1.25	—
1972 Proof	12	Value: 1,000				
1975	10,001,000	—	0.10	0.20	0.50	—
1975 Proof	10	Value: 1,000				
1977	—	—	—	800	1,500	—

Note: Circulation mintage melted, less than 10 surviving specimens known

Date	Mintage	F	VF	XF	Unc	BU
1977 Proof	10	Value: 1,500				

KM# 10 CENT

4.0000 g., Bronze, 22.5 mm. **Obv:** Value and date to upper left of sprig **Rev:** Arms with supporters **Designer:** Thomas Sasseen

Date	Mintage	F	VF	XF	Unc	BU
1970	25,000,000	—	0.10	0.50	1.00	—
1970 Proof	12	Value: 900				
1971	15,000,000	—	0.10	0.50	1.00	—
1972	10,000,000	—	0.10	0.50	1.00	—
1972 Proof	12	Value: 900				
1973	5,000,000	—	0.10	0.50	1.50	—
1973 Proof	10	Value: 900				
1974	—	—	0.10	0.50	1.00	—
1975	10,000,000	—	0.10	0.50	1.00	—
1975 Proof	10	Value: 900				
1976	20,000,000	—	0.10	0.20	0.50	—
1976 Proof	10	Value: 900				
1977	10,000,000	—	0.10	0.20	0.50	—

KM# 11 2-1/2 CENTS

Copper-Nickel **Obv:** Three spearpoints divides date below value **Rev:** Arms with supporters **Designer:** Thomas Sasseen

Date	Mintage	F	VF	XF	Unc	BU
1970	4,000,000	0.15	0.25	0.70	1.50	—
1970 Proof	12	Value: 950				

KM# 12 5 CENTS

3.0000 g., Copper-Nickel **Obv:** Flame lily divides date **Rev:** Arms with supporters **Designer:** Thomas Sasseen

Date	Mintage	F	VF	XF	Unc	BU
1973	—	0.25	0.75	1.50	3.00	—
1973 Proof	10	Value: 950				

KM# 13 5 CENTS

Copper-Nickel **Obv:** Flame lily **Rev:** Arms with supporters **Designer:** Thomas Sasseen

Date	Mintage	F	VF	XF	Unc	BU
1975	3,500,000	0.15	0.25	0.50	1.00	—
1975 Proof	10	Value: 900				
1976	8,038,000	0.15	0.25	0.50	1.00	—
1977	3,015,000	0.25	0.75	1.50	3.00	—

KM# 14 10 CENTS

Copper-Nickel **Obv:** Arms with supporters **Rev:** Shield, value and date **Designer:** Thomas Sasseen

Date	Mintage	F	VF	XF	Unc	BU
1975	2,003,000	0.15	0.30	0.60	1.50	—
1975 Proof	10	Value: 950				

KM# 15 20 CENTS

Copper-Nickel **Obv:** Arms with supporters **Rev:** Native headdress, value and date **Designer:** Thomas Sasseen

Date	Mintage	F	VF	XF	Unc	BU
1975	1,937,000	0.50	0.75	1.00	3.00	—
1975 Proof	10	Value: 950				
1977	—	0.50	0.75	1.50	3.50	—

KM# 16 25 CENTS

Copper-Nickel **Obv:** Arms with supporters **Rev:** Sable antelope, value and date **Designer:** Thomas Sasseen

Date	Mintage	F	VF	XF	Unc	BU
1975	1,011,000	0.50	1.00	2.00	5.00	7.50
1975 Proof	10	Value: 950				

RHODESIA & NYASALAND

The Federation of Rhodesia and Nyasaland was located in the east-central part of southern Africa. The multiracial federation has an area of about 487,000 sq. mi. (1,261,330 sq. km.) and a population of 6.8 million. Capital: Salisbury, in Southern Rhodesia.

The geographical unity of the three British possessions suggested the desirability of political and economic union as early as 1924. Despite objections by the African constituency of Northern Rhodesia and Nyasaland, who feared that African self-determination would be retarded by the dominant influence of prosperous and self-governing Southern Rhodesia. The Central African Federation was established in Sept. of 1953. As feared by the European constituency, Southern Rhodesia despite the fact that the three component countries largely retained their pre-federation political structure effectively and profitably dominated the Federation. It was dissolved at the end of 1963, largely because of the effective opposition of the Nyasaland African Congress. Northern Rhodesia and Nyasaland became the independent states of Zambia and Malawi in 1964. Southern Rhodesia unilaterally declared its independence the following year, which was not recognized by the British Government.

For earlier coinage refer to Southern Rhodesia. For later coinage refer to Malawi, Zambia, Rhodesia and Zimbabwe.

RULER

Elizabeth II, 1952-1964

MONETARY SYSTEM

12 Pence = 1 Shilling
5 Shillings = 1 Crown
20 Shillings = 1 Pound

FEDERATION

STANDARD COINAGE

KM# 1 1/2 PENNY

Bronze, 21 mm. **Ruler:** Elizabeth II **Obv:** Hole in center flanked by giraffes with crown above **Rev:** Value around hole in center flanked by sprigs

Date	Mintage	F	VF	XF	Unc	BU
1955	720,000	0.15	0.25	0.50	4.00	6.00
1955 Proof	2,010	Value: 5.00				
1956	480,000	0.20	0.50	1.00	4.00	6.00
1956 Proof	—	Value: 400				
1957	1,920,000	0.10	0.15	0.25	4.00	6.00
1957 Proof	—	Value: 400				
1958	2,400,000	0.10	0.15	0.25	4.00	6.00
1958 Proof	—	Value: 400				
1964	1,440,000	0.10	0.15	0.25	4.00	6.00

KM# 2 PENNY

6.3000 g., Bronze **Ruler:** Elizabeth II **Obv:** Hole in center and crown flanked by elephants **Rev:** Value around hole in center flanked by sprigs

Date	Mintage	F	VF	XF	Unc	BU
1955	2,040,000	0.15	0.25	0.75	4.50	7.50
1955 Proof	2,010	Value: 5.50				
1956	4,800,000	0.15	0.25	0.50	4.50	7.50
1956 Proof	—	Value: 400				
1957	7,200,000	0.10	0.15	0.25	4.50	7.50
1957 Proof	—	—	—	—	—	—
1958	2,880,000	0.10	0.15	0.25	4.50	7.50
1958 Proof	—	Value: 400				
1961	4,800,000	0.10	0.15	0.25	4.50	7.50
1961 Proof	—	—	—	—	—	—
1962	6,000,000	0.10	0.15	0.25	4.50	7.50
1963	6,000,000	0.10	0.15	0.25	4.50	7.50
1963 Proof	—	Value: 400				

KM# 3 3 PENCE

Copper-Nickel, 16.3 mm. **Ruler:** Elizabeth II **Obv:** Bust right **Obv. Designer:** Mary Gillick **Rev:** Flame lily divides date

Date	Mintage	F	VF	XF	Unc	BU
1955	1,200,000	0.20	0.50	1.00	4.00	—
1955 Proof	10	Value: 400				
1956	3,200,000	0.50	1.00	2.50	20.00	—
1956 Proof	—	Value: 600				
1957	6,000,000	0.20	0.50	0.75	3.00	—
1957 Proof	—	Value: 600				
1962	4,000,000	0.20	0.50	0.75	3.00	—
1962 Proof	—	—	—	—	—	—
1963	2,000,000	0.20	0.50	0.75	3.00	—
1963 Proof	—	—	—	—	—	—
1964	3,600,000	0.15	0.25	0.50	1.50	—

KM# 4 6 PENCE

Copper-Nickel **Ruler:** Elizabeth II **Obv:** Bust right **Obv. Designer:** Mary Gillick **Rev:** Lion standing on rock

Date	Mintage	F	VF	XF	Unc	BU
1955	400,000	0.50	1.00	2.50	7.50	10.00
1955 Proof	10	Value: 400				
1956	800,000	0.75	2.00	7.00	40.00	—
1956 Proof	—	—	—	—	—	—
1957	4,000,000	0.20	0.50	1.00	4.00	7.50
1957 Proof	—	—	—	—	—	—
1962	2,800,000	0.20	0.50	1.00	4.00	8.00
1962 Proof	—	—	—	—	—	—
1963	800,000	5.00	10.00	20.00	45.00	—
1963 Proof	—	—	—	—	—	—

KM# 5 SHILLING

Copper-Nickel **Ruler:** Elizabeth II **Obv:** Bust right **Obv. Designer:** Mary Gillick **Rev:** Sable antelope

Date	Mintage	F	VF	XF	Unc	BU
1955	200,000	1.50	2.50	7.00	18.00	—
1955 Proof	10	Value: 400				
1956	1,700,000	0.75	1.50	3.50	30.00	—
1956 Proof	—	—	—	—	—	—
1957	3,500,000	0.50	1.00	2.50	8.00	10.00
1957 Proof	—	—	—	—	—	—

KM# 6 2 SHILLINGS

Copper-Nickel **Ruler:** Elizabeth II **Obv:** Bust right **Obv. Designer:** Mary Gillick **Rev:** Eagle with talons in fish flanked by initials

Date	Mintage	F	VF	XF	Unc	BU
1955	1,750,000	1.25	2.50	5.00	12.50	—
1955 Proof	10	Value: 400				
1956	1,850,000	1.25	2.50	4.50	12.00	—
1956 Proof	—	—	—	—	—	—
1957	1,500,000	1.25	2.50	4.50	12.00	—
1957 Proof	—	—	—	—	—	—

KM# 7 1/2 CROWN

Copper-Nickel **Ruler:** Elizabeth II **Obv:** Bust right **Obv. Designer:** Mary Gillick **Rev:** Arms with supporters **Rev. Designer:** T.H. Paget

Date	Mintage	F	VF	XF	Unc	BU
1955	1,600,000	1.50	3.00	6.00	15.00	—
1955 Proof	10	Value: 550				
1956	160,000	7.50	15.00	35.00	250	—
1956 Proof	—	—	—	—	—	—
1957	2,400,000	7.50	15.00	35.00	75.00	—
1957 Proof	—	—	—	—	—	—

Romania (formerly the Socialist Republic of Romania), a country in southeast Europe, has an area of 91,699 sq. mi. (237,500 sq. km.) and a population of 23.2 million. Capital: Bucharest. Machinery, foodstuffs, raw minerals and petroleum products are exported. Heavy industry and oil have become increasingly important to the economy since 1959.

A new constitution was adopted in 1923. During this period in history, the Romanian government struggled with domestic problems, agrarian reform and economic reconstruction.

On August 23, 1944, King Mihai I proclaimed an armistice with the Allied Forces. The Romanian army drove out the Germans and Hungarians in northern Transylvania, but the country was subsequently occupied by the Soviet army. That monarchy was abolished on December 30, 1947, and Romania became a "People's Republic" based on the Soviet regime. The process of sovietization included Soviet regime. The anti-Communist combative resistance movement developed frequent purges of dissidents: mainly political but also clerical, cultural and peasants. Romanian elite disappeared into the concentration camps. The anti-Communist combative resistance movement developed in spite of the Soviet army presence until 1956. The partisans remained in the mountains until 1964. With the accession of N. Ceausescu to power, Romania began to exercise a considerable degree of independence, refusing to participate in the invasion of Czechoslovakia (August 1968). In 1965, it was proclaimed a "Socialist Republic". After 1977, an oppressed and impoverished domestic scene worsened.

On December 17, 1989, an anti-Communist revolt in Timisoara. On December 22, 1989 the Communist government was overthrown. Ceausescu and his wife were arrested and later executed. The new government established a republic, the constitutional name being Romania.

RULERS

Carol I (as Prince), 1866-81 (as King), 1881-1914
Ferdinand I, 1914-1927
Mihai I, 1927-1930
Carol II, 1930-1940
Mihai I, 1940-1947

MINT MARKS

(a) - Paris, privy marks only
(b) - Brussels, privy marks only
angel head (1872-1876),
no marks (1894-1924)
B - Bucharest (1870-1900)
B - Hamburg, Germany
C - Candescu, chief engineer of the Bucharest Mint (1870-)
FM - Franklin Mint, USA
H - Heaton, Birmingham, England
HF - Huguenin Freres & Co., Le Locle, Switzerland
J - Hamburg
KN - Kings Norton, Birmingham, England
(p) - Thunderbolt - Poissy, France
zig zag (1924)
V - Vienna, Austria
W - Watt (James Watt & Co.)
Huguenin - Le Locle, Switzerland
( ) - no marks, 1930 (10, 20 Lei),
1932 (100 Lei), Royal Mint – London

MINT OFFICIALS' INITIALS

Initials	Date	Name
BASSARAB		Costache Bassarab
IOANA BASSARAB	1941-45	Ioana Bassarab Starostescu
E.W. BECKER	1939-40	E.W. Becker
(wing)		Lucien Bazor
P.M. DAMMANN	1922	P.M. Dammann
C.D.	1990	C. Dumitrescu
V.G.	1990	Vasile Gabor
H.I.; H.IONESCU	1939-52	Haralamb Ionescu
I. Jalea	1935-41	Ion Jalea
LAVRILLIER	1930-32	A. Larrillier
A.M.; A. MICHAUX	1906	Alfons Michaux
A. MURNU	1940	A. Murnu
(torch)		Henry Auguste Jules Patey
A. ROMANESCU	1946	A.Rromanescu
A. SCHARFF	1894-1901	Anton Scharff
TASSET	1910-14	Ernst Paulini Tasset

MONETARY SYSTEM

100 Bani = 1 Leu

KINGDOM

STANDARD COINAGE

KM# 31 5 BANI

2.5000 g., Copper-Nickel, 19 mm. **Ruler:** Carol I **Obv:** Crown above banner and hole in center **Rev:** Hole in center flanked by designs with value above and date below **Designer:** A. Scharff

Date	Mintage	F	VF	XF	Unc	BU
1905	2,000,000	0.50	1.50	6.00	16.00	—
1905 Proof	—	Value: 42.00				
1906	48,000,000	0.25	0.50	2.00	8.00	—
1906J	24,000,000	0.25	0.50	2.50	9.00	—

KM# 32 10 BANI

4.0000 g., Copper-Nickel, 22 mm. **Ruler:** Carol I **Obv:** Crown above banner and hole in center **Rev:** Hole in center flanked by designs with value above and date below **Designer:** A. Scharff

Date	Mintage	F	VF	XF	Unc	BU
1905	10,820,000	0.50	1.50	5.00	16.00	—
1906	24,180,000	0.25	0.75	2.00	9.00	—
1906J	17,000,000	0.25	0.75	3.00	10.00	—

KM# 33 20 BANI

6.0000 g., Copper-Nickel, 25 mm. **Ruler:** Carol I **Obv:** Crown above banner and hole in center **Rev:** Hole in center flanked by designs with value above and date below **Designer:** A. Scharff

Date	Mintage	F	VF	XF	Unc	BU
1905	2,500,000	3.00	7.00	20.00	65.00	—
1906	3,000,000	2.00	4.50	16.00	48.00	—
1906J	2,500,000	2.00	4.50	14.00	40.00	—

KM# 44 25 BANI

0.8960 g., Aluminum, 19 mm. **Ruler:** Ferdinand I **Obv:** Eagle above hole in center **Rev:** Hole in center of value with crown at right **Note:** Center hole sizes vary from 4 to 4.5mm. No engraver's name.

Date	Mintage	F	VF	XF	Unc	BU
1921	20,000,000	0.50	1.50	3.00	8.00	—

KM# 23 50 BANI

2.5000 g., 0.8350 Silver 0.0671 oz. ASW **Ruler:** Carol I **Obv:** Head left **Rev:** Value, date within wreath **Designer:** Tasset

Date	Mintage	F	VF	XF	Unc	BU
1901	194,205	10.00	25.00	68.00	230	—

KM# 41 50 BANI

2.5000 g., 0.8350 Silver 0.0671 oz. ASW, 18 mm. **Ruler:** Carol I **Obv:** Head left **Rev:** Crown above design **Designer:** Tasset

Date	Mintage	F	VF	XF	Unc	BU
1910	3,600,000	1.50	3.00	8.00	19.00	—
Note: Edge varieties (round or flat) exist						
1910 Proof	—	Value: 160				
1911	3,000,000	2.00	4.00	12.00	26.00	—
1912	1,800,000	1.50	3.50	12.50	28.00	—
1914	1,600,000	1.25	2.00	5.00	14.00	—
Note: Edge varieties (round or flat) exist						
1914 Proof	—	Value: 120				

KM# 45 50 BANI
1.2030 g., Aluminum, 21 mm. **Ruler:** Ferdinand I **Obv:** Eagle above hole in center **Rev:** Hole in center of value with crown at right **Note:** Center hole size varies from 4 to 4.5mm.

Date	Mintage	F	VF	XF	Unc	BU
1921	30,000,000	0.50	1.50	4.00	9.00	—

KM# 24 LEU
5.0000 g., 0.8350 Silver 0.1342 oz. ASW, 23 mm. **Ruler:** Carol I **Designer:** A. Scharff

Date	Mintage	F	VF	XF	Unc	BU
1901	369,614	6.00	30.00	100	250	375
1901 Proof	—	Value: 1,000				

KM# 34 LEU
5.0000 g., 0.8350 Silver 0.1342 oz. ASW, 14 mm. **Ruler:** Carol I **Subject:** 40th Anniversary - Reign of Carol I **Obv:** Bearded head left **Rev:** Head left **Edge:** Reeded **Designer:** A. Michaux **Note:** Designer's name below truncation on reverse.

Date	Mintage	F	VF	XF	Unc	BU
ND(1906)	2,500,000	5.00	13.00	28.00	75.00	—
ND(1906) Proof	—	Value: 220				

KM# 42 LEU
5.0000 g., 0.8350 Silver 0.1342 oz. ASW **Ruler:** Carol I **Obv:** Bearded head left **Obv. Designer:** Tasset **Rev:** Standing figure walking right **Rev. Designer:** Bassarab

Date	Mintage	F	VF	XF	Unc	BU
1910	4,600,000	3.00	6.00	13.00	32.00	—
Note: Edge varieties (round or flat) exist						
1910 Proof	—	Value: 350				
1911	2,573,000	4.00	8.00	15.00	38.00	—
1912	3,540,000	3.00	5.00	9.50	28.00	—
1914	4,282,935	2.50	3.50	8.00	22.00	—
Note: Edge varieties (round or flat) exist						
1914 Proof	—	Value: 120				

KM# 46 LEU
3.5000 g., Copper-Nickel, 21 mm. **Ruler:** Ferdinand I **Obv:** Crowned arms with supporters flanked by stars **Rev:** Value above sprig **Edge:** Reeded

Date	Mintage	F	VF	XF	Unc	BU
1924(b) Thin	100,000,000	0.50	1.50	4.00	13.00	—
1924(p) Thick	100,006,000	0.50	1.50	5.00	15.00	—

KM# 56 LEU
2.7500 g., Nickel-Brass, 18 mm. **Ruler:** Carol II **Obv:** Crown and date above sprig **Rev:** Ear of corn divides value **Edge:** Plain **Designer:** I. Jalea **Note:** Without mint mark.

Date	Mintage	F	VF	XF	Unc	BU
1938	27,900,000	0.20	0.60	1.75	5.00	—
1939	72,200,000	0.20	0.50	1.50	3.00	—
1940	Inc. above	0.20	0.50	1.00	3.00	—
1941	Inc. above	0.20	0.50	1.50	3.50	—

KM# 25 2 LEI
10.0000 g., 0.8350 Silver 0.2684 oz. ASW **Ruler:** Carol I **Obv:** Head left **Obv. Inscription:** CAROL I.... **Obv. Designer:** Tasset **Rev:** Crowned arms with supporters within crowned mantle, divided value **Rev. Designer:** A. Scharff **Edge:** Reeded

Date	Mintage	F	VF	XF	Unc	BU
1901	12,476	420	680	1,250	2,600	—

KM# 43 2 LEI
10.0000 g., 0.8350 Silver 0.2684 oz. ASW **Ruler:** Carol I **Obv:** Bearded head left **Obv. Designer:** Tasset **Rev:** Standing figure walking right **Rev. Designer:** Bassarab

Date	Mintage	F	VF	XF	Unc	BU
1910	1,800,000	5.00	8.00	16.00	42.00	—
Note: Edge varieties (round and flat) exist						
1910 Proof	—	Value: 240				
1911	1,000,000	6.00	12.00	25.00	55.00	—
1912	1,500,000	5.00	7.50	13.50	36.00	—
1914	2,452,000	4.50	6.00	12.00	30.00	—
Note: Edge varieties (round and flat) exist						
1914 Proof	—	Value: 135				

KM# 47 2 LEI
7.0000 g., Copper-Nickel, 25 mm. **Ruler:** Ferdinand I **Obv:** Crowned arms with supporters flanked by stars **Rev:** Value above sprig **Edge:** Reeded

Date	Mintage	F	VF	XF	Unc	BU
1924(b)	50,000,000	1.00	1.75	4.50	14.00	—
1924(p)	50,008,000	1.00	1.75	5.00	16.00	—

KM# 58 2 LEI
3.2000 g., Zinc, 20 mm. **Ruler:** Mihai I **Obv:** Crown above date **Rev:** Value within wreath **Designer:** H. Ionescu

Date	Mintage	F	VF	XF	Unc	BU
1941	101,778,000	0.50	1.50	5.00	12.00	—

KM# 17.2 5 LEI
25.0000 g., 0.9000 Silver 0.7234 oz. ASW, 38 mm. **Ruler:** Carol I **Edge:** Reeded **Designer:** Kullrich

Date	Mintage	F	VF	XF	Unc	BU
1901B	82,460	75.00	150	500	1,200	—
1901B Proof	—	Value: 3,000				

KM# 35 5 LEI
25.0000 g., 0.9000 Silver 0.7234 oz. ASW, 38 mm. **Ruler:** Carol I **Subject:** 40th Anniversary - Reign of Carol I **Obv:** Bearded head left **Rev:** Head left **Edge:** Reeded **Designer:** A. Michaux

Date	Mintage	F	VF	XF	Unc	BU
ND(1906)	200,000	65.00	150	230	475	—
ND(1906) Proof	—	Value: 1,000				

KM# 48 5 LEI
3.5000 g., Nickel-Brass, 21 mm. **Ruler:** Mihai I **Obv:** Head left **Rev:** Crowned shield divides value flanked by stars **Edge:** Reeded **Designer:** A. J. Patey

Date	Mintage	F	VF	XF	Unc	BU
1930H	15,000,000	1.50	2.50	8.50	26.00	—
1930KN	15,000,000	1.50	3.50	9.00	28.00	—
1930(a)	30,000,000	1.00	2.50	6.50	22.00	—

KM# 61 5 LEI
4.5000 g., Zinc, 23 mm. **Ruler:** Mihai I **Obv:** Crown above date **Rev:** Oat sprigs to right of value **Designer:** H. Ionescu

Date	Mintage	F	VF	XF	Unc	BU
1942	140,000,000	0.50	1.25	3.00	8.00	—

KM# 49 10 LEI
5.0000 g., Nickel-Brass, 23 mm. **Ruler:** Carol II **Obv:** Head left **Rev:** Crowned eagle with crowned shield on chest divides value **Edge:** Reeded **Designer:** A. Lavrillier

Date	Mintage	F	VF	XF	Unc	BU
1930	15,000,000	1.00	3.50	9.00	28.00	—
1930 Proof	—	—	—	—	—	—
1930(a)	30,000,000	1.00	3.00	8.00	26.00	—
1930H	7,500,000	2.50	4.50	12.00	34.00	—
1930KN	7,500,000	3.00	7.00	16.00	40.00	—
1930(a) Proof	—	Value: 175				

KM# 36 12-1/2 LEI
4.0325 g., 0.9000 Gold 0.1167 oz. AGW, 19 mm. **Ruler:** Carol I **Subject:** 40th Anniversary - Reign of Carol I **Obv:** Bearded bust left **Rev:** Crowned eagle and banner **Designer:** A. Michaux

Date	Mintage	F	VF	XF	Unc	BU
1906	32,000	125	200	400	650	—

KM# 37 20 LEI
6.4516 g., 0.9000 Gold 0.1867 oz. AGW, 20 mm. **Ruler:** Carol I **Subject:** 40th Anniversary - Reign of Carol I **Obv:** Bearded head left **Rev:** Head left **Edge:** Reeded **Designer:** A. Michaux

Date	Mintage	F	VF	XF	Unc	BU
ND(1906)(b)	15,000	BV	240	400	700	—

KM# 50 20 LEI
7.5000 g., Nickel-Brass, 27 mm. **Ruler:** Mihai I **Obv:** Young head left **Rev:** Figures holding hands divides value **Rev. Designer:** Bassarab **Edge:** Reeded

Date	Mintage	F	VF	XF	Unc	BU
1930 London	40,000,000	2.50	7.00	20.00	40.00	—
1930 Proof	—	—	—	—	—	—
1930H	5,000,000	3.00	8.00	26.00	54.00	—
1930KN	5,000,000	3.50	12.00	32.00	75.00	—

KM# 51 20 LEI
7.5000 g., Nickel-Brass, 27 mm. **Ruler:** Carol II **Obv:** Head left **Rev:** Crowned eagle with crowned shield on chest divides value **Edge:** Reeded **Designer:** A. Lavrillier

Date	Mintage	F	VF	XF	Unc	BU
1930	6,750,000	2.00	4.00	14.00	26.00	—
1930 Proof	—	—	—	—	—	—
1930(a)	17,500,000	1.50	4.00	12.00	24.00	—
1930(a) Proof	—	Value: 180				
1930KN	7,750,000	3.00	6.50	26.00	58.00	—
1930KN Proof	—	Value: 200				
1930H	7,750,000	2.50	4.50	18.00	45.00	—
1930H Proof	—	Value: 220				

KM# 62 20 LEI
6.0000 g., Zinc, 26 mm. **Ruler:** Mihai I **Obv:** Crown above date **Rev:** Value within wreath **Edge:** Reeded **Designer:** H. Ionescu

Date	Mintage	F	VF	XF	Unc	BU
1942	44,000,000	0.75	1.50	3.00	8.50	—
1943	25,783,000	1.00	2.25	4.00	9.00	—
1944	5,034,000	1.50	3.00	5.00	13.00	—

KM# 38 25 LEI
8.0650 g., 0.9000 Gold 0.2334 oz. AGW, 30 mm. **Ruler:** Carol I **Subject:** 40th Anniversary - Reign of Carol I **Obv:** Uniformed bust left **Rev:** Crowned eagle and banner **Designer:** A. Michaux

Date	Mintage	F	VF	XF	Unc	BU
ND(1906)(b)	24,000	BV	355	595	880	—

KM# 39 50 LEI
16.1300 g., 0.9000 Gold 0.4667 oz. AGW, 35 mm. **Ruler:** Carol I **Subject:** 40th Anniversary - Reign of Carol I **Obv:** Uniformed bust left **Rev:** Equestrian **Designer:** A. Michaux

Date	Mintage	F	VF	XF	Unc	BU
ND(1906)(b)	28,000	BV	550	950	2,000	—

KM# 55 50 LEI
5.8300 g., Nickel, 24 mm. **Ruler:** Carol II **Obv:** Helmeted head left **Rev:** Crowned shield within sprigs divides value **Edge:** Reeded **Designer:** I. Jalea **Note:** 16,731 pieces melted.

Date	Mintage	F	VF	XF	Unc	BU
1937	12,000,000	1.25	2.50	6.00	14.00	—
1938	8,000,000	3.00	6.00	16.00	44.00	—

KM# 40 100 LEI
32.2600 g., 0.9000 Gold 0.9334 oz. AGW, 36 mm. **Ruler:** Carol I **Subject:** 40th Anniversary - Reign of Carol I **Designer:** Alfons Michaux **Note:** Similar to KM#35.

Date	Mintage	F	VF	XF	Unc	BU
ND(1906)(b)	3,000	BV	995	2,150	3,550	—

KM# 52 100 LEI
14.0000 g., 0.5000 Silver 0.2250 oz. ASW, 31 mm. **Ruler:** Carol II **Obv:** Head right **Rev:** Crowned eagle divides wreath with value within **Edge:** Reeded **Designer:** A. Lavrillier

Date	Mintage	F	VF	XF	Unc	BU
1932(a)	2,000,000	10.00	20.00	60.00	250	325
1932	16,400,000	5.00	10.00	30.00	180	250
1932 Proof	—	Value: 750				

KM# 54 100 LEI
8.2000 g., Nickel, 27 mm. **Ruler:** Carol II **Obv:** Head left **Rev:** Crowned shield within sprigs flanked by value **Edge:** Reeded **Designer:** I. Jalea **Note:** 17,030 pieces melted.

Date	Mintage	F	VF	XF	Unc	BU
1936	20,230,000	2.00	4.00	12.00	35.00	—
1938	3,250,000	3.00	7.50	16.00	46.00	—

KM# 64 100 LEI
8.5000 g., Nickel Clad Steel, 28 mm. **Ruler:** Mihai I **Obv:** Head right **Rev:** Crown divides wreath with date and value within **Edge:** Incuse lettering **Edge Lettering:** NIHIL SINE DEO **Designer:** H. Ionescu

Date	Mintage	F	VF	XF	Unc	BU
1943	40,590,000	0.25	0.50	2.00	7.00	—
Note: Portrait varieties exist						
1944	21,289,000	0.25	0.50	3.00	10.00	—

KM# 63 200 LEI
6.0000 g., 0.8350 Silver 0.1611 oz. ASW, 24 mm. **Ruler:** Mihai I **Obv:** Head right **Rev:** Crowned arms with supporters **Edge:** Incuse lettering **Edge Lettering:** NIHIL SINE DEO **Designer:** H. Ionescu

Date	Mintage	F	VF	XF	Unc	BU
1942	30,025,000	2.75	3.50	7.00	20.00	—

KM# 66 200 LEI
7.5000 g., Brass, 27 mm. **Ruler:** Mihai I **Obv:** Head right **Rev:** Crown divides wreath with date and value within **Designer:** H. Ionescu **Note:** Many were silver-plated privately.

Date	Mintage	F	VF	XF	Unc	BU
1945	1,399,000	1.00	2.00	6.00	16.00	—

KM# 53 250 LEI
13.5000 g., 0.7500 Silver 0.3255 oz. ASW, 29 mm. **Ruler:** Carol II **Obv:** Head left **Rev:** Crowned eagle with shield on chest **Designer:** I. Jalea

Date	Mintage	F	VF	XF	Unc	BU
1935	4,500,000	18.00	55.00	130	240	—

Note: Bank reports show that between 1937-39 4,490,670 pieces were withdrawn and remelted

KM# 57 250 LEI
12.0000 g., 0.8350 Silver 0.3221 oz. ASW, 30 mm. **Ruler:** Carol II **Obv:** Head right **Rev:** Crowned shield divides wreath with date and value within **Edge:** Incuse lettering, line interrupted by two rhombs **Edge Lettering:** MUNCA CREDINTA REGE NATIUNE **Designer:** H. Ionescu

Date	Mintage	F	VF	XF	Unc	BU
1939	10,000,000	6.00	12.00	30.00	76.00	—
1940	8,000,000	12.00	20.00	50.00	150	—

KM# 59.1 250 LEI
12.0000 g., 0.8350 Silver 0.3221 oz. ASW **Ruler:** Carol II **Obv:** Head left **Rev:** Date divided by portcullis **Edge:** Incuse lettering **Edge Lettering:** TOTUL PENTRU TARA **Designer:** H. Ionescu **Note:** Mintage unissued and reportedly melted.

Date	Mintage	F	VF	XF	Unc	BU
1940	—	—	—	3,000	4,000	—

KM# 59.2 250 LEI
12.0000 g., 0.8350 Silver 0.3221 oz. ASW **Ruler:** Mihai I **Obv:** Head left **Rev:** Crowned shield divides date with value and date within **Edge:** Incuse lettering **Edge Lettering:** TOTUL PENTRU TARA **Designer:** H. Ionescu

Date	Mintage	F	VF	XF	Unc	BU
1941	2,250,000	9.00	15.00	35.00	90.00	—

KM# 59.3 250 LEI
12.0000 g., 0.8350 Silver 0.3221 oz. ASW **Ruler:** Mihai I **Obv:** Head left **Edge:** Lettered **Edge Lettering:** NIHIL SINE DEO **Designer:** H. Ionescu

Date	Mintage	F	VF	XF	Unc	BU
1941B	13,750,000	6.50	9.50	16.00	30.00	—

KM# 60 500 LEI
25.0000 g., 0.8350 Silver 0.6711 oz. ASW, 37 mm. **Ruler:** Mihai I **Subject:** Basarabia Reunion **Obv:** Young head left **Rev:** Crowned kneeling figure presenting putna monastery to Lord **Edge:** Incuse lettering **Edge Lettering:** PRIN STATORNICIE LA IZBANADA + **Designer:** Ioana Bassarab

Date	Mintage	F	VF	XF	Unc	BU
1941	775,000	BV	11.50	16.50	36.00	—

KM# 65 500 LEI
12.0000 g., 0.7000 Silver 0.2701 oz. ASW, 32 mm. **Ruler:** Mihai I **Obv:** Head left **Rev:** Crowned arms with supporters within crowned mantle divides date **Edge:** Incuse lettering **Edge Lettering:** NIHIL SINE DEO **Designer:** H. Ionescu

Date	Mintage	F	VF	XF	Unc	BU
1944	9,731,000	BV	5.00	8.00	15.00	—

KM# 67 500 LEI
10.0000 g., Brass, 30 mm. **Ruler:** Mihai I **Obv:** Head left **Rev:** Crowned arms with supporters within crowned mantle divides date **Edge:** Reeded **Designer:** H. Ionescu **Note:** Many were silver-plated privately.

Date	Mintage	F	VF	XF	Unc	BU
1945	3,422,000	1.00	2.00	4.00	8.50	—

KM# 68 500 LEI
1.5000 g., Aluminum, 24 mm. **Ruler:** Mihai I **Obv:** Head right **Rev:** Value above sprig **Edge:** Reeded **Designer:** H. Ionescu **Note:** Without designer's name, the result of a filled die.

Date	Mintage	F	VF	XF	Unc	BU
1946	5,823,000	1.00	3.00	6.00	15.00	—

KM# 69 2000 LEI
5.1000 g., Brass, 24 mm. **Ruler:** Mihai I **Obv:** Head right **Rev:** Crowned arms with supporters **Edge:** Incuse lettering **Edge Lettering:** NIHIL SINE DEO **Designer:** H. Ionescu **Note:** Many were silver-plated privately.

Date	Mintage	F	VF	XF	Unc	BU
1946	24,619,000	0.50	1.00	3.00	8.00	—

KM# 76 10000 LEI
10.0000 g., Brass, 27 mm. **Ruler:** Mihai I **Obv:** Head right **Rev:** Crowned shield to left of value and sprigs **Edge:** Incuse lettering **Edge Lettering:** NIHIL SINE DEO **Designer:** H. Ionescu **Note:** Many were silver-plated privately.

Date	Mintage	F	VF	XF	Unc	BU
1947	11,850,000	1.00	2.00	4.00	9.00	—

KM# 70 25000 LEI
12.5000 g., 0.7000 Silver 0.2813 oz. ASW, 32 mm. **Ruler:** Mihai I **Obv:** Head right **Rev:** Crowned shield to left of value and sprigs **Edge:** Incuse lettering **Edge Lettering:** NIHIL SINE DEO **Designer:** H. Ionescu

Date	Mintage	F	VF	XF	Unc	BU
1946	2,372,000	BV	5.50	9.00	20.00	—

KM# 71 100000 LEI
25.0000 g., 0.7000 Silver 0.5626 oz. ASW, 37 mm. **Ruler:** Mihai I **Obv:** Head right **Obv. Designer:** H. Ionescu **Rev:** Standing figure releasing dove with crowned shield at lower right, value at lower left **Rev. Designer:** A. Romanescu **Edge:** Incuse lettering **Edge Lettering:** NIHIL SINE DEO

Date	Mintage	F	VF	XF	Unc	BU
1946	2,002,000	BV	9.50	12.50	25.00	—

REFORM COINAGE

Aug. 15, 1947; 100 Bani = 1 Leu

KM# 72 50 BANI
1.7000 g., Brass, 16 mm. **Ruler:** Mihai I **Obv:** Crown above date **Rev:** Value **Edge:** Plain **Designer:** H. Ionescu

Date	Mintage	F	VF	XF	Unc	BU
1947	13,266,000	1.00	2.00	4.00	11.00	—

KM# 73 LEU
2.5000 g., Brass, 18 mm. **Ruler:** Mihai I **Obv:** Crowned shield **Rev:** Value within oat sprig **Edge:** Plain **Designer:** H. Ionesw

Date	Mintage	F	VF	XF	Unc	BU
1947	88,341,000	1.00	2.25	4.50	12.00	—

KM# 74 2 LEI
3.5000 g., Bronze, 21 mm. **Ruler:** Mihai I **Obv:** Crowned shield and date **Rev:** Value within oat sprigs **Edge:** Plain **Designer:** H. Ionesw

Date	Mintage	F	VF	XF	Unc	BU
1947	40,000,000	1.00	2.50	6.00	18.00	—

KM# 75 5 LEI
1.5000 g., Aluminum, 23 mm. **Ruler:** Mihai I **Obv:** Head right **Rev:** Value to left of oat sprig **Designer:** H. Ionescu

Date	Mintage	F	VF	XF	Unc	BU
1947	56,026,000	1.50	2.50	8.50	25.00	—

PEOPLE'S REPUBLIC

STANDARD COINAGE

KM# 78 LEU

1.8300 g., Copper-Nickel-Zinc, 16 mm. **Obv:** Radiant sun and lighthouse **Rev:** Value and date **Edge:** Plain **Designer:** H. Ionescu

Date	Mintage	F	VF	XF	Unc	BU
1949	—	0.75	1.50	3.00	9.00	—
1950	—	0.75	1.50	4.00	12.00	—
1951	—	1.00	2.00	9.00	22.00	—

KM# 78a LEU

0.6100 g., Aluminum, 16 mm. **Obv:** Radiant sun and lighthouse **Rev:** Value and date **Designer:** H. Ionescu

Date	Mintage	F	VF	XF	Unc	BU
1951	—	1.00	2.00	5.00	12.00	—
1952	—	9.00	16.00	28.00	76.00	—

KM# 79 2 LEI

2.4400 g., Copper-Nickel-Zinc, 18 mm. **Obv:** Ear of corn flanked by oat and flower sprig **Rev:** Value and date **Edge:** Plain **Designer:** H. Ionescu

Date	Mintage	F	VF	XF	Unc	BU
1950	—	1.00	2.50	5.50	12.00	—
1951	—	2.00	5.00	11.00	24.00	—

KM# 79a 2 LEI

0.8400 g., Aluminum, 18 mm. **Obv:** Ear of corn flanked by oat and flower sprig **Rev:** Value and date **Designer:** H. Ionescu

Date	Mintage	F	VF	XF	Unc	BU
1951	—	0.75	2.00	5.50	13.50	—
1952	—	12.00	25.00	40.00	100	—

KM# 77 5 LEI

1.5000 g., Aluminum, 23 mm. **Obv:** National emblem **Rev:** Value within wreath **Edge:** Plain **Designer:** H. Ionescu

Date	Mintage	F	VF	XF	Unc	BU
1948	—	1.50	2.50	5.00	18.00	—
1949	—	1.25	2.00	4.00	14.00	—
1950	—	1.25	2.00	3.50	11.00	—
1951	—	1.25	2.00	5.50	18.00	—

KM# 80 20 LEI

2.1200 g., Aluminum, 26 mm. **Obv:** National emblem **Rev:** Blacksmith at anvil, factory in background **Edge:** Plain **Designer:** H. Ionescu

Date	Mintage	F	VF	XF	Unc	BU
1951	—	3.00	7.00	20.00	50.00	—

REFORM COINAGE

Jan. 26, 1952; 20 "old" Lei + 1 "new" Lei; 100 Bani = 1 Leu

KM# 81.1 BAN

1.0000 g., Copper-Nickel-Zinc, 16 mm. **Obv:** National emblem **Rev:** Value and date **Edge:** Reeded **Designer:** H. Ionescu

Date	Mintage	F	VF	XF	Unc	BU
1952	—	0.20	0.50	1.20	2.50	—

KM# 81.2 BAN

1.0000 g., Copper-Nickel-Zinc **Obv:** National emblem **Rev:** Value and date **Designer:** H. Ionescu

Date	Mintage	F	VF	XF	Unc	BU
1953	—	1.00	2.00	8.00	18.00	—
1954	—	3.00	8.00	20.00	50.00	—

KM# 82.1 3 BANI

2.0000 g., Copper-Nickel-Zinc, 18 mm. **Obv:** National emblem **Rev:** Value and date **Edge:** Reeded **Designer:** H. Ionescu

Date	Mintage	F	VF	XF	Unc	BU
1952	—	1.00	2.00	4.00	10.00	—

KM# 82.2 3 BANI

2.0000 g., Copper-Nickel-Zinc **Obv:** National emblem **Rev:** Value and date

Date	Mintage	F	VF	XF	Unc	BU
1953	—	0.50	1.00	2.50	9.50	—
1954	—	20.00	50.00	75.00	180	—

KM# 83.1 5 BANI

2.4000 g., Copper-Nickel-Zinc, 20 mm. **Obv:** National emblem **Rev:** Value and date **Edge:** Reeded **Designer:** H. Ionescu

Date	Mintage	F	VF	XF	Unc	BU
1952	—	0.50	1.00	3.00	8.00	—

KM# 83.2 5 BANI

2.4000 g., Copper-Nickel-Zinc, 20 mm. **Obv:** National emblem **Rev:** Value and date **Designer:** H. Ionescu

Date	Mintage	F	VF	XF	Unc	BU
1953	—	0.25	0.50	2.00	8.00	—
1954	—	0.25	0.50	1.50	6.00	—
1955	—	0.25	0.50	1.50	5.00	—
1956	—	0.25	0.50	1.25	4.50	—
1957	—	0.25	0.50	1.75	5.00	—

KM# 89 5 BANI

1.7000 g., Nickel Clad Steel, 16 mm. **Obv:** National emblem, RPR on ribbon **Rev:** Value and date **Edge:** Plain **Designer:** H. Ionescu

Date	Mintage	F	VF	XF	Unc	BU
1963	—	0.20	0.50	1.00	2.00	—

KM# 84.1 10 BANI

1.8000 g., Copper-Nickel, 17 mm. **Obv:** National emblem **Rev:** Value and date within wreath **Edge:** Reeded **Designer:** H. Ionescu

Date	Mintage	F	VF	XF	Unc	BU
1952	—	2.00	3.00	9.00	25.00	—

KM# 84.2 10 BANI

1.8000 g., Copper-Nickel **Obv:** National emblem **Obv. Legend:** ROMANA **Rev:** Value and date within wreath **Designer:** H. Ionescu

Date	Mintage	F	VF	XF	Unc	BU
1954	—	0.30	1.50	3.50	9.00	—

KM# 84.3 10 BANI

1.8000 g., Copper-Nickel **Obv:** National emblem **Obv. Legend:** ROMINA **Rev:** Value and date within wreath **Designer:** H. Ionescu

Date	Mintage	F	VF	XF	Unc	BU
1955	—	0.10	0.20	0.75	4.00	—
1956	—	0.10	0.20	0.75	3.50	—

KM# 87 15 BANI

2.8700 g., Nickel Clad Steel, 19.5 mm. **Obv:** National emblem **Rev:** Value within wreath **Edge:** Plain **Designer:** H. Ionescu

Date	Mintage	F	VF	XF	Unc	BU
1960	—	0.10	0.25	0.60	2.50	—

KM# 85.1 25 BANI

3.6000 g., Copper-Nickel, 22 mm. **Obv:** National emblem **Rev:** Value and date within wreath **Edge:** Reeded **Designer:** H. Ionescu

Date	Mintage	F	VF	XF	Unc	BU
1952	—	2.00	4.00	15.00	32.00	—

KM# 85.2 25 BANI

3.6000 g., Copper-Nickel **Obv:** National emblem **Obv. Legend:** ROMANA **Rev:** Value and date within wreath **Designer:** H. Ionescu

Date	Mintage	F	VF	XF	Unc	BU
1953	—	0.20	0.75	2.50	7.00	—
1954	—	0.20	0.60	2.00	6.00	—

KM# 88 25 BANI

3.3800 g., Nickel Clad Steel **Obv:** National emblem **Rev:** Value above tractor **Edge:** Plain **Designer:** H. Ionescu

Date	Mintage	F	VF	XF	Unc	BU
1960	—	0.15	0.30	1.00	4.00	—

KM# 86 50 BANI
4.5500 g., Copper-Nickel, 25 mm. **Obv:** National emblem **Rev:** Blacksmith at anvil, factory in background **Edge:** Reeded **Designer:** H. Ionescu

Date	Mintage	F	VF	XF	Unc	BU
1955	—	0.50	1.00	3.00	14.00	—
1956	—	0.50	1.00	4.00	16.00	—

KM# 90 LEU
5.0600 g., Nickel Clad Steel, 24 mm. **Obv:** National emblem **Rev:** Tractor **Edge:** Plain **Designer:** H. Ionescu

Date	Mintage	F	VF	XF	Unc	BU
1963	—	0.25	0.50	1.00	2.50	—

KM# 91 3 LEI
5.8600 g., Nickel Clad Steel, 27 mm. **Obv:** National emblem **Rev:** Oil refinery **Edge:** Plain **Designer:** H. Ionescu

Date	Mintage	F	VF	XF	Unc	BU
1963	—	0.25	0.50	1.50	4.00	—

SOCIALIST REPUBLIC

STANDARD COINAGE

KM# 92 5 BANI
1.7000 g., Nickel Clad Steel, 16 mm. **Obv:** National emblem, ROMANIA on ribbon **Rev:** Value and date **Edge:** Plain

Date	Mintage	F	VF	XF	Unc	BU
1966	—	0.10	0.50	1.00	2.00	—

KM# 92a 5 BANI
0.6000 g., Aluminum, 16 mm. **Obv:** National emblem, ROMANIA on ribbon **Rev:** Value and date **Edge:** Plain

Date	Mintage	F	VF	XF	Unc	BU
1975	—	—	0.10	0.50	1.00	—

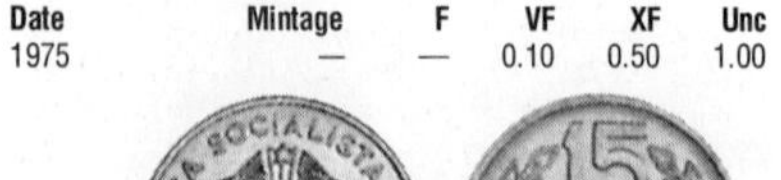

KM# 93 15 BANI
2.8800 g., Nickel Clad Steel, 19.5 mm. **Obv:** National emblem **Rev:** Value within wreath **Edge:** Plain

Date	Mintage	F	VF	XF	Unc	BU
1966	—	—	0.50	1.00	2.00	—

KM# 93a 15 BANI
1.0000 g., Aluminum, 19.5 mm. **Obv:** National emblem **Rev:** Value within wreath **Edge:** Plain

Date	Mintage	F	VF	XF	Unc	BU
1975	—	—	0.10	0.50	1.50	—

KM# 94 25 BANI
3.3800 g., Nickel Clad Steel, 22 mm. **Obv:** National emblem **Rev:** Value above tractor **Edge:** Plain

Date	Mintage	F	VF	XF	Unc	BU
1966	—	—	0.20	1.00	2.50	—

KM# 94a 25 BANI
1.3000 g., Aluminum, 22 mm. **Obv:** National emblem **Rev:** Value above tractor **Edge:** Plain

Date	Mintage	F	VF	XF	Unc	BU
1982	—	0.20	0.50	1.00	3.00	—

KM# 95 LEU
5.0600 g., Nickel Clad Steel, 24.6 mm. **Obv:** National emblem **Rev:** Tractor

Date	Mintage	F	VF	XF	Unc	BU
1966	—	0.10	0.25	0.75	2.00	—

KM# 96 3 LEI
5.8600 g., Nickel Clad Steel, 27 mm. **Obv:** National emblem **Rev:** Oil refinery **Edge:** Plain

Date	Mintage	F	VF	XF	Unc	BU
1966	—	0.25	0.50	1.20	4.00	—

KM# 97 5 LEI
2.8000 g., Aluminum, 29 mm. **Obv:** National emblem **Rev:** Value within design **Edge:** Security

Date	Mintage	F	VF	XF	Unc	BU
1978	—	0.25	0.50	1.50	5.00	—

REPUBLIC

STANDARD COINAGE

KM# 113 LEU
2.5000 g., Copper Clad Steel, 19 mm. **Subject:** National Bank of Romania **Obv:** Monogram above date and sprigs **Rev:** Value above oat sprigs **Edge:** Plain

Date	Mintage	F	VF	XF	Unc	BU
1992	Est. 60,000,000	0.20	0.50	1.25	3.50	—

KM# 115 LEU
2.5200 g., Copper Clad Steel, 19 mm. **Obv:** Value flanked by sprigs **Rev:** Shield divides date

Date	Mintage	F	VF	XF	Unc	BU
1993	Est. 61,000,000	—	0.10	0.25	1.50	—
1994	Est. 10,000,000	—	—	0.20	1.00	—
1995	2,000,000	—	—	0.10	1.00	—
1996	272,000	—	0.50	1.00	4.00	—
2000 Proof	4,500	Value: 4.50				
2002 Proof	1,500	Value: 5.00				
2003 Proof	2,000	Value: 5.00				
2004 Proof	2,000	Value: 5.00				
2005	—	—	—	—	1.00	—
2005 Proof	—	Value: 6.00				
2006 Proof	1,000	Value: 6.00				

KM# 114 5 LEI
3.3000 g., Nickel Plated Steel, 20.99 mm. **Obv:** Value flanked by oak leaves **Rev:** Shield divides date **Edge:** Plain

Date	Mintage	F	VF	XF	Unc	BU
1992 CD VG	Est. 30,000,000	—	0.25	0.60	3.00	—
1993 CD	Est. 70,000,000	—	—	0.30	2.00	—
1994	Est. 10,000,000	—	—	0.30	1.50	—
1995	25,000,000	—	—	0.20	1.00	—
1996	—	—	—	0.20	1.00	—
2000 Proof	4,500	Value: 4.50				
2002 Proof	1,500	Value: 5.00				
2003 Proof	2,000	Value: 5.00				
2004 Proof	—	Value: 5.00				
2005 Proof	—	Value: 5.00				

KM# 108 10 LEI
4.6500 g., Nickel-Clad Steel, 23 mm. **Subject:** Revolution Anniversary **Obv:** Flag and sprig **Rev:** Value within wreath **Edge:** Security scroll **Designer:** Vasile Gabor **Note:** Rotated die varieties exist.

Date	Mintage	F	VF	XF	Unc	BU
1990	30,000,000	—	0.50	1.00	3.00	—
1991	31,303,000	—	0.25	0.60	2.20	—
1992	60,000,000	—	0.25	0.50	1.50	—

KM# 116 10 LEI
4.7000 g., Nickel-Clad Steel, 23 mm. **Obv:** Value within sprigs **Rev:** Shield divides date **Edge:** Plain

Date	Mintage	F	VF	XF	Unc	BU
1993	Est. 6,000,000	—	0.75	1.50	3.50	—
1994	Est. 7,000,000	—	0.50	1.00	3.00	—
1995	30,000,000	—	—	0.30	1.50	—
1996	5,000	—	—	—	—	—
2000 Proof	4,500	Value: 4.50				
2002 Proof	1,500	Value: 6.00				
2003 Proof	2,000	Value: 6.00				

KM# 117.1 10 LEI
5.2000 g., Nickel Plated Steel, 23.2 mm. **Series:** F.A.O. **Subject:** 50 Years - F.A.O. **Obv:** Shield flanked by sprigs and diamonds above value **Rev:** F.A.O logo and dates **Edge:** Plain

Date	Mintage	F	VF	XF	Unc	BU
1995	200,000	—	—	3.50	8.00	—

KM# 117.2 10 LEI
Nickel Plated Steel, 23.3 mm. **Series:** F.A.O. **Subject:** 50 Years - F.A.O. **Obv:** Shield flanked by sprigs and diamonds **Rev:** F.A.O logo and dates **Note:** Obverse description: N in diamond at right for Numismatists

Date	Mintage	F	VF	XF	Unc	BU
1995	30,000	—	—	4.00	10.00	—

KM# 120 10 LEI
Nickel Plated Steel **Series:** 1996 Olympic Games - U.S.A. **Obv:** Shield above sprigs flanked by value **Rev:** Swimmer

Date	Mintage	F	VF	XF	Unc	BU
1996	10,000	—	—	6.00	14.00	—

KM# 121 10 LEI
Nickel Plated Steel **Series:** 1996 Olympic Games - U.S.A. **Obv:** Shield above sprig flanked by value **Rev:** Four Olympic scenes

Date	Mintage	F	VF	XF	Unc	BU
1996	10,000	—	—	6.00	14.00	—

KM# 122 10 LEI
Nickel Plated Steel **Series:** 1996 Olympic Games - U.S.A. **Obv:** Shield above sprig flanked by value **Rev:** Windsurfer

Date	Mintage	F	VF	XF	Unc	BU
1996	10,000	—	—	6.00	14.00	—

KM# 123 10 LEI
Nickel Plated Steel **Series:** 1996 Olympic Games - U.S.A. **Obv:** Shield above sprig flanked by value **Rev:** Sailboat with two racers

Date	Mintage	F	VF	XF	Unc	BU
1996	10,000	—	—	6.00	14.00	—

KM# 124 10 LEI
Nickel Plated Steel **Series:** 1996 Olympic Games - U.S.A. **Obv:** Shield above sprigs divide value **Rev:** Canoe with two racers

Date	Mintage	F	VF	XF	Unc	BU
1996	10,000	—	—	6.00	14.00	—

KM# 125 10 LEI
Nickel Plated Steel **Series:** 1996 Olympic Games - U.S.A. **Obv:** Shield above sprigs divide value **Rev:** Scullcraft with racers

Date	Mintage	F	VF	XF	Unc	BU
1996	10,000	—	—	6.00	14.00	—

KM# 126 10 LEI
Nickel Plated Steel **Subject:** World Food Summit - Rome **Obv:** Shield above value **Rev:** Logo above inscription

Date	Mintage	F	VF	XF	Unc	BU
1996	50,000	—	—	6.00	14.00	—

KM# 134 10 LEI
Nickel Plated Steel **Subject:** Euro Soccer **Obv:** Shield divides value **Rev:** Stylized soccer players

Date	Mintage	F	VF	XF	Unc	BU
1996	50,000	—	—	6.00	14.00	—

KM# 109 20 LEI
5.0000 g., Brass Clad Steel, 24 mm. **Obv:** Crowned bust of Prince Stefan Cel Mare facing, flanked by dots **Rev:** Value and date within half sprigs and dots **Edge:** Plain **Designer:** Constantin Dumitrescu **Note:** Date varieties exist.

Date	Mintage	F	VF	XF	Unc	BU
1991	Est. 43,200,000	—	—	1.00	3.00	—
1992	Est. 48,000,000	—	—	0.80	3.00	—
1993	Est. 33,800,000	—	—	0.80	3.00	—
1994	Est. 5,000,000	—	—	1.25	3.00	—
1995	8,000,000	—	—	0.75	3.00	—
1996	500,000	—	0.75	2.00	7.00	—
2000 Proof	4,500	Value: 6.00				
2002 Proof	1,500	Value: 7.50				
2003 Proof	2,000	Value: 7.50				

KM# 110 50 LEI
5.9000 g., Brass Clad Steel, 26 mm. **Obv:** Bust left flanked by dots **Rev:** Sprig divides date and value **Edge:** Plain **Designer:** Vasile Gabor

Date	Mintage	F	VF	XF	Unc	BU
1991	Est. 29,600,000	—	—	1.50	3.00	—
1992	Est. 70,800,000	—	—	1.00	2.00	—

Note: 1992 date varieties exist

Date	Mintage	F	VF	XF	Unc	BU
1993	Est. 34,600,000	—	—	1.00	2.00	—
1994	Est. 30,000,000	—	—	1.00	2.00	—
1995	20,000,000	—	—	1.00	2.20	—
1996	4,900,000	—	—	2.00	4.00	—
2000 Proof	4,500	Value: 7.00				
2002 Proof	1,500	Value: 8.00				
2003 Proof	2,000	Value: 8.00				

KM# 111 100 LEI
8.7500 g., Nickel Plated Steel, 29 mm. **Obv:** Bust with headdress 1/4 right **Rev:** Value within sprigs **Edge Lettering:** ROMANIA **Designer:** Vasile Gabor

Date	Mintage	F	VF	XF	Unc	BU
1991	Est. 12,600,000	—	—	2.50	6.00	—
1992	Est. 70,500,000	—	—	1.50	3.50	—

Note: Reported edge varieties for 1992 with TOTUL PENTRU TARA; without ROMANIA are presumed essais

Date	Mintage	F	VF	XF	Unc	BU
1993	Est. 78,000,000	—	—	1.50	3.00	—
1994	Est. 125,000,000	—	—	1.50	2.50	—
1995	30,000,000	—	—	1.50	3.50	—
1996	11,000,000	—	—	2.50	9.00	—
2000 Proof	4,500	Value: 7.50				
2002 Proof	1,500	Value: 8.00				
2003 Proof	2,000	Value: 8.00				
2004 Proof	2,000	Value: 8.00				
2005	—	—	—	—	2.50	—
2005 Proof	2,000	Value: 9.00				
2006 Proof	1,000	Value: 9.00				

KM# 145 500 LEI
3.7000 g., Aluminum, 25 mm. **Obv:** Shield within sprigs **Rev:** Value within 3/4 wreath **Edge:** Lettered **Edge Lettering:** ROMANIA (three times)

Date	Mintage	F	VF	XF	Unc	BU
1998	—	—	—	0.75	2.00	—
1999	—	—	—	0.75	2.00	—
2000	—	—	—	0.75	2.00	—
2000 Proof	4,500	Value: 6.00				
2001	—	—	—	0.75	2.00	—
2002 Proof	1,500	Value: 7.00				
2003 Proof	2,000	Value: 7.00				
2004 Proof	2,000	Value: 7.00				
2005	—	—	—	—	3.00	—
2005 Proof	1,000	Value: 8.00				
2006	—	—	—	—	3.00	—
2006 Proof	—	Value: 8.00				

KM# 153 1000 LEI
2.0000 g., Aluminum, 22.2 mm. **Subject:** Constantin Brancoveanu **Obv:** Value above shield within lined circle **Rev:** Bust with headdress facing **Edge:** Plain with serrated sections

Date	Mintage	VG	F	VF	XF	Unc
2000	—	—	—	—	0.50	3.00
2000 Proof	4,500	Value: 10.00				

Note: In proof sets only

Date	Mintage	VG	F	VF	XF	Unc
2001	—	—	—	—	0.25	2.50
2002	—	—	—	—	0.25	2.50
2002 Proof	1,500	Value: 12.00				

Note: In proof sets only

Date	Mintage	VG	F	VF	XF	Unc
2003	—	—	—	—	0.25	2.50
2003 Proof	2,000	Value: 12.00				

Note: In proof sets only

Date	Mintage	VG	F	VF	XF	Unc
2004	—	—	—	—	0.25	2.50
2004 Proof	2,000	Value: 12.00				

Note: In proof sets only

Date	Mintage	VG	F	VF	XF	Unc
2005	—	—	—	—	0.25	2.50
2005 Proof	—	Value: 13.00				

Note: In proof sets only

Date	Mintage	VG	F	VF	XF	Unc
2006 Proof	1,000	Value: 13.00				

KM# 158 5000 LEI
2.5200 g., Aluminum, 23.5 mm. **Obv:** Value and country name **Rev:** Sprig divides date and shield **Edge:** Plain **Shape:** 12-sided

Date	Mintage	F	VF	XF	Unc	BU
2001	—	—	—	—	0.50	—
2002 Proof	1,500	Value: 15.00				
2002	—	—	—	—	0.50	—
2003	—	—	—	—	0.25	—
2003 Proof	2,000	Value: 15.00				
2004 Proof	2,000	Value: 16.00				
2004	—	—	—	—	0.25	—
2005	—	—	—	—	0.25	—
2005 Proof	2,000	Value: 17.00				
2006 Proof	1,000	Value: 17.00				

REFORM COINAGE - 2005

10,000 Old Leu = 1 New Leu

KM# 189 BAN
2.4000 g., Copper-Plated-Steel, 16.8 mm. **Subject:** Monetary Reform of 2005 **Obv:** National arms flanked by stars **Rev:** Value **Edge:** Plain

Date	Mintage	F	VF	XF	Unc	BU
2005 Proof	—	Value: 2.50				
2005	—	—	—	—	0.30	0.50
2006 Proof	—	Value: 2.50				
2006	—	—	—	—	0.30	0.50
2007 Proof	—	Value: 2.50				
2007	—	—	—	—	0.30	0.50

KM# 190 5 BANI
2.8100 g., Copper Plated Steel, 18.2 mm. **Subject:** Monetary Reform of 2005 **Obv:** National arms flanked by stars **Obv. Legend:** ROMANIA **Rev:** Value **Edge:** Reeded

Date	Mintage	F	VF	XF	Unc	BU
2005	—	—	—	—	0.50	0.75
2005 Proof	—	Value: 5.00				
2006	—	—	—	—	0.50	0.65
2006 Proof	—	Value: 5.00				
2007	—	—	—	—	0.50	0.65
2007 Proof	—	Value: 5.00				

KM# 191 10 BANI
4.0000 g., Nickel Plated Steel, 20.4 mm. **Subject:** Monetary Reform of 2005 **Obv:** National arms flanked by stars **Obv. Legend:** ROMANIA **Rev:** Value **Edge:** Segmented reeding

Date	Mintage	F	VF	XF	Unc	BU
2005	—	—	—	—	0.65	0.85
2005 Proof	—	Value: 7.00				
2006	—	—	—	—	0.60	0.75
2006 Proof	—	Value: 7.00				
2007	—	—	—	—	0.50	0.65
2007 Proof	—	Value: 7.00				

KM# 192 50 BANI
6.1200 g., Brass, 23.6 mm. **Subject:** Monetary Reform of 2005 **Obv:** National arms flanked by stars **Obv. Legend:** ROMANIA **Rev:** Value **Edge:** Lettered **Edge Lettering:** "ROMANIA' twice

Date	Mintage	F	VF	XF	Unc	BU
2005	—	—	—	—	0.85	1.00
2005 Proof	—	Value: 10.00				
2006	—	—	—	—	0.75	0.85
2006 Proof	—	Value: 10.00				
2007	—	—	—	—	0.65	0.75
2007 Proof	—	Value: 10.00				

RUSSIA (U.S.S.R.)

Russia, formerly the central power of the Union of Soviet Socialist Republics and now of the Commonwealth of Independent States occupies the northern part of Asia and the eastern part of Europe, has an area of 17,075,400 sq. km. and a population of *146.2 million. Capital: Moscow. Exports include iron and steel, crude oil, timber, and nonferrous metals.

The first Russian dynasty was founded in Novgorod by the Viking Rurik in 862 A.D. under Yaroslav the Wise (1019-54). The subsequent Kievan state became one of the great commercial and cultural centers of Europe before falling to the Mongols of the Batu Khan, 13th century, who were suzerains of Russia until late in the 15th century when Ivan III threw off the Mongol yoke. The Russian Empire was enlarged, solidified and Westernized during the reigns of Ivan the Terrible, Peter the Great and Catherine the Great, and by 1881 extended to the Pacific and into Central Asia. Contemporary Russian history began in March of 1917 when Tsar Nicholas II abdicated under pressure and was replaced by a provisional government composed of both radical and conservative elements. This government rapidly lost ground to the Bolshevik wing of the Socialist Democratic Labor Party which attained power following the Bolshevik Revolution which began on Nov. 7, 1917. After the Russian Civil War, the regional governments, national states and armies became federal republics of the Russian Socialist Federal Soviet Republic. These autonomous republics united to form the Union of Soviet Socialist Republics that was established as a federation under the premiership of Lenin on Dec. 30, 1922.

In the fall of 1991, events moved swiftly in the Soviet Union. Estonia, Latvia and Lithuania won their independence and were recognized by Moscow, Sept. 6. The Commonwealth of Independent States was formed Dec. 8, 1991 in Mensk by Belarus, Russia and Ukraine. It was expanded at a summit Dec. 21, 1991 to include 11 of the 12 remaining republics (excluding Georgia) of the old U.S.S.R.

EMPIRE

RULER
Nicholas II, 1894-1917

MINT MARKS
Л – Leningrad, 1991
M – Moscow, 1990
СП – St. Petersburg, 1999
СПБ – St. Petersburg, 1724-1914
СПМД – St. Petersburg, 1999

(sp) (l) – LMD (ЛМД) monogram in oval, (Leningrad), (St. Petersburg) 1977-1997

MINT OFFICIALS' INITIALS

Leningrad Mint

Initials	Years	Mint Official
АГ	1921-22	A.F. Hartman
ПЛ	1922-27	P.V. Latishev

London Mint

Initials	Years	Mint Official
Т.Р.	1924	Thomas Ross
ФР	1924	Thomas Ross

St. Petersburg Mint

Initials	Years	Mint Official
ФЗ	1899-1901	Felix Zaleman
АР	1901-05	Alexander Redko
ЭБ	1906-13	Elikum Babayantz
ВС	1913-17	Victor Smirnov

NOTE: St. Petersburg Mint became Petrograd in 1914 and Leningrad in 1924. It was renamed St. Petersburg in 1991.

MONETARY SYSTEM
1/4 Kopek = Polushka ПОЛУШКА
1/2 Kopek = Denga, Denezhka ДЕНГА, ДЕНЕЖКА
Kopek = КОП_ИКА
(2, 3 & 4) Kopeks КОП_ИКИ
(5 and up) Kopeks КОП_ЕКЪ
(1924 – 5 and up) Kopeks КОПЕЕК
50 Kopeks = Poltina, Poltinnik ПОЛТИНА,...ПОЛРУБЛЪ
100 Kopeks = Rouble, Ruble РУБЛЪ
10 Roubles = Imperial ИМПЕРIАЛЪ
10 Roubles = Chervonetz ЧЕРВОНЕЦ

NOTE: Mintage figures for years after 1885 are for fiscal years and may or may not reflect actual rarity, the commemorative and 1917 silver figures being exceptions.

STANDARD COINAGE

Y# 47.1 1/4 KOPEK
0.8000 g., Copper **Ruler:** Nicholas II **Obv:** Crowned monogram above sprays **Rev:** Value, date **Edge:** Reeded

Date	Mintage	F	VF	XF	Unc	BU
1909СПБ	2,000,000	3.00	5.00	10.00	20.00	—
1910СПБ	8,000,000	4.00	8.00	15.00	30.00	—
1909-1910 Common date Proof	—	Value: 125				

Y# 47.2 POLUSHKA (1/4 Kopek)
0.8000 g., Copper **Ruler:** Nicholas II **Obv:** Crowned monogram above sprays **Rev:** Value, date

Date	Mintage	F	VF	XF	Unc	BU
1915	500,000	2.00	5.00	10.00	20.00	—
1916	1,200,000	40.00	80.00	150	300	—

Y# 48.1 1/2 KOPEK

1.6000 g., Copper, 16 mm. **Ruler:** Nicholas II **Obv:** Crowned monogram above sprays **Rev:** Value and date **Edge:** Reeded

Date	Mintage	F	VF	XF	Unc	BU
1908СПБ	8,000,000	3.00	5.00	10.00	20.00	—
1909СПБ	49,500,000	3.00	5.00	10.00	25.00	—
1910СПБ	24,000,000	2.00	5.00	10.00	20.00	30.00
1911СПБ	35,800,000	2.00	5.00	10.00	20.00	30.00
1912СПБ	28,000,000	2.00	5.00	10.00	20.00	30.00
1913СПБ	50,000,000	1.00	3.00	5.00	10.00	20.00
1914СПБ	14,000,000	3.00	5.00	10.00	25.00	35.00
1908-14 Common date Proof	—	Value: 200				

Y# 48.2 1/2 KOPEK

1.6000 g., Copper **Ruler:** Nicholas II **Obv:** Crowned monogram above sprays **Rev:** Value and date **Note:** Struck at Petrograd without mint mark.

Date	Mintage	F	VF	XF	Unc	BU
1915	12,000,000	3.00	6.00	12.00	25.00	30.00
1916	9,400,000	3.00	6.00	12.00	25.00	30.00

Y# 9.2 KOPEK

3.3000 g., Copper, 21.5 mm. **Ruler:** Nicholas II **Obv:** Crowned double-headed imperial eagle within circle **Rev:** Value flanked by stars within beaded circle **Edge:** Reeded

Date	Mintage	F	VF	XF	Unc	BU
1901СПБ	30,000,000	1.00	2.00	4.00	12.00	—
1902СПБ	20,000,000	2.00	8.00	15.00	30.00	—
1903СПБ	74,400,000	1.00	2.00	4.00	12.00	—
1904СПБ	30,600,000	1.00	2.00	4.00	12.00	—
1905СПБ	23,000,000	1.00	2.00	4.00	12.00	—
1906СПБ	20,000,000	1.00	2.00	4.00	12.00	—
1907СПБ	20,000,000	1.00	2.00	4.00	12.00	—
1908СПБ	40,000,000	1.00	2.00	4.00	12.00	—
1909СПБ	27,500,000	1.00	2.00	4.00	12.00	—
1910СПБ	36,500,000	1.00	2.00	4.00	12.00	—
1911СПБ	38,150,000	1.00	2.00	4.00	12.00	—
1912СПБ	31,850,000	1.00	2.00	4.00	12.00	—
1913СПБ	61,500,000	1.00	2.00	4.00	12.00	—
1914СПБ	32,500,000	1.00	2.00	4.00	12.00	—
1901-14 Common date Proof	—	Value: 150				

Y# 9.3 KOPEK

3.3000 g., Copper **Ruler:** Nicholas II **Obv:** Crowned double-headed imperial eagle within circle **Rev:** Value flanked by stars within beaded circle **Note:** Struck at Petrograd without mint mark.

Date	Mintage	F	VF	XF	Unc	BU
1915	58,000,000	1.00	2.00	4.00	12.00	—
1916	46,500,000	2.00	3.00	6.00	12.00	—
1917 Unique	—	—	—	—	—	—

Y# 10.2 2 KOPEKS

6.6000 g., Copper **Ruler:** Nicholas II **Obv:** Crowned double-headed imperial eagle within circle **Rev:** Value flanked by stars within circle **Edge:** Reeded

Date	Mintage	F	VF	XF	Unc	BU
1901СПБ	20,000,000	3.00	4.00	8.00	15.00	—
1902СПБ	10,000,000	3.00	4.00	8.00	15.00	—
1903СПБ	29,200,000	3.00	4.00	8.00	15.00	—
1904СПБ	13,300,000	3.00	4.00	8.00	15.00	—
1905СПБ	15,000,000	3.00	4.00	8.00	15.00	—
1906СПБ	6,250,000	3.00	4.00	8.00	15.00	—
1907СПБ	7,500,000	3.00	4.00	8.00	15.00	—
1908СПБ	19,000,000	3.00	4.00	8.00	15.00	—
1909СПБ	16,250,000	3.00	4.00	8.00	15.00	—
1910СПБ	12,000,000	3.00	4.00	8.00	15.00	—
1911СПБ	17,200,000	3.00	4.00	8.00	15.00	—
1912СПБ	17,050,000	3.00	4.00	8.00	15.00	—
1913СПБ	26,000,000	3.00	4.00	8.00	15.00	—
1914СПБ	20,000,000	3.00	4.00	8.00	15.00	—
1901-14 Common date proof	—	Value: 175				

Y# 10.3 2 KOPEKS

Copper **Ruler:** Nicholas II **Obv:** Crowned double-headed imperial eagle **Rev:** Value within circle **Note:** Struck at Petrograd without mint mark.

Date	Mintage	F	VF	XF	Unc	BU
1915	33,750,000	2.00	3.00	5.00	8.00	—
1916	31,500,000	2.00	3.00	5.00	8.00	—
Rare	—	—	—	—	—	—

Y# 11.2 3 KOPEKS

8.0000 g., Copper, 18.23 mm. **Ruler:** Nicholas II **Obv:** Crowned double imperial eagle within circle **Rev:** Value flanked by stars within beaded circle **Edge:** Reeded

Date	Mintage	F	VF	XF	Unc	BU
1901СПБ	10,000,000	3.00	5.00	10.00	20.00	—
1902СПБ	3,333,000	4.00	8.00	15.00	30.00	—
1903СПБ	11,400,000	3.00	5.00	10.00	20.00	—
1904СПБ	6,934,000	4.00	8.00	15.00	30.00	—
1905СПБ	3,333,000	4.00	8.00	15.00	30.00	—
1906СПБ	5,667,000	4.00	8.00	15.00	30.00	—
1907СПБ	2,500,000	4.00	8.00	15.00	30.00	—
1908СПБ	12,667,000	3.00	5.00	10.00	20.00	—
1909СПБ	6,733,000	3.00	5.00	10.00	20.00	—
1910СПБ	6,667,000	3.00	5.00	10.00	20.00	—
1911СПБ	9,467,000	3.00	5.00	10.00	20.00	—
1912СПБ	8,533,000	4.00	8.00	15.00	30.00	—
1913СПБ	15,333,000	3.00	5.00	10.00	20.00	—
1914СПБ	8,167,000	3.00	5.00	10.00	20.00	—
1901-14СПБ Common date proof	—	Value: 200				

Y# 11.3 3 KOPEKS

Copper **Ruler:** Nicholas II **Obv:** Crowned double-headed imperial eagle **Rev:** Value flanked by stars within beaded circle **Note:** Struck at Petrograd without mint mark.

Date	Mintage	F	VF	XF	Unc	BU
1915	19,833,000	2.00	5.00	10.00	30.00	—
1916	25,667,000	2.00	5.00	10.00	30.00	—
1917 Rare	—	—	—	—	—	—

Y# 19a.1 5 KOPEKS

0.8998 g., 0.5000 Silver 0.0145 oz. ASW **Ruler:** Nicholas II **Obv:** Crowned double-headed imperial eagle **Rev:** Crown above date and value within wreath **Edge:** Reeded

Date	Mintage	F	VF	XF	Unc	BU
1901СПБ АР	Inc. above	3.00	5.00	10.00	20.00	40.00
1901СПБ ФЗ	5,790,000	3.00	5.00	10.00	20.00	40.00
1902СПБ АР	6,000,000	3.00	5.00	10.00	20.00	40.00
1903СПБ АР	9,000,000	3.00	5.00	10.00	20.00	40.00
1904СПБ АР Rare	9	—	—	—	—	—
1905СПБ АР	10,000,000	3.00	5.00	10.00	30.00	90.00
1906СПБ ЭБ	4,000,000	3.00	5.00	10.00	30.00	90.00
1908СПБ ЭБ	400,000	3.00	5.00	10.00	30.00	90.00
1909СПБ ЭБ	3,100,000	3.00	5.00	10.00	30.00	90.00
1910СПБ ЭБ	2,500,000	3.00	5.00	10.00	30.00	90.00
1911СПБ ЭБ	2,700,000	3.00	5.00	10.00	30.00	90.00
1912СПБ ЭБ	3,000,000	3.00	5.00	10.00	30.00	90.00
1913СПБ ЭБ Proof	Inc. below	Value: 150				
1913СПБ ВС	1,300,000	3.00	5.00	10.00	30.00	90.00
1914СПБ ВС	4,200,000	3.00	5.00	10.00	30.00	90.00
1901-14 Common date proof	—	Value: 150				

Y# 19a.2 5 KOPEKS

0.8998 g., 0.5000 Silver 0.0145 oz. ASW **Ruler:** Nicholas II **Obv:** Crowned double-headed imperial eagle **Rev:** Crown above value and date within wreath **Note:** Struck at Petrograd without mint mark.

Date	Mintage	F	VF	XF	Unc	BU
1915 ВС	3,000,000	3.00	5.00	10.00	20.00	40.00

Y# 12.2 5 KOPEKS

16.4000 g., Copper, 32.6 mm. **Ruler:** Nicholas II **Obv:** Crowned double-headed imperial eagle within circle **Rev:** Value flanked by stars within beaded circle **Edge:** Reeded

Date	Mintage	F	VF	XF	Unc	BU
1911СПБ	3,800,000	10.00	20.00	35.00	70.00	—
1912СПБ	2,700,000	15.00	25.00	45.00	90.00	—

Y# 12.3 5 KOPEKS

Copper **Ruler:** Nicholas II **Obv:** Crowned double-headed imperial eagle **Rev:** Value flanked by stars within beaded circle **Note:** Struck at Petrograd without mint mark.

Date	Mintage	F	VF	XF	Unc	BU
1916	8,000,000	40.00	80.00	150	250	—
1917 Rare	—	—	—	—	—	—

Y# 20a.1 10 KOPEKS

1.7996 g., 0.5000 Silver 0.0289 oz. ASW **Ruler:** Nicholas II **Obv:** Crowned double-headed imperial eagle, ribbons on crown **Rev:** Crown above value and date within wreath **Note:** Struck at Osaka, Japan without mintmaster initials.

Date	Mintage	F	VF	XF	Unc	BU
1916	70,001,000	1.00	2.00	5.00	14.00	—

Y# 20a.2 10 KOPEKS

1.7996 g., 0.5000 Silver 0.0289 oz. ASW **Ruler:** Nicholas II **Obv:** Crowned double-headed imperial eagle, ribbons on crown **Rev:** Crown above value and date within wreath **Edge:** Reeded

Date	Mintage	F	VF	XF	Unc	BU
1901СПБ АР	Inc. above	2.00	4.00	10.00	20.00	—
1901СПБ ФЗ	15,000,000	2.00	4.00	10.00	20.00	—
1902СПБ АР	17,000,000	2.00	4.00	10.00	20.00	—
1903СПБ АР	28,500,000	2.00	40.00	10.00	20.00	—
1904СПБ АР	20,000,000	2.00	4.00	10.00	20.00	—
1905СПБ АР	25,000,000	2.00	4.00	10.00	20.00	—
1906СПБ ЭБ	17,500,000	2.00	4.00	10.00	20.00	—
1907СПБ ЭБ	—	2.00	4.00	10.00	20.00	—
1908СПБ ЭБ	8,210,000	2.00	4.00	10.00	20.00	—
1909СПБ ЭБ	25,290,000	2.00	4.00	10.00	20.00	—
1910СПБ ЭБ	20,000,000	2.00	4.00	10.00	20.00	—
1911СПБ ЭБ	19,180,000	2.00	4.00	10.00	20.00	—
1912СПБ ЭБ	20,000,000	2.00	4.00	10.00	20.00	—
1913СПБ ЭБ Proof	Inc. below	Value: 250				
1913СПБ ВС	7,250,000	2.00	4.00	10.00	20.00	—
1914СПБ ВС	51,250,000	2.00	4.00	10.00	20.00	—
1901-14 Common date proof	—	Value: 250				

Y# 20a.3 10 KOPEKS

1.7996 g., 0.5000 Silver 0.0289 oz. ASW **Ruler:** Nicholas II **Obv:** Crowned double-headed imperial eagle, ribbons on crown **Rev:** Crown above value and date within wreath **Edge:** Reeded **Note:** Struck at Petrograd without mintmaster initials.

Date	Mintage	F	VF	XF	Unc	BU
1915 ВС	82,500,000	2.00	3.00	5.00	10.00	—
1916 ВС	121,500,000	2.00	3.00	5.00	10.00	—
1917 ВС	17,600,000	—	30.00	50.00	100	—

Y# 21a.2 15 KOPEKS

2.6994 g., 0.5000 Silver 0.0434 oz. ASW **Ruler:** Nicholas II **Obv:** Crowned double-headed imperial eagle, ribbons on crown **Rev:** Crown above date and value within wreath **Edge:** Reeded

Date	Mintage	F	VF	XF	Unc	BU
1901СПБ ФЗ	6,670,000	5.00	10.00	15.00	30.00	—
1901СПБ АР	Inc. above	5.00	10.00	15.00	30.00	—
1902СПБ АР	28,667,000	3.00	5.00	10.00	20.00	—
1903СПБ АР	16,667,000	3.00	5.00	10.00	20.00	—
1904СПБ АР	15,600,000	3.00	5.00	10.00	20.00	—
1905СПБ АР	24,000,000	3.00	5.00	10.00	20.00	—
1906СПБ ЭБ	23,333,000	3.00	5.00	10.00	20.00	—
1907СПБ ЭБ	30,000,000	3.00	5.00	10.00	20.00	—
1908СПБ ЭБ	29,000,000	3.00	5.00	10.00	20.00	—
1909СПБ ЭБ	21,667,000	3.00	5.00	10.00	20.00	—
1911СПБ ЭБ	6,313,000	5.00	10.00	15.00	30.00	—

Date	Mintage	F	VF	XF	Unc	BU
1912СПБ ВС	Inc. above	6.00	10.00	20.00	50.00	—
1912СПБ ЭБ Rare	13,333,000	—	—	—	—	—
1913СПБ ЭБ Proof	Inc. below	Value: 250				
1913СПБ ВС	5,300,000	5.00	10.00	15.00	30.00	—
1914СПБ ВС	43,367,000	3.00	5.00	10.00	20.00	—
1901-14 Common date proof	—	Value: 250				

Y# 21a.3 15 KOPEKS

2.6994 g., 0.5000 Silver 0.0434 oz. ASW **Ruler:** Nicholas II **Obv:** Crowned double-headed imperial eagle, ribbons on crown **Rev:** Crown above value and date within wreath **Note:** Struck at Petrograd without mintmaster initials.

Date	Mintage	F	VF	XF	Unc	BU
1915 ВС	59,333,000	2.00	4.00	6.00	15.00	—
1916 ВС	96,773,000	2.00	4.00	6.00	15.00	—
1917 ВС	14,320,000	—	30.00	50.00	100	—

Y# 21a.1 15 KOPEKS

2.6994 g., 0.5000 Silver 0.0434 oz. ASW **Ruler:** Nicholas II **Obv:** Crowned double-headed imperial eagle, ribbons on crown **Rev:** Crown above value and date within wreath **Edge:** Reeded **Note:** Struck at Osaka, Japan without mintmaster initials.

Date	Mintage	F	VF	XF	Unc	BU
1916	96,666,000	BV	1.50	3.00	10.00	—

Y# 22a.1 20 KOPEKS

3.5992 g., 0.5000 Silver 0.0579 oz. ASW, 22 mm. **Ruler:** Nicholas II **Obv:** Crowned double-headed imperial eagle, ribbons on crown **Rev:** Crown above value and date within wreath

Date	Mintage	F	VF	XF	Unc	BU
1901СПБ ФЗ	7,750,000	3.00	5.00	10.00	20.00	—
1901СПБ АР Proof	Inc. above	Value: 300				
1902СПБ АР	10,000,000	3.00	5.00	10.00	20.00	—
1903СПБ АР	Inc. above	3.00	5.00	10.00	20.00	—
1904СПБ АР	13,000,000	3.00	5.00	10.00	20.00	—
1905СПБ АР	11,000,000	3.00	5.00	10.00	20.00	—
1906СПБ ЭБ	15,000,000	3.00	5.00	10.00	20.00	—
1907СПБ ЭБ	20,000,000	3.00	5.00	10.00	20.00	—
1908СПБ ЭБ	5,000,000	3.00	5.00	10.00	20.00	—
1909СПБ ЭБ	18,875,000	3.00	5.00	10.00	20.00	—
1910СПБ ЭБ	11,000,000	3.00	5.00	10.00	20.00	—
1911СПБ ЭБ	7,100,000	3.00	5.00	10.00	20.00	—
1912СПБ ЭБ	15,000,000	3.00	5.00	10.00	20.00	—
1912СПБ ВС Rare	Inc. above	—	—	—	—	—
1913СПБ ЭБ Proof	Inc. below	Value: 250				
1913СПБ ВС	4,250,000	3.00	5.00	10.00	20.00	—
1914СПБ ВС	52,750,000	2.00	3.00	8.00	15.00	20.00
1901-14 Common date proof	—	Value: 250				

Y# 22a.2 20 KOPEKS

3.5992 g., 0.5000 Silver 0.0579 oz. ASW **Ruler:** Nicholas II **Obv:** Crowned double-headed imperial eagle, ribbons on crown **Rev:** Crown above value and date within wreath **Note:** Struck at Petrograd without mint mark.

Date	Mintage	F	VF	XF	Unc	BU
1915 ВС	105,500,000	2.00	4.00	8.00	15.00	15.00
1916 ВС	131,670,000	2.00	4.00	8.00	15.00	20.00
1917 ВС	3,500,000	15.00	30.00	70.00	140	—
1915-17 Common date proof	—	Value: 250				

Y# 58.2 50 KOPEKS

9.9980 g., 0.9000 Silver 0.2893 oz. ASW **Ruler:** Nicholas II **Obv:** Head left **Rev:** Crowned double-headed imperial eagle, ribbons on crown **Note:** Without mint mark, moneyer's initials on edge.

Date	Mintage	F	VF	XF	Unc	BU
1901 АР	412,000	10.00	25.00	80.00	200	—
1901 ФЗ	Inc. above	10.00	25.00	80.00	200	—
1902 АР	36,000	15.00	30.00	70.00	250	—
1903 АР Proof	—	Value: 2,000				
1904 АР	4,010,000	100	200	400	1,200	—
1906 ЭБ	10,000	25.00	50.00	100	350	—
1907 ЭБ	200,000	10.00	20.00	50.00	200	—
1908 ЭБ	40,000	20.00	40.00	80.00	200	—
1909 ЭБ	50,000	20.00	40.00	80.00	200	—
1910 ЭБ	150,000	10.00	20.00	50.00	200	—
1911 ЭБ	800,000	10.00	20.00	40.00	150	—
1912 ЭБ	7,085,000	8.00	15.00	30.00	60.00	—

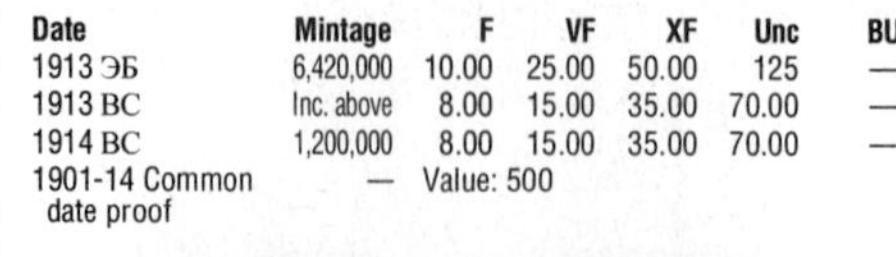

Date	Mintage	F	VF	XF	Unc	BU
1913 ЭБ	6,420,000	10.00	25.00	50.00	125	—
1913 ВС	Inc. above	8.00	15.00	35.00	70.00	—
1914 ВС	1,200,000	8.00	15.00	35.00	70.00	—
1901-14 Common date proof	—	Value: 500				

Y# 59.3 ROUBLE

19.9960 g., 0.9000 Silver 0.5786 oz. ASW **Ruler:** Nicholas II **Obv:** Head left **Rev:** Crowned double-headed imperial eagle, ribbons on crown **Note:** Without mint mark, moneyer's initials on edge.

Date	Mintage	F	VF	XF	Unc	BU
1901 ФЗ	2,608,000	25.00	50.00	100	300	600
1901 АР	Inc. above	60.00	120	300	700	4,000
1902 АР	140,000	90.00	100	200	600	1,200
1903 АР	56,000	90.00	150	350	800	—
1904 АР	12,000	120	220	500	1,100	—
1905 АР	21,000	30.00	150	850	900	—
1906 ЭБ	46,000	80.00	150	350	900	—
1907 ЭБ	400,000	40.00	80.00	200	600	2,000
1908 ЭБ	130,000	100	220	500	1,100	—
1909 ЭБ	51,000	70.00	140	300	800	—
1910 ЭБ	75,000	50.00	100	270	700	3,750
1911 ЭБ	129,000	50.00	100	200	600	2,750
1912 ЭБ	2,111,000	20.00	50.00	100	400	600
1913 ЭБ	22,000	100	200	400	900	—
1913 ВС	Inc. above	100	200	400	900	—
1914 ВС	536,000	40.00	100	250	600	2,000
1915 ВС	5,000	50.00	100	300	650	3,600

Note: Varieties exist with plain edge, these are mint errors and rare

Date	Mintage	F	VF	XF	Unc	BU
1901-15 Common date proof	—	Value: 4,000				

Y# 68 ROUBLE

19.9960 g., 0.9000 Silver 0.5786 oz. ASW, 34 mm. **Ruler:** Nicholas II **Subject:** Centennial - Napolean's Defeat **Obv:** Crowned double-headed imperial eagle with various crowned shields **Rev:** Inscription and date within beaded circle **Designer:** Alexander Vasulinskil

Date	Mintage	F	VF	XF	Unc	BU
1912 ЭБ	46,000	250	500	800	1,100	2,750
1912 ЭБ Proof	—	Value: 4,500				

Y# 69 ROUBLE

19.9960 g., 0.9000 Silver 0.5786 oz. ASW, 34 mm. **Ruler:** Nicholas II **Subject:** Alexander III Memorial **Obv:** Head left **Rev:** Monument **Designer:** Abraham Grilikez

Date	Mintage	F	VF	XF	Unc	BU
1912 ЭБ	2,100	750	1,600	2,750	5,000	9,500
1912 ЭБ Proof	—	Value: 10,000				

Y# 70 ROUBLE

19.9960 g., 0.9000 Silver 0.5786 oz. ASW, 34 mm. **Ruler:** Nicholas II **Subject:** 300th Anniversary - Romanov Dynasty **Obv:** Conjoined heads facing 1/4 right **Rev:** Crowned double-headed imperial eagle **Designer:** M.A. Kerzin **Note:** Struck at St. Petersburg without mint mark.

Date	Mintage	F	VF	XF	Unc	BU
1913 ВС	1,472,000	25.00	50.00	100	150	250

Y# 62 5 ROUBLES

4.3013 g., 0.9000 Gold 0.1245 oz. AGW **Ruler:** Nicholas II **Obv:** Head left **Rev:** Crowned double-headed imperial eagle, ribbons on crown **Note:** Struck at St. Petersburg without mint mark.

Date	Mintage	F	VF	XF	Unc	BU
1901 ФЗ	7,500,000	BV	260	280	300	400
1901 АР	Inc. above	BV	260	280	300	400
1902 АР	6,240,000	BV	260	280	300	400
1903 АР	5,148,000	BV	260	280	300	400
1904 АР	2,016,000	BV	260	280	300	400
1906 ЭБ	10	—	—	7,000	10,000	—
1907 ЭБ	109	—	—	4,000	7,500	—
1909 ЭБ	—	260	260	280	300	400
1910 ЭБ	200,000	260	260	280	300	400
1911 ЭБ	100,000	260	280	300	400	650
1901-11 Common date proof	—	Value: 2,500				

Y# 64 10 ROUBLES

8.6026 g., 0.9000 Gold 0.2489 oz. AGW **Ruler:** Nicholas II **Obv:** Head left **Rev:** Crowned double-headed imperial eagle, ribbons on crown **Note:** Without mint mark. Moneyer's initials on edge.

Date	Mintage	F	VF	XF	Unc	BU
1901 ФЗ	2,377,000	BV	260	280	300	500
1901 АР	Inc. above	BV	260	280	300	500
1902 АР	2,019,000	BV	260	280	300	500
1903 АР	2,817,000	BV	260	280	300	500
1904 АР	1,025,000	BV	260	280	300	500
1906 ЭБ Proof	10	Value: 15,000				
1909 ЭБ	50,000	260	280	300	400	600
1910 ЭБ	100,000	260	280	300	400	600
1911 ЭБ	50,000	260	280	300	400	600
1901-11 Common date proof	—	Value: 4,500				

РСФСР (R.S.F.S.R.)
(Russian Soviet Federated Socialist Republic)

STANDARD COINAGE

Y# 80 10 KOPEKS

1.8000 g., 0.5000 Silver 0.0289 oz. ASW **Obv:** National arms **Rev:** Value and date within beaded circle, star on top divides wreath

Date	Mintage	F	VF	XF	Unc	BU
1921	950,000	10.00	20.00	35.00	70.00	—
1921 Proof	—	Value: 375				
1922	18,640,000	3.00	5.00	15.00	25.00	—
1922 Proof	—	Value: 275				
1923	33,424,000	2.00	5.00	10.00	20.00	—
1923 Proof	—	Value: 225				

Y# 81 15 KOPEKS
2.7000 g., 0.5000 Silver 0.0434 oz. ASW **Obv:** National arms within circle **Rev:** Value and date within beaded circle, star on top divides wreath

Date	Mintage	F	VF	XF	Unc	BU
1921	933,000	10.00	20.00	40.00	80.00	—
1921 Proof	—	Value: 400				
1922	13,633,000	3.00	5.00	10.00	20.00	—
1922 Proof	—	Value: 250				
1923	28,504,000	2.00	4.00	8.00	15.00	—
1923 Proof	—	Value: 200				

Y# 82 20 KOPEKS
3.6000 g., 0.5000 Silver 0.0579 oz. ASW **Obv:** National arms within circle **Rev:** Value and date within beaded circle, star on top divides wreath **Note:** Varieties exist.

Date	Mintage	F	VF	XF	Unc	BU
1921	825,000	10.00	20.00	40.00	80.00	—
1921 Proof	—	Value: 500				
1922	14,220,000	4.00	8.00	15.00	30.00	—
1922 Proof	—	Value: 275				
1923	27,580,000	3.00	5.00	10.00	20.00	—
1923 Proof	—	Value: 225				

Y# 83 50 KOPEKS
9.9980 g., 0.9000 Silver 0.2893 oz. ASW **Obv:** National arms within beaded circle **Rev:** Value in center of star within beaded circle **Edge Lettering:** Mintmaster's initials

Date	Mintage	F	VF	XF	Unc	BU
1921 АГ	1,400,000	8.00	10.00	20.00	40.00	—
1921 АГ Proof	—	Value: 750				
1922 АГ	8,224,000	8.00	10.00	20.00	40.00	—
1922 АГ Proof	—	Value: 950				
1922 ПЛ	Inc. above	8.00	10.00	20.00	40.00	—
1922 ПЛ Proof	—	Value: 650				

Y# 84 ROUBLE
19.9960 g., 0.9000 Silver 0.5786 oz. ASW **Obv:** National arms within beaded circle **Rev:** Value in center of star within beaded circle **Edge Lettering:** Mintmaster's initials **Note:** Varieties exist.

Date	Mintage	F	VF	XF	Unc	BU
1921 АГ	1,000,000	15.00	25.00	50.00	100	140
1921 АГ Proof	—	Value: 2,250				
1922 АГ	2,050,000	20.00	35.00	70.00	140	200
1922 АГ Proof	—	Value: 3,000				
1922 ПЛ	Inc. above	20.00	35.00	70.00	140	200
1922 ПЛ Proof	—	Value: 2,750				

TRADE COINAGE

Y# 85 CHERVONETZ (10 Roubles)
8.6026 g., 0.9000 Gold 0.2489 oz. AGW **Obv:** National arms, PCØCP below arms **Rev:** Standing figure with head right **Edge Lettering:** Mintmaster's initials

Date	Mintage	F	VF	XF	Unc	BU
1923 ПЛ	2,751,000	275	400	600	750	1,250
1923 ПЛ Proof	—	Value: 8,000				
1975	250,000	—	—	—	BV+10%	—
1976 ЛМД	1,000,000	—	—	—	BV+10%	—
1976 Rare	—	—	—	—	—	—
1977 ММД	1,000,000	—	—	—	BV+10%	—
1977 ЛМД	1,000,000	—	—	—	BV+10%	—
1978 ММД	350,000	—	—	—	BV+10%	—
1979 ММД	1,000,000	—	—	—	BV+10%	—
1980 ЛМД	900,000	—	—	—	BV+10%	—
1980 ММД	—	—	—	—	—	—
1980 ММД Proof	100,000	Value: 195				
1981 ММД	1,000,000	—	—	—	BV+10%	—
1981 ЛМД Rare	—	—	—	—	—	—
1982 ММД	65,000	—	—	—	BV+10%	—
1982 ЛМД Rare	—	—	—	—	—	—

Y# A86 CHERVONETZ (10 Roubles)
8.6026 g., 0.9000 Gold 0.2489 oz. AGW **Obv:** National arms with CCCP below **Rev:** Standing figure with head right

Date	Mintage	F	VF	XF	Unc	BU
1925 Unique	600,000	—	—	—	—	—

Note: Chervonetz were first struck in 1923 under the R.S.F.S.R. government; in 1925 the U.S.S.R. government attempted a new issue of these coins, of which only one remaining coin is known; from 1975 to 1982 the U.S.S.R. government continued striking the original type with new dates

СССР (U.S.S.R.)

(Union of Soviet Socialist Republics)

STANDARD COINAGE

Y# 75 1/2 KOPEK
Copper **Obv:** CCCP within circle **Rev:** Value and date

Date	Mintage	F	VF	XF	Unc	BU
1925	45,380,000	10.00	15.00	30.00	50.00	—
1927	45,380,000	10.00	15.00	30.00	50.00	—
1927 Proof	—	Value: 350				
1928	—	10.00	20.00	30.00	60.00	—

Y# 76 KOPEK
3.2000 g., Bronze **Obv:** National arms within circle **Rev:** Value and date within oat sprigs

Date	Mintage	F	VF	XF	Unc	BU
1924	34,705,000	10.00	15.00	30.00	60.00	—
Note: Reeded edge						
1924 Proof	—	Value: 400				
Note: Reeded edge						
1924	Inc. above	50.00	100	150	500	—
Note: Plain edge						
1925	141,806,000	80.00	150	200	350	—

Y# 91 KOPEK
1.0300 g., Aluminum-Bronze, 15 mm. **Obv:** National arms within circle **Rev:** Value and date within oat sprigs **Note:** Varieties exist.

Date	Mintage	F	VF	XF	Unc	BU
1926	87,915,000	2.00	3.00	5.00	10.00	—
1926 Proof	—	Value: 200				
1927	—	2.00	3.00	5.00	10.00	—
1928	—	1.00	2.00	4.00	8.00	—
1929	95,950,000	1.00	2.00	4.00	8.00	—
1930	85,351,000	3.00	6.00	10.00	15.00	—
1931	106,100,000	1.00	2.00	4.00	8.00	—
1932	56,900,000	1.00	2.00	4.00	8.00	—
1933	111,257,000	1.00	2.00	4.00	8.00	—
1934	100,245	2.00	5.00	10.00	15.00	—
1935	66,405,000	1.00	2.00	5.00	10.00	—

Y# 98 KOPEK
Aluminum-Bronze **Obv:** National arms **Rev:** Value and date within oat sprigs

Date	Mintage	F	VF	XF	Unc	BU
1935	—	7.00	10.00	15.00	20.00	—
Note: Mintage inc.Y91						
1936	132,204,000	2.00	3.00	5.00	10.00	—

Y# 105 KOPEK
0.9400 g., Aluminum-Bronze, 15.20 mm. **Obv:** National arms **Rev:** Value and date within oat sprigs **Note:** Varieties exist.

Date	Mintage	F	VF	XF	Unc	BU
1937	—	1.00	2.00	3.00	6.00	—
1938	—	1.00	2.00	3.00	6.00	—
1939	—	1.00	2.00	3.00	6.00	—
1940	—	1.00	2.00	3.00	6.00	—
1941	—	2.00	3.00	5.00	10.00	—
1945	—	2.00	3.00	5.00	10.00	—
1946	—	2.00	3.00	5.00	10.00	—

Y# 112 KOPEK
1.0000 g., Aluminum-Bronze **Obv:** National arms **Rev:** Value and date within oat sprigs **Note:** Varieties exist.

Date	Mintage	F	VF	XF	Unc	BU
1948	—	2.00	3.00	5.00	10.00	—
1949	—	2.00	3.00	5.00	10.00	—
1950	—	2.00	3.00	5.00	12.00	—
1951	—	2.00	3.00	5.00	12.00	—
1952	—	1.00	2.00	3.00	5.00	—
1953	—	1.00	2.00	3.00	5.00	—
1954	—	1.00	2.00	3.00	4.00	—
1955	—	1.00	2.00	3.00	4.00	—
1956	—	1.00	2.00	3.00	4.00	—
1957 Rare	—	—	—	—	—	—

Y# 119 KOPEK
Aluminum-Bronze **Obv:** National arms **Rev:** Value and date within oat sprigs

Date	Mintage	F	VF	XF	Unc	BU
1957	—	2.00	4.00	8.00	16.00	—

Y# 126 KOPEK
Copper-Nickel **Obv:** National arms **Rev:** Value and date within oat sprigs

Date	Mintage	F	VF	XF	Unc	BU
1958	30,265,000	—	—	—	300	—

Note: Never officially released for circulation; majority of mintage remelted

Y# 126a KOPEK
1.0000 g., Brass, 15.05 mm. **Obv:** National arms **Rev:** Value and date above spray **Note:** Varieties exist.

Date	Mintage	F	VF	XF	Unc	BU
1961	—	0.10	0.25	0.50	2.00	—
1962	—	0.10	0.30	0.50	1.00	—
1963	—	0.10	0.30	0.50	1.00	—
1964	—	0.20	0.50	1.00	3.00	—
1965	—	0.10	0.30	0.50	1.00	—

Date	Mintage	F	VF	XF	Unc	BU
1966	—	0.10	0.30	0.50	1.00	—
1967	—	0.10	0.30	0.50	1.00	—
1968	—	0.10	0.30	0.50	1.00	—
1969	—	0.10	0.30	0.50	1.00	—
1970	—	0.10	0.30	0.50	1.00	—
1971	—	0.10	0.30	0.50	1.00	—
1972	—	0.20	0.30	0.50	1.00	—
1973	—	0.20	0.30	0.50	1.00	—
1974	—	0.20	0.30	0.50	1.00	—
1975	—	0.20	0.30	0.50	1.00	—
1976	—	0.20	0.30	0.50	1.00	—
1977	—	0.20	0.30	0.50	1.00	—
1978	—	0.20	0.30	0.50	1.00	—
1979	—	0.20	0.30	0.50	1.00	—
1980	—	0.20	0.30	0.50	1.00	—
1981	—	0.20	0.30	0.50	1.00	—
1982	—	0.20	0.30	0.50	1.00	—
1983	—	0.20	0.30	0.50	1.00	—
1984	—	0.20	0.30	0.50	1.00	—
1985	—	0.20	0.30	0.50	1.00	—
1986	—	0.20	0.30	0.50	1.00	—
1987	—	0.20	0.30	0.50	1.00	—
1988	—	0.20	0.30	0.50	1.00	—
1989	—	0.10	0.20	0.30	0.50	—
1990	—	0.10	0.20	0.30	0.50	—
1991 M	—	0.10	0.20	0.30	0.50	—
1991 Л	—	0.10	0.20	0.30	0.50	—

Y# 77 2 KOPEKS

Bronze **Obv:** National arms **Rev:** Value and date within oat sprigs **Note:** Varieties exist.

Date	Mintage	F	VF	XF	Unc	BU
1924	119,996,000	10.00	20.00	40.00	80.00	—
Note: Reeded edge						
1924	Inc. above	50.00	80.00	150	550	—
Note: Plain edge						
1925 Rare	Inc. above	—	—	—	800	—

Y# 92 2 KOPEKS

2.0000 g., Aluminum-Bronze **Obv:** National arms within circle **Rev:** Value and date within oat sprigs **Note:** Varieties exist.

Date	Mintage	F	VF	XF	Unc	BU
1926	105,053,000	1.00	2.00	3.00	6.00	—
1926 Proof	—	Value: 200				
1927 Rare	—	—	—	—	800	—
1928	—	1.00	2.00	3.00	6.00	—
1929	80,000,000	1.00	2.00	3.00	7.00	—
1930	134,186,000	1.00	2.00	3.00	6.00	—
1931	99,523,000	1.00	2.00	3.00	6.00	—
1932	39,573,000	1.00	2.00	3.00	6.00	—
1933	54,874,000	3.00	6.00	8.00	12.00	—
1934	61,574,000	1.00	2.00	4.00	7.00	—
1935	81,121,000	1.00	2.00	4.00	7.00	—

Y# 99 2 KOPEKS

Aluminum-Bronze **Obv:** National arms **Rev:** Value and date within oat sprigs **Note:** Varieties exist.

Date	Mintage	F	VF	XF	Unc	BU
1935	—	2.00	3.00	6.00	12.00	—
1936	94,354,000	2.00	3.00	5.00	9.00	—

Y# 106 2 KOPEKS

2.0000 g., Aluminum-Bronze **Obv:** National arms **Rev:** Value and date within oat sprigs

Date	Mintage	F	VF	XF	Unc	BU
1937	—	1.00	2.00	3.00	5.00	—
1938	—	1.00	2.00	3.00	5.00	—
1939	—	1.00	2.00	3.00	5.00	—
1940	—	1.00	2.00	3.00	4.00	—
1941	—	1.00	2.00	3.00	4.00	—
1945	—	1.00	2.00	4.00	7.00	—
1946	—	1.00	2.00	3.00	6.00	—
1948	—	40.00	70.00	130	225	—

Note: Five ribbons on each wreath

Y# 113 2 KOPEKS

1.8000 g., Aluminum-Bronze **Obv:** National arms **Rev:** Value and date within oat sprigs **Note:** Varieties exist.

Date	Mintage	F	VF	XF	Unc	BU
1948	—	1.00	2.00	3.00	4.00	—
1949	—	1.00	2.00	3.00	4.00	—
1950	—	1.00	2.00	3.00	4.00	—
1951	—	1.00	2.00	3.00	6.00	—
1952	—	0.50	1.00	2.00	3.00	—
1953	—	0.50	1.00	2.00	3.00	—
1954	—	0.50	1.00	2.00	3.00	—
1955	—	0.50	1.00	2.00	3.00	—
1956	—	0.50	1.00	2.00	3.00	—

Y# 120 2 KOPEKS

Aluminum-Bronze **Obv:** National arms **Rev:** Value and date within oat sprigs

Date	Mintage	F	VF	XF	Unc	BU
1957	—	1.00	3.00	6.00	12.00	—

Y# 127 2 KOPEKS

Copper-Nickel **Obv:** National arms **Rev:** Value and date within sprays

Date	Mintage	F	VF	XF	Unc	BU
1958	39,591,000	—	—	—	300	—

Note: Never officially released for circulation; majority of mintage remelted

Y# 127a 2 KOPEKS

2.0000 g., Brass, 18 mm. **Obv:** National arms **Rev:** Value and date within sprays **Note:** Varieties exist.

Date	Mintage	F	VF	XF	Unc	BU
1961	—	0.10	0.15	0.25	0.50	—
1962	—	0.10	0.15	0.25	0.50	—
1963	—	0.10	0.15	0.25	0.50	—
1964	—	0.15	0.25	0.50	1.00	—
1965	—	0.10	0.15	0.25	0.50	—
1966	—	0.10	0.15	0.25	0.50	—
1967	—	0.10	0.15	0.25	0.50	—
1968	—	0.10	0.15	0.25	0.50	—
1969	—	0.10	0.15	0.25	0.50	—
1970	—	0.10	0.15	0.25	0.50	—
1971	—	0.10	0.15	0.25	0.50	—
1972	—	0.10	0.15	0.25	0.50	—
1973	—	0.10	0.15	0.25	0.50	—
1974	—	0.10	0.15	0.25	0.50	—
1975	—	0.10	0.15	0.25	0.50	—
1976	—	0.10	0.15	0.25	0.50	—
1977	—	0.10	0.15	0.25	0.50	—
1978	—	0.10	0.15	0.25	0.50	—
1979	—	0.10	0.15	0.25	0.50	—
1980	—	0.10	0.15	0.25	0.50	—
1981	—	0.10	0.15	0.25	0.50	—
1982	—	0.10	0.15	0.25	0.50	—
1983	—	0.10	0.15	0.25	0.50	—
1984	—	0.10	0.15	0.25	0.50	—
1985	—	0.10	0.15	0.25	0.50	—
1986	—	0.10	0.15	0.25	0.50	—
1987	—	0.10	0.15	0.25	0.50	—
1988	—	0.10	0.15	0.25	0.50	—
1989	—	0.10	0.15	0.20	0.50	—
1990	—	0.10	0.15	0.20	0.50	—
1991 M	—	0.10	0.15	0.20	0.50	—
1991 Л	—	0.10	0.15	0.20	0.50	—

Y# 78 3 KOPEKS

Bronze **Obv:** National arms within circle **Rev:** Value and date within oat sprigs **Note:** Varieties exist.

Date	Mintage	F	VF	XF	Unc	BU
1924	101,283,000	50.00	100	175	275	—
Note: Reeded edge						
1924	Inc. above	6.00	12.50	25.00	65.00	—
Note: Plain edge						

Y# 93 3 KOPEKS

3.0900 g., Aluminum-Bronze, 22 mm. **Obv:** National arms within circle **Rev:** Value and date within oat sprigs **Note:** Varieties exist.

Date	Mintage	F	VF	XF	Unc	BU
1926	19,940,000	2.00	3.00	6.00	10.00	—
1926 Proof	—	Value: 225				
1926 Rare	—	—	—	—	—	—
Note: Obverse of Y#100						
1927	—	5.00	10.00	20.00	40.00	—
1928	—	2.00	3.00	6.00	8.00	—
1929	50,150,000	2.00	3.00	6.00	10.00	—
1930	74,159,000	1.00	2.00	3.00	6.00	—
1931	121,168,000	1.00	2.00	3.00	6.00	—
1931 Rare	—	—	—	—	—	—
Note: Without CCCP obverse						
1932	37,718,000	1.00	2.00	3.00	5.00	—
1933	44,764,000	1.00	2.00	4.00	6.00	—
1934	44,529,000	1.00	2.00	4.00	6.00	—
1935	58,303,000	1.00	2.00	5.00	7.00	—
1937 Rare	—	—	—	—	—	—

Y# 100 3 KOPEKS

Aluminum-Bronze **Obv:** National arms **Rev:** Value and date within oat sprigs **Note:** Varieties exist.

Date	Mintage	F	VF	XF	Unc	BU
1935	—	1.00	3.00	7.00	14.00	—
1936	62,757,000	1.00	2.00	5.00	10.00	—

Y# 107 3 KOPEKS

3.0000 g., Aluminum-Bronze **Obv:** National arms **Rev:** Value and date within oat sprigs **Note:** Varieties exist.

Date	Mintage	F	VF	XF	Unc	BU
1937	—	1.00	2.00	3.00	6.00	—
1938	—	1.00	2.00	3.00	6.00	—
1939	—	1.00	2.00	3.00	6.00	—
1940	—	1.00	2.00	3.00	9.00	—
1941	—	1.00	2.00	3.00	5.00	—
1943	—	1.00	2.00	3.00	5.00	—
1945	—	3.00	5.00	10.00	15.00	—
1946	—	1.00	2.00	3.00	6.00	—
1948 Five ribbons on each wreath	—	40.00	70.00	130	225	—

Y# 114 3 KOPEKS
Aluminum-Bronze **Obv:** National arms **Rev:** Value and date within oat sprigs **Note:** Varieties exist.

Date	Mintage	F	VF	XF	Unc	BU
1946 Rare	—	—	—	—	—	—
1948	—	1.00	2.00	3.00	6.00	—
1949	—	1.00	2.00	3.00	4.00	—
1950	—	1.00	2.00	3.00	4.00	—
1951	—	1.00	2.00	4.00	7.00	—
1952	—	1.00	2.00	3.00	4.00	—
1953	—	1.00	2.00	3.00	4.00	—
1954	—	1.00	2.00	3.00	4.00	—
1955	—	1.00	2.00	3.00	4.00	—
1956	—	1.00	2.00	3.00	4.00	—
1957	—	5.00	10.00	30.00	50.00	—

Y# 121 3 KOPEKS
Aluminum-Bronze **Obv:** National arms **Rev:** Value and date within oat sprigs

Date	Mintage	F	VF	XF	Unc	BU
1957	—	2.00	3.00	6.00	12.00	—

Y# 128 3 KOPEKS
Copper-Zinc **Obv:** National arms **Rev:** Value and date within sprigs

Date	Mintage	F	VF	XF	Unc	BU
1958	26,676,000	—	—	—	300	—

Note: Never officially released for circulation; majority of mintage remelted

Y# 128a 3 KOPEKS
3.0000 g., Aluminum-Bronze, 22.05 mm. **Obv:** National arms **Rev:** Value and date within sprigs **Note:** Varieties exist.

Date	Mintage	F	VF	XF	Unc	BU
1961	—	0.10	0.15	0.25	0.60	—
1962	—	0.25	0.50	1.00	2.00	—
1965	—	0.25	0.50	1.00	2.00	—
1966	—	0.10	0.15	0.25	0.60	—
1967	—	0.10	0.15	0.25	0.60	—
1968	—	0.10	0.15	0.25	0.60	—
1969	—	0.10	0.15	0.25	0.60	—
1970	—	0.10	0.15	0.25	0.60	—
1971	—	0.10	0.15	0.25	0.60	—
1972	—	0.10	0.15	0.25	0.60	—
1973	—	0.10	0.15	0.25	0.60	—
1974	—	0.10	0.15	0.25	0.60	—
1975	—	0.10	0.15	0.25	0.60	—
1976	—	0.10	0.15	0.25	0.60	—
1977	—	0.10	0.15	0.25	0.60	—
1978	—	0.10	0.15	0.25	0.60	—
1979	—	0.10	0.15	0.25	0.60	—
1980	—	0.10	0.15	0.25	0.60	—
1981	—	0.10	0.15	0.25	0.60	—
1982	—	0.10	0.15	0.25	0.60	—
1983	—	0.10	0.15	0.25	0.60	—
1984	—	0.10	0.15	0.25	0.60	—
1985	—	0.10	0.15	0.25	0.60	—
1986	—	0.10	0.15	0.25	0.60	—
1987	—	0.10	0.15	0.25	0.60	—
1988	—	0.10	0.15	0.25	0.60	—
1989	—	0.10	0.15	0.20	0.40	—
1990	—	0.10	0.15	0.20	0.40	—
1991 М	—	0.10	0.15	0.20	0.40	—
1991 Л	—	0.10	0.15	0.20	0.40	—

Y# 79 5 KOPEKS
Bronze **Obv:** National arms within circle **Rev:** Value and date within oat sprigs **Note:** Varieties exist.

Date	Mintage	F	VF	XF	Unc	BU
1924	88,510,000	50.00	100	175	275	—
Note: Reeded edge						
1924	Inc. above	7.00	15.00	30.00	75.00	—
Note: Plain edge						

Y# 94 5 KOPEKS
5.0000 g., Aluminum-Bronze **Obv:** National arms **Rev:** Value and date **Note:** Varieties exist.

Date	Mintage	F	VF	XF	Unc	BU
1926	14,697,000	3.00	5.00	10.00	20.00	—
1926 Proof	—	Value: 250				
1927	—	20.00	60.00	100	150	—
1928	—	3.00	5.00	10.00	15.00	—
1929	20,220,000	5.00	10.00	15.00	20.00	—
1930	44,490,000	2.00	3.00	4.00	8.00	—
1931	89,540,000	2.00	3.00	4.00	8.00	—
1932	65,100,000	2.00	3.00	4.00	8.00	—
1933	18,135,000	25.00	50.00	100	300	—
1934	5,354,000	25.00	50.00	90.00	120	—
1935	11,735,000	5.00	10.00	15.00	50.00	—

Y# 101 5 KOPEKS
Aluminum-Bronze **Obv:** National arms **Rev:** Value and date within oat sprigs **Note:** Varieties exist.

Date	Mintage	F	VF	XF	Unc	BU
1935	—	5.00	8.00	12.00	26.00	—
1936	5,242,000	5.00	8.00	12.00	28.00	—

Y# 108 5 KOPEKS
5.2100 g., Aluminum-Bronze, 25.1 mm. **Obv:** National arms **Rev:** Value and date within oat sprigs **Note:** Varieties exist.

Date	Mintage	F	VF	XF	Unc	BU
1937	—	5.00	9.00	15.00	30.00	—
1938	—	2.00	3.00	4.00	8.00	—
1939	—	2.00	3.00	4.00	8.00	—
1940	—	2.00	3.00	4.00	8.00	—
1941	—	2.00	3.00	4.00	8.00	—
1943	—	2.00	3.00	4.00	8.00	—
1945	—	5.00	8.00	15.00	20.00	—
1946	—	2.00	3.00	4.00	8.00	—

Y# 115 5 KOPEKS
4.8000 g., Aluminum-Bronze **Obv:** National arms **Rev:** Value and date withing oat sprigs **Note:** Varieties exist.

Date	Mintage	F	VF	XF	Unc	BU
1948	—	1.00	2.00	3.00	5.00	—
1949	—	1.00	2.00	3.00	4.00	—
1950	—	1.00	2.00	3.00	4.00	—
1951	—	4.00	6.00	8.00	12.00	—
1952	—	1.00	2.00	3.00	5.00	—
1953	—	1.00	2.00	3.00	5.00	—
1954	—	1.00	2.00	3.00	5.00	—
1955	—	1.00	2.00	3.00	5.00	—
1956	—	1.00	2.00	3.00	5.00	—

Y# 122 5 KOPEKS
4.9000 g., Aluminum-Bronze **Obv:** National arms **Rev:** Value and date within oat sprigs **Note:** Varieties exist.

Date	Mintage	F	VF	XF	Unc	BU
1957	—	3.00	6.00	8.00	12.00	—

Y# 129 5 KOPEKS
Copper-Zinc **Obv:** National arms **Rev:** Value and date within sprigs

Date	Mintage	F	VF	XF	Unc	BU
1958	61,119,000	—	—	—	600	—

Note: Never officially released for circulation; majority of mintage remelted

Y# 129a 5 KOPEKS
5.0000 g., Aluminum-Bronze, 25.1 mm. **Obv:** National arms **Rev:** Value and date within sprigs **Note:** Varieties exist.

Date	Mintage	F	VF	XF	Unc	BU
1961	—	0.20	0.30	0.50	1.00	—
1962	—	0.20	0.30	0.50	1.00	—
1965	—	3.00	5.00	8.00	12.00	—
1966	—	2.00	4.00	7.00	12.00	—
1967	—	0.50	1.00	1.50	3.00	—
1968	—	0.50	1.00	1.50	3.00	—
1969	—	2.00	4.00	6.00	10.00	—
1970	—	10.00	15.00	35.00	60.00	—
1971	—	2.00	4.00	6.00	10.00	—
1972	—	2.00	4.00	6.00	10.00	—
1973	—	1.00	1.50	2.00	3.00	—
1974	—	0.10	0.20	0.50	1.00	—
1975	—	0.10	0.20	0.50	1.00	—
1976	—	0.10	0.15	0.30	0.75	—
1977	—	0.10	0.15	0.30	0.75	—
1978	—	0.10	0.15	0.30	0.75	—
1979	—	0.10	0.15	0.30	0.75	—
1980	—	0.10	0.15	0.30	0.75	—
1981	—	0.10	0.15	0.30	0.75	—
1982	—	0.10	0.15	0.30	0.70	—
1983	—	0.10	0.15	0.30	0.75	—
1984	—	0.10	0.15	0.30	0.75	—
1985	—	0.10	0.15	0.30	0.75	—
1986	—	0.10	0.15	0.30	0.75	—
1987	—	0.10	0.15	0.30	0.75	—
1988	—	0.10	0.15	0.30	0.75	—
1989	—	0.10	0.15	0.25	0.50	—
1990	—	0.15	0.25	0.45	1.25	—
1990M	—	7.00	10.00	20.00	30.00	—
1991M	—	0.10	0.15	0.25	0.50	—
1991	—	0.10	0.15	0.25	0.50	—

Y# 86 10 KOPEKS

1.8000 g., 0.5000 Silver 0.0289 oz. ASW **Obv:** National arms within circle **Rev:** Value and date within oat sprigs **Note:** Varieties exist.

Date	Mintage	F	VF	XF	Unc	BU
1924	67,351,000	2.00	4.00	8.00	12.00	—
1924 Proof	—	Value: 450				
1925	101,013,000	2.00	4.00	8.00	12.00	—
1925 Proof	—	Value: 225				
1927	—	2.00	4.00	8.00	12.00	—
1927 Proof	—	Value: 225				
1928	—	1.00	2.00	5.00	10.00	—
1929	64,900,000	2.00	4.00	8.00	12.00	—
1930	163,424,000	1.00	2.00	5.00	10.00	—
1931 Rare	8,791,000	—	—	—	—	—

Y# 95 10 KOPEKS

1.8200 g., Copper-Nickel, 17.4 mm. **Obv:** National arms within circle **Rev:** Value on shield held by figure at left looking right **Note:** Varieties exist.

Date	Mintage	F	VF	XF	Unc	BU
1931	122,511,000	3.00	5.00	8.00	14.00	—
1932	171,641,000	2.00	3.00	4.00	6.00	—
1933	163,125,000	2.00	3.00	4.00	6.00	—
1934	104,059,000	2.00	3.00	4.00	7.00	—

Y# 102 10 KOPEKS

1.8000 g., Copper-Nickel **Obv:** National arms **Rev:** Value within octagon flanked by sprigs with date below

Date	Mintage	F	VF	XF	Unc	BU
1935	79,628,000	2.00	3.00	4.00	8.00	—
1936	122,260,000	1.00	2.00	3.00	6.00	—

Y# 109 10 KOPEKS

1.6900 g., Copper-Nickel, 17.5 mm. **Obv:** National arms **Rev:** Value within octagon flanked by sprigs with date below **Note:** Varieties exist.

Date	Mintage	F	VF	XF	Unc	BU
1937	—	2.00	3.00	4.00	8.00	—
1938	—	1.00	2.00	3.00	5.00	—
1939	—	1.00	2.00	3.00	5.00	—
1940	—	1.00	2.00	3.00	5.00	—
1941	—	1.00	2.00	3.00	5.00	—
1942	—	15.00	40.00	75.00	100	—
1943	—	1.00	2.00	3.00	5.00	—
1944	—	4.00	10.00	20.00	40.00	—
1945	—	1.00	2.00	3.00	5.00	—
1946	—	1.00	2.00	3.00	5.00	—

Y# A110 10 KOPEKS

Copper-Nickel **Obv:** National arms **Rev:** Value within octagon flanked by sprigs **Note:** Mule.

Date	Mintage	F	VF	XF	Unc	BU
1946 Rare	—	—	—	—	—	—

Y# 116 10 KOPEKS

1.8000 g., Copper-Nickel **Obv:** National arms, 8 and 7 ribbons on wreath **Rev:** Value within octagon flanked by sprigs with date below **Note:** Varieties exist.

Date	Mintage	F	VF	XF	Unc	BU
1948	—	1.00	2.00	3.00	5.00	—
1949	—	1.00	2.00	3.00	4.00	—
1950	—	1.00	2.00	3.00	4.00	—
1951	—	1.00	2.00	3.00	5.00	—
1952	—	1.00	2.00	3.00	4.00	—
1953	—	0.50	1.00	2.00	3.00	—
1954	—	0.50	1.00	2.00	3.00	—
1955	—	0.50	1.00	2.00	3.00	—
1956	—	0.50	1.00	2.00	3.00	—
1956	—	20.00	35.00	60.00	100	—

Note: Reverse of Y#123

Y# 123 10 KOPEKS

1.8000 g., Copper-Nickel **Obv:** National arms, 7 and 7 ribbons on wreath **Rev:** Value within octagon flanked by sprigs with date below

Date	Mintage	F	VF	XF	Unc	BU
1957	—	20.00	30.00	60.00	100	—

Note: Reverse of Y#116

Date	Mintage	F	VF	XF	Unc	BU
1957	—	1.00	2.00	3.00	6.00	—

Y# A130 10 KOPEKS

Copper-Nickel **Obv:** National arms **Rev:** Value and date within sprigs

Date	Mintage	F	VF	XF	Unc	BU
1958	108,023,000	—	—	—	300	—

Note: Never officially released for circulation; majority of mintage remelted

Y# 130 10 KOPEKS

1.6000 g., Copper-Nickel-Zinc, 17.35 mm. **Obv:** National arms **Rev:** Value and date flanked by sprigs

Date	Mintage	F	VF	XF	Unc	BU
1961	—	0.10	0.20	0.35	0.75	—
1962	—	0.10	0.20	0.35	0.75	—
1965	—	3.00	5.00	10.00	15.00	—
1966	—	1.00	2.50	5.00	10.00	—
1967	—	0.50	0.80	1.50	3.00	—
1968	—	0.10	0.20	0.35	0.75	—
1969	—	0.10	0.20	0.35	0.75	—
1970	—	0.10	0.20	0.35	0.75	—
1971	—	0.10	0.20	0.35	0.75	—
1972	—	0.10	0.20	0.35	0.75	—
1973	—	0.10	0.20	0.35	0.75	—
1974	—	0.10	0.20	0.35	0.75	—
1975	—	0.10	0.20	0.35	0.75	—
1976	—	0.10	0.20	0.35	0.75	—
1977	—	0.10	0.20	0.35	0.75	—
1978	—	0.10	0.20	0.35	0.75	—
1979	—	0.10	0.20	0.35	0.75	—
1980	—	0.10	0.20	0.35	0.75	—
1981	—	0.10	0.20	0.35	0.75	—
1982	—	0.10	0.20	0.35	0.75	—
1983	—	0.10	0.20	0.35	0.75	—
1984	—	0.10	0.20	0.35	0.75	—
1985	—	0.10	0.20	0.35	0.75	—
1986	—	0.10	0.20	0.35	0.75	—
1987	—	0.10	0.20	0.35	0.75	—
1988	—	0.10	0.20	0.35	0.75	—
1989	—	0.10	0.20	0.30	0.50	—
1990	—	0.25	0.50	1.00	2.50	—
1990 Л	—	0.10	0.20	0.30	0.50	—
1990 М	—	4.00	7.50	12.50	20.00	—
1991	—	0.15	0.25	0.50	1.25	—
1991 Л	—	0.10	0.20	0.30	0.50	—
1991 М	—	0.10	0.20	0.30	0.50	—

Y# 136 10 KOPEKS

Copper-Nickel-Zinc, 17 mm. **Subject:** 50th Anniversary of Revolution **Obv:** National arms within radiant circle with dates at right **Rev:** Value above radiant sun and design

Date	Mintage	F	VF	XF	Unc	BU
1967	49,789,000	—	0.20	0.30	1.00	—
1967 Prooflike	211,000	—	—	—	—	—

Y# 87 15 KOPEKS

2.7000 g., 0.5000 Silver 0.0434 oz. ASW **Obv:** National arms within circle **Rev:** Value and date within oat sprigs **Note:** Varieties exist.

Date	Mintage	F	VF	XF	Unc	BU
1924	72,426,000	2.00	3.00	6.00	12.00	—
1924 Proof	—	Value: 450				
1925	112,709,000	2.00	3.00	5.00	10.00	—
1925 Proof	—	Value: 225				
1927	—	2.00	3.00	5.00	10.00	—
1927 Proof	—	Value: 225				
1928	—	2.00	3.00	5.00	10.00	—
1929	46,400,000	2.00	3.00	5.00	10.00	—
1930	79,868,000	2.00	3.00	5.00	10.00	—
1931 Rare	5,099,000	—	—	—	—	—

Y# 96 15 KOPEKS

Copper-Nickel, 20 mm. **Obv:** National arms within circle **Rev:** Value on shield held by figure at left looking right **Note:** Varieties exist.

Date	Mintage	F	VF	XF	Unc	BU
1931	75,859,000	2.00	3.00	5.00	9.00	—
1932	136,046,000	1.00	2.00	3.00	5.00	—
1933	127,591,000	1.00	2.00	3.00	5.00	—
1934	58,367,000	2.00	3.00	4.00	7.00	—

Y# 103 15 KOPEKS

2.7000 g., Copper-Nickel, 20 mm. **Obv:** National arms **Rev:** Value within octagon flanked by sprigs with date below

Date	Mintage	F	VF	XF	Unc	BU
1935	51,308,000	2.00	3.00	4.00	7.00	—
1936	52,183,000	2.00	3.00	4.00	7.00	—

Y# 110 15 KOPEKS

2.6800 g., Copper-Nickel, 20 mm. **Obv:** National arms **Rev:** Value within octagon flanked by sprigs with date below **Note:** Varieties exist.

Date	Mintage	F	VF	XF	Unc	BU
1937	—	2.00	3.00	4.00	7.00	—
1938	—	1.00	2.00	3.00	5.00	—
1939	—	1.00	2.00	3.00	5.00	—
1940	—	1.00	2.00	3.00	5.00	—
1941	—	1.00	2.00	3.00	5.00	—
1942	—	18.00	50.00	80.00	100	—
1943	—	1.00	2.00	4.00	6.00	—
1944	—	2.00	4.00	8.00	12.00	—
1945	—	1.00	2.00	3.00	5.00	—
1946	—	1.00	2.00	3.00	4.00	—

Y# 117 15 KOPEKS

2.7000 g., Copper-Nickel, 20 mm. **Obv:** National arms, 8 and 7 ribbons on wreath **Rev:** Value within octagon flanked by sprigs with date below **Note:** Varieties exist.

Date	Mintage	F	VF	XF	Unc	BU
1948	—	1.00	2.00	3.00	5.00	—
1949	—	1.00	2.00	3.00	5.00	—
1950	—	0.50	1.00	2.00	3.00	—
1951	—	1.00	2.00	4.00	8.00	—
1952	—	1.00	2.00	3.00	4.00	—
1953	—	1.00	2.00	3.00	4.00	—
1954	—	1.00	2.00	3.00	4.00	—

Date	Mintage	F	VF	XF	Unc	BU
1955	—	1.00	2.00	3.00	4.00	—
1956	—	1.00	2.00	3.00	4.00	—

Y# 124 15 KOPEKS

Copper-Nickel, 20 mm. **Obv:** National arms **Rev:** Value within octagon flanked by sprigs with date below

Date	Mintage	F	VF	XF	Unc	BU
1957	—	2.00	3.00	6.00	8.00	—

Y# A131 15 KOPEKS

Copper-Nickel, 20 mm. **Obv:** National arms **Rev:** Value and date within sprigs

Date	Mintage	F	VF	XF	Unc	BU
1958	80,052,000	—	—	—	1,000	—

Note: Never officially released for circulation; majority of mintage remelted

Y# 131 15 KOPEKS

2.5000 g., Copper-Nickel-Zinc, 19.5 mm. **Obv:** National arms **Rev:** Value and date flanked by sprigs

Date	Mintage	F	VF	XF	Unc	BU
1961	—	0.10	0.20	0.40	0.75	—
1962	—	0.10	0.20	0.40	1.00	—
1965	—	1.00	2.00	4.00	7.50	—
1966	—	1.00	2.00	4.00	7.50	—
1967	—	0.50	1.00	2.00	4.00	—
1968	—	0.25	0.50	1.00	2.00	—
1969	—	0.10	0.20	0.40	0.75	—
1970	—	15.00	25.00	40.00	75.00	—
1971	—	1.00	3.00	5.00	10.00	—
1972	—	1.00	3.00	5.00	10.00	—
1973	—	1.00	3.00	5.00	10.00	—
1974	—	0.10	0.20	0.40	0.75	—
1975	—	0.10	0.20	0.40	0.75	—
1976	—	0.10	0.20	0.40	0.75	—
1977	—	0.10	0.20	0.40	0.75	—
1978	—	0.10	0.20	0.40	0.75	—
1979	—	0.10	0.20	0.40	0.75	—
1980	—	0.10	0.20	0.40	0.75	—
1981	—	0.10	0.20	0.40	0.75	—
1982	—	0.10	0.20	0.40	0.75	—
1983	—	0.10	0.20	0.40	0.75	—
1984	—	0.10	0.20	0.40	0.75	—
1985	—	0.10	0.20	0.40	0.75	—
1986	—	0.10	0.20	0.40	0.75	—
1987	—	0.10	0.20	0.40	0.75	—
1988	—	0.10	0.20	0.40	0.75	—
1989	—	0.10	0.20	0.30	0.50	—
1990	—	0.10	0.20	0.30	0.50	—
1991 М	—	0.10	0.20	0.30	0.50	—
1991 Л	—	0.10	0.20	0.30	0.50	—

Y# 137 15 KOPEKS

Copper-Nickel-Zinc, 20 mm. **Subject:** 50th Anniversary of Revolution **Obv:** National arms above value **Rev:** Statue of Laborers and dates **Rev. Designer:** Vera Muchina

Date	Mintage	F	VF	XF	Unc	BU
1967	49,789,000	0.30	0.50	1.00	2.00	—
1967 Prooflike	211,000	—	—	—	—	3.00

Y# 88 20 KOPEKS

3.6000 g., 0.5000 Silver 0.0579 oz. ASW **Obv:** National arms within circle **Rev:** Value and date within oat sprigs

Date	Mintage	F	VF	XF	Unc	BU
1924	93,810,000	3.00	5.00	10.00	18.00	—
1924 Proof	—	Value: 500				
1925	135,188,000	2.00	4.00	8.00	15.00	—
1925 Proof	—	Value: 225				
1927	—	2.00	4.00	8.00	15.00	—
1928	—	2.00	4.00	8.00	12.00	—
1929	67,250,000	2.00	4.00	8.00	12.00	—
1930	125,658,000	2.00	3.00	5.00	9.00	—
1931	9,530,000	—	—	—	800	—

Y# 97 20 KOPEKS

3.4800 g., Copper-Nickel, 22 mm. **Obv:** National arms within circle **Rev:** Value on shield held by figure at left looking right **Note:** Varieties exist.

Date	Mintage	F	VF	XF	Unc	BU
1931	82,200,000	2.00	3.00	4.00	8.00	—
1932	175,350,000	1.00	2.00	3.00	5.00	—
1933	143,927,000	1.00	2.00	4.00	6.00	—
1934	70,425,000	—	—	—	—	—

Y# 104 20 KOPEKS

Copper-Nickel **Obv:** National arms **Rev:** Value within octagon flanked by sprigs with date below **Note:** Varieties exist.

Date	Mintage	F	VF	XF	Unc	BU
1935	125,165,000	1.00	2.00	3.00	5.00	—
1936	52,968,000	1.00	2.00	3.00	6.00	—
1941 Rare	—	—	—	—	—	—

Y# 111 20 KOPEKS

3.6100 g., Copper-Nickel, 22.5 mm. **Obv:** National arms **Rev:** Value within octagon flanked by sprigs with date below **Note:** Varieties exist.

Date	Mintage	F	VF	XF	Unc	BU
1937	—	1.00	2.00	3.00	5.00	—
1938	—	1.00	2.00	3.00	5.00	—
1939	—	1.00	2.00	3.00	5.00	—
1940	—	1.00	2.00	3.00	5.00	—
1941	—	1.00	2.00	3.00	5.00	—
1942	—	1.00	2.00	3.00	6.00	—
1943	—	1.00	2.00	3.00	4.00	—
1944	—	1.00	3.00	4.00	6.00	—
1945	—	1.00	2.00	3.00	5.00	—
1946	—	1.00	2.00	4.00	6.00	—

Y# 118 20 KOPEKS

3.6000 g., Copper-Nickel **Obv:** National arms, 8 and 7 ribbons on wreath **Rev:** Value within octagon flanked by sprigs with date below **Note:** Varieties exist.

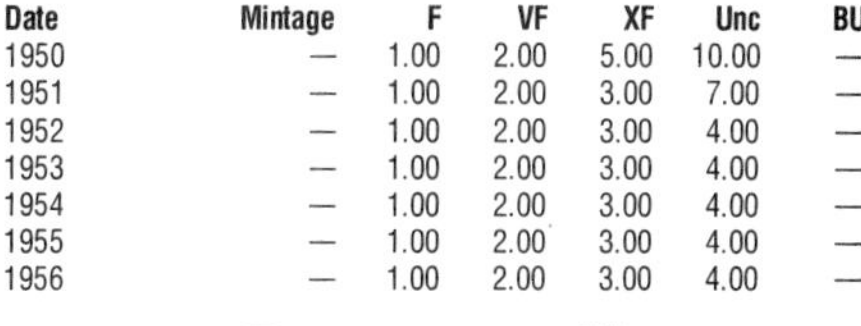

Date	Mintage	F	VF	XF	Unc	BU
1948	—	1.00	2.00	3.00	5.00	—
1949	—	1.00	2.00	3.00	5.00	—
1950	—	1.00	2.00	5.00	10.00	—
1951	—	1.00	2.00	3.00	7.00	—
1952	—	1.00	2.00	3.00	4.00	—
1953	—	1.00	2.00	3.00	4.00	—
1954	—	1.00	2.00	3.00	4.00	—
1955	—	1.00	2.00	3.00	4.00	—
1956	—	1.00	2.00	3.00	4.00	—

Y# 125 20 KOPEKS

Copper-Nickel **Obv:** National arms **Rev:** Value within octagon flanked by sprigs with date below

Date	Mintage	F	VF	XF	Unc	BU
1957	—	2.00	3.00	4.00	8.00	—

Y# A132 20 KOPEKS

Copper-Nickel **Obv:** National arms **Rev:** Value and date within sprigs

Date	Mintage	F	VF	XF	Unc	BU
1958	175,355,000	—	—	—	450	—

Note: Never officially released for circulation; majority of mintage remelted

Y# 132 20 KOPEKS

3.3000 g., Copper-Nickel-Zinc, 22 mm. **Obv:** National arms **Rev:** Value and date flanked by sprigs **Note:** Varieties exist.

Date	Mintage	F	VF	XF	Unc	BU
1961	—	0.15	0.30	0.50	1.00	—
1962	—	0.15	0.35	0.75	1.50	—
1965	—	1.00	3.00	5.00	10.00	—
1966	—	1.00	3.00	5.00	10.00	—
1967	—	0.50	1.00	2.00	3.00	—
1968	—	0.15	0.30	0.50	1.00	—
1969	—	0.50	1.00	2.00	4.00	—
1970	—	10.00	22.50	30.00	40.00	—
1971	—	0.50	1.00	2.00	3.00	—
1972	—	1.00	2.00	4.00	7.50	—
1973	—	10.00	15.00	25.00	40.00	—
1974	—	1.50	3.00	5.00	9.00	—
1975	—	1.00	3.00	4.00	7.50	—
1976	—	15.00	25.00	40.00	60.00	—
1977	—	0.15	0.30	0.50	1.00	—
1978	—	0.15	0.30	0.50	1.00	—
1979	—	0.15	0.30	0.50	1.00	—
1980	—	0.15	0.30	0.50	1.00	—
1981	—	0.15	0.30	0.50	1.00	—
1982	—	0.15	0.30	0.50	1.00	—
1983	—	0.15	0.30	0.50	1.00	—
1984	—	0.15	0.30	0.50	1.00	—
1985	—	0.15	0.30	0.50	1.00	—
1986	—	0.15	0.30	0.50	1.00	—
1987	—	0.15	0.30	0.50	1.00	—
1988	—	0.15	0.30	0.50	1.00	—
1989	—	0.10	0.20	0.30	0.75	—
1990	—	0.10	0.20	0.30	0.75	—
1991	—	30.00	70.00	100	300	—
1991 М	—	0.10	0.20	0.30	0.75	—
1991 Л	—	0.10	0.20	0.30	0.50	—

Y# 138 20 KOPEKS

Copper-Nickel-Zinc **Subject:** 50th Anniversary of Revolution **Obv:** National arms flanked by dates with inscription below **Rev:** Cruiser ship below value

Date	Mintage	F	VF	XF	Unc	BU
1967	49,789,000	1.00	2.00	3.00	4.00	—
1967 Prooflike	211,000	—	—	—	—	—

Y# 89.1 50 KOPEKS

9.9980 g., 0.9000 Silver 0.2893 oz. ASW **Obv:** National arms divide CCCP above inscription, circle surrounds all **Rev:** Blacksmith at anvil **Rev. Designer:** Thomas Ross **Edge Lettering:** Weight shown in old Russian units

Date	Mintage	F	VF	XF	Unc	BU
1924 ПЛ	26,559,000	10.00	15.00	20.00	40.00	—
1924 ПЛ Proof	—	Value: 550				
1924 ТР	40,000,000	10.00	15.00	20.00	40.00	—

Y# 89.2 50 KOPEKS

9.9980 g., 0.9000 Silver 0.2893 oz. ASW **Obv:** National arms divide CCCP above inscription, circle surrounds all **Rev:** Blacksmith at anvil **Rev. Designer:** Thomas Ross **Edge Lettering:** Weight shown in ЖУДПП (grams) only **Note:** Varieties exist.

Date	Mintage	F	VF	XF	Unc	BU
1925 ПЛ	43,558,000	10.00	15.00	20.00	40.00	—
1925 ПЛ Proof	—	Value: 400				
1926 ПЛ	24,374,000	10.00	15.00	20.00	40.00	—
1926 ПЛ Proof	—	Value: 400				
1927 ПЛ	—	15.00	20.00	30.00	50.00	—
1927 ПЛ Proof	—	Value: 500				

Y# 133 50 KOPEKS

Copper-Nickel **Obv:** National arms **Rev:** Value and date within sprigs

Date	Mintage	F	VF	XF	Unc	BU
1958	40,600,000	—	—	—	1,000	—

Note: Never officially released for circulation; majority of mintage remelted

Y# 133a.1 50 KOPEKS

4.6000 g., Copper-Nickel-Zinc **Obv:** National arms **Rev:** Value and date within sprigs **Edge:** Plain **Note:** Varieties exist.

Date	Mintage	F	VF	XF	Unc	BU
1961	—	2.00	4.00	8.00	15.00	—

Y# 133a.2 50 KOPEKS

4.4000 g., Copper-Nickel-Zinc, 24.05 mm. **Obv:** National arms **Rev:** Value and date within sprigs **Edge:** Lettered with date **Note:** Varieties exist for 1970, 1971, and 1975.

Date	Mintage	F	VF	XF	Unc	BU
1964	—	0.20	0.40	0.75	1.50	—
1965	—	0.20	0.40	0.75	1.50	—
1966	—	0.20	0.40	0.75	1.50	—
1967	—	1.00	1.50	3.00	5.00	—
1968	—	0.20	0.40	0.75	1.50	—
1969	—	0.20	0.40	0.75	1.50	—
1970	—	2.00	5.00	10.00	20.00	—
1971	—	2.00	5.00	10.00	10.00	—
1972	—	0.20	0.40	0.75	1.50	—
1973	—	0.20	0.40	0.75	1.50	—
1974	—	0.20	0.40	0.75	1.50	—
1975	—	1.00	2.50	5.00	10.00	—
1976	—	0.50	1.00	3.00	6.00	—
1977	—	0.20	0.40	0.75	1.50	—
1978	—	0.20	0.40	0.75	1.50	—
1979	—	0.20	0.40	0.75	1.50	—
1980	—	0.20	0.40	0.75	1.50	—
1981	—	0.20	0.40	0.75	1.50	—
1982	—	0.20	0.40	0.75	1.50	—
1983	—	0.20	0.40	0.75	1.50	—
1984	—	0.20	0.40	0.75	1.50	—
1985	—	0.20	0.40	0.75	1.50	—
1986	—	6.00	12.50	25.00	50.00	—
Note: With 1985 on edge						
1986	—	0.20	0.40	0.75	1.50	—
1987	—	0.20	0.40	0.75	1.50	—
1988	—	1.00	2.00	4.00	10.00	—
Note: With 1987 on edge						
1988	—	0.20	0.40	0.75	1.50	—
1989	—	6.00	12.50	25.00	50.00	—
Note: With 1988 on edge						
1989	—	0.15	0.25	0.50	1.00	—
1990	—	0.15	0.25	0.50	1.00	—
1990 Rare	—	—	—	—	—	—
Note: With 1989 on edge						
1991 М	—	0.15	0.25	0.50	1.00	—
1991 Л	—	0.15	0.25	0.50	1.00	—

Y# 139 50 KOPEKS

Copper-Nickel-Zinc, 25 mm. **Subject:** 50th Anniversary of Revolution **Obv:** National arms **Rev:** Lenin with right arm raised facing left, star at upper left

Date	Mintage	F	VF	XF	Unc	BU
ND(1967)	49,789,000	—	2.00	3.00	4.00	—
ND(1967) Prooflike	—	—	—	—	3.00	—

Y# 90.1 ROUBLE

19.9960 g., 0.9000 Silver 0.5786 oz. ASW **Obv:** National arms divides circle with inscription within **Rev:** Two figures walking right, radiant sun rising at right **Edge Lettering:** 18 ЖУДПП (grams) (43.21d) **Note:** Varieties exist.

Date	Mintage	F	VF	XF	Unc	BU
1924 ПЛ	12,998,000	15.00	30.00	50.00	100	150
1924 ПЛ Proof	—	Value: 2,500				

Y# 90.2 ROUBLE

19.9960 g., 0.9000 Silver 0.5786 oz. ASW **Obv:** National arms divides circle holding inscription **Rev:** Two figures walking right, sun rising at right **Edge:** 4 Zolotniks 21 Dolyas

Date	Mintage	F	VF	XF	Unc	BU
1924 Rare	—	—	—	—	—	—

Y# 134 ROUBLE

Copper-Nickel **Obv:** National arms **Rev:** Value and date within sprigs

Date	Mintage	F	VF	XF	Unc	BU
1958	30,700,000	—	—	—	900	—

Note: Never officially released for circulation; majority of mintage remelted

Y# 134a.1 ROUBLE

Copper-Nickel-Zinc **Obv:** National arms within circle **Rev:** Value and date within sprigs **Edge:** Plain

Date	Mintage	F	VF	XF	Unc	BU
1961	—	3.00	6.00	10.00	20.00	—

Y# 134a.2 ROUBLE

7.4000 g., Copper-Nickel-Zinc, 27 mm. **Obv:** National arms within circle **Rev:** Value and date within sprigs **Edge:** Lettered with date

Date	Mintage	F	VF	XF	Unc	BU
1964	—	0.40	0.75	1.50	2.50	—
1965	—	1.00	1.50	2.50	4.00	—
1966	—	0.40	0.75	1.50	2.50	—
1967 Rare	—	—	—	—	—	—
Note: With 1966 on edge						
1967	—	0.40	0.75	1.50	2.50	—
1968	—	0.40	0.75	1.50	2.50	—
1969	—	0.40	0.75	1.50	2.50	—
1970	—	0.40	0.75	1.50	2.50	—
1971	—	0.40	0.75	1.50	2.50	—
1972	—	0.40	0.75	1.50	2.50	—
1973	—	0.40	0.75	1.50	2.50	—
1974	—	0.40	0.75	1.50	2.50	—
1975	—	0.40	0.75	1.50	2.50	—
1976	—	0.40	0.75	1.50	2.50	—
1977	—	0.40	0.75	1.50	2.50	—
1978	—	0.40	0.75	1.50	2.50	—
1979	—	0.40	0.75	1.50	2.50	—
1980	—	0.40	0.75	1.50	2.50	—
1981	—	0.40	0.75	1.50	2.50	—
1982	—	0.40	0.75	1.50	2.50	—
1983	—	0.40	0.75	1.50	2.50	—
1984	—	0.40	0.75	1.50	2.50	—
1985	—	0.40	0.75	1.50	2.50	—
1986	—	0.40	0.75	1.50	2.50	—
1987	—	0.40	0.75	1.50	2.50	—
1988	—	0.40	0.75	1.50	2.50	—
1988	—	1.50	3.00	6.00	15.00	—
Note: With 1989 on edge						
1989	—	0.25	0.50	1.00	2.50	—
1990	—	1.50	3.00	6.00	15.00	—
Note: With 1989 on edge						
1990	—	0.25	0.50	1.00	2.50	—
1991 М	—	0.25	0.50	1.00	2.50	—
1991 Л	—	0.25	0.50	1.00	2.50	—

Y# 135.1 ROUBLE

Copper-Nickel-Zinc, 31 mm. **Subject:** 20th Anniversary of World War II Victory **Obv:** National arms divide CCCP with inscription below **Rev:** Statue by Vouchetic

Date	Mintage	F	VF	XF	Unc	BU
1965	59,989,000	—	1.00	2.00	3.00	—
1965 Prooflike	—	—	—	—	3.00	—
1965 Proof	—	Value: 30.00				

Y# 140.1 ROUBLE

Copper-Nickel-Zinc, 31 mm. **Subject:** 50th Anniversary of Revolution **Obv:** National arms **Rev:** Lenin with right arm raised facing left, star at upper left **Edge:** Lettered, with date

Date	Mintage	F	VF	XF	Unc	BU
1967	52,289,000	—	1.00	2.00	3.00	—
1967 Prooflike	—	—	—	—	3.00	—
1967 Proof	—	Value: 30.00				

Y# 141 ROUBLE

Copper-Nickel-Zinc, 31 mm. **Subject:** Centennial of Lenin's Birth **Obv:** National arms divide CCCP **Rev:** Head right

Date	Mintage	F	VF	XF	Unc	BU
ND(1970)	99,889,000	—	1.00	2.00	3.00	—
ND(1970) Prooflike	—	—	—	—	3.00	—
ND(1970) Proof	—	Value: 100				

Y# 142.1 ROUBLE

Copper-Nickel-Zinc, 31 mm. **Subject:** 30th Anniversary of World War II Victory **Obv:** National arms divide CCCP **Obv. Designer:** V. Ermokov **Rev:** Volgograd monument **Rev. Designer:** J. Komschicov **Edge:** Date **Note:** Date appears on the edge in English and Russian as "9 March 1975". Varieties exist.

Date	Mintage	F	VF	XF	Unc	BU
1975	14,989,000	—	1.00	2.00	3.00	—
1975 Prooflike	—	—	—	—	3.00	—
1975 Proof	—	Value: 30.00				

Y# 143.1 ROUBLE

Copper-Nickel-Zinc, 31 mm. **Subject:** 60th Anniversary of Bolshevik Revolution **Obv:** National arms divide CCCP **Rev:** Head left above ship, dates below

Date	Mintage	F	VF	XF	Unc	BU
ND(1977)	4,987,000	—	1.00	2.00	3.00	—
ND(1977) Prooflike	—	—	—	—	3.00	—
ND(1977) Proof	—	Value: 30.00				

Y# A144 ROUBLE

Copper-Nickel-Zinc, 31 mm. **Obv:** National arms divide CCCP above value **Rev:** Design with star on top with Olympic rings below **Note:** Mule

Date	Mintage	F	VF	XF	Unc	BU
1977 Rare	Inc. below	—	—	—	—	—

Y# 144 ROUBLE

Copper-Nickel-Zinc, 31 mm. **Series:** 1980 Olympics **Obv:** National arms divide CCCP above value **Rev:** Design with star on top with Olympic rings below **Rev. Designer:** V. Arsentiev

Date	Mintage	F	VF	XF	Unc	BU
1977	8,665,000	—	1.00	2.00	3.00	—
1977 Prooflike	—	—	—	—	3.00	—
1977 Proof	—	Value: 25.00				

Y# 153.1 ROUBLE

Copper-Nickel-Zinc, 31 mm. **Series:** 1980 Olympics **Obv:** National arms divide CCCP with value below **Rev:** Moscow Kremlin with stars on top of steeples **Rev. Designer:** Nikolay Nosov

Date	Mintage	F	VF	XF	Unc	BU
1978	6,490,000	—	1.00	2.00	3.00	—
1978 Prooflike	—	—	—	—	3.00	—
1978 Proof	—	Value: 60.00				

Y# 153.2 ROUBLE

Copper-Nickel-Zinc, 31 mm. **Obv:** National arms divide CCCP, value below **Rev:** Clock on tower shows Roman numeral 6 (VI) instead of 4 (IV)

Date	Mintage	F	VF	XF	Unc	BU
1978	Inc. above	—	8.00	16.00	25.00	—

Y# 165 ROUBLE

Copper-Nickel-Zinc, 31 mm. **Series:** 1980 Olympics **Obv:** National arms divide CCCP, value below **Rev:** Monument, Sputnik and Sojuz **Rev. Designer:** Nikolay Nosov

Date	Mintage	F	VF	XF	Unc	BU
1979	4,665,000	—	1.00	2.00	3.00	—
1979 Prooflike	—	—	—	—	3.00	—
1979 Proof	—	Value: 25.00				

Y# 164 ROUBLE

Copper-Nickel-Zinc, 31 mm. **Series:** 1980 Olympics **Obv:** National arms divide CCCP, value below **Rev:** Moscow University **Note:** Varieties in window arrangements exist.

Date	Mintage	F	VF	XF	Unc	BU
1979	4,665,000	—	1.00	2.00	3.00	—
1979 Prooflike	—	—	—	—	3.00	—
1979 Proof	—	Value: 25.00				

Y# 177 ROUBLE

Copper-Nickel, 31 mm. **Series:** 1980 Olympics **Obv:** National arms divide CCCP with value below **Rev:** Dolgorukij Monument **Rev. Designer:** Nikolay Nosov

Date	Mintage	F	VF	XF	Unc	BU
1980	4,490,000	—	1.00	2.00	3.00	—
1980 Prooflike	—	—	—	—	3.00	—
1980 Proof	—	Value: 25.00				

Y# 178 ROUBLE

Copper-Nickel, 31 mm. **Series:** 1980 Olympics **Obv:** National arms divide CCCP, value below **Rev:** Torch **Rev. Designer:** Nikolay Nosov

Date	Mintage	F	VF	XF	Unc	BU
1980	4,490,000	—	1.00	2.00	3.00	—
1980 Prooflike	—	—	—	—	3.00	—
1980 Proof	—	Value: 25.00				

Y# 188.1 ROUBLE

Copper-Nickel, 31 mm. **Subject:** 20th Anniversary of Manned Space Flights **Obv:** National arms divide CCCP with value below **Rev:** Cosmonaut facing flanked by rockets, hammer and sickle above

Date	Mintage	F	VF	XF	Unc	BU
ND(1981)	3,962,000	—	1.00	2.00	3.00	—
ND(1981) Proof	—	Value: 12.50				

Y# 189.1 ROUBLE

Copper-Nickel, 31 mm. **Subject:** Russian-Bulgarian Friendship **Obv:** National arms divide CCCP with value below **Rev:** Grasped hands divide flags above and sprigs below within beaded circle **Edge Lettering:** Cyrillic lettering

Date	Mintage	F	VF	XF	Unc	BU
1981	1,984,000	—	1.00	2.00	4.00	—
1981 Proof	16,000	Value: 22.50				

Note: The same reverse die was used for both Russia 1 Rouble KM #189 and Bulgaria 1 Lev KM#119

Y# 190.1 ROUBLE

Copper-Nickel, 31 mm. **Subject:** 60th Anniversary of the Soviet Union **Obv:** National arms divide CCCP with value below **Rev:** Radiant sun and standing statue facing left **Edge Lettering:** Cyrillic lettering

Date	Mintage	F	VF	XF	Unc	BU
ND(1982)	1,921,000	—	1.00	3.00	6.00	—
ND(1982) Proof	79,000	Value: 6.00				

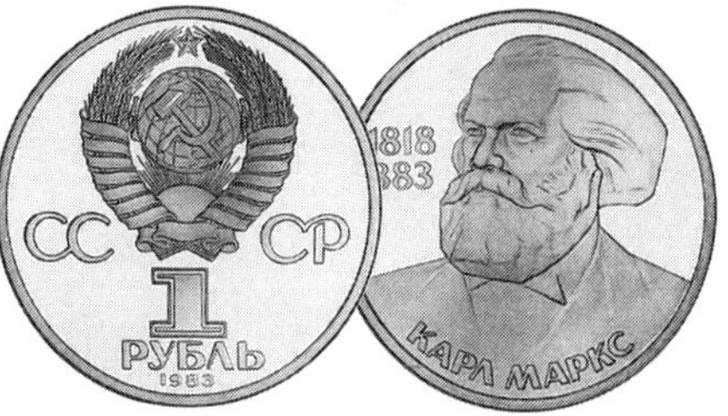

Y# 191.1 ROUBLE

Copper-Nickel, 31 mm. **Subject:** Death of Karl Marx Centennial **Obv:** National arms divide CCCP with value below **Rev:** Bust 3/4 left and dates **Edge:** Cyrillic lettering

Date	Mintage	F	VF	XF	Unc	BU
1983	1,921,000	—	1.00	2.00	4.00	—
1983 Proof	79,000	Value: 6.00				

Y# 192.1 ROUBLE

12.5000 g., Copper-Nickel, 31 mm. **Subject:** 20th Anniversary of First Woman in Space **Obv:** National arms divide CCCP with value below **Rev:** Cosmonaut head facing flanked by stars

Date	Mintage	F	VF	XF	Unc	BU
1983	1,945,000	—	1.00	2.00	4.00	—
1983 Proof	55,000	Value: 6.00				

Y# 193.1 ROUBLE

Copper-Nickel, 31 mm. **Subject:** First Russian Printer **Obv:** National arms divide CCCP with value below **Rev:** Ivan Fedorov **Edge:** Cyrillic lettering

Date	Mintage	F	VF	XF	Unc	BU
1983	1,965,000	—	1.00	2.00	4.00	—
1983 Proof	35,000	Value: 7.50				

Y# 194.1 ROUBLE

Copper-Nickel, 31 mm. **Subject:** 150th Anniversary - Birth of Dmitri Ivanovich Mendeleyev **Obv:** National arms divide CCCP with value below **Rev:** Head facing and dates **Edge:** Cyrillic lettering

Date	Mintage	F	VF	XF	Unc	BU
1984	1,965,000	—	1.00	2.00	4.00	—
1984 Proof	35,000	Value: 7.50				

Y# 195.1 ROUBLE

Copper-Nickel, 31 mm. **Subject:** 125th Anniversary - Birth of Alexander Popov **Obv:** National arms divide CCCP with value below **Rev:** Head facing and dates **Edge:** Cyrillic lettering

Date	Mintage	F	VF	XF	Unc	BU
1984	1,965,000	—	1.00	2.00	4.00	—
1984 Proof	35,000	Value: 6.00				

Y# 196.1 ROUBLE

Copper-Nickel, 31 mm. **Subject:** 185th Anniversary - Birth of Alexander Sergeyevich Pushkin **Obv:** National arms divide CCCP with value below **Rev. Designer:** Head left **Edge:** Cyrillic lettering

Date	Mintage	F	VF	XF	Unc	BU
1984	1,965,000	—	1.00	2.00	5.00	—
1984 Proof	35,000	Value: 7.50				

Y# 197.1 ROUBLE

Copper-Nickel, 31 mm. **Subject:** 115th Anniversary - Birth of Vladimir Lenin **Obv:** National arms divide CCCP with value below **Rev:** Bust left with dates **Edge:** Cyrillic lettering

Date	Mintage	F	VF	XF	Unc	BU
1985	1,960,000	—	1.00	3.00	6.00	—
1985 Proof	40,000	Value: 7.50				

Y# 198.1 ROUBLE

Copper-Nickel, 31 mm. **Subject:** 40th Anniversary - World War II Victory **Obv:** National arms divide CCCP with value below **Rev:** Hammer and sickle within radiant star, sprig and dates below **Edge:** Cyrillic lettering

Date	Mintage	F	VF	XF	Unc	BU
1985	5,960,000	—	1.00	2.00	5.00	—
1985 Proof	40,000	Value: 6.00				

Y# 199.1 ROUBLE

Copper-Nickel, 31 mm. **Subject:** 12th World Youth Festival in Moscow **Obv:** National arms divide CCCP with value below **Rev:** Festival emblem **Edge:** Cyrillic lettering

Date	Mintage	F	VF	XF	Unc	BU
1985	5,960,000	—	1.00	2.00	5.00	—
1985 Proof	40,000	Value: 6.00				

Y# 200.1 ROUBLE

Copper-Nickel, 31 mm. **Subject:** 165th Anniversary - Birth of Friedrich Engels **Obv:** National arms divide CCCP with value below **Rev:** Bust 3/4 left with dates **Rev. Designer:** Nikolay Nosov

Date	Mintage	F	VF	XF	Unc	BU
1985	1,960,000	—	1.00	3.00	6.00	—
1985 Proof	—	Value: 6.00				

Y# 201.1 ROUBLE

Copper-Nickel, 31 mm. **Subject:** International Year of Peace **Obv:** National arms divide CCCP with value below **Rev:** Hands within wreath releasing dove **Edge:** Cyrillic lettering **Note:** Rouble written with inverted "V" for ?.

Date	Mintage	F	VF	XF	Unc	BU
1986	—	—	—	—	12.00	—

Y# 201.3 ROUBLE

Copper-Nickel, 31 mm. **Subject:** International Year of Peace **Obv:** National arms divide CCCP with value below **Rev:** Hands within wreath releasing dove **Note:** Rouble written РУБЛЬ.

Date	Mintage	F	VF	XF	Unc	BU
1986	3,955,000	—	1.00	3.00	6.00	—
1986 Proof	45,000	Value: 6.00				

Y# 201.4 ROUBLE

Copper-Nickel, 31 mm. **Subject:** International Year of Peace **Obv:** National arms divide CCCP, value below **Rev:** Hands within wreath releasing dove **Edge Lettering:** 1988.N.

Date	Mintage	F	VF	XF	Unc	BU
1986	—	—	1.00	3.00	7.00	—
1986 Proof, rare	—	—	—	—	—	—

Y# 202.1 ROUBLE

Copper-Nickel, 31 mm. **Subject:** 275th Anniversary - Birth of Mikhail Lomonosov **Obv:** National arms divide CCCP with value below **Rev:** Bust 1/4 left **Edge:** Cyrillic lettering

Date	Mintage	F	VF	XF	Unc	BU
1986	1,965,000	—	1.00	2.00	4.00	—
1986 Proof	35,000	Value: 5.00				

Y# 205 ROUBLE

Copper-Nickel, 31 mm. **Subject:** 130th Anniversary - Birth of Constantin Tsiolkovsky **Obv:** National arms with CCCP and value below **Rev:** Seated figure facing left with stars and dates **Edge:** Cyrillic lettering

Date	Mintage	F	VF	XF	Unc	BU
1987	3,830,000	—	1.00	2.00	4.00	—
1987 Proof	170,000	Value: 5.00				

Y# 203 ROUBLE

Copper-Nickel, 31 mm. **Subject:** 175th Anniversary - Battle of Borodino **Obv:** National arms with CCCP and value below **Rev:** Group of soldiers **Edge:** Cyrillic lettering **Note:** Varieties with wheat in coat of arms.

Date	Mintage	F	VF	XF	Unc	BU
1987	3,780,000	—	1.00	2.00	4.00	—
1987 Proof	220,000	Value: 5.00				

Y# 204 ROUBLE

Copper-Nickel, 31 mm. **Subject:** 175th Anniversary - Battle of Borodino **Obv:** National arms with CCCP and value below **Rev:** Kutuzov Monument **Edge:** Cyrillic lettering **Note:** Varieties with wheat in coat of arms.

Date	Mintage	F	VF	XF	Unc	BU
1987	3,780,000	—	1.00	2.00	4.00	—
1987 Proof	220,000	Value: 5.00				

Y# 206 ROUBLE
Copper-Nickel, 31 mm. **Subject:** 70th Anniversary of Bolshevik Revolution **Obv:** National arms with CCCP and value below **Rev:** Hammer and sickle with ship on globe background at center of ribbon design, date and sprig below **Edge:** Cyrillic lettering **Note:** Varieties with wheat in coat of arms.

Date	Mintage	F	VF	XF	Unc	BU
1987	3,800,000	—	1.00	2.00	4.00	—
1987 Proof	200,000	Value: 6.00				

Y# 216 ROUBLE
Copper-Nickel, 31 mm. **Subject:** 160th Anniversary - Birth of Leo Tolstoi **Obv:** National arms with CCCP and value below **Rev:** Head facing **Edge:** Cyrillic lettering

Date	Mintage	F	VF	XF	Unc	BU
1987 Error	—	—	—	—	—	—
1988	3,775,000	—	1.00	2.00	4.00	—
1988 Proof	225,000	Value: 5.00				

Y# 209 ROUBLE
Copper-Nickel, 31 mm. **Subject:** 120th Anniversary - Birth of Maxin Gorky **Obv:** National arms with CCCP and value below **Rev:** Bust 1/4 right, designs and flying bird in background **Rev. Designer:** Albert Miroshnichenko **Edge:** Cyrillic lettering

Date	Mintage	F	VF	XF	Unc	BU
1988	3,775,000	—	1.00	2.00	4.00	—
1988 Proof	225,000	Value: 6.00				

Y# 220 ROUBLE
Copper-Nickel, 31 mm. **Subject:** 150th Anniversary - Birth of Musorgsky **Obv:** National arms with CCCP and value below **Rev:** Head 3/4 left divides dates **Edge:** Cyrillic lettering

Date	Mintage	F	VF	XF	Unc	BU
1989	2,700,000	—	1.00	3.00	5.00	—
1989 Proof	300,000	Value: 5.50				

Y# 228 ROUBLE
Copper-Nickel, 31 mm. **Subject:** 175th Anniversary - Birth of M.Y. Lermontov **Obv:** National arms with CCCP and value below **Rev:** Head 1/4 left, quill below, dates at right **Rev. Designer:** Nikolay Nosov **Edge:** Cyrillic lettering

Date	Mintage	F	VF	XF	Unc	BU
1989	2,700,000	—	1.00	3.00	5.00	—
1989 Proof	300,000	Value: 6.00				

Y# 232 ROUBLE
Copper-Nickel, 31 mm. **Subject:** 100th Anniversary - Birth of Hamza Hakim-zade Niyazi **Obv:** National arms with CCCP and value below **Rev:** Bust facing, dates at right **Edge:** Cyrillic lettering

Date	Mintage	F	VF	XF	Unc	BU
1989	1,800,000	—	2.00	4.00	7.00	—
1989 Proof	200,000	Value: 6.00				

Y# 233 ROUBLE
Copper-Nickel, 31 mm. **Subject:** 100th Anniversary - Death of Mihai Eminescu **Obv:** National arms with CCCP and value below **Rev:** Head 3/4 left flanked by dates **Edge:** Cyrillic lettering

Date	Mintage	F	VF	XF	Unc	BU
1989	1,800,000	—	2.00	4.00	7.00	—
1989 Proof	200,000	Value: 6.00				

Y# 235 ROUBLE
Copper-Nickel, 31 mm. **Subject:** 175th Anniversary - Birth of T.G. Shevchenko **Obv:** National arms with CCCP and value below **Rev:** Head looking down facing 3/4 left **Edge:** Cyrillic lettering

Date	Mintage	F	VF	XF	Unc	BU
1989	2,700,000	—	1.00	3.00	5.00	—
1989 Proof	300,000	Value: 5.50				

Y# 236 ROUBLE
Copper-Nickel, 31 mm. **Subject:** 100th Anniversary - Birth of Tschaikovsky - Composer **Obv:** National arms with CCCP and value below **Rev:** Seated figure left, musical notes in background **Edge:** Cyrillic lettering

Date	Mintage	F	VF	XF	Unc	BU
1990	2,600,000	—	—	—	3.00	—
1990 Proof	400,000	Value: 6.50				

Y# 237 ROUBLE
Copper-Nickel, 31 mm. **Subject:** Anniversary - Marshal Zhukov **Obv:** National arms with CCCP and value below **Rev:** Uniformed bust left **Edge:** Cyrillic lettering

Date	Mintage	F	VF	XF	Unc	BU
1990	1,600,000	—	—	—	8.00	—
1990 Proof	400,000	Value: 7.00				

Y# 240 ROUBLE
Copper-Nickel, 31 mm. **Subject:** 130th Anniversary - Birth of Anton Chekhov **Obv:** National arms with CCCP and value below **Rev:** Head 1/4 left divides design and dates **Edge:** Cyrillic lettering

Date	Mintage	F	VF	XF	Unc	BU
1990	2,600,000	—	—	—	5.00	—
1990 Proof	400,000	Value: 6.50				

Y# 257 ROUBLE
Copper-Nickel, 31 mm. **Subject:** 125th Anniversary - Birth of Janis Rainis **Obv:** National arms with CCCP and value below **Rev:** Head facing with dates at right **Edge:** Cyrillic lettering

Date	Mintage	F	VF	XF	Unc	BU
1990	2,600,000	—	—	—	5.00	—
1990 Proof	400,000	Value: 6.50				

Y# 258 ROUBLE
Copper-Nickel, 31 mm. **Subject:** 500th Anniversary - Birth of Francisk Scorina **Obv:** National arms with CCCP and value below **Rev:** Half figure facing **Edge:** Cyrillic lettering

Date	Mintage	F	VF	XF	Unc	BU
1990	2,600,000	—	—	—	5.00	—
1990 Proof	400,000	Value: 6.50				

Y# 260 ROUBLE
Copper-Nickel, 31 mm. **Subject:** 550th Anniversary - Birth of Alisher Navoi **Obv:** National arms with CCCP and value below **Rev:** Bust with hand on chin left **Edge:** Cyrillic lettering

Date	Mintage	F	VF	XF	Unc	BU
1990 Error	—	—	—	—	—	10.00
1991 Л	2,150,000	—	—	—	6.00	—
1991 Л Proof	350,000	Value: 3.50				
1991 M	—	—	—	—	6.00	—
1991 M Proof	—	Value: 3.50				

Y# 261 ROUBLE
Copper-Nickel, 31 mm. **Subject:** 125th Anniversary - Birth of P. N. Lebedev **Obv:** National arms with CCCP and value below **Rev:**

Half figure right with hand on book, designs on bottom, dates and fomulas at right **Edge:** Cyrillic lettering

Date	Mintage	F	VF	XF	Unc	BU
1990 Error, rare	—	—	—	—	—	—
1991	2,150,000	—	—	—	5.00	—
1991 Proof	350,000	Value: 5.50				

Y# 282 ROUBLE

Copper-Nickel, 31 mm. **Subject:** K.B. Ivanov **Obv:** National arms with CCCP and value below **Rev:** Head left **Edge:** Cyrillic lettering

Date	Mintage	F	VF	XF	Unc	BU
1991	3,150,000	—	—	—	5.00	—
1991 Proof	350,000	Value: 5.50				

Y# 283 ROUBLE

Copper-Nickel, 31 mm. **Subject:** Turkman Poet Makhtumkuli **Obv:** National arms with CCCP and value below **Rev:** Bust left **Edge:** Cyrillic lettering

Date	Mintage	F	VF	XF	Unc	BU
1991	2,150,000	—	—	—	6.00	—
1991 Proof	350,000	Value: 5.50				

Y# 284 ROUBLE

Copper-Nickel, 31 mm. **Subject:** 850th Anniversary - Birth of Nizami Gyanzhevi - Poet **Obv:** National arms with CCCP and value below **Rev:** Bust right writing with quill **Edge:** Cyrillic lettering

Date	Mintage	F	VF	XF	Unc	BU
1991	2,200,000	—	—	—	6.00	—
1991 Proof	300,000	Value: 5.50				

Y# 263.2 ROUBLE

Copper-Nickel, 31 mm. **Subject:** 100th Birthday of Sergey Prokofiev **Obv:** National arms with CCCP and value below **Rev:** Head right, dates below **Note:** Error death date: 1952.

Date	Mintage	F	VF	XF	Unc	BU
1991 Rare	—	—	—	—	—	—

Y# 263.1 ROUBLE

Copper-Nickel, 31 mm. **Subject:** 100th Birthday of Sergey Prokofiev **Obv:** National arms with CCCP and value below **Rev:** Head right **Edge:** Cyrillic lettering

Date	Mintage	F	VF	XF	Unc	BU
1991	2,150,000	—	—	—	3.00	—
1991 Proof	350,000	Value: 5.50				

GOVERNMENT BANK ISSUES

1991-1992

Y# 296 10 KOPEKS

Copper Clad Steel **Obv:** Kremlin Tower and Dome **Rev:** Value flanked by sprigs above date

Date	Mintage	F	VF	XF	Unc	BU
1991M	—	0.15	0.25	0.50	1.00	—

Y# 292 50 KOPEKS

Copper-Nickel **Obv:** Kremlin Tower and Dome **Rev:** Value flanked by sprigs above date

Date	Mintage	F	VF	XF	Unc	BU
1991Л	—	0.25	0.50	1.00	2.00	—

Y# 293 ROUBLE

Copper-Nickel **Obv:** Kremlin Tower and Dome **Rev:** Value flanked by sprigs above date

Date	Mintage	F	VF	XF	Unc	BU
1991Л	—	—	—	—	2.00	—
1991M	—	—	—	—	3.00	—

Y# 280 5 ROUBLES

Bi-Metallic Brass center in Copper-Nickel ring, 25 mm. **Series:** Wildlife **Obv:** Value flanked by sprigs within circle **Rev:** Owl flanked by grassy sprigs within circle **Edge:** Alternating reeded and smooth

Date	Mintage	F	VF	XF	Unc	BU
1991Л	500,000	—	—	—	4.00	7.00

Y# 281 5 ROUBLES

Bi-Metallic Brass center in Copper-Nickel ring, 25 mm. **Series:** Wildlife **Obv:** Value flanked by sprigs within circle **Rev:** Mountain Goat within circle **Edge:** Alternating reeded and smooth

Date	Mintage	F	VF	XF	Unc	BU
1991Л	500,000	—	—	—	3.00	6.00

Y# 294 5 ROUBLES

Copper-Nickel, 24 mm. **Obv:** Kremlin Tower and Dome **Rev:** Value flanked by sprigs above date **Edge:** Alternating reeded and smooth

Date	Mintage	F	VF	XF	Unc	BU
1991Л	—	—	—	—	4.00	—
1991M	—	—	—	—	6.00	—

Y# 295 10 ROUBLES

5.9700 g., Bi-Metallic Copper-Nickel ring, Aluminum-Bronze center, 25 mm. **Obv:** Kremlin Tower and Dome **Rev:** Value flanked by sprigs above date **Edge:** Alternating reeded and smooth

Date	Mintage	F	VF	XF	Unc	BU
1991(l)	—	0.50	2.00	3.00	4.00	—
1991(m)	—	2.00	5.00	8.00	15.00	—
1992(l) Error	—	—	30.00	50.00	80.00	—

RUSSIAN FEDERATION

Issued by РОССИЈСКИЈ БАНК (Russian Bank)

STANDARD COINAGE

Y# 303 ROUBLE

Copper-Nickel, 31 mm. **Subject:** Rebirth of Russian Sovereignty and Democracy **Obv:** Tower and steeples, value below **Rev:** Winged Victory and small building with flag on top

Date	Mintage	F	VF	XF	Unc	BU
1992Л	700,000	—	—	—	2.50	—
1992Л Proof	300,000	Value: 5.00				

Y# 305 ROUBLE

Copper-Nickel, 31 mm. **Subject:** 110th Anniversary - Birth of Jacob Kolas **Obv:** Tower and steeples, value below **Rev:** Head 1/4 right **Edge:** Cyrillic lettering

Date	Mintage	F	VF	XF	Unc	BU
1992Л	700,000	—	—	—	3.00	—
1992Л Proof	300,000	Value: 5.00				

Y# 306 ROUBLE

Copper-Nickel, 31 mm. **Subject:** 190th Anniversary - Birth of Admiral Nakhimov **Obv:** Tower and steeples, value below **Rev:** Uniformed bust with back facing, ship at right **Edge:** Cyrillic lettering

Date	Mintage	F	VF	XF	Unc	BU
1992Л	700,000	—	—	—	3.00	—
1992Л Proof	300,000	Value: 5.00				

Y# 311 ROUBLE
3.2500 g., Brass Clad Steel, 19.5 mm. **Obv:** Double headed eagle **Rev:** Value flanked by sprigs above date **Edge:** Plain

Date	Mintage	F	VF	XF	Unc	BU
1992	—	2.00	5.00	10.00	20.00	—
1992Л	—	—	—	—	2.00	—
1992М	—	—	—	—	2.00	—
1992Л	—	—	—	—	3.00	—
1992М	—	—	—	—	3.00	—

Y# 320 ROUBLE
Copper-Nickel, 31 mm. **Obv:** Tower and steeples, value below **Rev:** Head of Yanka Kupala left **Edge:** Cyrillic lettering

Date	Mintage	F	VF	XF	Unc	BU
1992Л	1,000,000	—	—	—	3.00	—
1992Л Prooflike	200,000	—	—	—	—	—
1992Л Proof	350,000	Value: 5.00				

Y# 321 ROUBLE
Copper-Nickel, 31 mm. **Obv:** Double-headed eagle within beaded circle **Rev:** N.I. Lobachevsky 1/4 right

Date	Mintage	F	VF	XF	Unc	BU
1992М	1,000,000	—	—	—	3.00	—
1992М Prooflike	500,000	—	—	—	—	—
1992М Proof	—	Value: 5.00				

Y# 319.1 ROUBLE
Copper-Nickel, 31 mm. **Subject:** Vladimir Ivanovich Vernadsky **Obv:** Double-headed eagle within beaded circle **Rev:** Head looking down with hand on head 1/4 right

Date	Mintage	F	VF	XF	Unc	BU
1993Л	450,000	—	—	—	3.00	—
1993 Proof	15,000	Value: 3.50				
1993Л Proof	35,000	Value: 5.50				

Y# 319.2 ROUBLE
Copper-Nickel, 31 mm. **Subject:** Vladimir Ivanovich Vernadsky **Obv:** Without mint mark below eagle's claw **Rev:** Head looking down with hand on head 1/4 right

Date	Mintage	F	VF	XF	Unc	BU
1993	—	—	—	—	3.00	—
1993 Proof	—	Value: 15.00				

Y# 325 ROUBLE
Copper-Nickel, 31 mm. **Subject:** Gavrila Romanovich Derzhavin **Obv:** Double-headed eagle within beaded circle **Rev:** Bust 1/4 left above date and objects

Date	Mintage	F	VF	XF	Unc	BU
1993М	500,000	—	—	—	3.00	—
1993М Proof	—	Value: 5.00				

Y# 326 ROUBLE
Copper-Nickel, 31 mm. **Subject:** K.A. Timiryazev **Obv:** Double-headed eagle within beaded circle **Rev:** Bust facing, plant in vase at upper left

Date	Mintage	F	VF	XF	Unc	BU
1993М	500,000	—	—	—	3.00	—
1993М Proof	—	Value: 5.00				

Y# 327 ROUBLE
Copper-Nickel, 31 mm. **Subject:** V. Maikovski **Obv:** Kremlin Tower and Dome within beaded circle **Rev:** Head 1/4 left

Date	Mintage	F	VF	XF	Unc	BU
1993Л	500,000	—	—	—	3.00	—
1993М Proof	—	Value: 5.00				

Y# 347 ROUBLE
Copper-Nickel, 31 mm. **Subject:** A.P. Borodin **Obv:** Double-headed eagle **Rev:** Bust facing 1/4 left, music notes and design in background

Date	Mintage	F	VF	XF	Unc	BU
1993М	500,000	—	—	—	3.00	—
1993М Proof	—	Value: 5.00				

Y# 348 ROUBLE
Copper-Nickel, 31 mm. **Subject:** I.S. Turgenev **Obv:** Double-headed eagle **Rev:** Head left

Date	Mintage	F	VF	XF	Unc	BU
1993Л	500,000	—	—	—	3.00	—
1993Л Proof	—	Value: 5.00				

Y# 312 5 ROUBLES
4.0500 g., Brass Clad Steel, 21.9 mm. **Obv:** Double-headed eagle **Rev:** Value flanked by sprigs above date

Date	Mintage	F	VF	XF	Unc	BU
1992Л	—	—	—	—	2.00	—
1992М	—	—	—	—	2.00	—
1992Л	—	—	—	—	3.00	—
1992М	—	—	—	—	3.00	—

Y# 400 5 ROUBLES
4.0500 g., Aluminum-Bronze, 21.9 mm. **Series:** WWII **Obv:** Double-headed eagle **Rev:** Infantry officer leading attack

Date	Mintage	F	VF	XF	Unc	BU
1995(l)	200,000	—	—	—	2.00	—

Note: In mint sets only

Y# 505 5 ROUBLES
4.0500 g., Brass, 21.9 mm. **Subject:** 300th Anniversary - Russian Fleet **Obv:** Double-headed eagle **Rev:** Sailing ship

Date	Mintage	F	VF	XF	Unc	BU
1996(l)	100,000	—	—	—	3.00	—

Note: In mint sets only

Y# 307 10 ROUBLES
5.9500 g., Bi-Metallic Aluminum-Bronze center in Copper-Nickel ring, 25 mm. **Series:** Wildlife **Obv:** Value **Rev:** Red-breasted Kazarka left **Edge:** Alternating reeded and smooth

Date	Mintage	F	VF	XF	Unc	BU
1992Л	300,000	—	—	—	3.00	7.00

Y# 308 10 ROUBLES
5.9500 g., Bi-Metallic Aluminum-Bronze center in Copper-Nickel ring, 25 mm. **Series:** Wildlife **Obv:** Value **Rev:** Tiger **Edge:** Alternating reeded and smooth

Date	Mintage	F	VF	XF	Unc	BU
1992Л	300,000	—	—	—	3.00	8.00

Y# 309 10 ROUBLES
5.9500 g., Bi-Metallic Aluminum-Bronze center in Copper-Nickel ring, 25 mm. **Series:** Wildlife **Obv:** Value **Rev:** Cobra **Edge:** Alternating reeded and smooth

Date	Mintage	F	VF	XF	Unc	BU
1992Л	300,000	—	—	—	3.00	7.50

Y# 313 10 ROUBLES

3.6500 g., Copper-Nickel, 21.1 mm. **Obv:** Double-headed eagle **Rev:** Value flanked by sprigs **Edge:** Reeded **Note:** St. Petersburg minted coins have a round-top 3 in date. Moscow minted coins have a flat-top 3 in date.

Date	Mintage	F	VF	XF	Unc	BU
1992Л	—	—	—	—	2.00	—
1992M	—	—	—	—	2.00	—
1993Л	—	—	—	—	2.00	—
1993M	—	—	—	—	10.00	—

Y# 313a 10 ROUBLES

3.3800 g., Copper-Nickel Clad Steel, 21.1 mm. **Obv:** Double-headed eagle **Rev:** Value flanked by sprigs **Edge:** Plain **Note:** St. Petersburg minted coins have a round-top 3 in date. Moscow minted coins have a flat-top 3 in date.

Date	Mintage	F	VF	XF	Unc	BU
1992(sp) (l)	—	—	—	—	2.00	—
1992M	—	—	—	—	12.00	—
1993Л	—	—	—	—	2.00	—
1993Л	—	—	—	—	2.00	—

Y# 401 10 ROUBLES

3.6500 g., Copper-Nickel, 21.1 mm. **Series:** WWII **Obv:** Double-headed eagle **Rev:** Munitions workers **Designer:** A. Baklanov

Date	Mintage	F	VF	XF	Unc	BU
1995(l)	200,000	—	—	—	3.00	—

Note: In mint sets only

Y# 314 20 ROUBLES

5.6000 g., Copper-Nickel, 24.1 mm. **Obv:** Double-headed eagle **Rev:** Value flanked by sprigs **Edge:** Reeded and plain sections

Date	Mintage	F	VF	XF	Unc	BU
1992Л	—	—	—	—	3.00	—
1992M	—	—	—	—	3.00	—
1992Л Rare	—	—	—	—	—	—
Note: Plain edge error						
1992M	—	—	—	—	20.00	—
Note: Plain edge error						

Y# 314a 20 ROUBLES

Copper-Nickel Clad Steel, 24.1 mm. **Obv:** Double-headed eagle **Rev:** Value flanked by sprigs **Edge:** Plain

Date	Mintage	F	VF	XF	Unc	BU
1993M	—	—	—	—	3.00	—

Y# 315 50 ROUBLES

5.9500 g., Bi-Metallic Aluminum-Bronze center in Copper-Nickel ring, 25 mm. **Obv:** Double-headed eagle **Rev:** Value flanked by sprigs **Note:** Off-metal strikes exist from both mints. The strike is on the planchet reserved for Y#316, 100 Roubles.

Date	Mintage	F	VF	XF	Unc	BU
1992Л	—	0.50	0.75	1.00	3.00	—
1992M	—	0.75	1.00	1.50	4.00	—

Y# 329.1 50 ROUBLES

Aluminum-Bronze, 25 mm. **Obv:** Double-headed eagle **Rev:** Value flanked by sprigs **Edge:** Alternating reeded and plain

Date	Mintage	F	VF	XF	Unc	BU
1993Л	—	—	—	—	3.00	—
1993M	—	—	—	—	3.00	—

Y# 329.2 50 ROUBLES

Brass Clad Steel, 25 mm. **Obv:** Double-headed eagle **Rev:** Value **Edge:** Plain

Date	Mintage	F	VF	XF	Unc	BU
1993(l)	—	—	—	—	4.00	—
1993(m)	—	—	—	—	3.00	—

Y# 330 50 ROUBLES

5.9500 g., Bi-Metallic Aluminum-Bronze center in Copper-Nickel ring, 25 mm. **Series:** Wildlife **Obv:** Double-headed eagle **Rev:** Black bear **Edge:** Alternating reeded and smooth

Date	Mintage	F	VF	XF	Unc	BU
1993Л	300,000	—	—	—	4.00	8.00

Y# 331 50 ROUBLES

5.9500 g., Bi-Metallic Aluminum-Bronze center in Copper-Nickel ring, 25 mm. **Series:** Wildlife **Obv:** Double-headed eagle **Rev:** Gecko **Edge:** Alternating reeded and smooth

Date	Mintage	F	VF	XF	Unc	BU
1993Л	300,000	—	—	—	5.00	9.00

Y# 332 50 ROUBLES

5.9500 g., Bi-Metallic Aluminum-Bronze center in Copper-Nickel ring, 25 mm. **Series:** Wildlife **Obv:** Double-headed eagle **Rev:** Grouse **Edge:** Alternating reeded and smooth

Date	Mintage	F	VF	XF	Unc	BU
1993Л	300,000	—	—	—	4.00	7.50

Y# 333 50 ROUBLES

5.9500 g., Bi-Metallic Aluminum-Bronze center in Copper-Nickel ring, 25 mm. **Series:** Wildlife **Obv:** Double-headed eagle **Rev:** Far Eastern Stork **Edge:** Alternating reeded and smooth

Date	Mintage	F	VF	XF	Unc	BU
1993Л	300,000	—	—	—	4.00	7.50

Y# 334 50 ROUBLES

5.9500 g., Bi-Metallic Aluminum-Bronze center in Copper-Nickel ring, 25 mm. **Series:** Wildlife **Obv:** Double-headed eagle **Rev:** Black Sea Porpoise **Edge:** Alternating reeded and smooth

Date	Mintage	F	VF	XF	Unc	BU
1993Л	300,000	—	—	—	4.00	10.00

Y# 367 50 ROUBLES

5.9500 g., Bi-Metallic Aluminum-Bronze center in Copper-Nickel ring, 25 mm. **Series:** Wildlife **Obv:** Double-headed eagle **Rev:** Blind mole rat **Edge:** Alternating reeded and smooth

Date	Mintage	F	VF	XF	Unc	BU
1994Л	300,000	—	—	—	5.00	7.50

Y# 368 50 ROUBLES

5.9500 g., Bi-Metallic Aluminum-Bronze center in Copper-Nickel ring, 25 mm. **Series:** Wildlife **Obv:** Double-headed eagle **Rev:** Bison **Edge:** Alternating reeded and smooth

Date	Mintage	F	VF	XF	Unc	BU
1994Л	300,000	—	—	—	5.00	7.00

Y# 369 50 ROUBLES

5.9500 g., Bi-Metallic Alunimum-Bronze center in Copper-Nickel ring, 25 mm. **Series:** Wildlife **Obv:** Double-headed eagle **Rev:** Goitered Gazelle **Edge:** Alternating reeded and smooth

Date	Mintage	F	VF	XF	Unc	BU
1994Л	300,000	—	—	—	5.00	7.00

Y# 370 50 ROUBLES

5.9500 g., Bi-Metallic Aluminum-Bronze center in Copper-Nickel ring, 25 mm. **Series:** Wildlife **Obv:** Double-headed eagle **Rev:** Peregrine Falcon **Edge:** Alternating reeded and smooth

Date	Mintage	F	VF	XF	Unc	BU
1994Л	300,000	—	—	—	5.00	8.00

Y# 371 50 ROUBLES
5.9500 g., Bi-Metallic Aluminum-Bronze center in Copper-Nickel ring, 25 mm. **Series:** Wildlife **Obv:** Double-headed eagle **Rev:** Two flamingos **Edge:** Alternating reeded and smooth

Date	Mintage	F	VF	XF	Unc	BU
1994Л	300,000	—	—	—	6.00	8.00

Y# 316 100 ROUBLES
6.0000 g., Bi-Metallic Copper-Nickel center in Aluminum-Bronze ring, 25.3 mm. **Obv:** Double-headed eagle **Rev:** Value flanked by sprigs **Note:** Off-metal strikes exist from the Moscow mint. The strike is on the planchet reserved for Y#315, 50 Roubles.

Date	Mintage	F	VF	XF	Unc	BU
1992Л	—	0.50	1.00	2.00	4.00	—
1992М	—	1.00	2.00	3.00	5.00	—

Y# 338 100 ROUBLES
Copper-Nickel-Zinc **Obv:** Double-headed eagle **Rev:** Value flanked by sprigs

Date	Mintage	F	VF	XF	Unc	BU
1993Л	—	0.25	1.00	2.00	4.00	—
1993М	—	0.25	1.00	2.00	4.00	—

REFORM COINAGE

January 1, 1998

1,000 Old Roubles = 1 New Rouble

Y# 600 KOPEK
1.5000 g., Nickel Plated Steel, 15.5 mm. **Obv:** St. George **Obv. Legend:** БАНК РОССИИ **Rev:** Value above vine sprig **Edge:** Plain **Shape:** Disc-like

Date	Mintage	F	VF	XF	Unc	BU
1997М	—	—	—	—	0.30	0.40
1997СП	—	—	—	—	0.30	0.40
1998М	—	—	—	—	0.30	0.40
1998СП	—	—	—	—	0.30	0.40
1999М	—	—	—	—	0.30	0.40
1999СП	—	—	—	—	0.30	0.40
2000М	—	—	—	—	0.30	0.40
2000СП	—	—	—	—	0.30	0.40
2001М	—	—	—	—	0.30	0.40
2001СП	—	—	—	—	0.30	0.40
2002М	—	—	—	—	0.30	0.40
2002СП	—	—	—	—	0.30	0.40
2003М	—	—	—	—	0.30	0.40
2003СП	—	—	—	—	0.30	0.40
2004М	—	—	—	—	0.30	0.40

Y# 601 5 KOPEKS
2.5000 g., Copper-Nickel Clad Steel, 18.5 mm. **Obv:** St. George **Obv. Legend:** БАНК РОССИИ **Rev:** Value above vine sprig **Edge:** Plain **Shape:** Disc-like

Date	Mintage	F	VF	XF	Unc	BU
1997М	—	—	—	—	0.35	0.50
1997СП	—	—	—	—	0.35	0.50
1998М	—	—	—	—	0.45	0.65
1998СП	—	—	—	—	0.45	0.65
1999М	—	—	—	—	0.35	0.50
1999СП	—	—	—	—	0.35	0.50
2000М	—	—	—	—	0.35	0.50
2000СП	—	—	—	—	0.35	0.50
2001М	—	—	—	—	0.40	0.50
2001СП	—	—	—	—	0.40	0.50
2002	—	—	—	—	15.00	17.00
2002М	—	—	—	—	0.40	0.50
2002СП	—	—	—	—	0.40	0.50
2003	—	—	—	—	10.00	12.00
2003М	—	—	—	—	0.35	0.50
2003СП	—	—	—	—	0.35	0.50
2004М	—	—	—	—	0.35	0.50
2004СП	—	—	—	—	0.35	0.50
2005М	—	—	—	—	0.35	0.50
2005СП	—	—	—	—	0.35	0.50
2006СП	—	—	—	—	0.35	0.50
2007	—	—	—	—	0.35	0.50

Y# 602 10 KOPEKS
2.0000 g., Brass **Obv:** St. George horseback right slaying dragon **Rev:** Value above vine sprig **Edge:** Reeded

Date	Mintage	F	VF	XF	Unc	BU
1997М	—	—	—	—	0.50	0.75
1997СП	—	—	—	—	0.50	0.75
1998М	—	—	—	—	0.65	1.00
1998СП	—	—	—	—	0.65	1.00
1999М	—	—	—	—	0.50	0.75
1999СП	—	—	—	—	0.50	0.75
2000М	—	—	—	—	0.50	0.75
2000СП	—	—	—	—	0.50	0.75
2001М	—	—	—	—	0.50	0.80
2001СП	—	—	—	—	0.50	0.80
2002М	—	—	—	—	0.50	0.80
2002СП	—	—	—	—	0.50	0.80
2003М	—	—	—	—	0.50	0.80
2003СП	—	—	—	—	0.50	0.80
2004М	—	—	—	—	0.50	0.80
2004СП	—	—	—	—	0.50	0.80
2005М	—	—	—	—	0.50	0.80
2005СП	—	—	—	—	0.50	0.80
2006М	—	—	—	—	0.50	0.80
2006СП	—	—	—	—	0.50	0.80
2007М	—	—	—	—	1.00	3.00
2007СП	—	—	—	—	1.00	3.00

Y# 602a 10 KOPEKS
Brass Plated Steel **Obv:** St. George on horseback slaying dragon to right **Obv. Legend:** БАНК РОССИИ **Rev:** Denomination above vine sprig **Edge:** Plain

Date	Mintage	F	VF	XF	Unc	BU
2006М	—	—	—	—	0.50	0.80
2006СП	—	—	—	—	0.50	0.80
2007М	—	—	—	—	0.50	0.80
2007СП	—	—	—	—	0.50	0.80

Y# 603 50 KOPEKS
2.9000 g., Brass, 19.5 mm. **Obv:** St. George on horseback slaying dragon right **Rev:** Value above vine sprig **Edge:** Reeded

Date	Mintage	F	VF	XF	Unc	BU
1997М	—	—	—	—	0.75	1.00
1997СП	—	—	—	—	0.75	1.00
1998М	—	—	—	—	1.00	1.50
1998СП	—	—	—	—	1.00	1.50
1999М	—	—	—	—	0.75	1.00
1999СП	—	—	—	—	0.75	1.00
2001М Rare	—	—	—	—	—	—
2002М	—	—	—	—	0.80	1.00
2002СП	—	—	—	—	0.80	1.00
2003М	—	—	—	—	0.80	1.00
2003СП	—	—	—	—	0.80	1.00
2004М	—	—	—	—	0.80	1.00
2004СП	—	—	—	—	0.80	1.00
2005СП	—	—	—	—	0.80	1.00
2006М	—	—	—	—	0.80	1.00
2006СП	—	—	—	—	0.80	1.00
2007М	—	—	—	—	2.50	4.00
2007СП	—	—	—	—	2.50	4.00

Y# 603a 50 KOPEKS
Brass Plated Steel **Obv:** St. George on horseback slaying dragon right **Rev:** Value above vine sprig **Edge:** Plain

Date	Mintage	F	VF	XF	Unc	BU
2006М	—	—	—	—	0.80	1.00
2006СП	—	—	—	—	0.80	1.00
2007М	—	—	—	—	0.80	1.00
2007СП	—	—	—	—	0.80	1.00

Y# 604 ROUBLE
3.2500 g., Copper-Nickel-Zinc, 20.6 mm. **Obv:** Double-headed eagle **Rev:** Value **Edge:** Reeded

Date	Mintage	F	VF	XF	Unc	BU
1997 (m)	—	—	—	—	1.00	1.50
1997 (sp)	—	—	—	—	1.00	1.50
1998 (m)	—	—	—	—	1.00	1.50
1998 (sp)	—	—	—	—	1.00	1.50
1999 (m)	—	—	—	—	1.00	1.50
1999 (sp)	—	—	—	—	1.00	1.50
2001 (m) Rare	—	—	—	—	—	—

Y# 640 ROUBLE
Copper-Nickel-Zinc, 20.5 mm. **Obv:** Double-headed eagle **Rev:** Stylized head of Pushkin left **Edge:** Reeded

Date	Mintage	F	VF	XF	Unc	BU
1999(m)	5,000,000	—	—	—	0.75	1.25
1999(sp)	5,000,000	—	—	—	0.75	1.25

Y# 731 ROUBLE
3.2100 g., Copper-Nickel, 20.7 mm. **Obv:** Double-headed eagle **Rev:** Stylized design above hologram **Edge:** Reeded

Date	Mintage	F	VF	XF	Unc	BU
2001СПМД	100,000,000	—	—	—	1.50	2.00

Y# 797 ROUBLE
3.2500 g., Copper-Nickel, 20.7 mm. **Obv:** Curved bank name below eagle

Date	Mintage	F	VF	XF	Unc	BU
2002	—	—	—	—	1.00	2.00

Y# 833 ROUBLE
3.2500 g., Copper-Nickel-Zinc, 20.6 mm. **Obv:** Two headed eagle above curved inscription **Rev:** Value and flower **Edge:** Reeded

Date	Mintage	F	VF	XF	Unc	BU
2002(sp)	—	—	—	—	2.00	3.00
2005(m)	—	—	—	—	2.00	3.00
2005(sp)	—	—	—	—	2.00	3.00
2006(m)	—	—	—	—	2.00	3.00

Y# 605 2 ROUBLES
5.1000 g., Copper-Nickel-Zinc, 23 mm. **Obv:** Double-headed eagle **Rev:** Value and vine sprig **Edge:** Alternating reeded and smooth

Date	Mintage	F	VF	XF	Unc	BU
1997(m)	—	—	—	—	2.00	3.00
1997(sp)	—	—	—	—	2.00	3.00
1998(m)	—	—	—	—	2.00	3.00
1998(sp)	—	—	—	—	2.00	3.00
1999(m)	—	—	—	—	2.00	4.00

Date	Mintage	F	VF	XF	Unc	BU
1999(sp)	—	—	—	—	2.00	4.00
2001(m)	—	—	—	—	5.00	7.00

Y# 663 2 ROUBLES

5.1000 g., Copper-Nickel-Zinc, 23 mm. **Series:** World War II **Obv:** Value **Rev:** Infantry assault at Stalingrad **Edge:** Reeded and plain sections

Date	Mintage	F	VF	XF	Unc	BU
2000(sp)	10,000,000	—	—	—	2.00	3.00

Y# 664 2 ROUBLES

Copper-Nickel-Zinc, 23 mm. **Obv:** Value at left of vine sprig **Rev:** Cannon manufacturing scene in Tula **Edge:** Alternating reeded and smooth

Date	Mintage	F	VF	XF	Unc	BU
2000(m)	10,000,000	—	—	—	2.00	3.00

Y# 665 2 ROUBLES

Copper-Nickel-Zinc, 23 mm. **Obv:** Value at left of vine sprig **Rev:** Truck-mounted rocket launchers in Smolensk **Edge:** Alternating reeded and smooth

Date	Mintage	F	VF	XF	Unc	BU
2000(m)	10,000,000	—	—	—	2.00	3.00

Y# 666 2 ROUBLES

5.1000 g., Copper-Nickel-Zinc, 23 mm. **Obv:** Value at left of vine sprig **Rev:** Murmansk ship convoy **Edge:** Alternating reeded and smooth

Date	Mintage	F	VF	XF	Unc	BU
2000(m)	10,000,000	—	—	—	2.00	3.00

Y# 667 2 ROUBLES

Copper-Nickel-Zinc, 23 mm. **Obv:** Value at left of vine sprig **Rev:** Defense of Moscow scene **Edge:** Alternating reeded and smooth

Date	Mintage	F	VF	XF	Unc	BU
2000(m)	10,000,000	—	—	—	2.00	3.00

Y# 668 2 ROUBLES

Copper-Nickel-Zinc, 23 mm. **Obv:** Value at left of vine sprig **Rev:** Marine landing scene in Novorusiisk **Edge:** Alternating reeded and smooth

Date	Mintage	F	VF	XF	Unc	BU
2000(sp)	10,000,000	—	—	—	2.00	3.00

Y# 669 2 ROUBLES

Copper-Nickel-Zinc, 23 mm. **Obv:** Value at left of vine sprig **Rev:** Siege of Leningrad truck convoy scene **Edge:** Alternating reeded and smooth

Date	Mintage	F	VF	XF	Unc	BU
2000(sp)	10,000,000	—	—	—	2.00	3.00

Y# 675 2 ROUBLES

5.2000 g., Copper-Nickel, 23 mm. **Subject:** Yuri Gagarin **Obv:** Value and date to left of vine sprig **Rev:** Uniformed bust facing **Edge:** Segmented reeding

Date	Mintage	F	VF	XF	Unc	BU
2001	—	—	—	—	15.00	18.00
2001(m)	10,000,000	—	—	—	2.00	4.00
2001(sp)	10,000,000	—	—	—	2.00	4.00

Y# 834 2 ROUBLES

5.1000 g., Copper-Nickel, 23 mm. **Obv:** Two headed eagle above curved inscription **Rev:** Value and flower **Edge:** Segmented reeding

Date	Mintage	F	VF	XF	Unc	BU
2002(sp)	—	—	—	—	4.00	5.00

Y# 606 5 ROUBLES

6.5000 g., Copper-Nickel Clad Copper, 25 mm. **Obv:** Double-headed eagle **Rev:** Value at left of vine sprig **Edge:** Reeded and plain sections

Date	Mintage	F	VF	XF	Unc	BU
1997(m)	—	—	—	—	3.00	4.00
1997(sp)	—	—	—	—	3.00	4.00
1998(m)	—	—	—	—	3.00	4.00
1998(sp)	—	—	—	—	3.00	4.00

Y# 799 5 ROUBLES

6.4500 g., Copper-Nickel Clad Copper, 25 mm. **Obv:** Curved bank name below eagle **Edge:** Segmented reeding

Date	Mintage	F	VF	XF	Unc	BU
2002	—	—	—	—	3.00	4.00

Y# 670 10 ROUBLES

8.2600 g., Bi-Metallic Copper-Nickel center in Brass ring, 27 mm. **Series:** WWII **Subject:** 55th Anniversary - Victorious Conclusion of WWII **Obv:** Value **Rev:** Infantry officer within star design **Edge:** Reeded and lettered

Date	Mintage	F	VF	XF	Unc	BU
2000(sp)	10,000,000	—	—	—	4.00	7.00
2000(m)	10,000,000	—	—	—	4.00	7.00

Y# 676 10 ROUBLES

8.2200 g., Bi-Metallic Copper-Nickel center in Brass ring, 27 mm. **Subject:** Yuri Gagarin **Obv:** Value with latent image in zero within circle and sprigs **Rev:** Helmeted bust 1/4 right **Edge:** Reeding over denomination

Date	Mintage	F	VF	XF	Unc	BU
2001(m)	10,000,000	—	—	—	4.00	5.00
2001(sp)	10,000,000	—	—	—	4.00	5.00

Y# 739 10 ROUBLES

8.2200 g., Bi-Metallic Copper-Nickel center in Brass ring, 27 mm. **Subject:** Ancient Towns - Derbent **Obv:** Value with latent image in zero within circle and sprigs **Rev:** Shield above walled city view **Edge:** Reeding over denomination

Date	Mintage	F	VF	XF	Unc	BU
2002	5,000,000	—	—	—	4.00	5.00

Y# 740 10 ROUBLES

8.2200 g., Bi-Metallic Copper-Nickel center in Brass ring, 27 mm. **Subject:** Ancient Towns - Kostroma **Obv:** Value with latent image in zero within circle and sprigs **Rev:** Cupola, shield and river view **Edge:** Reeding over denomination

Date	Mintage	F	VF	XF	Unc	BU
2002	5,000,000	—	—	—	4.00	6.00

Y# 741 10 ROUBLES

8.2200 g., Bi-Metallic Copper-Nickel center in Brass ring, 27 mm. **Subject:** Ancient Towns - Staraya Russa **Obv:** Value with latent image in zero within circle and sprigs **Rev:** Shield and cathedral **Edge:** Reeding over denomination

Date	Mintage	F	VF	XF	Unc	BU
2002(sp)	5,000,000	—	—	—	4.00	6.00

Y# 748 10 ROUBLES

8.2200 g., Bi-Metallic Copper-Nickel center in Brass ring, 27 mm. **Subject:** Ministry of Education **Obv:** Value with latent image in zero within circle and sprigs **Rev:** Seedling within open book **Edge:** Reeding over denomination

Date	Mintage	F	VF	XF	Unc	BU
2002(m)	5,000,000	—	—	—	4.00	6.00

Y# 749 10 ROUBLES

8.2200 g., Bi-Metallic Copper-Nickel center in Brass ring, 27 mm. **Subject:** Ministry of Finance **Obv:** Value with latent image in zero within circle and sprigs **Rev:** Caduceus within monogram **Edge:** Reeding over denomination

Date	Mintage	F	VF	XF	Unc	BU
2002(sp)	5,000,000	—	—	—	4.00	6.00

Y# 750 10 ROUBLES

8.2200 g., Bi-Metallic Copper-Nickel center in Brass ring, 27 mm. **Subject:** Ministry of Economic Development **Obv:** Value with latent image in zero within circle and sprigs **Rev:** Crowned double-headed eagle with cornucopia and caduceus **Edge:** Reeding over denomination

Date	Mintage	F	VF	XF	Unc	BU
2002(sp)	5,000,000	—	—	—	4.00	6.00

Y# 751 10 ROUBLES

8.2200 g., Bi-Metallic Copper-Nickel center in Brass ring, 27 mm. **Subject:** Ministry of Foreign Affairs **Obv:** Value with latent image in zero within circle and sprigs **Rev:** Crowned double-headed eagle above crossed sprigs **Edge:** Reeding over denomination

Date	Mintage	F	VF	XF	Unc	BU
2002(sp)	5,000,000	—	—	—	4.00	6.00

Y# 752 10 ROUBLES

8.2200 g., Bi-Metallic Copper-Nickel center in Brass ring, 27 mm. **Subject:** Ministry of Internal Affairs **Obv:** Value with latent image in zero within circle and sprigs **Rev:** Crowned double-headed eagle with round breast shield **Edge:** Reeding over denomination

Date	Mintage	F	VF	XF	Unc	BU
2002(sp)	5,000,000	—	—	—	4.00	6.00

Y# 753 10 ROUBLES

8.2200 g., Bi-Metallic Copper-Nickel center in Brass ring, 27 mm. **Subject:** Ministry of Justice **Obv:** Value with latent image in zero within circle and sprigs **Rev:** Crowned double-headed eagle with column on breast shield **Edge:** Reeding over denomination

Date	Mintage	F	VF	XF	Unc	BU
2002(sp)	5,000,000	—	—	—	4.00	6.00

Y# 754 10 ROUBLES

8.2200 g., Bi-Metallic Copper-Nickel center in Brass ring, 27 mm. **Subject:** Russian Armed Forces **Obv:** Value with latent image in zero within circle and sprigs **Rev:** Crowned double-headed eagle with crowned pointed top shield **Edge:** Reeding over denomination

Date	Mintage	F	VF	XF	Unc	BU
2002(m)	5,000,000	—	—	—	4.00	6.00

Y# 817 10 ROUBLES

8.3400 g., Bi-Metallic Copper-Nickel center in Brass ring, 27 mm. **Obv:** Value with latent image in zero within circle and sprigs **Rev:** Murom city view and tilted oval shields within circle **Edge:** Reeded and lettered

Date	Mintage	F	VF	XF	Unc	BU
2003(sp)	5,000,000	—	—	—	4.00	6.00

Y# 818 10 ROUBLES

8.3400 g., Bi-Metallic Copper-Nickel center in Brass ring, 27 mm. **Obv:** Value with latent image in zero within circle and sprigs **Rev:** Kasimov city view and shield within circle **Edge:** Reeded and lettered

Date	Mintage	F	VF	XF	Unc	BU
2003(sp)	5,000,000	—	—	—	4.00	6.00

Y# 819 10 ROUBLES

8.3400 g., Bi-Metallic Copper-Nickel center in Brass ring, 27 mm. **Obv:** Value with latent image in zero within circle and sprigs **Rev:** Monument, city view and shield within circle **Edge:** Reeded and lettered

Date	Mintage	F	VF	XF	Unc	BU
2003(m)	5,000,000	—	—	—	4.00	6.00

Y# 800 10 ROUBLES

8.4400 g., Bi-Metallic Copper-Nickel center in Brass ring, 27.1 mm. **Obv:** Value with latent image in zero within circle and sprigs **Rev:** Shield above walled city **Edge:** Reeding over lettering

Date	Mintage	F	VF	XF	Unc	BU
2003(sp)	—	—	—	—	4.00	6.00

Y# 824 10 ROUBLES

8.4600 g., Bi-Metallic Copper-Nickel center in Brass ring, 27.08 mm. **Subject:** Town of Ryazhsk **Obv:** Value with latent image in zero within circle and sprigs **Obv. Legend:** БАНК РОССИИ **Rev:** City view and crowned shield within circle **Edge:** Reeded and lettered

Date	Mintage	F	VF	XF	Unc	BU
2004ММД	—	—	—	—	4.00	6.00

Y# 825 10 ROUBLES

8.4600 g., Bi-Metallic, 27.08 mm. **Subject:** Town of Dmitrov **Obv:** Value with latent image in zero within circle and sprigs **Obv. Legend:** БАНК РОССИИ **Rev:** City view and crowned shield within circle **Edge:** Reeded and lettered

Date	Mintage	F	VF	XF	Unc	BU
2004ММД	—	—	—	—	4.00	6.00

Y# 826 10 ROUBLES

8.4600 g., Bi-Metallic, 27.08 mm. **Subject:** Town of Kem **Obv:** Value with latent image in zero within circle and sprigs **Obv. Legend:** БАНК РОССИИ **Rev:** City view and crowned shield within circle **Edge:** Reeded and lettered

Date	Mintage	F	VF	XF	Unc	BU
2004СПМД	—	—	—	—	4.00	6.00

Y# 827 10 ROUBLES

8.4000 g., Bi-Metallic Copper-Nickel center in brass ring, 27 mm. **Obv:** Value with latent image in zero within circle and sprigs **Rev:** WWII eternal flame monument above date and sprig within circle **Edge:** Reeded and Lettered

Date	Mintage	F	VF	XF	Unc	BU
2005	—	—	—	—	4.00	6.00

Y# 886 10 ROUBLES

8.2300 g., Bi-Metallic Copper-Nickel center in Brass ring, 27 mm. **Obv:** Value with latent image in zero within circle and sprigs **Rev:** Moscow coat of arms within circle **Edge:** Reeded and lettered

Date	Mintage	F	VF	XF	Unc	BU
2005	—	—	—	—	4.00	6.00

Y# 887 10 ROUBLES

8.2300 g., Bi-Metallic Copper-Nickel center in Brass ring, 27 mm. **Obv:** Value with latent image in zero within circle and sprigs **Rev:** Leningrad Oblast coat of arms within circle **Edge:** Reeded and lettered

Date	Mintage	F	VF	XF	Unc	BU
2005	—	—	—	—	4.00	6.00

Y# 888 10 ROUBLES

8.2300 g., Bi-Metallic Copper-Nickel center in Brass ring, 27 mm. **Obv:** Value with latent image in zero within circle and sprigs **Rev:** Tverskaya arms within circle **Edge:** Reeded and lettered

Date	Mintage	F	VF	XF	Unc	BU
2005	—	—	—	—	4.00	6.00

Y# 889 10 ROUBLES
8.2300 g., Bi-Metallic Copper-Nickel center in Brass ring, 27 mm. **Obv:** Value with latent image in zero within circle and sprigs **Rev:** Krasnodarskiy Kray coat of arms **Edge:** Reeded and lettered

Date	Mintage	F	VF	XF	Unc	BU
2005	—	—	—	—	4.00	6.00

Y# 890 10 ROUBLES
8.2300 g., Bi-Metallic Copper-Nickel center in Brass ring, 27 mm. **Obv:** Value with latent image in zero within circle and sprigs **Rev:** Orlovskaya Oblast coat of arms within circle **Edge:** Reeded and lettered

Date	Mintage	F	VF	XF	Unc	BU
2005	—	—	—	—	4.00	6.00

Y# 891 10 ROUBLES
8.2300 g., Bi-Metallic Copper-Nickel center in Brass ring, 27 mm. **Obv:** Value with latent image in zero within circle and sprigs **Rev:** Tatarstan Republic coat of arms within circle **Edge:** Reeded and lettered

Date	Mintage	F	VF	XF	Unc	BU
2005	—	—	—	—	4.00	6.00

Y# 956 10 ROUBLES
8.3000 g., Bi-Metallic Copper-Nickel center in Brass ring, 27 mm. **Obv:** Value with latent image in zero within circle and sprays **Rev:** Kaliningrad arms **Edge:** Reeded and lettered

Date	Mintage	F	VF	XF	Unc	BU
2005	—	—	—	—	4.00	6.00

Y# 957 10 ROUBLES
8.3000 g., Bi-Metallic Copper-Nickel center in Brass ring, 27 mm. **Obv:** Value with latent image in zero within circle and sprays **Rev:** Kasan arms **Edge:** Reeded and lettered

Date	Mintage	F	VF	XF	Unc	BU
2005	—	—	—	—	4.00	6.00

Y# 958 10 ROUBLES
8.3000 g., Bi-Metallic Copper-Nickel center in Brass ring, 27 mm. **Obv:** Value with latent image in zero within circle and sprays **Rev:** Mzensk arms **Edge:** Reeded and lettered

Date	Mintage	F	VF	XF	Unc	BU
2005	—	—	—	—	4.00	6.00

Y# 959 10 ROUBLES
8.3000 g., Bi-Metallic Copper-Nickel center in Brass ring, 27 mm. **Obv:** Value with latent image in zero within circle and sprays **Rev:** Borovsk arms **Edge:** Reeded and lettered

Date	Mintage	F	VF	XF	Unc	BU
2005	—	—	—	—	4.00	6.00

Y# 943 10 ROUBLES
Bi-Metallic Copper-Nickel center in Brass ring **Obv:** Double-headed eagle **Rev:** City of Kazan

Date	Mintage	F	VF	XF	Unc	BU
2005	—	—	—	—	4.00	6.00

Y# 944 10 ROUBLES
Bi-Metallic Copper-Nickel center in Brass ring **Obv:** Double-headed eagle **Rev:** City of Borobesk

Date	Mintage	F	VF	XF	Unc	BU
2005	—	—	—	—	4.00	6.00

Y# 945 10 ROUBLES
Bi-Metallic **Obv:** Double-headed eagle **Rev:** City of Machensk

Date	Mintage	F	VF	XF	Unc	BU
2005	—	—	—	—	4.00	6.00

Y# 946 10 ROUBLES
Bi-Metallic Copper-Nickel center in Brass ring **Obv:** Double-headed eagle **Rev:** City of Kaliningrad

Date	Mintage	F	VF	XF	Unc	BU
2005	—	—	—	—	4.00	6.00

Y# 947 10 ROUBLES
Bi-Metallic Copper-Nickel center in Brass ring **Obv:** Double-headed eagle **Rev:** City of Belgorod

Date	Mintage	F	VF	XF	Unc	BU
2006	—	—	—	—	4.00	6.00

Y# 948 10 ROUBLES
Bi-Metallic Copper-Nickel center in Brass ring **Obv:** Double-headed eagle **Rev:** City of Kargopol

Date	Mintage	F	VF	XF	Unc	BU
2006	—	—	—	—	4.00	6.00

Y# 949 10 ROUBLES
Bi-Metallic Copper-Nickel center in Brass ring **Obv:** Double-headed eagle **Rev:** City of Turzhok

Date	Mintage	F	VF	XF	Unc	BU
2006	—	—	—	—	4.00	6.00

Y# 950 10 ROUBLES
Bi-Metallic **Obv:** Double-headed eagle **Rev:** Coat of arms, Primorski Krai

Date	Mintage	F	VF	XF	Unc	BU
2006	—	—	—	—	4.00	6.00

Y# 951 10 ROUBLES
Bi-Metallic Copper-Nickel center in Brass ring **Obv:** Double-headed eagle **Rev:** Coat of arms, Chitinskaya Oblast

Date	Mintage	F	VF	XF	Unc	BU
2006	—	—	—	—	4.00	6.00

Y# 952 10 ROUBLES
Bi-Metallic Copper-Nickel center in Brass ring **Obv:** Double-headed eagle **Rev:** Coat of arms, Republic of Sakha (Yakotia)

Date	Mintage	F	VF	XF	Unc	BU
2006	—	—	—	—	4.00	6.00

Y# 953 10 ROUBLES
Bi-Metallic Copper-Nickel center in Brass ring **Obv:** Double-headed eagle **Rev:** Coat of arms, Republic of Altay

Date	Mintage	F	VF	XF	Unc	BU
2006	—	—	—	—	4.00	6.00

Y# 960 10 ROUBLES
8.3000 g., Bi-Metallic, 27 mm. **Obv:** Value with latent image in zero within circle and sprays **Rev:** Belgorod arms **Edge:** Reeded and lettered

Date	Mintage	F	VF	XF	Unc	BU
2006	—	—	—	—	4.00	6.00

Y# 961 10 ROUBLES
8.3000 g., Bi-Metallic Copper-Nickel center in Brass ring, 27 mm. **Obv:** Value with latent image in zero within circle and sprays **Rev:** Torzhok arms **Edge:** Reeded and lettered

Date	Mintage	F	VF	XF	Unc	BU
2006	—	—	—	—	4.00	6.00

Y# 962 10 ROUBLES
8.3000 g., Bi-Metallic Copper-Nickel center in Brass ring, 27 mm. **Obv:** Value with latent image in zero within circle and sprays **Rev:** Kargopol arms **Edge:** Reeded and lettered

Date	Mintage	F	VF	XF	Unc	BU
2006	—	—	—	—	4.00	6.00

Y# 938 10 ROUBLES
8.2300 g., Bi-Metallic Copper-Nickel center in Brass ring, 27 mm. **Obv:** Value with latent image in zero within circle and sprigs **Rev:** Republic of Altai arms **Edge:** Lettered and reeded

Date	Mintage	F	VF	XF	Unc	BU
2006(sp)	10,000,000	—	—	—	4.00	6.00

Y# 939 10 ROUBLES
8.2300 g., Bi-Metallic Copper-Nickel center in Brass ring, 27 mm. **Obv:** Value with latent image in zero within circle and sprigs **Rev:** Chita Region arms **Edge:** Lettered and reeded

Date	Mintage	F	VF	XF	Unc	BU
2006(sp)	10,000,000	—	—	—	4.00	6.00

Y# 940 10 ROUBLES
8.2300 g., Bi-Metallic Copper-Nickel center in Brass ring, 27 mm. **Obv:** Value with latent image in zero within circle and sprigs **Rev:** Primorskij Kraj Maritime Territory coat of arms **Edge:** Lettered and reeded

Date	Mintage	F	VF	XF	Unc	BU
2006(sp)	10,000,000	—	—	—	4.00	6.00

Y# 941 10 ROUBLES
8.2300 g., Bi-Metallic Copper-Nickel center in Brass ring, 27 mm. **Obv:** Value with latent image in zero within circle and sprigs **Rev:** Sakha Republic coat of arms **Edge:** Lettered and reeded

Date	Mintage	F	VF	XF	Unc	BU
2006(sp)	10,000,000	—	—	—	4.00	6.00

Y# 942 10 ROUBLES
8.2300 g., Bi-Metallic **Ring Composition:** Brass **Center Composition:** Copper-Nickel, 27 mm. **Obv:** Value with latent image in zero within circle and sprigs **Rev:** Sakhalin Region coat of arms **Edge:** Lettered and reeded

Date	Mintage	F	VF	XF	Unc	BU
2006(sp)	10,000,000	—	—	—	4.00	6.00

Y# 963 10 ROUBLES
8.3000 g., Bi-Metallic, 27 mm. **Obv:** Value with latent image in zero within circle and sprays **Rev:** Vologda arms **Edge:** Reeded and lettered

Date	Mintage	F	VF	XF	Unc	BU
2007	—	—	—	—	4.00	6.00

Y# 964 10 ROUBLES
8.3000 g., Bi-Metallic, 27 mm. **Obv:** Value with latent image in zero within circle and sprays **Rev:** Veliky Ustyug arms **Edge:** Reeded and lettered

Date	Mintage	F	VF	XF	Unc	BU
2007	—	—	—	—	4.00	6.00

Y# 965 10 ROUBLES
8.3000 g., Bi-Metallic, 27 mm. **Obv:** Value with latent image in zero within circle and sprays **Rev:** Gdov arms **Edge:** Reeded and lettered

Date	Mintage	F	VF	XF	Unc	BU
2007	—	—	—	—	4.00	6.00

Y# 970 10 ROUBLES
8.5700 g., Bi-Metallic, 27.08 mm. **Obv:** Value with latent image in zero within circle and sprays **Obv. Legend:** БАНК РОССИИ **Rev:** Rostov Region arms **Edge:** Reeded and lettered

Date	Mintage	F	VF	XF	Unc	BU
2007(sp)	—	—	—	—	4.00	6.00

Y# 971 10 ROUBLES

8.5700 g., Bi-Metallic, 27.08 mm. **Obv:** Value with latent image in zero within circle and sprays **Obv. Legend:** БАНК РОССИИ **Rev:** Caucasia Republic arms **Edge:** Reeded and lettered

Date	Mintage	F	VF	XF	Unc	BU
2007(sp)	—	—	—	—	4.00	6.00

Y# 972 10 ROUBLES

8.5700 g., Bi-Metallic, 27.08 mm. **Obv:** Value with latent image in zero within circle and sprays **Obv. Legend:** БАНК РОССИИ **Rev:** Bashkiria Republic arms **Edge:** Reeded and lettered

Date	Mintage	F	VF	XF	Unc	BU
2007(sp)	—	—	—	—	4.00	6.00

Y# 973 10 ROUBLES

8.5700 g., Bi-Metallic, 27.08 mm. **Obv:** Value with latent image in zero within circle and sprays **Obv. Legend:** БАНК РОССИИ **Rev:** Archangel region arms **Edge:** Reeded and lettered

Date	Mintage	F	VF	XF	Unc	BU
2007(sp)	—	—	—	—	4.00	6.00

Y# 974 10 ROUBLES

8.5700 g., Bi-Metallic Copper-Nickel center in brass ring., 27.08 mm. **Obv:** Value with latent image in zero within circle and sprays **Obv. Legend:** БАНК РОССИИ **Rev:** Novosibirsk region arms **Edge:** Reeded and lettered **Edge Lettering:** Denomination

Date	Mintage	F	VF	XF	Unc	BU
2007(sp)	—	—	—	—	4.00	6.00

Y# 975 10 ROUBLES

8.2000 g., Bi-Metallic Copper-Nickel center in brass ring., 27.09 mm. **Obv:** Value with latent image in zero within circle and sprays **Rev:** Udmurt Republic arms **Rev. Legend:** УДМУРТСКАЯ РЕСПУБЛИКА **Edge:** Reeded and lettered **Edge Lettering:** Denomination

Date	Mintage	F	VF	XF	Unc	BU
2008ММД	—	—	—	0.90	2.25	3.00

KM# 976 10 ROUBLES

8.2800 g., Bi-Metallic Copper-Nickel center in brass ring., 27.10 mm. **Series:** Ancient cities **Subject:** Vlaimir **Obv:** Value with latent image in zero within circle and sprays **Rev:** Small shield at upper left above city view **Rev. Legend:** < ВЛАДИМИР > **Edge:** Reeded and lettered **Edge Lettering:** Denomination

Date	Mintage	F	VF	XF	Unc	BU
2008ММД	—	—	—	0.90	2.25	3.00

RWANDA

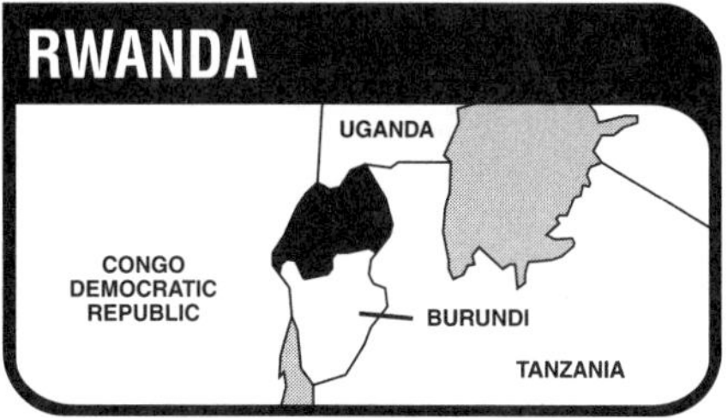

The Republic of Rwanda, located in central Africa between the Republic of the Congo and Tanzania, has an area of 10,169 sq. mi. (26,340 sq. km.) and a population of 7.3 million. Capital: Kigali. The economy is based on agriculture and mining. Coffee and tin are exported.

German Lieutenant Count von Goetzen was the first European to visit Rwanda, 1894. Four years later the court of the Mwami (the Tutsi king of Rwanda) willingly permitted the kingdom to become a protectorate of Germany. In 1916, during the African campaigns of World War I, Belgian troops from Congo occupied Rwanda. After the war it, together with Burundi, became a Belgian League of Nations mandate under the name of the Territory of Ruanda-Urundi. Following World War II, Ruanda-Urundi became a Belgian administered U.N. trust territory. The Tutsi monarchy was deposed by the U.N. supervised election of 1961, after which Belgium granted Rwanda internal autonomy. On July 1, 1962, the U.N. terminated the Belgian trusteeship and granted full independence to both Rwanda and Burundi.

For earlier coinage see Belgian Congo, and Rwanda and Burundi.

MINT MARKS

(a) - Paris, privy marks only
(b) - Brussels, privy marks only

MONETARY SYSTEM

100 Centimes = 1 Franc

REPUBLIC

STANDARD COINAGE

KM# 9 1/2 FRANC

0.7000 g., Aluminum, 16.1 mm. **Obv:** Value divides design within circle **Rev:** Inscription within circle

Date	Mintage	F	VF	XF	Unc	BU
1970	5,000,000	—	0.50	0.85	1.75	—

KM# 5 FRANC

Copper-Nickel, 21 mm. **Obv:** Head 1/4 right **Rev:** Value above flag draped arms **Edge:** Plain

Date	Mintage	F	VF	XF	Unc	BU
1964(b)	3,000,000	—	5.00	10.00	20.00	—
1965(b)	4,500,000	—	0.50	0.85	1.75	—

KM# 8 FRANC

1.0900 g., Aluminum, 21.1 mm. **Obv:** Head right **Rev:** Value above flag draped arms

Date	Mintage	F	VF	XF	Unc	BU
1969	5,000,000	—	0.50	1.50	3.50	—

KM# 12 FRANC

1.0200 g., Aluminum, 21.1 mm. **Obv:** Millet flower **Rev:** Value above flag draped arms

Date	Mintage	F	VF	XF	Unc	BU
1974	13,000,000	—	0.20	0.50	1.00	—
1977	15,000,000	—	0.15	0.25	0.75	—
1985	—	—	0.10	0.15	0.65	—

KM# 22 FRANC

0.0700 g., Aluminum, 16 mm. **Obv:** National arms **Rev:** Sorghum plant **Edge:** Plain

Date	Mintage	F	VF	XF	Unc	BU
2003(a)	—	—	—	0.25	0.65	1.00

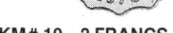

KM# 10 2 FRANCS

1.4900 g., Aluminum, 23.5 mm. **Series:** F.A.O. **Obv:** Seated figure facing above monogramed banner **Rev:** Value above flag draped arms **Shape:** Scalloped

Date	Mintage	F	VF	XF	Unc	BU
1970	5,000,000	—	0.10	0.20	0.50	—

KM# 6 5 FRANCS

Bronze **Obv:** Head 3/4 right **Rev:** Value above flag draped arms

Date	Mintage	F	VF	XF	Unc	BU
1964(b)	4,000,000	—	0.25	0.50	1.75	—
1965(b)	3,000,000	—	5.00	10.00	20.00	—

KM# 13 5 FRANCS

5.0000 g., Bronze, 26 mm. **Obv:** Coffee tree branch **Rev:** Value above flag draped arms

Date	Mintage	F	VF	XF	Unc	BU
1974	7,000,000	—	1.00	3.00	6.00	—
1977	7,002,000	—	1.00	2.00	4.00	—
1987	—	—	0.25	0.50	1.85	—

KM# 23 5 FRANCS

2.9600 g., Brass Plated Steel, 20 mm. **Obv:** National arms **Rev:** Coffee plant **Edge:** Plain

Date	Mintage	F	VF	XF	Unc	BU
2003(a)	—	—	—	0.25	0.65	1.00

KM# 7 10 FRANCS

10.2900 g., Copper-Nickel, 30.5 mm. **Obv:** Head 1/4 right **Rev:** Value above flag draped arms

Date	Mintage	F	VF	XF	Unc	BU
1964(b)	6,000,000	—	1.00	2.00	4.50	—

KM# 14.1 10 FRANCS
10.5000 g., Copper-Nickel, 30.1 mm. **Obv:** Coffee tree branch **Rev:** Value above flag draped arms

Date	Mintage	F	VF	XF	Unc	BU
1974	6,000,000	—	3.00	5.00	10.00	15.00

KM# 14.2 10 FRANCS
7.0000 g., Copper-Nickel **Obv:** Coffee tree branch **Rev:** Value above flag draped arms **Note:** Reduced size.

Date	Mintage	F	VF	XF	Unc	BU
1985	—	—	0.50	0.85	1.85	—

KM# 24 10 FRANCS
5.0000 g., Brass Plated Steel, 23.9 mm. **Obv:** National arms **Rev:** Banana tree **Edge:** Plain

Date	Mintage	F	VF	XF	Unc	BU
2003(a)	—	—	—	0.45	1.00	1.50

KM# 15 20 FRANCS
7.9500 g., Brass, 27 mm. **Obv:** Millet flower bud **Rev:** Value above flag draped arms

Date	Mintage	F	VF	XF	Unc	BU
1977(a)	22,000,000	—	1.00	2.00	4.00	—

KM# 25 20 FRANCS
3.5000 g., Nickel Clad Steel, 20 mm. **Obv:** National arms **Rev:** Coffee plant seedling **Edge:** Reeded

Date	Mintage	F	VF	XF	Unc	BU
2003(a)	—	—	—	—	1.75	2.00

KM# 16 50 FRANCS
9.9400 g., Brass, 28.88 mm. **Obv:** Leafy branch **Rev:** Value above flag draped arms

Date	Mintage	F	VF	XF	Unc	BU
1977(a)	9,000,000	—	2.50	3.50	7.00	—

KM# 26 50 FRANCS
5.8000 g., Nickel Clad Steel, 24 mm. **Obv:** National arms **Rev:** Ear of corn within husks **Edge:** Reeded

Date	Mintage	F	VF	XF	Unc	BU
2003(a)	—	—	—	—	4.50	5.00

RWANDA-BURUNDI

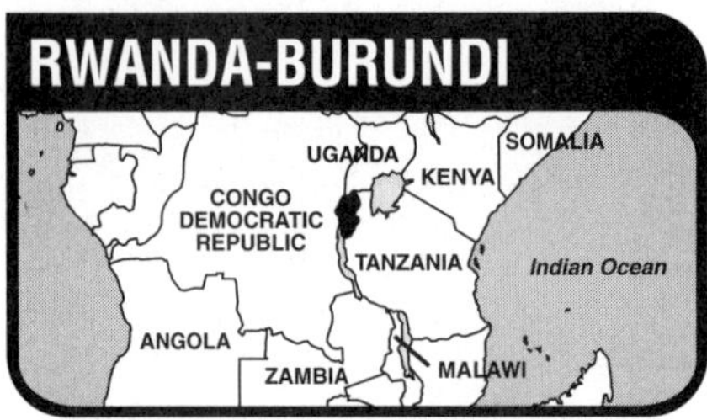

Rwanda-Burundi, a Belgian League of Nations mandate and United Nations trust territory comprising the provinces of Ruanda-Urundi of the former colony of German East Africa, was located in central Africa between the present Democratic Republic of the Congo, Uganda and mainland Tanzania. The mandate-trust territory had an area of 20,916 sq. mi. (54,272 sq. km.) and a population of 4.3 million.

For specific statistics and history of Ruanda and of Urundi see individual entries.

When Rwanda and Burundi were formed into a mandate for administration by Belgium, their names were combined as Ruanda-Urundi and they were organized as an integral part of the Belgian Congo. During the mandate-trust territory period, they utilized the coinage of the Belgian Congo, which from 1954 through 1960carried the appropriate dual identification. After the Belgian Congo acquired independence as the Democratic Republic of the Congo, the provinces of Ruanda and Urundi reverted to their former names of Rwanda and Burundi and utilized a common currency issued by a Central Bank (B.E.R.B.) established for that purpose until the time when, as independent republics, each issued its own national coinage.

For earlier coinage see Belgian Congo.

MONETARY SYSTEM
100 Centimes = 1 Franc

PROVINCES

STANDARD COINAGE

KM# 1 FRANC
Brass **Obv:** Value **Rev:** Lion

Date	Mintage	F	VF	XF	Unc	BU
1960	2,000,000	—	3.50	7.50	17.50	20.00
1961	16,000,000	—	0.50	1.00	3.50	6.00
1964	3,000,000	—	3.00	6.50	15.00	18.00

KM# 2 FRANC
Copper-Nickel **Obv:** Value **Rev:** Head left **Note:** Mule.

Date	Mintage	F	VF	XF	Unc	BU
1961	50	—	—	—	500	—

SAARLAND

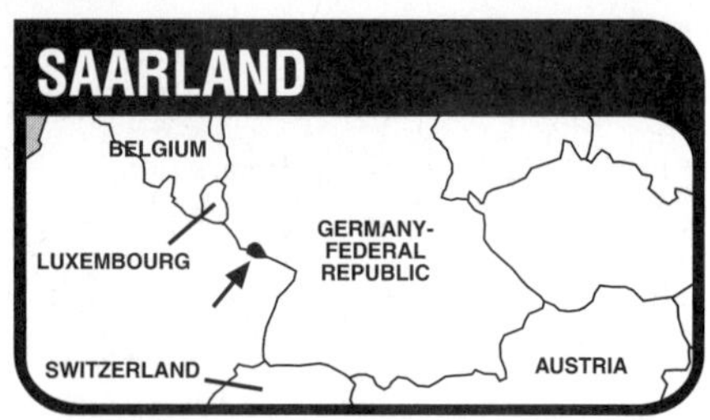

The Saar, the 10th state of the German Federal Republic, is located in the coal-rich Saar basin on the Franco-German frontier, and has an area of 991 sq. mi. and a population of 1.2 million. Capital: Saarbrucken. It is an important center of mining and heavy industry.

From the late 14th century until the fall of Napoleon, the city of Saarbrucken was ruled by the counts of Nassau-Saarbrucken, but the surrounding territory was subject to the political and cultural domination of France. At the close of the Napoleonic era, the Saarland came under the control of Prussia. France was awarded the Saar coal mines following World War I, and the Saarland was made an autonomous territory of the League of Nations, its future political affiliation to be determined by referendum. The plebiscite, 1935, chose re-incorporation into Germany. France reoccupied the Saarland, 1945, establishing strong economic ties and assuming the obligation of defense and foreign affairs. After sustained agitation by West Germany, France agreed, 1955, to there turn of the Saar to Germany by Jan. 1957.

MINT MARK
(a) - Paris - privy marks only

GERMAN REPUBLIC STATE

STANDARD COINAGE

KM# 1 10 FRANKEN
3.0400 g., Aluminum-Bronze, 20 mm. **Obv:** Industrial scene, arms at center **Rev:** Value and date **Designer:** Theo Siegal

Date	Mintage	F	VF	XF	Unc	BU
1954(a)	11,000,000	1.00	2.00	4.00	7.00	9.00

KM# 2 20 FRANKEN
4.0000 g., Aluminum-Bronze, 23.5 mm. **Obv:** Industrial scene, arms at center **Rev:** Value and date **Edge:** Plain **Designer:** Theo Siegal

Date	Mintage	F	VF	XF	Unc	BU
1954(a)	12,950,000	1.00	2.00	4.00	7.00	9.00

KM# 3 50 FRANKEN
8.0000 g., Aluminum-Bronze **Obv:** Industrial scene, arms in center **Rev:** Value and date **Designer:** Theo Siegal

Date	Mintage	F	VF	XF	Unc	BU
1954(a)	5,300,000	4.00	7.00	15.00	30.00	35.00

KM# 4 100 FRANKEN
6.0400 g., Copper-Nickel, 24 mm. **Obv:** Arms within circular design **Rev:** Value and date **Designer:** Theo Siegal

Date	Mintage	F	VF	XF	Unc	BU
1955(a)	11,000,000	2.00	4.00	7.00	17.50	22.50

SAINT HELENA & ASCENSION

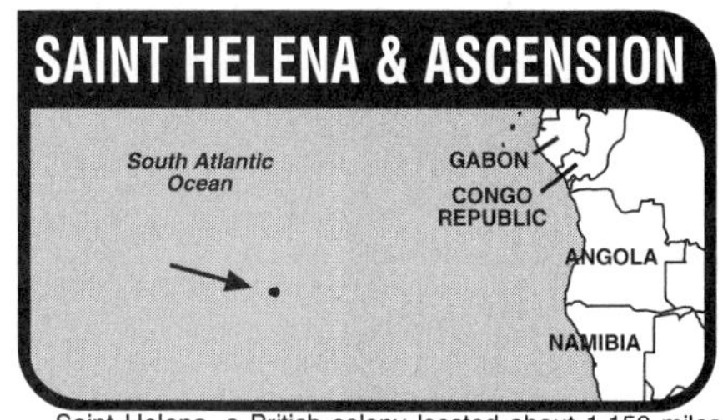

Saint Helena, a British colony located about 1,150 miles (1,850 km.) from the west coast of Africa, has an area of 47 sq. mi. (410 sq. km.) and a population of *7,000. Capital: Jamestown. Flax, lace, and rope are produced for export. Ascension and Tristan da Cunha are dependencies of Saint Helena.

The island was discovered and named by the Portuguese navigator Joao de Nova Castella in 1502. The Portuguese imported livestock, fruit trees, and vegetables but established no permanent settlement. The Dutch occupied the island temporarily, 1645-51. The original European settlement was founded by representatives of the British East India Company sent to annex the island after the departure of the Dutch. The Dutch returned and captured Saint Helena from the British on New Year's Day, 1673, but were in turn ejected by a British force under Sir Richard Munden. Thereafter Saint Helena was the undisputed possession of Great Britain. The island served as the place of exile for Napoleon, several Zulu chiefs, and an ex-sultan of Zanzibar.

RULER
British

MINT MARK
PM - Pobjoy Mint

MONETARY SYSTEM
12 Pence = 1 Shilling
100 Pence = 1 Pound

BRITISH OVERSEAS TERRITORY

STANDARD COINAGE

100 Pence = 1 Pound

KM# 1 PENNY
3.6000 g., Bronze, 20.32 mm. **Ruler:** Queen Elizabeth II **Obv:** Young bust right **Rev:** Tuna fish and value

Date	Mintage	F	VF	XF	Unc	BU
1984	—	—	—	0.20	0.50	1.25
1984 Proof	10,000	Value: 1.50				

KM# 13 PENNY
3.6000 g., Bronze, 20.32 mm. **Ruler:** Queen Elizabeth II **Obv:** Crowned head right **Obv. Designer:** Raphael David Maklouf **Rev:** Tuna fish and value

Date	Mintage	F	VF	XF	Unc	BU
1991	—	—	—	0.15	0.35	1.00

KM# 13a PENNY
3.5000 g., Copper Plated Steel Galvanized steel, 20.28 mm. **Ruler:** Queen Elizabeth II **Obv:** Crowned head right **Obv. Designer:** Raphael David Maklouf **Rev:** Tuna above value **Edge:** Plain

Date	Mintage	F	VF	XF	Unc	BU
1997	—	—	—	0.15	0.35	1.00
2003	—	—	—	0.15	0.35	0.75

KM# 2 2 PENCE
7.1000 g., Bronze, 25.91 mm. **Ruler:** Queen Elizabeth II **Obv:** Young bust right **Rev:** Donkey with firewood

Date	Mintage	F	VF	XF	Unc	BU
1984	—	—	—	0.25	0.65	1.25
1984 Proof	10,000	Value: 2.00				

KM# 12 2 PENCE
7.1000 g., Bronze, 25.91 mm. **Ruler:** Queen Elizabeth II **Obv:** Crowned head right **Obv. Designer:** Raphael David Maklouf **Rev:** Value below donkey

Date	Mintage	F	VF	XF	Unc	BU
1991	—	—	—	0.20	0.60	1.25

KM# 12a 2 PENCE
Copper Plated Steel **Ruler:** Queen Elizabeth II **Obv:** Crowned head right **Obv. Designer:** Raphael David Maklouf **Rev:** Value below donkey **Shape:** 25.91

Date	Mintage	F	VF	XF	Unc	BU
2003	—	—	—	0.20	0.60	1.25

KM# 3 5 PENCE
5.7000 g., Copper-Nickel, 23.59 mm. **Ruler:** Queen Elizabeth II **Obv:** Young bust right **Rev:** Rainpiper

Date	Mintage	F	VF	XF	Unc	BU
1984	—	—	—	0.25	0.65	1.25
1984 Proof	—	Value: 2.00				

KM# 14 5 PENCE
Copper-Nickel, 18 mm. **Ruler:** Queen Elizabeth II **Obv:** Crowned head right **Obv. Designer:** Raphael David Maklouf **Rev:** Value below rainpiper

Date	Mintage	F	VF	XF	Unc	BU
1991	—	—	—	0.20	0.50	1.00

KM# 22 5 PENCE
Copper-Nickel, 18 mm. **Ruler:** Queen Elizabeth II **Obv:** Crowned head right **Rev:** Giant tortoise

Date	Mintage	F	VF	XF	Unc	BU
1998	—	—	—	1.00	2.50	4.50
2003	—	—	—	1.00	2.50	4.50

KM# 4 10 PENCE
11.3000 g., Copper-Nickel, 28.5 mm. **Ruler:** Queen Elizabeth II **Obv:** Young bust right **Rev:** Value below arum lily

Date	Mintage	F	VF	XF	Unc	BU
1984	—	—	—	0.50	1.25	2.00
1984 Proof	—	Value: 3.00				

KM# 15 10 PENCE
11.3000 g., Copper-Nickel, 28.5 mm. **Ruler:** Queen Elizabeth II **Obv:** Crowned head right **Obv. Designer:** Raphael David Maklouf

Date	Mintage	F	VF	XF	Unc	BU
1991	—	—	—	0.30	1.00	1.50

KM# 23 10 PENCE
Copper-Nickel, 24.5 mm. **Ruler:** Queen Elizabeth II **Obv:** Crowned head right **Obv. Designer:** Raphael David Maklouf **Rev:** Dolphins

Date	Mintage	F	VF	XF	Unc	BU
1998	—	—	—	1.00	3.00	5.00
2003	—	—	—	1.00	3.00	5.00

KM# 21 20 PENCE
Copper-Nickel, 21.4 mm. **Ruler:** Queen Elizabeth II **Obv:** Crowned head right **Rev:** Flower **Shape:** 7-sided

Date	Mintage	F	VF	XF	Unc	BU
1998	—	—	—	0.75	1.50	2.50
2003	—	—	—	0.75	1.50	2.50

KM# 5 50 PENCE
13.5000 g., Copper-Nickel, 30 mm. **Ruler:** Queen Elizabeth II **Obv:** Young bust right **Rev:** Green sea turtle **Shape:** 7-sided

Date	Mintage	F	VF	XF	Unc	BU
1984	—	—	—	1.75	3.75	6.00
1984 Proof	—	Value: 7.50				

KM# 16 50 PENCE
13.5000 g., Copper-Nickel, 30 mm. **Ruler:** Queen Elizabeth II **Obv:** Crowned head right **Obv. Designer:** Raphael David Maklouf **Rev:** Green sea turtle **Shape:** 7-sided

Date	Mintage	F	VF	XF	Unc	BU
1991	—	—	—	1.50	3.50	5.00
2003	—	—	—	1.50	3.50	5.00

KM# 6 POUND
9.5000 g., Nickel-Brass, 22.5 mm. **Ruler:** Queen Elizabeth II **Obv:** Young bust right **Rev:** Flying birds

Date	Mintage	F	VF	XF	Unc	BU
1984	—	—	—	2.50	5.50	8.00
1984 Proof	—	Value: 9.00				

KM# 17 POUND
9.5000 g., Nickel-Brass, 22.5 mm. **Ruler:** Queen Elizabeth II **Obv:** Crowned head right **Obv. Designer:** Raphael David Maklouf **Rev:** Two birds in flight left

Date	Mintage	F	VF	XF	Unc	BU
1991	—	—	—	2.25	5.00	7.50
2003	—	—	—	2.25	5.00	7.50

KM# 26 2 POUNDS
11.8100 g., Nickel-Brass, 28.3 mm. **Obv:** Crowned bust right **Obv. Designer:** Raphael Maklouf **Rev:** National arms above value **Edge:** Reeded and lettered **Edge Lettering:** "500TH ANNIVERSARY"

Date	Mintage	F	VF	XF	Unc	BU
2002	—	—	—	6.00	10.00	12.50

KM# 25 2 POUNDS
12.0000 g., Bi-Metallic Copper-Nickel center in Brass ring, 28.4 mm. **Obv:** Crowned bust right **Obv. Designer:** Raphael Maklouf **Rev:** National Arms **Edge:** Reeded and lettered **Edge Lettering:** "LOYAL AND FAITHFUL"

Date	Mintage	F	VF	XF	Unc	BU
2003	—	—	—	9.00	15.00	17.50

SAINT PIERRE & MIQUELON

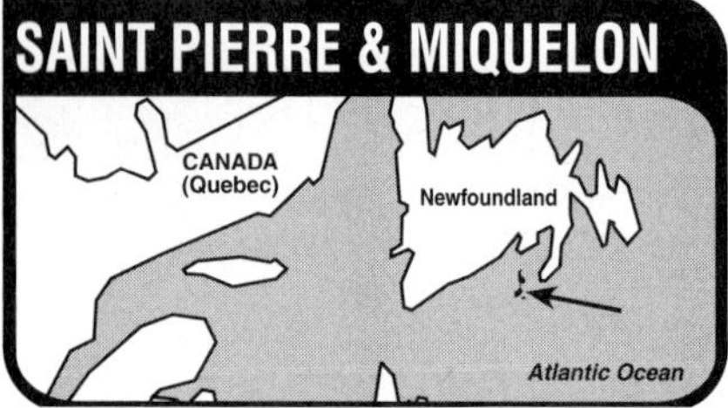

The Territorial Collectivity of Saint Pierre and Miquelon, a French overseas territory located 10 miles (16 km.) off the south coast of Newfoundland, has an area of 93 sq. mi. (242 sq. km.) and a population of *6,000. Capital: Saint Pierre. The economy of the barren archipelago is based on cod fishing and fur farming. Fish and fish products, and mink and silver fox pelts are exported.

The islands were occupied by the French in 1604, then were captured by the British in 1702 and held until 1763, at which time they were returned to the possession of France and employed as a fishing station. They passed between France and England on six more occasions between 1778 and 1814 when the Treaty of Paris awarded them permanently to France. The rugged, soil-poor granite islands, which will support only evergreen shrubs, are all that remain of France's extensive North American colonies. In 1958 Saint Pierre and Miquelon voted in favor of the new constitution of the Fifth Republic of France, thereby choosing to remain within the new French Community.

RULER
French

MINT MARK
(a) - Paris, privy marks only

MONETARY SYSTEM
100 Centimes = 1 Franc

FRENCH OVERSEAS DEPARTMENT

STANDARD COINAGE

KM# 1 FRANC
1.3200 g., Aluminum, 22.56 mm. **Obv:** Winged Liberty head left **Rev:** Ship above value **Edge:** Plain **Designer:** G.B.L. Bazor

Date	Mintage	F	VF	XF	Unc	BU
1948(a)	600,000	0.50	0.75	1.50	6.50	10.00

KM# 2 2 FRANCS
2.1400 g., Aluminum, 26.95 mm. **Obv:** Winged Liberty head left **Rev:** Ship above value **Edge:** Plain **Designer:** G.B.L. Bazor

Date	Mintage	F	VF	XF	Unc	BU
1948(a)	300,000	0.75	1.00	2.00	7.50	12.00

SAINT THOMAS & PRINCE

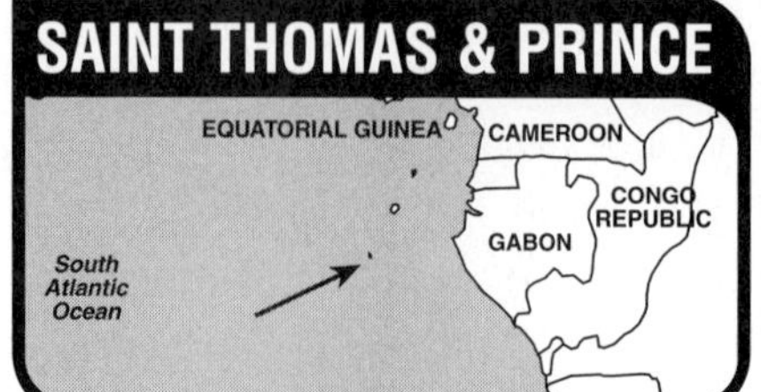

The Democratic Republic of St. Thomas & Prince (São Tomé e Príncipe) is located in the Gulf of Guinea 150 miles (241 km.) off the western coast of Africa. It has an area of 372 sq. mi. (960 sq. km.) and a population of *121,000. Capital: São Tomé. The economy of the islands is based on cocoa, copra and coffee.

Saint Thomas and Saint Prince were uninhabited when discovered by Portuguese navigators Joao de Santarem and Pedro de Escobar in 1470. After the failure of their initial settlement of 1485, the Portuguese successfully colonized St. Thomas with a colony of prisoners and exiled Jews in 1493. An initial prosperity based on the sugar trade gave way to a time of misfortune, 1567-1709, that saw the colony attacked and occupied or plundered by the French and Dutch, ravaged by the slave revolt of 1595; and finally rendered destitute by the transfer of the world sugar trade to Brazil. In the late 1800s, the colony turned from the production of sugar to cocoa, the basis of its present economy

The islands were designated a Portuguese overseas province in 1951. On April 25, 1974, the government of Portugal was seized by a military junta, which reached agreements providing for independence for the Portuguese overseas provinces of Portuguese Guinea (Guinea-Bissau), Mozambique, Cape Verde Islands, Angola, and Saint Thomas and Prince Islands. The Democratic Republic of São Tomé and Principe was declared on July 12, 1975.

RULERS
Portuguese, until 1975

MINT MARKS
R – Rio

MONETARY SYSTEM
100 Centavos = 1 Escudo

PORTUGUESE COLONY

REFORM COINAGE

100 Centavos = 1 Escudo

KM# 2 10 CENTAVOS
Nickel-Bronze **Obv:** Liberty head left **Rev:** Shield within globe above value

Date	Mintage	F	VF	XF	Unc	BU
1929	500,000	2.00	6.00	20.00	50.00	—

KM# 15 10 CENTAVOS
Bronze **Obv:** Value **Rev:** Shield within crowned globe

Date	Mintage	F	VF	XF	Unc	BU
1962	500,000	0.50	1.25	4.50	12.00	—

KM# 15a 10 CENTAVOS
Aluminum **Obv:** Value **Rev:** Shield within crowned globe

Date	Mintage	F	VF	XF	Unc	BU
1971	1,000,000	0.35	0.65	1.25	3.50	—

KM# 3 20 CENTAVOS
Nickel-Bronze **Obv:** Liberty head left **Rev:** Shield within globe above value

Date	Mintage	F	VF	XF	Unc	BU
1929	250,000	2.50	6.50	22.50	55.00	—

KM# 16.1 20 CENTAVOS
Bronze, 18 mm. **Obv:** Value **Rev:** Shield within crowned globe

Date	Mintage	F	VF	XF	Unc	BU
1962	250,000	0.50	1.25	5.50	15.00	—

KM# 16.2 20 CENTAVOS
Bronze, 16 mm. **Obv:** Value **Rev:** Shield within crowned globe

Date	Mintage	F	VF	XF	Unc	BU
1971	750,000	0.35	0.75	1.50	4.00	—

KM# 1 50 CENTAVOS
Nickel-Bronze **Obv:** Liberty head left **Rev:** Shield within globe above value

Date	Mintage	F	VF	XF	Unc	BU
1928	—	30.00	90.00	350	900	—
1929	400,000	4.00	12.00	50.00	150	—

KM# 8 50 CENTAVOS
Nickel-Bronze **Obv:** Value **Rev:** Shield within crowned globe

Date	Mintage	F	VF	XF	Unc	BU
1948	80,000	10.00	30.00	100	265	—

KM# 10 50 CENTAVOS
4.4500 g., Copper-Nickel, 22.64 mm. **Obv:** Value **Rev:** Shield within crowned globe

Date	Mintage	F	VF	XF	Unc	BU
1951	48,000	1.75	3.50	25.00	70.00	—

KM# 17.1 50 CENTAVOS
3.9500 g., Bronze, 20 mm. **Obv:** Value **Rev:** Shield within crowned globe

Date	Mintage	F	VF	XF	Unc	BU
1962	480,000	0.25	0.50	2.50	5.00	—

KM# 17.2 50 CENTAVOS
Bronze, 22 mm. **Obv:** Value **Rev:** Shield within crowned globe

Date	Mintage	F	VF	XF	Unc	BU
1971	600,000	0.20	0.35	1.50	3.00	—

KM# 4 ESCUDO

Copper-Nickel **Obv:** Value **Rev:** Shield within crowned globe

Date	Mintage	F	VF	XF	Unc	BU
1939	100,000	9.00	25.00	100	285	—

KM# 9 ESCUDO

Nickel-Bronze **Obv:** Value **Rev:** Shield within crowned globe

Date	Mintage	F	VF	XF	Unc	BU
1948	60,000	12.50	40.00	120	275	350

KM# 11 ESCUDO

Copper-Nickel **Obv:** Value **Rev:** Shield within crowned globe

Date	Mintage	F	VF	XF	Unc	BU
1951	18,000	3.50	12.00	60.00	175	—

KM# 18 ESCUDO

7.8500 g., Bronze, 26 mm. **Obv:** Value **Rev:** Shield within crowned globe

Date	Mintage	F	VF	XF	Unc	BU
1962	160,000	0.75	2.50	15.00	35.00	—
1971	350,000	0.35	0.75	1.50	3.50	—

KM# 5 2-1/2 ESCUDOS

3.5000 g., 0.6500 Silver 0.0731 oz. ASW **Obv:** Shield within globe on cross **Rev:** Shield within crowned globe

Date	Mintage	F	VF	XF	Unc	BU
1939	80,000	10.00	30.00	100	300	—
1948	120,000	15.00	35.00	100	300	—

KM# 12 2-1/2 ESCUDOS

3.5000 g., 0.6500 Silver 0.0731 oz. ASW **Obv:** Shield within globe on cross **Rev:** Shield within crowned globe

Date	Mintage	F	VF	XF	Unc	BU
1951	64,000	2.50	6.00	30.00	100	—

KM# 19 2-1/2 ESCUDOS

Copper-Nickel **Obv:** Shield within globe on cross **Rev:** Shield within crowned globe

Date	Mintage	F	VF	XF	Unc	BU
1962	140,000	0.75	1.50	5.00	15.00	—
1971	250,000	0.50	1.00	2.50	7.00	—

KM# 6 5 ESCUDOS

7.0000 g., 0.6500 Silver 0.1463 oz. ASW **Obv:** Shield within globe on cross **Rev:** Shield within crowned globe

Date	Mintage	F	VF	XF	Unc	BU
1939	60,000	12.50	35.00	100	300	—
1948	100,000	18.00	45.00	110	300	—

KM# 13 5 ESCUDOS

7.0000 g., 0.6500 Silver 0.1463 oz. ASW, 25 mm. **Obv:** Shield within globe on cross **Rev:** Shield within crowned globe

Date	Mintage	F	VF	XF	Unc	BU
1951	72,000	3.50	7.00	20.00	45.00	—

KM# 20 5 ESCUDOS

4.0000 g., 0.6000 Silver 0.0772 oz. ASW, 22 mm. **Obv:** Shield within globe **Rev:** Shield within crowned globe

Date	Mintage	F	VF	XF	Unc	BU
1962	88,000	1.50	2.50	6.00	12.50	—

KM# 22 5 ESCUDOS

Copper-Nickel **Obv:** Shield within globe on cross **Rev:** Shield within crowned globe

Date	Mintage	F	VF	XF	Unc	BU
1971	100,000	0.75	1.50	3.50	8.00	—

KM# 7 10 ESCUDOS

12.5000 g., 0.8350 Silver 0.3356 oz. ASW **Obv:** Shield within globe on cross **Rev:** Shield within crowned globe

Date	Mintage	F	VF	XF	Unc	BU
1939	40,000	12.00	25.00	65.00	250	—

KM# 14 10 ESCUDOS

12.5000 g., 0.7200 Silver 0.2893 oz. ASW **Obv:** Shield within globe on cross **Rev:** Shield within crowned globe

Date	Mintage	F	VF	XF	Unc	BU
1951	40,000	5.00	9.00	16.50	35.00	—

KM# 23 10 ESCUDOS

Copper-Nickel **Obv:** Shield within globe on cross **Rev:** Shield within crowned globe

Date	Mintage	F	VF	XF	Unc	BU
1971	100,000	1.25	2.50	5.50	12.50	—

KM# 24 20 ESCUDOS

Nickel **Obv:** Shield within globe **Rev:** Shield within circle

Date	Mintage	F	VF	XF	Unc	BU
1971	75,000	1.50	3.00	6.00	13.50	—

KM# 21 50 ESCUDOS

18.0000 g., 0.6500 Silver 0.3761 oz. ASW **Subject:** 500th Anniversary of Discovery **Obv:** Cross within designed circle **Rev:** Double shields flanked by dates, star design at top

Date	Mintage	F	VF	XF	Unc	BU
1970	150,000	—	—	—	8.00	10.00
1970 Matte proof	Est. 200	—	—	—	—	—

Note: Produced at the Lisbon Mint on private contract.

DEMOCRATIC REPUBLIC

STANDARD COINAGE

100 Centimos = 1 Dobra

KM# 25 50 CENTIMOS

Brass, 17 mm. **Series:** F.A.O. **Obv:** Arms with supporters **Rev:** Fish above value

Date	Mintage	F	VF	XF	Unc	BU
1977	2,000,000	—	0.10	0.20	0.75	1.00
1977 Proof	2,500	Value: 3.00				

KM# 26 DOBRA
Brass, 20 mm. **Series:** F.A.O. **Obv:** Arms with supporters **Rev:** Cocoa beans on stem and value

Date	Mintage	F	VF	XF	Unc	BU
1977	1,500,000	—	0.15	0.25	1.00	1.25
1977 Proof	2,500	Value: 3.00				

KM# 27 2 DOBRAS
Copper-Nickel, 18.5 mm. **Series:** F.A.O. **Obv:** Arms with supporters **Rev:** Goats

Date	Mintage	F	VF	XF	Unc	BU
1977	1,000,000	—	0.25	0.40	1.50	1.75
1977 Proof	2,500	Value: 3.50				

KM# 28 5 DOBRAS
Copper-Nickel, 24 mm. **Series:** F.A.O. **Obv:** Arms with supporters **Rev:** Corn and value

Date	Mintage	F	VF	XF	Unc	BU
1977	750,000	—	0.35	0.65	2.00	2.50
1977 Proof	2,500	Value: 5.00				

KM# 29 10 DOBRAS
6.4000 g., Copper-Nickel, 26 mm. **Series:** F.A.O. **Obv:** Arms with supporters **Rev:** Chickens with eggs in cartons

Date	Mintage	F	VF	XF	Unc	BU
1977	300,000	—	0.60	1.25	4.00	5.00
1977 Proof	2,500	Value: 7.00				

KM# 29a 10 DOBRAS
Copper-Nickel Clad Steel, 26 mm. **Series:** F.A.O. **Obv:** Arms with supporters **Rev:** Chickens with eggs in cartons

Date	Mintage	F	VF	XF	Unc	BU
1990	—	—	0.60	1.25	4.00	5.00

KM# 30 20 DOBRAS
7.9000 g., Copper-Nickel Clad Steel, 29 mm. **Series:** F.A.O. **Obv:** Arms with supporters **Rev:** Logo and value to right of various plants and produce

Date	Mintage	F	VF	XF	Unc	BU
1977	500,000	—	1.00	2.00	6.00	7.00
1977 Proof	2,500	Value: 10.00				

KM# 52 50 DOBRAS
Copper-Nickel Clad Steel **Series:** F.A.O. **Obv:** Arms with supporters **Rev:** Value within octogon design with bird above and snake below

Date	Mintage	F	VF	XF	Unc	BU
1990	—	—	—	—	6.00	9.00

KM# 87 100 DOBRAS
Chrome Clad Steel, 17.5 mm. **Obv:** Arms with supporters **Rev:** Value below bird

Date	Mintage	F	VF	XF	Unc	BU
1997	—	—	—	—	1.25	1.75

KM# 88 250 DOBRAS
Chrome Clad Steel **Obv:** Arms with supporters **Rev:** Value above bird

Date	Mintage	F	VF	XF	Unc	BU
1997	—	—	—	—	1.50	3.00

KM# 89 500 DOBRAS
Chrome Clad Steel **Obv:** Arms with supporters **Rev:** Monkey in trees **Shape:** 7-sided

Date	Mintage	F	VF	XF	Unc	BU
1997	—	—	—	—	2.00	3.00

KM# 90 1000 DOBRAS
6.3000 g., Chrome Clad Steel **Obv:** Arms with supporters **Rev:** Flowers and value **Shape:** 7-sided

Date	Mintage	F	VF	XF	Unc	BU
1997	—	—	—	—	2.75	3.75

KM# 91 2000 DOBRAS
Chrome Clad Steel **Obv:** Arms with supporters **Rev:** Tropical food plants within circle **Shape:** 7-sided

Date	Mintage	F	VF	XF	Unc	BU
1997	—	—	—	—	3.75	5.00

SAMOA

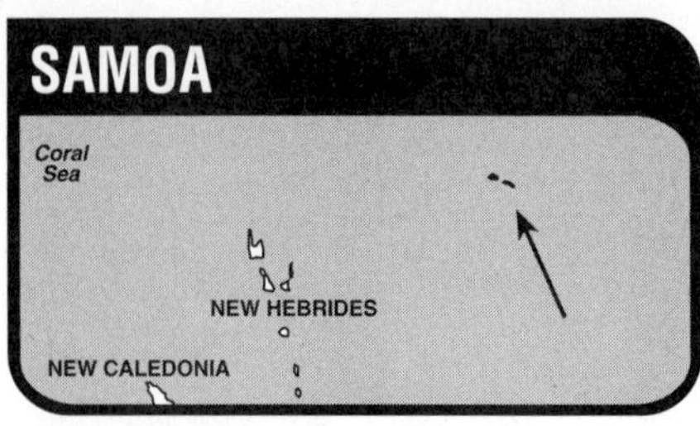

The Independent State of Samoa (formerly Western Samoa), located in the Pacific Ocean 1,600 miles (2,574 km.) northeast of New Zealand, has an area of 1,097 sq. mi. (2,860 sq. km.) and a population of *182,000. Capital: Apia. The economy is based on agriculture, fishing and tourism. Copra, cocoa and bananas are exported.

The first European to sight the Samoan group of islands was the Dutch navigator Jacob Roggeveen in 1722. Great Britain, the United States and Germany established consular representation at Apia in 1847, 1853 and 1861 respectively. The conflicting interests of the three powers produced the Berlin agreement of 1889, which declared Samoa neutral and had the effect of establishing a tripartite protectorate over the islands. A further agreement, 1899, recognized the rights of the United States in those islands east of 171 deg. west longitude (American Samoa) and of Germany in the other islands (Western Samoa).New Zealand occupied Western Samoa at the start of World War I and administered it as a League of Nations mandate and U. N. trusteeship until Jan. 1, 1962, when it became an independent state.

Samoa is a member of the Commonwealth of Nations. The Chief Executive is Chief of State. The prime minister is the Head of Government. The present Head of State, Malietoa Tanumafili II, holds his position for life. The Legislative Assembly will elect future Heads of State for 5-year terms.

Samoa, which had used New Zealand coinage, converted to a decimal coinage in 1967.

RULERS
British, until 1962
Malietoa Tanumafili II, 1962—

MONETARY SYSTEM
100 Sene = 1 Tala

CONSTITUTIONAL MONARCHY
Commonwealth of Nations

STANDARD COINAGE

KM# 1 SENE
1.7500 g., Bronze, 17.5 mm. **Obv:** Head left **Obv. Designer:** T.H. Paget **Rev:** Stars and value within wreath

Date	Mintage	F	VF	XF	Unc	BU
1967	915,000	—	0.10	0.15	0.30	—
1967 Proof	15,000	Value: 0.50				

KM# 12 SENE
1.7500 g., Bronze, 17.5 mm. **Obv:** Head left **Obv. Designer:** T.H. Paget **Rev:** Stars and value within wreath **Rev. Designer:** James Berry

Date	Mintage	F	VF	XF	Unc	BU
1974	3,380,000	—	—	0.10	0.25	—
1987	—	—	—	0.10	0.25	—
1988	—	—	—	0.10	0.25	—
1993	—	—	—	0.10	0.25	—
1996	—	—	—	0.10	0.25	—

KM# 2 2 SENE
3.2500 g., Bronze, 21.1 mm. **Obv:** Head left **Obv. Designer:** T.H. Paget **Rev:** Stars and value within wreath

Date	Mintage	F	VF	XF	Unc	BU
1967	465,000	—	0.10	0.20	0.40	—
1967 Proof	15,000	Value: 0.50				

KM# 13 2 SENE

3.2500 g., Bronze, 21.1 mm. **Obv:** Head left **Obv. Designer:** T.H. Paget **Rev:** Value below nut sprig **Rev. Designer:** James Berry

Date	Mintage	F	VF	XF	Unc	BU
1974	1,640,000	—	0.10	0.15	0.30	—
1988	—	—	0.10	0.15	0.30	—
1996	—	—	0.10	0.15	0.30	—

KM# 122 2 SENE

3.9400 g., Bronze, 19.25 mm. **Series:** F.A.O. **Obv:** Head left **Rev:** Stars and value within wreath **Edge:** Plain

Date	Mintage	F	VF	XF	Unc	BU
1999	—	—	—	—	0.35	—
2000	—	—	—	—	0.35	—

KM# 3 5 SENE

2.8000 g., Copper-Nickel, 19.4 mm. **Obv:** Head left **Rev:** Value and stars

Date	Mintage	F	VF	XF	Unc	BU
1967	495,000	—	0.15	0.25	0.50	—
1967 Proof	15,000	Value: 1.00				

KM# 14 5 SENE

2.8000 g., Copper-Nickel, 19.4 mm. **Obv:** Head left **Obv. Designer:** T.H. Paget **Rev:** Pineapple and value

Date	Mintage	F	VF	XF	Unc	BU
1974	1,736,000	—	0.10	0.20	0.40	—
1987	—	—	0.10	0.20	0.40	—
1988	—	—	0.10	0.20	0.40	—
1993	—	—	0.10	0.20	0.40	—
1996	—	—	0.10	0.20	0.40	—
2000	—	—	0.10	0.20	0.40	—

KM# 131 5 SENE

2.8400 g., Copper-Nickel, 19.5 mm. **Obv:** Head left **Obv. Designer:** T.H. Paget **Rev:** Pineapple and value **Rev. Designer:** James Berry **Edge:** Reeded **Note:** "Western" dropped from country name

Date	Mintage	F	VF	XF	Unc	BU
2002	—	—	—	—	0.50	0.75

KM# 4 10 SENE

5.6500 g., Copper-Nickel, 23.6 mm. **Obv:** Head left **Obv. Designer:** T.H. Paget **Rev:** National arms

Date	Mintage	F	VF	XF	Unc	BU
1967	400,000	—	0.20	0.35	0.70	—
1967 Proof	15,000	Value: 1.00				

KM# 15 10 SENE

5.6500 g., Copper-Nickel, 23.6 mm. **Obv:** Head left **Obv. Designer:** T.H. Paget **Rev:** Value to lower left of leafy plants **Rev. Designer:** James Berry

Date	Mintage	F	VF	XF	Unc	BU
1974	1,580,000	—	0.15	0.30	0.60	—
1987	—	—	0.15	0.30	0.60	—
1988	—	—	0.15	0.30	0.60	—
1993	—	—	0.15	0.30	0.60	—
1996	—	—	0.15	0.30	0.60	—
2000	—	—	0.15	0.30	0.60	—

KM# 132 10 SENE

5.6500 g., Copper-Nickel, 23.6 mm. **Obv:** Head left **Rev:** Taro leaves and value **Rev. Designer:** James Berry **Edge:** Reeded **Note:** "Western" dropped from country name

Date	Mintage	F	VF	XF	Unc	BU
2002	—	—	—	—	0.75	1.00

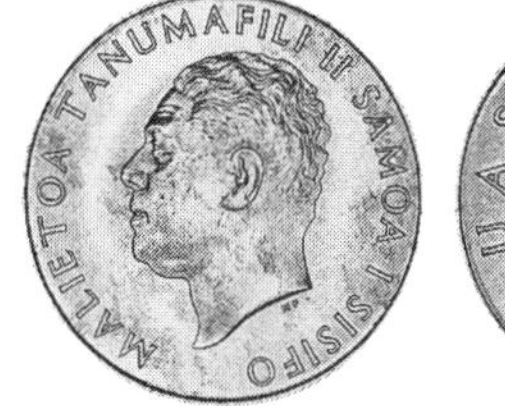

KM# 5 20 SENE

11.3000 g., Copper-Nickel, 28.5 mm. **Obv:** Head left **Obv. Designer:** T.H. Paget **Rev:** National arms

Date	Mintage	F	VF	XF	Unc	BU
1967	400,000	—	0.25	0.50	1.00	—
1967 Proof	15,000	Value: 1.50				

KM# 16 20 SENE

11.3000 g., Copper-Nickel, 28.5 mm. **Obv:** Head left **Obv. Designer:** T.H. Paget **Rev:** Breadfruit and value **Rev. Designer:** James Berry

Date	Mintage	F	VF	XF	Unc	BU
1974	1,380,000	—	0.20	0.40	0.80	—
1987	—	—	0.20	0.40	0.80	—
1988	—	—	0.20	0.40	0.80	—
1993	—	—	0.20	0.40	0.80	—
1996	—	—	0.20	0.40	0.80	—
2000	—	—	0.20	0.40	0.80	—

KM# 133 20 SENE

11.4000 g., Copper-Nickel, 28.45 mm. **Obv:** Head left **Obv. Designer:** T.H. Paget **Rev:** Breadfruits and value **Rev. Designer:** James Berry **Edge:** Reeded **Note:** "Western" dropped from country name

Date	Mintage	F	VF	XF	Unc	BU
2002	—	—	—	—	1.00	1.25

KM# 6 50 SENE

14.0000 g., Copper-Nickel, 32.4 mm. **Obv:** Head left **Obv. Designer:** T.H. Paget **Rev:** National arms

Date	Mintage	F	VF	XF	Unc	BU
1967	80,000	—	0.75	1.25	2.00	—
1967 Proof	15,000	Value: 2.50				

KM# 17 50 SENE

14.0000 g., Copper-Nickel, 32.4 mm. **Obv:** Head left **Obv. Designer:** T.H. Paget **Rev:** Banana tree and value **Rev. Designer:** James Berry

Date	Mintage	F	VF	XF	Unc	BU
1974	50,000	—	0.75	1.25	2.00	—
1988	—	—	0.75	1.25	2.00	—
1996	—	—	0.75	1.25	2.00	—
2000	—	—	0.75	1.25	2.00	—

KM# 80 50 SENE

14.0000 g., Copper-Nickel, 32.4 mm. **Subject:** 25th Anniversary of Independence **Obv:** Head left **Rev:** National arms

Date	Mintage	F	VF	XF	Unc	BU
1987	—	—	—	—	2.25	—

KM# 134 50 SENE

14.1300 g., Copper-Nickel, 32.3 mm. **Obv:** Head left **Rev:** Banana tree and value **Edge:** Reeded **Note:** "Western" dropped from country name

Date	Mintage	F	VF	XF	Unc	BU
2002	—	—	—	—	1.75	2.00

KM# 7 TALA

26.8500 g., Copper-Nickel, 38.71 mm. **Obv:** Head of Malietoa Tanumafili II left **Rev:** National arms, value **Edge:** Lettered **Edge Lettering:** DECIMAL CURRENCY INTRODUCED 10 JULY 1967

Date	Mintage	F	VF	XF	Unc	BU
1967	20,000	—	—	1.50	2.50	3.50
1967 Proof	15,000	Value: 5.00				

KM# 57 TALA

9.5000 g., Aluminum-Bronze, 30.6 mm. **Subject:** Circulation coinage **Obv:** Head left **Rev:** National arms **Shape:** 7-sided

Date	Mintage	F	VF	XF	Unc	BU
1984	1,000,000	—	0.50	0.75	1.00	1.50

KM# 135 TALA
9.5000 g., Brass, 30 mm. **Obv:** Head left **Obv. Designer:** T.H. Paget **Rev:** National arms above value and banner flanked by sprigs **Rev. Designer:** Nelson Eustis **Edge:** Reeded **Note:** "Western" dropped from country name

Date	Mintage	F	VF	XF	Unc	BU
2002	—	—	—	—	2.50	3.00

SAN MARINO

The Republic of San Marino, the oldest and smallest republic in the world is located in north central Italy entirely surrounded by the Province of Emilia-Romagna. It has an area of 24 sq. mi. (60 sq. km.) and a population of *23,000. Capital: San Marino. The principal economic activities are farming, livestock raising, cheese making, tourism and light manufacturing. Building stone, lime, wheat, hides and baked goods are exported. The government derives most of its revenue from the sale of postage stamps for philatelic purposes.

According to tradition, San Marino was founded about 350AD by a Christian stonecutter as a refuge against religious persecution. While gradually acquiring the institutions of an independent state, it avoided the factional fights of the Middle Ages and, except for a brief period in fief to Cesare Borgia, retained its freedom despite attacks on its sovereignty by the Papacy, the Lords of Rimini, Napoleon and Mussolini. In 1862 San Marino established a customs union with, and put itself under the protection of, Italy. A Communist-Socialist coalition controlled the Government for 12 years after World War II. The Christian Democratic Party has been the core of government since 1957. In 1978 a Communist-Socialist coalition again came into power and remained in control until 1991.

San Marino has its own coinage, but Italian and Vatican City coins and currency are also in circulation.

MINT MARKS
M - Milan
R – Rome

MONETARY SYSTEM
100 Centesimi = 1 Lira

REPUBLIC

STANDARD COINAGE

KM# 12 5 CENTESIMI
3.2000 g., Bronze **Obv:** Crowned pointed arms within wreath **Rev:** Value and date

Date	Mintage	F	VF	XF	Unc	BU
1935R	800,000	1.25	2.00	12.00	32.00	—
1936R	400,000	1.25	2.00	12.00	32.00	—
1937R	200,000	2.00	6.00	19.00	38.00	—
1938R	200,000	2.00	6.00	19.00	38.00	—

KM# 13 10 CENTESIMI
5.4000 g., Bronze **Obv:** Crowned pointed arms within wreath **Rev:** Value and date

Date	Mintage	F	VF	XF	Unc	BU
1935R	600,000	2.00	6.00	15.00	30.00	—
1936R	300,000	2.00	6.00	15.00	30.00	—
1937R	400,000	2.00	6.00	15.00	30.00	—
1938R	400,000	2.00	6.00	15.00	30.00	—

KM# 4 LIRA
5.0000 g., 0.8350 Silver 0.1342 oz. ASW **Obv:** Crowned arms within wreath **Obv. Legend:** RESPVBLICA S. MARINI **Rev:** Value, date within wreath

Date	Mintage	F	VF	XF	Unc	BU
1906R	30,000	15.00	22.50	40.00	228	—

KM# 14 LIRA
Aluminum **Obv:** Bust of Saint 1/4 left **Rev:** Value above arms without shield **Designer:** Monassi

Date	Mintage	F	VF	XF	Unc	BU
1972	291,000	—	—	0.10	0.20	—

KM# 22 LIRA
Aluminum **Obv:** Crowned shield **Rev:** Girl with national flag **Designer:** Guido Veroi

Date	Mintage	F	VF	XF	Unc	BU
1973	291,000	—	—	0.10	0.20	—

KM# 30 LIRA
Aluminum **Obv:** Smoking towers within circle **Rev:** Ant **Designer:** Luciano Minguzzi

Date	Mintage	F	VF	XF	Unc	BU
1974	276,000	—	—	0.25	1.25	2.00

KM# 40 LIRA
Aluminum **Obv:** Smoking towers within circle **Rev:** Spiders in web **Designer:** Bino Bini

Date	Mintage	F	VF	XF	Unc	BU
1975	291,000	—	—	0.25	1.25	2.10

KM# 51 LIRA
Aluminum **Obv:** Smoking towers **Rev:** Crossed flags flanked by hands **Designer:** Mario Molteni

Date	Mintage	F	VF	XF	Unc	BU
1976	195,000	—	—	0.10	0.20	—

KM# 63 LIRA
0.6500 g., Aluminum **Series:** F.A.O. **Obv:** Smoking towers within circle **Rev:** Globe in center of star wreath **Designer:** J. Vivarelli

Date	Mintage	F	VF	XF	Unc	BU
1977	1,180,000	—	—	0.10	0.20	—

KM# 76 LIRA
Aluminum **Obv:** Value below smoking towers **Rev:** Sitting figure within spider web

Date	Mintage	F	VF	XF	Unc	BU
1978	130,000	—	—	0.15	0.30	—

KM# 89 LIRA
Aluminum **Obv:** Crowned shield **Rev:** Sword handle divides value

Date	Mintage	F	VF	XF	Unc	BU
1979	125,000	—	—	0.15	0.30	—

KM# 102 LIRA
Aluminum **Series:** 1980 Olympics **Obv:** Olympic circles and date to left of smoking towers **Rev:** Ballerina

Date	Mintage	F	VF	XF	Unc	BU
1980	125,000	—	—	0.15	0.30	—

KM# 116 LIRA
Aluminum **Obv:** Crowned shield **Rev:** Value within design

Date	Mintage	F	VF	XF	Unc	BU
1981R	100,000	—	—	0.15	0.30	—

KM# 131 LIRA
Aluminum **Subject:** Social conquest **Obv:** Crown above smoking towers **Rev:** Back of standing figure divides date and value

Date	Mintage	F	VF	XF	Unc	BU
1982R	78,000	—	—	0.15	0.30	—

KM# 145 LIRA
Aluminum **Subject:** Nuclear war threat **Obv:** Crowned shield above sprig **Rev:** Beast of war

Date	Mintage	F	VF	XF	Unc	BU
1983R	72,000	—	—	0.20	0.40	—

KM# 159 LIRA
Aluminum **Obv:** Castle **Rev:** Bust facing flanked by value and caduceus

Date	Mintage	F	VF	XF	Unc	BU
1984R	65,000	—	—	0.20	0.40	—

KM# 173 LIRA

Aluminum **Subject:** War on drugs **Obv:** Shield **Rev:** Supine male 1/2 length figure below value and date

Date	Mintage	F	VF	XF	Unc	BU
1985R	60,000	—	—	0.10	0.25	—

KM# 187 LIRA

Aluminum **Subject:** Revolution of technology **Obv:** Crown above smoking towers on rock **Rev:** Footprints on the moon

Date	Mintage	F	VF	XF	Unc	BU
1986R	50,000	—	—	0.10	0.25	—

KM# 201 LIRA

Aluminum **Subject:** 15th Anniversary - Resumption of Coinage **Obv:** Crowned pointed arms within sprigs **Rev:** Tree flanked by value

Date	Mintage	F	VF	XF	Unc	BU
1987R	83,000	—	—	0.10	0.25	—

KM# 218 LIRA

Aluminum **Subject:** Fortifications **Obv:** Crowned ornate arms on shield **Rev:** Corner Tower **Designer:** Sergio Giandomenico

Date	Mintage	F	VF	XF	Unc	BU
1988R	38,000	—	—	0.10	0.25	—

KM# 231 LIRA

Aluminum **Subject:** History **Obv:** Crowned shield **Rev:** Stone Age tool

Date	Mintage	F	VF	XF	Unc	BU
1989R	37,000	—	—	0.10	0.25	—

KM# 248 LIRA

Aluminum **Subject:** 1,600 Years of History **Obv:** Stylized towers **Rev:** Stylized Saint **Designer:** Magdalena Dobrucka

Date	Mintage	F	VF	XF	Unc	BU
1990R	36,000	—	—	0.10	0.25	—

KM# 261 LIRA

Aluminum **Obv:** Date to upper left of smoking towers **Rev:** Hands holding hammer and chisel below value

Date	Mintage	F	VF	XF	Unc	BU
1991R	—	—	—	0.10	0.25	—

KM# 278 LIRA

Aluminum **Subject:** Columbus **Obv:** Towers with feather-like designs above within circle **Rev:** Potatoes and plant within design with value at left

Date	Mintage	F	VF	XF	Unc	BU
ND(1992)R	—	—	—	0.10	0.25	—

KM# 293 LIRA

Aluminum **Obv:** Stylized smoking towers **Rev:** Seedling divides date and value

Date	Mintage	F	VF	XF	Unc	BU
1993R	—	—	—	0.10	0.25	—

KM# 306 LIRA

Aluminum **Obv:** Bust facing with arms holding hammer and chisel, smoking towers at left **Rev:** Mother and child

Date	Mintage	F	VF	XF	Unc	BU
1994R	40,000	—	—	0.10	0.25	—

KM# 322 LIRA

Aluminum **Obv:** Banner around design **Rev:** Child on broken sword divides sprig and value **Designer:** Loredana Pancotto

Date	Mintage	F	VF	XF	Unc	BU
1995R	—	—	—	0.10	0.25	—

KM# 349 LIRA

Aluminum **Subject:** Talete - Child of the Universe **Obv:** Bust facing with flame within hands **Rev:** Value and date at left of head facing

Date	Mintage	F	VF	XF	Unc	BU
1996R	32,000	—	—	0.10	0.25	—

KM# 359 LIRA

Aluminum **Subject:** The Arts - Prehistoric **Obv:** Bust facing with flame within hands **Rev:** Elk

Date	Mintage	F	VF	XF	Unc	BU
1997R	28,000	—	—	0.10	0.25	0.75

KM# 5 2 LIRE

10.0000 g., 0.8350 Silver 0.2684 oz. ASW, 27 mm. **Obv:** Crowned arms within wreath **Obv. Legend:** RESPVBLICA S. MARINI **Rev:** Value, date within wreath

Date	Mintage	F	VF	XF	Unc	BU
1906R	15,000	25.00	40.00	175	380	—

KM# 15 2 LIRE

Aluminum, 18 mm. **Obv:** Value above stylized smoking towers **Rev:** Bust of Saint 1/4 right **Designer:** Monassi

Date	Mintage	F	VF	XF	Unc	BU
1972	291,000	—	—	0.10	0.30	—

KM# 23 2 LIRE

Aluminum, 18 mm. **Obv:** Crowned shield **Rev:** Pelican **Designer:** Guido Veroi

Date	Mintage	F	VF	XF	Unc	BU
1973	291,000	—	—	0.20	1.00	2.00

KM# 31 2 LIRE

Aluminum, 18 mm. **Obv:** Smoking towers within circle **Rev:** Beetle **Designer:** Lucaiano Minguzzi

Date	Mintage	F	VF	XF	Unc	BU
1974	276,000	—	—	0.25	1.25	2.50

KM# 41 2 LIRE

Aluminum, 18 mm. **Obv:** Smoking towers **Rev:** Seahorses **Designer:** Bino Bini

Date	Mintage	F	VF	XF	Unc	BU
1975	291,000	—	—	0.25	1.25	2.00

KM# 52 2 LIRE

Aluminum, 18 mm. **Obv:** Smoking towers **Rev:** Stylized sun, hills and sitting figure **Designer:** Mario Molteni

Date	Mintage	F	VF	XF	Unc	BU
1976	195,000	—	—	0.10	0.30	0.50

KM# 64 2 LIRE

Aluminum, 18 mm. **Obv:** Value and smoking towers within circle **Rev:** Stars above wave-like designs within circle **Designer:** J. Vivarelli

Date	Mintage	F	VF	XF	Unc	BU
1977	180,000	—	—	0.10	0.30	—

KM# 77 2 LIRE

Aluminum, 18 mm. **Obv:** Value below smoking towers **Rev:** Standing figure working

Date	Mintage	F	VF	XF	Unc	BU
1978	130,000	—	—	0.10	0.30	—

KM# 90 2 LIRE
Aluminum, 18 mm. **Obv:** Crowned shield **Rev:** Bugle with banner divides value

Date	Mintage	F	VF	XF	Unc	BU
1979	125,000	—	—	0.10	0.30	—

KM# 103 2 LIRE
Aluminum, 18 mm. **Series:** 1980 Olympics **Obv:** Olympic rings and date to left of smoking towers **Rev:** Soccer player

Date	Mintage	F	VF	XF	Unc	BU
1980	125,000	—	—	0.25	0.75	—

KM# 117 2 LIRE
Aluminum, 18 mm. **Obv:** Crowned shield **Rev:** Small head and hand left, date and value at upper left

Date	Mintage	F	VF	XF	Unc	BU
1981R	100,000	—	—	0.10	0.30	—

KM# 132 2 LIRE
Aluminum, 18 mm. **Subject:** Social Conquests **Obv:** Crown above smoking towers **Rev:** Value below stylized design

Date	Mintage	F	VF	XF	Unc	BU
1982R	78,000	—	—	0.10	0.30	—

KM# 146 2 LIRE
Aluminum, 18 mm. **Subject:** Nuclear war threat **Obv:** Crowned shield above sprig **Rev:** Two reaching arms

Date	Mintage	F	VF	XF	Unc	BU
1983R	72,000	—	—	0.20	0.40	—

KM# 160 2 LIRE
Aluminum, 18 mm. **Obv:** Castle **Rev:** Head facing

Date	Mintage	F	VF	XF	Unc	BU
1984R	65,000	—	—	0.20	0.40	—

KM# 174 2 LIRE
Aluminum, 18 mm. **Subject:** War on Drugs **Obv:** Shield **Rev:** Clenched fist

Date	Mintage	F	VF	XF	Unc	BU
1985R	60,000	—	—	0.10	0.25	—

KM# 188 2 LIRE
Aluminum, 18 mm. **Subject:** Revolution of Technology **Obv:** Crown above smoking towers on rock **Rev:** Astronaut walking in space

Date	Mintage	F	VF	XF	Unc	BU
1986R	50,000	—	—	0.10	0.25	—

KM# 202 2 LIRE
Aluminum, 18 mm. **Subject:** 15th Anniversary - Resumption of Coinage **Obv:** Crowned pointed shield within sprigs **Rev:** Flower designs

Date	Mintage	F	VF	XF	Unc	BU
1987R	83,000	—	—	0.10	0.25	—

KM# 219 2 LIRE
Aluminum, 18 mm. **Subject:** Fortifications **Obv:** Crowned ornate arms on shield **Rev:** Fortified archway **Designer:** Sergio Giandomenico

Date	Mintage	F	VF	XF	Unc	BU
1988R	38,000	—	—	0.10	0.25	—

KM# 232 2 LIRE
Aluminum, 18 mm. **Subject:** History **Obv:** Crowned shield **Rev:** Value divides wheat stalk and olive branch

Date	Mintage	F	VF	XF	Unc	BU
1989R	37,000	—	—	0.10	0.25	—

KM# 249 2 LIRE
Aluminum, 18 mm. **Subject:** 1,600 Years of History **Obv:** Stylized towers **Rev:** Stylized figure with spear **Designer:** Magdalena Dobrucka

Date	Mintage	F	VF	XF	Unc	BU
1990R	36,000	—	—	0.10	0.25	—

KM# 262 2 LIRE
Aluminum, 18 mm. **Obv:** Date to upper left of smoking towers **Rev:** Hands with interlocked fingers below value

Date	Mintage	F	VF	XF	Unc	BU
1991R	—	—	—	0.10	0.25	—

KM# 279 2 LIRE
Aluminum, 18 mm. **Subject:** Columbus **Obv:** Towers with feather-like designs on top within circle **Rev:** Ear of corn to left of value within design

Date	Mintage	F	VF	XF	Unc	BU
ND(1992)R	—	—	—	0.10	0.25	—

KM# 294 2 LIRE
Aluminum, 18 mm. **Obv:** Smoking towers **Rev:** Rose

Date	Mintage	F	VF	XF	Unc	BU
1993R	—	—	—	0.10	0.25	—

KM# 307 2 LIRE
Aluminum, 18 mm. **Obv:** Head with hands holding hammer and chisel, towers at left **Rev:** Standing stonecutter at work

Date	Mintage	F	VF	XF	Unc	BU
1994R	40,000	—	—	0.10	0.25	—

KM# 323 2 LIRE
Aluminum, 18 mm. **Obv:** Banner around bottom of design **Rev:** Child with toy castle **Designer:** Loredana Pancotto

Date	Mintage	F	VF	XF	Unc	BU
1995R	—	—	—	0.10	0.25	—

KM# 350 2 LIRE
Aluminum, 18 mm. **Obv:** Bust facing with flame within hands **Rev:** Head of Socrates

Date	Mintage	F	VF	XF	Unc	BU
1996R	32,000	—	—	0.10	0.25	—

KM# 360 2 LIRE
Aluminum, 18 mm. **Subject:** The Arts - Literature **Obv:** Bust facing with flame within hands **Rev:** Dante holding Divine Comedy

Date	Mintage	F	VF	XF	Unc	BU
1997R	28,000	—	—	0.10	0.25	—

KM# 9 5 LIRE
5.0000 g., 0.8350 Silver 0.1342 oz. ASW, 23 mm. **Obv:** Bust left within beaded circle **Rev:** Plant divides value above plow **Designer:** E. Saroldi

Date	Mintage	F	VF	XF	Unc	BU
1931R	50,000	3.50	5.50	10.00	100	—
1932R	50,000	3.50	5.50	10.00	100	—
1933R	50,000	3.50	5.50	8.50	30.00	—
1935R	200,000	3.50	5.50	8.50	20.00	—
1936R	100,000	3.50	5.50	8.50	50.00	—
1937R	100,000	3.50	5.50	8.50	50.00	—
1938R	120,000	3.50	5.50	8.50	50.00	—

KM# 16 5 LIRE
Aluminum, 20 mm. **Obv:** Bust of Saint 1/4 left **Rev:** Value above stylized smoking towers **Designer:** Monassi

Date	Mintage	F	VF	XF	Unc	BU
1972	291,000	—	—	0.10	0.35	—

KM# 24 5 LIRE
Aluminum, 20 mm. **Obv:** Crowned shield **Rev:** Heads within small circle on globe, radiant star border **Designer:** Guido Veroi

Date	Mintage	F	VF	XF	Unc	BU
1973	291,000	—	—	0.10	0.35	—

KM# 32 5 LIRE
Aluminum, 20 mm. **Obv:** Smoking towers within circle **Rev:** Porcupine **Designer:** Luciano Minguzzi

Date	Mintage	F	VF	XF	Unc	BU
1974	276,000	—	—	0.25	1.25	2.50

KM# 42 5 LIRE
Aluminum, 20 mm. **Obv:** Smoking towers **Rev:** Hedgehogs **Designer:** Bino Bini

Date	Mintage	F	VF	XF	Unc	BU
1975	291,000	—	—	0.20	1.00	2.50

KM# 53 5 LIRE
Aluminum, 20 mm. **Series:** F.A.O. **Obv:** Stylized smoking towers **Rev:** Stylized standing figures within design **Designer:** Mario Molteni

Date	Mintage	F	VF	XF	Unc	BU
1976	695,000	—	—	0.10	0.25	—

KM# 65 5 LIRE
Aluminum, 20 mm. **Obv:** Value below smoking towers within circle **Rev:** Stars within circle **Designer:** J. Vivarelli

Date	Mintage	F	VF	XF	Unc	BU
1977	180,000	—	—	0.10	0.35	—

KM# 78 5 LIRE
Aluminum, 20 mm. **Obv:** Value below smoking towers **Rev:** Standing figure holding water hose

Date	Mintage	F	VF	XF	Unc	BU
1978	130,000	—	—	0.10	0.35	—

KM# 91 5 LIRE
Aluminum, 20 mm. **Obv:** Crowned shield **Rev:** Crossbow divides value

Date	Mintage	F	VF	XF	Unc	BU
1979	125,000	—	—	0.10	0.35	—

KM# 104 5 LIRE
Aluminum, 20 mm. **Series:** 1980 Olympics **Obv:** Olympic rings and date to left of smoking towers **Rev:** Running figure right

Date	Mintage	F	VF	XF	Unc	BU
1980	125,000	—	—	0.25	0.75	—

KM# 118 5 LIRE
Aluminum, 20 mm. **Obv:** Crowned shield **Rev:** Goat divides value and date

Date	Mintage	F	VF	XF	Unc	BU
1981R	100,000	—	—	0.25	0.75	2.00

KM# 133 5 LIRE
Aluminum, 20 mm. **Subject:** Social Conquests **Obv:** Crown above smoking towers **Rev:** Stylized boats and plane

Date	Mintage	F	VF	XF	Unc	BU
1982R	78,000	—	—	0.10	0.30	—

KM# 147 5 LIRE
Aluminum, 20 mm. **Subject:** Nuclear War Threat **Obv:** Crown above shield and sprig **Rev:** Pair of reaching arms within barred window

Date	Mintage	F	VF	XF	Unc	BU
1983R	72,000	—	—	0.20	0.40	—

KM# 161 5 LIRE
Aluminum, 20 mm. **Obv:** Castle **Rev:** Bust of Galileo facing

Date	Mintage	F	VF	XF	Unc	BU
1984R	65,000	—	—	0.20	0.40	—

KM# 175 5 LIRE
Aluminum, 20 mm. **Subject:** War on Drugs **Obv:** Shield **Rev:** Face of addict

Date	Mintage	F	VF	XF	Unc	BU
1985R	60,000	—	—	0.10	0.30	—

KM# 189 5 LIRE
Aluminum, 20 mm. **Subject:** Revolution of Technology **Obv:** Crown above smoking towers on rock **Rev:** Human figure operating larger robot

Date	Mintage	F	VF	XF	Unc	BU
1986R	50,000	—	—	0.10	0.30	—

KM# 203 5 LIRE
Aluminum, 20 mm. **Subject:** 15th Anniversary - Resumption of Coinage **Obv:** Crowned pointed shield within sprigs **Rev:** Flowers in designed vase divide value

Date	Mintage	F	VF	XF	Unc	BU
1987R	83,000	—	—	0.10	0.30	—

KM# 220 5 LIRE
Aluminum, 20 mm. **Subject:** Fortification **Obv:** Crowned ornate arms on shield **Rev:** Round corner tower **Designer:** Sergio Giandomenico

Date	Mintage	F	VF	XF	Unc	BU
1988R	38,000	—	—	0.10	0.30	—

KM# 233 5 LIRE
Aluminum, 20 mm. **Subject:** History **Obv:** Crowned shield **Rev:** Cluster of grapes divide value

Date	Mintage	F	VF	XF	Unc	BU
1989R	37,000	—	—	0.10	0.30	—

KM# 250 5 LIRE
Aluminum, 20 mm. **Subject:** 1,600 Years of History **Obv:** Stylized towers above design **Rev:** Two stylized facing figures **Designer:** Magdalena Dobrucka

Date	Mintage	F	VF	XF	Unc	BU
1990R	36,000	—	—	0.10	0.30	—

KM# 263 5 LIRE
Aluminum, 20 mm. **Obv:** Date at upper left of smoking towers **Rev:** Hand holding quill below value

Date	Mintage	F	VF	XF	Unc	BU
1991R	—	—	—	0.10	0.30	—

KM# 280 5 LIRE
Aluminum, 20 mm. **Subject:** Columbus **Obv:** Towers with feather-like designs on top within circle **Rev:** Cotton plants and value within design

Date	Mintage	F	VF	XF	Unc	BU
ND(1992)R	—	—	—	0.10	0.30	—

KM# 295 5 LIRE
Aluminum, 20 mm. **Obv:** Stylized smoking towers **Rev:** Spade and hoe

Date	Mintage	F	VF	XF	Unc	BU
1993R	—	—	—	0.10	0.30	—

KM# 308 5 LIRE

Aluminum, 20 mm. **Obv:** Stone cutter holding hammer and chisel, towers at left **Rev:** Standing figures with tools

Date	Mintage	F	VF	XF	Unc	BU
1994R	40,000	—	—	0.10	0.30	—

KM# 324 5 LIRE

Aluminum, 20 mm. **Obv:** Banner wrapped around quills **Rev:** Child with 2 deer **Designer:** Loredana Pancotto

Date	Mintage	F	VF	XF	Unc	BU
1995R	—	—	—	0.10	0.30	—

KM# 351 5 LIRE

Aluminum, 20 mm. **Obv:** Bust facing with flame within hands **Rev:** Plato

Date	Mintage	F	VF	XF	Unc	BU
1996R	32,000	—	—	0.10	0.30	—

KM# 361 5 LIRE

Aluminum, 20 mm. **Subject:** The Arts - Theater **Obv:** Bust facing with flame within hands **Rev:** Hamlet with skull

Date	Mintage	F	VF	XF	Unc	BU
1997R	28,000	—	—	0.10	0.30	—

KM# 7 10 LIRE

3.2258 g., 0.9000 Gold 0.0933 oz. AGW **Obv:** Smoking towers within circle **Rev:** Standing Saint facing divides value **Note:** 16,000 coins melted at the mint.

Date	Mintage	F	VF	XF	Unc	BU
1925R	20,000	175	500	800	1,250	—

KM# 10 10 LIRE

10.0000 g., 0.8350 Silver 0.2684 oz. ASW **Obv:** Nine sided shield divides value within circle, crown at top divides circle **Rev:** Facing figure holding crown divides date within circle

Date	Mintage	F	VF	XF	Unc	BU
1931R	25,000	8.50	15.00	35.00	80.00	—
1932R	25,000	8.50	15.00	35.00	80.00	—
1933R	25,000	8.50	15.00	35.00	80.00	—
1935R	30,000	6.50	10.00	25.00	65.00	—
1936R	15,000	10.00	18.00	40.00	95.00	—
1937R	20,000	6.50	10.00	25.00	65.00	—
1938R	10,000	12.00	20.00	50.00	200	—

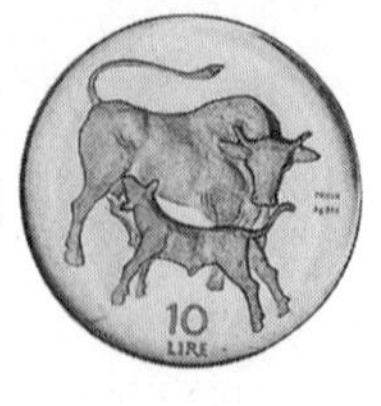

KM# 17 10 LIRE

1.6000 g., Aluminum, 23.3 mm. **Obv:** Stylized smoking towers **Rev:** Cow nursing calf

Date	Mintage	F	VF	XF	Unc	BU
1972	291,000	—	0.10	0.20	0.50	2.50

KM# 25 10 LIRE

1.6000 g., Aluminum, 23.3 mm. **Obv:** Crowned shield **Rev:** Man fighting four-headed dragon **Designer:** Guido Veroi

Date	Mintage	F	VF	XF	Unc	BU
1973	291,000	—	0.10	0.15	0.40	—

KM# 33 10 LIRE

1.6000 g., Aluminum, 23.3 mm. **Series:** F.A.O. **Obv:** Smoking towers within circle **Rev:** Bee **Designer:** Luciano Minguzzi

Date	Mintage	F	VF	XF	Unc	BU
1974	1,276,000	—	—	0.15	0.45	1.50

KM# 43 10 LIRE

1.6000 g., Aluminum, 23.3 mm. **Obv:** Smoking towers **Rev:** Rats divide value **Designer:** Bino Bini

Date	Mintage	F	VF	XF	Unc	BU
1975	291,000	—	0.10	0.25	1.00	2.00

KM# 54 10 LIRE

1.6000 g., Aluminum, 23.3 mm. **Obv:** Stylized smoking towers **Rev:** Fetus within circle, standing baby at left **Designer:** Mario Molteni

Date	Mintage	F	VF	XF	Unc	BU
1976	195,000	—	0.10	0.15	0.40	—

KM# 66 10 LIRE

1.6000 g., Aluminum, 23.3 mm. **Obv:** Stylized smoking towers within circle **Rev:** Foot above 1/2 designed star wreath **Designer:** J. Varelli

Date	Mintage	F	VF	XF	Unc	BU
1977	180,000	—	0.10	0.15	0.40	—

KM# 79 10 LIRE

1.6000 g., Aluminum, 23.3 mm. **Obv:** Smoking towers above value **Rev:** Seated figure

Date	Mintage	F	VF	XF	Unc	BU
1978	130,000	—	0.10	0.15	0.40	—

KM# 92 10 LIRE

1.6000 g., Aluminum, 23.3 mm. **Obv:** Crowned shield **Rev:** Date flanked by two crowned shields on stands

Date	Mintage	F	VF	XF	Unc	BU
1979	125,000	—	0.10	0.15	0.40	—

KM# 105 10 LIRE

1.6000 g., Aluminum, 23.3 mm. **Series:** 1980 Olympics **Obv:** Olympic rings and date to left of smoking towers **Rev:** Jumping equestrian

Date	Mintage	F	VF	XF	Unc	BU
1980	125,000	—	0.25	0.50	0.80	1.50

KM# 119 10 LIRE

1.6000 g., Aluminum, 23.3 mm. **Obv:** Crowned shield **Rev:** Value surrounded by nude figure

Date	Mintage	F	VF	XF	Unc	BU
1981R	100,000	—	0.10	0.20	0.50	—

KM# 134 10 LIRE

1.6000 g., Aluminum, 23.3 mm. **Subject:** Social Conquests **Obv:** Crown above smoking towers **Rev:** Stylized figures **Designer:** A. Biancini

Date	Mintage	F	VF	XF	Unc	BU
1982R	78,000	—	0.10	0.20	0.50	—

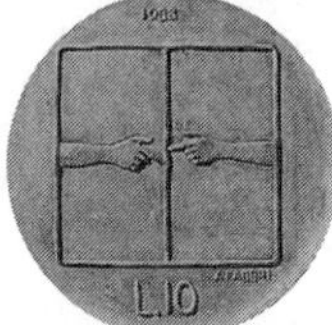

KM# 148 10 LIRE

1.6000 g., Aluminum, 23.3 mm. **Subject:** Nuclear War Threat **Obv:** Crown above shield and sprig **Rev:** Vertical line within square divides reaching arms

Date	Mintage	F	VF	XF	Unc	BU
1983R	72,000	—	0.10	0.25	0.75	—

KM# 162 10 LIRE

1.6000 g., Aluminum, 23.3 mm. **Subject:** Alessandro Volta **Obv:** Castle **Rev:** Bust 3/4 right

Date	Mintage	F	VF	XF	Unc	BU
1984R	65,000	—	0.10	0.25	0.75	—

KM# 176 10 LIRE

1.6000 g., Aluminum, 23.3 mm. **Subject:** War on Drugs **Obv:** Shield **Rev:** Mother lecturing son

Date	Mintage	F	VF	XF	Unc	BU
1985R	60,000	—	—	0.10	0.35	—

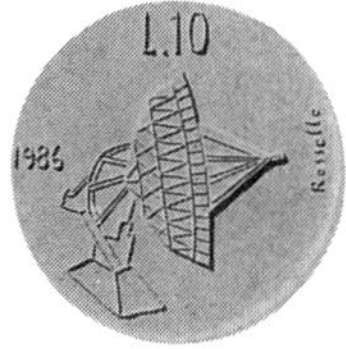

KM# 190 10 LIRE

1.6000 g., Aluminum, 23.3 mm. **Subject:** Revolution of Technology **Obv:** Crown above smoking towers on rock **Rev:** Radio receiver

Date	Mintage	F	VF	XF	Unc	BU
1986R	50,000	—	—	0.10	0.35	—

KM# 204 10 LIRE

1.6000 g., Aluminum, 23.3 mm. **Subject:** 15th Anniversary - Resumption of Coinage **Obv:** Crowned pointed shield within sprigs **Rev:** Tower divides value

Date	Mintage	F	VF	XF	Unc	BU
1987R	83,000	—	—	0.10	0.35	—

KM# 221 10 LIRE

1.6000 g., Aluminum, 23.3 mm. **Subject:** Fortifications **Obv:** Crowned ornate arms on shield **Rev:** Sloping fortress wall **Designer:** Sergio Giandomenico

Date	Mintage	F	VF	XF	Unc	BU
1988R	38,000	—	—	0.10	0.35	—

KM# 234 10 LIRE

1.6000 g., Aluminum, 23.3 mm. **Subject:** History **Obv:** Crowned shield **Rev:** Ancient pottery divides value

Date	Mintage	F	VF	XF	Unc	BU
1989R	37,000	—	—	0.10	0.35	—

KM# 251 10 LIRE

1.6000 g., Aluminum, 23.3 mm. **Subject:** 1,600 Years of History **Obv:** Stylized towers above design **Rev:** Stylized soldier **Designer:** Magdalena Dobrucka

Date	Mintage	F	VF	XF	Unc	BU
1990R	36,000	—	—	0.10	0.35	—

KM# 264 10 LIRE

1.6000 g., Aluminum, 23.3 mm. **Obv:** Date at left of smoking towers **Rev:** Value above hand holding castle tower

Date	Mintage	F	VF	XF	Unc	BU
1991R	—	—	—	0.10	0.35	—

KM# 281 10 LIRE

1.6000 g., Aluminum, 23.3 mm. **Subject:** Columbus **Obv:** Towers with feather-like designs on top within circle **Rev:** Dolphin, ship and value within globe design

Date	Mintage	F	VF	XF	Unc	BU
ND(1992)R	—	—	—	0.20	0.75	2.00

KM# 296 10 LIRE

1.6000 g., Aluminum, 23.3 mm. **Obv:** Smoking towers **Rev:** Value above corinthian column

Date	Mintage	F	VF	XF	Unc	BU
1993R	—	—	—	0.10	0.35	—

KM# 309 10 LIRE

1.6000 g., Aluminum, 23.3 mm. **Obv:** Stone cutter holding hammer and chisel, towers at left **Rev:** Marino and Leo working

Date	Mintage	F	VF	XF	Unc	BU
1994R	40,000	—	—	0.10	0.35	—

KM# 325 10 LIRE

1.6000 g., Aluminum, 23.3 mm. **Obv:** Banner wrapped around bottom of design **Rev:** Child holding two urns within square **Designer:** Loredana Pancotto

Date	Mintage	F	VF	XF	Unc	BU
1995R	—	—	—	0.10	0.35	—

KM# 352 10 LIRE

1.6000 g., Aluminum, 23.3 mm. **Obv:** Bust facing with flame within hands **Rev:** Aristotle

Date	Mintage	F	VF	XF	Unc	BU
1996R	28,000	—	—	0.10	0.35	—

KM# 362 10 LIRE

1.6000 g., Aluminum, 23.3 mm. **Subject:** The Arts - Architecture **Obv:** Bust facing with flame within hands **Rev:** Building on pillars

Date	Mintage	F	VF	XF	Unc	BU
1997R	28,000	—	—	0.10	0.35	—

KM# 378 10 LIRE

1.6000 g., Aluminum, 23.3 mm. **Subject:** Mathematics **Rev:** Hand and geometric shape

Date	Mintage	F	VF	XF	Unc	BU
1998R	—	—	—	0.10	0.35	—

KM# 389 10 LIRE

1.6000 g., Aluminum, 23.3 mm. **Subject:** Exploration **Obv:** Crowned shield **Rev:** Earth flat, as once envisioned

Date	Mintage	F	VF	XF	Unc	BU
1999R	—	—	—	0.10	0.35	—

KM# 399 10 LIRE

1.6000 g., Aluminum, 23.3 mm. **Subject:** Love **Obv:** Bust facing with flame within hands **Rev:** Child within poinsettia and globe design **Edge:** Plain **Note:** Struck at Rome.

Date	Mintage	F	VF	XF	Unc	BU
2000R	—	—	—	—	0.35	—

KM# 424 10 LIRE

1.6000 g., Aluminum, 23.3 mm. **Obv:** Three towers within circle **Rev:** Wheat stalks and value **Edge:** Plain

Date	Mintage	F	VF	XF	Unc	BU
2001R	—	—	—	—	0.35	—

KM# 8 20 LIRE
6.4516 g., 0.9000 Gold 0.1867 oz. AGW **Obv:** Smoking towers **Rev:** Standing Saint figure divides value **Note:** 7,334 coins were melted at the mint.

Date	Mintage	F	VF	XF	Unc	BU
1925R	9,334	400	700	1,200	2,300	—

KM# 11 20 LIRE
15.0000 g., 0.8000 Silver 0.3858 oz. ASW **Obv:** Upright stylized feathers above value with crown above **Rev:** Half length figure holding smoking towers within circle **Designer:** Saroldi

Date	Mintage	F	VF	XF	Unc	BU
1931R	10,000	25.00	45.00	90.00	200	—
1932R	10,000	35.00	60.00	110	235	—
1933R	10,000	30.00	50.00	100	220	—
1935R	10,000	30.00	50.00	100	220	—
1936R	5,000	60.00	125	200	425	—

KM# 11a 20 LIRE
20.0000 g., 0.8000 Silver 0.5144 oz. ASW **Obv:** Stylized upright feathers above value with crown above **Rev:** Half length figure holding smoking towers within circle

Date	Mintage	F	VF	XF	Unc	BU
1935R Rare	2	—	—	—	—	—
1937R	5,100	100	200	435	775	—
1938R	2,500	200	400	850	1,325	—

KM# 18 20 LIRE
3.6000 g., Aluminum-Bronze, 21.25 mm. **Obv:** Stylized feathers within towers **Rev:** Standing figures

Date	Mintage	F	VF	XF	Unc	BU
1972	291,000	—	0.10	0.25	0.60	—

KM# 26 20 LIRE
3.6000 g., Aluminum-Bronze, 21.25 mm. **Obv:** Crowned shield **Rev:** Man rescuing old man and baby from fire **Designer:** Guido Veroi

Date	Mintage	F	VF	XF	Unc	BU
1973	291,000	—	0.10	0.25	0.60	—

KM# 34 20 LIRE
3.6000 g., Aluminum-Bronze, 21.25 mm. **Obv:** Smoking towers within circle **Rev:** Lobster **Designer:** Luciano Minguzzi

Date	Mintage	F	VF	XF	Unc	BU
1974	276,000	—	0.10	0.30	1.50	2.50

KM# 44 20 LIRE
3.6000 g., Aluminum-Bronze, 21.25 mm. **Series:** F.A.O. **Obv:** Smoking towers **Rev:** Bird feeding babies **Designer:** Bino Bini

Date	Mintage	F	VF	XF	Unc	BU
1975	291,000	—	0.10	0.30	0.75	1.25

KM# 55 20 LIRE
3.6000 g., Aluminum-Bronze, 21.25 mm. **Obv:** Smoking towers **Rev:** Design flanked by stylized hands **Designer:** Mario Molteni

Date	Mintage	F	VF	XF	Unc	BU
1976	195,000	—	0.10	0.25	0.60	—

KM# 67 20 LIRE
3.6000 g., Aluminum-Bronze, 21.25 mm. **Obv:** Smoking towers **Rev:** Circular pattern within stylized hand **Designer:** J. Vivarelli

Date	Mintage	F	VF	XF	Unc	BU
1977	180,000	—	0.10	0.25	0.60	—

KM# 80 20 LIRE
3.6000 g., Aluminum-Bronze, 21.25 mm. **Obv:** Value below smoking towers **Rev:** Kneeling figure **Designer:** Monassi

Date	Mintage	F	VF	XF	Unc	BU
1978	130,000	—	0.10	0.25	0.60	—

KM# 93 20 LIRE
3.6000 g., Aluminum-Bronze, 21.25 mm. **Obv:** Crowned shield **Rev:** Crowned skeleton keys divide value

Date	Mintage	F	VF	XF	Unc	BU
1979	125,000	—	0.10	0.30	0.60	—

KM# 106 20 LIRE
3.6000 g., Aluminum-Bronze, 21.25 mm. **Series:** 1980 Olympics **Obv:** Olympic rings and date to left of smoking towers **Rev:** Pole vaulter

Date	Mintage	F	VF	XF	Unc	BU
1980	125,000	—	0.25	0.50	1.00	—

KM# 120 20 LIRE
3.6000 g., Aluminum-Bronze, 21.25 mm. **Obv:** Crowned shield **Rev:** Value above bird

Date	Mintage	F	VF	XF	Unc	BU
1981R	100,000	—	0.10	0.30	0.75	2.00

KM# 135 20 LIRE
3.6000 g., Aluminum-Bronze, 21.25 mm. **Subject:** Social conquests **Obv:** Crown above smoking towers **Rev:** Standing figures within design

Date	Mintage	F	VF	XF	Unc	BU
1982R	78,000	—	0.10	0.25	0.60	—

KM# 149 20 LIRE
3.6000 g., Aluminum-Bronze, 21.25 mm. **Subject:** Nuclear war threat **Obv:** Crown above shield and sprig **Rev:** Torch above man

Date	Mintage	F	VF	XF	Unc	BU
1983R	72,000	—	0.10	0.30	0.75	—

KM# 163 20 LIRE
3.6000 g., Aluminum-Bronze, 21.25 mm. **Obv:** Castle **Rev:** Bust of Louis Pasteur facing

Date	Mintage	F	VF	XF	Unc	BU
1984R	65,000	—	0.10	0.30	0.75	—

KM# 177 20 LIRE
3.6000 g., Aluminum-Bronze, 21.25 mm. **Subject:** War on drugs **Obv:** Shield **Rev:** Open hand flanked by value and date

Date	Mintage	F	VF	XF	Unc	BU
1985R	60,000	—	—	0.15	0.55	—

KM# 191 20 LIRE
3.6000 g., Aluminum-Bronze, 21.25 mm. **Subject:** Revolution of technology **Obv:** Crown above smoking towers on rock **Rev:**

Stylized figure at lower right of computer flanked by value and date

Date	Mintage	F	VF	XF	Unc	BU
1986R	50,000	—	—	0.15	0.55	—

KM# 205 20 LIRE

3.6000 g., Aluminum-Bronze, 21.25 mm. **Subject:** 15th Anniversary - Resumption of Coinage **Obv:** Crowned pointed arms within sprigs **Rev:** Volcanoes

Date	Mintage	F	VF	XF	Unc	BU
1987R	83,000	—	—	0.15	0.55	—

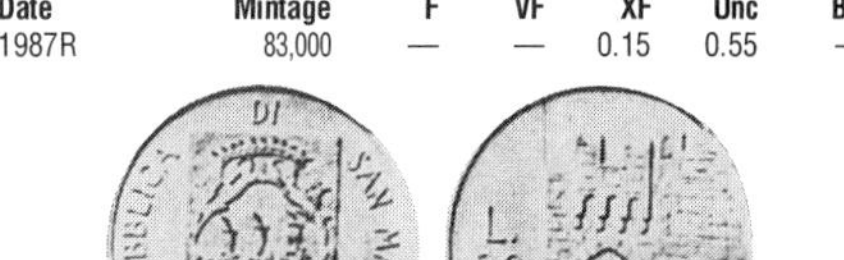

KM# 222 20 LIRE

3.6000 g., Aluminum-Bronze, 21.25 mm. **Subject:** Fortifications **Obv:** Crowned ornate arms on shield **Rev:** Small fortified gate **Designer:** Sergio Giandomenico

Date	Mintage	F	VF	XF	Unc	BU
1988R	38,000	—	—	0.15	0.55	—

KM# 235 20 LIRE

3.6000 g., Aluminum-Bronze, 21.25 mm. **Subject:** History **Obv:** Crowned shield **Rev:** Sword with value within flag

Date	Mintage	F	VF	XF	Unc	BU
1989R	37,000	—	—	0.15	0.55	—

KM# 252 20 LIRE

3.6000 g., Aluminum-Bronze, 21.25 mm. **Subject:** 1,600 Years of History **Obv:** Stylized towers above design **Rev:** Stylized large figure straddling value **Designer:** Magdalena Dobrucka

Date	Mintage	F	VF	XF	Unc	BU
1990R	96,000	—	—	0.15	0.55	—

KM# 265 20 LIRE

3.6000 g., Aluminum-Bronze, 21.25 mm. **Obv:** Date at upper left of smoking towers **Rev:** Value above gloved hand rejecting cardinal ring

Date	Mintage	F	VF	XF	Unc	BU
1991R	—	—	—	0.15	0.55	—

KM# 282 20 LIRE

3.6000 g., Aluminum-Bronze, 21.25 mm. **Obv:** Towers with feather-like designs on top within circle **Rev:** Columbus landing on Hispaniola **Designer:** L. Cretara

Date	Mintage	F	VF	XF	Unc	BU
1992R	—	—	—	0.10	0.55	—

KM# 297 20 LIRE

3.6000 g., Aluminum-Bronze, 21.25 mm. **Rev:** Scroll and arch

Date	Mintage	F	VF	XF	Unc	BU
1993R	—	—	—	0.10	0.55	—

KM# 310 20 LIRE

3.6000 g., Aluminum-Bronze, 21.25 mm. **Obv:** Stone cutter **Rev:** Workers pulling stone

Date	Mintage	F	VF	XF	Unc	BU
1994R	40,000	—	—	0.10	0.55	—

KM# 326 20 LIRE

3.6000 g., Aluminum-Bronze, 21.25 mm. **Obv:** Banner wrapped around quills **Rev:** Child straddling cornucopia **Designer:** Loredana Pancotto

Date	Mintage	F	VF	XF	Unc	BU
1995R	—	—	—	0.10	0.55	—

KM# 353 20 LIRE

3.6000 g., Aluminum-Bronze, 21.25 mm. **Obv:** Bust of Saint Thomas facing

Date	Mintage	F	VF	XF	Unc	BU
1996R	32,000	—	—	0.10	0.55	—

KM# 363 20 LIRE

3.6000 g., Aluminum-Bronze, 21.25 mm. **Subject:** The Arts - Cinema **Obv:** Bust facing with flame within hands **Rev:** Film strips

Date	Mintage	F	VF	XF	Unc	BU
1997R	28,000	—	—	0.10	0.55	—

KM# 379 20 LIRE

3.6000 g., Aluminum-Bronze, 21.25 mm. **Subject:** Communications **Rev:** Two profiles in silhouette left

Date	Mintage	F	VF	XF	Unc	BU
1998R	—	—	—	0.10	0.55	—

KM# 390 20 LIRE

3.6000 g., Aluminum-Bronze, 21.25 mm. **Subject:** Exploration **Obv:** Crowned shield **Rev:** Earth as known today **Designer:** Abd el-Kalik Yhia

Date	Mintage	F	VF	XF	Unc	BU
1999R	—	—	—	0.10	0.55	—

KM# 400 20 LIRE

3.6000 g., Aluminum-Bronze, 21.22 mm. **Subject:** Solidarity **Obv:** Bust facing with flame within hands **Rev:** Two hands about to grasp, globe design in background **Edge:** Plain

Date	Mintage	F	VF	XF	Unc	BU
2000R	—	—	—	0.10	0.55	—

KM# 425 20 LIRE

3.6000 g., Aluminum-Bronze, 21.8 mm. **Obv:** Three towers within circle **Rev:** Two dolphins and value **Edge:** Plain

Date	Mintage	F	VF	XF	Unc	BU
2001R	—	—	—	—	0.75	2.00

KM# 19 50 LIRE

6.2000 g., Steel, 24.8 mm. **Obv:** Stylized feathers within towers **Rev:** Female kneeling before St. Marinus

Date	Mintage	F	VF	XF	Unc	BU
1972	291,000	0.15	0.25	0.50	1.00	—

KM# 27 50 LIRE

6.2000 g., Steel, 24.8 mm. **Obv:** Crowned shield **Rev:** Stylized standing figure with sword and scale **Designer:** Guido Veroi **Note:** Depicts the balance of man, not as an individual but as a race

Date	Mintage	F	VF	XF	Unc	BU
1973	291,000	0.15	0.25	0.50	1.00	—

KM# 35 50 LIRE

6.2000 g., Steel, 24.8 mm. **Obv:** Smoking towers within circle **Rev:** Stylized chicken **Designer:** Luciano Minguzzi

Date	Mintage	F	VF	XF	Unc	BU
1974	276,000	0.15	0.25	0.60	1.25	2.10

KM# 45 50 LIRE

6.2000 g., Steel, 24.8 mm. **Obv:** Smoking towers **Rev:** Cluster of fish **Designer:** Bino Bini

Date	Mintage	F	VF	XF	Unc	BU
1975	831,000	0.15	0.25	0.60	1.25	2.00

KM# 56 50 LIRE
6.2000 g., Steel, 24.8 mm. **Obv:** Stylized smoking towers **Rev:** Face forward within triangle flanked by bottle-like designs **Designer:** Mario Molteni

Date	Mintage	F	VF	XF	Unc	BU
1976	195,000	0.15	0.25	0.50	1.00	—

KM# 68 50 LIRE
6.2000 g., Steel, 24.8 mm. **Obv:** Value below smoking towers within circle **Rev:** Fingers in center of circle of stars **Designer:** J. Vivarelli

Date	Mintage	F	VF	XF	Unc	BU
1977	180,000	0.15	0.25	0.50	1.00	—

KM# 81 50 LIRE
6.2000 g., Steel, 24.8 mm. **Obv:** Value below smoking towers **Rev:** Flowering plant below seated mother and child at desk

Date	Mintage	F	VF	XF	Unc	BU
1978	130,000	0.15	0.25	0.50	1.00	—

KM# 94 50 LIRE
6.2000 g., Steel, 24.8 mm. **Obv:** Crowned shield **Rev:** Liberty bell in front of building

Date	Mintage	F	VF	XF	Unc	BU
1979	125,000	0.15	0.25	0.50	1.00	—

KM# 107 50 LIRE
6.2000 g., Steel, 24.8 mm. **Series:** 1980 Olympics **Obv:** Olympic rings and date to upper left of smoking towers **Rev:** Downhill skier

Date	Mintage	F	VF	XF	Unc	BU
1980	125,000	0.25	0.50	1.00	2.00	—

KM# 121 50 LIRE
6.2000 g., Steel, 24.8 mm. **Obv:** Crowned shield **Rev:** Value at left of dancing figure

Date	Mintage	F	VF	XF	Unc	BU
1981R	100,000	0.15	0.25	0.50	1.00	—

KM# 136 50 LIRE
6.2000 g., Steel, 24.8 mm. **Subject:** Social conquests **Obv:** Crown above smoking towers **Rev:** Standing figures within design

Date	Mintage	F	VF	XF	Unc	BU
1982R	78,000	0.15	0.25	0.50	1.00	—

 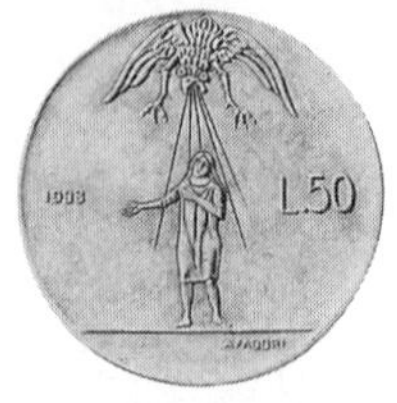

KM# 150 50 LIRE
6.2000 g., Steel, 24.8 mm. **Subject:** Nuclear war threat **Obv:** Crown above shield and sprig **Rev:** Beast of war above woman

Date	Mintage	F	VF	XF	Unc	BU
1983R	72,000	0.20	0.40	0.80	1.50	—

KM# 164 50 LIRE
6.2000 g., Steel, 24.8 mm. **Obv:** Castle **Rev:** Pierre and Marie Curie

Date	Mintage	F	VF	XF	Unc	BU
1984R	65,000	0.20	0.40	0.80	1.50	—

KM# 178 50 LIRE
6.2000 g., Steel, 24.8 mm. **Subject:** War on drugs **Obv:** Shield **Rev:** Stylized figures

Date	Mintage	F	VF	XF	Unc	BU
1985R	110,000	—	0.10	0.20	0.85	—

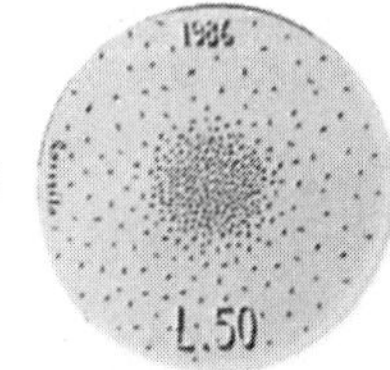

KM# 192 50 LIRE
6.2000 g., Steel, 24.8 mm. **Subject:** Revolution of technology **Obv:** Crown above smoking towers on rock **Rev:** Splitting the atom

Date	Mintage	F	VF	XF	Unc	BU
1986R	50,000	—	0.10	0.20	0.85	—

KM# 206 50 LIRE
6.2000 g., Steel, 24.8 mm. **Subject:** 15th Anniversary - Resumption of Coinage **Obv:** Crowned pointed shield within sprigs **Rev:** Animal in front of rock with tower at top

Date	Mintage	F	VF	XF	Unc	BU
1987R	93,000	—	0.10	0.20	0.85	—

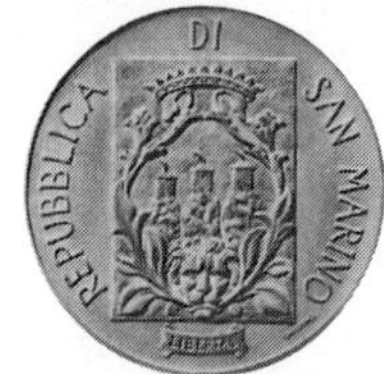 

KM# 223 50 LIRE
6.2000 g., Steel, 24.8 mm. **Subject:** Fortifications **Obv:** Crowned ornate arms on shield **Rev:** Ramp leading to gate house **Designer:** Sergio Giandomenico

Date	Mintage	F	VF	XF	Unc	BU
1988R	38,000	—	0.10	0.20	0.85	—

KM# 236 50 LIRE
6.2000 g., Steel, 24.8 mm. **Subject:** History **Obv:** Crowned shield **Rev:** Crossbow divides value

Date	Mintage	VG	F	VF	XF	Unc
1989R	87,000	—	—	0.10	0.20	0.85

KM# 253 50 LIRE
Steel, 17 mm. **Subject:** 1,600 Years of History **Obv:** Stylized towers above design **Rev:** Stylized bird **Designer:** Magdalena Dobrucka

Date	Mintage	F	VF	XF	Unc	BU
1990R	52,000	—	0.10	0.20	0.85	—

KM# 266 50 LIRE
Steel, 17 mm. **Obv:** Date at upper left of smoking towers **Rev:** Value above hand holding cannon barrels and wheat stalks

Date	Mintage	F	VF	XF	Unc	BU
1991R	—	—	0.10	0.20	0.85	—

KM# 283 50 LIRE
Steel, 17 mm. **Subject:** Columbus **Obv:** Towers with feather-like designs on top within circle **Rev:** Flying seagulls within radiant sun flanked by dates

Date	Mintage	F	VF	XF	Unc	BU
1992R	—	—	0.10	0.20	0.85	1.25

KM# 298 50 LIRE
Steel, 17 mm. **Obv:** Stylized feathers within towers **Rev:** Wheat growing through barbed wire

Date	Mintage	F	VF	XF	Unc	BU
1993R	—	—	0.10	0.20	0.85	—

KM# 311 50 LIRE
Stainless Steel, 17 mm. **Obv:** Stonecutter holding hammer and chisel, smoking towers at left **Rev:** Two stonecutters

Date	Mintage	F	VF	XF	Unc	BU
1994R	40,000	—	0.10	0.20	0.85	—

KM# 327 50 LIRE
Stainless Steel, 17 mm. **Obv:** Banner wrapped around bottom of design **Rev:** Child hugging bird **Designer:** Loredana Pancotto

Date	Mintage	F	VF	XF	Unc	BU
1995R	—	—	0.10	0.20	0.85	—

KM# 354 50 LIRE
Stainless Steel, 17 mm. **Obv:** Bust facing with flame within hands **Rev:** Descartes

Date	Mintage	F	VF	XF	Unc	BU
1996R	32,000	—	0.10	0.20	0.85	—

KM# 364 50 LIRE
Stainless Steel, 19 mm. **Subject:** The Arts - Sculpture **Obv:** Bust facing with flame within hands **Rev:** Han Dynasty Horse statue

Date	Mintage	F	VF	XF	Unc	BU
1997R	28,000	—	0.10	0.20	0.85	1.50

KM# 380 50 LIRE
Copper-Nickel, 19 mm. **Subject:** Engineering **Rev:** Cogwheel mind

Date	Mintage	F	VF	XF	Unc	BU
1998R	—	—	0.10	0.20	0.85	—

KM# 391 50 LIRE
Copper-Nickel, 19 mm. **Subject:** Exploration **Obv:** Crowned shield **Rev:** Ship sail, sun and waves

Date	Mintage	F	VF	XF	Unc	BU
1999R	—	—	0.10	0.20	0.85	—

KM# 401 50 LIRE
4.5000 g., Copper-Nickel, 19.2 mm. **Subject:** Equality **Obv:** Bust facing with flame within hands **Rev:** Five different plant leaves on 1 stem **Edge:** Plain **Note:** Struck at Rome.

Date	Mintage	F	VF	XF	Unc	BU
2000R	—	—	0.10	0.20	0.85	—

KM# 426 50 LIRE
4.5000 g., Stainless Steel, 19.2 mm. **Obv:** Three towers within circle **Rev:** Tree and value **Edge:** Plain

Date	Mintage	F	VF	XF	Unc	BU
2001R	—	—	—	—	0.85	—

KM# 20 100 LIRE
8.0000 g., Steel, 27.8 mm. **Obv:** Three smoking towers **Rev:** St. Marinus in a small boat **Designer:** Monassi

Date	Mintage	F	VF	XF	Unc	BU
1972	291,000	0.15	0.30	0.60	1.50	—

KM# 28 100 LIRE
8.0000 g., Steel, 27.8 mm. **Obv:** Crowned shield **Rev:** Ulysses passing the pillars of Hercules **Designer:** Guido Veroi

Date	Mintage	F	VF	XF	Unc	BU
1973	291,000	0.15	0.30	0.60	1.50	—

KM# 36 100 LIRE
8.0000 g., Steel, 27.8 mm. **Obv:** Smoking towers within circle **Rev:** Goat **Designer:** Luciano Minguzzi

Date	Mintage	F	VF	XF	Unc	BU
1974	276,000	0.15	0.30	0.65	1.75	3.00

KM# 46 100 LIRE
8.0000 g., Steel, 27.8 mm. **Obv:** Smoking towers **Rev:** Dog and cat lying together **Designer:** Bino Bini

Date	Mintage	F	VF	XF	Unc	BU
1975	821,000	0.15	0.30	0.65	1.75	3.50

KM# 57 100 LIRE
8.0000 g., Steel, 27.8 mm. **Obv:** Smoking towers **Rev:** Stylized seated figures within arch of building **Designer:** Mario Molteni

Date	Mintage	F	VF	XF	Unc	BU
1976	1,853,000	0.15	0.30	0.60	1.50	—

KM# 69 100 LIRE
8.0000 g., Steel, 27.8 mm. **Obv:** Value below smoking towers within circle **Rev:** Design within circular star wreath **Designer:** J. Vivarelli

Date	Mintage	F	VF	XF	Unc	BU
1977	565,000	0.15	0.30	0.60	1.50	—

KM# 70 100 LIRE
8.0000 g., Steel, 27.8 mm. **Obv:** Value below smoking towers within circle **Rev:** Stylized fish **Designer:** J. Vivarelli

Date	Mintage	F	VF	XF	Unc	BU
1977	565,000	0.15	0.30	0.60	2.00	—

KM# 82 100 LIRE
8.0000 g., Steel, 27.8 mm. **Series:** F.A.O. **Obv:** Value below smoking towers **Rev:** Standing figure using sickle

Date	Mintage	F	VF	XF	Unc	BU
1978	875,000	0.15	0.30	0.60	1.50	—

KM# 95 100 LIRE
8.0000 g., Steel, 27.8 mm. **Obv:** Crowned shield **Rev:** Design in center with assorted shields around border

Date	Mintage	F	VF	XF	Unc	BU
1979	665,000	0.15	0.30	0.60	1.50	—

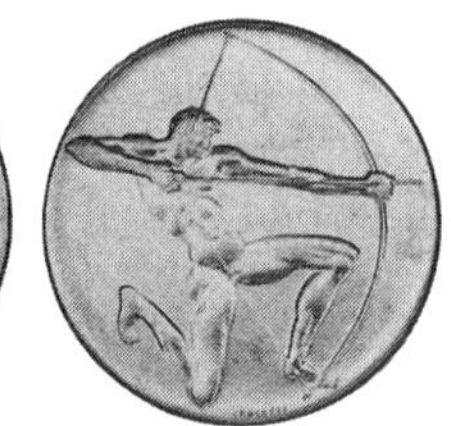

KM# 108 100 LIRE
8.0000 g., Steel, 27.8 mm. **Series:** 1980 Olympics **Obv:** Olympic rings and date to upper left of smoking towers **Rev:** Archery **Designer:** Crocetti

Date	Mintage	F	VF	XF	Unc	BU
1980	350,000	0.25	0.50	1.00	2.00	—

KM# 122 100 LIRE
8.0000 g., Steel, 27.8 mm. **Obv:** Crowned shield **Rev:** Stylized draped figure to left of value **Designer:** Crilli

Date	Mintage	F	VF	XF	Unc	BU
1981R	512,000	0.15	0.30	0.60	1.50	—

KM# 137 100 LIRE
8.0000 g., Steel, 27.8 mm. **Obv:** Crown above smoking towers **Rev:** Social conquests

Date	Mintage	F	VF	XF	Unc	BU
1982R	178,000	0.15	0.30	0.60	1.50	—

KM# 151 100 LIRE
8.0000 g., Steel, 27.8 mm. **Subject:** Nuclear War Threat **Obv:** Crown above shield and sprig **Rev:** Beast of war above man and woman

Date	Mintage	F	VF	XF	Unc	BU
1983R	172,000	0.15	0.30	0.60	1.50	—

KM# 165 100 LIRE
8.0000 g., Steel, 27.8 mm. **Obv:** Castle **Rev:** Bust of Guglielmo Marconi left

Date	Mintage	F	VF	XF	Unc	BU
1984R	165,000	0.15	0.30	0.60	1.50	—

KM# 179 100 LIRE
8.0000 g., Steel, 27.8 mm. **Subject:** War on Drugs **Obv:** Shield **Rev:** Three figures in discussion

Date	Mintage	F	VF	XF	Unc	BU
1985R	210,000	—	—	0.35	1.25	—

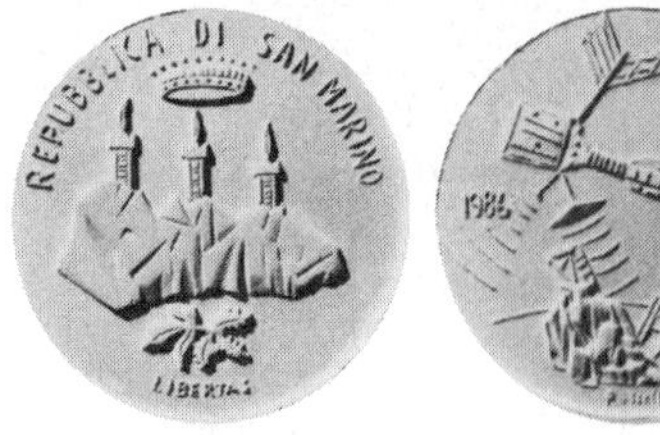

KM# 193 100 LIRE
8.0000 g., Steel, 27.8 mm. **Subject:** Revolution of Technology **Obv:** Crown above smoking towers on rock **Rev:** Satellite and receiving dishes divide date and value

Date	Mintage	F	VF	XF	Unc	BU
1986R	150,000	—	—	0.35	1.25	—

KM# 207 100 LIRE
8.0000 g., Steel, 27.8 mm. **Subject:** 15th Anniversary - Resumption of Coinage **Obv:** Crowned pointed shield within sprigs **Rev:** Sprig divides value

Date	Mintage	F	VF	XF	Unc	BU
1987R	143,000	—	—	0.35	1.25	—

KM# 224 100 LIRE
8.0000 g., Steel, 27.8 mm. **Subject:** Fortifications **Obv:** Crowned ornate arms on shield **Rev:** Gate tower **Designer:** Sergio Giandomenico

Date	Mintage	F	VF	XF	Unc	BU
1988R	38,000	—	—	0.35	1.25	—

KM# 237 100 LIRE
8.0000 g., Steel, 27.8 mm. **Subject:** History **Obv:** Crowned shield **Rev:** Teacher and student

Date	Mintage	F	VF	XF	Unc	BU
1989R	37,000	—	—	0.35	1.25	—

KM# 254 100 LIRE
Steel, 18 mm. **Subject:** 1,600 Years of History **Obv:** Towers above design **Rev:** Balance scales **Designer:** Magdalena Dobrncka

Date	Mintage	F	VF	XF	Unc	BU
1990R	1,086,000	—	—	0.35	1.25	—

KM# 267 100 LIRE
Steel, 18 mm. **Obv:** Date at upper left of smoking towers **Rev:** Value above clasped hands

Date	Mintage	F	VF	XF	Unc	BU
1991R	—	—	—	0.35	1.25	—

KM# 284 100 LIRE
Steel, 18 mm. **Subject:** Columbus **Obv:** Towers with feather-like designs on top within circle **Rev:** Value below three sailing ships

Date	Mintage	F	VF	XF	Unc	BU
1992R	—	—	—	0.35	1.25	—

KM# 299 100 LIRE
Copper-Nickel, 22 mm. **Obv:** Three towers above dentiled design **Rev:** Pan swallow above western Europe

Date	Mintage	F	VF	XF	Unc	BU
1993R	—	—	—	0.35	1.50	—

KM# 312 100 LIRE
Copper-Nickel, 22 mm. **Obv:** Stonecutter holding hammer and chisel, smoking towers at left **Rev:** Two stonecutters

Date	Mintage	F	VF	XF	Unc	BU
1994R	40,000	—	—	0.35	1.25	—

KM# 328 100 LIRE
Copper-Nickel, 22 mm. **Obv:** Banner wrapped around quills **Rev:** Three children **Designer:** Loredana Pancotto

Date	Mintage	F	VF	XF	Unc	BU
1995R	—	—	—	0.35	1.25	—

KM# 355 100 LIRE
Copper-Nickel, 22 mm. **Obv:** Bust facing with flame within hands **Rev:** Head of Rousseau 1/4 right

Date	Mintage	F	VF	XF	Unc	BU
1996R	32,000	—	—	0.35	1.25	—

KM# 365 100 LIRE
Copper-Nickel, 22 mm. **Subject:** The Arts - Dance **Obv:** Bust facing with flame within hands **Rev:** Ballet dancers

Date	Mintage	F	VF	XF	Unc	BU
1997R	28,000	—	—	0.35	1.25	—

KM# 381 100 LIRE
Copper-Nickel, 22 mm. **Subject:** Physics **Rev:** Human, crossbow

Date	Mintage	F	VF	XF	Unc	BU
1998R	—	—	—	0.35	1.25	—

KM# 402 100 LIRE
4.5000 g., Copper-Nickel, 22 mm. **Subject:** Ecology **Obv:** Bust facing with flame within hands **Rev:** Outline of house in center of leaf design, globe design in background **Edge:** Reeded and plain sectioned

Date	Mintage	F	VF	XF	Unc	BU
2000R	—	—	—	0.35	1.25	—

KM# 427 100 LIRE
4.5000 g., Copper-Nickel, 22 mm. **Obv:** Three towers within circle **Rev:** Grasping hands and value **Edge:** Plain and reeded sections

Date	Mintage	F	VF	XF	Unc	BU
2001R	—	—	—	—	1.25	—

KM# 83 200 LIRE

5.0000 g., Aluminum-Bronze, 24 mm. **Obv:** Value below smoking towers **Rev:** Seated figure weaving

Date	Mintage	F	VF	XF	Unc	BU
1978	530,000	—	0.25	0.75	1.75	—

KM# 96 200 LIRE

5.0000 g., Aluminum-Bronze, 24 mm. **Series:** F.A.O. **Obv:** Crowned shield **Rev:** Nude figure fighting lion flanked by value and date, F.A.O logo at upper right

Date	Mintage	F	VF	XF	Unc	BU
1979	675,000	—	0.25	0.75	1.75	2.50

KM# 109 200 LIRE

5.0000 g., Aluminum-Bronze, 24 mm. **Series:** 1980 Olympics **Obv:** Olympic rings and date at upper left of smoking towers **Rev:** Wrestlers

Date	Mintage	F	VF	XF	Unc	BU
1980	675,000	—	0.50	1.00	2.50	—

KM# 123 200 LIRE

5.0000 g., Aluminum-Bronze, 24 mm. **Series:** F.A.O. **Obv:** Crowned shield **Rev:** Stylized animal divides date and value **Designer:** Crilli

Date	Mintage	F	VF	XF	Unc	BU
1981R	700,000	—	0.25	0.75	1.75	2.50

KM# 138 200 LIRE

5.0000 g., Aluminum-Bronze, 24 mm. **Subject:** Social Conquests **Obv:** Crown above smoking towers **Rev:** Stylized figure within design

Date	Mintage	F	VF	XF	Unc	BU
1982R	178,000	—	0.25	0.75	1.75	—

KM# 152 200 LIRE

5.0000 g., Aluminum-Bronze, 24 mm. **Subject:** Nuclear War Threat **Obv:** Crown above shield and sprig **Rev:** Rider spearing victim

Date	Mintage	F	VF	XF	Unc	BU
1983R	172,000	—	0.25	0.75	1.75	—

KM# 166 200 LIRE

5.0000 g., Aluminum-Bronze, 24 mm. **Obv:** Castle **Rev:** Bust of Enrico Fermi facing

Date	Mintage	F	VF	XF	Unc	BU
1984R	165,000	—	0.25	0.75	1.75	—

KM# 180 200 LIRE

5.0000 g., Aluminum-Bronze, 24 mm. **Subject:** War on Drugs **Obv:** Shield **Rev:** Family group

Date	Mintage	F	VF	XF	Unc	BU
1985R	210,000	—	—	0.40	1.50	—

KM# 194 200 LIRE

5.0000 g., Aluminum-Bronze, 24 mm. **Subject:** Revolution of Technology **Obv:** Crown above smoking towers on rock **Rev:** Stylized hand holding microchip

Date	Mintage	F	VF	XF	Unc	BU
1986R	150,000	—	—	0.40	1.50	—

KM# 208 200 LIRE

5.0000 g., Aluminum-Bronze, 24 mm. **Subject:** 15th Anniversary - Resumption of Coinage **Obv:** Crowned pointed shield within sprigs **Rev:** Building in front of smoking towers

Date	Mintage	F	VF	XF	Unc	BU
1987R	143,000	—	—	0.40	1.50	—

KM# 225 200 LIRE

5.0000 g., Aluminum-Bronze, 24 mm. **Subject:** Fortifications **Obv:** Crowned ornate arms on shield **Rev:** Tower divides value **Designer:** Sergio Giandomenico

Date	Mintage	F	VF	XF	Unc	BU
1988R	38,000	—	—	0.40	1.50	—

KM# 238 200 LIRE

5.0000 g., Aluminum-Bronze, 24 mm. **Subject:** History **Obv:** Crowned shield **Rev:** Stylized view of San Marino **Designer:** J. Asselbergs

Date	Mintage	F	VF	XF	Unc	BU
1989R	1,037,000	—	—	0.40	1.50	—

KM# 255 200 LIRE

5.0000 g., Aluminum-Bronze, 24 mm. **Subject:** 1,600 Years of History **Obv:** Towers above design **Rev:** Stylized head left **Designer:** Magdalena Dobrucka

Date	Mintage	F	VF	XF	Unc	BU
1990R	36,000	—	—	0.40	1.50	—

KM# 268 200 LIRE

5.0000 g., Aluminum-Bronze, 24 mm. **Obv:** Date at upper left of smoking towers **Rev:** Value above hand holding coin die

Date	Mintage	F	VF	XF	Unc	BU
1991R	—	—	—	0.40	1.50	—

KM# 285 200 LIRE

5.0000 g., Aluminum-Bronze, 24 mm. **Obv:** Stylized feathers on top of towers within circle **Rev:** Columbus navigating by the stars **Designer:** L. Cretara

Date	Mintage	F	VF	XF	Unc	BU
ND(1992)R	—	—	—	0.40	1.50	—

KM# 300 200 LIRE

5.0000 g., Aluminum-Bronze, 24 mm. **Rev:** Door and arches

Date	Mintage	F	VF	XF	Unc	BU
1993R	—	—	—	0.40	1.50	—

KM# 313 200 LIRE

5.0000 g., Aluminum-Bronze, 24 mm. **Obv:** Stonecutter holding hammer and chisel, smoking towers at left **Rev:** Man and bear

Date	Mintage	F	VF	XF	Unc	BU
1994R	40,000	—	—	0.40	1.50	—

KM# 329 200 LIRE

5.0000 g., Aluminum-Bronze, 24 mm. **Obv:** Banner wrapped around quills **Rev:** Two children playing **Designer:** Loredana Pancotto

Date	Mintage	F	VF	XF	Unc	BU
1995R	—	—	—	0.40	1.50	—

KM# 356 200 LIRE

5.0000 g., Aluminum-Bronze, 24 mm. **Subject:** Kant **Obv:** Bust facing with flame within hands **Rev:** Head of Kant right within square above value

Date	Mintage	F	VF	XF	Unc	BU
1996R	32,000	—	—	0.40	1.50	—

KM# 366 200 LIRE
5.0000 g., Aluminum-Bronze, 24 mm. **Subject:** The Arts - Painting **Obv:** Bust facing with flame within hands **Rev:** Seated figure painting portrait of standing figure at left **Designer:** Galeabason

Date	Mintage	F	VF	XF	Unc	BU
1997R	28,000	—	—	0.40	1.50	—

KM# 382 200 LIRE
5.0000 g., Aluminum-Bronze, 24 mm. **Subject:** Zoology **Rev:** Stylized dolphins

Date	Mintage	F	VF	XF	Unc	BU
1998R	—	—	—	0.40	2.50	—

KM# 393 200 LIRE
5.0000 g., Aluminum-Bronze, 24 mm. **Subject:** Exploration **Obv:** Crowned shield **Rev:** Stonehenge beneath the sun and stars

Date	Mintage	F	VF	XF	Unc	BU
1999R	—	—	—	0.40	1.50	—

KM# 403 200 LIRE
5.0000 g., Aluminum-Bronze, 24 mm. **Subject:** Knowledge **Obv:** Bust facing with flame within hands **Rev:** Allegorical female head left within globe design **Edge:** Reeded **Note:** Struck at Rome.

Date	Mintage	F	VF	XF	Unc	BU
2000R	—	—	—	0.40	1.50	—

KM# 428 200 LIRE
5.0000 g., Aluminum-Bronze, 24 mm. **Obv:** Three towers within circle **Rev:** Broken chain, leaves, vines and value **Edge:** Reeded

Date	Mintage	F	VF	XF	Unc	BU
2001R	—	—	—	—	1.50	—

KM# 140 500 LIRE
6.8000 g., Bi-Metallic Aluminum-Bronze center in Stainless Steel ring, 25.8 mm. **Subject:** Social Conquests **Obv:** Crown above smoking towers within circle **Rev:** Stylized figures within circle **Designer:** A. Biancini

Date	Mintage	F	VF	XF	Unc	BU
1982R	1,900,000	—	—	2.00	4.00	—

KM# 153 500 LIRE
6.8000 g., Bi-Metallic Aluminum-Bronze center in Stainless Steel ring, 25.8 mm. **Subject:** Nuclear War Threat **Obv:** Crown above shield and sprig **Rev:** Three horses above two people **Designer:** A. Fabbri

Date	Mintage	F	VF	XF	Unc	BU
1983R	1,922,000	—	—	2.00	4.00	—

KM# 167 500 LIRE
6.8000 g., Bi-Metallic Aluminum-Bronze center in Stainless Steel ring, 25.8 mm. **Obv:** Castle within circle **Rev:** Bust of Albert Einstein facing within circle

Date	Mintage	F	VF	XF	Unc	BU
1984R	2,633,000	—	—	2.00	4.00	—

KM# 209 500 LIRE
6.8000 g., Bi-Metallic Aluminum-Bronze center in Stainless Steel ring, 25.8 mm. **Subject:** 15th Anniversary - Resumption of Coinage **Obv:** Crowned pointed shield within sprigs **Rev:** Smoking towers

Date	Mintage	F	VF	XF	Unc	BU
1987R	3,063,000	—	—	2.00	4.00	—

KM# 226 500 LIRE
6.8000 g., Bi-Metallic Aluminum-Bronze center in Stainless Steel ring, 25.8 mm. **Subject:** Fortifications **Obv:** Crowned ornate arms on shield **Rev:** Hilltop fortification **Designer:** Sergio Giandomenico

Date	Mintage	F	VF	XF	Unc	BU
1988R	3,526,000	—	—	2.00	4.00	—

KM# 239 500 LIRE
6.8000 g., Bi-Metallic Aluminum-Bronze center in Stainless Steel ring, 25.8 mm. **Subject:** History **Obv:** Crowned shield **Rev:** Stone carver **Designer:** J. Asselbergs

Date	Mintage	F	VF	XF	Unc	BU
1989R	3,145,000	—	—	2.00	4.00	—

KM# 269 500 LIRE
6.8000 g., Bi-Metallic Aluminum-Bronze center in Stainless Steel ring, 25.8 mm. **Obv:** Date at left of smoking towers within circle **Rev:** Value above hand holding flowers within circle **Designer:** Aparielo

Date	Mintage	F	VF	XF	Unc	BU
1991R	3,580,563	—	—	2.00	4.00	—

KM# 286 500 LIRE
6.8000 g., Bi-Metallic Aluminumn-Bronze center in Steel ring, 25.8 mm. **Subject:** Columbus **Obv:** Towers with feather-like designs on top within circle **Rev:** Winds blowing ship within circle

Date	Mintage	F	VF	XF	Unc	BU
1992R	4,554,864	—	—	—	3.50	—

KM# 301 500 LIRE
6.8000 g., Bi-Metallic Aluminum-Bronze center in Stainless Steel ring, 25.8 mm. **Obv:** Smoking towers within circle **Rev:** Growth from a tree stump **Designer:** G.P. Malison

Date	Mintage	F	VF	XF	Unc	BU
1993R	4,200,000	—	—	—	3.50	—

KM# 330 500 LIRE
6.8000 g., Bi-Metallic Aluminum-Bronze center in Stainless Steel ring, 25.8 mm. **Series:** F.A.O. **Subject:** 50th Anniversary - F.A.O. **Obv:** Banner wrapped around bottom of design **Rev:** Kneeling figure under sprig **Designer:** Loredana Pancotto

Date	Mintage	F	VF	XF	Unc	BU
1995R	3,000,000	—	—	—	3.50	—

KM# 357 500 LIRE
6.8000 g., Bi-Metallic Aluminum-Bronze center in Stainless Steel ring, 25.8 mm. **Obv:** Bust facing with flame within hands within circle **Obv. Designer:** Giulianelli **Rev:** Face within triangle and circle design **Rev. Designer:** Renka

Date	Mintage	F	VF	XF	Unc	BU
1996R	3,911,288	—	—	—	3.50	—

KM# 383 500 LIRE

6.8000 g., Bi-Metallic Aluminum-Bronze center in Stainless Steel ring, 25.8 mm. **Subject:** Chemistry **Obv:** Bust facing with flame within hands within circle **Obv. Designer:** Giulianelli **Rev:** Laboratory **Rev. Designer:** Magdalena Dobrucka

Date	Mintage	F	VF	XF	Unc	BU
1998R	1,300,000	—	—	—	3.50	—

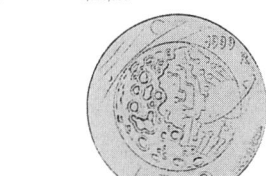

KM# 394 500 LIRE

6.8000 g., Bi-Metallic Aluminum-Bronze center in Stainless Steel ring, 25.8 mm. **Subject:** Exploration **Obv:** Bust facing with flame within hands within circle **Rev:** Moon's surface, radio waves and Saturn **Designer:** Y. Abd el-Kalik

Date	Mintage	F	VF	XF	Unc	BU
1999R	2,000,000	—	—	—	3.50	—

KM# 429 500 LIRE

Bi-Metallic Aluminum-Bronze center in Stainless Steel ring, 25.8 mm. **Obv:** Three towers within circle **Rev:** Three different plant stalks and value **Edge:** Reeded and plain sections **Note:** 6.8 grams.

Date	Mintage	F	VF	XF	Unc	BU
2001R	—	—	—	—	3.00	—

KM# 368 1000 LIRE

8.8200 g., Bi-Metallic Copper-Nickel center in Aluminum-Bronze ring, 27 mm. **Subject:** Millennium of building of the castle **Obv:** Heraldic lion within circle **Rev:** Statue, building and value within circle

Date	Mintage	F	VF	XF	Unc	BU
1997R	2,232,541	—	—	—	8.00	—

KM# 384 1000 LIRE

Bi-Metallic Copper-Nickel center in Aluminum-Bronze ring, 27 mm. **Subject:** Geology **Obv:** Child of the Universe **Rev:** Family standing on earth **Designer:** Magdalena Dobrucka

Date	Mintage	F	VF	XF	Unc	BU
1998R	2,061,275	—	—	—	8.00	—

KM# 395 1000 LIRE

Bi-Metallic Copper-Nickel center in Aluminum-Bronze ring, 27 mm. **Subject:** Exploration **Obv:** Child of the Universe **Rev:** Radiant north star design **Designer:** Y. Abd el-Kalik

Date	Mintage	F	VF	XF	Unc	BU
1999R	1,836,495	—	—	—	8.00	—

KM# 405 1000 LIRE

Bi-Metallic Copper-Nickel center in Aluminum-Bronze ring, 27 mm. **Subject:** Liberty **Obv:** Child of the Universe **Rev:** Barn Swallow flying over world globe **Edge:** Reeded and plain sectioned **Note:** Struck at Rome.

Date	Mintage	F	VF	XF	Unc	BU
2000R	2,898,805	—	—	—	10.00	—

KM# 430 1000 LIRE

8.8000 g., Bi-Metallic Stainless-Steel center in Aluminum-Bronze ring, 27 mm. **Obv:** Three towers within circle **Rev:** Value within circle of birds **Edge:** Reeded and plain sections

Date	Mintage	F	VF	XF	Unc	BU
2001R	—	—	—	—	7.50	—

EURO COINAGE

KM# 440 EURO CENT

2.2700 g., Copper Plated Steel, 16.2 mm. **Obv:** "Il Montale" **Obv. Designer:** M. Frantisek Chochola **Rev:** Value and globe **Rev. Designer:** Luc Luycx **Edge:** Plain

Date	Mintage	F	VF	XF	Unc	BU
2002R	120,000	—	—	—	—	40.00
2003R	70,000	—	—	—	—	42.00
2004R	1,500,000	—	—	—	—	20.00
2005R	70,000	—	—	—	—	20.00
2006R	2,730,000	—	—	—	—	18.00
2007R	—	—	—	—	—	18.00
2008R	—	—	—	—	—	18.00

KM# 441 2 EURO CENT

3.0300 g., Copper Plated Steel, 18.7 mm. **Obv:** Stefano Gallietti, Liberty fighter **Obv. Designer:** M. Frantisek Chochola **Rev:** Value and globe **Rev. Designer:** Luc Luycx **Edge:** Grooved

Date	Mintage	F	VF	XF	Unc	BU
2002R	120,000	—	—	—	—	40.00
2003R	70,000	—	—	—	—	42.00
2004R	1,395,000	—	—	—	—	20.00
2005R	150,000	—	—	—	—	20.00
2006R	2,730,000	—	—	—	—	18.00
2007R	—	—	—	—	—	18.00
2008R	—	—	—	—	—	18.00

KM# 442 5 EURO CENT

3.8600 g., Copper Plated Steel, 21.2 mm. **Obv:** "Guaita" tower **Obv. Designer:** M. Frantisek Chochola **Rev:** Value and globe **Rev. Designer:** Luc Luycx **Edge:** Plain

Date	Mintage	F	VF	XF	Unc	BU
2002R	120,000	—	—	—	—	40.00
2003R	70,000	—	—	—	—	42.00
2004R	1,000,000	—	—	—	—	20.00
2005R	70,000	—	—	—	—	20.00
2006R	2,880,000	—	—	—	—	18.00
2007R	—	—	—	—	—	18.00
2008R	—	—	—	—	—	18.00

KM# 443 10 EURO CENT

4.0700 g., Brass, 19.7 mm. **Obv:** Building Basilica del Santo Marinus **Obv. Designer:** M. Frantisek Chochola **Rev:** Map and value **Rev. Designer:** Luc Luycx **Edge:** Reeded

Date	Mintage	F	VF	XF	Unc	BU
2002R	120,000	—	—	—	—	40.00
2003R	70,000	—	—	—	—	42.00
2004R	180,000	—	—	—	—	22.00
2005R	70,000	—	—	—	—	22.00
2006R	65,000	—	—	—	—	20.00
2007R	—	—	—	—	—	18.00

KM# 444 20 EURO CENT

5.7300 g., Brass, 22.1 mm. **Obv:** St. Marinus from a portrait by van Guercino **Obv. Designer:** M. Frantisek Chochola **Rev:** Map and value **Rev. Designer:** Luc Luycx **Edge:** Notched

Date	Mintage	F	VF	XF	Unc	BU
2002R	302,400	—	—	—	18.00	20.00
2003R	430,000	—	—	—	15.00	18.00
2004R	70,000	—	—	—	15.00	18.00
2005R	310,000	—			15.00	18.00
2006R	65,000	—	—	—	15.00	18.00
2007R	—	—	—	—	14.00	16.00

KM# 445 50 EURO CENT

7.8100 g., Brass, 24.2 mm. **Obv:** Fortress of San Marino **Obv. Designer:** M. Frantisek Chochola **Rev:** Map and value **Rev. Designer:** Luc Luycx **Edge:** Reeded

Date	Mintage	F	VF	XF	Unc	BU
2002R	230,400	—	—	—	20.00	22.50
2003R	415,000	—	—	—	17.50	20.00
2004R	70,000	—	—	—	17.50	20.00
2005R	179,000	—	—	—	17.50	20.00
2006R	343,880	—	—	—	15.00	18.00
2007R	—	—	—	—	14.00	16.00

KM# 446 EURO

7.5000 g., Bi-Metallic Copper-Nickel center in Brass ring, 23.2 mm. **Obv:** Crowned arms within sprigs and circle within star border **Obv. Designer:** M. Frantisek Chochola **Rev:** Value and map **Rev. Designer:** Luc Luycx **Edge:** Reeded and plain sections

Date	Mintage	F	VF	XF	Unc	BU
2002R	360,800	—	—	—	22.00	25.00
2003R	70,000	—	—	—	—	45.00
2004R	180,000	—	—	—	—	25.00
2005R	70,000	—	—	—	—	25.00
2006R	150,000	—	—	—	—	20.00
2007R	—	—	—	—	—	18.00

KM# 447 2 EURO

8.5200 g., Bi-Metallic Brass center in Copper-Nickel ring, 25.7 mm. **Obv:** Government building **Obv. Designer:** M. Frantisek Chochola **Rev:** Value and map **Rev. Designer:** Luc Luycx **Edge:** Reeded with 2's and stars

Date	Mintage	F	VF	XF	Unc	BU
2002R	255,760	—	—	—	25.00	28.00
2003R	70,000	—	—	—	—	45.00
2004R	70,000	—	—	—	—	28.00
2005R	150,000	—	—	—	—	28.00
2006R	120,000	—	—	—	—	22.00
2007R	—	—	—	—	—	20.00

KM# 467 2 EURO

8.5000 g., Bi-Metallic Brass center in Copper-Nickel ring, 25.75 mm. **Obv:** Crowned arms within sprigs **Rev:** Bartolomeo Borghesi **Edge:** Alternating stars and 2's

Date	Mintage	F	VF	XF	Unc	BU
2004R	110,000	—	—	—	17.50	30.00

KM# 469 2 EURO

8.5000 g., Bi-Metallic, 25.75 mm. **Obv:** Galileo Galilei at telescope

Date	Mintage	F	VF	XF	Unc	BU
2005R	130,000	—	—	—	35.00	45.00

SARAWAK

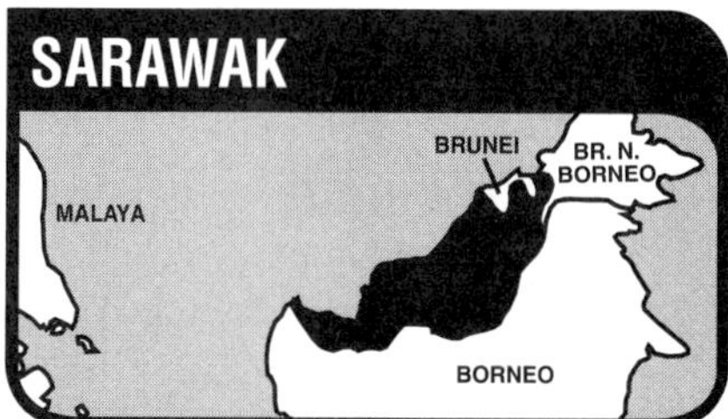

Sarawak is a former British protectorate located on the northwest coast of Borneo. The Japanese occupation during World War II so thoroughly devastated the economy that Rajah Sir Charles V. Brooke ceded it to Great Britain on July 1, 1946. In September, 1963 the colony joined the Federation of Malaysia. The capital is Kuching.

RULERS

Charles J. Brooke, Rajah, 1868-1917
Charles V. Brooke, Rajah, 1917-1946

MINT MARKS

H - Heaton, Birmingham

MONETARY SYSTEM

100 Cents = 1 Dollar

BRITISH PROTECTORATE

STANDARD COINAGE

100 Cents = 1 Dollar

KM# 20 1/2 CENT

Bronze 0 **Ruler:** Charles V. Brooke Rajah **Obv:** Head right **Rev:** Value within wreath

Date	Mintage	F	VF	XF	Unc	BU
1933H	2,000,000	5.00	8.00	20.00	30.00	—
1933H Proof	—	Value: 400				

KM# 12 CENT

Copper-Nickel **Ruler:** Charles V. Brooke Rajah **Obv:** Head right **Rev:** Value within wreath

Date	Mintage	F	VF	XF	Unc	BU
1920H	5,000,000	4.00	7.50	20.00	35.00	55.00

KM# 18 CENT

Bronze **Ruler:** Charles V. Brooke Rajah **Obv:** Head right **Rev:** Value within wreath

Date	Mintage	F	VF	XF	Unc	BU
1927H	5,000,000	1.25	3.00	6.00	15.00	—
1929H	2,000,000	1.25	3.00	6.00	15.00	—
1930H	3,000,000	1.25	3.00	6.00	15.00	—
1937H	3,000,000	1.25	3.00	6.00	15.00	—
1937H Proof	—	Value: 330				
1941H	3,000,000	350	700	1,000	1,600	—

Note: Estimate 50 pieces exist

KM# 8 5 CENTS

1.3500 g., 0.8000 Silver 0.0347 oz. ASW **Ruler:** Charles J. Brooke Rajah **Obv:** Head left **Obv. Legend:** C. BROOKE RAJAH **Rev:** Value within roped wreath

Date	Mintage	F	VF	XF	Unc	BU
1908H	40,000	45.00	120	200	350	—
1908H Proof	—	Value: 600				
1911H	40,000	45.00	120	200	350	—
1913H	100,000	50.00	95.00	190	300	—
1913H Proof	—	Value: 600				
1915H	100,000	50.00	95.00	150	300	—
1915H Proof	—	Value: 600				

KM# 13 5 CENTS

1.3500 g., 0.4000 Silver 0.0174 oz. ASW **Ruler:** Charles V. Brooke Rajah **Obv:** Head right **Rev:** Value within roped wreath

Date	Mintage	F	VF	XF	Unc	BU
1920H	100,000	70.00	140	215	400	—
1920H Proof	—	Value: 620				

KM# 14 5 CENTS

Copper-Nickel **Ruler:** Charles V. Brooke Rajah **Obv:** Head right **Rev:** Value within wreath

Date	Mintage	F	VF	XF	Unc	BU
1920H	400,000	2.00	4.00	10.00	25.00	—
1927H	600,000	2.00	4.00	10.00	22.00	—
1927H Proof	—	Value: 360				

KM# 9 10 CENTS

2.7100 g., 0.8000 Silver 0.0697 oz. ASW **Ruler:** Charles J. Brooke Rajah **Obv:** Head left **Obv. Legend:** C. BROOKE RAJAH **Rev:** Value within roped wreath

Date	Mintage	F	VF	XF	Unc	BU
1906H	50,000	35.00	50.00	95.00	230	—
1906H Proof	—	Value: 600				
1910H	50,000	35.00	50.00	95.00	230	—
1910H Proof	—	Value: 600				
1911H Proof	—	Value: 600				
1911H	100,000	28.00	45.00	85.00	220	—
1913H	100,000	28.00	45.00	85.00	190	—
1913H Proof	—	Value: 660				
1915H	100,000	70.00	120	200	400	—
1915H Proof	—	Value: 600				

KM# 15 10 CENTS

2.7100 g., 0.4000 Silver 0.0348 oz. ASW **Ruler:** Charles V. Brooke Rajah **Obv:** Head right **Rev:** Value within roped wreath

Date	Mintage	F	VF	XF	Unc	BU
1920H	150,000	35.00	70.00	120	200	—
1920H Proof	—	Value: 520				

KM# 16 10 CENTS

Copper-Nickel **Ruler:** Charles V. Brooke Rajah **Obv:** Head right **Rev:** Value within wreath

Date	Mintage	F	VF	XF	Unc	BU
1920H	800,000	2.00	4.00	9.00	20.00	—
1927H	1,000,000	2.00	3.00	7.00	19.00	—
1927H Proof	—	Value: 350				
1934H	2,000,000	2.00	3.00	7.00	19.00	—
1934H Proof	—	Value: 350				

KM# 10 20 CENTS

5.4300 g., 0.8000 Silver 0.1397 oz. ASW **Ruler:** Charles J. Brooke Rajah **Obv:** Head left **Obv. Legend:** C. BROOKE RAJAH **Rev:** Value within roped wreath

Date	Mintage	F	VF	XF	Unc	BU
1906H	25,000	60.00	120	300	550	—
1906H Proof	—	Value: 900				
1910H	25,000	60.00	120	300	550	—
1910H Proof	—	Value: 900				
1911H	15,000	60.00	120	300	550	—
1913H	25,000	60.00	120	300	550	—
1913H Proof	—	Value: 900				
1915H	25,000	310	410	650	1,000	—
1915H Proof	—	Value: 1,500				

KM# 17 20 CENTS

5.4300 g., 0.4000 Silver 0.0698 oz. ASW **Ruler:** Charles V. Brooke Rajah **Obv:** Head right **Rev:** Value within roped wreath

Date	Mintage	F	VF	XF	Unc	BU
1920H	25,000	140	280	415	760	—
1920H Proof	—	Value: 1,200				

KM# 17a 20 CENTS

5.0800 g., 0.4000 Silver 0.0653 oz. ASW **Ruler:** Charles V. Brooke Rajah **Obv:** Head right **Rev:** Value within roped wreath

Date	Mintage	F	VF	XF	Unc	BU
1927H	250,000	20.00	35.00	90.00	180	—
1927H Proof	—	Value: 680				

KM# 11 50 CENTS

13.5700 g., 0.8000 Silver 0.3490 oz. ASW **Ruler:** Charles V. Brooke Rajah **Obv:** Head left **Obv. Legend:** C. BROOKE RAJAH **Rev:** Value within roped wreath

Date	Mintage	F	VF	XF	Unc	BU
1906H	10,000	500	700	1,200	2,000	—
1906H Proof	—	Value: 3,000				

KM# 19 50 CENTS

10.3000 g., 0.5000 Silver 0.1656 oz. ASW **Ruler:** Charles V. Brooke Rajah **Obv:** Head right **Rev:** Value within roped wreath

Date	Mintage	F	VF	XF	Unc	BU
1927H	200,000	35.00	65.00	140	250	—
1927H Proof	—	Value: 650				

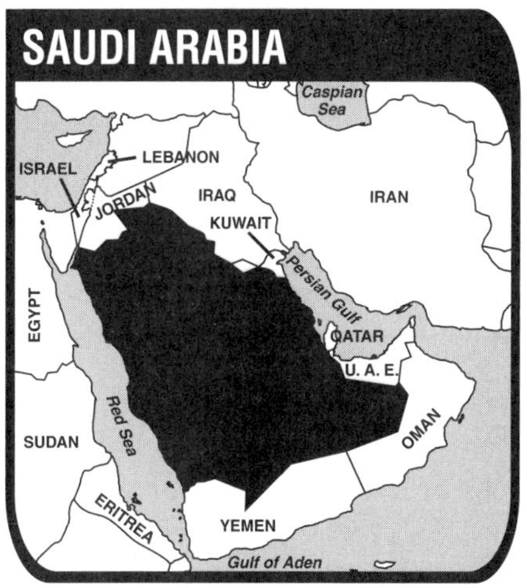

The Kingdom of Saudi Arabia, an independent and absolute hereditary monarchy comprising the former sultanate of Nejd, the old kingdom of Hejaz, Asir and Al Hasa, occupies four-fifths of the Arabian peninsula. The kingdom has an area of 830,000 sq. mi. (2,149,690 sq. km.) and a population of *16.1 million. Capital: Riyadh. The economy is based on oil, which provides 85 percent of Saudi Arabia's revenue.

Mohammed united the Arabs in the 7th century and his followers founded a great empire with its capital at Medina. The Turks established nominal rule over much of Arabia in the 16th and 17th centuries, and in the 18thcentury divided it into principalities.

The Kingdom of Saudi Arabia was created by King Abd Al-Aziz Bin Saud (1882-1953), a descendant of earlier Wahhabi rulers of the Arabian peninsula. In 1901 he seized Riyadh, capital of the Sultanate of Nejd, and in 1905 established himself as Sultan. In 1913 he captured the Turkish province of Al Hasa; took the Hejaz in 1925 and by 1926 most of Asir. In1932 he combined Nejd and Hejaz into the single kingdom of Saudi Arabia. Asir was incorporated into the kingdom a year later.

TITLES

العربية السعودية

Al-Arabiya(t) as-Sa'udiya(t)

المملكة العربية السعودية

Al-Mamlaka(t) al-'Arabiya(t) as-Sa'udiya(t)

RULERS

al Sa'ud Dynasty

Abd Al-Aziz Bin Sa'ud, (Ibn Sa'ud), AH1344-1373/1926-1953AD
Sa'ud Bin Abd Al-Aziz, AH1373-1383/1953-1964AD
Faisal Bin Abd Al-Aziz, AH1383-1395/1964-1975AD
Khalid Bin Abd Al-Aziz, AH1395-1403/1975-1982AD
Fahad Bin Abd Al-Aziz, AH1403-/1982-AD

MONETARY SYSTEM

Until 1960

20-22 Ghirsh = 1 Riyal
40 Riyals = 1 Guinea

NOTE: Copper-nickel, reeded-edge coins dated AH1356 and silver coins dated AH1354 were struck at the U. S. Mint in Philadelphia between 1944-1949.

HEJAZ & NEJD

Mecca, the metropolis of Islam and the capital of Hejaz, is located inland from the Red Sea due east of the port of Jidda. A center of non-political commercial, cultural and religious activities, Mecca remained virtually independent until 1259. Two centuries of Egyptian rule were followed by four centuries of Turkish rule which lasted until the Arab revolts which extinguished pretensions to sovereignty over any part of the Arabian peninsula.

MINT NAME

Makkah, Mecca

RULERS

Sharifs of Mecca

Ghalib b. Ma'sud, AH1219-1229
Yahya b. Surer, AH1230-1240
Abdul Muttalib and Ibn Awn, AH1240-1248

KINGDOM AND SULTANATE

Abd Al-Aziz bin Sa'ud as King of Hejaz and Sultan of Nejd

TRANSITIONAL COINAGE

Struck at the Mecca Mint during the occupation by Abd Al-Aziz Bin Sa'ud while establishing his kingdom.

KM# A3 1/2 GHIRSH

Bronze

Date	Mintage	Good	VG	F	VF	XF
AH1344//2	—	—	15.00	30.00	50.00	100

HEJAZ & NEJD SULTANATE

KINGDOM

REGULAR COINAGE

KM# 7 1/4 GHIRSH

Copper-Nickel **Obv:** Legend **Rev:** Value and date below legend

Date	Mintage	VG	F	VF	XF	Unc
AH1346	3,000,000	6.00	10.00	15.00	40.00	—

KM# 13 1/4 GHIRSH

Copper-Nickel **Obv:** Legend **Rev:** Value and date below legend

Date	Mintage	VG	F	VF	XF	Unc
AH1348	—	12.00	20.00	40.00	75.00	—
AH1348 Proof	1,000	—	—	—	—	—

KM# 8 1/2 GHIRSH

Copper-Nickel

Date	Mintage	VG	F	VF	XF	Unc
AH1346	3,000,000	10.00	15.00	25.00	60.00	—

KM# 14 1/2 GHIRSH

Copper-Nickel **Obv:** Legend **Rev:** Value and date below legend

Date	Mintage	VG	F	VF	XF	Unc
AH1348	—	12.00	25.00	40.00	100	—
AH1348 Proof	1,000	—	—	—	—	—

KM# 9 GHIRSH

Copper-Nickel **Obv:** Legend **Rev:** Value and date below legend

Date	Mintage	VG	F	VF	XF	Unc
AH1346	3,000,000	3.00	5.00	10.00	35.00	—

KM# 15 GHIRSH

Copper-Nickel **Obv:** Legend **Rev:** Value and date below inscription

Date	Mintage	VG	F	VF	XF	Unc
AH1348	—	12.00	20.00	30.00	75.00	—
AH1348 Proof	1,000	—	—	—	—	—

KM# 10 1/4 RIYAL

6.0500 g., 0.9170 Silver 0.1784 oz. ASW, 24 mm. **Obv:** Inscription within beaded circle, legend above, crossed swords below within design flanked by palms trees **Rev:** Inscription within beaded circle, legend above, value below within design flanked by palm trees

Date	Mintage	VG	F	VF	XF	Unc
AH1346	400,000	40.00	60.00	100	200	—
AH1346 Proof	—	Value: 750				
AH1348	200,000	60.00	90.00	150	350	—
AH1348 Proof	1,500	—	—	—	—	—

KM# 11 1/2 RIYAL

12.1000 g., 0.9170 Silver 0.3567 oz. ASW, 27 mm. **Obv:** Inscription within beaded circle, legend above, crossed swords below within design flanked by palm trees **Rev:** Inscription within beaded circle, legend above, value below within design flanked by palm trees and swords

Date	Mintage	VG	F	VF	XF	Unc
AH1346	200,000	100	175	250	500	—
AH1346 Proof	—	Value: 1,250				
AH1348	100,000	125	200	350	750	—
AH1348 Proof	2,000	—	—	—	—	—

KM# 12 RIYAL

24.1000 g., 0.9170 Silver 0.7105 oz. ASW, 37 mm. **Obv:** Inscription within beaded circle, legend above, crossed swords below within design flanked by palm trees **Rev:** Inscription within beaded circle, legend above, value below within design flanked by palm trees

Date	Mintage	VG	F	VF	XF	Unc
AH1346	800,000	40.00	60.00	90.00	150	—
AH1346 Proof	—	Value: 1,500				
AH1348	400,000	50.00	75.00	150	250	—
AH1348 Proof	2,000	—	—	—	—	—

UNITED KINGDOMS

KINGDOM

STANDARD COINAGE

KM# 19.1 1/4 GHIRSH

Copper-Nickel **Obv:** Legend **Rev:** Value and date below legend **Edge:** Plain

Date	Mintage	VG	F	VF	XF	Unc
AH1356 (1937)	1,000,000	2.00	5.00	10.00	35.00	—

KM# 19.2 1/4 GHIRSH

Copper-Nickel **Obv:** Legend **Rev:** Value and date below legend **Edge:** Reeded

Date	Mintage	VG	F	VF	XF	Unc
AH1356 (1937)	21,500,000	0.25	0.50	1.00	2.50	7.50

Note: Struck in 1947 (AH1366-67) at Philadelphia

KM# 20.1 1/2 GHIRSH

Copper-Nickel **Obv:** Legend **Rev:** Value and date below legend **Edge:** Plain

Date	Mintage	VG	F	VF	XF	Unc
AH1356 (1937)	1,000,000	3.00	8.00	20.00	45.00	—

KM# 20.2 1/2 GHIRSH

Copper-Nickel **Obv:** Legend **Rev:** Value and date below legend **Edge:** Reeded

Date	Mintage	VG	F	VF	XF	Unc
AH1356 (1937)	10,850,000	0.20	0.50	1.50	3.00	10.00

Note: Struck in 1947 (AH1366-67) at Philadelphia

KM# 21.1 GHIRSH

Copper-Nickel **Obv:** Legend **Rev:** Value and date below legend **Edge:** Plain

Date	Mintage	VG	F	VF	XF	Unc
AH1356 (1937)	4,000,000	3.00	8.00	15.00	40.00	—

KM# 21.2 GHIRSH

Copper-Nickel **Obv:** Legend **Rev:** Value and date below legend **Edge:** Reeded

Date	Mintage	VG	F	VF	XF	Unc
AH1356 (1937)	7,150,000	0.50	1.00	2.50	5.00	12.50

Note: Struck in 1947 (AH1366-67) at Philadelphia

KM# 40 GHIRSH

3.0000 g., Copper-Nickel, 22 mm. **Obv:** Palm above crossed swords at center of legend **Rev:** Value and date below legend **Edge:** Reeded

Date	Mintage	F	VF	XF	Unc	BU
AH1376 (1957)	10,000,000	0.15	0.25	0.50	3.00	—
AH1378 (1958)	50,000,000	0.15	0.25	0.50	2.00	—

KM# 41 2 GHIRSH

Copper-Nickel, 27 mm. **Obv:** Crossed swords below palm at center of legend **Rev:** Value and date below legend **Edge:** Reeded

Date	Mintage	F	VF	XF	Unc	BU
AH1376 (1957)	50,000,000	0.10	0.35	0.75	5.00	—
AH1379 (1959)	28,110,000	0.10	0.35	0.70	3.50	—

KM# 42 4 GHIRSH

Copper-Nickel, 30 mm. **Obv:** Crossed swords below palm at center of legend **Rev:** Value and date below legend **Edge:** Reeded

Date	Mintage	F	VF	XF	Unc	BU
AH1376 (1956)	49,100,000	0.25	0.50	1.00	6.00	—
AH1378 (1958)	10,000,000	0.25	0.50	1.00	5.00	—

KM# 16 1/4 RIYAL

3.1000 g., 0.9170 Silver 0.0914 oz. ASW **Obv:** Inscription within beaded circle, legend above, crossed swords below within design flanked by palm trees **Rev:** Inscription within beaded circle, legend above, value below within design flanked by palm trees

Date	Mintage	F	VF	XF	Unc	BU
AH1354 (1935)	900,000	1.75	2.50	3.00	5.50	—
AH1354 (1935) Proof	—	Value: 250				

KM# 37 1/4 RIYAL

2.9500 g., 0.9170 Silver 0.0870 oz. ASW **Obv:** Inscription within beaded circle, legend above, crossed swords below within design flanked by palm trees **Rev:** Inscription within beaded circle, legend above, value below within design flanked by palm trees

Date	Mintage	F	VF	XF	Unc	BU
AH1374 (1954)	4,000,000	BV	1.50	3.00	5.50	—

KM# 17 1/2 RIYAL

5.8500 g., 0.9170 Silver 0.1725 oz. ASW **Obv:** Inscription within beaded circle, legend above, crossed swords below within design flanked by palm trees **Rev:** Inscription within beaded circle, legend above, value below within design flanked by palm trees

Date	Mintage	F	VF	XF	Unc	BU
AH1354 (1935)	950,000	BV	3.00	8.00	20.00	—
AH1354 (1935) Proof	—	Value: 250				

KM# 38 1/2 RIYAL

5.9500 g., 0.9170 Silver 0.1754 oz. ASW **Obv:** Inscription within beaded circle, legend above, crossed swords below within design flanked by palm trees **Rev:** Inscription within beaded circle, legend above, value below within design flanked by palm trees

Date	Mintage	F	VF	XF	Unc	BU
AH1374 (1954)	2,000,000	BV	3.00	4.50	15.00	—

KM# 18 RIYAL

11.6000 g., 0.9170 Silver 0.3420 oz. ASW **Obv:** Inscription within beaded circle, legend above, crossed swords below within design flanked by palm trees **Rev:** Inscription within beaded circle, legend above, value below within design flanked by palm trees

Date	Mintage	F	VF	XF	Unc	BU
AH1354 (1935)	60,000,000	BV	5.50	6.50	12.50	—
AH1354 (1935) Proof	20,000,000	Value: 300				
AH1367 (1947)	Inc. above	BV	5.50	6.50	15.00	—
AH1370 (1950)	—	BV	5.50	6.50	17.50	—

KM# 39 RIYAL

11.6000 g., 0.9170 Silver 0.3420 oz. ASW **Obv:** Inscription within beaded circle, legend above, crossed swords below within design flanked by palm trees **Rev:** Inscription within beaded circle, legend above, value below within design flanked by palm trees

Date	Mintage	F	VF	XF	Unc	BU
AH1374 (1954)	48,000,000	BV	5.75	7.00	17.50	—

COUNTERMARKED COINAGE

70 = 65 Countermark

The following pieces are countermarked examples of earlier types bearing the Arabic numerals 65. They were countermarked in a move to break money changers' monopoly on small coins in AH1365 (1946AD). These countermarks vary in size and are found with the Arabic numbers raised in a circle. Incuse countermarks are considered a recent fabrication.

KM# 22 1/4 GHIRSH

Countermark: "65" **Note:** Countermark in Arabic numerals on 1/4 Ghirsh, KM#4.

CM Date	Host Date	Good	VG	F	VF	XF
AH1365	AH1344	6.00	12.00	30.00	65.00	—

KM# 23 1/4 GHIRSH

Countermark: "65" **Obv:** Countermark at center of legend **Rev:** Value and date below legend **Note:** Countermark in Arabic numerals on 1/4 Ghirsh, KM#7.

CM Date	Host Date	Good	VG	F	VF	XF
AH1365	AH1346	6.00	12.00	30.00	65.00	—

KM# 24 1/4 GHIRSH

Countermark: "65" **Note:** Countermark in Arabic numerals on 1/4 Ghirsh, KM#13.

CM Date	Host Date	Good	VG	F	VF	XF
AH1365	AH1348	20.00	30.00	50.00	100	—

KM# 25 1/4 GHIRSH

Countermark: "65" **Obv:** Countermark at center of legend **Rev:** Value and date below legend **Edge:** Plain **Note:** Countermark in Arabic numerals on 1/4 Ghirsh, KM#19.

CM Date	Host Date	Good	VG	F	VF	XF
AH1365	AH1356	2.50	5.00	15.00	30.00	—

KM# 26 1/2 GHIRSH

Countermark: "65" **Obv:** Countermark at center of legend **Rev:** Date below legend **Note:** Countermark in Arabic numerals on 1/2 Ghirsh, KM#5.

CM Date	Host Date	Good	VG	F	VF	XF
AH1365	AH1344	6.00	12.00	25.00	60.00	—

KM# 27 1/2 GHIRSH

Countermark: "65" **Obv:** Countermark at center of legend **Rev:** Date below legend **Note:** Countermark in Arabic numerals on 1/2 Ghirsh, KM#8.

CM Date	Host Date	Good	VG	F	VF	XF
AH1365	AH1346	6.00	12.00	25.00	60.00	—

KM# 28 1/2 GHIRSH

Countermark: "65" **Note:** Countermark in Arabic numerals on 1/2 Ghirsh, KM#14.

CM Date	Host Date	Good	VG	F	VF	XF
AH1365	AH1348	6.00	12.00	25.00	60.00	—

KM# 29 1/2 GHIRSH

Copper-Nickel **Countermark:** "65" **Obv:** Countermark at center of legend **Rev:** Date below legend **Edge:** Plain **Note:** Countermark in Arabic numerals on 1/2 Ghirsh, KM#20.1.

CM Date	Host Date	Good	VG	F	VF	XF
AH1365	AH1356	5.00	10.00	25.00	40.00	—

KM# 30 GHIRSH

Countermark: "65" **Obv:** Countermark at center of legend **Rev:** Value and date below legend **Note:** Countermark in Arabic numerals on 1 Ghirsh, KM#6.

CM Date	Host Date	Good	VG	F	VF	XF
AH1365	AH1344	6.00	12.00	35.00	65.00	—

KM# 31 GHIRSH

Countermark: "65" **Note:** Countermark in Arabic numerals on 1 Ghirsh, KM#9.

CM Date	Host Date	Good	VG	F	VF	XF
AH1365	AH1346	6.00	12.00	30.00	65.00	—

KM# 32 GHIRSH

Countermark: "65" **Obv:** Countermark at center of legend **Rev:** Value and date below legend **Note:** Countermark in Arabic numerals on 1 Ghirsh, KM#15.

CM Date	Host Date	Good	VG	F	VF	XF
AH1365	AH1348	10.00	20.00	35.00	65.00	—

KM# 33 GHIRSH

Copper-Nickel **Countermark:** "65" **Edge:** Plain **Note:** Countermark in Arabic numerals on 1 Ghirsh, KM#21.

CM Date	Host Date	Good	VG	F	VF	XF
AH1365	AH1356	6.00	10.00	20.00	30.00	—

REFORM COINAGE

5 Halala = 1 Ghirsh; 100 Halala = 1 Riyal

KM# 44 HALALA

Bronze **Obv:** Crossed swords and palm tree at center, legend above and below **Rev:** Value and date below legend

Date	Mintage	F	VF	XF	Unc	BU
AH1383 (1963)	5,000,000	0.50	0.60	0.85	3.00	—

KM# 60 HALALA

Bronze **Obv:** Different legend **Rev:** Value and date below legend

Date	Mintage	F	VF	XF	Unc	BU
AH1397 (1979)	—	—	—	—	—	175

Note: Not released for circulation

KM# 45 5 HALALA (Ghirsh)

2.5000 g., Copper-Nickel, 19.5 mm. **Obv:** Crossed swords and palm tree at center, legend above and below **Rev:** Legend above inscription in circle dividing value, date below

Date	Mintage	F	VF	XF	Unc	BU
AH1392 (1972)	130,000,000	0.10	0.15	0.30	0.50	—

KM# 53 5 HALALA (Ghirsh)

2.5000 g., Copper-Nickel, 19.5 mm. **Obv:** Crossed swords and palm tree at center, legend above and below **Rev:** Legend above inscription in circle dividing value, date below **Edge:** Reeded

Date	Mintage	F	VF	XF	Unc	BU
AH1397 (1976)	20,000,000	0.15	0.25	0.60	2.00	—
AH1400 (1979)	—	0.15	0.25	0.60	2.00	—

KM# 57 5 HALALA (Ghirsh)

2.5000 g., Copper-Nickel, 19.5 mm. **Series:** F.A.O. **Obv:** Crossed swords and palm tree at center, legend above and below **Rev:** Legend above inscription in circle dividing value, date below

Date	Mintage	F	VF	XF	Unc	BU
AH1398-1977	1,500,000	—	0.30	0.50	1.00	—

KM# 61 5 HALALA (Ghirsh)

2.5000 g., Copper-Nickel, 19.5 mm. **Obv:** Crossed swords and palm tree at center, legend above and below **Rev:** Legend above inscription in circle dividing value, date below

Date	Mintage	F	VF	XF	Unc	BU
AH1408 (1987)	80,000,000	—	0.30	0.50	1.00	—
AH1408 (1987) Proof	5,000	Value: 5.00				

KM# 46 10 HALALA (2 Ghirsh)

4.0000 g., Copper-Nickel, 21 mm. **Obv:** Crossed swords and palm tree at center, legend above and below **Rev:** Legend above inscription in circle dividing value, date below **Edge:** Reeded

Date	Mintage	F	VF	XF	Unc	BU
AH1392 (1972)	55,000,000	0.10	0.20	0.35	0.50	—

KM# 54 10 HALALA (2 Ghirsh)

4.0000 g., Copper-Nickel, 21 mm. **Obv:** Crossed swords and palm tree at center, legend above and below **Rev:** Legend above inscription in circle dividing value, date below

Date	Mintage	F	VF	XF	Unc	BU
AH1397 (1976)	50,000,000	0.15	0.25	1.00	2.50	—
AH1400 (1979)	29,500,000	0.25	0.75	1.00	3.00	—

KM# 58 10 HALALA (2 Ghirsh)

4.0000 g., Copper-Nickel, 21 mm. **Series:** F.A.O. **Obv:** Crossed swords and palm tree at center, legend above and below **Rev:** Legend above inscription in circle dividing value, date below

Date	Mintage	F	VF	XF	Unc	BU
AH1398-1977	1,000,000	—	0.25	0.50	1.00	—

KM# 62 10 HALALA (2 Ghirsh)

4.0000 g., Copper-Nickel, 21 mm. **Ruler:** Fahad Bin Abd Al-Aziz AH1403-1426/1982-2005AD **Obv:** National emblem at center, legend above and below **Rev:** Legend above inscription in circle dividing value, date below

Date	Mintage	F	VF	XF	Unc	BU
AH1408 (1987)	100,000,000	—	0.30	0.60	1.25	—
AH1408 (1987) Proof	5,000	Value: 6.00				
AH1423 (2002)	—	—	0.30	0.60	1.25	—

KM# 49 25 HALALA (1/4 Riyal)

5.0000 g., Copper-Nickel, 23 mm. **Series:** F.A.O. **Obv:** Crossed swords and palm tree at center, legend above and below **Rev:** Legend above inscription in circle dividing value, date below

Date	Mintage	F	VF	XF	Unc	BU
AH1392-1973	200,000	—	0.20	0.50	1.00	—

KM# 48 25 HALALA (1/4 Riyal)

5.0000 g., Copper-Nickel, 23 mm. **Obv:** Crossed swords and palm tree at center, legend above and below **Rev:** Legend above inscription in circle dividing value, date below **Note:** Corrected denomination; feminine gender.

Date	Mintage	F	VF	XF	Unc	BU
AH1392 (1972)	Inc. above	0.25	0.50	1.00	2.00	—

KM# 47 25 HALALA (1/4 Riyal)

5.0000 g., Copper-Nickel, 23 mm. **Obv:** Crossed swords and palm tree at center, legend above and below **Rev:** Legend above inscription in circle dividing value, date below **Note:** Error. Denomination in masculine gender.

Date	Mintage	F	VF	XF	Unc	BU
AH1392 (1972)	48,465,000	1.00	2.00	6.00	25.00	30.00

KM# 55 25 HALALA (1/4 Riyal)
5.0000 g., Copper-Nickel, 23 mm. **Obv:** Crossed swords and palm tree at center, legend above and below **Rev:** Legend above inscription in circle dividing value, date below

Date	Mintage	F	VF	XF	Unc	BU
AH1397 (1976)	20,000,000	0.35	0.50	1.00	3.00	—
AH1400 (1979)	57,000,000	0.35	0.50	0.85	2.50	—

KM# 63 25 HALALA (1/4 Riyal)
5.0000 g., Copper-Nickel, 23 mm. **Ruler:** Fahad Bin Abd Al-Aziz AH1403-1426/1982-2005AD **Obv:** National emblem at center, legend above and below **Rev:** Legend above inscription in circle dividing value, date below

Date	Mintage	F	VF	XF	Unc	BU
AH1408 (1987)	100,000,000	—	0.40	0.70	1.50	—
AH1408 (1987) Proof	5,000	Value: 7.50				
AH1423 (2002)	—	—	0.40	0.70	1.50	—

KM# 50 50 HALALA (1/2 Riyal)
6.5000 g., Copper-Nickel, 26 mm. **Series:** F.A.O. **Obv:** Crossed swords and palm tree at center, legend above and below **Rev:** Legend above inscription in circle dividing value, date below

Date	Mintage	F	VF	XF	Unc	BU
AH1392 (1972)	500,000	—	0.30	0.60	2.50	—

KM# 51 50 HALALA (1/2 Riyal)
6.5000 g., Copper-Nickel, 26 mm. **Obv:** Crossed swords and palm tree at center, legend above and below **Rev:** Legend above inscription in circle dividing value, date below

Date	Mintage	F	VF	XF	Unc	BU
AH1392 (1972)	16,000,000	0.20	0.35	0.60	2.00	—

KM# 56 50 HALALA (1/2 Riyal)
6.5000 g., Copper-Nickel, 26 mm. **Obv:** Crossed swords and palm tree at center, legend above and below **Rev:** Legend above inscription in circle dividing value, date below **Edge:** Reeded

Date	Mintage	F	VF	XF	Unc	BU
AH1397 (1976)	20,000,000	0.50	0.75	1.00	3.00	—
AH1400 (1979)	21,600,000	0.75	1.00	1.50	3.50	—

KM# 64 50 HALALA (1/2 Riyal)
6.5000 g., Copper-Nickel, 26 mm. **Ruler:** Fahad Bin Abd Al-Aziz AH1403-1426/1982-2005AD **Obv:** National emblem at center, legend above and below **Rev:** Legend above inscription in circle dividing value, date below

Date	Mintage	F	VF	XF	Unc	BU
AH1408 (1987)	70,000,000	0.20	0.50	2.25	3.50	—
AH1408 (1987) Proof	5,000	Value: 15.00				
AH1423 (2002)	—	0.20	0.50	2.25	3.50	—

KM# 68 50 HALALA (1/2 Riyal)
6.5000 g., Copper-Nickel **Ruler:** Abdullah bin Abdul Aziz AH1426-/2005-AD **Obv:** National emblem at center **Rev:** Legend above inscription in circle, dividing value, date below

Date	Mintage	F	VF	XF	Unc	BU
AH1428 (2007)	—	0.20	0.50	2.25	3.50	—

KM# 52 100 HALALA (1 Riyal)
10.0000 g., Copper-Nickel, 30 mm. **Obv:** Crossed swords and palm tree at center, legend above and below **Rev:** Legend above inscription in circle dividing value, date below

Date	Mintage	F	VF	XF	Unc	BU
AH1396 (1976)	250,000	—	0.65	1.00	3.50	—
AH1400 (1980)	30,000,000	—	0.65	1.00	3.00	—

KM# 59 100 HALALA (1 Riyal)
10.0000 g., Copper-Nickel, 30 mm. **Series:** F.A.O. **Obv:** Crossed swords and palm tree at center flanked by dates, legend above and below **Rev:** Legend above inscription in circle dividing value, date below

Date	Mintage	F	VF	XF	Unc	BU
AH1397 - 1977	—	—	—	150	275	325
Note: AH1397 date was struck as samples for the Saudi Arabia government by the British Royal Mint, but some escaped into circulation						
AH1398 - 1978	10,000,000	—	0.75	1.50	3.50	—

KM# 65 100 HALALA (1 Riyal)
10.0000 g., Copper-Nickel, 30 mm. **Obv:** Crossed swords and palm tree at center, legend above and below **Rev:** Legend above inscription in circle dividing value, date below

Date	Mintage	F	VF	XF	Unc	BU
AH1408 (1987)	40,000,000	—	1.00	2.00	3.00	—
AH1408 (1987) Proof	5,000	Value: 22.00				
AH1414 (1993)	5,000	—	1.00	2.00	4.00	—

KM# 66 100 HALALA (1 Riyal)
Bi-Metallic Brass center in Copper-Nickel ring, 23 mm. **Ruler:** Fahad Bin Abd Al-Aziz AH1403-1426/1982-2005AD **Obv:** National emblem at center, legend above and below **Rev:** Inscription at center, value at left, legend above, date below **Edge:** Reeded

Date	Mintage	F	VF	XF	Unc	BU
AH1419 (1998)	—	—	1.00	2.50	5.00	—

KM# 67 100 HALALA (1 Riyal)
Bi-Metallic Brass center in Copper-Nickel ring, 23 mm. **Ruler:** Fahad Bin Abd Al-Aziz AH1403-1426/1982-2005AD **Subject:** Centennial of Kingdom **Obv:** National emblem at center **Rev:** Inscription at center, legend above, value at left, date below **Edge:** Reeded

Date	Mintage	F	VF	XF	Unc	BU
AH1419 (1998)	—	—	1.50	3.50	6.50	—
AH1419 (1998) Proof	—	Value: 12.50				

TRADE COINAGE

KM# 36 GUINEA
7.9881 g., 0.9170 Gold 0.2355 oz. AGW **Obv:** Inscription within beaded circle, legend above, crossed swords below within design flanked by palm trees **Rev:** Inscription within beaded circle, legend above, value below within design flanked by palm trees

Date	Mintage	F	VF	XF	Unc	BU
AH1370 (1950)	2,000,000	—	—	BV	225	235

KM# 43 GUINEA
7.9881 g., 0.9170 Gold 0.2355 oz. AGW

Date	Mintage	F	VF	XF	Unc	BU
AH1377 (1957)	1,579,000	—	—	BV	225	250

SERBIA

Serbia, a former inland Balkan kingdom has an area of 34,116 sq. mi. (88,361 sq. km.). Capital: Belgrade.

Serbia emerged as a separate kingdom in the 12th century and attained its greatest expansion and political influence in the mid-14th century. After the Battle of Kosovo, 1389, Serbia became a vassal principality of Turkey and remained under Turkish suzerainty until it was re-established as an independent kingdom by the 1878 Treaty of Berlin. Following World War I, which had its immediate cause in the assassination of Austrian Archduke Francis Ferdinand by a Serbian nationalist, Serbia joined with the Croats and Slovenes to form the new Kingdom of the South Slavs with Peter I of Serbia as King. The name of the kingdom was later changed to Yugoslavia. Invaded by Germany during World War II, Serbia emerged as a constituent republic of the Socialist Federal Republic of Yugoslavia.

RULERS
Alexander I, 1889-1902
Peter I, 1903-1918

MINT MARKS
A - Paris
(a) - Paris, privy mark only
(g) - Gorham Mfg. Co., Providence, R.I.
H - Birmingham
V - Vienna
БП - (BP) Budapest

MONETARY SYSTEM
100 Para = 1 Dinara

DENOMINATIONS
ПАРА = Para
ПАРЕ = Pare
ДИНАР = Dinar
ДИНАРА = Dinara

KINGDOM

STANDARD COINAGE

KM# 23 2 PARE
2.0000 g., Bronze, 20 mm. **Ruler:** Peter I **Obv:** Crowned double-headed eagle **Rev:** Value **Note:** Medallic die alignment.

Date	Mintage	F	VF	XF	Unc	BU
1904	12,500,000	2.00	5.00	16.00	38.00	—

KM# 18 5 PARA
3.0000 g., Copper-Nickel, 17 mm. **Ruler:** Milan I as Prince **Obv:** Crowned double-headed eagle **Rev:** Value **Note:** Medallic die alignment.

Date	Mintage	F	VF	XF	Unc	BU
1904	8,000,000	1.00	2.50	7.00	18.00	—
1904 Proof	Inc. above	Value: 200				
1912	10,500,032	0.75	1.50	3.50	12.00	—
1912 Proof	—	Value: 130				
1917(g)	5,000,000	5.00	10.00	22.00	38.00	—

KM# 19 10 PARA
4.0000 g., Copper-Nickel, 20 mm. **Ruler:** Milan I as King **Obv:** Crowned double-headed eagle **Rev:** Value **Note:** Medallic die alignment.

Date	Mintage	F	VF	XF	Unc	BU
1904 Proof	—	Value: 350				
1912	7,700,032	0.75	1.25	4.00	14.00	—
1912 Proof	—	Value: 130				
1917(g)	5,000,000	1.00	2.50	10.00	28.00	—
1917(g) Proof	—	Value: 210				

KM# 20 20 PARA
6.0000 g., Copper-Nickel, 22 mm. **Ruler:** Milan I as King **Obv:** Crowned double-headed eagle **Rev:** Value **Note:** Medallic die alignment.

Date	Mintage	F	VF	XF	Unc	BU
1904 Proof	—	Value: 400				
1912	5,650,035	0.75	2.00	6.00	15.00	—
1912 Proof	—	Value: 140				
1917(g)	5,000,000	1.00	3.00	10.00	26.00	—

KM# 24.1 50 PARA
2.5000 g., 0.8350 Silver 0.0671 oz. ASW, 18 mm. **Ruler:** Peter I **Obv:** Head right with designer name **Rev:** Crown above value and date within wreath **Note:** Medallic die alignment.

Date	Mintage	F	VF	XF	Unc	BU
1904	1,400,031	2.00	6.00	14.00	35.00	—
1904 Proof	—	Value: 200				
1912	800,000	2.50	6.00	15.00	34.00	—
1915(a)	12,137,928	1.25	2.50	5.00	13.00	—

KM# 24.2 50 PARA
2.5000 g., 0.8350 Silver 0.0671 oz. ASW **Ruler:** Peter I **Obv:** Without designer's name **Rev:** Crown above value and date within wreath **Note:** Medallic die alignment

Date	Mintage	F	VF	XF	Unc	BU
1915(a)	1,862,071	8.00	14.00	36.00	96.00	—

KM# 24.5 50 PARA
Silver **Ruler:** Peter I **Obv:** With designer's signature **Rev:** Crown above value and date within wreath **Note:** Coin die alignment.

Date	Mintage	F	VF	XF	Unc	BU
1915(a)	—	—	—	—	—	—

KM# 25.1 DINAR
5.0000 g., 0.8350 Silver 0.1342 oz. ASW **Ruler:** Peter I **Obv:** Head right with designer's name below neck **Rev:** Crown above value and date within wreath **Note:** Medallic die alignment

Date	Mintage	F	VF	XF	Unc	BU
1904	2,000,086	4.50	13.00	26.00	76.00	—
1904 Proof	—	Value: 260				
1912	8,000,000	3.00	6.00	15.00	38.00	—
1915(a)	10,688,711	2.25	4.50	9.00	18.00	—

KM# 25.2 DINAR
5.0000 g., 0.8350 Silver 0.1342 oz. ASW **Ruler:** Peter I **Obv:** Without designer's name **Rev:** Crown above value and date within wreath **Note:** Medallic die alignment.

Date	Mintage	F	VF	XF	Unc	BU
1915(a)	2,312,304	5.00	15.00	35.00	96.00	—

KM# 26.1 2 DINARA
10.0000 g., 0.8350 Silver 0.2684 oz. ASW **Ruler:** Peter I **Obv:** Head right with designer's name below neck **Rev:** Crown above value and date within wreath **Note:** Medallic die alignment

Date	Mintage	F	VF	XF	Unc	BU
1904	1,150,044	7.50	15.00	32.00	86.00	—
1904 Proof	—	Value: 325				
1912	800,016	8.00	16.00	35.00	95.00	—
1915(a)	4,174,142	6.00	12.00	20.00	38.00	—

KM# 26.2 2 DINARA
10.0000 g., 0.8350 Silver 0.2684 oz. ASW **Ruler:** Peter I **Obv:** Without designer's name **Rev:** Crown above value and date within wreath **Note:** Medallic die alignment.

Date	Mintage	F	VF	XF	Unc	BU
1915(a)	825,858	9.00	24.00	52.00	140	—

KM# 26.3 2 DINARA
10.0000 g., 0.8350 Silver 0.2684 oz. ASW **Ruler:** Peter I **Obv:** Without designer's signature **Rev:** Crown above value and date within wreath **Note:** Coin die alignment.

Date	Mintage	VG	F	VF	XF	Unc
1915(a)	Inc. above	—	5.00	10.00	18.00	36.00
1915A	—	—	—	—	—	—

KM# 27 5 DINARA
25.0000 g., 0.9000 Silver 0.7234 oz. ASW, 37 mm. **Ruler:** Peter I **Subject:** 100th Anniversary - Karageorgevich Dynasty **Obv:** Conjoined heads right with designer name below neck **Obv. Designer:** Schwartz **Rev:** Crowned double-headed eagle on shield within crowned mantle **Edge:** Lettered, Type I **Edge Lettering:** • БОГ • ЧУВА • СРБИЈУ • **Note:** Edge lettered in Cyrillic: God Protect Serbia

Date	Mintage	F	VF	XF	Unc	BU
1904	200,000	35.00	75.00	230	680	—
1904 Proof	—	Value: 2,000				

KM# 28 5 DINARA
25.0000 g., 0.9000 Silver 0.7234 oz. ASW, 37 mm. **Ruler:** Peter I **Subject:** 100th Anniversary - Karageorgevich Dynasty **Edge:** Lettered, Type II **Edge Lettering:** • БОГ • СРБИЈУ • ЧУВА • **Note:** Edge lettered in Cyrillic: God Serbia Protect

Date	Mintage	F	VF	XF	Unc	BU
1904	Inc. above	150	300	700	1,800	—

GERMAN OCCUPATION

World War II

OCCUPATION COINAGE

KM# 30 50 PARA
Zinc **Obv:** Double-headed eagle **Rev:** Value and date within oat sprigs

Date	Mintage	F	VF	XF	Unc	BU
1942БП (BP)	20,000,000	2.00	4.50	10.00	20.00	—

KM# 31 DINAR
Zinc **Obv:** Double headed eagle **Rev:** Value and date within oat sprigs

Date	Mintage	F	VF	XF	Unc	BU
1942БП (BP)	50,000,000	0.70	2.00	6.00	18.00	—

KM# 32 2 DINARA
Zinc **Obv:** Double-headed eagle **Rev:** Value and date within oat sprigs

Date	Mintage	F	VF	XF	Unc	BU
1942БП (BP)	40,000,000	0.70	2.00	7.00	20.00	—

KM# 33 10 DINARA
Zinc **Obv:** Double-headed eagle **Rev:** Value and date within oat sprigs

Date	Mintage	F	VF	XF	Unc	BU
1943БП (BP)	50,000,000	1.00	2.50	8.00	22.00	—

REPUBLIC

STANDARD COINAGE

KM# 34 DINAR
4.3300 g., Copper-Zinc-Nickel, 20 mm. **Obv:** National Bank emblem within circle **Rev:** Bank building and value **Edge:** Reeded

Date	Mintage	F	VF	XF	Unc	BU
2003	10,320,000	—	—	0.25	1.00	1.50
2004	—	—	—	0.25	1.00	1.50
2005	—	—	—	0.25	1.00	1.50

KM# 39 DINAR
4.2600 g., Copper-Zinc-Nickel, 20 mm. **Obv:** Crowned and mantled arms **Rev:** National Bank and value **Edge:** Segmented reeding

Date	Mintage	F	VF	XF	Unc	BU
2005	—	—	—	0.25	1.00	1.50
2006	—	—	—	0.25	1.00	1.50
2007	—	—	—	0.25	1.00	1.50

KM# 35 2 DINARA
5.2400 g., Copper-Zinc-Nickel, 22 mm. **Obv:** National Bank emblem within circle **Rev:** Gracanica Monastery and value **Edge:** Reeded

Date	Mintage	F	VF	XF	Unc	BU
2003	4,688,500	—	—	0.50	2.00	2.50

KM# 46 2 DINARA
5.0000 g., Brass, 22 mm. **Obv:** Crowned and mantled arms **Rev:** Gracanica Monastery and value **Edge:** Segmented reeding

Date	Mintage	F	VF	XF	Unc	BU
2006	—	—	—	0.50	2.00	2.50
2007	—	—	—	0.50	2.00	2.50

KM# 36 5 DINARA
5.2400 g., Copper-Zinc-Nickel, 22 mm. **Obv:** National Bank emblem within circle **Rev:** Krusedol Monastery and value **Edge:** Reeded

Date	Mintage	F	VF	XF	Unc	BU
2003	15,170,000	—	0.50	1.00	2.25	3.25

KM# 40 5 DINARA
5.2500 g., Copper-Zinc-Nickel, 22 mm. **Obv:** Crowned and mantled arms **Rev:** Krusedol Monastery and value **Edge:** Segmented reeding

Date	Mintage	F	VF	XF	Unc	BU
2005	—	—	—	0.75	2.00	3.00
2006	—	—	—	0.75	2.00	3.00
2007	—	—	—	0.75	2.00	3.00

KM# 37 10 DINARA
7.7700 g., Copper-Zinc-Nickel, 26 mm. **Obv:** National Bank emblem within circle **Rev:** Studenica Monastery and value **Edge:** Reeded

Date	Mintage	F	VF	XF	Unc	BU
2003	10,160,500	—	0.50	1.00	2.50	3.50

KM# 41 10 DINARA
7.7700 g., Copper-Zinc-Nickel, 26 mm. **Obv:** Crowned and mantled arms **Rev:** Studenica Monastery and value **Edge:** Segmented reeding

Date	Mintage	F	VF	XF	Unc	BU
2005	—	—	—	0.75	2.25	3.50
2006	—	—	—	0.75	2.25	3.50
2007	—	—	—	—	2.00	3.25

KM# 38 20 DINARA
9.0000 g., Copper-Zinc-Nickel, 28 mm. **Obv:** National Bank emblem within circle **Rev:** Temple of St. Sava and value **Edge:** Reeded

Date	Mintage	F	VF	XF	Unc	BU
2003	25,491,500	—	—	0.75	2.00	3.00

KM# 42 20 DINARA
9.0000 g., Copper-Nickel-Zinc, 28 mm. **Obv:** Crowned and mantled Serbian royal arms **Rev:** Nikola Tesla **Edge:** Segmented reeding

Date	Mintage	F	VF	XF	Unc	BU
2006	1,000,000	—	—	0.75	2.25	3.50
2007	—	—	—	0.75	2.25	3.50

KM# 47 20 DINARA
9.1200 g., Copper-Nickel-Zinc, 27.93 mm. **Subject:** Dositej Obradovic, 1742-1811 **Obv:** National arms **Obv. Legend:** РЕПУБЛИКА СРБИЈА - REPUBLIKA SRBIJA **Rev:** Bast facing slightly left **Edge:** Segmented reeding

Date	Mintage	F	VF	XF	Unc	BU
2007	—	—	—	0.75	2.00	3.00

SEYCHELLES

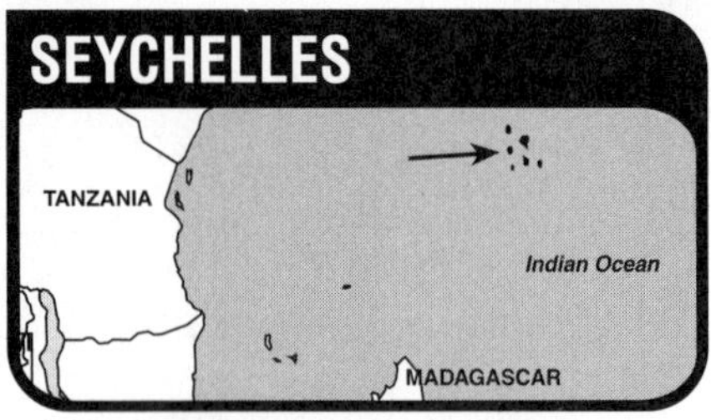

The Republic of Seychelles, an archipelago of 85 granite and coral islands situated in the Indian Ocean 600 miles (965 km.) northeast of Madagascar, has an area of 156 sq. mi. (455 sq. km.) and a population of *70,000. Among these islands are the Aldabra Islands, the Farquhar Group, and Ile Desroches, which the United Kingdom ceded to the Seychelles upon its independence. Capital: Victoria, on Mahe. The economy is based on fishing, a plantation system of agriculture, and tourism. Copra, cinnamon and vanilla are exported.

Although the Seychelles is marked on Portuguese charts of the early 16th century, the first recorded visit to the islands, by an English ship, occurred in 1609. The Seychelles were annexed to France by Captain Lazare Picault in 1743 and permanently settled in 1768, with the intention of establishing spice plantations to compete with the Dutch monopoly of the spice trade. British troops seized the islands in 1810, during the Napoleonic Wars; the Treaty of Paris, 1814, formally ceded them to Britain. The Seychelles was a dependency of Mauritius until Aug. 31, 1903, when they became a separate British Crown Colony. The colony was granted limited internal self-government in 1970, and attained independence on June 28, 1976, becoming Britain's last African possession to do so. Seychelles is a member of the Commonwealth of Nations. The president is the Head of State and of Government.

RULER
British, until 1976

MINT MARKS

(sa) - M in oval – South African Mint Co.
On coins dated 2000 and up in
Place of PM
PM - Pobjoy Mint
None - British Royal Mint

MONETARY SYSTEM
100 Cents = 1 Rupee

BRITISH CROWN COLONY

STANDARD COINAGE

KM# 5 CENT
Bronze **Obv:** Crowned head left **Obv. Designer:** Percy Metcalfe **Rev:** Value within beaded circle

Date	Mintage	F	VF	XF	Unc	BU
1948	300,000	—	0.25	0.50	1.25	—
1948 Proof	—	Value: 50.00				

KM# 14 CENT
Bronze **Obv:** Crowned head right **Obv. Designer:** Cecil Thomas **Rev:** Value within beaded circle

Date	Mintage	F	VF	XF	Unc	BU
1959	30,000	—	0.75	1.50	3.00	—
1959 Proof	—	—	—	—	—	—
1961	30,000	—	0.50	1.00	2.25	—
1961 Proof	—	—	—	—	—	—
1963	40,000	—	0.50	1.00	1.50	—
1963 Proof	—	—	—	—	—	—
1965	20,000	—	2.00	3.00	5.00	—
1969	Est. 5,000	15.00	20.00	30.00	65.00	—

Note: Latest reports indicate only 5,000 circulation strikes have been releasesd to date in addition to proof issues

Date	Mintage	F	VF	XF	Unc	BU
1969 Proof	—	Value: 5.00				

KM# 17 CENT

0.7000 g., Aluminum, 16 mm. **Series:** F.A.O. **Obv:** Young bust right **Obv. Designer:** Arnold Machin **Rev:** Cow head **Edge:** Plain

Date	Mintage	F	VF	XF	Unc	BU
1972	2,350,000	—	—	0.10	0.25	1.00

KM# 6 2 CENTS

Bronze **Obv:** Crowned head left **Obv. Designer:** Percy Metcalfe **Rev:** Value within beaded circle

Date	Mintage	F	VF	XF	Unc	BU
1948	350,000	—	0.35	0.60	1.50	—
1948 Proof	—	Value: 75.00				

KM# 15 2 CENTS

Bronze **Obv:** Crowned head right **Obv. Designer:** Cecil Thomas **Rev:** Value within beaded circle

Date	Mintage	F	VF	XF	Unc	BU
1959	30,000	—	0.50	1.00	2.75	—
1959 Proof	—	—	—	—	—	—
1961	30,000	—	0.50	1.00	2.75	—
1961 Proof	—	—	—	—	—	—
1963	40,000	—	0.75	1.25	2.50	—
1963 Proof	—	—	—	—	—	—
1965	20,000	—	2.00	3.00	4.50	—
1968	20,000	—	2.00	3.00	5.50	—
1969 Proof	5,000	Value: 4.00				

KM# 7 5 CENTS

Bronze **Obv:** Crowned head left **Obv. Designer:** Percy Metcalfe **Rev:** Value within circle

Date	Mintage	F	VF	XF	Unc	BU
1948	300,000	—	0.40	0.80	3.00	—
1948 Proof	—	Value: 100				

KM# 16 5 CENTS

Bronze **Obv:** Crowned head right **Obv. Designer:** Cecil Thomas **Rev:** Value within beaded circle

Date	Mintage	F	VF	XF	Unc	BU
1964	20,000	—	1.50	3.00	6.00	—
1964 Proof	—	—	—	—	—	—
1965	40,000	—	1.50	2.50	5.50	—
1967	20,000	—	2.50	5.00	9.00	—
1968	40,000	—	1.00	2.00	7.00	—
1969	100,000	—	0.50	1.00	5.00	—
1969 Proof	—	Value: 4.00				
1971	25,000	—	0.50	1.50	2.50	—

KM# 18 5 CENTS

0.7700 g., Aluminum, 18.5 mm. **Series:** F.A.O. **Obv:** Young bust right **Obv. Designer:** Arnold Machin **Rev:** Cabbage head **Shape:** Scalloped

Date	Mintage	F	VF	XF	Unc	BU
1972	2,200,000	—	—	0.10	0.25	—
1975	1,200,000	—	—	0.10	0.25	—

KM# 1 10 CENTS

Copper-Nickel **Obv:** Crowned head left **Obv. Designer:** Percy Metcalfe **Rev:** Value within sprig above date **Shape:** Scalloped

Date	Mintage	F	VF	XF	Unc	BU
1939	36,000	—	10.00	35.00	70.00	—
1939 Proof	—	Value: 150				
1943	36,000	—	10.00	22.00	40.00	—
1944	36,000	—	10.00	22.00	40.00	—
1944 Proof	—	Value: 175				

KM# 8 10 CENTS

Copper-Nickel **Obv:** Crowned head left **Obv. Designer:** Percy Metcalfe **Rev:** Value within sprig above date **Shape:** Scalloped

Date	Mintage	F	VF	XF	Unc	BU
1951	36,000	—	6.00	15.00	30.00	—
1951 Proof	—	Value: 135				

KM# 10 10 CENTS

6.0400 g., Nickel-Brass, 21.57 mm. **Obv:** Crowned head right **Obv. Designer:** Cecil Thomas **Rev:** Value within sprig above date **Shape:** 12-sided

Date	Mintage	F	VF	XF	Unc	BU
1953	130,000	—	0.50	1.00	3.00	—
1953 Proof	—	Value: 100				
1965	40,000	—	1.00	1.50	5.00	—
1967	20,000	—	4.00	7.50	15.00	—
1968	50,000	—	1.00	4.00	12.50	—
1969	60,000	—	1.00	2.00	7.00	—
1969 Proof	—	Value: 2.00				
1970	75,000	—	0.50	1.00	4.50	—
1971	100,000	—	0.50	1.00	1.75	—
1972	120,000	—	0.30	0.50	1.00	—
1973	100,000	—	0.15	0.25	1.00	—
1974	100,000	—	0.15	0.25	0.75	—

KM# 2 25 CENTS

2.9200 g., 0.5000 Silver 0.0469 oz. ASW **Obv:** Crowned head left **Obv. Designer:** Percy Metcalfe **Rev:** Value within sprig above date

Date	Mintage	F	VF	XF	Unc	BU
1939	36,000	—	7.50	35.00	125	—
1939 Proof	—	Value: 200				
1943	36,000	—	5.00	25.00	100	—
1944	36,000	—	3.50	20.00	85.00	—
1944 Proof	—	Value: 300				

KM# 9 25 CENTS

Copper-Nickel **Obv:** Crowned head left **Obv. Designer:** Percy Metcalfe **Rev:** Value within sprig above date

Date	Mintage	F	VF	XF	Unc	BU
1951	36,000	—	3.00	10.00	35.00	—
1951 Proof	—	Value: 160				

KM# 11 25 CENTS

3.0000 g., Copper-Nickel **Obv:** Crowned head right **Obv. Designer:** Cecil Thomas **Rev:** Value within sprig above date

Date	Mintage	F	VF	XF	Unc	BU
1954	124,000	—	0.75	1.25	3.50	—
1954 Proof	—	Value: 120				
1960	40,000	—	0.75	1.25	2.00	—
1960 Proof	—	—	—	—	—	—
1964	40,000	—	1.00	2.00	5.00	—
1965	40,000	—	1.00	2.00	5.00	—
1966	10,000	—	4.50	12.00	30.00	—
1967	20,000	—	2.50	4.00	15.00	—
1968	20,000	—	2.50	4.00	15.00	—
1969	100,000	—	1.00	2.00	4.00	—
1969 Proof	—	Value: 3.00				
1970	40,000	—	1.50	3.00	10.00	—
1972	120,000	—	0.50	0.75	1.50	—
1973	100,000	—	0.50	0.75	1.50	—
1974	100,000	—	0.50	0.75	1.50	—

KM# 3 1/2 RUPEE

5.8300 g., 0.5000 Silver 0.0937 oz. ASW **Obv:** Crowned head left **Obv. Designer:** Percy Metcalfe **Rev:** Value within sprig above date

Date	Mintage	F	VF	XF	Unc	BU
1939	36,000	—	22.00	80.00	175	—
1939 Proof	—	Value: 250				

KM# 12 1/2 RUPEE

Copper-Nickel **Obv:** Crowned head right **Obv. Designer:** Cecil Thomas **Rev:** Value within sprig above date

Date	Mintage	F	VF	XF	Unc	BU
1954	72,000	—	0.50	1.25	3.75	—
1954 Proof	—	Value: 150				
1960	60,000	—	0.50	3.00	6.00	—
1960 Proof	—	Value: 150				
1966	15,000	—	2.00	10.00	25.00	—
1967	20,000	—	3.00	12.00	25.00	—
1968	20,000	—	3.00	15.00	30.00	—
1969	60,000	—	0.75	5.00	12.00	—
1969 Proof	—	Value: 3.00				
1970	50,000	—	0.75	3.00	8.00	—
1971	100,000	—	0.75	2.00	6.00	—
1972	120,000	—	0.50	0.75	1.00	—
1974	100,000	—	0.50	0.75	1.00	—

KM# 4 RUPEE

11.6600 g., 0.5000 Silver 0.1874 oz. ASW, 30 mm. **Obv:** Crowned head left **Obv. Designer:** Percy Metcalfe **Rev:** Value within sprig above date **Edge:** Reeded

Date	Mintage	F	VF	XF	Unc	BU
1939	90,000	12.00	25.00	95.00	165	—
1939 Proof	—	Value: 400				

KM# 13 RUPEE

11.6400 g., Copper-Nickel, 30 mm. **Obv:** Crowned head right **Obv. Designer:** Cecil Thomas **Rev:** Value within sprig above date

Date	Mintage	F	VF	XF	Unc	BU
1954	150,000	—	0.50	1.00	3.00	—
1954 Proof	—	Value: 200				
1960	60,000	—	0.75	1.25	3.50	—
1960 Proof	—	—	—	—	—	—
1966	45,000	—	1.25	2.25	8.50	—
1967	10,000	—	6.00	12.50	30.00	—
1968	40,000	—	2.50	10.00	20.00	—
1969	50,000	—	1.50	5.00	12.50	—
1969 Proof	—	Value: 5.00				
1970	50,000	—	1.50	3.50	10.00	—
1971	100,000	—	0.75	1.50	5.00	—
1972	120,000	—	0.75	1.50	2.00	—
1974	100,000	—	—	—	1.50	—

KM# 19 5 RUPEES

Copper-Nickel, 30 mm. **Obv:** Young bust right **Obv. Designer:** Arnold Machin **Rev:** Palm tree, sailboats, giant tortoise and value **Edge:** Plain **Shape:** 7-sided

Date	Mintage	F	VF	XF	Unc	BU
1972	220,000	—	1.50	2.50	5.00	6.00

KM# 20 10 RUPEES

Copper-Nickel, 38.5 mm. **Obv:** Young bust right **Obv. Designer:** Arnold Machin **Rev:** Sea turtle and value **Rev. Designer:** Suzanne Danielli

Date	Mintage	F	VF	XF	Unc	BU
1974	—	—	2.00	4.00	12.00	14.00

REPUBLIC

STANDARD COINAGE

KM# 21 CENT

Aluminum, 16 mm. **Subject:** Declaration of Independence **Obv:** Head right **Rev:** Boueteur fish and value

Date	Mintage	F	VF	XF	Unc	BU
1976	109,000	—	0.10	0.20	0.75	1.00
1976 Proof	8,500	Value: 1.50				

KM# 30 CENT

0.7000 g., Aluminum, 16 mm. **Obv:** Arms with supporters **Rev:** Boueteur fish and value

Date	Mintage	F	VF	XF	Unc	BU
1977	—	—	—	0.15	0.75	1.00

KM# 46.1 CENT

Brass **Obv:** Arms with supporters **Rev:** Mud Crab and value

Date	Mintage	F	VF	XF	Unc	BU
1982	500,000	—	—	0.15	0.50	1.50
1982 Proof	—	Value: 2.25				

KM# 46.2 CENT

1.4300 g., Brass, 16.03 mm. **Obv:** Altered coat of arms **Rev:** Mud Crab **Edge:** Plain

Date	Mintage	F	VF	XF	Unc	BU
1990PM	—	—	—	0.15	0.45	0.60
1992PM	—	—	—	0.15	0.45	0.60
1992PM Proof	—	Value: 2.25				
1997	—	—	—	0.15	0.40	0.50
2004PM	—	—	—	0.15	0.25	0.35

KM# 22 5 CENTS

Aluminum **Subject:** Declaration of Independence **Obv:** Head right **Rev:** Fish above value and sprigs **Shape:** Scalloped **Note:** Varieties exist.

Date	Mintage	F	VF	XF	Unc	BU
1976	209,000	—	0.10	0.20	0.75	1.25
1976 Proof	8,500	Value: 1.50				

KM# 31 5 CENTS

Aluminum **Series:** F.A.O. **Obv:** Arms with supporters **Rev:** Fish above value and sprigs **Shape:** Scalloped

Date	Mintage	F	VF	XF	Unc	BU
1977	300,000	—	—	0.15	0.75	1.25

KM# 43 5 CENTS

1.9500 g., Brass, 18 mm. **Series:** World Food Day **Obv:** Arms with supporters **Rev:** Value at lower left of tapioca plant

Date	Mintage	F	VF	XF	Unc	BU
1981	720,000	—	—	0.15	0.45	1.00

KM# 47.1 5 CENTS

1.9500 g., Brass, 18 mm. **Obv:** Arms with supporters **Rev:** Value at lower left of tapioca plant

Date	Mintage	F	VF	XF	Unc	BU
1982	1,500,000	—	—	0.10	0.30	—
1982 Proof	Inc. above	Value: 2.50				

KM# 47.2 5 CENTS

1.9500 g., Brass, 18 mm. **Obv:** Altered coat of arms **Rev:** Tapioca plant

Date	Mintage	F	VF	XF	Unc	BU
1990PM	—	—	—	0.10	0.30	0.50
1992PM	—	—	—	0.10	0.30	0.50
1992PM Proof	—	Value: 2.50				
1995PM	—	—	—	0.10	0.30	0.50
1997PM	—	—	—	0.10	0.30	0.50
1997PM Proof	—	Value: 2.50				
2000 (sa)	—	—	—	0.10	0.30	0.50
2003PM	—	—	—	0.10	0.30	0.50

KM# 47a 5 CENTS

1.9700 g., Brass Plated Steel, 17.97 mm. **Obv:** National arms **Rev:** Tapioca plant **Edge:** Plain

Date	Mintage	F	VF	XF	Unc	BU
2007PM	—	—	—	0.10	0.30	0.50

KM# 23 10 CENTS

Nickel-Brass, 21 mm. **Subject:** Declaration of Independence **Obv:** Head right **Rev:** Sailfish and value **Edge:** Plain **Shape:** 12-sided

Date	Mintage	F	VF	XF	Unc	BU
1976	209,000	—	0.20	0.50	1.50	2.50
1976 Proof	8,500	Value: 2.50				

KM# 32 10 CENTS

Nickel-Brass, 21 mm. **Series:** F.A.O. **Obv:** Arms with supporters **Rev:** Sailfish and value

Date	Mintage	F	VF	XF	Unc	BU
1977	125,000	—	0.10	0.35	1.50	2.50

KM# 44 10 CENTS

3.2500 g., Brass, 21 mm. **Series:** World Food Day **Obv:** Arms with supporters **Rev:** Yellowfin tuna and value

Date	Mintage	F	VF	XF	Unc	BU
1981	145,000	—	0.10	0.25	1.00	1.50

KM# 48.1 10 CENTS

3.2500 g., Brass, 21 mm. **Obv:** Arms with supporters **Rev:** Yellowfin tuna and value

Date	Mintage	F	VF	XF	Unc	BU
1982	1,000,000	—	0.10	0.25	1.00	1.50
1982 Proof	Inc. above	Value: 2.75				

KM# 48.2 10 CENTS

3.2500 g., Brass, 21 mm. **Obv:** Altered coat of arms **Rev:** Yellowfin tuna **Edge:** Plain

Date	Mintage	F	VF	XF	Unc	BU
1990PM	—	—	0.10	0.25	1.00	1.50
1992PM	—	—	0.10	0.25	1.00	1.50
1992PM Proof	—	Value: 2.75				
1994PM	—	—	0.10	0.35	1.00	1.50
1997PM	—	—	0.10	0.35	1.00	1.50
2000 (sa)	—	—	0.10	0.35	1.00	1.50
2003PM	—	—	0.10	0.35	1.00	1.50

KM# 48a 10 CENTS

3.3700 g., Brass Plated Steel, 21 mm. **Obv:** National arms **Rev:** Black parrot, value **Edge:** Plain

Date	Mintage	F	VF	XF	Unc	BU
2007PM	—	—	—	0.30	0.75	1.00

KM# 24 25 CENTS

2.9000 g., Copper-Nickel, 19 mm. **Subject:** Declaration of Independence **Obv:** Head right **Rev:** Black Parrot and value

Date	Mintage	F	VF	XF	Unc	BU
1976	209,000	—	0.50	1.00	3.00	4.50
1976 Proof	8,500	Value: 3.50				

KM# 33 25 CENTS

2.9000 g., Copper-Nickel, 19 mm. **Obv:** Arms with supporters **Rev:** Black Parrot and value

Date	Mintage	F	VF	XF	Unc	BU
1977	—	—	0.25	0.75	3.00	4.50

KM# 49.1 25 CENTS

2.9000 g., Copper-Nickel, 19 mm. **Obv:** Arms with supporters **Rev:** Black Parrot and value **Edge:** Reeded

Date	Mintage	F	VF	XF	Unc	BU
1982	375,000	—	0.25	0.75	2.50	3.00
1982 Proof	Inc. above	Value: 4.00				

KM# 49.2 25 CENTS

2.9000 g., Copper-Nickel, 19 mm. **Obv:** Arms with supporters **Rev:** Black Parrot and value

Date	Mintage	F	VF	XF	Unc	BU
1989	1,500,000	—	0.25	0.75	2.25	4.00
1992PM	—	—	0.25	0.75	2.25	4.00
1992PM Proof	—	Value: 5.00				

KM# 49a 25 CENTS

2.9700 g., Nickel Clad Steel, 18.9 mm. **Obv:** National arms **Rev:** Black Parrot and value **Edge:** Plain

Date	Mintage	F	VF	XF	Unc	BU
1993PM	—	—	0.25	0.60	1.50	2.00
1997PM	—	—	0.25	0.60	1.50	2.00
2003PM	—	—	0.15	0.40	1.00	1.25
2007PM	—	—	—	0.40	1.00	1.25

KM# 49b 25 CENTS

Stainless Steel, 19 mm. **Obv:** Arms with supporters **Rev:** Black Parrot and value

Date	Mintage	F	VF	XF	Unc	BU
2000 (sa)	—	—	—	0.40	1.00	1.25

KM# 25 50 CENTS

5.8000 g., Copper-Nickel, 23.6 mm. **Subject:** Declaration of Independence **Obv:** Head right **Rev:** Orchid and value **Edge:** Reeded

Date	Mintage	F	VF	XF	Unc	BU
1976	209,000	—	0.50	1.00	2.50	—
1976 Proof	8,500	Value: 3.50				

KM# 34 50 CENTS

5.8000 g., Copper-Nickel, 23.6 mm. **Obv:** Arms with supporters **Rev:** Orchid and value

Date	Mintage	F	VF	XF	Unc	BU
1977	—	—	0.20	0.45	1.00	—

KM# 26 RUPEE

11.6500 g., Copper-Nickel, 30 mm. **Subject:** Declaration of Independence **Obv:** Head right **Rev:** Triton Conch shell and value **Edge:** Reeded

Date	Mintage	F	VF	XF	Unc	BU
1976	259,000	—	0.75	1.00	1.75	2.50
1976 Proof	8,500	Value: 3.50				

KM# 35 RUPEE

11.6500 g., Copper-Nickel, 30 mm. **Obv:** Arms with supporters **Rev:** Triton Conch shell and value

Date	Mintage	F	VF	XF	Unc	BU
1977	—	—	0.50	0.75	1.75	3.00

KM# 50.1 RUPEE

6.0500 g., Copper-Nickel, 25.3 mm. **Obv:** Arms with supporters **Rev:** Triton Conch shell and value

Date	Mintage	F	VF	XF	Unc	BU
1982	2,000,000	—	0.25	0.50	2.00	—
1982 Proof	Inc. above	Value: 5.00				
1983	—	—	0.50	1.00	2.00	—

KM# 50.2 RUPEE

6.1800 g., Copper-Nickel, 25.46 mm. **Obv:** Altered coat of arms **Rev:** Triton Conch Shell **Edge:** Reeded

Date	Mintage	F	VF	XF	Unc	BU
1992PM	—	—	0.25	0.60	1.50	2.00
1992PM Proof	—	Value: 5.00				
1995PM	—	—	0.25	0.60	1.50	2.00
1997PM	—	—	0.25	0.60	1.50	2.00
2007	—	—	—	0.45	1.10	1.50

KM# 27 5 RUPEES

13.5000 g., Copper-Nickel, 30 mm. **Subject:** Declaration of Independence **Obv:** Head right **Rev:** Palm tree and value **Shape:** 7-sided

Date	Mintage	F	VF	XF	Unc	BU
1976	50,000	—	1.25	1.75	3.00	—

KM# 36 5 RUPEES

13.5000 g., Copper-Nickel, 30 mm. **Obv:** Arms with supporters **Rev:** Palm tree and value **Shape:** 7-sided

Date	Mintage	F	VF	XF	Unc	BU
1977	—	—	1.00	1.50	2.25	—

KM# 51.1 5 RUPEES

13.5000 g., Copper-Nickel, 30 mm. **Obv:** Arms with supporters **Rev:** Palm tree and value

Date	Mintage	F	VF	XF	Unc	BU
1982	300,000	—	1.00	1.50	2.00	—
1982 Proof	Inc. above	Value: 5.00				

KM# 51.2 5 RUPEES

8.9700 g., Copper-Nickel, 28.8 mm. **Obv:** Altered arms **Rev:** Fruit tree divides value **Edge:** Reeded

Date	Mintage	F	VF	XF	Unc	BU
1992PM	—	—	0.35	0.80	2.00	2.75
1992PM Proof	—	Value: 5.00				
1997PM	—	—	0.35	0.80	2.00	2.75
2000 (sa) Thicker lettering	—	—	0.35	0.80	2.00	2.75
2007	—	—	0.30	0.70	1.75	2.25

KM# 28 10 RUPEES

18.1000 g., Copper-Nickel, 34.5 mm. **Subject:** Declaration of Independence **Obv:** Head right **Rev:** Green sea turtle and value **Rev. Designer:** Suzanne Danielli

Date	Mintage	F	VF	XF	Unc	BU
1976	50,000	—	2.00	2.75	6.00	10.00

KM# 37 10 RUPEES

18.1000 g., Copper-Nickel, 34.5 mm. **Series:** F.A.O. **Obv:** Arms with supporters **Rev:** Green sea turtle and value **Rev. Designer:** Suzanne Danielli

Date	Mintage	F	VF	XF	Unc	BU
1977	—	—	2.00	3.00	6.00	12.00
1977 Proof	—	Value: 12.00				

KM# 52 20 RUPEES

Copper-Nickel **Subject:** 5th Anniversary of Central Bank **Obv:** Arms with supporters **Rev:** Turtle at center of symbols of commerce

Date	Mintage	F	VF	XF	Unc	BU
1983	—	—	4.00	5.00	6.00	—

SIERRA LEONE

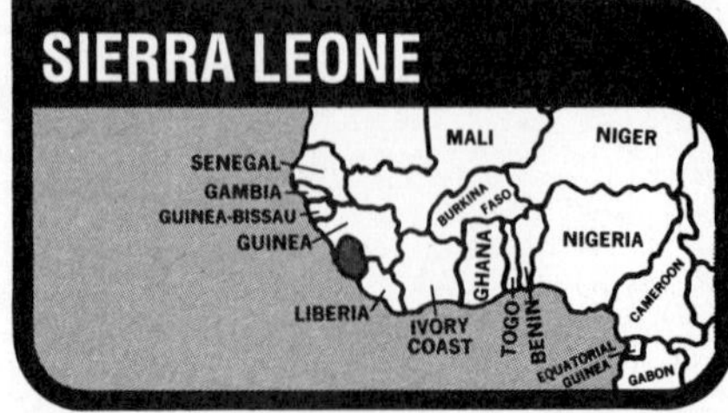

The Republic of Sierra Leone is located in western Africa between Guinea and Liberia, has an area of 27,699 sq. mi. (71,740 sq. km.) and a population of *4.1 million. Capital: Freetown. The economy is predominantly agricultural but mining contributes significantly to export revenues. Diamonds, iron ore, palm kernels, cocoa, and coffee are exported.

The coast of Sierra Leone was first visited by Portuguese and British slavers in the 15th and 16th centuries. The first settlement, at Freetown, 1787, was established as a refuge for freed slaves within the British Empire, runaway slaves from the United States and Negroes discharged from the British armed forces. The first settlers were virtually wiped out by tribal attacks and disease. The colony was re-established under the auspices of the Sierra Leone Company and transferred to the British Crown in 1807. The interior region was secured and established as a protectorate in 1896. Sierra Leone became independent on April 27, 1961, and adopted a republican constitution ten years later. It is a member of the Commonwealth of Nations. The president is Chief of State and Head of Government.

For similar coinage refer to British West Africa.

RULER

British, until 1961

MONETARY SYSTEM

Beginning 1964

100 Cents = 1 Leone

NOTE: Sierra Leone's official currency is the Leone. For previously listed Dollar Denominated Coinage, see the 5th Edition of Unusual World Coins.

REPUBLIC

STANDARD COINAGE

KM# 16 1/2 CENT

2.8500 g., Bronze, 20.2 mm. **Obv:** Value divides fish **Rev:** Head of right Sir Milton Margai **Edge:** Plain

Date	Mintage	F	VF	XF	Unc	BU
1964	600,000	—	—	0.15	0.25	0.75
1964 Proof	10,000	Value: 1.00				

KM# 31 1/2 CENT

2.8500 g., Bronze, 20.2 mm. **Obv:** Value above arms **Rev:** Head of Dr. Siaka Stevens right

Date	Mintage	F	VF	XF	Unc	BU
1980	—	—	0.15	0.30	1.00	—
1980 Proof	10,000	Value: 1.50				

KM# 17 CENT

5.7000 g., Bronze, 25.45 mm. **Obv:** Value within palm sprigs **Rev:** Head of Sir Milton Margai right **Edge:** Plain

Date	Mintage	F	VF	XF	Unc	BU
1964	35,000,000	—	—	0.15	0.25	—
1964 Proof	10,000	Value: 1.25				

KM# 32 CENT

5.7000 g., Bronze, 25.45 mm. **Obv:** Value above arms **Rev:** Head of Sir Milton Margai right

Date	Mintage	F	VF	XF	Unc	BU
1980	—	—	0.15	0.30	1.00	—
1980 Proof	10,000	Value: 1.50				

KM# 18 5 CENTS

2.5000 g., Copper-Nickel, 17.8 mm. **Obv:** Tree divides date within circle **Rev:** Head of right Sir Milton Margai

Date	Mintage	F	VF	XF	Unc	BU
1964	900,000	—	0.15	0.25	0.50	—
1964 Proof	10,000	Value: 1.50				

KM# 33 5 CENTS

2.5000 g., Copper-Nickel, 17.8 mm. **Obv:** Value above arms **Rev:** Head of Dr. Siaka Stevens right

Date	Mintage	F	VF	XF	Unc	BU
1980	—	—	0.15	0.30	0.75	—
1980 Proof	10,000	Value: 2.50				
1984	—	—	0.15	0.30	0.75	—

KM# 19 10 CENTS

4.9000 g., Copper-Nickel, 22.9 mm. **Obv:** Value within cocoa bean wreath **Rev:** Head of right Sir Milton Margai

Date	Mintage	F	VF	XF	Unc	BU
1964	24,000,000	—	0.25	0.40	0.65	—
1964 Proof	10,000	Value: 1.25				

KM# 34 10 CENTS

4.9000 g., Copper-Nickel, 22.9 mm. **Obv:** Value above arms **Rev:** Head of Dr. Siaka Stevens right

Date	Mintage	F	VF	XF	Unc	BU
1978	200,000	—	0.25	0.50	1.00	—
1980	—	—	0.20	0.40	0.75	—
1980 Proof	10,000	Value: 5.00				
1984	—	—	0.20	0.40	0.75	—

KM# 20 20 CENTS

8.2500 g., Copper-Nickel, 26.95 mm. **Obv:** Lion walking left **Rev:** Head of Sir Milton Margai right **Edge:** Reeded

Date	Mintage	F	VF	XF	Unc	BU
1964	11,000,000	—	0.35	0.60	1.25	—
1964 Proof	10,000	Value: 2.00				

KM# 30 20 CENTS

8.2500 g., Copper-Nickel, 26.95 mm. **Obv:** Value above arms **Rev:** Head of Dr. Siaka Stevens right

Date	Mintage	F	VF	XF	Unc	BU
1978	2,375,000	—	0.35	0.65	1.50	—
1980	—	—	0.35	0.60	1.25	—
1980 Proof	10,000	Value: 7.00				
1984	—	—	0.35	0.60	1.25	—

KM# 25 50 CENTS

11.6000 g., Copper-Nickel, 30 mm. **Obv:** Value above arms **Rev:** Head of Dr. Siaka Stevens right

Date	Mintage	F	VF	XF	Unc	BU
1972	1,000,000	—	1.00	1.75	3.00	—
1972 Proof	2,000	Value: 5.00				
1980	—	—	1.00	1.50	2.75	—
1980 Proof	10,000	Value: 10.00				
1984	—	—	1.00	1.50	2.75	—

KM# 26 LEONE

Copper-Nickel **Subject:** 10 Anniversary of Bank **Obv:** Lion right within circle **Rev:** Head of Dr. Siaka Stevens right

Date	Mintage	F	VF	XF	Unc	BU
ND(1974)	103,000	—	1.50	2.50	6.00	7.50

KM# 36 LEONE

Copper-Nickel **Subject:** O.A.U. Summit Conference **Obv:** Map within circle **Rev:** Head of Dr. Siaka Stevens right

Date	Mintage	F	VF	XF	Unc	BU
1980	75,000	—	1.75	2.75	6.00	—

KM# 43 LEONE
Nickel-Bronze **Obv:** Value above arms **Rev:** Bust of Dr. Joseph Saidu Momoh left **Shape:** Octagon

Date	Mintage	F	VF	XF	Unc	BU
1987	—	—	0.50	0.75	1.50	2.50
1988	—	—	0.50	0.75	1.50	2.50

KM# 29 2 LEONES
Copper-Nickel, 30 mm. **Series:** F.A.O. **Subject:** Regional Conference for Africa **Obv:** Farmer tilling field **Rev:** Head of Dr. Siaka Stevens right **Edge:** Plain **Shape:** 7-sided

Date	Mintage	F	VF	XF	Unc	BU
1976	20,000	—	1.00	2.50	5.50	6.50

KM# 44 10 LEONES
2.5000 g., Nickel-Bonded Steel, 17.99 mm. **Obv:** Value divides fish **Rev:** Bust of Mammy Yoko facing within circle **Edge:** Plain **Designer:** Avril Vaughan

Date	Mintage	F	VF	XF	Unc	BU
1996	—	—	—	—	0.75	1.00

KM# 295 20 LEONES
3.9200 g., Copper-Nickel, 21.7 mm. **Obv:** Value within fish and beaded circle **Rev:** Chimpanzee facing **Edge:** Plain

Date	Mintage	F	VF	XF	Unc	BU
2003	—	—	—	—	0.50	1.25

KM# 45 50 LEONES
Nickel-Bonded Steel **Obv:** Building above value **Rev:** Bust of Sir Henry Lightfoot facing **Shape:** Octagon **Designer:** Avril Vaughan

Date	Mintage	F	VF	XF	Unc	BU
1996	—	—	—	—	1.25	1.50

KM# 46 100 LEONES
Nickel-Bonded Steel **Obv:** Cocoa pods and value within beaded circle **Rev:** Head of Naimbana facing within beaded circle **Designer:** Avril Vaughan

Date	Mintage	F	VF	XF	Unc	BU
1996	—	—	—	—	1.75	2.00

KM# 302 100 LEONES
28.2800 g., Copper-Nickel, 38.6 mm. **Subject:** 40th Anniversary - Bank of Sierra Leone **Obv:** Bank President Kabbah **Rev:** Lion **Edge:** Reeded

Date	Mintage	F	VF	XF	Unc	BU
ND (2004)PM	5,000	—	—	—	15.00	18.00

KM# 296 500 LEONES
7.2000 g., Bi-Metallic Stainless Steel center in Brass ring, 24 mm. **Obv:** Building within circle **Rev:** Bust with hat facing within circle **Edge:** Plain **Shape:** 10-sided

Date	Mintage	F	VF	XF	Unc	BU
2004	—	—	—	—	7.50	9.00

KM# 346 500 LEONES
28.2800 g., Bronze, 38.6 mm. **Subject:** 40th Anniversary - Bank of Sierra Leone **Obv:** Bank President Kabbah **Rev:** Lion, denomination as "Le 500" **Edge:** Reeded

Date	Mintage	F	VF	XF	Unc	BU
ND(2004)PM	10,000	—	—	—	15.00	18.00

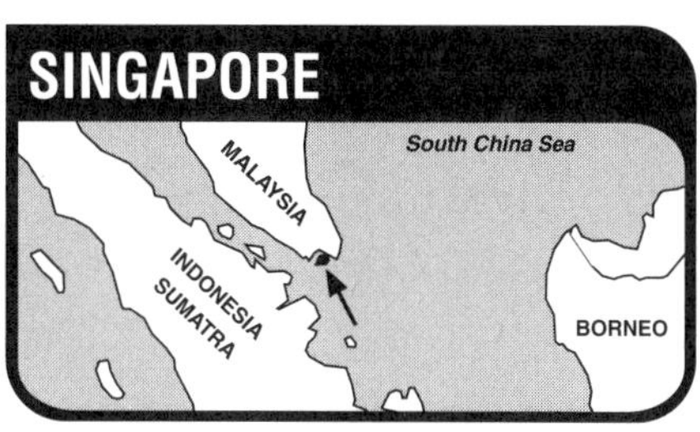

The Republic of Singapore, a member of the Commonwealth of Nations situated off the southern tip of the Malay peninsula, has an area of 224 sq. mi. (633 sq. km.) and a population of *2.7 million. Capital: Singapore. The economy is based on entrepôt trade, manufacturing and oil. Rubber, petroleum products, machinery and spices are exported.

Singapore's modern history - it was an important shipping center in the 14th century before the rise of Malacca and Penang - began in 1819 when Sir Thomas Stamford Raffles, an agent for the British East India Company, founded the town of Singapore. By 1825 its trade exceeded that of Malacca and Penang combined. The opening of the Suez Canal (1869) and the demand for rubber and tin created by the automobile and packaging industries combined to make Singapore one of the major ports of the world. In 1826 Singapore, Penang and Malacca were combined to form the Straits Settlements, which was made a Crown Colony in 1867. Singapore became a separate Crown Colony in 1946 when the Straits Settlements was dissolved. It joined in the formation of Malaysia in 1963, but broke away on Aug. 9, 1965, to become an independent republic. The President is Chief of State. The prime minister is Head of Government.

For earlier coinage see Straits Settlements, Malaya, Malaya and British Borneo.

MINT MARK
sm = ***"sm"*** - Singapore Mint monogram

MONETARY SYSTEM
100 Cents = 1 Dollar

REPUBLIC

STANDARD COINAGE

100 Cents = 1 Dollar

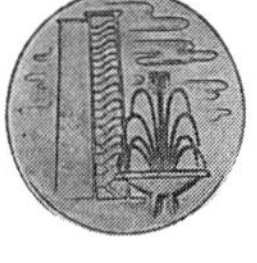

KM# 1 CENT
2.0000 g., Bronze, 17.8 mm. **Obv:** Value **Rev:** Apartment building **Edge:** Plain

Date	Mintage	F	VF	XF	Unc	BU
1967	7,500,000	—	—	0.30	0.60	—
1967 Proof	2,000	Value: 2.25				
1968	2,969,000	—	—	0.30	0.60	—
1968 Proof	5,000	Value: 2.00				
1969	7,220,000	—	—	1.20	2.00	—
1969 Proof	3,000	Value: 10.00				
1970	1,402,000	—	0.25	1.00	2.00	—
1971	9,731,000	—	—	0.25	0.60	—
1972	1,665,000	—	—	0.30	0.70	—
1972 Proof	749	Value: 40.00				
1973	6,377,000	—	—	0.20	0.30	—
1973 Proof	1,000	Value: 5.00				
1974	9,421,000	—	—	—	0.30	—
1974 Proof	1,500	Value: 4.00				
1975	24,226,000	—	—	—	0.30	—
1975 Proof	3,000	Value: 1.50				
1976	2,500,000	—	0.20	1.00	2.00	—
1976sm Proof	3,500	Value: 1.25				
1977sm Proof	3,500	Value: 1.25				
1978sm Proof	4,000	Value: 1.25				
1979sm Proof	3,500	Value: 1.25				
1980sm Proof	14,000	Value: 1.00				
1982sm Proof	20,000	Value: 1.00				
1983sm Proof	15,000	Value: 1.00				
1984sm Proof	15,000	Value: 1.00				

KM# 1a CENT
1.7500 g., Copper Clad Steel, 17.8 mm. **Obv:** Value **Rev:** Apartment building

Date	Mintage	F	VF	XF	Unc	BU
1976	13,665,000	—	—	0.20	0.30	—
1977	13,940,000	—	—	0.20	0.30	—
1978	5,931,000	—	—	—	0.30	—
1979	11,986,000	—	—	—	0.25	—
1980	19,922,000	—	—	—	0.25	—
1981	38,084,000	—	—	—	0.25	—
1982	24,105,000	—	—	—	0.25	—
1983	2,204,000	—	—	—	0.25	—
1984	5,695,000	—	—	—	0.25	—
1985	148,424	—	—	—	0.45	—

Note: In sets only

KM# 49 CENT
1.7500 g., Bronze, 17.8 mm. **Obv:** Arms with supporters **Rev:** Value divides plants **Edge:** Plain

Date	Mintage	F	VF	XF	Unc	BU
1986	20,000,000	—	—	—	0.10	0.15
1987	—	—	—	—	0.10	0.15
1988	—	—	—	—	0.10	0.15
1989	20,080,000	—	—	—	0.10	0.15
1990	10,000,000	—	—	—	0.10	0.15

KM# 49b CENT
Copper Plated Zinc, 17.8 mm. **Obv:** Arms with supporters **Rev:** Value divides plants

Date	Mintage	F	VF	XF	Unc	BU
1991	—	—	—	—	0.10	0.15

KM# 98 CENT
1.2750 g., Copper Plated Zinc, 15.96 mm. **Obv:** National arms **Rev:** Value divides plants **Edge:** Plain **Note:** Similar to KM#49 but motto ribbon on arms curves down at center.

Date	Mintage	F	VF	XF	Unc	BU
1992sm	20,000,000	—	—	—	0.10	0.15
1993sm	39,920,000	—	—	—	0.10	0.15
1994sm	130,810,000	—	—	—	0.10	0.15
1995sm	220,000,000	—	—	—	0.10	0.15
1996sm	—	—	—	—	0.20	0.30
1997sm	—	—	—	—	0.20	0.30
1998sm	48,940,000	—	—	—	0.20	0.30
1999sm	49,090,000	—	—	—	0.20	0.30
2000sm	52,360,000	—	—	—	0.10	0.15
2001sm	56,220,000	—	—	—	0.10	0.15
2002sm	19,003,000	—	—	—	0.10	0.15
2003sm	—	—	—	—	0.10	0.15
2003sm Proof	—	Value: 2.00				
2004sm	—	—	—	—	0.10	0.15
2004sm Proof	20,000	Value: 2.00				
2005sm	—	—	—	—	0.10	0.15
2006sm	—	—	—	—	0.10	0.15
2007sm	—	—	—	—	0.10	0.15

KM# 2 5 CENTS
1.4000 g., Copper-Nickel, 16.25 mm. **Obv:** Value and date **Rev:** Great White Egret **Edge:** Reeded

Date	Mintage	F	VF	XF	Unc	BU
1967	28,000,000	—	—	0.20	0.35	0.75
1967 Proof	2,000	Value: 3.25				
1968	4,217,000	—	—	0.25	0.40	0.80
1968 Proof	5,000	Value: 3.00				
1969	14,778,000	—	—	0.10	0.35	0.75
1969 Proof	3,000	Value: 15.00				
1970	4,065,000	—	—	0.20	0.40	0.80
1971	13,202,000	—	—	0.10	0.35	0.75
1972	9,817,000	—	—	0.10	0.35	0.75
1972 Proof	749	Value: 50.00				
1973	2,980,000	—	0.50	1.50	2.25	—
1973 Proof	1,000	Value: 7.50				
1974	10,868,000	—	—	0.10	0.35	0.75
1974 Proof	1,500	Value: 6.50				

Date	Mintage	F	VF	XF	Unc	BU
1975	1,729,000	—	—	0.40	1.00	1.25
1975 Proof	3,000	Value: 2.50				
1976	15,541,000	—	—	0.10	0.35	0.75
1976sm Proof	3,500	Value: 2.25				
1977	9,956,000	—	—	0.10	0.35	0.75
1977sm Proof	3,500	Value: 2.25				
1978	5,956,000	—	—	0.10	0.35	0.75
1978sm Proof	4,000	Value: 2.25				
1979	9,974,000	—	—	—	0.35	0.75
1979sm Proof	3,500	Value: 2.25				
1980	20,534,000	—	—	—	0.35	0.75
1980sm Proof	14,000	Value: 2.00				
1981	23,866,000	—	—	—	0.35	0.75
1982	24,413,000	—	—	—	0.35	0.75
1982sm Proof	20,000	Value: 2.00				
1983	4,016,000	—	—	—	0.35	0.75
1983sm Proof	15,000	Value: 2.00				
1984	18,880,000	—	—	—	0.35	0.75
1984sm Proof	15,000	Value: 2.00				
1985 In sets only	148,424	—	—	—	0.50	0.85

KM# 2a 5 CENTS

1.3000 g., Copper-Nickel Clad Steel, 16.25 mm. **Obv:** Value **Rev:** Great White Egret **Edge:** Reeded

Date	Mintage	F	VF	XF	Unc	BU
1980	12,001,000	—	—	—	0.35	0.50
1981	23,866,000	—	—	—	0.35	0.50
1982	24,413,000	—	—	—	0.35	0.50
1983	4,016,000	—	—	—	0.35	0.50
1984	—	—	—	—	0.35	0.50

KM# 8 5 CENTS

1.2700 g., Aluminum, 22 mm. **Series:** F.A.O. **Obv:** Value and date **Rev:** Pomfret fish **Edge:** Plain

Date	Mintage	F	VF	XF	Unc	BU
1971	3,049,000	—	0.10	0.30	1.00	1.25

KM# 50 5 CENTS

Aluminum-Bronze, 16.25 mm. **Obv:** Arms with supporters **Rev:** Fruit salad plant **Edge:** Reeded

Date	Mintage	F	VF	XF	Unc	BU
1985	14,840,000	—	—	—	0.20	0.30
1986	15,480,000	—	—	—	0.20	0.30
1987	31,040,000	—	—	—	0.20	0.30
1988	45,180,000	—	—	—	0.20	0.30
1989	69,988,000	—	—	—	0.20	0.30
1990	26,052,000	—	—	—	0.20	0.30
1991	—	—	—	—	0.20	0.30

KM# 99 5 CENTS

1.6000 g., Aluminum-Bronze, 16.25 mm. **Obv:** National arms **Rev:** Fruit salad plant **Edge:** Reeded **Note:** Similar to KM#50 but motto ribbon on arms curves down at center.

Date	Mintage	F	VF	XF	Unc	BU
1992sm	—	—	—	—	0.20	0.30
1993sm	5,996,000	—	—	—	0.20	0.30
1994sm	—	—	—	—	0.20	0.30
1995sm	90,000,000	—	—	—	0.20	0.30
1996sm	—	—	—	—	0.20	0.30
1997sm	60,000,000	—	—	—	0.20	0.30
1998sm	31,005,000	—	—	—	0.20	0.30
1999sm	35,630,000	—	—	—	0.20	0.30
2000sm	32,550,000	—	—	—	0.20	0.30
2001sm	35,005,000	—	—	—	0.20	0.30
2002sm	33,556,000	—	—	—	0.20	0.30
2003sm	35,930,000	—	—	—	0.20	0.30
2003sm Proof	—	Value: 3.00				
2004sm	38,040,000	—	—	—	0.20	0.30
2004sm Proof	20,000	Value: 3.00				
2005sm	56,832,000	—	—	—	0.20	0.30
2006sm	—	—	—	—	0.20	0.30
2007sm	—	—	—	—	0.20	0.30

KM# 3 10 CENTS

2.8500 g., Copper-Nickel, 19.4 mm. **Obv:** Value and date **Rev:** Stylized Great Crowned Seahorse **Edge:** Reeded

Date	Mintage	F	VF	XF	Unc	BU
1967	40,000,000	—	—	0.15	0.65	1.50
1967 Proof	2,000	Value: 5.00				
1968	36,261,000	—	—	0.20	0.65	1.50
1968 Proof	5,000	Value: 5.00				
1969	25,000,000	—	—	0.10	0.65	1.50
1969 Proof	3,000	Value: 20.00				
1970	21,304,000	—	—	0.20	0.65	1.50
1971	33,040,999	—	—	0.10	0.50	1.50
1972	2,675,000	—	0.20	0.75	1.50	2.00
1972 Proof	749	Value: 60.00				
1973	14,290,000	—	0.10	0.20	0.65	1.50
1973 Proof	1,000	Value: 10.00				
1974	13,450,000	—	0.10	0.20	0.65	1.50
1974 Proof	1,500	Value: 7.50				
1975	828,000	—	0.50	1.25	2.25	3.00
1975 Proof	3,000	Value: 4.00				
1976	29,718,000	—	—	0.15	0.35	1.50
1976sm Proof	3,500	Value: 3.50				
1977	11,776,000	—	—	0.10	0.35	1.50
1977sm Proof	3,500	Value: 3.50				
1978	5,936,000	—	—	0.10	0.35	1.50
1978sm Proof	4,000	Value: 3.50				
1979	12,001,000	—	—	0.10	0.35	1.50
1979sm Proof	3,500	Value: 3.50				
1980	40,299,000	—	—	0.10	0.35	1.50
1980sm Proof	14,000	Value: 3.00				
1981	58,600,000	—	—	0.10	0.35	1.50
1982	48,514,000	—	—	0.10	0.35	1.50
1982sm Proof	20,000	Value: 3.00				
1983	10,415,000	—	—	0.10	0.35	1.50
1983sm Proof	15,000	Value: 3.00				
1984	29,700,000	—	—	0.10	0.35	1.50
1984sm Proof	15,000	Value: 3.00				
1985 In sets only	148,424	—	—	0.10	0.35	1.50

KM# 51 10 CENTS

2.8500 g., Copper-Nickel, 19.4 mm. **Obv:** Arms with supporters **Rev:** Star Jasmine plant above value **Edge:** Reeded

Date	Mintage	F	VF	XF	Unc	BU
1985	45,040,000	—	—	—	0.20	0.30
1986	113,000,000	—	—	—	0.20	0.30
1987	90,000,000	—	—	—	0.20	0.30
1988	54,455,000	—	—	—	0.20	0.30
1989	134,190,000	—	—	—	0.20	0.30
1990	51,720,000	—	—	—	0.20	0.30
1991	159,770,000	—	—	—	0.20	0.30

KM# 100 10 CENTS

2.8500 g., Copper-Nickel, 19.4 mm. **Obv:** National arms **Rev:** Star Jasmine plant **Edge:** Reeded **Note:** Similar to KM#51 but motto ribbon on arms curves down at center.

Date	Mintage	F	VF	XF	Unc	BU
1992sm	—	—	—	—	0.20	0.30
1993sm	89,855,000	—	—	—	0.20	0.30
1994sm	—	—	—	—	0.20	0.30
1995sm	—	—	—	—	0.20	0.30
1996sm	—	—	—	—	0.20	0.30
1997sm	—	—	—	—	0.20	0.30
1998sm	89,840,000	—	—	—	0.20	0.30
1999sm	97,350,000	—	—	—	0.20	0.30
2000sm	80,370,000	—	—	—	0.20	0.30
2001sm	70,600,000	—	—	—	0.20	0.30
2002sm	61,670,000	—	—	—	0.20	0.30
2003sm	58,990,000	—	—	—	0.20	0.30
2003sm Proof	—	Value: 4.00				
2004sm	59,670,000	—	—	—	0.20	0.30
2004sm Proof	20,000	Value: 4.00				
2005sm	49,960,000	—	—	—	0.20	0.30
2006sm	—	—	—	—	0.20	0.30
2007sm	—	—	—	—	0.20	0.30

KM# 4 20 CENTS

5.6500 g., Copper-Nickel, 23.6 mm. **Obv:** Value and date **Rev:** Swordfish **Edge:** Reeded

Date	Mintage	F	VF	XF	Unc	BU
1967	36,500,000	—	0.15	0.35	0.75	1.50
1967 Proof	2,000	Value: 7.00				
1968	10,934,000	—	0.15	0.35	0.75	1.50
1968 Proof	5,000	Value: 6.00				
1969	8,460,000	—	0.15	0.35	0.75	1.50
1969 Proof	3,000	Value: 30.00				
1970	3,250,000	—	0.15	0.30	0.80	1.50
1971	1,732,000	—	0.15	0.70	2.00	3.00
1972	9,107,000	—	0.15	0.30	0.80	1.50
1972 Proof	749	Value: 70.00				
1973	8,838,000	—	0.15	0.30	0.80	1.50
1973 Proof	1,000	Value: 17.50				
1974	4,567,000	—	0.15	0.30	0.75	1.50
1974 Proof	1,500	Value: 12.50				
1975	1,546,000	0.15	0.35	1.20	2.00	2.50
1975 Proof	3,000	Value: 6.50				
1976	19,760,000	—	0.20	0.50	0.85	1.50
1976sm Proof	3,500	Value: 6.00				
1977	7,074,000	—	0.15	0.50	0.85	1.50
1977sm Proof	3,500	Value: 6.00				
1978	4,450,000	—	0.15	0.50	0.85	1.50
1978sm Proof	4,000	Value: 6.00				
1979	14,865,000	—	0.15	0.50	0.85	1.50
1979sm Proof	3,500	Value: 6.00				
1980	27,903,000	—	—	0.25	0.60	1.50
1980sm Proof	14,000	Value: 5.00				
1981	46,997,000	—	—	0.25	0.60	1.50
1982	25,234,000	—	—	0.25	0.60	1.50
1982sm Proof	20,000	Value: 4.00				
1983	6,424,000	—	—	0.25	0.60	1.50
1983sm Proof	15,000	Value: 4.00				
1984	9,290,000	—	—	0.25	0.60	1.50
1984sm Proof	15,000	Value: 4.00				
1985	148,424	—	—	—	0.60	1.50

Note: In sets only

KM# 52 20 CENTS

5.6500 g., Copper-Nickel, 23.6 mm. **Obv:** Arms with supporters **Rev:** Powder-puff plant above value

Date	Mintage	F	VF	XF	Unc	BU
1985	25,980,000	—	—	0.20	0.50	1.00
1986	47,560,000	—	—	0.20	0.50	1.00
1987	80,010,000	—	—	0.20	0.50	1.00
1988	35,783,000	—	—	0.20	0.50	1.00
1989	51,890,000	—	—	0.20	0.50	1.00
1990	49,958,000	—	—	0.20	0.50	1.00
1991	60,000,000	—	—	0.20	0.50	1.00

KM# 101 20 CENTS

5.6500 g., Copper-Nickel, 23.6 mm. **Obv:** National arms **Rev:** Powder puff plant above value **Edge:** Reeded **Note:** Similar to KM#52 but motto ribbon on arms curves down at center.

Date	Mintage	F	VF	XF	Unc	BU
1992sm	—	—	—	—	0.60	0.85
1993sm	24,998,000	—	—	—	0.50	0.70
1994sm	—	—	—	—	0.60	0.85
1995sm	—	—	—	—	0.60	0.85
1996sm	45,000,000	—	—	—	0.50	0.70
1997sm	90,000,000	—	—	—	0.50	0.70
1998sm	62,600,000	—	—	—	0.60	0.85
1999sm	64,590,000	—	—	—	0.60	0.85
2000sm	54,670,000	—	—	—	0.60	0.85
2001sm	52,050,000	—	—	—	0.60	0.75
2002sm	48,120,000	—	—	—	0.60	0.75
2003sm	45,470,000	—	—	—	0.60	0.75
2003sm	—	Value: 5.00				
2004sm	44,870,000	—	—	—	0.60	0.75
2004sm	20,000	Value: 5.00				
2005sm	—	—	—	—	0.60	0.75

Date	Mintage	F	VF	XF	Unc	BU
2006sm	23,310,000	—	—	—	0.60	0.75
2007sm	—	—	—	—	0.60	0.75

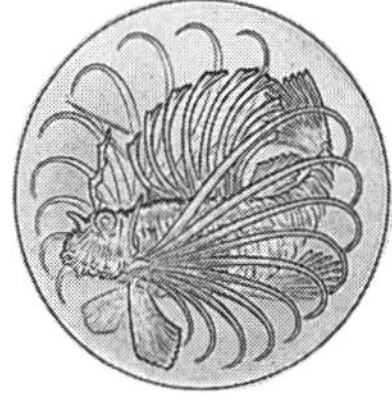

KM# 5 50 CENTS
9.3500 g., Copper-Nickel, 27.75 mm. **Obv:** Value and date **Rev:** Lion fish **Edge:** Reeded

Date	Mintage	F	VF	XF	Unc	BU
1967	11,000,000	—	0.30	0.65	2.00	2.50
1967 Proof	2,000	Value: 10.00				
1968	3,189,000	—	0.30	0.80	2.00	2.50
1968 Proof	5,000	Value: 8.50				
1969	2,008,000	—	0.30	1.00	2.00	2.50
1969 Proof	3,000	Value: 35.00				
1970	3,102,000	—	0.30	0.65	2.00	2.50
1971	3,933,000	—	0.30	0.65	1.80	2.00
1972	5,427,000	—	0.30	0.65	1.60	2.00
1972 Proof	749	Value: 90.00				
1973	4,474,000	—	0.30	0.60	1.10	1.50
1973 Proof	1,000	Value: 30.00				
1974	11,550,000	—	—	0.60	1.10	1.50
1974 Proof	1,500	Value: 22.50				
1975	1,432,000	0.25	0.60	2.00	3.00	4.00
1975 Proof	3,000	Value: 10.00				
1976	5,728,000	—	0.30	0.65	1.20	1.75
1976sm Proof	3,500	Value: 8.50				
1977	6,953,000	—	—	0.65	1.20	1.75
1977sm Proof	3,500	Value: 8.50				
1978	3,934,000	—	—	0.65	1.20	1.75
1978sm Proof	4,000	Value: 8.50				
1979	8,461,000	—	—	0.65	1.20	1.75
1979sm Proof	3,500	Value: 8.50				
1980	14,717,000	—	—	0.65	1.20	1.75
1980sm Proof	14,000	Value: 7.00				
1981	29,542,000	—	—	0.60	1.10	1.75
1982	13,756,000	—	—	0.60	1.10	1.75
1982sm Proof	20,000	Value: 5.00				
1983	4,482,000	—	—	0.85	1.50	1.85
1983sm Proof	15,000	Value: 5.00				
1984	3,658,000	—	—	0.85	1.50	1.85
1984sm Proof	15,000	Value: 5.00				
1985	148,424	—	—	—	1.50	1.85

Note: In sets only

KM# 53.1 50 CENTS
Copper-Nickel **Obv:** Arms with supporters within designed circle **Rev:** Yellow Allamanda plant above value **Edge:** Reeded

Date	Mintage	F	VF	XF	Unc	BU
1985	14,960,000	—	—	0.60	1.10	1.35
1986	15,022,000	—	—	0.60	1.10	1.35
1987	30,000,000	—	—	0.60	1.10	1.35
1988	25,000,000	—	—	0.60	1.10	1.35

KM# 53.2 50 CENTS
Copper-Nickel **Obv:** Arms with supporters **Rev:** Yellow Allamanda plant above value **Edge Lettering:** REPUBLIC OF SINGAPORE (lion's head)

Date	Mintage	F	VF	XF	Unc	BU
1989	20,046,000	—	—	0.45	0.85	2.00
1990	19,740,000	—	—	0.45	0.75	1.50
1991	19,946,000	—	—	0.45	0.75	1.50

KM# 102 50 CENTS
7.1900 g., Copper-Nickel, 24 mm. **Obv:** National arms **Rev:** Yellow Allamanda plant above value **Edge:** Plain **Edge Lettering:** REPUBLIC OF SINGAPORE (lion's head) **Note:** Similar to KM#53 but motto ribbon on arms curves down at center.

Date	Mintage	F	VF	XF	Unc	BU
1992sm	—	—	—	—	0.75	1.00
1993sm	4,878,000	—	—	—	0.75	1.00
1994sm	—	—	—	—	0.75	1.00
1995sm	49,440,000	—	—	—	0.75	1.00
1996sm	—	—	—	—	0.75	1.00
1997sm	30,000,000	—	—	—	0.75	1.00
1998sm	27,590,000	—	—	—	0.75	1.00
1999sm	28,960,000	—	—	—	0.75	1.00
2000sm	29,780,000	—	—	—	0.75	1.00
2001sm	30,020,000	—	—	—	0.75	1.00
2002sm	27,420,000	—	—	—	0.75	1.00
2003sm	23,650,000	—	—	—	0.75	1.00
2003sm Proof	—	Value: 6.00				
2004sm	24,640,000	—	—	—	0.75	1.00
2004sm Proof	20,000	Value: 6.00				
2005sm	24,996,000	—	—	—	0.75	1.00
2006sm	—	—	—	—	0.75	1.00
2007sm	7,680,000	—	—	—	0.75	1.00

KM# 6 DOLLAR
16.8500 g., Copper-Nickel, 33.3 mm. **Obv:** Value and date **Rev:** Statue flanked by sprigs **Edge:** Reeded

Date	Mintage	F	VF	XF	Unc	BU
1967	3,000,000	—	0.65	1.50	3.00	—
1967 Proof	2,000	Value: 22.50				
1968	2,194,000	—	0.65	1.50	3.00	—
1968 Proof	5,000	Value: 20.00				
1969	1,871,000	—	0.65	1.75	3.25	—
1969 Proof	3,000	Value: 75.00				
1970	560,000	—	0.65	1.75	3.25	—
1971	900,000	—	0.65	1.75	3.25	—
1972	458,000	—	0.75	2.00	5.00	—
1972 Proof	749	Value: 150				
1973	341,000	—	0.75	2.00	3.50	—
1973 Proof	1,000	Value: 50.00				
1974	352,000	—	0.75	2.00	3.50	—
1974 Proof	1,500	Value: 40.00				
1975	430,000	—	0.75	2.00	3.50	—
1975 Proof	3,000	Value: 20.00				
1976	165,000	—	2.00	3.00	6.00	—
1976sm Proof	3,500	Value: 13.50				
1977	132,000	—	2.00	4.00	8.00	—
1977sm Proof	3,500	Value: 13.50				
1978	37,000	—	5.00	10.00	20.00	—
1978sm Proof	4,000	Value: 13.50				
1979	100,000	—	—	4.00	8.00	—
1979sm Proof	3,500	Value: 13.50				
1980	166,000	—	—	2.25	4.00	—
1980sm Proof	14,000	Value: 11.50				
1981	1,230,000	—	—	2.25	4.00	—
1982	1,080,000	—	—	2.25	4.00	—
1983	101,000	—	—	3.00	5.25	—
1984	170,000	—	—	3.00	4.50	—
1985	148,424	—	—	0.65	1.25	—

Note: In sets only

KM# 54 DOLLAR
Copper-Nickel **Obv:** Arms with supporters **Rev:** Periwinkle flower

Date	Mintage	F	VF	XF	Unc	BU
1985	—	—	—	—	1.75	2.50
1986	120,000	—	—	—	1.75	2.50

Note: In sets only

Date	Mintage	F	VF	XF	Unc	BU
1987	120,000	—	—	—	1.75	2.50

Note: In sets only

KM# 54b DOLLAR
Aluminum-Bronze, 22.3 mm. **Obv:** Arms with supporters **Rev:** Periwinkle flower **Edge Lettering:** REPUBLIC OF SINGAPORE (lion's head)

Date	Mintage	F	VF	XF	Unc	BU
1987	21,772,000	—	—	0.75	1.50	2.25
1988	59,332,000	—	—	0.75	1.50	2.25
1989	62,586,000	—	—	0.75	1.50	2.25
1990	37,608,000	—	—	0.75	1.50	2.25
1991	—	—	—	0.75	1.50	2.25

KM# 103 DOLLAR
6.2900 g., Aluminum-Bronze, 22.3 mm. **Obv:** National arms **Rev:** Periwinkle flower **Edge:** Reeded **Note:** Similar to KM#54 but motto ribbon on arms curves down at center.

Date	Mintage	F	VF	XF	Unc	BU
1992sm	—	—	—	—	1.50	2.25
1993sm	—	—	—	—	1.50	2.25
1994sm	5,008,000	—	—	—	1.50	2.25
1995sm	65,000,000	—	—	—	1.50	2.25
1996sm	—	—	—	—	1.50	2.25
1997sm	129,856,000	—	—	—	1.50	2.25
1998sm	40,880,000	—	—	—	1.50	2.25
1999sm	38,300,000	—	—	—	1.50	2.25
2000sm	35,690,000	—	—	—	1.50	2.25
2001sm	40,840,000	—	—	—	1.50	2.25
2002sm	35,660,000	—	—	—	1.50	2.25
2003sm	31,900,000	—	—	—	1.50	2.25
2003sm Proof	—	Value: 10.00				
2004sm	34,380,000	—	—	—	1.50	2.25
2004sm Proof	20,000	Value: 10.00				
2005sm	—	—	—	—	1.50	2.25
2006sm	25,488,000	—	—	—	1.50	2.25
2007sm	—	—	—	—	1.50	2.25

KM# 104.1 5 DOLLARS
Bi-Metallic Aluminum-Bronze center in Copper-Nickel ring **Subject:** Vanda Miss Joaquim **Obv:** National arms, date and BCCS logo **Rev:** Flower and value within beaded circle **Shape:** Scalloped

Date	Mintage	F	VF	XF	Unc	BU
1992sm	—	—	—	—	—	15.00
Note: In mint sets only						
1993sm	—	—	—	—	—	15.00
Note: In mint sets only						
1994sm	—	—	—	—	—	15.00
Note: In mint sets only						
1995sm	—	—	—	—	—	15.00
Note: In mint sets only						
1996sm	—	—	—	—	—	15.00
Note: In mint sets only						
1997sm	—	—	—	—	—	15.00
Note: In mint sets only						
1998sm	—	—	—	—	—	15.00
Note: In mint sets only						
2002sm	—	—	—	—	—	15.00

KM# 138 5 DOLLARS
Bi-Metallic Aluminum-Bronze center in Copper-Nickel ring **Series:** 50th Anniversary - United Nations **Obv:** Arms with supporters within beaded circle **Rev:** UN logo within artistic design **Shape:** Scalloped

Date	Mintage	F	VF	XF	Unc	BU
1995	500,000	—	—	—	10.00	12.00

KM# 104.2 5 DOLLARS
Bi-Metallic **Ring Composition:** Copper-Nickel **Center Composition:** Aluminum-Bronze **Obv:** National arms, date and MAS logo **Rev:** Flower above value **Edge:** Plain

Date	Mintage	F	VF	XF	Unc	BU
1999sm	—	—	—	—	—	12.00
Note: In mint sets only						
2000sm	—	—	—	—	—	12.00
Note: In mint sets only						
2001sm	—	—	—	—	—	12.00
Note: In mint sets only						
2002sm	—	—	—	—	—	12.00
Note: In mint sets only						
2003sm	—	—	—	—	—	12.00
2004sm	—	—	—	—	—	12.00

Date	Mintage	F	VF	XF	Unc	BU
2005sm	—	—	—	—	—	12.00
2006sm	—	—	—	—	—	12.00

KM# 171 5 DOLLARS

Bi-Metallic Aluminum-Bronze center in Copper-Nickel ring **Obv:** Arms with supporters above latent date within beaded circle **Rev:** Millennium design **Edge:** Scalloped

Date	Mintage	F	VF	XF	Unc	BU
2000	406,000	—	—	—	6.50	10.00

KM# 104.3 5 DOLLARS

Bi-Metallic Aluminum-Bronze center in Copper-Nickel ring **Obv:** National arms above latent image "MAS" **Rev:** Flower and value **Shape:** Scalloped

Date	Mintage	F	VF	XF	Unc	BU
2002sm	—	—	—	—	—	10.00
2003sm	—	—	—	—	—	10.00
2003sm Proof	—	Value: 15.00				
2004sm	—	—	—	—	—	10.00
2004sm Proof	20,000	Value: 15.00				
2005sm	—	—	—	—	—	10.00
2006sm	—	—	—	—	—	10.00
2007sm	—	—	—	—	—	10.00

SLOVAKIA

The Republic of Slovakia has an area of 18,923 sq. mi. (49,035 sq. km.) and a population of 4.9 million. Capital: Bratislava. Textiles, steel, and wood products are exported.

The Slovak lands were united with the Czechs and the Czechoslovak State came into existence on Oct. 28, 1918 upon the dissolution of Austro-Hungarian Empire at the close of World War I. In March 1939, the German-influenced Slovak government proclaimed Slovakia independent and Germany incorporated the Czech lands into the Third Reich as the "Protectorate of Bohemia and Moravia". A Czechoslovak government-in-exile was setup in London in July 1940. The Soviet and USA forces liberated the area by May, 1945. At the close of World War II, Communist influence increased steadily while pressure for liberalization culminated in the overthrow of the Stalinist leader Antonin Novotn'y and his associates in 1968.The Communist Party then introduced far reaching reforms which received warnings from Moscow, followed by occupation by Warsaw Pact forces resulting in stationing of Soviet forces. Mass civilian demonstrations for reform began in Nov.1989 and the Federal Assembly abolished the Communist Party's sole right to govern. New governments followed on Dec. 3 and Dec. 10 and the Czech and Slovak Federal Republic was formed. The Movement for Democratic Slovakia was apparent in the June 1992 elections with the Slovak National Council adopting a declaration of sovereignty. Later, a constitution for an independent Slovakia with the Federal Assembly voting for the dissolution of the Republic came into effect on Dec. 31, 1992, and two new republics came into being on Jan. 1, 1993.

MINT MARK

Kremnica Mint

REPUBLIC
1939-45

STANDARD COINAGE

100 Halierov = 1 Koruna Slovenska (Ks)

KM# 8 5 HALIEROV

0.9400 g., Zinc, 14 mm. **Obv:** Double cross within shield **Obv. Designer:** Anton Ham **Rev:** Large value **Rev. Designer:** S. Grosch **Edge:** Plain

Date	Mintage	F	VF	XF	Unc	BU
1942	1,000,000	3.00	5.00	15.00	30.00	—

KM# 1 10 HALIEROV

1.6600 g., Bronze, 16 mm. **Obv:** Double cross within shield above sprigs **Obv. Designer:** Anton Ham **Rev:** Castle and large value **Rev. Designer:** A. Peter

Date	Mintage	F	VF	XF	Unc	BU
1939	15,000,000	1.50	2.00	4.00	8.00	—
1942	7,000,000	3.00	2.00	8.00	16.00	—

KM# 4 20 HALIEROV

2.5000 g., Bronze, 18 mm. **Obv:** Double cross on shield within flower sprig **Obv. Designer:** A. Ham **Rev:** Nitra Castle, large value **Rev. Designer:** A. Peter **Edge:** Plain

Date	Mintage	F	VF	XF	Unc	BU
1940	10,972,000	1.25	2.00	3.00	6.00	—
1941	4,028,000	2.50	6.00	10.00	30.00	—
1942	6,474,000	10.00	15.00	30.00	60.00	—

KM# 4a 20 HALIEROV

0.6500 g., Aluminum, 18 mm. **Obv:** Double cross on shield within flower sprigs **Obv. Designer:** A. Ham **Rev:** Nitra castle and large value **Rev. Designer:** A. Peter **Edge:** Plain **Note:** Varieties exist.

Date	Mintage	F	VF	XF	Unc	BU
1942	Inc. above	1.00	1.50	4.00	9.00	—
1943	15,000,000	1.00	1.50	4.00	9.00	—

KM# 5 50 HALIEROV

3.3300 g., Copper-Nickel, 20 mm. **Obv:** Double cross on shield and date **Rev:** Value above plow **Edge:** Plain **Designer:** Anton Ham, Andrej Peter, G. Angyal

Date	Mintage	F	VF	XF	Unc	BU
1940	Inc. above	30.00	40.00	50.00	100	—
1941	8,000,000	1.00	2.00	3.00	6.00	—

KM# 5a 50 HALIEROV

1.0000 g., Aluminum, 20 mm. **Obv:** Double cross on shield and date **Rev:** Value above plow **Edge:** Milled **Designer:** Anton ham, Andrej Peter, G. Angyal

Date	Mintage	F	VF	XF	Unc	BU
1943	4,400,000	1.00	1.50	2.50	5.00	—
1944	2,621,000	5.00	10.00	15.00	30.00	—

KM# 6 KORUNA

5.0000 g., Copper-Nickel, 22 mm. **Obv:** Double cross on shield within circle above date **Rev:** Value within oat sprigs and stalks **Edge:** Milled **Designer:** Gejza Angyal, Anton Ham, Andrej Peter **Note:** Open and closed 4.

Date	Mintage	F	VF	XF	Unc	BU
1940	2,350,000	0.75	1.25	2.25	6.00	—
1941	11,650,000	0.50	1.00	2.00	5.00	—
1942	6,000,000	0.50	1.00	2.00	5.00	—
Note: Varieties exist of 1942, in the numeral 4						
1944	884,000	10.00	15.00	30.00	60.00	—
1945	3,321,000	0.75	1.25	2.25	6.00	—

KM# 2 5 KORUN

Nickel, 27 mm. **Obv:** Double cross on shield within wheat sprigs below value with date below **Rev:** Head left **Edge:** Milled **Designer:** Anton Ham, Andrej Peter **Note:** Pointed top or flat top to the letter A in NAROD.

Date	Mintage	F	VF	XF	Unc	BU
1939	5,101,000	1.50	2.00	3.50	10.00	—

Note: Approximately 2,000,000 pieces were melted down by the Czechoslovak National Bank in 1947

KM# 9.1 10 KORUN

7.0000 g., 0.5000 Silver 0.1125 oz. ASW, 29 mm. **Obv:** Double cross on shield within radiant circle **Rev:** Standing figures facing divide value **Edge:** Plain **Designer:** Ladislav Majersky **Note:** Variety 1 - Cross atop church held by left figure.

Date	Mintage	F	VF	XF	Unc	BU
1944	1,381,000	2.00	4.00	5.00	12.00	—

KM# 9.2 10 KORUN

7.0000 g., 0.5000 Silver 0.1125 oz. ASW **Obv:** Double cross on shield within radiant circle **Rev:** Standing figure facing divides value **Designer:** Ladislav Majersky **Note:** Variety 2 - Without cross atop church held by left figure.

Date	Mintage	F	VF	XF	Unc	BU
1944	Inc. above	2.50	5.00	7.00	15.00	—

KM# 3 20 KORUN

15.0000 g., 0.5000 Silver 0.2411 oz. ASW, 31 mm. **Obv:** Double cross on shield within wreath flanked by value **Rev:** Head right **Edge:** Milled **Designer:** Anton Ham, Andrej Peter

Date	Mintage	F	VF	XF	Unc	BU
1939	200,000	5.00	10.00	20.00	40.00	—

KM# 7.1 20 KORUN

15.0000 g., 0.5000 Silver 0.2411 oz. ASW, 31 mm. **Subject:** St. Kyrill and St. Methodius **Obv:** Double cross on shield within sprigs **Rev:** Standing figures flanked by value **Edge:** Milled **Designer:** Frano Stefunko

Date	Mintage	F	VF	XF	Unc	BU
1941	2,500,000	4.00	5.00	7.00	16.00	—

KM# 7.2 20 KORUN

15.0000 g., 0.5000 Silver 0.2411 oz. ASW **Subject:** St. Kyrill and St. Methodius **Obv:** Double cross on shield within sprigs **Rev:** Variety 2 - Double bar cross **Designer:** Frano Stefunko

Date	Mintage	F	VF	XF	Unc	BU
1941	Inc. above	4.50	6.50	20.00	50.00	—

KM# 10 50 KORUN

16.5000 g., 0.7000 Silver 0.3713 oz. ASW, 34 mm. **Subject:** 5th Anniversary of Independence **Obv:** Double cross on shield within wreath flanked by value **Rev:** Head right **Edge:** Milled **Designer:** Anton Ham, Andrej Peter

Date	Mintage	F	VF	XF	Unc	BU
1944	2,000,000	6.00	7.00	9.00	18.00	—

REPUBLIC

STANDARD COINAGE

100 Halierov = 1 Slovak Koruna (Sk)

KM# 17 10 HALIEROV

0.7200 g., Aluminum, 17 mm. **Obv:** Double cross on shield above inscription **Rev:** Church steeple **Edge:** Plain **Designer:** Drahomir Zobek

Date	Mintage	F	VF	XF	Unc	BU
1993	32,200,000	—	—	—	0.35	—
Note: Varieties of cross on state emblem						
1994	89,130,000	—	—	—	0.35	—
1995	23,990,000	—	—	—	1.00	—
Note: In sets only						
1996	31,540,000	—	—	—	0.35	—
1997	10,000,000	—	—	—	0.35	—
1998	30,260,000	—	—	—	0.35	—
1999	31,420,000	—	—	—	0.35	—
1999	11,500	Value: 5.00				
2000	30,600,000	—	—	—	0.35	—
2000 Proof	12,500	Value: 5.00				
2001	20,330,000	—	—	—	0.35	—
2001 Proof	12,500	Value: 2.50				
2002	37,640,000	—	—	—	0.35	—
2002 Proof	16,100	Value: 1.50				
2003	3,000	—	—	—	2.50	—
Note: Mint sets only						

KM# 18 20 HALIEROV

0.9500 g., Aluminum, 19.5 mm. **Obv:** Double cross on shield above inscription **Rev:** Mountain peak and value **Edge:** Reeded **Designer:** Drahomir Zobek

Date	Mintage	F	VF	XF	Unc	BU
1993	37,410,000	—	—	—	0.45	—
1994	71,020,000	—	—	—	0.45	—
1995	32,390,000	—	—	—	1.00	—
Note: In sets only						
1996	19,800,000	—	—	—	0.45	—
1997	10,000,000	—	—	—	0.45	—
1998	21,000,000	—	—	—	0.45	—
1999	15,710,000	—	—	—	0.45	—
1999 Proof	11,500	Value: 5.00				
2000	31,120,000	—	—	—	0.45	—
2000 Proof	12,500	Value: 5.00				
2001	21,920,000	—	—	—	0.45	—
2001 Proof	12,500	Value: 2.50				
2002	36,300,000	—	—	—	0.45	—
2002 Proof	16,100	Value: 1.50				
2003	3,000	—	—	—	2.50	—
Note: Mint set only						

KM# 15 50 HALIEROV

1.2000 g., Aluminum, 22 mm. **Obv:** Double cross on shield above inscription **Rev:** Watch tower and value **Edge:** Plain **Designer:** Drahomir Zobek

Date	Mintage	F	VF	XF	Unc	BU
1993	35,130,000	—	—	—	0.55	—
1994	19,020,000	—	—	—	1.50	—
1995	12,000	—	—	—	1.50	—
Note: In sets only						

KM# 35 50 HALIEROV

2.8000 g., Copper Plated Steel, 18.7 mm. **Obv:** Double cross on shield above inscription **Rev:** Watch tower and value **Edge:** Milled and plain **Designer:** Drahomir Zobek

Date	Mintage	F	VF	XF	Unc	BU
1996	39,640,000	—	—	—	0.60	—
1997	11,500	—	—	—	1.50	—
Note: In sets only						
1998	15,000,000	—	—	—	0.60	—

Date	Mintage	F	VF	XF	Unc	BU
1999	11,500	—	—	—	1.50	—
Note: In sets only						
2000	20,212,000	—	—	—	0.60	—
2000 Proof	12,500	Value: 5.00				
2001	10,400,000	—	—	—	0.60	—
2001 Proof	12,500	Value: 2.50				
2002	11,000,000	—	—	—	0.60	—
2002 Proof	16,100	Value: 1.50				
2003	11,000,000	—	—	—	0.60	—
2004	16,500,000	—	—	—	0.60	—
2005	17,000,000	—	—	—	0.60	—
2006	22,050,000	—	—	—	0.60	—
2007	—	—	—	—	0.60	—

KM# 12 KORUNA

3.8500 g., Bronze Clad Steel, 21 mm. **Subject:** 15th Century of Madonna and Child **Obv:** Double cross on shield above inscription **Rev:** Madonna holding child and value **Edge:** Milled **Designer:** Drahomir Zobek

Date	Mintage	F	VF	XF	Unc	BU
1993	58,930,000	—	—	—	0.75	—
1994	44,320,000	—	—	—	0.75	—
1995	28,030,000	—	—	—	0.75	—
1996	15,000	—	—	—	1.50	—
Note: In sets only						
1997	15,000	—	—	—	1.50	—
Note: In sets only						
1998	12,000	—	—	—	1.50	—
Note: In sets only						
1999	11,500	—	—	—	1.50	—
Note: In sets only						
2000	12,500	—	—	—	1.50	—
Note: In sets only						
2000 Proof	900	Value: 10.00				
2001	12,500	—	—	—	1.50	—
Note: In sets only						
2001 Proof	—	Value: 3.00				
2002	11,000,000	—	—	—	0.75	—
2002 Proof	16,100	Value: 2.50				
2003	14,000	—	—	—	1.50	—
Note: In sets only						
2004	—	—	—	—	1.50	—
Note: In sets only						
2005	10,000,000	—	—	—	0.75	—
2006	9,605,000	—	—	—	0.75	—
2007	—	—	—	—	0.75	—

KM# 13 2 KORUNA

4.4000 g., Nickel Clad Steel, 21.5 mm. **Obv:** Double cross on shield above inscription **Rev:** Venus statue and value **Designer:** Drahomir Zobek

Date	Mintage	F	VF	XF	Unc	BU
1993	36,810,000	—	—	—	0.85	—
Note: Varieties of artist's initials						
1994	24,720,000	—	—	—	0.85	—
1995	30,510,000	—	—	—	0.85	—
1996	15,000	—	—	—	2.00	—
Note: In sets only						
1997	15,000	—	—	—	2.00	—
Note: In sets only						
1998	12,000	—	—	—	2.00	—
Note: In sets only						
1999	11,500	—	—	—	2.00	—
Note: In sets only						
2000	12,500	—	—	—	2.00	—
Note: In sets only						
2000 Proof	900	Value: 10.00				
2001	10,668,000	—	—	—	0.85	—
2001 Proof	12,500	Value: 5.00				
2002	11,000,000	—	—	—	0.85	—
2002 Proof	16,100	Value: 2.50				
2003	11,000,000	—	—	—	0.85	—
2004	—	—	—	—	2.00	—
Note: In sets only						
2005	—	—	—	—	2.00	—
Note: In sets only						
2006	—	—	—	—	2.00	—
Note: In sets only						
2007	—	—	—	—	2.00	—
Note: In sets only						

KM# 14 5 KORUNA

5.4000 g., Nickel Clad Steel, 24.75 mm. **Obv:** Double cross on shield above inscription **Rev:** Celtic coin of BIATEC at upper left of value **Edge:** Milled **Designer:** Drahomir Zobek

Date	Mintage	F	VF	XF	Unc	BU
1993	36,200,000	—	—	—	1.25	—
Note: Varieties in artist's initials						
1994	26,140,000	—	—	—	1.25	—
1995	16,530,000	—	—	—	1.25	—
1996	15,000	—	—	—	2.00	—
Note: In sets only						
1997	15,000	—	—	—	2.00	—
Note: In sets only						
1998	11,500	—	—	—	2.00	—
Note: In sets only						
1999	12,500	—	—	—	2.00	—
Note: In sets only						
2000	12,500	—	—	—	2.00	—
Note: In sets only						
2000 Proof	900	Value: 20.00				
2001 Proof	12,500	Value: 6.00				
2002 Proof	16,100	Value: 5.00				
2003	14,000	—	—	—	2.00	—
Note: In sets only						
2004	—	—	—	—	2.00	—
Note: In sets only						
2005	—	—	—	—	2.00	—
Note: In sets only						
2006	—	—	—	—	2.00	—
Note: In sets only						
2007	—	—	—	—	2.00	—
Note: In sets only						

KM# 11.1 10 KORUNA

6.6000 g., Brass, 26.5 mm. **Obv:** Double cross on shield above inscription **Rev:** Bronze cross and value **Designer:** Drahomir Zobek

Date	Mintage	F	VF	XF	Unc	BU
1993	40,934,000	—	—	—	2.50	—
1994	14,360,000	—	—	—	2.50	—
1995	42,204,000	—	—	—	2.50	—
1996	15,000	—	—	—	4.00	—
Note: In sets only						
1997	15,000	—	—	—	4.00	—
Note: In sets only						
1998	12,000	—	—	—	4.00	—
Note: In sets only						
1999	11,500	—	—	—	4.00	—
Note: In sets only						
2000	12,500	—	—	—	4.00	—
Note: In sets only						
2000 Proof	900	Value: 35.00				
2001 Proof	12,500	Value: 12.50				
2002 Proof	16,100	Value: 10.00				
2003	10,923,000	—	—	—	2.50	—
Note: In sets only						
2004	—	—	—	—	4.00	—
Note: In sets only						
2005	—	—	—	—	4.00	—
Note: In sets only						
2006	—	—	—	—	4.00	—
Note: In sets only						
2007	—	—	—	—	4.00	—

The Republic of Slovenia is located northwest of Yugoslavia in the valleys of the Danube River. It has an area of 7,819 sq. mi. and a population of *1.9 million. Capital: Ljubljana. Agriculture is the main industry with large amounts of hops and fodder crops grown as well as many varieties of fruit trees. Sheep raising, timber production and the mining of mercury from one of the country's oldest mines are also very important to the economy.

Slovenia was important as a land route between Europe and the eastern Mediterranean region. The Roman Catholic Austro-Hungarian Empire gained control of the area during the 14th century and retained its dominance until World War I. The United Kingdom of the Serbs, Croats and Slovenes (Yugoslavia) was founded in 1918 and consisted of various groups of South Slavs.

In 1929, King Alexander declared his assumption of power temporarily, however he was assassinated in 1934. His son Peter's regent, Prince Paul tried to settle internal problems, however, the Slovenes denounced the agreement he made. He resigned in 1941 and Peter assumed the throne. Peter was forced to flee when Yugoslavia was occupied. Slovenia was divided between Germany and Italy. Even though Yugoslavia attempted to remain neutral, the Nazis occupied the country and were resisted by guerilla armies, most notably Marshal Josif Broz Tito.

Under Marshal Tito, the Constitution of 1946 established 6 constituent republics which made up Yugoslavia. Each republic was permitted Liberties under supervision of the Communist Party.

In Oct. 1989 the Slovene Assembly voted a constitutional amendment giving it the right to secede from Yugoslavia. A referendum on Dec. 23, 1990 resulted in a majority vote for independence, which was formally declared on Dec. 26.

On June 25 Slovenia declared independence, but agreed to suspend this for 3 months at peace talks sponsored by the EC. Federal troops moved into Slovenia on June 27 to secure Yugoslavia's external borders, but after some fighting withdrew by the end of July. The 3-month moratorium agreed at the EC having expired, Slovenia (and Croatia) declared their complete independence of the Yugoslav federation on Oct.8, 1991.

MINT MARKS

Based on last digit in date.
(K) - Kremnitz (Slovakia): open 4, upturned 5
(BP) - Budapest (Hungary): closed 4, downturned 5

MONETARY SYSTEM

100 Stotinov = 1 Tolar

REPUBLIC

STANDARD COINAGE

100 Stotinow = 1 Tolar

KM# 7 10 STOTINOV

0.5500 g., Aluminum, 16 mm. **Obv:** Value within square **Rev:** Olm salamander **Edge:** Plain **Note:** Varieties exist.

Date	Mintage	F	VF	XF	Unc	BU
1992	2,515,000	—	—	—	0.35	0.75
1992 Proof	1,000	Value: 5.00				
1993	2,515,000	—	—	—	0.35	0.75
1993 Proof	1,000	Value: 5.00				
1994	1,000	—	—	—	—	3.00
Note: In sets only						
1994 Proof	1,000	Value: 5.00				
1995	1,000	—	—	—	—	3.00
Note: In sets only						
1995 Proof	1,000	Value: 5.00				
1996	1,000	—	—	—	—	3.00
Note: In sets only						
1996 Proof	800	Value: 5.00				
1997	1,000	—	—	—	—	3.00
Note: In sets only						
1997 Proof	800	Value: 5.00				
1998	1,000	—	—	—	—	3.00
Note: In sets only						
1998 Proof	800	Value: 5.00				
1999	1,000	—	—	—	—	3.00
Note: In sets only						
1999 Proof	800	Value: 5.00				
2000	1,000	—	—	—	—	3.00
Note: In sets only						
2000 Proof	800	Value: 5.00				
2001	1,000	—	—	—	—	3.00
Note: In sets only						
2001 Proof	800	Value: 5.00				
2002	1,000	—	—	—	—	3.00
Note: In sets only						
2002 Proof	800	Value: 5.00				
2003	1,000	—	—	—	—	3.00
Note: In sets only						
2003 Proof	800	Value: 5.00				
2004	1,000	—	—	—	—	3.00
Note: In sets only						
2004 Proof	800	Value: 5.00				
2005	3,000	—	—	—	—	2.00
Note: In sets only						
2005 Proof	1,000	Value: 5.00				
2006	4,000	—	—	—	—	2.00
Note: In sets only						
2006 Proof	1,000	Value: 5.00				

KM# 8 20 STOTINOV

0.7000 g., Aluminum, 18 mm. **Obv:** Value within square **Rev:** Small owl and value **Edge:** Plain

Date	Mintage	F	VF	XF	Unc	BU
1992	2,515,000	—	—	—	0.50	1.00
Note: Minor reverse varieties exist						
1992 Proof	1,000	Value: 6.00				
1993	2,515,000	—	—	—	0.50	1.00
Note: Minor reverse varieties exist						
1993 Proof	1,000	Value: 6.00				
1994	1,000	—	—	—	—	4.00
Note: In sets only						
1994 Proof	1,000	Value: 6.00				
1995	1,000	—	—	—	—	4.00
Note: In sets only						
1995 Proof	1,000	Value: 6.00				
1996	1,000	—	—	—	—	4.00
Note: In sets only						
1996 Proof	800	Value: 6.00				
1997	1,000	—	—	—	—	4.00
Note: In sets only						
1997 Proof	800	Value: 6.00				
1998	1,000	—	—	—	—	4.00
Note: In sets only						
1998 Proof	800	Value: 6.00				
1999	1,000	—	—	—	—	4.00
Note: In sets only						
1999 Proof	800	Value: 6.00				
2000	1,000	—	—	—	—	4.00
Note: In sets only						
2000 Proof	800	Value: 6.00				
2001	1,000	—	—	—	—	4.00
Note: In sets only						
2001 Proof	800	Value: 6.00				
2002	1,000	—	—	—	—	4.00
Note: In sets only						
2002 Proof	800	Value: 6.00				
2003	1,000	—	—	—	—	4.00
Note: In sets only						
2003 Proof	800	Value: 6.00				
2004	1,000	—	—	—	—	4.00
Note: In sets only						
2004 Proof	500	Value: 6.00				
2005	3,000	—	—	—	—	3.00
Note: In sets only						
2005 Proof	1,000	Value: 6.00				
2006	4,000	—	—	—	—	3.00
Note: In sets only						
2006 Proof	1,000	Value: 6.00				

KM# 3 50 STOTINOV

0.8500 g., Aluminum, 19.9 mm. **Obv:** Value within square **Rev:** Bee and value **Edge:** Plain

Date	Mintage	F	VF	XF	Unc	BU
1992	5,015,000	—	—	0.10	0.50	0.75
Note: Minor reverse varieties exist						
1992 Proof	1,000	Value: 7.50				
1993	18,315,000	—	—	0.10	0.50	0.75
1993 Proof	1,000	Value: 7.50				
1994	1,000	—	—	—	—	6.00
Note: In sets only						
1994 Proof	1,000	Value: 7.50				
1995	3,000,000	—	—	0.10	0.50	0.75
1995	1,000	—	—	—	—	6.00
Note: In sets only						
1995 Proof	1,000	Value: 7.50				
1996	3,000,000	—	—	0.10	0.50	0.75
1996 Proof	Est. 500	Value: 7.50				
1997	1,000	—	—	—	—	6.00
Note: In sets only						
1997 Proof	500	Value: 7.50				
1998	1,000	—	—	—	—	6.00
Note: In sets only						
1998 Proof	500	Value: 7.50				
1999	1,000	—	—	—	—	6.00
Note: In sets only						
1999 Proof	500	Value: 7.50				
2000	1,000	—	—	—	—	6.00
Note: In sets only						
2000 Proof	800	Value: 7.50				
2001	1,000	—	—	—	—	6.00
Note: In sets only						
2001 Proof	800	Value: 7.50				
2002	1,000	—	—	—	—	6.00
Note: In sets only						
2002 Proof	800	Value: 7.50				
2003	1,000	—	—	—	—	6.00
Note: In sets only						
2003 Proof	800	Value: 7.50				
2004	1,000	—	—	—	—	6.00
Note: In sets only						
2004 Proof	500	Value: 12.00				
2005	3,000	—	—	—	—	4.00
Note: In sets only						
2005 Proof	1,000	Value: 7.00				
2006	4,000	—	—	—	—	4.00
Note: In sets only						
2006 Proof	1,000	Value: 7.00				

KM# 4 TOLAR

4.5000 g., Brass, 21.9 mm. **Obv:** Value within circle **Rev:** Three brown trout **Edge:** Reeded **Note:** Date varieties exist: 1994 = closed or open "4"; 1995 = serif up and serif down in "5".

Date	Mintage	F	VF	XF	Unc	BU
1992	10,015,000	—	—	0.20	0.85	1.50
1992 Proof	1,000	Value: 7.50				
1993	30,015,000	—	—	0.20	0.85	1.50
1993 Proof	1,000	Value: 7.50				
1994 (K)	10,000,000	—	—	—	0.75	1.50
Note: 4 open to the top						
1994 (K) Proof	1,000	Value: 7.50				
Note: 4 open to right						
1994 (BP)	5,000,000	—	—	—	0.75	1.50
1995 (K)	10,000,000	—	—	—	0.75	1.50
1995 (K)	1,000	—	—	—	—	5.00
Note: In sets only						
1995 (K) Proof	1,000	Value: 7.50				
1995 (BP)	10,000,000	—	—	—	0.75	1.50
1996	Est. 21,800,000	—	—	—	0.75	1.50
1996 Proof	Est. 3,000	Value: 7.50				
1997	8,000,000	—	—	—	0.75	1.50
1997 Proof	500	Value: 10.00				
1998	12,000,000	—	—	—	0.75	1.50
1998 Proof	500	Value: 10.00				
1999	8,000,000	—	—	—	0.75	1.50
1999 Proof	500	Value: 10.00				
2000	15,001,000	—	—	—	0.75	1.50
2000 Proof	800	Value: 7.50				
2001	10,001,000	—	—	—	0.75	1.25
2001 Proof	800	Value: 7.50				
2002	1,000	—	—	—	—	5.00
Note: In sets only						
2002 Proof	800	Value: 7.50				
2003	1,000	—	—	—	—	5.00
Note: In sets only						
2003 Proof	800	Value: 7.50				
2004	10,001,000	—	—	—	0.75	1.25
2004 (K)	1,000	—	—	—	—	5.00
Note: 4 open to right; in sets only						
2004 Proof	500	Value: 8.50				
2005	3,000	—	—	—	—	4.00
Note: In sets only						
2005 Proof	1,000	Value: 7.50				
2006	4,000	—	—	—	—	4.00
Note: In sets only						
2006 Proof	1,000	Value: 7.50				

KM# 5 2 TOLARJA

5.4000 g., Brass, 24 mm. **Obv:** Value within circle **Rev:** Barn swallow in flight **Edge:** Reeded **Note:** Date varieties exist: 1994 = closed or open "4"; 1995 = serif up and serif down in "5".

Date	Mintage	F	VF	XF	Unc	BU
1992	5,015,000	—	—	0.25	0.85	1.75
1992 Proof	1,000	Value: 8.50				
1993	10,015,000	—	—	0.25	0.85	1.75
1993 Proof	1,000	Value: 8.50				
1994 (K)	10,000,000	—	—	—	0.75	1.75
Note: 4 open to the top						
1994 (K)	1,000	—	—	—	—	7.00
Note: 4 open to right; in sets only						
1994 (K) Proof	1,000	Value: 8.50				
Note: 4 open to right						
1994 (BP)	5,000,000	—	—	—	0.75	1.75
1995 (K)	10,000,000	—	—	—	0.75	1.75
1995 (K)	1,000	—	—	—	—	7.00
Note: In sets only						
1995 (K) Proof	1,000	Value: 8.50				
1995 (BP)	10,000,000	—	—	—	0.75	1.75
1996	Est. 16,600,000	—	—	—	0.75	1.75
1996 Proof	1,000	Value: 8.50				
1997	6,060,000	—	—	—	0.75	1.75
1997 Proof	500	Value: 12.00				
1998	5,000,000	—	—	—	0.75	1.75
1998 Proof	500	Value: 12.00				
1999	5,200,000	—	—	—	0.75	1.75
1999 Proof	500	Value: 12.00				
2000	15,001,000	—	—	—	0.75	1.75
2000 Proof	800	Value: 8.50				
2001	10,001,000	—	—	—	0.75	1.75
2001 Proof	800	Value: 8.50				
2002	1,000	—	—	—	—	7.00
Note: In sets only						
2002 Proof	800	Value: 8.50				
2003	1,000	—	—	—	—	7.00
Note: In sets only						
2003 Proof	800	Value: 8.50				
2004	10,001,000	—	—	—	0.75	1.50
2004 Proof	500	Value: 8.50				
2005	3,000	—	—	—	—	7.00
Note: In sets only						
2005 Proof	1,000	Value: 8.50				
2006	4,000	—	—	—	—	7.00
Note: In sets only						
2006 Proof	1,000	Value: 8.50				

KM# 6 5 TOLARJEV

6.3900 g., Brass, 26 mm. **Obv:** Value within circle **Rev:** Head and horns of ibex **Edge:** Reeded **Note:** Date varieties exist: 1994 = closed or open "4"; 1995 = serif up and serif down in "5".

Date	Mintage	F	VF	XF	Unc	BU
1992	10,015,000	—	—	0.35	1.00	2.00
1992 Proof	1,000	Value: 10.00				
1993	10,015,000	—	—	0.35	1.00	2.00
1993 Proof	1,000	Value: 10.00				
1994 (K)	10,000,000	—	—	—	0.85	2.00
Note: 4 open to the top						
1994 (K)	1,000	—	—	—	—	8.00
Note: 4 open to right; in sets only						
1994 (K) Proof	1,000	Value: 10.00				
Note: 4 open to right						
1994 (BP)	5,000,000	—	—	—	0.85	2.00
1995	5,000,000	—	—	—	0.85	2.00
1995 2 tip	—	—	—	—	0.85	2.00
1996	6,000,000	—	—	—	0.85	2.00
1996 Proof	Est. 3,000	Value: 10.00				
1997	8,000,000	—	—	—	0.85	2.00
1997 Proof	500	Value: 15.00				
1998	10,000,000	—	—	—	0.85	2.00
1998 Proof	500	Value: 15.00				
1999	6,403,000	—	—	—	0.85	2.00
1999 Proof	500	Value: 15.00				
2000	15,001,000	—	—	—	0.85	2.00
2000 Proof	800	Value: 10.00				
2001	1,000	—	—	—	—	8.00
Note: In sets only						
2001 Proof	800	Value: 10.00				
2002	1,000	—	—	—	—	8.00
Note: In sets only						
2002 Proof	800	Value: 10.00				
2003	1,000	—	—	—	—	8.00
Note: In sets only						
2003 Proof	800	Value: 10.00				
2004	1,000	—	—	—	—	8.00
Note: In sets only						
2004 Proof	500	Value: 15.00				
2005	3,000	—	—	—	—	7.00
Note: In sets only						
2005 Proof	1,000	Value: 10.00				
2006	4,000	—	—	—	—	7.00
Note: In sets only						
2006 Proof	1,000	Value: 10.00				

KM# 9 5 TOLARJEV

6.4000 g., Brass, 26 mm. **Subject:** 400th Anniversary - Battle of Sisek **Obv:** Value and date **Rev:** City view, arms, date, Andrej G. Turjaski **Edge:** Reeded **Designer:** Danilo Riznar

Date	Mintage	F	VF	XF	Unc	BU
1993	100,000	—	—	—	1.65	2.25

KM# 12 5 TOLARJEV

6.4000 g., Brass, 26 mm. **Subject:** 300th Anniversary - Establishment of Operosorum Labacensium Academy **Obv:** Value and date **Rev:** Beehive and bees **Edge:** Reeded **Designer:** Danilo Riznar

Date	Mintage	F	VF	XF	Unc	BU
1993	100,000	—	—	—	2.00	5.00

KM# 15 5 TOLARJEV

Brass, 26 mm. **Subject:** 50th Anniversary - Slovenian Bank **Obv:** Value and date **Rev:** Linden leaf and seed pod **Edge:** Reeded

Date	Mintage	F	VF	XF	Unc	BU
1994	100,000	—	—	—	1.65	2.25

KM# 16 5 TOLARJEV

Brass, 26 mm. **Subject:** 1,000th Anniversary - Glagolitic Alphabet **Obv:** Value and date **Rev:** Feather **Edge:** Reeded

Date	Mintage	F	VF	XF	Unc	BU
1994	200,000	—	—	—	1.65	2.25

KM# 21 5 TOLARJEV

Brass, 26 mm. **Series:** F.A.O. **Subject:** 50th Anniversary - F.A.O. **Obv:** Value within circle **Rev:** Hands holding F.A.O. logo **Edge:** Reeded

Date	Mintage	F	VF	XF	Unc	BU
ND(1995)	500,000	—	—	—	1.65	2.25

KM# 22 5 TOLARJEV

Brass, 26 mm. **Subject:** 50th Anniversary - Defeat of Fascism **Obv:** Value **Rev:** Vertical chain link design and dates **Edge:** Reeded

Date	Mintage	F	VF	XF	Unc	BU
1995	200,000	—	—	—	1.65	2.25

KM# 26 5 TOLARJEV

Brass, 26 mm. **Subject:** Aljazev Stolp **Obv:** Value within triangle design **Rev:** Head facing in front of mountains **Edge:** Reeded

Date	Mintage	F	VF	XF	Unc	BU
1995	200,000	—	—	—	1.65	2.25

KM# 29 5 TOLARJEV

Brass, 26 mm. **Subject:** 150th Anniversary - First Railway in Slovenia **Obv:** Date within design at upper right, value at far left **Rev:** Dates above train **Edge:** Reeded

Date	Mintage	F	VF	XF	Unc	BU
1996	Est. 300,000	—	—	—	1.65	2.25
1996 Proof	Inc. above	Value: 8.00				

KM# 32 5 TOLARJEV

Brass, 26 mm. **Subject:** 5th Anniversary of Independence **Obv:** Value and date at left **Rev:** Pink Carnation and dates **Edge:** Reeded

Date	Mintage	F	VF	XF	Unc	BU
1996	200,000	—	—	—	1.65	2.25
1996 Proof	—	Value: 8.00				

KM# 33 5 TOLARJEV

Brass, 26 mm. **Series:** Olympics **Subject:** Olympics Centennial **Obv:** Value above olympic rings and flag **Rev:** Gymnast above dates **Edge:** Reeded

Date	Mintage	F	VF	XF	Unc	BU
1996	200,000	—	—	—	1.65	2.25
1996 Proof	Est. 3,000	Value: 8.00				

KM# 38 5 TOLARJEV

Brass, 26 mm. **Subject:** Ziga Zois **Obv:** Value and date **Rev:** Zois ziga written within outline of face above dates **Edge:** Reeded

Date	Mintage	F	VF	XF	Unc	BU
1997	200,000	—	—	—	1.65	2.25

KM# 41 10 TOLARJEV

5.7500 g., Copper Nickel, 22 mm. **Obv:** Value within circle **Rev:** Stylized rearing horse **Edge:** Reeded

Date	Mintage	F	VF	XF	Unc	BU
2000	10,001,000	—	—	—	1.00	2.00
2000 Proof	800	Value: 12.00				
2001	29,441,000	—	—	—	1.00	2.00
2001 Proof	800	Value: 12.00				
2002	10,037,000	—	—	—	1.00	2.00
2002 Proof	800	Value: 12.00				
2003	1,000	—	—	—	—	4.00
Note: In sets only						
2003 Proof	800	Value: 12.00				
2004	10,001,000	—	—	—	1.00	2.00
2004 Proof	500	Value: 12.00				
2005	6,003,000	—	—	—	1.00	2.00
2005 Proof	1,000	Value: 12.00				
2006	6,001,000	—	—	—	1.00	2.00
2006 Proof	1,000	Value: 12.00				

KM# 51 20 TOLARJEV

6.8500 g., Copper-Nickel, 24 mm. **Obv:** Value within circle **Rev:** White Stork **Edge:** Reeded

Date	Mintage	F	VF	XF	Unc	BU
2003	10,001,000	—	—	—	3.50	5.00
2003 Proof	800	Value: 15.00				
2004	5,001,000	—	—	—	3.00	5.00
2004 Proof	500	Value: 15.00				
2005	8,003,000	—	—	—	3.50	5.00
2005 Proof	1,000	Value: 15.00				
2006	4,004,000	—	—	—	3.50	5.00
2006 Proof	1,000	Value: 15.00				

KM# 52 50 TOLARJEV

8.0000 g., Copper-Nickel, 26 mm. **Obv:** Value within circle **Rev:** Stylized bull **Edge:** Reeded and plain sections

Date	Mintage	F	VF	XF	Unc	BU
2003	10,001,000	—	—	—	2.00	4.00
2003 Proof	800	Value: 12.00				
2004	5,001,000	—	—	—	2.00	4.00
2004 Proof	500	Value: 15.00				
2005	8,003,000	—	—	—	2.00	4.00
2005 Proof	1,000	Value: 12.00				
2006	4,000	—	—	—	—	6.00
Note: In sets only						
2006 Proof	1,000	Value: 12.00				

KM# 42 100 TOLARJEV

9.1000 g., Copper-Nickel, 28 mm. **Subject:** 10th Anniversary of Slovenia and the Tolar **Obv:** Value **Rev:** Tree rings and inscription **Edge:** Reeded

Date	Mintage	F	VF	XF	Unc	BU
2001 Proof	800	Value: 10.00				
2001	500,000	—	—	—	3.00	4.00

KM# 45 500 TOLARJEV

8.5400 g., Bi-Metallic Copper-Nickel center in Brass ring, 28.1 mm. **Subject:** Soccer **Obv:** Value **Rev:** Soccer player and radiant sun **Edge:** Reeded

Date	Mintage	F	VF	XF	Unc	BU
2002	500,000	—	—	—	5.50	7.50
2002 Proof	800	Value: 12.50				

KM# 50 500 TOLARJEV

8.7200 g., Bi-Metallic Copper-Nickel center in Brass ring, 27.9 mm. **Subject:** European Year of the Disabled **Obv:** Stylized wheelchair **Rev:** Value **Edge:** Reeded

Date	Mintage	F	VF	XF	Unc	BU
2003 Proof	800	Value: 13.50				
2003	200,000	—	—	—	6.00	8.00

KM# 57 500 TOLARJEV

8.6000 g., Bi-Metallic Copper-Nickel center in Brass ring, 28 mm. **Obv:** Value **Rev:** Profile left looking down within mathematical graph **Edge:** Reeded

Date	Mintage	F	VF	XF	Unc	BU
2004	200,000	—	—	—	6.00	8.00
2004 Proof	500	Value: 20.00				

KM# 63 500 TOLARJEV

8.6500 g., Bi-Metallic Copper-Nickel center in Brass ring, 27.9 mm. **Obv:** Perched falcon and value **Rev:** Horizontal line in center divides partial suns **Edge:** Reeded

Date	Mintage	F	VF	XF	Unc	BU
2005	103,000	—	—	—	6.25	8.50
2005	1,000	Value: 12.00				

KM# 65 500 TOLARJEV

8.6000 g., Bi-Metallic Copper-Nickel center in Brass ring, 28 mm. **Obv:** Value **Rev:** Anton Tomaz Linhart's silhouette above life dates **Edge:** Reeded

Date	Mintage	F	VF	XF	Unc	BU
2006	104,000	—	—	—	—	6.00
2006 Proof	1,000	Value: 12.00				

EURO COINAGE

KM# 68 EURO CENT

2.2700 g., Copper Plated Steel, 16.2 mm. **Obv:** White Stork **Obv. Legend:** SLOVENIJA, star between each letter **Rev:** Value and globe **Edge:** Plain

Date	Mintage	F	VF	XF	Unc	BU
2007	—	—	—	—	0.25	—

KM# 69 2 EURO CENT

3.0000 g., Copper Plated Steel, 18.7 mm. **Obv:** Princely stone of power in consciousness **Obv. Legend:** SLOVENIJA, star between each letter **Rev:** Value and globe **Edge:** Grooved

Date	Mintage	F	VF	XF	Unc	BU
2007	—	—	—	—	0.50	—

KM# 70 5 EURO CENT

3.8600 g., Copper-Plated-Steel, 21.3 mm. **Obv:** Sower of Seeds - and stars **Obv. Legend:** SLOVENIJA, star between each letter **Rev:** Value and globe **Edge:** Plain

Date	Mintage	F	VF	XF	Unc	BU
2007	—	—	—	—	0.75	—

KM# 71 10 EURO CENT

4.0000 g., Brass, 19.7 mm. **Obv:** Plecnik's unrealised plans for Parliament building **Obv. Legend:** SLOVENIJA, star between each letter **Rev:** Value and map **Edge:** Reeded

Date	Mintage	F	VF	XF	Unc	BU
2007	—	—	—	—	1.00	—

KM# 72 20 EURO CENT

5.7300 g., Brass, 22.3 mm. **Obv:** Two Lipizzaner horses prancing left **Obv. Legend:** SLOVENIJA, star between each letter **Rev:** Value and map **Edge:** Notched

Date	Mintage	F	VF	XF	Unc	BU
2007	—	—	—	—	1.25	—

KM# 73 50 EURO CENT

7.8100 g., Brass, 24.2 mm. **Obv:** Mountain and stars **Rev:** Value and map **Edge:** Reeded

Date	Mintage	F	VF	XF	Unc	BU
2007	—	—	—	—	1.50	—

KM# 74 EURO

7.5000 g., Bi-Metallic Copper-Nickel center in Brass ring, 23.2 mm. **Obv:** Bearded Primoz Trubar **Rev:** Value and map **Edge:** Segmented reeding

Date	Mintage	F	VF	XF	Unc	BU
2007	—	—	—	—	2.50	—

KM# 75 2 EURO

8.5200 g., Bi-Metallic Brass center in Copper-Nickel ring, 25.7 mm. **Obv:** France Preseren silhouette and signature **Rev:** Value and map **Edge:** Reeded and lettered

Date	Mintage	F	VF	XF	Unc	BU
2007	—	—	—	—	4.00	—

SOLOMON ISLANDS

The Solomon Islands are made up of approximately 200 islands. They are located in the southwest Pacific east of Papua New Guinea, have an area of 10,983 sq. mi. (28,450 sq. km.) and a population of *552,000. Capital: Honiara. The most important islands of the Solomon chain are Guadalcanal (scene of some of the fiercest fighting of World War II), Malaitia, New Georgia, Florida, Vella Lavella, Choiseul, Rendova, San Cristobal, the Lord Howe group, the Santa Cruz islands, and the Duff group. Copra is the only important cash crop but it is hoped that timber will become an economic factor.

The Solomon Islands were discovered by Spanish navigator Alvaro de Mendana in 1567, and in 1569 he made an unsuccessful attempt to colonize them. European knowledge of the group would not be completed until the end of the 19th century. Germany declared a protectorate over the northern Solomon's in 1885. The British protectorate over the southern Solomons was established in 1893. In 1899 Germany transferred its claim to all Solomon Islands except Buka and Bougainville to Great Britain in exchange for recognition of German claims in Western Samoa. Australia occupied the two German islands in 1914, and administered them after 1920.

The Japanese invaded the Solomons during 1942-43, but were driven out by an American counteroffensive after a series of bloody clashes.

Following World War II, the islands returned to the status of a British protectorate. In 1976 the protectorate was abolished, and the Solomons became a self-governing dependency. Full independence was achieved on July 7,1978. Solomon Islands is a member of the Commonwealth of Nations. Queen Elizabeth II is Head of State, as Queen of the Solomon Islands.

RULER

British, until 1978

Queen Elizabeth II (see above)

MINT MARK

FM - Franklin Mint, U.S.A.*

NOTE: From 1977-1985 the Franklin Mint produced coinage in up to 3 different qualities. Qualities of issue are designated in ( ) after each date and are defined as follows:

(M) MATTE - Normal circulation strike or a dull finish produced by sandblasting special uncirculated (polish finish) or proof quality dies.

(U) SPECIAL UNCIRCULATED - Polished or proof-like in appearance without any frosted features.

(P) PROOF - The highest quality obtainable having mirror-like fields and frosted features.

MONETARY SYSTEM

100 Cents = 1 Dollar

COMMONWEALTH NATION

STANDARD COINAGE

KM# 1 CENT

2.6000 g., Bronze, 17.53 mm. **Ruler:** Elizabeth II **Series:** F.A.O. **Obv:** Young bust right **Obv. Legend:** ELIZABETH II - SOLOMON ISLANDS **Rev:** Food bowl divides value **Edge:** Plain

Date	Mintage	F	VF	XF	Unc	BU
1977	1,828,000	—	—	0.10	0.15	0.35
1977FM (M)	6,000	—	—	—	0.50	0.75
1977FM (U)	—	—	—	—	1.25	2.00
1977FM (P)	14,000	Value: 1.00				
1978FM (M)	6,000	—	—	—	0.50	0.75
1978FM (U)	544	—	—	—	1.25	2.00
1978FM (P)	5,122	Value: 1.00				
1979FM (M)	6,000	—	—	—	0.50	0.75
1979FM (U)	677	—	—	—	1.25	2.00
1979FM (P)	2,845	Value: 1.50				
1980FM (M)	6,000	—	—	—	0.50	0.75
1980FM (U)	624	—	—	—	1.25	2.00
1980FM (P)	1,031	Value: 1.50				
1981	—	—	—	—	0.50	0.75
1981FM (M)	6,000	—	—	—	0.50	0.75
1981FM (U)	212	—	—	—	2.00	3.00
1981FM (P)	448	Value: 1.50				
1982FM (U)	—	—	—	—	1.25	2.00
1982FM (P)	—	Value: 1.50				
1983FM (M)	—	—	—	—	0.50	0.75
1983FM (U)	200	—	—	—	2.00	3.00
1983FM (P)	—	Value: 1.50				

KM# 24 CENT

2.3000 g., Bronze Plated Steel, 17.53 mm. **Ruler:** Elizabeth II **Obv:** Crowned head right **Obv. Legend:** ELIZABETH II - SOLOMON ISLANDS **Rev:** Food bowl divides value **Edge:** Plain

Date	Mintage	F	VF	XF	Unc	BU
1987	—	—	—	—	0.35	0.75
1989	—	—	—	—	0.35	0.75
1996	—	—	—	—	0.35	0.75
2005	—	—	—	—	0.35	0.75

KM# 2 2 CENTS

5.2000 g., Bronze, 21.59 mm. **Subject:** Eagle Spirit of Malaita **Obv:** Young bust right **Rev:** Eagle spirit below value **Edge:** Plain

Date	Mintage	F	VF	XF	Unc	BU
1977	2,400,000	—	—	0.10	0.25	0.50
1977FM (M)	6,000	—	—	—	0.75	1.25
1977FM (U)	—	—	—	—	1.50	2.50
1977FM (P)	14,000	Value: 1.50				
1978FM (M)	6,000	—	—	—	0.75	1.25
1978FM (U)	544	—	—	—	1.50	2.50
1978FM (P)	5,122	Value: 1.50				
1979FM (M)	6,000	—	—	—	0.75	1.25
1979FM (U)	677	—	—	—	1.50	2.50
1979FM (P)	2,845	Value: 1.75				
1980FM (M)	6,000	—	—	—	0.75	1.25
1980FM (U)	624	—	—	—	1.50	2.50
1980FM (P)	1,031	—	—	—	1.25	2.00
1981FM (M)	6,000	—	—	—	0.75	1.25
1981FM (U)	212	—	—	—	1.50	2.50
1981FM (P)	448	Value: 2.00				
1982FM (U)	—	—	—	—	1.50	2.50
1982FM (P)	—	Value: 2.00				
1983FM (M)	—	—	—	—	0.75	1.25
1983FM (U)	200	—	—	—	1.50	2.50
1983FM (P)	—	Value: 2.00				

KM# 2a 2 CENTS

Bronze Plated Steel Galvanized steel planchet, 21.6 mm. **Ruler:** Elizabeth II **Subject:** Eagle Spirit of Malaita **Obv:** Crowned young bust right **Obv. Legend:** ELIZABETH II - SOLOMON ISLANDS **Rev:** Eagle spirit below value **Edge:** Plain

Date	Mintage	F	VF	XF	Unc	BU
1985	—	—	0.75	1.50	2.75	4.00

KM# 25 2 CENTS

Bronze Plated Steel, 21.6 mm. **Ruler:** Elizabeth II **Obv:** Crowned head right **Obv. Legend:** ELIZABETH II - SOLOMON ISLANDS **Rev:** Eagle spirit below value **Edge:** Plain

Date	Mintage	F	VF	XF	Unc	BU
1987	—	—	—	—	0.35	0.75
1989	—	—	—	—	0.35	0.75
1996	—	—	—	—	0.35	0.75
2005	—	—	—	—	0.35	0.75
2006	—	—	—	—	0.35	0.75

KM# 3 5 CENTS

2.8000 g., Copper-Nickel, 19.4 mm. **Subject:** Santa Ysabel **Obv:** Young bust right **Rev:** Native mask and value **Edge:** Reeded

Date	Mintage	F	VF	XF	Unc	BU
1977	1,200,000	—	—	0.15	0.35	0.75
1977FM (U)	—	—	—	—	1.50	2.50
1977FM (M)	6,000	—	—	—	1.00	1.50
1977FM (P)	14,000	Value: 1.75				
1978FM (M)	6,000	—	—	—	1.00	1.50
1978FM (U)	544	—	—	—	1.50	2.50
1978FM (P)	5,122	Value: 2.00				
1979FM (M)	6,000	—	—	—	1.00	1.50
1979FM (U)	677	—	—	—	1.50	2.50
1979FM (P)	2,845	Value: 2.25				
1980	—	—	—	—	—	—
1980FM (M)	6,000	—	—	—	1.00	1.50
1980FM (U)	624	—	—	—	1.50	2.50
1980FM (P)	1,031	Value: 2.50				
1981	—	—	—	—	—	—
1981FM (M)	6,000	—	—	—	1.00	1.50
1981FM (U)	212	—	—	—	1.50	2.50
1981FM (P)	448	Value: 2.50				
1982FM (U)	—	—	—	—	1.50	2.50
1982FM (P)	—	Value: 2.50				
1983FM (M)	—	—	—	—	1.00	1.50
1983FM (U)	200	—	—	—	2.00	3.50
1983FM (P)	—	Value: 2.50				
1985	—	—	—	—	0.30	0.50

KM# 26 5 CENTS

2.8000 g., Copper-Nickel, 19.4 mm. **Ruler:** Elizabeth II **Obv:** Crowned head right **Obv. Legend:** ELIZABETH II - SOLOMON ISLANDS **Rev:** Native mask and value **Edge:** Reeded

Date	Mintage	F	VF	XF	Unc	BU
1987	—	—	—	—	0.50	1.00
1988	—	—	—	—	0.50	1.00
1989	—	—	—	—	0.50	1.00

KM# 26a 5 CENTS

Nickel Plated Steel Galvanized steel planchet., 18.40 mm. **Ruler:** Elizabeth II **Obv:** Crowned bust right **Obv. Legend:** ELIZABETH II - SOLOMON ISLANDS **Rev:** Value at left, native mask at center right

Date	Mintage	F	VF	XF	Unc	BU
1993	—	—	—	—	0.50	1.00
1996	—	—	—	—	0.50	1.00
2005	—	—	—	—	0.50	1.00

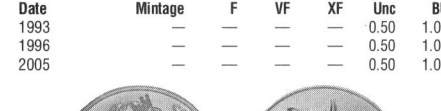

KM# 4 10 CENTS

5.6500 g., Copper-Nickel, 23.6 mm. **Subject:** Ngorieru **Obv:** Young bust right **Rev:** Sea spirit divides value **Edge:** Reeded

Date	Mintage	F	VF	XF	Unc	BU
1977	3,600,000	—	—	0.20	0.50	0.75
1977FM (M)	6,000	—	—	—	1.25	2.00
1977FM (U)	—	—	—	—	2.50	4.00
1977FM (P)	14,000	Value: 2.50				
1978FM (M)	6,000	—	—	—	1.25	2.00

Date	Mintage	F	VF	XF	Unc	BU
1978FM (U)	544	—	—	—	2.50	4.00
1978FM (P)	5,122	Value: 2.75				
1979FM (M)	6,000	—	—	—	1.25	2.00
1979FM (U)	677	—	—	—	2.50	4.00
1979FM (P)	2,845	Value: 3.50				
1980FM (M)	6,000	—	—	—	1.25	2.00
1980FM (U)	624	—	—	—	2.50	4.00
1980FM (P)	1,031	Value: 4.00				
1981FM (M)	6,000	—	—	—	1.25	2.00
1981FM (U)	212	—	—	—	2.50	4.00
1981FM (P)	448	Value: 4.00				
1982FM (U)	—	—	—	—	2.50	4.00
1982FM (P)	—	Value: 4.00				
1983FM (M)	—	—	—	—	1.25	2.00
1983FM (U)	200	—	—	—	3.50	5.00
1983FM (P)	—	Value: 4.00				

KM# 27 10 CENTS

5.6500 g., Copper-Nickel, 23.6 mm. **Subject:** Ngorieru **Obv:** Crowned head right **Rev:** Sea spirit divides value **Edge:** Reeded

Date	Mintage	F	VF	XF	Unc	BU
1988	—	—	—	—	0.65	1.00

KM# 27a 10 CENTS

Nickel Plated Steel Galvanized steel planchet., 23.6 mm. **Ruler:** Elizabeth II **Subject:** Ngorieru **Obv:** Crowned head right **Obv. Legend:** ELIZABETH II - SOLOMON ISLANDS **Rev:** Sea spirit divides value **Edge:** Reeded

Date	Mintage	F	VF	XF	Unc	BU
1990	—	—	—	—	0.65	1.00
1993	—	—	—	—	0.65	1.00
1996	—	—	—	—	0.65	1.00
2000	—	—	—	—	0.65	1.00
2005	—	—	—	—	0.65	1.00

KM# 5 20 CENTS

11.2500 g., Copper-Nickel, 28.5 mm. **Obv:** Young bust right **Rev:** Malaita pendant design within circle, denomination appears twice in legend **Edge:** Reeded

Date	Mintage	F	VF	XF	Unc	BU
1977	3,000,000	—	0.15	0.35	0.80	1.25
1977FM (M)	5,000	—	—	—	2.50	3.50
1977FM (P)	14,000	Value: 3.50				
1978	293,000	—	0.25	0.50	1.00	1.75
1978FM (M)	5,000	—	—	—	2.50	3.50
1978FM (U)	544	—	—	—	3.50	5.50
1978FM (P)	5,122	Value: 3.75				
1979FM (M)	5,000	—	—	—	2.50	3.50
1979FM (U)	677	—	—	—	3.50	5.00
1979FM (P)	2,845	Value: 3.75				
1980FM (M)	5,000	—	—	—	2.50	3.50
1980FM (U)	624	—	—	—	3.50	5.00
1980FM (P)	1,031	Value: 3.75				
1981FM (M)	5,000	—	—	—	2.50	3.50
1981FM (U)	212	—	—	—	4.00	6.00
1981FM (P)	448	Value: 4.00				
1982FM (U)	—	—	—	—	4.00	6.00
1982FM (P)	—	Value: 4.00				
1983FM (M)	—	—	—	—	2.50	3.50
1983FM (U)	200	—	—	—	5.00	7.00
1983FM (P)	—	Value: 4.00				

KM# 28 20 CENTS

11.2500 g., Nickel Plated Steel Galvanized steel planchet., 28.5 mm. **Ruler:** Elizabeth II **Obv:** Crowned head right **Obv. Legend:** ELIZABETH II _ SOLOMON ISLANDS **Rev:** Malaita pendant design within circle, denomination appears twice in legend **Edge:** Reeded

Date	Mintage	F	VF	XF	Unc	BU
1987	—	—	—	—	0.85	1.25
1989	—	—	—	—	0.85	1.25

Date	Mintage	F	VF	XF	Unc	BU
1993	—	—	—	—	0.85	1.25
1996	—	—	—	—	0.85	1.25
1997	—	—	—	—	0.85	1.25
2000	—	—	—	—	0.85	1.25
2005	—	—	—	—	0.85	1.25

KM# 82 20 CENTS

Nickel Plated Steel, 26 mm. **Obv:** Crowned bust right **Rev:** Native woman with basket on head **Edge:** Reeded

Date	Mintage	F	VF	XF	Unc	BU
1995	20,200	—	—	—	3.00	4.00

KM# 23 50 CENTS

Copper-Nickel, 29.5 mm. **Subject:** 10th Anniversary of Independence **Obv:** Crowned head right **Rev:** Arms with supporters **Edge:** Plain **Shape:** 12-sided

Date	Mintage	F	VF	XF	Unc	BU
1988	—	—	—	—	2.00	3.00

KM# 29 50 CENTS

10.0000 g., Copper-Nickel, 29.5 mm. **Ruler:** Elizabeth II **Obv:** Crowned head right **Obv. Legend:** ELIZABETH II - SOLOMON ISLANDS **Rev:** Arms with supporters **Edge:** Plain **Shape:** 12-sided **Note:** Circulation type.

Date	Mintage	F	VF	XF	Unc	BU
1990	—	—	—	—	2.00	3.00
1995	—	—	—	—	2.00	3.00
1996	—	—	—	—	2.00	3.00
1997	—	—	—	—	2.00	3.00
2005	—	—	—	—	2.00	3.00

KM# 6 DOLLAR

13.4000 g., Copper-Nickel, 30 mm. **Subject:** Nusu-Nusu head **Obv:** Young bust right **Rev:** Sea spirit statue divides value **Edge:** Plain **Shape:** 7-sided

Date	Mintage	F	VF	XF	Unc	BU
1977	1,500,000	—	—	1.00	2.00	3.00
1977FM (M)	3,000	—	—	—	3.00	5.00
1977FM (P)	14,000	Value: 4.50				
1978FM (M)	3,000	—	—	—	3.00	5.00
1978FM (U)	544	—	—	—	4.50	6.00
1978FM (P)	5,122	Value: 4.50				
1979FM (M)	3,000	—	—	—	3.00	5.00
1979FM (U)	677	—	—	—	4.50	6.00
1979FM (P)	2,845	Value: 5.00				
1980FM (M)	3,000	—	—	—	3.00	5.00
1980FM (U)	624	—	—	—	4.50	6.00
1980FM (P)	1,031	Value: 5.50				
1981FM (M)	3,000	—	—	—	3.00	5.00
1981FM (U)	212	—	—	—	7.00	10.00
1981FM (P)	448	Value: 6.00				
1982FM (U)	—	—	—	—	4.50	6.00
1982FM (P)	—	Value: 6.00				
1983FM (M)	—	—	—	—	3.00	5.00
1983FM (U)	200	—	—	—	7.00	10.00
1983FM (P)	—	Value: 5.50				

KM# 72 DOLLAR

13.4500 g., Copper-Nickel, 30 mm. **Ruler:** Elizabeth II **Obv:** Crowned head right **Obv. Legend:** ELIZABETH II - SOLOMON ISLANDS **Rev:** Sea spirit statue divides value **Edge:** Plain **Shape:** 7-sided

Date	Mintage	F	VF	XF	Unc	BU
1996	—	—	—	—	2.50	4.00
1997	—	—	—	—	2.50	4.00
2005	—	—	—	—	2.50	4.00

SOMALIA

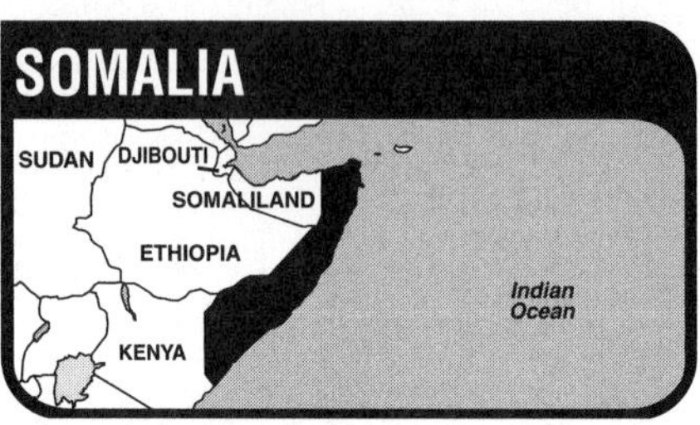

The Somali Democratic Republic, comprised of the former Italian Somaliland, is located on the coast of the eastern projection of the African continent commonly referred to as the "Horn". It has an area of 178,201 sq. mi. (461,657 sq. km.) and a population of *8.2 million. Capital: Mogadishu. The economy is pastoral and agricultural. Livestock, bananas and hides are exported.

The area of the British Somaliland Protectorate was known to the Egyptians at least 1,500 years B.C., and was occupied by the Arabs and Portuguese before British sea captains obtained trading and anchorage rights in 1827. The land of sandy clay and sporadic rainfall acquired a strategic importance with the opening of the Suez Canal in1869. After negotiating treaties with the tribes, Britain declared the area a protectorate in 1888. Italy acquired Italian Somaliland in 1895 by purchase from the Sultan of Zanzibar. Britain occupied Italian Somaliland in 1941 and administered it until April 1, 1950, when it was returned to Italy as a U.N. trusteeship. The British Somaliland protectorate became independent on June 26, 1960. Five days later it joined with Italian Somaliland to form the Somali Republic. The country was under a revolutionary military regime installed Oct. 21, 1969. After eleven years of civil war rebel forces fought their way into the capital. A.M. Muhammad became president in Aug. 1991,but inter-factional fighting continued. A UN-sponsored truce was signed in March 1992 and a peace plan and pact was signed Jan. 15, 1993.

The Northern Somali National Movement (SNM) declared a secession of the northwestern Somaliland Republic on May 17, 1991, which is not recognized by the Somali Democratic Republic.

TITLE

Al-Jumhuriya(t)as - Somaliya(t)

RULERS

Italian, until 1941
British, until 1950

MINT MARKS

Az - Arezzo (Italy)
R – Rome

U. N. TRUSTEESHIP UNDER ITALY

STANDARD COINAGE

100 Centesimi = 1 Scellino

KM# 1 CENTESIMO

3.0000 g., Copper, 21 mm. **Obv:** African elephant **Rev:** Value within circle with star flanked by crescents above **Edge:** Plain

Date	Mintage	F	VF	XF	Unc	BU
AH1369-1950	4,000,000	—	0.20	0.50	2.00	4.00

KM# 2 5 CENTESIMI
Copper **Obv:** African elephant **Rev:** Value within circle with star flanked by crescents above

Date	Mintage	F	VF	XF	Unc	BU
AH1369-1950	6,800,000	—	0.30	1.00	3.50	7.50

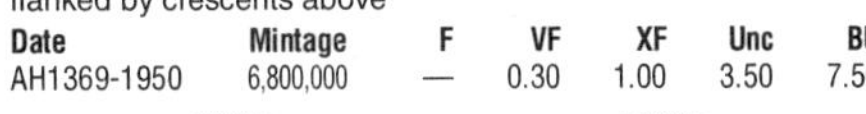

KM# 3 10 CENTESIMI
Copper **Rev:** Value within circle with star flanked by crescents above **Edge:** African elephant

Date	Mintage	F	VF	XF	Unc	BU
AH1369-1950	7,400,000	—	0.50	2.00	6.00	12.00

KM# 4 50 CENTESIMI
3.8000 g., 0.2500 Silver 0.0305 oz. ASW **Obv:** Star flanked by crescents above lion **Rev:** Value within beaded circle

Date	Mintage	F	VF	XF	Unc	BU
AH1369-1950	1,800,000	—	1.25	3.75	10.00	15.00

KM# 5 SOMALO
7.6000 g., 0.2500 Silver 0.0611 oz. ASW **Obv:** Star flanked by crescents above lion **Rev:** Value within beaded circle

Date	Mintage	F	VF	XF	Unc	BU
AH1369-1950	11,480,000	—	2.25	4.75	12.50	20.00

SOMALI REPUBLIC

STANDARD COINAGE

100 Centesimi = 1 Scellino

KM# 6 5 CENTESIMI
2.5000 g., Brass **Obv:** Crowned arms with supporters **Rev:** Value and star within circle **Designer:** Michael Rizzello

Date	Mintage	F	VF	XF	Unc	BU
1967	10,000,000	—	—	0.20	0.60	1.00

KM# 7 10 CENTESIMI
Brass **Obv:** Crowned arms with supporters **Rev:** Value and star within circle **Designer:** Michael Rizzello

Date	Mintage	F	VF	XF	Unc	BU
1967	15,000,000	—	0.15	0.25	0.70	1.25

KM# 8 50 CENTESIMI
Copper-Nickel **Obv:** Crowned arms with supporters **Rev:** Value and star within beaded circle **Designer:** Michael Rizzello

Date	Mintage	F	VF	XF	Unc	BU
1967	5,100,000	—	0.50	1.00	2.50	4.00

KM# 9 SCELLINO / SHILLING
7.6300 g., Copper-Nickel, 26.7 mm. **Obv:** Arms with supporters **Obv. Designer:** Michael Rizzello **Rev:** Value within beaded circle

Date	Mintage	F	VF	XF	Unc	BU
1967	8,150,000	—	1.00	3.00	6.00	9.00

DEMOCRATIC REPUBLIC

REFORM COINAGE

100 Senti = 1 Shilling

KM# A24 5 SENTI
Aluminum **Series:** F.A.O. **Obv:** Value within circle **Rev:** Corn ears and flower flanked by dates **Shape:** Round

Date	Mintage	F	VF	XF	Unc	BU
1976	—	—	—	—	200	—

KM# 24 5 SENTI
0.8700 g., Aluminum, 20 mm. **Series:** F.A.O. **Obv:** Crowned arms with supporters **Rev:** Value above fruit, grains and bread **Shape:** 12-sided

Date	Mintage	F	VF	XF	Unc	BU
1976	18,500,000	—	0.10	0.20	0.35	0.50

KM# 25 10 SENTI
1.3900 g., Aluminum, 23.5 mm. **Series:** F.A.O. **Obv:** Crowned arms with supporters **Rev:** Lamb flanked by dates below value **Edge:** Plain **Shape:** 12-sided

Date	Mintage	F	VF	XF	Unc	BU
1976	40,500,000	—	0.10	0.20	0.50	1.00

KM# 26 50 SENTI
3.8500 g., Copper-Nickel, 21 mm. **Series:** F.A.O. **Obv:** Crowned arms with supporters **Rev:** Value above grains and dates

Date	Mintage	F	VF	XF	Unc	BU
1976	10,080,000	—	0.15	0.25	0.75	1.00

KM# 26a 50 SENTI
3.8100 g., Nickel Plated Steel, 21 mm. **Series:** F.A.O. **Obv:** Crowned arms with supporters **Rev:** Value above grains and dates

Date	Mintage	F	VF	XF	Unc	BU
1984	—	—	1.00	2.00	5.00	—

KM# 27 SHILLING
6.2200 g., Copper-Nickel, 25.5 mm. **Series:** F.A.O. **Obv:** Crowned arms with supporters **Rev:** Lamb flanked by dates below value

Date	Mintage	F	VF	XF	Unc	BU
1976	20,040,000	—	0.35	0.65	2.25	2.50

KM# 27a SHILLING
6.1900 g., Nickel Plated Steel, 25.42 mm. **Series:** F.A.O. **Obv:** Crowned arms with supporters **Rev:** Lamb flanked by dates below value

Date	Mintage	F	VF	XF	Unc	BU
1984	—	—	2.00	4.00	10.00	—

REPUBLIC OF SOMALIA

STANDARD COINAGE

100 Centesimi = 1 Scellino

KM# 45 5 SHILLING / SCELLINI
1.2900 g., Aluminum, 21 mm. **Series:** F.A.O. **Obv:** Crowned arms with supporters **Rev:** Elephant **Edge:** Plain

Date	Mintage	F	VF	XF	Unc	BU
2000	—	—	—	—	1.50	1.75
2002	—	—	—	—	1.50	1.75

KM# 46 10 SHILLINGS / SCELLINI
1.2900 g., Aluminum, 21.92 mm. **Series:** F.A.O. **Obv:** Crowned arms with supporters **Rev:** Camel **Edge:** Plain

Date	Mintage	F	VF	XF	Unc	BU
1999	—	—	—	—	2.00	2.25
2000	—	—	—	—	2.00	2.25

KM# 103 25 SHILLINGS / SCELLINI
4.3700 g., Brass, 21.8 mm. **Subject:** Soccer **Obv:** Crowned arms with supporters **Rev:** Soccer player **Edge:** Plain

Date	Mintage	F	VF	XF	Unc	BU
2001	—	—	—	—	1.25	1.50

KM# 111 50 SHILLINGS
3.9000 g., Nickel-Clad Steel, 21.9 mm. **Obv:** Crowned arms with supporters **Rev:** Mandrill **Edge:** Plain

Date	Mintage	F	VF	XF	Unc	BU
2002	—	—	—	—	0.85	1.25

KM# 112 100 SHILLINGS
3.5400 g., Brass, 18.8 mm. **Obv:** Crowned arms with supporters above value **Rev:** Bust with headdress facing **Edge:** Plain

Date	Mintage	F	VF	XF	Unc	BU
2002	—	—	—	—	1.50	2.50

SOMALILAND

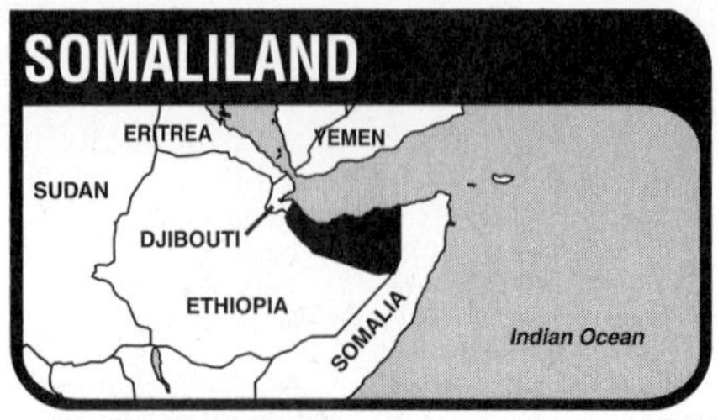

The Somaliland Republic, comprised of the former British Somaliland Protectorate is located on the coast of the northeastern projection of the African continent commonly referred to as the "Horn" on the southwestern end of the Gulf of Aden.

Bordered by Ethiopia to west and south and Somalia to the east. It has an area of 68,000* sq. mi. (176,000* sq. km). Capital: Hargeysa. It is mostly arid and mountainous except for the gulf shoreline.

The Protectorate of British Somaliland was established in 1888 and from 1905 a commissioner under the British Colonial Office administered the territory. Italian Somaliland was administered as a colony from1893 to 1941, when British forces occupied the territory. In 1950 the United Nations allowed Italy to resume control of Italian Somaliland under a trusteeship. In 1960 British and Italian Somaliland were united as Somalia, an independent republic outside the Commonwealth.

Civil war erupted in the late 1970's and continued until the capital of Somalia was taken in 1990. The United Nations provided aid and peacekeeping. A UN sponsored truce was signed in March 1992 and a peace plan and pact was signed Jan. 15, 1993. The northern Somali National Movement (SNM) declared a secession of the Somaliland Republic on May 17, 1991, which is not recognized by the Somali Democratic Republic.

The currency issued by the East African Currency Board was used in British Somaliland from 1945 to 1961; Somali currency was used later until 1995.

REPUBLIC

SHILLING COINAGE

KM# 1 SHILLING

1.0700 g., Aluminum, 20.5 mm. **Issuer:** Bank of Somaliland **Obv:** Bird **Obv. Legend:** REPUBLIC OF SOMALILAND **Rev:** Value **Rev. Legend:** • BAANKA SOMALILAND • **Edge:** Reeded

Date	Mintage	F	VF	XF	Unc	BU
1994PM	—	—	—	1.50	3.00	5.00

KM# 4 5 SHILLINGS

1.4500 g., Aluminum, 21.9 mm. **Obv:** Value **Rev:** Bust of Sir Richard F. Burton - explorer, divides dates **Edge:** Plain

Date	Mintage	F	VF	XF	Unc	BU
2002	—	—	—	—	1.25	1.50

KM# 5 5 SHILLINGS

1.4500 g., Aluminum, 21.9 mm. **Obv:** Value **Rev:** Rooster **Edge:** Plain

Date	Mintage	F	VF	XF	Unc	BU
2002	—	—	—	—	1.00	1.25

KM# 19 5 SHILLINGS

1.2400 g., Aluminum, 22 mm. **Obv:** Elephant with calf walking right **Obv. Legend:** REPUBLIC OF SOMALILAND **Rev:** Value **Rev. Legend:** BAANKA SOMALILAND **Edge:** Plain

Date	Mintage	F	VF	XF	Unc	BU
2005	—	—	—	—	1.25	1.50

SOUTH AFRICA

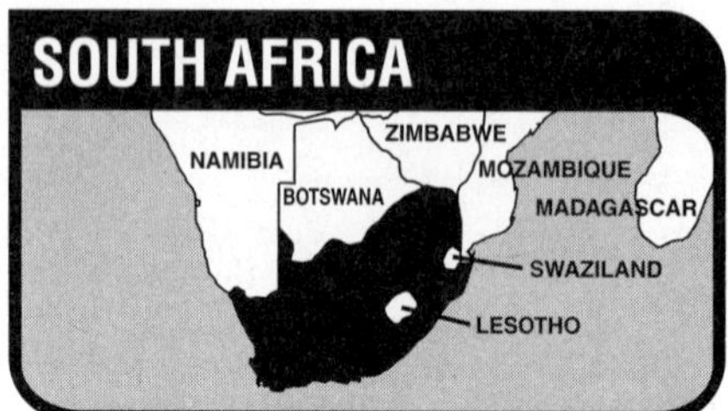

The Republic of South Africa, located at the southern tip of Africa, has an area of 471,445 sq. mi. (1,221,043 sq. km.) and a population of *30.2 million. Capitals: Administrative, Pretoria; Legislative, Cape Town; Judicial, Bloemfontein. Manufacturing, mining and agriculture are the principal industries. Exports include wool, diamonds, gold, and metallic ores.

Portuguese navigator Bartholomew Diaz became the first European to sight the region of South Africa when he rounded the Cape of Good Hope in 1488, but throughout the 16th century the only white men to come ashore were the survivors of ships wrecked while attempting the stormy Cape passage. Jan van Riebeeck of the Dutch East India Company established the first permanent settlement in 1652. In subsequent decades additional Dutch, German and Huguenot refugees from France settled in the Cape area to form the Afrikaner segment of today's population.

Great Britain captured the Cape colony in 1795, and again in 1806, receiving permanent title in 1814. To escape British political rule and cultural dominance, many Afrikaner farmers (Boers) migrated northward (the Great Trek) beginning in 1836, and established the independent Boer Republics of the Transvaal (the South African Republic, Zuid Afrikaansche Republic) in 1852, and the Orange Free State in 1854. British political intrigues against the two republics, coupled with the discovery of diamonds and gold in the Boer-settled regions, led to the bitter Boer Wars (1880-81, 1899-1902) and the incorporation of the Boer republics into the British Empire.

On May 31, 1910, the two former Boer Republics (Transvaal and Orange Free State) were joined with the British colonies of Cape of Good Hope and Natal to form the Union of South Africa, a dominion of the British Empire. In 1934 the Union achieved status as a sovereign state within the British Empire.

Political integration of the various colonies did not still the conflict between the Afrikaners and the English-speaking groups, which continued to have a significant impact on political developments. A resurgence of Afrikaner nationalism in the 1940s and 1950s led to a referendum in the white community authorizing the relinquishment of dominion status and the establishment of a republic. The decision took effect on May 31, 1961. The Republic of South Africa withdrew from the British Commonwealth in Oct. 1961.

The apartheid era ended April 27, 1994 with the first democratic election for all people of South Africa. Nelson Mandela was inaugurated President May 10, 1994, and South Africa was readmitted into the Commonwealth of Nations. Walvis Bay, former enclave of Cape Province, transferred to Namibia.

South African coins and currency bear inscriptions in tribal languages, Afrikaans and English.

RULERS

British, until 1934

MONETARY SYSTEM

Until 1961

12 Pence = 1 Shilling
2 Shillings = 1 Florin
20 Shillings = 1 Pound (Pond)

Commencing 1961

100 Cents = 1 Rand

REPUBLIK

STANDARD COINAGE

12 Pence = 1 Shilling; 20 Shillings = 1 Pond

KM# 11 1/2 POND

0.9990 Gold **Subject:** Veld-Boer War Siege Issue **Obv:** Monogram and date **Rev:** Inscription

Date	Mintage	F	VF	XF	Unc	BU
1902	986	750	1,350	2,750	5,000	—

UNION OF SOUTH AFRICA

Dominion under Great Britain

STANDARD COINAGE

12 Pence = 1 Shilling; 2 Shillings = 1 Florin;
20 Shillings 1 Pound

KM# 12.1 1/4 PENNY (Farthing)

Bronze, 20.20 mm. **Ruler:** George V **Obv:** Crowned bust left **Obv. Designer:** E.B. MacKennal **Rev:** Wheat sprig and berries divide birds within circle **Rev. Designer:** G.T. Kruger-Gray **Edge:** Plain

Date	Mintage	F	VF	XF	Unc	BU
1923	33,000	2.00	5.00	10.00	20.00	—
1923 Proof	1,402	Value: 285				
1924	95,000	1.50	3.50	9.00	20.00	—

KM# 12.2 1/4 PENNY (Farthing)

Bronze **Ruler:** George V **Obv:** Crowned bust left **Obv. Designer:** E.B. MacKennal **Rev:** Oat sprigs and berries divide birds within circle **Rev. Designer:** G.T. Kruger-Gray

Date	Mintage	F	VF	XF	Unc	BU
1926 Proof	16	Value: 6,000				
1928	64,000	1.50	3.00	5.00	12.50	—
1930	6,560	30.00	60.00	120	200	—
1930 Proof	14	Value: 1,200				
1931	154,000	1.00	1.50	4.00	6.00	—

KM# 12.3 1/4 PENNY (Farthing)

Bronze **Ruler:** George V **Obv:** Crowned bust left **Obv. Designer:** E.B. MacKennal **Rev:** Oat sprig and berries divide birds within circle **Rev. Designer:** G.T. Kruger-Gray

Date	Mintage	F	VF	XF	Unc	BU
1931	Inc. above	5.00	10.00	15.00	35.00	—
1931 Proof	62	Value: 200				
1932	105,000	1.00	1.50	3.50	7.00	—
1932 Proof	12	Value: 375				
1933	76	750	1,450	2,200	3,250	—
1933 Proof	20	Value: 4,000				
1934	52	750	1,450	2,200	3,250	—
1934 Proof	24	Value: 3,750				
1935	61,000	1.00	1.50	3.50	8.00	—
1935 Proof	20	Value: 3,000				
1936	43	350	750	1,100	2,000	—
1936 Proof	40	Value: 3,000				

KM# 23 1/4 PENNY (Farthing)
2.8400 g., Bronze, 20 mm. **Ruler:** George VI **Obv:** Head left **Obv. Designer:** T.H. Paget **Rev:** Oat sprig and berries divide birds within circle **Rev. Designer:** G.T. Kruger-Gray

Date	Mintage	F	VF	XF	Unc	BU
1937	38,000	1.50	3.00	6.00	12.50	—
1937 Proof	116	Value: 40.00				
1938	51,000	1.00	2.00	4.00	8.00	—
1938 Proof	44	Value: 100				
1939	102,000	0.50	1.50	3.00	7.50	—
1939 Proof	30	Value: 125				
1941	91,000	0.50	1.50	3.00	7.50	—
1942	3,756,000	0.25	0.50	1.00	2.00	—
1943	9,918,000	0.25	0.50	0.75	1.50	—
1943 Proof	104	Value: 40.00				
1944	4,468,000	0.25	0.50	0.75	2.00	—
1944 Proof	150	Value: 35.00				
1945	5,297,000	0.25	0.50	1.50	3.00	—
1945 Proof	150	Value: 35.00				
1946	4,378,000	0.25	0.50	1.50	4.00	—
1946 Proof	150	Value: 35.00				
1947	3,895,000	0.25	0.50	1.50	4.00	—
1947 Proof	2,600	Value: 4.00				

KM# 32.1 1/4 PENNY (Farthing)
Bronze **Ruler:** George VI **Obv:** Head left **Obv. Designer:** T.H. Paget **Rev:** Oat sprig and berries divide birds within circle **Rev. Designer:** G.T. Kruger-Gray

Date	Mintage	F	VF	XF	Unc	BU
1948	2,415,000	0.25	0.50	1.00	2.00	—
1948 Proof	1,120	Value: 3.00				
1949	3,568,000	0.25	0.50	1.00	2.50	—
1949 Proof	800	Value: 5.00				
1950	8,694,000	0.25	0.50	0.75	1.50	—
1950 Proof	500	Value: 8.00				

KM# 32.2 1/4 PENNY (Farthing)
2.7000 g., Bronze, 20.5 mm. **Ruler:** Edward VIII **Obv:** Head left **Obv. Designer:** T.H. Paget **Rev:** Oat sprig and berries divide birds within circle **Rev. Legend:** SUID AFRIKA-SOUTH AFRICA **Rev. Designer:** G.T. Kruger-Gray

Date	Mintage	F	VF	XF	Unc	BU
1951	3,511,000	0.15	0.35	0.75	2.50	—
1951 Proof	2,000	Value: 2.00				
1952	2,805,000	0.15	0.35	0.75	2.00	—
1952 Proof	16,000	Value: 2.00				

KM# 44 1/4 PENNY (Farthing)
2.8000 g., Bronze **Ruler:** Elizabeth II **Obv:** Laureate head right **Obv. Designer:** Mary Gillick **Rev:** Oat sprig and berries divide birds within circle **Rev. Designer:** G.T. Kruger-Gray

Date	Mintage	F	VF	XF	Unc	BU
1953	7,193,000	0.15	0.25	0.50	1.50	—
1953 Proof	5,000	Value: 2.00				
1954	6,568,000	0.15	0.25	0.50	1.50	—
1954 Proof	3,150	Value: 2.00				
1955	11,798,000	0.15	0.25	0.50	1.50	—
1955 Proof	2,850	Value: 2.00				
1956	1,287,000	0.15	0.25	0.50	2.50	—
1956 Proof	1,700	Value: 3.00				
1957	3,065,000	0.15	0.25	0.50	1.50	—
1957 Proof	1,130	Value: 4.00				
1958	5,452,000	0.15	0.25	0.50	1.50	—
1958 Proof	985	Value: 5.00				
1959	1,567,000	0.15	0.25	0.50	1.50	—
1959 Proof	900	Value: 6.00				
1960	1,022,999	0.15	0.25	0.50	2.00	—
1960 Proof	3,360	Value: 1.50				

KM# 13.1 1/2 PENNY
Bronze **Ruler:** George V **Subject:** Dromedaris (ship) **Obv:** Crowned bust left **Obv. Designer:** E.B. MacKennal **Rev:** Sailing ship **Rev. Designer:** G.T. Kruger-Gray

Date	Mintage	F	VF	XF	Unc	BU
1923	12,000	25.00	40.00	70.00	100	—
1923 Proof	1,402	Value: 100				
1924	64,000	7.50	12.50	30.00	60.00	—
1925	69,000	7.50	12.50	30.00	80.00	—
1926	65,000	10.00	15.00	35.00	100	—

KM# 13.2 1/2 PENNY
Bronze **Ruler:** George V **Subject:** Dromedaris (ship) **Obv:** Crowned bust left **Obv. Designer:** E.B. MacKennal **Rev:** Sailing ship **Rev. Designer:** G.T. Kruger-Gray

Date	Mintage	F	VF	XF	Unc	BU
1928	105,000	5.00	12.50	35.00	75.00	—
1929	272,000	2.50	5.00	15.00	35.00	—
1930	147,000	3.50	7.00	20.00	40.00	—
1930 Proof	14	Value: 400				
1930	Inc. above	4.00	8.00	25.00	50.00	—
Note: Without star after date						
1931	145,000	3.50	7.00	25.00	50.00	—

KM# 13.3 1/2 PENNY
Bronze **Ruler:** George V **Subject:** Dromedaris (ship) **Obv:** Crowned bust left **Obv. Designer:** E.B. MacKennal **Rev:** Sailing ship **Rev. Designer:** G.T. Kruger-Gray

Date	Mintage	F	VF	XF	Unc	BU
1931 Proof	62	Value: 1,000				
1932	106,000	5.00	10.00	30.00	75.00	—
1932 Proof	12	Value: 1,000				
1933	63,000	8.00	25.00	55.00	100	—
1933 Proof	20	Value: 500				
1934	326,000	1.50	5.00	15.00	45.00	—
1934 Proof	24	Value: 500				
1935	405,000	1.50	5.00	15.00	40.00	—
1935 Proof	20	Value: 500				
1936	407,000	1.50	5.00	15.00	30.00	—
1936 Proof	40	Value: 200				

KM# 24 1/2 PENNY
Bronze **Ruler:** George VI **Subject:** Dromedaris (ship) **Obv:** Head left **Obv. Designer:** T.H. Paget **Rev:** Sailing ship **Rev. Designer:** G.T. Kruger-Gray

Date	Mintage	F	VF	XF	Unc	BU
1937	638,000	1.00	2.00	9.00	15.00	—
1937 Proof	116	Value: 50.00				
1938	560,000	1.00	2.00	6.00	15.00	—
1938 Proof	44	Value: 125				
1939	271,000	2.50	5.00	10.00	20.00	—
1939 Proof	30	Value: 175				
1940	1,535,000	0.30	0.75	3.00	8.00	—
1941	2,053,000	0.30	0.75	3.00	8.00	—
1942	8,382,000	0.25	0.60	2.00	6.00	—
1943	5,135,000	0.25	0.60	2.00	6.00	—
1943 Proof	104	Value: 45.00				
1944	3,920,000	0.25	0.75	3.00	8.00	—
1944 Proof	150	Value: 35.00				
1945	2,357,000	0.25	0.60	2.50	7.00	—
1945 Proof	150	Value: 35.00				
1946	1,022,000	0.25	0.75	3.00	9.00	—
1946 Proof	150	Value: 35.00				
1947	258,000	1.00	3.00	6.00	17.50	—
1947 Proof	2,600	Value: 10.00				

KM# 33 1/2 PENNY
Bronze, 25 mm. **Ruler:** George VI **Subject:** Dromedaris (ship) **Obv:** Head left **Obv. Designer:** T.H. Paget **Rev:** Sailing ship **Rev. Designer:** G.T. Kruger-Gray

Date	Mintage	F	VF	XF	Unc	BU
1948	685,000	0.50	1.00	4.00	9.00	—
1948 Proof	1,120	Value: 15.00				
1949	1,850,000	0.25	0.50	1.75	4.00	—
1949 Proof	800	Value: 15.00				
1950	2,186,000	0.25	0.50	1.50	3.00	—
1950 Proof	500	Value: 6.00				
1951	3,746,000	0.25	0.50	1.25	3.00	—
1951 Proof	2,000	Value: 5.00				
1952	4,174,000	0.25	0.50	1.00	2.50	—
1952 Proof	1,550	Value: 4.00				

KM# 45 1/2 PENNY
5.6000 g., Bronze **Ruler:** Elizabeth II **Subject:** Dromedaris (ship) **Obv:** Laureate head right **Obv. Designer:** Mary Gillick **Rev:** Sailing ship **Rev. Designer:** G.T. Kruger-Gray

Date	Mintage	F	VF	XF	Unc	BU
1953	5,572,000	0.15	0.35	1.00	3.00	—
1953 Proof	5,000	Value: 4.00				
1954	101,000	2.00	4.00	7.50	12.50	—
1954 Proof	3,150	Value: 15.00				
1955	3,774,000	0.15	0.35	1.00	3.00	—
1955 Proof	2,850	Value: 4.00				
1956	1,305,000	0.15	0.35	1.00	3.00	—
1956 Proof	1,700	Value: 4.00				
1957	2,025,000	0.15	0.35	1.00	3.00	—
1957 Proof	1,130	Value: 4.00				
1958	2,171,000	0.15	0.35	1.00	2.50	—
1958 Proof	985	Value: 5.00				
1959	2,397,000	0.15	0.25	0.75	2.00	—
1959 Proof	900	Value: 6.00				
1960	2,552,000	0.15	0.25	0.75	2.00	—
1960 Proof	3,360	Value: 1.50				

KM# 14.1 PENNY
Bronze, 30.8 mm. **Ruler:** George V **Subject:** Dromedaris (ship) **Obv:** Crowned bust left **Obv. Designer:** E.B. MacKennal **Rev:** Sailing ship **Rev. Designer:** G.T. Kruger-Gray

Date	Mintage	F	VF	XF	Unc	BU
1923	91,000	3.00	7.00	17.50	35.00	—
1923 Proof	1,402	Value: 50.00				
1924	134,000	4.00	10.00	25.00	50.00	—

KM# 14.2 PENNY

Bronze, 30.8 mm. **Ruler:** George V **Subject:** Dromedaris (ship) **Obv:** Crowned bust left **Obv. Designer:** E.B. MacKennal **Rev:** Sailing ship **Rev. Designer:** G.T. Kruger-Gray

Date	Mintage	F	VF	XF	Unc	BU
1926	393,000	3.00	10.00	40.00	100	—
1926 Proof	16	Value: 600				
1927	285,000	3.00	10.00	40.00	90.00	—
1928	386,000	3.00	10.00	40.00	90.00	—
1929	1,093,000	1.00	5.00	15.00	35.00	—
1930	754,000	1.00	5.00	20.00	40.00	—
1930 Proof	14	Value: 600				

KM# 14.3 PENNY

9.5000 g., Bronze, 30.8 mm. **Ruler:** George V **Subject:** Dromedaris (ship) **Obv:** Crowned bust left **Obv. Designer:** E.B. MacKennal **Rev:** Sailing ship **Rev. Designer:** G.T. Kruger-Gray

Date	Mintage	F	VF	XF	Unc	BU
1931	284,000	1.00	5.00	17.50	40.00	—
1931 Proof	62	Value: 400				
1932	260,000	1.00	5.00	20.00	50.00	—
1932 Proof	12	Value: 800				
1933	225,000	2.00	10.00	30.00	45.00	—
1933 Proof	20	Value: 500				
1933	Inc. above	4.00	10.00	30.00	50.00	—
Note: Without star after date						
1934	2,089,999	0.50	1.50	8.00	22.50	—
1934 Proof	24	Value: 600				
1935	2,295,000	0.50	1.50	8.00	22.50	—
1935 Proof	20	Value: 600				
1936	1,819,000	0.35	1.00	5.00	20.00	—
1936 Proof	40	Value: 300				

KM# 25 PENNY

9.3000 g., Bronze, 30.8 mm. **Ruler:** George VI **Subject:** Dromedaris (ship) **Obv:** Head left **Rev:** Sailing ship **Rev. Designer:** G.T. Kruger-Gray

Date	Mintage	F	VF	XF	Unc	BU
1937	3,281,000	0.50	1.50	10.00	25.00	—
1937 Proof	116	Value: 75.00				
1938	1,840,000	0.50	1.50	8.00	30.00	—
1938 Proof	44	Value: 100				
1939	1,506,000	0.50	1.50	10.00	25.00	—
1939 Proof	30	Value: 175				
1940	3,592,000	0.35	1.00	4.00	10.00	—
1940	Inc. above	1.50	3.00	6.00	15.00	—
Note: Without star after date						
1941	7,871,000	0.25	0.75	2.50	7.00	—
1942	14,428,000	0.25	0.75	2.00	6.00	—
1942	Inc. above	3.00	6.00	12.50	30.00	—
Note: Without star after date						
1943	4,010,000	0.25	0.75	2.50	6.00	—
1943 Proof	104	Value: 55.00				
1944	6,425,000	0.25	0.75	2.50	7.00	—
1944 Proof	150	Value: 45.00				
1945	4,810,000	0.25	0.75	2.50	7.00	—
1945 Proof	150	Value: 45.00				
1946	2,605,000	0.25	0.75	3.00	8.00	—
1946 Proof	150	Value: 45.00				
1947	135,000	2.50	4.00	7.50	17.50	—
1947 Proof	2,600	Value: 7.00				

KM# 34.1 PENNY

Bronze, 30.8 mm. **Ruler:** George VI **Subject:** Dromedaris (ship) **Obv:** Head left **Obv. Designer:** T.H. Paget **Rev:** Sailing ship **Rev. Designer:** G.T. Kruger-Gray

Date	Mintage	F	VF	XF	Unc	BU
1948	2,398,000	0.25	0.75	2.50	6.00	—
1948 Proof	1,120	Value: 5.00				
1948	Inc. above	1.00	2.00	5.00	10.00	—
Note: Without star after date						
1949	3,634,000	0.25	0.75	2.00	6.00	—
1949 Proof	800	Value: 12.00				
1950	4,890,000	0.25	0.75	2.00	5.00	—
1950 Proof	500	Value: 10.00				

KM# 34.2 PENNY

Bronze, 30.8 mm. **Ruler:** George VI **Subject:** Dromedaris (ship) **Obv:** Head left **Obv. Designer:** T.H. Paget **Rev:** Sailing ship **Rev. Legend:** SUID AFRIKA-SOUTH AFRICA **Rev. Designer:** G.T. Kruger-Gray

Date	Mintage	F	VF	XF	Unc	BU
1951	3,787,000	0.25	0.75	1.50	4.00	—
1951 Proof	2,000	Value: 5.00				
1952	12,674,000	0.25	0.50	1.00	2.50	—
1952 Proof	16,000	Value: 4.00				

KM# 46 PENNY

9.6000 g., Bronze, 30.8 mm. **Ruler:** Elizabeth II **Subject:** Dromedaris (ship) **Obv:** Laureate head right **Obv. Designer:** Mary Gillick **Rev:** Sailing ship **Rev. Designer:** G.T. Kruger-Gray

Date	Mintage	F	VF	XF	Unc	BU
1953	5,491,000	0.20	0.35	0.75	2.00	—
1953 Proof	5,000	Value: 2.00				
1954	6,665,000	1.00	2.00	5.00	10.00	—
1954 Proof	3,150	Value: 15.00				
1955	6,508,000	0.20	0.35	0.75	3.00	—
1955 Proof	2,850	Value: 2.00				
1956	4,390,000	0.20	0.35	1.00	4.00	—
1956 Proof	1,700	Value: 3.00				
1957	3,973,000	0.20	0.35	0.75	3.00	—
1957 Proof	1,130	Value: 5.00				
1958	5,311,000	0.20	0.35	0.75	3.00	—
1958 Proof	985	Value: 6.00				
1959	5,066,000	0.20	0.35	0.75	2.00	—
1959 Proof	900	Value: 7.00				
1960	5,106,000	0.20	0.35	0.75	2.00	—
1960 Proof	3,360	Value: 2.00				

KM# 15A 3 PENCE

1.4100 g., 0.8000 Silver 0.0363 oz. ASW, 16.5 mm. **Ruler:** George V **Obv:** Crowned bust left **Obv. Designer:** E.B. MacKennal **Rev:** Value within wreath

Date	Mintage	F	VF	XF	Unc	BU
1923	302,000	4.00	8.00	20.00	45.00	—
1923 Proof	1,402	Value: 50.00				
1924	501,000	4.00	10.00	25.00	50.00	—
1925	—	10.00	35.00	200	475	—

KM# 15.1 3 PENCE

1.4100 g., 0.8000 Silver 0.0363 oz. ASW, 16.5 mm. **Ruler:** George V **Obv:** Crowned bust left **Obv. Designer:** E.B. MacKennal **Rev:** Protea flower in center, value as 3 PENCE **Rev. Designer:** G.T. Kruger-Gray

Date	Mintage	F	VF	XF	Unc	BU
1925	358,000	5.00	25.00	90.00	175	—
1926	1,572,000	1.00	3.50	20.00	50.00	—
1926 Proof	16	Value: 2,000				
1927	2,285,000	1.00	2.50	15.00	45.00	—
1928	919,000	1.50	3.50	20.00	50.00	—
1929	1,948,000	1.00	2.50	15.00	45.00	—
1930	981,000	1.00	3.50	20.00	50.00	—
1930 Proof	14	Value: 800				

KM# 15.2 3 PENCE

1.4100 g., 0.8000 Silver 0.0363 oz. ASW, 16.5 mm. **Ruler:** George V **Obv:** Crowned bust left **Obv. Designer:** E.B. MacKennal **Rev:** Protea flower in center, value as 3D **Rev. Designer:** G.T. Kruger-Gray

Date	Mintage	F	VF	XF	Unc	BU
1931	66	750	1,000	1,750	3,500	—
1931 Proof	62	Value: 3,500				
1932	2,622,000	1.00	2.50	15.00	30.00	—
1932 Proof	12	Value: 1,000				
1933	5,135,000	1.00	2.50	15.00	30.00	—
1933 Proof	20	Value: 1,000				
1934	2,357,000	1.00	2.50	15.00	30.00	—
1934 Proof	24	Value: 1,000				
1935	1,655,000	1.00	2.50	15.00	30.00	—
1935 Proof	20	Value: 1,000				
1936	1,095,000	1.00	2.50	15.00	35.00	—
1936 Proof	40	Value: 250				

KM# 26 3 PENCE

1.4100 g., 0.8000 Silver 0.0363 oz. ASW, 16.5 mm. **Ruler:** George VI **Obv:** Head left **Obv. Designer:** T.H. Paget **Rev:** Protea flower in center of designed bars shaped as a triangle **Rev. Designer:** G.T. Kruger-Gray

Date	Mintage	F	VF	XF	Unc	BU
1937	3,576,000	0.60	1.00	3.00	10.00	—
1937 Proof	116	Value: 80.00				
1938	2,394,000	0.60	1.50	7.00	20.00	—
1938 Proof	44	Value: 100				
1939	3,224,000	0.60	1.50	5.00	12.50	—
1939 Proof	30	Value: 250				
1940	4,887,000	0.60	1.00	3.00	12.50	—
1941	8,968,000	0.60	1.00	3.00	9.00	—
1942	8,055,999	0.60	1.00	3.00	9.00	—
1943	14,827,000	0.60	1.00	2.50	6.00	—
1943 Proof	104	Value: 70.00				
1944	3,331,000	0.60	1.00	3.00	9.00	—
1944 Proof	150	Value: 60.00				
1945/3	4,094,000	1.00	3.00	10.00	20.00	—
1945	Inc. above	0.60	1.00	3.00	9.00	—
1945 Proof	150	Value: 60.00				
1946	2,219,000	0.60	1.00	3.00	10.00	—
1946 Proof	150	Value: 65.00				
1947	1,127,000	0.60	1.00	2.50	8.00	—
1947 Proof	2,600	Value: 8.00				

KM# 35.1 3 PENCE

1.4100 g., 0.8000 Silver 0.0363 oz. ASW, 16.5 mm. **Ruler:** George VI **Obv:** Head left **Obv. Designer:** T.H. Paget **Rev:** Protea flower in center of designed bars shaped as a triangle **Rev. Designer:** G.T. Kruger-Gray

Date	Mintage	F	VF	XF	Unc	BU
1948	2,720,000	0.60	1.00	3.00	7.00	—
1948 Proof	1,120	Value: 5.00				
1949	1,904,000	0.60	1.00	3.00	7.00	—
1949 Proof	800	Value: 5.00				
1950	4,096,000	0.60	1.00	2.50	5.00	—
1950 Proof	500	Value: 7.00				

KM# 35.2 3 PENCE
1.4100 g., 0.5000 Silver 0.0227 oz. ASW, 16.5 mm. **Ruler:** George VI **Obv:** Head left **Obv. Designer:** T.H. Paget **Rev:** Protea flower in center of designed bars shaped as a triangle **Rev. Designer:** G.T. Kruger-Gray **Note:** Many varieties exist of George VI 3 Pence.

Date	Mintage	F	VF	XF	Unc	BU
1951	6,323,000	BV	0.50	1.00	3.00	—
1951 Proof	2,000	Value: 4.00				
1952	13,057,000	BV	0.50	1.00	2.00	—
1952 Proof	16,000	Value: 2.00				

KM# 47 3 PENCE
1.4100 g., 0.5000 Silver 0.0227 oz. ASW, 16.5 mm. **Ruler:** Elizabeth II **Obv:** Laureate head right **Obv. Designer:** Mark Gillick **Rev:** Protea flower in center of designed bars shaped as a triangle **Rev. Designer:** G.T. Kruger-Gray

Date	Mintage	F	VF	XF	Unc	BU
1953	5,483,000	BV	0.50	1.00	3.00	—
1953 Proof	5,000	Value: 3.00				
1954	3,898,000	BV	0.50	1.00	3.50	—
1954 Proof	3,150	Value: 4.00				
1955	4,720,000	BV	0.50	1.00	3.00	—
1955 Proof	2,850	Value: 3.00				
1956	6,189,000	BV	0.50	1.00	3.00	—
1956 Proof	1,700	Value: 4.00				
1957	1,893,000	BV	0.50	1.00	3.00	—
1957 Proof	1,130	Value: 5.00				
1958	3,227,000	BV	0.50	1.00	3.00	—
1958 Proof	985	Value: 6.00				
1959	2,552,000	BV	0.50	1.00	2.00	—
1959 Proof	900	Value: 7.00				
1959	Inc. above	2.00	3.00	5.00	10.00	—
Note: No K-G on reverse						
1960	18,000	1.00	2.50	4.00	7.00	—
1960 Proof	3,360	Value: 3.00				

KM# 16A 6 PENCE
2.8300 g., 0.8000 Silver 0.0728 oz. ASW, 19.5 mm. **Ruler:** George V **Obv:** Crowned bust left **Obv. Designer:** E.B. MacKennal **Rev:** Value within wreath

Date	Mintage	F	VF	XF	Unc	BU
1923	208,000	4.00	15.00	35.00	80.00	—
1923 Proof	1,402	Value: 80.00				
1924	326,000	3.50	12.50	30.00	70.00	—

KM# 16.1 6 PENCE
2.8300 g., 0.8000 Silver 0.0728 oz. ASW, 19.5 mm. **Ruler:** George V **Obv:** Crowned bust left **Obv. Designer:** E.B. MacKennal **Rev:** Protea flower in center, value as 6 PENCE **Rev. Designer:** G.T. Kruger-Gray

Date	Mintage	F	VF	XF	Unc	BU
1925	79,000	5.00	15.00	55.00	125	—
1926	722,000	2.00	10.00	45.00	100	—
1926 Proof	16	Value: 3,000				
1927	1,548,000	1.50	4.00	25.00	50.00	—
1929	784,000	2.00	8.00	30.00	60.00	—
1930	448,000	2.00	8.00	35.00	70.00	—
1930 Proof	14	Value: 1,000				

KM# 16.2 6 PENCE
2.8300 g., 0.8000 Silver 0.0728 oz. ASW, 19.5 mm. **Ruler:** George V **Obv:** Crowned bust left **Obv. Designer:** E.B. MacKennal **Rev:** Protea flower in center, value as 6D **Rev. Designer:** G.T. Kruger-Gray

Date	Mintage	F	VF	XF	Unc	BU
1931	4,743	75.00	150	250	550	—
1931 Proof	62	Value: 1,000				
1932	1,525,000	1.50	5.00	17.50	35.00	—
1932 Proof	12	Value: 1,200				
1933	2,819,000	1.50	5.00	17.50	35.00	—
1933 Proof	20	Value: 1,200				
1934	1,519,000	1.50	7.00	20.00	40.00	—
1934 Proof	24	Value: 1,200				
1935	573,000	2.00	8.00	30.00	100	—
1935 Proof	20	Value: 1,200				
1936	627,000	1.50	7.00	20.00	40.00	—
1936 Proof	40	Value: 275				

KM# 27 6 PENCE
2.8300 g., 0.8000 Silver 0.0728 oz. ASW, 19.5 mm. **Ruler:** George VI **Obv:** Head left **Obv. Designer:** T.H. Paget **Rev:** Protea flower in center of designed bars **Rev. Designer:** G.T. Kruger-Gray

Date	Mintage	F	VF	XF	Unc	BU
1937	1,696,000	1.20	2.00	7.00	17.50	—
1937 Proof	116	Value: 90.00				
1938	1,725,000	1.20	2.00	7.00	17.50	—
1938 Proof	44	Value: 125				
1939 Proof	30	Value: 3,750				
1940	1,629,000	1.20	1.50	5.00	10.00	—
1941	2,263,000	1.20	1.50	5.00	10.00	—
1942	4,936,000	BV	1.25	3.00	8.00	—
1943	3,776,000	BV	1.25	3.00	8.00	—
1943 Proof	104	Value: 85.00				
1944	228,000	2.00	7.00	15.00	30.00	—
1944 Proof	150	Value: 75.00				
1945	420,000	1.50	5.00	15.00	35.00	—
1945 Proof	150	Value: 75.00				
1946	290,000	1.50	6.00	15.00	30.00	—
1946 Proof	150	Value: 80.00				
1947	577,000	1.20	1.50	5.00	10.00	—
1947 Proof	2,600	Value: 10.00				

KM# 36.1 6 PENCE
2.8300 g., 0.8000 Silver 0.0728 oz. ASW, 19.5 mm. **Ruler:** George VI **Obv:** Head left **Obv. Designer:** T.H. Paget **Rev:** Protea flower in center of designed bars **Rev. Designer:** G.T. Kruger-Gray

Date	Mintage	F	VF	XF	Unc	BU
1948	2,266,000	BV	1.25	2.50	6.00	—
1948 Proof	1,120	Value: 10.00				
1949	196,000	3.00	7.50	15.00	30.00	—
1949 Proof	800	Value: 15.00				
1950	2,122,000	BV	1.20	2.00	5.00	—
1950 Proof	500	Value: 15.00				

KM# 36.2 6 PENCE
2.8300 g., 0.5000 Silver 0.0455 oz. ASW, 19.5 mm. **Ruler:** George VI **Obv:** Head left **Obv. Designer:** T.H. Paget **Rev:** Protea flower in center of designed bars **Rev. Designer:** G.T. Kruger-Gray

Date	Mintage	F	VF	XF	Unc	BU
1951	2,602,000	BV	1.00	2.00	4.00	—
1951 Proof	2,000	Value: 4.00				
1952	4,265,000	BV	0.75	1.25	3.00	—
1952 Proof	16,000	Value: 2.00				

KM# 48 6 PENCE
2.8300 g., 0.5000 Silver 0.0455 oz. ASW, 19 mm. **Ruler:** Elizabeth II **Obv:** Laureate head right **Obv. Designer:** Mary Gillick **Rev:** Protea flower in center of designed bars **Rev. Designer:** G.T. Kruger-Gray

Date	Mintage	F	VF	XF	Unc	BU
1953	2,496,000	BV	0.75	1.75	4.50	—
1953 Proof	5,000	Value: 3.00				
1954	2,196,000	BV	1.00	2.00	4.50	—
1954 Proof	3,150	Value: 4.00				
1955	1,969,000	BV	1.00	2.00	4.50	—
1955 Proof	2,850	Value: 3.00				
1956	1,772,000	BV	1.00	2.00	5.00	—
1956 Proof	1,700	Value: 4.00				
1957	3,288,000	BV	0.75	1.75	4.50	—
1957 Proof	1,130	Value: 6.00				
1958	1,172,000	BV	1.00	2.00	4.50	—
1958 Proof	985	Value: 6.00				
1959	261,000	1.00	2.00	4.00	12.00	—
1959 Proof	900	Value: 8.00				
1960	1,587,000	BV	0.75	1.25	2.50	—
1960 Proof	3,360	Value: 2.50				

KM# 17.1 SHILLING
5.6600 g., 0.8000 Silver 0.1456 oz. ASW, 23.5 mm. **Ruler:** George V **Obv:** Crowned bust left **Obv. Designer:** E.B. MacKennal **Rev:** Value as 1 SHILLING 1 **Rev. Designer:** G.T. Kruger-Gray

Date	Mintage	F	VF	XF	Unc	BU
1923	808,000	4.00	15.00	35.00	75.00	—
1923 Proof	1,402	Value: 80.00				
1924	1,269,000	3.50	12.50	30.00	75.00	—

KM# 17.2 SHILLING
5.6600 g., 0.8000 Silver 0.1456 oz. ASW, 23.5 mm. **Ruler:** George V **Obv:** Crowned bust left **Obv. Designer:** E.B. MacKennal **Rev:** Value as SHILLING **Rev. Designer:** G.T. Kruger-Gray

Date	Mintage	F	VF	XF	Unc	BU
1926	238,000	15.00	75.00	400	1,150	—
1926 Proof	16	Value: 3,000				
1927	488,000	10.00	25.00	150	375	—
1928	889,000	8.00	25.00	100	250	—
1929	926,000	5.00	10.00	30.00	175	—
1930	422,000	6.00	15.00	60.00	150	—
1930 Proof	14	Value: 1,000				

KM# 17.3 SHILLING
5.6600 g., 0.8000 Silver 0.1456 oz. ASW, 23.5 mm. **Ruler:** George V **Obv:** Crowned bust left **Obv. Designer:** E.B. MacKennal **Rev:** Standing female figure leaning on large anchor **Rev. Designer:** G.T. Kruger-Gray

Date	Mintage	F	VF	XF	Unc	BU
1931	6,541	80.00	165	375	600	—
1931 Proof	62	Value: 1,200				
1932	2,537,000	2.50	5.00	15.00	50.00	—
1932 Proof	12	Value: 1,400				
1933	1,463,000	3.50	7.00	30.00	70.00	—
1933 Proof	20	Value: 1,400				
1934	821,000	3.50	7.00	35.00	80.00	—
1934 Proof	24	Value: 1,400				
1935	685,000	4.00	8.50	45.00	90.00	—
1935 Proof	20	Value: 1,400				
1936	693,000	3.50	7.00	25.00	60.00	—
1936 Proof	40	Value: 500				

KM# 28 SHILLING
5.6600 g., 0.8000 Silver 0.1456 oz. ASW, 23.5 mm. **Ruler:** George VI **Obv:** Head left **Obv. Designer:** T.H. Paget **Rev:** Standing female figure leaning on large anchor **Rev. Designer:** G.T. Kruger-Gray

Date	Mintage	F	VF	XF	Unc	BU
1937	1,194,000	BV	3.00	10.00	25.00	—
1937 Proof	116	Value: 120				
1938	1,160,000	BV	3.00	10.00	25.00	—
1938 Proof	44	Value: 250				
1939 Proof	30	Value: 4,000				
1940	1,365,000	BV	2.50	7.50	17.50	—

Date	Mintage	F	VF	XF	Unc	BU
1941	1,826,000	BV	2.50	7.50	17.50	—
1942	3,867,000	BV	2.50	7.50	17.50	—
1943	4,187,999	BV	2.00	5.00	10.00	—
1943 Proof	104	Value: 165				
1944	48,000	8.00	20.00	40.00	70.00	—
1944 Proof	160	Value: 150				
1945	54,000	8.00	20.00	40.00	70.00	—
1945 Proof	150	Value: 150				
1946	27,000	10.00	30.00	60.00	120	—
1946 Proof	150	Value: 165				
1947	7,184	10.00	20.00	35.00	65.00	—
1947 Proof	2,600	Value: 70.00				

KM# 37.1 SHILLING

5.6600 g., 0.8000 Silver 0.1456 oz. ASW, 23.5 mm. **Ruler:** George VI **Obv:** Head left **Obv. Designer:** T.H. Paget **Rev:** Standing female figure leaning on large anchor **Rev. Designer:** G.T. Kruger-Gray

Date	Mintage	F	VF	XF	Unc	BU
1948	4,974	10.00	20.00	35.00	65.00	—
1948 Proof	1,120	Value: 70.00				
1949 Proof	800	Value: 225				
1950	1,704,000	BV	2.50	4.00	8.00	—
1950 Proof	500	Value: 40.00				

KM# 37.2 SHILLING

5.6600 g., 0.5000 Silver 0.0910 oz. ASW, 23.5 mm. **Ruler:** George VI **Obv:** Head left **Obv. Designer:** T.H. Paget **Rev:** Standing female figure, value as 1S **Rev. Designer:** G.T. Kruger-Gray

Date	Mintage	F	VF	XF	Unc	BU
1951	2,405,000	BV	1.50	4.00	8.00	—
1951 Proof	2,000	Value: 4.00				
1952	1,934,000	BV	1.50	3.50	7.00	—
1952 Proof	1,550	Value: 3.00				

KM# 49 SHILLING

5.6600 g., 0.5000 Silver 0.0910 oz. ASW, 23.5 mm. **Ruler:** Elizabeth II **Obv:** Laureate head right **Obv. Designer:** Mary Gillick **Rev:** Standing female figure leaning on large anchor **Rev. Designer:** G.T. Kruger-Gray

Date	Mintage	F	VF	XF	Unc	BU
1953	2,672,000	BV	1.50	2.50	5.50	—
1953 Proof	5,000	Value: 4.00				
1954	3,576,000	BV	1.50	2.50	5.50	—
1954 Proof	3,150	Value: 4.00				
1955	2,206,000	BV	1.50	2.50	5.50	—
1955 Proof	2,850	Value: 5.50				
1956	2,142,000	BV	1.50	2.50	6.00	—
1956 Proof	1,700	Value: 6.00				
1957	791,000	BV	2.50	5.00	10.00	—
1957 Proof	1,130	Value: 6.00				
1958	4,067,000	BV	1.50	2.50	5.50	—
1958 Proof	985	Value: 8.00				
1959	205,000	1.50	3.00	5.00	10.00	—
1959 Proof	900	Value: 10.00				
1960	2,187,000	BV	1.50	2.50	5.50	—
1960 Proof	3,360	Value: 3.00				

KM# 18 FLORIN

11.3100 g., 0.8000 Silver 0.2909 oz. ASW, 28.3 mm. **Ruler:** George V **Obv:** Crowned bust left **Obv. Designer:** E.B. MacKennal **Rev:** Shield divides date **Rev. Designer:** G.T. Kruger-Gray

Date	Mintage	F	VF	XF	Unc	BU
1923	695,000	6.00	20.00	40.00	80.00	—
1923 Proof	1,402	Value: 120				
1924	1,513,000	5.00	15.00	40.00	150	—
1925	50,000	125	350	1,000	2,200	—
1926	324,000	7.50	40.00	250	650	—
1927	399,000	7.50	35.00	200	600	—
1928	1,092,000	5.00	10.00	100	200	—
1929	648,000	6.00	15.00	120	225	—
1930	267,000	6.00	15.00	75.00	150	—
1930 Proof	14	Value: 1,200				

KM# 22 2 SHILLINGS

11.3100 g., 0.8000 Silver 0.2909 oz. ASW, 28.3 mm. **Ruler:** George V **Obv:** Crowned bust left **Obv. Designer:** E.B. MacKennal **Rev:** Shield divides date **Rev. Designer:** G.T. Kruger-Gray

Date	Mintage	F	VF	XF	Unc	BU
1931	383	250	450	700	1,200	—
1931 Proof	62	Value: 1,500				
1932	1,315,000	BV	6.00	18.00	75.00	—
1932 Proof	12	Value: 2,000				
1933	891,000	4.75	8.00	25.00	85.00	—
1933 Proof	20	Value: 2,000				
1934	559,000	4.75	8.00	25.00	60.00	—
1934 Proof	24	Value: 1,650				
1935	554,000	5.00	9.00	25.00	90.00	—
1935 Proof	20	Value: 1,650				
1936	669,000	4.75	8.00	25.00	65.00	—
1936 Proof	40	Value: 650				

KM# 29 2 SHILLINGS

11.3100 g., 0.8000 Silver 0.2909 oz. ASW, 28.3 mm. **Ruler:** George VI **Obv:** Head left **Obv. Designer:** T.H. Paget **Rev:** Shield divides date **Rev. Designer:** G.T. Kruger-Gray

Date	Mintage	F	VF	XF	Unc	BU
1937	1,495,000	BV	5.00	10.00	30.00	—
1937 Proof	116	Value: 150				
1938	214,000	5.00	10.00	20.00	50.00	—
1938 Proof	44	Value: 325				
1939	279,000	5.00	10.00	20.00	50.00	—
1939 Proof	30	Value: 1,000				
1940	2,600,000	BV	4.75	8.00	20.00	—
1941	1,764,000	BV	4.75	8.00	20.00	—
1942	2,847,000	—	BV	5.00	10.00	—
1943	3,125,000	—	BV	5.00	10.00	—
1943 Proof	104	Value: 135				
1944	225,000	4.75	7.00	17.50	40.00	—
1945	473,000	BV	6.00	15.00	35.00	—
1945 Proof	150	Value: 120				
1946	14,000	7.50	20.00	40.00	90.00	—
1946 Proof	150	Value: 135				
1947	2,892	15.00	25.00	40.00	85.00	—
1947 Proof	2,600	Value: 70.00				

KM# 38.1 2 SHILLINGS

11.3100 g., 0.8000 Silver 0.2909 oz. ASW, 28.3 mm. **Ruler:** George VI **Obv:** Head left **Obv. Designer:** T.H. Paget **Rev:** Shield divides date **Rev. Designer:** G.T. Kruger-Gray

Date	Mintage	F	VF	XF	Unc	BU
1948	6,773	10.00	15.00	30.00	70.00	—
1948 Proof	1,120	Value: 70.00				
1949	203,000	5.00	10.00	15.00	35.00	—
1949 Proof	800	Value: 60.00				
1950	4,945	20.00	40.00	80.00	140	—
1950 Proof	500	Value: 160				

KM# 38.2 2 SHILLINGS

11.3100 g., 0.5000 Silver 0.1818 oz. ASW, 28.3 mm. **Ruler:** George VI **Obv:** Head left **Obv. Designer:** T.H. Paget **Rev:** Shield, value as 2S **Rev. Designer:** G.T. Kruger-Gray

Date	Mintage	F	VF	XF	Unc	BU
1951	730,000	BV	3.50	5.00	10.00	—
1951 Proof	2,000	Value: 15.00				
1952	3,570,000	—	BV	3.50	6.50	—
1952 Proof	16,000	Value: 8.00				

KM# 50 2 SHILLINGS

11.3100 g., 0.5000 Silver 0.1818 oz. ASW, 28.3 mm. **Ruler:** Elizabeth II **Obv:** Laureate head right **Obv. Designer:** Mary Gillick **Rev:** Shield **Rev. Designer:** G.T. Kruger-Gray

Date	Mintage	F	VF	XF	Unc	BU
1953	3,274,000	BV	3.00	5.00	8.50	—
1953 Proof	5,000	Value: 6.50				
1954	5,866,000	BV	3.00	4.00	7.00	—
1954 Proof	3,150	Value: 6.50				
1955	3,745,000	BV	3.00	4.00	7.50	—
1955 Proof	2,850	Value: 6.50				
1956	2,549,000	BV	3.00	5.00	9.00	—
1956 Proof	1,700	Value: 7.50				
1957	2,507,000	BV	3.00	5.00	10.00	—
1957 Proof	1,130	Value: 7.50				
1958	2,821,000	BV	3.00	5.00	10.00	—
1958 Proof	985	Value: 15.00				
1959	1,219,000	BV	3.00	5.00	10.00	—
1959 Proof	900	Value: 20.00				
1960	1,951,000	BV	3.00	4.00	6.00	—
1960 Proof	3,360	Value: 4.00				

KM# 19.1 2-1/2 SHILLINGS

14.1400 g., 0.8000 Silver 0.3637 oz. ASW, 32.3 mm. **Ruler:** George V **Obv:** Crowned bust left **Obv. Designer:** E.B. MacKennal **Rev:** Value as 2-1/2 SHILLINGS 2-1/2 **Rev. Legend:** ZUID-AFRIKA **Rev. Designer:** G.T. Kruger-Gray

Date	Mintage	F	VF	XF	Unc	BU
1923	1,227,000	6.00	15.00	35.00	70.00	—
1923 Proof	1,402	Value: 125				
1924	2,556,000	BV	10.00	50.00	120	—
1925	460,000	9.00	30.00	180	600	—

KM# 19.2 2-1/2 SHILLINGS
14.1400 g., 0.8000 Silver 0.3637 oz. ASW, 32.3 mm. **Ruler:** George V **Obv:** Crowned bust left **Obv. Designer:** E.B. MacKennal **Rev:** Value as 2-1/2 SHILLINGS **Rev. Designer:** G.T. Kruger-Gray

Date	Mintage	F	VF	XF	Unc	BU
1926	205,000	10.00	40.00	250	650	—
1926 Proof	16	Value: 4,000				
1927	194,000	10.00	40.00	350	850	—
1928	984,000	6.50	25.00	125	325	—
1929	617,000	6.50	25.00	175	350	—
1930	324,000	6.50	15.00	100	250	—
1930 Proof	14	Value: 1,650				

KM# 19.3 2-1/2 SHILLINGS
14.1400 g., 0.8000 Silver 0.3637 oz. ASW, 32.3 mm. **Ruler:** George V **Obv:** Crowned bust left **Obv. Designer:** E.B. MacKennal **Rev:** Crowned shield divides date **Rev. Legend:** SUID. AFRIKA **Rev. Designer:** G.T. Kruger-Gray

Date	Mintage	F	VF	XF	Unc	BU
1931	790	225	450	700	1,300	—
1931 Proof	62	Value: 1,800				
1932	1,028,999	6.00	8.00	22.50	85.00	—
1932 Proof	12	Value: 2,400				
1933	136,000	9.00	40.00	185	300	—
1933 Proof	20	Value: 2,400				
1934	416,000	6.00	9.00	30.00	100	—
1934 Proof	24	Value: 1,650				
1935	345,000	6.50	12.50	32.50	125	—
1935 Proof	20	Value: 1,650				
1936	553,000	6.00	8.50	25.00	90.00	—
1936 Proof	40	Value: 800				

KM# 30 2-1/2 SHILLINGS
14.1400 g., 0.8000 Silver 0.3637 oz. ASW, 32.3 mm. **Ruler:** George VI **Obv:** Head left **Obv. Designer:** T.H. Paget **Rev:** Crowned shield divides date

Date	Mintage	F	VF	XF	Unc	BU
1937	1,154,000	BV	6.00	15.00	32.50	—
1937 Proof	116	Value: 175				
1938	534,000	6.00	8.00	20.00	60.00	—
1938 Proof	44	Value: 400				
1939	133,000	7.00	15.00	40.00	80.00	—
1939 Proof	30	Value: 800				
1940	2,976,000	BV	6.00	8.00	20.00	—
1941	1,988,000	BV	6.00	8.00	20.00	—
1942	3,180,000	BV	6.00	8.00	20.00	—
1943	2,098,000	BV	6.00	8.00	20.00	—
1943 Proof	104	Value: 150				
1944	1,360,000	BV	6.50	10.00	25.00	—
1944 Proof	150	Value: 130				
1945	183,000	BV	8.00	25.00	60.00	—
1945 Proof	150	Value: 130				
1946	11,000	15.00	30.00	50.00	90.00	—
1946 Proof	150	Value: 150				
1947	3,582	20.00	35.00	60.00	100	—
1947 Proof	2,600	Value: 110				

KM# 39.1 2-1/2 SHILLINGS
14.1400 g., 0.8000 Silver 0.3637 oz. ASW, 32.3 mm. **Ruler:** George VI **Obv:** Head left **Obv. Designer:** T.H. Paget **Rev:** Crowned shield divides date

Date	Mintage	F	VF	XF	Unc	BU
1948	1,600	25.00	45.00	75.00	100	—
1948 Proof	1,120	Value: 110				
1949	1,891	25.00	45.00	75.00	110	—
1949 Proof	800	Value: 120				
1950	5,076	25.00	45.00	75.00	140	—
1950 Proof	500	Value: 200				

KM# 39.2 2-1/2 SHILLINGS
14.1400 g., 0.5000 Silver 0.2273 oz. ASW, 32.3 mm. **Ruler:** George VI **Obv:** Head left **Obv. Designer:** T.H. Paget **Rev:** Crowned shield, value as 2-1/2 S **Rev. Designer:** G.T. Kruger-Gray

Date	Mintage	F	VF	XF	Unc	BU
1951	783,000	3.75	4.50	6.00	15.00	—
1951 Proof	2,000	Value: 9.00				
1952	1,996,000	BV	3.75	4.50	8.50	—
1952 Proof	16,000	Value: 5.00				

KM# 51 2-1/2 SHILLINGS
14.1400 g., 0.5000 Silver 0.2273 oz. ASW, 32.3 mm. **Ruler:** Elizabeth II **Obv:** Laureate head right **Obv. Designer:** Mary Gillick **Rev:** Crowned shield **Rev. Designer:** G.T. Kruger-Gray

Date	Mintage	F	VF	XF	Unc	BU
1953	2,513,000	BV	3.75	4.50	8.50	—
1953 Proof	6,000	Value: 6.00				
1954	4,249,000	BV	3.75	4.50	8.50	—
1954 Proof	3,150	Value: 7.50				
1955	3,863,000	BV	3.75	4.50	8.50	—
1955 Proof	2,850	Value: 7.50				
1956	2,437,000	BV	3.75	4.50	8.50	—
1956 Proof	1,700	Value: 8.50				
1957	2,137,000	BV	3.75	4.50	8.50	—
1957 Proof	1,130	Value: 8.50				
1958	2,260,000	BV	3.75	4.50	9.00	—
1958 Proof	985	Value: 14.00				
1959	46,000	3.75	4.50	7.00	12.50	—
1959 Proof	900	Value: 18.00				
1960	12,000	3.75	5.00	7.50	12.50	—
1960 Proof	3,360	Value: 5.00				

KM# 31 5 SHILLINGS
28.2800 g., 0.8000 Silver 0.7273 oz. ASW, 38.8 mm. **Ruler:** George VI **Subject:** Royal Visit **Obv:** Head left **Obv. Designer:** T.H. Paget **Rev:** Springbok **Rev. Designer:** Coert L. Steynberg

Date	Mintage	F	VF	XF	Unc	BU
1947	300,000	BV	12.50	15.00	20.00	—
1947 Proof	5,600	Value: 45.00				

KM# 40.1 5 SHILLINGS
28.2800 g., 0.8000 Silver 0.7273 oz. ASW, 38.8 mm. **Ruler:** George VI **Obv:** Head left **Obv. Designer:** T.H. Paget **Rev:** Springbok **Rev. Designer:** Coert L. Steynberg

Date	Mintage	F	VF	XF	Unc	BU
1948	780,000	—	BV	13.50	20.00	—
1948 Prooflike	1,000	—	—	—	22.50	—
1948 Proof	1,120	Value: 30.00				
1949	535,000	—	BV	13.50	20.00	—
1949 Prooflike	2,000	—	—	—	35.00	—
1949 Proof	800	Value: 50.00				
1950	83,000	BV	15.00	17.50	25.00	—
1950 Prooflike	1,200	—	—	—	60.00	—
1950 Proof	500	Value: 75.00				

KM# 40.2 5 SHILLINGS
28.2800 g., 0.5000 Silver 0.4546 oz. ASW, 38.8 mm. **Ruler:** George VI **Obv:** Head left **Obv. Designer:** T.H. Paget **Rev:** Springbok **Rev. Designer:** Coert L. Steynberg

Date	Mintage	F	VF	XF	Unc	BU
1951	363,000	BV	7.50	10.00	18.00	—
1951 Prooflike	1,483	—	—	—	25.00	—
1951 Proof	2,000	Value: 35.00				

KM# 41 5 SHILLINGS

28.2800 g., 0.5000 Silver 0.4546 oz. ASW, 38.8 mm. **Ruler:** George VI **Subject:** 300th Anniversary - Founding of Capetown **Obv:** Head left **Obv. Designer:** T.H. Paget **Rev:** Schooner in harbor **Rev. Designer:** Marion Walgate **Edge:** Reeded

Date	Mintage	F	VF	XF	Unc	BU
ND(1952)	1,698,000	BV	7.50	9.00	12.00	—
ND(1952) Prooflike	12,000	—	—	—	13.50	—
ND(1952) Proof	16,000	Value: 16.50				

KM# 52 5 SHILLINGS

28.2800 g., 0.5000 Silver 0.4546 oz. ASW, 38.8 mm. **Ruler:** Elizabeth II **Obv:** Laureate head right **Obv. Designer:** Mary Gillick **Rev:** Springbok **Rev. Designer:** Coert L. Steynberg

Date	Mintage	F	VF	XF	Unc	BU
1953	250,000	BV	7.50	10.00	16.00	—
1953 Prooflike	8,000	—	—	—	18.00	—
1953 Proof	5,000	Value: 22.00				
1953 Matte Proof	—	Value: 700				
1954	10,000	BV	8.50	12.50	20.00	—
1954 Prooflike	3,890	—	—	—	22.50	—
1954 Proof	3,150	Value: 25.00				
1955	40,000	BV	7.50	10.00	16.00	—
1955 Prooflike	2,230	—	—	—	20.00	—
1955 Proof	2,850	Value: 22.50				
1956	100,000	BV	7.00	9.00	12.50	—
1956 Prooflike	2,200	—	—	—	20.00	—
1956 Proof	1,700	Value: 25.00				
1957	154,000	BV	7.00	9.00	12.50	—
1957 Prooflike	1,600	—	—	—	25.00	—
1957 Proof	1,130	Value: 30.00				
1958	233,000	BV	7.00	9.00	12.50	—
1958 Prooflike	1,500	—	—	—	25.00	—
1958 Proof	985	Value: 30.00				
1959	2,989	20.00	35.00	65.00	100	—
1959 Prooflike	2,200	—	—	—	110	—
1959 Proof	950	Value: 120				

KM# 55 5 SHILLINGS

28.2800 g., 0.5000 Silver 0.4546 oz. ASW, 38.8 mm. **Ruler:** Elizabeth II **Subject:** 50th Anniversary - South African Union **Obv:** Shield **Obv. Designer:** G.T. Kruger-Gray **Rev:** Building and ship divides dates **Rev. Designer:** Hilda Mason **Edge:** Reeded **Note:** Many varieties exist of letters HM below building.

Date	Mintage	F	VF	XF	Unc	BU
1960	396,000	BV	7.00	8.50	11.50	—
1960 Prooflike	22,000	—	—	—	13.50	—
1960 Proof	3,360	Value: 16.50				

KM# 20 1/2 SOVEREIGN

3.9940 g., 0.9170 Gold 0.1177 oz. AGW **Ruler:** George V **Obv:** Head left **Rev:** Armored figure on rearing horse **Note:** British type with Pretoria mint mark: SA.

Date	Mintage	F	VF	XF	Unc	BU
1923 Proof	655	Value: 525				
1925	947,000	—	—	BV	150	—
1926	809,000	—	—	BV	150	—

KM# 21 SOVEREIGN

7.9881 g., 0.9170 Gold 0.2355 oz. AGW **Ruler:** George V **Obv:** Head left **Rev:** Armored figure on rearing horse **Note:** British type with Pretoria mint mark: SA.

Date	Mintage	F	VF	XF	Unc	BU
1923	64	BV	300	400	700	—
1923 Proof	655	Value: 650				
1924	3,184	700	1,350	2,250	4,500	—
1925	6,086,000	—	—	—	BV	230
1926	11,108,000	—	—	—	BV	230
1927	16,379,999	—	—	—	BV	230
1928	18,235,000	—	—	—	BV	230

KM# A22 SOVEREIGN

7.9881 g., 0.9170 Gold 0.2355 oz. AGW **Ruler:** George V **Obv:** Modified effigy, slightly smaller bust

Date	Mintage	F	VF	XF	Unc	BU
1929	12,024,000	—	—	—	BV	230
1930	10,028,000	—	—	—	BV	230
1931	8,512,000	—	—	—	BV	230
1932	1,067,000	—	—	—	BV	230

REPUBLIC

STANDARD COINAGE

100 Cents = 1 Rand

KM# 56 1/2 CENT

5.6000 g., Brass **Obv:** Oat sprig and berries divide birds **Obv. Designer:** G.T. Kruger-Gray **Rev:** Bust facing 1/4 right

Date	Mintage	F	VF	XF	Unc	BU
1961	39,189,000	—	0.15	0.25	1.25	2.00
1961 Proof	7,530	Value: 1.00				
1962	17,895,000	—	0.15	0.25	1.25	2.00
1962 Proof	3,844	Value: 1.00				
1963	11,611,000	—	0.15	0.25	2.00	2.50
1963 Proof	4,025	Value: 1.00				
1964	9,258,000	—	0.15	0.25	1.25	2.00
1964 Proof	16,000	Value: 1.00				

KM# 81 1/2 CENT

Bronze **Obv:** Arms with supporters **Rev:** Sparrows below value **Designer:** Tommy Sasseen **Note:** Bilingual.

Date	Mintage	F	VF	XF	Unc	BU
1970	Est. 57,721,000	—	0.10	0.25	0.50	—
Note: Coins dated 1970 were also struck for circulation in 1971, 1972 and 1973						
1970 Proof	10,000	Value: 2.50				
1971	8,000	—	—	—	2.50	—
1971 Proof	12,000	Value: 2.50				
1972	8,000	—	—	—	2.50	—
1972 Proof	12,000	Value: 2.50				
1973	20,000	—	0.10	0.20	2.50	—
1973 Proof	11,000	Value: 2.50				
1974	20,000	—	0.20	0.40	2.50	—
1974 Proof	15,000	Value: 2.50				
1975	20,000	—	0.10	0.20	2.50	—
1975 Proof	18,000	Value: 2.50				
1977	20,000	—	0.10	0.20	2.50	—
1977 Proof	19,000	Value: 2.50				
1978	18,000	—	0.10	0.20	2.50	—
1978 Proof	19,000	Value: 2.50				
1980 Proof	15,000	Value: 2.50				
1981 Proof	10,000	Value: 2.50				
1983 Proof	14,000	Value: 2.50				

KM# 90 1/2 CENT

Bronze **Obv:** President Fouche left **Rev:** Birds on branches **Note:** Similar to 1 Cent, KM#91.

Date	Mintage	F	VF	XF	Unc	BU
1976	20,000	—	—	—	1.00	—
1976 Proof	21,000	Value: 1.50				

KM# 97 1/2 CENT

Bronze **Obv:** Head of President Diederichs left **Rev:** Sparrows below value **Rev. Designer:** Tommy Sasseen

Date	Mintage	F	VF	XF	Unc	BU
1979	18,000	—	—	—	1.00	—
1979 Proof	17,000	Value: 1.50				

KM# 57 CENT

9.4200 g., Brass **Obv:** Covered wagon **Rev:** Bust 1/4 right

Date	Mintage	F	VF	XF	Unc	BU
1961	52,266,000	—	0.15	0.40	1.50	—
1961 Proof	7,530	Value: 0.75				
1962	21,929,000	—	0.15	0.40	1.50	—
1962 Proof	3,844	Value: 1.00				
1963	9,081,000	—	0.15	0.50	3.00	—
1963 Proof	4,025	Value: 1.00				

Date	Mintage	F	VF	XF	Unc	BU
1964	14,265,000	—	0.15	0.40	1.50	—
1964 Proof	16,000	Value: 2.00				

KM# 65.1 CENT

3.0000 g., Bronze, 19 mm. **Obv:** Head of Jan van Riebeeck right **Obv. Legend:** English legend **Rev:** Sparrows below value **Designer:** Tommy Sasseen

Date	Mintage	F	VF	XF	Unc	BU
1965	26,000	—	—	—	2.00	—
1965 Proof	25,000	Value: 2.50				
1966	50,157,000	—	—	0.10	0.50	—
1967	21,114,000	—	—	0.10	0.50	—
1969	10,196,000	—	—	0.10	0.50	—

KM# 65.2 CENT

3.0000 g., Bronze, 19 mm. **Obv:** Head of Jan van Riebeeck right **Obv. Legend:** Afrikaans legend **Rev:** Sparrows below value **Designer:** Tommy Sasseen

Date	Mintage	F	VF	XF	Unc	BU
1965	846	—	100	200	300	—
1965 Proof	185	Value: 350				
1966	50,157,000	—	—	0.10	0.50	—
1966 Proof	25,000	Value: 1.00				
1967	21,114,000	—	—	0.10	0.50	—
1967 Proof	25,000	Value: 1.00				
1969	10,196,000	—	—	0.10	0.50	—
1969 Proof	12,000	Value: 1.50				

KM# 74.1 CENT

3.0000 g., Bronze, 19 mm. **Subject:** President Charles Swart **Obv:** Head left **Obv. Legend:** English legend **Rev:** Sparrows below value **Designer:** Tommy Sasseen

Date	Mintage	F	VF	XF	Unc	BU
1968	6,000,000	—	—	0.10	0.50	—
1968 Proof	25,000	Value: 1.00				

KM# 74.2 CENT

3.0000 g., Bronze, 19 mm. **Subject:** President Charles Swart **Obv:** Head left **Obv. Legend:** Afrikaans legend **Rev:** Sparrows below value **Designer:** Tommy Sasseen

Date	Mintage	F	VF	XF	Unc	BU
1968	6,000,000	—	—	0.10	0.50	—

KM# 82 CENT

3.0000 g., Bronze, 19 mm. **Obv:** Arms with supporters **Obv. Legend:** Bilingual legend **Rev:** Sparrows below value **Designer:** Tommy Sasseen

Date	Mintage	F	VF	XF	Unc	BU
1970	37,072,000	—	—	—	0.30	0.50
1970 Proof	10,000	Value: 1.00				
1971	34,053,000	—	—	—	0.30	0.50
1971 Proof	12,000	Value: 1.00				
1972	35,662,000	—	—	—	0.30	0.50
1972 Proof	10,000	Value: 1.00				
1973	35,898,000	—	0.10	0.20	0.40	0.60
1973 Proof	11,000	Value: 1.00				
1974	54,940,000	—	—	—	0.25	0.50
1974 Proof	15,000	Value: 1.00				
1975	62,982,000	—	—	—	0.25	0.50
1975 Proof	18,000	Value: 1.00				
1977	72,444,000	—	—	—	0.25	0.50
1977 Proof	19,000	Value: 1.00				
1978	70,152,000	—	—	—	0.25	0.50

Date	Mintage	F	VF	XF	Unc	BU
1978 Proof	17,000	Value: 0.50				
1980	63,432,000	—	—	—	0.25	0.50
1980 Proof	15,000	Value: 0.50				
1981	63,444,000	—	—	—	0.25	0.50
1981 Proof	10,000	Value: 0.50				
1983	182,131,000	—	—	—	0.25	0.50
1983 Proof	14,000	Value: 0.50				
1984	107,155,000	—	—	—	0.25	0.50
1984 Proof	11,000	Value: 0.50				
1985	186,042,000	—	—	—	0.25	0.50
1985 Proof	9,859	Value: 0.50				
1986	169,734,000	—	—	—	0.25	0.50
1986 Proof	7,000	Value: 0.50				
1987	120,674,000	—	—	—	0.25	0.50
1987 Proof	6,781	Value: 0.50				
1988	240,272,000	—	—	—	0.25	0.50
1988 Proof	7,250	Value: 0.50				
1989	—	—	—	—	0.25	0.50
1989 Proof	—	Value: 0.50				

KM# 91 CENT

3.0000 g., Bronze, 19 mm. **Obv:** Head of President Fouche right **Rev:** Sparrows below value **Rev. Designer:** Tommy Sasseen

Date	Mintage	F	VF	XF	Unc	BU
1976	91,860,000	—	—	0.30	0.50	—
1976 Proof	21,000	Value: 0.75				

KM# 98 CENT

3.0000 g., Bronze, 19 mm. **Obv:** Head of President Diederichs left **Rev:** Sparrows below value **Rev. Designer:** Tommy Sasseen

Date	Mintage	F	VF	XF	Unc	BU
1979	63,432,000	—	—	0.30	0.50	—
1979 Proof	15,000	Value: 0.75				

KM# 109 CENT

3.0000 g., Bronze, 19 mm. **Obv:** Head of President Vorster 1/4 right **Rev:** Sparrows below value **Rev. Designer:** Tommy Sasseen

Date	Mintage	F	VF	XF	Unc	BU
1982	145,954,000	—	—	0.30	0.50	—
1982 Proof	12,000	Value: 0.75				

KM# 132 CENT

1.5000 g., Copper-Plated-Steel, 15 mm. **Obv:** Arms with supporters **Obv. Designer:** A.L. Sutherland **Rev:** Value divides sparrows **Rev. Designer:** W. Lumley

Date	Mintage	F	VF	XF	Unc	BU
1990	—	—	—	—	0.25	0.50
1990 Proof	—	Value: 0.50				
1991	—	—	—	—	0.25	0.50
1991 Proof	—	Value: 0.50				
1992	—	—	—	—	0.25	0.50
1992 Proof	—	Value: 0.50				
1993	—	—	—	—	0.25	0.50
1993 Proof	7,790	Value: 0.50				
1994	—	—	—	—	0.25	0.50
1994 Proof	5,804	Value: 0.50				
1995	—	—	—	—	0.25	0.50
1995 Proof	—	Value: 0.50				

KM# 158 CENT

1.5000 g., Copper-Plated-Steel, 15 mm. **Obv:** Arms with supporters **Obv. Legend:** Zulu legend **Obv. Designer:** A.L. Sutherland **Rev:** Value divides sparrows **Rev. Designer:** W. Lumley **Edge:** Plain

Date	Mintage	F	VF	XF	Unc	BU
1996	—	—	—	—	0.25	0.50
1996 Proof	10,000	Value: 0.50				

KM# 170 CENT

1.5000 g., Copper Plated Steel, 15 mm. **Obv:** Arms with supporters **Obv. Legend:** Ndebele legend **Obv. Designer:** A.L. Sutherland **Rev:** Value divides sparrows **Rev. Designer:** W. Lumley

Date	Mintage	F	VF	XF	Unc	BU
1997	—	—	—	—	0.25	0.50
1997 Proof	3,596	Value: 0.50				
1998	—	—	—	—	0.25	0.50
1998 Proof	—	Value: 0.50				
1999	—	—	—	—	0.25	0.50
1999 Proof	—	Value: 0.50				
2000	—	Value: 0.25				

KM# 221 CENT

1.5000 g., Copper Plated Steel, 15 mm. **Obv:** Crowned arms **Obv. Designer:** A.L. Sutherland **Rev:** Value divides sparrows **Rev. Designer:** W. Lumley **Edge:** Plain

Date	Mintage	F	VF	XF	Unc	BU
2000	—	—	—	—	0.35	0.50
2001	—	—	—	—	0.35	0.50

KM# 66.1 2 CENTS

4.0000 g., Bronze, 22.45 mm. **Obv:** English legend **Obv. Designer:** Tommy Sasseen **Rev:** Black Wildebeest

Date	Mintage	F	VF	XF	Unc	BU
1965	29,887,000	—	—	0.10	0.35	1.00
1966	9,267,000	—	—	0.10	0.40	1.00
1966 Proof	25,000	Value: 0.50				
1967	11,862,000	—	—	0.10	0.35	1.00
1967 Proof	25,000	Value: 0.50				
1969	5,817,000	—	—	0.10	0.40	1.00
1969 Proof	12,000	Value: 0.50				

KM# 66.2 2 CENTS

4.0000 g., Bronze, 22.45 mm. **Obv:** Afrikaans legend **Obv. Designer:** Tommy Sasseen **Rev:** Black Wildebeest

Date	Mintage	F	VF	XF	Unc	BU
1965	29,887,000	—	—	0.10	0.35	1.00
1965 Proof	25,000	Value: 0.50				
1966	9,267,000	—	—	0.10	0.35	1.00
1967	11,862,000	—	—	0.10	0.35	1.00
1969	5,817,000	—	—	0.10	0.40	1.00

KM# 75.1 2 CENTS

4.0000 g., Bronze, 22.45 mm. **Obv:** Head of President Charles Swart left **Obv. Legend:** English legend **Obv. Designer:** Tommy Sasseen **Rev:** Wildebeest

Date	Mintage	F	VF	XF	Unc	BU
1968	5,500,000	—	—	0.20	0.50	1.00

KM# 75.2 2 CENTS

4.0000 g., Bronze, 22.45 mm. **Obv:** Head of President Charles Swart left **Obv. Legend:** Afrikaans legend **Obv. Designer:** Tommy Sasseen **Rev:** Wildebeest

Date	Mintage	F	VF	XF	Unc	BU
1968	5,525,000	—	—	0.20	0.50	1.00
1968 Proof	25,000	Value: 1.00				

KM# 83 2 CENTS

4.0000 g., Bronze, 22.45 mm. **Obv:** Arms with supporters **Obv. Legend:** Bilingual legend **Obv. Designer:** Tommy Sasseen **Rev:** Wildebeest

Date	Mintage	F	VF	XF	Unc	BU
1970	35,217,000	—	—	0.15	0.50	1.00
1970 Proof	10,000	Value: 0.75				
1971	24,093,000	—	—	0.15	0.50	1.00
1971 Proof	12,000	Value: 0.75				
1972	7,304,000	—	—	0.15	0.50	1.00
1972 Proof	10,000	Value: 0.75				
1973	18,685,000	—	—	0.15	0.50	1.00
1973 Proof	11,000	Value: 0.75				
1974	25,301,000	—	—	0.15	0.50	1.00
1974 Proof	15,000	Value: 0.75				
1975	24,982,000	—	—	0.15	0.50	1.00
1975 Proof	18,000	Value: 0.75				
1977	45,116,000	—	—	0.15	0.50	1.00
1977 Proof	19,000	Value: 0.75				
1978	50,527,000	—	—	0.15	0.50	1.00
1978 Proof	17,000	Value: 0.75				
1980	37,795,000	—	—	0.15	0.50	1.00
1980 Proof	15,000	Value: 0.75				
1981	79,350,000	—	—	0.15	0.50	1.00
1981 Proof	10,000	Value: 0.75				
1983	112,575,000	—	—	0.15	0.50	1.00
1983 Proof	14,000	Value: 0.75				
1984	101,497,000	—	—	0.15	0.50	1.00
1984 Proof	11,000	Value: 0.75				
1985	102,708,000	—	—	0.15	0.50	1.00
1985 Proof	9,859	Value: 0.75				
1986	683,294,000	—	—	0.15	0.50	1.00
1986 Proof	7,100	Value: 0.75				
1987	104,981,000	—	—	0.15	0.50	1.00
1987 Proof	6,781	Value: 0.75				
1988	182,036,000	—	—	0.15	0.50	1.00
1988 Proof	7,250	Value: 0.75				
1989	—	—	—	0.15	0.50	1.00
1989 Proof	—	Value: 0.75				
1990	215,192,000	—	—	0.15	0.50	1.00

KM# 92 2 CENTS

4.0000 g., Bronze, 22.45 mm. **Obv:** Head of President Fouche right **Rev:** Wildebeest

Date	Mintage	F	VF	XF	Unc	BU
1976	51,474,000	—	—	0.25	0.50	1.00
1976 Proof	21,000	Value: 0.75				

KM# 99 2 CENTS

4.0000 g., Bronze, 22.45 mm. **Obv:** Head of President Diederichs left **Rev:** Wildebeest

Date	Mintage	F	VF	XF	Unc	BU
1979	40,043,000	—	—	0.25	0.50	1.00
1979 Proof	15,000	Value: 0.75				

KM# 110 2 CENTS

4.0000 g., Bronze, 22.45 mm. **Obv:** Head of President Vorster 1/4 right **Rev:** Wildebeest

Date	Mintage	F	VF	XF	Unc	BU
1982	53,962,000	—	—	0.25	0.50	1.00
1982 Proof	12,000	Value: 0.75				

KM# 133 2 CENTS

3.0000 g., Copper-Plated-Steel, 18 mm. **Obv:** Arms with supporters **Rev:** Eagle with fish in talons divides value **Designer:** A.L. Sutherland

Date	Mintage	F	VF	XF	Unc	BU
1990	—	—	—	—	1.50	1.75
1990 Proof	—	Value: 2.00				
1991	—	—	—	—	1.50	1.75
1991 Proof	12,000	Value: 2.00				
1992	—	—	—	—	0.50	0.75
1992 Proof	—	Value: 2.00				
1993	—	—	—	—	0.50	0.75
1993 Proof	7,790	Value: 2.00				
1994	—	—	—	—	0.50	0.75
1994 Proof	5,804	Value: 2.00				
1995	—	—	—	—	0.50	0.75
1995 Proof	—	Value: 2.00				

KM# 159 2 CENTS

3.0000 g., Copper-Plated-Steel, 18 mm. **Obv:** Arms with supporters **Obv. Legend:** AFURIKA TSHIPEMBE, Venda legend **Rev:** Eagle with fish in talons divides value **Designer:** A.L. Sutherland

Date	Mintage	F	VF	XF	Unc	BU
1996	—	—	—	—	0.50	0.75
1996 Proof	—	Value: 1.00				
1997	—	—	—	—	0.50	0.75
1997 Proof	3,596	Value: 1.00				
1998	—	—	—	—	0.50	0.75
1998 Proof	—	Value: 1.00				
1999	—	—	—	—	0.50	0.75
1999 Proof	—	Value: 1.00				
2000	—	—	—	—	0.50	0.75

KM# 222 2 CENTS

3.0000 g., Copper Plated Steel, 18 mm. **Obv:** Crowned arms **Rev:** Eagle with fish in talons divides value **Edge:** Plain **Designer:** A.L. Sutherland

Date	Mintage	F	VF	XF	Unc	BU
2000	—	—	—	—	0.50	0.75
2001	—	—	—	—	0.50	0.75

KM# 58 2-1/2 CENTS

1.4100 g., 0.5000 Silver 0.0227 oz. ASW **Obv:** Protea flower **Rev:** Bust facing

Date	Mintage	F	VF	XF	Unc	BU
1961	292,000	—	0.50	1.00	2.00	—
1961 Proof	7,530	Value: 4.00				
1962	8,745	—	2.00	4.00	8.00	—
1962 Proof	3,844	Value: 8.00				
1963	33,000	—	1.50	2.50	4.00	—
1963 Proof	4,025	Value: 6.00				
1964	14,000	—	2.00	4.00	6.00	—
1964 Proof	16,000	Value: 4.00				

KM# 59 5 CENTS

2.8300 g., 0.5000 Silver 0.0455 oz. ASW, 17.35 mm. **Obv:** Protea flower in center of designed bars **Rev:** Bust 1/4 right

Date	Mintage	F	VF	XF	Unc	BU
1961	1,479,000	—	BV	1.00	2.00	—
1961 Proof	7,530	Value: 2.50				
1962	4,187,999	—	BV	0.85	1.50	—
1962 Proof	3,844	Value: 3.00				
1963	8,054,000	—	BV	0.75	1.25	—
1963 Proof	4,025	Value: 3.00				
1964	3,567,000	—	BV	0.75	1.25	—
1964 Proof	16,000	Value: 1.50				

KM# 67.1 5 CENTS

2.5000 g., Nickel, 17.35 mm. **Obv:** English legend **Rev:** Blue Crane **Designer:** Tommy Sasseen

Date	Mintage	F	VF	XF	Unc	BU
1965	32,689,999	—	—	0.15	0.75	1.25
1965 Proof	25,000	Value: 0.80				
1966	4,101,000	—	—	0.15	0.75	1.25
1967	4,590,000	—	—	0.15	0.75	1.25
1969	5,020,000	—	—	0.15	0.75	1.25

KM# 67.2 5 CENTS

2.5000 g., Nickel, 17.35 mm. **Obv:** Afrikaans legend **Rev:** Blue Crane **Designer:** Tommy Sasseen

Date	Mintage	F	VF	XF	Unc	BU
1965	32,689,999	—	—	0.15	0.75	1.25
1966	4,101,000	—	—	0.15	0.75	1.25
1966 Proof	25,000	Value: 0.80				
1967	4,590,000	—	—	0.15	0.75	1.25
1967 Proof	25,000	Value: 0.80				
1969	5,020,000	—	—	0.15	0.75	1.25
1969 Proof	12,000	Value: 0.80				

KM# 76.1 5 CENTS

2.5000 g., Nickel, 17.35 mm. **Subject:** President Charles Swart **Obv:** Head left **Obv. Legend:** English legend **Rev:** Blue Crane **Designer:** Tommy Sasseen

Date	Mintage	F	VF	XF	Unc	BU
1968	6,000,000	—	—	0.15	0.75	1.00
1968 Proof	25,000	Value: 0.80				

KM# 76.2 5 CENTS

2.5000 g., Nickel, 17.35 mm. **Subject:** President Charles Swart **Obv:** Afrikaans legend **Rev:** Blue Crane **Designer:** Tommy Sasseen

Date	Mintage	F	VF	XF	Unc	BU
1968	6,000,000	—	—	0.15	0.75	1.00

KM# 84 5 CENTS

2.5000 g., Nickel, 17.35 mm. **Obv:** Arms with supporters **Obv. Legend:** Bilingual legend **Rev:** Blue Crane

Date	Mintage	F	VF	XF	Unc	BU
1970	6,652,000	—	—	0.15	0.75	1.00
1970 Proof	10,000	Value: 0.80				
1971	20,329,000	—	—	0.15	0.75	1.00

Date	Mintage	F	VF	XF	Unc	BU
1971 Proof	12,000	Value: 0.80				
1972	3,117,000	—	—	0.15	0.75	1.00
1972 Proof	9,000	Value: 0.80				
1973	17,092,000	—	—	0.15	0.75	1.00
1973 Proof	11,000	Value: 0.80				
1974	19,978,000	—	—	0.15	0.75	1.00
1974 Proof	15,000	Value: 0.80				
1975	21,982,000	—	—	0.15	0.75	1.00
1975 Proof	18,000	Value: 0.80				
1977	51,729,000	—	—	0.15	0.75	1.00
1977 Proof	19,000	Value: 0.80				
1978	30,050,000	—	—	0.15	0.75	1.00
1978 Proof	19,000	Value: 0.80				
1980	46,665,000	—	—	0.15	0.75	1.00
1980 Proof	15,000	Value: 0.80				
1981	40,351,000	—	—	0.15	0.75	1.00
1981 Proof	10,000	Value: 0.80				
1983	57,487,000	—	—	0.15	0.75	1.00
1983 Proof	14,000	Value: 0.80				
1984	67,345,000	—	—	0.15	0.75	1.00
1984 Proof	11,000	Value: 0.80				
1985	57,167,000	—	—	0.15	0.75	1.00
1985 Proof	9,859	Value: 0.80				
1986	54,226,000	—	—	0.15	0.75	1.00
1986 Proof	7,100	Value: 0.80				
1987	42,786,000	—	—	0.15	0.75	1.00
1987 Proof	5,297	Value: 0.80				
1988	110,164,000	—	—	0.15	0.75	1.00
1988 Proof	7,250	Value: 0.80				
1989	35,540,000	—	—	0.15	0.75	1.00
1989 Proof	Inc. above	Value: 1.50				

KM# 93 5 CENTS

2.5000 g., Nickel, 17.35 mm. **Obv:** Head of President Fouche right **Rev:** Blue Crane **Rev. Designer:** Tommy Sasseen

Date	Mintage	F	VF	XF	Unc	BU
1976	48,972,000	—	—	0.30	0.75	1.00
1976 Proof	19,000	Value: 1.50				

KM# 100 5 CENTS

2.5000 g., Nickel, 17.35 mm. **Obv:** Head of President Diederichs left **Rev:** Blue Crane

Date	Mintage	F	VF	XF	Unc	BU
1979	17,533,000	—	—	0.30	0.75	1.00
1979 Proof	17,000	Value: 1.50				

KM# 111 5 CENTS

2.5000 g., Nickel, 17.35 mm. **Obv:** Head of President Vorster 1/4 right **Rev:** Blue Crane **Rev. Designer:** Tommy Sasseen

Date	Mintage	F	VF	XF	Unc	BU
1982	47,236,000	—	—	0.30	0.75	1.00
1982 Proof	12,000	Value: 1.50				

KM# 134 5 CENTS

4.5000 g., Copper-Plated-Steel, 21 mm. **Obv:** Arms with supporters **Obv. Designer:** A.L. Sutherland **Rev:** Blue crane **Rev. Designer:** G. Richard

Date	Mintage	F	VF	XF	Unc	BU
1990	—	—	—	0.15	1.00	—
1990 Proof	—	Value: 1.25				
1991	—	—	—	0.15	1.00	—
1991 Proof	12,000	Value: 1.25				
1992	—	—	—	0.15	1.00	—
1992 Proof	—	Value: 1.25				
1993	—	—	—	0.15	1.00	—
1993 Proof	7,790	Value: 1.25				
1994	—	—	—	0.15	1.00	—
1994 Proof	5,804	Value: 1.25				
1995	—	—	—	0.15	1.00	—
1995 Proof	—	Value: 1.25				

KM# 160 5 CENTS

4.5000 g., Copper Plated Steel, 21 mm. **Obv:** Arms with supporters **Obv. Legend:** AFRIKA DZONGA, Tsonga legend **Obv. Designer:** A.L. Sutherland **Rev:** Blue crane **Rev. Designer:** G. Richard

Date	Mintage	F	VF	XF	Unc	BU
1996	—	—	—	0.15	0.75	1.00
1996 Proof	—	Value: 1.25				
1997	—	—	—	0.15	0.75	1.00
1997 Proof	3,596	Value: 1.25				
1998	—	—	—	0.15	0.75	1.00
1998 Proof	—	Value: 1.50				
1999	—	—	—	0.15	0.75	1.00
1999 Proof	—	Value: 1.50				
2000	—	—	—	0.15	0.75	1.00

KM# 223 5 CENTS

4.4300 g., Copper Plated Steel, 21 mm. **Obv:** Crowned arms **Obv. Designer:** A.L. Sutherland **Rev:** Blue crane **Rev. Designer:** G. Richard **Edge:** Plain

Date	Mintage	F	VF	XF	Unc	BU
2000	—	—	—	—	0.50	1.00
2001	—	—	—	—	0.50	1.00

KM# 268 5 CENTS

4.5000 g., Copper Plated Steel, 21 mm. **Obv:** Crowned arms **Obv. Legend:** Ningizimu Afrika **Obv. Designer:** A.L. Sutherland **Rev:** Blue Crane and value **Rev. Designer:** G. Richard **Edge:** Plain **Note:** Change in legend.

Date	Mintage	F	VF	XF	Unc	BU
2002 Proof	—	Value: 2.00				
2002	—	—	—	—	0.50	1.00

KM# 324 5 CENTS

4.5000 g., Copper-Plated-Steel, 21 mm. **Obv:** Crowned arms **Obv. Legend:** Afrika-Dzonga **Rev:** Blue crane and denomination

Date	Mintage	F	VF	XF	Unc	BU
2003	—	—	—	—	0.50	1.00

KM# 325 5 CENTS

4.5000 g., Copper-Plated-Steel, 21 mm. **Obv:** Crowned arms **Obv. Legend:** South Africa **Rev:** Blue crane and denomination

Date	Mintage	F	VF	XF	Unc	BU
2004	—	—	—	—	0.50	1.00

KM# 291 5 CENTS

4.5000 g., Copper-Plated-Steel, 21 mm. **Obv:** Crowned arms **Obv. Legend:** Aforika Borwa **Rev:** Crane and value **Edge:** Plain

Date	Mintage	F	VF	XF	Unc	BU
2005	—	—	—	—	—	1.00

KM# 60 10 CENTS

5.6600 g., 0.5000 Silver 0.0910 oz. ASW **Obv:** Standing female figure leaning on large anchor **Rev:** Bust 1/4 right **Designer:** G.E. Kruger-Gray

Date	Mintage	F	VF	XF	Unc	BU
1961	1,136,000	—	BV	1.50	2.50	—
1961 Proof	7,530	Value: 2.50				
1962	2,447,000	—	BV	1.50	2.50	—
1962 Proof	3,844	Value: 3.50				
1963	3,327,000	—	BV	1.50	2.50	—
1963 Proof	4,025	Value: 3.50				
1964	4,152,999	—	BV	1.50	2.00	—
1964 Proof	16,000	Value: 2.50				

KM# 68.1 10 CENTS

4.0000 g., Nickel, 20.7 mm. **Obv:** Head of Jan van Riebeeck right **Rev:** Aloe plant and value **Designer:** Tommy Sasseen

Date	Mintage	F	VF	XF	Unc	BU
1965	29,210,000	—	—	0.10	0.35	—
1966	3,685,000	—	—	0.10	0.45	—
1966 Proof	25,000	Value: 0.60				
1967	50,000	—	—	—	1.00	—
1967 Proof	25,000	Value: 0.60				
1969	558,000	—	—	0.10	0.50	—
1969 Proof	12,000	Value: 1.00				

KM# 68.2 10 CENTS

4.0000 g., Nickel, 20.7 mm. **Obv:** Head of Jan van Riebeeck right **Rev:** Aloe plant and value **Designer:** Tommy Sasseen

Date	Mintage	F	VF	XF	Unc	BU
1965	29,210,000	—	—	0.10	0.35	—
1965 Proof	25,000	Value: 0.60				
1966	3,685,000	—	—	0.10	0.45	—
1967	50,000	—	—	—	1.00	—
1969	558,000	—	0.10	0.20	2.50	—

KM# 77.1 10 CENTS

4.0000 g., Nickel, 20.7 mm. **Obv:** Head of President Charles Swart left **Rev:** Aloe plant and value **Designer:** Tommy Sasseen

Date	Mintage	F	VF	XF	Unc	BU
1968	50,000	—	—	—	2.00	—

KM# 77.2 10 CENTS

4.0000 g., Nickel, 20.7 mm. **Obv:** Afrikaans legend **Rev:** Aloe plant and value **Designer:** Tommy Sasseen

Date	Mintage	F	VF	XF	Unc	BU
1968	50,000	—	—	—	1.50	—
1968 Proof	25,000	Value: 0.60				

KM# 85 10 CENTS

4.0000 g., Nickel, 20.7 mm. **Obv:** Arms with supporters **Rev:** Aloe plant and value **Designer:** Tommy Sasseen

Date	Mintage	F	VF	XF	Unc	BU
1970	7,598,000	—	—	0.10	0.35	—
1970 Proof	10,000	Value: 0.60				
1971	6,440,000	—	—	0.10	0.35	—
1971 Proof	12,000	Value: 0.60				
1972	10,028,000	—	—	0.10	0.35	—
1972 Proof	10,000	Value: 0.60				
1973	1,760,000	—	—	0.10	0.35	—
1973 Proof	11,000	Value: 0.60				
1974	9,897,000	—	—	0.10	0.35	—
1974 Proof	15,000	Value: 0.60				
1975	12,982,000	—	—	0.10	0.35	—
1975 Proof	18,000	Value: 0.60				
1977	28,851,000	—	—	0.10	0.35	—
1977 Proof	19,000	Value: 0.60				

Date	Mintage	F	VF	XF	Unc	BU
1978	25,008,000	—	—	0.10	0.35	—
1978 Proof	19,000	Value: 0.60				
1980	5,040,000	—	—	0.10	0.35	—
1980 Proof	15,000	Value: 0.60				
1981	9,604,000	—	—	0.10	0.35	—
1981 Proof	10,000	Value: 0.60				
1983	26,495,000	—	—	0.10	0.35	—
1983 Proof	14,000	Value: 0.60				
1984	35,465,000	—	—	0.10	0.35	—
1984 Proof	11,000	Value: 0.60				
1985	29,270,000	—	—	0.10	0.35	—
1985 Proof	9,859	Value: 0.60				
1986	24,480,000	—	—	0.10	0.35	—
1986 Proof	7,100	Value: 0.60				
1987	43,234,000	—	—	0.10	0.35	—
1987 Proof	6,781	Value: 0.60				
1988	48,267,000	—	—	0.10	0.35	—
1988 Proof	7,250	Value: 0.60				
1989	—	—	—	—	0.35	—
1989 Proof	—	Value: 0.60				

KM# 94 10 CENTS
4.0000 g., Nickel, 20.7 mm. **Obv:** Head of President Fouche right **Rev:** Aloe plant and value **Rev. Designer:** Tommy Sasseen

Date	Mintage	F	VF	XF	Unc	BU
1976	30,986,000	—	—	0.40	1.00	—
1976 Proof	21,000	Value: 1.50				

KM# 101 10 CENTS
4.0000 g., Nickel, 20.7 mm. **Obv:** Head of President Diederichs left **Rev:** Aloe plant and value **Rev. Designer:** Tommy Sasseen

Date	Mintage	F	VF	XF	Unc	BU
1979	5,042,000	—	—	0.40	1.00	—
1979 Proof	17,000	Value: 1.50				

KM# 112 10 CENTS
4.0000 g., Nickel, 20.7 mm. **Obv:** Head of President Vorster 1/4 right **Rev:** Aloe plant and value **Rev. Designer:** Tommy Sasseen

Date	Mintage	F	VF	XF	Unc	BU
1982	15,806,000	—	—	0.40	1.00	—
1982 Proof	12,000	Value: 1.50				

KM# 135 10 CENTS
2.0000 g., Brass Plated Steel, 16 mm. **Obv:** Arms with supporters **Obv. Designer:** A.L. Sutherland **Rev:** Arum lily and value **Rev. Designer:** R.C. McFarlane

Date	Mintage	F	VF	XF	Unc	BU
1990	—	—	—	—	0.40	—
1990 Proof	—	Value: 0.60				
1991	—	—	—	—	0.40	—
1991 Proof	12,000	Value: 0.60				
1992	—	—	—	—	0.40	—
1992 Proof	—	Value: 0.60				
1993	—	—	—	—	0.40	—
1993 Proof	7,790	Value: 0.60				
1994	—	—	—	—	0.40	—
1994 Proof	5,804	Value: 0.60				
1995	—	—	—	—	0.40	—
1995 Proof	—	Value: 0.60				

KM# 161 10 CENTS
2.0000 g., Brass Plated Steel, 16 mm. **Obv:** English legend **Obv. Designer:** A.L. Sutherland **Rev:** Arum lily and value **Rev. Designer:** R.C. McFarlane

Date	Mintage	F	VF	XF	Unc	BU
1996	—	—	—	—	0.40	0.60
1996 Proof	—	Value: 0.75				
1997	—	—	—	—	0.40	0.60
1997 Proof	3,596	Value: 0.75				
1998	—	—	—	—	0.40	0.60
1998 Proof	—	Value: 1.75				
1999	—	—	—	—	0.40	0.60
1999 Proof	—	Value: 1.75				
2000	—	—	—	—	0.40	0.60

KM# 224 10 CENTS
2.0000 g., Brass Plated Steel, 16 mm. **Obv:** Crowned arms **Obv. Legend:** South Africa **Obv. Designer:** A.L. Sutherland **Rev:** Arum Lily and value **Rev. Designer:** R.C. McFarlane **Edge:** Reeded

Date	Mintage	F	VF	XF	Unc	BU
2000	—	—	—	—	0.60	0.85
2001	—	—	—	—	0.60	0.85

KM# 269 10 CENTS
2.0000 g., Copper Plated Steel, 16 mm. **Obv:** Crowned arms **Obv. Legend:** Afrika Dzonga **Obv. Designer:** A.L. Sutherland **Rev:** Arum Lily **Rev. Designer:** R.C. McFarlane **Edge:** Reeded **Note:** Change in legend.

Date	Mintage	F	VF	XF	Unc	BU
2002 Proof	—	Value: 3.00				
2002	—	—	—	—	0.60	1.00

KM# 326 10 CENTS
2.0000 g., Brass Plated Steel, 16 mm. **Obv:** Crowned arms **Obv. Legend:** Aforika Borwa **Rev:** Arum lily and denomination

Date	Mintage	F	VF	XF	Unc	BU
2004	—	—	—	—	0.40	0.60

KM# 292 10 CENTS
2.0000 g., Brass Plated Steel, 16 mm. **Obv:** Crowned arms **Obv. Legend:** Afrika Borwa **Rev:** Lily and value **Edge:** Reeded **Shape:** Round

Date	Mintage	F	VF	XF	Unc	BU
2005	—	—	—	—	—	0.60

KM# 61 20 CENTS
11.3100 g., 0.5000 Silver 0.1818 oz. ASW **Obv:** Shield **Obv. Designer:** G.E. Kruger-Gray **Rev:** Bust of Jan van Riebeeck 1/4 right

Date	Mintage	F	VF	XF	Unc	BU
1961	2,954,000	—	BV	3.00	3.50	—
1961 Proof	7,530	Value: 4.00				
1962 Small 2	3,568,000	—	BV	3.00	3.50	—
1962 Large 2	Inc. above	—	—	—	—	—
1962 Small 2; Proof	3,844	Value: 5.00				
1963	4,380,000	—	BV	3.00	3.50	—
1963 Proof	4,025	Value: 5.00				
1964	4,335,000	—	BV	3.00	3.50	—
1964 Proof	16,000	Value: 3.50				

KM# 69.1 20 CENTS
6.0000 g., Nickel, 24.2 mm. **Obv:** Head of Jan van Riebeeck, English legend **Obv. Legend:** English legend **Rev:** Protea flower within sprigs, value at left

Date	Mintage	F	VF	XF	Unc	BU
1965	29,210,000	—	0.15	0.20	0.40	—
1965 Proof	25,000	Value: 0.60				
1966	4,049,000	—	0.15	0.20	0.50	—
1967	58,000	—	—	—	1.00	—
1969	9,952	—	—	—	10.00	—

KM# 69.2 20 CENTS
6.0000 g., Nickel, 24.2 mm. **Obv:** Head of Jan van Riebeeck, Africaans legend **Obv. Legend:** Afrikaans legend **Rev:** Protea flower within sprigs, value at left

Date	Mintage	F	VF	XF	Unc	BU
1965	29,210,000	—	0.15	0.20	0.40	—
1966	4,049,000	—	0.15	0.20	0.50	—
1966 Proof	25,000	Value: 0.60				
1967	58,000	—	—	—	1.00	—
1967 Proof	25,000	Value: 0.60				
1969	9,952	—	—	—	6.00	—
1969 Proof	12,000	Value: 4.00				

KM# 78.1 20 CENTS
6.0000 g., Nickel, 24.2 mm. **Obv:** Head of President Charles Swart left, English legend **Obv. Designer:** Tommy Sasseen **Rev:** Protea flower within sprigs, value at left

Date	Mintage	F	VF	XF	Unc	BU
1968	50,000	—	—	—	3.00	—
1968 Proof	25,000	Value: 0.60				

KM# 78.2 20 CENTS
6.0000 g., Nickel, 24.2 mm. **Obv:** Africaans legend **Obv. Designer:** Tommy Sasseen **Rev:** Protea flower within sprigs, value at left

Date	Mintage	F	VF	XF	Unc	BU
1968	50,000	—	—	—	3.50	—

KM# 86 20 CENTS
6.0000 g., Nickel, 24.2 mm. **Obv:** Arms with supporters, bilingual legend **Obv. Legend:** Bilingual legend **Obv. Designer:** Tommy Sasseen **Rev:** Protea flower within sprigs, value at left **Note:** Varieties exist.

Date	Mintage	F	VF	XF	Unc	BU
1970	14,000	—	—	—	10.00	—
1970 Proof	10,000	Value: 1.50				
1971	5,893,000	—	0.15	0.25	0.60	—
1971 Proof	12,000	Value: 1.50				
1972	9,069,000	—	0.15	0.25	0.60	—
1972 Proof	10,000	Value: 1.50				
1973	20,000	—	—	—	5.00	—

Date	Mintage	F	VF	XF	Unc	BU
1973 Proof	11,000	Value: 1.50				
1974	2,436,000	—	0.15	0.35	0.75	—
1974 Proof	15,000	Value: 1.50				
1975	12,982,000	—	—	0.20	0.60	—
1975 Proof	18,000	Value: 1.00				
1977	30,650,000	—	—	0.20	0.60	—
1977 Proof	19,000	Value: 0.75				
1978	10,049,000	—	—	0.20	0.60	—
1978 Proof	19,000	Value: 0.75				
1980	13,335,000	—	—	0.20	0.60	—
1980 Proof	15,000	Value: 0.75				
1981	8,534,000	—	—	0.20	0.60	—
1981 Proof	10,000	Value: 0.75				
1983	25,667,000	—	—	0.20	0.60	—
1983 Proof	14,000	Value: 0.75				
1984	31,607,000	—	—	0.20	0.60	—
1984 Proof	11,000	Value: 0.75				
1985	29,329,000	—	—	0.20	0.60	—
1985 Proof	9,859	Value: 0.75				
1986	11,408,000	—	—	0.20	0.60	—
1986 Proof	7,100	Value: 0.75				
1987	36,904,000	—	—	0.20	0.60	—
1987 Proof	6,781	Value: 0.75				
1988	43,115,000	—	—	0.20	0.60	—
1988 Proof	7,250	Value: 0.75				
1989	—	—	—	0.20	0.60	—
1989 Proof	—	Value: 0.75				
1990	98,512,000	—	—	0.20	0.60	—

KM# 95 20 CENTS

6.0000 g., Nickel, 24.2 mm. **Obv:** Head of President Fouche right **Rev:** Protea flower within sprigs, value at left

Date	Mintage	F	VF	XF	Unc	BU
1976	18,826,000	—	—	0.70	1.50	—
1976 Proof	21,000	Value: 2.50				

KM# 102 20 CENTS

6.0000 g., Nickel, 24.2 mm. **Obv:** Head of President Diederichs left **Rev:** Protea flower within sprigs, value at left

Date	Mintage	F	VF	XF	Unc	BU
1979	5,032,000	—	—	0.70	1.50	—
1979 Proof	15,000	Value: 2.50				

KM# 113 20 CENTS

6.0000 g., Nickel, 24.2 mm. **Obv:** Head of President Vorster 1/4 right **Rev:** Protea flower within sprigs, value at left

Date	Mintage	F	VF	XF	Unc	BU
1982	18,083,000	—	—	0.70	1.50	—
1982 Proof	12,000	Value: 2.50				

KM# 136 20 CENTS

3.5000 g., Brass Plated Steel, 19 mm. **Obv:** Arms with supporters **Obv. Designer:** A.L. Sutherland **Rev:** Protea flower within sprigs, value at upper right **Rev. Designer:** S. Erasmus

Date	Mintage	F	VF	XF	Unc	BU
1990	—	—	—	—	4.00	—
1990 Proof	—	Value: 8.00				
1991	—	—	—	—	4.00	—
1991 Proof	11,800	Value: 8.00				
1992	—	—	—	—	0.60	—
1992 Proof	—	Value: 8.00				
1993	—	—	—	—	0.60	—
1993 Proof	7,790	Value: 8.00				
1994	—	—	—	—	0.60	—

Date	Mintage	F	VF	XF	Unc	BU
1994 Proof	5,804	Value: 8.00				
1995	—	—	—	—	0.60	—
1995 Proof	—	Value: 8.00				

KM# 162 20 CENTS

3.5000 g., Brass Plated Steel, 19 mm. **Obv:** Arms with supporters **Obv. Legend:** AFERIKA BORWA, Tswana legend above arms **Obv. Designer:** A.L. Sutherland **Rev:** Protea flower within sprigs, value at upper right **Rev. Designer:** S. Erasmus

Date	Mintage	F	VF	XF	Unc	BU
1996	—	—	—	—	0.60	0.85
1996 Proof	—	Value: 4.00				
1997	—	—	—	—	0.60	0.85
1997 Proof	3,596	Value: 4.00				
1998	—	—	—	—	0.60	0.85
1998 Proof	—	Value: 4.00				
1999	—	—	—	—	0.60	0.85
1999 Proof	—	Value: 4.00				
2000	—	—	—	—	0.60	0.85

KM# 225 20 CENTS

3.5000 g., Brass Plated Steel, 19 mm. **Obv:** Crowned arms **Obv. Designer:** A.L. Sutherland **Rev:** Protea flower within sprigs and value **Edge:** Reeded

Date	Mintage	F	VF	XF	Unc	BU
2000	—	—	—	—	0.75	1.00
2001	—	—	—	—	0.75	1.00

KM# 270 20 CENTS

3.5000 g., Bronze Plated Steel, 19 mm. **Obv:** Crowned arms **Obv. Legend:** South Africa **Obv. Designer:** A.L. Sutherland **Rev:** Protea flower and value **Rev. Designer:** S. Erasmus **Edge:** Reeded **Note:** Change in legend.

Date	Mintage	F	VF	XF	Unc	BU
2002	—	—	—	—	0.75	1.25
2002 Proof	—	Value: 4.00				

KM# 327 20 CENTS

3.5000 g., Brass Plated Steel, 19 mm. **Obv:** Crowned arms **Obv. Legend:** Aforika Borwa **Rev:** Protea flower within sprigs and value

Date	Mintage	F	VF	XF	Unc	BU
2003	—	—	—	—	—	0.75

KM# 328 20 CENTS

3.5000 g., Brass Plated Steel, 19 mm. **Obv:** Crowned arms **Obv. Legend:** Afrika Borwa **Rev:** Protea flower within sprigs and value

Date	Mintage	F	VF	XF	Unc	BU
2004	—	—	—	—	—	0.75

KM# 293 20 CENTS

3.5000 g., Brass Plated Steel, 19 mm. **Obv:** Crowned arms **Obv. Legend:** Suid-Afrika **Rev:** Protea flower and value **Edge:** Reeded **Shape:** Round

Date	Mintage	F	VF	XF	Unc	BU
2005	—	—	—	—	—	0.75

KM# 62 50 CENTS

28.2800 g., 0.5000 Silver 0.4546 oz. ASW **Obv:** Springbok **Obv. Designer:** C.L. Steynberg **Rev:** Bust of Jan van Riebeeck 1/4 right **Note:** Varieties exist with narrow, high relief and wide, low letters.

Date	Mintage	F	VF	XF	Unc	BU
1961	26,000	—	BV	7.50	10.00	—
1961 Prooflike	20,000	—	—	—	10.00	—
1961 Proof	8,530	Value: 18.00				
1962	15,000	—	BV	7.50	10.00	—
1962 Prooflike	6,024	—	—	—	12.50	—
1962 Proof	3,844	Value: 20.00				
1963	143,000	—	BV	7.50	10.00	—
1963 Prooflike	10,000	—	—	—	12.50	—
1963 Proof	4,025	Value: 20.00				
1964	86,000	—	BV	7.50	9.00	—
1964 Prooflike	25,000	—	—	—	10.00	—
1964 Proof	16,000	Value: 10.00				

KM# 70.1 50 CENTS

9.5000 g., Nickel, 27.8 mm. **Obv:** Head of Jan van Riebeeck right, English legend **Rev:** Flower and value **Designer:** Tommy Sasseen

Date	Mintage	F	VF	XF	Unc	BU
1965 Proof	—	Value: 3,500				
1966	8,055,999	—	—	0.50	2.50	—
1966 Proof	25,000	Value: 4.00				
1967	52,000	—	—	—	1.50	—
Note: In sets only						
1967 Proof	25,000	Value: 4.00				
1969	7,968	—	—	—	10.00	—
Note: In sets only						
1969 Proof	12,000	Value: 10.00				

KM# 70.2 50 CENTS

9.5000 g., Nickel, 27.8 mm. **Obv:** Head of Jan van Riebeeck right, Afrikaans legend **Rev:** Flower and value **Designer:** Tommy Sasseen

Date	Mintage	F	VF	XF	Unc	BU
1965	28,000	—	—	—	6.00	—
1965 Proof	25,000	Value: 6.00				
1966	8,055,999	—	—	0.50	2.50	—
1967	52,000	—	—	—	3.50	—
Note: In sets only						
1969	7,968	—	—	—	15.00	—
Note: In sets only						

KM# 79.1 50 CENTS

9.5000 g., Nickel, 27.8 mm. **Obv:** Head of President Charles Swart left, English legend **Rev:** Flowers and value **Designer:** Tommy Sasseen

Date	Mintage	F	VF	XF	Unc	BU
1968	750,000	—	—	0.50	1.50	—

KM# 79.2 50 CENTS

9.5000 g., Nickel, 27.8 mm. **Obv:** Head of President Charles Swart left, Afrikaans legend **Rev:** Flowers and value **Designer:** Tommy Sasseen

Date	Mintage	F	VF	XF	Unc	BU
1968	750,000	—	—	0.50	2.00	—
1968 Proof	25,000	Value: 3.50				

KM# 87 50 CENTS

9.5000 g., Nickel, 27.8 mm. **Obv:** Arms with supporters, bilingual legend **Rev:** Flowers and value **Designer:** Tommy Sasseen **Note:** Varieties exist.

Date	Mintage	F	VF	XF	Unc	BU
1970	4,098,000	—	—	0.50	1.50	—
1970 Proof	10,000	Value: 2.00				
1971	5,062,000	—	—	0.50	1.50	—
1971 Proof	12,000	Value: 2.00				
1972	771,000	—	—	0.50	1.50	—
1972 Proof	10,000	Value: 2.00				
1973	1,042,999	—	—	0.50	1.50	—
1973 Proof	11,000	Value: 2.00				
1974	1,942,000	—	—	0.50	1.50	—
1974 Proof	15,000	Value: 2.00				
1975	4,888,000	—	—	0.50	1.50	—
1975 Proof	18,000	Value: 2.00				
1977	10,196,000	—	—	0.50	1.50	—
1977 Proof	19,000	Value: 2.00				
1978	5,071,000	—	—	0.50	1.50	—
1978 Proof	17,000	Value: 2.00				
1980	4,268,000	—	—	0.50	1.50	—
1980 Proof	15,000	Value: 2.00				
1981	5,681,000	—	—	0.50	1.50	—
1981 Proof	10,000	Value: 2.00				
1983	5,150,000	—	—	0.40	1.00	—
1983 Proof	14,000	Value: 1.50				
1984	9,687,000	—	—	0.40	1.00	—
1984 Proof	11,000	Value: 1.50				
1985	13,339,000	—	—	0.40	1.00	—
1985 Proof	9,859	Value: 1.50				
1986	2,294,000	—	—	0.40	1.00	—
1986 Proof	7,100	Value: 1.50				
1987	19,071,000	—	—	0.40	1.00	—
1987 Proof	6,781	Value: 1.50				
1988	27,698,000	—	—	0.40	1.00	—
1988 Proof	7,250	Value: 1.50				
1989	—	—	—	0.40	1.00	—
1989 Proof	—	Value: 1.50				
1990	29,442,000	—	—	0.40	1.00	—

KM# 96 50 CENTS

9.5000 g., Nickel, 27.8 mm. **Obv:** Head of President Fouche right **Rev:** Flowers and value **Rev. Designer:** Tommy Sasseen

Date	Mintage	F	VF	XF	Unc	BU
1976	9,632,000	—	0.75	1.50	3.00	—
1976 Proof	21,000	Value: 5.00				

KM# 103 50 CENTS

9.5000 g., Nickel, 27.8 mm. **Obv:** Head of President Diederichs left **Rev:** Flowers and value **Rev. Designer:** Tommy Sasseen

Date	Mintage	F	VF	XF	Unc	BU
1979	5,051,000	—	0.75	1.50	3.50	—
1979 Proof	15,000	Value: 5.00				

KM# 114 50 CENTS

9.5000 g., Nickel, 27.8 mm. **Obv:** Head of President Vorster 1/4 right **Obv. Designer:** Tommy Sasseen **Rev:** Flowers and value

Date	Mintage	F	VF	XF	Unc	BU
1982	2,069,999	—	0.75	1.50	3.50	—
1982 Proof	12,000	Value: 5.00				

KM# 137 50 CENTS

5.0000 g., Brass Plated Steel, 22 mm. **Obv:** Arms with supporters **Obv. Designer:** A.L. Sutherland **Rev:** Plant and value **Rev. Designer:** C. Cogle

Date	Mintage	F	VF	XF	Unc	BU
1990	—	—	—	—	5.00	—
1990 Proof	—	Value: 10.00				
1991	—	—	—	—	5.00	—
1991 Proof	12,000	Value: 10.00				
1992	—	—	—	—	1.00	—
1992 Proof	—	Value: 10.00				
1993	—	—	—	—	1.00	—
1993 Proof	7,790	Value: 10.00				
1994	—	—	—	—	1.00	—
1994 Proof	5,804	Value: 10.00				
1995	—	—	—	—	1.00	—
1995 Proof	—	Value: 10.00				

KM# 163 50 CENTS

5.0000 g., Bronze Plated Steel, 22 mm. **Obv:** Arms with supporters **Obv. Legend:** AFRIKA BORWA, Sotho legend **Obv. Designer:** A.L. Sutherland **Rev:** Plant and value **Rev. Designer:** C. Cogle

Date	Mintage	F	VF	XF	Unc	BU
1996	—	—	—	—	1.00	1.25
1996 Proof	—	Value: 5.00				
1997	—	—	—	—	1.00	1.25
1997 Proof	—	Value: 5.00				
1998	—	—	—	—	1.00	1.25
1998 Proof	—	Value: 5.00				
1999	—	—	—	—	1.00	1.25
1999 Proof	—	Value: 5.00				
2000	—	—	—	—	1.00	1.25

KM# 226 50 CENTS

5.0000 g., Brass Plated Steel, 22 mm. **Obv:** Crowned arms **Obv. Designer:** A.L. Sutherland **Rev:** Plant and value **Rev. Designer:** C. Cogle **Edge:** Reeded

Date	Mintage	F	VF	XF	Unc	BU
2000	—	—	—	—	1.00	1.25
2001	—	—	—	—	1.00	1.25

KM# 329 50 CENTS

5.0000 g., Brass Plated Steel, 22 mm. **Obv:** Crowned arms **Obv. Legend:** Aforika Borwa **Rev:** Cricket player diving towards the wicket **Edge:** Reeded

Date	Mintage	F	VF	XF	Unc	BU
2002	—	—	—	—	2.25	2.50

KM# 271 50 CENTS

5.0000 g., Brass Plated Steel, 22 mm. **Obv:** Crowned arms **Obv. Legend:** Aforika Borwa **Obv. Designer:** A.L. Sutherland **Rev:** Strelitzia plant **Rev. Designer:** C. Cogle **Edge:** Reeded **Note:** Change in legend.

Date	Mintage	F	VF	XF	Unc	BU
2002 Proof	—	Value: 5.00				
2002	—	—	—	—	1.00	1.50

KM# 330 50 CENTS

5.0000 g., Brass Plated Steel, 22 mm. **Obv:** Crowned arms **Obv. Legend:** Afrika Borwa **Rev:** Stelitzia plant and denomination

Date	Mintage	F	VF	XF	Unc	BU
2003	—	—	—	—	2.25	2.50

KM# 276 50 CENTS

5.0000 g., Brass Plated Steel, 22 mm. **Obv:** Crowned arms **Obv. Legend:** Afrika Borwa **Obv. Designer:** A.L. Sutherland **Rev:** Cricket player diving towards the wicket **Edge:** Reeded

Date	Mintage	F	VF	XF	Unc	BU
2003	—	—	—	—	2.25	2.50

KM# 331 50 CENTS

5.0000 g., Brass Plated Steel, 22 mm. **Obv:** Crowned arms **Obv. Legend:** Suid Afrika **Rev:** Stelitzia plant and denomination

Date	Mintage	F	VF	XF	Unc	BU
2004	—	—	—	—	2.25	2.50

KM# 294 50 CENTS

5.0000 g., Brass Plated Steel, 22 mm. **Obv:** Crowned arms **Obv. Legend:** uMzantsi Afrika **Rev:** Plant and value **Edge:** Reeded **Shape:** Round

Date	Mintage	F	VF	XF	Unc	BU
2005	—	—	—	—	—	1.00

KM# 71.1 RAND

15.0000 g., 0.8000 Silver 0.3858 oz. ASW **Obv:** Head of Jan van Riebeeck right **Rev:** Springbok above value

Date	Mintage	F	VF	XF	Unc	BU
1965	—	—	—	BV	7.00	—
1965 Proof	25,000	Value: 20.00				
1966	1,434,000	—	—	BV	6.50	—
1966 Proof	20	Value: 1,250				
1968	50,000	—	—	BV	6.50	—
Note: In sets only						
1968 Proof	25,000	Value: 6.50				

KM# 71.2 RAND

15.0000 g., 0.8000 Silver 0.3858 oz. ASW **Obv:** Head of Jan van Riebeeck right, Afrikaans legend **Rev:** Springbok above value

Date	Mintage	F	VF	XF	Unc	BU
1965 V.I.P. Proof	—	—	—	—	1,000	—
1966	1,434,000	—	—	BV	6.50	—
1966 Proof	25,000	Value: 7.00				
1968	50,000	—	—	—	8.00	—
Note: In sets only						
1968 Proof	Est. 20	Value: 1,250				

KM# 72.1 RAND

15.0000 g., 0.8000 Silver 0.3858 oz. ASW **Subject:** 1st Anniversary - Death of Dr. Verwoerd **Obv:** Bust right, English legend **Obv. Designer:** Tommy Sasseen **Rev:** Springbok above value

Date	Mintage	F	VF	XF	Unc	BU
1967	1,544,000	—	—	BV	6.50	—
1967 Proof	Est. 20	Value: 1,250				

KM# 72.2 RAND

15.0000 g., 0.8000 Silver 0.3858 oz. ASW **Subject:** 1st Anniversary - Death of Dr. Verwoerd **Obv:** Bust right, Afrikaans legend **Obv. Designer:** Tommy Sasseen **Rev:** Springbok above value

Date	Mintage	F	VF	XF	Unc	BU
1967	1,544,000	—	—	BV	6.50	—
1967 Proof	25,000	Value: 7.50				

KM# 80.1 RAND

15.0000 g., 0.8000 Silver 0.3858 oz. ASW, 32.6 mm. **Subject:** Dr. T.E. Donges **Obv:** Bust right, English legend **Rev:** Springbok above value **Designer:** Tommy Sasseen **Note:** The South African mint does not acknowledge the existence of these 1 Rand pieces struck in proof.

Date	Mintage	F	VF	XF	Unc	BU
1969	506,000	—	—	BV	6.50	—
1969 Proof	Est. 20	Value: 1,250				

KM# 80.2 RAND

15.0000 g., 0.8000 Silver 0.3858 oz. ASW, 32.6 mm. **Subject:** Dr. T.E. Donges **Obv:** Bust right, Afrikaans legend **Rev:** Springbok above value **Designer:** Tommy Sasseen

Date	Mintage	F	VF	XF	Unc	BU
1969	506,000	—	—	BV	6.50	—
1969 Proof	12,000	Value: 7.50				

KM# 88 RAND

15.0000 g., 0.8000 Silver 0.3858 oz. ASW **Obv:** Arms with supporters, bilingual legend **Obv. Designer:** Tommy Sasseen **Rev:** Springbok

Date	Mintage	F	VF	XF	Unc	BU
1970	14,000	—	—	BV	6.50	—
1970 Proof	10,000	Value: 8.00				
1971	20,000	—	—	BV	6.50	—
1971 Proof	12,000	Value: 8.00				
1972	20,000	—	—	BV	6.50	—
1972 Proof	10,000	Value: 8.00				
1973	20,000	—	—	BV	6.50	—
1973 Proof	11,000	Value: 8.00				
1975	20,000	—	—	BV	6.50	—
1975 Proof	18,000	Value: 8.00				
1976	20,000	—	—	BV	6.50	—
1976 Proof	21,000	Value: 8.00				
1977 Proof	19,000	Value: 9.00				
1978 Proof	17,000	Value: 9.00				
1979 Proof	15,000	Value: 9.00				
1980 Proof	15,000	Value: 9.00				
1981 Proof	12,000	Value: 12.50				
1982 Proof	10,000	Value: 12.50				
1983 Proof	14,000	Value: 12.50				
1984 Proof	11,000	Value: 12.50				
1987	4,526	—	—	BV	15.00	—
1987 Proof	13,000	Value: 12.50				
1988	21	—	—	—	—	—
1988 Proof	7,250	Value: 15.00				
1989	3,684	—	—	BV	15.00	—
1989 Proof	15,000	Value: 12.50				
1990 Proof	—	Value: 25.00				

KM# 88a RAND

12.0000 g., Nickel, 31 mm. **Obv:** Arms with supporters, bilingual legend **Obv. Designer:** Tommy Sasseen **Rev:** Springbok above value

Date	Mintage	F	VF	XF	Unc	BU
1977	29,871,000	—	—	0.75	2.00	—
1977 Proof	10	Value: 1,500				
1978	12,021,000	—	—	0.75	2.00	—
1978 Proof	10	Value: 1,500				
1980	2,690,000	—	—	0.75	2.00	—
1981	2,035,000	—	—	0.75	2.00	—
1983	7,182,000	—	—	0.75	2.00	—
1983 Proof	10	Value: 1,500				
1984	5,736,000	—	—	0.75	2.00	—
1984 Proof	11,000	Value: 5.00				
1986	1,570,000	—	—	0.75	2.00	—
1986 Proof	7,000	Value: 5.00				
1987	12,152,000	—	—	0.75	2.00	—
1987 Proof	6,781	Value: 5.00				
1988	21,335,000	—	—	0.75	2.00	—
1988 Proof	7,250	Value: 5.00				
1989	—	—	—	—	2.00	—
1989 Proof	—	Value: 5.00				

KM# 104 RAND

12.0000 g., Nickel, 31 mm. **Obv:** Head of President Diederichs left **Rev:** Springbok above value

Date	Mintage	F	VF	XF	Unc	BU
1979	13,466,000	—	2.00	4.00	10.00	—
1979 Proof	5	Value: 2,000				

KM# 115 RAND

Nickel **Obv:** Head of President Vorster 1/4 right **Rev:** Springbok above value

Date	Mintage	F	VF	XF	Unc	BU
1982	7,685,000	—	2.50	5.00	10.00	—
1982 Proof	15	Value: 1,500				

KM# 117 RAND

Nickel **Obv:** Head of President Marais Viljoen left **Obv. Designer:** A.L. Sutherland **Rev:** Springbok above value

Date	Mintage	F	VF	XF	Unc	BU
1985	3,983,000	—	2.50	5.00	10.00	—
1985 Proof	9,859	Value: 5.00				

KM# 141 RAND

Nickel **Obv:** Head of President Botha facing **Rev:** Springbok above value

Date	Mintage	F	VF	XF	Unc	BU
1990	25,323,000	—	—	1.75	3.50	—
1990 Proof	15,000	Value: 10.00				

KM# 148 RAND

4.0000 g., Nickel Plated Copper, 20 mm. **Obv:** Head of President Botha facing **Obv. Designer:** A.L. Sutherland **Rev:** Springbok below value **Rev. Designer:** L. Lotriet

Date	Mintage	F	VF	XF	Unc	BU
1990	12,000	—	—	—	10.00	—
1990 Proof	10,000	Value: 15.00				

KM# 138 RAND

4.0000 g., Nickel Plated Copper, 20 mm. **Obv:** Arms with supporters **Obv. Designer:** A.L. Sutherland **Rev:** Springbok below value **Rev. Designer:** L. Lotriet

Date	Mintage	F	VF	XF	Unc	BU
1991	20,765,000	—	—	—	2.50	—
1991 Proof	12,000	Value: 15.00				
1992	59,571,000	—	—	—	2.50	—
1992 Proof	10,000	Value: 15.00				
1993	37,977,000	—	—	—	2.50	—
1993 Proof	7,790	Value: 20.00				
1994	54,633,000	—	—	—	2.50	—
1994 Proof	5,804	Value: 20.00				
1995	28,012,000	—	—	—	2.50	—
1995 Proof	5,816	Value: 20.00				

KM# 164 RAND

4.0000 g., Nickel Plated Copper, 20 mm. **Obv:** Arms with supporters, Afrikaans legend **Obv. Designer:** A.L. Sutherland **Rev:** Springbok and value **Rev. Designer:** L. Lotriet

Date	Mintage	F	VF	XF	Unc	BU
1996	12,199,000	—	—	—	1.75	—
1996 Proof	4,827	Value: 6.00				
1997	38,876,000	—	—	—	1.75	—
1997 Proof	3,596	Value: 6.00				
1998	—	—	—	—	1.75	—
1998 Proof	—	Value: 6.00				
1999	—	—	—	—	1.75	—
1999 Proof	—	Value: 6.00				
2000	—	—	—	—	1.75	—

KM# 227 RAND

4.0000 g., Nickel Plated Steel, 20 mm. **Obv:** Crowned arms **Obv. Designer:** A.L. Sutherland **Rev:** Springbok and value **Rev. Designer:** L. Lotriet **Edge:** Reeded and plain sections

Date	Mintage	F	VF	XF	Unc	BU
2000	—	—	—	—	1.75	2.75
2001	—	—	—	—	1.75	2.75

KM# 272 RAND

4.0000 g., Nickel Plated Copper, 20 mm. **Obv:** Crowned arms **Obv. Legend:** Suid-Afrika Afrika Borwa **Obv. Designer:** A.L. Sutherland **Rev:** Springbok **Rev. Designer:** L. Lotriet **Edge:** Reeded **Note:** Change in legend.

Date	Mintage	F	VF	XF	Unc	BU
2002	—	—	—	—	1.75	2.50
2002 Proof	—	Value: 6.00				

KM# 275 RAND

4.0000 g., Nickel-Plated Steel, 20 mm. **Subject:** Johannesburg World Summit on Sustainable Development **Obv:** Crowned arms **Obv. Designer:** A.L. Sutherland **Rev:** World globe and logo **Edge:** Reeded and plain sections

Date	Mintage	F	VF	XF	Unc	BU
2002	—	—	—	—	3.00	4.00

KM# 332 RAND

4.0000 g., Nickel Plated Copper, 20 mm. **Obv:** Crowned arms **Obv. Legend:** uMzantsi Afrika Suid-Afrika **Rev:** Springbok and denomination

Date	Mintage	F	VF	XF	Unc	BU
2003	—	—	—	—	—	1.75

KM# 333 RAND

4.0000 g., Nickel Plated Copper, 20 mm. **Obv:** Crowned arms **Obv. Legend:** iNingizimu Afrika uMzantsi Afrika **Rev:** Springbok and Denomination

Date	Mintage	F	VF	XF	Unc	BU
2004	—	—	—	—	—	1.75

KM# 295 RAND

4.0000 g., Nickel Plated Copper, 20 mm. **Obv:** Crowned arms **Obv. Legend:** iSewula Afrika iNingizimu Afrika **Rev:** Springbok and value **Edge:** Segmented reeding **Shape:** Round

Date	Mintage	F	VF	XF	Unc	BU
2005	—	—	—	—	—	1.75

KM# 139 2 RAND

5.5000 g., Nickel Plated Copper, 23 mm. **Obv:** Arms with supporters **Rev:** Greater Kudu **Designer:** A.L. Sutherland

Date	Mintage	F	VF	XF	Unc	BU
1989	65,233,000	—	—	—	2.00	—
1989 Proof	13,000	Value: 10.00				
1990	70,655,000	—	—	—	2.00	—
1990 Proof	10,000	Value: 7.50				
1991	39,243,000	—	—	—	2.00	—
1991 Proof	12,000	Value: 7.50				
1992	2,115,000	—	—	—	2.00	—
1992 Proof	10,000	Value: 7.50				
1993	92,000	—	—	—	2.00	—
1993 Proof	7,790	Value: 7.50				
1994	994,000	—	—	—	2.00	—
1994 Proof	5,804	Value: 7.50				
1995	13,213,000	—	—	—	2.00	—
1995 Proof	5,816	Value: 7.50				

KM# 165 2 RAND

5.5000 g., Nickel Plated Copper, 23 mm. **Obv:** Arms with supporters **Obv. Legend:** UMZANSTI AFRIKA, Xhosa legend **Rev:** Greater Kudu **Designer:** A.L. Sutherland

Date	Mintage	F	VF	XF	Unc	BU
1996	123,000	—	—	—	2.50	—
1996 Proof	4,827	Value: 8.00				
1997	1,804,000	—	—	—	2.50	—
1997 Proof	3,596	Value: 8.00				
1998	—	—	—	—	2.50	—
1998 Proof	—	Value: 8.00				
1999	—	—	—	—	2.50	—
1999 Proof	—	Value: 8.00				
2000	—	—	—	—	2.50	—

KM# 228 2 RAND

5.5000 g., Nickel Plated Steel, 23 mm. **Obv:** Crowned arms **Obv. Legend:** UMZANSTI AFRIKA, Xhosha legend **Rev:** Kudu and value **Edge:** Reeded and plain sections **Designer:** A.L. Sutherland

Date	Mintage	F	VF	XF	Unc	BU
2001	—	—	—	—	2.00	3.00

KM# 273 2 RAND

5.5000 g., Nickel Plated Copper, 23 mm. **Obv:** Crowned arms **Obv. Legend:** iNingizimu Afrika uMzantsi Afrika **Rev:** Kudu and value **Edge:** Reeded and plain sections **Designer:** A.L. Sutherland **Note:** Change in legend.

Date	Mintage	F	VF	XF	Unc	BU
2002 Proof	—	Value: 8.00				
2002	—	—	—	—	2.00	3.50

KM# 335 2 RAND

5.5000 g., Nickel Plated Copper, 23 mm. **Obv:** Crowned arms **Obv. Legend:** iNingizimu Afrika iSewula Afrika **Rev:** Kudu and denomination

Date	Mintage	F	VF	XF	Unc	BU
2003	—	—	—	—	2.00	3.50

KM# 336 2 RAND

5.5000 g., Nickel Plated Copper, 23 mm. **Obv:** Crowned arms **Obv. Legend:** Afurika Tshipembe iSewula Afrika **Rev:** Kudu and denomination

Date	Mintage	F	VF	XF	Unc	BU
2004	—	—	—	—	2.00	3.50

KM# 334 2 RAND

5.5000 g., Nickel Plated Copper, 23 mm. **Subject:** 10 Years of Freedom - 1994-2004 **Obv:** National arms, date and country name in English **Rev:** Denomination, flag logo and many people

Date	Mintage	F	VF	XF	Unc	BU
2004	—	—	—	—	—	2.00

KM# 296 2 RAND

5.5000 g., Nickel Plated Copper, 23 mm. **Obv:** Crowned arms **Obv. Legend:** Ningizimu Afrika Afurika Tshipembe **Rev:** Greater Kudu and value **Edge:** Segmented reeding **Shape:** Round

Date	Mintage	F	VF	XF	Unc	BU
2005	—	—	—	—	—	2.00

KM# 140 5 RAND
7.0000 g., Nickel Plated Copper, 26 mm. **Obv:** Arms with supporters **Rev:** Wildebeest **Designer:** A.L. Sutherland

Date	Mintage	F	VF	XF	Unc	BU
1994	45,212,000	—	—	—	4.50	5.50
1994 Proof	5,804	Value: 10.00				
1995	41,238,000	—	—	—	4.50	5.50
1995 Proof	5,816	Value: 10.00				

KM# 150 5 RAND
7.0000 g., Nickel Plated Copper, 26 mm. **Subject:** Presidential Inauguration **Obv:** Arms with supporters **Obv. Designer:** A.L. Sutherland **Rev:** Building below value **Rev. Designer:** S. Erasmus

Date	Mintage	F	VF	XF	Unc	BU
1994	10,095,000	—	—	—	5.50	6.50
1994 Proof	10,000	Value: 8.50				

KM# 166 5 RAND
7.0000 g., Nickel Plated Copper, 26 mm. **Obv:** Arms with supporters **Obv. Legend:** ININGIZIMU AFRIKA, Zulu/Swati legend **Rev:** Wildebeest **Designer:** A.L. Sutherland

Date	Mintage	F	VF	XF	Unc	BU
1996	15,435,000	—	—	—	4.50	—
1996 Proof	4,827	Value: 10.00				
1997	1,276,000	—	—	—	4.50	—
1997 Proof	3,596	Value: 10.00				
1998	—	—	—	—	4.50	—
1998 Proof	—	Value: 10.00				
1999	—	—	—	—	4.50	—
1999 Proof	—	Value: 10.00				
2000	—	—	—	—	4.50	—

KM# 230 5 RAND
7.0000 g., Nickel Plated Steel, 26 mm. **Obv:** Head of Nelson Mandela 1/4 right **Obv. Legend:** ININGIZIMU AFRIKA, Zulu legend **Rev:** Wildebeest **Edge:** Reeded and plain sections **Designer:** A.L. Sutherland

Date	Mintage	F	VF	XF	Unc	BU
2000	—	—	—	—	4.50	5.50
2000 Proof	—	Value: 10.00				

KM# 229 5 RAND
7.0000 g., Nickel Plated Steel, 26 mm. **Obv:** Crowned arms **Obv. Legend:** ININGIZIMU AFRIKA, Zulu legend **Rev:** Wildebeest and value **Edge:** Reeded and plain sections **Designer:** A.L. Sutherland

Date	Mintage	F	VF	XF	Unc	BU
2001	—	—	—	—	4.50	5.50

KM# 274 5 RAND
7.0000 g., Nickel Plated Copper, 26 mm. **Obv:** Crowned arms with Venda legend left, Ndebele legend right **Obv. Legend:** AFURIKA TSHIPEMBE - ISEWULA AFRIKA **Rev:** Wildebeest and value **Edge:** Reeded and plain sections **Designer:** A.L. Sutherland **Note:** Change in legend.

Date	Mintage	F	VF	XF	Unc	BU
2002	—	—	—	—	4.50	6.00
2002 Proof	—	Value: 10.00				

KM# 337 5 RAND
7.0000 g., Nickel Plated Copper, 26 mm. **Obv:** Crowned arms **Obv. Legend:** Afurika Tshipembe Ningizimu Afrika **Rev:** Wildebeest and denomination

Date	Mintage	F	VF	XF	Unc	BU
2003	—	—	—	—	4.50	6.00

KM# 281 5 RAND
9.5000 g., Bi-Metallic Brass center in Copper-Nickel ring, 26 mm. **Obv:** Crowned arms with Tsonga legend left, Zulu legend right **Obv. Legend:** AFRIKA DZONGA - NINGIZIMU AFRIKA **Rev:** Wildebeest and value **Edge:** Security type with lettering **Edge Lettering:** "SARB R5" repeated ten times

Date	Mintage	F	VF	XF	Unc	BU
2004	—	—	—	—	5.00	6.50

KM# 297 5 RAND
9.5000 g., Bi-Metallic Brass center in Copper-Nickel ring, 26 mm. **Obv:** Crowned arms **Obv. Legend:** Afrika Dzonga South Africa **Rev:** Wildebeest and value **Edge:** Security type with lettering **Edge Lettering:** "SARB R5" repeated ten times

Date	Mintage	F	VF	XF	Unc	BU
2005	—	—	—	—	—	5.00

SOUTH ARABIA

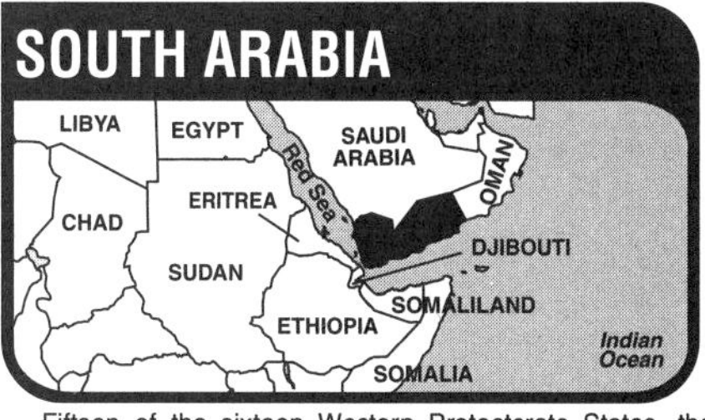

Fifteen of the sixteen Western Protectorate States, the Wahidi State of the Eastern Protectorate, and Aden Colony joined to form the Federation of South Arabia.

In 1959, Britain agreed to prepare South Arabia for full independence, which was achieved on Nov. 30, 1967, at which time South Arabia, including Aden, changed its name to the Peoples Republic of Southern Yemen. On Dec. 1, 1970, following the overthrow of the new government by the National Liberation Front, Southern Yemen changed its name to the Peoples Democratic Republic of Yemen.

TITLE

Al-Junubiya(t) al-Arabiya(t)

MONETARY SYSTEM

1000 Fils = 1 Dinar

FEDERATION

STANDARD COINAGE

KM# 1 FILS
Aluminum, 20 mm. **Obv:** Snowflake design **Rev:** Crossed swords

Date	Mintage	F	VF	XF	Unc	BU
1964	10,000,000	—	—	0.10	0.15	0.25
1964 Proof	—	Value: 1.50				

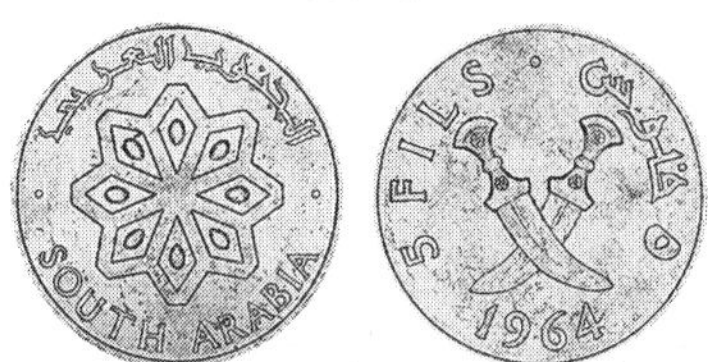

KM# 2 5 FILS
Bronze **Obv:** Snowflake design **Rev:** Crossed swords

Date	Mintage	F	VF	XF	Unc	BU
1964	10,000,000	—	0.15	0.25	0.50	0.65
1964 Proof	—	Value: 2.00				

KM# 3 25 FILS
Copper-Nickel **Obv:** Snowflake design **Rev:** Sailboat

Date	Mintage	F	VF	XF	Unc	BU
1964	4,000,000	—	0.25	0.45	0.85	1.00
1964 Proof	—	Value: 2.75				

KM# 4 50 FILS
Copper-Nickel **Obv:** Snowflake design **Rev:** Sailboat

Date	Mintage	F	VF	XF	Unc	BU
1964	6,000,000	—	0.45	0.65	1.25	1.50
1964 Proof	—	Value: 3.75				

SOUTHERN RHODESIA

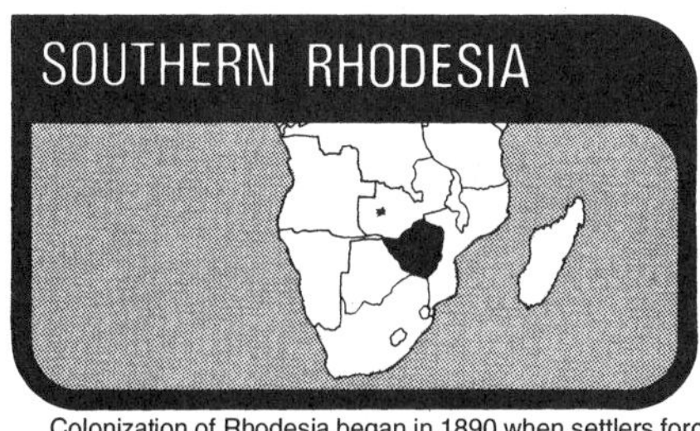

Colonization of Rhodesia began in 1890 when settlers forcibly acquired Shona lands and then Ndebele lands in 1893. It was named as Rhodesia, after Cecil Rhodes who led the build-up of the Colony.

Rhodesia became a self-governing colony under the name of Southern Rhodesia in 1923. Consequent upon later political difficulties and disagreement with the British authorities over common emancipation of the people, a unilateral declaration of independence (UDI) was declared on November 11, 1965.

Following United Nations sanctions against the country, various renamings as Rhodesia and Rhodesia-Zimbabwe, and elections in February 1980, the country became independent on April 18, 1980, as the Republic of Zimbabwe as a member of the Commonwealth of Nations.

RULER

British, until 1966

MONETARY SYSTEM

12 Pence = 1 Shilling
2 Shillings = 1 Florin
5 Shillings = 1 Crown
20 Shillings = 1 Pound

BRITISH COLONY

POUND COINAGE

KM# 6 1/2 PENNY

Copper-Nickel **Ruler:** George V **Obv:** Crowned flower design within circle, hole in center **Rev:** Value written within sprigs, hole in center

Date	Mintage	F	VF	XF	Unc	BU
1934	240,000	1.00	6.00	20.00	40.00	—
1934 Proof	—	Value: 125				
1936	240,000	5.00	40.00	80.00	150	—
1936 Proof	—	—	—	—	—	—

KM# 14 1/2 PENNY

Copper-Nickel **Ruler:** George VI **Obv:** Crowned flower design within circle, hole in center **Rev:** Value written within sprigs, hole in center

Date	Mintage	F	VF	XF	Unc	BU
1938	240,000	0.75	1.75	10.00	20.00	30.00
1938 Proof	—	—	—	—	—	—
1939	480,000	1.00	2.00	30.00	60.00	85.00
1939 Proof	—	—	—	—	—	—

KM# 14a 1/2 PENNY

Bronze **Ruler:** George VI **Obv:** Crowned flower design within circle, hole in center **Rev:** Value within sprigs, hole in center

Date	Mintage	F	VF	XF	Unc	BU
1942	480,000	0.60	1.50	13.50	25.00	—
1942 Proof	—	—	—	—	—	—
1943	960,000	0.35	0.75	2.25	6.50	18.00
1944	960,000	0.35	0.75	2.50	8.00	—
1944 Proof	—	—	—	—	—	—

KM# 26 1/2 PENNY

Bronze **Ruler:** George VI **Obv:** Crowned flower design within circle, hole in center **Obv. Legend:** KING GEORGE THE SIXTH **Rev:** Value witten within sprigs, hole in center

Date	Mintage	F	VF	XF	Unc	BU
1951	480,000	0.75	1.25	2.25	6.50	18.00
1951 Proof	—	—	—	—	—	—
1952	480,000	0.75	1.25	5.00	10.00	—
1952 Proof	—	—	—	—	—	—

KM# 28 1/2 PENNY

Bronze **Ruler:** Elizabeth II **Obv:** Crowned flower design within circle, hole in center **Rev:** Value written within sprigs, hole in center

Date	Mintage	F	VF	XF	Unc	BU
1954	960,000	0.75	2.00	35.00	65.00	—
1954 Proof	20	Value: 350				

KM# 7 PENNY

Copper-Nickel **Ruler:** George V **Obv:** Crowned flower design within circle, hole in center **Rev:** Value written within sprigs, hole in center

Date	Mintage	F	VF	XF	Unc	BU
1934	360,000	0.75	1.50	13.50	25.00	—
1934 Proof	—	Value: 125				
1935	492,000	1.50	15.00	75.00	125	250
1935 Proof	—	—	—	—	—	—
1936	1,044,000	0.60	1.25	13.50	30.00	—
1936 Proof	—	—	—	—	—	—

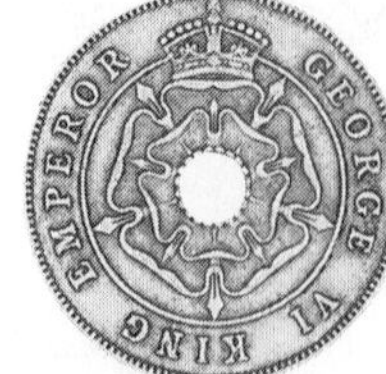
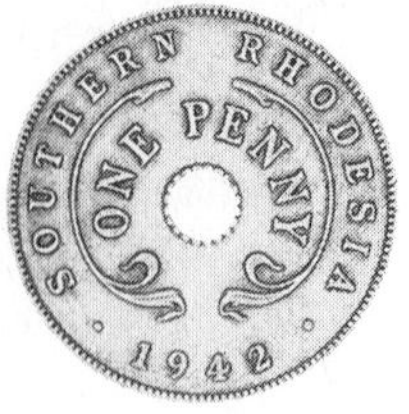

KM# 8 PENNY

Copper-Nickel **Ruler:** George VI **Obv:** Crowned flower design within circle, hole in center **Rev:** Value written within sprigs, hole in center

Date	Mintage	F	VF	XF	Unc	BU
1937	908,000	0.60	1.25	13.50	25.00	—
1937 Proof	—	Value: 300				
1938	240,000	1.50	3.00	27.50	50.00	—
1938 Proof	—	—	—	—	—	—
1939	1,284,000	0.45	1.00	23.50	37.50	—
1939 Proof	—	—	—	—	—	—
1940	1,080,000	0.45	1.00	23.50	37.50	—
1940 Proof	—	—	—	—	—	—
1941	720,000	0.50	1.25	24.50	40.00	—
1941 Proof	—	—	—	—	—	—
1942	960,000	0.50	1.25	34.50	65.00	—
1942 Proof	—	—	—	—	—	—

KM# 8a PENNY

Bronze **Ruler:** George VI **Obv:** Crowned flower design within circle, hole in center **Rev:** Written value within sprigs, hole in center

Date	Mintage	F	VF	XF	Unc	BU
1942	480,000	4.00	6.50	42.50	100	—
1942 Proof	—	Value: 400				
1943	3,120,000	0.50	0.80	6.50	15.00	30.00
1944	2,400,000	0.50	0.80	8.50	20.00	40.00
1944 Proof	—	—	—	—	—	—
1947	3,600,000	0.75	1.25	8.50	20.00	40.00
1947 Proof	—	—	—	—	—	—

KM# 25 PENNY

Bronze **Ruler:** George VI **Obv:** Crowned flower design within circle, hole in center **Rev:** Value written within sprigs, hole in center

Date	Mintage	F	VF	XF	Unc	BU
1949	1,440,000	0.50	1.00	12.50	25.00	—
1949 Proof	—	Value: 125				
1950	720,000	1.00	1.75	25.00	40.00	—
1950 Proof	—	Value: 125				
1951	4,896,000	0.50	0.75	3.25	10.00	18.00
1951 Proof	—	Value: 125				
1952	2,400,000	0.50	0.75	1.75	12.50	—
1952 Proof	—	—	—	—	—	—

KM# 29 PENNY

Bronze **Ruler:** Elizabeth II **Obv:** Crowned flower design within circle, hole in center **Rev:** Value written within sprigs, hole in center

Date	Mintage	F	VF	XF	Unc	BU
1954	960,000	4.00	27.50	115	250	350
1954 Proof	20	Value: 450				

KM# 1 3 PENCE

1.4100 g., 0.9250 Silver 0.0419 oz. ASW, 16 mm. **Ruler:** George V **Obv:** Crowned bust left **Obv. Designer:** E.B. MacKennal **Rev:** Three spearheads divide date **Rev. Designer:** G.E. Kruger-Gray

Date	Mintage	F	VF	XF	Unc	BU
1932	688,000	0.85	1.50	16.50	32.00	—
1932 Proof	—	Value: 60.00				
1934	628,000	0.85	2.00	40.00	60.00	—
1934 Proof	—	—	—	—	—	—
1935	840,000	0.85	2.00	27.50	45.00	—
1935 Proof	—	—	—	—	—	—
1936	1,052,000	0.85	2.00	27.50	45.00	65.00
1936 Proof	—	—	—	—	—	—

KM# 9 3 PENCE

1.4100 g., 0.9250 Silver 0.0419 oz. ASW, 16 mm. **Ruler:** George VI **Obv:** Crowned head left **Obv. Designer:** Percy Metcalfe **Rev:** Three spearheads divide date **Rev. Designer:** G.E. Kruger-Gray

Date	Mintage	F	VF	XF	Unc	BU
1937	1,228,000	0.85	2.00	20.00	40.00	—
1937 Proof	—	Value: 225				

KM# 16 3 PENCE

1.4100 g., 0.9250 Silver 0.0419 oz. ASW, 16 mm. **Ruler:** George VI **Obv:** Crowned head left **Obv. Designer:** Percy Metcalfe **Rev:** Three spearheads divide date **Rev. Designer:** G.E. Kruger-Gray

Date	Mintage	F	VF	XF	Unc	BU
1939	160,000	6.00	10.00	80.00	150	—
1939 Proof	—	Value: 300				
1940	1,200,000	0.85	2.00	27.50	40.00	—
1940 Proof	—	—	—	—	—	—
1941	600,000	2.50	5.00	30.00	50.00	—
1941 Proof	—	—	—	—	—	—
1942	2,000,000	0.75	1.50	16.50	30.00	—
1942 Proof	—	—	—	—	—	—

KM# 16a 3 PENCE

1.4100 g., 0.5000 Silver 0.0227 oz. ASW, 16 mm. **Ruler:** George VI **Obv:** Crowned head left **Obv. Designer:** Percy Metcalfe **Rev:** Three spearheads divide date **Rev. Designer:** G.E. Kruger-Gray **Edge:** Plain

Date	Mintage	F	VF	XF	Unc	BU
1944	1,600,000	0.65	1.50	30.00	60.00	—
1945	800,000	1.00	3.00	30.00	60.00	—
1945 Proof	—	—	—	—	—	—
1946	2,400,000	0.65	1.50	17.00	35.00	—
1946 Proof	—	—	—	—	—	—

KM# 16b 3 PENCE

Copper-Nickel, 16 mm. **Ruler:** George VI **Obv:** Crowned head left **Rev:** Three spearheads divide date

Date	Mintage	F	VF	XF	Unc	BU
1947	8,000,000	0.40	0.80	8.00	20.00	—
1947 Proof	—	Value: 250				

KM# 20 3 PENCE

Copper-Nickel, 16 mm. **Ruler:** George VI **Obv:** Crowned head left **Obv. Designer:** Percy Metcalfe **Rev:** Three spearheads divide date **Rev. Designer:** G.E. Kruger-Gray

Date	Mintage	F	VF	XF	Unc	BU
1948	2,000,000	0.40	2.00	13.50	30.00	45.00
1948 Proof	—	—	—	—	—	—
1949	4,000,000	0.40	2.00	13.00	25.00	—
1949 Proof	—	Value: 150				
1951	5,600,000	0.40	5.00	40.00	75.00	125
1951 Proof	—	—	—	—	—	—
1952	4,800,000	0.40	5.00	32.50	60.00	110
1952 Proof	—	Value: 150				

KM# 2 6 PENCE

2.8300 g., 0.9250 Silver 0.0842 oz. ASW **Ruler:** George V **Obv:** Crowned bust left **Obv. Designer:** E.B. MacKennal **Rev:** Crossed axes divide date and value **Rev. Designer:** G.E. Kruger-Gray

Date	Mintage	F	VF	XF	Unc	BU
1932	544,000	2.00	13.00	30.00	55.00	—
1932 Proof	—	Value: 65.00				
1934	214,000	3.00	17.00	55.00	90.00	—
1935	380,000	2.00	16.00	45.00	75.00	—
1935 Proof	—	—	—	—	—	—
1936	675,000	1.50	13.00	35.00	60.00	—
1936 Proof	—	—	—	—	—	—

KM# 10 6 PENCE

2.8300 g., 0.9250 Silver 0.0842 oz. ASW **Ruler:** George VI **Obv:** Crowned head left **Obv. Designer:** Percy Metcalfe **Rev:** Crossed axes divide date and value **Rev. Designer:** G.E. Kruger-Gray

Date	Mintage	F	VF	XF	Unc	BU
1937	823,000	2.50	15.00	30.00	55.00	—
1937 Proof	—	Value: 300				

KM# 17 6 PENCE

2.8300 g., 0.9250 Silver 0.0842 oz. ASW **Ruler:** George VI **Obv:** Crowned head left **Obv. Designer:** Percy Metcalfe **Rev:** Crossed axes divide date and value **Rev. Designer:** G.E. Kruger-Gray

Date	Mintage	F	VF	XF	Unc	BU
1939	200,000	3.00	27.00	125	200	300
1939 Proof	—	Value: 450				
1940	600,000	1.75	13.00	45.00	75.00	—
1940 Proof	—	—	—	—	—	—
1941	300,000	2.00	14.00	40.00	65.00	—
1941 Proof	—	—	—	—	—	—
1942	1,200,000	1.50	12.00	27.00	55.00	140
1942 Proof	—	Value: 200				

KM# 17a 6 PENCE

2.8300 g., 0.5000 Silver 0.0455 oz. ASW **Ruler:** George VI **Obv:** Crowned head left **Obv. Designer:** Percy Metcalfe **Rev:** Crossed axes divide date and value **Rev. Designer:** G.E. Kruger-Gray

Date	Mintage	F	VF	XF	Unc	BU
1944	800,000	1.25	2.50	55.00	90.00	150
1945	400,000	15.00	25.00	85.00	150	—
1945 Proof	—	—	—	—	—	—
1946	1,600,000	1.25	12.50	35.00	60.00	135
1946 Proof	—	—	—	—	—	—

KM# 17b 6 PENCE

Copper-Nickel **Ruler:** George VI **Obv:** Crowned head left **Obv. Designer:** Percy Metcalfe **Rev:** Crossed axes divide date and value **Rev. Designer:** G.E. Kruger-Gray

Date	Mintage	F	VF	XF	Unc	BU
1947	5,000,000	0.50	1.00	10.00	20.00	50.00
1947 Proof	—	Value: 250				

KM# 21 6 PENCE

Copper-Nickel **Ruler:** George VI **Obv:** Crowned head left **Obv. Designer:** Percy Metcalfe **Rev:** Crossed axes divide date and value **Rev. Designer:** G.E. Kruger-Gray

Date	Mintage	F	VF	XF	Unc	BU
1948	1,000,000	0.50	1.25	14.00	27.50	50.00
1948 Proof	—	—	—	—	—	—
1949	2,000,000	0.50	5.00	18.00	30.00	60.00
1949 Proof	—	Value: 250				
1950	2,000,000	0.50	6.00	24.00	55.00	95.00
1950 Proof	—	Value: 250				
1951	2,800,000	0.50	1.00	8.00	27.50	50.00
1951 Proof	—	—	—	—	—	—
1952	1,200,000	0.50	1.50	23.00	45.00	80.00
1952 Proof	—	—	—	—	—	—

KM# 3 SHILLING

5.6600 g., 0.9250 Silver 0.1683 oz. ASW **Ruler:** George V **Obv:** Crowned bust left **Obv. Designer:** E.B. MacKennal **Rev:** Bird sculpture divides date **Rev. Designer:** G.E. Kruger-Gray

Date	Mintage	F	VF	XF	Unc	BU
1932	896,000	2.75	20.00	42.00	80.00	—
1932 Proof	—	Value: 90.00				
1934	333,000	4.00	40.00	100	175	—
1935	830,000	2.75	24.00	70.00	120	—
1935 Proof	—	Value: 220				
1936	1,663,000	2.75	23.00	60.00	115	—
1936 Proof	—	—	—	—	—	—

KM# 11 SHILLING

5.6600 g., 0.9250 Silver 0.1683 oz. ASW **Ruler:** George VI **Obv:** Crowned head left **Obv. Designer:** Percy Metcalfe **Rev:** Bird sculpture divides date **Rev. Designer:** G.E. Kruger-Gray

Date	Mintage	F	VF	XF	Unc	BU
1937	1,700,000	2.75	24.00	55.00	90.00	—
1937 Proof	—	Value: 300				

KM# 18 SHILLING

5.6600 g., 0.9250 Silver 0.1683 oz. ASW **Ruler:** George VI **Obv:** Crowned head left **Obv. Designer:** Percy Metcalfe **Rev:** Bird sculpture divides date **Rev. Designer:** G.E. Kruger-Gray

Date	Mintage	F	VF	XF	Unc	BU
1939	420,000	7.00	45.00	150	275	—
1939 Proof	—	Value: 500				
1940	750,000	5.50	35.00	90.00	165	—
1940 Proof	—	—	—	—	—	—
1941	800,000	6.50	32.00	80.00	140	—
1941 Proof	—	—	—	—	—	—
1942	2,100,000	2.75	5.00	25.00	55.00	—
1942 Proof	—	—	—	—	—	—

KM# 18a SHILLING

5.6600 g., 0.5000 Silver 0.0910 oz. ASW **Ruler:** George VI **Obv:** Crowned head left **Rev:** Bird sculpture divides date

Date	Mintage	F	VF	XF	Unc	BU
1944	1,600,000	2.00	14.00	45.00	80.00	—
1946	1,700,000	3.50	18.00	70.00	120	—
1946 Proof	—	—	—	—	—	—

KM# 18b SHILLING

Copper-Nickel **Ruler:** George VI **Obv:** Crowned head left **Rev:** Bird sculpture divides date

Date	Mintage	F	VF	XF	Unc	BU
1947	8,000,000	0.75	1.50	24.00	40.00	80.00
1947 Proof	—	Value: 300				

KM# 22 SHILLING

Copper-Nickel **Ruler:** George VI **Obv:** Crowned head left **Obv. Designer:** Percy Metcalfe **Rev:** Bird sculpture divides date **Rev. Designer:** G.E. Kruger-Gray

Date	Mintage	F	VF	XF	Unc	BU
1948	1,500,000	0.75	1.50	16.00	30.00	60.00
1948 Proof	—	—	—	—	—	—
1949	4,000,000	0.75	8.00	18.00	35.00	65.00
1949 Proof	—	Value: 250				
1950	2,000,000	1.00	13.00	30.00	55.00	90.00
1950 Proof	—	Value: 225				
1951	3,000,000	0.75	4.00	14.00	20.00	40.00
1951 Proof	—	—	—	—	—	—
1952	2,600,000	0.75	8.00	30.00	55.00	90.00
1952 Proof	—	—	—	—	—	—

KM# 4 2 SHILLINGS

11.3100 g., 0.9250 Silver 0.3363 oz. ASW **Ruler:** George V **Obv:** Crowned bust left **Obv. Designer:** E.B. MacKennal **Rev:** Sable antelope **Rev. Designer:** G.E. Kruger-Gray

Date	Mintage	F	VF	XF	Unc	BU
1932	498,000	5.50	20.00	55.00	110	—
1932 Proof	—	Value: 125				
1934	154,000	12.50	40.00	140	225	—
1935	365,000	6.50	25.00	70.00	120	200
1935 Proof	—	—	—	—	—	—
1936	683,000	5.50	25.00	65.00	120	—
1936 Proof	—	—	—	—	—	—

KM# 12 2 SHILLINGS

11.3100 g., 0.9250 Silver 0.3363 oz. ASW **Ruler:** George VI **Obv:** Crowned head left **Obv. Designer:** Percy Metcalfe **Rev:** Sable antelope **Rev. Designer:** G.E. Kruger-Gray

Date	Mintage	F	VF	XF	Unc	BU
1937	552,000	7.50	30.00	75.00	135	—
1937 Proof	—	Value: 400				

KM# 19 2 SHILLINGS

11.3100 g., 0.9250 Silver 0.3363 oz. ASW **Ruler:** George VI **Obv:** Crowned head left **Obv. Designer:** Percy Metcalfe **Rev:** Sable antelope **Rev. Designer:** G.E. Kruger-Gray

Date	Mintage	F	VF	XF	Unc	BU
1939	120,000	50.00	225	450	650	—
1939 Proof	—	Value: 750				
1940	525,000	8.00	55.00	150	250	—
1940 Proof	—	—	—	—	—	—
1941	400,000	8.00	25.00	175	300	—
1941 Proof	—	—	—	—	—	—
1942	850,000	5.50	10.00	45.00	90.00	—

KM# 19a 2 SHILLINGS

11.3100 g., 0.5000 Silver 0.1818 oz. ASW **Ruler:** George VI **Obv:** Crowned head left **Rev:** Sable antelope

Date	Mintage	F	VF	XF	Unc	BU
1944	1,300,000	6.00	22.00	60.00	135	—
1946	700,000	100	300	400	650	—
1946 Proof	—	—	—	—	—	—

KM# 19b 2 SHILLINGS

Copper-Nickel **Ruler:** George VI **Obv:** Crowned head left **Rev:** Sable antelope

Date	Mintage	F	VF	XF	Unc	BU
1947	3,750,000	1.75	4.00	22.50	45.00	90.00
1947 Proof	—	Value: 300				

KM# 23 2 SHILLINGS
Copper-Nickel **Ruler:** George VI **Obv:** Crowned head left **Obv. Designer:** Percy Metcalfe **Rev:** Sable antelope **Rev. Designer:** G.E. Kruger-Gray

Date	Mintage	F	VF	XF	Unc	BU
1948	750,000	1.00	3.00	30.00	60.00	110
1948 Proof	—	—	—	—	—	—
1949	2,000,000	1.00	3.00	30.00	80.00	—
1949 Proof	—	Value: 350				
1950	1,000,000	1.00	4.00	35.00	115	—
1950 Proof	—	Value: 350				
1951	2,600,000	1.00	3.00	16.00	47.00	—
1951 Proof	—	—	—	—	—	—
1952	1,800,000	1.00	3.00	40.00	75.00	175
1952 Proof	—	—	—	—	—	—

KM# 30 2 SHILLINGS
Copper-Nickel **Ruler:** Elizabeth II **Obv:** Laureate bust right **Obv. Designer:** Mary Gillick **Rev:** Sable antelope **Rev. Designer:** G.E. Kruger-Gray

Date	Mintage	F	VF	XF	Unc	BU
1954	300,000	25.00	55.00	375	900	—
1954 Proof	20	Value: 1,250				

KM# 5 1/2 CROWN
14.1400 g., 0.9250 Silver 0.4205 oz. ASW, 32 mm. **Ruler:** George V **Obv:** Crowned bust left **Obv. Designer:** E.B. MacKennal **Rev:** Crowned shield **Rev. Designer:** G.E. Kruger-Gray

Date	Mintage	F	VF	XF	Unc	BU
1932	634,000	7.00	10.00	50.00	115	—
1932 Proof	—	Value: 125				
1934	419,000	7.50	30.00	145	240	—
1934 Proof	—	—	—	—	—	—
1935	512,000	7.00	25.00	85.00	175	—
1935 Proof	—	—	—	—	—	—
1936	518,000	7.00	28.00	70.00	145	260
1936 Proof	—	—	—	—	—	—

KM# 13 1/2 CROWN
14.1400 g., 0.9250 Silver 0.4205 oz. ASW, 32 mm. **Ruler:** George VI **Obv:** Crowned head left **Obv. Designer:** Percy Metcalfe **Rev:** Crowned shield **Rev. Designer:** G.E. Kruger-Gray

Date	Mintage	F	VF	XF	Unc	BU
1937	1,174,000	7.00	28.00	70.00	130	200
1937 Proof	—	Value: 350				

KM# 15 1/2 CROWN
14.1400 g., 0.9250 Silver 0.4205 oz. ASW, 32 mm. **Ruler:** George VI **Obv:** Crowned head left **Obv. Designer:** Percy Metcalfe **Rev:** Crowned shield **Rev. Designer:** G.E. Kruger-Gray

Date	Mintage	F	VF	XF	Unc	BU
1938	400,000	7.00	28.00	75.00	150	260
1938 Proof	—	—	—	—	—	—
1939	224,000	10.00	30.00	160	300	550
1939 Proof	—	Value: 500				
1940	800,000	7.00	10.00	37.50	80.00	—
1940 Proof	—	—	—	—	—	—
1941	1,240,000	BV	7.00	35.00	65.00	—
1941 Proof	—	—	—	—	—	—
1942	2,008,000	BV	7.00	35.00	70.00	140
1942 Proof	—	—	—	—	—	—

KM# 15a 1/2 CROWN
14.1400 g., 0.5000 Silver 0.2273 oz. ASW **Ruler:** George VI **Obv:** Crowned head left **Rev:** Crowned shield

Date	Mintage	F	VF	XF	Unc	BU
1944	800,000	3.75	7.00	40.00	90.00	—
1946	1,400,000	4.00	10.00	75.00	135	200
1946 Proof	—	—	—	—	—	—

KM# 15b 1/2 CROWN
Copper-Nickel, 32 mm. **Ruler:** George VI **Obv:** Crowned head left **Obv. Designer:** Percy Metcalfe **Rev:** Crowned shield **Rev. Designer:** G.E. Kruger-Gray

Date	Mintage	F	VF	XF	Unc	BU
1947	6,000,000	1.25	2.50	5.00	20.00	50.00
1947 Proof	—	Value: 300				

KM# 24 1/2 CROWN
Copper-Nickel, 32 mm. **Ruler:** George VI **Obv:** Crowned head left **Obv. Designer:** Percy Metcalfe **Rev:** Crowned shield **Rev. Designer:** G.E. Kruger-Gray

Date	Mintage	F	VF	XF	Unc	BU
1948	800,000	1.25	2.50	30.00	60.00	—
1948 Proof	—	—	—	—	—	—
1949	1,600,000	1.25	2.50	25.00	65.00	—
1949 Proof	—	Value: 450				
1950	1,200,000	1.25	2.50	35.00	75.00	—
1950 Proof	—	Value: 450				
1951	3,200,000	1.25	2.50	27.50	50.00	90.00
1951 Proof	—	Value: 350				
1952	2,800,000	1.25	2.50	30.00	70.00	100
1952 Proof	—	Value: 350				

KM# 31 1/2 CROWN
Copper-Nickel, 32 mm. **Ruler:** Elizabeth II **Obv:** Laureate bust right **Obv. Designer:** Mary Gillick **Rev:** Crowned shield **Rev. Designer:** G.E. Kruger-Gray

Date	Mintage	F	VF	XF	Unc	BU
1954	1,200,000	8.00	16.00	45.00	95.00	130
1954 Proof	20	Value: 450				

KM# 27 CROWN
28.2800 g., 0.5000 Silver 0.4546 oz. ASW, 38.5 mm. **Ruler:** Elizabeth II **Subject:** Birth of Cecil Rhodes Centennial **Obv:** Larueate bust right **Obv. Designer:** Mary Gillick **Rev:** Cameo flanked by sprigs with ribbon above assorted shields **Rev. Designer:** T.H. Paget **Edge Lettering:** 1853 OUT OF VISION CAME REALITY 1953 **Note:** Both upright and inverted edge varieties exist.

Date	Mintage	F	VF	XF	Unc	BU
1953	124,000	7.50	15.00	30.00	40.00	85.00
1953 Proof	1,500	Value: 85.00				
1953 Matte Proof	—	Value: 350				

SPAIN

The Spanish State, forming the greater part of the Iberian Peninsula of southwest Europe, has an area of 195,988 sq. mi. (504,714 sq. km.) and a population of 39.4 million including the Balearic and the Canary Islands. Capital: Madrid. The economy is based on agriculture, industry and tourism. Machinery, fruit, vegetables and chemicals are exported.

Discontent against the mother country increased after 1808 as colonists faced new imperialist policies from Napoleon or Spanish liberals. The revolutionary movement was established which resulted in the eventual independence of the Vice-royalties of New Spain, New Granada and Rio de la Plata within 2 decades.

The doomed republic was trapped in a tug-of-war between the right and left wing forces inevitably resulting in the Spanish

Civil War of 1936-38. The leftist Republicans were supported by the U.S.S.R. and the International Brigade, which consisted of mainly communist volunteers from all over the western world. The right wing Nationalists were supported by the Fascist governments of Italy and Germany. Under the leadership of Gen. Francisco Franco, the Nationalists emerged victorious and immediately embarked on a program of reconstruction and neutrality as dictated by the new "Caudillo"(leader) Franco.

The monarchy was reconstituted in 1947 under the regency of General Francisco Franco; the king designate to be crowned after Franco's death. Franco died on Nov. 20, 1975. Two days after his passing, Juan Carlos de Borbon, the grandson of Alfonso XIII, was proclaimed King of Spain.

RULERS

Alfonso XIII, 1886-1931
2nd Republic and Civil War, 1931-1939
Francisco Franco, 1939-1947
as Caudillo and regent, 1947-1975
Juan Carlos I, 1975-

NOTE: From 1868 to 1982, two dates may be found on most Spanish coinage. The larger date is the year of authorization and the smaller date incused on the two 6-pointed-stars found on most types is the year of issue. The latter appears in parentheses in these listings.

MINT MARKS

Until 1980
6-pointed star - Madrid

NOTE: Letters after date are initials of mint officials.

After 1982
Crowned M – Madrid

KINGDOM

THIRD DECIMAL COINAGE

10 Milesimas = 1 Centimo

100 Centesimos = 1 Peseta

KM# 724 20 PESETAS
6.4516 g., 0.9000 Gold 0.1867 oz. AGW **Obv:** Head right **Rev:** Crowned and mantled shield **Note:** Mint mark: 6-pointed star.

Date	Mintage	F	VF	XF	Unc	BU
1904 (04) SM-V	3,814	850	1,650	2,250	3,000	—

DECIMAL COINAGE

Peseta System

100 Centimos = 1 Peseta

KM# 726 CENTIMO
Bronze **Ruler:** Alfonso XIII **Obv:** Head right **Rev:** Crowned shield divides value within beaded circle **Note:** Mint mark: 6-pointed star.

Date	Mintage	F	VF	XF	Unc	BU
1906 (6) SL-V	7,500,000	0.35	0.75	1.50	3.50	5.00
1906 (6) SM-V	Inc. above	350	650	800	1,050	1,200

KM# 731 CENTIMO
Bronze **Ruler:** Alfonso XIII **Obv:** Head left **Rev:** Crowned shield divides value within beaded circle **Note:** Mint mark: 6-pointed star.

Date	Mintage	F	VF	XF	Unc	BU
1911 (1) PC-V	1,462,000	45.00	75.00	110	130	145
1912 (2) PC-V	2,109,000	2.00	3.50	7.00	13.50	20.00
1913 (3) PC-V	1,429,000	3.50	6.50	13.50	22.00	30.00

KM# 722 2 CENTIMOS
Copper **Ruler:** Alfonso XIII **Obv:** Head right **Rev:** Crowned shield divides value within beaded circle **Note:** Mint mark: 6-pointed star.

Date	Mintage	F	VF	XF	Unc	BU
1904 (04) SM-V	10,000,000	0.65	2.00	6.00	15.00	20.00
1905 (05) SM-V	5,000,000	0.75	3.00	8.00	20.00	25.00

KM# 732 2 CENTIMOS
Copper **Ruler:** Alfonso XIII **Obv:** Head left **Rev:** Crowned shield divides value within beaded circle **Note:** Mint mark: 6-pointed star.

Date	Mintage	F	VF	XF	Unc	BU
1911 (11) PC-V	2,284,000	0.65	1.75	6.00	15.00	20.00
1912 (12) PC-V	5,216,000	0.65	1.75	5.00	14.00	18.00

KM# 740 25 CENTIMOS
Copper-Nickel **Ruler:** Alfonso XIII **Obv:** Sailing ship **Rev:** Crowned value flanked by sprigs

Date	Mintage	F	VF	XF	Unc	BU
1925 PC-S	8,001,000	0.50	1.50	12.00	50.00	75.00

KM# 742 25 CENTIMOS
7.0000 g., Copper-Nickel, 25.2 mm. **Ruler:** Alfonso XIII **Obv:** Vine entwined on cross, crown and date, hole in center **Rev:** Value above oat sprigs, hole in center

Date	Mintage	F	VF	XF	Unc	BU
1927 PC-S	12,000,000	0.50	1.00	10.00	40.00	65.00

KM# 723 50 CENTIMOS
2.5000 g., 0.8350 Silver 0.0671 oz. ASW **Ruler:** Alfonso XIII **Obv:** Head left **Rev:** Crowned shield flanked by pillars with banner **Note:** Mint mark: 6-pointed star.

Date	Mintage	F	VF	XF	Unc	BU
1904 (04) SM-V	4,851,000	2.50	3.50	7.00	15.00	20.00
1904 (10) PC-V	1,303,000	2.75	4.00	8.00	20.00	25.00

KM# 730 50 CENTIMOS
2.5000 g., 0.8350 Silver 0.0671 oz. ASW **Ruler:** Alfonso XIII **Obv:** Head left **Rev:** Crowned shield flanked by pillars with banner **Note:** Mint mark: 6-pointed star.

Date	Mintage	F	VF	XF	Unc	BU
1910 (10) PC-V	4,526,000	2.75	4.00	8.00	24.00	30.00

KM# 741 50 CENTIMOS
2.5000 g., 0.8350 Silver 0.0671 oz. ASW **Ruler:** Alfonso XIII **Obv:** Head left **Rev:** Crowned shield within wreath

Date	Mintage	F	VF	XF	Unc	BU
1926 PC-S	4,000,000	2.75	3.50	6.50	12.00	16.00

KM# 706 PESETA
5.0000 g., 0.8350 Silver 0.1342 oz. ASW **Ruler:** Alfonso XIII **Obv:** Child's head left **Obv. Legend:** ALFONSO XIII... **Rev:** Crowned arms, pillars, value below **Rev. Legend:** REYCONST... **Note:** Mint mark: 6-pointed star. Prices are for coins with full right star dates. Partial right star dates sell for less. Examples with no visable right star date have limited collector appeal.

Date	Mintage	F	VF	XF	Unc	BU
1901 (01) SM-V	8,449,000	5.00	16.00	55.00	125	145
1902 (02) SM-V	2,599,000	25.00	80.00	175	350	400

KM# 721 PESETA
5.0000 g., 0.8350 Silver 0.1342 oz. ASW **Ruler:** Alfonso XIII **Obv:** Head left **Rev:** Crowned shield flanked by pillars with banner **Note:** Mint mark 6-pointed star.

Date	Mintage	F	VF	XF	Unc	BU
1903 (03) SM-V	10,602,000	4.00	14.00	40.00	90.00	100
1904 (04) SM-V	5,294,000	5.00	15.00	45.00	95.00	110
1905 (05) SM-V	492,000	45.00	135	550	950	1,100

KM# 725 2 PESETAS
10.0000 g., 0.8350 Silver 0.2684 oz. ASW **Ruler:** Alfonso XIII **Obv:** Head left **Rev:** Crowned shield flanked by pillars with banner **Note:** Mint mark: 6-pointed star.

Date	Mintage	F	VF	XF	Unc	BU
1905 (05) SM-V	3,589,000	4.50	15.00	28.00	50.00	55.00

REPUBLIC

1931 - 1939

DECIMAL COINAGE

Peseta System

100 Centimos = 1 Peseta

KM# 752 5 CENTIMOS
Iron **Obv:** Head left **Rev:** Value and date within wreath

Date	Mintage	F	VF	XF	Unc	BU
1937	10,000,000	0.35	1.00	2.00	5.00	10.00

KM# 756 10 CENTIMOS
Iron **Obv:** Crowned shield **Rev:** Value and date within wreath

Date	Mintage	F	VF	XF	Unc	BU
1938	1,000	—	600	1,050	2,100	3,000

Note: This coin was never released into circulation

KM# 751 25 CENTIMOS
Copper-Nickel **Obv:** Bust right holding sprig, hole in center **Rev:** Value above oat sprig and gear, hole in center

Date	Mintage	F	VF	XF	Unc	BU
1934	12,272,000	0.30	0.75	3.50	20.00	25.00

KM# 753 25 CENTIMOS
7.1100 g., Copper-Nickel, 25 mm. **Obv:** Inscription, date and arrow design, hole in center **Rev:** Crowned shield, value and sprig, hole in center

Date	Mintage	F	VF	XF	Unc	BU
1937	42,000,000	0.20	0.40	1.00	4.00	5.00

Note: This coin was issued by way of decree April 5, 1938, by the Governmant in Burgos. Franco and the Nationalist forces controlled the majority of Spain by this point in time

KM# 757 25 CENTIMOS
Copper **Obv:** Chain links around center hole **Rev:** Value and center hole divide sprigs

Date	Mintage	F	VF	XF	Unc	BU
1938	45,500,000	0.75	1.50	5.00	10.00	15.00

KM# 754.1 50 CENTIMOS
5.8000 g., Copper **Obv:** Seated figure holding sprig **Rev:** Value within beaded circle **Note:** Mint mark: 6-pointed star. Several varieties exist.

Date	Mintage	F	VF	XF	Unc	BU
1937 (34)	50,000,000	0.50	1.00	5.00	15.00	25.00
1937 (36)	1,000,000	0.65	1.50	5.00	11.00	20.00

KM# 754.2 50 CENTIMOS
Copper **Obv:** Seated allegorical figure left **Rev:** Border of rectangles **Note:** Mint mark: 6-pointed star.

Date	Mintage	F	VF	XF	Unc	BU
1937 (36)	Inc. above	1.50	3.00	8.00	20.00	30.00

KM# 750 PESETA
5.0000 g., 0.8350 Silver 0.1342 oz. ASW **Obv:** Seated figure holding sprig **Rev:** Crowned shield flanked by pillars with banner **Note:** Mint mark: 6-pointed star.

Date	Mintage	F	VF	XF	Unc	BU
1933 (3-4)	2,000,000	5.00	15.00	21.00	30.00	35.00

Note: Rotated reverse varieties exist, with values increasing by the degree of rotation.

KM# 755 PESETA
Brass **Obv:** Head left **Rev:** Value and grapes on vine

Date	Mintage	F	VF	XF	Unc	BU
1937	50,000,000	0.35	0.85	2.00	7.50	10.00

NATIONALIST GOVERNMENT
1939 - 1947
DECIMAL COINAGE
Peseta System

100 Centimos = 1 Peseta

KM# 765 5 CENTIMOS
Aluminum **Obv:** Armored figure on rearing horse **Rev:** Crowned shield within eagle flanked by pillars with banner **Note:** Mint mark: 6-pointed star. To realize the values below all Unc. and BU coins must have full strike including letters.

Date	Mintage	F	VF	XF	Unc	BU
1940 PLVS	175,000,000	1.50	5.00	15.00	40.00	55.00
1941	202,107,000	1.00	2.50	3.50	15.00	18.00
1945	221,500,000	—	1.00	3.00	9.00	12.00
1953	31,573,000	12.00	30.00	40.00	70.00	85.00

KM# 766 10 CENTIMOS
8.0700 g., Aluminum, 23 mm. **Obv:** Armored figure on rearing horse **Rev:** Crowned shield within eagle flanked by pillars with banner **Edge:** Coarse reeding **Designer:** Reeded **Note:** Varieties exist. To realize the values below all Unc. and BU coins must have full strike including letters.

Date	Mintage	F	VF	XF	Unc	BU
1940 PLUS	225,000,000	0.40	2.00	11.00	45.00	60.00
1940 PLVS	Inc. above	20.00	40.00	80.00	200	250
1941 PLUS	247,981,000	0.50	2.00	5.00	12.50	16.50
1941 PLVS	Inc. above	10.00	20.00	45.00	80.00	100
1945	250,000,000	—	0.60	3.00	11.00	14.00
1953	865,850,000	—	0.35	2.50	6.00	8.00

KM# 767 PESETA
Aluminum-Bronze **Obv:** Crowned shield within eagle flanked by pillars with banner **Rev:** Value in center of design **Note:** To realize the values below all Unc. and BU coins must have full strike including letters.

Date	Mintage	F	VF	XF	Unc	BU
1944	150,000,000	—	0.45	5.00	30.00	40.00

KINGDOM
1949 - Present
DECIMAL COINAGE
Peseta System

100 Centimos = 1 Peseta

KM# 790 10 CENTIMOS
Aluminum, 18 mm. **Ruler:** Caudillo and regent **Obv:** Head right **Rev:** Value within designed wreath **Edge:** Reeded

Date	Mintage	F	VF	XF	Unc	BU
1959	900,000,000	—	—	—	0.25	0.35
1959 Proof	101,000	Value: 3.00				

KM# 776 50 CENTIMOS
Copper-Nickel, 21 mm. **Ruler:** Caudillo and regent **Obv:** Anchor, date and part of captains wheel, hole in center **Rev:** Value, design with arrows pointing down and hole in center divide assorted shields **Edge:** Plain **Note:** Mint mark: 6-pointed star.

Date	Mintage	F	VF	XF	Unc	BU
1949 (51)	990,000	5.00	10.00	15.00	30.00	35.00

Note: Minting date "51" in incused star

KM# 777 50 CENTIMOS
Copper-Nickel, 21 mm. **Ruler:** Caudillo and regent **Obv:** Anchor, date and part of captains wheel, hole in center **Rev:** Value, design with arrows pointing up and hole in center divide assorted shields **Edge:** Plain **Note:** Mint mark: 6-pointed star.

Date	Mintage	F	VF	XF	Unc	BU
1949 (51)	8,010,000	—	2.00	3.00	18.50	25.00
1949 (E51)	Est. 5,000	—	—	—	600	750

Note: Issued to commemorate the 1st Ibero-American Numismatic Exposition December 2, 1951; An "E" replaces the "19" on the lower star

Date	Mintage	F	VF	XF	Unc	BU
1949 (52)	18,567,000	—	0.25	2.00	12.00	18.00
1949 (53)	17,500,000	—	0.50	5.00	25.00	30.00
1949 (54)	37,000,000	—	0.60	4.00	15.00	20.00
1949 (56)	38,000,000	—	0.15	2.00	12.00	15.00
1949 (62)	31,000,000	—	0.20	1.50	7.00	10.00
1963 (63)	4,000,000	1.50	5.50	9.00	30.00	35.00
1963 (64)	20,000,000	—	0.10	0.25	2.50	3.50
1963 (65)	14,000,000	—	0.10	0.20	1.50	2.50

KM# 795 50 CENTIMOS
1.1000 g., Aluminum, 20.1 mm. **Ruler:** Caudillo and regent **Obv:** Head right **Rev:** Sprig divides value **Edge:** Reeded **Note:** Mint mark: 6-pointed star. These coins generally suffer from oxidation and the values given are for perfect proof specimens.

Date	Mintage	F	VF	XF	Unc	BU
1966 (67)	80,000,000	—	—	0.15	0.75	1.00
1966 (68)	100,000,000	—	—	0.15	0.60	1.00
1966 (69)	50,000,000	—	—	0.25	2.50	3.00
1966 (70) Prooflike, in sets only	—	—	—	—	125	175
1966 (71)	99,000,000	—	—	0.15	0.35	0.75
1966 (72)	2,283,000	—	—	0.25	2.50	3.00
1966 (72) Proof	30,000	Value: 5.00				
1966 (73)	10,000,000	—	—	0.15	0.35	0.50
1966 (73) Proof	25,000	Value: 3.50				
1966 (74) Proof	23,000	Value: 50.00				
1966 (75) Proof	75,000	Value: 10.00				

KM# 805 50 CENTIMOS

Copper-Nickel **Ruler:** Juan Carlos I **Obv:** Head left **Rev:** Sprig divides value **Note:** Mint mark: 6-pointed star.

Date	Mintage	F	VF	XF	Unc	BU
1975 (76)	4,060,000	—	—	0.10	0.20	0.50
1975 (76) Proof	—	Value: 0.85				

KM# 815 50 CENTIMOS

Center Composition: Aluminum, 20 mm. **Ruler:** Juan Carlos I **Subject:** World Cup Soccer Games **Obv:** Head left **Rev:** Soccer balls above value **Edge:** Reeded **Note:** Mint mark: 6-pointed star.

Date	Mintage	F	VF	XF	Unc	BU
1980 (80)	15,000,000	—	—	0.10	0.20	0.35
1980 (80) Proof	—	Value: 0.75				

KM# 775 PESETA

Aluminum-Bronze, 21 mm. **Ruler:** Francisco Franco, caudillo **Obv:** Head right **Rev:** Crowned shield within eagle flanked by pillars with banner **Edge:** Reeded **Note:** Mint mark: 6-pointed star.

Date	Mintage	F	VF	XF	Unc	BU
1946 (48)	Est. 5,000	1,000	1,500	2,000	3,000	—
1947 (48)	15,000,000	—	1.00	15.00	150	200
1947 (49)	27,600,000	—	0.75	15.00	150	175
1947 (50)	4,000,000	1.50	6.00	50.00	450	650
1947 (51)	9,185,000	2.00	4.00	40.00	200	400
1947 (E51)	Est. 5,000	—	—	—	600	800
Note: Issued to commemorate the 2nd National Numismatic Exposition December 2, 1951; An "E" replaces the "19" on the lower star						
1947 (52)	19,195,000	—	1.00	10.00	60.00	150
1947 (53)	34,000,000	—	0.75	10.00	50.00	150
1947 (54)	50,000,000	—	1.00	15.00	75.00	200
1947 (56)	—	10.00	30.00	100	600	1,000
1953 (54)	40,272,000	—	3.00	30.00	250	325
1953 (56)	118,000,000	—	0.10	1.00	5.00	8.00
1953 (60)	45,160,000	—	0.70	10.50	75.00	125
1953 (61)	25,830,000	—	0.60	10.00	50.00	90.00
1953 (62)	66,252,000	—	0.10	1.00	3.00	7.00
1953 (63)	37,000,000	—	0.25	1.50	15.00	30.00
1963 (63)	36,000,000	—	0.35	2.25	20.00	25.00
1963 (64)	80,000,000	—	0.10	1.00	3.00	5.00
1963 (65)	70,000,000	—	0.10	1.00	3.00	5.00
1963 (66)	63,000,000	—	0.10	1.00	5.00	10.00
1963 (67)	11,300,000	—	2.00	10.00	50.00	100

KM# 796 PESETA

Aluminum-Bronze, 21 mm. **Ruler:** Caudillo and regent **Obv:** Head right **Rev:** Crowned shield within eagle flanked by pillars with banner **Edge:** Reeded **Note:** Mint mark: 6-pointed star.

Date	Mintage	F	VF	XF	Unc	BU
1966 (67)	59,000,000	—	0.15	0.30	1.50	4.50
1966 (68)	120,000,000	—	0.10	0.20	1.00	1.50
1966 (69)	120,000,000	—	0.10	0.20	1.00	1.50
1966 (70)	75,000,000	—	0.10	0.20	2.00	3.00
1966 (71)	115,270,000	—	0.10	0.15	0.75	1.50
1966 (72)	106,000,000	—	—	0.10	0.50	0.75
1966 (72) Proof	30,000	Value: 1.50				
1966 (73)	152,000,000	—	—	0.10	0.35	0.65
1966 (73) Proof	25,000	Value: 1.50				
1966 (74)	181,000,000	—	—	0.10	0.35	0.65
1966 (74) Proof	23,000	Value: 1.50				
1966 (75)	227,580,000	—	—	0.10	0.25	0.35
1966 (75) Proof	75,000	Value: 1.00				

KM# 806 PESETA

Aluminum-Bronze, 21 mm. **Ruler:** Juan Carlos I **Obv:** Head left **Rev:** Crowned shield within eagle flanked by pillars with banner **Edge:** Reeded

Date	Mintage	F	VF	XF	Unc	BU
1975 (76)	170,380,000	—	—	0.10	0.25	0.35
1975 (76) Proof	—	Value: 0.75				
1975 (77)	243,380,000	—	—	0.10	0.25	0.35
1975 (77) Proof	—	Value: 0.75				
1975 (78)	Est. 603,320,000	—	—	0.10	0.25	0.35
1975 (79)	507,000,000	—	—	0.10	0.25	0.35
Note: Two varieties of tilde size for the n in España exist of this date; Large is Madrid mint, small is Santiago de Chile						
1975 (79) Proof	—	Value: 0.75				
1975 (80)	590,000,000	—	—	0.10	0.25	0.50

KM# 816 PESETA

Aluminum-Bronze, 21 mm. **Ruler:** Juan Carlos I **Subject:** World Cup Soccer Games **Obv:** Head left **Rev:** Small crowned shield within eagle at left of value

Date	Mintage	F	VF	XF	Unc	BU
1980 (80)	—	—	—	0.10	0.15	0.30
1980 (80) Proof	—	Value: 0.75				
1980 (81)	385,000,000	—	—	0.10	0.25	0.35
1980 (82)	333,000,000	—	—	0.10	0.25	0.35

KM# 821 PESETA

1.2000 g., Aluminum, 21 mm. **Ruler:** Juan Carlos I **Obv:** Head left **Rev:** Crowned shield flanked by pillars with banner to right of value **Designer:** Plain

Date	Mintage	F	VF	XF	Unc	BU
1982	—	—	—	0.10	0.20	0.35
Note: Mintage included in KM#816, 1980 (82)						
1983	52,000,000	—	—	0.10	0.50	0.75
1984	131,000,000	—	—	0.10	0.20	0.35
1985	220,065,000	—	—	0.10	0.20	0.35
1986	299,960,000	—	—	0.10	0.20	0.35
1987	299,550,000	—	—	0.10	0.20	0.35
1988	223,460,000	—	—	0.10	0.20	0.35
1989	—	—	—	0.10	0.60	1.00
Note: Mintage included in KM#832, 1989						

KM# 832 PESETA

Aluminum, 14 mm. **Ruler:** Juan Carlos I **Obv:** Vertical line divides head left from value **Rev:** Crowned shield flanked by pillars with banner **Edge:** Plain

Date	Mintage	F	VF	XF	Unc	BU
1989	198,415,000	—	—	0.10	0.25	0.50
1990	197,700,000	—	—	0.10	0.25	0.50
1991	173,780,000	—	—	0.10	0.25	0.50
1992	168,870,000	—	—	0.10	0.20	0.25
1993	300,013,000	—	—	0.10	0.20	0.25
1994	162,860,000	—	—	0.10	0.20	0.25
1995	183,175,000	—	—	0.10	0.20	0.25
1996	101,885,000	—	—	0.10	0.20	0.25
1997	342,620,000	—	—	0.10	0.20	0.25
1998	411,614,000	—	—	0.10	0.20	0.25
1999	84,946,000	—	—	0.10	0.20	0.25
2000	—	—	—	0.10	0.20	0.25
2001	—	—	—	0.10	0.30	0.50

KM# 822 2 PESETAS

2.0000 g., Aluminum, 24 mm. **Ruler:** Juan Carlos I **Obv:** Head left **Rev:** Value within map

Date	Mintage	F	VF	XF	Unc	BU
1982	21,500,000	—	—	0.20	0.50	0.75
1984	47,650,000	—	—	0.20	0.45	0.65

KM# 785 2-1/2 PESETAS

Aluminum-Bronze **Ruler:** Caudillo and regent **Obv:** Head right **Rev:** Crowned shield within eagle flanked by pillars with banner

Date	Mintage	F	VF	XF	Unc	BU
1953 (54)	22,729,000	—	0.25	1.00	5.00	10.00
1953 (56)	30,322,000	—	0.25	1.00	5.00	10.00
1953 (56) Proof	—	Value: 100				
1953 (68)	1,000	—	—	—	—	1,200
Note: In sets only						
1953 (69)	2,000	—	—	—	—	1,000
Note: In sets only						
1953 (70)	6,000	—	—	—	—	140
Note: In sets only						
1953 (71)	10,000	—	—	—	—	150
Note: In sets only						

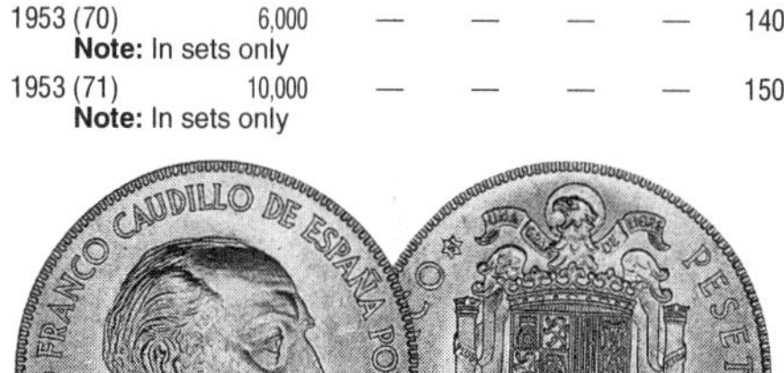

KM# 778 5 PESETAS

Nickel, 32 mm. **Ruler:** Caudillo and regent **Obv:** Head right **Rev:** Crowned shield within eagle flanked by pillars with banner **Edge:** Reeded

Date	Mintage	F	VF	XF	Unc	BU
1949 (49)	612,000	—	2.50	10.00	20.00	30.00
1949 (50)	21,000,000	—	0.85	2.00	5.00	10.00
1949 (E51)	Est. 6,000	—	—	—	1,500	2,250
Note: Issued to commemorate the Second National Numismatic Exposition December 2, 1951; An "E" replaces the "19" on the lower star						
1949 (51) Rare	145,000	—	—	—	—	—
1949 (52) Rare	Est. 200,000	—	—	—	—	—

KM# 786 5 PESETAS

5.7500 g., Copper-Nickel, 23 mm. **Ruler:** Caudillo and regent **Obv:** Head right **Rev:** Crowned shield within flying bird **Edge:** Reeded **Note:** Values in uncirculated drop by 50% or more when the PLUS in legend is not readable. This defect is most often seen on coins struck before 1968.

Date	Mintage	F	VF	XF	Unc	BU
1957 BA	Est. 43,000	—	100	150	225	300
Note: Issued to commemorate the 1958 2nd Ibero-American Numismatic Exposition in Barcelona with "BA" replacing the star on left side of reverse						
1957 (58)	13,000,000	—	0.45	3.00	50.00	100
1957 (59)	107,000,000	—	0.10	1.00	25.00	30.00
1957 (60)	26,000,000	—	0.10	1.00	10.00	20.00
1957 (61)	78,992,000	—	0.15	3.50	25.00	35.00
1957 (62)	40,963,000	—	0.10	1.00	10.00	20.00
1957 (63)	50,000,000	—	2.00	15.00	125	175
1957 (64)	51,000,000	—	0.10	1.00	10.00	20.00
1957 (65)	25,000,000	—	0.15	0.75	8.00	15.00
1957 (66)	28,000,000	—	0.15	3.50	25.00	35.00
1957 (67)	30,000,000	—	0.15	0.75	5.00	10.00
1957 (68)	60,000,000	—	0.20	0.60	3.00	4.00
1957 (69)	40,000,000	—	0.20	0.60	3.00	5.00

Date	Mintage	F	VF	XF	Unc	BU
1957 (70)	43,000,000	—	0.20	0.60	3.00	9.00
1957 (71)	77,000,000	—	0.20	0.60	1.50	3.00
1957 (72)	70,000,000	—	—	0.55	3.00	4.00
1957 (72) Proof	30,000	Value: 5.00				
1957 (73)	78,000,000	—	—	0.10	0.75	2.00
1957 (73) Proof	25,000	Value: 2.50				
1957 (74)	100,000,000	—	—	0.10	0.45	1.00
1957 (74) Proof	23,000	Value: 2.50				
1957 (75)	139,047,000	—	—	0.10	0.25	0.50
1957 (75) Proof	75,000	Value: 1.00				

KM# 811 5 PESETAS

Copper-Nickel **Ruler:** Juan Carlos I **Obv:** Head left **Rev:** World globe, soccerball, value and star with numeral 80 **Note:** Mule.

Date	Mintage	F	VF	XF	Unc	BU
1975 (80)	Est. 30,000	—	—	200	300	350

KM# 807 5 PESETAS

5.7500 g., Copper-Nickel, 23 mm. **Ruler:** Juan Carlos I **Obv:** Head left **Rev:** Crossed scepters and shield within wreath divides value, crown on top **Edge:** Reeded

Date	Mintage	F	VF	XF	Unc	BU
1975 (76)	150,560,000	—	—	0.10	0.25	0.35
1975 (76) Proof	—	Value: 1.00				
1975 (77)	154,982,000	—	—	0.10	0.25	0.35
1975 (77) Proof	Inc. above	Value: 1.00				
1975 (78)	412,610,000	—	—	0.10	0.35	0.50
1975 (79)	436,000,000	—	—	0.10	0.25	0.35
1975 (79) Proof	—	Value: 1.00				
1975 (80)	322,000,000	—	—	0.10	0.50	1.00

KM# 817 5 PESETAS

5.7500 g., Copper-Nickel, 23 mm. **Ruler:** Juan Carlos I **Subject:** World Cup Soccer Games **Obv:** Head left **Rev:** Numeral 82 on world globe, soccer ball above value

Date	Mintage	F	VF	XF	Unc	BU
1980 (80)	75,000,000	—	—	0.10	0.25	0.35
1980 (80) Proof	—	Value: 1.00				
1980 (81)	294,000,000	—	—	0.10	0.25	0.50
1980 (82)	291,000,000	—	—	0.10	0.25	0.50

KM# 823 5 PESETAS

5.7500 g., Copper-Nickel, 23 mm. **Ruler:** Juan Carlos I **Obv:** Head left **Rev:** Crossed scepters and shield within wreath divide value, crown on top **Note:** Mint mark: Crowned M.

Date	Mintage	F	VF	XF	Unc	BU
1982	—	—	—	0.10	1.00	1.50
Note: Mintage included in KM#817, 1980 (82)						
1983	200,000,000	—	—	0.10	0.50	0.65
1984	169,000,000	—	—	0.10	0.60	0.80
1989	—	—	—	0.10	0.75	1.00

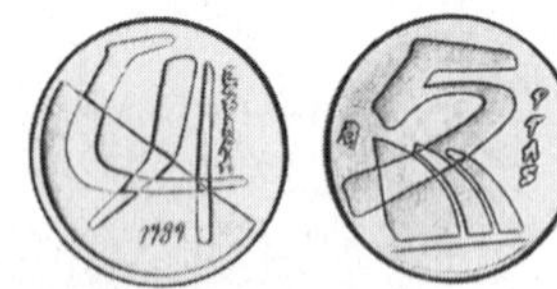

KM# 833 5 PESETAS

3.0500 g., Aluminum-Bronze, 18 mm. **Ruler:** Juan Carlos I **Obv:** Stylized design and date **Rev:** Value above stylized sailboats **Edge:** Plain

Date	Mintage	F	VF	XF	Unc	BU
1989	109,270,000	—	—	0.10	0.30	0.50
1990	191,740,000	—	—	0.10	0.50	1.00
1991	313,820,000	—	—	0.10	0.45	0.85
1992	493,224,000	—	—	0.10	0.35	0.50
1998	923,978,000	—	—	0.10	0.25	0.35
2000	—	—	—	0.10	0.25	0.35
2001	—	—	—	0.10	0.25	0.35

KM# 931 5 PESETAS

Nickel-Brass, 17.5 mm. **Ruler:** Juan Carlos I **Subject:** Aragon **Obv:** Front view of building **Rev:** Ballerina **Edge:** Plain **Note:** Wide rim variety exists.

Date	Mintage	F	VF	XF	Unc	BU
1994	199,678,000	—	—	—	0.25	0.40

KM# 946 5 PESETAS

Aluminum-Bronze, 17.5 mm. **Ruler:** Juan Carlos I **Subject:** Asturias **Obv:** Cross and date **Rev:** Value and design **Edge:** Plain

Date	Mintage	F	VF	XF	Unc	BU
1995	301,756,000	—	—	—	0.25	0.40

KM# 960 5 PESETAS

Aluminum-Bronze, 17.5 mm. **Ruler:** Juan Carlos I **Subject:** La Rioja **Obv:** Front view of building **Rev:** Figure on stilts, value and grapes **Edge:** Plain

Date	Mintage	F	VF	XF	Unc	BU
1996	674,168,000	—	—	—	0.15	0.25

KM# 981 5 PESETAS

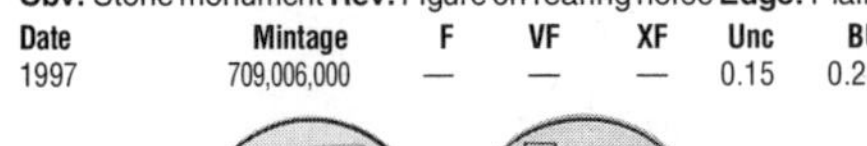

Brass, 17.5 mm. **Ruler:** Juan Carlos I **Subject:** Balearic Islands **Obv:** Stone monument **Rev:** Figure on rearing horse **Edge:** Plain

Date	Mintage	F	VF	XF	Unc	BU
1997	709,006,000	—	—	—	0.15	0.25

KM# 1008 5 PESETAS

Brass, 17.5 mm. **Ruler:** Juan Carlos I **Obv:** Crowned shield with supporters on arch **Rev:** Murcia waterwheel **Edge:** Plain

Date	Mintage	F	VF	XF	Unc	BU
1999	216,230,000	—	—	—	0.15	0.25

KM# 827 10 PESETAS

4.0000 g., Copper-Nickel, 18.5 mm. **Ruler:** Juan Carlos I **Obv:** Head left **Rev:** Crowned shield flanked by pillars with banner **Note:** Denomination "DIEZ".

Date	Mintage	F	VF	XF	Unc	BU
1983	149,000,000	—	—	0.25	0.35	0.40
1984	66,000,000	—	—	0.25	0.40	0.50
1985	45,706,000	—	—	0.25	0.50	0.60

KM# 903 10 PESETAS

4.0000 g., Copper-Nickel, 18.5 mm. **Ruler:** Juan Carlos I **Obv:** Head left **Rev:** Crowned shield flanked by pillars with banner **Edge:** Reeded

Date	Mintage	F	VF	XF	Unc	BU
1992	51,820,000	—	—	0.25	0.40	0.50

KM# 918 10 PESETAS

4.0000 g., Copper-Nickel, 18.5 mm. **Ruler:** Juan Carlos I **Subject:** Juan Miro **Obv:** Value, dates and inscription **Rev:** Head 3/4 right **Edge:** Plain

Date	Mintage	F	VF	XF	Unc	BU
1993	53,845,000	—	—	0.25	0.60	1.00

KM# 932 10 PESETAS

4.0000 g., Copper-Nickel, 18.5 mm. **Ruler:** Juan Carlos I **Subject:** Musician P. Sarasate **Obv:** Head right **Rev:** Violin **Edge:** Reeded

Date	Mintage	F	VF	XF	Unc	BU
1994	3,050,000	—	—	0.35	1.25	2.00

KM# 947 10 PESETAS

4.0000 g., Copper-Nickel, 18.5 mm. **Ruler:** Juan Carlos I **Subject:** Don Francisco de Quevedo **Obv:** Bust 1/4 left **Rev:** Quill in ink, book, glasses and value **Edge:** Reeded

Date	Mintage	F	VF	XF	Unc	BU
1995	1,050,000	—	—	1.00	4.00	5.00

KM# 961 10 PESETAS

4.0000 g., Copper-Nickel, 18.5 mm. **Ruler:** Juan Carlos I **Subject:** Emilia Pardo Bazan **Obv:** Monument and value **Rev:** Half length figure facing **Edge:** Reeded

Date	Mintage	F	VF	XF	Unc	BU
1996	1,060,000	—	—	0.30	1.75	2.50

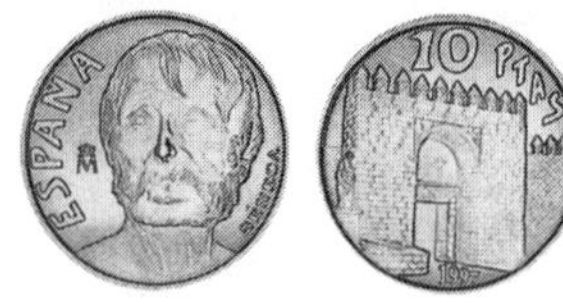

KM# 982 10 PESETAS

4.0000 g., Copper-Nickel, 18.5 mm. **Ruler:** Juan Carlos I **Subject:** Seneca **Obv:** Head facing **Rev:** Castle gate

Date	Mintage	F	VF	XF	Unc	BU
1997	—	—	—	0.25	0.40	0.50

KM# 1012 10 PESETAS

4.0000 g., Copper-Nickel, 18.5 mm. **Ruler:** Juan Carlos I **Obv:** Head left **Rev:** Value above national arms **Edge:** Reeded **Note:** Older portrait.

Date	Mintage	F	VF	XF	Unc	BU
1998	14,965,000	—	—	0.25	0.75	1.00
1999	2,125,000	—	—	0.35	0.85	1.00
2000	—	—	—	0.25	0.65	0.75

KM# 787 25 PESETAS

8.5000 g., Copper-Nickel, 26.5 mm. **Ruler:** Caudillo and regent **Obv:** Head right **Rev:** Crowned shield within flying bird **Edge Lettering:** UNA GRANDE LIBRE **Note:** Values in uncirculated drop by 50% or more when the "PLUS" in legend is not readable. This defect is most often seen on coins struck before 1968.

Date	Mintage	F	VF	XF	Unc	BU
1957 (58)	8,635,000	—	0.35	7.00	70.00	90.00
1957(BA)	43,000	—	25.00	55.00	85.00	100
Note: Issued to commemorate the 1958 Barcelona Exposition with "BA" replacing the star on left side of the reverse						
1957 (59)	42,185,000	—	0.30	1.50	30.00	35.00

Date	Mintage	F	VF	XF	Unc	BU
1957 (61)	24,120,000	—	2.00	20.00	160	200
1957 (64)	42,200,000	—	0.15	1.50	20.00	25.00
1957 (65)	20,000,000	—	0.20	1.00	3.50	10.00
1957 (66)	15,000,000	—	0.20	1.00	5.00	10.00
1957 (67)	20,000,000	—	0.15	1.50	12.00	20.00
1957 (68)	30,000,000	—	0.20	1.00	2.50	5.00
1957 (69)	24,000,000	—	0.30	0.75	2.00	3.00
1957 (70)	25,000,000	—	0.20	1.00	5.00	7.00
1957 (71)	7,800,000	—	1.00	5.00	35.00	50.00
1957 (72)	4,733,000	—	0.20	0.75	4.00	8.00
1957 (72) Proof	30,000	Value: 10.00				
1957 (73) Proof	25,000	Value: 80.00				
1957 (74)	5,000,000	—	0.30	0.65	4.00	6.00
1957 (74) Proof	23,000	Value: 10.00				
1957 (75)	10,270,000	—	0.30	0.65	2.25	3.00
1957 (75) Proof	75,000	Value: 3.50				

KM# 808 25 PESETAS

8.5000 g., Copper-Nickel, 26.5 mm. **Ruler:** Juan Carlos I **Obv:** Head left **Rev:** Crown above value **Edge Lettering:** UNA GRANDE LIBRE

Date	Mintage	F	VF	XF	Unc	BU
1975 (76)	35,707,000	—	0.20	0.25	0.75	1.00
1975 (76) Proof	—	Value: 1.00				
1975 (77)	46,690,000	—	0.20	0.25	0.75	1.00
1975 (77) Proof	Inc. above	Value: 1.00				
1975 (78)	97,555,000	—	0.20	0.25	2.00	3.00
1975 (79)	172,000,000	—	0.20	0.25	0.75	1.00
1975 (79) Proof	—	Value: 1.00				
1975 (80)	136,000,000	—	0.20	0.25	2.50	5.00

KM# 818 25 PESETAS

8.5000 g., Copper-Nickel, 26.5 mm. **Ruler:** Juan Carlos I **Subject:** World Cup Soccer Games **Obv:** Head left **Rev:** Soccer ball on net above value **Edge Lettering:** UNA GRANDE LIBRE

Date	Mintage	F	VF	XF	Unc	BU
1980 (80)	35,000,000	—	0.20	0.30	0.60	0.75
1980 (80) Proof	—	Value: 1.50				
1980 (81)	117,000,000	—	0.20	0.30	0.75	1.00
1980 (82)	100,000,000	—	0.20	0.30	1.00	2.00

KM# 824 25 PESETAS

8.5000 g., Copper-Nickel, 26.5 mm. **Ruler:** Juan Carlos I **Obv:** Head left **Rev:** Crown above value **Edge:** Reeded **Note:** Mint mark: Crowned M; Similar to KM#808.

Date	Mintage	F	VF	XF	Unc	BU
1982	146,000,000	—	0.20	0.30	2.00	3.00
1983	248,000,000	—	0.30	0.45	1.50	2.25
1984	242,000,000	—	0.20	0.30	3.50	5.00

KM# 850 25 PESETAS

Nickel-Bronze, 19.5 mm. **Ruler:** Juan Carlos I **Subject:** 1992 Olympics **Obv:** Discus thrower to right of center hole **Rev:** Center hole divides value, Olympic rings below

Date	Mintage	F	VF	XF	Unc	BU
1990	150,000,000	—	0.25	0.30	1.25	1.50
1991	Inc. above	—	0.20	0.25	3.50	6.50

KM# 851 25 PESETAS

Nickel-Bronze, 19.5 mm. **Ruler:** Juan Carlos I **Subject:** 1992 Olympics **Obv:** Center hole divides letters and bust left **Rev:** High jumper to upper right of center hole **Edge:** Plain

Date	Mintage	F	VF	XF	Unc	BU
1990	Inc. above	—	—	—	0.95	1.50
1991	87,000,000	—	—	—	2.50	3.00

KM# 904 25 PESETAS

Nickel-Bronze, 19.5 mm. **Ruler:** Juan Carlos I **Subject:** Giralda Tower of Sevilla **Obv:** Center hole divides letters and bust left **Rev:** Center hole divides tower and value

Date	Mintage	F	VF	XF	Unc	BU
1992	179,833,000	—	—	—	2.50	3.00

KM# 905 25 PESETAS

Nickel-Bronze, 19.5 mm. **Ruler:** Juan Carlos I **Subject:** Tower of Gold in Seville **Obv:** Globe design around center hole **Rev:** Center hole divides tower and vertical letters **Edge:** Plain

Date	Mintage	F	VF	XF	Unc	BU
1992	Inc. above	—	—	—	1.00	1.25

KM# 920 25 PESETAS

Nickel-Bronze, 19.5 mm. **Ruler:** Juan Carlos I **Subject:** Vasc Country **Obv:** Center hole divides inscription, date and design **Rev:** Center hole divides value and buildings

Date	Mintage	F	VF	XF	Unc	BU
1993	150,012,000	—	—	—	0.80	1.00

KM# 933 25 PESETAS

Nickel-Bronze, 19.5 mm. **Ruler:** Juan Carlos I **Subject:** Canary Islands **Obv:** Center hole divides inscription, date and flowers **Rev:** Center hole divides value, design and inscription **Edge:** Plain

Date	Mintage	F	VF	XF	Unc	BU
1994	242,566,000	—	—	—	0.60	0.75

KM# 948 25 PESETAS

Brass, 19.5 mm. **Ruler:** Juan Carlos I **Subject:** Castilla and Leon **Obv:** Center hole divides tower and inscription **Rev:** Center hole divides stylized animal figures, value and inscription **Edge:** Plain

Date	Mintage	F	VF	XF	Unc	BU
1995	221,963,000	—	—	—	1.00	1.25
1995 without Y	Inc. above	—	—	45.00	75.00	100

KM# 962 25 PESETAS

Copper-Zinc-Nickel, 19.5 mm. **Ruler:** Juan Carlos I **Subject:** Castilla - La Mancha - Don Quiote **Obv:** Center hole divides figure on horse, design and inscription **Rev:** Center hole divides design, inscription and value **Edge:** Plain

Date	Mintage	F	VF	XF	Unc	BU
1996	37,403,000	—	—	—	0.45	0.70

KM# 983 25 PESETAS

Brass, 19.5 mm. **Ruler:** Juan Carlos I **Subject:** Melilla **Obv:** Center hole divides towered buildings **Rev:** Center hole divides ancient amphora and dates **Edge:** Plain

Date	Mintage	F	VF	XF	Unc	BU
1997	461,688,000	—	—	—	0.45	0.70

KM# 990 25 PESETAS

Copper-Zinc-Nickel, 19.5 mm. **Ruler:** Juan Carlos I **Subject:** Ceuta **Obv:** Center hole right of ornamented building corner **Rev:** Center hole divides statue on wall shelf and value **Edge:** Plain

Date	Mintage	F	VF	XF	Unc	BU
1998	184,360,000	—	—	—	0.50	0.80

KM# 1007 25 PESETAS

4.3000 g., Nickel-Brass, 19.5 mm. **Ruler:** Juan Carlos I **Subject:** Navarra **Obv:** Center hole between castle towers **Rev:** Man running from bull, value and shield, all around center hole **Edge:** Plain

Date	Mintage	F	VF	XF	Unc	BU
1999	2,130,000	—	—	—	1.50	2.00

KM# 1013 25 PESETAS

4.2000 g., Nickel-Brass, 19.5 mm. **Ruler:** Juan Carlos I **Subject:** Navarra **Obv:** Center hole divides bust left and vertical letters **Rev:** Crowned above center hole, order collar at right, value at left **Edge:** Plain

Date	Mintage	F	VF	XF	Unc	BU
2000	—	—	—	—	1.00	1.50
2001	—	—	—	—	1.50	2.00

KM# 788 50 PESETAS

12.3500 g., Copper-Nickel, 30 mm. **Ruler:** Caudillo and regent **Obv:** Head right **Rev:** Crowned shield within flying bird **Edge Lettering:** UNA GRANDE LIBRE

Date	Mintage	F	VF	XF	Unc	BU
1957 (BA)	Est. 43,000	—	30.00	60.00	80.00	125
Note: Issued to commemorate the 1958 Barcelona Exposition with "BA" replacing the star on left side of reverse						
1957 (58)	21,471,000	—	0.50	0.75	2.50	3.50
1957 (58)	Inc. above	100	200	350	600	700
Note: Edge variety with UNA - LIBRE - GRANDE						

Date	Mintage	F	VF	XF	Unc	BU
1957 (59)	28,000,000	—	0.50	0.75	2.50	3.50
1957 (60)	24,800,000	—	0.50	0.75	2.50	3.50
1957 (67)	850,000	—	0.50	2.00	8.00	10.00
1957 (68)	1,000	—	—	—	—	1,250
Note: In sets only						
1957 (69)	1,200	—	—	—	—	1,100
Note: In sets only						
1957 (70)	19,000	—	—	—	—	250
Note: In sets only						
1957(71)	4,400,000	—	0.65	2.50	18.50	35.00
1957 (72) Proof	23,000	Value: 35.00				
1957 (73) Proof	28,000	Value: 60.00				
1957 (74) Proof	25,000	Value: 60.00				
1957 (75) Proof	75,000	Value: 15.00				

KM# 809 50 PESETAS
12.3500 g., Copper-Nickel, 30 mm. **Ruler:** Juan Carlos I **Obv:** Head left **Rev:** Crossed scepters and shield within order collar, crown above

Date	Mintage	F	VF	XF	Unc	BU
1975 (76)	4,400,000	—	0.50	0.60	1.00	1.25
1975 (76) Proof	—	Value: 2.00				
1975 (78)	17,555,000	—	0.50	0.75	2.50	3.00
1975 (79)	33,000,000	—	0.50	0.60	1.00	1.50
1975 (79) Proof	—	Value: 2.00				
1975 (80)	34,000,000	—	0.50	0.60	3.50	4.50

KM# 819 50 PESETAS
12.3500 g., Copper-Nickel, 30 mm. **Ruler:** Juan Carlos I **Subject:** World Cup Soccer Games **Obv:** Head left **Rev:** Soccer ball above value **Edge Lettering:** UNA GRANDE LIBRE

Date	Mintage	F	VF	XF	Unc	BU
1980 (80)	15,000,000	—	0.50	0.60	0.75	0.85
1980 (80) Proof	—	Value: 2.00				
1980 (81)	38,300,000	—	0.50	0.60	1.35	1.50
1980 (82)	30,950,000	—	0.50	0.60	2.00	2.50

KM# 825 50 PESETAS
12.3500 g., Copper-Nickel, 30 mm. **Ruler:** Juan Carlos I **Obv:** Head left **Rev:** Crossed scepters and shield within order collar, crown above **Note:** Mint mark: Crowned M.

Date	Mintage	F	VF	XF	Unc	BU
1982	27,000,000	—	0.50	1.00	2.50	4.50
1983	93,000,000	—	0.50	1.00	2.00	3.00
1984	17,500,000	5.00	12.00	20.00	40.00	70.00

KM# 852 50 PESETAS
Copper-Nickel, 20.3 mm. **Ruler:** Juan Carlos I **Subject:** Expo '92 **Obv:** Bust left **Rev:** Globe and value **Edge:** Notched

Date	Mintage	F	VF	XF	Unc	BU
1990	25,234,000	—	—	—	1.00	1.25

KM# 853 50 PESETAS
Copper-Nickel, 20.3 mm. **Ruler:** Juan Carlos I **Subject:** Expo '92 **Obv:** City view **Rev:** Globe and value **Edge:** Notched

Date	Mintage	F	VF	XF	Unc	BU
1990	7,916,000	—	—	—	1.00	1.25

KM# 906 50 PESETAS
Copper-Nickel, 20.3 mm. **Ruler:** Juan Carlos I **Subject:** 1992 Olympics **Obv:** "La Pedrera" building **Rev:** Pointed designs above Olympic rings, value at left **Edge:** Notched

Date	Mintage	F	VF	XF	Unc	BU
1992	40,370,000	—	—	—	1.00	1.25

KM# 907 50 PESETAS
Copper-Nickel, 20.3 mm. **Ruler:** Juan Carlos I **Subject:** 1992 Olympics **Obv:** Bust left **Rev:** Cathedral Sagrada Famillia (Gaudi) **Edge:** Notched

Date	Mintage	F	VF	XF	Unc	BU
1992	Inc. above	—	—	—	1.00	1.25

KM# 921 50 PESETAS
Copper-Nickel, 20.3 mm. **Ruler:** Juan Carlos I **Subject:** Extremadura **Obv:** Bridge **Rev:** Tower **Edge:** Notched

Date	Mintage	F	VF	XF	Unc	BU
1993	24,314,000	—	—	—	1.00	1.25

KM# 934 50 PESETAS
Copper-Nickel, 20.3 mm. **Ruler:** Juan Carlos I **Subject:** Altamira Cave Paintings **Obv:** Building **Rev:** Stylized design above value **Edge:** Notched

Date	Mintage	F	VF	XF	Unc	BU
1994	3,002,000	—	—	—	2.25	3.00

KM# 949 50 PESETAS
Copper-Nickel, 20.3 mm. **Ruler:** Juan Carlos I **Subject:** Alcala Gate **Obv:** Partial building and date **Rev:** Steepled buildings **Edge:** Notched

Date	Mintage	F	VF	XF	Unc	BU
1995	1,001,000	—	—	—	4.00	5.00

KM# 963 50 PESETAS
Copper-Nickel, 20.3 mm. **Ruler:** Juan Carlos I **Subject:** Philip V **Obv:** Head facing **Rev:** Shield divides value and letters, crown above divides date **Edge:** Notched

Date	Mintage	F	VF	XF	Unc	BU
1996	11,047,000	—	—	—	0.75	1.00

KM# 985 50 PESETAS
Copper-Nickel, 20.3 mm. **Ruler:** Juan Carlos I **Subject:** Juan De Herrera **Obv:** Head left **Rev:** Escorial Monastery **Edge:** Notched

Date	Mintage	F	VF	XF	Unc	BU
1997	17,496,000	—	—	—	1.00	1.25

KM# 991 50 PESETAS
Copper-Nickel, 20.3 mm. **Ruler:** Juan Carlos I **Obv:** Bust left **Rev:** Crossed scepters and shield within order chain, crown above, value at left **Edge:** Notched

Date	Mintage	F	VF	XF	Unc	BU
1998	17,496,000	—	—	—	1.00	1.50
1999	2,100,000	—	—	—	2.25	3.00
2000	—	—	—	—	2.00	2.50

KM# 797 100 PESETAS
19.0000 g., 0.8000 Silver 0.4887 oz. ASW **Ruler:** Caudillo and regent **Obv:** Head right **Rev:** Assorted emblems within flower design, crown on top **Edge Lettering:** UNA GRANDE LIBRE

Date	Mintage	F	VF	XF	Unc	BU
1966 (66)	15,045,000	—	BV	BV	7.50	9.00
1966 (67)	15,000,000	—	BV	BV	7.50	9.00
1966 (68)	24,000,000	—	BV	BV	7.50	9.00
1966 (69)	1,000,000	—	—	175	400	500
Note: 69 with straight 9 in star						
1966 (69)	Inc. above	—	—	75.00	150	175
Note: 69 with curved 9 in star						
1966 (70)	995,000	BV	7.50	10.00	20.00	25.00

Note: 1966(69) coins heavily altered; authentication recommended

KM# 810 100 PESETAS
Copper-Nickel **Ruler:** Juan Carlos I **Obv:** Head left **Rev:** Crowned shield flanked by pillars with banner

Date	Mintage	F	VF	XF	Unc	BU
1975 (76)	4,400,000	—	0.75	1.00	1.50	2.00
1975 (76) Proof	—	Value: 3.00				

KM# 820 100 PESETAS

Copper-Nickel **Ruler:** Juan Carlos I **Subject:** World Cup Soccer Games - Spain '82 **Obv:** Head left **Rev:** Value in center of assorted emblems

Date	Mintage	F	VF	XF	Unc	BU
1980 (80)	20,000,000	—	—	0.75	1.00	1.50
1980 (80) Proof	—	Value: 3.00				

KM# 826 100 PESETAS

9.3000 g., Aluminum-Bronze, 24.5 mm. **Ruler:** Juan Carlos I **Obv:** Head left **Rev:** Crowned shield flanked by pillars with banner **Edge:** Fleur-de-lis repeated

Date	Mintage	F	VF	XF	Unc	BU
1982	117,600,000	—	0.75	1.25	3.50	5.00
1982 Proof	—	Value: 5.00				
1983	—	—	0.75	1.25	30.00	45.00
1984	208,000,000	—	0.75	1.25	8.00	10.00
1985	118,000,000	—	0.75	1.25	10.00	15.00
1986	160,000,000	—	0.75	1.25	3.00	4.00
1988	125,674,000	—	0.75	1.25	4.00	6.00
1989	80,877,000	—	0.75	1.25	2.50	3.00
1990	25,636,000	—	0.75	1.25	6.00	8.00

Note: Varieties exist

KM# 908 100 PESETAS

9.3000 g., Aluminum-Bronze, 24.5 mm. **Ruler:** Juan Carlos I **Rev:** Crowned shield flanked by pillars with banner

Date	Mintage	F	VF	XF	Unc	BU
1992	22,661,000	—	—	—	4.00	5.00

Note: Edge varieties exist with positioning of fleur-de-lis

KM# 922 100 PESETAS

9.3000 g., Nickel-Brass, 24.5 mm. **Ruler:** Juan Carlos I **Subject:** European unity **Obv:** Value within map **Rev:** Radiant sun within star circle

Date	Mintage	F	VF	XF	Unc	BU
1993	39,723,000	—	—	—	3.00	5.00

KM# 935 100 PESETAS

9.3000 g., Nickel-Brass, 24.5 mm. **Ruler:** Juan Carlos I **Subject:** Museo del Prado **Obv:** Head left **Rev:** Statue in front of museum **Edge:** Fleur-de-lis repeated

Date	Mintage	F	VF	XF	Unc	BU
1994	24,853,000	—	—	—	2.50	3.50

KM# 950 100 PESETAS

9.3000 g., Copper-Nickel, 24.5 mm. **Ruler:** Juan Carlos I **Series:** F.A.O. **Obv:** Head left **Rev:** Oat sprig, value and F.A.O. logo **Edge:** Fleur-de-lis repeated

Date	Mintage	F	VF	XF	Unc	BU
1995	71,957,000	—	—	—	2.00	3.00

KM# 964 100 PESETAS

9.3000 g., Copper-Zinc-Nickel, 24.5 mm. **Ruler:** Juan Carlos I **Obv:** Head left **Rev:** National Library **Edge:** Fleur-de-lis repeated

Date	Mintage	F	VF	XF	Unc	BU
1996	21,466,000	—	—	—	2.50	3.50

KM# 984 100 PESETAS

9.3000 g., Copper-Zinc-Nickel, 24.5 mm. **Ruler:** Juan Carlos I **Subject:** Royal Theatre **Obv:** Head left **Rev:** Building

Date	Mintage	F	VF	XF	Unc	BU
1997	29,480,000	—	—	—	2.00	3.00

KM# 989 100 PESETAS

9.3000 g., Aluminum-Bronze, 24.5 mm. **Ruler:** Juan Carlos I **Obv:** Head left **Rev:** Crowned shield flanked by pillars with banner **Edge:** Fleur-de-lis repeated

Date	Mintage	F	VF	XF	Unc	BU
1998	—	—	—	—	1.50	2.00
2000	—	—	—	—	2.00	2.50

KM# 1006 100 PESETAS

9.3000 g., Brass, 24.5 mm. **Ruler:** Juan Carlos I **Obv:** Head left **Rev:** Design above sprig and value **Edge:** Fleur-de-lis repeated

Date	Mintage	F	VF	XF	Unc	BU
1999	60,332,000	—	—	—	1.50	2.00

KM# 1016 100 PESETAS

9.8000 g., Aluminum-Bronze, 24.4 mm. **Ruler:** Juan Carlos I **Subject:** 132nd Anniversary of the Peseta **Obv:** Head left **Rev:** Seated allegorical figure from an old coin design **Edge:** Ornamented

Date	Mintage	F	VF	XF	Unc	BU
2001	—	—	—	—	1.50	2.00

KM# 829 200 PESETAS

Copper-Nickel, 21.7 mm. **Ruler:** Juan Carlos I **Obv:** Head left **Rev:** Value divides sprigs

Date	Mintage	F	VF	XF	Unc	BU
1986	43,576,000	—	—	2.00	6.00	8.00
1987	66,718,000	—	—	2.00	12.00	16.00
1988	37,190,000	—	—	2.00	12.00	16.00

KM# 855 200 PESETAS

Copper-Nickel, 25.5 mm. **Ruler:** Juan Carlos I **Obv:** Conjoined busts of King and Crown Prince right **Rev:** Pair of lions pulling seated figure on barrel within circle

Date	Mintage	F	VF	XF	Unc	BU
1990	8,000,000	—	—	—	4.00	5.00

KM# 884 200 PESETAS

Copper-Nickel, 25.5 mm. **Ruler:** Juan Carlos I **Subject:** Madrid - European Culture Capital **Obv:** Conjoined busts of King and Crown Prince right **Rev:** Pair of lions pulling seated figure on barrel within circle

Date	Mintage	F	VF	XF	Unc	BU
1991	11,400,000	—	—	—	2.00	3.00

KM# 909 200 PESETAS

Copper-Nickel, 25.5 mm. **Ruler:** Juan Carlos I **Subject:** Madrid - European Culture Capital **Obv:** Conjoined busts of King and Crown Prince right **Rev:** Equestrian within circle

Date	Mintage	F	VF	XF	Unc	BU
1992	Inc. above	—	—	—	3.00	3.50

KM# 910 200 PESETAS

Copper-Nickel, 25.5 mm. **Ruler:** Juan Carlos I **Subject:** Madrid - European Culture Capital **Obv:** Conjoined busts of King and Crown Prince right **Rev:** Upright bear by tree within circle

Date	Mintage	F	VF	XF	Unc	BU
1992	Inc. above	—	—	—	3.00	3.50

KM# 923 200 PESETAS
Copper-Nickel, 25.5 mm. **Ruler:** Juan Carlos I **Subject:** Juan Luis Vives **Obv:** Feather and designs within circle **Rev:** Bust facing and crowned design within circle

Date	Mintage	F	VF	XF	Unc	BU
1993	2,811,000	—	—	—	6.00	7.00

KM# 936 200 PESETAS
Copper-Nickel, 25.5 mm. **Ruler:** Juan Carlos I **Subject:** Velasquez and Goya Paintings **Obv:** Three figures within circle **Rev:** Kneeling figures with umbrella within circle

Date	Mintage	F	VF	XF	Unc	BU
1994	2,997,000	—	—	—	4.00	5.00

KM# 951 200 PESETAS
Copper-Nickel, 25.5 mm. **Ruler:** Juan Carlos I **Subject:** Murillo and El Greco paintings **Obv:** Standing figures within circle **Rev:** Child and lamb within circle

Date	Mintage	F	VF	XF	Unc	BU
1995	1,022,000	—	—	—	20.00	30.00

KM# 965 200 PESETAS
Copper-Nickel, 25.5 mm. **Ruler:** Juan Carlos I **Subject:** Fortuny and Balleau paintings **Obv:** Seated figure blowing on instrument within circle **Rev:** Seated figure playing guitar within circle

Date	Mintage	F	VF	XF	Unc	BU
1996	9,206,000	—	—	—	2.00	3.00

KM# 986 200 PESETAS
Copper-Nickel, 25.5 mm. **Ruler:** Juan Carlos I **Subject:** Jacinto Benavente **Obv:** Stylized books within circle **Rev:** Bust left within circle

Date	Mintage	F	VF	XF	Unc	BU
1997	6,845,000	—	—	—	3.00	4.00

KM# 992 200 PESETAS
Copper-Nickel, 25.5 mm. **Ruler:** Juan Carlos I **Obv:** Conjoined busts of King and Crown Prince right **Rev:** Value within circle

Date	Mintage	F	VF	XF	Unc	BU
1998	5,008,000	—	—	—	2.00	3.50
1999	—	—	—	—	4.00	6.00
2000	—	—	—	—	5.00	7.00

KM# 831 500 PESETAS
Copper-Aluminum-Nickel **Ruler:** Juan Carlos I **Obv:** Conjoined heads of Juan Carlos and Sofia left **Rev:** Crowned shield flanked by pillars with banner, vertical value at right

Date	Mintage	F	VF	XF	Unc	BU
1987	400,000,000	—	—	3.50	10.00	12.00
1987 Proof	Inc. above	Value: 10.00				
1988	81,309,000	—	—	3.50	9.00	11.00
1989	103,861,000	—	—	3.50	5.00	6.00
1990	28,372,000	—	—	2.25	7.00	12.00

KM# 924 500 PESETAS
11.9000 g., Copper-Aluminum-Nickel **Ruler:** Juan Carlos I **Obv:** Conjoined heads of Juan Carlos and Sofia left **Rev:** Crowned shield flanked by pillars with banner, vertical value at right

Date	Mintage	F	VF	XF	Unc	BU
1993	3,059,000	—	—	—	30.00	40.00
1994	3,041,000	—	—	—	35.00	45.00
1995	1,015,000	—	—	—	30.00	40.00
1996	1,031,000	—	—	—	15.00	20.00
1997	4,881,000	—	—	—	12.00	15.00
1998	5,161,000	—	—	—	12.00	15.00
1999	2,030,000	—	—	—	12.00	15.00
2000	—	—	—	—	12.00	15.00
2001	—	—	—	—	12.00	15.00

EURO COINAGE

European Union Issues

KM# 1040 EURO CENT
2.2700 g., Copper Plated Steel, 16.2 mm. **Ruler:** Juan Carlos I **Obv:** Cathedral of Santiago de Compostela **Obv. Designer:** Garcilano Rollan **Rev:** Value and globe **Rev. Designer:** Luc Luycx **Edge:** Plain

Date	Mintage	F	VF	XF	Unc	BU
1999	721,000,000	—	—	—	0.25	0.35
2000	83,400,000	—	—	—	1.00	1.25
2001	130,900,000	—	—	—	0.25	0.30
2002	141,100,000	—	—	—	0.25	0.30
2003	670,500,000	—	—	—	0.25	0.30
2004	206,700,000	—	—	—	0.25	0.30
2005	444,200,000	—	—	—	0.25	0.30
2006	383,900,000	—	—	—	0.25	0.35
2007	—	—	—	—	0.25	0.35

KM# 1041 2 EURO CENT
3.0300 g., Copper Plated Steel, 18.7 mm. **Ruler:** Juan Carlos I **Obv:** Cathedral of Santiago de Compostela **Obv. Designer:** Garcilano Rollan **Rev:** Value and globe **Rev. Designer:** Luc Luycx **Edge:** Grooved

Date	Mintage	F	VF	XF	Unc	BU
1999	291,700,000	—	—	—	0.75	1.00
2000	711,300,000	—	—	—	0.25	0.35
2001	463,100,000	—	—	—	0.25	0.30
2002	4,100,000	—	—	—	1.25	1.50
2003	31,600,000	—	—	—	1.00	1.25
2004	206,700,000	—	—	—	0.25	0.30
2005	275,100,000	—	—	—	0.25	0.30
2006	262,200,000	—	—	—	0.25	0.30
2007	—	—	—	—	0.25	0.30

KM# 1042 5 EURO CENT
3.8600 g., Copper Plated Steel, 21.2 mm. **Ruler:** Juan Carlos I **Obv:** Cathedral of Santiago de Compostela **Obv. Designer:** Garcilano Rollan **Rev:** Value and globe **Rev. Designer:** Luc Luycx **Edge:** Plain

Date	Mintage	F	VF	XF	Unc	BU
1999	483,500,000	—	—	—	0.65	0.75
2000	399,900,000	—	—	—	0.65	0.75
2001	216,100,000	—	—	—	0.50	0.60
2002	8,300,000	—	—	—	1.00	1.50
2003	327,600,000	—	—	—	0.50	0.60
2004	258,700,000	—	—	—	0.40	0.50
2005	411,400,000	—	—	—	0.40	0.50
2006	142,800,000	—	—	—	0.40	0.50
2007	—	—	—	—	0.40	0.50

KM# 1043 10 EURO CENT
4.0700 g., Brass, 19.7 mm. **Ruler:** Juan Carlos I **Obv:** Head of Cervantes with ruffed collar 1/4 left within star border **Rev:** Value and map **Edge:** Reeded

Date	Mintage	F	VF	XF	Unc	BU
1999	588,100,000	—	—	—	0.65	0.75
2000	243,900,000	—	—	—	0.65	0.75
2001	160,100,000	—	—	—	0.60	0.75
2002	113,100,000	—	—	—	0.60	0.75
2003	292,500,000	—	—	—	0.75	0.90
2004	121,900,000	—	—	—	0.40	0.50
2005	321,300,000	—	—	—	0.40	0.50
2006	91,800,000	—	—	—	0.40	0.50

KM# 1044 20 EURO CENT
5.7300 g., Brass, 22.1 mm. **Ruler:** Juan Carlos I **Obv:** Head of Cervantes with ruffed collar 1/4 left within star border **Obv. Designer:** Begoña Castellanos **Rev:** Value and map **Rev. Designer:** Luc Luycx **Edge:** Notched

Date	Mintage	F	VF	XF	Unc	BU
1999	762,300,000	—	—	—	0.85	1.00
2000	29,300,000	—	—	—	2.75	3.50
2001	146,600,000	—	—	—	1.00	1.25
2002	91,500,000	—	—	—	0.60	0.75
2003	4,100,000	—	—	—	1.25	1.50
2004	3,900,000	—	—	—	0.60	0.75
2005	4,000,000	—	—	—	0.60	0.75
2006	102,000,000	—	—	—	0.60	0.75

KM# 1045 50 EURO CENT
7.8100 g., Brass, 24.2 mm. **Ruler:** Juan Carlos I **Obv:** Head of Cervantes with ruffed collar 1/4 left within star border **Obv. Designer:** Begoña Castellanos **Rev:** Value and map **Rev. Designer:** Luc Luycx **Edge:** Reeded

Date	Mintage	F	VF	XF	Unc	BU
1999	371,000,000	—	—	—	1.50	1.75
2000	519,600,000	—	—	—	1.25	1.50
2001	351,100,000	—	—	—	1.00	1.25
2002	9,800,000	—	—	—	3.00	3.50
2003	6,000,000	—	—	—	3.00	3.50
2004	4,400,000	—	—	—	1.50	2.00
2005	3,900,000	—	—	—	1.25	1.50
2006	4,000,000	—	—	—	1.25	1.50

KM# 1046 EURO
7.5000 g., Bi-Metallic Copper-Nickel center in Brass ring, 23.2 mm. **Ruler:** Juan Carlos I **Obv:** Head 1/4 left within circle and star border **Obv. Designer:** Luiz Jose Diaz **Rev:** Value and map within circle **Rev. Designer:** Luc Luycx **Edge:** Reeded and plain sections

Date	Mintage	F	VF	XF	Unc	BU
1999	100,200,000	—	—	—	3.00	3.50
2000	89,300,000	—	—	—	4.00	4.50
2001	259,100,000	—	—	—	3.00	4.00
2002	335,600,000	—	—	—	2.00	2.50
2003	297,400,000	—	—	—	2.00	2.50
2004	9,870,000	—	—	—	2.00	2.50
2005	77,800,000	—	—	—	2.00	2.50
2006	101,600,000	—	—	—	2.00	2.50

KM# 1047 2 EURO
8.5200 g., Bi-Metallic Brass center in Copper-Nickel ring, 25.7 mm. **Ruler:** Juan Carlos I **Obv:** Head 1/4 left within circle and star border **Obv. Designer:** Luis Jose Diaz **Rev:** Value and map within circle **Rev. Designer:** Luc Luycx **Edge:** Reeded **Edge Lettering:** 2's and stars

Date	Mintage	F	VF	XF	Unc	BU
1999	60,500,000	—	—	—	5.00	6.00
2000	36,600,000	—	—	—	5.00	6.00
2001	140,200,000	—	—	—	4.50	5.00
2002	164,000,000	—	—	—	3.50	4.00
2003	44,500,000	—	—	—	4.50	5.00
2004	4,100,000	—	—	—	4.50	5.00
2005	4,000,000	—	—	—	4.50	5.00
2006	4,000,000	—	—	—	4.50	5.00

KM# 1063 2 EURO
8.5200 g., Bi-Metallic Brass center in Copper-Nickel ring, 25.7 mm. **Ruler:** Juan Carlos I **Obv:** Stylized half length figure with hat holding spear within circle and star border **Rev:** Value and map within circle **Edge:** Reeding over stars and 2's **Note:** Mint mark: Crowned M.

Date	Mintage	F	VF	XF	Unc	BU
2005	8,000,000	—	—	—	5.00	6.00

KM# 1074 2 EURO
8.5200 g., Bi-Metallic Brass center in Copper-Nickel ring, 25.7 mm. **Ruler:** Juan Carlos I **Obv:** King's portrait **Obv. Designer:** Luis Jose Diaz **Rev:** Relief map of Western Europe, stars, lines and value **Rev. Designer:** Luc Luycx **Edge:** Reeded **Edge Lettering:** 2's and stars

Date	Mintage	F	VF	XF	Unc	BU
2007	—	—	—	—	4.75	5.00

KM# 1130 2 EURO
8.5300 g., Bi-Metallic **Ring Composition:** Copper-Nickel **Center Composition:** Brass, 25.70 mm. **Ruler:** Juan Carlos I **Subject:** 50th Anniversary Treaty of Rome **Obv:** Open treaty book **Obv. Legend:** ESPAÑA **Rev:** Large value at left, modified outline of Europe at right **Edge:** Reeded with 2's and stars

Date	Mintage	F	VF	XF	Unc	BU
2007	—	—	—	—	—	9.00

SRI (SHRI) LANKA

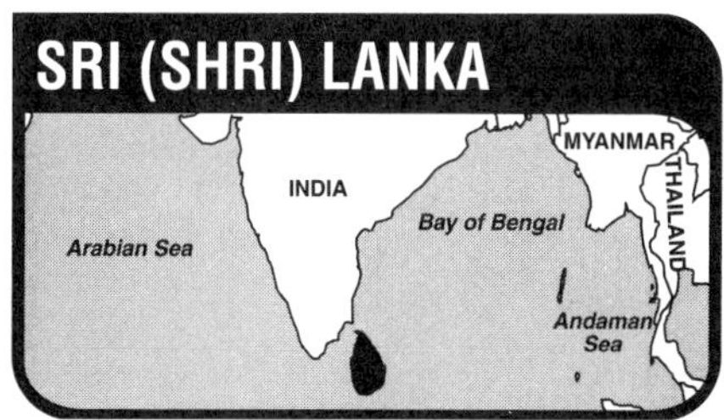

The Democratic Socialist Republic of Sri Lanka (formerly Ceylon) situated in the Indian Ocean 18 miles (29 km.) southeast of India, has an area of 25,332 sq. mi. (65,610 sq. km.) and a population of *16.9 million. Capital: Colombo. The economy is chiefly agricultural. Tea, coconut products and rubber are exported.

Sri Lanka is a member of the Commonwealth of Nations. The president is Chief of State. The prime minister is Head of Government. The present leaders of the country have reverted the country name back to Sri Lanka.

RULER
British, 1796-1948

DEMOCRATIC SOCIALIST REPUBLIC

DECIMAL COINAGE

100 Cents = 1 Rupee

KM# 137 CENT
Aluminum **Obv:** Value above designs within wreath **Rev:** National arms

Date	Mintage	F	VF	XF	Unc	BU
1975	52,778,000	—	—	0.10	0.25	0.45
1978	34,006,000	—	—	0.10	0.25	0.45
1978 Proof	20,000	Value: 2.50				
1989	6,000,000	—	—	0.10	0.25	0.45
1994	5,000,000	—	—	0.10	0.25	0.45

KM# 138 2 CENTS
0.7600 g., Aluminum, 18.5 mm. **Obv:** Value above designs within wreath **Rev:** National arms **Shape:** Scalloped

Date	Mintage	F	VF	XF	Unc	BU
1975	62,503,000	—	—	0.10	0.25	0.45
1978	23,425,000	—	—	0.10	0.25	0.45
1978 Proof	20,000	Value: 3.00				

KM# 139 5 CENTS
3.3000 g., Nickel-Brass **Obv:** Value above designs within wreath **Rev:** National arms **Shape:** Round-edged square

Date	Mintage	F	VF	XF	Unc	BU
1975	19,584,000	—	—	0.10	0.25	0.45

KM# 139a 5 CENTS
1.0000 g., Aluminum **Obv:** Value above designs within wreath **Rev:** National arms **Shape:** Round-edged square

Date	Mintage	F	VF	XF	Unc	BU
1978	272,308,000	—	—	0.10	0.25	0.45
1978 Proof	20,000	Value: 3.00				
1988	40,000,000	—	—	0.10	0.25	0.45
1991	50,000,000	—	—	0.10	0.25	0.45

KM# 140 10 CENTS
4.1000 g., Nickel-Brass **Obv:** Value above designs within wreath **Rev:** National arms **Shape:** Scalloped

Date	Mintage	F	VF	XF	Unc	BU
1975	10,800,000	—	—	0.10	0.25	0.45

KM# 140a 10 CENTS
1.2700 g., Aluminum, 23 mm. **Obv:** Value above designs within wreath **Rev:** National arms **Shape:** Scalloped

Date	Mintage	F	VF	XF	Unc	BU
1978	188,820,000	—	—	0.10	0.25	0.45
1978 Proof	20,000	Value: 3.50				
1988	40,000,000	—	—	0.10	0.25	0.45
1991	50,000,000	—	—	0.10	0.25	0.45

KM# 141.1 25 CENTS
Copper-Nickel **Obv:** Value above designs within wreath **Rev:** National arms **Edge:** Security

Date	Mintage	F	VF	XF	Unc	BU
1975	39,600,000	—	—	0.10	0.25	0.45
1975 Proof	1,431	Value: 4.00				
1978	65,009,000	—	—	0.10	0.25	0.45
1978 Proof	20,000	Value: 3.50				

KM# 141.2 25 CENTS
Copper-Nickel **Obv:** Value above designs within wreath **Rev:** National arms **Edge:** Reeded

Date	Mintage	F	VF	XF	Unc	BU
1982	90,000,000	—	—	0.10	0.25	0.45
1989	45,000,000	—	—	0.10	0.25	0.45
1991	50,000,000	—	—	0.10	0.25	0.45
1994	50,000,000	—	—	0.10	0.25	0.45

KM# 141a 25 CENTS
Nickel Clad Steel **Obv:** National arms **Rev:** Value **Edge:** Reeded

Date	Mintage	F	VF	XF	Unc	BU
1996	50,000,000	—	—	0.10	0.25	0.45
2001	10,000,000	—	—	0.10	0.25	0.45
2002	10,000,000	—	—	0.10	0.25	0.45

KM# 141.2b 25 CENTS
Copper Plated Steel, 16 mm. **Obv:** Denomination **Rev:** National arms

Date	Mintage	F	VF	XF	Unc	BU
2005	—	—	—	—	0.25	0.45

KM# 141b 25 CENTS
1.7000 g., Copper Plated Steel, 15.94 mm. **Obv:** National arms **Rev:** Value **Edge:** Plain

Date	Mintage	F	VF	XF	Unc	BU
2005	—	—	—	0.10	0.25	0.45
2006	—	—	—	0.10	0.25	0.45

KM# 135.1 50 CENTS
Copper-Nickel **Obv:** Value above designs within wreath **Rev:** National arms **Edge:** Security

Date	Mintage	F	VF	XF	Unc	BU
1972	11,000,000	—	0.15	0.30	0.75	1.25
1975	34,000,000	—	0.15	0.30	0.75	1.25
1978	66,010,000	—	0.15	0.30	0.75	1.25
1978 Proof	20,000	Value: 4.50				

KM# 135.2 50 CENTS
5.5000 g., Copper-Nickel **Obv:** Value above designs within wreath **Rev:** National arms **Edge:** Reeded

Date	Mintage	F	VF	XF	Unc	BU
1982	65,000,000	—	0.10	0.25	0.65	1.00
1991	40,000,000	—	0.10	0.25	0.65	1.00
1994	40,000,000	—	0.10	0.25	0.65	1.00

KM# 135a 50 CENTS
Nickel Clad Steel **Obv:** National arms **Rev:** Value **Edge:** Reeded

Date	Mintage	F	VF	XF	Unc	BU
1996	50,000,000	—	0.10	0.25	0.65	1.00
2001	30,000,000	—	0.10	0.25	0.65	1.00
2002	10,000,000	—	0.10	0.25	0.65	1.00

KM# 135.2b 50 CENTS
Copper Plated Steel **Obv:** Value above designs within wreath **Rev:** National arms **Edge:** Reeded

Date	Mintage	F	VF	XF	Unc	BU
2005	—	—	0.10	0.25	0.65	1.00

KM# 135b 50 CENTS
2.4900 g., Copper Plated Steel, 17.92 mm. **Obv:** National arms **Rev:** Value **Edge:** Reeded

Date	Mintage	F	VF	XF	Unc	BU
2005	—	—	—	0.25	0.60	1.00
2006	—	—	—	0.25	0.60	1.00

KM# 136.1 RUPEE
Copper-Nickel **Obv:** Inscription below designs within wreath **Rev:** National arms **Edge:** Security

Date	Mintage	F	VF	XF	Unc	BU
1972	7,000,000	—	0.30	0.60	1.25	1.75
1975	31,500,000	—	0.25	0.50	1.00	1.50
1978	37,018,000	—	0.25	0.50	1.00	1.50
1978 Proof	20,000	Value: 6.50				

KM# 136.2 RUPEE
Copper-Nickel **Obv:** Inscriptions below designs within wreath **Rev:** National arms **Edge:** Reeded

Date	Mintage	F	VF	XF	Unc	BU
1982	75,000,000	—	0.25	0.50	1.00	1.50
1994	50,000,000	—	0.25	0.50	1.00	1.50
2004	—	—	—	0.50	1.00	1.50

KM# 136a RUPEE
Nickel Clad Steel **Obv:** National arms **Rev:** Value **Edge:** Reeded

Date	Mintage	F	VF	XF	Unc	BU
1996	50,000,000	—	0.25	0.50	1.00	1.50
2000	30,000,000	—	0.25	0.50	1.00	1.50
2002	50,000,000	—	0.25	0.50	1.00	1.50

KM# 144 RUPEE
Copper-Nickel **Subject:** Inauguration of President Jayewardene **Obv:** National arms **Rev:** Head left

Date	Mintage	F	VF	XF	Unc	BU
1978	1,997,400	—	0.30	0.60	1.25	1.75
1978	2,600	—	—	—	—	50.00
Note: Right shoulder straight						
1978 Proof	20,000	Value: 6.50				

KM# 151 RUPEE
Copper-Nickel **Subject:** 3rd Anniversary of 2nd Executive President Premadusa **Obv:** Facing lions with swords above rectangular design **Rev:** Bust facing within wreath

Date	Mintage	F	VF	XF	Unc	BU
1992	25,000,000	—	0.30	0.65	1.75	2.50
1992 Proof	2,000	Value: 10.00				

KM# 157 RUPEE
Copper-Nickel **Subject:** UNICEF 50th Anniversary **Obv:** Inscription and value below designs within wreath **Rev:** Numeral 50 and UNICEF logo within circle

Date	Mintage	F	VF	XF	Unc	BU
1996	5,000,000	—	—	—	1.75	2.50

KM# 162 RUPEE
7.1300 g., Nickel Plated Steel, 25.4 mm. **Subject:** Army's 50th Anniversary **Obv:** National arms above crossed swords above dates within beaded circle **Rev:** Soldier giving dove to boy **Edge:** Reeded

Date	Mintage	F	VF	XF	Unc	BU
1999 Proof	8,000	Value: 10.00				
1999 Prooflike	127,000	—	—	—	—	6.00

KM# 164 RUPEE
7.1300 g., Nickel Plated Steel, 25.4 mm. **Subject:** Sri Lankan Navy 50 Years **Obv:** National arms within circle **Rev:** Patrol boat within circle **Edge:** Reeded

Date	Mintage	F	VF	XF	Unc	BU
2000	20,000	—	—	—	—	6.00

KM# 136.3 RUPEE
3.6200 g., Brass Plated Steel, 20 mm. **Obv:** National emblem **Rev:** Value and date **Edge:** Segmented reeding

Date	Mintage	F	VF	XF	Unc	BU
2005	—	—	—	—	0.75	1.00
2006	—	—	—	—	0.75	1.00

KM# 136b RUPEE
3.6700 g., Brass Plated Steel, 19.91 mm. **Obv:** National arms **Rev:** Value **Edge:** Segmented reeding

Date	Mintage	F	VF	XF	Unc	BU
2005	—	—	—	0.35	0.85	1.25
2006	—	—	—	0.35	0.85	1.25

KM# 142 2 RUPEES
Copper-Nickel, 30 mm. **Subject:** Non-Aligned Nations Conference **Obv:** Value within inscription, legend around border **Rev:** Conference building **Edge:** Plain **Shape:** 7-sided

Date	Mintage	F	VF	XF	Unc	BU
1976	2,000,000	—	0.50	1.50	2.25	3.50
1976 Proof	500	Value: 10.00				

KM# 145 2 RUPEES
Copper-Nickel **Subject:** Mahaweli Dam **Obv:** Numeral value within inscription, legend around border **Rev:** Dam within circle

Date	Mintage	F	VF	XF	Unc	BU
1981	45,000,000	—	0.35	0.75	2.50	3.75

KM# 147 2 RUPEES
Copper-Nickel **Obv:** National arms **Rev:** Value

Date	Mintage	F	VF	XF	Unc	BU
1984	25,000,000	—	0.25	0.50	1.00	1.50
1993	40,000,000	—	0.30	0.60	1.35	1.75
1996	50,000,000	—	0.30	0.60	1.35	1.75
2001	10,000,000	—	0.30	0.60	1.35	1.75
2002	40,000,000	—	0.30	0.60	1.35	1.75

KM# 155 2 RUPEES
Copper-Nickel **Series:** F.A.O. **Subject:** F.A.O. 50th Anniversary **Obv:** Value within inscription, legend around border **Rev:** F.A.O. logo and dates within circle

Date	Mintage	F	VF	XF	Unc	BU
1995	40,000,000	—	—	—	2.25	3.25

KM# 167 2 RUPEES
8.2500 g., Copper Nickel, 28.5 mm. **Subject:** Colombo Plan's 50th Anniversary **Obv:** Value within inscription above date **Rev:** Gear wheel **Edge:** Reeded

Date	Mintage	F	VF	XF	Unc	BU
2001	10,000,000	—	—	—	2.00	3.00

KM# 147a 2 RUPEES
7.0800 g., Nickel Clad Steel, 28.4 mm. **Obv:** National arms **Rev:** Value **Edge:** Reeded

Date	Mintage	F	VF	XF	Unc	BU
2005	—	—	—	0.45	1.10	1.50
2006	—	—	—	0.45	1.10	1.50

KM# 143 5 RUPEES
13.7000 g., Nickel **Subject:** Non-Aligned Nations Conference **Obv:** Value within inscription, legend around border **Rev:** Conference building **Shape:** 10-sided

Date	Mintage	F	VF	XF	Unc	BU
1976	1,000,000	—	0.75	1.50	3.00	4.50
1976 Proof	500	Value: 12.00				

KM# 146 5 RUPEES
Copper-Nickel **Subject:** 50th Anniversary - Universal Adult Franchise **Obv:** Value within inscription, legend around border **Rev:** Building with flag **Shape:** 10-sided

Date	Mintage	F	VF	XF	Unc	BU
1981	2,000,000	—	0.75	1.50	3.00	4.50

KM# 148.1 5 RUPEES
Aluminum-Bronze **Obv:** National arms **Rev:** Value within inscription, legend around border **Edge:** Lettered **Edge Lettering:** CBC - Central Bank of Ceylon

Date	Mintage	F	VF	XF	Unc	BU
1984	25,000,000	—	0.35	0.75	2.25	3.00

KM# 148.2 5 RUPEES
9.5000 g., Aluminum-Bronze **Obv:** National arms **Rev:** Value **Edge:** Lettered **Edge Lettering:** CBSL - Central Bank of Sri Lanka

Date	Mintage	F	VF	XF	Unc	BU
1986	60,000,000	—	0.35	0.75	2.25	3.00
1991	40,000,000	—	0.35	0.75	2.25	3.00
1994	50,000,000	—	0.35	0.65	2.00	2.75
2002	30,000,000	—	0.35	0.65	2.00	2.75
2004	—	—	—	0.65	2.00	2.75

KM# 148.2a 5 RUPEES
Bronze Plated Steel **Obv:** National arms **Rev:** Value

Date	Mintage	F	VF	XF	Unc	BU
2005	—	—	—	0.65	2.00	2.75

KM# 148a 5 RUPEES
7.6700 g., Brass Plated Steel, 23.49 mm. **Obv:** National arms **Rev:** Value **Edge:** Reeded and Lettered **Edge Lettering:** CBSL repeated in various languages

Date	Mintage	F	VF	XF	Unc	BU
2005	—	—	—	0.75	1.85	2.50
2006	—	—	—	0.75	1.85	2.50

KM# 156 5 RUPEES
Aluminum-Bronze **Subject:** 50th Anniversary - United Nations **Obv:** Value within inscription, legend around border **Rev:** Numeral 50 and UN logo within circle

Date	Mintage	F	VF	XF	Unc	BU
1995	50,000,000	—	—	—	2.50	3.50
1995 Proof	5,000	—	—	—	—	—

KM# 161 5 RUPEES
Aluminum-Bronze **Subject:** World Cricket Champions **Obv:** Trophy **Rev:** Batsman within circle

Date	Mintage	F	VF	XF	Unc	BU
1999	50,000,000	—	—	—	2.75	4.00

KM# 168 5 RUPEES
9.5200 g., Aluminum-Bronze, 23.4 mm. **Subject:** 250th Annniversary of the "Upasampada" Rite **Obv:** Value **Rev:** 1/2-length figure facing divides dates

Date	Mintage	F	VF	XF	Unc	BU
2003	—	—	—	—	3.00	4.50

KM# 169 5 RUPEES
9.5200 g., Aluminum-Bronze, 23.4 mm. **Subject:** 250th Anniversary - Upasampada **Obv:** Value **Rev:** Bust facing standing behind shield **Edge:** Reeded and lettered

Date	Mintage	F	VF	XF	Unc	BU
2003	—	—	—	—	3.00	4.50

KM# 170 5 RUPEES
7.6500 g., Brass, 23.5 mm. **Subject:** 2550th Anniversary of Buddha **Obv:** Value **Rev:** "Buddha Jayanthi", wheel above mountain **Edge:** Reeded and lettered

Date	Mintage	F	VF	XF	Unc	BU
2006	—	—	—	—	3.00	4.00

KM# 149 10 RUPEES
Copper-Nickel **Subject:** International Year of Shelter for Homeless **Obv:** Value within inscription, legend around border **Rev:** Logo, legend around border **Shape:** 4-sided

Date	Mintage	F	VF	XF	Unc	BU
1987	2,000,000	—	—	—	3.50	5.00
1987 Proof	200	—	—	—	—	—

KM# 158 10 RUPEES
8.9500 g., Bi-Metallic Brass center in Copper-Nickel ring, 27 mm. **Subject:** 50th Anniversary of Independence **Obv:** Value and dates within designed wreath **Rev:** Building within and outside of circle **Edge:** CBSL, (4 times) reeded

Date	Mintage	F	VF	XF	Unc	BU
1998	50,000,000	—	—	—	4.50	5.50

Straits Settlements, a former British crown colony situated on the Malay Peninsula of Asia, was formed in 1826 by combining the territories of Singapore, Penang and Malacca. The colony was administered by the East India Company until its abolition in 1858. Straits Settlements was a part of British India from 1858 to 1867 at which time it became a Crown Colony.

The Straits Settlements coinage gradually became acceptable legal tender in the neighboring Federated as well as the Unfederated Malay States. The Straits Settlements were dissolved in 1946, while the coinage continued to circulate until demonetized at the end of 1952.

RULER
British

MINT MARKS
H - Heaton, Birmingham
W - Soho Mint
B - Bombay

MONETARY SYSTEM
100 Cents = 1 Dollar

BRITISH CROWN COLONY
1867-1942

STANDARD COINAGE

KM# 14 1/4 CENT
Bronze **Ruler:** Victoria **Obv:** Crowned head left **Obv. Legend:** VICTORIA QUEEN **Obv. Designer:** G.W. DeSaulles **Rev:** Value within beaded circle **Rev. Legend:** STRAITS SETTLEMENTS.. **Edge:** Reeded

Date	Mintage	F	VF	XF	Unc	BU
1901	2,000,000	10.00	20.00	85.00	300	—

KM# 17 1/4 CENT
Bronze **Ruler:** Edward VII **Obv:** Crowned bust right **Obv. Designer:** E.B. MacKennal **Rev:** Value within beaded circle

Date	Mintage	F	VF	XF	Unc	BU
1904 Proof	—	Value: 1,800				
Note: Plain edge						
1905	2,008,000	10.00	25.00	80.00	180	—
1905 Proof	—	Value: 1,500				
1908	1,200,000	10.00	25.00	80.00	180	—

KM# 27 1/4 CENT
Bronze **Ruler:** George V **Obv:** Crowned bust left **Rev:** Value within beaded circle

Date	Mintage	F	VF	XF	Unc	BU
1916	4,000,000	6.00	12.50	22.00	40.00	—
1916 Proof	—	Value: 500				

KM# 18 1/2 CENT
Bronze **Ruler:** Edward VII **Obv:** Crowned bust right **Obv. Designer:** G.W. DeSaulles **Rev:** Value within beaded circle

Date	Mintage	F	VF	XF	Unc	BU
1904 Proof	—	Value: 3,000				
1908	2,000,000	15.00	27.50	80.00	210	—

KM# 28 1/2 CENT
Bronze **Ruler:** George V **Obv:** Crowned bust left **Obv. Designer:** E.B. MacKennal **Rev:** Value within beaded circle

Date	Mintage	F	VF	XF	Unc	BU
1916	3,000,000	6.00	10.00	20.00	32.00	—
1916 Proof	—	Value: 500				

KM# 37 1/2 CENT
Bronze **Ruler:** George V **Obv. Designer:** E.B. MacKennal **Rev:** Value within beaded circle **Edge:** Crowned bust left **Shape:** 4-sided

Date	Mintage	F	VF	XF	Unc	BU
1932	5,000,000	3.50	6.50	14.00	30.00	—
1932 Proof	—	Value: 420				

KM# 16 CENT
Bronze **Ruler:** Victoria **Obv:** Crowned head left **Obv. Legend:** VICTORIA QUEEN **Rev:** Value within beaded circle **Rev. Legend:** STRAITS SETTLEMENTS **Edge:** Reeded

Date	Mintage	F	VF	XF	Unc	BU
1901	15,230,000	1.25	10.00	70.00	260	—

KM# 19 CENT
Bronze **Ruler:** Edward VII **Obv:** Crowned bust right **Obv. Designer:** G.W. DeSaulles **Rev:** Value within beaded circle

Date	Mintage	F	VF	XF	Unc	BU
1903	7,053,000	2.00	10.00	70.00	250	—
1903 Proof, Rare	—	—	—	—	—	—
1904	6,647,000	2.00	10.00	70.00	250	—
1904 Proof, Rare	—	—	—	—	—	—
1906	7,504,000	10.00	60.00	150	350	—
1907	5,015,000	2.00	10.00	70.00	250	—

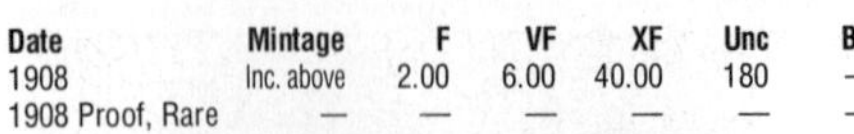

Date	Mintage	F	VF	XF	Unc	BU
1908	Inc. above	2.00	6.00	40.00	180	—
1908 Proof, Rare	—	—	—	—	—	—

KM# 32 CENT

Bronze, 21 mm. **Obv:** Crowned bust left **Obv. Designer:** E.B. MacKennal **Rev:** Value within beaded circle **Edge:** Plain **Shape:** 4-sided

Date	Mintage	F	VF	XF	Unc	BU
1919	20,165,000	0.50	1.50	10.00	42.00	—
1919 Proof	—	Value: 400				
1920	55,000,000	0.50	1.50	6.00	30.00	—
1920 Proof	—	Value: 400				
1926	5,000,000	0.50	1.50	12.00	60.00	—

KM# 10 5 CENTS

1.3600 g., 0.8000 Silver 0.0350 oz. ASW **Ruler:** Victoria **Obv:** Crowned head left **Obv. Legend:** VICTORIA QUEEN **Rev:** Value within beaded circle **Rev. Legend:** STRAITS SETTLEMENTS

Date	Mintage	F	VF	XF	Unc	BU
1901	3,000,000	6.00	9.00	60.00	300	—
1901 Proof	—	Value: 900				

KM# 20 5 CENTS

1.3600 g., 0.8000 Silver 0.0350 oz. ASW **Ruler:** Edward VII **Obv:** Crowned bust right **Obv. Designer:** G.W. DeSaulles **Rev:** Value within beaded circle

Date	Mintage	F	VF	XF	Unc	BU
1902	1,920,000	10.00	25.00	150	250	—
1902 Proof	—	Value: 1,000				
1903	2,270,000	10.00	25.00	150	250	—
1903 Proof	—	Value: 1,000				

KM# 31 5 CENTS

1.3600 g., 0.4000 Silver 0.0175 oz. ASW **Ruler:** George V **Obv:** Crowned bust left **Obv. Designer:** E.B. MacKennal **Rev:** Value within beaded circle

Date	Mintage	F	VF	XF	Unc	BU
1918	3,100,000	0.50	2.00	20.00	40.00	—
1919	6,900,000	0.50	2.00	20.00	40.00	—
1920	4,000,000	500	1,000	2,000	6,300	—

KM# 34 5 CENTS

Copper-Nickel **Ruler:** George V **Obv:** Crowned bust left **Obv. Designer:** E.B. MacKennal **Rev:** Value within beaded circle

Date	Mintage	F	VF	XF	Unc	BU
1920	20,000,000	1.50	20.00	90.00	180	—
1920 Proof, Rare	—	—	—	—	—	—

KM# 36 5 CENTS

1.3600 g., 0.6000 Silver 0.0262 oz. ASW **Ruler:** George V **Obv:** Smaller bust, broader rim **Obv. Designer:** E.B. MacKennal **Rev:** Value within beaded circle

Date	Mintage	F	VF	XF	Unc	BU
1926	10,000,000	0.65	1.00	8.00	20.00	—
1926 Proof	—	Value: 2,000				
1935	3,000,000	0.65	1.00	5.00	16.00	—
1935 Proof	—	Value: 2,000				

KM# 11 10 CENTS

2.7100 g., 0.8000 Silver 0.0697 oz. ASW **Ruler:** Victoria **Obv:** Crowned head left **Obv. Legend:** VICTORIA QUEEN **Rev:** Value within beaded circle **Rev. Legend:** STRAITS SETTLEMENTS

Date	Mintage	F	VF	XF	Unc	BU
1901	2,700,000	10.00	15.00	80.00	250	—

KM# 21 10 CENTS

2.7100 g., 0.8000 Silver 0.0697 oz. ASW **Ruler:** Edward VII **Obv:** Crowned bust right **Obv. Designer:** G.W. DeSaulles **Rev:** Value within beaded circle

Date	Mintage	F	VF	XF	Unc	BU
1902	6,118,000	8.00	20.00	90.00	280	—
1902 Proof, Rare	—	—	—	—	—	—
1903	1,401,000	8.00	25.00	110	280	—
1903 Proof, Rare	—	—	—	—	—	—

KM# 21a 10 CENTS

2.7100 g., 0.6000 Silver 0.0523 oz. ASW **Ruler:** Edward VII **Obv:** Crowned bust right **Obv. Designer:** G.W. DeSaulles **Rev:** Value within beaded circle

Date	Mintage	F	VF	XF	Unc	BU
1909B	11,088,000	15.00	40.00	120	400	—
1910B	1,657,000	2.00	5.00	15.00	40.00	—
1910B Proof, Rare	—	—	—	—	—	—

KM# 29 10 CENTS

2.7100 g., 0.6000 Silver 0.0523 oz. ASW **Ruler:** George V **Obv:** Crowned bust left **Obv. Designer:** E.B. MacKennal **Rev:** Value within beaded circle

Date	Mintage	F	VF	XF	Unc	BU
1916	600,000	5.00	12.00	60.00	160	—
1917	5,600,000	1.00	2.00	18.00	110	—

KM# 29a 10 CENTS

2.7100 g., 0.4000 Silver 0.0348 oz. ASW **Ruler:** George V **Obv:** Crowned bust left **Obv. Designer:** E.B. MacKennal **Rev:** Value within beaded circle

Date	Mintage	F	VF	XF	Unc	BU
1918	7,500,000	1.00	2.50	18.00	115	—
1919	11,500,000	1.00	2.50	18.00	110	—
1920	4,000,000	16.00	40.00	180	500	—

KM# 29b 10 CENTS

2.7100 g., 0.6000 Silver 0.0523 oz. ASW **Ruler:** George V **Obv:** Crowned bust left **Obv. Designer:** E.B. MacKennal **Rev:** Value within beaded circle

Date	Mintage	F	VF	XF	Unc	BU
1926	20,000,000	1.50	2.00	8.00	25.00	—
1926 Proof	—	Value: 550				
1927	23,000,000	1.50	2.00	4.00	7.00	—
1927 Proof	—	Value: 550				

KM# 12 20 CENTS

5.4300 g., 0.8000 Silver 0.1397 oz. ASW, 23 mm. **Ruler:** Victoria **Obv:** Crowned head left **Obv. Legend:** VICTORIA QUEEN **Rev:** Value within beaded circle **Rev. Legend:** STRAITS SETTLEMENTS

Date	Mintage	F	VF	XF	Unc	BU
1901	600,000	7.00	12.00	40.00	250	—

KM# 22 20 CENTS

5.4300 g., 0.8000 Silver 0.1397 oz. ASW, 23 mm. **Ruler:** Edward VII **Obv:** Crowned bust right **Obv. Designer:** G.W. DeSaulles **Rev:** Value within beaded circle

Date	Mintage	F	VF	XF	Unc	BU
1902	1,105,000	18.00	38.00	185	500	—
1902 Proof, Rare	—	—	—	—	—	—
1903	1,150,000	18.00	38.00	185	500	—
1903 Proof, Rare	—	—	—	—	—	—

KM# 22a 20 CENTS

5.4300 g., 0.6000 Silver 0.1047 oz. ASW, 23 mm. **Ruler:** Edward VII **Obv:** Crowned bust right **Obv. Designer:** G.W. DeSaulles **Rev:** Value within beaded circle

Date	Mintage	F	VF	XF	Unc	BU
1910B	3,276,000	7.00	10.00	50.00	150	—
1910B Proof, Rare	—	—	—	—	—	—

KM# 30 20 CENTS

5.4300 g., 0.6000 Silver 0.1047 oz. ASW, 23 mm. **Ruler:** George V **Obv:** Crowned bust left **Obv. Designer:** E.B. MacKennal **Rev:** Value within beaded circle

Date	Mintage	F	VF	XF	Unc	BU
1916B	545,000	10.00	20.00	110	260	—
1916B Proof, Rare	—	—	—	—	—	—
1917B	652,000	4.50	12.00	70.00	160	—

KM# 30a 20 CENTS

5.4300 g., 0.4000 Silver 0.0698 oz. ASW, 23 mm. **Ruler:** George V **Obv:** Crowned bust left **Obv. Designer:** E.B. MacKennal **Rev:** Value within beaded circle

Date	Mintage	F	VF	XF	Unc	BU
1919B	2,500,000	3.00	7.00	40.00	150	—
1919B Proof, Rare	—	—	—	—	—	—

KM# 30b 20 CENTS

5.4300 g., 0.6000 Silver 0.1047 oz. ASW, 23 mm. **Ruler:** George V **Obv:** Crowned bust left **Obv. Designer:** E.B. MacKennal **Rev:** Value within beaded circle

Date	Mintage	F	VF	XF	Unc	BU
1926	2,500,000	2.00	5.00	20.00	100	—
1926 Proof, Rare	—	—	—	—	—	—
1927	3,000,000	2.00	5.00	10.00	25.00	—
1927 Proof, Rare	—	—	—	—	—	—
1935 Round-top 3	1,000,000	2.50	4.00	10.00	15.00	—
1935 Flat-top 3	Inc. above	2.50	4.00	10.00	15.00	—

KM# 13 50 CENTS
13.5769 g., 0.8000 Silver 0.3492 oz. ASW **Ruler:** Victoria **Obv:** Crowned head left **Obv. Legend:** VICTORIA QUEEN **Rev:** Value within beaded circle **Rev. Legend:** STRAITS SETTLEMENTS

Date	Mintage	F	VF	XF	Unc	BU
1901	120,000	52.00	80.00	350	1,500	—

KM# 23 50 CENTS
13.5769 g., 0.8000 Silver 0.3492 oz. ASW, 31 mm. **Ruler:** Edward VII **Obv:** Crowned bust right **Obv. Designer:** G.W. DeSaulles **Rev:** Value within beaded circle

Date	Mintage	F	VF	XF	Unc	BU
1902	148,000	100	190	500	1,000	—
1902 Proof, Rare	—	—	—	—	—	—
1903	193,000	100	190	500	1,000	—
1903 Proof, Rare	—	—	—	—	—	—
1905B Raised	498,000	95.00	165	380	600	—
1905B Proof, raised, Rare	—	—	—	—	—	—
1905B Proof, incuse, Rare	—	—	—	—	—	—

KM# 24 50 CENTS
10.1000 g., 0.9000 Silver 0.2922 oz. ASW, 28 mm. **Ruler:** Edward VII **Obv:** Crowned bust right **Obv. Designer:** G.W. DeSaulles **Rev:** Value within beaded circle

Date	Mintage	F	VF	XF	Unc	BU
1907	464,000	17.50	30.00	90.00	180	—
1907H	2,667,000	17.50	30.00	90.00	180	—
1908	2,869,000	17.50	30.00	90.00	180	—
1908H	Inc. above	17.50	35.00	110	200	—

Note: Mintage included with 1907H

KM# 35.1 50 CENTS
8.4200 g., 0.5000 Silver 0.1353 oz. ASW **Ruler:** George V **Obv:** Crowned bust left **Obv. Designer:** E.B. MacKennal **Rev:** Value within beaded circle

Date	Mintage	F	VF	XF	Unc	BU
1920	3,900,000	5.00	7.50	10.00	20.00	—
1920 Proof, Rare	—	—	—	—	—	—
1921	2,579,000	5.00	8.00	12.00	25.00	—
1921 Proof, Rare	—	—	—	—	—	—

KM# 35.2 50 CENTS
8.4200 g., 0.5000 Silver 0.1353 oz. ASW **Ruler:** George V **Obv:** Crowned bust left with dot below bust **Obv. Designer:** E.B. MacKennal **Rev:** Value within beaded circle

Date	Mintage	F	VF	XF	Unc	BU
1920	Inc. above	200	350	560	1,000	—

KM# 25 DOLLAR
26.9500 g., 0.9000 Silver 0.7798 oz. ASW, 37 mm. **Ruler:** Edward VII **Obv:** Crowned bust right **Obv. Designer:** G.W. DeSaulles **Rev:** Artistic design within circle

Date	Mintage	F	VF	XF	Unc	BU
1903 Proof, Rare	—	—	—	—	—	—
1903B Incuse	15,010,000	40.00	62.50	165	280	—
1903B Raised	Inc. above	140	250	550	1,000	—
1903B Proof, raised, Rare	—	—	—	—	—	—
1904B	20,365,000	28.00	38.00	97.50	190	—
1904B Proof, Rare	—	—	—	—	—	—

KM# 26 DOLLAR
20.2100 g., 0.9000 Silver 0.5848 oz. ASW, 34.5 mm. **Ruler:** Edward VII **Obv:** Crowned bust right **Obv. Designer:** G.W. DeSaulles **Rev:** Artistic design within circle **Note:** Reduced size.

Date	Mintage	F	VF	XF	Unc	BU
1907	6,842,000	10.00	20.00	60.00	110	—
1907H	4,000,000	10.00	20.00	60.00	110	—
1907H Proof, Rare	—	—	—	—	—	—
1908	4,152,000	10.00	18.00	45.00	100	—
1908 Proof, Rare	—	—	—	—	—	—
1909	1,014,000	12.00	25.00	70.00	220	—
1909 Proof, Rare	—	—	—	—	—	—

KM# 33 DOLLAR
16.8500 g., 0.5000 Silver 0.2709 oz. ASW **Ruler:** George V **Obv:** Crowned bust left **Obv. Designer:** E.B. MacKennal **Rev:** Artistic design within circle

Date	Mintage	F	VF	XF	Unc	BU
1919	6,000,000	60.00	110	200	320	—
1919 Proof	—	Value: 200				
Note: Restrike						
1920	8,164,000	20.00	40.00	100	200	—
1920 Proof	—	Value: 200				
Note: Restrike						
1925	—	—	—	8,300	—	—
1925 Proof	—	Value: 10,000				
1925 Proof	—	Value: 3,000				
Note: Restrike						
1926	—	—	—	6,500	—	—
1926 Proof	—	Value: 10,000				
1926 Proof	—	Value: 3,000				
Note: Restrike						

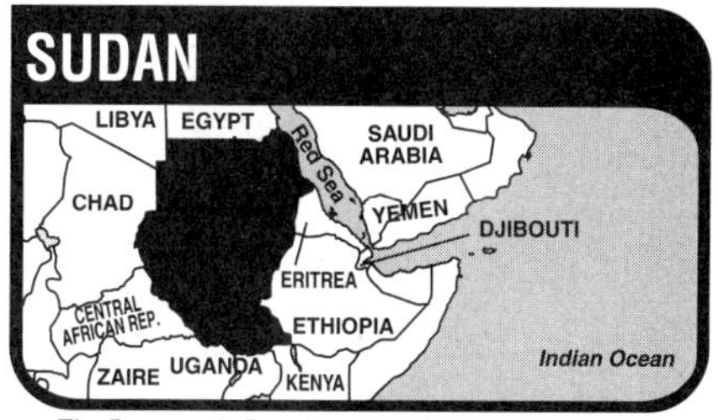

The Democratic Republic of the Sudan, located in northeast Africa on the Red Sea between Egypt and Ethiopia, has an area of 967,500 sq. mi. (2,505,810 sq. km.) and a population of *24.5 million. Capital: Khartoum. Agriculture and livestock raising are the chief occupations. Cotton, gum arabic and peanuts are exported.

The Sudan, site of the powerful Nubian kingdom of Roman times, was a collection of small independent states from the 14th century until 1820-22 when it was conquered and united by Mohammed Ali, Pasha of Egypt. Egyptian forces were driven from the area during the Mahdist revolt, 1881-98, but the Sudan was retaken by Anglo-Egyptian expeditions, 1896-98, and established as an Anglo-Egyptian condominium in 1899. Britain supplied the administrative apparatus and personnel, but the appearance of joint Anglo-Egyptian administration was continued until Jan. 9, 1954, when the first Sudanese self-government parliament was inaugurated. The Sudan achieved independence on Jan. 1, 1956 with the consent of the British and Egyptian government.

TITLES

جمهورية السودان

Jumhuriya(t) as-Sudan

الجمهورية السودان
الديمقراطية

Al-Arabiya(t) as-Sa'udiya(t)al-Jumhuriya(t) as-Sudan ad-Dimiqratiya(t)

MINT NAME

ام درمان

Omdurman

REPUBLIC

STANDARD COINAGE

KM# 29.1 MILLIM
1.7800 g., Bronze **Obv:** Large legend and value above flower sprigs **Rev:** Camel with rider running left

Date	Mintage	F	VF	XF	Unc	BU
AH1376-1956	5,000,000	—	—	0.15	0.30	0.75
AH1379-1960	1,300,000	—	—	0.15	0.35	0.75
AH1386-1966 Proof	—	—	—	—	—	—
AH1387-1967	—	—	—	0.15	0.30	0.75
AH1388-1968	—	—	—	0.15	0.30	0.75
AH1389-1969	—	—	—	0.15	0.30	0.75

KM# 39 MILLIM
Bronze **Obv:** New Arabic legend and value above flower sprigs **Rev:** Camel with rider running left

Date	Mintage	F	VF	XF	Unc	BU
AH1390-1970	—	—	—	—	—	—
AH1390-1970 Proof	1,646	Value: 1.00				
AH1391-1971 Proof	1,772	Value: 1.00				

KM# 30.1 2 MILLIM

Bronze **Obv:** Large written value with legend above flower sprigs **Rev:** Camel with rider running left **Edge:** Plain **Shape:** Scalloped

Date	Mintage	F	VF	XF	Unc	BU
AH1376-1956	5,000,000	—	—	0.15	0.50	1.00
AH1386-1966 Proof	—	Value: 1.00				
AH1387-1967	—	—	—	0.15	0.50	1.00
AH1388-1968	—	—	—	0.15	0.50	1.00
AH1389-1969	—	—	—	0.15	0.50	1.00

KM# 31.1 5 MILLIM

3.9500 g., Bronze **Obv:** Thin legend and narrow 5 **Rev:** Camel with rider running left **Shape:** Scalloped **Note:** Camel and rider, date size varieties exist, and with or without outlined bare line.

Date	Mintage	F	VF	XF	Unc	BU
AH1376-1956	30,000,000	—	0.10	0.20	0.50	1.00
AH1382-1962	6,000,000	—	0.10	0.20	0.50	1.00
AH1386-1966	4,000,000	—	0.10	0.15	0.50	1.00
AH1386-1966 Proof	—	—	—	—	—	—
AH1387-1967	4,000,000	—	0.10	0.15	0.35	1.00
AH1388-1968	—	—	0.10	0.15	0.35	1.00
AH1389-1969	—	—	0.10	0.15	0.35	1.00

KM# 41.1 5 MILLIM

Bronze **Obv:** New large Arabic legend narrow 5 **Rev:** Camel with rider running left **Shape:** Scalloped **Note:** Date heighth and size varieties exist

Date	Mintage	F	VF	XF	Unc	BU
AH1390-1970	—	—	0.20	0.45	1.25	1.75
AH1391-1971	3,000,000	—	0.20	0.45	1.25	1.75

KM# 47 5 MILLIM

Bronze **Subject:** 2nd Anniversary of Revolution **Obv:** Legend and value above flower sprigs **Rev:** Eagle divides dates below legend

Date	Mintage	F	VF	XF	Unc	BU
AH1391-1971	500,000	—	0.15	0.25	0.50	1.00

KM# 53 5 MILLIM

3.3200 g., Bronze, 21.5 mm. **Series:** F.A.O. **Obv:** Legend and value above flower sprigs **Rev:** Eagle divides dates below legend **Edge:** Plain

Date	Mintage	F	VF	XF	Unc	BU
AH1392-1972	6,000,000	—	—	0.15	0.35	—
AH1393-1973	9,000,000	—	—	0.15	0.35	—

KM# 54a.1 5 MILLIM

Brass **Obv:** Thick legend and written value **Rev:** Ribbon with 3 equal sections

Date	Mintage	F	VF	XF	Unc	BU
AH1395-1975	4,132,000	—	—	0.20	0.40	—
AH1398-1978	—	—	—	0.20	0.40	—

KM# 54 5 MILLIM

Bronze **Obv:** Legend and value **Rev:** Eagle divides AH and CE dates **Note:** Similar to 10 Millim, KM#55, but round.

Date	Mintage	F	VF	XF	Unc	BU
AH1392-1972	—	—	—	0.20	0.45	—

KM# 60 5 MILLIM

Brass **Series:** F.A.O. **Obv:** Legend and value above flower sprigs **Rev:** Eagle within sprigs divide legend and dates **Note:** Size varies 21.4 - 22.5 mm.

Date	Mintage	F	VF	XF	Unc	BU
AH1396-1976	7,868,000	—	—	0.10	0.20	—
AH1398-1978	7,000,000	—	—	0.10	0.20	—

KM# 94 5 MILLIM

Brass **Subject:** 20th Anniversary of Independence **Obv:** Legend and value above flower sprigs **Rev:** Eagle divides dates below legend

Date	Mintage	F	VF	XF	Unc	BU
AH1396-1976	—	—	0.15	0.20	0.25	—

KM# 54a.2 5 MILLIM

Brass **Obv:** Large legend and large 5 **Rev:** Eagle divides dates, ribbon with long center section

Date	Mintage	F	VF	XF	Unc	BU
AH1398-1978	—	—	—	0.20	0.40	—

KM# 32.1 10 MILLIM

Bronze **Obv:** Large written value **Rev:** Camel with rider running left **Shape:** Scalloped **Note:** Camel, rider and date size varieties exist.

Date	Mintage	F	VF	XF	Unc	BU
AH1376-1956	15,000,000	—	0.15	0.25	0.85	1.25
AH1380-1960	12,250,000	—	0.15	0.20	0.75	1.50
AH1381-1962 High date	—	—	0.15	0.20	0.75	1.00
AH1381-1962 Low date	—	—	0.15	0.20	0.75	1.00
AH1386-1966	1,000,000	—	0.15	0.25	0.85	1.50
AH1386-1966 Proof	—	—	—	—	—	—
AH1387-1967	1,000,000	—	0.15	0.20	0.75	1.00
AH1388-1968	—	—	0.15	0.20	0.75	1.50
AH1389-1969	—	—	0.15	0.20	0.75	1.50

KM# 42.1 10 MILLIM

Bronze **Obv:** New large Arabic legend and written value **Rev:** Camel with rider running left **Shape:** Scalloped

Date	Mintage	F	VF	XF	Unc	BU
AH1390-1970	—	—	0.20	0.40	1.00	1.50
AH1391-1971	3,000,000	—	0.20	0.40	1.00	1.50

KM# 48 10 MILLIM

Bronze **Subject:** 2nd Anniversary of the Revolution **Obv:** Legend and value above flower sprigs **Rev:** Eagle divides dates below legend

Date	Mintage	F	VF	XF	Unc	BU
AH1391-1971	500,000	—	10.00	15.00	25.00	—

KM# 55a.1 10 MILLIM

Brass **Obv:** Large legend and written value **Rev:** Ribbon with three equal sections **Shape:** Scalloped

Date	Mintage	F	VF	XF	Unc	BU
AH1395-1975	12,000,000	—	0.25	0.35	0.75	—
AH1398-1978	9,410,000	—	0.25	0.45	1.00	—

KM# 55a.3 10 MILLIM

Brass **Obv:** Small legend and written value **Rev:** Eagle divides dates, ribbon with 3 equal sections **Shape:** Scalloped

Date	Mintage	F	VF	XF	Unc	BU
AH1400-1980	2,490,000	—	0.25	0.45	1.00	—
AH1400-1980 Proof	—	Value: 2.50				

KM# 55 10 MILLIM

Bronze **Obv:** Legend and value above flower sprigs **Rev:** Eagle divides dates **Shape:** Scalloped

Date	Mintage	F	VF	XF	Unc	BU
AH1392-1972	6,500,000	—	0.15	0.25	0.50	—

KM# 55a.2 10 MILLIM

Brass, 25.5 mm. **Obv:** Large legend **Rev:** Ribbon with long center section, eagle divides AH and CE dates **Edge:** Plain **Shape:** Scalloped

Date	Mintage	F	VF	XF	Unc	BU
AH1398-1978	—	—	0.75	1.75	4.25	—

KM# 61 10 MILLIM

Brass **Series:** F.A.O. **Obv:** Legend and value above flower sprigs **Rev:** Eagle within sprigs divides date and legend **Shape:** Scalloped

Date	Mintage	F	VF	XF	Unc	BU
AH1396-1976	3,000,000	—	0.10	0.15	0.25	—
AH1398-1978	—	—	0.10	0.15	0.25	—

KM# 62 10 MILLIM

Brass **Subject:** 20th Anniversary of Independence **Obv:** Legend and value above flower sprigs **Rev:** Eagle divides dates below legend **Shape:** Scalloped

Date	Mintage	F	VF	XF	Unc	BU
AH1396-1976	3,610,000	—	0.10	0.20	0.40	—

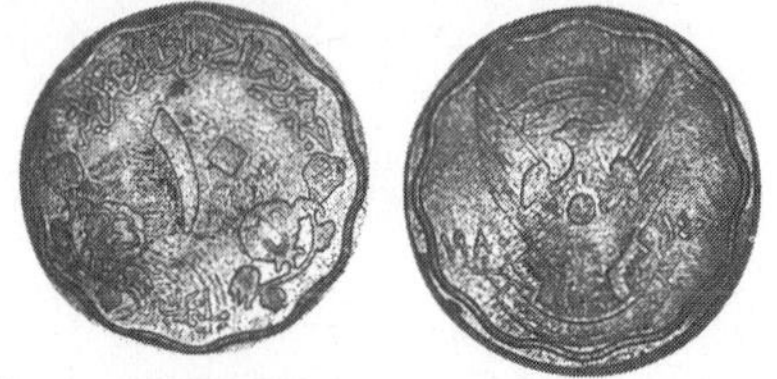

KM# 111 10 MILLIM

Brass, 24.5 mm. **Obv:** Legend and value above flower sprigs **Rev:** Eagle divides dates **Shape:** Round

Date	Mintage	F	VF	XF	Unc	BU
AH1400-1980	—	—	1.25	3.75	7.50	—

KM# 97 GHIRSH
Brass **Obv:** Legend and value above flower sprigs **Rev:** Eagle divides dates, ribbon with 3 equal sections

Date	Mintage	F	VF	XF	Unc	BU
AH1403-1983	1,140,000	—	0.25	0.65	2.00	—

KM# 99 GHIRSH
Aluminum-Bronze **Obv:** Legend and value above flower sprigs **Rev:** Building above inscription and crossed sprigs

Date	Mintage	F	VF	XF	Unc	BU
AH1408-1987	—	—	0.30	0.80	3.00	—

KM# 33 2 GHIRSH
Copper-Nickel, 17.5 mm. **Obv:** Legend and value above flower sprigs **Rev:** Camel with rider running left

Date	Mintage	F	VF	XF	Unc	BU
AH1376-1956	5,000,000	—	0.15	0.35	0.75	1.50
AH1381-1962	—	—	0.15	0.35	0.75	1.50

KM# 36 2 GHIRSH
Copper-Nickel, 20 mm. **Obv:** Legend and value above flower sprigs **Rev:** Camel with rider running left

Date	Mintage	F	VF	XF	Unc	BU
AH1382-1963	1,250,000	—	0.15	0.35	0.75	1.50
AH1386-1966 Proof	—	—	—	—	—	—
AH1387-1967	7,834	—	0.15	0.35	0.75	1.50
AH1387-1967 Proof	7,834	Value: 1.50				
AH1388-1968	5,251	—	0.15	0.35	0.75	1.50
AH1388-1968 Proof	5,251	Value: 1.50				
AH1389-1969	2,149	—	0.15	0.35	0.75	1.50
AH1389-1969 Proof	2,149	Value: 1.75				

KM# 43.1 2 GHIRSH
Copper-Nickel **Obv:** New large Arabic legend and written value **Rev:** Camel with rider running left

Date	Mintage	F	VF	XF	Unc	BU
AH1390-1970	—	—	0.30	0.60	1.25	2.00

KM# 49 2 GHIRSH
Copper-Nickel **Subject:** 2nd Anniversary of Revolution **Obv:** Legend and value above flower sprigs **Rev:** Eagle divides dates below legend

Date	Mintage	F	VF	XF	Unc	BU
AH1391-1971	500,000	—	0.25	0.45	0.80	—

KM# 57.1 2 GHIRSH
Copper-Nickel **Obv:** Thick legend and value above flower sprigs **Rev:** Eagle divides dates, ribbon with 3 equal sections

Date	Mintage	F	VF	XF	Unc	BU
AH1395-1975	1,000,000	—	0.20	0.35	0.75	—
AH1398-1978	1,250,000	—	0.20	0.35	0.75	—

KM# 57.2 2 GHIRSH
Copper-Nickel **Obv:** Large legend **Rev:** Ribbon with long center section, eagle divides AH and AD dates

Date	Mintage	F	VF	XF	Unc	BU
AH1398-1978	—	—	0.20	0.35	0.75	—
AH1400-1980	—	—	0.20	0.35	0.75	—

KM# 57.3 2 GHIRSH
Copper-Nickel, 20 mm. **Obv:** Thin legend and value above flower sprig **Rev:** Eagle divides dates, ribbon with 3 equal sections **Edge:** Reeded

Date	Mintage	F	VF	XF	Unc	BU
AH1399-1979	2,000,000	—	0.20	0.35	0.75	—
AH1400-1980	6,825,000	—	0.20	0.35	0.75	—
AH1400-1980 Proof	Inc. above	Value: 2.00				

KM# 57.2a 2 GHIRSH
Brass **Obv:** Legend with different style and value above flower sprigs **Rev:** Eagle divides dates

Date	Mintage	F	VF	XF	Unc	BU
AH1403-1983	100,000	—	0.75	1.50	3.50	—

KM# 63.1 2 GHIRSH
Copper-Nickel **Series:** F.A.O. **Obv:** Thick value **Rev:** Eagle within sprigs divides dates and legend

Date	Mintage	F	VF	XF	Unc	BU
AH1396-1976	500,000	—	0.20	0.35	0.75	—
AH1398-1978	Inc. above	—	0.20	0.35	0.75	—

KM# 63.2 2 GHIRSH
Copper-Nickel **Series:** F.A.O. **Obv:** Thin value **Rev:** Eagle divides AH and AD dates **Note:** Like KM#63.1.

Date	Mintage	F	VF	XF	Unc	BU
AH1398-1978	Inc. above	—	5.00	7.00	10.00	—

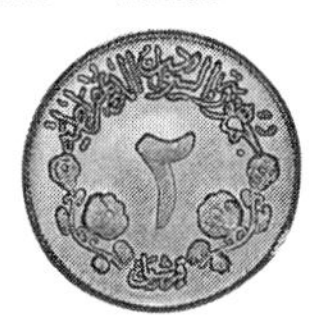 

KM# 64 2 GHIRSH
Copper-Nickel **Subject:** 20th Anniversary of Independence **Obv:** Legend and value above flower sprigs **Rev:** Eagle divides dates below legend

Date	Mintage	F	VF	XF	Unc	BU
AH1396-1976	1,750,000	—	0.20	0.30	0.60	—

KM# 34.1 5 GHIRSH
Copper-Nickel, 24 mm. **Obv:** Large written value **Rev:** Camel with rider running left **Edge:** Reeded

Date	Mintage	F	VF	XF	Unc	BU
AH1376-1956	40,000,000	—	0.20	0.40	1.20	1.50
AH1386-1966 Proof	—	Value: 2.00				
AH1387-1967	—	—	0.20	0.30	1.00	1.50
AH1388-1968	—	—	0.20	0.30	1.00	1.50
AH1389-1969	—	—	0.20	0.30	1.00	1.50

KM# 51 5 GHIRSH
Copper-Nickel **Subject:** 2nd Anniversary of Revolution **Obv:** Legend and value above flower sprigs **Rev:** Eagle divides dates below legend

Date	Mintage	F	VF	XF	Unc	BU
AH1391-1971	500,000	—	0.30	0.60	1.20	—

KM# 58.3 5 GHIRSH
Copper-Nickel, 23.5 mm. **Obv:** Small legend with different style and value above flower sprigs **Rev:** Ribbon with 3 equal sections, eagle divides dates **Edge:** Reeded

Date	Mintage	F	VF	XF	Unc	BU
AH1397-1977	2,000,000	—	0.25	0.45	0.85	—
AH1398-1978	1,000,000	—	0.25	0.45	0.85	—
AH1400-1980	1,000,000	—	0.25	0.45	0.85	—
AH1400-1980 Proof	Inc. above	Value: 3.00				

KM# 58.1 5 GHIRSH
Copper-Nickel **Obv:** Large legend and value **Rev:** Eagle divides dates, ribbon with 3 equal sections

Date	Mintage	F	VF	XF	Unc	BU
AH1395-1975	1,600,000	—	0.25	0.45	0.85	—

KM# 58.2 5 GHIRSH
Copper-Nickel **Obv:** Large legend style change, small value **Rev:** Eagle divides dates, ribbon with long center section **Note:** Edge varieties exist.

Date	Mintage	F	VF	XF	Unc	BU
AH1400-1980	—	—	0.25	0.45	0.85	—

Note: Mintage included with KM#58.1.

KM# 58.4 5 GHIRSH
Copper-Nickel **Obv:** Large legend in different style **Rev:** Ribbon with long center section, eagle divides AH and AD dates **Note:** Edge varieties exist.

Date	Mintage	F	VF	XF	Unc	BU
AH1400-1980	—	—	0.25	0.45	0.85	—

Note: Mintage included with KM#58.1.

KM# 65 5 GHIRSH

Copper-Nickel **Series:** F.A.O. **Obv:** Legend and value above flower sprigs **Rev:** Eagle within sprigs divides dates and legend

Date	Mintage	F	VF	XF	Unc	BU
AH1396-1976	500,000	—	0.20	0.30	0.65	—
AH1398-1978	—	—	0.20	0.30	0.65	—

KM# 66 5 GHIRSH

Copper-Nickel **Subject:** 20th Anniversary of Independence **Obv:** Legend and value above flower sprigs **Rev:** Eagle divides dates below legend

Date	Mintage	F	VF	XF	Unc	BU
AH1396-1976	3,940,000	—	0.25	0.50	1.00	—

KM# 74 5 GHIRSH

Copper-Nickel **Subject:** Council of Arab Economic Unity **Obv:** Clasped hands and legend within wreath **Rev:** Eagle divides dates **Note:** Edge varieties exist.

Date	Mintage	F	VF	XF	Unc	BU
AH1398-1978	5,040,000	—	0.15	0.25	0.50	—

KM# 84 5 GHIRSH

Copper-Nickel **Series:** F.A.O. **Obv:** Cow and calf flanked by designs **Rev:** Eagle divides dates **Note:** Edge varieties exist.

Date	Mintage	F	VF	XF	Unc	BU
AH1401-1981	1,000,000	—	0.20	0.40	0.75	—

KM# 110.1 5 GHIRSH

Brass **Obv:** Large value **Rev:** Ribbon with three equal sections, eagle divides AH and AD dates

Date	Mintage	F	VF	XF	Unc	BU
AH1403-1983	—	—	0.25	0.60	1.55	—

KM# 110.2 5 GHIRSH

Brass **Obv:** Legend and value above flower sprigs **Rev:** Eagle divides dates, ribbon with long center section

Date	Mintage	F	VF	XF	Unc	BU
AH1403-1983	—	—	0.50	1.25	2.25	—

KM# 110.3 5 GHIRSH

Brass **Obv:** Small value, legend in different style **Rev:** Ribbon with three equal sections, eagle divides AH and AD dates

Date	Mintage	F	VF	XF	Unc	BU
AH1403-1983	—	—	5.00	7.00	10.00	—

KM# 110.4 5 GHIRSH

Brass **Obv:** Large value and legend **Rev:** Ribbon with long center section, eagle divides AH and AD dates

Date	Mintage	F	VF	XF	Unc	BU
AH1403-1983	—	—	1.50	4.50	7.50	—

KM# 100 5 GHIRSH

Aluminum-Bronze **Obv:** Legend and value above flower sprigs **Rev:** Central bank building above inscription and crossed sprigs

Date	Mintage	F	VF	XF	Unc	BU
AH1408-1987	—	—	0.40	1.00	2.00	—

KM# 35.1 10 GHIRSH

Copper-Nickel, 28 mm. **Obv:** Large written value **Rev:** Camel with rider running left

Date	Mintage	F	VF	XF	Unc	BU
AH1376-1956	15,000,000	—	0.35	0.75	2.00	3.00
AH1386-1966 Proof	—	—	—	—	—	—
AH1387-1967	—	—	0.30	0.60	1.50	2.50
AH1388-1968	—	—	0.30	0.60	1.50	2.50
AH1389-1969	—	—	0.30	0.60	1.50	2.50

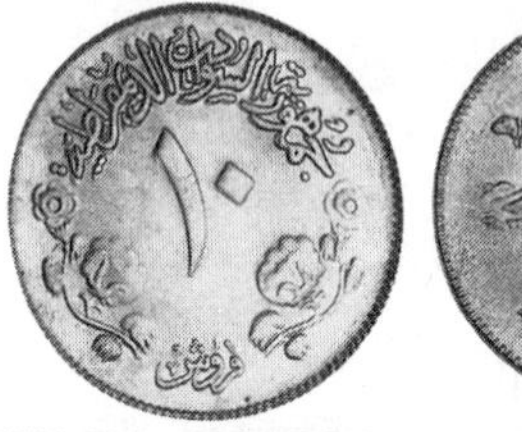

KM# 45.1 10 GHIRSH

Copper-Nickel, 28 mm. **Obv:** New large Arabic legend and written value **Rev:** Camel with rider running left

Date	Mintage	F	VF	XF	Unc	BU
AH1390-1970	—	—	0.60	1.25	3.00	—
AH1391-1971	385,000	—	0.60	1.25	3.00	—

KM# 52 10 GHIRSH

Copper-Nickel, 28 mm. **Subject:** 2nd Anniversary of Revolution **Obv:** Legend and value above flower sprigs **Rev:** Eagle divides dates below legend

Date	Mintage	F	VF	XF	Unc	BU
AH1391-1971	500,000	—	0.60	1.25	3.00	—

KM# 59.5 10 GHIRSH

Copper-Nickel, 28 mm. **Obv:** Thin legend, different style and value above flower sprigs **Rev:** Eagle divides dates **Edge:** Reeded

Date	Mintage	F	VF	XF	Unc	BU
AH1397-1977	1,000,000	—	0.50	1.00	2.75	—
AH1400-1980	2,965,000	—	0.50	1.00	2.75	—
AH1400-1980 Proof	—	Value: 4.50				

KM# 59.1 10 GHIRSH

Copper-Nickel, 28 mm. **Obv:** Legend and value above flower sprigs **Rev:** Eagle divides dates, ribbon with 3 equal sections **Edge:** Reeded

Date	Mintage	F	VF	XF	Unc	BU
AH1395-1975	1,000,000	—	0.50	1.00	2.50	—

KM# 59.2 10 GHIRSH

Copper-Nickel, 28 mm. **Obv:** Legend and value above flower sprigs **Rev:** Eagle divides dates, ribbon with long center section **Note:** Edge varieties exist.

Date	Mintage	F	VF	XF	Unc	BU
AH1400-1980	—	—	0.50	1.00	2.50	—

KM# 59.3 10 GHIRSH

Copper-Nickel **Obv:** Legend and value above flower sprigs **Rev:** Eagle divides dates **Note:** Reduced size. Edge varieties exist.

Date	Mintage	F	VF	XF	Unc	BU
AH1403-1983	—	—	0.50	1.00	2.50	—

KM# 59.4 10 GHIRSH

Copper-Nickel **Obv:** Value within flower sprigs below legend **Rev:** Ribbon with three equal sections, eagle divides AH and AD dates

Date	Mintage	F	VF	XF	Unc	BU
AH1403-1983	1,100,000	—	7.00	10.00	20.00	—

KM# 67 10 GHIRSH

Copper-Nickel, 28 mm. **Series:** F.A.O. **Obv:** Legend and value above flower sprigs **Rev:** Eagle within sprigs divides dates and legend

Date	Mintage	F	VF	XF	Unc	BU
AH1396-1976	500,000	—	0.30	0.65	1.50	—
AH1398-1978	—	—	0.30	0.65	1.50	—

KM# 68 10 GHIRSH

Copper-Nickel, 28 mm. **Subject:** 20th Anniversary of Independence **Obv:** Legend and value above flower sprigs **Rev:** Eagle divides dates below legend **Edge:** Reeded **Note:** Edge varieties exist.

Date	Mintage	F	VF	XF	Unc	BU
AH1396-1976	5,540,000	—	0.25	0.60	1.25	—

KM# 95 10 GHIRSH
Copper-Nickel, 28 mm. **Subject:** Council of Arab Economic Unity **Obv:** Clasped hands below inscription within wreath **Rev:** Eagle divides dates **Note:** Edge varieties exist.

Date	Mintage	F	VF	XF	Unc	BU
AH1398-1978	1,000,000	—	0.60	1.25	2.50	—

KM# 85 10 GHIRSH
Copper-Nickel, 28 mm. **Series:** F.A.O. **Obv:** Cow and calf flanked by designs **Rev:** Eagle divides dates **Edge:** Reeded **Note:** Edge varieties exist.

Date	Mintage	F	VF	XF	Unc	BU
AH1401-1981	1,000,000	—	0.60	1.25	2.50	—

KM# 107 10 GHIRSH
Aluminum-Bronze **Obv:** Legend and value above flower sprigs **Rev:** Central bank building above inscription and crossed sprigs

Date	Mintage	F	VF	XF	Unc	BU
AH1408-1987	—	—	0.75	1.50	3.00	—

KM# 98 20 GHIRSH
Copper-Nickel, 26.5 mm. **Obv:** Legend and value above flower sprigs **Rev:** Eagle divides dates

Date	Mintage	F	VF	XF	Unc	BU
AH1403-1983	72,000	—	—	—	5.00	—

KM# 96 20 GHIRSH
Copper-Nickel **Series:** F.A.O. **Obv:** Designs, value and F.A.O. letters **Rev:** Eagle divides dates

Date	Mintage	F	VF	XF	Unc	BU
AH1405-1985	—	—	—	—	3.00	—

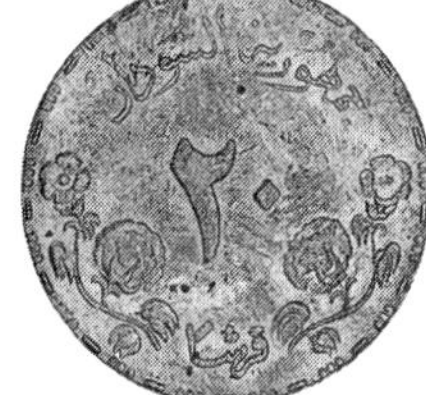

KM# 101.1 20 GHIRSH
Aluminum-Bronze **Obv:** Small value **Rev:** Central bank building above inscription and crossed sprigs **Note:** Denomination is 8 mm high.

Date	Mintage	F	VF	XF	Unc	BU
AH1408-1987	—	—	0.60	1.25	2.50	—

KM# 101.2 20 GHIRSH
Aluminum-Bronze **Obv:** Large value **Rev:** Central bank building **Note:** Denomination is 9.5 mm high.

Date	Mintage	F	VF	XF	Unc	BU
AH1408-1987	—	—	0.60	1.25	2.50	—

KM# 102.1 25 GHIRSH
Aluminum-Bronze **Obv:** Legend and value above flower sprigs **Rev:** Central bank building, inner ring of dashes only visible on the corners **Shape:** Square

Date	Mintage	F	VF	XF	Unc	BU
AH1408-1987	—	—	0.85	1.75	3.50	—

KM# 102.2 25 GHIRSH
Aluminum-Bronze **Obv:** Value **Rev:** Inner ring of dashes completely visible **Shape:** Square

Date	Mintage	F	VF	XF	Unc	BU
AH1408-1987	—	—	1.00	2.00	4.00	—

KM# 108 25 GHIRSH
Copper-Nickel Plated Steel **Obv:** Legend, value and dates **Rev:** Central bank building

Date	Mintage	F	VF	XF	Unc	BU
AH1409-1989	—	—	0.50	1.00	2.25	—

KM# 56.1 50 GHIRSH
Copper-Nickel **Series:** F.A.O. **Obv:** Eagle divides dates **Rev:** Large design

Date	Mintage	F	VF	XF	Unc	BU
AH1392-1972	1,000,000	—	1.50	3.00	6.50	—

KM# 56.2 50 GHIRSH
Copper-Nickel **Series:** F.A.O. **Obv:** Eagle divides dates **Rev:** Small design **Note:** Struck in 1976.

Date	Mintage	F	VF	XF	Unc	BU
AH1392-1972	30,000	—	5.00	10.00	20.00	—

KM# 69 50 GHIRSH
Copper-Nickel **Subject:** Establishment of Arab Cooperative **Obv:** Shield and value **Rev:** Legend above eagle and dates

Date	Mintage	F	VF	XF	Unc	BU
AH1396-1976	—	—	1.00	2.25	4.50	—

KM# 73 50 GHIRSH
Copper-Nickel **Subject:** 8th Anniversary of 1969 Revolt **Obv:** Eagle divides dates **Rev:** Cogwheel design with inscription on circular design at bottom

Date	Mintage	F	VF	XF	Unc	BU
AH1397-1977	100,000	—	1.00	2.25	4.50	—

KM# 103 50 GHIRSH
Aluminum-Bronze **Obv:** Legend and value above flower sprigs **Rev:** Central bank building above inscription and crossed sprigs **Shape:** 8-sided

Date	Mintage	F	VF	XF	Unc	BU
AH1408-1987	—	—	0.75	1.75	3.75	—

KM# 105 50 GHIRSH
Aluminum-Bronze **Subject:** 33rd Anniversary of Independence **Obv:** Legend and value above flower sprigs **Rev:** Inscription within map flanked by dates, designs below and legend above **Shape:** 8-sided

Date	Mintage	F	VF	XF	Unc	BU
AH1409-1989	—	—	0.75	1.75	3.75	—

KM# 109 50 GHIRSH
Copper-Nickel Plated Steel **Obv:** Value **Rev:** Central Bank building

Date	Mintage	F	VF	XF	Unc	BU
AH1409-1989	—	—	0.65	1.25	2.75	—

KM# 75 POUND
Copper-Nickel **Series:** F.A.O. **Subject:** Rural women **Obv:** Eagle divides dates **Rev:** Stylized designs **Shape:** 10-sided

Date	Mintage	F	VF	XF	Unc	BU
AH1398-1978	456,000	—	2.50	4.00	8.00	—

KM# 104 POUND
Aluminum-Bronze **Obv:** Legend and value above flower sprigs **Rev:** Central bank building

Date	Mintage	F	VF	XF	Unc	BU
AH1408-1987	—	—	2.00	3.00	7.00	—

KM# 106 POUND
Copper-Nickel Plated Steel **Obv:** Value **Rev:** Central Bank building

Date	Mintage	F	VF	XF	Unc	BU
AH1409-1989	—	—	0.75	1.50	3.75	—

REFORM COINAGE

100 Qurush (Piastres) = 1 Dinar

10 Pounds = 1 Dinar

KM# 117 1/4 DINAR
3.0000 g., Brass Plated Steel, 18 mm. **Obv:** Value **Rev:** Central Bank building **Edge:** Plain

Date	Mintage	F	VF	XF	Unc	BU
AH1415-1994 Rare	—	—	—	—	—	—

KM# 118 1/2 DINAR
4.0000 g., Brass Plated Steel, 20 mm. **Obv:** Value **Rev:** Central Bank building **Edge:** Plain

Date	Mintage	F	VF	XF	Unc	BU
AH1415-1994 Rare	—	—	—	—	—	—

KM# 112 DINAR
5.1400 g., Brass, 22.2 mm. **Obv:** Value **Rev:** Central Bank building **Edge:** Plain

Date	Mintage	F	VF	XF	Unc	BU
AH1415-1994	—	—	0.25	0.50	1.00	2.00

KM# 113 2 DINAR
Brass Plated Steel **Obv:** Value **Rev:** Central Bank building **Edge:** Plain **Note:** Varieties exist with finely spaced and widely spaced shading to the number "2" in the denomination.

Date	Mintage	F	VF	XF	Unc	BU
AH1415-1994	—	—	0.45	0.75	1.00	3.00

KM# 114 5 DINARS
Brass **Obv:** Value **Rev:** Central Bank building **Edge:** Plain

Date	Mintage	F	VF	XF	Unc	BU
AH1417-1996	—	—	1.00	2.00	4.50	7.00

KM# 119 5 DINARS
3.3500 g., Brass, 19 mm. **Obv:** Value **Rev:** Central Bank building

Date	Mintage	F	VF	XF	Unc	BU
AH1424-2003	—	—	0.75	1.50	3.00	5.00

KM# 115.1 10 DINARS
Brass **Obv:** Legend and value above designs **Rev:** Central Bank building, thin inscription below **Edge:** Plain

Date	Mintage	F	VF	XF	Unc	BU
AH1417-1996	—	—	1.00	2.00	3.50	6.00

KM# 115.2 10 DINARS
Brass **Obv:** Legend and value **Rev:** Central Bank building, thick inscription below **Edge:** Plain

Date	Mintage	F	VF	XF	Unc	BU
AH1417-1996	—	—	1.00	2.00	3.50	6.00

KM# 120.1 10 DINARS
4.6800 g., Brass, 22 mm. **Rev:** Central Bank building, "a" above "n" at the left end of the Arabic inscription, 64 border beads

Date	Mintage	F	VF	XF	Unc	BU
AH1424-2003	—	—	1.00	2.00	3.50	6.00

KM# 120.2 10 DINARS
4.5600 g., Brass, 22 mm. **Obv:** Value **Rev:** Larger Central Bank building, "a" to right of "n" at the left end of the Arabic inscription, 72 border beads

Date	Mintage	F	VF	XF	Unc	BU
AH1424-2003	—	—	1.00	2.00	3.50	6.00

KM# 116.1 20 DINARS
Copper-Nickel, 22 mm. **Obv:** Value **Rev:** Central Bank building, "a" to right of "n" at the left end of the Arabic inscription, 72 border beads **Edge:** Plain

Date	Mintage	F	VF	XF	Unc	BU
AH1417-1996	—	—	1.25	2.25	4.00	7.00

KM# 116.2 20 DINARS
4.6100 g., Copper-Nickel, 22.17 mm. **Obv:** Legend and value **Rev:** Smaller Central Bank building, "a" above "n" at the left end of the Arabic inscription, 64 border beads **Edge:** Plain

Date	Mintage	F	VF	XF	Unc	BU
AH1419-1999	—	—	1.25	2.25	4.00	7.00

KM# 121 50 DINARS
Copper-Nickel, 24 mm. **Rev:** Central Bank building

Date	Mintage	F	VF	XF	Unc	BU
AH1423-2002	—	—	2.00	3.50	6.00	9.00

REFORM COINAGE

100 Piastres = 1 Pound

2005 -

KM# 126 PIASTRE (Ghirsh)
2.2500 g., Aluminum-Bronze, 16 mm. **Obv:** Clay pot **Obv. Legend:** CENTRAL BANK OF SUDAN **Rev:** Value

Date	Mintage	F	VF	XF	Unc	BU
2006	—	—	—	0.90	2.25	3.00

KM# 125 5 PIASTRES
2.9200 g., Brass, 18.32 mm. **Obv:** National arms **Rev:** Large value **Edge:** Reeded

Date	Mintage	F	VF	XF	Unc	BU
2006	—	—	—	1.20	3.00	4.00

KM# 124 20 PIASTRES
5.0200 g., Bi-Metallic Copper-Nickel center in Brass ring., 22.19 mm. **Obv:** Water Buffalo **Obv. Legend:** CENTRAL BANK OF SUDAN **Rev:** large value **Edge:** Reeded

Date	Mintage	F	VF	XF	Unc	BU
2006	—	—	—	1.20	3.00	4.00

KM# 123 50 PIASTRES
5.8600 g., Bi-Metallic **Ring Composition:** Copper Nickel **Center Composition:** Brass, 24.27 mm. **Obv:** Dove in flight **Obv. Legend:** CENTRAL BANK OF SUDAN **Rev:** Value **Edge:** Reeded

Date	Mintage	F	VF	XF	Unc	BU
2006	—	—	—	0.90	2.25	3.00

SURINAME

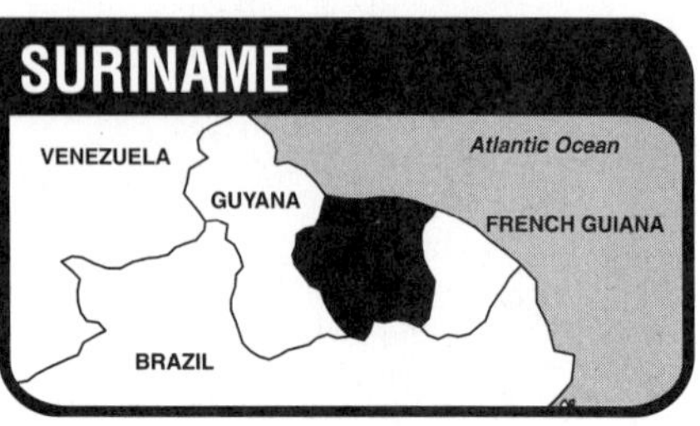

The Republic of Suriname also known as Dutch Guiana, located on the north central coast of South America between Guyana and French Guiana has an area of 63,037 sq. mi. (163,270 sq. km.) and a population of *433,000. Capital: Paramaribo. The country is rich in minerals and forests, and self-sufficient in rice, the staple food crop. The mining, processing and exporting of bauxite is the principal economic activity.

Lieutenants of Amerigo Vespucci sighted the Guiana coast in 1499. Spanish explorers of the 16th century, disappointed at finding no gold, departed leaving the area to be settled by the British in 1652. The colony prospered and the Netherlands acquired it in 1667 in exchange for the Dutch rights in Nieuw Nederland (state of New York). During the European wars of the 18th and 19th centuries, which were fought in part in the new world, Suriname was occupied by the British from 1781-1784 and 1796-1814.Suriname became an autonomous part of the Kingdom of the Netherlands on Dec. 15, 1954. Full independence was achieved on Nov. 25, 1975. In 1980, a coup installed a military government, which has since been dissolved.

RULER
Dutch, until 1975

MINT MARKS
(B) - British Royal Mint, no mint mark
FM - Franklin Mint, U.S.A.**
P - Philadelphia, U.S.A.
S - Sydney
(u) - Utrecht (privy marks only)

****NOTE**: From 1975-1985 the Franklin Mint produced coinage in up to 3 different qualities. Qualities of issue are designated in ( ) after each date and are defined as follows:

(M) MATTE - Normal circulation strike or a dull finish produced by sandblasting special uncirculated (polish finish) or proof quality dies.

(U) SPECIAL UNCIRCULATED - Polished or prooflike in appearance without any frosted features.

(P) PROOF - The highest quality obtainable having mirror-like fields and frosted features.

MONETARY SYSTEM
100 Cents = 1 Gulden (Guilders)

After January, 2004
1 Dollar = 100 Cents

DUTCH ADMINISTRATION

WORLD WAR II COINAGE

The 1942-1943 issues that follow are homeland coinage types of the Netherlands. KM#152, KM#163 and KM#164 were executed expressly for use in Suriname. Related issues produced for use in Curacao and Suriname are listed under Curacao. They are distinguished by a palm tree (acorn on homeland issues) and a mint mark (P-Philadelphia, D-Denver, S-San Francisco) flanking the date. See the Netherlands for similar issues. See Curacao for similar coins dated 1941-P, 1942-P and 1943-P.

KM# 10 CENT

2.5000 g., Brass, 18 mm. **Obv:** Upright lion with sword within beaded circle **Rev:** Value within orange wreath **Edge:** Reeded

Date	Mintage	F	VF	XF	Unc	BU
1943P Palm	4,000,000	0.85	3.75	7.50	15.00	20.00

KM# 10a CENT

2.5000 g., Bronze, 19 mm. **Obv:** Upright lion with sword within beaded circle **Rev:** Value within orange wreath **Edge:** Reeded

Date	Mintage	F	VF	XF	Unc	BU
1957(u)	1,200,000	—	1.00	2.00	4.50	7.00
1957(u) Proof	—	Value: 30.00				
1959(u)	1,800,000	—	1.00	2.00	4.50	7.00
1959(u) Proof	—	Value: 30.00				
1960(u)	1,200,000	—	1.00	2.00	4.50	7.00
1960(u) Proof	—	Value: 30.00				

KM# 9 10 CENTS

1.4000 g., 0.6400 Silver 0.0288 oz. ASW **Obv:** Head of Queen Wilhelmina left **Obv. Legend:** Value and date within orange wreath **Edge:** Reeded

Date	Mintage	F	VF	XF	Unc	BU
1942P Palm	1,500,000	6.00	12.50	15.00	30.00	35.00

REPUBLIC

MODERN COINAGE

KM# 11 CENT

2.5500 g., Bronze, 18 mm. **Obv:** Arms with supporters within wreath **Rev:** Value divides date within circle **Edge:** Plain

Date	Mintage	F	VF	XF	Unc	BU
1962(u) Fish	6,000,000	—	0.25	0.50	1.00	2.00
1962(u) S Proof	650	Value: 28.00				
1966(u)	6,500,000	—	0.25	0.50	1.00	2.00
1966(u) Proof	—	Value: 42.00				
1970(u) Cock	5,000,000	—	0.25	0.50	1.00	2.00
1972(u)	6,000,000	—	0.25	0.50	1.00	2.00

KM# 11a CENT

0.8000 g., Aluminum, 18 mm. **Obv:** Arms with supporters within wreath **Rev:** Value divides date within circle **Edge:** Plain

Date	Mintage	F	VF	XF	Unc	BU
1972 Proof	—	Value: 45.00				
1974(u)	1,000,000	—	0.10	0.25	0.50	1.00
1975(u)	1,000,000	—	0.10	0.25	0.50	1.00
1976(u)	3,000,000	—	0.10	0.25	0.50	1.00
1976 Proof	Est. 10	Value: 55.00				
1977(u)	10,000,000	—	—	0.25	0.50	1.00
1978(u)	6,000,000	—	—	0.25	0.50	1.00
1979(u)	10,000,000	—	—	0.25	0.50	1.00
1980(u)	8,000,000	—	—	0.25	0.50	1.00
Note: Cock and star privy marks						
1982(u) Anvil	8,000,000	—	—	0.25	0.50	1.00
1984	5,000,000	—	—	0.25	0.50	1.00
1985	2,000,000	—	—	0.25	0.50	1.00
1986	3,000,000	—	—	0.25	0.50	1.00

KM# 11b CENT

2.5000 g., Copper Plated Steel, 18 mm. **Obv:** Arms with supporters within wreath **Rev:** Value divides date within circle **Edge:** Plain

Date	Mintage	F	VF	XF	Unc	BU
1987(B)	—	—	—	0.20	0.80	1.25
1988(B)	—	—	—	0.20	0.80	1.25
1988(B) Proof	Est. 1,500	Value: 2.00				
1989(B)	—	—	—	0.20	0.80	1.25
2004(u)	4,000	—	—	—	1.00	1.50
Note: In sets only						
2005(u)	1,500	—	—	—	1.00	1.50
Note: In sets only						
2006(u)	1,500	—	—	—	1.00	1.50
Note: In sets only						
2007(u)	—	—	—	—	1.00	1.50
2008(u)	—	—	—	—	1.00	1.50

KM# 12.1 5 CENTS

4.0000 g., Nickel-Brass, 22 mm. **Obv:** Arms with supporters within circle **Rev:** Value divides date within circle **Shape:** 4-sided

Date	Mintage	F	VF	XF	Unc	BU
1962(u) Fish	2,200,000	—	0.50	1.00	2.00	4.00
1962(u) S Proof	650	Value: 25.00				
1966(u)	2,300,000	—	0.50	1.00	2.00	4.00
Note: With mint mark and mintmaster's mark						
1966(u) Proof	—	Value: 50.00				
1966(u)	400,000	—	1.75	3.50	7.00	10.00
Note: Without mint mark and mint master's mark						
1971(u) Cock	500,000	—	1.25	2.50	5.00	10.00
1972(u)	1,500,000	—	0.50	1.00	2.00	4.00

KM# 12.2 5 CENTS

4.0000 g., Nickel-Brass, 18 mm. **Obv:** Arms with supporters within circle **Rev:** Value divides date within circle **Shape:** Square **Note:** Medal turn.

Date	Mintage	F	VF	XF	Unc	BU
1966(u)	—	4.00	8.00	20.00	40.00	75.00
1966(u) Proof	—	Value: 450				

KM# 12.1a 5 CENTS

1.2000 g., Aluminum, 18 mm. **Obv:** Arms with supporters within circle **Rev:** Value divides date within circle **Shape:** Square

Date	Mintage	F	VF	XF	Unc	BU
1976(u)	5,500,000	—	0.10	0.25	0.50	1.00
1976 Proof	Est. 10	Value: 75.00				
1978(u)	3,000,000	—	0.10	0.25	0.50	1.00
1979(u)	2,000,000	—	0.10	0.25	0.50	1.00
1980(u)	1,000,000	—	0.10	0.25	0.50	1.00
Note: Cock and star privy marks						
1982(u) Anvil	1,000,000	—	0.10	0.25	0.50	1.00
1985(u)	1,000,000	—	0.10	0.25	0.50	1.00
1986(u)	1,500,000	—	0.10	0.25	0.50	1.00

KM# 12.1b 5 CENTS

3.0000 g., Copper Plated Steel, 18 mm. **Obv:** Arms with supporters within circle **Rev:** Value divides date within circle **Edge:** Plain **Shape:** Square

Date	Mintage	F	VF	XF	Unc	BU
1987(B)	—	—	—	0.30	0.60	1.00
1988(B)	—	—	—	0.30	0.60	1.00
1988(B) Proof	Est. 1,500	Value: 2.00				
1989(B)	—	—	—	0.30	0.60	1.00
2004(u)	4,000	—	—	—	1.00	1.50
Note: In sets only						
2005(u)	1,500	—	—	—	1.00	1.50
Note: In sets only						
2006(u)	1,500	—	—	—	1.00	1.50
Note: In sets only						
2007(u)	—	—	—	—	1.00	1.50
2008(u)	—	—	—	—	1.00	1.50

KM# 13 10 CENTS

2.0000 g., Copper-Nickel, 16 mm. **Obv:** Arms with supporters within wreath **Rev:** Value and date within circle

Date	Mintage	F	VF	XF	Unc	BU
1962(u) Fish	3,000,000	—	0.25	0.50	1.00	2.00
1962(u) S Proof	650	Value: 25.00				
1966(u)	2,500,000	—	0.25	0.50	1.00	2.00
1966(u) Proof	—	Value: 50.00				
1971(u) Cock	500,000	—	0.75	1.50	3.00	4.00
1972(u)	1,500,000	—	0.25	0.50	1.00	2.00
1974(u)	1,500,000	—	0.25	0.50	1.00	2.00
1976(u)	5,000,000	—	0.15	0.30	0.60	1.50
1976 Proof	Est. 10	Value: 100				
1978(u)	2,000,000	—	0.15	0.30	0.60	1.50
1979(u)	2,000,000	—	0.15	0.30	0.60	1.50
1982(u) Anvil	1,000,000	—	0.15	0.30	0.60	1.50
1985(u)	1,000,000	—	0.15	0.30	0.60	1.50
1986(u)	1,500,000	—	0.15	0.30	0.60	1.50

KM# 13a 10 CENTS

2.0000 g., Nickel Plated Steel, 16 mm. **Obv:** Arms with supporters within wreath **Rev:** Value and date within circle **Edge:** Reeded

Date	Mintage	F	VF	XF	Unc	BU
1987(B)	—	—	0.15	0.35	0.75	1.50
1988(B) Proof	Est. 1,500	Value: 3.00				
1989(B)	—	—	0.10	0.35	0.75	1.50
2004(u)	4,000	—	—	—	1.00	2.50
Note: In sets only						
2005(u)	1,500	—	—	—	1.00	2.50
Note: In sets only						
2006(u)	1,500	—	—	—	1.00	2.50
Note: In sets only						
2007(u)	—	—	—	—	1.00	2.50
2008(u)	—	—	—	—	1.00	2.50

KM# 14 25 CENTS

3.5000 g., Copper-Nickel, 20 mm. **Obv:** Arms with supporters within wreath **Rev:** Value and date within circle **Edge:** Reeded

Date	Mintage	F	VF	XF	Unc	BU
1962(u) Fish	2,300,000	0.25	0.30	0.50	1.00	2.00
1962(u) S Proof	650	Value: 20.00				
1966(u)	2,300,000	0.25	0.30	0.50	1.00	2.00
1966(u) Proof	—	Value: 50.00				
1972(u) Cock	1,800,000	0.25	0.30	0.50	1.00	2.50
1974(u)	1,500,000	0.30	0.30	0.50	1.00	2.50
1976(u)	5,000,000	0.20	0.30	0.50	1.00	2.00
1976 Proof	Est. 10	Value: 125				
1979(u)	2,000,000	0.20	0.30	0.50	1.00	2.00
1982(u) Anvil	2,000,000	0.20	0.30	0.50	1.00	2.00
1985(u)	1,000,000	0.20	0.30	0.50	1.00	2.50
1986(u)	1,500,000	0.20	0.30	0.50	1.00	2.50

KM# 14a 25 CENTS

3.5000 g., Nickel Plated Steel, 20 mm. **Obv:** Arms with supporters within wreath **Rev:** Value and date within circle **Edge:** Reeded

Date	Mintage	F	VF	XF	Unc	BU
1987(B)	—	0.20	0.30	0.50	1.00	2.00
1988(B)	—	0.20	0.30	0.50	1.00	2.00
1988(B) Proof	Est. 1,500	Value: 5.00				
1989(B)	—	0.20	0.35	0.65	1.25	2.50
2004(u)	4,000	—	—	—	2.00	4.00
Note: In sets only						
2005(u)	1,500	—	—	—	2.00	4.00
Note: In sets only						
2006(u)	1,500	—	—	—	2.00	4.00
Note: In sets only						
2007(u)	—	—	—	—	2.00	4.00
2008(u)	—	—	—	—	2.00	4.00

KM# 15 GULDEN
10.0000 g., 0.7200 Silver 0.2315 oz. ASW, 28 mm. **Obv:** Head of Queen Juliana right **Rev:** Arms with supporters within wreath **Edge Lettering:** JUSTITIA * PIETAS * FIDES *

Date	Mintage	F	VF	XF	Unc	BU
1962(u)	150,000	—	BV	6.00	10.00	15.00
1962(u) S Proof	650	Value: 50.00				
1966(u)	100,000	15.00	40.00	100	135	170

Note: Never officially released to circulation

Date	Mintage	F	VF	XF	Unc	BU
1966(u) Proof	—	Value: 250				

KM# 23 100 CENTS
Copper-Nickel, 23 mm. **Obv:** Arms with supporters within wreath **Rev:** Value and date within circle **Edge:** Reeded

Date	Mintage	F	VF	XF	Unc	BU
1987(B)	—	—	0.40	0.80	1.75	3.00
1988(B)	—	—	0.40	0.80	1.75	3.00
1988(B) Proof	Est. 1,500	Value: 12.00				
1989(B)	—	—	0.40	0.80	1.75	3.00
2004(u)	4,000	—	—	—	4.00	7.00
Note: In sets only						
2005(u)	1,500	—	—	—	4.00	7.00
Note: In sets only						
2006(u)	1,500	—	—	—	4.00	7.00
Note: In sets only						
2007(u)	—	—	—	—	4.00	7.00
2008(u)	—	—	—	—	4.00	7.00

KM# 24 250 CENTS
9.5700 g., Copper-Nickel, 28 mm. **Obv:** Arms with supporters within wreath **Rev:** Value and date within circle

Date	Mintage	F	VF	XF	Unc	BU
1987(B)	—	—	0.80	1.75	3.50	5.00
1988(B)	—	—	0.80	1.75	3.50	5.00
1988(B) Proof	Est. 1,500	Value: 17.50				
1989(B)	—	—	0.80	1.75	3.50	5.00
2004(u)	4,000	—	—	—	6.00	10.00
Note: In sets only						
2005(u)	1,500	—	—	—	6.00	10.00
Note: In sets only						
2006(u)	1,500	—	—	—	6.00	10.00
Note: In sets only						
2007(u)	—	—	—	—	6.00	10.00
2008(u)	—	—	—	—	6.00	10.00

SWAZILAND

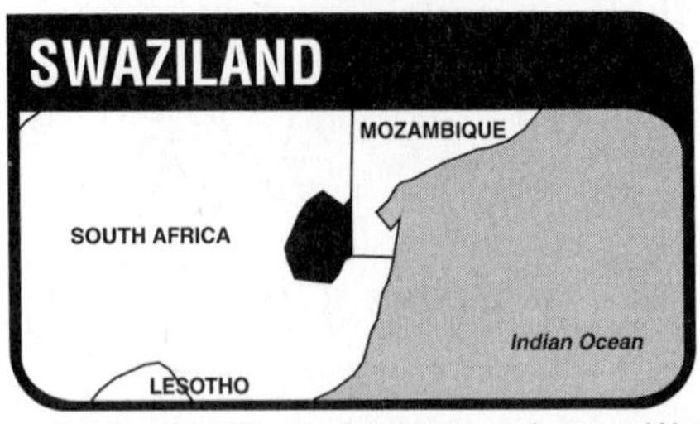

The Kingdom of Swaziland, located in southeastern Africa, has an area of 6,704 sq. mi. (17,360 sq. km.) and a population of *756,000. Capital: Mbabane (administrative); Lobamba (legislative). The diversified economy includes mining, agriculture, and light industry. Asbestos, iron ore, wood pulp, and sugar are exported.

The people of the present Swazi nation established themselves in an area including what is now Swaziland in the early 1800s. The first Swazi contact with the British came early in the reign of the extremely able Swazi leader Mswati when he asked the British for aid against Zulu raids into Swaziland. The British and Transvaal responded by guaranteeing the independence of Swaziland, 1881. South Africa assumed the power of protection and administration in 1894 and Swaziland continued under this administration until the conquest of the Transvaal during the Anglo-Boer War, when administration was transferred to the British government. After World War II, Britain began to prepare Swaziland for independence, which was achieved on Sept. 6, 1968. The Kingdom is a member of the Commonwealth of Nations. King Mswati III is Head of State. The prime minister is Head of Government.

RULERS
Sobhuza II, 1968-1982
Queen Dzeliwe, Regent for Prince Makhosetive, 1982-1986
King Msawati III, 1986-

MONETARY SYSTEM
100 Cents = 1 Luhlanga
25 Luhlanga = 1 Lilangeni
(plural - Emalangeni)

KINGDOM

DECIMAL COINAGE

100 Cents = 1 Lilangeni (plural emelangeni)

KM# 7 CENT
2.0000 g., Bronze, 18.3 mm. **Ruler:** Sobhuza II **Obv:** Head 1/4 right **Rev:** Pineapple and value **Designer:** Michael Rizzello

Date	Mintage	F	VF	XF	Unc	BU
1974	6,002,000	—	—	0.10	0.20	—
1974 Proof	13,000	Value: 0.75				
1979	500,000	—	—	0.10	0.25	—
1979 Proof	10,000	Value: 0.75				
1982	—	—	—	0.10	0.25	—
1983	1,100,000	—	—	0.10	0.25	—

KM# 21 CENT
2.0000 g., Bronze, 18.3 mm. **Ruler:** Sobhuza II **Series:** F.A.O. **Obv:** Head 1/4 right **Rev:** Pineapple and value **Shape:** 12-sided **Designer:** Michael Rizzello

Date	Mintage	F	VF	XF	Unc	BU
1975	2,500,000	—	—	0.10	0.25	—

KM# 39 CENT
Copper Plated Steel **Ruler:** Queen Dzeliwe Regent for Prince Makhosetive **Obv:** Bust facing **Rev:** Pineapple

Date	Mintage	F	VF	XF	Unc	BU
1986	12,000,000	—	—	0.10	0.25	—

KM# 39a CENT
Bronze **Ruler:** Queen Dzeliwe Regent for Prince Makhosetive **Obv:** Bust facing **Rev:** Pineapple

Date	Mintage	F	VF	XF	Unc	BU
1986	—	—	—	1.00	2.50	—

KM# 51 CENT
Bronze **Ruler:** King Msawati III **Obv:** Head 1/4 right **Rev:** Pineapple and value

Date	Mintage	F	VF	XF	Unc	BU
1995	—	—	—	—	0.25	—

KM# 8 2 CENTS
2.8000 g., Bronze, 18.6 mm. **Ruler:** Sobhuza II **Obv:** Head 1/4 right **Rev:** Trees and value **Shape:** Square **Designer:** Michael Rizzello

Date	Mintage	F	VF	XF	Unc	BU
1974	2,252,000	—	—	0.15	0.30	—
1974 Proof	13,000	Value: 0.75				
1979	1,000,000	—	—	0.15	0.30	—
1979 Proof	10,000	Value: 1.00				
1982	500,000	—	—	0.15	0.30	—

KM# 22 2 CENTS
2.8000 g., Bronze, 18.6 mm. **Ruler:** Sobhuza II **Series:** F.A.O. **Obv:** Head 1/4 right **Rev:** Trees and value **Edge:** Plain **Shape:** 4-sided **Designer:** Michael Rizzello

Date	Mintage	F	VF	XF	Unc	BU
1975	1,500,000	—	—	0.15	0.30	—

KM# 9 5 CENTS
2.1500 g., Copper-Nickel, 18.5 mm. **Ruler:** Sobhuza II **Obv:** Head 1/4 right **Rev:** Arum lily and value **Shape:** Scalloped **Designer:** Michael Rizzello

Date	Mintage	F	VF	XF	Unc	BU
1974	1,252,000	—	0.10	0.20	0.40	—
1974 Proof	13,000	Value: 1.00				
1975	1,500,000	—	0.10	0.20	0.40	—
1979	1,680,000	—	0.10	0.20	0.40	—
1979 Proof	10,000	Value: 1.75				

KM# 40.1 5 CENTS
2.1500 g., Copper-Nickel, 18.5 mm. **Ruler:** Queen Dzeliwe Regent for Prince Makhosetive **Obv:** Bust facing **Rev:** Arum lily and value **Edge:** Plain **Shape:** Scalloped

Date	Mintage	F	VF	XF	Unc	BU
1986	—	—	0.15	0.25	0.50	—

KM# 40.2 5 CENTS
Nickel Plated Steel, 18.5 mm. **Ruler:** King Msawati III **Obv:** Bust facing **Rev:** Arum lily **Edge:** Plain **Shape:** Scalloped

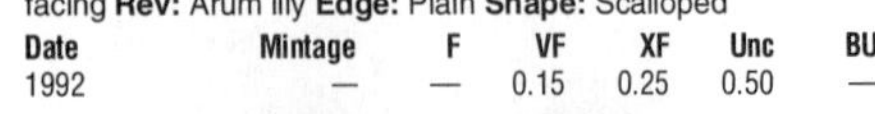

Date	Mintage	F	VF	XF	Unc	BU
1992	—	—	0.15	0.25	0.50	—

KM# 48 5 CENTS
2.1000 g., Nickel Plated Steel, 18.5 mm. **Ruler:** King Msawati III **Obv:** Head 1/4 right **Rev:** Arum lily and value **Edge:** Plain **Shape:** Scalloped

Date	Mintage	F	VF	XF	Unc	BU
1995	—	—	—	—	0.50	0.75
1996	—	—	—	—	0.50	0.75
1998	—	—	—	—	0.50	0.75
1999	—	—	—	—	0.50	0.75
2000	—	—	—	—	0.50	0.75

Date	Mintage	F	VF	XF	Unc	BU
Note: Thick inscription						
2000	—	—	—	—	0.50	0.75
Note: Thin inscription						
2001	—	—	—	—	0.50	0.75
2002	—	—	—	—	0.50	0.75
2006	—	—	—	—	0.50	0.75

KM# 48a 5 CENTS

Copper-Nickel, 18.5 mm. **Ruler:** King Msawati III **Obv:** Bust 1/4 right **Rev:** Arum lily and value

Date	Mintage	F	VF	XF	Unc	BU
1999	—	—	—	—	0.50	0.75

KM# 10 10 CENTS

Copper-Nickel, 22 mm. **Ruler:** Sobhuza II **Obv:** Head 1/4 right **Rev:** Sugar cane and value **Shape:** Scalloped **Designer:** Michael Rizzello

Date	Mintage	F	VF	XF	Unc	BU
1974	752,000	—	0.15	0.25	0.50	—
1974 Proof	13,000	Value: 1.00				
1979	500,000	—	0.15	0.25	0.50	—
1979 Proof	4,231	Value: 2.50				

KM# 23 10 CENTS

Copper-Nickel, 22 mm. **Ruler:** Sobhuza II **Series:** F.A.O. **Obv:** Head 1/4 right **Rev:** Sugar cane and value **Shape:** Scalloped

Date	Mintage	F	VF	XF	Unc	BU
1975	1,500,000	—	0.15	0.25	0.50	—

KM# 41 10 CENTS

3.6000 g., Copper-Nickel, 22 mm. **Ruler:** King Msawati III **Obv:** Head facing **Rev:** Sugar cane and value **Edge:** Plain **Shape:** Scalloped

Date	Mintage	F	VF	XF	Unc	BU
1986	—	—	0.15	0.25	0.50	—
1992	—	—	0.15	0.25	0.50	—

KM# 49 10 CENTS

Copper-Nickel, 22 mm. **Ruler:** King Msawati III **Obv:** Head 1/4 right **Rev:** Sugar cane and value **Shape:** Scalloped

Date	Mintage	F	VF	XF	Unc	BU
1995	—	—	—	—	0.50	0.75
1996	—	—	—	—	0.50	0.75
1998	—	—	—	—	0.50	0.75
2000	—	—	—	—	0.50	0.75
2001	—	—	—	—	0.50	0.75
2002	—	—	—	—	0.50	0.75
2006	—	—	—	—	0.50	0.75

KM# 11 20 CENTS

5.6000 g., Copper-Nickel, 25.2 mm. **Ruler:** Sobhuza II **Obv:** Head 1/4 right **Rev:** Elephant head and value **Shape:** Scalloped **Designer:** Michael Rizzello

Date	Mintage	F	VF	XF	Unc	BU
1974	502,000	—	0.35	0.75	2.50	4.50
1974 Proof	13,000	Value: 3.00				
1975	1,000,000	—	0.35	0.75	2.50	4.50

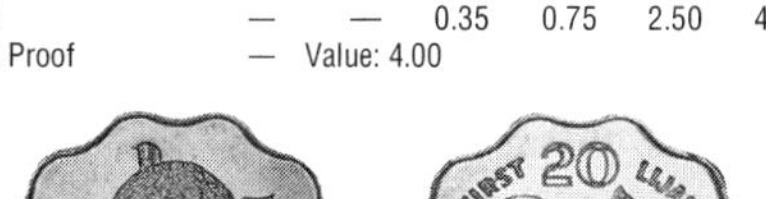

Date	Mintage	F	VF	XF	Unc	BU
1979	—	—	0.35	0.75	2.50	4.50
1979 Proof	—	Value: 4.00				

KM# 31 20 CENTS

5.6000 g., Copper-Nickel, 25.2 mm. **Ruler:** Sobhuza II **Series:** F.A.O. **Obv:** Head 1/4 right **Rev:** Sprigs and logo **Shape:** Scalloped

Date	Mintage	F	VF	XF	Unc	BU
1981	150,000	—	0.40	0.80	1.75	—

KM# 42 20 CENTS

5.6000 g., Copper-Nickel, 25.2 mm. **Ruler:** Queen Dzeliwe Regent for Prince Makhosetive **Obv:** Head facing **Rev:** Elephant head and value **Edge:** Plain **Shape:** Scalloped

Date	Mintage	F	VF	XF	Unc	BU
1986	—	—	0.40	0.80	3.00	5.00

KM# 50 20 CENTS

5.6000 g., Copper-Nickel, 25.2 mm. **Ruler:** King Msawati III **Obv:** Head 1/4 right **Rev:** Elephant head and value **Shape:** Scalloped **Note:** "Lg bust and legend": right tusk closer to rim; "Sm bust and legend": right tusk further from rim.

Date	Mintage	F	VF	XF	Unc	BU
1996	—	—	0.40	1.00	3.00	5.00
Note: Large bust and legend						
1998	—	—	0.40	1.00	3.00	5.00
Note: Small bust and legend						
2000	—	—	0.40	1.00	3.00	5.00
Note: Large bust and legend						
2001	—	—	0.40	0.80	3.00	5.00
Note: Small bust and legend						
2002	—	—	0.40	0.80	3.00	5.00
Note: Small bust and legend						
2003	—	—	0.40	0.80	3.00	5.00
Note: Small bust and legend						

KM# 12 50 CENTS

8.9000 g., Copper-Nickel, 29.45 mm. **Ruler:** Sobhuza II **Obv:** Head 1/4 right **Rev:** Arms with supporters **Shape:** 12-sided **Designer:** Michael Rizzello

Date	Mintage	F	VF	XF	Unc	BU
1974	252,000	—	1.00	1.50	2.75	—
1974 Proof	13,000	Value: 3.00				
1975	500,000	—	1.00	1.50	2.75	—
1979	—	—	0.50	1.00	2.50	—
1979 Proof	10,000	Value: 5.00				
1981	1,150,000	—	0.50	1.00	2.50	—

KM# 43 50 CENTS

8.9000 g., Copper-Nickel, 29.45 mm. **Ruler:** King Msawati III **Obv:** Head facing **Rev:** Arms with supporters **Edge:** Plain

Date	Mintage	F	VF	XF	Unc	BU
1986	1,000,000	—	0.50	1.50	3.50	—
1993	—	—	0.50	1.50	3.50	—

KM# 52 50 CENTS

8.9000 g., Copper-Nickel, 29.45 mm. **Ruler:** King Msawati III **Obv:** Head 1/4 right **Rev:** Arms with supporters

Date	Mintage	F	VF	XF	Unc	BU
1996	—	—	—	—	3.75	4.50
1998	—	—	—	—	3.75	4.50
2001	—	—	—	—	3.75	4.50
2003	—	—	—	—	3.75	4.50

KM# 13 LILANGENI

11.6500 g., Copper-Nickel, 30 mm. **Ruler:** Sobhuza II **Obv:** Head 1/4 right **Rev:** Female and child facing **Designer:** Michael Rizzello

Date	Mintage	F	VF	XF	Unc	BU
1974	127,000	—	1.50	2.50	4.50	—
1974 Proof	13,000	Value: 6.00				
1979	—	—	1.00	2.00	4.50	—
1979 Proof	110,000	Value: 7.50				

KM# 24 LILANGENI

Copper-Nickel, 30.5 mm. **Ruler:** Sobhuza II **Series:** F.A.O., International Women's Year **Obv:** Head 1/4 right **Rev:** Female and child facing

Date	Mintage	F	VF	XF	Unc	BU
1975	100,000	—	1.50	2.75	6.50	—

KM# 28 LILANGENI

11.6500 g., Copper-Nickel, 30 mm. **Ruler:** Sobhuza II **Series:** F.A.O. **Obv:** Head 1/4 right **Rev:** Female and child facing

Date	Mintage	F	VF	XF	Unc	BU
1976	100,000	—	1.50	2.75	6.50	—

KM# 32 LILANGENI
11.6500 g., Copper-Nickel, 30 mm. **Ruler:** Sobhuza II **Series:** F.A.O. **Obv:** Head 1/4 right **Rev:** Half length figure husking corn

Date	Mintage	F	VF	XF	Unc	BU
1981	871,000	—	1.50	3.00	7.00	—

KM# 44.1 LILANGENI
9.5000 g., Nickel-Brass, 22.5 mm. **Ruler:** Queen Dzeliwe Regent for Prince Makhosetive **Obv:** Head facing **Rev:** Bust facing **Edge:** Reeded

Date	Mintage	F	VF	XF	Unc	BU
1986	1,025,000	—	—	2.00	4.00	—

KM# 44.2 LILANGENI
Nickel-Brass Plated Steel, 22.5 mm. **Ruler:** King Msawati III **Obv:** Head facing **Rev:** Bust facing **Edge:** Reeded

Date	Mintage	F	VF	XF	Unc	BU
1992	—	—	—	1.50	3.50	—

KM# 45 LILANGENI
9.5000 g., Brass, 22.5 mm. **Ruler:** King Msawati III **Obv:** Head 1/4 right **Rev:** Bust facing

Date	Mintage	F	VF	XF	Unc	BU
1995	—	—	—	1.50	3.50	4.00
1996	—	—	—	1.50	3.50	4.00
1998	—	—	—	1.50	3.50	4.00
2002	—	—	—	1.50	3.25	3.75
2003	—	—	—	1.50	3.25	3.75

KM# 33a 2 EMALANGENI
Copper-Nickel **Ruler:** Sobhuza II **Subject:** Diamond Jubilee of King Sobhuza II **Obv:** Head 1/4 right **Rev:** Lilies and value

Date	Mintage	F	VF	XF	Unc	BU
1981	50,000	—	2.00	3.50	7.50	—

KM# 46 2 EMALANGENI
5.0000 g., Brass **Ruler:** King Msawati III **Obv:** Head 1/4 right **Rev:** Lilies and value

Date	Mintage	F	VF	XF	Unc	BU
1995 lg. bust	—	—	—	—	3.75	4.25
1996 sm. bust	—	—	—	—	3.75	4.25
1998 lg. bust	—	—	—	—	3.75	4.25
2003 sm. bust	—	—	—	—	3.75	4.25

KM# 47 5 EMALANGENI
7.6000 g., Brass **Ruler:** King Msawati III **Obv:** Head 1/4 right **Rev:** Arms with supporters above value that divides date

Date	Mintage	F	VF	XF	Unc	BU
1995 sm. bust	—	—	—	—	6.00	7.00
1996 sm. bust	—	—	—	—	6.00	7.00
1998 lg. bust	—	—	—	—	6.00	7.00
1999	—	—	—	—	6.00	7.00
2003 sm. bust	—	—	—	—	6.00	7.00

KM# 53 5 EMALANGENI
Brass **Ruler:** King Msawati III **Subject:** Central Bank's 25th Anniversary **Obv:** Head 1/4 right **Rev:** Bank seal within circle

Date	Mintage	F	VF	XF	Unc	BU
ND(1999)	—	—	—	—	5.50	6.50

SWEDEN

Norwegian Sea
ICELAND
North Atlantic Ocean
North
NORWAY
FINLAND
RUSSIA

The Kingdom of Sweden, a limited constitutional monarchy located in northern Europe between Norway and Finland, has an area of 173,732 sq. mi. (449,960 sq. km.) and a population of *8.5 million. Capital: Stockholm. Mining, lumbering and a specialized machine industry dominate the economy. Machinery, paper, iron and steel, motor vehicles and wood pulp are exported.

Olaf Skottkonung founded Sweden as a Christian stronghold late in the 10th century. After conquering Finland late in the 13th century, Sweden, together with Norway, came under the rule of Denmark, 1397-1523, in an association known as the Union of Kalmar. Modern Sweden had its beginning in 1523 when Gustaf Vasa drove the Danes out of Sweden and was himself chosen king. Under Gustaf Adolphus II and Charles XII, Sweden was one of the great powers of 17th century Europe – until Charles invaded Russia in 1708, and was defeated at the Battle of Pultowa in June, 1709. Early in the 18th century, a coalition of Russia, Poland and Denmark took away Sweden's Baltic empire and in 1809 Sweden was forced to cede Finland to Russia. The Treaty of Kiel ceded Norway to Sweden in January 1814. The Norwegians resisted for a time but later signed the Act of Union at the Convention of Moss in August 1814,The Union was dissolved in 1905 and Norway became independent. A new constitution that took effect on Jan. 1, 1975, restricts the function of the king largely to a ceremonial role.

RULERS
Oscar II, 1872-1907
Gustaf V, 1907-1950
Gustaf VI, 1950-1973
Carl XVI Gustaf, 1973-

MINT OFFICIALS' INITIALS

Letter	Date	Name
AL	1898-1916	Adolf Lindberg, engraver
B	1992-2005	Stefan Ingves
D	1986-1992	Bengt Dennis
EB	1876-1908	Emil Brusewitz
EL	1916-1944	Erik Lindberg, engraver
G	1927-1945	Alf Grabe
LH	1944-1974	Leo Holmberg, engraver
SI	2005-	Stefan Ingves
TS	1945-1961	Torsten Swensson
U	1961-1986	Benkt Ulvfot
W	1908-1927	Karl-August Wallroth

MONETARY SYSTEM
100 Ore = 1 Krona

KINGDOM

REFORM COINAGE

1873 - present

KM# 750 ORE
2.0000 g., Bronze, 16 mm. **Ruler:** Oscar II **Obv:** Monogram within crowned shield, legend lengthened **Rev:** Value and date flanked by 3 crowns

Date	Mintage	F	VF	XF	Unc	BU
1901	3,074,700	1.00	2.50	4.50	20.00	—
1902	2,685,400	1.00	2.50	4.50	22.50	—
1903	2,695,600	1.00	2.50	4.50	22.50	—
1904	2,032,700	1.00	2.50	4.50	20.00	—
1905	3,556,000	0.85	2.25	3.50	16.50	—

KM# 768 ORE
Bronze, 16 mm. **Ruler:** Oscar II **Obv:** Crowned shield **Rev:** Value and date flanked by crowns

Date	Mintage	F	VF	XF	Unc	BU
1906	1,783,300	2.00	4.00	10.00	65.00	—
1907	8,250,500	0.20	0.50	2.00	12.50	—

KM# 777.1 ORE
Bronze, 16 mm. **Ruler:** Gustaf V **Obv:** Crowned monogram with small cross on crown **Rev:** Value and crowns

Date	Mintage	F	VF	XF	Unc	BU
1909	3,805,600	6.00	9.00	18.00	100	—

KM# 777.2 ORE
2.0000 g., Bronze, 16 mm. **Ruler:** Gustaf V **Obv:** Large cross **Rev:** Value and crowns **Edge:** Plain

Date	Mintage	F	VF	XF	Unc	BU
1909	Inc. above	2.00	3.00	8.00	30.00	—
1910	1,582,600	3.00	6.00	10.00	50.00	—
1911	3,149,000	0.75	1.50	3.00	15.00	—
1912/1	3,170,000	8.50	20.00	47.50	250	—
1912	Inc. above	0.75	1.50	3.00	15.00	—
1913/12	3,197,300	4.00	10.00	22.50	125	—
1913	Inc. above	0.75	1.50	3.00	15.00	—
Note: Long and short-tailed 9						
1914 Open 4	2,214,050	35.00	60.00	125	435	—
1914 Closed 4	Inc. above	0.75	1.50	5.00	30.00	—
1915/3	4,471,300	2.25	6.00	10.00	37.50	—
1915	Inc. above	0.25	0.50	1.75	7.00	—
1916 Short 6	7,615,500	0.25	0.50	1.75	7.00	—
1916 Long 6	Inc. above	0.30	0.75	2.50	10.00	—
1919 Unique	—	—	—	—	—	—
1920	5,547,600	0.25	0.50	1.25	5.00	—
1921	7,441,510	0.25	0.50	1.25	5.00	—
1922	1,165,700	2.00	4.00	6.00	30.00	—
1923	4,511,800	0.35	0.75	1.75	7.00	—
1924	2,578,900	0.25	0.75	1.75	8.00	—
1925	4,714,900	0.15	0.35	0.60	3.00	—
1926	7,739,300	0.15	0.35	0.60	3.00	—
1927	3,601,600	0.15	0.35	0.60	3.00	—
1928	2,380,800	0.25	0.75	2.50	10.00	—
1929 Curved 2	6,090,500	0.20	0.35	0.85	4.00	—
1929 Straight 2	Inc. above	0.40	0.60	2.00	9.00	—
1930	5,477,300	0.20	0.35	0.85	4.00	—
1931	5,678,500	0.20	0.35	0.85	4.00	—
1932	3,339,000	—	0.45	1.75	7.00	—
1933	3,426,800	—	0.45	0.85	6.00	—
1934	6,120,500	—	0.30	0.60	3.00	—
1935	4,599,800	—	0.30	0.60	3.00	—
1936 Long 6	6,166,100	0.20	0.45	1.25	3.50	—
1936 Short 6	Inc. above	0.10	0.30	0.60	3.00	—
1937	7,738,200	0.10	0.25	0.60	1.75	—
1938	6,992,900	0.10	0.25	0.60	1.75	—
1939	6,562,300	0.10	0.25	0.60	1.75	—
1940	4,059,900	0.10	0.25	0.50	1.50	—
1941	11,599,090	0.10	0.25	0.50	1.50	—
1942	3,992,000	0.10	0.25	0.60	1.75	—
1950	22,421,200	0.10	0.25	0.50	1.50	—

KM# 789 ORE
Iron, 16 mm. **Ruler:** Gustaf V **Obv:** Crowned monogram divides date **Rev:** Value and crowns **Note:** World War I issues.

Date	Mintage	F	VF	XF	Unc	BU
1917	8,127,700	0.50	1.50	4.00	20.00	—
1918	9,706,100	1.00	2.25	6.50	27.50	—
1919	7,169,500	1.50	3.00	8.00	40.00	—

KM# 810 ORE

1.7000 g., Iron, 16 mm. **Ruler:** Gustaf V **Obv:** Crowned monogram divides date **Rev:** Value and crowns **Note:** World War II issues. Similar to KM#777.

Date	Mintage	F	VF	XF	Unc	BU
1942	10,053,000	0.10	0.25	0.75	3.50	—
1943	10,714,000	0.10	0.25	0.85	4.50	—
1944	8,648,500	0.10	0.25	0.75	4.50	—
1945	9,527,000	0.10	0.25	0.75	4.50	—
1945 Serif 4	Inc. above	3.50	6.50	15.00	30.00	—
1946	6,611,000	—	0.25	1.00	4.50	—
1947	14,244,500	—	0.20	0.40	1.50	—
1948	15,442,000	—	0.20	0.40	1.50	—
1949	11,778,900	—	0.20	0.40	1.50	—
1950	14,431,500	—	0.20	0.40	1.50	—

KM# 820 ORE

2.0000 g., Bronze, 16 mm. **Ruler:** Gustaf VI **Obv:** Crown above inscription **Rev:** Value within circle divides date below crown **Edge:** Plain **Note:** Varieties exist.

Date	Mintage	F	VF	XF	Unc	BU
1952 TS	3,819,000	—	0.20	0.75	3.50	—
1953 TS	22,635,800	—	—	0.30	2.00	—
1954 TS	15,492,000	—	—	0.30	2.00	—
1955 TS	24,008,000	—	—	0.30	2.00	—
1956 TS	20,792,000	—	—	0.30	2.00	—
1957 TS	21,018,500	—	—	0.30	2.00	—
1958 TS	20,220,000	—	—	0.30	2.00	—
1959 TS	14,027,500	—	—	0.30	2.00	—
1960 TS	21,840,000	—	—	0.25	2.00	—
1961 TS	11,457,500	—	—	0.35	2.25	—
1961 U	4,927,500	—	0.20	0.50	3.50	—
1962 U	19,692,500	—	—	0.30	2.00	—
1963 U	26,070,000	—	—	0.15	0.65	—
1964 U	19,290,000	—	—	0.15	0.65	—
1965 U	22,335,000	—	—	0.15	0.65	—
1966 U	24,092,500	—	—	0.15	0.30	—
1967 U	30,420,000	—	—	0.10	0.30	—
1968 U	20,760,000	—	—	0.10	0.30	—
1969 U	20,197,500	—	—	0.10	0.30	—
1970 U	44,400,000	—	—	0.10	0.30	—
1971 U	16,490,000	—	—	0.10	0.30	—

KM# 746 2 ORE

3.9100 g., Bronze, 21 mm. **Ruler:** Oscar II **Obv:** Large lettering **Rev:** Value, date and crowns within circle

Date	Mintage	F	VF	XF	Unc	BU
1901	1,415,200	0.50	1.25	3.50	22.50	—
1902	2,035,550	0.50	1.25	3.50	22.50	—
1904	698,050	0.50	1.25	4.50	30.00	—
1905	1,429,900	0.50	1.25	3.50	22.50	—

KM# 769 2 ORE

Bronze, 21 mm. **Ruler:** Oscar II **Obv:** Crowned shield **Rev:** Value, date and crowns within circle

Date	Mintage	F	VF	XF	Unc	BU
1906/5	994,250	100	200	420	875	—
1906	Inc. above	2.75	8.00	25.00	90.00	—
1907	3,807,350	0.30	0.60	2.50	15.00	—

KM# 778 2 ORE

4.0000 g., Bronze, 21 mm. **Ruler:** Gustaf V **Obv:** Crowned monogram divides date **Rev:** Value and crowns

Date	Mintage	F	VF	XF	Unc	BU
1909	1,584,550	0.50	2.00	8.00	47.50	—
1910	809,400	2.00	8.00	22.50	90.00	—
1912	445,750	2.50	10.00	32.50	100	—
1913	805,650	0.30	2.00	10.00	47.50	—
1914	1,196,900	0.30	2.00	10.00	47.50	—
1915/4	813,850	4.50	12.50	35.00	110	—
1915	Inc. above	0.30	2.00	10.00	47.50	—
1916/5	2,815,450	2.75	8.00	27.50	90.00	—
1916 Short 6	Inc. above	0.25	0.60	5.00	30.00	—
1916 Long 6	Inc. above	0.25	0.60	5.00	30.00	—
1919	1,202,700	0.25	0.60	4.00	22.50	—
1920	3,464,750	0.30	0.50	2.00	10.00	—
1921	2,958,250	0.30	0.50	2.00	10.00	—
1922	521,600	0.70	1.75	6.00	37.50	—
1923	769,200	1.00	2.50	7.00	47.50	—
1924	1,283,000	0.30	0.75	3.50	27.50	—
1925	3,903,350	0.20	0.50	1.75	15.00	—
1926	3,573,950	0.20	0.50	1.75	15.00	—
1927	2,190,250	0.20	0.50	1.75	15.00	—
1928	832,250	0.40	1.00	4.00	30.00	—
1929	2,384,350	0.20	0.30	1.75	10.00	—
1930	2,589,850	0.20	0.30	1.75	10.00	—
1931	2,295,200	0.20	0.30	1.75	10.00	—
1932	1,179,150	0.35	0.85	4.00	30.00	—
1933	1,721,300	0.20	0.35	1.75	10.00	—
1934	1,794,950	0.20	0.35	1.75	10.00	—
1935	3,677,750	0.20	0.30	1.25	7.00	—
1936 Short 6	2,244,100	0.20	0.30	1.00	6.00	—
1936 Long 6	Inc. above	0.65	1.25	3.75	18.50	—
1937	2,980,950	0.10	0.25	1.25	6.00	—
1938	3,224,800	0.10	0.25	0.75	6.00	—
1939	4,014,200	0.10	0.25	0.75	4.50	—
1940	3,304,750	0.10	0.25	0.75	4.50	—
1941	7,337,198	0.10	0.25	0.75	4.50	—
1942	1,614,000	0.30	0.75	1.50	10.00	—
1950	5,823,000	0.10	0.20	0.65	4.50	—

KM# 790 2 ORE

Iron, 21 mm. **Ruler:** Gustaf V **Obv:** Crowned monogram divides date **Rev:** Value and crowns **Note:** World War I issues. Similar to KM#553.

Date	Mintage	F	VF	XF	Unc	BU
1917	4,576,200	2.00	3.00	8.50	42.50	—
1918	4,981,750	2.50	5.00	12.50	57.50	—
1919	2,923,100	6.50	12.50	27.50	90.00	—
1920	1	—	—	—	—	—

KM# 811 2 ORE

3.5000 g., Iron, 21 mm. **Ruler:** Gustaf V **Obv:** Crowned monogram divides date **Rev:** Value and crowns **Note:** World War II issues.

Date	Mintage	F	VF	XF	Unc	BU
1942	9,343,350	0.15	0.30	1.50	10.00	—
1943	6,999,300	0.15	0.30	1.50	10.00	—
1944	6,125,900	0.15	0.30	1.50	10.00	—
1945	4,773,400	0.20	0.40	1.50	11.50	—
1946	5,854,000	0.15	0.30	1.50	10.00	—
1947	9,535,750	0.15	0.30	0.75	7.00	—
1948	11,424,250	0.15	0.30	0.75	7.00	—
1949 Long 9	10,599,750	0.15	0.30	0.75	7.00	—
1949 Short 9	Inc. above	0.15	0.30	0.75	7.00	—
1950	13,323,000	0.15	0.30	0.75	7.00	—

KM# 821 2 ORE

Bronze, 21 mm. **Ruler:** Gustaf VI **Obv:** Crown above inscription **Rev:** Value within circle divides date below crown **Edge:** Plain **Note:** Varieties exist.

Date	Mintage	F	VF	XF	Unc	BU
1952 TS	3,011,000	0.20	0.50	0.85	6.00	—
1953 TS	15,619,900	0.10	0.20	0.75	4.50	—
1954 TS	10,086,000	0.10	0.20	0.75	4.50	—
1955 TS	12,963,400	0.10	0.20	0.75	4.50	—
1956 TS	13,890,250	0.10	0.20	0.75	4.50	—
1957 TS	9,991,300	0.10	0.20	0.75	4.50	—
1958 TS	10,105,500	0.10	0.20	0.75	4.50	—
1959 TS	11,571,750	0.10	0.20	0.75	4.50	—
1960 TS	11,092,500	0.10	0.20	0.75	4.50	—
1961 TS	9,672,500	0.10	0.20	0.75	4.50	—
1961 U	1,075,000	0.70	1.50	3.00	15.00	—
1962 U	9,568,750	—	0.10	0.45	2.00	—
1963 U	13,337,500	—	0.10	0.45	2.00	—
1964 U	19,346,250	—	0.10	0.20	2.00	—
1964 U	Inc. above	0.60	1.25	2.50	10.00	—
Note: O in crown: first dot in crown on left with hollow center						
1965 U	23,356,000	—	0.10	0.20	0.75	—
1966 U	18,278,000	—	0.10	0.20	0.75	—
1967 U	23,931,000	—	—	0.10	0.45	—
1968 U	26,238,000	—	—	0.10	0.45	—
1969 U	16,843,000	—	—	0.10	0.45	—
1970 U	31,254,000	—	—	0.10	0.45	—
1971 U	19,179,000	—	—	0.10	0.45	—

KM# 757 5 ORE

Bronze, 27 mm. **Ruler:** Oscar II **Obv:** Large lettering **Rev:** Value, date and crowns within beaded circle

Date	Mintage	F	VF	XF	Unc	BU
1901	441,660	1.00	4.00	12.50	60.00	—
1902	652,420	1.00	4.00	12.50	60.00	—
1903	243,000	1.75	5.00	18.00	70.00	—
1904	414,240	1.00	4.00	12.50	50.00	—
1905	545,080	1.00	4.00	15.00	55.00	—

KM# 770 5 ORE

Bronze, 27 mm. **Ruler:** Oscar II **Obv:** Crowned shield **Rev:** Value, date and crowns within beaded circle

Date	Mintage	F	VF	XF	Unc	BU
1906	565,280	0.75	3.50	12.50	47.50	—
1907	1,953,260	0.50	2.00	6.00	25.00	—

KM# 779.1 5 ORE

8.0000 g., Bronze, 27 mm. **Ruler:** Gustaf V **Obv:** Small cross above crowned monograms **Rev:** Value above crowns

Date	Mintage	F	VF	XF	Unc	BU
1909	917,230	2.00	6.00	30.00	175	—

KM# 779.2 5 ORE

7.9400 g., Bronze, 27 mm. **Ruler:** Gustaf V **Obv:** Large cross above crowned monogram **Rev:** Value above crowns **Note:** Varieties exist.

Date	Mintage	F	VF	XF	Unc	BU
1909	Inc. above	7.00	45.00	265	875	—
1910	30,630	115	265	545	1,325	—
1911	778,000	0.85	3.50	25.00	135	—
Note: Narrow base mint mark						
1911	Inc. above	3.00	12.00	50.00	200	—
Note: Wide base mint mark						
1912	547,480	1.00	3.50	35.00	190	—
1913	761,780	0.85	2.25	22.50	125	—
1914	400,100	2.50	5.50	42.50	235	—
1915	1,122,820	0.50	2.50	18.50	65.00	—
1916/5	955,440	10.00	20.00	40.00	165	—
1916 Short 6	Inc. above	0.50	2.50	15.00	70.00	—
1916 Long 6	Inc. above	0.50	2.50	15.00	70.00	—
1917	1	—	—	—	—	—
1919	1,129,380	0.25	1.00	13.50	60.00	—
1920	2,360,920	0.25	1.00	8.00	35.00	—
1921	1,878,500	0.20	0.75	12.00	50.00	—
1922	763,420	0.25	2.50	27.50	125	—
1923	505,580	0.85	4.50	65.00	245	—
1924	899,500	0.25	1.50	17.50	90.00	—
1925	1,943,500	0.20	0.75	8.50	50.00	—
1926	1,742,100	0.20	0.75	8.50	50.00	—
1927	36,380	80.00	175	525	1,200	—
1928	987,900	0.20	1.00	12.00	65.00	—
1929	1,668,560	0.20	0.50	8.50	50.00	—
1930	1,716,040	0.20	0.50	8.50	50.00	—
1931	1,130,960	0.20	0.50	8.50	55.00	—
1932	1,165,220	0.20	0.50	8.50	55.00	—
1933	574,340	0.65	2.50	27.50	135	—
1934	1,710,260	0.20	0.40	5.00	37.50	—
1935	1,682,020	0.20	0.40	5.00	37.50	—
1936 Short 6	1,625,700	0.20	0.40	6.00	37.50	—
1936	Inc. above	0.25	0.75	7.00	47.50	—
1937	2,637,260	—	0.30	4.00	22.50	—
1938	2,354,240	—	0.30	4.00	22.50	—
1939	2,591,500	—	0.45	6.00	22.50	—
1940	2,729,580	—	0.35	3.50	20.00	—
1940 Serif 4	Inc. above	—	0.45	4.00	25.00	—
1941	2,054,540	—	0.35	2.50	17.50	—
1942	395,400	2.00	4.00	22.50	90.00	—
1950	12,559,100	—	0.25	0.75	6.00	—

KM# 791 5 ORE

Iron **Ruler:** Gustaf V **Obv:** Crowned monogram **Rev:** Value above crowns **Note:** World War I issues

Date	Mintage	F	VF	XF	Unc	BU
1917	2,953,320	4.00	8.00	18.00	70.00	—
1918	2,457,840	10.00	20.00	32.50	125	—
1919	2,302,480	10.00	20.00	32.50	120	—

KM# 812 5 ORE

7.0000 g., Iron, 27 mm. **Ruler:** Gustaf V **Obv:** Crowned monogram divides date **Rev:** Value above crowns **Note:** World War II issues.

Date	Mintage	F	VF	XF	Unc	BU
1942	4,343,420	0.20	0.75	4.00	30.00	—
1943	5,570,180	0.20	0.75	4.00	30.00	—
1944	4,561,980	0.20	0.75	4.00	30.00	—
1945	3,771,100	0.20	0.75	4.00	30.00	—
1946	2,375,080	—	0.50	3.00	20.00	—
1947	6,034,840	—	0.50	3.00	20.00	—
1948	6,246,000	—	0.50	3.00	20.00	—
1949	7,839,640	—	0.50	2.00	16.50	—
1950	5,289,500	—	0.50	2.00	16.50	—

KM# 822 5 ORE

8.0000 g., Bronze, 27 mm. **Ruler:** Gustaf VI **Obv:** Crown above inscription **Rev:** Value within circle divides date below crown **Edge:** Plain

Date	Mintage	F	VF	XF	Unc	BU
1952 TS	3,065,400	0.20	0.50	1.75	8.50	—
1953 TS	12,329,320	0.20	0.50	1.75	8.50	—
1954 TS	7,232,100	0.20	0.50	1.75	8.50	—
1955 TS	8,464,620	0.20	0.50	1.75	8.50	—
1956 TS	7,997,120	0.20	0.50	2.00	9.00	—
1957 TS	6,275,600	0.20	0.50	1.75	8.50	—
1958 TS	9,498,400	0.20	0.50	2.00	9.00	—
1959 TS	8,370,500	0.20	0.50	2.00	9.00	—
1960 TS	10,542,300	0.20	0.40	1.25	7.50	—
1961 TS	3,909,000	0.20	0.40	1.25	7.50	—
1961 U	2,451,500	0.20	0.50	1.25	8.50	—
1962 U	22,305,500	—	0.10	0.50	3.50	—
1963 U	17,156,500	—	0.10	0.50	3.50	—
1964 U	10,922,500	—	0.10	0.75	7.00	—
1964 U	Inc. above	2.75	5.50	11.50	30.00	—
Note: O in crown: first dot in crown on left with hollow center						
1965 U	22,635,000	—	0.10	0.20	1.00	—
1966 U	18,213,000	—	0.10	0.20	1.00	—
1967 U	20,776,000	—	0.10	0.20	1.00	—
1968 U	27,093,500	—	0.10	0.20	1.00	—
1969 U	26,886,500	—	0.10	0.20	1.00	—
1970 U	29,419,500	—	0.10	0.20	1.00	—
1971 U	15,749,000	—	0.10	0.20	1.00	—

KM# 845 5 ORE

2.7000 g., Bronze, 18 mm. **Ruler:** Gustaf VI **Obv:** Large crown above smaller crown **Rev:** Value divides date

Date	Mintage	F	VF	XF	Unc	BU
1972 U	107,894,000	—	—	0.10	0.25	0.60
1973 U	193,037,580	—	—	0.10	0.25	0.60

KM# 849 5 ORE

Copper-Tin-Zinc, 18 mm. **Ruler:** Carl XVI Gustaf **Obv:** Value **Rev:** Crowned monogram divides date **Edge:** Plain **Designer:** Lars Englund

Date	Mintage	F	VF	XF	Unc	BU
1976 U	4,672,350	—	—	0.10	0.40	0.60
1977 U	31,037,129	—	—	0.10	0.30	0.60
1978 U	46,021,707	—	—	0.10	0.30	0.60
1979 U	65,833,193	—	—	0.10	0.30	0.60
1980 U	60,996,699	—	—	0.10	0.25	0.60
1981 U	19,791,000	—	—	0.10	0.25	0.60

KM# 849a 5 ORE

Copper-Zinc, 18 mm. **Ruler:** Carl XVI Gustaf **Obv:** Value **Rev:** Crowned monogram divides date **Designer:** Lars Englund

Date	Mintage	F	VF	XF	Unc	BU
1981 U	34,960,593	—	—	0.10	0.20	0.60
1982 U	40,471,115	—	—	0.10	0.20	0.60
1983 U	36,304,042	—	—	0.10	0.20	0.60
1984 U	13,449,245	—	—	0.10	0.20	0.60

KM# 755 10 ORE

1.4500 g., 0.4000 Silver 0.0186 oz. ASW, 15 mm. **Ruler:** Oscar II **Obv:** Large lettering **Rev:** Value, date **Note:** Varieties exist.

Date	Mintage	F	VF	XF	Unc	BU
1902 EB	1,945,600	1.00	3.50	12.50	32.50	—
1903 EB	1,508,930	1.00	3.50	12.50	32.50	—
1904 EB	3,279,520	0.75	1.50	8.50	25.00	—

KM# 774 10 ORE

1.4500 g., 0.4000 Silver 0.0186 oz. ASW, 15 mm. **Ruler:** Oscar II **Obv:** Crowned shield flanked by crowns **Rev:** Value and date

Date	Mintage	F	VF	XF	Unc	BU
1907 EB	7,319,040	0.45	1.25	5.00	20.00	—

KM# 780 10 ORE

1.4500 g., 0.4000 Silver 0.0186 oz. ASW, 15 mm. **Ruler:** Gustaf V **Obv:** Three small crowns within crowned shield divides date **Rev:** Value

Date	Mintage	F	VF	XF	Unc	BU
1909 W	1,610,400	1.25	4.00	13.50	70.00	—
1911 W	3,180,650	0.35	2.00	8.50	32.50	—
1913 W	1,580,910	1.00	2.50	11.50	50.00	—
1914 W	1,571,330	0.75	3.00	8.50	32.50	—
1914 Serif 4	Inc. above	0.75	2.25	10.00	50.00	—
1915 W	1,546,950	0.50	2.25	8.00	47.50	—
1916/5 W	3,034,880	2.50	7.00	22.50	110	—
1916 W	Inc. above	0.75	1.75	6.50	32.50	—
1917 W	4,996,139	0.35	0.75	2.50	18.50	—
1918 W	4,114,180	0.35	0.75	2.50	18.50	—
1919 W	5,737,020	0.35	0.75	2.50	18.50	—
1927 W	2,509,590	0.30	0.60	2.50	22.50	—
1928 G	2,901,150	0.30	0.60	2.50	22.50	—
1929 G	5,505,200	0.30	0.60	1.75	11.50	—
1930 G	3,222,710	0.30	0.60	1.75	11.50	—
1931 G	4,272,073	0.30	0.60	1.75	11.50	—
1933 G	1,948,090	0.80	1.75	3.25	25.00	—
1934 G	4,059,293	0.30	0.50	1.25	6.50	—
1935 G	2,426,283	0.30	0.50	1.25	6.50	—
1936 G Short 6	5,099,270	1.75	4.50	20.00	60.00	—
1936 G Long 6	Inc. above	0.30	0.45	1.50	9.00	—
1937 G	5,116,920	0.30	0.40	1.00	6.50	—
1938 G	7,428,140	0.30	0.40	1.00	6.50	—
1938 G Proof	—	Value: 12.50				
1939/29 G	2,020,670	3.75	8.00	22.00	55.00	—
1939 G	Inc. above	0.30	0.60	2.25	13.50	—
1939 G Proof	—	Value: 17.50				
1940 G	3,017,320	0.30	0.50	1.25	6.00	—
1941 G	9,106,380	0.30	0.50	1.25	6.00	—
1942 G	3,691,640	0.30	0.50	1.25	6.00	—

KM# 795 10 ORE

1.5000 g., Nickel-Bronze, 15 mm. **Ruler:** Gustaf V **Obv:** Crowned monogram divides date **Rev:** Value

Date	Mintage	F	VF	XF	Unc	BU
1920 W	3,612,250	0.50	1.00	5.00	40.00	—
1920 W Large W	Inc. above	13.50	28.00	60.00	300	—
1921 W	2,269,950	0.50	1.25	6.00	40.00	—
1923 W	2,143,560	0.50	1.25	7.00	50.00	—
1924 W	1,600,000	0.50	1.50	8.00	70.00	—
1925 W	1,472,340	0.75	3.25	16.50	85.00	—
1940 G	3,373,200	0.20	0.50	2.00	16.00	—
1941	815,880	0.75	1.50	4.00	30.00	—
1946 TS	4,115,940	0.10	0.30	0.75	6.00	—
1947 TS	4,132,950	0.10	0.30	0.75	6.00	—

KM# 813 10 ORE

1.4400 g., 0.4000 Silver 0.0185 oz. ASW, 15 mm. **Ruler:** Gustaf V **Obv:** Crown **Rev:** Value **Note:** Varieties exist.

Date	Mintage	F	VF	XF	Unc	BU
1942 G	1,600,000	0.25	0.40	1.25	6.50	—
1942 G Proof	—	Value: 35.00				
1943 G	7,661,100	0.25	0.40	1.25	6.50	—
1944 G	12,276,900	BV	0.35	0.85	5.00	—
1945 G	11,702,510	BV	0.35	0.85	5.00	—
1945 TS	Inc. above	BV	0.35	0.85	5.00	—
1945 TS/G	Inc. above	BV	0.35	1.25	6.50	—
1946/5 TS Open 6	3,575,500	5.50	13.00	25.00	70.00	—
1946 TS Open 6	Inc. above	0.30	0.75	2.50	22.50	—
1946 TS Closed 6	Inc. above	BV	0.35	1.75	12.50	—
1947 TS	7,293,250	BV	0.30	0.85	5.00	—
1948 TS	10,418,650	BV	0.30	0.75	5.00	—
1949 TS	12,044,000	BV	0.30	0.75	5.00	—
1950 TS	31,823,870	BV	0.30	0.75	4.00	—

KM# 823 10 ORE
1.4400 g., 0.4000 Silver 0.0185 oz. ASW, 15 mm. **Ruler:** Gustaf VI **Obv:** Crown **Rev:** Value

Date	Mintage	F	VF	XF	Unc	BU
1952 TS	4,659,700	BV	0.40	0.85	4.50	—
1953 TS	28,484,040	—	BV	0.85	4.50	—
1954 TS	15,913,250	—	BV	0.85	4.50	—
1955 TS	16,687,200	—	BV	0.85	4.50	—
1956 TS	21,985,600	—	BV	0.60	3.50	—
1957 TS	21,294,400	—	BV	0.60	3.50	—
1958 TS	19,605,400	—	BV	0.60	3.50	—
1959 TS	18,523,000	—	BV	0.60	3.50	—
1960 TS	16,605,000	—	BV	0.60	3.50	—
1961 TS	8,283,000	—	BV	0.60	3.50	—
1961 U	7,843,000	—	BV	0.60	3.50	—
1962 U	8,619,000	—	BV	0.60	3.50	—

KM# 835 10 ORE
1.4000 g., Copper-Nickel, 15 mm. **Ruler:** Gustaf VI **Obv:** Crowned monogram divides date **Rev:** Value

Date	Mintage	F	VF	XF	Unc	BU
1962 U	8,814,000	0.10	0.25	0.60	3.50	7.50
1963 U	28,170,000	—	—	0.15	0.60	3.50
1964 U	36,895,000	—	—	0.15	0.60	3.50
1965 U	29,870,000	—	—	0.15	0.60	3.50
1966 U	20,435,000	—	—	0.15	0.60	3.50
1967 U	18,245,000	—	—	0.15	0.60	3.50
1968 U	51,490,000	—	—	0.15	0.50	3.50
1969 U	55,880,000	—	—	0.15	0.50	1.75
1970 U	60,910,000	—	—	0.15	0.50	1.75
1971 U	27,075,000	—	—	0.15	0.50	1.75
1972 U	36,766,500	—	—	0.15	0.25	1.00
1973 U	160,740,000	—	—	0.15	0.25	1.00

KM# 850 10 ORE
1.4500 g., Copper-Nickel, 14.54 mm. **Ruler:** Carl XVI Gustaf **Obv:** Crowned monogram divides date **Rev:** Value **Edge:** Plain **Designer:** Lars Englund

Date	Mintage	F	VF	XF	Unc	BU
1976 U	4,172,790	—	—	0.15	0.50	1.00
1977 U	44,517,287	—	—	0.10	0.35	0.75
1978 U	74,341,720	—	—	0.10	0.35	0.75
1979 U	75,305,608	—	—	0.10	0.15	0.40
1980 U	108,293,811	—	—	0.10	0.15	0.40
1981 U	102,453,931	—	—	0.10	0.15	0.30
1982 U	103,905,592	—	—	0.10	0.15	0.30
1983 U	773,149,400	—	—	0.10	0.15	0.40
1984 U	122,128,092	—	—	0.10	0.15	0.30
1985 U	79,154,951	—	—	0.10	0.15	0.40
1986 U	48,945,396	—	—	0.10	0.15	0.40
1986 D	48,945,220	—	—	0.10	0.15	0.40
1987 D	146,877,318	—	—	0.10	0.15	0.40
1988 D	194,986,479	—	—	0.10	0.15	0.30
1989 D	245,180,644	—	—	0.10	0.15	0.30
1990 D	139,298,404	—	—	0.10	0.15	0.30
1991 D	5,176,842	—	—	0.15	0.50	1.00

KM# 739 25 ORE
2.4200 g., 0.6000 Silver 0.0467 oz. ASW, 17 mm. **Ruler:** Oscar II **Obv:** Large lettering **Rev:** Value within wreath, date below

Date	Mintage	F	VF	XF	Unc	BU
1902 EB	1,259,039	2.00	7.00	22.50	80.00	—
1904 EB	691,888	2.00	7.00	22.50	82.00	—
1905 EB	732,000	1.75	5.50	18.50	70.00	—

KM# 775 25 ORE
2.4200 g., 0.6000 Silver 0.0467 oz. ASW, 17 mm. **Ruler:** Oscar II **Obv:** Crowned shield flanked by crowns **Rev:** Value within wreath

Date	Mintage	F	VF	XF	Unc	BU
1907 EB	3,222,580	0.80	2.00	6.00	42.50	—

KM# 785 25 ORE
2.4200 g., 0.6000 Silver 0.0467 oz. ASW, 17 mm. **Ruler:** Gustaf V **Obv:** Small crowns within crowned shield divides date **Rev:** Value above sprigs

Date	Mintage	F	VF	XF	Unc	BU
1910 W Large cross	2,043,936	0.75	2.00	6.00	50.00	—
1910 W Small cross	Inc. above	7.00	27.50	75.00	475	—
1912 W	1,013,740	0.75	2.75	15.00	70.00	—
1914 W	3,719,232	0.75	2.75	15.00	40.00	—
1916 W	1,269,120	0.75	2.75	15.00	70.00	—
1917 W	1,657,312	0.75	2.25	5.50	40.00	—
1918 W Small 8	2,364,784	0.75	2.25	7.50	50.00	—
1918 W Wide 8	Inc. above	0.75	2.25	9.50	58.00	—
1919 W	3,205,164	0.75	1.50	5.00	35.00	—
1927 W	1,687,984	0.75	1.75	5.00	35.00	—
1928 G	836,899	0.75	2.00	9.50	58.00	—
1929 G	1,124,932	0.75	1.75	6.00	40.00	—
1930 G	3,489,628	BV	1.50	3.00	18.50	—
1931 G	1,391,938	BV	1.50	3.00	18.50	—
1932 G	1,133,344	BV	1.50	3.00	18.50	—
1933 G	964,340	BV	1.50	8.00	35.00	—
1934 G	1,403,648	BV	1.50	3.00	11.50	—
1936 G	1,852,000	BV	1.50	3.00	11.50	—
1937 G Large G	Inc. above	0.75	2.00	4.50	18.50	—
1937 G Proof	Inc. above	Value: 20.00				
1937 G Small G	3,258,956	BV	1.50	4.50	12.50	—
1938	3,678,876	BV	1.25	2.75	7.50	—
1939	2,136,600	BV	1.00	2.75	7.50	—
1940	2,301,788	BV	1.00	2.50	7.00	—
1941	1,995,200	BV	1.00	2.50	7.00	—

KM# 798 25 ORE
2.4000 g., Nickel-Bronze, 17 mm. **Ruler:** Gustaf V **Obv:** Crowned monogram divides date **Rev:** Value within oat sprigs

Date	Mintage	F	VF	XF	Unc	BU
1921 W	1,354,656	1.50	3.00	13.50	85.00	—
1940 G	2,333,040	0.15	0.50	3.00	18.50	—
1941 G	1,056,680	0.15	0.50	3.00	27.50	—
1946 TS	2,066,048	0.15	0.30	1.25	9.00	—
1947 TS	1,594,200	0.15	0.30	1.25	9.00	—

KM# 816 25 ORE
2.3200 g., 0.4000 Silver 0.0298 oz. ASW, 17 mm. **Ruler:** Gustaf V **Obv:** Crown **Rev:** Value and date

Date	Mintage	F	VF	XF	Unc	BU
1943 G	9,854,640	BV	0.50	1.25	7.50	—
1944 G	9,532,148	BV	0.50	1.25	7.50	—
1945 G	5,362,800	BV	0.50	1.25	7.50	—
1945 TS	Inc. above	BV	0.75	2.50	11.50	—
1945 G/TS	Inc. above	BV	0.60	3.50	16.50	—
1946 TS	2,249,600	—	BV	2.50	11.50	—
1946 TS serif 6	Inc. above	2.00	4.00	14.50	42.50	—
1947 TS	5,332,800	—	BV	1.25	4.50	—
1948 TS	3,191,000	—	BV	1.25	4.50	—
1949 TS	5,812,180	—	BV	1.25	4.50	—
1950 TS	12,059,144	—	BV	1.25	3.50	—

KM# 824 25 ORE
2.3200 g., 0.4000 Silver 0.0298 oz. ASW, 17 mm. **Ruler:** Gustaf VI **Obv:** Value and date **Rev:** Crown

Date	Mintage	F	VF	XF	Unc	BU
1952 TS	2,113,890	—	BV	1.25	4.50	—
1953 TS	18,177,420	—	BV	1.00	2.50	—
1954 TS	9,491,740	—	BV	1.00	2.50	—
1955 TS	7,663,100	—	BV	1.25	4.00	—
1956 TS	10,930,800	—	BV	1.00	3.50	—
1957 TS	12,497,200	—	BV	1.00	3.50	—
1958 TS	6,883,940	—	BV	1.00	3.50	—
1959 TS	4,772,000	—	BV	1.00	3.50	—
1960 TS	4,374,000	BV	0.50	2.00	10.00	—
1961 TS	8,380,800	—	BV	1.00	3.50	—

KM# 836 25 ORE
2.2900 g., Copper-Nickel, 16.94 mm. **Ruler:** Gustaf VI **Obv:** Crowned monogram divides date **Rev:** Value **Edge:** Plain

Date	Mintage	F	VF	XF	Unc	BU
1962 U	4,426,000	—	0.25	1.00	3.25	—
1963 U	26,710,000	—	0.20	0.50	2.50	—
1964 U	17,300,000	—	0.20	0.50	2.50	—
1965 U	6,884,000	—	0.20	0.50	2.50	—
1966 U	12,932,000	—	—	0.25	1.25	—
1967 U	28,038,000	—	—	0.20	0.65	—
1968 U	14,366,000	—	—	0.20	0.65	—
1969 U	20,214,000	—	—	0.20	0.65	—
1970 U	23,780,000	—	—	0.20	0.65	—
1971 U	8,606,000	—	—	0.20	0.65	—
1972 U	1,323,200	—	—	0.20	0.65	—
1973 U	76,993,000	—	—	0.15	0.45	—

KM# 851 25 ORE
2.2000 g., Copper-Nickel, 17 mm. **Ruler:** Carl XVI Gustaf **Obv:** Crowned monogram divides date **Rev:** Value **Designer:** Lars Englund

Date	Mintage	F	VF	XF	Unc	BU
1976 U	2,515,285	—	—	0.15	0.65	—
1977 U	5,509,491	—	—	0.15	0.50	—
1978 U	54,593,293	—	—	0.10	0.30	—
1979 U	48,423,422	—	—	0.10	0.30	—
1980 U	38,889,325	—	—	0.10	0.30	—
1981 U	46,371,204	—	—	0.10	0.30	—
1982 U	43,212,638	—	—	0.10	0.30	—
1983 U	28,954,257	—	—	0.10	0.30	—
1984 U	7,293,722	—	—	0.10	0.30	—

KM# 771 50 ORE
5.0000 g., 0.6000 Silver 0.0964 oz. ASW, 22 mm. **Ruler:** Oscar II **Obv:** Crowned shield flanked by crowns **Rev:** Value and date within wreath

Date	Mintage	F	VF	XF	Unc	BU
1906 EB	319,452	2.75	8.00	35.00	190	—
1907 EB	803,340	2.00	5.00	32.50	125	—

KM# 788 50 ORE
5.0000 g., 0.6000 Silver 0.0964 oz. ASW, 22 mm. **Ruler:** Gustaf V **Obv:** Three small crowns within crowned shield divides date **Rev:** Value above sprigs

Date	Mintage	F	VF	XF	Unc	BU
1911 W	472,534	3.25	7.00	28.00	140	—
1912 W	483,062	4.50	8.50	30.00	165	—

Date	Mintage	F	VF	XF	Unc	BU
1914 W	378,448	4.50	8.50	30.00	165	—
1916 W	536,718	3.25	7.00	25.00	135	—
1919 W	458,296	3.25	7.00	28.00	120	—
1927 W	671,596	1.50	3.00	15.00	80.00	—
1928 G	1,135,054	BV	2.00	7.00	45.00	—
1929 G	470,990	1.50	3.00	15.00	80.00	—
1930 G	547,920	1.50	3.00	15.00	75.00	—
1931 G	671,457	BV	2.00	12.50	55.00	—
1933 G	547,606	BV	2.00	12.50	55.00	—
1934 G	613,124	BV	2.00	7.00	40.00	—
1935 G	690,792	BV	2.00	7.00	40.00	—
1936 G Short 6	823,176	BV	2.00	7.00	40.00	—
1936 G Long 6	Inc. above	BV	3.50	12.50	70.00	—
1938 G	441,546	BV	1.50	4.50	25.00	—
1939 G	921,750	—	BV	2.50	18.00	—
1939 G Proof	—	Value: 35.00				

KM# 796 50 ORE

Nickel-Bronze, 22 mm. **Ruler:** Gustaf V **Obv:** Crowned monogram divides date **Rev:** Value within oat sprigs **Note:** Varieties exist.

Date	Mintage	F	VF	XF	Unc	BU
1920 W Oval 0	479,500	1.75	8.00	40.00	200	—
1920 W Round 0	Inc. above	35.00	70.00	230	645	—
1921 W	214,922	2.75	20.00	110	385	—
1924 W	645,368	1.25	10.00	45.00	275	—
1940 G	1,340,750	0.25	1.00	4.50	35.00	—
1940 G large G	Inc. above	5.50	15.00	40.00	90.00	—
1946 TS	1,425,990	0.25	1.00	4.00	20.00	—
1947 TS	1,031,800	0.25	1.00	4.00	20.00	—

KM# 817 50 ORE

4.8000 g., 0.4000 Silver 0.0617 oz. ASW, 22 mm. **Ruler:** Gustaf V **Obv:** Crown **Rev:** Value and date

Date	Mintage	F	VF	XF	Unc	BU
1943 G	784,700	1.50	3.00	10.00	55.00	—
1944 G	1,540,296	BV	1.00	2.00	12.00	—
1945 G	2,584,800	BV	1.00	2.00	12.00	—
1946 TS	1,091,000	BV	1.00	2.00	12.00	—
1947 TS	1,770,500	BV	1.00	2.00	12.00	—
1948 TS	1,731,400	BV	1.00	2.00	12.00	—
1949 TS	1,883,100	BV	1.00	2.00	12.00	—
1950 TS	3,353,620	BV	1.00	1.50	10.00	—

KM# 825 50 ORE

4.8000 g., 0.4000 Silver 0.0617 oz. ASW, 22 mm. **Ruler:** Gustaf VI **Obv:** Value and date **Rev:** Crown

Date	Mintage	F	VF	XF	Unc	BU
1952 TS	1,197,760	BV	1.00	3.00	22.50	—
1953 TS	4,395,620	BV	1.00	2.50	20.00	—
1954 TS	5,778,850	BV	1.00	2.50	20.00	—
1955 TS	2,699,700	BV	1.00	4.00	18.50	—
1956 TS	7,056,670	—	BV	1.50	8.50	—
1957 TS	2,404,700	—	BV	2.50	18.50	—
1958 TS	1,659,800	—	BV	2.50	18.50	—
1961 TS	2,775,000	—	BV	1.50	11.50	—

KM# 837 50 ORE

4.5000 g., Copper-Nickel, 22 mm. **Ruler:** Gustaf VI **Obv:** Crowned monogram divides date **Rev:** Value

Date	Mintage	F	VF	XF	Unc	BU
1962 U	1,400,000	0.50	0.75	3.25	21.50	—
1963 U	5,808,000	0.15	0.25	1.25	11.50	—
1964 U	5,325,000	0.15	0.25	1.25	11.50	—
1965 U	6,453,000	0.15	0.25	0.60	7.50	—
1966 U	6,309,000	0.15	0.25	0.50	6.00	—
1967 U	7,890,000	0.15	0.25	0.50	6.00	—
1968 U	9,198,000	—	0.15	0.25	1.25	—
1969 U	7,265,000	—	0.15	0.25	1.25	—
1970 U	9,426,000	—	0.15	0.25	1.25	—
1971 U	7,218,000	—	0.15	0.25	1.25	—
1972 U	7,388,000	—	0.15	0.25	1.25	—
1973 U	52,467,000	—	0.15	0.20	0.60	—

KM# 855 50 ORE

4.5000 g., Copper-Nickel, 22 mm. **Ruler:** Carl XVI Gustaf **Obv:** Crowned monogram divides date **Rev:** Value **Edge:** Plain **Designer:** Lars Englund

Date	Mintage	F	VF	XF	Unc	BU
1976 U	2,588,575	—	0.15	0.25	1.00	—
1977 U	10,359,708	—	—	0.15	0.40	—
1978 U	33,282,476	—	—	0.15	0.40	—
1979 U	30,723,730	—	—	0.15	0.40	—
1980 U	28,665,662	—	—	0.15	0.40	—
1981 U	15,516,559	—	—	0.15	0.40	—
1982 U	14,778,358	—	—	0.15	0.40	—
1983 U	17,528,777	—	—	0.15	0.40	—
1984 U	27,527,534	—	—	0.15	0.40	—
1985 U	14,078,477	—	—	0.15	0.40	—
1986 U	937,214	—	—	0.20	0.75	—
1987 D	1,077,317	—	—	0.20	0.70	—
1988 D	531,669	—	—	0.20	0.75	—
1989 D	605,780	—	—	0.20	0.75	—
1990 D	31,934,675	—	—	0.10	0.20	—
1991 D	16,315,160	—	—	0.10	0.20	—

KM# 878 50 ORE

3.7000 g., Bronze, 18.7 mm. **Ruler:** Carl XVI Gustaf **Obv:** Value **Rev:** Three crowns and date **Edge:** Reeded

Date	Mintage	F	VF	XF	Unc	BU
1992 D	39,531,000	—	—	0.15	0.30	—
1992 B	39,531,000	—	—	0.15	0.40	—
1992 B	39,530,810	—	—	0.15	0.40	0.50
1993 B	643,520	—	—	0.20	0.65	0.85
1994 B	517,575	—	—	0.20	0.65	0.85
1995 B	486,538	—	—	0.10	0.20	0.35
1996 B	247,620	—	—	0.10	0.20	0.35
1997 B	69,995	—	—	0.10	0.20	0.35
1998 B	5,064,956	—	—	0.10	0.15	0.25
1999 B	22,076,128	—	—	0.10	0.15	0.25
2000 B	33,060,252	—	—	0.10	0.15	0.25
2001 B	30,120,532	—	—	0.10	0.15	0.25
2002 B	—	—	—	0.10	0.15	0.25
2003 B	—	—	—	0.10	0.15	0.25
2004 B	25,958,649	—	—	0.10	0.15	0.25
2005 B	—	—	—	0.10	0.15	0.25
2006 SI	—	—	—	0.10	0.15	0.25
2007 SI	—	—	—	0.10	0.15	0.25

KM# 760 KRONA

7.5000 g., 0.8000 Silver 0.1929 oz. ASW **Ruler:** Oscar II **Obv:** Head left **Obv. Legend:** OSCAR II SVERIGES... **Rev:** Crowned arms with supporters

Date	Mintage	F	VF	XF	Unc	BU
1901/898 EB	270,960	9.00	30.00	150	560	—
1901 EB	Inc. above	7.00	28.00	140	485	—
1903 EB	473,386	6.00	25.00	95.00	365	—
1904 EB	563,586	5.00	15.00	90.00	325	—

KM# 772 KRONA

7.5000 g., 0.8000 Silver 0.1929 oz. ASW **Ruler:** Oscar II **Obv:** Head left **Rev:** Crowned arms with supporters

Date	Mintage	F	VF	XF	Unc	BU
1906 EB	426,939	5.00	20.00	85.00	270	—
1907 EB	1,058,286	3.50	14.00	60.00	245	—

KM# 786.1 KRONA

7.5000 g., 0.8000 Silver 0.1929 oz. ASW **Ruler:** Gustaf V **Obv:** Head left **Rev:** Crowned arms within order chain

Date	Mintage	F	VF	XF	Unc	BU
1.9.1.0 W	643,065	3.25	12.50	45.00	175	—
1.9.1.2 W	303,420	7.00	22.50	110	420	—
1.9.1.3 W	353,051	3.50	12.50	42.50	190	—
1.9.1.4 W	622,217	3.25	11.50	40.00	180	—
1.9.1.5 W	1,415,956	3.00	7.00	25.00	145	—
1.9.1.6/5 W	1,139,245	4.00	13.50	55.00	230	—
1.9.1.6 W	Inc. above	3.25	11.50	40.00	190	—
1.9.1.8 W	258,091	3.25	8.50	30.00	200	—
1.9.2.3 W	746,277	3.00	8.00	27.50	135	—
1.9.2.4 W	2,066,155	BV	6.50	17.50	100	—

KM# 786.2 KRONA

7.5000 g., 0.8000 Silver 0.1929 oz. ASW **Ruler:** Gustaf V **Obv:** Head left **Rev:** Crowned arms within order chain

Date	Mintage	F	VF	XF	Unc	BU
1924 W	Inc. above	BV	4.50	22.50	90.00	—
1925 W	369,919	3.00	8.50	45.00	200	—
1926 W	465,467	3.00	7.50	28.00	135	—
1927 G	401,167	3.00	8.00	40.00	180	—
1928 G	739,189	BV	3.50	22.50	80.00	—
1929 G	1,345,647	BV	3.00	12.50	50.00	—
1930 G	1,743,783	—	BV	6.50	37.50	—
1931 G	1,007,523	—	BV	6.50	37.50	—
1932 G	1,035,877	—	BV	6.50	37.50	—
1933 G	1,044,634	—	BV	6.50	37.50	—
1934 G	585,673	—	3.00	12.50	60.00	—
1935 G	1,604,343	—	BV	3.00	12.50	—
1936 G	3,222,312	—	BV	3.00	10.00	—
1937 G	2,666,998	—	BV	3.00	10.00	—
1938 G	1,911,464	—	BV	3.00	10.00	—
1938 G Proof	—	Value: 25.00				
1939 G	7,589,316	—	BV	3.00	6.00	—
1940 G	6,917,460	—	BV	3.00	6.00	—
1941 G	Inc. above	—	BV	3.50	10.00	—
1941/4 G	2,183,338	BV	6.00	18.00	45.00	—
1942 G	240,000	20.00	40.00	90.00	345	—

KM# 814 KRONA

7.0000 g., 0.4000 Silver 0.0900 oz. ASW, 25 mm. **Ruler:** Gustaf V **Obv:** Head left **Rev:** Crowned arms within order chain divide value

Date	Mintage	F	VF	XF	Unc	BU
1942 G	5,644,990	—	BV	3.00	18.50	—
1943 G Plain 4	7,915,850	—	BV	3.00	18.50	—
1943 G Crosslet 4	Inc. above	—	BV	3.00	18.50	—
1944 G	7,423,463	—	BV	2.00	8.00	—
1945 G	7,359,360	—	BV	2.00	8.00	—
1945 TS	Inc. above	BV	1.50	2.75	15.00	—
1945 TS/G	Inc. above	BV	1.60	3.00	20.00	—
1946 TS	19,170,454	—	BV	1.75	6.00	—
1947 TS	9,124,335	—	BV	1.75	6.00	—
1948 TS	10,430,588	—	BV	1.75	6.00	—
1949 TS	7,981,162	—	BV	1.75	6.00	—
1950 TS	5,310,141	—	BV	1.75	8.00	—

KM# 826 KRONA

7.0000 g., 0.4000 Silver 0.0900 oz. ASW, 25 mm. **Ruler:** Gustaf VI **Obv:** Head left **Rev:** Crowned shield divides value

Date	Mintage	F	VF	XF	Unc	BU
1952 TS	1,101,625	—	BV	3.00	22.50	—
1953/2 TS	Inc. above	BV	1.50	4.50	20.00	—
1953 TS	3,305,843	—	BV	3.00	20.00	—
1954 TS	6,460,770	—	BV	3.00	15.00	—
1955 TS	4,140,904	—	BV	3.00	15.00	—
1956 TS	6,226,705	—	BV	3.00	8.00	—
1957 TS	3,544,268	—	BV	3.00	9.00	—
1958 TS	1,438,940	BV	1.50	4.50	20.00	—
1959 TS	1,187,000	1.50	2.75	7.50	35.00	—
1960 TS	4,085,250	—	BV	2.00	6.00	—
1961 TS	4,283,000	—	BV	2.00	6.00	—
1961 U	2,973,275	BV	1.50	3.00	20.00	—
1962 U	6,838,550	—	BV	2.00	6.00	—
1963 U	14,227,500	—	BV	1.50	3.50	—
1964 U	15,972,500	—	BV	1.50	3.00	—
1965 U	18,638,500	—	BV	1.50	3.00	—
1966 U	22,396,500	—	—	BV	2.25	—
1967 U	17,234,500	—	—	BV	2.25	—
1968 U	12,325,500	—	—	BV	2.25	—

KM# 826a KRONA

7.0000 g., Copper-Nickel Clad Copper, 25 mm. **Ruler:** Gustaf VI **Obv:** Head left **Rev:** Crowned shield divides value

Date	Mintage	F	VF	XF	Unc	BU
1968 U	5,177,000	—	0.30	1.00	3.50	—
1969 U	30,855,500	—	0.30	0.40	1.50	—
1970 U	25,314,500	—	0.30	0.40	1.50	—
1971 U	18,342,000	—	0.30	0.40	1.50	—
1972 U	21,941,000	—	0.30	0.40	1.50	—
1973 U	142,000,000	—	0.30	0.40	1.50	—

KM# 852 KRONA

7.0000 g., Copper-Nickel Clad Copper, 25 mm. **Ruler:** Carl XVI Gustaf **Obv:** Head left **Rev:** Three small crowns within crowned shield **Designer:** Lars Englund

Date	Mintage	F	VF	XF	Unc	BU
1976 U	4,320,811	—	0.30	0.50	1.25	—
1977 U	80,477,822	—	0.30	0.40	0.75	—
1978 U	81,407,892	—	0.30	0.40	0.75	—
1979 U	47,450,148	—	0.30	0.40	0.75	—
1980 U	51,694,323	—	0.30	0.40	0.75	—
1981 U	62,078,991	—	0.30	0.40	0.75	—

KM# 852a KRONA

7.0000 g., Copper-Nickel, 25 mm. **Ruler:** Carl XVI Gustaf **Obv:** Head left **Rev:** Three small crowns within crowned shield **Edge:** Reeded **Designer:** Lars Englund

Date	Mintage	F	VF	XF	Unc	BU
1982 U	24,836,789	—	—	0.30	0.65	—
1983 U	23,530,222	—	—	0.30	0.65	—
1984 U	37,811,592	—	—	0.30	0.65	—
1985 U	4,909,279	—	—	0.30	0.70	—
1986 U	901,095	—	—	0.50	1.25	—
1987 D	21,543,317	—	—	0.30	0.65	—
1988 D	30,341,842	—	—	0.30	0.45	—
1989 D	55,963,148	—	—	—	0.30	—
1990 D	54,469,545	—	—	—	0.30	—
1991 D	34,249,994	—	—	—	0.30	—
1992 B	16,770,810	—	—	—	0.30	—
1993 B	407,208	—	0.30	0.50	1.00	—
1994 B	567,137	—	0.30	0.50	1.00	—
1995 B	499,758	—	0.30	0.50	1.00	—
1996 B	323,656	—	—	1.00	2.00	—
1997 B	25,042,398	—	—	—	0.25	—
1998 B	39,747,941	—	—	—	0.25	—
1999 B	55,018,508	—	—	—	0.25	—
2000 B	104,213,074	—	—	—	0.25	—

KM# 897 KRONA

6.9800 g., Copper-Nickel, 24.9 mm. **Ruler:** Carl XVI Gustaf **Subject:** Millennium **Obv:** Head left **Rev:** Crowned monogram **Edge:** Reeded

Date	Mintage	F	VF	XF	Unc	BU
2000	2,978,113	—	—	—	2.00	3.00

KM# 894 KRONA

6.9800 g., Copper-Nickel, 24.9 mm. **Ruler:** Carl XVI Gustaf **Obv:** Head left **Rev:** Crown and value **Edge:** Reeded

Date	Mintage	F	VF	XF	Unc	BU
2001 B	23,905,454	—	—	—	0.65	1.00
2002 B	—	—	—	—	0.65	1.00
2003 B	—	—	—	—	0.65	1.00
2004 B	42,060,252	—	—	—	0.65	1.00
2005 B	—	—	—	—	0.65	1.00
2007 B	—	—	—	—	0.65	1.00

KM# 761 2 KRONOR

15.0000 g., 0.8000 Silver 0.3858 oz. ASW, 31 mm. **Ruler:** Oscar II **Obv:** Head left **Obv. Legend:** OSCAR II SVERIGES... **Rev:** Crowned arms with supporters

Date	Mintage	F	VF	XF	Unc	BU
1903 EB	64,308	25.00	85.00	240	865	—
1904 EB	175,029	12.00	40.00	145	465	—

KM# 773 2 KRONOR

15.0000 g., 0.8000 Silver 0.3858 oz. ASW, 31 mm. **Ruler:** Oscar II **Obv:** Head left **Rev:** Crowned arms with supporters

Date	Mintage	F	VF	XF	Unc	BU
1906 EB	112,468	9.00	22.50	90.00	320	—
1907 EB	300,573	6.50	18.50	75.00	320	—

KM# 776 2 KRONOR

15.0000 g., 0.8000 Silver 0.3858 oz. ASW, 31 mm. **Ruler:** Oscar II **Subject:** Golden Wedding Anniversary **Obv:** Busts of King Oscar II and Queen Sofia right **Rev:** Crowned arms within order chain **Edge:** Reeded **Designer:** Adolph Lindberg

Date	Mintage	F	VF	XF	Unc	BU
1907	251,000	BV	6.50	11.50	22.50	—

KM# 787 2 KRONOR

15.0000 g., 0.8000 Silver 0.3858 oz. ASW, 31 mm. **Ruler:** Gustaf V **Obv:** Head left **Rev:** Crowned arms within order chain

Date	Mintage	F	VF	XF	Unc	BU
1910 W Initial far from date	374,725	6.00	16.00	70.00	220	—
1910 W	Inc. above	37.50	100	365	900	—
1912 W	156,912	6.50	25.00	90.00	320	—
1913 W	304,616	BV	10.00	50.00	220	—
1914 W	191,905	6.00	13.50	68.00	240	—
1915 W	155,965	6.00	18.00	70.00	245	—
1922 W	201,821	BV	7.00	30.00	110	—
1924 W	199,314	BV	8.00	30.00	120	—
1926 W	221,577	BV	6.50	25.00	100	—
1928 G	160,319	BV	7.00	30.00	175	—
1929 G	184,458	BV	6.50	25.00	110	—
1930 G	178,387	BV	6.00	20.00	95.00	—
1931 G	210,576	—	BV	10.00	30.00	—
1934 G	273,419	—	BV	10.00	30.00	—
1935 G	211,059	—	BV	10.00	30.00	—
1936 G	491,296	—	BV	8.00	20.00	—
1937 G	129,760	—	BV	16.50	70.00	—
1937 G Proof	—	Value: 200				
1938 G	638,970	—	BV	7.00	18.00	—
1938 G Proof	—	Value: 30.00				
1939 G	1,200,329	—	BV	6.00	14.00	—
1939 G Proof	—	Value: 30.00				
1940 G	517,740	—	BV	7.00	15.00	—
1940 G Serif 4	Inc. above	BV	6.00	9.00	30.00	—

KM# 799 2 KRONOR

15.0000 g., 0.8000 Silver 0.3858 oz. ASW, 31 mm. **Ruler:** Gustaf V **Subject:** 400th Anniversary of Political Liberty **Obv:** Head right within decorative inner circle **Rev:** Crowned shield divides date within decorative inner circle **Designer:** Eric Lindberg

Date	Mintage	F	VF	XF	Unc	BU
1921 W	265,943	BV	6.00	8.50	20.00	—

KM# 805 2 KRONOR

15.0000 g., 0.8000 Silver 0.3858 oz. ASW, 31 mm. **Ruler:** Gustaf V **Subject:** 300th Anniversary - Death of Gustaf II Adolf **Obv:** Inscription within square with three small crowns within shield below **Rev:** Laureate bust right **Designer:** Eric Lindberg

Date	Mintage	F	VF	XF	Unc	BU
1932 G	253,770	BV	6.00	10.00	27.50	—

KM# 807 2 KRONOR
15.0000 g., 0.8000 Silver 0.3858 oz. ASW, 31 mm. **Ruler:** Gustaf V **Subject:** 300th Anniversary - Settlement of Delaware **Obv:** Head left **Rev:** The ship "Calmare Nyckel"

Date	Mintage	F	VF	XF	Unc	BU
ND(1938) G	508,815	BV	6.00	9.00	20.00	—

KM# 815 2 KRONOR
14.0000 g., 0.4000 Silver 0.1800 oz. ASW **Ruler:** Gustaf V **Obv:** Head left **Rev:** Crowned arms divides value

Date	Mintage	F	VF	XF	Unc	BU
1942 G	200,000	BV	3.75	6.50	32.50	—
1943 G	271,824	3.00	5.50	14.50	70.00	—
1944 G	627,200	BV	3.00	5.00	20.00	—
1945 G	969,675	BV	2.75	4.00	15.00	—
1945 G	Inc. above	6.50	13.50	28.00	90.00	—
Note: Without dots in motto						
1945 TS	Inc. above	BV	3.00	5.00	20.00	—
1945 TS/G	Inc. above	BV	3.50	7.00	27.50	—
1946 TS	978,000	—	BV	3.50	14.50	—
1947 TS	1,465,975	—	BV	3.50	14.50	—
1948 TS	281,660	BV	3.00	5.00	20.00	—
1949 TS	331,715	BV	3.00	5.00	20.00	—
1950/1 TS	3,727,465	—	BV	3.50	14.50	—
1950 TS	Inc. above	—	BV	3.50	8.50	—

KM# 827 2 KRONOR
14.0000 g., 0.4000 Silver 0.1800 oz. ASW **Ruler:** Gustaf VI **Obv:** Head left **Rev:** Crowned shield divides value

Date	Mintage	F	VF	XF	Unc	BU
1952 TS	315,325	BV	2.75	4.00	16.50	—
1953 TS	1,009,380	—	BV	3.00	8.00	—
1954 TS	2,300,835	—	BV	3.00	7.00	—
1955 TS	1,137,734	—	BV	3.50	9.00	—
1956 TS	1,709,468	—	BV	3.00	7.00	—
1957 TS	688,900	—	BV	3.50	15.00	—
1958 TS	1,104,555	—	BV	3.00	7.00	—
1959 TS	581,330	—	BV	3.50	15.00	—
1961 TS	533,220	—	BV	3.00	13.50	—
1963 U	1,468,750	—	—	BV	5.00	—
1964 U	1,212,750	—	—	BV	4.50	—
1965 U	1,189,500	—	—	BV	4.50	—
1966 U	989,250	—	—	BV	5.00	—

KM# 827a 2 KRONOR
Copper-Nickel **Ruler:** Gustaf VI **Obv:** Head left **Rev:** Crowned shield divides value

Date	Mintage	F	VF	XF	Unc	BU
1968 U	1,170,750	0.45	0.55	1.25	4.00	—
1969 U	1,148,250	0.45	0.55	0.70	2.25	—
1970 U	1,159,000	0.45	0.55	0.70	2.25	—
1971 U	1,213,250	0.45	0.55	0.85	2.75	—

KM# 766 5 KRONOR
2.2402 g., 0.9000 Gold 0.0648 oz. AGW **Ruler:** Oscar II **Obv:** Head right **Rev:** Value and crowns within wreath

Date	Mintage	F	VF	XF	Unc	BU
1901 EB	109,186	BV	60.00	75.00	100	—

KM# 797 5 KRONOR
2.2402 g., 0.9000 Gold 0.0648 oz. AGW **Ruler:** Gustaf V **Obv:** Head right **Rev:** Value and crowns above sprigs

Date	Mintage	F	VF	XF	Unc	BU
1920 W	103,000	BV	60.00	75.00	100	—

KM# 806 5 KRONOR
25.0000 g., 0.9000 Silver 0.7234 oz. ASW, 36 mm. **Ruler:** Gustaf V **Subject:** 500th Anniversary of Riksdag **Obv:** Head left **Rev:** Three small crowns within shield in center of cross design **Designer:** Eric Lindberg

Date	Mintage	F	VF	XF	Unc	BU
ND(1935) G	663,819	BV	11.50	14.50	22.50	—

KM# 828 5 KRONOR
22.7000 g., 0.4000 Silver 0.2919 oz. ASW, 36 mm. **Ruler:** Gustaf VI **Subject:** 70th Birthday of Gustaf VI Adolf **Obv:** Head left **Rev:** Crowned monogram divides value **Edge:** Plain **Designer:** Leo Holmgren

Date	Mintage	F	VF	XF	Unc	BU
ND(1952) TS	219,237	4.50	7.50	13.50	30.00	—

KM# 829 5 KRONOR
18.0000 g., 0.4000 Silver 0.2315 oz. ASW, 34 mm. **Ruler:** Gustaf VI **Obv:** Head left **Rev:** Crowned shield divides value **Edge Lettering:** PLIKTEN FRAMFOR ALLT **Note:** Regular issue.

Date	Mintage	F	VF	XF	Unc	BU
1954 TS	1,510,316	—	BV	3.75	7.00	—
1955 TS	3,568,985	—	BV	3.50	6.00	—
1971 U	712,500	—	BV	3.50	6.00	—

KM# 830 5 KRONOR
18.0000 g., 0.4000 Silver 0.2315 oz. ASW, 34 mm. **Ruler:** Gustaf VI **Subject:** Constitution Sesquicentennial **Obv:** Head left **Rev:** Standing figures with hats facing **Designer:** Leo Holmgren

Date	Mintage	F	VF	XF	Unc	BU
1959 TS	504,150	—	BV	4.50	8.50	—

KM# 838 5 KRONOR
18.0000 g., 0.4000 Silver 0.2315 oz. ASW, 34 mm. **Ruler:** Gustaf VI **Subject:** 80th Birthday of Gustaf VI Adolf **Obv:** Head left **Rev:** Pallas Athena left holding shield and owl

Date	Mintage	F	VF	XF	Unc	BU
ND(1962) U	256,000	4.00	7.50	13.50	35.00	—

Note: An additional 96,525 melted

KM# 839 5 KRONOR
18.0000 g., 0.4000 Silver 0.2315 oz. ASW, 34 mm. **Ruler:** Gustaf VI **Subject:** 100th Anniversary of Constitution Reform **Obv:** Head left **Rev:** Inscription within square flanked by sprigs **Edge:** Horizontal wavy lines **Designer:** Leo Holmgren

Date	Mintage	F	VF	XF	Unc	BU
1966 U	1,023,500	—	BV	3.50	6.00	—

KM# 846 5 KRONOR
Copper-Nickel Clad Nickel **Ruler:** Gustaf VI **Obv:** Head left **Rev:** Crowned shield divides value

Date	Mintage	F	VF	XF	Unc	BU
1972 U	21,736,000	—	—	1.25	2.00	—
1973 U	1,139,000	—	1.25	1.50	2.75	—

KM# 853 5 KRONOR
9.5000 g., Copper-Nickel, 28.5 mm. **Ruler:** Carl XVI Gustaf **Obv:** Crowned monogram **Rev:** Value **Designer:** Lars Englund

Date	Mintage	F	VF	XF	Unc	BU
1976 U	2,252,923	—	—	1.00	1.75	—
1977 U	3,985,381	—	—	1.00	1.75	—
1978 U	3,952,352	—	—	1.00	1.75	—
1979 U	3,164,051	—	—	1.00	1.75	—
1980 U	2,221,846	—	—	1.00	1.75	—
1981 U	5,507,222	—	—	1.00	1.75	—
1982 U	36,603,696	—	—	0.75	1.25	—
1983 U	31,364,320	—	—	0.85	1.50	—
1984 U	27,689,251	—	—	0.85	1.50	—
1985 U	10,603,060	—	—	0.75	1.25	—
1986 U	714,132	—	—	1.25	4.00	—
1987 D	15,117,317	—	—	0.75	1.25	—
1988 D	18,643,957	—	—	0.85	1.50	—
1989 D	960,667	—	—	1.25	3.50	—
1990 D	10,557,882	—	—	0.75	1.25	—
1991 D	15,792,139	—	—	0.75	1.25	—
1991 U	Est. 25,000	16.50	27.50	55.00	110	—
1992 D	5,350,810	—	—	1.00	1.50	—

KM# 853a 5 KRONOR
9.6000 g., Copper-Nickel Clad Nickel, 28.5 mm. **Ruler:** Carl XVI Gustaf **Obv:** Crowned monogram **Rev:** Value

Date	Mintage	F	VF	XF	Unc	BU
1993 B	274,932	—	—	—	1.75	2.00
1994 B	173,438	—	—	—	2.00	2.25
1995 B	186,687	—	—	—	1.00	1.25
1996 B	180,405	—	—	—	1.00	1.25
1997 B	174,455	—	—	—	1.00	1.25
1998 B	84,991	—	—	—	1.00	1.25
1999 B	96,035	—	—	—	1.00	1.25
2000 B	3,851,326	—	—	—	1.00	1.25
2001 B	6,001,481	—	—	—	1.00	1.25
2002 B	—	—	—	—	1.00	1.25
2003 B	—	—	—	—	1.00	1.25
2004 B	6,732,730	—	—	—	1.00	1.25

KM# 885 5 KRONOR
Copper-Nickel Clad Nickel, 28.5 mm. **Ruler:** Carl XVI Gustaf **Subject:** 50th Anniversary - United Nations **Obv:** Crowned monogram **Rev:** Numeral 50 and UN emblem

Date	Mintage	F	VF	XF	Unc	BU
ND(1995) B	300,000	—	—	1.00	3.50	4.50

KM# 767 10 KRONOR
4.4803 g., 0.9000 Gold 0.1296 oz. AGW **Ruler:** Oscar II **Obv:** Large head right **Rev:** Crowned and mantled arms

Date	Mintage	F	VF	XF	Unc	BU
1901 EB	213,286	—	BV	120	135	—
1901 EB Proof	Inc. above	Value: 525				

KM# 847 10 KRONOR
18.0000 g., 0.8300 Silver 0.4803 oz. ASW, 32 mm. **Ruler:** Gustaf VI **Subject:** 90th Birthday of Gustaf VI Adolf **Obv:** Head left **Rev:** Inscription and value

Date	Mintage	F	VF	XF	Unc	BU
1972 U	2,000,000	—	BV	7.50	9.50	—

Note: 652,907 were returned to the mint.

KM# 877 10 KRONOR
6.6700 g., Copper-Aluminum-Zinc, 20.46 mm. **Ruler:** Carl XVI Gustaf **Obv:** Head left **Rev:** Three crowns within value

Date	Mintage	F	VF	XF	Unc	BU
1991 D Medal	106,548,000	—	—	2.00	3.00	—
1991 D Coin	Inc. above	20.00	30.00	40.00	60.00	—
1992 D	42,506,792	—	—	—	1.75	—
1993 B	20,107,110	—	—	—	1.75	—
1994 B	573,243	—	—	—	2.00	—
1995 B	523,685	—	—	—	2.00	—
1996 B	295,053	—	—	—	2.00	—
1997 B	332,450	—	—	—	2.00	—
1998 B	332,000	—	—	—	2.00	—
1999 B	81,430	—	—	—	2.00	—
2000 B	8,520,983	—	—	—	1.75	—

KM# 895 10 KRONOR
6.5700 g., Copper-Aluminum-Zinc, 20.4 mm. **Ruler:** Carl XVI Gustaf **Obv:** Head left **Rev:** Three crowns and value **Edge:** Reeded and plain sections

Date	Mintage	F	VF	XF	Unc	BU
2001 B	4,171,757	—	—	—	1.75	2.00
2002 B	—	—	—	—	1.75	2.00
2003 B	—	—	—	—	1.75	2.00
2004 B	9,045,581	—	—	—	1.75	2.00
2005 B	—	—	—	—	1.75	2.00

KM# 765 20 KRONOR
8.9606 g., 0.9000 Gold 0.2593 oz. AGW **Ruler:** Oscar II **Obv:** Head right **Obv. Legend:** OSCAR II SVERIGES... **Rev:** Crowned and mantled arms

Date	Mintage	F	VF	XF	Unc	BU
1901 EB	226,679	—	BV	235	250	—
1902 EB	113,810	—	BV	245	275	—

KM# 800 20 KRONOR
8.9606 g., 0.9000 Gold 0.2593 oz. AGW **Ruler:** Gustaf V **Obv:** Head right **Rev:** Crowned arms within order chain divide value

Date	Mintage	F	VF	XF	Unc	BU
1925 W	387,257	245	325	465	765	—

The Swiss Confederation, located in central Europe north of Italy and south of Germany, has an area of 15,941 sq. mi. (41,290 sq. km.) and a population of *6.6 million. Capital: Bern. The economy centers about a well developed manufacturing industry. Machinery, chemicals, watches and clocks, and textiles are exported.

Switzerland, the habitat of lake dwellers in prehistoric times, was peopled by the Celtic Helvetians when Julius Caesar made it a part of the Roman Empire in 58 B.C. After the decline of Rome, Switzerland was invaded by Teutonic tribes, who established small temporal holdings which in the Middle Ages, became a federation of fiefs of the Holy Roman Empire. As a nation, Switzerland originated in 1291 when the districts of Nidwalden, Schwyz and Uri united to defeat Austria and attain independence as the Swiss Confederation. After acquiring new cantons in the 14th century, Switzerland was made independent from the Holy Roman Empire by the 1648 Treaty of Westphalia. The revolutionary armies of Napoleonic France occupied Switzerland and set up the Helvetian Republic, 1798-1803. After the fall of Napoleon, the Congress of Vienna, 1815, recognized the independence of Switzerland and guaranteed its neutrality. The Swiss Constitutions of 1848 and 1874 established a union modeled upon that of the United States.

MINT MARKS

B - Bern
BA - Basel
BB - Strasbourg
S – Solothurn

NOTE: The coinage of Switzerland has been struck at the Bern Mint since 1853 with but a few exceptions. All coins minted there carry a B mint mark through 1969, except for the 2-Centime and 2-Franc values where the mint mark was discontinued after 1968. In 1968 and 1969 some issues were struck at both Bern (B) and in London (no mint mark).

NOTE: The Swiss Shooting Fest coins, KM#S18-S68 previously listed here are actually medallic issues without legal tender status and as such are now listed in ***Unusual World Coins, 4th Edition***, by Krause Publications.

CONFEDERATION

Confoederatio Helvetica

MONETARY SYSTEM
100 Rappen (Centimes) = 1 Franc

DECIMAL COINAGE

KM# 3.2 RAPPEN
1.5000 g., Bronze, 16 mm. **Obv:** Thin cross in shield within sprigs **Rev:** Value within wreath

Date	Mintage	F	VF	XF	Unc	BU
1902B	950,000	35.00	65.00	100	150	350
1903B	1,000,000	22.00	35.00	55.00	85.00	180
1904B	1,000,000	22.00	35.00	60.00	85.00	160
1905B	2,000,000	5.00	13.00	19.00	30.00	40.00
1906B	1,000,000	16.00	30.00	45.00	60.00	110
1907B	2,000,000	5.00	9.00	12.50	30.00	45.00
1908B	3,000,000	4.50	7.50	12.50	18.00	27.00
1909B	1,000,000	12.50	20.00	30.00	45.00	70.00
1910B	1,500,000	9.00	15.00	22.00	30.00	40.00
1911B	1,500,000	9.00	15.00	22.00	30.00	40.00
1912B	2,000,000	4.00	8.50	12.50	20.00	30.00
1913B	3,000,000	1.25	4.00	6.00	9.00	15.00
1914B	3,500,000	1.75	4.50	9.50	22.00	35.00
1915B	3,000,000	2.50	6.00	11.00	30.00	45.00
1917B	2,000,000	3.50	8.50	16.00	28.00	40.00
1918B	3,000,000	1.50	3.00	5.00	13.00	30.00
1919B	3,000,000	1.50	3.50	6.00	13.00	30.00
1920B	1,000,000	3.00	8.00	13.00	18.00	30.00
1921B	3,000,000	1.50	4.00	5.50	18.00	27.00
1924B	2,000,000	3.00	8.00	18.00	22.00	28.00
1925/4B	2,500,000	2.50	6.00	12.00	25.00	35.00
1925B	Inc. above	2.00	4.50	9.00	13.00	22.00
1926B	2,000,000	2.00	4.50	9.00	18.00	30.00
1927B	1,500,000	4.00	9.00	13.00	17.00	30.00
1928B	2,000,000	2.00	5.00	7.50	13.00	25.00
1929B	4,000,000	0.55	1.25	2.00	7.50	15.00
1930B	2,500,000	1.75	3.50	6.50	10.00	25.00
1931B	5,000,000	0.55	1.00	1.50	6.50	12.50
1932B	5,000,000	0.55	1.00	1.50	6.50	12.50
1933B	3,000,000	0.75	1.50	3.00	9.00	18.00
1934B	3,000,000	0.75	1.50	2.50	9.00	18.00
1936B	2,000,000	1.50	3.50	9.00	13.00	25.00
1937B	2,400,000	0.75	1.50	2.50	6.50	9.00
1938B	5,300,000	0.75	1.50	2.50	6.50	9.00
1939B	10,000	18.00	45.00	50.00	75.00	100
1940B	3,027,000	1.50	4.50	5.00	13.50	22.00
1941B	12,794,000	—	0.50	1.00	5.00	7.00

KM# 3a RAPPEN
Zinc, 16 mm. **Obv:** Cross in shield **Rev:** Value within wreath

Date	Mintage	F	VF	XF	Unc	BU
1942B	17,969,000	—	0.50	1.50	9.50	16.00
1943B	8,647,000	0.55	1.25	3.00	9.50	19.00
1944B	11,825,000	—	0.50	2.50	9.50	16.00
1945B	2,800,000	4.00	9.50	12.00	25.00	45.00
1946B	12,063,000	—	0.50	1.50	6.50	12.50

KM# 46 RAPPEN
1.5400 g., Bronze, 15.95 mm. **Obv:** Cross **Rev:** Value and oat sprig **Edge:** Plain

Date	Mintage	F	VF	XF	Unc	BU
1948B	10,500,000	—	0.25	0.35	3.00	11.00
1949B	11,100,000	—	0.25	0.35	3.00	11.00
1950B	3,610,000	—	1.25	2.50	5.00	13.00
1951B	22,624,000	—	0.20	0.30	3.00	11.00
1952B	11,520,000	—	0.20	0.30	3.00	11.00
1953B	5,947,000	—	0.25	0.60	3.00	11.00
1954B	5,175,000	—	0.25	0.60	3.00	11.00
1955B	5,282,000	—	0.55	1.00	3.00	11.00
1956B	4,960,000	—	0.25	0.60	3.00	8.50
1957B	15,226,000	—	0.10	0.25	1.00	4.00
1958B	20,142,000	—	0.10	0.25	1.00	4.00
1959B	5,582,000	—	0.20	0.35	1.25	4.50
1962B	5,010,000	—	0.20	0.35	1.25	4.50
1963B	15,920,000	—	—	0.15	0.90	1.25
1966B	5,030,000	—	—	0.20	0.90	1.25

Date	Mintage	F	VF	XF	Unc	BU
1967B	3,020,000	—	—	0.30	0.90	1.25
1968B	4,920,000	—	—	0.20	0.50	1.00
1969B	4,810,000	—	—	0.20	0.50	1.00
1970	7,810,000	—	—	0.10	0.50	1.00
1971	5,030,000	—	—	0.10	0.50	1.00
1973	3,000,000	—	—	0.10	0.50	1.00
1974	3,007,000	—	—	0.10	0.50	1.00
1974 Proof	2,400	Value: 35.00				
1975	3,010,000	—	—	0.10	0.50	1.00
1975 Proof	10,000	Value: 2.50				
1976	3,005,000	—	—	0.10	0.50	1.00
1976 Proof	5,130	Value: 3.00				
1977	2,007,000	—	—	0.10	0.50	1.00
1977 Proof	7,030	Value: 3.00				
1978	2,010,000	—	—	0.10	0.50	1.00
1978 Proof	10,000	Value: 2.50				
1979	1,025,000	—	—	0.10	0.50	1.00
1979 Proof	10,000	Value: 2.50				
1980	1,030,000	—	—	0.10	0.50	1.00
1980 Proof	10,000	Value: 2.50				
1981	4,935,000	—	—	0.10	0.50	1.00
1981 Proof	10,000	Value: 2.50				
1982	6,655,000	—	—	0.10	0.50	1.00
1982 Proof	10,000	Value: 2.50				
1983	4,031,000	—	—	0.10	0.50	1.00
1983 Proof	11,000	Value: 2.50				
1984	3,995,000	—	—	0.10	0.50	1.00
1984 Proof	14,000	Value: 2.50				
1985	3,027,000	—	—	0.10	0.50	1.00
1985 Proof	12,000	Value: 2.50				
1986B	2,031,000	—	—	0.10	0.50	1.00
1986B Proof	10,000	Value: 2.50				
1987B	1,028,000	—	—	0.10	0.50	1.00
1987B Proof	8,800	Value: 3.00				
1988B	2,029,000	—	—	0.10	0.50	1.00
1988B Proof	9,000	Value: 3.00				
1989B	2,031,000	—	—	0.10	0.50	1.00
1989B Proof	8,800	Value: 3.00				
1990B	1,032,000	—	—	—	0.50	1.00
1990B Proof	8,900	Value: 3.00				
1991B	536,000	—	—	—	1.50	2.50
1991B Proof	9,900	Value: 3.00				
1992B	528,000	—	—	—	1.50	2.50
1992B Proof	7,450	Value: 3.00				
1993B	523,000	—	—	—	1.50	2.50
1993B Proof	6,200	Value: 3.00				
1994B	2,023,000	—	—	—	0.50	1.00
1994B Proof	6,100	Value: 3.00				
1995B	6,024,000	—	—	—	0.50	1.00
1995B Proof	6,100	Value: 3.00				
1996B	1,023,000	—	—	—	0.50	1.00
1996B Proof	6,100	Value: 3.00				
1997B	1,022,000	—	—	—	0.50	1.00
1997B Proof	5,500	Value: 3.00				
1998B	1,021,000	—	—	—	0.50	1.00
1998B Proof	4,800	Value: 3.00				
1999B	1,021,000	—	—	—	0.50	1.00
1999B Proof	5,000	Value: 3.00				
2000B	1,026,000	—	—	—	0.50	1.00
2000B Proof	5,500	Value: 3.00				
2001B Proof	6,000	Value: 2.00				
2001B	1,522,000	—	—	—	0.50	1.00
2002B Proof	5,500	Value: 2.00				
2002B	2,024,000	—	—	—	0.50	1.00
2003B	1,522,000	—	—	—	0.50	1.00
2003B Proof	5,500	Value: 2.00				
2004B Proof	5,000	Value: 2.00				
2004B	1,526,000	—	—	—	0.50	1.00
2005B	1,524,000	—	—	—	0.50	1.00
2005B Proof	4,500	Value: 2.00				
2006B	26,000	—	—	—	—	135
Note: In sets only, circulatin strikes not released						
2006B Proof	4,000	Value: 175				

KM# 4.2 2 RAPPEN

3.0000 g., Bronze, 20 mm. **Obv:** Cross in shield within sprigs **Rev:** Value within wreath

Date	Mintage	F	VF	XF	Unc	BU
1902B	500,000	21.00	45.00	75.00	125	250
1903B	500,000	18.00	35.00	60.00	100	150
1904B	500,000	16.00	35.00	45.00	60.00	125
1906B	500,000	16.00	35.00	45.00	65.00	150
1907B	1,000,000	2.50	12.00	16.00	22.00	45.00
1908B	1,000,000	2.50	9.50	15.00	22.00	35.00
1909B	1,000,000	2.50	6.00	13.00	18.00	32.00
1910B	500,000	18.00	35.00	50.00	70.00	100
1912B	1,000,000	6.50	11.00	19.00	23.00	35.00
1913B	1,000,000	6.50	16.00	21.00	45.00	70.00
1914B	1,000,000	6.50	16.00	21.00	28.00	65.00
1915B	1,000,000	5.00	12.50	19.00	25.00	45.00
1918B	1,000,000	5.00	9.50	12.00	14.00	25.00
1919B	2,000,000	1.75	3.50	5.00	13.00	20.00
1920B	500,000	23.00	45.00	65.00	75.00	145

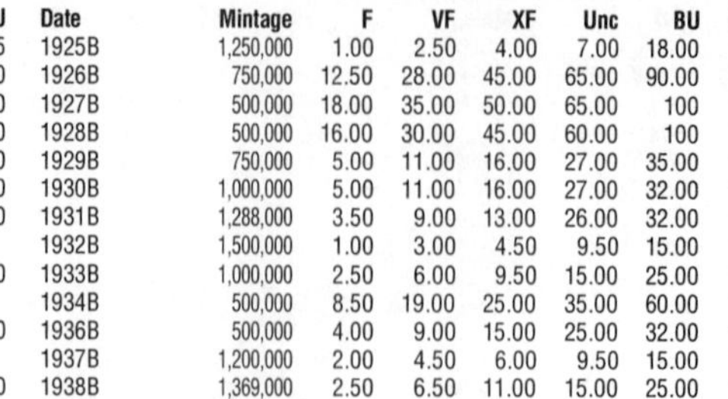

Date	Mintage	F	VF	XF	Unc	BU
1925B	1,250,000	1.00	2.50	4.00	7.00	18.00
1926B	750,000	12.50	28.00	45.00	65.00	90.00
1927B	500,000	18.00	35.00	50.00	65.00	100
1928B	500,000	16.00	30.00	45.00	60.00	100
1929B	750,000	5.00	11.00	16.00	27.00	35.00
1930B	1,000,000	5.00	11.00	16.00	27.00	32.00
1931B	1,288,000	3.50	9.00	13.00	26.00	32.00
1932B	1,500,000	1.00	3.00	4.50	9.50	15.00
1933B	1,000,000	2.50	6.00	9.50	15.00	25.00
1934B	500,000	8.50	19.00	25.00	35.00	60.00
1936B	500,000	4.00	9.00	15.00	25.00	32.00
1937B	1,200,000	2.00	4.50	6.00	9.50	15.00
1938B	1,369,000	2.50	6.50	11.00	15.00	25.00
1941B	3,448,000	—	1.00	1.50	2.50	6.50

KM# 4.2a 2 RAPPEN

2.4000 g., Zinc, 20 mm. **Obv:** Cross on shield within sprigs **Rev:** Value within wreath

Date	Mintage	F	VF	XF	Unc	BU
1942B	8,954,000	—	0.75	1.50	7.00	15.00
1943B	4,499,000	—	2.50	6.00	16.00	30.00
1944B	8,086,000	—	0.75	1.50	7.00	15.00
1945B	3,640,000	2.00	4.00	10.00	20.00	40.00
1946B	1,393,000	7.50	22.00	30.00	40.00	65.00

KM# 47 2 RAPPEN

3.0200 g., Bronze, 20 mm. **Obv:** Cross **Rev:** Value and oat sprig

Date	Mintage	F	VF	XF	Unc	BU
1948B	10,197,000	—	0.25	0.50	5.00	11.00
1951B	9,622,000	—	0.25	0.50	5.00	11.00
1952B	1,916,000	—	0.50	1.75	7.00	17.00
1953B	2,007,000	—	0.50	1.75	5.00	14.00
1954B	2,539,000	—	0.50	1.00	4.50	9.00
1955B	2,493,000	—	0.25	1.00	4.50	9.00
1957B	8,099,000	—	0.10	0.25	2.50	5.50
1958B	6,078,000	—	0.10	0.25	2.50	5.50
1963B	10,065,000	—	0.10	0.25	1.50	2.50
1966B	2,510,000	—	0.10	0.25	1.50	2.00
1967B	1,510,000	—	0.20	0.95	1.50	2.25
1968B	2,865,000	—	0.10	0.25	0.75	1.50
1969	6,200,000	—	0.10	0.20	0.50	1.00
1970	3,115,000	—	0.10	0.20	0.50	1.00
1974	3,540,000	—	0.10	0.20	0.50	1.00
1974 Proof	2,400	Value: 50.00				

KM# 26 5 RAPPEN

2.0000 g., Copper-Nickel, 17.1 mm. **Obv:** Crowned head right **Obv. Legend:** CONFOEDERATIO HELVETICA **Rev:** Value within wreath **Edge:** Plain

Date	Mintage	F	VF	XF	Unc	BU
1901B	3,000,000	0.50	3.00	5.00	25.00	75.00
1902B	1,000,000	7.50	10.00	40.00	75.00	225
1902B	Inc. above	9.00	12.00	45.00	100	250
Note: "T" over "L" in HELVETICA						
1902B	Inc. above	7.50	10.00	45.00	100	225
Note: "I" over tilted "I" in Helvetica						
1903B	2,000,000	1.00	2.50	12.00	65.00	150
1904B	1,000,000	4.00	10.00	28.00	110	250
1905B	1,000,000	3.00	7.00	12.00	60.00	150
1906B	3,000,000	0.50	2.50	9.50	20.00	40.00
1907B	5,000,000	0.50	2.50	6.00	13.00	25.00
1908B	3,000,000	0.50	2.50	6.00	13.00	30.00
1909B	2,000,000	0.50	2.50	6.00	15.00	35.00
1910B	1,000,000	2.00	5.00	10.00	50.00	90.00
1911B	2,000,000	0.50	1.00	3.00	13.00	30.00
1912B	3,000,000	0.50	1.00	3.00	13.00	30.00
1913B	3,000,000	0.50	1.00	3.00	13.00	30.00
1914B	3,000,000	0.50	1.00	7.00	75.00	200
1915B	3,000,000	0.50	1.00	12.50	110	350
1917B	1,000,000	1.50	2.50	10.00	100	300
1919B	6,000,000	—	0.50	2.50	23.00	40.00
1920B	5,000,000	—	0.50	2.50	13.00	30.00
1921B	3,000,000	—	0.50	2.50	13.00	30.00
1922B	4,000,000	—	0.50	1.75	12.00	22.00
1925B	3,000,000	—	0.50	2.00	13.00	25.00
1926B	3,000,000	—	0.50	2.00	13.00	25.00
1927B	2,000,000	—	0.50	4.50	14.00	35.00
1928B	2,000,000	—	0.50	2.50	13.00	30.00
1929B	2,000,000	—	0.50	1.75	13.00	30.00
1930B	3,000,000	—	0.50	1.75	13.00	30.00
1931B	5,037,000	—	0.50	1.75	13.00	20.00
1940B	1,416,000	—	0.50	5.00	50.00	225
1942B	5,078,000	—	0.25	0.50	12.50	26.00
1943B	6,591,000	—	0.25	0.50	12.00	26.00
1944B	9,981,000	—	0.25	0.50	12.50	26.00
1945B	985,000	—	1.00	12.00	100	325
1946B	6,179,000	—	0.25	0.50	12.50	25.00
1947B	5,125,000	—	0.25	0.50	12.50	25.00
1948B	4,710,000	—	0.25	0.50	7.00	9.50
1949B	4,589,000	—	0.25	0.50	5.00	7.00
1950B	920,000	—	0.50	1.50	6.00	8.50
1951B	2,141,000	—	0.50	2.50	40.00	70.00
1952B	4,690,000	—	0.20	0.35	3.50	8.00
1953B	9,131,000	—	0.20	0.35	3.00	8.00
1954B	8,038,000	—	0.20	0.35	6.00	16.00
1955B	19,943,000	—	0.20	0.30	2.25	11.00
1957B	10,147,000	—	0.20	0.30	2.25	11.00
1958B	10,217,000	—	0.20	0.30	2.25	11.00
1959B	11,085,000	—	0.20	0.30	2.25	11.00
1962B	23,840,000	—	0.10	0.20	0.90	7.50
1963B	29,730,000	—	0.10	0.20	0.50	4.00
1964B	17,080,000	—	0.10	0.20	0.50	3.50
1965B	1,430,000	—	0.25	1.00	1.50	3.00
1966B	10,010,000	—	—	0.15	0.50	1.00
1967B	13,010,000	—	—	0.55	1.25	1.75
1968B	10,020,000	—	—	0.15	0.50	1.00
1969B	32,990,000	—	—	0.10	0.50	1.00
1970	34,800,000	—	—	0.10	0.50	1.00
1971	40,020,000	—	—	0.10	0.50	1.00
1974	30,002,000	—	—	0.10	0.50	1.00
1974 Proof	2,400	Value: 35.00				
1975	34,005,000	—	—	0.10	0.50	1.00
1975 Proof	10,000	Value: 3.00				
1976	12,005,000	—	—	0.10	0.50	1.00
1976 Proof	5,130	Value: 4.00				
1977	14,012,000	—	—	0.10	0.50	1.00
1977 Proof	7,030	Value: 4.00				
1978	16,415,000	—	—	0.10	0.50	1.00
1978 Proof	10,000	Value: 3.00				
1979	27,010,000	—	—	0.10	0.50	1.00
1979 Proof	10,000	Value: 3.00				
1980	15,500,000	—	—	0.10	0.50	1.00
1980 Proof	10,000	Value: 3.00				

KM# 26a 5 RAPPEN

Brass, 17.1 mm. **Obv:** Crowned head right **Rev:** Value within wreath

Date	Mintage	F	VF	XF	Unc	BU
1918B	6,000,000	4.00	7.00	20.00	25.00	30.00

KM# 26b 5 RAPPEN

Nickel, 17.1 mm. **Obv:** Crowned head right **Rev:** Value within wreath **Edge:** Plain **Note:** Retired legal tender status as of January 1, 2004, removed from circulation.

Date	Mintage	F	VF	XF	Unc	BU
1932B	6,000,000	—	0.50	1.50	7.00	15.00
1933B	3,000,000	—	0.50	1.50	7.50	30.00
1934B	4,000,000	—	0.50	1.50	7.00	40.00
1936B	1,000,000	—	0.75	2.50	8.50	30.00
1937B	2,000,000	—	0.50	1.00	10.00	28.00
1938B	1,000,000	—	0.50	1.50	9.00	30.00
1939B	10,048,000	—	0.50	1.00	7.00	18.00
1941B	3,087,000	—	1.75	5.00	60.00	90.00

KM# 26c 5 RAPPEN

2.0000 g., Aluminum-Brass, 17.1 mm. **Obv:** Crowned head right **Rev:** Value within wreath **Edge:** Plain

Date	Mintage	F	VF	XF	Unc	BU
1981	79,020,000	—	—	—	0.50	1.00
1981 Proof	10,000	Value: 3.00				
1982	75,340,000	—	—	—	0.50	1.00
1982 Proof	10,000	Value: 3.00				
1983	92,746,000	—	—	—	0.50	1.00
1983 Proof	11,000	Value: 3.00				
1984	69,960,000	—	—	—	0.50	1.00
1984 Proof	14,000	Value: 3.00				
1985	60,032,000	—	—	—	0.50	1.00
1985 Proof	12,000	Value: 3.00				
1986B	55,041,000	—	—	—	0.50	1.00
1986B Proof	10,000	Value: 3.00				
1987B	39,828,000	—	—	—	0.50	1.00
1987B Proof	8,800	Value: 4.00				
1988B	55,044,000	—	—	—	0.50	1.00
1988B Proof	9,000	Value: 4.00				
1989B	45,031,000	—	—	—	0.50	1.00
1989B Proof	8,800	Value: 4.00				
1990B	16,042,000	—	—	—	0.50	1.00
1990B Proof	8,900	Value: 4.00				
1991B	35,036,000	—	—	—	0.50	1.00
1991B Proof	9,900	Value: 3.00				
1992B	35,028,000	—	—	—	0.50	1.00
1992B Proof	7,450	Value: 4.00				
1993B	38,023,000	—	—	—	0.50	1.00
1993B Proof	6,200	Value: 4.00				
1994B	35,023,000	—	—	—	0.50	1.00

Date	Mintage	F	VF	XF	Unc	BU
1994B Proof	6,100	Value: 4.00				
1995B	20,024,000	—	—	—	0.50	1.00
1995B Proof	6,100	Value: 4.00				
1996B	25,023,000	—	—	—	0.50	1.00
1996B Proof	6,100	Value: 4.00				
1997B	25,022,000	—	—	—	0.50	1.00
1997B Proof	5,500	Value: 4.00				
1998B	10,021,000	—	—	—	0.50	1.00
1998B Proof	4,800	Value: 4.00				
1999B	8,021,000	—	—	—	0.50	1.00
1999B Proof	5,000	Value: 4.00				
2000B	5,026,000	—	—	—	0.50	1.00
2000B Proof	5,500	Value: 4.00				
2001B	5,022,000	—	—	—	0.50	1.00
2001B Proof	6,000	Value: 2.00				
2002B	12,024,000	—	—	—	0.50	1.00
2002B Proof	6,000	Value: 2.00				
2003B	10,022,000	—	—	—	0.50	1.00
2003B Proof	5,500	Value: 2.00				
2004B	10,026,000	—	—	—	0.50	1.00
2004B Proof	5,000	Value: 2.00				
2005B	13,024,000	—	—	—	0.50	1.00
2005B Proof	4,500	Value: 2.00				
2006B	12,026,000	—	—	—	0.50	1.00
2006B Proof	4,000	Value: 2.00				
2007B	13,024,000	—	—	—	0.50	1.00
2007B Proof	4,000	Value: 2.00				

KM# 27 10 RAPPEN

3.0000 g., Copper-Nickel, 19.1 mm. **Obv:** Crowned head right **Obv. Legend:** CONFOEDERATIO HELVETICA **Rev:** Value within wreath **Edge:** Plain

Date	Mintage	F	VF	XF	Unc	BU
1901B	1,000,000	1.50	6.50	19.00	65.00	175
1902B	1,000,000	1.50	6.50	12.00	60.00	125
1903B	1,000,000	1.50	6.50	10.00	90.00	200
1904B	1,000,000	1.50	5.00	26.00	140	450
1906B	1,000,000	1.50	5.00	10.00	40.00	125
1907B	2,000,000	1.00	2.00	5.00	24.00	60.00
1908B	2,000,000	1.00	2.00	5.00	24.00	60.00
1909B	2,000,000	1.00	2.00	5.00	24.00	55.00
1911B	1,000,000	1.50	3.00	8.00	40.00	90.00
1912B	1,500,000	0.50	1.50	5.00	38.00	85.00
1913B	2,000,000	0.50	1.00	5.00	45.00	115
1914B	2,000,000	0.50	1.50	7.00	70.00	225
1915B	1,200,000	1.00	2.00	25.00	190	475
1919B	3,000,000	—	0.50	3.00	27.00	55.00
1920B	3,500,000	—	0.50	3.00	27.00	40.00
1921B	3,000,000	—	0.50	3.00	27.00	40.00
1922B	2,000,000	—	0.50	3.00	35.00	55.00
1924B	2,000,000	—	0.50	3.00	35.00	60.00
1925B	3,000,000	—	0.50	3.00	18.00	35.00
1926B	3,000,000	—	0.50	3.00	16.00	35.00
1927B	2,000,000	—	0.50	3.00	16.00	40.00
1928B	2,000,000	—	0.50	3.00	16.00	35.00
1929B	2,000,000	—	0.50	3.00	26.00	35.00
1930B	2,000,000	—	0.50	3.00	30.00	50.00
1931B	2,244,000	—	0.50	3.00	30.00	50.00
1940B	2,000,000	—	0.75	10.00	75.00	350
1942B	2,110,000	—	0.75	10.00	50.00	100
1943B	3,176,000	—	0.50	5.00	37.50	65.00
1944B	6,133,000	—	0.50	2.50	16.00	25.00
1945B	993,000	—	1.00	12.00	120	350
1946B	4,010,000	—	0.50	2.50	24.00	50.00
1947B	3,152,000	—	0.50	2.50	24.00	55.00
1948B	1,000,000	0.50	1.00	15.00	200	475
1949B	2,269,000	—	0.50	1.00	30.00	50.00
1950B	3,200,000	—	0.35	0.70	2.50	6.00
1951B	3,430,000	—	0.35	0.70	7.00	25.00
1952B	4,451,000	—	0.35	0.70	7.00	22.00
1953B	6,149,000	—	0.35	0.70	7.00	22.00
1954B	3,200,000	—	0.35	0.70	15.00	45.00
1955B	11,795,000	—	0.35	0.70	7.00	20.00
1957B	10,092,000	—	0.35	0.70	9.50	27.00
1958B	10,040,000	—	0.35	0.70	7.00	20.00
1959B	13,053,000	—	0.35	0.70	6.00	10.00
1960B	4,040,000	—	0.35	0.70	6.00	9.00
1961B	7,949,000	—	—	0.50	2.00	4.50
1962B	34,965,000	—	—	0.20	1.00	3.00
1964B	16,340,000	—	—	0.20	1.00	3.00
1965B	14,190,000	—	—	0.20	1.00	3.00
1966B	4,025,000	—	—	0.50	1.00	1.50
1967B	10,000,000	—	—	0.50	1.00	1.50
1968B	14,065,000	—	—	0.25	0.50	1.00
1969B	28,855,000	—	—	0.25	0.50	1.00
1970	40,020,000	—	—	0.25	0.40	1.00
1972	7,877,000	—	—	0.25	0.40	1.00
1973	30,350,000	—	—	—	0.40	0.75
1974	30,007,000	—	—	—	0.40	0.75
1974 Proof	2,400	Value: 60.00				
1975	25,002,000	—	—	—	0.40	0.75
1975 Proof	10,000	Value: 4.00				
1976	19,012,000	—	—	—	0.40	0.75
1976 Proof	5,130	Value: 5.00				
1977	10,007,000	—	—	—	0.40	0.75
1977 Proof	7,030	Value: 5.00				
1978	19,957,000	—	—	—	0.40	0.75
1978 Proof	10,000	Value: 4.00				
1979	18,010,000	—	—	—	0.40	0.75
1979 Proof	10,000	Value: 4.00				
1980	18,005,000	—	—	—	0.50	1.00
1980 Proof	10,000	Value: 4.00				
1981	30,140,000	—	—	—	0.50	1.00
1981 Proof	10,000	Value: 4.00				
1982	50,110,000	—	—	—	0.50	1.00
1982 Proof	10,000	Value: 4.00				
1983	40,033,000	—	—	—	0.50	1.00
1983 Proof	11,000	Value: 4.00				
1984	22,022,000	—	—	—	0.50	1.00
1984 Proof	14,000	Value: 4.00				
1985	3,032,000	—	—	—	0.50	1.00
1985 Proof	12,000	Value: 4.00				
1986B	2,324,000	—	—	—	0.50	1.00
1986B Proof	10,000	Value: 4.00				
1987B	5,028,000	—	—	—	0.50	1.00
1987B Proof	8,800	Value: 5.00				
1988B	5,029,000	—	—	—	0.50	1.00
1988B Proof	9,000	Value: 5.00				
1989B	41,031,000	—	—	—	0.50	1.00
1989B Proof	8,800	Value: 5.00				
1990B	40,032,000	—	—	—	0.50	1.00
1990B Proof	8,900	Value: 5.00				
1991B	35,046,000	—	—	—	0.50	1.00
1991B Proof	9,900	Value: 4.00				
1992B	18,028,000	—	—	—	0.50	1.00
1992B Proof	7,450	Value: 5.00				
1993B	27,022,000	—	—	—	0.50	1.00
1993B Proof	6,200	Value: 5.00				
1994B	18,023,000	—	—	—	0.50	1.00
1994B Proof	6,100	Value: 5.00				
1995B	5,024,000	—	—	—	0.50	1.00
1995B Proof	6,100	Value: 5.00				
1996B	18,023,000	—	—	—	0.50	1.00
1996B Proof	6,100	Value: 5.00				
1997B	15,022,000	—	—	—	0.50	1.00
1997B Proof	5,500	Value: 5.00				
1998B	10,021,000	—	—	—	0.50	1.00
1998B Proof	4,800	Value: 5.00				
1999B	7,021,000	—	—	—	0.50	1.00
1999B Proof	5,000	Value: 5.00				
2000B	5,026,000	—	—	—	0.50	1.00
2000B Proof	5,500	Value: 5.00				
2001B	7,022,000	—	—	—	0.50	1.00
2001B Proof	6,000	Value: 2.00				
2002B	15,024,000	—	—	—	0.50	1.00
2002B Proof	6,000	Value: 2.00				
2003B	12,022,000	—	—	—	0.50	1.00
2003B Proof	5,500	Value: 2.00				
2004B	5,026,000	—	—	—	0.50	1.00
2004B Proof	5,000	Value: 2.00				
2005B	7,024,000	—	—	—	0.50	1.00
2005B Proof	4,500	Value: 2.00				
2006B	2,026,000	—	—	—	0.50	1.00
2006B Proof	4,000	Value: 2.00				
2007B	18,024,000	—	—	—	0.50	1.00
2007B Proof	4,000	Value: 2.00				

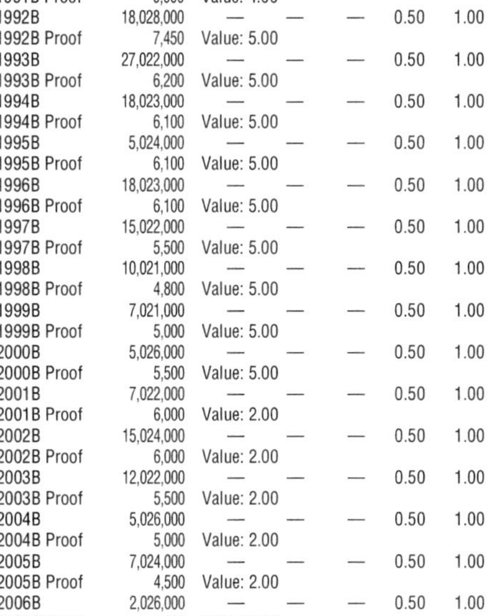

KM# 27a 10 RAPPEN

Brass, 19.1 mm. **Obv:** Crowned head right **Rev:** Value within wreath

Date	Mintage	F	VF	XF	Unc	BU
1918B	6,000,000	7.50	12.00	20.00	30.00	60.00
1919B	3,000,000	35.00	75.00	95.00	125	200

KM# 27b 10 RAPPEN

Nickel, 19.1 mm. **Obv:** Crowned head right **Rev:** Value within wreath **Edge:** Plain **Note:** Retired legal tender status as of January 1, 2004, removed from circulation.

Date	Mintage	F	VF	XF	Unc	BU
1932B	3,500,000	—	0.50	1.00	13.00	25.00
1933B	2,000,000	—	0.50	1.00	13.00	40.00
1934B	3,000,000	—	0.50	1.00	19.00	40.00
1936B	1,500,000	—	0.50	1.00	14.00	45.00
1937B	1,000,000	0.40	0.75	1.50	22.00	55.00
1938B	1,000,000	0.40	0.75	1.50	13.00	35.00
1939B	10,022,000	—	0.50	1.50	13.00	30.00

KM# 29 20 RAPPEN

4.0000 g., Nickel, 21 mm. **Obv:** Crowned head right **Obv. Legend:** CONFOEDERATIO HELVETICA **Rev:** Value within wreath **Note:** Retired legal tender status as of January 1, 2004, removed from circulation.

Date	Mintage	F	VF	XF	Unc	BU
1901B	1,000,000	0.50	1.00	8.00	150	400
1902B	1,000,000	0.50	1.00	8.00	75.00	200
1903B	1,000,000	0.50	1.00	8.00	50.00	210
1906B	1,000,000	0.50	1.00	8.00	50.00	175
1907B	1,000,000	0.50	1.00	7.00	32.00	100
1908B	1,500,000	0.50	1.00	5.00	38.00	100
1909B	2,000,000	0.50	1.00	5.00	32.00	80.00
1911B	1,000,000	0.50	1.00	6.00	65.00	200
1912B	2,000,000	0.35	0.75	5.00	75.00	145
1913B	1,500,000	0.35	0.75	5.00	100	225
1919B	1,500,000	0.35	0.75	5.00	38.00	85.00
1920B	3,100,000	—	0.50	2.00	30.00	65.00
1921B	2,500,000	—	0.50	2.00	22.00	60.00
1924B	1,100,000	—	0.50	2.00	65.00	125
1925B	1,500,000	—	0.50	2.00	20.00	60.00
1926B	1,500,000	—	0.50	2.00	30.00	70.00
1927B	500,000	1.00	2.50	12.00	110	300
1929B	2,000,000	—	0.50	1.00	20.00	40.00
1930B	2,000,000	—	0.50	1.00	20.00	50.00
1931B	2,250,000	—	0.50	1.00	20.00	50.00
1932B	2,000,000	—	0.50	1.00	20.00	70.00
1933B	1,500,000	—	0.50	1.00	28.00	75.00
1934B	2,000,000	—	0.50	1.00	30.00	85.00
1936B	1,000,000	0.50	1.00	2.00	32.00	100
1938B	2,805,000	—	0.50	1.50	32.00	100

KM# 29a 20 RAPPEN

4.2000 g., Copper-Nickel, 21 mm. **Obv:** Crowned head right **Rev:** Value within wreath **Edge:** Plain

Date	Mintage	F	VF	XF	Unc	BU
1939B	8,100,000	—	0.50	18.00	150	400
1943B	10,173,000	—	0.50	1.00	28.00	60.00
1944B	7,139,000	—	0.50	1.00	10.00	30.00
1945B	1,992,000	—	1.00	10.00	75.00	350
1947B	5,131,000	—	0.50	0.75	25.00	65.00
1947B	Inc. above	1.00	2.00	4.00	30.00	70.00
Note: Dot over 4 in date						
1950B	5,970,000	—	0.50	0.75	6.00	15.00
1951B	3,640,000	—	0.50	0.75	13.00	35.00
1952B	3,075,000	—	0.50	0.75	13.00	35.00
1953B	6,958,000	—	0.50	0.75	6.00	25.00
1954B	1,504,000	—	1.00	4.00	32.00	250
1955B	9,103,000	—	0.50	0.75	13.00	45.00
1956B	5,111,000	—	0.50	0.75	13.00	35.00
1957B	2,535,000	—	0.50	1.25	28.00	200
1958B	5,037,000	—	0.50	0.75	13.00	40.00
1959B	10,136,000	—	—	0.50	3.50	30.00
1960B	15,469,000	—	—	0.50	3.50	16.00
1961B	8,234,000	—	—	0.50	3.50	16.00
1962B	30,145,000	—	—	0.50	3.00	16.00
1963B	9,020,000	—	—	0.50	3.50	11.00
1964B	14,370,000	—	—	0.50	2.00	8.00
1965B	15,005,000	—	—	0.50	2.00	8.00
1966B	10,785,000	—	—	0.50	1.00	3.50
1967B	8,995,000	—	—	0.50	1.00	4.50
1968B	10,540,000	—	—	0.50	1.00	2.00
1969B	39,875,000	—	—	0.40	1.00	2.00
1970	45,605,000	—	—	—	1.00	2.00
1971	25,160,000	—	—	—	1.00	2.00
1974	30,025,000	—	—	—	1.00	2.00
1974 Proof	2,400	Value: 75.00				
1975	50,060,000	—	—	—	1.00	2.00
1975 Proof	10,000	Value: 5.00				
1976	23,150,000	—	—	—	1.00	2.00
1976 Proof	5,130	Value: 6.00				
1977	14,012,000	—	—	—	1.00	2.00
1977 Proof	7,030	Value: 6.00				
1978	14,815,000	—	—	—	1.00	2.00
1978 Proof	10,000	Value: 5.00				
1979	18,378,000	—	—	—	1.00	2.00
1979 Proof	10,000	Value: 5.00				
1980	24,560,000	—	—	—	1.00	2.00
1980 Proof	10,000	Value: 5.00				
1981	22,020,000	—	—	—	1.00	2.00
1981 Proof	10,000	Value: 5.00				
1982	25,035,000	—	—	—	1.00	2.00
1982 Proof	10,000	Value: 5.00				
1983	10,026,000	—	—	—	1.00	2.00
1983 Proof	11,000	Value: 5.00				
1984	22,055,000	—	—	—	1.00	2.00
1984 Proof	14,000	Value: 5.00				
1985	40,027,000	—	—	—	1.00	2.00
1985 Proof	12,000	Value: 5.00				
1986B	10,299,000	—	—	—	1.00	1.50
1986B Proof	10,000	Value: 5.00				
1987B	10,028,000	—	—	—	1.00	1.50
1987B Proof	8,800	Value: 6.00				
1988B	25,029,000	—	—	—	1.00	1.50
1988B Proof	9,000	Value: 6.00				
1989B	20,031,000	—	—	—	1.00	1.50
1989B Proof	8,800	Value: 6.00				
1990B	6,534,000	—	—	—	1.00	1.50
1990B Proof	8,900	Value: 6.00				
1991B	48,076,000	—	—	—	1.00	1.50
1991B Proof	9,900	Value: 6.00				
1992B	12,628,000	—	—	—	1.00	1.50
1992B Proof	7,450	Value: 6.00				

Date	Mintage	F	VF	XF	Unc	BU
1993B	32,523,000	—	—	—	1.00	1.50
1993B Proof	6,200	Value: 6.00				
1994B	20,023,000	—	—	—	1.00	1.50
1994B Proof	6,100	Value: 6.00				
1995B	8,024,000	—	—	—	1.00	1.50
1995B Proof	6,100	Value: 6.00				
1996B	4,023,000	—	—	—	1.00	1.50
1996B Proof	6,100	Value: 6.00				
1997B	6,022,000	—	—	—	1.00	1.50
1997B Proof	5,500	Value: 6.00				
1998B	7,021,000	—	—	—	1.00	1.50
1998B Proof	4,800	Value: 6.00				
1999B	4,021,000	—	—	—	1.00	1.50
1999B Proof	5,000	Value: 6.00				
2000B	3,026,000	—	—	—	1.00	1.50
2000B Proof	5,500	Value: 6.00				
2001B	7,022,000	—	—	—	1.00	2.00
2001B Proof	6,000	Value: 3.00				
2002B	12,024,000	—	—	—	1.00	2.00
2002B Proof	6,000	Value: 3.00				
2003B	10,022,000	—	—	—	1.00	2.00
2003B Proof	5,500	Value: 3.00				
2004B	10,026,000	—	—	—	1.00	2.00
2004B Proof	5,000	Value: 3.00				
2005B	6,024,000	—	—	—	1.00	2.00
2005B Proof	4,500	Value: 3.00				
2006B	5,026,000	—	—	—	1.00	2.00
2006B Proof	4,000	Value: 3.00				
2007B	22,024,000	—	—	—	1.00	2.00
2007B Proof	4,000	Value: 3.00				

KM# 23 1/2 FRANC

2.5000 g., 0.8350 Silver 0.0671 oz. ASW, 18.1 mm. **Obv:** Standing Helvetia with lance and shield within star border **Rev:** Value, date within wreath **Edge:** Reeded **Designer:** A. Bovy

Date	Mintage	F	VF	XF	Unc	BU
1901B	200,000	15.00	50.00	175	750	2,250
1901B Specimen	—	—	—	—	—	3,500
1903B	800,000	1.00	3.00	15.00	95.00	225
1903B Specimen	—	—	—	—	—	1,500
1904B	400,000	2.00	5.00	75.00	600	2,000
1904B Specimen	—	—	—	—	—	4,000
1905B	600,000	1.00	3.00	23.00	125	250
1905B Specimen	—	—	—	—	—	1,250
1906B	1,000,000	1.00	3.00	23.00	125	250
1906B Specimen	—	—	—	—	—	1,250
1907B	1,200,000	1.00	3.00	15.00	100	2,250
1907B Specimen	—	—	—	—	—	1,000
1908B	800,000	1.00	3.00	15.00	100	250
1908B Specimen	—	—	—	—	—	1,000
1909B	1,000,000	1.00	3.00	10.00	95.00	250
1909B Specimen	—	—	—	—	—	1,000
1910B	1,000,000	1.00	3.00	10.00	65.00	175
1910B Specimen	—	—	—	—	—	1,000
1913B	800,000	1.00	3.00	7.50	65.00	150
1913B Specimen	—	—	—	—	—	750
1914B	2,000,000	1.00	3.00	5.00	32.00	70.00
1914B Specimen	—	—	—	—	—	425
1916B	800,000	1.00	3.00	5.00	95.00	175
1916B Specimen	—	—	—	—	—	650
1920B	5,400,000	1.00	3.00	4.00	14.00	60.00
1920B Specimen	—	—	—	—	—	300
1921B	6,000,000	1.00	3.00	4.00	14.00	50.00
1921B Specimen	—	—	—	—	—	300
1928B	1,000,000	1.00	3.00	9.50	55.00	200
1928B Specimen	—	—	—	—	—	425
1929B	2,000,000	1.00	3.00	5.00	14.00	35.00
1929B Specimen	—	—	—	—	—	225
1931B	1,000,000	1.00	2.00	9.50	32.00	80.00
1931B Specimen	—	—	—	—	—	300
1932B	1,000,000	1.00	2.00	6.50	30.00	60.00
1932B Specimen	—	—	—	—	—	300
1934B	2,000,000	1.00	2.00	6.50	14.00	35.00
1934B Specimen	—	—	—	—	—	200
1936B	400,000	1.50	3.00	9.50	32.00	100
1936B Specimen	—	—	—	—	—	300
1937B	1,000,000	1.00	2.00	5.00	14.00	45.00
1937B Specimen	—	—	—	—	—	250
1939B	1,001,000	1.00	2.00	5.00	23.00	50.00
1939B Specimen	—	—	—	—	—	150
1940B	2,002,000	—	2.00	4.00	12.00	30.00
1940B Specimen	—	—	—	—	—	120
1941B	200,000	1.50	3.00	8.00	20.00	40.00
1941B Specimen	—	—	—	—	—	90.00
1942B	2,969,000	—	1.50	2.50	5.00	18.00
1942B Specimen	—	—	—	—	—	90.00
1943B	4,573,000	—	1.50	2.50	5.00	18.00
1943B Specimen	—	—	—	—	—	90.00
1944B	7,455,000	—	1.50	2.50	5.00	8.00
1944B Specimen	—	—	—	—	—	90.00
1945B	4,928,000	—	1.50	2.50	5.00	16.00
1945B Specimen	—	—	—	—	—	90.00
1946B	6,817,000	—	1.50	2.50	4.00	8.00
1946B	Inc. above	50.00	110	160	250	750
Note: Medal alignment						
1946B Specimen	—	—	—	—	—	90.00
1948B	6,113,000	—	1.50	2.50	4.00	7.00
1948B Specimen	—	—	—	—	—	90.00
1950B	7,148,000	—	1.50	2.50	4.00	7.00
1950B Specimen	—	—	—	—	—	90.00
1951B	8,530,000	—	1.50	2.50	4.00	7.00
1951B Specimen	—	—	—	—	—	90.00
1952B	14,023,000	—	1.50	2.50	4.00	7.00
1952B Specimen	—	—	—	—	—	75.00
1953B	3,567,000	—	1.50	2.50	4.50	7.50
1953B Specimen	—	—	—	—	—	90.00
1955B	1,320,000	—	1.50	3.00	8.00	12.00
1955B Specimen	—	—	—	—	—	110
1956B	4,250,000	—	1.50	2.50	4.50	7.50
1956B Specimen	—	—	—	—	—	60.00
1957B	12,085,000	—	1.50	2.50	4.00	7.00
1957B Specimen	—	—	—	—	—	30.00
1958B	11,558,000	—	1.50	2.50	4.00	7.00
1958B Specimen	—	—	—	—	—	30.00
1959B	12,581,000	—	1.50	2.50	4.00	7.00
1959B Specimen	—	—	—	—	—	30.00
1960B	14,528,000	—	1.50	2.50	4.00	7.00
1960B Specimen	—	—	—	—	—	30.00
1961B	6,906,000	—	1.50	2.50	4.00	7.00
1961B Specimen	—	—	—	—	—	30.00
1962B	18,272,000	—	1.50	2.50	3.50	6.00
1962B Specimen	—	—	—	—	—	30.00
1963B	25,168,000	—	1.50	2.50	5.00	6.00
1963B Specimen	—	—	—	—	—	30.00
1964B	22,720,000	—	1.50	2.50	5.00	6.00
1964B Specimen	—	—	—	—	—	30.00
1965B	17,920,000	—	1.50	2.50	5.00	6.00
1965B Specimen	—	—	—	—	—	30.00
1966B	10,008,000	—	1.50	2.50	5.00	6.00
1966B Specimen	—	—	—	—	—	30.00
1967B	16,096,000	—	1.50	2.50	5.00	6.00
1967B Specimen	—	—	—	—	—	30.00

KM# 23a.1 1/2 FRANC

2.2000 g., Copper-Nickel, 18.1 mm. **Obv:** Standing Helvetia with lance and shield within star border **Rev:** Value within wreath

Date	Mintage	F	VF	XF	Unc	BU
1968	20,000,000	—	—	—	2.50	4.00
1968B	44,920,000	—	—	—	2.50	4.00
1969	31,400,000	—	—	—	2.50	4.00
1969B	51,704,000	—	—	—	2.50	4.00
1970	52,620,000	—	—	—	2.50	4.00
1971	34,472,000	—	—	—	2.50	4.00
1972	9,996,000	—	—	—	2.50	4.00
1973	5,000,000	—	—	—	4.00	7.00
1974	45,006,000	—	—	—	2.50	4.00
1974 Proof	2,400	Value: 85.00				
1975	27,234,000	—	—	—	2.50	3.50
1975 Proof	10,000	Value: 6.00				
1976	10,009,000	—	—	—	2.50	3.50
1976 Proof	5,130	Value: 6.00				
1977	19,011,000	—	—	—	2.50	3.50
1977 Proof	7,030	Value: 6.00				
1978	20,818,000	—	—	—	2.50	3.50
1978 Proof	10,000	Value: 6.00				
1979	27,014,000	—	—	—	2.50	3.50
1979 Proof	10,000	Value: 6.00				
1980	31,064,000	—	—	—	2.50	3.50
1980 Proof	10,000	Value: 6.00				
1981	30,155,000	—	—	—	2.50	3.50
1981 Proof	10,000	Value: 6.00				

KM# 23a.2 1/2 FRANC

2.2000 g., Copper-Nickel, 18.1 mm. **Obv:** 22 Stars around figure **Rev:** Value within wreath **Note:** Medal alignment.

Date	Mintage	F	VF	XF	Unc	BU
1982	30,151,000	—	—	—	2.50	3.50
1982 Proof	10,000	Value: 6.00				

KM# 23a.3 1/2 FRANC

2.2000 g., Copper-Nickel, 18.1 mm. **Obv:** 23 Stars around figure **Rev:** Value within wreath **Edge:** Reeded **Designer:** A. Bovy

Date	Mintage	F	VF	XF	Unc	BU
1983	22,020,000	—	—	—	1.75	2.75
1983 Proof	11,000	Value: 6.00				
1984	22,036,000	—	—	—	1.75	2.75
1984 Proof	14,000	Value: 6.00				
1985	6,026,000	—	—	—	2.50	3.50
1985 Proof	12,000	Value: 6.00				
1986B	5,031,000	—	—	—	2.50	3.50
1986B Proof	10,000	Value: 6.00				
1987B	10,028,000	—	—	—	1.75	2.75
1987B Proof	8,800	Value: 6.00				
1988B	5,029,000	—	—	—	2.50	3.50
1988B Proof	9,000	Value: 6.00				
1989B	10,031,000	—	—	—	1.75	2.75
1989B Proof	8,800	Value: 6.00				
1990B	20,032,000	—	—	—	1.75	2.75
1990B Proof	8,900	Value: 6.00				
1991B	10,036,000	—	—	—	1.75	2.75
1991B Proof	9,900	Value: 6.00				
1992B	30,028,000	—	—	—	1.75	2.75
1992B Proof	7,450	Value: 7.00				
1993B	13,023,000	—	—	—	1.75	2.75
1993B Proof	6,200	Value: 7.00				
1994B	15,023,000	—	—	—	1.75	3.00
1994B Proof	6,100	Value: 7.00				
1995B	10,024,000	—	—	—	2.50	3.50
1995B Proof	6,000	Value: 7.00				
1996B	8,023,000	—	—	—	2.50	3.50
1996B Proof	6,100	Value: 7.00				
1997B	6,022,000	—	—	—	2.50	3.50
1997B Proof	5,500	Value: 8.00				
1998B	6,021,000	—	—	—	2.50	3.50
1998B Proof	4,800	Value: 8.00				
1999B	5,021,000	—	—	—	2.50	3.50
1999B Proof	5,000	Value: 8.00				
2000B	4,026,000	—	—	—	2.50	3.50
2000B Proof	5,500	Value: 8.00				
2001B Proof	6,000	Value: 5.00				
2001B	6,022,000	—	—	—	2.50	3.50
2002B	2,024,000	—	—	—	2.50	3.50
2002B Proof	6,000	Value: 5.00				
2003B	2,022,000	—	—	—	2.50	3.50
2003B Proof	5,500	Value: 5.00				
2004B Proof	5,000	Value: 5.00				
2004B	2,026,000	—	—	—	2.50	3.50
2005B	1,024,000	—	—	—	2.50	3.50
2005B Proof	4,500	Value: 5.00				
2006B	2,025,000	—	—	—	2.50	3.50
2006B Proof	4,500	Value: 5.00				
2007B	18,024,000	—	—	—	2.50	3.50
2007B Proof	4,000	Value: 5.00				

KM# 24 FRANC

5.0000 g., 0.8350 Silver 0.1342 oz. ASW **Obv:** Standing Helvetia with lance and shield within star border **Rev:** Value, date within wreath **Edge:** A. Bovy

Date	Mintage	F	VF	XF	Unc	BU
1901B	400,000	3.00	8.00	75.00	400	1,750
1901B Specimen	—	—	—	—	—	3,500
1903B	1,000,000	2.00	3.50	20.00	120	300
1903B Specimen	—	—	—	—	—	1,500
1904B	400,000	5.00	10.00	150	1,300	2,750
1904B Specimen	—	—	—	—	—	5,000
1905B	700,000	2.00	3.50	25.00	180	400
1905B Specimen	—	—	—	—	—	1,500
1906B	700,000	2.00	3.50	40.00	275	700
1906B Specimen	—	—	—	—	—	1,500
1907B	800,000	2.00	3.50	40.00	275	750
1907B Specimen	—	—	—	—	—	1,500
1908B	1,200,000	2.00	3.50	10.00	110	275
1908B Specimen	—	—	—	—	—	1,200
1909B	900,000	2.00	3.50	10.00	110	250
1909B Specimen	—	—	—	—	—	1,200
1910B	1,000,000	2.00	3.50	9.50	75.00	225
1910B Specimen	—	—	—	—	—	1,200
1911B	1,200,000	2.00	3.50	9.50	70.00	175
1911B Specimen	—	—	—	—	—	900
1912B	1,200,000	2.00	3.50	6.00	65.00	135
1912B Specimen	—	—	—	—	—	750
1913B	1,200,000	2.00	3.50	6.00	65.00	135
1913B Specimen	—	—	—	—	—	900
1914B	4,200,000	2.00	3.50	5.00	25.00	70.00
1914B Specimen	—	—	—	—	—	600
1916B	1,000,000	2.00	3.50	7.00	90.00	175
1916B Specimen	—	—	—	—	—	1,200
1920B	3,300,000	2.00	3.00	5.00	20.00	60.00
1920B Specimen	—	—	—	—	—	300
1921B	3,800,000	2.00	3.00	5.00	20.00	55.00
1921B Specimen	—	—	—	—	—	300
1928B	1,500,000	2.00	3.00	5.00	20.00	40.00
1928B Specimen	—	—	—	—	—	250
1931B	1,000,000	2.00	3.00	5.00	30.00	50.00
1931B Specimen	—	—	—	—	—	250
1932B	500,000	2.00	3.00	7.00	65.00	225
1932B Specimen	—	—	—	—	—	600
1934B	500,000	2.00	3.00	9.50	65.00	225
1934B Specimen	—	—	—	—	—	600
1936B	500,000	2.00	3.00	9.50	65.00	150
1936B Specimen	—	—	—	—	—	500
1937B	1,000,000	2.00	3.00	5.00	20.00	55.00
1937B Specimen	—	—	—	—	—	250
1939B	2,106,000	2.00	3.00	5.00	13.00	23.00
1939B Specimen	—	—	—	—	—	175
1940B	2,003,000	2.00	3.00	5.00	13.00	23.00
1940B Specimen	—	—	—	—	—	150
1943B	3,526,000	2.00	3.00	4.00	7.00	18.00
1943B Specimen	—	—	—	—	—	150
1944B	6,225,000	2.00	3.00	4.00	7.00	16.00
1944B Specimen	—	—	—	—	—	150

Date	Mintage	F	VF	XF	Unc	BU
1945B	7,794,000	2.00	3.00	4.00	7.00	18.00
1945B Specimen	—	—	—	—	—	150
1946B	2,539,000	2.00	3.00	4.00	13.00	22.00
1946B Specimen	—	—	—	—	—	150
1947B	624,000	2.50	3.00	5.00	15.00	28.00
1947B Specimen	—	—	—	—	—	150
1952B	2,853,000	2.00	3.00	4.00	6.50	10.00
1952B Specimen	—	—	—	—	—	120
1953B	786,000	2.50	3.00	5.00	15.00	30.00
1953B Specimen	—	—	—	—	—	120
1955B	194,000	3.00	4.00	10.00	20.00	35.00
1955B Specimen	—	—	—	—	—	150
1956B	2,500,000	—	—	3.00	6.50	9.00
1956B Specimen	—	—	—	—	—	90.00
1957B	6,421,000	—	—	3.00	6.50	9.00
1957B Specimen	—	—	—	—	—	45.00
1958B	3,580,000	—	—	3.00	6.50	9.00
1958B Specimen	—	—	—	—	—	45.00
1959B	1,859,000	—	—	3.00	6.50	10.00
1959B Specimen	—	—	—	—	—	45.00
1960B	3,523,000	—	—	2.00	6.50	9.00
1960B Specimen	—	—	—	—	—	45.00
1961B	6,549,000	—	—	2.50	6.50	9.00
1961B Specimen	—	—	—	—	—	45.00
1962B	6,220,000	—	—	2.50	6.00	8.00
1962B Specimen	—	—	—	—	—	45.00
1963B	13,476,000	—	—	2.50	6.00	8.00
1963B Specimen	—	—	—	—	—	45.00
1964B	12,560,000	—	—	2.50	6.00	8.00
1964B Specimen	—	—	—	—	—	45.00
1965B	5,032,000	—	—	2.50	6.00	8.00
1965B Specimen	—	—	—	—	—	45.00
1966B	3,032,000	—	—	2.50	6.00	9.00
1966B Specimen	—	—	—	—	—	45.00
1967B	2,088,000	—	—	2.50	6.00	9.00
1967B Specimen	—	—	—	—	—	45.00

KM# 24a.1 FRANC

4.4000 g., Copper-Nickel, 23.1 mm. **Obv:** Standing Helvetia with lance and shield within star border **Rev:** Value within wreath **Edge:** Reeded **Designer:** A. Bovy

Date	Mintage	F	VF	XF	Unc	BU
1968	15,000,000	—	—	1.00	3.00	5.00
1968B	40,864,000	—	—	—	3.00	5.00
1969B	37,598,000	—	—	—	3.00	5.00
1970	24,240,000	—	—	—	3.00	5.00
1971	11,496,000	—	—	—	3.00	5.00
1973	5,000,000	—	—	—	4.00	7.00
1974	15,012,000	—	—	—	3.00	5.00
1974 Proof	2,400	Value: 85.00				
1975	13,012,000	—	—	—	3.00	5.00
1975 Proof	10,000	Value: 7.00				
1976	5,009,000	—	—	—	4.00	7.00
1976 Proof	5,130	Value: 8.00				
1977	6,019,000	—	—	—	4.00	7.00
1977 Proof	7,030	Value: 8.00				
1978	13,548,000	—	—	—	3.00	5.00
1978 Proof	10,000	Value: 7.00				
1979	10,800,000	—	—	—	3.00	5.00
1979 Proof	10,000	Value: 7.00				
1980	11,002,000	—	—	—	3.00	5.00
1980 Proof	10,000	Value: 7.00				
1981	18,013,000	—	—	—	3.00	5.00
1981 Proof	10,000	Value: 7.00				

KM# 24a.2 FRANC

4.4000 g., Copper-Nickel, 23.1 mm. **Obv:** 22 Stars around figure **Rev:** Value and date within wreath **Note:** Medal alignment.

Date	Mintage	F	VF	XF	Unc	BU
1982	15,039,000	—	—	—	3.50	6.00
1982 Proof	10,000	Value: 8.00				

KM# 24a.3 FRANC

4.4000 g., Copper-Nickel, 23.1 mm. **Obv:** 23 Stars around figure **Rev:** Value and date within wreath **Edge:** Reeded **Designer:** A. Bovy

Date	Mintage	F	VF	XF	Unc	BU
1983	7,018,000	—	—	—	3.00	5.00
1983 Proof	11,000	Value: 7.00				
1984	3,028,000	—	—	—	3.00	5.00
1984 Proof	14,000	Value: 7.00				
1985	20,042,000	—	—	—	3.00	5.00
1985 Proof	12,000	Value: 7.00				
1986B	17,997,000	—	—	—	3.00	5.00
1986B Proof	10,000	Value: 7.00				
1987B	17,028,000	—	—	—	3.00	5.00
1987B Proof	8,800	Value: 7.00				
1988B	18,029,000	—	—	—	3.00	5.00
1988B Proof	9,000	Value: 7.00				
1989B	15,031,000	—	—	—	3.00	5.00
1989B Proof	8,800	Value: 7.00				
1990B	2,032,000	—	—	—	4.00	7.00
1990B Proof	8,900	Value: 7.00				
1991B	9,036,000	—	—	—	3.00	5.00
1991B Proof	9,900	Value: 7.00				
1992B	12,028,000	—	—	—	3.00	5.00
1992B Proof	7,450	Value: 7.00				
1993B	12,023,000	—	—	—	3.00	5.00
1993B Proof	6,200	Value: 8.00				
1994B	10,023,000	—	—	—	3.00	5.00
1994B Proof	6,100	Value: 8.00				
1995B	13,024,000	—	—	—	3.00	5.00
1995B Proof	6,100	Value: 8.00				
1996B	3,023,000	—	—	—	3.50	6.00
1996B Proof	6,100	Value: 8.00				
1997B	3,022,000	—	—	—	3.50	6.00
1997B Proof	5,500	Value: 8.00				
1998B	3,021,000	—	—	—	3.50	6.00
1998B Proof	4,800	Value: 8.00				
1999B	3,021,000	—	—	—	3.50	6.00
1999B Proof	5,000	Value: 8.00				
2000B	4,026,000	—	—	—	3.50	6.00
2000B Proof	5,500	Value: 8.00				
2001B	3,022,000	—	—	—	3.00	5.00
2001B Proof	6,000	Value: 7.00				
2002B	1,024,000	—	—	—	3.00	5.00
2002B Proof	6,000	Value: 7.00				
2003B	2,022,000	—	—	—	3.00	5.00
2003B Proof	5,500	Value: 7.00				
2004B	2,026,000	—	—	—	3.00	5.00
2004B Proof	5,000	Value: 7.00				
2005B	1,024,000	—	—	—	3.00	5.00
2005B Proof	4,500	Value: 7.00				
2006B	2,026,000	—	—	—	3.00	5.00
2006B Proof	4,000	Value: 7.00				
2007B	3,024,000	—	—	—	3.00	5.00
2007B Proof	4,000	Value: 7.00				

KM# 21 2 FRANCS

10.0000 g., 0.8350 Silver 0.2684 oz. ASW **Obv:** Standing Helvetia with lance and shield within star border **Rev:** Value, date within wreath **Edge:** Reeded **Designer:** A. Bovy

Date	Mintage	F	VF	XF	Unc	BU
1901B	50,000	80.00	135	1,600	6,500	9,000
1901B Specimen; Rare	—	—	—	—	—	—
1903B	300,000	4.50	10.00	80.00	600	1,500
1903B Specimen	—	—	—	—	—	3,000
1904B	200,000	6.00	15.00	225	1,250	3,250
1904B Specimen	—	—	—	—	—	6,000
1905B	300,000	4.50	10.00	75.00	600	1,750
1905B Specimen	—	—	—	—	—	3,000
1906B	400,000	4.00	8.00	100	500	1,700
1906B Specimen	—	—	—	—	—	3,500
1907B	300,000	4.50	12.00	160	1,000	3,000
1907B Specimen	—	—	—	—	—	4,500
1908B	200,000	6.00	15.00	300	1,400	4,000
1908B Specimen	—	—	—	—	—	7,500
1909B	300,000	4.50	10.00	65.00	400	2,000
1909B Specimen	—	—	—	—	—	4,500
1910B	250,000	5.00	7.00	130	650	2,000
1910B Specimen	—	—	—	—	—	4,500
1911B	400,000	4.00	6.00	50.00	250	500
1911B Specimen	—	—	—	—	—	2,000
1912B	400,000	4.00	6.00	50.00	150	400
1912B Specimen	—	—	—	—	—	1,500
1913B	300,000	4.00	6.00	65.00	200	400
1913B Specimen	—	—	—	—	—	2,100
1914B	1,000,000	4.00	5.00	20.00	150	225
1914B Specimen	—	—	—	—	—	1,500
1916B	250,000	4.00	6.00	110	425	1,500
1916B Specimen	—	—	—	—	—	2,500
1920B	2,300,000	4.00	5.00	12.00	30.00	75.00
1920B Specimen	—	—	—	—	—	600
1921B	2,000,000	4.00	5.00	12.00	30.00	75.00
1921B Specimen	—	—	—	—	—	600
1922B	400,000	4.00	6.00	27.50	200	450
1922B Specimen	—	—	—	—	—	1,500
1928B	750,000	4.00	5.00	12.00	30.00	85.00
1928B Specimen	—	—	—	—	—	600
1931B	500,000	4.00	5.00	12.00	40.00	90.00
1931B Specimen	—	—	—	—	—	600
1932B	250,000	4.00	5.00	30.00	210	500
1932B Specimen	—	—	—	—	—	1,200
1936B	250,000	4.00	5.00	20.00	150	225
1936B Specimen	—	—	—	—	—	650
1937B	250,000	4.00	5.00	14.00	85.00	150
1937B Specimen	—	—	—	—	—	500
1939B	1,455,000	—	4.00	7.50	13.00	30.00
1939B Specimen	—	—	—	—	—	1,000
1940B	2,503,000	—	4.00	7.50	13.00	28.00
1940B Specimen	—	—	—	—	—	180
1941B	1,192,000	—	4.00	7.50	15.00	30.00
1941B Specimen	—	—	—	—	—	180
1943B	2,089,000	—	4.00	7.50	14.00	25.00
1943B Specimen	—	—	—	—	—	180
1944B	6,276,000	—	4.00	7.50	13.00	20.00
1944B Specimen	—	—	—	—	—	180
1945B	1,134,000	—	4.00	12.00	21.00	40.00
1945B Specimen	—	—	—	—	—	180
1946B	1,629,000	—	4.00	12.00	22.00	30.00
1946B Specimen	—	—	—	—	—	180
1947B	500,000	4.00	5.00	10.00	30.00	50.00
1947B Specimen	—	—	—	—	—	180
1948B	920,000	—	4.00	11.00	15.00	30.00
1948B Specimen	—	—	—	—	—	180
1953B	438,000	4.00	5.00	10.00	32.00	55.00
1953B Specimen	—	—	—	—	—	200
1955B	1,032,000	—	4.00	6.50	10.00	27.00
1955B Specimen	—	—	—	—	—	150
1957B	2,298,000	—	4.00	6.50	9.00	19.00
1957B Specimen	—	—	—	—	—	60.00
1958B	650,000	—	4.00	6.50	9.00	19.00
1958B Specimen	—	—	—	—	—	60.00
1959B	2,905,000	—	4.00	6.50	9.00	27.00
1959B Specimen	—	—	—	—	—	60.00
1960B	1,980,000	—	—	6.50	9.00	27.00
1960B Specimen	—	—	—	—	—	60.00
1961B	4,653,000	—	—	6.50	8.00	13.00
1961B Specimen	—	—	—	—	—	60.00
1963B	8,030,000	—	—	6.50	8.00	13.00
1963B Specimen	—	—	—	—	—	60.00
1964B	4,558,000	—	—	6.50	8.00	13.00
1964B Specimen	—	—	—	—	—	60.00
1965B	8,526,000	—	—	6.50	8.00	13.00
1965B Specimen	—	—	—	—	—	60.00
1967B	4,132,000	—	—	6.50	8.00	13.00
1967B Specimen	—	—	—	—	—	60.00

KM# 21a.1 2 FRANCS

8.8000 g., Copper-Nickel, 27.4 mm. **Obv:** Standing Helvetia with lance and shield within star border **Rev:** Value within wreath **Edge:** Reeded **Designer:** A. Bovy

Date	Mintage	F	VF	XF	Unc	BU
1968	10,000,000	—	—	—	5.00	8.00
1968B	31,588,000	—	—	—	4.50	7.50
1969B	17,296,000	—	—	—	4.50	7.50
1970	10,350,000	—	—	—	4.50	7.50
1972	5,003,000	—	—	—	4.50	7.50
1973	5,996,000	—	—	—	4.50	7.50
1974	15,009,000	—	—	—	5.00	8.00
1974 Proof	2,400	Value: 85.00				
1975	7,061,000	—	—	—	5.00	8.00
1975 Proof	10,000	Value: 12.00				
1976	5,011,000	—	—	—	5.00	8.00
1976 Proof	5,130	Value: 15.00				
1977	2,010,000	—	—	—	6.00	10.00
1977 Proof	7,030	Value: 15.00				
1978	12,812,000	—	—	—	5.00	8.00
1978 Proof	10,000	Value: 12.00				
1979	10,995,000	—	—	—	5.00	8.00
1979 Proof	10,000	Value: 12.00				
1980	10,001,000	—	—	—	5.00	6.00
1980 Proof	10,000	Value: 12.00				
1981	13,852,000	—	—	—	5.00	8.00
1981 Proof	10,000	Value: 12.00				

KM# 21a.2 2 FRANCS

8.8000 g., Copper-Nickel, 27.4 mm. **Obv:** 22 Stars around figure **Rev:** Value within wreath **Note:** Medal alignment.

Date	Mintage	F	VF	XF	Unc	BU
1982	5,912,000	—	—	—	4.50	7.50
1982 Proof	10,000	Value: 15.00				

KM# 21a.3 2 FRANCS

8.8000 g., Copper-Nickel, 27.4 mm. **Obv:** 23 Stars around figure **Rev:** Value within wreath **Edge:** Reeded **Designer:** A. Bovy

Date	Mintage	F	VF	XF	Unc	BU
1983	3,023,000	—	—	—	5.00	8.00
1983 Proof	11,000	Value: 12.00				
1984	2,029,000	—	—	—	5.00	8.00
1984 Proof	14,000	Value: 12.00				
1985	2,022,000	—	—	—	5.00	8.00
1985 Proof	12,000	Value: 12.00				
1986B	3,032,000	—	—	—	5.00	8.00
1986B Proof	10,000	Value: 12.00				
1987B	8,028,000	—	—	—	3.50	6.00
1987B Proof	8,800	Value: 15.00				
1988B	10,029,000	—	—	—	3.50	6.00
1988B Proof	9,000	Value: 12.00				
1989B	8,031,000	—	—	—	3.50	6.00
1989B Proof	8,800	Value: 12.00				
1990B	5,045,000	—	—	—	4.00	7.00
1990B Proof	8,900	Value: 12.00				
1991B	12,036,000	—	—	—	3.50	6.00
1991B Proof	9,900	Value: 12.00				
1992B	10,028,000	—	—	—	3.50	6.00
1992B Proof	7,450	Value: 15.00				
1993B	13,050,000	—	—	—	3.50	6.00
1993B Proof	6,200	Value: 15.00				
1994B	16,023,000	—	—	—	3.50	6.00
1994B Proof	6,100	Value: 15.00				
1995B	7,024,000	—	—	—	3.50	6.00
1995B Proof	6,100	Value: 15.00				
1996B	5,023,000	—	—	—	4.00	7.00
1996B Proof	6,100	Value: 15.00				
1997B	5,022,000	—	—	—	4.00	7.00
1997B Proof	5,500	Value: 15.00				
1998B	4,021,000	—	—	—	4.00	7.00
1998B Proof	4,800	Value: 15.00				
1999B	3,021,000	—	—	—	5.00	8.00
1999B Proof	5,000	Value: 15.00				
2000B	3,026,000	—	—	—	5.00	8.00
2000B Proof	5,500	Value: 15.00				
2001B	4,022,000	—	—	—	4.00	7.00
2001B Proof	6,000	Value: 10.00				
2002B	1,024,000	—	—	—	4.50	7.50
2002B Proof	6,000	Value: 10.00				
2003B	1,022,000	—	—	—	4.50	7.50
2003B Proof	5,500	Value: 10.00				
2004B	1,026,000	—	—	—	4.50	7.50
2004B Proof	5,000	Value: 10.00				
2005B	2,024,000	—	—	—	4.00	7.00
2005B Proof	4,500	Value: 10.00				
2006B	7,026,000	—	—	—	4.50	7.50
2006B Proof	4,000	Value: 10.00				
2007B	16,024,000	—	—	—	4.50	7.50
2007B Proof	4,000	Value: 10.00				

KM# 34 5 FRANCS

25.0000 g., 0.9000 Silver 0.7234 oz. ASW **Obv:** Laureate head left **Obv. Legend:** CONFOEDERATIO HELVETICA **Rev:** Shield divides value within wreath, star above

Date	Mintage	F	VF	XF	Unc	BU
1904B	40,000	300	600	1,300	3,250	6,000
1904B Specimen	—	—	—	—	—	10,000
1907B	277,000	60.00	100	200	750	2,500
1907B Specimen	—	—	—	—	—	5,000
1908B	200,000	75.00	125	250	900	2,500
1908B Specimen	—	—	—	—	—	5,000
1909B	120,000	150	200	300	1,100	2,500
1909B Specimen	—	—	—	—	—	5,000
1912B	11,000	1,500	3,000	4,000	6,000	12,500
1912B Specimen	—	—	—	—	—	17,500
1916B	22,000	500	900	1,250	2,250	4,500
1916B Specimen	—	—	—	—	—	9,000

KM# 37 5 FRANCS

25.0000 g., 0.9000 Silver 0.7234 oz. ASW **Obv:** William Tell right **Rev:** Shield flanked by sprigs

Date	Mintage	F	VF	XF	Unc	BU
1922B	2,400,000	40.00	60.00	100	225	500
1922B	Inc. above	—	—	1,500	2,250	3,000
Note: Dot between Confoederatio and Helvetica						
1922B Specimen	—	—	—	—	—	3,000
1923B	11,300,000	30.00	50.00	80.00	175	350
1923B Specimen	—	—	—	—	—	3,000

KM# 38 5 FRANCS

25.0000 g., 0.9000 Silver 0.7234 oz. ASW **Obv:** William Tell right **Rev:** Shield flanked by sprigs

Date	Mintage	F	VF	XF	Unc	BU
1924B	182,000	225	300	400	750	2,250
1924B Specimen	—	—	—	—	—	3,500
1925B	2,830,000	40.00	60.00	90.00	200	500
1925B Specimen	—	—	—	—	—	1,500
1926B	2,000,000	50.00	90.00	125	250	550
1926B Specimen	—	—	—	—	—	1,500
1928B	24,000	3,500	6,500	8,500	12,000	25,000
1928B Specimen; Rare	—	—	—	—	—	—

KM# 40 5 FRANCS

15.0000 g., 0.8350 Silver 0.4027 oz. ASW, 31.5 mm. **Obv:** William Tell right **Rev:** Shield flanked by sprigs **Edge:** Lettered; two variations **Edge Lettering:** Lettering starts with vertical dividing line and group of three stars. Type I; "3 stars/DOMINUS/PROVIDEBIT/10 stars" Type II; "3 stars/DOMINUS/10 stars/PROVIDEBIT" **Note:** Raised edge lettering.

Date	Mintage	F	VF	XF	Unc	BU
1931B	Inc. above	—	50.00	100	200	300
Note: Edge lettering type II starts at 6 o'clock						
1931B	3,520,000	6.00	8.00	25.00	70.00	150
Note: Edge lettering type I starts at 6 o'clock						
1931B Specimen	Inc. above	—	—	—	—	1,500
Note: Edge lettering type I starts at 6 o'clock						
1931B	Inc. above	—	16.00	45.00	125	450
Note: Edge lettering type I starts at 2 o'clock						
1931B	Inc. above	—	1,000	1,250	1,750	2,500
Note: Edge lettering type II starts at 10 o'clock						
1932B	10,580,000	6.00	7.50	12.00	26.00	45.00
1932B Specimen	—	—	—	—	—	500
1933B	5,900,000	6.00	7.50	13.00	22.00	45.00
1933B Specimen	—	—	—	—	—	500
1935B	3,000,000	6.00	9.00	15.00	35.00	60.00
1935B Specimen	—	—	—	—	—	500
1937B	645,000	6.00	9.00	17.00	40.00	125
1937B Specimen	—	—	—	—	—	900
1939B	2,197,000	6.00	9.00	12.00	18.00	32.00
1939B Specimen	—	—	—	—	—	450
1940B	1,601,000	6.00	9.00	20.00	40.00	60.00
1940B Specimen	—	—	—	—	—	600
1948B	416,000	6.00	10.00	22.00	50.00	100
1948B Specimen	—	—	—	—	—	600
1949B	407,000	6.00	9.00	18.00	55.00	100
1949B Specimen	—	—	—	—	—	600
1950B	482,000	5.50	9.00	20.00	40.00	80.00
1950B Specimen	—	—	—	—	—	600
1951B	1,096,000	6.00	9.00	16.00	30.00	45.00
1951B Specimen	—	—	—	—	—	300
1952B	155,000	20.00	40.00	80.00	125	300
1952B Specimen	—	—	—	—	—	750
1953B	3,403,000	6.00	9.00	15.00	18.00	25.00
1953B Specimen	—	—	—	—	—	150
1954B	6,600,000	6.00	8.00	12.00	18.00	24.00
1954B Specimen	—	—	—	—	—	150
1965B	5,021,000	6.00	8.00	10.00	13.00	17.00
1965B Specimen	—	—	—	—	—	120
1966B	9,016,000	6.00	7.00	8.00	11.00	15.00
1966B Specimen	—	—	—	—	—	120
1967B	13,817,000	6.00	7.00	8.00	11.00	15.00
Note: Edge lettering type I starts at 6 o'clock						
1967B Specimen	—	—	—	—	—	120
Note: Edge lettering type I starting at 6 o'clock						
1967B	Inc. above	35.00	65.00	100	145	210
Note: Edge lettering type II starts at 2 o'clock						
1969B	8,637,000	6.00	7.00	8.00	11.00	15.00
1969B Specimen	—	—	—	—	—	120

KM# 40a.1 5 FRANCS

13.2000 g., Copper-Nickel, 31.3 mm. **Obv:** William Tell right **Rev:** Shield flanked by sprigs **Edge Lettering:** DOMINUS PROVIDEBIT

Date	Mintage	F	VF	XF	Unc	BU
1968B	33,871,000	—	—	—	7.00	10.00
1970	6,306,000	—	—	—	8.00	12.00
1973	5,002,000	—	—	—	8.00	12.00
1974	6,007,000	—	—	—	8.00	12.00
1974 Proof	2,400	Value: 125				
1975	4,015,000	—	—	—	8.00	12.00
1975 Proof	10,000	Value: 20.00				
1976	3,007,000	—	—	—	8.00	12.00
1976 Proof	5,130	Value: 20.00				
1977	2,009,000	—	—	—	9.00	14.00
1977 Proof	7,030	Value: 20.00				
1978	4,411,000	—	—	—	8.00	12.00
1978 Proof	10,000	Value: 16.00				
1979	4,011,000	—	—	—	8.00	12.00
1979 Proof	10,000	Value: 16.00				
1980	4,026,000	—	—	—	8.00	12.00
1980 Proof	10,000	Value: 16.00				
1981	6,018,000	—	—	—	8.00	12.00
1981 Proof	10,000	Value: 16.00				

KM# 40a.2 5 FRANCS

13.2000 g., Copper-Nickel, 31.3 mm. **Obv:** William Tell right **Rev:** Cross on shield flanked by sprigs **Note:** Medal alignment.

Date	Mintage	F	VF	XF	Unc	BU
1982	5,050,000	—	—	—	8.00	12.00
1982 Proof	10,000	Value: 20.00				
1983	4,033,000	—	—	—	8.00	12.00
1983 Proof	11,000	Value: 20.00				
1984	3,953,000	—	—	—	8.00	12.00
1984 Proof	14,000	Value: 16.00				

KM# 40a.3 5 FRANCS

13.2000 g., Copper-Nickel, 31.3 mm. **Obv:** William Tell right **Rev:** Shield flanked by sprigs **Note:** Incuse edge lettering. Retired legal tender status as of January 1, 2004, 1985-1993 removed from circulation.

Date	Mintage	F	VF	XF	Unc	BU
1985	4,050,000	—	—	—	8.00	12.00
1985 Proof	12,000	Value: 16.00				
1986B	7,083,000	—	—	—	8.00	12.00
1986B Proof	10,000	Value: 16.00				
1987B	7,028,000	—	—	—	8.00	12.00
1987B Proof	8,800	Value: 20.00				
1988B	7,029,000	—	—	—	8.00	12.00
1988B Proof	9,000	Value: 20.00				
1989B	5,031,000	—	—	—	8.00	12.00
1989B Proof	8,800	Value: 20.00				
1990B	1,049,000	—	—	—	8.00	12.00
1990B Proof	8,900	Value: 20.00				
1991B	26,100	—	—	—	—	145
Note: In sets only; 5,000,000 were minted and destroyed						
1991B Proof	9,900	Value: 175				
1992B	5,035,000	—	—	—	8.00	12.00
1992B Proof	7,450	Value: 20.00				
1993B Variety 1 closed shirt	16,400	—	—	—	—	145
Note: In sets only; 5,000,000 were minted and destroyed						
1993B Variety 2 open shirt	Inc. above	—	—	—	—	145
1993B Proof	6,200	Value: 175				

KM# 40a.4 5 FRANCS
13.2000 g., Copper-Nickel, 31.3 mm. **Obv:** William Tell right **Rev:** Shield flanked by sprigs **Edge:** DOMINUS PROVIDEBIT and 13 stars raised **Designer:** Paul Burkhard

Date	Mintage	F	VF	XF	Unc	BU
1994B	12,023,000	—	—	—	7.00	10.00
1994B Proof	6,100	Value: 20.00				
1995B	12,024,000	—	—	—	7.00	10.00
1995B Proof	6,100	Value: 20.00				
1996B	12,023,000	—	—	—	7.00	10.00
1996B Proof	6,100	Value: 20.00				
1997B	9,022,000	—	—	—	7.00	10.00
1997B Proof	5,500	Value: 20.00				
1998B	9,021,000	—	—	—	7.00	10.00
1998B Proof	4,800	Value: 22.50				
1999B	9,021,000	—	—	—	7.00	10.00
1999B Proof	5,000	Value: 22.50				
2000B	7,026,000	—	—	—	7.00	10.00
2000B Proof	5,500	Value: 20.00				
2001B	1,022,000	—	—	—	6.50	9.50
2001B Proof	6,000	Value: 15.00				
2002B	1,024,000	—	—	—	6.50	9.50
2002B Proof	6,000	Value: 15.00				
2003B	1,022,000	—	—	—	6.50	9.50
2003B Proof	5,500	Value: 15.00				
2004B	526,000	—	—	—	7.50	11.00
2004B Proof	5,000	Value: 15.00				
2005B	524,000	—	—	—	7.50	11.00
2005B Proof	4,500	Value: 15.00				
2006B	526,000	—	—	—	7.50	11.00
2006B Proof	4,000	Value: 15.00				
2007B	524,000	—	—	—	7.50	11.00
2007B Proof	4,000	Value: 15.00				

KM# 36 10 FRANCS
3.2258 g., 0.9000 Gold 0.0933 oz. AGW **Obv:** Young bust left **Rev:** Radiant cross above date and sprigs **Designer:** Fritz Ulysse Landry

Date	Mintage	F	VF	XF	Unc	BU
1911B	100,000	100	200	300	375	600
1912B	200,000	—	BV	100	150	175
1913B	600,000	—	BV	100	150	175
1914B	200,000	—	BV	100	150	175
1915B	400,000	—	BV	100	150	175
1916B	130,000	—	BV	100	150	175
1922B	1,020,000	—	—	BV	90.00	110

KM# 35.1 20 FRANCS
6.4516 g., 0.9000 Gold 0.1867 oz. AGW **Obv:** Young head left **Obv. Legend:** HELVETIA **Rev:** Shield within oak branches divides value **Designer:** Fritz Ulysse Landry

Date	Mintage	F	VF	XF	Unc	BU
1901B	500,000	—	BV	170	180	210
1902B	600,000	—	BV	170	180	210
1903B	200,000	—	BV	185	210	235
1904B	100,000	—	180	215	245	325
1905B	100,000	—	170	195	225	300
1906B	100,000	—	BV	185	210	235
1907B	150,000	—	BV	170	190	220
1908B	355,000	—	BV	170	180	200
1909B	400,000	—	BV	170	180	200
1910B	375,000	—	BV	170	180	200
1911B	350,000	—	BV	170	180	200
1912B	450,000	—	BV	170	180	200
1913B	700,000	—	BV	170	180	200
1914B	700,000	—	BV	170	180	200
1915B	750,000	—	BV	170	180	200
1916B	300,000	—	BV	170	180	200
1922B	2,783,678	—	—	BV	170	190
1925B	400,000	—	BV	170	180	200
1926B	50,000	—	170	180	210	235
1927B	5,015,000	—	—	BV	170	190
1930B	3,371,764	—	—	BV	170	190
1935B	175,000	—	BV	170	180	200
1935L-B	20,008,813	—	—	BV	170	190

Note: The 1935L-B issue was struck in 1945, 1946 and 1947

KM# 35.2 20 FRANCS
6.4516 g., 0.9000 Gold 0.1867 oz. AGW **Obv:** Bust left **Rev:** Shield within oak branches divides value **Edge Lettering:** AD LEGEM ANNI MCMXXXI

Date	Mintage	F	VF	XF	Unc	BU
1947B	9,200,000	—	—	BV	170	190
1949B	10,000,000	—	—	BV	170	190

KM# 39 100 FRANCS
32.2581 g., 0.9000 Gold 0.9334 oz. AGW **Obv:** Young bust left **Rev:** Radiant cross above value, date and sprigs **Designer:** Fritz Ulysse Landry

Date	Mintage	F	VF	XF	Unc	BU
1925B	5,000	—	6,000	7,500	9,000	12,500

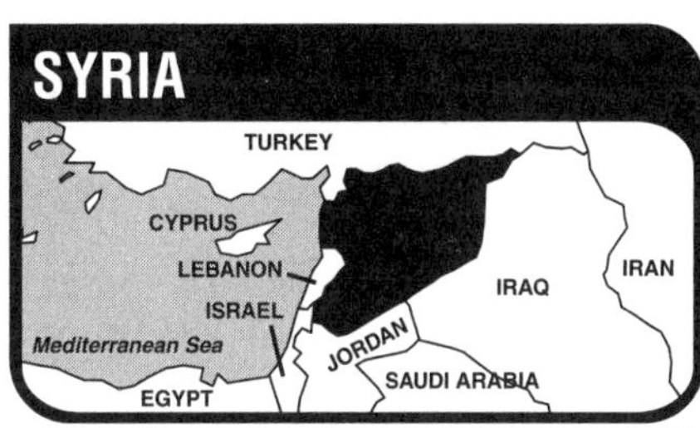

The Syrian Arab Republic, located in the Near East at the eastern end of the Mediterranean Sea, has an area of 71,498 sq. mi. (185,180 sq. km.) and a population of *12 million. Capital: Greater Damascus. Agriculture and animal breeding are the chief industries. Cotton, crude oil and livestock are exported.

Ancient Syria, a land bridge connecting Europe, Africa and Asia, has spent much of its history in thrall to the conqueror's whim. Its subjection by Egypt about 1500 B.C. was followed by successive conquests by the Hebrews, Phoenicians, Babylonians, Assyrians, Persians, Macedonians, Romans, Byzantines and finally, in 636 A.D., by the Moslems. The Arabs made Damascus, one of the oldest continuously inhabited cities of the world, the trade center and capital of an empire stretching from India to Spain. In 1516, following the total destruction of Damascus by the Mongols of Tamerlane, Syria fell to the Ottoman Turks and remained a part of Turkey until the end of World War I. The League of Nations gave France a mandate to the Levant states of Syria and Lebanon in 1920. In 1930, following a series of uprisings, France recognized Syria as an independent republic, but still subject to the mandate. Lebanon became fully independent on Nov. 22, 1943, and Syria on Jan. 1,1944.

TITLES

الجمهورية السورية

al-Jumhuriya(t) al-Suriya(t)

الجمهورية لعربية السورية

al-Jumhuriya(t) al-Arabiya(t) as-Suriya(t)

RULERS
Ottoman, until 1918
Faysal, 1918-1920

MINT MARK
(a)- Paris, privy marks only

MINT NAMES

د مشق

Damascus (Dimask)

حلب

Haleb (Aleppo)

FRENCH PROTECTORATE

STANDARD COINAGE

KM# 68 1/2 PIASTRE
4.0000 g., Copper-Nickel **Obv:** Value within roped wreath flanked by oat sprigs **Rev:** Value within wreath

Date	Mintage	F	VF	XF	Unc	BU
1921(a)	4,000,000	0.50	2.00	5.00	15.00	—

KM# 75 1/2 PIASTRE
Nickel-Brass **Obv:** Value within roped circle **Rev:** Value within oat sprigs

Date	Mintage	F	VF	XF	Unc	BU
1935(a)	600,000	1.00	4.00	12.00	42.50	—
1936(a)	800,000	1.00	4.00	9.00	30.00	—

KM# 71 PIASTRE
5.1000 g., Nickel-Brass **Obv:** Hole in center of wreath flanked by stars **Rev:** Hole in center of sprigs flanked by lion heads

Date	Mintage	F	VF	XF	Unc	BU
1929(a)	750,000	1.00	3.00	7.00	32.50	—
1933(a)	600,000	1.50	4.00	10.00	40.00	—
1935(a)	1,900,000	0.75	2.50	5.00	22.50	—
1936(a)	1,400,000	0.75	2.50	7.00	25.00	—

KM# 71a PIASTRE
3.5000 g., Zinc **Obv:** Hole in center of wreath flanked by stars **Rev:** Hole in center flanked by lion heads

Date	Mintage	F	VF	XF	Unc	BU
1940(a)	2,000,000	2.00	5.00	15.00	60.00	—

KM# 69 2 PIASTRES
Aluminum-Bronze **Obv:** Inscription divides dates within design **Rev:** Crossed oat sprigs divide value

Date	Mintage	F	VF	XF	Unc	BU
1926(a)	600,000	5.00	10.00	25.00	75.00	—
1926	Inc. above	5.00	10.00	25.00	75.00	—

Note: Without privy marks by date

KM# 76 2-1/2 PIASTRES
Aluminum-Bronze **Obv:** Hole in center of wreath flanked by stars **Rev:** Hole in center of sprigs flanked by lion heads

Date	Mintage	F	VF	XF	Unc	BU
1940(a)	2,000,000	1.25	4.00	8.00	27.50	—

KM# 70 5 PIASTRES
3.9000 g., Aluminum-Bronze **Obv:** Inscription divides dates within design **Rev:** Crossed oat sprigs divide value

Date	Mintage	F	VF	XF	Unc	BU
1926(a)	300,000	0.75	2.00	8.00	25.00	—
1926	600,000	0.75	3.00	12.00	35.00	—
1933(a)	1,200,000	0.40	2.00	12.50	40.00	—
1935(a)	2,000,000	0.30	1.50	8.00	25.00	—
1936(a)	900,000	0.50	2.00	10.00	30.00	—
1940(a)	500,000	0.50	1.50	4.00	15.00	—

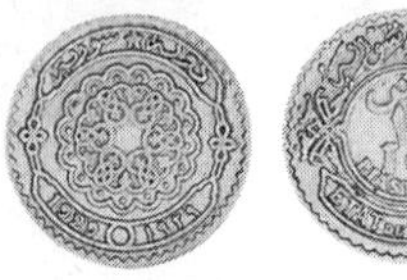

KM# 72 10 PIASTRES
2.0000 g., 0.6800 Silver 0.0437 oz. ASW **Obv:** Star in center of flower design **Rev:** Value within circle

Date	Mintage	F	VF	XF	Unc	BU
1929	1,000,000	4.00	12.00	28.00	90.00	—

KM# 73 25 PIASTRES
5.0000 g., 0.6800 Silver 0.1093 oz. ASW **Obv:** Value within circle **Rev:** Star in center of flower design

Date	Mintage	F	VF	XF	Unc	BU
1929	1,000,000	3.00	5.00	27.50	85.00	—
1933(a)	500,000	4.00	12.00	40.00	160	—
1936(a)	897,000	3.50	7.00	30.00	100	—
1937(a)	393,000	5.00	10.00	35.00	140	—

KM# 74 50 PIASTRES
10.0000 g., 0.6800 Silver 0.2186 oz. ASW **Obv:** Value within circle **Rev:** Star in center of flower design

Date	Mintage	F	VF	XF	Unc	BU
1929	880,000	4.00	8.00	35.00	140	—
1933(a)	250,000	6.00	10.00	45.00	190	—
1936(a)	400,000	5.00	10.00	40.00	160	—
1937(a)	Inc. above	7.00	12.00	50.00	200	—

WORLD WAR II EMERGENCY COINAGE

KM# 77 PIASTRE
Brass **Obv:** English value **Rev:** Arabic value

Date	Mintage	F	VF	XF	Unc	BU
ND	—	2.50	5.00	10.00	20.00	—

KM# 78 2-1/2 PIASTRES
Aluminum **Obv:** English value **Rev:** Arabic value

Date	Mintage	F	VF	XF	Unc	BU
ND	—	10.00	20.00	35.00	65.00	—

REPUBLIC

STANDARD COINAGE

KM# 81 2-1/2 PIASTRES
Copper-Nickel **Obv:** Imperial eagle **Rev:** Inscription within rectangle below value

Date	Mintage	F	VF	XF	Unc	BU
AH1367-1948	2,500,000	0.75	1.50	3.00	6.00	—
AH1375-1956	5,000,000	0.75	1.50	3.00	6.00	—

KM# 82 5 PIASTRES
3.0000 g., Copper-Nickel **Obv:** Imperial eagle **Rev:** Value within diamond shape above design flanked by stars **Designer:** Gilroy Roberts

Date	Mintage	F	VF	XF	Unc	BU
AH1367-1948	8,000,000	0.75	1.50	3.00	6.00	—
AH1375-1956	4,000,000	0.75	1.50	3.00	6.00	—

KM# 83 10 PIASTRES
Copper-Nickel **Obv:** Imperial eagle **Rev:** Value above 1/2 designed wreath **Designer:** Gilroy Roberts

Date	Mintage	F	VF	XF	Unc	BU
AH1367-1948	—	0.75	1.50	3.00	6.00	—
AH1375-1956	4,000,000	0.75	1.50	3.00	6.00	—

KM# 79 25 PIASTRES
2.5000 g., 0.6000 Silver 0.0482 oz. ASW **Obv:** Imperial eagle **Rev:** Value within circle of design flanked by oat sprigs

Date	Mintage	F	VF	XF	Unc	BU
AH1366-1947	6,300,000	1.50	2.50	6.00	20.00	—

KM# 80 50 PIASTRES
5.0000 g., 0.6000 Silver 0.0964 oz. ASW **Obv:** Imperial eagle **Rev:** Value in center circle of design

Date	Mintage	F	VF	XF	Unc	BU
AH1366-1947	4,500,000	2.50	5.00	10.00	25.00	—

KM# 84 1/2 POUND
3.3793 g., 0.9000 Gold 0.0978 oz. AGW **Obv:** Imperial eagle **Rev:** Inscription within rectangle above sprigs

Date	Mintage	F	VF	XF	Unc	BU
AH1369-1950	100,000	BV	90.00	100	125	175

KM# 85 LIRA
10.0000 g., 0.6800 Silver 0.2186 oz. ASW **Obv:** Imperial eagle **Rev:** Inscription and value within center of rectangle and sprigs

Date	Mintage	F	VF	XF	Unc	BU
AH1369-1950	7,000,000	3.50	6.50	12.50	25.00	—

KM# 86 POUND
6.7586 g., 0.9000 Gold 0.1956 oz. AGW **Obv:** Imperial eagle **Rev:** Inscription and value within rectangle above sprigs

Date	Mintage	F	VF	XF	Unc	BU
AH1369-1950	250,000	—	BV	185	200	245

UNITED ARAB REPUBLIC

STANDARD COINAGE

KM# 90 2-1/2 PIASTRES
2.0000 g., Aluminum-Bronze, 17 mm. **Obv:** Imperial eagle flanked by dates **Rev:** Inscription within rectangle below value

Date	Mintage	F	VF	XF	Unc	BU
AH1380-1960	1,100,000	0.10	0.20	0.35	0.75	—

KM# 91 5 PIASTRES
3.0000 g., Aluminum-Bronze, 19 mm. **Obv:** Imperial eagle **Rev:** Value, inscription

Date	Mintage	F	VF	XF	Unc	BU
AH1380-1960	4,240,000	0.10	0.20	0.35	0.75	—

KM# 92 10 PIASTRES
4.0000 g., Aluminum-Bronze, 21 mm. **Obv:** Imperial eagle flanked by dates **Rev:** Value in center of 1/2 wreath

Date	Mintage	F	VF	XF	Unc	BU
AH1380-1960	2,800,000	0.10	0.20	0.40	1.00	—

KM# 87 25 PIASTRES
0.3500 g., 0.6000 Silver 0.0068 oz. ASW, 20.3 mm. **Obv:** Imperial eagle **Rev:** Value flanked by oat sprigs in center of gear

Date	Mintage	F	VF	XF	Unc	BU
AH1377-1958	2,300,000	1.00	2.00	3.00	7.00	—

KM# 88 50 PIASTRES
5.0000 g., 0.6000 Silver 0.0964 oz. ASW, 23.4 mm. **Obv:** Imperial eagle **Rev:** Sword divides value within wreath

Date	Mintage	F	VF	XF	Unc	BU
AH1377-1958	120,000	2.00	3.50	7.00	18.00	—

KM# 89 50 PIASTRES
5.0000 g., 0.6000 Silver 0.0964 oz. ASW **Subject:** 1st Anniversary - Founding of United Arab Republic **Obv:** Imperial eagle **Rev:** Value

Date	Mintage	F	VF	XF	Unc	BU
AH1378-1959	1,500,000	1.75	2.75	5.00	12.00	—

SYRIAN ARAB REPUBLIC

STANDARD COINAGE

KM# 93 2-1/2 PIASTRES
2.0000 g., Aluminum-Bronze, 17 mm. **Obv:** Imperial eagle **Rev:** Inscription within rectangle below value

Date	Mintage	F	VF	XF	Unc	BU
AH1382-1962	8,000,000	—	0.10	0.20	0.50	—
AH1385-1965	8,000,000	—	0.10	0.20	0.50	—

KM# 104 2-1/2 PIASTRES
2.0000 g., Aluminum-Bronze, 17 mm. **Obv:** Imperial eagle **Rev:** Inscription within rectangle below value

Date	Mintage	F	VF	XF	Unc	BU
AH1393-1973	10,000,000	—	0.10	0.15	0.25	—

KM# 94 5 PIASTRES
3.0000 g., Aluminum-Bronze, 19 mm. **Obv:** Imperial eagle **Rev:** Value within diamond shape above design flanked by stars

Date	Mintage	F	VF	XF	Unc	BU
AH1382-1962	7,000,000	—	0.10	0.15	0.35	—
AH1385-1965	18,000,000	—	0.10	0.15	0.35	—

KM# 100 5 PIASTRES
3.0000 g., Aluminum-Bronze, 19 mm. **Series:** F.A.O. **Obv:** Imperial eagle **Rev:** Upright oat sprig within sprigs **Rev. Designer:** Khalid Asali

Date	Mintage	F	VF	XF	Unc	BU
AH1391-1971	15,000,000	—	0.10	0.15	0.25	—

KM# 105 5 PIASTRES
3.0000 g., Aluminum-Bronze, 19 mm. **Obv:** Imperial eagle **Rev:** Value within diamond shape above design flanked by stars

Date	Mintage	F	VF	XF	Unc	BU
AH1394-1974	—	—	0.10	0.15	0.25	—

KM# 110 5 PIASTRES
3.0000 g., Aluminum-Bronze, 19 mm. **Series:** F.A.O. **Obv:** Imperial eagle **Rev:** Euphrates dam within 1/2 gear and 1/2 oat sprig

Date	Mintage	F	VF	XF	Unc	BU
AH1396-1976	2,000,000	—	0.10	0.15	0.25	—

KM# 116 5 PIASTRES
3.0000 g., Aluminum-Bronze, 19 mm. **Obv:** Imperial eagle with heavy neck feathers **Rev:** Value within diamond shape above design flanked by stars **Note:** Similar to KM#94 but heavier neck feathers

Date	Mintage	F	VF	XF	Unc	BU
AH1399-1979	—	—	0.10	0.15	0.25	—

KM# 95 10 PIASTRES
4.0000 g., Aluminum-Bronze, 21 mm. **Obv:** Imperial eagle **Rev:** Value within 1/2 designed wreath **Note:** Varieties exist with fine (narrow) and course (widely spaced) reeding.

Date	Mintage	F	VF	XF	Unc	BU
AH1382-1962	6,000,000	—	0.10	0.20	0.45	—
AH1385-1965	22,000,000	—	0.10	0.20	0.45	—

Note: Reeding varieties exist

KM# 106 10 PIASTRES
4.0000 g., Aluminum-Bronze, 21 mm. **Obv:** Imperial eagle **Rev:** Value within 1/2 designed wreath

Date	Mintage	F	VF	XF	Unc	BU
AH1394-1974	—	—	0.10	0.15	0.30	—

KM# 111 10 PIASTRES
4.0000 g., Brass, 21 mm. **Series:** F.A.O. **Obv:** Imperial eagle with heavy neck feathers **Rev:** Euphrates dam within 1/2 gear and 1/2 oat sprig **Note:** Similar to 5 Piastres, KM#110.

Date	Mintage	F	VF	XF	Unc	BU
AH1396-1976	500,000	—	0.10	0.15	0.25	—

KM# 117 10 PIASTRES
4.0000 g., Copper-Nickel, 21 mm. **Obv:** Imperial eagle **Rev:** Value within 1/2 designed wreath

Date	Mintage	F	VF	XF	Unc	BU
AH1399-1979	—	—	0.10	0.15	0.30	—

KM# 96 25 PIASTRES
3.5000 g., Nickel, 20.3 mm. **Obv:** Imperial eagle **Rev:** Inscription within rectangle flanked by dates below value

Date	Mintage	F	VF	XF	Unc	BU
AH1387-1968	15,000,000	—	0.20	0.30	0.60	—

KM# 101 25 PIASTRES
3.5000 g., Nickel, 20.3 mm. **Subject:** 25th Anniversary - Al-Ba'ath Party **Obv:** Imperial eagle **Rev:** Flaming torch divides value within oat sprigs

Date	Mintage	F	VF	XF	Unc	BU
AH1392-1972	—	—	0.15	0.25	0.60	—

KM# 107 25 PIASTRES
3.5000 g., Nickel, 20.3 mm. **Obv:** Imperial eagle **Rev:** Inscription within rectangle below value

Date	Mintage	F	VF	XF	Unc	BU
AH1394-1974	—	—	0.10	0.25	0.50	—

KM# 112 25 PIASTRES
3.5000 g., Nickel, 20.5 mm. **Series:** F.A.O. **Obv:** Imperial eagle **Rev:** Euphrates dam within 1/2 gear and 1/2 oat sprig

Date	Mintage	F	VF	XF	Unc	BU
AH1396-1976	1,000,000	—	0.10	0.25	0.50	—

KM# 118 25 PIASTRES
3.5000 g., Copper-Nickel, 20.3 mm. **Obv:** Imperial eagle **Rev:** Inscription within rectangle below value

Date	Mintage	F	VF	XF	Unc	BU
AH1399-1979	—	—	0.10	0.25	0.50	—

KM# 97 50 PIASTRES
5.0000 g., Nickel, 23.4 mm. **Obv:** Imperial eagle **Rev:** Value in center square of design above dates and oat sprigs

Date	Mintage	F	VF	XF	Unc	BU
AH1387-1968	10,000,000	—	0.25	0.50	0.85	—

KM# 102 50 PIASTRES
5.0000 g., Nickel, 23.4 mm. **Subject:** 25th Anniversary - Al-Ba'ath Party **Obv:** Imperial eagle **Rev:** Inscription, dates, value and flames

Date	Mintage	F	VF	XF	Unc	BU
AH1392-1972	—	—	0.50	1.00	2.00	—

KM# 108 50 PIASTRES
5.0000 g., Nickel, 23.4 mm. **Obv:** Imperial eagle **Rev:** Value within center square of design above sprigs

Date	Mintage	F	VF	XF	Unc	BU
AH1394-1974	—	—	0.20	0.30	0.75	—

KM# 113 50 PIASTRES
5.0000 g., Nickel, 23.4 mm. **Series:** F.A.O. **Obv:** Imperial eagle **Rev:** Euphrates dam within 1/2 gear and 1/2 oat sprig

Date	Mintage	F	VF	XF	Unc	BU
AH1396-1976	1,000,000	—	0.20	0.50	1.00	—

KM# 119 50 PIASTRES
5.0000 g., Copper-Nickel, 23.4 mm. **Obv:** Imperial eagle **Rev:** Value in center square of design above sprigs

Date	Mintage	F	VF	XF	Unc	BU
AH1399-1979	—	—	0.20	0.30	0.75	—

KM# 98 POUND
7.5000 g., Nickel, 27 mm. **Obv:** Imperial eagle **Rev:** Value in diamond shape within rectangle **Edge:** Reeded

Date	Mintage	F	VF	XF	Unc	BU
AH1387-1968	10,000,000	—	0.30	0.75	1.25	—
AH1391-1971	10,000,000	—	0.30	0.75	1.25	—

KM# 99 POUND
7.5000 g., Nickel, 27 mm. **Series:** F.A.O. **Obv:** Imperial eagle **Rev:** Hands holding rectangle, oat sprig bouquet above **Designer:** Khalid Asali

Date	Mintage	F	VF	XF	Unc	BU
AH1388-1968	500,000	—	1.00	2.00	3.50	—

KM# 103 POUND
7.5000 g., Nickel, 27 mm. **Subject:** 25th Anniversary - Al-Ba'ath Party **Obv:** Imperial eagle **Rev:** Stylized map and flaming torch

Date	Mintage	F	VF	XF	Unc	BU
AH1392-1972	10,000,000	—	0.50	1.00	2.50	—

KM# 109 POUND
7.5000 g., Nickel, 27 mm. **Obv:** Imperial eagle **Rev:** Value in diamond shape at center of rectangle

Date	Mintage	F	VF	XF	Unc	BU
AH1394-1974	—	—	0.30	0.75	2.00	—

KM# 114 POUND
7.5000 g., Nickel, 27 mm. **Series:** F.A.O. **Obv:** Imperial eagle **Rev:** Euphrates dam within 1/2 gear and 1/2 oat sprig

Date	Mintage	F	VF	XF	Unc	BU
AH1396-1976	500,000	—	0.50	1.00	2.50	—

KM# 115 POUND
7.5000 g., Nickel, 27 mm. **Subject:** Re-election of President **Obv:** Imperial eagle within circle **Rev:** Head left within circle

Date	Mintage	F	VF	XF	Unc	BU
AH1398-1978	—	—	1.50	2.50	5.00	—

KM# 120.1 POUND
7.5000 g., Copper-Nickel, 27 mm. **Obv:** Imperial eagle **Rev:** Value in diamond shape at center of rectangle **Edge:** Reeded

Date	Mintage	F	VF	XF	Unc	BU
AH1399-1979	—	—	0.30	0.70	1.50	—

KM# 120.2 POUND
4.9400 g., Stainless Steel, 21 mm. **Obv:** Imperial eagle **Rev:** Value in diamond shape at center of rectangle **Note:** Reduced size and weight.

Date	Mintage	F	VF	XF	Unc	BU
AH1412-1991	—	—	0.30	0.70	1.50	2.00

KM# 121 POUND
5.0000 g., Stainless Steel **Obv:** Imperial eagle **Rev:** Value in diamond shape at center of rectangle

Date	Mintage	F	VF	XF	Unc	BU
AH1414-1994	—	—	0.30	0.70	1.50	2.00
AH1416 1996	—	—	0.30	0.75	1.50	2.00

KM# 132 POUND
5.0000 g., Stainless Steel, 25.4 mm. **Obv:** Flowers to left of dates below heraldic bird **Rev:** Value and ornamentation **Edge:** Reeded

Date	Mintage	F	VF	XF	Unc	BU
AH1416-1996	—	—	—	—	1.50	2.00

KM# 125 2 POUNDS
6.0000 g., Stainless Steel, 23 mm. **Obv:** Imperial eagle flanked by dates **Rev:** Ancient ruins and value

Date	Mintage	F	VF	XF	Unc	BU
AH1416-1996	—	—	—	0.85	1.75	2.50

KM# 123 5 POUNDS
5.0100 g., Copper-Nickel, 24.4 mm. **Obv:** Imperial eagle within birdhouse design **Rev:** Palace above value within birdhouse design

Date	Mintage	F	VF	XF	Unc	BU
AH1416-1996	—	—	—	1.00	2.00	3.00

KM# 129 5 POUNDS
7.5300 g., Nickel-Clad Steel, 24.5 mm. **Obv:** National arms within design and beaded border **Rev:** Old fort and latent image above value within design and beaded border **Edge:** Reeded and lettered **Edge Lettering:** "CENTRAL BANK 5 SYP"

Date	Mintage	F	VF	XF	Unc	BU
AH1424-2003	—	—	—	—	1.00	1.50

KM# 124 10 POUNDS
7.0000 g., Copper-Nickel, 26.40 mm. **Obv:** Imperial eagle within circle **Rev:** Ancient ruins above value within circle

Date	Mintage	F	VF	XF	Unc	BU
AH1416-1996	—	—	—	1.25	2.50	3.50
AH1417-1997(a)	—	—	—	1.25	2.50	3.50

KM# 128 10 POUNDS
7.0000 g., Copper-Nickel, 26.5 mm. **Subject:** 50th Anniversary of Al Ba'ath Party **Obv:** Imperial eagle within circle **Rev:** Map and flag above sprigs within circle **Edge:** Reeded

Date	Mintage	F	VF	XF	Unc	BU
AH1417-1997	100,000	—	—	1.25	2.50	3.50

KM# 130 10 POUNDS
9.5300 g., Copper-Nickel-Zinc, 27.4 mm. **Obv:** National arms within beaded border **Rev:** Ancient ruins with latent image within beaded border **Edge:** Reeded and lettered **Edge Lettering:** "10 SYRIAN POUNDS"

Date	Mintage	F	VF	XF	Unc	BU
AH1424-2003	—	—	—	—	2.00	3.00

KM# 122 25 POUNDS

Bi-Metallic Stainless Steel center in Aluminum-Bronze ring **Obv:** Imperial eagle within circle **Rev:** Head left within circle

Date	Mintage	F	VF	XF	Unc	BU
ND(1995)	—	—	—	2.50	7.00	9.00

KM# 126 25 POUNDS

6.4500 g., Bi-Metallic Stainless Steel center in Aluminum-Bronze ring, 25 mm. **Obv:** Imperial eagle within designed wreath **Rev:** Central Bank building within circle

Date	Mintage	F	VF	XF	Unc	BU
AH1416-1996	—	—	—	2.00	6.00	7.50

KM# 131 25 POUNDS

8.4000 g., Bi-Metallic Copper-Nickel in Nickel-Brass ring, 25 mm. **Obv:** National arms within beaded border **Rev:** Building and latent image within beaded border **Edge:** Reeded and lettered **Edge Lettering:** "CENTRAL BANK OF SYRIA 25"

Date	Mintage	F	VF	XF	Unc	BU
AH1424-2003	—	—	—	—	4.50	6.00

TAJIKISTAN

The Republic of Tajikistan (Tadjiquistan), was formed from those regions of Bukhara and Turkestan where the population consisted mainly of Tajiks. Is bordered in the north and west by Uzbekistan and Kyrgyzstan, in the east by China and in the south by Afghanistan. It has an area of 55,240 sq. miles (143,100 sq. km.) and a population of 5.95 million. It includes 2 provinces of Khudzand and Khatlon together with the Gorno-Badakhshan Autonomous Region with a population of 5,092,603. Capital: Dushanbe. Tajikistan was admitted as a constituent republic of the Soviet Union on Dec. 5, 1929. In August 1990 the Tajik Supreme Soviet adopted a declaration of republican sovereignty, and in Dec. 1991 the republic became a member of the CIS.

After demonstrations and fighting, the Communist government was replaced by a Revolutionary Coalition Council on May 7, 1992. Following further demonstrations President Nabiev was ousted on Sept. 7, 1992. Civil war broke out, and the government resigned on Nov. 10, 1992. On Nov. 30, 1992 it was announced that a CIS peacekeeping force would be sent to Tajikistan. A state of emergency was imposed in Jan. 1993. A ceasefire was signed in 1996 and a peace agreement signed in June 1997.

MONETARY SYSTEM

1 Ruble = 100 Tanga

REPUBLIC

DECIMAL COINAGE

KM# 2.1 5 DRAMS

2.0500 g., Brass Clad Steel, 16.5 mm. **Obv:** Crown within 1/2 star border **Rev:** Value within design **Edge:** Plain

Date	Mintage	F	VF	XF	Unc	BU
2001(sp)	—	—	—	—	0.50	0.75
2006(sp)	—	—	—	—	0.50	0.75

KM# 3.1 10 DRAMS

2.4700 g., Brass Clad Steel, 17.5 mm. **Obv:** Crown within 1/2 star border **Rev:** Value within design **Edge:** Plain

Date	Mintage	F	VF	XF	Unc	BU
2001(sp)	—	—	—	—	0.75	1.00
2006(sp)	—	—	—	—	0.75	1.00

KM# 4.1 20 DRAMS

2.7300 g., Brass Clad Steel, 18.5 mm. **Obv:** Crown within 1/2 star border **Rev:** Value within design **Edge:** Plain

Date	Mintage	F	VF	XF	Unc	BU
2001(sp)	—	—	—	—	1.00	1.25
2006(sp)	—	—	—	—	1.00	1.25

KM# 5.1 25 DRAMS

2.8000 g., Brass, 19.1 mm. **Obv:** Crown within 1/2 star border **Rev:** Value within design **Edge:** Plain

Date	Mintage	F	VF	XF	Unc	BU
2001(sp)	—	—	—	—	1.50	1.75
2006(sp)	—	—	—	—	1.50	1.75

KM# 6.1 50 DRAMS

3.5500 g., Brass, 21 mm. **Obv:** Crown within 1/2 star border **Rev:** Value within design **Edge:** Plain

Date	Mintage	F	VF	XF	Unc	BU
2001(sp)	—	—	—	—	1.75	2.00

KM# 7 SOMONI

5.1500 g., Copper-Nickel-Zinc, 23.9 mm. **Obv:** King's bust 1/2 right **Rev:** Value **Edge:** Reeded and plain sections

Date	Mintage	F	VF	XF	Unc	BU
2001(sp)	—	—	—	—	3.50	5.00

KM# 12 SOMONI

5.2100 g., Copper-Nickel-Zinc, 24 mm. **Subject:** Year of Aryan Civilization **Obv:** National arms above value **Rev:** Ancient archer in war chariot **Edge:** Segmented reeding

Date	Mintage	F	VF	XF	Unc	BU
2006(sp)	100,000	—	—	—	—	4.00

KM# 13 SOMONI

5.2100 g., Copper-Nickel-Zinc, 24 mm. **Subject:** Year of Aryan Civilization **Obv:** National arms above value **Rev:** Two busts left **Edge:** Segmented reeding

Date	Mintage	F	VF	XF	Unc	BU
2006(sp)	100,000	—	—	—	—	4.00

KM# 16 SOMONI

5.2400 g., Copper-Nickel-Zinc, 23.95 mm. **Subject:** 800th Anniversary Birth of Jaloliddini Rumi **Obv:** Small arms above value in cartouche **Rev:** 1/2 length figure facing **Edge:** Segmented reeding

Date	Mintage	F	VF	XF	Unc	BU
2007	—	—	—	—	3.00	4.00

KM# 8 3 SOMONI

6.3200 g., Copper-Nickel-Zinc, 25.5 mm. **Obv:** National arms **Rev:** Crown above value within design **Edge:** Lettered

Date	Mintage	F	VF	XF	Unc	BU
2001(sp)	—	—	—	—	5.00	7.00

KM# 10 3 SOMONI

Bi-Metallic, 25.5 mm. **Subject:** 80th Year - Dushanbe City **Obv:** Value below arms within circle **Rev:** Statue in arch within circle

Date	Mintage	F	VF	XF	Unc	BU
2004(sp)	—	—	—	—	6.50	9.00

KM# 14 3 SOMONI

6.3000 g., Bi-Metallic Copper-Nickel center in Brass ring, 25.5 mm. **Subject:** 2700th Anniversary of Kulyab **Obv:** National arms above value **Rev:** Kulyab city arms **Edge:** Lettered

Date	Mintage	F	VF	XF	Unc	BU
2006(sp)	100,000	—	—	—	6.00	7.50

KM# 9 5 SOMONI

7.1000 g., Copper-Nickel-Zinc, 26.4 mm. **Obv:** Turbaned head right **Rev:** Crown above value within design **Edge:** Reeded and plain sections with a star

Date	Mintage	F	VF	XF	Unc	BU
2001(sp)	—	—	—	—	7.50	9.00

KM# 11 5 SOMONI
6.9400 g., Bi-Metallic Copper-Nickel center in Brass ring, 26.5 mm. **Subject:** 10th Anniversary - Constitution **Obv:** Arms above value within circle **Rev:** Flag and book within circle **Edge:** Lettered

Date	Mintage	F	VF	XF	Unc	BU
2004(sp)	—	—	—	—	7.50	10.00

KM# 15 5 SOMONI
7.0000 g., Bi-Metallic Copper-Nickel center in Brass ring, 26.5 mm. **Subject:** 15th Anniversary of Independence **Obv:** National arms above value **Rev:** Government building **Edge:** Lettered

Date	Mintage	F	VF	XF	Unc	BU
2006(sp)	100,000	—	—	—	7.50	10.00

TANNU TUVA

The Tannu-Tuva Peoples Republic (Tuva), an autonomous part of Russia located in central Asia on the northwest border of Outer Mongolia, has an area of 64,000 sq. mi. (165,760 sq. km.) and a population of about 175,000. Capital: Kyzyl. The economy is based on herding, forestry and mining.

As Urianghi, Tuva was part of Outer Mongolia of the Chinese Empire when tsarist Russia, after fomenting a separatist movement, extended its protection to the mountainous country in 1914. Tuva declared its independence as the Tannu-Tuva Peoples Republic in 1921 under the auspices of the Tuva Peoples Revolutionary Party. In 1926, following Russia's successful mediation of the resultant Tuvinian-Mongolian territorial dispute, Tannu-Tuva and Outer Mongolia formally recognized each other's independence. The Tannu-Tuva Peoples Republic became an autonomous region of the U.S.S.R. on Oct. 13, 1944.

MONETARY SYSTEM
100 Kopejek (Kopeks) = 1 Aksha

REPUBLIC

STANDARD COINAGE

KM# 1 KOPEJEK
Aluminum-Bronze **Obv:** Inscription within circle **Rev:** Value and date

Date	Mintage	VG	F	VF	XF	Unc
1934	—	20.00	30.00	50.00	85.00	—

KM# 2 2 KOPEJEK
Aluminum-Bronze **Obv:** Inscription within circle **Rev:** Value and date

Date	Mintage	VG	F	VF	XF	Unc
1933	—	—	—	—	—	—
1934	—	22.50	35.00	65.00	100	—

KM# 3 3 KOPEJEK
Aluminum-Bronze **Obv:** Inscription within circle **Rev:** Value and date

Date	Mintage	VG	F	VF	XF	Unc
1933	—	—	—	—	—	—
1934	—	20.00	30.00	50.00	85.00	—

KM# 4 5 KOPEJEK
Aluminum-Bronze **Obv:** Inscription within circle **Rev:** Value and date

Date	Mintage	VG	F	VF	XF	Unc
1934	—	22.50	35.00	65.00	100	—

KM# 5 10 KOPEJEK
Copper-Nickel **Obv:** Inscription within circle **Rev:** Value and date

Date	Mintage	VG	F	VF	XF	Unc
1934	—	22.50	35.00	65.00	100	—

KM# 6 15 KOPEJEK
Copper-Nickel **Obv:** Inscription within circle **Rev:** Value and date

Date	Mintage	VG	F	VF	XF	Unc
1934	—	22.50	35.00	65.00	100	—

KM# 7 20 KOPEJEK
Copper-Nickel **Obv:** Inscription within circle **Rev:** Value and date

Date	Mintage	VG	F	VF	XF	Unc
1934	—	22.50	35.00	65.00	100	—

TANZANIA

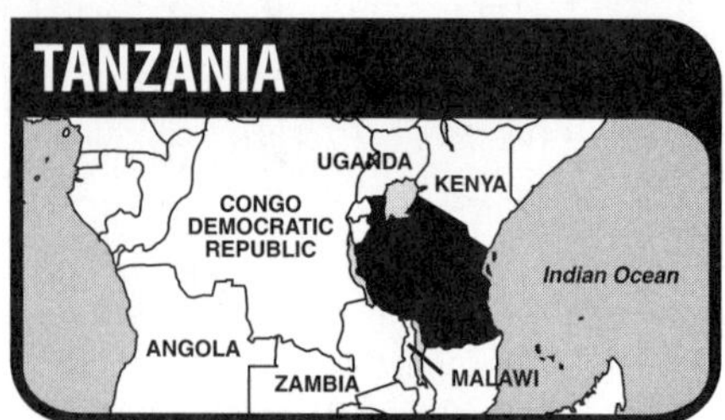

The United Republic of Tanzania, located on the east coast of Africa between Kenya and Mozambique, consists of Tanganyika and the islands of Zanzibar and Pemba. It has an area of 364,900 sq. mi. (945,090 sq. km.) and a population of *25.2 million. Capital: Dar es Salaam (Haven of Peace). The chief exports are cotton, coffee, diamonds, sisal, cloves, petroleum products, and cashew nuts.

Tanzania is a member of the Commonwealth of Nations. The President is Chief of State.

NOTE: For earlier coinage see East Africa.

REPUBLIC

STANDARD COINAGE

100 Senti = 1 Shilingi

KM# 1 5 SENTI
4.0000 g., Bronze, 22.5 mm. **Obv:** Head of President J.K. Nyerere left **Rev:** Sailfish above value **Shape:** 12-sided **Designer:** Christopher Ironside

Date	Mintage	F	VF	XF	Unc	BU
1966	55,250,000	—	0.10	0.20	0.50	1.25
1966 Proof	5,500	Value: 1.25				
1971	5,000,000	—	0.10	0.20	0.50	1.25
1972	—	—	0.10	0.20	0.50	1.25
1973	20,000,000	—	0.10	0.20	0.50	1.25
1974	12,500,000	—	0.10	0.20	0.50	1.25
1975	—	—	0.10	0.20	0.50	1.25
1976	37,500,000	—	0.10	0.20	0.50	1.25
1977	10,000,000	—	0.10	0.20	0.50	1.25
1979	7,200,000	—	0.10	0.20	0.50	1.25
1980	10,000,000	—	0.10	0.20	0.50	1.25
1981	13,650,000	—	0.10	0.20	0.50	1.25
1982	—	—	0.10	0.20	0.50	1.25
1983	18,000	—	0.10	0.20	0.50	1.25
1984	—	—	0.10	0.20	0.50	1.25

KM# 11 10 SENTI
4.8000 g., Nickel-Brass, 25 mm. **Obv:** Head of President J.K. Nyerere left **Rev:** Zebra running right **Shape:** Scalloped **Designer:** Christopher Ironside

Date	Mintage	F	VF	XF	Unc	BU
1977	19,505,000	—	0.75	1.50	4.00	6.00
1979	8,000,000	—	0.75	1.50	4.00	6.00
1980	10,000,000	—	0.75	1.50	4.00	6.00
1981	10,000,000	—	0.75	1.50	4.00	6.00
1984	—	—	0.75	1.50	4.00	6.00

KM# 2 20 SENTI
5.0000 g., Nickel-Brass, 24 mm. **Obv:** Head of President J.K. Nyerere left **Rev:** Ostrich running left **Edge:** Plain **Designer:** Christopher Ironside

Date	Mintage	F	VF	XF	Unc	BU
1966	26,500,000	—	0.20	0.40	1.50	2.00
1966 Proof	5,500	Value: 2.25				
1970	5,000,000	—	0.20	0.40	1.50	2.00
1973	20,100,000	—	0.20	0.40	1.50	2.00
1975	—	—	0.20	0.40	1.50	2.00
1976	10,000,000	—	0.20	0.40	1.50	2.00

Date	Mintage	F	VF	XF	Unc	BU
1977	10,000,000	—	0.20	0.40	1.50	2.00
1979	10,000,000	—	0.20	0.40	1.50	2.00
1980	10,000,000	—	0.20	0.40	1.50	2.00
1981	10,000,000	—	0.20	0.40	1.50	2.00
1982	—	—	0.20	0.40	1.50	2.00
1983	50,000	—	0.20	0.40	1.50	2.00
1984	—	—	0.20	0.40	1.50	2.00

KM# 3 50 SENTI

4.0000 g., Copper-Nickel, 21 mm. **Obv:** Head of President J.K. Nyerere left **Rev:** Rabbit left **Designer:** Christopher Ironside

Date	Mintage	F	VF	XF	Unc	BU
1966	6,250,000	—	0.20	0.40	2.00	2.50
1966 Proof	5,500	Value: 3.00				
1970	10,000,000	—	0.20	0.40	2.00	2.50
1973	10,000,000	—	0.25	0.50	2.00	2.50
1980	10,000,000	—	0.25	0.50	2.00	2.50
1981	—	—	0.25	0.50	2.00	2.50
1982	10,000,000	—	0.25	0.50	2.00	2.50
1983	—	—	0.25	0.50	2.00	2.50
1984	10,000,000	—	0.25	0.50	2.00	2.50

KM# 26 50 SENTI

4.0000 g., Nickel Clad Steel, 19.20 mm. **Obv:** President Mwinyi right flanked by flowers **Rev:** Rabbit left **Edge:** Reeded

Date	Mintage	F	VF	XF	Unc	BU
1988	10,000,000	—	0.25	0.75	1.50	2.00
1989	—	—	0.25	0.75	1.50	2.00
1990	—	—	0.25	0.75	1.50	2.00

KM# 4 SHILINGI

8.0000 g., Copper-Nickel, 27.5 mm. **Obv:** Head of President J.K. Nyerere left **Rev:** Hand holding torch **Designer:** Christopher Ironside

Date	Mintage	F	VF	XF	Unc	BU
1966	48,000,000	—	0.25	0.50	1.50	2.00
1966 Proof	5,500	Value: 5.00				
1972	10,000,000	—	0.25	0.50	1.50	2.00
1974	15,000,000	—	0.30	0.60	1.75	2.25
1975	—	—	0.30	0.60	1.75	2.25
1977	5,000,000	—	0.30	0.60	1.75	2.25
1980	10,000,000	—	0.25	0.50	1.50	2.00
1981	—	—	0.30	0.60	1.75	2.25
1982	10,000,000	—	0.30	0.60	1.75	2.25
1983	10,000,000	—	0.30	0.60	1.75	2.25
1984	10,000,000	—	0.30	0.60	1.75	2.25

KM# 22 SHILINGI

6.5000 g., Nickel Clad Steel, 23.5 mm. **Obv:** President Mwinyi right flanked by flowers **Rev:** Hand holding torch **Edge:** Reeded

Date	Mintage	F	VF	XF	Unc	BU
1987	5,000,000	—	0.40	0.80	2.00	2.50
1988	10,000,000	—	0.40	0.80	2.00	2.50
1989	—	—	0.40	0.80	2.00	2.50
1990	—	—	0.20	0.40	1.25	1.75
1991	—	—	0.20	0.40	1.25	1.75
1992	—	—	0.20	0.40	1.25	1.75

KM# 5 5 SHILINGI

Copper-Nickel, 31.5 mm. **Series:** F.A.O. **Subject:** 10th Anniversary of Independence **Obv:** Head of President J.K. Nyerere left **Rev:** Value in center circle, food sources in frames surround **Shape:** 10-sided **Designer:** Christopher Ironside

Date	Mintage	F	VF	XF	Unc	BU
ND(1971)	1,000,000	—	0.75	1.50	3.50	4.50

KM# 6 5 SHILINGI

13.8000 g., Copper-Nickel, 31.5 mm. **Series:** F.A.O. **Obv:** Head of President J.K. Nyerere left **Rev:** Value in center circle, food sources in frames surround **Shape:** 10-sided **Designer:** Christopher Ironside

Date	Mintage	F	VF	XF	Unc	BU
1972	8,000,000	—	0.75	1.50	3.50	4.00
1973	5,000,000	—	0.75	1.75	4.00	4.50
1980	5,000,000	—	0.75	1.75	4.00	4.50

KM# 10 5 SHILINGI

Copper-Nickel, 31.5 mm. **Subject:** 10th Anniversary - Bank of Tanzania **Obv:** Head of President J.K. Nyerere left **Rev:** Bank building above sprigs and value **Shape:** 10-sided **Designer:** Christopher Ironside

Date	Mintage	F	VF	XF	Unc	BU
ND(1976)	1,000,000	—	0.75	1.50	3.50	4.50
ND(1976) Proof	200	Value: 40.00				

KM# 12 5 SHILINGI

Copper-Nickel, 31.5 mm. **Series:** F.A.O. **Subject:** Regional Conference for Africa **Obv:** President J.K. Nyerere left flanked by oat sprigs **Rev:** Farmer working with tractor **Shape:** 10-sided **Designer:** Christopher Ironside

Date	Mintage	F	VF	XF	Unc	BU
1978	50,000	—	0.75	1.50	2.75	3.75
1978 Proof	2,000	Value: 11.50				

KM# 23 5 SHILINGI

Copper-Nickel **Obv:** President Mwinyi right flanked by flowers **Rev:** Value within center circle, food sources in frames surround **Shape:** 10-sided

Date	Mintage	F	VF	XF	Unc	BU
1987	5,000,000	—	0.75	1.50	3.00	3.50
1988	10,000,000	—	0.75	1.50	3.00	3.50
1989	—	—	0.75	1.50	3.00	3.50

KM# 23a.1 5 SHILINGI

8.5000 g., Nickel Clad Steel, 26.5 mm. **Obv:** Small (17mm) head right flanked by flowers **Rev:** Value within center circle, food sources in frames surround **Edge:** Reeded

Date	Mintage	F	VF	XF	Unc	BU
1990	—	—	0.60	1.20	1.85	2.25

KM# 23a.2 5 SHILINGI

8.5000 g., Nickel Clad Steel, 26.5 mm. **Obv:** Large (18mm) head right flanked by flowers **Rev:** Value within center circle, food sources in frames surround

Date	Mintage	F	VF	XF	Unc	BU
1991	—	—	0.60	1.20	1.85	2.25
1992	—	—	0.50	1.00	1.50	2.00
1993	—	—	0.50	1.00	1.50	2.00

KM# 20 10 SHILINGI

9.7000 g., Copper-Nickel, 29 mm. **Obv:** President J.K. Nyerere 1/4 left within circle **Rev:** National arms **Designer:** Philip Nathan

Date	Mintage	F	VF	XF	Unc	BU
1987	10,000,000	—	1.00	1.50	3.25	3.75
1988	10,000,000	—	1.00	1.50	3.25	3.75
1989	—	—	1.00	1.50	3.25	3.75

KM# 20a 10 SHILINGI

10.0000 g., Nickel Clad Steel, 29 mm. **Obv:** Bust of President J.K. Nyerere 1/4 left within circle **Rev:** National arms

Date	Mintage	F	VF	XF	Unc	BU
1990	—	—	1.00	1.50	2.25	2.75
1991	—	—	1.00	1.50	2.25	2.75
1992	—	—	0.85	1.25	2.00	2.50
1993	—	—	0.85	1.25	2.00	2.50

KM# 20a.1 10 SHILINGI

10.0000 g., Nickel Clad Steel, 29 mm. **Obv:** Bust of President J.K. Nyerere 1/4 left within circle **Rev:** 4 mm "10"; inscription near edge

Date	Mintage	F	VF	XF	Unc	BU
1990	—	—	0.60	1.20	1.85	2.25

KM# 20a.2 10 SHILINGI

10.0000 g., Nickel Clad Steel, 29 mm. **Obv:** Bust of President J.K. Nyerere 1/4 left within circle **Rev:** 3 mm "10"; inscription away from edge

Date	Mintage	F	VF	XF	Unc	BU
1991	—	—	0.60	1.20	1.85	2.25
1992	—	—	0.60	1.20	1.85	2.25
1993	—	—	0.60	1.20	1.85	2.25

KM# 13 20 SHILINGI

Copper-Nickel **Subject:** 20th Anniversary of Independence **Obv:** President J.K. Nyerere 1/4 left within circle **Rev:** National arms **Designer:** Philip Nathan

Date	Mintage	F	VF	XF	Unc	BU
ND(1981)	997,000	—	2.50	4.50	10.00	12.00

KM# 27.1 20 SHILINGI

Nickel Bonded Steel **Obv:** President Mwinyi right flanked by flowers **Rev:** Elephants **Shape:** 7-sided

Date	Mintage	F	VF	XF	Unc	BU
1990	—	—	1.50	2.00	3.50	3.75
1991	—	—	1.50	2.00	3.50	3.75

KM# 27.2 20 SHILINGI

13.0000 g., Nickel Bonded Steel, 31 mm. **Obv:** President Mwinyi right flanked by flowers **Rev:** Elephant with calf **Shape:** 7-sided **Note:** Reduced size.

Date	Mintage	F	VF	XF	Unc	BU
1992	—	—	1.25	1.75	3.25	4.50

KM# 33 50 SHILINGI

Brass Plated Steel **Subject:** Conservation **Obv:** Head of Ali Nassan Mwinyi right within circle **Rev:** Mother rhino and calf **Shape:** 7-sided **Designer:** Philip Nathan

Date	Mintage	F	VF	XF	Unc	BU
1996	—	—	—	—	4.00	5.00

KM# 32 100 SHILINGI

Brass Plated Steel **Subject:** Conservation **Obv:** Bust of President J.K. Nyerere left **Obv. Designer:** Philip Nathan **Rev:** Four Impalas running right

Date	Mintage	F	VF	XF	Unc	BU
1993	—	—	—	—	4.00	5.00
1994	—	—	—	—	4.00	5.00

KM# 34 200 SHILINGI

8.0000 g., Copper-Nickel-Zinc **Obv:** Head of Sheikh Karume 1/4 left within circle **Rev:** Two lions **Edge:** Plain and reeded sections

Date	Mintage	F	VF	XF	Unc	BU
1998	—	—	—	—	5.00	7.50

THAILAND

The Kingdom of Thailand (formerly Siam), a constitutional monarchy located in the center of mainland Southeast Asia between Burma and Laos, has an area of 198,457 mi. (514,000 sq. km.) and a population of *55.5 million. Capital: Bangkok. The economy is based on agriculture and mining. Rubber, rice, teakwood, tin and tungsten are exported.

The history of The Kingdom of Siam, the only country in south and Southeast Asia that was never colonized by an European power, dates from the 6th century A.D. when Thai people started to migrate into the area a process that accelerated with the Mongol invasion of China in the 13th century. After 400 years of sporadic warfare with the neighboring Burmese, King Taskin won the last battle in 1767. He founded a new capital, Dhonburi, on the west bank of the Chao Praya River. King Rama I moved the capital to Bangkok in 1782, thus initiating the so-called Bangkok Period of Siamese coinage characterized by Pot Duang money (bullet coins) stamped with regal symbols.

The Portuguese, who were followed by the Dutch, British and French, introduced the Thai to the Western world. Rama III of the present ruling dynasty negotiated a treaty of friendship and commerce with Britain in 1826, and in 1896 the independence of the kingdom was guaranteed by an Anglo-French accord.

In 1909 Siam ceded to Great Britain its suzerain rights over the dependencies of Kedah, Kelantan, Trengganu and Perlis, Malay states situated in southern Siam just north of British Malaya, which eliminated any British jurisdiction in Siam proper.

The absolute monarchy was changed into a constitutional monarchy in 1932.

On Dec. 8, 1941, after five hours of fighting, Thailand agreed to permit Japanese troops passage through the country to invade Northern British Malaysia. This eventually led to increased Japanese intervention and finally occupation of the country. On Jan. 25, 1942, Thailand declared war on Great Britain and the United States. A free Thai guerilla movement was soon organized to counteract the Japanese. In July 1943 Japan transferred the four northern Malay States back to Thailand. These were returned to Great Britain after peace treaties were signed in 1946.

RULERS

Rama V (Phra Maha Chulalongkorn), 1868-1910
Rama VI (Phra Maha Vajiravudh), 1910-1925
Rama VII (Phra Maha Prajadhipok), 1925-1935
Rama VIII (Phra Maha Ananda Mahidol), 1935-1946
Rama IX (Phra Maha Bhumifhol Adulyadej), 1946-

MONETARY SYSTEM

Old currency system

2 Solos = 1 Att
2 Att = 1 Sio (Pai)
2 Sio = 1 Sik
2 Sik = 1 Fuang
2 Fuang = 1 Salung (not Sal'ung)
4 Salung = 1 Baht
4 Baht = 1 Tamlung
20 Tamlung = 1 Chang

UNITS OF OLD THAI CURRENCY

Chang -	ชั่ง	Sik -	ซีก
Tamlung -	ตำลึง	Sio (Pai) -	เสี้ยว
Baht -	บาท	Att -	อัฐ
Salung -	สลึง	Solos -	โสฬส
Fuang -	เฟื้อง		

MINT MARKS

H-Heaton Birmingham

DATING

Typical BE Dating

1 2 3 8 1244

Typical CS Dating

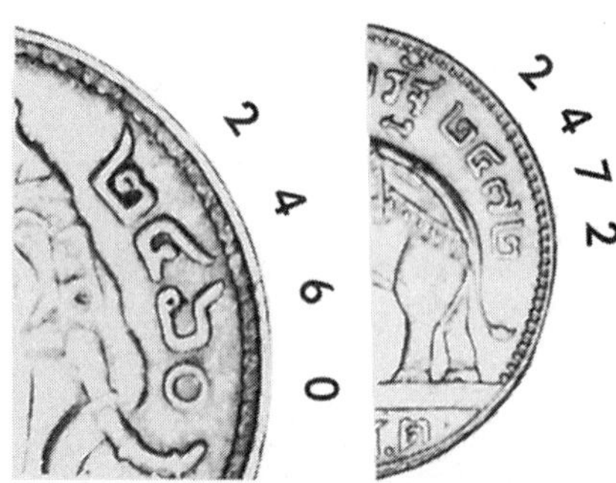

NOTE: Sometimes the era designator *BE* or *CS* will actually appear on the coin itself.

Denomination

2-1/2 (Satang) RS Dating

2 5 0 9

DATE CONVERSION TABLES

B.E. date - 543 = A.D. date
Ex: 2516 - 543 = 1973
R.S. date + 1781 = A.D. date
Ex: 127 + 1781 = 1908
C.S. date + 638 = A.D. date
Ex 1238 + 638 = 1876

Primary denominations used were 1 Baht, 1/4 and 1/8 Baht up to the reign of Rama IV. Other denominations are much scarcer.

KINGDOM OF SIAM
until 1939

STANDARD COINAGE

Y# 21 1/2 ATT (1 Solot)

Bronze **Ruler:** Rama V **Obv:** Uniformed bust left **Rev:** Crowned seated figure right

Date	Mintage	F	VF	XF	Unc	BU
RS124 (1905)	—	1.50	2.50	8.50	85.00	—

Note: These coins were also minted in RS114, RS115, RS121 and RS122. The last year had a mintage of 5,120,000. Coins with these dates have not been observed and were probably additional mintings of coins dated RS109 and RS118. A nickel pattern dated RS114 does exist. Varieties in numeral size and rotated dies exist

Y# 22 ATT

Bronze **Ruler:** Rama V **Obv:** Uniformed bust left **Rev:** Crowned seated figure right **Note:** Full red uncirculated coins of this type carry a substantial premium.

Date	Mintage	F	VF	XF	Unc	BU
RS121 (1902)	11,251,000	3.50	5.00	30.00	170	—
RS122 (1903)	4,109,000	4.50	10.00	50.00	200	—
Note: Exists with large (greater than 1mm) and small (less than 1mm) numerals						
RS124 (1905)	—	3.50	5.00	30.00	170	—

Y# 23 2 ATT (1/32 Baht = 1 Sio)

Bronze **Ruler:** Rama V **Obv:** Uniformed bust left **Rev:** Crowned seated figure right **Note:** Varieties in numeral size and rotated dies exist. Full red uncirculated coins of this type carry a substantial premium.

Date	Mintage	F	VF	XF	Unc	BU
RS121 (1902)	2,797,000	1.50	3.00	25.00	200	—
RS122 (1903)	2,323,000	1.50	3.00	25.00	200	—
RS124 (1905)	—	1.50	3.00	25.00	200	—

Y# 32a FUANG (1/8 Baht)

Silver **Ruler:** Rama V **Obv:** Bust left **Rev:** National arms **Note:** Weight range: 1.7-2.01 g.

Date	Mintage	F	VF	XF	Unc	BU
RS120 (1901)	—	3.00	15.00	60.00	120	—
RS121 (1902)	380,000	3.00	15.00	60.00	120	—
RS122 (1903)	460,000	3.00	15.00	60.00	130	—
RS123 (1904)	310,000	3.00	15.00	60.00	120	—
RS124 (1905)	410,000	3.00	15.00	60.00	130	—
RS125 (1906)	—	3.00	15.00	60.00	120	—
RS126 (1907)	—	3.00	15.00	60.00	120	—
RS127 (1908)	480,000	3.00	15.00	80.00	180	—

Y# 32c FUANG (1/8 Baht)

Gold **Ruler:** Rama V **Obv:** Bust left **Rev:** National arms

Date	Mintage	F	VF	XF	Unc	BU
RS122 (1903)	—	500	1,000	1,500	2,800	—
RS123 (1904)	—	1,500	3,000	5,000	7,000	—
RS124 (1905)	—	1,500	3,000	5,000	7,000	—
RS125 (1906)	—	1,500	3,000	5,000	7,000	—
RS126 (1907)	—	1,500	3,000	5,000	7,000	—
RS127 (1908)	—	1,500	3,000	5,000	7,000	—
RS128 (1909)	—	1,500	3,000	5,000	7,000	—
RS129 (1910)	—	1,500	3,000	5,000	7,000	—

Y# 33a SALUNG = 1/4 BAHT

Silver **Ruler:** Rama V **Obv:** Bust left **Rev:** National arms **Note:** Weight range: 3.60-4.02g.

Date	Mintage	F	VF	XF	Unc	BU
RS120 (1901)	—	100	200	300	4,000	—
RS121 (1902)	560,000	20.00	40.00	60.00	180	—
RS122 (1903)	340,000	30.00	60.00	80.00	240	—
RS123 (1904)	190,000	30.00	40.00	60.00	180	—
RS125 (1906)	—	20.00	40.00	60.00	180	—
RS126 (1907)	—	20.00	40.00	60.00	180	—
RS127 (1908)	270,000	20.00	60.00	80.00	200	—

Y# 43 SALUNG = 1/4 BAHT

3.7500 g., 0.8000 Silver 0.0964 oz. ASW **Ruler:** Rama VI **Obv:** Bust right **Rev:** Elephant heads flank facing elephant

Date	Mintage	F	VF	XF	Unc	BU
BE2458 (1915)	2,040,000	—	5.00	10.00	20.00	—

Y# 43a SALUNG = 1/4 BAHT

3.7500 g., 0.6500 Silver 0.0784 oz. ASW **Ruler:** Rama VI **Obv:** Bust right **Rev:** Elephant heads flank facing elephant

Date	Mintage	F	VF	XF	Unc	BU
BE2460 (1917)	1,100,000	—	4.00	8.00	18.50	—
BE2461 (1918)	2,170,000	—	4.00	8.00	18.50	—
BE2462 (1919)	7,860,000	—	3.00	6.50	15.00	—
BE2467 (1924)	2,100,000	—	4.00	8.00	18.50	—
BE2468 (1925)	—	—	4.00	8.00	18.50	—

Y# 43b SALUNG = 1/4 BAHT

3.7500 g., 0.5000 Silver 0.0603 oz. ASW **Ruler:** Rama VI **Obv:** Bust right **Rev:** Elephant heads flank facing elephant

Date	Mintage	F	VF	XF	Unc	BU
BE2462 (1919) Dot after legend	Inc. above	—	40.00	65.00	120	—

Y# 34a BAHT

Silver, 31.5 mm. **Ruler:** Rama V **Obv:** Bust left **Rev:** National arms, flags flanking **Edge:** Plain

Date	Mintage	F	VF	XF	Unc	BU
RS120 (1901)	—	100	200	400	1,500	—
RS121 (1902)	4,070,000	20.00	40.00	90.00	300	—
Note: There are two varieties, large and small date						
RS122 (1903)	19,150,000	30.00	50.00	80.00	240	—
RS123 (1904)	4,790,000	20.00	40.00	60.00	180	—
RS124 (1905)	6,770,000	20.00	40.00	60.00	180	—
RS125 (1906)	—	20.00	40.00	60.00	180	—
RS126 (1907)	—	40.00	60.00	150	380	—

DECIMAL COINAGE

25 Satang = 1 Salung; 100 Satang = 1 Baht

Y# 50 1/2 SATANG

Bronze **Ruler:** Rama VIII **Obv:** Hole in center divides inscription **Rev:** Hole in center of design

Date	Mintage	F	VF	XF	Unc	BU
BE2480 (1937)	—	—	0.75	1.75	3.50	—

Y# 35 SATANG

Bronze **Ruler:** Rama VI **Obv:** Hole in center divides inscription **Rev:** Hole in center of design **Edge:** Plain **Note:** Variations in lettering exist.

Date	Mintage	F	VF	XF	Unc	BU
RS127 (1908)	17,000,000	—	2.50	35.00	100	—
RS128 (1909)	150,000	—	3.50	35.00	100	—
RS129 (1910)	9,000,000	—	1.50	35.00	100	—
RS130 (1911)	30,000,000	—	1.50	25.00	50.00	—
RS132 (1913) Rare	—	—	—	—	—	—
BE2456 (1913)	10,000,000	—	1.00	1.50	4.00	—
BE2457 (1914)	1,000,000	—	2.00	4.00	12.50	—
BE2458 (1915)	5,000,000	—	0.75	1.00	2.75	—
BE2461 (1918)	18,880,000	—	0.65	1.25	3.00	—
BE2462 (1919)	6,400,000	—	0.65	1.00	2.75	—
BE2463 (1920)	17,240,000	—	1.00	1.50	3.50	—
BE2464 (1921)	6,360,000	—	15.00	25.00	100	—
BE2466 (1923)	14,000,000	—	0.75	1.00	2.75	—
BE2467 (1924)	Inc. above	—	1.00	1.50	3.50	—
BE2469 (1926)	20,000,000	—	0.50	0.75	2.50	—
BE2470 (1927)	—	—	0.50	0.75	2.50	—
BE2472 (1929)	—	—	0.50	1.00	2.75	—
BE2478 (1935)	—	—	0.50	0.70	2.00	—
BE2480 (1937)	—	—	0.50	0.70	2.00	—

Y# 51 SATANG

Bronze **Ruler:** Rama VIII **Obv:** Hole in center divides inscription **Rev:** Hole in center of design **Edge:** Plain

Date	Mintage	F	VF	XF	Unc	BU
BE2482 (1939)	24,400,000	—	1.50	3.00	6.00	—

Y# 36 5 SATANG

Nickel, 18 mm. **Ruler:** Rama VI **Obv:** Hole in center divides inscription **Rev:** Center hole within design

Date	Mintage	F	VF	XF	Unc	BU
RS127 (1908)	7,000,000	—	3.00	35.00	100	—
RS128 (1909)	4,000,000	—	3.50	35.00	100	—
RS129 (1910)	4,000,000	—	1.50	35.00	100	—
RS131 (1912)	2,000,000	—	1.50	25.00	50.00	—
RS132 (1913) Rare	—	—	—	—	—	—
BE2456 (1913)	2,000,000	—	1.50	2.50	6.00	—
BE2457 (1914)	2,000,000	—	1.50	2.50	6.00	—
BE2461 (1918)	2,000,000	—	1.50	2.50	6.00	—
BE2462 (1919)	2,000,000	—	1.00	2.00	6.00	—
BE2463 (1920)	9,900,000	—	1.00	1.50	4.50	—
BE2464 (1921)	13,000,000	—	0.60	1.25	3.00	—
BE2469 (1926)	20,000,000	—	0.60	1.25	3.00	—
BE2478 (1935)	10,000,000	—	0.60	1.25	3.00	—
BE2480 (1937)	20,000,000	—	0.60	1.25	3.00	—

Y# 37 10 SATANG

3.3000 g., Nickel **Ruler:** Rama VI **Obv:** Hole in center divides inscription **Rev:** Hole in center of design **Edge:** Plain **Note:** Variations in lettering exist.

Date	Mintage	F	VF	XF	Unc	BU
RS127 (1908)	7,000,000	—	1.50	35.00	120	—
RS129 (1910)	5,000,000	—	1.50	35.00	120	—
RS130 (1911)	500,000	—	2.00	5.00	12.00	—
RS131 (1912)	1,500,000	—	1.50	3.00	10.00	—
BE2456 (1913)	1,000,000	—	1.25	2.00	6.00	—
BE2457 (1914)	1,000,000	—	1.25	2.00	6.00	—
BE2461 (1918)	770,000	—	2.50	3.50	9.00	—
BE2462 (1919)	774,000	—	1.25	1.50	3.50	—
BE2463 (1920)	Inc. above	—	1.25	1.50	3.50	—
BE2464 (1921)	21,727,000	—	1.00	1.25	3.00	—
BE2478 (1935)	5,000,000	—	1.00	1.25	3.00	—
BE2480 (1937)	5,000,000	—	0.75	1.00	2.50	—

Y# 48 25 SATANG = 1/4 BAHT
3.7500 g., 0.6500 Silver 0.0784 oz. ASW **Ruler:** Rama VII **Obv:** Uniformed bust left **Rev:** Elephant

Date	Mintage	F	VF	XF	Unc	BU
BE2472 (1929)	—	—	4.50	9.00	22.50	—

Y# 49 50 SATANG = 1/2 BAHT
7.5000 g., 0.6500 Silver 0.1567 oz. ASW **Ruler:** Rama VII **Obv:** Uniformed bust left **Rev:** Elephant

Date	Mintage	F	VF	XF	Unc	BU
BE2472 (1929)	17,008,000	—	7.00	16.50	35.00	45.00

Y# 44 2 SALUNG = 1/2 BAHT
7.5000 g., 0.8000 Silver 0.1929 oz. ASW **Ruler:** Rama VI **Obv:** Uniformed bust right **Rev:** Elephant heads flank facing elephant

Date	Mintage	F	VF	XF	Unc	BU
BE2458 (1915)	2,740,000	—	7.50	18.50	40.00	—

Y# 44b 2 SALUNG = 1/2 BAHT
7.5000 g., 0.5000 Silver 0.1206 oz. ASW **Ruler:** Rama VI **Obv:** Uniformed bust right **Rev:** Elephant heads flank facing elephant

Date	Mintage	F	VF	XF	Unc	BU
BE2462 (1919)	Inc. above	—	7.50	16.50	32.50	—
Note: Large dot after legend						
BE2462 (1919)	Inc. above	—	7.50	16.50	32.50	—
Note: Small dot after legend						

Y# 44a 2 SALUNG = 1/2 BAHT
7.5000 g., 0.6500 Silver 0.1567 oz. ASW **Ruler:** Rama VI **Obv:** Uniformed bust right **Rev:** Elephant heads flank facing elephant **Note:** Date varieties exist.

Date	Mintage	F	VF	XF	Unc	BU
BE2462 (1919)	3,230,000	—	6.00	14.00	30.00	—
BE2463 (1920)	4,970,000	—	6.00	14.00	30.00	—
BE2464 (1921)	—	—	6.00	14.00	30.00	—

Y# 39 BAHT
15.0000 g., 0.9000 Silver 0.4340 oz. ASW **Ruler:** Rama V **Obv:** Uniformed bust left **Rev:** Elephant heads flank facing elephant

Date	Mintage	F	VF	XF	Unc	BU
RS127 (1908)	1,037,000	—	2,500	3,750	6,750	—

Y# 45 BAHT
15.0000 g., 0.9000 Silver 0.4340 oz. ASW **Ruler:** Rama VI **Obv:** Uniformed bust right **Rev:** Elephant heads flank facing elephant

Date	Mintage	F	VF	XF	Unc	BU
BE2456 (1913)	2,690,000	—	12.50	18.50	40.00	—
Note: BE2456 is often found weakly struck so it does appear similar to a counterfeit						
BE2457 (1914)	490,000	—	14.50	25.00	50.00	—
BE2458 (1915)	5,000,000	—	12.50	18.50	40.00	—
BE2459 (1916)	9,080,000	—	12.50	18.50	32.00	—
BE2460 (1917)	14,340,000	—	12.50	18.50	32.00	—
BE2461 (1918)	3,840,000	—	12.50	18.50	45.00	—

KINGDOM OF THAILAND
1939-

DECIMAL COINAGE

25 Satang = 1 Salung; 100 Satang = 1 Baht

Y# 54 SATANG
Bronze **Ruler:** Rama VIII **Obv:** Hole in center of design **Rev:** Hole in center of design **Edge:** Plain

Date	Mintage	F	VF	XF	Unc	BU
BE2484 (1941)	—	—	0.50	1.50	3.00	—

Y# 57 SATANG
1.5000 g., Tin **Ruler:** Rama VIII **Obv:** Center hole within design **Rev:** Center hole within design **Edge:** Plain **Note:** BE date and denomination in Thai numerals, without hole.

Date	Mintage	F	VF	XF	Unc	BU
BE2485 (1942)	20,700,000	—	0.30	0.50	1.00	—
Note: Approximately 790,000 coins were struck for circulation 1967-73						

Y# 60 SATANG
Tin **Ruler:** Rama VIII **Obv:** Hole in center of design **Rev:** Hole in center of design **Edge:** Plain **Note:** BE date and denomination in Western numerals. No hole.

Date	Mintage	F	VF	XF	Unc	BU
BE2487 (1944)	500,000	—	0.10	0.20	0.50	—

Y# 186 SATANG
0.5000 g., Aluminum, 14.58 mm. **Ruler:** Bhumipol Adulyadej (Rama IX) **Obv:** Head left **Rev:** Steepled building **Edge:** Plain

Date	Mintage	F	VF	XF	Unc	BU
BE2530 (1987)	93,000	—	—	—	0.10	—
BE2531 (1988)	200,000	—	—	—	0.10	—
BE2533 (1990)	—	—	—	—	0.10	—
BE2534 (1991)	—	—	—	—	0.10	—
BE2535 (1992)	—	—	—	—	0.10	—
BE2536 (1993)	—	—	—	—	0.10	—
BE2537 (1994)	—	—	—	—	0.10	—
BE2538 (1995)	—	—	—	—	0.10	—

Y# 342 SATANG
Aluminum **Ruler:** Bhumipol Adulyadej (Rama IX) **Subject:** 50th Anniversary - Reign of King Rama IX **Obv:** Uniformed bust facing **Rev:** Arms

Date	Mintage	F	VF	XF	Unc	BU
BE2539 (1996)	—	—	—	—	0.15	—

Y# 55 5 SATANG
1.5000 g., 0.6500 Silver 0.0313 oz. ASW **Ruler:** Rama VIII **Obv:** Center hole within design **Rev:** Center hole within design

Date	Mintage	F	VF	XF	Unc	BU
BE2484 (1941)	—	—	1.50	3.00	4.50	—

Y# 58 5 SATANG
Tin **Ruler:** Rama VIII **Obv:** Hole in center of design **Rev:** Hole in center of design **Note:** BE date and denomination in Thai numerals.

Date	Mintage	F	VF	XF	Unc	BU
BE2485 (1942)	—	—	0.50	1.50	3.00	—

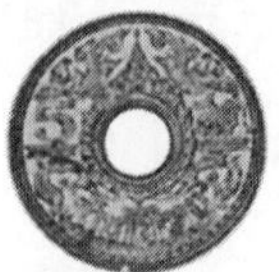

Y# 61 5 SATANG
Tin **Ruler:** Rama VIII **Obv:** Hole in center of design **Rev:** Hole in center of design **Note:** Thick (2.2mm) planchet. BE date and denomination in Western numerals.

Date	Mintage	F	VF	XF	Unc	BU
BE2487 (1944)	—	—	0.50	1.25	3.00	—
BE2488 (1945)	—	—	0.50	1.25	3.00	—

Y# 61a 5 SATANG
Tin **Ruler:** Rama VIII **Obv:** Hole in center of design **Rev:** Hole in center of design **Note:** Thin (2mm) planchet.

Date	Mintage	F	VF	XF	Unc	BU
BE2488 (1945)	—	—	0.50	1.25	3.00	—

Y# 61b 5 SATANG
Tin **Ruler:** Rama VIII **Obv:** Hole in center of design **Rev:** Hole in center of design **Note:** Medium planchet.

Date	Mintage	F	VF	XF	Unc	BU
BE2488 (1945)	—	—	0.50	1.25	3.00	—

Y# 64 5 SATANG
Tin **Ruler:** Rama VIII **Obv:** King Ananda, youth head left **Rev:** Mythical creature "Garuda"

Date	Mintage	F	VF	XF	Unc	BU
BE2489 (1946)	—	—	0.50	1.00	2.00	—

Y# 68 5 SATANG
1.1000 g., Tin **Ruler:** Rama VIII **Obv:** King Ananda, youth head left **Rev:** Mythical creature "Garuda"

Date	Mintage	F	VF	XF	Unc	BU
BE2489 (1946)	24,480,000	—	0.15	0.50	1.00	—

Y# 72 5 SATANG
Tin **Ruler:** Bhumipol Adulyadej (Rama IX) **Obv:** Uniformed bust left with one medal **Rev:** Mantled arms

Date	Mintage	F	VF	XF	Unc	BU
BE2493 (1950)	Est. 6,480,000	—	0.50	0.75	1.25	—
Note: Coins bearing this date were also struck in 1954, 58, 59, and 73. Mintages are included here						

Y# 72a 5 SATANG
Aluminum-Bronze **Ruler:** Bhumipol Adulyadej (Rama IX) **Obv:** Uniformed bust left **Rev:** Mantled arms **Edge:** Plain

Date	Mintage	F	VF	XF	Unc	BU
BE2493 (1950)	15,500,000	—	0.25	1.00	2.00	—

Y# 78 5 SATANG
Aluminum-Bronze **Ruler:** Bhumipol Adulyadej (Rama IX) **Obv:** Smaller head, 3 medals on uniform **Rev:** Mantled arms **Edge:** Plain

Date	Mintage	F	VF	XF	Unc	BU
BE2500 (1957)	Est. 46,440,000	—	—	0.10	0.25	—
Note: Minted without date change until 1987						

Y# 78a 5 SATANG
Bronze **Ruler:** Bhumipol Adulyadej (Rama IX) **Obv:** Uniformed bust left **Rev:** Mantled arms **Edge:** Plain

Date	Mintage	F	VF	XF	Unc	BU
BE2500 (1957)	Est. 6,240,000	—	0.50	1.50	2.00	—

Y# 78b 5 SATANG
Tin **Ruler:** Bhumipol Adulyadej (Rama IX) **Obv:** Uniformed bust left **Rev:** Mantled arms

Date	Mintage	F	VF	XF	Unc	BU
BE2500 (1957)	—	—	1.75	3.00	5.00	—
Note: The above coins were struck to replace Y#72 in mint sets						

Y# 208 5 SATANG

0.6000 g., Aluminum, 15.95 mm. **Ruler:** Bhumipol Adulyadej (Rama IX) **Obv:** Bust left **Rev:** Phra Patom Temple **Edge:** Plain

Date	Mintage	F	VF	XF	Unc	BU
BE2530 (1987)	—	—	—	—	20.00	—
BE2531 (1988)	704,000	—	—	—	0.10	—
BE2533 (1990)	—	—	—	—	0.10	—
BE2534 (1991)	—	—	—	—	0.10	—
BE2535 (1992)	—	—	—	—	0.10	—
BE2536 (1993)	—	—	—	—	0.10	—
BE2537 (1994)	—	—	—	—	0.10	—
BE2538 (1995)	—	—	—	—	0.10	—

Y# 343 5 SATANG

Aluminum **Ruler:** Bhumipol Adulyadej (Rama IX) **Subject:** 50th Anniversary - Reign of King Rama IX **Obv:** Bust facing **Rev:** Arms

Date	Mintage	F	VF	XF	Unc	BU
BE2539 (1996)	—	—	—	—	0.25	—

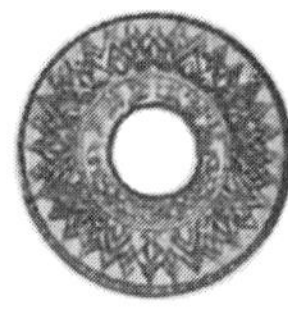

Y# 56 10 SATANG

2.5000 g., 0.6500 Silver 0.0522 oz. ASW **Ruler:** Rama VIII **Obv:** Hole in center of design **Rev:** Hole in center of design **Edge:** Plain

Date	Mintage	F	VF	XF	Unc	BU
BE2484 (1941)	—	—	2.00	4.00	8.00	—

Y# 59 10 SATANG

Tin **Ruler:** Rama VIII **Obv:** Hole in center of design **Rev:** Hole in center of design **Note:** BE date and denomination in Thai numerals.

Date	Mintage	F	VF	XF	Unc	BU
BE2485 (1942)	230,000	—	1.00	2.00	5.00	—

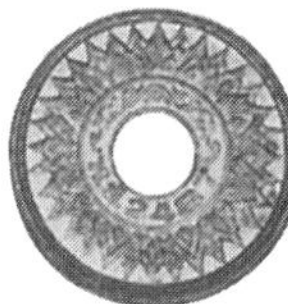

Y# 62 10 SATANG

Tin **Ruler:** Rama VIII **Obv:** Hole in center of design **Rev:** Hole in center of design **Note:** Thick (2.5mm) planchet. BE date and denomination in Western numerals.

Date	Mintage	F	VF	XF	Unc	BU
BE2487 (1944)	—	—	1.00	2.00	3.50	—
BE2488 (1945)	—	—	3.50	7.00	15.00	—

Y# 62a 10 SATANG

Tin **Ruler:** Bhumipol Adulyadej (Rama IX) **Obv:** Hole in center of design **Rev:** Hole in center of design **Note:** Thin (2mm) planchet.

Date	Mintage	F	VF	XF	Unc	BU
BE2488 (1945)	—	—	1.00	2.50	4.00	—

Y# 65 10 SATANG

Tin **Ruler:** Bhumipol Adulyadej (Rama IX) **Obv:** King Ananda, child head **Rev:** Mythical creature "Garuda"

Date	Mintage	F	VF	XF	Unc	BU
BE2489 (1946)	—	—	0.50	1.25	2.25	—

Y# 69 10 SATANG

Tin **Ruler:** Bhumipol Adulyadej (Rama IX) **Obv:** Youth head **Rev:** Mythical creature "Garuda" **Edge:** Plain

Date	Mintage	F	VF	XF	Unc	BU
BE2489 (1946)	40,470,000	—	0.50	1.25	2.00	—

Y# 73 10 SATANG

Tin **Ruler:** Bhumipol Adulyadej (Rama IX) **Obv:** King Bhumiphol, one medal on uniform **Rev:** Arms **Edge:** Plain

Date	Mintage	F	VF	XF	Unc	BU
BE2493 (1950)	139,695,000	—	0.40	1.00	1.50	—

Note: These coins were also struck in 1954-1973 and the mintages are also included here

Y# 73a 10 SATANG

Aluminum-Bronze **Ruler:** Bhumipol Adulyadej (Rama IX) **Obv:** King Bhumiphol left **Rev:** Arms

Date	Mintage	F	VF	XF	Unc	BU
BE2493 (1950)	4,060,000	—	0.75	1.50	2.50	—

Y# 79 10 SATANG

Aluminum-Bronze **Ruler:** Bhumipol Adulyadej (Rama IX) **Obv:** Smaller head, 3 medals on uniform **Rev:** Mantled arms with thin style legend

Date	Mintage	F	VF	XF	Unc	BU
BE2500 (1957)	Est. 55,410,000	—	0.10	0.25	0.50	—

Note: Minted without date change until 1987

Y# 79a 10 SATANG

Bronze **Ruler:** Bhumipol Adulyadej (Rama IX) **Obv:** Uniformed bust left **Rev:** Mantled arms with thick style legend **Edge:** Plain

Date	Mintage	F	VF	XF	Unc	BU
BE2500 (1957)	13,365,000	—	0.25	0.75	1.25	—
BE2501 (1958)	—	—	0.25	0.75	1.25	—

Y# 79b 10 SATANG

Tin **Ruler:** Bhumipol Adulyadej (Rama IX) **Obv:** Uniformed bust left **Rev:** Mantled arms with thick style legend

Date	Mintage	F	VF	XF	Unc	BU
BE2500 (1957)	—	—	—	—	20.00	—

Y# 79c 10 SATANG

Bronze **Ruler:** Bhumipol Adulyadej (Rama IX) **Obv:** Uniformed bust left **Rev:** Mantled arms with thin style legend

Date	Mintage	F	VF	XF	Unc	BU
BE2500 (1957)	Inc. above	—	100	200	400	—

Y# 79d 10 SATANG

Aluminum-Bronze **Ruler:** Bhumipol Adulyadej (Rama IX) **Obv:** Uniformed bust left **Rev:** Mantled arms with thick style legend **Edge:** Plain

Date	Mintage	F	VF	XF	Unc	BU
BE2500 (1957)	—	—	0.10	0.25	0.50	—

Y# 209 10 SATANG

0.8000 g., Aluminum, 16.47 mm. **Ruler:** Bhumipol Adulyadej (Rama IX) **Obv:** Young bust left **Rev:** Steepled building **Edge:** Plain

Date	Mintage	F	VF	XF	Unc	BU
BE2530 (1987)	—	—	—	—	20.00	—
BE2531 (1988)	900,000	—	—	—	0.10	—
BE2533 (1990)	—	—	—	—	0.10	—
BE2534 (1991)	—	—	—	—	0.10	—
BE2535 (1992)	—	—	—	—	0.10	—
BE2536 (1993)	—	—	—	—	0.10	—
BE2537 (1994)	—	—	—	—	0.10	—
BE2538 (1995)	—	—	—	—	0.10	—

Y# 344 10 SATANG

Aluminum **Ruler:** Bhumipol Adulyadej (Rama IX) **Subject:** 50th Anniversary - Reign of King Rama IX **Obv:** Bust facing **Rev:** Arms

Date	Mintage	F	VF	XF	Unc	BU
BE2539 (1996)	—	—	—	—	0.35	—

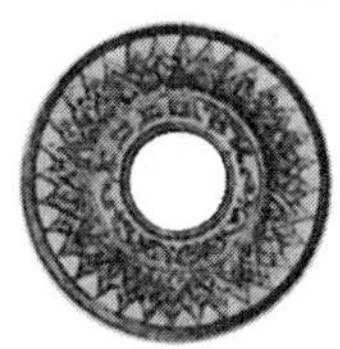

Y# A56 20 SATANG

3.0000 g., 0.6500 Silver 0.0627 oz. ASW **Ruler:** Rama VIII **Obv:** Hole in center of design **Rev:** Hole in center of design **Note:** BE date and denomination in Thai numerals

Date	Mintage	F	VF	XF	Unc	BU
BE2485 (1942)	—	—	3.00	6.00	12.00	—

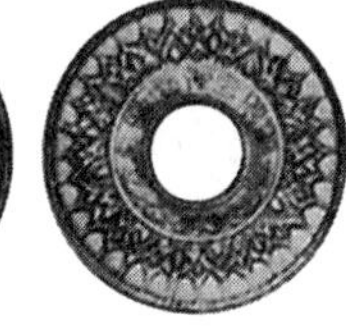

Y# 63 20 SATANG

Tin **Ruler:** Rama VIII **Obv:** Hole in center of design **Rev:** Hole in center of design **Edge:** Plain **Note:** BE date and denomination in Western numerals.

Date	Mintage	F	VF	XF	Unc	BU
BE2488 (1945)	—	—	1.00	2.50	5.00	—

Y# 66 25 SATANG = 1/4 BAHT

Tin **Ruler:** Rama VIII **Obv:** King Ananda, childs head **Rev:** Mythical creature "Garuda"

Date	Mintage	F	VF	XF	Unc	BU
BE2489 (1946)	—	—	2.50	4.50	12.50	—

Y# 70 25 SATANG = 1/4 BAHT

Tin **Ruler:** Rama VIII **Obv:** Youth's head left **Rev:** Mythical creature "Garuda" **Edge:** Reeded

Date	Mintage	F	VF	XF	Unc	BU
BE2489 (1946)	Est. 226,348,000	—	0.20	0.40	0.75	—

Note: These coins were also struck 1954-64 and mintage figure is a total

Y# 76 25 SATANG = 1/4 BAHT

Aluminum-Bronze **Ruler:** Bhumipol Adulyadej (Rama IX) **Obv:** Young bust left, one medal on uniform **Rev:** Mantled arms

Date	Mintage	F	VF	XF	Unc	BU
BE2493 (1950)	23,170,000	—	0.75	1.75	4.00	—

Y# 80 25 SATANG = 1/4 BAHT

Aluminum-Bronze **Ruler:** Bhumipol Adulyadej (Rama IX) **Obv:** Smaller head, 3 medals on uniform **Rev:** Mantled arms **Edge:** Reeded **Note:** Dot after the letters for "Satang" are found with raised and incuse varieties.

Date	Mintage	F	VF	XF	Unc	BU
BE2500 (1957)	620,480,000	—	0.10	0.15	0.25	—

Note: Minted without date change and with and without reeded edges until 1987

Y# 109 25 SATANG = 1/4 BAHT
Brass **Ruler:** Bhumipol Adulyadej (Rama IX) **Obv:** Bust left **Rev:** Value and inscription **Note:** Date varieties exist.

Date	Mintage	F	VF	XF	Unc	BU
BE2520 (1977)	183,356,000	—	—	0.10	0.15	—

Y# 187 25 SATANG = 1/4 BAHT
1.9000 g., Aluminum-Bronze, 15.93 mm. **Ruler:** Bhumipol Adulyadej (Rama IX) **Obv:** Head left **Rev:** Steepled building **Edge:** Reeded

Date	Mintage	F	VF	XF	Unc	BU
BE2530 (1987)	5,108,000	—	—	—	0.20	—
BE2531 (1988)	42,096,000	—	—	—	0.10	—
BE2532 (1989)	—	—	—	—	0.10	—
BE2533 (1990)	—	—	—	—	0.10	—
BE2534 (1991)	—	—	—	—	0.10	—
BE2535 (1992)	—	—	—	—	0.10	—
BE2536 (1993)	—	—	—	—	0.10	—
BE2537 (1994)	—	—	—	—	0.10	—
BE2538 (1995)	—	—	—	—	0.10	—
BE2539 (1996)	—	—	—	—	0.10	—
BE2540 (1997)	—	—	—	—	0.10	—
BE2541 (1998)	—	—	—	—	0.10	—
BE2545 (2002)	—	—	—	—	0.10	—
BE2547 (2004)	—	—	—	—	0.10	—
BE2549 (2006)	—	—	—	—	0.10	—

Y# 345 25 SATANG = 1/4 BAHT
1.9000 g., Brass **Ruler:** Bhumipol Adulyadej (Rama IX) **Subject:** Golden Jubilee - Reign of King Rama IX **Obv:** Bust facing **Rev:** Arms with supporters

Date	Mintage	F	VF	XF	Unc	BU
BE2539 (1996)	—	—	—	—	0.50	—

Y# 67 50 SATANG = 1/2 BAHT
Tin **Ruler:** Rama VIII **Obv:** King Ananda, child's head left **Rev:** Mythical creature "Garuda"

Date	Mintage	F	VF	XF	Unc	BU
BE2489 (1946)	—	—	40.00	75.00	180	—

Y# 71 50 SATANG = 1/2 BAHT
Tin **Ruler:** Rama VIII **Obv:** Youth's head left **Rev:** Mythical creature "Garuda" **Edge:** Reeded

Date	Mintage	F	VF	XF	Unc	BU
BE2489 (1946)	17,008,000	—	0.75	1.50	4.00	—

Note: These coins were minted from 1954-1957 and mintage figure is a total

Y# 77 50 SATANG = 1/2 BAHT
Aluminum-Bronze **Ruler:** Bhumipol Adulyadej (Rama IX) **Obv:** Young bust left, 1 medal on uniform **Rev:** Mantled arms

Date	Mintage	F	VF	XF	Unc	BU
BE2493 (1950)	20,710,000	—	—	—	20.00	—

Y# 81 50 SATANG = 1/2 BAHT
Aluminum-Bronze **Ruler:** Bhumipol Adulyadej (Rama IX) **Obv:** Smaller head, 3 medals on uniform **Rev:** Mantled arms **Edge:** Reeded

Date	Mintage	F	VF	XF	Unc	BU
BE2500 (1957)	439,874,000	—	0.10	0.15	0.25	—

Note: Minted without date change until 1987

Y# 168 50 SATANG = 1/2 BAHT
Aluminum-Bronze **Ruler:** Bhumipol Adulyadej (Rama IX) **Obv:** Bust left **Rev:** Value and inscription **Edge:** Plain

Date	Mintage	F	VF	XF	Unc	BU
BE2523 (1980)	122,260,000	—	0.10	0.15	0.25	—

Y# 203 50 SATANG = 1/2 BAHT
2.4000 g., Brass **Ruler:** Bhumipol Adulyadej (Rama IX) **Obv:** Head left **Rev:** Steepled building divides value

Date	Mintage	F	VF	XF	Unc	BU
BE2530 (1987)	—	—	—	—	15.00	—
BE2531 (1988)	23,776,000	—	—	—	0.10	—
BE2532 (1989)	—	—	0.20	0.30	1.00	—
BE2533 (1990)	—	—	—	—	0.10	—
BE2534 (1991)	—	—	—	—	0.10	—
BE2535 (1992)	—	—	—	—	0.10	—
BE2536 (1993)	—	—	—	—	0.10	—
BE2537 (1994)	—	—	—	—	0.10	—
BE2538 (1995)	—	—	—	—	0.10	—
BE2539 (1996)	—	—	—	—	0.10	—
BE2541 (1998)	—	—	—	—	0.10	—
BE2543 (2000)	—	—	—	—	0.10	—
BE2544 (2001)	—	—	—	—	0.10	—
BE2545 (2002)	—	—	—	—	0.10	—
BE2547 (2004)	—	—	—	—	0.10	—

Y# 329 50 SATANG = 1/2 BAHT
Aluminum-Bronze **Ruler:** Bhumipol Adulyadej (Rama IX) **Subject:** 50th Year of Reign - King Rama IX **Obv:** Bust facing **Rev:** Arms

Date	Mintage	F	VF	XF	Unc	BU
BE2539 (1996)	—	—	—	—	0.35	—

Y# 82.1 BAHT
7.1500 g., Copper-Nickel-Silver-Zinc, 26.9 mm. **Ruler:** Bhumipol Adulyadej (Rama IX) **Obv:** Bust left, three medals on uniform **Rev:** National arms **Edge:** Reeded

Date	Mintage	F	VF	XF	Unc	BU
BE2500 (1957)	3,143,000	—	0.75	1.50	6.00	—

Note: These coins were minted from 1958-60 and mintage figure is a total

Y# 82.2 BAHT
Copper-Nickel, 26.9 mm. **Ruler:** Bhumipol Adulyadej (Rama IX) **Obv:** Bust left, one medal on uniform **Rev:** National arms

Date	Mintage	F	VF	XF	Unc	BU
BE2500 (1957)	—	—	0.75	1.50	6.00	—

Y# 82a BAHT
Silver, 26.9 mm. **Ruler:** Bhumipol Adulyadej (Rama IX) **Obv:** Bust left **Rev:** National arms

Date	Mintage	F	VF	XF	Unc	BU
BE2500 (1957) Rare	—	—	—	—	—	—

Y# 83 BAHT
Copper-Nickel, 26.9 mm. **Ruler:** Bhumipol Adulyadej (Rama IX) **Subject:** King Rama IX and Queen Sirikit return from abroad **Obv:** Conjoined busts left flanked by diamonds **Rev:** Mantled arms **Edge:** Reeded

Date	Mintage	F	VF	XF	Unc	BU
BE2504 (1961)	4,430,000	—	0.40	0.75	2.00	—

Y# 84 BAHT
Copper-Nickel, 26.9 mm. **Ruler:** Bhumipol Adulyadej (Rama IX) **Obv:** Young bust left **Rev:** Mantled arms **Edge:** Reeded

Date	Mintage	F	VF	XF	Unc	BU
BE2505 (1962)	883,086,000	—	0.10	0.15	0.50	—

Note: These coins were minted from 1962-82 and mintage figure is a total

Y# 85 BAHT
Copper-Nickel, 26.9 mm. **Ruler:** Bhumipol Adulyadej (Rama IX) **Subject:** 36th Birthday - King Rama IX **Obv:** Uniformed bust left **Rev:** Design in center circle of design **Edge:** Reeded

Date	Mintage	F	VF	XF	Unc	BU
ND(1963)	3,000,000	—	0.25	0.75	2.00	—

Y# 87 BAHT

Copper-Nickel, 26.9 mm. **Ruler:** Bhumipol Adulyadej (Rama IX) **Subject:** 5th Asian Games Bangkok **Obv:** Conjoined busts right **Rev:** Star design **Edge:** Reeded

Date	Mintage	F	VF	XF	Unc	BU
BE2509 (1966)	9,000,000	—	0.25	0.75	3.00	—

Y# 91 BAHT

Copper-Nickel, 26.9 mm. **Ruler:** Bhumipol Adulyadej (Rama IX) **Subject:** 6th Asian Games Bangkok **Obv:** Conjoined busts right **Rev:** Star design **Edge:** Reeded

Date	Mintage	F	VF	XF	Unc	BU
BE2513 (1970)	9,000,000	—	0.25	0.75	1.50	—

Y# 96 BAHT

Copper-Nickel, 26.9 mm. **Ruler:** Bhumipol Adulyadej (Rama IX) **Series:** F.A.O. **Obv:** Head left **Rev:** State ploughing ceremony **Edge:** Reeded **Note:** Released on May 7, 1973.

Date	Mintage	F	VF	XF	Unc	BU
BE2515 (1972)	9,000,000	—	0.10	0.25	0.75	—

Y# 97 BAHT

Copper-Nickel, 26.9 mm. **Ruler:** Bhumipol Adulyadej (Rama IX) **Subject:** Prince Vajiralongkorn Investiture **Obv:** Young head left **Rev:** Crowned monogram **Edge:** Reeded

Date	Mintage	F	VF	XF	Unc	BU
BE2515 (1972)	9,000,000	—	0.15	0.40	1.00	—

Y# 99 BAHT

Copper-Nickel, 26.9 mm. **Ruler:** Bhumipol Adulyadej (Rama IX) **Subject:** 25th Anniversary - World Health Organization **Obv:** Head left **Rev:** Arms within wreath **Edge:** Reeded

Date	Mintage	F	VF	XF	Unc	BU
BE2516 (1973)	1,000,000	—	0.25	0.65	1.25	—

Y# 100 BAHT

Copper-Nickel, 25 mm. **Ruler:** Bhumipol Adulyadej (Rama IX) **Obv:** Head left **Rev:** Mythical creature "Garuda" **Edge:** Reeded

Date	Mintage	F	VF	XF	Unc	BU
BE2517 (1974)	248,978,000	—	0.15	0.40	1.00	—

Y# 105 BAHT

7.0000 g., Copper-Nickel, 25 mm. **Ruler:** Bhumipol Adulyadej (Rama IX) **Subject:** 8th SEAP Games **Obv:** Conjoined heads right **Rev:** Flower design within center circle of poinsettia design

Date	Mintage	F	VF	XF	Unc	BU
BE2518 (1975)	3,000,000	—	0.25	0.65	1.25	—

Y# 107 BAHT

7.0000 g., Copper-Nickel, 25 mm. **Ruler:** Bhumipol Adulyadej (Rama IX) **Subject:** 75th Birthday of Princess Mother October 21st **Obv:** Bust facing **Rev:** Monogram **Edge:** Reeded

Date	Mintage	F	VF	XF	Unc	BU
BE2518 (1975)	9,000,000	—	0.15	0.40	1.00	—

Y# 110 BAHT

7.0000 g., Copper-Nickel **Ruler:** Bhumipol Adulyadej (Rama IX) **Obv:** Head left **Rev:** Suphannahong, with Wat Aran Temple **Edge:** Reeded **Note:** Varieties exist.

Date	Mintage	F	VF	XF	Unc	BU
BE2520 (1977)	506,460,000	—	0.10	0.20	0.50	—

Y# 112 BAHT

7.0000 g., Copper-Nickel, 25 mm. **Ruler:** Bhumipol Adulyadej (Rama IX) **Series:** F.A.O. **Obv:** Figures scattering rice **Rev:** Seated female figure left

Date	Mintage	F	VF	XF	Unc	BU
BE2520 (1977)	2,000,000	—	0.15	0.40	1.00	—

Y# 114 BAHT

7.0000 g., Copper-Nickel, 25 mm. **Ruler:** Bhumipol Adulyadej (Rama IX) **Subject:** Princess Sirindhorn, 1st Thai Royal graduate of a great university **Obv:** Bust left **Rev:** Radiant crown **Edge:** Reeded

Date	Mintage	F	VF	XF	Unc	BU
BE2520 (1977)	8,998,000	—	0.15	0.40	1.00	—

Y# 114a BAHT

Bronze, 25 mm. **Ruler:** Bhumipol Adulyadej (Rama IX) **Subject:** Princess Sirindhorn, 1st Thai Royal graduate of a great university **Obv:** Bust left **Rev:** Radiant crown

Date	Mintage	F	VF	XF	Unc	BU
BE2520 (1977)	—	—	—	—	—	—

Y# 124 BAHT

7.0000 g., Copper-Nickel **Ruler:** Bhumipol Adulyadej (Rama IX) **Subject:** Investiture of Princess Sirindhorn, May 12, female counterpart to the crown prince **Obv:** Bust right **Rev:** Crowned monogram

Date	Mintage	F	VF	XF	Unc	BU
BE2520 (1977)	5,000,000	—	0.15	0.40	1.00	—

Y# 127 BAHT

7.0000 g., Copper-Nickel, 25 mm. **Ruler:** Bhumipol Adulyadej (Rama IX) **Subject:** Graduation of Crown Prince Vajiralongkorn September 15, with the rank of "Panturi" **Obv:** Bust left **Rev:** Crown within oval design **Edge:** Reeded

Date	Mintage	F	VF	XF	Unc	BU
BE2521 (1978)	5,000,000	—	0.10	0.20	0.50	—

Y# 130 BAHT

7.0000 g., Copper-Nickel, 25 mm. **Ruler:** Bhumipol Adulyadej (Rama IX) **Subject:** 8th Asian Games **Obv:** Conjoined busts right **Rev:** Small radiant sun within design **Edge:** Reeded

Date	Mintage	F	VF	XF	Unc	BU
BE2521 (1978)	5,000,000	—	0.10	0.20	0.50	—

Y# 157 BAHT

7.0000 g., Copper-Nickel, 25 mm. **Ruler:** Bhumipol Adulyadej (Rama IX) **Series:** World Food Day October 16 **Obv:** Bust left **Rev:** F.A.O. logo above wheat sprigs

Date	Mintage	F	VF	XF	Unc	BU
BE2525 (1982)	1,500,000	—	0.10	0.20	0.50	—

Y# 159.1 BAHT

7.0000 g., Copper-Nickel, 25 mm. **Ruler:** Bhumipol Adulyadej (Rama IX) **Obv:** Large bust with collar touching hairline **Rev:** The Grand Palace **Edge:** Reeded **Note:** 2527 and 2528 are frozen dates, with the Thai numerals for 27 and 28 in the Finance Ministry decal at the bottom of the reverse.

Date	Mintage	F	VF	XF	Unc	BU
BE2525 (1982)	123,585,000	—	0.10	0.20	0.50	—
BE2525 (1984)	—	—	0.10	0.20	0.50	—
BE2525 (1985)	—	—	0.10	0.20	0.50	—

Y# 159.2 BAHT

7.0000 g., Copper-Nickel **Ruler:** Bhumipol Adulyadej (Rama IX) **Obv:** Small bust with space between collar and lower hairline **Rev:** The Grand Palace **Edge:** Reeded

Date	Mintage	F	VF	XF	Unc	BU
BE2525 (1982)	Inc. above	—	2.50	5.00	10.00	—

Y# 183 BAHT
3.4500 g., Copper-Nickel, 20 mm. **Ruler:** Bhumipol Adulyadej (Rama IX) **Obv:** Head left **Rev:** Palace **Edge:** Reeded **Note:** Varieties exist.

Date	Mintage	F	VF	XF	Unc	BU
BE2529 (1986)	—	—	0.20	0.30	1.00	—
BE2530 (1987)	325,271,000	—	—	—	0.10	—
BE2531 (1988)	391,442,000	—	—	—	0.10	—
BE2532 (1989)	—	—	—	—	0.10	—
BE2533 (1990)	—	—	—	—	0.10	—
BE2534 (1991)	—	—	—	—	0.10	—
BE2535 (1992)	—	—	—	—	0.10	—
BE2536 (1993)	—	—	—	—	0.10	—
BE2537 (1994)	—	—	—	—	0.10	—
BE2538 (1995)	—	—	—	—	0.10	—
BE2539 (1996)	—	—	—	—	0.10	—
BE2540 (1997)	—	—	—	—	0.10	—
BE2541 (1998)	—	—	—	—	0.10	—
BE2542 (1999)	—	—	—	—	0.10	—
BE2543 (2000)	—	—	—	—	0.10	—
BE2544 (2001)	—	—	—	—	0.10	—
BE2545 (2002)	—	—	—	—	0.10	—
BE2546 (2003)	—	—	—	—	0.10	—
BE2547 (2004)	—	—	—	—	0.10	—
BE2548 (2005)	—	—	—	—	0.10	—
BE2549 (2006)	—	—	—	—	0.10	—

Y# 330 BAHT
Copper-Nickel, 20 mm. **Ruler:** Bhumipol Adulyadej (Rama IX) **Subject:** 50th Anniversary - Reign of King Rama IX June 8 **Obv:** Bust facing **Rev:** Arms with supporters **Edge:** Reeded

Date	Mintage	F	VF	XF	Unc	BU
BE2539 (1996)	—	—	—	—	0.35	—

Y# 134 2 BAHT
Copper-Nickel, 27 mm. **Ruler:** Bhumipol Adulyadej (Rama IX) **Subject:** Graduation of Princess Chulabhorn from Gusaehit University July 19 **Obv:** Bust 1/4 left **Rev:** Design within circle **Edge:** Plain **Note:** Science of Agriculture University.

Date	Mintage	F	VF	XF	Unc	BU
BE2522 (1979)	5,000,000	—	0.20	0.40	1.00	—

Y# 176 2 BAHT
Copper-Nickel Clad Copper, 22 mm. **Ruler:** Bhumipol Adulyadej (Rama IX) **Subject:** International Youth Year **Obv:** Bust left **Rev:** Conjoined profiles right within wreath **Edge:** Reeded

Date	Mintage	F	VF	XF	Unc	BU
BE2528 (1985)	10,000,000	—	0.20	0.40	1.00	—

Y# 177 2 BAHT
Copper-Nickel Clad Copper, 22 mm. **Ruler:** Bhumipol Adulyadej (Rama IX) **Subject:** XII SEAP Games Bangkok December 8-17 **Obv:** Half length bust facing **Rev:** Games logo flanked by value **Edge:** Reeded

Date	Mintage	F	VF	XF	Unc	BU
BE2528 (1985)	5,000,000	—	0.20	0.40	1.00	—

Y# 178 2 BAHT
Copper-Nickel Clad Copper, 22 mm. **Ruler:** Bhumipol Adulyadej (Rama IX) **Subject:** National Years of the Trees 2528-2531 **Obv:** Bust left **Rev:** Inscription within tree flanked by emblems below **Edge:** Reeded

Date	Mintage	F	VF	XF	Unc	BU
ND (1986)	3,000,000	—	0.50	1.00	3.50	—

Y# 180 2 BAHT
Copper-Nickel Clad Copper, 22 mm. **Ruler:** Bhumipol Adulyadej (Rama IX) **Subject:** Year of Peace **Obv:** Bust left **Rev:** Dove divides wreath below inscription **Note:** Australia, Russia and Mongolia issued coins with identical motif.

Date	Mintage	F	VF	XF	Unc	BU
BE2529 (1986)	5,000,000	—	—	—	0.50	—

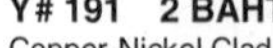

Y# 191 2 BAHT
Copper-Nickel Clad Copper, 22 mm. **Ruler:** Bhumipol Adulyadej (Rama IX) **Subject:** Princess Chulabhorn Awarded Einstein Medal for research October 24 **Obv:** Bust in cap and gown 1/4 left **Rev:** Head left within center circle of hexagon design

Date	Mintage	F	VF	XF	Unc	BU
BE2529 (1986)	3,000,000	—	—	—	0.50	—

Y# 188 2 BAHT
Copper-Nickel Clad Copper, 22 mm. **Ruler:** Bhumipol Adulyadej (Rama IX) **Subject:** 100th Year of "Nairoi" Chulalongkorn Military Academy **Obv:** Conjoined busts left **Rev:** Flagged arms

Date	Mintage	F	VF	XF	Unc	BU
BE2530 (1987)	3,000,000	—	—	—	0.50	—

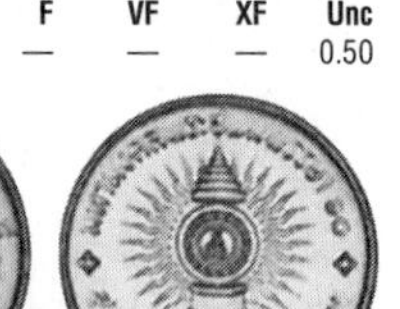

Y# 194 2 BAHT
Copper-Nickel Clad Copper, 22 mm. **Ruler:** Bhumipol Adulyadej (Rama IX) **Subject:** 60th Birthday - King Rama IX, December 5 **Obv:** Bust facing **Rev:** Radiant crown

Date	Mintage	F	VF	XF	Unc	BU
BE2530 (1987)	10,000	—	—	—	0.50	—

Y# 204 2 BAHT
Copper-Nickel Clad Copper, 22 mm. **Ruler:** Bhumipol Adulyadej (Rama IX) **Subject:** 72nd Anniversary of Thai Cooperatives February 26 **Obv:** Conjoined busts left **Rev:** Inscription **Edge:** Reeded

Date	Mintage	F	VF	XF	Unc	BU
BE2531 (1988)	3,000,000	—	—	—	0.50	—

Y# 210 2 BAHT
Copper-Nickel Clad Copper, 22 mm. **Ruler:** Bhumipol Adulyadej (Rama IX) **Subject:** 42nd Anniversary - Reign of King Rama IX July 2 **Obv:** Bust facing **Rev:** Crowned monogram **Edge:** Reeded

Date	Mintage	F	VF	XF	Unc	BU
BE2531 (1988)	5,000,000	—	—	—	0.50	—

Y# 220 2 BAHT
Copper-Nickel Clad Copper, 22 mm. **Ruler:** Bhumipol Adulyadej (Rama IX) **Subject:** 100th Anniversary of Siriraj Hospital April 26 **Obv:** Conjoined busts left **Rev:** Radiant crown above design

Date	Mintage	F	VF	XF	Unc	BU
BE2531 (1988)	3,412,000	—	—	—	0.50	—

Y# 222 2 BAHT
Copper-Nickel Clad Copper, 22 mm. **Ruler:** Bhumipol Adulyadej (Rama IX) **Subject:** Crown Prince's 36th birthday **Obv:** Head 1/4 left **Rev:** Crowned monogram within lightning bolts

Date	Mintage	F	VF	XF	Unc	BU
BE2531 (1988)	2,000,000	—	—	—	0.50	—

Y# 225 2 BAHT
Copper-Nickel Clad Copper, 22 mm. **Ruler:** Bhumipol Adulyadej (Rama IX) **Subject:** 72nd Anniversary of Chulalongkorn University March 26 **Obv:** Conjoined busts left **Rev:** Radiant crown **Edge:** Reeded

Date	Mintage	F	VF	XF	Unc	BU
BE2532 (1989)	3,000,000	—	—	—	0.50	—

Y# 230 2 BAHT
Copper-Nickel Clad Copper, 22 mm. **Ruler:** Bhumipol Adulyadej (Rama IX) **Subject:** Centennial of First Medical College, Siriraj, September 5 2433-2533 **Obv:** Conjoined uniformed busts facing **Rev:** First medical college **Edge:** Reeded

Date	Mintage	F	VF	XF	Unc	BU
BE2533 (1990)	1,000,000	—	—	—	0.50	—

Y# 232 2 BAHT
Copper-Nickel Clad Copper, 22 mm. **Ruler:** Bhumipol Adulyadej (Rama IX) **Subject:** 90th Birthday of Queen Mother October 21 **Obv:** Crown on stand flanked by others **Rev:** Bust 1/4 left **Edge:** Reeded

Date	Mintage	F	VF	XF	Unc	BU
BE2533 (1990)	2,000,000	—	—	—	0.50	—

Y# 235 2 BAHT

Copper-Nickel Clad Copper, 22 mm. **Ruler:** Bhumipol Adulyadej (Rama IX) **Subject:** 100th Anniversary - Office of the Comptroller General 2433-2533 **Obv:** Conjoined uniformed busts 1/4 left **Rev:** Building above computer, typewriter and phone **Edge:** Reeded

Date	Mintage	F	VF	XF	Unc	BU
BE2533 (1990)	1,000,000	—	—	—	0.50	—

Y# 243 2 BAHT

Copper-Nickel Clad Copper, 22 mm. **Ruler:** Bhumipol Adulyadej (Rama IX) **Subject:** World Health Organization **Obv:** Bust of Queen Mother 1/4 left **Rev:** Gold medal for good health, December 17 **Edge:** Reeded

Date	Mintage	F	VF	XF	Unc	BU
BE2533 (1990)	2,000,000	—	—	—	1.00	—

Y# 237 2 BAHT

Copper-Nickel Clad Copper, 22 mm. **Ruler:** Bhumipol Adulyadej (Rama IX) **Subject:** 36th Birthday of Princess Sirindhorn April 2 **Obv:** Uniformed bust 1/4 left **Rev:** Crowned monogram flanked by stars above sprigs **Edge:** Reeded

Date	Mintage	F	VF	XF	Unc	BU
BE2534 (1991)	2,300,000	—	—	—	0.50	—

Y# 240 2 BAHT

Copper-Nickel Clad Copper, 22 mm. **Ruler:** Bhumipol Adulyadej (Rama IX) **Subject:** 80th Anniversary of Thai Boy Scouts July 1 2454-2534 **Obv:** Conjoined young busts 1/4 left in scout uniforms **Rev:** Scouting emblem and phrase "Better to die than to lie" **Edge:** Reeded

Date	Mintage	F	VF	XF	Unc	BU
BE2534 (1991)	2,000,000	—	—	—	1.50	—

Y# 255 2 BAHT

Copper-Nickel Clad Copper, 22 mm. **Ruler:** Bhumipol Adulyadej (Rama IX) **Subject:** Princess Sirindhorn's Magsaysay Foundation Award for public administration August 31 **Obv:** Seated figures within circle **Rev:** Shield within sprig and circle below cameo **Edge:** Reeded

Date	Mintage	F	VF	XF	Unc	BU
BE2534 (1991)	12,000,000	—	—	—	0.50	—

Y# 248 2 BAHT

Copper-Nickel Clad Copper, 22 mm. **Ruler:** Bhumipol Adulyadej (Rama IX) **Subject:** Centenary Celebration of Mahitorn - Father of King Rama IX, January 1 **Obv:** Head facing **Rev:** Crown on stand flanked by others **Edge:** Reeded

Date	Mintage	F	VF	XF	Unc	BU
BE2535 (1992)	2,308,000	—	—	—	0.50	—

Y# 251 2 BAHT

Copper-Nickel Clad Copper, 22 mm. **Ruler:** Bhumipol Adulyadej (Rama IX) **Subject:** Ministry of Justice Centennial March 25 **Obv:** Conjoined busts left **Rev:** Balance scales within design **Edge:** Reeded

Date	Mintage	F	VF	XF	Unc	BU
BE2535 (1992)	1,500,000	—	—	—	0.50	—

Y# 253 2 BAHT

Copper-Nickel Clad Copper, 22 mm. **Ruler:** Bhumipol Adulyadej (Rama IX) **Subject:** Ministry of Justice Centennial April 1 2435-2535 **Obv:** Conjoined busts facing **Rev:** Mythical animal within circle **Edge:** Reeded

Date	Mintage	F	VF	XF	Unc	BU
1992 (1992)	1,500,000	—	—	—	0.50	—

Y# 259 2 BAHT

Copper-Nickel Clad Copper, 22 mm. **Ruler:** Bhumipol Adulyadej (Rama IX) **Subject:** Queen's 60th Birthday August 12 (Thai Mother's Day) **Obv:** Crowned bust facing **Rev:** Crowned monogram **Edge:** Reeded

Date	Mintage	F	VF	XF	Unc	BU
BE2535 (1992)	1,700,000	—	—	—	0.50	—

Y# 268 2 BAHT

Copper-Nickel Clad Copper, 22 mm. **Ruler:** Bhumipol Adulyadej (Rama IX) **Subject:** 60th Anniversary of the National Assembly - June 28 **Obv:** Conjoined busts left **Rev:** Anatasamakhom Throne Hall **Edge:** Reeded

Date	Mintage	F	VF	XF	Unc	BU
BE2535 (1992)	1,000,000	—	—	—	0.50	—

Y# 270 2 BAHT

Copper-Nickel Clad Copper, 22 mm. **Ruler:** Bhumipol Adulyadej (Rama IX) **Subject:** 100th Anniversary Ministry of Agriculture April 1 2435-2535 **Obv:** Conjoined busts 1/4 left **Rev:** Emblem within sprigs **Edge:** Reeded

Date	Mintage	F	VF	XF	Unc	BU
BE2535 (1992)	1,000,000	—	—	—	0.50	—

Y# 276 2 BAHT

Copper-Nickel Clad Copper, 22 mm. **Ruler:** Bhumipol Adulyadej (Rama IX) **Subject:** Centennial of Thai Teacher Training October 12 **Obv:** Conjoined busts left **Rev:** Emblem **Edge:** Reeded

Date	Mintage	F	VF	XF	Unc	BU
BE2535 (1992)	1,200,000	—	—	—	0.50	—

Y# 277 2 BAHT

Copper-Nickel Clad Copper, 22 mm. **Ruler:** Bhumipol Adulyadej (Rama IX) **Subject:** 50th Year of Thai National Bank December 10 **Obv:** Conjoined busts facing **Rev:** Seated figure

Date	Mintage	F	VF	XF	Unc	BU
BE2535 (1992)	1,000,000	—	—	—	0.50	—

Y# 272 2 BAHT

Copper-Nickel Clad Copper, 22 mm. **Ruler:** Bhumipol Adulyadej (Rama IX) **Subject:** King's 64th Birthday November 18 **Obv:** Conjoined busts 1/4 left **Rev:** Crowned monograms **Edge:** Reeded **Note:** In honor of the King reaching the lifespan of his great-grandfather.

Date	Mintage	F	VF	XF	Unc	BU
BE2535 (1992)	1,000,000	—	—	—	0.50	—

Y# 278 2 BAHT

Copper-Nickel Clad Copper, 22 mm. **Ruler:** Bhumipol Adulyadej (Rama IX) **Subject:** Centennial of Attorney General's Office April 1 2436-2536 **Obv:** Conjoined busts facing **Rev:** Crowned balance scale **Edge:** Reeded

Date	Mintage	F	VF	XF	Unc	BU
BE2536 (1993)	1,000,000	—	—	—	0.50	—

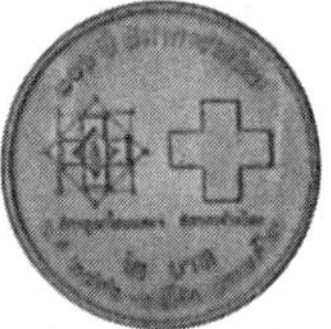

Y# 279 2 BAHT

Copper-Nickel Clad Copper, 22 mm. **Ruler:** Bhumipol Adulyadej (Rama IX) **Subject:** Centennial of Thai Red Cross 2436-2536 **Obv:** Conjoined busts 1/4 left **Rev:** Symbols **Edge:** Reeded

Date	Mintage	F	VF	XF	Unc	BU
BE2536 (1993)	1,200,000	—	—	—	0.50	—

Y# 282 2 BAHT

Copper-Nickel Clad Copper, 22 mm. **Ruler:** Bhumipol Adulyadej (Rama IX) **Subject:** 60th Year of the Treasury Department May 23 **Obv:** Conjoined busts left **Rev:** Emblem within circle **Edge:** Reeded

Date	Mintage	F	VF	XF	Unc	BU
BE2536 (1993)	1,200,000	—	—	—	0.50	—

Y# 288 2 BAHT

Copper-Nickel Clad Copper, 22 mm. **Ruler:** Bhumipol Adulyadej (Rama IX) **Subject:** 100th Anniversary of Rama VII

November 8 **Obv:** Bust left **Rev:** Crown and designs within oval circle **Edge:** Reeded

Date	Mintage	F	VF	XF	Unc	BU
BE2536 (1993)	1,500,000	—	—	—	0.50	—

Y# 292 2 BAHT

Copper-Nickel Clad Copper, 22 mm. **Ruler:** Bhumipol Adulyadej (Rama IX) **Subject:** 60th Anniversary - Royal Thai Language Academy March 31 **Obv:** Conjoined busts left **Rev:** Crowned emblem **Edge:** Reeded

Date	Mintage	F	VF	XF	Unc	BU
BE2537 (1994)	1,200,000	—	—	—	0.50	—

Y# 294 2 BAHT

Copper-Nickel Clad Copper, 22 mm. **Ruler:** Bhumipol Adulyadej (Rama IX) **Subject:** 120th Anniversary - Council of Advisors to the King - Royal decree 2417-2537 **Obv:** Conjoined busts facing **Rev:** Building **Edge:** Reeded

Date	Mintage	F	VF	XF	Unc	BU
BE2537 (1994)	1,200,000	—	—	—	0.50	—

Y# 296 2 BAHT

Copper-Nickel Clad Copper, 22 mm. **Ruler:** Bhumipol Adulyadej (Rama IX) **Subject:** 60th Anniversary - Thammasat University June 27 **Obv:** Conjoined busts left **Rev:** University emblem within circle **Edge:** Reeded

Date	Mintage	F	VF	XF	Unc	BU
BE2537 (1994)	1,250,000	—	—	—	0.50	—

Y# 307 2 BAHT

Copper-Nickel Clad Copper, 22 mm. **Ruler:** Bhumipol Adulyadej (Rama IX) **Series:** F.A.O. 50th Year, 1945-1995 **Obv:** Bust left **Rev:** Emblem and dates **Edge:** Reeded

Date	Mintage	F	VF	XF	Unc	BU
BE2538 (1995)	—	—	—	—	0.65	—

Y# 313 2 BAHT

Copper-Nickel Clad Copper, 22 mm. **Ruler:** Bhumipol Adulyadej (Rama IX) **Subject:** Information Technology Year **Obv:** Bust 3/4 left **Rev:** Symbols on globe background **Edge:** Reeded

Date	Mintage	F	VF	XF	Unc	BU
BE2538 (1995)	—	—	—	—	0.50	—

Y# 315 2 BAHT

Copper-Nickel Clad Copper, 22 mm. **Ruler:** Bhumipol Adulyadej (Rama IX) **Subject:** ASEAN Environment Year "Greenland Clean" **Obv:** Conjoined busts left **Rev:** Design within circle flanked by sprig and arrow **Edge:** Reeded

Date	Mintage	F	VF	XF	Unc	BU
BE2538 (1995)	—	—	—	—	0.50	—

Y# 317 2 BAHT

Copper-Nickel Clad Copper, 22 mm. **Ruler:** Bhumipol Adulyadej (Rama IX) **Subject:** Siriraj Nursing and Midwifery School Centennial January 12 **Obv:** Bust facing **Rev:** Crowned monogram **Edge:** Reeded

Date	Mintage	F	VF	XF	Unc	BU
BE2539 (1996)	—	—	—	—	0.65	—

Y# 319 2 BAHT

Copper-Nickel Clad Copper, 22 mm. **Ruler:** Bhumipol Adulyadej (Rama IX) **Subject:** King's 50th Year of Reign June 9 **Obv:** Bust facing **Rev:** National arms **Edge:** Reeded

Date	Mintage	F	VF	XF	Unc	BU
BE2539 (1996)	—	—	—	—	1.25	—

Y# 98 5 BAHT

Copper-Nickel **Ruler:** Bhumipol Adulyadej (Rama IX) **Obv:** Head left **Rev:** Mythical creature "Garuda" **Edge:** Plain **Shape:** 9-sided

Date	Mintage	F	VF	XF	Unc	BU
BE2515 (1972)	30,016,000	—	0.30	0.60	1.20	—

Y# 111 5 BAHT

Copper-Nickel Clad Copper **Ruler:** Bhumipol Adulyadej (Rama IX) **Obv:** Head left **Rev:** Mythical creature "Garuda" **Edge:** Lettered

Date	Mintage	F	VF	XF	Unc	BU
BE2520 (1977)	27,257,000	—	0.30	0.60	1.20	—
BE2522 (1979)	72,740,000	—	0.30	0.60	1.20	—

Y# 120 5 BAHT

Copper-Nickel Clad Copper, 29.5 mm. **Ruler:** Bhumipol Adulyadej (Rama IX) **Subject:** 50th Birthday - Rama IX December 5 **Obv:** Head left **Obv. Legend:** PRATHET THAI **Rev:** Crowned monogram **Edge:** Reeded

Date	Mintage	F	VF	XF	Unc	BU
BE2520 (1977)	500,000	—	0.35	0.75	1.50	—

Y# 121 5 BAHT

Copper-Nickel Clad Copper, 29.5 mm. **Ruler:** Bhumipol Adulyadej (Rama IX) **Subject:** 50th Birthday - Rama IX December 5 **Obv:** Bust left **Obv. Legend:** "SIAM MINTA" **Rev:** Crowned monogram **Edge:** Reeded **Note:** Error legend

Date	Mintage	F	VF	XF	Unc	BU
BE2520 (1977)	—	—	7.00	15.00	30.00	—

Y# 131 5 BAHT

Copper-Nickel Clad Copper, 30 mm. **Ruler:** Bhumipol Adulyadej (Rama IX) **Subject:** 8th ASEAN Games Bangkok **Obv:** Conjoined busts right **Rev:** Small radiant sun within designs **Edge:** Reeded

Date	Mintage	F	VF	XF	Unc	BU
BE2521 (1978)	500,000	—	1.50	3.50	6.50	—

Y# 132 5 BAHT

Copper-Nickel Clad Copper, 30 mm. **Ruler:** Bhumipol Adulyadej (Rama IX) **Subject:** Royal Cradle Ceremony January 11 **Obv:** Small child head right **Rev:** Inscription within designed wreath **Edge:** Reeded

Date	Mintage	F	VF	XF	Unc	BU
BE2522 (1979)	1,000,000	—	0.50	1.00	2.00	—

Y# 137 5 BAHT

Copper-Nickel Clad Copper, 30 mm. **Ruler:** Bhumipol Adulyadej (Rama IX) **Subject:** Queen's Birthday August 12 and F.A.O. Ceres Medal **Obv:** Crowned head 1/4 left **Rev:** Figures working within football-like designs **Edge:** Reeded

Date	Mintage	F	VF	XF	Unc	BU
BE2523 (1980)	9,000,000	—	0.25	0.50	1.50	—

Y# 140 5 BAHT

Copper-Nickel Clad Copper, 30 mm. **Ruler:** Bhumipol Adulyadej (Rama IX) **Subject:** 80th Birthday of King's Mother October 21 **Obv:** Bust with hat left **Rev:** Crown on stand flanked by others **Edge:** Reeded

Date	Mintage	F	VF	XF	Unc	BU
BE2523 (1980)	3,504,000	—	0.25	0.50	1.50	—

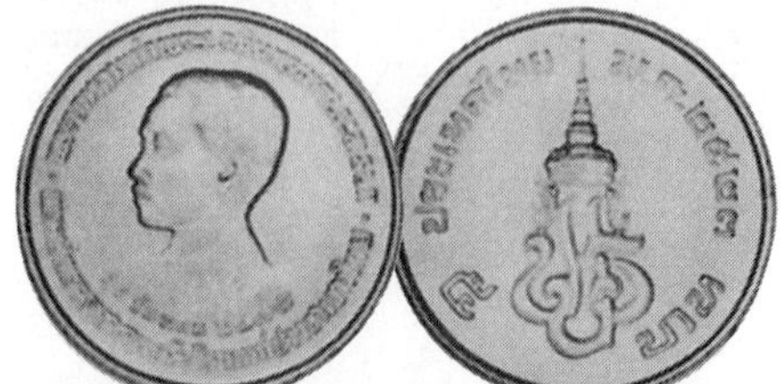

Y# 144 5 BAHT

Copper-Nickel Clad Copper, 30 mm. **Ruler:** Bhumipol Adulyadej (Rama IX) **Subject:** Rama VII Constitutional Monarchy December 10 2475-2523 **Obv:** Head left **Rev:** Crowned monogram **Edge:** Reeded

Date	Mintage	F	VF	XF	Unc	BU
BE2523 (1980)	2,113,000	—	0.25	0.50	1.50	—

Y# 142 5 BAHT
Copper-Nickel Clad Copper, 30 mm. **Ruler:** Bhumipol Adulyadej (Rama IX) **Subject:** Centennial - Birth of King Rama VI January 3 **Obv:** Bust right **Rev:** Design **Edge:** Reeded

Date	Mintage	F	VF	XF	Unc	BU
BE2524 (1981)	2,222,000	—	0.25	0.50	1.50	—

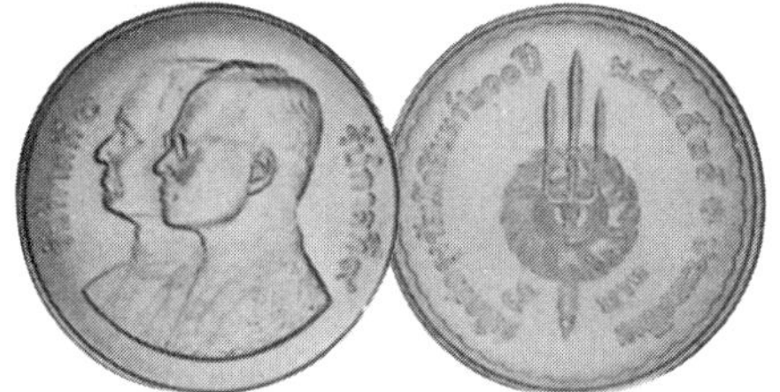

Y# 149 5 BAHT
Copper-Nickel Clad Copper, 30 mm. **Ruler:** Bhumipol Adulyadej (Rama IX) **Subject:** Bicentennial of the Chakri Dynasty **Obv:** Conjoined busts left **Rev:** Emblem **Edge:** Reeded

Date	Mintage	F	VF	XF	Unc	BU
BE2525 (1982)	5,000,000	—	0.25	0.50	1.50	—

Y# 158 5 BAHT
Copper-Nickel Clad Copper, 30 mm. **Ruler:** Bhumipol Adulyadej (Rama IX) **Series:** World Food Day **Obv:** Uniformed bust left **Rev:** Emblem above wheat sprigs **Edge:** Reeded

Date	Mintage	F	VF	XF	Unc	BU
BE2525 (1982)	400,000	—	0.35	0.75	1.50	—

Y# 161 5 BAHT
Copper-Nickel Clad Copper, 30 mm. **Ruler:** Bhumipol Adulyadej (Rama IX) **Subject:** 75th Anniversary of Boy Scouts **Obv:** Bust left in scout uniform **Rev:** Stylized banner and flag

Date	Mintage	F	VF	XF	Unc	BU
BE2525 (1982)	206,000	—	1.50	3.50	6.50	—

Y# 160 5 BAHT
12.0000 g., Copper-Nickel Clad Copper **Ruler:** Bhumipol Adulyadej (Rama IX) **Obv:** Bust left **Rev:** Mythical creature "Garuda" **Note:** 2525 is a frozen date, with the Thai numerals for the first 2 digits of the actual year (25, 28, 29) in the Finance Ministry decal at the bottom of the reverse

Date	Mintage	F	VF	XF	Unc	BU
BE2525 (25) (1982)	200,000	—	0.50	1.00	2.00	—
BE2526 (1983)	—	—	0.60	1.25	2.25	—
BE2527 (1984)	—	—	0.60	1.25	2.25	—
BE2525 (1985)	—	—	5.00	10.00	25.00	—
BE2528 (1985)	—	—	1.00	2.00	5.00	—

Date	Mintage	F	VF	XF	Unc	BU
BE2525 (1986)	—	—	0.20	0.50	1.00	—
BE2529 (1986)	—	—	0.20	0.50	1.00	—

Y# 171 5 BAHT
Copper-Nickel Clad Copper **Ruler:** Bhumipol Adulyadej (Rama IX) **Subject:** 84th Birthday of King's Mother October 21 **Obv:** Crown on stand flanked by others **Rev:** Bust 3/4 left

Date	Mintage	F	VF	XF	Unc	BU
BE2527 (1984)	600,000	—	1.00	2.00	4.50	—

Y# 184 5 BAHT
Copper-Nickel Clad Copper, 24 mm. **Ruler:** Bhumipol Adulyadej (Rama IX) **Subject:** 200th Anniversary - Birth of Rama III 2330-2530 **Obv:** Bust facing **Rev:** Design within circle **Edge:** Reeded

Date	Mintage	F	VF	XF	Unc	BU
BE2530 (1987)	2,000,000	—	—	—	0.75	—

Y# 195 5 BAHT
Copper-Nickel Clad Copper, 30 mm. **Ruler:** Bhumipol Adulyadej (Rama IX) **Subject:** 60th Birthday - King Rama IX December 5 **Obv:** Uniformed bust facing **Rev:** Crowned emblem within lightning bolts **Edge:** Reeded

Date	Mintage	F	VF	XF	Unc	BU
BE2530 (1987)	1,500,000	—	—	—	2.00	—

Y# 185 5 BAHT
7.5000 g., Copper-Nickel Clad Copper **Ruler:** Bhumipol Adulyadej (Rama IX) **Obv:** Head left **Rev:** Suphannahong, royal grand palace **Note:** Circulation coinage.

Date	Mintage	F	VF	XF	Unc	BU
BE2530 (1987)	14,000,000	—	—	—	0.75	—
BE2531 (1988)	—	—	—	—	0.75	—

Y# 219 5 BAHT
7.4600 g., Copper-Nickel Clad Copper, 24 mm. **Ruler:** Bhumipol Adulyadej (Rama IX) **Obv:** Head left **Rev:** Penjahwat **Edge:** Coarse reeding **Note:** Circulation coinage.

Date	Mintage	F	VF	XF	Unc	BU
BE2531 (1988)	—	—	—	—	0.50	—
BE2532 (1989)	—	—	—	—	0.50	—
BE2533 (1990)	—	—	—	—	0.50	—
BE2534 (1991)	—	—	—	—	0.50	—
BE2535 (1992)	—	—	—	—	0.50	—
BE2536 (1993)	—	—	—	—	0.50	—
BE2537 (1994)	—	—	—	—	0.50	—

Date	Mintage	F	VF	XF	Unc	BU
BE2538 (1995)	—	—	—	—	0.50	—
BE2539 (1996)	—	—	—	—	0.50	—
BE2540 (1997)	—	—	—	—	0.50	—
BE2541 (1998)	—	—	—	—	0.50	—
BE2542 (1999)	—	—	—	—	0.50	—
BE2543 (2000)	—	—	—	—	0.50	—
BE2549 (2006)	—	—	—	—	0.50	—

Y# 211 5 BAHT
Copper-Nickel, 30 mm. **Ruler:** Bhumipol Adulyadej (Rama IX) **Subject:** 42nd Anniversary - Reign of King Rama IX July 2 **Obv:** Uniformed bust facing **Rev:** Crowned monogram **Edge:** Reeded

Date	Mintage	F	VF	XF	Unc	BU
BE2531 (1988)	1,500,000	—	—	—	2.00	—

Y# 260 5 BAHT
Copper-Nickel Clad Copper, 24 mm. **Ruler:** Bhumipol Adulyadej (Rama IX) **Subject:** Queen's 60th Birthday August 12 **Obv:** Crowned bust facing **Rev:** Crowned monogram **Edge:** Reeded

Date	Mintage	F	VF	XF	Unc	BU
BE2535 (1992)	1,000,000	—	—	—	1.25	—

Y# 306 5 BAHT
Copper-Nickel Clad Copper, 24 mm. **Ruler:** Bhumipol Adulyadej (Rama IX) **Subject:** 18th SEA Games December 9-17 held at Ching My **Obv:** Half length bust facing **Rev:** Designs and inscription within circle above designed sprigs **Edge:** Reeded

Date	Mintage	F	VF	XF	Unc	BU
BE2538 (1995)	—	—	—	—	1.25	—

Y# 320 5 BAHT
Copper-Nickel Clad Copper, 24 mm. **Ruler:** Bhumipol Adulyadej (Rama IX) **Subject:** King's 50th Year of Reign June 9 **Obv:** Bust facing **Rev:** National arms **Edge:** Reeded

Date	Mintage	F	VF	XF	Unc	BU
BE2539 (1996)	—	—	—	—	1.50	—

Y# 92 10 BAHT
5.0000 g., 0.8000 Silver 0.1286 oz. ASW, 20 mm. **Ruler:** Bhumipol Adulyadej (Rama IX) **Subject:** 25th Anniversary - Reign of King Rama IX June 9 **Obv:** Head right **Rev:** Radiant crowned monogram **Edge:** Reeded

Date	Mintage	F	VF	XF	Unc	BU
BE2514 (1971)	2,000,000	—	BV	2.50	4.50	—

Y# 115 10 BAHT

Nickel, 32 mm. **Ruler:** Bhumipol Adulyadej (Rama IX) **Subject:** Graduation of Princess Sirindhorn 1st royal graduate **Obv:** Bust left **Rev:** Radiant crown **Edge:** Reeded

Date	Mintage	F	VF	XF	Unc	BU
BE2520 (1977)	2,097,000	—	0.50	1.00	2.50	—

Y# 115a 10 BAHT

Bronze, 32 mm. **Ruler:** Bhumipol Adulyadej (Rama IX) **Subject:** Graduation of Princess Sirindhorn 1st royal graduate **Obv:** Bust left **Rev:** Radiant crown

Date	Mintage	F	VF	XF	Unc	BU
BE2520 (1977)	—	—	—	—	20.00	—

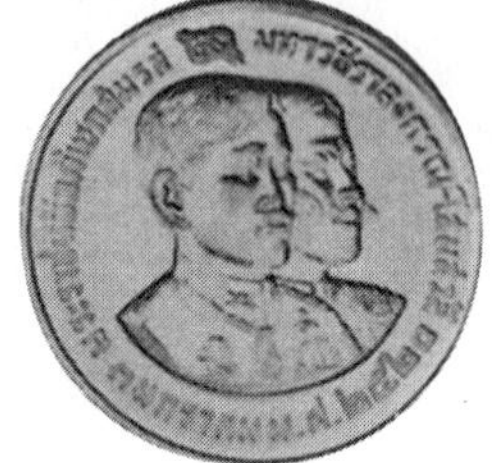

Y# 117 10 BAHT

Nickel, 32 mm. **Ruler:** Bhumipol Adulyadej (Rama IX) **Subject:** Crown Prince Vajiralongkorn and Princess Soamsawali Wedding January 3 **Obv:** Conjoined busts right **Rev:** Crowned monogram **Edge:** Reeded

Date	Mintage	F	VF	XF	Unc	BU
BE2520 (1977)	1,890,000	—	0.50	1.00	2.50	—

Y# 135 10 BAHT

Nickel, 32 mm. **Ruler:** Bhumipol Adulyadej (Rama IX) **Subject:** Graduation of Princess Chulabhorn **Obv:** Bust 3/4 left **Rev:** Graduation emblem within circle

Date	Mintage	F	VF	XF	Unc	BU
BE2522 (1979)	1,196,000	—	0.50	1.00	2.50	—

Y# 141 10 BAHT

Nickel, 32 mm. **Ruler:** Bhumipol Adulyadej (Rama IX) **Subject:** 80th Birthday of King's Mother October 21 **Obv:** Bust with hat left **Rev:** Crown on stand flanked by others **Edge:** Reeded

Date	Mintage	F	VF	XF	Unc	BU
BE2523 (1980)	1,288,000	—	0.50	1.00	2.50	—

Y# 145 10 BAHT

Nickel, 32 mm. **Ruler:** Bhumipol Adulyadej (Rama IX) **Subject:** 30th Anniversary of Buddhist Fellowship **Obv:** Bust left **Rev:** Design within circle and wreath **Edge:** Reeded

Date	Mintage	F	VF	XF	Unc	BU
BE2523 (1980)	1,035,000	—	0.50	1.00	2.50	—

Y# 146 10 BAHT

Nickel, 32 mm. **Ruler:** Bhumipol Adulyadej (Rama IX) **Subject:** King Rama IX Anniversary of Reign, twice as long on the throne - June 19 **Obv:** Conjoined busts left **Rev:** Crowns and emblems **Edge:** Reeded

Date	Mintage	F	VF	XF	Unc	BU
BE2524 (1981)	2,039,000	—	0.50	1.00	2.50	—

Y# 154 10 BAHT

Nickel, 32 mm. **Ruler:** Bhumipol Adulyadej (Rama IX) **Subject:** 50th Birthday of Queen Sirikit August 12 **Obv:** Crowned head 1/4 left **Rev:** Crowned monogram **Edge:** Reeded

Date	Mintage	F	VF	XF	Unc	BU
BE2525 (1982)	500,000	—	0.75	1.50	3.50	—
BE2525 (1982) Proof	9,999	Value: 22.50				

Y# 162 10 BAHT

Nickel, 32 mm. **Ruler:** Bhumipol Adulyadej (Rama IX) **Subject:** 75th Anniversary of Boy Scouts **Obv:** Bust left in scouting uniform **Rev:** Stylized banner and flag **Edge:** Reeded **Note:** Similar to 5 Baht, Y#161.

Date	Mintage	F	VF	XF	Unc	BU
BE2525 (1982)	100,000	—	1.25	2.50	5.00	—
BE2525 (1982) Proof	1,500	Value: 45.00				

Y# 163 10 BAHT

Nickel, 32 mm. **Ruler:** Bhumipol Adulyadej (Rama IX) **Subject:** 100th Anniversary of Postal Service August 4 **Obv:** Bust left **Rev:** Radiant crown above inscription

Date	Mintage	F	VF	XF	Unc	BU
BE2526 (1983)	300,000	—	0.75	1.50	3.50	—
BE2526 (1983) Proof	5,000	Value: 27.50				

Y# 165 10 BAHT

Nickel, 32 mm. **Ruler:** Bhumipol Adulyadej (Rama IX) **Subject:** 700th Anniversary of Thai Alphabet **Obv:** Seated figure, Ramkamhaeng the Great, pre-Bangkok era **Rev:** Six-line inscription

Date	Mintage	F	VF	XF	Unc	BU
BE2526 (1983)	500,000	—	0.75	1.50	3.50	—
BE2526 (1983) Proof	5,167	Value: 25.00				

Y# 172 10 BAHT

Nickel, 32 mm. **Ruler:** Bhumipol Adulyadej (Rama IX) **Subject:** 84th Birthday of King's Mother October 21 **Obv:** Three crowns on stands **Rev:** Bust left **Note:** Similar to 5 Baht, Y#171.

Date	Mintage	F	VF	XF	Unc	BU
BE2527 (1984)	200,000	—	1.25	2.50	5.50	—
BE2527 (1984) Proof	3,492	Value: 37.50				

Y# 175 10 BAHT

Nickel, 32 mm. **Ruler:** Bhumipol Adulyadej (Rama IX) **Subject:** 72nd Anniversary of Government Savings Bank April 1 **Obv:** Conjoined uniformed busts 1/4 left **Rev:** Designs within sectioned circle **Edge:** Reeded

Date	Mintage	F	VF	XF	Unc	BU
BE2528 (1985)	500,000	—	0.50	1.00	2.50	—
BE2528 (1985) Proof	3,000	Value: 37.50				

Y# 179 10 BAHT

Nickel, 32 mm. **Ruler:** Bhumipol Adulyadej (Rama IX) **Subject:** National Years of the Trees 2528-2531 **Obv:** Bust left **Rev:** Circular design below inscription within tree, emblems flank tree below

Date	Mintage	F	VF	XF	Unc	BU
ND (1986)	100,000	—	4.00	9.00	18.00	—
ND (1986) Proof	2,100	Value: 45.00				

Y# 181 10 BAHT

Nickel, 32 mm. **Ruler:** Bhumipol Adulyadej (Rama IX) **Subject:** 6th ASEAN Orchid Congress November 7-14 **Obv:** Bust left **Rev:** Symbols of congress meeting **Edge:** Reeded

Date	Mintage	F	VF	XF	Unc	BU
BE2529 (1986)	200,000	—	—	—	2.50	—
BE2529 (1986) Proof	3,000	Value: 37.50				

Y# 192 10 BAHT

Nickel, 32 mm. **Ruler:** Bhumipol Adulyadej (Rama IX) **Subject:** Princess Chulabhorn Awarded Einstein Medal October 24 **Obv:** Graduate's bust 1/4 left **Rev:** Head left within center circle of hexagon design

Date	Mintage	F	VF	XF	Unc	BU
BE2529 (1986)	200,000	—	—	—	2.50	—
BE2529 (1986) Proof	1,080	Value: 50.00				

Y# 196 10 BAHT

Nickel, 32 mm. **Ruler:** Bhumipol Adulyadej (Rama IX) **Subject:** 60th Birthday of King Rama IX December 5 **Obv:** Uniformed bust facing **Rev:** Crowned emblem within lightning bolts **Edge:** Reeded

Date	Mintage	F	VF	XF	Unc	BU
BE2530 (1987)	500,000	—	—	—	2.50	—
BE2530 (1987) Proof	5,000	Value: 32.50				

Y# 189 10 BAHT

Nickel, 32 mm. **Ruler:** Bhumipol Adulyadej (Rama IX) **Subject:** Chulachomklao Royal Military Academy August 5 **Obv:** Conjoined busts left **Rev:** Flagged arms

Date	Mintage	F	VF	XF	Unc	BU
BE2530 (1987)	300,000	—	—	—	2.50	—
BE2530 (1987) Proof	2,060	Value: 45.00				

Y# 190 10 BAHT

Nickel, 32 mm. **Ruler:** Bhumipol Adulyadej (Rama IX) **Subject:** Rural Development Leadership July 21 **Obv:** Kneeling figure facing left talking to seated figures **Rev:** Emblem above inscription **Edge:** Reeded

Date	Mintage	F	VF	XF	Unc	BU
BE2530 (1987)	300,000	—	—	—	2.50	—
BE2530 (1987) Proof	2,100	Value: 45.00				

Y# 227 10 BAHT

8.5400 g., Bi-Metallic Aluminum-bronze center in Stainless steel ring, 26 mm. **Ruler:** Bhumipol Adulyadej (Rama IX) **Obv:** Head left within circle **Rev:** Temple of the Dawn within circle **Edge:** Segmented reeding **Note:** Varieties exist.

Date	Mintage	F	VF	XF	Unc	BU
BE2531 (1988) Prooflike; Rare	100,000	—	—	—	—	—

Note: The BE2531 (1988) pieces were not released to general circulation and are very scarce in the numismatic community

Date	Mintage	F	VF	XF	Unc	BU
BE2532 (1989)	200,000,000	—	—	—	2.50	—
BE2533 (1990)	100	—	—	—	2,500	—
BE2534 (1991)	—	—	—	—	2.50	—
BE2535 (1992)	—	—	—	—	2.50	—
BE2536 (1993)	—	—	—	—	2.50	—
BE2537 (1994)	—	—	—	—	3.00	—
BE2538 (1995)	—	—	—	—	3.00	—
BE2539 (1996)	—	—	—	—	3.00	—
BE2544 (2001)	—	—	—	—	3.00	—
BE2545 (2002)	—	—	—	—	3.00	—
BE2546 (2003)	—	—	—	—	3.00	—
BE2547 (2004)	—	—	—	—	3.00	—
BE2548 (2005)	—	—	—	—	3.00	—
BE2549 (2006)	—	—	—	—	3.00	—

Y# 205 10 BAHT

Nickel, 32 mm. **Ruler:** Bhumipol Adulyadej (Rama IX) **Subject:** 72nd Anniversary of Thai Cooperatives February 26 **Obv:** Conjoined busts left **Rev:** Inscription

Date	Mintage	F	VF	XF	Unc	BU
BE2531 (1988)	143,000	—	—	—	2.50	—
BE2530 (1988) Proof	3,000	Value: 32.50				

Y# 212 10 BAHT

Nickel, 32 mm. **Ruler:** Bhumipol Adulyadej (Rama IX) **Subject:** 42nd Anniversary - Reign of King Rama IX July 2 **Obv:** Bust facing **Rev:** Crowned monogram

Date	Mintage	F	VF	XF	Unc	BU
BE2531 (1988)	500,000	—	—	—	2.50	—
BE2531 (1988) Proof	8,110	Value: 25.00				

Y# 221 10 BAHT

Nickel, 32 mm. **Ruler:** Bhumipol Adulyadej (Rama IX) **Subject:** 100th Anniversary of Siriraj Hospital April 26 **Obv:** Crowned busts left **Rev:** Crown above design

Date	Mintage	F	VF	XF	Unc	BU
BE2531 (1988)	290,000	—	—	—	2.50	—
BE2531 (1988) Proof	5,000	Value: 27.50				

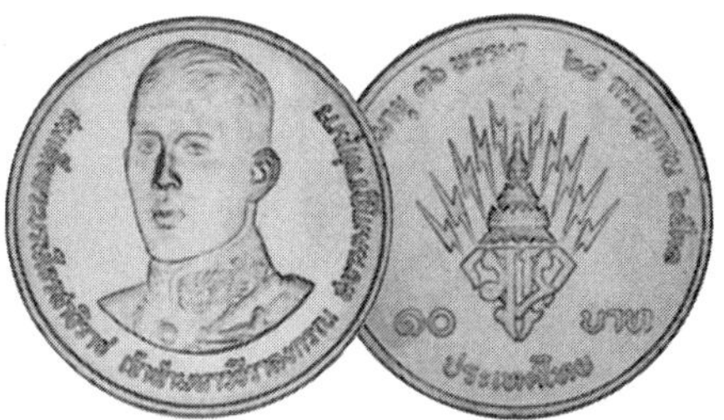

Y# 223 10 BAHT

Nickel, 32 mm. **Ruler:** Bhumipol Adulyadej (Rama IX) **Subject:** Crown Prince's Birthday **Obv:** Head 1/4 left **Rev:** Crowned monogram within lightning bolts **Edge:** Reeded

Date	Mintage	F	VF	XF	Unc	BU
BE2531 (1988)	200,000	—	—	—	2.50	—
BE2531 (1988) Proof	3,000	Value: 32.50				

Y# 228 10 BAHT

Nickel, 32 mm. **Ruler:** Bhumipol Adulyadej (Rama IX) **Subject:** 72nd Anniversary Chulalongkorn University March 26 **Obv:** 3 Conjoined busts left **Rev:** Radiant crown

Date	Mintage	F	VF	XF	Unc	BU
BE2532 (1989)	500,000	—	—	—	2.50	—

Y# 231 10 BAHT

Copper-Nickel, 32 mm. **Ruler:** Bhumipol Adulyadej (Rama IX) **Subject:** Centennial of First Medical College September 5 2433 to September 5 2533 **Obv:** Conjoined busts facing **Rev:** Building **Edge:** Reeded

Date	Mintage	F	VF	XF	Unc	BU
BE2533 (1990)	300,000	—	—	—	2.50	—
BE2533 (1990) Proof	3,772	Value: 32.50				

Y# 233 10 BAHT

Copper-Nickel, 32 mm. **Ruler:** Bhumipol Adulyadej (Rama IX) **Subject:** 90th Birthday of the King's Mother October 21 **Obv:** Crown on stand flanked by others **Rev:** Bust 1/4 left **Edge:** Reeded

Date	Mintage	F	VF	XF	Unc	BU
BE2533 (1990)	500,000	—	—	—	2.50	—
BE2533 (1991) Proof	6,076	Value: 32.50				

Y# 236 10 BAHT

Copper-Nickel, 32 mm. **Ruler:** Bhumipol Adulyadej (Rama IX) **Subject:** 100th Anniversary - Office of Comptroller General **Obv:**

Conjoined busts 1/4 left **Rev:** Building above computer, typewriter and phone

Date	Mintage	F	VF	XF	Unc	BU
BE2533 (1990)	300,000	—	—	—	2.50	—

Y# 244 10 BAHT

Copper-Nickel, 32 mm. **Ruler:** Bhumipol Adulyadej (Rama IX) **Subject:** World Health Organization December 17 **Obv:** Bust 1/4 left **Rev:** Gold medal for good health **Edge:** Reeded

Date	Mintage	F	VF	XF	Unc	BU
BE2533 (1990)	800,000	—	—	—	3.00	—
BE2533 (1990) Proof	34,041	Value: 45.00				

Y# 238 10 BAHT

Copper-Nickel, 32 mm. **Ruler:** Bhumipol Adulyadej (Rama IX) **Subject:** 36th Birthday of Princess Sirindhorn April 2 **Obv:** Uniformed bust 1/4 left **Rev:** Crowned monogram flanked by stars above sprigs **Edge:** Reeded

Date	Mintage	F	VF	XF	Unc	BU
BE2534 (1991)	1,100,000	—	—	—	2.50	—
BE2534 (1991) Proof	3,300	Value: 35.00				

Y# 241 10 BAHT

Copper-Nickel, 32 mm. **Ruler:** Bhumipol Adulyadej (Rama IX) **Subject:** 80th Anniversary of Thai Boy Scouts July 1 2454-2534 **Obv:** Conjoined busts 1/4 left in scouting uniform **Rev:** Scout emblem and motto "Better to die than to lie" **Edge:** Reeded

Date	Mintage	F	VF	XF	Unc	BU
BE2534 (1991)	650,000	—	—	—	3.00	—
BE2534 (1991) Proof	3,237	Value: 35.00				

Y# 256 10 BAHT

Copper-Nickel, 32 mm. **Ruler:** Bhumipol Adulyadej (Rama IX) **Subject:** Princess Sirindhorn's Magsaysay Foundation Award August 31 **Obv:** Seated and kneeling figures within circle **Rev:** Foundation Award medal below cameo **Edge:** Reeded

Date	Mintage	F	VF	XF	Unc	BU
BE2534 (1991)	800,000	—	—	—	2.50	—
BE2534 (1991) Proof	2,111	Value: 37.50				

Y# 249 10 BAHT

Copper-Nickel, 32 mm. **Ruler:** Bhumipol Adulyadej (Rama IX) **Subject:** Centenary Celebration - Father of King Rama IX Mahidon - January 1 **Obv:** Crown on stand flanked by others **Rev:** Bust facing **Edge:** Reeded

Date	Mintage	F	VF	XF	Unc	BU
BE2535 (1992)	800,000	—	—	—	2.50	—
BE2535 (1992) Proof	5,314	Value: 25.00				

Y# 252 10 BAHT

Copper-Nickel, 32 mm. **Ruler:** Bhumipol Adulyadej (Rama IX) **Subject:** Ministry of Justice Centennial March 25 **Obv:** Conjoined busts left **Rev:** Balance scales within design **Edge:** Reeded

Date	Mintage	F	VF	XF	Unc	BU
BE2535 (1992)	800,000	—	—	—	2.50	—
BE2535 (1992) Proof	—	Value: 22.50				

Y# 254 10 BAHT

Copper-Nickel, 32 mm. **Ruler:** Bhumipol Adulyadej (Rama IX) **Subject:** Ministry of Interior Centennial April 1 2435 to 2535 **Obv:** Conjoined uniformed busts facing **Rev:** Mythical animal within circle **Edge:** Reeded

Date	Mintage	F	VF	XF	Unc	BU
BE2535 (1992)	800,000	—	—	—	2.50	—
BE2535 (1992) Proof	10,000	Value: 17.50				

Y# 261 10 BAHT

Copper-Nickel, 32 mm. **Ruler:** Bhumipol Adulyadej (Rama IX) **Subject:** Queen's 60th Birthday August 12 (Thai Mother's Day) **Obv:** Crowned bust facing **Rev:** Crowned monogram **Edge:** Reeded

Date	Mintage	F	VF	XF	Unc	BU
BE2535 (1992)	1,100,000	—	—	—	3.00	—
BE2535 (1992) Proof	18,000	Value: 17.50				

Y# 269 10 BAHT

Copper-Nickel, 32 mm. **Ruler:** Bhumipol Adulyadej (Rama IX) **Subject:** 60th Anniversary of National Assembly June 28 **Obv:** Conjoined busts left **Rev:** Ratasapa - Paraliment building **Edge:** Reeded

Date	Mintage	F	VF	XF	Unc	BU
BE2535 (1992)	44,000	—	—	—	2.50	—

Y# 271 10 BAHT

Copper-Nickel, 32 mm. **Ruler:** Bhumipol Adulyadej (Rama IX) **Subject:** Ministry of Agriculture April 1 **Obv:** Conjoined busts 1/4 left **Rev:** Emblem above designed sprigs **Edge:** Reeded

Date	Mintage	F	VF	XF	Unc	BU
BE2535 (1992)	550,000	—	—	—	2.50	—
BE2535 (1992) Proof	—	Value: 25.00				

Y# 284 10 BAHT

Copper-Nickel, 32 mm. **Ruler:** Bhumipol Adulyadej (Rama IX) **Subject:** Centennial of Thai Teacher Training October 12 **Obv:** Conjoined busts left **Rev:** Emblem **Edge:** Reeded

Date	Mintage	F	VF	XF	Unc	BU
BE2535 (1992)	700,000	—	—	—	2.50	—

Y# 285 10 BAHT

Copper-Nickel, 32 mm. **Ruler:** Bhumipol Adulyadej (Rama IX) **Subject:** Centennial of Thai National Bank December 10 **Obv:** Conjoined busts facing **Rev:** Seated figure **Edge:** Reeded

Date	Mintage	F	VF	XF	Unc	BU
BE2535 (1992)	700,000	—	—	—	2.50	—
BE2535 (1992) Proof	6,927	Value: 20.00				

Y# 273 10 BAHT

Copper-Nickel, 32 mm. **Ruler:** Bhumipol Adulyadej (Rama IX) **Subject:** King's 64th Birthday November 18 **Obv:** Conjoined busts 1/4 left **Rev:** Crowned monograms **Edge:** Reeded **Note:** In honor of the King reaching the life span of his great grandfather.

Date	Mintage	F	VF	XF	Unc	BU
BE2535 (1992)	550,000	—	—	—	2.50	—
BE2535 (1992) Proof	3,711	Value: 25.00				

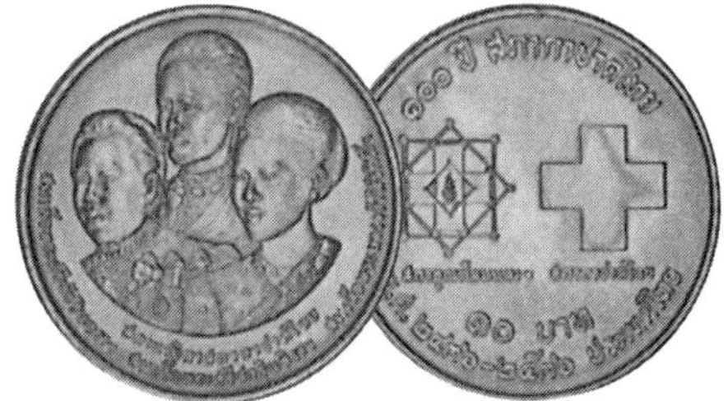

Y# 280 10 BAHT

Copper-Nickel, 32 mm. **Ruler:** Bhumipol Adulyadej (Rama IX) **Subject:** Centennial of Thai Red Cross 2436-2536 **Obv:** Conjoined busts 1/4 left **Rev:** Symbols **Edge:** Reeded

Date	Mintage	F	VF	XF	Unc	BU
BE2536 (1993)	700,000	—	—	—	2.50	—
BE2535 (1993) Proof	14,000	Value: 18.50				

Y# 283 10 BAHT

Copper-Nickel, 32 mm. **Ruler:** Bhumipol Adulyadej (Rama IX) **Subject:** 60th Anniversary Treasury Department May 23 **Obv:** Conjoined busts left **Rev:** Emblem within circle **Edge:** Reeded

Date	Mintage	F	VF	XF	Unc	BU
BE2536 (1993)	600,000	—	—	—	2.50	—
BE2535 (1993) Proof	10,000	Value: 22.50				

Y# 286 10 BAHT

Copper-Nickel, 32 mm. **Ruler:** Bhumipol Adulyadej (Rama IX) **Subject:** Centennial of Attorney General's Office April 1 2436-2536 **Obv:** Conjoined busts facing **Rev:** Crowned balance scales above sprigs **Edge:** Reeded

Date	Mintage	F	VF	XF	Unc	BU
BE2536 (1993)	700,000	—	—	—	2.50	—

Y# 289 10 BAHT

Copper-Nickel, 32 mm. **Ruler:** Bhumipol Adulyadej (Rama IX) **Subject:** 100th Anniversary of Rama VII November 8 **Obv:** Bust left **Rev:** Crown and designs within oval circle **Edge:** Reeded

Date	Mintage	F	VF	XF	Unc	BU
BE2536 (1993)	800,000	—	—	—	2.50	—
BE2536 (1993) Proof	10,000	Value: 22.50				

Y# 293 10 BAHT

Copper-Nickel, 32 mm. **Ruler:** Bhumipol Adulyadej (Rama IX) **Subject:** 60th Anniversary - Royal Thai Language Academy March 31 **Obv:** Conjoined busts left **Rev:** Crowned emblem **Edge:** Reeded

Date	Mintage	F	VF	XF	Unc	BU
BE2537 (1994)	700,000	—	—	—	2.50	—
BE2537 (1994) Proof	10,000	Value: 22.50				

Y# 295 10 BAHT

Copper-Nickel, 32 mm. **Ruler:** Bhumipol Adulyadej (Rama IX) **Subject:** 120th Anniversary Council of Advisors to the King - Royal decree 2417-2537 **Obv:** Conjoined busts facing **Rev:** Building **Edge:** Reeded

Date	Mintage	F	VF	XF	Unc	BU
BE2537 (1994)	800,000	—	—	—	2.50	—
BE2537 (1994) Proof	12,000	Value: 22.50				

Y# 297 10 BAHT

Copper-Nickel, 32 mm. **Ruler:** Bhumipol Adulyadej (Rama IX) **Subject:** 60th Anniversary - Thammasat University June 27 **Obv:** Conjoined busts left **Rev:** Emblem within circle and wreath **Edge:** Reeded

Date	Mintage	F	VF	XF	Unc	BU
BE2537 (1994)	800,000	—	—	—	2.50	—
BE2537 (1994) Proof	12,000	Value: 22.50				

Y# 339 10 BAHT

8.4200 g., Bi-Metallic Brass center in Copper-Nickel ring, 26 mm. **Ruler:** Bhumipol Adulyadej (Rama IX) **Subject:** International Rice Award June 5 **Obv:** Half length figure with camera left within circle **Rev:** Rice plant within circle **Edge:** Alternating reeded and plain

Date	Mintage	F	VF	XF	Unc	BU
BE2538 (1996)	—	—	—	—	3.50	—

Y# 328.1 10 BAHT

Bi-Metallic Brass center in Copper-Nickel ring, 26 mm. **Ruler:** Bhumipol Adulyadej (Rama IX) **Subject:** 50th Anniversary - Reign of King Rama IX June 9 **Obv:** Bust facing within circle **Rev:** National arms within circle **Edge:** Alternating reeded and plain

Date	Mintage	F	VF	XF	Unc	BU
BE2539 (1996)	—	—	—	—	3.00	—

Y# 328.2 10 BAHT

Bi-Metallic Brass center in Copper-Nickel ring, 26 mm. **Ruler:** Bhumipol Adulyadej (Rama IX) **Subject:** 50th Anniversary - Reign of King Rama IX June 9 **Obv:** Bust facing within circle **Rev:** National arms within circle **Edge:** Alternating reeded and plain

Date	Mintage	F	VF	XF	Unc	BU
BE2539 (1996)	—	—	—	—	3.00	—

Y# 334 10 BAHT

Bi-Metallic Brass center in Copper-Nickel ring, 26 mm. **Ruler:** Bhumipol Adulyadej (Rama IX) **Subject:** F.A.O. World Summit December 2 **Obv:** Bust left within circle **Rev:** Seated and kneeling figures within circle **Edge:** Alternating reeded and plain

Date	Mintage	F	VF	XF	Unc	BU
BE2538 (1996)	—	—	—	—	3.50	—

Y# 347 10 BAHT

Bi-Metallic Brass center in Copper-Nickel ring, 26 mm. **Ruler:** Bhumipol Adulyadej (Rama IX) **Subject:** 100th Anniversary of Chulalongkorn's European Tour **Obv:** Bust right within circle **Rev:** Design and inscription divides circle **Edge:** Alternating reeded and plain

Date	Mintage	F	VF	XF	Unc	BU
BE2540 (1997)	—	—	—	—	2.50	—

Y# 346 10 BAHT

Bi-Metallic Brass center in Copper-Nickel ring, 26 mm. **Ruler:** Bhumipol Adulyadej (Rama IX) **Subject:** 100th Anniversary - Central General Hospital - Medication Office 2441-2541 **Obv:** Conjoined busts facing within circle **Rev:** Figure seated on facing elephant within circle **Edge:** Alternating reeded and plain

Date	Mintage	F	VF	XF	Unc	BU
BE2541 (1998)	—	—	—	—	4.00	—

Y# 348 10 BAHT

Bi-Metallic Brass center in Copper-Nickel ring, 26 mm. **Ruler:** Bhumipol Adulyadej (Rama IX) **Subject:** 13th Asian Games Bangkok December 6-20 **Obv:** Bust left within circle **Rev:** Symbols within circle **Edge:** Alternating reeded and plain

Date	Mintage	F	VF	XF	Unc	BU
BE2541 (1998)	10,000,000	—	—	—	2.50	—

Y# 352 10 BAHT

Bi-Metallic Brass center in Copper-Nickel ring, 26 mm. **Ruler:** Bhumipol Adulyadej (Rama IX) **Subject:** Rama III honored with the title "Great" March 31 **Obv:** Head facing within circle **Rev:** Crowned arms within circle **Edge:** Alternating reeded and plain

Date	Mintage	F	VF	XF	Unc	BU
BE2541 (1998)	—	—	—	—	2.50	—

Y# 349 10 BAHT

Bi-Metallic Brass center in Copper-Nickel ring, 26 mm. **Ruler:** Bhumipol Adulyadej (Rama IX) **Subject:** 125th Anniversary of the Customer's Department July 4 **Obv:** Conjoined busts 1/4 right **Rev:** Buildings below emblem **Edge:** Alternating reeded and plain

Date	Mintage	F	VF	XF	Unc	BU
BE2542 (1999)	—	—	—	—	2.50	—

Y# 350 10 BAHT

Bi-Metallic Brass center in Copper-Nickel ring, 26 mm. **Ruler:** Bhumipol Adulyadej (Rama IX) **Subject:** King's 72nd Birthday December 5 **Obv:** Head left within circle **Rev:** Crowned emblem within circle **Edge:** Alternating reeded and plain

Date	Mintage	F	VF	XF	Unc	BU
BE2542 (1999)	10,000,000	—	—	—	1.75	—

Y# 354 10 BAHT

Bi-Metallic Brass center in Copper-Nickel ring, 26 mm. **Ruler:** Bhumipol Adulyadej (Rama IX) **Subject:** 100th Anniversary Army Medical Department January 7 2443-2543 **Obv:** Conjoined busts facing **Rev:** Emblem within circle **Edge:** Alternating reeded and plain

Date	Mintage	F	VF	XF	Unc	BU
ND (2000)	—	—	—	—	2.00	—

Y# 358 10 BAHT

8.4900 g., Bi-Metallic Brass center in Copper-Nickel ring, 26 mm. **Ruler:** Bhumipol Adulyadej (Rama IX) **Subject:** 80th Anniversary - Commerce Ministry August 20 **Obv:** Head facing within circle **Rev:** Ministry logo within square and circle **Edge:** Segmented reeding

Date	Mintage	F	VF	XF	Unc	BU
BE2543 (2000)	—	—	—	—	2.00	—

Y# 361 10 BAHT

Bi-Metallic Brass center in Copper-Nickel ring, 26 mm. **Ruler:** Bhumipol Adulyadej (Rama IX) **Subject:** 100th Birthday - King's Mother October 21 **Obv:** Bust left within circle **Rev:** Emblem within circle **Edge:** Alternating reeded and plain

Date	Mintage	F	VF	XF	Unc	BU
BE2543 (2000)	—	—	—	—	2.00	—

Y# 373 10 BAHT

8.5000 g., Bi-Metallic Brass center in Copper-Nickel ring, 26 mm. **Ruler:** Bhumipol Adulyadej (Rama IX) **Subject:** Department of Lands Centennial February 17 2444-2544 **Obv:** Conjoined busts facing divides circle **Rev:** Department seal within circle **Edge:** Alternating reeded and plain

Date	Mintage	F	VF	XF	Unc	BU
BE2545(2001)	—	—	—	—	2.50	—

Y# 381 10 BAHT

8.5500 g., Bi-Metallic Brass center in Copper-Nickel ring, 26 mm. **Ruler:** Bhumipol Adulyadej (Rama IX) **Subject:** Centennial of Irrigation Department June 13 **Obv:** Conjoined busts facing divides circle **Rev:** Department logo **Edge:** Alternating reeded and plain

Date	Mintage	F	VF	XF	Unc	BU
BE2545(2002)	—	—	—	—	2.00	—

Y# 382 10 BAHT

8.5500 g., Bi-Metallic Brass center in Copper-Nickel ring, 26 mm. **Ruler:** Bhumipol Adulyadej (Rama IX) **Subject:** Department of Internal Trade 60th Anniversary May 5 **Obv:** Head left **Rev:** Department logo **Edge:** Alternating reeded and plain

Date	Mintage	F	VF	XF	Unc	BU
BE2545(2002)	—	—	—	—	2.00	—

Y# 383 10 BAHT

8.5500 g., Bi-Metallic Brass center in Copper-Nickel ring, 26 mm. **Ruler:** Bhumipol Adulyadej (Rama IX) **Subject:** State Highway Department 90th Anniversary April 1 **Obv:** Conjoined busts facing divides circle **Rev:** Department logo **Edge:** Alternating reeded and plain

Date	Mintage	F	VF	XF	Unc	BU
BE2545(2002)	—	—	—	—	2.00	—

Y# 384 10 BAHT

8.5500 g., Bi-Metallic Brass center in Copper-Nickel ring, 26 mm. **Ruler:** Bhumipol Adulyadej (Rama IX) **Subject:** Vajira Hospital 90th Anniversary January 2 **Obv:** Conjoined busts facing divides circle **Rev:** Hospital logo **Edge:** Alternating reeded and plain

Date	Mintage	F	VF	XF	Unc	BU
BE2545(2002)	—	—	—	—	2.00	—

Y# 385 10 BAHT

8.5500 g., Bi-Metallic Brass center in Copper-Nickel ring, 26 mm. **Ruler:** Bhumipol Adulyadej (Rama IX) **Subject:** 20th World Scouting Jamboree **Obv:** Rama IX wearing a scouting uniform **Rev:** Jamboree logo **Edge:** Alternating reeded and plain

Date	Mintage	F	VF	XF	Unc	BU
BE2545(2002)	—	—	—	—	2.00	—

Y# 387 10 BAHT

8.5500 g., Bi-Metallic Brass center in Copper-Nickel ring, 26 mm. **Ruler:** Bhumipol Adulyadej (Rama IX) **Subject:** King's 75th Birthday December 5 **Obv:** Head left **Rev:** Royal crown in radiant oval **Edge:** Alternating reeded and plain

Date	Mintage	F	VF	XF	Unc	BU
BE2545(2002)	—	—	—	—	2.00	—

Y# 400 10 BAHT

8.5500 g., Bi-Metallic Brass center in Copper-Nickel ring, 26 mm. **Ruler:** Bhumipol Adulyadej (Rama IX) **Obv:** Head left **Rev:** APEC logo **Edge:** Segmented reeding

Date	Mintage	F	VF	XF	Unc	BU
BE2546-2003	—	—	—	—	3.00	—

Y# 405 10 BAHT

8.5400 g., Bi-Metallic Brass center in Copper-Nickel ring, 26 mm. **Ruler:** Bhumipol Adulyadej (Rama IX) **Subject:** "CITES COP" **Obv:** Bust 3/4 left within circle **Rev:** "CITES" logo **Edge:** Segmented reeding

Date	Mintage	F	VF	XF	Unc	BU
ND(2003)	—	—	—	—	2.00	—

Y# 409 10 BAHT

Bi-Metallic **Ruler:** Bhumipol Adulyadej (Rama IX) **Subject:** 150th Anniversary of King Rama V

Date	Mintage	F	VF	XF	Unc	BU
BE2546(2003)	—	—	—	—	2.50	—

Y# 391 10 BAHT

8.5000 g., Bi-Metallic Brass center in Copper-Nickel ring, 26 mm. **Ruler:** Bhumipol Adulyadej (Rama IX) **Subject:** Inspector General's Department Centennial May 6 **Obv:** Head left within circle **Rev:** Department seal within circle and design **Edge:** Alternating reeded and plain

Date	Mintage	F	VF	XF	Unc	BU
BE2546(2003)	—	—	—	—	1.75	—

Y# 392 10 BAHT

8.5000 g., Bi-Metallic Brass center in Copper-Nickel ring, 26 mm. **Ruler:** Bhumipol Adulyadej (Rama IX) **Subject:** 80th Birthday of Princess May 6 **Obv:** Bust 1/4 right **Rev:** Crowned emblem and value **Edge:** Alternating reeded and plain **Note:** This is the king's sister.

Date	Mintage	F	VF	XF	Unc	BU
BE2546(2003)	—	—	—	—	1.75	—

Y# 396 10 BAHT

8.5500 g., Bi-Metallic Brass center in Copper-Nickel ring, 26 mm. **Ruler:** Bhumipol Adulyadej (Rama IX) **Subject:** 90th Anniversary of the Government Savings Bank April 1 **Obv:** Uniformed bust facing within circle **Rev:** Bank emblem **Edge:** Alternating reeded and plain

Date	Mintage	F	VF	XF	Unc	BU
BE2546(2003)	—	—	—	—	2.00	—

Y# 411 10 BAHT

Bi-Metallic **Ruler:** Bhumipol Adulyadej (Rama IX) **Subject:** 70th Anniversary Royal Institute

Date	Mintage	F	VF	XF	Unc	BU
BE2547(2004)	—	—	—	—	2.50	—

Y# 412 10 BAHT

Bi-Metallic **Ruler:** Bhumipol Adulyadej (Rama IX) **Subject:** 72nd Anniversary of Queen's Birthday

Date	Mintage	F	VF	XF	Unc	BU
BE2547(2004)	—	—	—	—	2.50	—

Y# 413 10 BAHT

Bi-Metallic **Ruler:** Bhumipol Adulyadej (Rama IX) **Subject:** World Conservation Congress

Date	Mintage	F	VF	XF	Unc	BU
BE2547(2004)	—	—	—	—	2.50	—

Y# 414 10 BAHT

Bi-Metallic **Ruler:** Bhumipol Adulyadej (Rama IX) **Subject:** Anti Drugs

Date	Mintage	F	VF	XF	Unc	BU
BE2547(2004)	—	—	—	—	2.50	—

Y# 415 10 BAHT

Bi-Metallic **Ruler:** Bhumipol Adulyadej (Rama IX) **Subject:** Bicentennial of King Rama IV

Date	Mintage	F	VF	XF	Unc	BU
BE2547(2004)	—	—	—	—	2.50	—

Y# 410 10 BAHT

8.4500 g., Bi-Metallic Brass center in Copper-Nickel ring, 25.9 mm. **Obv:** King in uniform **Rev:** Thammasat University arms **Edge:** Segmented reeding **Note:** 70th Anniversary of Thammasat University

Date	Mintage	F	VF	XF	Unc	BU
BE2547 (2004)	—	—	—	—	2.50	—

Y# 416 10 BAHT

Bi-Metallic **Ruler:** Bhumipol Adulyadej (Rama IX) **Subject:** 100th Anniversary of Army Transportation

Date	Mintage	F	VF	XF	Unc	BU
BE2548(2005)	—	—	—	—	2.50	—

Y# 417 10 BAHT

Bi-Metallic **Ruler:** Bhumipol Adulyadej (Rama IX) **Obv:** Baby head

Date	Mintage	F	VF	XF	Unc	BU
BE2548(2005)	—	—	—	—	2.50	—

Y# 402 10 BAHT

8.4400 g., Bi-Metallic Brass center in Copper-Nickel ring, 26 mm. **Ruler:** Bhumipol Adulyadej (Rama IX) **Obv:** Bust 1/4 left within circle **Rev:** Treasury Department seal within circle **Edge:** Segmented reeding

Date	Mintage	F	VF	XF	Unc	BU
BE2548(2005)	—	—	—	—	2.50	—

Y# 418 10 BAHT

Bi-Metallic **Ruler:** Bhumipol Adulyadej (Rama IX) **Subject:** 25th Asia-Pacific Scout Jamboree

Date	Mintage	F	VF	XF	Unc	BU
BE2550(2006)	—	—	—	—	2.50	—

Y# 424 10 BAHT

8.4300 g., Bi-Metallic Brass center in Copper-Nickel ring, 25.98 mm. **Ruler:** Bhumipol Adulyadej (Rama IX) **Subject:** 150th Birthday of Prince Jaturon Ratsamee **Obv:** Bust of Prince facing 3/4 right **Rev:** Radiant badge **Edge:** Segmented reeding

Date	Mintage	F	VF	XF	Unc	BU
BE2549(2006)	—	—	—	—	2.50	—

Y# 425 10 BAHT

8.4300 g., Bi-Metallic Brass center in Copper-Nickel ring, 25.98 mm. **Ruler:** Bhumipol Adulyadej (Rama IX) **Subject:** Centenary of Royal Mounted Army **Obv:** Conjoined kings' busts left **Rev:** Royal crown above emblem **Edge:** Segmented reeding

Date	Mintage	F	VF	XF	Unc	BU
BE2550(2007)	—	—	—	—	2.50	—

Y# 426 10 BAHT

8.4300 g., Bi-Metallic Brass center in Copper-Nickel ring, 25.98 mm. **Ruler:** Bhumipol Adulyadej (Rama IX) **Subject:** Centenary of 1st Thai Commercial Bank **Obv:** Conjoined kings' busts left **Rev:** Garuda Bird **Edge:** Segmented reeding

Date	Mintage	F	VF	XF	Unc	BU
BE2550(2007)	—	—	—	—	2.50	—

Y# 407 20 BAHT

15.0200 g., Copper Nickel, 32 mm. **Ruler:** Bhumipol Adulyadej (Rama IX) **Subject:** 60th Anniversary of Reign **Obv:** Head left **Rev:** Royal Crown on display **Edge:** Reeded

Date	Mintage	F	VF	XF	Unc	BU
BE2549(2006)	—	—	—	—	—	4.00
BE2549(2006) Proof	—	Value: 18.50				

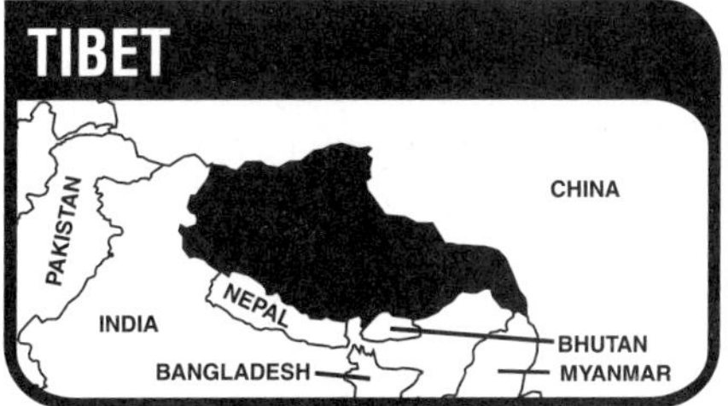

Tibet, an autonomous region of China located in central Asia between the Himalayan and Kunlun Mts. has an area of 471,660 sq. mi. (1,221,599 sq. km.) and a population of*1.9 million. Capital: Lhasa. The economy is based on agriculture and livestock raising. Wool, livestock, salt and hides are exported.

Lamaism, a form of Buddhism, developed in Tibet in the 8th century. From that time until the 1900s, the Tibetan rulers virtually isolated the country from the outside world. The British in India achieved some influence in the early 20th century. British troops were sent with the Young Husband mission to extend trade in the north of India in December 1903; leaving during September 1904. The 13th Dalai Lama had fled to Urga where he remained until 1907. In April 1905 a revolt broke out and spread through southwestern Szechuan and northwestern Yunnan. Chao Erh-feng was appointed to subdue this rebellion and entered Lhasa in January 1910 with 2,000 troops. The Dalai Lama fled to India until he returned in June 1912., The British encouraged Tibet to declare its independence from China in 1913. The Communist revolution in China marked a new era in Tibetan history. Chinese Communist troops invaded Tibet in Oct., 1950. After a token resistance, Tibet signed an agreement with China in which China recognized the spiritual and temporal leadership of the Dalai Lama, and Tibet recognized the suzerainty of China. In 1959, a nationwide revolt triggered by Communist-initiated land reform broke out. The revolt was ruthlessly crushed. The dalai lama fled to India, and on Sept. 1,1965, the Chinese made Tibet an autonomous region of China.

The first coins to circulate in Tibet were those of neighboring Nepal from about 1570. Shortly after 1720, the Nepalese government began striking specific issues for use in Tibet. These coins had a lower silver content than those struck for use in Nepal and were exchanged with the Tibetans for an equal weight in silver bullion. Around 1763 the Tibetans struck their own coins for the first time in history. The number of coins struck at that time must have been very small. Larger quantities of coins were struck by the Tibetan government mint, which opened in 1791 with the permission of the Chinese. Operations of this mint however were suspended two years later. The Chinese opened a second mint in Lhasa in 1792. It produced a coinage until 1836. Shortly thereafter, the Tibetan mint was reopened and the government of Tibet continued to strike coins until 1953.

DATING

Based on the Tibetan calendar, Tibetan coins are dated by the cycle which contains 60 years. To calculate the western date use the following formula: Number of cycles -1, x 60 + number of years + 1026.Example 15th cycle 25th year = 1891 AD. Example: 15th cycle, 25th year 15 - 1 x 60 + 25 + 1026 = 1891AD.

13/30 = 1776	14/30 = 1836	15/30 = 1896
13/40 = 1786	14/40 = 1846	15/40 = 1906
13/50 = 1796	14/50 = 1856	15/50 = 1916
13/60 = 1806	14/60 = 1866	15/60 = 1926
14/10 = 1816	15/10 = 1876	16/10 = 1936
14/20 = 1826	15/20 = 1886	16/20 = 1946

Certain Sino-Tibetan issues are dated in the year of reign of the Emperor of China.

MONETARY SYSTEM

15 Skar = 1-1/2 Sho = 1 Tangka
10 Sho = 1 Srang

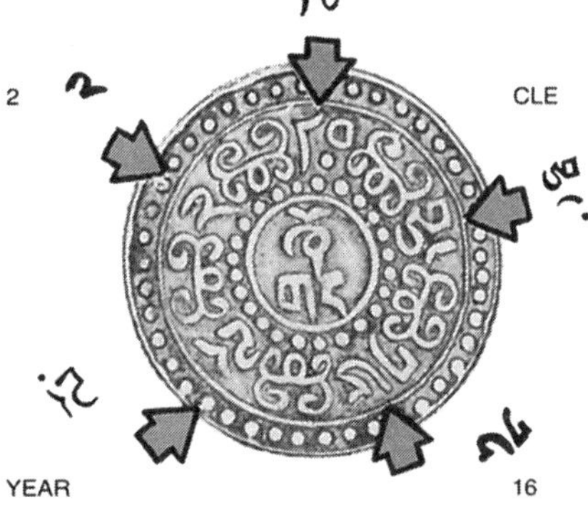

16(th)CYCLE 2(nd)YEAR = 1928AD

16(th) CYCLE 7(th) YEAR = 1933AD

NUMERALS

1	༡	གཅིག་
2	༢	གཉིས་
3	༣	གསུམ་
4	༤	བཞི་
5	༥	ལྔ་
6	༦	དྲུག་
7	༧	བདུན་
8	༨	བརྒྱད་
9	༩	དགུ་
10	༡༠	བཅུ་ or བཅུ་ཐམ་པ་
11	༡༡	བཅུག་ or བཅུ་གཅིག་
12	༡༢	བཅུས་ or བཅུ་གཉིས་
13	༡༣	བཅུ མ་ or བཅུ་གསུམ་
14	༡༤	བཅུ་བཞི་
15	༡༥	བཅོ་ལྔ་
16	༡༦	བཅུ་དྲུག་
17	༡༧	བཅུ་བདུན་
18	༡༨	བཅོ་བརྒྱད་
19	༡༩	བཅུ་དགུ་
20	༢༠	ཉི་ཤུ
21	༢༡	ཉི་ཤུ་རྩ་གཅིག་ or ཉེར་གཅིག་
22	༢༢	ཉེར་གཉིས་
23	༢༣	ཉེར་གསུམ་
24	༢༤	ཉེར་ བཞི་

25 ༢༥ ཉེར་ལྔ

26 ༢༦ ཉེར་དྲུག

27 ༢༧ ཉེར་བདུན

28 ༢༨ ཉེར་བརྒྱད

CHINESE AUTHORITY

SINO-TIBETAN COINAGE

Milled

Y# A4 1/2 SKAR

Copper **Ruler:** Hsüan-t'ung **Edge:** Plain **Note:** Weight varies: 3.10-3.60 grams.

Date	Mintage	Good	VG	F	VF	XF
ND(1910)	—	300	500	700	1,000	—

Y# 4 SKAR

Copper, 27 mm. **Ruler:** Hsüan-t'ung **Rev. Inscription:** Hsüan-t'ung.... **Edge:** Plain **Note:** Weight varies: 5.40-6.60 grams. Varieties exist. Modern counterfeits exist.

Date	Mintage	Good	VG	F	VF	XF
ND(1910)	—	90.00	150	250	400	—

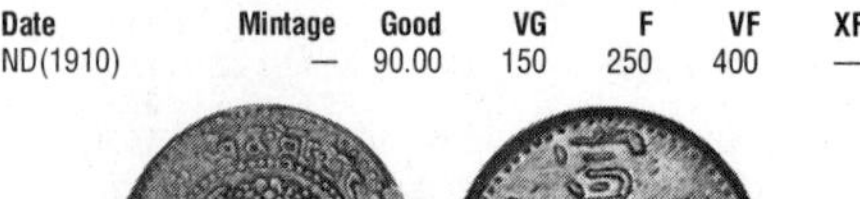

Y# 5 SHO

Silver, 22 mm. **Ruler:** Hsüan-t'ung **Rev. Inscription:** Hsüan-t'ung.... **Edge:** Reeded **Note:** Weight varies: 3.30-4.10 grams. Varieties exist, one having the inner circle of dots, on the Chinese side, connected by lines. Modern counterfeits exist.

Date	Mintage	Good	VG	F	VF	XF
ND(1910)	—	20.00	30.00	50.00	75.00	125

Y# 6 2 SHO

Silver, 25 mm. **Ruler:** Hsüan-t'ung **Rev. Inscription:** Hsüan-t'ung.... **Edge:** Reeded **Note:** Weight varies: 5.20-8.40 grams. Varieties with different dragon claws and lotus exist. Modern counterfeits exist.

Date	Mintage	Good	VG	F	VF	XF
ND(1910)	—	25.00	40.00	80.00	125	175

TANGKA COINAGE

Kong-par Tangka

The legend of this so called Ranjana Tangka appears to be in ornamental Lansa script and represents a mantra alluding to wealth and luck. The type is a copy of the Nepalese debased Tangka of Pratap Simha. Struck unofficially by Nepalese traders in Tibet between 1880 and 1912, it was legal tender, due to an edict issued in 1881 ordering that no distinction be made between false and genuine coins. The Tangka, C#27 was cut in parts of 3, 4, and 5 petals to make change and the resulting fractions are occasionally encountered.

C# 27.1 TANGKA

Silver **Obv:** Crescent and moon at top **Note:** Weight varies: 4.60-5.40 grams. Prev. #C27.

Date	Mintage	Good	VG	F	VF	XF
BE15-40 (1906)	—	8.00	15.00	25.00	40.00	70.00

Note: In addition to the meaningful dates, the following meaningless ones exist: 13-16, 13-31, 13-92, 15-40, 16-16, 16-61, 16-64, 16-69, 16-92, 16-93, 92-34, 92-39, 96-61 (sixes maybe reversed threes and nines reversed ones); These are of silver, varying from 3.9 to 5.2 grams

C# 27.2 TANGKA

Silver **Obv:** Crescent and swastika at top **Note:** Weight varies: 4.60-5.40 grams. See note for C#27.1.

Date	Mintage	Good	VG	F	VF	XF
BE15-46 (1912)	—	60.00	80.00	100	150	225

GA-DEN TANGKA COINAGE

Hammered

The Ga-den Tangkas are among the most common and perhaps most beautiful of all Tibetan silver coins. The obverse shows a stylized Lotus flower within a circle surrounded by the 8 Buddhist lucky symbols in radiating petals. The reverse shows an 8-petalled wheel (flower) within a star surrounded by a Tibetan inscription (reading Ga-den Palace, victorious in all directions), which is broken up into 8 oval frames. The Ga-den Palace is the former residence of the Dala Lamas, located in Drepung Monastery near Lhasa. On Tibetan coins the name "Ga-den Palace" is used as epithet for "Tibetan Government". Compass directions indicate the location of the Buddhist emblems.

Numbers for Obverse Types A & B

Numbers for Obverse Types C thru H

1. Umbrella of sovereignty.
2. Two golden fish of good fortune.
3. Amphora of ambrosia.
4. Lotus.
5. Conch shell.
6. Emblem of endless birth.
7. Banner of victory.
8. Wheel of empire.

Reverse - All Types

དགའ་	dGa'	"Ga-"
ལྡན་	lDan	"den"
ཕོ་	Pho	Po-
བྲང་	Brañ	dang
ཕྱོགས་	Phyogs	Tschog-
ལས་	Las	le
རྣམ་	rNam	Nam-
རྒྱལ་	rGyal	gyel

Based on the ornamentation in the outer angles between the petals on both sides of the coin, the Ga-Den Tangkas can be differentiated in the following 8 types, A-H.

Type	Outer Obv.	Water-line	Outer Rev.	Rev. Ctr.
A	∵	None	〰	Pellet
B	∵	2 lines	〰	3 Crescents
C	∵	1 line	〰	2 Crescents
D	∵	1 line	∵	2 Crescents
E	〰	1 line	∵	2 Crescents
F	•	1 line	∵	2 Crescents
G	None	1 line	None	2 Crescents
H	•	1 line	•	3 Crescents

Within these types, changes in the order, design, and style of the 8 lucky signs or significant errors constitute subtypes. The sutypes appearing in this catalog are not the only ones. Some subtypes show a wide range of styles and die varieties. Weights given include 95 percent of the indicated types.

Error strikes with muled reverses exist. Specimens of Types D, E, and F with lumps are known, reportedly containing gold, probably used by high lamas in their offerings.

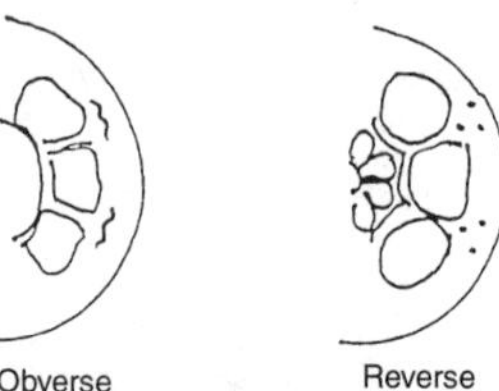

Obverse has wavy water line in outer angles. New style lotus without three small leaves to left and right. Reverse has three dots in outer angles, wheel with spokes.

Y# E13.1 TANGKA

Silver **Obv:** Dot to left and right of lotus **Edge:** Plain **Note:** Weight varies: 4.60-4.80 grams. Prev. Y#13.4.

Date	Mintage	VG	F	VF	XF	Unc
ND(ca.1899-1907)	—	3.00	4.00	7.00	12.00	35.00

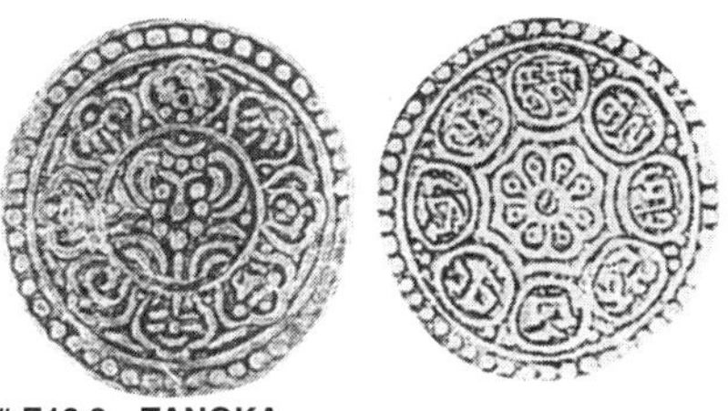

Y# E13.3 TANGKA

Silver **Obv:** Four dots (NE), one dot (E) **Edge:** Plain **Note:** Weight varies: 3.80-5.70 grams. Similar to Y#E13.1 but obverse emblems rotated by one position clockwise (error).

Date	Mintage	Good	VG	F	VF	XF
ND(ca.1899-1907)	—	75.00	100	150	200	300

Y# E13.4 TANGKA

3.8000 g., Silver **Obv:** 7.5-8.0mm lotus circle, no dot at left and right of lotus **Edge:** Plain **Note:** Prev. Y#E13.8 (Y#13.5).

Date	Mintage	VG	F	VF	XF	Unc
ND(ca.1904)	—	60.00	85.00	120	180	250

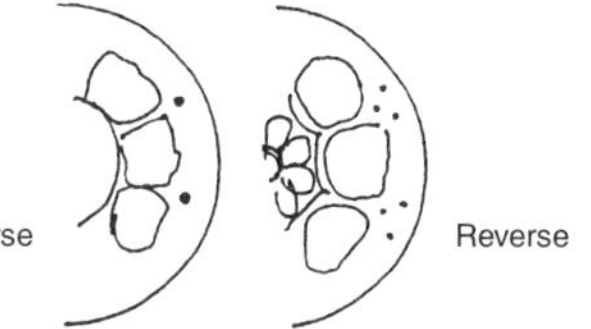

Y# F13.1 TANGKA

Billon **Obv:** Nine dots within lotus circle **Rev:** Flower buds full or outlined **Edge:** Plain **Note:** Six varieties exist. Weight varies: 4.10-4.70 grams. Prev. Y#13.6.

Date	Mintage	VG	F	VF	XF	Unc
ND(ca.1907-09)	—	4.00	6.00	10.00	16.00	40.00

Y# F13.4 TANGKA

Billon **Obv:** Dot to left and right of lotus; northeast symbol two fish with dots; south symbol with 3 dots; northwest symbol circle with 4 dots around center dot **Edge:** Plain **Note:** Weight varies: 4.10-4.70 grams. Varieties exist including 34-78 dots for outer circles. Prev. Y#13.7.

Date	Mintage	VG	F	VF	XF	Unc
ND(ca.1912-22)	—	8.00	12.00	20.00	32.00	60.00

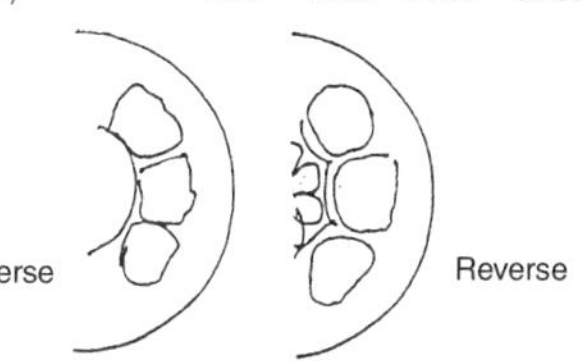

Y# G13 TANGKA

Billon **Rev:** No outer angles at inner circle **Edge:** Plain **Note:** Weight varies: 3.30-4.60 grams. Prev. Y#13.9.

Date	Mintage	VG	F	VF	XF	Unc
ND(ca.1921)	—	4.00	6.00	9.00	15.00	45.00

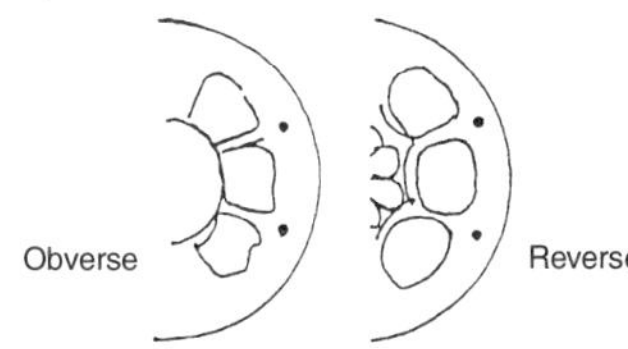

Y# H13.1 TANGKA

Billon **Obv:** Dot between symbols at inner circle, lotus petals joined **Rev:** Dot between characters at inner circle **Edge:** Plain **Note:** Weight varies: 4.00-4.20 grams. Two minor die varieties exist. Prev. Y#13.10.

Date	Mintage	VG	F	VF	XF	Unc
ND(1929)	—	10.00	14.00	20.00	30.00	50.00

Y# H13.2 TANGKA

Billon **Obv:** Similar to Y#H13.1 **Rev:** Similar to Y#H13.1 but Northeast character in retrograde **Edge:** Plain **Note:** Weight varies: 4.00-4.20 grams. Machine struck.

Date	Mintage	VG	F	VF	XF	Unc
ND(ca.1929-30)	—	60.00	90.00	120	150	—

Y# 15 2 TANGKA

Billon **Note:** Weight varies: 7.80-10.50 grams. Varieties exist.

Date	Mintage	VG	F	VF	XF	Unc
ND(ca.1912)	—	125	200	400	500	—

PRESENTATION TANGKA COINAGE

Y# 14 TANGKA

Silver **Edge:** Plain **Note:** Weight varies: 2.70-5.00 grams. Fifteen obverse varieties exist with combinations of none or up to two dots inside trapezoids enclosing the legend.

Date	Mintage	VG	F	VF	XF	Unc
ND(1910)	600,000	10.00	15.00	25.00	50.00	60.00

Y# 31 TANGKA

Silver **Edge:** Reeded **Note:** Weight varies: 3.10-5.30 grams. Varieties exist, the two "commas" in central circle are in either vertical or horizontal alignment.

Date	Mintage	VG	F	VF	XF	Unc
ND(1953)	—	7.00	10.00	15.00	22.00	—
ND(1953)	331,292	7.00	10.00	15.00	22.00	40.00

Note: Struck for presentation to Monks; Circulated later but briefly with value of 5 and then 10 Srang

SHO-SRANG COINAGE

Y# A7 1/8 SHO

Copper, 22 mm. **Note:** Two reverse varieties exist, one with a dot between the upper two syllables of the legend, the other is without a dot.

Date	Mintage	Good	VG	F	VF	XF
1 (1909)	—	85.00	150	225	350	—

Note: A silver striking of this type exists (rare), possibly a pattern; Year 1 of the reign of Hsuan T'ung

Y# B7 1/4 SHO

Copper, 26 mm.

Date	Mintage	Good	VG	F	VF	XF
1(1909)	—	50.00	100	150	250	—

Note: This coin struck in silver is a forgery; Modern forgeries struck in copper and copper-nickel exist; Year 1 of the reign of Husan T'ung

Y# 10 2-1/2 SKAR

Copper, 22 mm. **Obv:** Lion standing left, looking backwards **Edge:** Plain **Note:** Lion varieties exist.

Date	Mintage	Good	VG	F	VF	XF
BE15-43 (1909)	—	150	250	350	500	—

Y# 16.1 2-1/2 SKAR

Copper **Obv:** Lion crouching and looking upwards **Edge:** Plain **Note:** Weight varies: 3.70-6.00 grams. Varieties exist.

Date	Mintage	Good	VG	F	VF	XF
BE15-47 (1913)	—	5.00	12.00	20.00	50.00	—
BE15-48 (1914)	—	5.00	12.00	20.00	50.00	—
BE15-49 (1915)	—	15.00	30.00	60.00	120	—
BE15-50 (1916)	—	8.00	16.00	30.00	70.00	—
BE15-51 (1917)	—	30.00	60.00	120	240	—
BE15-52 (1918)	—	6.50	14.00	25.00	60.00	—

Y# A19 2-1/2 SKAR

Copper **Obv:** Lion standing left, looking back and upwards **Shape:** Scalloped

Date	Mintage	Good	VG	F	VF	XF
BE15-52 (1918)	—	50.00	85.00	110	150	—
BE15-53 (1918)	—	50.00	90.00	120	165	—
BE15-55 (1921)	—	50.00	90.00	120	165	—

Y# A10 5 SKAR

Copper, 25 mm. **Obv:** Lion standing left, looking back and upwards **Edge:** Plain

Date	Mintage	Good	VG	F	VF	XF
BE15-43 (1909)	—	150	250	350	500	—

Y# 17 5 SKAR

Copper **Obv:** Lion standing left and looking upward **Edge:** Plain

Date	Mintage	Good	VG	F	VF	XF
BE15-47 (1913)	—	6.00	10.00	25.00	55.00	—
BE15-48 (1914)	—	4.00	7.00	15.00	35.00	—

Date	Mintage	Good	VG	F	VF	XF
BE15-49 (1915)	—	5.00	8.00	18.00	40.00	—
BE15-50 (1916)	—	5.00	8.00	18.00	40.00	—
BE15-51 (1917)	—	3.50	6.00	12.00	30.00	—
BE15-52 (1918)	—	25.00	55.00	120	250	—

Y# 17.1 5 SKAR

Copper **Obv:** Lion standing left, looking back **Edge:** Plain **Note:** Size of obverse circle and weight of coin vary considerably.

Date	Mintage	Good	VG	F	VF	XF
BE15-49 (1914)	—	4.00	7.00	15.00	32.00	—
Note: Obverse varieties (lion) exist						
BE15-50 (1916)	—	4.00	7.00	15.00	32.00	—
BE15-51 (1917)	—	4.00	7.00	15.00	32.00	—
BE15-52 (1918)	—	5.00	8.00	18.00	40.00	—

Y# 17.2 5 SKAR

Copper **Obv:** Lion standing left looking back and upwards **Edge:** Plain

Date	Mintage	Good	VG	F	VF	XF
BE15-48 (1914)	—	5.00	9.00	20.00	45.00	—
BE15-49 (1915)	—	8.00	14.00	35.00	70.00	—

Y# 17.3 5 SKAR

Copper **Obv:** Lion standing left looking back and upwards **Rev:** Flower with eight petals rather than wheel with eight spokes **Edge:** Plain

Date	Mintage	Good	VG	F	VF	XF
BE15-48 (1914)	—	6.00	10.00	25.00	55.00	—

Y# 19 5 SKAR

Copper **Obv:** Lion standing left **Edge:** Reeded **Note:** Varieties exist.

Date	Mintage	Good	VG	F	VF	XF
BE15-52 (1918)	—	2.25	3.50	6.00	12.00	—
BE15-53 (1919)	—	2.00	3.00	5.50	11.00	—
BE15-54 (1920)	—	1.50	2.50	5.00	10.00	—
BE15-55 (1921)	—	5.00	10.00	20.00	40.00	—
BE15-56 (1922)	—	1.50	2.50	5.00	10.00	—
BE56-15 (1922) Error	—	25.00	40.00	70.00	110	—
Note: Reverse inscription reads counterclockwise on error date coin						

Y# 19.1 5 SKAR

Copper **Obv:** Lion standing left **Rev:** Dot added above center **Edge:** Reeded

Date	Mintage	Good	VG	F	VF	XF
BE15-55 (1921)	—	10.00	20.00	35.00	65.00	—
BE15-56 (1922)	—	4.00	8.00	15.00	25.00	—

Y# 11 7-1/2 SKAR

Copper, 28 mm. **Obv:** Lion standing left, looking back and upwards **Edge:** Plain **Note:** Modern counterfeits exist.

Date	Mintage	Good	VG	F	VF	XF
BE15-43 (1909)	—	150	250	350	500	—

Y# 20 7-1/2 SKAR

Copper **Edge:** Plain **Note:** Some 15-52, 15-53, and 15-55 specimens have the reverse central "whirlwind" in a counterclockwise direction. Many varieties exist with size of inner circle on reverse.

Date	Mintage	Good	VG	F	VF	XF
BE15-52 (1918)	—	2.00	3.00	5.00	8.50	—
BE15-53 (1919)	—	1.50	2.50	4.00	7.00	—
BE15-54 (1920)	—	1.50	2.50	4.00	7.00	—
BE15-55 (1921)	—	1.50	2.50	4.00	7.00	—
BE15-56 (1922)	—	1.50	2.50	4.00	7.00	—
BE15-60 (1926)	—	20.00	30.00	50.00	100	—

Y# 21 SHO

Copper **Obv:** Lion standing left, looking upwards **Rev:** Central legend horizontal

Date	Mintage	Good	VG	F	VF	XF
BE15-52 (1918)	—	30.00	45.00	75.00	120	—

Y# 21.1 SHO

Copper, 24 mm. **Obv:** Lion standing left, looking backwards, without dot in reverse arabesque **Note:** Weight varies: 3.95-7.13 grams. Varieties exist.

Date	Mintage	Good	VG	F	VF	XF
BE15-52 (1918)	—	1.50	2.00	3.25	7.00	—
BE15-53/52 (1919)	—	—	—	—	—	—
BE15-53 (1919)	—	1.00	1.50	2.50	5.00	—
BE15-54 (1920)	—	1.00	1.50	2.50	5.00	—
BE15-55 (1921)	—	1.00	1.50	2.50	5.00	—
BE15-56 (1922)	—	1.00	1.50	2.50	5.00	—
BE15-57 (1923)	—	1.50	2.00	3.25	7.00	—
BE15-57 (1923) Without dots (obverse)	—	5.00	10.00	20.00	30.00	—
BE15-58 (1924)	—	1.00	1.50	2.50	5.00	—
BE58-15 (1924) (error) year and cycle transposed	—	—	—	—	—	—
BE15-59 (1925)	—	1.00	1.50	2.50	5.00	—
BE15-59 (1925) Without dots (obverse)	—	5.00	10.00	20.00	30.00	—
BE15-60 (1926)	—	1.00	1.50	2.50	5.00	—
BE15-6 (1926) (error) for 15-60	—	—	—	—	—	—
BE16-1 (1927)	—	1.00	1.50	2.50	5.00	—
BE16-2 (1928)	—	1.00	1.50	2.50	5.00	—

Y# 21.2 SHO

Copper **Obv:** Lion looking upwards, with dot in reverse arabesque. **Note:** Varieties exist.

Date	Mintage	Good	VG	F	VF	XF
BE15-54 (1920)	—	2.00	3.00	5.00	9.00	—
Note: Specimens dated 15-54 may all be contemporary forgeries						
BE54-15 (1920) (Error) year and cycle transposed	—	25.00	40.00	65.00	100	—

Date	Mintage	Good	VG	F	VF	XF
BE15/51-54 (1920) (error) cycle transposed	—	25.00	40.00	65.00	100	—
BE15-55 (1921)	—	1.50	2.50	4.50	7.00	—
BE55-15 (1921) Error; "year" and "cycle" transposed	—	25.00	40.00	65.00	100	—
BE15-56/5 (1921)	—	1.00	1.50	2.50	5.00	—
BE15-56 (1922)	—	1.00	1.50	2.50	5.00	—
BE15-57 (1923)	—	1.25	1.75	3.25	7.00	—
BE15-58 (1924)	—	1.00	1.50	2.50	5.00	—
BE15-59 (1925)	—	1.00	1.50	2.50	5.00	—
BE15-60 (1926)	—	1.00	1.50	2.50	5.00	—
BE16-1/15-60 (1927)	—	15.00	25.00	40.00	65.00	—
BE16-1 (1927)	—	1.00	1.50	2.50	5.00	—
BE16-2/1 (1928)	—	1.00	1.50	2.50	5.00	—
BE16-2 (1928)	—	1.00	1.50	2.50	5.00	—

Y# 21a SHO

Copper **Rev:** Central legend vertical **Note:** Two varieties (lion) exist for each of the following dates: 15-56, 15-57, 15-58, and 16-2. Overstrikes on 5 Skar, Y#17 exist.

Date	Mintage	VG	F	VF	XF	Unc
BE15-56 (1922)	—	8.00	13.50	20.00	30.00	—
BE15-57 (1923)	—	2.00	3.50	6.00	10.00	—
BE57-15 (1923) Error; year and cycle transposed	—	25.00	40.00	65.00	100	—
BE15-58 (1924)	—	2.00	3.50	6.00	10.00	—
BE15-59/8 (1925)	—	1.25	2.25	4.00	8.00	—
BE15-59 (1925)	—	1.25	2.25	4.00	8.00	—
BE15-60 (1925)	—	1.25	2.25	4.00	8.00	—
BE15-60/59 (1926)	—	1.25	2.25	4.00	8.00	—
BE16-1 (1927)	—	1.25	2.25	4.00	8.00	—
BE16-1 (1927) Dot below 0 above denomination	—	1.25	2.25	4.00	8.00	—
BE(16-2/1) (1927) Reported, not confirmed	—	—	—	—	—	—
BE16-2 (1928)	—	2.00	3.50	6.00	10.00	—
Note: A scarce 16-2 variety features a reversed 2						
BE16-2 (1928) dot below syllable "rab"	—	—	—	—	—	—

Y# 21b SHO

Copper **Obv:** Lion looking backwards

Date	Mintage	Good	VG	F	VF	XF
BE15-52 (1923)	—	40.00	60.00	80.00	140	—

Y# 23 SHO

Copper **Edge:** Reeded **Note:** Weight varies: 4.02-6.09 grams. Dates 16-10, 16-11, 16-12, and 16-16 exist struck on thick and thin planchets and many lion obverse varieties.Several mint marks are known in reverse.

Date	Mintage	VG	F	VF	XF	Unc
BE16-6 (1932) (a)	6,000,000	3.00	5.00	9.00	15.00	—
BE16-7 (1933) (a)	Inc. above	3.00	5.00	9.00	15.00	—
BE16-8 (1934) (a)	Inc. above	3.00	5.00	9.00	15.00	—
Note: Two varieties exist						
BE16-9 (1935) (a)	Inc. above	2.00	3.50	6.00	11.00	—
Note: Two varieties exist						
BE16-9 (1935) (b)	Inc. above	1.50	3.00	5.00	10.00	—
Note: A scarce 16-9 variety features a hook ("bird") on the Sengi's (lion's) back						
BE16-10 (1936) (a)	Inc. above	5.00	10.00	15.00	25.00	—
BE16-10 (1936) (b)	Inc. above	5.00	10.00	15.00	25.00	—
BE16-10 (1936) (c)	Inc. above	1.50	3.00	5.00	10.00	—
BE16-11 (1937) (a)	Inc. above	2.50	4.00	9.00	15.00	—
BE16-11 (1937) (b)	Inc. above	5.00	10.00	15.00	25.00	—
BE16-11 (1937) (c)	Inc. above	2.50	4.00	9.00	15.00	—
BE16-11 (1937) (d)	Inc. above	2.50	4.00	9.00	15.00	—
BE16-11 (1937) (e)	Inc. above	1.50	3.00	5.00	10.00	—
BE16-11 (1937) (f)	Inc. above	5.00	10.00	15.00	25.00	—
BE16-11 (1937) (g)	Inc. above	5.00	10.00	15.00	25.00	—
BE16-12 (1938) (c)	Inc. above	5.00	10.00	15.00	25.00	—

Date	Mintage	VG	F	VF	XF	Unc
BE16-12 (1938) (d)	Inc. above	5.00	10.00	15.00	25.00	—
BE16-12 (1938) (f)	Inc. above	4.00	8.00	12.00	20.00	—
BE16-12 (1938) (g)	Inc. above	4.00	8.00	12.00	20.00	—
BE16-16 (1942) (f) Rare	Inc. above	—	—	—	—	—

Y# 27.1 3 SHO

Copper **Note:** Single cloud line. Four varieties of conch shell on reverse.

Date	Mintage	VG	F	VF	XF	Unc
BE16-20 (1946)	—	8.00	15.00	25.00	50.00	—

Y# 27.2 3 SHO

Copper **Note:** Double cloud line.

Date	Mintage	VG	F	VF	XF	Unc
BE16-20 (1946)	—	15.00	30.00	50.00	85.00	—

Y# 8 5 SHO

Silver **Ruler:** Hsüan-t'ung **Edge:** Reeded **Note:** Weight varies: 9.4-9.7 grams.

Date	Mintage	VG	F	VF	XF	Unc
BE1 (1909)	—	600	1,200	2,000	2,500	—

Note: A forgery exists with some of the stars blundered and letters inaccurate

Y# 18 5 SHO

Silver **Obv:** Lion looking upwards **Edge:** Reeded **Note:** Weight varies: 8.4-11.4 grams.

Date	Mintage	VG	F	VF	XF	Unc
BE15-47 (1913)	—	50.00	70.00	100	150	—
BE15-48 (1914)	—	35.00	50.00	80.00	125	—
BE15-49 (1915)	—	35.00	50.00	80.00	125	—
BE15-50 (1916)	—	35.00	50.00	80.00	125	—
Note: Two BE15-50 varieties exist; small and large lions, or 13.5mm vs. 14.5mm obverse circle, short or long flowers on reverse						
BE15-58 (1924) Rare	—	—	—	—	—	—
BE15-59 (1925)	—	150	250	350	500	—
BE15-60 (1926)	—	125	240	400	600	—

Y# 18.1 5 SHO

Silver **Obv:** Lion looking backwards **Edge:** Reeded **Note:** Weight varies: 7.40-9.80 grams. Varieties exist.

Date	Mintage	VG	F	VF	XF	Unc
BE15-49 (1915)	—	35.00	50.00	80.00	125	—
BE15-50 (1916)	—	35.00	50.00	80.00	125	—

Date	Mintage	VG	F	VF	XF	Unc
BE15-51 (1917)	—	35.00	50.00	80.00	125	—
BE15-52 (1918)	—	35.00	50.00	80.00	125	—
BE15-53 (1919)	—	100	175	275	400	—
BE15-56 (1922)	—	100	175	275	400	—
BE15-59 (1925)	—	350	450	600	800	—
BE15-60 (1926)	—	200	350	500	700	—
BE16-1 (1927)	—	125	225	350	500	—

Y# 18.2 5 SHO

Silver **Edge:** Reeded **Note:** Weight varies: 8.00-9.70 grams.

Date	Mintage	VG	F	VF	XF	Unc
BE15-52 (1920)	—	125	175	250	350	—

Y# 32 5 SHO

Silver **Edge:** Reeded **Note:** Weight varies: 5.43-6.55 grams. Two obverse varieties exist. Considered a pattern by some authorities.

Date	Mintage	VG	F	VF	XF	Unc
ND(1928-29)	—	500	750	1,000	1,400	—

Y# 28.1 5 SHO

Copper **Obv:** Three mountains with two suns **Edge:** Reeded **Note:** Die varieties involving tail hairs (5-8), leg hairs (2-5) and yin-yang features (S, reversed S or the incuse of either) include 5 of 16-21, 38 of 16-22 and 30 of 16-23.

Date	Mintage	VG	F	VF	XF	Unc
BE16-21 (1947)	—	2.00	3.50	6.00	10.00	—
Note: A modern medallic series dated 16-21 (1947) exists struck in copper, silver, and gold which were authorized by the Dalai Lama while in exile; Refer to Unusual World Coins, 4th edition, KP Books, 2005						
BE16-22 (1948)	—	2.50	4.00	7.50	12.50	—
Note: Dots a and c						
BE16-22 (1948)	—	23.00	30.00	40.00	50.00	—
Note: Without dot after "16"						
BE16-23 (1949)	—	5.00	8.00	14.00	25.00	—
Note: With 8 sun rays						
BE16-23 (1949)	—	1.50	3.00	5.00	8.50	—
Note: With dot after 16; Unclear overdates and varieties of BE16-23 exist						
BE16-24 (1950)	—	30.00	40.00	50.00	65.00	—
BE16-24/3 (1950)	—	40.00	60.00	80.00	100	—

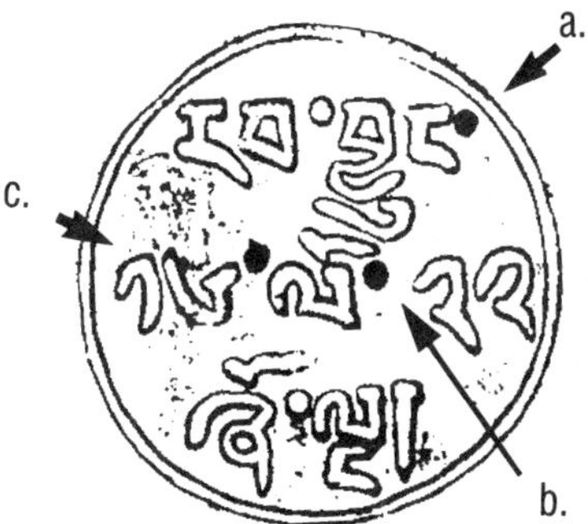

a. "CYCLE"

b. "YEAR"

c. "16"

Y# 28 5 SHO

Copper **Obv:** Two mountains with two suns **Edge:** Reeded **Note:** Three lion die varieties exist. Modern counterfiets made of yellowish copper exist.

Date	Mintage	VG	F	VF	XF	Unc
BE16-21 (1947)	—	4.00	7.50	10.00	20.00	—

Y# 28.2 5 SHO

Copper **Obv:** Cloud above middle mountain missing **Edge:** Reeded

Date	Mintage	VG	F	VF	XF	Unc
BE16-22 (1948)	—	35.00	60.00	95.00	150	—

Y# 9 SRANG

Silver **Edge:** Reeded **Note:** 17.2-19.9 g. Obverse varieties exist

Date	Mintage	VG	F	VF	XF	Unc
BE1 (1909)	—	125	185	275	425	—

Y# 12 SRANG

Silver **Obv:** Lion standing left, looking backwards **Edge:** Plain **Note:** Weight varies: 18.00-18.30 grams. Varieties exist.

Date	Mintage	VG	F	VF	XF	Unc
BE15-43 (1909)	—	140	225	325	475	—

Y# A18 SRANG

18.1000 g., Silver **Obv:** Lion standing left looking back and upwards **Edge:** Reeded **Note:** Varieties exist.

Date	Mintage	VG	F	VF	XF	Unc
BE15-48 (1914)	—	400	700	1,200	1,750	—

Y# A18.1 SRANG

Silver **Obv:** Lion looking backwards **Edge:** Reeded **Note:** Weight varies: 17.80-18.30 grams

Date	Mintage	VG	F	VF	XF	Unc
BE15-52 (1918)	—	350	650	850	1,200	—
BE15-53 (1919)	—	275	450	700	1,000	—

Y# 24 1-1/2 SRANG

5.0000 g., Silver **Edge:** Reeded **Note:** Dates are written in words, not numerals. Obverse varieties exist.

Date	Mintage	F	VF	XF	Unc	BU
BE16-10 (1936)	—	3.50	6.00	10.00	20.00	—
BE16-11 (1937)	—	3.00	5.00	9.00	17.00	—
BE16-12 (1938)	—	3.50	6.00	10.00	20.00	—
BE16-20 (1946)	—	20.00	40.00	70.00	90.00	—

Y# 25 3 SRANG

11.3000 g., Silver **Edge:** Reeded **Note:** Dates are written in words, not numerals. Varieties exist in lion.

Date	Mintage	F	VF	XF	Unc	BU
BE16-7 (1933)	—	8.00	12.00	20.00	35.00	—
Note: 7 or 8-tail plume variety						
BE16-8 (1934)	—	8.00	12.00	20.00	35.00	—

Y# 26 3 SRANG

Silver **Edge:** Reeded **Note:** Dates are written in words, not numerals. Varieties in circular obverse and reverse legends exist.

Date	Mintage	F	VF	XF	Unc	BU
BE16-9 (1935)	—	7.00	10.00	18.00	30.00	—
BE16-10 (1936)	—	6.00	9.00	15.00	25.00	—
BE16-10/9 (1936)	—	7.00	10.00	18.00	30.00	—
BE16-11 (1937)	—	6.00	9.00	15.00	25.00	—
BE16-12 (1938)	—	6.00	9.00	15.00	25.00	—
BE16-20 (1946)	—	20.00	40.00	70.00	110	—

Y# 29 10 SRANG

Billon **Obv:** Two suns **Rev:** Numerals for denomination at center right **Edge:** Reeded

Date	Mintage	F	VF	XF	Unc	BU
BE16-22 (1948)	—	4.50	9.00	18.00	40.00	—

Y# 29a 10 SRANG

Billon **Obv:** Moon and sun **Edge:** Reeded **Note:** The "dot" is after the denomination. A modern medallic series dated 16-24 (1950) exists struck in copper-nickel, silver, and gold which were authorized by the Dalai Lama while in exile. Refer to "Unusual World Coins", 4th edition, KP Books, 2005.

Date	Mintage	F	VF	XF	Unc	BU
BE16-23 (1949)	—	20.00	45.00	100	175	—
Note: With dot						
BE16-24/23 (1950)	—	7.00	15.00	30.00	60.00	—
Note: With dot						
BE16-24/23 (1950)	—	20.00	40.00	80.00	140	—
Note: With dot and moon cut over sun						
BE16-24/22 (1950)	—	9.00	18.00	35.00	70.00	—
BE16-24 (1950)	—	10.00	20.00	40.00	70.00	—
Note: Moon cut over sun, denomination in words						
BE16-24 (1950)	—	12.00	22.00	50.00	90.00	—
Note: With dot						
BE16-25/24 (1951)	—	7.00	15.00	30.00	60.00	—
Note: With dot						
BE16-25/24 (1951)	—	10.00	20.00	40.00	70.00	—
Note: Without dot						
BE16-25 (1951)	—	7.00	15.00	30.00	60.00	—
Note: With dot						
BE16-26/25 (1952)	—	7.00	15.00	30.00	60.00	—
Note: Without dot						
BE16-26 (1952)	—	7.00	15.00	30.00	60.00	—
Note: With dot						

Y# 29.1 10 SRANG

Billon **Rev:** Words for denomination at center right

Date	Mintage	F	VF	XF	Unc	BU
BE16-23 (1949)	—	6.00	10.00	20.00	40.00	—
Note: With dot before and after ten						
BE16-23 (1949)	—	6.00	10.00	20.00	40.00	—
Note: Without dot after ten						
BE16-23/22 (1949)	—	12.00	20.00	35.00	70.00	—

Y# 30 10 SRANG

Billon **Rev:** Cycle and year in words **Edge:** Reeded **Note:** Said to be struck for payment of Tibetan Army members

Date	Mintage	F	VF	XF	Unc	BU
BE16-24 (1950)	—	6.00	12.00	25.00	55.00	—
Note: Without dot after year						
BE16-24 (1950)	—	7.00	15.00	30.00	65.00	—
Note: With dot						
BE16-25/4 (1951)	—	5.00	10.00	20.00	45.00	—
Note: With dot						
BE16-25 (1951)	—	5.00	10.00	20.00	45.00	—
Note: With dot						

TRADE COINAGE

1 Rupee = 3 Tangka

Total mintage of the 1 Rupee between 1902 and 1942 was between 25.5 and 27.5 million according to Chinese sources. In addition to the types illustrated above, large quantities of the following coins also circulated in Tibet: China Dollars, Y#318a, 329, and 345 plus Szechuan issues Y#449 and 459, and Indian Rupees, KM#473, 492, and 508.

Rupees exist with local merchant countermarks in Chinese, Tibetan, and other scripts. Examples of crown-size rupees struck in silver (26.30-27.50 grams) and gold (36.30 grams) are considered fantasies and are listed in Unusual World Coins.

Y# 1 1/4 RUPEE

2.8000 g., 0.9350 Silver 0.0842 oz. ASW, 19 mm. **Edge:** Reeded **Note:** Varieties exist

Date	Mintage	F	VF	XF	Unc	BU
ND(1904-05)	120,000	40.00	60.00	90.00	150	—
ND(1904-05, 1912)	120,000	45.00	65.00	100	175	—

Y# 2 1/2 RUPEE

5.6000 g., 0.9350 Silver 0.1683 oz. ASW, 24 mm. **Edge:** Reeded **Note:** Varieties exist

Date	Mintage	F	VF	XF	Unc	BU
ND(1904-05, 1907, 1912)	130,000	60.00	85.00	145	250	—

Y# A1.1 RUPEE

11.5000 g., Silver **Ruler:** Hsüan-t'ung **Edge:** Plain **Note:** Prev. #C20.

Date	Mintage	Good	VG	F	VF	XF
ND(1902-03)	—	750	1,000	1,500	2,250	—

Note: Struck in or near Tachienlu (today Kang Ting) and known as Lu Kuan Rupee. It was meant to replace the Indian Rupee which was used in eastern Tibet and western Szechuan (Sichuan) in the 19th century and is considered the forerunner of the Szechuan Rupee (Y#3). Varieties exist.

Y# A1.2 RUPEE

Silver **Ruler:** Hsüan-t'ung **Note:** Obverse and reverse inscriptions deviating in style. Kann#1285

Date	Mintage	Good	VG	F	VF	XF
ND(1902-03)	—	750	1,000	1,500	2,250	—

Y# 3 RUPEE

11.2000 g., Silver **Obv:** Small bust without collar **Rev:** Vertical rosette **Edge:** Reeded **Note:** Two reverse varieties exist. Finenesses vary: .8350-9350.

Date	Mintage	F	VF	XF	Unc	BU
ND(1902-11)	—	30.00	50.00	80.00	125	—

Y# 3.1 RUPEE

11.2000 g., Silver **Rev:** Horizontal rosette **Edge:** Reeded **Note:** Two reverse varieties exist. Finenesses vary: .8350-.9350.

Date	Mintage	F	VF	XF	Unc	BU
ND(1902-11)	—	20.00	40.00	60.00	100	—

Y# 3.2 RUPEE

0.7000 Silver **Obv:** Small bust with collar **Rev:** Vertical rosette **Note:** Struck at Chengdu (Szechuan) Mint before 1930, then at Kangding (Tachienlu) Mint after 1930. Two reverse varieties exist.

Date	Mintage	F	VF	XF	Unc	BU
ND(1911-16, 1930-33)	—	15.00	25.00	45.00	75.00	—

Note: An example with two obverses exists

Y# 3.3 RUPEE

Silver **Obv:** Large bust **Rev:** Vertical rosette **Note:** Finenesses vary .4200-.5000. Varieties exist.

Date	Mintage	F	VF	XF	Unc	BU
ND(1939-42)	—	20.00	35.00	65.00	110	—

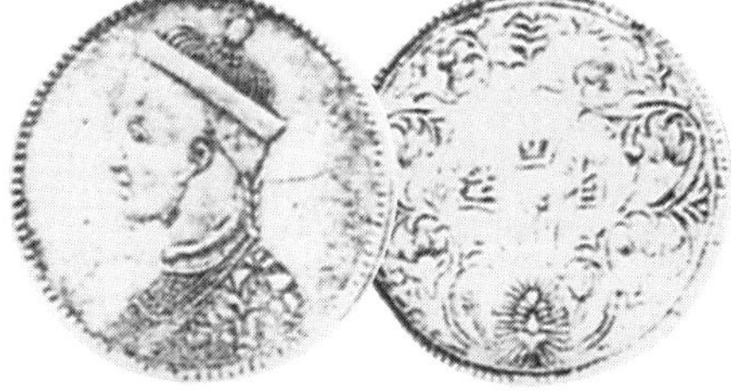

Y# 3.4 RUPEE

Silver **Obv:** Small bust with flat nose, revised non-floral gown. **Rev:** Vertical rosette **Note:** .650-.500 silver

Date	Mintage	F	VF	XF	Unc	BU
ND(1933-39)	—	20.00	35.00	65.00	110	—

Y# 3.5 RUPEE

Silver **Obv:** Small bust similar to Y#3.4 **Rev:** Horizontal rosette **Note:** .650-.500 silver.

Date	Mintage	F	VF	XF	Unc	BU
ND(1933-39)	—	30.00	50.00	90.00	160	—

Y# 3a RUPEE

Debased Silver/Billon

Date	Mintage	F	VF	XF	Unc	BU
ND(1939-42)	—	10.00	20.00	40.00	70.00	—

Note: Coins with copper base and silver wash exist

TIMOR

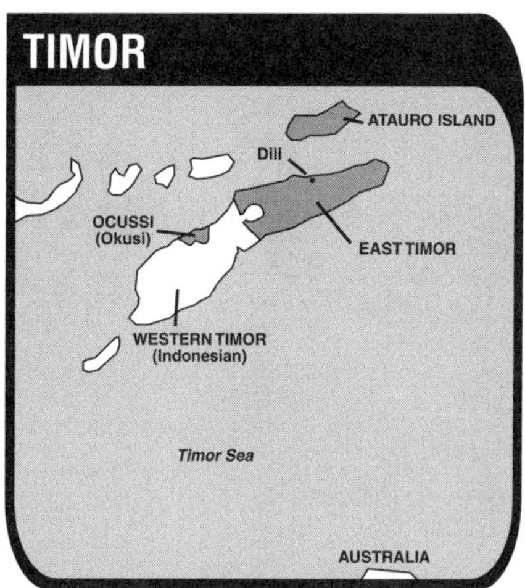

(East Timor)

Timor is an island between the Savu and Timor Seas. It has an area, including the former colony of Portuguese Timor, of 11,883 sq. mi. (30,775 sq. km.) and a population of 1.5 million. Western Timor is administered as part of Nusa Tenggara Timur (East Nusa Tenggara) province. Capital: Kupang. The eastern half of the island, the former Portuguese colony, forms a single province, Timor Timur (East Timor). Originally the Portuguese colony also included the area around Ocussi-Ambeno and the small island of Atauro (Pulau Kambing) located north of Dili. Capital: Dili. Timor exports sandalwood, coffee, tea, hides, rubber and copra.

Portuguese traders reached Timor about 1520, and moved to the north and east when the Dutch established themselves in Kupang, a sheltered bay at the southwestern tip in 1613. Treaties effective in 1860 and 1914 established the boundaries between the two colonies. Japan occupied the entire island during World War II. The former Dutch colony in the western part of the island became part of Indonesia in 1950.

For later coinage see East Timor.

MONETARY SYSTEM

100 Avos = 1 Pataca

PORTUGUESE COLONY

MILLED COINAGE

100 Avos = 1 Pataca

KM# 5 10 AVOS

Bronze **Obv:** Small circles within cross design **Obv. Legend:** REPUBLICA PORTUGUESA **Rev:** Value above sprigs **Rev. Legend:** COLONIA DE TIMOR

Date	Mintage	F	VF	XF	Unc	BU
1945	50,000	120	220	400	1,000	—
1948	500,000	3.50	8.00	17.00	35.00	—
1951	6,250,000	1.50	3.50	7.50	15.00	—

KM# 6 20 AVOS

Nickel-Bronze **Obv:** Laureate liberty head right **Obv. Legend:** REPUBLICA PORTUGUESA **Rev:** Shield within globe and wreath **Rev. Legend:** COLONIA DE TIMOR

Date	Mintage	F	VF	XF	Unc	BU
1945	50,000	16.00	35.00	70.00	175	—

KM# 7 50 AVOS

3.5000 g., 0.6500 Silver 0.0731 oz. ASW **Obv:** Shield within globe on maltese cross **Obv. Legend:** REPUBLICA PORTUGUESA **Rev:** Value above sprigs **Rev. Legend:** COLONIA DE TIMOR

Date	Mintage	F	VF	XF	Unc	BU
1945	100,000	45.00	90.00	135	275	—
1948	500,000	3.00	5.50	12.00	30.00	—
1951	6,250,000	2.00	4.00	9.00	18.00	—

1958 REFORM COINAGE

100 Centavos = 1 Escudo

KM# 10 10 CENTAVOS

Bronze **Obv:** Value **Obv. Legend:** REPUBLICA PORTUGUESA **Rev:** Shield within crowned globe, flowers in legend, date below **Rev. Legend:** TIMOR

Date	Mintage	F	VF	XF	Unc	BU
1958	1,000,000	1.00	3.00	15.00	35.00	—

KM# 17 20 CENTAVOS

Bronze **Obv:** Value **Obv. Legend:** REPUBLICA PORTUGUESA **Rev:** Shield within crowned globe, flowers in legend, date below **Rev. Legend:** TIMOR

Date	Mintage	F	VF	XF	Unc	BU
1970	1,000,000	0.45	1.00	2.50	5.00	7.50

KM# 11 30 CENTAVOS

Bronze **Obv:** Value **Obv. Legend:** REPUBLICA PORTUGUESA **Rev:** Shield within crowned globe, flowers in legend, date below **Rev. Legend:** TIMOR

Date	Mintage	F	VF	XF	Unc	BU
1958	2,000,000	0.75	1.50	12.00	30.00	—

KM# 18 50 CENTAVOS

4.0000 g., Bronze, 19.8 mm. **Obv:** Value **Obv. Legend:** REPUBLICA PORTUGUESA **Rev:** Shield within crowned globe, flowers in legend, date below **Rev. Legend:** TIMOR

Date	Mintage	F	VF	XF	Unc	BU
1970	1,000,000	0.45	1.00	2.00	4.50	6.50

KM# 12 60 CENTAVOS

Copper-Nickel-Zinc **Obv:** Shield within globe on maltese cross, date below **Obv. Legend:** REPUBLICA PORTUGUESA **Rev:** Shield within crowned globe, flowers in legend, value below **Rev. Legend:** TIMOR

Date	Mintage	F	VF	XF	Unc	BU
1958	1,000,000	1.25	2.75	12.00	30.00	—

KM# 13 ESCUDO
Copper-Nickel-Zinc **Obv:** Shield within globe on maltese cross, date below **Obv. Legend:** REPUBLICA PORTUGUESA **Rev:** Shield within crowned globe, flowers in legend, value below **Rev. Legend:** TIMOR

Date	Mintage	F	VF	XF	Unc	BU
1958	1,200,000	2.00	4.00	40.00	75.00	—

KM# 19 ESCUDO
7.8700 g., Bronze, 25.7 mm. **Obv:** Value **Obv. Legend:** REPUBLICA PORTUGUESA **Rev:** Shield within crowned globe, flowers in legend, date below **Rev. Legend:** TIMOR

Date	Mintage	F	VF	XF	Unc	BU
1970	1,200,000	1.50	3.00	7.00	15.00	—

KM# 20 2-1/2 ESCUDOS
Copper-Nickel **Obv:** Shield within globe on maltese cross, date below **Obv. Legend:** REPUBLICA PORTUGUESA **Rev:** Shield within crowned globe, flowers in legend, value below **Rev. Legend:** TIMOR

Date	Mintage	F	VF	XF	Unc	BU
1970	1,000,000	0.75	1.50	3.50	8.00	14.00

KM# 14 3 ESCUDOS
3.5000 g., 0.6500 Silver 0.0731 oz. ASW **Obv:** Shield within globe on maltese cross, date below **Obv. Legend:** REPUBLICA PORTUGUESA **Rev:** Shield within crowned globe, flowers in legend, value below **Rev. Legend:** TIMOR

Date	Mintage	F	VF	XF	Unc	BU
1958	1,000,000	3.00	5.00	10.00	25.00	—

KM# 21 5 ESCUDOS
6.9300 g., Copper-Nickel, 24 mm. **Obv:** Shield within globe on maltese cross, date below **Obv. Legend:** REPUBLICA PORTUGUESA **Rev:** Shield within crowned globe, flowers in legend, value below **Rev. Legend:** TIMOR

Date	Mintage	F	VF	XF	Unc	BU
1970	1,200,000	1.50	3.00	6.50	12.00	—

KM# 15 6 ESCUDOS
7.0000 g., 0.6500 Silver 0.1463 oz. ASW **Obv:** Shield within globe on maltese cross, date below **Obv. Legend:** REPUBLICA PORTUGUESA **Rev:** Shield within crowned globe, flowers in legend, value below **Rev. Legend:** TIMOR

Date	Mintage	F	VF	XF	Unc	BU
1958	1,000,000	3.50	6.00	12.50	25.00	—

KM# 16 10 ESCUDOS
7.0000 g., 0.6500 Silver 0.1463 oz. ASW **Obv:** Shield within globe on maltese cross, date below **Obv. Legend:** REPUBLICA PORTUGUESA **Rev:** Shield within crowned globe, flowers in legend, value below **Rev. Legend:** TIMOR

Date	Mintage	F	VF	XF	Unc	BU
1964	600,000	3.50	6.00	12.50	25.00	—

KM# 22 10 ESCUDOS
9.0000 g., Copper-Nickel, 28 mm. **Obv:** Shield within globe on maltese cross, date below **Obv. Legend:** REPUBLICA PORTUGUESA **Rev:** Shield within crowned globe, flowers in legend, value below **Rev. Legend:** TIMOR

Date	Mintage	F	VF	XF	Unc	BU
1970	700,000	3.00	5.50	12.00	24.00	—

TOGO

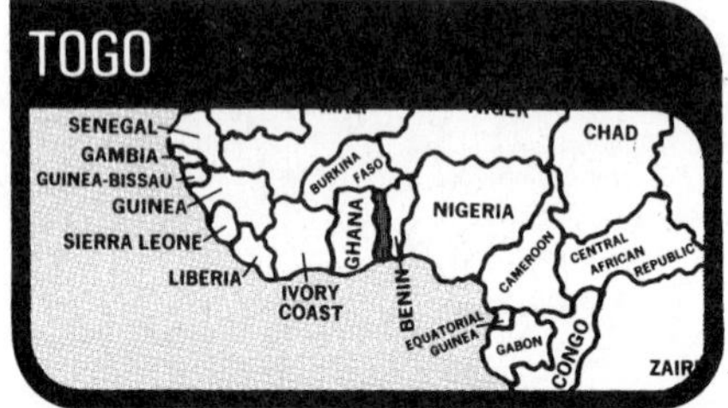

The Republic of Togo (formerly part of German Togoland), situated on the Gulf of Guinea in West Africa between Ghana and Dahomey, has an area of 21,622 sq.mi. (56,790 sq. km.) and a population of *3.4 million. Capital: Lome. Agriculture and herding, the production of dyewoods, and the mining of phosphates and iron ore are the chief industries. Copra, phosphates and coffee are exported.

Although Brazilians were the first traders to settle in Togo, Germany achieved possession, in 1884, by inducing coastal chiefs to place their territories under German protection. The German protectorate was extended international recognition at the Berlin conference of 1885 and its ultimate boundaries delimited by treaties with France in 1897 and with Britain in 1904. Anglo-French forces occupied Togoland in 1914, subsequently becoming a League of Nations mandate and a U.N. trusteeship divided, for administrative purpose, between Great Britain and France. The British portion voted in 1957 for incorporation with Ghana. The French portion became the independent Republic of Togo on April 27, 1960.

RULERS
German, 1884-1914
Anglo - French, 1914-1957
French, 1957-1960

MINT MARK
(a) - Paris, privy marks only

MONETARY SYSTEM
100 Centimes = 1 Franc

FRENCH MANDATE

U.N. Trusteeship

STANDARD COINAGE

100 Centimes = 1 Franc

KM# 1 50 CENTIMES
Aluminum-Bronze **Obv:** Laureate head left **Rev:** Value within upright sprigs **Designer:** A. Patay

Date	Mintage	F	VF	XF	Unc	BU
1924(a)	3,691,000	4.00	20.00	50.00	80.00	—
1925(a)	2,064,000	5.00	22.00	55.00	100	—
1926(a)	445,000	20.00	50.00	100	300	—

KM# 2 FRANC
Aluminum-Bronze **Obv:** Laureat head left **Rev:** Value within upright sprigs **Designer:** A. Patay

Date	Mintage	F	VF	XF	Unc	BU
1924(a)	3,472,000	3.50	27.50	60.00	125	—
1925(a)	2,768,000	4.00	19.00	65.00	140	—

KM# 4 FRANC
Aluminum **Obv:** Winged head left **Rev:** Slender-horned gazelle head divides value within sprigs **Designer:** G.B.L. Bazor

Date	Mintage	F	VF	XF	Unc	BU
1948(a)	5,000,000	5.00	12.00	30.00	70.00	125

KM# 3 2 FRANCS
Aluminum-Bronze **Obv:** Laureate head left **Rev:** Value within upright sprigs **Designer:** A. Patay

Date	Mintage	F	VF	XF	Unc	BU
1924(a)	750,000	6.00	35.00	110	250	—
1925(a)	580,000	7.00	38.00	120	275	—

KM# 5 2 FRANCS
2.1000 g., Aluminum **Obv:** Winged head left **Rev:** Slender-horned gazelle head divides value within sprigs **Designer:** G.B.L. Bazor **Note:** Similar to 1 Franc, KM#4.

Date	Mintage	F	VF	XF	Unc	BU
1948(a)	5,000,000	6.00	15.00	35.00	80.00	150

KM# 6 5 FRANCS
Aluminum-Bronze, 20 mm. **Obv:** Head left **Rev:** Slender-horned gazelle head divides value within sprigs

Date	Mintage	F	VF	XF	Unc	BU
1956(a)	10,000,000	3.00	6.00	12.00	25.00	—

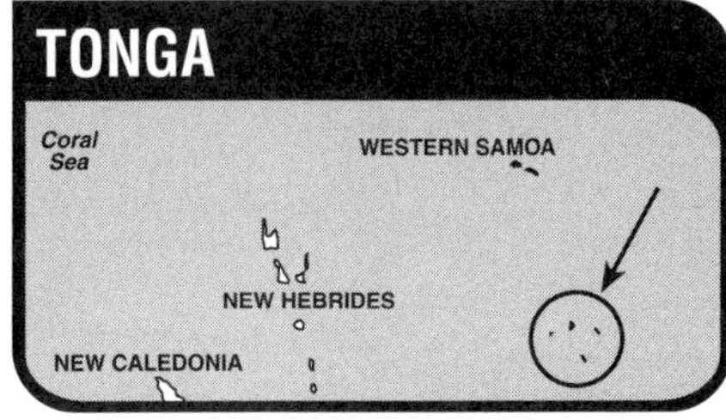

The Kingdom of Tonga (or Friendly Islands) is an archipelago situated in the southern Pacific Ocean south of Western Samoa and east of Fiji comprised of 150 islands. Tonga has an area of 270 sq. mi. (748 sq. km.) and a population of *100,000. Capital: Nuku'alofa. Primarily agricultural, the kingdom exports bananas and copra.

Dutch navigators Willem Schouten and Jacob Lemaire were the first Europeans to visit Tonga in 1616. The noted Dutch explorer Abel Tasman who visited the Tongatapu group in 1643 followed them. No further European contact was made until 1773 when British navigator Capt. James Cook arrived and, impressed by the peaceful deportment of the natives, named the islands the Friendly Islands. Within a few years of Cook's visit, Tonga was embroiled in a civil war that lasted until the great chief Taufa'ahau, who reigned as Siasoi Tupou I (1845-93), was converted to Christianity and brought unity and peace to the islands. Tonga became a self-governing protectorate of Great Britain in 1900 and a fully independent state on June 4, 1970. The monarchy is a member of the Commonwealth of Nations. King Taufa'ahau is Head of State and Government.

RULERS
Queen Salote, 1918-1965
King Taufa'ahau IV, 1967—2006

MONETARY SYSTEM
12 Pence = 1 Shilling
20 Shillings = 1 Pound

KINGDOM

DECIMAL COINAGE

100 Senti = 1 Pa'anga; 100 Pa'anga = 1 Hau

KM# 4 SENITI
1.8500 g., Bronze, 17.5 mm. **Ruler:** King Taufa'ahau Tupou IV **Obv:** Head right **Rev:** Giant Tortoise **Edge:** Plain

Date	Mintage	F	VF	XF	Unc	BU
1967	500,000	—	0.10	0.15	1.00	2.50
1967 Proof	—	Value: 2.00				

KM# 27 SENITI
1.8500 g., Bronze, 17.5 mm. **Ruler:** King Taufa'ahau Tupou IV **Obv:** Head right **Rev:** Giant tortoise **Edge:** Plain

Date	Mintage	F	VF	XF	Unc	BU
1968	500,000	—	0.10	0.15	1.00	2.00
1968 Proof	—	Value: 2.50				

KM# 27a SENITI
1.6900 g., Brass, 17.5 mm. **Ruler:** King Taufa'ahau Tupou IV **Obv:** Head right **Rev:** Giant tortoise **Edge:** Plain

Date	Mintage	F	VF	XF	Unc	BU
1974	500,000	—	0.10	0.15	0.75	1.50

KM# 42 SENITI
1.8500 g., Bronze, 17.5 mm. **Ruler:** King Taufa'ahau Tupou IV **Series:** F.A.O. **Obv:** Ear of corn **Rev:** Sow right **Edge:** Plain

Date	Mintage	F	VF	XF	Unc	BU
1975	1,000,000	—	—	0.10	0.45	1.25
1979	1,000,000	—	—	0.10	0.45	1.25

KM# 66 SENITI
1.8000 g., Bronze, 16.51 mm. **Ruler:** King Taufa'ahau Tupou IV **Series:** World Food Day **Obv:** Ear of corn **Rev:** Vanilla plant **Edge:** Plain

Date	Mintage	F	VF	XF	Unc	BU
1981	1,544,000	—	—	0.10	0.45	0.80
1990	—	—	—	0.10	0.35	0.75
1991	—	—	—	0.10	0.35	0.75
1994	500,000	—	—	0.10	0.35	0.75
1996	—	—	—	0.10	0.35	0.75
2005	—	—	—	0.10	0.35	0.75

KM# 66a SENITI
Copper Plated Steel, 17.5 mm. **Ruler:** King Taufa'ahau Tupou IV **Series:** World Food Day **Obv:** Ear of corn **Obv. Legend:** TONGA **Rev:** Vanilla plant **Rev. Legend:** FAKALAHI ME'AKAI **Edge:** Plain

Date	Mintage	F	VF	XF	Unc	BU
2002	—	—	—	0.10	0.35	0.75
2003	—	—	—	0.10	0.35	0.75
2004	—	—	—	0.10	0.35	0.75

KM# 5 2 SENITI
3.9000 g., Bronze, 21 mm. **Ruler:** King Taufa'ahau Tupou IV **Obv:** Head right **Rev:** Giant Tortoise **Edge:** Plain

Date	Mintage	F	VF	XF	Unc	BU
1967	500,000	—	0.10	0.20	1.50	3.00
1967 Proof	—	Value: 3.00				

KM# 28 2 SENITI
3.9000 g., Bronze, 21 mm. **Ruler:** King Taufa'ahau Tupou IV **Obv:** Head right **Rev:** Giant tortoise **Edge:** Plain

Date	Mintage	F	VF	XF	Unc	BU
1968	200,000	—	0.10	0.20	1.75	3.00
1968 Proof	—	Value: 3.80				
1974	25,000	—	0.10	0.20	1.75	3.00

KM# 43 2 SENITI
3.9000 g., Bronze, 21 mm. **Ruler:** King Taufa'ahau Tupou IV **Series:** F.A.O. **Obv:** Two watermelons **Rev:** Paper doll cutouts form design in center circle of wreath **Edge:** Plain

Date	Mintage	F	VF	XF	Unc	BU
1975	400,000	—	—	0.15	0.65	1.50
1979	500,000	—	—	0.15	0.65	1.50

KM# 67 2 SENITI
3.8700 g., Bronze, 19.46 mm. **Ruler:** King Taufa'ahau Tupou IV **Series:** World Food Day **Obv:** Taro Plants **Rev:** Paper doll cutouts form design in center circle of wreath **Edge:** Plain

Date	Mintage	F	VF	XF	Unc	BU
1981	1,102,000	—	—	0.15	0.65	1.35
1990	—	—	—	0.15	0.50	1.25
1991	—	—	—	0.15	0.50	1.25
1994	250,000	—	—	0.15	0.50	1.25
1996	—	—	—	0.15	0.50	1.25

KM# 67a 2 SENITI
Copper Plated Steel, 21 mm. **Ruler:** King Taufa'ahau Tupou IV **Series:** World Food Day **Obv:** Taro plants **Obv. Legend:** TONGA **Rev:** Paper doll cutouts form design in center circle of sprays **Rev. Legend:** PLANNED FAMILIES • FOOD FOR ALL

Date	Mintage	F	VF	XF	Unc	BU
2002	—	—	—	0.15	0.65	1.25
2003	—	—	—	0.15	0.65	1.25
2004	—	—	—	0.15	0.65	1.25

KM# 6 5 SENITI
2.8000 g., Copper-Nickel, 19.5 mm. **Ruler:** King Taufa'ahau Tupou IV **Obv:** Head right **Rev:** Value and stars flanked by sprigs **Edge:** Plain

Date	Mintage	F	VF	XF	Unc	BU
1967	300,000	—	0.10	0.25	1.75	2.50
1967 Proof	—	Value: 3.50				

KM# 29 5 SENITI
2.8000 g., Copper-Nickel, 19.5 mm. **Ruler:** King Taufa'ahau Tupou IV **Obv:** Head right **Rev:** Value and stars flanked by sprigs

Date	Mintage	F	VF	XF	Unc	BU
1968	100,000	—	0.10	0.25	1.50	2.25
1968 Proof	—	Value: 2.50				
1974	75,000	—	0.10	0.25	1.50	2.25

KM# 44 5 SENITI
2.8000 g., Copper-Nickel, 19.5 mm. **Ruler:** King Taufa'ahau Tupou IV **Series:** F.A.O. **Obv:** Hen with chicks **Rev:** Banana bunch

Date	Mintage	F	VF	XF	Unc	BU
1975	100,000	—	0.10	0.25	1.00	1.75
1977	110,000	—	0.10	0.25	1.00	1.75
1979	100,000	—	0.10	0.25	1.00	1.75

KM# 68 5 SENITI
2.8000 g., Copper-Nickel, 19.5 mm. **Ruler:** King Taufa'ahau Tupou IV **Series:** World Food Day **Obv:** Hen with chicks **Rev:** Coconuts above sprig **Edge:** Reeded

Date	Mintage	F	VF	XF	Unc	BU
1981	941,000	—	0.10	0.25	0.85	1.50
1990	—	—	0.10	0.25	0.85	1.50
1991	—	—	—	0.25	0.85	1.50
1994	200,000	—	0.10	0.25	0.85	1.50
1996	—	—	0.10	0.25	0.75	1.25
2005	—	—	0.10	0.25	0.75	1.25

KM# 68a 5 SENITI
2.7900 g., Nickel Plated Steel, 19.39 mm. **Ruler:** King Taufa'ahau Tupou IV **Series:** World Food Day **Obv:** Hen with chicks **Obv. Legend:** TONGA **Rev:** Coconuts **Rev. Legend:** FAKALAHI ME'AKAI **Edge:** Reeded

Date	Mintage	F	VF	XF	Unc	BU
2002	—	—	—	0.25	0.75	1.35
2003	—	—	—	0.25	0.75	1.35
2004	—	—	—	0.25	0.75	1.35
2005	—	—	—	0.25	0.75	1.35

KM# 7 10 SENITI
5.6500 g., Copper-Nickel, 23.5 mm. **Ruler:** King Taufa'ahau Tupou IV **Obv:** Head right **Rev:** Value and stars flanked by sprigs

Date	Mintage	F	VF	XF	Unc	BU
1967	300,000	—	0.20	0.35	1.85	2.50
1967 Proof	—	Value: 3.50				

KM# 30 10 SENITI
5.6500 g., Copper-Nickel, 23.5 mm. **Ruler:** King Taufa'ahau Tupou IV **Obv:** Head right **Rev:** Value and stars flanked by sprigs

Date	Mintage	F	VF	XF	Unc	BU
1968	100,000	—	0.20	0.40	1.75	2.25
1968 Proof	—	Value: 3.00				
1974	50,000	—	0.25	0.50	1.75	2.25

KM# 45 10 SENITI
5.6500 g., Copper-Nickel, 23.5 mm. **Ruler:** King Taufa'ahau Tupou IV **Series:** F.A.O. **Obv:** Uniformed bust facing **Rev:** Cows in pasture

Date	Mintage	F	VF	XF	Unc	BU
1975	75,000	—	0.20	0.30	1.25	2.00
1977	25,000	—	0.20	0.30	1.25	2.00
1979	100,000	—	0.20	0.30	1.25	2.00

KM# 69 10 SENITI
5.6500 g., Copper-Nickel, 23.5 mm. **Ruler:** King Taufa'ahau Tupou IV **Series:** World Food Day **Obv:** Uniformed bust facing **Rev:** Banana tree **Edge:** Reeded

Date	Mintage	F	VF	XF	Unc	BU
1981	712,000	—	0.20	0.30	1.25	2.00
1990	—	—	0.20	0.30	1.00	1.75
1991	—	—	0.20	0.30	1.00	1.75
1994	140,000	—	0.20	0.30	1.00	1.75
1996	—	—	0.20	0.30	1.00	1.75

KM# 69a 10 SENITI
Nickel Plated Steel, 23.5 mm. **Ruler:** King Taufa'ahau Tupou IV **Series:** World Food Day **Obv:** Uniformed bust facing **Obv. Legend:** F•A•O - TONGA **Rev:** Banana tree **Rev. Legend:** FAKALAHI ME'AKAI

Date	Mintage	F	VF	XF	Unc	BU
2002	—	—	—	0.30	1.00	1.75
2003	—	—	—	0.30	1.00	1.75
2004	—	—	—	0.30	1.00	1.75

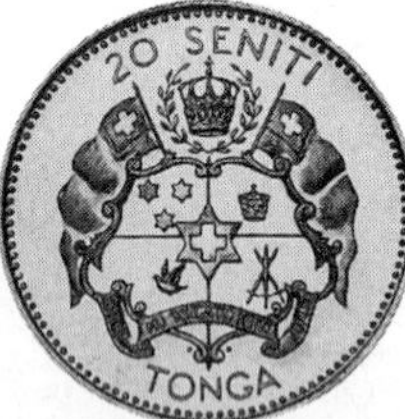

KM# 8 20 SENITI
11.3000 g., Copper-Nickel, 28.5 mm. **Ruler:** King Taufa'ahau Tupou IV **Obv:** Head right **Rev:** Crowned arms

Date	Mintage	F	VF	XF	Unc	BU
1967	150,000	—	0.25	0.50	2.25	3.50
1967 Proof	—	Value: 4.50				

KM# 13 20 SENITI
11.3000 g., Copper-Nickel, 28.5 mm. **Ruler:** King Taufa'ahau Tupou IV **Subject:** Coronation of Taufa'ahau Tupou IV **Obv:** Head right, small crowns around border **Obv. Designer:** Maurice Meers **Rev:** Crowned arms **Rev. Designer:** Ernest Hyde **Edge:** Reeded

Date	Mintage	F	VF	XF	Unc	BU
ND(1967)	15,000	—	0.50	1.25	2.25	3.50
ND(1967) Proof	—	Value: 3.50				

KM# 31 20 SENITI
11.3000 g., Copper-Nickel, 28.5 mm. **Ruler:** King Taufa'ahau Tupou IV **Obv:** Head right **Rev:** Crowned arms

Date	Mintage	F	VF	XF	Unc	BU
1968	35,000	—	0.25	0.50	2.00	2.75
1968 Proof	—	Value: 3.00				
1974	50,000	—	0.25	0.50	2.00	2.75

KM# 46 20 SENITI
11.3000 g., Copper-Nickel, 28.5 mm. **Ruler:** King Taufa'ahau Tupou IV **Series:** F.A.O. **Obv:** Uniformed bust facing **Rev:** Box hive and 20 bees

Date	Mintage	F	VF	XF	Unc	BU
1975	75,000	—	0.25	0.60	2.00	3.00
1977	25,000	—	0.25	0.60	2.00	3.00
1979	50,000	—	0.25	0.60	2.00	3.00

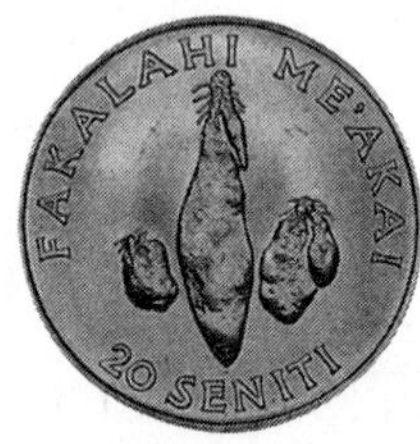

KM# 70 20 SENITI
11.3000 g., Copper-Nickel, 28.5 mm. **Ruler:** King Taufa'ahau Tupou IV **Series:** World Food Day **Obv:** Uniformed bust facing **Obv. Legend:** TONGA **Rev:** Yams **Rev. Legend:** FAKALAHI ME'AKAI **Edge:** Reeded

Date	Mintage	F	VF	XF	Unc	BU
1981	610,000	—	0.25	0.50	1.50	2.50
1990	610,000	—	0.25	0.50	1.25	2.25
1991	—	—	0.25	0.50	1.25	2.25
1994	680,000	—	0.25	0.50	1.25	2.00
1996	—	—	0.25	0.50	1.25	2.00
2003	—	—	0.25	0.50	1.25	2.00
2004	—	—	0.25	0.50	1.25	2.00

KM# 9 50 SENITI
18.0000 g., Copper-Nickel, 34.5 mm. **Ruler:** King Taufa'ahau Tupou IV **Obv:** Head right **Rev:** Crowned arms

Date	Mintage	F	VF	XF	Unc	BU
1967	75,000	—	0.75	1.25	2.75	4.00
1967 Proof	—	Value: 5.00				

KM# 15 50 SENITI
Copper-Nickel, 34.5 mm. **Ruler:** King Taufa'ahau Tupou IV **Subject:** Coronation of Taufa'ahau Tupou IV **Obv:** Head right **Obv. Designer:** Maurice Meers **Rev:** Crowned arms **Rev. Designer:** Ernest Hyde

Date	Mintage	F	VF	XF	Unc	BU
ND(1967)	15,000	—	1.00	1.75	3.00	4.50
ND(1967) Proof	—	Value: 6.00				

KM# 32 50 SENITI
17.8000 g., Copper-Nickel, 34.5 mm. **Ruler:** King Taufa'ahau Tupou IV **Obv:** Head right **Rev:** Crowned arms

Date	Mintage	F	VF	XF	Unc	BU
1968	25,000	—	0.75	1.25	2.25	3.50
1968 Proof	—	Value: 4.00				

KM# 41 50 SENITI
14.6000 g., Copper-Nickel, 32.5 mm. **Ruler:** King Taufa'ahau Tupou IV **Obv:** Head right **Rev:** Crowned arms **Edge:** Plain **Shape:** 12-sided

Date	Mintage	F	VF	XF	Unc	BU
1974	50,000	—	0.75	1.25	2.00	3.50

KM# 47 50 SENITI
14.6000 g., Copper-Nickel, 32.5 mm. **Ruler:** King Taufa'ahau Tupou IV **Series:** F.A.O. **Obv:** Uniformed bust facing **Rev:** 50 Fish swimming in circle formation **Edge:** Plain **Shape:** 12-sided

Date	Mintage	F	VF	XF	Unc	BU
1975	40,000	—	0.50	1.00	2.25	3.00
1977	20,000	—	0.75	1.25	2.75	3.25
1978	60,000	—	0.50	1.00	2.25	3.00

KM# 71 50 SENITI
14.6000 g., Copper-Nickel, 32.5 mm. **Ruler:** King Taufa'ahau Tupou IV **Series:** World Food Day **Obv:** Uniformed bust facing

Obv. Legend: TONGA **Rev:** Tomatoe plants **Rev. Legend:** FAKALAHI ME'AKAI **Edge:** Plain **Shape:** 12-sided

Date	Mintage	F	VF	XF	Unc	BU
1981	555,000	—	0.45	0.75	1.75	3.00
1990	—	—	0.45	0.75	1.50	3.00
1991	—	—	0.45	0.75	1.50	2.75
1994	41,000	—	0.45	0.75	1.50	2.75
1996	—	—	0.45	0.75	1.50	2.50
2002	—	—	0.45	0.75	1.50	2.50
2003	—	—	0.45	0.75	1.50	2.50
2004	—	—	0.45	0.75	1.50	2.50

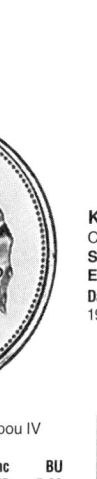

KM# 11 PA'ANGA

Copper-Nickel, 38.5 mm. **Ruler:** King Taufa'ahau Tupou IV **Obv:** Head right **Rev:** Crowned arms **Edge:** Reeded

Date	Mintage	F	VF	XF	Unc	BU
1967	78,000	—	1.00	2.00	3.75	5.00
1967 Proof	—	Value: 6.00				

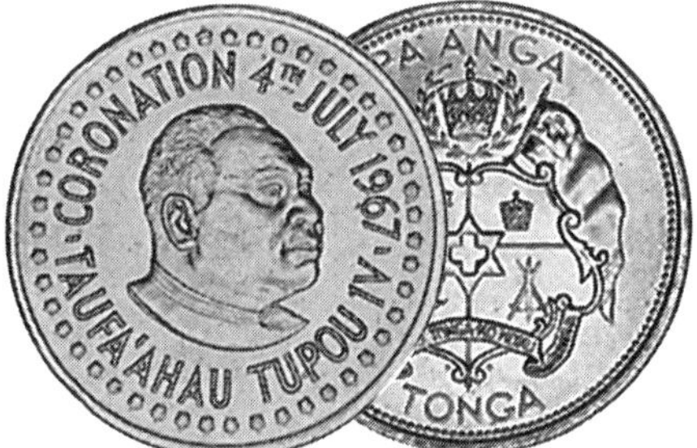

KM# 17 PA'ANGA

Copper-Nickel, 38.5 mm. **Ruler:** King Taufa'ahau Tupou IV **Subject:** Coronation of Taufa'ahau Tupou IV **Obv:** Head right, small crowns around border **Obv. Designer:** Maurice Meers **Rev:** Crowned arms **Rev. Designer:** Ernest Hyde **Edge:** Reeded

Date	Mintage	F	VF	XF	Unc	BU
ND(1967)	13,000	—	1.00	2.00	4.00	5.50
ND(1967) Proof	1,923	Value: 6.50				

KM# 33 PA'ANGA

Copper-Nickel, 38.5 mm. **Ruler:** King Taufa'ahau Tupou IV **Obv:** Head right **Rev:** Crowned arms **Edge:** Reeded

Date	Mintage	F	VF	XF	Unc	BU
1968	14,000	—	1.00	2.00	4.00	5.50
1968 Proof	—	Value: 6.50				
1974	10,000	—	1.00	2.00	4.00	4.00

KM# 48 PA'ANGA

Copper-Nickel, 38.5 mm. **Ruler:** King Taufa'ahau Tupou IV **Series:** F.A.O. **Obv:** Uniformed bust facing **Rev:** 100 Palm trees **Edge:** Reeded

Date	Mintage	F	VF	XF	Unc	BU
1975	13,000	—	1.25	2.50	4.50	6.00

TONKIN

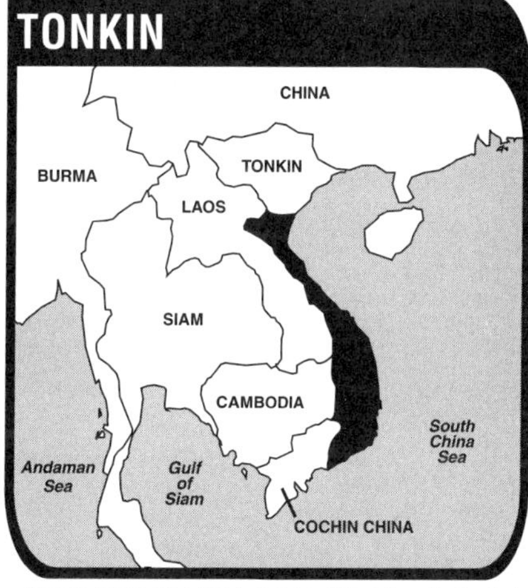

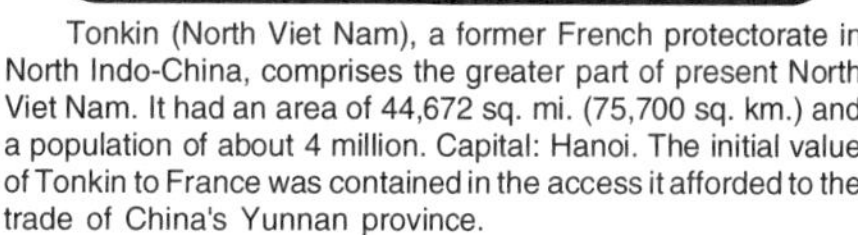

Tonkin (North Viet Nam), a former French protectorate in North Indo-China, comprises the greater part of present North Viet Nam. It had an area of 44,672 sq. mi. (75,700 sq. km.) and a population of about 4 million. Capital: Hanoi. The initial value of Tonkin to France was contained in the access it afforded to the trade of China's Yunnan province.

France established a protectorate over Annam and Tonkin by the treaties of Tientsin and Hue negotiated in 1884. Tonkin was incorporated in the independent state of Viet Nam (within the French Union) and upon the defeat of France by the Viet Minh became the body of ***North Viet Nam***.

MINT MARK

(a) - Paris, privy marks only

FRENCH PROTECTORATE

MILLED COINAGE

KM# 1 1/600 PIASTRE

2.1000 g., Zinc **Obv:** Legend around square center hole **Obv. Legend:** PROTECTORAT DU TONKIN **Rev:** Value above and below, "Thong-bao" at left and right **Note:** 0.9 mm thick planchet.

Date	Mintage	F	VF	XF	Unc	BU
1905(a)	60,000,000	3.50	7.50	18.00	45.00	—

TRANSNISTRIA

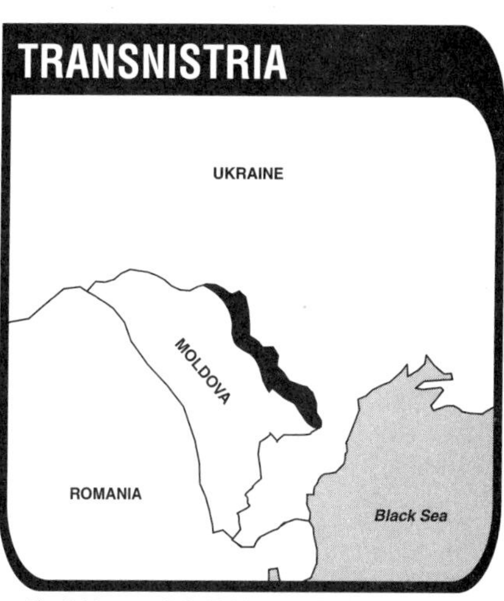

The Pridnestrovskaia Moldavskaia Respublica was formed in 1990, even before the separation of Moldavia from Russia. It has an area of 11,544 sq. mi. (29,900 sq. km.) and a population of 555,000. Capital: Tiraspol.

The area was conquered from the Turks in the last half of the 18th century, and in 1792 the capital city of Bessarabia (present Moldova and part of the Ukraine) became part of the Russian Empire. During the Russian Revolution, in 1918, the area was taken by Romanian troops, and in 1924 the Moldavian Autonomous SSR was formed on the left bank of the Dniester River. On June 22, 1941, Romania declared war on the U.S.S.R. and Romanian troops fought alongside the Germans up to Stalingrad. A Romanian occupation area between the Dniester and Bug Rivers called Transnistria was established in October 1941. Its center was the port of Odessa.

Once the Moldavian SSR declared independence in August 1991, Transnistria did not want to be part of Moldavia. In 1992, Moldova tried to solve the issue militarily with battles in Bendery and Doubossary. The conflict was ended with Russian mediation and Russian peacekeeping forces were stationed there.

Transnistria (or Transdniestra) has a president, parliament, army and police forces, but as yet it is lacking international recognition.

MOLDAVIAN REPUBLIC

STANDARD COINAGE

1 Rublei = 100 Kopeek

KM# 1 KOPEEK

0.6200 g., Aluminum, 15.9 mm. **Obv:** State arms **Obv. Legend:** ПРИДНЕСТРОВСКАЯ МОЛДАВСКАЯ РЕСПУБЛИКА **Rev:** Value between wheat stalks **Edge:** Plain

Date	Mintage	F	VF	XF	Unc	BU
2000	—	—	—	—	0.25	0.40

KM# 2 5 KOPEEK

0.7000 g., Aluminum, 17.9 mm. **Obv:** State arms **Obv. Legend:** ПРИДНЕСТРОВСКАЯ МОЛДАВСКАЯ РЕСПУБЛИКА **Rev:** Value flanked by wheat stalks **Edge:** Plain

Date	Mintage	F	VF	XF	Unc	BU
2000	—	—	—	—	0.50	0.65
	—	—	—	—	0.50	0.65

KM# 3 10 KOPEEK

1.0000 g., Aluminum, 20 mm. **Obv:** State arms **Obv. Legend:** ПРИДНЕСТРОВСКАЯ МОЛДАВСКАЯ РЕСПУБЛИКА **Rev:** Value flanked by wheat stalks **Edge:** Plain

Date	Mintage	F	VF	XF	Unc	BU
2000	—	—	—	—	0.75	0.90
2005	—	—	—	—	0.75	0.90

KM# 5 25 KOPEEK
2.1500 g., Brass, 17 mm. **Obv:** National arms **Rev:** Value flanked by wheat stalks **Edge:** Plain

Date	Mintage	F	VF	XF	Unc	BU
2002	—	—	—	—	1.00	1.20
2005	—	—	—	—	1.00	1.20

KM# 4 50 KOPEEK
2.7500 g., Brass, 19 mm. **Obv:** State arms **Obv. Legend:** ПРИДНЕСТРОВСКАЯ МОЛДАВСКАЯ РЕСПУБЛИКА **Rev:** Value within wreath **Edge:** Plain

Date	Mintage	F	VF	XF	Unc	BU
2000	—	—	—	—	1.25	1.50
2005	—	—	—	—	1.25	1.50

TRINIDAD & TOBAGO

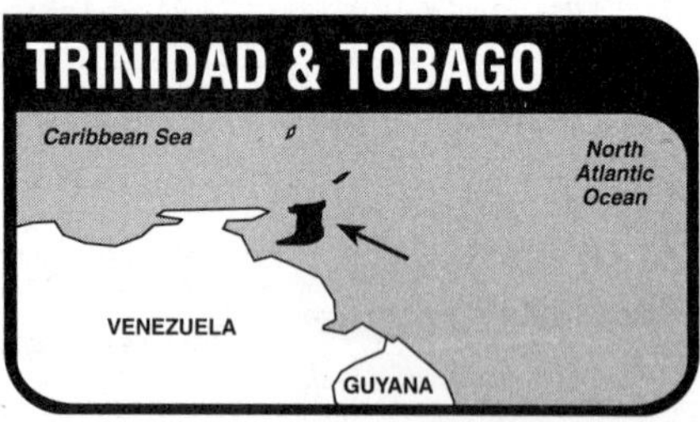

The Republic of Trinidad and Tobago is situated 7 miles (11 km.) off the coast of Venezuela, has an area of 1,981 sq. mi. (5,130 sq. km.) and a population of *1.2 million. Capital: Port-of-Spain. The island of Trinidad contains the world's largest natural asphalt bog. Birds of Paradise live on little Tobago, the only place outside of their native New Guinea where they can be found in a wild state. Petroleum and petroleum products are the mainstay of the economy. Petroleum products, crude oil and sugar are exported.

Columbus discovered Trinidad and Tobago in 1498. Trinidad remained under Spanish rule from the time of its settlement in 1592 until its capture by the British in 1797. It was ceded to the British in 1802. Tobago was occupied at various times by the French, Dutch and English before being ceded to Britain in 1814. Trinidad and Tobago were merged into a single colony in 1888. The colony was part of the Federation of the West Indies until Aug. 31, 1962, when it became independent. A new constitution establishing a republican form of government was adopted on Aug. 1, 1976. Trinidad and Tobago is a member of the Commonwealth of Nations. The President is Chief of State. The Prime Minister is Head of Government.

RULER
British, until 1976

MINT MARKS
FM - Franklin Mint, U.S.A.*

***NOTE**: From 1975-1985 the Franklin Mint produced coinage in up to 3 different qualities. Qualities of issue are designated in ( ) after each date and are defined as follows:

(M) MATTE - Normal circulation strike or a dull finish produced by sandblasting special uncirculated (polish finish) or proof quality dies.

(U) SPECIAL UNCIRCULATED - Polished or proof-like in appearance without any frosted features.

(P) PROOF - The highest quality obtainable having mirror-like fields and frosted features.

MONETARY SYSTEM
100 Cents = 1 Dollar

BRITISH COLONIAL

STANDARD COINAGE

KM# 1 CENT
1.9500 g., Bronze, 17.8 mm. **Obv:** Value **Rev:** National arms **Edge:** Plain

Date	Mintage	F	VF	XF	Unc	BU
1966	24,500,000	—	—	—	0.15	0.30
1966 Proof	8,000	Value: 1.00				
1967	4,000,000	—	—	—	0.25	0.50
1968	5,000,000	—	—	—	0.25	0.50
1970	5,000,000	—	—	—	0.25	0.50
1970 Proof	2,104	Value: 1.50				
1971	10,600,000	—	—	—	0.15	0.30
1971FM (M)	286,000	—	—	—	0.20	0.40
1971FM (P)	12,000	Value: 0.50				
1972	16,500,000	—	—	—	0.15	0.30
1973	10,000,000	—	—	—	0.15	0.30

KM# 9 CENT
1.9500 g., Bronze, 17.8 mm. **Subject:** 10th Anniversary of Independence **Obv:** Value and date **Rev:** National arms **Edge:** Plain

Date	Mintage	F	VF	XF	Unc	BU
1972	5,000,000	—	—	0.10	0.15	0.30
1972FM (M)	125,000	—	—	—	0.25	0.50
1972FM (P)	16,000	Value: 0.50				

KM# 17 CENT
1.9500 g., Bronze, 17.8 mm. **Obv:** Value and date **Rev:** National arms **Edge:** Plain

Date	Mintage	F	VF	XF	Unc	BU
1973FM (M)	127,000	—	—	—	0.50	1.00
1973FM (P)	20,000	Value: 1.50				

KM# 25 CENT
1.9500 g., Bronze, 17.8 mm. **Obv:** National arms **Rev:** Hummingbird and value **Edge:** Plain

Date	Mintage	F	VF	XF	Unc	BU
1974FM (M)	128,000	—	—	—	0.50	1.00
1974FM (P)	14,000	Value: 0.80				
1975	10,000,000	—	—	—	0.50	1.00
1975FM (M)	125,000	—	—	—	0.50	1.00
1975FM (U)	1,111	—	—	—	1.25	2.50
1975FM (P)	24,000	Value: 0.80				
1976	15,050,000	—	—	—	0.50	1.00

KM# 2 5 CENTS
3.2500 g., Bronze, 21.15 mm. **Obv:** Value **Rev:** National arms

Date	Mintage	F	VF	XF	Unc	BU
1966	7,500,000	—	—	0.10	0.25	0.50
1966 Proof	8,000	Value: 1.25				
1967	3,000,000	—	—	0.10	0.50	1.00
1970 Proof	2,104	Value: 1.75				
1971	2,400,000	—	—	0.10	0.50	1.00
1971FM (M)	57,000	—	—	—	0.15	0.30
1971FM (P)	12,000	Value: 0.75				
1972	2,250,000	—	—	0.10	0.50	1.00

KM# 10 5 CENTS
3.2500 g., Bronze, 21.15 mm. **Subject:** 10th Anniversary of Independence **Obv:** Value and date **Rev:** National arms

Date	Mintage	F	VF	XF	Unc	BU
1972	15,000	—	—	—	0.35	0.70
1972FM (M)	25,000	—	—	—	0.25	0.50
1972FM (P)	16,000	Value: 0.75				

KM# 57 5 CENTS
3.2500 g., Bronze, 21.15 mm. **Obv:** Value **Rev:** National arms

Date	Mintage	F	VF	XF	Unc	BU
1973FM (M)	27,000	—	—	—	0.50	1.00
1973FM (P)	20,000	Value: 1.50				

KM# 26 5 CENTS
3.2500 g., Bronze, 21.15 mm. **Obv:** National arms **Rev:** Bird of Paradise and value

Date	Mintage	F	VF	XF	Unc	BU
1974FM (M)	28,000	—	—	—	0.50	1.00
1974FM (P)	14,000	Value: 0.75				
1975	1,500,000	—	—	0.10	0.45	0.90
1975FM (M)	25,000	—	—	—	0.45	0.90
1975FM (U)	1,111	—	—	—	2.50	5.00
1975FM (P)	24,000	Value: 0.75				
1976	7,500,000	—	—	0.10	0.45	0.90

KM# 3 10 CENTS
1.4000 g., Copper-Nickel, 16.3 mm. **Obv:** Value and date **Rev:** National arms **Edge:** Reeded

Date	Mintage	F	VF	XF	Unc	BU
1966	7,800,000	—	—	0.10	0.30	0.60
1966 Proof	8,000	Value: 1.50				
1967	4,000,000	—	—	0.10	0.45	0.90
1970 Proof	2,104	Value: 2.00				
1971	—	—	—	0.10	0.45	0.90
1971FM (M)	29,000	—	—	—	0.35	0.70
1971FM (P)	12,000	Value: 1.00				
1972	4,000,000	—	—	0.10	0.30	0.60

KM# 11 10 CENTS
1.4000 g., Copper-Nickel, 16.3 mm. **Subject:** 10th Anniversary of Independence **Obv:** Value **Rev:** National arms **Edge:** Reeded

Date	Mintage	F	VF	XF	Unc	BU
1972	41,000	—	—	—	0.40	0.80
1972FM (M)	13,000	—	—	—	0.60	1.20
1972FM (P)	16,000	Value: 1.00				

KM# 58 10 CENTS
1.4000 g., Copper-Nickel, 16.3 mm. **Obv:** Value **Rev:** National arms **Edge:** Reeded

Date	Mintage	F	VF	XF	Unc	BU
1973FM (M)	14,000	—	—	—	1.00	2.00
1973FM (P)	20,000	Value: 2.50				

KM# 27 10 CENTS
1.4000 g., Copper-Nickel, 16.3 mm. **Obv:** National arms **Rev:** Flaming Hibiscus and value **Edge:** Reeded

Date	Mintage	F	VF	XF	Unc	BU
1974FM (M)	16,000	—	—	—	1.00	2.00
1974FM (P)	14,000	Value: 1.00				
1975	4,000,000	—	—	0.10	0.25	0.50
1975FM (M)	13,000	—	—	—	0.50	1.00
1975FM (U)	1,111	—	—	—	2.50	5.00
1975FM (P)	24,000	Value: 1.00				
1976	14,720,000	—	—	0.10	0.20	0.40

KM# 4 25 CENTS
3.5000 g., Copper-Nickel, 20 mm. **Obv:** Value **Rev:** National arms **Edge:** Reeded

Date	Mintage	F	VF	XF	Unc	BU
1966	7,200,000	—	0.10	0.15	0.35	0.70
1966 Proof	8,000	Value: 1.75				
1967	1,800,000	—	0.10	0.15	0.50	1.00
1970 Proof	2,014	Value: 2.50				
1971	1,500,000	—	0.10	0.15	0.50	1.00
1971FM (M)	11,000	—	—	—	0.65	1.30
1971FM (P)	12,000	Value: 1.25				
1972	3,000,000	—	0.10	0.15	0.35	0.70

KM# 12 25 CENTS
3.5000 g., Copper-Nickel, 20 mm. **Subject:** 10th Anniversary of Independence **Obv:** Value and date **Rev:** National arms **Edge:** Reeded

Date	Mintage	F	VF	XF	Unc	BU
1972	14,000	—	0.20	0.65	1.00	2.00
1972FM (M)	5,000	—	—	—	1.50	3.00
1972FM (P)	16,000	Value: 1.25				

KM# 59 25 CENTS
3.5000 g., Copper-Nickel, 20 mm. **Obv:** Value **Rev:** National arms **Edge:** Reeded

Date	Mintage	F	VF	XF	Unc	BU
1973FM (M)	6,575	—	—	—	2.25	4.50
1973FM (P)	20,000	Value: 3.00				

KM# 28 25 CENTS
3.5000 g., Copper-Nickel, 20 mm. **Obv:** National arms **Rev:** Chaconia and value **Edge:** Reeded

Date	Mintage	F	VF	XF	Unc	BU
1974FM (M)	8,258	—	—	—	1.75	3.50
1974FM (P)	14,000	Value: 1.25				
1975	3,000,000	—	0.10	0.15	0.30	0.60
1975FM (M)	5,000	—	—	—	1.50	3.00
1975FM (U)	1,111	—	—	—	2.00	4.00
1975FM (P)	24,000	Value: 1.25				
1976	9,000,000	—	0.10	0.15	0.30	0.60

KM# 5 50 CENTS
7.0000 g., Copper-Nickel, 26 mm. **Obv:** Value **Rev:** National arms **Edge:** Reeded

Date	Mintage	F	VF	XF	Unc	BU
1966	975,000	—	0.25	0.60	1.50	3.00
1966 Proof	8,000	Value: 2.50				
1967	750,000	—	0.25	0.50	1.25	2.50
1970 Proof	2,104	Value: 3.00				
1971FM (M)	5,714	—	—	—	2.50	5.00
1971FM (P)	12,000	Value: 1.75				

KM# 13 50 CENTS
7.0000 g., Copper-Nickel, 26 mm. **Subject:** 10th Anniversary of Independence **Obv:** Value **Rev:** National arms **Edge:** Reeded

Date	Mintage	F	VF	XF	Unc	BU
1972	375,000	—	0.50	0.75	1.50	3.00
1972FM (M)	2,500	—	—	—	5.00	10.00
1972FM (P)	16,000	Value: 1.75				

KM# 22 50 CENTS
7.0000 g., Copper-Nickel, 26 mm. **Obv:** National arms **Rev:** Kettle drums and value **Edge:** Reeded

Date	Mintage	F	VF	XF	Unc	BU
1973FM (M)	4,075	—	—	—	2.50	5.00
1973FM (P)	20,000	Value: 2.25				
1974FM (M)	5,758	—	—	—	2.50	5.00
1974FM (P)	14,000	Value: 2.25				
1975FM (M)	2,500	—	—	—	4.00	8.00
1975FM (U)	1,111	—	—	—	2.50	5.00
1975FM (P)	24,000	Value: 2.00				
1976	750,000	—	0.50	0.75	1.50	3.00

KM# 6 DOLLAR
12.7000 g., Nickel, 32 mm. **Series:** F.A.O. **Obv:** National arms **Rev:** Value in front of leaves

Date	Mintage	F	VF	XF	Unc	BU
1969	250,000	—	0.75	1.50	3.50	7.00

KM# 7 DOLLAR
12.7000 g., Copper-Nickel, 32 mm. **Obv:** Value **Rev:** National arms

Date	Mintage	F	VF	XF	Unc	BU
1971FM (M)	2,857	—	—	—	5.00	10.00
1971FM (P)	12,000	Value: 3.00				

KM# 7a DOLLAR
Nickel, 36 mm. **Obv:** Value **Rev:** National arms

Date	Mintage	F	VF	XF	Unc	BU
1970 Proof	2,014	Value: 6.00				

KM# 14 DOLLAR
Copper-Nickel, 36 mm. **Subject:** 10th Anniversary of Independence **Obv:** National arms **Rev:** Bird on branch and value

Date	Mintage	F	VF	XF	Unc	BU
1972	9,700	—	—	—	6.00	12.00
1972FM (M)	1,250	—	—	—	12.50	20.00
1972FM (P)	16,000	Value: 4.00				

KM# 23 DOLLAR
Copper-Nickel, 36 mm. **Obv:** National arms **Rev:** Bird on branch and value

Date	Mintage	F	VF	XF	Unc	BU
1973FM (M)	2,825	—	—	—	5.50	10.00
1973FM (P)	20,000	Value: 4.00				
1974FM (M)	4,508	—	—	—	5.50	10.00
1974FM (P)	14,000	Value: 4.00				
1975FM (M)	1,250	—	—	—	6.50	12.00
1975FM (U)	1,111	—	—	—	6.50	12.00
1975FM (P)	24,000	Value: 4.00				

REPUBLIC

STANDARD COINAGE

KM# 29 CENT
1.9500 g., Bronze, 17.76 mm. **Obv:** National arms **Rev:** Hummingbird and value **Edge:** Plain

Date	Mintage	F	VF	XF	Unc	BU
1976	—	—	—	—	—	—
1976FM (M)	150,000	—	—	0.20	0.35	1.00
1976FM (U)	582	—	—	1.00	2.50	3.50
1976FM (P)	10,000	Value: 0.60				
1977FM	25,000,000	—	—	0.20	0.35	1.00
1977FM (M)	150,000	—	—	0.20	0.35	1.00
1977FM (U)	633	—	—	1.00	2.50	3.50
1977FM (P)	5,337	Value: 0.60				
1978FM	12,500,000	—	—	0.20	0.35	1.00
1978FM (M)	150,000	—	—	0.20	0.35	1.00
1978FM (U)	472	—	—	1.00	2.50	3.50
1978FM (P)	4,845	Value: 1.00				
1979FM	30,200,000	—	—	0.20	0.35	1.00
1979FM (M)	150,000	—	—	0.20	0.35	1.00
1979FM (U)	518	—	—	1.00	2.50	3.50
1979FM (P)	3,270	Value: 1.00				
1980FM	12,500,000	—	—	0.20	0.35	1.00
1980FM (M)	75,000	—	—	0.20	0.35	1.00
1980FM (U)	796	—	—	1.00	2.50	3.50
1980FM (P)	2,393	Value: 1.00				
1981FM	—	—	—	0.20	0.35	1.00
1981FM (M)	—	—	—	0.20	0.35	1.00
1981FM (U)	—	—	—	1.00	2.50	3.50
1981FM (P)	—	Value: 1.00				
1982FM	—	—	—	0.20	0.35	1.00
1983FM	—	—	—	0.20	0.35	1.00
1984FM	—	—	—	0.20	0.35	1.00
1985FM	25,400,000	—	—	0.20	0.35	1.00
1986FM	10,000,000	—	—	0.20	0.35	1.00
1987FM	10,000,000	—	—	0.20	0.35	1.00
1988FM	5,000,000	—	—	0.20	0.35	1.00
1989FM	—	—	—	0.20	0.35	1.00
1990FM	—	—	—	0.20	0.35	1.00
1991FM	—	—	—	0.20	0.35	1.00
1993FM	—	—	—	0.20	0.35	1.00
1994FM	—	—	—	0.20	0.35	1.00
1995FM	—	—	—	0.20	0.35	1.00

Date	Mintage	F	VF	XF	Unc	BU
1996FM	—	—	—	0.20	0.35	1.00
1997FM	—	—	—	0.20	0.35	1.00
1998	—	—	—	0.20	0.35	1.00
1999	—	—	—	0.20	0.35	1.00
1999 Proof	3,000	Value: 0.60				
2000	—	—	—	0.20	0.35	1.00
2001	—	—	—	0.10	0.30	0.40
2002	—	—	—	0.10	0.30	0.40
2003FM	—	—	—	0.10	0.30	0.40
2005	—	—	—	0.10	0.30	0.40
2006FM	—	—	—	0.10	0.30	0.40

KM# 42 CENT

1.9500 g., Bronze, 17.8 mm. **Subject:** 20th Anniversary of Independence **Obv:** National arms **Rev:** Flaming hibiscus and value **Edge:** Plain

Date	Mintage	F	VF	XF	Unc	BU
1982FM (M)	—	—	—	—	0.15	0.30
1982FM (U)	—	—	—	—	1.50	3.00
1982FM (P)	—	Value: 1.00				

KM# 51 CENT

1.9500 g., Bronze, 17.8 mm. **Obv:** National arms **Rev:** Flaming hibiscus and value **Edge:** Plain

Date	Mintage	F	VF	XF	Unc	BU
1983FM (M)	—	—	—	—	1.50	3.00
1983FM (P)	—	Value: 1.00				
1984FM (P)	—	Value: 1.00				

KM# 30 5 CENTS

3.3100 g., Bronze, 21.2 mm. **Obv:** National arms **Rev:** Bird of paradise and value **Edge:** Plain

Date	Mintage	F	VF	XF	Unc	BU
1976FM (M)	30,000	—	—	—	0.25	1.00
1976FM (U)	582	—	—	—	1.75	3.50
1976FM (P)	10,000	Value: 0.75				
1977	12,000,000	—	—	0.10	0.25	1.00
1977FM (M)	30,000	—	—	—	0.25	1.00
1977FM (U)	633	—	—	—	1.75	3.50
1977FM (P)	5,337	Value: 0.75				
1978	1,500,000	—	—	0.10	0.25	1.00
1978FM (M)	30,000	—	—	—	0.25	1.00
1978FM (U)	472	—	—	—	1.75	3.50
1978FM (P)	4,845	Value: 1.25				
1979	—	—	—	0.10	0.25	1.00
1979FM (M)	30,000	—	—	—	0.25	1.00
1979FM (U)	518	—	—	—	1.75	3.50
1979FM (P)	3,270	Value: 1.25				
1980	15,000,000	—	—	0.10	0.25	1.00
1980FM (M)	15,000	—	—	—	0.25	1.00
1980FM (U)	796	—	—	—	5.00	7.50
1980FM (P)	2,393	Value: 1.25				
1981	—	—	—	0.10	0.25	1.00
1981FM (M)	—	—	—	—	0.25	1.00
1981FM (U)	—	—	—	—	1.75	2.50
1981FM (P)	—	Value: 1.25				
1983	—	—	—	0.10	0.25	1.00
1984	4,094,999	—	—	0.10	1.00	1.25
1988	20,000,000	—	—	0.10	0.25	1.00
1990	—	—	—	0.10	0.25	1.00
1992	—	—	—	0.10	0.25	1.00
1995	—	—	—	0.10	0.25	1.00
1996	—	—	—	0.10	0.25	1.00
1997	—	—	—	0.10	0.25	1.00
1998	—	—	—	0.10	0.25	1.00
1999	—	—	—	0.10	0.25	1.00
1999 Proof	3,000	Value: 1.00				
2000	—	—	—	0.10	0.25	1.00
2001	—	—	—	0.15	0.45	0.60
2002	—	—	—	0.15	0.45	0.60
2003	—	—	—	0.15	0.45	0.60
2004	—	—	—	0.15	0.45	0.60
2005	—	—	—	0.15	0.45	0.60
2007	—	—	—	0.15	0.45	0.60

KM# 43 5 CENTS

3.2500 g., Bronze, 21.15 mm. **Subject:** 20th Anniversary of Independence **Obv:** National arms **Rev:** Butterfly and value

Date	Mintage	F	VF	XF	Unc	BU
1982FM (M)	—	—	—	—	1.50	5.00
1982FM (U)	—	—	—	—	3.00	6.00
1982FM (P)	—	Value: 5.00				

KM# 52 5 CENTS

3.2500 g., Bronze, 21.15 mm. **Obv:** National arms **Rev:** Butterfly

Date	Mintage	F	VF	XF	Unc	BU
1983FM (M)	—	—	—	—	2.50	5.00
1983FM (P)	—	Value: 6.00				
1984FM (P)	—	Value: 6.00				

KM# 31 10 CENTS

1.4000 g., Copper-Nickel, 16.2 mm. **Obv:** National arms **Rev:** Hibiscus and value **Edge:** Reeded

Date	Mintage	F	VF	XF	Unc	BU
1976FM (M)	15,000	—	—	—	0.50	1.00
1976FM (U)	582	—	—	5.00	7.50	10.00
1976FM (P)	10,000	Value: 1.00				
1977	17,280,000	—	—	0.10	0.20	0.40
1977FM (M)	15,000	—	—	—	0.50	1.00
1977FM (U)	633	—	—	5.00	7.50	10.00
1977FM (P)	5,337	Value: 1.00				
1978	10,000,000	—	—	0.10	0.20	0.40
1978FM (M)	15,000	—	—	—	0.50	1.00
1978FM (U)	472	—	—	5.00	7.50	9.00
1978FM (P)	4,845	Value: 1.50				
1979	1,970,000	—	—	0.10	0.30	0.60
1979FM (M)	15,000	—	—	—	0.50	1.00
1979FM (U)	518	—	—	5.00	7.50	9.00
1979FM (P)	3,270	Value: 1.50				
1980	20,000,000	—	—	0.10	0.30	0.60
1980FM (M)	7,500	—	—	—	0.50	1.00
1980FM (U)	796	—	—	5.00	7.50	9.00
1980FM (P)	2,393	Value: 1.50				
1981	—	—	—	0.10	0.30	0.60
1981FM (M)	—	—	—	—	0.50	1.00
1981FM (U)	—	—	—	5.00	7.50	9.00
1981FM (P)	—	Value: 1.50				
1990	—	—	—	0.10	0.30	0.60
1997	—	—	—	0.20	0.50	1.00
1998	—	—	—	0.20	0.50	1.00
1999	—	—	—	0.20	0.50	1.00
1999 Proof	—	Value: 2.00				
2000	—	—	—	0.20	0.50	1.00
2001	—	—	—	0.25	0.60	0.80
2002	—	—	—	0.25	0.60	0.80
2003	—	—	—	0.25	0.60	0.80
2004	—	—	—	0.25	0.60	0.80
2005	—	—	—	0.25	0.60	0.80
2006	—	—	—	0.25	0.60	0.80

KM# 44 10 CENTS

1.4000 g., Copper-Nickel, 16.3 mm. **Subject:** 20th Anniversary of Independence **Obv:** National arms **Rev:** Hummingbird and value **Edge:** Reeded

Date	Mintage	F	VF	XF	Unc	BU
1982FM (M)	—	—	—	—	3.00	7.00
1982FM (U)	—	—	—	—	4.00	7.00
1982FM (P)	—	Value: 2.50				

KM# 53 10 CENTS

1.4000 g., Copper-Nickel, 16.3 mm. **Obv:** National arms **Rev:** Hummingbird and value

Date	Mintage	F	VF	XF	Unc	BU
1983FM (M)	—	—	—	—	3.00	6.00
1983FM (P)	—	Value: 2.00				
1984FM (P)	—	Value: 2.00				

KM# 32 25 CENTS

3.5700 g., Copper-Nickel, 20 mm. **Obv:** National arms **Rev:** Chaconia and value **Edge:** Reeded

Date	Mintage	F	VF	XF	Unc	BU
1976FM (M)	6,000	—	—	—	1.00	2.00
1976FM (U)	582	—	—	5.00	7.50	10.00
1976FM (P)	10,000	Value: 1.25				
1977	9,000,000	—	0.10	0.15	0.30	0.60
1977FM (M)	6,000	—	—	—	1.00	2.00
1977FM (U)	633	—	—	5.00	7.50	10.00
1977FM (P)	5,337	Value: 1.25				
1978	5,470,000	—	0.10	0.15	0.30	0.60
1978FM (M)	6,000	—	—	—	1.00	2.00
1978FM (U)	472	—	—	5.00	7.50	10.00
1978FM (P)	4,845	Value: 1.75				
1979	—	—	0.10	0.15	0.40	0.80
1979FM (M)	6,000	—	—	—	1.00	2.00
1979FM (U)	518	—	—	5.00	7.50	10.00
1979FM (P)	3,270	Value: 2.00				
1980	15,000,000	—	0.10	0.15	0.40	0.80
1980FM (M)	3,000	—	—	—	1.00	2.00
1980FM (U)	796	—	—	5.00	7.50	10.00
1980FM (P)	2,393	Value: 2.00				
1981	—	—	0.10	0.15	0.40	0.80
1981FM (M)	—	—	—	—	1.00	2.00
1981FM (U)	—	—	—	5.00	7.50	10.00
1981FM (P)	—	Value: 2.00				
1983	—	—	0.10	0.15	0.40	0.80
1983FM (M)	—	—	—	—	2.00	4.00
1983FM (P)	—	Value: 2.00				
1984	—	—	0.10	0.15	0.40	0.80
1984	—	Value: 2.00				
1993	—	—	—	0.15	0.40	0.80
1997	—	—	—	0.15	0.40	0.80
1998	—	—	—	0.15	0.40	0.80
1999	—	—	—	0.15	0.40	0.80
1999 Proof	—	Value: 3.00				
2001	—	—	—	0.30	0.75	1.00
2002	—	—	—	0.30	0.75	1.00
2003	—	—	—	0.30	0.75	1.00
2004	—	—	—	0.30	0.75	1.00
2005	—	—	—	0.30	0.75	1.00
2006	—	—	—	0.30	0.75	1.00
2007	—	—	—	0.30	0.75	1.00

KM# 45 25 CENTS

3.5000 g., Copper-Nickel, 20 mm. **Subject:** 20th Anniversary of Independence **Obv:** National arms **Rev:** Chaconia and value **Edge:** Reeded

Date	Mintage	F	VF	XF	Unc	BU
1982FM (M)	—	—	—	—	1.00	2.00
1982FM (U)	—	—	—	—	2.25	4.50
1982FM (P)	—	Value: 2.00				

KM# 33 50 CENTS

7.0000 g., Copper-Nickel, 26 mm. **Obv:** National arms **Rev:** Kettle drums and value **Edge:** Reeded

Date	Mintage	F	VF	XF	Unc	BU
1976FM (M)	3,000	—	—	—	3.25	5.00
1976FM (U)	582	—	—	5.00	7.50	15.00
1976FM (P)	10,000	Value: 1.50				

Date	Mintage	F	VF	XF	Unc	BU
1977	1,500,000	—	0.25	0.50	1.00	2.00
1977FM (M)	3,000	—	—	—	3.00	6.00
1977FM (U)	633	—	—	5.00	7.50	15.00
1977FM (P)	5,337	Value: 1.50				
1978	563,000	—	0.50	0.75	1.50	3.50
1978FM (M)	3,000	—	—	—	3.00	6.00
1978FM (U)	472	—	—	5.00	7.50	15.00
1978FM (P)	4,845	Value: 2.00				
1979	750,000	—	0.50	0.75	1.50	3.50
1979FM (M)	3,000	—	—	—	3.25	6.00
1979FM (U)	518	—	—	5.00	7.50	15.00
1979FM (P)	3,270	Value: 2.00				
1980	3,750,000	—	0.25	0.50	1.00	2.00
1980FM (M)	1,500	—	—	—	3.00	6.00
1980FM (U)	796	—	—	5.00	7.50	15.00
1980FM (P)	2,393	Value: 2.00				
1981FM (M)	—	—	—	—	3.00	6.00
1981FM (U)	—	—	—	5.00	7.50	10.00
1981FM (P)	—	Value: 2.00				
1999	—	—	—	—	2.00	4.00
1999 Proof	3,000	Value: 4.00				
2003	—	—	—	—	—	—

KM# 46 50 CENTS

7.0000 g., Copper-Nickel, 26 mm. **Subject:** 20th Anniversary of Independence **Obv:** National arms **Rev:** Kettle drums and player **Edge:** Reeded

Date	Mintage	F	VF	XF	Unc	BU
1982FM (M)	—	—	—	—	3.00	6.00
1982FM (U)	—	—	—	—	2.50	5.00
1982FM (P)	—	Value: 2.00				

KM# 54 50 CENTS

7.0000 g., Copper-Nickel, 26 mm. **Obv:** National arms **Rev:** Kettle drums and player

Date	Mintage	F	VF	XF	Unc	BU
1983FM (M)	—	—	—	—	4.00	8.00
1983FM (P)	—	Value: 2.00				
1984FM (P)	—	Value: 2.00				

KM# 34 DOLLAR

Copper-Nickel, 36 mm. **Obv:** National arms **Rev:** Bird on branch and value

Date	Mintage	F	VF	XF	Unc	BU
1976FM (M)	1,500	—	—	—	6.00	10.00
1976FM (U)	582	—	—	8.00	10.00	15.00
1976FM (P)	10,000	Value: 2.00				
1977FM (M)	1,500	—	—	—	6.00	10.00
1977FM (U)	633	—	—	8.00	10.00	15.00
1977FM (P)	5,337	Value: 2.00				
1978FM (M)	1,500	—	—	—	6.00	10.00
1978FM (U)	472	—	—	8.00	10.00	15.00
1978FM (P)	4,845	Value: 3.00				
1979FM (M)	1,500	—	—	—	6.00	10.00
1979FM (U)	518	—	—	8.00	10.00	15.00
1979FM (P)	3,270	Value: 3.00				
1980FM (M)	750	—	—	8.00	10.00	15.00
1980FM (U)	796	—	—	8.00	10.00	15.00
1980FM (P)	2,393	Value: 5.00				
1981FM (M)	—	—	—	—	5.00	10.00
1981FM (U)	—	—	—	—	3.00	6.00
1981FM (P)	—	Value: 2.50				
1983FM (M)	—	—	—	—	6.00	10.00
1983FM (P)	—	Value: 2.50				
1984FM (P)	—	Value: 2.50				

KM# 38 DOLLAR

12.7000 g., Copper Nickel, 32 mm. **Series:** F.A.O. **Obv:** National arms **Rev:** Value in front of leaves

Date	Mintage	F	VF	XF	Unc	BU
1979	—	—	0.75	1.50	3.50	6.50

KM# 47 DOLLAR

Copper-Nickel, 36 mm. **Subject:** 20th Anniversary of Independence **Obv:** National arms **Rev:** Bird on branch and value within circle

Date	Mintage	F	VF	XF	Unc	BU
1982FM (M)	—	—	—	—	9.00	12.50
1982FM (U)	—	—	—	—	6.00	9.00
1982FM (P)	—	Value: 5.00				

KM# 61 DOLLAR

8.4000 g., Copper-Nickel **Subject:** 50th Anniversary - F.A.O. **Obv:** National arms **Rev:** Sprig, value and logo

Date	Mintage	F	VF	XF	Unc	BU
1995	—	—	—	1.00	1.75	2.75
1999	—	—	—	1.00	1.75	2.75
1999 Proof	3,000	Value: 5.00				

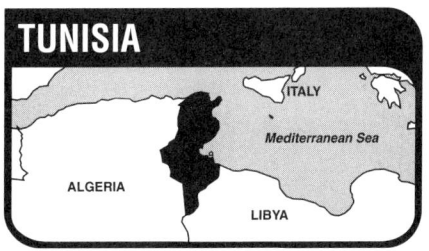

TUNISIA

ITALY
Mediterranean Sea
ALGERIA
LIBYA

The Republic of Tunisia, located on the northern coast of Africa between Algeria and Libya, has an area of 63,170sq. mi. (163,610 sq. km.) and a population of *7.9 million. Capital: Tunis. Agriculture is the backbone of the economy. Crude oil, phosphates, olive oil, and wine are exported.

Tunisia, settled by the Phoenicians in the 12th century B.C., was the center of the seafaring Carthaginian Empire. After the total destruction of Carthage, Tunisia became part of Rome's African province. It remained a part of the Roman Empire (except for the 439-533 interval of Vandal conquest) until taken by the Arabs, 648, who administered it until the Turkish invasion of 1570. Under Turkish control, the public revenue was heavily dependent upon the piracy of Mediterranean shipping, an endeavor that wasn't abandoned until 1819 when a coalition of powers threatened appropriate reprisal. Deprived of its major source of income, Tunisia underwent a financial regression that ended in bankruptcy, enabling France to establish a protectorate over the country in 1881. National agitation and guerrilla fighting forced France to grant Tunisia internal autonomy in 1955 and to recognize Tunisian independence on March20, 1956. Tunisia abolished the monarchy and established a republic on July 25, 1957.

TITLES

المملكة التونسية

al-Mamlaka al-Tunisiya

الجمهورية التونسية

al-Jumhuriya al-Tunisiya

al-Amala al-Tunisiya
(Tunisian Protectorate)

MINT MARKS

A - Paris, AH1308/1891-AH1348/1928
(a) - Paris, privy marks, AH1349/1929-AH1376/1957
FM - Franklin Mint, Franklin Center, PA
Numismatic Italiana, Arezzo, Italy

TUNIS

Tunis, the capital and major seaport of Tunisia, existed in the Carthaginian era, but its importance dates only from the Moslem conquest, following which it became a major center of Arab power and prosperity. Spain seized it in 1535, lost it in 1564, retook it in 1573 and ceded it to the Turks in 1574. Thereafter the history of Tunis merged with that of Tunisia.

Local Rulers

Ali Bey, AH1299-1320/1882-1902AD
Muhammad Al-Hadi Bey, AH1320-1324/1902-1906AD
Muhammad Al-Nasir Bey, AH1324-1340/1906-1922AD
Muhammad Al-Habib Bey, AH1340-1348/1922-1929AD
Ahmad Pasha Bey, AH1348-1361/1929-1942AD
Muhammad Al-Munsif Bey, AH1361-1362/1942-1943AD
Muhammad Al-Amin Bey, AH1362-1376/1943-1957AD

NOTE: All coins struck until AH1298/1881AD bear the name of the Ottoman Sultan; the name of the Bey of Tunis was added in AH1272/1855AD. After AH1298, when the French established their protectorate, only the Bey's name appears on the coin until AH1376/1956AD.

TUNISIA

FRENCH PROTECTORATE

Ali Bey

"Struck in his name"

DECIMAL COINAGE

100 Centimes = 1 Franc

The following coins all bear French inscriptions on one side, Arabic on the other, and usually have both AH and AD dates. Except for KM#246-48, they are struck in the name of the Tunisian Bey.

KM# 223 50 CENTIMES

2.5000 g., 0.8350 Silver 0.0671 oz. ASW **Obv:** Legend flanked by sprigs **Obv. Legend:** ALI **Rev:** Value, date in center circle of ornate design

Date	Mintage	F	VF	XF	Unc	BU
AH1319/1901A	1,000	—	—	150	250	—
AH1320/1902A	1,000	—	—	150	250	—

KM# 224 FRANC

5.0000 g., 0.8350 Silver 0.1342 oz. ASW **Obv:** Legend flanked by sprigs **Obv. Legend:** ALI **Rev:** Value, date in center circle of ornate design

Date	Mintage	F	VF	XF	Unc	BU
AH1319/1901A	700	—	—	175	275	—
AH1320/1902A	703	—	—	175	275	—

KM# 225 2 FRANCS

10.0000 g., 0.8350 Silver 0.2684 oz. ASW **Obv:** Legend flanked by sprigs **Obv. Legend:** ALI **Rev:** Value, date within center circle of ornate design

Date	Mintage	F	VF	XF	Unc	BU
AH1319/1901A	300	—	—	200	350	—
AH1320/1902A	300	—	—	200	350	—

KM# 226 10 FRANCS

3.2258 g., 0.9000 Gold 0.0933 oz. AGW **Obv:** Legend flanked by sprigs **Obv. Legend:** ALI **Rev:** Value, date in center circle of ornate design

Date	Mintage	F	VF	XF	Unc	BU
AH1319/1901A	80	—	—	450	850	—
AH1319/1901A	80	—	—	450	850	—
AH1320/1902A	83	—	—	450	850	—

KM# 227 20 FRANCS

6.4516 g., 0.9000 Gold 0.1867 oz. AGW **Obv:** Legend flanked by sprigs **Obv. Legend:** ALI **Rev:** Value, date in center circle of ornate design

Date	Mintage	F	VF	XF	Unc	BU
AH1319/1901A	150,000	—	—	BV	195	—
AH1320/1902A	20	—	—	550	1,000	—

Muhammad al-Hadi Bey

"Struck in his name"

DECIMAL COINAGE

100 Centimes = 1 Franc

The following coins all bear French inscriptions on one side, Arabic on the other, and usually have both AH and AD dates. Except for KM#246-48, they are struck in the name of the Tunisian Bey.

KM# 228 5 CENTIMES

Bronze **Obv:** Inscription within sprigs **Obv. Legend:** MUHAMMAD AL-HADI **Rev:** Value and date within center circle

Date	Mintage	F	VF	XF	Unc	BU
AH1321/1903A	500,000	—	8.00	12.00	25.00	—
AH1322/1904A	1,000,000	—	8.00	12.00	25.00	—

KM# 229 10 CENTIMES

Bronze **Obv:** Inscription within sprigs **Obv. Legend:** MUHAMMAD AL-HADI **Rev:** Value and date within center circle

Date	Mintage	F	VF	XF	Unc	BU
AH1321/1903A	250,000	—	10.00	20.00	30.00	—
AH1322/1904A	500,000	—	10.00	20.00	30.00	—

KM# 230 50 CENTIMES

2.5000 g., 0.8350 Silver 0.0671 oz. ASW **Obv. Legend:** MUHAMMAD AL-HADI

Date	Mintage	F	VF	XF	Unc	BU
AH1321/1903A	1,003	—	—	150	250	—
AH1322/1904A	1,003	—	—	150	250	—
AH1323/1905A	1,003	—	—	150	250	—
AH1324/1906A	1,003	—	—	150	250	—

KM# 231 FRANC

5.0000 g., 0.8350 Silver 0.1342 oz. ASW **Obv. Legend:** MUHAMMAD AL-HADI

Date	Mintage	F	VF	XF	Unc	BU
AH1321/1903A	703	—	—	150	250	—
AH1322/1904A	300,000	—	75.00	100	150	—
AH1323/1905A	703	—	—	150	250	—
AH1324/1906A	703	—	—	150	250	—

KM# 232 2 FRANCS

10.0000 g., 0.8350 Silver 0.2684 oz. ASW **Obv. Legend:** MUHAMMAD AL-HADI

Date	Mintage	F	VF	XF	Unc	BU
AH1321/1903A	303	—	—	150	250	—
AH1322/1904A	150,000	—	100	150	220	—
AH1323/1905A	303	—	—	150	250	—
AH1324/1906A	303	—	—	150	250	—

KM# 233 10 FRANCS

3.2258 g., 0.9000 Gold 0.0933 oz. AGW **Obv. Legend:** MUHAMMAD AL-HADI

Date	Mintage	F	VF	XF	Unc	BU
AH1321/1903A	83	—	—	450	900	—
AH1322/1904A	83	—	—	450	900	—
AH1323/1905A	83	—	—	450	900	—
AH1324/1906A	83	—	—	450	900	—

KM# 234 20 FRANCS

6.4516 g., 0.9000 Gold 0.1867 oz. AGW **Obv:** Inscription within sprigs **Obv. Legend:** MUHAMMAD AL-HADI **Rev:** Value and date within center circle

Date	Mintage	F	VF	XF	Unc	BU
AH1321/1903A	300,000	—	—	BV	190	—
AH1321/1904A	600,000	—	—	BV	190	—
AH1322/1904A	Inc. above	—	—	BV	190	—
AH1323/1905A	23	—	—	550	1,000	—
AH1324/1906A	23	—	—	550	1,000	—

Muhammad al-Nasir Bey

"Struck in his name"

DECIMAL COINAGE

100 Centimes = 1 Franc

The following coins all bear French inscriptions on one side, Arabic on the other, and usually have both AH and AD dates. Except for KM#246-48, they are struck in the name of the Tunisian Bey.

KM# 235 5 CENTIMES

Bronze, 26 mm. **Obv:** Inscription within sprigs **Obv. Legend:** MUHAMMAD AL-NASIR **Rev:** Value and date within center circle **Edge:** Plain

Date	Mintage	F	VF	XF	Unc	BU
AH1325/1907A	1,000,000	—	3.00	6.00	17.00	—
AH1326/1908A	1,000,000	—	3.00	6.00	17.00	—
AH1330/1912A	1,000,000	—	3.00	6.00	17.00	—
AH1332/1914A	1,000,000	—	3.00	6.00	17.00	—
AH1334/1916A	2,000,000	—	3.00	6.00	12.00	—
AH1336/1917A	2,021,000	—	3.00	6.00	12.00	—

KM# 242 5 CENTIMES

Nickel-Bronze, 19 mm. **Obv:** Hole in center of inscription **Obv. Legend:** MOHAMMED AL-NASIR **Rev:** Value above hole in center, date and sprigs

Date	Mintage	F	VF	XF	Unc	BU
AH1337/1918(a)	1,549,000	—	4.00	10.00	25.00	—
AH1337/1919(a)	4,451,000	—	3.00	8.00	20.00	—
AH1338/1920(a)	Inc. above	—	3.00	8.00	20.00	—
AH1338/6/1920(a)	2,206,000	—	4.00	10.00	25.00	—
AH1338/7/1920(a)	Inc. above	—	4.00	10.00	25.00	—
AH1339/1920(a)	Inc. above	—	3.00	8.00	20.00	—

KM# 245 5 CENTIMES

Nickel-Bronze, 17 mm. **Obv:** Hole in center of inscription **Rev:** Value above hole in center, date and sprigs **Note:** Reduced size.

Date	Mintage	F	VF	XF	Unc	BU
AH1339/1920(a)	1,794,000	—	20.00	40.00	75.00	—

KM# 236 10 CENTIMES

9.4000 g., Bronze **Obv:** Inscription within sprigs **Obv. Legend:** MUHAMMAD AL-NASIR **Rev:** Value and date within center circle

Date	Mintage	F	VF	XF	Unc	BU
AH1325/1907A	500,000	—	3.00	8.00	20.00	—
AH1326/1908A	500,000	—	3.00	8.00	20.00	—
AH1329/1911A	500,000	—	3.00	8.00	20.00	—
AH1330/1912A	500,000	—	3.00	8.00	20.00	—
AH1332/1914A	500,000	—	3.00	8.00	20.00	—
AH1334/1916A	1,000,000	—	3.00	8.00	20.00	—
AH1336/1917A	1,050,000	—	3.00	8.00	20.00	—

KM# 243 10 CENTIMES

Nickel-Bronze **Obv:** Hole in center of inscription **Obv. Legend:** MUHAMMAD AL-NASIR **Rev:** Value above hole in center, date and sprigs

Date	Mintage	F	VF	XF	Unc	BU
AH1337/1918(a)	1,288,000	—	3.00	8.00	25.00	—
AH1337/1919(a)	2,712,000	—	3.00	8.00	20.00	—
AH1338/1920(a)	3,000,000	—	3.00	8.00	20.00	—

KM# 244 25 CENTIMES

Nickel-Bronze **Obv:** Hole in center of inscription **Obv. Legend:** MUHAMMAD AL-NASIR **Rev:** Value above hole in center, date and sprigs

Date	Mintage	F	VF	XF	Unc	BU
AH1337/1918(a)	2,000,000	—	5.00	12.00	35.00	—
AH1337/1919(a)	Inc. above	—	4.00	10.00	25.00	—
AH1338/1920(a)	2,000,000	—	4.00	10.00	25.00	—

KM# 237 50 CENTIMES

2.5000 g., 0.8350 Silver 0.0671 oz. ASW **Obv:** Inscription within sprigs **Obv. Legend:** MUHAMMAD AL-NASIR **Rev:** Value and date within center circle

Date	Mintage	F	VF	XF	Unc	BU
AH1325/1907A	201,000	—	10.00	20.00	40.00	—
AH1326/1908A	2,006	—	—	100	150	—
AH1327/1909A	1,003	—	—	100	175	—
AH1328/1910A	1,003	—	—	100	175	—
AH1329/1911A	1,003	—	—	100	175	—
AH1330/1912A	201,000	—	10.00	20.00	40.00	—
AH1331/1913A	1,003	—	—	100	175	—
AH1332/1914A	201,000	—	10.00	20.00	40.00	—
AH1334/1915A	707,000	—	8.00	15.00	30.00	—
AH1334/1916A	3,614,000	—	7.00	12.00	25.00	—
AH1335/1916A	Inc. above	—	7.00	12.00	25.00	—
AH1335/1917A	2,139,000	—	7.00	12.00	25.00	—
AH1336/1917A	Inc. above	—	7.00	12.00	25.00	—
AH1337/1918A	1,003	—	—	100	175	—
AH1338/1919A	1,003	—	—	100	175	—

Date	Mintage	F	VF	XF	Unc	BU
AH1339/1920A	1,003	—	—	100	175	—
AH1340/1921A	1,003	—	—	100	175	—

KM# 238 FRANC

5.0000 g., 0.8350 Silver 0.1342 oz. ASW **Obv:** Inscription within sprigs **Obv. Legend:** MUHAMMAD AL-NASIR **Rev:** Value and date within center circle

Date	Mintage	F	VF	XF	Unc	BU
AH1325/1907A	301,000	—	10.00	20.00	35.00	—
AH1326/1908A	401,000	—	10.00	15.00	35.00	—
AH1327/1909A	703	—	—	135	225	—
AH1328/1910A	703	—	—	135	225	—
AH1329/1911A	1,051,000	—	7.00	12.00	30.00	—
AH1330/1912A	501,000	—	8.00	15.00	30.00	—
AH1331/1913A	703	—	—	135	225	—
AH1332/1914A	201,000	—	8.00	15.00	25.00	—
AH1333/1914A	Inc. above	—	8.00	15.00	25.00	—
AH1334/1915A	1,060,000	—	7.00	12.00	20.00	—
AH1334/1916A	3,270,000	—	7.00	12.00	20.00	—
AH1335/1916A	Inc. above	—	7.00	12.00	20.00	—
AH1335/1917A	1,628,000	—	7.00	12.00	20.00	—
AH1336/1918A	804,000	—	7.00	12.00	18.00	—
AH1337/1918A	Inc. above	—	7.00	12.00	18.00	—
AH1338/1919A	703	—	—	135	225	—
AH1339/1920A	703	—	—	135	225	—
AH1340/1921A	703	—	—	135	225	—

KM# 239 2 FRANCS

10.0000 g., 0.8350 Silver 0.2684 oz. ASW **Obv:** Inscription within sprigs **Obv. Legend:** MUHAMMAD AL-NASIR **Rev:** Value and date within center circle

Date	Mintage	F	VF	XF	Unc	BU
AH1325/1907A	306	—	—	150	250	—
AH1326/1908A	101,000	—	20.00	40.00	100	—
AH1327/1909A	303	—	—	150	250	—
AH1328/1910A	303	—	—	150	250	—
AH1329/1911A	475,000	—	20.00	30.00	50.00	—
AH1330/1912A	200,000	—	20.00	30.00	50.00	—
AH1331/1913A	303	—	—	150	250	—
AH1332/1914A	100,000	—	20.00	30.00	50.00	—
AH1333/1914A	Inc. above	—	20.00	30.00	50.00	—
AH1334/1915A	408,000	—	20.00	30.00	50.00	—
AH1334/1916A	1,000,000	—	20.00	30.00	50.00	—
AH1335/1916A	Inc. above	—	20.00	30.00	50.00	—
AH1336/1917A	303	—	—	150	250	—
AH1337/1918A	303	—	—	150	250	—
AH1338/1919A	303	—	—	150	250	—
AH1339/1920A	303	—	—	150	250	—
AH1340/1921A	303	—	—	150	250	—

KM# 240 10 FRANCS

3.2258 g., 0.9000 Gold 0.0933 oz. AGW **Obv. Legend:** MUHAMMAD AL-NASIR

Date	Mintage	F	VF	XF	Unc	BU
AH1325/1907A	36	—	—	500	900	—
AH1326/1908A	166	—	—	300	500	—
AH1327/1909A	83	—	—	450	850	—
AH1328/1910A	83	—	—	450	850	—
AH1329/1911A	83	—	—	450	850	—
AH1330/1912A	83	—	—	450	850	—
AH1331/1913A	83	—	—	450	850	—
AH1332/1914A	83	—	—	450	850	—
AH1334/1915A	83	—	—	450	850	—
AH1334/1916A	83	—	—	450	850	—
AH1336/1917A	83	—	—	450	850	—
AH1337/1918A	83	—	—	450	850	—
AH1338/1919A	83	—	—	450	850	—
AH1339/1920A	83	—	—	450	850	—
AH1340/1921A	83	—	—	450	850	—

KM# 241 20 FRANCS

6.4516 g., 0.9000 Gold 0.1867 oz. AGW **Obv. Legend:** MUHAMMAD AL-NASIR

Date	Mintage	F	VF	XF	Unc	BU
AH1325/1907A	26	—	—	550	1,000	—
AH1326/1908A	46	—	—	450	850	—
AH1327/1909A	23	—	—	550	1,000	—
AH1328/1910A	23	—	—	550	1,000	—
AH1329/1911A	23	—	—	550	1,000	—
AH1330/1912A	23	—	—	550	1,000	—
AH1331/1913A	23	—	—	550	1,000	—
AH1332/1914A	23	—	—	550	1,000	—

Date	Mintage	F	VF	XF	Unc	BU
AH1334/1915A	23	—	—	550	1,000	—
AH1334/1916A	23	—	—	550	1,000	—
AH1336/1917A	23	—	—	550	1,000	—
AH1337/1918A	23	—	—	550	1,000	—
AH1338/1919A	23	—	—	550	1,000	—
AH1339/1920A	23	—	—	550	1,000	—
AH1340/1921A	23	—	—	550	1,000	—

Muhammad al-Habib Bey

"Struck in his name"

DECIMAL COINAGE

100 Centimes = 1 Franc

The following coins all bear French inscriptions on one side, Arabic on the other, and usually have both AH and AD dates. Except for KM#246-48, they are struck in the name of the Tunisian Bey.

KM# 254 10 CENTIMES

4.0000 g., Nickel-Bronze **Obv:** Hole in center of inscription **Obv. Legend:** MUHAMMAD AL-HABIB **Rev:** Value above hole in center, date and sprigs

Date	Mintage	F	VF	XF	Unc	BU
AH1345/1926(a)	1,000,000	—	20.00	50.00	100	—

KM# 249 50 CENTIMES

2.5000 g., 0.8350 Silver 0.0671 oz. ASW **Obv:** Inscription within sprigs **Obv. Legend:** MUHAMMAD AL-HABIB **Rev:** Value and date within center circle

Date	Mintage	F	VF	XF	Unc	BU
AH1341/1922A	1,003	—	—	100	200	—
AH1342/1923A	2,009	—	—	100	200	—
AH1343/1924A	1,003	—	—	100	200	—
AH1344/1925A	1,003	—	—	100	200	—
AH1345/1926A	1,003	—	—	100	200	—
AH1346/1927A	1,003	—	—	100	200	—
AH1347/1928A	1,003	—	—	100	200	—

KM# 250 FRANC

5.0000 g., 0.8350 Silver 0.1342 oz. ASW **Obv. Legend:** MUHAMMAD AL-HABIB

Date	Mintage	F	VF	XF	Unc	BU
AH1341/1922A	703	—	—	135	275	—
AH1342/1923A	1,409	—	—	100	250	—
AH1343/1924A	703	—	—	135	275	—
AH1344/1925A	703	—	—	135	275	—
AH1345/1926A	703	—	—	135	275	—
AH1346/1927A	703	—	—	135	275	—
AH1347/1928A	703	—	—	135	275	—

KM# 250a FRANC

5.5000 g., 0.8350 Silver 0.1476 oz. ASW

Date	Mintage	F	VF	XF	Unc	BU
AH1347/1928A	Inc. above	—	—	135	275	—

KM# 251 2 FRANCS

10.0000 g., 0.8350 Silver 0.2684 oz. ASW **Obv. Legend:** MUHAMMAD AL-HABIB

Date	Mintage	F	VF	XF	Unc	BU
AH1341/1922A	303	—	—	150	325	—
AH1342/1923A	690	—	—	135	275	—
AH1343/1924A	303	—	—	150	325	—
AH1344/1925A	303	—	—	150	325	—
AH1345/1926A	303	—	—	150	325	—
AH1346/1927A	303	—	—	150	325	—

KM# 251a 2 FRANCS

8.6000 g., 0.8350 Silver 0.2309 oz. ASW

Date	Mintage	F	VF	XF	Unc	BU
AH1347/1928A	303	—	—	150	325	—

KM# 252 10 FRANCS

3.2258 g., 0.9000 Gold 0.0933 oz. AGW **Obv. Legend:** MUHAMMAD AL-HABIB BEY

Date	Mintage	F	VF	XF	Unc	BU
AH1341/1922A	83	—	—	450	850	—
AH1342/1923A	169	—	—	300	500	—
AH1343/1924A	83	—	—	450	850	—
AH1344/1925A	83	—	—	450	850	—
AH1345/1926A	83	—	—	450	850	—
AH1346/1927A	83	—	—	450	850	—
AH1347/1928A	83	—	—	450	850	—

KM# 253 20 FRANCS

6.4516 g., 0.9000 Gold 0.1867 oz. AGW **Obv. Legend:** MUHAMMAD AL-HABIB

Date	Mintage	F	VF	XF	Unc	BU
AH1341/1922A	23	—	—	650	1,100	—
AH1342/1923A	49	—	—	450	850	—
AH1343/1924A	23	—	—	550	1,000	—
AH1344/1925A	23	—	—	550	1,000	—
AH1345/1926A	23	—	—	550	1,000	—
AH1346/1927A	23	—	—	550	1,000	—
AH1347/1928A	23	—	—	550	1,000	—

Ahmad Pasha Bey

"Struck in his name"

DECIMAL COINAGE

100 Centimes = 1 Franc

The following coins all bear French inscriptions on one side, Arabic on the other, and usually have both AH and AD dates. Except for KM#246-48, they are struck in the name of the Tunisian Bey.

KM# 258 5 CENTIMES

2.0000 g., Nickel-Bronze **Obv:** Hole in center of inscription **Obv. Legend:** AHMAD **Rev:** Value above hole in center, date and sprigs

Date	Mintage	F	VF	XF	Unc	BU
AH1350/1931(a)	2,000,000	—	4.00	10.00	25.00	—
AH1352/1933(a)	1,000,000	—	5.00	12.00	30.00	—
AH1357/1938(a)	1,200,000	—	4.00	10.00	25.00	—

KM# 259 10 CENTIMES

Nickel-Bronze **Obv:** Hole in center of inscription **Obv. Legend:** AHMAD **Rev:** Value above hole in center, date and sprigs

Date	Mintage	F	VF	XF	Unc	BU
AH1350/1931(a)	750,000	—	6.00	15.00	35.00	—
AH1352/1933(a)	1,000,000	—	6.00	15.00	35.00	—
AH1357/1938(a)	1,200,000	—	5.00	12.00	25.00	—

KM# 267 10 CENTIMES

2.5000 g., Zinc **Obv. Legend:** AHMAD

Date	Mintage	F	VF	XF	Unc	BU
AH1360/1941(a)	5,000,000	—	2.50	6.00	25.00	—
AH1361/1942(a)	10,000,000	—	1.50	4.00	20.00	—

KM# 268 20 CENTIMES

3.6000 g., Zinc **Obv:** Hole in center of inscription **Obv. Legend:** AHMAD **Rev:** Value above hole in center, date and sprigs

Date	Mintage	F	VF	XF	Unc	BU
AH1361/1942A	5,000,000	—	20.00	35.00	50.00	—

KM# 260 25 CENTIMES

5.0000 g., Nickel-Aluminum-Bronze **Obv:** Hole in center of inscription **Obv. Legend:** AHMAD **Rev:** Value above hole in center, date and sprigs

Date	Mintage	F	VF	XF	Unc	BU
AH1350/1931(a)	300,000	—	8.00	15.00	35.00	—
AH1352/1933(a)	400,000	—	8.00	15.00	35.00	—
AH1357/1938(a)	480,000	—	4.00	10.00	25.00	—

KM# 261 5 FRANCS
5.0000 g., 0.6800 Silver 0.1093 oz. ASW **Obv:** Inscription and date within sprigs **Obv. Legend:** AHMAD **Rev:** Value flanked by designs

Date	Mintage	F	VF	XF	Unc	BU
AH1353 (1934) (a)	2,000,000	—	10.00	18.00	25.00	—
AH1355 (1936) (a)	2,000,000	—	10.00	18.00	25.00	—

KM# 264 5 FRANCS
5.0000 g., 0.6800 Silver 0.1093 oz. ASW **Obv:** Inscription and date within sprigs **Obv. Legend:** AHMAD **Rev:** Value in center of circular inscription and design

Date	Mintage	F	VF	XF	Unc	BU
AH1358/1939(a)	1,600,000	—	15.00	25.00	40.00	—

KM# 255 10 FRANCS
10.0000 g., 0.6800 Silver 0.2186 oz. ASW **Obv:** Inscription within oblong design flanked by sprigs **Obv. Legend:** AHMAD **Rev:** Value and date within center circle of design

Date	Mintage	F	VF	XF	Unc	BU
AH1349/1930(a)	60,000	—	45.00	70.00	110	—
AH1350/1931(a)	1,103	—	150	250	350	—
AH1351/1932(a)	60,000	—	60.00	100	200	—
AH1352/1933(a)	1,103	—	150	250	350	—
AH1353/1934(a)	30,000	—	45.00	70.00	110	—

KM# 262 10 FRANCS
10.0000 g., 0.6800 Silver 0.2186 oz. ASW **Obv:** Inscription and date within sprigs **Rev:** Value flanked by designs

Date	Mintage	F	VF	XF	Unc	BU
AH1353 (1934) (a)	1,501,000	—	10.00	20.00	35.00	—
AH1354 (1935) (a)	1,103	—	—	225	350	—
AH1355 (1936) (a)	2,006	—	—	225	350	—
AH1356 (1937) (a)	1,103	—	—	225	350	—
AH1357 (1938)	—	—	—	400	600	—
AH1358 (1939)	—	—	—	400	600	—

KM# 265 10 FRANCS
10.0000 g., 0.6800 Silver 0.2186 oz. ASW **Obv:** Inscription and date within sprigs **Rev:** Value and date within circular inscription and design

Date	Mintage	F	VF	XF	Unc	BU
AH1358/1939(a)	501,000	—	7.00	15.00	35.00	—
AH1359/1940(a)	—	—	—	225	350	—
AH1360/1941(a)	1,103	—	—	225	350	—
AH1361/1942(a)	1,103	—	—	225	350	—

KM# 256 20 FRANCS
20.0000 g., 0.6800 Silver 0.4372 oz. ASW **Obv:** Inscription within oblong design flanked by sprigs **Obv. Legend:** AHMAD **Rev:** Value and date within center circle of design

Date	Mintage	F	VF	XF	Unc	BU
AH1349/1930(a)	20,000	—	60.00	100	175	—
AH1350/1931(a)	53	—	200	300	500	—
AH1351/1932(a)	20,000	—	75.00	150	275	—
AH1352/1933(a)	53	—	200	300	500	—
AH1353/1934(a)	9,500	—	60.00	100	175	—

Note: It is believed that an additional number of coins dated AH1353/1934(a) were struck and included in mintage figures of KM#263 of the same date

KM# 263 20 FRANCS
20.0000 g., 0.6800 Silver 0.4372 oz. ASW **Obv:** Inscription and date within sprigs **Rev:** Value flanked by designs

Date	Mintage	F	VF	XF	Unc	BU
AH1353 (1934) (a)	1,250,000	—	12.00	25.00	60.00	—
AH1354 (1935) (a)	53	—	—	275	450	—
AH1355 (1936) (a)	106	—	—	225	375	—
AH1356 (1937) (a)	53	—	—	275	450	—

KM# 266 20 FRANCS
20.0000 g., 0.6800 Silver 0.4372 oz. ASW **Obv:** Inscription and date within sprigs **Rev:** Value and date within circular inscription and design

Date	Mintage	F	VF	XF	Unc	BU
AH1358/1939(a)	100,000	—	20.00	40.00	90.00	—
AH1359/1940(a)	—	—	—	—	—	—

Note: Reported, not confirmed

Date	Mintage	F	VF	XF	Unc	BU
AH1360/1941(a)	53	—	—	275	450	—
AH1361/1942(a)	53	—	—	275	450	—

KM# 257 100 FRANCS
6.5500 g., 0.9000 Gold 0.1895 oz. AGW **Obv:** Inscription within oblong design flanked by sprigs **Obv. Legend:** AHMAD **Rev:** Value and date within center circle of design

Date	Mintage	F	VF	XF	Unc	BU
AH1349/1930(a)	3,000	—	—	BV	190	—
AH1350/1931(a)	33	—	—	500	900	—
AH1351/1932(a)	3,000	—	—	BV	190	—
AH1352/1933(a)	33	—	—	500	900	—
AH1353/1934(a)	133	—	—	300	400	—
AH1354/1935(a)	3,000	—	—	BV	190	—
AH1355/1936(a)	33	—	—	500	900	—
AH1356/1937(a)	33	—	—	500	900	—

Muhammad al-Amin Bey

"Struck in his name"

DECIMAL COINAGE

100 Centimes = 1 Franc

The following coins all bear French inscriptions on one side, Arabic on the other, and usually have both AH and AD dates. Except for KM#246-48, they are struck in the name of the Tunisian Bey.

KM# 271 10 CENTIMES
1.6000 g., Nickel-Aluminum-Bronze **Obv:** Hole in center of inscription **Obv. Legend:** MUHAMMAD AL AMIN **Rev:** Value above hole in center, date and sprigs

Date	Mintage	F	VF	XF	Unc	BU
AH1364/1945(a)	10,000,000	—	40.00	75.00	140	—

Note: Most were probably melted

KM# 272 20 CENTIMES
Zinc **Obv:** Hole in center of inscription **Obv. Legend:** MUHAMMAD AL-AMIN **Rev:** Value above hole in center, date and sprigs

Date	Mintage	F	VF	XF	Unc	BU
AH1364/1945(a)	5,205,000	—	60.00	120	200	—

Note: A large quantity was remelted

KM# 273 5 FRANCS
Aluminum-Bronze **Obv:** Inscription and date within sprigs **Obv. Legend:** MUHAMMAD AL-AMIN **Rev:** Value and date within circular inscription and design

Date	Mintage	F	VF	XF	Unc	BU
AH1365/1946(a)	10,000,000	—	1.50	5.00	10.00	—

KM# 277 5 FRANCS
Copper-Nickel **Obv:** Dates within crescent below design **Rev:** Value and date within upper circle

Date	Mintage	F	VF	XF	Unc	BU
AH1373/1954(a)	18,000,000	—	1.00	2.50	5.00	—
AH1376/1957(a)	4,000,000	—	2.00	4.00	7.00	—

KM# 269 10 FRANCS
10.0000 g., 0.6800 Silver 0.2186 oz. ASW **Obv:** Inscription and date within sprigs **Rev:** Value and date within circular inscription and design

Date	Mintage	F	VF	XF	Unc	BU
AH1363/1943(a)	1,503	—	—	225	350	—
AH1364/1944(a)	2,206	—	—	200	300	—

KM# 270 20 FRANCS
20.0000 g., 0.6800 Silver 0.4372 oz. ASW **Obv. Legend:** MUHAMMAD AL-AMIN

Date	Mintage	F	VF	XF	Unc	BU
AH1363/1943(a)	103	—	—	300	500	—
AH1364/1944(a)	106	—	—	300	500	—

KM# 274 20 FRANCS
Copper-Nickel **Obv:** Dates within crescent below design **Rev:** Value and date within upper circle

Date	Mintage	F	VF	XF	Unc	BU
AH1370/1950(a)	10,000,000	—	0.60	2.25	6.50	—
AH1376/1957(a)	4,000,000	—	0.45	1.25	4.50	—

KM# 275 50 FRANCS
Copper-Nickel **Obv:** Dates within crescent below design **Obv. Legend:** MUHAMMAD AL-AMIN **Rev:** Value and date within upper circle

Date	Mintage	F	VF	XF	Unc	BU
AH1370/1950(a)	5,000,000	—	0.60	2.25	6.50	—
AH1376/1957(a)	600,000	—	1.25	2.75	6.50	—

KM# 276 100 FRANCS
Copper-Nickel **Obv:** Dates within crescent below design **Obv. Legend:** MUHAMMAD AL-AMIN **Rev:** Value and date within upper circle

Date	Mintage	F	VF	XF	Unc	BU
AH1370/1950(a)	8,000,000	—	2.25	5.50	11.50	—
AH1376/1957(a)	1,000,000	—	2.25	4.50	10.00	—

Anonymous Ruler

TOKEN COINAGE

KM# 246 50 CENTIMES
1.9500 g., Aluminum-Bronze, 18 mm. **Obv:** Date within wreath **Rev:** Value within wreath **Rev. Inscription:** BON POUR (Good For) 50 CENTIMES

Date	Mintage	F	VF	XF	Unc	BU
AH1340/1921(a)	4,000,000	—	2.00	7.00	20.00	—
AH1345/1926(a)	1,000,000	—	3.00	10.00	25.00	—
AH1352/1933(a)	500,000	—	6.00	17.00	50.00	—
AH1360/1941(a)	4,646,000	—	1.00	3.00	10.00	—
AH1364/1945(a)	11,180,000	—	1.00	2.00	10.00	—

KM# 247 FRANC
Aluminum-Bronze, 23.5 mm. **Obv:** Date within wreath **Rev:** Value within wreath **Rev. Inscription:** BON POUR (Good For) 1 FRANC

Date	Mintage	F	VF	XF	Unc	BU
AH1340/1921(a)	5,000,000	—	2.00	7.00	20.00	—
AH1344/1926(a)	1,000,000	—	2.00	15.00	35.00	—
AH1345/1926(a)	1,000,000	—	4.00	17.00	40.00	—
AH1360/1941(a)	6,612,000	—	1.00	4.00	10.00	—
AH1364/1945(a)	10,699,000	—	1.00	3.00	10.00	—

KM# 248 2 FRANCS
8.1000 g., Aluminum-Bronze **Obv:** Date within wreath **Rev:** Value within wreath **Rev. Inscription:** BON POUR (Good For) 2 FRANCS

Date	Mintage	F	VF	XF	Unc	BU
AH1340/1921(a)	1,500,000	—	3.00	15.00	35.00	—
AH1343/1924(a)	500,000	—	8.00	20.00	50.00	—
AH1345/1926(a)	500,000	—	8.00	20.00	50.00	—
AH1360/1941(a)	1,976,000	—	3.00	8.00	15.00	—
AH1364/1945(a)	6,464,000	—	3.00	6.00	15.00	—

REPUBLIC

DECIMAL COINAGE

1000 Millim = 1 Dinar

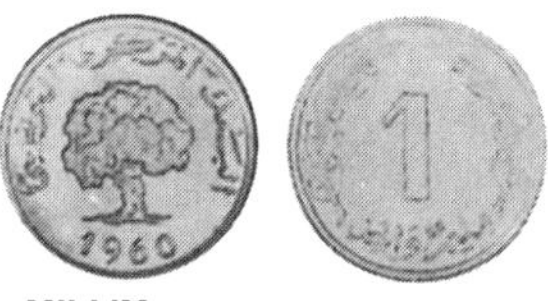

KM# 280 MILLIM
0.6500 g., Aluminum, 18 mm. **Obv:** Oak tree and date **Rev:** Value within sprigs

Date	Mintage	F	VF	XF	Unc	BU
1960	—	—	—	0.10	0.25	—

KM# 349 MILLIM
1.2000 g., Aluminum **Series:** F.A.O. **Obv:** Oak tree and date **Rev:** Value within sprigs

Date	Mintage	F	VF	XF	Unc	BU
1999	—	—	—	—	0.75	—
2000	—	—	—	—	0.75	—

KM# 281 2 MILLIM
1.0000 g., Aluminum, 21 mm. **Obv:** Oak tree and date **Rev:** Value within sprigs

Date	Mintage	F	VF	XF	Unc	BU
1960	—	—	—	0.10	0.25	—

KM# 282 5 MILLIM
1.5000 g., Aluminum, 24 mm. **Obv:** Oak tree and date **Rev:** Value within sprigs

Date	Mintage	F	VF	XF	Unc	BU
1960	—	—	—	0.10	0.25	—
1983	—	—	—	0.10	0.25	—
1993	—	—	—	0.10	0.25	—
1996	—	—	—	0.10	0.25	—

KM# 348 5 MILLIM
1.4900 g., Aluminum, 24 mm. **Obv:** Oak tree and dates **Rev:** Value within sprigs

Date	Mintage	F	VF	XF	Unc	BU
AH1418-1997	—	—	—	—	0.50	—
AH1426-2005	—	—	—	—	0.50	—

KM# 306 10 MILLIM
3.5000 g., Brass, 19 mm. **Obv:** Inscription and dates within inner circle of design **Rev:** Value in center of design **Edge:** Reeded

Date	Mintage	F	VF	XF	Unc	BU
AH1380-1960	—	—	0.15	0.25	0.50	—
AH1414-1993	—	—	0.15	0.25	0.50	—
AH1416-1996	—	—	0.15	0.25	0.50	—
AH1418-1997	—	—	0.15	0.25	0.50	—
AH1426-2005	—	—	0.15	0.25	0.50	—

KM# 307 20 MILLIM
4.5000 g., Brass, 22 mm. **Obv:** Inscription and dates within center circle of design **Rev:** Value within center of design

Date	Mintage	F	VF	XF	Unc	BU
AH1380-1960	—	—	0.30	0.50	0.80	—
AH1403-1983	—	—	0.30	0.50	0.80	—
Note: Large and small date varieties exist.						
AH1414-1993	—	—	0.30	0.50	0.80	—
AH1416-1996	—	—	0.30	0.50	0.80	—
AH1418-1997	—	—	0.30	0.50	0.80	—
AH1426-2005	—	—	0.30	0.50	0.80	—
AH1428-2007	—	—	0.30	0.50	0.80	—

KM# 308 50 MILLIM
6.0000 g., Brass, 25 mm. **Obv:** Inscription and dates within center circle of design **Rev:** Value in center of design

Date	Mintage	F	VF	XF	Unc	BU
AH1380-1960	—	—	0.65	0.85	1.25	—
AH1403-1983	—	—	0.65	0.85	1.25	—
Note: Large and small date varieties exist.						
AH1414-1993	—	—	0.65	0.85	1.25	—
AH1416-1996	—	—	0.65	0.85	1.25	—
AH1418-1997	—	—	0.65	0.85	1.25	—
AH1428-2007	—	—	0.65	0.85	1.25	—

KM# 309 100 MILLIM
7.5000 g., Brass, 27 mm. **Obv:** Inscription and dates within center circle of design **Rev:** Value in center of design

Date	Mintage	F	VF	XF	Unc	BU
AH1380-1960	—	—	1.25	1.50	2.00	—
AH1403-1983	—	—	1.25	1.50	2.00	—
Note: Large and small date varieties exist.						
AH1414-1993	—	—	1.25	1.50	2.00	—
AH1416-1996	—	—	1.25	1.50	2.00	—
AH1418-1997	—	—	1.25	1.50	2.00	—

Date	Mintage	F	VF	XF	Unc	BU
AH1421-2000	—	—	1.25	1.50	2.00	—
AH1426-2005	—	—	1.25	1.50	2.00	—

KM# 291 1/2 DINAR

Nickel **Obv:** Head left **Rev:** Value and date

Date	Mintage	F	VF	XF	Unc	BU
1968(a)	500,000	—	1.00	2.00	4.50	—

KM# 303 1/2 DINAR

Copper-Nickel **Series:** F.A.O. **Obv:** Head left **Rev:** 2 Hands with fruit and wheat sprig

Date	Mintage	F	VF	XF	Unc	BU
1976	700,000	—	1.50	3.50	6.50	—
Note: Variations exist with large and small designer's name						
1983	400,000	—	1.50	3.50	6.50	—

KM# 318 1/2 DINAR

Copper-Nickel **Series:** F.A.O. **Obv:** Map and date **Rev:** 2 Hands with fruit and wheat sprig

Date	Mintage	F	VF	XF	Unc	BU
1988	—	—	1.00	3.00	5.50	—
1990	300,000	—	1.00	3.00	5.50	—

KM# 346 1/2 DINAR

Copper-Nickel **Obv:** Shield within circle **Rev:** 2 Hands with fruit and wheat sprig **Note:** Rim varieties exist.

Date	Mintage	F	VF	XF	Unc	BU
AH1416-1996	5,000,000	—	1.00	2.50	4.50	—
AH1418-1997	—	—	1.00	2.50	4.50	—
AH1418-1998	—	—	1.00	2.50	4.50	—
AH1426-2005	—	—	1.00	2.50	4.50	—
AH1428-2007	—	—	1.00	2.50	4.50	—

KM# 302 DINAR

18.0000 g., 0.6800 Silver 0.3935 oz. ASW **Series:** F.A.O. **Obv:** Head of Habib Bourguiba left **Rev:** Coconut tree, oxen and figure, tractor in background at left

Date	Mintage	F	VF	XF	Unc	BU
1970(a)	100,000	—	6.00	8.00	12.00	—
1970(a) Proof	1,250	Value: 40.00				

KM# 304 DINAR

Copper-Nickel **Series:** F.A.O. **Obv:** Head of Habib Bourguiba left **Rev:** Female half figure right **Note:** Varieties exist. Coins dated 1976 exist with or without dots (error) below iy of Tunisiya.

Date	Mintage	F	VF	XF	Unc	BU
1976	12,000,000	—	2.00	4.00	8.00	—
1983	4,000,000	—	2.00	4.00	8.00	—

KM# 319 DINAR

Copper-Nickel **Series:** F.A.O. **Obv:** Map and date **Rev:** Female half figure right

Date	Mintage	F	VF	XF	Unc	BU
1988	—	—	2.00	4.00	8.00	—
1989	—	—	2.00	4.00	8.00	—
1990	8,000,000	—	2.00	4.00	8.00	—

KM# 347 DINAR

Copper-Nickel **Series:** F.A.O. **Obv:** Shield within circle **Rev:** Female half figure right

Date	Mintage	F	VF	XF	Unc	BU
AH1416-1996	—	—	2.00	4.00	7.50	—
AH1418-1997	—	—	2.00	4.00	7.50	—
AH1428-2007	—	—	2.00	4.00	7.50	—

KM# 350 5 DINARS

10.0000 g., Bi-Metallic Copper-Nickel center in Brass ring, 29 mm. **Obv:** National arms **Rev:** Former president Habib Bourguiba **Edge:** Six reeded and six plain sections **Shape:** 12-sided

Date	Mintage	F	VF	XF	Unc	BU
AH1423-2002	—	—	—	—	6.50	8.00

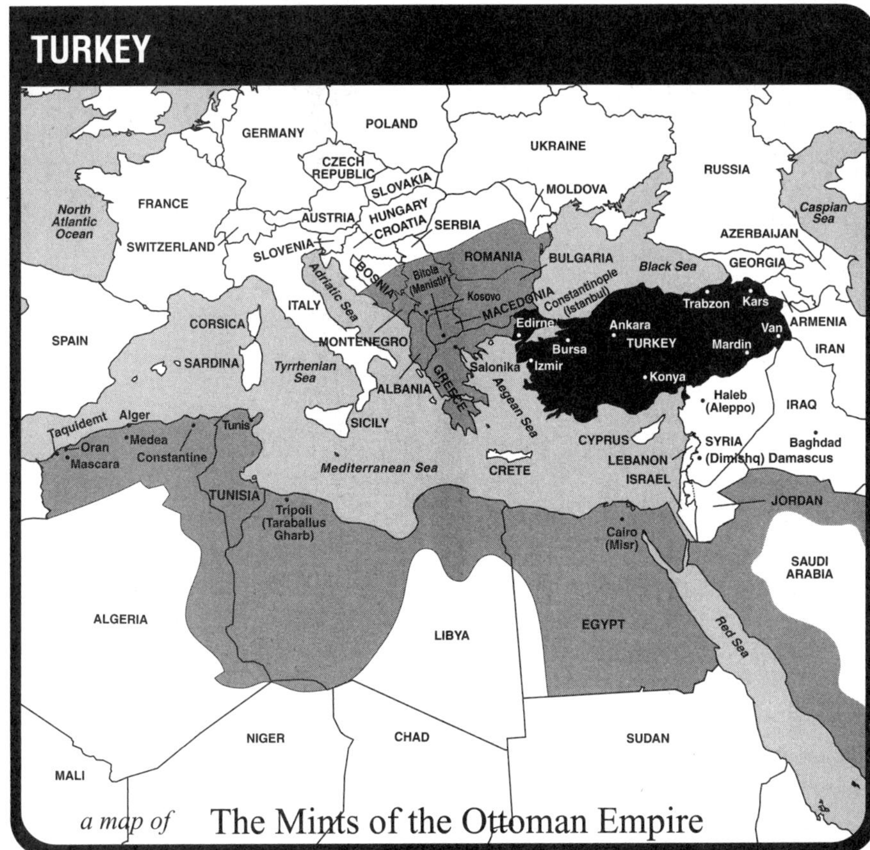

a map of The Mints of the Ottoman Empire

The Republic of Turkey, a parliamentary democracy of the Near East located partially in Europe and partially in Asia between the Black and the Mediterranean Seas, has an area of 301,382 sq. mi. (780,580 sq. km.) and a population of *55.4 million. Capital: Ankara. Turkey exports cotton, hazelnuts, and tobacco, and enjoys a virtual monopoly in meerschaum.

The Ottoman Turks, a tribe from Central Asia, first appeared in the early 13th century, and by the 17th century had established the Ottoman Empire which stretched from the Persian Gulf to the southern frontier of Poland, and from the Caspian Sea to the Algerian plateau. The defeat of the Turkish navy by the Holy League in 1571, and of the Turkish forces besieging Vienna in 1683, began the steady decline of the Ottoman Empire which, accelerated by the rise of nationalism, contracted its European border, and by the end of World War I deprived it of its Arab lands. The present Turkish boundaries were largely fixed by the Treaty of Lausanne in 1923. The sultanate and caliphate, the political and spiritual ruling institutions of the old empire, were separated and the sultanate abolished in 1922. On Oct. 29, 1923, Turkey formally became a republic.

RULERS

Abdul Hamid II, AH1293-1327/1876-1909AD
Muhammad V, AH1327-1336/1909-1918AD
Muhammad VI, AH1336-1341/1918-1923AD
Republic, AH1341/AD1923-

MINT NAMES

قسطنطنية

Constantinople
(Qustantiniyah)

مصر

Misr
See Egypt

MONETARY EQUIVALENTS

3 Akche = 1 Para
5 Para = Beshlik (Beshparalik)
10 Para = Onluk
20 Para = Yirmilik
30 Para = Zolota
40 Para = Kurush (Piastre)
1-1/2 Kurush (Piastres) = Altmishlik

MONETARY SYSTEM

Silver Coinage

40 Para = 1 Kurush (Piastre)
2 Kurush (Piastres) = 1 Ikilik
2-1/2 Kurush (Piastres) = Yuzluk
3 Kurush (Piastres) = Uechlik
5 Kurush (Piastres) = Beshlik
6 Kurush (Piastres) = Altilik

Gold Coinage

100 Kurush (Piastres) = 1 Turkish Pound (Lira)

This system has remained essentially unchanged since its introduction by Ahmad III in 1688, except that the Asper and Para have long since ceased to be coined. The Piastre, established as a crown-sized silver coin approximately equal to the French Ecu of Louis XIV, has shrunk to a tiny copper coin, worth about 1/15 of a U.S. cent. Since the establishment of the Republic in 1923, the Turkish terms, Kurus and Lira, have replaced the European names Piastres and Turkish Pounds.

MINT VISIT ISSUES

From time to time, certain cities of the Ottoman Empire, such as Bursa, Edirne, Kosova, Manistir and Salonika were honored by having special coins struck at Istanbul, but with inscriptions stating that they were struck in the city of honor. These were produced on the occasion of the Sultan's visit to that city. The coins were struck in limited, but not small quantities, and were probably intended for distribution to the notables of the city and the Sultan's own followers. Because they were of the same size and type as the regular circulation issues struck at Istanbul, many specimens found their way into circulation and worn or mounted specimens are found today, although some have been preserved in XF or better condition. Mintage statistics are not known.

MONNAIE DE LUXE

In the 23rd year of the reign of Abdul Hamid II, two parallel series of gold coins were produced, regular mint issues and monnaies de luxe', which were intended primarily for presentation and jewelry purposes. The Monnaie de Luxe' were struck to a slightly less weight and the same fineness as regular issues, but were broader and thinner, and from more ornate dies.

Coins are listed by type, followed by a list of reported years. Most of the reported years have never been confirmed and other years may also exist. Mintage figures are known for the AH1293 and 1327 series, but are unreliable and of little utility.

Although some years are undoubtedly much rarer than others, there is at present no date collecting of Ottoman gold and therefore little justification for higher prices for rare dates.

There is no change in design in the regular series. Only the toughra, accessional date and regnal year vary. The deluxe series show ornamental changes. The standard coins generally do not bear the denomination.

HONORIFIC TITLES

El Ghazi

Reshat

The first coinage of Abdul Hamid II has a flower right of the toughra while the second coinage has *el Ghazi* (The Victorious). The first coinage of Mohammad Reshat V has *Reshat* right of the toughra while his second coinage has *el Ghazi.*

SULTANATE

Abdul Hamid II

AH1293-1327/1876-1909AD

MILLED COINAGE

Gold Issues

KM# 745 12-1/2 KURUSH

0.8770 g., 0.9170 Gold 0.0259 oz. AGW **Series:** Monnaie de Luxe **Obv:** Toughra **Mint:** Qustantiniyah

Date	Mintage	VG	F	VF	XF	Unc
AH1293//27	720	—	—	—	—	—
AH1293//28	800	40.00	120	200	300	—
AH1293//29	11,696	30.00	70.00	150	220	—
AH1293//30	13,208	30.00	70.00	150	220	—
AH1293//31	24,504	30.00	70.00	150	220	—
AH1293//32	14,392	30.00	70.00	150	220	—
AH1293//33	13,032	30.00	70.00	150	220	—
AH1293//34	—	40.00	120	200	300	—

KM# 729 25 KURUSH

1.8040 g., 0.9170 Gold 0.0532 oz. AGW **Obv:** Toughra; "el-Ghazi" to right **Rev:** Text, value and date within wreath, star above **Mint:** Qustantiniyah

Date	Mintage	VG	F	VF	XF	Unc
AH1293//27	99,500	—	BV	55.00	70.00	—
AH1293//28	77,300	—	BV	55.00	70.00	—
AH1293//29	101,548	—	BV	55.00	70.00	—
AH1293//30	156,280	—	BV	55.00	70.00	—
AH1293//31	58,404	—	BV	55.00	70.00	—
AH1293//32	112,000	—	BV	55.00	70.00	—
AH1293//33	15,535	—	BV	55.00	70.00	—
AH1293//34	115,484	—	BV	55.00	70.00	—

KM# 739 25 KURUSH

1.7540 g., 0.9170 Gold 0.0517 oz. AGW **Series:** Monnaie de Luxe **Obv:** Toughra; "el-Ghazi" to right **Rev:** Text, value and date in beaded circle within circular text **Mint:** Qustantiniyah

Date	Mintage	VG	F	VF	XF	Unc
AH1293//27	7,620	55.00	70.00	120	180	—
AH1293//28	9,268	55.00	70.00	120	180	—
AH1293//29	29,056	55.00	70.00	120	180	—
AH1293//30	27,964	55.00	70.00	120	180	—
AH1293//31	39,192	55.00	70.00	120	180	—
AH1293//32	41,696	55.00	70.00	120	180	—
AH1293//33	17,728	55.00	70.00	120	180	—
AH1293//34	—	55.00	95.00	150	200	—

KM# 731 50 KURUSH

3.6080 g., 0.9170 Gold 0.1064 oz. AGW **Obv:** Toughra; "el-Ghazi" to right **Rev:** Text, value and date within wreath, star above **Mint:** Qustantiniyah

Date	Mintage	VG	F	VF	XF	Unc
AH1293//27	14,200	—	—	BV	110	—
AH1293//28	33,450	—	—	BV	110	—
AH1293//29	24,244	—	—	BV	110	—
AH1293//30	66,000	—	—	BV	110	—
AH1293//31	58,612	—	—	BV	110	—
AH1293//32	48,000	—	—	BV	110	—
AH1293//33	16,145	—	—	BV	110	—
AH1293//34	6,276	—	—	BV	150	—

KM# 740 50 KURUSH

3.5080 g., 0.9170 Gold 0.1034 oz. AGW **Series:** Monnaie de Luxe **Obv:** Toughra; "el-Ghazi" to right **Rev:** Text, value and date in beaded circle within circular text **Mint:** Qustantiniyah

Date	Mintage	VG	F	VF	XF	Unc
AH1293//27	6,630	—	BV	140	200	—
AH1293//28	8,660	—	BV	140	200	—

Date	Mintage	VG	F	VF	XF	Unc
AH1293//29	14,924	—	BV	140	200	—
AH1293//30	18,812	—	BV	140	200	—
AH1293//31	22,460	—	BV	140	200	—
AH1293//32	27,542	—	BV	140	200	—
AH1293//33	12,886	—	BV	140	200	—
AH1293//34	—	—	BV	180	250	—

KM# 730 100 KURUSH

7.2160 g., 0.9170 Gold 0.2127 oz. AGW **Obv:** Toughra; "el-Ghazi" to right **Rev:** Text, value and date within wreath, star above **Mint:** Qustantiniyah

Date	Mintage	VG	F	VF	XF	Unc
AH1293//27	48,200	—	—	BV	210	—
AH1293//28	865,011	—	—	BV	210	—
AH1293//29	1,026,275	—	—	BV	210	—
AH1293//30	1,643,795	—	—	BV	210	—
AH1293//31	2,748,448	—	—	BV	210	—
AH1293//32	1,951,611	—	—	BV	210	—
AH1293//33	962,672	—	—	BV	210	—
AH1293//34	1,715,274	—	BV	210	250	—

KM# 741 100 KURUSH

7.0160 g., 0.9170 Gold 0.2068 oz. AGW **Series:** Monnaie de Luxe **Obv:** Toughra; "el-Ghazi" to right **Rev:** Text, value and date in beaded circle within circular text **Mint:** Qustantiniyah

Date	Mintage	VG	F	VF	XF	Unc
AH1293//27	9,580	—	—	BV	220	—
AH1293//28	13,638	—	—	BV	220	—
AH1293//29	18,129	—	—	BV	220	—
AH1293//30	22,796	—	—	BV	220	—
AH1293//31	31,126	—	—	BV	220	—
AH1293//32	42,662	—	—	BV	220	—
AH1293//33	18,716	—	—	BV	220	—
AH1293//34	—	—	—	BV	250	—

KM# 732 250 KURUSH

18.0400 g., 0.9170 Gold 0.5318 oz. AGW **Obv:** Toughra; "el-Ghazi" to right **Rev:** Text, value and date within wreath, star above **Mint:** Qustantiniyah

Date	Mintage	VG	F	VF	XF	Unc
AH1293//27	1,450	—	—	BV	525	—
AH1293//28	7,027	—	—	BV	525	—
AH1293//29	7,522	—	—	BV	525	—
AH1293//30	4,900	—	—	BV	525	—
AH1293//31	8,552	—	—	BV	525	—
AH1293//32	8,729	—	—	BV	525	—
AH1293//33	2,669	—	—	BV	525	—
AH1293//34	6,478	—	—	BV	600	—

KM# 742 250 KURUSH

17.5400 g., 0.9170 Gold 0.5171 oz. AGW **Series:** Monnaie de Luxe **Obv:** Toughra; "el-Ghazi" to right **Rev:** Text, value and date within beaded circle, designed wreath **Mint:** Qustantiniyah

Date	Mintage	VG	F	VF	XF	Unc
AH1293//27	1,770	—	BV	500	750	—
AH1293//28	1,520	—	BV	500	750	—
AH1293//29	1,631	—	BV	500	750	—
AH1293//30	1,922	—	BV	500	750	—
AH1293//31	1,778	—	BV	500	750	—
AH1293//32	2,650	—	BV	500	750	—
AH1293//33	931	—	BV	800	1,000	—
AH1293//34 Rare	—	—	—	—	—	—

KM# 733 500 KURUSH

36.0800 g., 0.9170 Gold 1.0637 oz. AGW **Obv:** Toughra; "el-Ghazi" to right **Rev:** Text, value and date within wreath, star above **Mint:** Qustantiniyah

Date	Mintage	VG	F	VF	XF	Unc
AH1293//27	22,450	—	—	BV	1,025	—
AH1293//28	35,918	—	—	BV	1,025	—
AH1293//29	16,621	—	—	BV	1,025	—
AH1293//30	33,129	—	—	BV	1,025	—
AH1293//31	40,953	—	—	BV	1,025	—
AH1293//32	32,516	—	—	BV	1,025	—
AH1293//33	16,403	—	—	BV	1,025	—
AH1293//34	39,028	—	—	BV	1,025	—

KM# 746 500 KURUSH

35.0800 g., 0.9170 Gold 1.0342 oz. AGW **Series:** Monnaie de Luxe **Obv:** Radiant Toughra above crossed flags, ornamental base **Rev:** Inscription and date within star and designed border **Mint:** Qustantiniyah

Date	Mintage	VG	F	VF	XF	Unc
AH1293//27	1,428	—	BV	1,100	1,200	—
AH1293//28	858	—	BV	1,100	1,200	—
AH1293//29	804	—	BV	1,100	1,200	—
AH1293//30	1,204	—	BV	1,100	1,200	—
AH1293//31	1,021	—	BV	1,100	1,200	—
AH1293//32	1,334	—	BV	1,100	1,200	—
AH1293//33	812	—	BV	1,100	1,200	—
AH1293//34	—	—	BV	1,100	1,200	—

STANDARD COINAGE

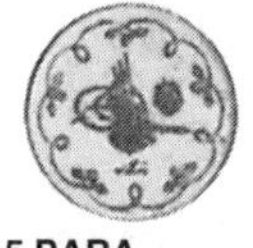

KM# 743 5 PARA

1.0023 g., 0.1000 Silver 0.0032 oz. ASW **Obv:** Toughra; "el-Ghazi" to right **Rev:** Text within crescent below value, date and star **Mint:** Qustantiniyah

Date	Mintage	VG	F	VF	XF	Unc
AH1293//27 (1901)	—	0.25	0.50	1.25	4.00	—
AH1293//28 (1902)	—	0.50	1.00	3.00	12.00	—
AH1293//30 (1904)	—	6.00	12.00	20.00	40.00	—

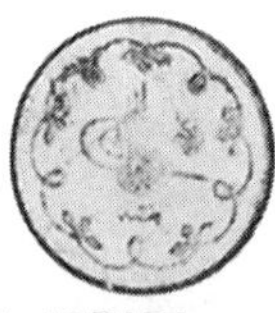

KM# 744 10 PARA

2.0046 g., 0.1000 Silver 0.0064 oz. ASW **Obv:** Toughra; "el-Ghazi" to right **Rev:** Text within crescent below date, value and star **Mint:** Qustantiniyah

Date	Mintage	VG	F	VF	XF	Unc
AH1293//27 (1901)	—	0.25	0.50	1.00	4.00	—
Note: Varieties exist in size of regnal year 27						
AH1293//28 (1902)	—	0.25	0.50	1.50	6.00	—
AH1293//30 (1904)	—	1.00	2.00	5.00	15.00	—

KM# 735 KURUSH

1.2027 g., 0.8300 Silver 0.0321 oz. ASW **Obv:** Toughra; "el-Ghazi" to right **Rev:** Text, value and date within circle of stars **Mint:** Qustantiniyah **Note:** Varieties exist in the size of year and inscription.

Date	Mintage	VG	F	VF	XF	Unc
AH1293//27 (1901)	9,945,000	1.00	2.00	3.00	5.00	—
AH1293//28 (1902)	16,139,000	1.00	2.00	3.00	5.00	—
AH1293//29 (1903)	7,076,000	1.00	2.00	3.00	5.00	—
AH1293//30 (1904)	707,000	2.00	4.00	8.00	15.00	—
AH1293//31 (1905)	1,366,000	1.00	2.00	3.00	5.00	—
AH1293//32 (1906)	1,140,000	1.00	2.00	3.00	5.00	—
AH1293//33 (1907)	1,700,000	1.00	2.00	3.00	5.00	—
AH1293//34 (1908)	—	150	200	230	260	—

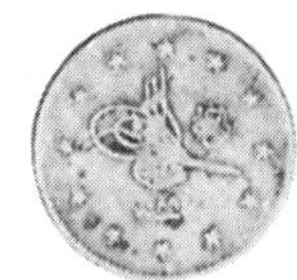
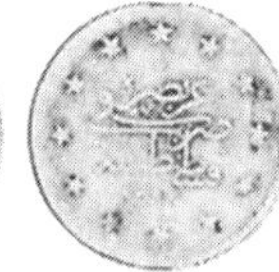

KM# 736 2 KURUSH

2.4055 g., 0.8300 Silver 0.0642 oz. ASW **Obv:** Toughra; "el-Ghazi" to right **Rev:** Text, value and date within circle of stars **Mint:** Qustantiniyah **Note:** Varieties exist in the size of toughra and year.

Date	Mintage	VG	F	VF	XF	Unc
AH1293//27 (1901)	4,689,000	1.50	2.00	4.00	7.00	—
AH1293//28 (1902)	7,567,000	1.50	2.00	4.00	7.00	—
AH1293//29 (1903)	7,775,000	1.50	2.00	4.00	7.00	—
AH1293//30 (1904)	1,366,000	1.50	2.00	4.00	7.00	—
AH1293//31 (1905)	3,014,000	1.50	2.00	4.00	7.00	—
AH1293//32 (1906)	1,625,000	1.50	2.00	4.00	7.00	—
AH1293//33 (1907)	2,173,000	1.50	2.00	4.00	7.00	—
AH1293//34 (1908)	—	150	225	250	300	—

KM# 737 5 KURUSH

6.0130 g., 0.8300 Silver 0.1605 oz. ASW **Obv:** Toughra; "el-Ghazi" to right **Rev:** Text, value and date within circle of stars and crescent border **Mint:** Qustantiniyah **Note:** Varieties exist in the size of toughra, inscription, and date.

Date	Mintage	VG	F	VF	XF	Unc
AH1293//27 (1901)	16,000	15.00	30.00	45.00	75.00	—
AH1293//28 (1902)	6,000	100	150	175	200	—
AH1293//29 (1903)	7,000	100	150	175	200	—
AH1293//30 (1904)	38,000	5.00	10.00	15.00	30.00	—
AH1293//31 (1905)	Inc. above	3.50	4.50	7.00	15.00	—
AH1293//31/0 (1905)	3,175,000	6.00	13.00	25.00	35.00	—
AH1293//32 (1906)	3,334,000	2.50	3.75	5.00	9.50	—
AH1293//33 (1907)	907,000	3.00	5.00	9.00	16.00	—
AH1293//34 (1908)	—	200	225	275	350	—

KM# 738 10 KURUSH

12.0270 g., 0.8300 Silver 0.3209 oz. ASW **Obv:** Toughra; "el-Ghazi" to right **Rev:** Text, value and date within circle of stars and crescent border

Date	Mintage	VG	F	VF	XF	Unc
AH1293//31 (1905)	51,000	60.00	100	120	150	—
AH1293//32 (1906)	575,000	7.50	12.50	18.00	30.00	—
AH1293//33 (1907)	274,000	6.50	11.50	20.00	35.00	—

Muhammad V
AH1327-36/1909-18AD

MILLED COINAGE
Gold Issues

KM# 762 12-1/2 KURUSH

0.9020 g., 0.9170 Gold 0.0266 oz. AGW **Series:** Monnaie de Luxe **Obv:** Toughra; "Reshat" to right **Rev:** Value and date within designed wreath **Mint:** Qustantiniyah

Date	Mintage	VG	F	VF	XF	Unc
AH1327//2	43,568	30.00	50.00	90.00	130	—
AH1327//3	50,368	30.00	50.00	90.00	130	—
AH1327//4	19,344	30.00	50.00	90.00	130	—
AH1327//5	9,160	30.00	50.00	90.00	130	—
AH1327//6	11,880	30.00	50.00	90.00	130	—

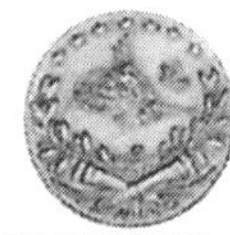

KM# 752 25 KURUSH

1.8040 g., 0.9170 Gold 0.0532 oz. AGW **Obv:** Toughra; "Reshat" to right **Rev:** Inscription and date within wreath, star on top **Mint:** Qustantiniyah

Date	Mintage	VG	F	VF	XF	Unc
AH1327//1	115,484	—	—	BV	55.00	—
AH1327//2	194,740	—	—	BV	55.00	—
AH1327//3	249,416	—	—	BV	55.00	—
AH1327//4	338,172	—	—	BV	55.00	—
AH1327//5	167,592	—	—	BV	55.00	—
AH1327//6	72,872	—	—	BV	55.00	—

KM# 763 25 KURUSH

1.7540 g., 0.9170 Gold 0.0517 oz. AGW **Series:** Monnaie de Luxe **Obv:** Toughra within designed wreath **Rev:** Inscription and date within designed wreath **Mint:** Qustantiniyah

Date	Mintage	VG	F	VF	XF	Unc
AH1327//2	47,788	BV	60.00	90.00	120	—
AH1327//3	70,775	BV	60.00	90.00	120	—
AH1327//4	47,088	BV	60.00	90.00	120	—
AH1327//5	25,964	55.00	80.00	110	140	—
AH1327//6	23,348	55.00	80.00	110	140	—

KM# 773 25 KURUSH

1.8040 g., 0.9170 Gold 0.0532 oz. AGW **Obv:** Toughra; "el-Ghazi" to right **Rev:** Inscription and date within wreath, star on top **Mint:** Qustantiniyah

Date	Mintage	VG	F	VF	XF	Unc
AH1327//7	22,420	—	—	55.00	75.00	—
AH1327//8	5,926	—	—	55.00	75.00	—
AH1327//9	4,060	—	—	55.00	75.00	—
AH1327//10	53,524	1,000	1,500	2,000	—	—

KM# 774 25 KURUSH

1.7540 g., 0.9170 Gold 0.0517 oz. AGW **Series:** Monnaie de Luxe **Obv:** Toughra **Mint:** Qustantiniyah

Date	Mintage	VG	F	VF	XF	Unc
AH1327//8	10,612	1,750	2,500	3,500	5,000	—

KM# 753 50 KURUSH

3.6080 g., 0.9170 Gold 0.1064 oz. AGW **Obv:** Toughra; "Reshat" to right **Rev:** Inscription and date within wreath, star on top **Mint:** Qustantiniyah

Date	Mintage	VG	F	VF	XF	Unc
AH1327//1	6,276	1,000	1,500	2,000	3,000	—
AH1327//2	89,712	—	—	BV	110	—
AH1327//3	75,442	—	—	BV	110	—
AH1327//4	96,030	—	—	BV	110	—
AH1327//5	40,618	—	—	BV	110	—
AH1327//6	26,408	—	—	BV	110	—

KM# 764 50 KURUSH

3.5080 g., 0.9170 Gold 0.1034 oz. AGW **Series:** Monnaie de Luxe **Obv:** Toughra within designed wreath **Rev:** Inscription and date within designed wreath **Mint:** Qustantiniyah

Date	Mintage	VG	F	VF	XF	Unc
AH1327//2	25,224	—	BV	140	180	—
AH1327//3	23,971	—	BV	140	180	—
AH1327//4	15,716	—	BV	140	180	—
AH1327//5	17,118	—	BV	140	180	—
AH1327//6	8,706	—	BV	180	250	—

KM# 775 50 KURUSH

3.6080 g., 0.9170 Gold 0.1064 oz. AGW **Obv:** Toughra; "el-Ghazi" to right **Mint:** Qustantiniyah

Date	Mintage	VG	F	VF	XF	Unc
AH1327//7	9,175	—	BV	150	250	—
AH1327//8	7,330	—	BV	150	250	—
AH1327//9	2,000	—	BV	150	250	—
AH1327//10	53,524	1,000	1,500	2,000	3,000	—

KM# 781 50 KURUSH

3.5080 g., 0.9170 Gold 0.1034 oz. AGW **Series:** Monnaie de Luxe **Obv:** Toughra **Mint:** Qustantiniyah

Date	Mintage	VG	F	VF	XF	Unc
AH1327//8	3,291	250	500	800	1,200	—

KM# 754 100 KURUSH

7.2160 g., 0.9170 Gold 0.2127 oz. AGW **Obv:** Toughra; "Reshat" to right **Rev:** Inscription and date within wreath, star on top **Mint:** Qustantiniyah

Date	Mintage	VG	F	VF	XF	Unc
AH1327//1	1,715,274	—	—	BV	210	—
AH1327//2	3,376,679	—	—	BV	210	—
AH1327//3	4,627,115	—	—	BV	210	—
AH1327//4	3,591,676	—	—	BV	210	—
AH1327//5	881,895	—	—	BV	210	—
AH1327//6	3,769,100	—	—	BV	210	—
AH1327//7	2,989,609	—	—	BV	210	—

KM# 755 100 KURUSH

7.0160 g., 0.9170 Gold 0.2068 oz. AGW **Series:** Monnaie de Luxe **Obv:** Toughra within designed wreath **Rev:** Inscription and date within designed wreath

Date	Mintage	VG	F	VF	XF	Unc
AH1327//1	—	—	—	BV	250	—
AH1327//2	37,110	—	—	BV	250	—
AH1327//3	53,738	—	—	BV	250	—
AH1327//4	41,507	—	—	BV	250	—
AH1327//5	58,819	—	—	BV	250	—
AH1327//6	19,768	—	—	BV	250	—

KM# 776 100 KURUSH

7.2160 g., 0.9170 Gold 0.2127 oz. AGW **Obv:** Toughra; "el-Ghazi" to right **Rev:** Inscription and date within wreath, star on top **Mint:** Qustantiniyah

Date	Mintage	VG	F	VF	XF	Unc
AH1327//7	1,232,090	—	—	BV	210	—
AH1327//8	Inc. above	—	—	BV	210	—
AH1327//9	3,582,005	—	—	BV	210	—
AH1327//10	—	—	—	BV	210	—

KM# 756 250 KURUSH

18.0400 g., 0.9170 Gold 0.5318 oz. AGW **Obv:** Toughra; "Reshat" to right **Rev:** Inscription and date within wreath, star on top **Mint:** Qustantiniyah

Date	Mintage	VG	F	VF	XF	Unc
AH1327//1	6,878	—	—	BV	510	—
AH1327//2	9,207	—	—	BV	510	—
AH1327//3	9,990	—	—	BV	510	—
AH1327//4	13,400	—	—	BV	510	—
AH1327//5	18,143	—	—	BV	510	—
AH1327//6	6,155	—	—	BV	510	—

KM# 757 250 KURUSH

17.5400 g., 0.9170 Gold 0.5171 oz. AGW **Series:** Monnaie de Luxe **Obv:** Toughra within designed wreath **Rev:** Inscription and date within designed wreath **Mint:** Qustantiniyah

Date	Mintage	VG	F	VF	XF	Unc
AH1327//1	—	BV	500	600	800	—
AH1327//2	6,995	BV	500	600	800	—
AH1327//3	12,084	BV	500	600	800	—
AH1327//4	10,250	BV	500	600	800	—
AH1327//5	16,879	BV	500	600	800	—
AH1327//6	9,039	BV	500	600	800	—

KM# 777 250 KURUSH

18.0400 g., 0.9170 Gold 0.5318 oz. AGW **Obv:** Toughra; "el-Ghazi" to right **Rev:** Inscription and date within wreath, star on top **Mint:** Qustantiniyah

Date	Mintage	VG	F	VF	XF	Unc
AH1327//7	30	1,250	1,750	2,800	4,000	—
AH1327//8	21	1,750	2,500	3,500	5,000	—
AH1327//9	28	1,750	2,500	3,500	5,000	—

KM# 783 250 KURUSH

17.5400 g., 0.9170 Gold 0.5171 oz. AGW **Series:** Monnaie de Luxe **Obv:** Toughra within designed wreath **Rev:** Inscription and date within designed wreath **Mint:** Qustantiniyah

Date	Mintage	VG	F	VF	XF	Unc
AH1327//8	3,107	1,250	1,750	2,500	3,500	—

KM# 758 500 KURUSH

17.5400 g., 0.9170 Gold 0.5171 oz. AGW **Obv:** Toughra; "Reshat" to right **Rev:** Inscription and date within wreath, star on top **Mint:** Qustantiniyah

Date	Mintage	VG	F	VF	XF	Unc
AH1327//1	39,028	—	BV	525	650	—
AH1327//2	37,474	—	BV	525	650	—
AH1327//3	53,900	—	BV	525	650	—
AH1327//4	41,863	—	BV	525	650	—
AH1327//5	36,996	—	BV	525	650	—
AH1327//6	17,792	—	BV	525	650	—

KM# 765 500 KURUSH

35.0800 g., 0.9170 Gold 1.0342 oz. AGW **Series:** Monnaie de Luxe **Obv:** Radiant Toughra above crossed flags, ornamental base **Rev:** Inscription and date within designed wreath **Mint:** Qustantiniyah

Date	Mintage	VG	F	VF	XF	Unc
AH1327//2	1,718	—	BV	1,000	1,350	—
AH1327//3	4,631	—	BV	1,000	1,350	—
AH1327//4	3,887	—	BV	1,000	1,350	—
AH1327//5	5,145	—	BV	1,000	1,350	—
AH1327//6	2,401	—	BV	1,000	1,350	—

KM# 784 500 KURUSH

36.0800 g., 0.9170 Gold 1.0637 oz. AGW **Obv:** Toughra; "el-Ghazi" to right **Rev:** Inscription and date within wreath, star on top **Mint:** Qustantiniyah

Date	Mintage	VG	F	VF	XF	Unc
AH1327//7	484	1,750	2,500	3,500	5,000	—
AH1327//8	19	1,750	2,750	4,250	6,000	—
AH1327//9	22	1,750	2,750	4,250	6,000	—
AH1327//10	—	1,750	2,500	3,500	5,000	—

KM# 778 500 KURUSH

35.0800 g., 0.9170 Gold 1.0342 oz. AGW **Series:** Monnaie de Luxe **Obv:** Radiant Toughra above crossed flags, ornamental base **Rev:** Inscription and date within designed wreath **Mint:** Qustantiniyah **Note:** Struck at Qustantiniyah.

Date	Mintage	VG	F	VF	XF	Unc
AH1327//7	295	1,200	1,750	2,500	3,500	—
AH1327//8	1,618	1,000	1,500	2,200	3,000	—

MILLED COINAGE

Gold Mint Visit Issues

Muhammad V's visit to Bursa

KM# 787 25 KURUSH

1.8040 g., 0.9170 Gold 0.0532 oz. AGW **Obv:** Toughra in center of sprigs and stars **Rev:** Inscription and date within wreath, star on top **Mint:** Bursa

Date	Mintage	F	VF	XF	Unc	BU
AH1327//1	—	185	275	400	800	—

KM# 788 50 KURUSH

3.6080 g., 0.9170 Gold 0.1064 oz. AGW **Obv:** Toughra in center of sprigs and stars **Rev:** Inscription and date within wreath, star on top **Mint:** Bursa

Date	Mintage	F	VF	XF	Unc	BU
AH1327//1	—	165	275	350	650	—

KM# 789 100 KURUSH

7.2160 g., 0.9170 Gold 0.2127 oz. AGW **Obv:** Toughra in center of sprigs and stars **Rev:** Inscription and date within wreath, star on top **Mint:** Bursa

Date	Mintage	F	VF	XF	Unc	BU
AH1327//1	—	215	325	400	700	—

MILLED COINAGE

Gold Mint Visit Issues

Muhammad V visit to Edirne

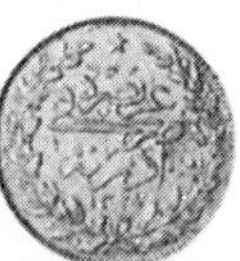

KM# 793 50 KURUSH

3.6080 g., 0.9170 Gold 0.1064 oz. AGW **Obv:** Toughra in center of sprigs and stars **Rev:** Inscription and date within wreath, star on top **Mint:** Edirne

Date	Mintage	F	VF	XF	Unc	BU
AH1327//2	—	200	275	350	600	—

KM# 794 100 KURUSH
7.2160 g., 0.9170 Gold 0.2127 oz. AGW **Obv:** Toughra in center of sprigs and stars **Rev:** Inscription and date within wreath, star on top **Mint:** Edirne

Date	Mintage	F	VF	XF	Unc	BU
AH1327//2	—	250	350	475	700	—

KM# 795 500 KURUSH
36.0800 g., 0.9170 Gold 1.0637 oz. AGW **Obv:** Toughra in center of sprigs and stars **Rev:** Inscription and date within wreath, star on top **Mint:** Edirne

Date	Mintage	F	VF	XF	Unc	BU
AH1327//2	—	1,500	2,500	3,500	4,000	—

MILLED COINAGE

Gold Mint Visit Issues

Muhammad Vs visit to Kosova

KM# 799 50 KURUSH
3.6080 g., 0.9170 Gold 0.1064 oz. AGW **Obv:** Toughra in center of sprigs and stars **Rev:** Inscription and date within wreath, star on top **Mint:** Kosova

Date	Mintage	F	VF	XF	Unc	BU
AH1327//3	1,200	225	275	400	700	—

KM# 800 100 KURUSH
7.2160 g., 0.9170 Gold 0.2127 oz. AGW **Obv:** Toughra in center of stars and sprigs **Rev:** Inscription and date within wreath, star on top **Mint:** Kosova

Date	Mintage	F	VF	XF	Unc	BU
AH1327//3	750	250	300	450	750	—

KM# 801 500 KURUSH
36.0800 g., 0.9170 Gold 1.0637 oz. AGW **Obv:** Toughra in center of stars and sprigs **Rev:** Inscription and date within wreath, star on top **Mint:** Kosova

Date	Mintage	F	VF	XF	Unc	BU
AH1327//3	20	3,000	4,000	5,000	6,000	—

MILLED COINAGE

Gold Mint Visit Issues

Muhammad V's visit to Manastir

KM# 805 50 KURUSH
3.6080 g., 0.9170 Gold 0.1064 oz. AGW **Obv:** Toughra in center of sprigs and stars **Rev:** Inscription and date within wreath, star on top **Mint:** Manastir

Date	Mintage	F	VF	XF	Unc	BU
AH1327//3	1,200	200	325	450	700	—

KM# 806 100 KURUSH
7.2160 g., 0.9170 Gold 0.2127 oz. AGW **Obv:** Toughra in center of sprigs and stars **Rev:** Inscription and date within wreath, star on top **Mint:** Manastir

Date	Mintage	F	VF	XF	Unc	BU
AH1327//3	750	225	350	450	750	—

KM# 807 500 KURUSH
36.0800 g., 0.9170 Gold 1.0637 oz. AGW **Obv:** Toughra in center of sprigs and stars **Rev:** Inscription and date within wreath, star on top **Mint:** Manastir

Date	Mintage	F	VF	XF	Unc	BU
AH1327//3	20	2,500	4,000	5,000	6,250	—

MILLED COINAGE

Gold Mint Visit Issues

Muhammad V's visit to Salonika

KM# 811 50 KURUSH
3.6080 g., 0.9170 Gold 0.1064 oz. AGW **Obv:** Toughra in center of sprigs and stars **Rev:** Inscription and date within wreath, star on top **Mint:** Salonika

Date	Mintage	F	VF	XF	Unc	BU
AH1327//3	1,200	200	325	400	700	—

KM# 812 100 KURUSH
7.2160 g., 0.9170 Gold 0.2127 oz. AGW **Obv:** Toughra in center of sprigs and stars **Rev:** Inscription and date within wreath, star on top **Mint:** Salonika

Date	Mintage	F	VF	XF	Unc	BU
AH1327//3	750	225	350	450	750	—

KM# 813 500 KURUSH
36.0800 g., 0.9170 Gold 1.0637 oz. AGW **Obv:** Toughra in center of sprigs and stars **Rev:** Inscription and date within wreath, star on top **Mint:** Salonika

Date	Mintage	F	VF	XF	Unc	BU
AH1327//3	20	2,500	4,000	5,250	6,750	—

STANDARD COINAGE

KM# 759 5 PARA
Nickel **Obv:** Toughra; "Reshat" to right **Rev:** Value within beaded circle above sprigs **Mint:** Qustantiniyah

Date	Mintage	Good	VG	F	VF	XF
AH1327//2 (1910)	1,664,000	—	2.00	4.00	6.00	9.00
AH1327//3 (1911)	21,760,000	—	0.50	1.00	2.00	4.00
AH1327//4 (1912)	21,392,000	—	0.50	1.00	2.00	4.00
AH1327//5 (1913)	30,579,000	—	0.50	1.00	2.00	4.00
AH1327//6 (1914)	15,751,000	—	0.50	1.00	2.00	4.00
AH1327//7 (1915)	2,512,000	—	10.00	15.00	20.00	30.00

KM# 767 5 PARA
Nickel **Obv:** Toughra; "el-Ghazi" to right **Rev:** Value within beaded circle above sprigs **Mint:** Qustantiniyah

Date	Mintage	Good	VG	F	VF	XF
AH1327//7 (1915)	740,000	—	10.00	12.50	15.00	20.00

KM# 760 10 PARA
2.6000 g., Nickel **Obv:** Toughra; "Reshat" to right **Rev:** Value within beaded circle above sprigs **Mint:** Qustantiniyah

Date	Mintage	Good	VG	F	VF	XF
AH1327//2 (1910)	2,576,000	—	0.25	0.50	2.00	5.00
AH1327//3 (1911)	18,992,000	—	0.15	0.25	1.00	3.00
AH1327//4 (1912)	18,576,000	—	0.15	0.25	1.00	3.00
AH1327//5 (1913)	31,799,000	—	0.15	0.25	1.00	3.00
AH1327//6 (1914)	17,024,000	—	0.15	0.25	1.00	3.00
AH1327//7 (1915)	21,680,000	—	0.30	0.65	1.50	4.00

KM# 768 10 PARA
2.6000 g., Nickel **Obv:** Toughra; "el-Ghazi" to right **Rev:** Value within beaded circle above sprigs **Mint:** Qustantiniyah

Date	Mintage	Good	VG	F	VF	XF
AH1327//7 (1915)	—	—	0.30	0.60	1.50	4.00
Note: Mintage included in KM760						
AH1327//8 (1916)	7,590,000	—	0.50	1.00	4.00	10.00

KM# 761 20 PARA
Nickel **Obv:** Toughra; "Reshat" to right **Rev:** Value within beaded circle above sprigs **Mint:** Qustantiniyah

Date	Mintage	Good	VG	F	VF	XF
AH1327 (1909) No regnal year	—	—	5.00	8.50	15.00	25.00
AH1327//2 (1910)	1,524,000	—	0.25	0.50	2.00	8.00

Date	Mintage	Good	VG	F	VF	XF
AH1327//3 (1911)	11,418,000	—	0.15	0.35	1.50	6.00
AH1327//4 (1912)	10,848,000	—	0.15	0.25	1.00	5.00
AH1327//5 (1913)	24,350,000	—	0.15	0.25	1.00	5.00
AH1327//6 (1914)	20,663,000	—	0.15	0.25	1.00	5.00
AH1327//7 (1915) Rare	—	—	500	700	900	1,200

KM# 769 20 PARA

Nickel **Obv:** Toughra; "el-Ghazi" to right **Mint:** Qustantiniyah

Date	Mintage	Good	VG	F	VF	XF
AH1327//7 (1915) Rare	—	—	400	600	750	1,000

KM# 766 40 PARA

5.9200 g., Nickel **Obv:** Toughra; "Reshat" to right **Mint:** Qustantiniyah **Note:** Struck at Qustantiniyah.

Date	Mintage	Good	VG	F	VF	XF
AH1327//3 (1910)	1,992,000	—	0.50	1.00	3.00	10.00
AH1327//4 (1911)	8,716,000	—	0.15	0.30	2.00	5.00
AH1327//5 (1912)	9,248,000	—	0.15	0.30	2.00	5.00

KM# 779 40 PARA

Copper-Nickel **Obv:** Toughra; "el-Ghazi" to right **Rev:** Value within beaded circle above sprigs **Mint:** Qustantiniyah

Date	Mintage	Good	VG	F	VF	XF
AH1327//8 (1916)	16,339,000	—	0.15	0.30	2.00	5.00
AH1327//9 (1917)	3,034,000	—	1.00	2.00	10.00	25.00

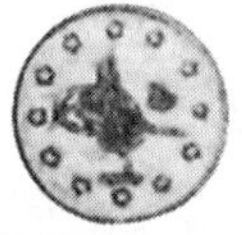
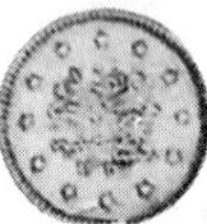

KM# 748 KURUSH

1.2027 g., 0.8300 Silver 0.0321 oz. ASW **Obv:** Toughra within star border **Rev:** Inscription and date within star border **Mint:** Qustantiniyah

Date	Mintage	Good	VG	F	VF	XF
AH1327//1 (1909)	1,270,000	—	1.25	2.50	3.50	6.00
AH1327//2 (1910)	8,770,000	—	1.00	2.00	3.00	5.00
AH1327//3 (1911)	840,000	—	1.50	3.00	6.00	12.50

KM# 749 2 KURUSH

2.4055 g., 0.8300 Silver 0.0642 oz. ASW **Obv:** Toughra; "Reshat" to right **Rev:** Inscription and date within star border **Mint:** Qustantiniyah **Note:** Varieties exist in the size of date.

Date	Mintage	Good	VG	F	VF	XF
AH1327//1 (1909)	5,157,000	—	1.75	2.25	3.50	7.50
AH1327//2 (1910)	11,120,000	—	1.50	2.00	3.00	6.50
AH1327//3 (1911)	6,110,000	—	1.50	2.00	3.00	6.50
AH1327//4 (1912)	4,031,000	—	1.50	2.00	3.00	6.50
AH1327//5 (1913)	301,000	—	2.50	5.00	10.00	20.00
AH1327//6 (1914)	1,884,000	—	2.00	2.50	4.00	8.00
AH1327//6/2 (1914)	Inc. above	—	2.00	2.50	4.00	8.00

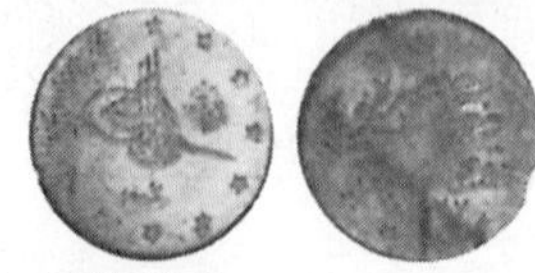

KM# 770 2 KURUSH

2.4055 g., 0.8300 Silver 0.0642 oz. ASW **Obv:** Toughra; "el-Ghazi" to right **Rev:** Inscription and date within star border **Mint:** Qustantiniyah **Note:** Varieties exist in the size of date.

Date	Mintage	Good	VG	F	VF	XF
AH1327//7 (1915)	17,000	—	12.50	25.00	40.00	75.00
AH1327//8 (1916)	398,000	—	20.00	30.00	50.00	100
AH1327//9 (1917)	8,000	—	250	350	450	600

KM# 750 5 KURUSH

6.0130 g., 0.8300 Silver 0.1605 oz. ASW **Obv:** Toughra; "Reshat" to right **Rev:** Inscription and date within star border and design **Mint:** Qustantiniyah

Date	Mintage	Good	VG	F	VF	XF
AH1327//1 (1909)	1,558,000	—	BV	3.50	6.00	10.00
AH1327//2 (1910)	1,886,000	—	BV	3.50	6.00	10.00
AH1327//3 (1911)	1,273,000	—	BV	3.50	6.00	10.00
AH1327//4 (1912)	1,635,000	—	BV	3.50	6.00	10.00
AH1327//5 (1913)	194,000	—	6.00	9.00	15.00	28.00
AH1327//6 (1914)	664,000	—	3.00	3.50	5.00	9.00
AH1327//7 (1915)	834,000	—	3.00	3.50	5.00	9.00

KM# 771 5 KURUSH

6.0130 g., 0.8300 Silver 0.1605 oz. ASW **Obv:** Toughra; "el-Ghazi" to right **Rev:** Inscription and date within star border and design **Mint:** Qustantiniyah

Date	Mintage	Good	VG	F	VF	XF
AH1327//7 (1915)	—	—	3.50	4.50	7.00	10.00
Note: Mintage included in KM750						
AH1327//8 (1916)	648,000	—	4.00	7.00	10.00	20.00
AH1327//9 (1917)	3,938	—	100	200	250	350

KM# 751 10 KURUSH

12.0270 g., 0.8300 Silver 0.3209 oz. ASW **Obv:** Toughra; "Reshat" to right **Rev:** Inscription and date within star border and design **Mint:** Qustantiniyah

Date	Mintage	Good	VG	F	VF	XF
AH1327//1 (1909)	110,000	—	12.50	25.00	50.00	100
AH1327//2 (1910)	Inc. above	—	10.00	20.00	50.00	100
AH1327//3 (1911)	8,000	—	70.00	125	1,000	1,600
AH1327//4 (1912)	96,000	—	5.00	8.00	15.00	25.00
AH1327//5 (1913)	34,000	—	10.00	20.00	50.00	100
AH1327//6 (1914)	81,000	—	7.50	12.50	17.50	30.00
AH1327//7 (1915)	582,000	—	6.00	10.00	16.50	32.00

KM# 772 10 KURUSH

12.0270 g., 0.8300 Silver 0.3209 oz. ASW **Obv:** Toughra; "el-Ghazi" to right **Rev:** Inscription and date within star border and design **Mint:** Qustantiniyah

Date	Mintage	Good	VG	F	VF	XF
AH1327//7 (1915)	—	—	5.00	8.00	15.00	28.00
Note: Mintage included in KM751						
AH1327//8 (1916)	408,000	—	7.00	9.00	17.50	32.00
AH1327//9 (1917)	299,000	—	10.00	20.00	35.00	50.00
AH1327//10 (1918)	666,000	—	12.50	25.00	50.00	85.00

KM# 780 20 KURUSH

24.0550 g., 0.8300 Silver 0.6419 oz. ASW **Obv:** Toughra within star border and cresent wreath **Rev:** Inscription and date within star border and crescent wreath **Mint:** Qustantiniyah

Date	Mintage	Good	VG	F	VF	XF
AH1327//8 (1916)	713,000	—	10.00	12.00	20.00	35.00
AH1327//9 (1917)	5,962,000	—	BV	10.00	15.00	30.00
AH1327//10 (1918)	11,025,000	—	10.00	12.00	20.00	35.00

Muhammad VI

AH1336-41/1918-23AD

MILLED COINAGE

Gold Issues

KM# 819 25 KURUSH

1.8040 g., 0.9170 Gold 0.0532 oz. AGW **Obv:** Toughra in center of sprigs and stars **Rev:** Inscription and date within wreath, star on top **Mint:** Qustantiniyah

Date	Mintage	VG	F	VF	XF	Unc
AH1336//1	53,524	55.00	60.00	80.00	120	—
AH1336//2	62,253	55.00	60.00	80.00	120	—
AH1336//3	52,421	55.00	80.00	150	200	—
AH1336//4	400	55.00	90.00	200	300	—
AH1336//5	819	80.00	140	240	375	—

KM# 825 25 KURUSH

1.7540 g., 0.9170 Gold 0.0517 oz. AGW **Series:** Monnaie de Luxe **Obv:** Toughra **Mint:** Qustantiniyah

Date	Mintage	VG	F	VF	XF	Unc
AH1336//2	8,400	60.00	100	120	200	—
AH1336//3	11,179	60.00	100	120	200	—

KM# 820 50 KURUSH

3.6080 g., 0.9170 Gold 0.1064 oz. AGW **Obv:** Toughra in center of sprigs and stars **Rev:** Inscription and date within wreath, star on top **Mint:** Qustantiniyah

Date	Mintage	VG	F	VF	XF	Unc
AH1336//1	162,363	110	125	150	300	—
AH1336//2	346	110	125	150	300	—
AH1336//3	447	150	200	250	500	—
AH1336//4	200	250	450	750	1,500	—
AH1336//5	204	200	300	450	1,000	—

KM# 821 100 KURUSH

7.2160 g., 0.9170 Gold 0.2127 oz. AGW **Obv:** Toughra in center of sprigs and stars **Rev:** Inscription and date within wreath, star on top **Mint:** Qustantiniyah

Date	Mintage	VG	F	VF	XF	Unc
AH1336//1	5,036,830	—	—	BV	210	—
AH1336//2	37,634	—	—	BV	210	—
AH1336//3	30,313	—	BV	225	450	—
AH1336/4	200	400	600	800	1,000	—
AH1336//5	—	400	600	800	1,000	—

KM# 826 100 KURUSH
7.0160 g., 0.9170 Gold 0.2068 oz. AGW **Series:** Monnaie de Luxe **Obv:** Toughra in center of legend **Rev:** Inscription and date in center of legend **Mint:** Qustantiniyah

Date	Mintage	VG	F	VF	XF	Unc
AH1336//2	33,077	250	300	400	500	—
AH1336//3	20,248	250	300	400	500	—

KM# 822 250 KURUSH
18.0400 g., 0.9170 Gold 0.5318 oz. AGW **Obv:** Toughra in center of sprigs and stars **Rev:** Inscription and date within wreath, star on top **Mint:** Qustantiniyah

Date	Mintage	VG	F	VF	XF	Unc
AH1336//1	39	1,750	3,000	4,500	6,500	—
AH1336//2	26	1,750	3,000	4,500	6,500	—
AH1336//3	31	1,750	3,000	4,500	6,500	—
AH1336/4	20	1,750	3,000	4,500	6,500	—
AH1336/5	21	1,750	3,000	4,500	6,500	—

KM# 827 250 KURUSH
17.5400 g., 0.9170 Gold 0.5171 oz. AGW **Series:** Monnaie de Luxe **Obv:** Toughra within beaded circle **Rev:** Inscription and date within beaded circle **Mint:** Qustantiniyah

Date	Mintage	VG	F	VF	XF	Unc
AH1336//2	5,995	BV	500	800	1,200	—
AH1336//3	12,739	BV	500	800	1,200	—

KM# 824 500 KURUSH
35.0800 g., 0.9170 Gold 1.0342 oz. AGW **Series:** Monnaie de Luxe **Obv:** Radiant Toughra above crossed flags, ornamental base **Rev:** Inscription and date within designed wreath **Mint:** Qustantiniyah

Date	Mintage	VG	F	VF	XF	Unc
AH1336//1	—	1,000	1,250	1,750	2,400	—
AH1336//2	—	—	BV	1,000	1,300	—
AH1336//3	5,207	—	BV	1,000	1,300	—
AH1336//4	88	1,500	2,000	2,500	3,200	—

KM# 823 500 KURUSH
36.0800 g., 0.9170 Gold 1.0637 oz. AGW **Obv:** Toughra in center of sprigs and stars **Rev:** Inscription and date within wreath, star on top **Mint:** Qustantiniyah **Note:** Beware of counterfeits

Date	Mintage	VG	F	VF	XF	Unc
AH1336//1	26,984	1,050	1,200	1,450	1,800	—
AH1336//2	22,192	1,050	1,200	1,450	1,800	—
AH1336//3	16,424	1,050	1,200	1,450	1,800	—
AH1336//4	23	2,000	4,000	6,000	8,000	—
AH1336//5	22	2,000	4,000	6,000	8,000	—

STANDARD COINAGE

KM# 828 40 PARA
Copper-Nickel **Obv:** Toughra within beaded circle above sprigs **Rev:** Value within beaded circle above sprigs **Mint:** Qustantiniyah

Date	Mintage	Good	VG	F	VF	XF
AH1336//4 (1920)	6,520,000	—	1.75	2.50	4.00	10.00

KM# 815 2 KURUSH
2.4055 g., 0.8300 Silver 0.0642 oz. ASW **Obv:** Toughra within star border **Rev:** Inscription and date within star border **Mint:** Qustantiniyah

Date	Mintage	Good	VG	F	VF	XF
AH1336//1 (1918)	25,000	—	50.00	100	150	220
AH1336//2 (1918)	3,000	—	75.00	125	200	350

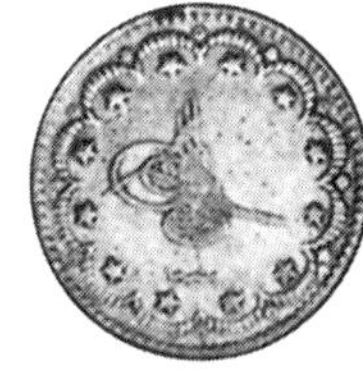

KM# 816 5 KURUSH
6.0130 g., 0.8300 Silver 0.1605 oz. ASW **Obv:** Toughra within star border and crescent wreath **Rev:** Inscription and date within star border and crescent wreath **Mint:** Qustantiniyah

Date	Mintage	Good	VG	F	VF	XF
AH1336//1 (1917)	10,000	—	50.00	125	175	265
AH1336//2 (1918)	2,000	—	75.00	150	225	385

KM# 817 10 KURUSH
12.0270 g., 0.8300 Silver 0.3209 oz. ASW **Obv:** Toughra within star border and crescent wreath **Rev:** Inscription and date within star border and crescent wreath **Mint:** Qustantiniyah

Date	Mintage	Good	VG	F	VF	XF
AH1336//1 (1917)	10,000	—	120	250	400	600
AH1336//2 (1918)	2,000	—	200	400	600	1,000

KM# 818 20 KURUSH
24.0550 g., 0.8300 Silver 0.6419 oz. ASW **Obv:** Toughra within star bordr and crescent wreath **Rev:** Inscription and date within star border and crescent wreath **Mint:** Qustantiniyah

Date	Mintage	Good	VG	F	VF	XF
AH1336//1 (1917)	—	—	30.00	60.00	125	185
AH1336//2 (1918)	1,530	—	350	525	650	925

REPUBLIC

STANDARD COINAGE

Old Monetary System

KM# 830 100 PARA
2.0000 g., Aluminum-Bronze **Obv:** Inscription and date to left of oat sprig **Rev:** Value to left of sprig, crescent and star at top

Date	Mintage	F	VF	XF	Unc	BU
AH1340 (1921)	1,798,026	3.00	5.00	10.00	60.00	—
AH1341 (1922)	5,582,846	1.00	2.50	5.00	30.00	—

KM# 834 100 PARA
Aluminum-Bronze **Obv:** Inscription and date to left of oat sprig **Rev:** Value to left of sprig, crescent and star on top

Date	Mintage	F	VF	XF	Unc	BU
1926	4,388,266	1.00	2.50	6.00	32.00	—
1928	4,000	150	225	400	600	—

KM# 831 5 KURUS
4.0000 g., Aluminum-Bronze **Obv:** Inscription and date to left of oat sprig **Rev:** Value to left of sprig, crescent and star on top

Date	Mintage	F	VF	XF	Unc	BU
AH1340 (1921)	5,023,238	1.00	2.50	7.00	32.00	—
AH1341 (1922)	23,544,591	1.00	2.50	7.00	32.00	—

KM# 835 5 KURUS
Aluminum-Bronze **Obv:** Inscription and date to left of oat sprig **Rev:** Value to left of sprig, crescent and star on top

Date	Mintage	F	VF	XF	Unc	BU
1926	355,910	1.00	2.50	7.00	32.00	—
1928	2,000	175	250	500	700	—

KM# 832 10 KURUS
Aluminum-Bronze **Obv:** Inscription and date to left of oat sprig **Rev:** Value to left of sprig, crescent and star on top **Note:** Varieties exist.

Date	Mintage	F	VF	XF	Unc	BU
AH1340 (1921)	4,836,483	1.50	3.00	8.00	35.00	—
AH1341 (1922)	14,223,098	1.50	3.00	8.00	35.00	—

KM# 836 10 KURUS
Aluminum-Bronze **Obv:** Inscription and date to left of oat sprig **Rev:** Value to left of sprigs, crescent and star on top

Date	Mintage	F	VF	XF	Unc	BU
1926	855,982	1.50	3.00	8.00	35.00	—
1928	1,000	125	200	375	575	—

KM# 833 25 KURUS
Nickel **Obv:** Inscription and date to left of oat sprig **Rev:** Value to left of sprigs, crescent and star on top

Date	Mintage	F	VF	XF	Unc	BU
AH1341 (1922)	4,972,686	2.00	4.00	10.00	30.00	—

KM# 837 25 KURUS
Nickel **Obv:** Inscription and date to left of oat sprig **Rev:** Value to left of sprigs, crescent and star on top **Note:** Varieties exist.

Date	Mintage	F	VF	XF	Unc	BU
1926	26,869	175	275	475	675	—
1928	5,794,000	1.50	3.00	8.00	30.00	—

DECIMAL COINAGE

Western numerals and Latin alphabet

40 Para = 1 Kurus; 100 Kurus = 1 Lira

Mintage figures of the 1930s and early 1940s may not be exact. It is suspected that in some cases, figures for a particular year may include quantities struck with the previous year's date.

KM# 868 10 PARA (1/4 Kurus)
Aluminum-Bronze **Obv:** Crescent and star **Rev:** Value and date

Date	Mintage	VG	F	VF	XF	Unc
1940	30,800,000	0.25	0.75	2.50	5.00	—
1941	22,400,000	0.25	0.75	2.50	5.00	—
1942	26,800,000	0.25	0.75	2.50	5.00	—

KM# 884 1/2 KURUS (20 Para)
Brass **Obv:** Center hole and date **Rev:** Center hole divides oat sprig and value

Date	Mintage	F	VF	XF	Unc	BU
1948	150	—	—	800	1,000	—

Note: Not released to circulation

KM# 861 KURUS
Copper-Nickel **Obv:** Star above crescent **Rev:** Value within designed sprigs

Date	Mintage	VG	F	VF	XF	Unc
1935	784,000	2.00	4.00	6.00	15.00	—
1936	5,300,000	2.50	3.50	5.00	10.00	—
1937	4,500,000	2.50	3.50	5.00	10.00	—

KM# 867 KURUS
2.4000 g., Copper-Nickel **Obv:** Star above crescent **Rev:** Value within designed sprigs

Date	Mintage	VG	F	VF	XF	Unc
1938	16,400,000	0.25	0.50	1.50	4.00	—
1939	21,600,000	0.25	0.50	1.50	4.00	—
1940	8,800,000	0.50	1.00	2.00	8.00	—
1941	6,700,000	0.25	0.75	1.75	5.00	—
1942	10,800,000	0.25	0.50	1.50	4.00	—
1943	4,000,000	0.25	0.75	1.75	5.00	—
1944	6,000,000	0.25	0.75	1.75	5.00	—

KM# 881 KURUS
2.2000 g., Brass, 18.5 mm. **Obv:** Date below hole in center **Rev:** Hole in center flanked by oat sprig and value **Edge:** Plain

Date	Mintage	F	VF	XF	Unc	BU
1947	890,000	1.00	1.50	2.50	5.00	—
1948	35,470,000	0.15	0.25	0.50	1.50	—
1949	29,530,000	0.15	0.25	0.50	1.25	—
1950	32,800,000	0.15	0.25	0.50	1.25	—
1951	6,310,000	0.15	0.30	0.75	2.25	—

KM# 895 KURUS
1.0000 g., Brass **Obv:** Crescent and star **Rev:** Olive branch divides value and date

Date	Mintage	F	VF	XF	Unc	BU
1961	1,180,000	—	—	0.10	5.00	—
1962	3,620,000	—	—	0.10	5.00	—
1963	1,085,000	—	—	0.10	5.00	—

KM# 895a KURUS
1.0000 g., Bronze, 14 mm. **Obv:** Crescent and star **Rev:** Olive branch divides value and date **Edge:** Plain

Date	Mintage	F	VF	XF	Unc	BU
1963	1,180,000	—	—	0.10	1.50	—
1964	2,520,000	—	—	0.10	1.50	—
1965	1,860,000	—	—	0.10	1.50	—
1966	1,820,000	—	—	0.10	1.50	—
1967	2,410,000	—	—	0.10	1.50	—
1968	1,040,000	—	—	0.10	1.50	—
1969	900,000	—	—	0.10	1.50	—
1970	1,960,000	—	—	0.10	1.50	—
1971	2,940,000	—	—	0.10	1.50	—
1972	720,000	—	—	0.10	1.50	—
1973	540,000	—	—	0.10	1.50	—
1974	510,000	—	—	0.10	1.50	—

KM# 895b KURUS
Aluminum, 14 mm. **Obv:** Crescent and star **Rev:** Olive branch divides date and value

Date	Mintage	F	VF	XF	Unc	BU
1975	690,000	—	0.10	0.25	1.00	—
1976	200,000	—	0.10	0.25	1.50	—
1977	110,000	—	0.10	0.25	4.00	—

KM# 924 KURUS
Bronze **Series:** F.A.O. **Obv:** Anatolic bride's head left **Rev:** Olive branch divides value and date

Date	Mintage	F	VF	XF	Unc	BU
1979	15,000	—	0.25	1.00	3.00	—

KM# 924a KURUS
Aluminum **Series:** F.A.O. **Obv:** Head left **Rev:** Olive branch divides date and value

Date	Mintage	F	VF	XF	Unc	BU
1979	15,000	—	0.25	1.00	3.00	—

KM# 885 2-1/2 KURUS
3.2000 g., Brass, 21 mm. **Obv:** Date below center hole **Rev:** Center hole divides oat sprig and value

Date	Mintage	F	VF	XF	Unc	BU
1948	24,720,000	0.25	0.50	1.00	3.00	—
1949	23,720,000	0.25	0.50	1.00	3.00	—
1950	11,560,000	3.00	5.00	8.00	15.00	—
1951	2,000,000	12.50	25.00	50.00	100	—

KM# 862 5 KURUS
4.0000 g., Copper-Nickel **Obv:** Star within crescent **Rev:** Value within designed sprigs

Date	Mintage	VG	F	VF	XF	Unc
1935	100,000	2.00	5.00	10.00	50.00	100
1936	2,900,000	0.50	1.00	2.00	8.00	25.00

Date	Mintage	VG	F	VF	XF	Unc
1937	4,060,000	0.30	0.75	1.50	8.00	22.50
1938	13,380,000	0.25	0.50	1.00	5.00	12.50
1939	12,520,000	0.25	0.50	1.00	5.00	12.50
1940	4,340,000	0.30	0.75	1.50	5.00	15.00
1942	10,160,000	0.20	0.40	1.00	5.00	12.50
1943	15,360,000	0.20	0.40	1.00	5.00	12.50

KM# 887 5 KURUS

Brass, 16.3 mm. **Obv:** Crescent, star and date **Rev:** Value within wreath **Edge:** TURMITE CUMHURITETI

Date	Mintage	F	VF	XF	Unc	BU
1949	4,500,000	0.25	0.50	1.00	4.00	—
1950	45,900,000	0.15	0.35	0.75	3.00	—
1951	29,600,000	0.15	0.35	0.75	3.00	—
1955	15,300,000	0.15	0.35	0.75	3.00	—
1956	21,380,000	0.15	0.35	0.75	3.00	—
1957	3,320,000	0.25	0.50	1.00	4.00	—

KM# 890.1 5 KURUS

2.5000 g., Bronze, 17 mm. **Obv:** Crescent and star **Rev:** Oak branch divides value and date

Date	Mintage	F	VF	XF	Unc	BU
1958	25,870,000	0.10	0.25	0.50	20.00	—
1959	21,580,000	—	—	0.10	20.00	—
1960	17,150,000	—	—	0.10	15.00	—
1961	11,110,000	—	—	0.10	15.00	—
1962	15,280,000	—	—	0.10	6.00	—
1963	17,680,000	—	—	0.10	6.00	—
1964	18,190,000	—	—	0.10	5.00	—
1965	19,170,000	—	—	0.10	3.00	—
1966	19,840,000	—	—	0.10	3.00	—
1967	16,170,000	—	—	0.10	2.00	—
1968	26,050,000	—	—	0.10	2.00	—

KM# 890.2 5 KURUS

2.0000 g., Bronze **Obv:** Crescent and star **Rev:** Oak branch divides value and date **Note:** Reduced weight.

Date	Mintage	F	VF	XF	Unc	BU
1969	33,630,000	—	—	0.10	2.00	—
1970	29,360,000	—	—	0.10	1.00	—
1971	17,440,000	—	—	0.10	1.00	—
1972	22,670,000	—	—	0.10	1.00	—
1973	17,370,000	—	—	0.10	1.00	—

KM# 890.3 5 KURUS

1.3500 g., Bronze **Obv:** Crescent and star **Rev:** Oak branch divides value and date **Note:** Varieties exist.

Date	Mintage	F	VF	XF	Unc	BU
1974	13,540,000	—	—	0.10	1.00	—
1974 Unconiferous	Inc. above	—	—	50.00	125	—

KM# 890a 5 KURUS

1.6900 g., Aluminum, 21 mm. **Obv:** Crescent and star **Rev:** Oak branch divides value and date

Date	Mintage	F	VF	XF	Unc	BU
1975	1,560,000	—	—	0.10	1.00	—
1976	1,321,000	—	—	0.10	1.00	—
1977	190,000	—	0.10	0.20	5.00	—

KM# 906 5 KURUS

0.9100 g., Aluminum, 17 mm. **Series:** F.A.O. **Obv:** Anatolic bride's head left **Rev:** Oak branch divides date and value

Date	Mintage	F	VF	XF	Unc	BU
1975	1,019,000	—	0.50	1.50	3.00	—

KM# 907 5 KURUS

Aluminum **Series:** F.A.O. **Obv:** Mother breastfeading infant **Rev:** Oak branch divides value and date

Date	Mintage	F	VF	XF	Unc	BU
1976	17,000	—	0.50	1.50	10.00	—

KM# 934 5 KURUS

Bronze **Series:** F.A.O. **Obv:** Fisherman within flounder **Rev:** Oak branch divides value and date

Date	Mintage	F	VF	XF	Unc	BU
1980	13,000	—	0.25	0.75	7.00	—

KM# 863 10 KURUS

5.8000 g., Copper-Nickel **Obv:** Star within crescent **Rev:** Star above value and date within designed sprigs

Date	Mintage	VG	F	VF	XF	Unc
1935	60,000	2.00	5.00	8.00	20.00	—
1936	3,580,000	0.75	2.00	5.00	12.50	—
1937	3,020,000	0.50	1.00	4.00	8.00	—
1938	6,610,000	0.50	1.00	4.00	8.00	—
1939	4,610,000	0.50	1.00	2.50	5.00	—
1940	6,960,000	0.50	1.00	2.50	5.00	—

KM# 888 10 KURUS

Brass **Obv:** Star, crescent and date **Rev:** Value within wreath

Date	Mintage	F	VF	XF	Unc	BU
1949	27,000,000	0.10	0.25	0.75	3.00	—
1951	6,200,000	0.10	0.25	0.75	3.00	—
1955	10,090,000	0.10	0.25	0.75	3.00	—
1956	9,910,000	0.10	0.25	0.75	3.00	—

KM# 891.1 10 KURUS

4.0000 g., Bronze, 21.3 mm. **Obv:** Star and crescent **Rev:** Oat stalks divide date and value

Date	Mintage	F	VF	XF	Unc	BU
1958	14,770,000	—	0.10	0.25	30.00	—
1959	11,160,000	—	—	0.10	30.00	—
1960	9,450,000	—	—	0.10	20.00	—
1961	5,370,000	—	—	0.10	20.00	—
1962	9,250,000	—	—	0.10	10.00	—
1963	10,390,000	—	—	0.10	4.00	—
1964	9,890,000	—	—	0.10	4.00	—
1965	10,480,000	—	—	0.10	3.00	—
1966	12,200,000	—	—	0.10	3.00	—
1967	11,410,000	—	—	0.10	2.00	—
1968	1,862,000	—	—	0.10	2.00	—

KM# 891a 10 KURUS

1.3800 g., Aluminum **Obv:** Star and crescent **Rev:** Oat stalks divide date and value

Date	Mintage	F	VF	XF	Unc	BU
1975	2,165,000	—	—	0.10	1.00	—
1976	559,000	—	0.10	0.20	1.00	—
1977	106,000	—	0.10	0.50	10.00	—

KM# 891.2 10 KURUS

3.5000 g., Bronze **Obv:** Star and crescent **Rev:** Oat stalks divide date and value **Note:** Reduced weight.

Date	Mintage	F	VF	XF	Unc	BU
1969	21,190,000	—	—	0.10	2.00	—
1970	19,930,000	—	—	0.10	1.00	—
1971	14,780,000	—	—	0.10	1.00	—
1972	17,960,000	—	—	0.10	1.00	—
1973	11,930,000	—	—	0.10	1.00	—

KM# 891.3 10 KURUS

2.5000 g., Bronze **Obv:** Star and crescent **Rev:** Oat stalks divide date and value **Note:** Varieties exist.

Date	Mintage	F	VF	XF	Unc	BU
1974	9,280,000	—	—	1.00	1.50	—
1974 Open 4	Inc. above	—	—	40.00	75.00	—

KM# 898.1 10 KURUS

3.5000 g., Bronze **Series:** F.A.O. **Obv:** Atatürk driving a tractor **Obv. Designer:** M. Duyer **Rev:** Oat stalks divide value and date

Date	Mintage	F	VF	XF	Unc	BU
1971	1,140,000	—	0.50	1.00	2.00	—
1972	500,000	—	1.00	2.00	4.00	—
1973	10,000	—	100	250	500	—

KM# 898.2 10 KURUS

2.5000 g., Bronze **Obv:** Atatürk driving tractor **Rev:** Oat stalks divide date and value

Date	Mintage	F	VF	XF	Unc	BU
1974	605,000	—	1.00	2.00	4.00	—

KM# 898a 10 KURUS

Aluminum **Obv:** Atatürk driving tractor **Rev:** Oat stalks divide date and value

Date	Mintage	F	VF	XF	Unc	BU
1975	517,000	—	0.50	1.00	2.00	—

KM# 908 10 KURUS

Aluminum **Series:** F.A.O. **Obv:** Mother breastfeading infant **Rev:** Oat stalks divide value and date

Date	Mintage	F	VF	XF	Unc	BU
1976	17,000	—	0.50	2.00	10.00	—

KM# 935 10 KURUS

Bronze **Series:** F.A.O. **Obv:** Anatolic bride's head left **Rev:** Oat stalks divide date and value

Date	Mintage	F	VF	XF	Unc	BU
1980	13,000	—	0.25	1.00	6.00	—

KM# 864 25 KURUS

3.0000 g., 0.8300 Silver 0.0801 oz. ASW **Obv:** Head of Kemal Atatürk left **Rev:** Oat sprig divides date, value at left

Date	Mintage	VG	F	VF	XF	Unc
1935	888,000	1.35	2.25	6.00	15.00	—
1936	10,576,000	1.35	2.50	10.00	20.00	—
1937	8,536,000	1.35	2.50	10.00	20.00	—

KM# 880 25 KURUS

2.8700 g., Nickel-Bronze **Obv:** Crescent and star **Rev:** Oat sprig divides date, value at left

Date	Mintage	VG	F	VF	XF	Unc
1944	20,000,000	0.25	0.50	1.00	2.50	—
1945	5,328,000	0.50	1.00	1.50	3.00	—
1946	2,672,000	0.50	1.25	2.00	4.00	—

KM# 886 25 KURUS

Brass **Obv:** Crescent and star **Rev:** Value within wreath

Date	Mintage	F	VF	XF	Unc	BU
1948	18,000,000	0.10	0.20	0.40	1.25	—
1949	21,000,000	0.10	0.20	0.40	1.25	—
1951	2,000,000	5.00	10.00	25.00	50.00	—
1955	9,624,000	0.10	0.20	0.40	1.25	—
1956	14,376,000	0.10	0.20	0.40	1.25	—

KM# 892.1 25 KURUS

5.0000 g., Stainless Steel, 22.5 mm. **Obv:** Smooth ground under standing figure facing **Rev:** Value within wreath

Date	Mintage	F	VF	XF	Unc	BU
1959	21,864,000	0.10	0.15	0.30	10.00	—

KM# 892.2 25 KURUS

5.0000 g., Stainless Steel, 22.5 mm. **Obv:** Rough ground under standing figure facing **Rev:** Value within wreath

Date	Mintage	F	VF	XF	Unc	BU
1960	14,778,000	—	0.10	0.15	10.00	—
1961	7,248,000	—	0.10	0.15	15.00	—
1962	10,722,000	—	0.10	0.15	10.00	—
1963	11,016,000	—	0.10	0.15	10.00	—
1964	13,962,000	—	0.10	0.15	8.00	—
1965	9,816,000	—	0.10	0.15	5.00	—
1966	2,424,000	—	0.10	0.15	5.00	—

KM# 892.3 25 KURUS

4.0000 g., Stainless Steel **Obv:** Standing figure facing **Rev:** Value within wreath **Note:** Reduced weight

Date	Mintage	F	VF	XF	Unc	BU
1966	7,596,000	—	—	0.10	5.00	—
1967	17,022,000	—	—	0.10	4.00	—
1968	31,482,000	—	—	0.10	3.00	—
1969	34,566,000	—	—	0.10	3.00	—
1970	32,960,000	—	—	0.10	2.00	—
1973	20,496,000	—	—	0.10	2.00	—
1974	16,602,000	—	—	0.10	1.00	—
1977	10,204,000	—	—	0.10	1.00	—
1978	185,000	0.35	0.75	1.25	3.00	—

KM# 865 50 KURUS

6.0000 g., 0.8300 Silver 0.1601 oz. ASW **Obv:** Head of Kemal Atatürk left **Rev:** Oat sprig divides date, value at left

Date	Mintage	VG	F	VF	XF	Unc
1935	630,000	3.25	6.50	10.00	25.00	—
1936	5,082,000	2.75	5.00	8.00	17.00	—
1937	4,270,000	12.00	30.00	50.00	100	—

KM# 882 50 KURUS

4.0000 g., 0.6000 Silver 0.0772 oz. ASW **Obv:** Crescent, star and date **Rev:** Value within wreath **Note:** Edge varieties exist.

Date	Mintage	F	VF	XF	Unc	BU
1947	9,296,000	1.25	2.50	3.50	6.00	—
1948	12,704,000	1.25	2.50	3.50	6.00	—

KM# 899 50 KURUS

Stainless Steel, 24 mm. **Obv:** Anatolic bride's head left **Rev:** Value within wreath

Date	Mintage	F	VF	XF	Unc	BU
1971	16,756,000	—	0.10	0.15	1.00	—
1972	22,152,000	—	0.10	0.15	1.00	—
1973	18,928,000	—	0.10	0.15	1.00	—
1974	14,480,000	—	0.10	0.15	1.00	—
1975	27,714,000	—	0.10	0.15	1.00	—
1976	27,476,000	—	0.10	0.15	1.00	—
1977	5,062,000	—	0.10	0.15	1.00	—
1979	3,714,000	—	0.10	0.15	1.00	—

KM# 913 50 KURUS

Stainless Steel, 24 mm. **Series:** F.A.O. **Obv:** Mother breastfeeding child **Rev:** Value and date within wreath

Date	Mintage	F	VF	XF	Unc	BU
1978	10,000	—	2.00	4.00	6.00	—

KM# 925 50 KURUS

Stainless Steel, 24 mm. **Series:** F.A.O. **Obv:** Atatürk driving tractor **Obv. Designer:** M. Duyer **Rev:** Value and date within wreath

Date	Mintage	F	VF	XF	Unc	BU
1979	20,000	—	2.00	4.00	6.00	—

KM# 936 50 KURUS

Stainless Steel, 24 mm. **Series:** F.A.O. **Obv:** Anatolic bride's head left **Rev:** Value and date within wreath

Date	Mintage	F	VF	XF	Unc	BU
1980	13,000	—	2.00	4.00	6.00	—

KM# 860.1 100 KURUS (Lira)

12.0000 g., 0.8300 Silver 0.3202 oz. ASW **Obv:** Head of Kemal Atatürk left **Rev:** High star above value within crescent, date below

Date	Mintage	VG	F	VF	XF	Unc
1934	718,000	30.00	40.00	75.00	150	—

KM# 860.1a 100 KURUS (Lira)

13.5000 g., 0.9250 Silver 0.4015 oz. ASW, 29.5 mm. **Series:** Nostalgia **Obv:** Head of Kemal Atatürk left **Rev:** High star above value within crescent, date below **Edge:** Plain **Mint:** Istanbul

Date	Mintage	F	VF	XF	Unc	BU
1934 Matte	684	—	—	—	40.00	—

KM# 860.2 100 KURUS (Lira)

12.0000 g., 0.8300 Silver 0.3202 oz. ASW **Obv:** Head of Kemal Atatürk left **Rev:** Low star above value within crescent, date below

Date	Mintage	VG	F	VF	XF	Unc
1934	Inc. above	15.00	30.00	50.00	80.00	—

KM# 866 LIRA

12.0000 g., 0.8300 Silver 0.3202 oz. ASW **Obv:** Head of Kemal Atatürk left **Rev:** Value and date within crescent below star

Date	Mintage	VG	F	VF	XF	Unc
1937	1,624,000	5.50	10.00	15.00	32.00	—
1938	8,282,000	25.00	50.00	75.00	150	—
1939	376,000	5.50	10.00	15.00	32.00	—

KM# 869 LIRA

12.0000 g., 0.8300 Silver 0.3202 oz. ASW **Obv:** Head of Ismet Inonu left **Rev:** Star above value and date within crescent

Date	Mintage	VG	F	VF	XF	Unc
1940	253,000	7.50	12.50	15.00	25.00	—
1941	6,167,000	5.00	10.00	12.50	22.50	—

KM# 883 LIRA

7.5000 g., 0.6000 Silver 0.1447 oz. ASW **Obv:** Crescent, star and date **Rev:** Value within wreath **Note:** Edge varieties exist.

Date	Mintage	F	VF	XF	Unc	BU
1947	11,104,000	BV	3.50	5.00	8.50	—
1948	16,896,000	BV	3.00	4.00	7.50	—

KM# 889 LIRA

Copper-Nickel **Obv:** Head of Kemal Atatürk left **Rev:** Value and date within wreath

Date	Mintage	F	VF	XF	Unc	BU
1957	25,000,000	0.25	0.50	1.00	7.00	—

KM# 889a.1 LIRA

8.0000 g., Stainless Steel **Obv:** Head of Kemal Atatürk left **Rev:** Value and date within wreath

Date	Mintage	F	VF	XF	Unc	BU
1959	7,452,000	—	0.10	0.20	25.00	—
1960	11,436,000	—	0.10	0.20	25.00	—
1961	2,100,000	—	0.10	0.20	75.00	—
1962	4,228,000	—	0.10	0.20	20.00	—
1963	4,316,000	—	0.10	0.20	20.00	—
1964	4,976,000	—	0.10	0.20	15.00	—
1965	5,348,000	—	0.10	0.20	10.00	—
1966	8,040,000	—	0.10	0.20	10.00	—
1967	—	—	25.00	50.00	80.00	—

KM# 889a.2 LIRA

7.0000 g., Stainless Steel, 27 mm. **Obv:** Head of Kemal Atatürk left **Rev:** Value and date within wreath **Note:** Reduced weight.

Date	Mintage	F	VF	XF	Unc	BU
1967	10,444,000	—	0.10	0.20	10.00	—
1968	12,728,000	—	0.10	0.20	5.00	—
1969	6,612,000	—	0.10	0.20	5.00	—
1970	8,652,000	—	0.10	0.20	3.00	—
1971	10,504,000	—	0.10	0.20	3.00	—
1972	26,512,000	—	0.10	0.20	3.00	—
1973	12,596,000	—	0.10	0.20	3.00	—
1974	11,596,000	—	0.10	0.20	3.00	—
1975	20,348,000	—	0.10	0.20	2.00	—
1976	23,144,000	—	0.10	0.20	1.00	—
1977	30,244,000	—	0.10	0.20	1.00	—
1978	22,156,000	—	0.10	0.20	1.00	—
1979	9,289,000	—	0.10	0.20	1.00	—
1980	3,585,000	—	0.10	0.20	1.00	—

KM# 914 LIRA

8.0000 g., Stainless Steel **Series:** F.A.O. **Obv:** Mother breastfeeding infant **Rev:** Value and date within wreath

Date	Mintage	F	VF	XF	Unc	BU
1978	20,000	—	2.00	4.00	6.00	—

KM# 926 LIRA

8.0000 g., Stainless Steel **Series:** F.A.O. **Obv:** Atatürk driving tractor **Rev:** Value and date within wreath

Date	Mintage	F	VF	XF	Unc	BU
1979	20,000	—	2.00	4.00	6.00	—

KM# 937 LIRA

8.0000 g., Stainless Steel **Series:** F.A.O. **Obv:** Anatolic bride's head left **Rev:** Value and date within wreath

Date	Mintage	F	VF	XF	Unc	BU
1980	13,000	—	2.00	4.00	6.00	—

KM# 943 LIRA

1.1000 g., Aluminum, 17 mm. **Obv:** Head of Kemal Atatürk left **Rev:** Value and date within wreath

Date	Mintage	F	VF	XF	Unc	BU
1981	14,432,000	—	—	0.10	0.50	—

KM# 990 LIRA

1.1000 g., Aluminum, 17 mm. **Obv:** Head of Kemal Atatürk left **Rev:** Crescent opens right with thin "1"

Date	Mintage	F	VF	XF	Unc	BU
1982	799,000	—	—	1.00	2.00	—

KM# 962.1 LIRA

1.1000 g., Aluminum, 17 mm. **Obv:** Head of Kemal Atatürk left **Rev:** Large (5mm) "1"

Date	Mintage	F	VF	XF	Unc	BU
1984	498,000	—	—	0.10	0.50	—

KM# 962.2 LIRA

1.1000 g., Aluminum, 17 mm. **Obv:** Head of Kemal Atatürk left **Rev:** Small (3.5mm) "1" **Note:** Varieties exist.

Date	Mintage	F	VF	XF	Unc	BU
1985	712,000	—	—	0.10	0.50	—
1986	504,000	—	—	0.10	0.50	—
1987	500,000	—	—	0.10	0.50	—
1988	75,000	—	—	0.10	0.50	—
1989	10,000	—	—	0.10	4.00	—

KM# 893.1 2-1/2 LIRA

12.0000 g., Stainless Steel, 30 mm. **Obv:** Standing figure facing right **Rev:** Value and date within wreath

Date	Mintage	F	VF	XF	Unc	BU
1960	4,015,000	—	0.25	1.00	100	—
1961	1,222,000	—	0.25	1.00	150	—
1962	3,636,000	—	0.25	1.00	150	—
1963	3,108,000	—	0.25	1.00	100	—
1964	2,710,000	—	0.25	1.00	50.00	—
1965	1,246,000	—	0.25	1.00	10.00	—
1966	1,788,000	—	0.25	1.00	40.00	—
1967	5,333,000	—	0.25	1.00	20.00	—
1968	2,707,000	—	0.25	1.00	10.00	—

KM# 893.2 2-1/2 LIRA

9.0000 g., Stainless Steel, 30 mm. **Obv:** Standing figure facing right **Rev:** Value and date within wreath **Note:** Reduced weight. Varieties exist with landscape and number of beads in laurel.

Date	Mintage	F	VF	XF	Unc	BU
1969	1,378,000	—	0.15	0.75	10.00	—
1970	3,777,000	—	0.15	0.75	5.00	—
1971	2,170,000	—	0.15	0.75	4.00	—
1972	9,147,000	—	0.15	0.50	4.00	—
1973	4,348,000	—	0.15	0.50	4.00	—
1974	3,816,000	—	0.15	0.50	4.00	—
1975	9,811,000	—	0.15	0.50	2.50	—
1976	3,952,000	—	0.15	0.50	2.50	—
1977	21,473,000	—	0.10	0.25	2.00	—
1978	15,738,000	—	0.10	0.25	2.00	—
1979	6,074,000	—	0.10	0.25	2.00	—
1980	2,621,000	—	0.10	0.25	2.00	—

KM# 896 2-1/2 LIRA

9.0000 g., Stainless Steel, 30 mm. **Series:** F.A.O. **Obv:** Atatürk driving tractor **Obv. Designer:** M. Duyer **Rev:** Value and date within wreath

Date	Mintage	F	VF	XF	Unc	BU
1970	200,000	—	0.75	1.00	1.50	—

KM# 910 2-1/2 LIRA

Stainless Steel, 30 mm. **Series:** F.A.O. **Obv:** Stylized standing figures **Rev:** Value and date within wreath

Date	Mintage	F	VF	XF	Unc	BU
1977	25,000	—	1.00	1.50	2.00	—

KM# 915 2-1/2 LIRA

Stainless Steel, 30 mm. **Series:** F.A.O. **Obv:** Mother breastfeeding infant **Rev:** Value and date within wreath

Date	Mintage	F	VF	XF	Unc	BU
1978	10,000	—	2.50	5.00	10.00	—

KM# 927 2-1/2 LIRA

Stainless Steel, 30 mm. **Series:** F.A.O. **Obv:** Head of Kemal Atatürk left **Rev:** Value and date within wreath

Date	Mintage	F	VF	XF	Unc	BU
1979	20,000	—	4.00	6.00	8.00	—

KM# 938 2-1/2 LIRA

Stainless Steel, 30 mm. **Series:** F.A.O. **Obv:** Fisherman within flounder **Rev:** Value and date within wreath

Date	Mintage	F	VF	XF	Unc	BU
1980	13,000	—	3.00	5.00	10.00	—

KM# 905 5 LIRA
11.1000 g., Stainless Steel, 32.5 mm. **Obv:** Atatürk on horseback **Rev:** Value and date within wreath

Date	Mintage	F	VF	XF	Unc	BU
1974	2,842,000	—	0.15	0.75	5.00	—
1975	10,855,000	—	0.15	0.25	2.00	—
1976	17,532,000	—	0.15	0.25	2.00	—
1977	6,172,000	—	0.15	0.75	3.00	—
1978	76,000	1.50	2.50	3.50	8.00	—
1979	6,054,000	—	0.15	0.30	1.00	—

KM# 909 5 LIRA
Stainless Steel **Series:** International Women's Year; F.A.O. **Obv:** Mother breastfeeding infant **Rev:** Value and date within wreath

Date	Mintage	F	VF	XF	Unc	BU
1976	17,000	—	3.00	6.00	12.00	—

KM# 911 5 LIRA
Stainless Steel **Series:** F.A.O. **Obv:** Stylized standing figures **Rev:** Value and date within wreath

Date	Mintage	F	VF	XF	Unc	BU
1977	25,000	—	1.75	2.50	3.50	—

KM# 916 5 LIRA
Stainless Steel **Series:** F.A.O. **Obv:** Atatürk driving tractor **Obv. Designer:** M. Duyer **Rev:** Value and date within wreath

Date	Mintage	F	VF	XF	Unc	BU
1978	10,000	—	5.00	8.00	12.00	—

KM# 928 5 LIRA
Stainless Steel **Series:** F.A.O. **Obv:** Anatolic bride's head left **Rev:** Value and date within wreath

Date	Mintage	F	VF	XF	Unc	BU
1979	20,000	—	3.00	6.00	12.00	—

KM# 939 5 LIRA
Stainless Steel **Series:** F.A.O. **Obv:** Fisherman within flounder **Rev:** Value and date within wreath

Date	Mintage	F	VF	XF	Unc	BU
1980	13,000	—	6.00	8.00	12.00	—

KM# 944 5 LIRA
Aluminum **Obv:** Atatürk on horseback **Rev:** Crescent opens left

Date	Mintage	F	VF	XF	Unc	BU
1981	61,605,000	—	—	0.15	1.00	—

KM# 949.1 5 LIRA
1.7000 g., Aluminum, 19.42 mm. **Obv:** Atatürk on horseback **Rev:** Crescent opens right **Edge:** Reeded

Date	Mintage	F	VF	XF	Unc	BU
1982	69,975,000	—	—	0.15	1.00	—

KM# 949.2 5 LIRA
Aluminum **Obv:** Atatürk on horseback **Rev:** Smaller, bolder "5"

Date	Mintage	F	VF	XF	Unc	BU
1983	90,310,000	—	—	0.15	1.00	—

KM# 963 5 LIRA
1.6700 g., Aluminum, 19.46 mm. **Obv:** Head left **Rev:** Value and date within wreath **Edge:** Reeded **Note:** Varieties exist.

Date	Mintage	F	VF	XF	Unc	BU
1984	17,316,000	—	—	0.15	1.00	—
1985	9,405,000	—	—	0.15	1.00	—
1986	9,575,000	—	—	0.20	1.00	—
1987	500,000	—	—	0.20	1.00	—
1988	100,000	—	—	0.20	1.00	—
1989	10,000	—	—	0.20	4.00	—

KM# 894 10 LIRA
15.0000 g., 0.8300 Silver 0.4003 oz. ASW **Subject:** 27th May Revolution **Obv:** Head of Atatürk left **Rev:** Radiant crescent and star above torch, balance scales, crossed flag and wing

Date	Mintage	F	VF	XF	Unc	BU
ND(1960)	4,000,000	—	BV	6.50	10.00	—
ND(1960) Prooflike	—	—	—	—	12.50	—

KM# 945 10 LIRA
Aluminum **Obv:** Half-length figure right **Rev:** Value and date within wreath, crescent opens left

Date	Mintage	F	VF	XF	Unc	BU
1981	25,520,000	—	0.10	0.25	0.50	—

KM# 950.1 10 LIRA
Aluminum **Obv:** Half-length figure right **Rev:** Value and date within wreath, crescent opens right

Date	Mintage	F	VF	XF	Unc	BU
1982	17,092,000	—	0.10	0.25	0.50	—

KM# 950.2 10 LIRA
Aluminum **Obv:** Half-length figure right **Rev:** Value and date within wreath

Date	Mintage	F	VF	XF	Unc	BU
1983	2,228,000	—	0.10	1.00	4.00	—

KM# 964 10 LIRA
2.3000 g., Aluminum, 25 mm. **Obv:** Head of Atatürk left **Rev:** Value and date within wreath **Note:** Varieties exist.

Date	Mintage	F	VF	XF	Unc	BU
1984	23,360,000	—	0.10	0.25	0.50	—
1985	41,736,000	—	—	0.15	0.50	—
1986	78,224,000	—	—	0.15	0.50	—
1987	62,340,000	—	—	0.15	0.50	—
1988	17,620,000	—	—	0.15	1.00	—
1989	10,000	—	—	0.15	4.00	—

KM# 946 20 LIRA
Aluminum **Series:** World Food Day **Obv:** Value and date within wreath **Rev:** Stylized design below sprig

Date	Mintage	F	VF	XF	Unc	BU
1981	10,000	—	—	2.50	4.00	—

KM# 965 20 LIRA
7.2000 g., Copper-Nickel **Obv:** Head of Atatürk left **Rev:** Value and date within wreath

Date	Mintage	F	VF	XF	Unc	BU
1984	1,644,000	—	0.10	0.25	2.00	—
1989	—	—	0.10	0.25	2.00	—

KM# 975 25 LIRA
2.8500 g., Aluminum, 27 mm. **Obv:** Head of Atatürk left **Rev:** Value and date within wreath **Note:** Varieties exist.

Date	Mintage	F	VF	XF	Unc	BU
1985	37,014,000	—	—	0.15	0.50	—
1986	49,611,000	—	—	0.15	0.50	—
1987	61,335,000	—	—	0.15	0.50	—
1988	39,540,000	—	—	0.15	1.00	—
1989	10,000	—	—	0.15	4.00	—

KM# 966 50 LIRA
Copper-Nickel-Zinc, 26.8 mm. **Obv:** Head of Atatürk left **Rev:** Value and date within wreath **Edge:** Reeded **Note:** Varieties exist.

Date	Mintage	F	VF	XF	Unc	BU
1984	14,731,000	—	0.10	0.25	0.60	—
1985	52,658,000	—	0.10	0.20	0.50	—
1986	80,656,000	—	0.10	0.20	0.50	—
1987	32,078,000	—	0.10	0.20	0.50	—

KM# 987 50 LIRA
3.2500 g., Aluminum-Bronze, 18.7 mm. **Obv:** Head of Atatürk left **Rev:** Value and date within wreath **Note:** Varieties exist.

Date	Mintage	F	VF	XF	Unc	BU
1988	3,396,000	—	—	—	0.15	—
1989	25,463,000	—	—	—	0.15	—
1990	500,000	—	—	—	0.15	—
1991	10,000	—	—	—	0.15	—
1992	10,000	—	—	—	0.15	—
1993	5,000	—	—	—	0.35	—
1994	2,500	—	—	—	0.50	—

KM# 967 100 LIRA
11.0500 g., Copper-Nickel-Zinc, 29.65 mm. **Obv:** Head of Atatürk left **Rev:** Value and date within wreath **Note:** Varieties exist.

Date	Mintage	F	VF	XF	Unc	BU
1984	758,000	—	0.20	0.40	0.85	—
1985	866,000	—	0.20	0.40	0.85	—
1986	12,064,000	—	0.20	0.40	0.85	—
1987	91,400,000	—	0.15	0.25	0.65	—
1988	16,184,000	—	0.15	0.25	0.65	—

KM# 988 100 LIRA
4.1500 g., Aluminum-Bronze, 20.8 mm. **Obv:** Head of Atatürk left **Rev:** Value and date within wreath **Note:** Varieties exist.

Date	Mintage	F	VF	XF	Unc	BU
1988	10,000,000	—	—	—	0.20	—
1989	233,750,000	—	—	—	0.20	—
1990	152,230,000	—	—	—	0.20	—
1991	49,160,000	—	—	—	0.20	—
1992	22,930,000	—	—	—	0.20	—

Date	Mintage	F	VF	XF	Unc	BU
1993	3,700,000	—	—	—	0.20	—
1994	2,500	—	—	—	0.50	—

KM# 989 500 LIRA
6.1500 g., Aluminum-Bronze, 24 mm. **Obv:** Head of Atatürk left **Rev:** Value and date within wreath **Edge:** Reeded **Note:** Varieties exist.

Date	Mintage	F	VF	XF	Unc	BU
1989	141,813,000	—	—	—	0.60	—
1990	100,114,000	—	—	—	0.60	—
1991	30,006,000	—	—	—	0.60	—
1992	10,000	—	—	—	0.60	—
1993	5,000	—	—	—	0.75	—
1994	2,500	—	—	—	0.85	—
1995	2,500	—	—	—	0.85	—
1996	10,000	—	—	—	0.60	—
1997	—	—	—	—	0.60	—

KM# 997 1000 LIRA
Copper-Zinc-Nickel, 25.8 mm. **Obv:** Head of Atatürk left **Rev:** Value and date within oat sprigs **Edge:** Reeded

Date	Mintage	F	VF	XF	Unc	BU
1990	136,480,000	—	0.15	0.25	2.00	—
1991	110,245,000	—	0.15	0.25	2.00	—
1992	15,820,000	—	0.15	0.25	2.00	—
1993	11,675,000	—	0.15	0.25	2.00	—
1994	61,515,000	—	0.15	0.25	2.00	—

KM# 1028 1000 LIRA
3.0700 g., Bronze Clad Brass, 16.93 mm. **Obv:** Head of Atatürk left **Rev:** Value and date within oat sprigs

Date	Mintage	F	VF	XF	Unc	BU
1995	36,820,000	—	—	—	1.00	—
1996	3,900,000	—	—	—	1.00	—
1997	—	—	—	—	1.00	—

KM# 1015 2500 LIRA
Nickel-Bronze, 26.5 mm. **Obv:** Head of Atatürk left **Rev:** Value to lower right of oak leaf branch **Edge Lettering:** TURKIYE CUMHURIYETI

Date	Mintage	F	VF	XF	Unc	BU
1991	22,938,000	0.10	0.25	0.50	3.00	—
1992	48,784,000	0.10	0.25	0.50	3.00	—
1993	2,310,000	0.10	0.25	0.50	3.00	—
1994	2,500	0.10	0.25	0.50	4.50	—
1995	2,500	0.10	0.25	0.50	4.50	—
1996	10,000	0.10	0.25	0.50	3.00	—
1997	—	0.10	0.25	0.50	3.00	—

KM# 1025 5000 LIRA
Nickel-Bronze, 28.5 mm. **Obv:** Head of Atatürk left **Rev:** Flower sprigs to left of value and date **Edge Lettering:** TURKIYE CUMHURIYETI

Date	Mintage	F	VF	XF	Unc	BU
1992	24,904,000	0.10	0.25	0.50	3.00	—
1992 Proof	—	Value: 6.50				
1993	15,872,000	0.10	0.25	0.50	3.00	—
1994	69,504,000	0.10	0.25	0.50	3.00	—

KM# 1029.1 5000 LIRA
5.9800 g., Brass, 19.5 mm. **Obv:** Head of Atatürk left **Rev:** Flower sprigs to left of value and date

Date	Mintage	F	VF	XF	Unc	BU
1995 Large date	69,550,000	—	—	—	1.50	—
1995 Small date	Inc. above	—	—	—	0.75	—
1996	80,506,000	—	—	—	0.75	—
1997	—	—	—	—	0.75	—
1998	—	—	—	—	0.75	—

KM# 1029.2 5000 LIRA
3.4800 g., Brass, 19.5 mm. **Obv:** Head of Atatürk left **Rev:** Flower sprigs to left of value and date **Edge:** Reeded **Note:** Reduced weight version of KM#1029.1

Date	Mintage	F	VF	XF	Unc	BU
1998	—	—	—	—	0.75	—
1999	—	—	—	—	0.75	—

KM# 1027.1 10000 LIRA (10 Bin Lira)
9.7500 g., Copper-Nickel-Zinc, 23.5 mm. **Obv:** Head of Kemal Atat?rk left **Rev:** Value to left of flower sprig, large lettering **Edge:** Reeded with legend **Edge Lettering:** TURKIYE CUMHURIYETI, dates 1994 and 1995

Date	Mintage	F	VF	XF	Unc	BU
1994	17,319,000	—	0.10	0.25	3.00	—
1995	56,584,000	—	0.10	0.25	3.00	—
1996	119,572,000	—	0.10	0.25	3.00	—
1997	—	—	0.10	0.25	3.00	—

KM# 1042 10000 LIRA (10 Bin Lira)
9.7500 g., Copper-Nickel-Zinc, 23.5 mm. **Series:** 1994 Olympics **Obv:** Value to left of flower sprig **Rev:** Radiant Olympic rings

Date	Mintage	F	VF	XF	Unc	BU
1994	500,000	—	—	—	3.75	—

KM# 1027.2 10000 LIRA (10 Bin Lira)
9.7500 g., Copper-Nickel-Zinc, 23.5 mm. **Obv:** Head of Kemal Atatürk left **Rev:** Value to left of flower sprig, small lettering **Edge:** Reeded with incuse legend **Edge Lettering:** TURKIYE CUMHURIYETI, dates 1996 and 1997 **Note:** Thin planchet. Edge varieties exist.

Date	Mintage	F	VF	XF	Unc	BU
1997	—	—	0.10	0.25	3.00	—
1998	—	—	0.10	0.25	3.00	—
1999	—	—	0.10	0.25	3.00	—

KM# 1041 25000 LIRA (25 Bin Lira)
Copper-Nickel-Zinc, 26.5 mm. **Obv:** Head of Atatürk left **Rev:** Value to left of rose **Edge:** Lettered TC and flower five times

Date	Mintage	F	VF	XF	Unc	BU
1995	13,740,000	0.20	0.30	0.50	3.00	—
1996	59,742,000	0.20	0.30	0.50	3.00	—
1997	—	0.20	0.30	0.50	3.00	—
1998	—	0.20	0.30	0.50	3.00	—
1999	—	0.20	0.30	0.50	3.00	—
2000	—	0.20	0.30	0.50	3.00	—

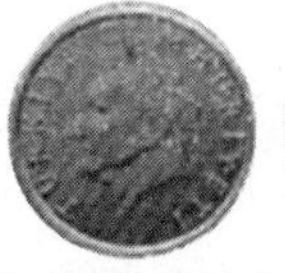

KM# 1104 25000 LIRA (25 Bin Lira)
2.7000 g., Copper-Zinc, 17 mm. **Obv:** Head left **Rev:** Value **Edge:** Plain **Mint:** Istanbul

Date	Mintage	F	VF	XF	Unc	BU
2001	—	—	—	—	2.00	—
2002	—	—	—	—	2.00	—
2003	—	—	—	—	2.00	—

KM# 1050 50000 LIRA (50 Bin Lira)
11.7800 g., Copper-Nickel-Zinc, 28 mm. **Series:** F.A.O. **Obv:** Globe within center of designs, single sprig at left **Rev:** Value **Edge:** "T.C." and four fleur-de-lis repeated four times

Date	Mintage	F	VF	XF	Unc	BU
ND(1996)	500,000	—	—	—	4.50	—

KM# 1056 50000 LIRA (50 Bin Lira)
11.6000 g., Copper-Nickel-Zinc, 28 mm. **Obv:** Head of Atatürk left **Rev:** Value

Date	Mintage	F	VF	XF	Unc	BU
1996	11,916,000	—	—	—	3.50	—
1997	—	—	—	—	3.50	—
1998	—	—	—	—	3.50	—
1999	—	—	—	—	3.50	—
2000	—	—	—	—	3.50	—

KM# 1105 50000 LIRA (50 Bin Lira)
3.2000 g., Copper-Nickel-Zinc, 17.75 mm. **Obv:** Head left within circle **Rev:** Value **Edge:** Plain **Mint:** Istanbul

Date	Mintage	F	VF	XF	Unc	BU
2001	—	—	—	—	0.50	—
2002	—	—	—	—	0.50	—
2003	—	—	—	—	0.50	—
2004	—	—	—	—	0.50	—

KM# 1078 100000 LIRA (100 Bin Lira)
Copper-Nickel-Zinc **Subject:** 75th Anniversary of Republic **Obv:** Value below crescent and star **Rev:** Bust of Mustafa Kemal Atatürk left

Date	Mintage	F	VF	XF	Unc	BU
1999	—	—	—	—	3.00	—
2000	—	—	—	—	3.00	—

KM# 1079 100000 LIRA (100 Bin Lira)
Copper-Nickel-Zinc **Subject:** 75th Anniversary of Republic **Obv:** Value below crescent and star **Rev:** Anniversary logo and dates

Date	Mintage	F	VF	XF	Unc	BU
1999	—	—	—	—	4.00	—
2000	—	—	—	—	4.00	—

KM# 1106 100000 LIRA (100 Bin Lira)
4.6000 g., Copper-Nickel-Zinc, 21 mm. **Obv:** Head with hat right within circle **Rev:** Value **Edge:** Plain **Mint:** Istanbul

Date	Mintage	F	VF	XF	Unc	BU
2001	—	—	—	—	0.75	—
2002	—	—	—	—	0.75	—
2003	—	—	—	—	0.75	—
2004	—	—	—	—	0.75	—

KM# 1137 250000 LIRA
6.4200 g., Copper-Nickel-Zinc, 23.4 mm. **Obv:** Bust facing within circle **Rev:** Value **Edge Lettering:** "T.C." six times dividing reeded sections **Mint:** Istanbul

Date	Mintage	F	VF	XF	Unc	BU
2002	—	—	—	—	1.00	—
2003	—	—	—	—	1.00	—
2004	—	—	—	—	1.00	—

KM# 1161 500000 LIRA
4.6000 g., Copper-Nickel, 21 mm. **Obv:** Value and date within sprigs **Rev:** One sheep **Edge:** Plain **Mint:** Istanbul

Date	Mintage	F	VF	XF	Unc	BU
2002	—	—	—	—	2.50	—

KM# 1162 750000 LIRA
6.4000 g., Copper-Nickel, 23.5 mm. **Obv:** Value and date within sprigs **Rev:** Angora Ram **Edge:** Plain **Mint:** Istanbul

Date	Mintage	F	VF	XF	Unc	BU
2002	—	—	—	—	3.50	—

REFORM DECIMAL COINAGE

2005 - 100,000 Old Lira = 1 New Lira

KM# 1164 NEW KURUS
2.7200 g., Brass, 17 mm. **Obv:** Head left within circle **Rev:** Value **Edge:** Plain **Mint:** Istanbul

Date	Mintage	F	VF	XF	Unc	BU
2005	—	—	—	—	0.15	—
2006	—	—	—	—	0.15	—
2007	Est. 3,000	—	—	—	—	—
2008	—	—	—	—	—	—

KM# 1165 5 NEW KURUS
2.9500 g., Copper-Nickel, 17.1 mm. **Obv:** Head left within circle **Rev:** Value **Edge:** Plain **Mint:** Istanbul

Date	Mintage	F	VF	XF	Unc	BU
2005	—	—	—	—	0.25	—
2006	—	—	—	—	0.25	—
2007	—	—	—	—	0.25	—

KM# 1166 10 NEW KURUS
3.8300 g., Copper-Nickel, 19.4 mm. **Obv:** Head with hat right within circle **Rev:** Value **Edge:** Plain **Mint:** Istanbul

Date	Mintage	F	VF	XF	Unc	BU
2005	—	—	—	—	0.50	—
2006	—	—	—	—	0.50	—
2007	—	—	—	—	0.50	—

KM# 1167 25 NEW KURUS
5.3000 g., Copper-Nickel, 21.5 mm. **Obv:** Head facing within circle **Rev:** Value **Edge:** Reeded **Mint:** Istanbul

Date	Mintage	F	VF	XF	Unc	BU
2005	—	—	—	—	0.50	—
2006	—	—	—	—	1.00	—
2007	—	—	—	—	0.60	—

KM# 1168 50 NEW KURUS
7.0000 g., **Ring Composition:** Brass **Center Composition:** Copper-Nickel, 23.8 mm. **Obv:** Head right within circle **Rev:** Value within circle **Edge:** Reeded **Mint:** Istanbul

Date	Mintage	F	VF	XF	Unc	BU
2005	—	—	—	—	2.00	—
2006	—	—	—	—	2.00	—
2007	—	—	—	—	1.00	—

KM# 1169 NEW LIRA
8.5000 g., Bi-Metallic Brass center in Copper-Nickel ring, 26 mm. **Obv:** Head 1/4 left within circle **Rev:** Value within circle **Edge:** Segmented Reeding **Mint:** Istanbul **Note:** Varieties of weights and other details exist.

Date	Mintage	F	VF	XF	Unc	BU
2005	—	—	—	—	2.50	—
2006	—	—	—	—	2.50	—

Date	Mintage	F	VF	XF	Unc	BU
2007	—	—	—	—	2.50	—
2008	—	—	—	—	2.50	—

KM# 1171 5 NEW LIRA
12.0000 g., Bi-Metallic Brass center in Copper-Nickel ring, 32 mm. **Subject:** 23rd Universiade in red holder **Obv:** Stylized bird within circle **Rev:** Logo within circle **Mint:** Istanbul

Date	Mintage	F	VF	XF	Unc	BU
ND (2005)	10,000	—	—	—	12.50	—

TURKMENISTAN

The Turkmenistan Republic (formerly the Turkmen Soviet Socialist Republic) covers the territory of the Trans-Caspian Region of Turkestan, the Charjiui Vilayet of Bukhara and the part of Khiva located on the right bank of the Oxus. Bordered on the north by the Autonomous Kara-Kalpak Republic (a constituent of Uzbekistan), by Iran and Afghanistan on the south, by the Usbek Republic on the east and the Caspian Sea on the west. It has an area of 186,400 sq. mi. (488,100 sq. km.) and a population of 3.5 million. Capital: Ashkhabad (formerly Poltoratsk). Main occupation is agricultural products including cotton and maize. It is rich in minerals, oil, coal, sulphur and salt and is also famous for its carpets, Turkoman horses and Karakui sheep.

The Turkomans arrived in Trancaspia as nomadic Seluk Turks in the 11th century. It often became subjected to one of the neighboring states. Late in the 19th century the Czarist Russians invaded with their first victory at Kyzyl Arvat in 1877, arriving in Ashkhabad in 1882 resulting in submission of the Turkmen tribes. By March 18,1884 the Transcaspian province of Russian Turkestan was formed. During WW I the Czarist government tried to conscript the Turkmen; this led to a revolt in Oct. 1916 under the leadership of Aziz Chapykov. In 1918 the Turks captured Baku from the Red army and the British sent a contingent to Merv to prevent a German-Turkish offensive toward Afghanistan and India. In mid-1919 a Bureau of Turkestan Moslem Communist Organization was formed in Moscow hoping to develop one large republic including all surrounding Turkic areas within a Soviet federation. A Turkestan Autonomous Soviet Socialist Republic was formed and plans to partition Turkestan into five republics according to the principle of nationalities was quickly implemented by Joseph Stalin. On Oct. 27, 1924 Turkmenistan became a Soviet Socialist Republic and was accepted as a member of the U.S.S.R. on Jan. 29, 1925. The Bureau of T.M.C.O. was disbanded in 1934. In Aug. 1990 the Turkmen Supreme Soviet adopted a declaration of sovereignty followed by a declaration of independence in Oct. 1991 joining the Commonwealth of Independent States in Dec. A new constitution was adopted in 1992 providing for an executive presidency.

REPUBLIC

STANDARD COINAGE

100 Tenge = 1 Manat

KM# 1 TENGE
1.9000 g., Copper Plated Steel, 16 mm. **Obv:** Value in center of flower-like design within circle **Rev:** Head of President Saparmyrat Nyyazow left **Edge:** Plain

Date	Mintage	F	VF	XF	Unc	BU
1993	—	—	—	—	0.25	0.35

KM# 2 5 TENGE
3.0000 g., Copper Plated Steel, 19.5 mm. **Obv:** Value in center of flower-like design within circle **Rev:** Head of President Saparmyrat Nyyazow left **Edge:** Plain

Date	Mintage	F	VF	XF	Unc	BU
1993	—	—	—	—	0.35	0.45

KM# 3 10 TENGE
4.5000 g., Copper Plated Steel, 22.5 mm. **Obv:** Value in center of designs within circle **Rev:** Head of President Saparmyrat Nyyazow left **Edge:** Plain

Date	Mintage	F	VF	XF	Unc	BU
1993	—	—	—	—	0.60	0.75

KM# 4 20 TENGE
3.6000 g., Nickel Plated Steel, 20.9 mm. **Obv:** Value within ornate circle **Rev:** Head of President Saparmyrat Nyyazow left **Edge:** Plain

Date	Mintage	F	VF	XF	Unc	BU
1993	—	—	—	—	1.25	1.50

KM# 5 50 TENGE
4.9000 g., Nickel Plated Steel, 24 mm. **Obv:** Value above animal leaning on horn at right **Rev:** Head of President Saparmyrat Nyyazow left **Edge:** Plain

Date	Mintage	F	VF	XF	Unc	BU
1993	—	—	—	—	2.75	3.00

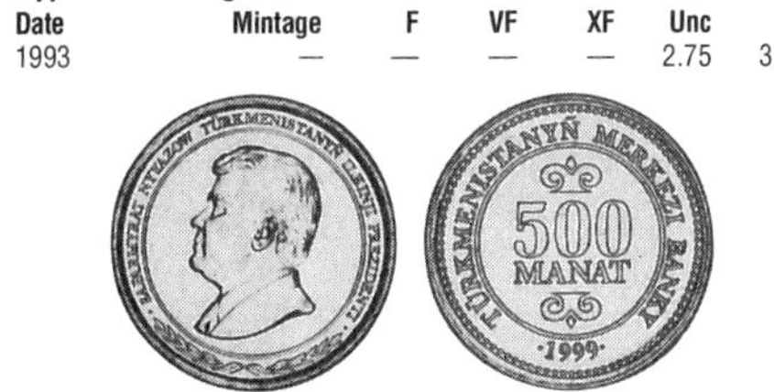

KM# 12 500 MANAT
Nickel Clad Steel **Obv:** Head of President Saparmyrat Nyyazow left **Rev:** Crown and value within circle **Edge:** Reeded

Date	Mintage	F	VF	XF	Unc	BU
1999	Est. 5,000	—	—	—	1.25	1.50

TUVALU

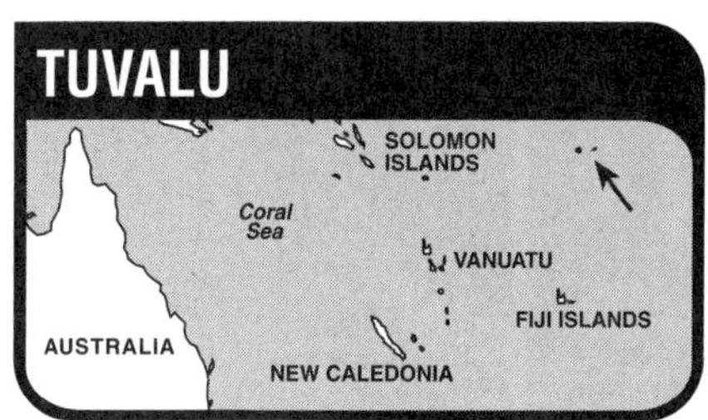

Tuvalu (formerly the Ellice or Lagoon Islands of the Gilbert and Ellice Islands), located in the South Pacific north of the Fiji Islands, has an area of 10 sq. mi. (26 sq.km.) and a population of *9,000. Capital: Funafuti. The independent state includes the islands of Nanumanga, Nanumea, Nui, Niutao, Viatupa, Funafuti, Nukufetau, Nukulailai and Nurakita. The latter four islands were claimed by the United States until relinquished by the Feb. 7, 1979, Treaty of Friendship signed by the United States and Tuvalu. The principal industries are copra production and phosphate mining.

The islands were discovered in 1764 by John Byron, a British navigator, and annexed by Britain in 1892. In 1915 they became part of the crown colony of the Gilbert and Ellice Islands. In 1974 the islanders voted to separate from the Gilberts, becoming on Jan. 1, 1976, the separate constitutional dependency of Tuvalu. Full independence was attained on Oct. 1, 1978. Tuvalu is a member of the Commonwealth of Nations. Elizabeth II is Head of State as Queen of Tuvalu.

RULER
British, until 1978

MONETARY SYSTEM
100 Cents = 1 Dollar

CONSTITUTIONAL MONARCHY WITHIN THE COMMONWEALTH

STANDARD COINAGE

KM# 1 CENT
2.6000 g., Bronze, 17.5 mm. **Obv:** Young bust right **Rev:** Sea shell and value

Date	Mintage	F	VF	XF	Unc	BU
1976	93,000	—	—	0.10	0.50	1.00
1976 Proof	20,000	Value: 1.00				
1981	—	—	—	0.10	0.50	1.00
1981 Proof	—	Value: 1.00				
1985	—	—	—	0.10	0.50	1.00

KM# 26 CENT
2.6000 g., Bronze, 17.5 mm. **Obv:** Crowned head right **Obv. Designer:** Raphael Maklouf **Rev:** Sea shell and value

Date	Mintage	F	VF	XF	Unc	BU
1994	—	—	—	—	0.50	1.00

KM# 2 2 CENTS
5.2000 g., Bronze, 21.6 mm. **Obv:** Young bust right **Rev:** Stingray and value

Date	Mintage	F	VF	XF	Unc	BU
1976	51,000	—	0.10	0.15	1.00	2.50
1976 Proof	20,000	Value: 1.75				
1981	—	—	0.10	0.15	1.00	2.50
1981 Proof	—	Value: 1.75				
1985	—	—	0.10	0.15	1.00	2.50

KM# 30 2 CENTS
5.2000 g., Bronze, 21.6 mm. **Obv:** Crowned head right **Obv. Designer:** Raphael Maklouf

Date	Mintage	F	VF	XF	Unc	BU
1994	—	—	—	—	1.00	2.00

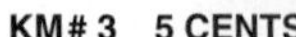

KM# 3 5 CENTS

2.8000 g., Copper-Nickel, 19.4 mm. **Obv:** Young bust right **Rev:** Tiger shark and value

Date	Mintage	F	VF	XF	Unc	BU
1976	26,000	—	0.10	0.25	1.50	3.50
1976 Proof	20,000	Value: 4.00				
1981	—	—	0.10	0.25	1.50	3.50
1981 Proof	—	Value: 4.00				
1985	—	—	0.10	0.25	1.50	3.50

KM# 31 5 CENTS

2.8000 g., Copper-Nickel, 19.4 mm. **Obv:** Crowned head right **Obv. Designer:** Raphael Maklouf

Date	Mintage	F	VF	XF	Unc	BU
1994	—	—	—	—	1.50	4.00

KM# 4 10 CENTS

5.6000 g., Copper-Nickel, 23.5 mm. **Obv:** Young bust right **Rev:** Crab and value

Date	Mintage	F	VF	XF	Unc	BU
1976	26,000	0.15	0.20	0.35	1.50	4.00
1976 Proof	20,000	Value: 4.00				
1981	—	0.15	0.20	0.35	1.50	4.00
1981 Proof	—	Value: 4.00				
1985	—	0.15	0.20	0.35	1.50	4.00

KM# 32 10 CENTS

5.6000 g., Copper-Nickel, 23.5 mm. **Obv:** Crowned head right **Obv. Designer:** Raphael Maklouf

Date	Mintage	F	VF	XF	Unc	BU
1994	—	—	—	—	1.50	4.00

KM# 5 20 CENTS

11.2500 g., Copper-Nickel, 28.45 mm. **Obv:** Young bust right **Rev:** Flying fish and value

Date	Mintage	F	VF	XF	Unc	BU
1976	36,000	0.30	0.40	0.60	2.50	4.50
1976 Proof	20,000	Value: 6.00				
1981	—	0.30	0.40	0.60	2.50	4.50
1981 Proof	—	Value: 6.00				
1985	—	0.30	0.40	0.60	2.50	4.50

KM# 33 20 CENTS

11.2500 g., Copper-Nickel, 28.45 mm. **Obv:** Crowned head right **Obv. Designer:** Raphael Maklouf

Date	Mintage	F	VF	XF	Unc	BU
1994	—	—	—	—	2.00	3.50

KM# 6 50 CENTS

15.5000 g., Copper-Nickel, 31.65 mm. **Obv:** Young bust right **Rev:** Octopus and value

Date	Mintage	F	VF	XF	Unc	BU
1976	19,000	0.50	0.75	1.50	5.00	8.50
1976 Proof	20,000	Value: 8.00				
1981	—	0.50	0.75	1.50	5.00	8.50
1981 Proof	—	Value: 8.00				
1985	—	0.50	0.75	1.50	5.00	8.50

KM# 34 50 CENTS

15.5000 g., Copper-Nickel, 31.65 mm. **Obv:** Crowned head right **Obv. Designer:** Raphael Maklouf

Date	Mintage	F	VF	XF	Unc	BU
1994	—	—	—	—	5.00	8.00

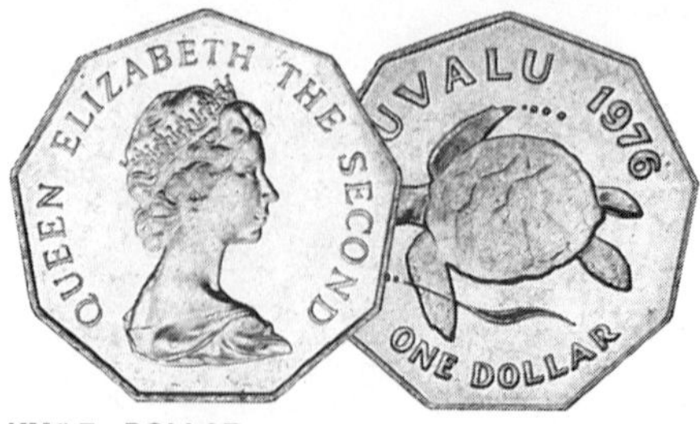

KM# 7 DOLLAR

16.0000 g., Copper-Nickel, 33 mm. **Obv:** Young bust right **Rev:** Sea turtle and value **Shape:** 9-sided

Date	Mintage	F	VF	XF	Unc	BU
1976	21,000	1.00	1.50	2.00	6.00	10.00
1976 Proof	20,000	Value: 11.50				
1981	—	1.00	1.50	2.00	6.00	10.00
1981 Proof	—	Value: 11.50				
1985	—	1.00	1.50	2.00	6.00	10.00

KM# 35 DOLLAR

16.0000 g., Copper-Nickel, 33 mm. **Obv:** Crowned head right **Obv. Designer:** Raphael Maklouf

Date	Mintage	F	VF	XF	Unc	BU
1994	—	—	—	—	6.00	10.00

UGANDA

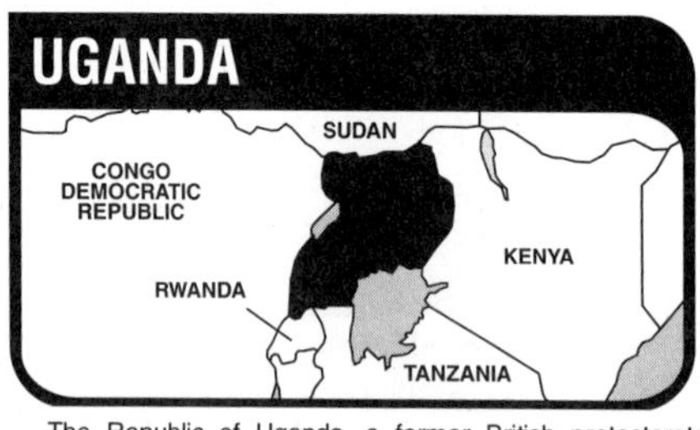

The Republic of Uganda, a former British protectorate located astride the equator in east-central Africa, has an area of 91,134 sq. mi. (236,040 sq. km.) and a population of *17 million. Capital: Kampala. Agriculture, including livestock, is the basis of the economy; there is some mining of copper, tin, gold and lead. Coffee, cotton, copper and tea are exported.

Uganda was first visited by Arab slavers in the 1830s. They were followed in the 1860s by British explorers searching for the headwaters of the Nile. The explorers, and the missionaries who followed them into the Lake Victoria region of south central Africa in 1877-79, found well-developed African kingdoms dating back several centuries. In 1894 the local native Kingdom of Buganda was established as a British protectorate that was extended in 1896 to encompass an area substantially the same as the present Republic of Uganda. The protectorate was given a ministerial form of government in 1955, full internal self-government on March 1, 1962, and complete independence on Oct. 9, 1962. Uganda is a member of the Commonwealth of Nations. The president is Chief of State and Head of Government.

For earlier coinage refer to East Africa.

RULER

British, until 1962

MONETARY SYSTEM

100 Cents = 1 Shilling

REPUBLIC

STANDARD COINAGE

KM# 1 5 CENTS

3.2100 g., Bronze, 20 mm. **Obv:** Value above crossed tusks within circle **Rev:** Value within circular sprig **Edge:** Plain

Date	Mintage	F	VF	XF	Unc	BU
1966	41,000,000	—	0.10	0.15	0.30	1.00
1966 Proof	—	Value: 1.00				
1974	8,624,000	—	0.20	0.30	0.75	1.00
1975	14,784,000	—	0.20	0.30	0.75	1.00

KM# 1a 5 CENTS

Copper Plated Steel **Obv:** Value above crossed tusks within circle **Rev:** Value within circular sprig

Date	Mintage	F	VF	XF	Unc	BU
1976	10,000,000	—	0.20	0.30	0.75	—

KM# 2 10 CENTS

5.0000 g., Bronze, 24.5 mm. **Obv:** Value above crossed tusks within circle **Rev:** Value within circular sprig

Date	Mintage	F	VF	XF	Unc	BU
1966	19,100,000	—	0.10	0.15	0.35	1.00
1966 Proof	—	Value: 1.00				
1968	20,000,000	—	0.10	0.15	0.35	1.00
1970	6,000,000	—	0.20	0.30	0.75	1.00
1972	6,000,000	—	0.20	0.30	0.75	1.00
1974	4,110,000	—	0.20	0.30	0.75	1.25
1975	14,000,000	—	0.20	0.30	0.75	1.25

KM# 2a 10 CENTS

Copper-Plated-Steel **Obv:** Value above crossed tusks within circle **Rev:** Value within circular sprig

Date	Mintage	F	VF	XF	Unc	BU
1976	10,000,000	—	0.20	0.30	0.75	1.25

KM# 3 20 CENTS

Bronze **Obv:** Value above crossed tusks within circle **Rev:** Value within circular sprig

Date	Mintage	F	VF	XF	Unc	BU
1966	7,000,000	—	0.30	0.70	1.65	2.00
1966 Proof	—	Value: 2.00				
1974	2,000,000	—	0.50	1.00	2.25	3.00

KM# 4 50 CENTS

Copper-Nickel **Obv:** National arms **Rev:** East African crowned crane, mountains and value

Date	Mintage	F	VF	XF	Unc	BU
1966	16,000,000	—	0.20	0.40	2.00	3.50
1966 Proof	—	Value: 3.50				
1970	3,000,000	—	0.25	0.75	3.00	3.50
1974	10,000,000	—	0.25	0.65	2.00	3.50

KM# 4a 50 CENTS

Copper-Nickel Plated Steel **Obv:** National arms **Rev:** East African crowned crane within circular sprig above value and date

Date	Mintage	F	VF	XF	Unc	BU
1976	10,000,000	—	0.25	0.65	2.00	3.00

KM# 5 SHILLING

Copper-Nickel **Obv:** National arms **Rev:** East African crowned crane within circular sprig above date and value

Date	Mintage	F	VF	XF	Unc	BU
1966	24,500,000	—	0.25	0.50	2.50	4.50
1966 Proof	—	Value: 4.50				
1968	10,000,000	—	0.35	0.85	2.75	4.50
1972	4,040,000	—	0.35	0.85	2.75	4.50
1975	15,500,000	—	0.35	0.85	2.50	4.50

KM# 5a SHILLING

Copper-Nickel Plated Steel **Obv:** National arms **Rev:** East African crowned crane within circular sprig above date and value

Date	Mintage	F	VF	XF	Unc	BU
1976	10,000,000	—	0.35	0.85	2.50	4.00

KM# 27 SHILLING
4.3000 g., Copper Plated Steel, 19.85 mm. **Obv:** National arms **Rev:** Flowers 3/4 surround value within center circle, sack below above date **Edge:** Plain **Shape:** 12-sided

Date	Mintage	F	VF	XF	Unc	BU
1987	—	—	—	—	0.25	0.40
1987 Proof	—	Value: 2.50				

KM# 6 2 SHILLINGS
Copper-Nickel **Obv:** National arms **Rev:** East African crowned crane within circular sprig above date and value

Date	Mintage	F	VF	XF	Unc	BU
1966	4,000,000	—	1.00	2.00	5.00	7.50
1966 Proof	—	Value: 9.00				

KM# 28 2 SHILLINGS
8.1000 g., Copper Plated Steel, 24.37 mm. **Obv:** National arms **Rev:** Value in center circle of flowered sprigs **Edge:** Plain **Shape:** 12-sided

Date	Mintage	F	VF	XF	Unc	BU
1987	—	—	—	—	1.00	1.50
1987 Proof	—	Value: 4.00				

KM# 7 5 SHILLINGS
Copper-Nickel, 37.8 mm. **Series:** F.A.O. **Obv:** National arms **Rev:** Cow and calf

Date	Mintage	F	VF	XF	Unc	BU
ND(1968)	100,000	—	1.50	2.50	5.00	7.00
ND(1968) Proof	5,000	Value: 8.50				

KM# 18 5 SHILLINGS
Copper-Nickel, 30 mm. **Obv:** National arms **Rev:** East African crowned crane within circular sprig **Edge:** Plain **Shape:** 7-sided
Note: Withdrawn from circulation. Almost entire mintage was melted.

Date	Mintage	F	VF	XF	Unc	BU
1972	Est. 8,000,000	—	25.00	45.00	90.00	125

KM# 29 5 SHILLINGS
3.5000 g., Stainless Steel, 20.23 mm. **Obv:** National arms **Rev:** Value within center circle of sprigs **Edge:** Plain **Shape:** 7-sided

Date	Mintage	F	VF	XF	Unc	BU
1987	—	—	—	—	2.50	3.00
1987 Proof	—	Value: 6.50				

KM# 30 10 SHILLINGS
5.8000 g., Stainless Steel, 25.91 mm. **Obv:** National arms **Rev:** Value in center circle of sprigs **Edge:** Plain **Shape:** 7-sided

Date	Mintage	F	VF	XF	Unc	BU
1987	—	—	—	—	3.50	4.50
1987 Proof	—	Value: 12.50				

KM# 66 50 SHILLINGS
Nickel Plated Steel **Obv:** National arms **Rev:** Antelope head facing

Date	Mintage	F	VF	XF	Unc	BU
1998	—	—	—	—	1.00	1.25
2003	—	—	—	—	1.00	1.25

KM# 67 100 SHILLINGS
7.0000 g., Copper-Nickel, 26.9 mm. **Obv:** National arms **Rev:** African bull **Edge:** Reeded

Date	Mintage	F	VF	XF	Unc	BU
1998	—	—	—	—	1.50	1.75
2003	—	—	—	—	1.50	1.75

KM# 129 100 SHILLINGS
3.5000 g., Stainless Steel, 24 mm. **Obv:** National arms **Rev:** Monkey with elf-like ears **Edge:** Plain

Date	Mintage	F	VF	XF	Unc	BU
2004	—	—	—	—	1.50	—

KM# 188 100 SHILLINGS
3.5300 g., Nickel Plated Steel, 24 mm. **Series:** Zodiac **Obv:** National arms **Obv. Legend:** BANK OF UGANDA **Rev:** Head of a rat **Rev. Legend:** BANK OF UGANDA **Edge:** Plain

Date	Mintage	F	VF	XF	Unc	BU
2004	—	—	—	—	1.50	—

KM# 189 100 SHILLINGS
3.5300 g., Nickel Plated Steel, 24 mm. **Series:** Zodiac **Obv:** National arms **Obv. Legend:** BANK OF UGANDA **Rev:** Head of an ox **Rev. Legend:** BANK OF UGANDA **Edge:** Plain

Date	Mintage	F	VF	XF	Unc	BU
2004	—	—	—	—	1.50	—

KM# 190 100 SHILLINGS
3.5300 g., Nickel Plated Steel, 24 mm. **Series:** Zodiac **Obv:** National arms **Obv. Legend:** BANK OF UGANDA **Rev:** Head of a tiger **Rev. Legend:** BANK OF UGANDA **Edge:** Plain

Date	Mintage	F	VF	XF	Unc	BU
2004	—	—	—	—	1.50	—

KM# 191 100 SHILLINGS
3.5300 g., Nickel Plated Steel, 24 mm. **Series:** Zodiac **Obv:** National arms **Obv. Legend:** BANK OF UGANDA **Rev:** Head of a rabbit **Rev. Legend:** BANK OF UGANDA **Edge:** Plain

Date	Mintage	F	VF	XF	Unc	BU
2004	—	—	—	—	1.50	—

KM# 192 100 SHILLINGS
3.5300 g., Nickel Plated Steel, 24 mm. **Series:** Zodiac **Obv:** National arms **Obv. Legend:** BANK OF UGANDA **Rev:** Head of a dragon **Rev. Legend:** BANK OF UGANDA **Edge:** Plain

Date	Mintage	F	VF	XF	Unc	BU
2004	—	—	—	—	1.50	—

KM# 193 100 SHILLINGS
3.5300 g., Nickel Plated Steel, 24 mm. **Series:** Zodiac **Obv:** National arms **Obv. Legend:** BANK OF UGANDA **Rev:** Head and hood of Cobra snake **Rev. Legend:** BANK OF UGANDA **Edge:** Plain

Date	Mintage	F	VF	XF	Unc	BU
2004	—	—	—	—	1.50	—

KM# 194 100 SHILLINGS
3.5300 g., Nickel Plated Steel, 24 mm. **Series:** Zodiac **Obv:** National arms **Obv. Legend:** BANK OF UGANDA **Rev:** Head of a horse **Rev. Legend:** BANK OF UGANDA **Edge:** Plain

Date	Mintage	F	VF	XF	Unc	BU
2004	—	—	—	—	1.50	—

KM# 195 100 SHILLINGS
3.5300 g., Nickel Plated Steel, 24 mm. **Series:** Zodiac **Obv:** National arms **Obv. Legend:** BANK OF UGANDA **Rev:** Head of a goat **Rev. Legend:** BANK OF UGANDA **Edge:** Plain

Date	Mintage	F	VF	XF	Unc	BU
2004	—	—	—	—	1.50	—

KM# 196 100 SHILLINGS
3.5300 g., Nickel Plated Steel, 24 mm. **Series:** Zodiac **Obv:** National arms **Obv. Legend:** BANK OF UGANDA **Rev:** Head of a monkey **Rev. Legend:** BANK OF UGANDA **Edge:** Plain

Date	Mintage	F	VF	XF	Unc	BU
2004	—	—	—	—	1.50	—

KM# 197 100 SHILLINGS
3.5300 g., Nickel Plated Steel, 24 mm. **Series:** Zodiac **Obv:** National arms **Obv. Legend:** BANK OF UGANDA **Rev:** Forepart of a rooster **Rev. Legend:** BANK OF UGANDA **Edge:** Plain

Date	Mintage	F	VF	XF	Unc	BU
2004	—	—	—	—	1.50	—

KM# 198 100 SHILLINGS
3.5300 g., Nickel Plated Steel, 24 mm. **Series:** Zodiac **Obv:** National arms **Obv. Legend:** BANK OF UGANDA **Rev:** Head of a dog **Rev. Legend:** BANK OF UGANDA **Edge:** Plain

Date	Mintage	F	VF	XF	Unc	BU
2004	—	—	—	—	1.50	—

KM# 199 100 SHILLINGS
3.5300 g., Nickel Plated Steel, 24 mm. **Series:** Zodiac **Obv:** National arms **Obv. Legend:** BANK OF UGANDA **Rev:** Head of a pig **Rev. Legend:** BANK OF UGANDA **Edge:** Plain

Date	Mintage	F	VF	XF	Unc	BU
2004	—	—	—	—	1.50	—

KM# 148 200 SHILLINGS
7.6000 g., Aluminum-Bronze, 26 mm. **Series:** Food For All **Obv:** National arms **Obv. Legend:** BANK OF UGANDA **Rev:** Fish

Date	Mintage	F	VF	XF	Unc	BU
1995	20,000	—	—	—	—	18.00

KM# 68 200 SHILLINGS
8.0500 g., Copper-Nickel, 24.9 mm. **Obv:** National arms **Rev:** Cichlid fish above value and date **Edge:** Plain

Date	Mintage	F	VF	XF	Unc	BU
1998	—	—	—	—	2.00	2.25
2003	—	—	—	—	2.00	2.25

KM# 69 500 SHILLINGS
9.0000 g., Aluminum-Brass, 23.5 mm. **Obv:** National arms **Rev:** East African crowned crane head left **Edge:** Reeded

Date	Mintage	F	VF	XF	Unc	BU
1998	—	—	—	—	2.50	3.00
2003	—	—	—	—	2.50	3.00

UKRAINE

BELARUS
POLAND
RUSSIA
TRANSDNIESTRA
SLOVAKIA
HUNGARY
MOLDOVA
ROMANIA
Black Sea

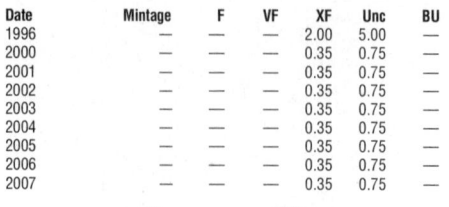

Ukraine (formerly the Ukrainian Soviet Socialist Republic) is bordered by Russia to the east, Russia and Belarus to the north, Poland, Slovakia and Hungary to the west, Romania and Moldova to the southwest and in the south by the Black Sea and the Sea of Azov. It has an area of 233,088 sq. mi. (603,700 sq. km.) and a population of 51.9 million. Capital: Kyiv (Kiev). Coal, grain, vegetables and heavy industrial machinery are major exports.

The territory of Ukraine has been inhabited for over 30,000 years. As the result of its location, Ukraine has served as the gateway to Europe for millennia and its early history has been recorded by Arabic, Greek, Roman, as well as Ukrainian historians.

Ukraine, which was known as *Rus'* until the sixteenth century (and from which the name Russia was derived in the 17th century) became the major political and cultural center of Eastern Europe in the 9th century. The Rus' Kingdom, under a dynasty of Varangian origin, due to its position on the intersection of the north-south Scandinavia to Byzantium and the east-west Orient to Europe trade routes, became a focal point of world trade. At its apex Rus' stretched from the Baltic to the Black Sea and from the upper Volga River in the east, almost to the Vistula River in the west. It has family ties to many European dynasties. In 988 knyaz (king) Volodymyr adopted Christianity from Byzantium. With it came church books written in the Cyrillic alphabet, which originated in Bulgaria. The Mongol invasion in 1240 brought an end to the might of the Rus' Kingdom.

In the seventeenth century, after almost four hundred years of Mongol, Lithuanian, Polish, and Turkish domination, the Cossack State under Hetman Bohdan Khmelnytsky regained Ukrainian independence. The Hetman State lasted until the mid-eighteenth century and was followed by a period of foreign rule. Eastern Ukraine was controlled by Russia, which enforced russification through introduction of the Russian language and prohibiting the use of the Ukrainian language in schools, books and public life. Western Ukraine came under relatively benign Austro-Hungarian rule.

With the disintegration of the Russian and Austro-Hungarian Empires in 1917 and 1918. Eastern Ukraine declared its full independence on January 22,1918 and Western Ukraine followed suit on November 1 of that year. On January 22, 1919 both parts united into one state that had to defend itself on three fronts: from the "Red Bolsheviks"and their puppet Ukrainian Soviet Republic formed in Kharkiv, from the "White" czarist Russian forces, and from Poland. Ukraine lost the war. In 1920 Eastern Ukraine was occupied by the Bolsheviks and in 1922 was incorporated into the Soviet Union. There followed a brief resurgence of Ukrainian language and culture which Stalin suppressed in 1928. The artificial famine-genocide of 1932-33 killed 7-10 million Ukrainians, and Stalinist purges in the mid-1930s took a heavy toll. Western Ukraine was partitioned between Poland, Romania, Hungary and Czechoslovakia.

On August 24, 1991 Ukraine once again declared its independence. On December 1, 1991 over 90% of Ukraine's electorate approved full independence from the Soviet Union. On December 5, 1991 the Ukrainian Parliament abrogated the 1922 treaty which incorporated Ukraine into the Soviet Union. Later, Leonid Kravchuk was elected president by a 65% majority.

Ukraine is a charter member of the United Nations and has inherited the third largest nuclear arsenal in the world.

RULERS

Russian (Eastern, Northern, Southern, Central Ukraine), 1654-1917
Austrian (Western Ukraine), 1774-1918

MINT

Without mm - Lugansk; Kiev (1997-1998)

MONETARY SYSTEM

(1) Kopiyka
(2) Kopiyky КОПІЙКИ
(5 and up) Kopiyok КОПІЙОК
100 Kopiyok = 1 Hrynia ГРИВЕНЬ
100,000 Karbovanetsiv = 1 Hryni or Hryven)

REPUBLIC

REFORM COINAGE

September 2, 1996

100,000 Karbovanets = 1 Hryvnia; 100 Kopiyok = 1 Hryvnia; The Kopiyok has replaced the Karbovanet

KM# 6 KOPIYKA

1.5300 g., Stainless Steel, 15.96 mm. **Obv:** National arms **Rev:** Value within wreath **Edge:** Plain

Date	Mintage	F	VF	XF	Unc	BU
1992	—	—	—	0.15	0.35	—
1994	—	—	—	5.00	10.00	—
1996	—	—	—	2.00	5.00	—
2000	—	—	—	0.35	0.75	—
2001	—	—	—	0.35	0.75	—
2002	—	—	—	0.35	0.75	—
2003	—	—	—	0.35	0.75	—
2004	—	—	—	0.35	0.75	—
2005	—	—	—	0.35	0.75	—
2006	—	—	—	0.35	0.75	—
2007	—	—	—	0.35	0.75	—

KM# 4a 2 KOPIYKY

0.6400 g., Aluminum, 17.3 mm. **Obv:** National arms **Rev:** Value within wreath **Edge:** Plain **Note:** Prev. KM#4.

Date	Mintage	F	VF	XF	Unc	BU
1992	—	—	—	—	200	—
1993	—	—	0.20	0.50	1.00	—
1994	—	—	0.20	0.50	1.00	—
1996	—	—	0.40	2.00	3.00	—

KM# 4b 2 KOPIYKY

1.8000 g., Stainless Steel, 17.3 mm. **Obv:** National arms **Rev:** Value in wreath **Edge:** Plain

Date	Mintage	F	VF	XF	Unc	BU
2001	—	—	0.20	0.50	1.00	—
2002	—	—	0.20	0.50	1.00	—
2004	—	—	0.20	0.50	1.00	—
2005	—	—	0.20	0.50	1.00	—
2006	—	—	0.20	0.50	1.00	—
2007	—	—	0.20	0.50	1.00	—

KM# 7 5 KOPIYOK

4.3000 g., Stainless Steel, 23.91 mm. **Obv:** National arms **Rev:** Value within wreath **Edge:** Reeded

Date	Mintage	F	VF	XF	Unc	BU
1992	—	—	—	0.35	0.65	—
1994	—	—	—	—	100	—
2001	—	—	0.50	3.00	6.00	—
2003	—	—	—	0.50	1.00	—
2004	—	—	—	0.50	1.00	—
2005	—	—	—	0.50	1.00	—
2006	—	—	—	0.50	1.00	—
2007	—	—	—	0.50	1.00	—

KM# 1.1a 10 KOPIYOK

1.7000 g., Brass, 16.3 mm. **Obv:** National arms **Rev:** Five dots right of final "K" in value **Edge:** Reeded **Note:** Fine or coarse reeded edge varieties exist. Prev. KM#1.1.

Date	Mintage	F	VF	XF	Unc	BU
1992	—	—	0.50	1.00	2.25	—
1994	—	—	0.50	1.00	2.25	—
1996	—	—	0.60	1.25	2.50	—

KM# 1.1b 10 KOPIYOK

1.7000 g., Aluminum-Bronze, 16.24 mm. **Obv:** National arms **Rev:** Value within wreath

Date	Mintage	F	VF	XF	Unc	BU
2001	—	—	2.00	5.00	6.00	—
2002	—	—	0.60	1.25	2.50	—
2003	—	—	0.50	1.00	2.25	—
2004	—	—	0.50	1.00	2.25	—
2005	—	—	0.50	1.00	2.25	—
2006	—	—	0.50	1.00	2.25	—
2007	—	—	0.50	1.00	2.25	—

KM# 1.2 10 KOPIYOK

Brass **Obv:** National arms **Rev:** Six dots right of "K"

Date	Mintage	F	VF	XF	Unc	BU
1992	—	—	0.50	1.00	2.25	—

KM# 2.1a 25 KOPIYOK

2.9000 g., Brass, 20.8 mm. **Obv:** National arms **Rev:** Value within wreath **Note:** Prev. KM#2.1.

Date	Mintage	F	VF	XF	Unc	BU
1992	—	—	0.60	1.25	2.50	—
1994	—	—	0.60	1.25	2.50	—
1995	—	—	1.50	3.00	6.00	—
1996	—	—	0.80	2.25	4.00	—

KM# 2.1b 25 KOPIYOK

Aluminum-Bronze

Date	Mintage	F	VF	XF	Unc	BU
2001	—	—	0.80	3.00	6.00	—
2006	—	—	0.80	3.00	6.00	—
2007	—	—	0.80	3.00	6.00	—

KM# 2.2 25 KOPIYOK

Brass **Obv:** National arms **Rev:** Berries with dots inside

Date	Mintage	F	VF	XF	Unc	BU
1992	—	—	0.60	1.25	2.50	—

KM# 3.1 50 KOPIYOK

4.2000 g., Brass, 23 mm. **Obv:** National arms **Rev:** Five dots grouped i wreath to right of final letter "K" in value **Edge:** Reeded sections of 16 grooves each

Date	Mintage	F	VF	XF	Unc	BU
1992	—	—	0.85	1.75	3.50	—
1994	—	—	0.85	1.75	3.50	—

KM# 3.3a 50 KOPIYOK

Brass **Obv:** National arms **Rev:** Five dots grouped in wreath to right of final letter "K" in value **Note:** Prev. KM#3.3.

Date	Mintage	F	VF	XF	Unc	BU
1992	—	—	0.85	1.75	3.50	—
1994	—	—	0.85	1.75	3.50	—
1995	—	—	3.00	5.00	10.00	—
1996	—	—	1.00	2.50	4.50	—

KM# 3.3b 50 KOPIYOK

Aluminum-Bronze

Date	Mintage	F	VF	XF	Unc	BU
2001	—	—	1.00	2.00	4.00	—
2006	—	—	1.00	2.00	4.00	—
2007	—	—	1.00	2.00	4.00	—

KM# 3.2 50 KOPIYOK

Brass **Obv:** National arms **Rev:** Four dots grouped in wreath to right of final letter "K" in value **Edge:** Reeded sections of seven grooves each

Date	Mintage	F	VF	XF	Unc	BU
1992	—	—	0.85	1.75	3.50	—

KM# 8a HRYVNIA

7.1000 g., Brass, 26 mm. **Obv:** National arms **Rev:** Value, sprigs and designs **Note:** Prev. KM#8.

Date	Mintage	F	VF	XF	Unc	BU
1992	—	—	—	80.00	200	—
1995	—	—	—	5.00	10.00	—
1996	—	—	—	2.50	4.50	—
2006	—	—	—	2.50	4.50	—

KM# 8b HRYVNIA

6.9000 g., Aluminum-Bronze

Date	Mintage	F	VF	XF	Unc	BU
2001	—	—	—	2.50	4.50	—
2002	—	—	—	3.50	6.50	—
2003	—	—	—	2.50	4.50	—

KM# 208 HRYVNIA

6.8000 g., Aluminum-Bronze, 26 mm. **Subject:** 60th Anniversary - Victory over the Nazis **Obv:** National arms above value **Rev:** Uniform lapel with Soviet military medals group **Edge:** Lettered **Edge Lettering:** Date and denomination

Date	Mintage	F	VF	XF	Unc	BU
2004	5,000,000	—	—	—	4.00	—

KM# 209 HRYVNIA

6.7400 g., Aluminum-Bronze, 26 mm. **Obv:** National arms above value **Rev:** Half length figure of Volodymyr the Great facing holding church model building and staff **Edge:** Lettered **Edge Lettering:** Date and denomination

Date	Mintage	F	VF	XF	Unc	BU
2004	10,000,000	—	—	—	3.50	—
2005	—	—	—	—	3.00	—
2006	—	—	—	—	3.00	—

KM# 228 HRYVNIA

6.8000 g., Aluminum-Bronze, 26 mm. **Subject:** WW II Victory 60th Anniversary **Obv:** Value **Rev:** Soldiers in a "V" of search lights **Edge:** Reeded

Date	Mintage	F	VF	XF	Unc	BU
2005	5,000,000	—	—	—	4.00	—

KM# 104 5 HRYVEN

9.4000 g., Bi-Metallic Brass center in Copper-Nickel ring, 28 mm. **Subject:** Third Millennium **Obv:** National arms **Rev:** Figure sowing seeds within circle **Edge:** Reeded and plain sections

Date	Mintage	F	VF	XF	Unc	BU
2000	50,000	—	—	—	50.00	—

KM# 140 5 HRYVEN

9.4000 g., Bi-Metallic Brass center in Copper-Nickel ring, 28 mm. **Subject:** 10th Anniversary of Military forces **Obv:** Crossed maces, arms and date within wreath and circle **Rev:** Circle in center of cross within wreath and circle **Edge:** Reeded and plain sections

Date	Mintage	F	VF	XF	Unc	BU
2001	30,000	—	—	—	60.00	—

KM# 158 5 HRYVEN

9.4300 g., Bi-Metallic Brass center in Copper-Nickel ring, 28 mm. **Subject:** 70th Anniversary of Dnipro Hydroelectric Power Station **Obv:** Turbine within circle **Rev:** Large dam within circle **Edge:** Reeded and plain sections

Date	Mintage	F	VF	XF	Unc	BU
2002	30,000	—	—	—	30.00	—

KM# 200 5 HRYVEN

9.4000 g., Bi-Metallic Brass center in Copper-Nickel ring, 28 mm. **Obv:** Bandura strings over ornamental design **Rev:** Bandura divides circle and wreath **Edge:** Segmented reeding

Date	Mintage	F	VF	XF	Unc	BU
2003	30,000	—	—	—	15.00	—

KM# 185 5 HRYVEN

9.4000 g., Bi-Metallic Brass center in Copper-Nickel ring, 28 mm. **Subject:** 150th Anniversary of the Central Ukrainian Archives **Obv:** Value, signature and seal **Rev:** Hourglass divides books and circle **Edge:** Segmented reeding

Date	Mintage	F	VF	XF	Unc	BU
2003	30,000	—	—	—	15.00	—

KM# 220 5 HRYVEN

9.4300 g., Bi-Metallic BRASS center in COPPER-NICKEL ring, 28 mm. **Subject:** 50 Years of Ukraine's Membership in UNESCO **Obv:** National arms in center of sprigs and circle **Rev:** Building within sprigs and circle **Edge:** Segmented reeding

Date	Mintage	F	VF	XF	Unc	BU
2004	50,000	—	—	—	12.00	—

KM# 333 5 HRYVEN

9.4000 g., Bi-Metallic Brass center in Copper-Nickel ring, 28 mm. **Obv:** Horizontal lines across flowery design **Rev:** Cossack-style lyre within circle and wreath **Edge:** Segmented reeding

Date	Mintage	F	VF	XF	Unc	BU
2004	30,000	—	—	—	14.00	—

KM# 336 5 HRYVEN

9.4000 g., Bi-Metallic Brass center in Copper-Nickel ring, 28 mm. **Subject:** 50th Anniversary of Crimean Union With Ukraine **Obv:** National arms on wheat sheaf on map **Rev:** Crowned lion on shield flanked by pillars within rope wreath **Edge:** Segmented reeding

Date	Mintage	F	VF	XF	Unc	BU
2004	30,000	—	—	—	14.00	—

KM# 402 5 HRYVEN

9.4200 g., Bi-Metallic Brass center in Copper-Nickel ring, 28 mm. **Obv:** Symbolic sound of music **Rev:** Tsimbal stringed musical instrument **Edge:** Segmented reeding

Date	Mintage	F	VF	XF	Unc	BU
2006	100,000	—	—	—	10.00	—

UNITED ARAB EMIRATES

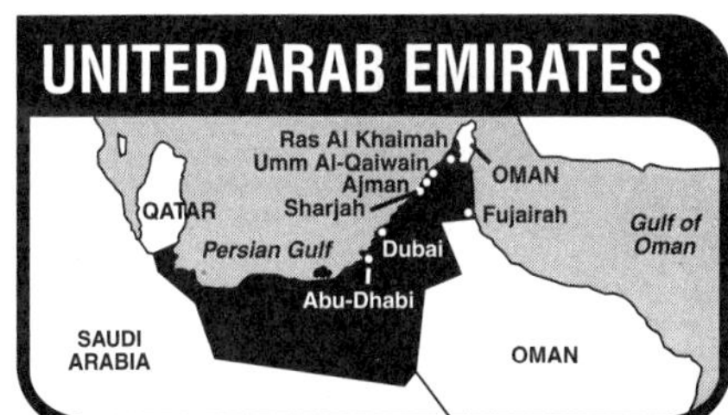

The seven United Arab Emirates (formerly known as the Trucial Sheikhdoms or States), located along the southern shore of the Persian Gulf, are comprised of the Sheikhdoms of Abu Dhabi, Dubai, al-Sharjah, Ajman, Umm al Qaiwain, Ras al-Khaimah and al-Fujairah. They have a combined area of about 32,000 sq. mi. (83,600 sq. km.) and a population of *2.1 million. Capital: Abu Zaby (Abu Dhabi). Since the oil strikes of 1958-60, the economy has centered about petroleum.

The Trucial States came under direct British influence in 1892 when the Maritime Truce Treaty enacted after the supression of pirate activity along the Trucial Coast was enlarged to enjoin the states from disposing of any territory, or entering into any foreign agreements, without British consent in return for British protection from external aggression. In March of 1971 Britain reaffirmed its decision to terminate its treaty relationships with the Trucial Sheikhdoms, whereupon the seven states joined with Bahrain and Qatar in an effort to form a union of Arab Emirates under British protection. When the prospective members failed to agree on terms of union, Bahrain and Qatar declared their respective independence, Aug. and Sept. of 1971. Six of the sheikhdoms united to form the United Arab Emirates on Dec. 2, 1971. Ras al-Khaimah joined a few weeks later.

TITLE

al-Imara(t) al-Arabiya(t) al-Muttahida(t)

MONETARY SYSTEM

Falus, Fulus Fals, Fils Falsan

100 Fils = 1 Dirham

UNITED EMIRATES

STANDARD COINAGE

KM# 1 FILS

1.5000 g., Bronze, 15 mm. **Series:** F.A.O. **Obv:** Value **Rev:** Date palms above dates **Edge:** Plain **Designer:** Geoffrey Colley

Date	Mintage	F	VF	XF	Unc	BU
AH1393-1973	4,000,000	—	0.10	0.20	0.45	0.75
AH1395-1975	—	—	0.20	0.30	0.50	0.75
AH1408-1988	—	—	0.20	0.30	0.50	0.75
AH1409-1989	—	—	0.20	0.30	0.50	0.75
AH1418-1997	—	—	0.20	0.30	0.50	0.75

KM# 2.1 5 FILS

3.7500 g., Bronze, 22 mm. **Series:** F.A.O. **Obv:** Value **Rev:** Fish above dates **Edge:** Plain **Designer:** Geoffrey Colley

Date	Mintage	F	VF	XF	Unc	BU
AH1393-1973	11,400,000	—	0.10	0.15	0.30	1.00
AH1402-1982	—	—	0.10	0.20	0.35	1.00
AH1407-1987	—	—	0.10	0.20	0.35	1.00
AH1408-1988	—	—	0.10	0.20	0.35	1.00
AH1409-1989	—	—	0.10	0.20	0.35	1.00

KM# 2.2 5 FILS

Bronze **Series:** F.A.O. **Obv:** Value **Rev:** Fish above dates **Note:** Reduced size.

Date	Mintage	F	VF	XF	Unc	BU
AH1416-1996	—	—	0.10	0.15	0.30	1.00
AH1422-2001	—	—	0.10	0.15	0.30	1.00

KM# 3.1 10 FILS

7.5000 g., Bronze, 27 mm. **Obv:** Value **Rev:** Arab dhow above dates

Date	Mintage	F	VF	XF	Unc	BU
AH1393-1973	6,400,000	—	0.25	0.40	0.95	1.25
AH1402-1982	—	—	0.25	0.45	1.00	1.25
AH1404-1984	—	—	0.25	0.45	1.00	1.25
AH1407-1987	—	—	0.25	0.45	1.00	1.25
AH1408-1988	—	—	0.25	0.45	1.00	1.25
AH1409-1989	—	—	0.25	0.45	1.00	1.25

KM# 3.2 10 FILS

Bronze **Obv:** Value **Rev:** Arab dhow above dates **Note:** Reduced size.

Date	Mintage	F	VF	XF	Unc	BU
AH1416-1996 (1996)	—	—	0.20	0.35	0.80	1.20
1422 (2001)	—	—	0.20	0.35	0.80	1.20

KM# 4 25 FILS

3.5000 g., Copper-Nickel, 20 mm. **Obv:** Value **Rev:** Gazelle above dates

Date	Mintage	F	VF	XF	Unc	BU
AH1393-1973	10,400,000	—	0.15	0.35	0.70	1.00
AH1402-1982	—	—	0.20	0.40	0.75	1.00
AH1403-1983	—	—	0.20	0.40	0.75	1.00
AH1404-1984	—	—	0.20	0.40	0.75	1.00
AH1406-1986	—	—	0.20	0.40	0.75	1.00
AH1407-1987	—	—	0.20	0.40	0.75	1.00
AH1408-1988	—	—	0.20	0.40	0.75	1.00
AH1409-1989	—	—	0.20	0.40	0.75	1.00
AH1410-1990	—	—	0.20	0.40	0.75	1.00
AH1415-1995	—	—	0.20	0.40	0.75	1.00
AH1416-1996	—	—	0.20	0.40	0.75	1.00
AH1419-1998	—	—	0.20	0.40	0.75	1.00
AH1425-2005	—	—	0.20	0.40	0.75	1.00

KM# 5 50 FILS

Copper-Nickel, 24.8 mm. **Obv:** Value **Rev:** Oil derricks above dates **Edge:** Reeded

Date	Mintage	F	VF	XF	Unc	BU
AH1393-1973	8,400,000	—	0.35	0.50	1.50	2.00
AH1402-1982	—	—	0.35	0.55	1.65	2.00
AH1404-1984	—	—	0.35	0.55	1.65	2.00
AH1407-1987	—	—	0.35	0.55	1.65	2.00
AH1408-1988	—	—	0.35	0.55	1.65	2.00
Note: Coarser edge reeding						
AH1409-1989	—	—	0.35	0.55	1.65	2.00

KM# 16 50 FILS

4.3000 g., Copper-Nickel, 21 mm. **Obv:** Value **Rev:** Oil derricks above dates **Shape:** 7-sided **Note:** Reduced size.

Date	Mintage	F	VF	XF	Unc	BU
AH1415-1995	—	—	0.25	0.45	1.35	1.85
AH1419-1998	—	—	0.25	0.45	1.35	1.85
AH1425-2005	—	—	0.25	0.45	1.35	1.85

KM# 6.1 DIRHAM

11.3000 g., Copper-Nickel, 28.5 mm. **Obv:** Value **Rev:** Jug above dates **Edge:** Reeded

Date	Mintage	F	VF	XF	Unc	BU
AH1393-1973	13,000,000	—	0.50	0.75	2.00	2.50
AH1402-1982	—	—	0.50	0.80	2.25	2.75
AH1404-1984	—	—	0.50	0.80	2.25	2.75
AH1406-1986	—	—	0.50	0.80	2.25	2.75
AH1407-1987	—	—	0.50	0.80	2.25	2.75
AH1408-1988	—	—	0.50	0.80	2.25	2.75
AH1409-1989	—	—	0.50	0.80	2.25	2.75

KM# 6.2 DIRHAM

6.4000 g., Copper-Nickel, 24 mm. **Obv:** Value **Rev:** Jug above dates **Edge:** Reeded **Note:** Reduced size.

Date	Mintage	F	VF	XF	Unc	BU
AH1415-1995	—	—	0.35	0.65	1.85	2.25
AH1419-1998	—	—	0.35	0.65	1.85	2.25
AH1425-2005	—	—	0.35	0.65	1.85	2.25
AH1428-2007	—	—	0.35	0.65	1.85	2.25

KM# 10 DIRHAM

11.3100 g., Copper-Nickel, 28.5 mm. **Subject:** 27th Chess Olympiad in Dubai **Obv:** Value **Rev:** Chess pieces and olympic rings

Date	Mintage	F	VF	XF	Unc	BU
ND(1986)	200,000	—	2.00	4.50	9.00	—

KM# 11 DIRHAM

Copper-Nickel, 28.5 mm. **Subject:** 25th Anniversary - Offshore Oil Drilling **Obv:** Value **Rev:** Offshore oil drilling rig

Date	Mintage	F	VF	XF	Unc	BU
ND(1987)	300,000	—	2.00	4.50	9.00	—

KM# 14 DIRHAM

Copper-Nickel, 28.5 mm. **Subject:** 10th Anniversary - al-Ain University **Obv:** Value **Rev:** Emblem above map and book within radiant design

Date	Mintage	F	VF	XF	Unc	BU
ND(1987)	200,000	—	1.75	4.00	8.00	—

KM# 15 DIRHAM

Copper-Nickel, 28.5 mm. **Subject:** U.A.E. Soccer Team - Qualification for WC - 1990 **Obv:** Value **Rev:** Stylized winged soccer player

Date	Mintage	F	VF	XF	Unc	BU
ND(1991)	250,000	—	1.50	3.00	6.50	—

KM# 32 DIRHAM

Copper-Nickel, 24 mm. **Subject:** Bank of Dubai 35th Anniversary **Obv:** Value **Rev:** Towered bank building divides dates

Date	Mintage	F	VF	XF	Unc	BU
ND(1998)	500,000	—	—	—	3.50	—

KM# 35 DIRHAM

Copper-Nickel, 24 mm. **Subject:** 10th Anniversary - College of Technology **Obv:** Value **Rev:** Bird viewed through window frame

Date	Mintage	F	VF	XF	Unc	BU
ND(1998)	250,000	—	—	—	3.50	—

KM# 38 DIRHAM

Copper-Nickel, 24 mm. **Subject:** 15th Anniversary - Rashid bin Humaid Award for Culture **Obv:** Value **Rev:** Logo within circle

Date	Mintage	F	VF	XF	Unc	BU
ND(1998)	250,000	—	—	—	3.50	—

KM# 39 DIRHAM

Copper-Nickel, 24 mm. **Subject:** Sharjah Cultural City **Obv:** Value **Rev:** Stylized flame within beaded circle

Date	Mintage	F	VF	XF	Unc	BU
ND(1998)	—	—	—	—	3.50	—
ND(1999)	200,000	—	—	—	3.50	—

KM# 40 DIRHAM

6.3700 g., Copper-Nickel, 24 mm. **Subject:** 25 Years - Oil Production on Abu Al Bukhoosh Oil Field **Obv:** Value **Rev:** Offshore oil drilling rig **Edge:** Reeded

Date	Mintage	F	VF	XF	Unc	BU
ND(1999)	200,000	—	—	—	3.50	—

KM# 41 DIRHAM

6.3700 g., Copper-Nickel, 24 mm. **Subject:** Islamic Personality of 1999 - Sheikh Zayed **Obv:** Value **Rev:** Square design

Date	Mintage	F	VF	XF	Unc	BU
ND(2000)	500,000	—	—	—	3.50	—

KM# 43 DIRHAM

6.3700 g., Copper-Nickel, 24 mm. **Subject:** 25th Anniversary - Dubai Islamic Bank **Obv:** Value **Rev:** Bank name within circle

Date	Mintage	F	VF	XF	Unc	BU
ND(2000)	250,000	—	—	—	3.50	—

KM# 46 DIRHAM

6.3700 g., Copper-Nickel, 24 mm. **Subject:** 25th Anniversary - General Women's Union (1975-2000) **Obv:** Value **Rev:** Stylized gazelle

Date	Mintage	F	VF	XF	Unc	BU
ND(2000)	500,000	—	—	—	3.50	—

KM# 49 DIRHAM

6.3700 g., Copper-Nickel, 24 mm. **Subject:** 25th Anniversary - Armed Forces Unification **Obv:** Value **Rev:** Heraldic eagle within rope wreath **Edge:** Reeded

Date	Mintage	F	VF	XF	Unc	BU
ND (2001)	250,000	—	—	—	3.50	4.00

KM# 73 DIRHAM

6.4100 g., Copper-Nickel, 23.93 mm. **Subject:** Dubai 2003 **Obv:** Denomination **Rev:** Mosaic arc **Edge:** Reeded

Date	Mintage	F	VF	XF	Unc	BU
2003	—	—	—	0.90	2.25	3.00

KM# 51 DIRHAM

6.3300 g., Copper-Nickel, 24 mm. **Subject:** 50 Years of Formal Education **Obv:** Value **Rev:** Symbolic design **Edge:** Reeded

Date	Mintage	F	VF	XF	Unc	BU
ND (2003)	—	—	—	—	3.50	4.00

KM# 52 DIRHAM

6.4000 g., Copper-Nickel, 24 mm. **Subject:** Abu Dhabi National Bank 35th Anniversary **Obv:** Value **Rev:** Towers divide dates within circle **Edge:** Reeded

Date	Mintage	F	VF	XF	Unc	BU
ND (2003)	—	—	—	—	3.50	4.00

KM# 54 DIRHAM

6.4000 g., Copper-Nickel, 24 mm. **Subject:** 40th Anniversary of Crude Oil Exports **Obv:** Value **Rev:** "ADCO" logo **Edge:** Reeded

Date	Mintage	F	VF	XF	Unc	BU
ND (2003)	—	—	—	—	3.50	4.00

KM# 74 DIRHAM

6.5400 g., Copper-Nickel, 24 mm. **Subject:** 25th Anniversary First Gulf Bank **Obv:** Denomination **Rev:** Bank logo **Edge:** Reeded

Date	Mintage	F	VF	XF	Unc	BU
ND(2004)	—	—	—	0.90	2.25	3.00

KM# 81 DIRHAM

6.3000 g., Copper-Nickel **Subject:** First National Bank - 25 Years of Excellence

Date	Mintage	F	VF	XF	Unc	BU
ND(2004)	—	—	—	—	3.50	4.00

KM# 83 DIRHAM

6.4700 g., Copper-Nickel, 24.02 mm. **Subject:** Honoring Mother of Nations **Obv:** Large value **Rev:** Inscription in flower bud at center **Rev. Legend:** Sheikha Fatima Bint Mubarak **Edge:** Reeded

Date	Mintage	F	VF	XF	Unc	BU
2005	—	—	—	0.90	2.25	3.00

KM# 75 DIRHAM

Copper-Nickel, 24 mm. **Subject:** Honoring the Mother of the Nation

Date	Mintage	F	VF	XF	Unc	BU
2005	—	—	—	—	3.50	4.00

KM# 77 DIRHAM

6.3000 g., Copper-Nickel, 24 mm. **Obv:** Value **Rev:** Zakum Development Co. logo **Edge:** Reeded

Date	Mintage	F	VF	XF	Unc	BU
ND(2007)	—	—	—	—	3.50	4.00

KM# 76 DIRHAM

6.4000 g., Copper-Nickel, 24 mm. **Subject:** 75th Anniversary Sharjah International Airport **Obv:** Value **Obv. Legend:** UNITED ARAB EMIRATES **Rev:** Three birds in flight under arc **Edge:** Reeded

Date	Mintage	F	VF	XF	Unc	BU
ND(2007)	—	—	—	1.20	3.00	4.00

KM# 78 DIRHAM

6.4000 g., Copper-Nickel, 23.95 mm. **Obv:** Value **Obv. Legend:** UNITED ARAB EMIRATES **Rev:** Large "50" with Police badge in "0" **Rev. Legend:** ABU DHABI POLICE GOLDEN JUBILEE **Edge:** Reeded

Date	Mintage	F	VF	XF	Unc	BU
ND(2007)	—	—	—	—	3.50	4.00

KM# 79 DIRHAM

6.4300 g., Copper-Nickel, 24.03 mm. **Obv:** Value **Obv. Legend:** UNITED ARAB EMIRATES **Rev:** Large "30" and logo **Rev. Legend:** 30TH ANNIVERSARY OF THE 1ST LNG SHIPMENT **Rev. Inscription:** ADGAS **Edge:** Reeded

Date	Mintage	F	VF	XF	Unc	BU
ND(2007)	—	—	—	—	3.50	4.00

KM# 9 5 DIRHAMS

Copper-Nickel **Subject:** 1500th Anniversary - al-Hegira **Obv:** Value flanked by dates **Rev:** Perched eagle **Shape:** 15-sided

Date	Mintage	F	VF	XF	Unc	BU
AH1401-1981	2,000,000	—	2.00	4.00	15.00	—

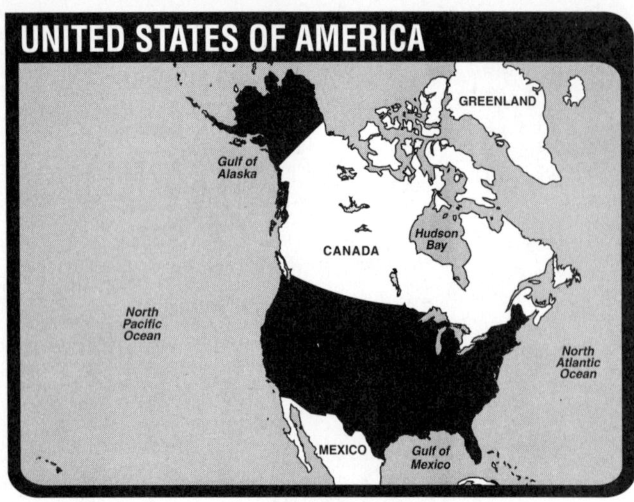

CIRCULATION COINAGE

CENT

Lincoln Cent

Wheat Ears

KM# 132 BRONZE 19 mm. 3.1100 g. **Designer:** Victor D. Brenner **Notes:** The 1909 "VDB" varieties have the designer's initials inscribed at the 6 o'clock position on the reverse. The initials were removed until 1918, when they were restored on the obverse • MS60 prices are for Brown coins and MS65 prices are for coins that are at least 90% original red.

Date	Mintage	G-4	VG-8	F-12	VF-20	XF-40	AU-50	MS-60	MS-65	Prf-65
1909 VDB	27,995,000	12.00	12.50	12.75	13.00	14.00	16.00	21.00	125	—
1909 VDB Doubled Die Obverse	Inc. above	—	—	55.00	75.00	100.00	120	150	1,900	—
1909S VDB	484,000	760	895	1,010	1,150	1,290	1,450	1,650	6,900	—
1909	72,702,618	4.25	4.40	4.75	5.00	6.00	12.00	15.00	85.00	520
1909S	1,825,000	115	120	130	170	245	265	360	1,325	—
1909S/S S over horizontal S	Inc. above	125	132	145	190	280	325	385	1,600	—
1910	146,801,218	.50	.60	.75	1.50	4.50	10.00	17.50	250	700
1910S	6,045,000	17.00	19.00	21.50	29.00	49.00	75.00	105	800	—
1911	101,177,787	.60	.80	2.00	2.50	7.00	11.50	20.00	375	600
1911D	12,672,000	5.25	6.00	10.00	18.50	54.00	74.00	92.00	1,550	—
1911S	4,026,000	45.00	48.00	51.00	55.00	80.00	112	180	3,300	—
1912	68,153,060	1.75	2.00	2.50	6.00	14.00	26.00	34.00	550	950
1912D	10,411,000	7.00	9.50	12.00	27.00	74.00	112	165	2,800	—
1912S	4,431,000	23.00	25.00	30.00	42.00	83.00	120	185	4,400	—
1913	76,532,352	1.00	1.20	1.75	3.40	18.50	29.50	36.00	400	550
1913D	15,804,000	3.00	3.50	4.00	11.00	50.00	65.00	98.00	2,100	—
1913S	6,101,000	13.50	17.50	20.00	32.00	56.00	108	195	6,650	—
1914	75,238,432	.75	1.10	2.25	6.50	19.00	40.00	47.50	415	600
1914D	1,193,000	220	260	4,000	495	975	1,475	1,975	24,000	—
1914S	4,137,000	24.50	27.00	28.00	39.00	92.00	170	295	11,500	—
1915	29,092,120	1.65	2.85	4.10	18.50	60.00	73.00	84.00	1,150	600
1915D	22,050,000	1.75	2.40	3.60	6.75	24.00	44.00	70.00	1,350	—
1915S	4,833,000	20.00	23.00	27.00	30.00	82.00	98.00	175	4,800	—
1916	131,833,677	.35	.60	1.25	2.60	8.00	13.00	18.00	385	1,650
1916D	35,956,000	1.75	2.25	3.00	6.00	15.50	36.00	72.00	3,300	—
1916S	22,510,000	2.25	3.25	4.50	7.00	25.00	38.00	84.00	8,500	—
1917	196,429,785	.35	.45	.55	2.00	5.00	13.50	16.00	480	—
1917 Doubled Die Obverse	Inc. above	100.00	125	210	375	900	1,750	2,500	25,000	—
1917D	55,120,000	1.50	1.75	2.50	5.50	39.00	45.00	62.00	3,000	—
1917S	32,620,000	.80	1.20	1.75	2.65	11.00	25.00	62.00	7,200	—
1918	288,104,634	.35	.40	.50	1.25	4.50	10.00	14.00	400	—
1918D	47,830,000	1.60	2.00	2.65	5.50	16.50	32.00	72.00	3,650	—
1918S	34,680,000	.50	1.20	1.75	3.65	11.50	32.00	61.00	8,450	—
1919	392,021,000	.30	.40	.50	.80	1.75	6.00	8.50	175	—
1919D	57,154,000	1.25	1.60	2.00	5.00	13.00	34.00	54.00	2,700	—
1919S	139,760,000	.40	.70	1.80	2.65	6.00	17.00	40.00	4,300	—
1920	310,165,000	.35	.40	.90	1.50	2.80	7.00	13.50	235	—
1920D	49,280,000	1.25	1.65	3.00	7.00	19.50	38.00	74.00	2,750	—
1920S	46,220,000	.90	1.00	1.50	2.75	13.00	38.00	112	9,350	—
1921	39,157,000	.60	1.00	1.25	3.00	13.00	22.50	44.00	375	—
1921S	15,274,000	1.65	2.10	2.85	6.00	35.00	70.00	110	6,700	—
1922D	7,160,000	17.50	20.00	22.50	25.00	38.00	76.00	108	2,450	—
1922D Weak Rev	Inc. above	16.00	17.00	20.00	22.00	32.00	63.00	90.00	1,950	—
1922D Weak D	Inc. above	32.00	45.00	65.00	110	235	300	550	—	—
1922 No D Die 2 Strong Rev	Inc. above	750	840	1,275	1,700	3,150	6,600	11,000	200,000	—
1922 No D Die 3 Weak Rev	Inc. above	300	400	685	885	1,750	3,500	8,500	—	—
1923	74,723,000	.60	.80	1.00	1.50	6.00	11.00	14.00	480	—
1923S	8,700,000	3.00	4.00	5.00	8.00	38.00	86.00	195	15,500	—
1924	75,178,000	.35	.50	.60	1.10	5.50	11.00	20.00	390	—
1924D	2,520,000	37.00	43.00	48.00	60.00	115	180	270	9,500	—
1924S	11,696,000	1.75	2.00	2.80	5.50	32.00	72.00	115	11,000	—
1925	139,949,000	.30	.40	.50	.70	2.85	7.00	10.50	100.00	—
1925D	22,580,000	1.50	2.00	3.00	6.00	16.50	30.00	62.00	5,000	—
1925S	26,380,000	1.20	1.50	2.00	3.00	12.50	32.00	90.00	10,000	—
1926	157,088,000	.25	.40	.50	.70	1.65	6.00	7.75	75.00	—
1926D	28,020,000	1.50	1.70	3.50	5.50	14.50	34.00	85.00	4,350	—
1926S	4,550,000	8.50	10.00	11.50	16.00	35.00	72.00	140	100,000	—
1927	144,440,000	.20	.30	.40	.70	1.60	5.50	7.40	95.00	—
1927D	27,170,000	1.50	1.75	2.25	3.50	8.00	26.50	62.00	2,000	—
1927S	14,276,000	1.50	1.85	3.00	5.50	16.00	43.00	66.00	6,650	—
1928	134,116,000	.20	.30	.40	.70	1.25	4.25	7.50	90.00	—
1928D	31,170,000	1.10	1.40	2.25	3.75	6.50	19.50	35.00	1,100	—
1928S Small S	17,266,000	1.20	1.65	2.75	4.00	9.50	30.00	74.00	4,650	—
1928S Large S	Inc. above	2.00	2.85	4.25	6.75	6.00	44.00	140	5,500	—
1929	185,262,000	.20	.30	.40	.60	1.00	5.50	7.00	85.00	—
1929D	41,730,000	.70	1.20	1.50	2.85	6.50	14.00	24.00	625	—
1929S	50,148,000	.80	1.25	2.00	3.00	7.00	15.00	19.00	550	—
1930	157,415,000	.20	.30	.40	.60	1.25	2.75	3.75	32.50	—
1930D	40,100,000	.35	.45	.65	.90	2.00	6.00	11.00	95.00	—
1930S	24,286,000	.35	.45	.60	.80	1.50	7.00	10.00	50.00	—
1931	19,396,000	.70	.80	1.30	2.00	4.00	10.50	20.00	135	—
1931D	4,480,000	5.00	6.00	6.75	8.00	13.50	36.00	52.00	1,000	—
1931S	866,000	122	124	130	133	140	148	163	725	—
1932	9,062,000	1.75	2.00	3.00	3.50	7.00	13.50	22.00	100.00	—
1932D	10,500,000	1.40	2.00	2.50	2.85	4.15	11.00	17.50	150	—
1933	14,360,000	1.40	1.80	2.50	3.00	7.00	12.00	17.50	100.00	—
1933D	6,200,000	3.50	4.25	5.20	6.50	12.00	16.50	23.50	135	—
1934	219,080,000	.20	.30	.40	.60	1.25	4.00	8.00	30.00	—
1934D	28,446,000	.40	.60	1.00	1.65	4.00	10.00	20.00	52.00	—
1935	245,338,000	.20	.30	.40	.55	.90	1.50	3.50	28.00	—
1935D	47,000,000	.15	.20	.30	.40	.95	2.50	4.50	30.00	—
1935S	38,702,000	.25	.35	.60	1.75	3.00	5.00	12.00	55.00	—
1936 (Proof in Satin Finish)	309,637,569	.20	.30	.40	.55	.85	1.40	2.00	7.50	1,200
1936 Brilliant Proof	Inc. above	—	—	—	—	—	—	—	—	—
1936D	40,620,000	.20	.30	.40	.55	.90	1.50	3.50	22.00	—
1936S	29,130,000	.20	.30	.45	.60	1.00	1.75	3.00	18.00	—
1937	309,179,320	.20	.30	.40	.55	.85	1.40	1.60	20.00	125
1937D	50,430,000	.20	.30	.40	.60	.95	1.00	2.20	24.00	—
1937S	34,500,000	.20	.30	.40	.55	.90	1.25	2.40	22.50	—
1938	156,696,734	.20	.30	.40	.55	.85	1.20	3.00	16.50	85.00
1938D	20,010,000	.20	.30	.45	.60	1.00	1.50	3.50	17.00	—
1938S	15,180,000	.30	.40	.50	.70	1.00	2.00	2.80	26.00	—
1939	316,479,520	.20	.30	.40	.55	.75	.90	1.00	15.00	78.00
1939D	15,160,000	.35	.45	.50	.60	.85	1.90	2.50	20.00	—
1939S	52,070,000	.30	.40	.50	.60	.80	1.10	2.00	19.00	—
1940	586,825,872	.10	.20	.30	.40	.50	.75	1.00	17.00	70.00
1940D	81,390,000	.20	.30	.40	.55	.75	.50	1.20	11.50	—
1940S	112,940,000	.20	.30	.40	.55	.90	1.25	1.40	14.00	—
1941	887,039,100	.10	.20	.30	.40	.50	.70	.85	17.00	65.00
1941 Doubled Die Obv	Inc. above	35.00	50.00	70.00	80.00	95.00	135	200	2,800	—
1941D	128,700,000	.20	.30	.40	.55	.75	1.25	2.25	20.00	—
1941S	92,360,000	.20	.30	.40	.55	.75	1.75	2.75	23.50	—
1942	657,828,600	.10	.20	.30	.40	.50	.70	.85	17.00	78.00
1942D	206,698,000	.20	.25	.30	.35	.40	.50	.65	22.00	—
1942S	85,590,000	.25	.35	.45	.85	1.25	2.50	4.50	26.00	—

KM# 132a ZINC COATED STEEL 19 mm. 2.7000 g. **Designer:** Victor D. Brenner

Date	Mintage	G-4	VG-8	F-12	VF-20	XF-40	AU-50	MS-60	MS-65	Prf-65
1943	684,628,670	.25	.30	.35	.45	.60	.85	1.25	4.75	—
1943D	217,660,000	.35	.40	.45	.50	.70	1.00	1.25	8.50	—
1943D/D RPM	—	30.00	38.00	50.00	65.00	90.00	125	200	—	—
1943S	191,550,000	.45	.45	.50	.65	.90	1.40	3.00	13.50	—

KM# A132 COPPER-ZINC 19 mm. 3.1100 g. **Designer:** Victor D. Brenner **Notes:** KM#132 design and composition resumed • MS60 prices are for Brown coins and MS65 prices are for coins that are at least 90% original red.

Date	Mintage	XF-40	MS-65	Prf-65
1944	1,435,400,000	.40	8.00	—
1944D	430,578,000	.50	12.50	—
1944D/S Type 1	Inc. above	235	3,750	—
1944D/S Type 2	Inc. above	175	1,600	—
1944S	282,760,000	.40	12.00	—
1945	1,040,515,000	.40	15.00	—
1945D	226,268,000	.40	13.50	—
1945S	181,770,000	.40	12.00	—
1946	991,655,000	.30	13.00	—
1946D	315,690,000	.30	6.00	—

Date	Mintage	XF-40	MS-65	Prf-65
1946S	198,100,000	.30	5.50	—
1946S/D	—	70.00	600	—
1947	190,555,000	.45	16.00	—
1947D	194,750,000	.40	10.00	—
1947S	99,000,000	.35	12.00	—
1948	317,570,000	.40	14.00	—
1948D	172,637,000	.40	6.75	—
1948S	81,735,000	.40	6.50	—
1949	217,775,000	.40	15.00	—
1949D	153,132,000	.40	12.00	—
1949S	64,290,000	.50	10.00	—
1950	272,686,386	.40	13.50	40.00
1950D	334,950,000	.35	9.00	—
1950S	118,505,000	.40	8.00	—
1951	295,633,500	.40	14.00	40.00
1951D	625,355,000	.30	8.00	—
1951S	136,010,000	.40	10.00	—
1952	186,856,980	.40	16.00	34.00
1952D	746,130,000	.30	8.00	—
1952S	137,800,004	.60	9.00	—
1953	256,883,800	.30	18.00	28.00
1953D	700,515,000	.30	11.00	—
1953S	181,835,000	.40	11.50	—
1954	71,873,350	.25	17.50	9.00
1954D	251,552,500	.25	10.00	—
1954S	96,190,000	.25	12.00	—
1955	330,958,000	.25	15.00	13.00
1955 Doubled Die	Inc. above	1,650	43,500	—

Note: The 1955 "doubled die" has distinct doubling of the date and lettering on the obverse.

Date	Mintage	XF-40	MS-65	Prf-65
1955D	563,257,500	.20	12.00	—
1955S	44,610,000	.35	7.50	—
1956	421,414,384	.20	16.00	3.00
1956D	1,098,201,100	.20	8.00	—
1957	283,787,952	.20	9.00	2.00
1957D	1,051,342,000	.20	8.00	—
1958	253,400,652	.20	9.00	3.00
1958D	800,953,300	.20	8.00	—

Lincoln Memorial

KM# 201 COPPER-ZINC 3.1100 g. **Rev. Designer:** Frank Gasparro **Notes:** MS60 prices are for Brown coins and MS65 prices are for coins that are at least 90% original red. The dates were modified in 1960, 1970 and 1982, resulting in large-date and small-date varieties for those years. The 1972 "doubled die" shows doubling of "In God We Trust." The 1979-S and 1981-S Type II proofs have a clearer mint mark than the Type I proofs of those years. Some 1982 cents have the predominantly copper composition; others have the predominantly zinc composition. They can be distinguished by weight.

Small date Large date

Large date

Small date

Date	Mintage	XF-40	MS-65	Prf-65
1959	610,864,291	—	18.00	1.50
1959D	1,279,760,000	—	16.00	—
1960 small date, low 9	588,096,602	2.10	12.00	16.00
1960 large date, high 9	Inc. above	—	10.00	1.25
1960D small date, low 9	1,580,884,000	—	10.00	—
1960D large date, high 9	Inc. above	—	11.00	—
1960D/D small over large date	—	—	300	—
1961	756,373,244	—	6.50	1.00
1961D	1,753,266,700	—	15.00	—
1962	609,263,019	—	8.00	1.00
1962D	1,793,148,400	—	14.00	—
1963	757,185,645	—	10.00	1.00
1963D	1,774,020,400	—	12.00	—
1964	2,652,525,762	—	6.50	1.00
1964D	3,799,071,500	—	7.00	—
1965	1,497,224,900	—	10.00	—
1965 SMS	—	—	7.50	—
1966	2,188,147,783	—	10.00	—
1966 SMS	—	—	8.00	—
1967	3,048,667,100	—	10.00	—
1967 SMS	—	—	8.00	—
1968	1,707,880,970	—	12.00	—
1968D	2,886,269,600	—	12.00	—
1968S	261,311,510	—	8.00	1.00
1969	1,136,910,000	—	6.50	—
1969D	4,002,832,200	—	10.00	—

Date	Mintage	XF-40	MS-65	Prf-65
1969S	547,309,631	—	8.00	1.10
1969S Doubled Die Obverse	—	—	—	—
1970	1,898,315,000	—	8.00	—
1970D	2,891,438,900	—	6.00	—
1970S	693,192,814	—	—	1.20
1970S small date, level 7	Inc. above	—	75.00	60.00
1970S large date, low 7	—	—	16.00	—
1970S Doubled Die Obverse	—	—	—	—
1971	1,919,490,000	—	25.00	—
1971D	2,911,045,600	—	5.50	—
1971S	528,354,192	—	6.00	1.20
1971S Doubled Die Obverse	—	—	—	—
1972	2,933,255,000	—	6.00	—
1972 Doubled Die Obverse	—	240	775	—
1972D	2,665,071,400	—	10.00	—
1972S	380,200,104	—	30.00	1.15
1973	3,728,245,000	—	8.00	—
1973D	3,549,576,588	—	11.00	—
1973S	319,937,634	—	8.00	0.80
1974	4,232,140,523	—	12.00	—
1974D	4,235,098,000	—	12.00	—
1974S	412,039,228	—	10.00	0.75
1975	5,451,476,142	—	8.00	—
1975D	4,505,245,300	—	13.50	—
1975S	(2,845,450)	—	—	5.50
1976	4,674,292,426	—	18.00	—
1976D	4,221,592,455	—	20.00	—
1976S	(4,149,730)	—	—	5.00
1977	4,469,930,000	—	14.00	—
1977D	4,149,062,300	—	14.00	—
1977S	(3,251,152)	—	—	3.00
1978	5,558,605,000	—	14.00	—
1978D	4,280,233,400	—	12.00	—
1978S	(3,127,781)	—	—	3.50
1979	6,018,515,000	—	12.00	—
1979D	4,139,357,254	—	8.00	—
1979S type I, proof	(3,677,175)	—	—	4.00
1979S type II, proof	Inc. above	—	—	4.25
1980	7,414,705,000	—	6.50	—
1980D	5,140,098,660	—	10.00	—
1980S	(3,554,806)	—	—	2.25
1981	7,491,750,000	—	7.50	—
1981D	5,373,235,677	—	9.00	—
1981S type I, proof	(4,063,083)	—	—	3.50
1981S type II, proof	Inc. above	—	—	60.00
1982 large date	10,712,525,000	—	6.00	—
1982 small date	Inc. above	—	8.00	—
1982D large date	6,012,979,368	—	6.00	—
1982S	3,857,479	—	—	—

KM# 201a COPPER PLATED ZINC 19 mm. 2.5000 g. **Notes:** MS60 prices are for brown coins and MS65 prices are for coins that are at least 90% original red.

Date	Mintage	XF-40	MS-65	Prf-65
1982 large date	—	—	6.00	—
1982 small date	—	—	9.00	—
1982D large date	—	—	8.00	—
1982D small date	—	—	6.00	—

KM# 201b COPPER PLATED ZINC 19 mm. **Notes:** MS60 prices are for brown coins and MS65 prices are for coins that are at least 90% original red. The 1983 "doubled die reverse" shows doubling of "United States of America." The 1984 "doubled die" shows doubling of Lincoln's ear on the obverse.

Date	Mintage	XF-40	MS-65	Prf-65
1982S	(3,857,479)	—	—	3.00
1983	7,752,355,000	—	7.00	—
1983 Doubled Die	Inc. above	—	400	—
1983D	6,467,199,428	—	5.50	—
1983S	(3,279,126)	—	—	4.00
1984	8,151,079,000	—	7.50	—
1984 Doubled Die	Inc. above	—	275	—
1984D	5,569,238,906	—	5.50	—
1984S	(3,065,110)	—	—	4.50
1985	5,648,489,887	—	4.50	—
1985D	5,287,399,926	—	4.50	—
1985S	(3,362,821)	—	—	6.00
1986	4,491,395,493	—	5.00	—
1986D	4,442,866,698	—	8.00	—
1986S	(3,010,497)	—	—	7.50
1987	4,682,466,931	—	8.50	—
1987D	4,879,389,514	—	6.00	—
1987S	(4,227,728)	—	—	5.00
1988	6,092,810,000	—	8.50	—
1988D	5,253,740,443	—	5.50	—
1988S	(3,262,948)	—	—	4.00
1989	7,261,535,000	—	5.00	—
1989D	5,345,467,111	—	5.00	—
1989S	(3,220,194)	—	—	6.00
1990	6,851,765,000	—	5.00	—
1990D	4,922,894,533	—	5.00	—
1990S	(3,299,559)	—	—	5.00
1990 no S, Proof only	Inc. above	—	—	2,750
1991	5,165,940,000	—	6.00	—
1991D	4,158,442,076	—	5.00	—

Date	Mintage	XF-40	MS-65	Prf-65
1991S	(2,867,787)	—	—	5.00
1992	4,648,905,000	—	5.50	—
1992D	4,448,673,300	—	5.50	—
1992D Close AM, Proof Reverse Die	Inc. above	—	—	—
1992S	(4,176,560)	—	—	5.00
1993	5,684,705,000	—	5.50	—
1993D	6,426,650,571	—	5.50	—
1993S	(3,394,792)	—	—	7.00
1994	6,500,850,000	—	10.00	—
1994D	7,131,765,000	—	5.50	—
1994S	(3,269,923)	—	—	4.00
1995	6,411,440,000	—	4.50	—
1995 Doubled Die Obverse	Inc. above	20.00	50.00	—
1995D	7,128,560,000	—	5.00	—
1995S	(2,707,481)	—	—	9.50
1996	6,612,465,000	—	5.00	—
1996D	6,510,795,000	—	5.00	—
1996S	(2,915,212)	—	—	6.50
1997	4,622,800,000	—	5.00	—
1997D	4,576,555,000	—	5.00	—
1997S	(2,796,678)	—	—	11.50
1998	5,032,155,000	—	5.00	—
1998 Wide AM Reverse For Proof Die	Inc. above	—	—	—
1998D	5,255,353,500	—	5.00	—
1998S	(2,957,286)	—	—	9.50
1999	5,237,600,000	—	5.00	—
1999 Wide AM Reverse For Proof Die	Inc. above	—	—	—
1999D	6,360,065,000	—	5.00	—
1999S	(3,362,462)	—	—	5.00
2000 Wide AM Reverse For Proof Die	Inc. above	—	—	—
2000	5,503,200,000	—	4.00	—
2000D	8,774,220,000	—	4.00	—
2000S	(4,063,361)	—	—	4.00
2001	4,959,600,000	—	4.00	—
2001D	5,374,990,000	—	4.00	—
2001S	(3,099,096)	—	—	4.00
2002	3,260,800,000	—	4.00	—
2002D	4,028,055,000	—	4.00	—
2002S	(3,157,739)	—	—	4.00
2003	3,300,000,000	—	3.50	—
2003D	3,548,000,000	—	3.50	—
2003S	(3,116,590)	—	—	4.00
2004	3,379,600,000	—	3.50	—
2004D	3,456,400,000	—	3.50	—
2004S	2,992,069	—	—	4.00
2005	3,935,600,000	—	3.50	—
2005D	3,764,450,000	—	3.50	—
2005S	3,273,000	—	—	4.00
2006	4,290,000,000	—	2.00	—
2006D	3,944,000,000	—	2.50	—
2006S	2,923,105	—	—	4.00
2007	—	—	1.50	—
2007D	—	—	1.50	—
2007S	—	—	—	4.00

5 CENTS

Liberty Nickel

Liberty head left, within circle of stars, date below Roman numeral value within wreath, "Cents" below

KM# 112 COPPER-NICKEL 5.0000 g.

Date	Mintage	G-4	VG-8	F-12	VF-20	XF-40	AU-50	MS-60	MS-65	Prf-65
1901	26,480,213	1.85	2.50	7.50	15.00	34.00	69.00	88.00	720	675
1902	31,480,579	1.85	2.50	4.50	15.00	31.00	69.00	94.00	720	675
1903	28,006,725	1.85	2.50	5.00	15.00	31.00	69.00	85.00	725	675
1904	21,404,984	1.85	2.50	5.00	12.50	29.00	69.00	88.00	750	700
1905	29,827,276	1.85	2.50	4.50	12.50	29.00	69.00	88.00	720	675
1906	38,613,725	1.85	2.50	4.50	12.50	29.00	69.00	88.00	950	675
1907	39,214,800	1.85	2.25	4.50	12.50	29.00	69.00	88.00	1,400	675
1908	22,686,177	1.85	2.25	4.50	12.50	29.00	69.00	93.00	1,300	675
1909	11,590,526	2.20	2.50	4.50	13.50	32.00	85.00	105	1,350	675
1910	30,169,353	1.85	2.25	4.50	11.00	29.00	55.00	72.00	720	675
1911	39,559,372	1.85	2.25	4.50	11.00	29.00	55.00	72.00	720	675
1912	26,236,714	1.85	2.25	4.50	11.00	29.00	55.00	72.00	720	675
1912D	8,474,000	2.70	4.00	12.00	38.00	74.00	175	290	2,600	—
1912S	238,000	175	245	280	500	850	1,350	1,550	7,500	—
1913 5 known	—	—	—	—	—	—	—	—	—	—

Note: 1913, Superior Sale, March 2001, Proof, $1,840,000.

Buffalo Nickel

Buffalo standing on a mound

KM# 133 COPPER-NICKEL 21.2 mm. 5.0000 g. **Designer:** James Earle Fraser

Date	Mintage	G-4	VG-8	F-12	VF-20	XF-40	AU-50	MS-60	MS-65	Prf-65
1913	30,993,520	8.00	11.00	11.75	12.50	18.50	25.00	32.50	200	3,500
1913D	5,337,000	16.00	19.50	21.00	25.00	35.00	57.00	62.50	330	—
1913S	2,105,000	43.00	47.00	50.00	60.00	75.00	100.00	125	725	—

American Bison standing on a line

KM# 134 COPPER-NICKEL 21.2 mm. 5.0000 g. **Designer:** James Earle Fraser **Notes:** In 1913 the reverse design was modified so the ground under the buffalo was represented as a line rather than a mound. On the 1937D 3-legged variety, the buffalo's right front leg is missing, the result of a damaged die.

1918/17D

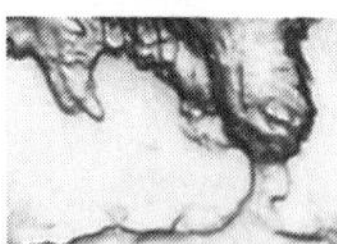
1937D 3-legged

Date	Mintage	G-4	VG-8	F-12	VF-20	XF-40	AU-50	MS-60	MS-65	Prf-65
1913	29,858,700	8.00	11.00	11.50	12.50	18.50	25.00	34.00	375	2,600
1913D	4,156,000	125	155	180	190	205	240	285	1,575	—
1913S	1,209,000	365	425	445	475	575	675	850	4,300	—
1914	20,665,738	17.00	21.00	22.00	23.00	27.50	37.50	49.00	450	2,250
1914/3	Inc. above	150	300	425	525	700	1,050	2,750	24,000	—
1914D	3,912,000	92.00	130	155	220	315	395	450	1,850	—
1914/3D	Inc. above	—	—	—	—	—	—	—	—	—
1914S	3,470,000	26.00	37.50	45.00	62.50	90.00	145	160	2,350	—
1914/3S	Inc. above	250	500	750	1,000	1,450	2,200	4,300	—	—
1915	20,987,270	5.50	7.00	7.75	11.00	21.50	38.50	50.00	325	2,100
1915D	7,569,500	21.50	31.00	41.50	66.00	115	150	225	2,500	—
1915S	1,505,000	47.00	74.00	105	185	320	490	625	3,400	—
1916	63,498,066	5.00	6.40	7.00	8.00	13.50	24.00	43.50	350	3,650
1916/16	Inc. above	2,000	4,250	8,000	12,000	17,000	38,000	55,000	395,000	—
1916D	13,333,000	15.00	26.50	29.00	38.50	82.50	110	150	2,500	—
1916S	11,860,000	11.00	13.50	20.00	35.00	75.00	125	175	2,650	—
1917	51,424,029	5.00	7.00	8.00	10.00	16.00	32.50	60.00	580	—
1917D	9,910,800	20.00	31.00	55.00	80.00	135	255	345	3,750	—
1917S	4,193,000	23.00	42.00	80.00	110	180	285	395	5,250	—
1918	32,086,314	5.00	6.50	8.00	15.00	31.00	48.50	110	1,700	—
1918/17D	8,362,314	1,150	1,650	2,850	6,250	10,000	11,800	28,500	365,000	—
1918D	Inc. above	22.50	39.00	66.00	135	220	330	430	5,000	—
1918S	4,882,000	14.00	27.50	55.00	100.00	175	300	495	28,500	—
1919	60,868,000	2.20	3.40	3.80	7.00	16.00	32.00	60.00	595	—
1919D	8,006,000	15.50	31.00	66.00	115	235	335	570	7,750	—
1919S	7,521,000	8.00	20.00	50.00	110	225	360	540	26,000	—
1920	63,093,000	1.50	2.75	3.25	8.00	16.00	30.00	59.00	850	—
1920D	9,418,000	8.50	19.00	35.00	125	275	340	555	7,600	—
1920S	9,689,000	4.50	12.75	30.00	100.00	200	300	525	28,500	—
1921	10,663,000	3.75	6.25	8.50	25.00	53.50	73.00	125	850	—
1921S	1,557,000	67.50	120	200	545	845	1,100	1,500	8,000	—
1923	35,715,000	1.70	3.25	4.25	7.00	14.00	37.50	60.00	750	—
1923S	6,142,000	8.00	11.00	27.00	125	275	335	595	12,500	—
1924	21,620,000	1.25	2.40	4.50	10.00	19.00	41.00	73.50	950	—
1924D	5,258,000	8.00	12.00	30.00	90.00	215	315	375	5,600	—
1924S	1,437,000	16.50	32.00	96.00	455	1,100	1,700	2,300	13,500	—
1925	35,565,100	2.50	3.00	3.75	8.50	18.00	32.00	44.00	525	—
1925D	4,450,000	10.00	20.00	38.00	80.00	160	240	380	6,400	—
1925S	6,256,000	4.50	9.00	17.50	77.50	170	250	440	42,500	—
1926	44,693,000	1.50	2.00	2.80	5.40	11.50	20.00	31.50	200	—
1926D	5,638,000	10.00	17.50	28.50	100.00	170	295	315	6,400	—
1926S	970,000	20.00	42.00	100.00	450	900	2,750	5,000	125,000	—
1927	37,981,000	1.40	1.75	2.50	4.50	12.50	20.00	35.00	300	—
1927D	5,730,000	3.00	6.00	7.00	27.50	75.00	115	150	9,000	—
1927S	3,430,000	2.00	3.00	6.00	31.00	80.00	160	485	22,500	—
1928	23,411,000	1.40	1.75	2.50	4.50	12.50	25.00	32.50	325	—
1928D	6,436,000	1.90	2.50	3.75	16.00	40.00	46.50	50.00	950	—
1928S	6,936,000	1.75	2.35	3.00	12.00	27.50	105	215	5,350	—
1929	36,446,000	1.40	1.75	2.50	4.50	13.00	21.00	35.00	375	—
1929D	8,370,000	1.50	1.85	3.00	6.75	32.50	42.50	55.00	1,950	—
1929S	7,754,000	1.50	1.85	2.25	4.00	12.50	25.00	47.50	525	—
1930	22,849,000	1.40	1.75	2.50	4.50	12.00	21.00	32.50	250	—
1930S	5,435,000	1.50	2.00	3.00	4.50	16.00	37.50	55.00	550	—
1931S	1,200,000	16.00	18.00	20.00	22.00	33.00	50.00	65.00	315	—
1934	20,213,003	1.40	1.75	2.50	4.50	11.00	19.00	48.50	425	—
1934D	7,480,000	2.00	3.00	4.75	9.60	22.00	50.00	82.50	1,000	—
1935	58,264,000	1.25	1.60	2.25	3.00	4.00	11.00	20.00	145	—
1935 Double Die Rev.	Inc. above	50.00	75.00	125	250	600	1,800	3,500	35,000	—

Date	Mintage	G-4	VG-8	F-12	VF-20	XF-40	AU-50	MS-60	MS-65	Prf-65
1935D	12,092,000	1.60	2.50	3.00	9.00	20.00	48.00	75.00	525	—
1935D/S	Inc. above	—	—	—	—	—	—	—	—	—
1935S	10,300,000	1.35	1.75	2.50	3.50	4.50	17.50	50.00	260	—
1936	119,001,420	1.25	1.60	2.25	3.00	4.00	6.75	15.00	110	1,750
1936 Brilliant	—	—	—	—	—	—	—	—	—	2,800
1936D	24,814,000	1.35	1.75	2.75	4.00	5.35	11.50	35.00	118	—
1936S	14,930,000	1.35	1.75	2.50	3.50	4.50	11.00	35.00	115	—
1937	79,485,769	1.25	1.60	2.25	3.00	4.00	6.75	14.50	74.00	2,100
1937D	17,826,000	1.35	1.75	2.50	3.50	4.50	9.00	30.00	75.00	—
1937D 3-legged	Inc. above	560	650	950	1,100	1,300	1,500	2,650	26,500	—
1937S	5,635,000	1.35	1.75	2.50	3.50	4.50	10.00	27.50	70.00	—
1938D	7,020,000	3.50	3.75	3.90	4.00	4.50	8.00	20.00	70.00	—
1938D/D	—	4.00	4.50	6.00	8.00	10.00	17.00	28.00	125	—
1938D/S	Inc. above	4.50	6.75	9.00	12.50	19.00	32.50	50.00	185	—

Jefferson Nickel

Monticello, mintmark to right side

KM# 192 COPPER-NICKEL 21.2 mm. 5.0000 g. **Designer:** Felix Schlag **Notes:** Some 1939 strikes have doubling of the word "Monticello" on the reverse.

Date	Mintage	VG-8	F-12	VF-20	XF-40	MS-60	MS-65	-65FS	Prf-65
1938	19,515,365	.50	.75	1.00	2.00	6.00	12.00	125	130
1938D	5,376,000	1.00	1.25	1.50	2.00	4.00	10.00	95.00	—
1938S	4,105,000	1.75	2.00	2.50	3.00	5.25	12.00	165	—
1939 T I, wavy steps, Rev. of 1939	—	—	—	—	—	—	—	300	70.00
1939 T II, even steps, Rev. of 1940	120,627,535	—	.20	.25	.30	1.75	3.50	40.00	130
1939 doubled Monticello T II	—	40.00	60.00	90.00	165	300	1,250	2,000	—
1939D T IT I, wavy steps, Rev. of 1939	—	—	—	—	—	—	—	275	—
1939D T IIT II, even steps, Rev. of 1940	3,514,000	4.00	5.00	8.00	14.00	44.00	125	250	—
1939S T IT I, wavy steps, Rev. of 1939	—	—	—	—	—	—	—	250	—
1939S T IIT II, even steps, Rev. of 1940	6,630,000	.45	.60	1.50	4.00	17.00	45.00	275	—
1940	176,499,158	—	—	—	.25	1.00	3.00	35.00	135
1940D	43,540,000	—	.20	.30	.40	1.50	2.75	25.00	—
1940S	39,690,000	—	.20	.25	.50	2.50	6.00	45.00	—
1941	203,283,720	—	—	—	.20	.75	2.50	40.00	130
1941D	53,432,000	—	.20	.30	.50	2.50	6.00	25.00	—
1941S	43,445,000	—	.20	.30	.50	3.75	6.75	60.00	—
1942	49,818,600	—	—	—	.40	5.00	8.50	75.00	115
1942D	13,938,000	1.00	1.50	3.00	5.00	32.00	60.00	70.00	—

Note: Fully Struck Full Step nickels command higher prices. Bright, Fully Struck coins command even higher prices. 1938 thru 1989 - 5 Full Steps. 1990 to date - 6 Full Steps. Without bag marks or nicks on steps.

Date	Mintage	VG-8	F-12	VF-20	XF-40	MS-60	MS-65	-65FS	Prf-65
1942D horiz./D	—	35.00	60.00	100.00	165	750	10,000	25,000	—

Monticello, mint mark above

KM# 192a 0.3500 **COPPER-SILVER-MANGANESE** 21.2 mm. **Designer:** Felix Schlag **Notes:** War-time composition nickels have the mint mark above Monticello on the reverse.

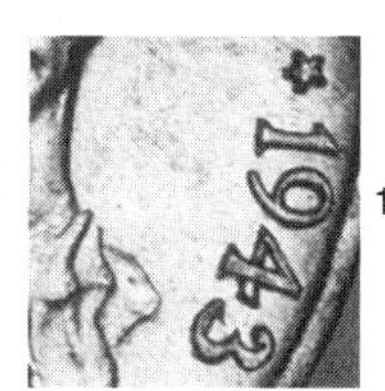
1943/2P

Date	Mintage	VG-8	F-12	VF-20	XF-40	MS-60	MS-65	-65FS	Prf-65
1942P	57,900,600	1.20	1.30	1.50	2.00	8.00	22.50	70.00	205
1942S	32,900,000	1.20	1.30	1.50	2.50	14.00	20.00	125	—
1943P	271,165,000	1.20	1.30	1.50	2.00	4.00	15.00	35.00	—
1943/2P	Inc. above	35.00	50.00	75.00	110	250	650	1,000	—
1943D	15,294,000	1.50	1.50	1.70	2.10	5.00	13.00	30.00	—
1943S	104,060,000	1.20	1.30	1.50	2.00	6.00	13.00	55.00	—
1944P	119,150,000	1.20	1.30	1.50	2.00	10.00	22.50	100.00	—
1944D	32,309,000	1.30	1.30	1.50	2.30	10.00	17.50	30.00	—
1944S	21,640,000	1.30	1.30	1.50	2.10	7.00	14.00	185	—
1945P	119,408,100	1.20	1.30	1.50	2.00	6.00	13.50	125	—
1945D	37,158,000	1.30	1.40	1.60	2.20	5.50	13.00	40.00	—
1945S	58,939,000	1.20	1.30	1.50	2.00	5.00	14.00	250	—

Note: Fully Struck Full Step nickels command higher prices. Bright, Fully Struck coins command even higher prices. 1938 thru 1989 - 5 Full Steps. 1990 to date - 6 Full Steps. Without bag marks or nicks on steps.

Pre-war design resumed

KM# A192 COPPER-NICKEL 19.53 mm. 5.0000 g. **Designer:** Felix Schlag **Notes:** KM#192 design and composition resumed. The 1979-S and 1981-S Type II proofs have clearer mint marks than the Type I proofs of those years.

Date	Mintage	VG-8	F-12	VF-20	XF-40	MS-60	MS-65	-65FS	Prf-65
1946	161,116,000	—	—	.20	.25	.80	3.50	40.00	—
1946D	45,292,200	—	—	.25	.35	.95	3.50	30.00	—
1946S	13,560,000	—	—	.30	.40	.50	2.00	45.00	—
1947	95,000,000	—	—	.20	.25	.75	2.00	30.00	—
1947D	37,822,000	—	—	.20	.30	.90	2.50	55.00	—
1947S	24,720,000	—	—	.20	.25	1.00	2.25	60.00	—
1948	89,348,000	—	—	.20	.25	.50	2.50	30.00	—
1948D	44,734,000	—	—	.25	.35	1.20	4.50	45.00	—
1948S	11,300,000	—	—	.25	.50	1.20	3.50	200	—
1949	60,652,000	—	—	.25	.30	2.25	6.00	200	—
1949D	36,498,000	—	—	.30	.40	1.25	5.00	75.00	—
1949D/S	Inc. above	—	35.00	40.00	65.00	170	325	1,750	—
1949S	9,716,000	.25	.35	.45	.90	1.50	3.50	145	—
1950	9,847,386	.20	.30	.35	.75	1.50	4.75	150	70.00
1950D	2,630,030	12.00	12.50	13.00	14.00	16.00	30.00	45.00	—
1951	28,609,500	—	—	.40	.50	1.50	9.00	90.00	70.00
1951D	20,460,000	.25	.30	.40	.50	3.00	10.00	45.00	—
1951S	7,776,000	.30	.40	.50	1.10	1.75	5.00	150	—
1952	64,069,980	—	—	.20	.25	.85	4.50	125	37.50
1952D	30,638,000	—	—	.30	.45	2.00	7.00	65.00	—
1952S	20,572,000	—	—	.20	.25	.75	3.50	195	—
1953	46,772,800	—	—	.20	.25	.40	1.50	200	37.50
1953D	59,878,600	—	—	.20	.25	.40	1.50	100.00	—
1953S	19,210,900	—	—	.20	.25	.60	2.50	1,750	—
1954	47,917,350	—	—	—	.20	.60	2.00	95.00	20.00
1954D	117,136,560	—	—	—	.20	.35	2.00	175	—
1954S	29,384,000	—	—	—	.25	1.00	3.00	1,000	—
1954S/D	Inc. above	—	9.00	14.00	30.00	50.00	500	—	—
1955	8,266,200	.25	.35	.40	.50	.75	2.00	85.00	13.50
1955D	74,464,100	—	—	—	.15	.20	1.00	150	—
1955D/S	Inc. above	—	10.00	16.00	40.00	65.00	135	185	—
1956	35,885,384	—	—	—	.20	.30	.70	35.00	2.50
1956D	67,222,940	—	—	—	.15	.25	.60	90.00	—
1957	39,655,952	—	—	—	.15	.25	.60	40.00	1.50
1957D	136,828,900	—	—	—	.15	.25	.60	55.00	—
1958	17,963,652	—	—	.15	.25	.30	.65	80.00	7.00
1958D	168,249,120	—	—	—	.15	.25	.60	30.00	—

Note: Fully Struck Full Step nickels command higher prices. Bright, Fully Struck coins command even higher prices. 1938 thru 1989 - 5 Full Steps. 1990 to date - 6 Full Steps. Without bag marks or nicks on steps.

Date	Mintage	VG-8	F-12	VF-20	XF-40	MS-60	MS-65	-65FS	Prf-65
1959	28,397,291	—	—	—	—	.30	.65	30.00	1.25
1959D	160,738,240	—	—	—	—	.25	.55	45.00	—
1960	57,107,602	—	—	—	—	.25	2.00	60.00	1.00
1960D	192,582,180	—	—	—	—	.25	.55	650	—
1961	76,668,244	—	—	—	—	.25	.55	100.00	1.00
1961D	229,342,760	—	—	—	—	.25	.55	800	—
1962	100,602,019	—	—	—	—	.25	1.50	75.00	1.00
1962D	280,195,720	—	—	—	—	.25	.55	60.00	—
1963	178,851,645	—	—	—	—	.25	.55	45.00	1.00
1963D	276,829,460	—	—	—	—	.25	.55	650	—
1964	1,028,622,762	—	—	—	—	.25	.55	55.00	1.00
1964D	1,787,297,160	—	—	—	—	.25	.50	500	—
1965	136,131,380	—	—	—	—	.25	.50	225	—
1966	156,208,283	—	—	—	—	.25	.50	350	—
1967	107,325,800	—	—	—	—	.25	.50	275	—
1968 none minted	—	—	—	—	—	—	—	—	—
1968D	91,227,880	—	—	—	—	.25	.50	750	—
1968S	103,437,510	—	—	—	—	.25	.50	300	0.75
1969 none minted	—	—	—	—	—	—	—	—	—
1969D	202,807,500	—	—	—	—	.25	.50	—	—
1969S	123,099,631	—	—	—	—	.25	.50	450	0.75
1970 none minted	—	—	—	—	—	—	—	—	—
1970D	515,485,380	—	—	—	—	.25	.50	500	—
1970S	241,464,814	—	—	—	—	.25	.50	125	0.75
1971	106,884,000	—	—	—	—	.85	2.00	35.00	—
1971D	316,144,800	—	—	—	—	.25	.50	25.00	—
1971S	(3,220,733)	—	—	—	—	—	—	—	2.00
1972	202,036,000	—	—	—	—	.25	.50	35.00	—
1972D	351,694,600	—	—	—	—	.25	.50	25.00	—
1972S	(3,260,996)	—	—	—	—	—	—	—	2.00
1973	384,396,000	—	—	—	—	—	.50	20.00	—
1973D	261,405,000	—	—	—	—	—	.50	20.00	—
1973S	(2,760,339)	—	—	—	—	—	—	—	1.75
1974	601,752,000	—	—	—	—	—	.50	75.00	—
1974D	277,373,000	—	—	—	—	—	.50	50.00	—
1974S	(2,612,568)	—	—	—	—	—	—	—	2.00
1975	181,772,000	—	—	—	—	—	.75	65.00	—
1975D	401,875,300	—	—	—	—	—	.50	60.00	—
1975S	(2,845,450)	—	—	—	—	—	—	—	2.25
1976	367,124,000	—	—	—	—	—	.75	150	—
1976D	563,964,147	—	—	—	—	—	.60	55.00	—
1976S	(4,149,730)	—	—	—	—	—	—	—	2.00
1977	585,376,000	—	—	—	—	—	.40	65.00	—
1977D	297,313,460	—	—	—	—	—	.55	35.00	—

Date	Mintage	VG-8	F-12	VF-20	XF-40	MS-60	MS-65	-65FS	Prf-65
1977S	(3,251,152)	—	—	—	—	—	—	—	1.75
1978	391,308,000	—	—	—	—	—	.40	40.00	—
1978D	313,092,780	—	—	—	—	—	.40	35.00	—
1978S	(3,127,781)	—	—	—	—	—	—	—	1.75
1979	463,188,000	—	—	—	—	—	.40	95.00	—
1979D	325,867,672	—	—	—	—	—	.40	35.00	—
1979S type I, proof	(3,677,175)	—	—	—	—	—	—	—	1.50
1979S type II, proof	Inc. above	—	—	—	—	—	—	—	1.75
1980P	593,004,000	—	—	—	—	—	.40	30.00	—
1980D	502,323,448	—	—	—	—	.25	.40	25.00	—
1980S	(3,554,806)	—	—	—	—	—	—	—	1.50
1981P	657,504,000	—	—	—	—	.25	.40	70.00	—
1981D	364,801,843	—	—	—	—	.25	.40	40.00	—
1981S type I,, proof	(4,063,083)	—	—	—	—	—	—	—	2.00
1981S type II, proof	Inc. above	—	—	—	—	—	—	—	2.50
1982P	292,355,000	—	—	—	—	2.00	12.50	80.00	—
1982D	373,726,544	—	—	—	—	1.50	3.50	45.00	—
1982S	(3,857,479)	—	—	—	—	—	—	—	3.50
1983P	561,615,000	—	—	—	—	1.50	4.00	45.00	—
1983D	536,726,276	—	—	—	—	.75	2.50	35.00	—
1983S	(3,279,126)	—	—	—	—	—	—	—	4.00
1984P	746,769,000	—	—	—	—	1.25	3.00	65.00	—
1984D	517,675,146	—	—	—	—	.30	.85	30.00	—
1984S	(3,065,110)	—	—	—	—	—	—	—	5.00
1985P	647,114,962	—	—	—	—	.35	.75	60.00	—
1985D	459,747,446	—	—	—	—	.35	.75	35.00	—
1985S	(3,362,821)	—	—	—	—	—	—	—	4.00
1986P	536,883,483	—	—	—	—	.40	1.00	70.00	—
1986D	361,819,140	—	—	—	—	1.00	2.00	60.00	—
1986S	(3,010,497)	—	—	—	—	—	—	—	7.00
1987P	371,499,481	—	—	—	—	.25	.75	30.00	—
1987D	410,590,604	—	—	—	—	.25	.75	25.00	—
1987S	(4,227,728)	—	—	—	—	—	—	—	3.50
1988P	771,360,000	—	—	—	—	.25	.75	30.00	—
1988D	663,771,652	—	—	—	—	—	.75	25.00	—
1988S	(3,262,948)	—	—	—	—	—	—	—	6.50
1989P	898,812,000	—	—	—	—	.25	.75	75.00	—
1989D	570,842,474	—	—	—	—	.25	.75	25.00	—
1989S	(3,220,194)	—	—	—	—	—	—	—	5.50
1990P	661,636,000	—	—	—	—	.25	.75	25.00	—
1990D	663,938,503	—	—	—	—	.25	.75	25.00	—
1990S	(3,299,559)	—	—	—	—	—	—	—	5.50
1991P	614,104,000	—	—	—	—	.25	.75	25.00	—
1991D	436,496,678	—	—	—	—	.25	.75	25.00	—
1991S	(2,867,787)	—	—	—	—	—	—	—	5.00
1992P	399,552,000	—	—	—	—	.65	2.00	25.00	—
1992D	450,565,113	—	—	—	—	.25	.75	25.00	—
1992S	(4,176,560)	—	—	—	—	—	—	—	4.00
1993P	412,076,000	—	—	—	—	.25	.75	25.00	—
1993D	406,084,135	—	—	—	—	.25	.75	25.00	—
1993S	(3,394,792)	—	—	—	—	—	—	—	4.50
1994P	722,160,000	—	—	—	—	.25	.75	25.00	—
1994P matte proof	(167,703)	—	—	—	—	—	—	—	75.00
1994D	715,762,110	—	—	—	—	.25	.75	25.00	—
1994S	(3,269,923)	—	—	—	—	—	—	—	4.00
1995P	774,156,000	—	—	—	—	.25	.75	25.00	—
1995D	888,112,000	—	—	—	—	.35	.85	25.00	—
1995S	(2,707,481)	—	—	—	—	—	—	—	4.00
1996P	829,332,000	—	—	—	—	.25	.75	25.00	—
1996D	817,736,000	—	—	—	—	.25	.75	25.00	—
1996S	(2,915,212)	—	—	—	—	—	—	—	4.00
1997P	470,972,000	—	—	—	—	.25	.75	25.00	—
1997P matte proof	(25,000)	—	—	—	—	—	—	—	200
1997D	466,640,000	—	—	—	—	.30	2.00	25.00	—
1997S	(1,975,000)	—	—	—	—	.25	—	—	5.00
1998P	688,272,000	—	—	—	—	.25	.80	25.00	—
1998D	635,360,000	—	—	—	—	.25	.80	25.00	—
1998S	(2,957,286)	—	—	—	—	—	—	—	4.50
1999P	1,212,000,000	—	—	—	—	.25	.80	20.00	—
1999D	1,066,720,000	—	—	—	—	.25	.80	20.00	—
1999S	(3,362,462)	—	—	—	—	—	—	—	3.50
2000P	846,240,000	—	—	—	—	.25	.80	20.00	—
2000D	1,509,520,000	—	—	—	—	.25	.80	20.00	—
2000S	(4,063,361)	—	—	—	—	—	—	—	2.00
2001P	675,704,000	—	—	—	—	.25	.50	20.00	—
2001D	627,680,000	—	—	—	—	.25	.50	20.00	—
2001S	(3,099,096)	—	—	—	—	—	—	—	2.00
2002P	539,280,000	—	—	—	—	.25	.50	—	—
2002D	691,200,000	—	—	—	—	.25	.50	—	—
2002S	(3,157,739)	—	—	—	—	—	—	—	2.00
2003P	441,840,000	—	—	—	—	.25	.50	—	—
2003D	383,040,000	—	—	—	—	.25	.50	—	—
2003S	(3,116,590)	—	—	—	—	—	—	—	2.00

Jefferson era peace medal design: two clasped hands, pipe and hatchet

KM# 360 COPPER NICKEL 21.2 mm. 5.0000 g. **Obv. Designer:** Felix Schlag **Rev. Designer:** Norman E. Nemeth

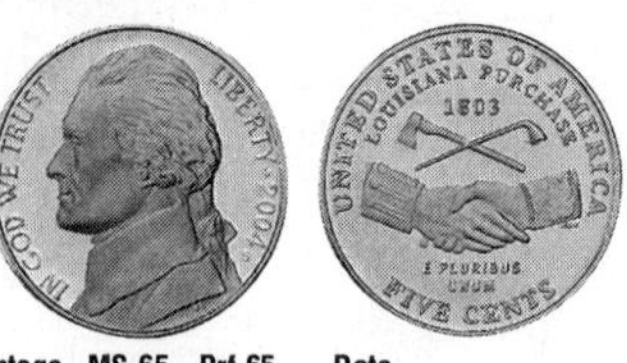

Date	Mintage	MS-65	Prf-65	Date	Mintage	MS-65	Prf-65
2004P	361,440,000	1.00	—	2004S	—	—	13.00
2004D	372,000,000	1.00	—				

Lewis and Clark's Keelboat

KM# 361 COPPER NICKEL 21.2 mm. 5.0000 g. **Obv. Designer:** Felix Schlag **Rev. Designer:** Al Maletsky

Date	Mintage	MS-65	Prf-65	Date	Mintage	MS-65	Prf-65
2004P	366,720,000	1.00	—	2004S	—	—	13.00
2004D	344,880,000	1.00	—				

Thomas Jefferson large profile right American Bison right

KM# 368 COPPER NICKEL 21.2 mm. 5.0000 g. **Obv. Designer:** Joe Fitzgerald and Don Everhart II **Rev. Designer:** Jamie Franki and Norman E. Nemeth

Date	Mintage	MS-65	Prf-65	Date	Mintage	MS-65	Prf-65
2005P	448,320,000	1.00	—	2005S	—	—	7.50
2005D	487,680,000	1.00	—				

Pacific coastline

KM# 369 COPPER NICKEL 21.2 mm. 5.0000 g. **Obv. Designer:** Joe Fitzgerald and Don Everhart **Rev. Designer:** Joe Fitzgerald and Donna Weaver

Date	Mintage	MS-65	Prf-65	Date	Mintage	MS-65	Prf-65
2005P	394,080,000	1.00	—	2005S	—	—	6.50
2005D	411,120,000	1.00	—				

Large facing portrait Monticello, enhanced design

KM# 381 COPPER-NICKEL 21 mm. 5.0000 g. **Obv. Designer:** Jamie N. Franki and Donna Weaver **Rev. Designer:** Felix Schlag and John Mercanti

Date	Mintage	MS-65	Prf-65	Date	Mintage	MS-65	Prf-65
2006P	693,120,000	1.00	—	2007P	—	1.00	—
2006D	809,280,000	1.00	—	2007D	—	1.00	—
2006S	—	—	4.00	2007S	—	—	4.00

DIME

Barber Dime

Laureate head right, date at angle below
Value within wreath

KM# 113 0.9000 **SILVER** 0.0723 oz. ASW. 17.9 mm. 2.5000 g. **Designer:** Charles E. Barber

Date	Mintage	G-4	VG-8	F-12	VF-20	XF-40	AU-50	MS-60	MS-65	Prf-65
1901	18,860,478	2.50	3.75	6.50	10.00	27.50	65.00	110	850	1,450
1901O	5,620,000	3.75	5.25	16.00	27.50	67.50	180	450	4,500	—
1901S	593,022	80.00	150	360	450	520	675	1,000	5,500	—
1902	21,380,777	3.00	3.75	5.50	8.00	23.00	65.00	100.00	700	1,450
1902O	4,500,000	3.45	5.25	15.00	32.50	62.50	135	340	4,650	—
1902S	2,070,000	8.00	21.00	55.00	85.00	135	200	385	4,000	—
1903	19,500,755	2.50	3.75	4.40	8.00	25.00	65.00	110	1,150	1,450
1903O	8,180,000	3.50	5.00	13.50	23.50	50.00	110	250	5,100	—
1903S	613,300	84.00	130	340	490	770	845	1,150	3,750	—
1904	14,601,027	2.50	3.75	6.25	9.50	25.00	65.00	110	1,950	1,450
1904S	800,000	45.00	75.00	160	240	345	480	750	4,500	—
1905	14,552,350	2.80	3.45	5.60	8.00	25.00	65.00	110	700	1,450
1905O	3,400,000	4.00	10.00	34.00	57.50	96.00	155	285	1,900	—
1905S	6,855,199	3.50	3.85	9.00	18.50	45.00	100.00	220	800	—
1906	19,958,406	1.75	2.20	3.75	6.75	22.00	62.50	100.00	700	1,450
1906D	4,060,000	2.75	3.85	7.00	15.00	36.00	80.00	175	1,600	—
1906O	2,610,000	5.50	13.00	47.50	75.00	100.00	135	200	1,300	—
1906S	3,136,640	2.80	5.25	12.50	22.00	46.00	115	240	1,300	—
1907	22,220,575	1.75	2.20	3.40	6.75	22.00	62.50	110	700	1,450
1907D	4,080,000	2.50	4.00	8.50	17.50	45.00	115	280	4,600	—
1907O	5,058,000	3.45	6.75	31.50	47.50	62.50	110	210	1,350	—
1907S	3,178,470	3.45	5.50	16.00	27.50	67.50	150	420	2,500	—
1908	10,600,545	2.20	2.50	3.40	6.75	22.00	62.50	110	700	1,450
1908D	7,490,000	2.15	2.50	4.65	9.50	30.00	62.50	130	1,150	—
1908O	1,789,000	5.00	11.00	42.50	61.00	96.00	150	300	1,700	—
1908S	3,220,000	3.45	5.25	11.50	22.00	47.50	175	325	2,750	—
1909	10,240,650	2.20	2.50	3.40	6.75	22.00	62.50	110	700	1,700
1909D	954,000	7.50	19.50	60.00	96.00	135	230	500	3,600	—
1909O	2,287,000	4.00	7.50	12.50	22.00	50.00	96.00	190	2,000	—
1909S	1,000,000	9.00	20.00	85.00	125	190	330	535	3,200	—
1910	11,520,551	1.85	2.20	3.40	9.50	23.00	62.50	110	700	1,450
1910D	3,490,000	2.50	4.00	8.50	19.50	47.50	110	220	1,550	—
1910S	1,240,000	5.25	10.00	50.00	71.00	110	200	435	2,600	—
1911	18,870,543	1.75	2.10	3.40	6.75	22.00	62.50	110	700	1,700
1911D	11,209,000	1.75	2.10	3.40	6.75	25.00	62.50	110	750	—
1911S	3,520,000	2.80	3.75	8.50	19.00	41.50	110	200	1,300	—
1912	19,350,700	1.75	2.10	3.40	6.75	22.00	62.50	110	700	1,700
1912D	11,760,000	1.75	2.10	3.75	6.75	22.00	62.50	110	700	—
1912S	3,420,000	2.20	2.75	5.60	12.50	34.00	96.00	160	850	—
1913	19,760,622	1.75	2.10	3.00	6.50	22.00	62.50	110	700	1,450
1913S	510,000	30.00	47.50	110	170	240	330	480	1,350	—
1914	17,360,655	1.75	2.10	3.00	6.50	22.00	62.50	110	700	1,700
1914D	11,908,000	1.75	2.10	3.40	6.50	22.00	62.50	110	700	—
1914S	2,100,000	3.00	4.00	8.00	17.50	41.50	80.00	150	1,350	—
1915	5,620,450	2.20	2.50	3.00	7.00	22.00	62.50	110	700	2,000
1915S	960,000	7.00	12.00	32.50	47.50	70.00	135	250	1,600	—
1916	18,490,000	1.75	2.15	3.40	8.00	22.00	62.50	110	700	—
1916S	5,820,000	1.75	2.65	4.00	8.00	23.50	65.00	110	850	—

Mercury Dime

KM# 140 0.9000 **SILVER** 0.0723 oz. ASW. 17.9 mm. 2.5000 g. **Designer:** Adolph A. Weinman **Notes:** All specimens listed as -65FSB are for fully struck MS-65 coins with fully split and rounded horizontal bands on the fasces.

Mint mark

1942/41

Full split bands

Date	Mintage	G-4	VG-8	F-12	VF-20	XF-40	AU-50	MS-60	MS-63	MS-65	-65FSB
1916	22,180,080	3.45	4.70	6.25	7.00	12.00	22.50	30.00	43.00	110	120
1916D	264,000	1,000	1,600	2,700	3,850	6,200	9,250	13,750	18,400	26,500	44,500
1916S	10,450,000	4.00	5.50	9.75	15.00	25.00	30.00	46.00	60.00	210	600
1917	55,230,000	1.85	2.25	2.50	5.50	8.00	12.50	28.00	55.00	155	400
1917D	9,402,000	4.00	6.00	11.00	26.00	51.00	92.50	120	300	1,100	6,000
1917S	27,330,000	1.80	2.40	3.50	6.50	14.00	28.00	64.00	170	470	1,150
1918	26,680,000	2.50	3.20	5.75	12.00	34.00	42.00	70.00	95.00	420	1,150
1918D	22,674,800	2.65	3.25	5.00	12.00	32.00	46.00	105	210	600	33,500
1918S	19,300,000	2.40	3.00	3.85	10.00	24.00	38.50	96.00	230	660	6,600
1919	35,740,000	1.90	2.50	3.00	5.50	12.00	23.00	37.00	105	315	700
1919D	9,939,000	3.50	6.50	12.00	25.00	46.00	72.00	180	420	2,100	38,500
1919S	8,850,000	2.90	3.25	8.00	17.00	42.00	72.00	180	450	1,250	13,000
1920	59,030,000	1.50	1.75	2.25	4.00	8.50	14.00	28.00	67.00	235	515
1920D	19,171,000	2.50	2.85	4.50	8.00	24.00	46.00	110	310	750	4,000
1920S	13,820,000	2.40	2.75	4.00	8.50	21.00	42.00	110	300	1,300	8,000
1921	1,230,000	60.00	75.00	125	280	550	875	1,175	1,465	3,100	4,400
1921D	1,080,000	78.00	125	205	380	675	1,175	1,325	1,650	3,250	5,600
1923	50,130,000	1.50	2.00	2.25	4.00	7.00	15.00	28.00	42.00	115	295
1923S	6,440,000	2.60	3.00	7.50	18.00	75.00	100.00	160	375	1,150	6,900
1924	24,010,000	1.50	2.00	2.75	4.50	13.50	26.50	42.00	88.00	175	520
1924D	6,810,000	3.00	4.25	6.50	22.00	63.00	100.00	175	460	1,050	1,400
1924S	7,120,000	2.90	3.75	4.25	12.00	60.00	95.00	170	450	1,100	14,000
1925	25,610,000	1.50	1.75	2.35	4.00	9.00	16.00	28.00	75.00	210	1,000
1925D	5,117,000	4.00	4.25	12.00	44.00	135	190	350	725	1,750	3,500
1925S	5,850,000	2.50	2.75	7.00	14.00	85.00	100.00	185	475	1,400	4,400
1926	32,160,000	1.50	1.75	2.00	3.00	6.00	12.00	25.00	55.00	240	525
1926D	6,828,000	2.90	4.00	5.00	10.00	32.00	43.00	125	260	550	2,650
1926S	1,520,000	10.50	12.50	29.00	70.00	290	410	900	1,425	3,000	6,500
1927	28,080,000	1.50	1.75	2.00	3.50	6.00	11.00	26.00	48.00	138	400
1927D	4,812,000	2.90	5.00	7.50	21.00	88.00	92.50	175	360	1,285	8,500
1927S	4,770,000	2.25	3.75	5.00	9.00	32.00	48.00	285	550	1,400	7,700
1928	19,480,000	1.50	1.75	1.85	3.50	4.50	16.00	27.50	48.00	120	300
1928D	4,161,000	3.75	4.00	9.00	22.00	55.00	85.00	175	315	875	2,500
1928S Large S	7,400,000	2.75	3.25	4.50	10.00	30.00	60.00	200	385	640	—
1928S Small S	Inc. above	2.00	2.25	3.00	6.50	19.00	37.00	125	280	425	1,900
1929	25,970,000	1.50	1.75	2.10	3.00	4.50	10.00	21.00	28.00	60.00	265
1929D	5,034,000	2.00	3.00	4.00	8.00	15.00	22.00	27.00	30.00	75.00	225
1929S	4,730,000	1.50	1.85	2.25	5.00	7.00	20.00	32.50	42.00	90.00	525
1929S Doubled Die Obv	Inc. above	5.00	9.00	16.00	25.00	40.00	60.00	90.00	140	275	—
1930	6,770,000	1.50	1.75	2.10	3.75	7.00	13.00	26.00	48.00	120	525
1930S	1,843,000	2.50	3.50	4.80	6.50	19.00	45.00	82.00	122	200	565
1931	3,150,000	2.25	3.00	3.35	4.25	12.50	22.50	33.00	62.50	135	—
1931D	1,260,000	9.00	11.00	15.00	18.00	45.00	56.00	100.00	125	285	350
1931 Doubled Die Obv & Rev	Inc. above	—	—	—	50.00	70.00	90.00	135	200	485	—
1931S	1,800,000	4.00	5.00	5.50	11.00	22.00	45.00	96.00	135	275	2,100
1931S Doubled Die Obv	—	7.50	10.00	13.00	25.00	35.00	60.00	140	200	425	—
1934	24,080,000	—	1.45	1.75	3.00	6.50	10.00	29.00	33.00	42.00	150
1934D	6,772,000	1.60	2.10	3.25	7.50	14.00	27.50	50.00	60.00	78.00	360
1935	58,830,000	—	1.35	1.50	2.15	4.25	7.50	10.00	15.00	30.00	70.00
1935D	10,477,000	1.50	1.90	2.85	6.50	13.00	25.00	37.00	46.00	84.00	600
1935S	15,840,000	1.35	1.65	2.00	3.00	5.50	14.00	24.00	28.00	37.00	500
1936	87,504,130	—	—	1.50	2.50	3.50	6.50	9.00	15.00	26.50	90.00
1936 Doubled Die Obv	Inc. above	—	—	8.00	15.00	25.00	35.00	50.00	100.00	165	—
1936D	16,132,000	—	1.65	2.10	4.25	8.50	17.00	28.00	36.00	53.00	295
1936S	9,210,000	—	1.50	1.90	3.00	6.00	12.50	20.00	30.00	33.00	85.00
1937	56,865,756	—	—	1.50	2.00	3.75	6.00	8.00	12.00	24.00	42.00
1937 Doubled Die Obv	Inc. above	—	—	—	6.00	9.00	12.00	20.00	40.00	60.00	—
1937D	14,146,000	—	1.40	1.80	3.00	6.00	12.50	22.00	30.00	43.00	100.00

Date	Mintage	G-4	VG-8	F-12	VF-20	XF-40	AU-50	MS-60	MS-63	MS-65	-65FSB
1937S	9,740,000	—	1.50	2.00	3.00	5.50	10.00	22.00	27.00	36.00	195
1937S Doubled Die Obv	Inc. above	—	—	—	5.00	7.00	9.00	24.00	40.00	80.00	—
1938	22,198,728	—	—	1.50	2.25	3.75	7.50	13.00	15.00	25.00	80.00
1938D	5,537,000	1.75	2.25	3.25	5.00	6.00	12.00	18.00	24.00	34.00	65.00
1938S	8,090,000	1.50	2.00	2.75	3.25	5.00	12.00	21.00	27.50	37.00	135
1939	67,749,321	—	—	1.50	2.00	3.25	4.50	9.00	11.00	25.00	170
1939 Doubled Die Obv	Inc. above	—	—	—	4.00	6.00	8.00	14.00	20.00	35.00	—
1939D	24,394,000	—	1.25	1.50	2.00	3.50	5.50	7.50	10.00	26.00	45.00
1939S	10,540,000	1.50	1.75	2.25	3.50	6.75	14.00	25.00	32.00	50.00	750
1940	65,361,827	—	—	—	1.25	2.50	4.00	6.00	11.00	30.00	57.50
1940D	21,198,000	—	—	—	1.40	3.00	5.00	8.00	13.00	32.00	55.00
1940S	21,560,000	—	—	—	1.40	3.00	4.50	8.50	12.50	32.00	95.00
1941	175,106,557	—	—	—	1.25	1.60	2.75	6.00	10.00	30.00	42.00
1941 Doubled Die Obv	Inc. above	—	—	—	10.00	16.00	30.00	55.00	80.00	140	—
1941D	45,634,000	—	—	—	1.40	2.00	4.00	8.00	13.00	23.00	40.00
1941D Doubled Die Obv	Inc. above	—	—	—	9.00	14.00	20.00	30.00	60.00	90.00	—
1941S Small S	43,090,000	—	—	—	1.40	2.00	4.50	7.00	10.00	30.00	50.00
1941S Large S	Inc. above	2.50	4.00	8.00	15.00	25.00	60.00	110	145	250	—
1941S Doubled Die Rev	—	1.75	2.50	3.00	4.00	5.00	7.50	18.00	25.00	50.00	—
1942	205,432,329	—	—	—	1.25	1.60	2.00	6.00	11.00	24.00	52.50
1942/41	Inc. above	525	525	625	735	800	1,500	2,250	4,000	12,500	38,500
1942D	60,740,000	—	—	—	1.40	2.00	4.00	8.00	12.75	27.50	40.00
1942/41D	Inc. above	500	595	680	840	920	1,400	2,650	4,500	7,000	19,500
1942S	49,300,000	—	—	—	1.40	2.00	4.50	9.50	16.00	24.00	140
1943	191,710,000	—	—	—	1.25	1.60	2.25	6.00	10.00	31.00	50.00
1943D	71,949,000	—	—	—	1.40	2.00	3.00	7.75	12.00	30.00	40.00
1943S	60,400,000	—	—	—	1.40	2.00	4.50	9.00	13.00	26.50	66.00
1944	231,410,000	—	—	—	1.25	1.60	2.25	6.00	10.00	23.00	80.00
1944D	62,224,000	—	—	—	1.40	2.00	3.00	7.50	15.00	23.00	40.00
1944S	49,490,000	—	—	—	1.40	2.00	4.00	7.50	16.00	30.00	50.00
1945	159,130,000	—	—	—	1.25	1.60	2.25	6.00	10.00	23.00	8,000
1945D	40,245,000	—	—	—	1.40	2.00	2.75	6.50	10.00	24.00	40.00
1945S	41,920,000	—	—	—	1.40	2.00	4.00	7.00	10.00	24.00	135
1945S micro S	Inc. above	3.00	4.00	6.00	9.00	13.00	20.00	28.00	38.00	115	650

Roosevelt Dime

KM# 195 0.9000 **SILVER** 0.0723 oz. ASW. 17.9 mm. 2.5000 g. **Designer:** John R. Sinnock

Mint mark 1946-64

Date	Mintage	G-4	VG-8	F-12	VF-20	XF-40	AU-50	MS-60	MS-65	Prf-65
1946	225,250,000	—	—	—	—	1.50	2.00	2.00	14.00	—
1946D	61,043,500	—	—	—	—	1.50	2.20	2.25	15.00	—
1946S	27,900,000	—	—	—	—	1.50	2.25	2.35	17.00	—
1947	121,520,000	—	—	—	—	1.50	2.00	4.00	15.00	—
1947D	46,835,000	—	—	—	—	1.70	2.25	5.00	17.00	—
1947S	34,840,000	—	—	—	—	1.50	2.00	5.00	16.00	—
1948	74,950,000	—	—	—	—	1.60	2.00	4.50	15.00	—
1948D	52,841,000	—	—	—	—	1.90	2.50	6.00	17.00	—
1948S	35,520,000	—	—	—	—	1.80	2.25	5.00	14.00	—
1949	30,940,000	—	—	1.50	2.00	3.00	8.00	16.00	50.00	—
1949D	26,034,000	—	—	1.35	1.75	2.25	5.00	9.00	22.00	—
1949S	13,510,000	—	1.60	2.00	3.50	7.50	14.00	40.00	65.00	—
1950	50,181,500	—	—	—	1.75	2.25	3.50	10.00	25.00	55.00
1950D	46,803,000	—	—	—	—	—	2.50	5.00	12.00	—
1950S	20,440,000	—	1.20	1.80	2.00	3.75	9.00	32.00	60.00	—
1951	102,937,602	—	—	—	—	—	2.10	2.50	10.00	60.00
1951D	56,529,000	—	—	—	—	—	2.00	2.50	8.00	—
1951S	31,630,000	—	—	—	1.70	2.00	4.00	10.00	26.00	—
1952	99,122,073	—	—	—	—	—	1.90	2.50	9.00	40.00
1952D	122,100,000	—	—	—	—	—	1.90	2.50	10.00	—
1952S	44,419,500	—	—	—	1.75	1.90	2.75	5.50	15.00	—
1953	53,618,920	—	—	—	—	—	1.90	2.25	8.00	45.00
1953D	136,433,000	—	—	—	—	—	1.90	2.45	8.00	—
1953S	39,180,000	—	—	—	—	—	2.30	3.00	15.00	—
1954	114,243,503	—	—	—	—	—	1.90	2.10	7.00	20.00
1954D	106,397,000	—	—	—	—	—	1.90	2.10	7.00	—
1954S	22,860,000	—	—	—	—	—	1.90	2.20	10.00	—
1955	12,828,381	—	—	—	1.75	1.50	2.30	2.75	10.00	18.00
1955D	13,959,000	—	—	—	1.75	1.60	2.45	2.75	10.00	—
1955S	18,510,000	—	—	—	1.75	1.55	2.35	2.25	9.00	—
1956	109,309,384	—	—	—	—	—	1.90	2.10	9.00	8.00
1956D	108,015,100	—	—	—	—	—	1.90	2.20	10.00	—
1957	161,407,952	—	—	—	—	—	1.90	2.10	8.00	6.00
1957D	113,354,330	—	—	—	—	—	1.90	2.10	8.00	—
1958	32,785,652	—	—	—	—	—	1.90	2.10	8.50	6.00
1958D	136,564,600	—	—	—	—	—	1.90	2.10	9.00	—
1959	86,929,291	—	—	—	—	—	1.90	2.10	8.00	5.00
1959D	164,919,790	—	—	—	—	—	1.90	2.10	8.00	—
1960	72,081,602	—	—	—	—	—	1.90	2.10	7.50	5.00
1960D	200,160,400	—	—	—	—	—	1.90	2.10	7.50	—
1961	96,758,244	—	—	—	—	—	1.90	2.10	6.50	4.50
1961D	209,146,550	—	—	—	—	—	1.90	2.10	6.50	—
1962	75,668,019	—	—	—	—	—	1.90	2.10	7.00	4.50
1962D	334,948,380	—	—	—	—	—	1.90	2.10	7.00	—
1963	126,725,645	—	—	—	—	—	1.90	2.10	6.50	4.00
1963D	421,476,530	—	—	—	—	—	1.90	2.10	6.50	—
1964	933,310,762	—	—	—	—	—	1.90	2.10	6.00	4.00
1964D	1,357,517,180	—	—	—	—	—	1.90	2.10	6.00	—

KM# 195a COPPER-NICKEL CLAD COPPER 17.9 mm. 2.2700 g. **Designer:** John R. Sinnock **Notes:** The 1979-S and 1981-S Type II proofs have clearer mint marks than the Type I proofs of those years. On the 1982 no-mint-mark variety, the mint mark was inadvertently left off.

Mint mark 1968-present

1982 No mint mark

Date	Mintage	MS-65	Prf-65
1965	1,652,140,570	1.00	—
1966	1,382,734,540	1.00	—
1967	2,244,007,320	1.50	—
1968	424,470,000	1.00	—
1968D	480,748,280	1.00	—
1968S	(3,041,506)	—	1.00
1969	145,790,000	3.00	—
1969D	563,323,870	1.00	—
1969S	(2,934,631)	—	0.80
1970	345,570,000	1.00	—
1970S No S	—	—	1,300
1970D	754,942,100	1.00	—
1970S	(2,632,810)	—	1.00
1971	162,690,000	2.00	—
1971D	377,914,240	1.00	—
1971S	(3,220,733)	—	1.00
1972	431,540,000	1.00	—
1972D	330,290,000	1.00	—
1972S	(3,260,996)	—	1.00
1973	315,670,000	1.00	—
1973D	455,032,426	1.00	—
1973S	(2,760,339)	—	1.00
1974	470,248,000	1.00	—
1974D	571,083,000	1.00	—
1974S	(2,612,568)	—	1.00
1975	585,673,900	1.00	—
1975D	313,705,300	1.00	—
1975S	(2,845,450)	—	2.00
1976	568,760,000	1.50	—
1976D	695,222,774	1.00	—
1976S	(4,149,730)	—	1.00
1977	796,930,000	1.00	—
1977D	376,607,228	1.00	—
1977S	(3,251,152)	—	2.00
1978	663,980,000	1.00	—
1978D	282,847,540	1.00	—
1978S	(3,127,781)	—	1.00
1979	315,440,000	1.00	—
1979D	390,921,184	1.00	—
1979 type I	—	—	1.00
1979S type I	(3,677,175)	—	1.00
1979S type II	Inc. above	—	2.00
1980P	735,170,000	1.00	—
1980D	719,354,321	.70	—
1980S	(3,554,806)	—	1.00
1981P	676,650,000	1.00	—
1981D	712,284,143	1.00	—
1981S type I	—	—	1.00
1981S type II	—	—	2.00
1982P	519,475,000	8.50	—
1982 no mint mark	—	300	—
1982D	542,713,584	3.00	—
1982S	(3,857,479)	—	2.00
1983P	647,025,000	7.00	—
1983D	730,129,224	2.50	—
1983S	(3,279,126)	—	2.00
1984P	856,669,000	1.00	—
1984D	704,803,976	2.00	—
1984S	(3,065,110)	—	2.00
1985P	705,200,962	1.00	—
1985D	587,979,970	1.00	—
1985S	(3,362,821)	—	1.00
1986P	682,649,693	2.00	—
1986D	473,326,970	2.00	—
1986S	(3,010,497)	—	2.75
1987P	762,709,481	1.00	—
1987D	653,203,402	1.00	—
1987S	(4,227,728)	—	1.00
1988P	1,030,550,000	1.00	—
1988D	962,385,488	1.00	—
1988S	(3,262,948)	—	3.00
1989P	1,298,400,000	1.00	—
1989D	896,535,597	1.00	—
1989S	(3,220,194)	—	4.00
1990P	1,034,340,000	1.00	—
1990D	839,995,824	1.00	—
1990S	(3,299,559)	—	2.00
1991P	927,220,000	1.00	—
1991D	601,241,114	1.00	—
1991S	(2,867,787)	—	3.00
1992P	593,500,000	1.00	—
1992D	616,273,932	1.00	—
1992S	(2,858,981)	—	4.00
1993P	766,180,000	1.00	—
1993D	750,110,166	1.50	—
1993S	(2,633,439)	—	7.00
1994P	1,189,000,000	1.00	—
1994D	1,303,268,110	1.00	—
1994S	(2,484,594)	—	5.00
1995P	1,125,500,000	1.50	—
1995D	1,274,890,000	2.00	—
1995S	(2,010,384)	—	20.00
1996P	1,421,163,000	1.00	—
1996D	1,400,300,000	1.00	—
1996W	1,457,949	25.00	—
1996S	(2,085,191)	—	2.50
1997P	991,640,000	2.00	—
1997D	979,810,000	1.00	—
1997S	(1,975,000)	—	11.00
1998P	1,163,000,000	1.00	—
1998D	1,172,250,000	1.25	—
1998S	(2,078,494)	—	4.00
1999P	2,164,000,000	1.00	—
1999D	1,397,750,000	1.00	—
1999S	(2,557,897)	—	4.00
2000P	1,842,500,000	1.00	—
2000D	1,818,700,000	1.00	—
2000S	(3,097,440)	—	1.00
2001P	1,369,590,000	1.00	—
2001D	1,412,800,000	1.00	—
2001S	(2,249,496)	—	1.00
2002P	1,187,500,000	1.00	—
2002D	1,379,500,000	1.00	—
2002S	(2,268,913)	—	2.00
2003P	1,085,500,000	1.00	—
2003D	986,500,000	1.00	—
2003S	(2,076,165)	—	2.00
2004P	1,328,000,000	1.00	—
2004D	1,159,500,000	1.00	—
2004S	(1,804,396)	—	4.75
2005P	1,412,000,000	1.00	—
2005D	1,423,500,000	1.00	—
2005S	—	—	2.25
2006P	1,381,000,000	1.00	—
2006D	1,447,000,000	1.00	—
2006S	—	—	2.25
2007P	—	1.00	—
2007D	—	1.00	—
2007S	—	—	2.25

QUARTER

Barber Quarter

Laureate head right, flanked by stars, date below Heraldic eagle

KM# 114 0.9000 **SILVER** 0.1808 oz. ASW. 24.3 mm. 6.2500 g. **Designer:** Charles E. Barber

Date	Mintage	G-4	VG-8	F-12	VF-20	XF-40	AU-50	MS-60	MS-65	Prf-65
1901	8,892,813	11.00	13.00	25.00	41.50	80.00	135	215	2,250	2,200
1901O	1,612,000	40.00	60.00	135	275	470	685	900	5,750	—
1901S	72,664	7,000	11,000	16,500	21,000	28,500	38,000	42,000	100,000	—
1902	12,197,744	6.00	8.00	19.50	33.50	70.00	125	220	1,300	2,100
1902O	4,748,000	8.50	16.00	52.50	82.50	150	245	485	5,000	—
1902S	1,524,612	13.50	22.00	55.00	95.00	170	260	540	3,600	—
1903	9,670,064	6.75	8.00	19.00	33.50	66.00	115	215	2,600	2,000
1903O	3,500,000	8.00	12.50	41.50	65.00	125	260	450	5,800	—
1903S	1,036,000	15.50	25.00	46.00	80.00	145	285	450	2,900	—
1904	9,588,813	8.00	9.75	20.00	36.00	72.50	125	225	1,475	2,000
1904O	2,456,000	11.00	21.50	62.50	100.00	225	460	850	3,250	—
1905	4,968,250	11.00	13.00	27.50	41.50	75.00	125	215	1,650	2,000
1905O	1,230,000	18.50	32.50	82.50	160	260	375	515	6,600	—
1905S	1,884,000	11.00	15.00	43.50	66.00	115	225	350	3,650	—
1906	3,656,435	6.75	8.00	19.00	33.50	70.00	115	215	1,300	2,000
1906D	3,280,000	7.00	8.00	25.00	42.50	71.50	155	220	2,200	—
1906O	2,056,000	7.00	9.00	41.50	60.00	105	200	300	1,400	—
1907	7,192,575	5.25	8.00	17.50	33.50	66.00	115	215	1,300	2,000
1907D	2,484,000	6.00	9.00	29.00	52.50	80.00	180	250	2,750	—
1907O	4,560,000	5.25	8.00	19.00	38.50	70.00	135	220	2,600	—
1907S	1,360,000	10.00	18.50	47.50	75.00	135	275	480	3,500	—
1908	4,232,545	5.00	6.25	18.50	33.50	70.00	115	215	1,300	2,200
1908D	5,788,000	5.00	6.25	17.50	32.50	70.00	120	250	1,750	—
1908O	6,244,000	5.00	8.50	17.50	38.50	75.00	125	215	1,300	—
1908S	784,000	20.00	40.00	92.50	160	320	520	775	5,100	—
1909	9,268,650	5.00	6.25	17.50	33.50	66.00	115	215	1,300	2,000
1909D	5,114,000	6.25	8.00	22.00	41.50	90.00	160	215	2,350	—
1909O	712,000	25.00	60.00	175	400	900	1,250	1,700	9,000	—
1909S	1,348,000	8.00	11.00	37.50	57.50	96.00	200	300	2,400	—
1910	2,244,551	7.75	10.00	30.00	46.00	80.00	140	215	1,300	2,000
1910D	1,500,000	8.00	11.00	47.50	75.00	130	260	375	2,250	—
1911	3,720,543	5.25	8.00	17.50	33.50	72.50	125	215	1,300	2,000
1911D	933,600	8.00	19.00	95.00	215	330	500	700	6,250	—
1911S	988,000	7.00	12.00	51.50	80.00	160	300	400	1,500	—
1912	4,400,700	5.75	8.00	17.50	33.50	70.00	115	215	1,300	2,000
1912S	708,000	10.00	13.00	46.00	77.50	125	230	390	2,750	—
1913	484,613	15.00	25.00	75.00	185	415	535	960	5,000	2,200
1913D	1,450,800	12.50	13.50	38.50	58.50	94.00	185	275	1,400	—
1913S	40,000	1,500	2,150	4,000	5,600	6,500	7,000	9,000	24,000	—
1914	6,244,610	5.00	6.25	17.50	30.00	57.50	115	215	1,300	2,200
1914D	3,046,000	5.00	6.25	17.50	30.00	57.50	115	215	1,300	—
1914S	264,000	70.00	105	200	315	520	700	940	3,550	—
1915	3,480,450	5.00	6.25	17.50	30.00	66.00	115	215	1,300	2,200
1915D	3,694,000	5.00	6.25	17.50	30.00	66.00	115	215	1,300	—
1915S	704,000	9.00	13.00	35.00	57.50	110	220	285	1,300	—
1916	1,788,000	5.00	9.50	17.50	27.50	57.50	115	215	1,300	—
1916D	6,540,800	5.00	6.25	17.50	30.00	57.50	115	215	1,300	—
1916D/D	—	15.00	22.00	30.00	50.00	125	—	—	—	—

Standing Liberty Quarter

Right breast exposed; Type 1

KM# 141 0.9000 **SILVER** 0.1808 oz. ASW. 24.3 mm. 6.2500 g. **Designer:** Hermon A. MacNeil

Right breast exposed

Date	Mintage	G-4	VG-8	F-12	VF-20	XF-40	AU-50	MS-60	MS-65	-65FH
1916	52,000	3,500	6,350	9,500	13,000	14,500	16,500	18,500	30,000	37,500
1917	8,792,000	24.00	40.00	52.00	70.00	95.00	175	200	750	1,500
1917D	1,509,200	28.00	42.00	55.00	85.00	125	195	235	950	2,550
1917S	1,952,000	30.00	44.00	60.00	90.00	160	210	240	1,200	4,100

Right breast covered; Type 2 Three stars below eagle

KM# 145 0.9000 **SILVER** 0.1808 oz. ASW. 24.3 mm. 6.2500 g. **Designer:** Hermon A. MacNeil

Right breast covered

Mint mark

Date	Mintage	G-4	VG-8	F-12	VF-20	XF-40	AU-50	MS-60	MS-65	-65FH
1917	13,880,000	22.00	33.00	42.50	54.00	75.00	105	165	575	950
1917D	6,224,400	40.00	45.00	65.00	78.00	110	160	225	1,325	3,500
1917S	5,522,000	40.00	45.00	63.00	75.00	108	155	215	1,100	3,650
1918	14,240,000	17.00	21.00	29.00	35.00	46.00	80.00	135	560	1,750
1918D	7,380,000	26.00	36.00	66.00	78.00	122	195	250	1,485	4,850
1918S	11,072,000	17.00	21.00	32.00	35.00	48.00	95.00	185	1,250	13,500
1918/17S	Inc. above	1,550	2,250	3,850	5,200	7,500	13,500	17,850	110,000	320,000
1919	11,324,000	33.00	44.00	55.00	74.00	80.00	118	175	600	1,650
1919D	1,944,000	85.00	110	195	345	565	695	825	2,950	28,500
1919S	1,836,000	80.00	105	185	285	510	585	750	4,200	30,000
1920	27,860,000	15.00	18.00	25.00	37.00	51.00	90.00	165	600	2,100
1920D	3,586,400	48.00	65.00	88.00	120	160	215	325	2,250	7,200
1920S	6,380,000	19.00	25.00	30.00	37.00	57.00	110	235	2,650	24,000
1921	1,916,000	185	220	450	625	750	1,100	1,500	3,850	5,500
1923	9,716,000	15.00	18.00	35.00	37.00	55.00	95.00	155	620	4,000
1923S	1,360,000	300	425	675	985	1,250	1,650	2,300	4,750	6,500
1924	10,920,000	15.00	18.00	25.00	34.00	45.00	90.00	170	585	1,650
1924D	3,112,000	56.00	68.00	108	135	185	220	300	610	5,750
1924S	2,860,000	27.00	32.00	43.00	57.00	105	220	315	1,850	6,500
1925	12,280,000	4.00	4.75	7.00	18.50	44.00	90.00	150	575	950
1926	11,316,000	3.50	4.00	6.00	14.00	37.00	80.00	140	585	2,250
1926D	1,716,000	6.50	10.00	20.00	40.00	75.00	118	170	545	22,500
1926S	2,700,000	4.50	5.40	11.00	30.00	110	225	325	2,175	28,000
1927	11,912,000	3.50	4.00	6.00	12.00	32.00	70.00	105	550	1,300
1927D	976,400	14.00	19.00	32.00	70.00	140	210	250	600	2,650
1927S	396,000	35.00	48.00	110	285	1,000	2,650	4,750	12,000	165,000
1928	6,336,000	3.50	4.75	6.00	12.00	32.00	65.00	100.00	540	2,150
1928D	1,627,600	4.75	6.00	7.50	20.00	42.50	90.00	135	540	5,650
1928S Large S	2,644,000	6.00	7.50	10.00	25.00	65.00	115	200	—	—
1928S Small S	Inc. above	4.50	5.50	6.50	16.50	38.00	79.00	125	560	900
1929	11,140,000	3.50	4.75	6.00	12.00	32.00	65.00	100.00	540	900
1929D	1,358,000	4.25	5.50	6.75	16.00	38.50	79.00	135	540	5,850
1929S	1,764,000	4.00	5.50	6.50	15.00	34.00	75.00	120	540	875
1930	5,632,000	3.50	4.00	6.00	12.00	32.00	65.00	100.00	540	875
1930S	1,556,000	4.00	5.50	6.50	15.00	34.00	70.00	115	550	925

Washington Quarter

KM# 164 **SILVER** 24.3 mm. 6.2000 g. **Designer:** John Flanagan

Mint mark 1932-64

Date	Mintage	G-4	VG-8	F-12	VF-20	XF-40	AU-50	MS-60	MS-65	Prf-65
1932	5,404,000	4.00	5.20	6.00	7.50	9.75	15.00	26.00	435	—
1932D	436,800	165	180	205	240	345	500	1,000	24,500	—
1932S	408,000	195	200	205	240	285	300	500	7,000	—
1934 Medium Motto	31,912,052	4.40	4.80	5.40	6.30	6.80	10.00	27.50	110	—
1934 Heavy Motto	Inc. above	4.50	5.75	7.00	12.50	18.00	30.00	50.00	225	—
1934 Light motto	Inc. above	4.00	5.00	6.00	10.00	15.00	26.00	45.00	400	—
1934 Doubled Die Obverse	Inc. above	75.00	100.00	165	200	320	450	800	8,000	—
1934D Medium Motto	3,527,200	5.00	6.00	8.50	13.50	28.00	95.00	245	1,550	—
1934D Heavy Motto	Inc. above	6.00	8.00	11.00	16.00	37.00	110	295	1,900	—
1935	32,484,000	4.10	4.20	4.40	4.80	5.00	10.00	21.50	145	—
1935D	5,780,000	4.40	4.90	7.50	14.00	30.00	130	255	975	—
1935S	5,660,000	4.40	4.90	5.00	7.50	15.00	38.50	100.00	465	—
1936	41,303,837	4.10	4.20	4.40	4.80	4.80	9.50	22.50	115	1,950
1936D	5,374,000	5.00	6.50	8.50	22.00	55.00	275	625	1,850	—
1936S	3,828,000	4.40	4.90	4.40	6.25	13.50	52.50	115	420	—
1937	19,701,542	4.10	4.20	4.40	4.80	4.50	16.00	23.50	94.00	665
1937D	7,189,600	4.40	4.90	5.00	6.25	13.50	34.00	67.00	175	—
1937S	1,652,000	4.00	5.00	7.00	15.00	34.00	100.00	170	415	—
1938	9,480,045	4.00	4.75	5.25	6.25	16.00	46.00	94.00	250	405
1938S	2,832,000	4.75	5.25	6.00	9.75	22.50	57.50	112	300	—
1939	33,548,795	4.10	4.20	4.40	4.80	4.00	7.00	16.00	56.00	345
1939D	7,092,000	4.40	4.90	4.50	5.25	11.00	20.00	45.00	125	—

Date	Mintage	G-4	VG-8	F-12	VF-20	XF-40	AU-50	MS-60	MS-65	Prf-65
1939S	2,628,000	4.00	4.40	5.25	9.00	22.00	60.00	110	375	—
1940	35,715,246	4.10	4.20	4.40	4.80	4.00	5.50	18.50	57.50	250
1940D	2,797,600	3.50	4.25	7.00	12.50	27.50	70.00	135	350	—
1940S	8,244,000	4.40	4.90	5.00	6.50	9.00	18.00	28.00	62.50	—
1941	79,047,287	—	—	—	—	4.00	4.40	9.75	45.00	205
1941D	16,714,800	—	—	—	3.50	4.50	15.00	35.00	70.00	—
1941S	16,080,000	—	—	—	3.50	6.50	12.50	31.00	70.00	—
1942	102,117,123	—	—	—	—	4.00	4.10	5.50	37.50	190
1942D	17,487,200	—	—	—	3.50	6.00	11.00	19.00	45.00	—
1942S	19,384,000	—	—	—	3.75	9.00	24.00	80.00	180	—
1943	99,700,000	—	—	—	—	4.00	4.10	5.00	44.00	—
1943D	16,095,600	—	—	—	3.75	8.00	16.50	31.00	52.50	—
1943S	21,700,000	—	—	3.00	5.00	7.50	15.00	28.00	60.00	—
1943S Double Die Obv.	Inc. above	40.00	75.00	125	175	225	275	500	3,500	—
1944	104,956,000	—	—	—	—	4.00	4.10	5.00	37.50	—
1944D	14,600,800	—	—	—	3.50	4.25	10.00	20.00	37.50	—
1944S	12,560,000	—	—	—	3.50	4.00	9.00	15.00	37.50	—
1945	74,372,000	—	—	—	—	4.00	4.10	5.00	45.00	—
1945D	12,341,600	—	—	—	3.50	6.50	11.50	19.00	47.50	—
1945S	17,004,001	—	—	—	3.50	3.75	6.00	9.00	38.50	—
1946	53,436,000	—	—	—	—	4.00	4.10	5.00	47.50	—
1946D	9,072,800	—	—	—	3.50	4.25	5.50	10.00	46.00	—
1946S	4,204,000	—	—	—	3.50	4.00	5.00	9.00	40.00	—
1947	22,556,000	—	—	—	—	4.30	5.00	11.50	47.50	—
1947D	15,338,400	—	—	—	3.50	4.10	4.50	11.00	44.00	—
1947S	5,532,000	—	—	—	3.50	4.10	4.50	10.00	40.00	—
1948	35,196,000	—	—	—	3.50	4.00	4.00	5.50	45.00	—
1948D	16,766,800	—	—	—	3.50	4.10	7.00	13.50	56.00	—
1948S	15,960,000	—	—	—	3.50	4.00	5.00	8.00	50.00	—
1949	9,312,000	—	—	—	3.50	6.50	15.00	38.50	65.00	—
1949D	10,068,400	—	—	—	3.40	5.00	10.00	18.00	51.00	—
1950	24,971,512	—	—	—	—	4.00	4.10	5.50	32.00	65.00
1950D	21,075,600	—	—	—	—	4.00	4.10	5.00	34.00	—
1950D/S	Inc. above	30.00	33.00	40.00	60.00	140	215	275	3,400	—
1950S	10,284,004	—	—	—	—	3.50	4.50	9.00	42.00	—
1950S/D	Inc. above	32.00	36.00	44.00	70.00	180	315	400	850	—
1950S/S	Inc. above	—	—	—	—	—	—	—	—	—
1951	43,505,602	—	—	—	—	4.00	3.50	6.00	32.00	65.00
1951D	35,354,800	—	—	—	—	4.00	4.10	7.00	38.00	—
1951S	9,048,000	—	—	3.00	4.50	6.00	9.00	24.00	52.00	—
1952	38,862,073	—	—	—	—	4.00	4.10	5.50	36.00	46.00
1952D	49,795,200	—	—	—	—	4.00	4.10	5.00	32.00	—
1952S	13,707,800	—	—	—	4.00	7.50	12.50	22.00	47.00	—
1953	18,664,920	—	—	—	—	—	4.10	5.50	42.00	46.00
1953D	56,112,400	—	—	—	—	—	4.10	4.25	29.00	—
1953S	14,016,000	—	—	—	—	4.00	4.10	5.00	38.00	—
1954	54,645,503	—	—	—	—	—	4.10	5.00	30.00	21.00
1954D	42,305,500	—	—	—	—	—	4.10	4.75	30.00	—
1954S	11,834,722	—	—	—	—	—	4.10	4.00	26.00	—
1955	18,558,381	—	—	—	—	—	4.10	3.50	25.00	24.00
1955D	3,182,400	—	—	—	—	5.10	5.30	6.50	42.00	—
1956	44,813,384	—	—	—	—	—	4.10	4.00	24.00	23.00
1956 Double Bar 5	Inc. above	—	4.00	4.50	5.00	6.50	9.00	20.00	—	—
1956 Type B rev, proof rev die	Inc. above	—	—	8.00	12.00	20.00	30.00	40.00	100.00	—
1956D	32,334,500	—	—	—	—	4.00	4.10	3.50	26.00	—
1957	47,779,952	—	—	—	—	—	4.10	3.50	23.00	10.00
1957 Type B rev, proof rev die	Inc. above	—	—	—	6.50	10.00	16.00	30.00	110	—
1957D	77,924,160	—	—	—	—	—	4.10	3.40	26.00	—
1958	7,235,652	—	—	—	—	4.00	4.10	4.60	20.00	6.00
1958 Type B rev, proof rev die	Inc. above	—	—	—	6.50	10.00	16.00	24.00	90.00	—
1958D	78,124,900	—	—	—	—	—	4.10	4.60	22.00	—
1959	25,533,291	—	—	—	—	—	4.10	4.60	20.00	10.00
1959 Type B rev, proof rev die	Inc. above	—	—	—	5.00	10.00	14.00	20.00	70.00	—
1959D	62,054,232	—	—	—	—	—	4.10	4.60	25.00	—
1960	30,855,602	—	—	—	—	—	4.10	4.60	17.00	8.00
1960 Type B rev, proof rev die	Inc. above	—	—	—	6.50	10.00	16.00	24.00	90.00	—
1960D	63,000,324	—	—	—	—	—	4.10	4.60	17.00	—
1961	40,064,244	—	—	—	—	—	4.10	4.60	22.50	8.00
1961 Type B rev, proof rev die	Inc. above	—	—	—	5.00	10.00	14.00	20.00	70.00	—
1961D	83,656,928	—	—	—	—	—	4.10	4.60	16.00	—
1962	39,374,019	—	—	—	—	—	4.10	4.60	18.00	6.00
1962 Type B rev, proof rev die	Inc. above	—	—	—	10.00	15.00	25.00	60.00	175	—
1962D	127,554,756	—	—	—	—	—	4.10	4.60	16.00	—
1963	77,391,645	—	—	—	—	—	4.10	4.60	15.00	6.00
1963 Type B rev, proof rev die	Inc. above	—	—	—	5.00	10.00	14.00	20.00	70.00	—
1963D	135,288,184	—	—	—	—	—	4.10	4.60	15.00	—
1964	564,341,347	—	—	—	—	—	4.10	4.60	15.00	6.00
1964 Type B rev, proof rev die	Inc. above	—	—	—	5.00	10.00	14.00	20.00	70.00	—
1964D	704,135,528	—	—	—	—	—	4.10	4.60	15.00	—
1964D Type C rev, clad rev die	Inc. above	—	—	—	40.00	55.00	75.00	125	450	—

Washington Quarter

KM# 164a COPPER-NICKEL CLAD COPPER 24.3 mm. 5.6700 g. **Designer:** John Flanagan

Date	Mintage	MS-65	Prf-65
1965	1,819,717,540	9.00	—
1965 SMS	—	7.50	—
1966	821,101,500	7.50	—
1966 SMS	—	9.00	—
1967 SMS	—	10.00	—
1967	1,524,031,848	8.00	—
1968	220,731,500	7.50	—
1968D	101,534,000	9.00	—
1968S	(3,041,506)	—	6.50
1969	176,212,000	14.00	—
1969D	114,372,000	12.00	—
1969S	(2,934,631)	—	7.00
1970	136,420,000	12.00	—
1970D	417,341,364	9.50	—
1970S	(2,632,810)	—	7.00
1971	109,284,000	9.00	—
1971D	258,634,428	8.00	—
1971S	(3,220,733)	—	4.00
1972	215,048,000	7.50	—
1972D	311,067,732	10.00	—
1972S	(3,260,996)	—	3.50
1973	346,924,000	10.00	—
1973D	232,977,400	12.50	—
1973S	(2,760,339)	—	3.00
1974	801,456,000	12.00	—
1974D	353,160,300	18.00	—
1974S	(2,612,568)	—	6.50
1975 none minted	—	—	—
1975D none minted	—	—	—
1975S none minted	—	—	—

Bicentennial design, drummer boy

KM# 204 COPPER-NICKEL CLAD COPPER 24.3 mm. 5.6700 g. **Rev. Designer:** Jack L. Ahr

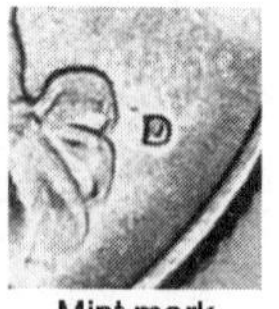

Mint mark 1968-present

Date	Mintage	G-4	VG-8	F-12	VF-20	XF-40	MS-60	MS-65	Prf-65
1976	809,784,016	—	—	—	—	—	.60	10.00	—
1976D	860,118,839	—	—	—	—	—	.60	10.00	—
1976S	(4,149,730)	—	—	—	—	—	—	—	3.25

Regular design resumed

KM# A164a COPPER-NICKEL CLAD COPPER 24.3 mm. 5.6700 g. **Notes:** KM#164 design and composition resumed. The 1979-S and 1981 Type II proofs have clearer mint marks than the Type I proofs for those years.

Date	Mintage	MS-65	Prf-65
1977	468,556,000	10.00	—
1977D	256,524,978	9.00	—
1977S	(3,251,152)	—	5.00
1978	521,452,000	10.00	—
1978D	287,373,152	11.00	—
1978S	(3,127,781)	—	5.00
1979	515,708,000	10.00	—
1979D	489,789,780	9.00	—
1979S T-I	—	—	4.00
1979S T-II	—	—	8.00
1980P	635,832,000	11.00	—
1980D	518,327,487	8.50	—
1980S	(3,554,806)	—	5.00
1981P	601,716,000	10.00	—
1981D	575,722,833	9.00	—
1981S T-I	—	—	5.00
1981S T-II	—	—	7.50
1982P	500,931,000	32.50	—
1982D	480,042,788	22.00	—
1982S	(3,857,479)	—	7.00
1983P	673,535,000	45.00	—
1983D	617,806,446	40.00	—
1983S	(3,279,126)	—	5.00
1984P	676,545,000	16.00	—
1984D	546,483,064	12.50	—
1984S	(3,065,110)	—	4.50
1985P	775,818,962	32.00	—
1985D	519,962,888	10.00	—
1985S	(3,362,821)	5.00	6.00
1986P	551,199,333	12.00	—
1986D	504,298,660	15.00	—
1986S	(3,010,497)	—	5.00
1987P	582,499,481	10.50	—
1987D	655,594,696	10.00	—
1987S	(4,227,728)	—	5.00
1988P	562,052,000	16.00	—
1988D	596,810,688	14.00	—
1988S	(3,262,948)	—	6.50
1989P	512,868,000	18.00	—
1989D	896,535,597	5.50	—
1989S	(3,220,194)	—	5.00
1990P	613,792,000	17.00	—
1990D	927,638,181	7.00	—
1990S	(3,299,559)	—	6.00
1991P	570,968,000	15.00	—
1991D	630,966,693	14.00	—
1991S	(2,867,787)	—	5.00
1992P	384,764,000	20.00	—
1992D	389,777,107	27.50	—
1992S	(2,858,981)	—	4.50
1993P	639,276,000	11.00	—
1993D	645,476,128	14.00	—
1993S	(2,633,439)	—	5.00
1994P	825,600,000	18.00	—
1994D	880,034,110	8.00	—
1994S	(2,484,594)	—	13.50
1995P	1,004,336,000	22.00	—
1995D	1,103,216,000	20.00	—
1995S	(2,010,384)	—	12.50
1996P	925,040,000	15.00	—
1996D	906,868,000	14.00	—
1996S	—	—	4.50
1997P	595,740,000	12.50	—
1997D	599,680,000	16.00	—
1997S	(1,975,000)	—	10.00
1998P	896,268,000	13.50	—
1998D	821,000,000	13.50	—
1998S	—	—	10.00

50 State Quarters

Connecticut

KM# 297 COPPER-NICKEL CLAD COPPER

Date	Mintage	MS-63	MS-65	Prf-65
1999P	688,744,000	1.00	10.00	—
1999D	657,480,000	1.00	9.00	—
1999S	(3,713,359)	—	—	12.00

Delaware

KM# 293 COPPER-NICKEL CLAD COPPER 24.3 mm. 5.6700 g.

Date	Mintage	MS-63	MS-65	Prf-65
1999P	373,400,000	1.40	8.00	—
1999D	401,424,000	1.25	20.00	—
1999S	(3,713,359)	—	—	12.00

Georgia

KM# 296 COPPER-NICKEL CLAD COPPER

Date	Mintage	MS-63	MS-65	Prf-65
1999P	451,188,000	1.20	14.00	—
1999D	488,744,000	1.20	14.00	—
1999S	(3,713,359)	—	—	12.00

New Jersey

KM# 295 COPPER-NICKEL CLAD COPPER

Date	Mintage	MS-63	MS-65	Prf-65
1999P	363,200,000	1.00	10.00	—
1999D	299,028,000	1.00	9.00	—
1999S	(3,713,359)	—	—	12.00

Pennsylvania

KM# 294 COPPER-NICKEL CLAD COPPER 24.3 mm. 5.6700 g.

Date	Mintage	MS-63	MS-65	Prf-65
1999P	349,000,000	1.00	15.00	—
1999D	358,332,000	1.00	20.00	—
1999S	(3,713,359)	—	—	12.00

Maryland

KM# 306 COPPER-NICKEL CLAD COPPER

Date	Mintage	MS-63	MS-65	Prf-65
2000P	678,200,000	1.00	11.00	—
2000D	556,526,000	1.00	11.00	—
2000S	(4,078,747)	—	—	3.50

KM# 306a 0.9000 **SILVER** 0.1808 oz. ASW. 6.2500 g.

Date	Mintage	MS-63	MS-65	Prf-65
2000S	(965,921)	—	—	5.50

Massachusetts

KM# 305 COPPER-NICKEL CLAD COPPER

Date	Mintage	MS-63	MS-65	Prf-65
2000P	629,800,000	1.00	10.00	—
2000D	535,184,000	1.00	12.00	—
2000S	(4,078,747)	—	—	3.50

KM# 305a 0.9000 **SILVER** 0.1808 oz. ASW. 6.2500 g.

Date	Mintage	MS-63	MS-65	Prf-65
2000S	(965,921)	—	—	5.50

New Hampshire

KM# 308 COPPER-NICKEL CLAD COPPER

Date	Mintage	MS-63	MS-65	Prf-65
2000P	673,040,000	1.00	12.50	—
2000D	495,976,000	1.00	10.00	—
2000S	(4,078,747)	—	—	3.50

KM# 308a 0.9000 **SILVER** 0.1808 oz. ASW. 6.2500 g.

Date	Mintage	MS-63	MS-65	Prf-65
2000S	(965,921)	—	—	5.50

South Carolina

KM# 307 COPPER-NICKEL CLAD COPPER

Date	Mintage	MS-63	MS-65	Prf-65
2000P	742,756,000	1.40	9.00	—
2000P	742,756,000	1.40	9.00	—
2000D	566,208,000	1.40	12.00	—
2000D	566,208,000	1.40	12.00	—
2000S	(4,078,747)	—	—	3.50
2000S	(4,078,747)	—	—	3.50

KM# 307a 0.9000 **SILVER** 0.1808 oz. ASW. 6.2500 g.

Date	Mintage	MS-63	MS-65	Prf-65
2000S	(965,921)	—	—	5.50

Virginia

KM# 309 COPPER-NICKEL CLAD COPPER

Date	Mintage	MS-63	MS-65	Prf-65
2000P	943,000,000	1.00	8.00	—
2000D	651,616,000	1.00	8.00	—
2000S	(4,078,747)	—	—	3.35

KM# 309a 0.9000 **SILVER** 0.1808 oz. ASW. 6.2500 g.

Date	Mintage	MS-63	MS-65	Prf-65
2000S	(965,921)	—	—	5.50

Kentucky

KM# 322 COPPER-NICKEL CLAD COPPER

Date	Mintage	MS-63	MS-65	Prf-65
2001P	353,000,000	1.20	7.00	—
2001D	370,564,000	1.00	8.00	—
2001S	(3,009,800)	—	—	11.00

KM# 322a 0.9000 **SILVER** 0.1808 oz. ASW. 6.2500 g.

Date	Mintage	MS-63	MS-65	Prf-65
2001S	(849,500)	—	—	21.00

New York

KM# 318 COPPER-NICKEL CLAD COPPER

Date	Mintage	MS-63	MS-65	Prf-65
2001P	655,400,000	1.00	8.50	—
2001D	619,640,000	1.00	8.50	—
2001S	(3,009,800)	—	—	11.00

KM# 318a 0.9000 **SILVER** 0.1808 oz. ASW. 6.2500 g.

Date	Mintage	MS-63	MS-65	Prf-65
2001S	(849,600)	—	—	24.00

North Carolina

KM# 319 COPPER-NICKEL CLAD COPPER

Date	Mintage	MS-63	MS-65	Prf-65
2001P	627,600,000	1.00	7.50	—
2001D	427,876,000	1.00	8.50	—
2001S	(3,009,800)	—	—	11.00

KM# 319a 0.9000 **SILVER** 0.1808 oz. ASW. 6.2500 g.

Date	Mintage	MS-63	MS-65	Prf-65
2001S	(849,600)	—	—	22.00

Rhode Island

KM# 320 COPPER-NICKEL CLAD COPPER 5.6000 g.

Date	Mintage	MS-63	MS-65	Prf-65
2001P	423,000,000	1.00	6.50	—
2001D	447,100,000	1.00	8.00	—
2001S	(3,009,800)	—	—	11.00

KM# 320a 0.9000 **SILVER** 0.1808 oz. ASW. 6.2500 g.

Date	Mintage	MS-63	MS-65	Prf-65
2001S	(849,600)	—	—	19.00

Vermont

KM# 321 COPPER-NICKEL CLAD COPPER

Date	Mintage	MS-63	MS-65	Prf-65
2001P	423,400,000	1.20	7.00	—
2001D	459,404,000	1.00	7.00	—
2001S	(3,009,800)	—	—	11.00

KM# 321a 0.9000 **SILVER** 0.1808 oz. ASW. 6.2500 g.

Date	Mintage	MS-63	MS-65	Prf-65
2001S	(849,600)	—	—	19.00

Indiana

KM# 334 COPPER-NICKEL CLAD COPPER 5.6700 g.

Date	Mintage	MS-63	MS-65	Prf-65
2002P	362,600,000	1.00	6.00	—
2002D	327,200,000	1.00	6.50	—
2002S	(3,084,185)	—	—	4.00

KM# 334a 0.9000 **SILVER** 0.1808 oz. ASW. 6.2500 g.

Date	Mintage	MS-63	MS-65	Prf-65
2002S	(892,229)	—	—	9.00

Louisiana

KM# 333 COPPER-NICKEL CLAD COPPER

Date	Mintage	MS-63	MS-65	Prf-65
2002P	362,000,000	1.00	6.50	—
2002D	402,204,000	1.00	7.00	—
2002S	(3,084,185)	—	—	4.00

KM# 333a 0.9000 **SILVER** 0.1808 oz. ASW. 6.2500 g.

Date	Mintage	MS-63	MS-65	Prf-65
2002S	(892,229)	—	—	9.00

Mississippi

KM# 335 COPPER-NICKEL CLAD COPPER 5.6700 g.

Date	Mintage	MS-63	MS-65	Prf-65
2002P	290,000,000	1.00	5.00	—
2002D	289,600,000	1.00	6.00	—
2002S	(3,084,185)	—	—	4.00

KM# 335a 0.9000 **SILVER** 0.1808 oz. ASW. 6.2500 g.

Date	Mintage	MS-63	MS-65	Prf-65
2002S	(892,229)	—	—	9.00

Ohio

KM# 332 COPPER-NICKEL CLAD COPPER

Date	Mintage	MS-63	MS-65	Prf-65
2002P	217,200,000	1.00	6.50	—
2002D	414,832,000	1.00	7.00	—
2002S	(3,084,185)	—	—	4.00

KM# 332a 0.9000 **SILVER** 0.1808 oz. ASW. 6.2500 g.

Date	Mintage	MS-63	MS-65	Prf-65
2002S	(892,229)	—	—	9.00

Tennessee

KM# 331 COPPER-NICKEL CLAD COPPER

Date	Mintage	MS-63	MS-65	Prf-65
2002P	361,600,000	1.40	6.50	—
2002D	286,468,000	1.40	7.00	—
2002S	(3,084,185)	—	—	4.00

KM# 331a 0.9000 **SILVER** 0.1808 oz. ASW. 6.2500 g.

Date	Mintage	MS-63	MS-65	Prf-65
2002S	(892,229)	—	—	9.00

Alabama

KM# 344 COPPER-NICKEL CLAD COPPER 5.6700 g.

Date	Mintage	MS-63	MS-65	Prf-65
2003P	225,000,000	1.00	7.00	—
2003D	232,400,000	1.00	7.00	—
2003S	(3,270,603)	—	—	3.50

KM# 344a 0.9000 **SILVER** 0.1808 oz. ASW. 6.2500 g.

Date	Mintage	MS-63	MS-65	Prf-65
2003S	—	—	—	5.25

Arkansas

KM# 347 COPPER-NICKEL CLAD COPPER

Date	Mintage	MS-63	MS-65	Prf-65
2003P	228,000,000	1.00	7.00	—
2003D	229,800,000	1.00	7.00	—
2003S	(3,270,603)	—	—	3.50

KM# 347a 0.9000 **SILVER** 0.1808 oz. ASW. 6.2500 g.

Date	Mintage	MS-63	MS-65	Prf-65
2003S	—	—	—	5.25

Illinois

KM# 343 COPPER-NICKEL CLAD COPPER 5.6700 g.

Date	Mintage	MS-63	MS-65	Prf-65
2003P	225,800,000	1.10	7.00	—
2003D	237,400,000	1.10	6.00	—
2003S	(3,270,603)	—	—	3.50

KM# 343a 0.9000 **SILVER** 0.1808 oz. ASW. 6.2500 g.

Date	Mintage	MS-63	MS-65	Prf-65
2003S	—	—	—	5.25

Maine

KM# 345 COPPER-NICKEL CLAD COPPER

Date	Mintage	MS-63	MS-65	Prf-65
2003P	217,400,000	1.00	6.50	—
2003D	213,400,000	1.00	8.00	—
2003S	(3,270,603)	—	—	3.50

KM# 345a 0.9000 **SILVER** 0.1808 oz. ASW. 6.2500 g.

Date	Mintage	MS-63	MS-65	Prf-65
2003S	—	—	—	5.25

Missouri

KM# 346 COPPER-NICKEL CLAD COPPER

Date	Mintage	MS-63	MS-65	Prf-65
2003P	225,000,000	1.00	7.00	—
2003D	228,200,000	1.00	7.00	—
2003S	(3,270,603)	—	—	3.50

KM# 346a 0.9000 **SILVER** 0.1808 oz. ASW. 6.2500 g.

Date	Mintage	MS-63	MS-65	Prf-65
2003S	—	—	—	5.25

Florida

KM# 356 COPPER-NICKEL CLAD COPPER 5.6700 g.

Date	Mintage	MS-63	MS-65	Prf-65
2004P	240,200,000	.75	6.50	—
2004D	241,600,000	.75	7.00	—
2004S	—	—	—	5.00

KM# 356a 0.9000 **SILVER** 0.1808 oz. ASW. 6.2500 g.

Date	Mintage	MS-63	MS-65	Prf-65
2004S	—	—	—	6.00

Iowa

KM# 358 COPPER-NICKEL CLAD COPPER 5.6700 g.

Date	Mintage	MS-63	MS-65	Prf-65
2004P	213,800,000	.75	6.50	—
2004D	251,800,000	.75	7.00	—
2004S	—	—	—	5.00

KM# 358a 0.9000 **SILVER** 0.1808 oz. ASW. 6.2500 g.

Date	Mintage	MS-63	MS-65	Prf-65
2004S	—	—	—	6.00

Michigan

KM# 355 COPPER-NICKEL CLAD COPPER 5.6700 g.

Date	Mintage	MS-63	MS-65	Prf-65
2004P	233,800,000	.75	6.50	—
2004D	225,800,000	.75	6.50	—
2004S	—	—	—	5.00

KM# 355a 0.9000 **SILVER** 0.1808 oz. ASW. 6.2500 g.

Date	Mintage	MS-63	MS-65	Prf-65
2004S	—	—	—	6.00

Texas

KM# 357 COPPER-NICKEL CLAD COPPER 5.6700 g.

Date	Mintage	MS-63	MS-65	Prf-65
2004P	278,800,000	.75	7.00	—
2004D	263,000,000	.75	7.00	—
2004S	—	—	—	5.00

KM# 357a 0.9000 **SILVER** 0.1808 oz. ASW. 6.2500 g.

Date	Mintage	MS-63	MS-65	Prf-65
2004S	—	—	—	6.00

Wisconsin

KM# 359 COPPER-NICKEL CLAD COPPER 5.6700 g.

Date	Mintage	MS-63	MS-65	Prf-65
2004P	226,400,000	1.00	8.00	—
2004D	226,800,000	1.00	10.00	—
2004D Extra Leaf Low	Est. 9,000	300	600	—
2004D Extra Leaf High	Est. 3,000	400	900	—
2004S	—	—	—	5.00

KM# 359a 0.9000 **SILVER** 0.1808 oz. ASW. 6.2500 g.

Date	Mintage	MS-63	MS-65	Prf-65
2004S	—	—	—	6.00

California

KM# 370 COPPER-NICKEL CLAD COPPER 5.7000 g.

Date	Mintage	MS-63	MS-65	Prf-65
2005P	257,200,000	.75	5.00	—
2005P Satin Finish	Inc. above	3.50	6.00	—
2005D	263,200,000	.75	5.00	—
2005D Satin Finish	Inc. above	3.50	6.00	—
2005S	—	—	—	3.00

KM# 370a 0.9000 **SILVER** 0.1808 oz. ASW. 6.2500 g.

Date	Mintage	MS-63	MS-65	Prf-65
2005S	—	—	—	5.50

Kansas

KM# 373 COPPER-NICKEL CLAD COPPER

Date	Mintage	MS-63	MS-65	Prf-65
2005P	263,400,000	.75	5.00	—
2005P Satin Finish	Inc. above	3.50	6.00	—
2005D	300,000,000	.75	5.00	—
2005D Satin Finish	Inc. above	3.50	6.00	—
2005S	—	—	—	3.00

KM# 373a 0.9000 **SILVER** 0.1808 oz. ASW. 6.2500 g.

Date	Mintage	MS-63	MS-65	Prf-65
2005S	—	—	—	5.50

Minnesota

KM# 371 COPPER-NICKEL CLAD COPPER 5.7000 g.

Date	Mintage	MS-63	MS-65	Prf-65
2005P	226,400,000	.75	5.00	—
2005P Satin Finish	Inc. above	3.50	6.00	—
2005D	226,800,000	.75	5.00	—
2005D Satin Finish	Inc. above	3.50	6.00	—
2005S	—	—	—	3.00

KM# 371a 0.9000 **SILVER** 0.1808 oz. ASW. 6.2500 g.

Date	Mintage	MS-63	MS-65	Prf-65
2005S	—	—	—	5.50

Oregon

KM# 372 COPPER-NICKEL CLAD COPPER 5.6700 g.

Date	Mintage	MS-63	MS-65	Prf-65
2005P	316,200,000	.75	5.00	—
2005P Satin Finish	Inc. above	3.50	6.00	—
2005D	404,000,000	.75	5.00	—
2005D Satin Finish	Inc. above	3.50	6.00	—
2005S	—	—	—	3.00

KM# 372a 0.9000 **SILVER** 0.1808 oz. ASW. 6.2500 g.

Date	Mintage	MS-63	MS-65	Prf-65
2005S	—	—	—	5.50

West Virginia

KM# 374 COPPER-NICKEL CLAD COPPER 5.6700 g.

Date	Mintage	MS-63	MS-65	Prf-65
2005P	365,400,000	.75	5.00	—
2005P Satin Finish	Inc. above	3.50	6.00	—
2005D	356,200,000	.75	5.00	—
2005D Satin Finish	Inc. above	3.50	6.00	—
2005S	—	—	—	3.00

KM# 374a 0.9000 **SILVER** 0.1808 oz. ASW. 6.2500 g.

Date	Mintage	MS-63	MS-65	Prf-65
2005S	—	—	—	5.50

Colorado

KM# 384 COPPER-NICKEL CLAD COPPER 24 mm. 5.6400 g.

Date	Mintage	MS-63	MS-65	Prf-65
2006P	274,800,000	.75	5.00	—
2006P Satin Finish	Inc. above	3.00	5.00	—
2006D	294,200,000	.75	5.00	—
2006D Satin Finish	Inc. above	3.00	5.00	—
2006S	—	—	—	5.00

KM# 384a 0.9000 **SILVER** 0.1808 oz. ASW. 6.2500 g.

Date	Mintage	MS-63	MS-65	Prf-65
2006S	—	—	—	5.75

Nebraska

KM# 383 COPPER-NICKEL CLAD COPPER 24.16 mm. 5.7300 g.

Date	Mintage	MS-63	MS-65	Prf-65
2006P	318,000,000	.75	6.00	—
2006P Satin Finish	Inc. above	3.00	5.00	—
2006D	273,000,000	.75	6.00	—
2006D Satin Finish	Inc. above	3.00	5.00	—
2006S	—	—	—	5.00

KM# 383a 0.9000 **SILVER** 0.1808 oz. ASW. 6.2500 g.

Date	Mintage	MS-63	MS-65	Prf-65
2006S	—	—	—	5.75

Nevada

KM# 382 COPPER-NICKEL CLAD COPPER 24.21 mm. 5.6800 g.

Date	Mintage	MS-63	MS-65	Prf-65
2006P	277,000,000	.75	6.00	—
2006P Satin Finish	Inc. above	3.00	5.00	—
2006D	312,800,000	.75	6.00	—
2006D Satin Finish	Inc. above	3.00	5.00	—
2006S	—	—	—	5.00

KM# 382a 0.9000 **SILVER** 0.1808 oz. ASW. 6.2500 g.

Date	Mintage	MS-63	MS-65	Prf-65
2006S	—	—	—	5.75

North Dakota

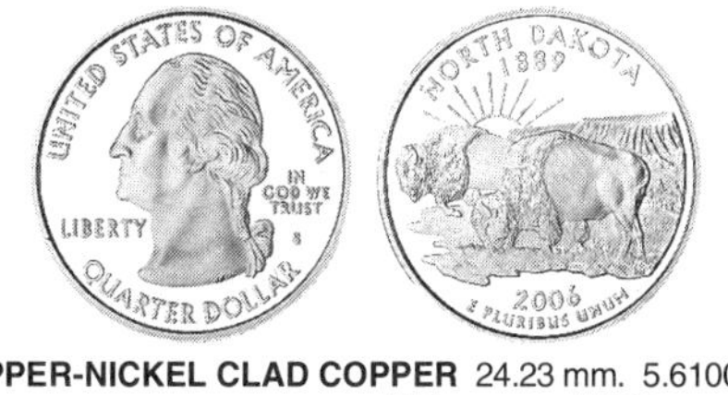

KM# 385 COPPER-NICKEL CLAD COPPER 24.23 mm. 5.6100 g.

Date	Mintage	MS-63	MS-65	Prf-65
2006P	305,800,000	.75	5.00	—
2006P Satin Finish	Inc. above	3.00	5.00	—
2006D	359,000,000	.75	5.00	—
2006D Satin Finish	Inc. above	3.00	5.00	—
2006S	—	—	—	5.00

KM# 385a 0.9000 **SILVER** 0.1808 oz. ASW. 6.2500 g.

Date	Mintage	MS-63	MS-65	Prf-65
2006S	—	—	—	5.75

South Dakota

KM# 386 COPPER-NICKEL CLAD COPPER 24.18 mm. 5.6400 g.

Date	Mintage	MS-63	MS-65	Prf-65
2006P	245,000,000	.75	5.00	—
2006P Satin Finish	Inc. above	3.00	5.00	—
2006D	265,800,000	.75	5.00	—
2006D Satin Finish	Inc. above	3.00	5.00	—
2006S	—	—	—	5.00

KM# 386a 0.9000 **SILVER** 0.1808 oz. ASW. 6.2500 g.

Date	Mintage	MS-63	MS-65	Prf-65
2006S	—	—	—	5.75

Idaho

KM# 398 COPPER-NICKEL CLAD COPPER

Date	Mintage	MS-63	MS-65	Prf-65
2007P	294,600,000	.75	8.00	—
2007D	286,800,000	.75	8.00	—
2007S	—	—	—	4.00

KM# 398a 0.9000 **SILVER** 0.1808 oz. ASW. 6.2500 g.

Date	Mintage	MS-63	MS-65	Prf-65
2007S	Inc. above	—	—	6.50

Montana

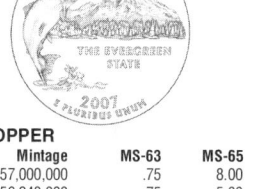

KM# 396 COPPER-NICKEL CLAD COPPER

Date	Mintage	MS-63	MS-65	Prf-65
2007P	257,000,000	.75	8.00	—
2007D	256,240,000	.75	5.00	—
2007S	—	—	—	4.00

KM# 396a 0.9000 **SILVER** 0.1808 oz. ASW. 6.2500 g.

Date	Mintage	MS-63	MS-65	Prf-65
2007S	Inc. above	—	—	6.50

Utah

KM# 400 COPPER-NICKEL CLAD COPPER

Date	Mintage	MS-63	MS-65	Prf-65
2007P	—	.75	8.00	—
2007D	—	.75	8.00	—
2007S	—	—	—	4.00

KM# 400a 0.9000 **SILVER** 0.1808 oz. ASW. 6.2500 g.

Date	Mintage	MS-63	MS-65	Prf-65
2007S	Inc. above	—	—	6.50

Washington

KM# 397 COPPER-NICKEL CLAD COPPER

Date	Mintage	MS-63	MS-65	Prf-65
2007P	265,200,000	.75	8.00	—
2007D	280,000,000	.75	8.00	—
2007S	—	—	—	4.00

KM# 397a 0.9000 **SILVER** 0.1808 oz. ASW. 6.2500 g.

Date	Mintage	MS-63	MS-65	Prf-65
2007S	Inc. above	—	—	6.50

Wyoming

KM# 399 COPPER-NICKEL CLAD COPPER

Date	Mintage	MS-63	MS-65	Prf-65
2007P	—	.75	8.00	—
2007D	—	.75	8.00	—
2007S	—	—	—	4.00

KM# 399a 0.9000 **SILVER** 0.1808 oz. ASW. 6.2500 g.

Date	Mintage	MS-63	MS-65	Prf-65
2007S	Inc. above	—	—	6.50

Alaska

KM# 424 COPPER-NICKEL CLAD COPPER

Date	Mintage	MS-63	MS-65	Prf-65
2008P	—	.75	8.00	—
2008D	—	.75	8.00	—
2008S	—	—	—	4.00

Arizona

KM# 423 COPPER-NICKEL CLAD COPPER

Date	Mintage	MS-63	MS-65	Prf-65
2008P	—	.75	8.00	—
2008D	—	.75	8.00	—
2008S	—	—	—	4.00

Hawaii

KM# 425 COPPER-NICKEL CLAD COPPER

Date	Mintage	MS-63	MS-65	Prf-65
2008P	—	.75	8.00	—
2008D	—	.75	8.00	—
2008S	—	—	—	4.50

New Mexico

KM# 422 COPPER-NICKEL CLAD COPPER

Date	Mintage	MS-63	MS-65	Prf-65
2008P	—	.75	8.00	—
2008D	—	.75	8.00	—
2008S	—	—	—	4.00

Oklahoma

KM# 421 COPPER-NICKEL CLAD COPPER

Date	Mintage	MS-63	MS-65	Prf-65
2008P	—	.75	8.00	—
2008D	—	.75	8.00	—
2008S	—	—	—	4.00

HALF DOLLAR

Barber Half Dollar

Laureate head right, flanked by stars, date below Heraldic eagle

KM# 116 0.9000 **SILVER** 0.3617 oz. ASW. 30.6 mm. 12.5000 g. **Designer:** Charles E. Barber

Mint mark

Date	Mintage	G-4	VG-8	F-12	VF-20	XF-40	AU-50	MS-60	MS-65	Prf-65
1901	4,268,813	13.50	16.00	38.50	96.00	180	300	510	4,400	3,500
1901O	1,124,000	16.50	26.50	80.00	205	350	475	1,350	16,500	—
1901S	847,044	34.00	55.00	160	355	610	1,050	1,850	19,500	—
1902	4,922,777	12.50	13.50	32.50	86.00	175	295	475	4,850	3,500
1902O	2,526,000	13.50	17.00	52.50	105	225	360	725	12,500	—
1902S	1,460,670	16.00	19.00	62.50	150	260	420	750	8,400	—
1903	2,278,755	13.50	16.00	47.50	100.00	200	325	500	11,000	3,500
1903O	2,100,000	13.00	17.00	54.00	115	210	335	665	10,000	—
1903S	1,920,772	15.00	18.00	55.00	125	235	380	610	8,800	—
1904	2,992,670	12.00	13.50	34.00	85.00	155	300	475	6,000	3,500
1904O	1,117,600	20.00	32.50	80.00	220	385	590	1,100	12,500	—
1904S	553,038	38.50	70.00	260	565	1,075	1,775	6,250	38,500	—
1905	662,727	22.50	29.50	95.00	180	270	345	565	7,500	3,500
1905O	505,000	30.00	50.00	125	235	340	440	760	5,250	—
1905S	2,494,000	15.50	18.00	50.00	125	230	365	615	9,800	—
1906	2,638,675	11.75	13.25	31.00	85.00	165	290	475	3,800	3,500
1906D	4,028,000	11.75	13.25	32.50	93.50	160	300	485	4,500	—
1906O	2,446,000	11.75	13.25	44.00	100.00	185	310	600	6,500	—
1906S	1,740,154	13.00	16.50	57.50	110	215	310	610	6,500	—
1907	2,598,575	11.75	13.25	30.00	85.00	155	300	470	3,650	3,500
1907D	3,856,000	11.75	13.25	30.00	78.50	155	300	470	3,600	—
1907O	3,946,000	11.75	13.25	32.00	93.50	165	325	575	3,700	—
1907S	1,250,000	16.00	22.00	80.00	170	310	650	1,275	13,500	—
1908	1,354,545	11.75	13.25	30.00	83.00	155	285	470	4,350	3,500
1908D	3,280,000	11.75	13.25	30.00	83.00	155	295	485	3,700	—
1908O	5,360,000	11.75	13.25	30.00	93.50	155	315	540	3,600	—
1908S	1,644,828	18.50	27.00	75.00	160	285	435	850	6,600	—
1909	2,368,650	12.50	16.00	32.50	84.00	160	275	470	3,600	3,500
1909O	925,400	16.00	23.50	58.00	140	300	510	775	4,950	—
1909S	1,764,000	12.00	13.50	37.50	100.00	190	395	600	4,650	—
1910	418,551	20.00	28.50	90.00	170	330	415	610	3,900	3,500
1910S	1,948,000	13.50	16.50	37.50	100.00	190	350	650	6,850	—
1911	1,406,543	11.75	13.25	30.00	83.00	155	290	475	3,600	3,500
1911D	695,080	13.00	16.00	41.00	94.00	195	285	550	3,800	—
1911S	1,272,000	13.50	16.50	41.00	98.00	180	325	580	6,100	—
1912	1,550,700	11.75	13.25	30.00	83.00	160	295	480	4,350	3,500
1912D	2,300,800	13.00	13.50	30.00	83.00	155	310	470	3,600	—
1912S	1,370,000	15.00	20.00	41.50	100.00	195	330	535	6,250	—
1913	188,627	78.00	90.00	235	420	600	850	1,150	5,250	3,500
1913D	534,000	17.00	21.00	44.00	100.00	200	300	485	5,250	—
1913S	604,000	20.00	25.00	53.50	110	225	365	610	4,850	—
1914	124,610	155	175	325	550	775	1,025	1,400	8,500	3,500
1914S	992,000	15.00	19.00	41.00	98.00	190	315	575	5,000	—
1915	138,450	118	175	285	380	575	900	1,250	6,400	3,500
1915D	1,170,400	11.75	13.25	30.00	80.00	155	285	470	3,600	—
1915S	1,604,000	15.50	20.00	41.50	99.00	170	295	485	3,675	—

Walking Liberty Half Dollar

KM# 142 SILVER 30.6 mm. 12.5000 g. **Designer:** Adolph A. Weinman **Notes:** The mint mark appears on the obverse below the word "Trust" on 1916 and some 1917 issues. Starting with some 1917 issues and continuing through the remainder of the series, the mint mark was changed to the reverse, at about the 8 o'clock position near the rim.

Obverse mint mark   Reverse mint mark

Date	Mintage	G-4	VG-8	F-12	VF-20	XF-40	AU-50	MS-60	MS-65	Prf-65
1916	608,000	45.00	52.50	100.00	180	250	285	350	1,800	—
1916D	1,014,400	45.00	52.50	80.00	140	225	265	375	2,400	—
1916S	508,000	110	130	285	470	650	750	1,100	6,250	—
1917D obv.	765,400	22.00	31.50	80.00	160	235	350	640	8,000	—
1917S obv.	952,000	27.50	44.00	135	375	720	1,225	2,300	19,500	—
1917	12,292,000	7.40	7.60	9.00	20.00	44.00	75.00	135	1,000	—
1917D rev.	1,940,000	10.00	16.50	45.00	135	275	575	975	18,500	—
1917S rev.	5,554,000	7.40	8.00	16.50	33.00	65.00	160	345	13,000	—
1918	6,634,000	7.40	8.00	16.00	70.00	160	275	580	3,800	—
1918D	3,853,040	8.00	13.00	36.00	96.00	235	500	1,350	25,000	—
1918S	10,282,000	7.40	7.60	15.00	35.00	65.00	200	525	18,000	—
1919	962,000	19.00	32.50	78.50	275	550	920	1,350	7,500	—
1919D	1,165,000	18.00	38.50	100.00	325	765	1,550	6,250	130,000	—
1919S	1,552,000	17.50	30.00	75.00	325	850	1,800	3,450	20,500	—
1920	6,372,000	7.40	7.60	16.00	44.00	75.00	160	350	5,250	—
1920D	1,551,000	12.00	20.00	70.00	250	475	960	1,550	12,000	—
1920S	4,624,000	7.40	8.00	20.00	80.00	235	520	850	12,500	—
1921	246,000	185	225	350	780	1,550	2,750	4,350	18,000	—
1921D	208,000	315	39.00	550	940	2,200	3,400	5,300	27,500	—
1921S	548,000	46.00	70.00	220	750	4,800	8,600	14,000	105,000	—
1923S	2,178,000	8.50	11.50	27.50	115	315	700	1,400	15,000	—
1927S	2,392,000	7.40	8.00	13.50	47.50	160	415	1,050	10,000	—
1928S	1,940,000	10.00	12.50	24.00	110	300	600	1,650	—	—
1928S	Inc. above	6.75	7.25	15.00	70.00	195	450	1,000	10,750	—
1929D	1,001,200	8.00	12.00	19.00	60.00	110	210	415	3,500	—
1929S	1,902,000	7.40	8.00	12.50	28.50	115	230	425	3,550	—
1933S	1,786,000	8.50	11.00	12.50	20.00	60.00	260	625	4,500	—
1934	6,964,000	7.10	7.60	7.70	8.00	11.00	26.00	85.00	625	—
1934D	2,361,400	7.40	8.00	8.10	10.00	29.00	90.00	155	1,700	—
1934S	3,652,000	7.10	7.80	8.10	8.50	27.00	105	395	5,200	—
1935	9,162,000	7.10	7.60	7.70	8.00	8.50	22.50	45.00	585	—
1935D	3,003,800	7.10	7.80	8.10	10.00	32.50	70.00	140	3,150	—
1935S	3,854,000	7.10	7.80	8.10	8.50	29.00	100.00	295	3,700	—
1936	12,617,901	7.10	7.60	7.70	8.00	8.50	21.50	38.50	300	6,600
1936D	4,252,400	7.10	7.80	8.10	8.50	20.00	55.00	80.00	700	—

Date	Mintage	G-4	VG-8	F-12	VF-20	XF-40	AU-50	MS-60	MS-65	Prf-65
1936S	3,884,000	7.10	7.80	8.10	8.50	21.50	62.50	135	1,050	—
1937	9,527,728	7.10	7.60	7.70	8.00	8.50	22.50	40.00	335	1,700
1937D	1,676,000	7.10	8.00	8.50	14.00	33.50	110	225	850	—
1937S	2,090,000	7.10	7.80	8.10	8.50	25.50	65.00	175	850	—
1938	4,118,152	7.10	7.80	8.10	8.50	9.50	41.50	70.00	550	1,275
1938D	491,600	90.00	100.00	115	135	220	260	525	1,550	—
1939	6,820,808	7.10	7.30	6.50	7.00	8.50	22.50	42.50	230	1,150
1939D	4,267,800	7.10	7.60	7.70	8.00	8.50	26.00	47.50	275	—
1939S	2,552,000	7.10	7.80	8.10	9.00	25.00	80.00	150	370	—
1940	9,167,279	7.10	7.30	7.00	7.50	9.00	11.00	30.00	210	1,000
1940S	4,550,000	7.10	7.60	7.70	8.00	12.00	22.00	52.50	420	—
1941	24,207,412	7.10	7.30	7.00	7.50	9.00	11.00	32.50	160	850
1941D	11,248,400	7.10	7.60	7.70	8.00	10.00	18.00	38.50	200	—
1941S	8,098,000	7.10	7.60	7.70	8.00	12.00	27.50	75.00	1,175	—
1942	47,839,120	7.10	7.30	7.00	7.50	9.00	11.00	32.50	150	850
1942D	10,973,800	7.10	7.60	7.70	8.00	10.00	19.00	38.50	345	—
1942S	12,708,000	7.10	7.60	7.70	8.00	10.00	17.50	38.50	700	—
1943	53,190,000	7.10	7.30	7.00	7.50	9.00	11.00	33.50	150	—
1943D	11,346,000	7.10	7.60	7.70	8.00	10.00	25.00	43.50	330	—
1943D Double Die Obverse	—	7.30	7.50	9.00	12.00	15.00	30.00	55.00	450	—
1943S	13,450,000	7.10	7.60	7.70	8.00	10.00	18.50	43.50	485	—
1944	28,206,000	7.10	7.30	7.00	7.50	9.00	11.00	33.50	220	—
1944D	9,769,000	7.10	7.60	7.70	8.00	10.00	20.00	37.50	240	—
1944S	8,904,000	7.10	7.60	7.70	8.00	10.00	16.00	38.50	490	—
1945	31,502,000	7.10	7.30	7.00	7.50	9.00	11.00	32.50	160	—
1945D	9,966,800	7.10	7.60	7.70	8.00	10.00	19.00	34.00	160	—
1945S	10,156,000	7.10	7.60	7.70	8.00	10.00	17.50	35.00	220	—
1946	12,118,000	7.10	7.30	7.00	7.50	9.00	11.00	32.50	250	—
1946D	2,151,000	7.10	7.80	7.70	8.00	25.50	38.50	50.00	150	—
1946S	3,724,000	7.10	7.60	7.70	8.00	12.00	19.00	43.50	165	—
1947	4,094,000	7.10	7.25	7.75	8.00	11.00	22.00	52.50	230	—
1947D	3,900,600	7.10	7.80	7.70	8.00	14.00	31.50	52.50	150	—

Franklin Half Dollar

KM# 199 0.9000 **SILVER** 0.3617 oz. ASW. 30.6 mm. 12.5000 g. **Designer:** John R. Sinnock

Mint mark

Date	Mintage	G-4	VG-8	F-12	VF-20	XF-40	AU-50	MS-60	MS-65	-65FBL	-65CAM
1948	3,006,814	—	5.00	6.00	7.00	8.50	11.50	15.50	75.00	190	—
1948D	4,028,600	—	5.00	6.00	7.00	8.00	11.00	15.00	125	260	—
1949	5,614,000	—	—	—	—	8.00	12.00	38.50	145	300	—
1949D	4,120,600	—	—	—	—	8.00	25.00	43.50	900	1,750	—
1949S	3,744,000	—	—	—	7.00	11.00	30.00	62.50	155	650	—
1950	7,793,509	—	—	—	—	8.00	10.00	26.00	110	250	3,700
1950D	8,031,600	—	—	—	—	9.00	11.50	22.00	425	1,150	—
1951	16,859,602	—	—	—	—	—	8.00	11.00	75.00	235	2,200
1951D	9,475,200	—	—	—	—	12.00	17.50	26.00	170	525	—
1951S	13,696,000	—	—	—	—	—	15.00	23.50	125	775	—
1952	21,274,073	—	—	—	—	—	8.00	8.50	80.00	200	1,100
1952D	25,395,600	—	—	—	—	—	8.00	8.50	135	450	—
1952S	5,526,000	—	—	6.00	12.00	20.00	32.00	50.00	100.00	1,500	—
1953	2,796,920	—	—	—	—	10.00	16.00	25.00	125	850	475
1953D	20,900,400	—	—	—	—	—	8.00	15.00	160	400	—
1953S	4,148,000	—	—	—	—	—	15.00	25.00	65.00	16,000	—
1954	13,421,503	—	—	—	—	—	8.00	8.50	80.00	250	250
1954D	25,445,580	—	—	—	—	—	8.00	8.50	110	200	—
1954S	4,993,400	—	—	—	—	—	8.50	13.50	105	425	—
1955	2,876,381	—	18.00	20.00	21.00	22.00	23.00	24.00	65.00	185	195
1955 Bugs Bunny	—	—	20.00	22.00	23.00	25.00	26.00	28.00	100.00	750	—
1956	4,701,384	—	7.25	7.50	7.75	8.00	8.50	13.50	50.00	95.00	75.00
1957	6,361,952	—	—	—	—	—	8.00	8.50	62.50	95.00	135
1957D	19,966,850	—	—	—	—	—	8.00	8.50	65.00	100.00	—
1958	4,917,652	—	—	—	—	—	8.00	8.50	60.00	100.00	250
1958D	23,962,412	—	—	—	—	—	8.00	8.50	62.50	75.00	—
1959	7,349,291	—	—	—	—	—	8.00	8.50	105	250	475
1959D	13,053,750	—	—	—	—	—	8.00	8.50	135	190	—
1960	7,715,602	—	—	—	—	—	8.00	8.50	135	350	75.00
1960D	18,215,812	—	—	—	—	—	8.00	8.50	475	1,250	—
1961	11,318,244	—	—	—	—	—	8.00	8.50	145	1,750	75.00
1961D	20,276,442	—	—	—	—	—	8.00	8.50	200	875	—
1962	12,932,019	—	—	—	—	—	8.00	8.50	160	1,850	50.00
1962D	35,473,281	—	—	—	—	—	8.00	8.50	225	775	—
1963	25,239,645	—	—	—	—	—	8.00	8.50	55.00	775	50.00
1963D	67,069,292	—	—	—	—	—	8.00	8.50	70.00	125	—

Kennedy Half Dollar

KM# 202 0.9000 **SILVER** 0.3617 oz. ASW. 30.6 mm. 12.5000 g. **Obv. Designer:** Gilroy Roberts **Rev. Designer:** Frank Gasparro

Mint mark 1964

Date	Mintage	G-4	VG-8	F-12	VF-20	XF-40	MS-60	MS-65	Prf-65
1964	277,254,766	—	—	—	—	—	7.50	20.00	12.00
1964 Accented Hair	Inc. above	—	—	—	—	—	—	—	40.00
1964D	156,205,446	—	—	—	—	—	7.50	24.00	—

KM# 202a SILVER 30.6 mm. 11.5000 g. **Obv. Designer:** Gilroy Roberts **Rev. Designer:** Frank Gasparro

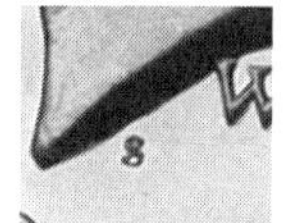
Mint mark 1968 - present

Date	Mintage	G-4	VG-8	F-12	VF-20	XF-40	MS-60	MS-65	Prf-65
1965	65,879,366	—	—	—	—	—	3.00	18.00	—
1965 SMS	2,360,000	—	—	—	—	—	—	15.00	—
1966	108,984,932	—	—	—	—	—	3.00	14.00	—
1966 SMS	2,261,583	—	—	—	—	—	—	17.00	—
1967	295,046,978	—	—	—	—	—	3.00	22.00	—
1967 SMS	18,633,440	—	—	—	—	—	—	18.00	—
1968D	246,951,930	—	—	—	—	—	3.00	18.00	—
1968S	3,041,506	—	—	—	—	—	—	—	7.00
1969D	129,881,800	—	—	—	—	—	3.00	20.00	—
1969S	2,934,631	—	—	—	—	—	—	—	7.50
1970D	2,150,000	—	—	—	—	—	13.00	38.00	—
1970S	2,632,810	—	—	—	—	—	—	—	20.00

KM# 202b COPPER-NICKEL CLAD COPPER 30.6 mm. 11.3400 g. **Obv. Designer:** Gilroy Roberts **Rev. Designer:** Frank Gasparro

Date	Mintage	G-4	VG-8	F-12	VF-20	XF-40	MS-60	MS-65	Prf-65
1971	155,640,000	—	—	—	—	—	1.00	15.00	—
1971D	302,097,424	—	—	—	—	—	1.00	15.00	—
1971S	3,244,183	—	—	—	—	—	—	—	8.00
1972	153,180,000	—	—	—	—	—	1.00	20.00	—
1972D	141,890,000	—	—	—	—	—	1.00	14.00	—
1972S	3,267,667	—	—	—	—	—	—	—	7.00
1973	64,964,000	—	—	—	—	—	1.00	14.00	—
1973D	83,171,400	—	—	—	—	—	—	12.00	—
1973S	(2,769,624)	—	—	—	—	—	—	—	7.00
1974	201,596,000	—	—	—	—	—	1.00	18.00	—
1974D	79,066,300	—	—	—	—	—	1.00	20.00	—
1974S	(2,617,350)	—	—	—	—	—	—	—	5.00
1975 none minted	—	—	—	—	—	—	—	—	—
1975D none minted	—	—	—	—	—	—	—	—	—
1975S none minted	—	—	—	—	—	—	—	—	—

Bicentennial design, Independence Hall

KM# 205 COPPER NICKEL 11.1000 g. **Rev. Designer:** Seth Huntington

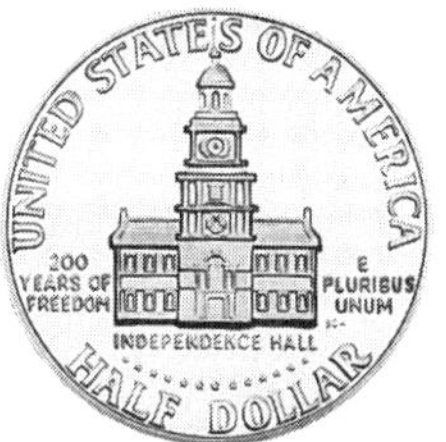

Date	Mintage	G-4	VG-8	F-12	VF-20	XF-40	MS-60	MS-65	Prf-65
1976	234,308,000	—	—	—	—	—	1.00	22.00	—
1976D	287,565,248	—	—	—	—	—	1.00	9.00	—
1976S	(7,059,099)	—	—	—	—	—	—	—	4.00

Regular design resumed

KM# A202b COPPER-NICKEL CLAD COPPER 30.6 mm. 11.3400 g. **Notes:** KM#202b design and composition resumed. The 1979-S and 1981-S Type II proofs have clearer mint marks than the Type I proofs of those years.

Date	Mintage	MS-65	Prf-65
1977	43,598,000	18.00	—
1977D	31,449,106	20.00	—
1977S	(3,251,152)	—	4.50
1978	14,350,000	12.00	—
1978D	13,765,799	10.00	—
1978S	(3,127,788)	—	6.00
1979	68,312,000	11.00	—
1979D	15,815,422	9.00	—
1979S type I, proof	3,677,175	—	6.00
Note: type I, proof			
1979S type II, proof	Inc. above	—	20.00
Note: type II, proof			
1980P	44,134,000	9.00	—
1980D	33,456,449	6.50	—
1980S	(3,547,030)	—	6.00
1981P	29,544,000	8.00	—
1981D	27,839,533	8.50	—
1981S type I, proof	(4,063,083)	—	5.00
Note: type I, proof			
1981S type II, proof	Inc. above	—	17.50
Note: type II, proof			
1982P	10,819,000	10.00	—
1982P no initials FG	Inc. above	40.00	—
1982D	13,140,102	9.00	—
1982S	(38,957,479)	—	6.50
1983P	34,139,000	20.00	—
1983D	32,472,244	10.00	—
1983S	(3,279,126)	—	6.50
1984P	26,029,000	10.00	—
1984D	26,262,158	15.00	—
1984S	(3,065,110)	—	7.00
1985P	18,706,962	10.00	—
1985D	19,814,034	12.00	—
1985S	(3,962,138)	—	6.00
1986P	13,107,633	25.00	—
1986D	15,336,145	17.00	—
1986S	(2,411,180)	—	8.00
1987P	2,890,758	14.00	—
1987D	2,890,758	10.00	—
1987S	(4,407,728)	—	6.50
1988P	13,626,000	16.00	—
1988D	12,000,096	12.00	—
1988S	(3,262,948)	—	6.00
1989P	24,542,000	18.00	—
1989D	23,000,216	14.00	—
1989S	(3,220,194)	—	8.00
1990P	22,780,000	20.00	—
1990D	20,096,242	15.00	—
1990S	(3,299,559)	—	7.00
1991P	14,874,000	15.00	—
1991D	15,054,678	18.00	—
1991S	(2,867,787)	—	16.00
1992P	17,628,000	18.00	—
1992D	17,000,106	8.00	—
1992S	(2,858,981)	—	8.00
1993P	15,510,000	15.00	—
1993D	15,000,006	14.00	—
1993S	(2,633,439)	—	14.00
1994P	23,718,000	8.00	—
1994D	23,828,110	8.00	—
1994S	(2,484,594)	—	11.00
1995P	26,496,000	9.00	—
1995D	26,288,000	8.00	—
1995S	(2,010,384)	—	35.00
1996P	24,442,000	11.00	—
1996D	24,744,000	8.00	—
1996S	(2,085,191)	—	16.00
1997P	20,882,000	14.00	—
1997D	19,876,000	10.00	—
1997S	(1,975,000)	—	34.00
1998P	15,646,000	14.00	—
1998D	15,064,000	14.00	—
1998S	(2,078,494)	—	22.00
1999P	8,900,000	9.00	—
1999D	10,682,000	9.00	—
1999S	(2,557,897)	—	24.00
2000P	22,600,000	9.00	—
2000D	19,466,000	7.00	—
2000S	(3,082,944)	—	8.00
2001P	21,200,000	9.00	—
2001D	19,504,000	9.00	—
2001S	(2,235,000)	—	10.00
2002P	3,100,000	10.00	—
2002D	2,500,000	10.00	—
2002S	(2,268,913)	—	8.00
2003P	2,500,000	14.00	—
2003D	2,500,000	14.00	—
2003S	2,076,165	—	6.00
2004P	2,900,000	14.00	—
2004D	2,900,000	14.00	—
2004S	1,789,488	—	13.00
2005P	3,800,000	9.00	—
2005P Satin finish	1,160,000	8.00	—
2005D	3,500,000	9.00	—
2005D Satin finish	1,160,000	10.00	—
2005S	2,275,000	—	7.00
2006P	2,400,000	12.00	—
2006P Satin finish	847,361	12.00	—
2006D	2,000,000	20.00	—
2006D Satin finish	847,361	14.00	—
2006S	1,934,965	—	10.00
2007P	—	7.00	—
2007P Satin finish	—	—	—
2007D	—	7.00	—
2007D Satin finish	—	—	—
2007S	—	—	10.00

KM# B202b SILVER

Date	Mintage	Prf-65
1992S	(1,317,579)	12.00
1993S	(761,353)	32.00
1994S	(785,329)	36.00
1995S	(838,953)	92.00
1996S	(830,021)	40.00
1997S	(821,678)	75.00
1998S	(878,792)	25.00
1998S Matte Proof	(62,350)	325
1999S	(804,565)	38.00
2000S	(965,921)	9.00
2001S	(849,600)	20.00
2002S	(888,816)	14.00
2003S	(1,040,425)	14.50
2004S	1,175,935	14.00
2005S	1,069,679	9.00
2006S	988,140	11.00
2007S	—	12.00

DOLLAR

Morgan Dollar

Laureate head left, date below flanked by stars Eagle within 1/2 wreath

KM# 110 0.9000 **SILVER** 0.7734 oz. ASW. 38.1 mm. 26.7300 g. **Designer:** George T. Morgan **Notes:** "65DMPL" values are for coins grading MS-65 deep-mirror prooflike. The 1878 "8 tail feathers" and "7 tail feathers" varieties are distinguished by the number of feathers in the eagle's tail. On the "reverse of 1878" varieties, the top of the top feather in the arrows held by the eagle is straight across and the eagle's breast is concave. On the "reverse of 1879 varieties," the top feather in the arrows held by the eagle is slanted and the eagle's breast is convex. The 1890-CC "tail-bar variety has a bar extending from the arrow feathers to the wreath on the reverse, the result of a die gouge. The Pittman Act of 1918 authorized the melting of 270 Million pieces of various dates. They were not indivudually recorded.

Date	Mintage	VG-8	F-12	VF-20	XF-40	AU-50	MS-60	MS-63	MS-64	MS-65	65DMPL	Prf-65
1901	6,962,813	27.50	36.00	57.50	110	395	2,185	17,000	56,000	235,000	—	7,850
1901 doubled die reverse	Inc. above	275	450	900	2,000	3,850	—	—	—	—	—	—
1901O	13,320,000	18.80	18.90	19.10	20.10	25.30	31.00	48.00	68.00	205	9,750	—
1901S	2,284,000	19.50	21.00	31.50	46.00	220	470	700	1,075	3,750	18,950	—
1902	7,994,777	19.30	18.90	19.00	22.10	25.00	44.00	100.00	138	475	19,500	7,350
1902O	8,636,000	18.80	18.90	19.10	20.10	22.30	31.00	48.00	65.00	170	13,250	—
1902S	1,530,000	60.00	82.00	160	220	315	425	625	1,135	3,050	15,000	—
1903	4,652,755	48.00	50.00	52.00	58.00	60.00	75.00	92.00	125	320	32,500	7,350
1903O	4,450,000	325	350	375	410	418	425	450	475	735	5,950	—
1903S	1,241,000	95.00	130	215	425	2,100	4,400	7,000	8,500	10,850	40,000	—
1903S Micro S	Inc. above	135	225	450	1,150	3,000	—	—	—	—	—	—
1904	2,788,650	21.00	23.00	25.00	27.00	32.00	78.00	280	715	3,650	41,500	7,350
1904O	3,720,000	21.00	23.00	25.00	27.00	59.00	37.00	48.00	65.00	170	965	—
1904S	2,304,000	35.00	47.50	87.00	230	570	1,075	4,350	6,250	9,850	19,000	—
1921	44,690,000	17.80	17.90	18.10	18.10	20.30	23.00	35.00	44.00	175	11,000	—
1921D	20,345,000	17.80	17.90	18.10	18.60	21.00	45.00	56.00	155	420	10,000	—
1921S	21,695,000	17.80	17.90	18.10	18.10	20.00	45.00	69.00	170	965	31,000	—

Peace Dollar

Liberty Head left Eagle facing right pearched on rock

KM# 150 0.9000 **SILVER** 0.7734 oz. ASW. 38.1 mm. 26.7300 g. **Designer:** Anthony DeFrancisci **Notes:** Commonly called Peace dollars.

Mint mark

Date	Mintage	G-4	VG-8	F-12	VF-20	XF-40	AU-50	MS-60	MS-63	MS-64	MS-65
1921	1,006,473	100.00	125	135	140	150	170	245	545	885	2,450
1922	51,737,000	17.30	17.60	17.80	17.90	18.10	18.40	21.80	32.00	50.00	180
1922D	15,063,000	17.30	17.80	17.80	17.90	18.10	19.30	26.50	53.00	98.00	510
1922S	17,475,000	17.30	17.80	17.80	17.90	18.10	19.30	26.50	69.00	300	2,500
1923	30,800,000	17.30	17.60	17.80	17.90	18.10	18.40	21.80	32.00	50.00	170
1923D	6,811,000	17.30	16.00	16.50	17.00	18.00	22.00	52.00	135	295	1,300
1923S	19,020,000	17.30	17.80	17.80	17.90	18.10	19.30	28.50	74.00	375	7,850
1924	11,811,000	17.30	17.60	16.50	17.90	18.10	18.40	21.80	32.00	50.00	200
1924S	1,728,000	25.00	30.00	31.00	33.00	44.00	66.50	200	600	1,725	11,250
1925	10,198,000	17.30	17.60	16.50	17.90	18.10	18.40	23.00	32.00	50.00	200
1925S	1,610,000	18.20	19.50	21.00	25.00	29.00	46.00	75.00	210	1,050	25,000

Date	Mintage	G-4	VG-8	F-12	VF-20	XF-40	AU-50	MS-60	MS-63	MS-64	MS-65
1926	1,939,000	18.20	18.50	18.90	19.20	19.60	22.50	43.00	82.00	125	485
1926D	2,348,700	18.20	18.50	18.70	19.00	22.00	32.50	66.00	190	325	895
1926S	6,980,000	17.90	18.20	18.40	18.50	18.70	21.40	44.00	110	290	1,250
1927	848,000	25.00	29.00	32.00	33.00	38.00	50.00	70.00	185	485	3,650
1927D	1,268,900	24.00	28.00	30.00	31.00	34.00	80.00	145	365	1,025	5,700
1927S	866,000	24.00	28.00	31.00	32.00	35.00	80.00	135	445	1,575	11,350
1928	360,649	355	435	445	455	465	475	525	925	1,450	4,600
1928S Lg S	1,632,000	30.00	36.00	40.00	46.00	54.00	90.00	220	800	2,100	18,500
1928S Sm S	Inc. above	28.00	33.00	34.00	38.00	43.50	66.00	155	595	1,500	24,000
1934	954,057	18.20	19.50	21.00	21.00	22.50	46.00	120	245	465	965
1934D Lg D	1,569,500	17.00	20.00	23.50	23.00	26.00	60.00	165	600	900	3,000
1934D Sm D	Inc. above	18.20	18.50	21.00	21.00	22.00	46.00	135	500	740	1,990
1934S	1,011,000	26.00	31.00	48.00	85.00	200	500	1,750	3,850	6,250	8,650
1935	1,576,000	17.60	18.00	21.00	21.50	22.00	30.00	60.00	115	212	750
1935S	1,964,000	17.60	18.00	21.00	20.00	23.00	92.00	235	380	630	1,350

Eisenhower Dollar

KM# 203 COPPER-NICKEL CLAD COPPER 38.1 mm. 22.6800 g. **Designer:** Frank Gasparro

Date	Mintage	Proof	MS-63	Prf-65
1971	47,799,000	—	10.00	—
1971D	68,587,424	—	8.00	—
1972 Low Relief	75,890,000	—	6.50	—
1972 High Relief	Inc. above	—	175	—
1972 Modified High Relief	Inc. above	—	40.00	—
1972D	92,548,511	—	5.50	—
1973	2,000,056	—	14.00	—
1973D	2,000,000	—	15.00	—
1973S	—	(2,769,624)	—	12.00
1974	27,366,000	—	5.50	—
1974D	35,466,000	—	7.00	—
1974S	—	(2,617,350)	—	11.00

Bicentennial design, moon behind Liberty Bell

KM# 206 COPPER-NICKEL CLAD COPPER 38.1 mm. 22.6800 g. **Rev. Designer:** Dennis R. Williams **Notes:** In 1976 the lettering on the reverse was changed to thinner letters, resulting in the Type II variety for that year. The Type I variety was minted 1975 and dated 1976.

Type I

Type II

Date	Mintage	Proof	MS-63	Prf-65
1976 type I	117,337,000	—	9.00	—
1976 type II	Inc. above	—	5.00	—
1976D type I	103,228,274	—	6.00	—
1976D type II	Inc. above	—	5.00	—
1976S type I	—	(2,909,369)	—	13.00
1976S type II	—	(4,149,730)	—	9.00

Regular design resumed

KM# A203 COPPER-NICKEL CLAD COPPER 38.1 mm.

Date	Mintage	Proof	MS-63	Prf-65
1977	12,596,000	—	7.00	—
1977D	32,983,006	—	7.00	—
1977S	—	(3,251,152)	—	10.00
1978	25,702,000	—	5.00	—
1978D	33,012,890	—	5.00	—
1978S	—	(3,127,788)	—	12.00

Susan B. Anthony Dollar

Susan B. Anthony bust right Eagle landing on moon, symbolic of Apollo manned moon landing

KM# 207 COPPER-NICKEL CLAD COPPER 26.5 mm. 8.1000 g. **Designer:** Frank Gasparro **Notes:** The 1979-S and 1981-S Type II coins have a clearer mint mark than the Type I varieties for those years.

Date	Mintage	MS-63	Prf-65	Date	Mintage	MS-63	Prf-65
1979P Near date	360,222,000	70.00	—	1981P	3,000,000	7.50	—
1979P	Inc. above	2.50	—	1981D	3,250,000	7.50	—
1979D	288,015,744	3.00	—	1981S	3,492,000	7.50	—
1979S Proof, Type I	(3,677,175)	—	8.00	1981S Proof, Type I	4,063,083	—	8.00
1979S Proof, Type II	Inc. above	—	110	1981S Proof, Type II	Inc. above	—	230
1979S	109,576,000	3.00	—	1999P	29,592,000	4.00	—
1980P	27,610,000	3.00	—	1999P Proof; *maximum mintage	(750,000)	—	25.00
1980D	41,628,708	2.00	—	1999D	11,776,000	4.00	—
1980S	20,422,000	3.50	—				
1980S Proof	3,547,030	—	8.00				

Sacagawea Dollar

Sacagawea bust right, with baby on back Eagle in flight left

KM# 310 COPPER-ZINC-MANGANESE-NICKEL CLAD COPPER 26.4 mm. 8.0700 g.

Date	Mintage	MS-63	Prf-65	Date	Mintage	MS-63	Prf-65
2000P	767,140,000	2.00	—	2004P	2,660,000	2.50	—
2000D	518,916,000	2.00	—	2004D	2,660,000	2.50	—
2000S	4,048,865	—	10.00	2004S	—	—	22.50
2001P	62,468,000	2.00	—	2005P	2,520,000	2.50	—
2001D	70,909,500	2.00	—	2005D	2,520,000	2.50	—
2001S	(3,084,600)	—	100.00	2005S	—	—	22.50
2002P	3,865,610	2.00	—	2006P	4,900,000	2.50	—
2002D	3,732,000	2.00	—	2006D	2,800,000	5.00	—
2002S	(3,157,739)	—	28.50	2006S	—	—	22.50
2003P	3,090,000	3.00	—	2007P	—	2.50	—
2003D	3,090,000	3.00	—	2007D	—	2.50	—
2003S	(3,116,590)	—	20.00	2007S	—	—	22.50

Presidents

George Washington

KM# 401 COPPER-ZINC-MANGANESE-NICKEL CLAD COPPER 26.4 mm. 8.0700 g. **Notes:** Date and mint mark incuse on edge.

Date	Mintage	MS-63	MS-65	Prf-65
2007P	176,680,000	2.00	—	—
(2007) Plain edge error	Inc. above	75.00	—	—
2007D	163,680,000	2.00	—	—
2007S	—	—	—	—

James Madison

KM# 404 COPPER-ZINC-MANGANESE-NICKEL CLAD COPPER 26.4 mm. 8.0700 g. **Notes:** Date and mint mark incuse on edge.

Date	Mintage	MS-63	MS-65	Prf-65
2007P	—	2.00	3.00	—
2007D	—	2.00	3.00	—
2007S	—	—	—	—

John Adams

KM# 402 **COPPER-ZINC-MANGANESE-NICKEL CLAD COPPER** 26.4 mm. 8.0700 g. **Notes:** Date and mint mark incuse on edge.

Date	Mintage	MS-63	MS-65	Prf-65
2007P	112,420,000	2.00	5.00	—
2007P Double edge lettering	Inc. above	250	—	—
2007D	102,810,000	2.00	5.00	—
2007S	—	—	—	8.00

Thomas Jefferson

KM# 403 **COPPER-ZINC-MANGANESE-NICKEL CLAD COPPER** 26.4 mm. 8.0700 g. **Notes:** Date and mint mark incuse on edge.

Date	Mintage	MS-63	MS-65	Prf-65
2007P	—	2.00	3.00	—
2007D	—	2.00	3.00	—
2007S	—	—	—	—

Andrew Jackson

KM# 428 **COPPER-ZINC-MANGANESE-NICKEL CLAD COPPER** 8.0700 g.

Date	Mintage	MS-63	MS-65	Prf-65
2008P	—	2.00	3.00	—
2008D	—	2.00	3.00	—
2008S	—	2.00	3.00	—

James Monroe

KM# 426 **COPPER-ZINC-MANGANESE-NICKEL CLAD COPPER** 8.0700 g.

Date	Mintage	MS-63	MS-65	Prf-65
2008P	—	2.00	3.00	—
2008D	—	2.00	3.00	—
2008S	—	—	—	—

John Quincy Adams

KM# 427 **COPPER-ZINC-MANGANESE-NICKEL CLAD COPPER** 8.0700 g.

Date	Mintage	MS-63	MS-65	Prf-65
2008P	—	2.00	5.00	—
2008D	—	2.00	5.00	—
2008S	—	—	—	8.00

Martin van Buren

KM# 429 **COPPER-ZINC-MANGANESE-NICKEL CLAD COPPER** 8.0700 g.

Date	Mintage	MS-63	MS-65	Prf-65
2008P	—	2.00	5.00	—
2008D	—	2.00	5.00	—
2008S	—	—	—	8.00

$2.50 (QUARTER EAGLE)

Coronet Head

Coronet head left within circle of stars
No motto above eagle

KM# 72 0.9000 **GOLD** 0.1209 oz. AGW. 18 mm. 4.1800 g. **Designer:** Christian Gobrecht **Notes:** Varieties for 1843 are distinguished by the size of the numerals in the date. One 1848 variety has "Cal." inscribed on the reverse, indicating it was made from California gold. The 1873 "closed-3" and "open-3" varieties are distinguished by the amount of space between the upper left and lower left serifs in the 3 in the date.

Date	Mintage	F-12	VF-20	XF-40	AU-50	MS-60	Prf-65
1901	91,322	150	175	200	235	275	12,500
1902	133,733	150	170	200	235	275	12,500
1903	201,257	150	170	200	235	275	13,000
1904	160,960	150	170	200	240	275	12,500
1905	217,944	150	170	200	240	275	12,500
1906	176,490	150	170	200	240	275	12,500
1907	336,448	150	170	200	240	275	12,500

Indian Head

KM# 128 0.9000 **GOLD** 0.1209 oz. AGW. 18 mm. 4.1800 g. **Designer:** Bela Lyon Pratt

Date	Mintage	VF-20	XF-40	AU-50	MS-60	MS-63	MS-65	Prf-65
1908	565,057	165	220	230	275	1,800	8,500	16,000
1909	441,899	175	220	230	275	2,600	11,000	30,000
1910	492,682	175	220	230	275	2,600	12,500	18,000
1911	704,191	175	220	230	280	1,600	12,500	16,000
1911D	55,680	2,500	3,650	5,000	9,850	24,500	90,000	16,000
1912	616,197	175	220	230	275	2,800	16,000	16,000
1913	722,165	175	220	230	280	1,725	14,000	16,500
1914	240,117	175	235	260	480	8,500	34,000	16,500
1914D	448,000	175	220	230	300	2,650	40,000	23,000
1915	606,100	175	220	230	275	1,650	13,500	15,250
1925D	578,000	175	220	230	275	1,450	7,000	—
1926	446,000	175	220	230	275	1,450	7,000	—
1927	388,000	175	220	230	275	1,450	7,000	—
1928	416,000	175	220	230	275	1,450	7,000	—
1929	532,000	180	230	250	340	1,600	10,000	—

$5 (HALF EAGLE)

Coronet Head

Coronet head, left, within circle of stars
"In God We Trust" above eagle

KM# 101 0.9000 **GOLD** 0.2419 oz. AGW. 21.6 mm. 8.3590 g. **Designer:** Christian Gobrecht **Notes:** The 1873 "closed-3" and "open-3" varieties are known and are distinguished by the amount of space between the upper left and lower left serifs of the 3 in the date.

Date	Mintage	VF-20	XF-40	AU-50	MS-60	MS-63	MS-65	Prf-65
1901	616,040	215	220	225	235	750	3,650	27,000
1901S	3,648,000	215	220	225	235	730	3,600	—
1902	172,562	215	220	225	235	730	4,400	27,000
1902S	939,000	215	220	225	235	730	3,600	—
1903	227,024	215	220	225	235	730	4,000	27,000
1903S	1,855,000	215	220	225	235	730	3,600	—
1904	392,136	215	220	225	235	730	3,600	27,000
1904S	97,000	215	240	285	900	3,850	9,600	—
1905	302,308	215	220	225	235	740	4,000	27,000
1905S	880,700	215	225	250	235	1,500	9,600	—
1906	348,820	215	220	225	235	745	3,600	26,000
1906D	320,000	215	220	225	235	930	3,200	—
1906S	598,000	215	220	230	240	900	4,400	—
1907	626,192	215	220	225	235	730	3,400	23,000
1907D	888,000	215	220	225	235	730	3,400	—
1908	421,874	215	220	225	235	730	3,400	—

Indian Head

KM# 129 0.9000 **GOLD** 0.2419 oz. AGW. 21.6 mm. 8.3590 g. **Designer:** Bela Lyon Pratt

Date	Mintage	VF-20	XF-40	AU-50	MS-60	MS-63	MS-65	Prf-65
1908	578,012	330	355	385	460	4,350	25,000	25,500
1908D	148,000	330	355	385	460	4,350	27,500	—
1908S	82,000	330	415	430	1,275	4,350	24,000	—
1909	627,138	330	355	385	460	4,350	25,000	36,000
1909D	3,423,560	330	355	385	460	4,350	25,000	—
1909O	34,200	2,000	3,400	6,000	21,000	66,000	260,000	—
1909S	297,200	330	355	385	1,400	11,000	45,000	—
1910	604,250	330	355	385	460	4,350	25,000	37,000
1910D	193,600	330	355	385	460	4,350	42,500	—
1910S	770,200	330	355	385	1,000	6,000	44,000	—
1911	915,139	330	355	385	460	4,350	25,000	28,500
1911D	72,500	475	535	515	4,500	37,000	241,500	—
1911S	1,416,000	340	355	385	560	4,350	41,500	—
1912	790,144	330	355	385	460	4,350	25,000	28,500
1912S	392,000	330	365	400	1,700	13,500	93,500	—
1913	916,099	330	355	385	460	4,350	25,000	28,000
1913S	408,000	340	350	385	1,400	11,500	120,000	—
1914	247,125	330	355	385	460	4,350	25,000	28,500

Date	Mintage	VF-20	XF-40	AU-50	MS-60	MS-63	MS-65	Prf-65
1914D	247,000	335	355	385	460	4,350	26,000	—
1914S	263,000	340	365	400	1,375	13,500	100,000	—
1915	588,075	330	355	385	460	4,350	25,000	39,000
1915S	164,000	340	400	385	2,000	17,000	110,000	—
1916S	240,000	330	355	385	560	4,350	25,000	—
1929	662,000	4,200	9,600	10,500	13,250	17,500	45,000	—

$10 (EAGLE)

Coronet Head

New-style head, left, within circle of stars "In God We Trust" above eagle

KM# 102 0.9000 **GOLD** 0.4837 oz. AGW. 27 mm. 16.7180 g. **Designer:** Christian Gobrecht **Notes:** The 1873 "closed-3" and "open-3" varieties are distinguished by the amount of space between the upper left and lower left serifs of the 3 in the date.

Date	Mintage	VF-20	XF-40	AU-50	MS-60	MS-63	MS-65	Prf-65
1901	1,718,825	466	472	479	514	1,325	7,900	43,500
1901O	72,041	494	510	517	634	3,750	12,500	—
1901S	2,812,750	466	472	479	514	1,325	7,900	—
1902	82,513	466	472	479	524	2,800	11,750	43,500
1902S	469,500	466	472	479	514	1,325	7,900	—
1903	125,926	466	472	479	524	2,450	13,500	43,500
1903O	112,771	494	510	517	624	3,250	18,000	—
1903S	538,000	466	472	479	524	1,350	7,900	—
1904	162,038	466	472	479	524	2,000	9,500	46,000
1904O	108,950	494	510	517	624	3,700	16,500	—
1905	201,078	466	472	479	514	1,450	8,500	43,500
1905S	369,250	494	505	544	1,100	5,600	22,500	—
1906	165,497	466	472	479	524	2,450	10,000	43,500
1906D	981,000	466	472	479	514	1,325	7,000	—
1906O	86,895	494	510	517	664	4,900	14,500	—
1906S	457,000	494	505	517	674	5,000	15,500	—
1907	1,203,973	466	472	479	514	1,325	7,900	43,500
1907D	1,030,000	466	472	479	524	2,250	—	—
1907S	210,500	494	505	539	714	5,450	17,000	—

Indian Head

No motto next to eagle

KM# 125 0.9000 **GOLD** 0.4837 oz. AGW. 27 mm. 16.7180 g. **Designer:** Augustus Saint-Gaudens **Notes:** 1907 varieties are distinguished by whether the edge is rolled or wired, and whether the legend "E Pluribus Unum" has periods between each word.

Date	Mintage	VF-20	XF-40	AU-50	MS-60	MS-63	MS-65	Prf-65
1907 wire edge, periods before and after legend	500	9,500	14,900	16,900	22,000	36,500	65,000	—
1907 same, without stars on edge, unique	—	—	—	—	—	—	—	—
1907 rolled edge, periods	42	26,000	38,500	49,000	66,500	98,500	250,000	—
1907 without periods	239,406	580	600	630	775	3,100	11,450	—
1908 without motto	33,500	565	585	615	720	4,650	14,500	—
1908D without motto	210,000	565	585	615	760	6,250	38,500	—

"In God We Trust" left of eagle

KM# 130 0.9000 **GOLD** 0.4837 oz. AGW. 27 mm. 16.7180 g. **Designer:** Augustus Saint-Gaudens

Date	Mintage	VF-20	XF-40	AU-50	MS-60	MS-63	MS-65	Prf-65
1908	341,486	560	580	610	700	3,150	9,450	52,500
1908D	836,500	565	585	615	705	6,850	29,000	—
1908S	59,850	575	635	665	2,950	8,650	25,500	—
1909	184,863	560	580	610	700	3,500	12,750	54,500
1909D	121,540	565	585	615	775	4,650	34,500	—
1909S	292,350	565	585	615	775	5,350	13,900	—
1910	318,704	560	580	610	700	2,350	8,950	54,500
1910D	2,356,640	555	575	610	700	2,185	8,600	—
1910S	811,000	565	585	615	705	7,450	55,000	—
1911	505,595	555	575	605	695	2,185	8,800	52,500
1911D	30,100	610	675	950	4,200	21,500	120,000	—
1911S	51,000	595	555	645	1,050	7,950	14,500	—
1912	405,083	560	580	610	700	2,350	9,650	52,500
1912S	300,000	565	585	615	705	5,850	38,500	—
1913	442,071	560	580	610	700	2,350	8,800	52,500
1913S	66,000	610	600	775	3,900	28,500	100,000	—
1914	151,050	560	580	610	700	2,400	9,850	52,500
1914D	343,500	560	580	610	700	2,650	15,500	—
1914S	208,000	570	590	620	720	6,500	32,500	—
1915	351,075	560	580	610	700	2,350	9,850	55,000
1915S	59,000	610	725	775	3,150	14,850	65,000	—
1916S	138,500	595	615	645	735	5,150	18,500	—
1920S	126,500	7,800	11,000	14,500	28,500	71,500	275,000	—
1926	1,014,000	555	575	605	695	1,650	7,450	—
1930S	96,000	7,500	10,000	13,500	21,500	41,500	68,500	—
1932	4,463,000	555	575	605	695	1,650	7,500	—
1933	312,500	110,000	140,000	150,000	185,000	245,000	650,000	—

$20 (DOUBLE EAGLE)

Liberty

Coronet head, left, within circle of stars "Twenty Dollars" below eagle

KM# 74.3 0.9000 **GOLD** 0.9675 oz. AGW. 33.4360 g.

Date	Mintage	VF-20	XF-40	AU-50	MS-60	MS-63	MS-65	Prf-65
1901	111,526	963	973	988	1,018	1,175	5,500	82,500
1901S	1,596,000	963	973	988	1,018	3,350	20,000	—
1902	31,254	1,063	1,173	1,050	1,400	11,250	37,500	95,000
1902S	1,753,625	963	973	988	1,018	2,900	24,000	—
1903	287,428	963	973	988	1,018	1,150	5,500	95,000
1903S	954,000	963	973	988	1,018	1,385	13,500	—
1904	6,256,797	963	973	988	1,018	1,150	4,650	95,000
1904S	5,134,175	963	973	988	1,018	1,175	5,400	—
1905	59,011	968	993	1,028	1,250	15,500	—	95,000
1905S	1,813,000	963	973	988	1,018	3,250	20,500	—
1906	69,690	968	978	993	1,118	6,850	22,500	82,500
1906D	620,250	963	973	988	1,018	3,250	19,000	—
1906S	2,065,750	963	973	988	1,018	2,350	19,500	—
1907	1,451,864	963	973	988	1,018	1,155	8,200	82,500
1907D	842,250	963	973	988	1,018	2,650	7,350	—
1907S	2,165,800	963	973	988	1,018	2,375	27,000	—

Saint-Gaudens

Roman numerals in date No motto below eagle

KM# 126 0.9000 **GOLD** 0.9675 oz. AGW. 34 mm. 33.4360 g. **Designer:** Augustus Saint-Gaudens

Date	Mintage	VF-20	XF-40	AU-50	MS-60	MS-63	MS-65	Prf-65
MCMVII (1907) high relief, unique, AU-55, $150,000	—	—	—	—	—	—	—	—
MCMVII (1907) high relief, wire rim	11,250	7,500	8,500	10,800	13,500	21,700	46,500	—
MCMVII (1907) high relief, flat rim	Inc. above	7,750	8,850	11,250	15,000	24,650	49,500	—

Arabic numerals in date No motto below eagle

KM# 127 0.9000 **GOLD** 0.9675 oz. AGW. 34 mm. 33.4360 g. **Designer:** Augustus Saint-Gaudens

Date	Mintage	VF-20	XF-40	AU-50	MS-60	MS-63	MS-65	Prf-65
1907 large letters on edge, unique	—	—	—	—	—	—	—	—
1907 small letters on edge	361,667	957	967	992	1,042	1,332	3,350	—
1908	4,271,551	947	957	972	1,002	1,222	1,750	—
1908D	663,750	957	967	982	1,027	1,332	9,000	—

"In God We Trust" below eagle

KM# 131 0.9000 **GOLD** 0.9675 oz. AGW. 34 mm. 33.4360 g. **Designer:** Augustus Saint-Gaudens

Date	Mintage	VF-20	XF-40	AU-50	MS-60	MS-63	MS-65	Prf-65
1908	156,359	952	962	982	1,052	1,750	21,500	49,500
Note: 34500								
1908 Roman finish; Prf64 Rare	—	—	—	—	—	—	—	—
1908D	349,500	957	967	992	1,042	1,352	5,350	—

Date	Mintage	VF-20	XF-40	AU-50	MS-60	MS-63	MS-65	Prf-65
1908S	22,000	1,450	2,050	4,650	10,500	22,500	43,000	—
1909/8	161,282	957	967	1,032	1,850	6,950	32,500	—
1909	Inc. above	967	987	1,002	1,102	3,350	42,500	49,000
1909D	52,500	997	1,007	1,127	3,100	8,850	39,500	—
1909S	2,774,925	957	967	992	1,022	1,307	5,500	—
1910	482,167	952	962	982	1,052	1,322	7,350	49,000
1910D	429,000	952	962	982	1,027	1,292	2,600	—
1910S	2,128,250	957	967	997	1,032	1,357	8,000	—
1911	197,350	957	967	1,002	1,042	1,875	15,500	39,500
1911D	846,500	952	962	982	1,027	1,292	1,850	—
1911S	775,750	952	962	982	1,032	1,292	6,200	—
1912	149,824	957	967	997	1,067	2,050	19,500	44,000
1913	168,838	957	967	997	1,072	2,850	33,000	44,000
1913D	393,500	952	962	982	1,027	1,332	6,500	—
1913S	34,000	1,007	1,017	1,032	2,000	4,350	36,500	—
1914	95,320	967	977	1,032	1,275	3,900	25,000	41,500
1914D	453,000	952	962	982	1,027	1,302	3,250	—
1914S	1,498,000	952	962	982	1,027	1,292	2,000	—
1915	152,050	957	967	992	1,032	2,200	28,500	47,500
1915S	567,500	952	962	982	1,027	1,292	2,000	—
1916S	796,000	957	967	992	1,067	1,322	2,700	—
1920	228,250	947	957	972	1,027	1,352	62,500	—
1920S	558,000	12,500	15,500	22,500	44,500	98,500	225,000	—
1921	528,500	17,500	29,500	43,500	100,000	240,000	950,000	—
1922	1,375,500	947	957	972	1,002	1,242	2,450	—
1922S	2,658,000	1,025	1,150	1,300	2,450	4,850	42,500	—
1923	566,000	947	957	972	1,002	1,242	4,750	—
1923D	1,702,250	957	967	982	1,012	1,242	1,850	—
1924	4,323,500	947	957	972	1,002	1,222	1,750	—
1924D	3,049,500	1,050	1,550	1,800	3,100	9,150	76,500	—
1924S	2,927,500	1,025	1,550	1,850	3,000	9,850	54,500	—
1925	2,831,750	947	957	972	1,002	1,222	1,950	—
1925D	2,938,500	1,550	2,100	2,375	4,450	11,500	96,000	—
1925S	3,776,500	1,350	1,950	3,450	9,000	24,500	105,000	—
1926	816,750	947	957	972	1,002	1,222	1,750	—
1926D	481,000	8,500	12,500	16,000	28,500	43,500	115,000	—
1926S	2,041,500	1,050	1,550	1,725	3,150	5,650	31,500	—
1927	2,946,750	947	957	972	1,002	1,222	1,750	—
1927D	180,000	155,000	220,000	265,000	340,000	1,500,000	2,100,000	—
1927S	3,107,000	5,850	8,250	12,750	26,500	57,500	130,000	—
1928	8,816,000	947	957	972	1,002	1,222	1,750	—
1929	1,779,750	5,750	9,000	12,500	18,500	39,500	105,000	—
1930S	74,000	15,500	26,500	30,000	39,000	125,000	235,000	—
1931	2,938,250	9,800	14,500	18,850	30,000	68,500	110,000	—
1931D	106,500	9,000	11,850	21,500	42,500	95,000	130,000	—
1932	1,101,750	8,000	14,500	16,850	26,500	72,500	110,000	—
1933	445,500	—	—	—	—	—	9,000,000	—

Note: Sotheby/Stack's Sale, July 2002. Thirteen known, only one currently available.

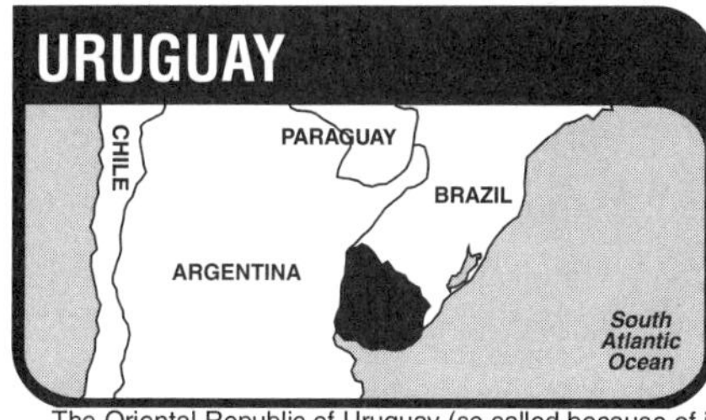

The Oriental Republic of Uruguay (so called because of its location on the east bank of the Uruguay River) is situated on the Atlantic coast of South America between Argentina and Brazil. This South American country has an area of 68,536 sq. mi. (176,220 sq. km.) and a population of *3 million. Capital: Montevideo. Uruguay's chief economic assets are the rich, rolling grassy plains. Meat, wool, hides and skins are exported.

Uruguay was discovered in 1516 by Juan Diaz de Solis, a Spaniard, but settled by the Portuguese who founded Colonia in 1680. Spain contested Portuguese possession and, after a long struggle, gained control of the country in 1778. During the general South American struggle for independence, Uruguay 's first attempt was led by Gaucho soldier Jose Gervasio Artigas leading the Banda Oriental which was quelled by Spanish and Portuguese forces in 1811. The armistice was soon broken and Argentine force from Buenos Aires cast off the Spanish bond in the Plata region in 1814 only to be conquered again by the Portuguese from Brazil in the struggle of 1816-20. Revolt flared anew in 1825 and independence was reasserted in 1828 with the help of Argentina. The Uruguayan Republic was established in 1830.

MINT MARKS

A - Paris, Berlin, Vienna
(a) Paris, privy marks only
D - Lyon (France)
H - Birmingham
Mx, Mo - Mexico City
(p) - Poissy, France
So - Santiago (Small O above S)
(u) – Utrecht

MONETARY SYSTEM

100 Centesimo = 1 Peso
1975-1993
1000 Old Pesos = 1 Nuevo (New) Peso
Commencing 1994
1000 Nuevos Pesos = 1 Peso Uruguayo

REPUBLIC

DECIMAL COINAGE

KM# 19 CENTESIMO

2.0000 g., Copper-Nickel **Obv:** Radiant sun design **Rev:** Value within wreath

Date	Mintage	F	VF	XF	Unc	BU
1901A	6,000,000	1.00	5.00	20.00	50.00	—
1901A Proof	—	Value: 225				
1909A	5,000,000	0.50	2.00	6.00	15.00	—
1924(p)	3,000,000	0.50	2.00	8.00	20.00	—
1936A	2,000,000	0.50	2.00	8.00	20.00	—

KM# 32 CENTESIMO

1.5000 g., Copper-Nickel **Obv:** Artigas bust right, 'HP' below **Obv. Designer:** T.H. Paget **Rev:** Value within wreath **Rev. Designer:** Gilroy Roberts **Note:** Medal rotation.

Date	Mintage	F	VF	XF	Unc	BU
1953	5,000,000	0.25	0.50	1.00	3.00	—
1953 Proof	—	Value: 150				

KM# 20 2 CENTESIMOS

3.5000 g., Copper-Nickel, 20 mm. **Obv:** Radiant sun design **Rev:** Value within wreath

Date	Mintage	F	VF	XF	Unc	BU
1901A	7,500,000	1.00	4.00	12.00	30.00	—
1909A	10,000,000	1.00	2.00	9.00	20.00	—
1924(p)	11,000,000	1.00	2.00	7.00	15.00	—
1936A	6,500,000	1.00	3.00	11.00	25.00	—
1941So	10,000,000	1.00	2.00	10.00	22.00	—

KM# 20a 2 CENTESIMOS

3.5000 g., Copper, 20 mm. **Obv:** Radiant sun design **Rev:** Value within wreath

Date	Mintage	F	VF	XF	Unc	BU
1943So	5,000,000	0.25	1.00	3.00	10.00	—
1944So	3,500,000	0.25	1.00	3.00	10.00	—
1945So	2,500,000	0.25	1.00	3.00	10.00	—
1946So	2,500,000	0.25	0.50	3.00	10.00	—
1947So	5,000,000	0.25	0.50	1.50	7.00	—
1948So	7,500,000	0.25	0.50	1.00	6.00	—
1949So	7,400,000	0.25	0.50	1.00	6.00	—
1951So	12,500,000	0.25	0.50	1.00	6.00	—

KM# 33 2 CENTESIMOS

2.5000 g., Copper-Nickel **Obv:** Artigas, 'HP' below **Obv. Designer:** T.H. Paget **Rev:** Value within wreath **Rev. Designer:** Gilroy Roberts **Note:** Medal rotation.

Date	Mintage	F	VF	XF	Unc	BU
1953	50,000,000	0.15	0.30	1.00	5.00	—
1953 Proof	—	Value: 65.00				

KM# 37 2 CENTESIMOS

2.0000 g., Nickel-Brass **Obv:** Artigas, 'HP' below **Obv. Designer:** T.H. Paget **Rev:** Value within wreath **Rev. Designer:** Gilroy Roberts **Note:** Medal rotation.

Date	Mintage	F	VF	XF	Unc	BU
1960	17,500,000	—	0.15	0.25	1.00	—
1960 Proof	—	Value: 40.00				

KM# 21 5 CENTESIMOS

5.0000 g., Copper-Nickel, 23.3 mm. **Obv:** Radiant sun design **Rev:** Value within wreath

Date	Mintage	F	VF	XF	Unc	BU
1901A	6,000,000	1.00	4.00	12.00	30.00	—
1901A Proof	—	Value: 325				
1909A	5,000,000	1.00	3.00	10.00	22.00	—
1909A Proof	—	Value: 175				
1924(p)	5,000,000	0.50	2.00	6.00	15.00	—
1936A	3,000,000	0.50	2.00	6.00	15.00	—
1941So	2,400,000	0.25	1.00	4.00	10.00	—
1941So Proof	—	Value: 200				

KM# 21a 5 CENTESIMOS

5.0000 g., Copper, 22.8 mm. **Obv:** Radiant sun design **Rev:** Value within wreath

Date	Mintage	F	VF	XF	Unc	BU
1944So	4,000,000	0.25	1.00	3.00	10.00	—
1946So	2,000,000	0.20	1.00	4.00	12.00	—
1947So	2,000,000	0.20	1.00	4.00	12.00	—
1948So	3,000,000	0.20	0.75	3.00	10.00	—
1949So	2,800,000	0.20	0.75	3.00	10.00	—
1951So	15,000,000	0.20	0.50	2.00	7.00	—

KM# 34 5 CENTESIMOS

3.5000 g., Copper-Nickel **Obv:** Artigas, 'HP' below **Obv. Designer:** T.H. Paget **Rev:** Value within wreath **Rev. Designer:** Gilroy Roberts **Note:** Medal rotation.

Date	Mintage	F	VF	XF	Unc	BU
1953	17,500,000	0.20	0.30	0.50	1.00	—
1953 Proof	—	Value: 75.00				

KM# 38 5 CENTESIMOS

3.5000 g., Nickel-Brass **Obv:** Artigas, 'HP' below **Obv. Designer:** T.H. Paget **Rev:** Value within wreath **Rev. Designer:** Gilroy Roberts **Note:** Medal rotation.

Date	Mintage	F	VF	XF	Unc	BU
1960	88,000,000	—	0.15	0.25	1.00	—
1960 Proof	—	Value: 75.00				

KM# 25 10 CENTESIMOS

8.0000 g., Aluminum-Bronze, 27 mm. **Subject:** Constitutional Centennial **Obv:** MORLON behind neck **Rev:** Puma walking left in front of sun rays above value

Date	Mintage	F	VF	XF	Unc	BU
1930(a)	5,000,000	2.00	4.00	12.00	50.00	—

KM# 28 10 CENTESIMOS

6.0000 g., Aluminum-Bronze, 25 mm. **Obv:** Head laureate right **Rev:** Puma walking left in front of sunrays above value

Date	Mintage	F	VF	XF	Unc	BU
1936A	2,000,000	1.50	3.50	10.00	45.00	—

KM# 35 10 CENTESIMOS

4.5000 g., Copper-Nickel **Obv:** Artigas, 'HP' below **Obv. Designer:** T.H. Paget **Rev:** Value within wreath **Rev. Designer:** Gilroy Roberts **Note:** Medal rotation.

Date	Mintage	F	VF	XF	Unc	BU
1953	28,250,000	0.15	0.20	0.30	1.00	—
1953 Proof	—	Value: 75.00				
1959	10,000,000	0.20	0.30	1.00	3.00	—

KM# 39 10 CENTESIMOS

4.5000 g., Nickel-Brass **Obv:** Artigas, 'HP' below **Obv. Designer:** T.H. Paget **Rev:** Value within wreath **Rev. Designer:** Gilroy Roberts **Note:** Medal rotation.

Date	Mintage	F	VF	XF	Unc	BU
1960	72,500,000	0.15	0.20	0.30	1.00	—
1960 Proof	—	Value: 100				

KM# 24 20 CENTESIMOS

5.0000 g., 0.8000 Silver 0.1286 oz. ASW **Obv:** Radiant sun peeks out over arms within wreath **Rev:** Head left

Date	Mintage	F	VF	XF	Unc	BU
1920	2,500,000	2.50	5.50	12.00	35.00	—

KM# 26 20 CENTESIMOS

5.0000 g., 0.8000 Silver 0.1286 oz. ASW, 25 mm. **Subject:** Constitutional Centennial **Obv:** Seated figure left above date **Rev:** Wheat stalks divide value, mint marks flank stems

Date	Mintage	F	VF	XF	Unc	BU
1930(a)	2,500,000	2.25	4.50	10.00	30.00	—

KM# 29 20 CENTESIMOS

3.0000 g., 0.7200 Silver 0.0694 oz. ASW, 19 mm. **Obv:** Head laureate right **Rev:** Wheat stalks divide value

Date	Mintage	F	VF	XF	Unc	BU
1942So	18,000,000	1.50	2.50	4.50	7.00	—

KM# 36 20 CENTESIMOS

3.0000 g., 0.7200 Silver 0.0694 oz. ASW, 19 mm. **Obv:** Head right **Rev:** Wheat stalks divide value

Date	Mintage	F	VF	XF	Unc	BU
1954(u)	10,000,000	1.25	1.75	2.50	5.00	—

KM# 44 20 CENTESIMOS

1.4000 g., Aluminum **Obv:** Head right **Rev:** Value within wreath **Note:** Medal rotation.

Date	Mintage	F	VF	XF	Unc	BU
1965So	40,000,000	0.15	0.20	0.35	1.00	—

KM# 40 25 CENTESIMOS

3.0000 g., Copper-Nickel **Obv:** 'HP' below bust **Rev:** Radiant sun peeking out above arms within wreath, value divides circle of stars **Note:** Medal rotation.

Date	Mintage	F	VF	XF	Unc	BU
1960	48,000,000	0.20	0.35	0.50	1.00	—
1960 Proof	—	Value: 80.00				

KM# 22 50 CENTESIMOS

12.5000 g., 0.9000 Silver 0.3617 oz. ASW

Date	Mintage	F	VF	XF	Unc	BU
1916	400,000	8.50	20.00	50.00	300	—
1917	5,600,000	6.50	12.00	30.00	150	—

KM# 31 50 CENTESIMOS

7.0000 g., 0.7000 Silver 0.1575 oz. ASW **Obv:** Head right **Rev:** Date below value

Date	Mintage	F	VF	XF	Unc	BU
1943So	10,800,000	BV	2.75	4.75	12.00	—

KM# 41 50 CENTESIMOS

Copper-Nickel **Obv:** Artigas bust right, 'HP' below **Rev:** Radiant sun peeking out above arms within wreath, value divides circle of stars **Note:** Medal rotation.

Date	Mintage	F	VF	XF	Unc	BU
1960	18,000,000	0.20	0.50	1.00	2.00	—
1960 Proof	—	Value: 80.00				

KM# 45 50 CENTESIMOS

Aluminum **Obv:** Artigas head right **Rev:** Value within wreath **Note:** Medal rotation.

Date	Mintage	F	VF	XF	Unc	BU
1965So	50,000,000	0.15	0.25	0.40	1.00	—

KM# 23 PESO

25.0000 g., 0.9000 Silver 0.7234 oz. ASW **Obv:** Radiant sun peeking out above arms within wreath **Rev:** Bust left

Date	Mintage	F	VF	XF	Unc	BU
1917	2,000,000	12.00	20.00	50.00	250	—

KM# 30 PESO

9.0000 g., 0.7200 Silver 0.2083 oz. ASW **Obv:** Artigas head right **Rev:** Puma walking left, sunrays behind

Date	Mintage	F	VF	XF	Unc	BU
1942So	9,000,000	BV	4.50	10.00	40.00	—

KM# 42 PESO

Copper-Nickel **Obv:** Artigas head right **Rev:** Radiant sun peeking out above arms within wreath, value divides circle of stars **Note:** Medal rotation.

Date	Mintage	F	VF	XF	Unc	BU
1960	8,000,000	0.25	0.50	0.75	2.00	—
1960 Proof	—	Value: 75.00				

KM# 46 PESO

Aluminum-Bronze **Obv:** Artigas head right **Rev:** Radiant sun peeking out above arms within wreath, value divides circle of stars **Note:** Medal rotation.

Date	Mintage	F	VF	XF	Unc	BU
1965So	60,000,000	—	0.15	0.35	1.00	—
1965So Proof	25	Value: 65.00				

KM# 49 PESO

Nickel-Brass, 17.3 mm. **Obv:** Artigas head right **Rev:** Flower and value **Note:** Medal rotation.

Date	Mintage	F	VF	XF	Unc	BU
1968So	103,200,000	—	—	0.15	0.75	—
1968So Proof	50	Value: 50.00				

KM# 52 PESO

Aluminum-Brass **Obv:** Radiant sun with face **Rev:** Flower and value **Note:** Medal rotation.

Date	Mintage	F	VF	XF	Unc	BU
1969So	51,800,000	—	—	0.15	0.75	—

KM# 47 5 PESOS

Aluminum-Bronze **Obv:** Artigas head right **Rev:** Radiant sun peeking out above arms within wreath, value divides circle of stars **Note:** Medal rotation.

Date	Mintage	F	VF	XF	Unc	BU
1965So	18,000,000	0.20	0.30	0.50	1.00	—
1965So Proof	25	Value: 75.00				

KM# 50 5 PESOS

3.0000 g., Nickel-Brass **Obv:** Artigas head right **Rev:** Flower and value **Note:** Medal rotation.

Date	Mintage	F	VF	XF	Unc	BU
1968So	42,680,000	0.10	0.20	0.30	0.40	—
1968So Proof	50	Value: 65.00				

KM# 53 5 PESOS

Aluminum-Bronze **Obv:** Radiant sun with face **Rev:** Flower and value **Note:** Medal rotation.

Date	Mintage	F	VF	XF	Unc	BU
1969So	42,320,000	—	—	0.10	0.30	—

KM# 43 10 PESOS

12.5000 g., 0.9000 Silver 0.3617 oz. ASW **Subject:** Sesquicentennial of Revolution Against Spain **Obv:** M.G. Rizzello bust right with hat **Rev:** Value within wreath

Date	Mintage	F	VF	XF	Unc	BU
1961	3,000,000	—	BV	9.00	8.00	10.00
1961 Proof	—	Value: 600				

KM# 48 10 PESOS

Aluminum-Bronze **Obv:** Artigas head right **Rev:** Radiant sun peeking out above arms within wreath, value divides circle of stars **Note:** Medal rotation.

Date	Mintage	F	VF	XF	Unc	BU
1965So	18,000,000	0.15	0.20	0.35	1.00	—

KM# 51 10 PESOS

Nickel-Brass, 23 mm. **Obv:** Artigas head right **Rev:** Flower and value **Note:** Medal rotation.

Date	Mintage	F	VF	XF	Unc	BU
1968So	90,000,000	0.15	0.20	0.35	0.65	—
1968So Proof	50	Value: 80.00				

KM# 54 10 PESOS

4.1000 g., Aluminum-Bronze, 23 mm. **Obv:** Radiant sun with face **Rev:** Flower and value **Note:** Medal rotation.

Date	Mintage	F	VF	XF	Unc	BU
1969So	10,000,000	0.15	0.20	0.35	0.65	—

KM# 56 20 PESOS

Copper-Nickel **Obv:** Radiant sun peeking out above arms within wreath **Rev:** Spears of wheat and value **Note:** Medal rotation.

Date	Mintage	F	VF	XF	Unc	BU
1970So	50,000,000	0.15	0.25	0.40	0.75	—
1970So Proof	—	Value: 80.00				

KM# 57 50 PESOS

Copper-Nickel **Obv:** Radiant sun peeking out above arms within wreath **Rev:** Spears of wheat and value **Note:** Medal rotation.

Date	Mintage	F	VF	XF	Unc	BU
1970So	20,000,000	0.20	0.40	0.60	1.50	—
1970So Proof	—	Value: 80.00				

KM# 58 50 PESOS

5.2000 g., Nickel-Brass **Subject:** Centennial - Birth of Rodo **Obv:** Rodo facing **Rev:** Feather, value and date **Note:** Medal rotation.

Date	Mintage	F	VF	XF	Unc	BU
1971So	15,000,000	0.20	0.50	1.00	2.00	—

KM# 59 100 PESOS

8.0000 g., Copper-Nickel **Obv:** Artigas head 1/4 left **Rev:** Value, date and sprig **Note:** Coin rotation.

Date	Mintage	F	VF	XF	Unc	BU
1973Mx	20,000,000	0.25	0.50	1.00	2.50	—

REFORM COINAGE

1000 Old Pesos = 1 Nuevo (New) Peso

KM# 71 CENTESIMO

1.0000 g., Aluminum, 19 mm. **Obv:** Radiant sun with face **Rev:** Value in front of supine wheat stalk **Shape:** 12-sided **Note:** Medal rotation.

Date	Mintage	F	VF	XF	Unc	BU
1977So	10,000,000	—	—	0.15	0.25	—

KM# 72 2 CENTESIMOS

Aluminum, 21 mm. **Obv:** Radiant sun with face **Rev:** Value in front of supine wheat stalk **Shape:** 12-sided **Note:** Medal rotation.

Date	Mintage	F	VF	XF	Unc	BU
1977So	17,000,000	—	—	0.15	0.25	—
1978So	3,000,000	—	—	0.15	0.25	—

KM# 73 5 CENTESIMOS

Aluminum, 23 mm. **Obv:** Steer left **Rev:** Value in front of supine wheat stalk **Shape:** 12-sided **Note:** Medal rotation.

Date	Mintage	F	VF	XF	Unc	BU
1977So	11,000,000	—	—	0.15	0.50	—
1978So	19,000,000	—	—	0.15	0.50	—

KM# 66 10 CENTESIMOS

3.1000 g., Aluminum-Bronze, 19 mm. **Obv:** Horse left **Rev:** Value flanked by sprigs **Shape:** 12-sided **Note:** Medal rotation.

Date	Mintage	F	VF	XF	Unc	BU
1976So	127,400,000	—	—	0.30	0.80	1.50
1976So Proof	—	—	—	—	—	—
1977So	12,700,000	—	—	0.35	0.85	1.50
1978So	19,900,000	—	—	0.35	0.85	1.50
1981So	—	—	—	0.35	0.85	1.50

KM# 67 20 CENTESIMOS

5.1000 g., Aluminum-Bronze, 22 mm. **Obv:** Small building on top of hill **Rev:** Value flanked by sprigs **Shape:** 12-sided **Note:** Medal rotation.

Date	Mintage	F	VF	XF	Unc	BU
1976So	40,000,000	—	—	0.20	0.45	0.85
1976So Proof	—	—	—	—	—	—
1977So	4,700,000	—	—	0.20	0.60	1.00
1978So	15,300,000	—	—	0.20	0.45	0.85
1981So	—	—	—	0.20	0.45	0.85

KM# 68 50 CENTESIMOS

7.0000 g., Aluminum-Bronze, 25.5 mm. **Obv:** Scale **Rev:** Value flanked by sprigs **Shape:** 12-sided

Date	Mintage	F	VF	XF	Unc	BU
1976So	30,000,000	—	—	0.20	0.50	1.00
1976So Proof	—	—	—	—	—	—
1977So	9,800,000	—	—	0.20	0.50	1.00
1981So	200,000	—	—	0.25	0.60	1.25

KM# 69 NUEVO PESO

11.1000 g., Aluminum-Bronze, 30 mm. **Obv:** Head of Jose Gervasio Artigas left **Rev:** Value in front of supine wheat stalk **Edge:** Plain **Shape:** 12-sided **Note:** Medal rotation.

Date	Mintage	F	VF	XF	Unc	BU
1976So	65,540,000	—	—	0.30	0.60	1.25
1976So Proof	—	—	—	—	—	—
1977So	7,360,000	—	—	0.30	0.65	1.45
1978So	27,100,000	—	—	0.30	0.65	1.45

KM# 74 NUEVO PESO

5.9000 g., Copper-Nickel, 24 mm. **Obv:** Radiant sun peeking over arms within wreath **Rev:** Flower and value **Note:** Medal rotation.

Date	Mintage	F	VF	XF	Unc	BU
1980So	50,000,000	—	0.20	0.35	0.65	1.00

KM# 95 NUEVO PESO

Stainless Steel **Obv:** Radiant sun **Rev:** Value within wreath **Note:** Medal rotation.

Date	Mintage	F	VF	XF	Unc	BU
1989	—	—	—	0.15	0.35	0.65

KM# 77 2 NUEVO PESOS

7.1000 g., Copper-Nickel-Zinc, 25 mm. **Subject:** World Food Day **Obv:** Wheat stalks divide date and country name **Rev:** Value **Edge:** Plain **Shape:** 12-sided

Date	Mintage	F	VF	XF	Unc	BU
1981	95,000,000	—	0.25	0.50	1.00	1.50

KM# 65 5 NUEVO PESOS

14.4000 g., Copper-Nickel-Aluminum **Subject:** 150th Anniversary - Revolutionary Movement **Obv:** Artigas head facing within square above inscription **Rev:** Upright design **Note:** Medal rotation.

Date	Mintage	F	VF	XF	Unc	BU
ND(1975)So	3,000,000	0.50	0.75	1.25	3.50	5.00

KM# 70 5 NUEVO PESOS

Copper-Aluminum **Subject:** 250th Anniversary - Founding of Montevideo **Obv:** Head facing to left of value **Rev:** Crowned shield within wreath **Note:** Medal rotation.

Date	Mintage	F	VF	XF	Unc	BU
1976So	300,000	0.75	1.00	1.50	4.00	5.50

KM# 75 5 NUEVO PESOS

7.9000 g., Copper-Nickel, 26.15 mm. **Obv:** National flag **Rev:** Flower and value **Note:** Medal rotation.

Date	Mintage	F	VF	XF	Unc	BU
1980So	50,000,000	—	0.20	0.40	1.50	2.00
1981So	—	—	0.20	0.40	1.50	2.00

KM# 92 5 NUEVO PESOS

Stainless Steel **Obv:** Radiant sun **Rev:** Value and date within wreath **Note:** Medal rotation.

Date	Mintage	F	VF	XF	Unc	BU
1989	65,000,000	—	—	0.15	0.35	0.65

KM# 79 10 NUEVO PESOS

9.8000 g., Copper-Nickel, 28 mm. **Obv:** Bust of Jose Gervasio Artigas half left **Rev:** Flower and value **Note:** Medal rotation.

Date	Mintage	F	VF	XF	Unc	BU
1981So	—	—	0.20	0.50	1.75	2.25

KM# 93 10 NUEVO PESOS

Stainless Steel **Obv:** Radiant sun **Rev:** Value and date within wreath **Note:** Medal rotation.

Date	Mintage	F	VF	XF	Unc	BU
1989	79,000,000	—	—	0.20	0.45	0.75

KM# 94 50 NUEVO PESOS

4.7000 g., Stainless Steel **Obv:** Radiant sun **Rev:** Value and date within wreath **Note:** Medal rotation.

Date	Mintage	F	VF	XF	Unc	BU
1989	—	—	—	0.20	0.50	0.85

KM# 96 100 NUEVO PESOS

Stainless Steel **Obv:** Gaucho with hat right **Rev:** Value and date within wreath **Note:** Medal rotation.

Date	Mintage	F	VF	XF	Unc	BU
1989	—	—	—	0.35	0.75	1.50

KM# 97 200 NUEVO PESOS

Copper-Nickel **Obv:** Unchained Liberty **Rev:** Value and date within wreath **Note:** Medal rotation.

Date	Mintage	F	VF	XF	Unc	BU
1989	—	—	—	—	1.50	2.50

KM# 98 500 NUEVO PESOS

Copper Nickel **Obv:** Bust of Jose Gervasio Artigas half right **Rev:** Value and date within wreath **Note:** Medal rotation.

Date	Mintage	F	VF	XF	Unc	BU
1989	—	—	—	—	3.00	4.50

REFORM COINAGE

March 1993

1,000 Nuevos Pesos = 1 Uruguayan Peso; 100 Centesimos = 1 Uruguayan Peso (UYP)

KM# 102 10 CENTESIMOS

1.6900 g., Stainless Steel, 14.48 mm. **Obv:** Artigas head right **Rev:** Value, date and sprig **Edge:** Plain **Note:** Coin rotation.

Date	Mintage	F	VF	XF	Unc	BU
1994	—	—	—	0.25	0.50	0.65

KM# 105 20 CENTESIMOS

Stainless Steel **Obv:** Artigas head right **Rev:** Value, date and sprig **Note:** Coin rotation.

Date	Mintage	F	VF	XF	Unc	BU
1994	—	—	—	0.30	0.60	0.75

KM# 106 50 CENTESIMOS

2.9400 g., Stainless Steel, 20.97 mm. **Obv:** Bust of Artigas right **Obv. Legend:** REPUBLICA ORIENTAL DEL URUGUAY **Rev:** Value, date and sprig **Edge:** Plain **Note:** Coin rotation.

Date	Mintage	F	VF	XF	Unc	BU
1994	—	—	—	0.35	0.75	1.00
1998	—	—	—	0.35	0.75	1.00
2002	—	—	—	0.35	0.75	1.00
2005	—	—	—	0.35	0.75	1.00

KM# 103.1 UN PESO URUGUAYO

3.5000 g., Aluminum-Bronze, 20 mm. **Obv:** Artigas head right **Rev:** Value and date **Note:** Left point of bust shoulder points at "U" in Republic.

Date	Mintage	F	VF	XF	Unc	BU
1994	—	—	—	—	0.60	1.00

KM# 103.2 UN PESO URUGUAYO

3.5000 g., Aluminum-Bronze, 19.95 mm. **Obv:** Bust of Artigas right **Obv. Legend:** REPUBLICA ORIENTAL DEL URUGUAY **Rev:** Value and date **Edge:** Plain **Note:** Medal rotation; left point of bust shoulder points at "P" in Republic.

Date	Mintage	F	VF	XF	Unc	BU
1998So	—	—	—	—	0.50	0.75
2005So	—	—	—	—	0.50	0.75

KM# 104.1 2 PESOS URUGUAYOS

4.5000 g., Aluminum-Bronze, 23 mm. **Obv:** Artigas head right **Rev:** Value and date **Note:** Medal rotation. Left point of bust shoulder points at "U" in "Republic".

Date	Mintage	F	VF	XF	Unc	BU
1994	—	—	—	0.75	1.50	2.00

KM# 104.2 2 PESOS URUGUAYOS

4.4900 g., Aluminum-Bronze, 23.0 mm. **Obv:** Bust of Artigas right **Obv. Legend:** REPUBLICA ORIENTAL DEL URUGUAY **Rev:** Value and date **Edge:** Plain **Note:** Medal rotation. Left point of bust shoulder points at "P" in "Republic".

Date	Mintage	F	VF	XF	Unc	BU
1998So	—	—	—	0.75	1.50	2.00
Note: Mint mark under bust						
2007So	—	—	—	0.75	1.50	2.00

KM# 120.1 5 PESOS URUGUAYOS

6.2400 g., Aluminum-Bronze, 26 mm. **Obv:** Bust of Antigas right **Obv. Legend:** REPUBLICA ORIENTAL DEL URUGUAY **Rev:** Value **Edge:** Plain **Note:** Left point of bust shoulder points at "U" in "Republic".

Date	Mintage	F	VF	XF	Unc	BU
2003	—	—	—	—	2.50	3.00

KM# 120.2 5 PESOS URUGUAYOS

6.3000 g., Aluminum-Bronze, 26 mm. **Obv:** Bust of Antigas right **Obv. Legend:** REPUBLICA ORIENTAL DEL URUGUAY • **Rev:** Value, date **Note:** Left point of bust shoulder points at "P" in "Republic".

Date	Mintage	F	VF	XF	Unc	BU
2005So	—	—	—	—	2.50	3.00

KM# 121 10 PESOS URUGUAYOS

10.4000 g., Bi-Metallic Aluminum-Bronze center in Stainless Steel ring, 28 mm. **Obv:** Artigas head right within circle **Rev:** Value above signature within circle **Edge:** Plain

Date	Mintage	F	VF	XF	Unc	BU
2000	—	—	—	—	3.50	5.00
2000 (RCM)	—	—	—	—	3.50	5.00
Note: 5-pointed star to each side of date, issued 2006						

The Republic of Uzbekistan (formerly the Uzbek S.S.R.), is bordered on the north by Kazakhstan, to the east by Kirghizia and Tajikistan, on the south by Afghanistan and on the west by Turkmenistan. The republic is comprised of the regions of Andizhan, Bukhara, Dzhizak, Ferghana, Kashkadar, Khorezm (Khiva), Namangan, Navoi, Samarkand, Surkhan-Darya, Syr-Darya, Tashkent and the Karakalpak Autonomous Republic. It has an area of 172,741 sq. mi. (447,400 sq. km.) and a population of 20.3 million. Capital: Tashkent.

Crude oil, natural gas, coal, copper, and gold deposits make up the chief resources, while intensive farming, based on artificial irrigation, provides an abundance of cotton.

On the eve of WW I, Khiva and Bukhara were enclaves within a Russian Turkestan divided into five provinces or oblasti. The czarist government did not attempt to Russify the indigenous Turkic or Tajik populations. The revolution of March 1917 created a confused situation in the area. In Tashkent there was a Turkestan committee of the provisional government; a Communist-controlled council of workers', soldiers' and peasants' deputies; also a Moslem Turkic movement, Shuro-i-Islamiya, and a young Turkestan or Jaddidi (Renovation) party. The last named party claimed full political autonomy for Turkestan and the abolition of the emirate of Bukhara and the khanate of Khiva. After the Communist *coup d'etat in* Petrograd, the council of people's commissars on Nov. 24 (Dec. 7), 1917, published an appeal to "all toiling Moslems in Russia and in the east" proclaiming their right to build their national life "freely and unhindered". In response, the Moslem and Jaddidi organizations in Dec. 1917 convoked a national congress in Khokand, which appointed a provisional government headed by Mustafa Chokayev (or Chokaigolu; 1890-1941) and resolved to elect a constituent assembly to decide whether Turkestan should remain within a Russian federal state or proclaim its independence. In the spring of 1919 a Red army group defeated Kolchak and in September its commander, M.V. Frunze, arrived in Tashkent with V.V.Kuibyshev as political commissar. The Communists were still much too weak in Turkestan to proclaim the country part of Soviet Russia. Faizullah Khojayev organized a young Bukhara movement, which on Sept. 14, 1920, proclaimed the dethronement of Emir Mir Alim. Bukhara was then made a S.S.R. In 1920 the Tashkent Communist government declared war on Junaid, who took to flight, and Khiva became another S.S.R. In Oct. 1921, Enver Pasha, the former leader of the young Turks, appeared in Bukhara and assumed command of the Basmachi movement. In Aug. 1922 he was forced to retreat into Tajikistan and died on Aug. 4, in a battle near Baljuvan. Khiva concluded a treaty of alliance with the Russian S.F.S.R. in Sept. 1920, and Bukhara followed suit in March 1921. Theoretically, a Turkestan Autonomous Soviet Socialist Republic had existed since May 1, 1918; in 1920 this "Turk republic", as it was called, was proclaimed part of the R.S.F.S.R. On Sept. 18, 1924, the Uzbek and Turkmen peoples were authorized to form S.S.R.'s of their own, and the Kazakhs, Kirghiz, and Tajiks to form autonomous S.S.R.'s. On Oct.27, 1924, the Uzbek and Turkmen S.S.R. were officially constituted and the former was formally accepted on Jan.15, 1925, as a member of the U.S.S.R. Tajikistan was an autonomous soviet republic within Uzbekistan until Dec.5, 1929, when it became a S.S.R. On Dec. 5, 1936, incorporating the Kara-Kalpak A.S.S.R., which had belonged to Kazakhstan until 1930 and afterward had come under direct control of the R.S.F.S.R, increased the Uzbekistan territory.

On June 20, 1990 the Uzbek Supreme Soviet adopted a declaration of sovereignty, and in Aug. 1991, following an unsuccessful coup, declared itself independent as the "Republic of Uzbekistan", which was confirmed by referendum in Dec. That same month Uzbekistan became a member of the CIS.

MONETARY SYSTEM

100 Tiyin = 1 Som

REPUBLIC

STANDARD COINAGE

KM# 1.1 TIYIN

1.7500 g., Brass Clad Steel, 16.9 mm. **Obv:** Arms within wreath below stars **Rev:** Value and date flanked by sprigs **Edge:** Plain

Date	Mintage	F	VF	XF	Unc	BU
1994	—	—	—	—	0.30	—

KM# 1.2 TIYIN

1.7500 g., Brass Clad Steel, 16.9 mm. **Obv:** Arms within wreath below stars **Rev:** Value and date flanked by sprigs **Edge:** Plain

Date	Mintage	F	VF	XF	Unc	BU
1994	—	—	—	—	0.30	—

KM# 2.1 3 TIYIN

2.7000 g., Brass Plated Steel, 19.9 mm. **Obv:** Arms within wreath below stars **Rev:** Value and date flanked by sprigs **Edge:** Reeded

Date	Mintage	F	VF	XF	Unc	BU
1994	—	—	—	—	3.00	—

KM# 2.2 3 TIYIN

2.7000 g., Brass Plated Steel, 19.9 mm. **Obv:** Arms within wreath below stars **Rev:** Value and date flanked by sprigs **Edge:** Reeded

Date	Mintage	F	VF	XF	Unc	BU
1994	—	—	—	—	1.00	—

KM# 3.1 5 TIYIN

3.4000 g., Brass Plated Steel, 21.4 mm. **Obv:** Arms within wreath below stars **Rev:** Value and date flanked by sprigs **Edge:** Reeded

Date	Mintage	F	VF	XF	Unc	BU
1994	—	—	—	—	2.00	—

KM# 3.2 5 TIYIN

3.4000 g., Brass Plated Steel, 21.4 mm. **Obv:** Arms within wreath below stars **Rev:** Value and date flanked by sprigs **Edge:** Reeded

Date	Mintage	F	VF	XF	Unc	BU
1994	—	—	—	—	0.50	—

KM# 4.1 10 TIYIN

2.8500 g., Nickel Clad Steel, 18.7 mm. **Obv:** Arms within wreath below stars **Rev:** Value and date flanked by sprigs **Edge:** Reeded **Note:** Two varieties of sunray arrangements exist; die varieties exist with slightly larger or smaller denomination, plain rim.

Date	Mintage	F	VF	XF	Unc	BU
1994	—	—	—	—	0.60	—
1994PM Rare	—	—	—	—	—	—

KM# 4.2 10 TIYIN

2.8500 g., Nickel Clad Steel, 18.7 mm. **Obv:** Arms within wreath below stars **Rev:** Value and date flanked by sprigs **Edge:** Reeded **Note:** Beaded rim.

Date	Mintage	F	VF	XF	Unc	BU
1994	—	—	—	—	5.00	—

KM# 5.1 20 TIYIN

4.0000 g., Nickel Clad Steel, 22 mm. **Obv:** Arms within wreath below stars **Rev:** Date and value flanked by sprigs **Edge Lettering:** Cyrillic denomination twice

Date	Mintage	F	VF	XF	Unc	BU
1994	—	—	—	—	0.75	—

KM# 5.5 20 TIYIN

4.0000 g., Nickel Clad Steel, 22 mm. **Obv:** Arms within wreath below stars **Rev:** Date and large denomination flanked by sprigs **Edge Lettering:** Cyrillic

Date	Mintage	F	VF	XF	Unc	BU
1994	—	—	—	—	0.75	—

KM# 5.2 20 TIYIN

4.0000 g., Nickel Clad Steel, 22 mm. **Obv:** Arms within wreath below stars **Rev:** Date and value flanked by sprigs **Note:** Two sun ray varieties exist, varieties exist with wide and narrow edge lettering.

Date	Mintage	F	VF	XF	Unc	BU
1994	—	—	—	—	1.00	—
1994PM Rare	—	—	—	—	—	—

KM# 5.3 20 TIYIN

4.0000 g., Nickel Clad Steel, 22 mm. **Obv:** Arms within wreath below stars **Rev:** Date and value flanked by sprigs **Edge:** Lettering in Cyrillic **Note:** Two varieties of sunray arrangements exist.

Date	Mintage	F	VF	XF	Unc	BU
1994	—	—	—	—	0.75	—

KM# 5.4 20 TIYIN

4.0000 g., Nickel Clad Steel, 22 mm. **Obv:** Arms within wreath below stars **Rev:** Date and value flanked by sprigs **Edge:** Lettering in Cyrillic

Date	Mintage	F	VF	XF	Unc	BU
1994 Scarce	—	—	—	—	20.00	—

KM# 6.1 50 TIYIN

4.8000 g., Nickel Clad Steel, 23.9 mm. **Obv:** Arms within wreath below stars **Rev:** Small denomination and date flanked by sprigs **Edge:** Lettering in Cyrillic **Note:** 2 varieties of sunray arrangements exist; all coins show orthographic error in 1st letter of "ellik" within edge inscription.

Date	Mintage	F	VF	XF	Unc	BU
1994	—	—	—	—	1.00	—
1994PM	—	—	—	—	50.00	—

KM# 6.2 50 TIYIN

4.8000 g., Nickel Clad Steel, 23.9 mm. **Obv:** Arms within wreath below stars **Rev:** Large denomination, date flanked by sprigs **Edge:** Lettering in Cyrillic **Note:** All coins show orthographic error in 1st letter of "ellik" within edge inscription.

Date	Mintage	F	VF	XF	Unc	BU
1994	—	—	—	—	1.00	—

KM# 8 SOM

2.8000 g., Nickel Clad Steel **Obv:** Arms within wreath below stars **Rev:** Value and date flanked by sprigs **Note:** Edge varieties exist.

Date	Mintage	F	VF	XF	Unc	BU
1997	—	—	—	—	1.35	—
1998 Rare	—	—	—	—	—	—
1999	—	—	—	—	1.35	—
2000	—	—	—	—	1.35	—

KM# 12 SOM

2.8300 g., Nickel-Clad Steel, 18.8 mm. **Obv:** National arms **Rev:** Value and map **Edge:** Reeded

Date	Mintage	F	VF	XF	Unc	BU
2000	—	—	—	—	1.00	1.25

KM# 9 5 SOM

4.0000 g., Nickel Clad Steel **Obv:** Arms within wreath below stars **Rev:** Value and date flanked by sprigs

Date	Mintage	F	VF	XF	Unc	BU
1997	—	—	—	—	1.50	—
Note: Edge varieties exist						
1998 Rare	—	—	—	—	—	—
1999	—	—	—	—	1.50	—

KM# 13 5 SOM
3.3500 g., Brass Plated Steel, 21.2 mm. **Obv:** National arms **Rev:** Value and map **Edge:** Plain

Date	Mintage	F	VF	XF	Unc	BU
2001	—	—	—	—	1.35	1.75

Note: 2 reverse map varieties known

KM# 10 10 SOM
4.7000 g., Nickel Clad Steel **Obv:** Arms within wreath below stars **Rev:** Value and date flanked by sprigs

Date	Mintage	F	VF	XF	Unc	BU
1997	—	—	—	—	2.00	—
Note: Edge varieties exist						
1998 Rare	—	—	—	—	—	—
1999	—	—	—	—	2.00	—
2000	—	—	—	—	2.00	—

KM# 14 10 SOM
2.7100 g., Nickel-Clad Steel, 19.75 mm. **Obv:** National arms **Rev:** Value and map **Edge:** Plain

Date	Mintage	F	VF	XF	Unc	BU
2001	—	—	—	—	2.00	2.50

Note: 2 reverse map varieties exist

VANUATU

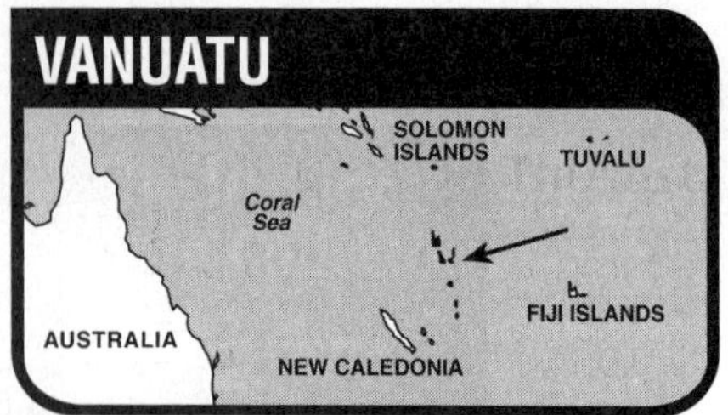

The Republic of Vanuatu, formerly New Hebrides Condominium, a group of islands located in the South Pacific 500 miles (800 km.) west of Fiji, were under the joint sovereignty of Great Britain and France. The islands have an area of 5,700 sq. mi. (14,760 sq. km.) and a population of 165,000, mainly Melanesians of mixed blood. Capital: Port-Vila. The volcanic and coral islands, while malarial land subject to frequent earthquakes, are extremely fertile, and produce copra, coffee, tropical fruits and timber for export.

The New Hebrides were discovered by Portuguese navigator Pedro de Quiros (sailing under orders by the King of Spain) in 1606, visited by French explorer Bougainville in 1768, and named by British navigator Capt. James Cook in 1774. Ships of all nations converged on the islands to trade for sandalwood, prompting France and Britain to relinquish their individual claims and declare the islands a neutral zone in 1878. The New Hebrides were placed under the control of a mixed Anglo-French commission of naval officers during the native uprisings of 1887, and established as a condominium under the joint sovereignty of France and Great Britain in 1906.

Vanuatu became an independent republic within the Commonwealth in July 1980. A president is Head of State and the Prime Minister is Head of Government.

MINT MARK
(a) - Paris, privy marks only

MONETARY SYSTEM
Francs until 1983
Vatu to Present

REPUBLIC

STANDARD COINAGE

KM# 3 VATU
1.9900 g., Nickel-Brass, 16.95 mm. **Obv:** National arms **Rev:** Shell and value **Edge:** Plain

Date	Mintage	F	VF	XF	Unc	BU
1983	—	—	—	0.10	0.50	0.75
1983 Proof	—	Value: 1.00				
1990	—	—	—	0.10	0.50	0.75
1999	—	—	—	0.10	0.50	0.75

KM# 4 2 VATU
3.0000 g., Nickel-Brass, 20 mm. **Obv:** National arms **Rev:** Shell and value **Edge:** Plain

Date	Mintage	F	VF	XF	Unc	BU
1983	—	—	—	0.15	0.50	1.00
1983 Proof	—	Value: 1.50				
1990	—	—	—	0.15	0.50	1.00
1995	—	—	—	0.15	0.50	1.00

KM# 5 5 VATU
4.1000 g., Nickel-Brass, 23.5 mm. **Obv:** National arms **Rev:** Shell and value **Edge:** Plain

Date	Mintage	F	VF	XF	Unc	BU
1983	—	—	—	0.20	0.75	1.50
1983 Proof	—	Value: 1.75				
1990	—	—	—	0.20	0.75	1.50
1995	—	—	—	0.20	0.75	1.50

KM# 6 10 VATU
6.1000 g., Copper-Nickel, 23.95 mm. **Series:** F.A.O. **Obv:** National arms **Rev:** Crab and value, palm trees **Edge:** Plain

Date	Mintage	F	VF	XF	Unc	BU
1983	—	—	—	0.25	1.00	2.00
1983 Proof	—	Value: 2.00				
1990	—	—	—	0.25	1.00	2.00
1995	—	—	—	0.25	1.00	2.00

KM# 7 20 VATU
10.2000 g., Copper-Nickel, 28.45 mm. **Series:** F.A.O. **Obv:** National arms **Rev:** Crab, value, palm trees **Edge:** Reeded **Note:** Similar 10 Vatu, KM#6.

Date	Mintage	F	VF	XF	Unc	BU
1983	—	—	—	0.35	1.50	2.50
1983 Proof	—	Value: 3.00				
1990	—	—	—	0.35	1.50	2.50
1995	—	—	—	0.35	1.50	2.50

KM# 1 50 VATU
15.0000 g., Nickel, 32.9 mm. **Subject:** 1st Anniversary of Independence **Obv:** National arms **Rev:** Figures working in fields

Date	Mintage	F	VF	XF	Unc	BU
1981	—	—	—	0.75	2.00	3.00

VATICAN CITY

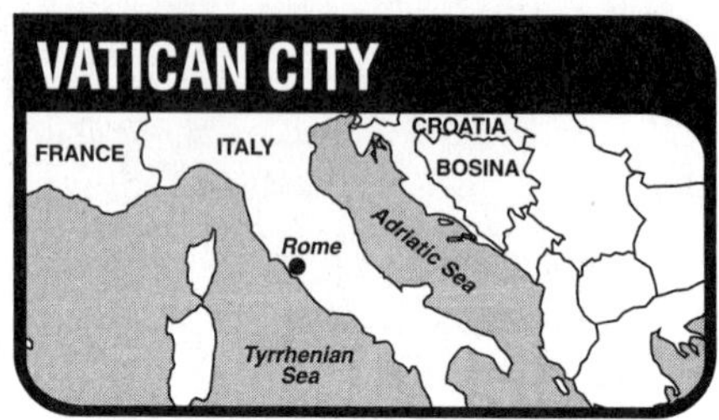

The State of the Vatican City, a papal state on the right bank of the Tiber River within the boundaries of Rome, has an area of 0.17 sq. mi. (0.44 sq. km.) and a population of *775. Capital: Vatican City.

Vatican City State, comprising the Vatican, St. Peter's, extra-territorial right to Castel Gandolfo and 13 buildings throughout Rome, is all that remains of the extensive Papal States over which the Pope exercised temporal power in central Italy. During the struggle for Italian unification, the Papal States, including Rome, were forcibly incorporated into the Kingdom of Italy in 1870. The resultant confrontation of crozier and sword remained unresolved until the signing of the Lateran Treaty, Feb. 11, 1929, between the Vatican and the Kingdom of Italy which recognized the independence and sovereignty of the State of the Vatican City, defined the relationship between the government and the church within Italy, and financially compensated the Holy See for the territorial losses from 1870.

Today the Pope exercises supreme legislative, executive and judicial power within the Vatican City, and the State of the Vatican City is recognized by many nations as an independent sovereign state under the temporal jurisdiction of the Pope, even to the extent of ambassadorial exchange. The Pope, is of course, the head of the Roman Catholic Church.

PONTIFFS
Pius XI, 1922-1939
Sede Vacante, Feb. 10 - Mar. 2, 1939
Pius XII, 1939-1958
Sede Vacante, Oct. 9 - 28, 1958
John XXIII, 1958-1963
Sede Vacante, June 3 - 21,1963
Paul VI, 1963-1978
Sede Vacante, Aug. 6 - 26, 1978
John Paul I, Aug. 26 - Sept. 28, 1978
Sede Vacante, Sept. 28 - Oct. 16, 1978
John Paul II, 1978-2005
Sede Vacante, April 2 - 19, 2005
Benedict XVI, 2005-

MINT MARK
Commencing 1981
R – Rome

MONETARY SYSTEM
100 Centesimi = 1 Lira (thru 2002)
100 Euro Cent = 1 Euro

DATING
Most Vatican coins indicate the regnal year of the pope preceded by the word *Anno* (or an abbreviation), even if the *anno domini* date is omitted.

CITY STATE

Pius XI

DECIMAL COINAGE

100 Centesimi = 1 Lira

KM# 1 5 CENTESIMI

Bronze **Obv:** Crowned shield divides date **Rev:** Olive branch divides value **Designer:** Aurelio Mistruzzi

Date	Mintage	F	VF	XF	Unc	BU
1929/VIII	10,000	—	7.50	12.50	30.00	—
1930/IX	100,000	—	5.00	7.50	15.00	—
1931/X	100,000	—	5.00	7.50	15.00	—
1932/XI	100,000	—	5.00	7.50	15.00	—
1934/XIII	100,000	—	5.00	7.50	15.00	—
1935/XIV	44,000	—	7.50	12.50	30.00	—
1936/XV	62,000	—	5.00	7.50	15.00	—
1937/XVI	62,000	—	5.00	7.50	15.00	—
1938/XVII Rare	—	—	—	—	—	—

KM# 11 5 CENTESIMI

Bronze, 20 mm. **Subject:** Jubilee **Obv:** Crowned shield flanked by date **Rev:** Olive branch divides value **Designer:** Aurelio Mistruzzi

Date	Mintage	F	VF	XF	Unc	BU
1933-34	100,000	—	7.50	12.50	30.00	—

KM# 2 10 CENTESIMI

Bronze **Obv:** Crowned shield divides date **Rev:** St. Peter bust right **Designer:** Aurelio Mistruzzi

Date	Mintage	F	VF	XF	Unc	BU
1929/VIII	10,000	—	7.50	12.50	30.00	—
1930/IX	90,000	—	5.00	7.50	15.00	—
1931/X	90,000	—	5.00	7.50	15.00	—
1932/XI	90,000	—	5.00	7.50	15.00	—
1934/XIII	90,000	—	5.00	7.50	15.00	—
1935/XIV	90,000	—	5.00	7.50	15.00	—
1936/XV	81,000	—	5.00	7.50	15.00	—
1937/XVI	81,000	—	5.00	7.50	15.00	—
1938/XVII	—	—	450	900	1,500	—

KM# 12 10 CENTESIMI

Bronze, 22 mm. **Subject:** Jubilee **Obv:** Crowned shield flanked by dates **Rev:** St. Peter bust right **Designer:** Aurelio Mistruzzi

Date	Mintage	F	VF	XF	Unc	BU
1933-34	90,000	—	7.50	12.50	30.00	—

KM# 3 20 CENTESIMI

Nickel **Obv:** Crowned Arms **Rev:** St. Paul bust left **Designer:** Aurelio Mistruzzi

Date	Mintage	F	VF	XF	Unc	BU
1929/VIII	10,000	—	7.50	12.50	30.00	—
1930/IX	80,000	—	5.00	7.50	15.00	—
1931/X	80,000	—	5.00	7.50	15.00	—
1932/XI	80,000	—	5.00	7.50	15.00	—
1934/XIII	80,000	—	5.00	7.50	15.00	—
1935/XIV	11,000	—	25.00	50.00	75.00	—

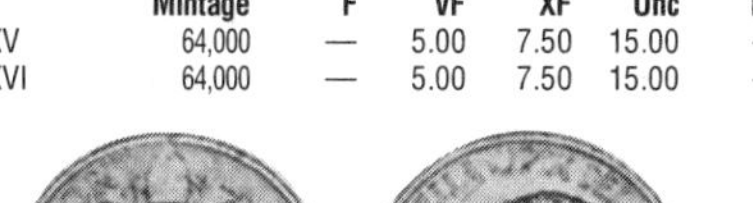

Date	Mintage	F	VF	XF	Unc	BU
1936/XV	64,000	—	5.00	7.50	15.00	—
1937/XVI	64,000	—	5.00	7.50	15.00	—

KM# 13 20 CENTESIMI

Nickel, 21 mm. **Subject:** Jubilee **Obv:** Crowned Arms **Rev:** St. Paul bust left **Designer:** Aurelio Mistruzzi

Date	Mintage	F	VF	XF	Unc	BU
1933-34	80,000	—	7.50	12.50	30.00	—

KM# 4 50 CENTESIMI

Nickel **Obv:** Crowned Arms **Rev:** Archangel Michael divides value **Designer:** Aurelio Mistruzzi

Date	Mintage	F	VF	XF	Unc	BU
1929/VIII	10,000	—	7.50	12.50	30.00	—
1930/IX	80,000	—	5.00	7.50	15.00	—
1931/X	80,000	—	5.00	7.50	15.00	—
1932/XI	80,000	—	5.00	7.50	15.00	—
1934/XIII	80,000	—	5.00	7.50	15.00	—
1935/XIV	14,000	—	6.00	15.00	30.00	—
1936/XV	52,000	—	5.00	7.50	15.00	—
1937/XVI	52,000	—	5.00	7.50	15.00	—

KM# 14 50 CENTESIMI

Nickel, 24 mm. **Subject:** Jubilee **Obv:** Crowned Arms **Rev:** Archangel Michael divides value **Designer:** Aurelio Mistruzzi

Date	Mintage	F	VF	XF	Unc	BU
1933-34	80,000	—	6.00	12.00	20.00	—

KM# 5 LIRA

Nickel **Obv:** Crowned Arms **Rev:** Virgin Mary standing on globe and crescent **Designer:** Aurelio Mistruzzi

Date	Mintage	F	VF	XF	Unc	BU
1929/VIII	10,000	—	7.50	12.50	30.00	—
1930/IX	80,000	—	5.00	7.50	15.00	—
1931/X	80,000	—	5.00	7.50	15.00	—
1932/XI	80,000	—	5.00	7.50	15.00	—
1934/XIII	80,000	—	5.00	7.50	15.00	—
1935/XIV	40,000	—	5.00	7.50	15.00	—
1936/XV	40,000	—	5.00	7.50	15.00	—
1937/XVI	70,000	—	5.00	7.50	15.00	—

KM# 15 LIRA

Nickel, 27 mm. **Subject:** Jubilee **Obv:** Crowned Arms **Rev:** Virgin Mary standing on globe and crescent **Designer:** Aurelio Mistruzzi **Note:** Enlargement of date area.

Date	Mintage	F	VF	XF	Unc	BU
1933-34	80,000	—	7.50	12.50	30.00	—

KM# 6 2 LIRE

Nickel, 29 mm. **Obv:** Crowned Arms **Rev:** Lamb on shoulders of young shepard **Designer:** Aurelio Mistruzzi

Date	Mintage	F	VF	XF	Unc	BU
1929/VIII	10,000	—	7.50	12.50	30.00	—
1930/IX	50,000	—	5.00	7.50	15.00	—
1931/X	50,000	—	5.00	7.50	15.00	—
1932/XI	50,000	—	5.00	7.50	15.00	—
1934/XIII	50,000	—	5.00	7.50	15.00	—
1935/XIV	70,000	—	5.00	7.50	15.00	—
1936/XV	40,000	—	5.00	7.50	15.00	—
1937/XVI	70,000	—	5.00	7.50	15.00	—

KM# 16 2 LIRE

Nickel, 30 mm. **Subject:** Jubilee **Obv:** Crowned Arms **Rev:** Lamb on shoulders of young shepard

Date	Mintage	F	VF	XF	Unc	BU
1933-34	50,000	—	5.00	7.50	15.00	—

KM# 7 5 LIRE

5.0000 g., 0.8350 Silver 0.1342 oz. ASW **Obv:** Bust left **Rev:** St. Peter in a boat **Designer:** Aurelio Mistruzzi

Date	Mintage	F	VF	XF	Unc	BU
1929/VIII	10,000	—	10.00	20.00	35.00	—
1930/IX	50,000	—	7.50	12.50	30.00	—
1931/X	50,000	—	7.50	12.50	30.00	—
1932/XI	50,000	—	7.50	12.50	30.00	—
1934/XIII	30,000	—	7.50	12.50	30.00	—
1935/XIV	20,000	—	10.00	20.00	35.00	—
1936/XV	40,000	—	7.50	12.50	30.00	—
1937/XVI	40,000	—	7.50	12.50	30.00	—

KM# 17 5 LIRE

5.0000 g., 0.8350 Silver 0.1342 oz. ASW, 23 mm. **Subject:** Jubilee **Obv:** Bust left **Rev:** St. Peter in a boat **Designer:** Aurelio Mistruzzi

Date	Mintage	F	VF	XF	Unc	BU
1933-34	50,000	—	10.00	20.00	35.00	—

KM# 8 10 LIRE

10.0000 g., 0.8350 Silver 0.2684 oz. ASW **Obv:** Bust left **Rev:** Mary, Queen of Peace holding infant **Designer:** Aurelio Mistruzzi

Date	Mintage	F	VF	XF	Unc	BU
1929/VIII	10,000	—	20.00	35.00	50.00	—
1930/IX	50,000	—	10.00	17.50	30.00	—
1931/X	50,000	—	10.00	17.50	30.00	—
1932/XI	50,000	—	10.00	17.50	30.00	—
1934/XIII	60,000	—	10.00	17.50	30.00	—
1935/XIV	50,000	—	10.00	17.50	30.00	—
1936/XV	40,000	—	10.00	17.50	30.00	—
1937/XVI	40,000	—	10.00	17.50	30.00	—

KM# 18 10 LIRE

10.0000 g., 0.8350 Silver 0.2684 oz. ASW, 27 mm. **Subject:** Jubilee **Obv:** Bust left **Rev:** Seated crowned figure of Mary, Queen of peace facing holding infant **Designer:** Aurelio Mistruzzi

Date	Mintage	F	VF	XF	Unc	BU
1933-34	50,000	—	10.00	17.50	30.00	—

KM# 9 100 LIRE

8.8000 g., 0.9000 Gold 0.2546 oz. AGW, 23.5 mm. **Obv:** Bust right **Rev:** Standing Jesus facing with child at feet **Designer:** Aurelio Mistruzzi

Date	Mintage	F	VF	XF	Unc	BU
1929/VIII	10,000	—	350	550	700	—
1930/IX	2,621	—	300	500	800	—
1931/X	3,343	—	BV	375	500	—
1932/XI	5,073	—	BV	375	500	—
1934/XIII	2,533	—	BV	375	500	—
1935/XIV	2,015	—	BV	375	500	—

KM# 19 100 LIRE

8.8000 g., 0.9000 Gold 0.2546 oz. AGW, 23.5 mm. **Subject:** Jubilee **Obv:** Bust right **Rev:** Standing Jesus facing with child at feet **Designer:** Aurelio Mistruzzi

Date	Mintage	F	VF	XF	Unc	BU
1933-34	23,000	—	BV	375	500	—

KM# 10 100 LIRE

5.1900 g., 0.9000 Gold 0.1502 oz. AGW, 20.5 mm. **Obv:** Bust right **Rev:** Standing Jesus facing with child at feet

Date	Mintage	F	VF	XF	Unc	BU
1936/XV	8,239	—	225	375	500	—
1937/XVI	2,000	—	—	2,000	3,000	—
1938 Rare	6	—	—	—	—	—

Sede Vacante

DECIMAL COINAGE

100 Centesimi = 1 Lira

KM# 20 5 LIRE

5.0000 g., 0.8350 Silver 0.1342 oz. ASW **Subject:** Sede Vacante **Obv:** Arms of Cardinal Pacelli **Rev:** Dove within 1/2 sun

Date	Mintage	F	VF	XF	Unc	BU
1939	40,000	—	15.00	30.00	45.00	—

KM# 21 10 LIRE

10.0000 g., 0.8350 Silver 0.2684 oz. ASW **Obv:** Arms of Cardinal Eugenio Pacelli **Rev:** Dove within 1/2 sun

Date	Mintage	F	VF	XF	Unc	BU
1939	30,000	—	20.00	35.00	50.00	—

Pius XII

DECIMAL COINAGE

100 Centesimi = 1 Lira

KM# 22 5 CENTESIMI

Aluminum-Bronze **Obv:** Crowned shield divides date

Date	Mintage	F	VF	XF	Unc	BU
1939/I	62,000	—	5.00	7.50	12.50	—
1940/II	62,000	—	5.00	7.50	12.50	—
1941/III	5,000	—	10.00	17.50	40.00	—

KM# 31 5 CENTESIMI

Brass **Obv:** Bust left **Rev:** Dove

Date	Mintage	F	VF	XF	Unc	BU
1942/IV	5,000	—	25.00	40.00	75.00	—
1943/V	1,000	—	35.00	60.00	95.00	—
1944/VI	1,000	—	45.00	65.00	110	—
1945/VII	1,000	—	45.00	65.00	110	—
1946/VIII	1,000	—	45.00	65.00	110	—

KM# 23 10 CENTESIMI

Aluminum-Bronze **Obv:** Crowned shield divides date **Rev:** St. Peter bust right **Rev. Designer:** Aurelio Mistruzzi

Date	Mintage	F	VF	XF	Unc	BU
1939/I	81,000	—	5.00	7.50	12.50	—
1940/II	81,000	—	5.00	7.50	12.50	—
1941/III	7,500	—	17.50	17.50	40.00	—

KM# 32 10 CENTESIMI

Brass **Obv:** Bust left **Rev:** Dove **Designer:** Aurelio Mistruzzi

Date	Mintage	F	VF	XF	Unc	BU
1942/IV	7,500	—	25.00	40.00	75.00	—
1943/V	1,000	—	40.00	60.00	110	—
1944/VI	1,000	—	50.00	75.00	125	—
1945/VII	1,000	—	50.00	75.00	125	—
1946/VIII	1,000	—	50.00	75.00	125	—

KM# 24 20 CENTESIMI

Nickel **Obv:** Crowned Arms **Rev:** St. Paul bust left **Rev. Designer:** Aurelio Mistruzzi

Date	Mintage	F	VF	XF	Unc	BU
1939/I	64,000	—	2.00	4.00	6.00	—

KM# 24a 20 CENTESIMI

Stainless Steel **Obv:** Crowned Arms **Rev:** St. Pual bust left

Date	Mintage	F	VF	XF	Unc	BU
1940/II	64,000	—	2.00	4.00	6.00	—
1941/III	125,000	—	2.00	4.00	6.00	—

KM# 33 20 CENTESIMI

Stainless Steel **Obv:** Crowned shield divides date and beaded circle **Rev:** Justice seated with tablets of the Law **Designer:** Aurelio Mistruzzi

Date	Mintage	F	VF	XF	Unc	BU
1942/IV	125,000	—	2.00	3.00	4.50	—
1943/V	1,000	—	50.00	75.00	125	—
1944/VI	1,000	—	50.00	75.00	125	—
1945/VII	1,000	—	50.00	75.00	125	—
1946/VIII	1,000	—	50.00	75.00	125	—

KM# 25 50 CENTESIMI

Nickel **Obv:** Crowned Arms **Rev:** Archangel Michael facing, divides value **Rev. Designer:** Aurelio Mistruzzi

Date	Mintage	F	VF	XF	Unc	BU
1939/I	52,000	—	2.50	4.00	6.00	—

KM# 25a 50 CENTESIMI

Stainless Steel **Obv:** Crowned Arms **Rev:** Archangel Michael facing, divides value

Date	Mintage	F	VF	XF	Unc	BU
1940/II	52,000	—	2.00	4.00	6.00	—
1941/III	180,000	—	2.00	4.00	6.00	—

KM# 34 50 CENTESIMI

Stainless Steel **Obv:** Crowned shield divides date and beaded circle **Rev:** Justice seated with tablets of the Law **Designer:** Aurelio Mistruzzi

Date	Mintage	F	VF	XF	Unc	BU
1942/IV	180,000	—	2.00	3.25	4.50	—
1943/V	1,000	—	50.00	75.00	125	—
1944/VI	1,000	—	50.00	75.00	125	—
1945/VII	1,000	—	50.00	75.00	125	—
1946/VIII	1,000	—	50.00	75.00	125	—

KM# 26 LIRA

Nickel **Rev:** Virgin Mary standing on globe and crescent **Rev. Designer:** Aurelio Mistruzzi

Date	Mintage	F	VF	XF	Unc	BU
1939/I	70,000	—	5.00	10.00	20.00	—

KM# 26a LIRA

7.8600 g., Stainless Steel, 26.65 mm. **Obv:** Papal arms **Rev:** Virgin Mary standing on globe and crescent **Rev. Designer:** Aurelio Mistruzzi **Edge:** Reeded

Date	Mintage	F	VF	XF	Unc	BU
1940/II	70,000	—	3.00	5.00	7.50	—
1941/III	284,000	—	1.00	2.00	4.50	—

KM# 35 LIRA

Stainless Steel **Obv:** Crowned shield divides date and beaded circle **Rev:** Justice seated with tablets of the Law **Designer:** Aurelio Mistruzzi

Date	Mintage	F	VF	XF	Unc	BU
1942/IV	284,000	—	1.00	2.00	4.50	—
1943/V	1,000	—	50.00	75.00	125	—
1944/VI	1,000	—	50.00	75.00	125	—
1945/VII	1,000	—	50.00	75.00	125	—
1946/VIII	1,000	—	50.00	75.00	125	—

KM# 40 LIRA

Aluminum **Obv:** Crowned shield divides date and beaded circle **Rev:** Justice seated with tablet of the Law **Designer:** Aurelio Mistruzzi

Date	Mintage	F	VF	XF	Unc	BU
1947/IX	120,000	—	1.00	2.00	4.00	—
1948/X	10,000	—	2.00	4.00	7.00	—
1949/XI	10,000	—	2.00	4.00	7.00	—

KM# 44 LIRA

Aluminum **Subject:** Holy Year **Obv:** Crowned shield **Rev:** Holy Year Door **Designer:** Giampaoli

Date	Mintage	F	VF	XF	Unc	BU
1950	50,000	—	1.00	2.00	3.50	—

KM# 49.1 LIRA

0.6200 g., Aluminum, 17 mm. **Obv:** Crowned shield **Obv. Legend:** ANNO **Rev:** Temperance standing pouring libation in bowl **Edge:** Plain **Designer:** Giampaoli

Date	Mintage	F	VF	XF	Unc	BU
1951/XIII	400,000	—	0.25	0.50	1.50	—
1952/XIV	400,000	—	0.25	0.50	1.50	—
1953/XV	400,000	—	0.25	0.50	1.50	—
1955/XVII	10,000	—	1.50	3.00	6.00	—
1957/XIX	30,000	—	0.75	2.00	3.50	—
1958/XX	30,000	—	0.75	2.00	3.50	—

KM# 49.2 LIRA

Aluminum, 17 mm. **Obv:** Crowned shield **Obv. Legend:** A **Edge:** Plain

Date	Mintage	F	VF	XF	Unc	BU
1956/XVIII	10,000	—	1.50	3.00	6.00	—

KM# 27 2 LIRE

Nickel, 29 mm. **Obv:** Crowned Arms **Rev:** Lamb on shoulders of shepard **Rev. Designer:** Aurelio Mistruzzi

Date	Mintage	F	VF	XF	Unc	BU
1939/I	40,000	—	4.00	6.00	12.50	—

KM# 27a 2 LIRE

Stainless Steel, 29 mm. **Obv:** Crowned Arms **Rev:** Lamb on shoulders of shepard

Date	Mintage	F	VF	XF	Unc	BU
1940/II	40,000	—	0.75	2.00	4.00	—
1941/III	270,000	—	0.50	1.00	3.00	—

KM# 36 2 LIRE

Stainless Steel, 29 mm. **Obv:** Crowned shield divides date and beaded circle **Rev:** Justice seated with tablets of the Law **Designer:** Aurelio Mistruzzi

Date	Mintage	F	VF	XF	Unc	BU
1942/IV	270,000	—	0.50	1.00	3.00	—
1943/V	1,000	—	50.00	75.00	125	—
1944/VI	1,000	—	50.00	75.00	125	—
1945/VII	1,000	—	50.00	75.00	125	—
1946/VIII	1,000	—	50.00	75.00	125	—

KM# 41 2 LIRE

Aluminum **Obv:** Crowned shield divides date and beaded circle **Rev:** Justice seated with tablets of the Law **Designer:** Aurelio Mistruzzi

Date	Mintage	F	VF	XF	Unc	BU
1947/IX	65,000	—	2.00	4.00	8.00	—
1948/X	110,000	—	1.50	3.50	5.00	—
1949/XI	10,000	—	4.00	8.00	17.50	—

KM# 45 2 LIRE

Aluminum **Subject:** Holy Year **Obv:** Bust right **Rev:** Dove and St. Peter's Basilica Dome **Designer:** Giampaoli

Date	Mintage	F	VF	XF	Unc	BU
1950	50,000	—	1.25	2.50	4.00	—

KM# 50 2 LIRE

Aluminum **Obv:** Crowned shield **Rev:** Fortude standing with lion at feet **Designer:** Giampaoli

Date	Mintage	F	VF	XF	Unc	BU
1951/XIII	400,000	—	0.25	0.50	1.50	—
1952/XIV	400,000	—	0.25	0.50	1.50	—
1953/XV	400,000	—	0.25	0.50	1.50	—
1955/XVII	20,000	—	1.00	2.00	4.00	—
1956/XVIII	20,000	—	1.00	2.00	4.00	—
1957/XIX	30,000	—	0.75	1.25	3.00	—
1958/XX	30,000	—	0.75	1.25	3.00	—

KM# 28 5 LIRE

5.0000 g., 0.8350 Silver 0.1342 oz. ASW **Obv:** Bust left **Rev:** St. Peter in a boat **Designer:** Aurelio Mistruzzi

Date	Mintage	F	VF	XF	Unc	BU
1939/I	100,000	—	4.00	10.00	20.00	—
1940/II	100,000	—	4.00	10.00	20.00	—
1941/III	4,000	—	25.00	40.00	65.00	—

KM# 37 5 LIRE

5.0000 g., 0.8350 Silver 0.1342 oz. ASW **Obv:** Bust left **Rev:** Caritas figure facing flanked by children **Designer:** Aurelio Mistruzzi

Date	Mintage	F	VF	XF	Unc	BU
1942/IV	4,000	—	25.00	40.00	65.00	—
1943/V	1,000	—	60.00	90.00	140	—
1944/VI	1,000	—	60.00	90.00	140	—
1945/VII	1,000	—	60.00	90.00	140	—
1946/VIII	1,000	—	60.00	90.00	140	—

KM# 42 5 LIRE

Aluminum **Obv:** Bust left **Rev:** Caritas figure facing flanked by children **Designer:** Aurelio Mistruzzi

Date	Mintage	F	VF	XF	Unc	BU
1947/IX	50,000	—	2.00	4.00	7.50	—
1948/X	74,000	—	2.00	4.00	7.50	—
1949/XI	74,000	—	2.00	4.00	7.50	—

KM# 46 5 LIRE

Aluminum **Subject:** Holy Year **Obv:** Bust left **Rev:** Standing Pope with staff flanked by figures within Holy Year Door **Designer:** Giampaoli

Date	Mintage	F	VF	XF	Unc	BU
1950	50,000	—	3.00	5.00	10.00	—

KM# 51.1 5 LIRE
1.0000 g., Aluminum, 20 mm. **Obv:** Bust right **Obv. Legend:** AN **Rev:** Justice standing with sword and scales **Designer:** Giampaoli

Date	Mintage	F	VF	XF	Unc	BU
1951/XIII	1,500,000	—	0.25	0.50	1.50	—
1952/XIV	1,500,000	—	0.25	0.50	1.50	—
1953/XV	1,500,000	—	0.25	0.50	1.50	—
1955/XVII	30,000	—	0.50	0.75	2.00	—
1956/XVIII	60,000	—	0.50	0.75	2.00	—
1957/XIX	30,000	—	0.50	0.75	2.00	—
1958/XX	30,000	—	0.50	0.75	2.00	—

KM# 51.2 5 LIRE
Aluminum, 20 mm. **Obv:** Bust right **Obv. Legend:** A

Date	Mintage	F	VF	XF	Unc	BU
1956/XVIII	30,000	—	0.50	1.00	2.50	—
1957/XIX	30,000	—	0.50	1.00	2.50	—
1958/XX	30,000	—	0.50	1.00	2.50	—

KM# 29 10 LIRE
10.0000 g., 0.8350 Silver 0.2684 oz. ASW **Obv:** Bust left **Rev:** Mary, Queen of Peace holding child **Designer:** Aurelio Mistruzzi

Date	Mintage	F	VF	XF	Unc	BU
1939/I	10,000	—	15.00	25.00	45.00	—
1940/II	10,000	—	15.00	25.00	45.00	—
1941/III	4,000	—	20.00	40.00	80.00	—

KM# 38 10 LIRE
10.0000 g., 0.8350 Silver 0.2684 oz. ASW **Obv:** Bust left **Rev:** Caritas figure facing flanked by children **Designer:** Aurelio Mistruzzi

Date	Mintage	F	VF	XF	Unc	BU
1942/IV	4,000	—	25.00	50.00	90.00	—
1943/V	1,000	—	60.00	85.00	125	—
1944/VI	1,000	—	60.00	85.00	125	—
1945/VII	1,000	—	60.00	85.00	125	—
1946/VIII	1,000	—	60.00	85.00	125	—

KM# 43 10 LIRE
Aluminum **Obv:** Bust left **Rev:** Caritas figure facing flanked by children **Designer:** Aurelio Mistruzzi

Date	Mintage	F	VF	XF	Unc	BU
1947/IX	50,000	—	3.00	5.00	8.00	—
1948/X	60,000	—	3.00	5.00	8.00	—
1949/XI	60,000	—	3.00	5.00	8.00	—

KM# 47 10 LIRE
Aluminum **Subject:** Holy Year **Obv:** Bust right **Rev:** Procession thru Holy Year door

Date	Mintage	F	VF	XF	Unc	BU
1950	60,000	—	3.00	5.00	8.00	—

KM# 52.1 10 LIRE
1.0000 g., Aluminum, 23 mm. **Obv:** Bust left **Obv. Legend:** AN **Rev:** Prudence standing and date divides value **Designer:** Giampaoli

Date	Mintage	F	VF	XF	Unc	BU
1951/XIII	1,130,000	—	0.50	0.75	1.50	—
1952/XIV	1,130,000	—	0.50	0.75	1.50	—
1953/XV	1,130,000	—	0.50	0.75	1.50	—
1955/XVII	80,000	—	0.75	1.50	3.00	—
1957/XIX	—	—	0.75	1.50	3.00	—
1958/XX	—	—	0.75	1.50	3.00	—

KM# 52.2 10 LIRE
Aluminum, 23 mm. **Obv:** Bust left **Obv. Legend:** A **Rev:** Prudence standing date divides value

Date	Mintage	F	VF	XF	Unc	BU
1956/XVIII	80,000	—	0.75	1.50	3.00	—

KM# A52.1 20 LIRE
3.6000 g., Aluminum-Bronze, 21.25 mm. **Obv:** Bust left **Obv. Legend:** A **Rev:** Caritas standing holding child with another at feet

Date	Mintage	F	VF	XF	Unc	BU
1957/XIX	20,000	—	0.75	1.25	2.50	—

KM# A52.2 20 LIRE
5.6000 g., Aluminum-Bronze, 21.25 mm. **Obv:** Bust left **Obv. Legend:** AN **Rev:** Caritas standing holding child with another at feet

Date	Mintage	F	VF	XF	Unc	BU
1958/XX	60,000	—	0.75	1.25	2.50	—

KM# 54.1 50 LIRE
6.2000 g., Stainless Steel, 24.8 mm. **Obv:** Bust right **Obv. Legend:** AN **Rev:** Spes standing with large anchor which divides date and value

Date	Mintage	F	VF	XF	Unc	BU
1955/XVII	180,000	—	1.00	1.50	3.00	—
1956/XVIII	—	—	1.00	1.50	3.00	—
1957/XIX	—	—	1.00	1.50	3.00	—
1958/XX	—	—	1.00	1.50	3.00	—

KM# 54.2 50 LIRE
6.2000 g., Stainless Steel, 24.8 mm. **Obv:** Bust right **Obv. Legend:** A **Rev:** Spes standing facing with large anchor which divides date and value

Date	Mintage	F	VF	XF	Unc	BU
1956/XVIII	180,000	—	1.00	1.50	3.00	—
1957/XIX	180,000	—	1.00	1.50	3.00	—
1958/XX	60,000	—	1.00	1.50	3.00	—

KM# 30.1 100 LIRE
5.1900 g., 0.9000 Gold 0.1502 oz. AGW **Obv:** Head right **Obv. Legend:** AN **Rev:** Standing Jesus divides value **Designer:** Aurelio Mistruzzi

Date	Mintage	F	VF	XF	Unc	BU
1939/I	2,700	—	—	350	600	—
1940/II	2,000	—	—	350	600	—

KM# 30.2 100 LIRE
5.1900 g., 0.9000 Gold 0.1502 oz. AGW **Obv:** Head right **Obv. Legend:** A **Rev:** Standing Jesus divides value

Date	Mintage	F	VF	XF	Unc	BU
1941/III	2,000	—	—	350	650	—

KM# 39 100 LIRE
5.1900 g., 0.9000 Gold 0.1502 oz. AGW **Obv:** Head right **Rev:** Caritas seated facing flanked by children

Date	Mintage	F	VF	XF	Unc	BU
1942/IV	2,000	—	—	300	550	—
1943/V	1,000	—	—	350	600	—
1944/VI	1,000	—	—	350	600	—
1945/VII	1,000	—	—	350	600	—
1946/VIII	1,000	—	—	350	600	—
1947/IX	1,000	—	—	350	600	—
1948/X	5,000	—	—	300	500	—
1949/XI	1,000	—	—	350	600	—

KM# 48 100 LIRE
5.1900 g., 0.9000 Gold 0.1502 oz. AGW **Subject:** Holy Year **Obv:** Crowned bust left **Rev:** Opening of the Holy Year Door

Date	Mintage	F	VF	XF	Unc	BU
MCML (1950)	20,000	—	—	300	500	—

KM# 53.1 100 LIRE
5.1900 g., 0.9000 Gold 0.1502 oz. AGW **Obv:** Bust right **Obv. Legend:** AN **Rev:** Caritas standing facing holding child with another at feet

Date	Mintage	F	VF	XF	Unc	BU
1951/XIII	1,000	—	—	350	550	—
1952/XIV	1,000	—	—	350	550	—
1953/XV	1,000	—	—	350	550	—
1954/XVI	1,000	—	—	350	550	—
1955/XVII	1,000	—	—	350	550	—

KM# 53.2 100 LIRE
5.1900 g., 0.9000 Gold 0.1502 oz. AGW **Obv:** Bust right **Obv. Legend:** A **Rev:** Caritas standing facing holding child with another at feet

Date	Mintage	F	VF	XF	Unc	BU
1956/XVIII	1,000	—	—	350	550	—

KM# 55 100 LIRE
8.0000 g., Stainless Steel, 27.75 mm. **Obv:** Bust left **Rev:** Fides standing with large cross divides value and date **Designer:** Giampaoli

Date	Mintage	F	VF	XF	Unc	BU
1955/XVII	1,300,000	—	0.50	1.00	2.00	—
1956/XVII	1,400,000	—	0.50	1.00	2.00	—
1957/XIX	900,000	—	0.50	1.00	2.00	—
1958/XX	852,000	—	0.50	1.00	2.00	—

KM# A53 100 LIRE
5.1900 g., 0.9000 Gold 0.1502 oz. AGW **Obv:** Bust right **Rev:** Crowned shield divides value

Date	Mintage	F	VF	XF	Unc	BU
1957/XIX	2,000	—	—	300	500	—
1958/XX	3,000	—	—	300	500	—

KM# 56 500 LIRE
11.0000 g., 0.8350 Silver 0.2953 oz. ASW, 29 mm. **Obv:** Bust left **Rev:** Crowned shield divides value **Designer:** Pietro Giampaoli

Date	Mintage	F	VF	XF	Unc	BU
1958/XX	20,000	—	7.50	15.00	25.00	—

Sede Vacante

DECIMAL COINAGE

100 Centesimi = 1 Lira

KM# 57 500 LIRE
11.0000 g., 0.8350 Silver 0.2953 oz. ASW, 29.3 mm. **Obv:** Descending dove divides sun above value **Rev:** Arms of Cardinal Benedetto Aloisi-Masella **Designer:** Pietro Giampaoli

Date	Mintage	F	VF	XF	Unc	BU
1958	100,000	—	10.00	40.00	70.00	—

John XXIII

DECIMAL COINAGE

100 Centesimi = 1 Lira

KM# 58.1 LIRA
Aluminum, 17 mm. **Obv:** Crowned shield **Obv. Legend:** AN **Rev:** Temperance kneeling pouring libation into bowl **Edge:** Plain **Designer:** Giampaoli

Date	Mintage	F	VF	XF	Unc	BU
1959/I	25,000	—	1.00	3.00	6.00	—
1960/II	25,000	—	1.00	2.00	4.00	—

KM# 58.2 LIRA
Aluminum, 17 mm. **Obv:** Crowned shield **Obv. Legend:** A **Rev:** Temperance kneeling pouring libation into bowl **Edge:** Plain

Date	Mintage	F	VF	XF	Unc	BU
1961/III	25,000	—	1.00	2.00	4.00	—
1962/IV	25,000	—	1.00	2.00	4.00	—

KM# 67 LIRA
Aluminum, 17 mm. **Subject:** Second Ecumenical Council **Obv:** Crowned shield **Rev:** Radiant dove in rays **Edge:** Plain

Date	Mintage	F	VF	XF	Unc	BU
1962/IV	50,000	—	1.00	1.50	3.00	—

KM# 59.1 2 LIRE
Aluminum, 18 mm. **Obv:** Crowned shield **Obv. Legend:** AN **Rev:** Fortude seated facing and lion divides value and date

Date	Mintage	F	VF	XF	Unc	BU
1959/I	25,000	—	1.50	4.00	6.00	—
1960/II	25,000	—	1.50	4.00	6.00	—

KM# 59.2 2 LIRE
Aluminum, 18 mm. **Obv:** Crowned shield **Obv. Legend:** A **Rev:** Fortude seated facing and lion divides value and date

Date	Mintage	F	VF	XF	Unc	BU
1961/III	25,000	—	1.50	4.00	6.00	—
1962/IV	25,000	—	1.50	4.00	6.00	—

KM# 68 2 LIRE
Aluminum, 18 mm. **Subject:** Second Ecumenical Council **Obv:** Crowned shield **Rev:** Radiant dove in rays

Date	Mintage	F	VF	XF	Unc	BU
1962/IV	50,000	—	1.00	1.50	3.00	—

KM# 60.1 5 LIRE
Aluminum, 20 mm. **Obv:** Bust right **Obv. Legend:** AN **Rev:** Kneeling figure holding sword and scales divides value and date

Date	Mintage	F	VF	XF	Unc	BU
1959/I	25,000	—	1.50	4.00	7.00	—

KM# 60.2 5 LIRE
Aluminum, 20 mm. **Obv:** Bust right **Obv. Legend:** A **Rev:** Kneeling figure holding sword and scales divides date and value

Date	Mintage	F	VF	XF	Unc	BU
1960/II	25,000	—	1.50	4.00	7.00	—
1961/III	25,000	—	1.50	4.00	7.00	—
1962/IV	25,000	—	1.00	2.00	4.00	—

KM# 69 5 LIRE
Aluminum, 20 mm. **Subject:** Second Ecumenical Council **Obv:** Bust right **Rev:** Radiant dove

Date	Mintage	F	VF	XF	Unc	BU
1962/IV	50,000	—	0.40	0.75	2.00	—

KM# 61.1 10 LIRE
Aluminum, 23 mm. **Obv:** Bust left **Obv. Legend:** AN **Rev:** Prudence kneeling holding snake and object divides value and date

Date	Mintage	F	VF	XF	Unc	BU
1959/I	50,000	—	1.00	3.00	6.00	—

KM# 61.2 10 LIRE
Aluminum, 23 mm. **Obv:** Bust left **Obv. Legend:** A **Rev:** Prudence kneeling

Date	Mintage	F	VF	XF	Unc	BU
1960/II	50,000	—	1.00	3.00	6.00	—
1961/III	50,000	—	1.00	3.00	6.00	—
1962/IV	50,000	—	1.00	2.00	4.00	—

KM# 70 10 LIRE
Aluminum, 23 mm. **Subject:** Second Ecumenical Council **Obv:** Bust left **Rev:** Radiant dove

Date	Mintage	F	VF	XF	Unc	BU
1962/IV	100,000	—	1.00	2.00	4.00	—

KM# 62.1 20 LIRE
3.6000 g., Aluminum-Bronze, 21.25 mm. **Obv:** Helmeted bust left **Obv. Legend:** AN **Rev:** Caritas seated facing flanked by children

Date	Mintage	F	VF	XF	Unc	BU
1959/I	50,000	—	0.75	1.25	2.50	—

KM# 62.2 20 LIRE
3.6000 g., Aluminum-Bronze, 21.25 mm. **Obv:** Capped bust left **Obv. Legend:** A **Rev:** Seated figure with children

Date	Mintage	F	VF	XF	Unc	BU
1960/II	50,000	—	0.75	1.25	2.50	—
1961/III	50,000	—	0.75	1.00	2.50	—
1962/IV	50,000	—	0.75	1.00	2.50	—

KM# 71 20 LIRE
3.6000 g., Aluminum-Bronze, 21.25 mm. **Subject:** Second Ecumenical Council **Obv:** Capped bust left **Rev:** Radiant dove

Date	Mintage	F	VF	XF	Unc	BU
1962/IV	100,000	—	0.75	1.00	2.00	—

KM# 63.1 50 LIRE
6.2000 g., Stainless Steel, 24.8 mm. **Obv:** Bust right **Rev:** Spes standing facing with large anchor divides date and value

Date	Mintage	F	VF	XF	Unc	BU
1959/I	100,000	—	1.00	2.50	6.50	—

KM# 63.2 50 LIRE
6.2000 g., Stainless Steel, 24.8 mm. **Obv:** Bust right **Rev:** Spes standing facing and large anchor divides date and value

Date	Mintage	F	VF	XF	Unc	BU
1960/II	100,000	—	1.00	2.50	5.50	—
1961/III	100,000	—	1.00	2.00	4.50	—
1962/IV	100,000	—	1.00	2.00	4.50	—

KM# 72 50 LIRE

6.2000 g., Stainless Steel, 24.8 mm. **Subject:** Second Ecumenical Council **Obv:** Bust right **Rev:** Bishops at council meeting with radiant dove above **Designer:** Giampaoli

Date	Mintage	F	VF	XF	Unc	BU
1962/IV	200,000	—	0.50	1.25	3.00	—

KM# 66 100 LIRE

5.1900 g., 0.9000 Gold 0.1502 oz. AGW **Obv:** Bust right **Rev:** Crowned shield divides value

Date	Mintage	F	VF	XF	Unc	BU
1959/I	3,000	—	1,100	1,500	2,280	—

KM# 64.1 100 LIRE

8.0000 g., Stainless Steel, 27.75 mm. **Obv:** Bust left **Rev:** Fides standing, cross divides value and date **Designer:** Giampaoli

Date	Mintage	F	VF	XF	Unc	BU
1959/I	783,000	—	1.25	2.00	4.00	—

KM# 64.2 100 LIRE

8.0000 g., Stainless Steel, 27.75 mm. **Obv:** Regnal year under bust facing left **Rev:** Fides standing, cross divides value and date

Date	Mintage	F	VF	XF	Unc	BU
1960/II	783,000	—	1.75	3.00	6.50	—
1961/III	783,000	—	0.75	1.00	2.50	—
1962/IV	783,000	—	0.75	1.00	2.50	—

KM# 73 100 LIRE

8.0000 g., Stainless Steel, 27.75 mm. **Subject:** Second Ecumenical Council **Obv:** Bust left **Rev:** Bishops at council meeting with radiant doves **Designer:** Giampaoli

Date	Mintage	F	VF	XF	Unc	BU
1962/IV	1,566,000	—	0.40	1.00	2.00	—

KM# 65.1 500 LIRE

11.0000 g., 0.8350 Silver 0.2953 oz. ASW, 29.3 mm. **Obv:** Bust left with continuous legend **Rev:** Crowned shield divides value **Designer:** Pietro Giampaoli

Date	Mintage	F	VF	XF	Unc	BU
1959/I	30,000	—	7.50	15.00	30.00	—

KM# 65.2 500 LIRE

11.0000 g., 0.8350 Silver 0.2953 oz. ASW, 29.3 mm. **Obv:** Regnal year under bust facing left **Rev:** Crowned shield divides value

Date	Mintage	F	VF	XF	Unc	BU
1960/II	30,000	—	10.00	20.00	35.00	—
1961/III	30,000	—	7.00	15.00	30.00	—
1962/IV	30,000	—	7.00	15.00	30.00	—

KM# 74 500 LIRE

11.0000 g., 0.8350 Silver 0.2953 oz. ASW, 29.3 mm. **Subject:** Second Ecumenical Council **Obv:** Crowned bust left **Rev:** Bishops at council meeting with radiant doves

Date	Mintage	F	VF	XF	Unc	BU
1962/IV	60,000	—	7.00	17.50	30.00	—

Sede Vacante

DECIMAL COINAGE

100 Centesimi = 1 Lira

KM# 75 500 LIRE

11.0000 g., 0.8350 Silver 0.2953 oz. ASW, 29.3 mm. **Obv:** Descending dove divides sun above value **Rev:** Arms of Cardinal Benedetto Aloisi-Masella

Date	Mintage	F	VF	XF	Unc	BU
1963	200,000	—	6.00	10.00	17.50	—

Paul VI

DECIMAL COINAGE

100 Centesimi = 1 Lira

KM# 76.1 LIRA

Aluminum, 17 mm. **Obv:** Crowned shield **Obv. Legend:** AN **Rev:** Temperance seated pouring libation divides value and date **Edge:** Plain

Date	Mintage	F	VF	XF	Unc	BU
1963/I	60,000	—	0.75	2.00	3.50	—

KM# 76.2 LIRA

Aluminum, 17 mm. **Obv:** Crowned shield **Obv. Legend:** A **Rev:** Temperance seated pouring libation divides value and date **Edge:** Plain

Date	Mintage	F	VF	XF	Unc	BU
1964/II	60,000	—	0.50	1.00	2.00	—
1965/III	60,000	—	0.50	1.00	2.00	—

KM# 84 LIRA

Aluminum, 17 mm. **Obv:** Crowned head left **Rev:** Sheep on shoulders of shepard **Edge:** Plain **Designer:** E. Greco

Date	Mintage	F	VF	XF	Unc	BU
1966/IV	90,000	—	0.25	0.75	1.25	—

KM# 92 LIRA

Aluminum, 17 mm. **Obv:** Crowned shield **Rev:** Crossed keys within radiant sword **Edge:** Plain

Date	Mintage	F	VF	XF	Unc	BU
1967/V	100,000	—	0.25	0.75	1.25	—

KM# 100 LIRA

Aluminum, 17 mm. **Series:** F.A.O. **Obv:** Bust left **Rev:** Wheat ears forming radiant cross **Edge:** Plain **Designer:** G. Pirrone

Date	Mintage	F	VF	XF	Unc	BU
ND(1968)/VI	100,000	—	0.25	0.75	1.25	—

KM# 108 LIRA

Aluminum, 17 mm. **Series:** F.A.O. **Obv:** Crowned head 1/4 left divides inscription **Rev:** Stylized angel in flight **Edge:** Plain **Designer:** C. Ruffini

Date	Mintage	F	VF	XF	Unc	BU
1969/VII	100,000	—	0.25	0.75	1.25	—

KM# 116 LIRA

Aluminum, 17 mm. **Series:** F.A.O. **Obv:** Crowned shield **Rev:** Palm sprigs **Designer:** Tomaso Gismondi

Date	Mintage	F	VF	XF	Unc	BU
1970/VIII	100,000	—	0.25	0.50	1.00	—
1971/IX	110,000	—	0.25	0.50	1.00	—
1972/X	110,000	—	0.25	0.50	1.00	—
1973/XI	132,000	—	0.25	0.50	1.00	—
1974/XII	132,000	—	0.25	0.50	1.00	—
1975/XIII	150,000	—	0.25	0.50	1.00	—
1976/XIV	150,000	—	0.25	0.50	1.00	—
1977/XV	135,000	—	0.25	0.50	1.00	—

KM# 124 LIRA

Aluminum, 17 mm. **Subject:** Holy Year - Faith in the Lord on Part of Man Afflicted by Evil **Obv:** Crowned shield **Rev:** Mother and child playing **Designer:** Guido Veroi

Date	Mintage	F	VF	XF	Unc	BU
1975	170,000	—	0.25	0.50	1.00	—

KM# 77.1 2 LIRE

Aluminum, 18 mm. **Obv:** Crowned shield **Obv. Legend:** AN **Rev:** Fortude standing with shield, lion at side, value

Date	Mintage	F	VF	XF	Unc	BU
1963/I	60,000	—	0.75	2.00	3.00	—

KM# 77.2 2 LIRE

Aluminum, 18 mm. **Obv:** Crowned shield **Obv. Legend:** A **Rev:** Fortude standing with shield, lion at side, value

Date	Mintage	F	VF	XF	Unc	BU
1964/II	60,000	—	0.75	2.00	3.00	—
1965/III	60,000	—	0.75	3.00	3.00	—

KM# 85 2 LIRE

Aluminum, 18 mm. **Obv:** Crowned head left **Rev:** Sheep on shoulder of shepard **Designer:** E. Greco

Date	Mintage	F	VF	XF	Unc	BU
1966/IV	90,000	—	0.25	0.75	1.25	—

KM# 93 2 LIRE

Aluminum, 18 mm. **Obv:** Crowned shield **Rev:** Papal tiara above inverted cross, keys flanking

Date	Mintage	F	VF	XF	Unc	BU
1967/V	100,000	—	0.25	0.75	1.25	—

KM# 101 2 LIRE

Aluminum, 18 mm. **Series:** F.A.O. **Subject:** Feeding of the 5,000 **Obv:** Bust right **Rev:** Standing figure flanked by others **Designer:** G. Pirrone

Date	Mintage	F	VF	XF	Unc	BU
ND(1968)/VI	100,000	—	0.25	0.75	1.25	—

KM# 109 2 LIRE

Aluminum, 18 mm. **Obv:** Crowned head 1/4 left divides inscription **Rev:** Stylized angel in flight **Designer:** C. Ruffini

Date	Mintage	F	VF	XF	Unc	BU
1969/VII	100,000	—	0.25	0.75	1.25	—

KM# 117 2 LIRE

Aluminum, 18 mm. **Obv:** Crowned shield **Rev:** Lamb standing **Designer:** Tomaso Gismondi

Date	Mintage	F	VF	XF	Unc	BU
1970/VIII	100,000	—	0.25	0.50	1.00	—
1971/IX	110,000	—	0.25	0.50	1.00	—
1972/X	110,000	—	0.25	0.50	1.00	—
1973/XI	132,000	—	0.25	0.50	1.00	—
1974/XII	132,000	—	0.25	0.50	1.00	—
1975/XIII	150,000	—	0.25	0.50	1.00	—
1976/XIV	150,000	—	0.25	0.50	1.00	—
1977/XV	135,000	—	0.25	0.50	1.00	—

KM# 125 2 LIRE

Aluminum, 18 mm. **Subject:** Holy Year - Reconciliation among brothers **Obv:** Crowned shield **Rev:** Two men embracing **Designer:** Guido Veroi

Date	Mintage	F	VF	XF	Unc	BU
1975	180,000	—	0.25	0.50	1.00	—

KM# 78.1 5 LIRE

Aluminum, 20 mm. **Obv:** Bust right **Obv. Legend:** AN **Rev:** Justice seated with sword and scales

Date	Mintage	F	VF	XF	Unc	BU
1963/I	60,000	—	1.00	2.00	4.00	—

KM# 78.2 5 LIRE

Aluminum, 20 mm. **Obv:** Bust right **Obv. Legend:** A **Rev:** Justice seated with sword and scales

Date	Mintage	F	VF	XF	Unc	BU
1964/II	60,000	—	8.00	16.00	32.00	—
1965/III	60,000	—	8.00	16.00	32.00	—

KM# 86 5 LIRE

Aluminum, 20 mm. **Obv:** Crowned head left **Rev:** Sheep on shoulder of shepard

Date	Mintage	F	VF	XF	Unc	BU
1966/IV	90,000	—	0.25	0.50	1.25	—

KM# 94 5 LIRE

Aluminum, 20 mm. **Obv:** Bust right **Rev:** Crossed keys within radiant sword

Date	Mintage	F	VF	XF	Unc	BU
1967/V	100,000	—	0.25	0.50	1.25	—

KM# 102 5 LIRE

Aluminum, 20 mm. **Series:** F.A.O. **Subject:** Lady of the Harvest **Obv:** Bust right **Rev:** Our Lady of the Harvest within wheat sprigs **Designer:** G. Pirrone

Date	Mintage	F	VF	XF	Unc	BU
ND(1968)/VI	100,000	—	0.25	0.50	1.25	—

KM# 110 5 LIRE

Aluminum, 20 mm. **Obv:** Crowned head 1/4 left divides inscription **Rev:** Stylized angel in flight **Designer:** G. Ruffini

Date	Mintage	F	VF	XF	Unc	BU
1969/VII	100,000	—	0.25	0.50	1.25	—

KM# 118 5 LIRE

Aluminum, 20 mm. **Obv:** Crowned shield **Rev:** Pelican feeding young **Designer:** Tomaso Gismondi

Date	Mintage	F	VF	XF	Unc	BU
1970/VIII	100,000	—	0.25	0.60	1.25	—
1971/IX	110,000	—	0.25	0.60	1.25	—
1972/X	110,000	—	0.25	0.60	1.25	—
1973/XI	132,000	—	0.25	0.60	1.25	—
1974/XII	132,000	—	0.25	0.60	1.25	—
1975/XIII	150,000	—	0.25	0.60	1.25	—
1976/XIV	150,000	—	0.25	0.60	1.25	—
1977/XV	135,000	—	0.25	0.60	1.25	—

KM# 126 5 LIRE

Aluminum, 20 mm. **Subject:** Holy Year - Redemption of the Woman of Bethany **Obv:** Crowned shield **Rev:** Female kneeling receiving blessing from seated figure **Designer:** Guido Veroi

Date	Mintage	F	VF	XF	Unc	BU
1975	380,000	—	0.25	0.50	1.25	—

KM# 133 5 LIRE

Aluminum, 20 mm. **Obv:** Crowned shield **Rev:** Stylized standing figure divides value **Designer:** Nicola Morelli

Date	Mintage	F	VF	XF	Unc	BU
1978/XVI	120,000	—	0.25	0.50	1.25	—

KM# 79.1 10 LIRE

Aluminum, 23 mm. **Obv:** Bust left **Obv. Legend:** AN **Rev:** Prudence standing dividing date and value

Date	Mintage	F	VF	XF	Unc	BU
1963/I	90,000	—	1.00	1.50	3.00	—

KM# 79.2 10 LIRE

Aluminum, 23 mm. **Obv:** Bust left **Obv. Legend:** A **Rev:** Prudence standing dividing date and value

Date	Mintage	F	VF	XF	Unc	BU
1964/II	90,000	—	0.75	1.00	2.00	—
1965/III	90,000	—	0.75	1.00	2.00	—

KM# 87 10 LIRE

Aluminum, 23 mm. **Obv:** Crowned head left **Rev:** Shepard with sheep on his shoulders

Date	Mintage	F	VF	XF	Unc	BU
1966/IV	100,000	—	0.25	1.00	2.00	—

KM# 95 10 LIRE

Aluminum, 23 mm. **Obv:** Bust left **Rev:** Papal taira above inverted cross, keys flanking

Date	Mintage	F	VF	XF	Unc	BU
ND(1967)/V	110,000	—	0.25	0.75	1.25	—

KM# 103 10 LIRE

Aluminum, 23 mm. **Series:** F.A.O. **Obv:** Bust left **Rev:** Feeding of the 5,000 **Designer:** G. Pirrone

Date	Mintage	F	VF	XF	Unc	BU
ND(1968)/VI	110,000	—	0.25	0.75	1.50	—

KM# 111 10 LIRE

Aluminum, 23 mm. **Obv:** Crowned head 1/4 left divides inscription **Rev:** Stylized angel in flight **Designer:** G. Ruffini

Date	Mintage	F	VF	XF	Unc	BU
1969/VII	110,000	—	0.25	0.50	1.25	—

KM# 119 10 LIRE

Aluminum, 23 mm. **Obv:** Crowned shield **Rev:** Fish **Designer:** Tomaso Gismondi

Date	Mintage	F	VF	XF	Unc	BU
1970/VIII	110,000	—	0.25	0.50	1.25	—
1971/IX	160,000	—	0.25	0.50	1.25	—
1972/X	160,000	—	0.25	0.50	1.25	—
1973/XI	170,000	—	0.25	0.50	1.25	—
1974/XII	170,000	—	0.25	0.50	1.25	—
1975/XIII	200,000	—	0.25	0.50	1.25	—
1976/XIV	200,000	—	0.25	0.50	1.25	—
1977/XV	200,000	—	0.25	0.50	1.25	—

KM# 127 10 LIRE

Aluminum, 23 mm. **Subject:** Holy Year - Reconciliation between God and man **Obv:** Crowned shield **Rev:** Noah's ark **Designer:** Guido Veroi

Date	Mintage	F	VF	XF	Unc	BU
1975	400,000	—	0.25	0.75	1.50	—

KM# 134 10 LIRE

Aluminum, 23 mm. **Obv:** Crowned shield **Rev:** Figure kneeling left **Designer:** Nicola Morelli

Date	Mintage	F	VF	XF	Unc	BU
1978/XVI	250,000	—	0.25	0.50	1.00	—

KM# 80.1 20 LIRE

3.6000 g., Aluminum-Bronze, 21.25 mm. **Obv:** Bust left **Obv. Legend:** AN **Rev:** Caritas seated flanked by children

Date	Mintage	F	VF	XF	Unc	BU
1963/I	90,000	—	1.00	2.00	4.00	—
1964/II	90,000	—	1.00	2.00	4.00	—

KM# 80.2 20 LIRE

3.6000 g., Aluminum-Bronze, 21.25 mm. **Obv:** Bust left **Obv. Legend:** A **Rev:** Caritas seated flanked by children

Date	Mintage	F	VF	XF	Unc	BU
1965/III	90,000	—	0.75	1.00	2.00	—

KM# 88 20 LIRE

3.6000 g., Aluminum-Bronze, 21.25 mm. **Obv:** Crowned head left **Rev:** Shepard with sheep on his shoulders

Date	Mintage	F	VF	XF	Unc	BU
1966/IV	100,000	—	0.25	0.75	1.25	—

KM# 96 20 LIRE

3.6000 g., Aluminum-Bronze, 21.25 mm. **Obv:** Bust right **Rev:** Saints Peter and Paul, sword between **Designer:** G. Pirrone

Date	Mintage	F	VF	XF	Unc	BU
ND(1967)/V	105,000	—	0.25	0.75	1.25	—

KM# 104 20 LIRE

3.6000 g., Aluminum-Bronze, 21.25 mm. **Series:** F.A.O. **Obv:** Bust right **Rev:** Wheat ears forming radiant cross **Designer:** G. Pirrone

Date	Mintage	F	VF	XF	Unc	BU
ND(1968)/VI	105,000	—	0.25	0.75	1.50	—

KM# 112 20 LIRE

3.6000 g., Aluminum-Bronze, 21.25 mm. **Obv:** Crowned head 1/4 left divides inscription **Rev:** Stylized angel in flight **Designer:** C. Ruffini

Date	Mintage	F	VF	XF	Unc	BU
1969/VII	105,000	—	0.25	0.60	1.25	—

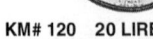

KM# 120 20 LIRE

3.6000 g., Aluminum-Bronze, 21.25 mm. **Obv:** Crowned shield **Rev:** Red deer **Designer:** Tomas Gismondi

Date	Mintage	F	VF	XF	Unc	BU
1970/VIII	105,000	—	0.25	0.50	1.50	2.00
1971/IX	170,000	—	0.25	0.50	1.50	2.00
1972/X	170,000	—	0.25	0.50	1.50	2.00
1973/XI	—	—	0.25	0.50	1.50	2.00
1974/XII	—	—	0.25	0.50	1.50	2.00
1975/XIII	250,000	—	0.25	0.50	1.50	2.00
1976/XIV	250,000	—	0.25	0.50	1.50	2.00
1977/XV	250,000	—	0.25	0.50	1.50	2.00

KM# 128 20 LIRE

3.6000 g., Aluminum-Bronze, 21.25 mm. **Subject:** Holy Year - Man's Confidence in the Lord **Obv:** Crowned shield **Rev:** Standing figure facing right and value **Designer:** Guido Veroi

Date	Mintage	F	VF	XF	Unc	BU
1975	400,000	—	0.25	0.50	1.25	—

KM# 135 20 LIRE

3.6000 g., Aluminum-Bronze, 21.25 mm. **Subject:** Prodigal Son Parable **Obv:** Crowned shield **Rev:** Standing figures facing each other above value **Designer:** Nicola Morelli

Date	Mintage	F	VF	XF	Unc	BU
1978/XVI	120,000	—	0.25	0.50	1.25	—

KM# 81.1 50 LIRE

6.2000 g., Stainless Steel, 24.8 mm. **Obv:** Bust right **Obv. Legend:** AN **Rev:** Spes standing with anchor date and value are divided

Date	Mintage	F	VF	XF	Unc	BU
1963/I	120,000	—	1.00	2.00	4.00	—
1964/II	120,000	—	0.75	1.50	3.00	—

KM# 81.2 50 LIRE

6.2000 g., Stainless Steel, 24.8 mm. **Obv:** Bust right **Obv. Legend:** A **Rev:** Spes standing with anchor, date and value divided

Date	Mintage	F	VF	XF	Unc	BU
1965/III	120,000	—	0.50	1.00	2.00	—

KM# 89 50 LIRE

6.2000 g., Stainless Steel, 24.8 mm. **Obv:** Crowned head left **Rev:** Shepard with sheep on shoulders

Date	Mintage	F	VF	XF	Unc	BU
1966/IV	150,000	—	0.50	1.00	2.00	—

KM# 97 50 LIRE

6.2000 g., Stainless Steel, 24.8 mm. **Subject:** Conversion of Saint Paul **Obv:** Bust right **Rev:** Rearing equestrian **Designer:** G. Pirrone

Date	Mintage	F	VF	XF	Unc	BU
1967/V	190,000	—	0.50	1.00	2.00	—

KM# 105 50 LIRE
6.2000 g., Stainless Steel, 24.8 mm. **Series:** F.A.O. **Obv:** Bust right **Rev:** Our Lady of Harvest standing within wheat sprigs **Designer:** G. Pirrone

Date	Mintage	F	VF	XF	Unc	BU
ND(1968)/VI	190,000	—	0.50	1.00	2.00	—

KM# 113 50 LIRE
6.2000 g., Stainless Steel, 24.8 mm. **Obv:** Crowned head 1/4 left divides inscription **Rev:** Stylized angel

Date	Mintage	F	VF	XF	Unc	BU
1969/VII	190,000	—	0.50	1.00	2.00	—

KM# 121 50 LIRE
6.2000 g., Stainless Steel, 24.8 mm. **Obv:** Crowned shield **Rev:** Olive branch **Designer:** Tomas Gismondi

Date	Mintage	F	VF	XF	Unc	BU
1970/VIII	190,000	—	0.25	0.75	1.75	—
1971/IX	700,000	—	0.25	0.75	1.50	—
1972/X	700,000	—	0.25	0.75	1.50	—
1973/XI	750,000	—	0.25	0.75	1.50	—
1974/XII	750,000	—	0.25	0.75	1.50	—
1975/XIII	600,000	—	0.25	0.75	1.50	—
1976/XIV	600,000	—	0.25	0.75	1.50	—

KM# 129 50 LIRE
6.2000 g., Stainless Steel, 24.8 mm. **Subject:** Holy Year - The Peace of the Lord **Obv:** Crowned shield **Rev:** Stylized figure in fetal position within design with hand above **Designer:** Guido Veroi

Date	Mintage	F	VF	XF	Unc	BU
1975	500,000	—	0.40	0.75	1.50	—

KM# A121 50 LIRE
6.2000 g., Stainless Steel, 24.8 mm. **Obv:** Crowned shield **Rev:** Wheat and grapes

Date	Mintage	F	VF	XF	Unc	BU
1977/XV	600,000	—	0.25	0.50	1.25	—

KM# 136 50 LIRE
6.2000 g., Stainless Steel, 24.8 mm. **Obv:** Crowned shield **Rev:** Child and kneeling adult **Designer:** Nicola Morelli

Date	Mintage	F	VF	XF	Unc	BU
1978/XVI	223,000	—	0.25	0.50	1.25	—

KM# 82.1 100 LIRE
8.0000 g., Stainless Steel, 27.75 mm. **Obv:** Bust left **Obv. Legend:** AN **Rev:** Fides standing figure divides value and date

Date	Mintage	F	VF	XF	Unc	BU
1963/I	558,000	—	1.00	2.00	3.75	—

KM# 82.2 100 LIRE
8.0000 g., Stainless Steel, 27.75 mm. **Obv:** Bust left **Obv. Legend:** A **Rev:** Fides standing figure divides value and date

Date	Mintage	F	VF	XF	Unc	BU
1964/II	558,000	—	0.50	1.00	2.50	—
1965/III	558,000	—	0.50	1.00	2.50	—

KM# 90 100 LIRE
8.0000 g., Stainless Steel, 27.75 mm. **Obv:** Crowned head left **Rev:** Shepard with sheep on shoulders **Designer:** E. Greco

Date	Mintage	F	VF	XF	Unc	BU
1966/IV	388,000	—	0.50	1.00	2.50	—

KM# 98 100 LIRE
8.0000 g., Stainless Steel, 27.75 mm. **Obv:** Bust left **Rev:** St. Peter seated on throne facing **Designer:** G. Pirrone

Date	Mintage	F	VF	XF	Unc	BU
1967/V	315,000	—	0.50	1.00	2.50	—

KM# 106 100 LIRE
8.0000 g., Stainless Steel, 27.75 mm. **Series:** F.A.O. **Obv:** Bust left **Rev:** Feeding of the 5,000 **Designer:** G. Pirrone

Date	Mintage	F	VF	XF	Unc	BU
ND(1968)/VI	315,000	—	0.50	1.00	2.50	—

KM# 114 100 LIRE
8.0000 g., Stainless Steel, 27.75 mm. **Obv:** Crowned head 1/4 left divides inscription **Rev:** Stylized angel in flight **Designer:** C. Ruffini

Date	Mintage	F	VF	XF	Unc	BU
1969/VII	315,000	—	0.50	1.00	2.50	—

KM# 122 100 LIRE
8.0000 g., Stainless Steel, 27.75 mm. **Obv:** Crowned shield **Rev:** Dove in flight with olive branch **Designer:** Tomas Gismondi

Date	Mintage	F	VF	XF	Unc	BU
1970/VIII	315,000	—	0.50	1.00	2.50	—
1971/IX	966,000	—	0.40	0.75	1.50	—
1972/X	966,000	—	0.40	0.75	1.50	—
1973/XI	830,000	—	0.40	0.75	1.50	—
1974/XII	830,000	—	0.40	0.75	1.50	—
1975/XIII	808,000	—	0.40	0.75	1.50	—
1976/XIV	808,000	—	0.40	0.75	1.50	—
1977/XV	819,000	—	0.40	0.75	1.50	—

KM# 130 100 LIRE
8.0000 g., Stainless Steel, 27.75 mm. **Subject:** Holy Year - Symbolic Baptism of Man **Obv:** Crowned shield **Rev:** Hands pulling up net filled with fish **Designer:** Guido Veroi

Date	Mintage	F	VF	XF	Unc	BU
1975	605,000	—	0.60	1.25	2.00	—

KM# 137 100 LIRE
8.0000 g., Stainless Steel, 27.75 mm. **Obv:** Crowned shield **Rev:** Stylized figure standing in courtyard **Designer:** Nicola Morelli

Date	Mintage	F	VF	XF	Unc	BU
1978/XVI	399,000	—	0.50	1.00	2.00	—

KM# 138 200 LIRE
5.0000 g., Aluminum-Bronze, 24 mm. **Obv:** Crowned shield **Rev:** Stylized figure above value

Date	Mintage	F	VF	XF	Unc	BU
1978/XVI	355,000	—	0.50	1.00	2.50	—

KM# 83.1 500 LIRE

11.0000 g., 0.8350 Silver 0.2953 oz. ASW, 29.3 mm. **Obv:** Bust right **Obv. Legend:** AN **Rev:** Crowned shield divides value **Designer:** Pietro Giampaoli

Date	Mintage	F	VF	XF	Unc	BU
1963/I	70,000	—	8.00	16.00	32.00	—

KM# 83.2 500 LIRE

11.0000 g., 0.8350 Silver 0.2953 oz. ASW, 29.3 mm. **Obv:** Bust right **Obv. Legend:** A **Rev:** Crowned shield divides value

Date	Mintage	F	VF	XF	Unc	BU
1964/II	70,000	—	7.00	15.00	25.00	—
1965/III	70,000	—	7.00	15.00	25.00	—

KM# 91 500 LIRE

11.0000 g., 0.8350 Silver 0.2953 oz. ASW, 29.3 mm. **Obv:** Crowned head left **Rev:** Shepard with sheep on shoulders **Designer:** E. Greco

Date	Mintage	F	VF	XF	Unc	BU
1966/IV	100,000	—	7.00	15.00	25.00	—

KM# 99 500 LIRE

11.0000 g., 0.8350 Silver 0.2953 oz. ASW, 29.3 mm. **Obv:** Bust left **Rev:** Saint Peter and Paul, cross between, keys below **Designer:** G. Pirrone

Date	Mintage	F	VF	XF	Unc	BU
ND(1967)/V	110,000	—	6.00	12.00	18.00	—

KM# 107 500 LIRE

11.0000 g., 0.8350 Silver 0.2953 oz. ASW, 29.3 mm. **Series:** F.A.O. **Obv:** Bust left **Rev:** Wheat ears forming radiant cross **Designer:** G. Pirrone

Date	Mintage	F	VF	XF	Unc	BU
ND(1968)/VI	110,000	—	6.00	12.00	18.00	—

KM# 115 500 LIRE

11.0000 g., 0.8350 Silver 0.2953 oz. ASW, 29.3 mm. **Obv:** Crowned head 1/4 left divides inscription **Rev:** Stylized angel in flight **Designer:** C. Ruffini

Date	Mintage	F	VF	XF	Unc	BU
1969/VII	110,000	—	6.00	12.00	18.00	—

KM# 123 500 LIRE

11.0000 g., 0.8350 Silver 0.2953 oz. ASW, 29.3 mm. **Obv:** Crowned shield **Rev:** Wheat and grapes **Designer:** Tomas Gismondi

Date	Mintage	F	VF	XF	Unc	BU
1970/VIII	110,000	—	—	6.00	15.00	—
1971/IX	125,000	—	—	6.00	15.00	—
1972/X	125,000	—	—	6.00	15.00	—
1973/XI	145,000	—	—	6.00	15.00	—
1974/XII	145,000	—	—	6.00	15.00	—
1975/XIII	162,000	—	—	6.00	15.00	—
1976/XIV	162,000	—	—	6.00	15.00	—

KM# 131 500 LIRE

11.0000 g., 0.8350 Silver 0.2953 oz. ASW, 29.3 mm. **Subject:** Holy Year - Forgiveness **Obv:** Crowned shield **Rev:** Stylized father embracing son **Designer:** Guido Veroi

Date	Mintage	F	VF	XF	Unc	BU
1975	200,000	—	—	7.00	16.00	—

KM# 132 500 LIRE

11.0000 g., 0.8350 Silver 0.2953 oz. ASW, 29.3 mm. **Subject:** Book of the Evangelists **Obv:** Crowned shield **Rev:** Assorted animal heads within cross window frame

Date	Mintage	F	VF	XF	Unc	BU
1977/XV	160,000	—	—	8.00	16.50	—

KM# 139 500 LIRE

11.0000 g., 0.8350 Silver 0.2953 oz. ASW, 29.3 mm. **Obv:** Crowned shield **Rev:** Stylized Jesus walking on water reaching for figure in boat

Date	Mintage	F	VF	XF	Unc	BU
1978/XVI	145,000	—	—	8.00	16.50	—

Sede Vacante

DECIMAL COINAGE

100 Centesimi = 1 Lira

KM# 140 500 LIRE

11.0000 g., 0.8350 Silver 0.2953 oz. ASW, 29.3 mm. **Obv:** Descending stylized dove above value **Rev:** Arms of Cardinal Jean Villot **Rev. Legend:** SEDE VACANTE MCMLXXVIII **Designer:** Cismondi **Note:** First 1978 Sede Vacante issue

Date	Mintage	F	VF	XF	Unc	BU
1978	500,000	—	—	10.00	20.00	—

KM# 141 500 LIRE

11.0000 g., 0.8350 Silver 0.2953 oz. ASW **Obv:** Descending radiant dove **Rev:** Arms of Cardinal Jean Villot **Rev. Legend:** SEDE VACANTE SEPTEMBER MCMLXXVIII **Note:** Second 1978 Sede Vacante issue

Date	Mintage	F	VF	XF	Unc	BU
1978	—	—	6.00	10.00	20.00	—

Note: Mintage included with Y#140

John Paul II

DECIMAL COINAGE

100 Centesimi = 1 Lira

KM# 143 10 LIRE

Aluminum, 23 mm. **Obv:** Bust left **Rev:** Cardinal Virtues - Temperance **Designer:** Guido Veroi

Date	Mintage	F	VF	XF	Unc	BU
1979/I	250,000	—	0.25	0.50	2.00	—
1980/II	170,000	—	0.25	0.50	2.00	—

KM# 155 10 LIRE

Aluminum, 23 mm. **Obv:** Head left **Rev:** Jesus given water at the well **Mint:** Rome **Designer:** Guido Veroi

Date	Mintage	F	VF	XF	Unc	BU
1981/IIIR	170,000	—	0.25	0.50	2.00	—

KM# 161 10 LIRE

Aluminum, 23 mm. **Subject:** Creation of Woman **Obv:** Bust right **Rev:** Standing figure facing to right of value **Mint:** Rome **Designer:** Enrico Manfrini

Date	Mintage	F	VF	XF	Unc	BU
1982/IVR	220,000	—	0.25	0.50	2.00	—

KM# 170 10 LIRE

Aluminum, 23 mm. **Subject:** Work and Teaching **Obv:** Head left at lower right of cross **Rev:** Teacher, student and value **Mint:** Rome **Designer:** Nicola Morelli

Date	Mintage	F	VF	XF	Unc	BU
1983/VR	110,000	—	0.25	0.50	2.00	—

KM# 177 10 LIRE
Aluminum, 23 mm. **Subject:** Year of Peace **Obv:** Bust left **Rev:** Hand holding bouquet **Mint:** Rome **Designer:** Ennio Tesei

Date	Mintage	F	VF	XF	Unc	BU
1984/VIR	110,000	—	0.25	0.50	2.00	—

KM# 185 10 LIRE
Aluminum, 23 mm. **Obv:** Head left **Rev:** Angel with gospel of St. Matthew **Designer:** Guido Veroi

Date	Mintage	F	VF	XF	Unc	BU
1985/VII	90,000	—	0.25	0.50	2.00	—

KM# 192 10 LIRE
Aluminum, 23 mm. **Rev:** Mary seated, value **Designer:** Guido Veroi

Date	Mintage	F	VF	XF	Unc	BU
1986/VIII	90,000	—	0.25	0.50	2.00	—

KM# 199 10 LIRE
Aluminum, 23 mm. **Obv:** Bust right **Rev:** Basilica behind Pieta Statue **Designer:** Angelo Canevari

Date	Mintage	F	VF	XF	Unc	BU
1987/IX	—	—	0.25	0.50	2.00	—

KM# 206 10 LIRE
Aluminum, 23 mm. **Subject:** Temptation of Adam and Eve **Obv:** Bust right **Rev:** Tree with snake divides standing figures **Designer:** Guido Veroi

Date	Mintage	F	VF	XF	Unc	BU
1988/X	—	—	0.25	0.50	2.00	—

KM# 213 10 LIRE
Aluminum, 23 mm. **Subject:** Jesus the Teacher **Rev:** Seated figure facing standing figure **Designer:** Enrico Manfrini

Date	Mintage	F	VF	XF	Unc	BU
1989/XI	—	—	0.25	0.50	2.00	—

KM# 220 10 LIRE
Aluminum, 23 mm. **Subject:** Saints Peter and Paul **Obv:** Bust 3/4 left **Rev:** Saints Peter and Paul facing **Designer:** Angelo Canevari

Date	Mintage	F	VF	XF	Unc	BU
1990/XII	—	—	0.25	0.50	2.00	—

KM# 228 10 LIRE
Aluminum, 23 mm. **Obv:** Head left **Rev:** Standing figure with book to right of value **Designer:** Nicola Morelli

Date	Mintage	F	VF	XF	Unc	BU
1991/XIII	—	—	0.25	0.50	2.00	—

KM# 236 10 LIRE
Aluminum, 23 mm. **Obv:** Bust right **Rev:** Bee on flower **Designer:** Sergio Giandomenico

Date	Mintage	F	VF	XF	Unc	BU
1992/XIV	—	—	0.25	0.50	2.00	—

KM# 244 10 LIRE
Aluminum, 23 mm. **Obv:** Head facing **Rev:** Sailboat divides inscription **Designer:** Guido Veroi

Date	Mintage	F	VF	XF	Unc	BU
1993/XV	—	—	0.25	0.50	2.00	—

KM# 252 10 LIRE
Aluminum, 23 mm. **Obv:** Bust left **Rev:** Figures planting trees **Designer:** Angelo Canevari

Date	Mintage	F	VF	XF	Unc	BU
1994/XVI	—	—	0.25	0.50	2.00	—

KM# 262 10 LIRE
Aluminum, 23 mm. **Rev:** Preaching **Designer:** Enrico Manfrini

Date	Mintage	F	VF	XF	Unc	BU
1995/XVII	—	—	0.25	0.50	2.00	—

KM# 272 10 LIRE
Aluminum, 23 mm. **Subject:** Child Carried to Peace **Obv:** Head left **Rev:** Stylized standing figure holding infant walking left **Designer:** Orietta Rossi

Date	Mintage	F	VF	XF	Unc	BU
1996/XVIII	—	—	0.25	0.50	3.00	—

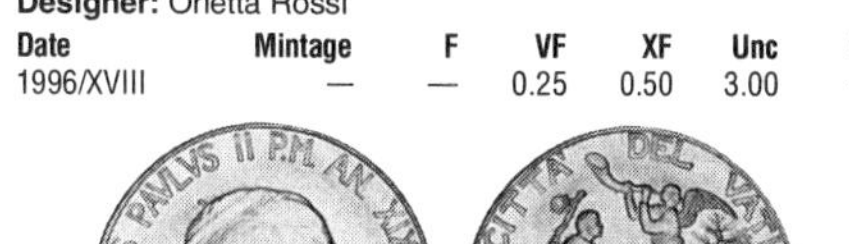

KM# 280 10 LIRE
Aluminum, 23 mm. **Obv:** Head right **Rev:** Angel blowing horn to upper right of man sowing seeds **Designer:** Gabriella Titotto

Date	Mintage	F	VF	XF	Unc	BU
1997/XIX	—	—	0.50	0.75	2.00	—

KM# 293 10 LIRE
1.6000 g., Aluminum, 23 mm. **Obv:** Bust right holding crucifix **Rev:** Standing figure flanked by seated figures **Designer:** Paolo Borghi

Date	Mintage	F	VF	XF	Unc	BU
1998/XX	—	—	0.50	0.75	3.00	—

KM# 305 10 LIRE
1.6000 g., Aluminum, 23.3 mm. **Subject:** Right to Life - Motherhood **Obv:** Bust right **Rev:** Mother with baby and child below tree **Edge:** Plain **Mint:** Rome **Designer:** Angelo Canevari

Date	Mintage	F	VF	XF	Unc	BU
1999/XXI	—	—	0.50	0.75	3.00	—

KM# 323 10 LIRE
1.6000 g., Aluminum, 23.2 mm. **Obv:** Papal arms within circle **Rev:** Pope lifting child **Edge:** Plain **Mint:** Rome **Designer:** Cecco Bonanotte

Date	Mintage	F	VF	XF	Unc	BU
2000/XXII	—	—	0.50	0.75	3.00	—

KM# 144 20 LIRE
3.6000 g., Aluminum-Bronze, 21.25 mm. **Rev:** Fortitude **Designer:** Guido Veroi

Date	Mintage	F	VF	XF	Unc	BU
1979/I	120,000	—	0.50	0.75	3.00	—
1980/II	265,000	—	0.50	0.75	3.00	—

KM# 156 20 LIRE
3.6000 g., Aluminum-Bronze, 21.25 mm. **Obv:** Head left **Rev:** Open door flanked by standing figures **Designer:** Guido Veroi

Date	Mintage	F	VF	XF	Unc	BU
1981/III	265,000	—	0.50	0.75	3.00	—

KM# 162 20 LIRE
3.6000 g., Aluminum-Bronze, 21.25 mm. **Subject:** Marriage **Obv:** Bust right **Rev:** Standing figures shaking hands **Designer:** Enrico Manfrini

Date	Mintage	F	VF	XF	Unc	BU
1982/IV	360,000	—	0.50	0.75	3.00	—

KM# 171 20 LIRE
3.6000 g., Aluminum-Bronze, 21.25 mm. **Subject:** Incarnation of the Word **Obv:** Head left to lower right of cross **Rev:** Radiant dove above stylized kneeling figures within triangle shape **Designer:** Nicola Morelli

Date	Mintage	F	VF	XF	Unc	BU
1983/V	170,000	—	0.50	0.75	3.00	—

KM# 178 20 LIRE
3.6000 g., Aluminum-Bronze, 21.25 mm. **Subject:** Year of Peace **Obv:** Bust left **Rev:** Child and sheep **Designer:** Ennio Tesei

Date	Mintage	F	VF	XF	Unc	BU
1984/VI	170,000	—	0.50	0.75	3.00	—

KM# 186 20 LIRE
3.6000 g., Aluminum-Bronze, 21.25 mm. **Obv:** Head left **Rev:** Stylized eagle holding gospel of St. John **Designer:** Guido Veroi

Date	Mintage	F	VF	XF	Unc	BU
1985/VII	255,000	—	0.50	0.75	3.00	—

KM# 193 20 LIRE
3.6000 g., Aluminum-Bronze, 21.25 mm. **Obv:** Bust right **Rev:** Stylized standing angel **Designer:** Guido Veroi

Date	Mintage	F	VF	XF	Unc	BU
1986/VIII	100,000	—	0.50	0.75	3.00	—

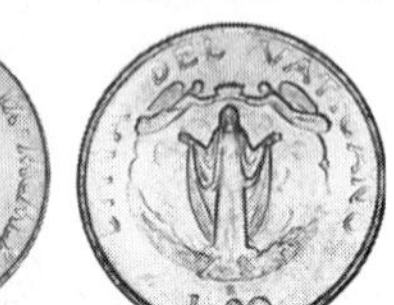

KM# 200 20 LIRE
3.6000 g., Aluminum-Bronze, 21.25 mm. **Obv:** Bust right **Rev:** Assumption of Mother Mary into heaven **Designer:** Angelo Canevari

Date	Mintage	F	VF	XF	Unc	BU
1987/IX	—	—	0.50	0.75	3.00	—

KM# 207 20 LIRE
3.6000 g., Aluminum-Bronze, 21.25 mm. **Subject:** Temptation of Adam and Eve **Rev:** Apple tree flanked by standing figures and pair of hands **Designer:** Guido Veroi **Note:** Similar to 200 Lire, KM#210.

Date	Mintage	F	VF	XF	Unc	BU
1988/X	—	—	0.50	0.75	3.00	—

KM# 214 20 LIRE
3.6000 g., Aluminum-Bronze, 21.25 mm. **Subject:** The Harvest **Rev:** Standing and kneeling figures **Designer:** Enrico Manfrini

Date	Mintage	F	VF	XF	Unc	BU
1989/XI	—	—	0.50	0.75	3.00	—

KM# 221 20 LIRE
3.6000 g., Aluminum-Bronze, 21.25 mm. **Obv:** Bust 3/4 left **Rev:** Pope John Paul II and Eastern Rite Bishop **Designer:** Angelo Canevari

Date	Mintage	F	VF	XF	Unc	BU
1990/XII	—	—	0.50	0.75	3.00	—

KM# 229 20 LIRE
3.6000 g., Aluminum-Bronze, 21.25 mm. **Obv:** Head left **Rev:** Crane and buildings **Designer:** Nicola Morelli

Date	Mintage	F	VF	XF	Unc	BU
1991/XIII	—	—	0.50	0.75	3.00	—

KM# 237 20 LIRE
3.6000 g., Aluminum-Bronze, 21.25 mm. **Obv:** Bust right **Rev:** Three children above value **Designer:** Sergio Giandomenico

Date	Mintage	F	VF	XF	Unc	BU
1992/XIV	—	—	0.50	0.75	3.00	—

KM# 245 20 LIRE
3.6000 g., Aluminum-Bronze, 21.25 mm. **Obv:** Head facing **Rev:** Crucifix, as on papal croizer **Designer:** Guido Veroi

Date	Mintage	F	VF	XF	Unc	BU
1993/XV	—	—	0.50	0.75	3.00	—

KM# 253 20 LIRE
3.6000 g., Aluminum-Bronze, 21.25 mm. **Obv:** Bust left **Rev:** Hospital patient with visitors **Designer:** Angelo Canaveri

Date	Mintage	F	VF	XF	Unc	BU
1994/XVI	—	—	0.50	0.75	3.00	—

KM# 263 20 LIRE
3.6000 g., Aluminum-Bronze, 21.25 mm. **Subject:** Euthanasia **Designer:** Enrico Manfrini

Date	Mintage	F	VF	XF	Unc	BU
1995/XVII	—	—	0.50	0.75	3.00	—

KM# 273 20 LIRE
3.6000 g., Aluminum-Bronze, 21.25 mm. **Obv:** Head left **Rev:** Parents praising child **Designer:** Orietta Rossi

Date	Mintage	F	VF	XF	Unc	BU
1996/XVIII	—	—	0.50	0.75	3.00	—

KM# 281 20 LIRE
3.6000 g., Aluminum-Bronze, 21.25 mm. **Obv:** Bust right **Rev:** Jesus teaching with book **Designer:** Gabriella Titotto

Date	Mintage	F	VF	XF	Unc	BU
1997/XIX	—	—	0.50	0.75	3.00	—

KM# 294 20 LIRE
3.6000 g., Aluminum-Bronze, 21.25 mm. **Obv:** Bust right holding crucifix **Rev:** Family and sun **Designer:** Paolo Borghi

Date	Mintage	F	VF	XF	Unc	BU
1998/XX	—	—	0.50	0.75	3.00	—

KM# 306 20 LIRE
3.6000 g., Aluminum-Bronze, 21.3 mm. **Subject:** Work - The Right to Fulfill One's Potential **Obv:** Bust right **Rev:** Workers **Edge:** Plain **Mint:** Rome **Designer:** Angelo Canevari

Date	Mintage	F	VF	XF	Unc	BU
1999/XXI	—	—	0.50	0.75	3.00	—

KM# 324 20 LIRE
3.5700 g., Brass, 21.2 mm. **Obv:** Papal arms within circle **Rev:** Head of Pope stargazing **Edge:** Plain **Mint:** Rome **Designer:** Cecco Bonanotte

Date	Mintage	F	VF	XF	Unc	BU
2000/XXII	—	—	0.50	0.75	3.00	—

KM# 332 20 LIRE
3.5700 g., Brass, 21.2 mm. **Obv:** Bust left **Rev:** Papal arms **Edge:** Plain **Mint:** Rome **Designer:** Laura Cretella

Date	Mintage	F	VF	XF	Unc	BU
2001/XXIII	—	—	0.50	0.75	3.00	—

KM# 145 50 LIRE
6.2000 g., Stainless Steel, 24.8 mm. **Obv:** Bust left **Rev:** Justice seated right with sword and scales **Designer:** Guido Veroi

Date	Mintage	F	VF	XF	Unc	BU
1979/I	223,000	—	0.50	0.75	3.00	—
1980/II	250,000	—	0.50	0.75	3.00	—

KM# 157 50 LIRE
6.2000 g., Stainless Steel, 24.8 mm. **Obv:** Head left **Rev:** Upright design flanked by standing figures **Designer:** Guido Veroi

Date	Mintage	F	VF	XF	Unc	BU
1981/III	240,000	—	0.50	0.75	3.00	—

KM# 163 50 LIRE

6.2000 g., Stainless Steel, 24.8 mm. **Subject:** Motherhood **Obv:** Bust right **Rev:** Seated figure with infant on lap **Designer:** Enrico Manfrini

Date	Mintage	F	VF	XF	Unc	BU
1982/IV	400,000	—	0.50	0.75	3.00	—

KM# 172 50 LIRE

6.2000 g., Stainless Steel, 24.8 mm. **Subject:** Banishment of Adam and Eve **Obv:** Head left to lower right of cross **Rev:** Stylized figure **Designer:** Nicola Morelli

Date	Mintage	F	VF	XF	Unc	BU
1983/V	300,000	—	0.50	0.75	3.00	—

KM# 179 50 LIRE

6.2000 g., Stainless Steel, 24.8 mm. **Subject:** Year of Peace **Obv:** Bust left **Rev:** Doves **Designer:** Ennio Tesei

Date	Mintage	F	VF	XF	Unc	BU
1984/VI	300,000	—	0.50	0.75	3.00	—

KM# 187 50 LIRE

6.2000 g., Stainless Steel, 24.8 mm. **Obv:** Head left **Rev:** Winged lion holding gospel of St. Mark **Designer:** Guido Veroi

Date	Mintage	F	VF	XF	Unc	BU
1985/VII	360,000	—	0.50	0.75	3.00	—

KM# 194 50 LIRE

6.2000 g., Stainless Steel, 24.8 mm. **Obv:** Bust right **Rev:** Moses seated on rock **Designer:** Guido Veroi

Date	Mintage	F	VF	XF	Unc	BU
1986/VIII	100,000	—	0.50	0.75	3.00	—

KM# 201 50 LIRE

6.2000 g., Stainless Steel, 24.8 mm. **Obv:** Bust right **Rev:** Mother Mary protecting kneeling sinners **Designer:** Angelo Canevari

Date	Mintage	F	VF	XF	Unc	BU
1987/IX	—	—	0.50	0.75	3.00	—

KM# 208 50 LIRE

6.2000 g., Stainless Steel, 24.8 mm. **Subject:** Creation of Eve From Adam's Rib **Obv:** Bust right **Rev:** Face profile to right of female figure rising out of male figure on ground **Designer:** Guido Veroi

Date	Mintage	F	VF	XF	Unc	BU
VS1988/X	—	—	0.50	0.75	3.00	—

KM# 215 50 LIRE

6.2000 g., Stainless Steel, 24.8 mm. **Subject:** Human Solidarity **Rev:** Standing figures **Designer:** Enrico Manfrini

Date	Mintage	F	VF	XF	Unc	BU
1989/XI	—	—	0.50	0.75	3.00	—

KM# 222 50 LIRE

Stainless Steel, 16.3 mm. **Obv:** Bust 3/4 left **Rev:** Radiant cross in open door **Designer:** Angelo Canevari

Date	Mintage	F	VF	XF	Unc	BU
1990/XII	—	—	0.50	0.75	3.00	—

KM# 230 50 LIRE

Stainless Steel, 16.3 mm. **Obv:** Head left **Rev:** Baptism scene **Designer:** Nicola Morelli

Date	Mintage	F	VF	XF	Unc	BU
1991/XIII	—	—	0.50	0.75	3.00	—

KM# 238 50 LIRE

Stainless Steel, 16.3 mm. **Obv:** Bust right **Rev:** Cross as balance scale between agriculture and industry **Designer:** Sergio Giandomenico

Date	Mintage	F	VF	XF	Unc	BU
1992/XIV	—	—	0.50	0.75	3.00	—

KM# 246 50 LIRE

Stainless Steel, 16.3 mm. **Obv:** Head facing **Rev:** Chalice divides inscription **Designer:** Guido Veroi

Date	Mintage	F	VF	XF	Unc	BU
1993/XV	—	—	0.50	0.75	3.00	—

KM# 254 50 LIRE

Stainless Steel, 16.3 mm. **Obv:** Bust left **Rev:** Hands and prison bars **Designer:** Angelo Canevari

Date	Mintage	F	VF	XF	Unc	BU
1994/XVI	—	—	0.50	0.75	3.00	—

KM# 264 50 LIRE

Stainless Steel, 16.3 mm. **Rev:** Dragon on Prone Woman (Abortion) **Designer:** Enrico Manfrini

Date	Mintage	F	VF	XF	Unc	BU
1995/XVII	—	—	0.50	0.75	3.00	—

KM# 274 50 LIRE

Copper-Nickel, 19.2 mm. **Obv:** Head left **Rev:** Guardian angel protecting child **Designer:** Orietta Rossi

Date	Mintage	F	VF	XF	Unc	BU
1996/XVIII	—	—	0.50	0.75	3.00	—

KM# 282 50 LIRE

Copper-Nickel, 19.2 mm. **Obv:** Head right **Rev:** One man with lowered sword, the other with dove **Designer:** Gabriella Titotto

Date	Mintage	F	VF	XF	Unc	BU
1997/XIX	—	—	0.50	0.75	3.00	—

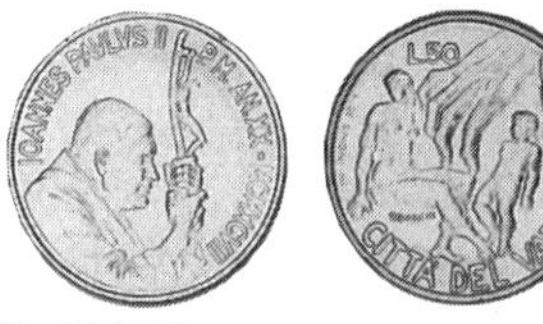

KM# 295 50 LIRE

Copper-Nickel, 19.2 mm. **Obv:** Pope with crucifix croizer **Rev:** Two figures and hand **Designer:** Paolo Borghi

Date	Mintage	F	VF	XF	Unc	BU
1998/XX	—	—	0.50	0.75	3.00	—

KM# 307 50 LIRE

4.4600 g., Copper-Nickel, 19.2 mm. **Subject:** Ecosystem - Agriculture **Obv:** Bust right **Rev:** Agricultural workers **Edge:** Plain **Mint:** Rome **Designer:** Angelo Canevari

Date	Mintage	F	VF	XF	Unc	BU
1999/XXI	—	—	0.50	0.75	3.00	—

KM# 325 50 LIRE

4.5000 g., Copper-Nickel, 19.2 mm. **Obv:** Papal arms within circle **Rev:** Pope about to kiss ground **Edge:** Plain **Mint:** Rome **Designer:** Cecco Bonanotte

Date	Mintage	F	VF	XF	Unc	BU
2000/XXII	—	—	0.50	0.75	3.00	—

KM# 333 50 LIRE

4.5000 g., Copper-Nickel, 19.2 mm. **Obv:** Pius XII bust left **Rev:** Papal arms **Edge:** Plain **Mint:** Rome **Designer:** Laura Cretella

Date	Mintage	F	VF	XF	Unc	BU
2001/XXIII	—	—	0.50	0.75	3.00	—

KM# 146 100 LIRE
8.0000 g., Stainless Steel, 27.75 mm. **Obv:** Bust left **Rev:** Prudence seated **Designer:** Guido Veroi

Date	Mintage	F	VF	XF	Unc	BU
1979/I	399,000	—	0.75	1.25	3.50	—
1980/II	485,000	—	0.75	1.25	3.50	—

KM# 158 100 LIRE
8.0000 g., Stainless Steel, 27.75 mm. **Obv:** Head left **Rev:** Angel offering food to seated figure **Designer:** Guido Veroi

Date	Mintage	F	VF	XF	Unc	BU
1981/III	550,000	—	0.75	1.25	3.50	—

KM# 164 100 LIRE
8.0000 g., Stainless Steel, 27.75 mm. **Subject:** Family Unit **Obv:** Bust right **Rev:** Standing and seated figure divides value **Designer:** Enrico Manfrini

Date	Mintage	F	VF	XF	Unc	BU
1982/IV	656,000	—	0.75	1.25	3.50	—

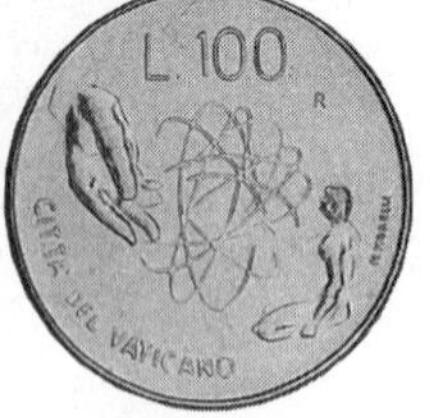

KM# 173 100 LIRE
8.0000 g., Stainless Steel, 27.75 mm. **Subject:** God Gives World to Mankind **Obv:** Head left to lower right of cross **Rev:** Design flanked by hand and kneeling figure **Designer:** Nicola Morelli

Date	Mintage	F	VF	XF	Unc	BU
1983/V	455,000	—	0.75	1.25	3.50	—

KM# 180 100 LIRE
8.0000 g., Stainless Steel, 27.75 mm. **Subject:** Year of Peace **Obv:** Bust left **Rev:** Cross divides lamb and value **Designer:** Ennio Tesei

Date	Mintage	F	VF	XF	Unc	BU
1984/VI	400,000	—	0.75	1.25	3.50	—

KM# 188 100 LIRE
8.0000 g., Stainless Steel, 27.75 mm. **Obv:** Head left **Rev:** Small airplane in flight over map **Designer:** Guido Veroi

Date	Mintage	F	VF	XF	Unc	BU
1985/VII	800,000	—	0.75	1.25	3.50	—

KM# 195 100 LIRE
8.0000 g., Stainless Steel, 27.75 mm. **Obv:** Bust right **Rev:** Christ seated on rocks **Designer:** Guido Veroi

Date	Mintage	F	VF	XF	Unc	BU
1986/VIII	100,000	—	0.75	1.25	3.50	—

KM# 202 100 LIRE
8.0000 g., Stainless Steel, 27.75 mm. **Subject:** Angel and Mary, The Annunciation **Obv:** Bust right **Rev:** Dove above angel and seated figure **Designer:** Angelo Canevari

Date	Mintage	F	VF	XF	Unc	BU
1987/IX	—	—	0.75	1.25	3.50	—

KM# 209 100 LIRE
8.0000 g., Stainless Steel, 27.75 mm. **Subject:** Adam naming the Animals **Obv:** Bust right **Rev:** Standing figure in palm of hand to left of assorted animals **Designer:** Guido Veroi

Date	Mintage	F	VF	XF	Unc	BU
1988/X	—	—	0.75	1.25	3.50	—

KM# 216 100 LIRE
8.0000 g., Stainless Steel, 27.75 mm. **Rev:** Pelican feeding young **Designer:** Enrico Manfrini

Date	Mintage	F	VF	XF	Unc	BU
1989/XI	—	—	0.75	1.25	3.50	—

KM# 223 100 LIRE
Stainless Steel, 18 mm. **Subject:** Early Bishop **Obv:** Bust 3/4 left **Rev:** Hooded half-figure facing **Designer:** Angelo Canevari

Date	Mintage	F	VF	XF	Unc	BU
1990/XII	—	—	0.75	1.25	3.50	—

KM# 231 100 LIRE
Stainless Steel, 18 mm. **Obv:** Head left **Rev:** Depiction of the risen Christ **Designer:** Nicola Morelli

Date	Mintage	F	VF	XF	Unc	BU
1991/XIII	—	—	0.75	1.25	3.50	—

KM# 239 100 LIRE
Stainless Steel, 18 mm. **Obv:** Bust right **Rev:** Open book above value **Designer:** Sergio Giandomenico

Date	Mintage	F	VF	XF	Unc	BU
1992/XIV	—	—	0.75	1.25	3.50	—

KM# 247 100 LIRE
Copper-Nickel, 21.8 mm. **Obv:** Head facing **Rev:** Portrait of Jesus facing divides inscription above value **Designer:** Guido Veroi

Date	Mintage	F	VF	XF	Unc	BU
1993/XV	—	—	0.75	1.25	3.50	—

KM# 255 100 LIRE
Copper-Nickel, 21.8 mm. **Obv:** Bust left **Rev:** Basketball players with one in wheelchair **Designer:** Angelo Canevari

Date	Mintage	F	VF	XF	Unc	BU
1994/XVI	—	—	0.75	1.25	3.50	—

KM# 265 100 LIRE
Copper-Nickel, 21.8 mm. **Rev:** Guard and prisoners **Designer:** Enrico Manfrini

Date	Mintage	F	VF	XF	Unc	BU
1995/XVII	—	—	0.75	1.25	3.50	—

KM# 275 100 LIRE
Copper-Nickel, 21.8 mm. **Obv:** Head left **Rev:** Women helping children **Designer:** Orietta Rossi

Date	Mintage	F	VF	XF	Unc	BU
1996/XVIII	—	—	0.75	1.25	3.50	—

KM# 283 100 LIRE
Copper-Nickel, 21.8 mm. **Obv:** Bust right **Rev:** Woman filling birdbath and doves **Designer:** Gabriella Titotto

Date	Mintage	F	VF	XF	Unc	BU
1997/XIX	—	—	0.75	1.25	2.50	—

KM# 296 100 LIRE
Copper-Nickel, 21.8 mm. **Obv:** Pope with crucifix croizer **Rev:** Female figure in front of globe **Designer:** Paolo Borghi

Date	Mintage	F	VF	XF	Unc	BU
1998/XX	—	—	0.75	1.25	2.50	—

KM# 308 100 LIRE
4.5000 g., Copper-Nickel, 22 mm. **Subject:** The Right to Peace **Obv:** Bust right within circle **Rev:** Children of the world gathered in peace **Edge:** Reeded and plain sections **Mint:** Rome **Designer:** Angelo Canevari

Date	Mintage	F	VF	XF	Unc	BU
1999/XXI	—	—	0.75	1.25	2.50	—

KM# 326 100 LIRE
4.5000 g., Copper-Nickel, 22 mm. **Obv:** Papal arms within circle **Rev:** Pope resting head on hand within window frame design **Edge:** Plain and reeded sections **Mint:** Rome **Designer:** Cecco Bonanotte

Date	Mintage	F	VF	XF	Unc	BU
2000/XXII	—	—	0.75	1.25	2.50	—

KM# 334 100 LIRE
4.5000 g., Copper-Nickel, 22 mm. **Obv:** Bust left **Rev:** Papal arms within circle **Edge:** Reeded and plain sections **Mint:** Rome **Designer:** Laura Cretella

Date	Mintage	F	VF	XF	Unc	BU
2001/XXIII	—	—	0.50	1.00	2.50	—

KM# 147 200 LIRE
5.0000 g., Aluminum-Bronze, 24 mm. **Obv:** Bust left **Rev:** Peace seated flanked by value and sprig **Designer:** Guido Veroi

Date	Mintage	F	VF	XF	Unc	BU
1979/I	355,000	—	0.50	1.00	2.50	—
1980/II	200,000	—	0.50	1.00	2.50	—

KM# 159 200 LIRE
5.0000 g., Aluminum-Bronze, 24 mm. **Subject:** Corporal acts of Mercy - Bury the dead **Obv:** Head left **Rev:** Standing figures carrying supine figure **Designer:** Guido Veroi

Date	Mintage	F	VF	XF	Unc	BU
1981/III	170,000	—	0.50	1.00	2.50	—

KM# 165 200 LIRE
5.0000 g., Aluminum-Bronze, 24 mm. **Subject:** Farm labor **Obv:** Bust right **Rev:** Workers and ox **Designer:** Enrico Manfrini

Date	Mintage	F	VF	XF	Unc	BU
1982/IV	500,000	—	0.50	1.00	2.50	—

KM# 174 200 LIRE
5.0000 g., Aluminum-Bronze, 24 mm. **Subject:** Creation of Man **Obv:** Head left to lower right of cross **Rev:** Stylized figure above hands **Designer:** Nicola Morelli

Date	Mintage	F	VF	XF	Unc	BU
1983/V	300,000	—	0.50	1.00	2.25	—

KM# 181 200 LIRE
5.0000 g., Aluminum-Bronze, 24 mm. **Subject:** Year of Peace **Obv:** Bust left **Rev:** Sailboat and cross **Designer:** Ennio Tesei

Date	Mintage	F	VF	XF	Unc	BU
1984/VI	250,000	—	0.50	1.00	2.25	—

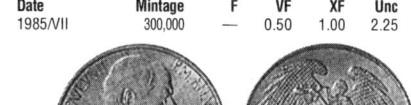

KM# 189 200 LIRE
5.0000 g., Aluminum-Bronze, 24 mm. **Obv:** Head left **Rev:** Winged Ox holding gospel **Designer:** Guido Veroi

Date	Mintage	F	VF	XF	Unc	BU
1985/VII	300,000	—	0.50	1.00	2.25	—

KM# 196 200 LIRE
5.0000 g., Aluminum-Bronze, 24 mm. **Obv:** Bust right **Rev:** Archangel Michael and value **Designer:** Guido Veroi

Date	Mintage	F	VF	XF	Unc	BU
1986/VIII	100,000	—	0.50	1.00	2.25	—

KM# 203 200 LIRE
5.0000 g., Aluminum-Bronze, 24 mm. **Subject:** Mary, Queen of Peace **Obv:** Bust right **Rev:** Seated figure in front of trees **Designer:** Angelo Canevari

Date	Mintage	F	VF	XF	Unc	BU
1987/IX	—	—	0.50	1.00	2.25	—

KM# 210 200 LIRE
5.0000 g., Aluminum-Bronze, 24 mm. **Subject:** Creation of Adam **Obv:** Bust right **Rev:** Face profile at left of figure within palm of hand **Designer:** Guido Veroi

Date	Mintage	F	VF	XF	Unc	BU
1988/X	—	—	0.50	1.00	2.25	—

MB# 217 200 LIRE
5.0000 g., Aluminum-Bronze, 24 mm. **Obv:** Bust 3/4 right **Rev:** Group of standing figures **Designer:** Enrico Manfrini

Date	Mintage	F	VF	XF	Unc	BU
1989/XI	—	—	0.50	1.00	2.25	—

KM# 224 200 LIRE
5.0000 g., Aluminum-Bronze, 24 mm. **Subject:** Blessed Virgin Mary **Obv:** Bust 3/4 left **Rev:** Standing figure facing and value **Designer:** Angelo Canevari

Date	Mintage	F	VF	XF	Unc	BU
1990/XII	—	—	0.50	1.00	2.25	—

KM# 232 200 LIRE
5.0000 g., Aluminum-Bronze, 24 mm. **Obv:** Head left **Rev:** Stylized figure to left of city **Designer:** Nicola Morelli

Date	Mintage	F	VF	XF	Unc	BU
1991/XIII	—	—	0.50	1.00	2.25	—

KM# 240 200 LIRE
5.0000 g., Aluminum-Bronze, 24 mm. **Obv:** Bust right **Rev:** Mother nursing child **Designer:** Sergio Giandomenico

Date	Mintage	F	VF	XF	Unc	BU
1992/XIV	—	—	0.50	1.00	2.25	—

KM# 248 200 LIRE
5.0000 g., Aluminum-Bronze, 24 mm. **Subject:** Ten Commandments **Obv:** Head facing **Rev:** 10 commandment stone divides name above value **Designer:** Guido Veroi

Date	Mintage	F	VF	XF	Unc	BU
1993/XV	—	—	0.50	1.00	2.25	—

KM# 256 200 LIRE
5.0000 g., Aluminum-Bronze, 24 mm. **Subject:** Helping Victims of Drug Abuse **Obv:** Bust left **Rev:** Group of standing figures **Designer:** Angelo Canevari

Date	Mintage	F	VF	XF	Unc	BU
1994/XVI	—	—	0.50	1.00	2.25	—

KM# 266 200 LIRE
5.0000 g., Aluminum-Bronze, 24 mm. **Rev:** Family and farming scene **Designer:** Enrico Manfrini

Date	Mintage	F	VF	XF	Unc	BU
1995/XVII	—	—	0.50	1.00	2.25	—

KM# 276 200 LIRE
5.0000 g., Aluminum-Bronze, 24 mm. **Obv:** Head left **Rev:** Display of family togetherness **Designer:** Orietta Rossi

Date	Mintage	F	VF	XF	Unc	BU
1996/XVIII	—	—	0.50	1.00	2.25	—

KM# 284 200 LIRE
5.0000 g., Aluminum-Bronze, 24 mm. **Obv:** Bust right **Rev:** Angel guiding two people **Designer:** Gabriella Titotto

Date	Mintage	F	VF	XF	Unc	BU
1997/XIX	—	—	0.50	1.00	2.25	—

KM# 297 200 LIRE
5.0000 g., Aluminum-Bronze, 24 mm. **Obv:** Bust left **Rev:** Group of standing figures **Designer:** Paolo Borghi

Date	Mintage	F	VF	XF	Unc	BU
1998/XX	—	—	0.50	1.00	2.25	—

KM# 309 200 LIRE
5.0000 g., Aluminum-Bronze, 24 mm. **Obv:** Bust right **Rev:** Christ among the poor and outcast **Edge:** Reeded **Mint:** Rome **Designer:** Angelo Canevari

Date	Mintage	F	VF	XF	Unc	BU
1999/XXI	—	—	0.50	1.00	2.25	—

KM# 327 200 LIRE
5.0000 g., Brass, 22 mm. **Obv:** Papal arms within circle **Rev:** Pope praying **Edge:** Reeded **Mint:** Rome **Designer:** Cecco Bonanotte

Date	Mintage	F	VF	XF	Unc	BU
2000/XXII	—	—	0.50	1.00	2.25	—

KM# 335 200 LIRE
5.0000 g., Brass, 22 mm. **Obv:** Bust right **Rev:** Papal arms within circle **Edge:** Reeded **Mint:** Rome **Designer:** Laura Cretella

Date	Mintage	F	VF	XF	Unc	BU
2001/XXIII	—	—	0.50	1.00	2.25	—

KM# 148 500 LIRE
11.0000 g., 0.8350 Silver 0.2953 oz. ASW, 29.3 mm. **Obv:** Head left **Rev:** Crowned shield **Designer:** Celestino Giampaoli

Date	Mintage	F	VF	XF	Unc	BU
1979/I	145,000	—	—	10.00	22.50	—
1980/II	184,000	—	—	10.00	22.50	—

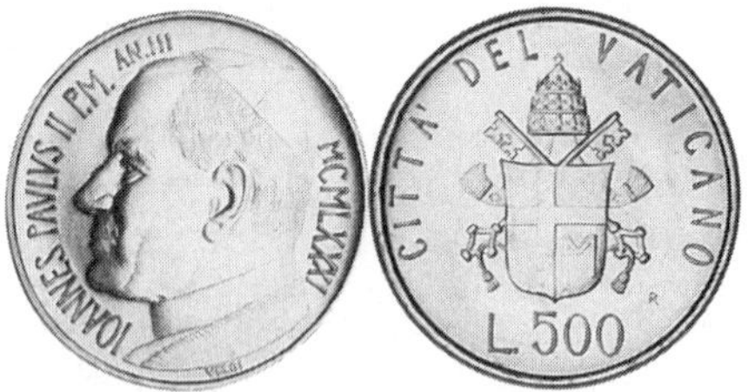

KM# 160 500 LIRE
11.0000 g., 0.8350 Silver 0.2953 oz. ASW, 29.3 mm. **Obv:** Head left **Rev:** Crowned shield **Designer:** Guido Veroi

Date	Mintage	F	VF	XF	Unc	BU
1981/III	184,000	—	—	10.00	22.50	—

KM# 166 500 LIRE
6.8000 g., Bi-Metallic Aluminum-Bronze center in Stainless Steel ring, 25.8 mm. **Subject:** Education **Obv:** Bust right within circle **Rev:** Seated figure flanked by children within circle **Designer:** Enrico Manfrini

Date	Mintage	F	VF	XF	Unc	BU
1982/IV	1,852,000	—	—	3.50	7.00	—

KM# 175 500 LIRE
6.8000 g., Bi-Metallic Aluminum-Bronze center in Stainless Steel ring, 25.8 mm. **Subject:** Creation of the Universe **Obv:** Head left to lower right of cross within circle **Rev:** Hand reaching in globe within circle **Designer:** Nicola Morelli

Date	Mintage	F	VF	XF	Unc	BU
1983/V	—	—	—	3.50	7.00	—

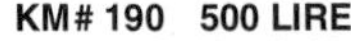

KM# 182 500 LIRE
6.8000 g., Bi-Metallic Aluminum-Bronze center in Stainless Steel ring, 25.8 mm. **Subject:** Year of Peace **Obv:** Head left within circle **Rev:** Sprig within clasped hands within circle **Designer:** Ennio Tesei

Date	Mintage	F	VF	XF	Unc	BU
1984/VI	270,000	—	—	3.50	7.00	—

KM# 190 500 LIRE
6.8000 g., Bi-Metallic Aluminum-Bronze center in Stainless Steel ring, 25.8 mm. **Obv:** Head left within circle **Rev:** St. Paul in boat within circle **Designer:** Guido Veroi

Date	Mintage	F	VF	XF	Unc	BU
1985/VII	300,000	—	—	2.50	6.00	—

KM# 197 500 LIRE
6.8000 g., Bi-Metallic Aluminum-Bronze center in Stainless Steel ring, 25.8 mm. **Obv:** Bust right within circle **Rev:** Seated Mary and Jesus within circle

Date	Mintage	F	VF	XF	Unc	BU
1986/VIII	300,000	—	—	2.50	6.00	—

KM# 204 500 LIRE
6.8000 g., Bi-Metallic Aluminum-Bronze center in Stainless Steel ring, 25.8 mm. **Obv:** Bust left within circle **Rev:** Mary before Crucified Jesus within circle **Designer:** Angelo Canevari

Date	Mintage	F	VF	XF	Unc	BU
1987/IX	—	—	—	2.50	6.00	—

KM# 211 500 LIRE
6.8000 g., Bi-Metallic Aluminum-Bronze center in Stainless Steel ring, 25.8 mm. **Obv:** Head right within circle **Rev:** Dove at center, conjoined busts within circle **Designer:** Guido Veroi

Date	Mintage	F	VF	XF	Unc	BU
1988/X	—	—	—	2.50	6.00	—

KM# 218 500 LIRE

6.8000 g., Bi-Metallic Aluminum-Bronze center in Stainless Steel ring, 25.8 mm. **Obv:** Bust right within circle **Rev:** Grapevine within circle **Designer:** Enrico Manfrini

Date	Mintage	F	VF	XF	Unc	BU
1989/XI	—	—	—	2.50	6.00	—

KM# 225 500 LIRE

6.8000 g., Bi-Metallic Aluminum-Bronze center in Stainless Steel ring, 25.8 mm. **Obv:** Bust left within circle **Rev:** Jesus flanked by kneeling figures within circle **Designer:** Angelo Canevari

Date	Mintage	F	VF	XF	Unc	BU
1990/XII	—	—	—	2.25	5.00	—

KM# 233 500 LIRE

6.8000 g., Bi-Metallic Aluminum-Bronze center in Stainless Steel ring, 25.8 mm. **Obv:** Head left within circle **Rev:** Redeemer sending out missionaries within circle **Designer:** Nicola Morelli

Date	Mintage	F	VF	XF	Unc	BU
1991/XIII	—	—	—	2.25	5.00	—

KM# 241 500 LIRE

6.8000 g., Bi-Metallic Aluminum-Bronze center in Stainless Steel ring, 25.8 mm. **Obv:** Bust right within circle **Rev:** Hands holding loaf of bread within globe **Designer:** Sergio Giandomenico

Date	Mintage	F	VF	XF	Unc	BU
1992/XIV	—	—	—	2.25	5.00	—

KM# 249 500 LIRE

6.8000 g., Bi-Metallic Aluminum-Bronze center in Stainless Steel ring, 25.8 mm. **Rev:** Thurible **Designer:** Guido Veroi

Date	Mintage	F	VF	XF	Unc	BU
1993/XV	—	—	—	2.25	5.00	—

KM# 257 500 LIRE

6.8000 g., Bi-Metallic Aluminum-Bronze center in Stainless Steel ring, 25.8 mm. **Obv:** Bust left within circle **Rev:** People meeting, Golgotha in background **Designer:** Angelo Caevari

Date	Mintage	F	VF	XF	Unc	BU
1994/XVI	—	—	—	2.25	5.00	—

KM# 267 500 LIRE

6.8000 g., Bi-Metallic, 25.8 mm. **Rev:** Cain slaying Abel within circle **Designer:** Enrico Manfrini

Date	Mintage	F	VF	XF	Unc	BU
1995/XVII	460,000	—	—	2.25	5.00	—

KM# 277 500 LIRE

6.8000 g., Bi-Metallic Aluminum-Bronze center in Stainless Steel ring, 25.8 mm. **Obv:** Head left within circle **Rev:** Seated figures within circle, serpent at left of circle **Designer:** Orietta Rossi

Date	Mintage	F	VF	XF	Unc	BU
1996/XVIII	100,000	—	—	2.25	5.00	—

KM# 285 500 LIRE

6.8000 g., Bi-Metallic Aluminum-Bronze center in Stainless Steel ring, 25.8 mm. **Obv:** Head right within circle **Rev:** One man freeing another from thorns **Designer:** Gabriella Titotto

Date	Mintage	F	VF	XF	Unc	BU
1997/XIX	160,000	—	—	2.25	5.00	—

KM# 298 500 LIRE

6.8000 g., Bi-Metallic Aluminum-Bronze center in Stainless Steel ring, 25.8 mm. **Obv:** Bust right holding crucifix within circle **Rev:** Two figures within circle **Designer:** Paolo Borghi

Date	Mintage	F	VF	XF	Unc	BU
1998/XX	103,500	—	—	2.25	5.00	—

KM# 310 500 LIRE

6.7000 g., Bi-Metallic Aluminum-Bronze center in Stainless Steel ring, 25.9 mm. **Subject:** Time of Choices, Time of Hope **Obv:** Bust right within circle **Rev:** God's hand above young parent's with baby **Edge:** Reeded **Mint:** Rome **Designer:** Angelo Canevari

Date	Mintage	F	VF	XF	Unc	BU
1999/XXI	161,000	—	—	2.25	5.50	—

KM# 322 500 LIRE

11.0000 g., 0.8350 Silver 0.2953 oz. ASW, 29.3 mm. **Subject:** 70th Anniversary - Vatican City Arms of Six Popes **Obv:** Bust right **Rev:** Dates in center of assorted crowned shields

Date	Mintage	F	VF	XF	Unc	BU
1999/XXI	—	—	—	30.00	40.00	—
1999/XXI Proof	—	Value: 65.00				

KM# 328 500 LIRE

6.7700 g., Bi-Metallic Aluminum-Bronze center in Stainless Steel ring, 25.7 mm. **Obv:** Papal arms within circle **Rev:** Bust right turning a page within circle **Edge:** Reeded and plain sections **Mint:** Rome **Designer:** Cecco Bonanotte

Date	Mintage	F	VF	XF	Unc	BU
2000/XXII	—	—	—	3.00	6.50	—

KM# 336 500 LIRE

6.7700 g., Bi-Metallic Aluminum-Bronze center in Stainless steel ring, 25.7 mm. **Obv:** Head left **Rev:** Papal arms within circle **Edge:** Reeded and plain sections **Mint:** Rome **Designer:** Laura Cretella

Date	Mintage	F	VF	XF	Unc	BU
2001/XXIII	—	—	—	3.50	7.00	—

KM# 286 1000 LIRE

Bi-Metallic Stainless Steel center in Aluminum-Bronze ring, 26.9 mm. **Obv:** Head right within circle **Rev:** Crowned shield within circle **Designer:** Gabriella Titotto

Date	Mintage	F	VF	XF	Unc	BU
1997/XIX	270,000	—	—	3.50	7.00	—

KM# 299 1000 LIRE

Bi-Metallic Stainless Steel center in Aluminum-Bronze ring, 26.9 mm. **Obv:** Head left within circle **Rev:** Papal coat-of-arms within circle **Designer:** Paolo Borghi

Date	Mintage	F	VF	XF	Unc	BU
1998/XX	306,500	—	—	3.50	8.50	—

KM# 311 1000 LIRE

8.8500 g., Bi-Metallic Stainless Steel center in Aluminum-Bronze ring, 26.9 mm. **Obv:** Pope's arms within circle **Rev:** Couple at base of Christ on cross within circle **Edge:** Reeded and plain sections **Mint:** Rome **Designer:** Angelo Canevari

Date	Mintage	F	VF	XF	Unc	BU
1999/XXI	126,100	—	—	4.00	8.50	—

KM# 329 1000 LIRE

8.8500 g., Bi-Metallic Stainless Steel center in Aluminum-Bronze ring, 26.9 mm. **Obv:** Papal arms within circle **Rev:** Pope and Eastern Orthodox Patriarch within circle **Edge:** Reeded and plain sections **Mint:** Rome **Designer:** Cecco Bonanotte

Date	Mintage	F	VF	XF	Unc	BU
2000/XXII	—	—	—	4.00	8.50	—

KM# 337 1000 LIRE

8.8500 g., Copper-Nickel, 26.9 mm. **Obv:** Bust right **Rev:** Crowned shield **Edge:** Reeded and plain sections **Mint:** Rome **Designer:** Laura Cretella

Date	Mintage	F	VF	XF	Unc	BU
2001/XIV	—	—	—	5.50	7.00	—

EURO COINAGE

John Paul II

KM# 341 EURO CENT

2.2700 g., Copper Plated Steel, 16.2 mm. **Obv:** Bust 1/4 left **Obv. Designer:** Guido Veroi **Rev:** Value and globe **Rev. Designer:** Luc Luycx **Edge:** Plain **Mint:** Rome

Date	Mintage	F	VF	XF	Unc	BU
2002R	80,000	—	—	—	115	—
2002R Proof	9,000	Value: 175				
2003R	65,000	—	—	—	55.00	—
2003R Proof	13,000	Value: 145				
2004R	65,000	—	—	—	25.00	—
2004R Proof	13,000	Value: 145				
2005R	85,000	—	—	—	25.00	—
2005R Proof	16,000	Value: 140				

KM# 342 2 EURO CENT

3.0300 g., Copper Plated Steel, 18.7 mm. **Obv:** Bust 1/4 left **Obv. Designer:** Guido Veroi **Rev:** Value and globe **Edge:** Grooved **Mint:** Rome

Date	Mintage	F	VF	XF	Unc	BU
2002R	80,000	—	—	—	115	—
2002R Proof	9,000	Value: 175				
2003R	65,000	—	—	—	55.00	—
2003R Proof	13,000	Value: 145				
2004R	65,000	—	—	—	25.00	—
2004R Proof	13,000	Value: 145				
2005R	85,000	—	—	—	25.00	—
2005R Proof	16,000	Value: 140				

KM# 343 5 EURO CENT

3.8600 g., Copper Plated Steel, 21.2 mm. **Obv:** Bust 1/4 left **Obv. Designer:** Guido Veroi **Rev:** Value and globe **Edge:** Plain **Mint:** Rome

Date	Mintage	F	VF	XF	Unc	BU
2002R	80,000	—	—	—	115	—
2002R Proof	9,000	Value: 175				
2003R	65,000	—	—	—	55.00	—
2003R Proof	13,000	Value: 145				
2004R	65,000	—	—	—	28.00	—
2004R Proof	13,000	Value: 145				
2005R	85,000	—	—	—	28.00	—
2005R Proof	16,000	Value: 140				

KM# 344 10 EURO CENT

4.0700 g., Brass, 19.7 mm. **Obv:** Bust 1/4 left **Obv. Designer:** Guido Veroi **Rev. Designer:** Luc Luycx **Edge:** Reeded **Mint:** Rome

Date	Mintage	F	VF	XF	Unc	BU
2002R	80,000	—	—	—	115	—
2002R Proof	9,000	Value: 175				
2003R	65,000	—	—	—	55.00	—
2003R Proof	13,000	Value: 145				
2004R	65,000	—	—	—	35.00	—
2004R Proof	13,000	Value: 145				
2005R	85,000	—	—	—	35.00	—
2005R Proof	16,000	Value: 140				

KM# 345 20 EURO CENT

5.7300 g., Brass, 22.1 mm. **Obv:** Bust 1/4 left **Obv. Designer:** Guido Veroi **Rev:** Map and value **Rev. Designer:** Luc Luycx **Edge:** Notched **Mint:** Rome

Date	Mintage	F	VF	XF	Unc	BU
2002R	80,000	—	—	—	115	—
2002R Proof	9,000	Value: 175				
2003R	65,000	—	—	—	55.00	—
2003R Proof	13,000	Value: 145				
2004R	65,000	—	—	—	38.00	—
2004R Proof	13,000	Value: 145				
2005R	85,000	—	—	—	38.00	—
2005R Proof	16,000	Value: 140				

KM# 346 50 EURO CENT

7.8100 g., Brass, 24.2 mm. **Obv:** Bust 1/4 left **Obv. Designer:** Guido Veroi **Rev:** Map and value **Rev. Designer:** Luc Luycx **Edge:** Reeded **Mint:** Rome

Date	Mintage	F	VF	XF	Unc	BU
2002R	80,000	—	—	—	115	—
2002R Proof	9,000	Value: 175				
2003R	65,000	—	—	—	55.00	—
2003R Proof	13,000	Value: 145				
2004R	65,000	—	—	—	42.00	—
2004R Proof	13,000	Value: 145				
2005R	85,000	—	—	—	42.00	—
2005R Proof	16,000	Value: 140				

KM# 347 EURO

7.5000 g., Bi-Metallic Copper-Nickel center in Brass ring, 23.2 mm. **Obv:** Bust 1/4 left **Obv. Designer:** Guido Veroi **Rev:** Value and map **Rev. Designer:** Luc Luycx **Edge:** Reeded and plain sections **Mint:** Rome

Date	Mintage	F	VF	XF	Unc	BU
2002R	80,000	—	—	—	100	—
2002R Proof	9,000	Value: 185				
2003R	65,000	—	—	—	75.00	—
2003R Proof	13,000	Value: 145				
2004R	65,000	—	—	—	60.00	—
2004R Proof	13,000	Value: 145				
2005R	85,000	—	—	—	60.00	—
2005R Proof	16,000	Value: 140				

KM# 348 2 EURO

8.5200 g., Bi-Metallic Brass center in Copper-Nickel ring, 25.7 mm. **Obv:** Bust 1/4 left **Obv. Designer:** Guido Veroi **Rev:** Value and map **Rev. Designer:** Luc Luycx **Edge:** Reeded **Edge Lettering:** 2's and stars **Mint:** Rome

Date	Mintage	F	VF	XF	Unc	BU
2002R	80,000	—	—	—	165	—
2002R Proof	9,000	Value: 215				
2003R	65,000	—	—	—	100	—
2003R Proof	13,000	Value: 185				
2004R	65,000	—	—	—	80.00	—
2004R Proof	13,000	Value: 185				
2005R	85,000	—	—	—	80.00	—
2005R Proof	16,000	Value: 180				

KM# 358 2 EURO

8.5000 g., Bi-Metallic Brass center in Copper-Nickel ring, 25.75 mm. **Subject:** 75th Anniversary of the Founding of the Vatican City State **Obv:** St. Peter's Square within city walls, dates 1929-2004 **Rev:** Value and map **Edge:** Reeding over 2's and stars **Mint:** Rome **Designer:** Luciana de Simoni

Date	Mintage	F	VF	XF	Unc	BU
2004R	85,000	—	—	—	25.00	—

VENEZUELA

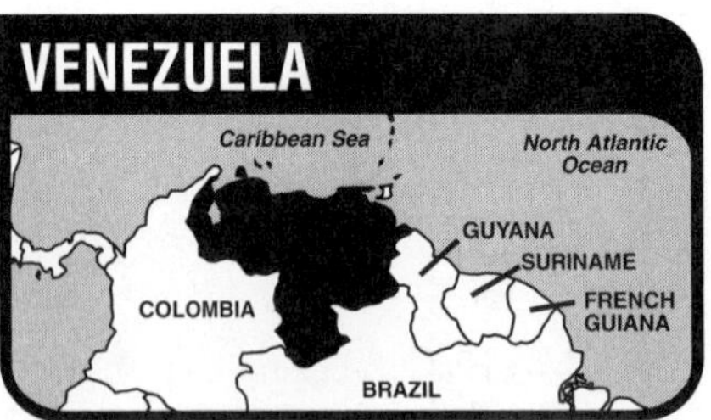

The Republic of Venezuela ("Little Venice"), located on the northern coast of South America between Colombia and Guyana, has an area of 352,145 sq. mi.(912,050 sq. km.) and a population of 20 million. Capital: Caracas. Petroleum and mining provide a significant portion of Venezuela's exports. Coffee, grown on 60,000 plantations, is the chief crop. Metalurgy, refining, oil, iron and steel production are the main employment industries.

Columbus discovered Venezuela on his third voyage in 1498. Initial exploration did not reveal Venezuela to be a land of great wealth. An active pearl trade operated on the offshore islands and slavers raided the interior in search of Indians to be sold into slavery, but no significant mainland settlements were made before 1567 when Caracas was founded. Venezuela, the home of Bolivar, was among the first South American colonies to rebel against Spain in 1810. The declaration of Independence of Venezuela was signed by seven provinces which are represented by the seven stars of the Venezuelan flag. Coinage of Caracas and Margarita use the seven stars in their designs. These original provinces were: Barcelona, Barinas, Caracas, Cumana, Margarita, Merida and Trujillo. The Provinces of Coro, Guyana and Maracaibo were added to Venezuela during the Independence War. Independence was attained in 1821 but not recognized by Spain until 1845. Together with Ecuador, Panama and Colombia, Venezuela was part of "Gran Colombia" until 1830, when it became a sovereign and independent state.

RULER

Republic, 1823-present

MINT MARKS

A - Paris
(a) - Paris, privy marks only
(aa) - Altena
(b) - Berlin
(bb) - Brussels
(cc) – Canada

(c) - Caracas
(d) - Denver
H, Heaton - Heaton, Birmingham
(l) - London
(m) - Madrid
(mm) - Mexico
(o) - Ontario
(p) - Philadelphia
(s) - San Francisco
(sc) - Schwerte - Vereinigte Deutsche Nickelwerke
(w) - Werdohl - Vereinigte Deutsche Metalwerke

MONETARY SYSTEM

100 Centimos = 1 Bolivar

REPUBLIC

REFORM COINAGE

1896; 100 Centimos = 1 Bolivar

Y# 27 5 CENTIMOS

2.3000 g., Copper-Nickel **Obv:** National arms, stars above **Obv. Legend:** ESTADOS UNIDOS DE VENEZUELA **Rev:** Value within wreath

Date	Mintage	F	VF	XF	Unc	BU
1915(p)	2,000,000	1.00	4.00	50.00	150	300
1921(p)	2,000,000	0.50	4.00	70.00	200	300
1925(p)	2,000,000	0.30	1.00	10.00	20.00	40.00
1927(p)	2,000,000	0.30	1.00	10.00	20.00	40.00
1929(p)	2,000,000	0.25	1.00	10.00	20.00	40.00
1936(p)	5,000,000	0.15	0.50	4.00	10.00	20.00
1938(p)	6,000,000	0.10	0.20	4.00	10.00	20.00

Y# 29 5 CENTIMOS

2.4300 g., Brass **Obv:** National arms, stars above **Rev:** Denomination within wreath

Date	Mintage	F	VF	XF	Unc	BU
1944(d)	4,000,000	0.50	1.00	6.00	20.00	60.00

Y# 29a 5 CENTIMOS

2.4000 g., Copper-Nickel, 19.1 mm. **Obv:** National arms, stars above **Rev:** Denomination within wreath

Date	Mintage	F	VF	XF	Unc	BU
1945(p)	12,000,000	0.10	0.20	0.50	4.00	6.00
1946(p)	12,000,000	0.10	0.20	0.50	4.00	6.00
1948(p)	18,000,000	0.10	0.20	0.50	3.00	5.00

Y# 38.1 5 CENTIMOS

Copper-Nickel **Obv:** National arms, stars above **Rev:** Denomination within wreath

Date	Mintage	F	VF	XF	Unc	BU
1958(p)	25,000,000	—	—	—	0.75	1.25

Y# 38.2 5 CENTIMOS

2.5000 g., Copper-Nickel, 19.8 mm. **Obv:** National arms, stars above **Rev:** Denomination within wreath

Date	Mintage	F	VF	XF	Unc	BU
1964(m)	40,000,000	—	—	—	0.50	1.00
1965(m)	60,000,000	—	—	—	0.50	1.00

Y# 38.3 5 CENTIMOS

Copper-Nickel **Obv:** National arms, stars above **Rev:** Denomination within wreath

Date	Mintage	F	VF	XF	Unc	BU
1971(o)	40,000,000	—	—	—	0.50	1.00

Y# 49 5 CENTIMOS

Copper Clad Steel **Obv:** National arms, stars above **Rev:** Denomination below spray

Date	Mintage	F	VF	XF	Unc	BU
1974(w)	200,000,000	—	—	—	1.00	5.00
1976(w)	200,000,000	—	—	—	1.00	4.00
1977(l)	600,000,000	—	—	—	0.15	1.00

Y# 49a 5 CENTIMOS

Nickel Clad Steel **Obv:** National arms, stars above **Rev:** Denomination below spray

Date	Mintage	F	VF	XF	Unc	BU
1983(w)	600,000,000	—	—	—	0.10	0.20

Y# 49b 5 CENTIMOS

Copper-Nickel Clad Steel **Obv:** National arms, stars above **Rev:** Denomination below spray

Date	Mintage	F	VF	XF	Unc	BU
1986(w)	500,000,000	—	—	—	0.10	0.20

Y# A40 10 CENTIMOS

Copper-Nickel **Obv:** National arms, stars above **Rev:** Denomination within wreath

Date	Mintage	F	VF	XF	Unc	BU
1971(o)	60,000,000	—	—	0.10	0.25	0.50

Y# 28 12-1/2 CENTIMOS

Copper-Nickel **Obv:** National arms, stars above **Obv. Legend:** ESTADOS UNIDOS DE VENEZUELA **Rev:** Value within wreath **Note:** Varieties exist.

Date	Mintage	F	VF	XF	Unc	BU
1925(p)	800,000	2.50	6.50	45.00	200	400
1927(p)	800,000	1.00	2.00	15.00	100	150
1929(p)	800,000	0.15	0.50	10.00	75.00	100
1936(p)	1,200,000	0.15	0.30	5.00	35.00	75.00
1938(p)	1,600,000	0.15	0.30	2.00	25.00	50.00

Y# 30 12-1/2 CENTIMOS

Brass **Obv:** National arms, stars above **Rev:** Denomination within wreath

Date	Mintage	F	VF	XF	Unc	BU
1944(d)	800,000	2.50	4.50	15.00	75.00	150

Y# 30a 12-1/2 CENTIMOS

Copper-Nickel **Obv:** National arms, stars above **Rev:** Denomination within wreath

Date	Mintage	F	VF	XF	Unc	BU
1945(p)	11,200,000	0.10	0.20	0.35	9.00	15.00
1946(p)	9,200,000	0.10	0.20	0.35	12.00	20.00
1948(s)	6,000,000	0.10	0.20	0.35	12.00	20.00

Y# 39 12-1/2 CENTIMOS

Copper-Nickel **Obv:** National arms, stars above **Rev:** Denomination within wreath, knobbed 2

Date	Mintage	F	VF	XF	Unc	BU
1958(p)	10,000,000	—	—	0.20	2.00	4.00

Y# A39.1 12-1/2 CENTIMOS

Copper-Nickel **Obv:** National arms, flat stars **Rev:** Denomination within wreath, plain 2

Date	Mintage	F	VF	XF	Unc	BU
1969(m)	2,000,000	—	—	—	75.00	100

Y# A39.2 12-1/2 CENTIMOS

Copper-Nickel **Obv:** National arms, raised stars **Rev:** Denomination within wreath, outlined stem ends

Date	Mintage	F	VF	XF	Unc	BU
1969(m)	Inc. above	—	—	—	100	200

Y# A39.3 12-1/2 CENTIMOS

Copper-Nickel **Obv:** National arms, stars above **Rev:** Denomination within wreath, solid stem ends

Date	Mintage	F	VF	XF	Unc	BU
1969(m)	Inc. above	—	—	—	100	200

Note: 1969 dated strikes were not released into circulation, but the Central Bank has been selling limited quantities on occasion

Y# 20 GR 1.250 (1/4 Bolivar)

1.2500 g., 0.8350 Silver 0.0336 oz. ASW **Obv:** National arms **Obv. Legend:** ESTADOS UNIDOS DE VENEZUELA. **Rev:** Head left **Rev. Legend:** BOLIVAR LIBERTADOR **Rev. Designer:** Albert Barre

Date	Mintage	F	VF	XF	Unc	BU
1901	393,000	7.00	25.00	55.00	300	600
1903(p)	400,000	6.00	20.00	50.00	200	375
1911	600,000	2.50	5.00	12.00	75.00	125
1912	800,000	3.00	6.00	15.00	100	200
1919(p)	400,000	2.50	5.00	12.00	100	300
1921(p) High 2	800,000	2.00	4.00	10.00	50.00	125
1921(p) Low 2	Inc. above	1.00	3.00	10.00	50.00	125
1924(p)	400,000	1.00	3.00	10.00	35.00	100
1929(p)	1,200,000	—	BV	1.00	6.00	15.00
1935(p)	3,400,000	—	BV	1.00	3.00	10.00
1936(p)	2,800,000	—	BV	1.00	3.00	10.00
1944(p)	1,800,000	—	BV	1.00	2.00	5.00
1945(p)	8,000,000	—	—	BV	1.50	2.50
1946(p)	8,000,000	—	—	BV	1.00	2.00
1948(s)	8,638,000	—	—	BV	1.00	2.00

Y# 35 25 CENTIMOS

1.2500 g., 0.8350 Silver 0.0336 oz. ASW **Obv:** National arms **Rev:** Head of Bolivar left **Rev. Designer:** Albert Barre

Date	Mintage	F	VF	XF	Unc	BU
1954(p)	36,000,000	—	—	BV	1.00	1.50

Y# 35a 25 CENTIMOS

1.2500 g., 0.8350 Silver 0.0336 oz. ASW **Obv:** National arms **Rev:** Head of Bolivar left

Date	Mintage	F	VF	XF	Unc	BU
1960	48,000,000	—	—	BV	0.75	1.50

Y# 40 25 CENTIMOS

Nickel, 17 mm. **Obv:** National arms **Rev:** Head of Bolivar left **Rev. Designer:** Albert Barre

Date	Mintage	F	VF	XF	Unc	BU
1965(l)	240,000,000	—	—	0.10	0.35	1.00

Y# 50.1 25 CENTIMOS

1.7500 g., Nickel, 17 mm. **Obv:** National arms **Rev:** Head of Bolivar left **Rev. Designer:** Albert Barre **Note:** 1.18mm thick.

Date	Mintage	F	VF	XF	Unc	BU
1977(w)	240,000,000	—	—	0.10	0.25	0.50
1978	—	—	—	0.10	0.25	0.50

Y# 50.2 25 CENTIMOS

1.5000 g., Nickel, 17 mm. **Obv:** National arms **Rev:** Head of Bolivar left **Note:** Dies vary for each date; thin.

Date	Mintage	F	VF	XF	Unc	BU
1977(w)	Inc. above	—	—	0.10	0.25	0.50
1978(w)	200,000,000	—	—	0.10	0.25	0.50
1987	150,000,000	—	—	0.10	0.25	0.50

Y# 50a 25 CENTIMOS

2.4800 g., Nickel Clad Steel, 16.06 mm. **Obv:** National arms **Rev:** Head of Bolivar left **Edge:** Reeded **Note:** Varieties exist.

Date	Mintage	F	VF	XF	Unc	BU
1989(sc)	510,000,000	—	—	0.10	0.25	0.50
1990(mm)	400,000,000	—	—	0.10	0.25	0.50

Y# 21 GR 2.500 (1/2 Bolivar)

2.5000 g., 0.8350 Silver 0.0671 oz. ASW **Obv:** Arms within sprigs above banner, cornucopias above **Obv. Legend:** ESTADOS UNIDOS DE VENEZUELA **Rev:** Head of Bolivar left **Rev. Legend:** BOLIVAR LIBERTADOR **Rev. Designer:** Albert Barre

Date	Mintage	F	VF	XF	Unc	BU
1901	600,000	20.00	50.00	175	750	1,000
Note: Privy mark placement varies with 1901						
1903(p)	200,000	75.00	200	600	2,000	3,250
1911	300,000	30.00	60.00	200	600	1,200
Note: Privy mark placement varies with 1911						
1912	1,920,000	5.00	15.00	50.00	300	600
1919(p)	400,000	6.00	20.00	80.00	300	800
1921(p) Normal date	600,000	2.50	7.00	16.00	100	250
1921(p) Narrow date	Inc. above	3.50	9.00	27.50	125	300
1921(p) Wide date	Inc. above	3.50	9.00	27.50	125	300
1924(p)	800,000	2.50	7.00	16.00	85.00	200
1929(p)	400,000	1.35	2.00	6.00	55.00	135
1935(p)	1,000,000	—	BV	1.35	12.00	30.00
1936(p)	600,000	BV	1.35	5.00	50.00	125

Y# 21a GR 2.500 (1/2 Bolivar)

2.5000 g., 0.8350 Silver 0.0671 oz. ASW **Obv:** National arms above ribbon, plants flank, cornucopias above **Rev:** Head of Bolivar left **Rev. Designer:** Albert Barre

Date	Mintage	F	VF	XF	Unc	BU
1944(d)	500,000	1.35	3.00	5.00	15.00	30.00
Note: Accent in Bolivar						
1944(d)	Inc. above	1.50	5.00	10.00	25.00	50.00
Note: Without accent in Bolivar						
1945(p)	4,000,000	—	BV	1.35	5.00	10.00
1946(p)	2,500,000	—	BV	1.35	5.00	10.00

Y# 36 50 CENTIMOS

2.5000 g., 0.8350 Silver 0.0671 oz. ASW, 18 mm. **Obv:** National arms **Rev:** Head of Bolivar left **Rev. Designer:** Albert Barre

Date	Mintage	F	VF	XF	Unc	BU
1954 (p)	15,000,000	—	—	BV	3.00	5.00

Y# 36a 50 CENTIMOS

2.5000 g., 0.8350 Silver 0.0671 oz. ASW, 18 mm. **Obv:** National arms **Rev:** Head of Bolivar left **Rev. Designer:** Albert Barre

Date	Mintage	F	VF	XF	Unc	BU
1960(a)	20,000,000	—	—	BV	2.00	3.00

Y# 41 50 CENTIMOS

Nickel, 20 mm. **Obv:** National arms **Rev:** Head of Bolivar left **Rev. Designer:** Albert Barre

Date	Mintage	F	VF	XF	Unc	BU
1965(l)	180,000,000	—	0.10	0.15	0.35	1.00
1985(o)	50,000,000	—	0.10	0.15	0.35	1.00

Y# 41a 50 CENTIMOS

3.2000 g., Nickel Clad Steel, 20 mm. **Obv:** National arms **Rev:** Head of Bolivar left

Date	Mintage	F	VF	XF	Unc	BU
1988(w)	80,000,000	—	0.10	0.15	0.30	0.50
1989(w)	260,000,000	—	0.10	0.15	0.30	0.50
1990(l)	300,000,000	—	0.10	0.15	0.30	0.50

Note: Die varieties exist for 1990 dated strikes

Y# 22 GRAM 5 (Bolivar)

5.0000 g., 0.8350 Silver 0.1342 oz. ASW **Obv:** Arms within sprigs above banner, cornucopias above **Obv. Legend:** ESTADOS UNIDOS DE VENEZUELA **Rev:** Head of Bolivar left **Rev. Legend:** BOLIVAR LIBERTADOR **Rev. Designer:** Albert Barre

Date	Mintage	F	VF	XF	Unc	BU
1901	323,000	20.00	55.00	150	650	1,000
1903(p)	800,000	5.00	15.00	90.00	350	850
1911	1,500,000	3.00	5.00	40.00	200	650
1912 Wide date	820,000	6.00	16.50	75.00	300	800
1912 Narrow date	Inc. above	6.00	16.50	75.00	300	800
1919(p)	1,000,000	2.50	3.50	12.00	60.00	150
1921(p)	1,000,000	2.50	3.50	12.00	60.00	150
1924(p)	1,500,000	BV	2.50	6.00	50.00	100
1926(p)	1,000,000	BV	2.50	6.00	50.00	100
1929(p)	2,500,000	—	BV	2.50	10.00	30.00
1935(p)	5,000,000	—	BV	2.50	5.00	12.50
1936(p)	5,000,000	—	BV	2.25	5.00	12.50

Y# 22a GRAM 5 (Bolivar)

5.0000 g., 0.8350 Silver 0.1342 oz. ASW **Obv:** National arms above ribbon, plants flank, cornucopias above **Rev:** Head of Bolivar left **Rev. Designer:** Albert Barre

Date	Mintage	F	VF	XF	Unc	BU
1945(p)	8,000,000	—	—	BV	3.50	5.00

Y# 37 BOLIVAR

5.0000 g., 0.8350 Silver 0.1342 oz. ASW **Obv:** National arms above ribbon, plants flank, cornucopias above **Rev:** Head of Bolivar left **Rev. Designer:** Albert Barre

Date	Mintage	F	VF	XF	Unc	BU
1954(p)	13,500,000	—	—	BV	2.75	4.00

Y# 37a BOLIVAR

5.0000 g., 0.8350 Silver 0.1342 oz. ASW **Obv:** National arms above ribbon, plants flank, cornucopias above **Rev:** Head of Bolivar left **Rev. Designer:** Albert Barre

Date	Mintage	F	VF	XF	Unc	BU
1960	30,000,000	—	—	BV	2.50	4.00
Note: Thin letters						
1960	Inc. above	—	—	BV	2.50	4.00
Note: Thick letters						
1965(l)	20,000,000	—	—	BV	2.50	4.00

Y# 42 BOLIVAR

Nickel, 23 mm. **Obv:** National arms above ribbon, plants flank, cornucopias above **Rev:** Head of Bolivar left **Rev. Designer:** Albert Barre

Date	Mintage	F	VF	XF	Unc	BU
1967(l)	180,000,000	—	0.10	0.15	0.75	1.00

Y# 52 BOLIVAR

Nickel, 23 mm. **Obv:** National arms above ribbon, plants flank, cornucopias above **Rev:** Head of Bolivar left **Rev. Designer:** Albert Barre **Note:** Dies vary for each date.

Date	Mintage	F	VF	XF	Unc	BU
1977(l)	200,000,000	—	0.10	0.15	0.65	1.00
1986(w)	200,000,000	—	0.10	0.15	0.50	1.00
1986(w) Prooflike	50,000,000	—	0.10	0.15	0.60	1.50

Y# 52a.2 BOLIVAR

4.2000 g., Nickel Clad Steel, 23 mm. **Obv:** National arms above ribbon, plants flank, cornucopias above **Rev:** Head of Bolivar left **Note:** Dies vary for each date. Obverse has large letters and date

Date	Mintage	F	VF	XF	Unc	BU
1989(sc)	600,000,000	—	0.10	0.15	0.45	0.60
1990(mm)	600,000,000	—	0.10	0.15	0.45	0.60

Y# 52a.1 BOLIVAR

4.2000 g., Nickel Clad Steel, 23 mm. **Obv:** National arms above ribbon, plants flank, cornucopias above **Rev:** Head of Bolivar left **Note:** Both sides of coin have small letters and date

Date	Mintage	F	VF	XF	Unc	BU
1989(w)	370,000,000	—	0.10	0.15	0.45	0.60

Knobbed 6 Pointed 6

Y# 23 GRAM 10 (2 Bolivares)

10.0000 g., 0.8350 Silver 0.2684 oz. ASW **Obv:** Arms within sprigs above banner, cornucopias above **Obv. Legend:** ESTADOS UNIDOS DE VENEZUELA **Rev:** Head of Bolivar left **Rev. Legend:** BOLIVAR LIBERTADOR **Rev. Designer:** Albert Barre

Date	Mintage	F	VF	XF	Unc	BU
1902(p)	500,000	11.50	45.00	200	500	1,000
1903(p)	500,000	12.50	50.00	250	550	1,100
1904 Large 0, small 4	550,000	11.50	40.00	175	500	1,000
1904 Large 0, large 4	Inc. above	11.50	40.00	175	500	1,000
1904 Small 0, large 4	Inc. above	11.50	45.00	185	550	1,000
1904 Small 0, large slant 4	Inc. above	11.50	45.00	185	550	1,000
1904 Small 0, small 4	50,000	20.00	55.00	200	600	1,000
1905 Upright 5	750,000	4.50	16.50	100	400	800
1905 Slant 5	Inc. above	4.50	16.50	100	400	800
1911	750,000	4.50	16.50	60.00	275	650
1912	500,000	4.50	16.50	140	400	1,000
1913 Normal date	210,000	40.00	250	500	1,000	2,000
1913 Raised 3	Inc. above	40.00	250	500	1,000	2,000
1919(p)	1,000,000	BV	4.50	11.50	125	300
1922(p) Narrow date	1,000,000	BV	4.50	11.50	100	250
1922(p) Wide date	Inc. above	BV	4.50	11.50	100	250
1922(p) Low first 2	Inc. above	BV	4.50	11.50	100	250
1924(p)	1,250,000	BV	4.50	11.50	85.00	200
1926(p)	1,000,000	BV	4.50	11.50	85.00	200
1929(p)	1,500,000	—	BV	8.00	20.00	50.00
1930(p)	425,000	BV	7.00	25.00	130	300
1935(p)	3,000,000	—	BV	4.50	8.00	25.00
1936(p)	2,500,000	—	BV	4.50	8.00	25.00

Y# 23a GRAM 10 (2 Bolivares)

10.0000 g., 0.8350 Silver 0.2684 oz. ASW **Obv:** National arms above ribbon, plants flank, cornucopias above **Rev:** Head of Bolivar left **Rev. Designer:** Albert Barre

Date	Mintage	F	VF	XF	Unc	BU
1945(p)	3,000,000	—	—	BV	5.50	7.50

Y# A37 2 BOLIVARES

10.0000 g., 0.8350 Silver 0.2684 oz. ASW **Obv:** National arms above ribbon, plants flank, cornucopias above **Rev:** Head of Bolivar left **Rev. Designer:** Albert Barre

Date	Mintage	F	VF	XF	Unc	BU
1960	4,000,000	—	—	BV	5.00	6.50
1965(l)	7,170,000	—	—	BV	5.00	6.50

Y# 43 2 BOLIVARES

Nickel, 27 mm. **Obv:** National arms above ribbon, plants flank, cornucopias above **Rev:** Head of Bolivar left **Rev. Designer:** Albert Barre **Note:** Dies vary for each date.

Date	Mintage	F	VF	XF	Unc	BU
1967(l)	50,000,000	—	—	0.25	0.50	1.50
1986(w)	50,000,000	—	—	0.25	0.50	1.50
Note: Die varieties exist for 1986 strikes						
1986(w) Prooflike	—	—	—	0.25	0.50	1.50
Note: Die varieties exist for 1986 strikes						
1988(c)	80,000,000	—	—	0.25	0.50	1.50

Y# 43a.1 2 BOLIVARES

7.5000 g., Nickel Clad Steel, 27 mm. **Obv:** Small letters in legend, raised motto in ribbon, lines beneath horse, "R" in 'Libertador' 2mm away from truncation **Rev:** Head of Bolivar left, small letters

Date	Mintage	F	VF	XF	Unc	BU
1989(sc)	200,000,000	—	—	0.20	0.75	1.50
1990(c)	400,000,000	—	—	0.20	0.75	1.50
Note: Two varieties of 1990 exist						

Y# 43a.2 2 BOLIVARES

7.5000 g., Nickel Clad Steel, 27 mm. **Obv:** Large letters in legend, no lines beneath horse, "R" in 'Libertador' touching truncation **Rev:** Head of Bolivar left, large letters

Date	Mintage	F	VF	XF	Unc	BU
1989(w)	100,000,000	—	—	0.20	0.75	1.50
1989(c)	95,000,000	—	—	0.20	0.75	1.50

Y# 44 5 BOLIVARES

Nickel, 31 mm. **Obv:** National arms above ribbon, plants flank, cornucopias above **Rev:** Head of Bolivar left **Rev. Designer:** Albert Barre

Date	Mintage	F	VF	XF	Unc	BU
1973(m)	20,000,000	—	0.45	0.75	1.75	15.00

Y# 53.1 5 BOLIVARES

Nickel, 31 mm. **Obv:** National arms above ribbon, plants flank, cornucopias above, six pointed stars **Rev:** Head of Bolivar left **Rev. Designer:** Albert Barre

Date	Mintage	F	VF	XF	Unc	BU
1977(m)	60,000,000	—	—	0.50	1.50	2.00

Y# 53.2 5 BOLIVARES

Nickel **Obv:** National arms above ribbon, plants flank, cornucopias above, date and denomination below, five pointed stars **Rev:** Head of Bolivar left

Date	Mintage	F	VF	XF	Unc	BU
1987(c)	25,000,000	—	—	0.50	1.50	2.00
1987(c) Prooflike	Inc. above	—	—	—	—	30.00
1988(w)	20,000,000	—	—	1.00	5.00	10.00

Y# 53a.1 5 BOLIVARES

13.3000 g., Nickel Clad Steel, 31 mm. **Obv:** National arms above ribbon, plants flank, cornucopias above, small letters **Rev:** Head of Bolivar left, large letters **Rev. Designer:** Albert Barre

Date	Mintage	F	VF	XF	Unc	BU
1989(w)	55,000,000	—	—	0.50	1.50	2.00
1989(w) Prooflike	26,000,000	—	—	1.00	2.00	3.00

Y# 53a.2 5 BOLIVARES

13.3000 g., Nickel Clad Steel, 31 mm. **Obv:** Large letters **Rev:** Small letters

Date	Mintage	F	VF	XF	Unc	BU
1989(sc)	100,000,000	—	—	0.50	1.50	3.00
1990(c)	200,000,000	—	—	0.50	1.50	3.00

Y# 53a.3 5 BOLIVARES

13.3000 g., Nickel Clad Steel, 31 mm. **Obv:** National arms above ribbon, plants flank, cornucopias above **Rev:** Head of Bolivar left **Rev. Designer:** Albert Barre **Note:** Large letters in legends.

Date	Mintage	F	VF	XF	Unc	BU
1990	—	—	—	0.65	1.75	3.00

Y# 31 GR 3.2258 (10 Bolivares)

3.2258 g., 0.9000 Gold 0.0933 oz. AGW **Obv:** National arms above ribbon, plants flank, cornucopias above **Rev:** Head of Bolivar right **Rev. Designer:** Albert Barre

Date	Mintage	F	VF	XF	Unc	BU
1930(p)	Est. 500,000	—	BV	95.00	110	125
Note: Only 10% of the total mintage was released; the balance remaining as part of the nation's gold reserve						

Y# 75 10 BOLIVARES

Nickel Clad Steel, 17 mm. **Obv:** National arms **Rev:** Head of Bolivar left within 7-sided outline **Rev. Designer:** Albert Barre **Note:** Struck at Ceska Mincova and Budapest mints.

Date	Mintage	F	VF	XF	Unc	BU
1998	—	—	—	—	0.25	0.50

Y# 32 GR 6.4516 (20 Bolivares)

6.4516 g., 0.9000 Gold 0.1867 oz. AGW **Obv:** Arms within sprigs above banner, cornucopias above **Obv. Legend:** ESTRADOS UNIDOS DE VENEZUELA **Rev:** Head of Bolivar right **Rev. Legend:** BOLIVAR LIBERTADOR **Rev. Designer:** Albert Barre

Date	Mintage	F	VF	XF	Unc	BU
1904	100,000	—	BV	180	190	210
1905	100,000	—	BV	180	190	210
1910	70,000	—	BV	180	200	250
Note: Die varieties exist in the placement of dot between date and Lei, Type 1 is evenly spaced, Type 2 had dot closer to L of Lei						
1911	80,000	—	BV	180	190	210
Note: Die varieties exist in the placement of dot between date and Lei, Type 1 is evenly spaced, Type 2 had dot closer to L of Lei						
1912	150,000	—	BV	180	190	210
Note: Die varieties exist in the placement of the torch privy mark in relation to bust truncation; Type 1 is well below truncation, Type 2 is slightly below truncation and Type 3 is in line with the truncation						

Y# 76.1 20 BOLIVARES

Nickel Clad Steel, 20 mm. **Obv:** National arms **Rev:** Head of Bolivar left within 7-sided outline **Rev. Designer:** Albert Barre **Note:** Struck at Ceska Mincova and Budapest mints.

Date	Mintage	F	VF	XF	Unc	BU
1998	—	—	—	—	0.25	0.50

Y# 76.2 20 BOLIVARES

4.3200 g., Nickel Clad Steel, 20 mm. **Obv:** National arms **Rev:** Head of Bolivar left within 7-sided outline **Edge:** Plain

Date	Mintage	F	VF	XF	Unc	BU
1999	—	—	—	0.30	0.60	—

Y# 77.1 50 BOLIVARES

6.6000 g., Nickel Clad Steel **Obv:** National arms **Rev:** Head of Bolivar left within 7-sided outline **Rev. Designer:** Albert Barre **Note:** Struck at Ceska Mincova and Budapest mints.

Date	Mintage	F	VF	XF	Unc	BU
1998	—	—	—	—	0.35	0.70

Y# 77.2 50 BOLIVARES

6.6500 g., Nickel Clad Steel, 23 mm. **Obv:** National arms **Rev:** Head of Bolívar left and mint mark, in 7-sided outline **Rev. Designer:** Albert Barre **Edge:** Reeded

Date	Mintage	F	VF	XF	Unc	BU
1999	—	—	—	0.40	0.80	—

Y# 78.1 100 BOLIVARES

6.8000 g., Nickel Clad Steel, 25 mm. **Obv:** National arms **Rev:** Head of Bolívar left in 7-sided outline **Rev. Designer:** Albert Barre **Note:** Struck at Ceska Mincova and Budapest mints.

Date	Mintage	F	VF	XF	Unc	BU
1998	—	—	—	—	0.50	1.00

Y# 78.2 100 BOLIVARES

6.8200 g., Nickel-Clad Steel, 25 mm. **Obv:** National arms **Rev:** Head of Bolívar right in 7-sided outline **Rev. Designer:** Albert Barre **Edge:** Plain

Date	Mintage	F	VF	XF	Unc	BU
1999	—	—	—	0.60	1.20	—

Y# 79.1 500 BOLIVARES

8.4000 g., Nickel Clad Steel, 28.5 mm. **Obv:** National arms **Rev:** Head of Bolívar left in 7-sided outline **Rev. Designer:** Albert Barre **Note:** Struck at Ceska Mincova and Budapest mints.

Date	Mintage	F	VF	XF	Unc	BU
1998	—	—	—	0.50	1.20	1.60

REPUBLIC

Bolivariana

REFORM COINAGE

1896; 100 Centimos = 1 Bolivar

Y# 80 10 BOLIVARES

2.3300 g., Nickel Clad Steel, 17 mm. **Obv:** National arms left of denomination **Obv. Legend:** REPÚBLICA BOLIVARIANA DE VENEZUELA **Rev:** Head of Bolívar left in 7-sided outline **Rev. Legend:** BOLÍVAR - LIBERTADOR **Rev. Designer:** Albert Barre **Edge:** Reeded

Date	Mintage	F	VF	XF	Unc	BU
2000	—	—	—	—	0.25	0.50
2001	—	—	—	—	0.25	0.50
2002	—	—	—	—	0.25	0.50

Y# 80a 10 BOLIVARES

1.7390 g., Aluminum-Zinc, 16.92 mm. **Obv:** National arms and value **Obv. Legend:** REPÚBLICA BOLIVARIANA DE VENEZUELA **Rev:** Head of Bolívar left in 7-sided outline **Rev. Legend:** BOLÍVAR - LIBERTADOR **Rev. Designer:** Albert Barre **Edge:** Reeded

Date	Mintage	F	VF	XF	Unc	BU
2001	—	—	—	0.15	0.45	0.60
2002	—	—	—	0.15	0.45	0.60
2004	—	—	—	0.15	0.45	0.60

Y# 81 20 BOLIVARES

4.3200 g., Nickel Clad Steel, 20 mm. **Obv:** National arms left of denomination **Obv. Legend:** REPÚBLICA BOLIVARIANA DE VENEZUELA **Rev:** Head of Bolivar left in 7-sided outline **Rev. Legend:** BOLÍVAR - LIBERTADOR **Rev. Designer:** Albert Barre **Edge:** Plain

Date	Mintage	F	VF	XF	Unc	BU
2000	—	—	—	—	0.25	0.50
2001	—	—	—	—	0.25	0.50
2002	—	—	—	—	0.25	0.50

Y# 81a.1 20 BOLIVARES

3.2650 g., Aluminum-Zinc, 20 mm. **Obv:** National arms and value with wavy based "2" **Obv. Legend:** REPÚBLICA BOLÍVARIANA DE VENEZUELA **Rev:** Head of Bolívar left in 7-sided outline **Rev. Legend:** BOLÍVAR - LIBERTADOR **Rev. Designer:** Albert Barre **Edge:** Plain

Date	Mintage	F	VF	XF	Unc	BU
2001	—	—	—	—	0.65	1.00

Y# 81a.2 20 BOLIVARES

3.2400 g., Aluminum-Zinc, 20 mm. **Obv:** National arms and value with flat based "2" **Obv. Legend:** REPÚBLICA BOLIVARIANA DE VENEZUELA **Rev:** Head of Bolívar left in 7-sided outline **Rev. Legend:** BOLÍVAR - LIBERTADOR **Rev. Designer:** Albert Barre **Edge:** Plain

Date	Mintage	F	VF	XF	Unc	BU
2002	—	—	—	0.25	0.60	0.80
2004	—	—	—	0.25	0.60	0.80

Y# 82 50 BOLIVARES

6.5800 g., Nickel Clad Steel, 23 mm. **Obv:** National arms left of denomination **Obv. Legend:** REPÚBLICA BOLIVARIANA DE VENEZUELA **Rev:** Head of Bolivar left in 7-sided outline **Rev. Legend:** BOLÍVAR - LIBERTADOR **Rev. Designer:** Albert Barre **Edge:** Reeded

Date	Mintage	F	VF	XF	Unc	BU
2000	—	—	—	0.30	0.75	1.00
2001	—	—	—	0.30	0.75	1.00
2004	—	—	—	0.30	0.75	1.00

Y# 83 100 BOLIVARES

6.8200 g., Nickel Clad Steel, 25 mm. **Obv:** National arms and value **Obv. Legend:** REPÚBUBLICA BOLIVARIANA DE VENEZUELA **Rev:** Head of Bolívar left in 7-sided ouline **Rev. Legend:** BOLÍVAR - LIBERTADO **Rev. Designer:** Albert Barre **Edge:** Plain

Date	Mintage	F	VF	XF	Unc	BU
2001	—	—	—	0.45	1.10	1.50
2002	—	—	—	0.45	1.10	1.50
2004	—	—	—	0.45	1.10	1.50

Y# 79.2 500 BOLIVARES

8.4000 g., Nickel Clad Steel, 28.5 mm. **Obv:** National arms **Obv. Legend:** REPÚBLICA BOLIVARIANA DA VENEZUELA **Rev:** Head of Bolívar left in 7-sided outline **Rev. Legend:** BOLÍVAR - LIBERTADOR **Rev. Designer:** Albert Barre **Edge:** Segmented reeding **Note:** Prev. KM# 84.

Date	Mintage	F	VF	XF	Unc	BU
1999	—	—	—	0.60	1.50	2.00

Y# 94 500 BOLIVARES

8.5000 g., Nickel Plated Steel, 28.40 mm. **Obv:** National arms and denomination **Obv. Legend:** REPÚBLICA BOLIVARIANA DE VENEZUELA **Rev:** Head of Bolívar left in 7-sided outline **Rev. Legend:** BOLÍVAR - LIBERTADOR **Rev. Designer:** Albert Barre **Edge:** Segmented reeding

Date	Mintage	F	VF	XF	Unc	BU
2004	—	—	—	0.60	1.50	2.00

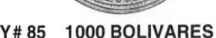

Y# 85 1000 BOLIVARES

8.3500 g., Bi-Metallic Copper-Nickel center in Brass ring, 24 mm. **Obv:** National arms and value in center **Obv. Legend:** REPÚBLICA BOLIVARIANA DE VENEZUELA **Rev:** Head of Bolívar left **Rev. Legend:** BOLÍVAR - LIBERTADOR **Rev. Designer:** Albert Barre **Edge:** Lettered **Edge Lettering:** "BCV 1000" four times

Date	Mintage	F	VF	XF	Unc	BU
2005	9,000,000	—	—	0.90	2.25	3.00

REFORM COINAGE

2007-

1000 Bolivares = 1 Bolivar Fuerte

Y# 87 CENTIMO

1.3600 g., Copper Plated Steel, 14.94 mm. **Obv:** National arms **Obv. Legend:** REPÚBLICA BOLIVARIANA DE VENEZUELA **Rev:** Eight stars at left, large value at right **Edge:** Reeded

Date	Mintage	F	VF	XF	Unc	BU
2007	—	—	—	—	—	0.25

Y# 88 5 CENTIMOS

2.0300 g., Copper Plated Steel, 16.94 mm. **Obv:** National arms **Obv. Legend:** REPÚBLICA BOLIVARIANA DE VENEZUELA **Rev:** Eight stars at left, large value at right **Edge:** Plain

Date	Mintage	F	VF	XF	Unc	BU
2007	—	—	—	—	—	0.50

Y# 89 10 CENTIMOS

2.6200 g., Nickel Plated Steel, 18 mm. **Obv:** National arms **Obv. Legend:** REPÚBLICA BOLIVARIANA DE VENEZUELA **Rev:** Eight stars at left, large value at right **Edge:** Reeded

Date	Mintage	F	VF	XF	Unc	BU
2007	—	—	—	—	—	0.75

Y# 90 12-1/2 CENTIMOS

3.9300 g., Nickel Plated Steel, 23 mm. **Obv:** National arms **Obv. Legend:** REPÚBLICA BOLIVARIANA DE VENEZUELA **Rev:** Large value, eight stars below in sprays **Edge:** Plain

Date	Mintage	F	VF	XF	Unc	BU
2007	—	—	—	—	—	1.50

Y# 91 25 CENTIMOS

3.8600 g., Nickel Plated Steel, 20 mm. **Obv:** National arms **Obv. Legend:** REPÚBLICA BOLIVARIANA DE VENEZUELA **Rev:** Eight stars at left, large value at center right **Edge:** Plain

Date	Mintage	F	VF	XF	Unc	BU
2007	—	—	—	—	—	2.00

Y# 92 50 CENTIMOS

4.3000 g., Nickel Plated Steel, 21.9 mm. **Obv:** National arms **Obv. Legend:** REPÚBLICA BOLIVARIANA DE VENEZUELA **Rev:** Eight stars at left, large value at center right **Edge:** Segmented reeding

Date	Mintage	F	VF	XF	Unc	BU
2007	—	—	—	—	—	3.00

Y# 93 BOLIVAR

8.0400 g., Bi-Metallic Nickel center in Aluminum-Bronze ring, 24 mm. **Obv:** Eight stars at left of national arms, large value at right **Obv. Legend:** REPÚBLICA BOLIVARIANA DE VENEZUELA **Rev:** Head of Bolívar left **Rev. Designer:** Albert Barre **Edge:** Lettered **Edge Lettering:** "BCV 1" repeated

Date	Mintage	F	VF	XF	Unc	BU
2007	—	—	—	—	—	5.00

VIET NAM

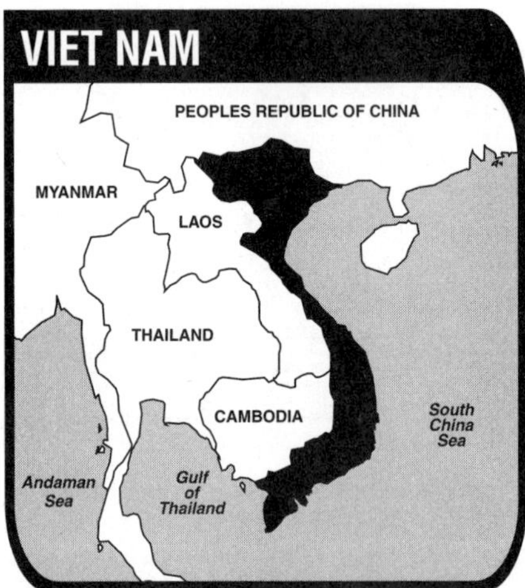

The Socialist Republic of Viet Nam, located in Southeast Asia west of the South China Sea, has an area of 127,300 sq. mi. (329,560 sq. km.) and a population of *66.8 million. Capital: Hanoi. Agricultural products, coal, and mineral ores are exported.

At the start of World War II, Vietnamese Communists fled to China's Kwangsi provinces where Ho Chi Minh organized the Revolution to free Viet Nam of French rule. The Japanese occupied Viet Nam during World War II. As the end of the war drew near, they ousted the Vichy French administration and granted Viet Nam independence under a puppet government headed by Bao Dai, Emperor of Annam. The Bao Dai government collapsed at the end of the war, and on Sept. 2, 1945, Ho Chi Minh proclaimed the existence of an independent Viet Nam consisting of Cochin-China, Annam, and Tonkin, and set up a Communist government. France recognized the new government as a free state, but reneged and in 1949 reinstalled Bao Dai as Ruler of Viet Nam and extended the regime independence within the French Union. Ho Chi Minh led a guerrilla war, in the first Indochina war, against the French which raged on to the disastrous defeat of the French at Dien Bien Phu on May 7,1954.

An agreement signed at Geneva on July 21, 1954, provided for a temporary division of Viet Nam at the 17th parallel of latitude, between a Communist-supported North and a U.S. supported South. In Oct. 1955, South Viet Nam deposed Bao Dai by referendum and authorized the establishment of a republic with Ngo Dinh Diem as president. The Republic of South Viet Nam was proclaimed on Oct. 26, 1955, and was immediately recognized by some Western Powers.

The activities of Communists in South Viet Nam led to the second Indochina war which came to a brief halt in 1973 (when a cease-fire was arranged and U.S. forces withdrew), but it didn't end until April 30, 1975 when South Viet Nam surrendered unconditionally. The two Viet Nams were reunited as the Socialist Republic of Viet Nam on July 2, 1976.

NOTE: For earlier coinage refer to French Indo-China or Tonkin.

MONETARY SYSTEM
10 Xu = 1 Hao
10 Hao = 1 Dong

EMPERORS

成泰
Thanh Thai, 1888-1907

維新
Duy Tan, 1907-1916

啓定
Khai Dinh, 1916-1925

保大
Bao Dai, 1926-1945

IDENTIFICATION

CYCLICAL DATES

	庚	辛	壬	癸	甲	乙	丙	丁	戊	己
戌	1850 1910		1862 1922		1874 1934		1886 1946		1838 1898	
亥		1851 1911		1863 1923		1875 1935		1887 1947		1839 1899
子	1840 1900		1852 1912		1864 1924		1876 1936		1888 1948	
丑		1841 1901		1853 1913		1865 1925		1877 1937		1889 1949
寅	1830 1890		1842 1902		1854 1914		1866 1926		1878 1938	
卯		1831 1891		1843 1903		1855 1915		1867 1927		1879 1939
辰	1880 1940		1832 1892		1844 1904		1856 1916		1868 1928	
巳		1881 1941		1833 1893		1845 1905		1857 1917		1869 1929
午	1870 1930		1882 1942		1834 1894		1846 1906		1858 1918	
未		1871 1931		1883 1943		1835 1895		1847 1907		1859 1919
申	1860 1920		1872 1932		1884 1944		1836 1896		1848 1908	
酉		1861 1921		1873 1933		1885 1945		1837 1897		1849 1909

NOTE: This table has been adapted from *Chinese Bank Notes* by Ward Smith and Brian Matravers.

Cyclical dates consist of a pair of characters one of which indicates the animal associated with that year. Every 60 years, this pair of characters is repeated. The first character of a cyclical date corresponds to a character in the first row of the chart above. The second character is taken from the column at left. In this catalog where a cyclical date is used, the abbreviation CD appears before the A.D. date.

Annamese silver and gold coins were sometimes dated according to the year of the emperor's reign. In this case, simply add the year of reign to the year in which the reign would be 1849 (1847 plus 3 = 1850 -1 = 1849 or 1847 = 1; 1848 = 2; 1849 = 3). In this catalog the A.D. date appears in parenthesis followed by the year of reign.

MONETARY SYSTEM
10 Dong (zinc) = 1 Dong (copper)
600 Dong (zinc) = 1 Quan (string of ¬¬cash)
Approx. 2600 Dong (zinc) = 1 Piastre

NOTE: Ratios between metals changed frequently, therefore the above is given as an approximate relationship.

SILVER and GOLD
2-1/2 Quan = 1 Lang
10 Tien (Mace) = 1 Lang (Tael)
14 to 17 Piastres (silver) = 1 Piastre (gold)
14 to 17 Lang (silver) = 1 Lang (gold)

The real currency of Dai Nam and An Nam consisted of copper and zinc coins similar to Chinese cash-style coins and were called sapeques and dongs by the French.

The smaller gold pieces saw a limited circulation, mainly among the local merchants and foreign traders. The larger gold pieces were used mainly for hoarding, while most of these were intended as rewards and gifts. Many of these gold pieces appear to have been struck from silver coin dies or vice-versa.

NOTE. Sch# are in reference to Albert Schroeder's *Annam, Etudes Numismatiques* or to the same numbering system used in *Gold and Silver Coins of Annam"*, by Bernard Permar and John Novak.

CHARACTER IDENTIFICATION

The Vietnamese used Chinese-style characters for official documents and coins and bars. Some were modified to their liking and will sometimes not match the Chinese character for the same word. The above identification and this table will translate most of the Vietnamese characters (Chinese-style) on their coins and bars described herein.
Chinese/French
Vietnamese/English

安南
An Nam = name of the French protectorate

大南
Dai Nam = name of the country under Gia Long's Nguyen dynasty

越南
Viet Nam = name used briefly during Minh Mang's reign and became the modern name of the country

河內
Ha Noi = city and province in north Dai NamTonkin

內帑
Noi Thang = court treasury in the capital of Hue

年
Nien = year

造
Tao = made

銀
Ngan = silver

金
Kim = gold

錢
Tien = a weight of about 3.78 grams

兩
Lang = a weight of about 37.78 grams

貫
Quan = a string of cash-style coins

分
Phan = a weight of about .38 grams

文
Van = cash-style coins

中平
Trung Binh = a name of weight standard

FRENCH PROTECTORATE OF ANNAM

CAST COINAGE

KM# 654 PHAN
Cast Copper Alloys **Ruler:** Khai Dinh **Obv. Inscription:** "Khai Dinh Thong Bao" **Note:** Prev. Y#4.

Date	Mintage	Good	VG	F	VF	XF
ND(1916-25)	—	5.50	9.00	15.00	25.00	—

KM# 661 PHAN
Cast Brass **Ruler:** Bao Dai **Obv. Inscription:** Bao-dai Thong bao **Note:** Prev. Y#6a.

Date	Mintage	Good	VG	F	VF	XF
ND(1926-45)	—	2.50	5.00	7.50	12.50	—

KM# 652 10 VAN
Cast Brass **Ruler:** Duy Tan **Obv. Inscription:** "Duy Tan Thong Bao" **Rev. Inscription:** "10 Van" **Note:** Prev. Y#3.

Date	Mintage	Good	VG	F	VF	XF
ND(1907-16)	—	0.50	0.75	1.25	2.50	—

KM# 664 10 VAN
Copper Alloys **Ruler:** Bao Dai **Obv. Inscription:** "Bao Dai Thong Bao" **Rev. Inscription:** "10 Van" **Note:** Prev. Y#7.

Date	Mintage	Good	VG	F	VF	XF
ND(1926-45)	—	2.00	3.50	7.50	12.50	—

MILLED COINAGE

Brass

 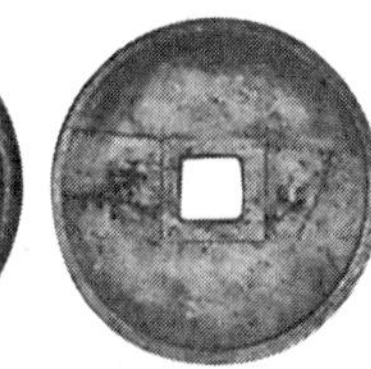

KM# 656 PHAN
Brass **Ruler:** Khai Dinh **Obv:** Characters slightly different **Obv. Inscription:** "Khai Dinh Thong Bao" **Note:** Prev. Y#5.2.

Date	Mintage	Good	VG	F	VF	XF
ND(1916-25)	—	2.00	3.50	6.00	10.00	—

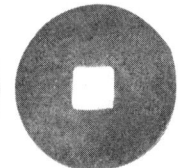

KM# 655 PHAN
Brass **Ruler:** Khai Dinh **Obv. Inscription:** "Khai Dinh Thong Bao" **Note:** Uniface. Prev. Y#5.1.

Date	Mintage	Good	VG	F	VF	XF
ND(1916-25)	—	1.75	2.75	4.50	7.50	—

KM# 662 PHAN
Copper Alloys, 18 mm. **Ruler:** Bao Dai **Obv. Inscription:** "Bao Dai Thong Bao" **Note:** Prev. Y#6.

Date	Mintage	Good	VG	F	VF	XF
ND(1926-45)	—	2.50	5.00	7.50	12.50	—

REBEL COMMUNIST STATE

MILLED COINAGE

KM# 1 20 XU
Aluminum **Ruler:** Bao Dai **Obv:** Star, date below **Obv. Legend:** VIET NAM DAN CHU CHONG HOA **Rev:** Denomination **Rev. Inscription:** 20 XU

Date	Mintage	F	VF	XF	Unc	BU
1945(v)	—	40.00	125	175	250	—

KM# 2.1 5 HAO
Aluminum **Obv:** Ceremonial pot **Obv. Legend:** VIET-NAM DAN-CHU CONG-HAO **Rev:** Value incused in star **Rev. Inscription:** 5 HAO

Date	Mintage	F	VF	XF	Unc	BU
1946(v)	—	4.00	10.00	20.00	60.00	—

Note: Commonly encountered with rotated dies

KM# 2.2 5 HAO
Aluminum **Obv:** Ceremonial pot **Obv. Legend:** VIET-NAM DAN-CHU CONG-HOA **Rev:** Value raised in star

Date	Mintage	F	VF	XF	Unc	BU
1946(v)	—	—	50.00	125	250	—

KM# 3 DONG
Aluminum **Obv:** Head right **Obv. Legend:** VIET-NAM DAN-CHU CONG-HOA **Rev:** Value to right of spray **Rev. Inscription:** 1 DONG

Date	Mintage	F	VF	XF	Unc	BU
1946(v)	—	15.00	35.00	85.00	160	—

KM# 4 2 DONG
Bronze **Obv:** Bust of Ho Chi Minh 3/4 facing **Obv. Legend:** CHU TICH HO MIHN **Rev:** Value above and below in wreath, Nam II at bottom **Rev. Legend:** VIET-NAM DAN CHU CONG HOA **Rev. Inscription:** HAI DONG **Note:** Varieties exist.

Date	Mintage	F	VF	XF	Unc	BU
1946(v)	—	7.50	15.00	40.00	150	—

NORTH VIET NAM

INDEPENDENT COMMUNIST STATE

REFORM COINAGE

KM# 5 XU
Aluminum **Obv:** Center hole within arms **Obv. Legend:** "NUOC VIET NAM DAN CHU CONG HOA" **Rev:** Center hole divides date and denomination **Rev. Legend:** "NGAN HANG QUOC GIA VIET NAM" **Rev. Inscription:** Value: "MOT XU"

Date	Mintage	F	VF	XF	Unc	BU
1958(s)	—	1.25	2.50	5.00	8.00	—

KM# 6 2 XU
Aluminum **Obv:** Center hole within arms **Obv. Legend:** "NUOC VIET NAM DAN CHU CONG HOA" **Rev:** Center hole divides denomination and date **Rev. Legend:** "NGAN HANG QUOC GIA VIET NAM" **Rev. Inscription:** Value: "HAI XU"

Date	Mintage	F	VF	XF	Unc	BU
1958(s)	—	1.50	3.00	6.00	10.00	—

KM# 7 5 XU
Aluminum **Obv:** Center hole within arms **Obv. Legend:** "NUOC VIET NAM DAN CHU CONG HOA" **Rev:** Center hole divides denomination and date **Rev. Legend:** "NGAN HANG QUOC GIA VIET NAM" **Rev. Inscription:** Value: "NAM XU"

Date	Mintage	F	VF	XF	Unc	BU
1958(s)	—	2.00	4.00	8.00	15.00	—

SOCIALIST REPUBLIC

SOCIALIST REPUBLIC

STANDARD COINAGE

KM# 11 HAO
Aluminum **Obv:** Arms **Rev:** Spray divides denomination **Rev. Legend:** "NGAN HANG NHA NUOC VIET NAM" **Rev. Inscription:** "1 HAO"

Date	Mintage	F	VF	XF	Unc	BU
1976(s)	—	1.25	2.50	5.00	10.00	—

KM# 12 2 HAO
1.4100 g., Aluminum **Obv:** Arms **Rev:** Spray divides denomination **Rev. Legend:** "NGAN HANG NHA HUOC VIET NAM" **Rev. Inscription:** "2 HOA"

Date	Mintage	F	VF	XF	Unc	BU
1976(s)	—	1.25	2.50	5.00	10.00	—

KM# 13 5 HAO
Aluminum **Obv:** Arms **Rev:** Denomination above ornament

Date	Mintage	F	VF	XF	Unc	BU
1976	—	1.50	3.00	6.00	12.00	—

KM# 14 DONG
Aluminum **Obv:** Arms **Rev:** Ornaments flank thick denomination **Rev. Legend:** "NGAN HANG NHA NUOC VIET NAM" **Rev. Inscription:** "1 DONG"

Date	Mintage	F	VF	XF	Unc	BU
1976(s)	—	4.00	8.00	16.00	35.00	—

KM# 71 200 DONG
3.1000 g., Nickel Clad Steel, 20.75 mm. **Obv:** National emblem **Rev:** Denomination

Date	Mintage	F	VF	XF	Unc	BU
2003	125,000,000	0.10	0.15	0.25	0.35	0.50

KM# 74 500 DONG
4.5000 g., Nickel-Clad Steel, 21.86 mm. **Obv:** National emblem **Rev:** Denomination **Edge:** Segmented reeding

Date	Mintage	F	VF	XF	Unc	BU
2003	175,000,000	0.15	0.20	0.35	0.50	1.00

KM# 72 1000 DONG
3.7000 g., Brass Plated Steel, 19.75 mm. **Obv:** National emblem **Rev:** Bat De Pagoda in Hanoi **Edge:** Reeded

Date	Mintage	F	VF	XF	Unc	BU
2003	250,000,000	0.20	0.35	0.50	0.75	1.50

KM# 75 2000 DONG

5.0000 g., Brass Plated Steel, 23.92 mm. **Obv:** National emblem **Rev:** Highland Stilt House in Tay Nguyen above value **Edge:** Segmented reeding

Date	Mintage	F	VF	XF	Unc	BU
2003	—	—	—	—	2.25	2.75

KM# 73 5000 DONG

7.6000 g., Brass, 25 mm. **Obv:** National emblem **Rev:** Chua Mot Cot Pagoda in Hanoi

Date	Mintage	F	VF	XF	Unc	BU
2003	500,000,000	0.50	0.75	1.00	1.25	2.50

STATE OF SOUTH VIET NAM

DEMOCRATIC STATE

STANDARD COINAGE

KM# 1 10 SU

Aluminum **Obv:** Three conjoined busts left **Obv. Legend:** "QUOC-GIA VIET-NAM" **Rev:** Rice plant (oryza sativa - Gramineae) dividing value **Rev. Legend:** "VIET-NAM"

Date	Mintage	F	VF	XF	Unc	BU
1953(a)	20,000,000	0.50	1.00	2.00	4.00	—

KM# 2 20 SU

Aluminum **Obv:** Three conjoined busts left **Obv. Legend:** "QUOC-GIA VIET-NAM" **Rev:** Rice plant dividing value **Rev. Legend:** "VIET-NAM"

Date	Mintage	F	VF	XF	Unc	BU
1953(a)	15,000,000	0.40	0.75	1.50	3.00	—

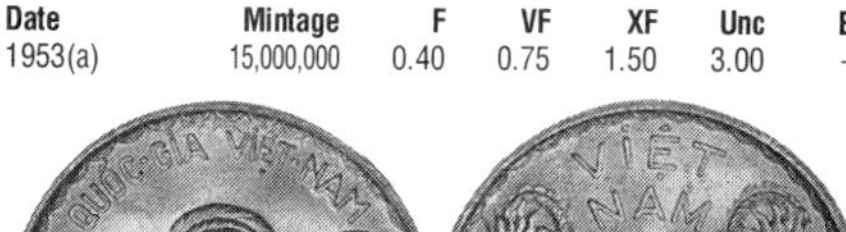

KM# 3 50 XU

Aluminum **Obv:** Three busts; 3/4 left, facing and 3/4 right **Obv. Legend:** "QUOC-GIA VIET-NAM" **Rev:** Dragons flank denomination **Rev. Legend:** "VIET-NAM"

Date	Mintage	F	VF	XF	Unc	BU
1953(a)	15,000,000	3.00	6.00	12.00	25.00	—

REPUBLIC OF VIET NAM

STANDARD COINAGE

KM# 4 50 SU

Aluminum **Obv:** Bust of Ngo Dihn Diem left **Obv. Legend:** "VIET-NAM CONG-HOA" **Rev:** Bamboo plants divide denomination **Note:** The 1960 50 Su coin was minted by the Paris Mint with the French spelling Su for Xu. The coin was restruck with the correct Xu, a new date of 1963, and is cataloged as KM#6.

Date	Mintage	F	VF	XF	Unc	BU
1960(a)	10,000,000	1.00	2.00	4.00	8.00	—
1960(a) Proof	—	Value: 80.00				

KM# 6 50 XU

2.9400 g., Aluminum **Obv:** Bust of Ngo Dihn Diem left **Obv. Legend:** "VIET-NAM CONG-HOA" **Rev:** Bamboo plants divide denomination

Date	Mintage	F	VF	XF	Unc	BU
1963	20,000,000	0.40	0.80	1.50	4.00	—
1963 Proof	—	Value: 80.00				

KM# 5 DONG

Copper-Nickel, 22 mm. **Obv:** Bust of Ngo Dihn Diem left **Obv. Legend:** "VIET-NAM CONG-HAO" **Rev:** Bamboo plants divide denomination

Date	Mintage	F	VF	XF	Unc	BU
1960(a)	105,000,000	0.20	0.50	1.25	2.50	6.50
1960(a) Proof	—	Value: 80.00				

KM# 7 DONG

3.9500 g., Copper-Nickel, 22.3 mm. **Obv:** Denomination **Obv. Legend:** "VIET-NAM CONG-HAO" **Rev:** Rice stalks

Date	Mintage	F	VF	XF	Unc	BU
1964	190,000,000	0.20	0.35	0.75	1.50	3.50
1964 Proof	—	—	—	—	—	—

KM# 7a DONG

3.6000 g., Nickel-Clad Steel **Obv:** Denomination **Obv. Legend:** "VIET-NAM CONG-HAO" **Rev:** Rice stalks

Date	Mintage	F	VF	XF	Unc	BU
1971	—	0.10	0.15	0.35	1.00	3.00

KM# 12 DONG

1.2000 g., Aluminum, 22.40 mm. **Series:** F.A.O. **Obv:** Denomination **Obv. Legend:** "VIET-NAM CONG-HAO" **Rev:** Rice stalks **Rev. Legend:** "TANG-GIA SAN-NUAT LUONG-THUC"

Date	Mintage	F	VF	XF	Unc	BU
1971	30,000,000	0.25	0.50	1.00	2.50	5.50

KM# 9 5 DONG

Copper-Nickel **Obv:** Denomination **Obv. Legend:** "VIET-NAM CONG-HAO" **Rev:** Rice stalks **Rev. Legend:** "NGAN-HANG VIET-NAM CONG-HOA" **Shape:** Scalloped

Date	Mintage	F	VF	XF	Unc	BU
1966	100,000,000	0.25	0.50	1.00	2.00	4.00

KM# 9a 5 DONG

Nickel-Clad Steel **Obv:** Denomination **Obv. Legend:** "VIET-NAM CONG-HAO" **Rev:** Rice stalks **Rev. Legend:** "NGAN-HANG VIET-NAM CONG-HOA"

Date	Mintage	F	VF	XF	Unc	BU
1971	15,000,000	0.40	0.75	1.50	3.00	7.50

KM# 8 10 DONG

Copper-Nickel, 25.5 mm. **Obv:** Denomination **Obv. Legend:** "VIET-NAM CONG-HAO" **Rev:** Rice stalks

Date	Mintage	F	VF	XF	Unc	BU
1964	45,000,000	0.25	0.50	1.00	2.00	6.00

KM# 8a 10 DONG

Nickel-Clad Steel **Obv:** Denomination **Obv. Legend:** "VIET-NAM CONG-HAO" **Rev:** Rice stalks

Date	Mintage	F	VF	XF	Unc	BU
1968	30,000,000	0.25	0.50	1.00	2.00	6.00
1970	50,000,000	0.25	0.50	1.00	2.00	6.00

KM# 13 10 DONG

4.3900 g., Brass-Clad Steel, 24 mm. **Series:** F.A.O. **Obv:** Denomination **Obv. Legend:** "VIET-NAM CONG-HAO, NGAN-HUAN QUOC-GIA VIET-NAM" **Rev:** Farmers in rice paddy **Rev. Legend:** "TANG-GIA SAM-XUAT NONG-PHAN"

Date	Mintage	F	VF	XF	Unc	BU
1974	30,000,000	0.25	0.50	1.00	2.00	4.00

KM# 10 20 DONG

Nickel-Clad Steel **Obv:** Denomination **Obv. Legend:** "VIET-NAM CONG-HAO" **Rev:** Farmer in rice paddy **Rev. Legend:** "NGAN-HANG QUOC-GIA VIET-NAM" **Designer:** Lu'u Tri

Date	Mintage	F	VF	XF	Unc	BU
1968	—	0.75	1.50	3.00	6.00	10.00

KM# 11 20 DONG

8.7600 g., Nickel-Clad Steel, 29.6 mm. **Series:** F.A.O. **Obv:** Denomination **Obv. Legend:** "VIET-NAM CONG-HAO" **Rev:** Farmer in rice paddy **Rev. Legend:** "CHIEN-TICH THE-GIOI CHONG NAM DOI" **Shape:** 12-sided **Designer:** Lu'u Tri

Date	Mintage	F	VF	XF	Unc	BU
1968	500,000	1.00	2.00	4.00	8.00	12.00

KM# 14 50 DONG

Nickel Clad Steel **Series:** F.A.O. **Obv:** Denomination **Obv. Legend:** "VIET-NAM CONG-HAO, NGAN-HANG QUOC-GIA VIET-NAM" **Rev:** Farmers in rice paddy **Rev. Legend:** "TANG-GIA SAM-XUAT NONG-PHAN"

Date	Mintage	F	VF	XF	Unc	BU
1975	1,010,000	—	—	450	650	800

Note: It is reported that all but a few examples were disposed of as scrap metal

PEOPLE'S REVOLUTIONARY GOVERNMENT

STANDARD COINAGE

KM# A8 XU

Aluminum **Obv:** Star above center hole, spray below **Obv. Legend:** "NGAN HANG VIET NAM" **Rev:** 1 above center hole, MOT XU below, grain stalks flank

Date	Mintage	F	VF	XF	Unc	BU
ND(1975)	—	1.00	2.50	5.00	12.00	—

KM# A9 2 XU

Aluminum **Obv:** Wreath surrounds center hole, HAI XU below **Obv. Legend:** "NGAN HANG VIET NAM" **Rev:** Ornaments surround center hole, 2 above, XU below ornamentation

Date	Mintage	F	VF	XF	Unc	BU
1975	—	2.00	4.00	7.00	20.00	—

KM# A10 5 XU

Aluminum **Obv:** Denomination below center hole **Obv. Legend:** "NGAN HANG VIET NAM" **Rev:** "NAM XU" above, 5 below in stylized sprays

Date	Mintage	F	VF	XF	Unc	BU
ND(1975)	—	2.00	4.00	9.00	25.00	—

WEST AFRICAN STATES

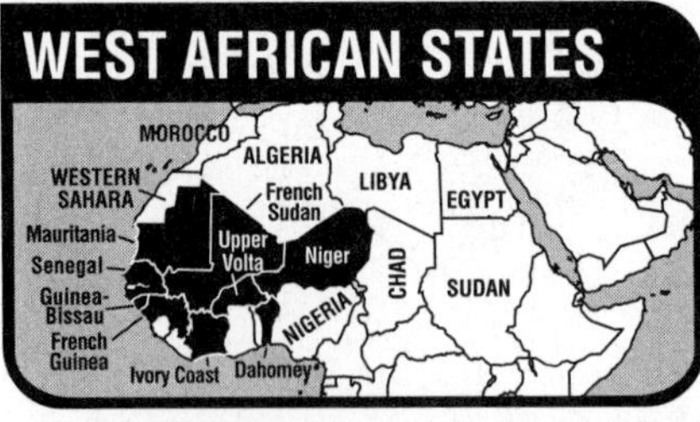

The West African States, a former federation of eight French colonial territories on the northwest coast of Africa, has an area of 1,831,079 sq. mi. (4,742,495 sq. km.) and a population of about 17 million. Capital: Dakar. The constituent territories were Mauritania, Senegal, Dahomey, French Sudan, Ivory Coast, Upper Volta, Niger and French Guinea.

The members of the federation were overseas territories within the French Union until Sept. of 1958 when all but French Guinea approved the constitution of the Fifth French Republic, thereby electing to become autonomous members of the new French Community. French Guinea voted to become the fully independent Republic of Guinea. The other seven attained independence in 1960. The French West Africa territories were provided with a common currency, a practice which was continued as the monetary union of the West African States which provides a common currency to the autonomous republics of Dahomey (now Benin), Senegal, Upper Volta (now Burkina Faso), Ivory Coast, Mali, Togo, Niger, and Guinea-Bissau.

For earlier coinage refer to Togo, and French West Africa.

MINT MARK

(a)- Paris, privy marks only

MONETARY SYSTEM

100 Centimes = 1 Franc

FEDERATION

STANDARD COINAGE

KM# 3.1 FRANC

1.3000 g., Aluminum, 23 mm. **Obv:** Taku symbol divides denomination **Rev:** Gazelle head facing (gazella leptoceros - bovidae) **Designer:** G.B.L. Bazor

Date	Mintage	F	VF	XF	Unc	BU
1961(a)	3,000,000	—	0.15	0.30	0.60	0.85
1964(a)	10,500,000	—	0.15	0.30	0.60	0.85
1965(a)	6,000,000	—	0.15	0.30	0.60	0.85
1967(a)	2,500,000	—	0.15	0.30	0.60	0.85
1971(a)	8,000,000	—	0.15	0.30	0.60	0.85
1972(a)	4,000,000	—	0.15	0.30	0.60	0.85
1973(a)	4,500,000	—	0.15	0.30	0.60	0.85
1974(a)	4,500,000	—	0.15	0.30	0.60	0.85
1975(a)	18,000,000	—	0.15	0.30	0.60	0.85

KM# 3.2 FRANC

Aluminum, 23 mm. **Obv:** Taku symbol divides denomination **Rev:** Engraver general's name

Date	Mintage	F	VF	XF	Unc	BU
1962(a)	2,000,000	—	2.00	5.00	10.00	12.00
1963(a)	4,500,000	—	1.50	4.00	7.00	9.00

KM# 8 FRANC

1.6000 g., Steel **Obv:** Taku - Ashanti gold weight **Rev:** Value and date **Designer:** R. Joly

Date	Mintage	F	VF	XF	Unc	BU
1976(a)	8,000,000	—	—	0.10	0.35	0.60
1977(a)	14,700,000	—	—	0.10	0.35	0.60
1978(a)	21,800,000	—	—	0.10	0.35	0.60
1979(a)	16,600,000	—	—	0.10	0.35	0.60
1980(a)	13,000,000	—	—	0.10	0.35	0.60
1981(a)	2,000,000	—	—	0.10	0.35	0.60
1982(a)	6,000,000	—	—	0.10	0.35	0.60
1984(a)	33,400,000	—	—	0.10	0.35	0.60
1985(a)	26,900,000	—	—	—	—	—
1988(a)	—	—	—	0.10	0.35	0.60
1990(a)	10,000,000	—	—	0.10	0.35	0.60
1991(a)	3,500,000	—	—	0.10	0.35	0.60
1992(a)	6,000,000	—	—	0.10	0.35	0.60
1995(a)	3,000,000	—	—	0.10	0.35	0.60
1996(a)	3,000,000	—	—	0.10	0.35	0.60
1997(a)	1,500,000	—	—	0.10	0.35	0.60
1999(a)	1,000,000	—	—	0.10	0.35	0.60
2000(a)	—	—	—	0.10	0.35	0.60

Date	Mintage	F	VF	XF	Unc	BU
2001(a)	—	—	—	0.10	0.35	0.60
2002(a)	—	—	—	0.10	0.35	0.60

KM# 2 5 FRANCS

2.9400 g., Aluminum-Bronze, 20.2 mm. **Obv:** Taku symbol divides denomination **Rev:** Gazelle head facing **Designer:** G.B.L. Bazor

Date	Mintage	F	VF	XF	Unc	BU
1960(a)	5,000,000	—	0.20	0.40	0.70	1.00

KM# 2a 5 FRANCS

3.0000 g., Aluminum-Nickel-Bronze, 20 mm. **Obv:** Taku - Ashanti gold weight divides value value **Rev:** Gazelle head facing

Date	Mintage	F	VF	XF	Unc	BU
1965(a)	12,500,000	—	0.20	0.40	0.70	1.00
1967(a)	6,500,000	—	0.20	0.40	0.70	1.00
1968(a)	6,000,000	—	0.20	0.45	0.75	1.10
1969(a)	8,000,000	—	0.20	0.40	0.70	1.00
1970(a)	10,005,000	—	0.20	0.40	0.70	1.00
1971(a)	10,000,000	—	0.20	0.40	0.70	1.00
1972(a)	5,000,000	—	0.20	0.40	0.70	1.00
1973(a)	6,000,000	—	0.20	0.45	0.75	1.10
1974(a)	13,326,000	—	0.10	0.15	0.30	0.50
1975(a)	16,840,000	—	0.20	0.40	0.70	1.00
1976(a)	20,010,000	—	0.20	0.30	0.60	0.85
1977(a)	22,000,000	—	0.20	0.30	0.60	0.85
1978(a)	40,000,000	—	0.20	0.30	0.60	0.85
1979(a)	11,000,000	—	0.10	0.20	0.40	0.60
1980(a)	18,000,000	—	0.10	0.20	0.40	0.60
1981(a)	18,000,000	—	0.10	0.20	0.40	0.60
1982(a)	25,000,000	—	0.10	0.20	0.40	0.60
1984(a)	31,700,000	—	0.10	0.20	0.40	0.60
1985(a)	16,000,000	—	0.10	0.20	0.40	0.60
1986(a)	8,000,000	—	0.10	0.20	0.40	0.60
1987(a)	26,500,000	—	0.10	0.20	0.40	0.60
1989(a)	44,500,000	—	0.10	0.20	0.40	0.60
1990(a)	—	—	0.10	0.20	0.40	0.60
1991(a)	19,000,000	—	0.10	0.20	0.40	0.60
1992(a)	—	—	0.10	0.20	0.40	0.60
1993(a)	—	—	0.10	0.20	0.40	0.60
1994(a)	20,000,000	—	0.10	0.20	0.40	0.60
1995(a)	—	—	0.10	0.20	0.40	0.60
1996(a)	21,500,000	—	0.10	0.20	0.40	0.60
1997(a)	18,000,000	—	0.10	0.20	0.40	0.60
1999(a)	36,900,000	—	0.10	0.20	0.40	0.60
2000(a)	—	—	0.10	0.20	0.40	0.60
2001(a)	—	—	0.10	0.20	0.40	0.60
2002(a)	—	—	0.10	0.20	0.40	0.60
2003(a)	—	—	0.10	0.20	0.40	0.60
2004(a)	—	—	0.10	0.20	0.40	0.60
2005(a)	—	—	0.10	0.20	0.40	0.60

KM# 1 10 FRANCS

Aluminum-Bronze **Obv:** Taku symbol divides denomination **Designer:** G.B.L. Bazor

Date	Mintage	F	VF	XF	Unc	BU
1959(a)	10,000,000	—	0.15	0.30	0.60	0.85
1964(a)	10,000,000	—	0.20	0.40	0.70	1.00

KM# 1a 10 FRANCS

Aluminum-Nickel-Bronze **Obv:** Taku symbol divides denomination **Rev:** Gazelle head facing

Date	Mintage	F	VF	XF	Unc	BU
1966(a)	6,000,000	—	0.20	0.40	0.70	1.00
1967(a)	3,500,000	—	0.25	0.50	0.90	1.25
1968(a)	6,000,000	—	0.20	0.40	0.70	1.00
1969(a)	7,000,000	—	0.25	0.50	0.90	1.25
1970(a)	7,000,000	—	0.15	0.30	0.60	0.85
1971(a)	8,000,000	—	0.15	0.30	0.60	0.85
1972(a)	5,500,000	—	0.20	0.40	0.70	1.00
1973(a)	3,000,000	—	0.20	0.40	0.70	1.00
1974(a)	10,000,000	—	0.15	0.30	0.60	0.85
1975(a)	17,000,000	—	0.15	0.30	0.60	0.85
1976(a)	18,000,000	—	0.15	0.30	0.60	0.85
1977(a)	11,000,000	—	0.15	0.25	0.50	0.75
1978(a)	21,000,000	—	0.15	0.25	0.50	0.75
1979(a)	11,000,000	—	0.15	0.25	0.50	0.75
1980(a)	16,000,000	—	0.15	0.25	0.50	0.75
1981(a)	12,000,000	—	0.15	0.25	0.50	0.75

KM# 10 10 FRANCS

4.0400 g., Brass, 23.4 mm. **Series:** F.A.O. **Obv:** Taku - Ashanti gold weight divides value **Rev:** People getting water **Designer:** R. Joly

Date	Mintage	F	VF	XF	Unc	BU
1981(a)	2,000,000	—	0.25	0.50	1.25	1.50
1982(a)	23,000,000	—	0.25	0.50	1.25	1.50
1983(a)	6,000,000	—	0.25	0.50	1.25	1.50
1984(a)	10,000,000	—	0.25	0.50	1.25	1.50
1985(a)	5,000,000	—	0.25	0.50	1.25	1.50
1986(a)	7,500,000	—	0.25	0.50	1.25	1.50
1987(a)	28,000,000	—	0.25	0.50	1.25	1.50
1989(a)	40,500,000	—	0.25	0.50	1.25	1.50
1990(a)	18,000,000	—	0.25	0.50	1.25	1.50
1991(a)	18,000,000	—	0.25	0.50	1.25	1.50
1992(a)	5,000,000	—	0.25	0.50	1.25	1.50
1993(a)	4,400,000	—	0.25	0.50	1.25	1.50
1994(a)	19,900,000	—	0.25	0.50	1.25	1.50
1995(a)	3,700,000	—	0.25	0.50	1.25	1.50
1996(a)	33,300,000	—	0.25	0.50	1.25	1.50
1997(a)	38,200,000	—	0.25	0.50	1.25	1.50
1999(a)	33,000,000	—	0.25	0.50	1.25	1.50
2000(a)	6,500,000	—	0.25	0.50	1.25	1.50
2002(a)	—	—	0.25	0.50	1.25	1.50
2003(a)	—	—	0.25	0.50	1.25	1.50
2004(a)	—	—	0.25	0.50	1.00	1.50
2005(a)	—	—	0.25	0.50	1.00	1.50

KM# 5 25 FRANCS

Aluminum-Bronze, 27 mm. **Obv:** Taku divides denomination **Rev:** Gazelle head facing **Designer:** G.B.L. Bazor

Date	Mintage	F	VF	XF	Unc	BU
1970(a)	7,000,000	—	0.25	0.45	1.00	1.25
1971(a)	7,000,000	—	0.50	0.75	1.25	1.50
1972(a)	2,000,000	—	1.50	2.50	4.50	6.00
1975(a)	5,035,000	—	0.25	0.45	1.00	1.25
1976(a)	3,365,000	—	0.25	0.45	1.00	1.25
1977(a)	3,288,000	—	0.25	0.45	1.00	1.25
1978(a)	6,800,000	—	0.25	0.45	1.00	1.25
1979(a)	5,200,000	—	0.25	0.45	1.00	1.25

KM# 9 25 FRANCS

7.9500 g., Aluminum-Bronze, 27 mm. **Series:** F.A.O. **Obv:** Taku - Ashanti gold weight divides value **Rev:** Figure filling tube

Date	Mintage	F	VF	XF	Unc	BU
1980(a)	7,800,000	—	0.25	0.75	1.75	2.00
1981(a)	4,000,000	—	0.25	0.75	1.75	2.00
1982(a)	8,000,000	—	0.25	0.75	1.75	2.00
1984(a)	15,300,000	—	0.25	0.75	1.75	2.00
1985(a)	8,587,000	—	0.25	0.75	1.75	2.00
1987(a)	9,000,000	—	0.25	0.75	1.75	2.00
1989(a)	17,600,000	—	0.25	0.75	1.75	2.00
1990(a)	6,000,000	—	0.25	0.75	1.75	2.00
1991(a)	1,700,000	—	0.25	0.75	1.75	2.00
1992(a)	6,000,000	—	0.25	0.75	1.75	2.00
1994(a)	8,200,000	—	0.25	0.75	1.75	2.00
1995(a)	—	—	0.25	0.75	1.75	2.00
1996(a)	18,300,000	—	0.25	0.75	1.75	2.00
1997(a)	22,000,000	—	0.25	0.75	1.75	2.00
1999(a)	16,700,000	—	0.25	0.75	1.75	2.00
2000(a)	16,800,000	—	0.25	0.75	1.75	2.00
2001(a)	—	—	0.25	0.75	1.75	2.00
2002(a)	—	—	0.25	0.75	1.75	2.00
2003(a)	—	—	0.25	0.75	1.75	2.00
2004(a)	—	—	0.25	0.75	1.50	2.00
2005(a)	—	—	0.25	0.75	1.50	2.00

KM# 6 50 FRANCS

5.0900 g., Copper-Nickel, 22 mm. **Series:** F.A.O. **Obv:** Taku - Ashanti gold weight **Rev:** Value within mixed beans, grains and nuts **Designer:** R. Joly

Date	Mintage	F	VF	XF	Unc	BU
1972(a)	20,000,000	—	0.35	0.50	1.25	1.50
1974(a)	3,000,000	—	0.50	0.75	1.50	1.75
1975(a)	9,000,000	—	0.25	0.40	1.00	1.25
1976(a)	6,002,000	—	0.35	0.50	1.25	1.50
1977(a)	4,832,000	—	0.35	0.50	1.25	1.50
1978(a)	7,200,000	—	0.35	0.50	1.25	1.50
1979(a)	4,200,000	—	0.35	0.50	1.25	1.50
1980(a)	7,200,000	—	0.35	0.50	1.25	1.50
1981(a)	6,000,000	—	0.35	0.50	1.25	1.50
1982(a)	12,000,000	—	0.35	0.50	1.25	1.50
1984(a)	25,500,000	—	0.35	0.50	1.25	1.50
1985(a)	4,120,000	—	0.35	0.50	1.25	1.50
1986(a)	—	—	0.35	0.50	1.25	1.50
1987(a)	10,000,000	—	0.35	0.50	1.25	1.50
1989(a)	17,000,000	—	0.35	0.50	1.25	1.50
1990(a)	7,500,000	—	0.35	0.50	1.25	1.50
1991(a)	5,600,000	—	0.35	0.50	1.25	1.50
1992(a)	7,000,000	—	0.35	0.50	1.25	1.50
1993(a)	2,800,000	—	0.35	0.50	1.25	1.50
1995(a)	40,000,000	—	0.35	0.50	1.25	1.50
1996(a)	20,500,000	—	0.35	0.50	1.25	1.50
1997(a)	25,800,000	—	0.35	0.50	1.25	1.50
1999(a)	25,200,000	—	0.35	0.50	1.25	1.50
2000(a)	14,400,000	—	0.35	0.50	1.25	1.50
2001(a)	—	—	0.35	0.50	1.25	1.50
2002(a)	—	—	0.35	0.50	1.25	1.50
2003(a)	—	—	0.35	0.50	1.25	1.50
2004(a)	—	—	0.35	0.50	1.25	1.50
2005(a)	—	—	0.35	0.50	1.25	1.50

KM# 4 100 FRANCS

7.0700 g., Nickel, 26 mm. **Obv:** Taku - Ashanti gold weight **Rev:** Value within flowers **Designer:** R. Joly

Date	Mintage	F	VF	XF	Unc	BU
1967(a)	—	—	0.75	1.00	2.50	3.00
1968(a)	25,000,000	—	0.75	1.00	2.50	3.00
1969(a)	25,000,000	—	0.75	1.00	2.50	3.00
1970(a)	4,510,000	—	0.80	1.50	3.50	5.00
1971(a)	12,000,000	—	0.50	0.75	1.85	2.25
1972(a)	5,000,000	—	0.60	0.85	2.00	2.50
1973(a)	5,000,000	—	0.60	0.85	2.00	2.50
1974(a)	8,500,000	—	0.60	0.75	1.85	2.25
1975(a)	16,000,000	—	0.60	0.75	1.85	2.25
1976(a)	11,575,000	—	0.60	0.75	1.85	2.25
1977(a)	6,200,000	—	0.60	0.75	1.85	2.25
1978(a)	12,000,000	—	0.60	0.75	1.85	2.25
1979(a)	12,400,000	—	0.60	0.85	2.00	2.50
1980(a)	13,000,000	—	0.60	0.75	2.00	2.50
1981(a)	8,000,000	—	0.60	0.75	2.00	2.50
1982(a)	18,000,000	—	0.60	0.75	2.00	2.50
1984(a)	2,500,000	—	0.65	0.85	2.25	2.75
1985(a)	1,460,000	—	0.65	0.85	2.25	2.75
1987(a)	9,000,000	—	0.65	0.85	2.25	2.75
1989(a)	16,500,000	—	0.65	0.85	2.25	2.75
1990(a)	6,500,000	—	0.65	0.85	2.25	2.75
1991(a)	1,000,000	—	0.65	0.85	2.25	2.75
1992(a)	4,000,000	—	0.65	0.85	2.25	2.75
1996(a)	24,000,000	—	0.65	0.85	2.25	2.75
1997(a)	69,000,000	—	0.65	0.85	2.25	2.75
2000(a)	1,800,000	—	0.60	0.85	2.25	2.75
2001(a)	—	—	0.60	0.85	2.25	2.75
2002(a)	—	—	0.60	0.85	2.25	2.75
2003(a)	—	—	0.60	0.85	2.25	2.75
2004(a)	—	—	0.60	0.75	2.00	2.75
2005(a)	—	—	0.60	0.75	2.00	2.75

KM# 14 200 FRANCS

6.9000 g., Bi-Metallic Brass center in Copper-Nickel ring, 24.4 mm. **Obv:** Taku - Ashanti gold weight **Rev:** Agricultural produce and value **Edge:** Segmented reeding **Designer:** Raymond Joly

Date	Mintage	F	VF	XF	Unc	BU
2003	—	—	1.00	1.60	4.00	6.00
2004(a)	—	—	1.00	1.60	4.00	6.00
2005(a)	—	—	1.00	1.60	4.00	6.00

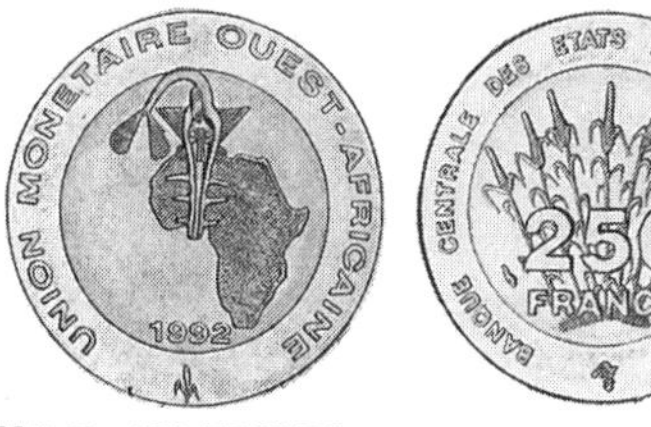

KM# 13 250 FRANCS

Bi-Metallic Brass center in Copper-Nickel ring **Obv:** Map on globe, Taku symbol at top **Rev:** Stalks behind denomination, circle surrounds

Date	Mintage	F	VF	XF	Unc	BU
1992(a)	9,000,000	—	1.75	2.75	7.00	8.00
1993(a)	10,000,000	—	1.75	2.75	7.00	8.00
1996(a)	7,500,000	—	2.00	3.00	8.00	9.00

KM# 15 500 FRANCS

10.6000 g., Bi-Metallic Copper-Nickel center in Brass ring, 27.9 mm. **Obv:** Taku - Ashanti gold weight **Rev:** Agricultural produce and value **Edge:** Segmented reeding **Designer:** Raymond Joly

Date	Mintage	F	VF	XF	Unc	BU
2003	—	—	2.25	4.00	10.00	12.00
2004(a)	—	—	2.25	4.00	10.00	12.00
2005(a)	—	—	2.25	4.00	10.00	12.00

YEMEN

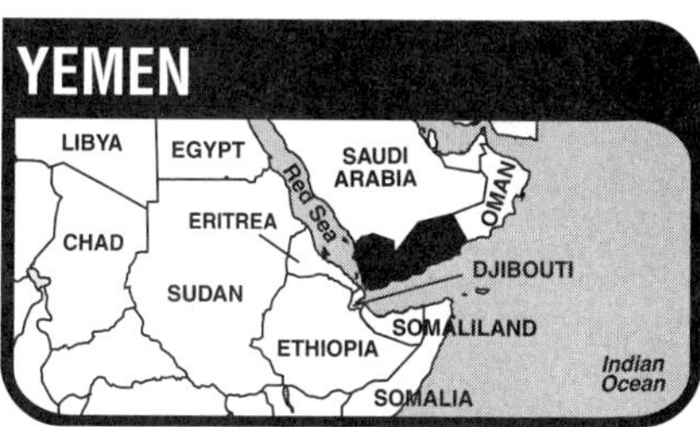

One of the oldest centers of civilization in the Middle East, Yemen was once part of the Minaean Kingdom and of the ancient Kingdom of Sheba, after which it was captured successively by Egyptians, Ethiopians and Romans. It was converted to Islam in 628 A.D. and administered as a caliphate until 1538, when it came under Ottoman occupation in 1849. The second Ottoman occupation which began in 1872 was maintained until 1918 when autonomy was achieved through revolution.

TITLE

المملكة المتوكلية اليمنية

al-Mamlaka(t) al-Mutawakkiliya(t) al-Yamaniya(t)

RULER

Ottoman, until 1625

QASIMID IMAMS

al-Mansur Muhammad bin Yahya, (Imam Mansur) AH1307-1322/1890-1904AD

al Hadi al-Hasan bin Yahya (Counter Imam, in Sa'da) AH1322/1904AD

al-Mutawakkil Yahya bin Muhammad (Imam Yahya) AH1322-1367/1904-1948AD

al-Nasir Ahmad bin Yahya, (Imam Ahmad) AH1367-1382/ 1948-1962AD

al-Badr Muhammad bin Ahmad, (Imam Badr) AH1382-1388/ 1962-1968AD (mostly in exile)

MINT NAME

San'a

NETARY SYSTEM

ter Accession of Iman Yahya
AH1322/1904AD

1 Zalat = 1/160 Riyal
2 Zalat = 1 Halala = 1/80 Riyal
2 Halala = 1 Buqsha = 1/40 Riyal
40 Buqsha = 1 Riyal

NOTE: The Riyal was called an IMADI (RIYAL) during the reign of Imam Yahya "Imadi" honorific name for Yahyawi and an AHMADI (RIYAL) during the reign of Imam Ahmad. The 1 Zalat, Y#2.1, D1, A3, A4 and all Imam Yahya gold strikes except Y#F10, bear no indication of value. Many of the Mutawakkilite coins after AH1322/1904AD bear the denomination expressed as fraction of the Riyal as follows.

BRONZE and ALUMINUM

Thumn ushr = 1/80 Riyal = 1/2 Buqsha = 1 Halala
Rub ushr = 1/40 Riyal = 1 Buqsha
Nisf ushr = 1/20 Riyal = 2 Buqsha = 1/2 Bawlah
Nisf thumn = 1/16 Riyal = 2-1/2 Buqsha
Ushr = 1/10 Riyal = 4 Buqsha = 1 Bawlah
Thumn = 1/8 Riyal = 5 Buqsha
Rub = 1/4 Riyal = 10 Buqsha
Nisf = 1/2 Riyal = 20 Buqsha
1 Riyal (Imadi, Ahmadi) = 40 Buqsha

DATING

All coins of Imam Yahya have accession date AH1322 on obverse and actual date of issue on reverse. All coins of Imam Ahmad bear accession date AH1367 on obverse and actual date on reverse.

If not otherwise noted, all coins of Imam Yahya and Imam Ahad as well as the early issues of the Republic (Y#20 through Y#A25 and Y#32), were struck at the mint in Sana'a. The Sana'a Mint was essentially a medieval mint, using hand-cut dies and crudely machined blanks. There is a large amount of variation from one die to the next in arrangement of legends and ornaments, form of crescents, number of stars, size of the circle, etc., and literally hundreds of subtypes could be identified. Types are divided only when there are changes in the inscriptions, or major variations in the basic type, such as the presence or absence of "Rabb al-Alamin" in the legend or the position of the word *Sana* (= year) in relation to the year.

NOTE: All "ZALAT" coins are without mint name or denomination.

KINGDOM

HAMMERED COINAGE

KM# 403 HARF

Bronze **Ruler:** al-Mansur Muhammad bin Yahya (Imam Mansur) AH1307-1322 / 1890-1904AD **Note:** Similar to 1 Kabir, KM#410.

Date	Mintage	Good	VG	F	VF	XF
AH1320	—	—	—	—	—	—

KM# 410 KABIR

Silver, 15-16 mm. **Ruler:** al-Mansur Muhammad bin Yahya (Imam Mansur) AH1307-1322 / 1890-1904AD **Obv:** Similar to KM#409 **Rev:** "Allah/Abd/" date, divided by ornament, wtih four circular segments **Note:** Weight varies: 0.60-1.00 gram. Size varies. Varieties with three and four stars on reverse exist. Varieties of planchet thickness exist.

Date	Mintage	Good	VG	F	VF	XF
AH1319	—	15.00	30.00	50.00	150	—
AH1320	—	15.00	30.00	50.00	150	—
AH1321	—	15.00	30.00	50.00	150	—

MILLED COINAGE

Y# C1 HALALA

1.9300 g., Bronze **Ruler:** al-Hadi al-Hasan AH1322 / 1904AD **Obv:** Al-Hasan/bin Yahya/Sana 1322 **Rev:** Al-Hadi/Li-din Allah

Date	Mintage	Good	VG	F	VF	XF
AH1322	—	—	—	—	—	—

Y# 1.1 ZALAT

Bronze **Ruler:** al-Mutawakkil Yahya bin Muhammad (Imam Yahya) AH1322-1367 / 1904-1948AD **Obv:** Inscription in three lines above accession date AH1322 **Edge:** Plain **Note:** Weight varies: 0.90-1.60 grams. Obverse varieties with no stars or two stars. Reverse with eight stars. Size of inner circle varies, various planchet thicknesses.

Date	Mintage	Good	VG	F	VF	XF
AH1341	—	15.00	30.00	100	160	—
AH1342	—	5.00	12.00	30.00	50.00	—
AH1343	—	4.00	10.00	20.00	40.00	—

Note: 1343 also known with seven stars

Date	Mintage	Good	VG	F	VF	XF
AH1344	—	5.00	12.00	30.00	50.00	—

Note: 1344 also exists with traces of reeded edges

Date	Mintage	Good	VG	F	VF	XF
AH1345	—	10.00	25.00	75.00	125	—
AH1346	—	4.00	10.00	20.00	40.00	—

Y# 1.2 ZALAT

Bronze **Ruler:** al-Mutawakkil Yahya bin Muhammad (Imam Yahya) AH1322-1367 / 1904-1948AD **Obv:** Inscription in two lines above accession date AH1322

Date	Mintage	Good	VG	F	VF	XF
AH1342	—	5.00	12.00	30.00	50.00	—

Note: Obverse varieties with 1, 2, and 4 stars, and reverse with 8, 11, 12, 13, 14, 15, 16, 17, 20, and 22 stars exist; Some specimens show traces of reeded edges; Various planchet thicknesses exist

Y# 1.4 ZALAT

Bronze **Ruler:** al-Mutawakkil Yahya bin Muhammad (Imam Yahya) AH1322-1367 / 1904-1948AD **Obv:** Crescent below accession date AH1322

Date	Mintage	Good	VG	F	VF	XF
AH1342	—	300	425	650	1,000	—

Note: Varieties exist with 11, 14, 15, 16, and 17 stars on reverse and with 1, 2, and 4 stars on obverse; Various planchet thicknesses

Y# 1.7 ZALAT

Bronze **Ruler:** al-Mutawakkil Yahya bin Muhammad (Imam Yahya) AH1322-1367 / 1904-1948AD **Obv:** Inscription in three lines above accession date AH1322 **Rev:** Date in margin at bottom

Date	Mintage	Good	VG	F	VF	XF
AH1342 Rare	—	—	—	—	—	—

Note: Obverse varieties with 1 and 2 stars, Reverse with 11 stars, various planchet thicknesses

Y# 1.8 ZALAT

Bronze **Ruler:** al-Mutawakkil Yahya bin Muhammad (Imam Yahya) AH1322-1367 / 1904-1948AD **Obv:** Inscription in three lines above accession date AH1322

Date	Mintage	Good	VG	F	VF	XF
AH1344	—	—	—	—	—	—

Y# B1 ZALAT

Bronze **Ruler:** al-Mutawakkil Yahya bin Muhammad (Imam Yahya) AH1322-1367 / 1904-1948AD **Obv:** Inscription in two lines above accession date AH1322 **Note:** Probably struck at Shaharah about 1925. Dies were reportedly prepared in Italy. For silver strikes, see Y#A4.

Date	Mintage	Good	VG	F	VF	XF
NDAH1322(ca.1925)	—	30.00	60.00	125	200	—

Note: This issue is believed to be a pattern

Date	Mintage	Good	VG	F	VF	XF
ND(ca.1925)	—	30.00	60.00	125	200	—

Note: Possibly a pattern

Y# D1 1/80 RIYAL (1/2 Buqsha)

Bronze **Ruler:** al-Mutawakkil Yahya bin Muhammad (Imam Yahya) AH1322-1367 / 1904-1948AD **Obv:** Crescent below accession date AH1322 **Obv. Inscription:** Rabb al-Alamin **Rev:** Toughra **Note:** Without denomination or mint name.

Date	Mintage	Good	VG	F	VF	XF
ND(ca.1911) Rare; Accessional date only	—	—	—	—	—	—

Y# 2.1 1/80 RIYAL (1/2 Buqsha)

Bronze **Ruler:** al-Mutawakkil Yahya bin Muhammad (Imam Yahya) AH1322-1367 / 1904-1948AD **Note:** Accession date AH1322 above crescent on obverse and within crescent on reverse.

Date	Mintage	Good	VG	F	VF	XF
ND(ca.1911)	—	12.50	25.00	50.00	85.00	—

Note: Probably struck at Shaharah

Y# 2.2 1/80 RIYAL (1/2 Buqsha)

Bronze **Ruler:** al-Mutawakkil Yahya bin Muhammad (Imam Yahya) AH1322-1367 / 1904-1948AD **Obv:** Crescent below accession date AH1322 **Note:** Thin flan, 1.50-3.00 grams. The number and arrangement of stars and the size of the circle on the reverse vary as well as the exact arrangement of the legends which sometimes vary within each year. The reverse exists with 10, 12, 14, 20, 22, 24, 28, and 34 stars. Obverse varieties exist with 1, 2, 3 or 4 stars and without stars. Accession date: AH(1)322 or 1322. Struck at Shaharah.

Date	Mintage	Good	VG	F	VF	XF
AH1330	—	20.00	35.00	60.00	100	—
AH1331	—	20.00	35.00	75.00	150	—
AH1332	—	10.00	15.00	25.00	40.00	—
AH1333	—	10.00	15.00	25.00	40.00	—
AH1337	—	10.00	15.00	25.00	40.00	—
AH1338	—	10.00	15.00	25.00	40.00	—
AH1339	—	10.00	15.00	25.00	40.00	—

Y# 2.3 1/80 RIYAL (1/2 Buqsha)

Bronze **Ruler:** al-Mutawakkil Yahya bin Muhammad (Imam Yahya) AH1322-1367 / 1904-1948AD **Rev:** "Duriba Bi Sana'a" added

Date	Mintage	Good	VG	F	VF	XF
AH1340	—	10.00	20.00	40.00	75.00	—

Note: AH1340 exists with 4 and 8 stars on reverse

Date	Mintage	Good	VG	F	VF	XF
AH1341	—	10.00	20.00	40.00	75.00	—

Note: AH1341 exists with 4 stars on reverse

Y# 2.4 1/80 RIYAL (1/2 Buqsha)

Bronze **Ruler:** al-Mutawakkil Yahya bin Muhammad (Imam Yahya) AH1322-1367 / 1904-1948AD **Obv:** Without "Rabb al-Alamin" with crescent below accession date AH1322 **Note:** Weight and diameter varies.

Date	Mintage	Good	VG	F	VF	XF
AH1341	—	12.00	25.00	50.00	85.00	—

Note: AH1341 exists with 4 stars on reverse

Date	Mintage	Good	VG	F	VF	XF
AH1342	—	12.00	25.00	50.00	85.00	—

Note: AH1342 coins exist with 4 and 6 stars on reverse

Y# 2.5 1/80 RIYAL (1/2 Buqsha)

Bronze (Red To Yellow) **Ruler:** al-Mutawakkil Yahya bin Muhammad (Imam Yahya) AH1322-1367 / 1904-1948AD **Obv:** Crescent below accession date AH1332 **Obv. Inscription:** Rabb al-alamin **Rev:** "Sana" above date **Note:** Number and arrangement of stars on reverse (4, 5, 6, 7, or 8) as well as the size of the inner circle vary. Varieties exist in the form of crescent and arrangement of legends and planchet thicknesses.

Date	Mintage	Good	VG	F	VF	XF
AH1339	—	7.00	12.00	25.00	40.00	—
AH1341	—	7.00	12.00	25.00	40.00	—
AH1342	—	2.00	5.00	12.00	20.00	—
AH1343	—	2.00	5.00	12.00	20.00	—
AH1344	—	2.00	5.00	12.00	20.00	—
AH1345	—	1.50	4.00	8.00	15.00	—

Date	Mintage	Good	VG	F	VF	XF
AH1346	—	1.50	3.00	6.00	12.00	—

Note: Some examples of AH1346 show the 6 re-engraved over low I

Date	Mintage	Good	VG	F	VF	XF
AH1347	—	1.50	4.00	8.00	15.00	—
AH1348	—	1.50	4.00	8.00	15.00	—
AH1349	—	1.50	4.00	8.00	15.00	—
AH1350	—	1.50	4.00	8.00	15.00	—
AH135x	—	1.50	4.00	8.00	15.00	—
AH1351	—	2.00	6.00	12.00	20.00	—
AH1352	—	2.00	6.00	12.00	20.00	—
AH1353	—	2.00	6.00	12.00	20.00	—
AH1358	—	—	—	—	—	—

Note: Reported, not confirmed

Date	Mintage	Good	VG	F	VF	XF
AH1359	—	2.50	6.00	12.00	20.00	—
AH1360	—	2.50	4.00	8.00	15.00	—
AH1361	—	4.00	8.00	15.00	25.00	—

Y# 2.6 1/80 RIYAL (1/2 Buqsha)

3.0000 g., Bronze **Ruler:** al-Mutawakkil Yahya bin Muhammad (Imam Yahya) AH1322-1367 / 1904-1948AD **Rev:** "Sana" below date **Note:** Thin flan. Struck at Shaharah.

Date	Mintage	Good	VG	F	VF	XF
AH1333	—	80.00	100	200	300	—

Y# 2.7 1/80 RIYAL (1/2 Buqsha)

Bronze **Ruler:** al-Mutawakkil Yahya bin Muhammad (Imam Yahya) AH1322-1367 / 1904-1948AD **Note:** Thick flan. Weight varies: 4-5.4 grams. Varieties with 10 and 14 stars on reverse. Obverse with 1, 2, 3, 4, or no stars. Varieties of legend distribution. Some coins occur with light silver wash. Struck at Shaharah.

Date	Mintage	Good	VG	F	VF	XF
AH1332	—	10.00	15.00	25.00	40.00	—
AH1333	—	10.00	15.00	25.00	40.00	—
AH1338	—	10.00	15.00	25.00	40.00	—

Y# 2.8 1/80 RIYAL (1/2 Buqsha)

Bronze **Ruler:** al-Mutawakkil Yahya bin Muhammad (Imam Yahya) AH1322-1367 / 1904-1948AD **Note:** Mule, two obverses.

Date	Mintage	Good	VG	F	VF	XF
ND(ca.1911-21)	—	20.00	30.00	60.00	100	—

Y# 11.1 1/80 RIYAL (1 Halala = 1/2 Buqsha)

Bronze (Red To Yellow) **Ruler:** al-Nasir Ahmad bin Yahya (Imam Ahmad) AH1367-1382 / 1948-1962AD **Obv:** Crescent below accession date AH1367 which may vary as 1367/1267, 1367/1777, etc. **Rev:** "Sana" above date **Note:** There is a variation in the number of stars on reverse, as follows: AH1368 - 8 stars; AH1371-74 and some AH1381 (not overdate) - 7 stars; AH1375-81 including some AH1381, some AH1382, and all AH1381 overdates - 8 stars. Varieties of arrangement of legends, form of crescent, and size of circle on reverse exist. Some earlier dates exist on thinner planchets.

Date	Mintage	VG	F	VF	XF	Unc
AH1368	—	1.00	2.00	5.00	10.00	—
AH1371	—	0.30	1.00	3.00	8.00	—
AH1372	—	0.30	1.00	3.00	8.00	—
AH1373	—	0.30	0.60	1.00	3.00	—
AH1374	—	0.30	1.00	3.00	8.00	—
AH1275 Error for 1375	—	1.00	2.00	6.00	12.00	—
AH1375	—	—	—	—	—	—
AH1376	—	—	—	—	—	—
AH1376/86 Error	—	—	—	—	—	—
AH1278 Error for 1378	—	1.00	2.00	6.00	12.00	—
AH1378	—	—	—	—	—	—
AHx379	—	1.00	2.00	6.00	12.00	—
AH1379	—	0.50	1.00	2.50	5.00	—
AH1380/1	—	1.00	2.00	6.00	12.00	—
AH1380/79	—	0.50	1.00	2.50	5.00	—
AH1380/9	—	0.50	1.00	2.50	5.00	—
AH1380	—	0.50	1.00	2.50	5.00	—
AH1381/80/79	—	0.40	0.85	1.50	2.50	—
AH1381/79	—	0.40	0.85	1.50	2.50	—
AH1381	—	0.20	0.40	0.75	1.25	—
AH1382	—	5.00	10.00	15.00	20.00	—

Y# 11.2 1/80 RIYAL (1 Halala = 1/2 Buqsha)

Bronze **Ruler:** al-Nasir Ahmad bin Yahya (Imam Ahmad) AH1367-1382 / 1948-1962AD **Rev:** Without "Sana"

Date	Mintage	VG	F	VF	XF	Unc
AH1373 Rare	—	—	—	—	—	—

Y# 11a 1/80 RIYAL (1 Halala = 1/2 Buqsha)

Aluminum **Ruler:** al-Nasir Ahmad bin Yahya (Imam Ahmad) AH1367-1382 / 1948-1962AD **Obv:** Crescent below accession date AH1367 **Rev:** "Sana" above date **Note:** AH1374 and some AH1380 have 7 stars, the rest have 8 stars on reverse. Dies of 1/80 Riyal, Y#11.1, were used.

Date	Mintage	VG	F	VF	XF	Unc
AH1374	—	0.25	1.00	2.50	5.00	—
AH1375	—	0.75	2.50	5.50	10.00	—
AH1376	—	0.25	1.50	4.00	8.00	—
AH1377	—	0.75	2.50	5.50	10.00	—
AH1378	—	0.25	1.00	2.50	5.00	—
AH1378/6	—	0.25	1.00	2.50	5.00	—
AH1379	—	0.25	1.00	2.50	5.00	—
AH1379/5	—	0.75	2.50	5.50	10.00	—
AH1379/8	—	0.75	2.50	5.50	10.00	—
AH1380	—	0.25	1.00	2.50	5.00	—

Y# 11.3 1/80 RIYAL (1 Halala = 1/2 Buqsha)

Bronze **Ruler:** al-Nasir Ahmad bin Yahya (Imam Ahmad) AH1367-1382 / 1948-1962AD **Obv:** Crescent below accession date AH1367 **Note:** Struck with dies of 1/4 Ahmadi Riyal, Y#15 on 1/80 Riyal planchet.

Date	Mintage	VG	F	VF	XF	Unc
AH(13)80 Rare	—	—	—	—	—	—

Y# 18 1/80 RIYAL (1 Halala = 1/2 Buqsha)

Aluminum **Ruler:** al-Nasir Ahmad bin Yahya (Imam Ahmad) AH1367-1382 / 1948-1962AD **Note:** Accession date: AH1367.

Date	Mintage	VG	F	VF	XF	Unc
ND	—	0.15	0.25	0.50	1.00	—

Note: Struck privately in Lebanon in 1955 and 1956 and released into circulation in 1956

Y# A3 1/40 RIYAL (1 Buqsha)

Billon Silver **Ruler:** al-Mutawakkil Yahya bin Muhammad (Imam Yahya) AH1322-1367 / 1904-1948AD **Note:** Weight varies: 0.65-1.25 grams. Size varies: 15-16 mm. Accession date: AH1322.

Date	Mintage	VG	F	VF	XF	Unc
ND(ca.1911-21)	—	275	550	1,100	1,650	—

Note: Minted at Qaflat Idhar, without mint name or denomination

Y# 3.1 1/40 RIYAL (1 Buqsha)

Bronze **Ruler:** al-Mutawakkil Yahya bin Muhammad (Imam Yahya) AH1322-1367 / 1904-1948AD **Obv:** Without "Rabb al-Alamin", with crescent below accession date AH1322 **Rev:** "Sana" below date

Date	Mintage	VG	F	VF	XF	Unc
AH1341	—	10.00	20.00	40.00	80.00	—

Note: Varieties of borders, arrangement of legends, and thickness of planchets exist

Y# 3.2 1/40 RIYAL (1 Buqsha)

Bronze (Red To Yellow) **Ruler:** al-Mutawakkil Yahya bin Muhammad (Imam Yahya) AH1322-1367 / 1904-1948AD **Obv:** Crescent below accession date AH1322 **Obv. Inscription:** Rabb al-Alamin **Rev:** "Sana" above date, small "Sana'a" and three leaf ornaments plus star in border legend

Date	Mintage	VG	F	VF	XF	Unc
AH1342	—	4.00	10.00	20.00	60.00	—

Note: AH1342 exists with 4 leaf ornaments and without star in border legend

Date	Mintage	VG	F	VF	XF	Unc
AH13442	—	65.00	125	—	—	—
AH1343	—	4.00	10.00	20.00	60.00	—
AH1344	—	15.00	30.00	50.00	75.00	—

Y# 3.3 1/40 RIYAL (1 Buqsha)

Bronze (Red To Yellow) **Ruler:** al-Mutawakkil Yahya bin Muhammad (Imam Yahya) AH1322-1367 / 1904-1948AD **Obv:** Crescent below accession date AH1322 **Rev:** Large "Sana'a" in legend **Note:** Varieties in arrangement of legends, ornaments, form of the crescent, and size of the circle on reverse exist; weight varies.

Date	Mintage	VG	F	VF	XF	Unc
AH1344	—	12.00	20.00	35.00	100	—
AH1345	—	12.00	20.00	35.00	100	—
AH1349	—	1.50	3.50	10.00	25.00	—
AH1353	—	—	—	—	—	—

Note: Reported, not confirmed

Date	Mintage	VG	F	VF	XF	Unc
AH1358	—	2.00	4.00	10.00	25.00	—
AH1359	—	2.00	4.00	10.00	25.00	—
AH1360	—	2.00	4.00	10.00	25.00	—
AH1361/0	—	10.00	20.00	50.00	75.00	—
AH1362/0	—	2.50	5.00	10.00	35.00	—
AH1362	—	1.50	3.50	10.00	30.00	—
AH1363	—	1.50	5.00	12.00	35.00	—
AH1364	—	1.50	5.00	12.00	35.00	—
AH1365/4	—	2.25	5.00	12.00	35.00	—
AH1365	—	2.50	5.00	12.00	35.00	—
AH1366	—	1.50	3.50	12.00	30.00	—
AH1366/x	—	2.50	5.00	12.00	35.00	—
AH1367	—	10.00	20.00	50.00	75.00	—

Y# 12.1 1/40 RIYAL (1 Buqsha)

Bronze (Red To Yellow) **Ruler:** al-Nasir Ahmad bin Yahya (Imam Ahmad) AH1367-1382 / 1948-1962AD **Obv:** Crescent below accession date AH1367 **Rev:** "Sana" above date, large "Sana'a" in border legend **Note:** Some dates exist on thinner planchets and weight varies.

Date	Mintage	VG	F	VF	XF	Unc
AH1368	—	0.50	1.00	4.00	12.00	—

Note: AH1368 also exists with accession date 13776 (error) known

Date	Mintage	VG	F	VF	XF	Unc
AH1369	—	0.75	1.25	5.00	15.00	—
AH1370	—	0.35	0.75	3.00	6.00	—
AH1371	—	0.35	0.75	3.00	6.00	—
AH1372	—	0.35	0.75	2.00	4.00	—
AH1373/1	—	—	—	—	—	—
AH1373/2	—	0.85	1.80	3.00	6.00	—
AH1373	—	0.35	0.75	2.00	4.00	—
AH1374	—	0.35	0.75	2.00	4.00	—
AH1375/4	—	0.50	1.00	3.00	6.00	—
AH1377	—	—	—	—	—	—

Note: Reported, not confirmed

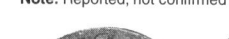

Y# 12.2 1/40 RIYAL (1 Buqsha)

Bronze (Red To Yellow) **Ruler:** al-Nasir Ahmad bin Yahya (Imam Ahmad) AH1367-1382 / 1948-1962AD **Obv:** Crescent below accession date AH1367 **Rev:** Small "Sana'a" in legend **Note:** Varieties of arrangement of legends, form of crescent, and size of circle exist.

Date	Mintage	VG	F	VF	XF	Unc
AH1371	—	0.35	0.75	3.00	6.00	—
AH1374	—	0.35	0.75	2.00	4.00	—
AH1375	—	0.35	0.75	2.00	4.00	—
AH1376	—	0.50	1.00	5.00	12.00	—

Note: Exists with accession date 1376 instead of 1367 on obverse

Date	Mintage	VG	F	VF	XF	Unc
AH1377/6	—	0.85	1.75	4.00	8.00	—

Note: Exists with accession date 1376 instead of 1367 on obverse

Date	Mintage	VG	F	VF	XF	Unc
AH1377	—	0.85	1.75	5.00	10.00	—
AH1378/5	—	—	—	—	—	—

Date	Mintage	VG	F	VF	XF	Unc
379/7	—	0.85	1.75	4.00	8.00	—
1380/79	—	0.85	1.75	4.00	8.00	—
AH1380	—	10.00	20.00	50.00	75.00	—

Y# 12a.1 1/40 RIYAL (1 Buqsha)
Aluminum **Ruler:** al-Nasir Ahmad bin Yahya (Imam Ahmad) AH1367-1382 / 1948-1962AD **Obv:** Crescent below accession date AH1367 **Rev:** "Sana" above date, large "Sana'a" in border legend **Note:** Dies of 1/40 Riyal, Y#12.1, were used.

Date	Mintage	VG	F	VF	XF	Unc
AH1371	—	0.50	1.00	4.00	10.00	—
AH1373	—	0.50	1.00	4.00	10.00	—
AH1374	—	0.50	1.00	4.00	10.00	—
AH1375	—	0.50	1.00	4.00	10.00	—
AH1377	—	15.00	30.00	50.00	90.00	—

Y# 12.3 1/40 RIYAL (1 Buqsha)
Bronze (Red To Yellow) **Ruler:** al-Nasir Ahmad bin Yahya (Imam Ahmad) AH1367-1382 / 1948-1962AD **Obv:** Crescent below accession date AH1367 **Rev:** Large "Sana'a" in legend, without "Sana" above date

Date	Mintage	VG	F	VF	XF	Unc
AH1371	—	0.50	1.00	4.00	12.00	—

Y# 12a.2 1/40 RIYAL (1 Buqsha)
Aluminum **Ruler:** al-Nasir Ahmad bin Yahya (Imam Ahmad) AH1367-1382 / 1948-1962AD **Obv:** Crescent below accession date AH1367 **Rev:** Small "Sana'a" in legend **Note:** Dies of 1/40 Riyal, Y#12.2, were used. AH1376 and AH1377 plain dates also exist with accession date AH1376 instead of AH1367 on obverse. Varieties exist.

Date	Mintage	VG	F	VF	XF	Unc
AH1375	—	0.50	1.00	4.00	10.00	—
AH1376	—	0.50	1.00	4.00	10.00	—
AH1377/6	—	10.00	20.00	40.00	75.00	—
AH1377	—	15.00	30.00	50.00	90.00	—

Y# 19 1/40 RIYAL (1 Buqsha)
Aluminum **Ruler:** al-Nasir Ahmad bin Yahya (Imam Ahmad) AH1367-1382 / 1948-1962AD **Note:** Accession date: AH1367 at bottom.

Date	Mintage	VG	F	VF	XF	Unc
ND	—	0.25	0.45	0.65	1.00	2.50

Note: Struck privately in Lebanon in 1955 and 1956 and released into circulation in 1956

Y# A4 1/20 IMADI RIYAL
Silver **Ruler:** al-Mutawakkil Yahya bin Muhammad (Imam Yahya) AH1322-1367 / 1904-1948AD **Obv:** Inscription in two lines above

Date	Mintage	VG	F	VF	XF	Unc
ND(1911-21)	—	60.00	120	250	400	—

Note: Dated accessionally on obverse without mint name or denomination; Probably struck at Shaharah about 1925; dies were reportedly prepared in Italy; Strikes in nickel reported; See Y#B1;This issue is believed to be a pattern

Y# B4 1/20 IMADI RIYAL
Silver **Ruler:** al-Mutawakkil Yahya bin Muhammad (Imam Yahya) AH1322-1367 / 1904-1948AD **Obv:** Crescent below accession date AH1322 **Rev:** Without "Sana"

Date	Mintage	VG	F	VF	XF	Unc
AH1337 Rare	—	—	—	—	—	—

Note: Three stars on reverse

Y# 4.1 1/20 IMADI RIYAL
Silver **Ruler:** al-Mutawakkil Yahya bin Muhammad (Imam Yahya) AH1322-1367 / 1904-1948AD **Obv:** Without "Rabb al-Alamin", with crescent below accession date AH1322 **Note:** Varieties in arrangement of legends, size of circle, and with 3 and 4 stars on reverse exist. Variety of Y#4 dated with 2 digits AH(13)22 of the accessional year are considered local contemporary counterfeits by leading authorities. They are reported having been produced by the Zaraing tribe at Bait Al-Faqih.

Date	Mintage	VG	F	VF	XF	Unc
AH1337	—	40.00	80.00	150	250	—
AH1338 Rare	—	—	—	—	—	—
AH1339	—	40.00	80.00	150	250	—
Note: Some strikes show accessional year as 322 only						
AH1340	—	20.00	30.00	60.00	100	—
Note: Some strikes show accessional year as 322 only						
AH1342	—	5.00	12.00	30.00	60.00	—
AH1343	—	4.00	10.00	25.00	50.00	—
AH1344	—	4.00	10.00	25.00	50.00	—
AH1345	—	4.00	10.00	25.00	50.00	—
AH1345/2	—	4.00	10.00	25.00	50.00	—
AH1347	—	5.00	12.00	30.00	60.00	—
AH1348	—	4.00	10.00	25.00	50.00	—
AH1349	—	4.00	10.00	25.00	50.00	—
AH1350	—	4.00	12.00	30.00	60.00	—
AH1351	—	5.00	15.00	35.00	75.00	—
AH1352	—	4.00	12.00	30.00	60.00	—
AH1353	—	4.00	12.00	30.00	60.00	—
AH1358	—	3.00	8.00	20.00	40.00	—
AH1359	—	3.00	8.00	20.00	40.00	—
AH1362/58	—	5.00	15.00	30.00	60.00	—
AH1362/59	—	5.00	15.00	30.00	60.00	—
AH1363	—	4.00	10.00	30.00	60.00	—
AH1364/46	—	3.00	8.00	20.00	40.00	—
AH1364	—	3.00	8.00	20.00	40.00	—
AHx364	—	3.00	8.00	20.00	40.00	—
AH1365	—	3.00	10.00	25.00	50.00	—
AH1366/44	—	4.00	12.00	30.00	60.00	—
AH1366	—	4.00	12.00	30.00	60.00	—

Y# 4.4 1/20 IMADI RIYAL
Silver **Ruler:** al-Mutawakkil Yahya bin Muhammad (Imam Yahya) AH1322-1367 / 1904-1948AD **Rev:** Border legend shifted to left **Note:** Accession date AH1322.

Date	Mintage	VG	F	VF	XF	Unc
AH1340 Rare	—	—	—	—	—	—

Note: Three stars on reverse

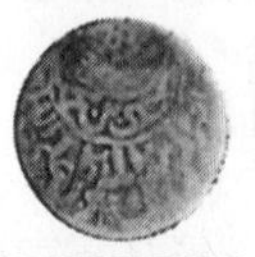 

Y# 4.2 1/20 IMADI RIYAL
Silver **Ruler:** al-Mutawakkil Yahya bin Muhammad (Imam Yahya) AH1322-1367 / 1904-1948AD **Obv:** Crescent **Rev:** "Sana" below date, normal legend position **Note:** Four stars on reverse.

Date	Mintage	VG	F	VF	XF	Unc
AH1341	—	40.00	80.00	150	250	—
AHx341	—	40.00	80.00	150	250	—

Y# 5.1 1/10 IMADI RIYAL
Silver **Ruler:** al-Mutawakkil Yahya bin Muhammad (Imam Yahya) AH1322-1367 / 1904-1948AD **Obv:** Crescent below accession date AH1322 **Obv. Inscription:** Rabb al-Alamin **Rev:** Without "Sana"

Date	Mintage	VG	F	VF	XF	Unc
AH1337	—	30.00	60.00	100	175	—

Note: Reverse varieties with 3, 4, and 5 stars. Size of circle and form of crescent varies

Y# 5.2 1/10 IMADI RIYAL
Silver **Ruler:** al-Mutawakkil Yahya bin Muhammad (Imam Yahya) AH1322-1367 / 1904-1948AD **Obv:** Without "Rabb al-Alamin", with crescent below accession date AH1322

Date	Mintage	VG	F	VF	XF	Unc
AH1339	—	20.00	40.00	75.00	150	—
Note: Some AH1339 strikes show accession date as 322						
AH1340	—	20.00	40.00	75.00	150	—
Note: AH1340 also exists with three stars, others with six stars on reverse						
AH1341	—	20.00	40.00	75.00	150	—
AH1348	—	100	150	350	500	—

Y# 5.3 1/10 IMADI RIYAL
Silver **Ruler:** al-Mutawakkil Yahya bin Muhammad (Imam Yahya) AH1322-1367 / 1904-1948AD **Obv:** Crescent below accession date AH1322 **Rev:** "Sana" below date **Note:** Varieties with three and six stars on the reverse exist.

Date	Mintage	VG	F	VF	XF	Unc
AH1341	—	20.00	40.00	75.00	150	—
AH1342	—	20.00	40.00	75.00	150	—

Y# 5.5 1/10 IMADI RIYAL
Silver **Ruler:** al-Mutawakkil Yahya bin Muhammad (Imam Yahya) AH1322-1367 / 1904-1948AD **Obv:** Without "Rabb al-Alamin" **Rev:** "Sana" above date **Note:** Form of crescent, size of circle on reverse, and arrangement of legends vary. Normal reverse contains 6 stars though varieties with 7, 8, 9, 10, and 12 stars on reverse exist. Some earlier dates show varying amounts of edge reeding.

Date	Mintage	VG	F	VF	XF	Unc
AH1342	—	4.00	10.00	25.00	50.00	—
AH1343	—	4.00	10.00	25.00	50.00	—
AH1344	—	3.00	8.00	20.00	40.00	—
AH1345	—	3.00	8.00	20.00	40.00	—
AH1347	—	3.00	8.00	20.00	40.00	—
AH1348	—	3.00	8.00	20.00	35.00	—
AH1349	—	3.00	6.00	15.00	30.00	—
AH1350	—	—	—	—	—	—
Note: Reported, not confirmed						
AH1351	—	4.00	10.00	25.00	40.00	—
AH1352	—	4.00	10.00	25.00	40.00	—
AH1358/49	—	3.00	8.00	15.00	30.00	—
AH1358	—	3.00	8.00	15.00	30.00	—
AH1359/3	—	3.00	8.00	15.00	30.00	—
AH1359/49	—	3.00	8.00	15.00	30.00	—
AH1362/44	—	4.00	10.00	25.00	40.00	—
AH1362/59	—	4.00	10.00	25.00	40.00	—
AH1363	—	3.00	8.00	25.00	45.00	—
AH1364/43	—	3.00	8.00	20.00	40.00	—
AH1364/3	—	3.00	8.00	25.00	45.00	—
AH1364/52	—	3.00	8.00	25.00	45.00	—
AH1364	—	3.00	8.00	15.00	35.00	—
AH1365	—	3.00	8.00	15.00	35.00	—
AH1366/5	—	3.00	10.00	20.00	50.00	—
AH1366/5x	—	3.00	10.00	20.00	50.00	—

Y# 5.4 1/10 IMADI RIYAL
Silver **Ruler:** al-Mutawakkil Yahya bin Muhammad (Imam Yahya) AH1322-1367 / 1904-1948AD **Obv:** Crescent below accession date AH1322 **Obv. Inscription:** Rabb al-Alamin **Rev:** "Sana" above date **Note:** Varieties with 8, 9, and 10 stars on reverse exist.

Date	Mintage	VG	F	VF	XF	Unc
AH1342	—	20.00	40.00	75.00	150	—

Y# 8 1/8 IMADI RIYAL

Silver **Ruler:** al-Mutawakkil Yahya bin Muhammad (Imam Yahya) AH1322-1367 / 1904-1948AD **Obv:** One or no stars in crescent below accession date AH1322 **Rev:** "Thumn" in place of "Ushr" below date, 6 stars

Date	Mintage	VG	F	VF	XF	Unc
AH1339	—	325	550	1,100	1,650	—

Y# 6.1 1/4 IMADI RIYAL

Silver **Ruler:** al-Mutawakkil Yahya bin Muhammad (Imam Yahya) AH1322-1367 / 1904-1948AD **Obv:** Without "Rabb al-Alamin", with crescent below accession date AH1322 **Rev:** "Sana" below date

Date	Mintage	VG	F	VF	XF	Unc
AH1341	—	20.00	45.00	75.00	150	—
Note: AH1341 with 4 stars on reverse						
AH1342	—	25.00	50.00	100	175	—
Note: AH1342 with 4 stars on reverse and 2 stars flanking date						

Y# 6.2 1/4 IMADI RIYAL

Silver **Ruler:** al-Mutawakkil Yahya bin Muhammad (Imam Yahya) AH1322-1367 / 1904-1948AD **Obv:** Crescent below accession date AH1322 **Obv. Inscription:** Rabb al-Alamin **Rev:** "Sana" above date, two stars and two ornaments in border

Date	Mintage	VG	F	VF	XF	Unc
AH1342	—	70.00	100	300	450	—

Y# 6.5 1/4 IMADI RIYAL

Silver **Ruler:** al-Mutawakkil Yahya bin Muhammad (Imam Yahya) AH1322-1367 / 1904-1948AD **Obv:** Crescent below accession date AH1322 **Rev:** "Sana" below date, eight stars in border

Date	Mintage	VG	F	VF	XF	Unc
AH1342	—	100	150	300	500	—

Y# 6.6 1/4 IMADI RIYAL

Silver **Ruler:** al-Mutawakkil Yahya bin Muhammad (Imam Yahya) AH1322-1367 / 1904-1948AD **Obv:** Crescent below accession date AH1322 **Rev:** "Sana" below date, one star in border

Date	Mintage	VG	F	VF	XF	Unc
AH1342	—	100	150	300	500	—
Note: Obverse varieties with one and two stars exist						

Y# 10 1/4 IMADI RIYAL

Silver **Ruler:** al-Mutawakkil Yahya bin Muhammad (Imam Yahya) AH1322-1367 / 1904-1948AD **Obv:** Crescent below accession date AH1322 **Rev:** Redesigned, date moved to margin **Edge:** Plain, traces of reeding to full reeding known **Note:** The size of the reverse inner circle varies, 12 to 16 crescents on obverse.

Date	Mintage	VG	F	VF	XF	Unc
AH1342	—	20.00	40.00	75.00	150	—
AH1343	—	20.00	60.00	100	175	—
AH1344	—	4.25	10.00	25.00	75.00	—
AH1345	—	4.25	10.00	25.00	60.00	—
AH1349	—	—	—	—	—	—
Note: Reported, not confirmed						
AH1351	—	20.00	30.00	50.00	100	—
AH1352	—	5.00	12.00	20.00	40.00	—
AH1358	—	3.50	5.50	15.00	35.00	—
AH1359	—	3.50	5.50	15.00	35.00	—
AH1363	—	3.50	8.00	20.00	40.00	—
AH1364/3	—	4.25	8.00	20.00	40.00	—
AH1364	—	3.50	5.00	20.00	40.00	—
AH1365/4	—	4.25	6.00	20.00	40.00	—
AH1365	—	3.50	5.00	20.00	40.00	—
AH1366	—	3.50	5.00	20.00	40.00	—

Y# 7 IMADI RIYAL

28.0700 g., Silver **Ruler:** al-Mutawakkil Yahya bin Muhammad (Imam Yahya) AH1322-1367 / 1904-1948AD **Obv:** Double crescent below accession date AH1322 **Note:** Several die varieties exist, possibly struck over a number of years with frozen date AH1344. Edge varieties exist.

Date	Mintage	VG	F	VF	XF	Unc
AH1342	—	—	—	—	—	—
Note: Reported, not confirmed						
AH1344	—	7.00	12.00	18.00	28.00	40.00
Note: Copper trial strikes dated AH1344 reported						
AH1365 Two known	—	—	—	—	—	2,000

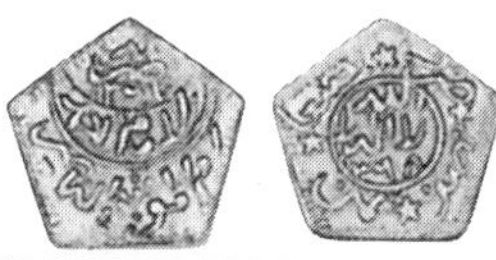

Y# 13 1/16 AHMADI RIYAL

Silver **Ruler:** al-Nasir Ahmad bin Yahya (Imam Ahmad) AH1367-1382 / 1948-1962AD **Obv:** Crescent below accession date AH1367 **Obv. Inscription:** Amir al-Mu'minin **Shape:** 5-sided **Note:** Arrangement of legends and size of inner circle on reverse vary.

Date	Mintage	VG	F	VF	XF	Unc
AH1367	—	1.00	2.00	6.00	12.00	—
AH1368	—	1.00	1.75	5.00	10.00	—
AH1371	—	1.00	1.75	5.00	10.00	—
AH1374	—	1.00	1.50	4.00	8.00	—

Y# 13.1 1/16 AHMADI RIYAL

Silver **Ruler:** al-Nasir Ahmad bin Yahya (Imam Ahmad) AH1367-1382 / 1948-1962AD **Obv:** Crescent below accession date AH1367, 1/8 Ahmadi Riyal, Y#14 **Rev:** Y#13 **Shape:** 5-sided **Note:** Mule. Ends of crescents cut off on reverse.

Date	Mintage	VG	F	VF	XF	Unc
AH1374	—	20.00	40.00	100	150	—

Y# A14 1/10 AHMADI RIYAL

Silver **Ruler:** al-Nasir Ahmad bin Yahya (Imam Ahmad) AH1367-1382 / 1948-1962AD **Obv:** Crescent below accession date AH1367

Date	Mintage	VG	F	VF	XF	Unc
AH1370	—	400	750	1,250	1,500	—

Y# 14a 1/8 AHMADI RIYAL

Silver **Ruler:** al-Nasir Ahmad bin Yahya (Imam Ahmad) AH1367-1382 / 1948-1962AD **Shape:** Hexagonal

Date	Mintage	VG	F	VF	XF	Unc
AH1368	—	350	650	1,250	1,850	—

Y# 14 1/8 AHMADI RIYAL

Silver **Ruler:** al-Nasir Ahmad bin Yahya (Imam Ahmad) AH1367-1382 / 1948-1962AD **Obv:** Crescent below accession date AH1367 **Note:** Pentagonal planchet. Arrangement of legends and size of inner circle on reverse vary.

Date	Mintage	VG	F	VF	XF	Unc
AH1367	—	4.00	8.00	15.00	30.00	—
AH1368	—	2.75	4.00	8.00	20.00	—
AH1370	—	2.75	4.00	8.00	20.00	—
AH1371	—	2.00	3.50	6.00	15.00	—
AH1372	—	2.00	2.75	4.00	10.00	—
AH1373	—	2.00	2.75	4.00	10.00	—
AH1374	—	2.00	3.00	5.00	15.00	—
AH1375/1	—	4.00	10.00	40.00	80.00	—
AH1379/x	—	2.00	3.00	5.00	15.00	—
AH1379/5	—	2.00	3.00	5.00	15.00	—
AH1379	—	2.00	3.50	6.00	15.00	—
AH1380	—	2.00	3.75	7.00	20.00	—

Y# 15 1/4 AHMADI RIYAL

Silver **Ruler:** al-Nasir Ahmad bin Yahya (Imam Ahmad) AH1367-1382 / 1948-1962AD **Obv:** Crescent below accession date AH1367 **Edge:** Reeded **Note:** The size of inner circle as well as the arrangement of legends on reverse vary. All dates have only the final 2 digits on the coin.

Date	Mintage	VG	F	VF	XF	Unc
AH(13)67	—	3.75	5.50	7.50	15.00	—
AH(13)68	—	3.75	5.50	7.50	15.00	—
AH(13)70	—	3.25	4.50	6.00	12.00	—
AH(13)71/68	—	6.00	8.00	12.50	20.00	—
AH(13)71/0	—	4.50	6.50	9.00	15.00	—
AH(13)71	—	3.25	4.50	6.00	10.00	—
AH(13)72	—	3.25	4.50	6.00	10.00	—
AH(13)74	—	3.25	4.50	6.00	10.00	—
AH(13)75/3	—	4.50	6.50	9.00	15.00	—
AH(13)75	—	3.25	4.50	6.00	10.00	—
AH(13)77/5	—	4.50	6.50	9.00	15.00	—
AH(13)80	—	30.00	60.00	100	175	—

Y# 15a 1/4 AHMADI RIYAL

Copper **Ruler:** al-Nasir Ahmad bin Yahya (Imam Ahmad) AH1367-1382 / 1948-1962AD

Date	Mintage	VG	F	VF	XF	Unc
AH(13)81d Rare	—	—	—	—	—	—
Note: This issue is considered a pattern						

Y# 16.1 1/2 AHMADI RIYAL

Silver **Ruler:** al-Nasir Ahmad bin Yahya (Imam Ahmad) AH1367-1382 / 1948-1962AD **Obv:** Double crescent below accession date AH1367 **Rev:** Full dates; denomination and mint name read inward

Date	Mintage	VG	F	VF	XF	Unc
AH1367	—	7.00	10.00	15.00	35.00	—
AH1368	—	7.00	10.00	15.00	35.00	—
AH1369	—	6.00	8.00	12.50	20.00	—
AH1370	—	8.00	12.50	20.00	40.00	—
AH1371	—	8.00	12.50	20.00	40.00	—
AH1372/68	—	7.00	10.00	15.00	30.00	—
AH1373	—	9.00	15.00	25.00	45.00	—
AH1375	—	—	—	—	—	—
Note: Reported, not confirmed						
AH(13)75	—	30.00	50.00	80.00	100	—
AH1377	—	—	—	—	—	—

Y# 16.2 1/2 AHMADI RIYAL

Silver **Ruler:** al-Nasir Ahmad bin Yahya (Imam Ahmad) AH1367-1382 / 1948-1962AD **Obv:** Double crescent below accession date AH1367 **Rev:** Full dates; denomination and mint name read outward **Edge:** Reeded **Note:** Arrangement of legends and size of circle on reverse vary. These coins were struck over blanks punched from Maria Theresa Thalers. The outer rings are reported to have circulated as currency, but this is doubtful, as they are found only counterstamped "Void" in Arabic.

Date	Mintage	VG	F	VF	XF	Unc
AH1377	—	6.00	8.00	12.50	20.00	—
AH1378	—	7.00	10.00	15.00	25.00	—
AH1379	—	6.00	8.00	12.50	20.00	—
AH1380	—	17.50	30.00	40.00	75.00	—
AH1381	—	12.50	22.50	30.00	50.00	—
AH1382	—	8.00	12.50	25.00	40.00	—

Y# 16a 1/2 AHMADI RIYAL

Copper **Ruler:** al-Nasir Ahmad bin Yahya (Imam Ahmad) AH1367-1382 / 1948-1962AD

Date	Mintage	VG	F	VF	XF	Unc
AH1381 Rare	—	—	—	—	—	—

Note: This issue is considered a pattern

Y# 17 AHMADI RIYAL

Silver, 39.5 mm. **Ruler:** al-Nasir Ahmad bin Yahya (Imam Ahmad) AH1367-1382 / 1948-1962AD **Obv:** Double crescent below accession date AH1367 **Note:** These are usually found struck over Austrian Maria Theresa Talers and occasionally over other foreign crowns. All Y-17s have 1367 in the center obverse. The date for each piece is located in the lower left of the reverse. Varieties exist.

Date	Mintage	F	VF	XF	Unc	BU
AH1367	—	20.00	30.00	45.00	80.00	—
AH1370	—	15.00	20.00	30.00	55.00	—
AH1371	—	15.00	20.00	30.00	55.00	—
AH1372/68	—	—	—	—	—	—
Note: Reported, not confirmed						
AH1373	—	12.50	15.00	22.50	35.00	—
Note: Most AH1373 Riyals appear to be weakly struck from recut AH1372 dies, and the dates are easily confused						
AH1374	—	13.50	16.50	25.00	45.00	—
AH1375	—	13.50	16.50	25.00	45.00	—
AH1377	—	13.50	16.50	25.00	45.00	—
Note: Reported, not confirmed						
AH1378	—	13.50	16.50	25.00	45.00	—
AH1380	—	13.50	16.50	25.00	45.00	—
AH1381	—	13.50	16.50	25.00	45.00	—

The northwestern region of present day Yemen was dominated by Ottoman Turks until 1918. Formal boundaries were established in 1934 and a Republic was formed in 1962 leading to an eight year civil war between royalist imam and new republican forces.

REPUBLIC

MILLED COINAGE

Y# 20 1/80 RIYAL (1/2 Buqsha)

Bronze **Obv:** Denomination within circle **Rev:** Hand holding torch within circle **Note:** Varieties exist.

Date	Mintage	F	VF	XF	Unc	BU
AH1382	—	—	0.50	2.00	5.00	—

Y# 21.1 1/80 RIYAL (1/2 Buqsha)

Bronze **Obv:** Denomination within circle **Rev:** Full star between lines within circle

Date	Mintage	F	VF	XF	Unc	BU
AH1382	—	—	2.00	6.00	15.00	—

Y# 21.2 1/80 RIYAL (1/2 Buqsha)

Bronze **Obv:** Denomination within circle **Rev:** Outlined star between lines within circle **Note:** Varieties exist.

Date	Mintage	F	VF	XF	Unc	BU
AH13882 (sic)	—	—	—	—	—	—
AH1382	—	—	2.00	6.00	15.00	—

Y# 26 1/2 BUQSHA

Copper-Aluminum **Obv:** Denomination within circle **Rev:** Leafy branch within wreath **Mint:** Cairo **Note:** Varieties exist.

Date	Mintage	F	VF	XF	Unc	BU
AH1382-1963	10,000,000	—	0.15	0.20	0.35	0.75

Y# 32 1/2 BUQSHA

Bronze **Obv:** Denomination within circle **Rev:** Full star between lines within circle **Note:** Varieties exist.

Date	Mintage	F	VF	XF	Unc	BU
AH1382	—	—	3.00	5.00	9.00	—

Y# 22 1/40 RIYAL (1 Buqsha)

Brass Or Bronze **Obv:** Denomination within circle **Rev:** Hand holding torch within circle **Note:** Dated both sides; AH1382, AH1383 and AH1384/3 are dated AH1382 on obverse, actual date on reverse; AH1384 and AH1384/284 dated AH1384 on both sides. There are varieties of date size and design.

Date	Mintage	F	VF	XF	Unc	BU
AH1382	—	—	0.75	1.00	2.25	—
AH1383/282	—	—	0.75	1.00	2.25	—
AH1383	—	—	1.50	2.25	6.00	—
AH1384/284	—	—	0.75	1.00	2.25	—
AH1384/3	—	—	0.75	1.00	2.25	—
AH1384	—	—	4.00	7.50	20.00	—

Y# 27 BUQSHA

Copper-Aluminum **Obv:** Denomination within circle **Rev:** Leafy branch within wreath **Mint:** Cairo

Date	Mintage	F	VF	XF	Unc	BU
AH1382-1963	10,377,000	—	0.20	0.40	1.00	2.00

Y# 23.1 1/20 RIYAL (2 Buqsha)

0.7200 Silver **Obv:** Denomination within circle **Rev:** Three stones on top row of wall within circle **Note:** Thick variety, 1.10-1.60 grams

Date	Mintage	F	VF	XF	Unc	BU
AH1382	—	20.00	35.00	60.00	125	—

Y# 23.2 1/20 RIYAL (2 Buqsha)

0.7200 Silver **Obv:** Denomination within circle **Rev:** Two stones on top row of wall within circle **Note:** Thin variety, 0.60-0.90 grams

Date	Mintage	F	VF	XF	Unc	BU
AH1382	—	15.00	30.00	50.00	100	—

Y# A27 2 BUQSHA

4.9100 g., Copper-Aluminum, 23 mm. **Obv:** Denomination within circle **Rev:** Leafy branch within wreath

Date	Mintage	F	VF	XF	Unc	BU
AH1382-1963	—	—	0.25	0.60	1.25	2.50

Y# 24.1 1/10 RIYAL (4 Buqsha)

0.7200 Silver **Rev:** Three or four stones in top row of wall within circle **Note:** Thick variety, 2.40-3.00 grams

Date	Mintage	F	VF	XF	Unc	BU
AH1382	—	5.00	15.00	25.00	50.00	—

Y# 24.2 1/10 RIYAL (4 Buqsha)

0.7200 Silver **Obv:** Denomination within circle **Rev:** Four stones in top row of wall within circle **Note:** Thin variety, 1.40-1.80 grams. Edge varieties, varying number of stones in wall, exist.

Date	Mintage	F	VF	XF	Unc	BU
AH1382	—	—	2.50	6.00	15.00	—

Y# 28 5 BUQSHA

0.7200 Silver **Obv:** Denomination within circle **Rev:** Leafy branch within wreath, dates below **Mint:** Cairo

Date	Mintage	F	VF	XF	Unc	BU
AH1382-1963	1,600,000	—	1.50	1.75	2.50	4.50

Y# 25.1 2/10 RIYAL (8 Buqsha)
0.7200 Silver **Obv:** Denomination within circle **Rev:** Tree and wall within circle **Note:** Thick variety, 5.80-6.50 grams.

Date	Mintage	F	VF	XF	Unc	BU
AH1382	—	6.00	15.00	25.00	50.00	—

Y# 25.2 2/10 RIYAL (8 Buqsha)
0.7200 Silver **Obv:** Denomination within circle **Rev:** Tree and wall within circle **Note:** Thin variety, 4.90-5.10 grams.

Date	Mintage	F	VF	XF	Unc	BU
AH1382	—	—	75.00	150	250	—

Y# A25.1 1/4 RIYAL (10 Buqsha)
0.7200 Silver **Obv:** Denomination within circle **Rev:** Tree and wall within circle **Note:** Thick variety, 6.00-7.30 grams.

Date	Mintage	F	VF	XF	Unc	BU
AH1382	—	250	500	1,000	1,750	—

Y# A25.2 1/4 RIYAL (10 Buqsha)
0.7200 Silver **Obv:** Denomination within circle **Rev:** Tree and wall within circle **Note:** Thin variety, 4.00-4.60 grams. Overstrikes over earlier 1/4 Riyal coins exist.

Date	Mintage	F	VF	XF	Unc	BU
AH1382	—	250	500	1,000	1,750	—

Y# 29 10 BUQSHA
5.0000 g., 0.7200 Silver 0.1157 oz. ASW **Obv:** Denomination within circle **Rev:** Leafy branch within wreath

Date	Mintage	F	VF	XF	Unc	BU
AH1382-1963	1,024,000	—	2.50	3.00	5.00	8.00

Y# 30 20 BUQSHA
9.8500 g., 0.7200 Silver 0.2280 oz. ASW **Obv:** Denomination within circle **Rev:** Leafy branch within wreath

Date	Mintage	F	VF	XF	Unc	BU
AH1382-1963	1,016,000	—	4.50	6.00	8.00	12.00

Y# 31 RIYAL
19.7500 g., 0.7200 Silver 0.4572 oz. ASW **Obv:** Denomination within wreath **Rev:** Leafy branch within wreath

Date	Mintage	F	VF	XF	Unc	BU
AH1382-1963	4,614,000	—	7.50	9.00	13.50	16.00

DECIMAL COINAGE

100 Fils = 1 Riyal/Rial

Y# 33 FILS
Aluminum **Obv:** National arms **Rev:** Denomination within circle

Date	Mintage	F	VF	XF	Unc	BU
AH1394-1974	Est. 1,000,000	—	3.00	5.00	10.00	—

Note: It is doubtful that the entire mintage was released for circulation

Date	Mintage	F	VF	XF	Unc	BU
AH1394-1974 Proof	5,024	Value: 1.50				
AH1400-1980 Proof	10,000	Value: 1.50				

Y# 43 FILS
Aluminum **Series:** F.A.O. **Obv:** National arms **Rev:** Denomination within circle

Date	Mintage	F	VF	XF	Unc	BU
AH1398-1978	7,050	—	—	1.25	3.00	—

Y# 34 5 FILS
2.7500 g., Brass, 21 mm. **Obv:** National arms **Rev:** Denomination within circle

Date	Mintage	F	VF	XF	Unc	BU
AH1394-1974	10,000,000	—	0.50	1.00	2.50	—
AH1394-1974 Proof	—	Value: 2.50				
AH1400-1980 Proof	—	Value: 2.00				

Y# 38 5 FILS
2.7500 g., Brass, 21 mm. **Series:** F.A.O. **Obv:** National arms **Rev:** Denomination within circle

Date	Mintage	F	VF	XF	Unc	BU
AH1394-1974	500,000	—	—	0.10	0.25	—

Y# 35 10 FILS
4.2500 g., Brass, 23 mm. **Obv:** National arms **Rev:** Denomination within circle

Date	Mintage	F	VF	XF	Unc	BU
AH1394-1974	20,000,000	—	0.50	1.00	2.50	—
AH1394-1974 Proof	5,024	Value: 2.50				
AH1400-1980 Proof	10,000	Value: 2.00				

Y# 39 10 FILS
4.2500 g., Brass, 23 mm. **Series:** F.A.O. **Obv:** National arms **Rev:** Denomination within circle

Date	Mintage	F	VF	XF	Unc	BU
AH1394-1974	200,000	—	—	0.10	0.25	—

Y# 36 25 FILS
3.0000 g., Copper-Nickel, 20 mm. **Obv:** National arms **Rev:** Denomination within circle

Date	Mintage	F	VF	XF	Unc	BU
AH1394-1974	15,000,000	—	0.25	0.50	3.00	—
AH1394-1974 Proof	5,024	Value: 3.00				
AH1399-1979	11,000,000	—	0.25	0.50	2.00	—
AH1400-1980 Proof	10,000	Value: 2.25				

Y# 40 25 FILS
3.0000 g., Copper-Nickel, 20 mm. **Series:** F.A.O. **Obv:** National arms **Rev:** Denomination within circle

Date	Mintage	F	VF	XF	Unc	BU
AH1394-1974	40,000	—	0.20	0.40	1.00	—

Y# 37 50 FILS
5.3000 g., Copper-Nickel, 24 mm. **Obv:** National arms **Rev:** Denomination within circle

Date	Mintage	F	VF	XF	Unc	BU
AH1394-1974	10,000,000	—	0.35	0.75	2.50	—
AH1394-1974 Proof	5,024	Value: 3.50				
AH1399-1979	4,000,000	—	0.35	0.75	2.50	—
AH1400-1980 Proof	10,000	Value: 2.50				
AH1405-1985	—	—	0.35	0.75	2.50	—

Y# 41 50 FILS
5.3000 g., Copper-Nickel, 24 mm. **Series:** F.A.O. **Obv:** National arms **Rev:** Denomination within circle

Date	Mintage	F	VF	XF	Unc	BU
AH1394-1974	25,000	—	0.25	0.50	1.25	—

Y# 42 RIYAL

8.0000 g., Copper-Nickel, 28 mm. **Obv:** National arms **Rev:** Denomination within circle

Date	Mintage	F	VF	XF	Unc	BU
AH1396-1976	7,800,000	—	0.50	1.25	2.50	—
AH1400-1980 Proof	—	Value: 5.00				
AH1405-1985	—	—	0.50	1.25	2.50	—
AH1414-1993	—	—	0.50	1.25	2.50	—

Y# 44 RIYAL

8.0000 g., Copper-Nickel, 28 mm. **Series:** F.A.O. **Obv:** National arms **Rev:** Denomination within circle

Date	Mintage	F	VF	XF	Unc	BU
AH1398-1978	7,050	—	—	2.00	5.00	—

YEMEN REPUBLIC

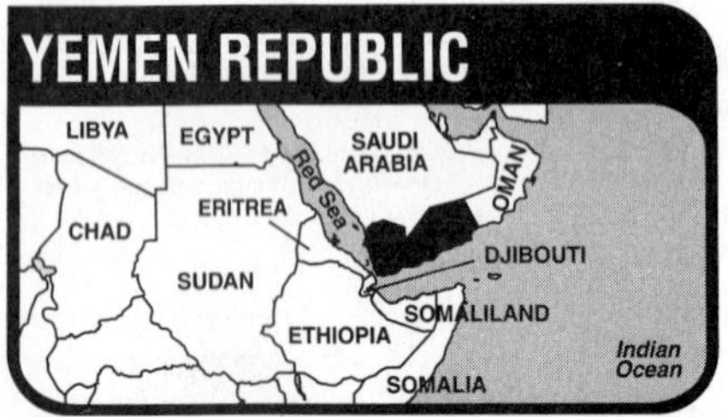

The Republic of Yemen, formerly Yemen Arab Republic and Peoples Democratic Republic of Yemen, is located on the southern coast of the Arabian Peninsula. It has an area of 205,020 sq. mi. (531,000 sq. km.) and a population of 12 million. Capital: San'a. The port of Aden is the main commercial center and the area's most valuable natural resource. Recent oil and gas finds and a developing petroleum industry have improved their economic prospects. Agriculture and local handicrafts are the main industries. Cotton, fish, coffee, rock salt and hides are exported.

On May 22, 1990, the Yemen Arab Republic (North Yemen) and Peoples Democratic Republic of Yemen (South Yemen) merged into a unified Republic of Yemen. Disagreements between the two former governments simmered until civil war erupted in 1994, with the northern forces of the old Yemen Arab Republic eventually prevailing.

TITLE

دار الخلافة

Dar al-Khilafa(t)

REPUBLIC

MILLED COINAGE

KM# 25 RIYAL

2.6500 g., Stainless Steel, 19.95 mm. **Obv:** Denomination within circle **Rev:** National arms **Edge:** Multi-sided **Shape:** 21-sided

Date	Mintage	F	VF	XF	Unc	BU
AH1414-1993	—	—	—	—	1.25	1.75

KM# 26 5 RIYALS

4.5000 g., Stainless Steel, 22.85 mm. **Obv:** Denomination within circle **Rev:** Building **Shape:** 21-sided

Date	Mintage	F	VF	XF	Unc	BU
AH1414-1993	—	—	—	—	1.75	2.25
AH1420-2000	—	—	—	—	1.75	2.25
AH1421-2001	—	—	—	—	1.75	2.25
AH1425-2004	—	—	—	—	1.75	2.25

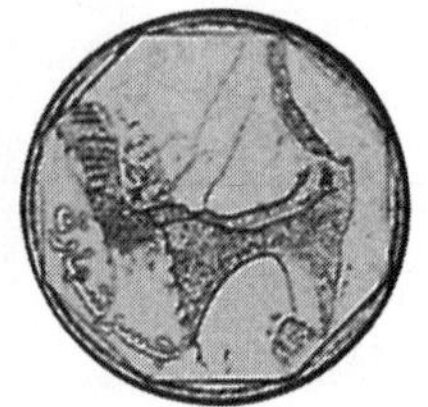

KM# 27 10 RIYALS

6.0500 g., Stainless Steel, 26 mm. **Obv:** Denomination within circle **Rev:** Bridge at Shaharah

Date	Mintage	F	VF	XF	Unc	BU
AH1416-1995	—	—	—	—	2.75	3.50
AH1424-2003	—	—	—	—	2.75	3.50

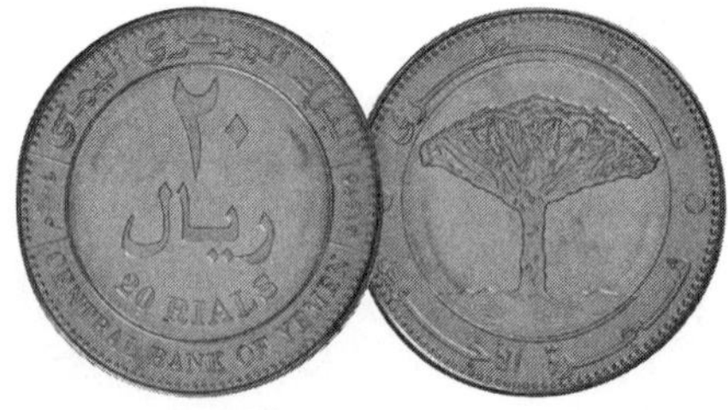

KM# 29 20 RIALS

7.1000 g., Bi-Metallic Brass plated Steel center in Stainless Steel ring, 29.85 mm. **Obv:** Value within circle **Rev:** Tree within circle **Edge:** Reeded

Date	Mintage	F	VF	XF	Unc	BU
AH1425-2004	—	—	—	—	4.00	5.00

YEMEN, DEMOCRATIC REPUBLIC

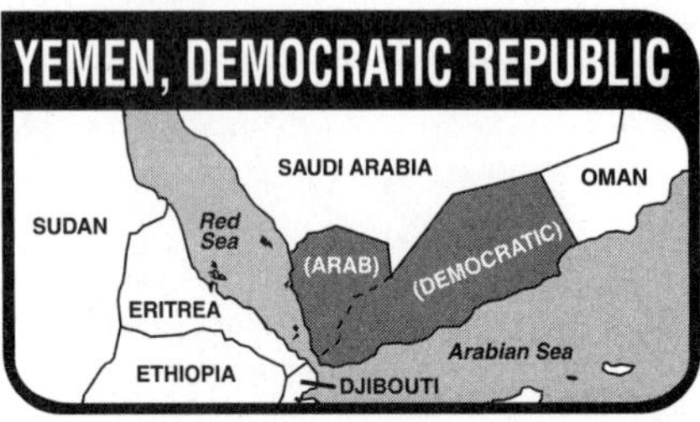

The southeast region of present day Yemen was predominately controlled by the British since their occupation of Aden in 1839. Independence was declared November 30, 1967 after the collapse of the Federation of South Arabia and the withdrawal of the British.

TITLES

Al-Jumhuriya(t) al-Yamaniya(t)
ad-Dimiqratiya(t) ash-Sha'biya(t)

MONETARY SYSTEM

Falus, Fulus — Fals, Fils — Falsan, Filsan

1000 Fils = 1 Dinar

PEOPLES DEMOCRATIC REPUBLIC

DECIMAL COINAGE

KM# 3 2-1/2 FILS

0.6500 g., Aluminum, 17 mm. **Obv:** Denomination and dates **Rev:** Leafy plant

Date	Mintage	F	VF	XF	Unc	BU
AH1393-1973	20,000,000	—	0.25	0.65	1.50	2.50

KM# 2 5 FILS

1.3500 g., Bronze, 23.1 mm. **Obv:** 8-sided star design **Rev:** Crossed daggers

Date	Mintage	F	VF	XF	Unc	BU
1971	2,000,000	—	0.30	0.60	1.00	1.50

KM# 4 5 FILS

1.3500 g., Aluminum, 23.1 mm. **Obv:** Denomination and dates **Rev:** Spiny lobster

Date	Mintage	F	VF	XF	Unc	BU
AH1393-1973	20,000,000	—	0.15	0.30	1.00	1.50
AH1404-1984	—	—	0.15	0.30	1.00	1.50

KM# 9 10 FILS

2.2000 g., Aluminum, 25.6 mm. **Obv:** Monument **Rev:** Denomination within circle **Shape:** Scallop

Date	Mintage	F	VF	XF	Unc	BU
1981	—	—	0.35	0.75	2.00	3.00

KM# 5 25 FILS

4.5500 g., Copper-Nickel, 20 mm. **Obv:** 8-sided star design **Rev:** Dhow

Date	Mintage	F	VF	XF	Unc	BU
1976	2,000,000	—	0.25	0.50	1.25	2.25
1977	1,000,000	—	0.25	0.50	1.50	2.50
1979	—	—	0.25	0.50	1.50	2.50
1982	—	—	0.25	0.50	1.50	2.50
1984	—	—	0.25	0.50	1.75	2.75

KM# 6 50 FILS

9.1000 g., Copper-Nickel, 27.8 mm. **Obv:** 8-sided star design **Rev:** Dhow

Date	Mintage	F	VF	XF	Unc	BU
1976	2,000,000	—	0.35	0.75	2.50	3.50
1977	2,000,000	—	0.35	0.75	2.50	3.50

Date	Mintage	F	VF	XF	Unc	BU
1979	—	—	0.35	0.75	2.50	3.50
1984	—	—	0.35	0.75	2.50	3.50

KM# 10 100 FILS
10.0000 g., Copper-Nickel, 23.1 mm. **Obv:** Monument **Rev:** Denomination within circle **Shape:** 8-sided

Date	Mintage	F	VF	XF	Unc	BU
1981	—	—	0.50	1.00	3.00	4.50

KM# 7 250 FILS
11.2000 g., Copper-Nickel, 31 mm. **Subject:** 10th Anniversary of Independence **Obv:** Monument **Rev:** Ship at sea with date below

Date	Mintage	F	VF	XF	Unc	BU
1977	30,000	2.50	5.00	10.00	25.00	—

KM# 11 250 FILS
11.2000 g., Copper-Nickel, 31 mm. **Obv:** Monument **Rev:** Denomination within circle

Date	Mintage	F	VF	XF	Unc	BU
1981	—	—	1.50	3.00	5.50	7.00

YUGOSLAVIA

The Federal Republic of Yugoslavia, formerly the Socialist Federal Republic of Yugoslavia, a Balkan country located on the east shore of the Adriatic Sea, has an area of 39,450 sq. mi. (102,173 sq. km.) and a population of 10.5 million. Capital: Belgrade. The chief industries area agriculture, mining, manufacturing and tourism. Machinery, nonferrous metals, meat and fabrics are exported.

Yugoslavia was proclaimed on Dec. 1, 1918, after the union of the Kingdom of Serbia, Montenegro and the South Slav territories of Austria-Hungary; and changed its official name from the Kingdom of the Serbs, Croats and Slovenes to the Kingdom of Yugoslavia on Oct. 3, 1929.The republic was composed of six autonomous republics -Serbia, Croatia, Slovenia, Bosnia-Herzegovina, Macedonia and Montenegro - and two autonomous provinces within Serbia: Kosovo-Melohija and Vojvodina. The government of Yugoslavia attempted to remain neutral in World War II but, yielding to German pressure, aligned itself with the Axis powers in March of 1941; a few days later it was overthrown by revolutionary forces and its neutrality reasserted. The Nazis occupied the country on April 6, and throughout the remaining war years were resisted by a number of guerrilla armies, notably that of Marshal Josip Broz Tito. After the defeat of the Axis powers, a leftist coalition headed by Tito abolished the monarchy and, on Jan. 31, 1946, established a "People's Republic". The collapse of the Federal Republic during 1991-1992 has resulted in the autonomous republics of Croatia, Slovenia, Bosnia-Herzegovina and Macedonia declaring their respective independence. Bosnia-Herzegovina is under military contest with the Serbian, Croat and Muslim populace opposing each other. Besides the remainder of the older Serbian sectors, a Serbian enclave in Knin located in southern Croatia has emerged called REPUBLIKE SRPSKEKRAJINE or Serbian Republic - Krajina whose capital is Knin and has also declared its independence in1992 when the former Republics of Serbia and Montenegro became the Federal Republic of Yugoslavia.

The name Yugoslavia appears on the coinage in letters of the Cyrillic alphabet alone until formation of the Federated Peoples Republic of Yugoslavia in 1953, after which both the Cyrillic and Latin alphabets are employed. From 1965, the coin denomination appears in the 4 different languages of the federated republics in letters of both the Cyrillic and Latin alphabets.

DENOMINATIONS
Para ПАРА
Dinar, ДИНАР, Dinara ДИНАРА
Dinari ДИНАРИ, Dinarjev

RULERS
Petar I, 1918-1921
Alexander I, 1921-1934
Petar II, 1934-1945

MINT MARKS
(a) - Paris, privy marks only
(b) - Brussels
(k) - КОВНИЦА,...А.Д. = Kovnica, A.D. (Akcionarno Drustvo) Belgrade
(l) - London
(p) - Poissy (thunderbolt)
(v) – Vienna

MONETARY SYSTEM
100 Para = 1 Dinar

KINGDOM OF THE SERBS, CROATS AND SLOVENES

STANDARD COINAGE

KM# 1 5 PARA
Zinc, 18.8 mm. **Ruler:** Petar I **Obv:** Crowned and mantled arms on shield **Obv. Designer:** Adolf Hoffmann **Rev:** Denomination above date **Rev. Designer:** Joseph Prinz **Edge:** Plain

Date	Mintage	F	VF	XF	Unc	BU
1920(v)	3,825,514	3.00	7.50	15.00	42.00	—

KM# 2 10 PARA
Zinc, 20.85 mm. **Ruler:** Petar I **Obv:** Crowned and mantled arms on shield **Obv. Designer:** Adolf Hoffmann **Rev:** Denomination above date **Rev. Designer:** Joseph Prinz **Edge:** Plain

Date	Mintage	F	VF	XF	Unc	BU
1920(v)	58,946,122	1.50	3.50	9.00	24.00	—

KM# 3 25 PARA
Nickel-Bronze, 24 mm. **Ruler:** Petar I **Obv:** Crowned and mantled arms on shield **Obv. Designer:** Adolf Hoffmann **Rev:** Denomination above date **Rev. Designer:** Joseph Prinz **Edge:** Plain

Date	Mintage	F	VF	XF	Unc	BU
1920(v)	48,173,138	1.50	3.50	9.50	25.00	—

KM# 4 50 PARA
Nickel-Bronze, 18 mm. **Ruler:** Alexander I **Obv:** Head left **Rev:** Denomination and date within crowned wreath **Edge:** Milled **Designer:** A. Patey **Note:** Mint mark: lightning bolt.

Date	Mintage	F	VF	XF	Unc	BU
1925(b)	24,500,000	0.50	1.00	2.00	7.00	—
1925(p)	25,000,000	0.50	1.50	3.00	8.00	—

KM# 5 DINAR
4.9200 g., Nickel-Bronze, 23 mm. **Ruler:** Alexander I **Obv:** Head left **Rev:** Denomination and date within crowned wreath **Edge:** Milled **Designer:** A. Patey **Note:** Mint mark: lightning bolt.

Date	Mintage	F	VF	XF	Unc	BU
1925(b)	37,000,000	0.50	1.00	2.50	7.50	—
1925(p)	37,500,410	0.75	1.50	3.00	8.00	—

KM# 6 2 DINARA
Nickel-Bronze, 27 mm. **Ruler:** Alexander I **Obv:** Head left **Rev:** Denomination and date within crowned wreath **Edge:** Milled **Designer:** A. Patey **Note:** Mint mark: lightning bolt.

Date	Mintage	F	VF	XF	Unc	BU
1925(b)	29,500,000	1.00	2.00	5.00	13.00	—
1925(p)	25,004,177	1.00	2.50	5.50	15.00	—

KM# 7 20 DINARA
6.4516 g., 0.9000 Gold 0.1867 oz. AGW, 21 mm. **Ruler:** Alexander I **Obv:** Head left **Rev:** Denomination and date within crowned wreath **Edge:** Milled

Date	Mintage	F	VF	XF	Unc	BU
1925	1,000,000	—	BV	200	250	—
1925 Proof	—	—	—	—	—	—

KINGDOM OF YUGOSLAVIA

STANDARD COINAGE

KM# 17 25 PARA
Bronze, 20 mm. **Ruler:** Petar II **Obv:** Center hole within crowned wreath **Rev:** Center hole divides denomination **Edge:** Plain **Note:** 4 mm hole in center of coin.

Date	Mintage	F	VF	XF	Unc	BU
1938	40,000,000	1.25	2.50	5.50	14.00	—
1938 Proof	—	—	—	—	—	—

KM# 18 50 PARA
Aluminum-Bronze, 18 mm. **Ruler:** Petar II **Obv:** Crown **Rev:** Denomination above date **Edge:** Plain

Date	Mintage	F	VF	XF	Unc	BU
1938	100,000,000	0.50	1.00	2.50	7.50	—

KM# 19 DINAR
Aluminum-Bronze, 21 mm. **Ruler:** Petar II **Obv:** Crown **Rev:** Denomination above date **Edge:** Plain

Date	Mintage	F	VF	XF	Unc	BU
1938	100,000,000	0.50	0.75	2.00	6.00	—
1938 Proof	—	—	—	—	—	—

KM# 20 2 DINARA
5.1000 g., Aluminum-Bronze, 24.5 mm. **Ruler:** Petar II **Obv:** Crown **Rev:** Denomination above date, large numeral **Edge:** Plain

Date	Mintage	F	VF	XF	Unc	BU
1938	74,250,000	0.50	1.00	3.50	9.00	—
1938 Proof	—	—	—	—	—	—

KM# 21 2 DINARA
Aluminum-Bronze, 24.5 mm. **Ruler:** Petar II **Obv:** 12 mm crown **Rev:** Denomination above date, large numeral **Edge:** Plain

Date	Mintage	F	VF	XF	Unc	BU
1938	750,000	6.00	10.00	19.00	38.00	—
1938 Proof	—	—	—	—	—	—

KM# 10 10 DINARA
7.0000 g., 0.5000 Silver 0.1125 oz. ASW **Ruler:** Alexander I **Obv:** Head left **Rev:** Crowned double eagle with shield on breast **Edge:** Milled

Date	Mintage	F	VF	XF	Unc	BU
1931(l)	19,000,000	2.00	4.00	8.00	18.00	—
1931(l) Proof	—	—	—	—	—	—
1931(a)	4,000,000	3.50	7.00	15.00	32.00	—
1931(a) Proof	—	—	—	—	—	—

KM# 22 10 DINARA
Nickel, 23 mm. **Ruler:** Petar II **Obv:** Head right **Rev:** Denomination and date within crowned wreath **Edge:** Milled **Designer:** F. Dincic

Date	Mintage	F	VF	XF	Unc	BU
1938	25,000,000	0.50	1.00	2.00	4.50	—

KM# 11 20 DINARA
14.0000 g., 0.5000 Silver 0.2250 oz. ASW, 31 mm. **Ruler:** Alexander I **Obv:** Head left **Rev:** Crowned double eagle with shield on breast **Edge:** Milled **Designer:** Percy Metcalfe

Date	Mintage	F	VF	XF	Unc	BU
1931(k)	12,500,000	BV	6.00	12.50	33.00	—
1931(k) Proof	—	—	—	—	—	—

KM# 23 20 DINARA
9.0000 g., 0.7500 Silver 0.2170 oz. ASW **Ruler:** Petar II **Obv:** Head left **Rev:** Crowned double eagle with shield on breast **Edge Lettering:** BOG CUVA JUGOSLAVIJU ***

Date	Mintage	F	VF	XF	Unc	BU
1938	15,000,000	BV	3.50	6.00	12.50	—

KM# 16 50 DINARA
23.3300 g., 0.7500 Silver 0.5625 oz. ASW, 36 mm. **Ruler:** Alexander I **Obv:** Head left **Rev:** Crowned double eagle with shield on breast **Edge Lettering:** BOG CUVA JUGOSLAVIJU

Date	Mintage	F	VF	XF	Unc	BU
1932(k)	5,500,000	10.00	22.00	45.00	180	—
1932(l)	5,500,000	10.00	25.00	50.00	200	—
1932(l) Proof	—	Value: 2,200				

KM# 24 50 DINARA
15.0000 g., 0.7500 Silver 0.3617 oz. ASW, 31 mm. **Ruler:** Petar II **Obv:** Head right **Rev:** Crowned double eagle with shield on breast

Date	Mintage	F	VF	XF	Unc	BU
1938	10,000,000	BV	6.00	9.00	18.00	—

TRADE COINAGE

Trade-coinage countermarks were applied by the Yugoslav Control Office for Noble Metals to confirm gold purity. The initial countermark displayed a sword, but part way through the first production year, this was retired and the second countermark, showing an ear of corn, was used.

KM# 12.1 DUKAT
3.4900 g., 0.9860 Gold 0.1106 oz. AGW **Ruler:** Alexander I **Countermark:** Birds **Obv:** Head left, small legend with КОВНИА, А.Д. below head **Obv. Designer:** Richard Plecht **Rev:** Crowned double eagle with shield on breast **Rev. Designer:** Joseph Prinz **Edge:** Milled

Date	Mintage	F	VF	XF	Unc	BU
1931(k)	Est. 50,000	—	BV	150	200	—
1932(k) Rare	Inc. below	—	—	—	—	—

Note: The 1932(k) examples with sword countermark are believed to be mint sports

KM# 12.2 DUKAT
3.4900 g., 0.9860 Gold 0.1106 oz. AGW **Ruler:** Alexander I **Countermark:** Ear of corn **Obv:** Head left **Rev:** Crowned double eagle with shield on breast **Note:** Forgeries bearing no countermark exist for 1932 and possibly other dates. Small legend on both sides

Date	Mintage	F	VF	XF	Unc	BU
1931(k)	Est. 150,000	—	BV	140	185	—
1932(k)	Est. 70,000	—	BV	145	195	—
1933(k)	Est. 40,000	—	135	185	300	—
1934(k)	Est. 2,000	—	500	850	1,250	—

KM# 12.3 DUKAT
3.4900 g., 0.9860 Gold 0.1106 oz. AGW **Ruler:** Alexander I **Countermark:** Sword **Obv:** Head left **Rev:** Crowned double eagle with shield on breast **Note:** Mule.

Date	Mintage	F	VF	XF	Unc	BU
1931(k)	—	—	—	3,000	5,000	—

KM# 13.1 DUKAT
3.4900 g., 0.9860 Gold 0.1106 oz. AGW **Ruler:** Alexander I **Obv:** Head left **Rev:** Crowned double eagle with shield on breast **Note:** Large legend on both sides.

Date	Mintage	F	VF	XF	Unc	BU
1931(k)	2,869	—	—	3,500	5,500	—

KM# 13.2 DUKAT
3.4900 g., 0.9860 Gold 0.1106 oz. AGW **Ruler:** Alexander I **Countermark:** Sword **Obv:** Head left **Rev:** Crowned double eagle with shield on breast **Note:** Large-letter varieties bear the Kovnica, A.D. mint mark but were actually struck in Vienna.

Date	Mintage	F	VF	XF	Unc	BU
1931(k)	Inc. above	—	—	4,000	6,500	—

KM# 14.1 4 DUKATA
13.9600 g., 0.9860 Gold 0.4425 oz. AGW **Ruler:** Alexander I **Countermark:** Sword **Obv:** Jugate busts of royal couple left **Obv. Designer:** Richard Placht **Rev:** Crowned double eagle with shield on breast **Rev. Designer:** Joseph Prinz **Edge:** Milled **Note:** Small legend on both sides. The 1932(k) examples with birds countermark are believed to be mint sports.

Date	Mintage	F	VF	XF	Unc	BU
1931(k)	Est. 10,000	—	475	750	950	—
1932(k) Rare	Inc. below	—	—	—	—	—

KM# 14.2 4 DUKATA
13.9600 g., 0.9860 Gold 0.4425 oz. AGW **Ruler:** Alexander I **Countermark:** Ear of corn **Obv:** Conjoined busts of royal couple left **Rev:** Crowned double eagle with shield on breast

Date	Mintage	F	VF	XF	Unc	BU
1931(k)	Est. 15,000	—	475	750	950	—
1932(k)	Est. 10,000	—	475	725	1,000	—
1933(k)	Est. 2,000	—	1,000	1,600	2,500	—

POST WAR COINAGE

KM# 25 50 PARA
Zinc, 18 mm. **Obv:** State emblem, nine stars below **Rev:** Denomination surrounded by stars **Edge:** Milled

Date	Mintage	F	VF	XF	Unc	BU
1945	40,000,000	0.50	1.00	3.00	9.00	—

KM# 26 DINAR
Zinc, 20 mm. **Obv:** State emblem, nine stars below **Rev:** Stars surround denomination **Edge:** Milled

Date	Mintage	F	VF	XF	Unc	BU
1945	90,000,000	0.50	1.00	2.50	7.00	—

KM# 27 2 DINARA
Zinc, 22 mm. **Obv:** State emblem, nine stars below **Rev:** Stars surround denomination **Edge:** Milled

Date	Mintage	F	VF	XF	Unc	BU
1945	70,000,000	0.50	1.25	3.00	9.00	—

KM# 28 5 DINARA
Zinc, 26.5 mm. **Obv:** State emblem, nine stars below **Rev:** Stars surround denomination **Edge:** Milled

Date	Mintage	F	VF	XF	Unc	BU
1945	50,000,000	1.00	2.00	4.00	12.00	—

FEDERAL PEOPLE'S REPUBLIC

STANDARD COINAGE

KM# 29 50 PARA
Aluminum, 17.4 mm. **Obv:** State emblem **Rev:** Denomination divides date, seven stars above **Edge:** Plain

Date	Mintage	F	VF	XF	Unc	BU
1953	—	—	—	0.10	0.50	—

KM# 30 DINAR
Aluminum, 19.8 mm. **Obv:** State emblem **Rev:** Denomination divides date, seven stars above **Edge:** Plain

Date	Mintage	F	VF	XF	Unc	BU
1953	—	—	0.10	0.15	0.50	—

KM# 31 2 DINARA
Aluminum, 22.2 mm. **Obv:** State emblem **Rev:** Denomination divides date, seven stars above **Edge:** Plain

Date	Mintage	F	VF	XF	Unc	BU
1953	—	—	0.10	0.25	0.75	—

KM# 32 5 DINARA
Aluminum, 24.6 mm. **Obv:** State emblem **Rev:** Denomination divides date, seven stars above **Edge:** Plain

Date	Mintage	F	VF	XF	Unc	BU
1953	—	0.10	0.25	0.50	1.00	—

KM# 33 10 DINARA
Aluminum-Bronze, 21 mm. **Obv:** State emblem **Rev:** Hand holding grain stalks below head left **Edge:** Milled **Designer:** F. M. Dincic

Date	Mintage	F	VF	XF	Unc	BU
1955	—	0.15	0.30	0.75	1.50	—

KM# 34 20 DINARA
Aluminum-Bronze, 25.5 mm. **Obv:** State emblem **Rev:** Head at left looking right, cogwheel lower right **Edge:** Milled **Designer:** F. M. Dincic

Date	Mintage	F	VF	XF	Unc	BU
1955	—	0.25	0.50	1.00	2.00	—

KM# 35 50 DINARA
Aluminum-Bronze, 25.5 mm. **Obv:** State emblem **Rev:** Two jugate heads right, cogwheel below **Edge:** Milled **Designer:** F. M. Dincic

Date	Mintage	F	VF	XF	Unc	BU
1955	—	0.25	0.75	2.00	4.50	—

SOCIALIST FEDERAL REPUBLIC

STANDARD COINAGE

KM# 42 5 PARA
1.5900 g., Copper-Zinc, 16 mm. **Obv:** State emblem **Rev:** Denomination above date within wreath, six stars above **Edge:** Milled

Date	Mintage	F	VF	XF	Unc	BU
1965	23,839,900	—	0.10	0.20	0.40	—

KM# 43 5 PARA
1.5500 g., Copper-Zinc, 16 mm. **Obv:** State emblem **Rev:** Denomination divides date **Edge:** Milled

Date	Mintage	F	VF	XF	Unc	BU
1965	16,200,000	—	—	0.10	0.20	—
1973	36,384,000	—	—	0.10	0.15	—
1974	3,628,000	—	—	0.10	0.25	—
1975	20,272,000	—	—	0.10	0.15	—
1976	30,490,000	—	—	0.10	0.15	—
1977	10,270,000	—	—	0.10	0.15	—
1978	12,000,000	—	—	0.10	0.15	—
1979	20,414,000	—	—	0.10	0.15	—
1980	22,412,000	—	—	0.10	0.15	—
1981	630,000	—	0.10	0.25	0.50	—

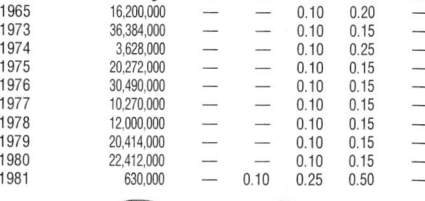

KM# 44 10 PARA
2.9700 g., Copper-Zinc, 21 mm. **Obv:** State emblem **Rev:** Denomination divides date **Edge:** Milled

Date	Mintage	F	VF	XF	Unc	BU
1965	15,400,000	—	—	0.10	0.20	—
1973	15,647,000	—	—	0.10	0.20	—
1974	60,139,000	—	—	0.10	0.20	—
1975	36,139,000	—	—	0.10	0.15	—
1976	36,111,000	—	—	0.10	0.15	—
1977	40,451,000	—	—	0.10	0.15	—
1978	50,129,000	—	—	0.10	0.15	—
Note: Two varieties of "7" exist						
1979	89,738,000	—	—	0.10	0.15	—
1980	90,111,000	—	—	0.10	0.15	—
1981	14,090,000	—	—	0.10	0.15	—

KM# 139 10 PARA
3.1300 g., Copper-Zinc, 18.01 mm. **Obv:** State emblem **Rev:** Denomination **Edge:** Plain

Date	Mintage	F	VF	XF	Unc	BU
1990	174,028,000	—	—	0.10	0.15	—
1991	60,828,000	—	—	0.15	0.35	—

KM# 45 20 PARA

Copper-Zinc, 23.2 mm. **Obv:** State emblem **Rev:** Denomination divides date **Edge:** Milled **Note:** Thickness varies: 1.3-1.5 mm.

Date	Mintage	F	VF	XF	Unc	BU
1965	—	—	—	0.10	0.30	—
1973	30,448,000	—	—	0.10	0.30	—
1974	31,364,000	—	—	0.10	0.30	—
1975	44,683,000	—	—	0.10	0.30	—
1976	33,312,000	—	—	0.10	0.30	—
1977	40,782,000	—	—	0.10	0.30	—
1978	39,999,000	—	—	0.10	0.30	—
1979	49,121,000	—	—	0.10	0.30	—
1980	73,757,000	—	—	0.10	0.30	—
1981	96,144,000	—	—	0.10	0.30	—

KM# 140 20 PARA

3.8000 g., Copper-Zinc **Obv:** State emblem **Rev:** Denomination above date

Date	Mintage	VG	F	VF	XF	Unc
1990	174,028,500	—	—	0.10	0.20	0.50
1991	60,828,000	—	—	0.10	0.20	0.50

KM# 84 25 PARA

Bronze, 17 mm. **Obv:** State emblem **Rev:** Denomination above date **Edge:** Plain

Date	Mintage	F	VF	XF	Unc	BU
1982	185,316,000	—	—	0.10	0.25	—
1983	65,290,000	—	—	0.15	0.30	—

KM# 46.1 50 PARA

Copper-Zinc, 25.5 mm. **Obv:** State emblem **Rev:** Denomination divides date **Edge:** Milled

Date	Mintage	F	VF	XF	Unc	BU
1965	—	—	0.10	0.20	0.65	—
1973	23,739,000	—	0.10	0.20	0.65	—
1974	33,000	1.00	1.50	2.50	5.00	—
1975	10,220,000	—	0.10	0.20	0.80	—
1976	8,438,000	—	0.10	0.20	1.00	—
1977	17,864,000	—	0.10	0.20	0.75	—
1978	40,177,000	—	0.10	0.20	0.65	—
Note: Two varieties of "7" exist						
1979	3,021,000	0.50	1.00	2.00	5.00	—

KM# 46.2 50 PARA

Copper-Zinc **Obv:** State emblem **Rev:** Denomination divides date

Date	Mintage	F	VF	XF	Unc	BU
1979	12,278,000	0.20	0.50	1.00	2.50	—
1980	24,974,000	—	0.10	0.20	0.65	—
1981	40,319,000	—	0.10	0.20	0.65	—

KM# 85 50 PARA

2.8500 g., Bronze, 19 mm. **Obv:** State emblem **Rev:** Denomination above date **Edge:** Plain

Date	Mintage	F	VF	XF	Unc	BU
1982	79,584,000	—	—	0.10	0.20	—
1983	72,100,000	—	—	0.10	0.20	—
1984	59,642,000	0.25	0.50	1.00	1.50	—

KM# 141 50 PARA

Copper-Zinc **Obv:** State emblem **Rev:** Denomination

Date	Mintage	F	VF	XF	Unc	BU
1990	137,873,000	—	—	0.10	0.20	—
1991	42,152,000	—	0.20	0.40	1.00	—

KM# 36 DINAR

0.9000 g., Aluminum, 19.8 mm. **Obv:** State emblem **Rev:** Denomination divides date, seven stars above **Edge:** Plain

Date	Mintage	F	VF	XF	Unc	BU
1963	—	—	—	0.10	0.15	—

KM# 47 DINAR

Copper-Nickel, 21.8 mm. **Obv:** State emblem **Rev:** Denomination and date within wreath, six stars above **Edge:** Milled

Date	Mintage	F	VF	XF	Unc	BU
1965	75,822,000	0.10	0.15	0.30	0.60	—

KM# 48 DINAR

Copper-Nickel, 21.8 mm. **Obv:** State emblem **Rev:** Denomination above date within wreath, six stars above **Edge:** Milled

Date	Mintage	F	VF	XF	Unc	BU
1968	35,497,000	0.10	0.20	0.40	0.80	—

KM# 59 DINAR

Copper-Nickel-Zinc, 21.8 mm. **Obv:** State emblem **Rev:** Text surrounds denomination within wreath, six stars above **Edge:** Milled

Date	Mintage	F	VF	XF	Unc	BU
1973	18,974,000	—	0.10	0.15	0.40	—
1974	42,724,000	—	0.10	0.15	0.35	—
1975	30,260,000	—	0.10	0.15	0.35	—
1976	21,849,000	—	0.10	0.15	0.35	—
1977	30,468,000	—	0.10	0.15	0.35	—
Note: Two varieties of wreath						
1977 Proof	—	Value: 40.00				
1978	35,032,000	—	0.10	0.15	0.35	—
1979	39,844,000	—	0.10	0.15	0.35	—
1980	60,630,000	—	0.10	0.15	0.35	—
1981	56,650,000	—	0.10	0.15	0.35	—

KM# 61 DINAR

Copper-Nickel-Zinc, 21.8 mm. **Series:** F.A.O. **Obv:** State emblem **Rev:** Text surrounds denomination, stylized grain stalks at sides **Edge:** Milled

Date	Mintage	F	VF	XF	Unc	BU
1976	500,000	—	0.10	0.30	1.00	—

KM# 86 DINAR

3.6000 g., Nickel-Brass, 20 mm. **Obv:** State emblem **Rev:** Text surrounds denomination **Edge:** Milled

Date	Mintage	F	VF	XF	Unc	BU
1982	70,105,000	—	—	0.10	0.30	—
1983	114,180,000	—	—	0.10	0.20	—
1984	172,185,000	—	—	0.10	0.20	—
1985	64,436,000	—	—	0.10	0.25	—
1986	122,643,000	—	—	0.10	0.20	—

KM# 142 DINAR

Copper-Nickel-Zinc **Obv:** State emblem **Rev:** Text surrounds denomination **Edge:** Milled

Date	Mintage	F	VF	XF	Unc	BU
1990	172,105,000	—	—	0.10	0.25	—
1991	79,549,000	—	0.15	0.25	0.75	—

KM# 37 2 DINARA

Aluminum, 22.2 mm. **Obv:** State emblem **Rev:** Denomination divides date, seven stars above **Edge:** Plain

Date	Mintage	F	VF	XF	Unc	BU
1963	—	—	0.10	0.15	0.25	—

KM# 55 2 DINARA

Copper-Nickel-Zinc, 24.5 mm. **Series:** F.A.O. **Obv:** State emblem **Rev:** Text surrounds denomination, grain stalks at sides **Edge:** Milled

Date	Mintage	F	VF	XF	Unc	BU
1970	500,000	—	0.20	0.40	1.00	—

KM# 57 2 DINARA

Copper-Nickel-Zinc, 24.5 mm. **Obv:** State emblem **Rev:** Text encircles denomination, wreath surrounds, six stars above **Edge:** Milled

Date	Mintage	F	VF	XF	Unc	BU
1971	10,413,000	—	0.10	0.30	0.70	—
1972	18,446,000	—	0.10	0.20	0.50	—
1973	31,848,000	—	0.10	0.20	0.45	—
1974	10,989,000	—	0.10	0.20	0.50	—

Date	Mintage	F	VF	XF	Unc	BU
1975	92,000	2.00	4.00	7.50	15.00	—
1976	6,092,000	—	0.10	0.20	0.50	—
1977	19,335,000	—	0.10	0.20	0.50	—
1978	13,035,000	—	0.10	0.20	0.50	—
1979	20,069,000	—	0.10	0.20	0.45	—
1980	36,088,000	—	0.10	0.20	0.45	—
1981	42,599,000	—	0.10	0.20	0.45	—

KM# 87 2 DINARA

4.4000 g., Nickel-Brass, 22 mm. **Obv:** State emblem **Rev:** Text surrounds denomination **Edge:** Milled

Date	Mintage	F	VF	XF	Unc	BU
1982	40,632,000	—	0.10	0.15	0.35	—
1983	35,468,000	—	0.10	0.15	0.35	—
1984	51,500,000	—	0.10	0.15	0.35	—
1985	81,100,000	—	0.10	0.15	0.35	—
1986	50,453,000	—	0.10	0.15	0.35	—

KM# 143 2 DINARA

Copper-Nickel-Zinc **Obv:** State emblem **Rev:** Text surrounds denomination

Date	Mintage	F	VF	XF	Unc	BU
1990	15,936,000	0.15	0.30	0.60	2.00	—
1991	32,836,000	—	0.20	0.40	1.00	—
1992	14,155,000	2.50	3.50	7.00	12.50	—

KM# 38 5 DINARA

Aluminum, 24.6 mm. **Obv:** State emblem **Rev:** Denomination divides date, seven stars above **Edge:** Plain

Date	Mintage	F	VF	XF	Unc	BU
1963	—	0.10	0.20	0.35	0.50	—

KM# 56 5 DINARA

Copper-Nickel-Zinc, 27.5 mm. **Series:** F.A.O. **Obv:** State emblem **Rev:** Text surrounds denomination, grain stalks at sides **Edge:** Milled

Date	Mintage	F	VF	XF	Unc	BU
1970	500,000	0.20	0.50	1.00	2.50	—

KM# 58 5 DINARA

6.9000 g., Copper-Nickel-Zinc, 27.5 mm. **Obv:** State emblem **Rev:** Text encircles denomination, wreath surrounds, six stars above **Edge:** Milled **Note:** Regular issue.

Date	Mintage	F	VF	XF	Unc	BU
1971	10,224,000	0.20	0.40	0.60	1.00	—
Note: Two varieties of wreath						
1972	27,974,000	0.10	0.20	0.35	0.60	—
Note: Two varieties of 2 in date						
1973	12,705,000	0.20	0.40	0.60	1.00	—

Date	Mintage	F	VF	XF	Unc	BU
1974	6,054,000	0.25	0.50	1.00	2.00	—
1975	13,533,000	0.10	0.20	0.35	0.60	—
1976	4,965,383	0.10	0.25	0.40	0.80	—
1977	922,000	0.30	0.60	1.20	2.50	—
1978	1,000,000	0.10	0.25	0.50	1.50	—
1979	3,000,000	0.10	0.25	0.40	0.80	—
1980	9,977,000	0.10	0.20	0.35	0.60	—
1981	15,450,000	0.10	0.20	0.35	0.60	—

KM# 60 5 DINARA

Copper-Nickel-Zinc, 27.5 mm. **Subject:** 30th Anniversary of Nazi Defeat **Obv:** State emblem **Rev:** Denomination, six stars

Date	Mintage	F	VF	XF	Unc	BU
1975	1,020,000	0.25	0.50	1.00	2.50	—

KM# 88 5 DINARA

5.5000 g., Nickel-Brass, 24 mm. **Obv:** State emblem **Rev:** Denomination **Edge:** Milled

Date	Mintage	F	VF	XF	Unc	BU
1982	40,956,000	—	0.10	0.15	0.50	—
1983	40,156,000	—	0.10	0.15	0.50	—
1984	33,023,000	—	0.10	0.15	0.50	—
1985	94,422,000	—	0.10	0.15	0.50	—
1986	37,199,000	—	0.10	0.15	0.50	—

KM# 144 5 DINARA

Copper-Nickel-Zinc **Obv:** State emblem **Rev:** Denomination

Date	Mintage	F	VF	XF	Unc	BU
1990	9,354,000	0.25	0.45	1.00	2.50	—
1991	113,420,000	—	0.25	0.50	1.25	—
1992	15,970,000	1.50	2.50	4.00	7.00	—

KM# 39 10 DINARA

Aluminum-Bronze, 21 mm. **Obv:** State emblem **Rev:** Hand holding grain stalks below head left **Edge:** Milled **Designer:** F. Dincic

Date	Mintage	F	VF	XF	Unc	BU
1963	—	0.15	0.30	0.75	1.25	—

KM# 62 10 DINARA

9.8000 g., Copper-Nickel, 30 mm. **Obv:** State emblem **Rev:** Text encircles denomination, wreath surrounds, six stars above **Edge:** Milled

Date	Mintage	F	VF	XF	Unc	BU
1976	10,549,500	0.30	0.60	0.75	1.25	—
1977	39,645,000	0.30	0.60	0.75	1.00	—
Note: Two varieties of wreath						
1978	29,834,000	0.30	0.60	0.75	1.00	—
1979	4,969,000	0.30	0.60	0.75	1.00	—

Date	Mintage	F	VF	XF	Unc	BU
1980	10,139,000	0.30	0.60	0.75	1.00	—
1981	20,166,000	0.30	0.60	0.75	1.00	—

KM# 63 10 DINARA

Copper-Nickel-Zinc, 30 mm. **Series:** F.A.O. **Obv:** State emblem **Rev:** Text surrounds denomination, grain stalks at sides, six stars above

Date	Mintage	F	VF	XF	Unc	BU
1976	500,000	0.50	0.75	1.00	2.50	—

KM# 89 10 DINARA

5.2000 g., Copper-Nickel, 23 mm. **Obv:** State emblem **Rev:** Text surrounds denomination **Edge:** Milled

Date	Mintage	F	VF	XF	Unc	BU
1982	8,862,000	—	0.10	0.20	0.80	—
1983	42,400,000	—	0.10	0.20	0.75	—
1984	30,900,000	—	0.10	0.20	0.75	—
1985	31,647,000	—	0.10	0.20	0.75	—
1986	40,739,000	—	0.10	0.20	0.75	—
1987	104,988,000	—	0.10	0.20	0.75	—
1988	27,614,000	—	0.10	0.20	0.75	—

KM# 96 10 DINARA

Copper-Nickel, 30 mm. **Subject:** 40th Anniversary - Battle of Neretva River **Obv:** State emblem within flat bottomed circle **Rev:** Bridge over the River Neretva **Edge:** Milled

Date	Mintage	F	VF	XF	Unc	BU
ND(1983)	900,000	—	1.00	2.00	4.00	6.00
ND(1983) Proof	100,000	Value: 8.00				

KM# 97.1 10 DINARA

Copper-Nickel, 30 mm. **Subject:** 40th Anniversary - Battle of Sutjeska River **Obv:** State emblem within flat bottom circle **Rev:** Pathway divides monument **Edge:** Milled

Date	Mintage	F	VF	XF	Unc	BU
ND(1983)	900,000	—	1.00	1.50	3.00	5.00
ND(1983) Proof	100,000	Value: 7.50				

KM# 97.2 10 DINARA

Copper-Nickel **Subject:** 40th Anniversary - Battle of Sutjeska River **Obv:** State emblem within flat bottom circle **Rev:** Without pathway in front of monument

Date	Mintage	F	VF	XF	Unc	BU
ND(1983)	—	—	3.00	6.00	10.00	12.00

KM# 131 10 DINARA

Brass **Obv:** Text surrounds state emblem within square **Rev:** Denomination within square, text on four sides **Edge:** Plain

Date	Mintage	F	VF	XF	Unc	BU
1988	35,992,000	—	—	0.10	0.25	0.35
1989	75,000,000	—	—	0.10	0.25	0.35

KM# 40 20 DINARA
3.7000 g., Aluminum-Bronze, 23.2 mm. **Obv:** State emblem **Rev:** Head at left looking right, cogwheel below **Edge:** Milled **Designer:** F. Dincic

Date	Mintage	F	VF	XF	Unc	BU
1963	—	0.50	1.00	1.75	3.50	—

KM# 112 20 DINARA
Copper-Zinc-Nickel, 25 mm. **Obv:** State emblem **Rev:** Denomination **Edge:** Milled

Date	Mintage	F	VF	XF	Unc	BU
1985	5,000,000	—	0.10	0.15	0.50	—
1986	20,235,000	—	0.10	0.15	0.35	—
1987	39,514,000	—	0.10	0.15	0.35	—

KM# 132 20 DINARA
Brass **Obv:** Text surrounds state emblem within square **Rev:** Denomination within square, text on four sides **Edge:** Plain

Date	Mintage	F	VF	XF	Unc	BU
1988	29,775,000	—	—	0.10	0.25	0.35
1989	12,994,000	—	—	0.10	0.25	0.35

KM# 41 50 DINARA
Aluminum-Bronze, 25.5 mm. **Obv:** State emblem **Rev:** Conjoined heads looking right, cogwheel below **Edge:** Milled **Designer:** Dincic **Note:** Exists with filled letter in denomination. Two varieties of the letter "P" in ANHAPA.

Date	Mintage	F	VF	XF	Unc	BU
1963	—	1.00	2.50	6.00	16.00	—

KM# 113 50 DINARA
Copper-Zinc-Nickel, 27 mm. **Obv:** State emblem **Rev:** Denomination **Edge:** Milled

Date	Mintage	F	VF	XF	Unc	BU
1985	25,488,000	—	0.10	0.25	0.75	—
1986	20,353,000	—	0.10	0.25	0.75	—
1987	21,792,000	—	0.10	0.25	0.75	—
1988	28,370,000	—	0.10	0.25	0.75	—

KM# 133 50 DINARA
Brass **Obv:** Text surrounds state emblem within square **Rev:** Denomination within square, text on four sides

Date	Mintage	F	VF	XF	Unc	BU
1988	46,973,000	—	—	0.10	0.25	0.35
1989	2,999,000	—	0.50	1.00	2.00	3.50

Note: Not issued

KM# 134 100 DINARA
Brass **Obv:** Text surrounds state emblem within square **Rev:** Denomination within square, text on four sides

Date	Mintage	F	VF	XF	Unc	BU
1988	12,610,000	—	—	0.15	0.30	0.50
1989	124,260,000	—	—	0.15	0.30	0.50

FEDERAL REPUBLIC

STANDARD COINAGE

KM# 161 PARA
Brass **Obv:** Monogram on shield **Rev:** Denomination and date

Date	Mintage	F	VF	XF	Unc	BU
1994	25,350,000	—	—	—	0.35	0.50

KM# 164.1 5 PARA
Brass **Obv:** Monogram on shield **Rev:** Denomination and date

Date	Mintage	F	VF	XF	Unc	BU
1994	30,408,000	—	—	—	0.50	0.65
1995	3,400,000	—	—	—	0.60	0.85

KM# 164.2 5 PARA
2.7200 g., Brass, 17 mm. **Obv:** Monogram on shield **Rev:** Denomination and date **Note:** Reduced size.

Date	Mintage	F	VF	XF	Unc	BU
1996	9,951,000	—	—	—	0.50	0.70

KM# 162.1 10 PARA
Copper-Nickel-Zinc **Obv:** Monogram on shield **Rev:** Denomination and date

Date	Mintage	F	VF	XF	Unc	BU
1994	52,161,000	—	—	—	0.50	0.65

KM# 162.2 10 PARA
Brass **Obv:** Monogram on shield **Rev:** Denomination and date **Note:** Reduced size.

Date	Mintage	F	VF	XF	Unc	BU
1995	31,041,000	—	—	—	0.65	0.85

KM# 173 10 PARA
3.3600 g., Brass **Obv:** National arms **Rev:** Denomination and date

Date	Mintage	F	VF	XF	Unc	BU
1996	18,129,000	—	—	—	0.50	0.65
1997	21,384,000	—	—	—	0.50	0.65
1998	5,153,000	—	—	—	0.50	0.70

KM# 163 50 PARA
Copper-Nickel-Zinc **Obv:** Monogram on shield **Rev:** Date and denomination

Date	Mintage	F	VF	XF	Unc	BU
1994	45,013,000	—	—	—	0.75	0.90

KM# 163a 50 PARA
Brass **Obv:** Monogram on shield **Rev:** Date and denomination

Date	Mintage	F	VF	XF	Unc	BU
1995	19,193,000	—	—	—	1.00	1.20

KM# 174 50 PARA
Brass **Obv:** National arms **Rev:** Date and denomination

Date	Mintage	F	VF	XF	Unc	BU
1996	3,520,000	—	—	—	1.00	1.25
1997	14,742,000	—	—	—	1.00	1.20
1998	20,050,000	—	—	—	1.00	1.20
1999	18,140,000	—	—	—	1.00	1.20

KM# 179 50 PARA
3.3000 g., Brass, 18 mm. **Obv:** Head 3/4 facing **Rev:** National arms above denomination **Edge:** Plain

Date	Mintage	F	VF	XF	Unc	BU
2000	23,821,000	—	—	—	0.25	0.45

KM# 165 NOVI DINAR
Copper-Nickel-Zinc **Obv:** Monogram on shield **Rev:** Date and denomination

Date	Mintage	F	VF	XF	Unc	BU
1994	47,755,000	—	—	—	1.00	1.20
1995	10,359,000	—	—	—	1.25	1.50

KM# 168 NOVI DINAR
Copper-Nickel-Zinc **Obv:** National arms **Rev:** Date and denomination **Note:** Reduced size.

Date	Mintage	F	VF	XF	Unc	BU
1996	80,122,000	—	—	—	1.00	1.20
1999	21,686,000	—	—	—	1.00	1.20

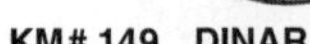

KM# 149 DINAR
Copper-Zinc **Obv:** Monogram on shield **Rev:** Date and denomination

Date	Mintage	F	VF	XF	Unc	BU
1992	49,269,000	—	0.10	0.30	0.60	0.75

KM# 154 DINAR
3.1000 g., Copper-Zinc-Nickel **Obv:** Monogram on shield **Rev:** Date and denomination

Date	Mintage	F	VF	XF	Unc	BU
1993	20,249,000	—	0.10	0.20	0.50	0.65

KM# 160 DINAR
Copper-Zinc-Nickel **Obv:** Monogram on shield **Rev:** Date and denomination

Date	Mintage	F	VF	XF	Unc	BU
1994	10,747,000	—	—	—	1.00	1.20

KM# 180 DINAR
4.4000 g., Copper-Zinc-Nickel, 20 mm. **Obv:** National arms within circle **Rev:** Building **Edge:** Reeded

Date	Mintage	F	VF	XF	Unc	BU
2000	20,076,000	—	—	—	0.25	0.50
2002	60,780,000	—	—	—	0.25	0.45

KM# 150 2 DINARA
4.1800 g., Copper-Zinc **Obv:** Monogram on shield **Rev:** Large, thick denomination, date below

Date	Mintage	F	VF	XF	Unc	BU
1992	10,571,000	—	0.20	0.40	1.00	1.25

KM# 155 2 DINARA
3.8000 g., Copper-Zinc-Nickel **Obv:** Monogram on shield **Rev:** Denomination and date

Date	Mintage	F	VF	XF	Unc	BU
1993	10,263,000	—	0.10	0.20	0.50	0.70

KM# 181 2 DINARA
5.2000 g., Copper-Nickel-Zinc, 21.9 mm. **Obv:** National arms within circle **Rev:** Church **Edge:** Reeded

Date	Mintage	F	VF	XF	Unc	BU
2000	10,071,000	—	—	—	0.25	0.50
2002	71,053,000	—	—	—	0.25	0.45

KM# 151 5 DINARA
5.0000 g., Copper-Zinc **Obv:** Monogram on shield **Rev:** Large, thick denomination, date below

Date	Mintage	F	VF	XF	Unc	BU
1992	26,658,000	—	0.15	0.30	0.75	0.90

KM# 156 5 DINARA
Copper-Zinc-Nickel **Obv:** Monogram on shield **Rev:** Denomination and date

Date	Mintage	F	VF	XF	Unc	BU
1993	10,135,000	—	0.10	0.20	0.50	0.65

KM# 182 5 DINARA
6.3000 g., Copper-Nickel-Zinc, 24 mm. **Obv:** National arms **Rev:** Domed building, denomination and date at left **Edge:** Reeded

Date	Mintage	F	VF	XF	Unc	BU
2000	32,762,500	—	—	—	1.25	1.50
2002	30,966,000	—	—	—	1.25	1.50

KM# 152 10 DINARA
Copper-Zinc-Nickel **Obv:** Monogram on shield **Rev:** Large, thick denomination, date below

Date	Mintage	F	VF	XF	Unc	BU
1992	76,607,000	—	0.10	0.25	0.60	0.75

KM# 157 10 DINARA
6.0000 g., Copper-Zinc-Nickel **Obv:** Monogram on shield **Rev:** Large denomination, date below

Date	Mintage	F	VF	XF	Unc	BU
1993	20,461,000	—	0.15	0.30	0.70	1.00

KM# 153 50 DINARA
Copper-Zinc-Nickel **Obv:** Monogram on shield **Rev:** Large, thick denomination, date below

Date	Mintage	F	VF	XF	Unc	BU
1992	50,571,000	—	0.25	0.50	1.00	1.25

KM# 158 50 DINARA
7.0000 g., Copper-Zinc-Nickel **Obv:** Monogram on shield **Rev:** Large denomination, date below

Date	Mintage	F	VF	XF	Unc	BU
1993	10,823,000	—	0.20	0.40	0.80	1.00

KM# 159 100 DINARA
Brass **Obv:** Monogram on shield **Rev:** Denomination and date

Date	Mintage	F	VF	XF	Unc	BU
1993	14,294,500	—	0.25	0.50	1.00	1.25

KM# 167 500 DINARA
Brass **Obv:** Monogram on shield **Rev:** Denomination and date
Note: All but 1,000 reported melted. Not released for circulation.

Date	Mintage	F	VF	XF	Unc	BU
1993	—	—	—	—	6.50	7.00

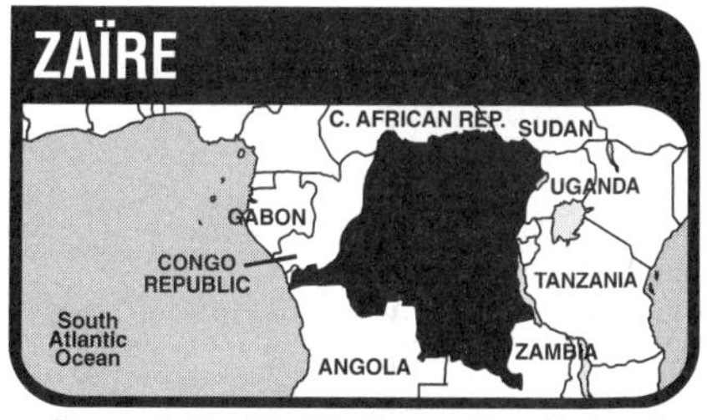

Democratic Republic of the Congo achieved independence on June 30, 1960. It followed the same monetary system as when under the Belgians. Monetary Reform of 1967 introduced new denominations and coins. The name of the country was changed to **Zaire** in 1971.

Under the command of Laurent Kabila, rebel forces overthrew ruler Sese Seko Mobutu in May of 1997. Self appointed President Kabila has officially renamed the country the Democratic Republic of Congo.

MONETARY SYSTEM
100 Makuta = 1 Zaire

1993 -
3,000,000 old Zaires = 1 Nouveau Zaire

REPUBLIC

DECIMAL COINAGE

KM# 12 5 MAKUTA
Copper-Nickel **Obv:** Denomination **Rev:** Mobuto bust left

Date	Mintage	F	VF	XF	Unc	BU
1977	8,000,000	—	0.50	1.00	3.50	—

KM# 7 10 MAKUTA
8.9500 g., Copper-Nickel **Obv:** Mobuto bust 1/4 right **Rev:** Arms below denomination

Date	Mintage	F	VF	XF	Unc	BU
1973	5,000,000	—	2.25	4.00	8.00	—
1975	—	—	2.25	4.00	8.00	—
1976	—	—	2.50	4.50	9.00	—
1978	—	—	2.50	4.50	9.00	—

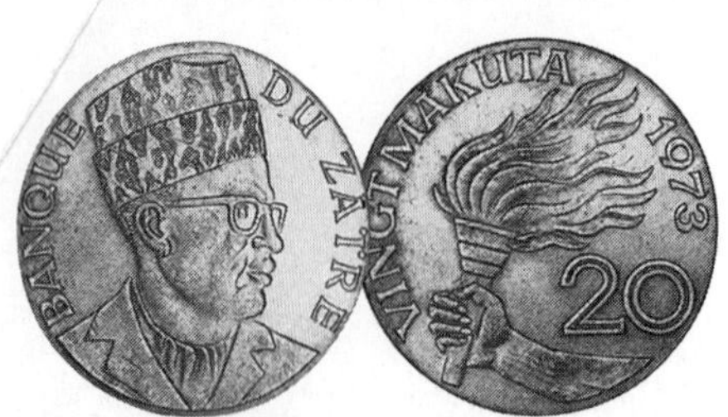

KM# 8 20 MAKUTA

Copper-Nickel **Obv:** Mobuto bust right **Rev:** Hand with torch

Date	Mintage	F	VF	XF	Unc	BU
1973	—	—	3.00	5.50	12.00	—
1976	—	—	3.50	6.50	14.00	—

KM# 13 ZAIRE

Brass **Obv:** Denomination **Rev:** Bust facing

Date	Mintage	F	VF	XF	Unc	BU
1987	—	—	0.50	1.00	2.00	—
1987 Specimen, coin rotation	—	—	—	—	—	—
1987 Specimen, medal rotation	—	—	—	—	—	—

KM# 14 5 ZAIRES

Brass, 24 mm. **Obv:** Denomination **Rev:** Mobuto bust facing

Date	Mintage	F	VF	XF	Unc	BU
1987	—	—	0.65	1.25	2.50	—

KM# 19 10 ZAIRES

7.9200 g., Brass **Obv:** Denomination **Rev:** Mobuto bust facing

Date	Mintage	F	VF	XF	Unc	BU
1988	—	—	2.00	4.50	9.00	—

ZAMBIA

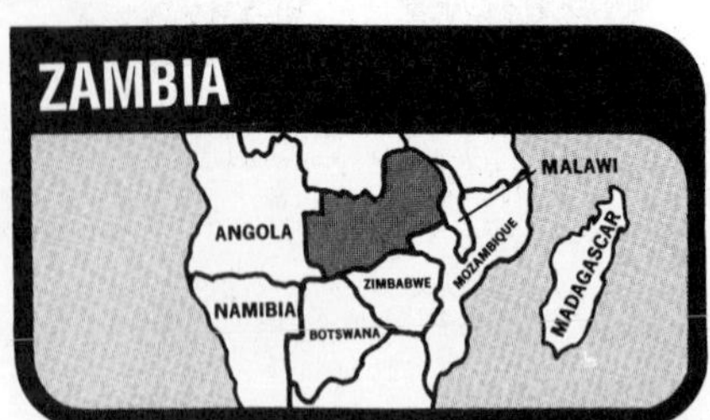

The Republic of Zambia (formerly Northern Rhodesia), a landlocked country in south-central Africa, has an area of 290,586 sq. mi. (752,610 sq. km.) and a population of*7.9 million. Capital: Lusaka. The economy of Zambia is based principally on copper, of which Zambia is the world's third largest producer. Copper, zinc, lead, cobalt and tobacco are exported.

The area that is now Zambia was brought within the British sphere of influence in 1888 by empire builder Cecil Rhodes, who obtained mining concessions in south-central Africa from indigenous chiefs. The territory was ruled by the British South Africa Company, which Rhodes established, until 1924 when its administration was transferred to the British government as a protectorate. In1953, Northern Rhodesia was joined with Nyasaland and the colony of Southern Rhodesia to form the Federation of Rhodesia and Nyasaland. Northern Rhodesia seceded from the Federation on Oct. 24, 1964, and became the independent Republic of Zambia. Zambia is a member of the Commonwealth of Nations. The president is Chief of State.

Zambia converted to a decimal coinage on January 16, 1969. For earlier coinage refer to Rhodesia and Nyasaland.

RULER
British, until 1964

MONETARY SYSTEM
12 Pence = 1 Shilling
20 Shillings = 1 Pound

REPUBLIC

STANDARD COINAGE

KM# 5 PENNY

Bronze **Obv:** Date below center hole **Rev:** Denomination below center hole

Date	Mintage	F	VF	XF	Unc	BU
1966	7,200,000	0.25	0.45	0.85	1.75	2.75
1966 Proof	60	—	—	—	—	—

KM# 1 6 PENCE

Copper-Nickel-Zinc **Obv:** National arms divide date **Rev:** Morning Glory (Ipomoea sp. convolvulaceae), denomination below

Date	Mintage	F	VF	XF	Unc	BU
1964	3,500,000	0.15	0.30	0.60	1.20	1.50
1964 Proof	5,000	Value: 1.75				

KM# 6 6 PENCE

Copper-Nickel-Zinc **Obv:** Head of K.D. Kaunda right, date below **Rev:** Morning glory, denomination below

Date	Mintage	F	VF	XF	Unc	BU
1966	7,200,000	0.25	0.50	1.00	2.00	2.50
1966 Proof	60	—	—	—	—	—

KM# 2 SHILLING

Copper-Nickel **Obv:** National arms divides date **Rev:** Crowned Hornbill, oribi and denomination

Date	Mintage	F	VF	XF	Unc	BU
1964	3,510,000	0.25	0.50	1.00	2.00	2.50
1964 Proof	5,000	Value: 3.50				

KM# 7 SHILLING

Copper-Nickel **Obv:** Head of K.D. Kaunda right, date below **Rev:** Crowned hornbill and denomination

Date	Mintage	F	VF	XF	Unc	BU
1966	5,000,000	0.35	0.75	1.50	3.25	4.00
1966 Proof	60	—	—	—	—	—

KM# 3 2 SHILLINGS

Copper-Nickel **Obv:** National arms divides date **Rev:** Bohor Reedbuck right and denomination

Date	Mintage	F	VF	XF	Unc	BU
1964	3,770,000	0.35	0.75	1.50	3.00	5.00
1964 Proof	5,000	Value: 6.00				

KM# 8 2 SHILLINGS

Copper-Nickel **Obv:** Head of K.D. Kaunda right, date below **Rev:** Bohor Reedbuck right and denomination

Date	Mintage	F	VF	XF	Unc	BU
1966	5,000,000	0.45	1.00	2.25	4.50	5.00
1966 Proof	60	—	—	—	—	—

KM# 4 5 SHILLINGS

Copper-Nickel, 38.8 mm. **Subject:** 1st Anniversary of Independence **Obv:** National arms with supporters, denomination below **Rev:** Head of K.D. Kaunda right, date below **Edge Lettering:** ONE ZAMBIA ONE NATION * 24.10.1964 * **Designer:** D.A.H. Byatt **Note:** Two edge ltter varieties.

Date	Mintage	F	VF	XF	Unc	BU
1965	10,000	—	2.50	3.50	6.50	8.00
1965 Proof	20,000	Value: 9.00				

DECIMAL COINAGE

100 Ngwee = 1 Kwacha

KM# 9 NGWEE

2.1000 g., Bronze, 17.5 mm. **Obv:** Head of K.D. Kaunda right, date below **Rev:** Aardvark left, denomination below

Date	Mintage	F	VF	XF	Unc	BU
1968	8,000,000	—	0.10	0.30	1.50	2.50
1968 Proof	4,000	Value: 1.50				
1969	16,000,000	—	0.10	0.20	1.00	2.00
1972	21,000,000	—	0.10	0.20	1.00	2.00
1978	23,976,000	—	0.10	0.20	1.00	2.00
1978 Proof	24,000	Value: 1.50				

KM# 9a NGWEE

2.1000 g., Copper-Clad Steel, 16.47 mm. **Obv:** Head of K.D. Kaunda right, date below **Rev:** Aardvark left, denomination below **Edge:** Plain

Date	Mintage	F	VF	XF	Unc	BU
1982	10,000,000	—	0.10	0.20	1.00	1.50
1983	60,000,000	—	0.10	0.20	1.00	1.50

KM# 10 2 NGWEE

4.2000 g., Bronze, 21 mm. **Obv:** Head of K.D. Kaunda right, date below **Rev:** Martial Eagle, denomination at right

Date	Mintage	F	VF	XF	Unc	BU
1968	19,000,000	—	0.10	0.20	1.00	1.50
1968 Proof	4,000	Value: 2.00				

Date	Mintage	F	VF	XF	Unc	BU
1978	—	—	0.15	0.25	1.25	2.00
1978 Proof	24,000	Value: 2.00				

KM# 10a 2 NGWEE

4.1900 g., Copper-Clad Steel, 19.39 mm. **Obv:** Head of K.D. Kaunda right, date below **Rev:** Martial Eagle, denomination at right **Edge:** Plain

Date	Mintage	F	VF	XF	Unc	BU
1982	7,500,000	—	0.10	0.20	1.00	—
1983	60,000,000	—	0.10	0.15	0.75	—

KM# 11 5 NGWEE

2.8000 g., Copper-Nickel, 19.4 mm. **Obv:** Head of K.D. Kaunda right, date below **Rev:** Morning Glory, denomination below

Date	Mintage	F	VF	XF	Unc	BU
1968	12,000,000	—	0.20	0.30	0.60	—
1968 Proof	4,000	Value: 1.75				
1972	9,000,000	—	0.20	0.30	0.60	—
1978	1,976,000	—	0.20	0.30	0.60	—
1978 Proof	24,000	Value: 2.00				
1982	12,000,000	—	0.20	0.30	0.60	—
1987	10,000,000	—	0.20	0.30	0.60	—

KM# 12 10 NGWEE

5.6500 g., Copper-Nickel-Zinc, 23.6 mm. **Obv:** K.D. Kaunda head right **Rev:** Crowned Hornbill and denomination

Date	Mintage	F	VF	XF	Unc	BU
1968	1,000,000	—	0.40	0.85	1.75	—
1968 Proof	4,000	Value: 2.00				
1972	1,000,000	—	0.30	0.50	1.00	—
1978	1,976,000	—	0.30	0.50	1.00	—
1978 Proof	24,000	Value: 2.25				
1982	8,000,000	—	0.30	0.50	1.00	—
1983	2,500	—	0.30	0.50	1.00	—
1987	6,000,000	—	0.30	0.50	1.00	—

KM# 13 20 NGWEE

11.3000 g., Copper-Nickel, 28.5 mm. **Obv:** Head of K.D. Kaunda right, date below **Rev:** Bohur Reedbuck right and denomination

Date	Mintage	F	VF	XF	Unc	BU
1968	1,500,000	—	0.75	1.50	2.50	—
1968 Proof	4,000	Value: 2.75				
1972	7,500,000	—	0.50	1.00	2.00	—
1978 Proof	24,000	Value: 3.00				
1983	998,000	—	0.75	1.50	2.50	—
1987	—	—	0.50	1.00	2.00	—
1988	3,000,000	—	0.50	1.00	2.00	—

KM# 22 20 NGWEE

11.3000 g., Copper-Nickel, 28.5 mm. **Series:** F.A.O. - World Food Day **Obv:** Head of K.D. Kaunda right, date below **Rev:** Corn plant, date and denomination within inner circle

Date	Mintage	F	VF	XF	Unc	BU
1981	970,000	—	0.75	1.50	2.75	—

KM# 23 20 NGWEE

11.3000 g., Copper-Nickel, 28.5 mm. **Subject:** 20th Anniversary - Bank of Zambia **Obv:** Head of K.D. Kaunda right, date below **Rev:** Bank building divides dates, denomination above

Date	Mintage	F	VF	XF	Unc	BU
1985	—	—	0.50	1.00	1.50	—

KM# 29 25 NGWEE

2.5100 g., Nickel Plated Steel, 19.93 mm. **Obv:** National arms with supporters, date below **Rev:** Crowned Hornbill and denomination **Edge:** Plain

Date	Mintage	F	VF	XF	Unc	BU
1992	—	—	—	—	1.00	—

KM# 14 50 NGWEE

11.6000 g., Copper-Nickel, 30 mm. **Series:** F.A.O. **Obv:** Head of K.D. Kaunda right, date below **Rev:** Ear of corn divides denomination **Shape:** 12-sided

Date	Mintage	F	VF	XF	Unc	BU
ND(1969)	70,000	—	2.00	3.50	5.50	—

KM# 15 50 NGWEE

11.6000 g., Copper-Nickel, 30 mm. **Series:** F.A.O. **Obv:** Head of K.D. Kaunda right, date below **Rev:** Ear of corn divides denomination **Shape:** 12-sided

Date	Mintage	F	VF	XF	Unc	BU
1972	510,000	—	1.25	2.50	4.50	—

KM# 16 50 NGWEE

11.6000 g., Copper-Nickel, 30 mm. **Subject:** Second Republic, 13 December 1972 **Obv:** Head of K.D. Kaunda right, date below **Rev:** National arms with supporters, denomination below **Shape:** 12-sided

Date	Mintage	F	VF	XF	Unc	BU
1972	6,000,000	—	1.00	2.00	4.00	—
1972 Proof	2,000	Value: 14.00				
1978 Proof	24,000	Value: 8.00				
1983	998,000	—	1.00	2.00	4.00	—

KM# 24 50 NGWEE

11.6000 g., Copper-Nickel, 30 mm. **Subject:** 40th Anniversary of United Nations **Obv:** Head of K.D. Kaunda right, date below **Rev:** United Nations logo **Shape:** 12-sided

Date	Mintage	F	VF	XF	Unc	BU
1985	—	—	1.00	1.25	2.50	—

KM# 30 50 NGWEE

4.0500 g., Nickel Plated Steel, 22.55 mm. **Obv:** National arms with supporters, date below **Rev:** Kafue Lechwe and denomination **Edge:** Plain

Date	Mintage	F	VF	XF	Unc	BU
1992	—	—	—	—	1.50	2.00

KM# 26 KWACHA

Nickel-Brass **Obv:** Head of K.D. Kaunda right, date below **Rev:** Two falcons on branch divided by denomination

Date	Mintage	F	VF	XF	Unc	BU
1989	8,000,000	—	0.75	1.50	4.00	5.00

KM# 38 KWACHA

3.0000 g., Brass, 19.2 mm. **Obv:** National arms with supporters, date below **Rev:** Two falcons on branch divided by denomination

Date	Mintage	F	VF	XF	Unc	BU
1992	—	—	—	—	1.50	2.50

KM# 31 5 KWACHA

3.5000 g., Brass **Obv:** National arms with supporters, date below **Rev:** Oryx right and denomination

Date	Mintage	F	VF	XF	Unc	BU
1992	—	—	—	—	2.00	2.50

KM# 32 10 KWACHA

5.1000 g., Brass **Obv:** National arms, date below **Rev:** Rhinoceros facing and denomination

Date	Mintage	F	VF	XF	Unc	BU
1992	—	—	—	—	2.50	3.00

ZANZIBAR

The British protectorate of Zanzibar and adjacent small islands, located in the Indian Ocean 22 miles (35 km.) off the coast of Tanganyika, comprised a portion of British East Africa. Zanzibar was also the name of a sultanate which included the Zanzibar and Kenya protectorates. Zanzibar has an area of 637 sq. mi. (1,651 sq. km.). Chief city: Zanzibar. The islands are noted for their cloves, of which Zanzibar is the world's foremost producer.

Zanzibar came under Portuguese control in 1503, was conquered by the Omani Arabs in 1698, became independent of Oman in 1860, and (with Pemba) came under British control in 1890. Britain granted the protectorate self-government in 1961, and independence within the British Commonwealth on Dec. 19, 1963. On April 26,1964, Tanganyika and Zanzibar (with Pemba) united to form the United Republic of Tanganyika and Zanzibar. The name of the country, which remained within the British Commonwealth was changed to Tanzania on Oct. 29,1964.

TITLE

زنجباراه

Zanjibara

RULER

Sultan Ali Bin Hamud, 1902-1911AD

MONETARY SYSTEM

64 Pysa (Pice) = 1 Rupee
136 Pysa = 1 Ryal (to 1908)
100 Cents = 1 Rupee (to 1909)

BRITISH PROTECTORATE

DECIMAL COINAGE

100 Cents = 1 Rupee

KM# 8 CENT

Bronze **Ruler:** Sultan Ali Bin Hamud **Obv:** Inscription **Rev:** Palm tree divides value

Date	Mintage	F	VF	XF	Unc	BU
1908	1,000,000	75.00	150	300	450	—

KM# 9 10 CENTS

Bronze **Ruler:** Sultan Ali Bin Hamud **Obv:** Inscription **Rev:** Palm tree divides value

Date	Mintage	F	VF	XF	Unc	BU
1908	100,000	100	225	400	750	—

KM# 10 20 CENTS

Nickel **Ruler:** Sultan Ali Bin Hamud **Obv:** Inscription **Rev:** Palm tree divides value

Date	Mintage	F	VF	XF	Unc	BU
1908	100,000	150	300	500	950	—

ZIMBABWE

The Republic of Zimbabwe (formerly the Republic of Rhodesia or Southern Rhodesia), located in the east-central part of southern Africa, has an area of 150,804 sq. mi. (390,580sq. km.) and a population of *10.1 million. Capital: Harare (formerly Salisbury). The economy is based on agriculture and mining. Tobacco, sugar, asbestos, copper, chrome, ore and coal are exported.

The Rhodesian area contains extensive evidence of the habitat of Paleolithic man and earlier civilizations, notably the world-famous ruins of Zimbabwe, a gold-trading center that flourished about the 14th or 15th century A.D. The Portuguese of the 16th century were the first Europeans to attempt to develop south-central Africa, but it re-mained for Cecil Rhodes and the British South Africa Co. to open the hinterlands. Rhodes obtained a concession for mineral rights from local chiefs in 1888 and administered his African empire (named Southern Rhodesia in 1895) through the British South Africa Co. until 1923, when the British government annexed the area after the white settlers voted for existence as a separate entity, rather than for incorporation into the Union of South Africa. From Sept. of 1953 through 1963 Southern Rhodesia was joined with the British Protectorates of Northern Rhodesia and Nyasaland into a multiracial federation, known as the Federation of Rhodesia and Nyasaland. When the federation was dissolved at the end of 1963, Northern Rhodesia and Nyasaland became the independent states of Zambia and Malawi.

Britain was prepared to grant independence to Southern Rhodesia but declined to do so when the politically dominant white Rhodesians refused to give assurances of representative government. On Nov. 11, 1965, following two years of unsuccessful negotiation with the British government, Prime Minister Ian Smith issued an unilateral declaration of independence. Britain responded with economic sanctions supported by the United Nations. After further futile attempts to effect an accommodation, the Rhodesian Parliament severed all ties with Britain and on March 2, 1970, established the Republic of Rhodesia.

On March 3, 1978, Prime Minister Ian Smith and three moderate black nationalist leaders signed an agreement providing for black majority rule. The name of the country was changed to Zimbabwe Rhodesia. Following a conference in London in December 1979, the opposition government conceded and it was agreed that the British Government should resume control. A British Governor soon returned to Southern Rhodesia. One of his first acts was to affirm the nullification of the purported declaration of independence. On April 18, 1980 pursuant to an act of the British Parliament, the colony of Southern Rhodesia became independent as the Republic of Zimbabwe, a member of the British Commonwealth of Nations, until recently suspended.

MONETARY SYSTEM

100 Cents = 1 Dollar

MINT

Harare

REPUBLIC

DECIMAL COINAGE

KM# 1 CENT

3.1000 g., Bronze, 18.45 mm. **Obv:** Bird statue above date **Rev:** Value within garland of flame lily leaves **Designer:** Jeff Huntly

Date	Mintage	F	VF	XF	Unc	BU
1980	10,000,000	—	0.10	0.20	0.40	0.65
1980 Proof	15,000	Value: 1.50				
1982	—	—	0.10	0.20	0.40	0.65
1983	—	—	0.10	0.20	0.40	0.65
1986	—	—	0.10	0.20	0.40	0.65
1988	—	—	0.10	0.20	0.40	0.65

KM# 1a CENT

2.9800 g., Bronze Plated Steel, 18.45 mm. **Obv:** Bird statue above date **Rev:** Denomination within wreath **Edge:** Plain **Designer:** Jeff Huntly

Date	Mintage	F	VF	XF	Unc	BU
1989	—	—	0.10	0.20	0.50	0.75
1990	—	—	0.10	0.20	0.50	0.75
1991	—	—	0.10	0.20	0.50	0.75
1994	—	—	0.10	0.20	0.50	0.75
1995	—	—	0.10	0.20	0.50	0.75
1997	—	—	0.10	0.20	0.50	0.75
1997 Proof	5,500	Value: 1.00				
1999	—	—	0.10	0.20	0.50	0.75

KM# 2 5 CENTS

2.6000 g., Copper-Nickel, 17.04 mm. **Obv:** Bird statue above date **Rev:** Hare left, value **Edge:** Plain **Designer:** Jeff Huntly

Date	Mintage	F	VF	XF	Unc	BU
1980	—	—	0.15	0.30	1.00	1.25
1980 Proof	15,000	Value: 1.50				
1982	—	—	0.15	0.30	1.00	1.25
1983	—	—	0.15	0.30	1.00	1.25
1988	—	—	0.15	0.30	1.00	1.25
1989	—	—	0.15	0.30	1.00	1.25
1990	—	—	0.15	0.30	1.00	1.25
1991	—	—	0.15	0.30	1.00	1.25
1995	—	—	0.15	0.30	1.00	1.25
1996	—	—	0.15	0.30	1.00	1.25
1997	—	—	0.15	0.30	1.00	1.25
1997 Proof	Est. 5,500	Value: 2.00				
1999	—	—	0.15	0.30	1.00	1.25

KM# 3 10 CENTS

3.8200 g., Copper-Nickel, 19.98 mm. **Obv:** Bird statue above date **Rev:** Baobab tree, value at right **Edge:** Plain **Designer:** Jeff Huntly

Date	Mintage	F	VF	XF	Unc	BU
1980	—	—	0.15	0.30	0.75	1.00
1980 Proof	15,000	Value: 2.00				
1983	—	—	0.15	0.30	0.75	1.00
1987	—	—	0.15	0.30	0.75	1.00
1988	—	—	0.15	0.30	0.75	1.00
1989	—	—	0.15	0.30	0.75	1.00
1991	—	—	0.15	0.30	0.75	1.00
1994	—	—	0.15	0.30	0.75	1.00
1997	—	—	0.15	0.30	0.75	1.00
1997 Proof	Est. 5,500	Value: 3.00				
1999	—	—	0.15	0.30	0.75	1.00

KM# 3a 10 CENTS

Nickel-Plated Steel, 20 mm. **Obv:** National emblem **Rev:** Baobab tree, value **Edge:** Plain **Designer:** Jeff Huntly

Date	Mintage	F	VF	XF	Unc	BU
2001	—	—	0.15	0.30	0.75	1.00
2002	—	—	0.15	0.30	0.75	1.00
2003	—	—	0.15	0.30	0.45	1.00

KM# 4 20 CENTS

5.7000 g., Copper-Nickel, 22.95 mm. **Obv:** Bird statue above date **Rev:** Birchenough Bridge over the Sabi River, value below **Edge:** Plain **Designer:** Jeff Huntly

Date	Mintage	F	VF	XF	Unc	BU
1980	—	—	0.25	0.50	1.50	1.75
1980 Proof	15,000	Value: 2.50				
1983	—	—	0.25	0.50	1.50	1.75
1987	—	—	0.20	0.40	1.25	1.50
1988	—	—	0.20	0.40	1.25	1.50
1989	—	—	0.20	0.40	1.25	1.50
1990	—	—	0.20	0.40	1.25	1.50
1991	—	—	0.20	0.40	1.25	1.50
1994	—	—	0.20	0.40	1.25	1.50
1996	—	—	0.20	0.40	1.25	1.50
1997	—	—	0.20	0.40	1.25	1.50
1997 Proof	Est. 5,500	Value: 4.00				

KM# 4a 20 CENTS

Nickel-Plated Steel, 23 mm. **Obv:** National emblem **Rev:** Birchenough Bridge over the Sabi River, value below **Edge:** Plain **Designer:** Jeff Huntly

Date	Mintage	F	VF	XF	Unc	BU
2001	—	—	0.20	0.40	1.25	1.50
2002	—	—	0.20	0.40	1.25	1.50
2003	—	—	0.20	0.40	1.25	1.50

KM# 5 50 CENTS

7.5200 g., Copper-Nickel, 25.95 mm. **Obv:** Bird statue above date **Rev:** Radiant sun rising, symbolic of independence, value **Edge:** Plain **Designer:** Jeff Huntly

Date	Mintage	F	VF	XF	Unc	BU
1980	—	—	0.60	1.25	2.25	2.50
1980 Proof	15,000	Value: 4.50				
1988	—	—	0.40	1.00	1.75	2.00
1989	—	—	0.40	1.00	1.75	2.00
1990	—	—	0.40	1.00	1.75	2.00
1993	—	—	0.40	1.00	1.75	2.00
1995	—	—	0.40	1.00	1.75	2.00
1997	—	—	0.40	1.00	1.75	2.00
1997 Proof	Est. 5,500	Value: 8.00				

KM# 5a 50 CENTS

Nickel-Plated Steel, 26 mm. **Obv:** National emblem **Rev:** Radiant sun rising, symbolic of independence, value **Edge:** Plain **Designer:** Jeff Huntly

Date	Mintage	F	VF	XF	Unc	BU
2001	—	—	0.40	1.00	1.75	2.00
2002	—	—	0.40	1.00	1.75	2.00
2003	—	—	0.40	1.00	1.75	2.00

KM# 6 DOLLAR

10.0000 g., Copper-Nickel, 28.95 mm. **Obv:** Bird statue above date **Rev:** Zimbabwe Ruins, value **Edge:** Reeded **Designer:** Jeff Huntly

Date	Mintage	F	VF	XF	Unc	BU
1980	—	—	1.00	1.50	3.00	3.50
1980 Proof	15,000	Value: 6.50				
1993	—	—	1.00	1.50	3.00	3.50
1997	—	—	1.00	1.50	3.00	3.50
1997 Proof	Est. 5,500	Value: 12.00				

KM# 6a DOLLAR

Nickel-Plated Steel, 29 mm. **Obv:** National emblem **Rev:** Zimbabwe ruins amongst trees, value **Edge:** Reeded **Designer:** Jeff Huntly

Date	Mintage	F	VF	XF	Unc	BU
2001	—	—	1.00	1.50	3.00	3.50
2002	—	—	1.00	1.50	3.00	3.50
2003	—	—	1.00	1.50	3.00	3.50

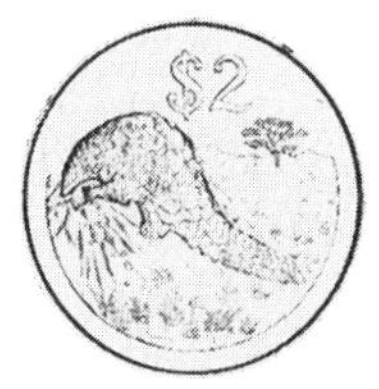

KM# 12 2 DOLLARS

9.5200 g., Brass, 24.5 mm. **Obv:** Bird statue above date **Rev:** Pangolin below denomination **Edge:** Reeded **Designer:** Jeff Huntly

Date	Mintage	F	VF	XF	Unc	BU
1997	—	—	1.25	2.25	5.00	6.00
1997 Proof	Est. 5,500	Value: 20.00				

KM# 12a 2 DOLLARS

Brass Plated Steel, 24.5 mm. **Obv:** National emblem **Rev:** Pangolin below value **Edge:** Reeded

Date	Mintage	F	VF	XF	Unc	BU
2001	—	—	1.25	2.25	5.00	6.00
2002	—	—	1.25	2.25	5.00	6.00
2003	—	—	1.25	2.25	5.00	6.00

KM# 13 5 DOLLARS

9.0500 g., Bi-Metallic Nickel-plated-Steel center in Brass ring, 27.4 mm. **Obv:** Bird on nest within circle **Rev:** Rhinoceros within circle **Edge:** Reeded

Date	Mintage	F	VF	XF	Unc	BU
2001	—	—	—	—	7.50	8.50
2002	—	—	—	—	7.50	8.50
2003	—	—	—	—	7.50	8.50

NUMISMATIC SOCIETIES

American Numismatic Association
818 North Cascade Ave.
Colorado Springs, CO 80903
U.S.A.

American Numismatic Society
75 Varick St., 11th Floor
New York, NY 10013

Amigos de la Casa de la Moneda de Segovia
(Friends of the Segovia Mint)
Apartado 315
40080 Segovia
Spain

Asociación Numismática de Costa Rica
Apartado 2075-1002
San José
Costa Rica

Asociación Numismática Española
Gran via de les Corts Catalanes 627 Pral. 1ª
08010 Barcelonia
Spain

Asociación Numismática de Chile "ANUCH"
Luis Thayer Ojeda 0115
Local 35-36
Providencia, Santiago
Chile

Canadian Numismatic Association
5694 Hwy #7 East, Suite 432
Markham ON Canada L3P 1B4

Centro Numismatico Buenos Aires
Av. San Juan 2630 (C1232AAV)
Buenos Aires
Argentina

Commission Internationale Numismatique
(C.I.N)
Rutimeyer Strasse 12
CH-4054 Basel
Switzerland

Deutsche Numismatische Gesellschaft
Dr. R. Albert
Hans-Purrman-Allee 26
D-67346 Speyer
Germany

Hellenic Numismatic Society
A.Metaxa 28
p.c 106 81 Athens
Greece

Lithuanian Numismatic Association
P.O. Box 22696
Baltimore, MD 21203
U.S.A.

Malaysia Numismatic Society
G. P.O. 12367
50776 Kuala Lumpur
Malaysia

Nordisk Numismatisk Unions Medlemsblad
%Den Lgl. Mont-og Medaillesamng
Nationalmuseet/Frederiksholms
Kanal 12
DK-1220 Kobenhaven
Denmark

Numismatic Association of Australia
Box 1920
GPO Melbourne
Victoria 3001
Australia

Numismatics International
P.O. Box 570842
Dallas, TX 75357-0842
U.S.A.

Numismatic Society of India
Nisar Ahmed
Banaras Hindu University
Varanasi 221-005
India

Oriental Numismatic Society
Regional Secretary O.N.S.
J. Lingen
Dr. A. Schweitzerstraat 29
2861 XZ BERGAMBACHT
Netherlands
Or
Oriental Numismatic Society
Charlie Karukstis
P.O. Box 1528
Claremont, CA 91711

Polish Numismatic Society
P.O. Box 1873
Chicago, IL 60690
U.S.A.

Royal Numismatic Society
C/o Dept. Coins and Medals
British Museum
Great Russell Street
London, WC1B 3DG
United Kingdom

Royal Numismatic Society of New Zealand
P.O. Box 2023
Wellington 6015
New Zealand

Russian Numismatic Society
RNS Secretary
P.O. Box 3684
Santa Rosa, CA 95402
U.S.A.

Sarawak Philatelic and Numismatic Society
P.O. Box 376
96007 Sibu
Sarawak
Malaysia

Sociedad Numismatica de Mexico
Eugenia 13-301 Col. Napoles
C.P. 03810 Mexico D.F.

Sociedad Numismatica de Puerto Rico
Box 194636
San Juan, Puerto Rico 00919-4636

Sociedad Portuguesa de Numismática
Rue de Costa Cabral 664
4200-211 Porto
Portugal

Sociedade Numismática Brasileira
Rua 24 de Maio, 247 2º And.
Centro San Paulo SP
Brazil

Sodiedade Portugesa de Numismatica
Rua de Costa Cabral, 664
4200 Porto
Portugal

Societe Royale de Numismatique de Belgique
Ave. Leopold 28A
B-1330 Rixensart
Belgium

South Africa Numismatic Society
P.O. Box 1689
Cape Town 8000
South Africa

Turkish Numismatic Society
Haci Emin Efendi Sok. No 7
Murat Apt. Daire 4
Tesvkive Istanbul
Turkey

Ukranian Philatelic and Numismatic Society
P.O. Box 303
Southfields, NY 10975-0303

U.S. Mexican Numismatic Association
USMexNA c/o Don Bailey
P.O. Box 98
Homer, MI 49245-0098

Verband der Deutschen Munzvereine
(Association of German Numismatic Societies)
Reisenbergstr. 58A
D-8000 Munich 60
Germany